CONTENTS (Cont.) WITHDRAWN

16.0

AUTOMATIC TRANSMISSIONS & TRANSAXLES INDEX (Cont.)

Manufacturer & Transmission	Oil Circuit Diagram	Transmission Servicing	Transmission Removal	Electronic Controls	Diagnosis & Overhaul
Mazda					
FA4A-EL & GF4A-EL	1-130, 150	2-27	2-83	3-863	3-830
LA4A-EL		2-27	2-83	[1]	3-908
LJ4A-EL		2-27	2-83	3-930	3-911
NC4A-EL	1-161	2-27	2-83	3-960	3-944
RA4A-EL, RA4AX-EL & RB4A-EL	1-174	2-27	2-83	3-998	3-973
4R44E & 4R55E		2-27	2-83	[2]	[2] 3-1031
Mazda Shift Lock System				3-1033	3-1033
Mercedes-Benz					
722 Series (W4A020, W4A040 & W5A030)		2-33	2-87	3-1040	3-1040
Mitsubishi					
F3A20 & F4A20 Series	1-112	2-36	2-88	3-1128	3-1065
F4AC1		2-36	2-88	3-1086	[3]
F4A33, W4A32 & W4A33		2-36	2-88	3-1103	3-1103
F4A20, F4A30 & W4A30 Series		2-36	2-88	3-1128	3-1128
V4AW2	1-29	2-36	2-88	3-1147	3-1147
V4AW3	1-198	2-36	2-88	3-1181	3-1164
Nissan					
RE4F03A/V		2-40	2-89	3-1214	3-1192
RE4F04A & RE4F04V		2-40	2-89	3-1246	3-1223
RE4R01A, RE4R03A & RL4R01A		2-40	2-89	3-1283	3-1261
RL4F03A/V		2-40	2-89	3-1303	3-1303
Porsche					
A50/05		2-43	2-93	3-1345	3-1325
Rover					
ZF4HP22 & ZF4HP24		2-45	2-94		
Saab					
AW50-40LE		2-51	2-95	3-1360	3-1360
ZF 4HP 18		2-51	2-95	3-1369	3-1369
Subaru					
4-Speed	1-206	2-52	2-96	3-1397	3-1380
Suzuki					
Aisin Warner AW03-72LE	1-29	2-53	2-97	3-217	3-202
ECC 3-Speed		2-53	2-97	3-1429, 3-1437	3-1417
Esteem 4-Speed	1-218	2-53	2-97	3-1460, 3-1468	3-1443
Hydra-Matic 3L30		2-53	2-97	3-541	3-541
Toyota					
A-43D, A-46DE & A-46DF		2-57	2-98	3-1497, 3-1500	3-1477
A-131L & A-132L	1-224	2-57	2-98	3-1509	3-1509
A-140E	1-233	2-57	2-98	3-1547	3-1527
A-240 "E" & "L" Series	1-242	2-57	2-98	3-1592, 3-1614	3-1560
A-340 & A-350 Series	1-251	2-57	2-98	3-1657, 3-1682	3-1615
A-340E & A-340F Previa	1-251	2-57	2-98	3-1717	3-1615
A-343F		2-57	2-98	3-1727	3-1615
A-540H & A-541E		2-57	2-98	3-1765, 3-1774	3-1737
Toyota Shift Lock System				3-1787	3-1787
Volkswagen					
Model 096		2-62	2-116	3-1796	3-1796
Type 01M		2-62	2-116	3-1827	3-1827
Volvo					
AW40 Series		2-63	2-117	3-1858	3-1858
AW50-42LE		2-63	2-117	3-1875	3-1875
AW-71		2-63	2-117	3-1897	3-1897

[1] – For additional repair information, see FORD CD4E article in MITCHELL® 1995-96 TRANSMISSION SERVICE & REPAIR manual for DOMESTIC CARS, LIGHT TRUCKS & VANS.

[2] – For additional repair information, see FORD 4R44E & 4R55E article in MITCHELL® 1995-96 TRANSMISSION SERVICE & REPAIR manual for DOMESTIC CARS, LIGHT TRUCKS & VANS.

[3] – For diagnosis and overhaul information, see CHRYSLER 41TE/AE article in MITCHELL® 1995-96 TRANSMISSION SERVICE & REPAIR manual for DOMESTIC CARS, LIGHT TRUCKS & VANS.

D0941148

CONTENTS (Cont.)

MANUAL TRANSMISSIONS & TRANSAXLES INDEX

Manufacturer Transmission	Transmission Servicing	Transmission Removal	Transmission Overhaul
Acura			
K4A6	2-119	2-136	4-3
K4F6	2-119	2-136	4-3
YS1	2-119	2-136	4-19
Y80	2-119	2-136	4-19
MUA5CT	2-119	2-136	4-110
Audi			
01A	2-119	2-138	4-32
012	2-119	2-138	4-43
01E	2-119	2-138	4-54
BMW (Getrag)			
260	2-121	2-139	[1]
Geo			
Metro (Suzuki)	2-121	2-140	4-64
Prizm (C52 Toyota)	2-121	2-140	4-233
Tracker (Suzuki)	2-121	2-140	4-72
Honda			
P2U5	2-122	2-142	4-78
M2F4	2-122	2-142	4-78
M2L5	2-122	2-142	4-78
M2S4	2-122	2-142	4-78
P2A5	2-122	2-142	4-78
P2U5	2-122	2-142	4-78
S20	2-122	2-142	4-86
Y21	2-122	2-142	4-19
Hyundai			
M5A Series	2-123	2-143	4-104
Infiniti			
RS5F32A & RS5F32V	2-123	2-144	4-178
RS5F50A/V	2-123	2-144	4-184
Isuzu			
MUA Series	2-124	2-145	4-110
Kia			
Kia (Getrag) 5-Speed	2-125	2-147	4-116
Lexus			
W58 (Toyota)	2-125	2-147	4-279
Mazda			
F25M-R	2-126	2-148	4-122
G25M-R	2-126	2-148	4-122
M15M-D	2-126	2-148	4-131
R15M-D	2-126	2-148	4-134
Mitsubishi			
F5M21	2-127	2-150	4-145
F5M22	2-127	2-150	4-145
F5M31	2-127	2-150	4-145
F5M33	2-127	2-150	4-145
R5M21	2-127	2-150	4-152
V5MT1	2-127	2-150	4-156
W5M33	2-127	2-150	4-160
W6MG1	2-127	2-150	4-160
Nissan			
FS5R30A	2-128	2-152	4-168
FS5W71C	2-128	2-152	4-173
RS5F31A	2-128	2-152	4-178
RS5F32A	2-128	2-152	4-178
RS5F32V	2-128	2-152	4-178
RS5F50A	2-128	2-152	4-184
RS5F50V	2-128	2-152	4-184
RS5R30A	2-128	2-152	4-168
Porsche			
G50/20 6-Speed	2-129	2-156	4-190
Rover			
R380	2-129	2-156	4-201

[1] – Overhaul information is not available.

CONTENTS (Cont.)

MANUAL TRANSMISSIONS & TRANSAXLES INDEX (Cont.)

Manufacturer Transmission	Transmission Servicing	Transmission Removal	Transmission Overhaul
Saab			
FM5 Series	2-130	2-156	4-207
Subaru			
5-Speed (Impreza & Legacy)	2-131	2-158	4-216
Suzuki			
5-Speed (Samurai)	2-132	2-158	4-229
5-Speed (Sidekick & X90)	2-132	2-158	4-72
5-Speed (Swift)	2-132	2-158	4-64
Toyota			
C50	2-133	2-159	4-233
C52	2-133	2-159	4-233
C141	2-133	2-159	4-233
C151	2-133	2-159	4-233
E153	2-133	2-159	4-238
E250F (RAV4)	2-133	2-159	4-254
G58	2-133	2-159	4-248
R150 & R150F	2-133	2-159	4-265
S51 & S54	2-133	2-159	4-273
W55	2-133	2-159	4-279
W56	2-133	2-159	4-279
W58	2-133	2-159	4-279
W59	2-133	2-159	4-279
Volkswagen			
02A	2-134	2-166	4-287
020	2-134	2-166	4-293
Volvo			
850	2-135	2-168	[1]

[1] – Overhaul information is not available.

AXLE SHAFTS & TRANSFER CASES INDEX

Manufacturer	Axle Shafts	Transfer Cases
Acura	5-3	5-82
Audi	5-5	
BMW	5-6	
Geo	5-7	5-90
Honda	5-9	5-82
Hyundai	5-12	
Infiniti	5-14, 5-17	
Isuzu	5-20	5-82
Kia	5-21	[1]
Lexus	5-22, 5-24	5-123
Mazda	5-28, 5-32	5-116
Mitsubishi	5-36, 5-39	5-107
Nissan	5-42, 5-46, 5-48	5-116
Porsche	5-50	
Saab	5-52	
Subaru	5-53, 5-55	
Suzuki	5-57	5-120
Toyota	5-61, 5-66, 5-71, 5-74	5-123, 5-130, 5-159, 5-163, 5-169
Volkswagen	5-79	
Volvo	5-80	

[1] – See appropriate transmission article for transfer case information.

LATEST CHANGES & CORRECTIONS

NOTE: Latest changes and corrections represents a collection of last minute information. Read this section and make notations in appropriate 1994 and earlier manuals for easy reference.

AUTOMATIC TRANSMISSIONS

HYUNDAI

[1] *INCORRECT REFERENCE* – Please note that FAULT CODE IDENTIFICATION table on page 3-537 contains an incorrect reference. Several words are misspelled in the first tariff line. The line should read as follows:

¹ – To check items, see ELECTRONIC SYSTEM & COMPONENT TESTING under ELECTRONIC TROUBLE SHOOTING. Also see ADJUSTMENTS.

This correction applies to the following publication:
1993-94 TRANSMISSION SERVICE & REPAIR manual for IMPORT CARS, LIGHT TRUCKS & VANS.

ISUZU

[1] *REVISED HYDRA-MATIC 4L30-E ELECTRONIC CONTROLS DIANOSTICS* – Please note that pages 3-396 through 3-477 diagnostic charts have been revised by manufacturer. Use 1995 HYDRA-MATIC 4L30-E ELECTRONIC CONTROLS diagnostic charts for correct procedures.

This correction applies to the following publication:
1993-94 TRANSMISSION SERVICE & REPAIR manual for IMPORT CARS, LIGHT TRUCKS & VANS.

MAZDA

[1] *MISSING FIGURE* – Please note that MAZDA NA4A-HL & NC4A-EL article is missing an exploded view of the upper valve body. *See Fig. 33* in MAZDA NC4A-EL article in this manual.

This correction applies to the following publication:
1993-94 TRANSMISSION SERVICE & REPAIR manual for IMPORT CARS, LIGHT TRUCKS & VANS.

TOYOTA

[1] *INCOMPLETE FIGURE INFORMATION* – Please note that page 3-1306, TOYOTA A-240 "E" & "L" SERIES ELECTRONIC CONTROLS article, Fig. 9 contains incomplete information. This figure does not provide terminal identification for the Corolla combination meter harness connector. Please refer to *Fig. 13* in TOYOTA A-240 "E" SERIES ELECTRONIC CONTROLS article in this manual.

This correction applies to the following publication:
1993-94 TRANSMISSION SERVICE & REPAIR manual for IMPORT CARS, LIGHT TRUCKS & VANS.

[2] *INCORRECT FIGURE CALLOUT* - Please note that page 3-1202, TOYOTA A-43D, A-46DE & A-46DF article, Fig 53 contains incorrect information. Callout No. 1 reads "1-2 Shift Valve". Callout No. 1 should read "2-3 Shift Valve".

This correction applies to the following publication:
1993-94 TRANSMISSION SERVICE & REPAIR manual for IMPORT CARS, LIGHT TRUCKS & VANS.

[3] *INCORRECT FIGURE CALLOUT* – Please note that page 3-1202, TOYOTA A-43D, A-46DE & A-46DF article, Fig 55 contains incorrect information. The "1-2 Shift Valve Retainer" should read "3-4 Shift Valve Retainer".

This correction applies to the following publication:
1993-94 TRANSMISSION SERVICE & REPAIR manual for IMPORT CARS, LIGHT TRUCKS & VANS.

[4] *INCORRECT FIGURE CALLOUT* – Please note that page 3-1437, TOYOTA A-540E & A541E article, *Fig. 29* contains incorrect callout information. The legend lists Nos. 1-7 callouts which are not pointed out in the figure. Disregard Nos. 1-7 callouts in the legend. The remaining callouts are correct.

This correction applies to the following publication:
1993-94 TRANSMISSION SERVICE & REPAIR manual for IMPORT CARS, LIGHT TRUCKS & VANS.

[5] *INCORRECT FIGURE CALLOUT* – Please note that page 3-1435, TOYOTA A-540E & A541E article, *Fig. 26* contains incorrect callout information. The legend lists No. 1-3 callouts which are not pointed out in the figure. Disregard No. 1-3 callouts in the legend. The remaining callouts are correct.

This correction applies to the following publication:
1993-94 TRANSMISSION SERVICE & REPAIR manual for IMPORT CARS, LIGHT TRUCKS & VANS.

MANUAL TRANSMISSIONS

HONDA

[1] *INCORRECT FIGURE CALLOUT* – Please note that page 4-91, HONDA S20 manual transmission article, *Fig. 2* contains incorrect callout information. Please use *Fig. 2* in HONDA S20 article in this manual for correct callout information.

This correction applies to the following publication:
1993-94 TRANSMISSION SERVICE & REPAIR manual for IMPORT CARS, LIGHT TRUCKS & VANS.

TOYOTA

[1] *INCORRECT LABOR TIMES* – Please note that page 4-303 lists incorrect labor times for the TOYOTA S51, S53 & S54 5-SPEED manual transmission. The following table includes correct labor times:

APPLICATION & LABOR TIMES

APPLICATION & LABOR TIMES

Vehicle Application	Labor Times		Trans. Model
	¹ R & I	² Overhaul	
Camry			
2.2L (5S-FE)	6.3	6.3	S51
Celica			
1993 FWD	5.2	6.3	S53
1994 2.2L	5.8	6.3	S54
MR2			
2.2L Non-Turbo	5.4	6.3	S54

¹ – Removal and installation of transmission from vehicle chassis.
² – Bench overhaul time for transmission and differential. DOES NOT include removal and installation.

This correction applies to the following publication:
1993-94 TRANSMISSION SERVICE & REPAIR manual for IMPORT CARS, LIGHT TRUCKS & VANS.

Acura – Volvo

TRANSMISSION SERVICE & REPAIR

1995-96 Imported Vehicles

APPLICATIONS & IDENTIFICATION

OIL CIRCUIT DIAGRAMS
Section 1

TRANSMISSION SERVICING
Section 2

AUTOMATIC TRANSMISSION
Section 3

MANUAL TRANSMISSION
Section 4

AXLE SHAFTS & TRANSFER CASES
Section 5

ACKNOWLEDGMENT

Mitchell Repair Information Company thanks the domestic and import automobile and light truck manufacturers, distributors, and dealers for their generous cooperation and assistance which make this manual possible.

MARKETING

Senior Vice President
David Peterson

Directors
David R. Koontz
Daniel Ramirez

Product Managers
Catherine Smith
Victor Addison
Nick DiVerde
Robert Gardner

EDITORIAL

Director, Annual Data Editorial
Gary Nicks

Manager, Annual Data Editorial
Thomas L. Landis

Manager, Special Product Editorial
Ronald E. Garrett

Senior Editors
Chuck Vedra
Ramiro Gutierrez
John M. Fisher
Tom L. Hall
James A. Hawes
Serge G. Pirino
Eddie Santangelo

Technical Editors
Scott A. Olsen
Bob Reel
David W. Himes
Alex A. Solis
Donald T. Pellettera
Michael C. May
James R. Warren
Bobby R. Gifford
Linda M. Murphy
Donald Lawler
Wayne D. Charbonneau
Sal Caloca
Charles "Bud" Gardner
Dan Hankins
Robert L. Eller
Julia A. Gillis
John Schartz
Richard C. Hamilton
Leonid A. Shneyder
Brian Yockey
Robert Henry
John Howard
Todd Mercer
James Barrow

WIRING DIAGRAMS

Manager
Matthew M. Krimple

TECHNICAL LIBRARIAN
Charlotte "Charlie" Norris

Assoc. Tech. Librarian
Debbie Hickman

PRODUCT SUPPORT

Product Specialists
James A. Wafford
Tim Flannery
Kevin Oehrke
Phillip Groudas
Anthony Romano

GRAPHICS

Manager
Judith A. LaPierre
Supervisor
Ann Klimetz

> This publication is dedicated in memory of
> **Carrie Neal**

Published By

MITCHELL REPAIR INFORMATION COMPANY
9889 Willow Creek Road
P.O. Box 26260
San Diego, California 92196-0260

ISBN 0-8470-1840-7

©1997 Mitchell Repair Information Company, LLC
All Rights Reserved

Printed in U.S.A.

COPYRIGHT: No part of this publication may be reproduced, stored in a retrieval system, or transmitted in any form or by any means, electronic, mechanical, photocopying, recording, or otherwise, without the prior written permission of the copyright holder.

Customer Service Numbers
For Subscription, Billing or Technical Information call:
1-888-724-6742 Toll Free or 619-549-7809

Or Write: P.O. Box 26260, San Diego, CA 92196-0260

DISCLAIMER OF WARRANTIES: Although the information contained within this volume has been obtained from sources generally believed to be reliable, no warranty (expressed or implied) can be made as to its accuracy or completeness, nor is any responsibility assumed by Mitchell Repair Information Company or anyone connected with it for loss or damages suffered through reliance on any information contained in this volume.
SPECIFICALLY, NO WARRANTY OF MERCHANTABILITY, FITNESS FOR A PARTICULAR PURPOSE OR ANY OTHER WARRANTY IS MADE OR TO BE IMPLIED WITH RESPECT TO THIS VOLUME AND ITS CONTENTS.
In no event will Mitchell Repair Information Company be liable for any damages, direct or indirect, consequential or compensatory, including, without limitation, lost profits, for any representations, breaches or defaults arising out of the use of this volume. Customer agrees to indemnify Mitchell Repair Information Company and hold it harmless against all claims and damages, including without limitation, reasonable attorney's fees arising out of the use of this volume, unless such claims or damages result from the infringement of any copyright or other proprietary right of any third party.

APPLICATIONS & IDENTIFICATION

Page

Automatic Transmission Applications
  Acura-To-Mazda 2
  Mercedes-To-Suzuki 3
  Toyota-To-Volvo 4
Manual Transmission Applications
  Acura-To-Chrysler Corp. & Eagle 4
  Geo-To-Subaru 5
  Suzuki-To-Volvo 6
Transfer Case Applications 6
Computer Relearn Procedures 7
Gear Tooth Contact Pattern 8
Air Bag Servicing 9

APPLICATIONS & IDENTIFICATION
Automatic Transmissions

ACURA AUTOMATIC TRANSMISSION APPLICATIONS

Vehicle Year & Model	Transmission Model
1995	
Integra	SP7A
Legend	MPYA
1995-96	
2.5TL	M1WA
1996	
Integra	SX4A
SLX	Hydra-Matic 4L30-E
3.2TL	M5HA
3.5RL	M5DA

AUDI AUTOMATIC TRANSMISSION APPLICATIONS

Vehicle Year & Model	Transmission Model
1995-96	
A6	01N
Cabriolet & 90	097
1996	
A4 & A4 AWD	01V

BMW AUTOMATIC TRANSMISSION APPLICATIONS

Vehicle Year & Model	Transmission Model
1995	
M3	ZF 5HP18
318	Hydra-Matic 4L30-E
325	Hydra-Matic 4L30-E
525	Hydra-Matic 4L30-E
530i & 530iT	ZF 5HP18
540i	ZF 5HP18
740i & 840Ci	ZF 5HP30
1996	
318	Hydra-Matic 4L30-E
328	Hydra-Matic 4L30-E
740i & 840Ci	ZF 5HP30
Z3	Hydra-Matic 4L30-E

GEO AUTOMATIC TRANSMISSION APPLICATIONS

Vehicle Year & Model	Transmission Model
1995-96	
Metro	Suzuki ECC 3-Speed
Prizm	Toyota A-131L
Prizm LSi	Toyota A-245E
Tracker	Hydra-Matic 3L30
1996	
Tracker	Aisin Warner AW03-72LE

HONDA AUTOMATIC TRANSMISSION APPLICATIONS

Vehicle Year & Model	Transmission Model
1995	
Civic	A24A
1995-96	
Accord	
Except V6	AOYA Or MPOA
V6	MPZA
Civic Del Sol	S24A
Odyssey	MPJA
Passport	Hydra-Matic 4L30-E
Prelude	MP1A
1996	
Civic	
4-Speed	A4RA
CVT	M4VA

HYUNDAI AUTOMATIC TRANSMISSION APPLICATIONS

Vehicle Year & Model	Transmission Model
1995	
Elantra	KM175
Scoupe	A4AF
1995-96	
Accent	A4AF2
Sonata	
4-Cyl.	KM175
V6	F4A33
1996	
Elantra	A4BF1

INFINITI AUTOMATIC TRANSMISSION APPLICATIONS

Vehicle Year & Model	Transmission Model
1995-96	
G20	RE4F03A/V
J30	RE4R01A
Q45	RE4R03A
1996	
I30	RE4F04A/V

ISUZU AUTOMATIC TRANSMISSION APPLICATIONS

Vehicle Year & Model	Transmission Model
1995-96	
Oasis	MPJA
Rodeo & Trooper (V6)	Hydra-Matic 4L30-E

JAGUAR AUTOMATIC TRANSMISSION APPLICATIONS

Vehicle Year & Model	Transmission Model
1995	
XJR, XJS & XJ12	[1] Hydra-Matic 4L80-E
1995-96	
XJS & XJ6	ZF 4HP 24-E
1996	
XJR & XJ12	[1] Hydra-Matic 4L80-E

[1] – For diagnosis and overhaul information, see MITCHELL® 1995-96 TRANSMISSION SERVICE & REPAIR manual for DOMESTIC CARS, LIGHT TRUCKS & VANS.

KIA AUTOMATIC TRANSMISSION APPLICATION

Vehicle Year & Model	Transmission Model
1995-96	
Sephia	FA4A-EL
Sportage	AW372LE

LEXUS AUTOMATIC TRANSMISSION APPLICATIONS

Vehicle Year & Model	Transmission Model
1995	
GS300	A-340E
1995-96	
ES300	A-541E
LS400	A-340E
SC300	A-340E
SC400	A-340E
1996	
GS300	A-350E
LX450	A-343F

MAZDA AUTOMATIC TRANSMISSION APPLICATIONS

Vehicle Year & Model	Transmission Model
1995	
RX7	RB4A-EL
929	RA4A-EL
MX-3	FA4A-EL
1995-96	
B2300 & B3000	[1] 4R44E
B4000	[1] 4R55E
Miata	NC4A-EL
Millenia	
2.3L	LJ4A-EL
2.5L	GF4A-EL
MPV	
2WD	RA4A-EL
4WD	RA4AX-EL
MX-6 & 626	
2.0L	[2] LA4A-EL
2.5L	GF4A-EL
Protege	FA4A-EL

[1] – For diagnosis and overhaul information, see FORD 4R44E & 4R55E article in MITCHELL® 1995-96 TRANSMISSION SERVICE & REPAIR manual for DOMESTIC CARS, LIGHT TRUCKS & VANS.

[2] – For diagnosis and overhaul information, see FORD CD4E article in MITCHELL® 1995-96 TRANSMISSION SERVICE & REPAIR manual for DOMESTIC CARS, LIGHT TRUCKS & VANS.

MERCEDES-BENZ AUTOMATIC TRANSMISSION APPLICATIONS

Vehicle Year & Model	Series	Transmission
1995		
C220	722.423	W4A020
C280	722.424	W4A020
C36	722.424	W4A020
E300D	722.435	W4A020
E320	722.369	W4A040
E420	722.366	W4A040
S320	722.508	W5A030
S350D	722.367	W4A040
S500	722.370	W4A040
S600	722.362	W4A040
SL320	722.507	W5A030
SL500	722.364	W4A040
SL600	722.362	W4A040
1996		
C220	722.423	W4A020
C280	722.424	W4A020
C36	722.424	W4A020
E320	722.369	W4A040
E300D	722.438	W4A020
S320	722.508	W5A030
SL320	722.507	W5A030

MITSUBISHI AUTOMATIC TRANSMISSION APPLICATIONS

Vehicle Year & Model	Transmission Model
1995	
Expo	
AWD	W4A32
FWD	
1.8L	F4A22
2.4L	F4A23
1995-96	
Diamante	F4A33
Eclipse	
2.0L Non-Turbo	[1] F4AC1
2.0L Turbo	
AWD	W4A33
FWD	F4A33
2.4L	F4A23
Galant	F4A23
Mirage	
1.5L	F3A21
1.8L	F4A22
Montero	
3.0L	V4AW2
3.0L & 3.5L	V4AW3
Pickup	[2] R4AC1
3000GT	F4A33

[1] – For diagnosis and overhaul information, see CHRYSLER 41TE/AE article in MITCHELL® 1995-96 TRANSMISSION SERVICE & REPAIR manual for DOMESTIC CARS, LIGHT TRUCKS & VANS.

[2] – For diagnosis and overhaul information, see MITCHELL® 1993-94 TRANSMISSION SERVICE & REPAIR manual for IMPORT CARS, LIGHT TRUCKS & VANS.

NISSAN AUTOMATIC TRANSMISSION APPLICATIONS

Vehicle Year & Model	Transmission Model
1995-96	
Altima	RE4F04A & RE4F04V
Maxima	RE4F04A & RE4F04V
Pathfinder	RE4R01A
Pickup	
2.4L	RL4R01A
3.0L	RE4R01A
Quest	RE4F04A
Sentra	RL4F03A
200SX	RE4F03V
240SX	RE4R01A
300ZX	
Non-Turbo	RE4R01A
Turbo	RE4R03A

PORSCHE AUTOMATIC TRANSMISSION APPLICATION

Vehicle Year & Model	Transmission Model
1995	
911 Carrera 2	A50/05 Tiptronic

ROVER AUTOMATIC TRANSMISSION APPLICATIONS

Vehicle Year & Model	Transmission Model
1995-96	
Discovery	ZF4HP22
Range Rover	ZF4HP24

SAAB AUTOMATIC TRANSMISSION APPLICATIONS

Vehicle Year & Model	Transmission Model
1995-96	
900 & 9000 4-Cyl.	AW50-40LE
9000 V6	ZF 4HP 18

SUBARU AUTOMATIC TRANSMISSION APPLICATIONS

Vehicle Year & Model	Transmission Model
1995-96	
Impreza	4-Speed
Legacy	4-Speed
SVX	4-Speed

SUZUKI AUTOMATIC TRANSMISSION APPLICATIONS

Vehicle Year & Model	Transmission Model
1995-96	
Esteem	Suzuki 4-Speed
Sidekick	
2-Door	Hydra-Matic 3L30
4-Door	AW03-72LE
Swift	Suzuki ECC 3-Speed
1996	
X90	AW03-72LE

TOYOTA AUTOMATIC TRANSMISSION APPLICATIONS

Vehicle Year & Model	Transmission Model
1995	
Pickup	
2WD	
4-Cyl.	A-43D
V6	A-340E
4WD	
4-Cyl.	A-340F
V6	A-340H
MR2	A-241E
4Runner	
2WD	
V6	A-340E
4WD	
2.4L 4-Cyl.	A-340F
V6	A-340H
1995-96	
Avalon	A-541E
Camry	
4-Cyl.	A-140E
V6	A-541E
Corolla	
1.6L (4A-FE)	A-131L
1.8L (7A-FE)	A-245E
Celica	
1.8L (4A-FE)	A-246L
2.2L (5S-FE)	A-140E
Land Cruiser	A-343F
Paseo	A-244E
Previa	
Non-Supercharged	
AWD	A-46DF
2WD	A-46DE
Supercharged	
AWD	A-340F
2WD	A-340E
Supra	A-340E
Tacoma	
2WD (4-Cyl.)	A-43D
V6	
2WD	A-340E
4WD	A-340F
Tercel	
3-Speed	A-132L
4-Speed	A-242L
T100	
2WD (2.7L 4-Cyl.)	A-340E
V6	
2WD	A-340E
4WD	A-340F

TOYOTA AUTOMATIC TRANSMISSION APPLICATIONS (Cont.)

Vehicle Year & Model	Transmission Model
1996	
RAV4	
2WD	A-241E
4WD	A-540H
4Runner	
2WD	
2.7L 4-Cyl.	A-340E
V6	A-340E
4WD	
2.7L 4-Cyl.	A-340F
V6	A-340F

VOLKSWAGEN AUTOMATIC TRANSMISSION APPLICATIONS

Vehicle Year & Model	Transmission Model
1995	
Cabrio	096
Golf III	096
GTI VR6	096
Jetta III	096
Passat	096
1995-96	
Cabrio	01M
Golf	01M
Golf III	01M
GTI	01M
Jetta & Jetta III	01M
Passat	01M

VOLVO AUTOMATIC TRANSMISSION APPLICATIONS

Vehicle Year & Model	Transmission Model
1995	
940 & 940 Turbo	AW-71
1995-96	
850	AW50-42LE
960	AW40

Manual Transmissions

1995-96 ACURA MANUAL TRANSMISSIONS

Vehicle Application	Transmission Model
Integra	
1995	Y80
1996	S80
Legend (1995)	
5-Speed	K4A6
6-Speed	K4F6
SLX (4WD)	[1] MUA5CT

[1] – For SLX models, see ISUZU MUA SERIES 5-SPEED article.

1995-96 AUDI MANUAL TRANSMISSIONS

Vehicle Application	Transmission Model
1995	
A4, A6 & A90	012
A6 AWD	01A
S6	01E
90 AWD	01A
1996	
A4	012
A4 AWD	01A
S6	01E

1995-96 CHRYSLER CORP. & EAGLE MANUAL TRANSMISSIONS

Vehicle Application	Transmission Model
Colt & Summit	
1.5L	F5M21
1.8L	F5M22
Colt Vista & Summit Wagon	
AWD	W5M33
FWD	
1.8L	F5M22
2.4L	F5M31
Stealth	
Non-Turbo	F5M33
Turbo	W6MG1 (6-Speed)
Talon	
AWD	W5M33
FWD	
Non-Turbo	F5MC1
Turbo	F5M33

1995-96 GEO MANUAL TRANSMISSIONS

Vehicle Application	Transmission Model
Metro	Suzuki 5-Speed
Prizm	[1] Toyota C52 5-Speed
Tracker	Suzuki 5-Speed

[1] – See TOYOTA "C" SERIES – 4 & 5-SPEED transmissions.

1995-96 HONDA MANUAL TRANSMISSIONS

Vehicle Application	Transmission Model
1995-96 Accord	
F22B1 Engine	P2U5
F22B2 Engine	P2A5
Civic & Civic Del Sol	
With B16A3 Engine	Y21
Without B16A3 Engine	S21
Passport	[1] MUA Series
Prelude	
F22A1 Engine	M2L5
H22A2 Engine (VTEC)	M2F4
H23A1 Engine	M2S4

[1] – For Passport models, see ISUZU MUA SERIES 5-SPEED article.

1995-96 HYUNDAI MANUAL TRANSMISSIONS

Vehicle Application	Transmission Model
Accent	M5AF3 5-Speed
Elantra	M5BF1 5-Speed
Scoupe	M5AF 5-Speed

1995-96 INFINITI MANUAL TRANSMISSIONS

Vehicle Application	Transmission Model
G20	RS5F32A Or RS5F32V
I30	RS5F50A/V

1995-96 ISUZU MANUAL TRANSMISSIONS

Vehicle Application	Transmission Model
Pickup & Hombre	
2WD (2.3L)	MUA5C
4WD (2.6L)	MUA5CT
Rodeo	
2WD	MUA5C
4WD	MUA5CT
Trooper	MUA5CT

1995-96 KIA MANUAL TRANSMISSIONS

Vehicle Application	Transmission Model
Sephia	
1.6L	[1] Mazda F25M-R
1.8L	[1] Mazda G25M-R
Sportage	Kia (Getrag) 5-Speed

[1] – See MAZDA F25M-R & G25M-R transmission.

1995-96 LAND ROVER MANUAL TRANSMISSIONS

Vehicle Application	Transmission Series
Defender (1995)	Rover R380 5-Speed
Discovery	Rover R380 5-Speed

1995-96 LEXUS MANUAL TRANSMISSIONS

Vehicle Application	Transmission Model
SC300	[1] Toyota W58

[1] – See TOYOTA "W" SERIES 5-SPEED transmission article.

1995-96 MAZDA MANUAL TRANSMISSIONS

Vehicle Application	Transmission Model
"B" Series Pickups	[1] M5OD
Miata	M15M-D
MX-3	F25M-R
MX-6 & 626	G25M-R
Protege	
1.5L SOHC	F25M-R
1.8L DOHC	G25M-R
RX7	R15M-D

[1] – For "B" Series Pickup models, see FORD (MAZDA) M5OD transmission article in MITCHELL® 1995-96 TRANSMISSION SERVICE & REPAIR manual for DOMESTIC CARS, LIGHT TRUCKS & VANS.

1995-96 MITSUBISHI MANUAL TRANSMISSIONS

Vehicle Application	Transmission Series
Eclipse	
2.0L Non-Turbo	F5MC1
2.0L Turbo	F5M33
2.4L	F5M31
AWD	W5M33
Expo	
FWD	
1.8L	F5M22
2.4L	F5M31
AWD	W5M33
Galant	F5M31
Mirage	
1.5L	F5M21
1.8L	F5M22
Montero (3.0L)	V5MT1-6
Pickup	
RWD (4-Cyl.)	R5M21
4WD	V5MT1-2
3000GT	
AWD	W6MG1
FWD	F5M33

1995-96 NISSAN MANUAL TRANSMISSIONS

Vehicle Application	Transmission Series
Altima	RS5F50A/V
Maxima	RS5F50A/V
Pathfinder & Pickup (3.0L)	FS5R30A
Pickup (2.4L)	FS5W71C
Sentra & 200SX	
1.6L	RS5F31A
2.0L	RS5F32V
240SX	FS5W71C
300ZX	RS5R30A

1995-96 PORSCHE MANUAL TRANSMISSIONS

Vehicle Application	Transmission Series
911 Carrera 2	G50/20 6-Speed
911 Carrera 4	[1] G64

[1] – Information not available.

1995-96 SAAB MANUAL TRANSMISSIONS

Vehicle Application	Transmission Series
900 & 9000 Series	FM5

1995-96 SUBARU MANUAL TRANSMISSIONS

Vehicle Application	Transmission Model
Impreza	
FWD	5MT-1
AWD	5MT-2
Legacy	
FWD	5MT-1
AWD	5MT-2

1995-96 SUZUKI MANUAL TRANSMISSIONS

Vehicle Application	Transmission Model
Swift	[1] Suzuki 5-Speed
Sidekick	[2] Suzuki 5-Speed
Samurai	Suzuki Samurai 5-Speed
X90	[2] Suzuki 5-Speed

[1] – See GEO METRO & SUZUKI SWIFT transmission article.
[2] – See GEO TRACKER & SUZUKI SIDEKICK transmission article.

1995-96 TOYOTA MANUAL TRANSMISSIONS

Vehicle Application	Transmission Model
Camry	
4-Cylinder	S51
V6	E53
Celica	
1.8L (7A-FE)	C52
2.2L (5S-FE)	S54
Corolla	
1.6L	C50
1.8L	C52
MR2	
Turbo (1995)	E153
Non-Turbo (1995)	S54
Paseo (1.5L)	C150
Pickup (1995)	
4-Cylinder (22R-E)	
2WD	G58 Or W55
4WD	G58 Or W56
V6	
2WD	R150
4WD	R150F
RAV4 (1996)	E250F
Supra (3.0L)	W58
T100	
2.7L 4-Cylinder	
1995	W56
1996	W59
V6	
2WD	R150
4WD	R150F

1995-96 TOYOTA MANUAL TRANSMISSIONS (Cont.)

Vehicle Application	Transmission Model
Tacoma	
1995	
2WD	R150
4WD	R150F
1996	W59
4Runner	
1995	
2.4L 4-Cylinder	G58
V6	R150F
1996	
2.7L 4-Cylinder	W59
V6	R150F
Tercel (1.5L)	
4-Speed	C141
5-Speed	C151

[1] – Overhaul information is not available.

1995-96 VOLKSWAGEN MANUAL TRANSMISSIONS

Vehicle Application	Transmission Model
4-Cylinder	
Golf III, Cabriolet & Jetta III	VAG 020
V6	
GTI VR6, Jetta & Passat	02A

1995-96 VOLVO MANUAL TRANSMISSIONS

Vehicle Application	Transmission Model
850	[1] M56

[1] – Overhaul information is not available.

Transfer Cases

1995-96 ACURA TRANSFER CASE APPLICATIONS

Vehicle Model	Transfer Case Model
SLX	See ISUZU

1995-96 GEO TRANSFER CASE APPLICATIONS

Vehicle Application	Transfer Case Model
Geo & Suzuki	[1]

[1] – Transfer case model number is not available.

1995-96 HONDA TRANSFER CASE APPLICATIONS

Vehicle Model	Transfer Case Model
Passport	See ISUZU

1995-96 LEXUS TRANSFER CASE APPLICATIONS

Vehicle Application	Transfer Case Model
LX450	Toyota HF2AV

1995-96 MAZDA TRANSFER CASE APPLICATIONS

Vehicle Application	Transfer Case Model
MPV	RA4AX-EL
Pickup Models	[1] BW 1354

[1] – See article in MITCHELL® 1995-96 TRANSMISSION SERVICE & REPAIR manual for DOMESTIC CARS, LIGHT TRUCKS & VANS.

1995-96 MITSUBISHI TRANSFER CASE APPLICATIONS

Vehicle Application	Transfer Case Model
Montero	[1]
Pickup	[1]

[1] – Transfer case model number not available from manufacturer.

1995-96 NISSAN TRANSFER CASE APPLICATIONS

Vehicle Application	Transfer Case Model
Pathfinder	TX-10A
Pickup	TX-10A

1995-96 SUZUKI TRANSFER CASE APPLICATIONS

Vehicle Application	Transfer Case Model
Samurai	1
Sidekick	1
X90	1

1 – Transfer case model number not available.

1995-96 TOYOTA TRANSFER CASE APPLICATIONS

Vehicle Application	Transfer Case Model
Land Cruiser	HF2AV
Pickup, Tacoma, T100 & 4Runner	
Automatic Transmission	
A340F	
1995	VF1A
1996	1
A340H	2
Manual Transmission	
G58	RF1A
R150F	VF1A
W59	3
Previa	TF1AV
RAV4	
With A/T	4 A540H
With M/T	4 E250F

1 – A340F is available on 1996 Tacoma and 4Runner with One-Touch 2-4 Selector System. No additional transfer case model number is available.

2 – A340H is only available on 1995 4Runner. A340H is only available with 2-speed electronically controlled transfer case. No additional transfer case model number is available.

3 – W59 is available on 1996 Tacoma and 4Runner with One-Touch 2-4 Selector System. No additional transfer case model number is available.

4 – Transmission code, transfer case model code not available.

Computer Relearn Procedures

INTRODUCTION

Vehicles equipped with engine or transmission computers may require a relearn procedure after the vehicle battery is disconnected. Many vehicle computers memorize and store vehicle operation patterns for optimum driveability and performance. When the vehicle battery is disconnected, this memory is lost. The computer will use default data until new data from each key start is stored. As the computer memorizes vehicle operation for each new key start, driveability is restored. Vehicle computers may memorize vehicles operation patterns for 40 or more key starts.

Customers often complain of driveability problems during the relearn stage because the vehicle acts differently then before being serviced. Depending on the type and make of vehicle and how it is equipped, the following complaints (driveability problems) may exist:

• Harsh Or Poor Shift Quality
• Rough Or Unstable Idle
• Hesitation Or Stumble
• Rich Or Lean Running
• Poor Fuel Mileage

These symptoms and complaints should disappear after a number of drive cycles have been memorized. To reduce the possibility of complaints, after any service which requires battery power to be disconnected, vehicle should be road tested. If a specific relearn procedure is not available, the following procedure may be used:

Automatic Transmission

• Set parking brake, and start engine in "P" or "N" position. Warm-up vehicle to normal operating temperature or until cooling fan cycles.
• Allow vehicle to idle for one minute in "N" position. Select "D" and allow engine to idle for one minute.
• Accelerate at normal throttle position (20-50%) until vehicle shifts into top gear.
• Cruise at light to medium throttle.
• Decelerate to a stop, allowing vehicle to downshift, and use brakes normally.
• Process may be repeated as necessary.

Manual Transmission

• Place transmission in Neutral position.
• Ensure the emergency brake has been set and all accessories are turned off.
• Start engine and bring to normal operating temperature.
• Allow vehicle to idle in Neutral for one minute.
• Initial relearn is complete; process will be completed during normal driving.

Some manufacturers identify a specific relearn procedure which will help establish suitable driveability during the relearn stage. These procedures are especially important if the vehicle is equipped with an electronically controlled automatic transmission or transaxle. Always complete the procedure before returning the vehicle to the customer.

APPLICATIONS & IDENTIFICATION
Gear Tooth Contact Patterns

The following chart should be used when adjusting differential gears for correct contact pattern. Always follow manufacturers procedures and specifications to establish correct preload and end play.

➡ :ADJUSTING DIRECTION OF DRIVE PINION   ⇨ :ADJUSTING DIRECTION DIRECTION OF RING GEAR

CONDITION	CONTACT PATTERN	CORRECTIVE ACTION
CORRECT TOOTH CONTACT. Tooth contact pattern slightly shifted toward toe under no-load rotation. (When loaded, contact pattern moves toward heel)	Toe Side 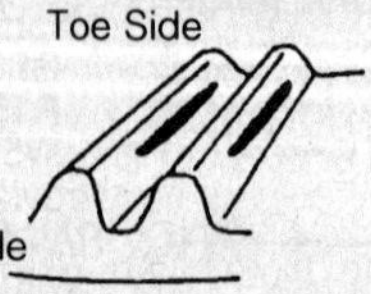 / Heel Side	
FACE CONTACT Backlash is too small.	 This may cause noise and chipping at tooth ends.	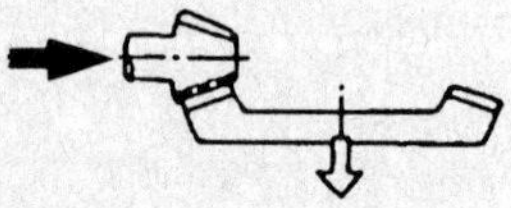 Increase thickness of drive pinion height adjusting shim in order to move drive pinion closer to ring gear.
FLANK CONTACT Backlash is too small.	 This may cause noise and stepped wear on tooth surface	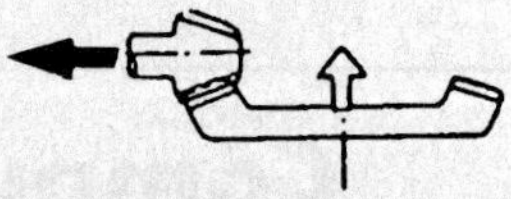 Decrease thickness of drive pinion height adjusting shim in order to move drive pinion away from ring gear.
TOE CONTACT Contact only at inside end.	 Contact area is too small. This may cause chipping at toe ends.	Procedure same as FLANK CONTACT. 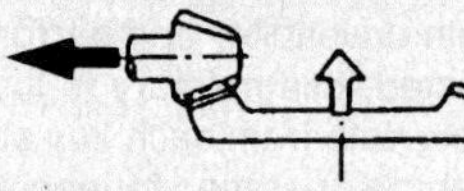
HEEL CONTACT Contact only at outside.	Contact area is too small. This may cause chipping at heel ends. 	Procedure same as FACE CONTACT. 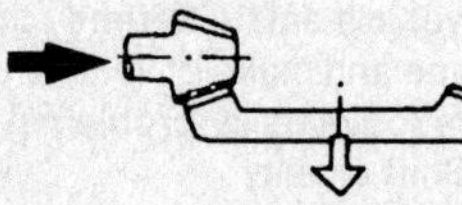

Courtesy of Subaru of America, Inc.

Gear Tooth Contact Patterns

WARNING: To avoid injury from accidental air bag deployment, read and carefully follow all SERVICE PRECAUTIONS and DISABLING & ACTIVATING AIR BAG SYSTEM procedures.

NOTE: References to SRS and SIR by manufacturers refer to Supplemental Restraint Systems (SRS) and Supplemental Inflatable Restraints (SIR).

SPECIAL CARE DURING MECHANICAL REPAIRS

NOTE: For information on air bag DIAGNOSIS & TESTING or DISPOSAL PROCEDURES, see MITCHELL® AIR BAG SERVICE & REPAIR MANUAL, DOMESTIC & IMPORTED MODELS.

Observe manufacturer service precautions when working on a vehicle equipped with an air bag system. See appropriate manufacturer's SERVICE PRECAUTIONS.

Electrical sources should never be allowed near inflator on back of air bag module. Never probe air bag system electrical wires with analog volt-ohmmeter or test light. Always disable air bag system before servicing vehicle. See appropriate DISABLING & ACTIVATING AIR BAG SYSTEM procedure. Failure to do so could result in accidental air bag deployment and possible personal injury.

If air bag system is not fully functional for any reason, DO NOT drive vehicle until system is repaired and is again operational. DO NOT remove bulbs, modules, sensors or other components, or in any way disable system from operating normally. If air bag system is not functional, park vehicle until system is repaired and functions properly.

ACURA

NOTE: For Acura SLX information see ISUZU Trooper.

SYSTEM OPERATION CHECK

When ignition is turned on, SRS indicator light should come on for about 6 seconds and then go off. While vehicle is driven, light should not come on or flash. If SRS indicator light does not operate as specified, system must be inspected/repaired as soon as possible.

SERVICE PRECAUTIONS

Observe these precautions when working with air bag systems and seat belt pretensioners (if equipped):

- Disable SRS before servicing any SRS or steering column component. Failure to do this could result in accidental air bag deployment, possibly causing personal injury. See DISABLING & ACTIVATING AIR BAG SYSTEM.
- Wait about 3 minutes after disabling air bag system. A back-up power circuit capacitor (in SRS control unit) maintains system voltage for about 3 minutes after battery is disconnected. Servicing air bag system or seat belt pretensioners before 3 minutes may cause accidental deployment and possible personal injury.
- After an accident, all SRS components, including wiring harness and brackets, must be inspected. If any components are damaged or bent, they must be replaced, even if air bag did not deploy. Check steering column, knee bolster, instrument panel steering column reinforcement plate and lower brace for damage. DO NOT service/repair any component or wiring. If components or wiring are damaged or defective, replacement is required.
- Always wear safety glasses when servicing SRS or handling an air bag or seat belt pretensioner (if equipped).
- DO NOT attempt to disassemble air bag assembly or seat belt pretensioner (if equipped). Neither component has any serviceable or reusable parts.
- A replacement air bag assembly must be stored in its original special container until used for service. Special container must be stored in a clean, dry place, away from sources of extreme heat, sparks and high electrical energy.

- When placing a live air bag assembly on a bench or other surface, always face air bag and trim cover up, away from surface. This will reduce motion of air bag assembly if accidentally deployed.
- After deployment, air bag assembly is very hot. Wait 30 minutes before handling.
- After deployment, air bag surface may contain deposits of sodium azide and potassium nitrate, which can irritate skin. Always wear safety glasses, rubber gloves and long-sleeved shirt during clean-up, and wash hands using mild soap and water. Follow correct disposal procedures.
- DO NOT allow any electrical source near inflator on back of air bag assembly or near 3-pin connector of seat belt pretensioner.
- When carrying a live air bag assembly, trim cover pad should be pointed away from your body to minimize injury in case of accidental air bag deployment.
- DO NOT probe any wire through insulator; this will damage wire and eventually cause failure due to corrosion.
- When performing electrical tests, always use test harnesses recommended by manufacturer. DO NOT connect tester probes directly to component connector pins or wires.
- DO NOT use any type of electrical equipment other than that specified by manufacturer.
- If SRS is not fully functional for any reason, vehicle should not be driven until system is repaired. DO NOT remove any component or in any way disable system from operating normally. If SRS is not functional, park vehicle until repairs can be made.

DISABLING & ACTIVATING AIR BAG SYSTEM

WARNING: Wait about 3 minutes after disabling air bag system. A back-up power circuit capacitor (in SRS control unit) maintains system voltage for about 3 minutes after battery is disconnected. Servicing air bag system before 3 minutes may cause accidental air bag deployment, possibly causing personal injury.

Disabling Driver-Side Air Bag (Integra) – 1) Turn ignition off. Disconnect both battery cables. Remove access panel from steering wheel. *See Fig. 1.* Remove Red short connector from holder on access panel. **2)** Disconnect air bag connector from cable reel connector. Connect Red short connector to air bag connector. Driver-side air bag is now disabled. Disable passenger-side air bag.

WARNING: If SRS Red short connectors are not properly installed, static electricity can deploy air bags and seat belt pretensioners (if equipped).

Disabling Passenger-Side Air Bag (Integra) – Remove glove box. Disconnect harness connector from passenger-side air bag connector. Connect Red short connector to passenger-side air bag connector. *See Fig. 2.* Passenger-side air bag is now disabled.

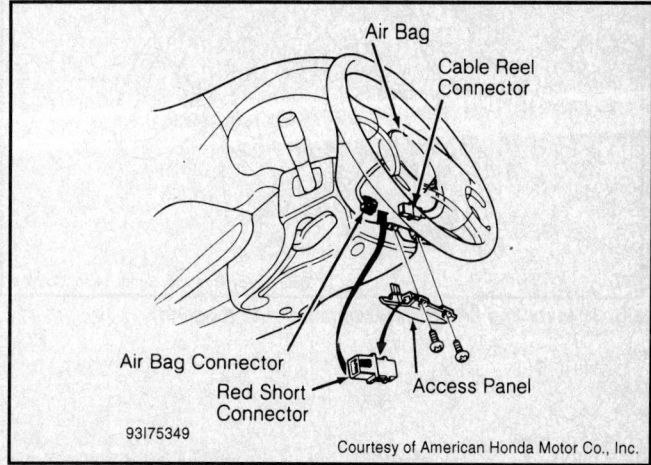

93I75349

Courtesy of American Honda Motor Co., Inc.

Fig. 1: Disabling Driver-Side Air Bag (Integra)

Activating System (Integra) – Ensure ignition switch is in OFF position and both battery cables are disconnected. Remove Red short connector(s) installed during DISABLING SYSTEM. Install Red short connector(s) in holder(s). Reconnect connectors as necessary. Install access panel to steering wheel (install glove box as necessary). Reconnect battery cables. Ensure system is functioning properly. See SYSTEM OPERATION CHECK.

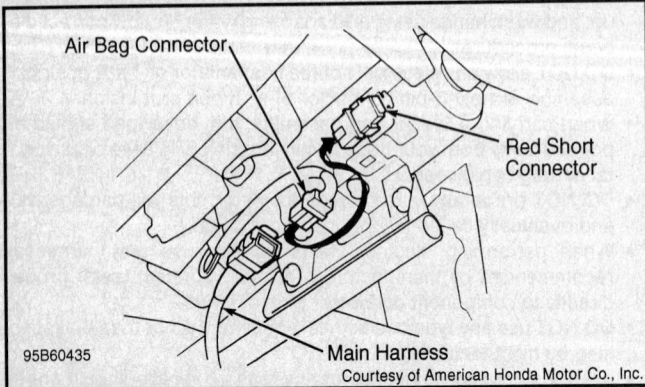

Fig. 2: Disabling Passenger-Side Air Bag (Integra)

Disabling System (Legend) – **1)** Ensure ignition switch is in OFF position. Disconnect both battery cables. From bottom rear of steering wheel and below air bag assembly, remove access panel. Remove Red short connector from access panel.

2) Disconnect driver-side air bag connector from cable reel connector. Connect Red short connector to driver-side air bag connector. See Fig. 3. Connect SRS Short Connector "A" (07MAZ-SP0020A) to cable reel connector.

3) Remove glove box. Disconnect passenger-side air bag connector from SRS main harness. Connect passenger-side air bag connector to Red short connector. See Fig. 4. Connect another SRS short connector "A" to SRS main harness 3-pin connector.

4) Access both seat belt pretensioner connectors. Locate and remove Red short connector from connector holder on seat belt pretensioner. See Fig. 5. Disconnect SRS seat belt pretensioner harness connector. Install SRS Red short connector to SRS seat belt pretensioner connector.

5) Cover seat belt pretensioner harness connector to keep terminals clean. Repeat procedure for remaining seat belt pretensioner. SRS is disabled when all Red short connectors are installed to both air bags and both seat belt pretensioners.

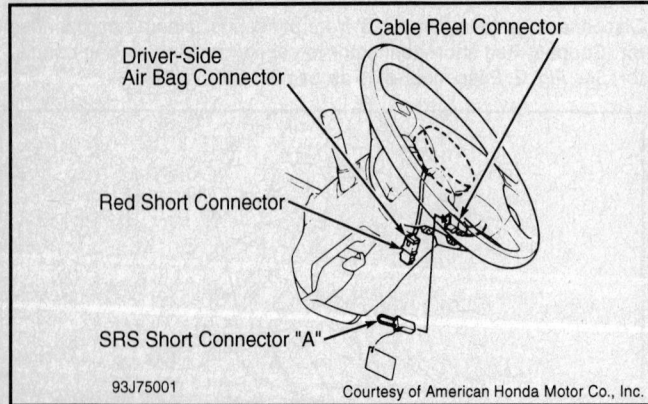

Fig. 3: Installing SRS Short Connector "A" (Legend)

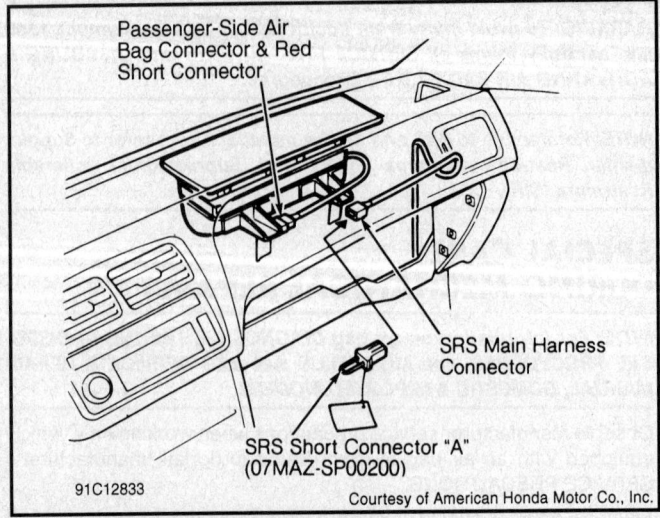

Fig. 4: Installing Short Connector "A"
To SRS Main Harness (Legend)

Activating System (Legend) – **1)** Ensure ignition switch is in OFF position and both battery cables are disconnected. Remove SRS short connector "A" from passenger-side air bag SRS main harness connector.

2) Remove passenger-side air bag connector from Red short connector in connector holder. Reconnect passenger-side air bag connector to SRS main harness connector. Reinstall glove box.

3) Remove Red short connectors from seat belt pretensioners, and install Red short connectors to their holders. See Fig. 5. Reconnect harness connectors to seat belt pretensioner connectors. Reinstall quarter trim panels ("B" pillar trim panels on Sedan).

4) Remove Red short connector from driver-side air bag connector. Remove SRS short connector "A" from cable reel connector. Reconnect driver-side air bag connector to cable reel connector. Install short connector to access panel. Reinstall access panel to steering wheel.

5) Reconnect battery. Check SRS indicator light to ensure system is functioning properly. See SYSTEM OPERATION CHECK.

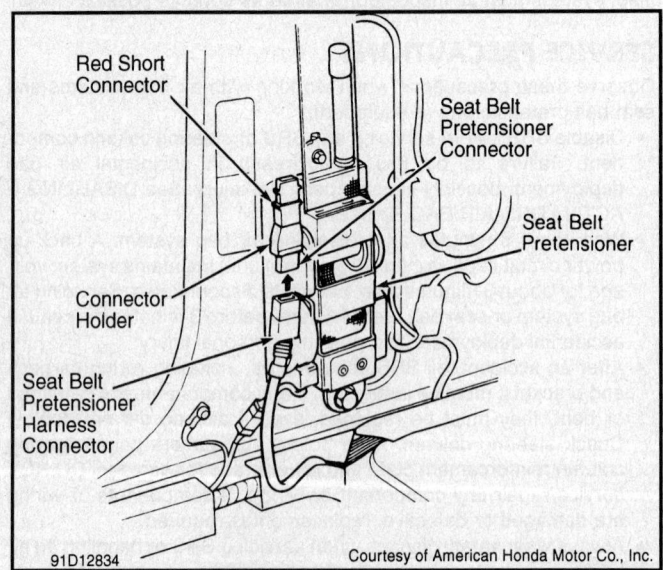

Fig. 5: Locating Seat Belt Pretensioner Short Connector (Legend)

Disabling System (2.5TL & 3.2TL) – **1)** Ensure ignition switch is in OFF position. Disconnect both battery cables. From bottom rear of steering wheel and below air bag assembly, remove access panel.

2) Disconnect driver-side air bag connector from cable reel connector. Driver-side air bag is now disabled. Remove glove box. Remove Red short connector from holder. Disconnect passenger-side air bag connector from SRS main harness. Connect passenger-side air bag connector to Red short connector. See Fig. 6. Passenger-side air bag is now disabled.

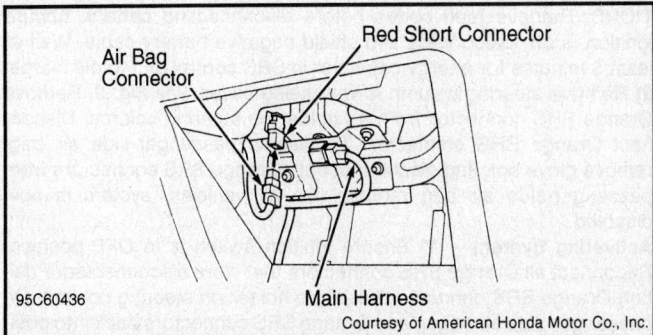

95C60436
Courtesy of American Honda Motor Co., Inc.

Fig. 6: Disabling Passenger-Side Air Bag Module (2.5TL & 3.2TL)

Activating System (2.5TL & 3.2TL) – Ensure ignition switch is in OFF position and both battery cables are disconnected. Remove Red short connector installed during DISABLING SYSTEM. Install Red short connector into holder. Reconnect connectors as necessary. Install access panel to steering wheel. Install glove box. Reconnect battery cables. Ensure system is functioning properly. See SYSTEM OPERATION CHECK.

AUDI

SYSTEM OPERATION CHECK

Turn ignition switch to ON position. AIRBAG indicator light should come on for about 10 seconds and then go out. If light flashes and then remains on, control unit has detected a system fault. If light does not glow, check bulb. If bulb is okay, diagnose air bag system. See MITCHELL® AIR BAG SERVICE & REPAIR MANUAL, DOMESTIC & IMPORTED MODELS.

SERVICE PRECAUTIONS

Observe these precautions when working with air bag systems:

- Before disconnecting battery cable(s) and disabling air bag system, obtain radio security code from vehicle owner.
- Before installing computer memory saver on vehicles with electronic radio lock, disconnect air bag voltage supply connector. See DISABLING & ACTIVATING AIR BAG SYSTEM. Failure to do so may cause air bag activation.
- Disable air bag system before servicing any air bag system or steering column component. See DISABLING & ACTIVATING AIR BAG SYSTEM.
- Because of critical operating requirements of system, DO NOT attempt to service any air bag system component.
- DO NOT leave air bag parts unattended. Install air bag parts in vehicle immediately after they are obtained.
- DO NOT use air bag components that have been dropped from heights of approximately 20" or higher.
- DO NOT allow chemical cleaners, oil or grease to contact vinyl covering on air bag unit.
- DO NOT place stickers or covers on steering wheel.
- Disable SRS before performing electric welding on vehicle.
- DO NOT expose air bag unit to temperatures greater than 212°F (100°C).

DISABLING & ACTIVATING AIR BAG SYSTEM

NOTE: *On 1996 A6 models with AIRBAG III system, the single-pin air bag voltage supply connector has been eliminated. It is only necessary to disconnect negative battery cable.*

1) Disconnect and shield negative battery cable. Disconnect air bag voltage supply connector. On A4, Cabriolet and 90, voltage supply connector is located on a clip behind inspection cover, on driver-side lower instrument panel cover. See Fig. 7.

2) On 1995 A6, connector is located in passenger-side footwell, above electronic box (marked with a warning tag). See Fig. 8. Driver-side air bag is now disabled. To disable passenger-side air bag, disconnect passenger-side air bag voltage supply connector(s). Passenger-side air bag is now disabled.

3) To activate system, reconnect negative battery cable and voltage supply connector. Perform system operation check to ensure system is functioning properly. See SYSTEM OPERATION CHECK.

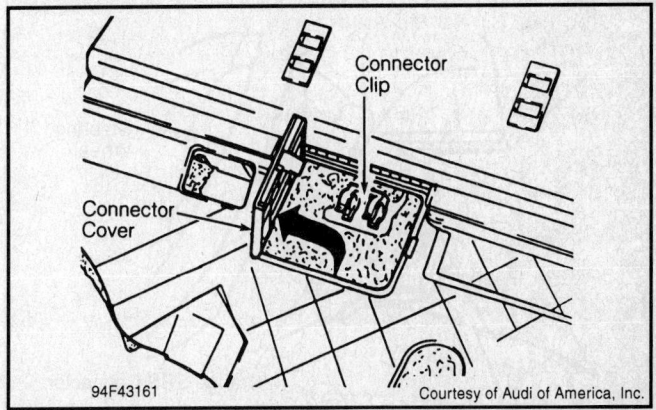

94F43161
Courtesy of Audi of America, Inc.

Fig. 7: Locating Voltage Supply Connector (A4, Cabriolet & 90)

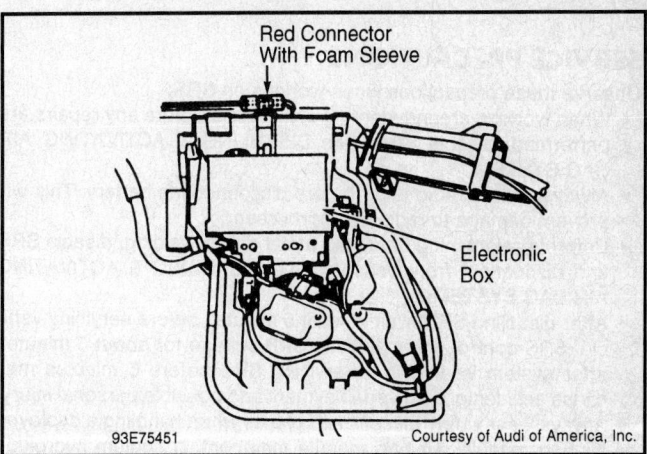

93E75451
Courtesy of Audi of America, Inc.

Fig. 8: Locating Voltage Supply Connector (1995 A6)

BMW

SYSTEM OPERATION CHECK

Turn ignition switch to ON position. If SRS warning light does not come on, SRS warning light bulb or circuit is faulty. If SRS warning light comes on and then goes out after about 6 seconds, SRS is okay at this time. If SRS warning light does not respond as specified, SRS is malfunctioning and must be repaired.

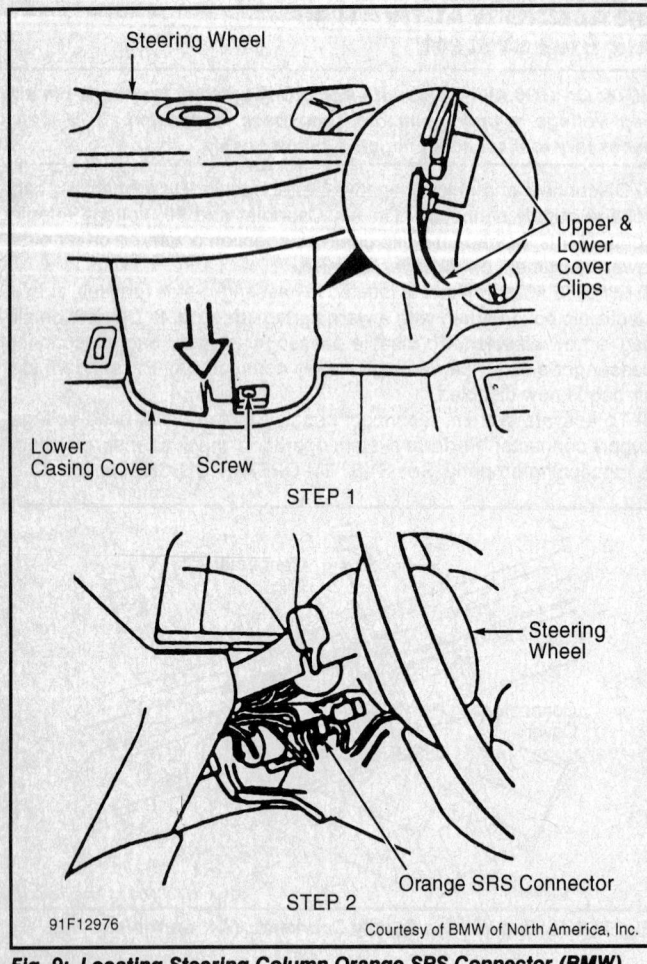

STEP 1

Labels: Steering Wheel; Upper & Lower Cover Clips; Lower Casing Cover; Screw

STEP 2

Labels: Steering Wheel; Orange SRS Connector

91F12976   Courtesy of BMW of North America, Inc.

Fig. 9: Locating Steering Column Orange SRS Connector (BMW)

SERVICE PRECAUTIONS

Observe these precautions when working on SRS:

- When working around steering column and before any repairs are performed, disable SRS. See DISABLING & ACTIVATING AIR BAG SYSTEM.
- Always ensure radio is off before disconnecting battery. This will prevent damage to radio microprocessor.
- Before straightening damaged metal or arc-welding, disable SRS and disconnect front sensors. See DISABLING & ACTIVATING AIR BAG SYSTEM.
- After disabling SRS, wait at least 5 minutes before servicing vehicle. SRS control unit maintains SRS voltage for about 5 minutes after system is disabled. Servicing SRS before 5 minutes may cause accidental air bag deployment and possible personal injury.
- Always wear safety glasses and gloves when handling a deployed air bag module. Air bag module may contain sodium hydroxide deposits, which irritates skin.
- Handle sensors carefully. Never strike or jar sensors. All sensors and mounting bracket bolts must be tightened to specification to ensure proper sensor operation.
- Never use any SRS component that has been dropped from 2 feet or higher.
- DO NOT repair any part of SRS wiring harness.
- Always handle air bag module with trim cover away from your body. Always place air bag module on workbench with trim cover up, away from loose objects.
- Never expose SRS components to temperatures greater than 212°F (100°C).
- Never expose any SRS system components to cleaning agents such as solvents, gasoline, lye, etc.

DISABLING & ACTIVATING AIR BAG SYSTEM

WARNING: After disabling system, wait at least 5 minutes before servicing vehicle. Energy capacitor in SRS control unit maintains system voltage for about 5 minutes after system is disabled. Servicing system before 5 minutes may cause accidental air bag deployment and possible personal injury.

Disabling System – 1) Before proceeding, see SERVICE PRECAUTIONS. Retrieve fault codes before disconnecting battery. Ensure ignition is off. Disconnect and shield negative battery cable. Wait at least 5 minutes for energy capacitor in SRS control unit to discharge. 2) Remove steering column lower casing cover. *See Fig. 9.* Remove Orange SRS connector from its holder on steering column. Disconnect Orange SRS connector. To disable passenger-side air bag, remove glove box and disconnect both Orange SRS connectors from passenger-side air bag module. On all vehicles, system is now disabled.

Activating System – 1) Ensure ignition switch is in OFF position. Reconnect all Orange SRS connectors that were disconnected. Position Orange SRS connector back into holder on steering column. On passenger-side air bag, place Orange SRS connectors back into position near passenger air bag module. Install glove box. 2) On all models, install steering column lower casing cover. Connect negative battery cable. System is now activated. Perform system operation check to ensure system is functioning properly and no fault codes are set. See SYSTEM OPERATION CHECK.

CHRYSLER CORP. & MITSUBISHI
SYSTEM OPERATION CHECK

WARNING: After servicing vehicle, turn ignition on from outside of vehicle (driver side).

Turn ignition on. SRS warning light on instrument panel should come on for about 7 seconds then turn off. This indicates SRS is functioning properly. If SRS warning light does not come on, stays on, or comes on while driving, SRS is malfunctioning and needs repair. See MITCHELL® AIR BAG SERVICE & REPAIR MANUAL, DOMESTIC & IMPORTED MODELS.

SERVICE PRECAUTIONS

Observe the following precautions when working with SRS:

- Disable SRS before servicing any SRS or steering column component. Failure to do this may result in accidental air bag deployment and possible personal injury. See DISABLING & ACTIVATING AIR BAG SYSTEM.
- For about 60 seconds after air bag system is disabled, it retains enough voltage to deploy air bags. After disabling system, wait at least 60 seconds before servicing.
- After servicing, check SRS warning light to verify system operation. See SYSTEM OPERATION CHECK.
- Always wear safety glasses when servicing or handling an air bag.
- The SRS Diagnostic Unit (SDU) must be stored in its original special container until used for service. It must be stored in a clean, dry place, away from sources of extreme heat, sparks and high electrical energy.
- DO NOT expose air bag module and clockspring to temperatures greater than 200°F (93°C).
- When placing a live air bag module on a bench or other surface, always face air bag module and trim cover up, away from surface. This will reduce motion of module if air bag accidentally deploys.
- After air bag deploys, air bag surface may contain deposits of sodium hydroxide, which irritates skin. Always wear safety glasses, rubber gloves and long-sleeved shirt during clean-up. Wash hands using mild soap and water. Follow correct clean-up and disposal procedures.

- Because of critical system operating requirements, DO NOT service any SRS components. Repairs are only made by replacing defective part(s).
- DO NOT allow any electrical source near inflator on the back of air bag module.
- When carrying a live (undeployed) air bag module, trim cover must be pointed away from body to minimize injury in case of accidental air bag deployment.
- DO NOT probe a wire through insulator, as this will damage it and eventually cause failure due to corrosion.
- If SRS is not fully functional for any reason, DO NOT drive vehicle until system is repaired and is fully functional. DO NOT remove bulbs, modules, sensors or other components, or in any way disable system from operating normally. If SRS is not functional, park vehicle until repairs are made.

DISABLING & ACTIVATING AIR BAG SYSTEM

WARNING: SRS system voltage is maintained for about 60 seconds after battery cable is disconnected. After disconnecting battery cable, wait at least 60 seconds before servicing SRS. Failure to wait may cause accidental air bag deployment and possible personal injury.

To disable system, turn ignition switch to LOCK position. Disconnect negative battery cable. Shield cable end. Wait at least 60 seconds before servicing vehicle. To activate system, reconnect negative battery cable.

FORD MOTOR CO.

SYSTEM OPERATION CHECK

1) Turn ignition switch to RUN position. If AIR BAG warning light glows 4-8 seconds and then goes out, SRS is functioning properly and no fault codes exist.
2) If a fault code is detected in SRS during initial system check, AIR BAG warning light will fail to light, stay on continuously or flash a code sequence. If AIR BAG warning light flashes, indicating a fault in system, count number of flashes after fault code has cycled twice. Number of flashes represents a code number used to diagnose SRS.
3) If a system fault code exists and AIR BAG warning light fails to light, an audible tone will be heard indicating AIR BAG warning light is out and service is required.

SERVICE PRECAUTIONS

These precautions should be observed when working with SRS:
- Disable SRS before servicing any SRS or steering column components. Failure to do so may result in accidental air bag deployment and personal injury. See DISABLING & ACTIVATING AIR BAG SYSTEM.
- Wait one minute after disabling SRS before working on vehicle. Back-up power supply holds a deployment charge for approximately one minute after positive battery cable is disconnected. Servicing SRS before one minute may cause accidental air bag deployment and possible personal injury.
- Because of critical system operating requirements, DO NOT service impact sensors, clockspring, diagnostic monitor or air bag modules. Repairs are made by replacement only.
- Always wear safety glasses whenever servicing an air bag equipped vehicle or handling an air bag.
- When carrying a live air bag module, ensure air bag module and trim cover are pointed away from your body. This minimizes chance of injury in the event of an accidental deployment.
- When placing a live air bag module on a bench or other surface, always face air bag module and trim cover facing up, away from surface. This will reduce motion of module if it is accidentally deployed.

- After deployment, air bag surface may contain deposits of sodium hydroxide, which may irritate skin. Sodium hydroxide is a product of gas generant combustion. Always wear gloves and safety glasses when handling a deployed air bag. Wash your hands using mild soap and water. Follow correct disposal procedures.
- If scrapping a vehicle with an undeployed air bag module, air bag must be deployed.
- Never probe connectors on air bag module. Doing so may cause air bag deployment and/or personal injury.
- Instruction to disconnect always refers to connector. DO NOT remove component from vehicle if instructed to disconnect.
- After any servicing, ensure AIR BAG warning light does not indicate any fault codes. See SYSTEM OPERATION CHECK.
- Replace air bag module if trim cover (deployment doors) is marred or damaged. DO NOT repaint trim cover; paint may degrade cover material. Replace air bag module as necessary.

DISABLING & ACTIVATING AIR BAG SYSTEM

WARNING: Wait one minute after disabling SRS before working on vehicle. Back-up power supply holds a deployment charge for approximately one minute after positive battery cable is disconnected. Servicing SRS before one minute may cause accidental air bag deployment and possible personal injury.

Disabling System – Disconnect negative and then positive battery cables. Shield both cables. SRS contains a back-up power supply built into air bag diagnostic monitor. Wait at least one minute before servicing any air bag components. System is now disabled. To activate SRS, see ACTIVATING SYSTEM.

WARNING: Disabling procedure should be used for vehicle servicing or component replacement purposes only. If vehicle was involved in a collision and air bag did not deploy or if SRS is not functioning properly, and if vehicle needs to be driven, complete system deactivation is required. For information on COMPLETE SYSTEM DEACTIVATION, see MITCHELL® AIR BAG SERVICE & REPAIR MANUAL, DOMESTIC & IMPORTED MODELS.

Activating System – Connect positive and negative battery cables. System is now activated. From outside of vehicle (driver side), turn ignition switch to RUN position. Check AIR BAG warning light for system fault codes. Perform system operation check to ensure SRS is functioning properly. See SYSTEM OPERATION CHECK.

GEO

SYSTEM OPERATION CHECK

On Prizm, if system is functioning normally, AIR BAG indicator light should light steadily for about 6 seconds when ignition switch is first turned to ACC or ON position. On Metro and Tracker, if system is functioning normally, AIR BAG indicator should flash 7 times. If AIR BAG indicator light does not function as described, service air bag system. See MITCHELL® AIR BAG SERVICE & REPAIR MANUAL, DOMESTIC & IMPORTED MODELS.

SERVICE PRECAUTIONS

These precautions should be observed when working with SIR systems:
- Disable SIR system before servicing any SIR system or steering column component. Failure to do this could result in accidental air bag deployment and possible personal injury. See DISABLING & ACTIVATING AIR BAG SYSTEM.
- Wait about 2 minutes after disabling SIR system before servicing vehicle. System maintains SIR system voltage for about 2 minutes. Servicing SIR system before 2 minutes have passed may cause accidental air bag deployment and possible personal injury.
- After repairs, ensure AIR BAG indicator light is working properly and no system faults are indicated. See SYSTEM OPERATION CHECK.

- Always wear safety glasses when servicing or handling an air bag.
- Inflator module must be stored in its original special container until used for service. It must be stored in a clean, dry place, away from sources of extreme heat, sparks or high electrical energy.
- When placing a live inflator module (air bag module) on a bench or other surface, always face air bag and trim cover up, away from surface. This will reduce motion of module if accidentally deployed.
- After deployment, air bag surface may contain deposits of sodium hydroxide, which can irritate skin. Always wear safety glasses, rubber gloves and long-sleeved shirt during clean-up, and wash hands using mild soap and water. Follow correct disposal procedures.
- At no time should any electrical source be allowed near inflator or back of inflator module.
- When carrying a live inflator module, trim cover should be pointed away from your body to minimize injury in case of accidental deployment.
- DO NOT probe a wire through insulator; this will damage wire and eventually cause failure due to corrosion.
- If SIR system is not fully functional for any reason, vehicle should not be driven until system is repaired. DO NOT remove bulbs, modules, sensors or other components or in any way disable system from operating normally. If SIR system is not functional, park vehicle until repairs can be made.

DISABLING & ACTIVATING AIR BAG SYSTEM

WARNING: Wait about 10 minutes after disabling SIR system before servicing. System maintains SIR system voltage for about 10 minutes. Servicing SIR system before 10 minutes have passed may cause accidental air bag deployment and possible personal injury.

Metro & Tracker – 1) Remove AIR BAG-IG fuse from fuse block near base of steering column. Remove steering wheel side cover. Remove Connector Position Assurance (CPA) clip and disconnect Yellow 2-pin SIR lower steering column connector.
2) Remove glove box assembly. Remove Connector Position Assurance (CPA) clip and disconnect Yellow 4-pin SIR passenger inflator module connector.

NOTE: When AIR BAG-IG fuse is removed and ignition switch is ON, AIR BAG indicator light will remain ON. This is normal operation and does not indicate a SIR system malfunction.

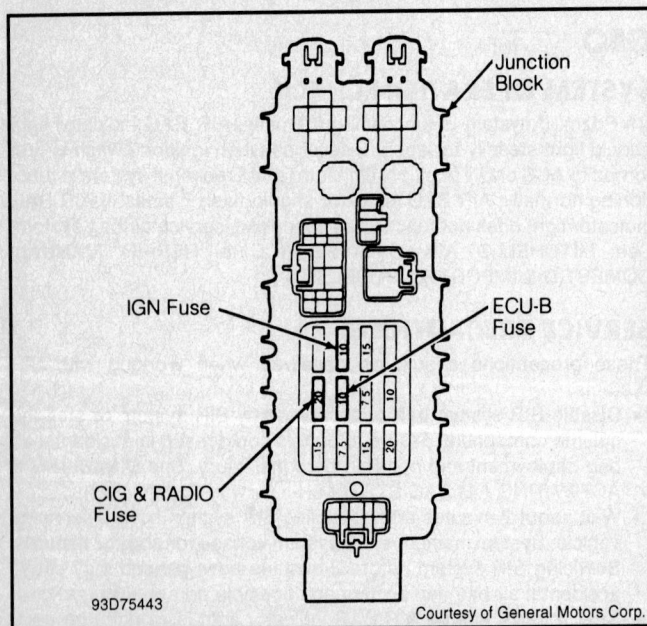

Fig. 10: Locating IGN, CIG & RADIO Fuses (Prizm)

3) To activate SIR system, turn ignition switch to LOCK position. Connect 4-pin connector and CPA clip behind glove box. Reinstall glove box. Connect 2-pin connector and CPA clip at base of steering column. Install AIR BAG-IG fuse into fuse block. Turn ignition switch to ON and ensure AIR BAG indicator light flashes 7 times, then turns off.

Prizm – 1) Ensure front wheels face straight ahead. Turn ignition switch to LOCK. Remove IGN fuse, and CIG and RADIO fuse from junction block. *See Fig. 10.* Remove Connector Position Assurance (CPA) clip and disconnect Yellow 2-pin SIR lower steering column connector. *See Fig. 11.*
2) Open glove box door. Carefully pry off passenger inflator module connector retainer. *See Fig. 12.* Remove Connector Position Assurance (CPA) clip and disconnect Yellow 2-pin SIR passenger inflator module connector.
3) To activate SIR system, turn ignition switch to LOCK position. Connect 2-pin connector and CPA clip at base of steering column and behind glove box. Install IGN, CIG and RADIO fuses to junction block. Turn ignition switch to ACC or ON and ensure air bag indicator illuminates steady for approximately 6 seconds, then turns off.

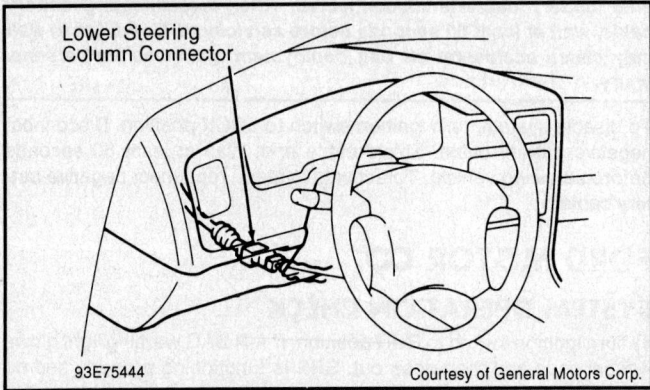

Fig. 11: Locating 2-Pin Lower Steering Column Connector (Prizm)

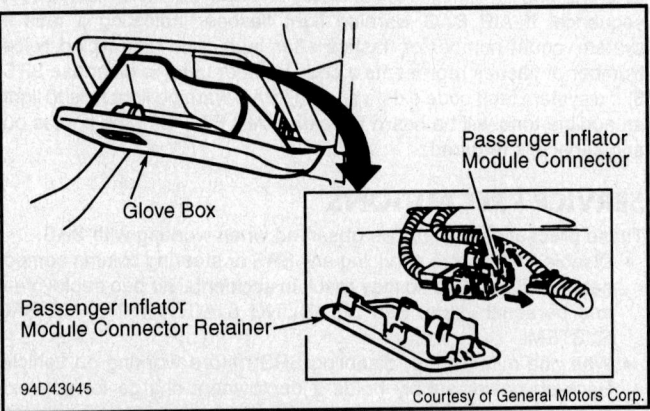

Fig. 12: Locating Passenger Inflator Module 2-Pin Connector (Prizm)

HONDA

NOTE: For Honda Passport information see ISUZU Rodeo.

SYSTEM OPERATION CHECK

When ignition is turned on, SRS indicator light will glow for about 6 seconds and then go off. If indicator does not glow, does not go off after about 6 seconds or glows while driving, system must be inspected as soon as possible. See MITCHELL® AIR BAG SERVICE & REPAIR MANUAL, DOMESTIC & IMPORTED MODELS.

SERVICE PRECAUTIONS

NOTE: On vehicles with radio theft protection system, obtain 5-digit stereo security code from vehicle owner before disconnecting battery cable.

Observe these precautions when working with air bag systems:

- Disable SRS before servicing any SRS or steering column component. Failure to do this could result in accidental air bag deployment and possible personal injury. See DISABLING & ACTIVATING AIR BAG SYSTEM.
- After an accident, all SRS components, including harness and brackets, must be inspected. If any components are damaged or bent, they must be replaced, even if a deployment did not occur. Check steering column, knee bolster, instrument panel steering column reinforcement plate and lower brace for damage. DO NOT service any component or wiring. If components or wiring are damaged or defective, replacement is necessary. DO NOT use components from another vehicle. Only use new replacement parts.
- After repairs, turn ignition on while ensuring any accidental air bag deployment will not cause injury. Ensure SRS indicator light is working properly and no system faults are indicated. See SYSTEM OPERATION CHECK.
- Always wear safety glasses when servicing or handling an air bag.
- Air bag module must be stored in its original special container until used for service. It must be stored in a clean, dry place, away from sources of extreme heat, sparks and high electrical energy.
- When placing a live air bag module on a bench or other surface, always face air bag and trim cover up, away from surface. This will reduce motion of module if it is accidentally deployed.
- After deployment, air bag surface may contain deposits of sodium hydroxide, which can irritate skin. Always wear safety glasses, rubber gloves and long-sleeved shirt during clean-up, and wash hands using mild soap and water. Follow correct disposal procedures.
- NEVER allow any electrical source near inflator on back of air bag module.
- When carrying a live air bag module, trim cover should be pointed away from your body to minimize injury in case of deployment.
- DO NOT probe a wire through insulator; this will damage wire and eventually cause failure due to corrosion.
- When performing electrical tests, always use SRS test harnesses recommended by manufacturer. DO NOT use test probes directly on component connector pins or wires.
- When installing SRS wiring harnesses, ensure they will not be pinched or interfere with other vehicle components.
- Inspect all ground connections. Ensure they are clean and tight.
- DO NOT use any type of electrical equipment not specified by manufacturer.
- If SRS is not fully functional for any reason, vehicle should not be driven until system is repaired. DO NOT remove any component or in any way disable system from operating normally. If SRS is not functional, park vehicle until repairs can be made.

DISABLING & ACTIVATING AIR BAG SYSTEM

NOTE: Passenger-side air bag modules in 1996 models, DO NOT require a separate short connector. Module is automatically shorted when connector is unplugged.

Disabling Driver-Side Air Bag – Disconnect both battery cables. Remove access panel from steering wheel. *See Fig. 13.* Remove Red short connector, located on inside of access panel. Disconnect air bag connector from cable reel connector. Connect Red short connector to air bag connector. Disable passenger-side air bag (if equipped).

Disabling Passenger-Side Air Bag – Remove glove box. Disconnect passenger-side air bag connector. *See Figs. 14-18.* Connect Red short connector to air bag connector (1995 models only).

Activating System – Remove Red short connectors that were installed at air bags during disabling procedure. Reconnect air bag connectors. Return Red short connector to storage location. Check AIR BAG indicator light to ensure system is functioning properly. See SYSTEM OPERATION CHECK.

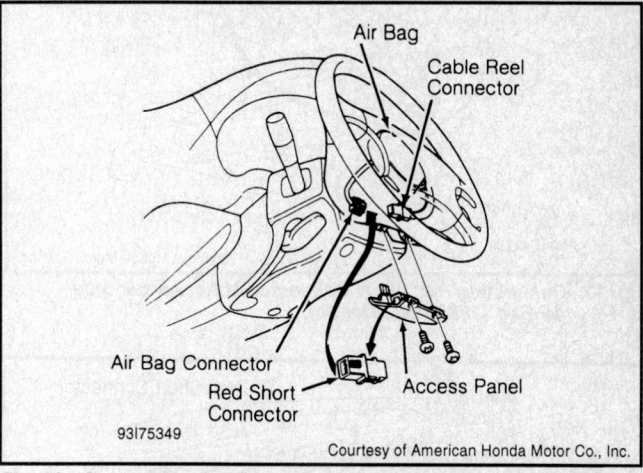

93I75349

Courtesy of American Honda Motor Co., Inc.

Fig. 13: Connecting Red Short Connector At Driver-Side Air Bag (Accord Shown; Other Models Are Similar)

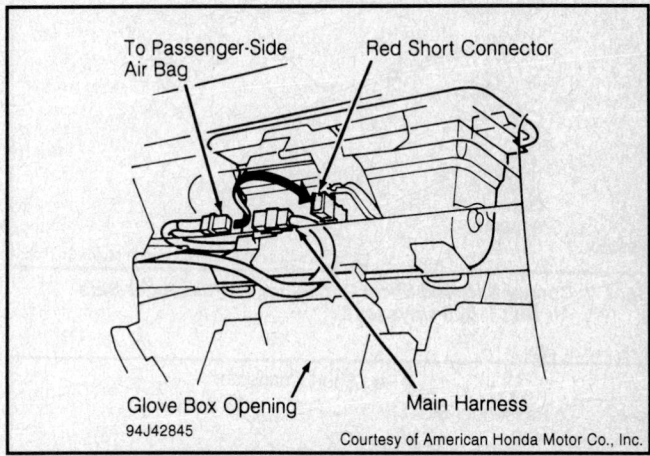

94J42845

Courtesy of American Honda Motor Co., Inc.

Fig. 14: Connecting Red Short Connector At Passenger-Side Air Bag (1995 Accord)

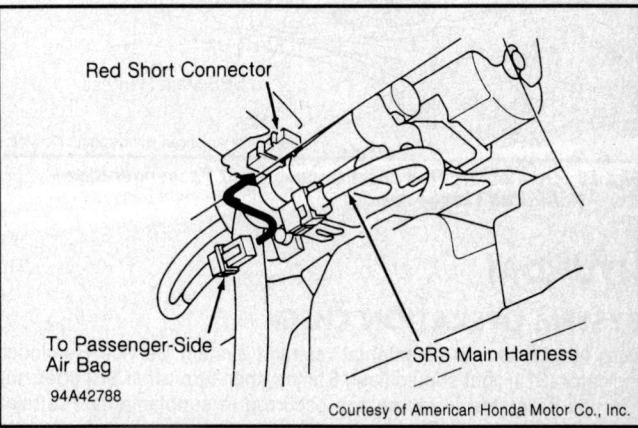

94A42788

Courtesy of American Honda Motor Co., Inc.

Fig. 15: Connecting Red Short Connector At Passenger-Side Air Bag (1995 Civic)

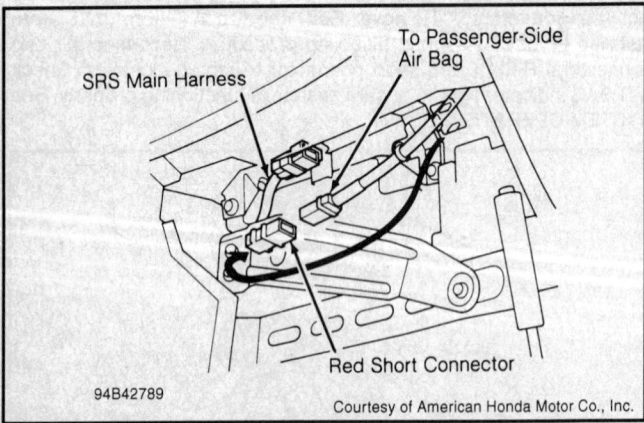

Fig. 16: Connecting Red Short Connector At Passenger-Side Air Bag (1995 Civic Del Sol)

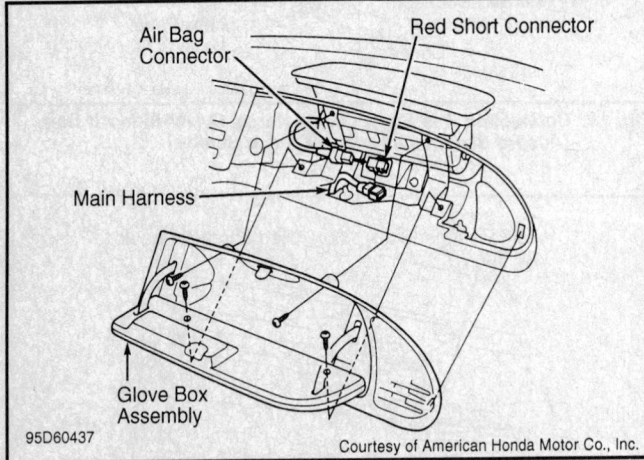

Fig. 17: Connecting Red Short Connector At Passenger-Side Air Bag (1995 Odyssey)

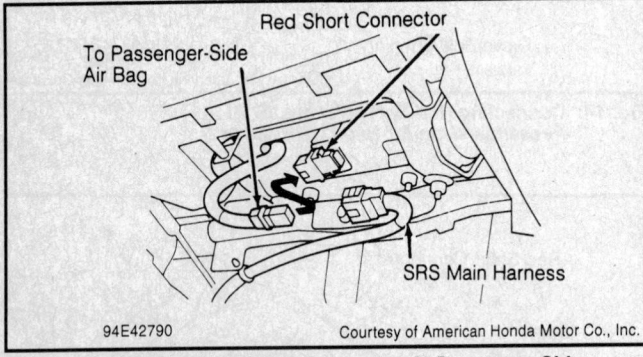

Fig. 18: Connecting Red Short Connector At Passenger-Side Air Bag (1995 Prelude)

HYUNDAI

SYSTEM OPERATION CHECK

Turn ignition on. Supplemental restraint system Service Reminder Indicator (SRI) light should flash 6 times, then turn off. If SRI does not function as stated, a failure has occurred in supplemental restraint system and must be repaired.

SERVICE PRECAUTIONS

These precautions should be observed when working with air bag systems:

- Disable air bag system before servicing any air bag system or steering column component. See DISABLING & ACTIVATING AIR BAG SYSTEM.
- After turning ignition switch to LOCK position and disconnecting negative battery cable, wait at least 30 seconds before working on SRS. SRS is equipped with a back-up power source that may allow air bag to deploy up to 30 seconds after negative battery cable is disconnected.
- During servicing of air bag module, store where ambient temperature is less than 200°F (93°C), without high humidity and away from electrical noise.
- When placing a live air bag on a bench or other surface, ensure pad top surface is facing up, away from surface. This will reduce motion of module if it is accidentally deployed.
- If electric welding is necessary to repair vehicle, disconnect Red 2-pin air bag connector located under steering column near multi-function switch connector before starting work.
- Because of critical operating requirements of system, DO NOT attempt to service air bag module, clockspring, wiring harness or SRS Control Module (SRSCM). Corrections are made by replacement with new parts only. NEVER use parts from another vehicle.
- If air bag module or SRSCM have been dropped, or there are cracks, dents or other defects visible, replace with new parts.
- DO NOT attempt to measure resistance across air bag module squib connector. Accidental air bag deployment is possible which could cause personal injury.
- After deployment, air bag surface may contain deposits of sodium hydroxide, which irritates skin, from gas generant combustion. Always wear safety glasses, rubber gloves and long-sleeved shirt during clean-up, and wash hands using mild soap and water.
- After deployment of an air bag, replace clockspring with a new one.
- After work is complete on SRS, ensure system is functioning properly. See SYSTEM OPERATION CHECK.

DISABLING & ACTIVATING AIR BAG SYSTEM

WARNING: Back-up power supply maintains SRS voltage for about 30 seconds after battery is disconnected. After disabling SRS, wait at least 30 seconds before servicing SRS to prevent accidental air bag deployment and possible personal injury.

To disable SRS, turn ignition switch to LOCK position. Disconnect negative battery cable. Wait at least 30 seconds before servicing SRS. To activate SRS, reconnect negative battery cable. Perform SYSTEM OPERATING CHECK.

INFINITI

G20, I30, J30 & Q45 – See NISSAN.

ISUZU

NOTE: For Isuzu Oasis information see HONDA Odyssey.

SYSTEM OPERATION CHECK

If system is functioning normally, AIR BAG indicator light should flash 7 times when ignition switch is first turned to ACC or ON position. If AIR BAG indicator light does not function as described, perform diagnostics. See MITCHELL® AIR BAG SERVICE & REPAIR MANUAL, DOMESTIC & IMPORTED MODELS.

SERVICE PRECAUTIONS

These precautions should be observed when working with SRS systems:

- Disable SRS system before servicing any SRS system or steering column component. Failure to do this could result in accidental air bag deployment and possible personal injury. See DISABLING & ACTIVATING AIR BAG SYSTEM.
- Wait about 2 minutes after disabling SRS system before servicing. System maintains SRS system voltage for about 2 minutes. Servicing SRS system before 2 minutes have passed may cause accidental air bag deployment and possible personal injury.
- After repairs, ensure AIR BAG indicator light is working properly and no system faults are indicated. See SYSTEM OPERATION CHECK.
- Always wear safety glasses when servicing or handling an air bag.
- Inflator module must be stored in its original special container until used for service. It must be stored in a clean, dry place, away from sources of extreme heat, sparks or high electrical energy.
- When placing a live inflator module (air bag module) on a bench or other surface, always face air bag and trim cover up, away from surface. This will reduce motion of module if accidentally deployed.
- After deployment, air bag surface may contain deposits of sodium hydroxide, which can irritate skin. Always wear safety glasses, rubber gloves and long-sleeved shirt during clean-up, and wash hands using mild soap and water. Follow correct disposal procedures.
- At no time should any electrical source be allowed near inflator on back of inflator module.
- When carrying a live inflator module, trim cover should be pointed away from your body to minimize injury in case of accidental deployment.
- DO NOT probe a wire through insulator; this will damage wire and eventually cause failure due to corrosion.
- If SRS system is not fully functional for any reason, vehicle should not be driven until system is repaired. DO NOT remove bulbs, modules, sensors or other components or in any way disable system from operating normally. If SRS system is not functional, park vehicle until repairs can be made.

DISABLING & ACTIVATING AIR BAG SYSTEM

WARNING: Wait about 2 minutes after disabling SRS system before servicing. System maintains SRS system voltage for about 2 minutes. Servicing SRS system before 2 minutes have passed may cause accidental air bag deployment and possible personal injury.

Disabling System (Except Hombre) – 1) Disconnect negative battery cable. Shield cable end. Remove SRS-1 fuse (No. 21) and SRS-2 fuse (No. 22) from instrument panel fuse block.
2) Unplug Yellow SRS connector at base of steering column. Remove glove box assembly. Unplug Yellow SRS connector from behind glove box assembly. SRS system is now disabled.
Activating System (Except Hombre) – 1) Ensure ignition switch is in LOCK position, and remove key. Reconnect passenger-side Yellow SRS connector. Install glove box assembly. Reconnect driver-side Yellow SRS connector.
2) Install SRS-1 fuse (No. 21) and SRS-2 fuse (No. 22). Reconnect negative battery cable. System is now activated. From outside of vehicle (driver side), turn ignition switch to RUN position. Check AIR BAG indicator light to ensure it flashes 7 times, then turns off.
Disabling System (Hombre) – 1) Turn steering wheel to place vehicle wheels in straight ahead position. Turn ignition switch to LOCK position. Disconnect negative battery cable. Shield cable end.
2) Remove AIR BAG fuse (No. 22) from fuse block. Remove CPA clip and disconnect Yellow SRS connector at base of steering column (it may be necessary to remove left sound insulator). Wait 2 minutes before servicing vehicle. SRS system is now disabled.

Activating System (Hombre) – 1) Ensure ignition switch is in LOCK position, and remove key. Reconnect Yellow SRS connector. Install left sound insulator (if removed).
2) Install AIR BAG fuse (No. 22). Reconnect negative battery cable. System is now activated. From outside of vehicle (driver side), turn ignition switch to RUN position. Check AIR BAG indicator light to ensure it flashes 7 times, then turns off.

JAGUAR

SYSTEM OPERATION CHECK

Except XJS – When ignition is turned on, SRS indicator light will glow for about 5 seconds and then go off. If indicator does not glow, does not go off after about 5 seconds or glows while driving, system must be inspected as soon as possible. See MITCHELL® AIR BAG SERVICE & REPAIR MANUAL, DOMESTIC & IMPORTED MODELS.

SERVICE PRECAUTIONS

Observe these precautions when working with air bag systems:
- Disable air bag system before servicing any air bag system or steering column component. See DISABLING & ACTIVATING AIR BAG SYSTEM.
- After turning ignition switch to LOCK position and disconnecting negative battery cable, wait at least 1 minute before working on SRS. SRS is equipped with a back-up power source that may allow air bag to deploy within 1 minute after disconnecting negative battery cable.
- Because of critical operating requirements of system, DO NOT attempt to service air bag components.
- DO NOT attempt to dismantle air bag module. DO NOT puncture, incinerate or bring into contact with electricity or electrical devices.
- DO NOT remove steering column mountings or steering wheel from vehicle before disarming and removing air bag module.
- Air bag module must be stored in its original special container until used for service. It must be stored in a clean, dry place, away from sources of extreme heat, sparks and high electrical energy.
- To prevent inadvertently arming module, DO NOT tamper with safety shaft in center on rear of module after removal.
- DO NOT cut open inflator/sensor assembly or in any way repair module.
- DO NOT hit module or apply force on steering wheel.
- DO NOT install module to steering wheel and arm module until column and wheel are firmly installed into vehicle.
- DO NOT store module at temperatures above 168°F (75°C).
- DO NOT transfer air bag module to another vehicle.
- When carrying air bag module, hold module to one side of your body with deployment side of module facing either to front or rear.

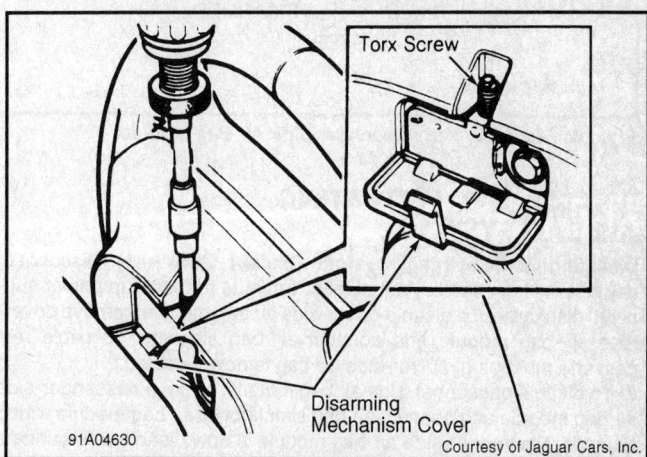

91A04630   Courtesy of Jaguar Cars, Inc.

Fig. 19: Disabling XJS Driver-Side Air Bag Module

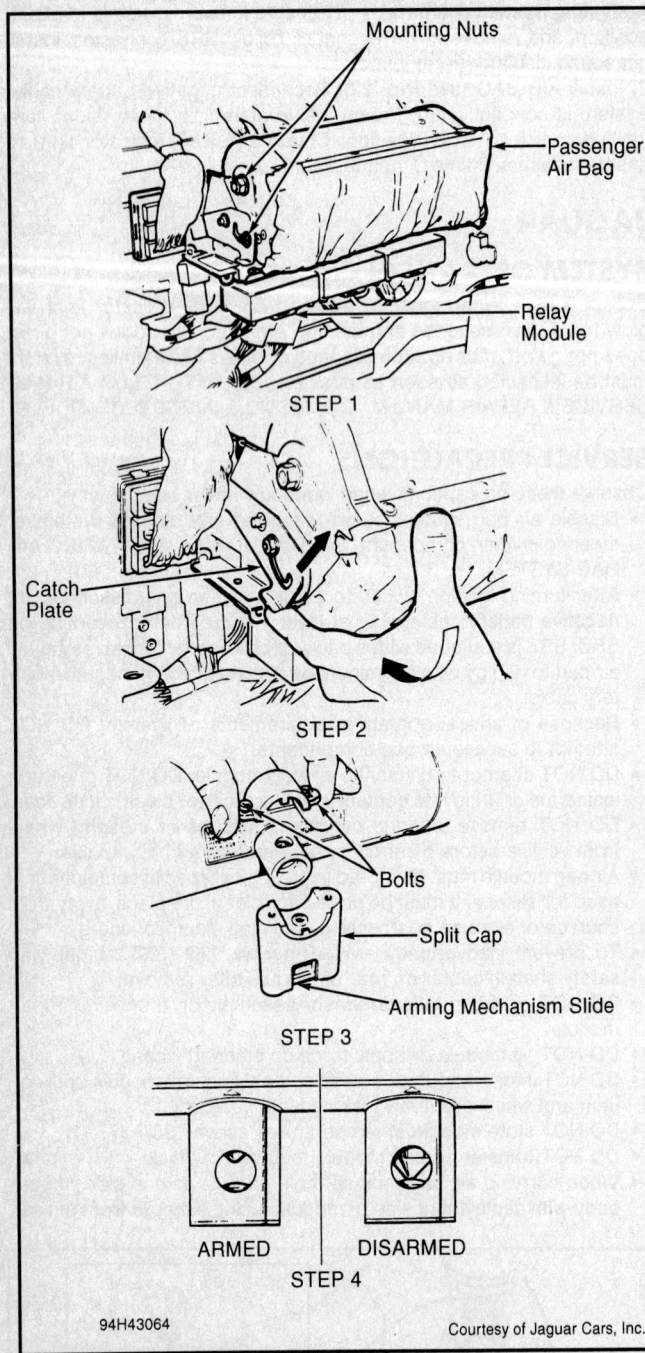

STEP 1

Mounting Nuts

Passenger Air Bag

Relay Module

Catch Plate

STEP 2

Bolts

Split Cap

Arming Mechanism Slide

STEP 3

ARMED   DISARMED

STEP 4

94H43064   Courtesy of Jaguar Cars, Inc.

Fig. 20: Disabling XJS Passenger-Side Air Bag Module

DISABLING & ACTIVATING AIR BAG SYSTEM

Disabling & Activating System (Except XJS) – 1) Disconnect negative battery cable. Wait at least 1 minute for back-up power supply to discharge. To disable driver-side air bag module, remove driver-side air bag module and connect air bag simulator to cable reel cassette multi-plug. Driver-side air bag is now disabled.
2) To disable passenger-side air bag module, remove passenger-side air bag module and connect air bag simulator to air bag module wiring harness. Passenger-side air bag module is now disabled. Reconnect negative battery cable (if necessary).
3) Disconnect negative battery cable (if reconnected). Remove driver-side and passenger-side air bag simulators from air bag modules. Reconnect negative battery cable. Turn ignition on. Ensure SRS indicator light glows for about 5 seconds and then turns off.

Disabling & Activating System (XJS Driver-Side Air Bag) – 1) Disconnect negative battery cable. To disable air bag module, open disarming mechanism cover on back of steering wheel. Using Torx screwdriver, turn arming screw counterclockwise until it stops (approximately 12 turns). See Fig. 19. Air bag module is now disabled.
2) To activate air bag module, turn arming screw clockwise approximately 12 turns until it stops. Tighten screw to 8-18 INCH lbs. (1-2 N.m). Reconnect negative battery cable.

Disabling & Activating System (XJS Passenger-Side Air Bag) – 1) Remove fascia board from instrument panel. Loosen air bag module mounting nuts. See Fig. 20. Lift catch plates and carefully pivot air bag module downwards to disarmed position.

WARNING: As catch plates are released, air bag arming mechanism will apply considerable force. DO NOT allow air bag assembly to snap down. Fully support air bag module with both hands and ease module downward to disarmed position.

---

2) Remove mounting bolts and reposition relay module aside. Remove outer bracket-to-dash rail and crossbar assembly fasteners. Remove air bag module mounting nuts. Remove air bag module and outer bracket assembly from vehicle. Ensure arming mechanism slide is fully down in the disarmed position. See Fig. 20.
3) If air bag module is not in the disarmed position, place air bag module on work bench with air bag module and trim cover facing up, away from surface. Using finger pressure, slide arming mechanism downwards. If arming mechanism will not slide downwards, place air bag module in a safe place and contact manufacturer for further instructions.
4) On disarmed air bag modules only, remove split cap bolts and carefully remove arming mechanism from air bag module. To activate air bag module, reverse disarming procedure.

KIA

SYSTEM OPERATION CHECK

Turn ignition on. AIR BAG warning light in instrument cluster should glow for 4-8 seconds and then turn off. If AIR BAG warning light does not function as described, a failure has occurred in Supplemental Restraint System (SRS). Repair malfunctioning SRS. See MITCHELL® AIR BAG SERVICE & REPAIR MANUAL, DOMESTIC & IMPORTED MODELS.

SERVICE PRECAUTIONS

Observe the following precautions when servicing SRS:
- Disable SRS before servicing any SRS or steering column component. Failure to do this could result in accidental air bag deployment and possible personal injury. See DISABLING & ACTIVATING AIR BAG SYSTEM.
- After turning ignition switch to LOCK position and disconnecting negative battery cable, wait at least 30 minutes before working on SRS. SRS is equipped with a back-up power source that may allow air bag to deploy within 30 minutes after disconnecting negative battery cable.
- In a minor collision in which air bags did not deploy, inspect front air bag sensors and steering wheel pad.
- NEVER use air bag parts from another vehicle. Replace air bag parts with new parts.
- Never disassemble or repair system components. Replace cracked, dented or otherwise damaged system component.
- DO NOT expose front air bag sensors, center air bag sensor assembly, steering wheel pad, passenger-side air bag or seat belt pretensioner to heat or flame.
- After servicing SRS, check air bag warning light to ensure system is functioning properly. See SYSTEM OPERATION CHECK.
- Always wear safety glasses when servicing or handling an air bag.
- When placing a live air bag on a bench or other surface, always face air bag and trim cover upward, away from surface. This will reduce motion of module if it is accidentally deployed.

- After deployment, air bag surface may contain deposits of sodium hydroxide, which irritates skin. Always wear safety glasses, rubber gloves and long-sleeved shirt during clean-up. After clean-up, wash hands using mild soap and water.
- When carrying a live air bag module, trim cover must be pointed away from your body to minimize injury in case of accidental deployment.
- If SRS is not fully functional for any reason, vehicle should not be driven until system is repaired and again becomes operational. DO NOT remove bulbs, modules, sensors or other components or in any way disable system from operating normally. If SRS is not functional, park vehicle until it is repaired and functions properly.

DISABLING & ACTIVATING
AIR BAG SYSTEM

WARNING: Back-up power supply maintains SRS voltage for about 30 minutes after battery is disconnected. After disabling SRS, wait at least 30 minutes before servicing SRS to prevent accidental air bag deployment and possible personal injury.

To disable SRS, turn ignition switch to LOCK position. Disconnect negative battery cable. Wait at least 30 minutes before servicing SRS. To activate SRS, reconnect negative battery cable. Perform SYSTEM OPERATION CHECK.

LAND ROVER

SYSTEM OPERATION CHECK

Turn ignition on. AIR BAG warning light should come on for about 7 seconds and then go off, indicating SRS is okay. If AIR BAG warning light does not come on, service Supplemental Restraint System (SRS). If AIR BAG warning light comes on for about 7 seconds, then starts flashing, a fault code is set in memory. See MITCHELL® AIR BAG SERVICE & REPAIR MANUAL, DOMESTIC & IMPORTED MODELS.

SERVICE PRECAUTIONS

These precautions should be observed when working with air bag systems:

- Disable SRS before servicing any SRS or steering column component. Failure to do this could result in accidental air bag deployment and possible personal injury. See DISABLING & ACTIVATING AIR BAG SYSTEM.
- Wait about 20 minutes after disabling SRS before servicing vehicle. System maintains SRS voltage for about 2 minutes. Servicing SRS before 20 minutes have passed may cause accidental air bag deployment and possible personal injury.
- Always disconnect and shield both battery cables before working near any SRS components. Disconnect negative battery cable first.
- Always remove key from ignition switch before beginning any work on SRS.
- Always wear safety glasses when servicing or handling an air bag.
- DO NOT repair, splice or modify any SRS wiring harness. If harness is damaged, it must be replaced.
- DO NOT use a circuit tester to check SRS components or wiring harness connector. Only use manufacturer recommended procedures and equipment when testing SRS.
- DO NOT install any used SRS components to replace used or damaged parts. Use only new SRS components when repairing system.
- Airbag modules contain sodium azide which is a poisonuos and flamable gas. Contact with water, acid or heavy metals may produce harmful or explosive compounds. DO NOT dismantle or incinerate air bag modules. Always dispose of air bag modules properly.
- When placing a live air bag module on a bench or other surface, always face air bag and trim cover up, away from surface. This will reduce motion of module if accidentally deployed.

- Wash hand thoroughly after handling deployed air bags.
- DO NOT subject air bag modules to temperatures more than 185°F (85°C) or electrical equipment.
- DO NOT allow grease, oil, cleaning solutions, or similar products to come in contact with air bag module.
- When carrying a live air bag module, trim cover should be pointed away from your body to minimize injury in case of accidental deployment.

DISABLING & ACTIVATING
AIR BAG SYSTEM

WARNING: Back-up power supply maintains SRS voltage for about 20 minutes after battery is disconnected. After disabling SRS, wait at least 20 minutes before servicing SRS to prevent accidental air bag deployment and possible personal injury.

To disable SRS, turn ignition switch to LOCK position. Disconnect negative battery cable. Wait at least 20 minutes before servicing SRS. To activate SRS, reconnect negative battery cable. Perform SYSTEM OPERATION CHECK.

LEXUS

SYSTEM OPERATION CHECK

Turn ignition switch to ACC or ON position. Air bag warning light in instrument cluster should come on for about 6 seconds, then go out. If light does not respond as specified, SRS is malfunctioning and needs repair. See MITCHELL® AIR BAG SERVICE & REPAIR MANUAL, DOMESTIC & IMPORTED MODELS.

SERVICE PRECAUTIONS

Observe the following precautions when servicing SRS:

- Disable SRS before servicing any SRS or steering column component. Failure to do this could result in accidental air bag deployment and possible personal injury. See DISABLING & ACTIVATING AIR BAG SYSTEM.
- After turning ignition switch to LOCK position and disconnecting negative battery cable, wait at least 90 seconds before working on SRS. SRS is equipped with a back-up power source that may allow air bag to deploy within 90 seconds after disconnecting negative battery cable.
- In a minor collision in which air bags did not deploy, inspect front air bag sensors and steering wheel pad.
- NEVER use air bag parts from another vehicle. Replace air bag parts with new parts.
- Remove air bag sensors if shocks are likely to be applied to sensors during repair.
- Center air bag sensor contains mercury. After replacement, DO NOT destroy old part. When scrapping vehicle or replacing center air bag sensor, remove center air bag sensor and dispose of it as toxic waste.
- Never disassemble or repair system components. Replace cracked, dented or otherwise damaged system components.
- DO NOT expose front air bag sensors, center air bag sensor assembly, steering wheel pad, passenger-side air bag or seat belt pretensioner to heat or flame.
- Information labels are attached to air bag components. Follow all notices on labels.
- After servicing SRS, check air bag warning light to ensure system is functioning properly. See SYSTEM OPERATION CHECK.
- Always wear safety glasses when servicing or handling an air bag.
- When placing a live air bag on a bench or other surface, always face air bag and trim cover upward, away from surface. This will reduce motion of module if it is accidentally deployed.
- After deployment, air bag surface may contain deposits of sodium hydroxide, which irritates skin. Always wear safety glasses, rubber gloves and long-sleeved shirt during clean-up. After clean-up, wash hands using mild soap and water.

- When carrying a live air bag module, trim cover must be pointed away from your body to minimize injury in case of accidental deployment.
- If SRS is not fully functional for any reason, vehicle should not be driven until system is repaired and again becomes operational. DO NOT remove bulbs, modules, sensors or other components or in any way disable system from operating normally. If SRS is not functional, park vehicle until it is repaired and functions properly.

DISABLING & ACTIVATING AIR BAG SYSTEM

WARNING: Back-up power supply maintains SRS voltage for about 90 seconds after battery is disconnected. After disabling SRS, wait at least 90 seconds before servicing SRS to prevent accidental air bag deployment and possible personal injury.

Disabling System – 1) Turn ignition switch to LOCK position. Disconnect and shield negative battery cable. Wait at least 90 seconds before working on system.
2) Remove steering wheel pad (air bag). Open glove box. Disconnect passenger-side air bag connector, accessible through finish plate on left side of glove box.
Activating System – Reconnect passenger-side air bag connector. Install steering wheel pad. Reconnect negative battery cable. Perform SYSTEM OPERATION CHECK.

MAZDA

SYSTEM OPERATION CHECK

Turn ignition on. AIR BAG warning light in instrument cluster should glow for 4-8 seconds and then turn off. If AIR BAG warning light does not function as described, a failure has occurred in Supplemental Restraint System (SRS). Repair malfunctioning SRS.

SERVICE PRECAUTIONS

Following precautions should be observed when working with air bag systems.
- Disable air bag system before servicing any air bag system or steering column component. See DISABLING & ACTIVATING AIR BAG SYSTEM.
- Wait at least 10 minutes after disabling air bag system before servicing. Air bag system voltage is maintained for about 10 minutes after system is disabled. Failure to wait at least 10 minutes before servicing system may cause accidental air bag deployment and possible personal injury.
- Obtain radio code from vehicle owner or deactivate radio anti-theft function (if equipped) before disconnecting vehicle battery.
- Because of critical system operating requirements, DO NOT service any air bag system component or wiring harness. Corrections are made by replacement only.
- DO NOT use an ohmmeter to check resistance of air bag module, as it may cause air bag deployment.
- When carrying a live (undeployed) module, ensure trim cover is pointed away from your body. This minimizes chance of injury in event of accidental air bag deployment.
- When placing a live air bag module on any surface, always face trim cover upward to reduce motion of module if it is accidentally deployed.
- Crash sensors must always be installed with arrow on sensor facing front of vehicle. Also, check sensors for cracks, defects and rust before installation. Replace crash sensor(s) as necessary.
- Air bag system clockspring MUST be aligned in neutral position, since its rotation ability is limited. DO NOT turn steering wheel or column after removal of steering gear.
- A double-lock mechanism is used on clockspring connectors. DO NOT use excessive force when disconnecting connectors, as damage to connector may occur.

DISABLING & ACTIVATING AIR BAG SYSTEM

WARNING: After disabling air bag system, wait at least 10 minutes before servicing. Air bag system voltage is maintained for about 10 minutes after system is disabled. Failure to wait at least 10 minutes may cause accidental air bag deployment and possible personal injury.

CAUTION: When battery is disconnected, radio will go into anti-theft protection mode (if equipped). Obtain radio anti-theft protection code from owner prior to servicing vehicle or deactivate radio anti-theft function before disconnecting vehicle battery.

Disabling System (Miata, Millenia, MPV, MX-6, Pickup, Protege & 626) – Disconnect and shield negative battery cable. Wait at least 10 minutes for back-up power supply to be depleted. Remove cover panel below left side of instrument panel. Disconnect Orange and Blue clockspring connectors for driver air bag. *See Fig. 21 or 22.* Remove glove box. Disconnect Orange and Blue passenger air bag module connectors (if equipped). *See Fig. 23.*
Activating System (Miata, Millenia, MPV, MX-6, Pickup, Protege & 626) – Ensure negative battery cable is disconnected. Connect Orange and Blue passenger air bag module connectors (if equipped). Install glove box. Connect driver air bag Orange and Blue clockspring connectors. Install lower cover panel. Connect negative battery cable. See SYSTEM OPERATION CHECK.

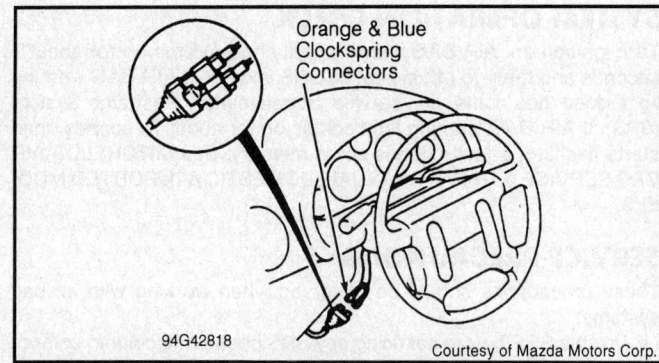

94G42818   Courtesy of Mazda Motors Corp.

Fig. 21: Locating Driver Air Bag Clockspring Connectors (Miata Shown; Other Models Are Similar)

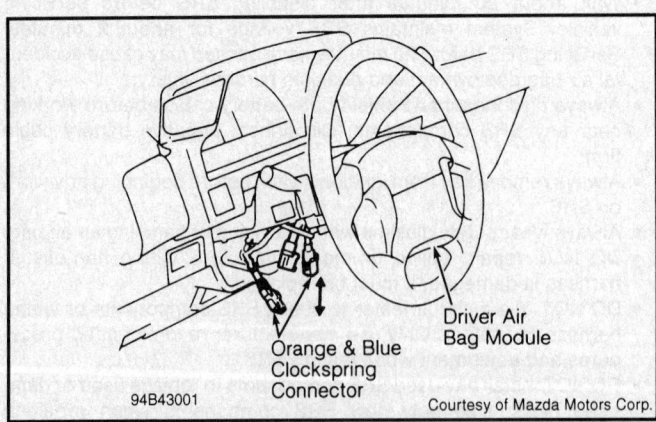

94B43001   Courtesy of Mazda Motors Corp.

Fig. 22: Locating Driver Air Bag Clockspring Connectors (MPV)

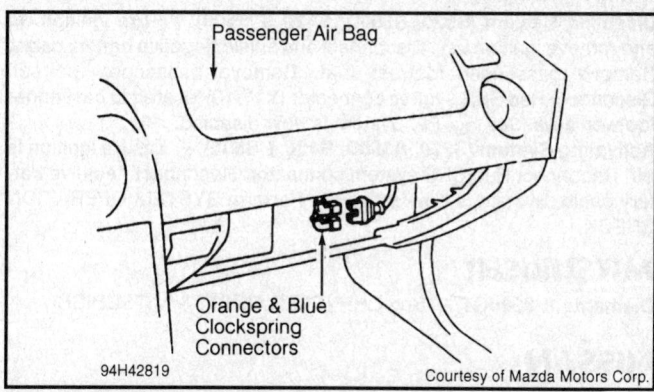

Fig. 23: Locating Passenger Air Bag Clockspring Connectors (Miata Shown; Other Models Are Similar)

Disabling System (MX-3, RX7 & 929) – Disconnect and shield negative battery cable. Wait at least 10 minutes for back-up power supply to be depleted. Disconnect harness connectors from diagnostic module, located behind left side of instrument panel. Connect Short Circuit Connectors (49-H066-004) to diagnostic module harness connectors. See Fig. 24 or 25.

Activating System (MX-3, RX7 & 929) – Ensure negative battery cable is disconnected. Remove short circuit connectors from diagnostic module harness connectors. Reconnect diagnostic module connectors. Connect negative battery cable. See SYSTEM OPERATION CHECK.

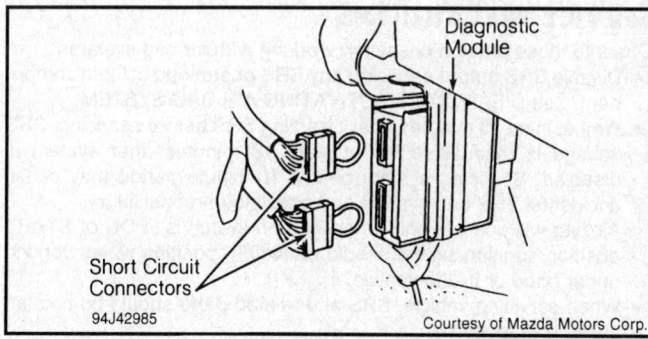

Fig. 24: Disabling Air Bag System (MX-3 Shown; 929 Is Similar)

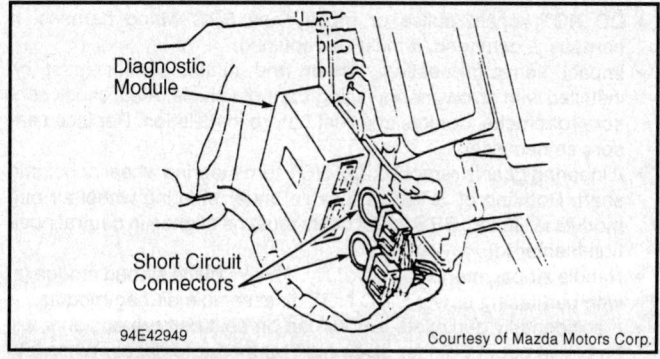

Fig. 25: Disabling Air Bag System (RX7)

MERCEDES-BENZ

SYSTEM OPERATION CHECK

The Supplemental Restraint System (SRS) warning light indicates air bag and seat belt Emergency Tensioning Retractor (ETR) system readiness. Turn ignition on. SRS warning light will light, and then go out after approximately 4 seconds indicating system is functioning properly.

If SRS warning light does not light, lights up while driving or lights all the time (for crash related faults), there is a system fault. IF SRS warning light stays on for a duration of approximately 2 minutes, a non-crash related faults is present. Repair malfunctioning system. See MITCHELL® AIR BAG SERVICE & REPAIR MANUAL, DOMESTIC & IMPORTED MODELS.

SERVICE PRECAUTIONS

Observe following precautions when working with air bag systems:
- When working around steering column components and before any repairs are performed, disable air bag system.
- Before straightening any damage to body, or before performing electrical arc-welding, disable air bag system.
- Always wear safety glasses and gloves when handling a deployed air bag module. Air bag module may contain sodium hydroxide deposits which are irritating to the skin.
- DO NOT repair any portion of SRS wiring harness.
- Always handle air bag module with trim cover away from your body. Always place air bag module on workbench with trim cover up, away from loose objects.
- DO NOT expose any SRS component to temperatures in excess of 212°F (100°C).
- DO NOT expose any SRS component to cleaning agents such as solvents, gasoline, lye, etc.

DISABLING & ACTIVATING AIR BAG SYSTEM

Disabling System (C220 & C280) – 1) Turn ignition off and remove ignition key. Disconnect and shield negative battery cable. Remove covers as necessary to access horn/air bag clockspring connector (A45x1) located at base of steering column. See Fig. 26.

2) Disconnect horn/air bag clockspring connector. Remove passenger floor covering and door sill covers as necessary to access passenger air bag connector (X28/12). See Fig. 27. Disconnect passenger air bag connector. System is now disabled.

Activating System (C220 & C280) – Ensure ignition is off. Reconnect horn/air bag clockspring connector. Reconnect passenger air bag connector. Reconnect negative battery cable. System is now activated. Perform SYSTEM OPERATION CHECK.

Disabling System (E300D, E320, E420 & E500) – Turn ignition off and remove ignition key. Disconnect and shield negative battery cable. Remove passenger foot mat. Remove passenger footrest. Disconnect SRS system connector (X29/9) located at passenger footwell area. See Fig. 28. System is now disabled.

Activating System (E300D, E320, E420 & E500) – Ensure ignition is off. Reconnect SRS system connector. Reconnect negative battery cable. System is now activated. Perform SYSTEM OPERATION CHECK.

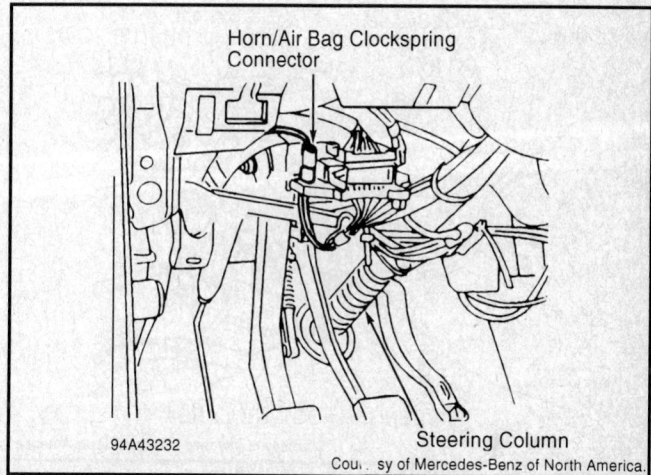

Fig. 26: Locating Air Bag Clockspring Connector (C220 & C280)

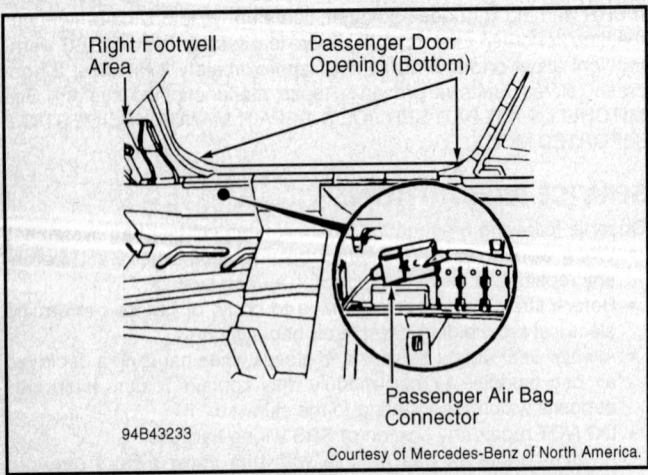

Fig. 27: Locating Passenger Air Bag Connector (C220 & C280)

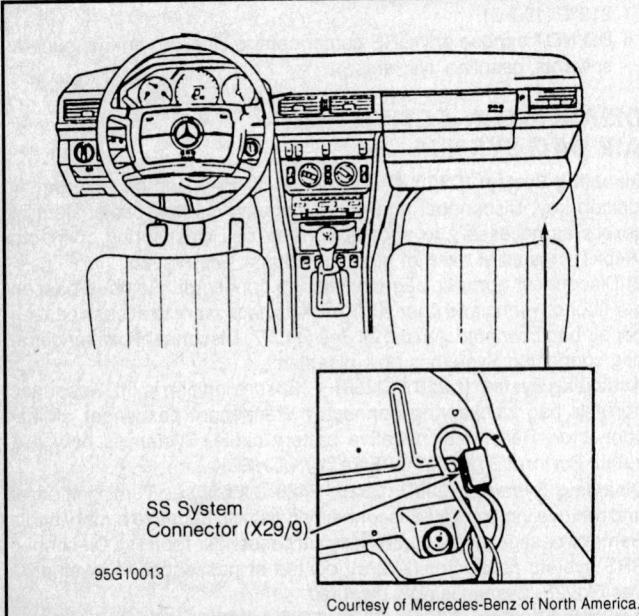

Fig. 28: Locating SRS System Connector (E300D, E320, E420 & E500)

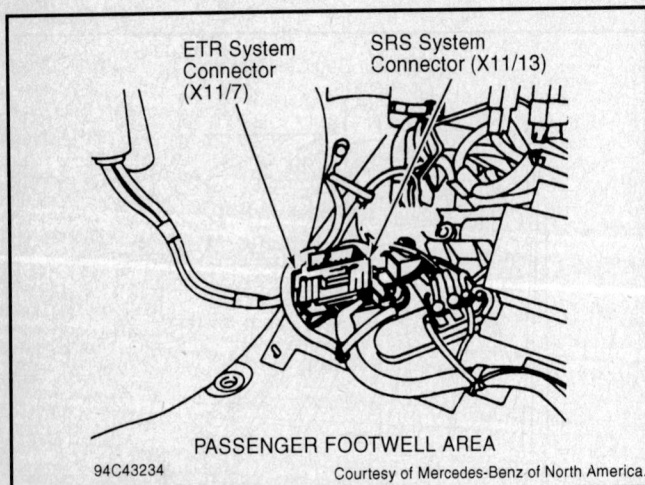

Fig. 29: Locating Red SRS System Connector (S320, S350D, S420 & S500)

Disabling System (S320, S350D, S420 & S500) – Turn ignition off and remove ignition key. Disconnect and shield negative battery cable. Remove passenger footrest mat. Remove passenger footrest. Disconnect Red SRS system connector (X11/13) located at passenger footwell area. *See Fig. 29.* System is now disabled.

Activating System (S320, S350D, S420 & S500) – Ensure ignition is off. Reconnect Red SRS system connector. Reconnect negative battery cable. System is now activated. Perform SYSTEM OPERATION CHECK.

MITSUBISHI

Diamante & 3000GT – See CHRYSLER CORP. & MITSUBISHI.

NISSAN

SYSTEM OPERATION CHECK

Turn ignition on. AIR BAG warning light should come on for about 7 seconds and then go off, indicating SRS is okay. If AIR BAG warning light does not come on, service Supplemental Restraint System (SRS). If AIR BAG warning light stays on constantly, service SRS. If AIR BAG warning light comes on for about 7 seconds, goes off, then starts flashing, a fault code is set in memory. See MITCHELL® AIR BAG SERVICE & REPAIR MANUAL, DOMESTIC & IMPORTED MODELS.

NOTE: On seat belt pre-tensioner equipped vehicles, the seat belt warning light should also come on for about 7 seconds and then go off (with seat belt fastened).

SERVICE PRECAUTIONS

Observe these precautions when working with air bag systems:
- Disable SRS before servicing any SRS or steering column component. See DISABLING & ACTIVATING AIR BAG SYSTEM.
- Wait at least 10 minutes after disabling SRS before servicing. SRS voltage is maintained for at least 10 minutes after system is disabled. Servicing system before 10-minute period may cause accidental SRS deployment and possible personal injury.
- Air bag will operate only when ignition switch is in ON or START position. Ignition switch should be in OFF position when working under hood or inside vehicle.
- When servicing vehicle, SRS and related parts should be pointed away from technician.
- DO NOT use a circuit tester to check air bag harness connectors. SRS wiring harness and connectors have Yellow insulation for easy identification. Keep all ground points clean.
- DO NOT repair, splice or modify any SRS wiring harness. If harness is damaged, it must be replaced.
- Impact sensor(s), safing sensor and tunnel sensor must be installed with arrow marks facing front of vehicle. Also, check sensors for cracks, defects and rust before installation. Replace sensors as necessary.
- If steering gear is removed, DO NOT turn steering wheel or column shaft. Rotation of SRS spiral cable under steering wheel air bag module is limited. SRS spiral cable must be aligned in neutral position (centered).
- Handle air bag module(s) carefully. Always place air bag module(s) with pad facing upward. DO NOT disassemble air bag module.
- If accidentally deployed, rubber cap on seat belt pretensioner will be blown out of cylinder tip by high temperature gases. When laying aside seat belt pretensioner, ensure cylinder tip points away from people (place pretensioners in a box if possible).
- After servicing, perform SYSTEM OPERATION CHECK.
- DO NOT expose air bag module to temperatures exceeding 194°F (90°C). DO NOT allow oil, grease or water to contact module.
- If front of vehicle is damaged in collision, check impact sensor(s), tunnel and safing sensors and related wiring harnesses.
- Before discarding an air bag module or seat belt pretensioner (including scrapping a vehicle with air bag system), always deploy air bag(s) and seat belt pretensioners.
- Replace used mounting bolts with NEW mounting bolts.

DISABLING & ACTIVATING AIR BAG SYSTEM

WARNING: SRS voltage is maintained for at least 10 minutes after system is disabled. Wait at least 10 minutes after disabling SRS before servicing. Servicing system before 10-minute period may cause accidental air bag deployment and possible personal injury.

To disable SRS, turn ignition off. Disconnect and shield BOTH battery cables. Wait at least 10 minutes before working on or near SRS components. To activate SRS, connect negative battery cable. Turn ignition on. Ensure AIR BAG indicator light operates as specified. See SYSTEM OPERATION CHECK.

PORSCHE

SYSTEM OPERATION CHECK

Turn ignition switch to ON position. AIR BAG light on instrument panel should come on for about 2-5 seconds and then go off. If AIR BAG light fails to come on, remains on after 2-5 seconds or comes on while driving, air bag system requires servicing. See MITCHELL® AIR BAG SERVICE & REPAIR MANUAL, DOMESTIC & IMPORTED MODELS.

SERVICE PRECAUTIONS

Observe the following precautions when servicing air bag system:
- Before servicing any air bag system or steering column component, disable air bag system. See DISABLING & ACTIVATING AIR BAG SYSTEM.
- After disabling air bag system, wait at least 20 minutes before servicing. Air bag system voltage is maintained for about 20 minutes after system is disabled. Failure to wait at least 20 minutes before servicing system may cause accidental air bag deployment and possible personal injury.
- Because of critical operating requirements of system, DO NOT service any air bag component. Correction is made by replacement only.
- DO NOT allow grease, oil, cleaning solutions, or similar products to come in contact with air bag units.
- DO NOT subject air bag units to temperatures greater than 194°F (90°C).
- Replace air bag units, crash sensors, and air bag control units that have fallen from a height of 1.5 feet or more.
- DO NOT install additional trim, labels or stickers on steering wheel, or in area of passenger-side air bag.
- DO NOT repair or modify air bag system wiring.
- Disable air bag system before electric-welding vehicle.
- DO NOT route wires from other electrical equipment in the vicinity of air bag wire harness.
- Wash hands thoroughly after handling deployed air bags.

DISABLING & ACTIVATING AIR BAG SYSTEM

WARNING: Wait at least 20 minutes after disabling air bag system before servicing. Air bag system voltage is maintained for about 20 minutes after system is disabled. Servicing system before 20 minutes has elapsed may cause accidental air bag deployment and possible personal injury.

To disable air bag system, turn ignition off. Disconnect and shield negative battery cable. To activate air bag system, reconnect negative battery cable. Perform a system operation check to ensure system is functioning properly. See SYSTEM OPERATION CHECK.

SAAB

SYSTEM OPERATION CHECK

Turn ignition on. Supplemental Restraint System (SRS) warning light should come on for 3-4 seconds, then go out. The SRS is not functional for the first 6 seconds. If light remains on, or does not come on at all, a fault exists in system. See MITCHELL® AIR BAG SERVICE & REPAIR MANUAL, DOMESTIC & IMPORTED MODELS.

WARNING: Saab vehicles are equipped with seat belt pre-tensioners. The SRS system controls both air bags and seat belt pre-tensioners.

SERVICE PRECAUTIONS

Observe these precautions when working with air bag systems:
- Disable Supplemental Restraint System (SRS) before servicing any SRS or steering column component. See DISABLING & ACTIVATING AIR BAG SYSTEM.
- Because of critical operating requirements of system, DO NOT attempt to service air bag components. Corrections are made by replacement only.
- Always wear safety glasses when servicing or handling an air bag.
- Handle air bag components carefully. Avoid exposing components to impact, heat, moisture, etc.
- Air bag module must be installed immediately after it is taken out of storage. If work is interrupted, module must be returned to storage. Air bag modules must never be left unattended out of storage.
- Air bag module is a sealed unit. DO NOT attempt to dismantle or repair it.
- When placing a live air bag module on a bench or other surface, always face air bag and trim cover up, away from surface. This will reduce motion of module if accidentally deployed.
- After deployment, air bag surface may contain deposits of sodium hydroxide, which can irritate skin. Always wear safety glasses, rubber gloves and long-sleeved shirt during clean-up, and wash hands using mild soap and water. Follow correct disposal procedures.
- Never allow any electrical source near inflator on back of air bag module.
- When carrying a live air bag module, trim cover should be pointed away from your body to minimize injury in case of accidental deployment.
- Never apply grease to SRS connectors.

DISABLING & ACTIVATING AIR BAG SYSTEM

To disable SRS, disconnect and shield negative battery cable. To activate system, reconnect negative battery cable. Perform a system operation check. See SYSTEM OPERATION CHECK.

SUBARU

SYSTEM OPERATION CHECK

Turn ignition on. AIR BAG warning light in instrument cluster should come on and then go out after approximately 8 seconds. If AIR BAG warning light stays on for longer than 8 seconds, or does not come on, SRS is malfunctioning. See MITCHELL® AIR BAG SERVICE & REPAIR MANUAL, DOMESTIC & IMPORTED MODELS.

SERVICE PRECAUTIONS

Observe following precautions when working with air bag system:
- Disable SRS before servicing any SRS or steering column component. Failure to disable system could result in accidental air bag deployment and possible personal injury. See DISABLING & ACTIVATING AIR BAG SYSTEM.
- Wait at least 20 seconds after disconnecting battery cable before servicing SRS. See DISABLING & ACTIVATING AIR BAG SYSTEM. Back-up power supply maintains SRS power for a few sec-

onds after battery is disconnected. Servicing SRS before 20 seconds have elapsed may cause accidental air bag deployment and possible personal injury.

- Whenever possible when working near, removing, or installing an undeployed air bag module, DO NOT position yourself directly in front of air bag.
- In a minor collision in which air bag does not deploy, front air bag impact sensors and steering wheel pad should be inspected.
- DO NOT use air bag parts from another vehicle. Replace air bag parts with new parts.
- Remove front impact sensors if shocks are likely to be applied to sensors during repairs.
- DO NOT repair damage or opens found in SRS harnesses. Manufacturer recommends replacement of any defective SRS harness with a new part.
- DO NOT disassemble and attempt repair of front impact sensors or steering wheel pad.
- If front impact sensors, control unit, or steering wheel pad is dropped, or if there are cracks, dents, or other defects in the case or connector, replace parts with new ones.
- DO NOT expose front impact sensors, control unit, or steering wheel pad to temperatures greater than 194°F (90°C).
- DO NOT apply tester probes directly to any SRS harness connector terminal. Use specified test harness during circuit testing.
- Information labels are attached to air bag components. Follow all notices on labels.
- After work on SRS is completed, verify system is functioning properly. See SYSTEM OPERATION CHECK.
- Always wear safety glasses when servicing or handling an air bag.
- DO NOT check for air bag module continuity with air bag removed from vehicle.
- When placing a live air bag on a bench or other surface, always face air bag and trim cover up, away from surface. This will reduce motion of module if it is accidentally deployed.
- After deployment, air bag surface may contain deposits of sodium hydroxide, which irritates skin. Always wear safety glasses, rubber gloves, and long sleeves shirt during cleanup. Wash hands with mild soap and water.
- When carrying a live air bag module, point trim cover away from your body to minimize injury in case of deployment.
- If SRS is not fully functional for any reason, vehicle should not be driven until system is repaired and again becomes operational. DO NOT remove bulbs, modules, sensors, or other components or in any way disable system from operating normally. If SRS is not functional, park vehicle until it is repaired and functions properly.

DISABLING & ACTIVATING AIR BAG SYSTEM

WARNING: Wait at least 20 seconds after disconnecting negative battery cable before servicing SRS. Back-up power supply maintains SRS power for a few seconds after battery is disconnected. Servicing SRS before 20 seconds may cause accidental air bag deployment and possible personal injury.

To disable SRS, turn ignition off. Disconnect and shield negative battery cable. After battery cable has been disconnected, wait at least 20 seconds before servicing SRS. To activate SRS, reconnect negative battery cable. Observe AIR BAG warning light to verify system is functioning properly. See SYSTEM OPERATION CHECK.

SUZUKI

SYSTEM OPERATION CHECK

Turn ignition switch to ON position. If system is functioning normally, AIR BAG indicator should flash 7 times (6 times on Esteem). If air bag warning light does not operate as specified, service air bag system. See MITCHELL® AIR BAG SERVICE & REPAIR MANUAL, DOMESTIC & IMPORTED MODELS.

SERVICE PRECAUTIONS

Observe the following precautions when servicing SRS:

- Disable air bag system before servicing any air bag or steering column component. Failure to disable air bag could result in accidental air bag deployment and possible personal injury. See DISABLING & ACTIVATING AIR BAG SYSTEM.
- After turning ignition switch to LOCK position and removing AIR BAG or AIR BAG-IG fuse, wait at least 10 seconds before working on air bag system. Sensing and Diagnostic Module (SDM) maintains a reserve voltage for up to 10 seconds.
- Always wear safety glasses when servicing or handling an air bag.
- Handle air bag module(s) carefully. Always place air bag module(s) with pad facing upward. DO NOT disassemble air bag module.
- If the air bag system and another vehicle system both need repair, the air bag system must be repaired first to avoid unintended air bag deployment.
- DO NOT modify steering wheel, dashboard, or any other air bag system component. Modifications can adversely affect air bag system performance and lead to personal injury.
- Never use air bag parts from another vehicle. Replace air bag parts with new parts.
- Remove air bag modules and SDM if repairing the vehicle requires exposing the vehicle to temperatures over 200°F (93°C). Never expose air bag system components directly to hot air or flames.
- Remove air bag components if repairing the vehicle requires impacting (shocking) the vehicle.
- When using electric welding, always disconnect air bag module connectors.
- If painting vehicle, DO NOT expose air bag harness or connectors to paint mist.

DISABLING & ACTIVATING AIR BAG SYSTEM

NOTE: With AIR BAG or AIR BAG-IG fuse removed and ignition on, AIR BAG warning light will be on. This is normal and does not indicate an air bag system malfunction.

Disabling System – 1) Ensure wheels are in straight-ahead position. Turn ignition switch to LOCK position. Remove ignition key. Remove AIR BAG or AIR BAG-IG fuse from fuse block, located on left kick panel. Remove left side cap from steering wheel. Release locking lever and disconnect Yellow connector for driver-side air bag module.

2) Pull out glove box while pushing in both right and left sides. Release locking lever and disconnect Yellow connector for passenger-side air bag module (located in glove box opening).

Activating System – Reconnect driver-side air bag module and passenger-side air bag module connector. Install AIR BAG or AIR BAG-IG fuse. Perform SYSTEM OPERATION CHECK.

TOYOTA

SYSTEM OPERATION CHECK

Turn ignition switch to ACC or ON position. Air bag warning light should come on for about 6 seconds, then go out. If air bag warning light does not operate as specified, service air bag system. See MITCHELL® AIR BAG SERVICE & REPAIR MANUAL, DOMESTIC & IMPORTED MODELS.

SERVICE PRECAUTIONS

Observe the following precautions when servicing SRS:

- Disable SRS before servicing any SRS or steering column component. Failure to disable air bag could result in accidental air bag deployment and possible personal injury. See DISABLING & ACTIVATING AIR BAG SYSTEM.
- After turning ignition switch to LOCK position and disconnecting negative battery cable, wait at least 90 seconds before working on SRS. SRS is equipped with a back-up power source that may allow air bag to deploy until 90 seconds after disconnecting negative battery cable.

- If vehicle was in a minor collision but air bags did not deploy, inspect front air bag sensors and steering wheel pad.
- Never use air bag parts from another vehicle. Replace air bag parts with new parts.
- Remove center air bag sensor and front air bag sensors if repairing the vehicle requires impacting (shocking) the vehicle.
- Center air bag sensor contains mercury. After replacement, DO NOT destroy old part. When scrapping vehicle or replacing center air bag sensor, remove center air bag sensor and dispose of it as toxic waste.
- Never disassemble and repair front air bag sensors, center air bag sensor or steering wheel pad.
- Replace dropped, cracked, dented or otherwise damaged component.
- DO NOT expose front air bag sensors, center air bag sensor or steering wheel pad directly to heat or flame.
- Information labels are attached to air bag components. Follow all notices on labels.
- After work on SRS is completed, check air bag warning light to ensure system is functioning properly. See SYSTEM OPERATION CHECK.
- Always wear safety glasses when servicing or handling an air bag.
- When placing a live air bag on a bench or other surface, always face air bag and trim cover upward, away from surface. This will reduce motion of module if it is accidentally deployed.
- After deployment, air bag surface may contain deposits of sodium hydroxide, which irritates skin. Always wear safety glasses, rubber gloves and long-sleeved shirt during clean-up. After clean-up, wash hands using mild soap and water.
- Carry a live air bag module with trim cover (air bag) pointed away from your body to minimize injury in case of accidental deployment.
- If SRS is not fully functional for any reason, vehicle should not be driven until system is repaired and again becomes operational. DO NOT remove bulbs, modules, sensors or other components or in any way disable system from operating normally. If SRS is not functional, park vehicle until it is repaired and functions properly.

DISABLING & ACTIVATING AIR BAG SYSTEM

WARNING: Back-up power supply maintains SRS voltage for about 90 seconds after battery is disconnected. After disabling SRS, wait at least 90 seconds before servicing SRS to prevent accidental air bag deployment and possible personal injury.

Disabling System – Turn ignition switch to LOCK position. Disconnect and shield negative battery cable. Wait at least 90 seconds before working on system. Remove steering wheel pad (air bag). On vehicles equipped with passenger-side air bag, disconnect passenger-side air bag connector, accessible through finish plate in glove box.

Activating System – Reconnect passenger-side air bag connector (if equipped). Install steering wheel pad. Reconnect negative battery cable. Perform SYSTEM OPERATION CHECK.

VOLKSWAGEN

SYSTEM OPERATION CHECK

An air bag light is located on left side of instrument cluster. Air bag light is used to indicate readiness of system. This light, which glows when ignition switch is on or engine is started, will stay on approximately 3 seconds while air bag control unit performs an electronic test cycle of system.

If air bag light does not glow when ignition is on or does not go out after 3 seconds, a fault probably exists in system. If a fault occurs while ignition is on, it is stored in fault memory. Warning light will then glow and air bag system will be switched off. If warning light glows or flickers while driving, air bag system should be tested. See MITCHELL® AIR BAG SERVICE & REPAIR MANUAL, DOMESTIC & IMPORTED MODELS.

SERVICE PRECAUTIONS

Observe these precautions when working with air bag systems:
- Before disconnect battery cable(s) and disabling air bag system, obtain radio security code from vehicle owner.
- DO NOT use computer memory saver tool. Using computer memory saver tool will keep air bag system active and may cause accidental deployment of air bag unit.
- Disable air bag system before servicing any air bag system or steering column component. See DISABLING & ACTIVATING AIR BAG SYSTEM.
- Because of critical operating requirements of system, DO NOT attempt to service any air bag system component.
- Air bag parts should not be left unattended. They should be installed in vehicle immediately after obtaining them.
- Air bag components which have been dropped more than 20 inches should not be used.
- Chemical cleaners, oil and grease should not contact vinyl covering on air bag unit.
- DO NOT place stickers or covers on steering wheel.
- Always disable air bag system before performing electric welding on vehicle.

DISABLING & ACTIVATING AIR BAG SYSTEM

To disable air bag system, disconnect and shield negative battery cable. To activate system, reconnect negative battery cable. Perform a system operational check to ensure proper system operation. See SYSTEM OPERATION CHECK.

VOLVO

SYSTEM OPERATION CHECK

Turn ignition switch to ON position (engine not running). If no fault codes are present, SRS warning light will go out after 10 seconds. If SRS is malfunctioning, SRS fault code will be stored in crash sensor memory during the following conditions:
- SRS warning light does not glow.
- SRS warning light does not go out after 10 seconds.
- SRS warning light does not go out after engine is started.
- SRS warning light comes on while driving.

If SRS warning light indicates a malfunction, enter self-diagnostics and retrieve fault codes.

Seat Belt Tensioner Inspection – 1) There are 2 methods of determining seat belt tensioner activation. Start by pulling seat belt out and releasing it. If belt normally extends easily to full length, tensioner has not been activated. If either belt sticks, jerks when reeling and unreeling or fails to reel, both belts must be replaced.

2) If seat belt tensioner activation can not be determined, turn ignition switch to OFF position. Disconnect negative battery cable. Remove "B" post inner panel. Insert a steel rod into tensioner tube to establish position of plunger.

3) On 850 models, if plunger position is near bottom of tensioner tube, seat belt tensioner has been activated and both belts must be replaced. If plunger position is near top of tensioner tube, seat belt tensioner has not deployed.

4) On 960 models, if plunger position is near bottom of tensioner tube, seat belt tensioner has not deployed. If plunger position is near top of tensioner tube, seat belt tensioner has been activated and both belts must be replaced.

SERVICE PRECAUTIONS

Observe these precautions when working with air bag systems:
- Always disable SRS before performing any air bag repairs. See DISABLING & ACTIVATING AIR BAG SYSTEM.
- Before disconnect battery cable(s) and disabling air bag system, obtain radio security code from vehicle owner.
- Always ensure radio is off before disconnecting battery. This will prevent damage to radio microprocessor.

- Always wear safety glasses and gloves when handling a deployed air bag module and/or seat belt tensioners. Air bag module and/or seat belt tensioners may contain sodium hydroxide deposits, which irritate skin.
- Use caution when handling sensors. Never strike or jar sensors. All sensors and mounting bracket bolts must be tightened carefully to ensure proper sensor operation.
- Never apply power to SRS if any SRS crash sensor is not securely mounted to vehicle.
- Never make any measurement directly on air bag module(s) or seat belt tensioners.
- Wiring repairs should not be performed on any portion of SRS wiring harness.
- Always handle air bag modules with trim cover away from your body. Always place air bag module on workbench with trim cover facing up, away from loose objects.

DISABLING & ACTIVATING AIR BAG SYSTEM

WARNING: DO NOT disconnect crash sensor connector or standby power unit to disable system. This action could cause air bag to deploy.

Disabling System – 1) Before proceeding, see SERVICE PRECAUTIONS. Before performing any repairs, turn ignition switch to OFF position. Disconnect and shield negative battery cable. Locate and disconnect air bag module and seat belt tensioner connectors and passenger-side air bag module connector.

2) On 1995-96 850 & 1996 960 models with side air bags, remove cover from side seat compartment. Remove transport safety device from inside of cover. Install transport safety device onto side impact sensor. *See Fig. 30.* Repeat procedure for opposite front seat. SRS system is now disabled.

Activating System – After repairs are performed, ensure all wiring and component connectors are connected. Turn ignition switch to ON position. Connect negative battery cable. Ensure vehicle is not occupied when connecting battery cable. Ensure system is functioning properly. See SYSTEM OPERATION CHECK.

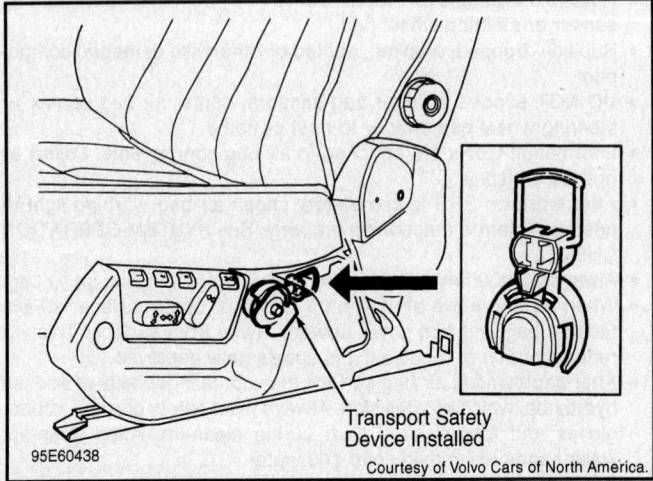

Transport Safety Device Installed

95E60438

Courtesy of Volvo Cars of North America.

Fig. 30: Disabling Side Air Bags (960 Shown; 850 Is Similar)

SECTION 1

OIL CIRCUIT DIAGRAMS

MANUFACTURER & MODEL	Page
Acura M1WA	1-2
Acura MPYA, M5DA & M5HA	1-11
Acura SP7A	1-20
Aisin Warner AW03-72L & Mitsubishi V4AW2	1-29
Honda Accord 2.7L MPZA	1-41
Honda Civic A4RA	1-50
Honda Civic CVT	1-57
Honda AOYA, MPJA & MPOA	1-66
Honda MP1A	1-75
Honda S24A	1-84
Hydra-Matic 3L30	1-93
Hydra-Matic 4L30	1-101
Hyundai A4AF & Mitsubishi F4A20 Series	1-112
Hyundai KM175	1-121
Mazda FA4A-EL	1-130
Mazda GF4A-EL	1-150
Mazda NC4A-EL	1-161
Mazda RA4A-EL & RA4AX-EL	1-174
Mitsubishi R4AC1	1-187
Mitsubishi V4AW3	1-198
Subaru 4-Speed	1-206
Suzuki Esteem	1-218
Toyota A-132L	1-224
Toyota A-140E	1-233
Toyota A-240E & A-241E	1-242
Toyota A-340E & A-340H	1-251

OIL CIRCUIT DIAGRAMS
Acura M1WA

NO.	DESCRIPTION OF PRESSURE	NO.	DESCRIPTION OF PRESSURE	NO.	DESCRIPTION OF PRESSURE
1	LINE	15	1ST-HOLD CLUTCH	42	4TH CLUTCH
2	LINE	16	1ST-HOLD CLUTCH	55	THROTTLE B
3	LINE	18	LINE	56	THROTTLE B
3'	LINE	20	2ND CLUTCH	90	TORQUE CONVERTER
3"	LINE	21	2ND CLUTCH	91	TORQUE CONVERTER
4	LINE	22	2ND CLUTCH	92	TORQUE CONVERTER
4'	LINE	25	LINE	93	OIL COOLER
5	LINE	30	3RD CLUTCH	94	TORQUE CONVERTER
6	MODULATOR	31	3RD CLUTCH	95	LUBRICATION
6'	MODULATOR (DUTY CONTROL)	32	3RD CLUTCH	96	TORQUE CONVERTER
9	LINE	40	4TH CLUTCH	99	SUCTION
10	1ST CLUTCH	41	4TH CLUTCH	X	BLEED

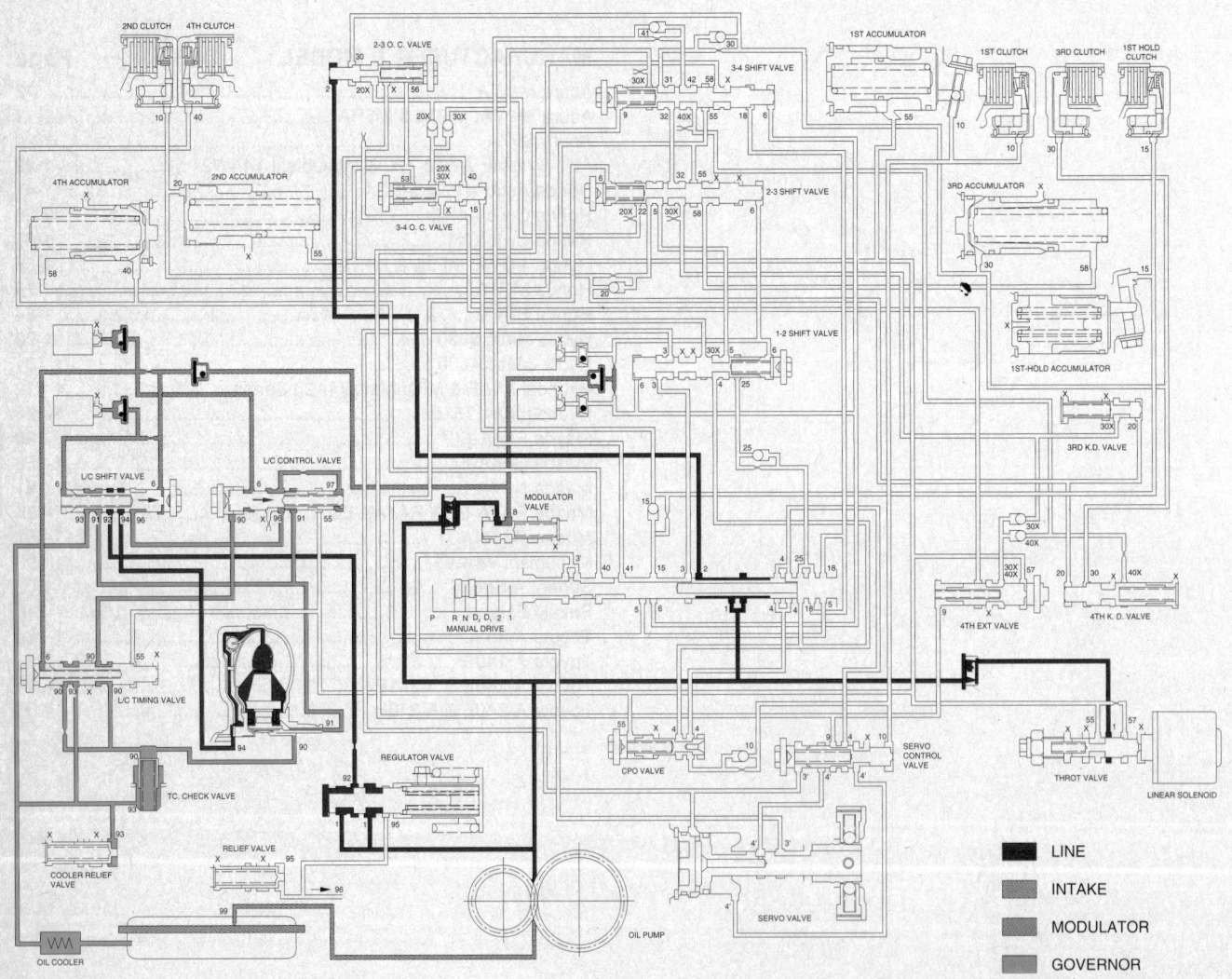

Fig. 1: "N" Position — Neutral

Courtesy of American Honda Motor Co., Inc.

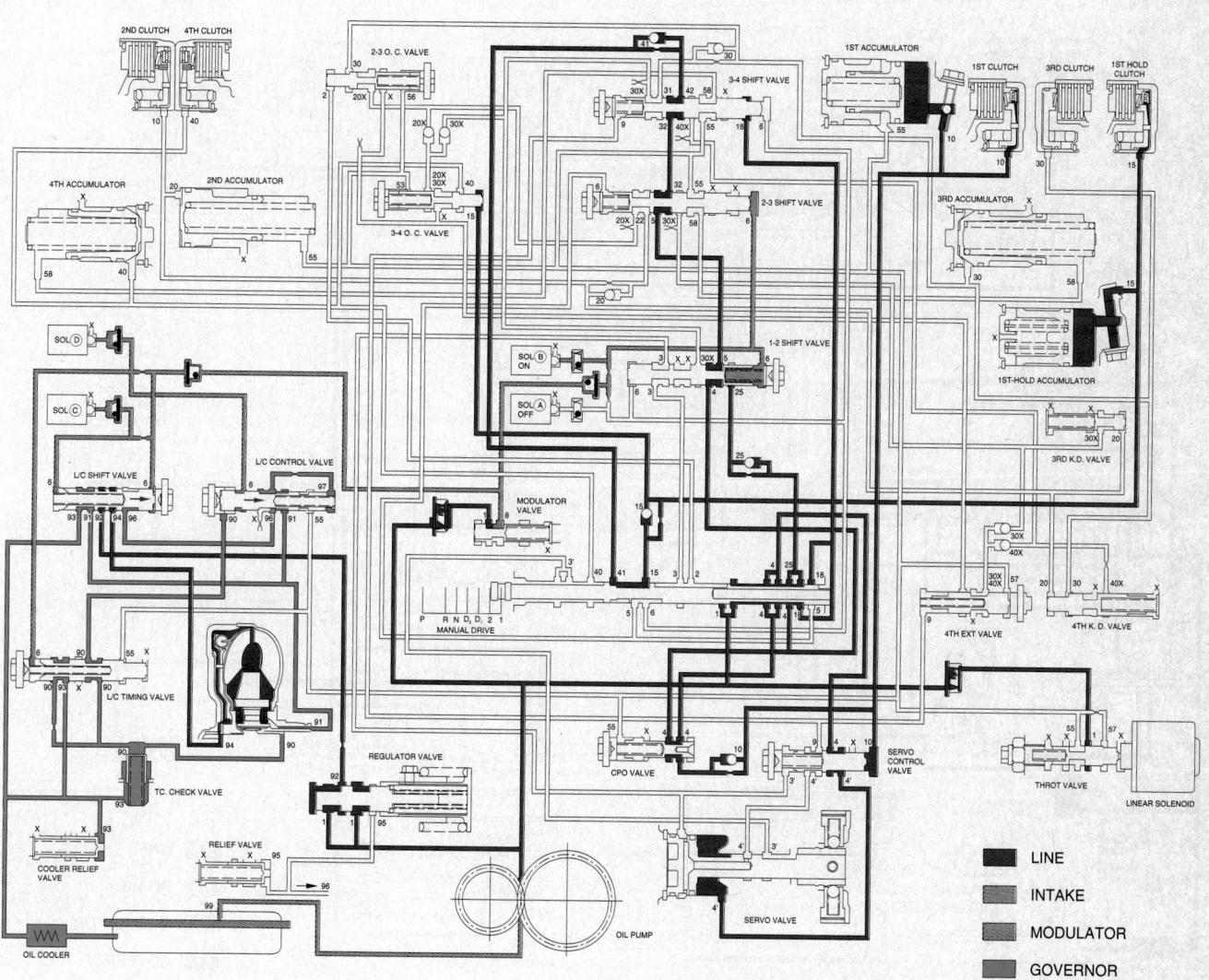

Fig. 2: "1" Position — 1st Gear

Courtesy of American Honda Motor Co., Inc.

OIL CIRCUIT DIAGRAMS
Acura M1WA (Cont.)

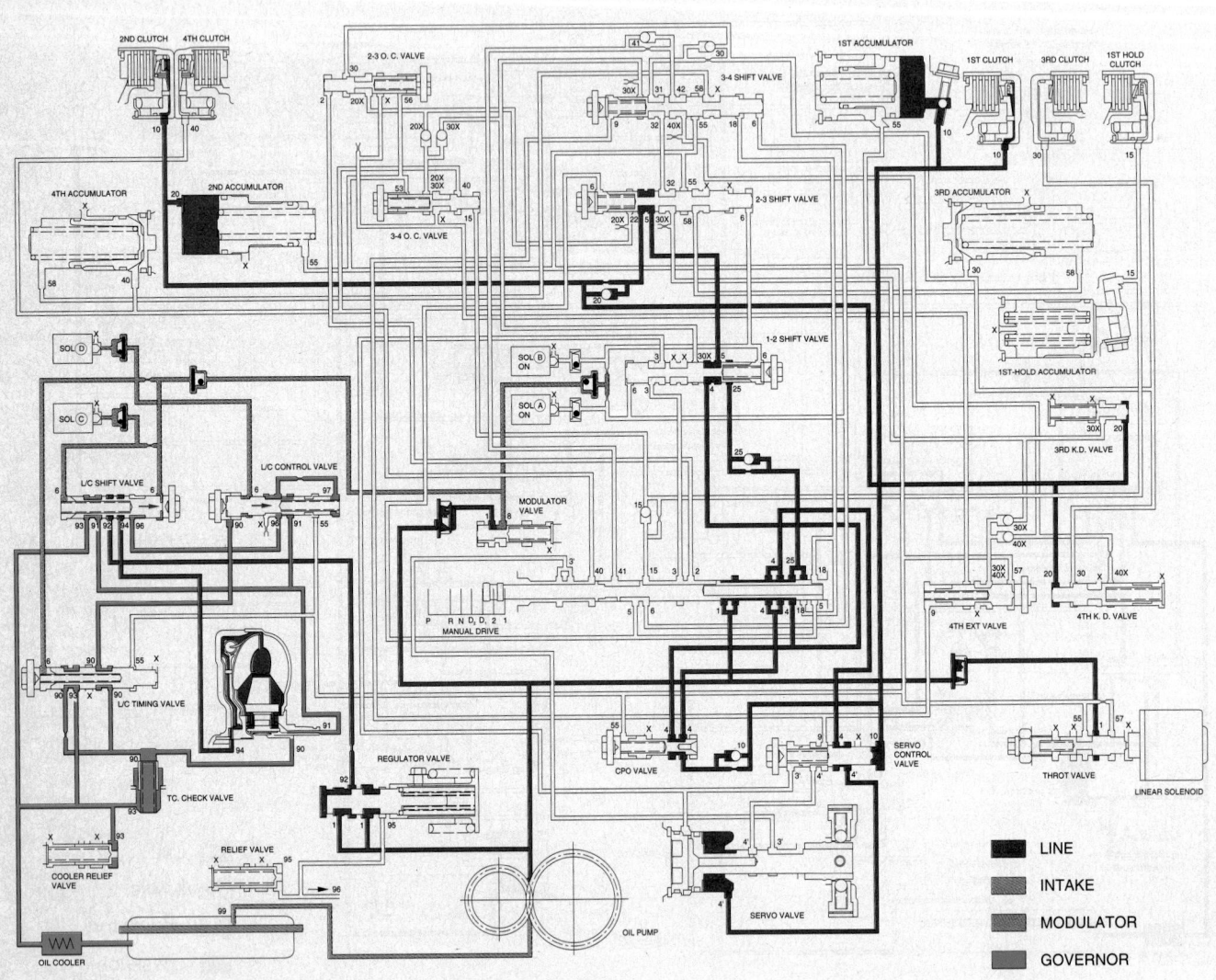

Courtesy of American Honda Motor Co., Inc.

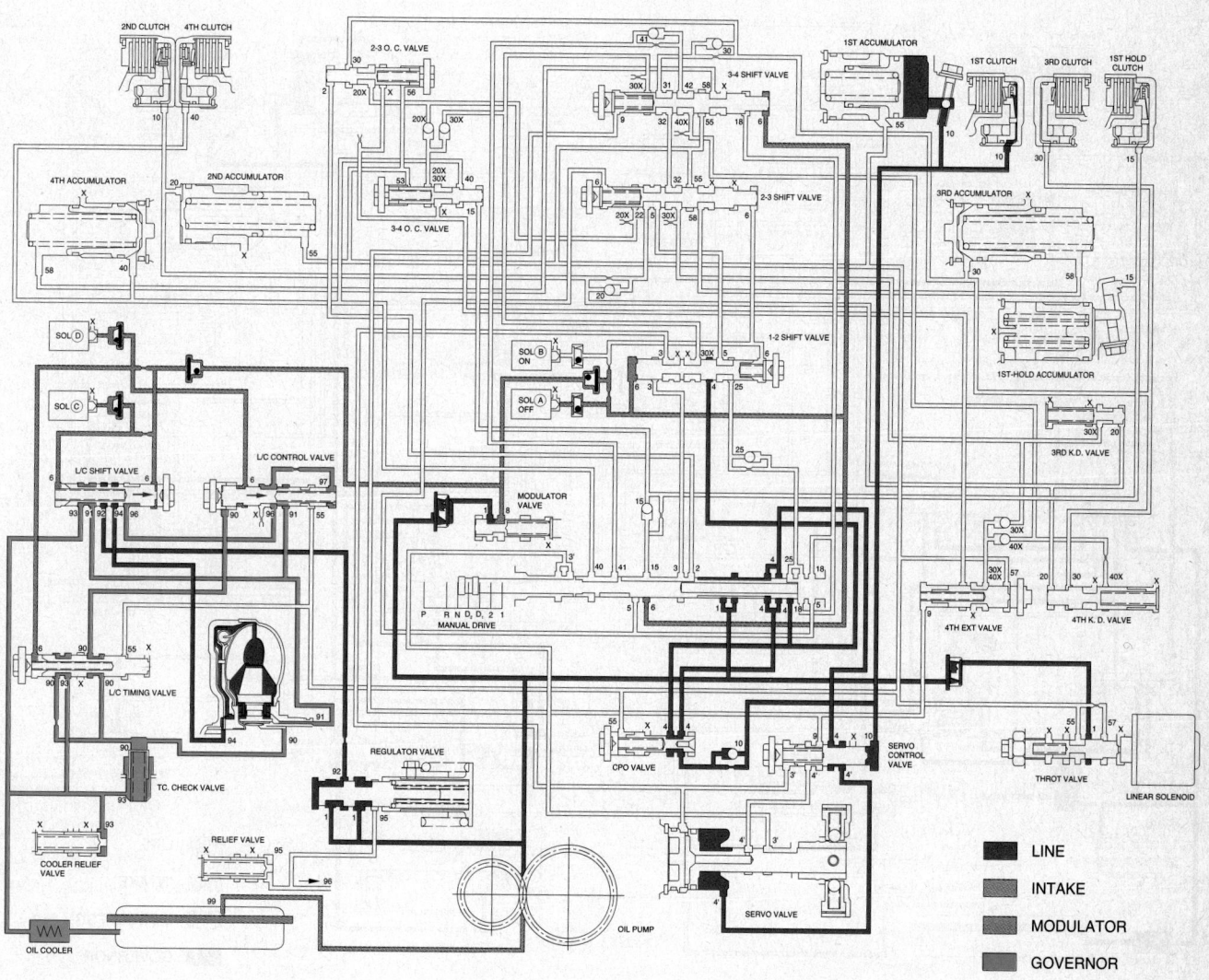

Fig. 4: "D₄" Or "D₃" Position — 1st Gear

Courtesy of American Honda Motor Co., Inc.

OIL CIRCUIT DIAGRAMS
Acura M1WA (Cont.)

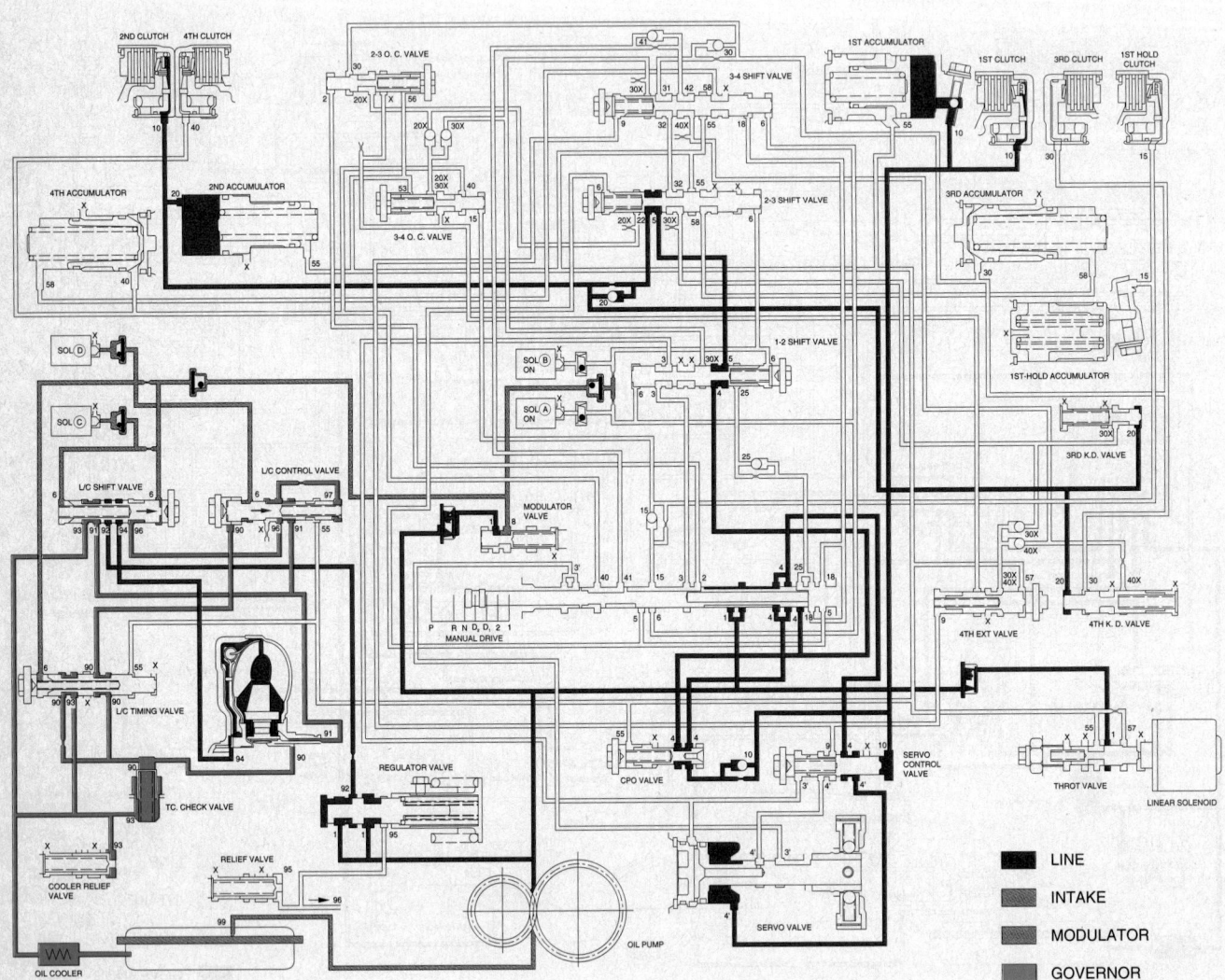

Fig. 5: "D₄" Or "D₃" Position — 2nd Gear

Courtesy of American Honda Motor Co., Inc.

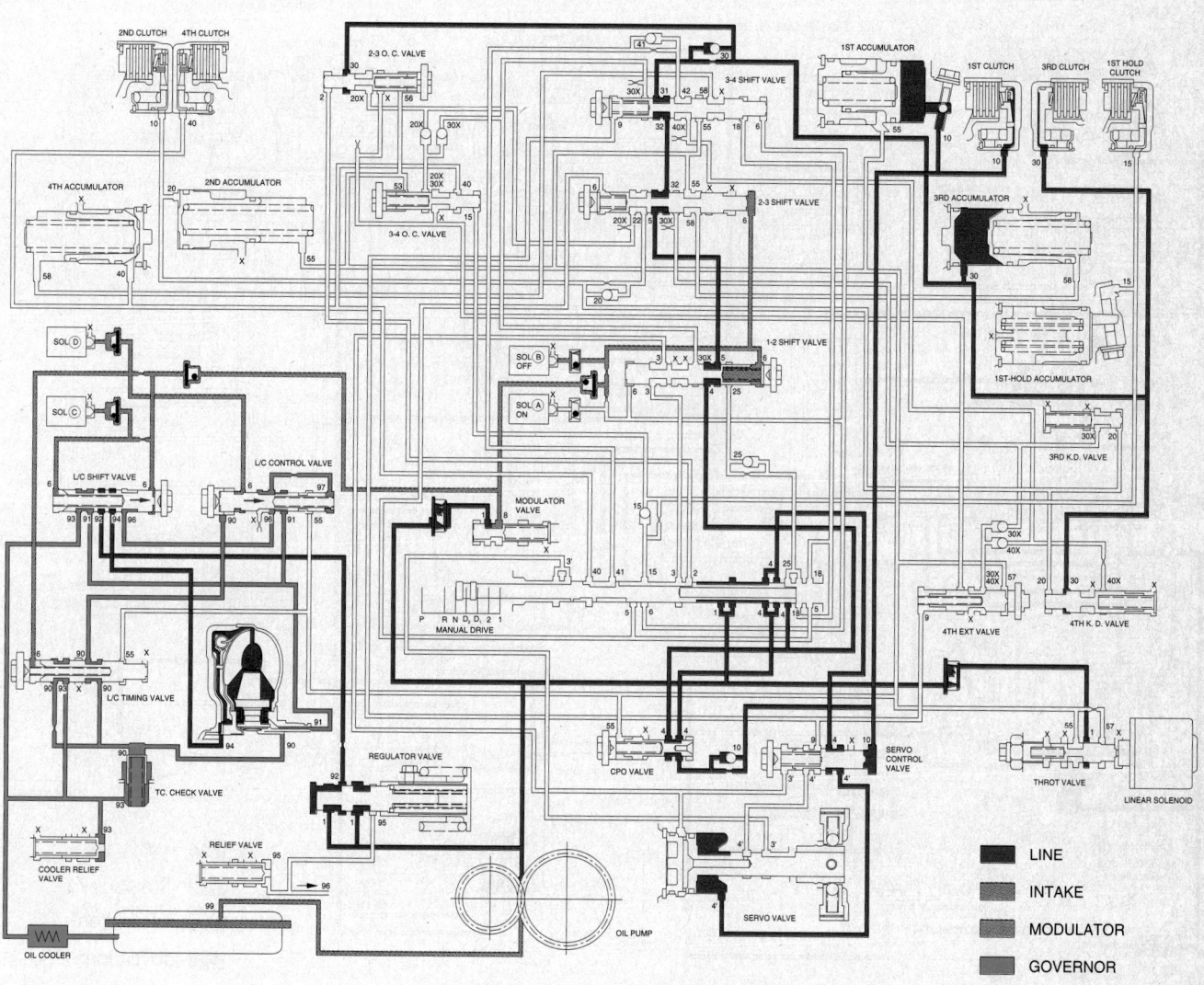

Fig. 6: "D₄" Or "D₃" Position — 3rd Gear

Courtesy of American Honda Motor Co., Inc.

OIL CIRCUIT DIAGRAMS
Acura M1WA (Cont.)

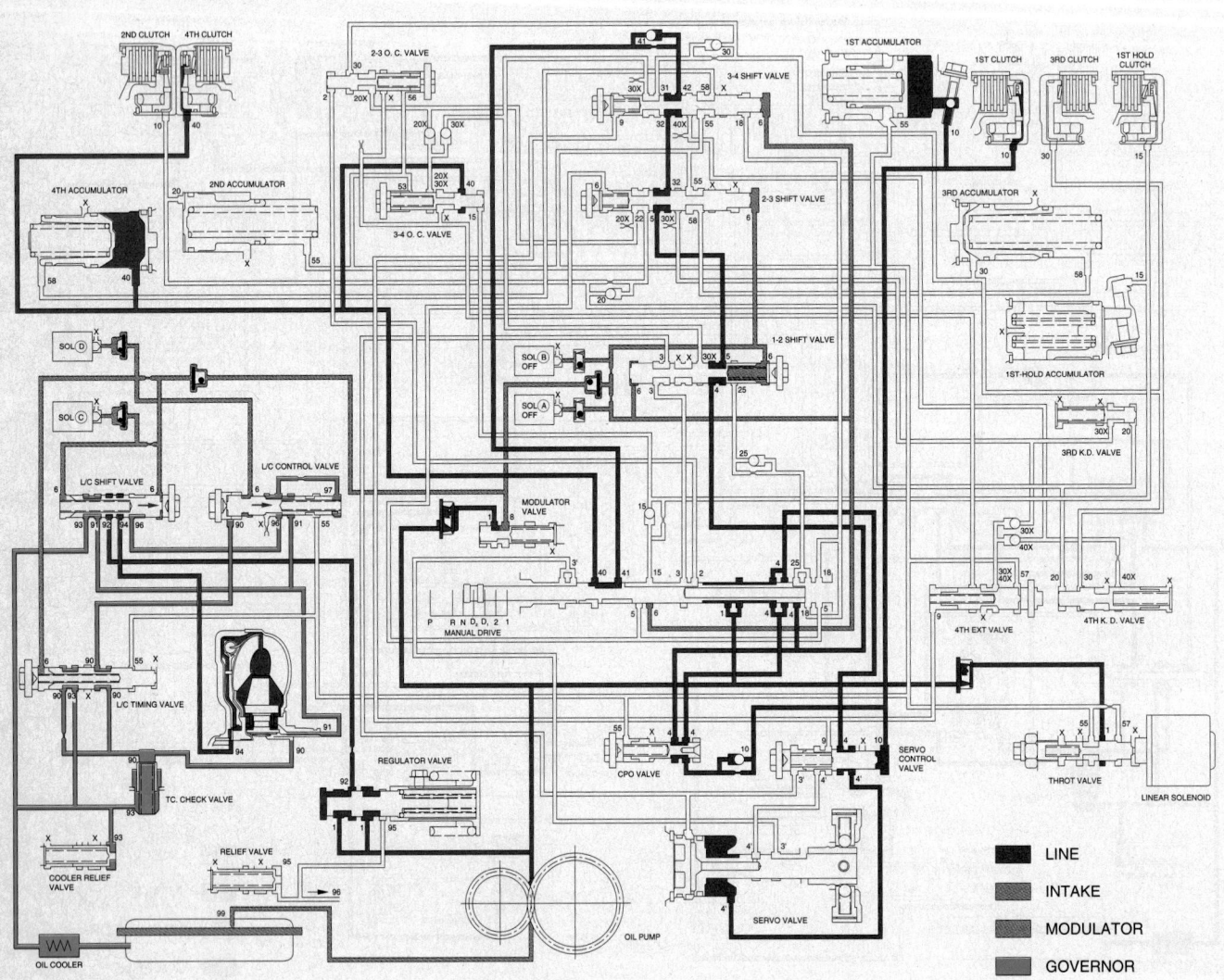

Fig. 7: "D₄" Or "D₃" Position — 4th Gear

Courtesy of American Honda Motor Co., Inc.

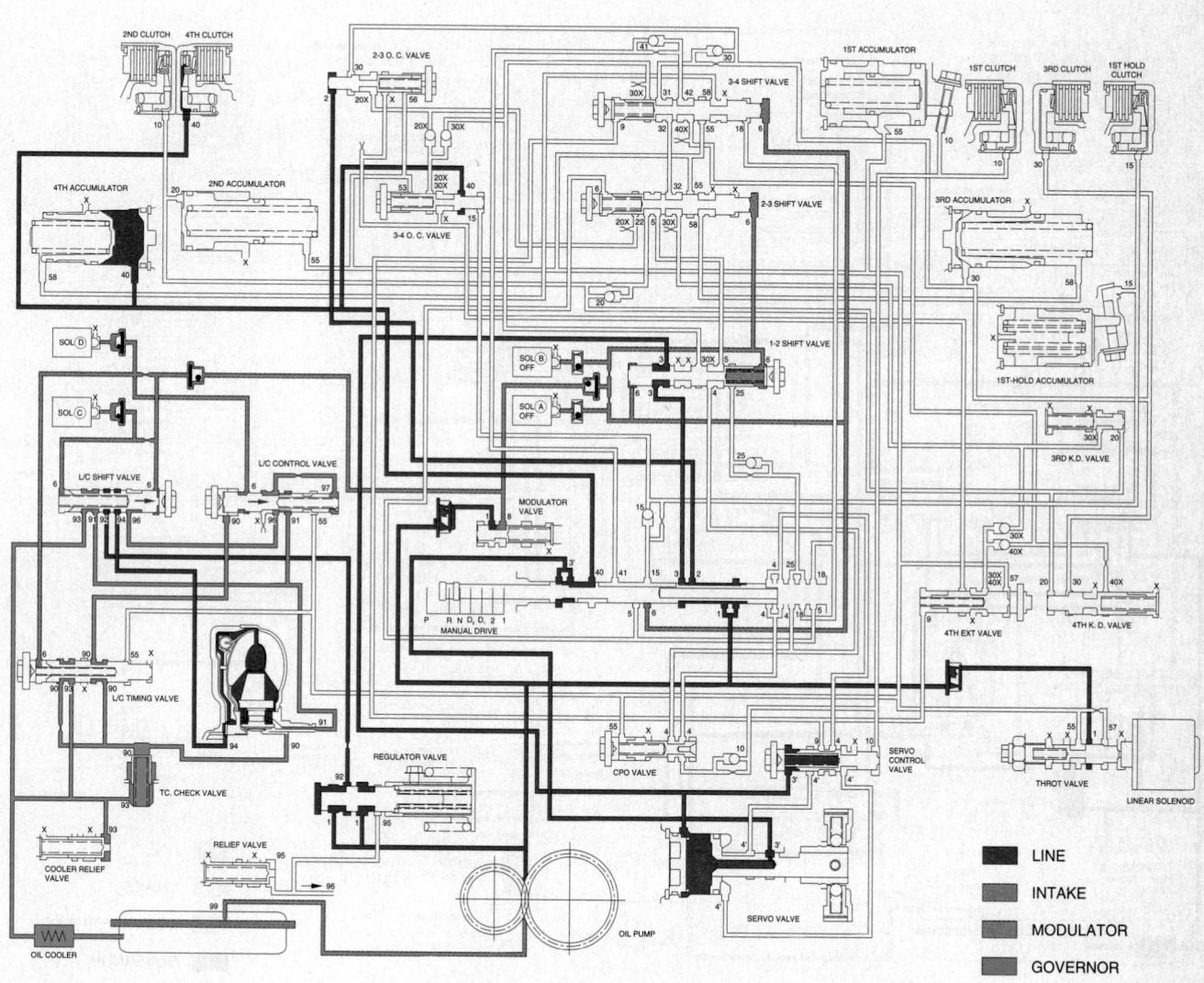

Fig. 8: "R" Position — Reverse

Courtesy of American Honda Motor Co., Inc.

OIL CIRCUIT DIAGRAMS
Acura M1WA (Cont.)

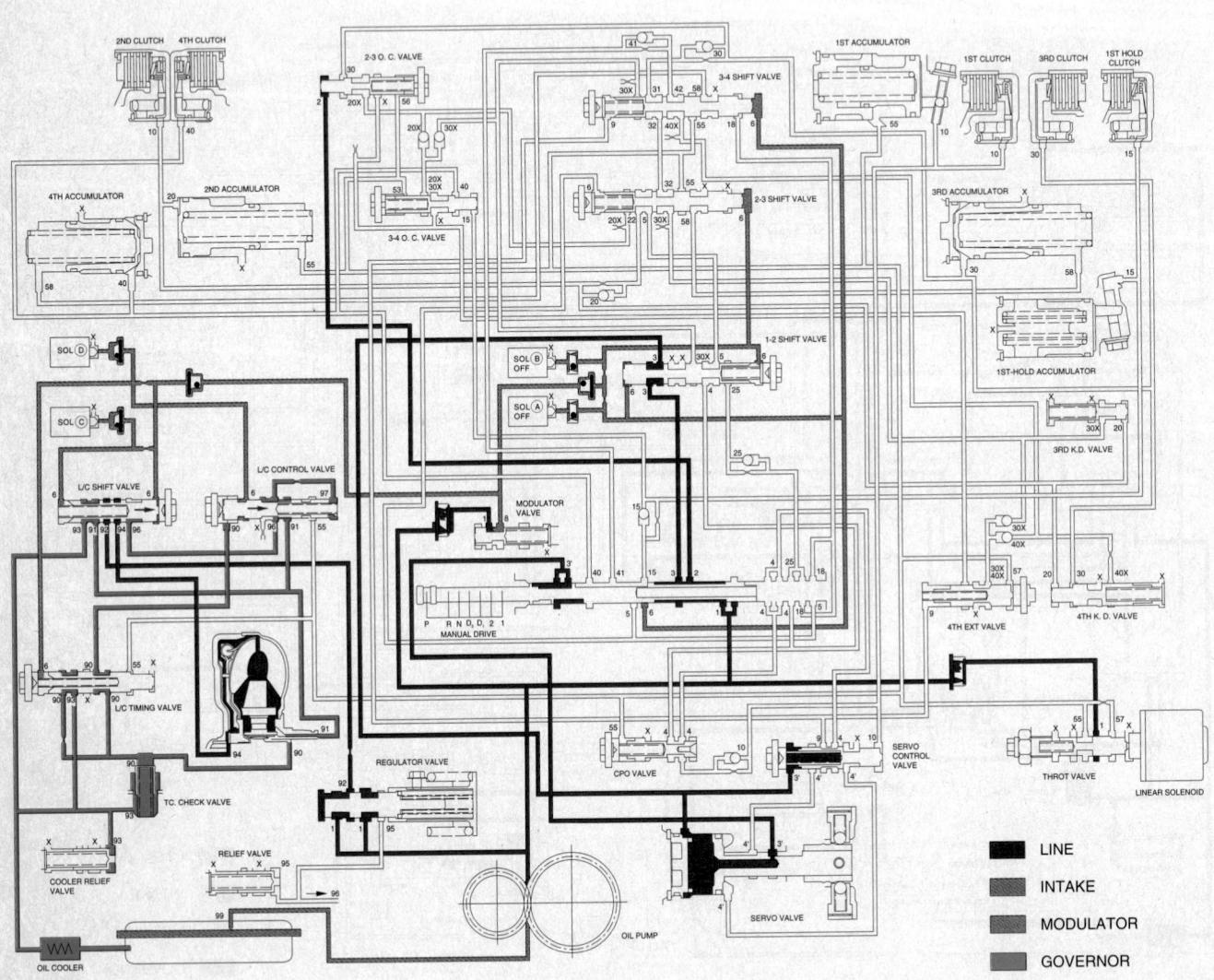

Fig. 9: "P" Position — Park

Courtesy of American Honda Motor Co., Inc.

OIL CIRCUIT DIAGRAMS
Acura MPYA, M5DA & M5HA

NO.	DESCRIPTION OF PRESSURE	NO.	DESCRIPTION OF PRESSURE	NO.	DESCRIPTION OF PRESSURE
1	LINE	10	1ST CLUTCH	71	1ST-HOLD CLUTCH
2	LINE	10'	1ST CLUTCH	72	1ST-HOLD CLUTCH
4	LINE	11	1ST CLUTCH	90	TORQUE CONVERTER
4'	LINE	20	2ND CLUTCH	91	TORQUE CONVERTER
5	LINE	30	3RD CLUTCH	93	OIL COOLER
6	MODULATOR	40	4TH CLUTCH	94	TORQUE CONVERTER
6A	MODULATOR (SHIFT SOL A)	50	REVERSE CLUTCH	95	LUBRICATION
6B	MODULATOR (SHIFT SOL B)	55	THROTTLE B	96	TORQUE CONVERTER
6C	MODULATOR (L/C SOL A)	56	THROTTLE B	99	SUCTION
6D	MODULATOR (L/C SOL B)	57	THROTTLE B	X	BLEED
7	LINE	70	1ST-HOLD CLUTCH		

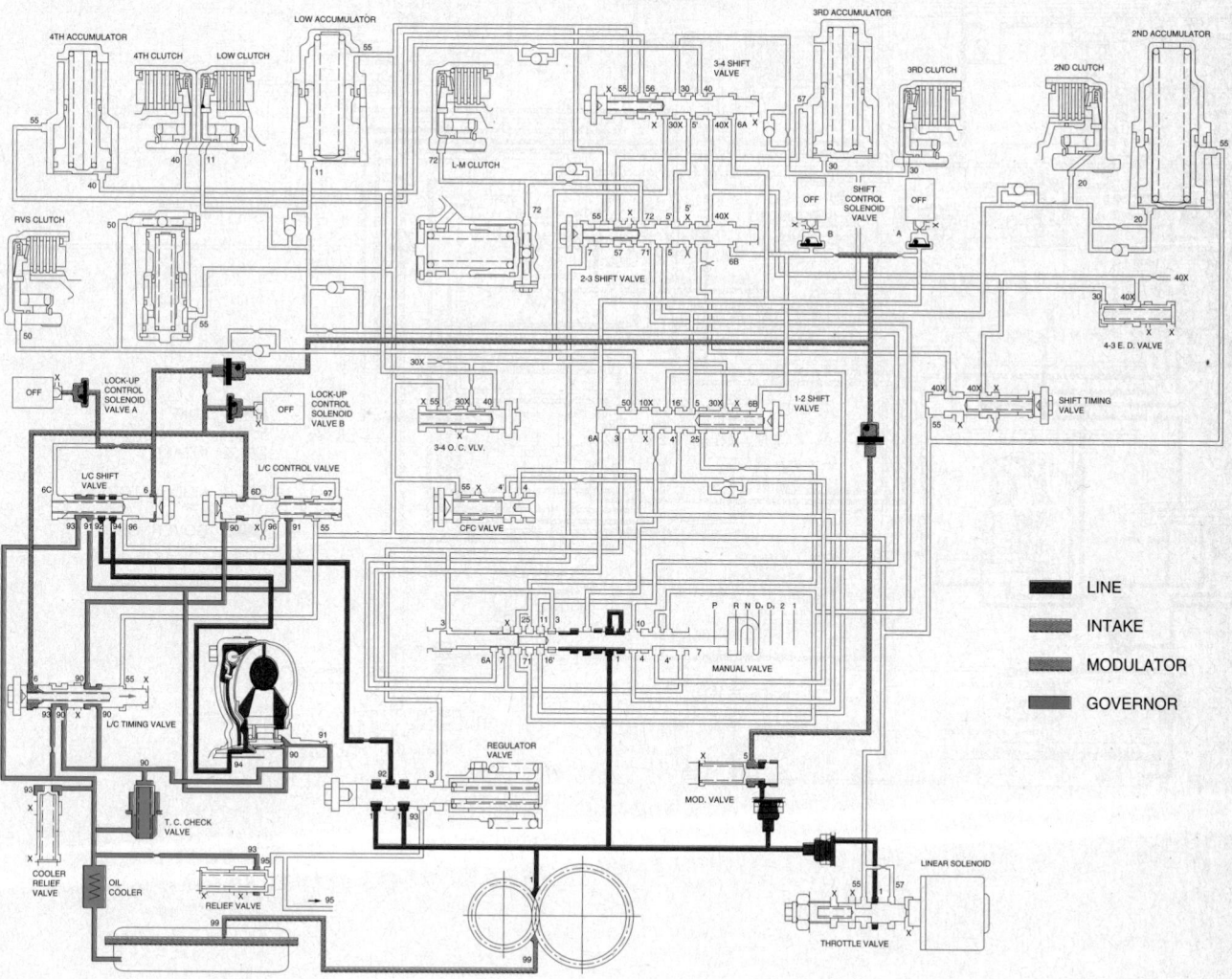

Fig. 1: "N" Position — Neutral

Courtesy of American Honda Motor Co., Inc.

OIL CIRCUIT DIAGRAMS
Acura MPYA, M5DA & M5HA (Cont.)

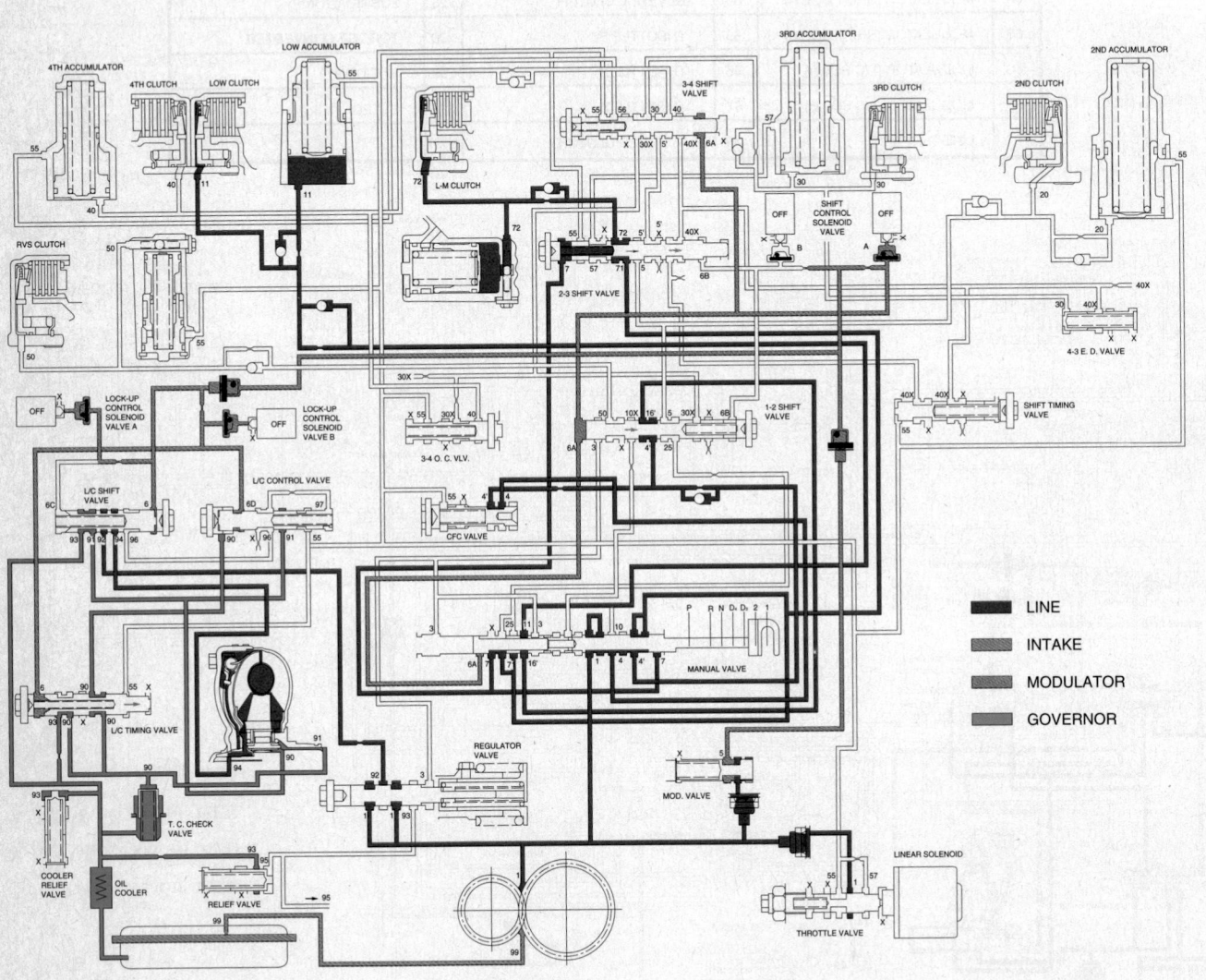

LINE
INTAKE
MODULATOR
GOVERNOR

Fig. 2: "1" Position — 1st Gear

Courtesy of American Honda Motor Co., Inc.

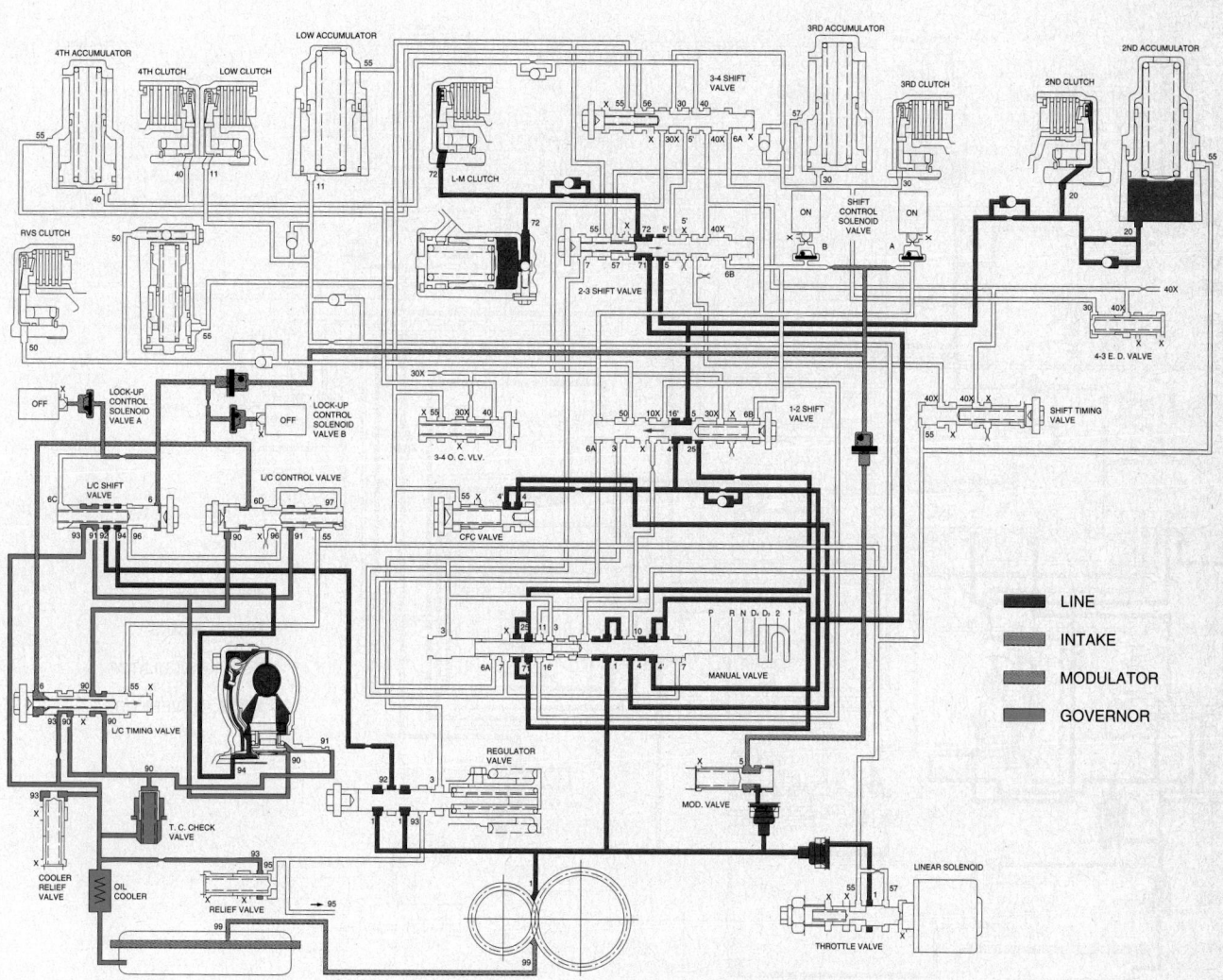

LINE
INTAKE
MODULATOR
GOVERNOR

Fig. 3: "2" Position — 1st Gear

Courtesy of American Honda Motor Co., Inc.

OIL CIRCUIT DIAGRAMS
Acura MPYA, M5DA & M5HA (Cont.)

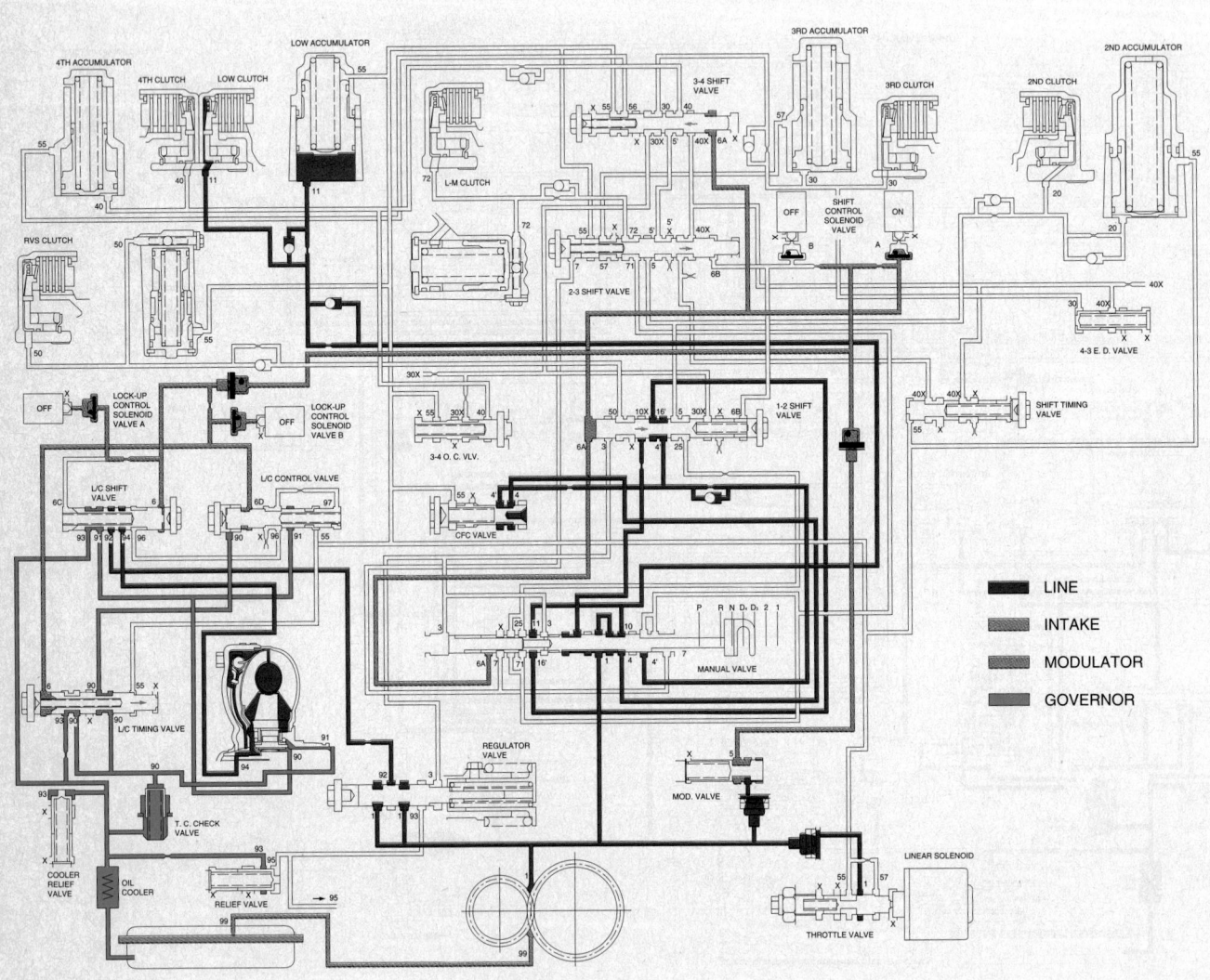

Fig. 4: "D₄" Or "D₃" Position — 1st Gear

Courtesy of American Honda Motor Co., Inc.

OIL CIRCUIT DIAGRAMS
Acura MPYA, M5DA & M5HA (Cont.)

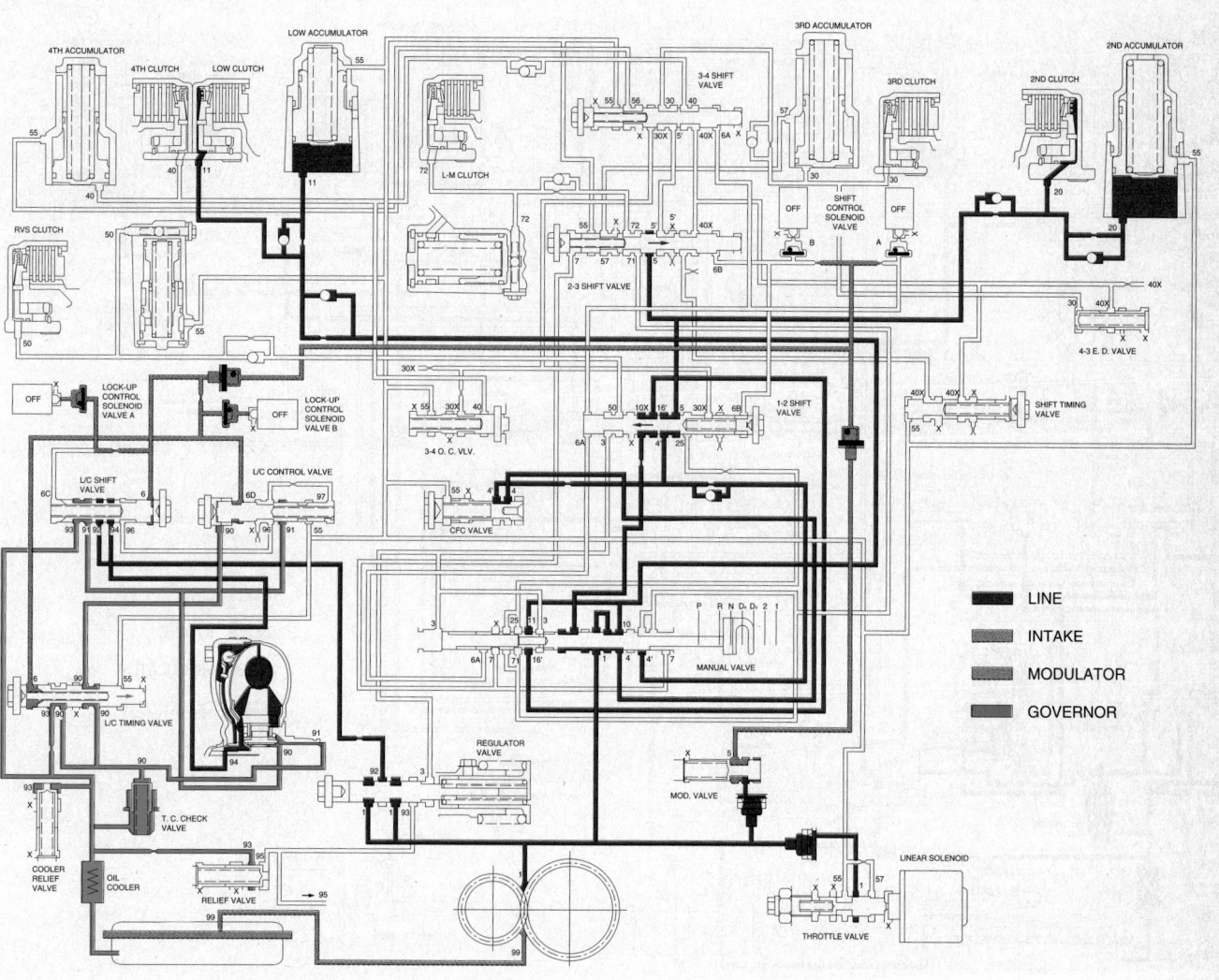

Fig. 5: "D₄" Or "D₃" Position — 2nd Gear

Courtesy of American Honda Motor Co., Inc.

OIL CIRCUIT DIAGRAMS
Acura MPYA, M5DA & M5HA (Cont.)

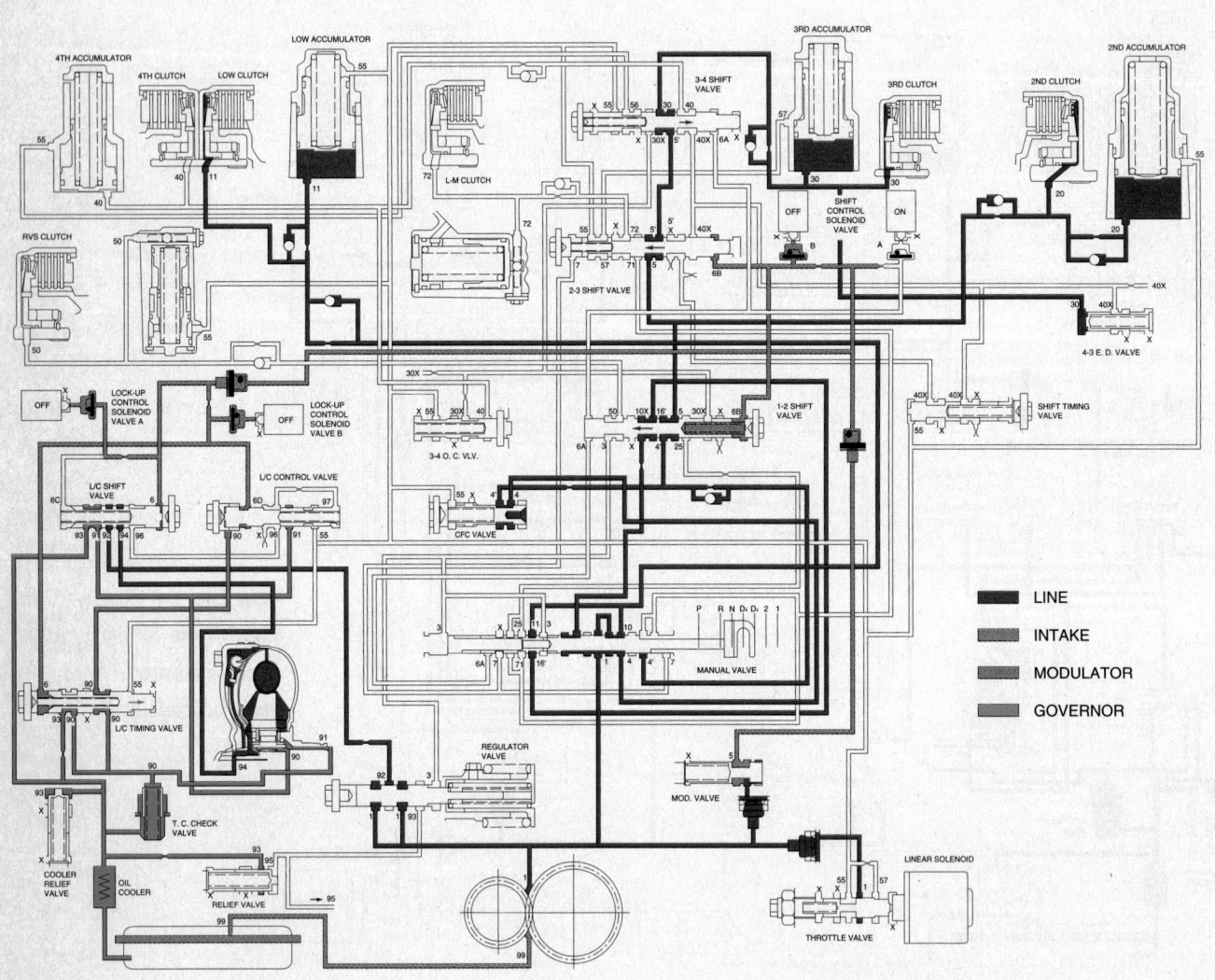

LINE

INTAKE

MODULATOR

GOVERNOR

Fig. 6: "D₄" Or "D₃" Position — 3rd Gear

Courtesy of American Honda Motor Co., Inc.

OIL CIRCUIT DIAGRAMS
Acura MPYA, M5DA & M5HA (Cont.)

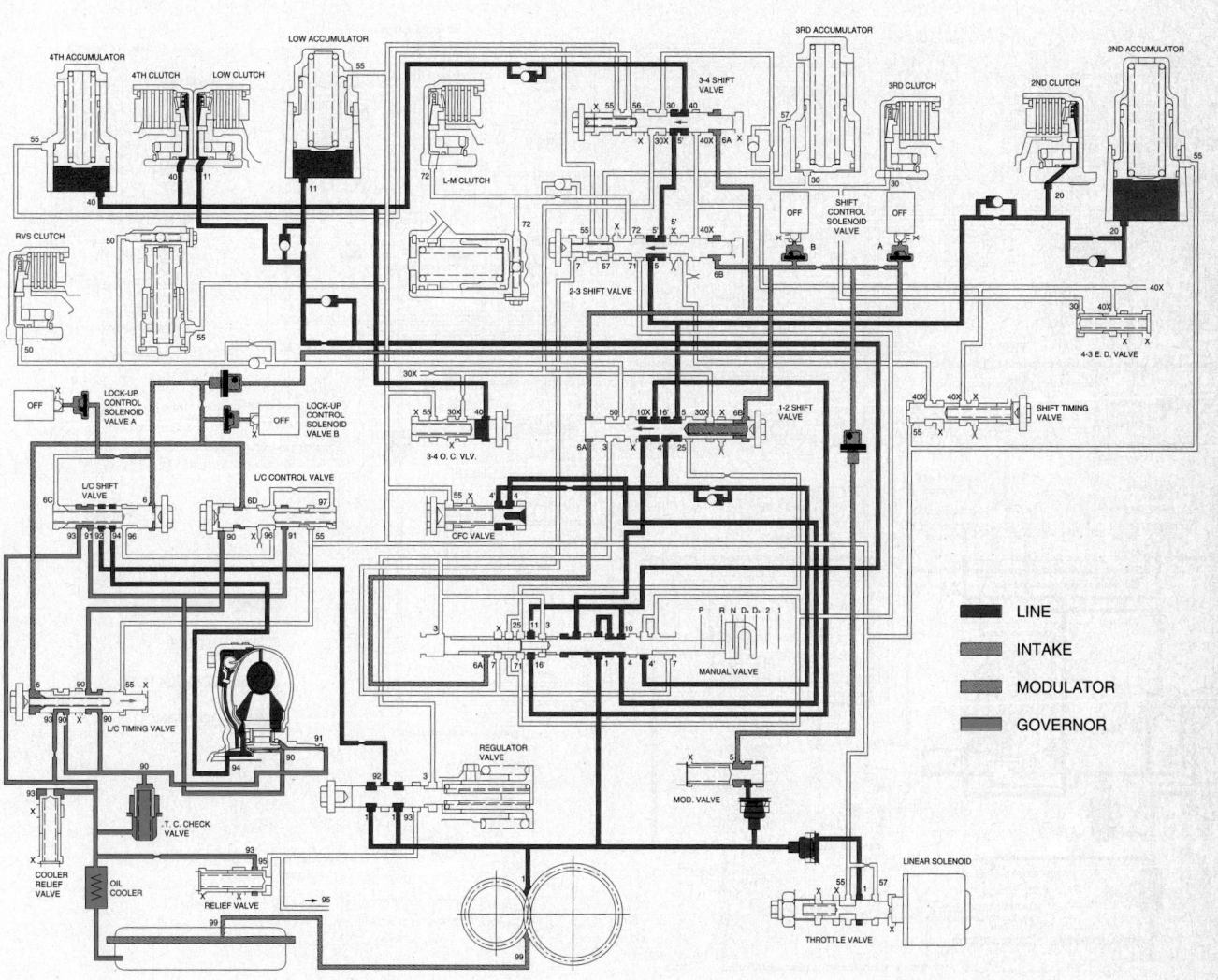

LINE

INTAKE

MODULATOR

GOVERNOR

Fig. 7: *"D₄" Or "D₃" Position — 4th Gear*

Courtesy of American Honda Motor Co., Inc.

OIL CIRCUIT DIAGRAMS
Acura MPYA, M5DA & M5HA (Cont.)

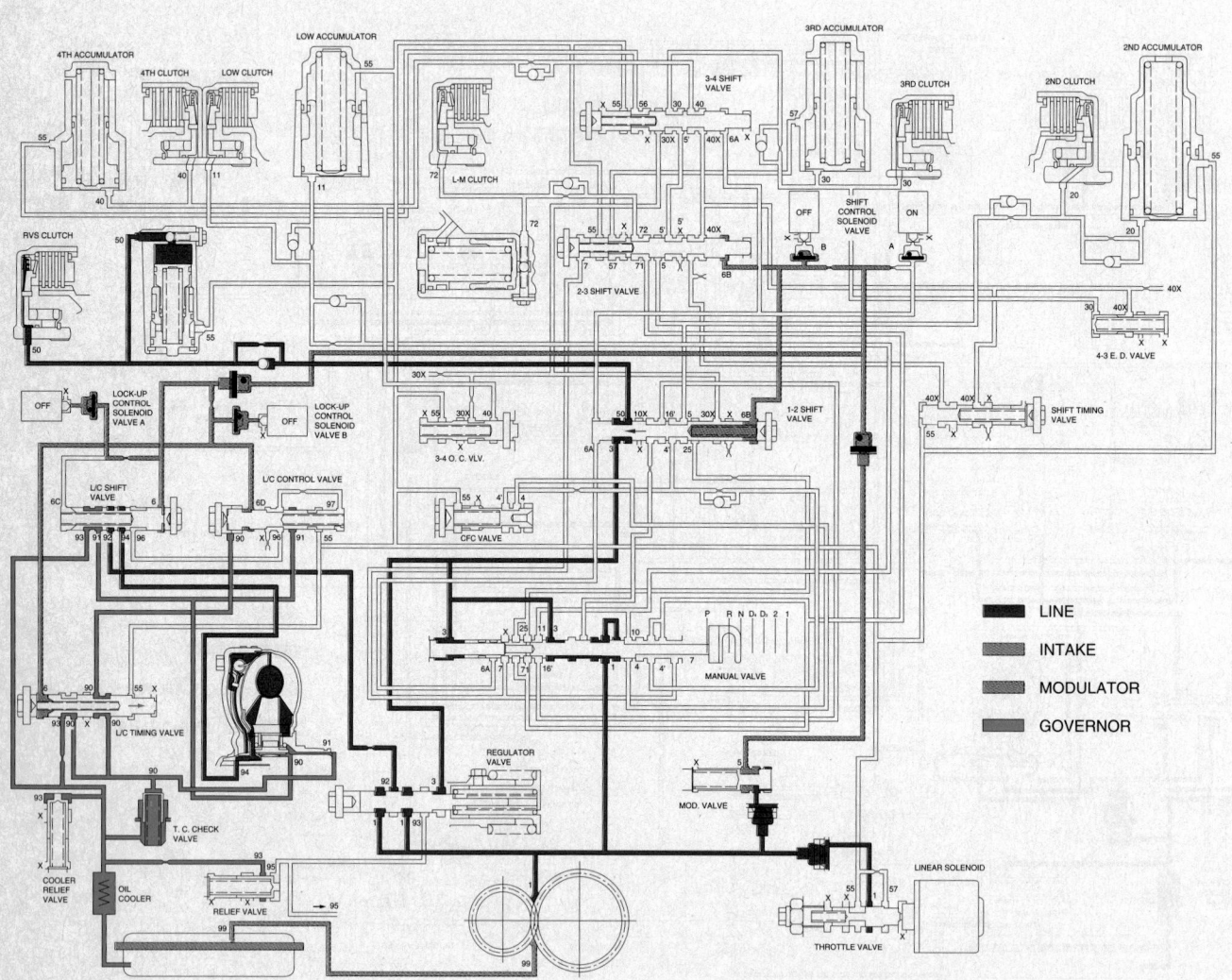

LINE

INTAKE

MODULATOR

GOVERNOR

Fig. 8: "R" Position — Reverse   Courtesy of American Honda Motor Co., Inc.

OIL CIRCUIT DIAGRAMS
Acura MPYA, M5DA & M5HA (Cont.)

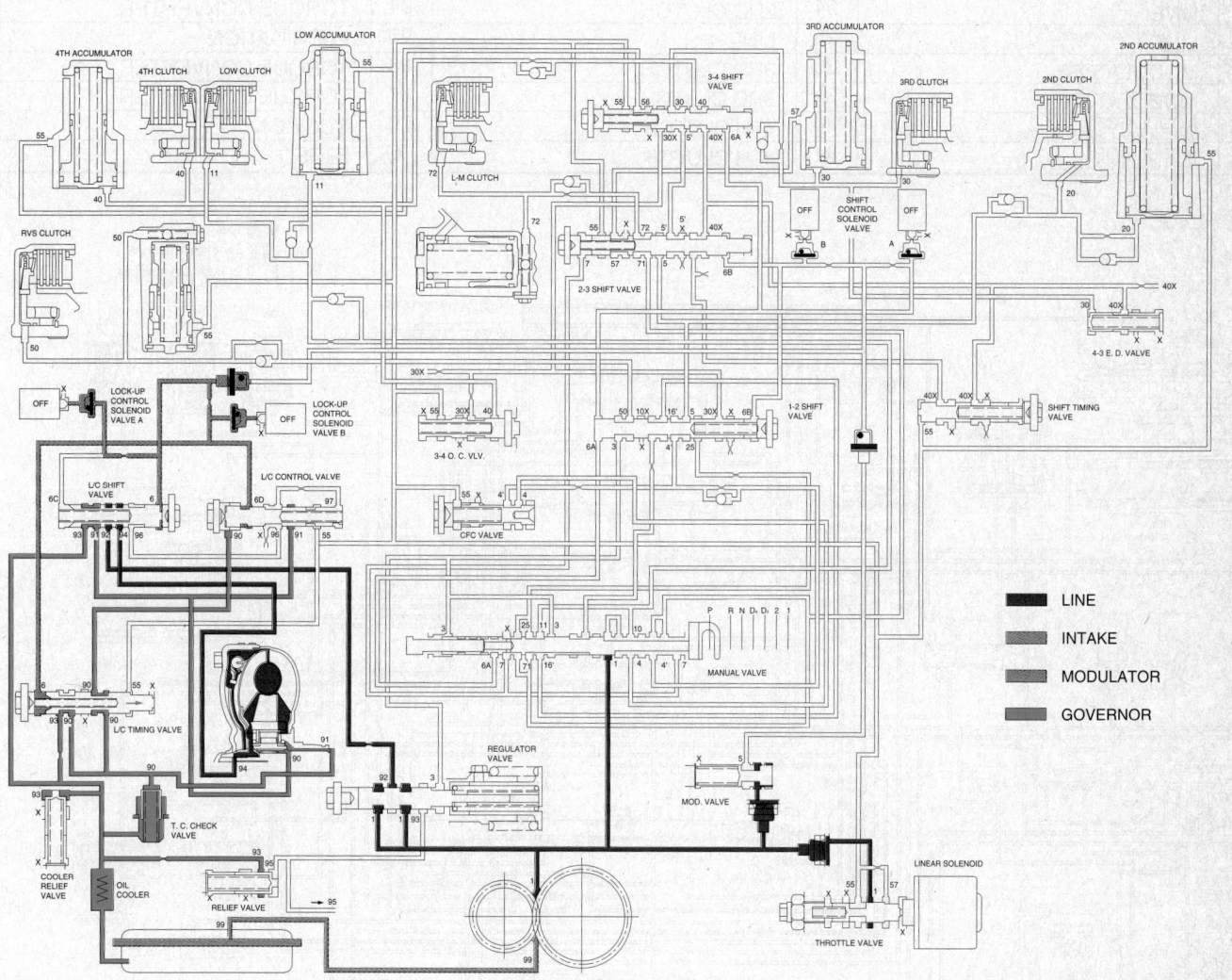

Fig. 9: "P" Position — Park

Courtesy of American Honda Motor Co., Inc.

OIL CIRCUIT DIAGRAMS
Acura SP7A

NO.	DESCRIPTION OF PRESSURE	NO.	DESCRIPTION OF PRESSURE	NO.	DESCRIPTION OF PRESSURE
1	LINE	6C	MODULATOR (LOCK-UP CONTROL SOLENOID VALVE A)	55	THROTTLE B
2	LINE	6D	MODULATOR (LOCK-UP CONTROL SOLENOID VALVE B)	56	THROTTLE B
3	LINE	9	LINE	57	THROTTLE B
3'	LINE	10	1ST CLUTCH	58	THROTTLE B
3"	LINE	15	1ST-HOLD CLUTCH	90	TORQUE CONVERTER
4	LINE	16	1ST-HOLD CLUTCH	91	TORQUE CONVERTER
4'	LINE	18	LINE	92	TORQUE CONVERTER
5	LINE	20	2ND CLUTCH	93	OIL COOLER
5'	LINE	21	2ND CLUTCH	94	TORQUE CONVERTER
5"	LINE	25	LINE	95	LUBRICATION
6	MODULATOR	30	3RD CLUTCH	96	TORQUE CONVERTER
6'	MODULATOR	31	3RD CLUTCH	97	TORQUE CONVERTER
6A	MODULATOR (SHIFT CONTROL SOLENOID VALVE A)	40	4TH CLUTCH	99	SUCTION
6B	MODULATOR (SHIFT CONTROL SOLENOID VALVE B)	41	4TH CLUTCH	X	BLEED

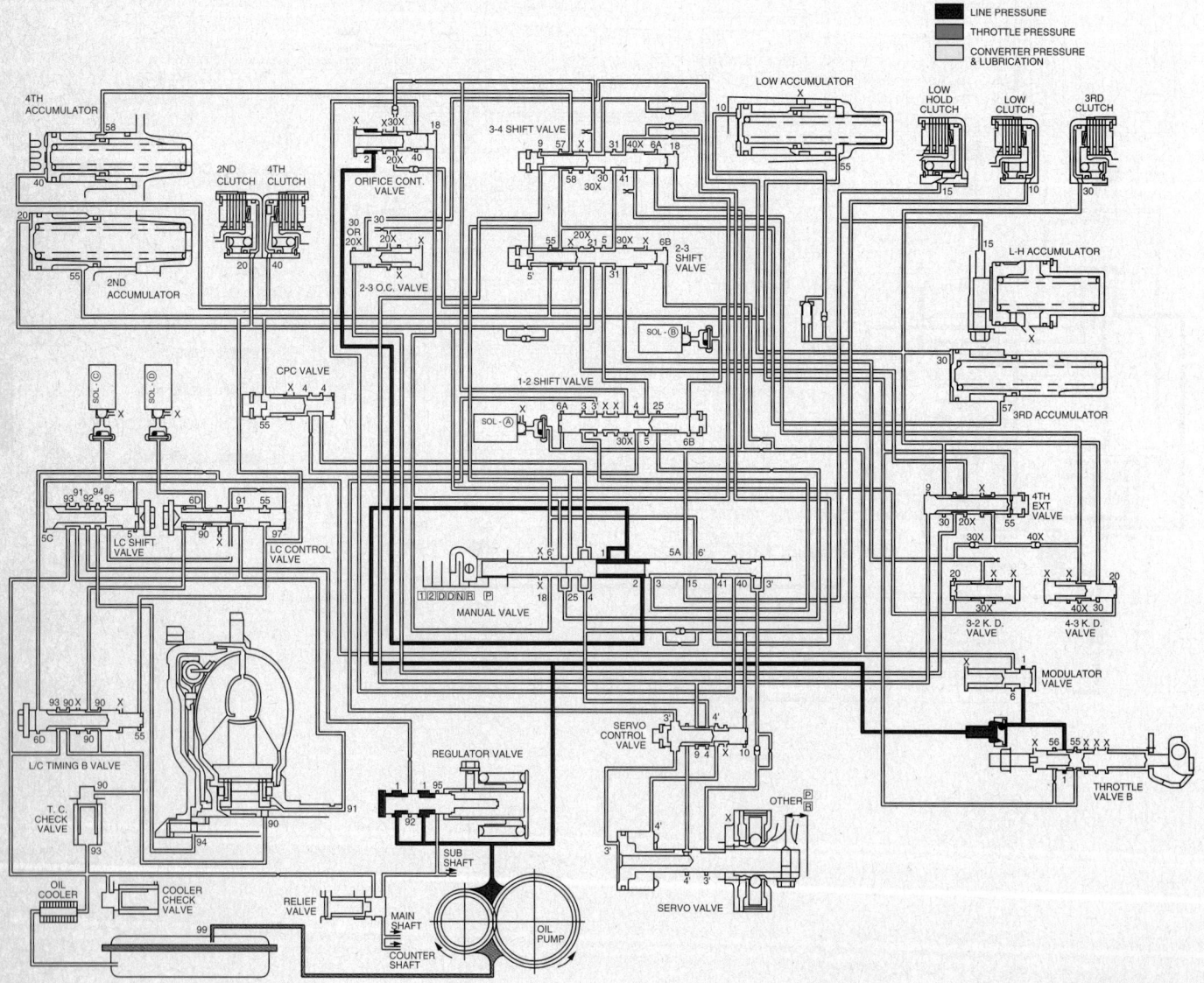

Fig. 1: "N" Position — Neutral

Courtesy of American Honda Motor Co., Inc.

OIL CIRCUIT DIAGRAMS
Acura SP7A (Cont.)

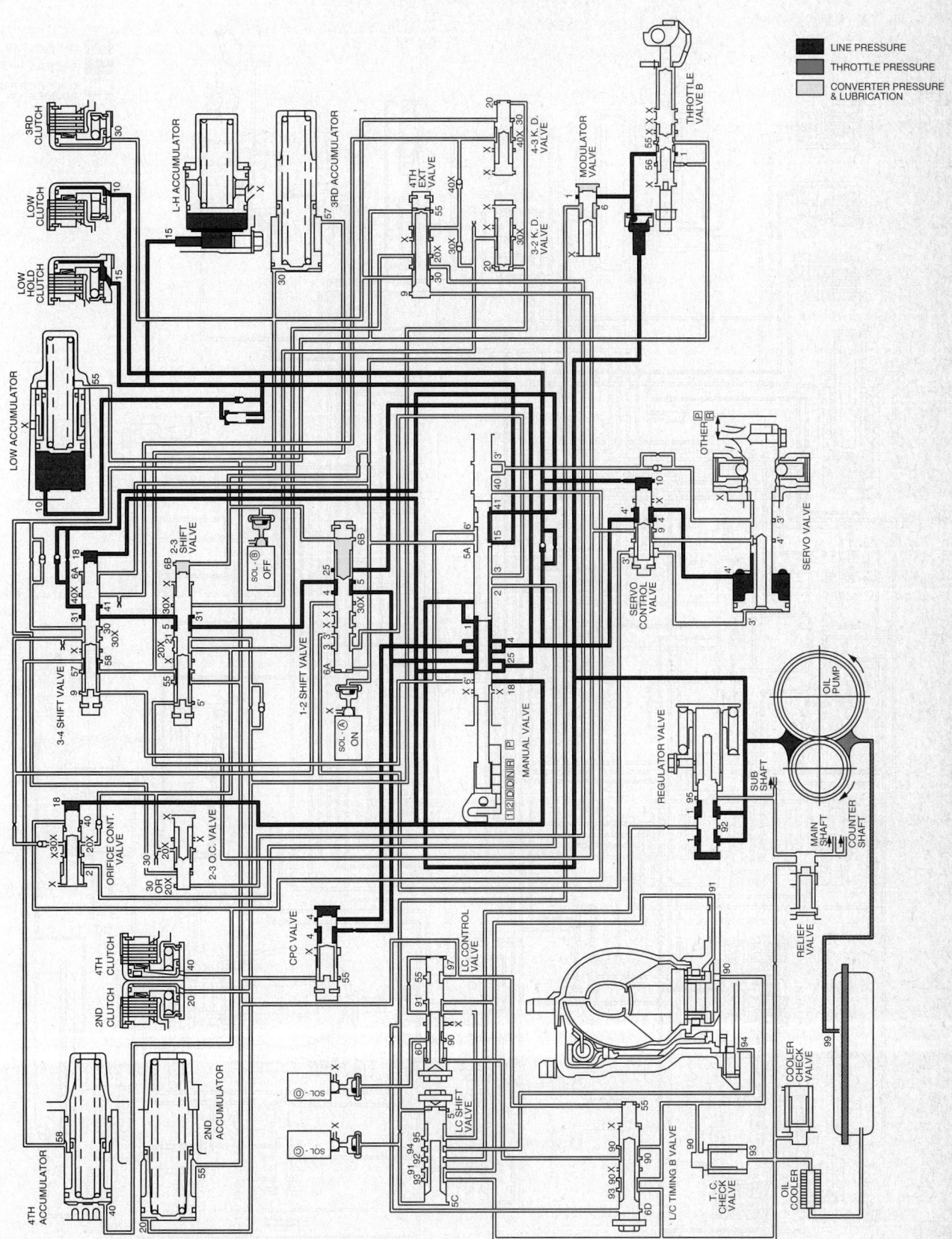

Fig. 2: "1" Position — 1st Gear

Courtesy of American Honda Motor Co., Inc.

OIL CIRCUIT DIAGRAMS
Acura SP7A (Cont.)

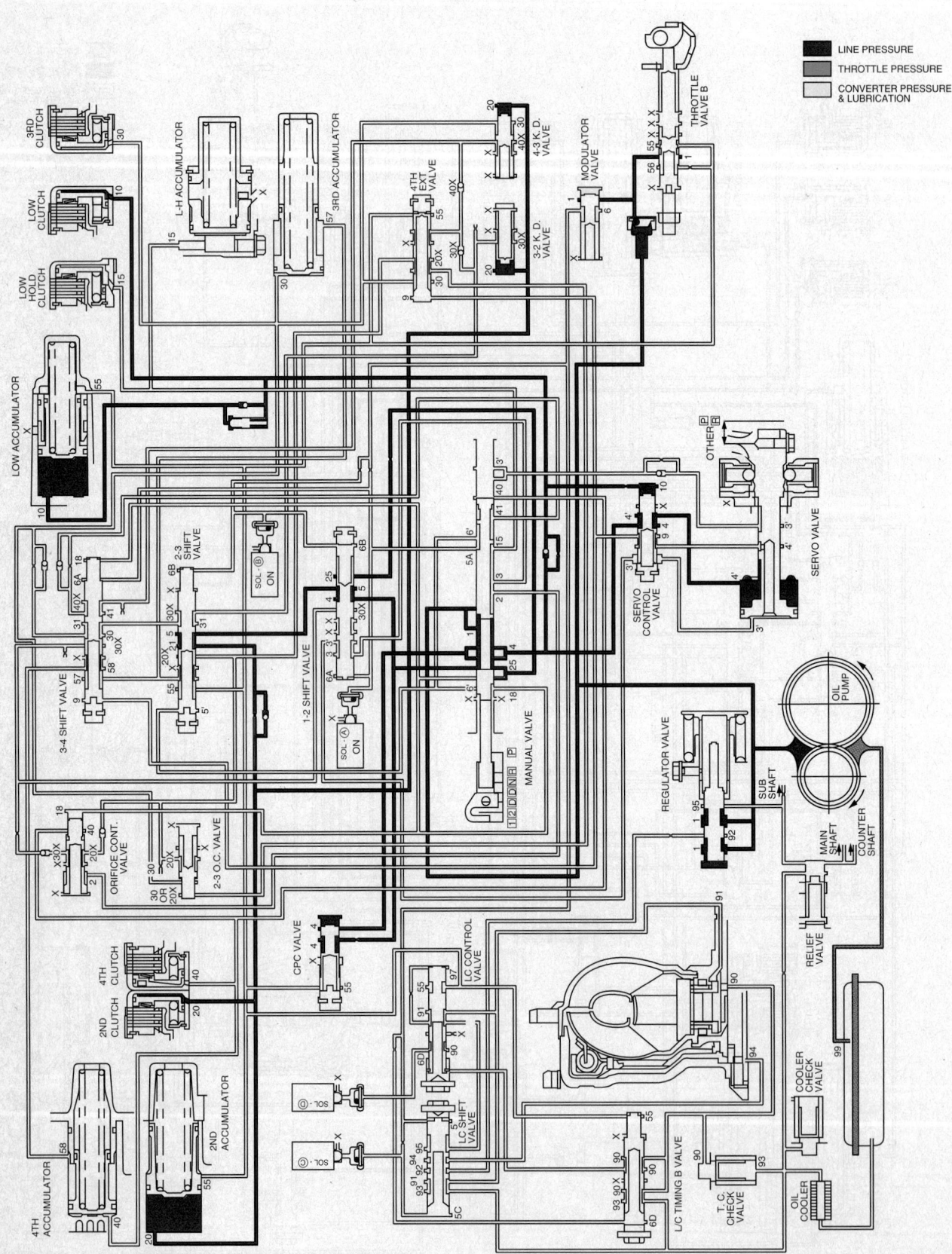

Fig. 3: *"2" Position — 2nd Gear*

Courtesy of American Honda Motor Co., Inc.

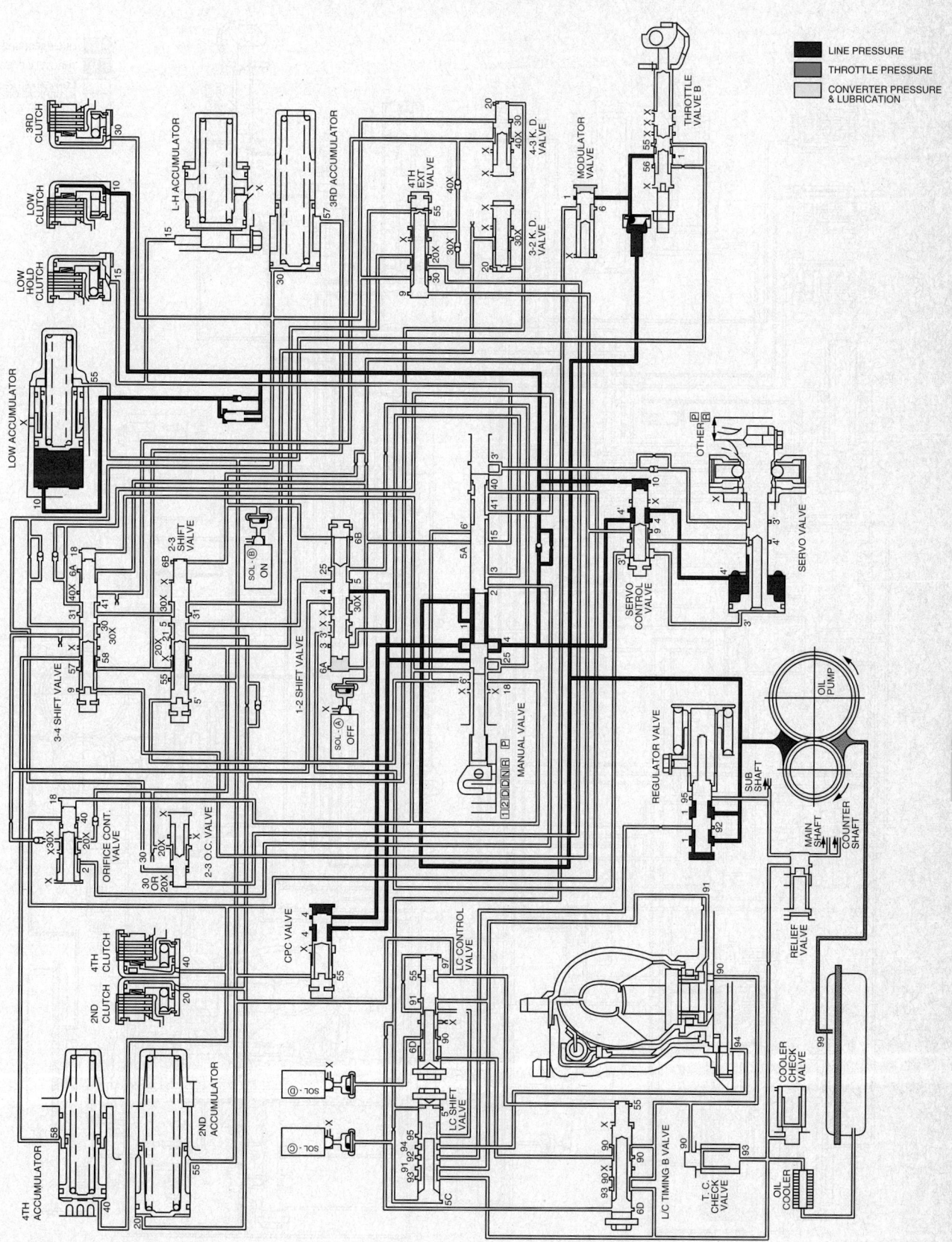

Fig. 4: "D₃" Or "D₄" Position — 1st Gear

Courtesy of American Honda Motor Co., Inc.

OIL CIRCUIT DIAGRAMS
Acura SP7A (Cont.)

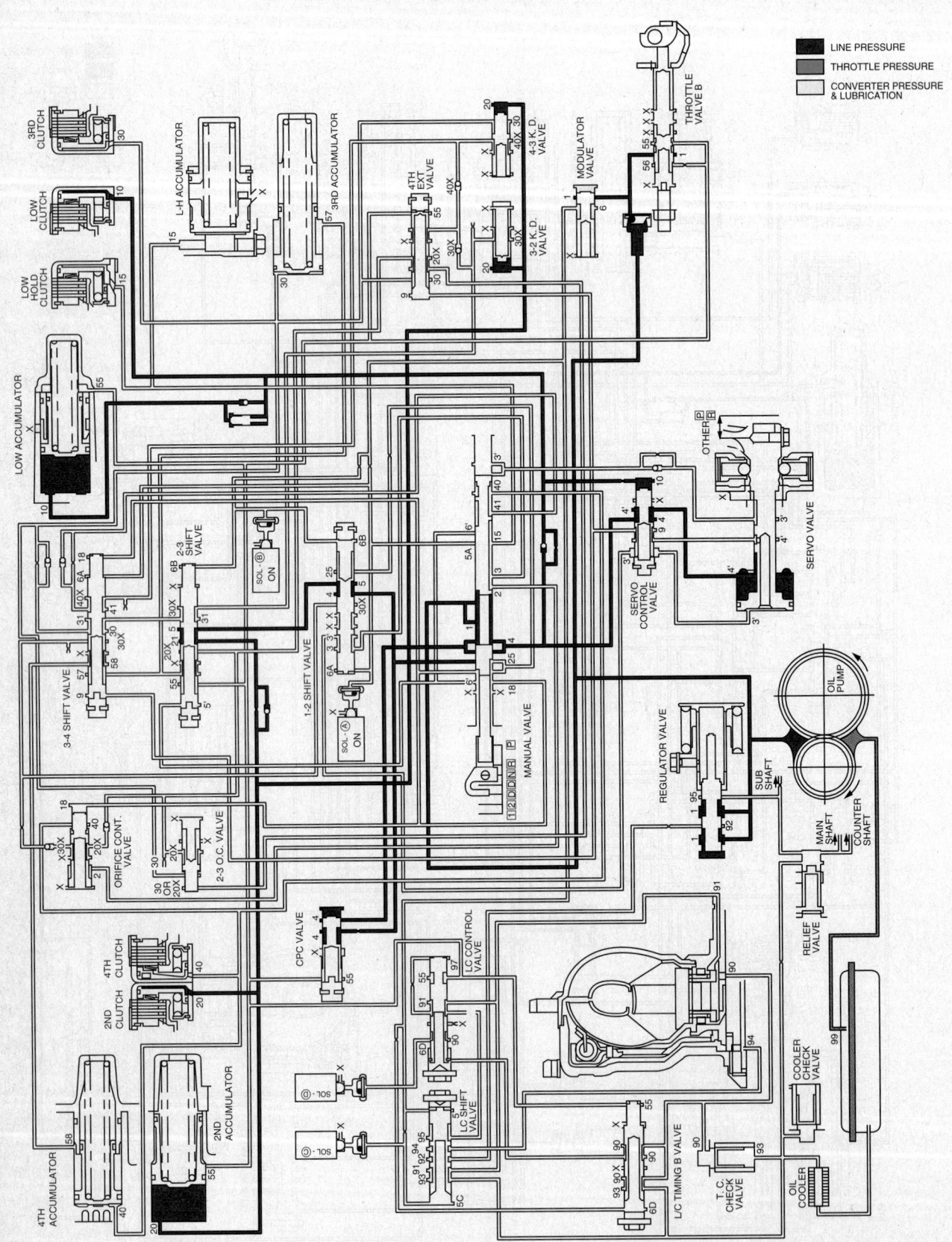

■	LINE PRESSURE
■	THROTTLE PRESSURE
□	CONVERTER PRESSURE & LUBRICATION

Fig. 5: "D₃" Or "D₄" Position — 2nd Gear

Courtesy of American Honda Motor Co., Inc.

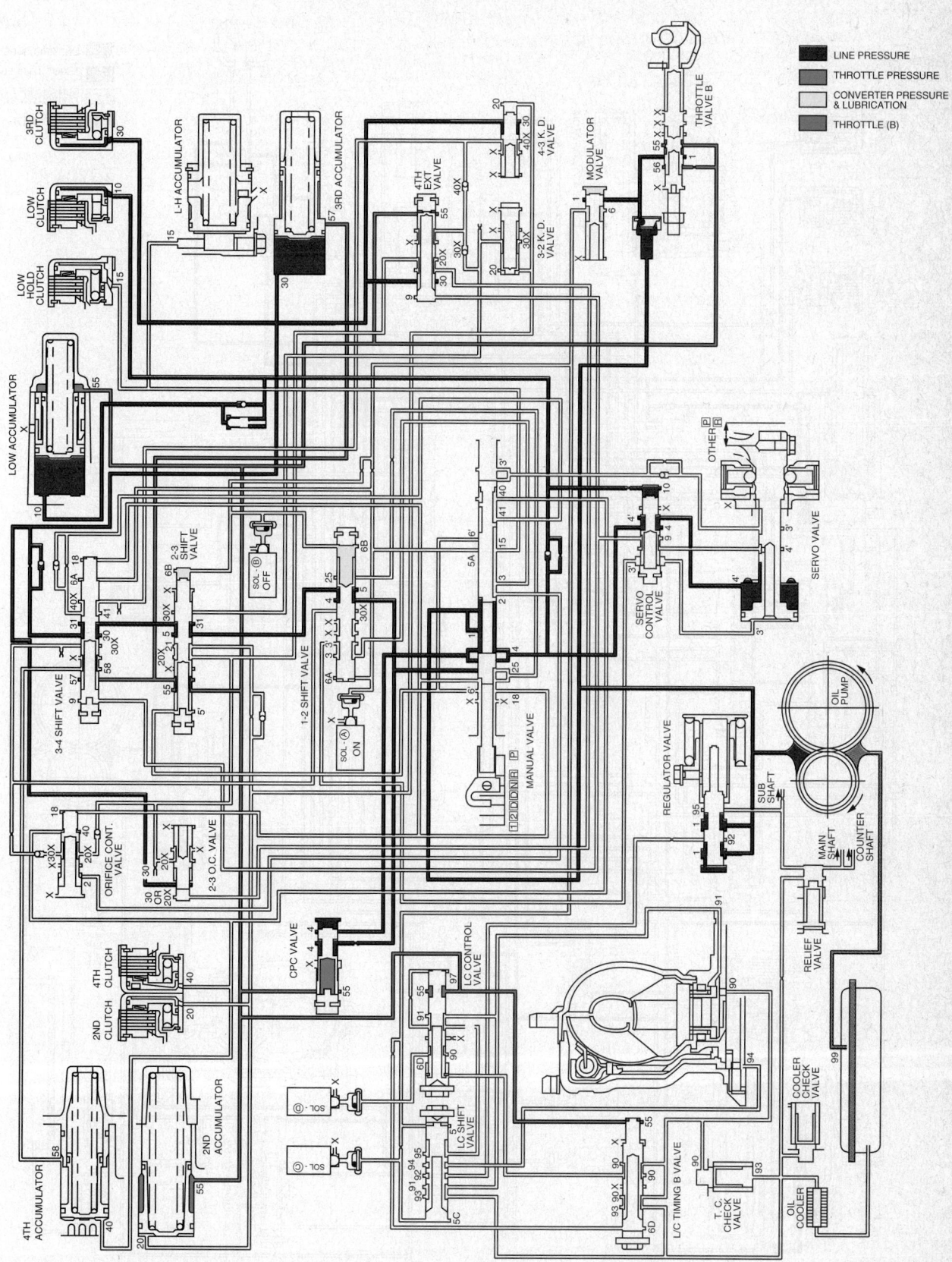

OIL CIRCUIT DIAGRAMS
Acura SP7A (Cont.)

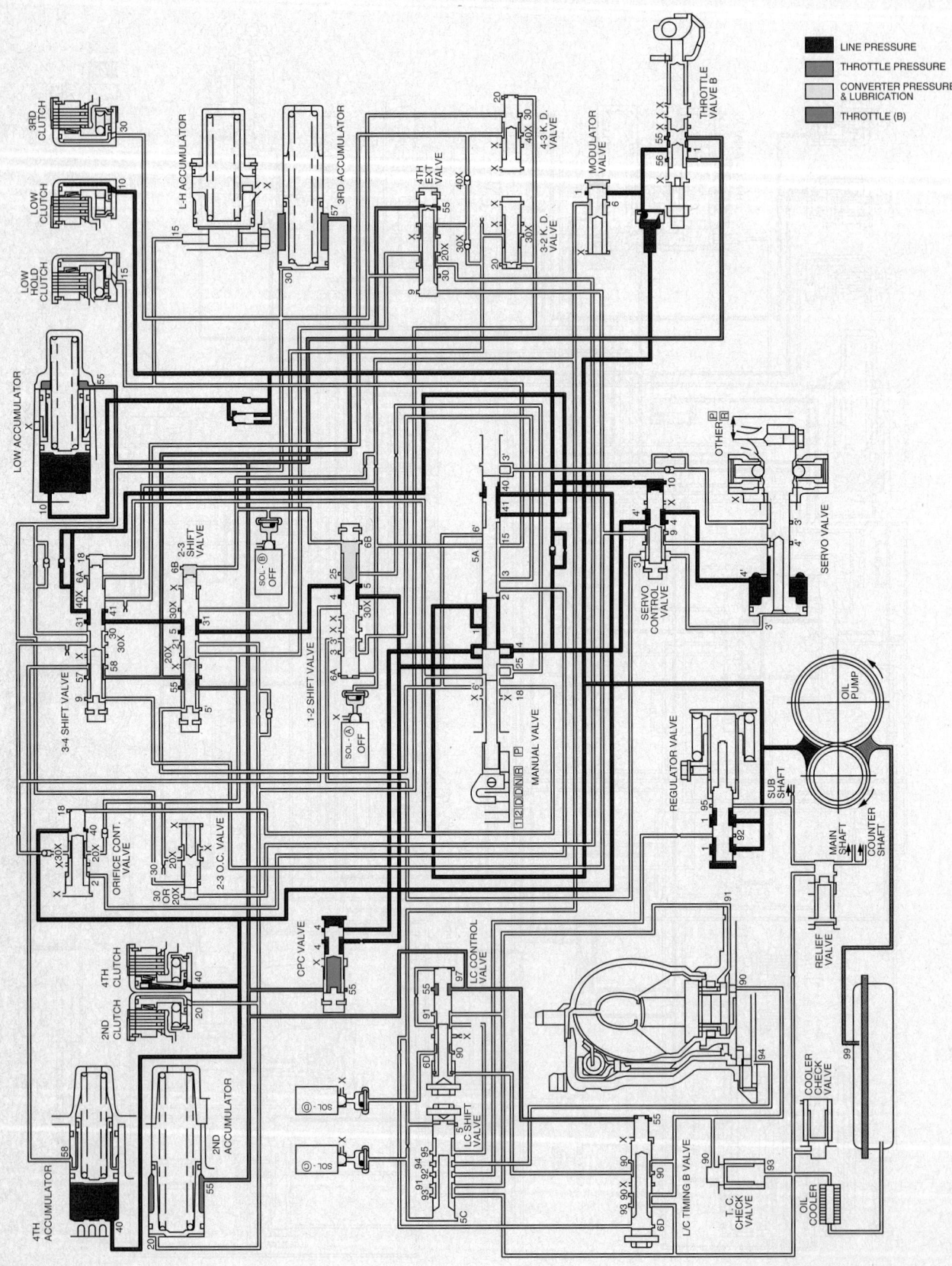

Fig. 7: "D₄" Position — 4th Gear

Courtesy of American Honda Motor Co., Inc.

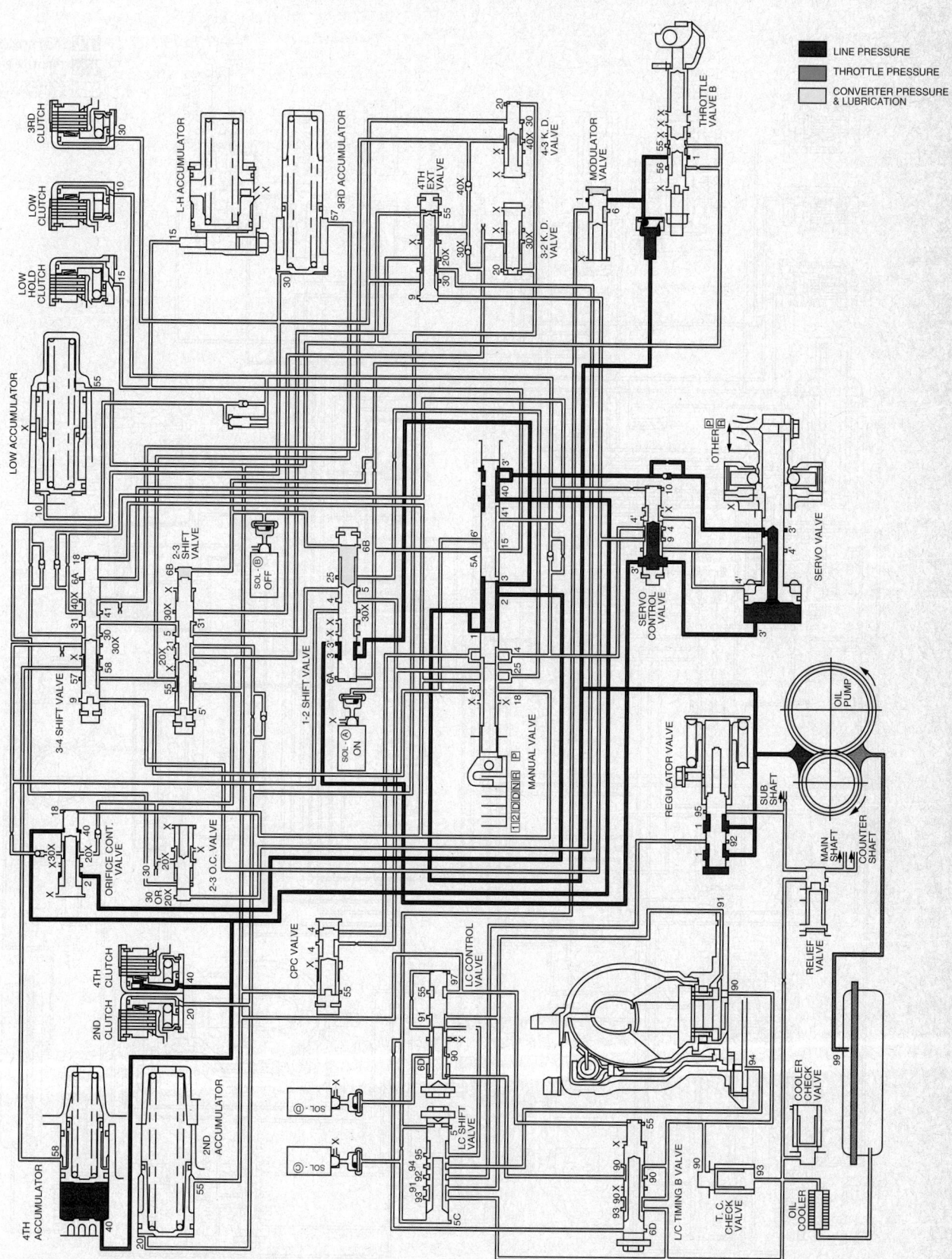

LINE PRESSURE

THROTTLE PRESSURE

CONVERTER PRESSURE & LUBRICATION

Fig. 8: "R" Position — Reverse

Courtesy of American Honda Motor Co., Inc.

OIL CIRCUIT DIAGRAMS
Acura SP7A (Cont.)

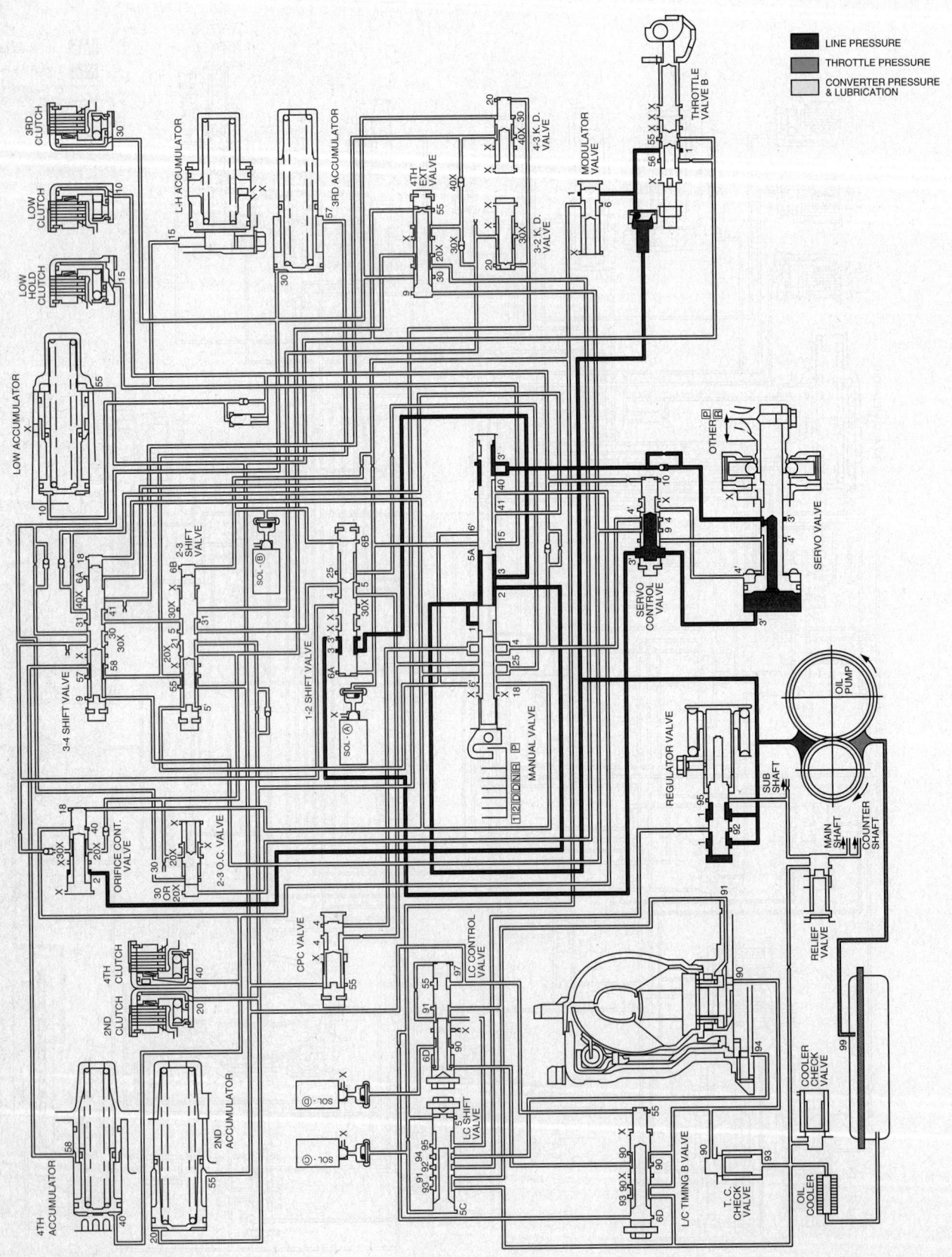

Fig. 9: "P" Position — Park

Courtesy of American Honda Motor Co., Inc.

OIL CIRCUIT DIAGRAMS
Aisin Warner AW03-72L & Mitsubishi V4AW2

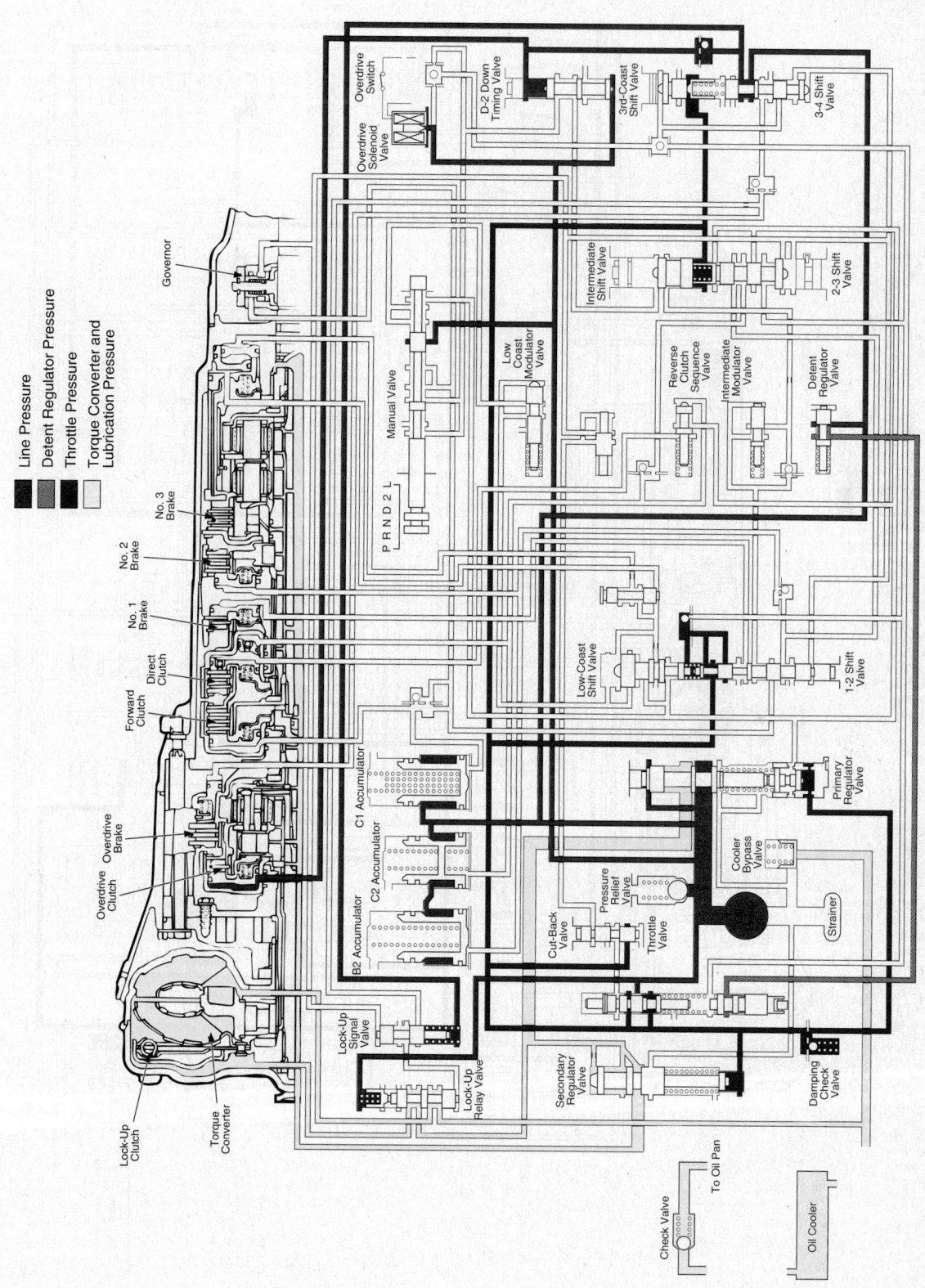

Fig. 1: "N" Position — Neutral

Courtesy of Isuzu Motor Co.

OIL CIRCUIT DIAGRAMS
Aisin Warner AW03-72L & Mitsubishi V4AW2 (Cont.)

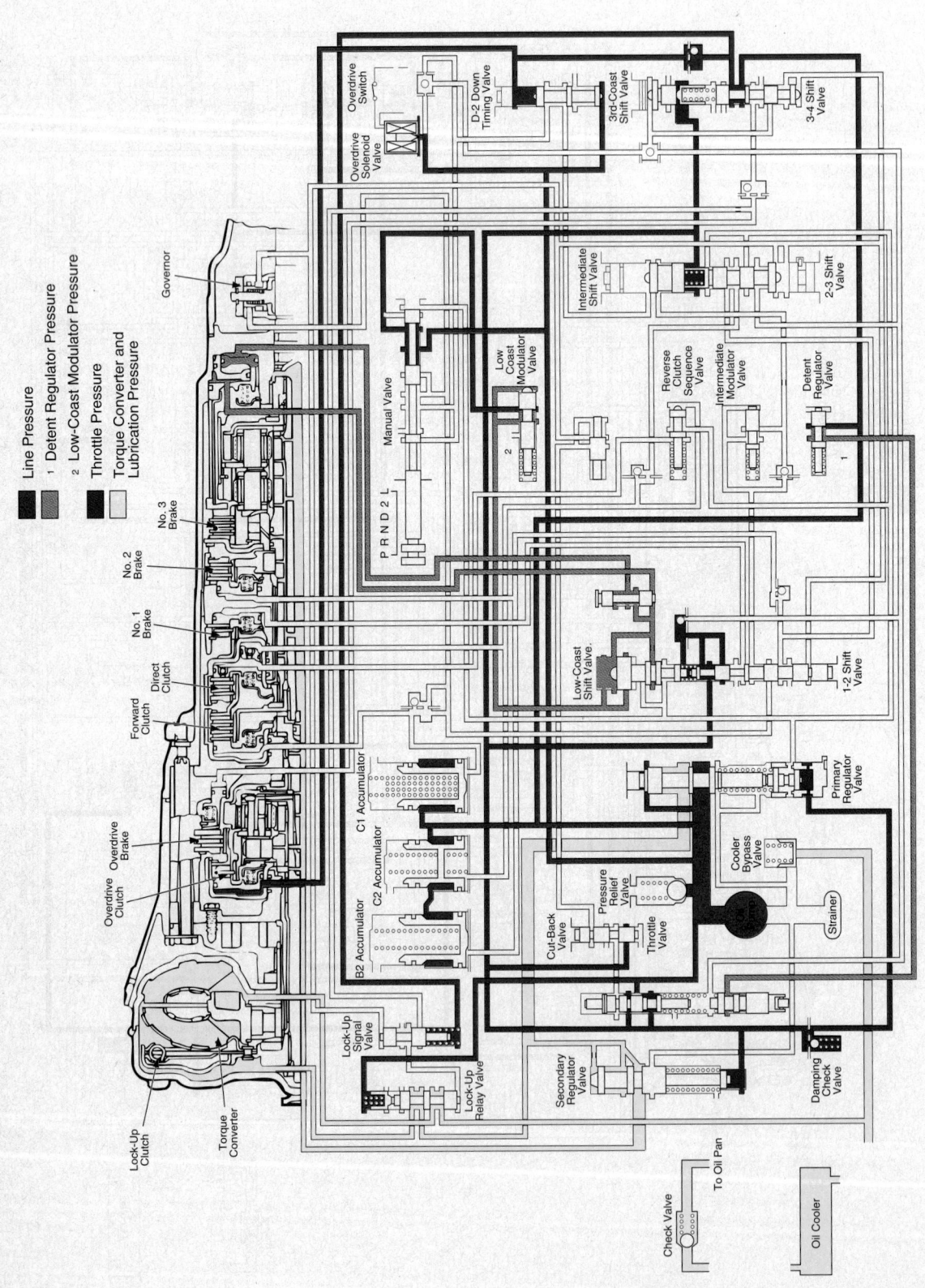

Fig. 2: "P" Position — Park

Courtesy of Isuzu Motor Co.

OIL CIRCUIT DIAGRAMS
Aisin Warner AW03-72L & Mitsubishi V4AW2 (Cont.)

1-31

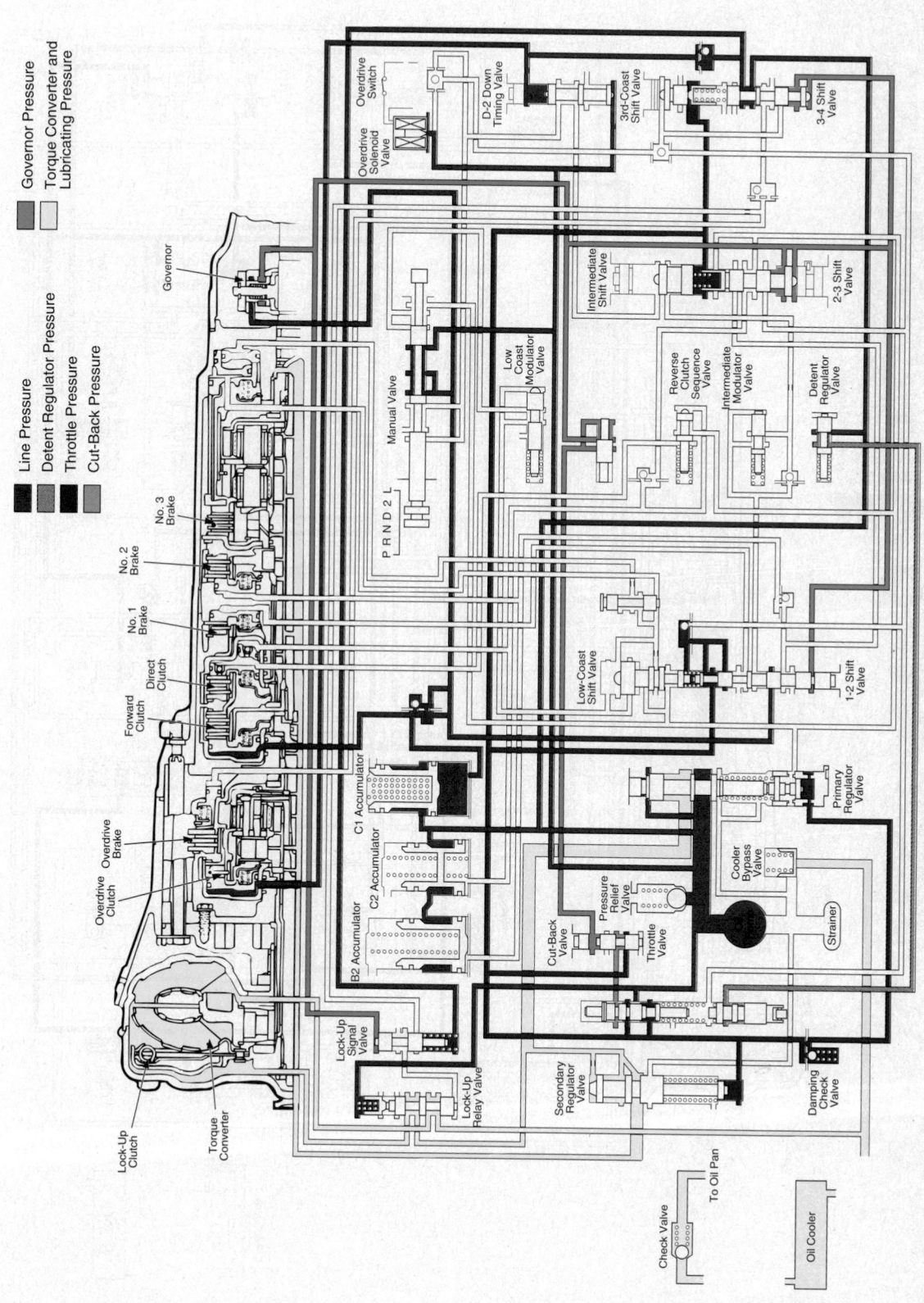

Fig. 3: "D" Position — 1st Gear

Courtesy of Isuzu Motor Co.

OIL CIRCUIT DIAGRAMS
Aisin Warner AW03-72L & Mitsubishi V4AW2 (Cont.)

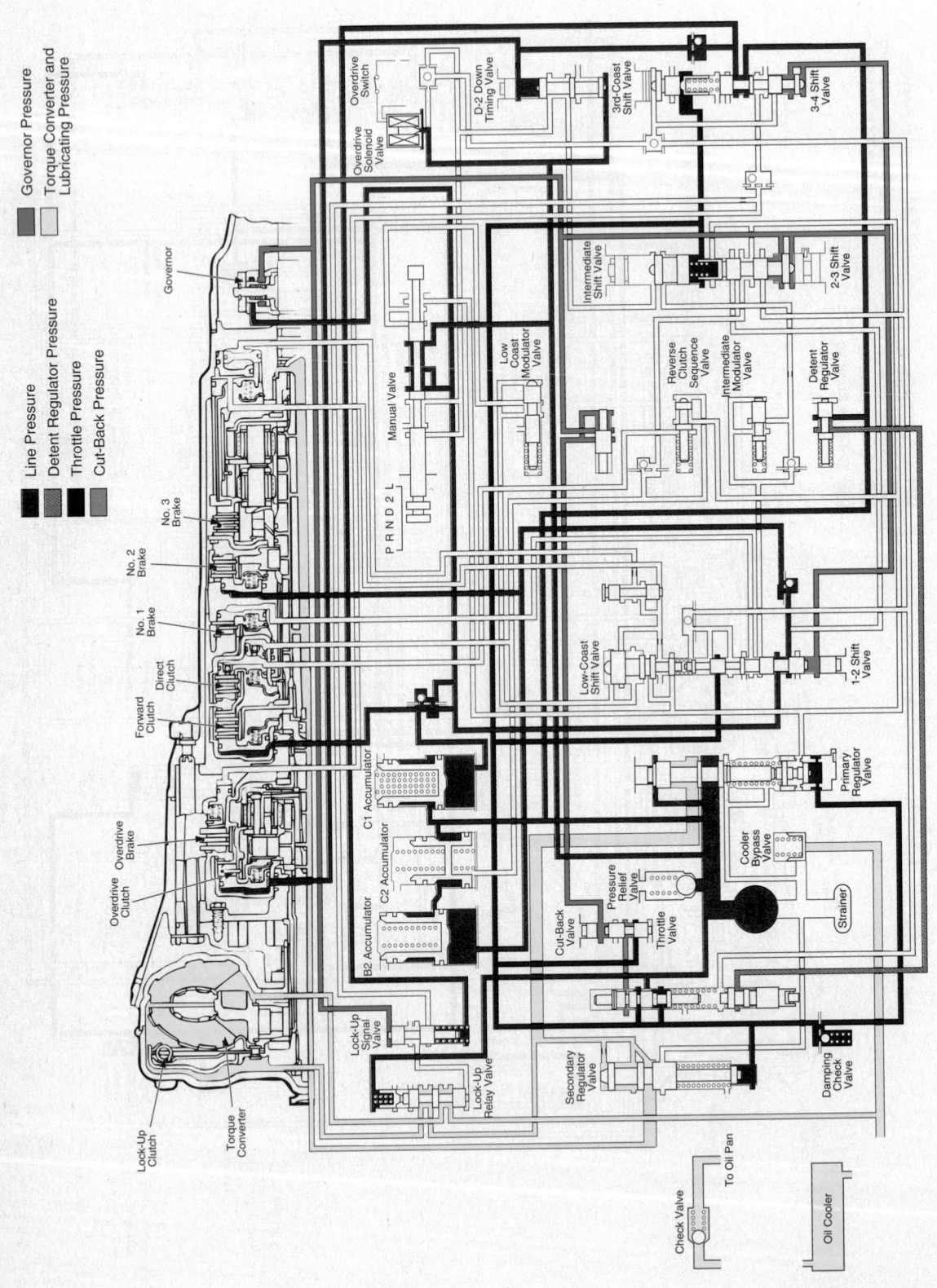

Fig. 4: "D" Position — 2nd Gear

Courtesy of Isuzu Motor Co.

OIL CIRCUIT DIAGRAMS
Aisin Warner AW03-72L & Mitsubishi V4AW2 (Cont.)

1-33

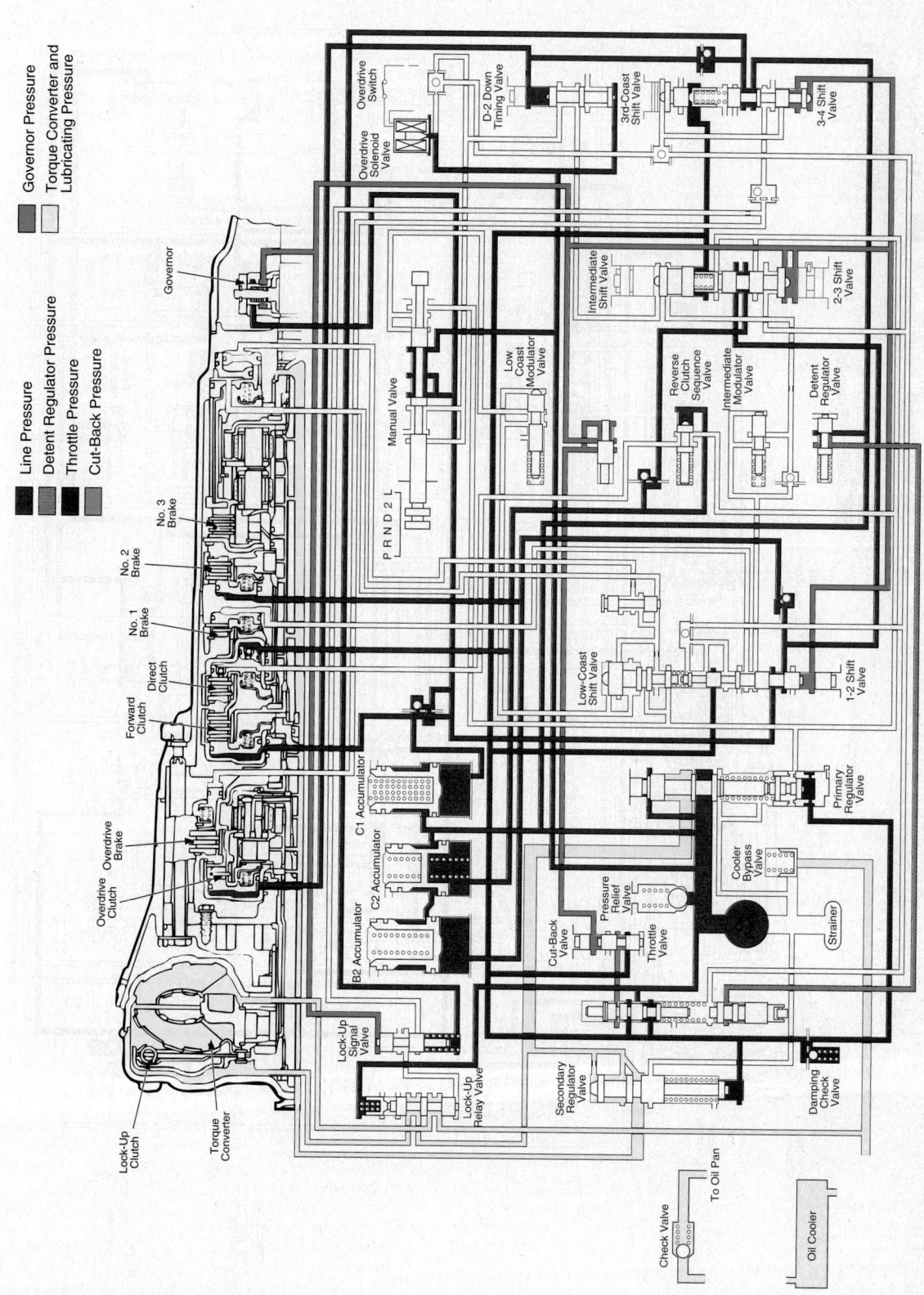

Fig. 5: "D" Position — 3rd Gear

Courtesy of Isuzu Motor Co.

OIL CIRCUIT DIAGRAMS
Aisin Warner AW03-72L & Mitsubishi V4AW2 (Cont.)

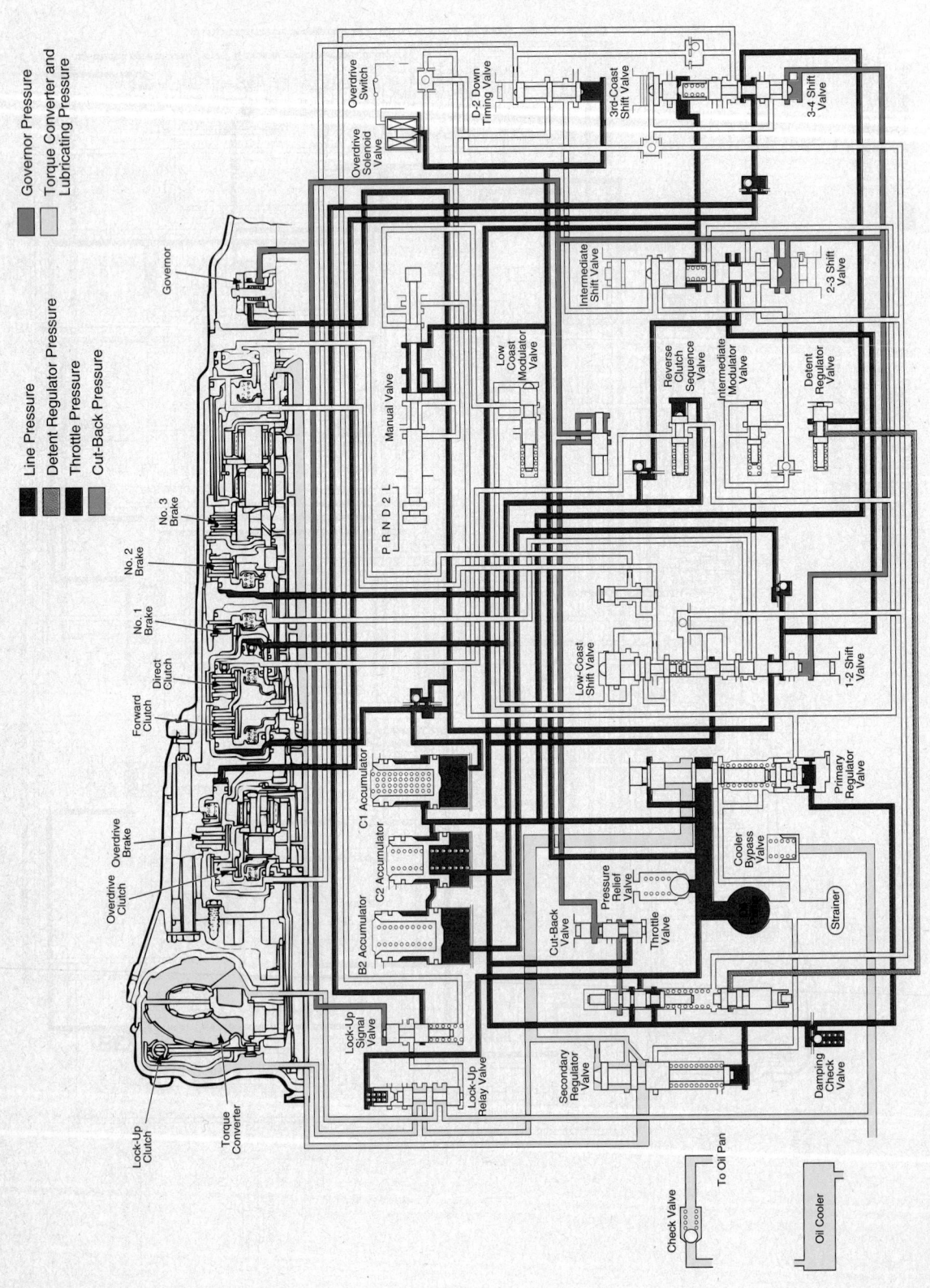

Governor Pressure

Torque Converter and Lubricating Pressure

Line Pressure

Detent Regulator Pressure

Throttle Pressure

Cut-Back Pressure

Fig. 6: "D" Position — 4th Gear (Lock-Up OFF)

Courtesy of Isuzu Motor Co.

OIL CIRCUIT DIAGRAMS
Aisin Warner AW03-72L & Mitsubishi V4AW2 (Cont.)

1-35

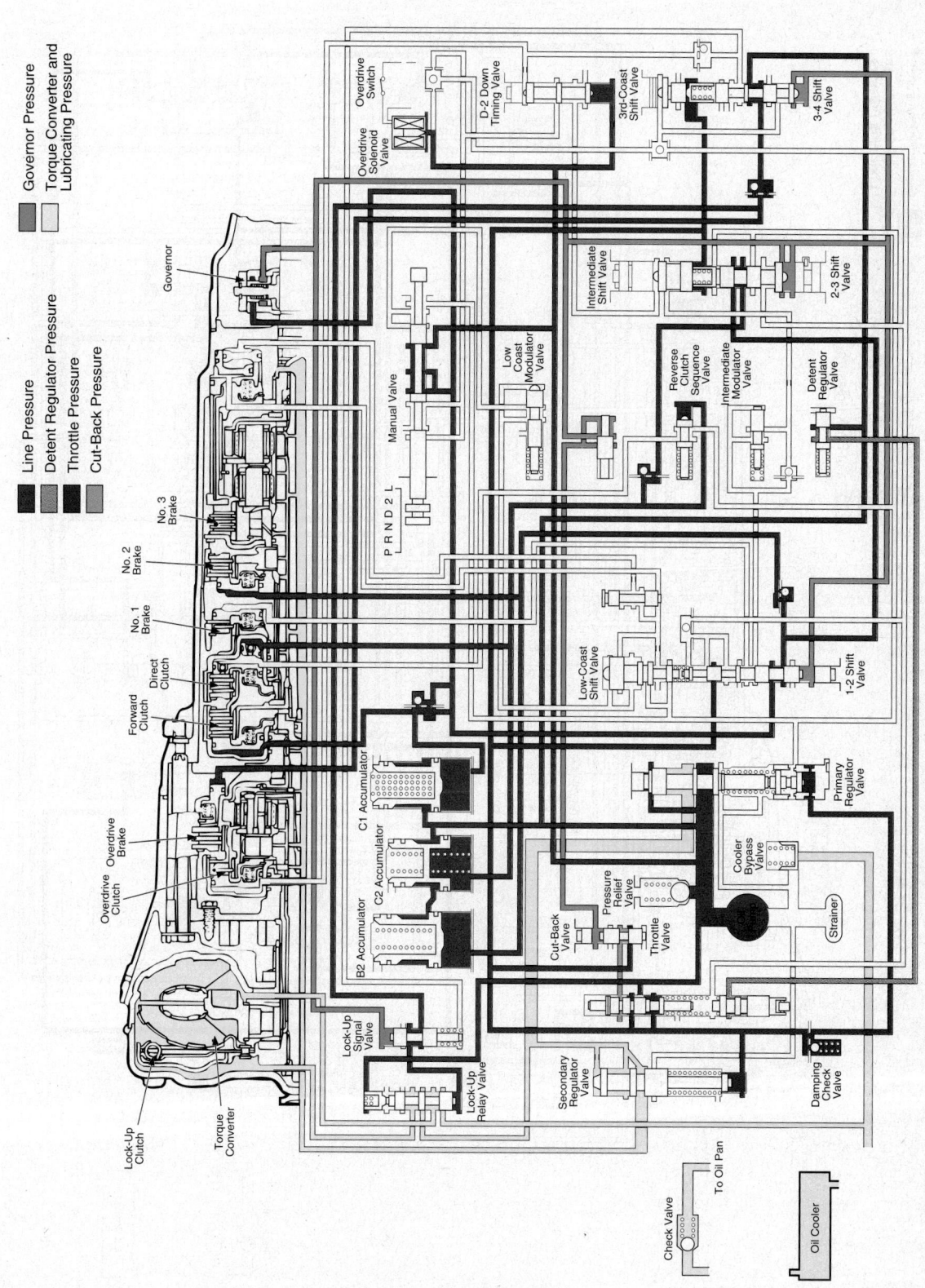

Fig. 7: "D" Position — 4th Gear (Lock-Up ON)

Courtesy of Isuzu Motor Co.

OIL CIRCUIT DIAGRAMS
Aisin Warner AW03-72L & Mitsubishi V4AW2 (Cont.)

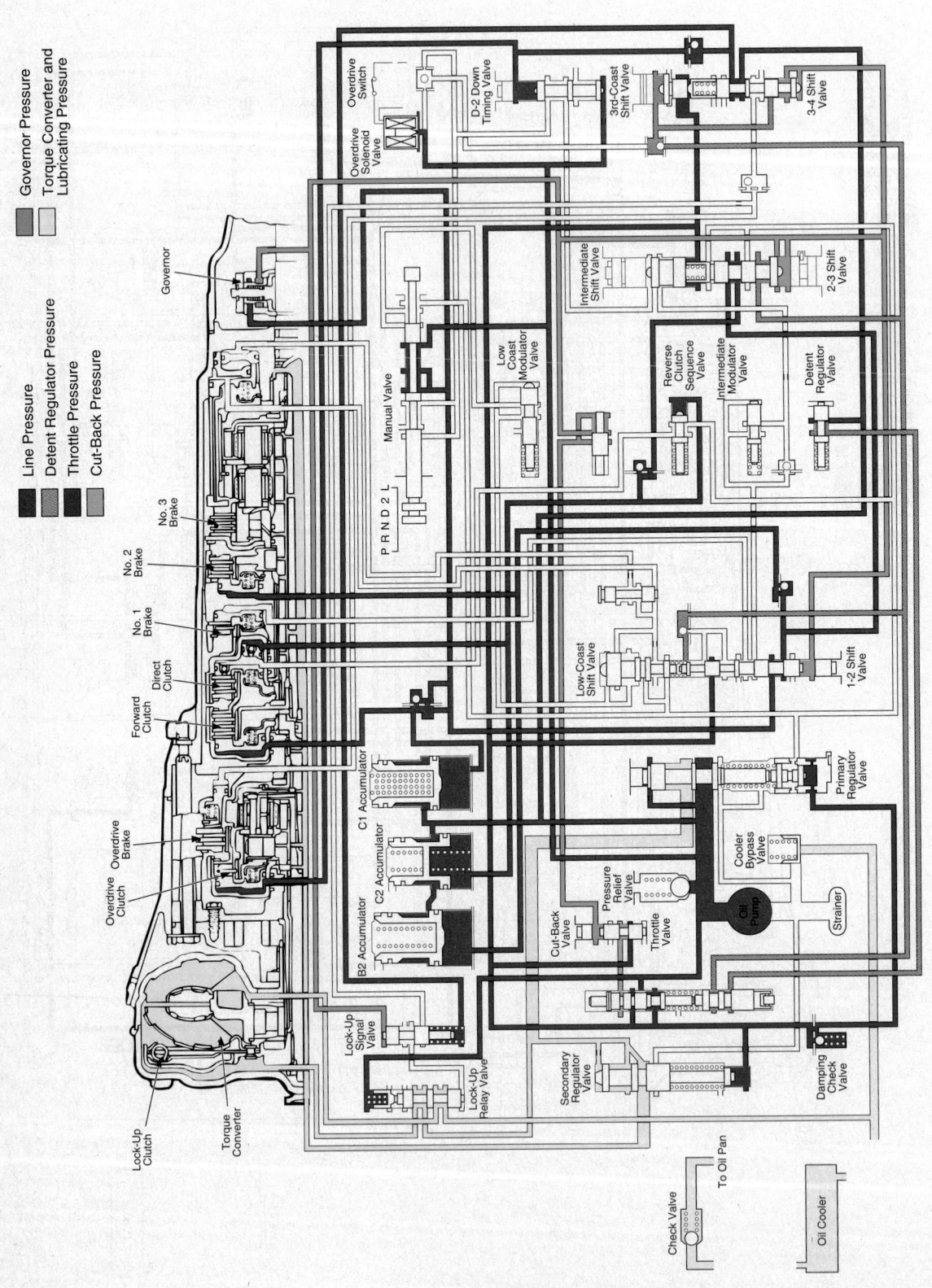

Fig. 8: "D" Position — 4-3 Downshift

Courtesy of Isuzu Motor Co.

OIL CIRCUIT DIAGRAMS
Aisin Warner AW03-72L & Mitsubishi V4AW2 (Cont.)

1-37

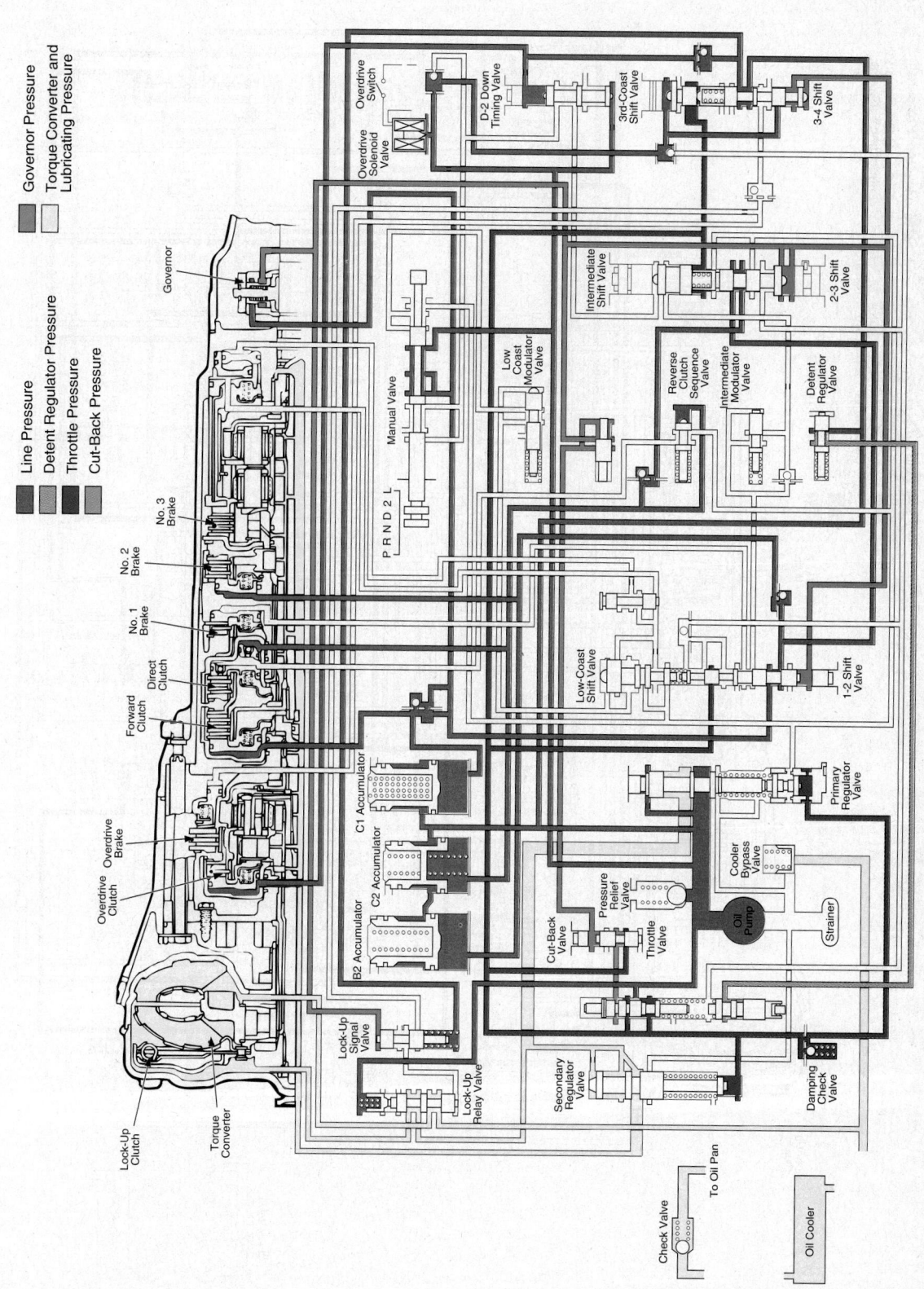

Fig. 9: "D" Position — 3rd Gear (OD Switch OFF)

Courtesy of Isuzu Motor Co.

OIL CIRCUIT DIAGRAMS
Aisin Warner AW03-72L & Mitsubishi V4AW2 (Cont.)

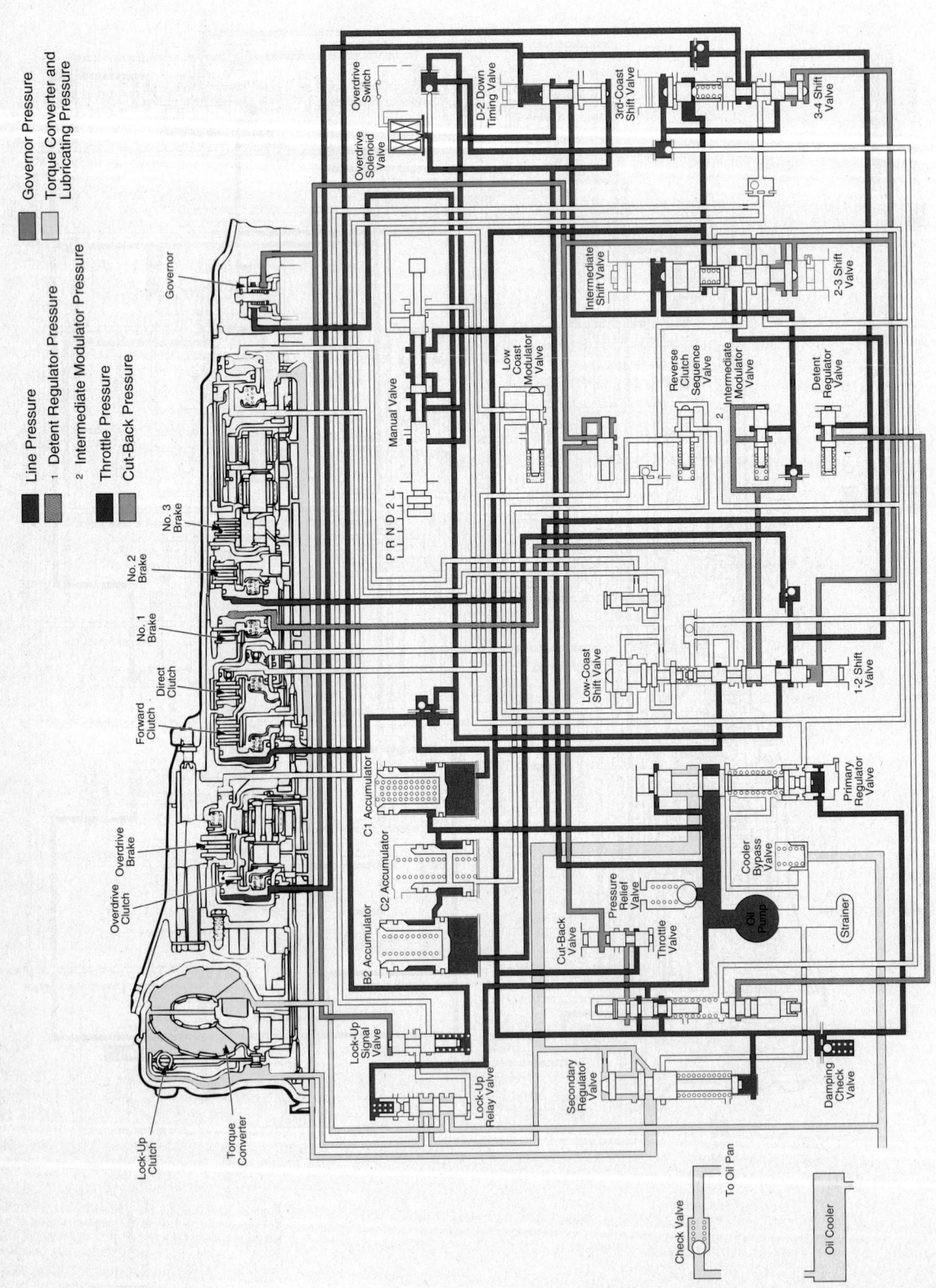

Fig. 10: "2" Position — 2nd Gear

Courtesy of Isuzu Motor Co.

OIL CIRCUIT DIAGRAMS
Aisin Warner AW03-72L & Mitsubishi V4AW2 (Cont.)

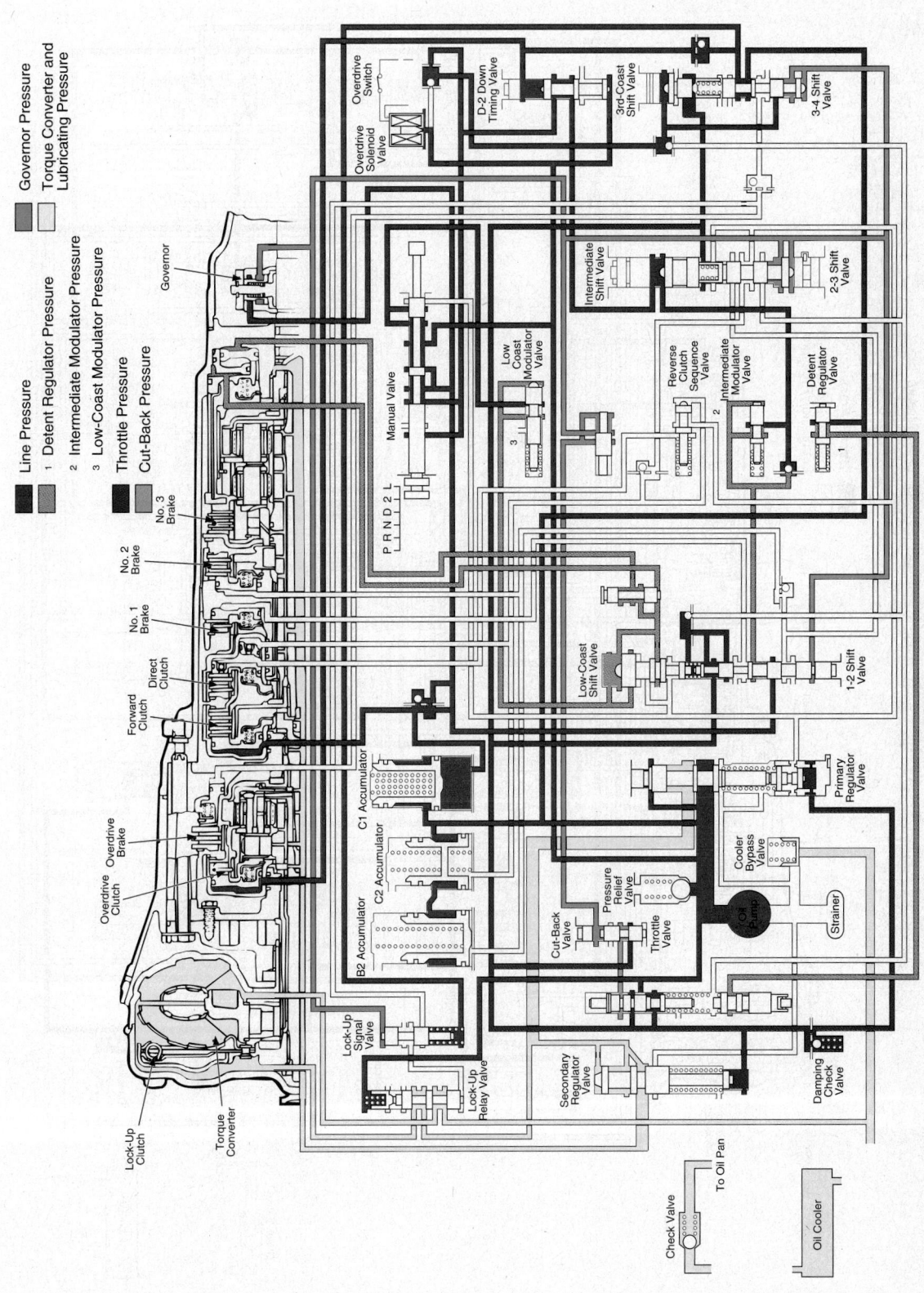

Fig. 11: "L" Position — 1st Gear

Courtesy of Isuzu Motor Co.

OIL CIRCUIT DIAGRAMS
Aisin Warner AW03-72L & Mitsubishi V4AW2 (Cont.)

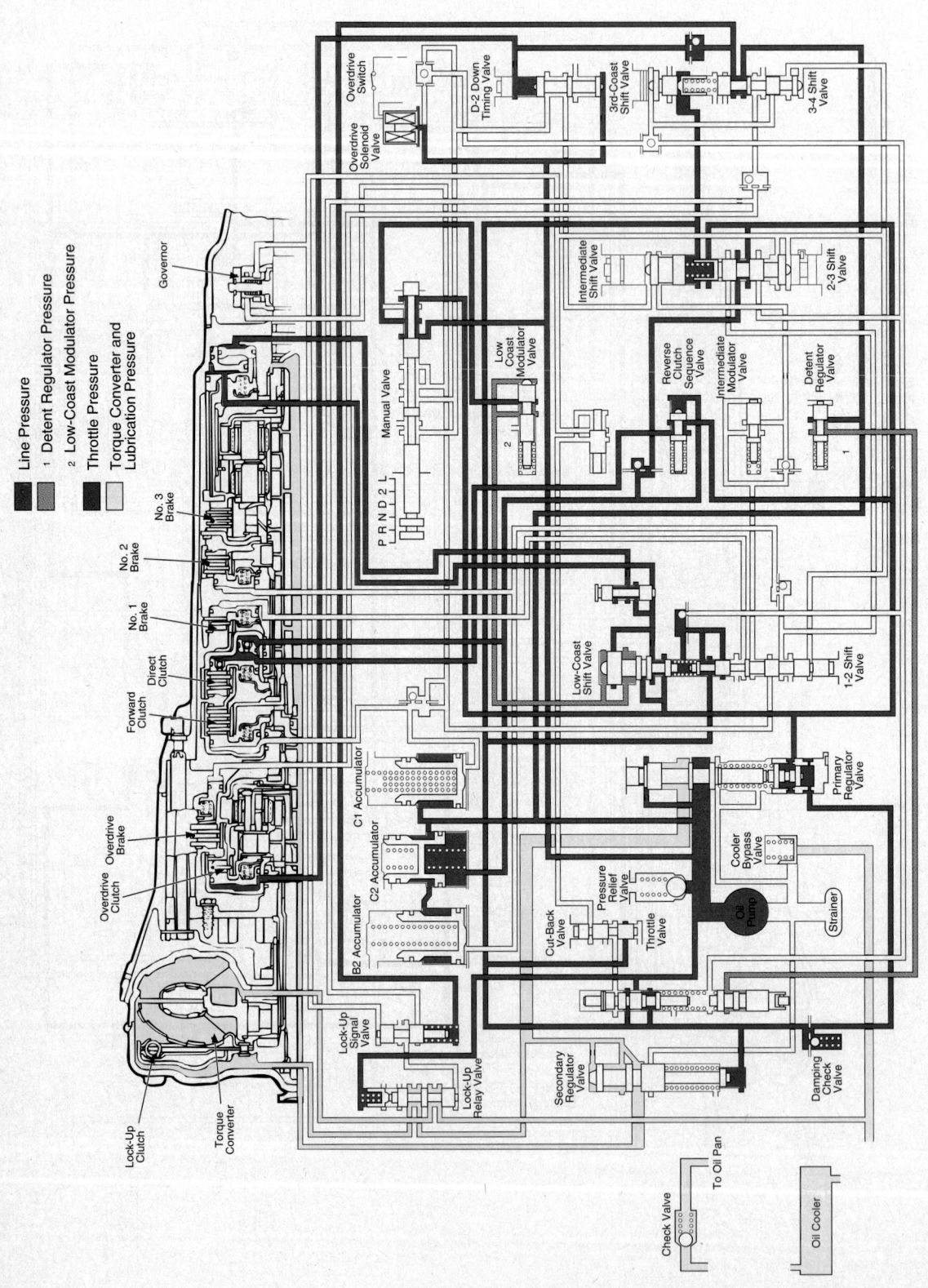

Fig. 12: "R" Position — Reverse

Courtesy of Isuzu Motor Co.

OIL CIRCUIT DIAGRAMS
Honda Accord 2.7L MPZA

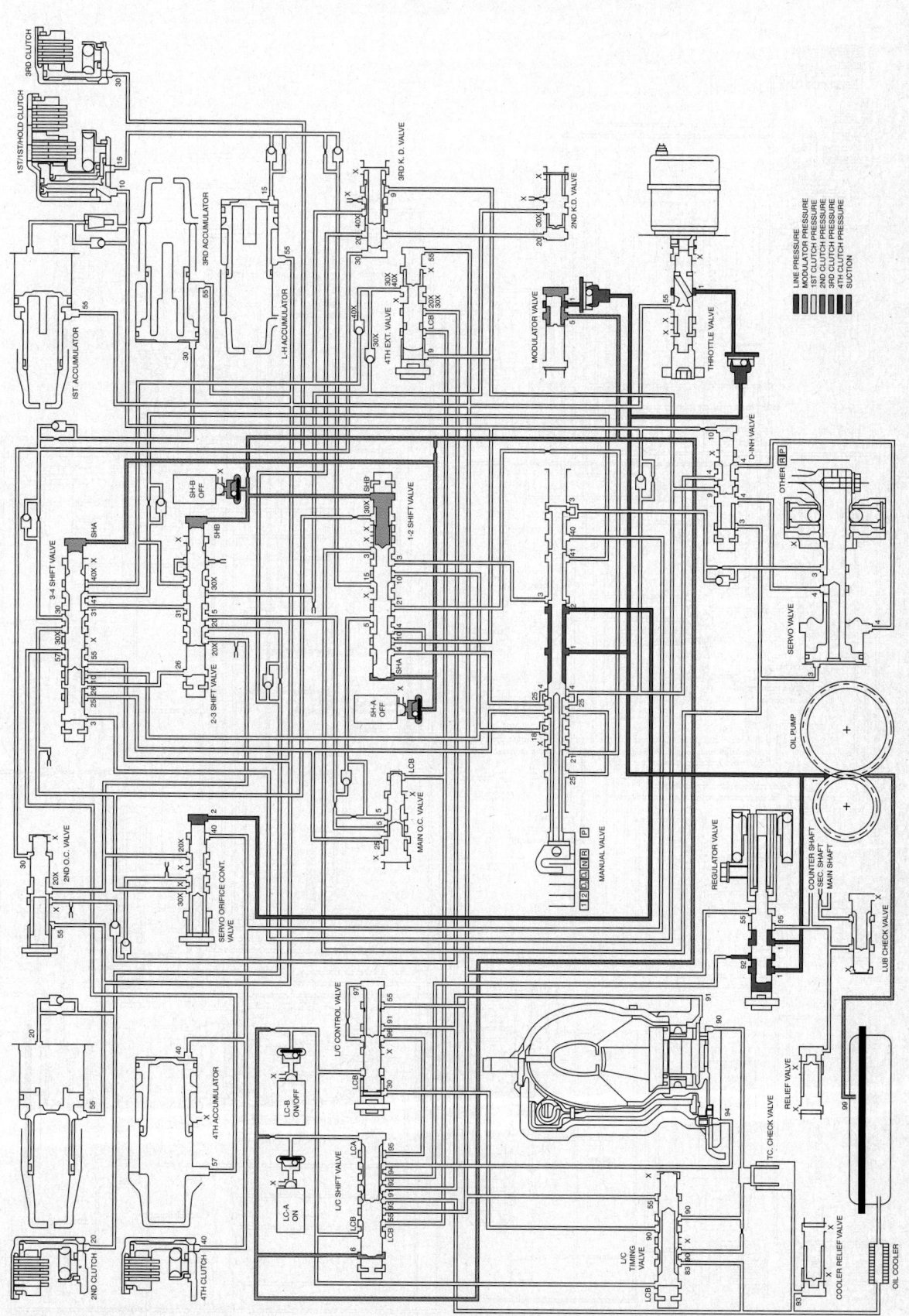

Fig. 1: "N" Position — Neutral

Courtesy of American Honda Motor Co., Inc.

OIL CIRCUIT DIAGRAMS
Honda Accord 2.7L MPZA (Cont.)

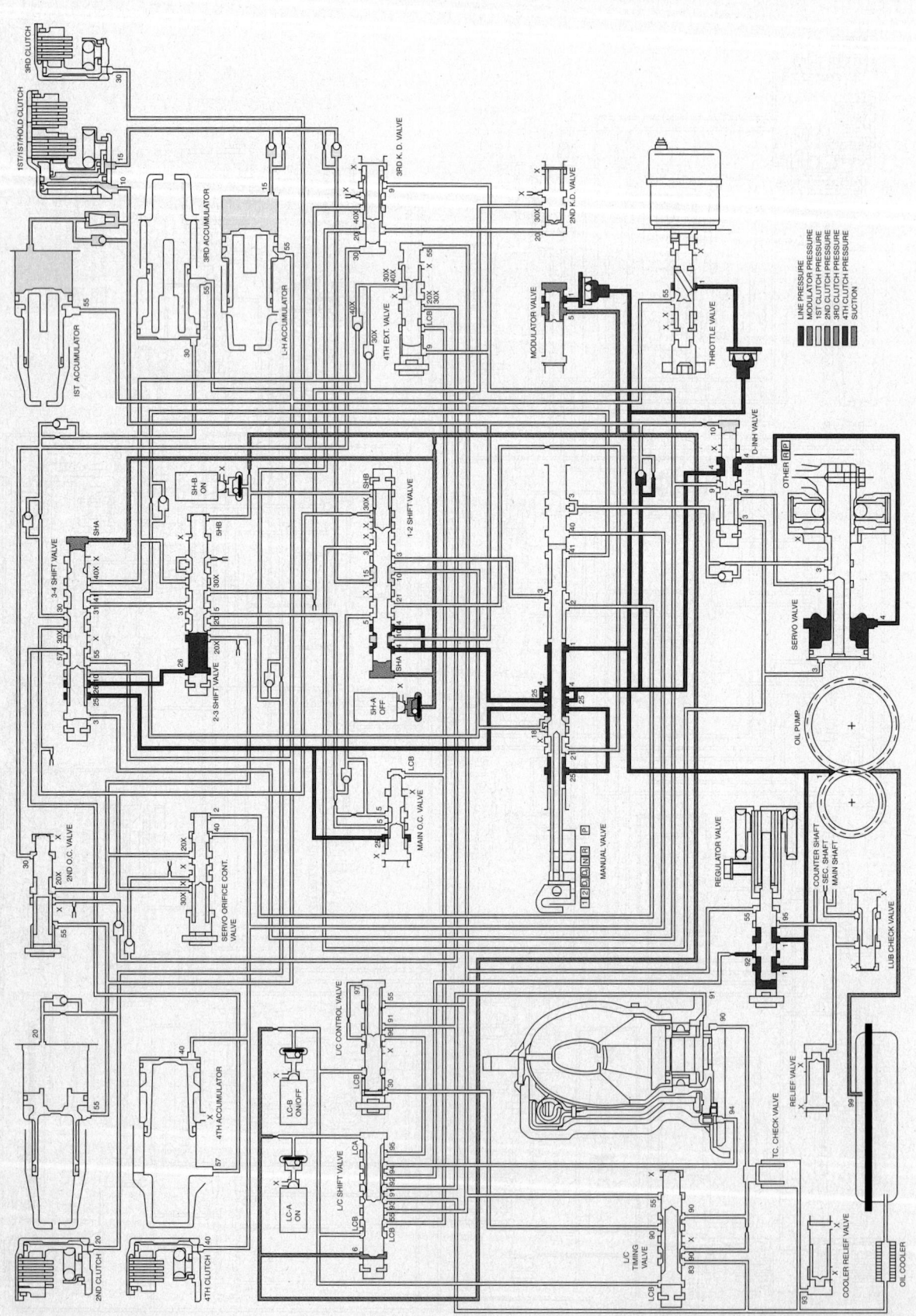

Fig. 2: "1" Position — 1st Gear

Courtesy of American Honda Motor Co., Inc.

OIL CIRCUIT DIAGRAMS
Honda Accord 2.7L MPZA (Cont.)

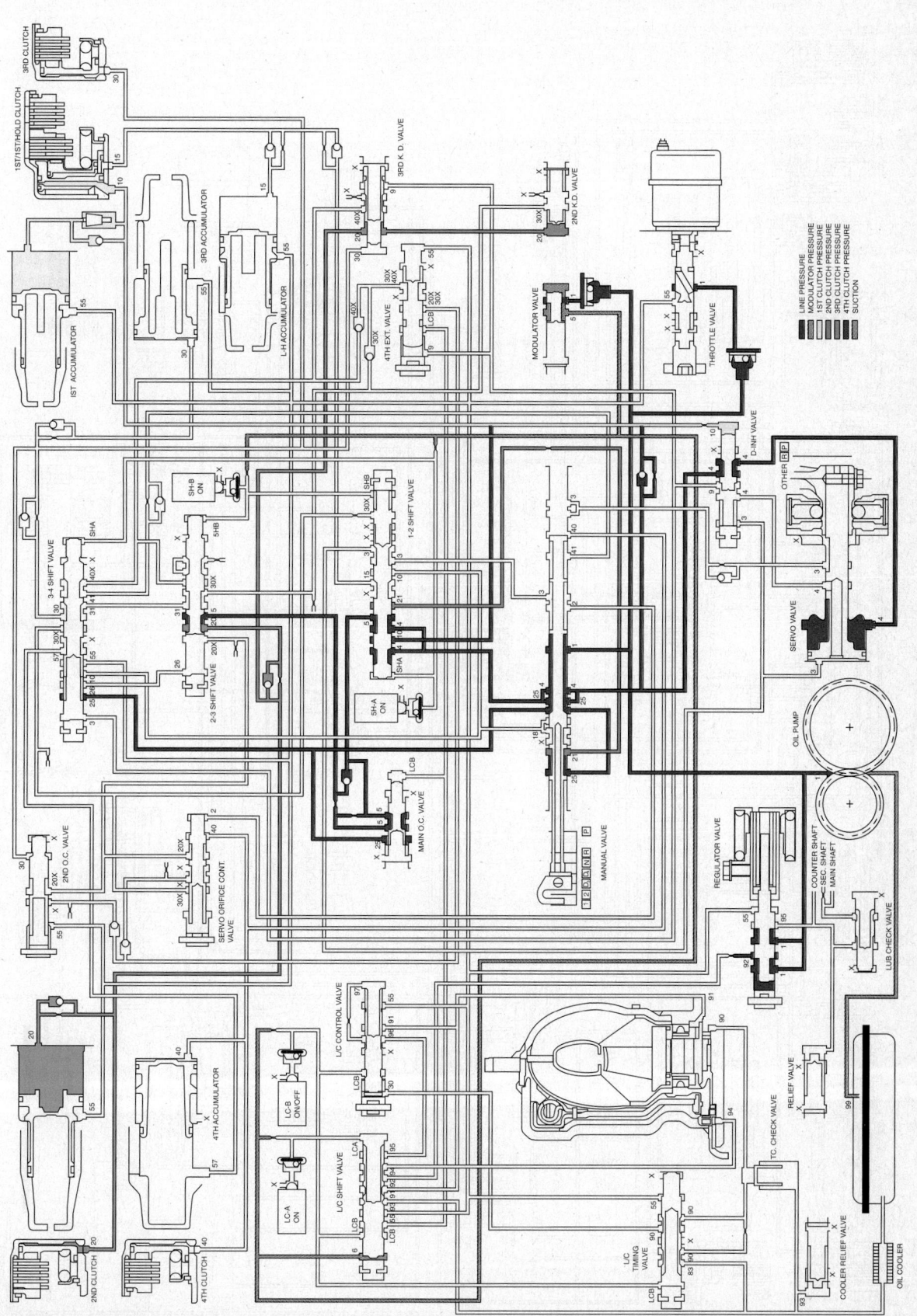

Fig. 3: "2" Position — 2nd Gear

Courtesy of American Honda Motor Co., Inc.

OIL CIRCUIT DIAGRAMS
Honda Accord 2.7L MPZA (Cont.)

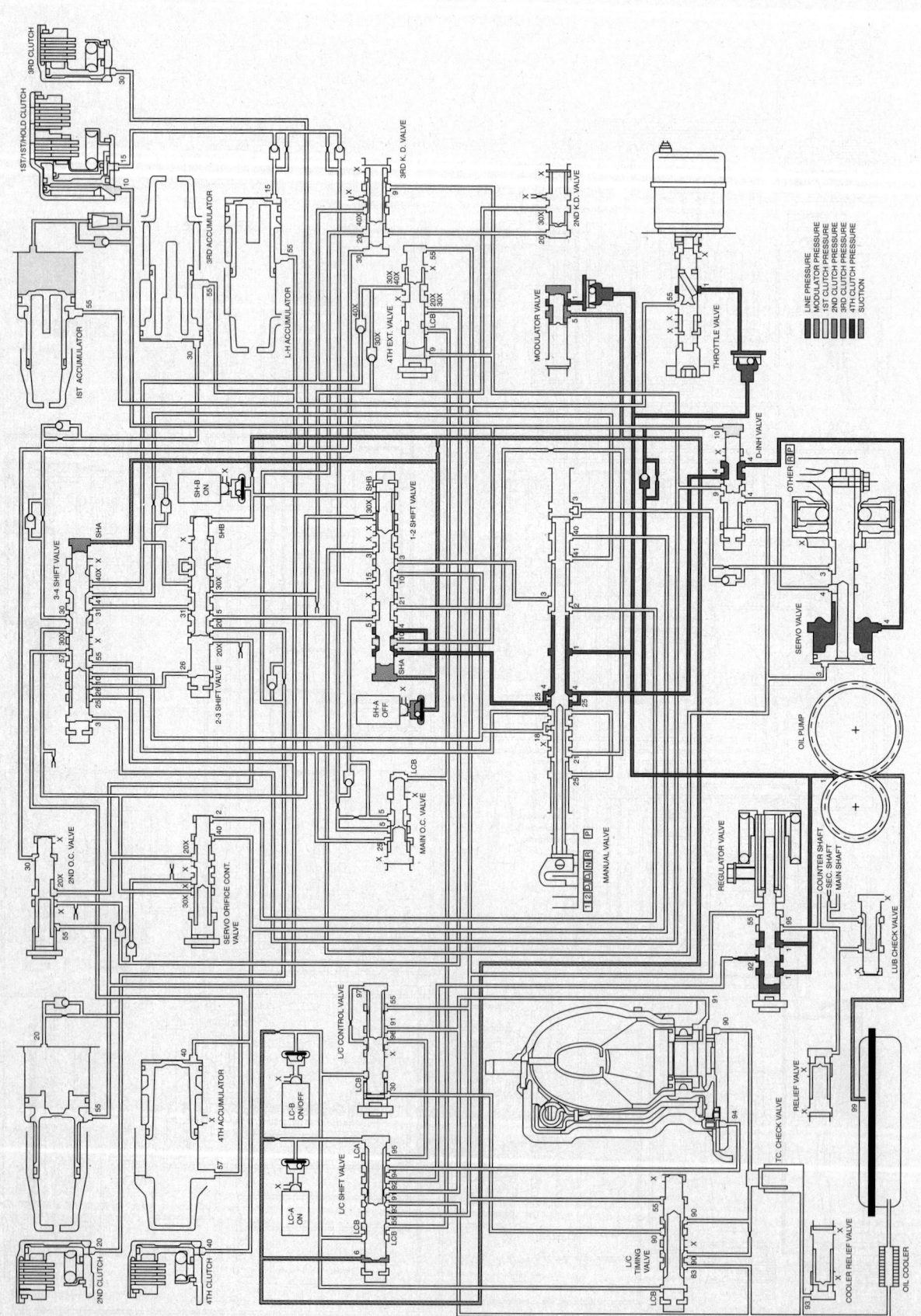

Fig. 4: "D₃" Or "D₄" Position — 1st Gear

Courtesy of American Honda Motor Co., Inc.

OIL CIRCUIT DIAGRAMS
Honda Accord 2.7L MPZA (Cont.)

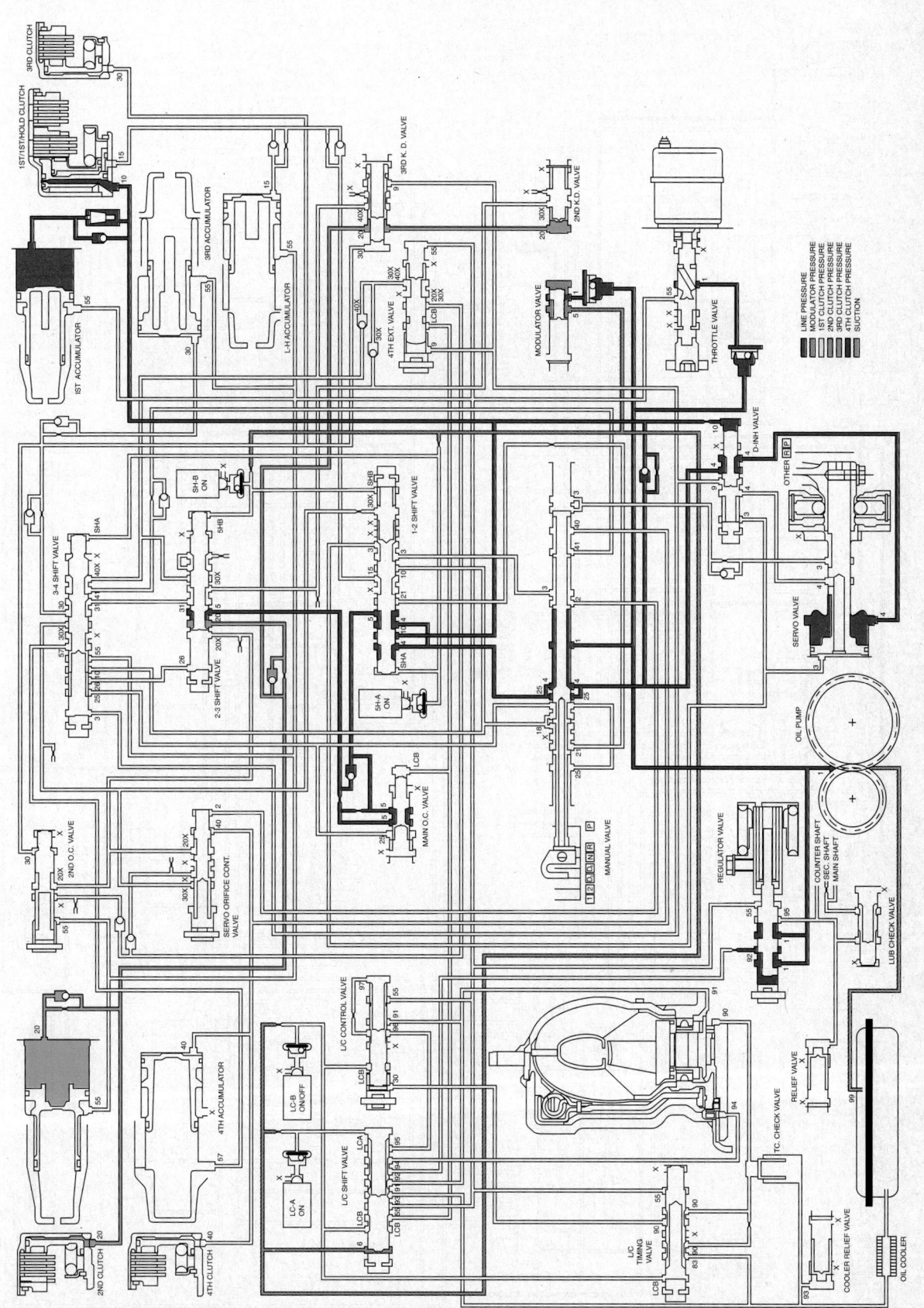

Fig. 5: "D₃" Or "D₄" Position — 2nd Gear

Courtesy of American Honda Motor Co., Inc.

OIL CIRCUIT DIAGRAMS
Honda Accord 2.7L MPZA (Cont.)

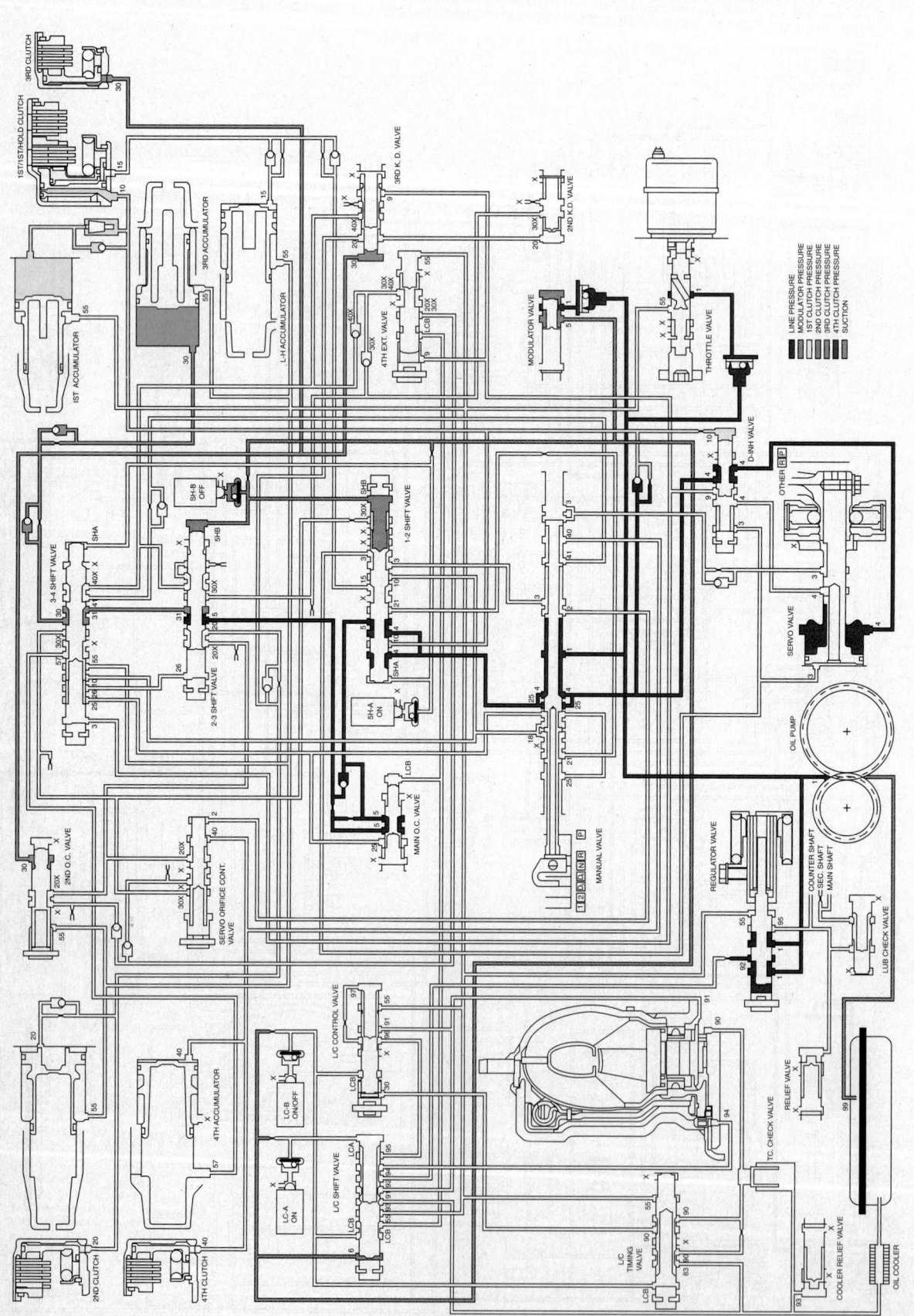

Fig. 6: "D₃" Or "D₄" Position — 3rd Gear

Courtesy of American Honda Motor Co., Inc.

OIL CIRCUIT DIAGRAMS
Honda Accord 2.7L MPZA (Cont.)

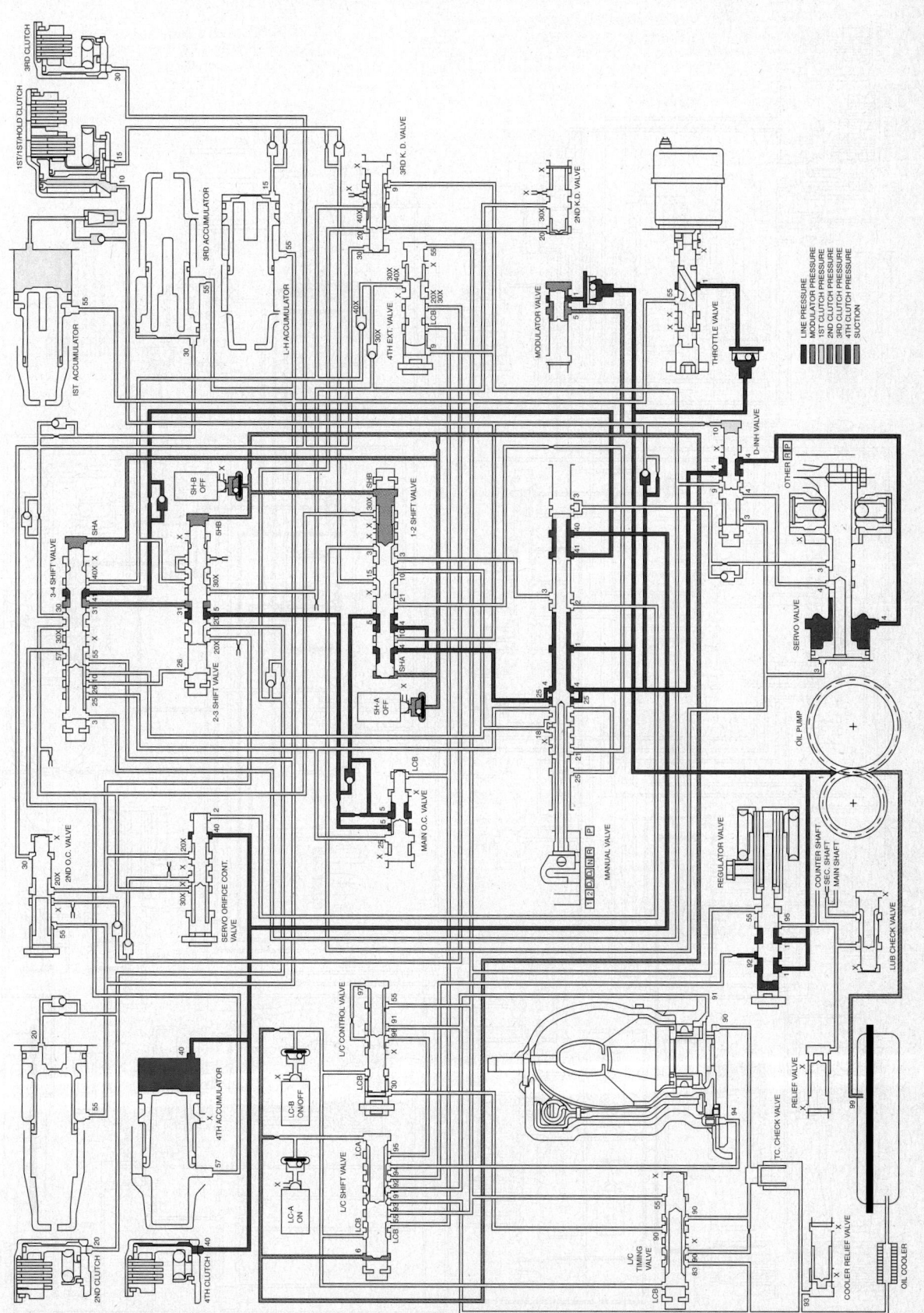

Fig. 7: "D₄" Position — 4th Gear

Courtesy of American Honda Motor Co., Inc.

OIL CIRCUIT DIAGRAMS
Honda Accord 2.7L MPZA (Cont.)

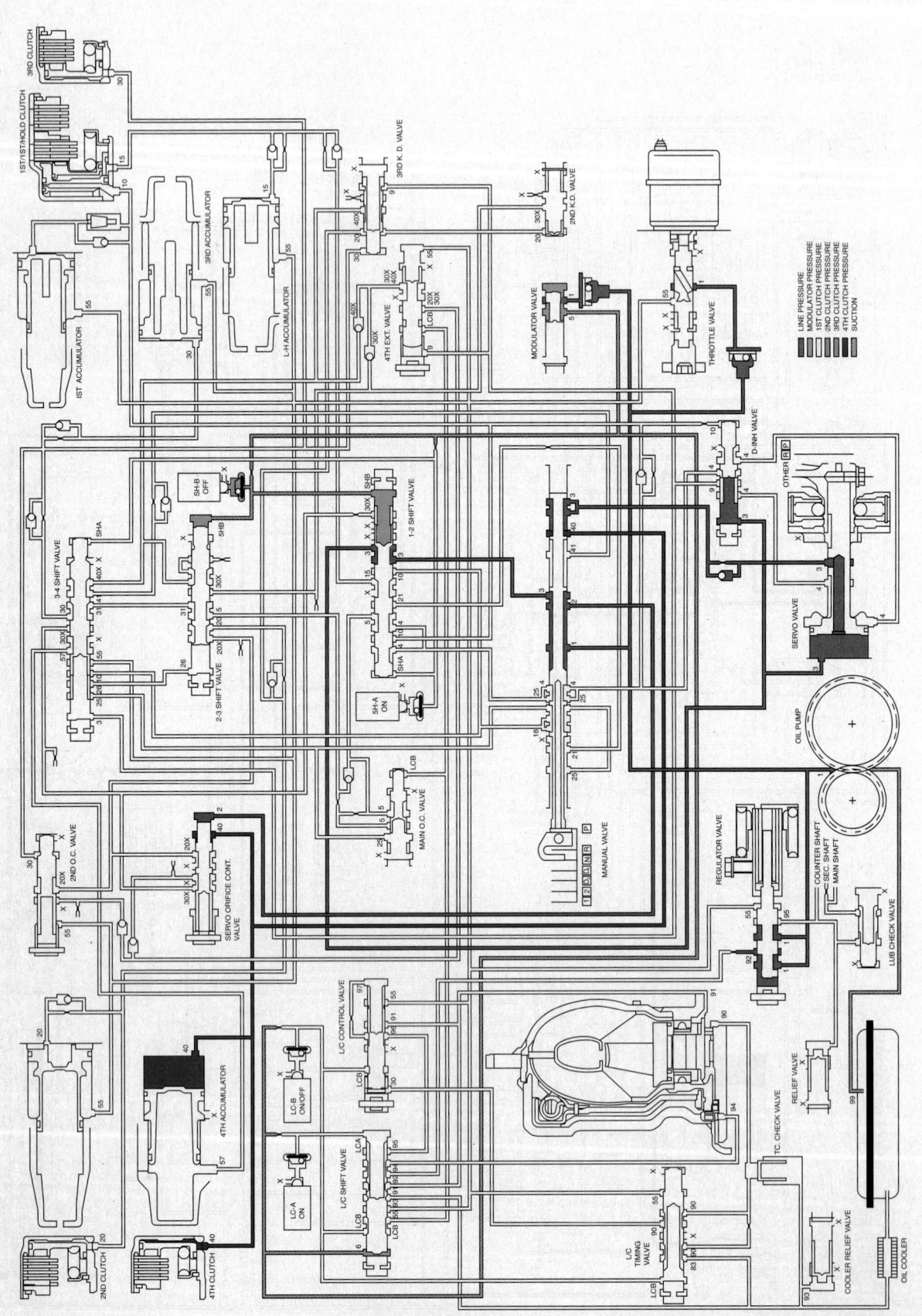

Fig. 8: "R" Position — Reverse

Courtesy of American Honda Motor Co., Inc.

OIL CIRCUIT DIAGRAMS
Honda Accord 2.7L MPZA (Cont.)

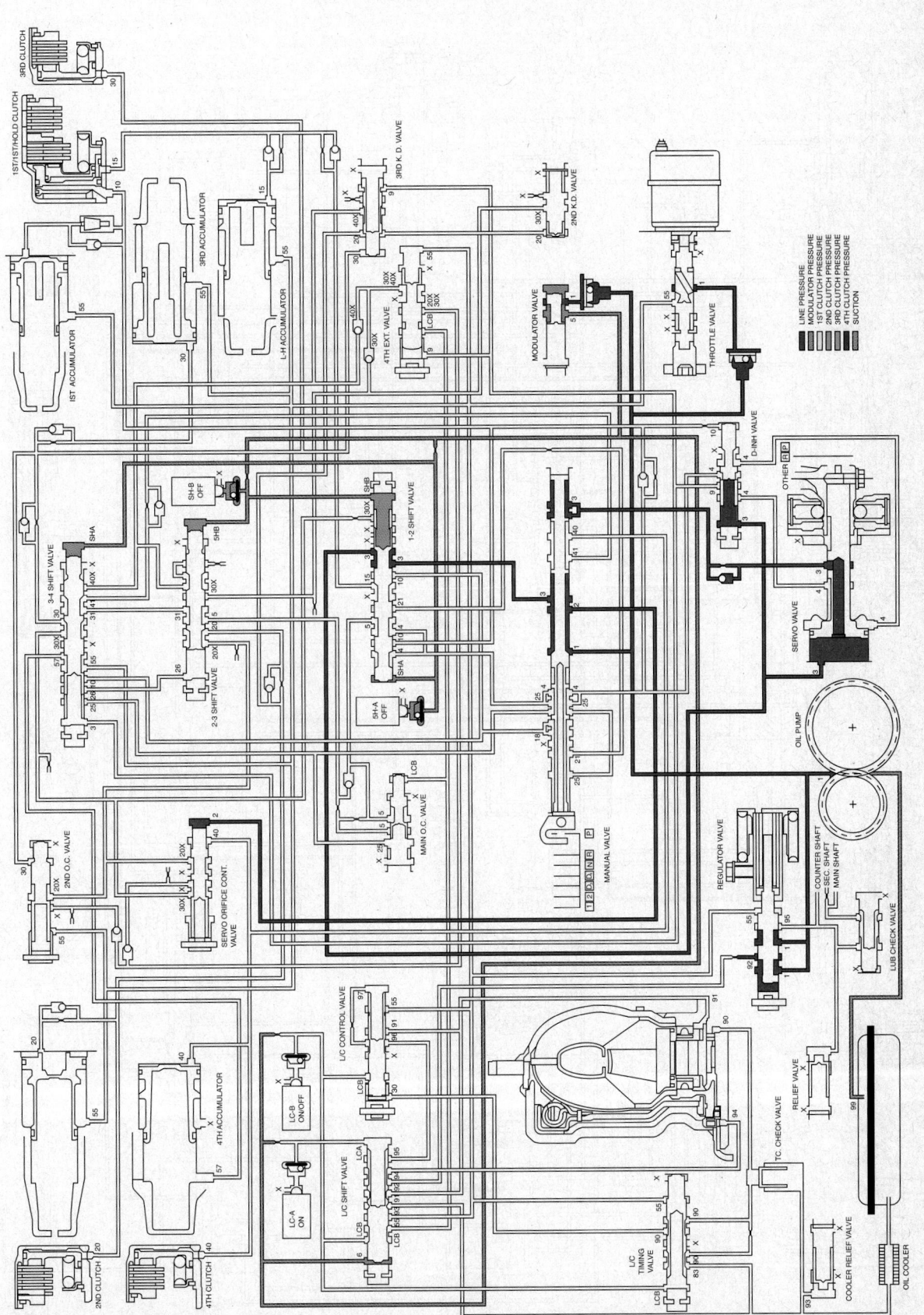

Fig. 9: "P" Position — Park

Courtesy of American Honda Motor Co., Inc.

OIL CIRCUIT DIAGRAMS
Honda Civic A4RA

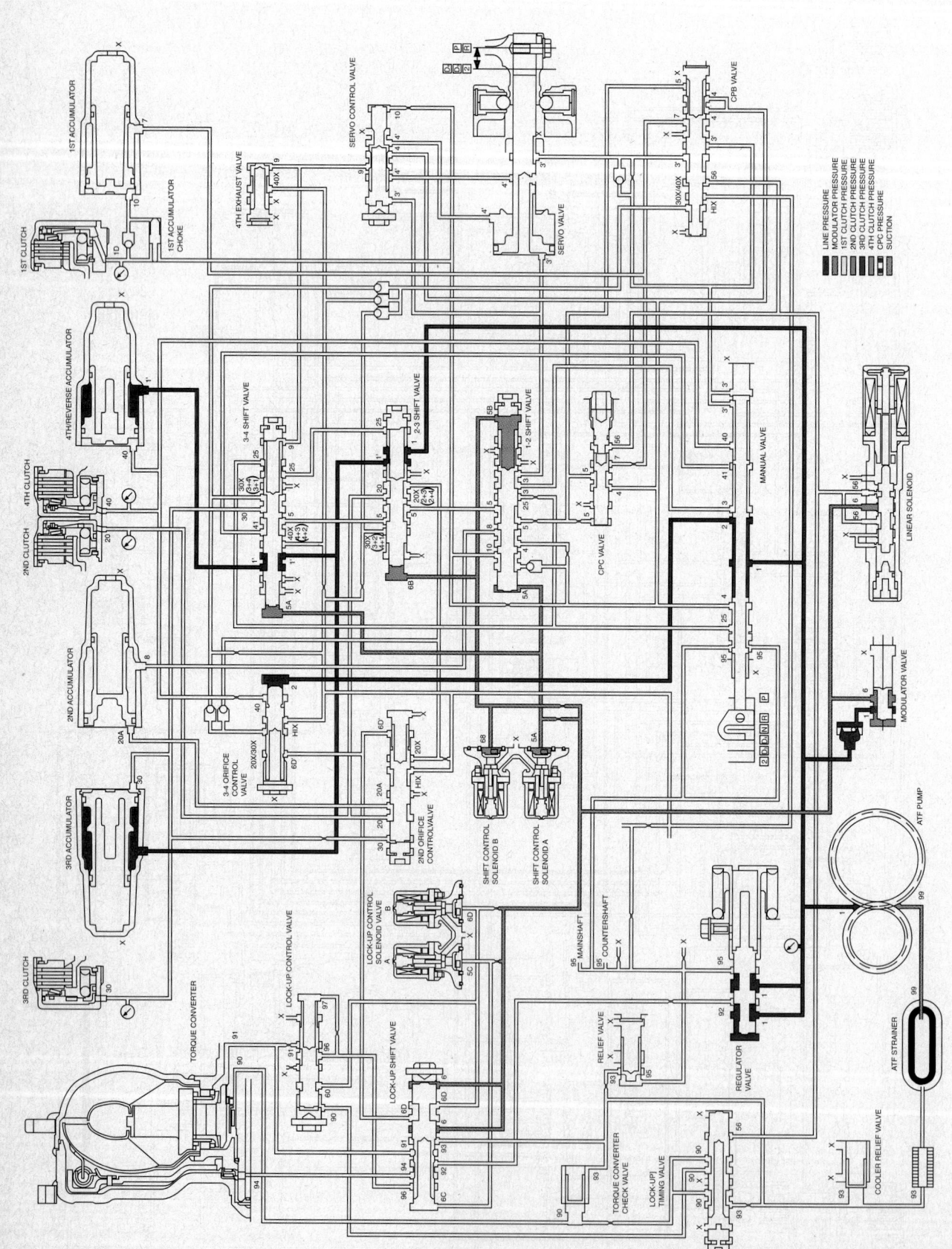

Fig. 1: "N" Position — Neutral

Courtesy of American Honda Motor Co., Inc.

OIL CIRCUIT DIAGRAMS
Honda Civic A4RA (Cont.)

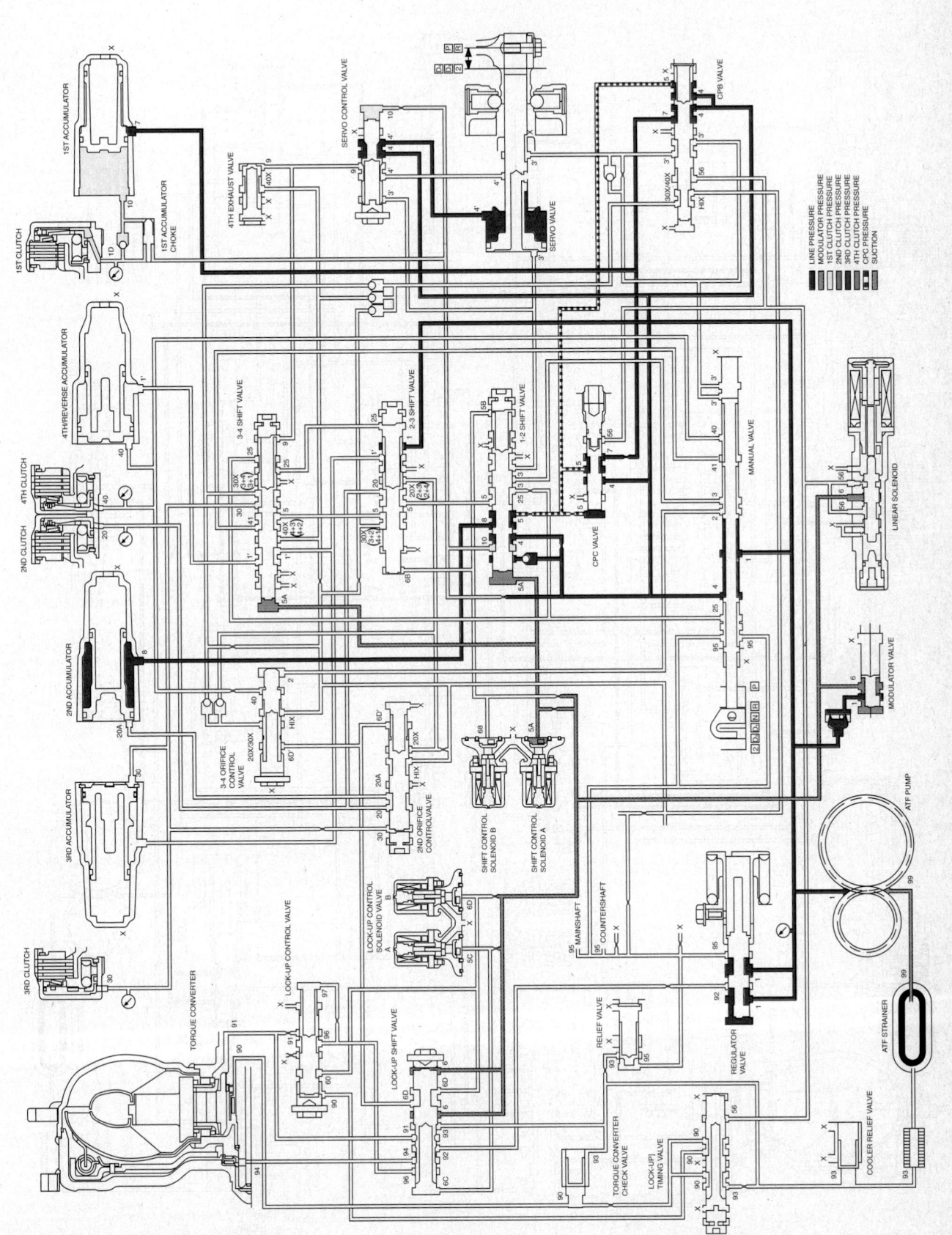

Fig. 2: "D₃" Or "D₄" Position — 1st Gear

Courtesy of American Honda Motor Co., Inc.

OIL CIRCUIT DIAGRAMS
Honda Civic A4RA (Cont.)

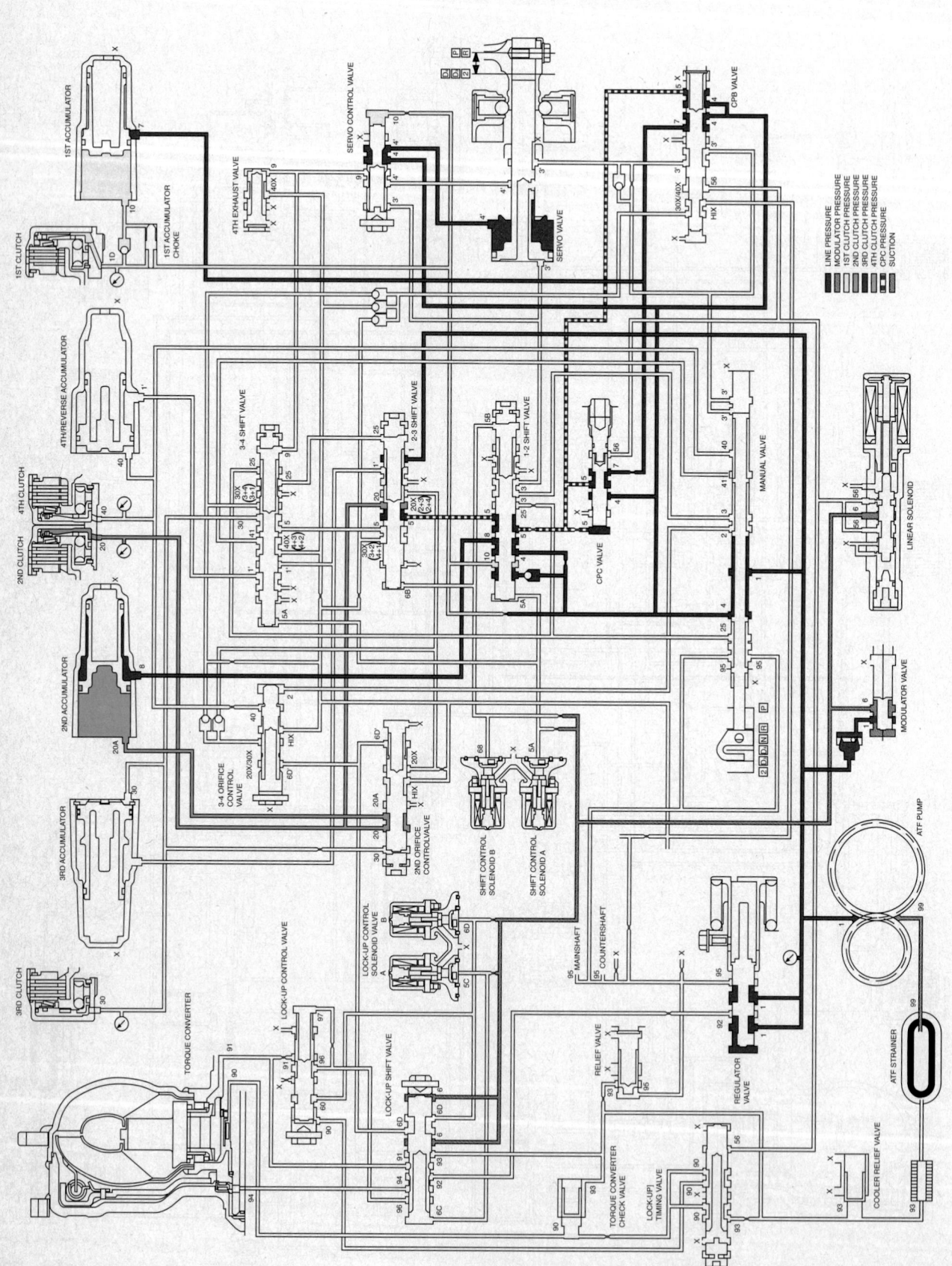

Fig. 3: "D₃" Or "D₄" Position — 2nd Gear

Courtesy of American Honda Motor Co., Inc.

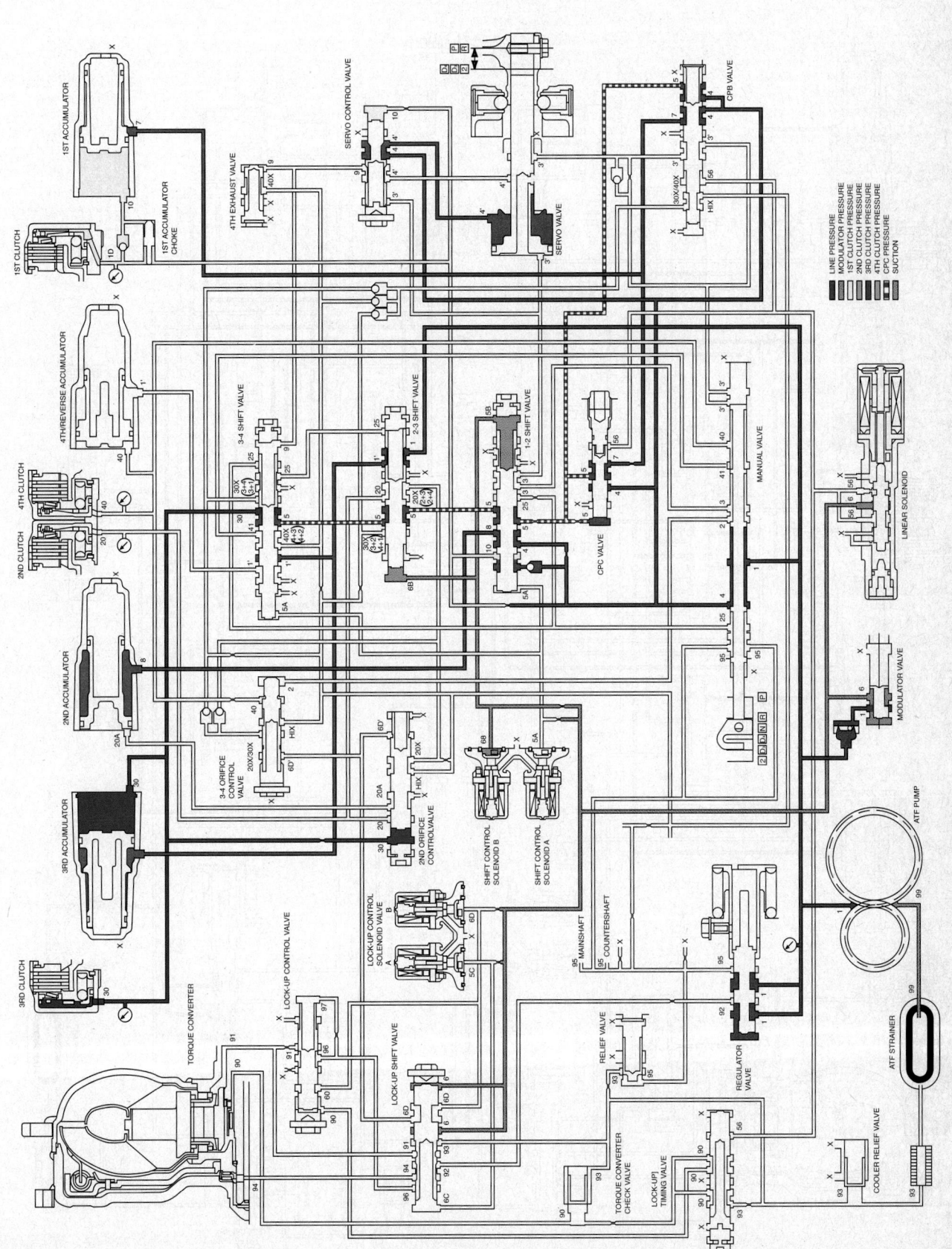

Fig. 4: "D₃" Or "D₄" Position — 3rd Gear

Courtesy of American Honda Motor Co., Inc.

OIL CIRCUIT DIAGRAMS
Honda Civic A4RA (Cont.)

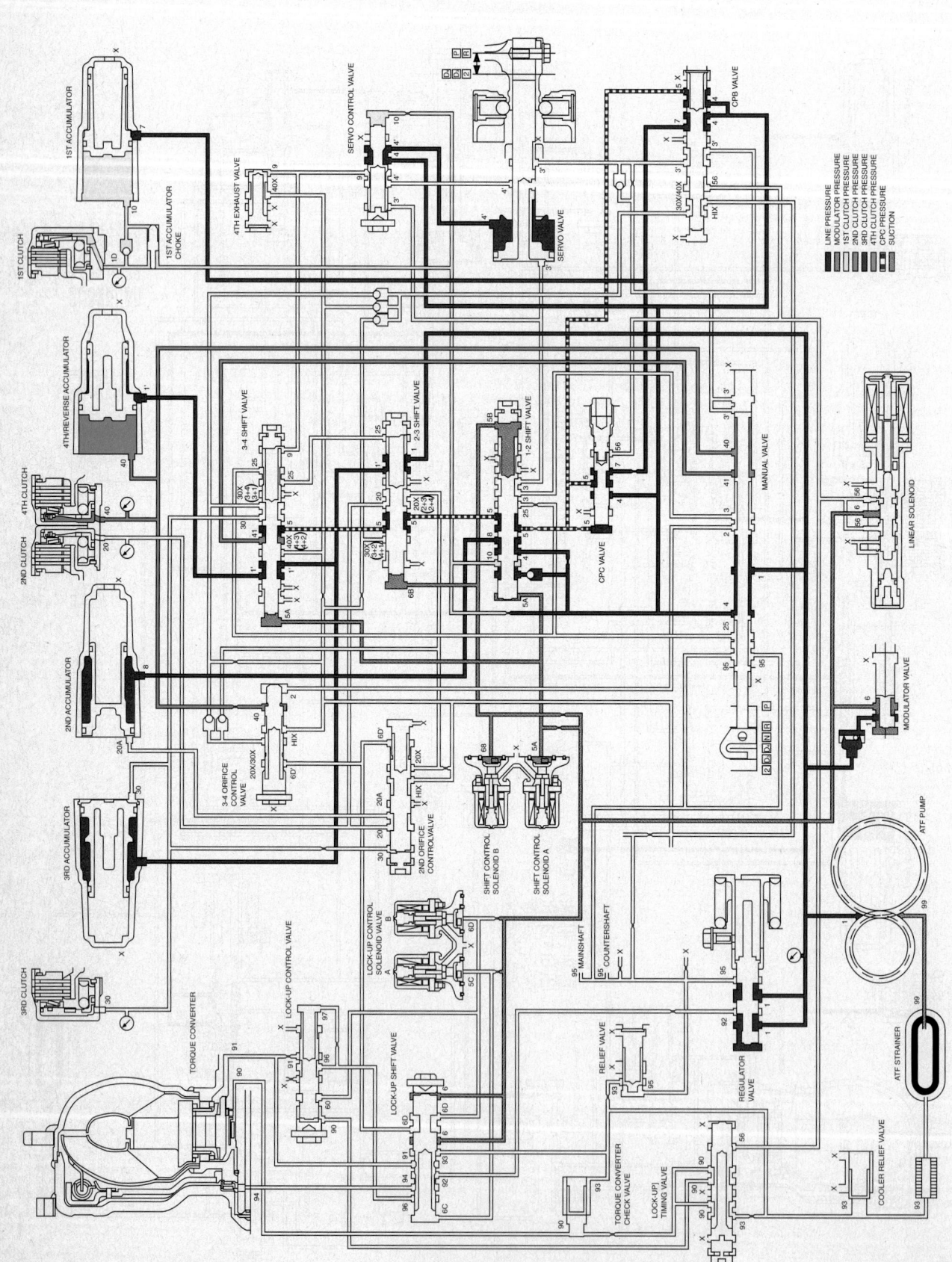

Fig. 5: "D₄" Position — 4th Gear

Courtesy of American Honda Motor Co., Inc.

OIL CIRCUIT DIAGRAMS
Honda Civic A4RA (Cont.)

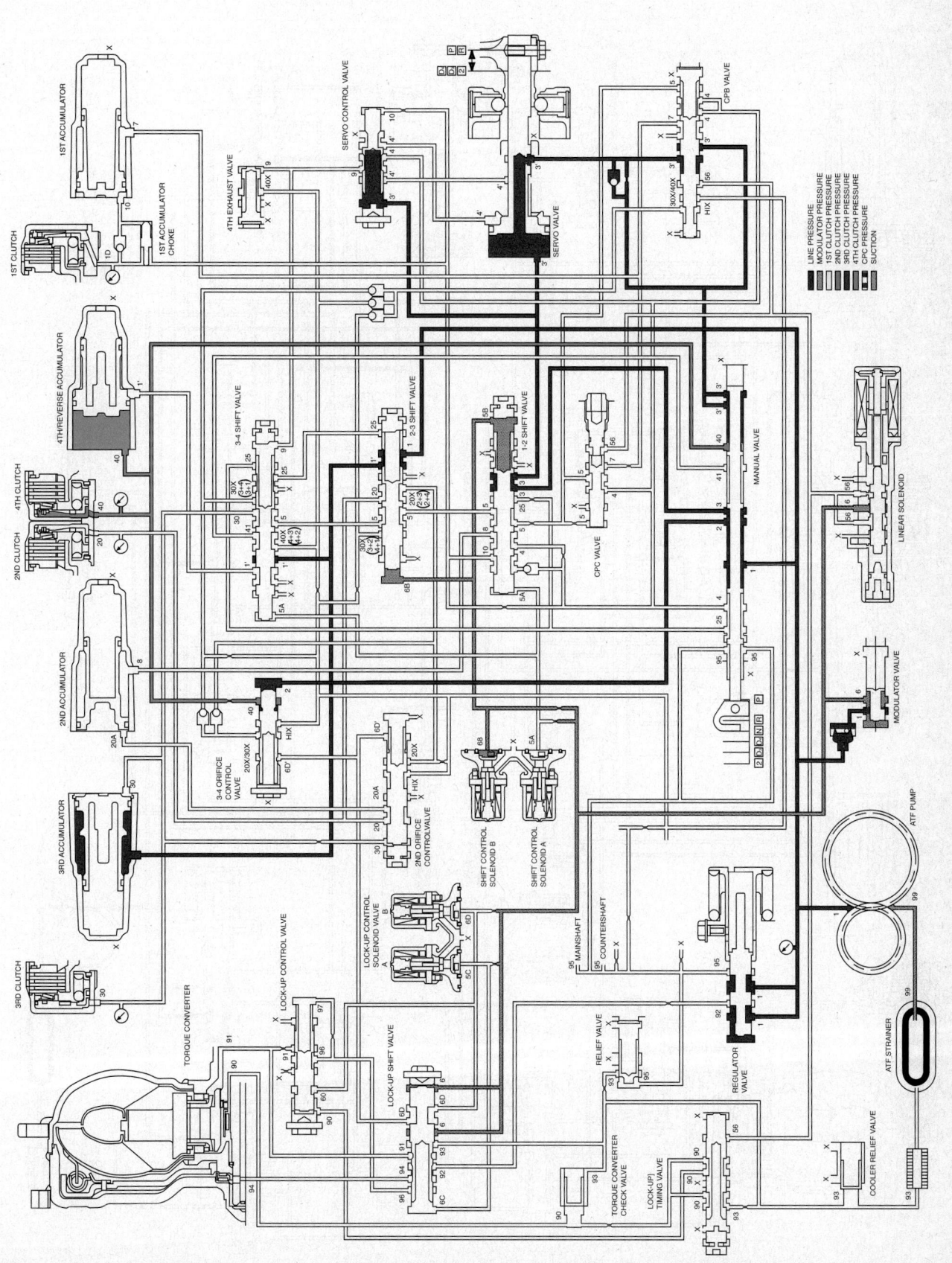

Fig. 6: "R" Position — Reverse

Courtesy of American Honda Motor Co., Inc.

OIL CIRCUIT DIAGRAMS
Honda Civic A4RA (Cont.)

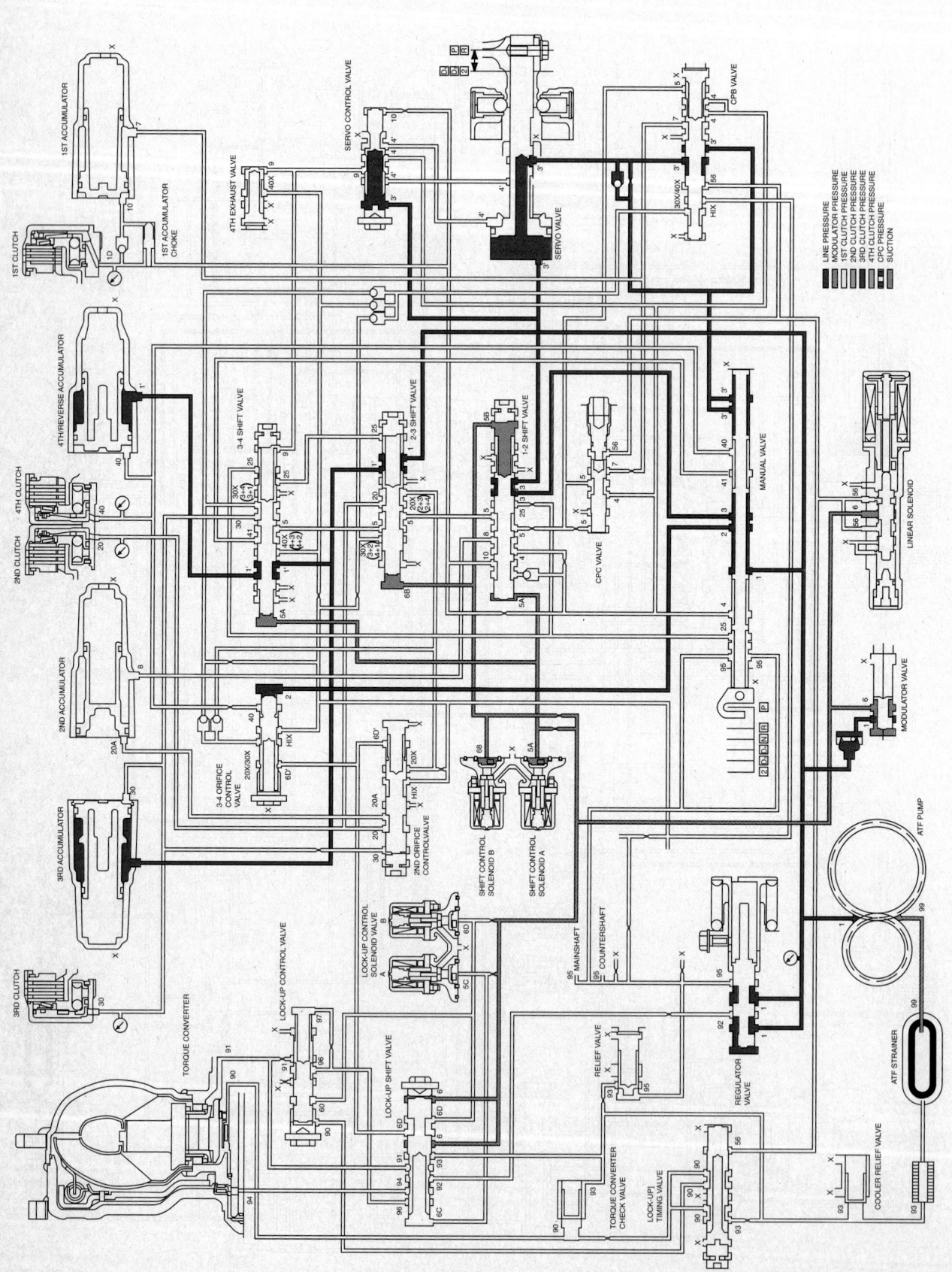

Fig. 7: "P" Position — Park

Courtesy of American Honda Motor Co., Inc.

OIL CIRCUIT DIAGRAMS
Honda Civic M4VA CVT

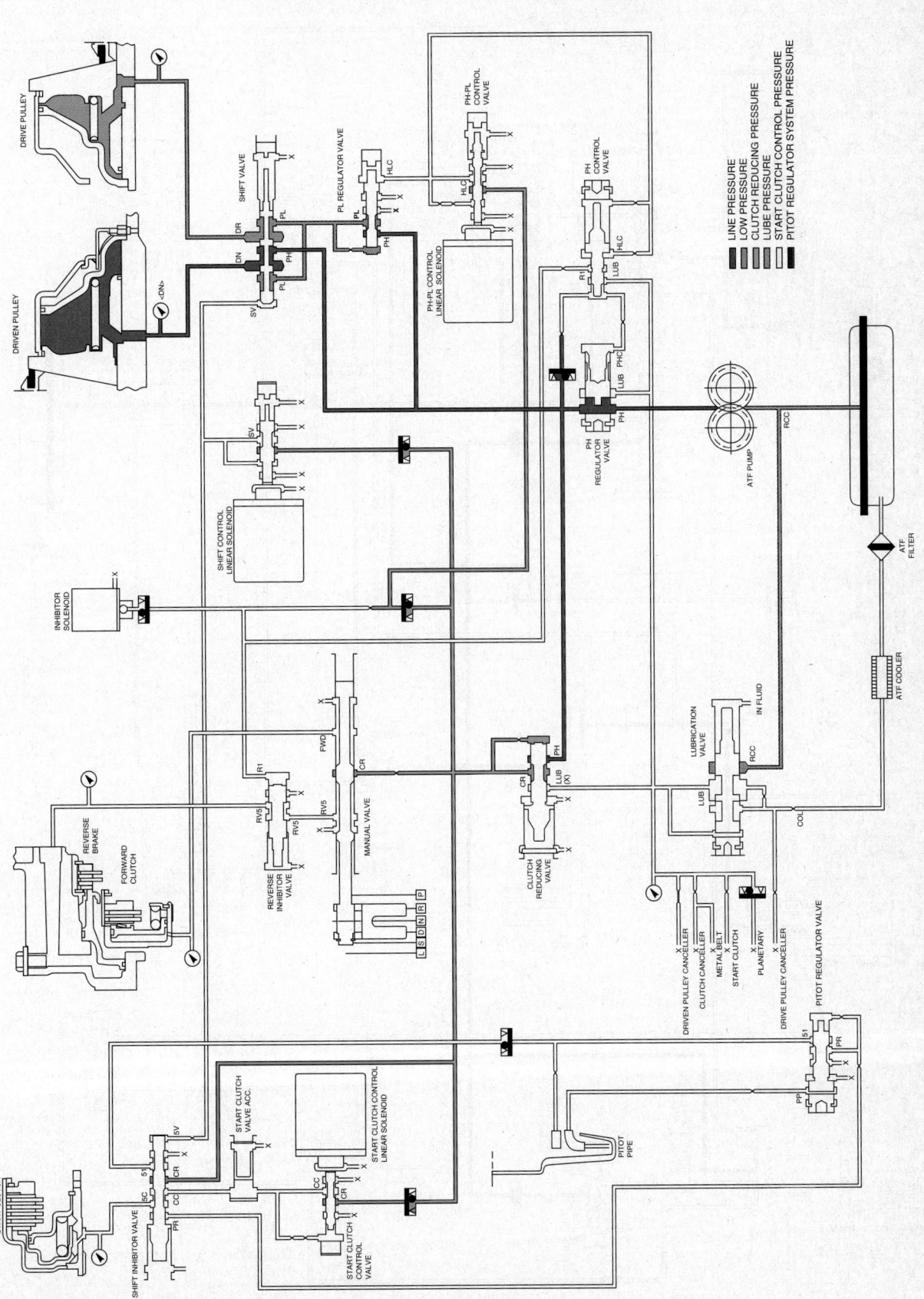

Fig. 1: "N" Position — Neutral

Courtesy of American Honda Motor Co., Inc.

OIL CIRCUIT DIAGRAMS
Honda Civic M4VA CVT (Cont.)

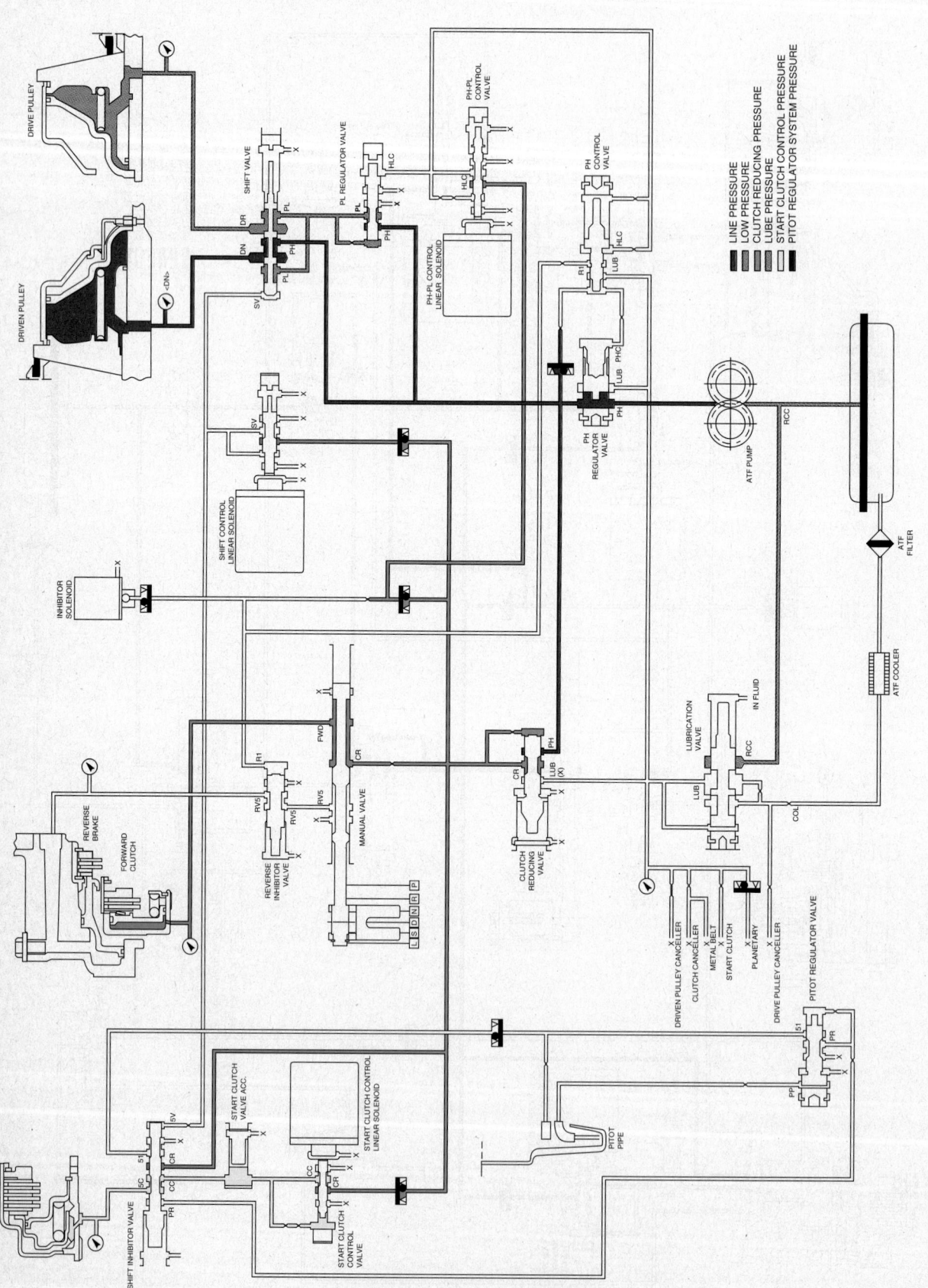

Fig. 2: "D" Position — Low Speed

Courtesy of American Honda Motor Co., Inc.

OIL CIRCUIT DIAGRAMS
Honda Civic M4VA CVT (Cont.)

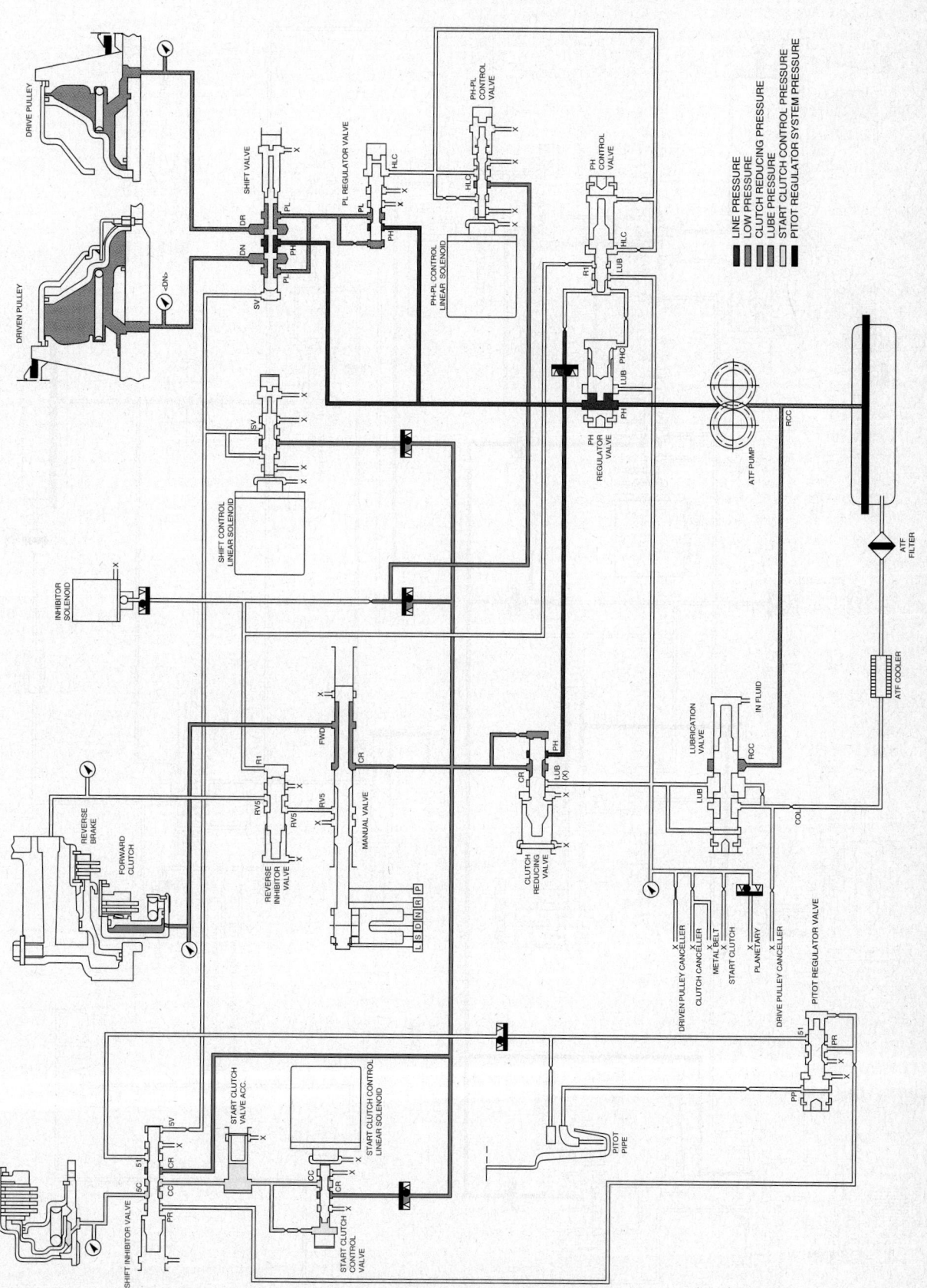

Fig. 3: "D" Position — Middle Speed

Courtesy of American Honda Motor Co., Inc.

OIL CIRCUIT DIAGRAMS
Honda Civic M4VA CVT (Cont.)

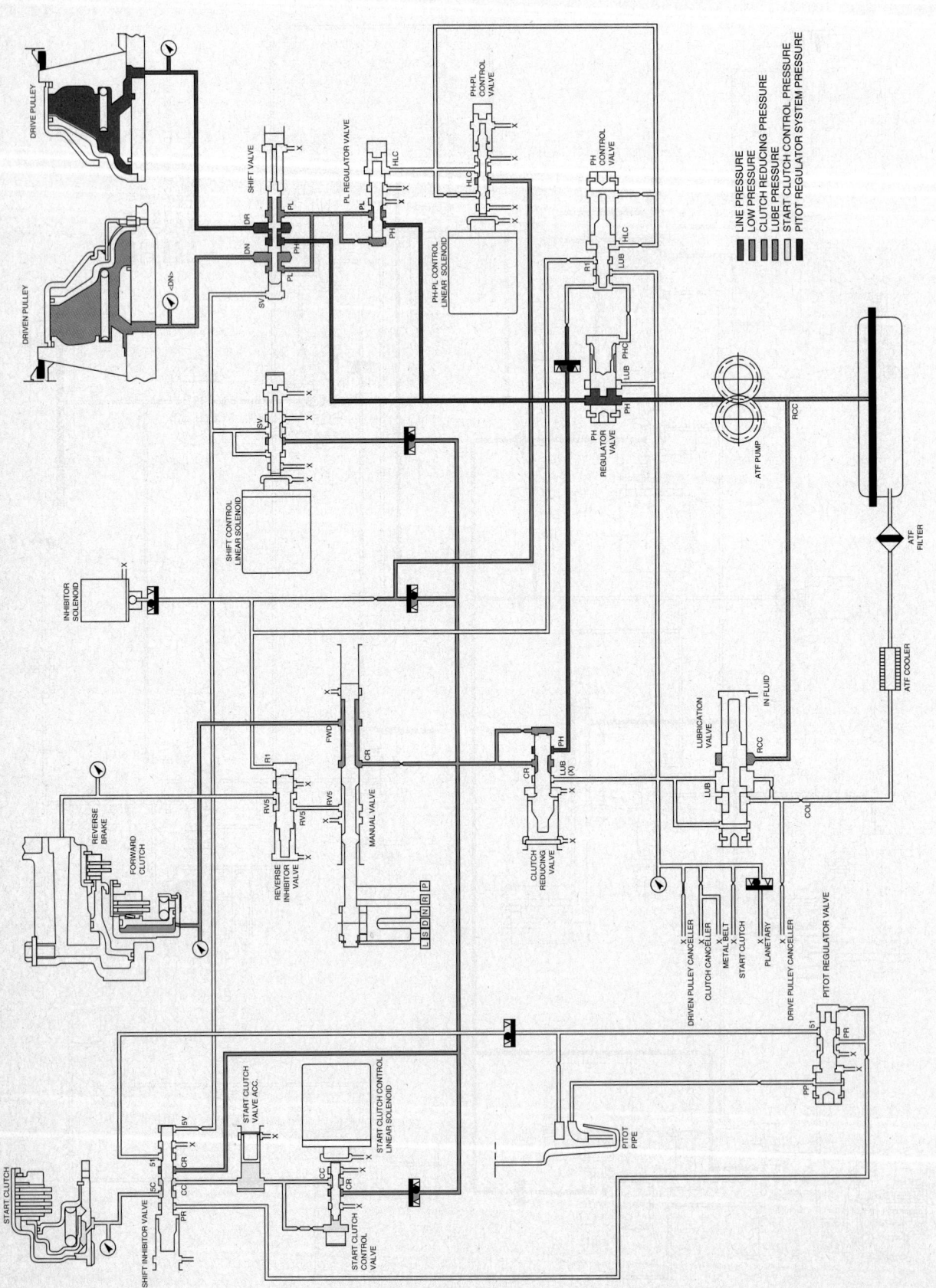

Fig. 4: "D" Position — High Speed

Courtesy of American Honda Motor Co., Inc.

OIL CIRCUIT DIAGRAMS
Honda Civic M4VA CVT (Cont.)

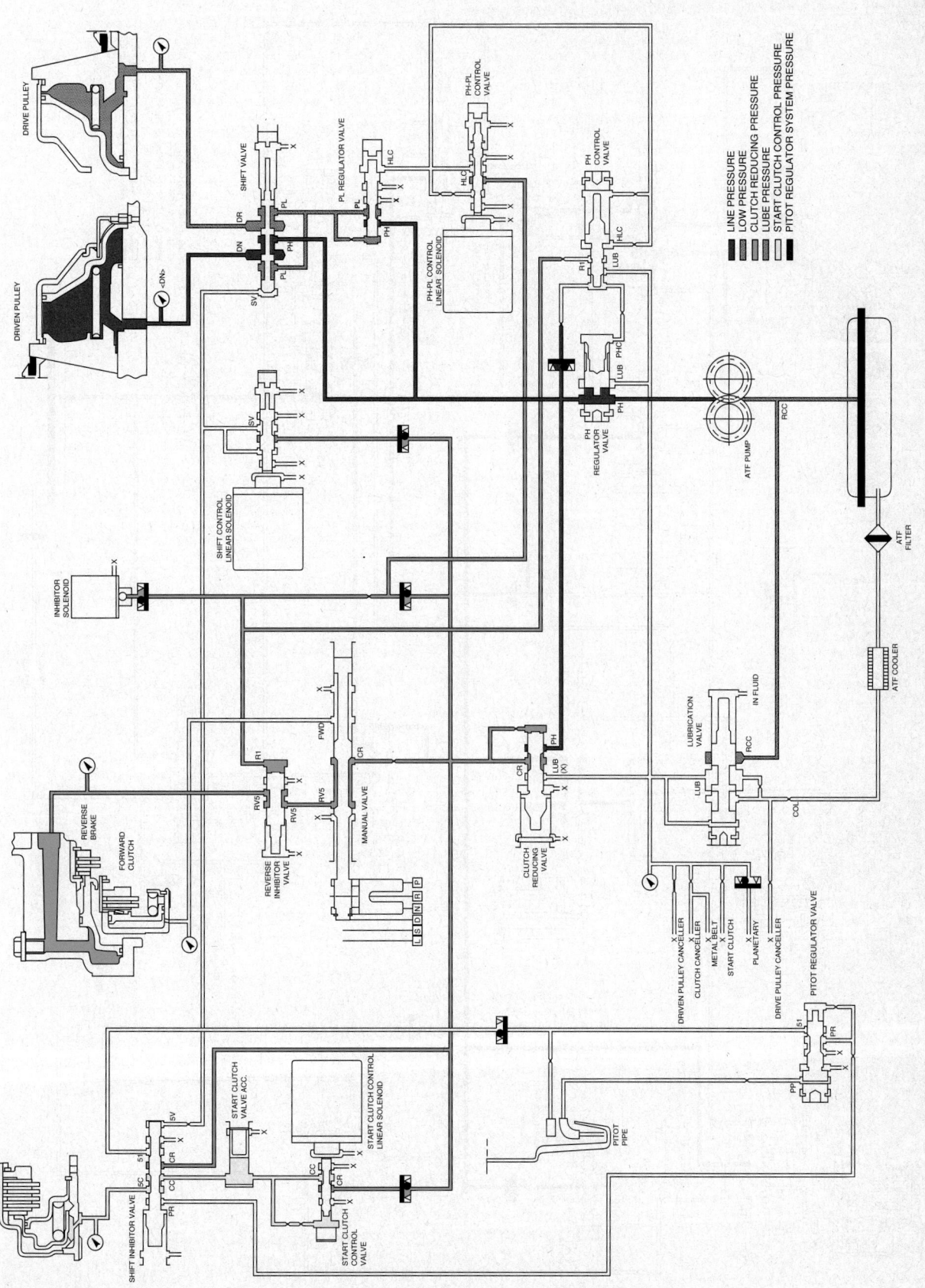

Fig. 5: "R" Position — Reverse

Courtesy of American Honda Motor Co., Inc.

OIL CIRCUIT DIAGRAMS
Honda Civic M4VA CVT (Cont.)

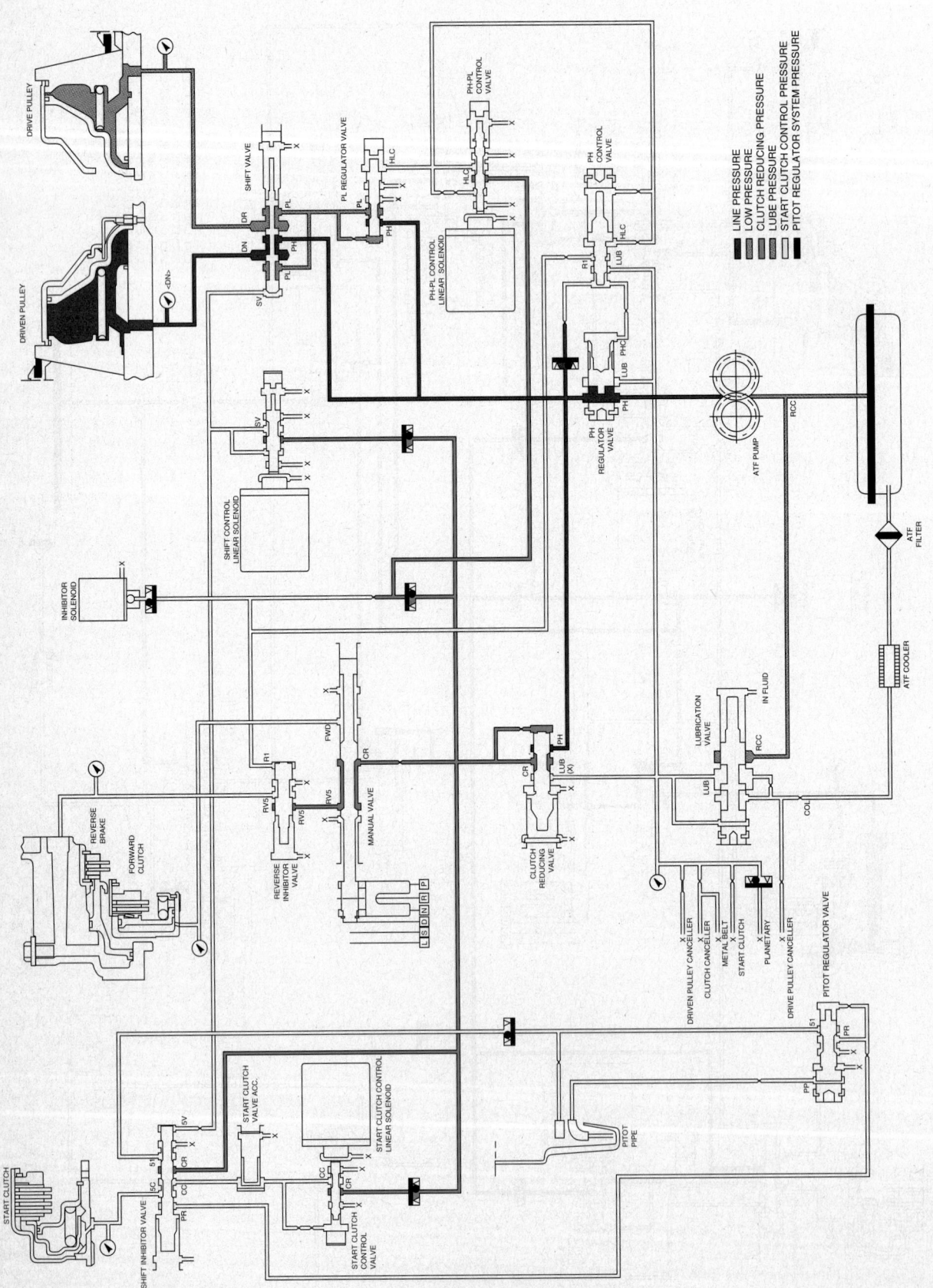

Fig. 6: "R" Position — When Selected While Moving Forward

Courtesy of American Honda Motor Co., Inc.

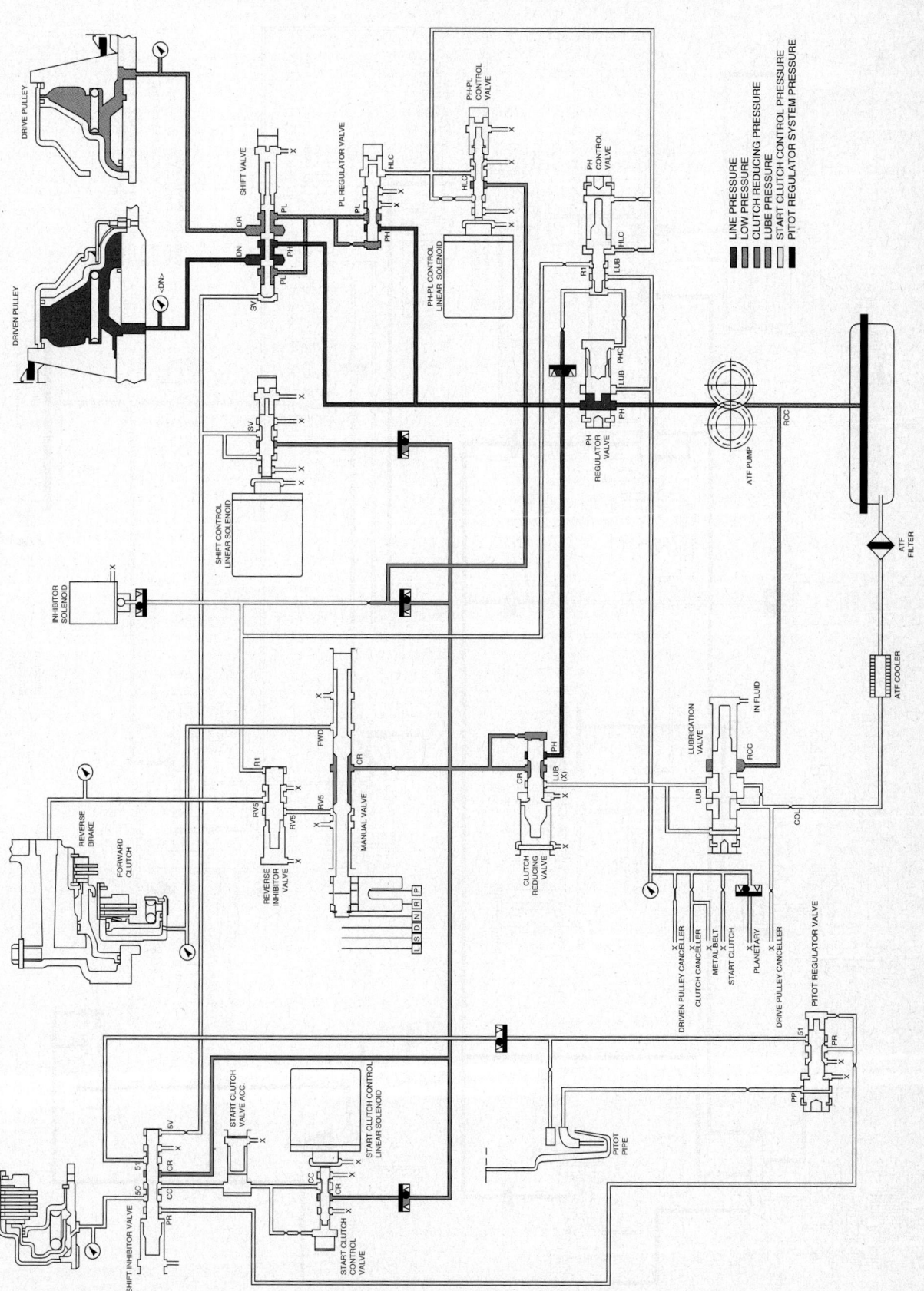

Fig. 7: "P" Position — Park

Courtesy of American Honda Motor Co., Inc.

OIL CIRCUIT DIAGRAMS
Honda Civic M4VA CVT (Cont.)

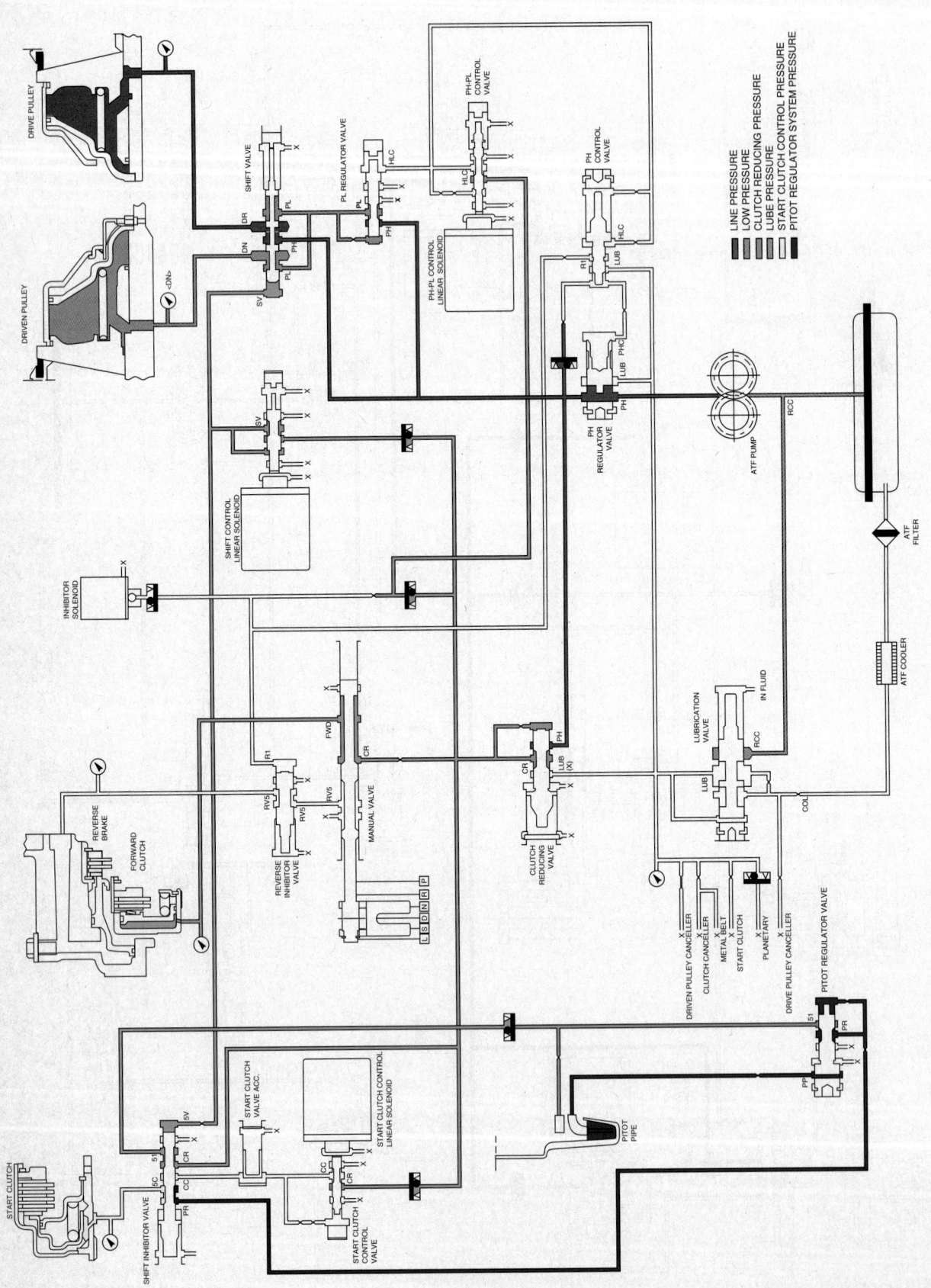

Fig. 8: "D" Position — Default Mode With Faulty ECU

Courtesy of American Honda Motor Co., Inc.

OIL CIRCUIT DIAGRAMS
Honda Civic M4VA CVT (Cont.)

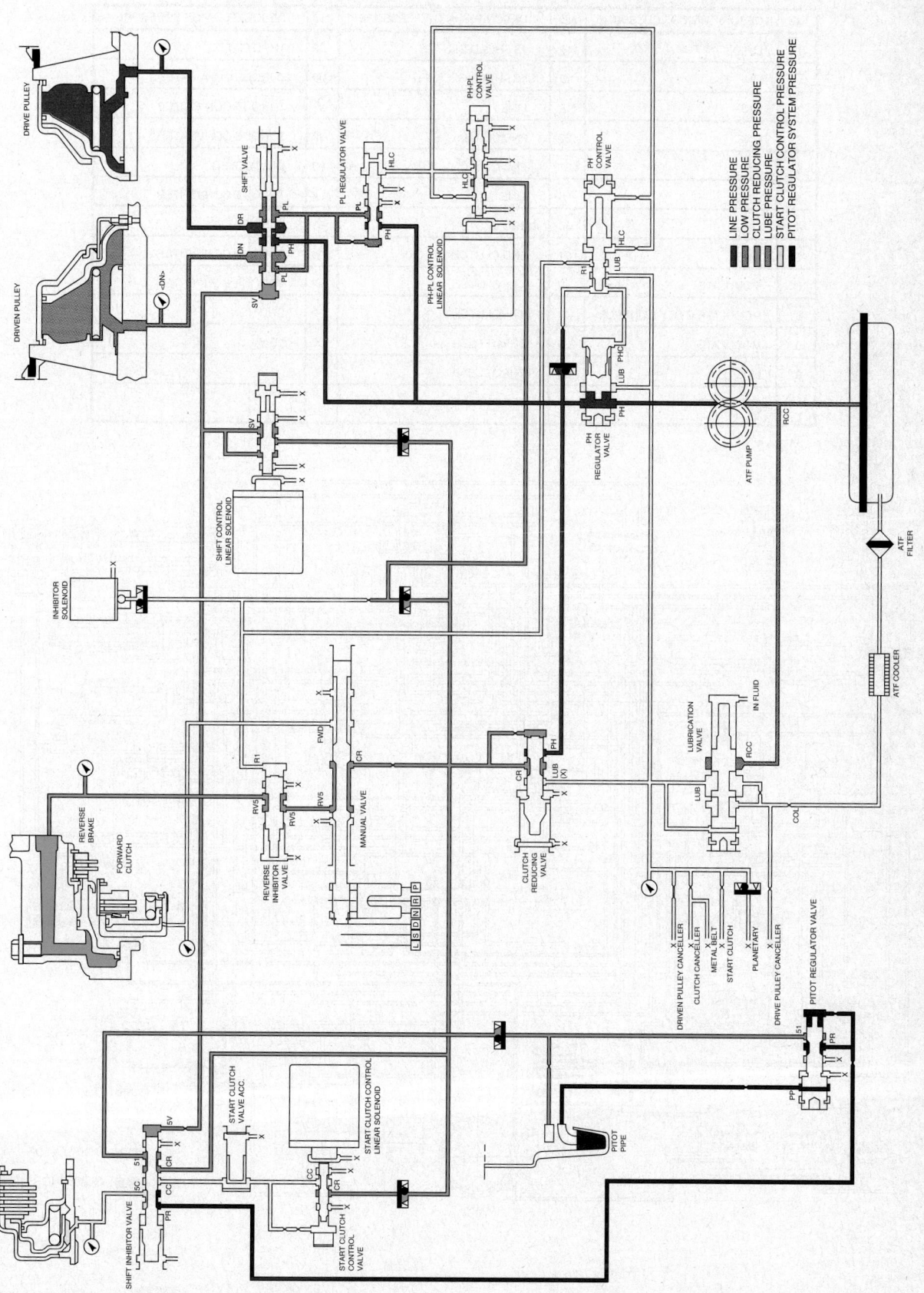

Fig. 9: "R" Position — Default Mode With Faulty ECU

Courtesy of American Honda Motor Co., Inc.

OIL CIRCUIT DIAGRAMS
Honda AOYA, MPJA & MPOA

NO.	DESCRIPTION OF PRESSURE	NO.	DESCRIPTION OF PRESSURE	NO.	DESCRIPTION OF PRESSURE
1	LINE	15	1ST-HOLD CLUTCH	58	THROTTLE B
2	LINE	16	1ST-HOLD CLUTCH	90	TORQUE CONVERTER
3	LINE	18	LINE	91	TORQUE CONVERTER
3'	LINE	20	2ND CLUTCH	92	TORQUE CONVERTER
3"	LINE	21	2ND CLUTCH	93	OIL COOLER
4	LINE	25	LINE	94	TORQUE CONVERTER
4'	LINE	30	3RD CLUTCH	95	LUBRICATION
5	LINE	31	3RD CLUTCH	96	TORQUE CONVERTER
6	MODULATE	40	4TH CLUTCH	97	TORQUE CONVERTER
6'	MODULATE (DUTY CONTROL)	41	4TH CLUTCH	99	SUCTION
6"	MODULATE	55	THROTTLE B	X	LEAK
9	LINE	56	THROTTLE B		
10	1ST CLUTCH	57	THROTTLE B		

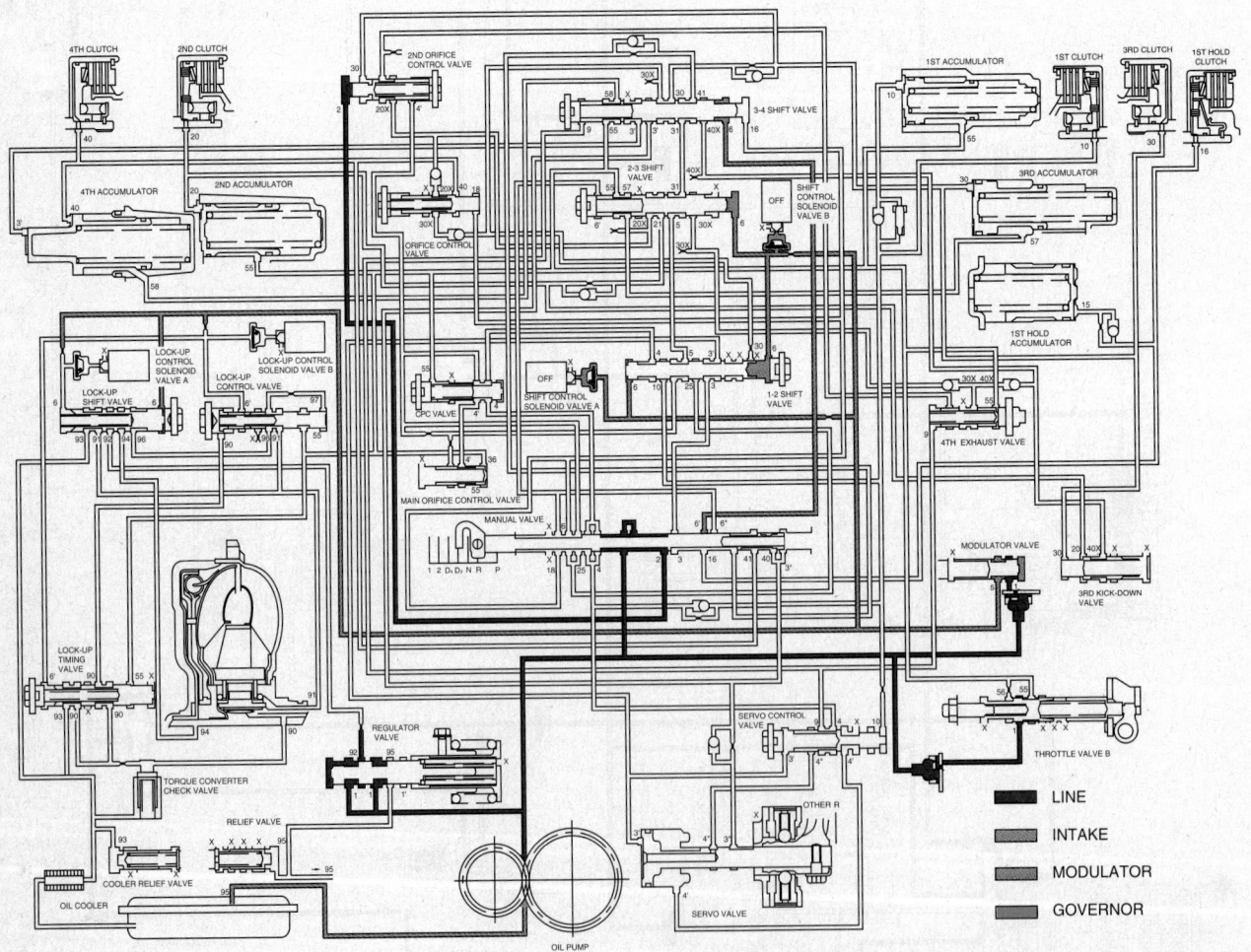

Courtesy of American Honda Motor Co., Inc.

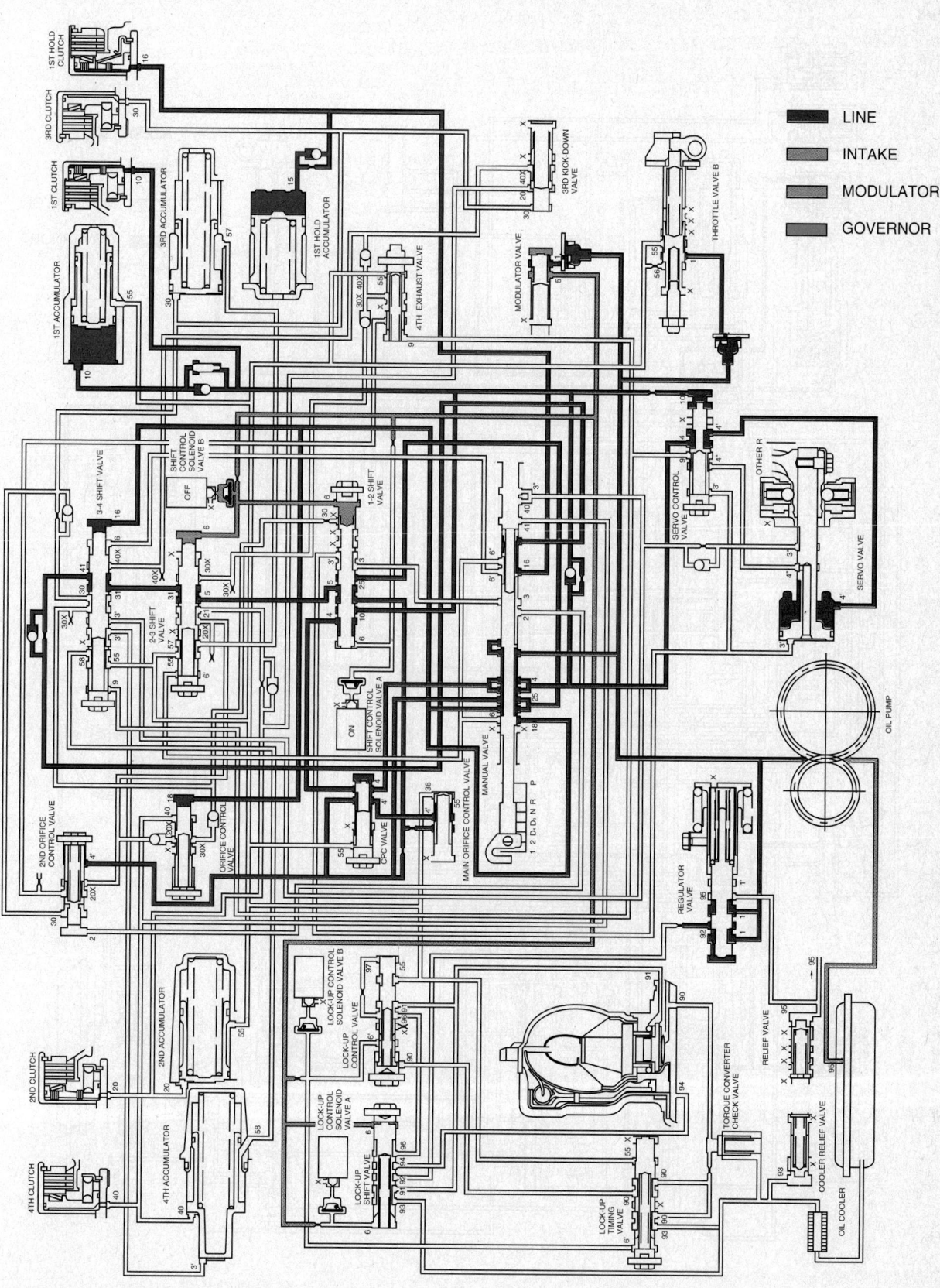

LINE

INTAKE

MODULATOR

GOVERNOR

Fig. 2: "1" Position — 1st Gear

Courtesy of American Honda Motor Co., Inc.

OIL CIRCUIT DIAGRAMS
Honda AOYA, MPJA & MPOA (Cont.)

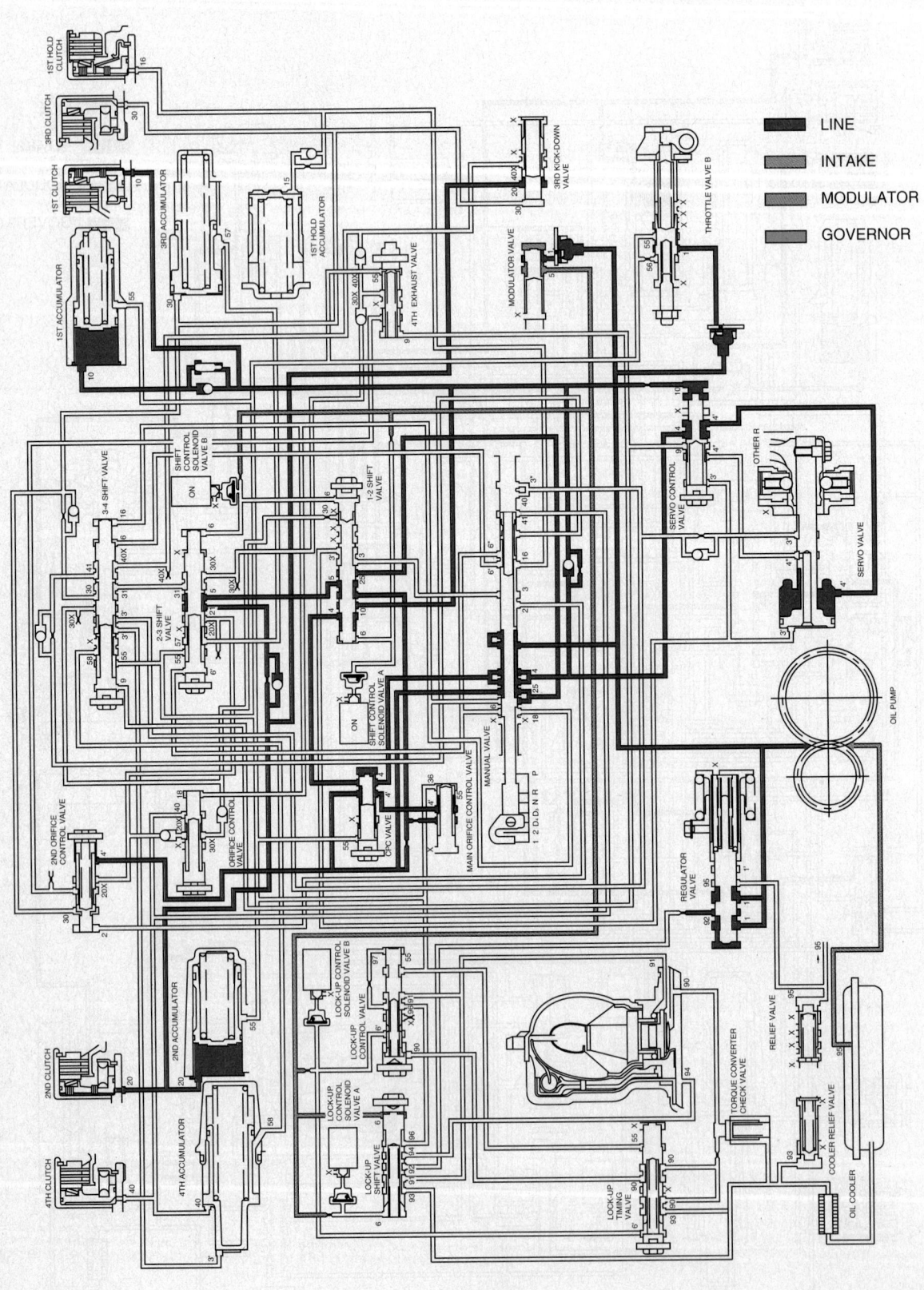

LINE

INTAKE

MODULATOR

GOVERNOR

Fig. 3: "2" Position — 1st Gear

Courtesy of American Honda Motor Co., Inc.

OIL CIRCUIT DIAGRAMS
Honda AOYA, MPJA & MPOA (Cont.)

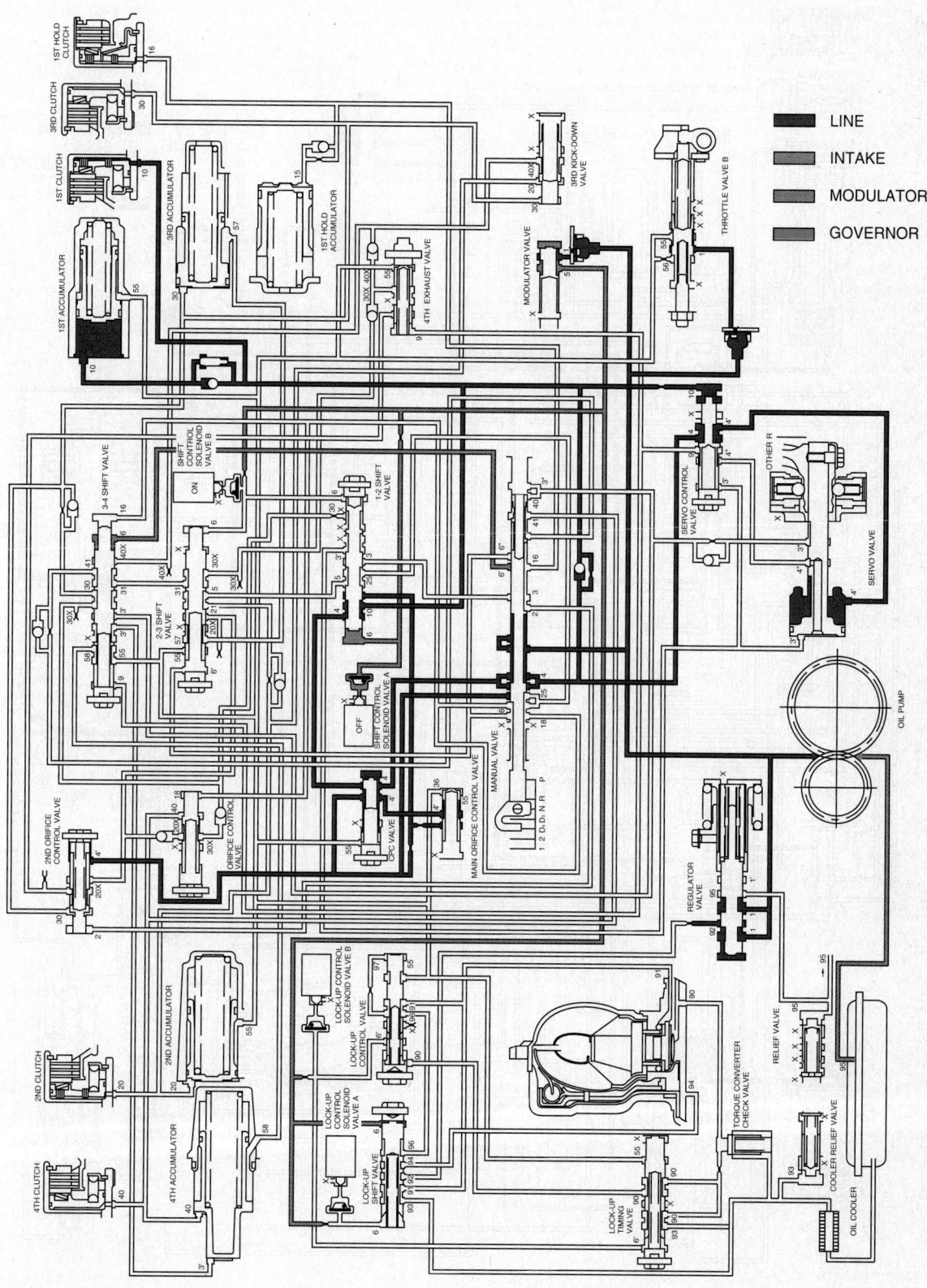

LINE
INTAKE
MODULATOR
GOVERNOR

Fig. 4: "D₃" Or "D₄" Position — 1st Gear

Courtesy of American Honda Motor Co., Inc.

OIL CIRCUIT DIAGRAMS
Honda AOYA, MPJA & MPOA (Cont.)

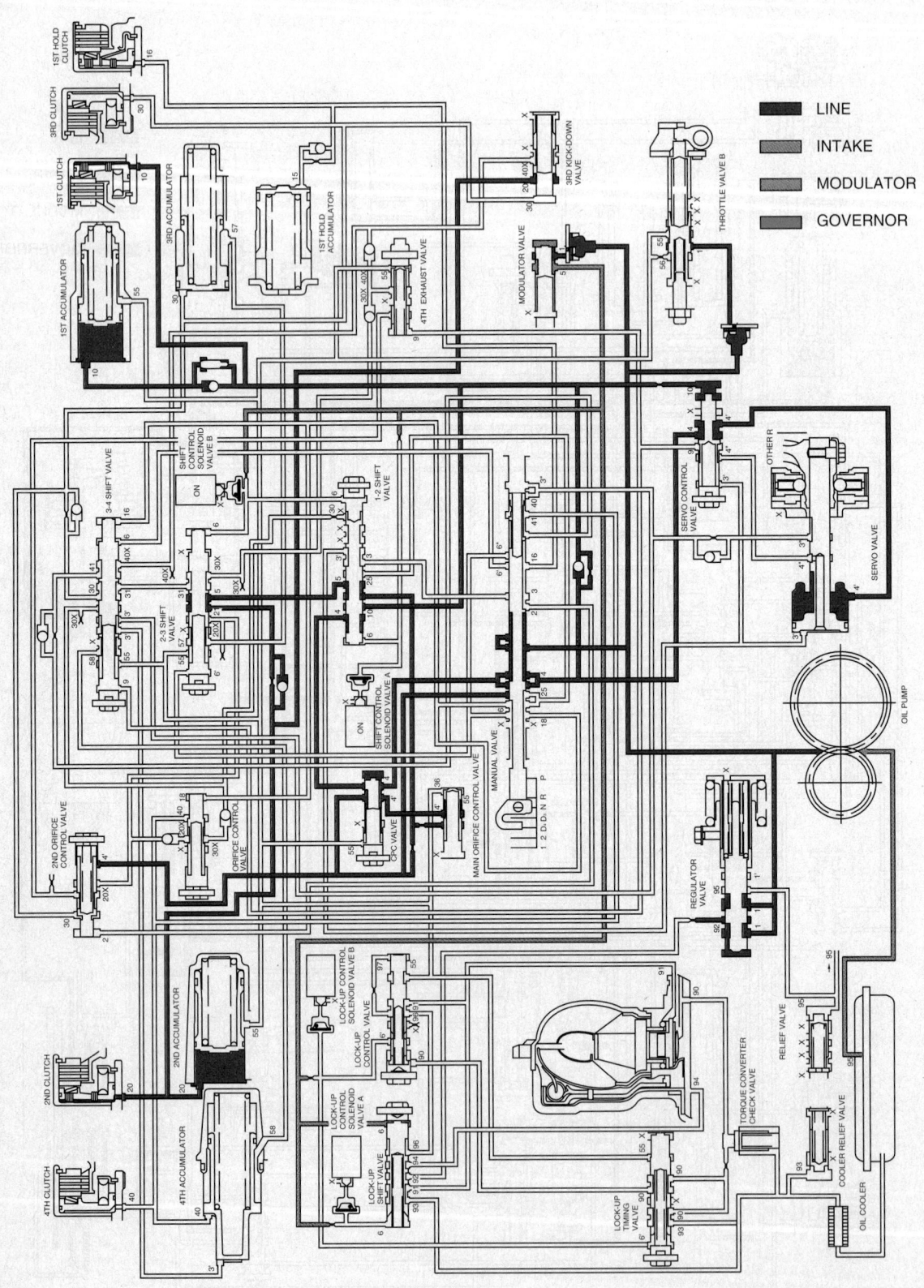

Fig. 5: "D₃" Or "D₄" Position — 2nd Gear

Courtesy of American Honda Motor Co., Inc.

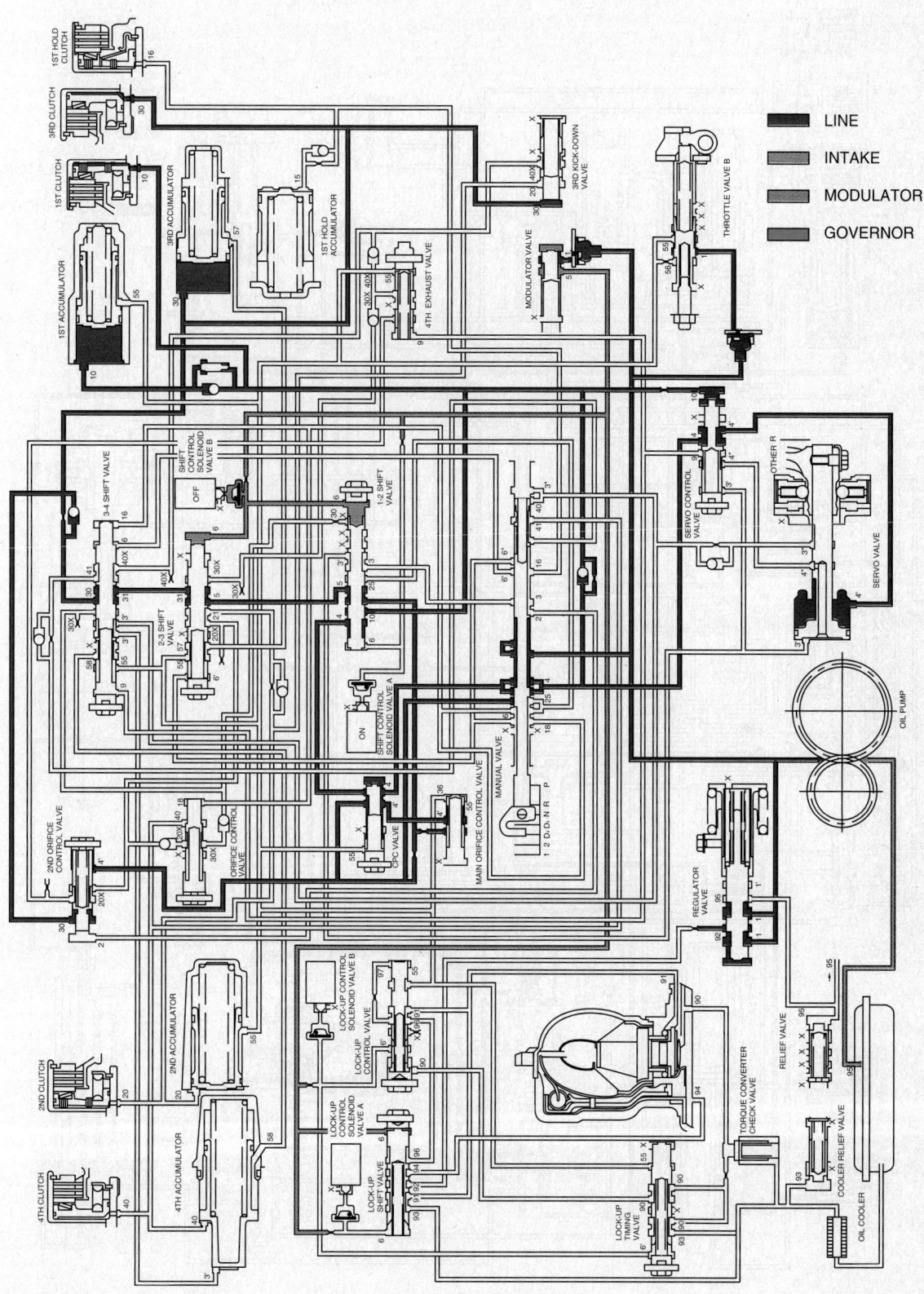

Fig. 6: "D₃" Or "D₄" Position — 3rd Gear

Courtesy of American Honda Motor Co., Inc.

OIL CIRCUIT DIAGRAMS
Honda AOYA, MPJA & MPOA (Cont.)

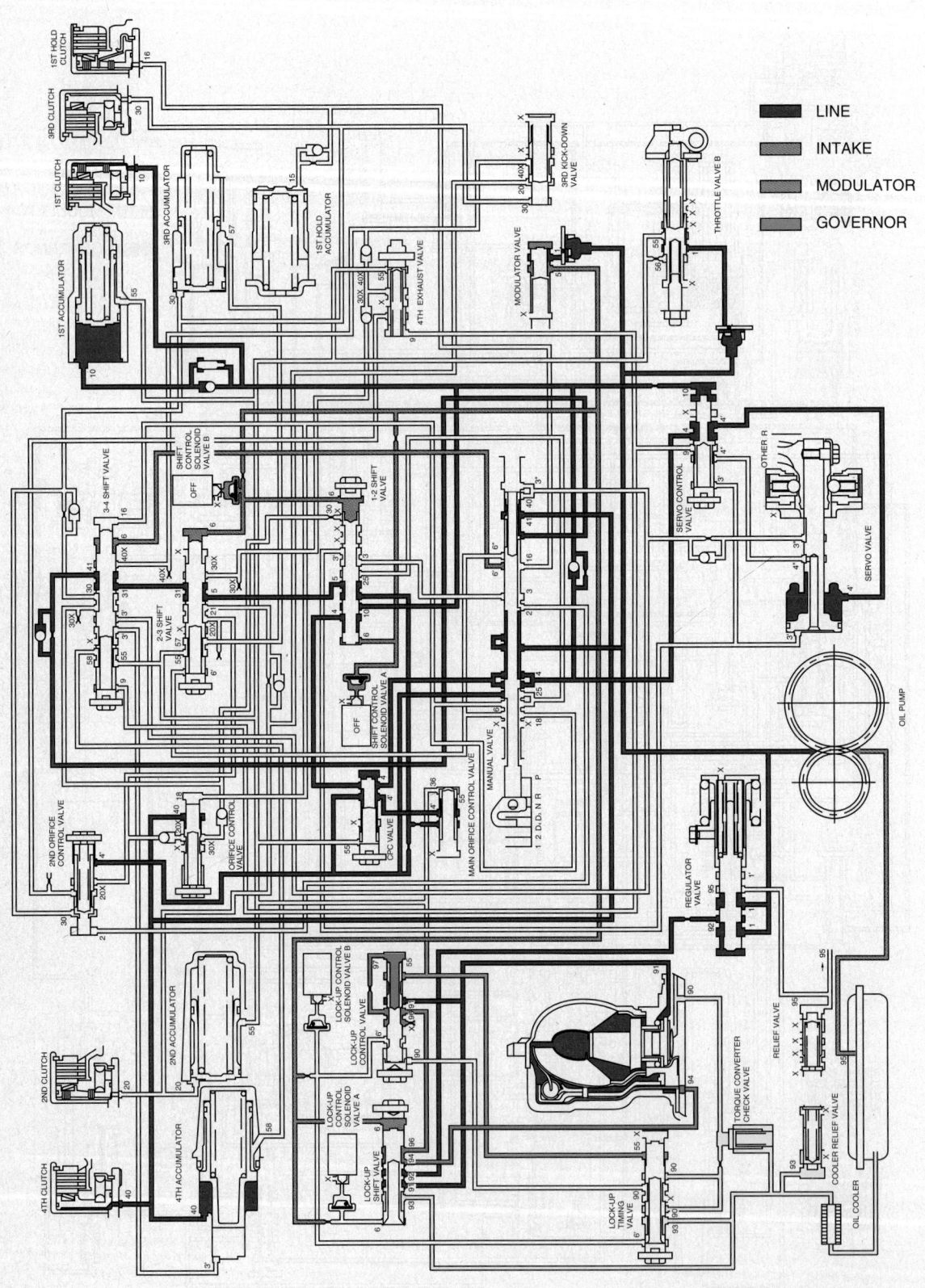

LINE

INTAKE

MODULATOR

GOVERNOR

Fig. 7: "D₄" Position — 4th Gear

Courtesy of American Honda Motor Co., Inc.

OIL CIRCUIT DIAGRAMS
Honda AOYA, MPJA & MPOA (Cont.)

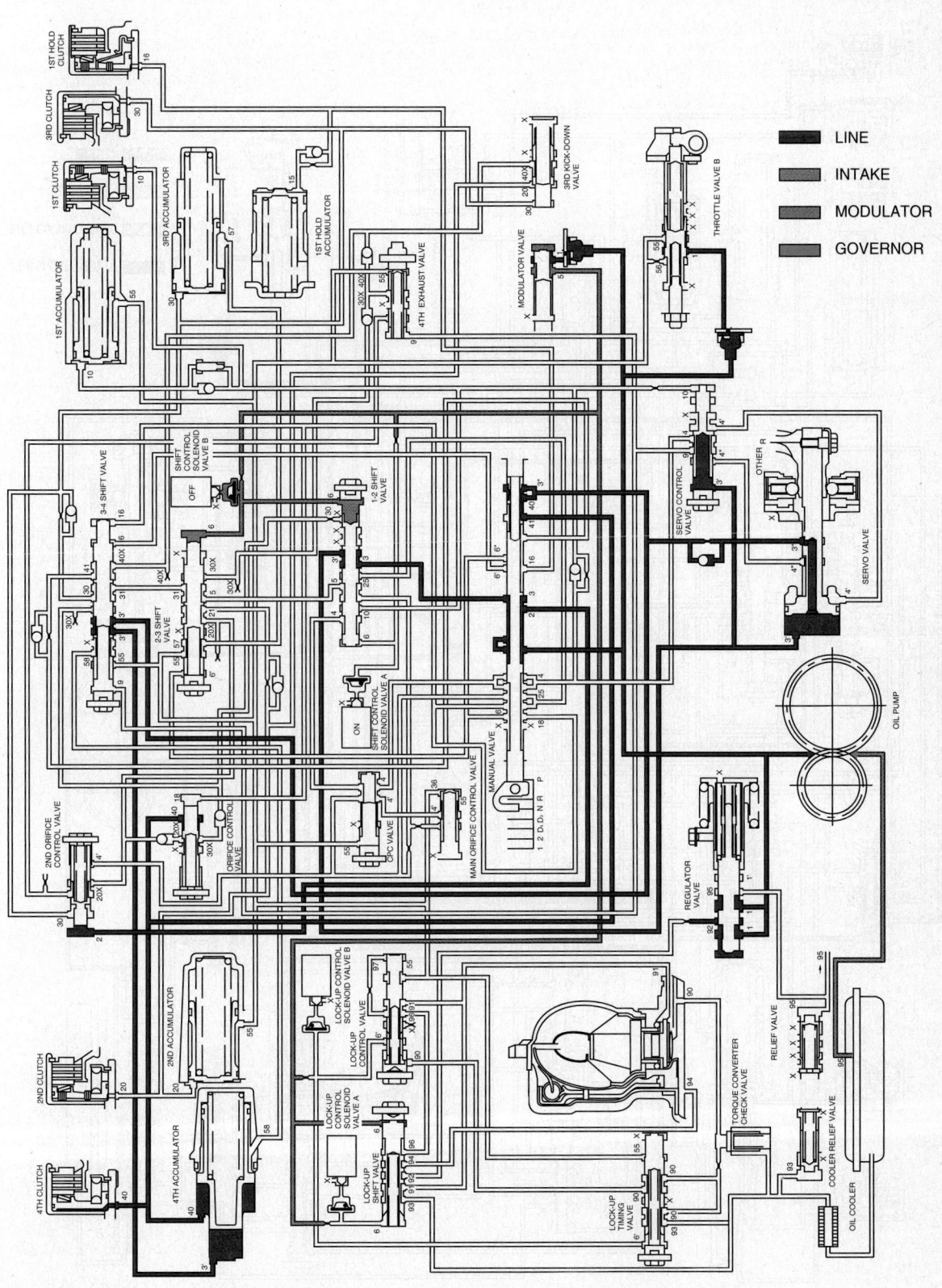

LINE

INTAKE

MODULATOR

GOVERNOR

Fig. 8: "R" Position — Reverse

Courtesy of American Honda Motor Co., Inc.

OIL CIRCUIT DIAGRAMS
Honda AOYA, MPJA & MPOA (Cont.)

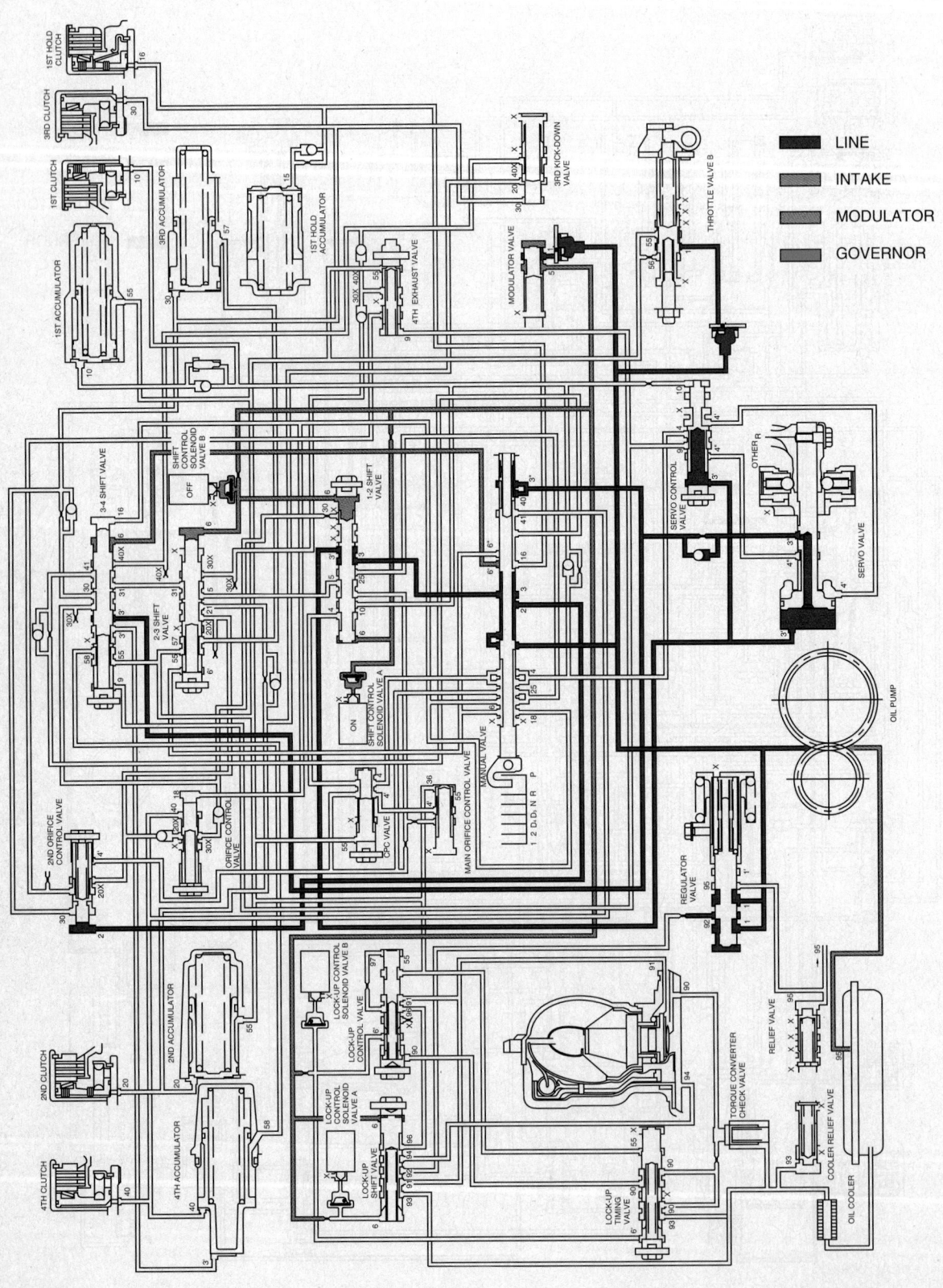

▮ LINE	
▮ INTAKE	
▮ MODULATOR	
▮ GOVERNOR	

Fig. 9: "P" Position — Park

Courtesy of American Honda Motor Co., Inc.

OIL CIRCUIT DIAGRAMS
Honda MP1A

NO.	DESCRIPTION OF PRESSURE	NO.	DESCRIPTION OF PRESSURE	NO.	DESCRIPTION OF PRESSURE	NO.	DESCRIPTION OF PRESSURE
1	LINE	6'	MODULATE (DUTY CONTROL)	30	3RD CLUTCH	93	OIL COOLER
2	LINE	9	LINE	31	3RD CLUTCH	94	TORQUE CONVERTER
3	LINE	10	1ST CLUTCH	40	4TH CLUTCH	95	LUBRICATION
3'	LINE	15	1ST HOLD CLUTCH	41	4TH CLUTCH	96	TORQUE CONVERTER
3"	LINE	16	1ST LINE CLUTCH	55	THROTTLE B	99	SUCTION
4	LINE	18	LINE	56	THROTTLE B	X	BLEED
4'	LINE	20	2ND CLUTCH	90	TORQUE CONVERTER		
5	LINE	21	2ND CLUTCH	91	TORQUE CONVERTER		
6	MODULATE	25	LINE	92	TORQUE CONVERTER		

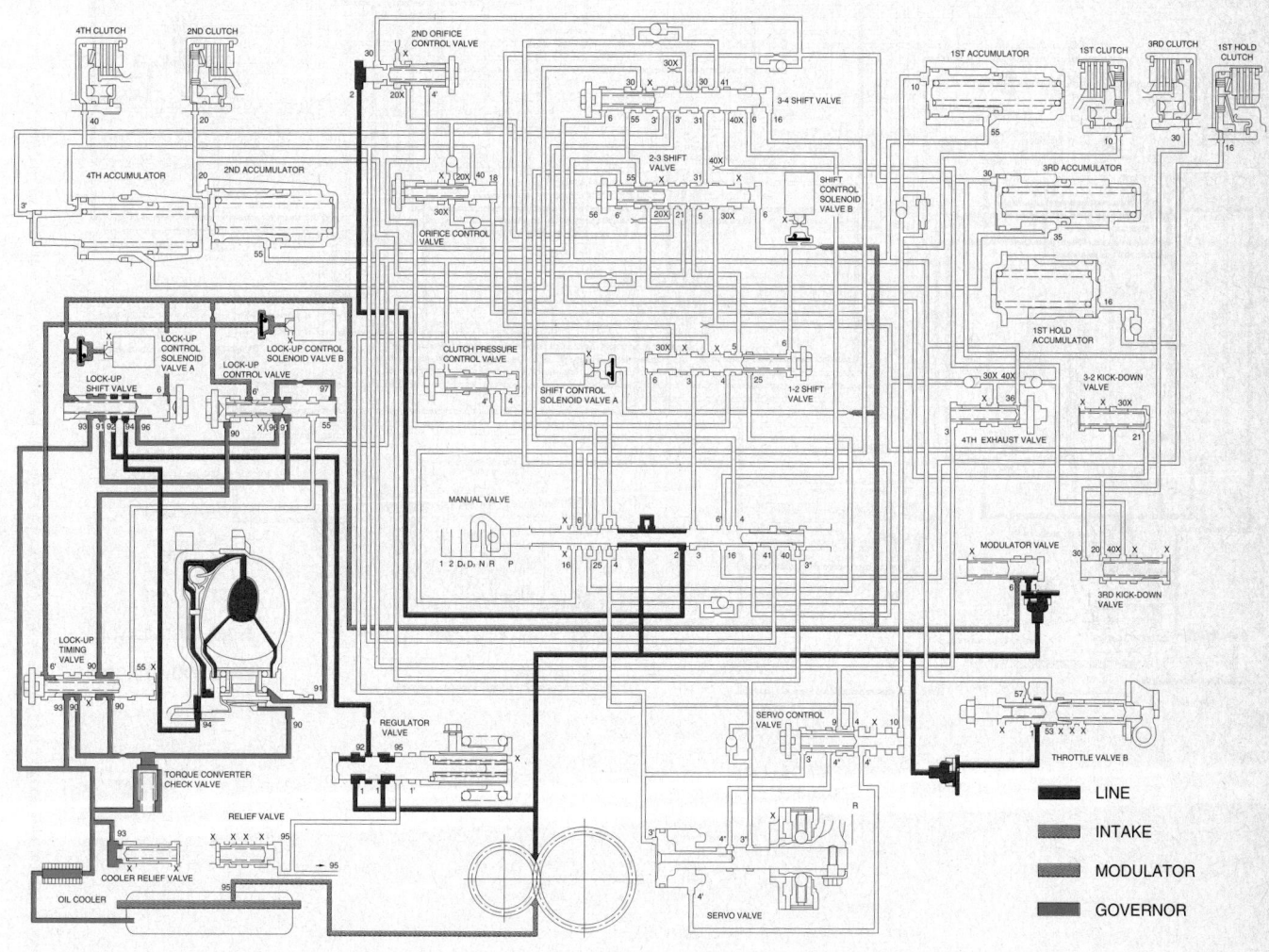

Fig. 1: "N" Position — Neutral

Courtesy of American Honda Motor Co., Inc.

OIL CIRCUIT DIAGRAMS
Honda MP1A (Cont.)

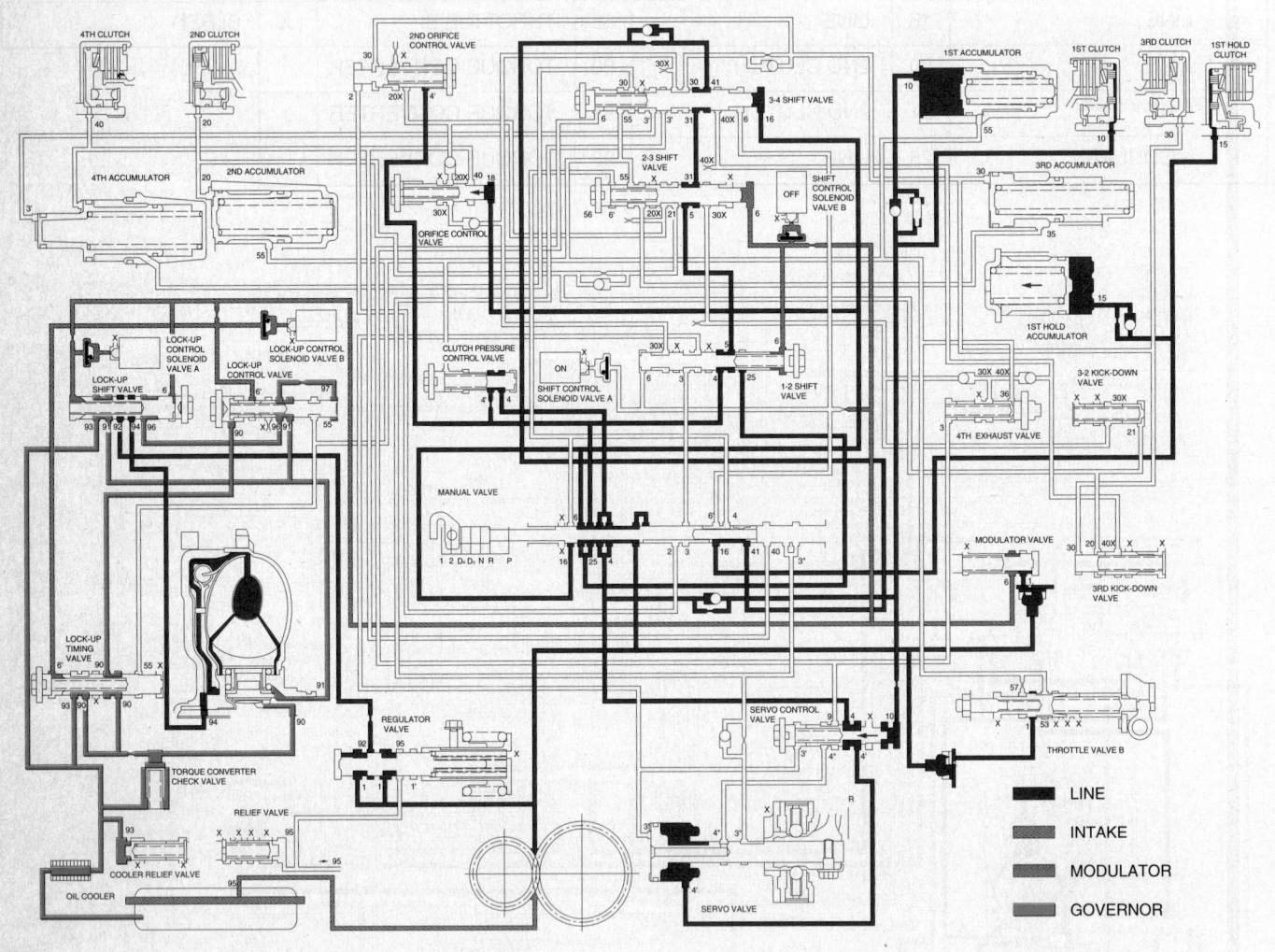

Fig. 2: "1" Position — 1st Gear

Courtesy of American Honda Motor Co., Inc.

OIL CIRCUIT DIAGRAMS
Honda MP1A (Cont.)

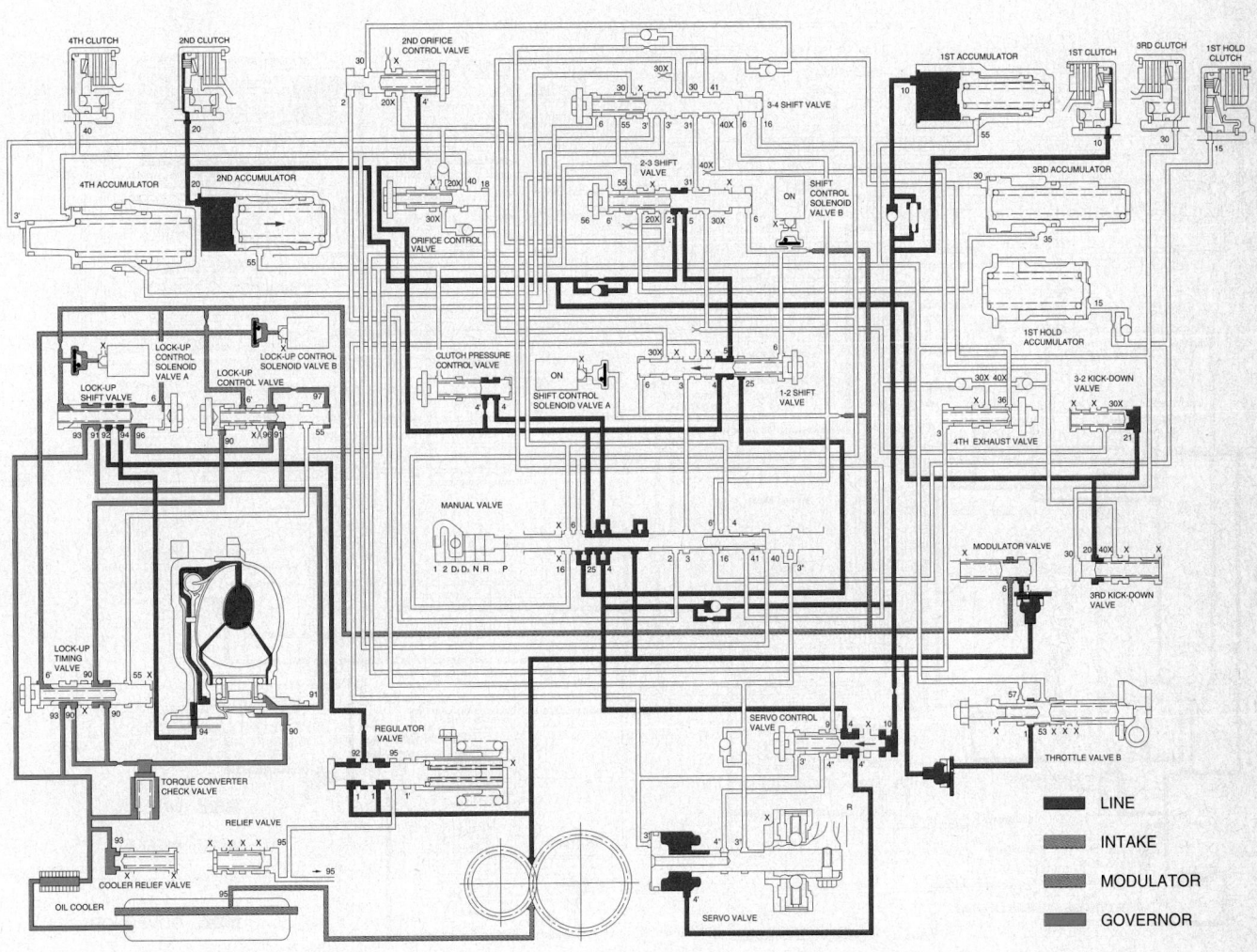

Courtesy of American Honda Motor Co., Inc.

OIL CIRCUIT DIAGRAMS
Honda MP1A (Cont.)

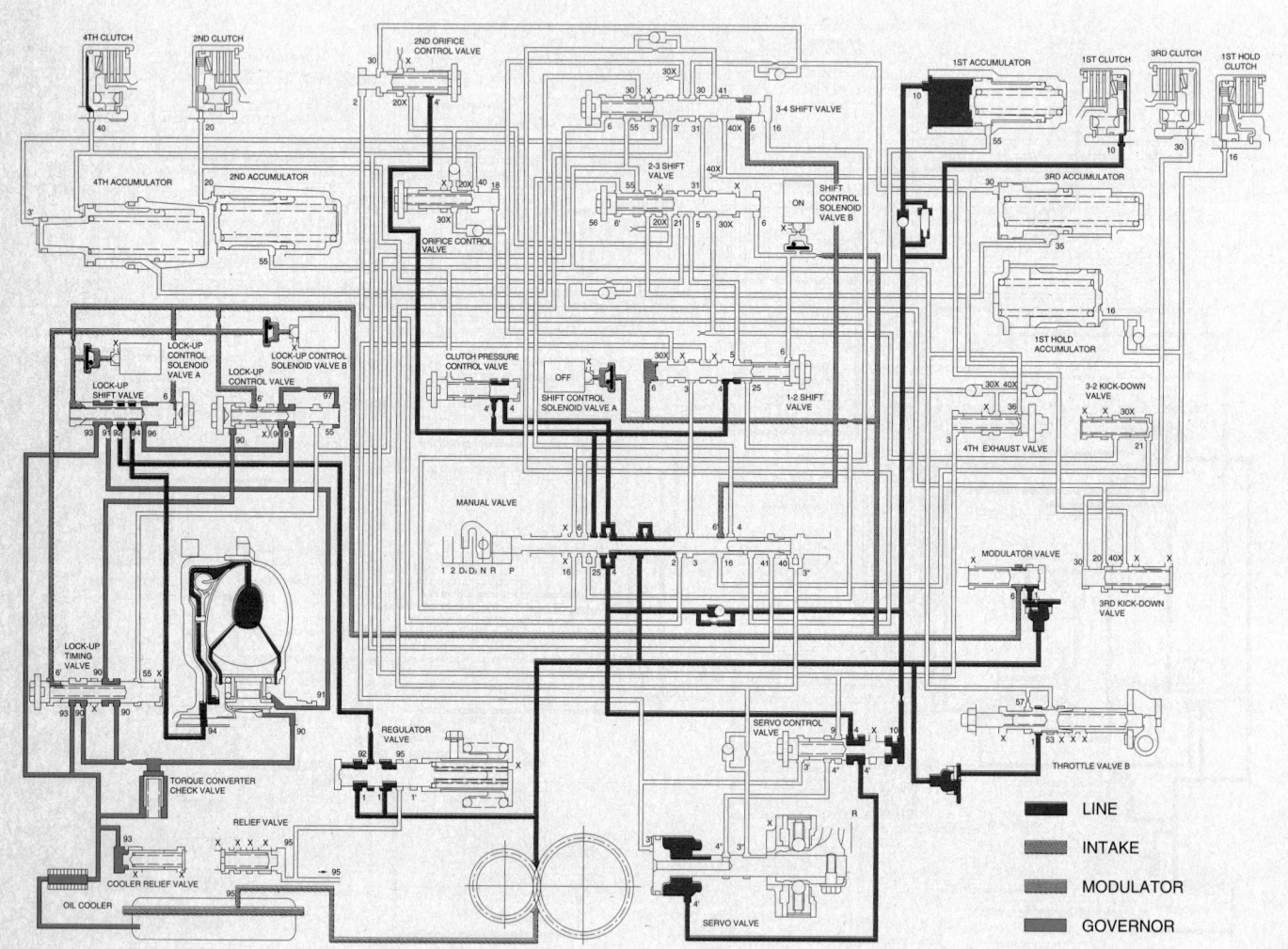

Fig. 4: *"D₃" Or "D₄" Position — 1st Gear*

Courtesy of American Honda Motor Co., Inc.

OIL CIRCUIT DIAGRAMS
Honda MP1A (Cont.)

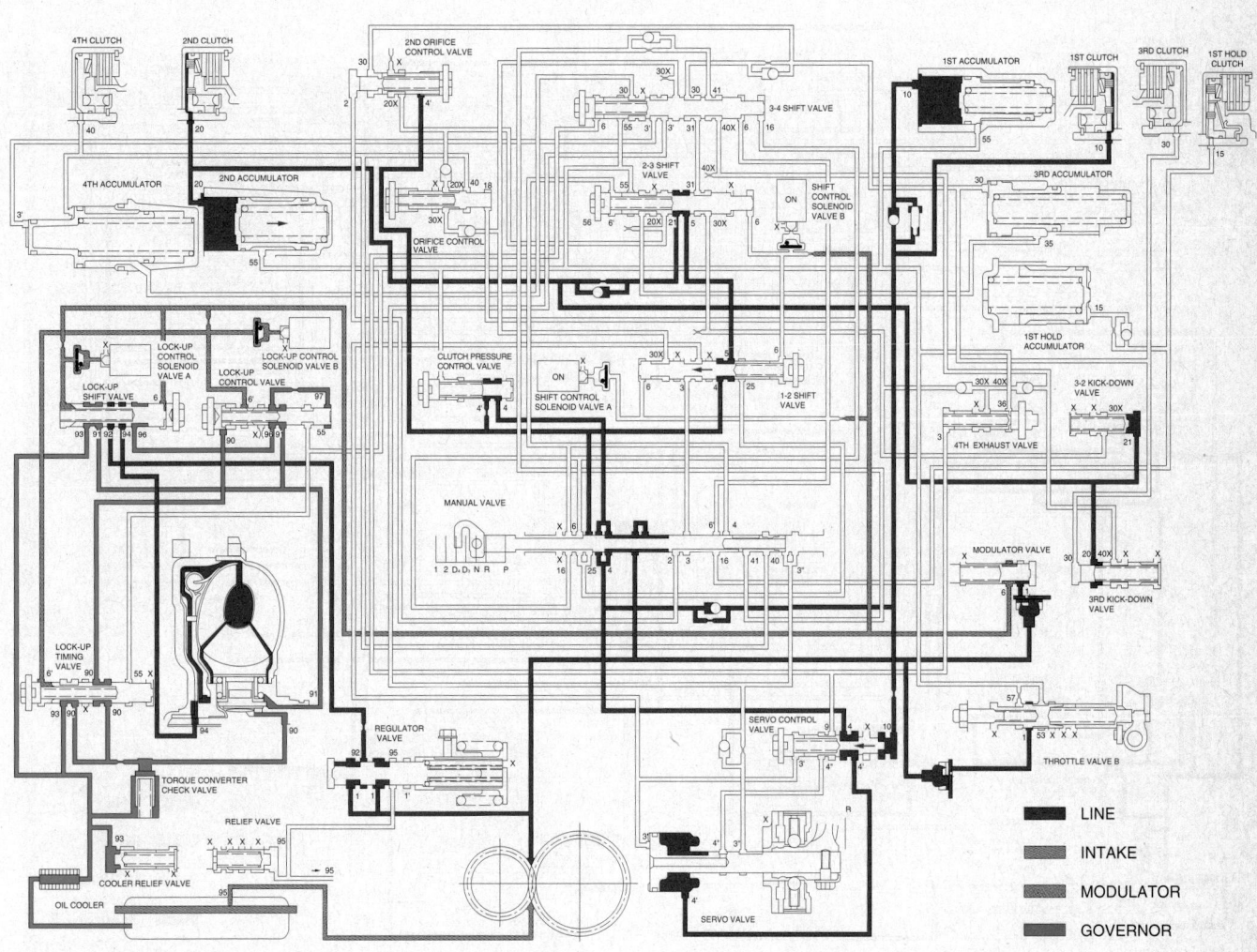

Fig. 5: "D₃" Or "D₄" Position — 2nd Gear

Courtesy of American Honda Motor Co., Inc.

OIL CIRCUIT DIAGRAMS
Honda MP1A (Cont.)

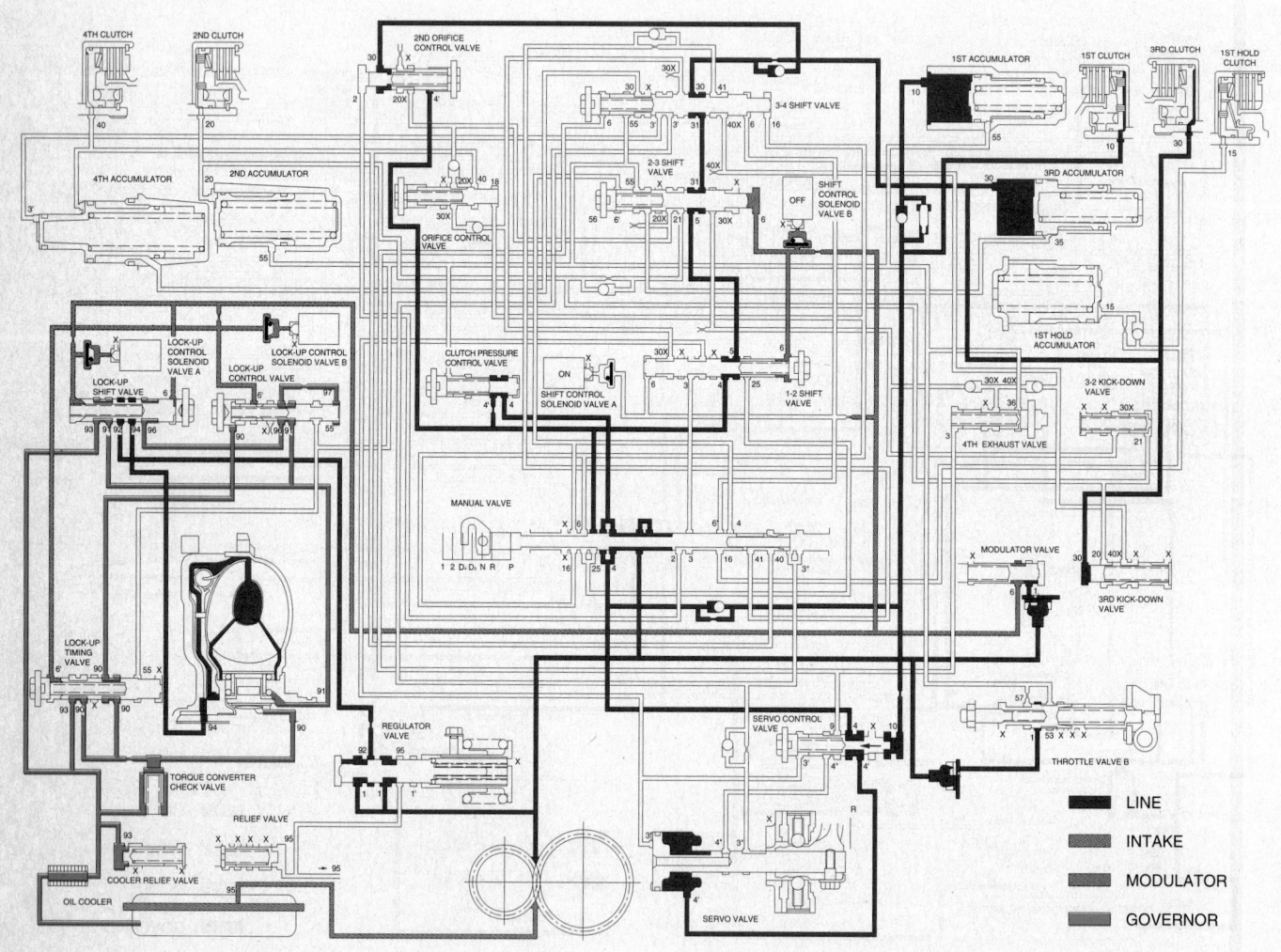

Fig. 6: "D₃" Or "D₄" Position — 3rd Gear

Courtesy of American Honda Motor Co., Inc.

OIL CIRCUIT DIAGRAMS
Honda MP1A (Cont.)

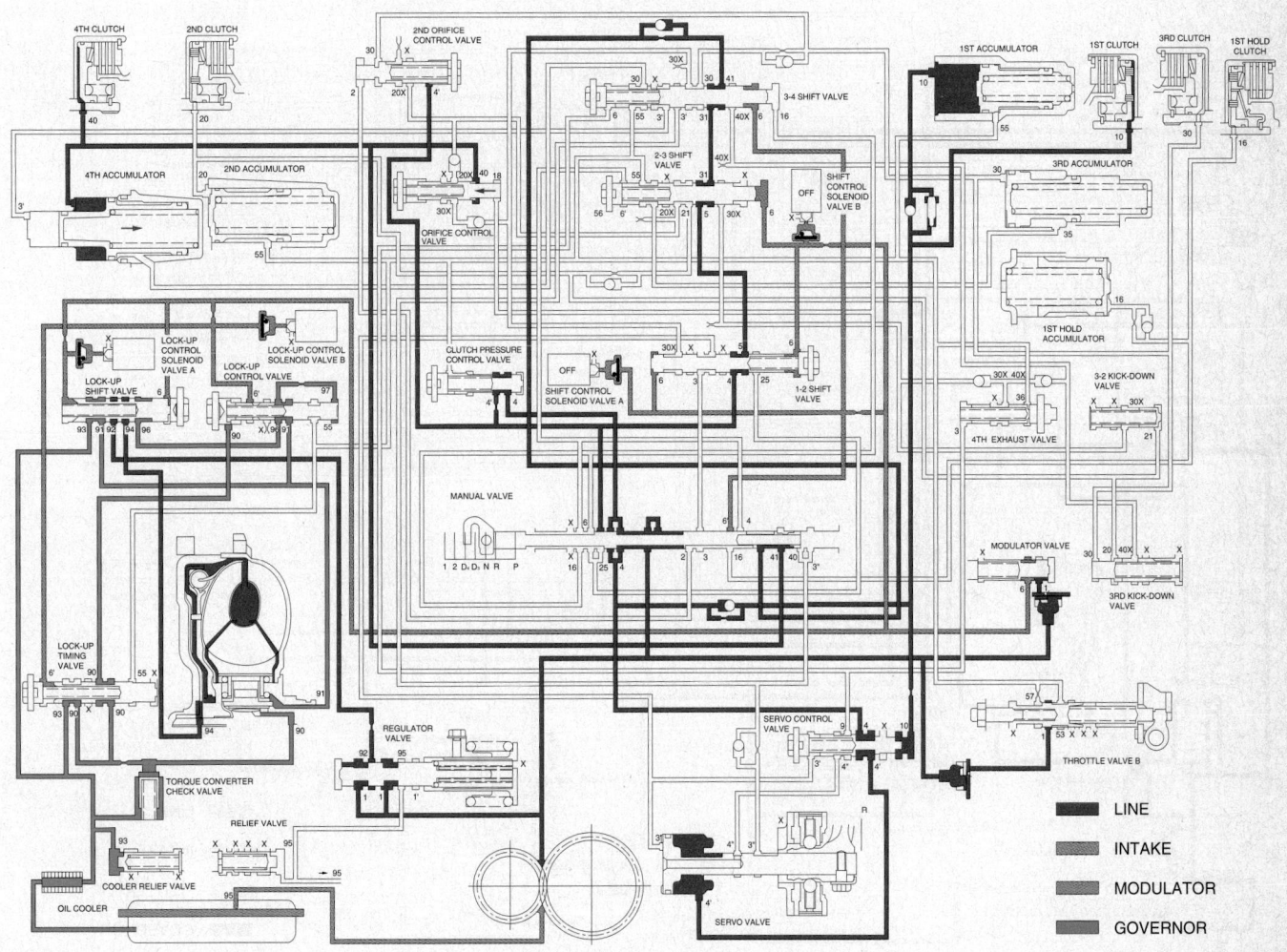

Fig. 7: "D₄" Position — 4th Gear

Courtesy of American Honda Motor Co., Inc.

OIL CIRCUIT DIAGRAMS
Honda MP1A (Cont.)

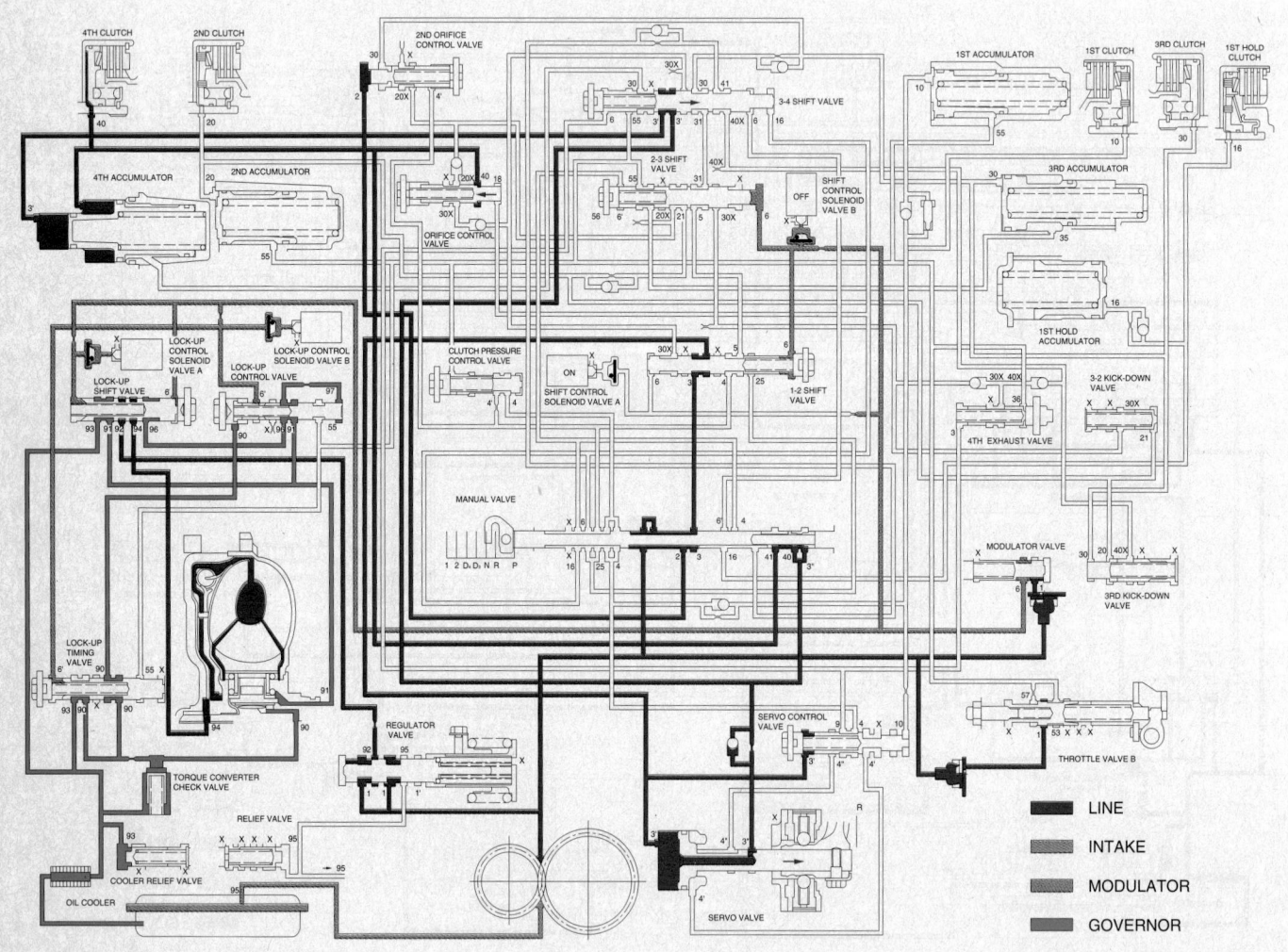

Fig. 8: "R" Position — Reverse

Courtesy of American Honda Motor Co., Inc.

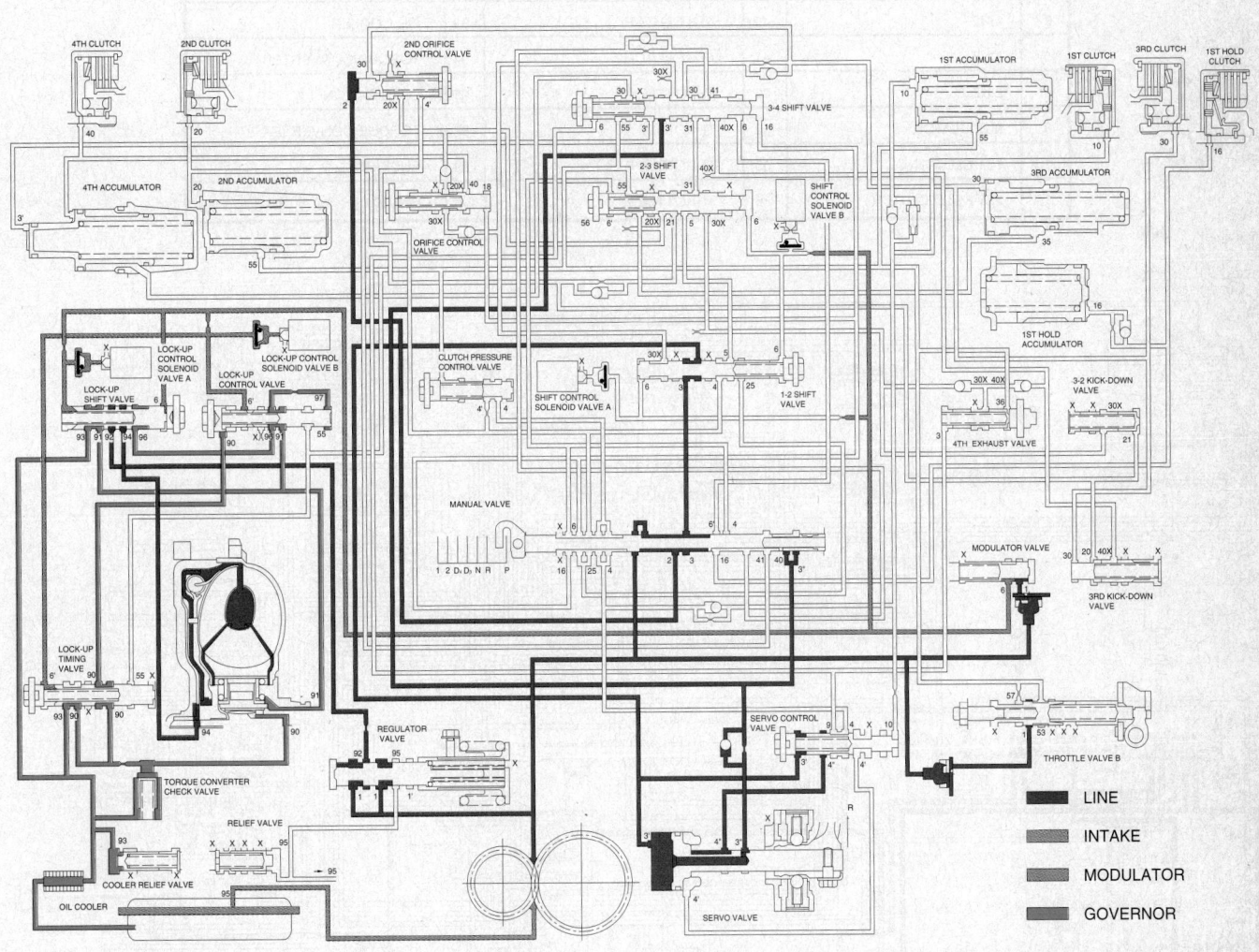

OIL CIRCUIT DIAGRAMS
Honda S24A

NO.	DESCRIPTION OF PRESSURE	NO.	DESCRIPTION OF PRESSURE	NO.	DESCRIPTION OF PRESSURE
1	LINE	16	1ST-HOLD CLUTCH	57	THROTTLE B
2	LINE	18	LINE	58	THROTTLE B
3	LINE	20	2ND CLUTCH	60	GOVERNOR
3'	LINE	21	2ND CLUTCH	61	GOVERNOR
3"	LINE	25	LINE	90	TORQUE CONVERTER
4	LINE	30	3RD CLUTCH	91	TORQUE CONVERTER
4'	LINE	31	3RD CLUTCH	92	TORQUE CONVERTER
5	LINE	40	4TH CLUTCH	93	OIL COOLER
5'	LINE	41	4TH CLUTCH	94	TORQUE CONVERTER
5"	LINE	50	THROTTLE A	95	LUBRICATION
6'	MODULATOR	52	THROTTLE A	97	TORQUE CONVERTER
10	1ST CLUTCH	55	THROTTLE B	99	SUCTION
15	1ST-HOLD CLUTCH	56	THROTTLE B	X	BLEED

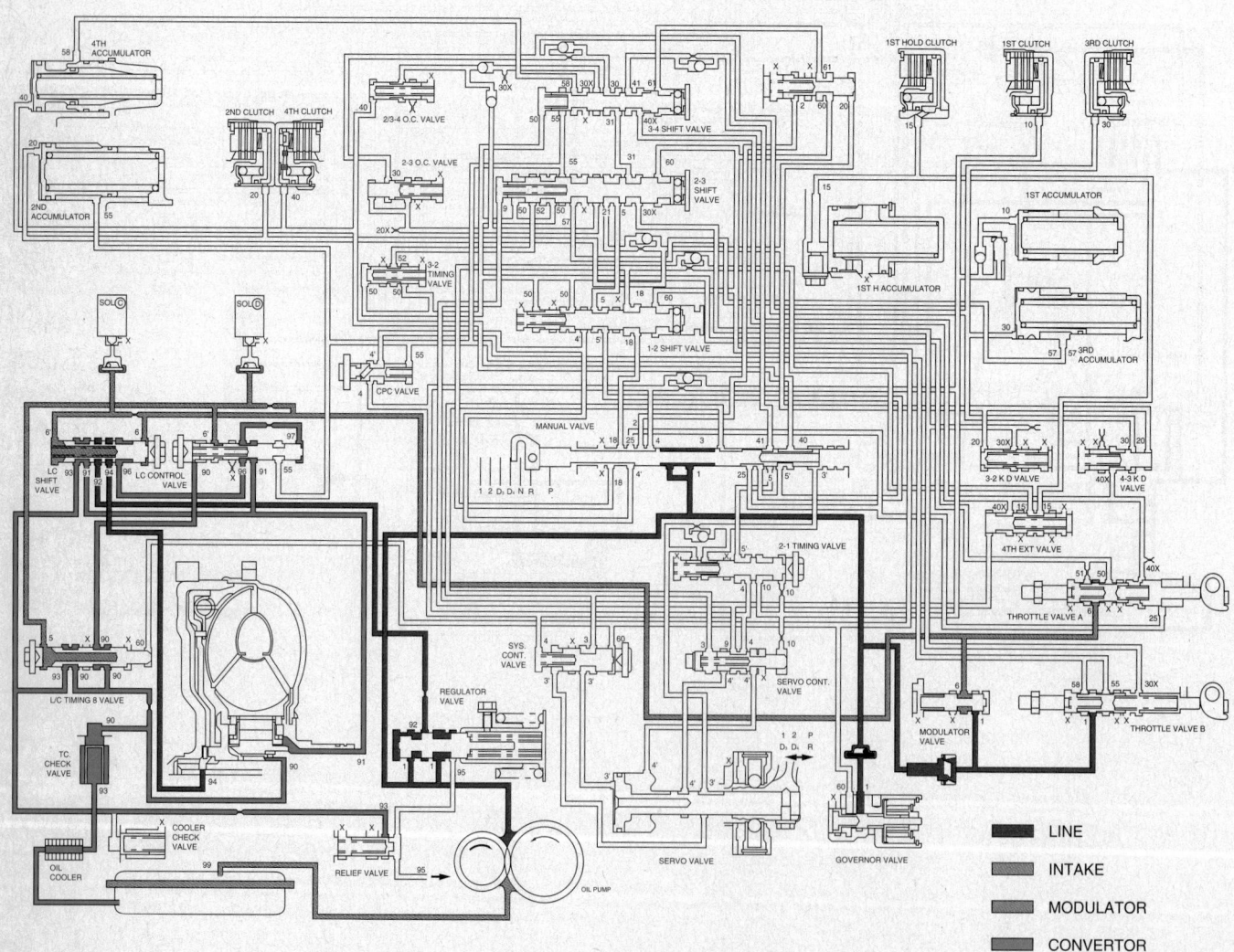

LINE

INTAKE

MODULATOR

CONVERTOR

Fig. 1: "N" Position — Neutral

Courtesy of American Honda Motor Co., Inc.

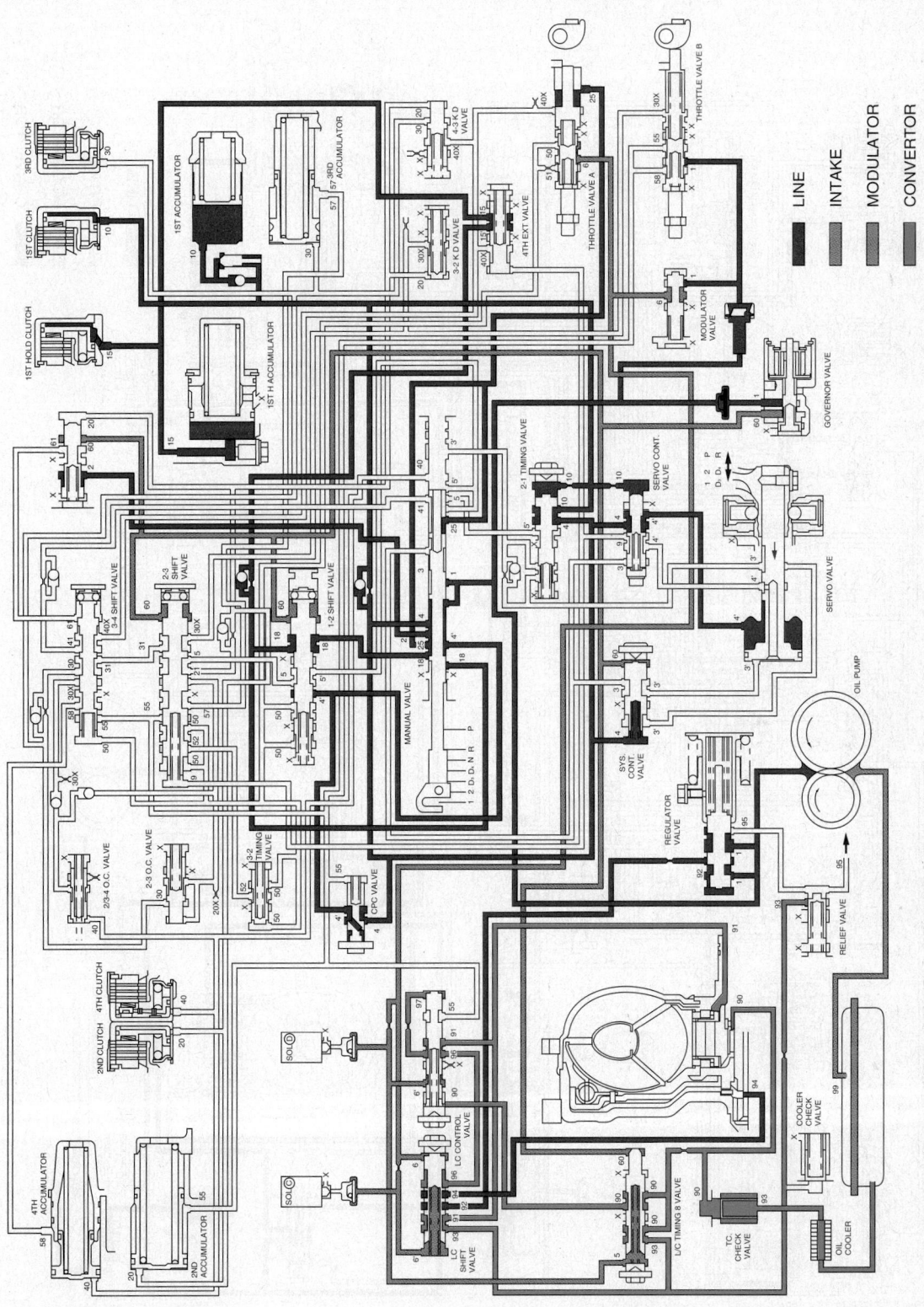

OIL CIRCUIT DIAGRAMS
Honda S24A (Cont.)

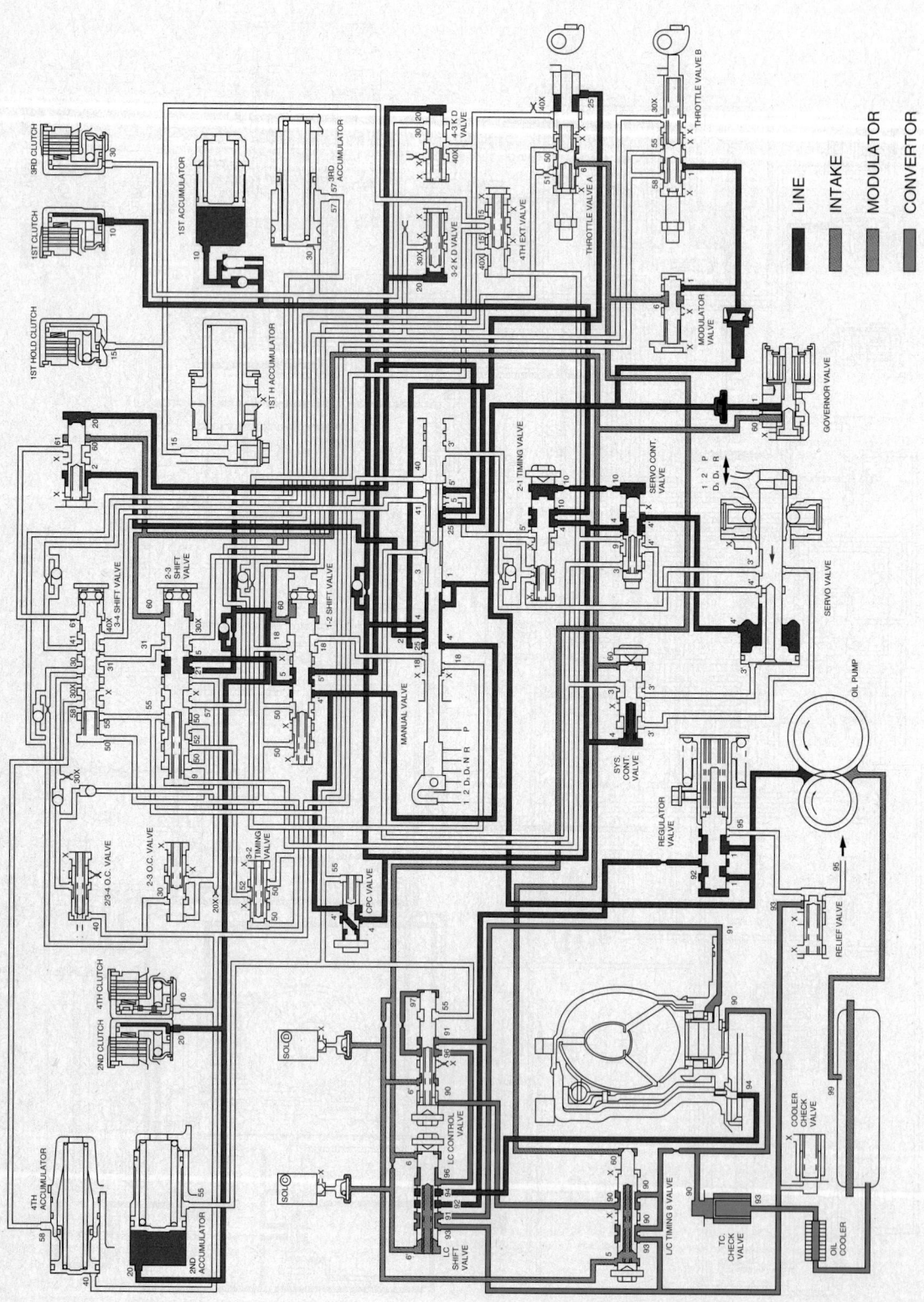

Fig. 3: "2" Position — 1st Gear

Courtesy of American Honda Motor Co., Inc.

OIL CIRCUIT DIAGRAMS
Honda S24A (Cont.)

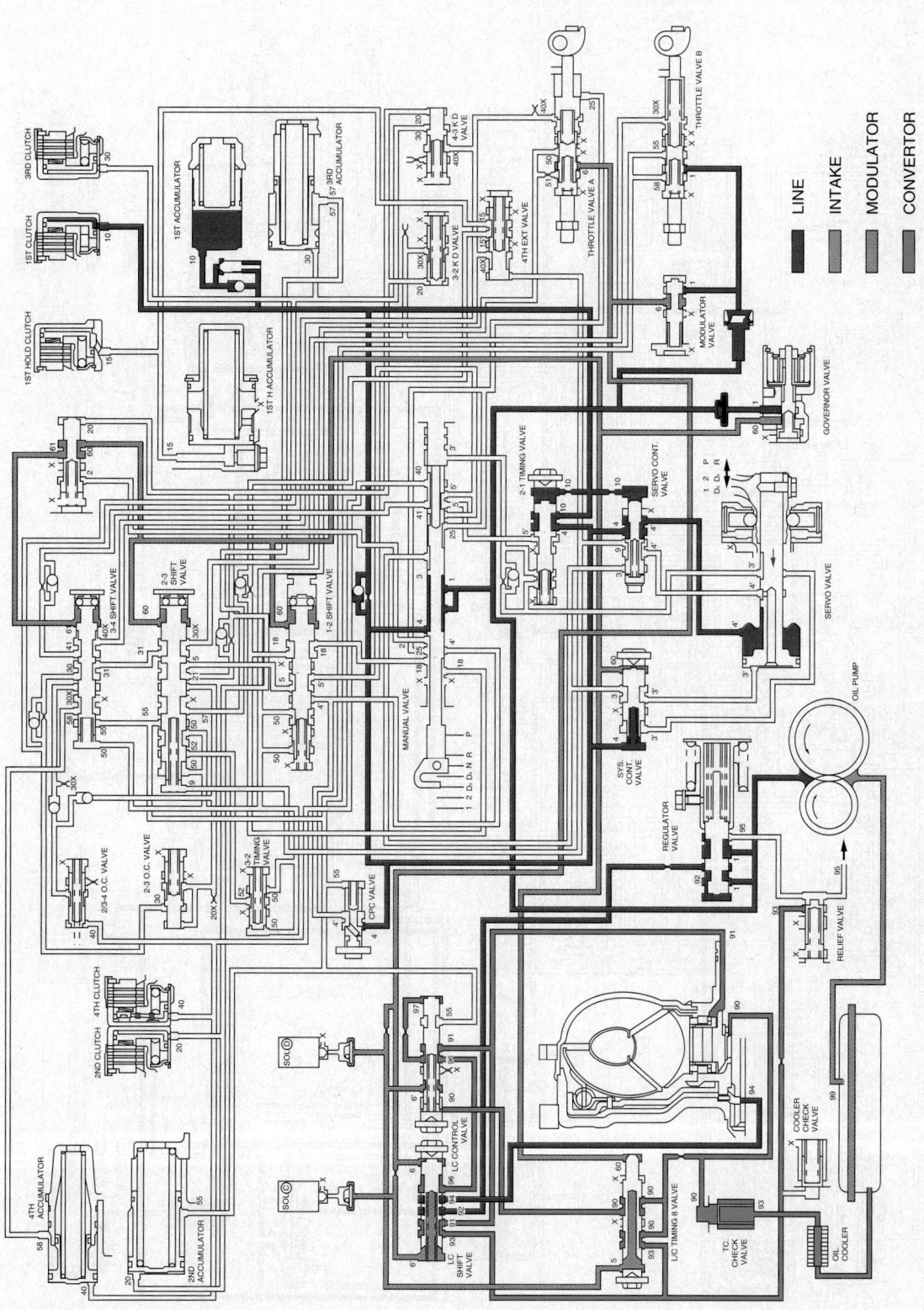

Fig. 4: "D₄" Or "D₃" Position — 1st Gear

Courtesy of American Honda Motor Co., Inc.

OIL CIRCUIT DIAGRAMS
Honda S24A (Cont.)

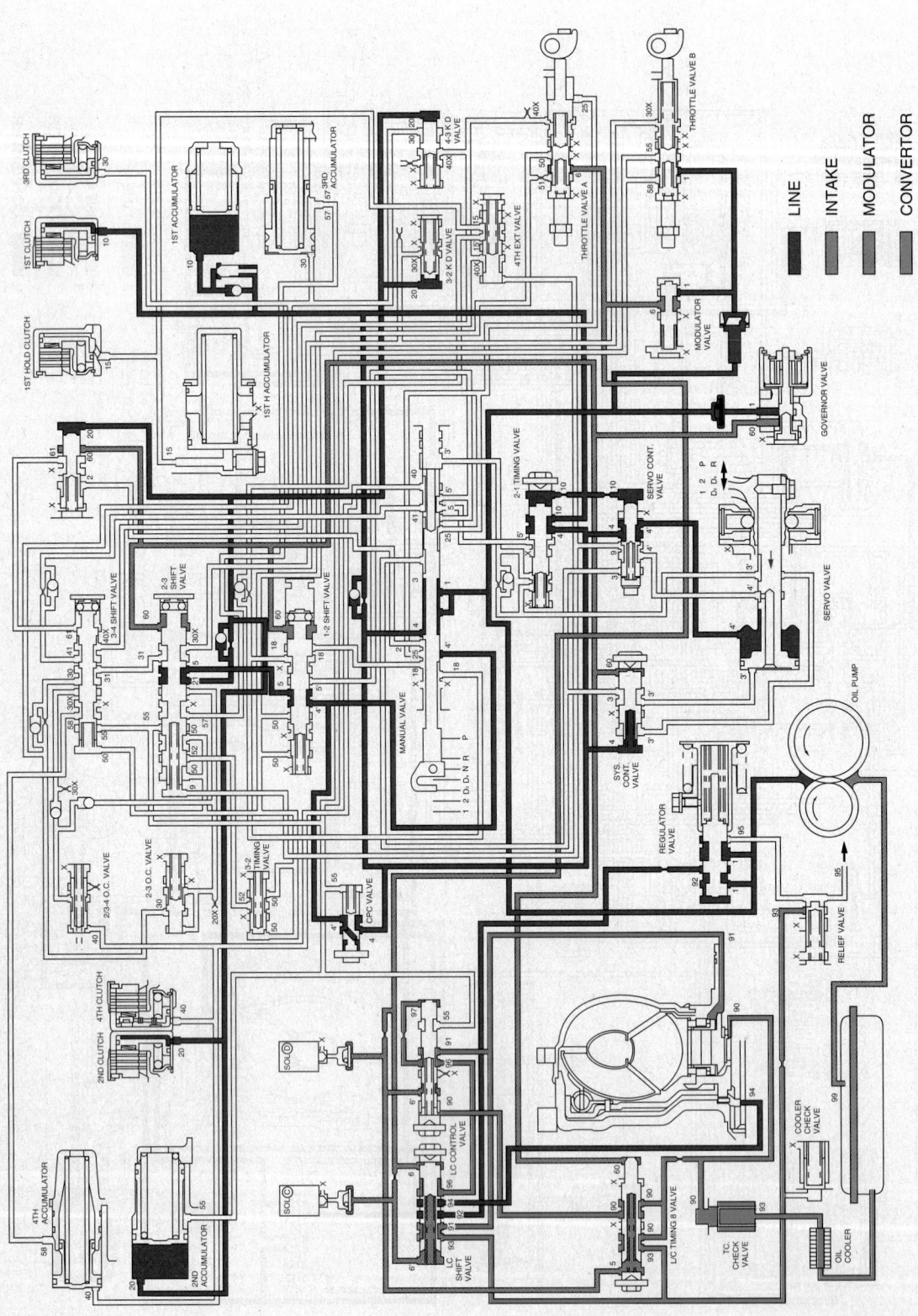

Fig. 5: "D₄" Or "D₃" Position — 2nd Gear

Courtesy of American Honda Motor Co., Inc.

OIL CIRCUIT DIAGRAMS
Honda S24A (Cont.)

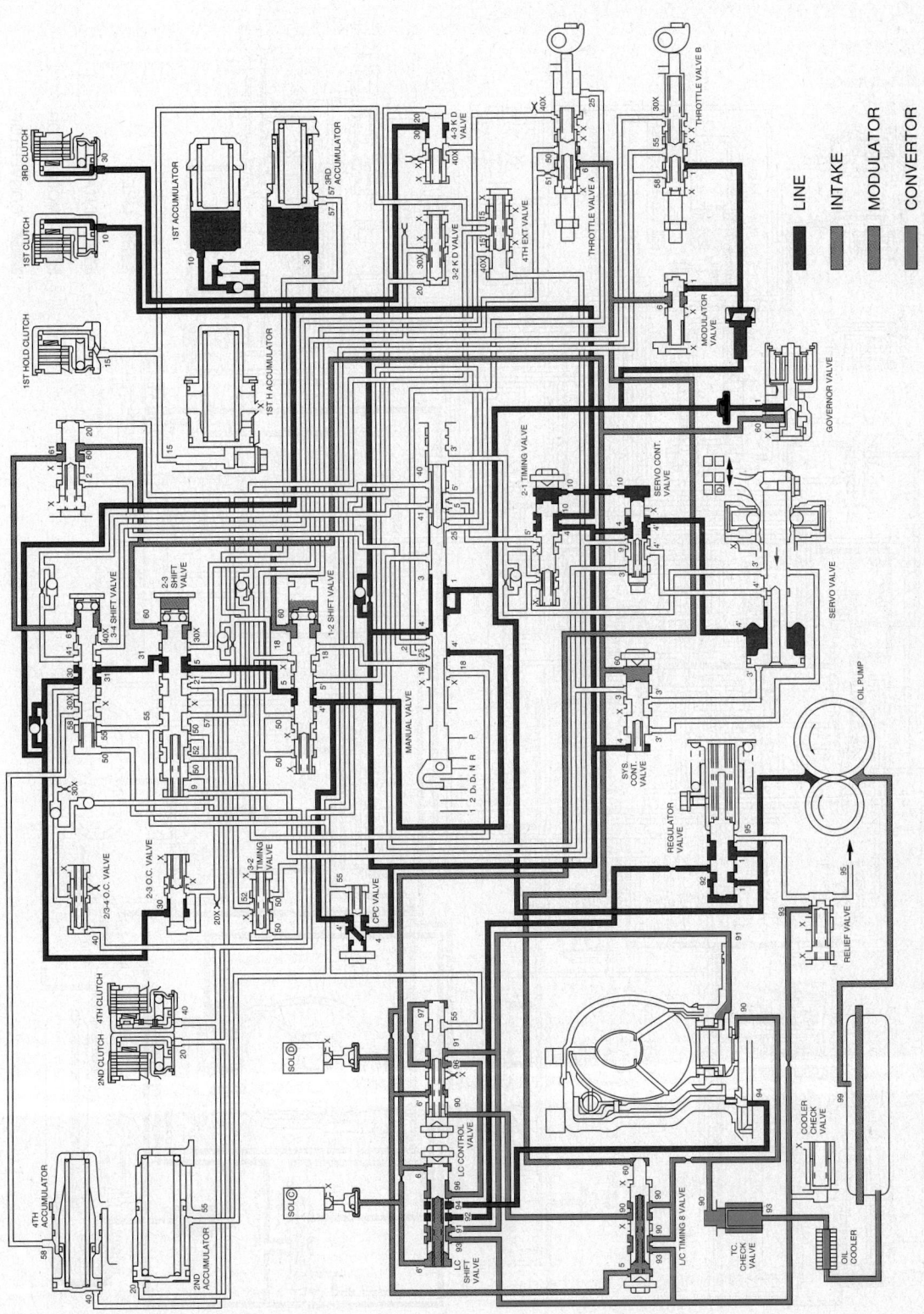

Fig. 6: *"D₄" Or "D₃" Position — 3rd Gear*

Courtesy of American Honda Motor Co., Inc.

OIL CIRCUIT DIAGRAMS
Honda S24A (Cont.)

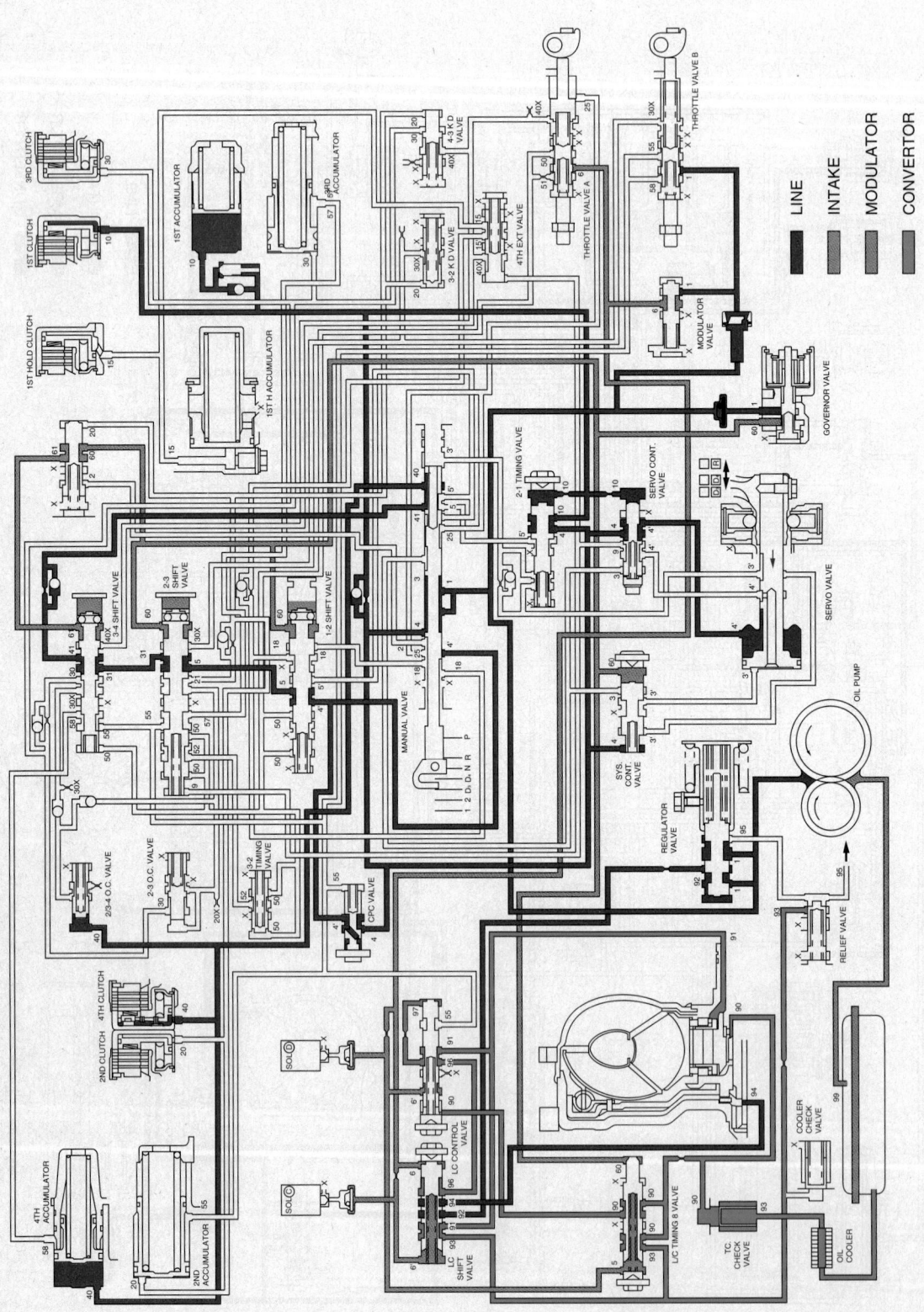

Fig. 7: "D₄" Or "D₃" Position — 4th Gear

Courtesy of American Honda Motor Co., Inc.

OIL CIRCUIT DIAGRAMS
Honda S24A (Cont.)

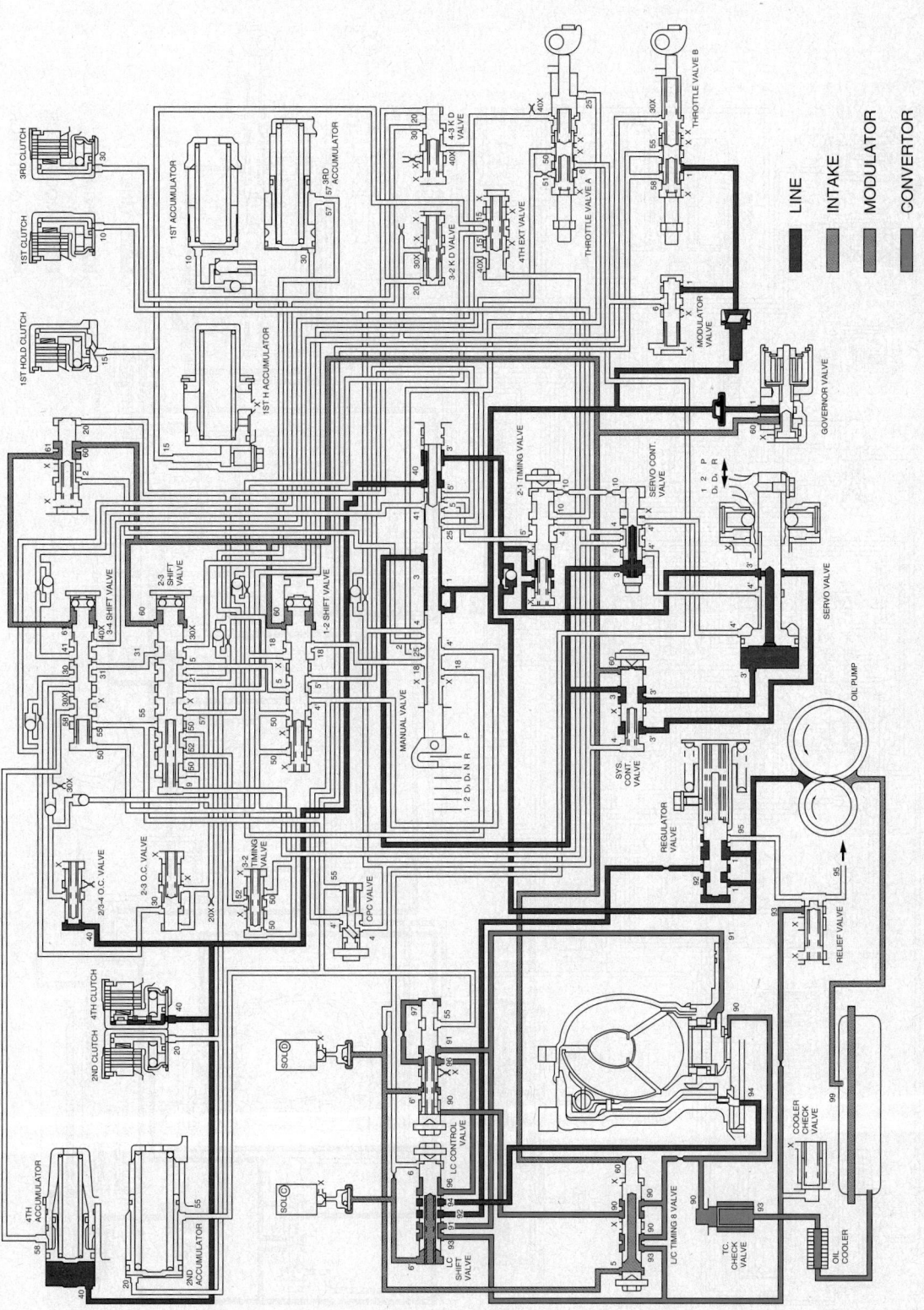

Fig. 8: "R" Position — Reverse

Courtesy of American Honda Motor Co., Inc.

OIL CIRCUIT DIAGRAMS
Honda S24A (Cont.)

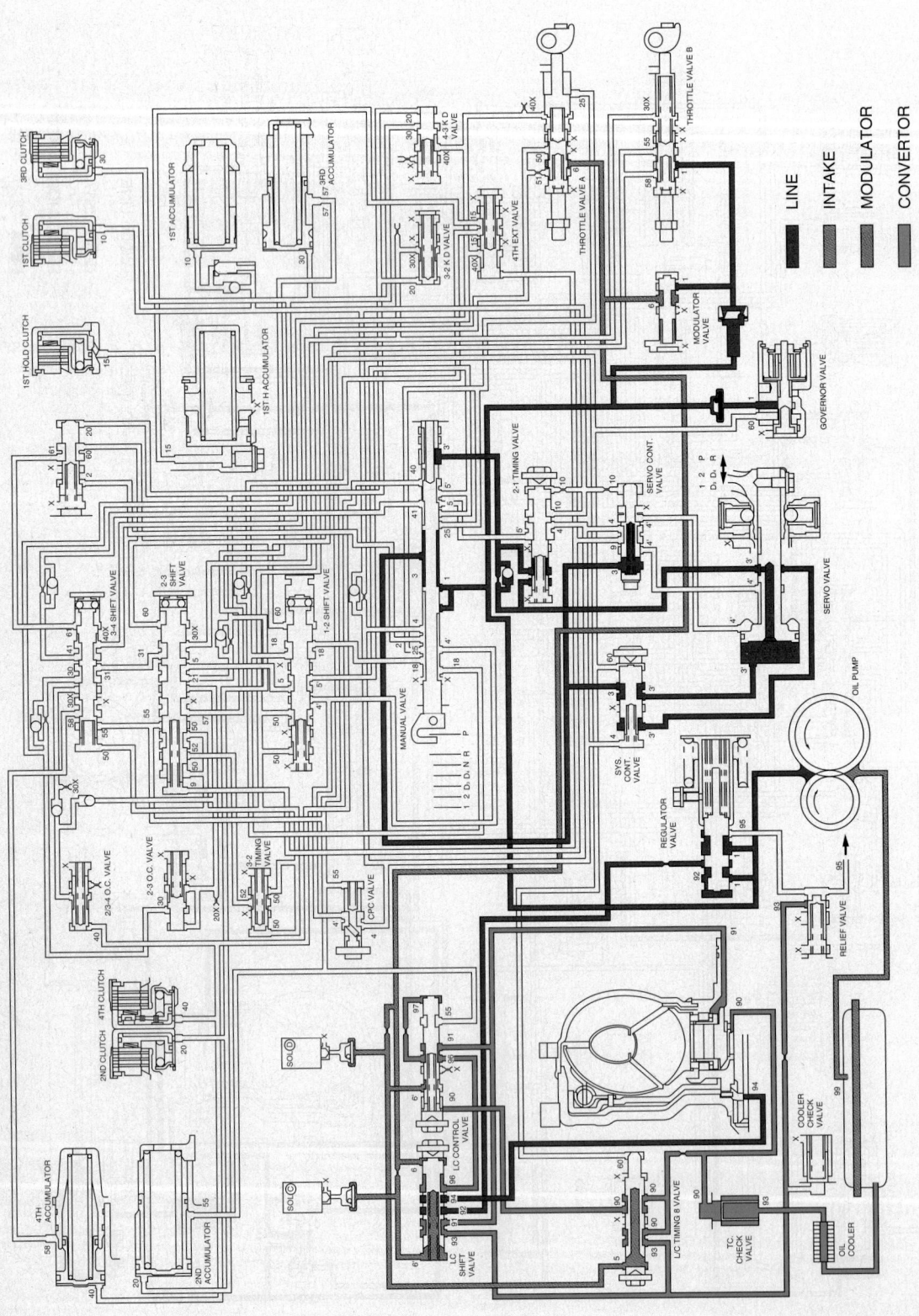

Fig. 9: "P" Position — Park

Courtesy of American Honda Motor Co., Inc.

OIL CIRCUIT DIAGRAMS
Hydra-Matic 3L30

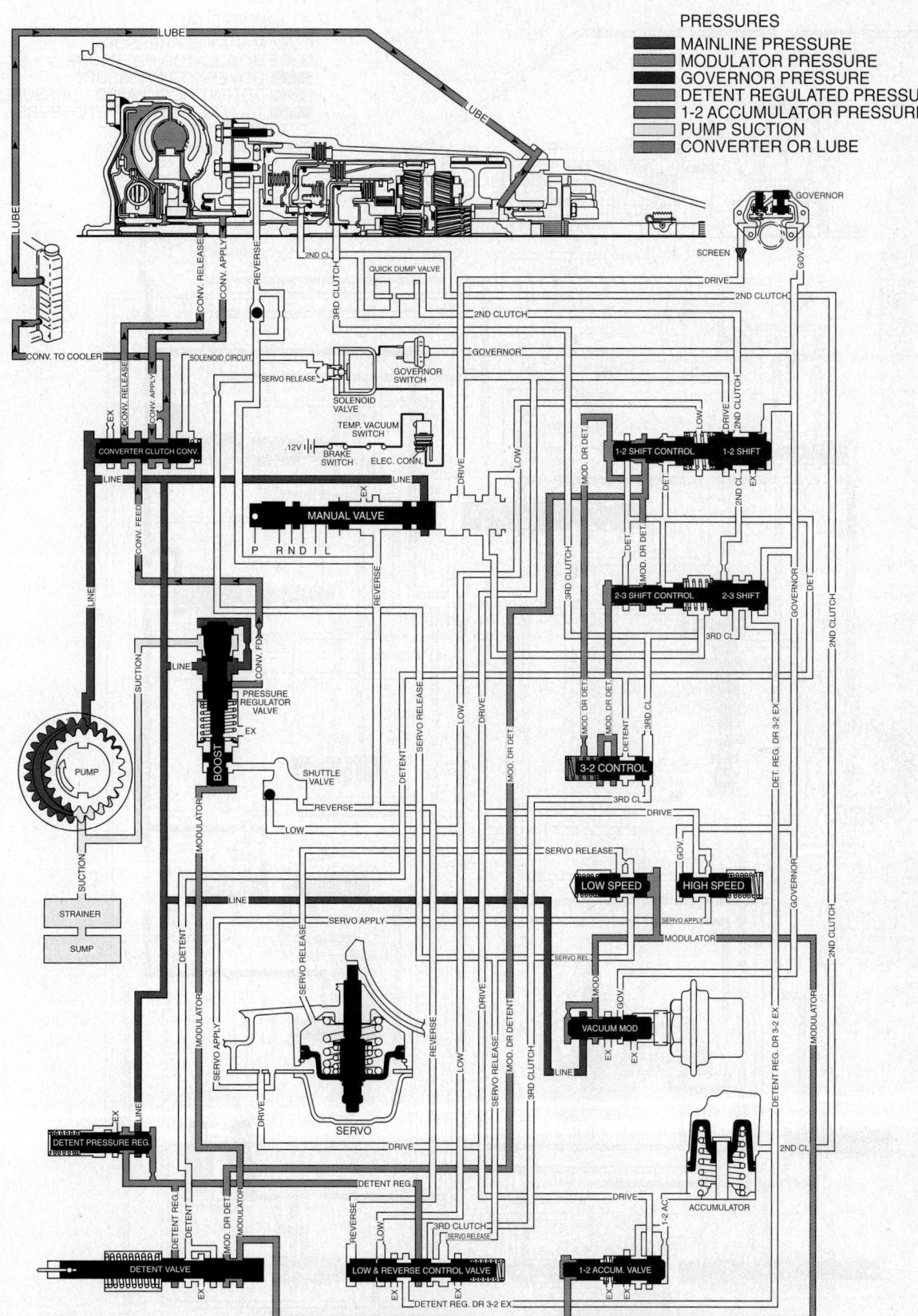

PRESSURES
- MAINLINE PRESSURE
- MODULATOR PRESSURE
- GOVERNOR PRESSURE
- DETENT REGULATED PRESSURE
- 1-2 ACCUMULATOR PRESSURE
- PUMP SUCTION
- CONVERTER OR LUBE

Fig. 1: "P" & "N" Position — Park & Neutral At Idle

Courtesy of General Motors Corp.

OIL CIRCUIT DIAGRAMS
Hydra-Matic 3L30 (Cont.)

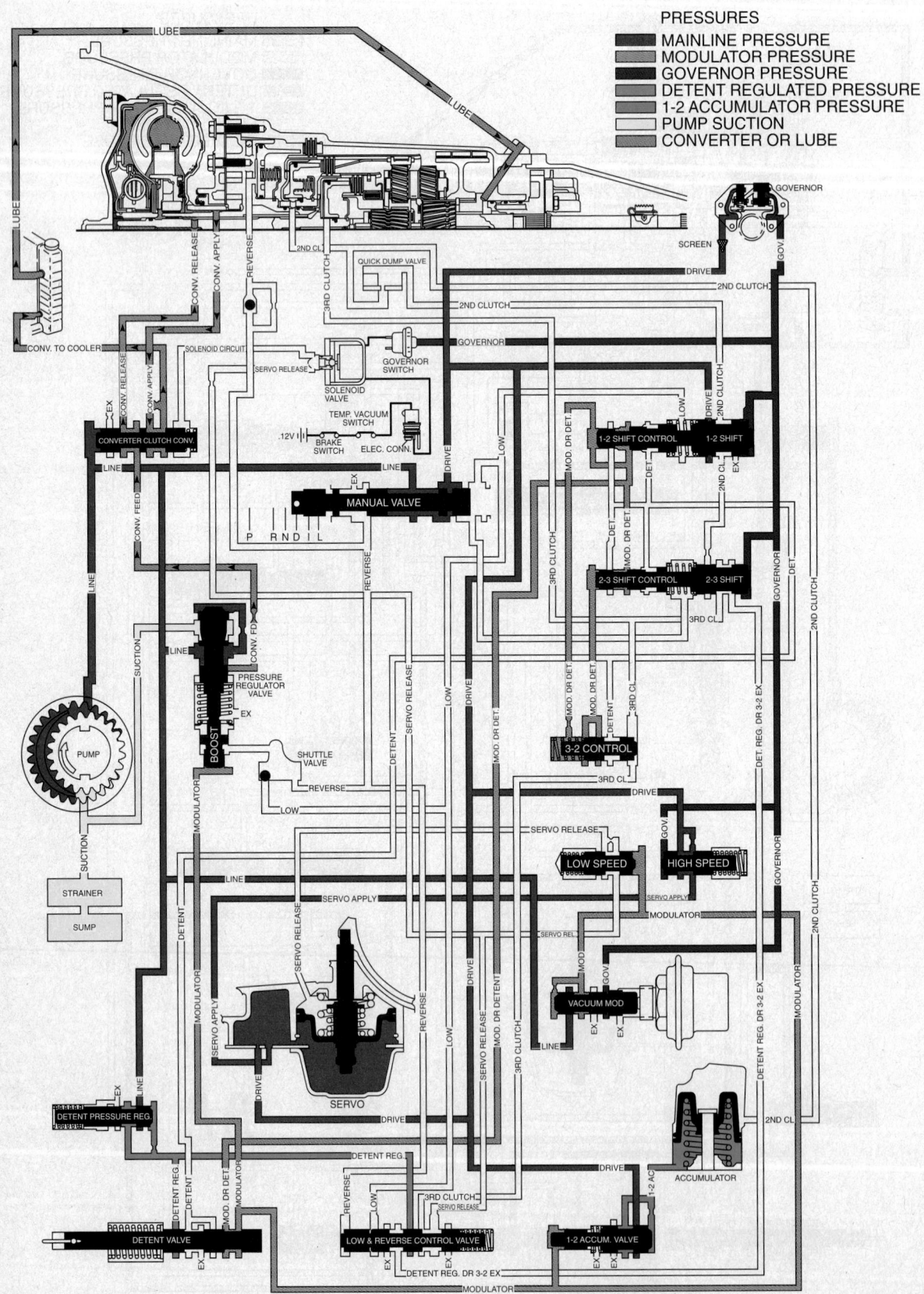

PRESSURES
- MAINLINE PRESSURE
- MODULATOR PRESSURE
- GOVERNOR PRESSURE
- DETENT REGULATED PRESSURE
- 1-2 ACCUMULATOR PRESSURE
- PUMP SUCTION
- CONVERTER OR LUBE

Fig. 2: "D" Position — 1st Gear

Courtesy of General Motors Corp.

OIL CIRCUIT DIAGRAMS
Hydra-Matic 3L30 (Cont.)

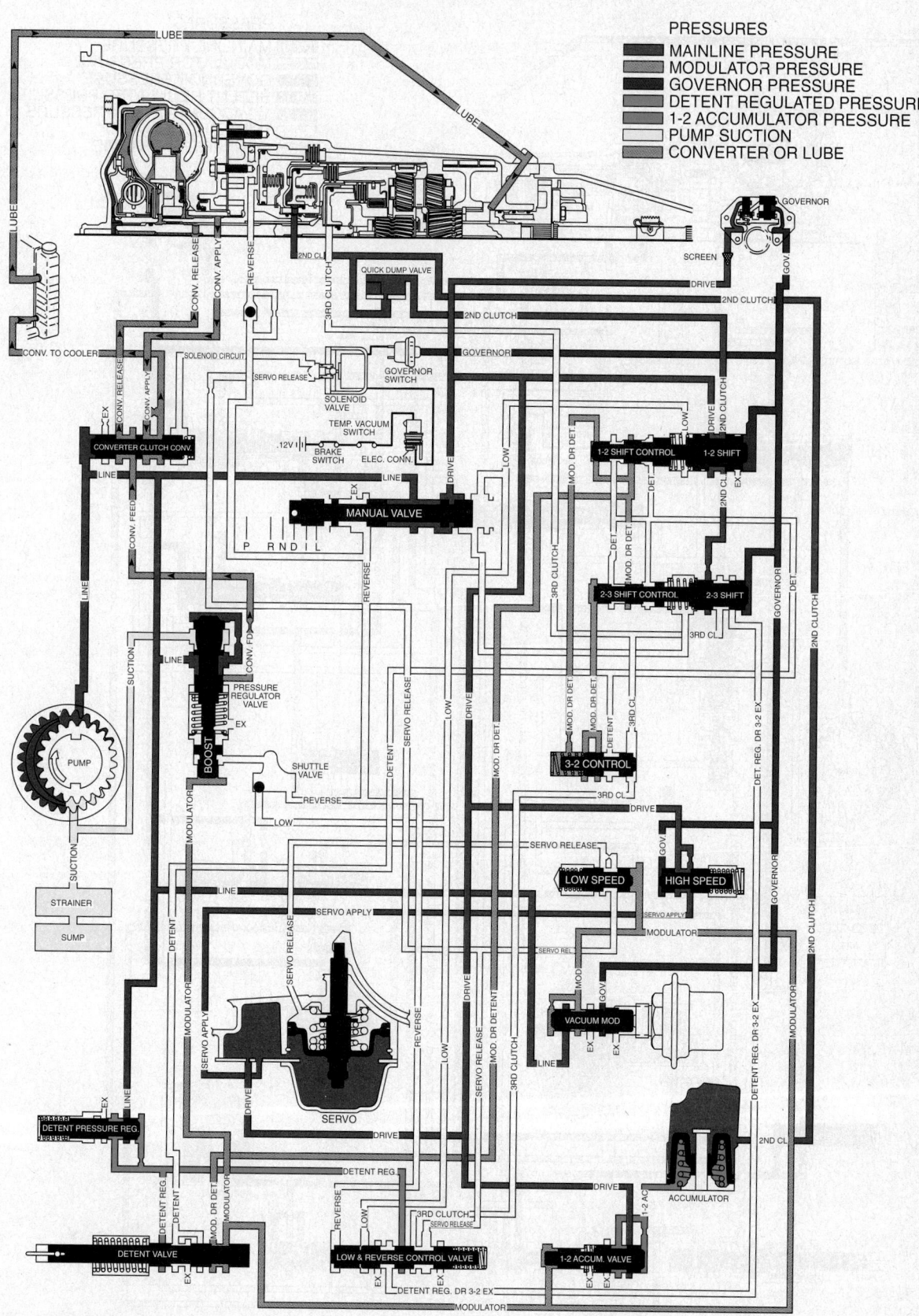

PRESSURES
- MAINLINE PRESSURE
- MODULATOR PRESSURE
- GOVERNOR PRESSURE
- DETENT REGULATED PRESSURE
- 1-2 ACCUMULATOR PRESSURE
- PUMP SUCTION
- CONVERTER OR LUBE

Fig. 3: "D" Position — 2nd Gear

Courtesy of General Motors Corp.

OIL CIRCUIT DIAGRAMS
Hydra-Matic 3L30 (Cont.)

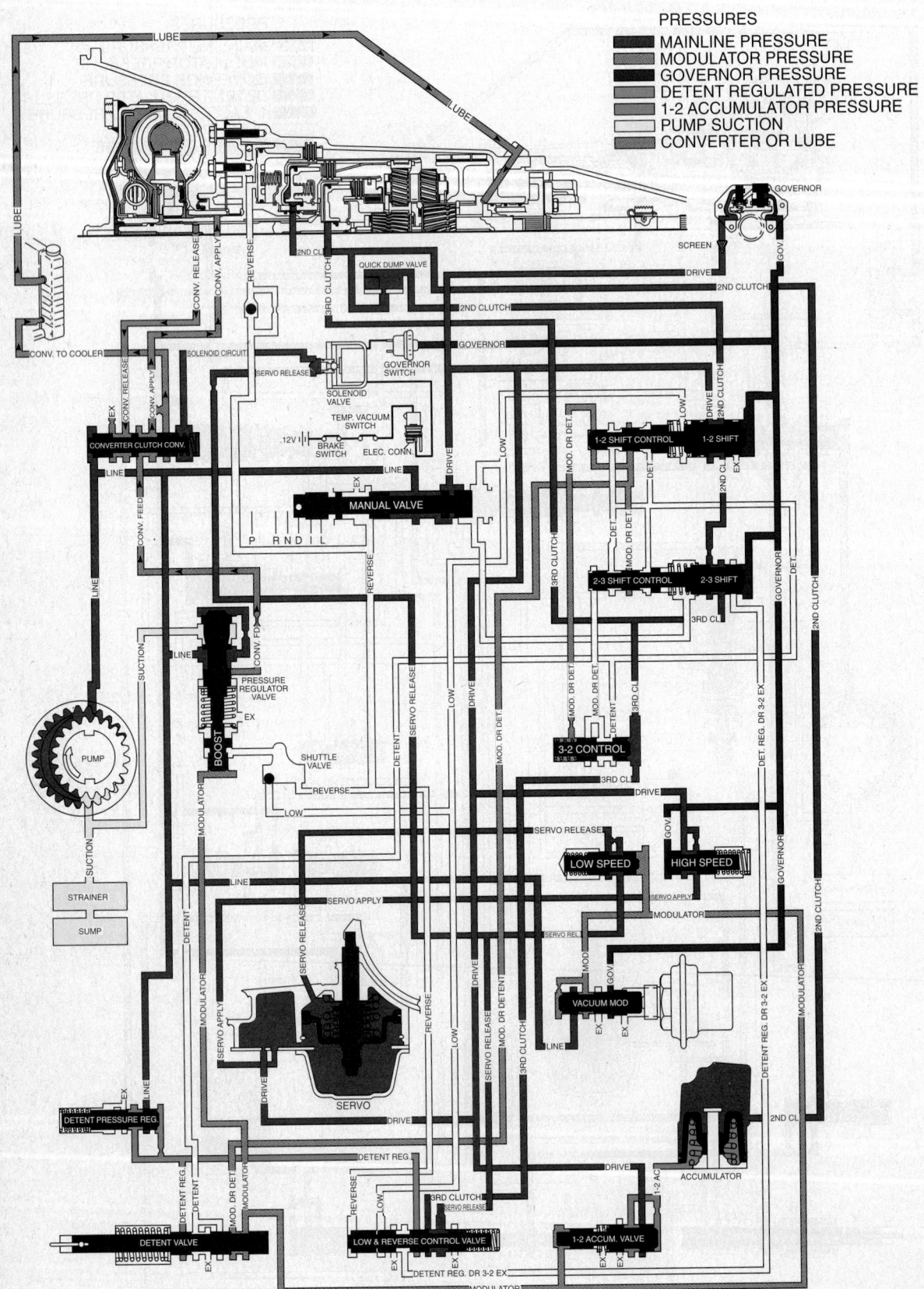

PRESSURES
- MAINLINE PRESSURE
- MODULATOR PRESSURE
- GOVERNOR PRESSURE
- DETENT REGULATED PRESSURE
- 1-2 ACCUMULATOR PRESSURE
- PUMP SUCTION
- CONVERTER OR LUBE

Fig. 4: "D" Position — 3rd Gear

Courtesy of General Motors Corp.

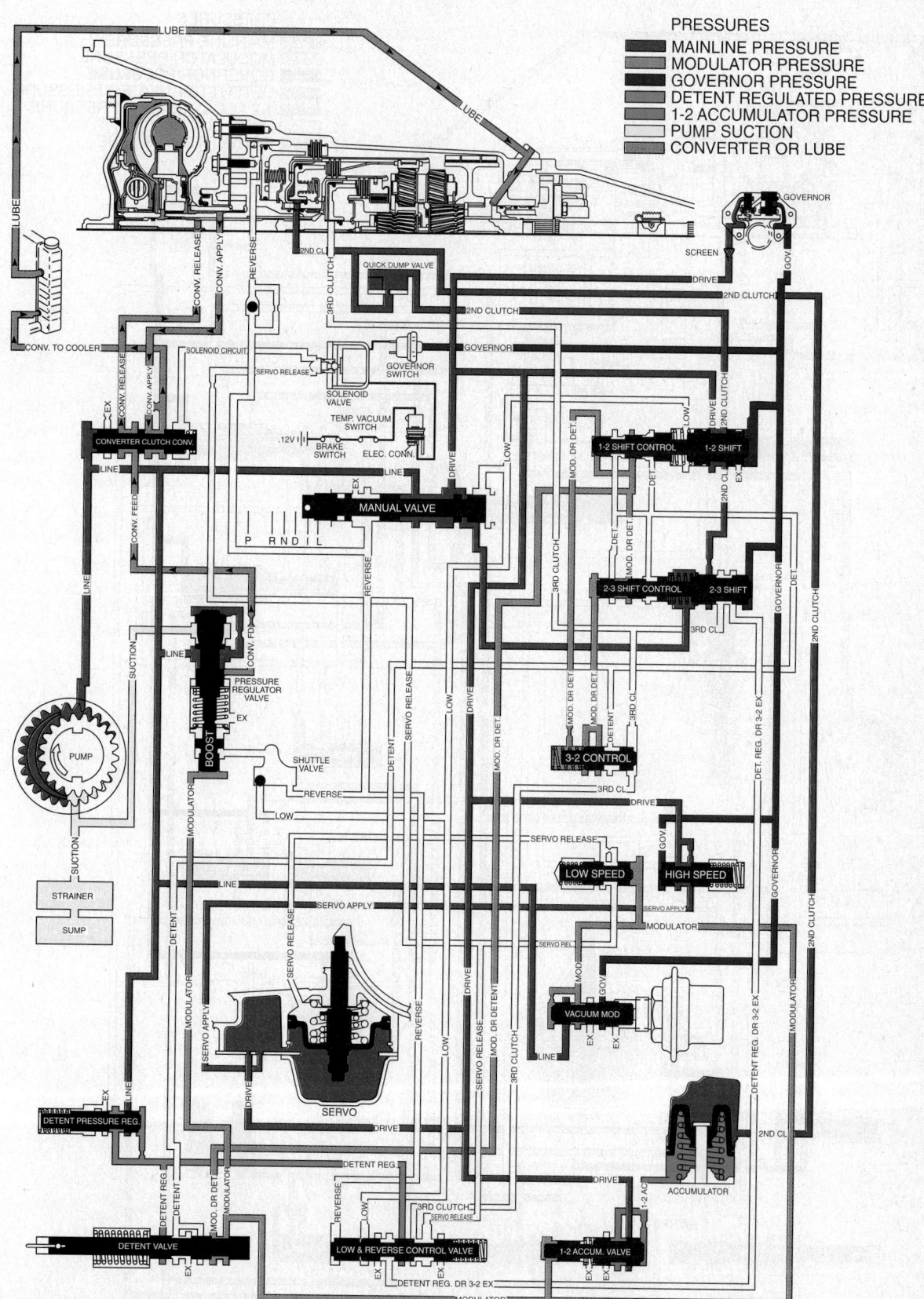

Fig. 5: "2" Position — 2nd Gear (Manual Select)

Courtesy of General Motors Corp.

OIL CIRCUIT DIAGRAMS
Hydra-Matic 3L30 (Cont.)

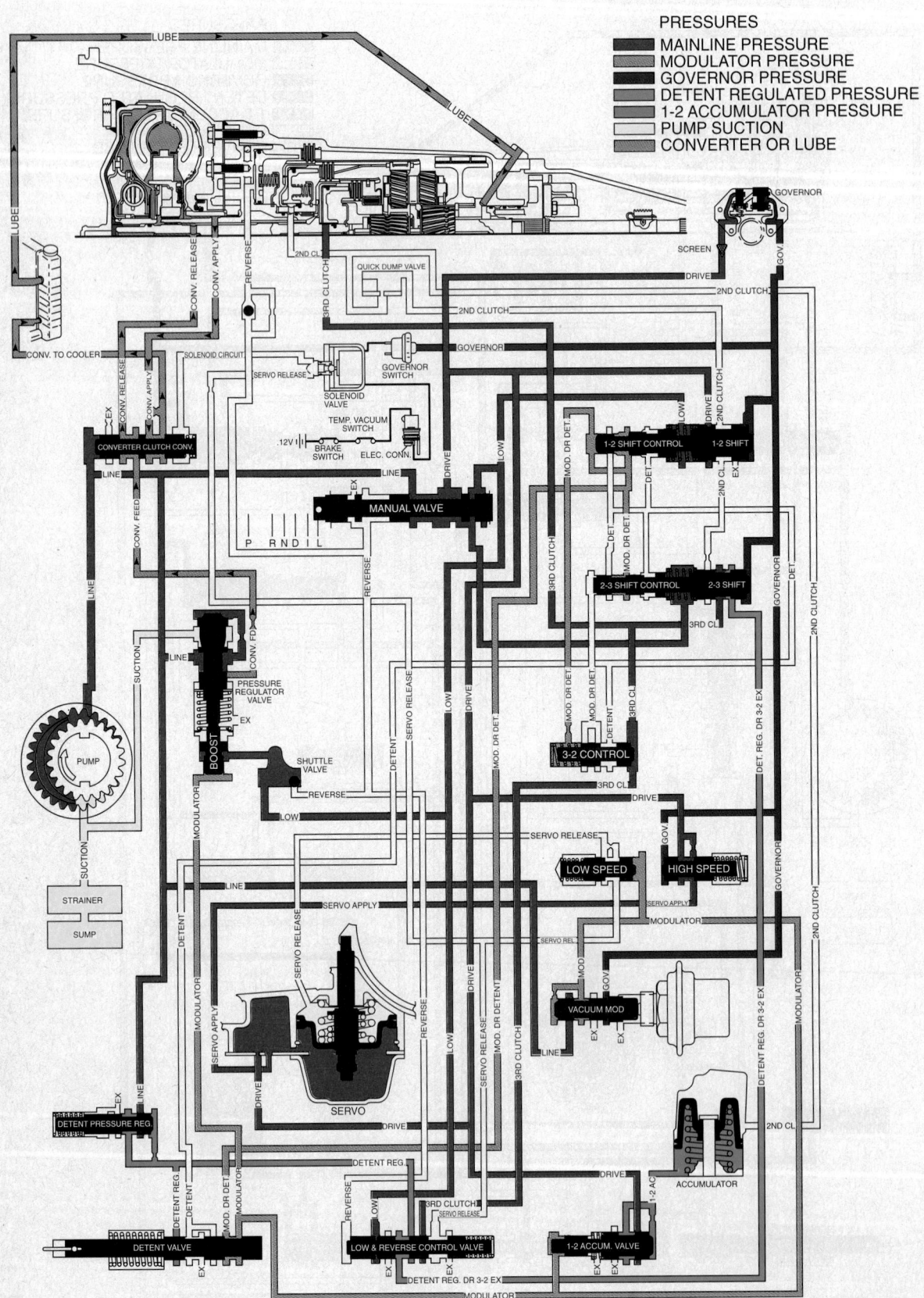

PRESSURES
- MAINLINE PRESSURE
- MODULATOR PRESSURE
- GOVERNOR PRESSURE
- DETENT REGULATED PRESSURE
- 1-2 ACCUMULATOR PRESSURE
- PUMP SUCTION
- CONVERTER OR LUBE

Fig. 6: "1" Position — 1st Gear (Manual Select)

Courtesy of General Motors Corp.

OIL CIRCUIT DIAGRAMS
Hydra-Matic 3L30 (Cont.)

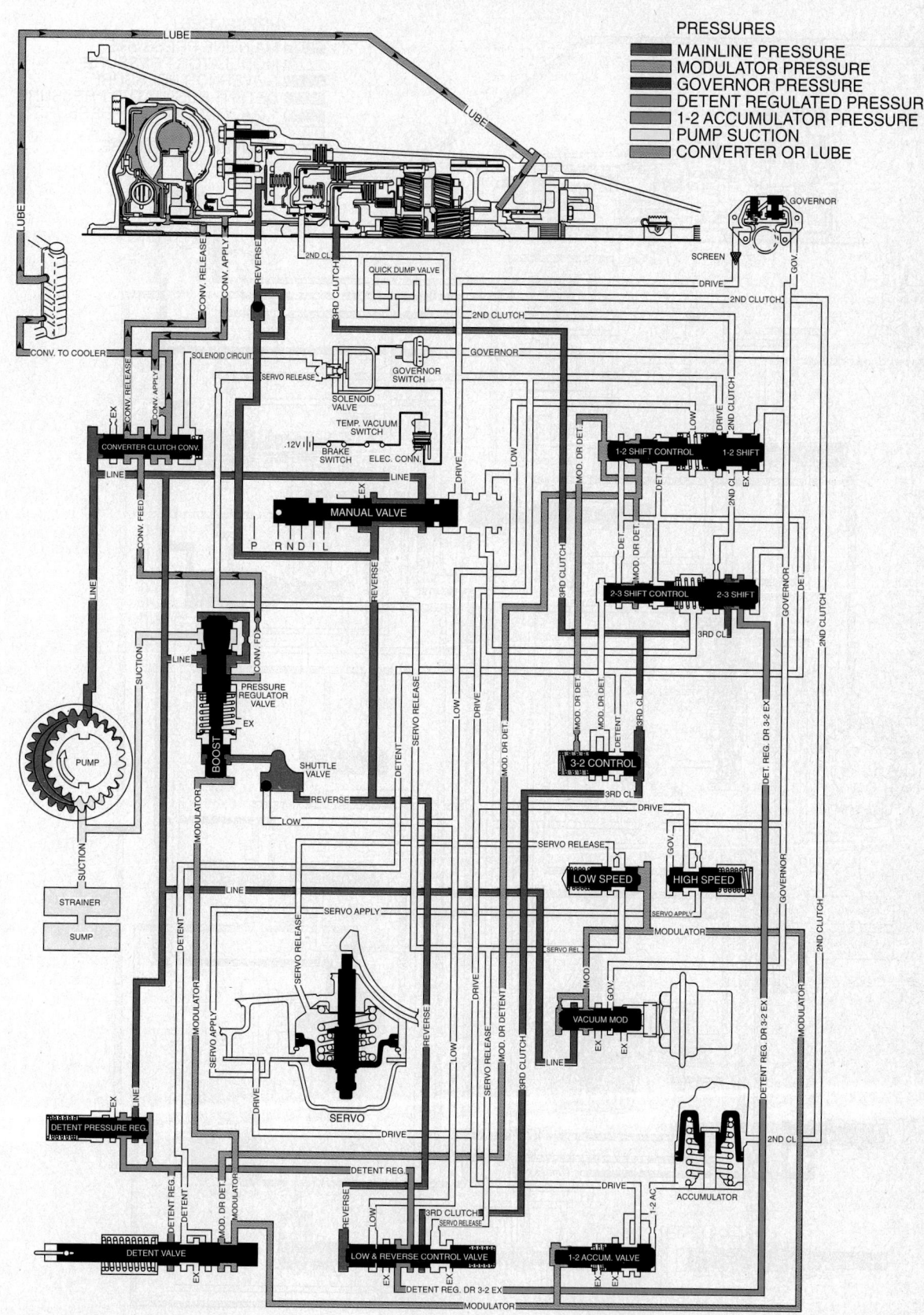

Fig. 7: "R" Position — Reverse Gear

Courtesy of General Motors Corp.

OIL CIRCUIT DIAGRAMS
Hydra-Matic 3L30 (Cont.)

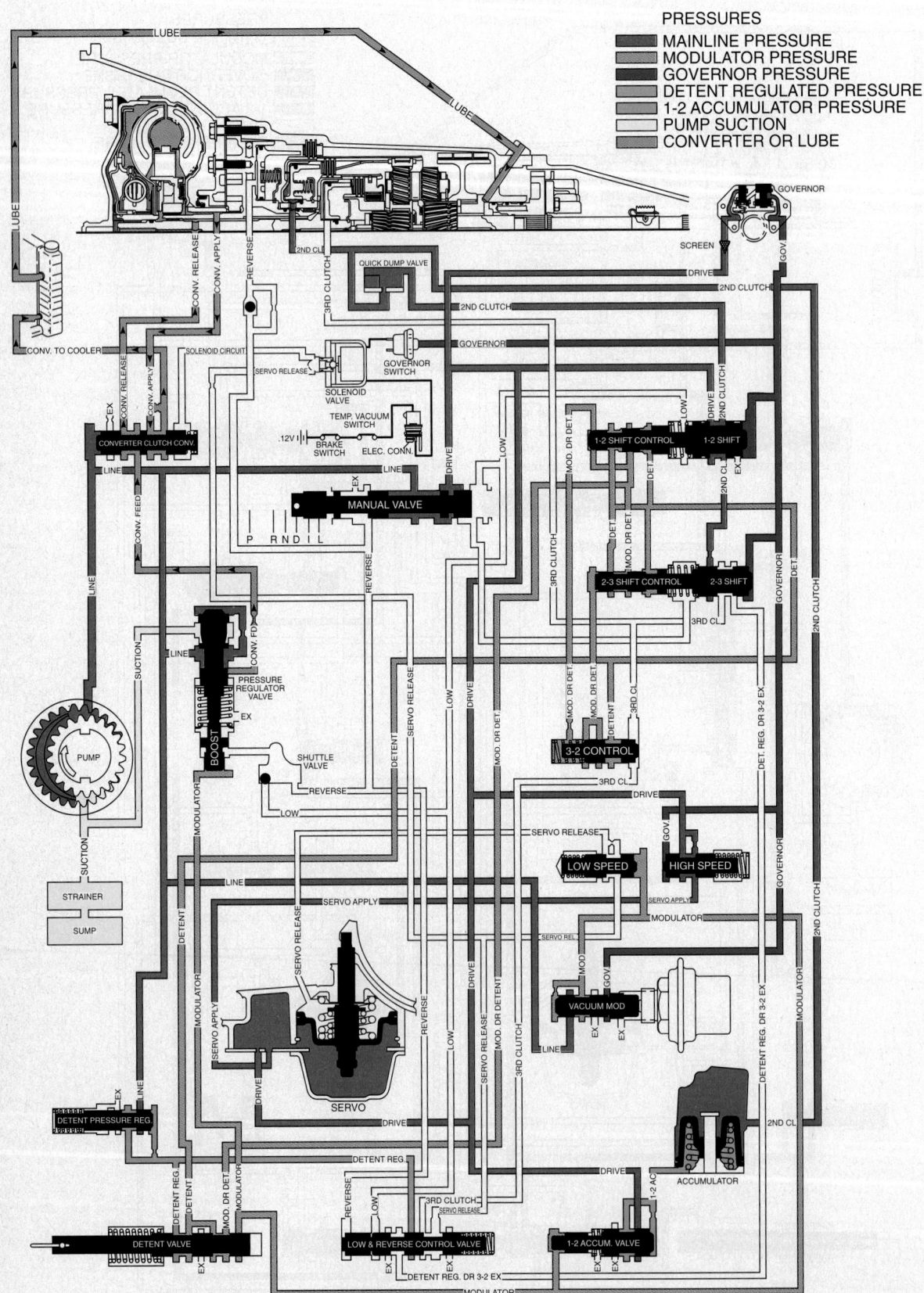

PRESSURES
- MAINLINE PRESSURE
- MODULATOR PRESSURE
- GOVERNOR PRESSURE
- DETENT REGULATED PRESSURE
- 1-2 ACCUMULATOR PRESSURE
- PUMP SUCTION
- CONVERTER OR LUBE

Fig. 8: "D" Position — Kickdown (Passing Gear)

Courtesy of General Motors Corp.

OIL CIRCUIT DIAGRAMS
Hydra-Matic 4L30-E

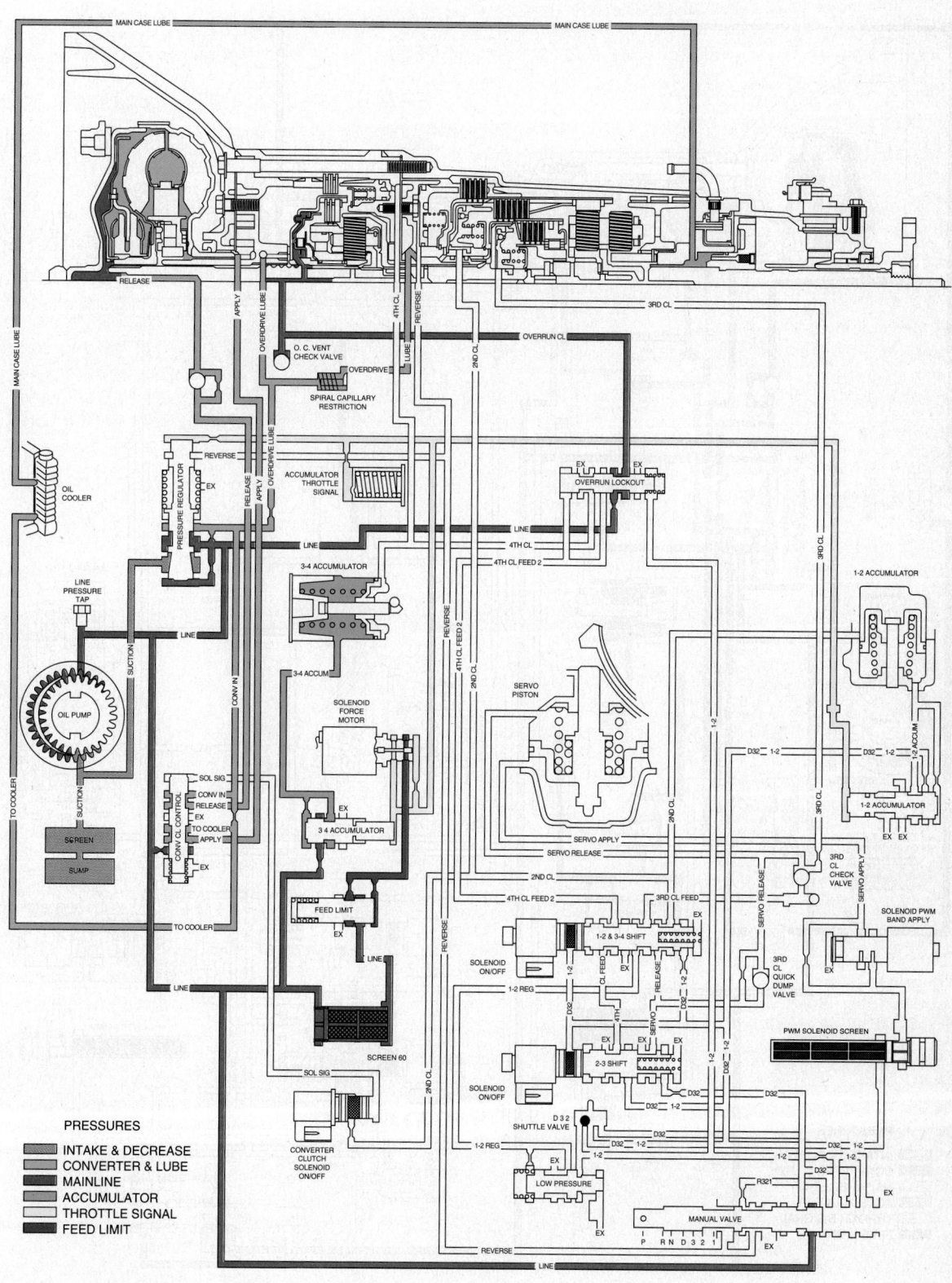

PRESSURES
- INTAKE & DECREASE
- CONVERTER & LUBE
- MAINLINE
- ACCUMULATOR
- THROTTLE SIGNAL
- FEED LIMIT

Fig. 1: "P" Position — Park

Courtesy of Isuzu Motor Co.

OIL CIRCUIT DIAGRAMS
Hydra-Matic 4L30-E (Cont.)

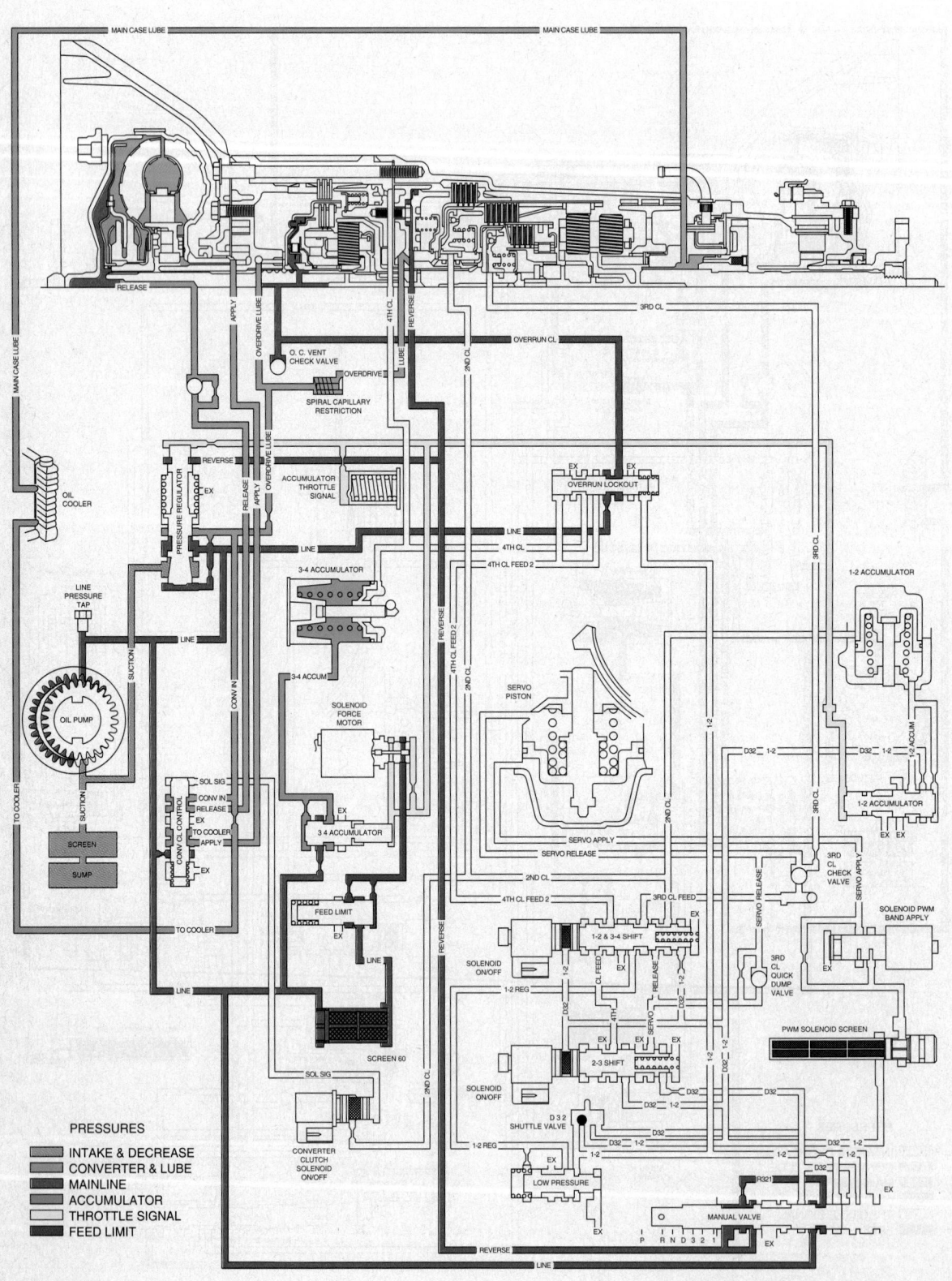

Fig. 2: "R" Position — Reverse

Courtesy of Isuzu Motor Co.

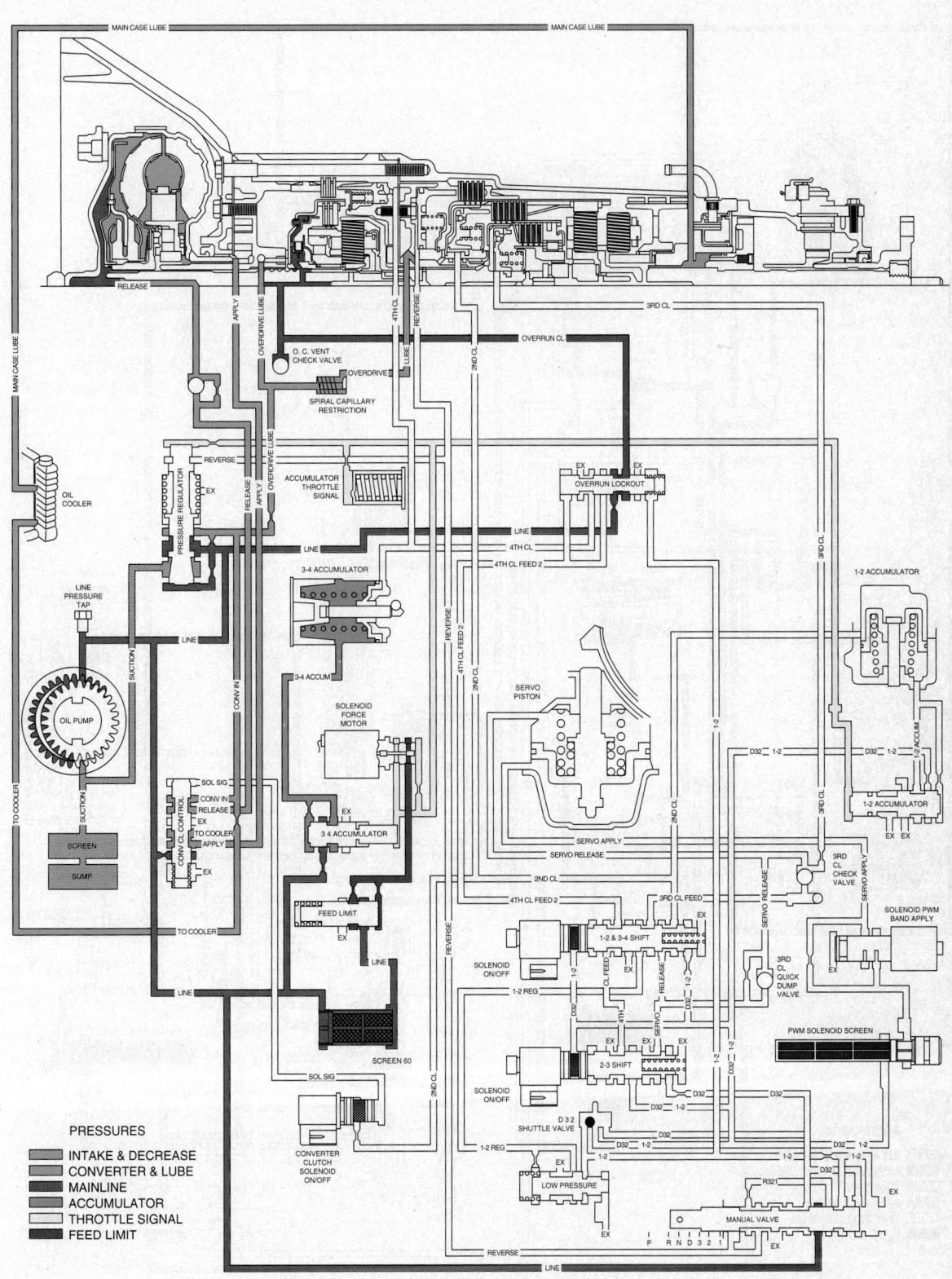

Fig. 3: "N" Position — Neutral

Courtesy of Isuzu Motor Co.

OIL CIRCUIT DIAGRAMS
Hydra-Matic 4L30-E (Cont.)

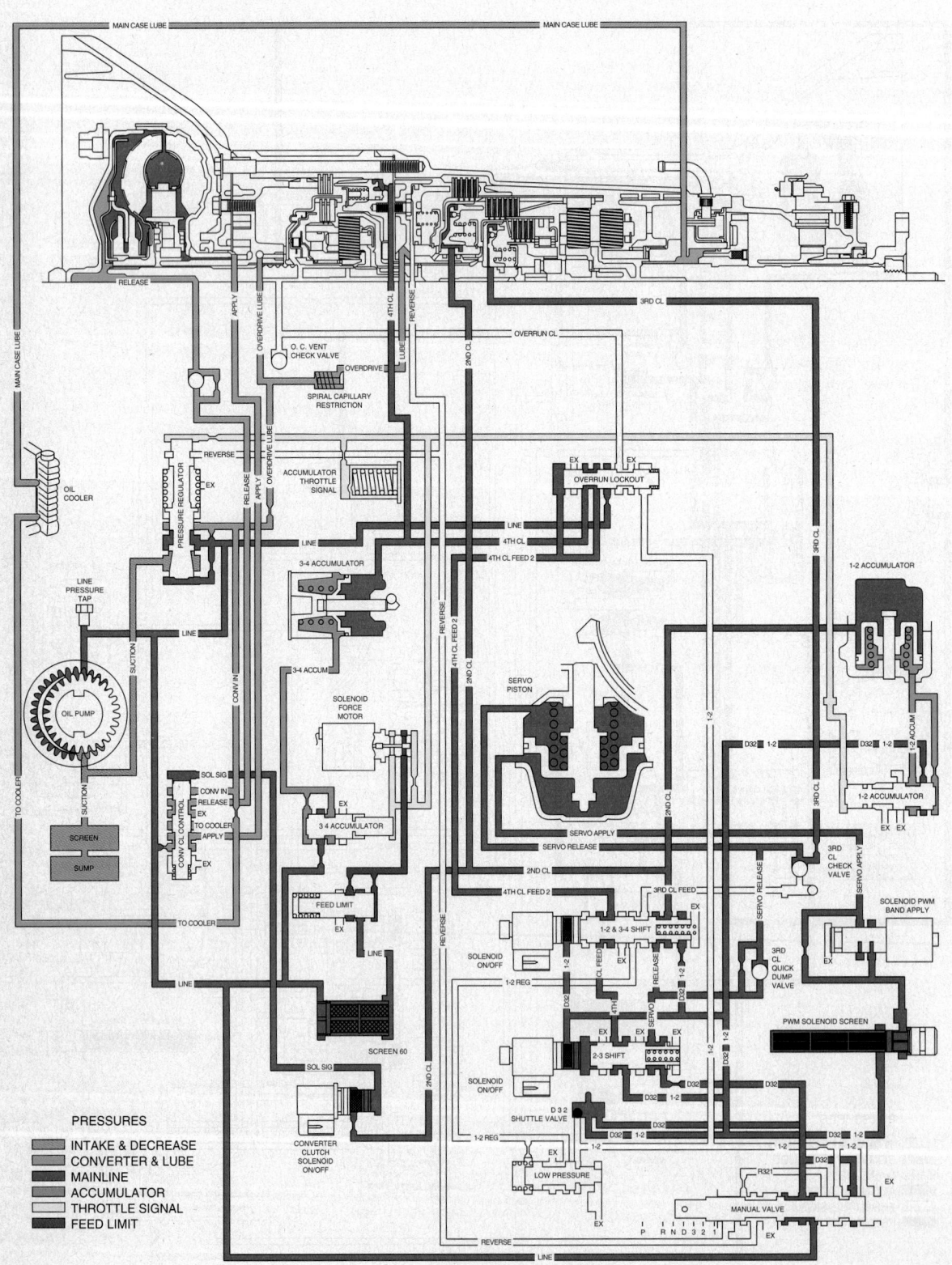

PRESSURES

- INTAKE & DECREASE
- CONVERTER & LUBE
- MAINLINE
- ACCUMULATOR
- THROTTLE SIGNAL
- FEED LIMIT

Fig. 4: "D" Position — 4th Gear (Lock-Up ON)

Courtesy of Isuzu Motor Co.

OIL CIRCUIT DIAGRAMS
Hydra-Matic 4L30-E (Cont.)

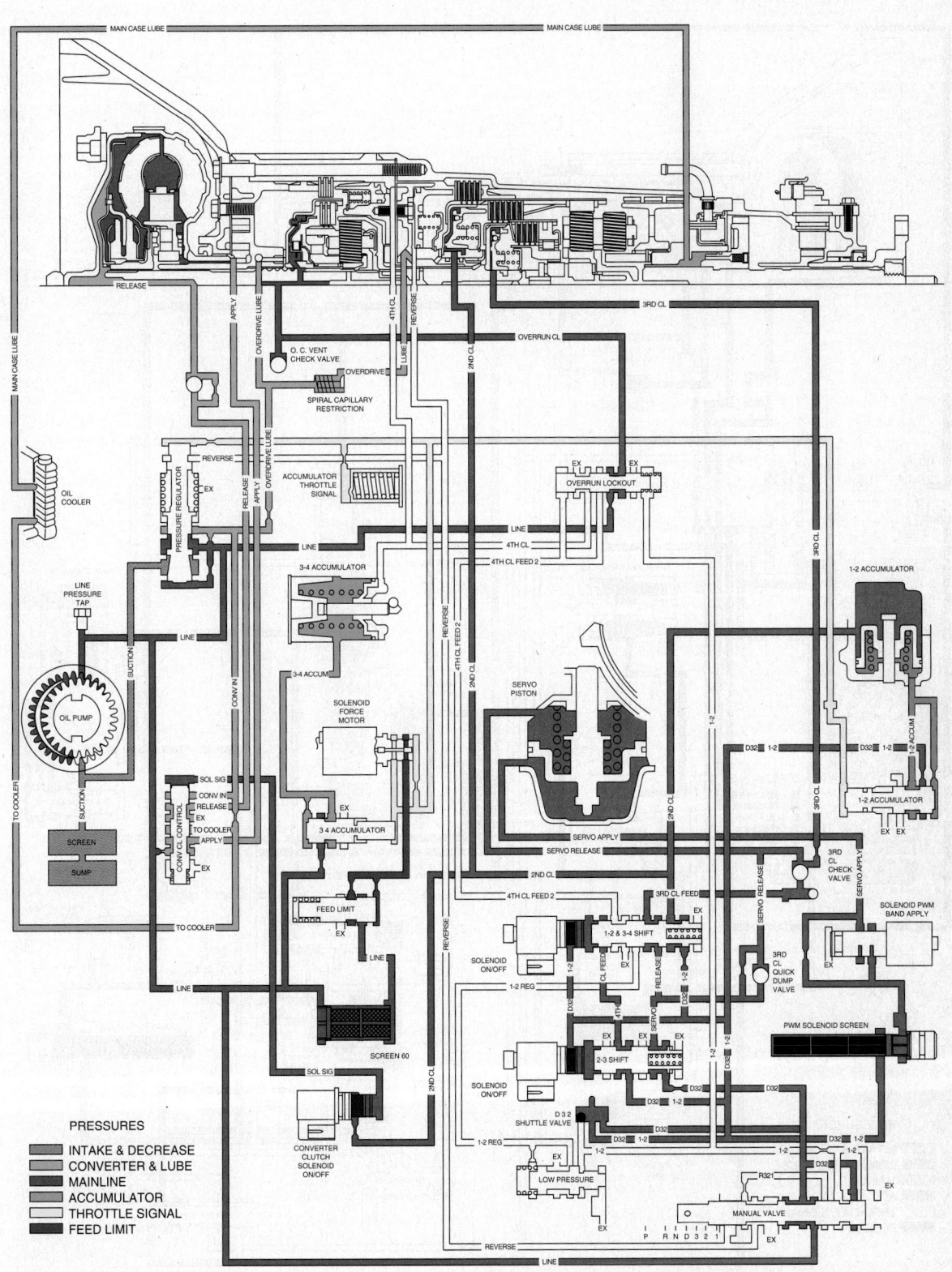

PRESSURES

- INTAKE & DECREASE
- CONVERTER & LUBE
- MAINLINE
- ACCUMULATOR
- THROTTLE SIGNAL
- FEED LIMIT

Fig. 5: "D" Position — 3rd Gear (Lock-Up ON)

Courtesy of Isuzu Motor Co.

OIL CIRCUIT DIAGRAMS
Hydra-Matic 4L30-E (Cont.)

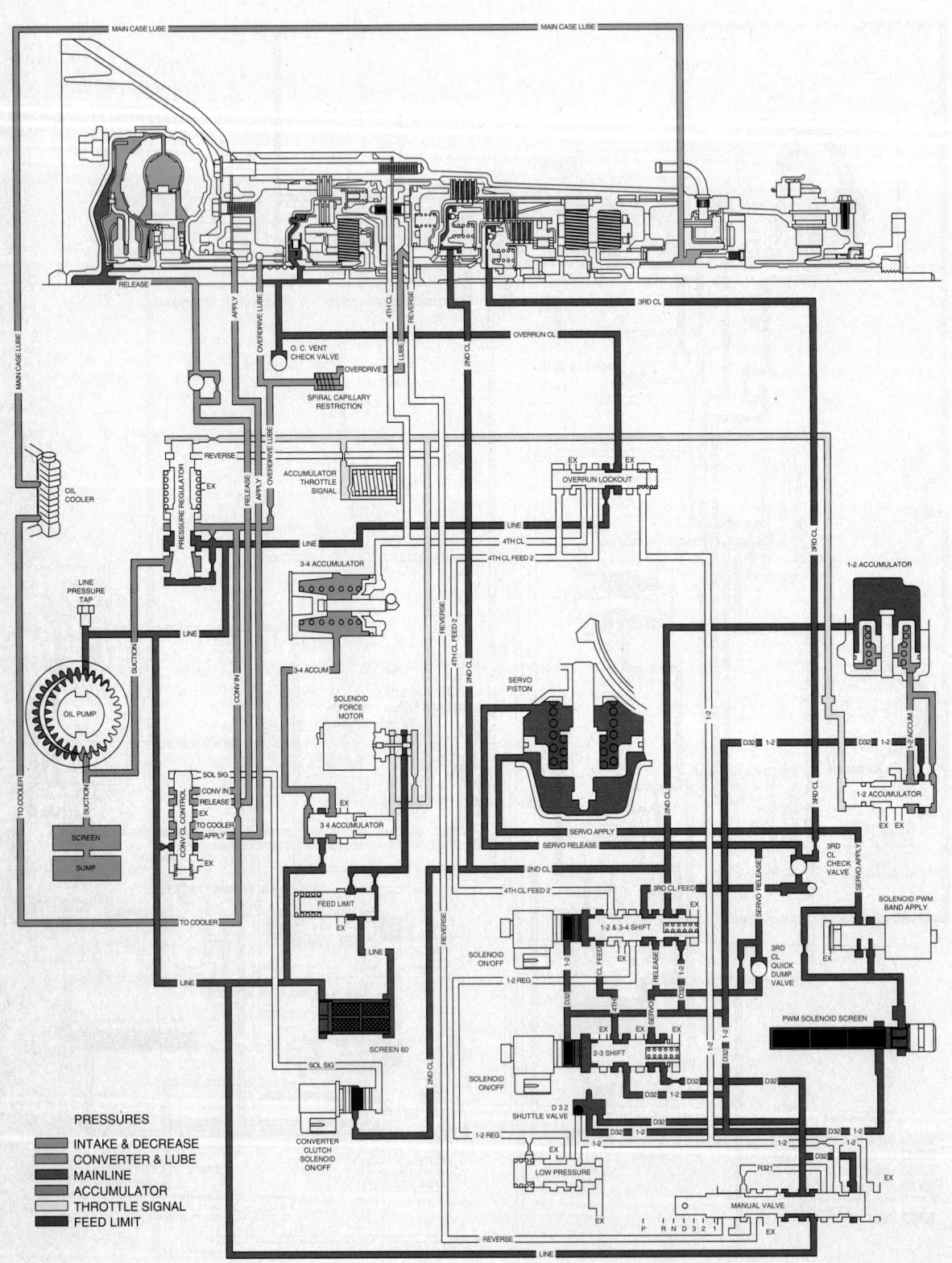

PRESSURES

- INTAKE & DECREASE
- CONVERTER & LUBE
- MAINLINE
- ACCUMULATOR
- THROTTLE SIGNAL
- FEED LIMIT

Fig. 6: "D" Position — 3rd Gear (Lock-Up OFF)

Courtesy of Isuzu Motor Co.

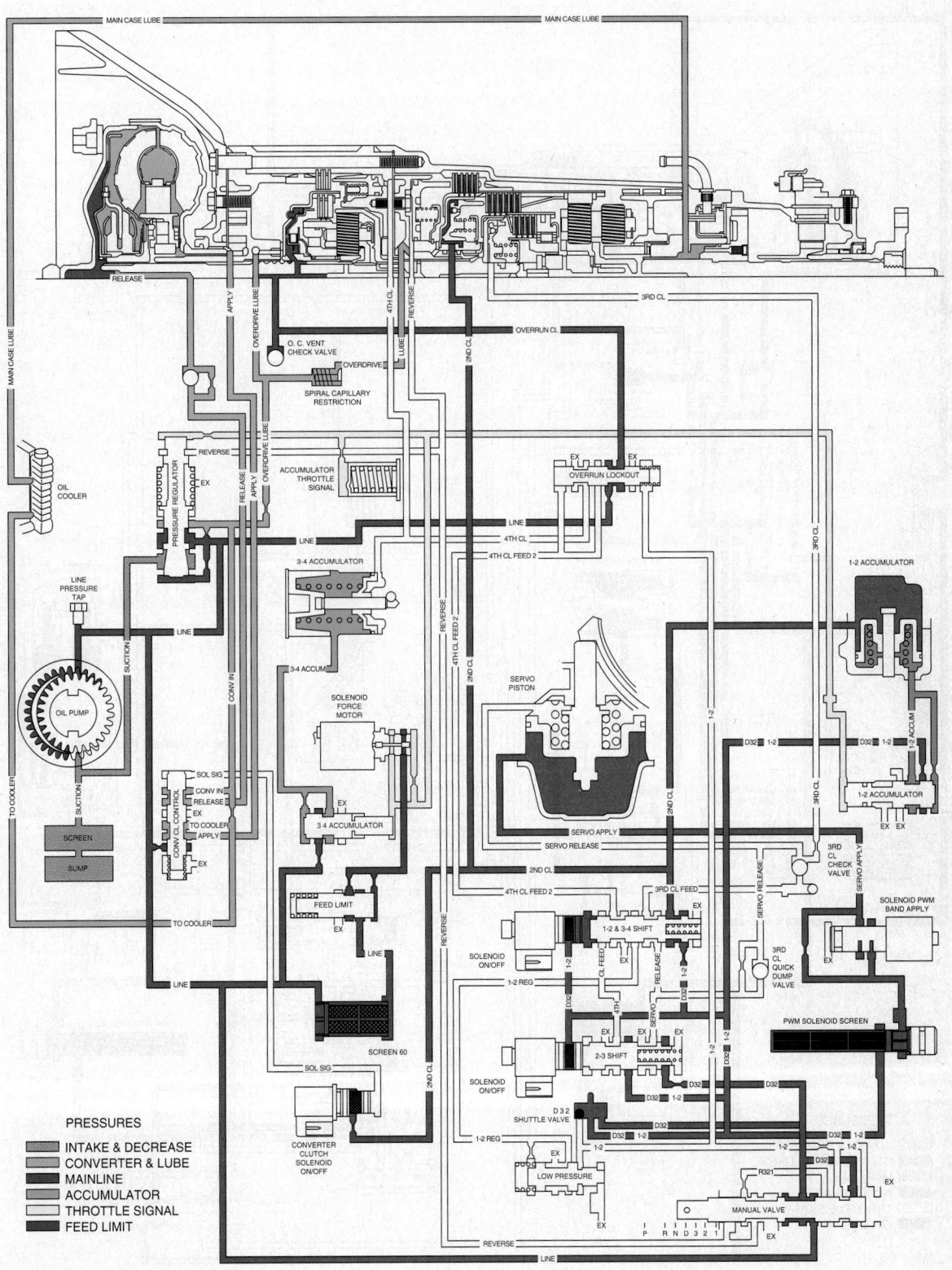

Fig. 7: "D" Position — 2nd Gear

Courtesy of Isuzu Motor Co.

OIL CIRCUIT DIAGRAMS
Hydra-Matic 4L30-E (Cont.)

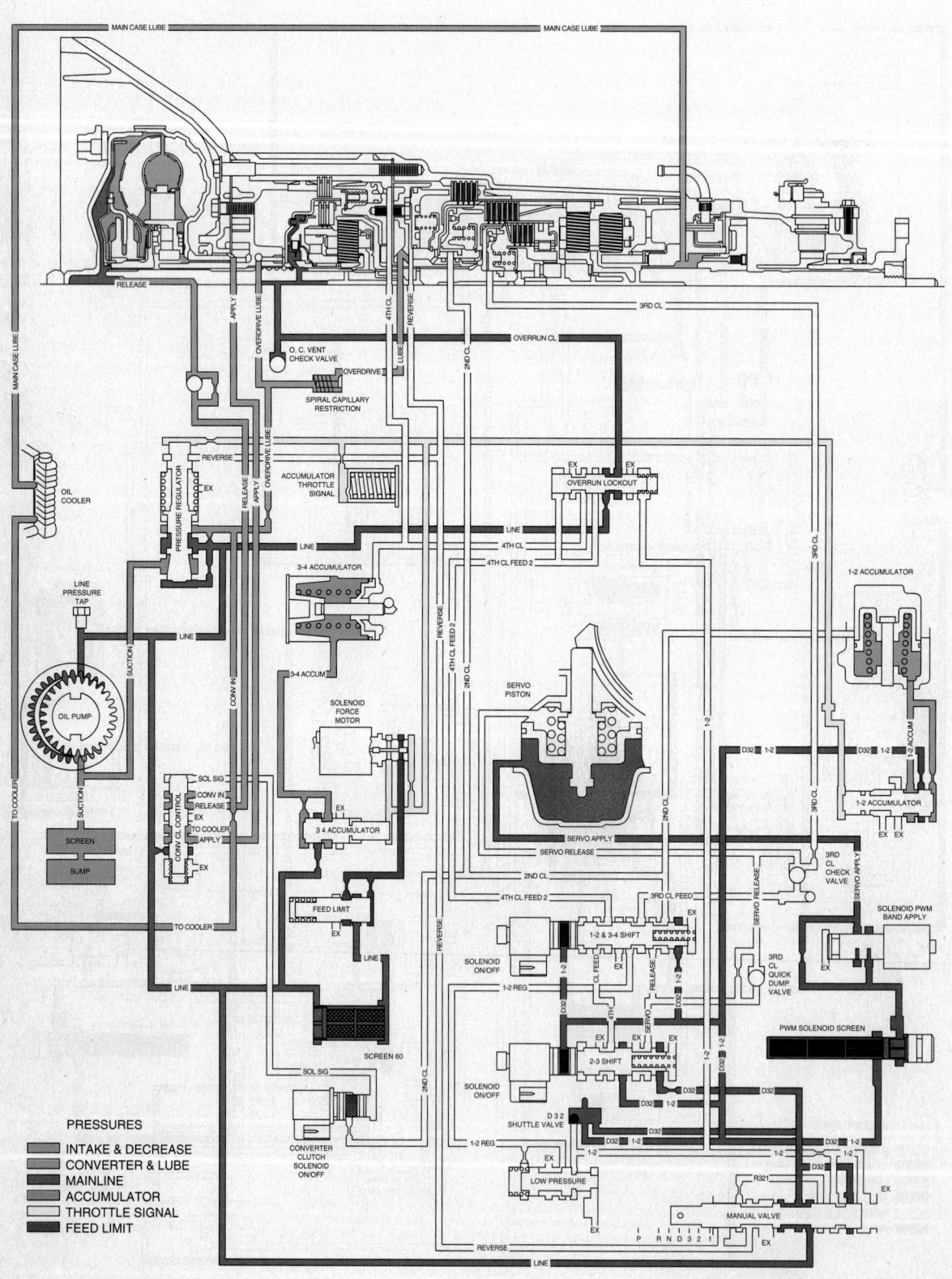

Fig. 8: "D" Position — 1st Gear

Courtesy of Isuzu Motor Co.

OIL CIRCUIT DIAGRAMS
Hydra-Matic 4L30-E (Cont.)

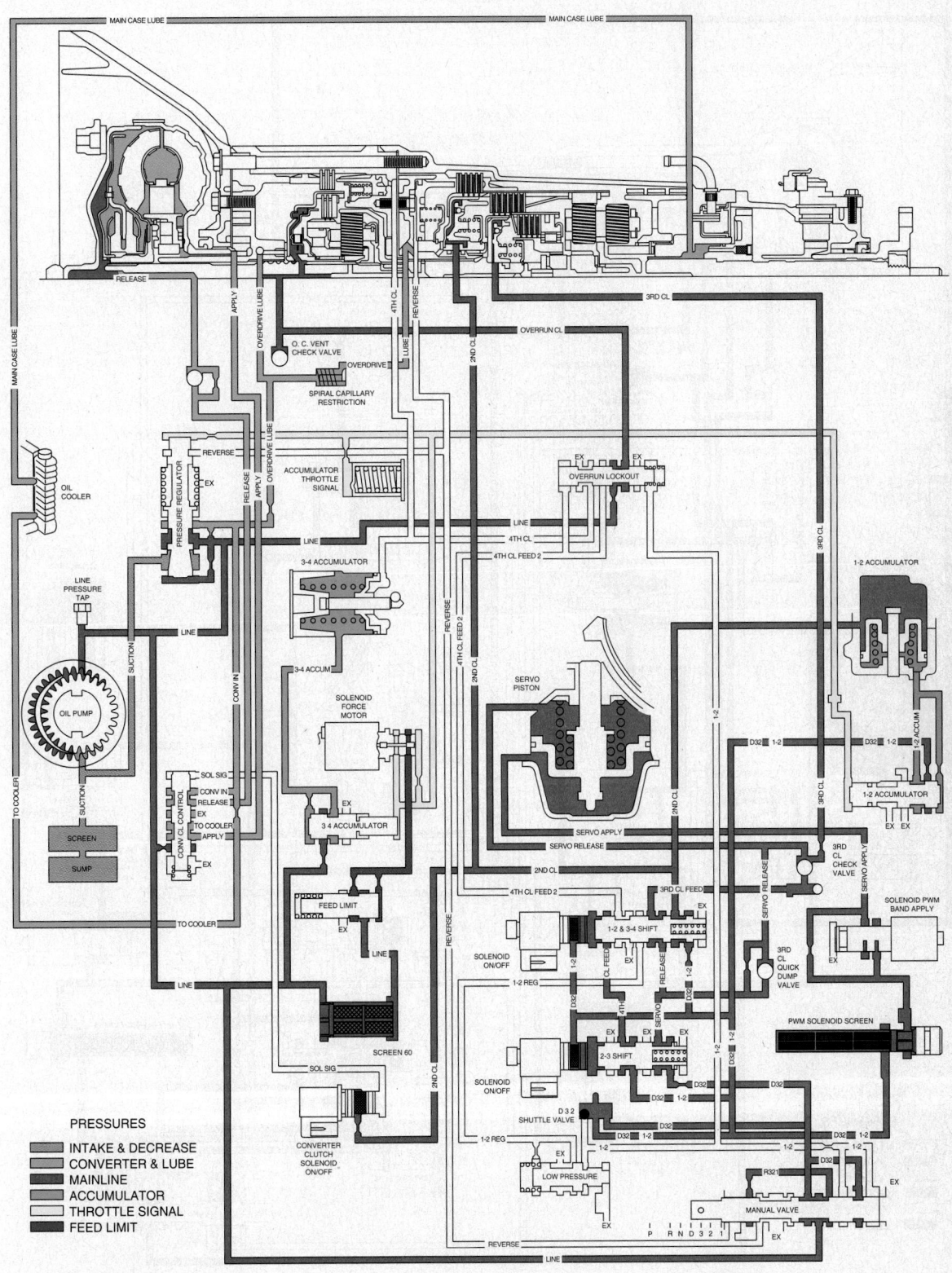

Fig. 9: "3" Position — 3rd Gear (Lock-Up OFF)

Courtesy of Isuzu Motor Co.

OIL CIRCUIT DIAGRAMS
Hydra-Matic 4L30-E (Cont.)

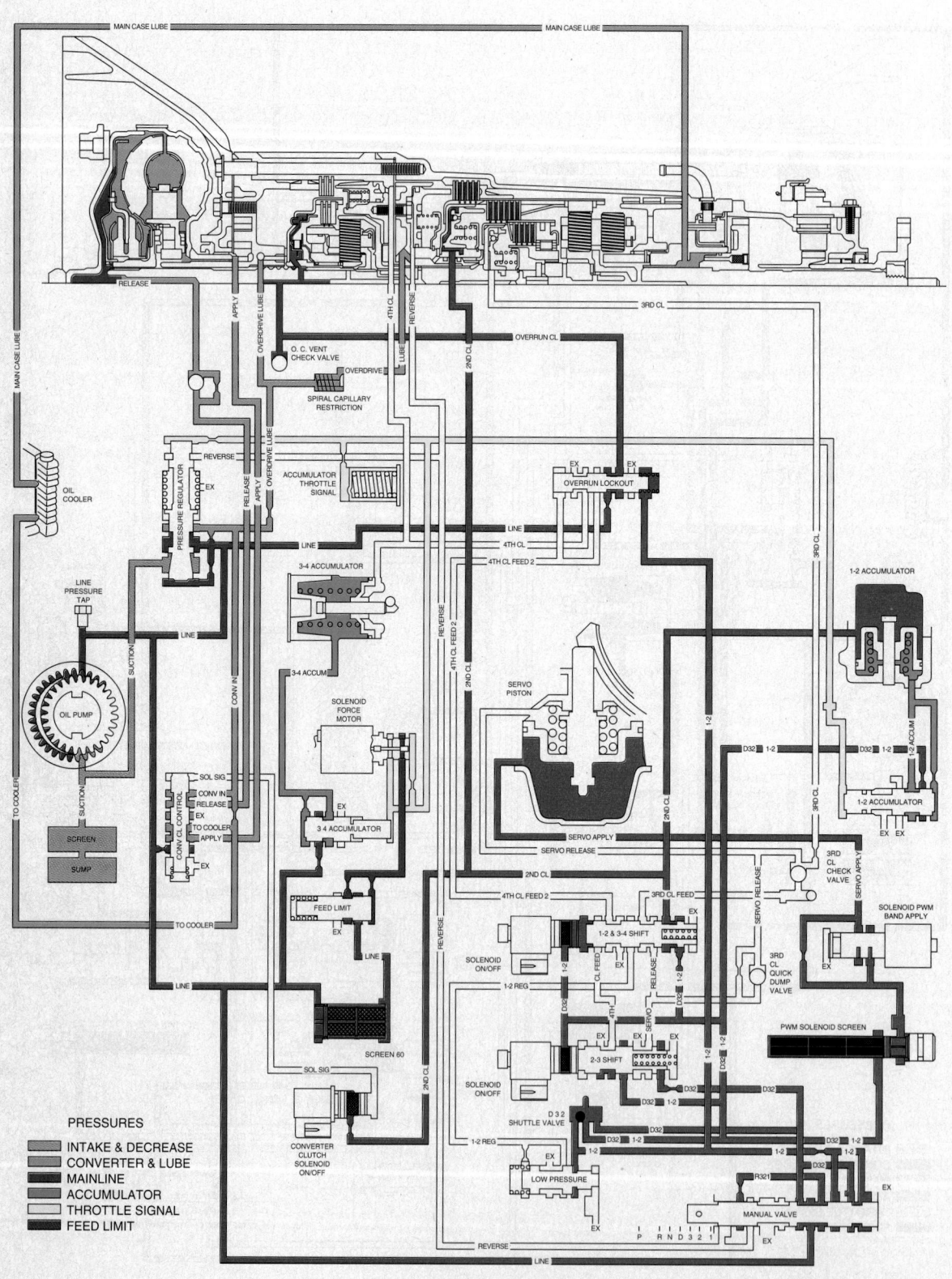

Fig. 10: "2" Position — 2nd Gear

Courtesy of Isuzu Motor Co.

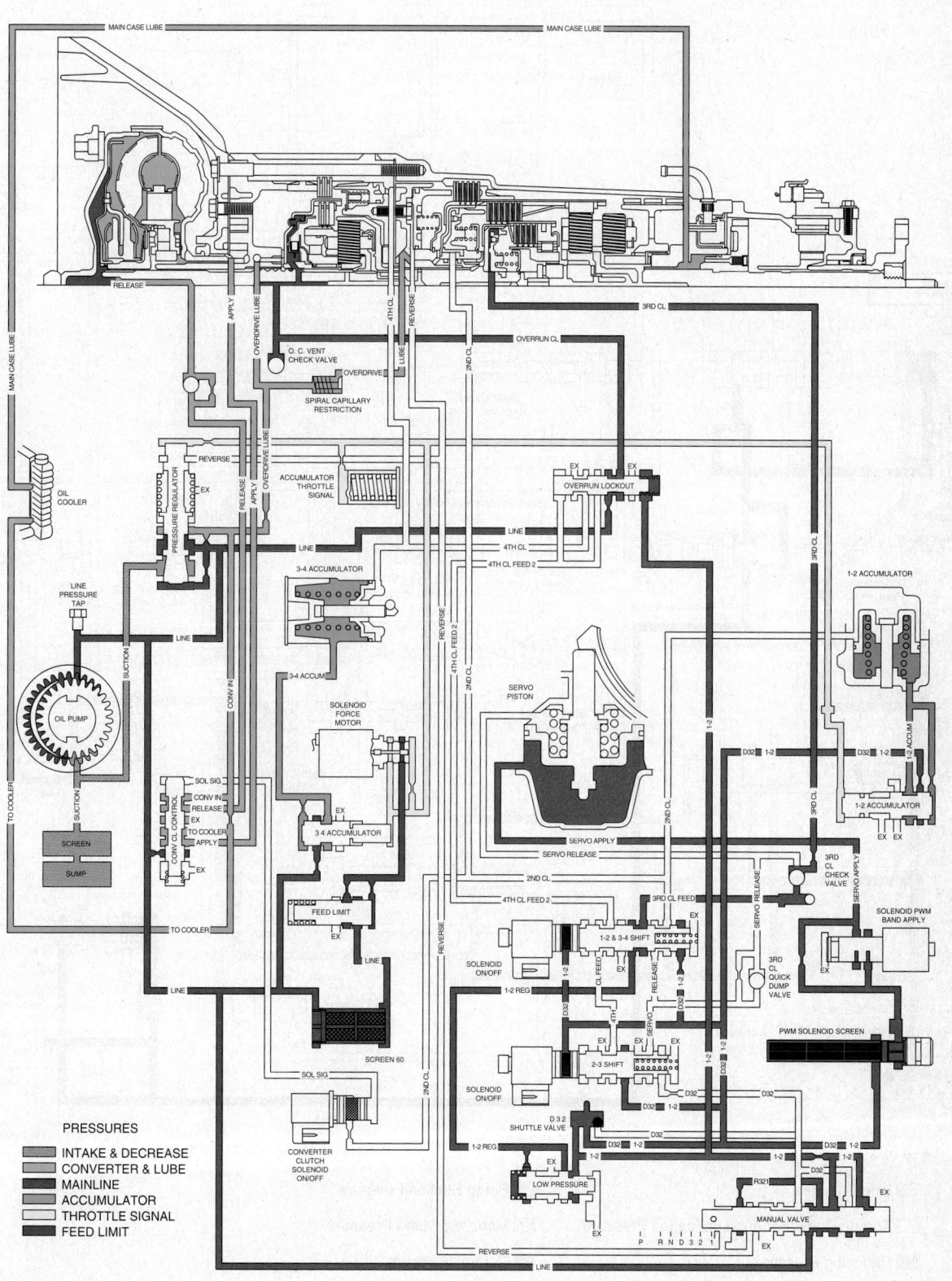

Fig. 11: "1" Position — 1st Gear

Courtesy of Isuzu Motor Co.

OIL CIRCUIT DIAGRAMS
Hyundai A4AF & Mitsubishi F4A20 Series

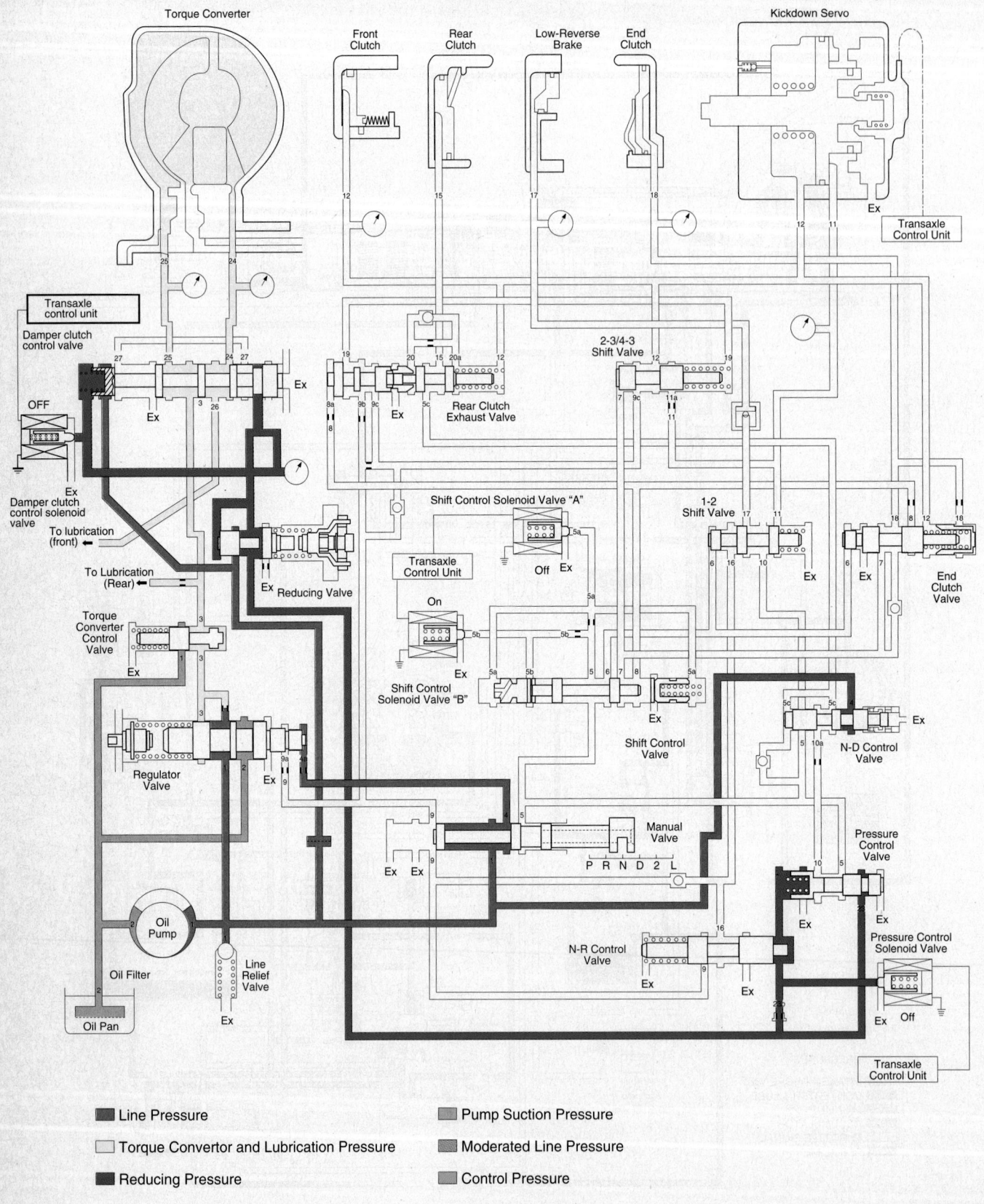

Line Pressure

Torque Convertor and Lubrication Pressure

Reducing Pressure

Pump Suction Pressure

Moderated Line Pressure

Control Pressure

Fig. 1: "N" Position — Neutral

Courtesy of Chrysler Corp.

OIL CIRCUIT DIAGRAMS
Hyundai A4AF & Mitsubishi F4A20 Series (Cont.)

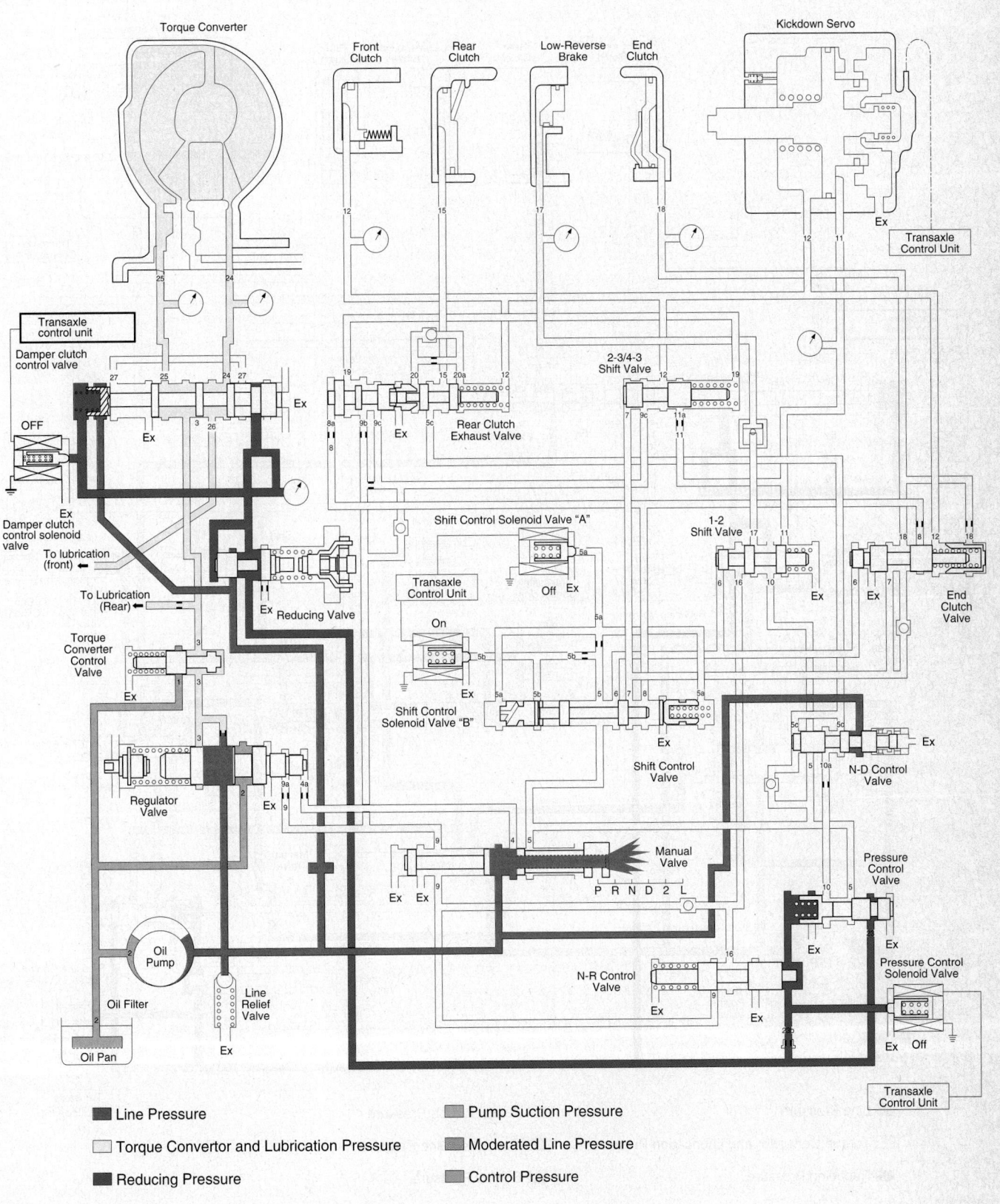

■ Line Pressure

□ Torque Convertor and Lubrication Pressure

■ Reducing Pressure

■ Pump Suction Pressure

■ Moderated Line Pressure

■ Control Pressure

Fig. 2: "P" Position — Park

Courtesy of Chrysler Corp.

OIL CIRCUIT DIAGRAMS
Hyundai A4AF & Mitsubishi F4A20 Series (Cont.)

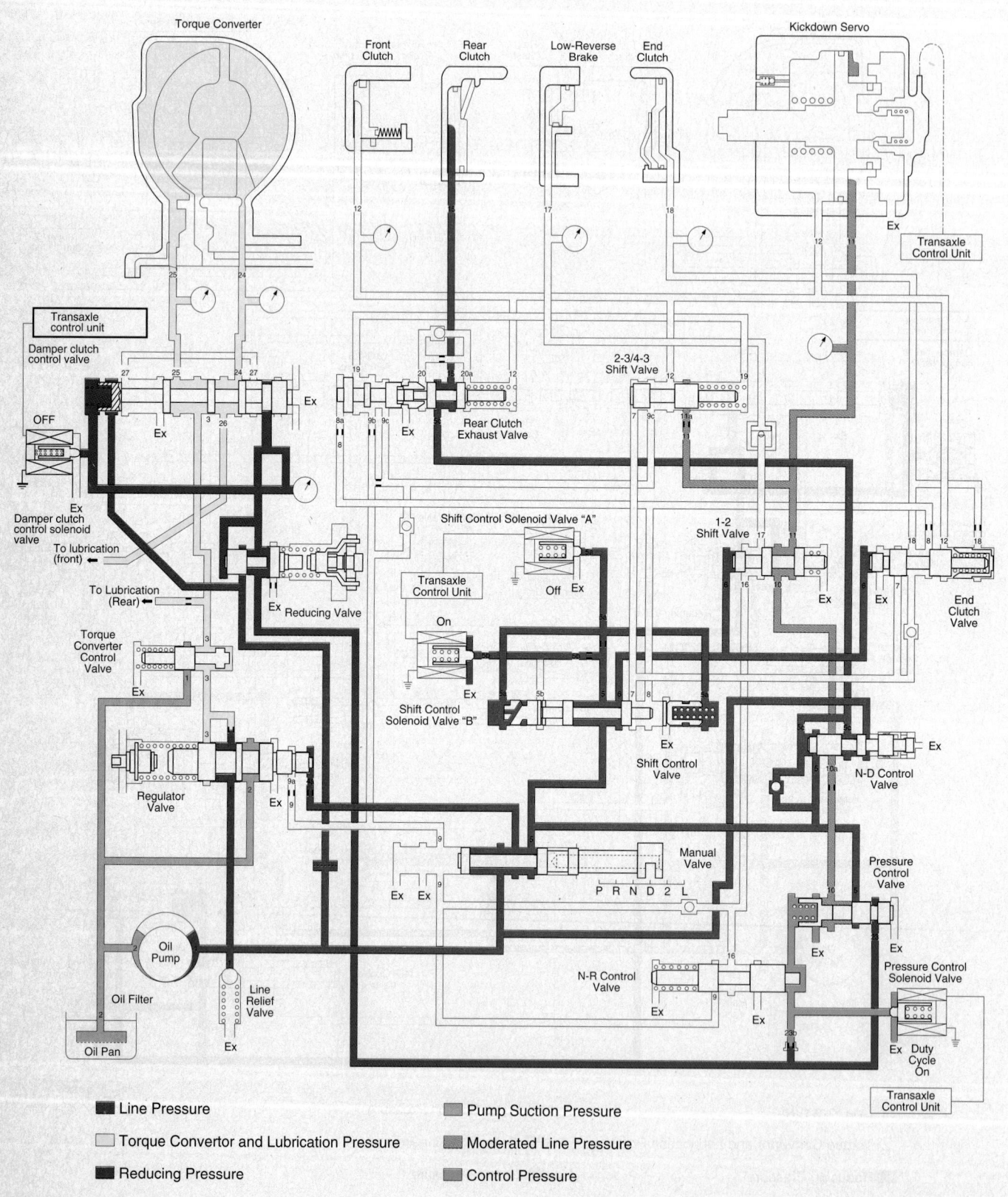

Fig. 3: "D" Position — Stopped At Idle

Courtesy of Chrysler Corp.

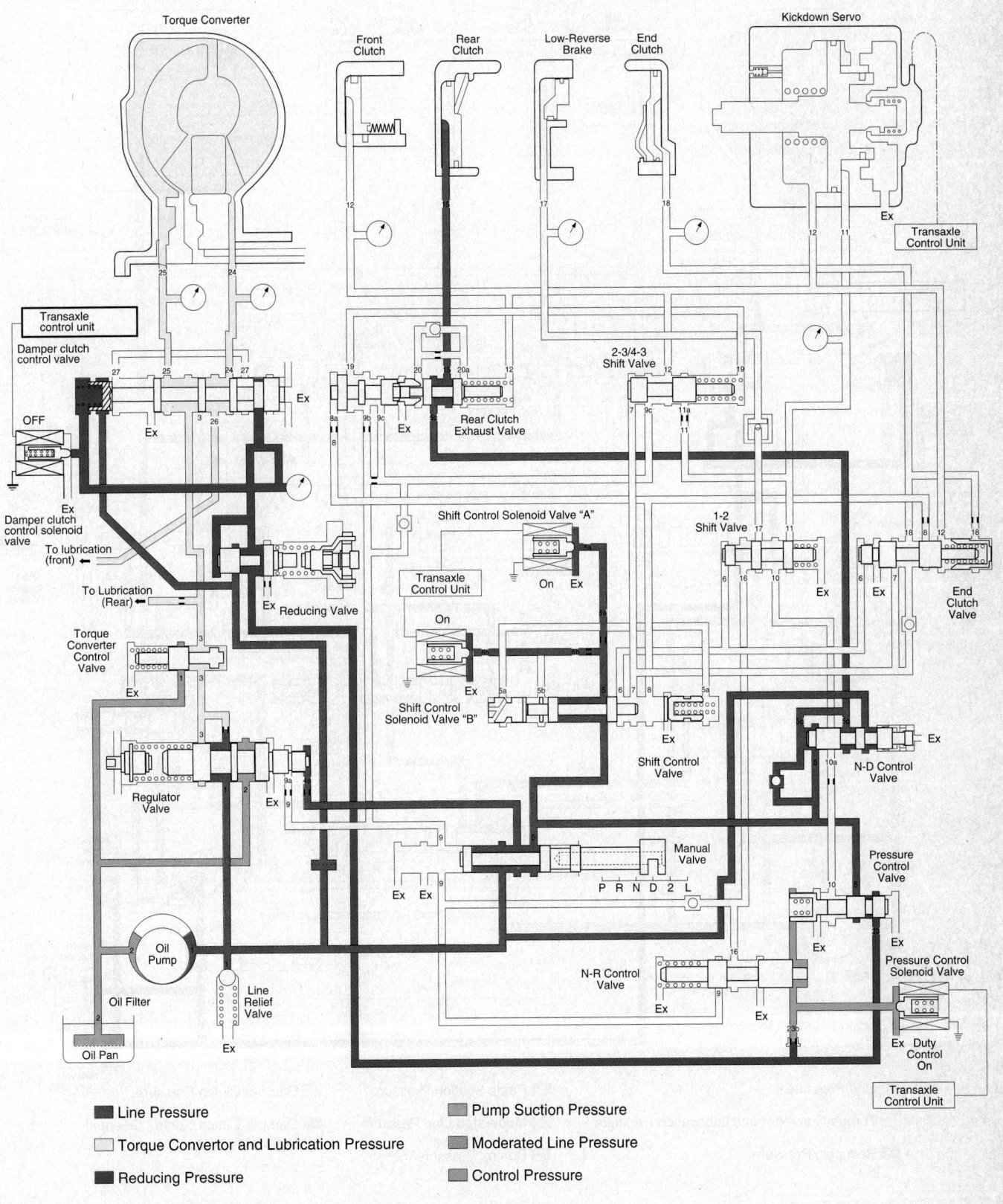

Line Pressure

Torque Convertor and Lubrication Pressure

Reducing Pressure

Pump Suction Pressure

Moderated Line Pressure

Control Pressure

Fig. 4: "D" Position — 1st Gear

Courtesy of Chrysler Corp.

OIL CIRCUIT DIAGRAMS
Hyundai A4AF & Mitsubishi F4A20 Series (Cont.)

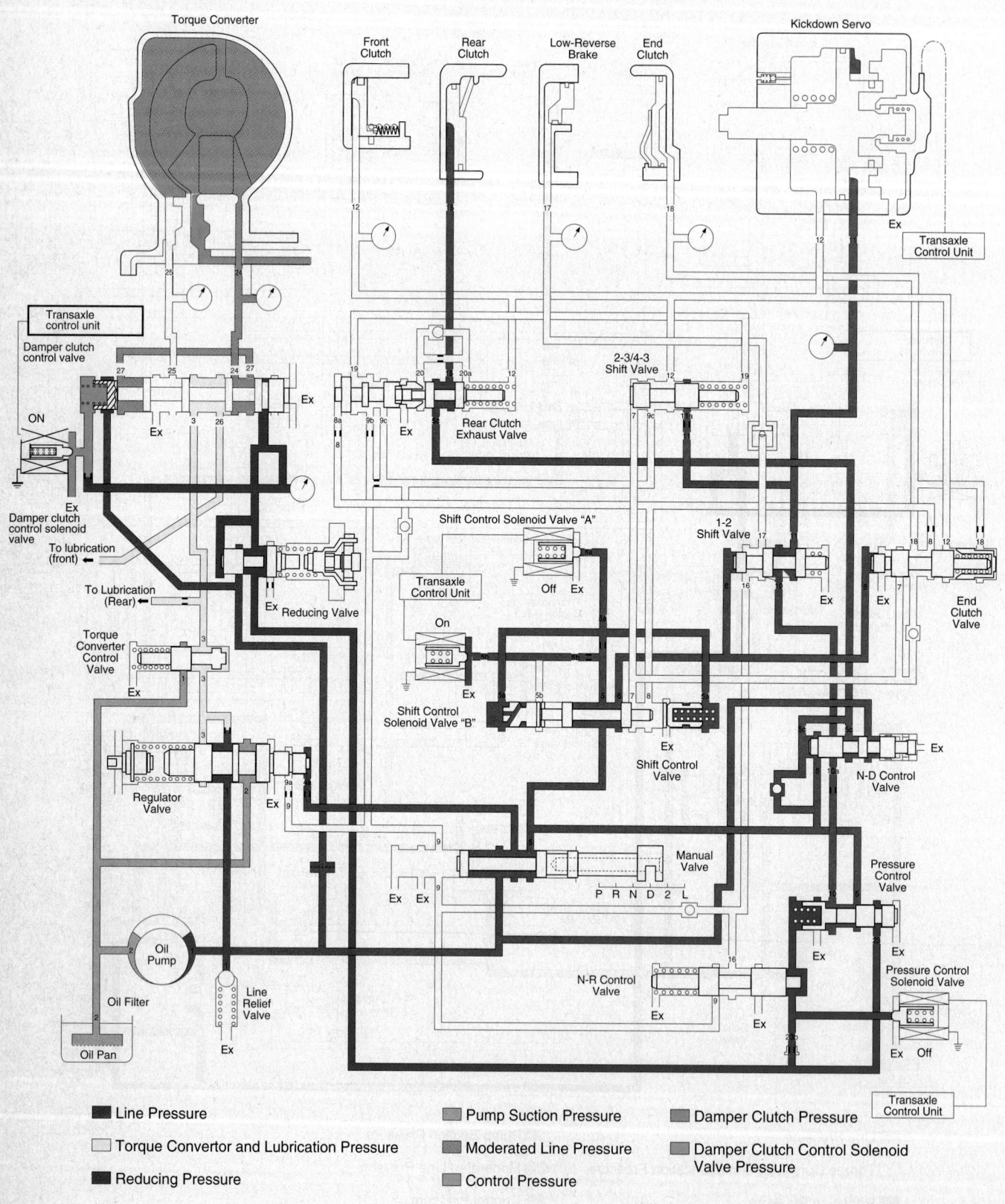

Fig. 5: "D" Position — 2nd Gear

Courtesy of Chrysler Corp.

OIL CIRCUIT DIAGRAMS
Hyundai A4AF & Mitsubishi F4A20 Series (Cont.)

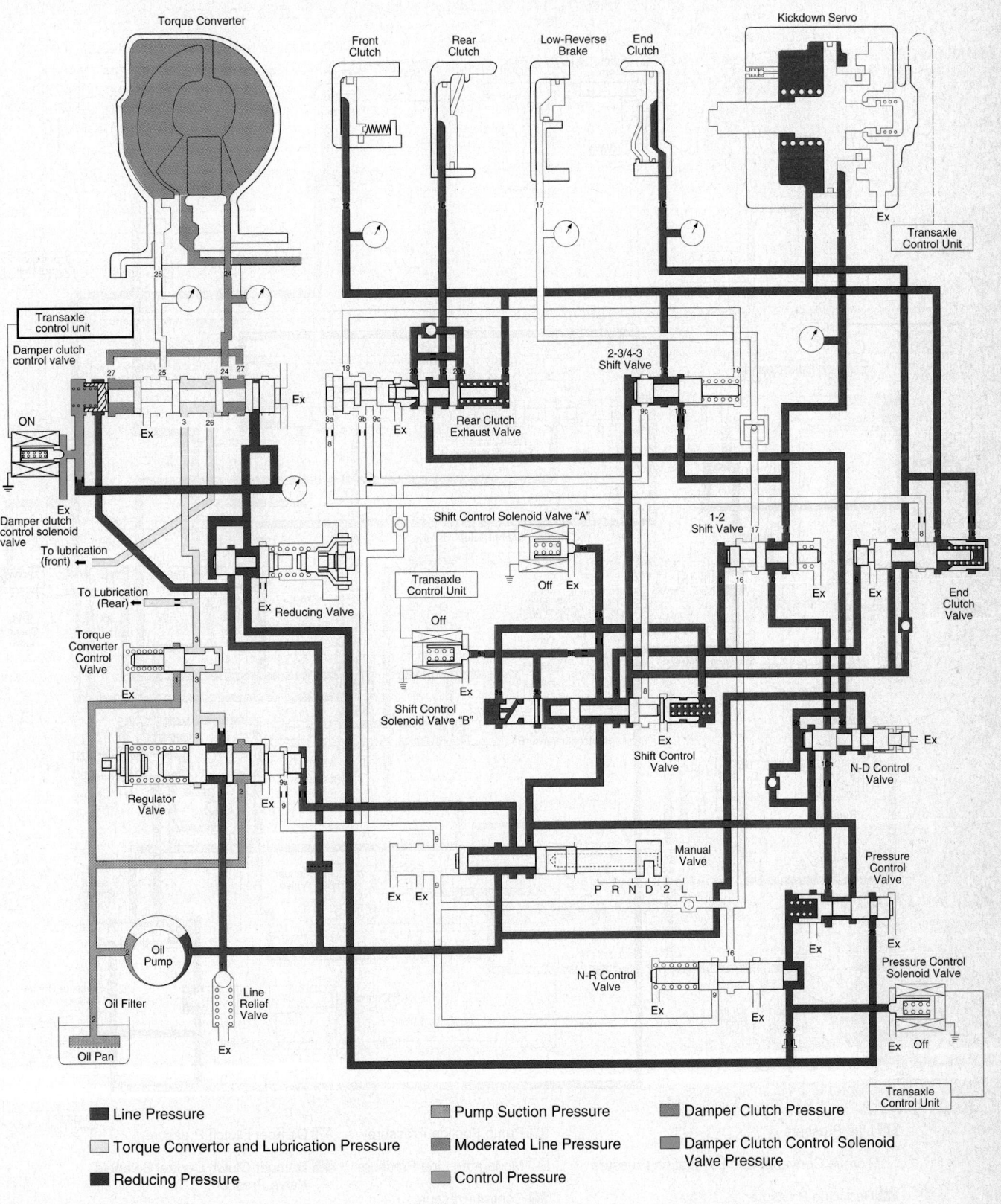

Fig. 6: "D" Position — 3rd Gear

Courtesy of Chrysler Corp.

OIL CIRCUIT DIAGRAMS
Hyundai A4AF & Mitsubishi F4A20 Series (Cont.)

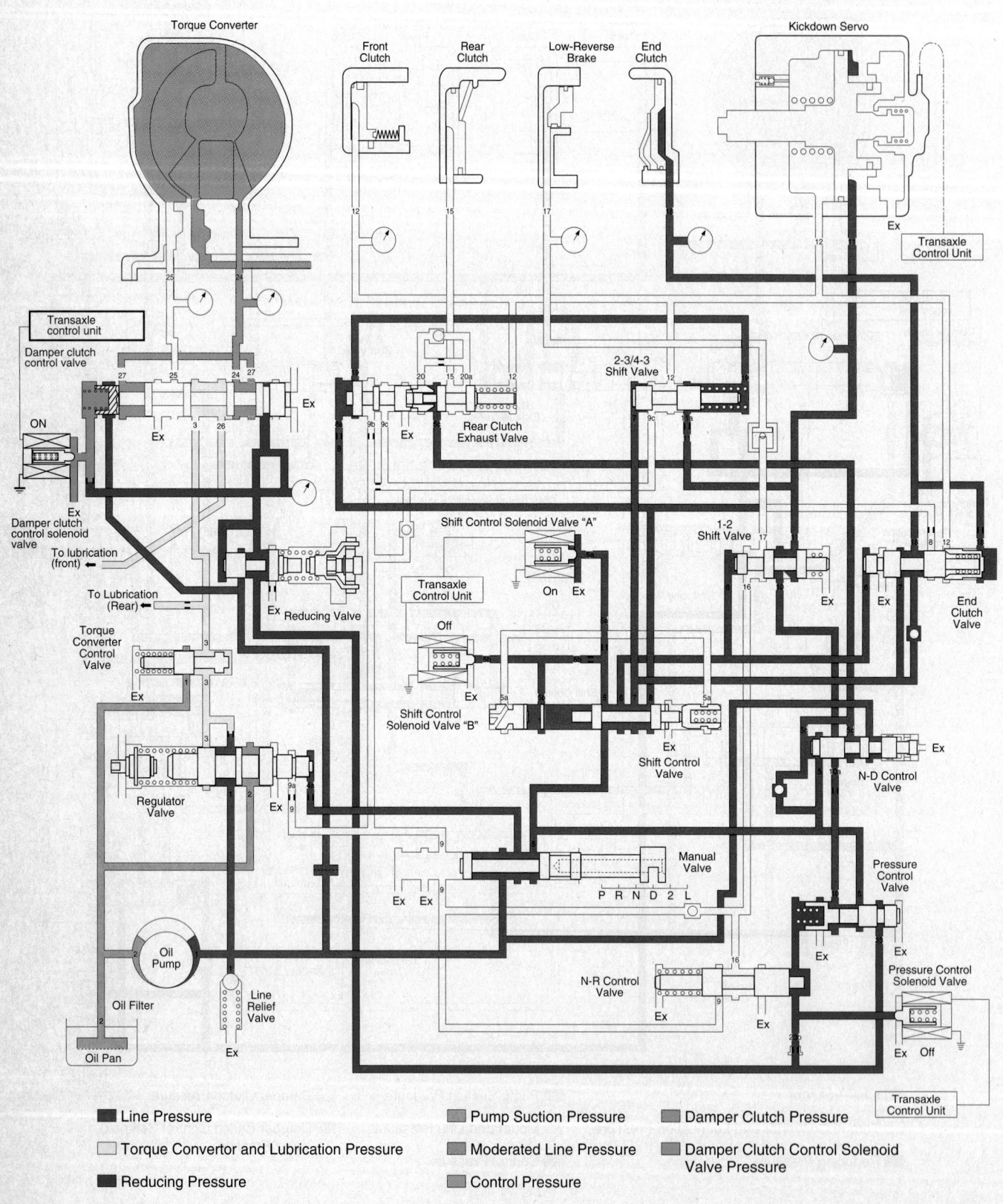

Fig. 7: "D" Position — 4th Gear

Courtesy of Chrysler Corp.

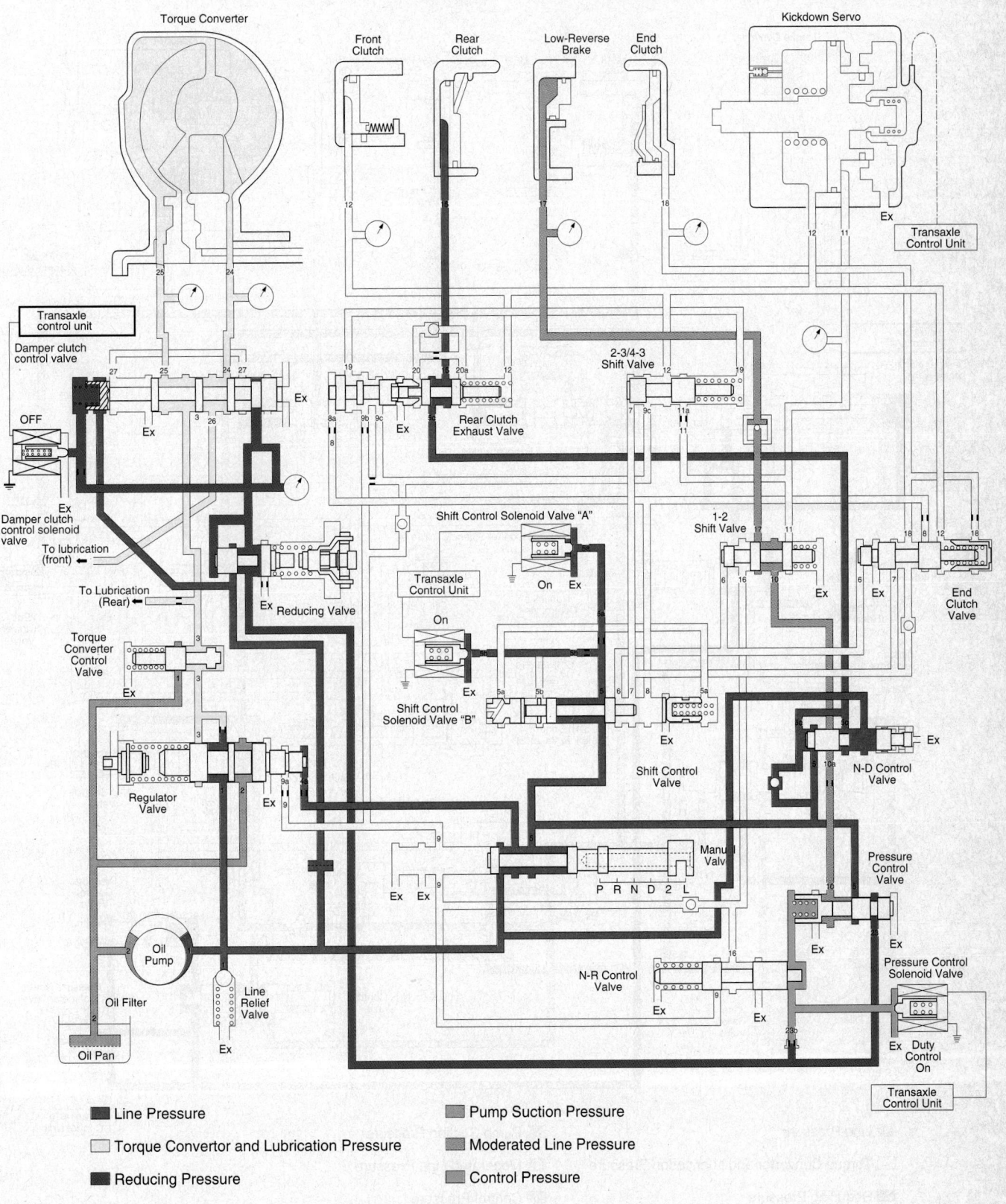

Fig. 8: "L" Position — 1st Gear

Courtesy of Chrysler Corp.

OIL CIRCUIT DIAGRAMS
Hyundai A4AF & Mitsubishi F4A20 Series (Cont.)

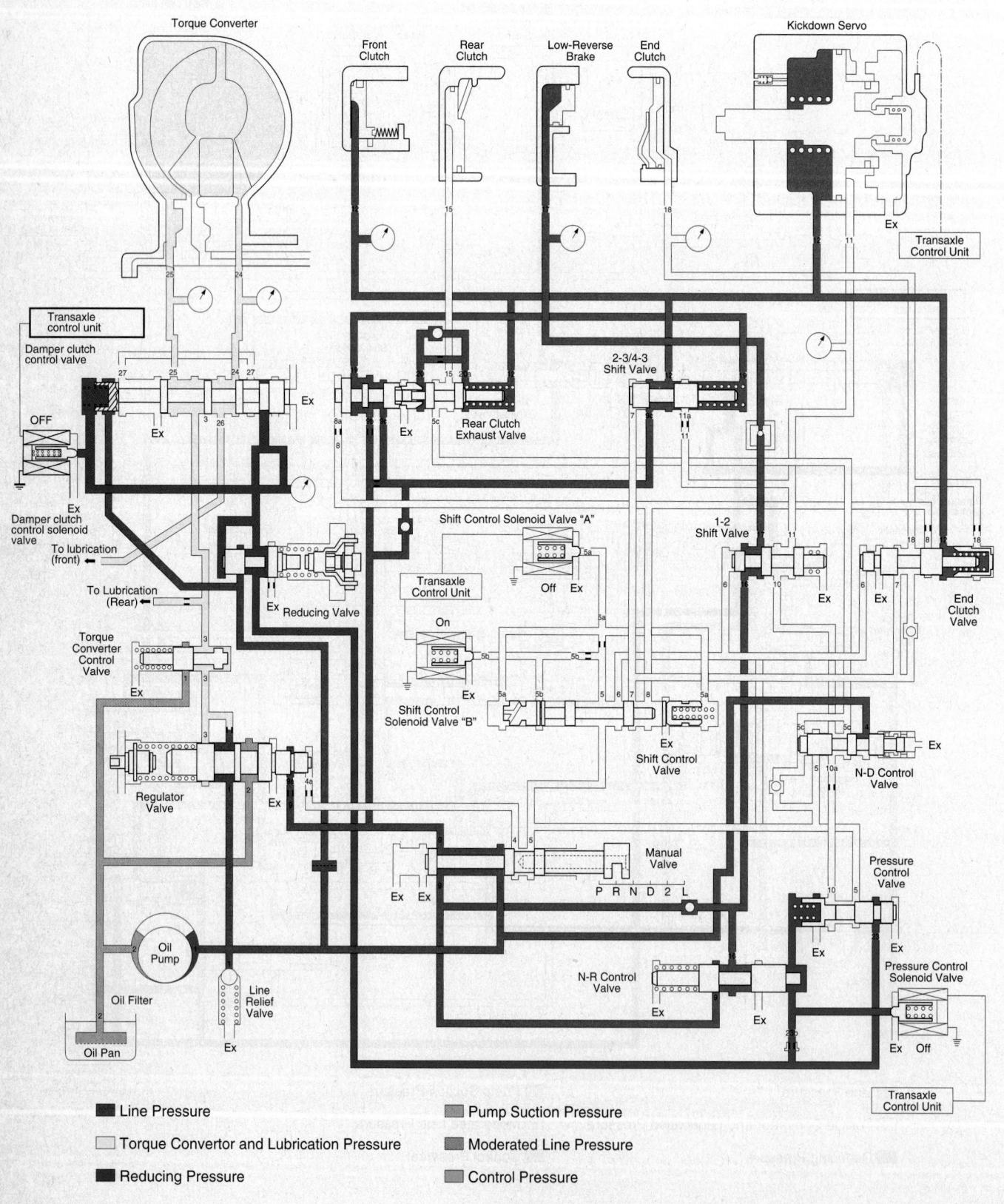

Line Pressure

Torque Convertor and Lubrication Pressure

Reducing Pressure

Pump Suction Pressure

Moderated Line Pressure

Control Pressure

Fig. 9: "R" Position — Reverse

Courtesy of Chrysler Corp.

OIL CIRCUIT DIAGRAMS
Hyundai KM175 Series

■ Line Pressure   ■ Reducing Pressure

□ Torque Convertor and   ■ Pump Suction Pressure
  Lubrication Pressure

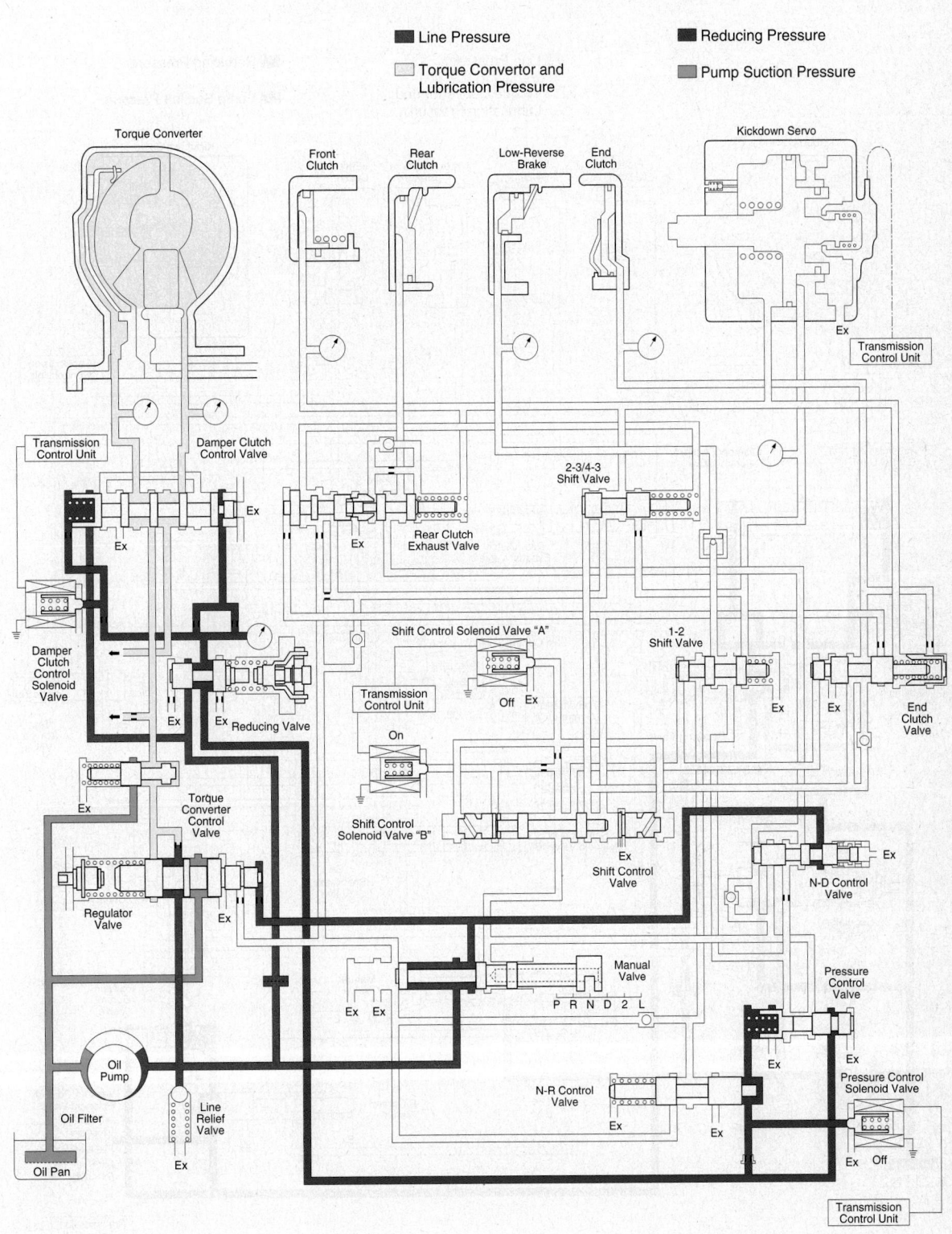

Fig. 1: "N" Position — Neutral

Courtesy of Hyundai Motor Co.

OIL CIRCUIT DIAGRAMS
Hyundai KM175 Series (Cont.)

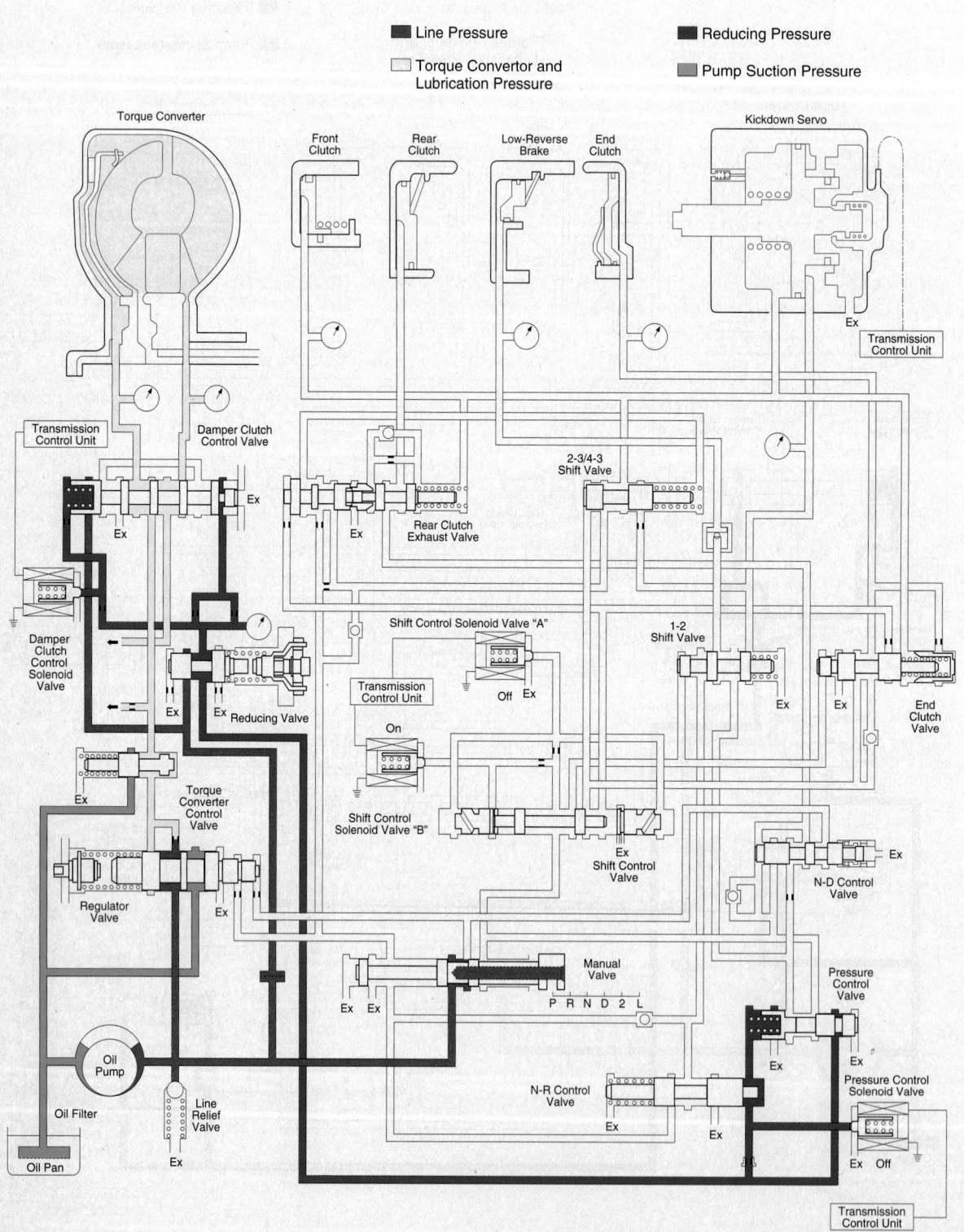

Fig. 2: "P" Position — Park

Courtesy of Hyundai Motor Co.

OIL CIRCUIT DIAGRAMS
Hyundai KM175 Series (Cont.)

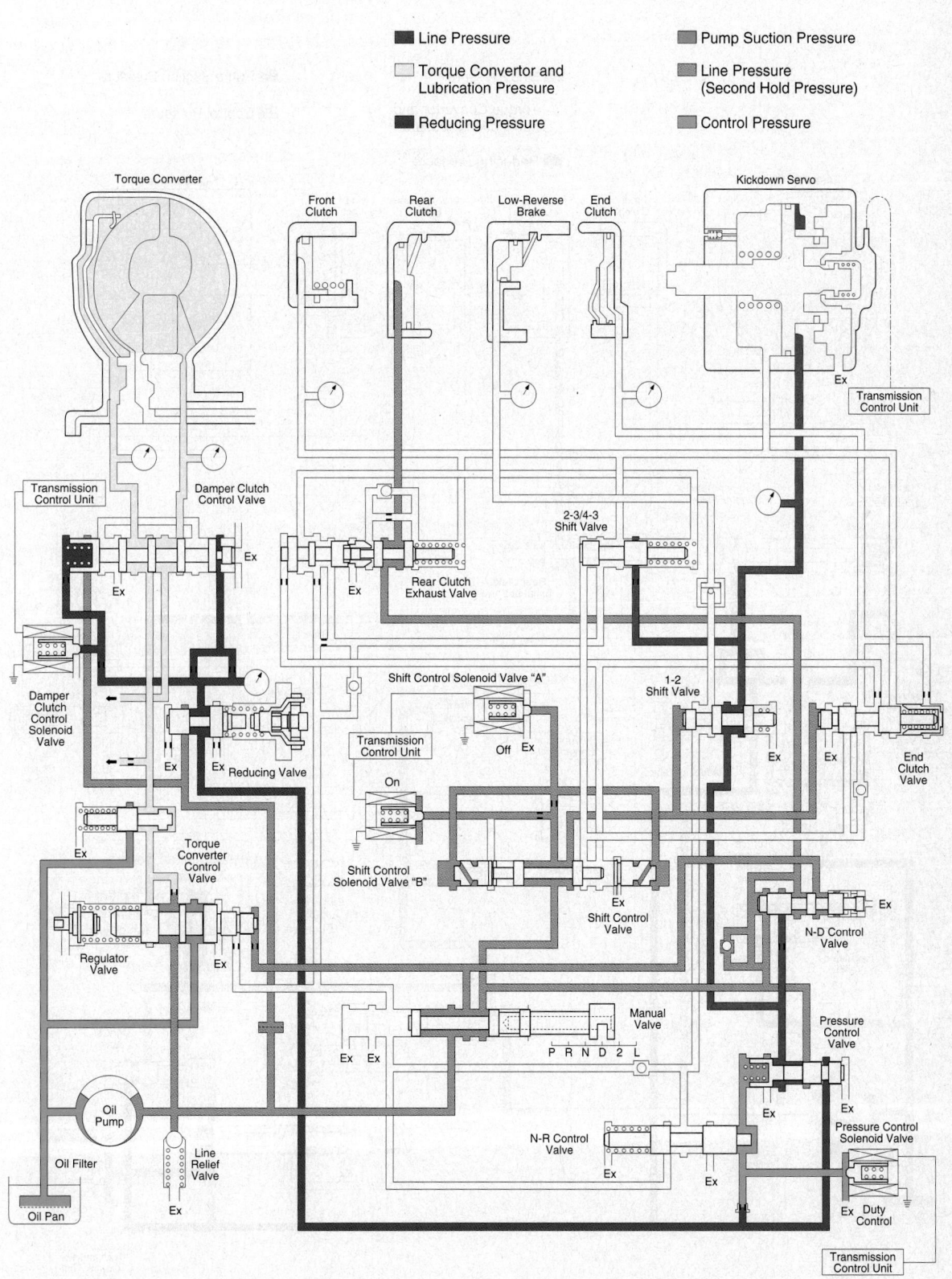

■ Line Pressure

■ Pump Suction Pressure

□ Torque Convertor and Lubrication Pressure

■ Line Pressure (Second Hold Pressure)

■ Reducing Pressure

■ Control Pressure

Fig. 3: "D" Position — Vehicle Stopped

Courtesy of Hyundai Motor Co.

OIL CIRCUIT DIAGRAMS
Hyundai KM175 Series (Cont.)

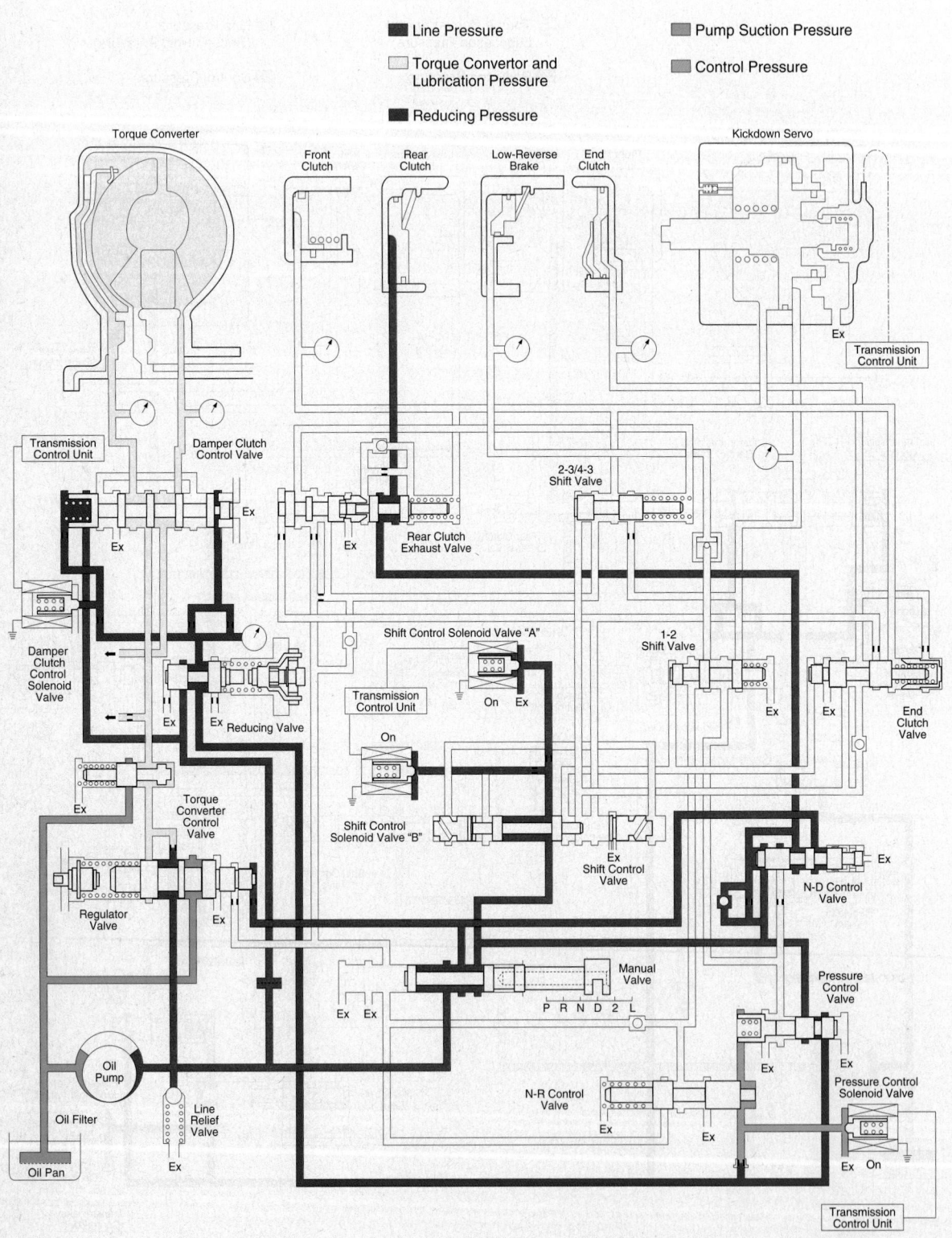

■ Line Pressure

□ Torque Convertor and Lubrication Pressure

■ Reducing Pressure

■ Pump Suction Pressure

■ Control Pressure

Fig. 4: "D" Position — 1st Gear

Courtesy of Hyundai Motor Co.

OIL CIRCUIT DIAGRAMS
Hyundai KM175 Series (Cont.)

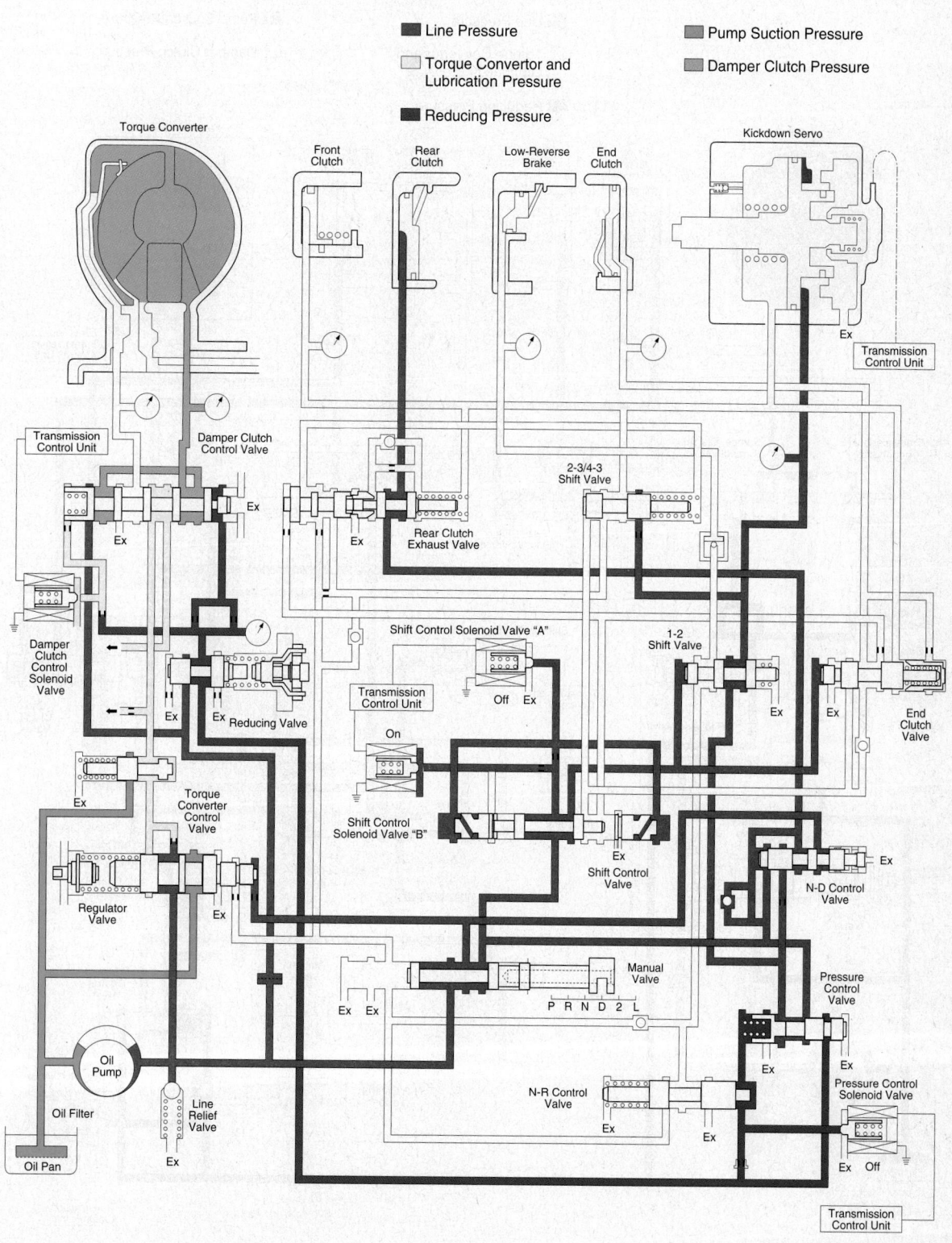

Fig. 5: "D" Position — 2nd Gear

Courtesy of Hyundai Motor Co.

OIL CIRCUIT DIAGRAMS
Hyundai KM175 Series (Cont.)

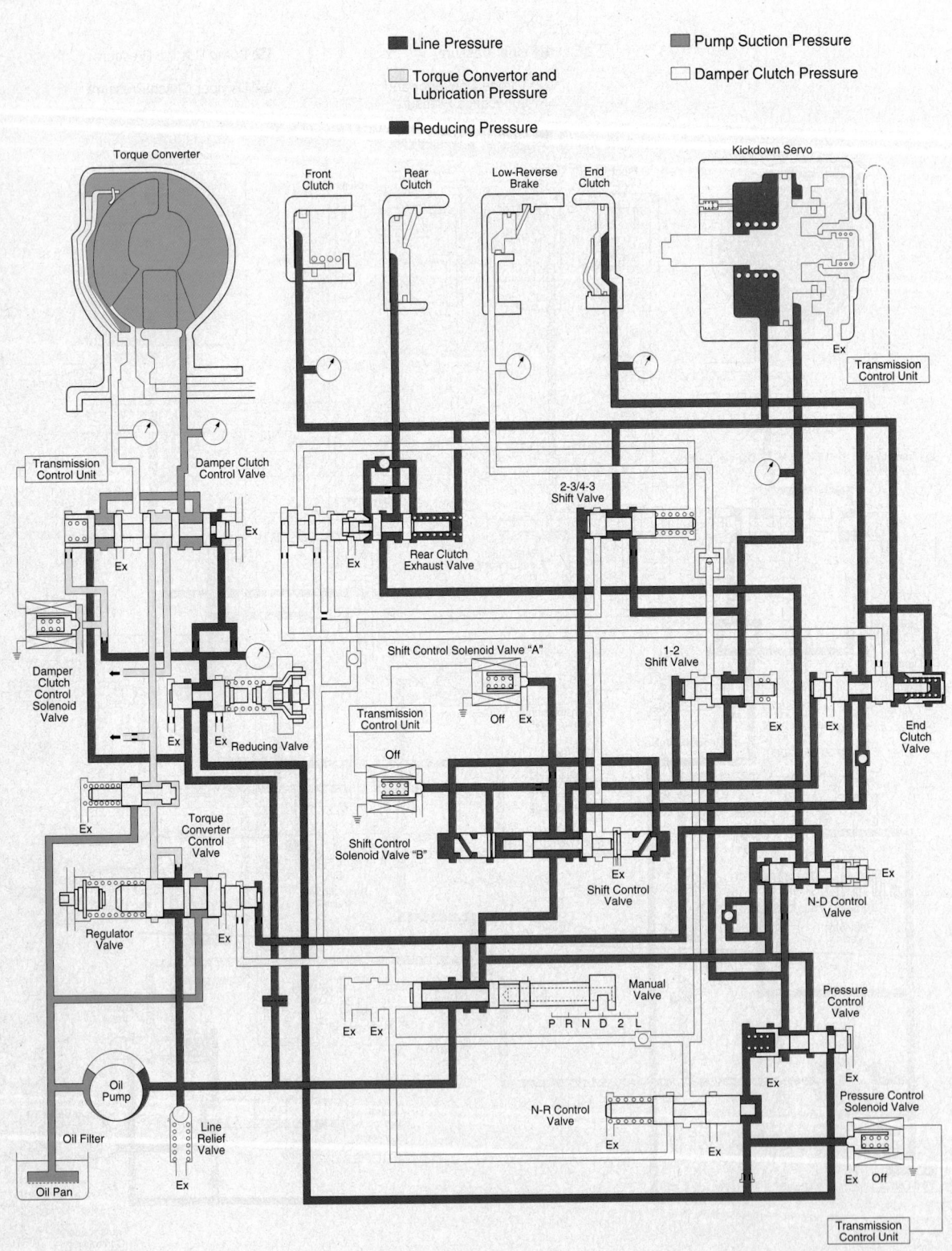

- ■ Line Pressure
- □ Torque Convertor and Lubrication Pressure
- ■ Reducing Pressure
- ■ Pump Suction Pressure
- □ Damper Clutch Pressure

Fig. 6: "D" Position — 3rd Gear

Courtesy of Hyundai Motor Co.

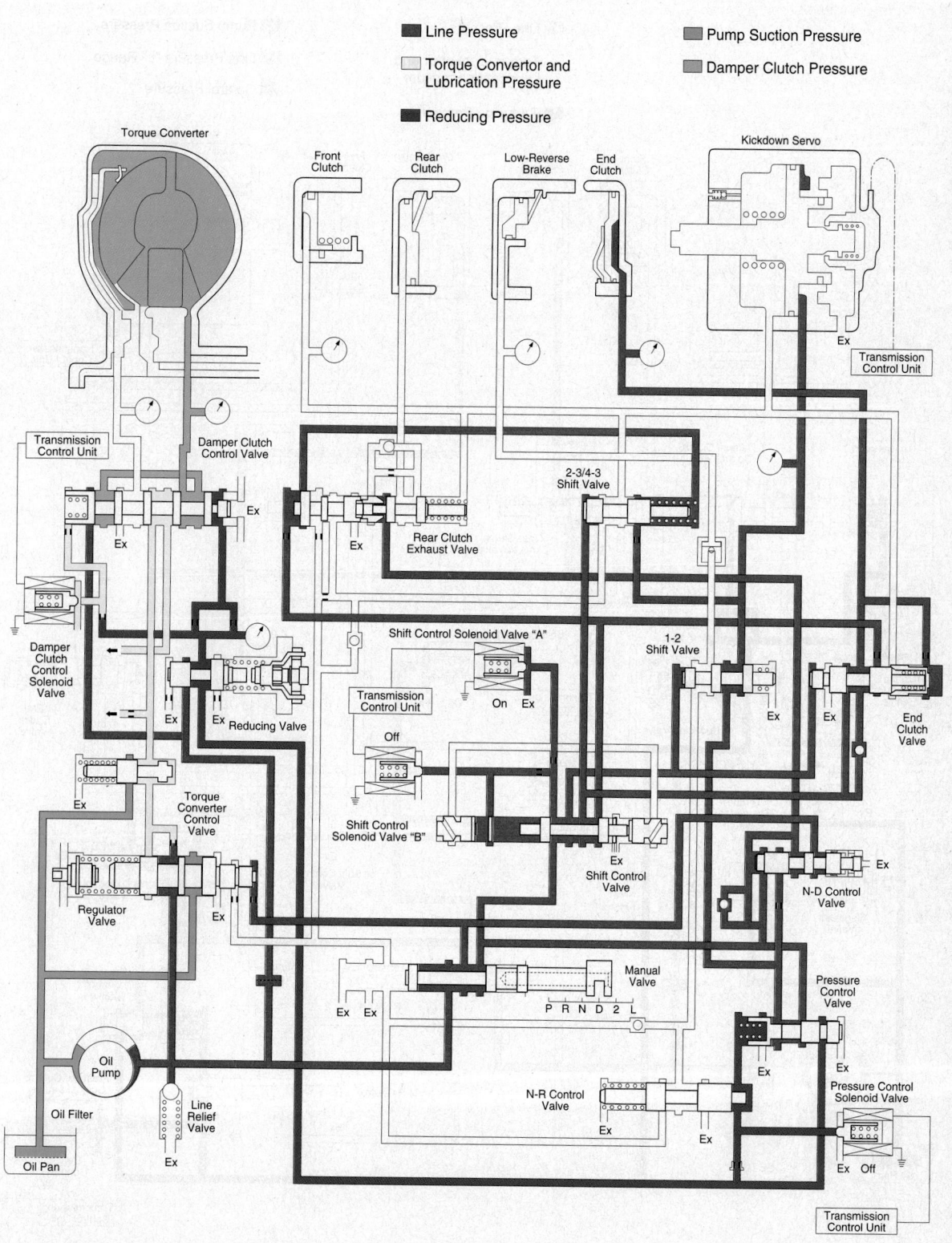

Fig. 7: "D" Position — 4th Gear (Lock-Up OFF)

Courtesy of Hyundai Motor Co.

OIL CIRCUIT DIAGRAMS
Hyundai KM175 Series (Cont.)

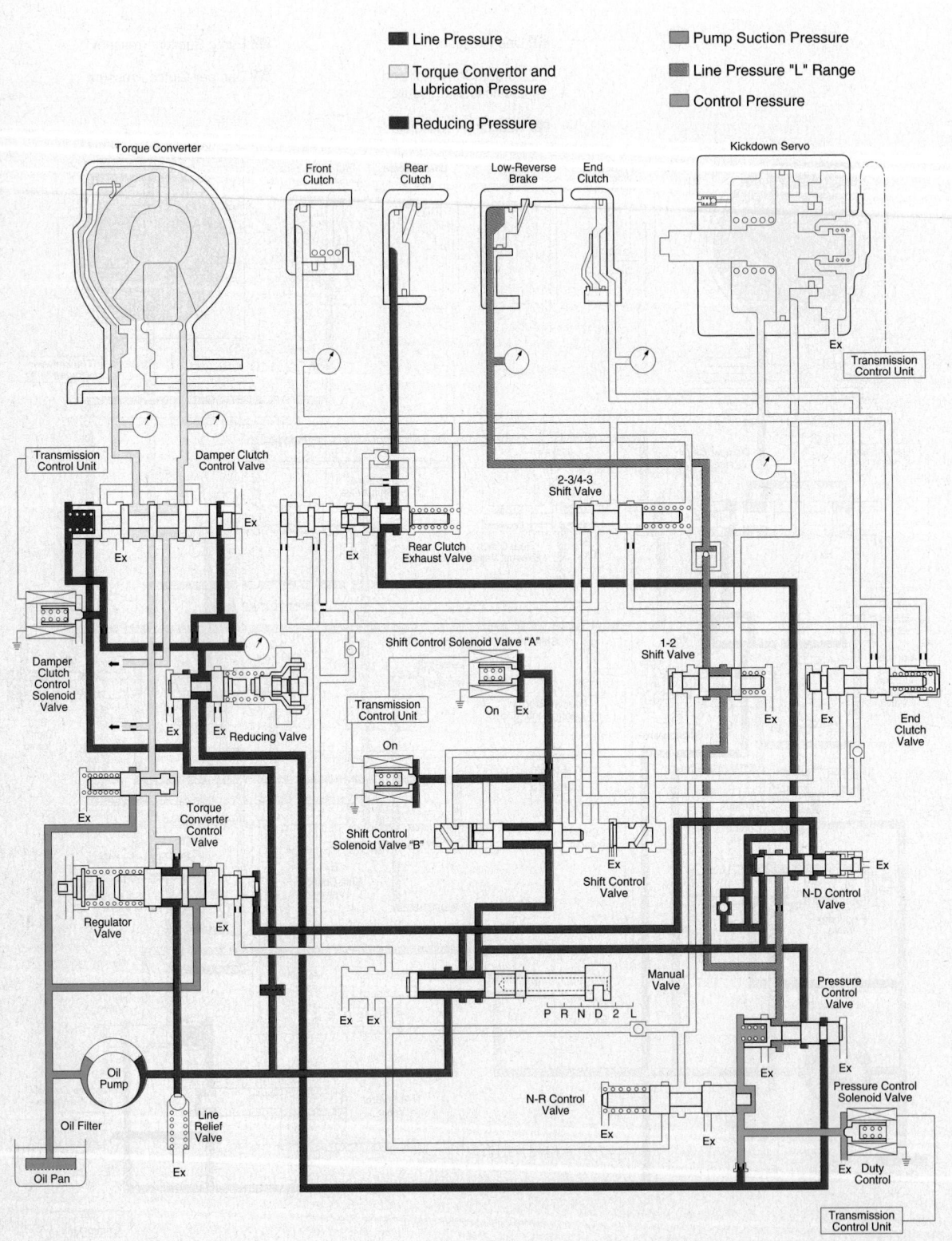

Fig. 8: "D" Position — 4th Gear (Lock-Up ON)

Courtesy of Hyundai Motor Co.

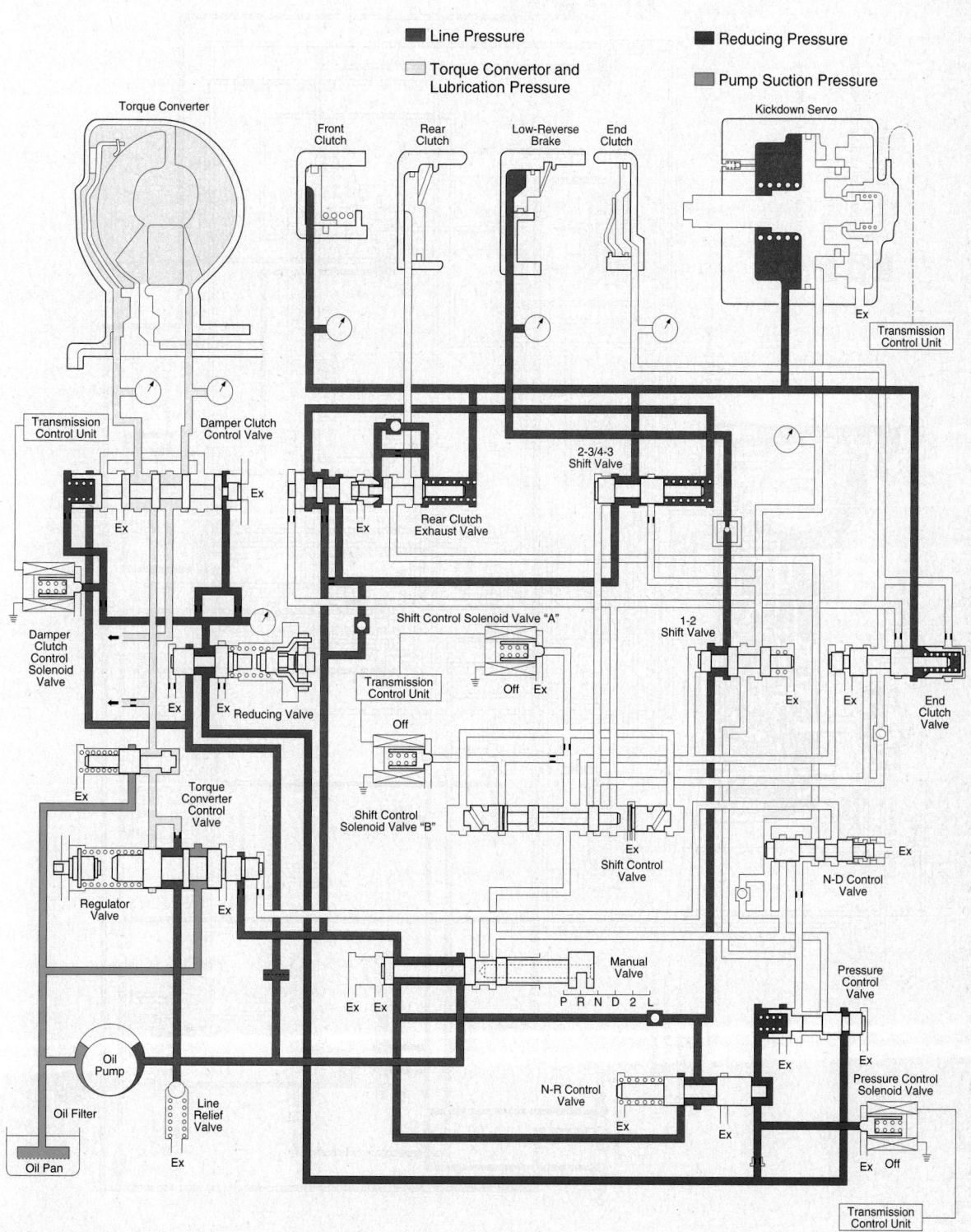

Fig. 9: "R" Position — Reverse

Courtesy of Hyundai Motor Co.

OIL CIRCUIT DIAGRAMS
Mazda FA4A-EL

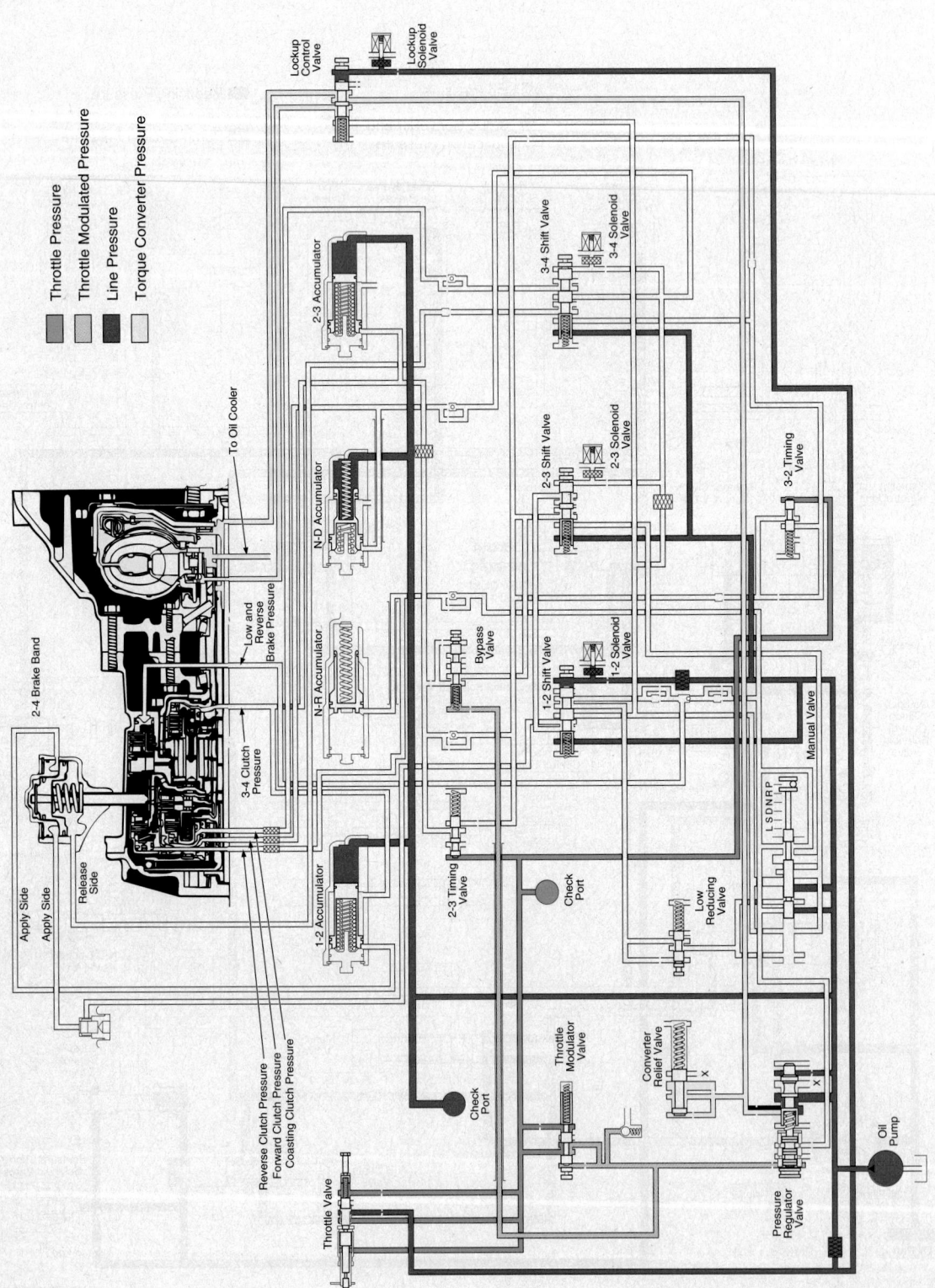

OIL CIRCUIT DIAGRAMS
Mazda FA4A-EL (Cont.)

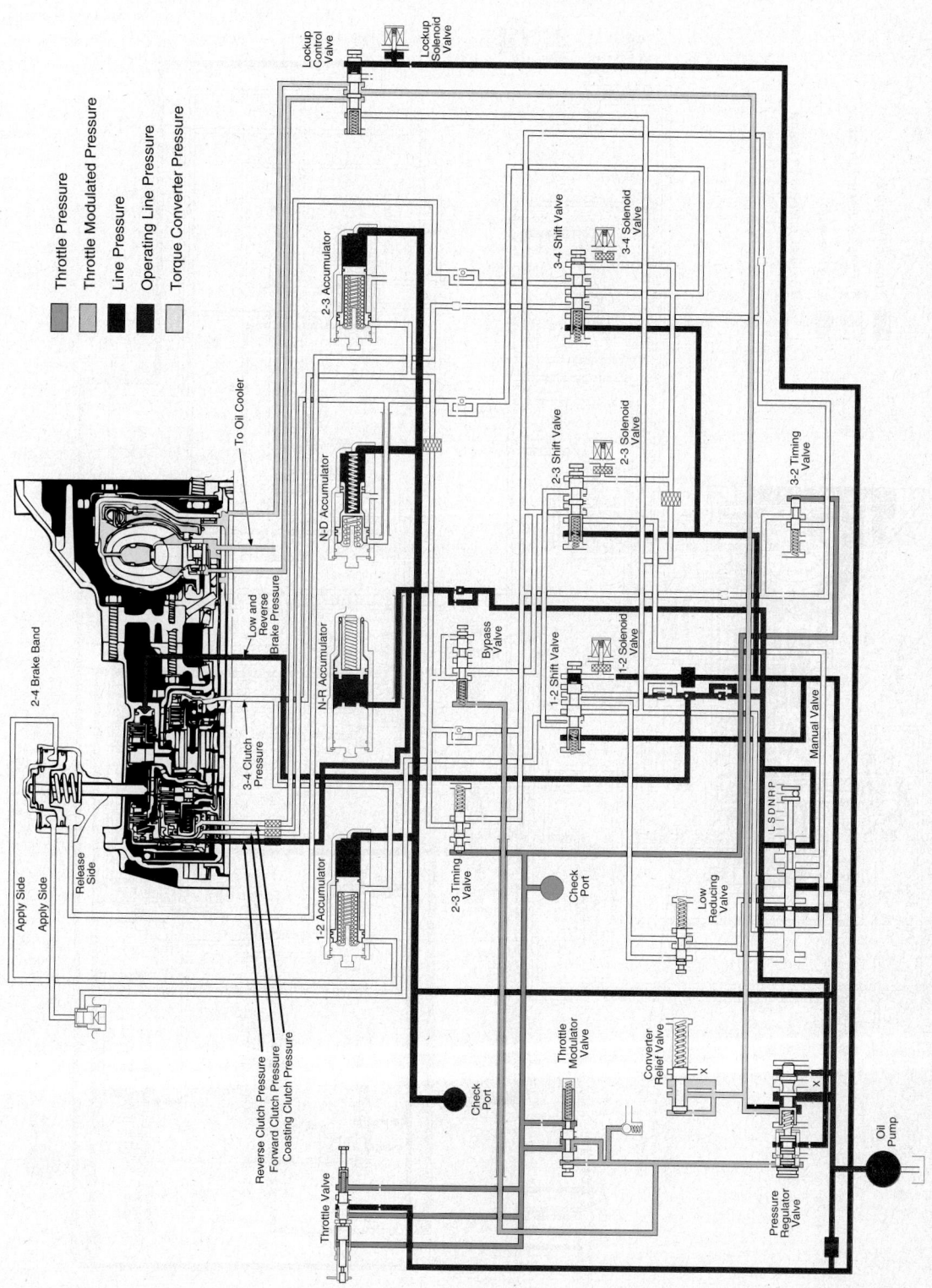

Throttle Pressure
Throttle Modulated Pressure
Line Pressure
Operating Line Pressure
Torque Converter Pressure

Fig. 2: "R" Position — Reverse

Courtesy of Mazda Motors Corp.

OIL CIRCUIT DIAGRAMS
Mazda FA4A-EL (Cont.)

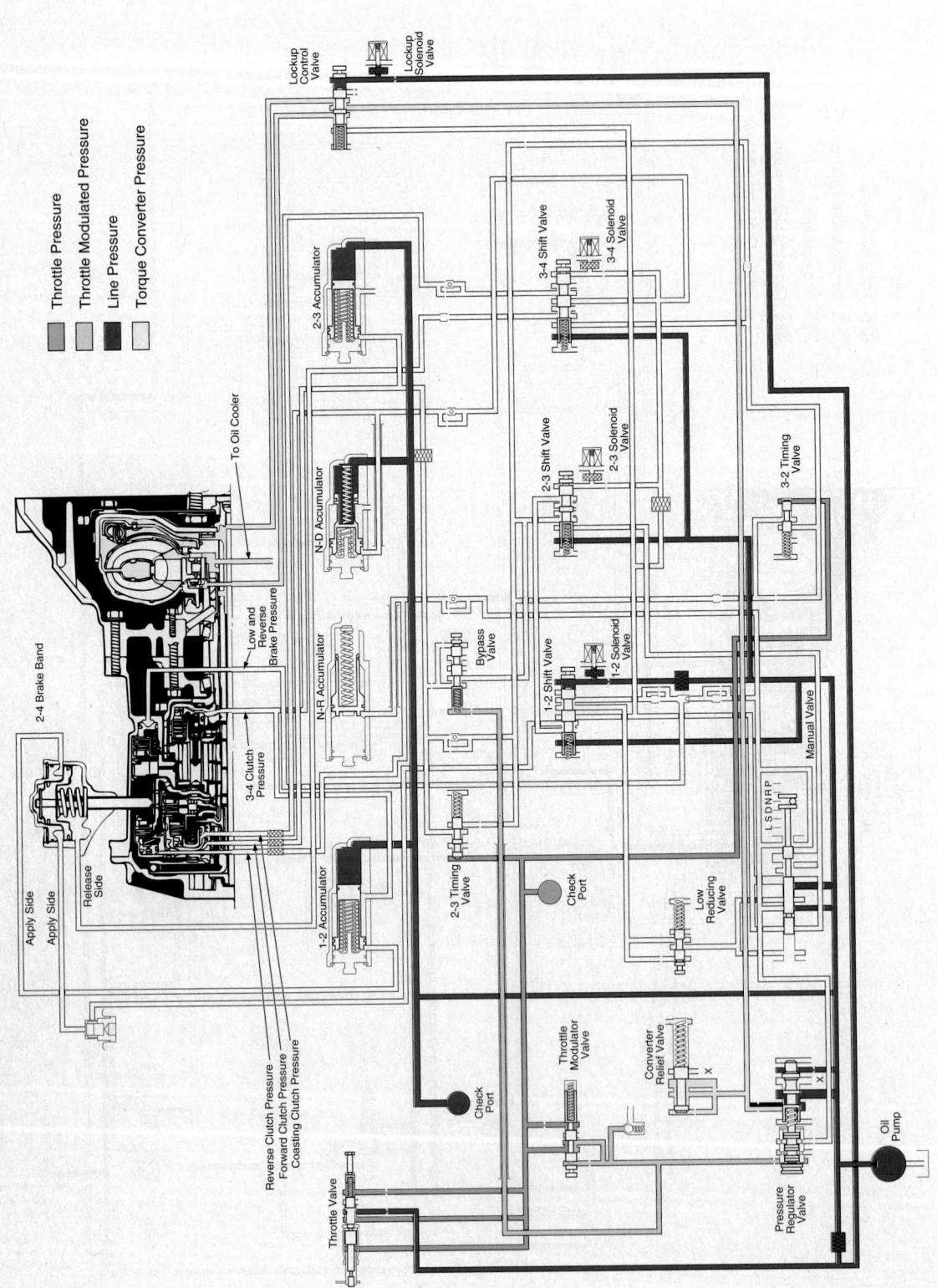

Fig. 3: "N" Position — Neutral (Speed Less Than 2.5 MPH)

Courtesy of Mazda Motors Corp.

OIL CIRCUIT DIAGRAMS
Mazda FA4A-EL (Cont.)

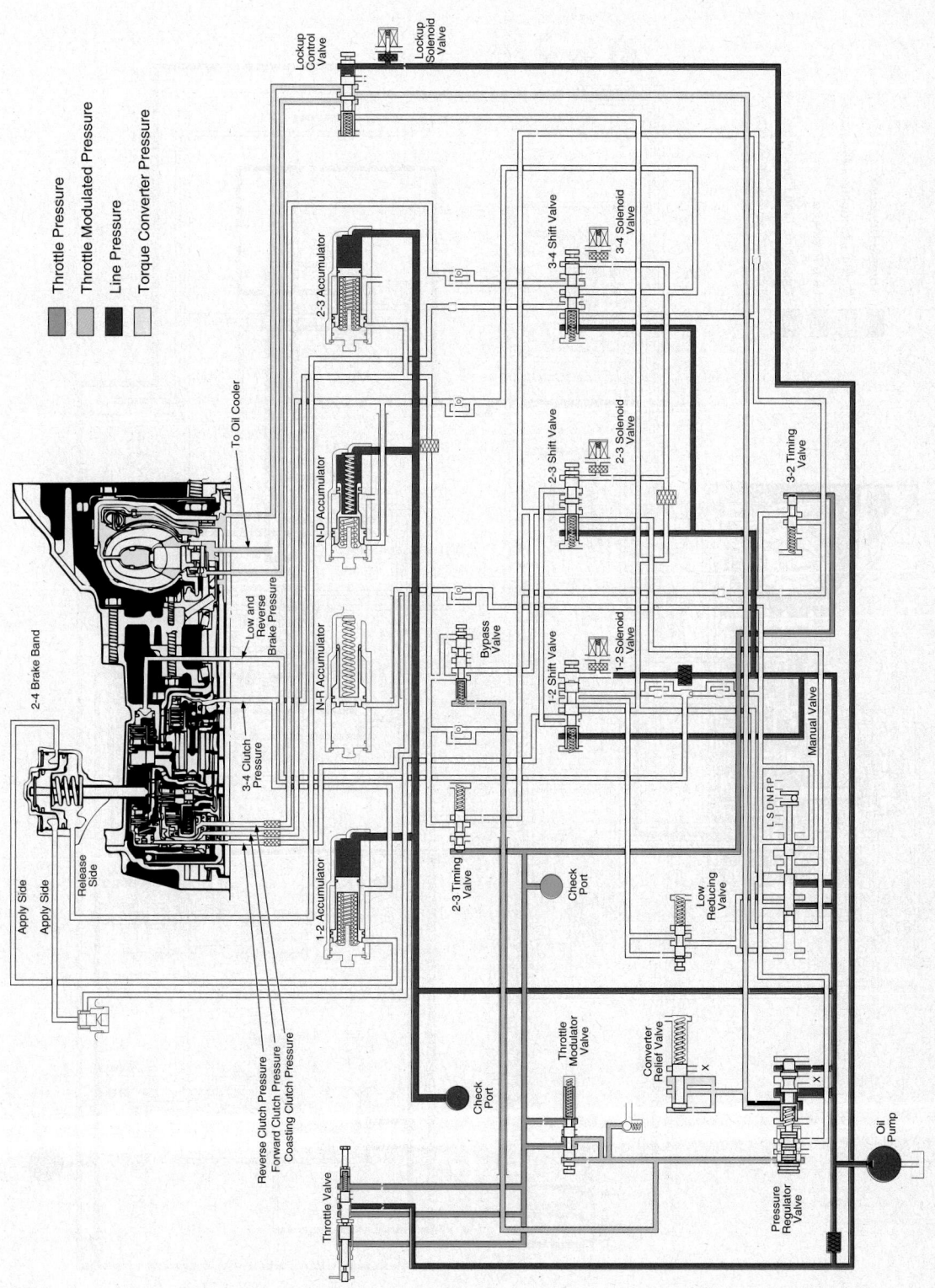

Fig. 4: "N" Position — Neutral (Speed Greater Than 3 MPH)

Courtesy of Mazda Motors Corp.

OIL CIRCUIT DIAGRAMS
Mazda FA4A-EL (Cont.)

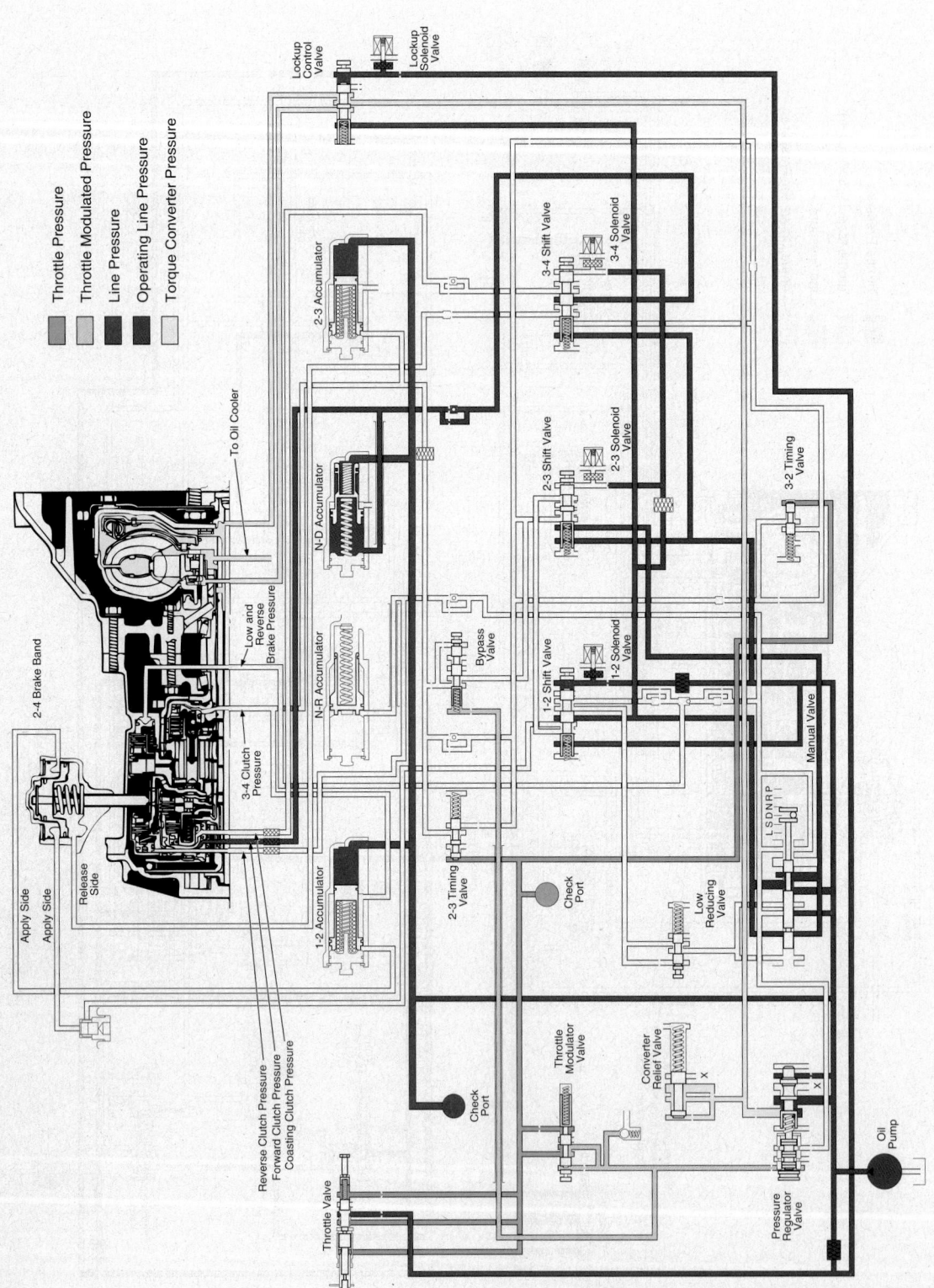

Fig. 5: "D" Position — 1st Gear (Hold)

Courtesy of Mazda Motors Corp.

OIL CIRCUIT DIAGRAMS
Mazda FA4A-EL (Cont.)

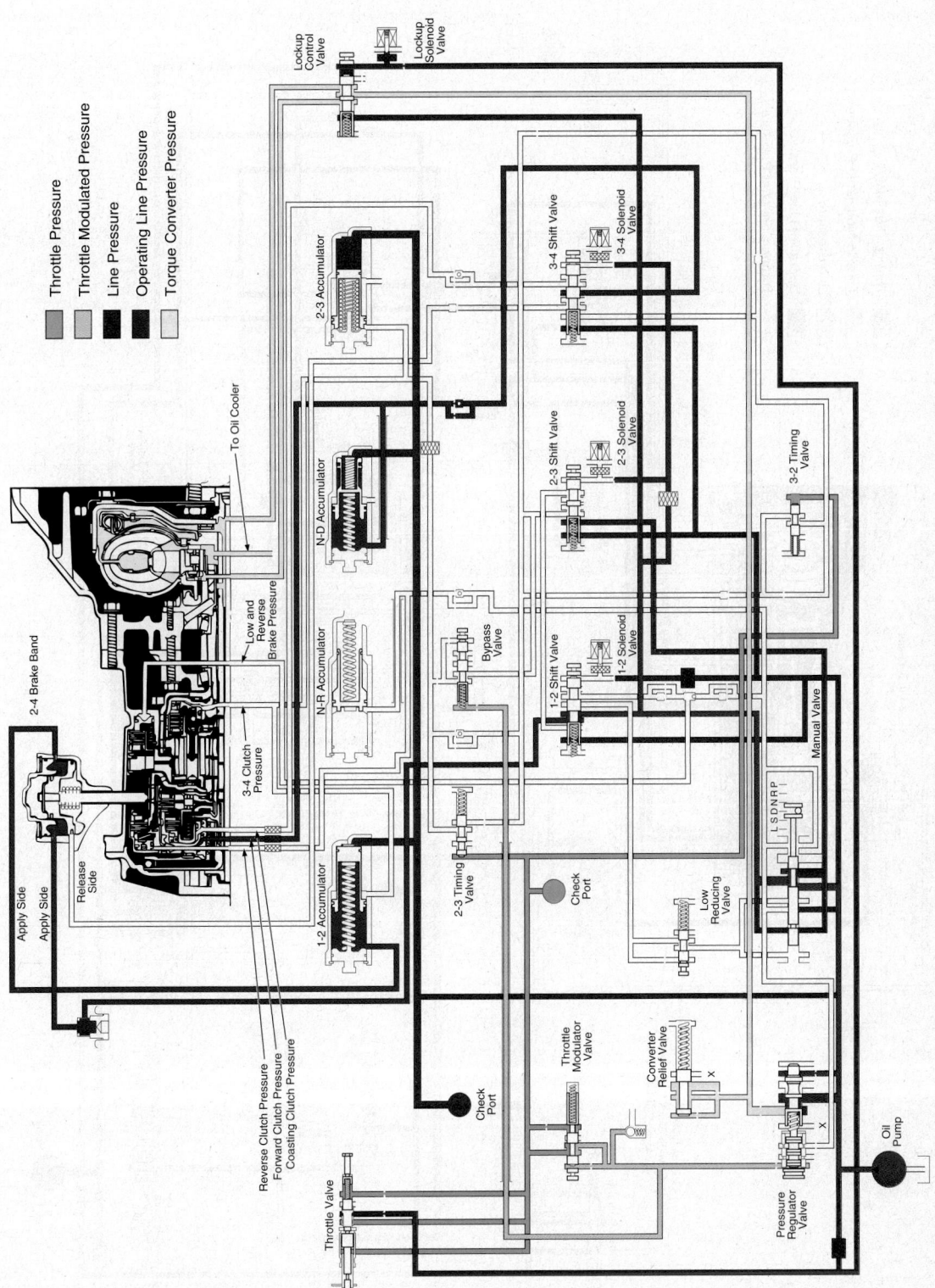

Fig. 6: "D" Position — 2nd Gear (Hold)

Courtesy of Mazda Motors Corp.

OIL CIRCUIT DIAGRAMS
Mazda FA4A-EL (Cont.)

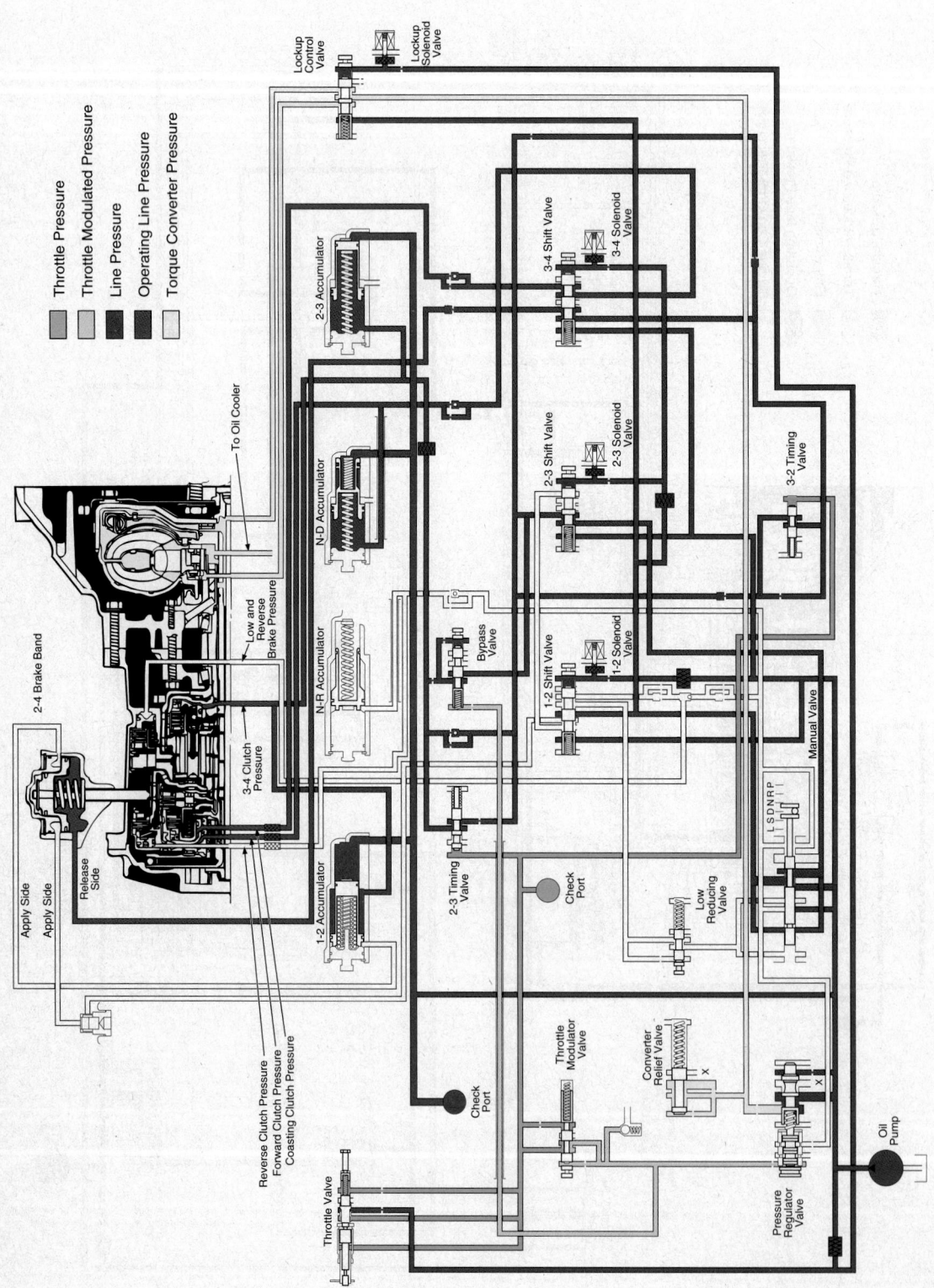

Fig. 7: "D" Position — 3rd Gear (With Speed Less Than 3.1 MPH)

Courtesy of Mazda Motors Corp.

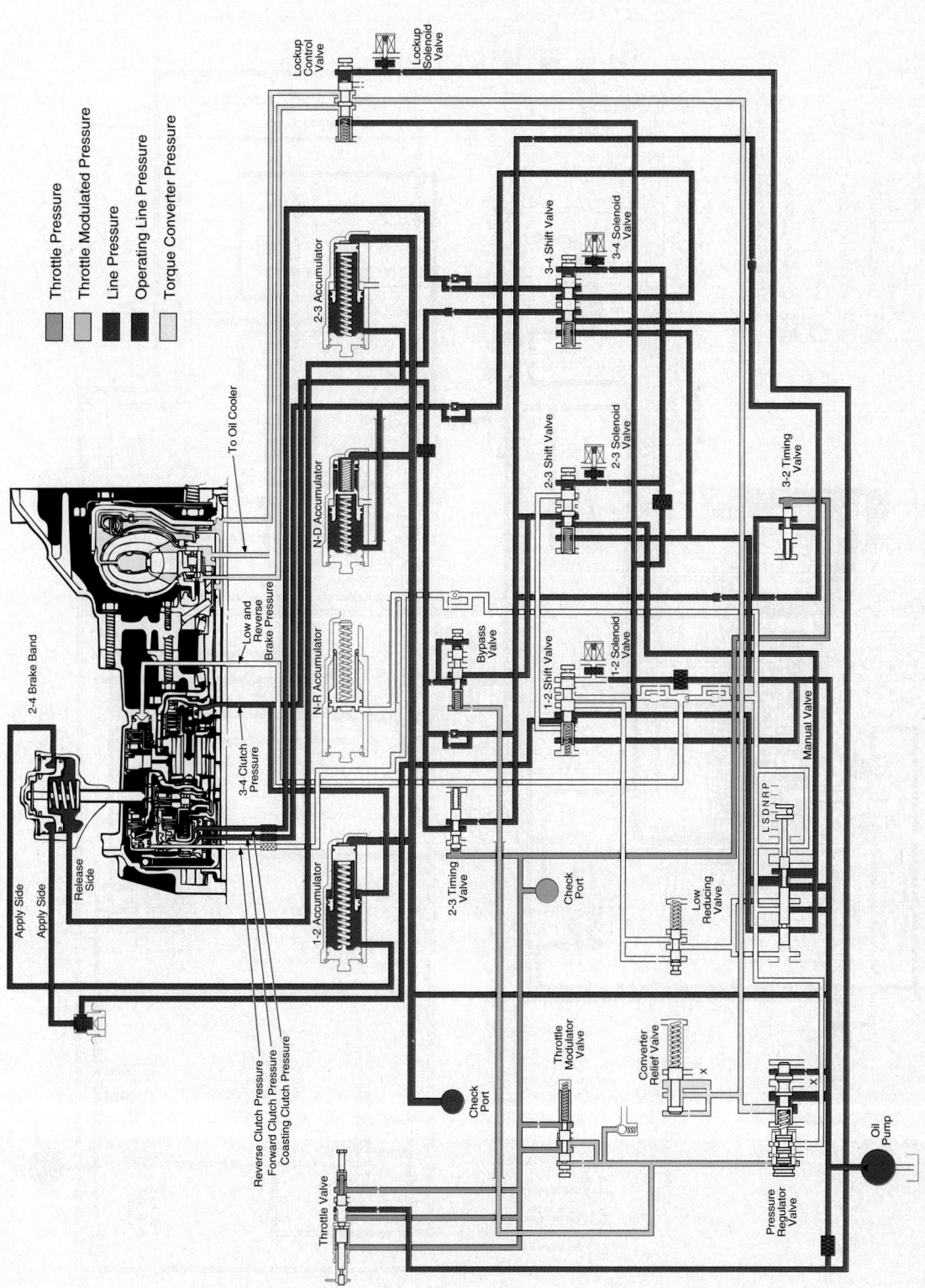

OIL CIRCUIT DIAGRAMS
Mazda FA4A-EL (Cont.)

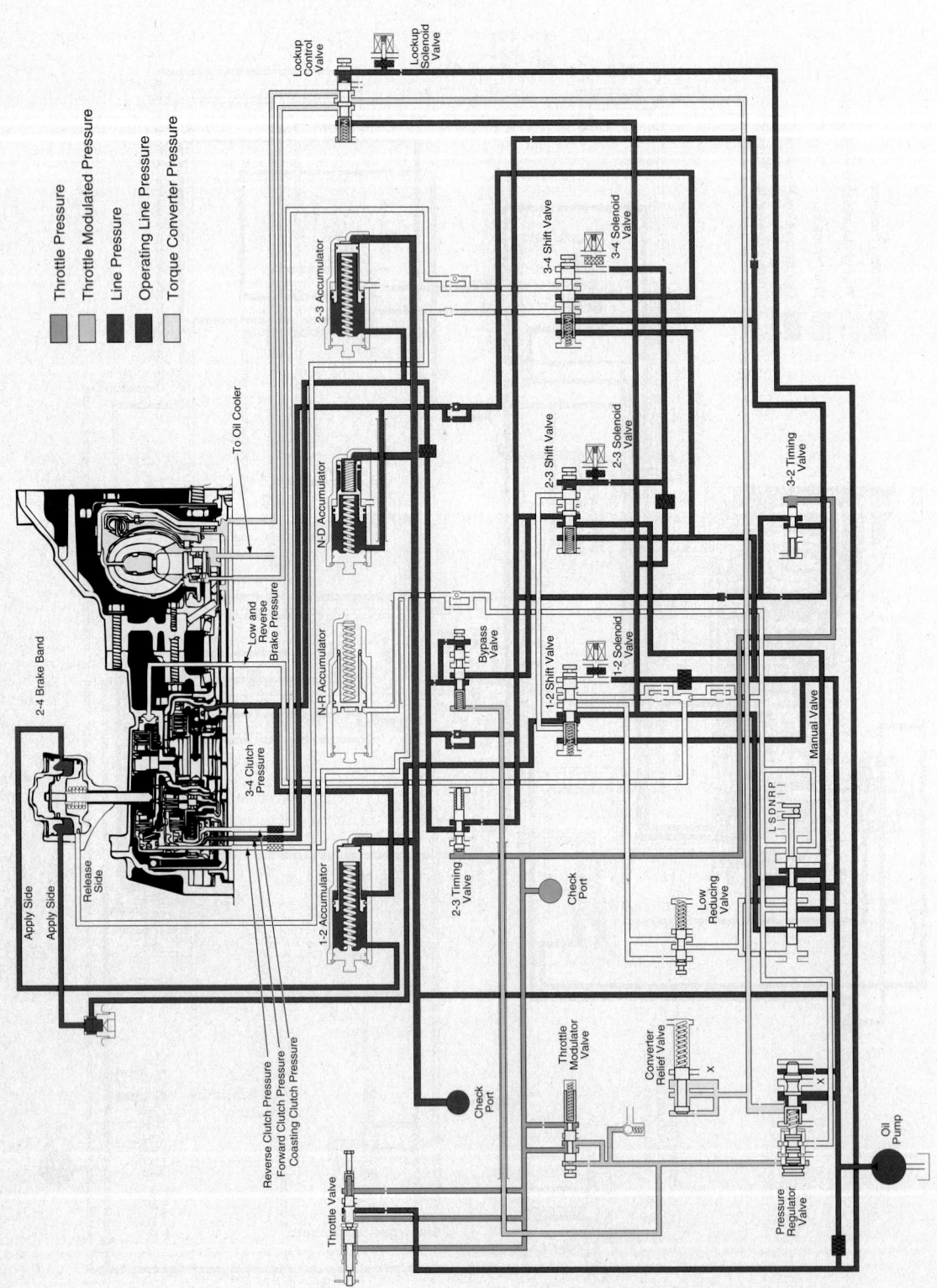

Fig. 9: "D" Position — 4th Gear (Lock-Up OFF)   Courtesy of Mazda Motors Corp.

OIL CIRCUIT DIAGRAMS
Mazda FA4A-EL (Cont.)

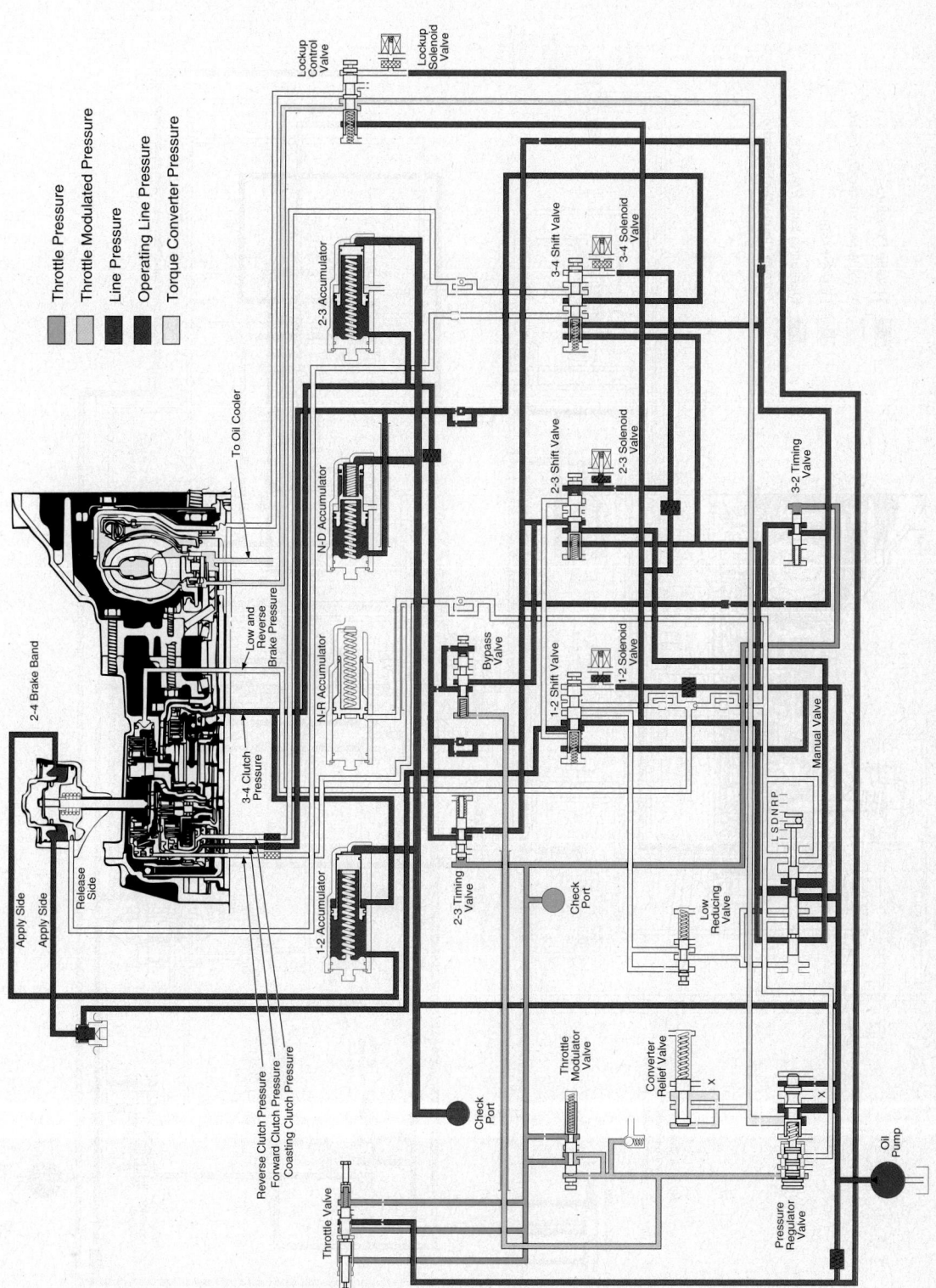

Fig. 10: "D" Position — 4th Gear (Lock-Up ON)

Courtesy of Mazda Motors Corp.

OIL CIRCUIT DIAGRAMS
Mazda FA4A-EL (Cont.)

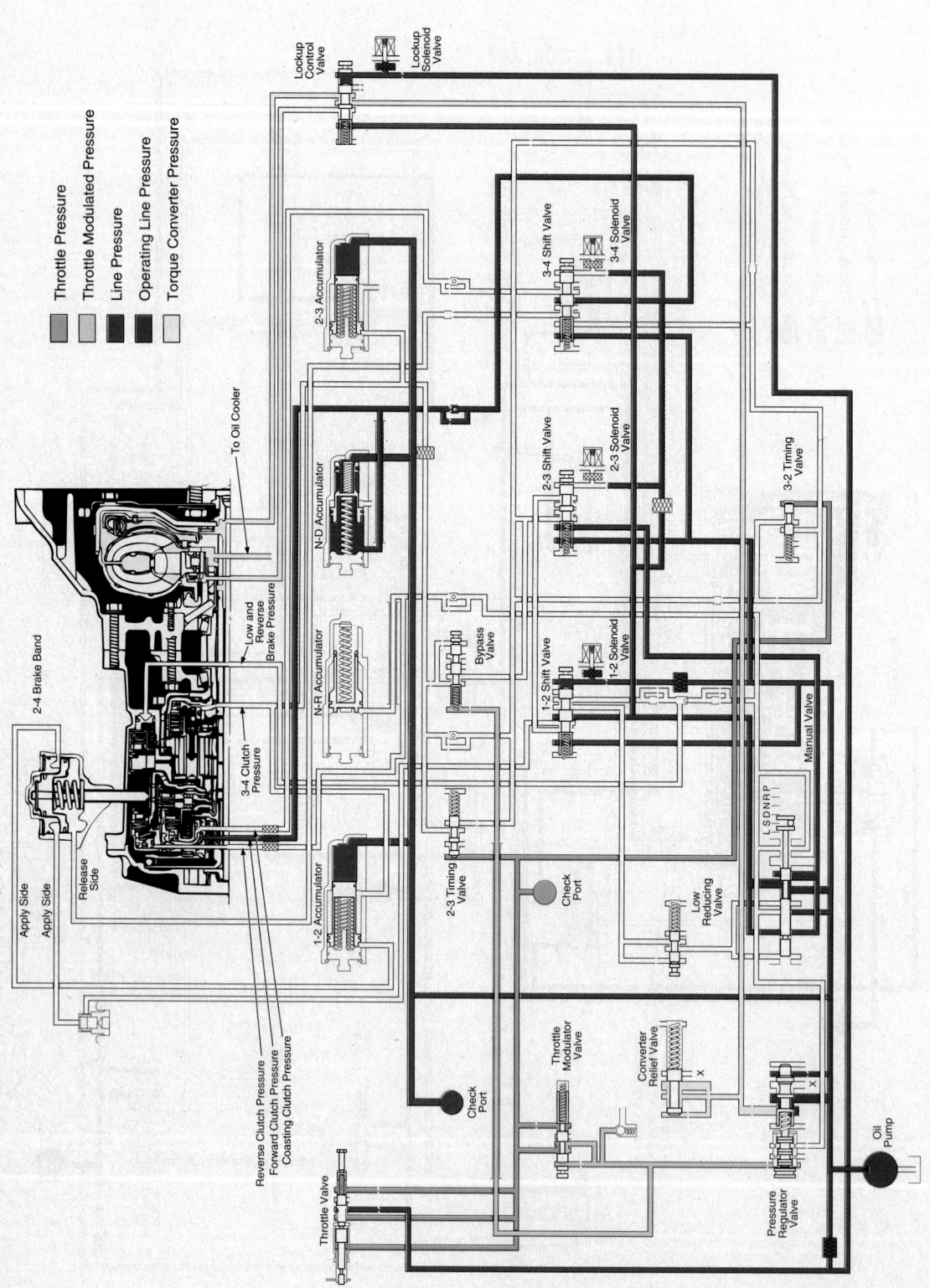

Fig. 11: "S" Position — 1st Gear

Courtesy of Mazda Motors Corp.

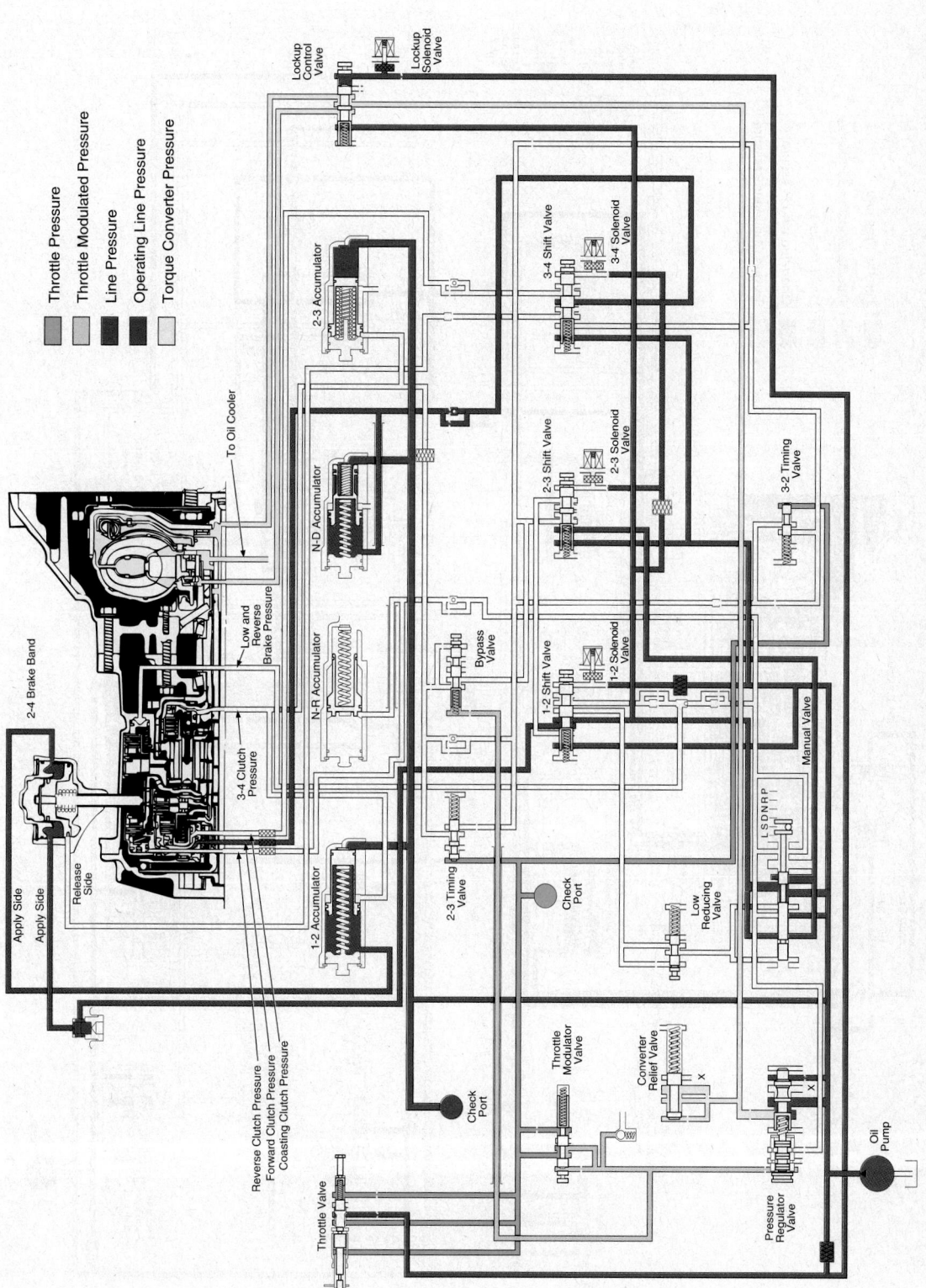

Fig. 12: "S" Position — 2nd Gear

Courtesy of Mazda Motors Corp.

OIL CIRCUIT DIAGRAMS
Mazda FA4A-EL (Cont.)

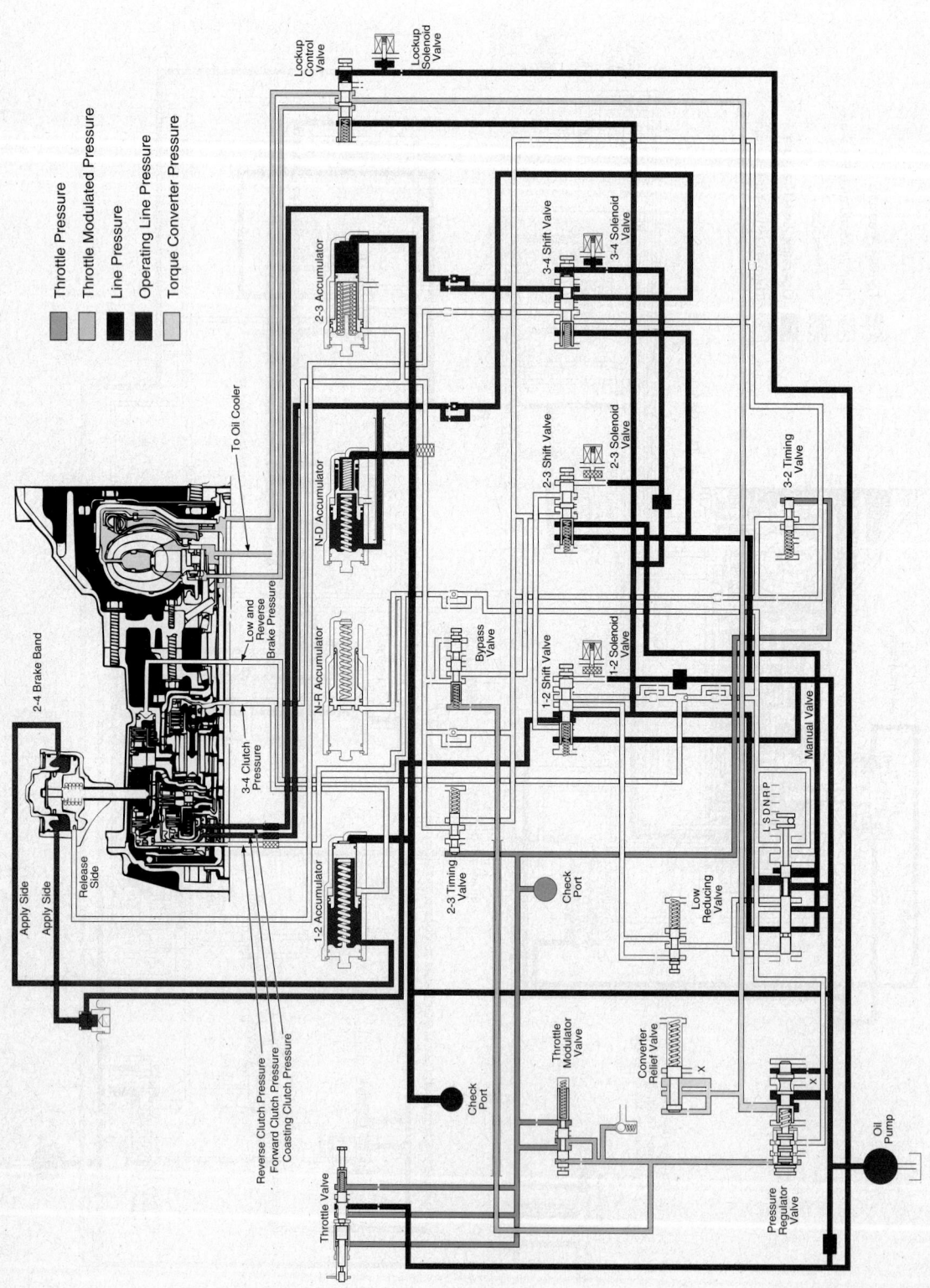

Fig. 13: "S" Position — 2nd Gear (Hold)

Courtesy of Mazda Motors Corp.

OIL CIRCUIT DIAGRAMS
Mazda FA4A-EL (Cont.)

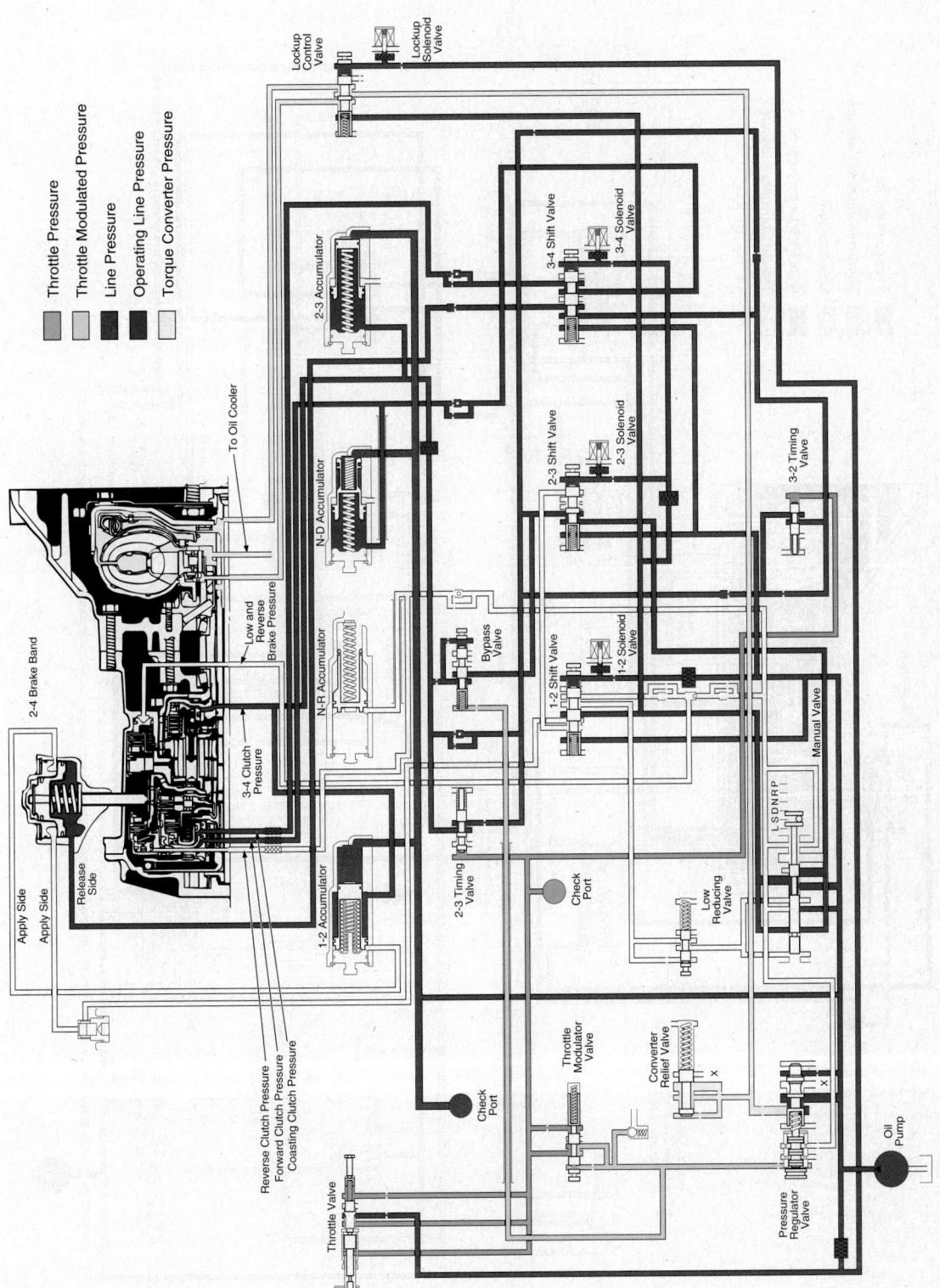

Throttle Pressure
Throttle Modulated Pressure
Line Pressure
Operating Line Pressure
Torque Converter Pressure

Lockup Control Valve
Lockup Solenoid Valve

3-4 Shift Valve
3-4 Solenoid Valve

2-3 Accumulator

2-3 Shift Valve
2-3 Solenoid Valve

3-2 Timing Valve

To Oil Cooler

N-D Accumulator

Bypass Valve

1-2 Shift Valve
1-2 Solenoid Valve

3-2 Timing Valve

Low and Reverse Brake Pressure

N-R Accumulator

Manual Valve

2-4 Brake Band

3-4 Clutch Pressure

1-2 Accumulator

2-3 Timing Valve

Check Port

L.S.D.N.R.P

Apply Side
Apply Side
Release Side

Reverse Clutch Pressure
Forward Clutch Pressure
Coasting Clutch Pressure

Check Port

Throttle Valve

Throttle Modulator Valve

Converter Relief Valve

Low Reducing Valve

Pressure Regulator Valve

Oil Pump

Fig. 14: "S" Position — 3rd Gear (Hold With Speed Less Than 3.1 MPH)

Courtesy of Mazda Motors Corp.

OIL CIRCUIT DIAGRAMS
Mazda FA4A-EL (Cont.)

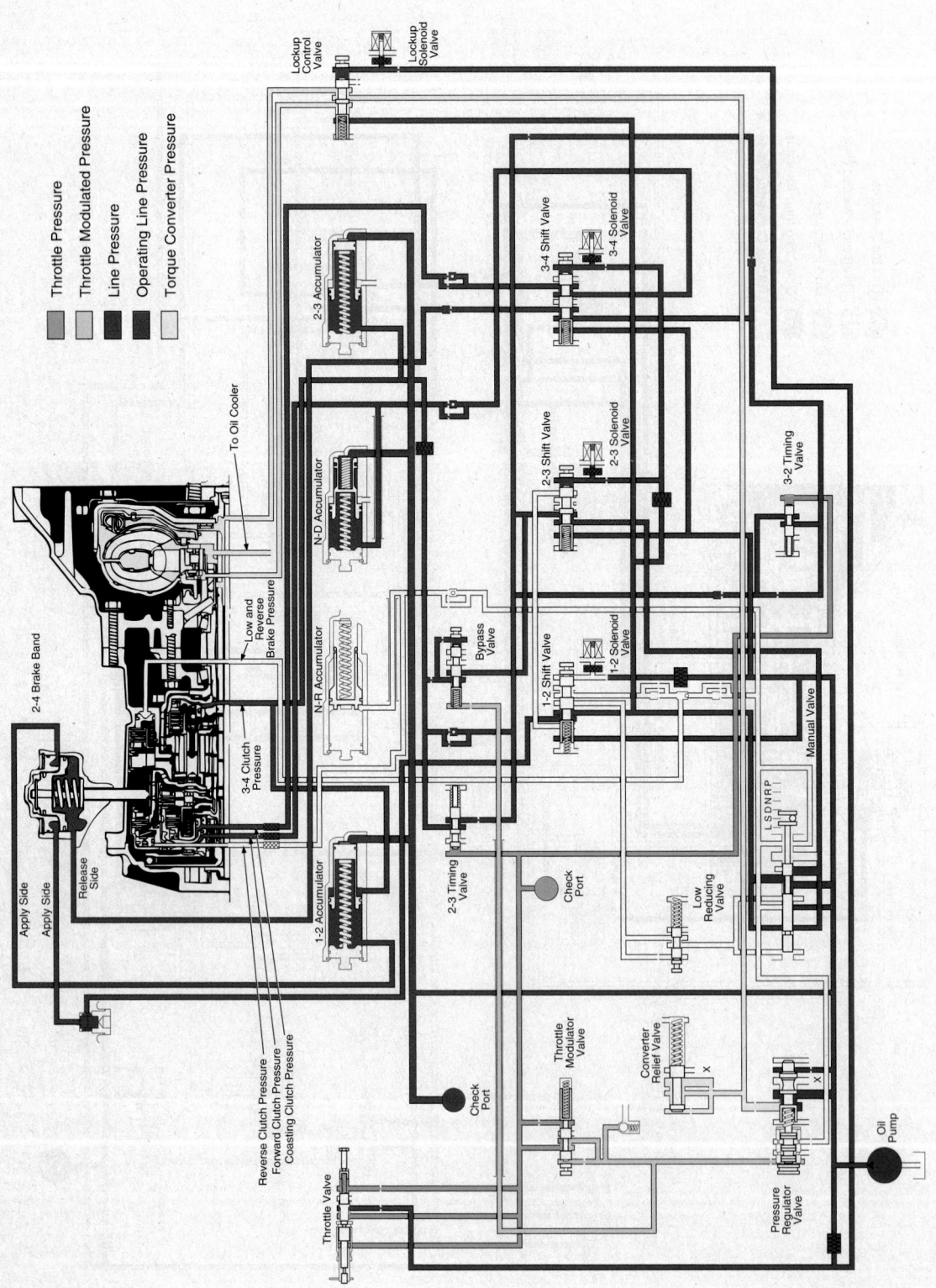

Fig. 15: "S" Position — 3rd Gear (Hold With Speed Above 3.1 MPH)

Courtesy of Mazda Motors Corp.

OIL CIRCUIT DIAGRAMS
Mazda FA4A-EL (Cont.)

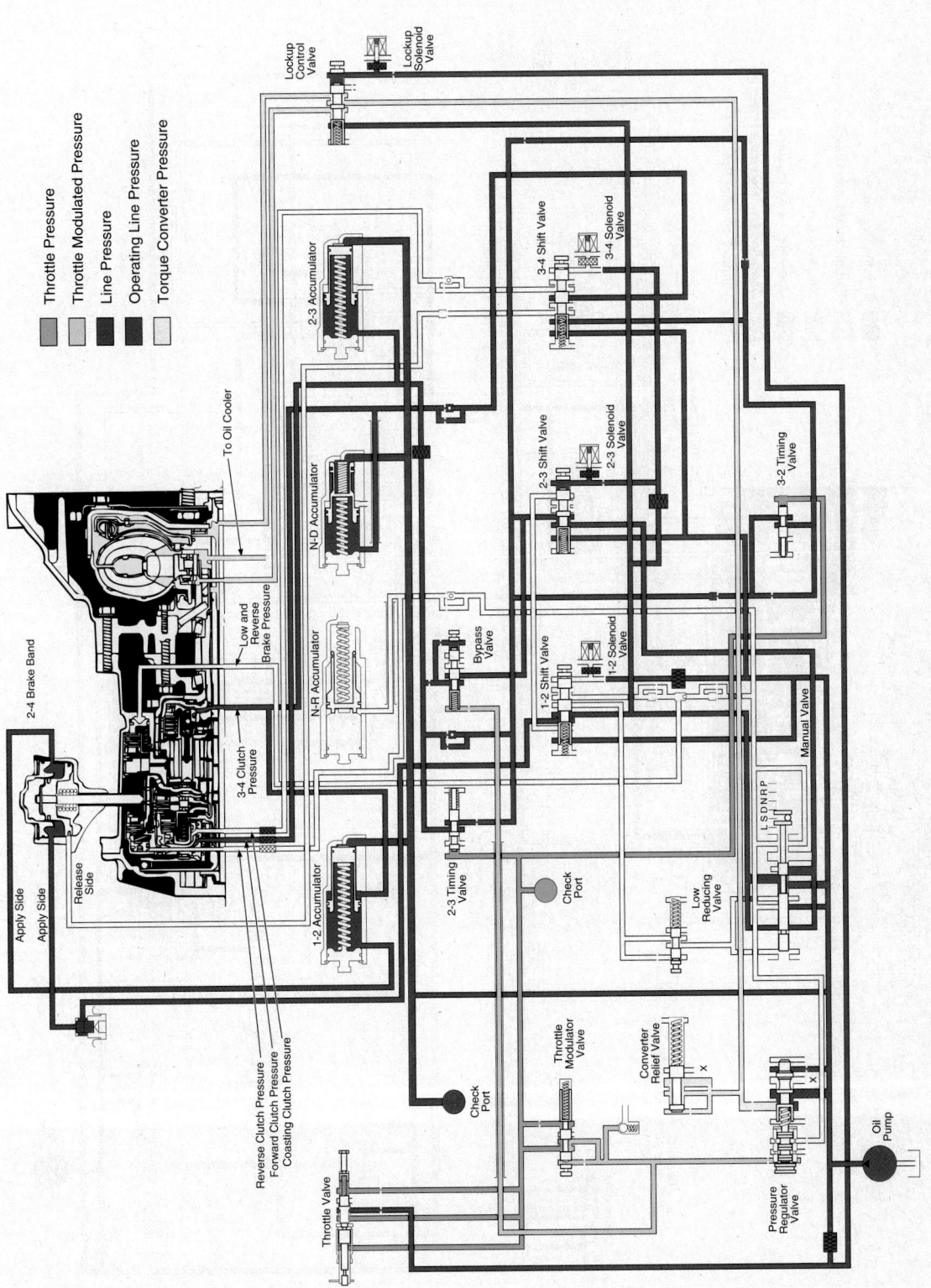

Fig. 16: "S" Position — 4th Gear

Courtesy of Mazda Motors Corp.

OIL CIRCUIT DIAGRAMS
Mazda FA4A-EL (Cont.)

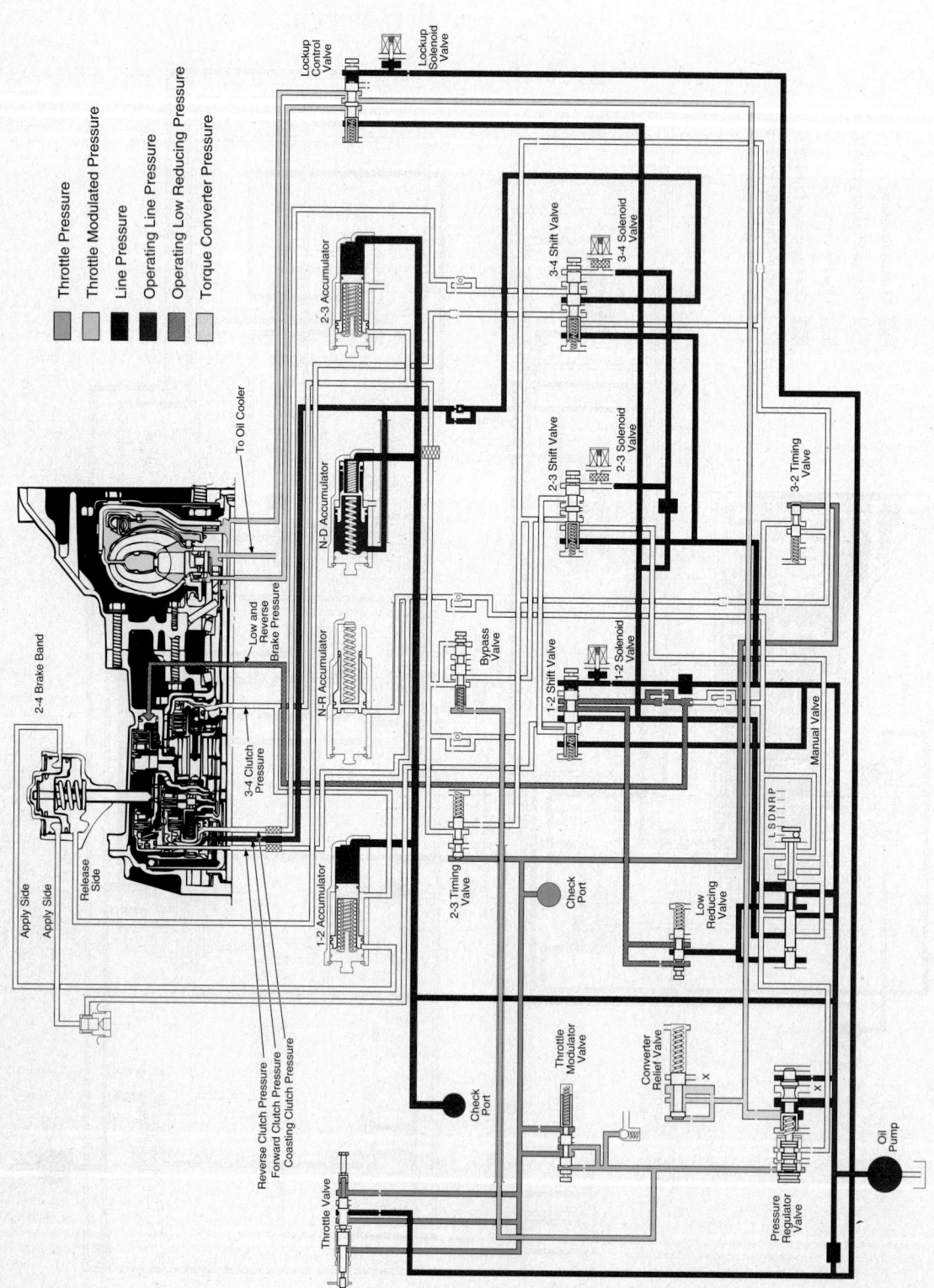

Courtesy of Mazda Motors Corp.

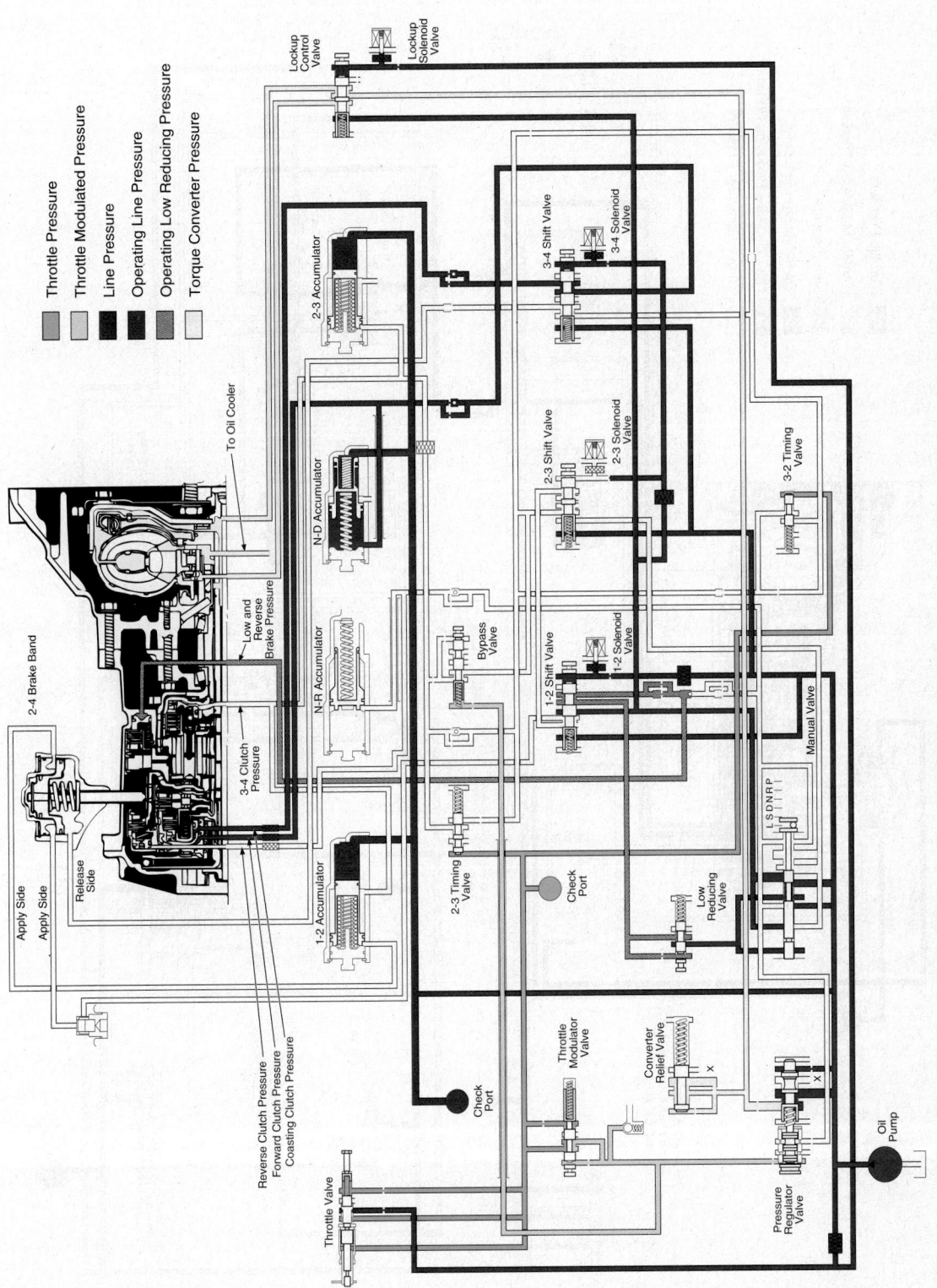

Fig. 18: "L" Position — 1st Gear (Hold)

Courtesy of Mazda Motors Corp.

OIL CIRCUIT DIAGRAMS
Mazda FA4A-EL (Cont.)

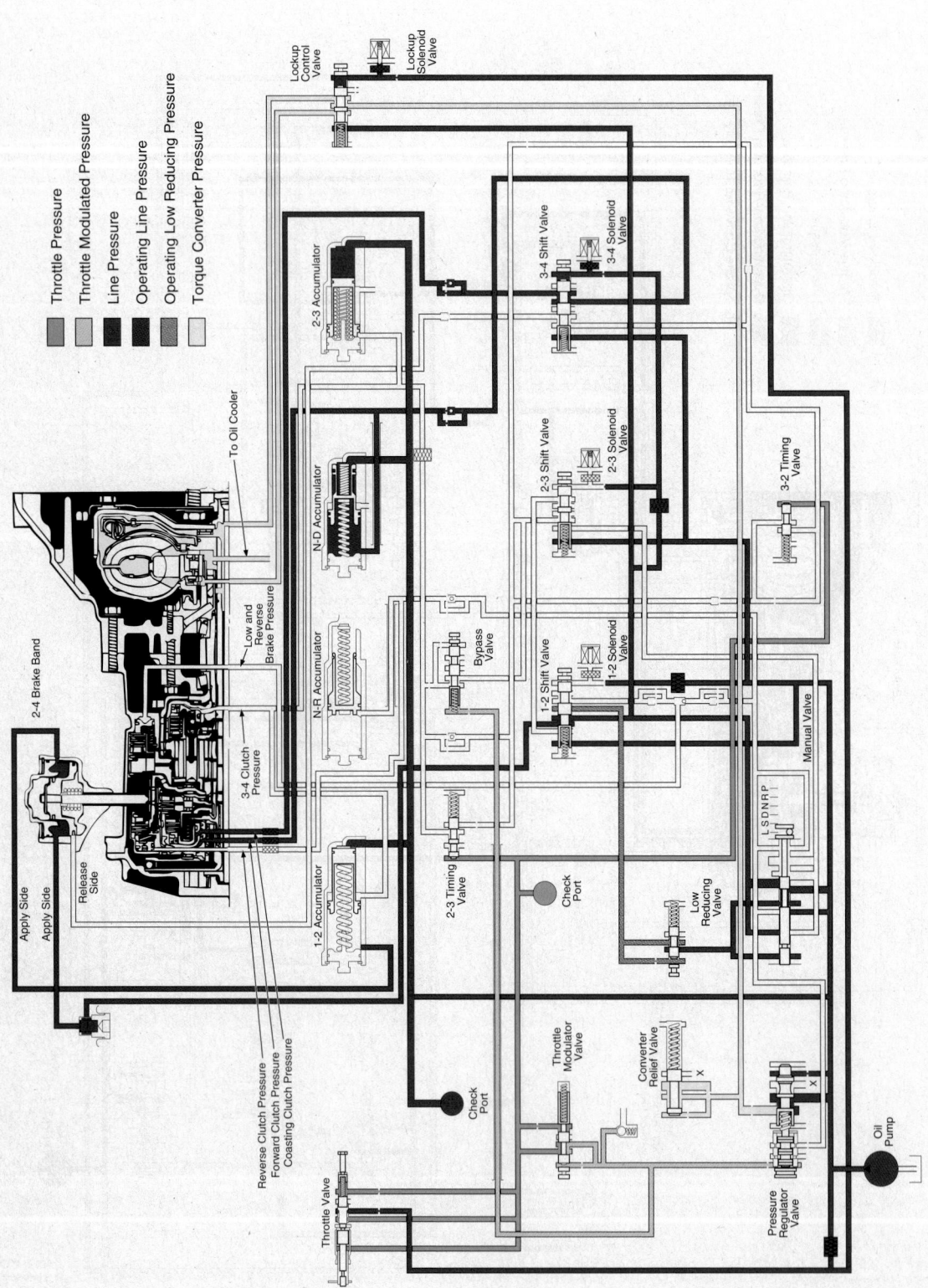

Fig. 19: "L" Position — 2nd Gear (With Speed Less Than 68 MPH)

Courtesy of Mazda Motors Corp.

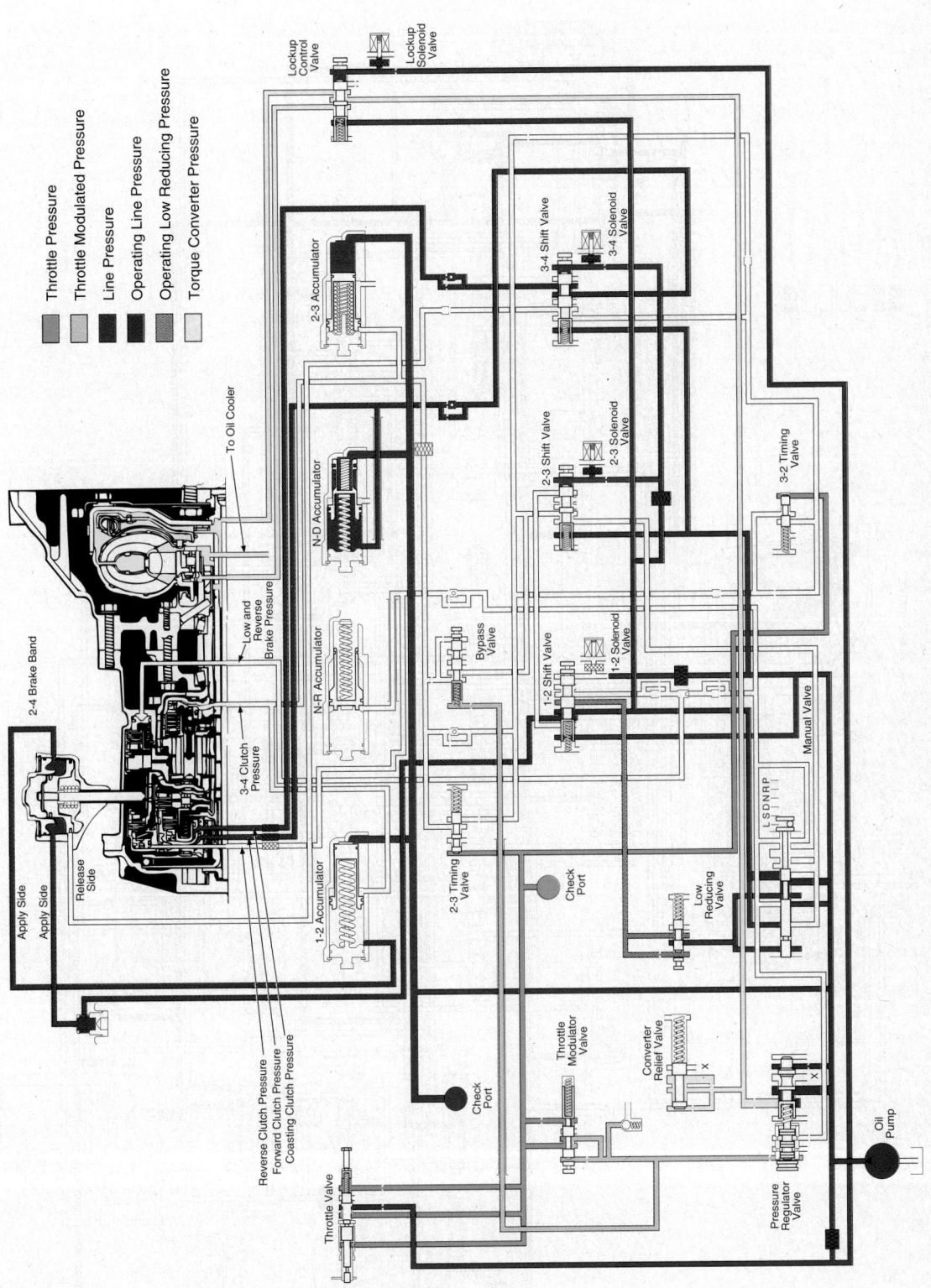

Fig. 20: "L" Position — 2nd Gear (Hold With Speed Above 68 MPH)

Courtesy of Mazda Motors Corp.

OIL CIRCUIT DIAGRAMS
Mazda GF4A-EL

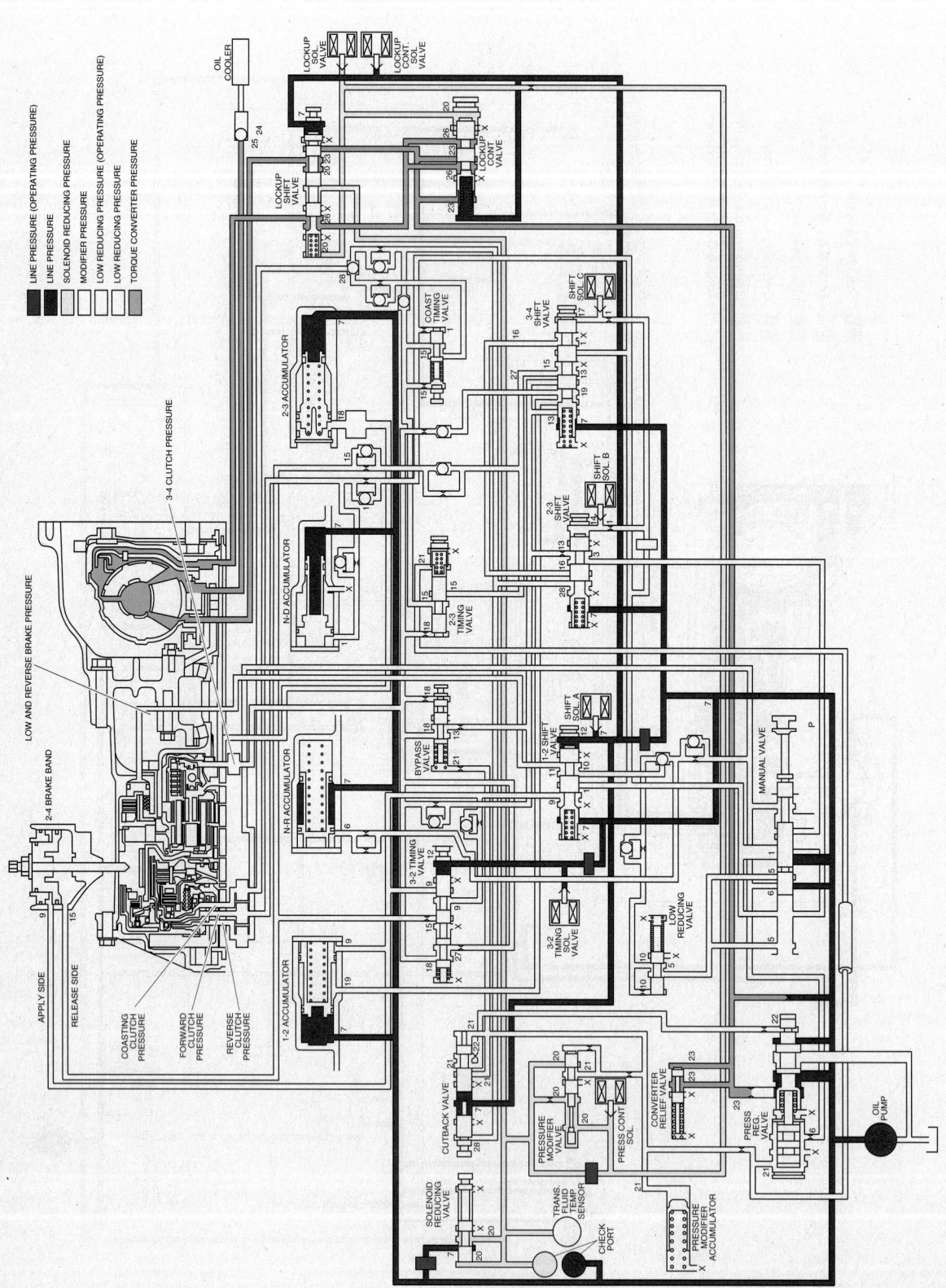

Fig. 1: "P" Or "N" Position — Park

OIL CIRCUIT DIAGRAMS
Mazda GF4A-EL (Cont.)

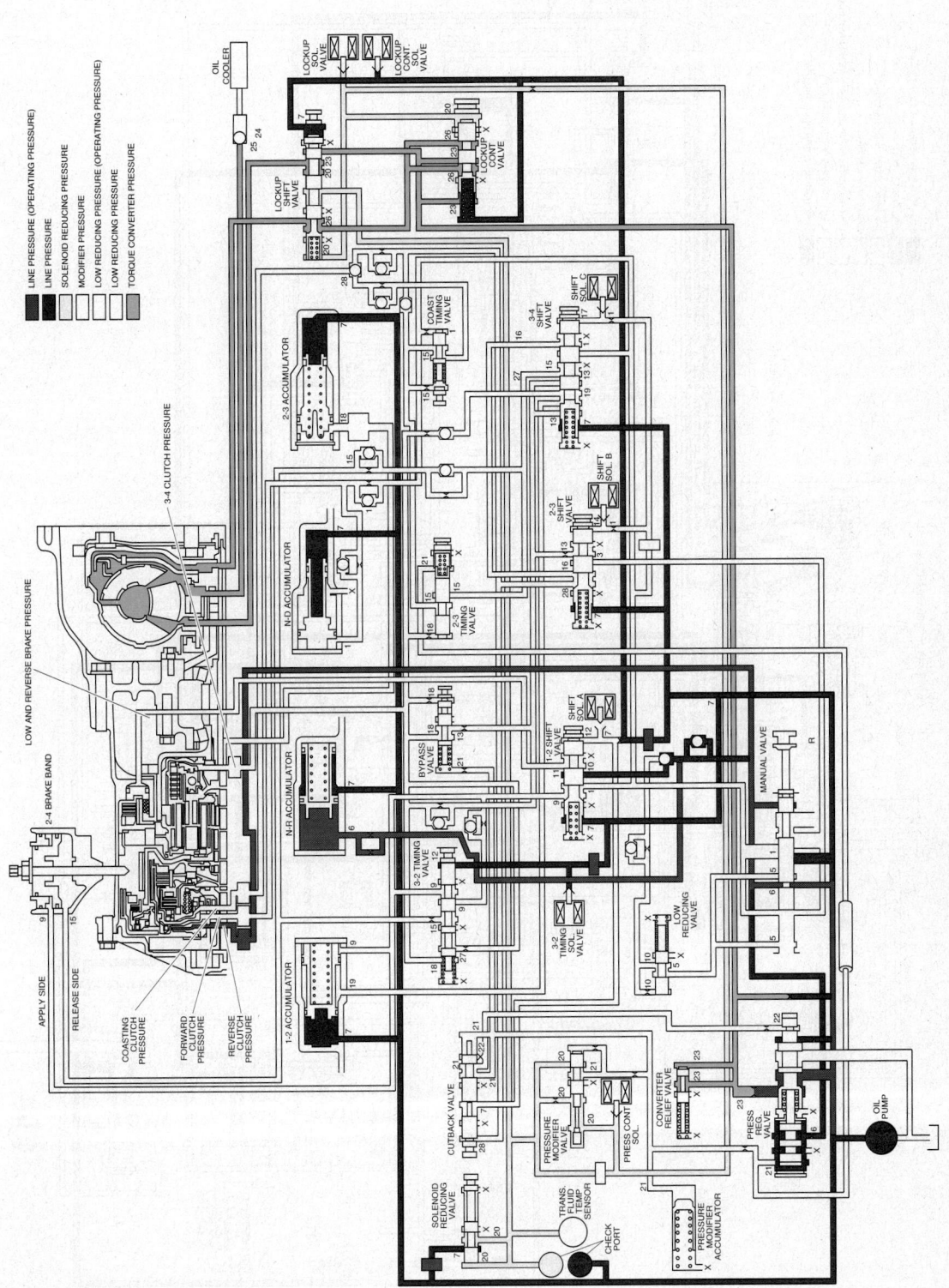

Fig. 2: "R" Position — Reverse (Speed Above 19 MPH)

Courtesy of Mazda Motors Corp.

OIL CIRCUIT DIAGRAMS
Mazda GF4A-EL (Cont.)

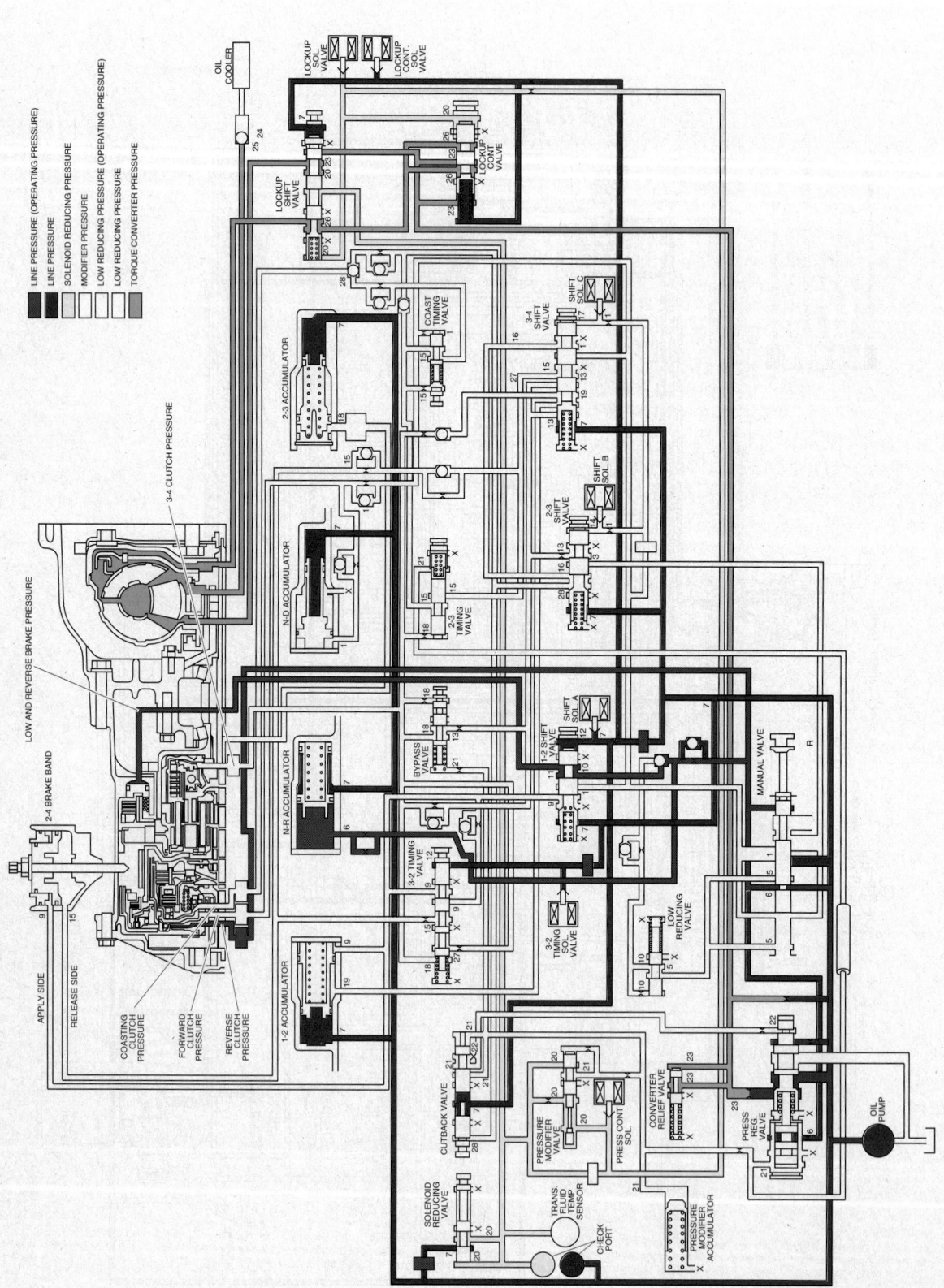

Fig. 3: "R" Position — Reverse (Speed Below Approx. 2.5 MPH)　　　　Courtesy of Mazda Motors Corp.

OIL CIRCUIT DIAGRAMS
Mazda GF4A-EL (Cont.)

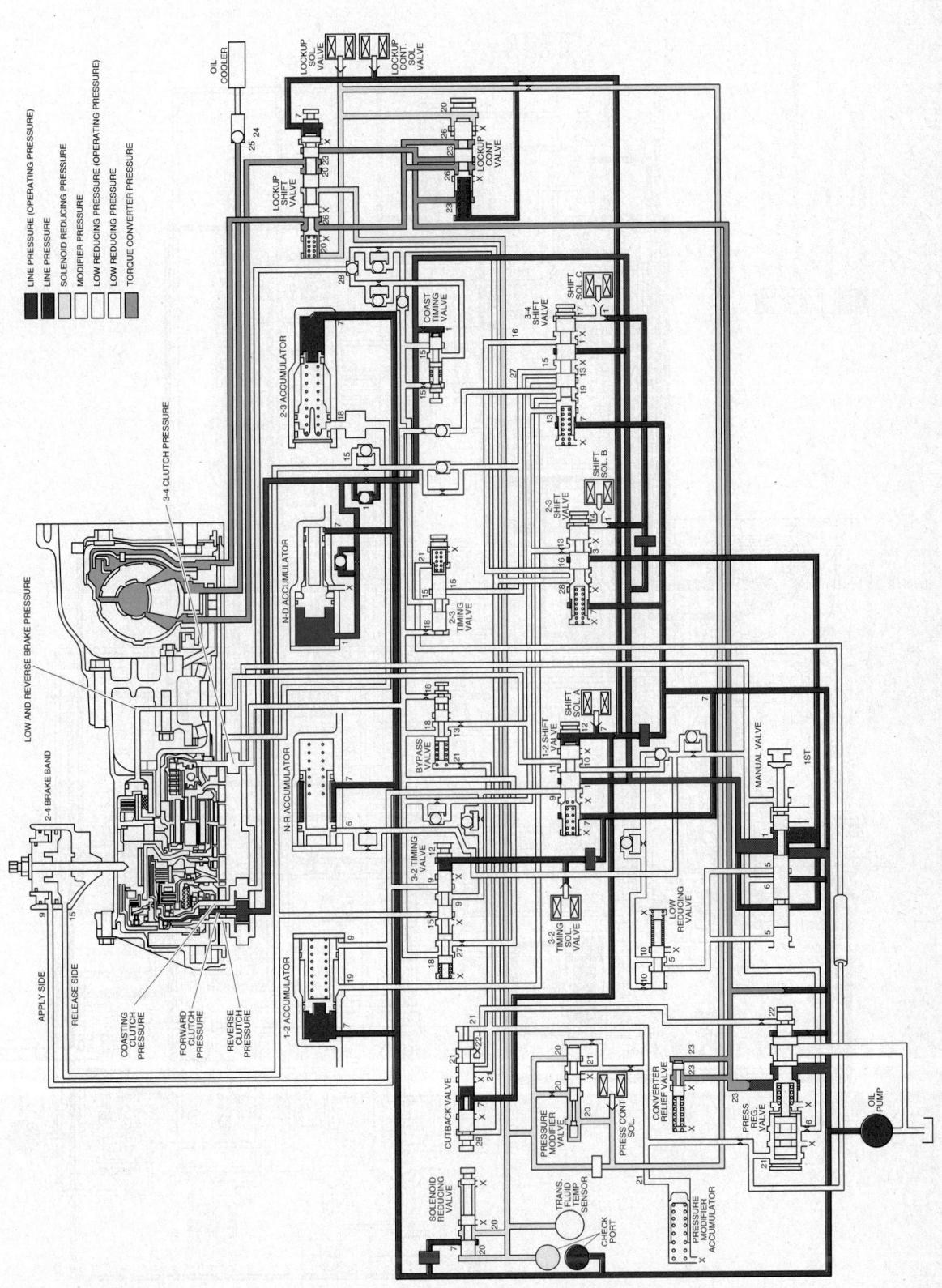

Fig. 4: "1" Or "L" Position — 1st Gear

Courtesy of Mazda Motors Corp.

OIL CIRCUIT DIAGRAMS
Mazda GF4A-EL (Cont.)

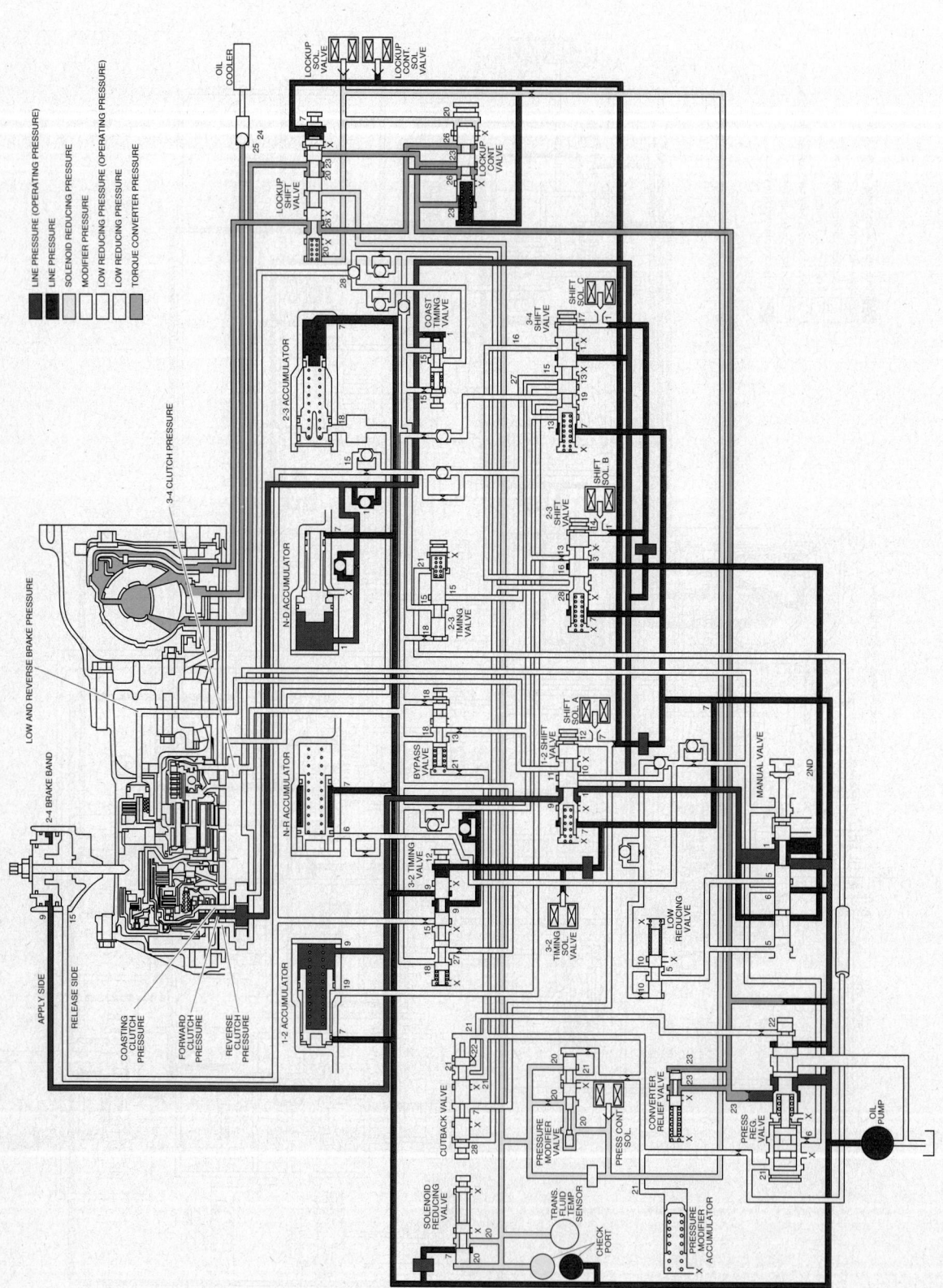

Fig. 5: "2" Or "S" Position — 2nd Gear — Power, Normal & Hold (Speed Above 10.5 MPH)   Courtesy of Mazda Motors Corp.

OIL CIRCUIT DIAGRAMS
Mazda GF4A-EL (Cont.)

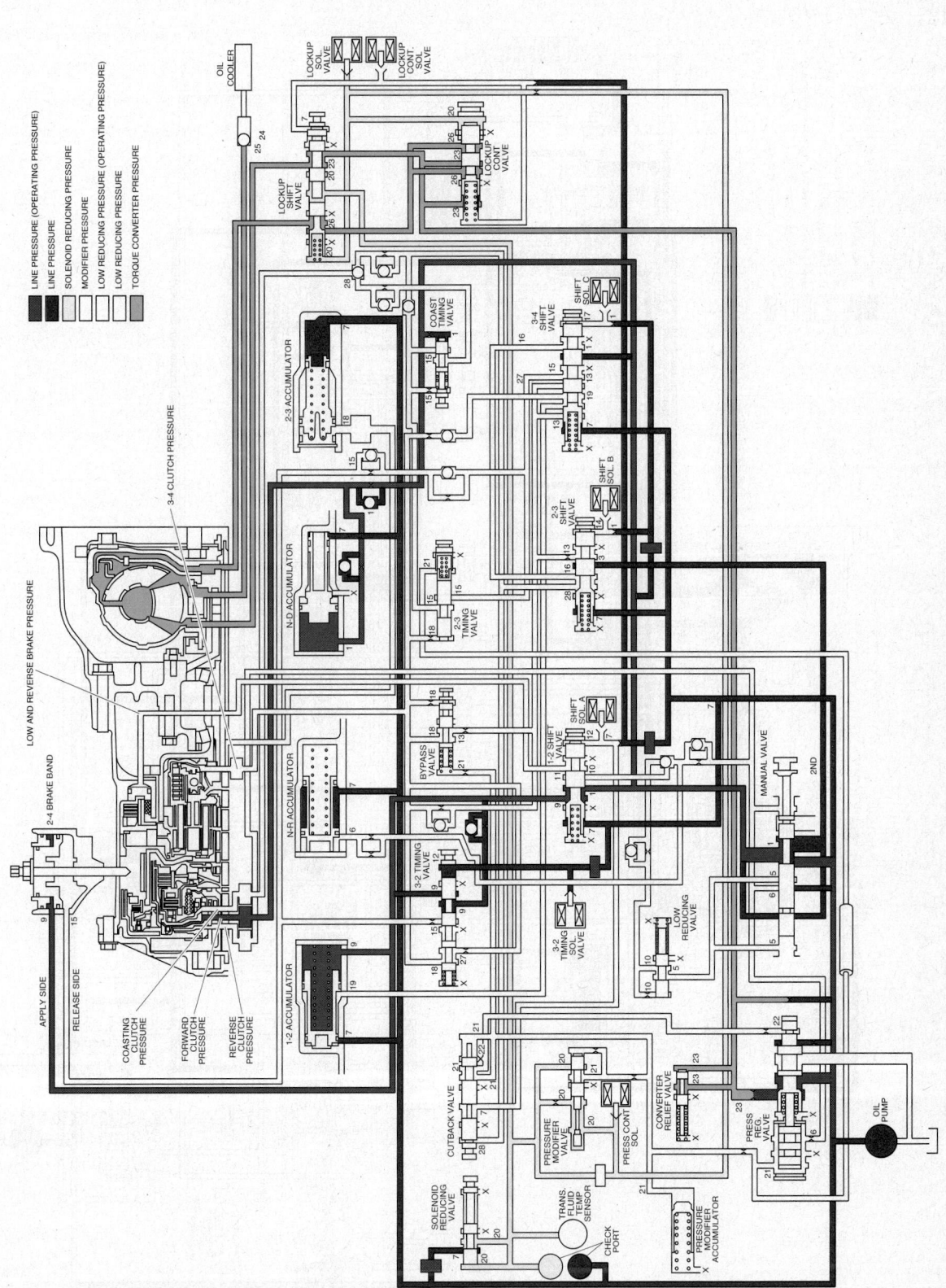

Fig. 6: "2" Or "S" Position — 2nd Gear — Slip Lock-Up (No Engine Braking)   Courtesy of Mazda Motors Corp.

OIL CIRCUIT DIAGRAMS
Mazda GF4A-EL (Cont.)

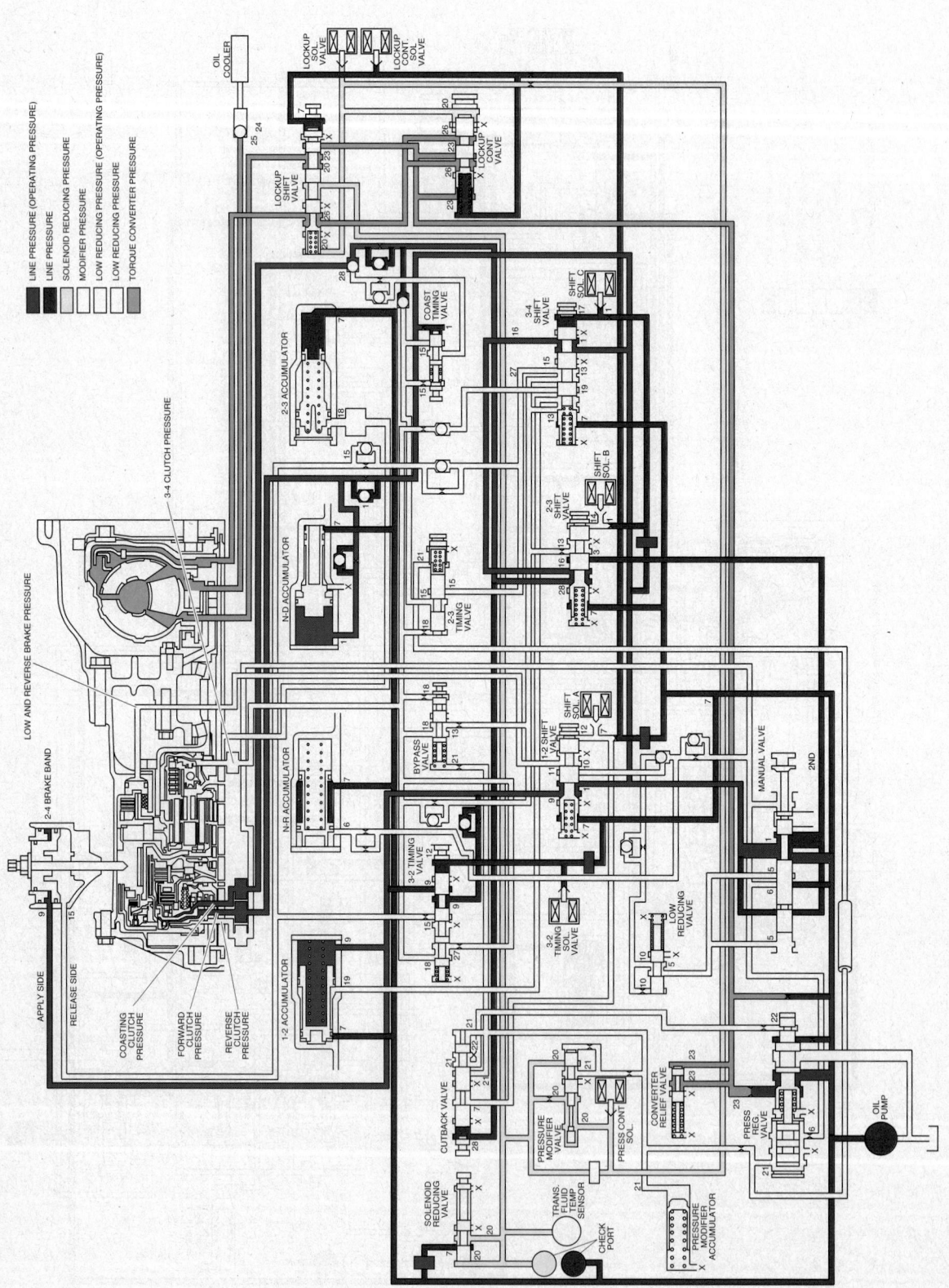

Fig. 7: "2" Or "S" Position — 2nd Gear — Hold (Speed Below 8.7 MPH — Engine Braking)

Courtesy of Mazda Motors Corp.

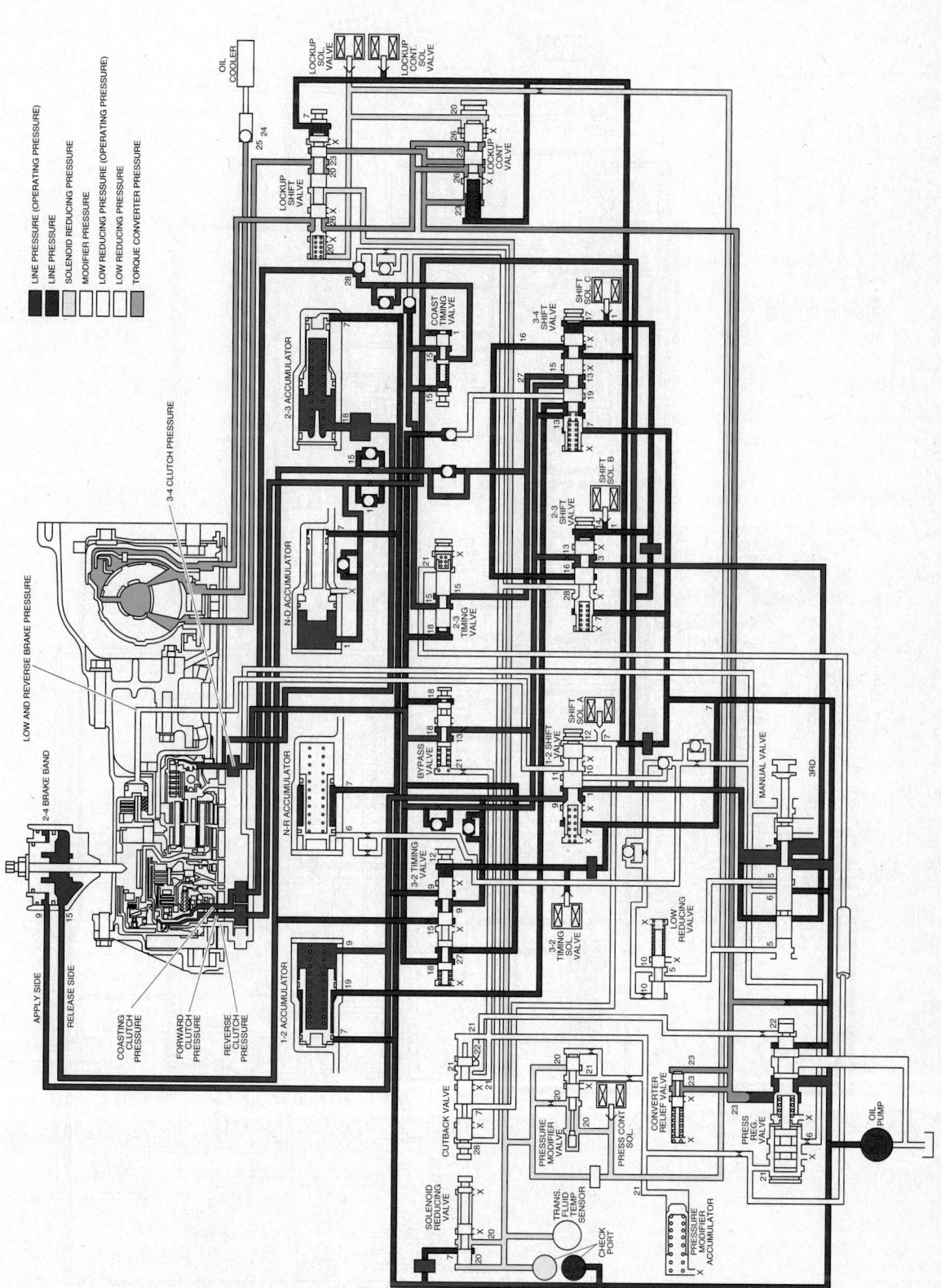

Fig. 8: "D" Position — 3rd Gear — Power, Normal, Hold (TCC OFF)

Courtesy of Mazda Motors Corp.

OIL CIRCUIT DIAGRAMS
Mazda GF4A-EL (Cont.)

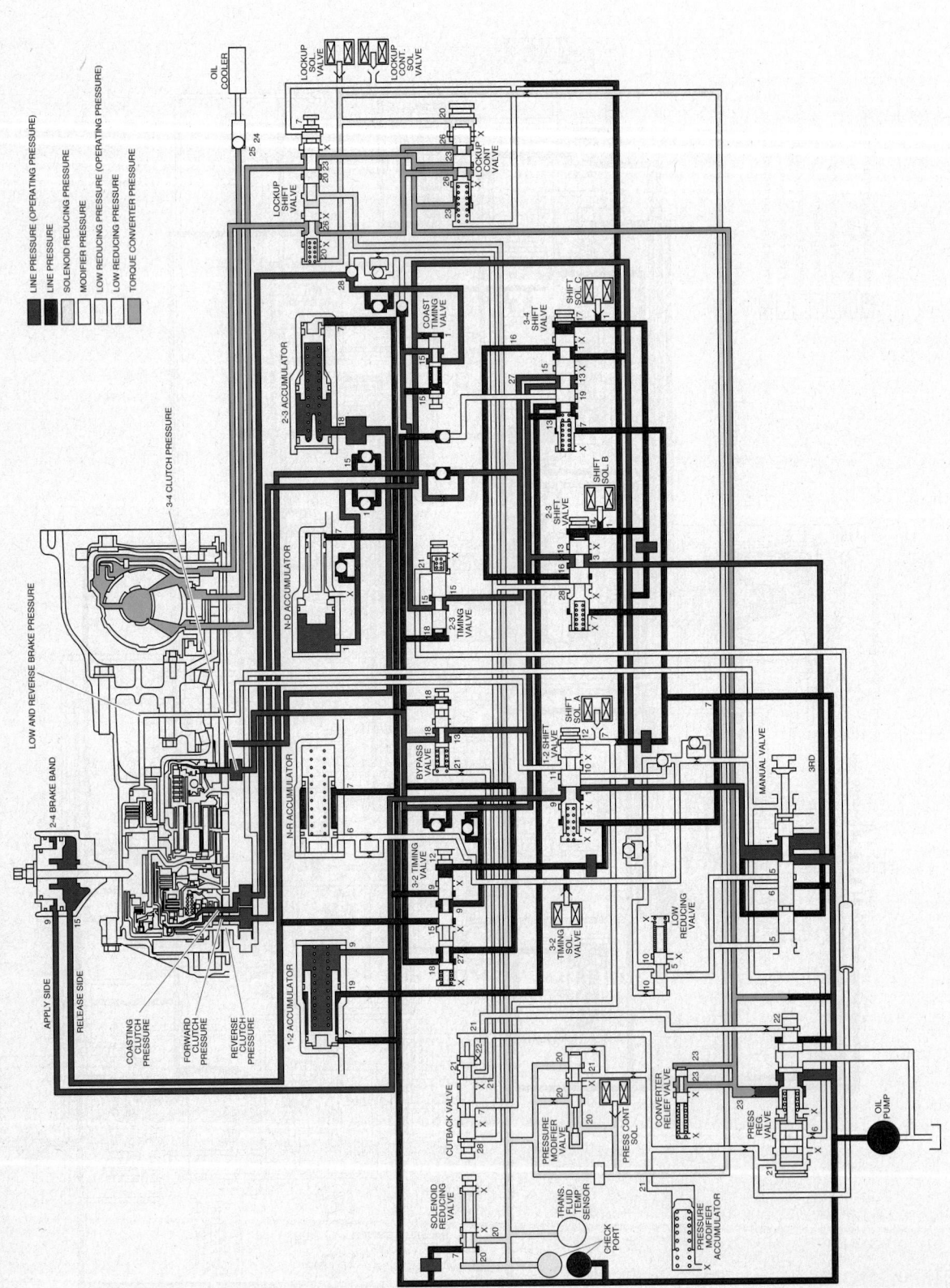

Fig. 9: "D" Position — 3rd Gear — Slip Lock-Up (TCC ON)

Courtesy of Mazda Motors Corp.

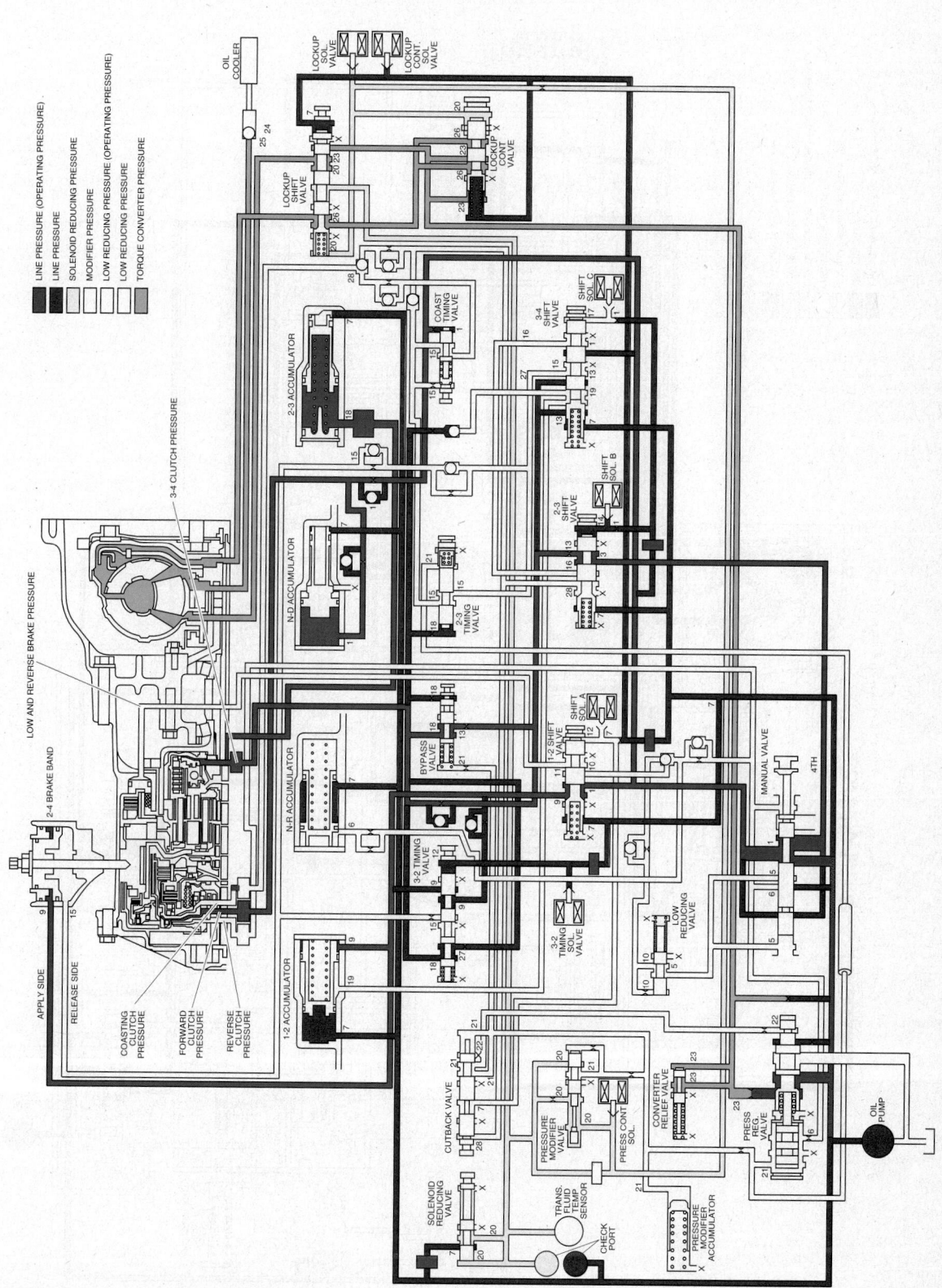

Fig. 10: "D" Position — 4th Gear — Power, Normal (TCC OFF)

Courtesy of Mazda Motors Corp.

OIL CIRCUIT DIAGRAMS
Mazda GF4A-EL (Cont.)

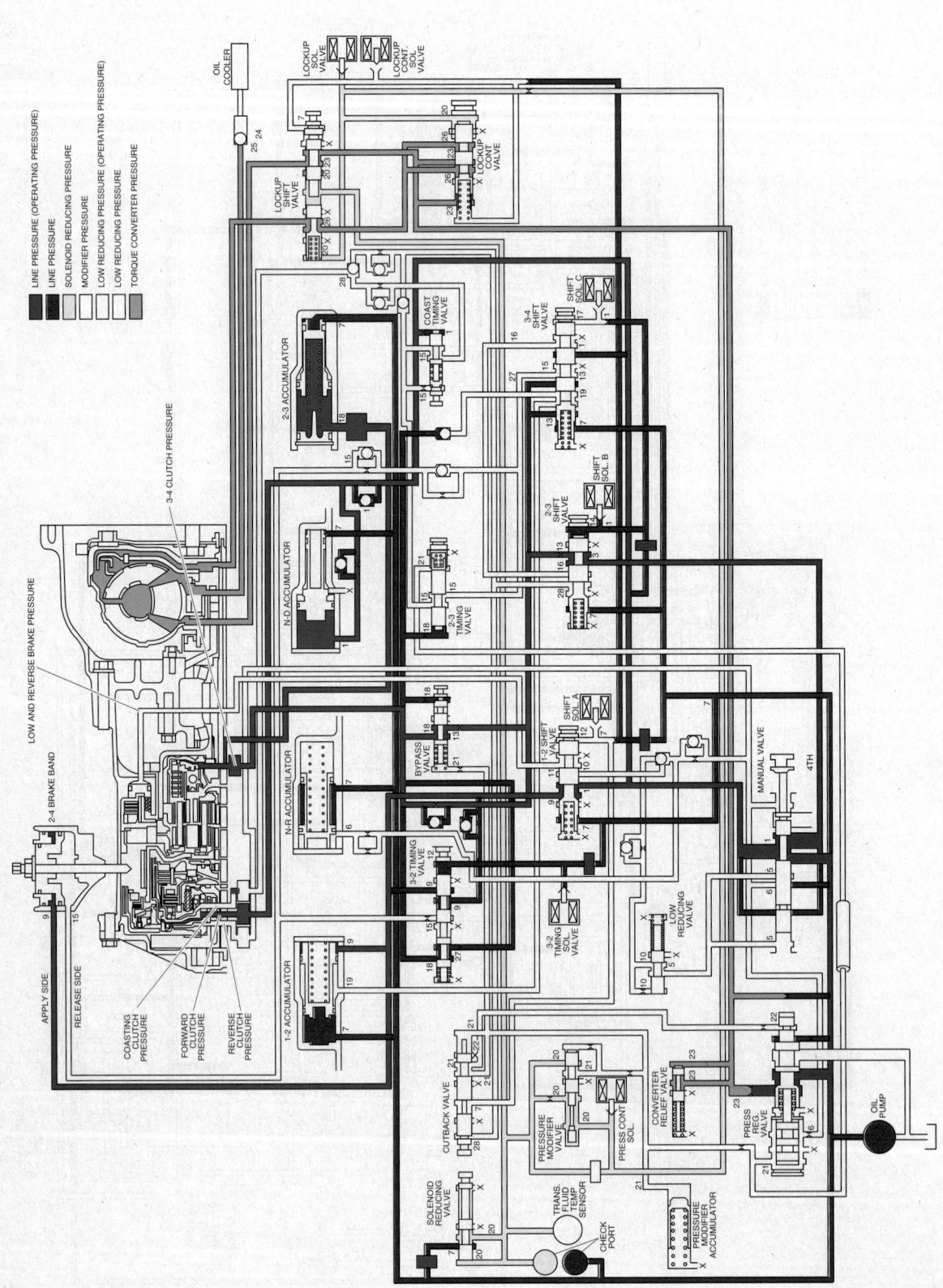

Fig. 11: "D" Position — 4th Gear — Slip Lock-Up, Complete Lock-Up (TCC ON)

Courtesy of Mazda Motors Corp.

OIL CIRCUIT DIAGRAMS
Mazda NC4A-EL

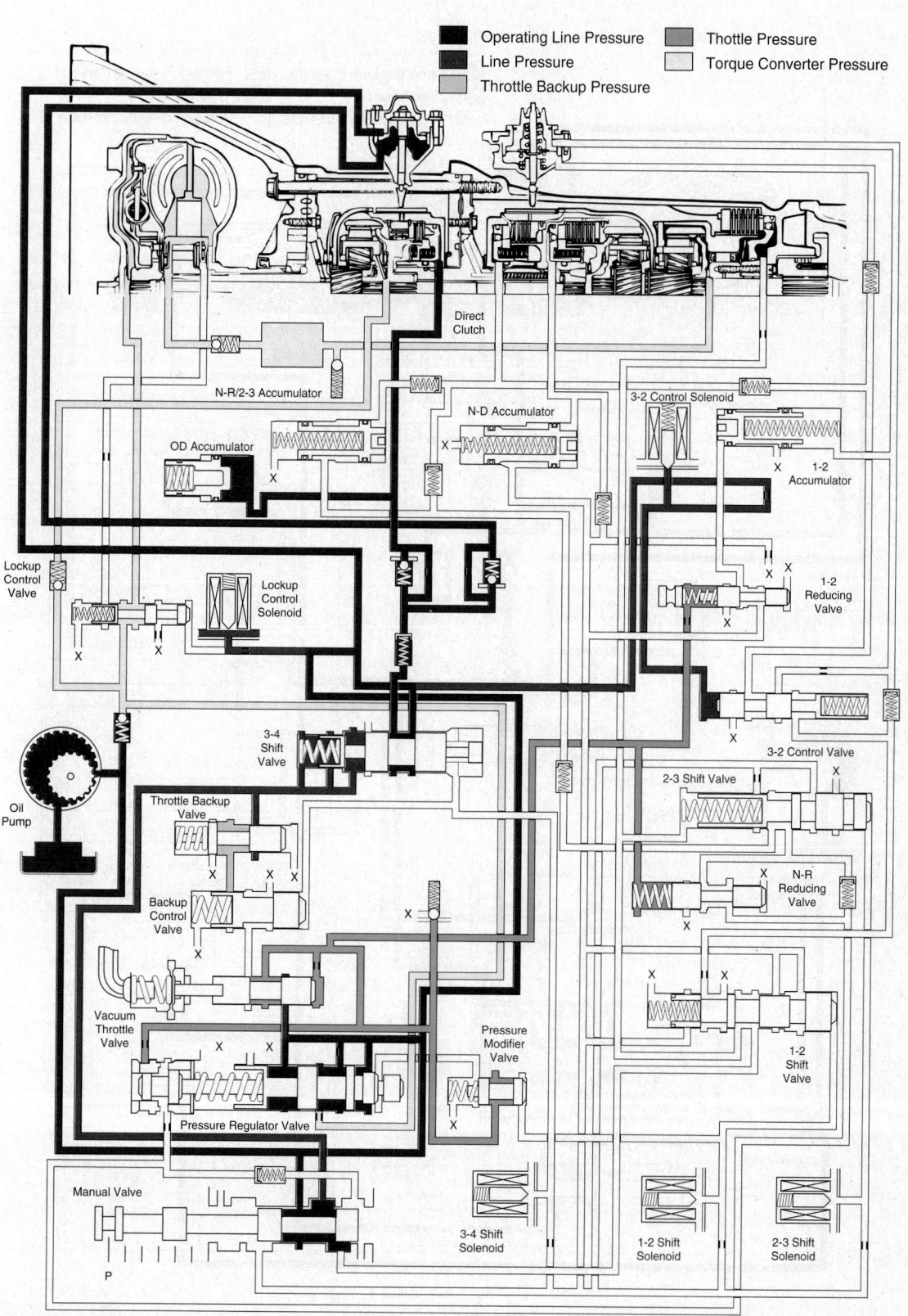

Operating Line Pressure
Line Pressure
Throttle Backup Pressure
Thottle Pressure
Torque Converter Pressure

Direct Clutch

N-R/2-3 Accumulator

N-D Accumulator

3-2 Control Solenoid

OD Accumulator

1-2 Accumulator

Lockup Control Valve

Lockup Control Solenoid

1-2 Reducing Valve

Oil Pump

3-4 Shift Valve

3-2 Control Valve

2-3 Shift Valve

Throttle Backup Valve

N-R Reducing Valve

Backup Control Valve

Vacuum Throttle Valve

Pressure Modifier Valve

1-2 Shift Valve

Pressure Regulator Valve

Manual Valve

P

3-4 Shift Solenoid

1-2 Shift Solenoid

2-3 Shift Solenoid

Fig. 1: "P" Position — Park

Courtesy of Mazda Motors Corp.

OIL CIRCUIT DIAGRAMS
Mazda NC4A-EL (Cont.)

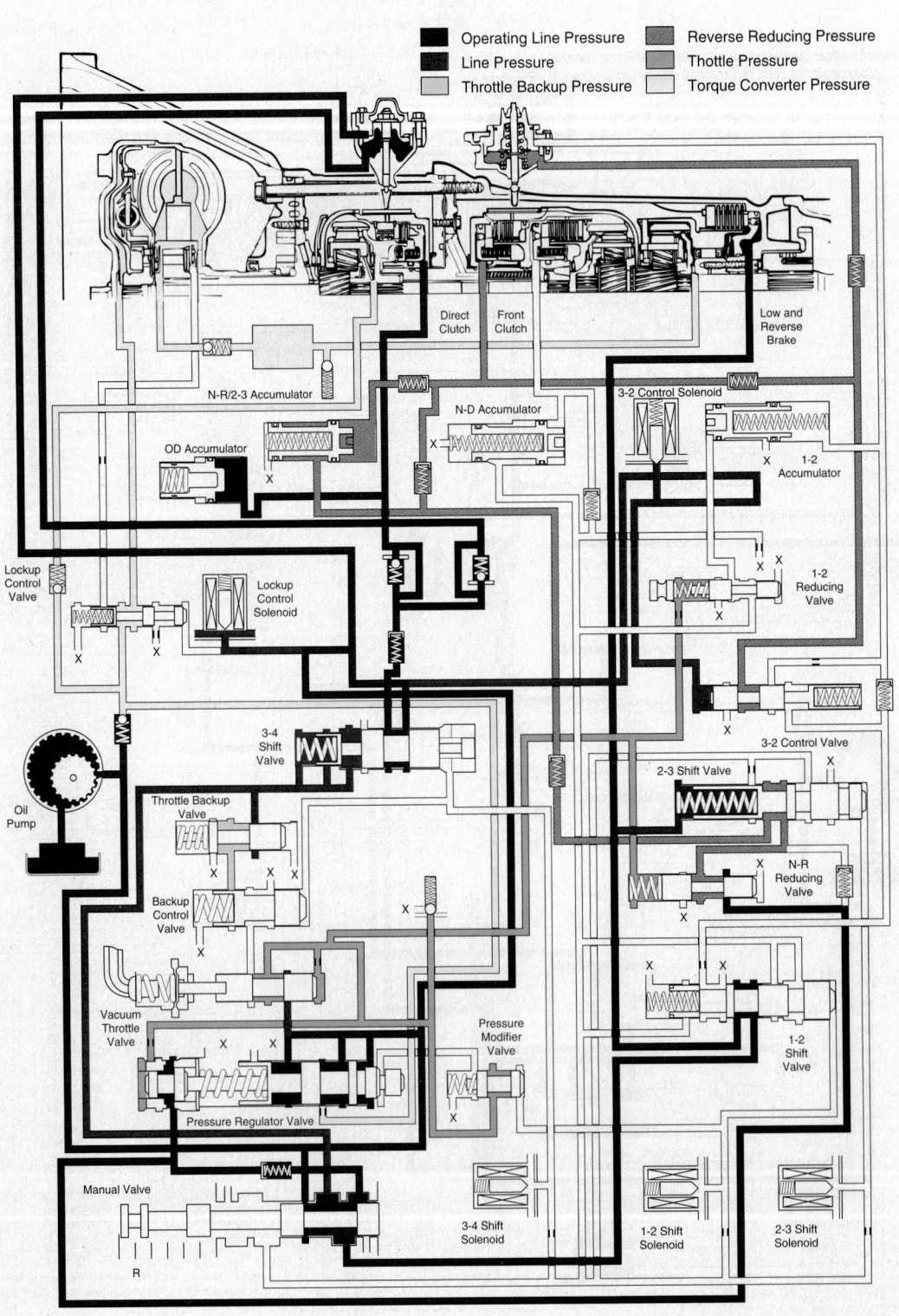

Operating Line Pressure
Line Pressure
Throttle Backup Pressure
Reverse Reducing Pressure
Thottle Pressure
Torque Converter Pressure

Direct Clutch
Front Clutch
Low and Reverse Brake

N-R/2-3 Accumulator
OD Accumulator
N-D Accumulator
3-2 Control Solenoid
1-2 Accumulator

Lockup Control Valve
Lockup Control Solenoid
1-2 Reducing Valve

Oil Pump
3-4 Shift Valve
3-2 Control Valve
2-3 Shift Valve
N-R Reducing Valve

Throttle Backup Valve
Backup Control Valve

Vacuum Throttle Valve
Pressure Modifier Valve
1-2 Shift Valve

Pressure Regulator Valve

Manual Valve
3-4 Shift Solenoid
1-2 Shift Solenoid
2-3 Shift Solenoid

R

Fig. 2: "R" Position — Reverse

Courtesy of Mazda Motors Corp.

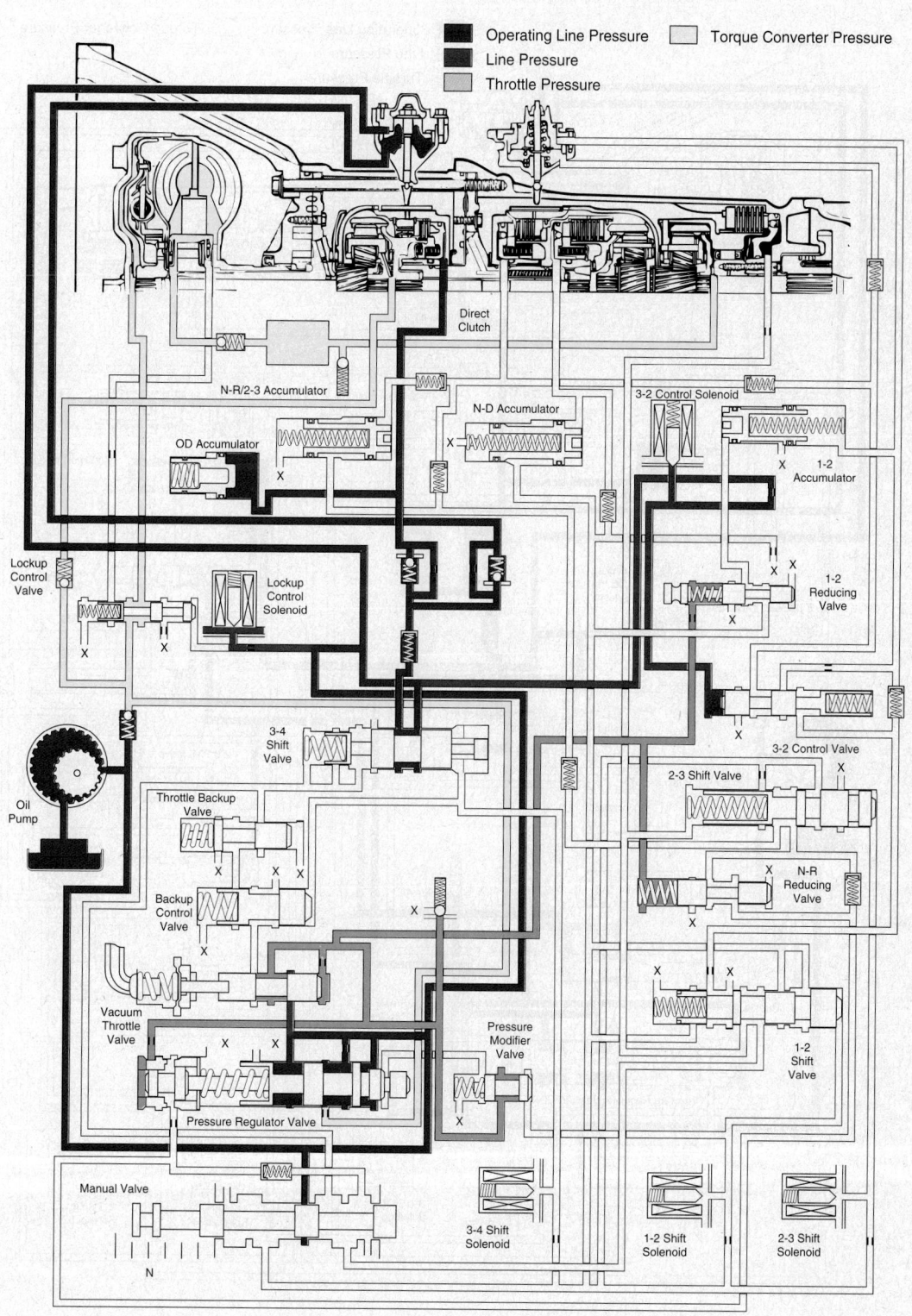

Operating Line Pressure · Torque Converter Pressure
Line Pressure
Throttle Pressure

Direct Clutch

N-R/2-3 Accumulator

N-D Accumulator

3-2 Control Solenoid

OD Accumulator

1-2 Accumulator

Lockup Control Valve

Lockup Control Solenoid

1-2 Reducing Valve

3-4 Shift Valve

Oil Pump

Throttle Backup Valve

3-2 Control Valve

2-3 Shift Valve

Backup Control Valve

N-R Reducing Valve

Vacuum Throttle Valve

Pressure Modifier Valve

1-2 Shift Valve

Pressure Regulator Valve

Manual Valve

N

3-4 Shift Solenoid

1-2 Shift Solenoid

2-3 Shift Solenoid

Fig. 3: "N" Position — Neutral (With Speed Less Than 4.5 MPH)

Courtesy of Mazda Motors Corp.

OIL CIRCUIT DIAGRAMS
Mazda NC4A-EL (Cont.)

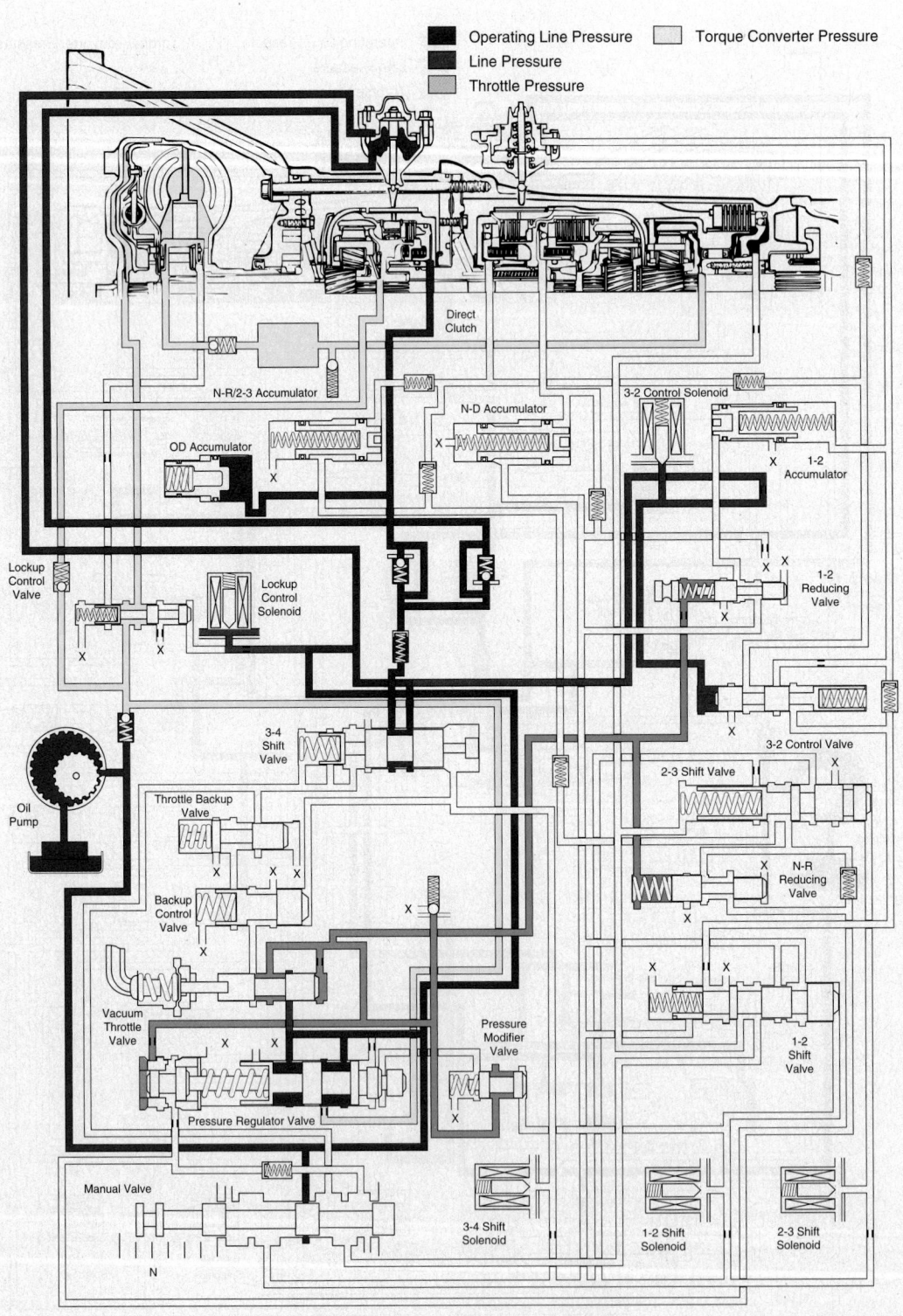

Operating Line Pressure
Line Pressure
Throttle Pressure
Torque Converter Pressure

Direct Clutch

N-R/2-3 Accumulator

N-D Accumulator

3-2 Control Solenoid

OD Accumulator

1-2 Accumulator

Lockup Control Valve

Lockup Control Solenoid

1-2 Reducing Valve

3-2 Control Valve

2-3 Shift Valve

Oil Pump

3-4 Shift Valve

Throttle Backup Valve

N-R Reducing Valve

Backup Control Valve

Vacuum Throttle Valve

Pressure Modifier Valve

1-2 Shift Valve

Pressure Regulator Valve

Manual Valve

N

3-4 Shift Solenoid

1-2 Shift Solenoid

2-3 Shift Solenoid

Fig. 4: "N" Position — Neutral (With Speed Greater Than 5.5 MPH)

Courtesy of Mazda Motors Corp.

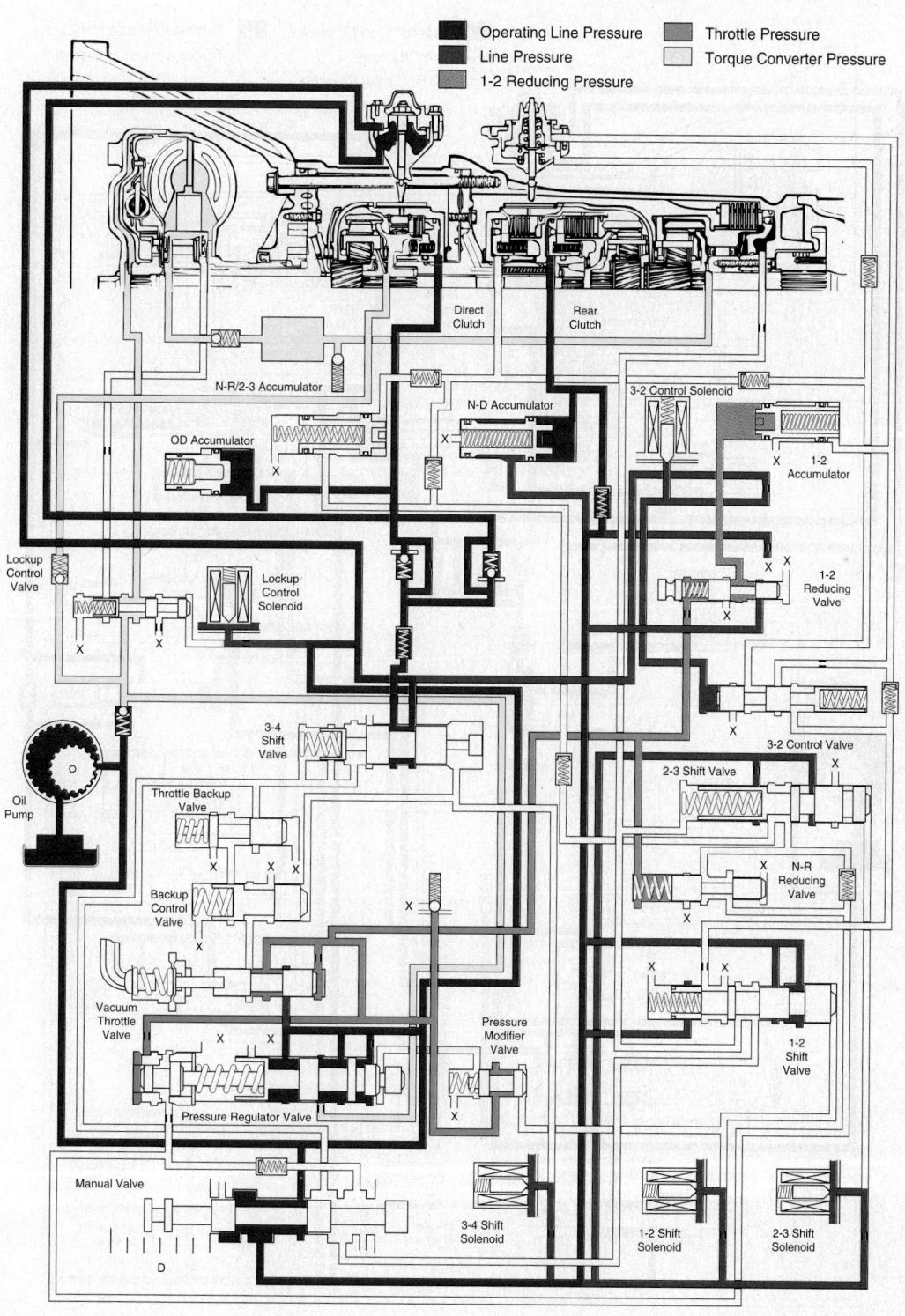

Fig. 5: "D" Position — 1st Gear

Courtesy of Mazda Motors Corp.

OIL CIRCUIT DIAGRAMS
Mazda NC4A-EL (Cont.)

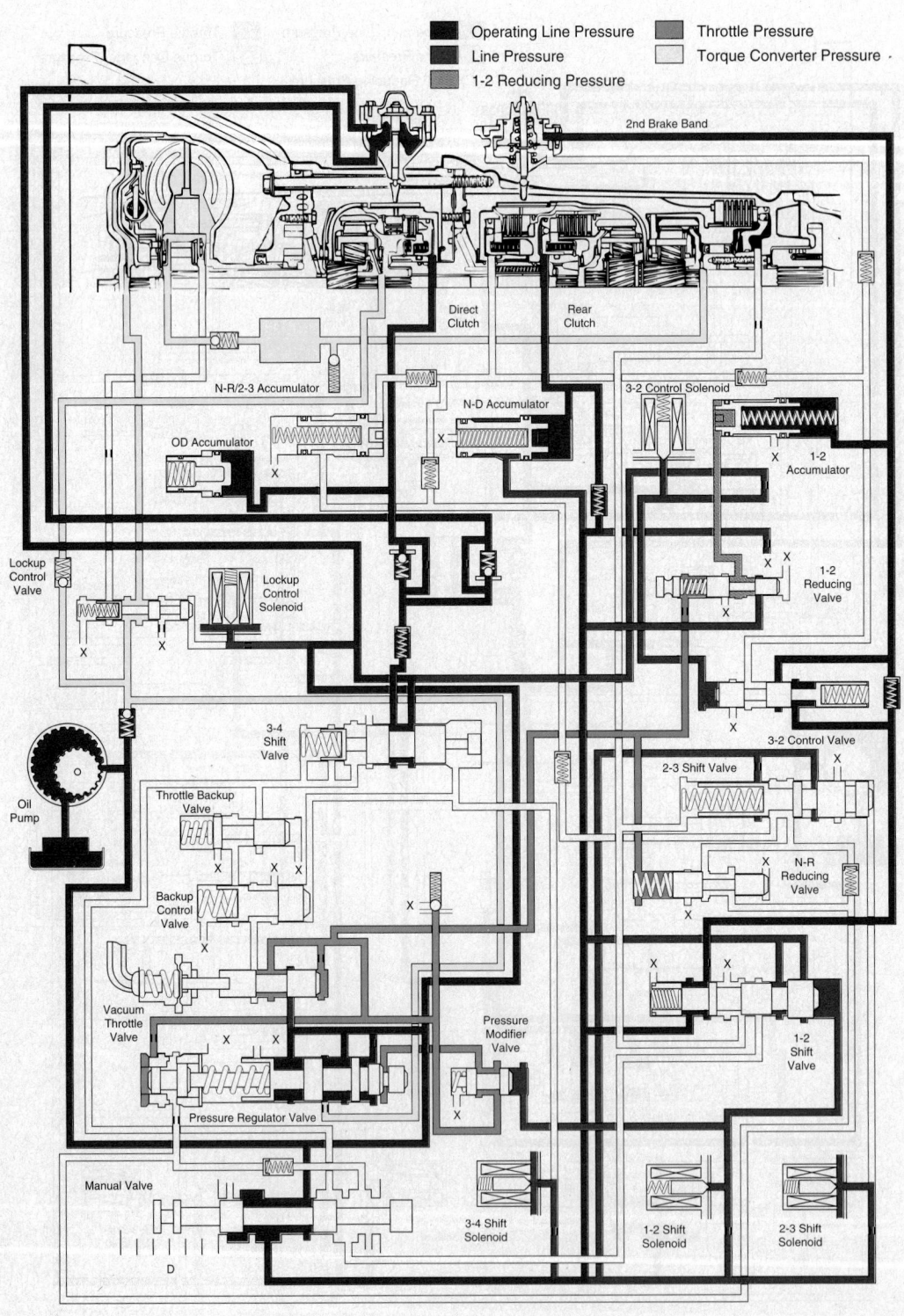

■ Operating Line Pressure	▨ Throttle Pressure
■ Line Pressure	□ Torque Converter Pressure
▨ 1-2 Reducing Pressure	

Fig. 6: "D" Position — 2nd Gear

Courtesy of Mazda Motors Corp.

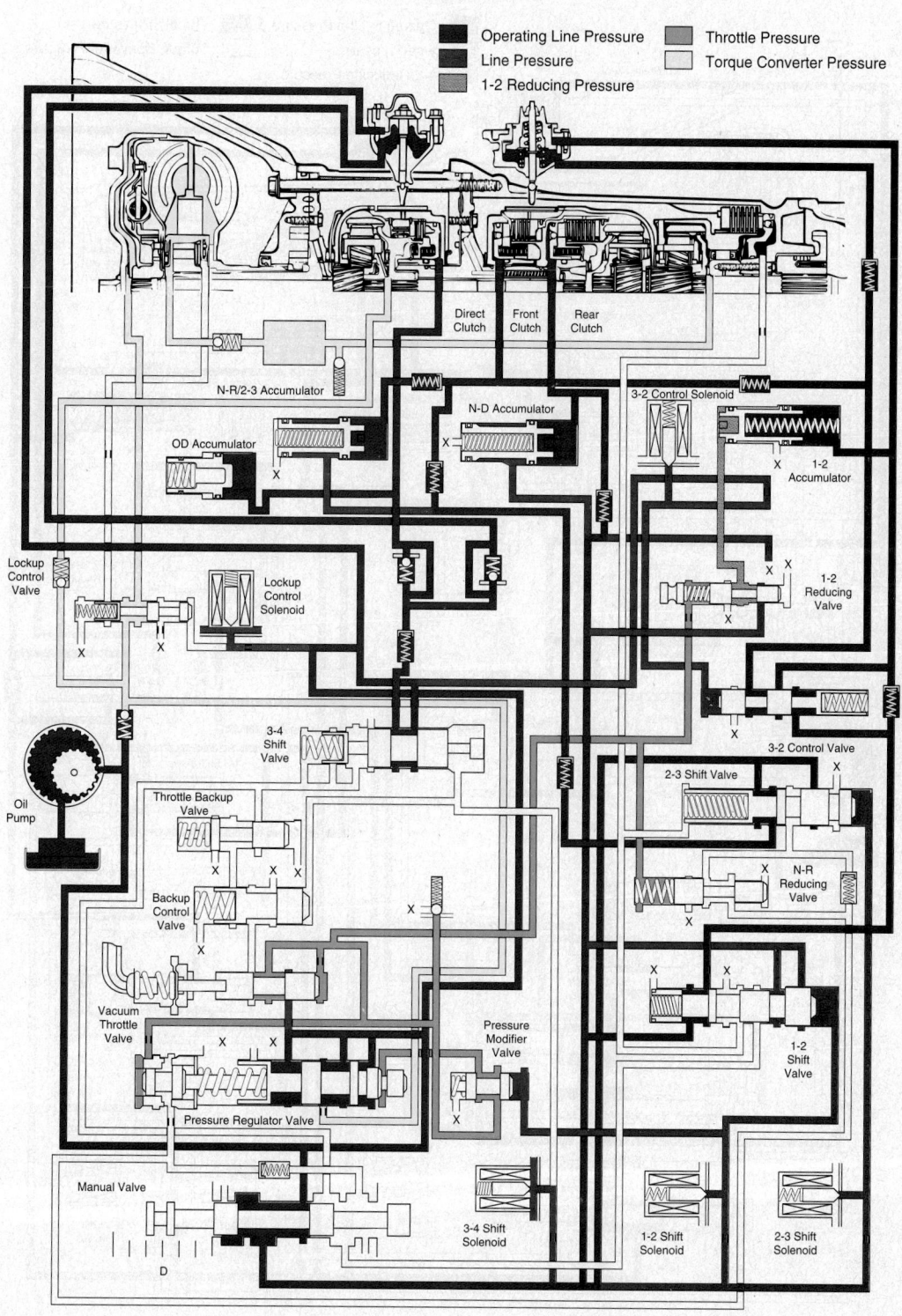

Fig. 7: "D" Position — 3rd Gear

Courtesy of Mazda Motors Corp.

OIL CIRCUIT DIAGRAMS
Mazda NC4A-EL (Cont.)

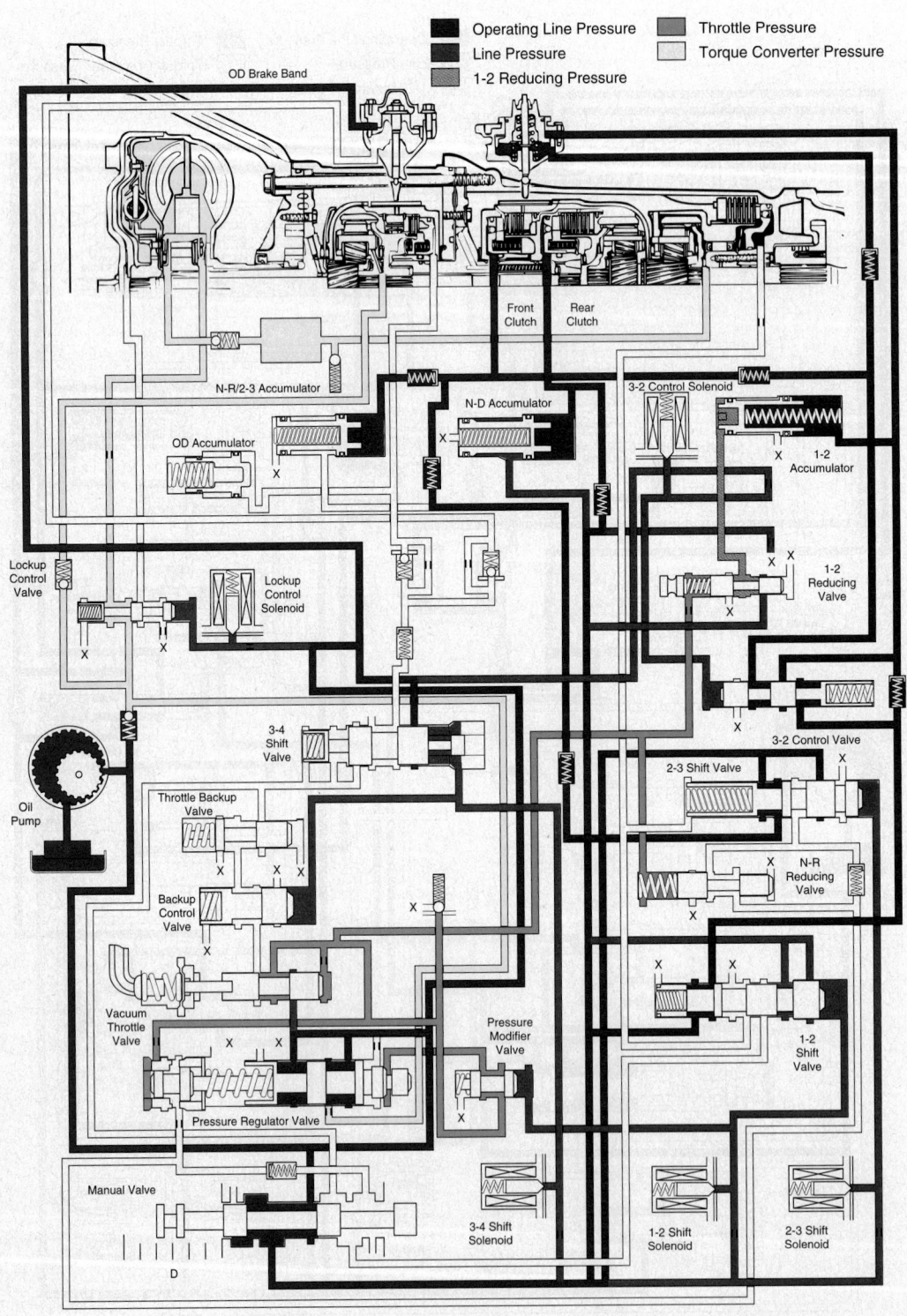

Fig. 8: "D" Position — Overdrive (Lock-Up ON)

Courtesy of Mazda Motors Corp.

OIL CIRCUIT DIAGRAMS
Mazda NC4A-EL (Cont.)

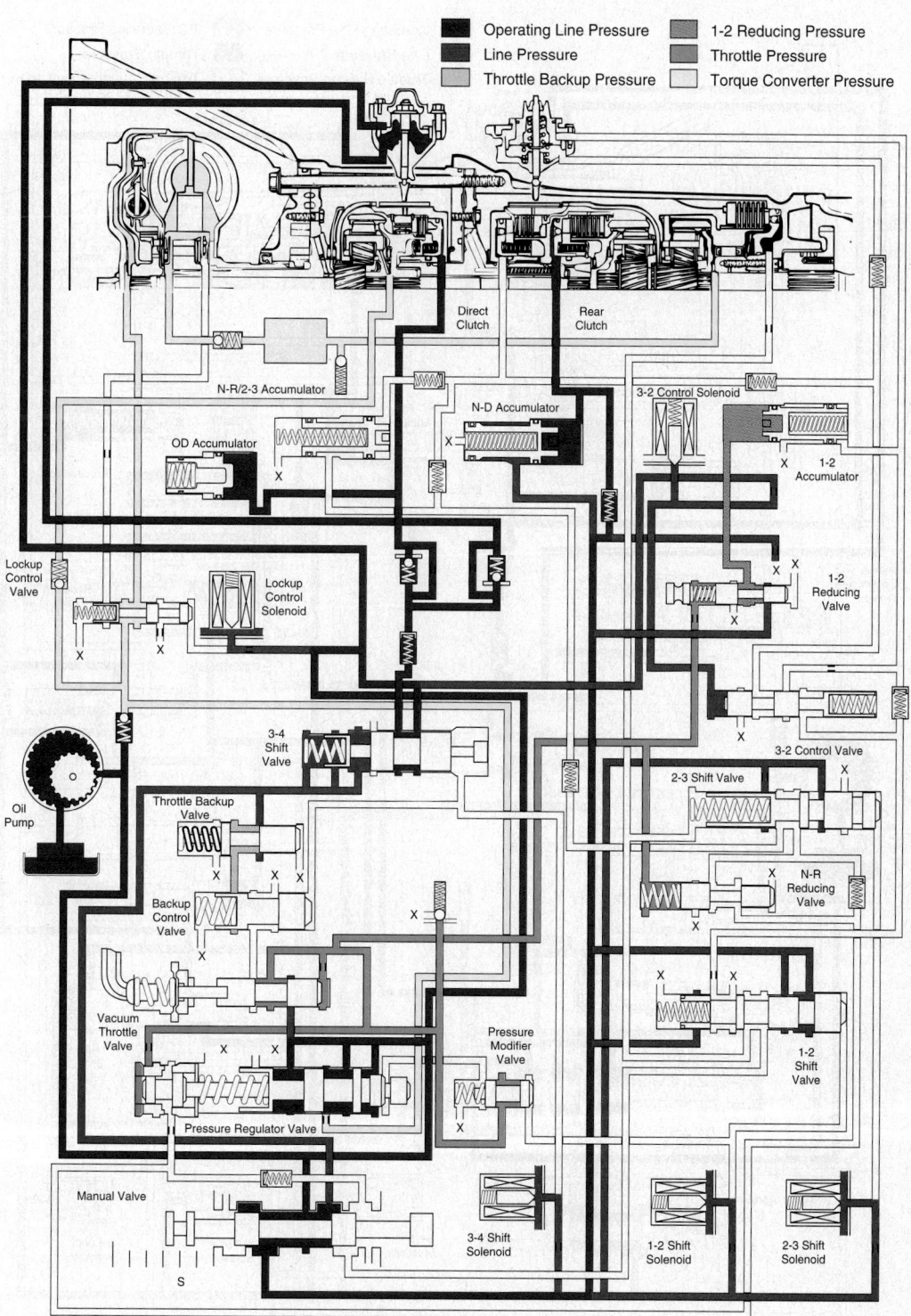

Fig. 9: "S" Position — 1st Gear

Courtesy of Mazda Motors Corp.

OIL CIRCUIT DIAGRAMS
Mazda NC4A-EL (Cont.)

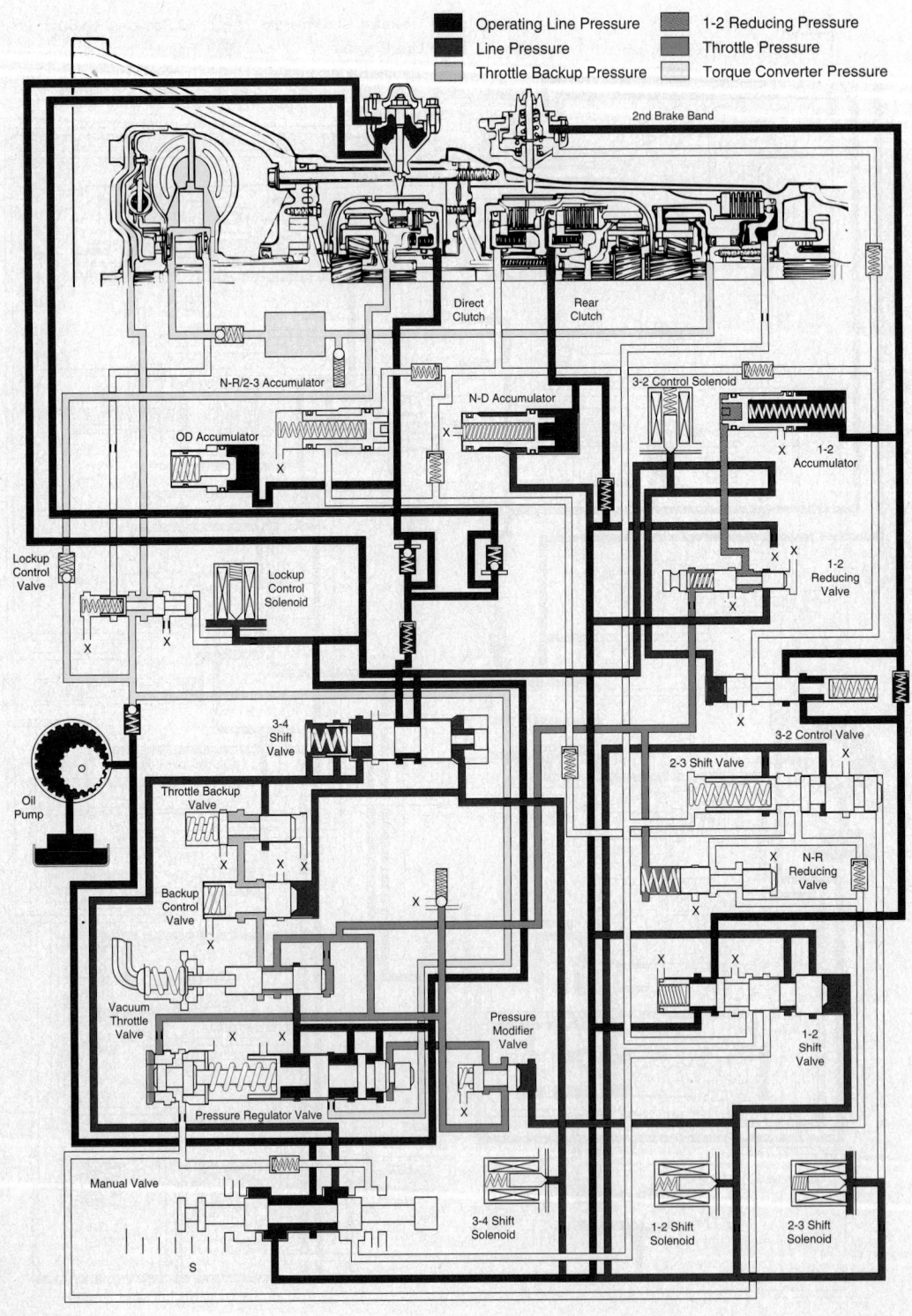

	Operating Line Pressure		1-2 Reducing Pressure
	Line Pressure		Throttle Pressure
	Throttle Backup Pressure		Torque Converter Pressure

Fig. 10: "S" Position — 1st Gear

Courtesy of Mazda Motors Corp.

OIL CIRCUIT DIAGRAMS
Mazda NC4A-EL (Cont.)

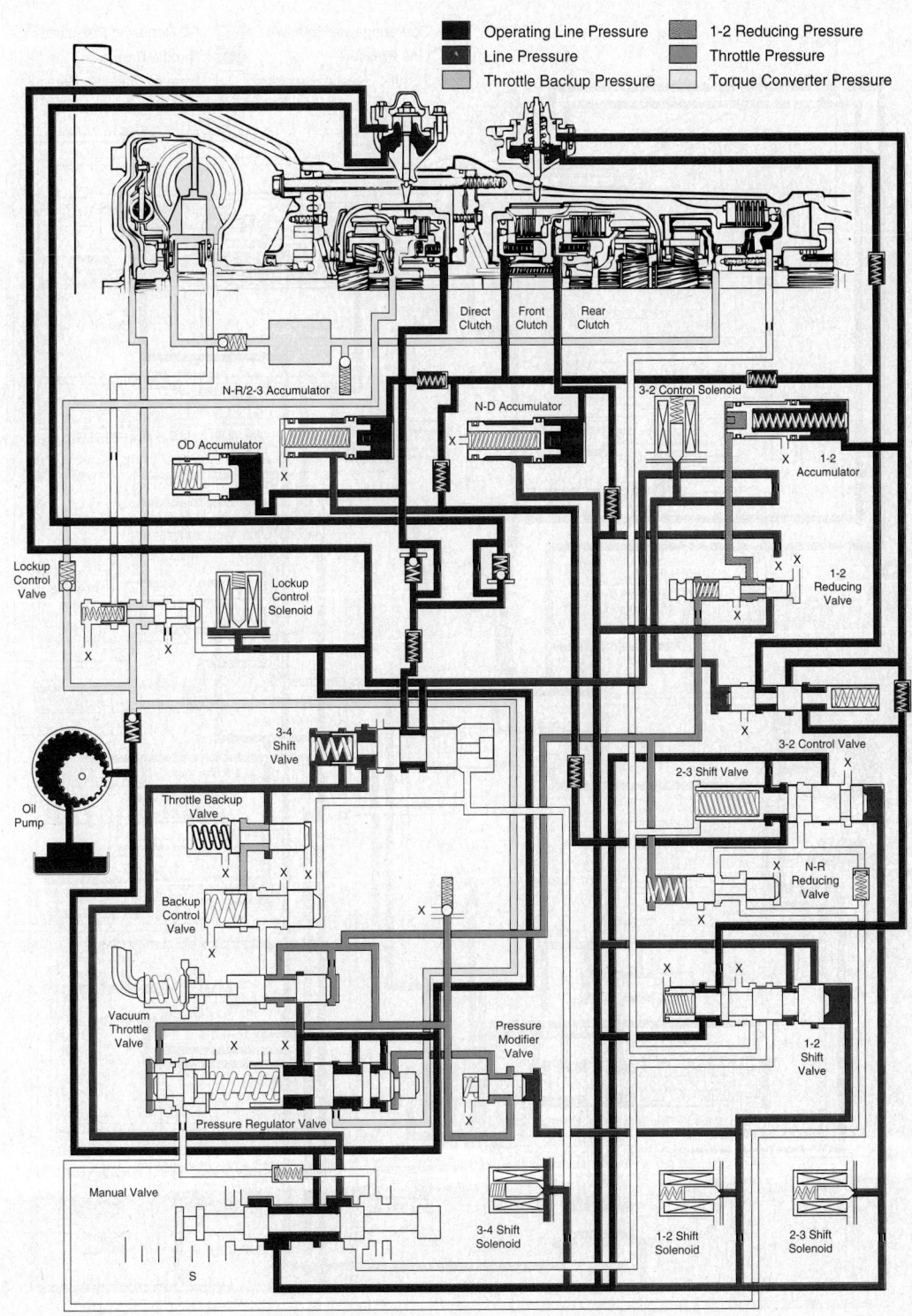

Legend:
- Operating Line Pressure
- Line Pressure
- Throttle Backup Pressure
- 1-2 Reducing Pressure
- Throttle Pressure
- Torque Converter Pressure

Direct Clutch
Front Clutch
Rear Clutch

N-R/2-3 Accumulator
OD Accumulator
N-D Accumulator
3-2 Control Solenoid
1-2 Accumulator

Lockup Control Valve
Lockup Control Solenoid
1-2 Reducing Valve

3-4 Shift Valve
3-2 Control Valve
2-3 Shift Valve

Oil Pump
Throttle Backup Valve
N-R Reducing Valve

Backup Control Valve
Vacuum Throttle Valve
Pressure Modifier Valve
1-2 Shift Valve

Pressure Regulator Valve

Manual Valve
3-4 Shift Solenoid
1-2 Shift Solenoid
2-3 Shift Solenoid

NC4A-EL Fig. 11 "S" 3RD GR

Fig. 11: "S" Position — 3rd Gear

Courtesy of Mazda Motors Corp.

OIL CIRCUIT DIAGRAMS
Mazda NC4A-EL (Cont.)

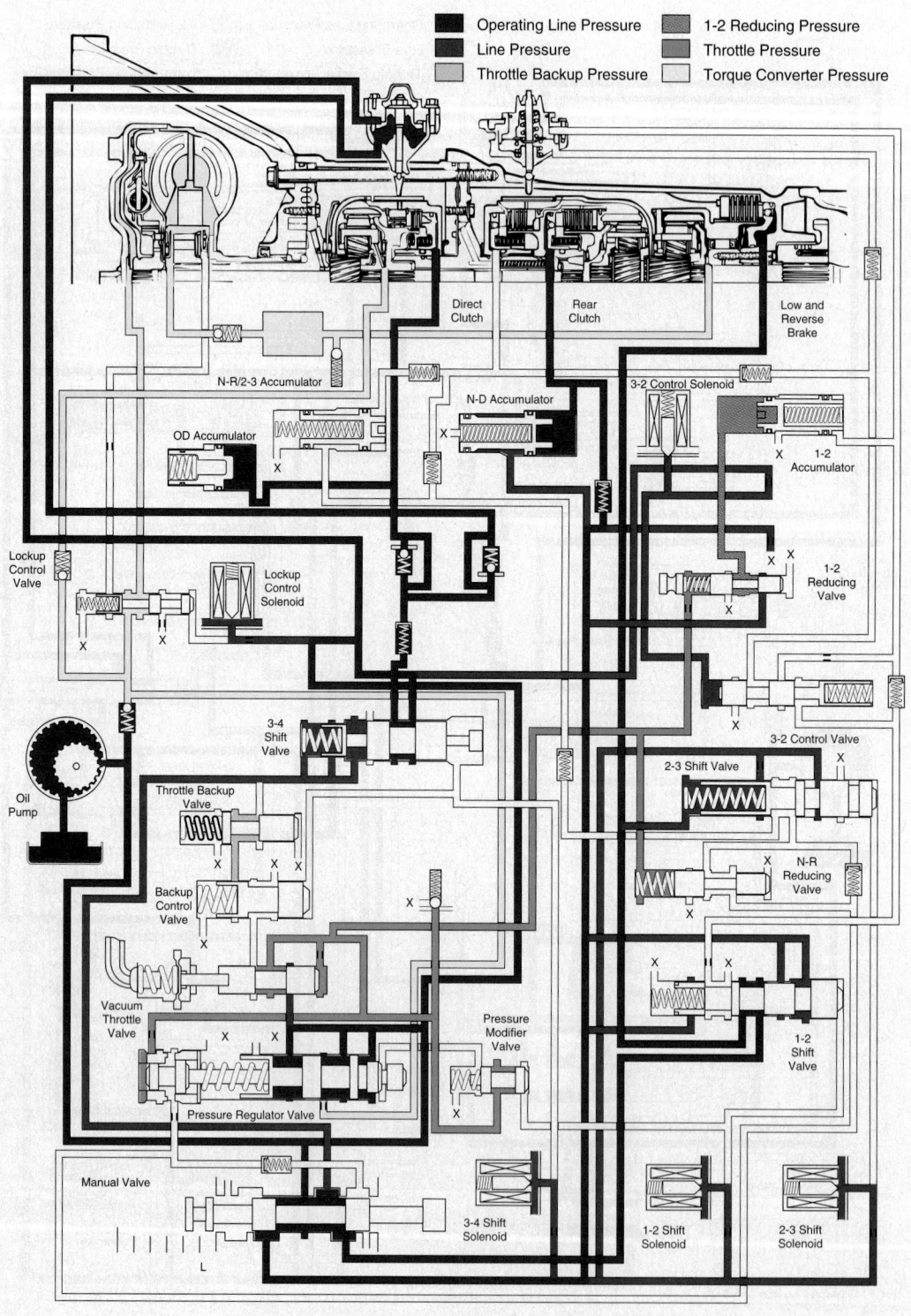

Fig. 12: "L" Position — 1st Gear

Courtesy of Mazda Motors Corp.

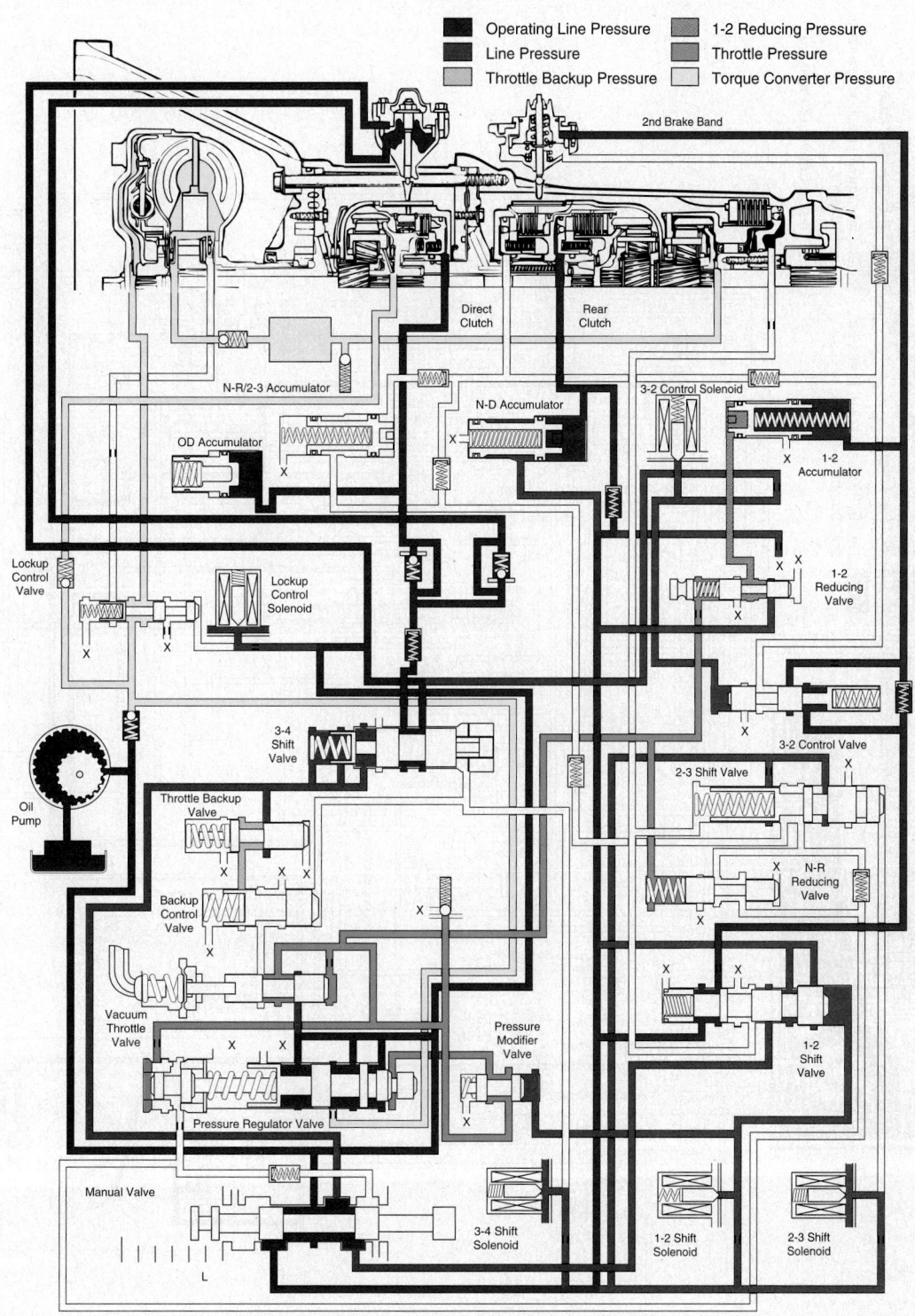

Operating Line Pressure **1-2 Reducing Pressure**
Line Pressure **Throttle Pressure**
Throttle Backup Pressure **Torque Converter Pressure**

Fig. 13: "L" Position — 2nd Gear

Courtesy of Mazda Motors Corp.

OIL CIRCUIT DIAGRAMS
Mazda RA4A-EL & RA4AX-EL

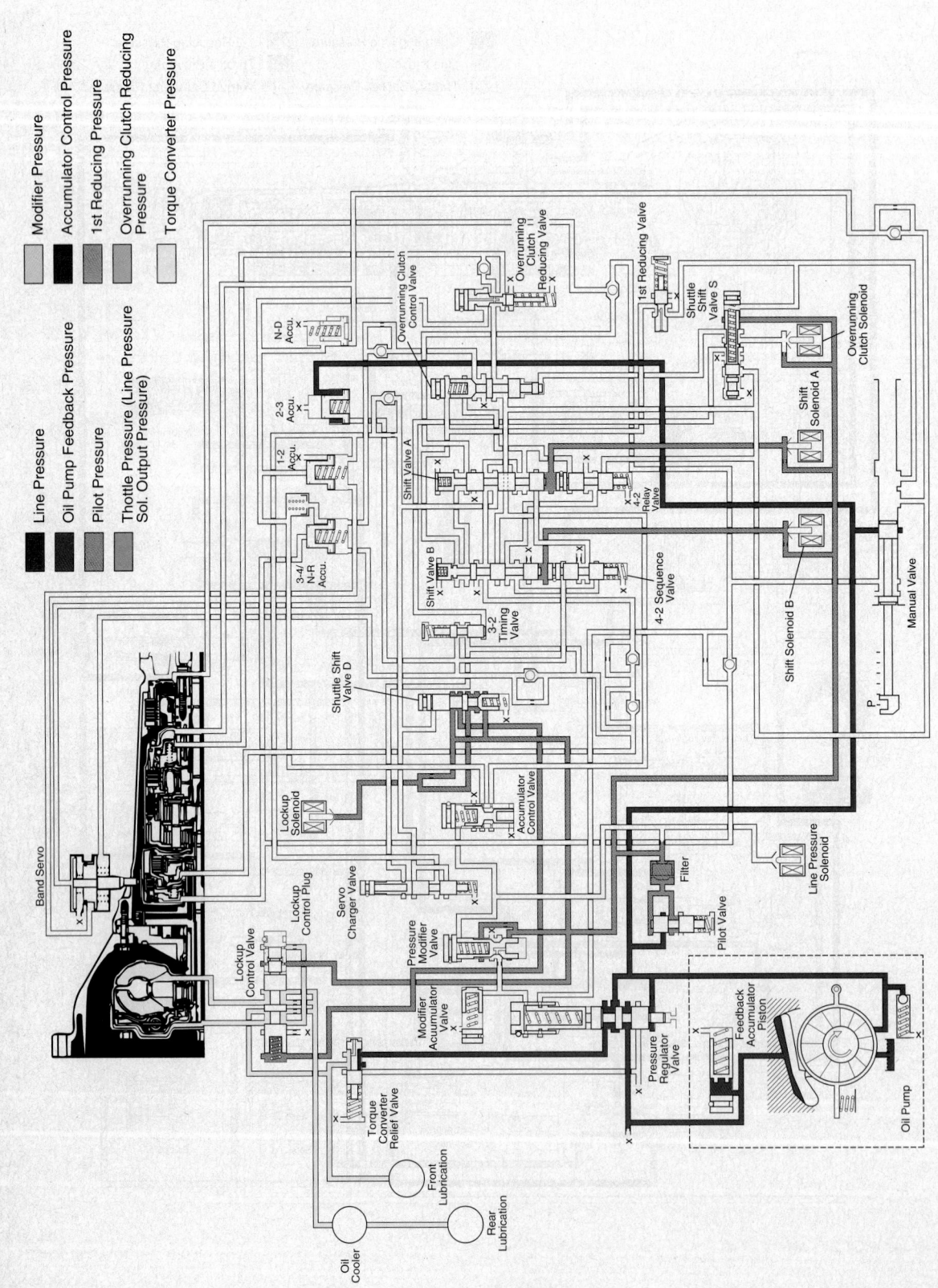

Fig. 1: "P" Position — Park

Courtesy of Mazda Motors Corp.

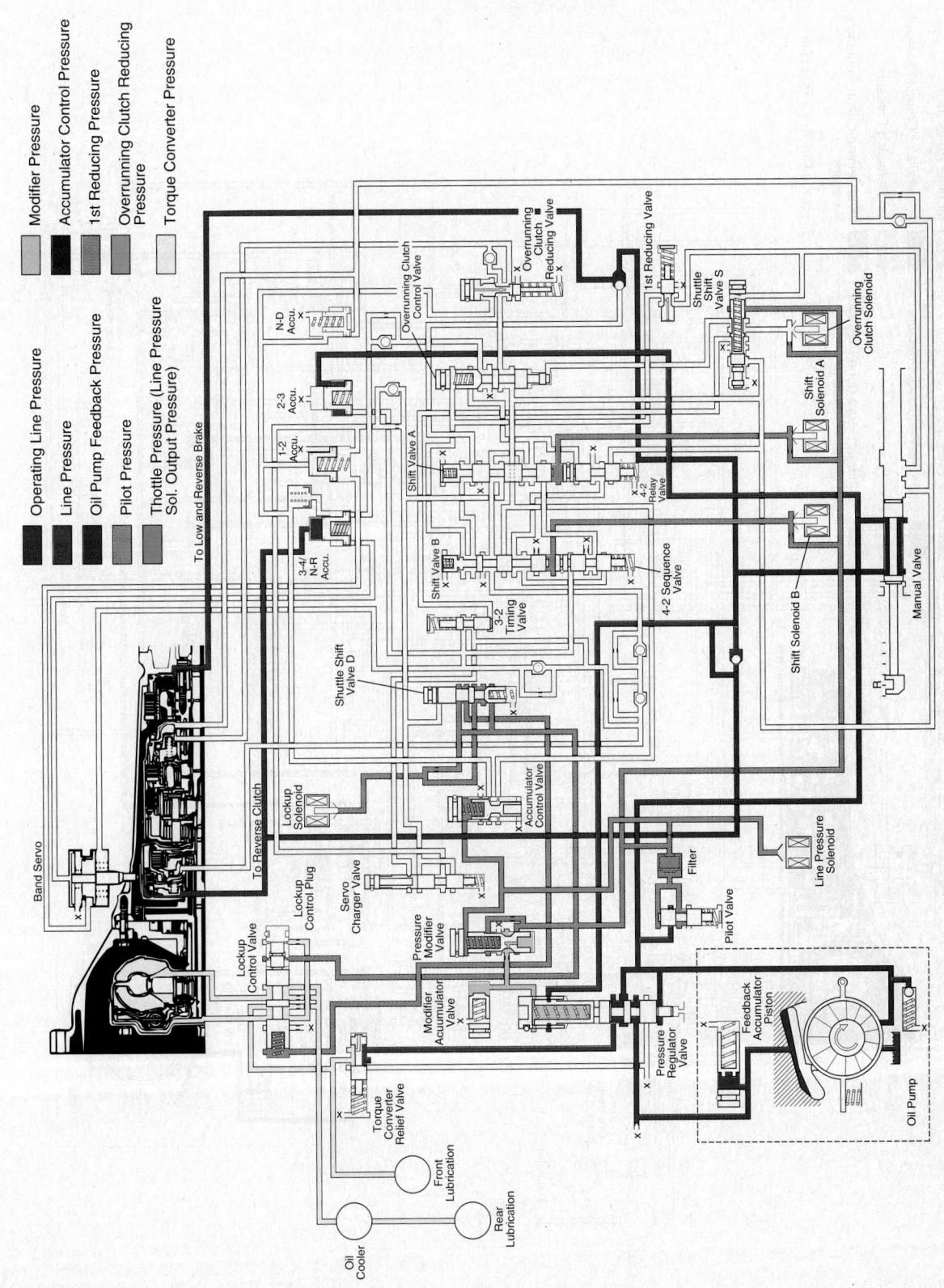

OIL CIRCUIT DIAGRAMS
Mazda RA4A-EL & RA4AX-EL (Cont.)

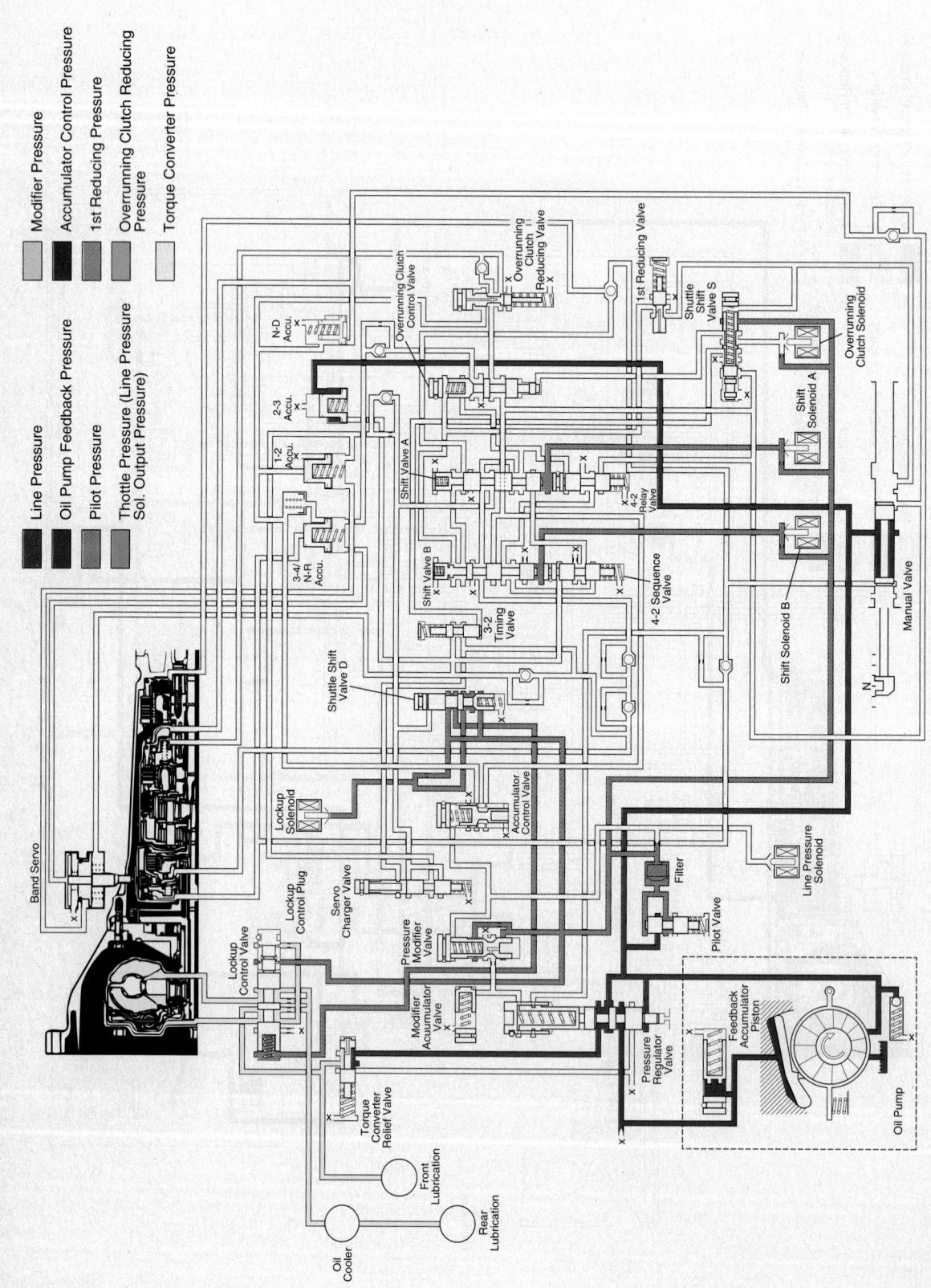

Fig. 3: "N" Position — Neutral

Courtesy of Mazda Motors Corp.

OIL CIRCUIT DIAGRAMS
Mazda RA4A-EL & RA4AX-EL (Cont.)

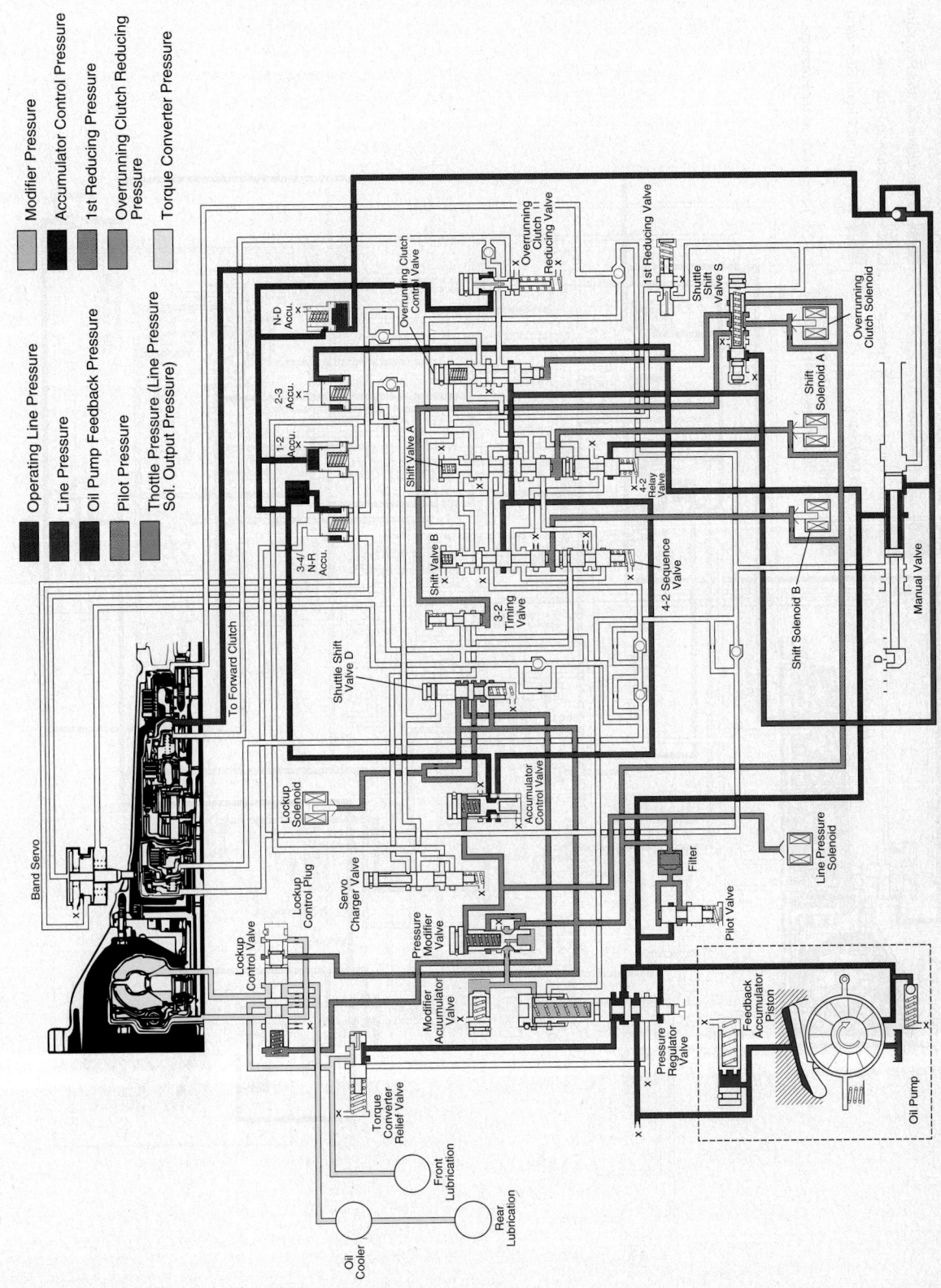

Fig. 4: "D" Position — 1st Gear

Courtesy of Mazda Motors Corp.

OIL CIRCUIT DIAGRAMS
Mazda RA4A-EL & RA4AX-EL (Cont.)

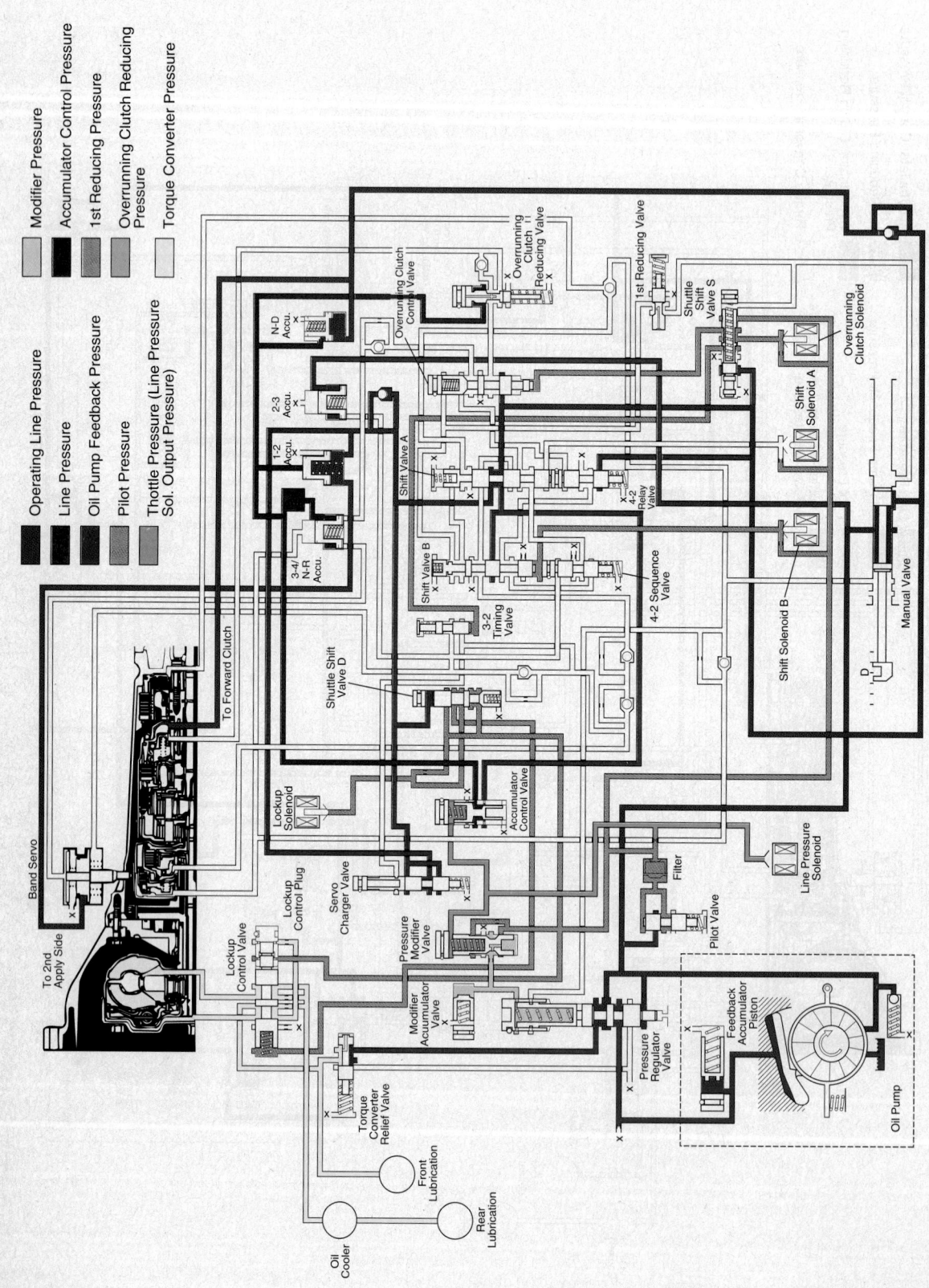

Fig. 5: "D" Position — 2nd Gear

Courtesy of Mazda Motors Corp.

OIL CIRCUIT DIAGRAMS
Mazda RA4A-EL & RA4AX-EL (Cont.)

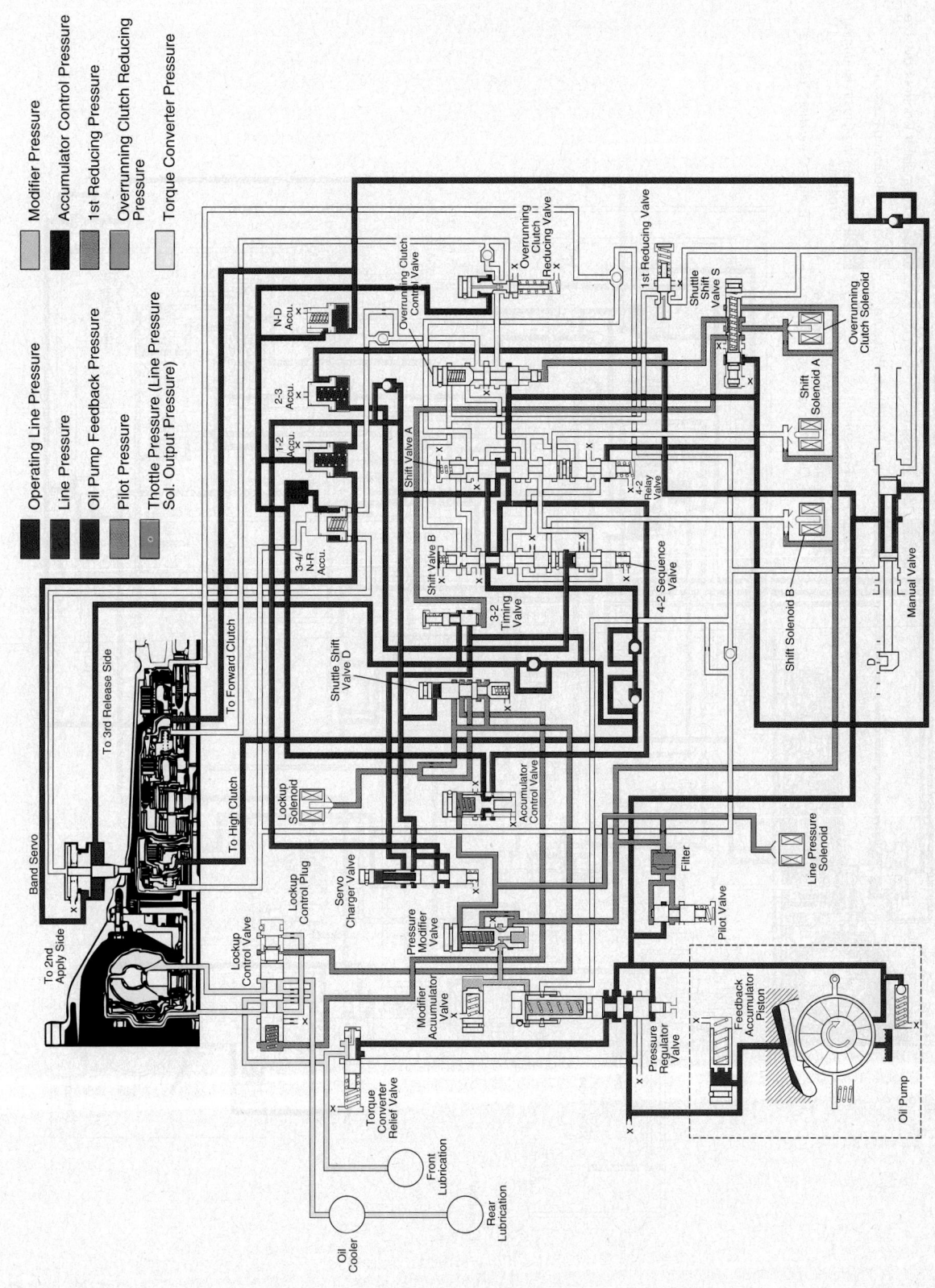

Fig. 6: "D" Position — 3rd Gear

Courtesy of Mazda Motors Corp.

OIL CIRCUIT DIAGRAMS
Mazda RA4A-EL & RA4AX-EL (Cont.)

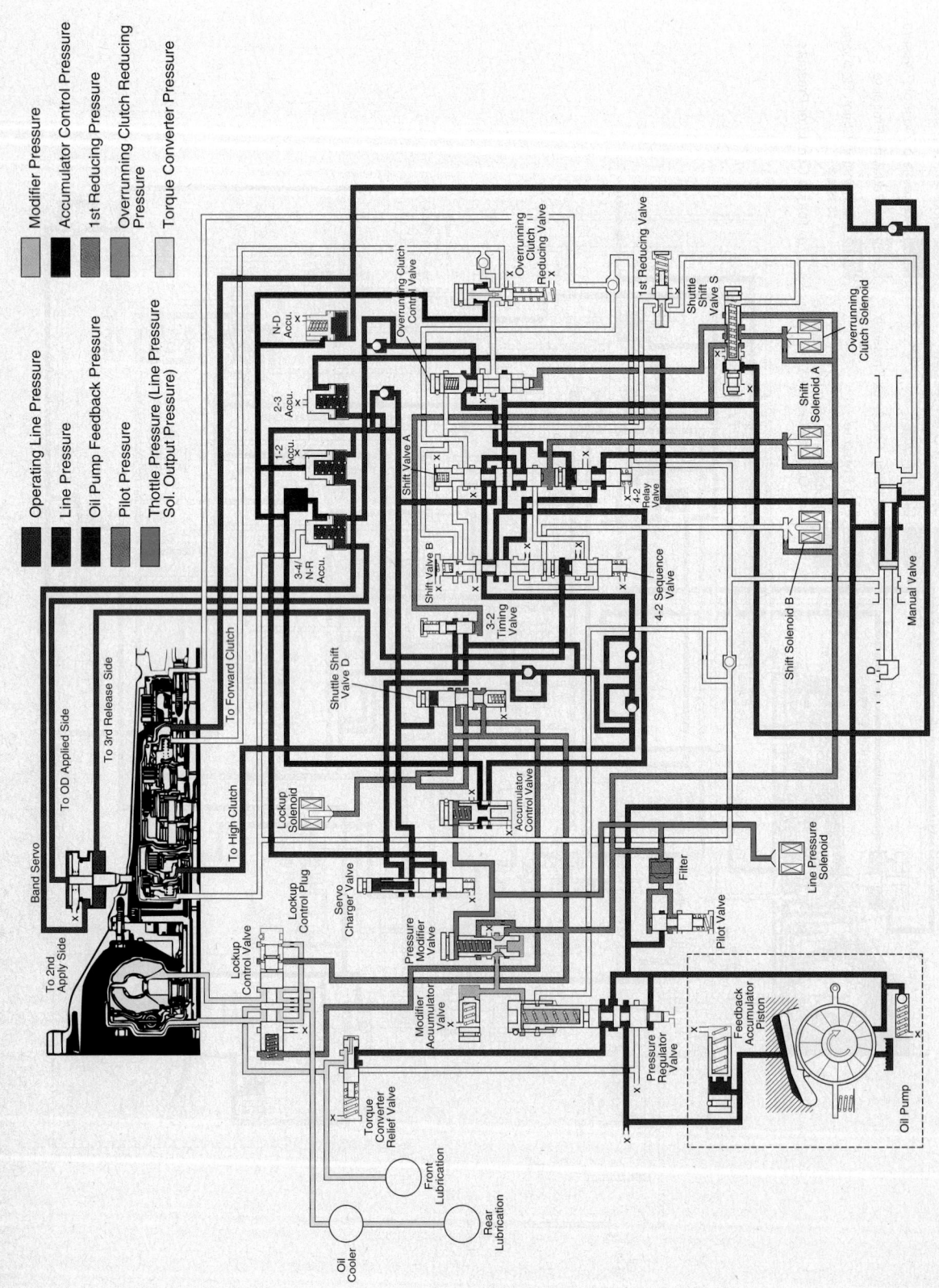

Fig. 7: "D" Position — Overdrive (Lock-Up OFF)

Courtesy of Mazda Motors Corp.

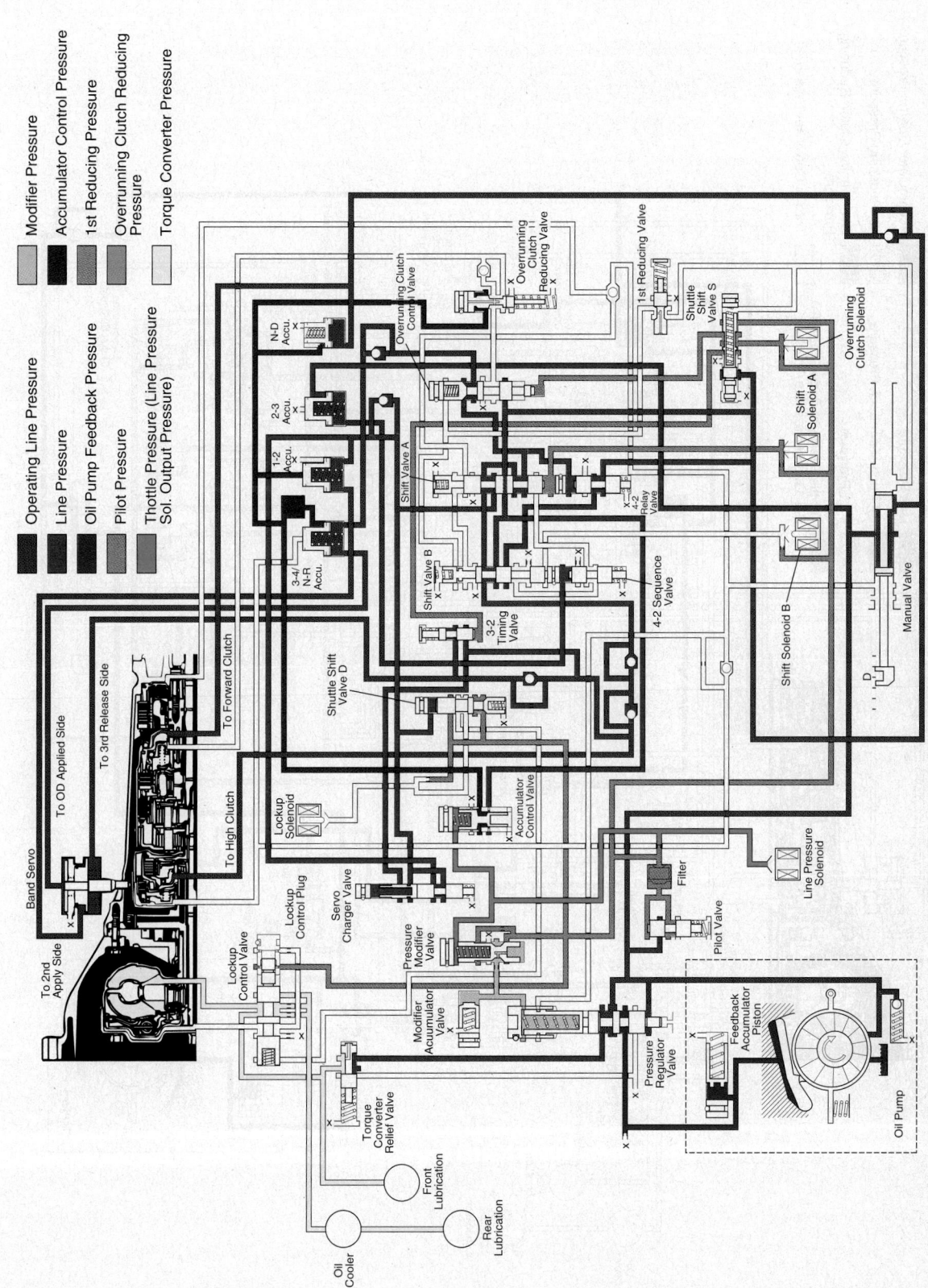

Fig. 8: "D" Position — Overdrive (Lock-Up ON)

Courtesy of Mazda Motors Corp.

OIL CIRCUIT DIAGRAMS
Mazda RA4A-EL & RA4AX-EL (Cont.)

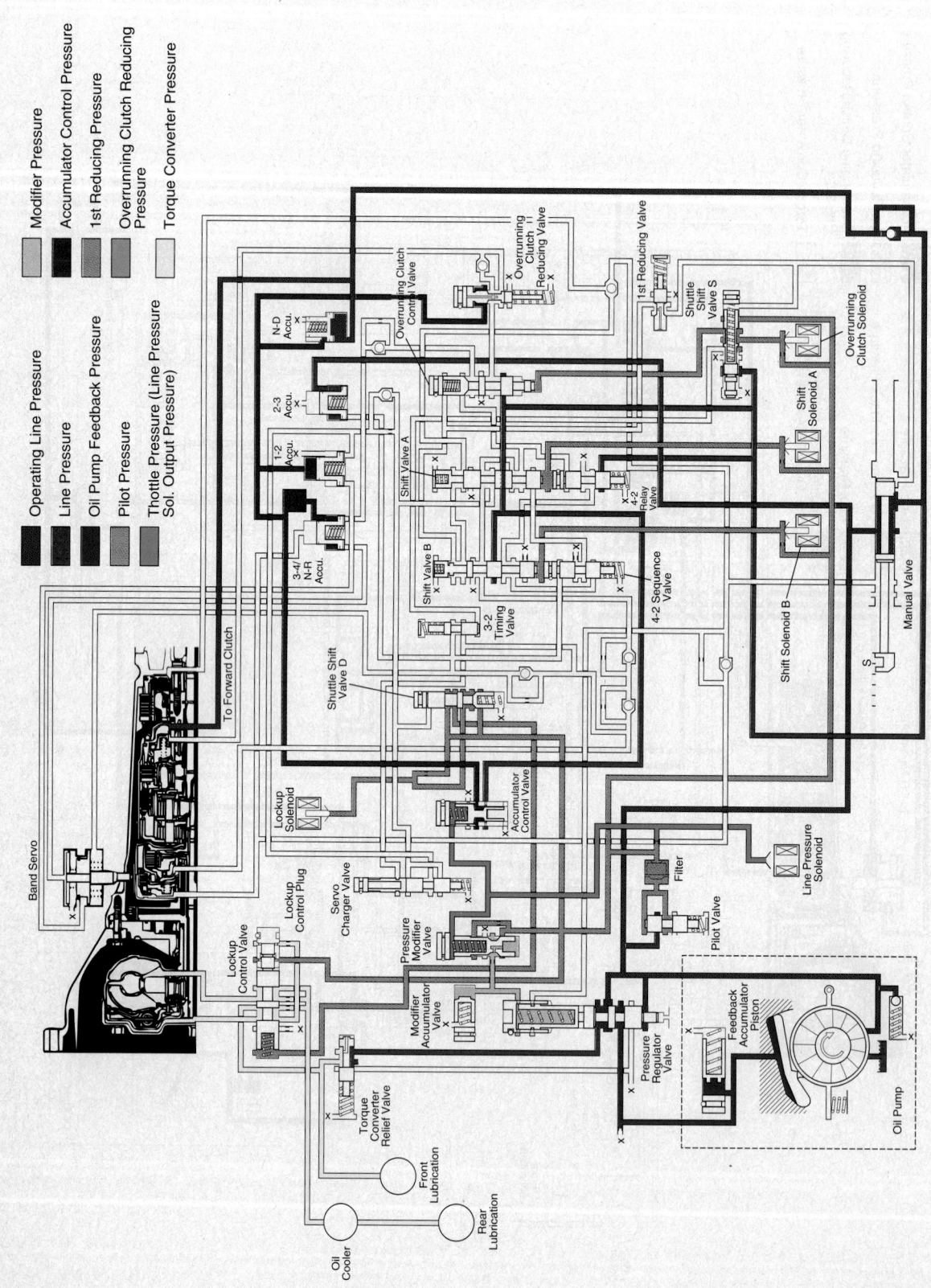

Fig. 9: "S" Position — 1st Gear

Courtesy of Mazda Motors Corp.

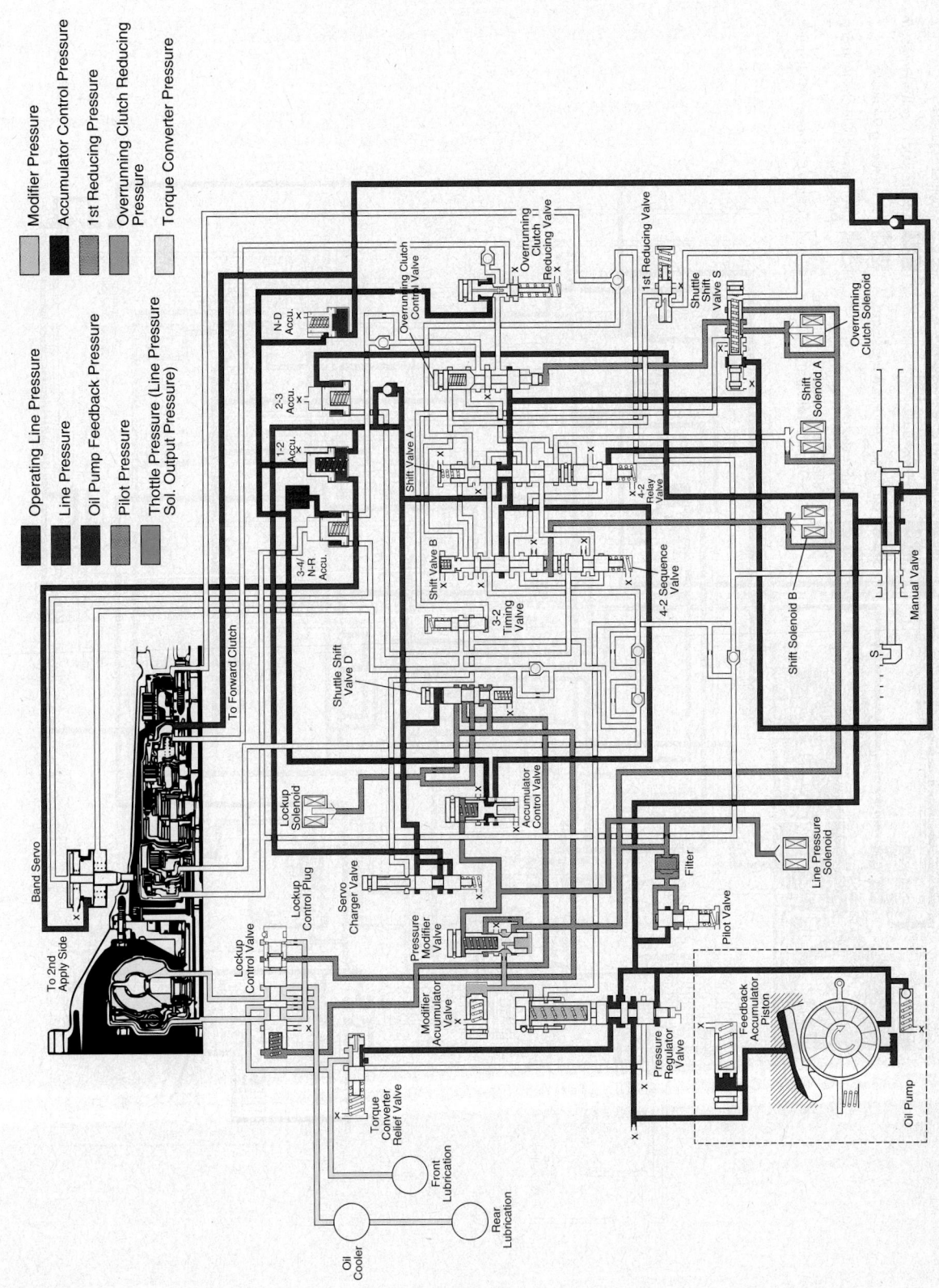

OIL CIRCUIT DIAGRAMS
Mazda RA4A-EL & RA4AX-EL (Cont.)

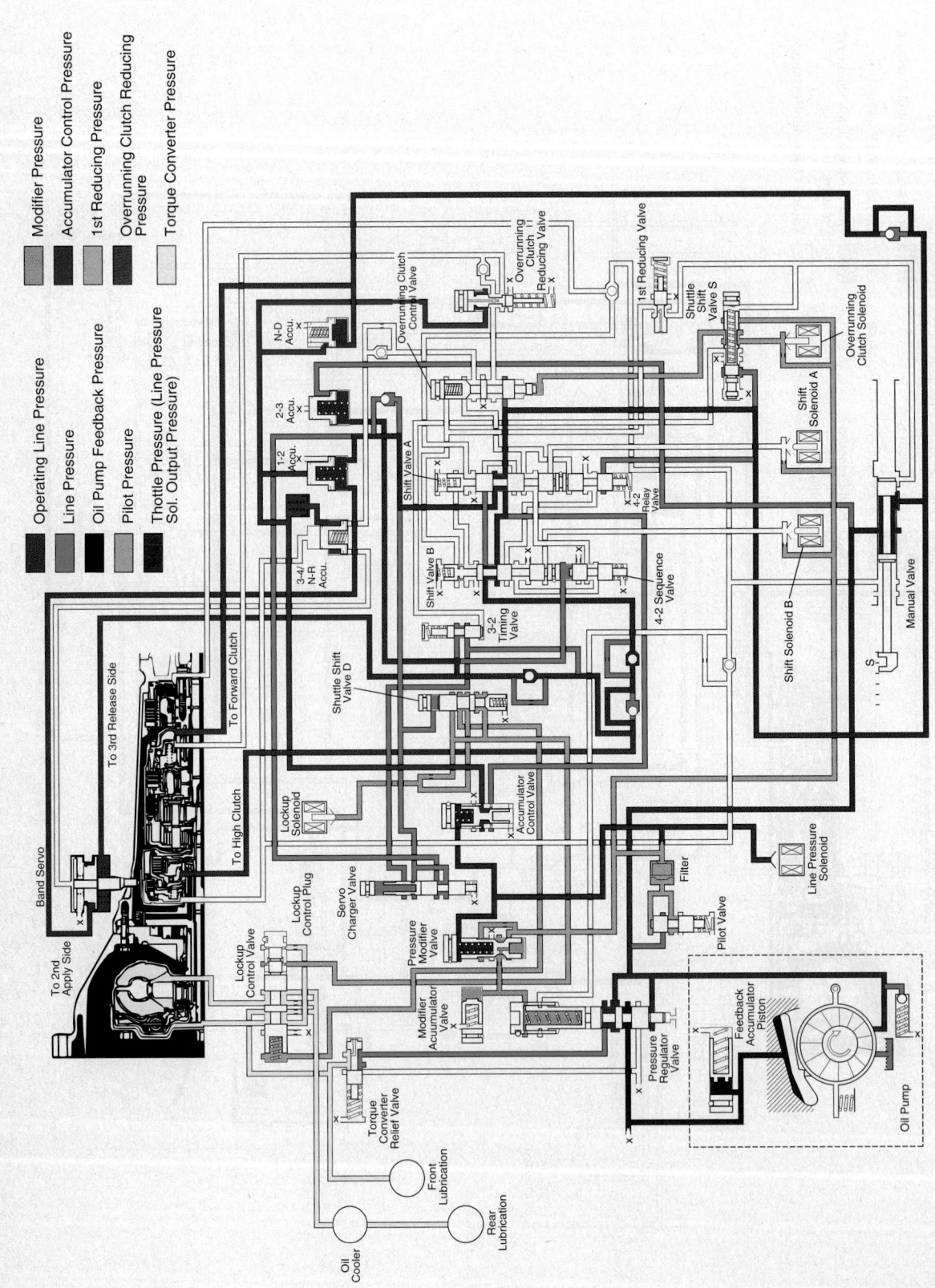

Fig. 11: "S" Position — 3rd Gear

Courtesy of Mazda Motors Corp.

OIL CIRCUIT DIAGRAMS
Mazda RA4A-EL & RA4AX-EL (Cont.)

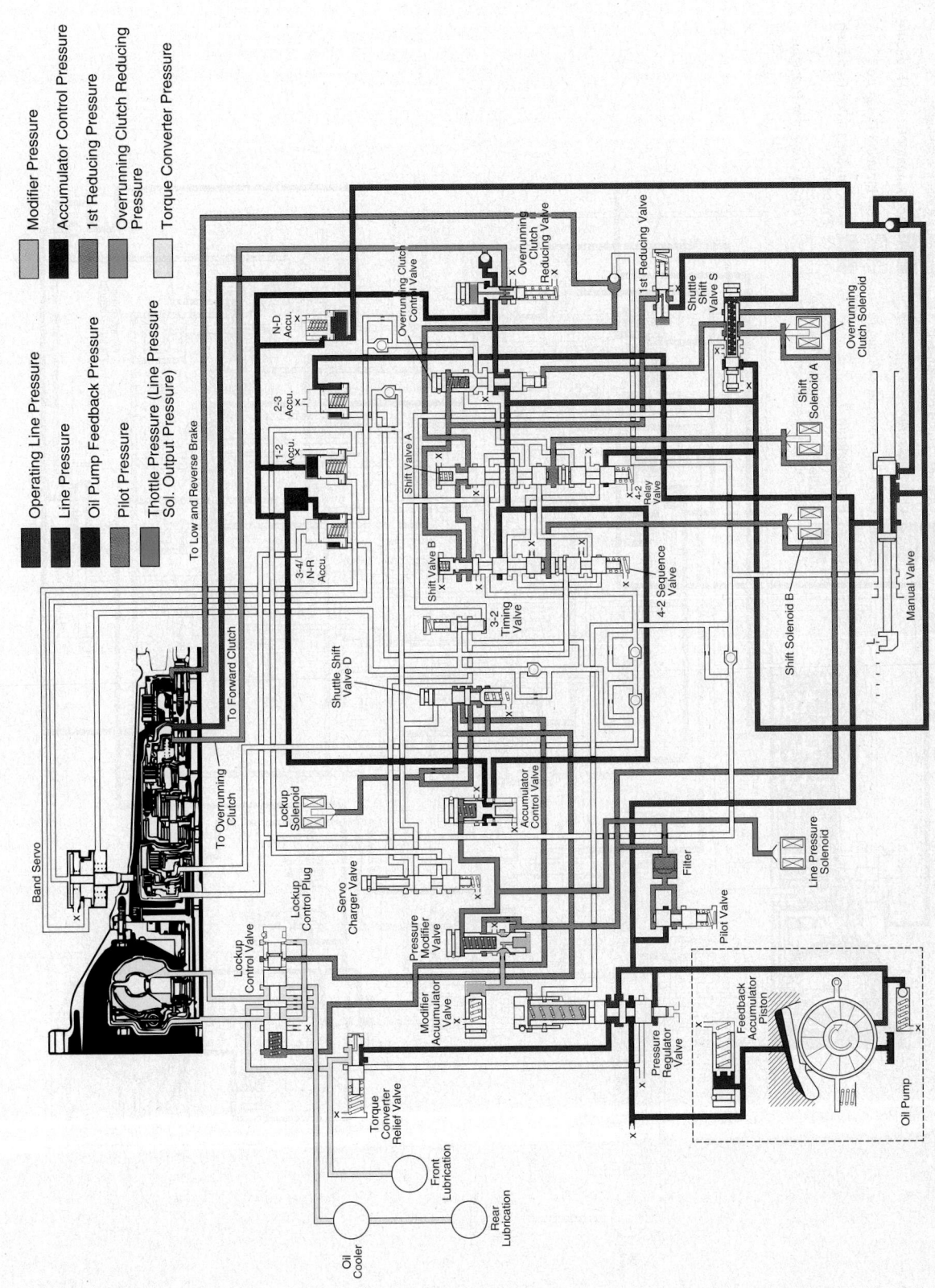

Fig. 12: "L" Position — 1st Gear

Courtesy of Mazda Motors Corp.

OIL CIRCUIT DIAGRAMS
Mazda RA4A-EL & RA4AX-EL (Cont.)

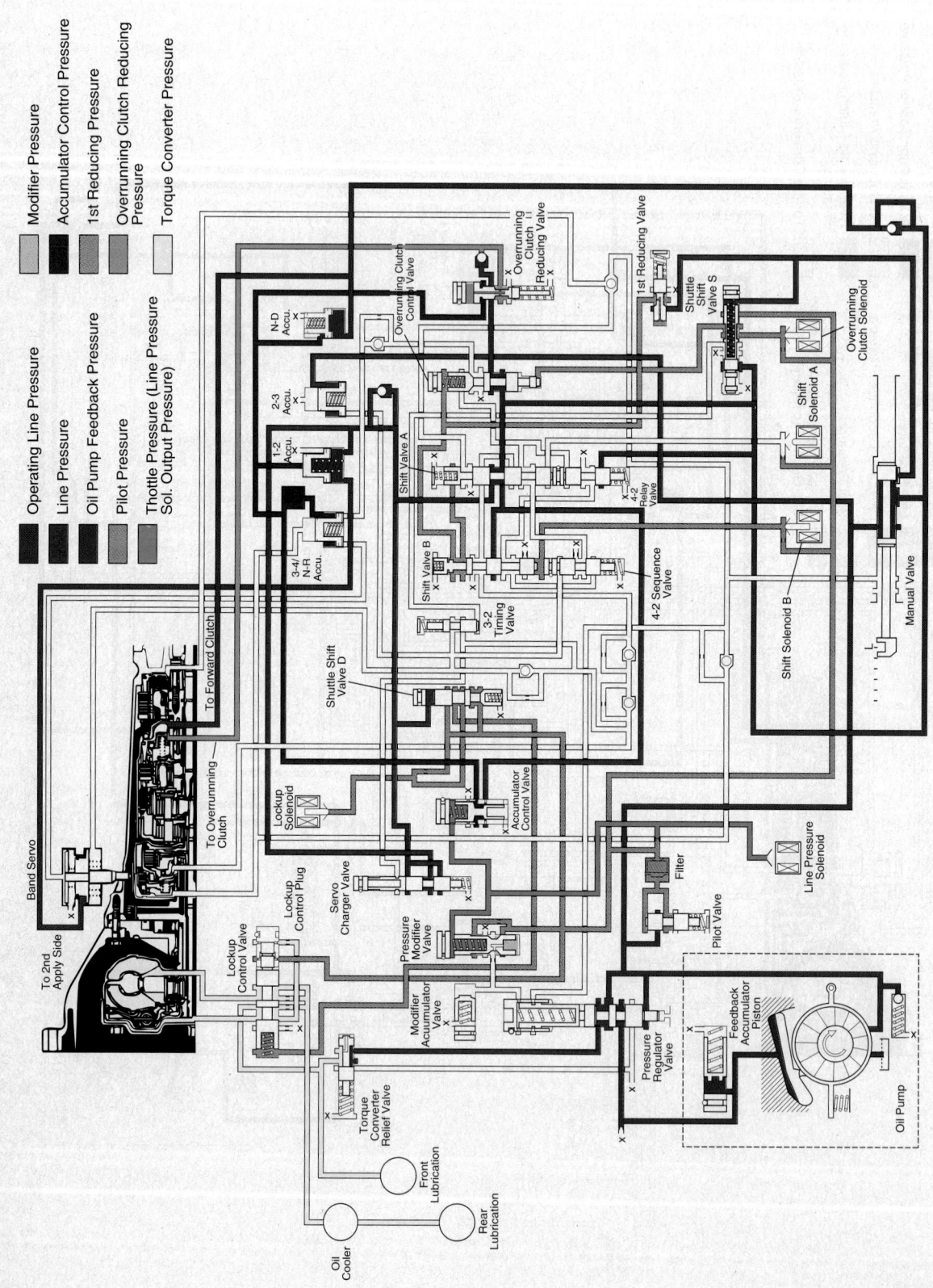

Fig. 13: "L" Position — 2nd Gear

Courtesy of Mazda Motors Corp.

OIL CIRCUIT DIAGRAMS
Mitsubishi R4AC1

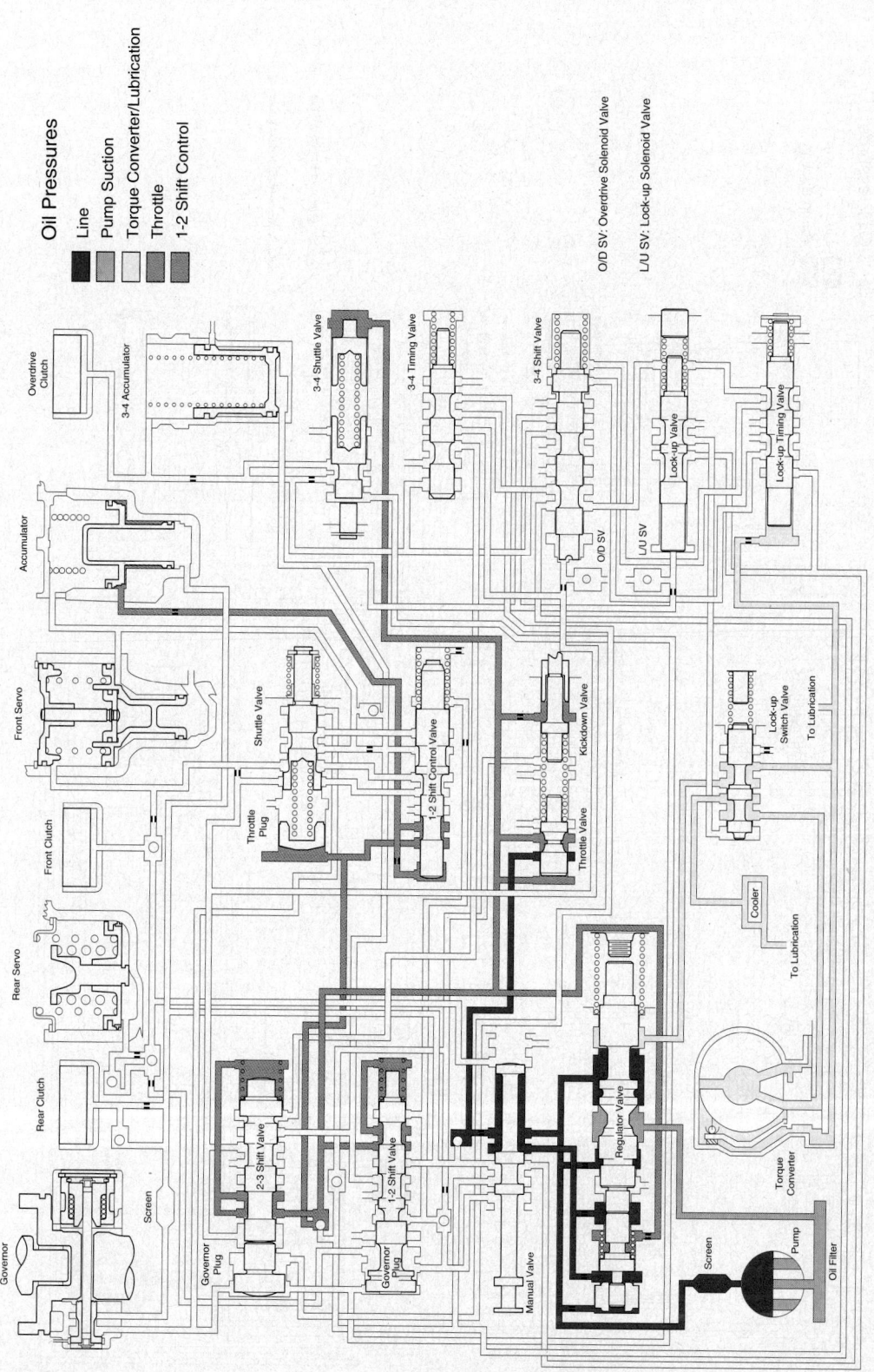

Fig. 1: "N" Position — Neutral

Courtesy of Mitsubishi Motor Sales of America

OIL CIRCUIT DIAGRAMS
Mitsubishi R4AC1 (Cont.)

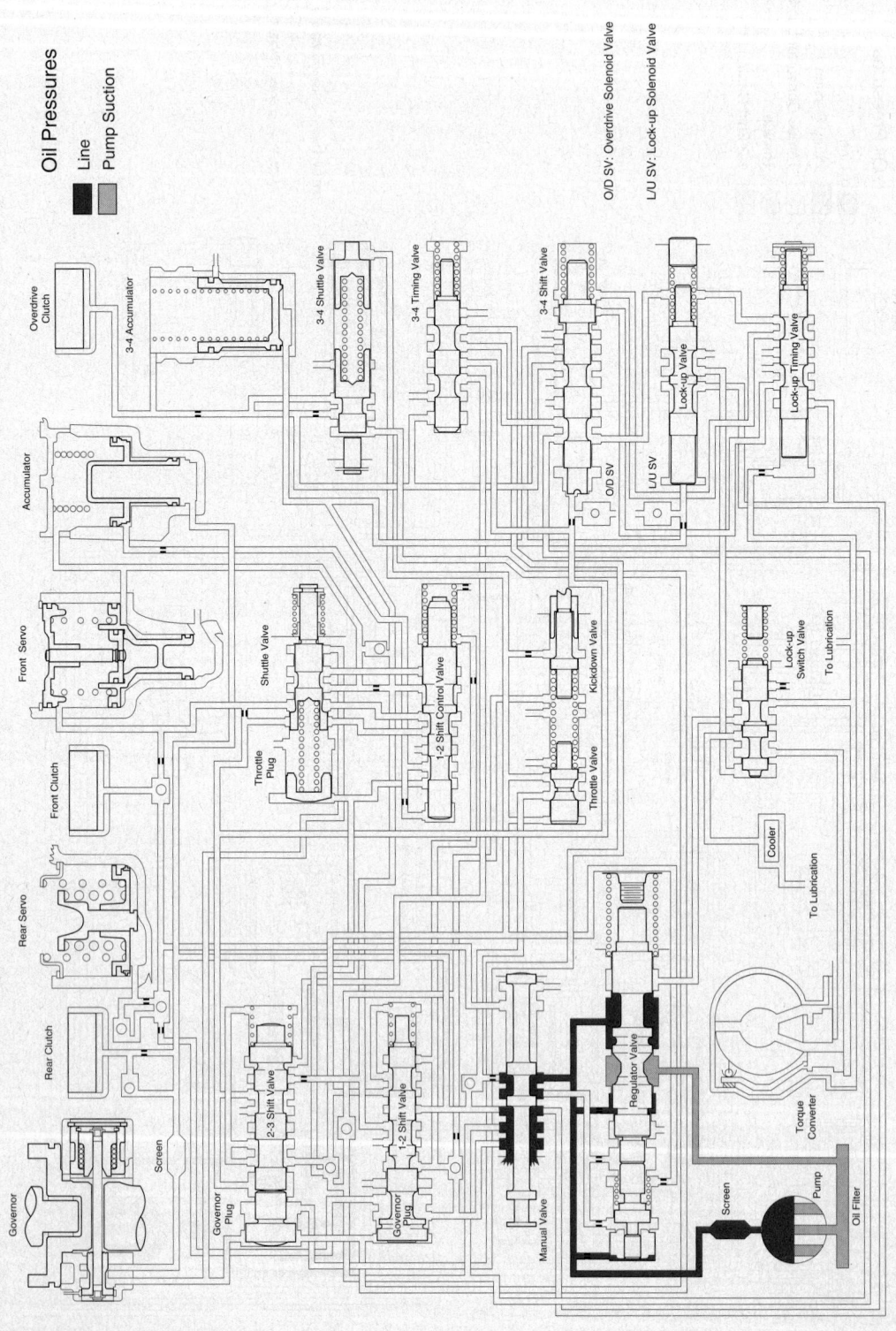

Fig. 2: "P" Position — Park

Courtesy of Mitsubishi Motor Sales of America

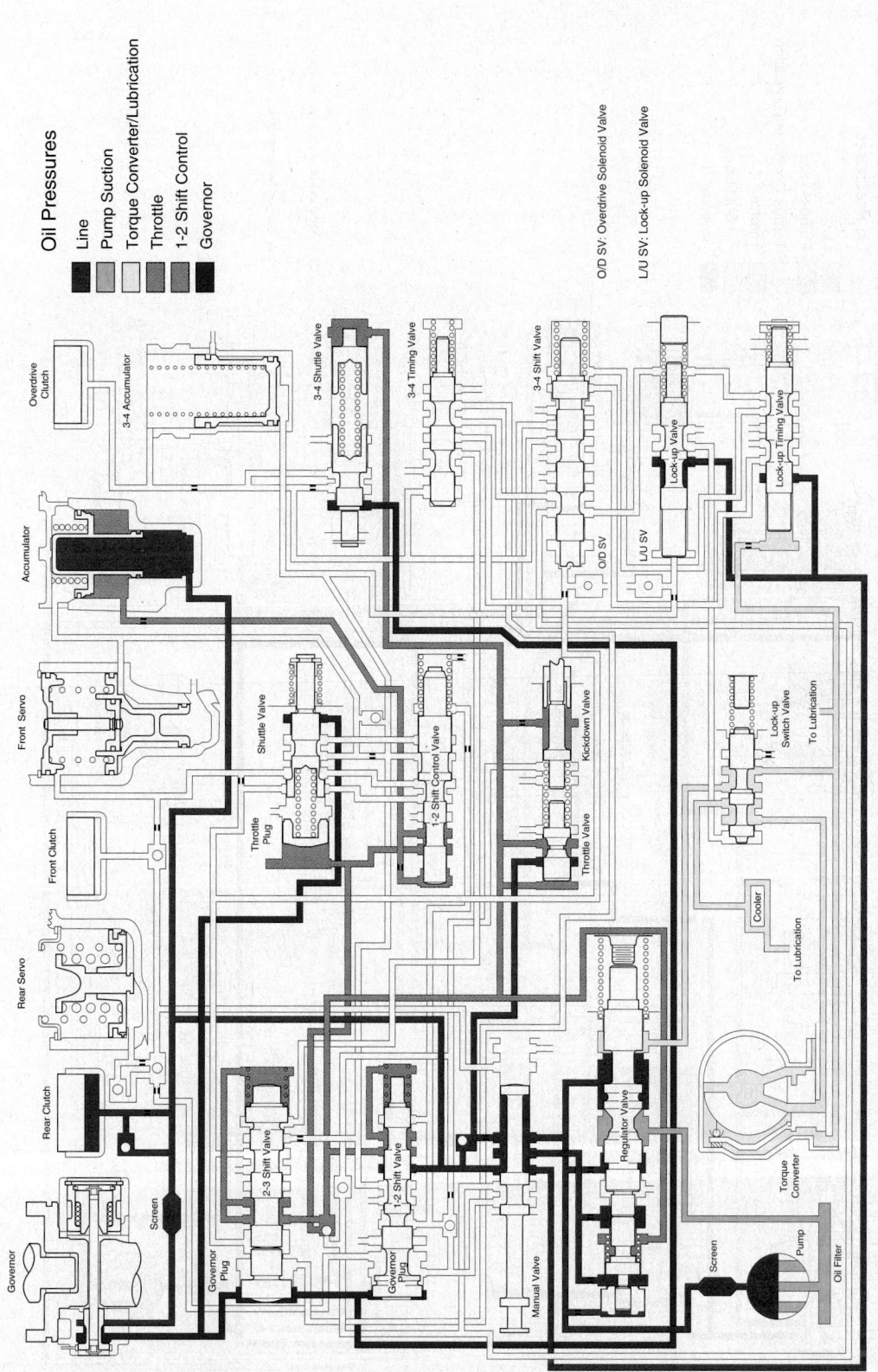

Oil Pressures

- Line
- Pump Suction
- Torque Converter/Lubrication
- Throttle
- 1-2 Shift Control
- Governor

O/D SV: Overdrive Solenoid Valve

L/U SV: Lock-up Solenoid Valve

Fig. 3: "D" Position — 1st Gear

Courtesy of Mitsubishi Motor Sales of America

OIL CIRCUIT DIAGRAMS
Mitsubishi R4AC1 (Cont.)

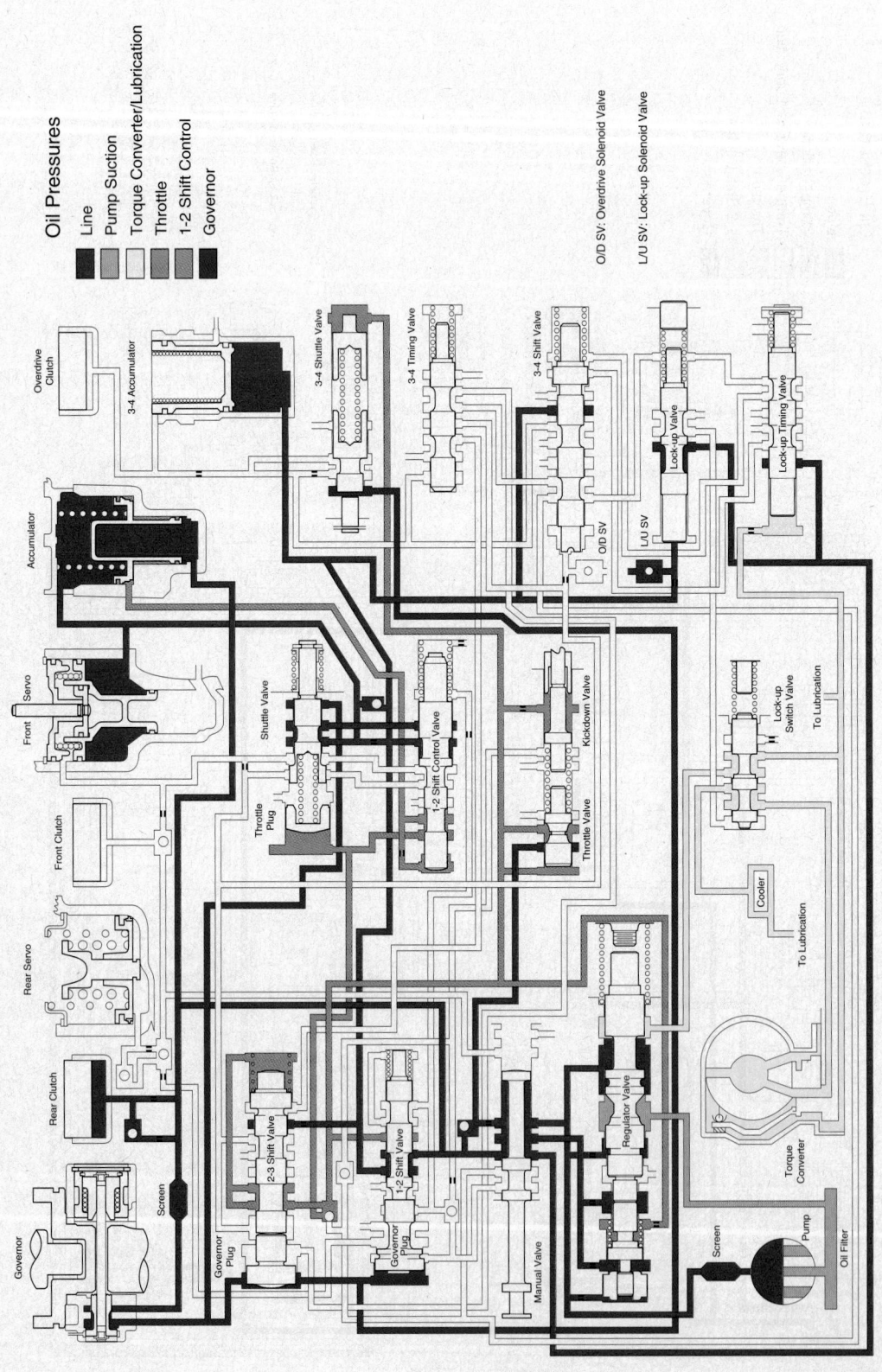

Fig. 4: "D" Position — 2nd Gear

Courtesy of Mitsubishi Motor Sales of America

OIL CIRCUIT DIAGRAMS
Mitsubishi R4AC1 (Cont.)

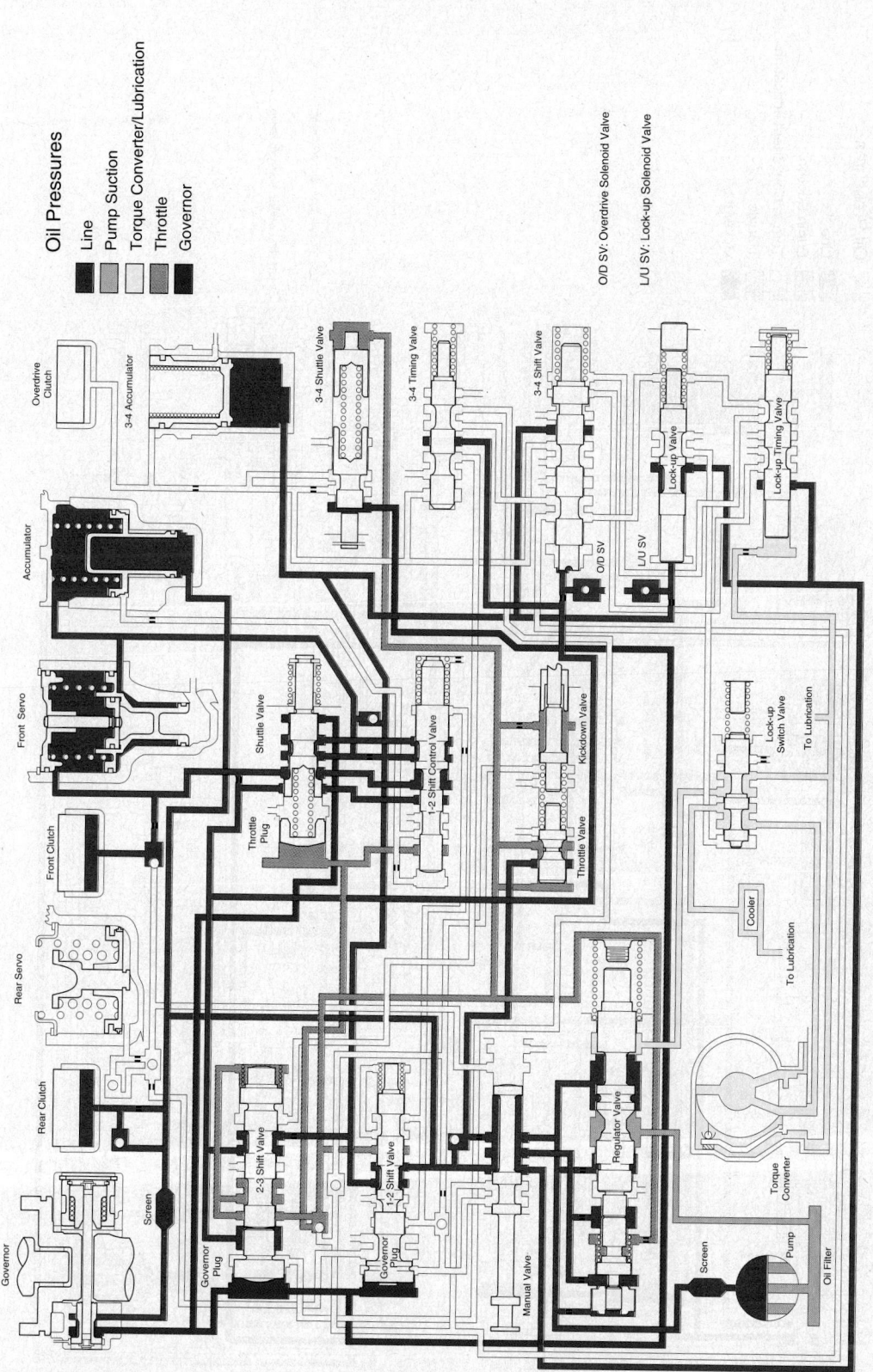

OIL CIRCUIT DIAGRAMS
Mitsubishi R4AC1 (Cont.)

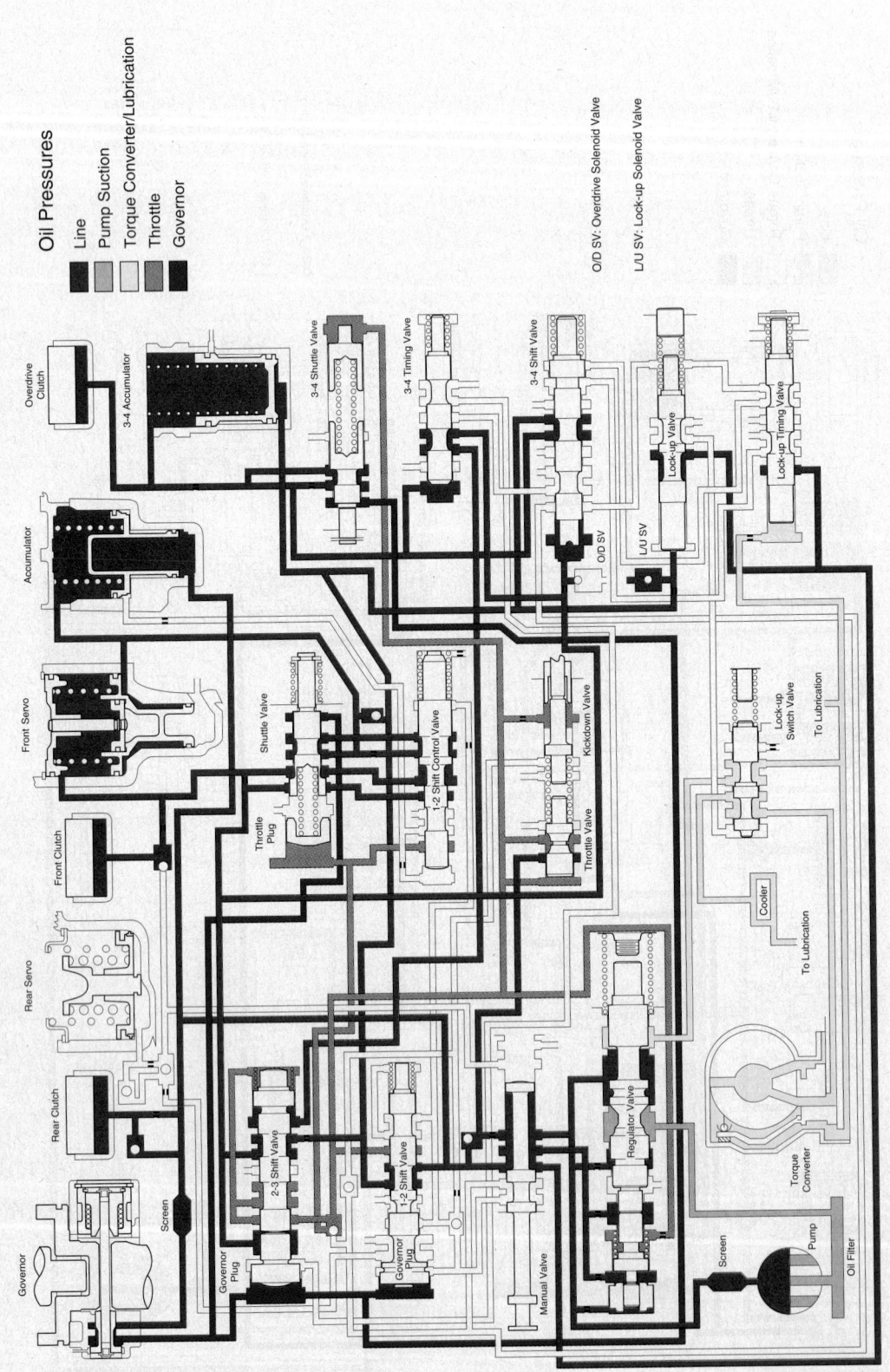

Oil Pressures
- Line
- Pump Suction
- Torque Converter/Lubrication
- Throttle
- Governor

O/D SV: Overdrive Solenoid Valve
L/U SV: Lock-up Solenoid Valve

Overdrive Clutch

3-4 Accumulator

Accumulator

Front Servo

Front Clutch

Rear Servo

Rear Clutch

Governor

Screen

Governor Plug

Governor Plug

Manual Valve

Screen

Pump

Oil Filter

Torque Converter

Regulator Valve

Throttle Valve

Kickdown Valve

1-2 Shift Valve

2-3 Shift Valve

Throttle Plug

Shuttle Valve

1-2 Shift Control Valve

3-4 Shuttle Valve

3-4 Timing Valve

3-4 Shift Valve

O/D SV

L/U SV

Lock-up Valve

Lock-up Timing Valve

Lock-up Switch Valve

Cooler

To Lubrication

To Lubrication

Fig. 6: "D" Position — 4th Gear (Lock-Up OFF)

Courtesy of Mitsubishi Motor Sales of America

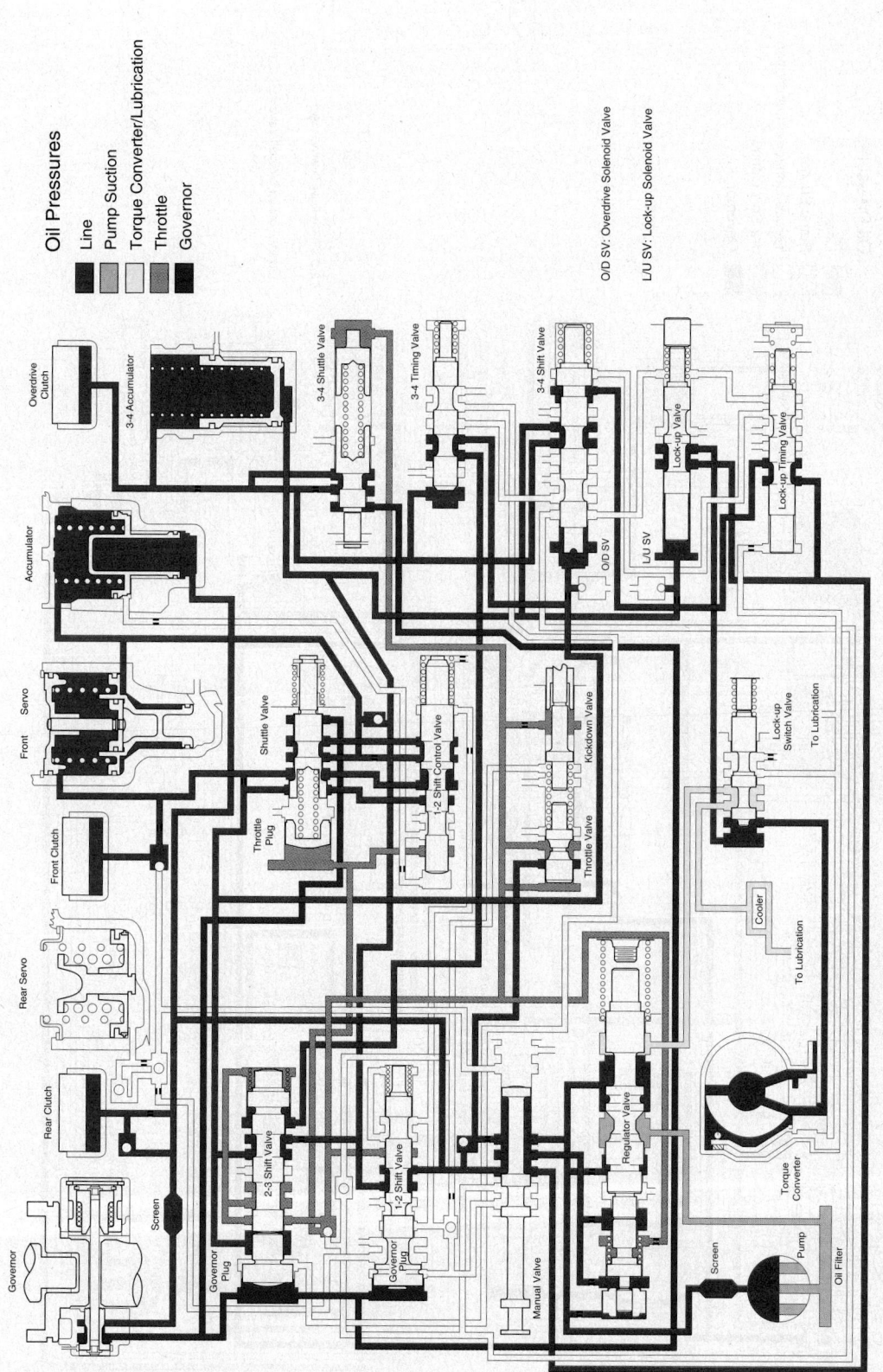

Oil Pressures
Line
Pump Suction
Torque Converter/Lubrication
Throttle
Governor

O/D SV: Overdrive Solenoid Valve
L/U SV: Lock-up Solenoid Valve

Fig. 7: *"D" Position — 4th Gear (Lock-Up ON)*

Courtesy of Mitsubishi Motor Sales of America

OIL CIRCUIT DIAGRAMS
Mitsubishi R4AC1 (Cont.)

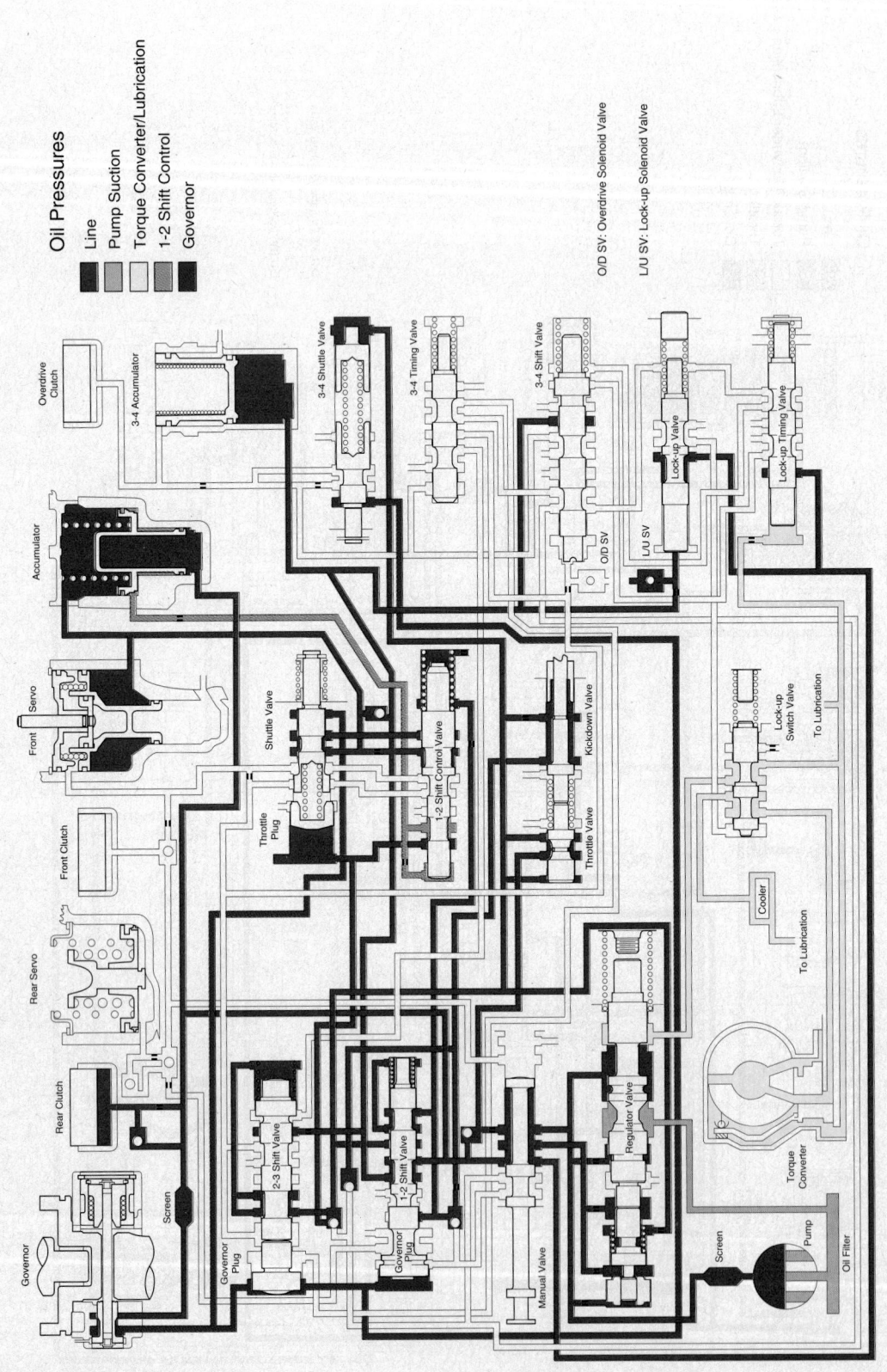

Fig. 8: "D" Position — Kickdown

Courtesy of Mitsubishi Motor Sales of America

OIL CIRCUIT DIAGRAMS
Mitsubishi R4AC1 (Cont.)

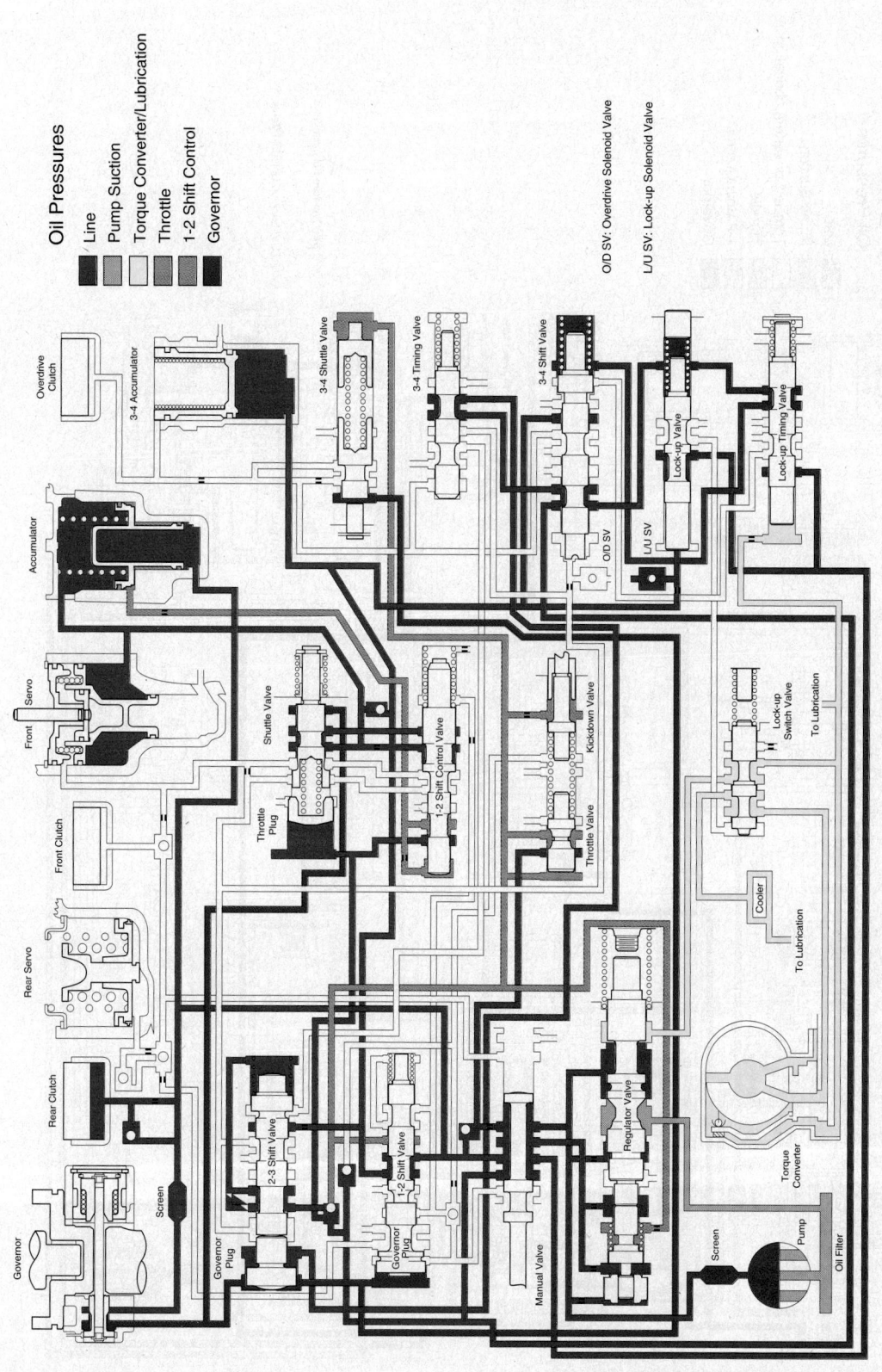

Oil Pressures
- Line
- Pump Suction
- Torque Converter/Lubrication
- Throttle
- 1-2 Shift Control
- Governor

O/D SV: Overdrive Solenoid Valve
L/U SV: Lock-up Solenoid Valve

Fig. 9: "2" Position — 2nd Gear

Courtesy of Mitsubishi Motor Sales of America

OIL CIRCUIT DIAGRAMS
Mitsubishi R4AC1 (Cont.)

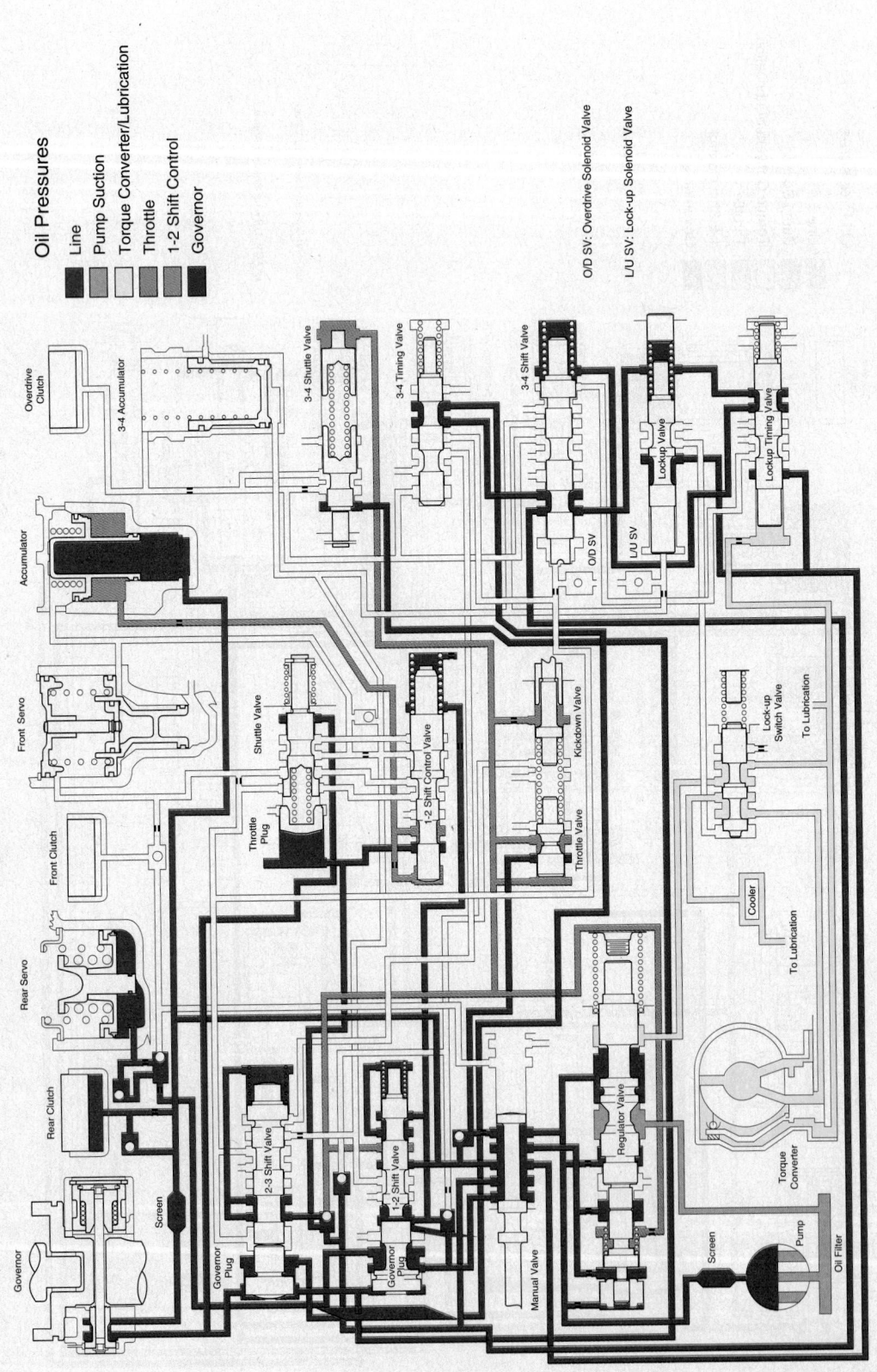

OIL CIRCUIT DIAGRAMS
Mitsubishi R4AC1 (Cont.)

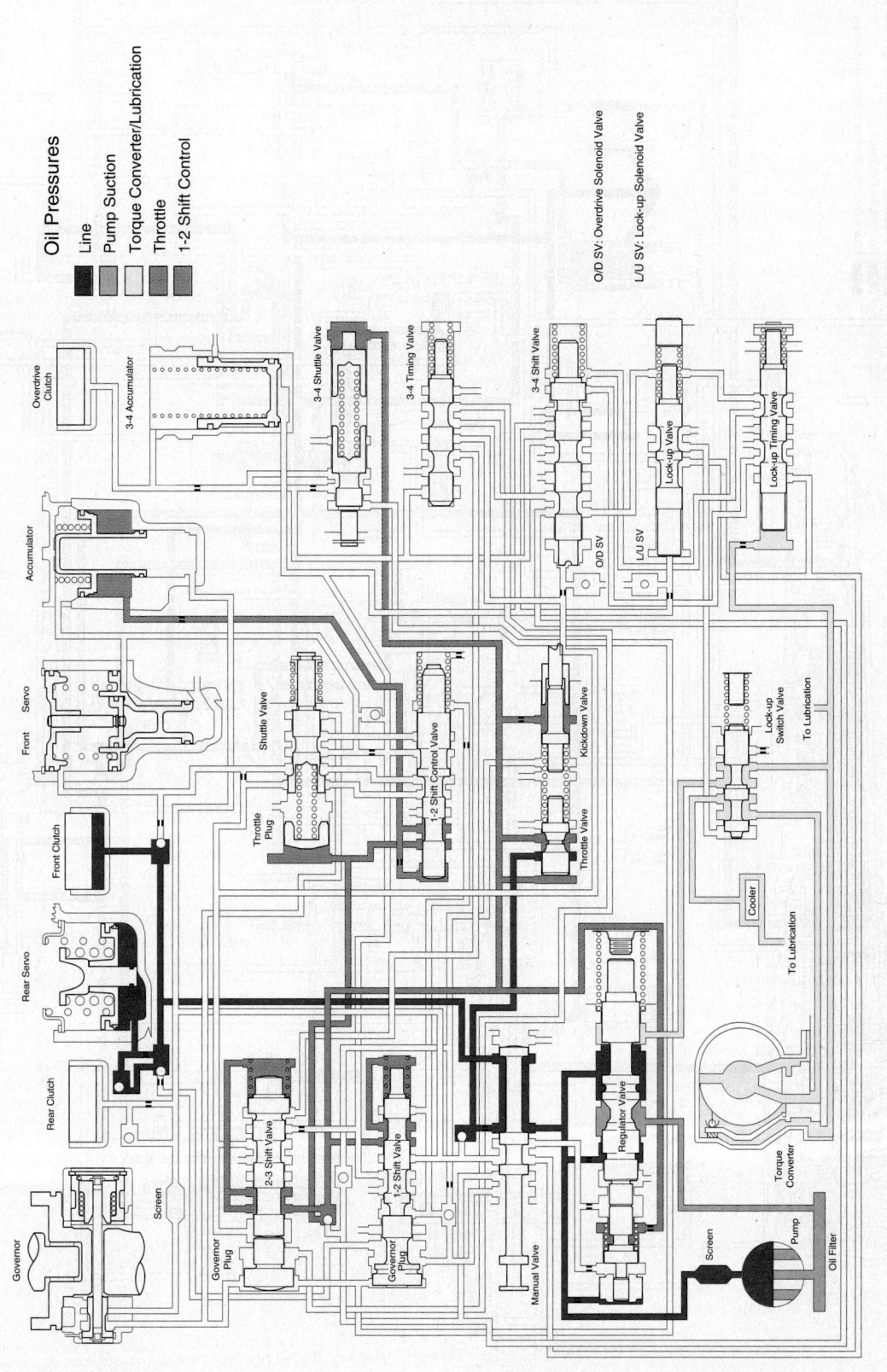

Fig. 11: "R" Position — Reverse

Courtesy of Mitsubishi Motor Sales of America

OIL CIRCUIT DIAGRAMS
Mitsubishi V4AW3

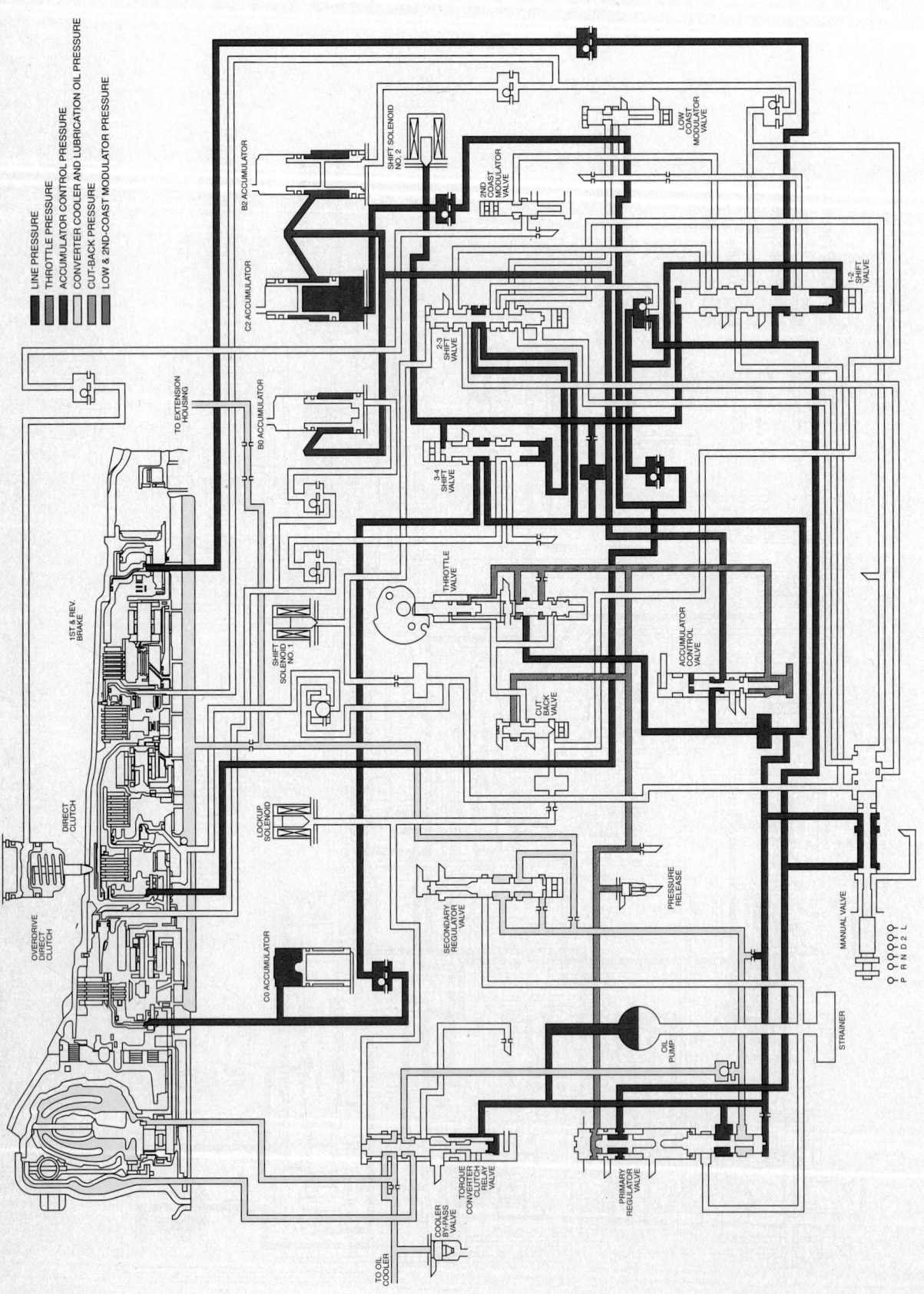

Fig. 1: "R" Position — Reverse

Courtesy of Mitsubishi Motor Sales of America

OIL CIRCUIT DIAGRAMS
Mitsubishi V4AW3 (Cont.)

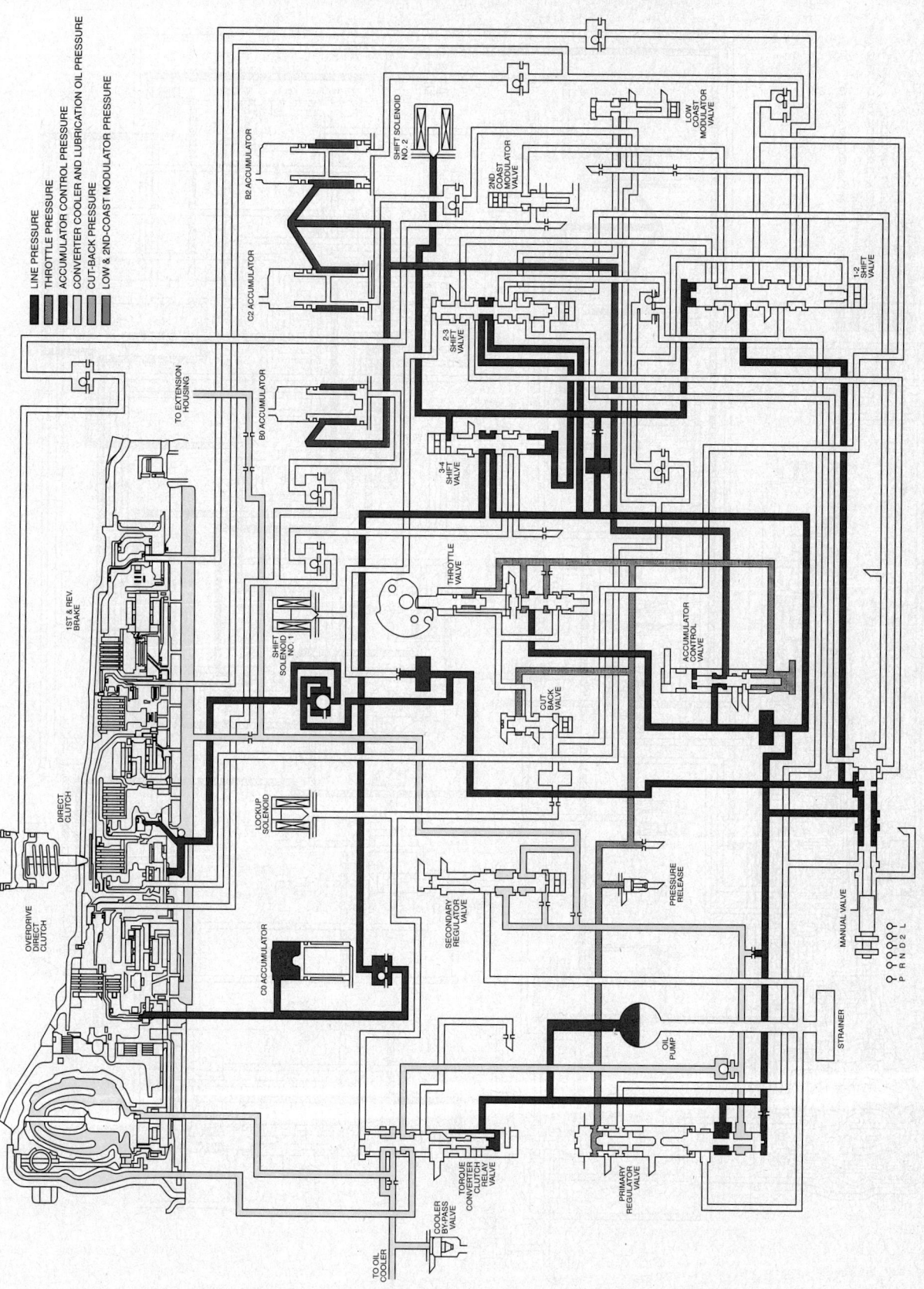

Fig. 2: "D" Position — 1st Gear

Courtesy of Mitsubishi Motor Sales of America

OIL CIRCUIT DIAGRAMS
Mitsubishi V4AW3 (Cont.)

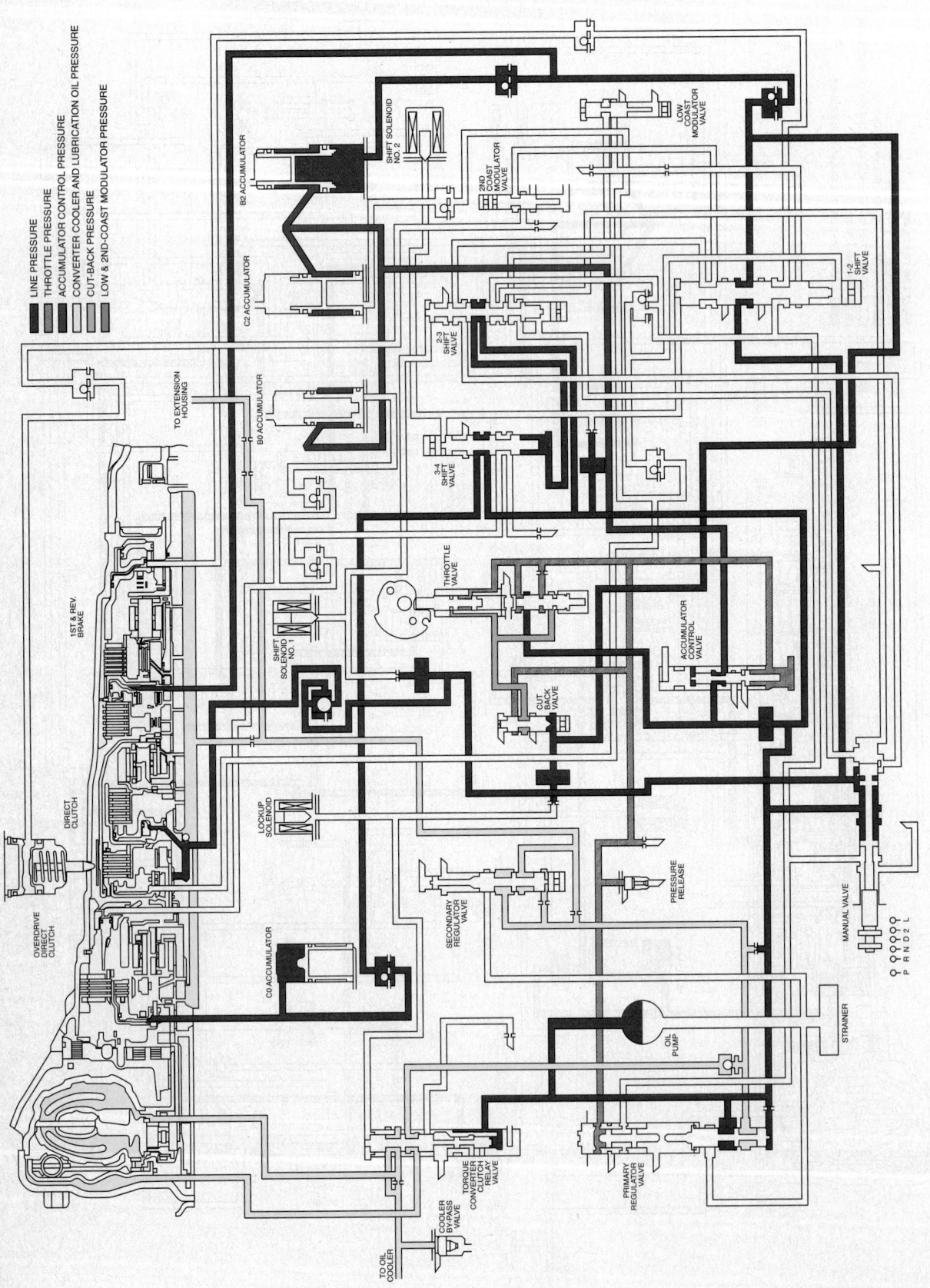

Fig. 3: "D" Position — 2nd Gear

Courtesy of Mitsubishi Motor Sales of America

OIL CIRCUIT DIAGRAMS
Mitsubishi V4AW3 (Cont.)

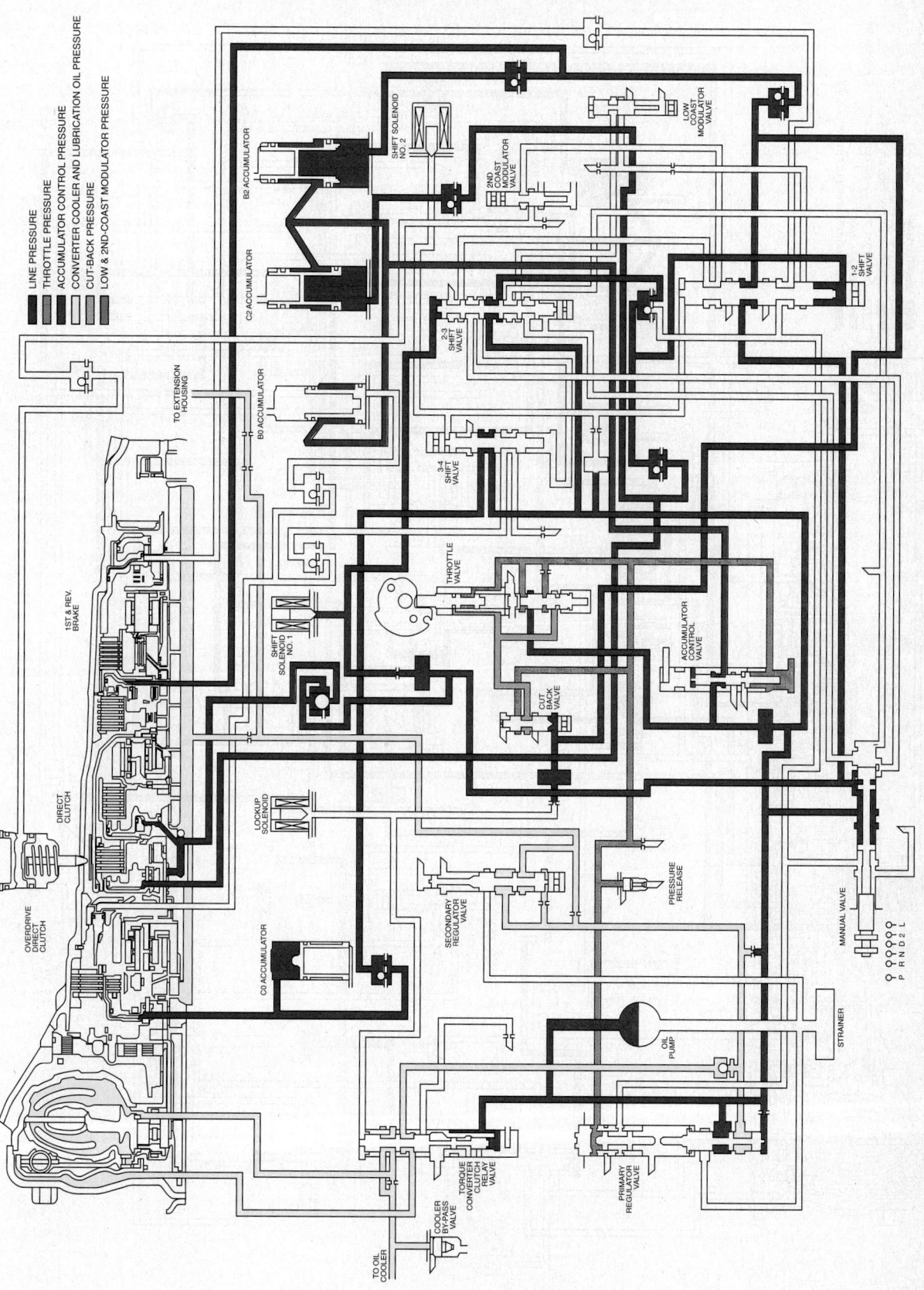

Fig. 4: "D" Position — 3rd Gear

Courtesy of Mitsubishi Motor Sales of America

OIL CIRCUIT DIAGRAMS
Mitsubishi V4AW3 (Cont.)

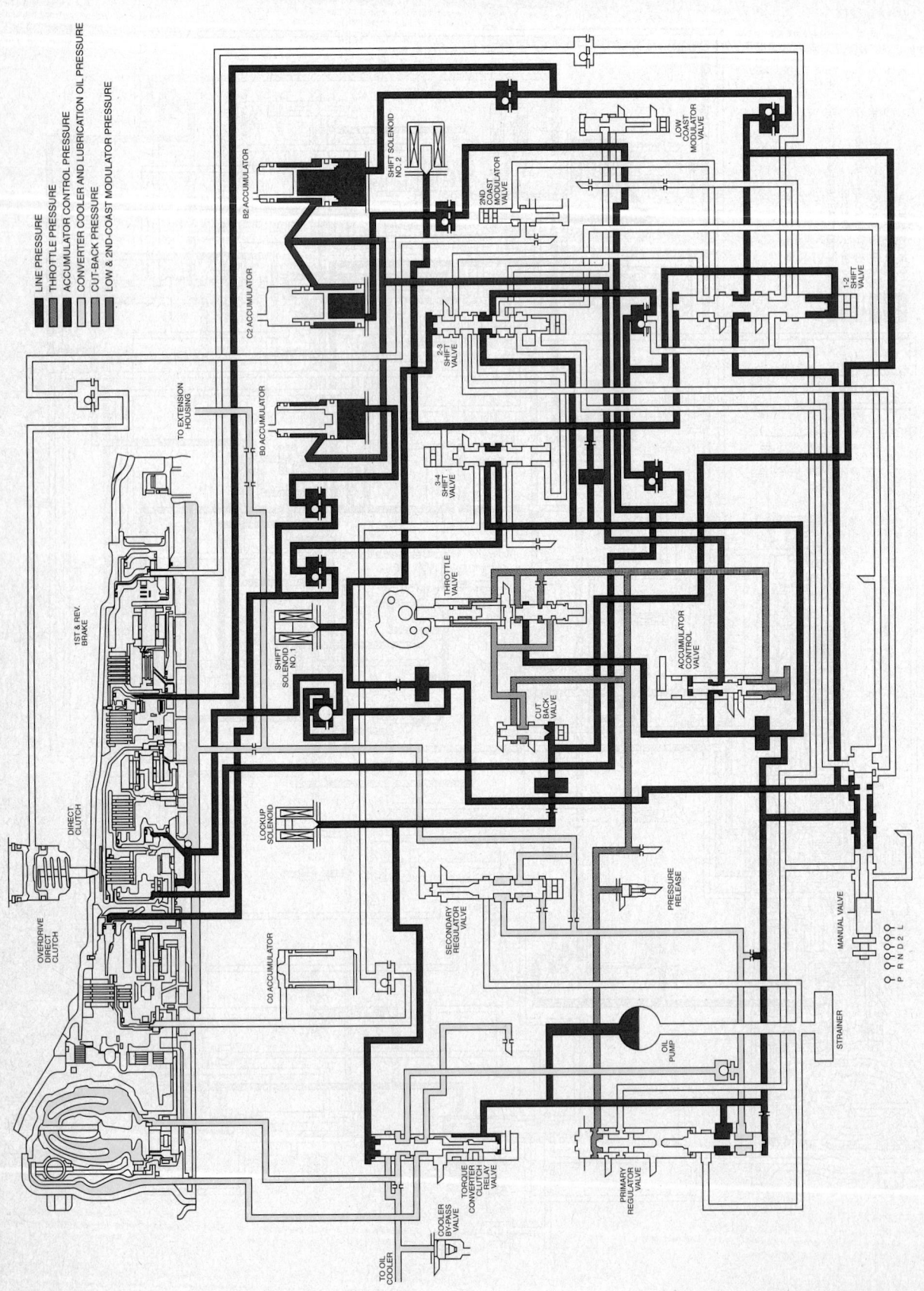

Fig. 5: "D" Position — 4th Gear (Lock-Up)

Courtesy of Mitsubishi Motor Sales of America

OIL CIRCUIT DIAGRAMS
Mitsubishi V4AW3 (Cont.)

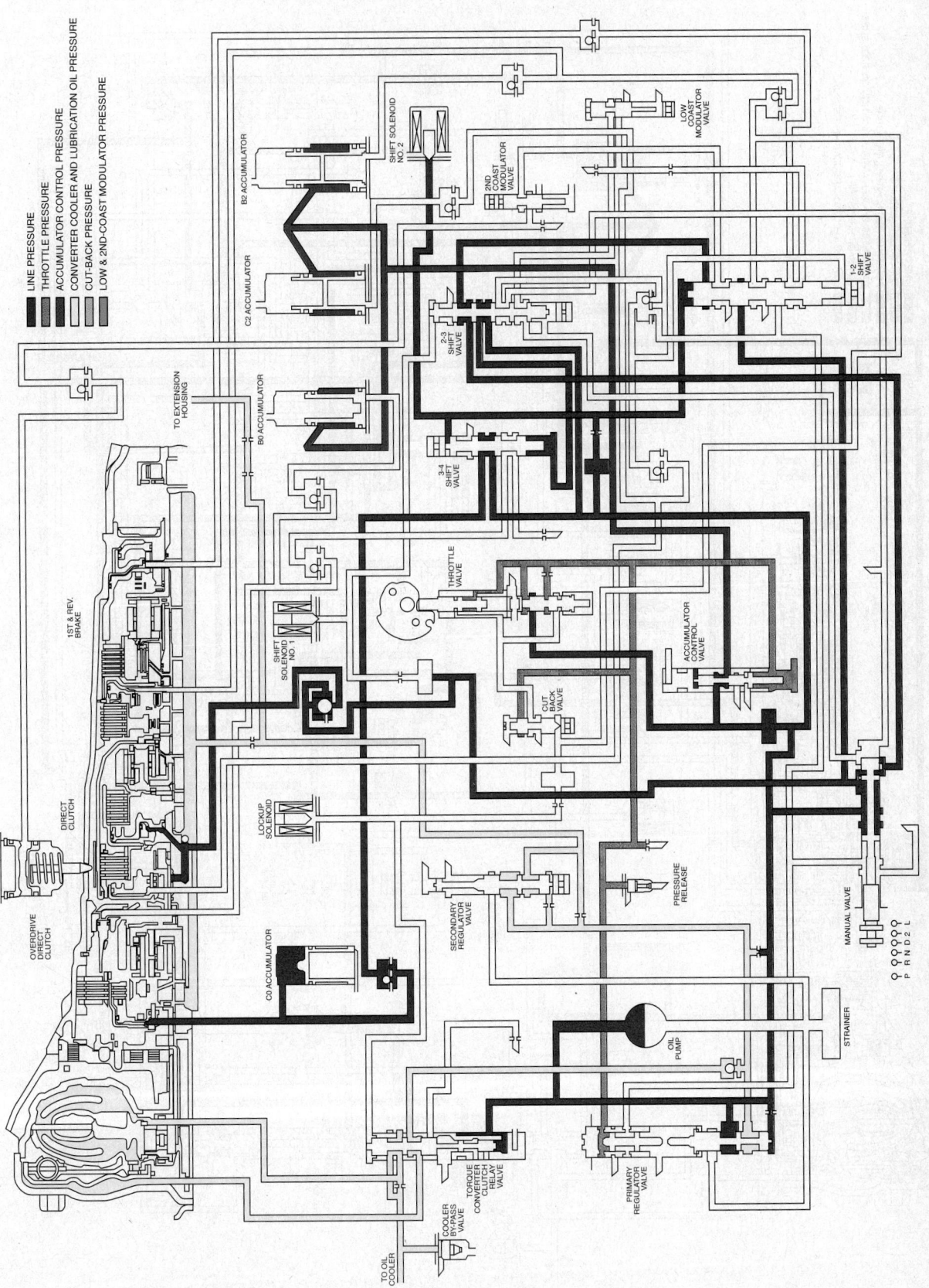

Fig. 6: "2" Position — 1st Gear

Courtesy of Mitsubishi Motor Sales of America

OIL CIRCUIT DIAGRAMS
Mitsubishi V4AW3 (Cont.)

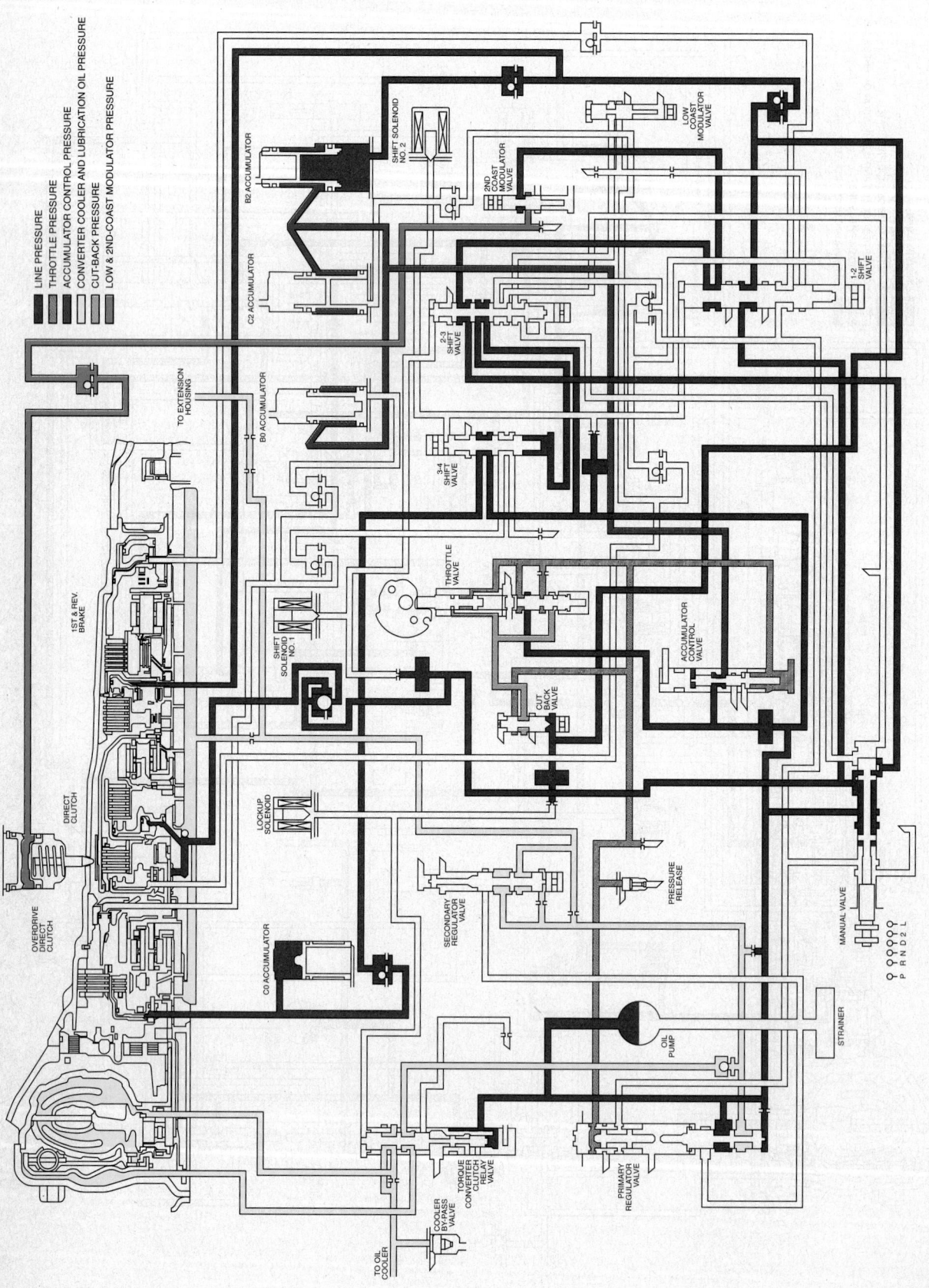

Fig. 7: "2" Position — 2nd Gear

Courtesy of Mitsubishi Motor Sales of America

OIL CIRCUIT DIAGRAMS
Mitsubishi V4AW3 (Cont.)

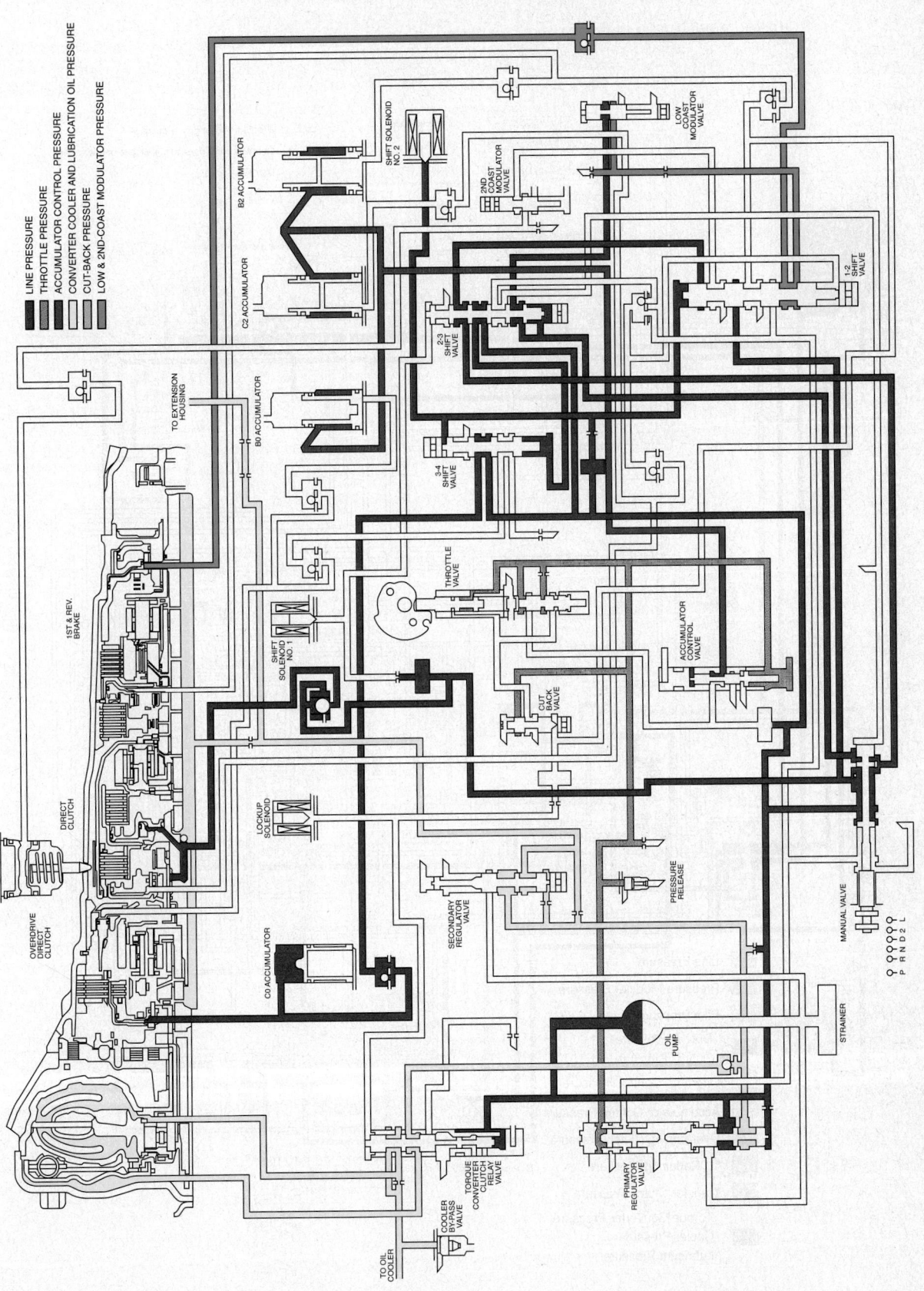

Fig. 8: "L" Position — 1st Gear

Courtesy of Mitsubishi Motor Sales of America

OIL CIRCUIT DIAGRAMS
Subaru 4-Speed

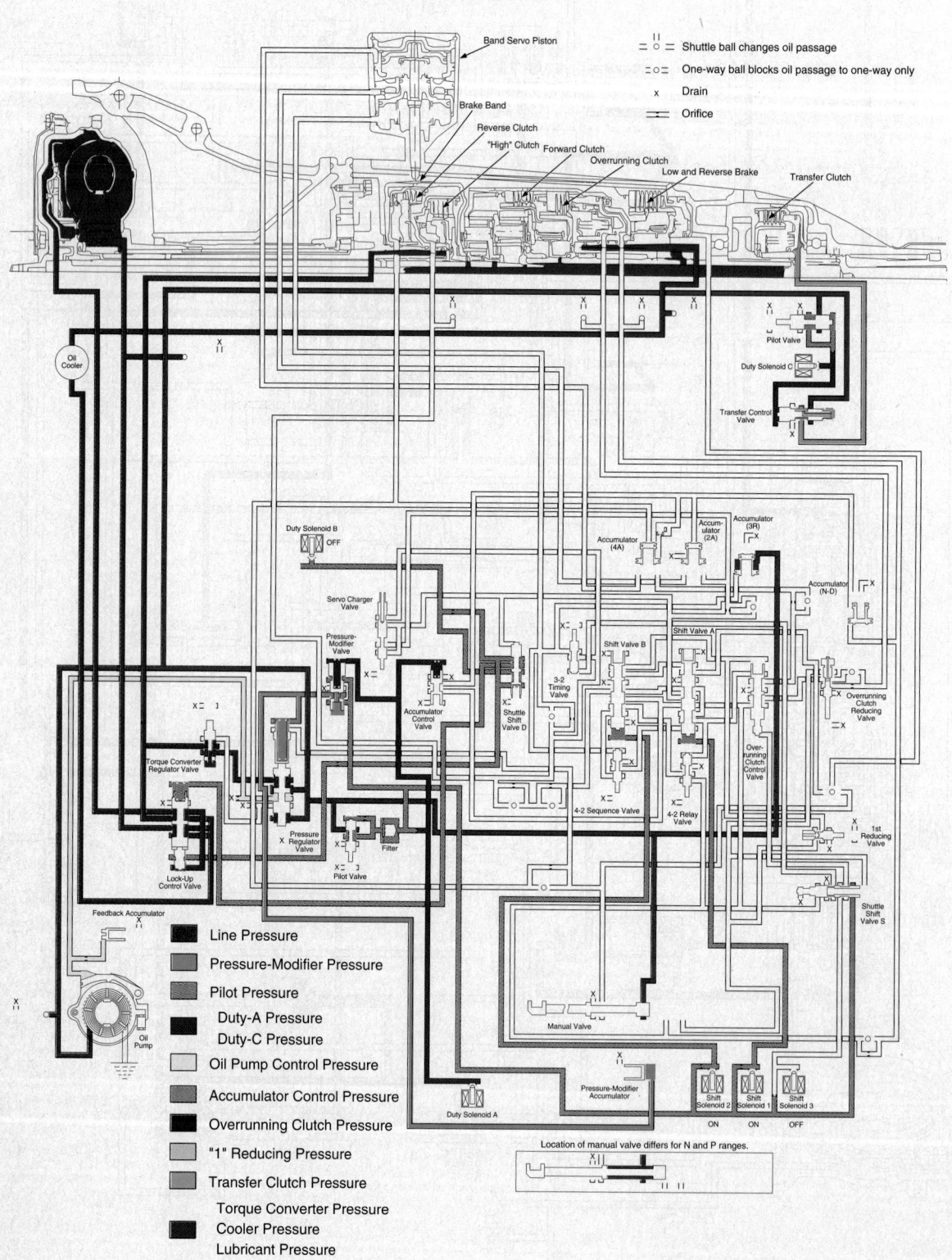

⬛	Line Pressure	
	Pressure-Modifier Pressure	
	Pilot Pressure	
	Duty-A Pressure	
	Duty-C Pressure	
	Oil Pump Control Pressure	
	Accumulator Control Pressure	
	Overrunning Clutch Pressure	
	"1" Reducing Pressure	
	Transfer Clutch Pressure	
	Torque Converter Pressure	
	Cooler Pressure	
	Lubricant Pressure	

Shuttle ball changes oil passage
One-way ball blocks oil passage to one-way only
x   Drain
Orifice

Band Servo Piston
Brake Band
Reverse Clutch
"High" Clutch
Forward Clutch
Overrunning Clutch
Low and Reverse Brake
Transfer Clutch

Oil Cooler
Pilot Valve
Duty Solenoid C
Transfer Control Valve

Duty Solenoid B   OFF
Accumulator (4A)
Accumulator (2A)
Accumulator (3R)
Accumulator (N-D)

Servo Charger Valve
Pressure-Modifier Valve
Shift Valve B
Shift Valve A
Overrunning Clutch Reducing Valve

Accumulator Control Valve
Shuttle Shift Valve D
3-2 Timing Valve
Overrunning Clutch Control Valve

Torque Converter Regulator Valve

Pressure Regulator Valve
Filter
4-2 Sequence Valve
4-2 Relay Valve
1st Reducing Valve

Lock-Up Control Valve
Pilot Valve
Shuttle Shift Valve S

Feedback Accumulator

Oil Pump

Manual Valve

Pressure-Modifier Accumulator

Duty Solenoid A

Shift Solenoid 2   ON
Shift Solenoid 1   ON
Shift Solenoid 3   OFF

Location of manual valve differs for N and P ranges.

Fig. 1: "P" & "N" Positions — Park & Neutral

Courtesy of Subaru of America, Inc.

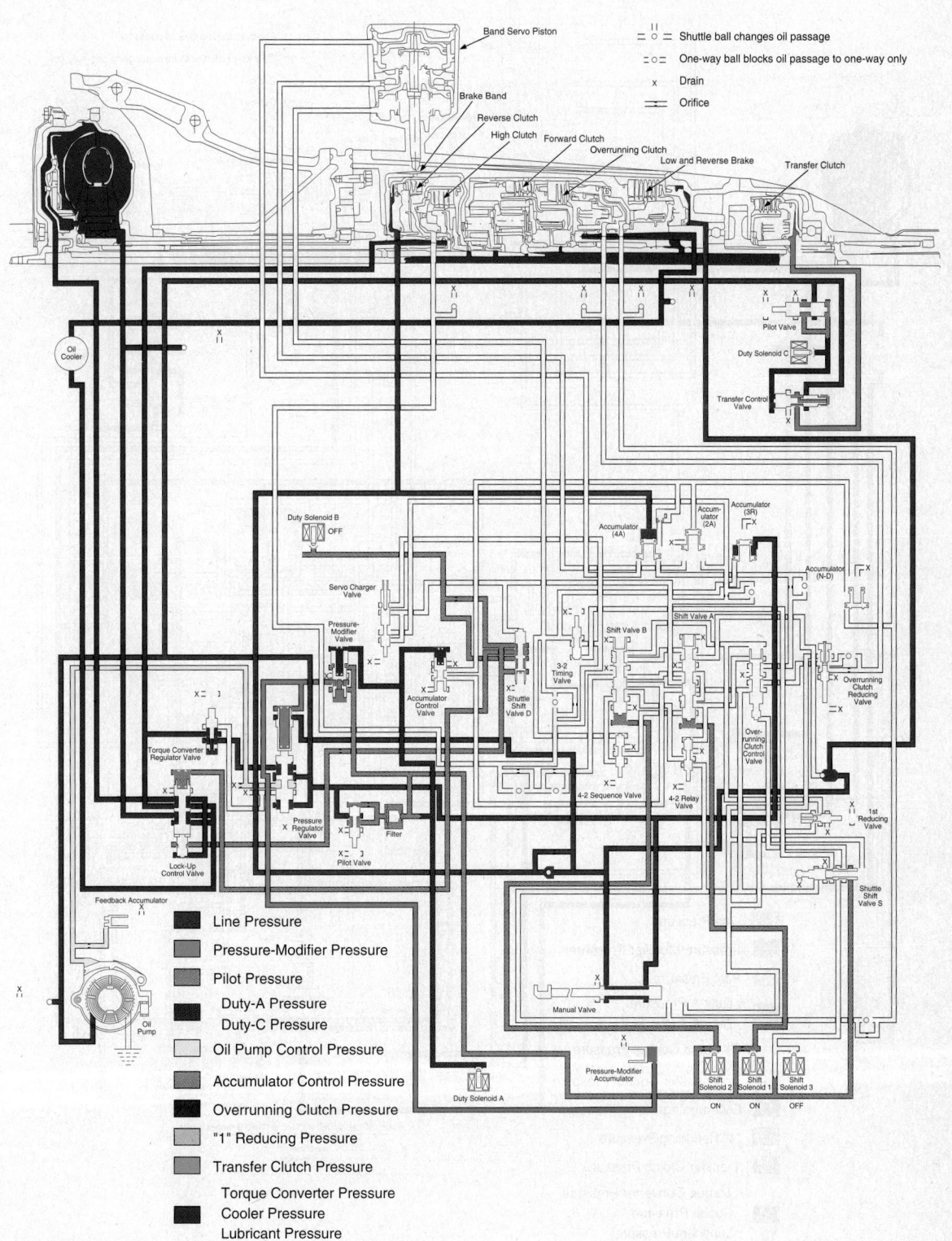

Band Servo Piston

Brake Band
Reverse Clutch
High Clutch
Forward Clutch
Overrunning Clutch
Low and Reverse Brake
Transfer Clutch

= ‖ ○ = Shuttle ball changes oil passage
= ○ = One-way ball blocks oil passage to one-way only
x Drain
≣≣ Orifice

Pilot Valve
Duty Solenoid C
Transfer Control Valve

Oil Cooler

Duty Solenoid B OFF

Accumulator (4A)
Accumulator (2A)
Accumulator (3R)
Accumulator (N-D)

Servo Charger Valve

Pressure-Modifier Valve

Shift Valve B
Shift Valve A

Accumulator Control Valve

3-2 Timing Valve

Shuttle Shift Valve D

Overrunning Clutch Reducing Valve

Overrunning Clutch Control Valve

Torque Converter Regulator Valve

Pressure Regulator Valve

Filter

Pilot Valve

4-2 Sequence Valve

4-2 Relay Valve

1st Reducing Valve

Lock-Up Control Valve

Shuttle Shift Valve S

Feedback Accumulator

Oil Pump

Manual Valve

Pressure-Modifier Accumulator

Duty Solenoid A

Shift Solenoid 2 ON
Shift Solenoid 1 ON
Shift Solenoid 3 OFF

Line Pressure
Pressure-Modifier Pressure
Pilot Pressure
Duty-A Pressure
Duty-C Pressure
Oil Pump Control Pressure
Accumulator Control Pressure
Overrunning Clutch Pressure
"1" Reducing Pressure
Transfer Clutch Pressure
Torque Converter Pressure
Cooler Pressure
Lubricant Pressure

Fig. 2: "R" Position — Reverse

Courtesy of Subaru of America, Inc.

OIL CIRCUIT DIAGRAMS
Subaru 4-Speed (Cont.)

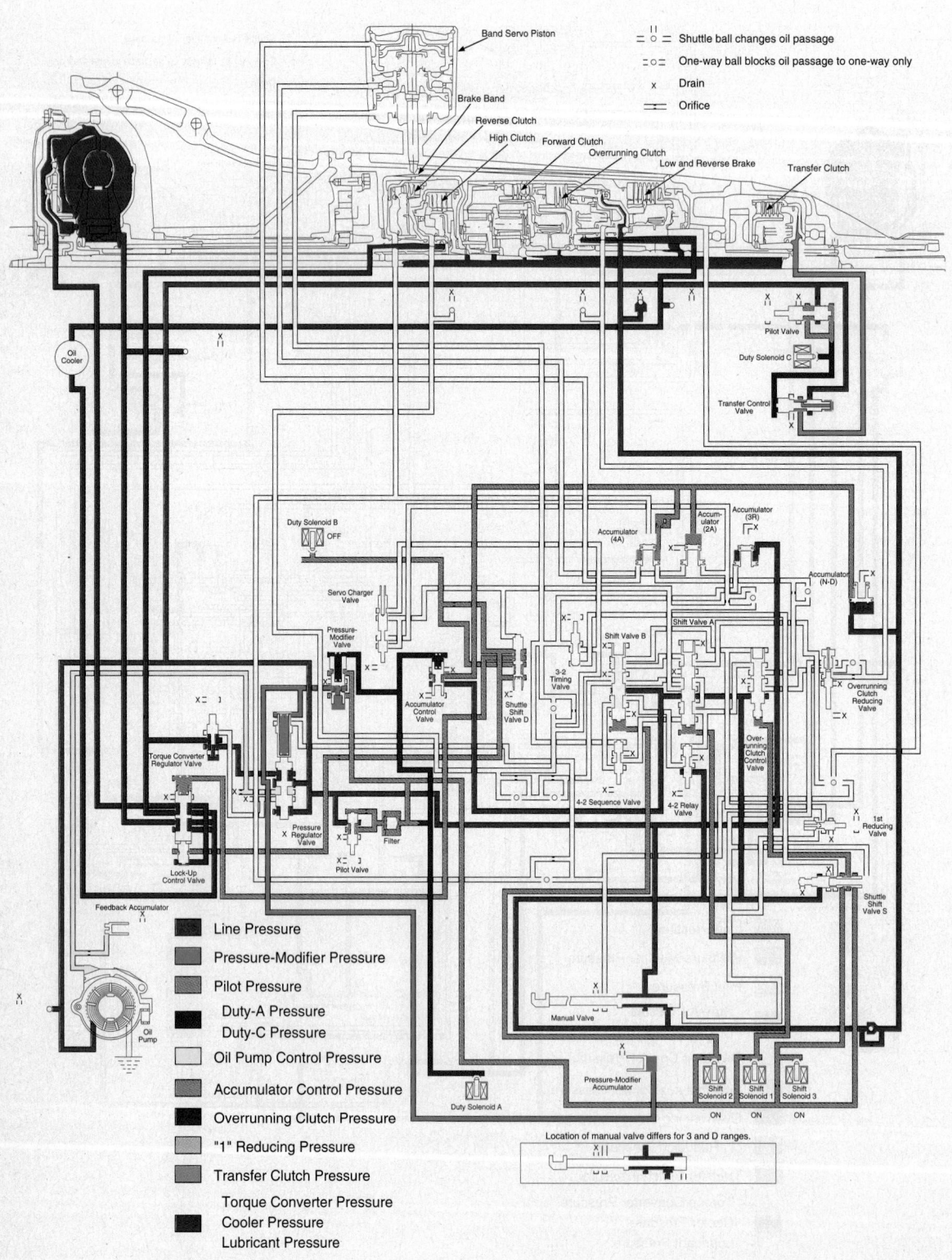

Band Servo Piston

= ‖‖ = ○ = Shuttle ball changes oil passage

= ○ = One-way ball blocks oil passage to one-way only

x Drain

Orifice

Brake Band

Reverse Clutch

High Clutch Forward Clutch

Overrunning Clutch

Low and Reverse Brake

Transfer Clutch

Pilot Valve

Duty Solenoid C

Transfer Control Valve

Oil Cooler

Duty Solenoid B OFF

Accumulator (4A)

Accumulator (2A)

Accumulator (3R)

Accumulator (N-D)

Servo Charger Valve

Pressure-Modifier Valve

Shift Valve A

Shift Valve B

3-2 Timing Valve

Overrunning Clutch Reducing Valve

Accumulator Control Valve

Shuttle Shift Valve D

Torque Converter Regulator Valve

Overrunning Clutch Control Valve

Pressure Regulator Valve

Filter

4-2 Sequence Valve

4-2 Relay Valve

1st Reducing Valve

Lock-Up Control Valve

Pilot Valve

Shuttle Shift Valve S

Feedback Accumulator

Oil Pump

Manual Valve

Pressure-Modifier Accumulator

Duty Solenoid A

Shift Solenoid 2 Shift Solenoid 1 Shift Solenoid 3

ON ON ON

Location of manual valve differs for 3 and D ranges.

Line Pressure

Pressure-Modifier Pressure

Pilot Pressure

Duty-A Pressure

Duty-C Pressure

Oil Pump Control Pressure

Accumulator Control Pressure

Overrunning Clutch Pressure

"1" Reducing Pressure

Transfer Clutch Pressure

Torque Converter Pressure
Cooler Pressure
Lubricant Pressure

Fig. 3: "D" Or "3" Position — 1st Gear   Courtesy of Subaru of America, Inc.

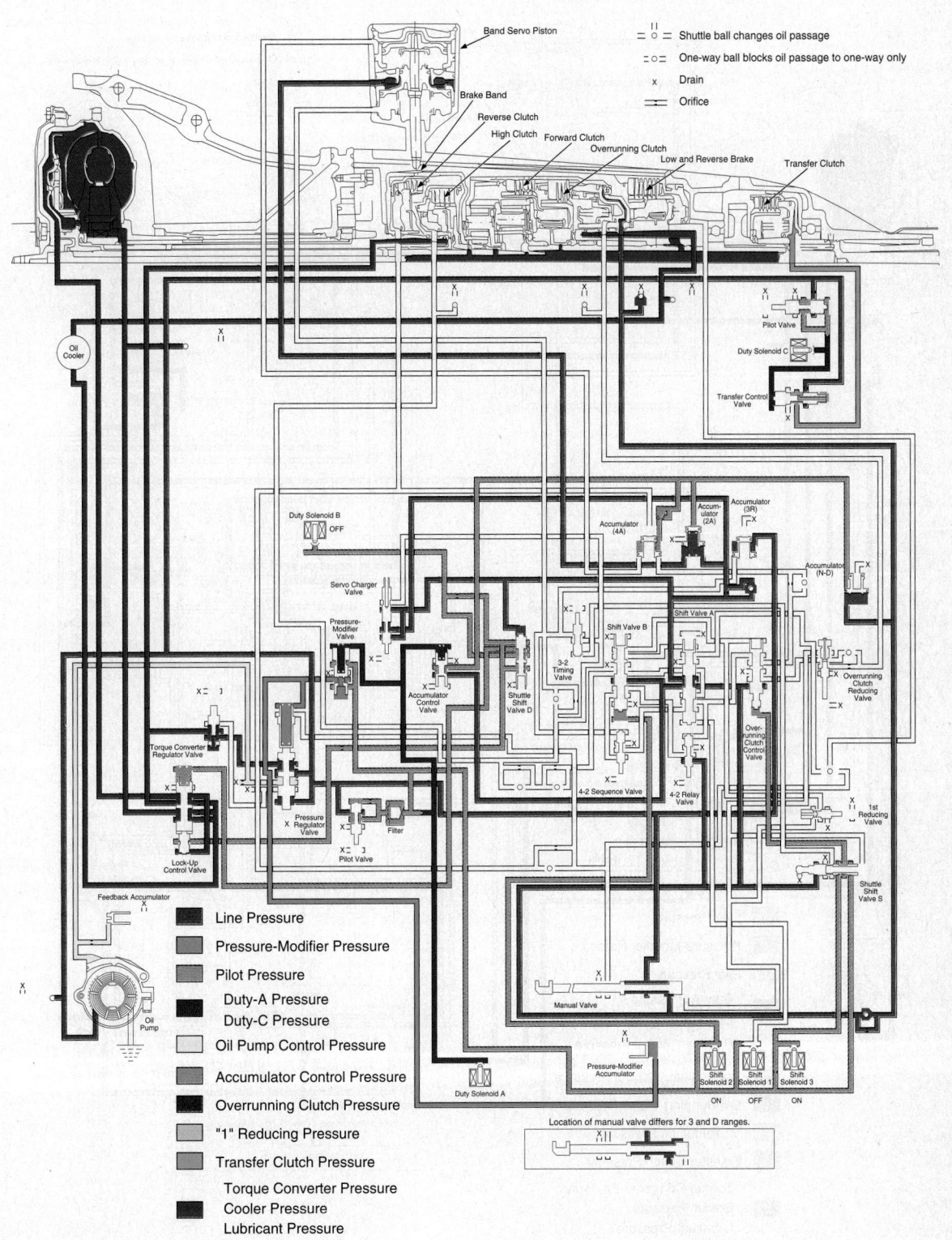

Fig. 4: "D" Or "3" Position — 2nd Gear (Lock-Up OFF)

Courtesy of Subaru of America, Inc.

OIL CIRCUIT DIAGRAMS
Subaru 4-Speed (Cont.)

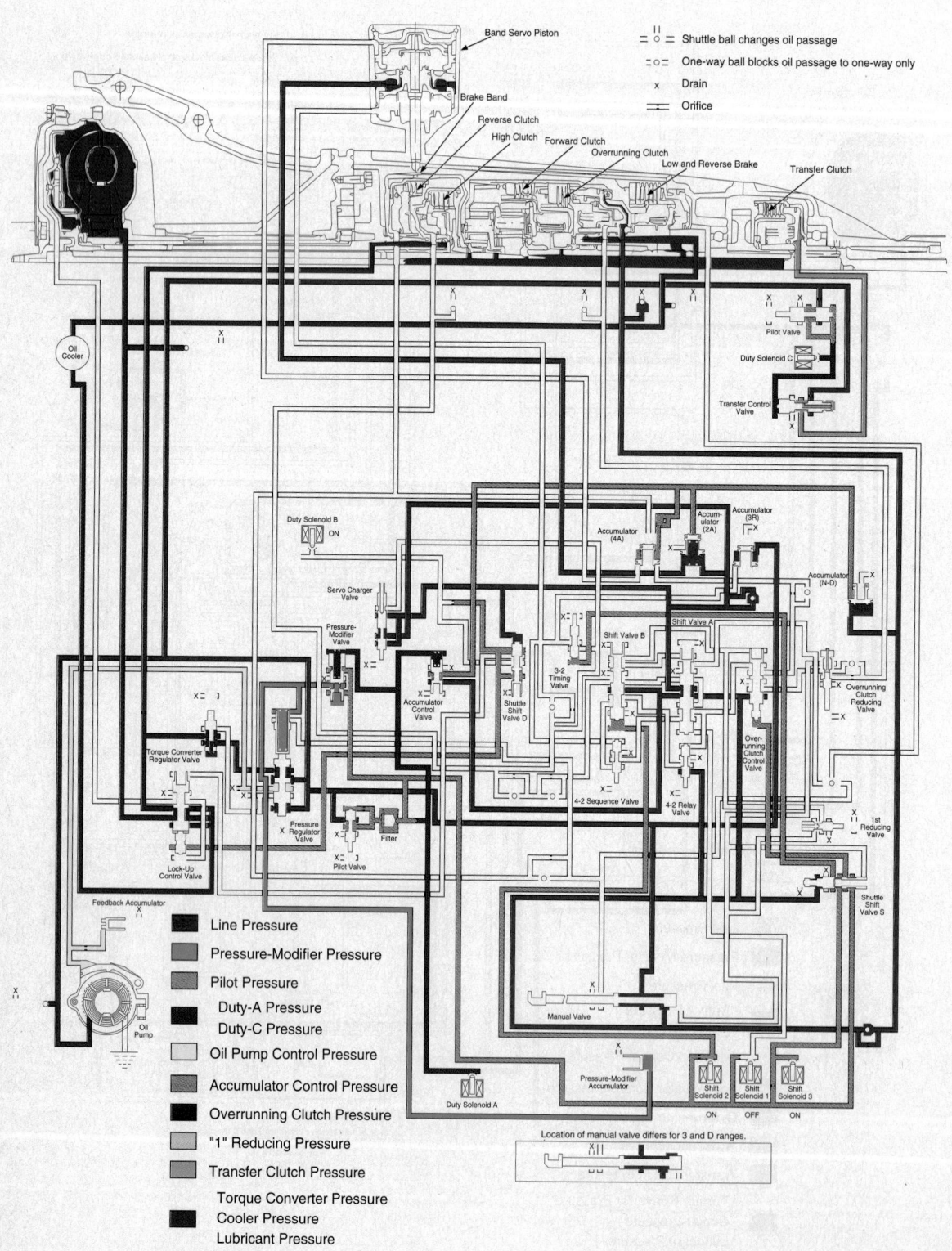

Fig. 5: "D" Or "3" Position — 2nd Gear (Lock-Up ON)

Courtesy of Subaru of America, Inc.

OIL CIRCUIT DIAGRAMS
Subaru 4-Speed (Cont.)

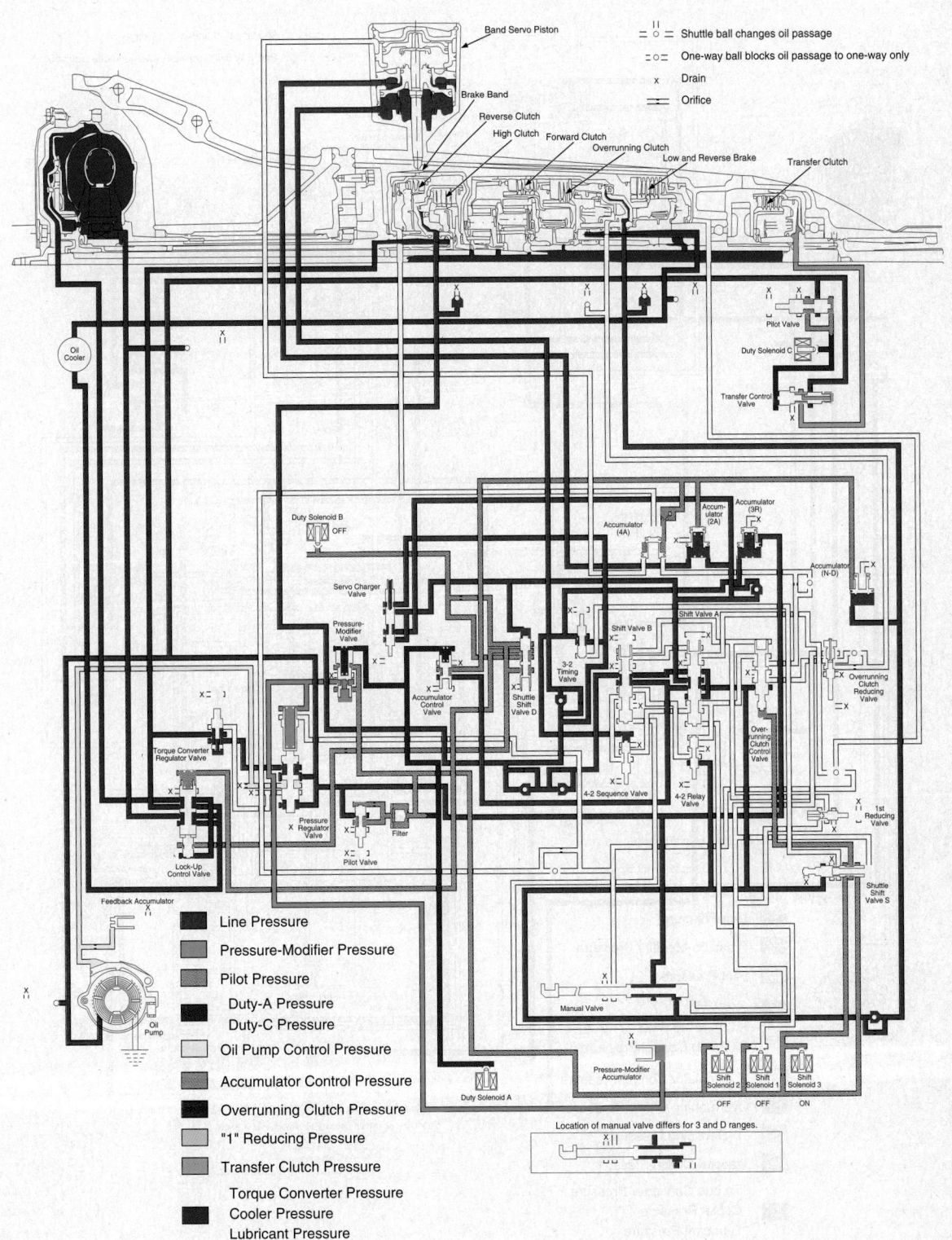

Band Servo Piston

Brake Band
Reverse Clutch
High Clutch   Forward Clutch
Overrunning Clutch
Low and Reverse Brake   Transfer Clutch

≡ ‖
= ○ ‖   Shuttle ball changes oil passage
‖≡ ○ ≡‖   One-way ball blocks oil passage to one-way only
x   Drain
≡≡   Orifice

Oil Cooler

Pilot Valve
Duty Solenoid C
Transfer Control Valve

Duty Solenoid B   OFF

Accumulator (4A)   Accumulator (2A)   Accumulator (3R)   Accumulator (N-D)

Servo Charger Valve
Pressure-Modifier Valve
Shift Valve A
Shift Valve B
Accumulator Control Valve
3-2 Timing Valve
Shuttle Shift Valve D
Overrunning Clutch Reducing Valve

Torque Converter Regulator Valve
Pressure Regulator Valve
Filter
Pilot Valve
4-2 Sequence Valve
4-2 Relay Valve
Overrunning Clutch Control Valve
1st Reducing Valve

Lock-Up Control Valve
Feedback Accumulator
Shuttle Shift Valve S

Oil Pump

Manual Valve

Pressure-Modifier Accumulator

Shift Solenoid 2   Shift Solenoid 1   Shift Solenoid 3
OFF   OFF   ON

Duty Solenoid A

Location of manual valve differs for 3 and D ranges.

- Line Pressure
- Pressure-Modifier Pressure
- Pilot Pressure
- Duty-A Pressure
- Duty-C Pressure
- Oil Pump Control Pressure
- Accumulator Control Pressure
- Overrunning Clutch Pressure
- "1" Reducing Pressure
- Transfer Clutch Pressure
- Torque Converter Pressure
- Cooler Pressure
- Lubricant Pressure

Fig. 6: "D" Or "3" Position — 3rd Gear (Lock-Up OFF)   Courtesy of Subaru of America, Inc.

OIL CIRCUIT DIAGRAMS
Subaru 4-Speed (Cont.)

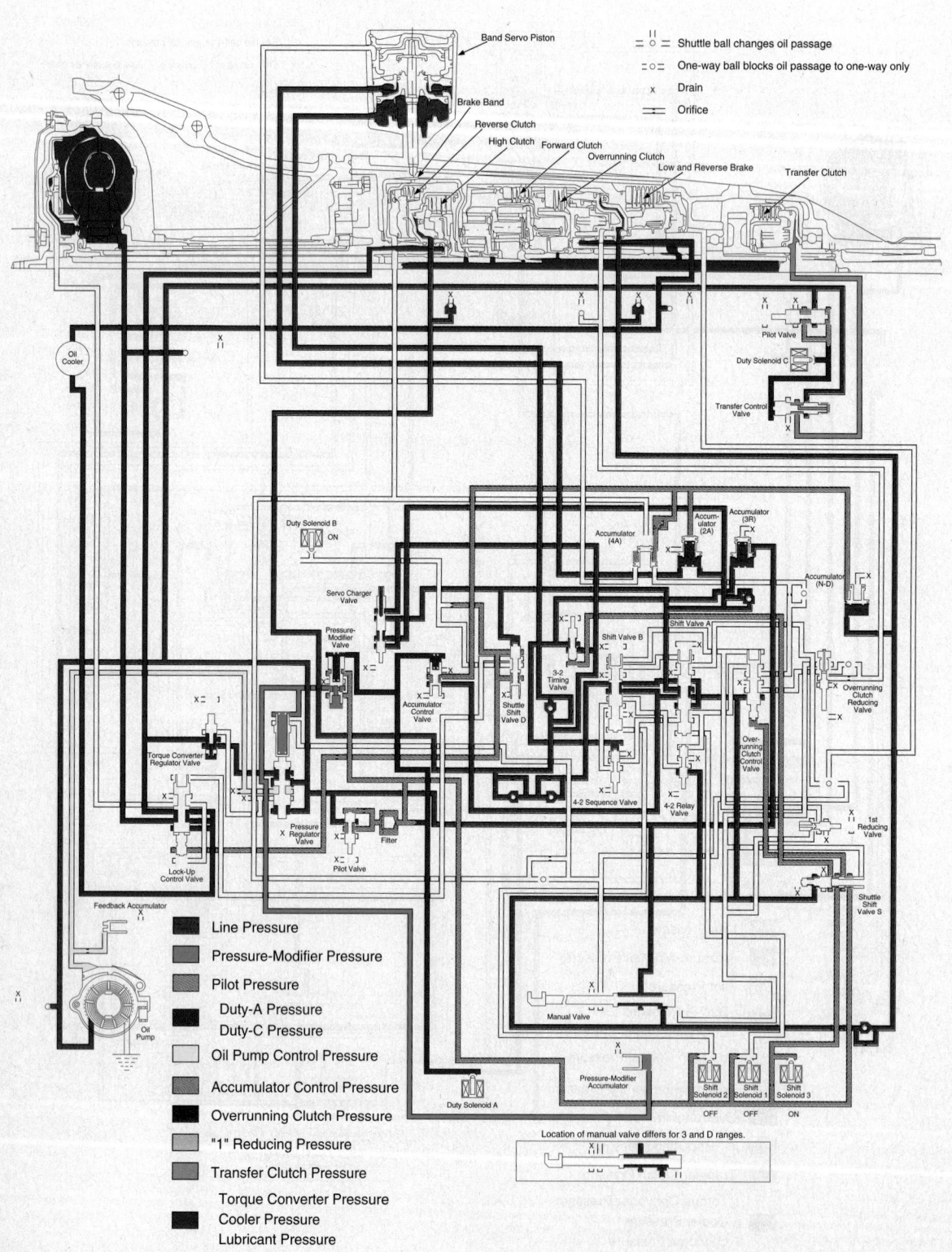

☰∘☰	Shuttle ball changes oil passage
☲∘☲	One-way ball blocks oil passage to one-way only
x	Drain
=	Orifice

Legend:
- Line Pressure
- Pressure-Modifier Pressure
- Pilot Pressure
- Duty-A Pressure
- Duty-C Pressure
- Oil Pump Control Pressure
- Accumulator Control Pressure
- Overrunning Clutch Pressure
- "1" Reducing Pressure
- Transfer Clutch Pressure
- Torque Converter Pressure
- Cooler Pressure
- Lubricant Pressure

Fig. 7: "D" Or "3" Position — 3rd Gear (Lock-Up ON)

Courtesy of Subaru of America, Inc.

OIL CIRCUIT DIAGRAMS
Subaru 4-Speed (Cont.)

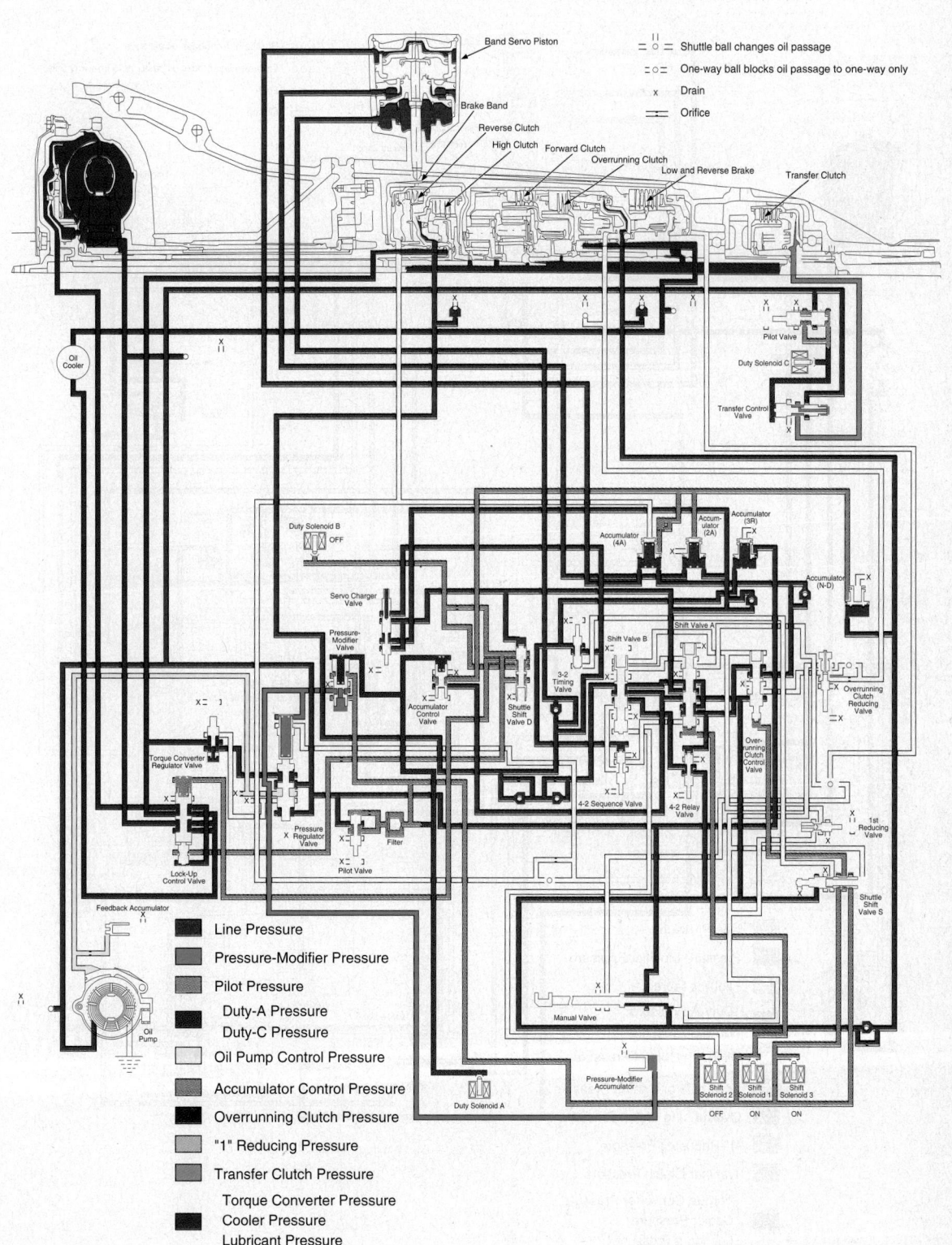

Band Servo Piston

Brake Band
Reverse Clutch
High Clutch
Forward Clutch
Overrunning Clutch
Low and Reverse Brake
Transfer Clutch

= ‖ = Shuttle ball changes oil passage
⊏ ○ ⊐ One-way ball blocks oil passage to one-way only
x Drain
=ⅠⅠ= Orifice

Oil Cooler

Pilot Valve
Duty Solenoid C
Transfer Control Valve

Duty Solenoid B   OFF

Accumulator (4A)
Accumulator (2A)
Accumulator (3R)
Accumulator (N-D)

Servo Charger Valve
Pressure-Modifier Valve
Accumulator Control Valve
Shuttle Shift Valve D
3-2 Timing Valve
Shift Valve B
Shift Valve A
Overrunning Clutch Reducing Valve
Overrunning Clutch Control Valve

Torque Converter Regulator Valve
Pressure Regulator Valve
Filter
Pilot Valve
4-2 Sequence Valve
4-2 Relay Valve
1st Reducing Valve

Lock-Up Control Valve
Shuttle Shift Valve S

Feedback Accumulator

Oil Pump

Manual Valve

Line Pressure
Pressure-Modifier Pressure
Pilot Pressure
Duty-A Pressure
Duty-C Pressure
Oil Pump Control Pressure
Accumulator Control Pressure
Overrunning Clutch Pressure
"1" Reducing Pressure
Transfer Clutch Pressure
Torque Converter Pressure
Cooler Pressure
Lubricant Pressure

Duty Solenoid A

Pressure-Modifier Accumulator

Shift Solenoid 2   OFF
Shift Solenoid 1   ON
Shift Solenoid 3   ON

Fig. 8: "D" Position — 4th Gear (Lock-Up OFF)   Courtesy of Subaru of America, Inc.

OIL CIRCUIT DIAGRAMS
Subaru 4-Speed (Cont.)

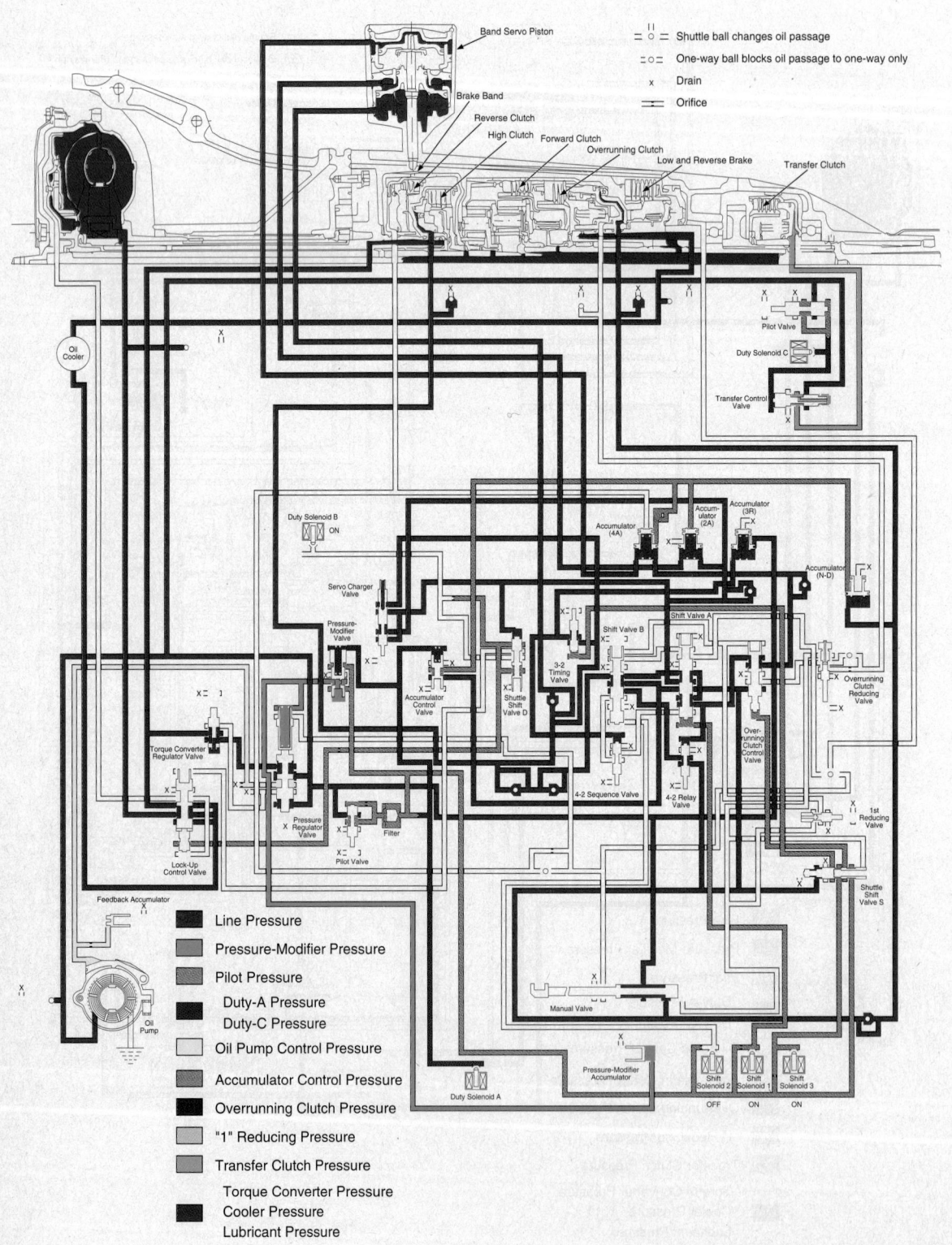

Band Servo Piston

Brake Band

Reverse Clutch

High Clutch

Forward Clutch

Overrunning Clutch

Low and Reverse Brake

Transfer Clutch

Shuttle ball changes oil passage

One-way ball blocks oil passage to one-way only

x   Drain

Orifice

Pilot Valve

Duty Solenoid C

Transfer Control Valve

Oil Cooler

Duty Solenoid B   ON

Accumulator (4A)

Accumulator (2A)

Accumulator (3R)

Accumulator (N-D)

Servo Charger Valve

Pressure-Modifier Valve

Accumulator Control Valve

3-2 Timing Valve

Shift Valve B

Shift Valve A

Overrunning Clutch Reducing Valve

Shuttle Shift Valve D

Overrunning Clutch Control Valve

Torque Converter Regulator Valve

Pressure Regulator Valve

Filter

4-2 Sequence Valve

4-2 Relay Valve

1st Reducing Valve

Lock-Up Control Valve

Pilot Valve

Shuttle Shift Valve S

Feedback Accumulator

Oil Pump

Manual Valve

Pressure-Modifier Accumulator

Duty Solenoid A

Shift Solenoid 2   OFF

Shift Solenoid 1   ON

Shift Solenoid 3   ON

Line Pressure

Pressure-Modifier Pressure

Pilot Pressure

Duty-A Pressure

Duty-C Pressure

Oil Pump Control Pressure

Accumulator Control Pressure

Overrunning Clutch Pressure

"1" Reducing Pressure

Transfer Clutch Pressure

Torque Converter Pressure

Cooler Pressure

Lubricant Pressure

Fig. 9: "D" Position — 4th Gear (Lock-Up ON)   Courtesy of Subaru of America, Inc.

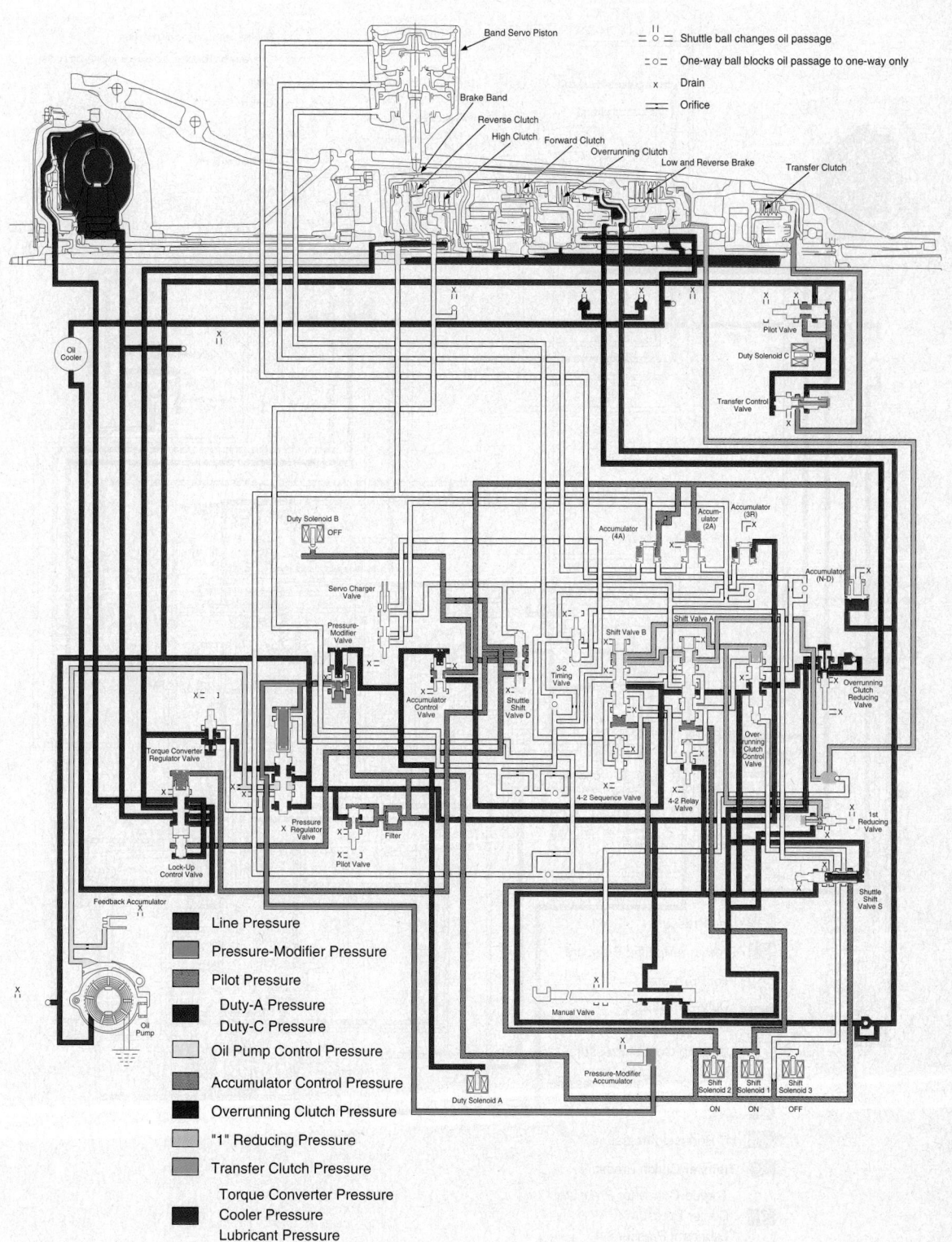

OIL CIRCUIT DIAGRAMS
Subaru 4-Speed (Cont.)

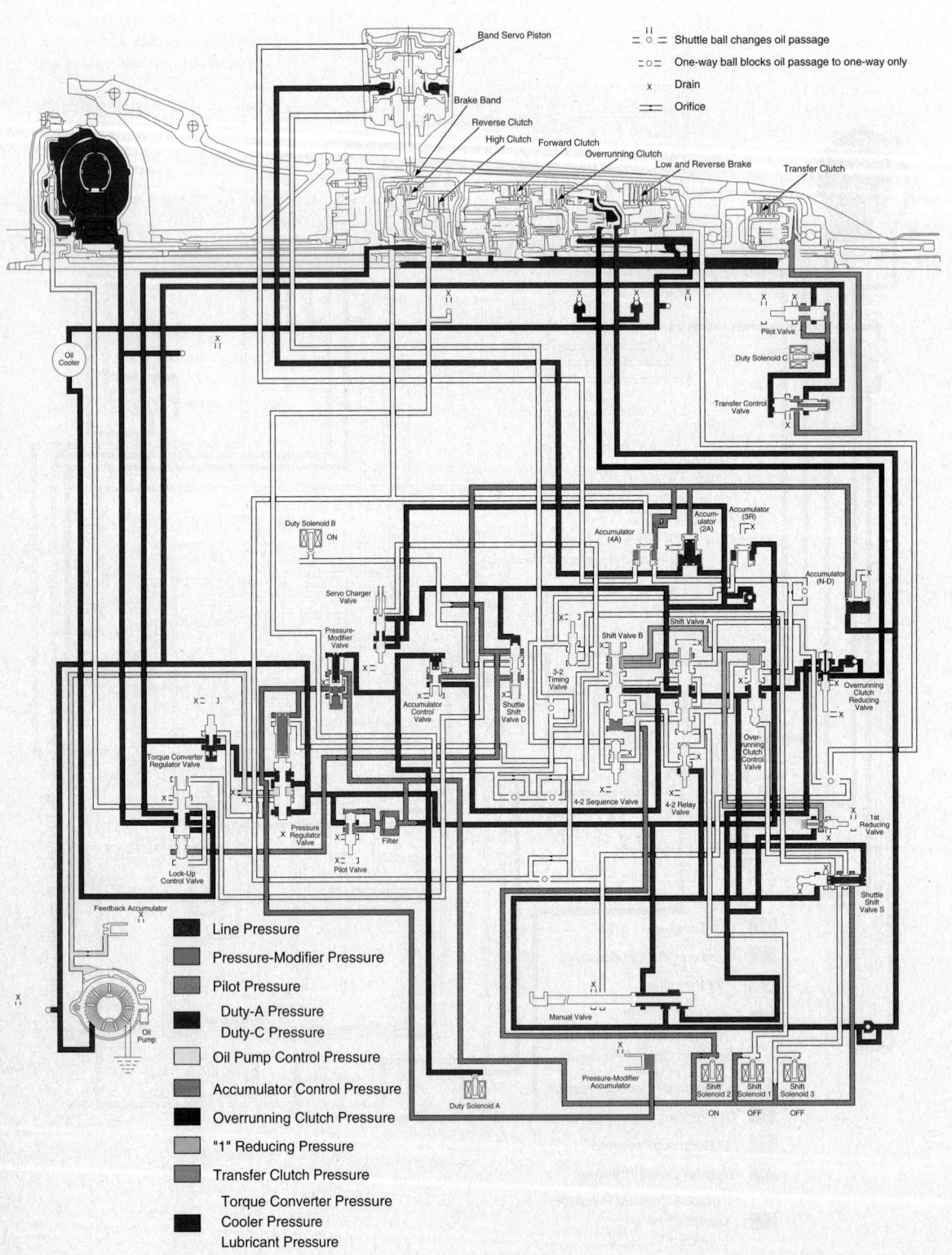

Band Servo Piston

⊟ ⊙ ⊟ Shuttle ball changes oil passage

⊟ ⊙ ⊟ One-way ball blocks oil passage to one-way only

x Drain

⊟⊟ Orifice

Brake Band
Reverse Clutch
High Clutch
Forward Clutch
Overrunning Clutch
Low and Reverse Brake
Transfer Clutch

Pilot Valve
Duty Solenoid C
Transfer Control Valve

Oil Cooler

Duty Solenoid B ON

Accumulator (4A)
Accumulator (2A)
Accumulator (3R)
Accumulator (N-D)

Servo Charger Valve
Pressure-Modifier Valve

Shift Valve B
Shift Valve A

3-2 Timing Valve
Shuttle Shift Valve D
Accumulator Control Valve

Overrunning Clutch Reducing Valve
Overrunning Clutch Control Valve

Torque Converter Regulator Valve

Pressure Regulator Valve
Filter

4-2 Sequence Valve
4-2 Relay Valve

1st Reducing Valve

Lock-Up Control Valve
Pilot Valve

Shuttle Shift Valve S

Feedback Accumulator

Manual Valve

Oil Pump

■	Line Pressure
■	Pressure-Modifier Pressure
■	Pilot Pressure
■	Duty-A Pressure
	Duty-C Pressure
▫	Oil Pump Control Pressure
■	Accumulator Control Pressure
■	Overrunning Clutch Pressure
▨	"1" Reducing Pressure
■	Transfer Clutch Pressure
■	Torque Converter Pressure
	Cooler Pressure
	Lubricant Pressure

Duty Solenoid A

Pressure-Modifier Accumulator

Shift Solenoid 2 ON
Shift Solenoid 1 OFF
Shift Solenoid 3 OFF

Fig. 11: "2" Or "1st Hold" Position — 2nd Gear (Lock-Up ON)

Courtesy of Subaru of America, Inc.

OIL CIRCUIT DIAGRAMS
Subaru 4-Speed (Cont.)

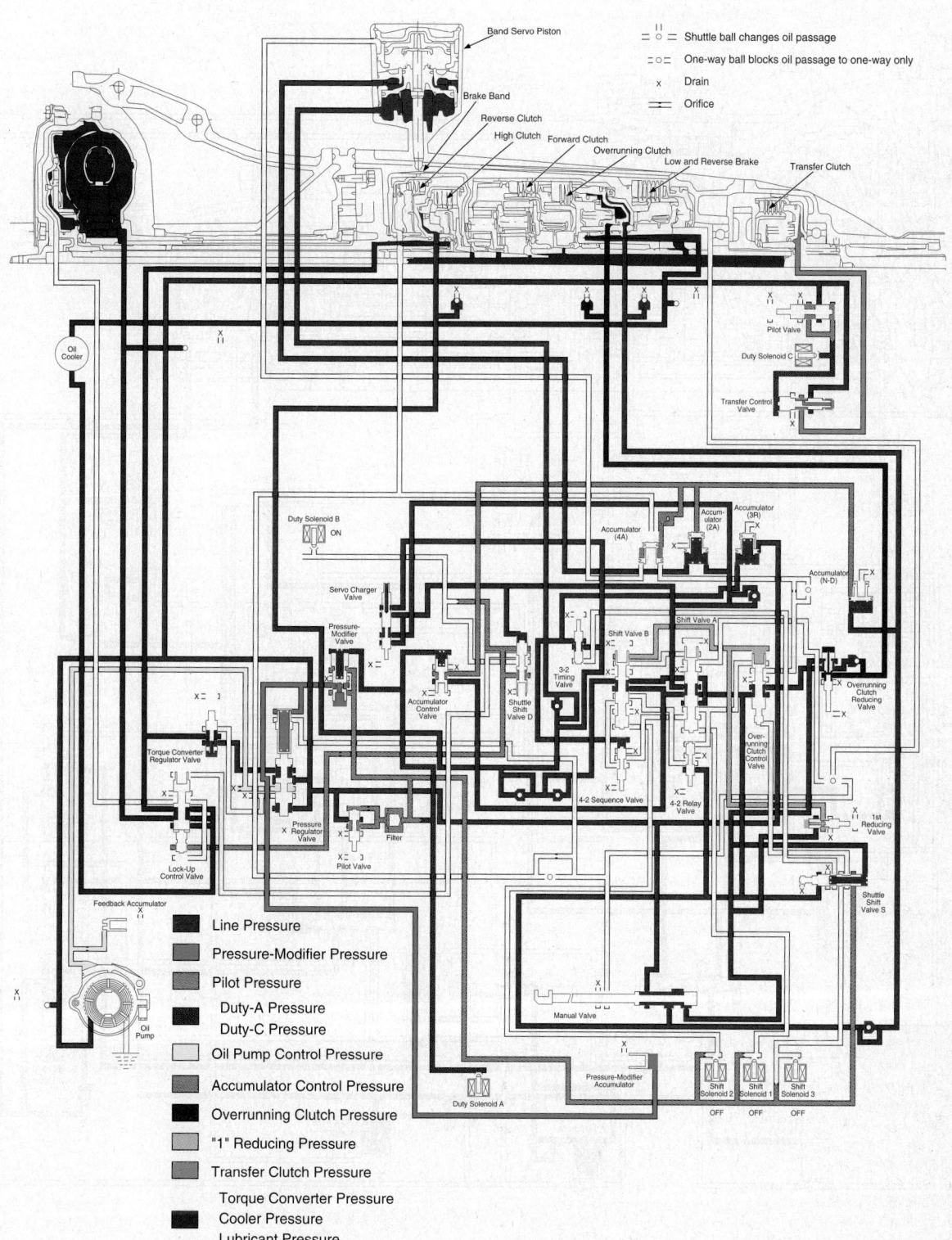

Fig. 12 "2" Or "1st Hold" Position — 3rd Gear (Lock-Up ON)

Courtesy of Subaru of America, Inc.

OIL CIRCUIT DIAGRAMS
Suzuki Esteem

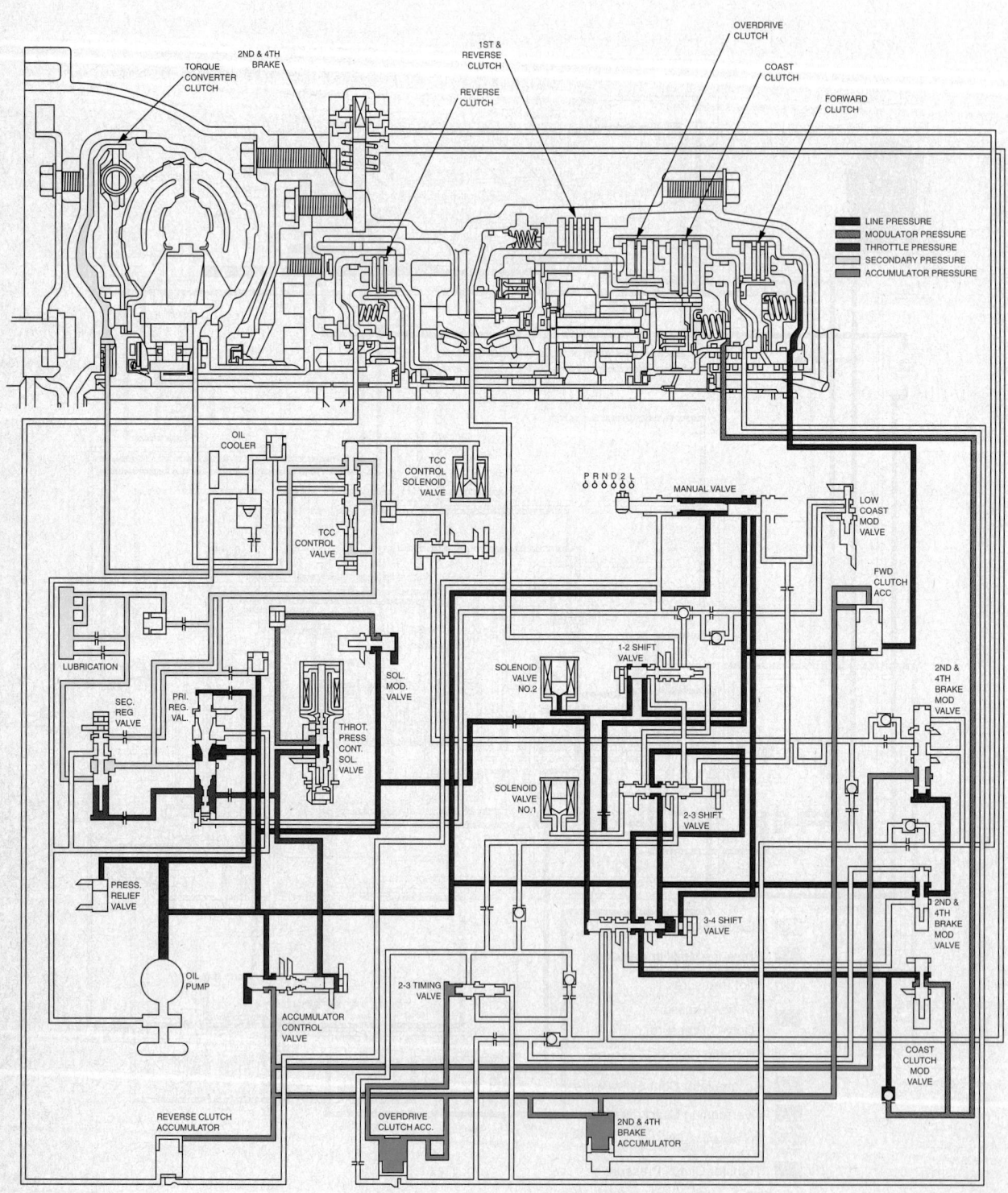

LINE PRESSURE
MODULATOR PRESSURE
THROTTLE PRESSURE
SECONDARY PRESSURE
ACCUMULATOR PRESSURE

Fig. 1: "D" Or "2" Position — 1st Gear

Courtesy of Suzuki of America Corp.

OIL CIRCUIT DIAGRAMS
Suzuki Esteem (Cont.)

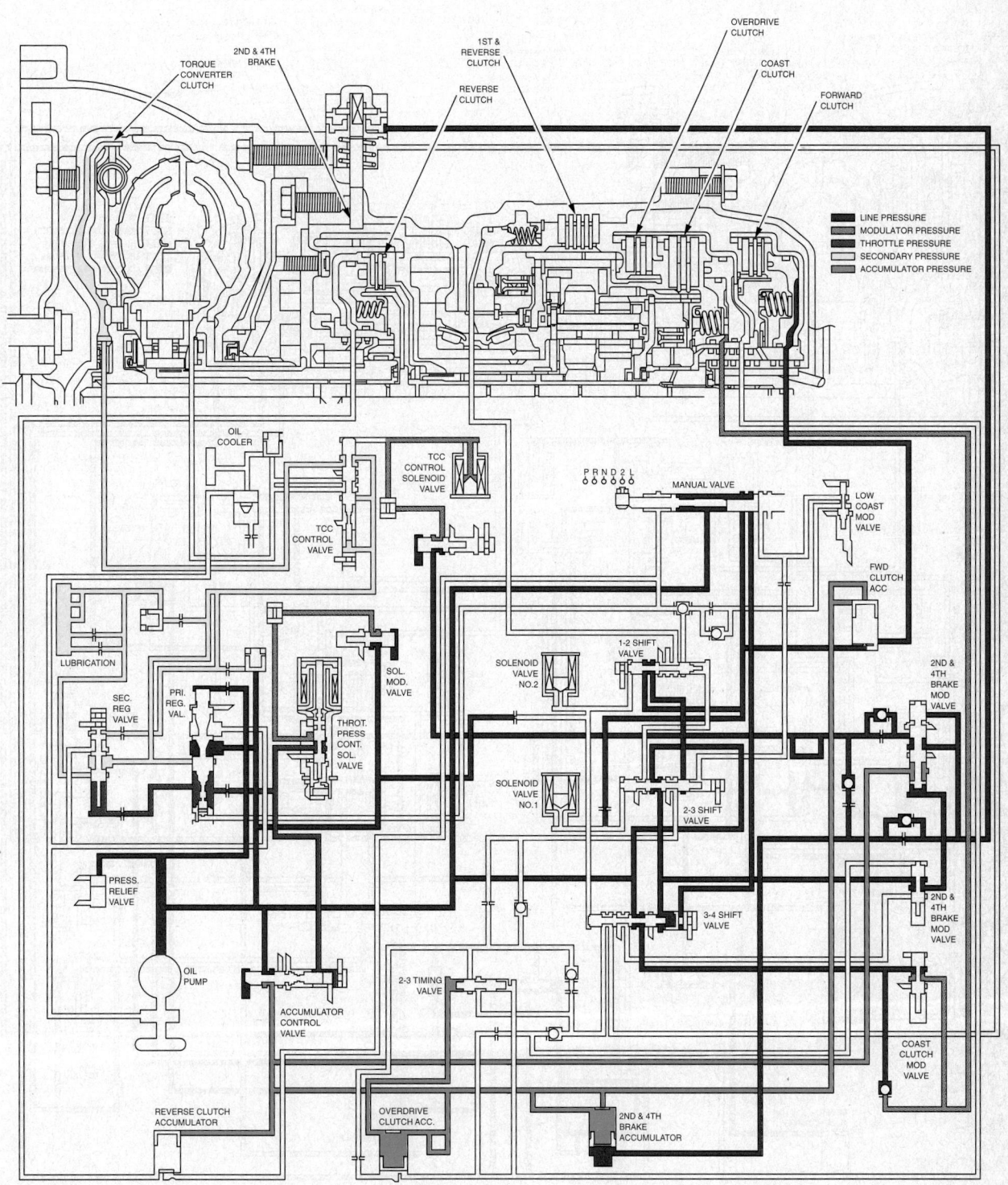

Fig. 2: "D" Or "2" Position — 2nd Gear

Courtesy of Suzuki of America Corp.

OIL CIRCUIT DIAGRAMS
Suzuki Esteem (Cont.)

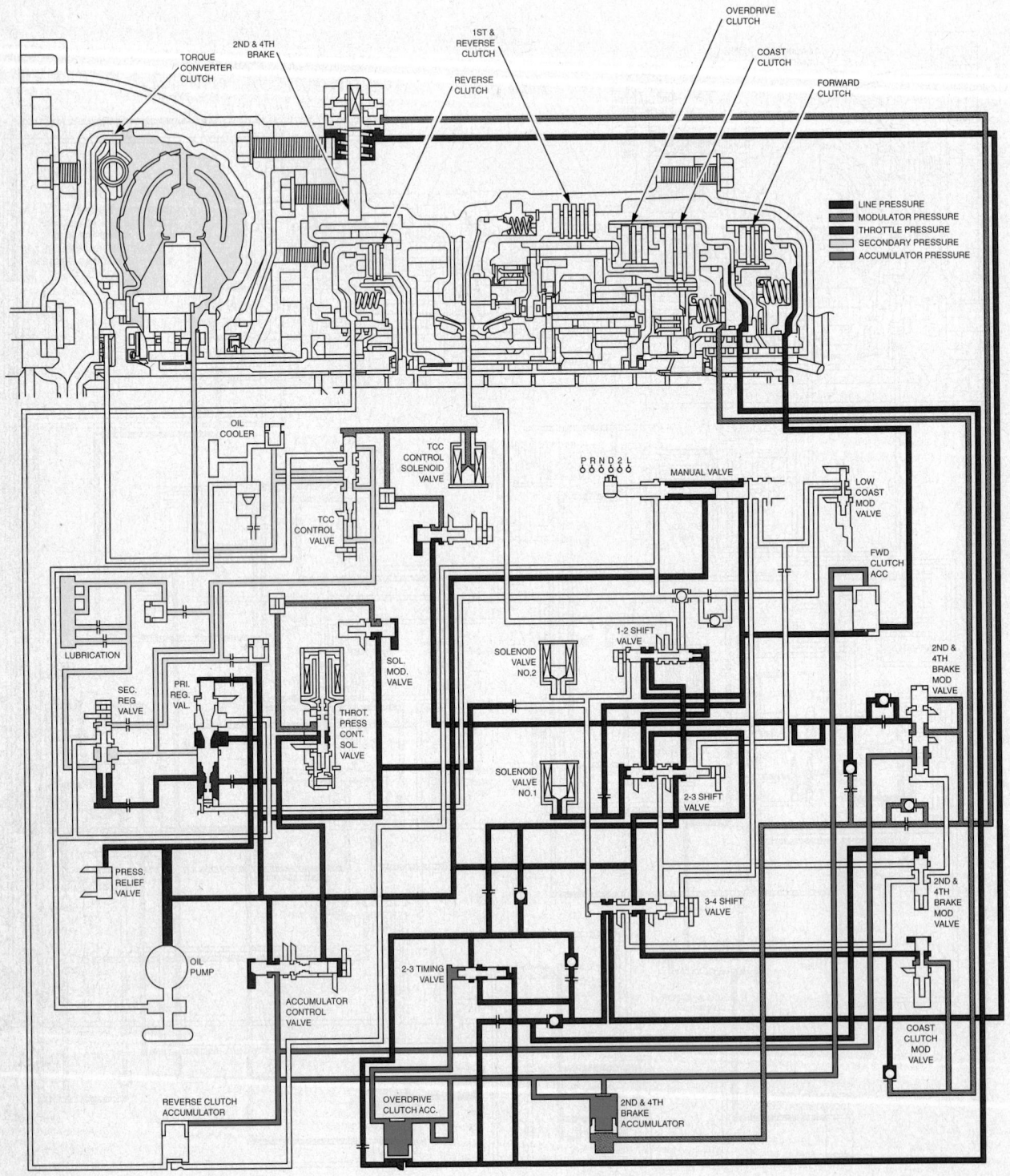

Fig. 3: "D" Position — 3rd Gear

Courtesy of Suzuki of America Corp.

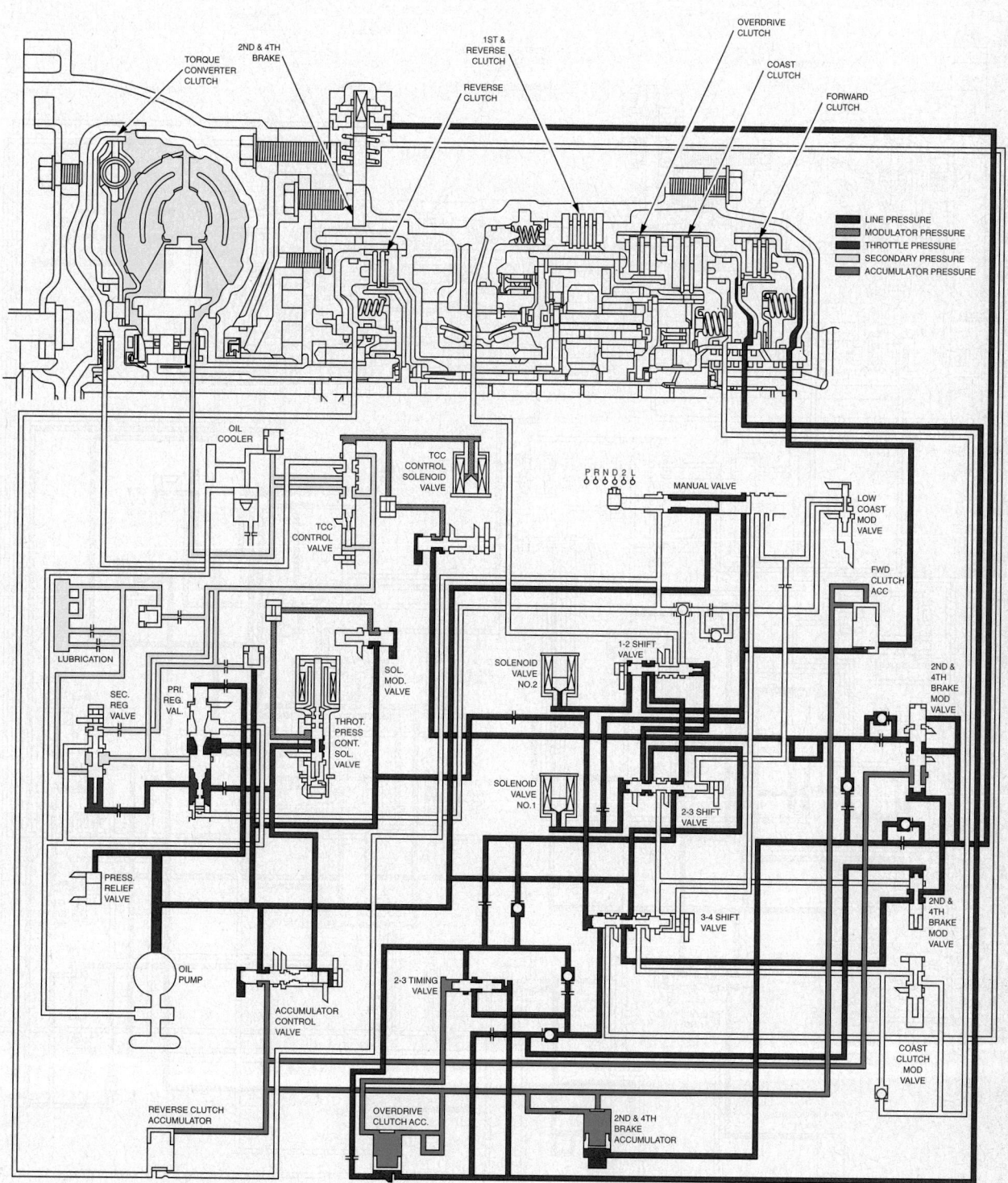

Fig. 4: "D" Position — 4th Gear

Courtesy of Suzuki of America Corp.

OIL CIRCUIT DIAGRAMS
Suzuki Esteem (Cont.)

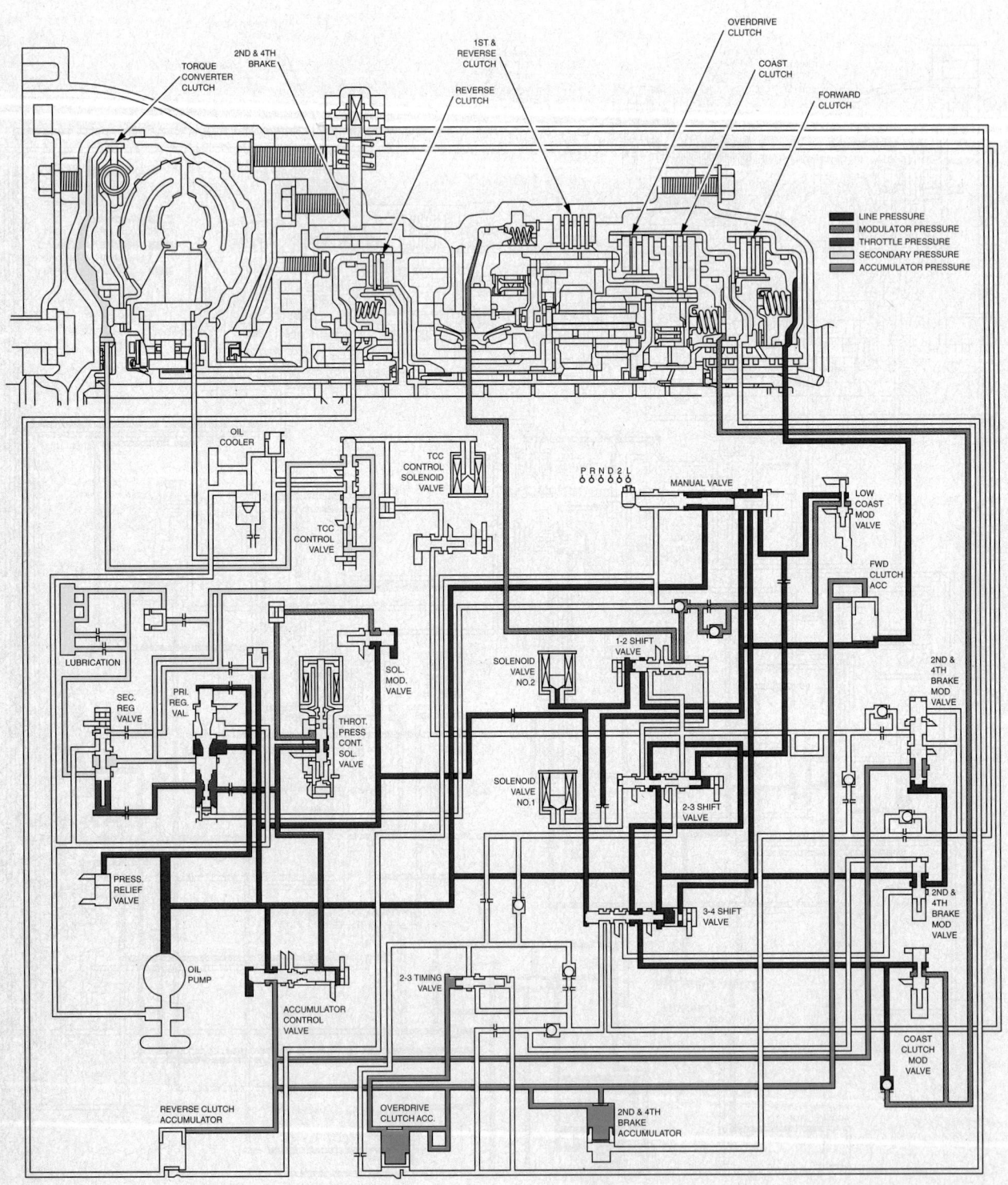

Fig. 5: "L" Position — 1st Gear

Courtesy of Suzuki of America Corp.

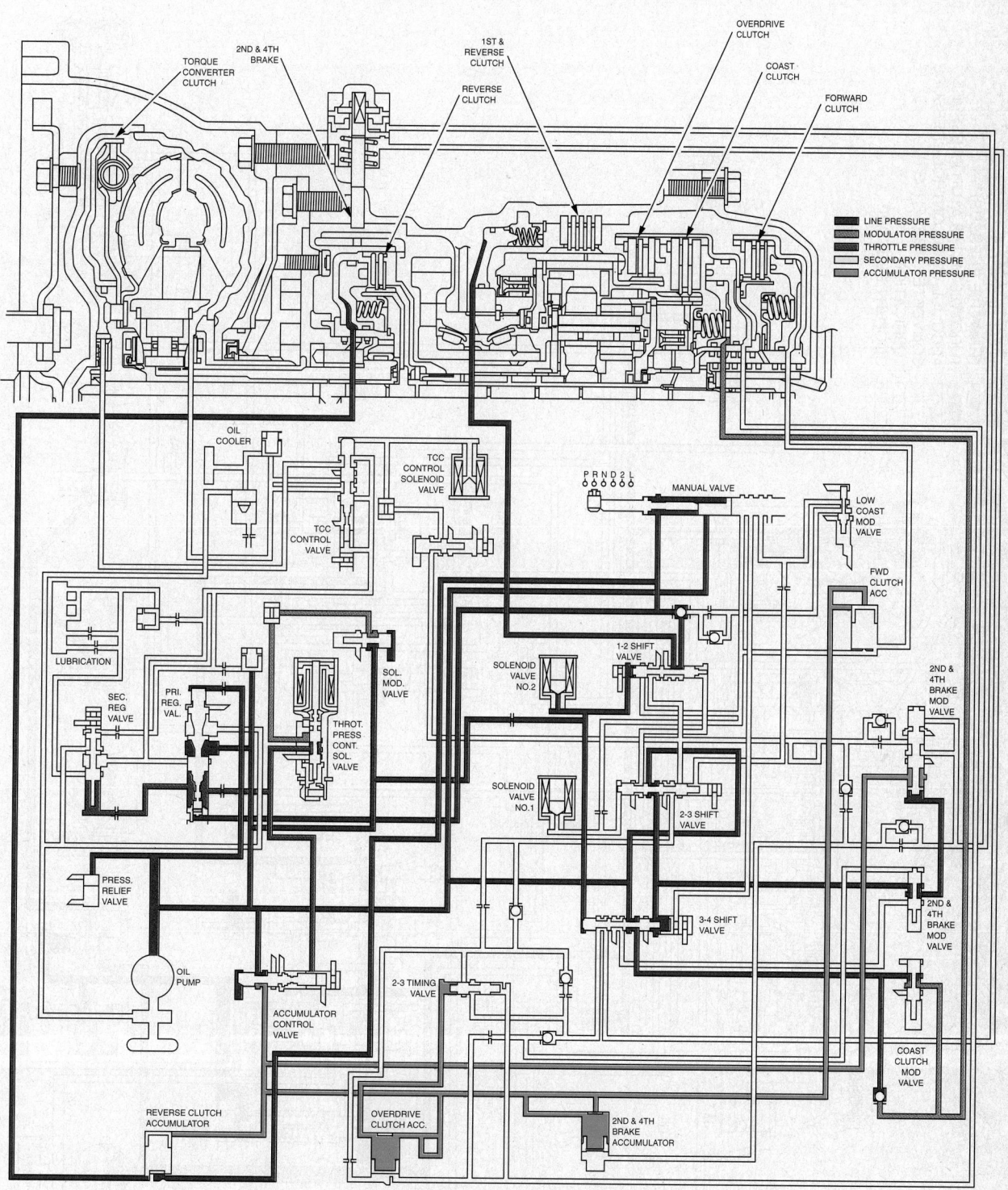

Fig. 6: "R" Position — Reverse

Courtesy of Suzuki of America Corp.

OIL CIRCUIT DIAGRAMS
Toyota A-132L

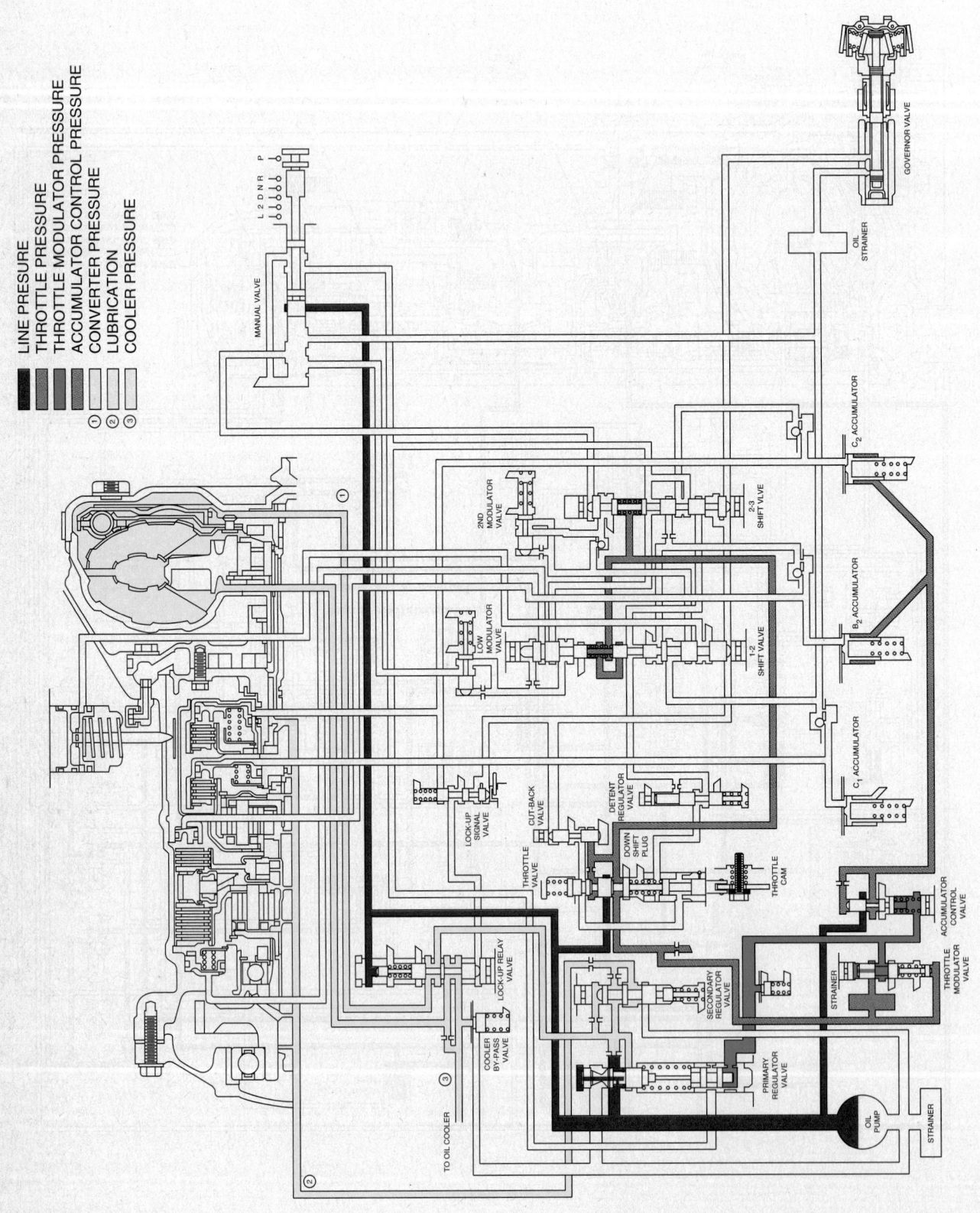

LINE PRESSURE
THROTTLE PRESSURE
THROTTLE MODULATOR PRESSURE
ACCUMULATOR CONTROL PRESSURE
CONVERTER PRESSURE
LUBRICATION
COOLER PRESSURE

GOVERNOR VALVE

OIL STRAINER

MANUAL VALVE

2ND MODULATOR VALVE

2-3 SHIFT VALVE

C_2 ACCUMULATOR

LOW MODULATOR VALVE

1-2 SHIFT VALVE

B_2 ACCUMULATOR

C_1 ACCUMULATOR

LOCK-UP SIGNAL VALVE

CUT-BACK VALVE

DETENT REGULATOR VALVE

THROTTLE VALVE

DOWN SHIFT PLUG

THROTTLE CAM

ACCUMULATOR CONTROL VALVE

LOCK-UP RELAY VALVE

STRAINER

THROTTLE MODULATOR VALVE

COOLER BY-PASS VALVE

SECONDARY REGULATOR VALVE

TO OIL COOLER

PRIMARY REGULATOR VALVE

OIL PUMP

STRAINER

Fig. 1: "P" Position — Park

Courtesy of Toyota Motor Sales, U.S.A., Inc.

OIL CIRCUIT DIAGRAMS
Toyota A-132L (Cont.)

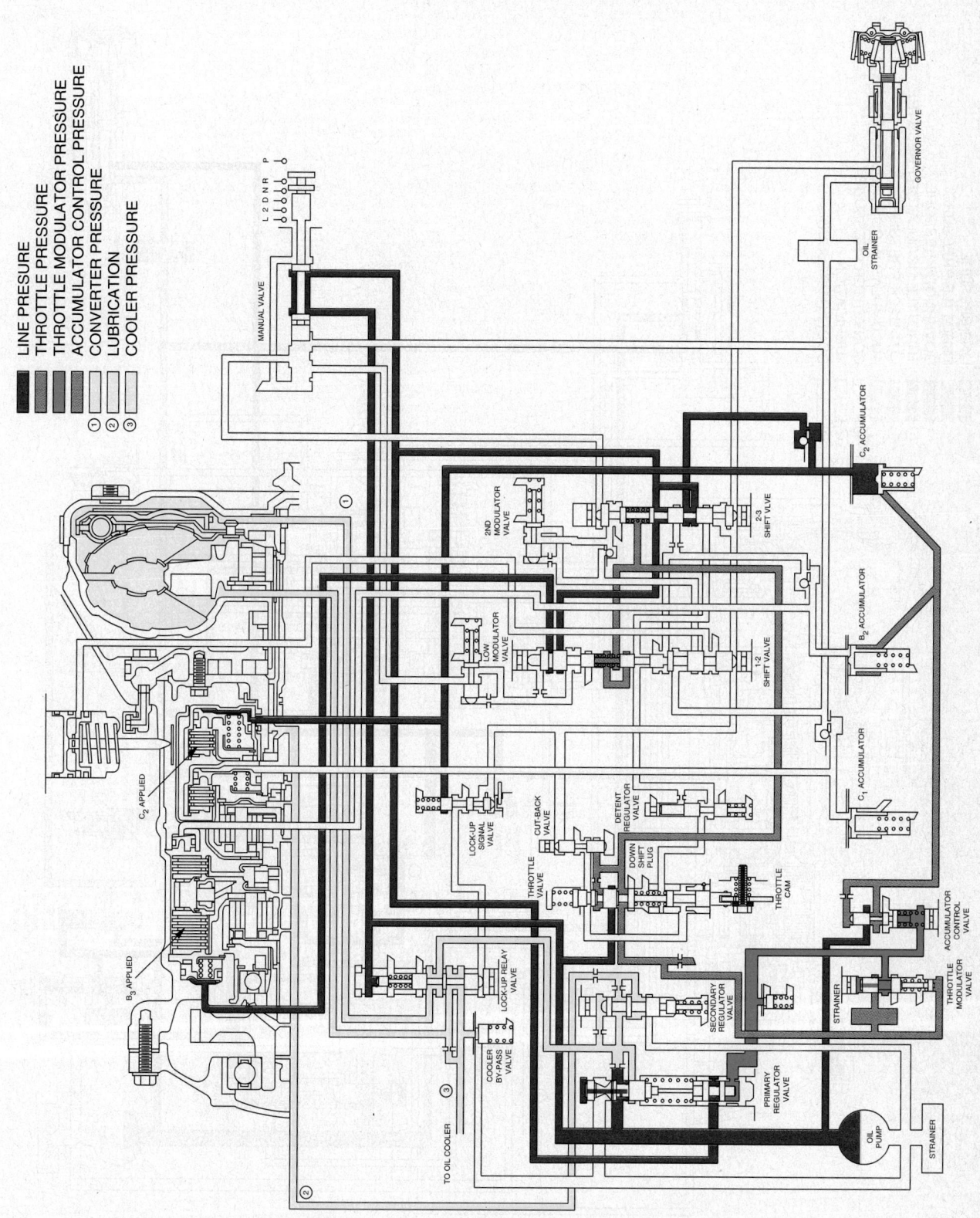

Fig. 2: "R" Position — Reverse

Courtesy of Toyota Motor Sales, U.S.A., Inc.

OIL CIRCUIT DIAGRAMS
Toyota A-132L (Cont.)

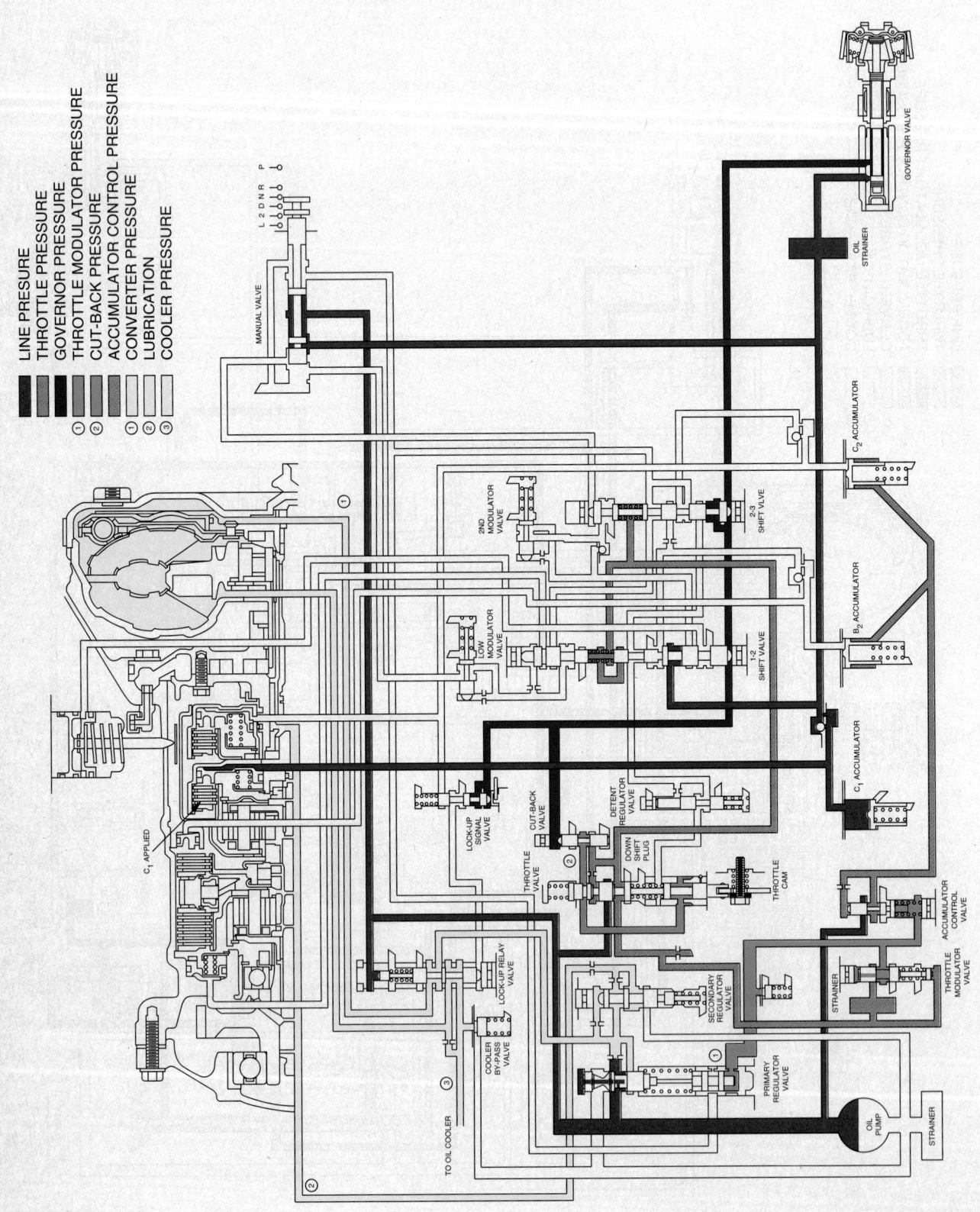

Fig. 3: "D" Position — 1st Gear

Courtesy of Toyota Motor Sales, U.S.A., Inc.

OIL CIRCUIT DIAGRAMS
Toyota A-132L (Cont.)

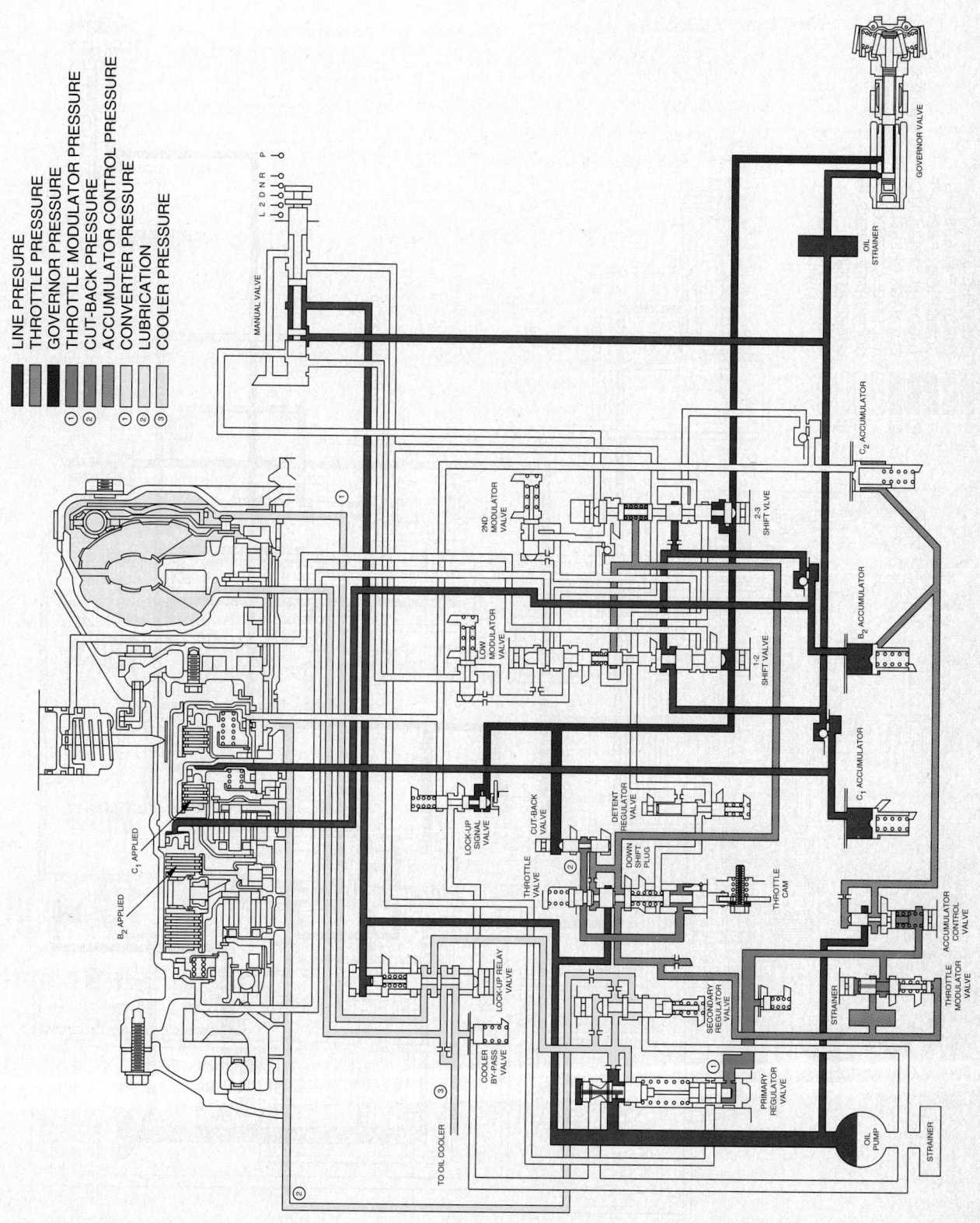

Fig. 4: "D" Position — 2nd Gear

Courtesy of Toyota Motor Sales, U.S.A., Inc.

OIL CIRCUIT DIAGRAMS
Toyota A-132L (Cont.)

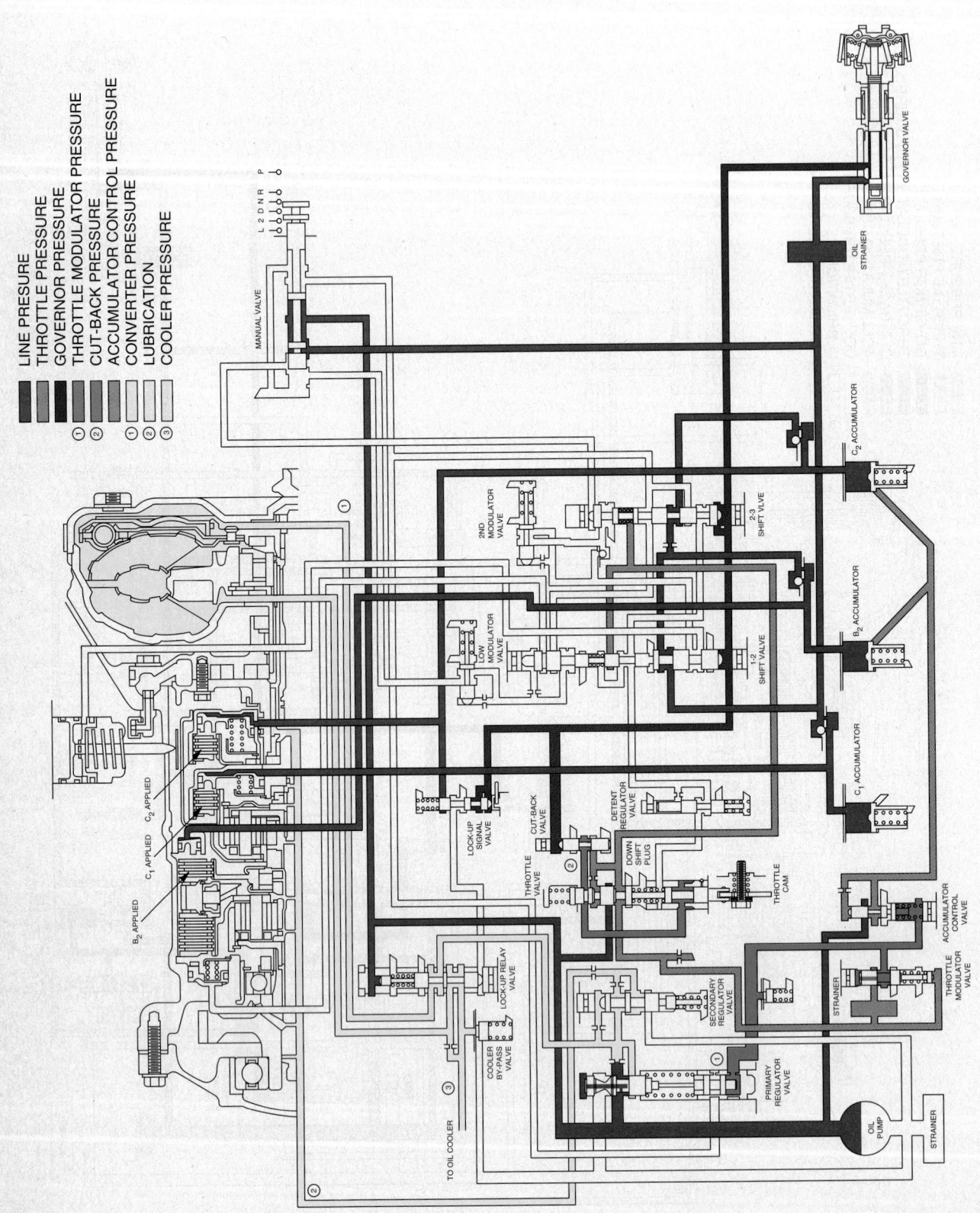

Fig. 5: "D" Position — 3rd Gear

Courtesy of Toyota Motor Sales, U.S.A., Inc.

OIL CIRCUIT DIAGRAMS
Toyota A-132L (Cont.)

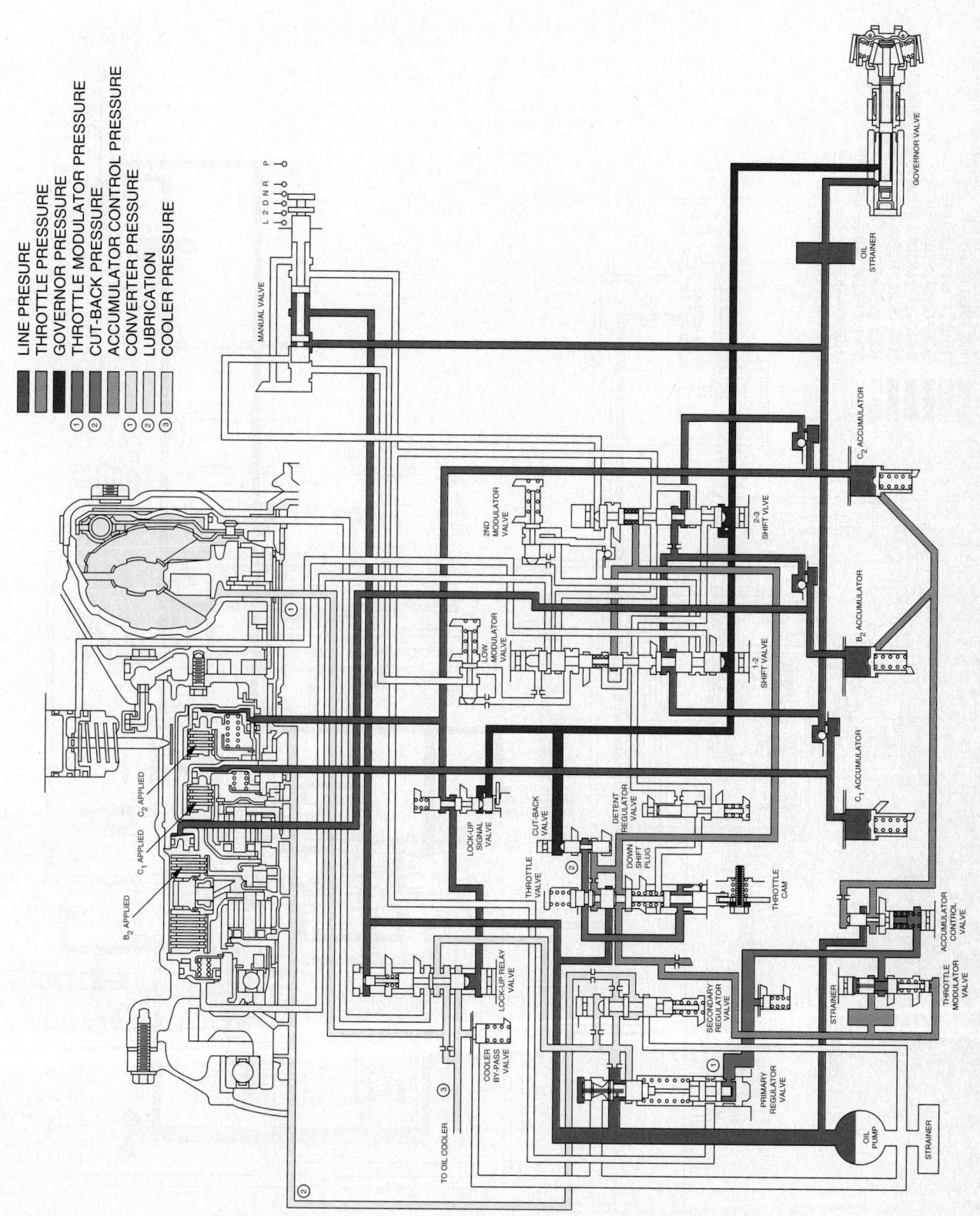

Fig. 6: "D" Position — 3rd Gear (Lock-Up ON)

Courtesy of Toyota Motor Sales, U.S.A., Inc.

OIL CIRCUIT DIAGRAMS
Toyota A-132L (Cont.)

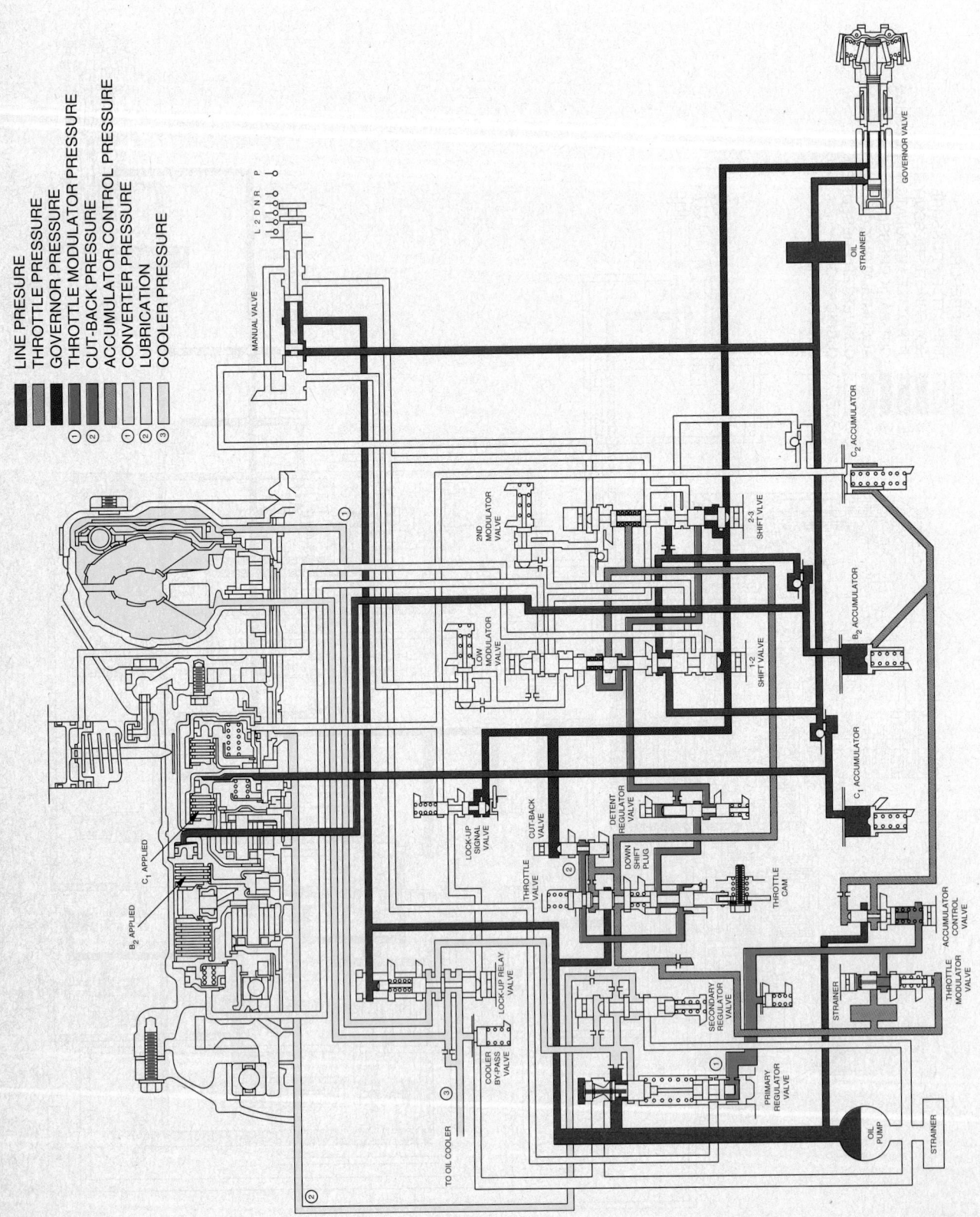

Fig. 7: "D" Position — 2nd Gear—Kickdown

Courtesy of Toyota Motor Sales, U.S.A., Inc.

OIL CIRCUIT DIAGRAMS
Toyota A-132L (Cont.)

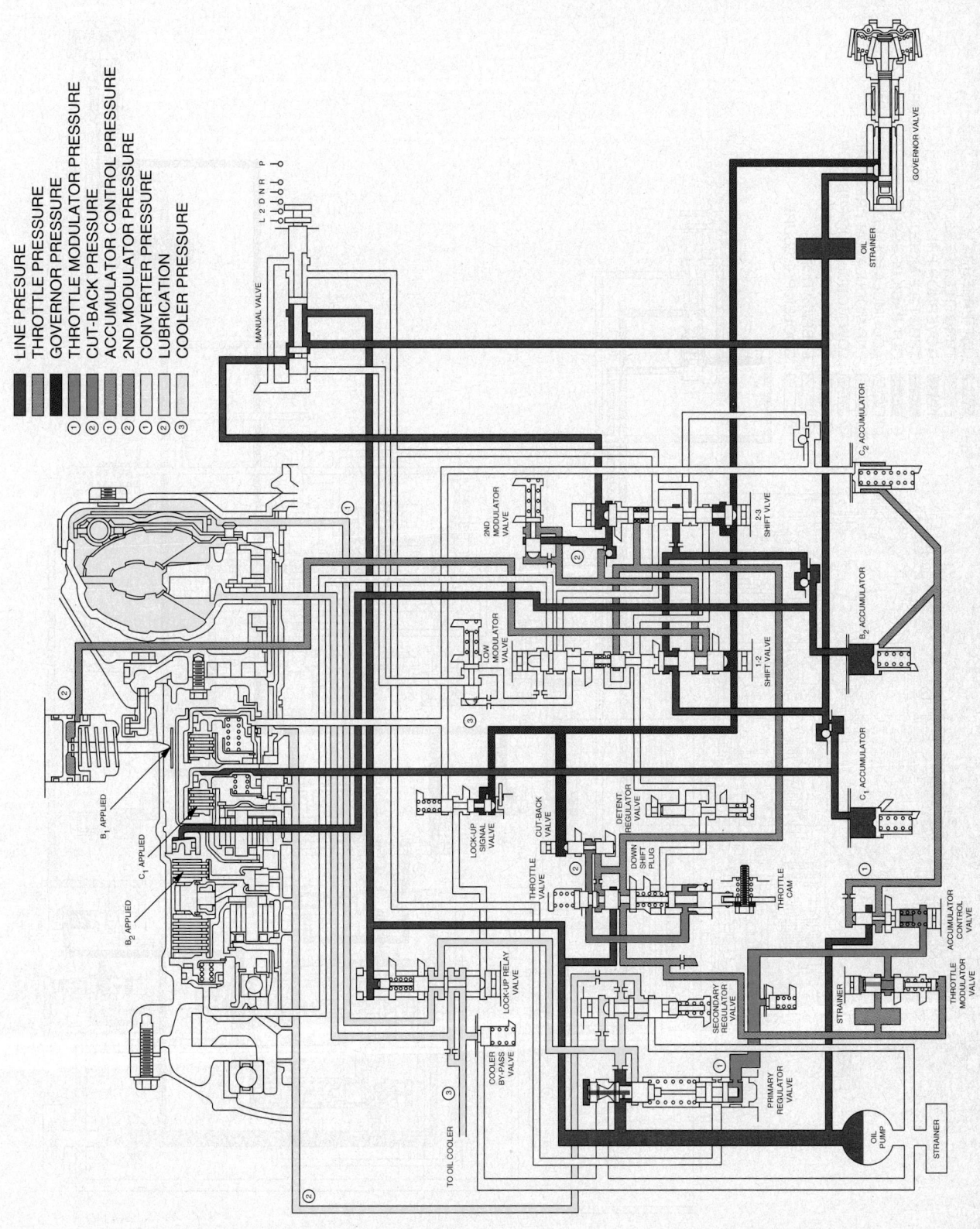

Fig. 8: "2" Position — 2nd Gear

Courtesy of Toyota Motor Sales, U.S.A., Inc.

OIL CIRCUIT DIAGRAMS
Toyota A-132L (Cont.)

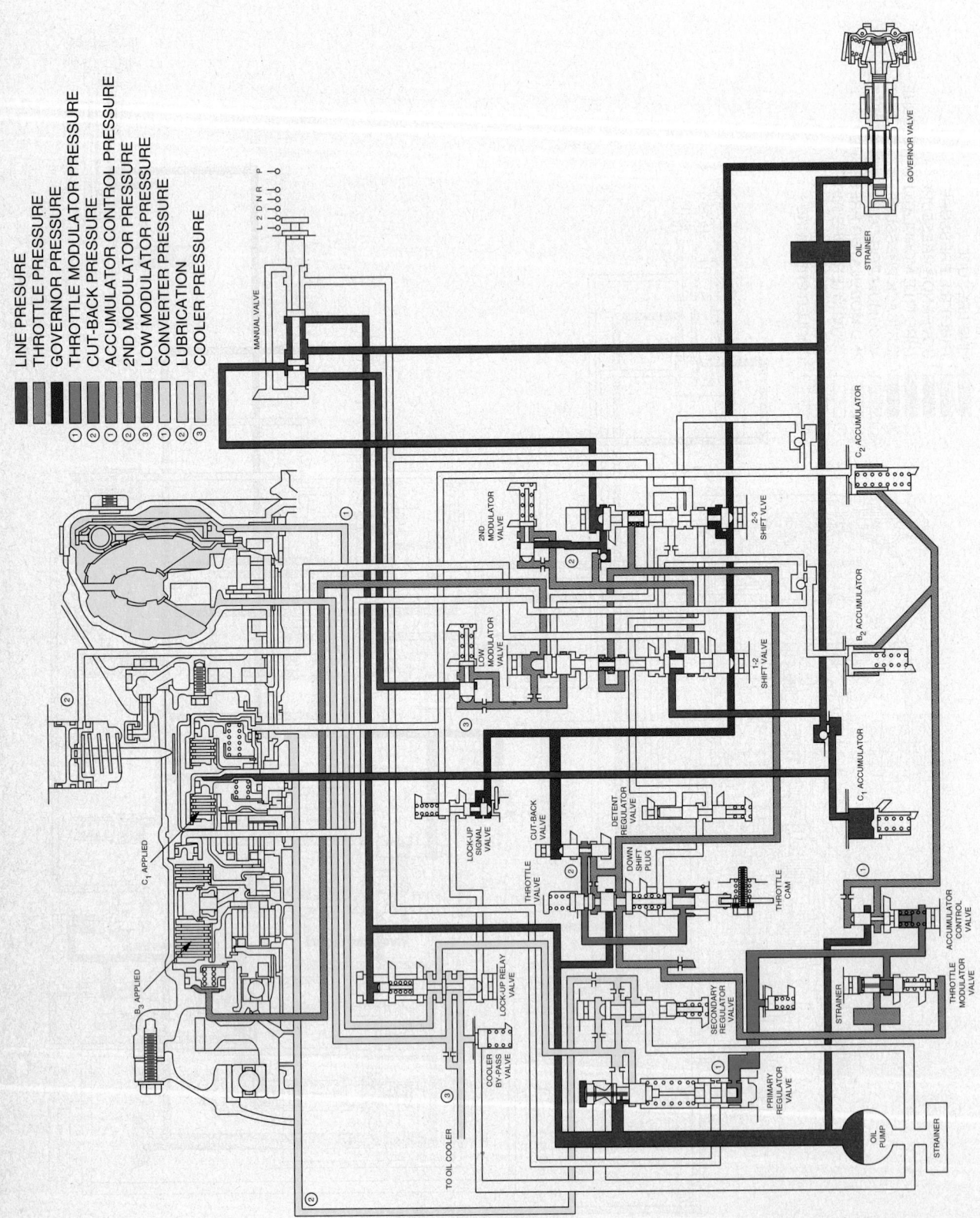

Fig. 9: "L" Position — 1st Gear

Courtesy of Toyota Motor Sales, U.S.A., Inc.

OIL CIRCUIT DIAGRAMS
Toyota A-140E

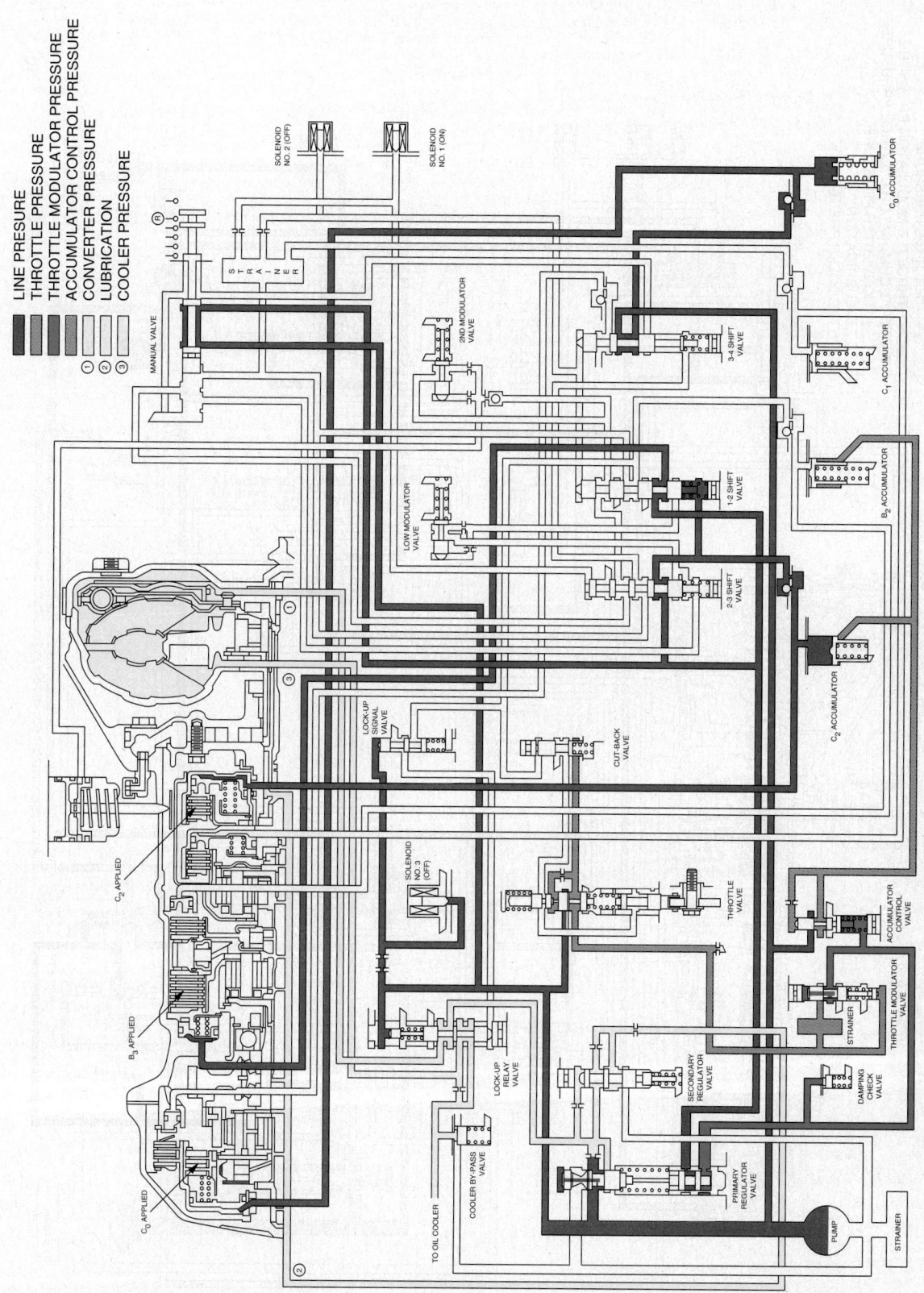

Fig. 1: "R" Position — Reverse

Courtesy of Toyota Motor Sales, U.S.A., Inc.

OIL CIRCUIT DIAGRAMS
Toyota A-140E (Cont.)

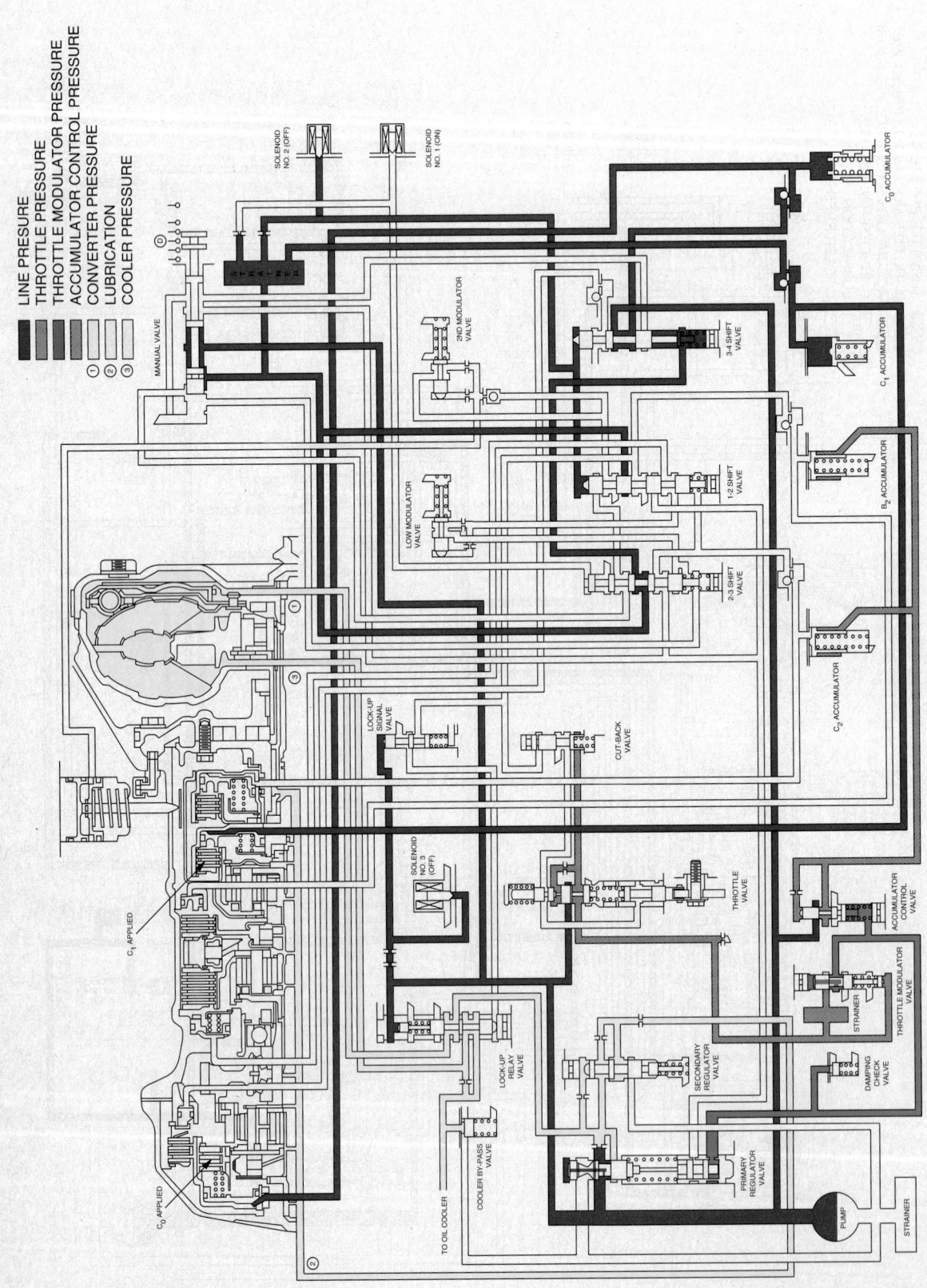

Fig. 2: "D" Position — 1st Gear

Courtesy of Toyota Motor Sales, U.S.A., Inc.

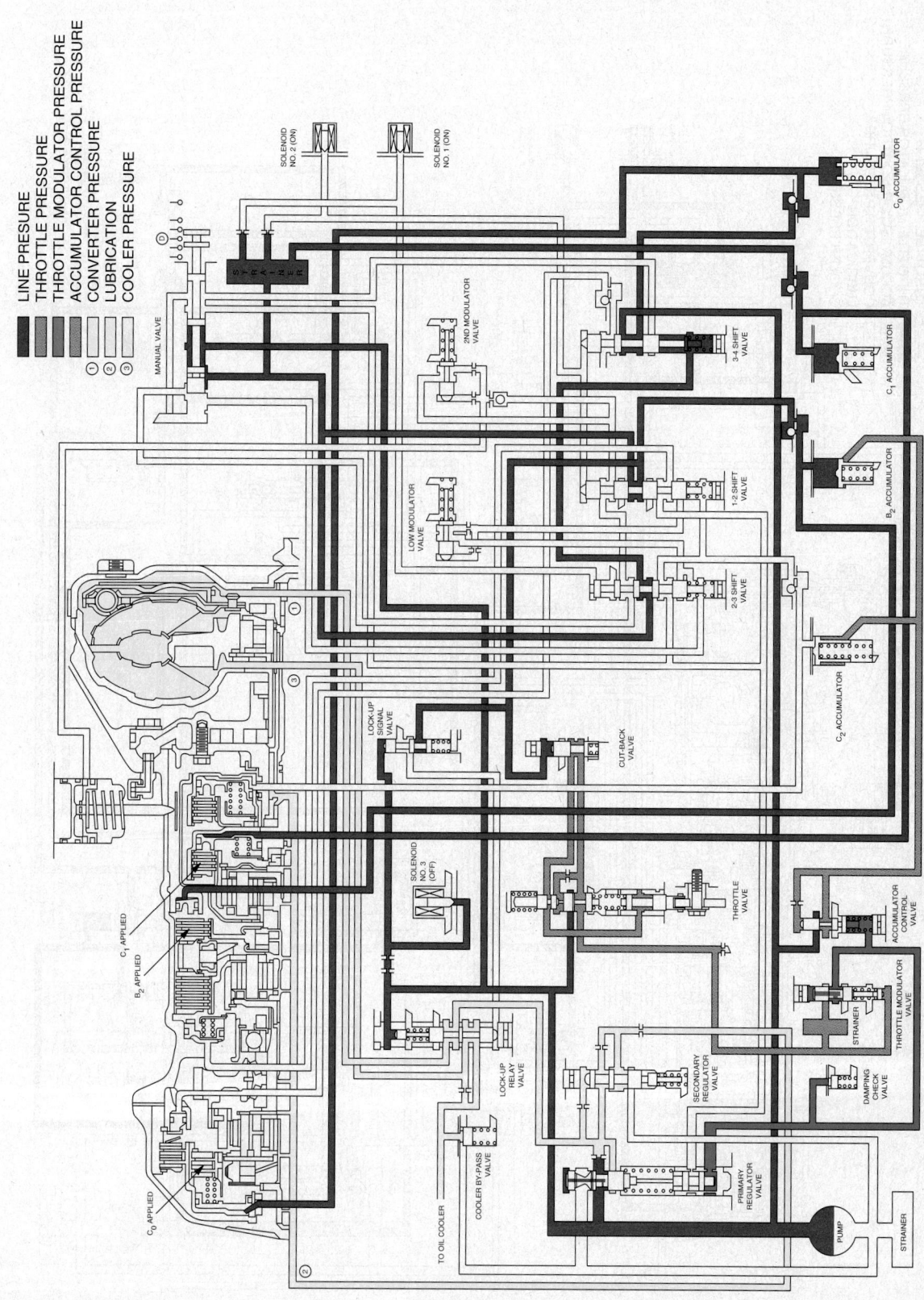

Fig. 3: "D" Position — 2nd Gear

Courtesy of Toyota Motor Sales, U.S.A., Inc.

OIL CIRCUIT DIAGRAMS
Toyota A-140E (Cont.)

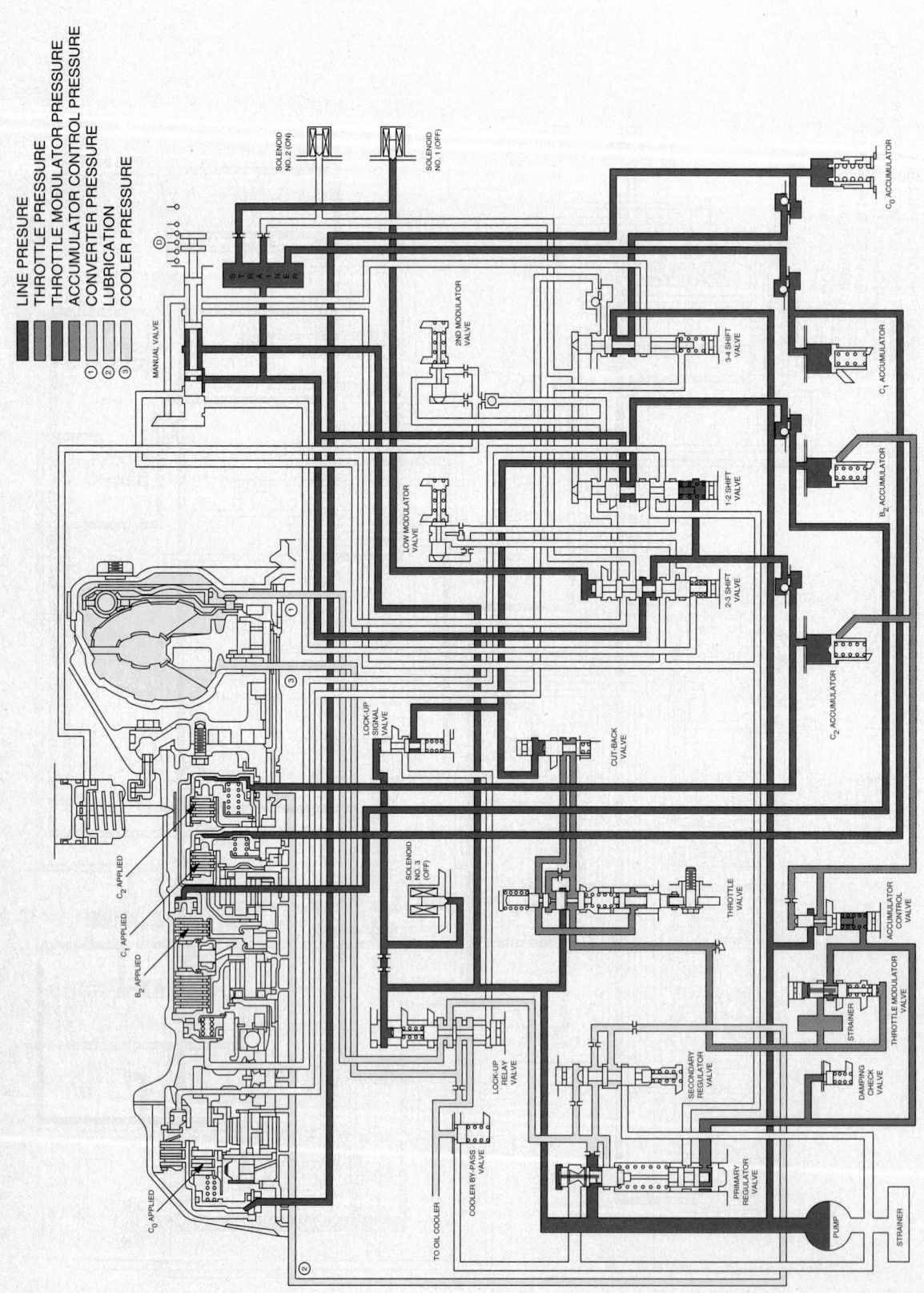

Fig. 4: "D" Position — 3rd Gear

Courtesy of Toyota Motor Sales, U.S.A., Inc.

OIL CIRCUIT DIAGRAMS
Toyota A-140E (Cont.)

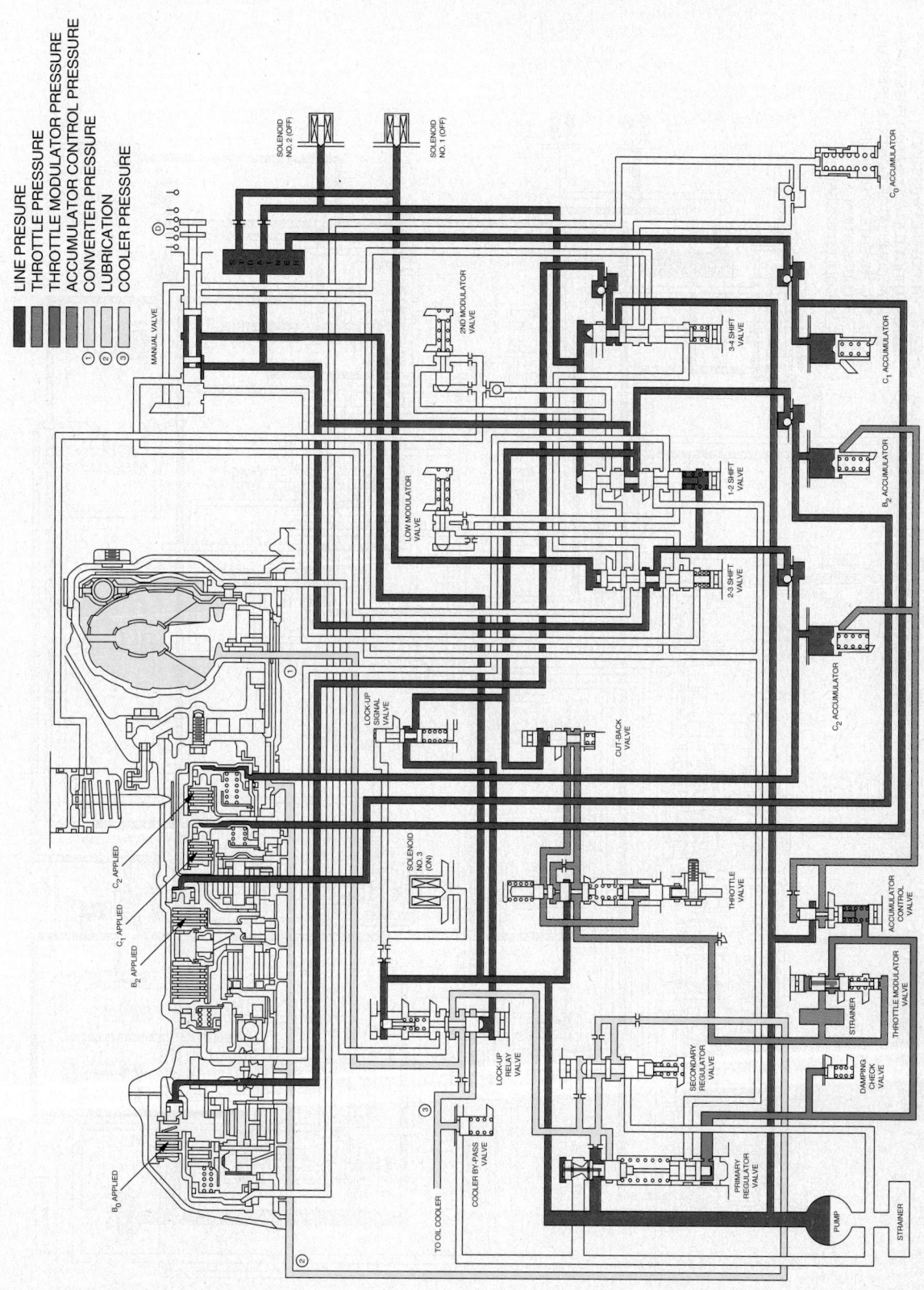

Fig. 5: "OD" Position — (Lock-Up ON)

Courtesy of Toyota Motor Sales, U.S.A., Inc.

OIL CIRCUIT DIAGRAMS
Toyota A-140E (Cont.)

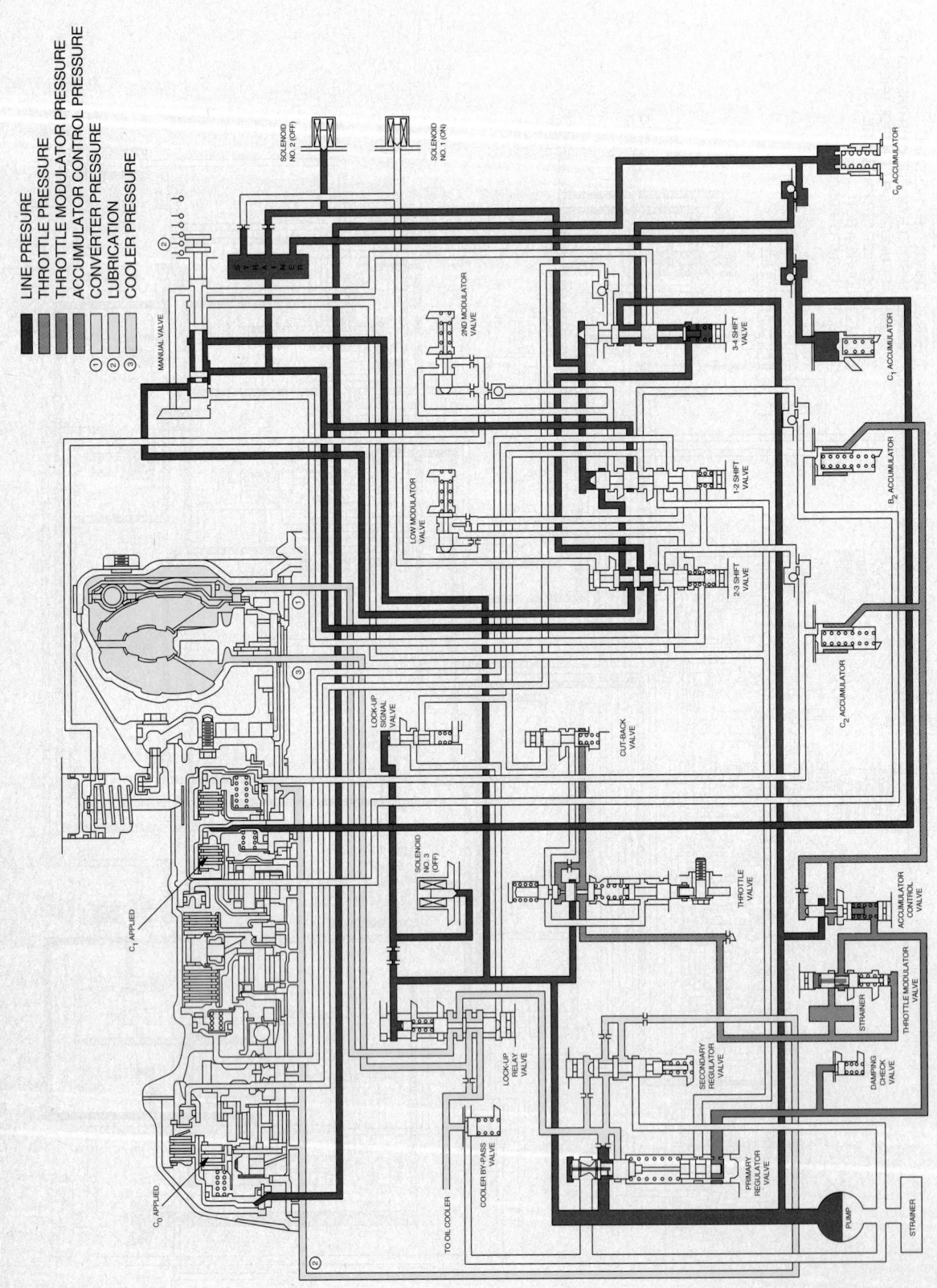

Fig. 6: "2" Position — 1st Gear

Courtesy of Toyota Motor Sales, U.S.A., Inc.

OIL CIRCUIT DIAGRAMS
Toyota A-140E (Cont.)

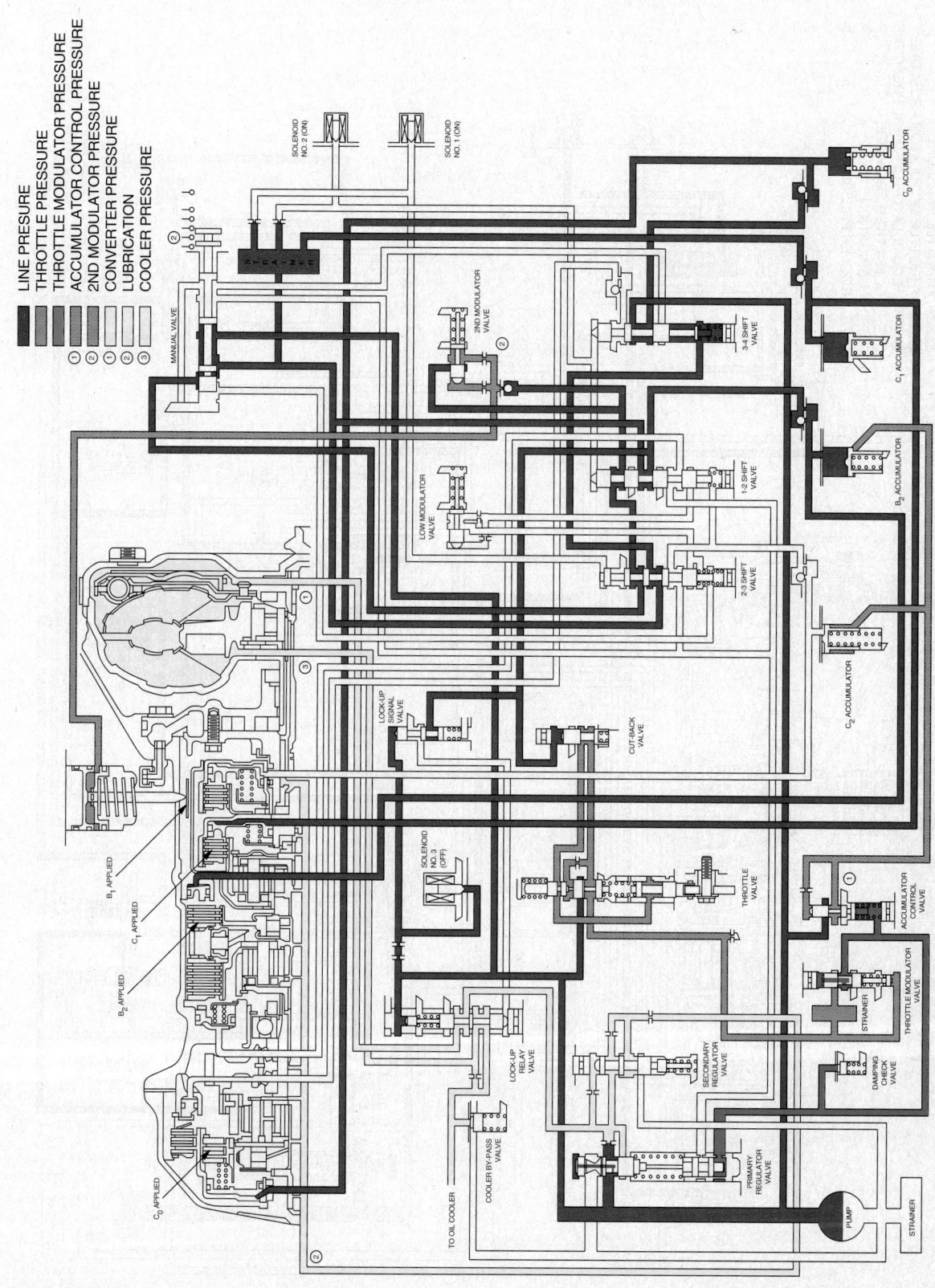

Fig. 7: "2" Position — 2nd Gear

Courtesy of Toyota Motor Sales, U.S.A., Inc.

OIL CIRCUIT DIAGRAMS
Toyota A-140E (Cont.)

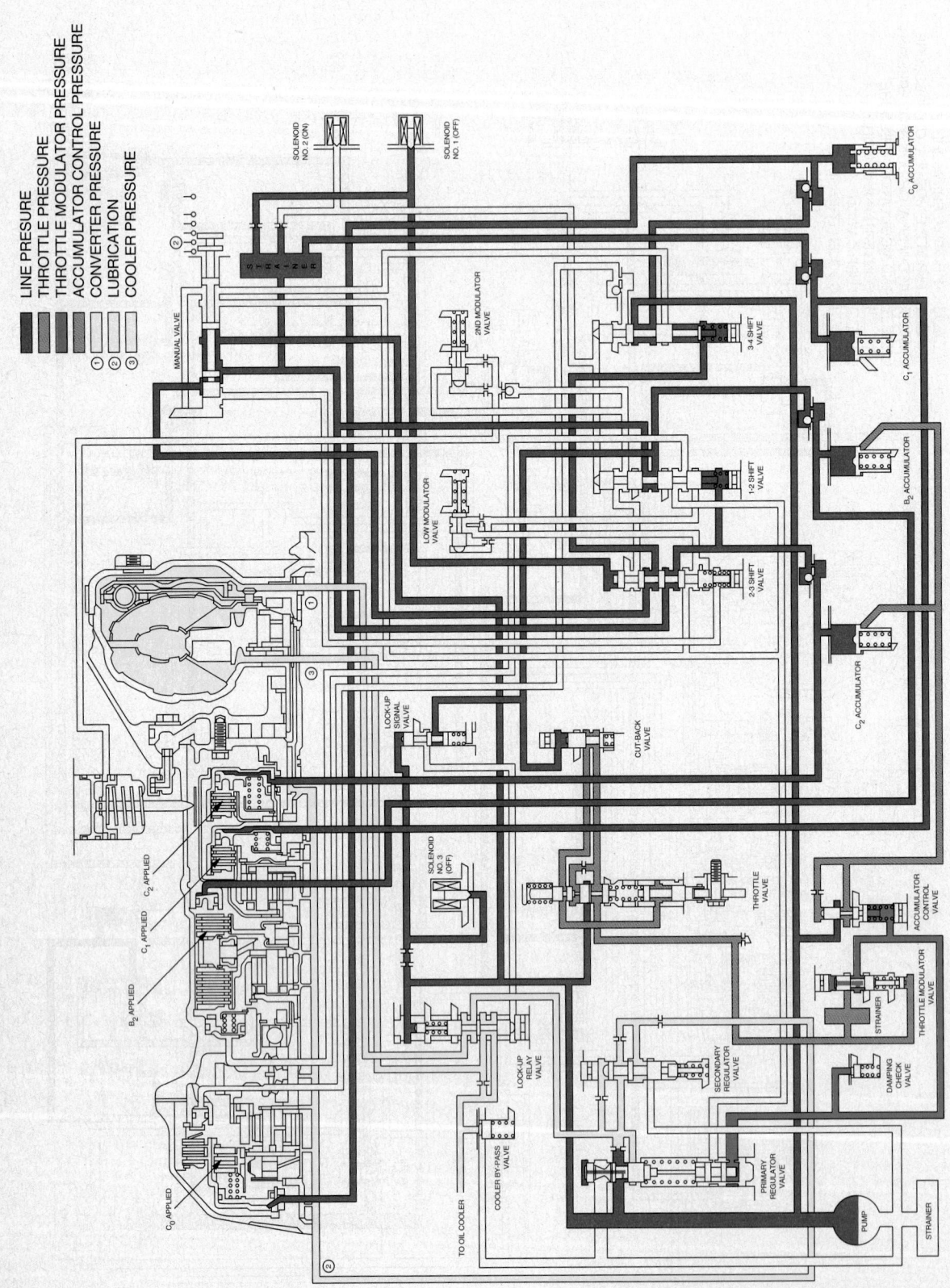

Fig. 8: "2" Position — 3rd Gear

Courtesy of Toyota Motor Sales, U.S.A., Inc.

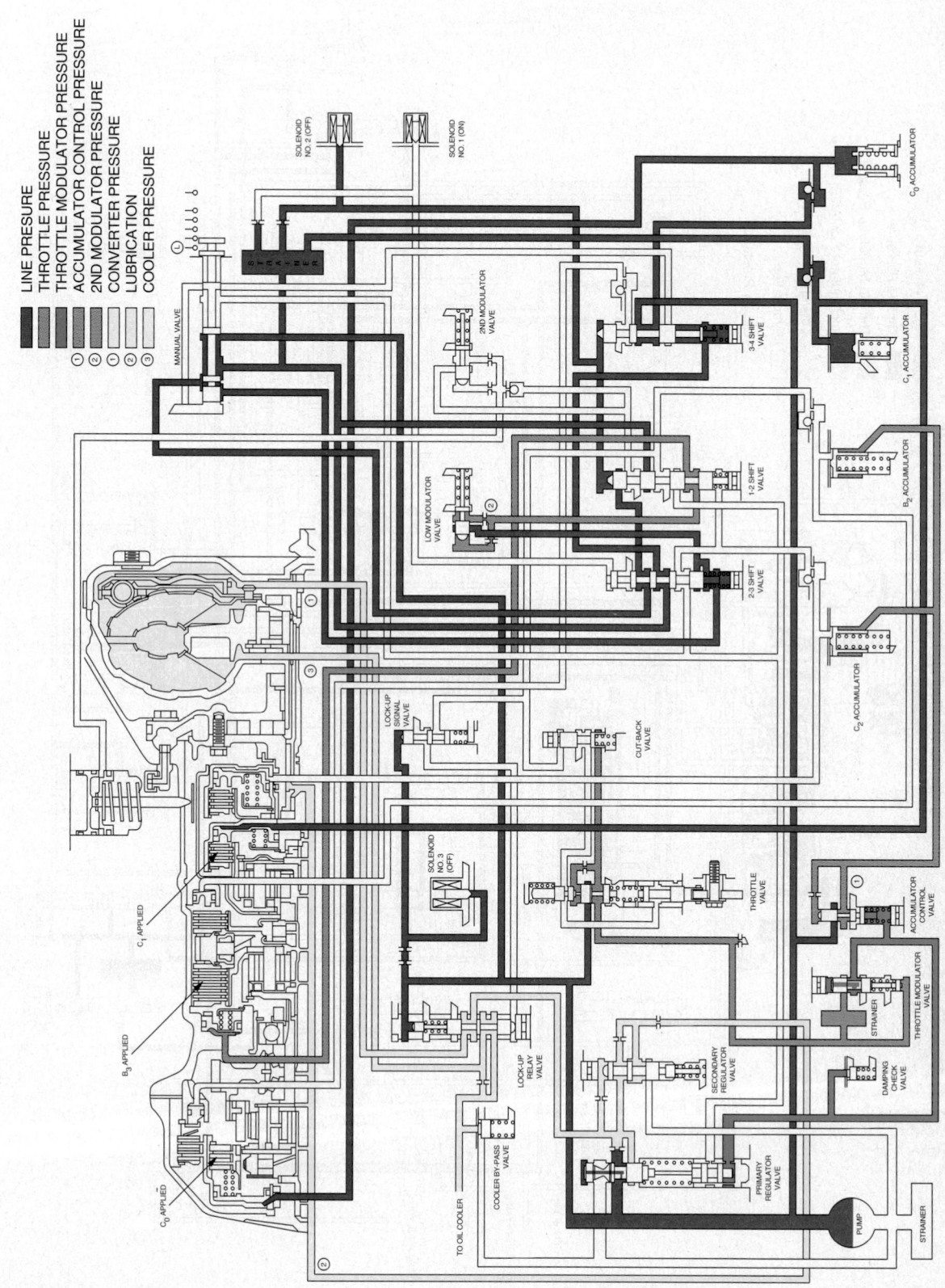

OIL CIRCUIT DIAGRAMS
Toyota A-240E & A-241E

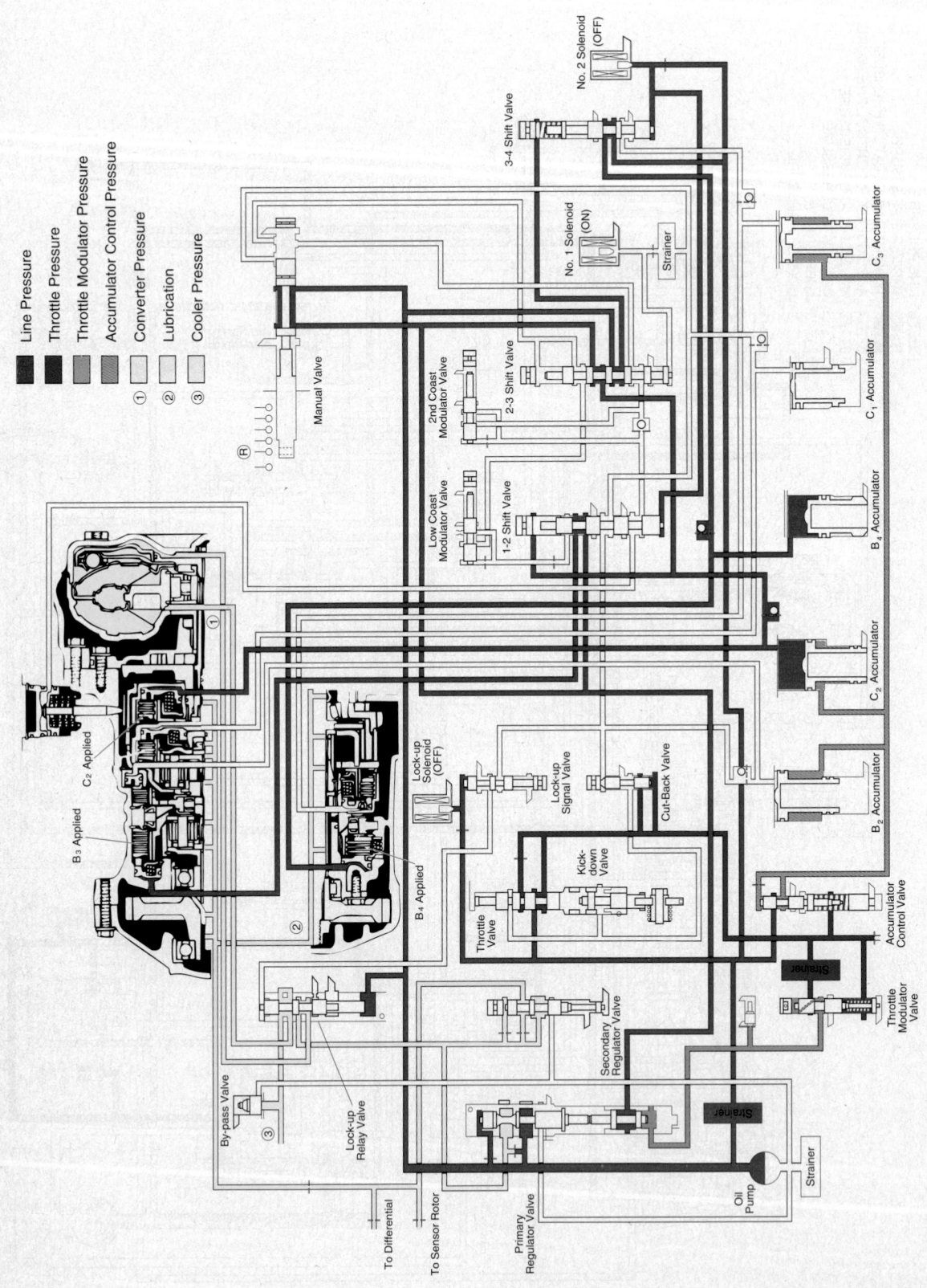

Line Pressure
Throttle Pressure
Throttle Modulator Pressure
Accumulator Control Pressure
Converter Pressure
Lubrication
Cooler Pressure
① ② ③

No. 2 Solenoid (OFF)
3-4 Shift Valve
No. 1 Solenoid (ON)
Strainer
C_3 Accumulator
C_1 Accumulator
Manual Valve
2nd Coast Modulator Valve
2-3 Shift Valve
Low Coast Modulator Valve
1-2 Shift Valve
B_4 Accumulator
C_2 Applied
B_3 Applied
Lock-up Solenoid (OFF)
Lock-up Signal Valve
Cut-Back Valve
C_2 Accumulator
B_2 Accumulator
B_4 Applied
Throttle Valve
Kick-down Valve
Accumulator Control Valve
By-pass Valve
Lock-up Relay Valve
Secondary Regulator Valve
Throttle Modulator Valve
Strainer
To Differential
To Sensor Rotor
Primary Regulator Valve
Strainer
Oil Pump
Strainer

Fig. 1: "R" Position — Reverse

Courtesy of Toyota Motor Sales, U.S.A., Inc.

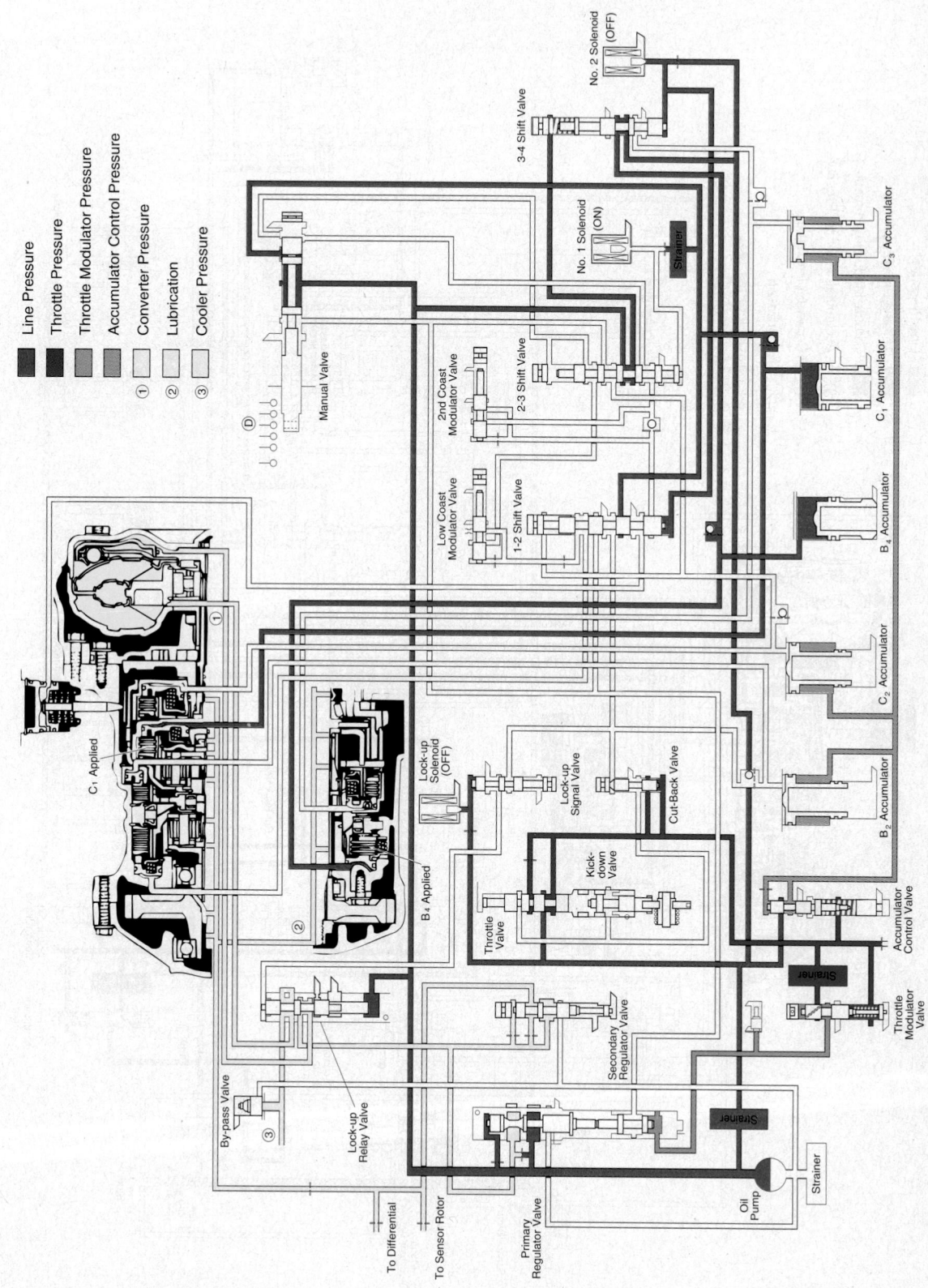

Fig. 2: "D" Position — 1st Gear

Courtesy of Toyota Motor Sales, U.S.A., Inc.

OIL CIRCUIT DIAGRAMS
Toyota A-240E & A-241E (Cont.)

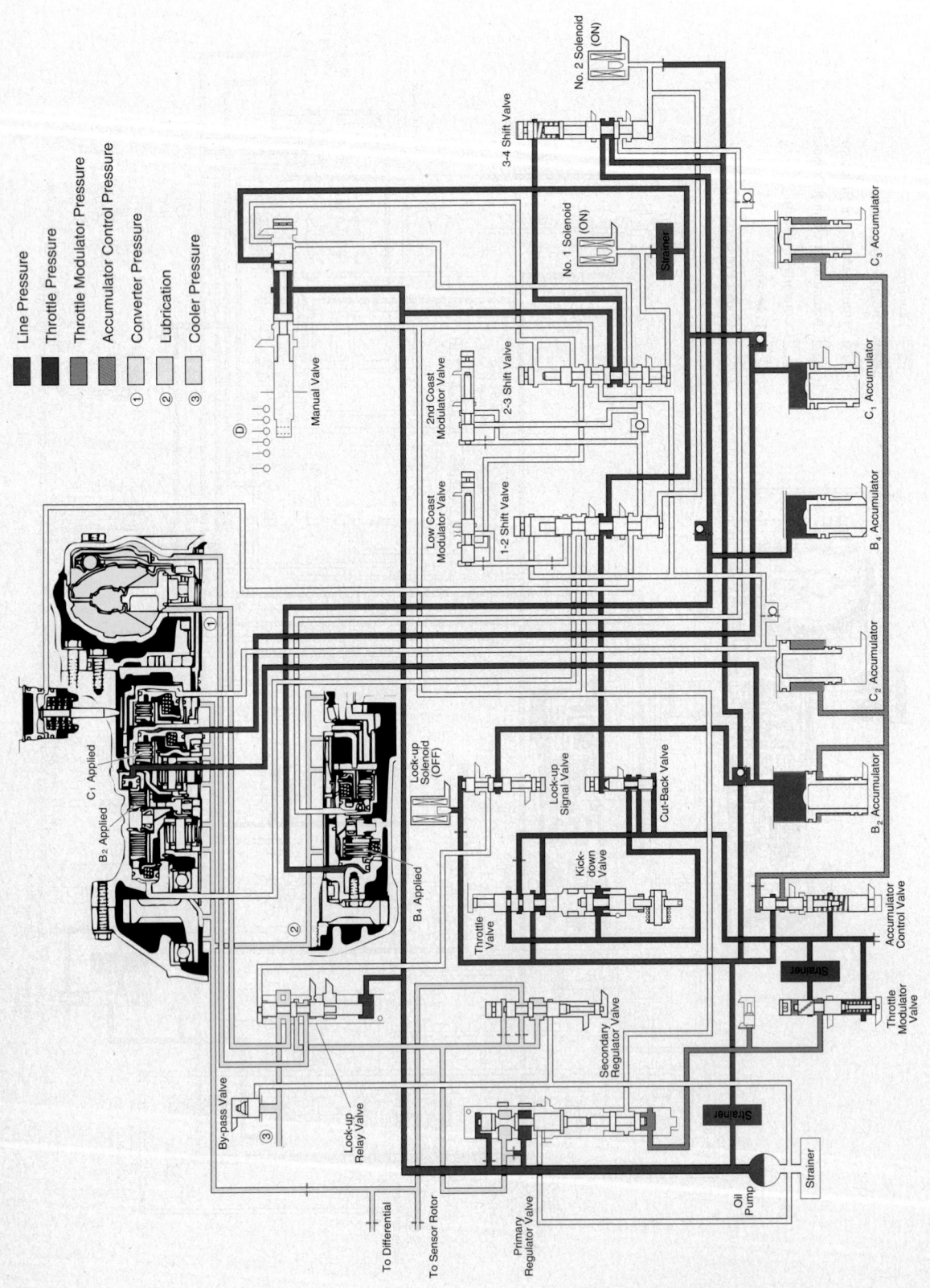

Fig. 3: *"D" Position — 2nd Gear*

Courtesy of Toyota Motor Sales, U.S.A., Inc.

OIL CIRCUIT DIAGRAMS
Toyota A-240E & A-241E (Cont.)

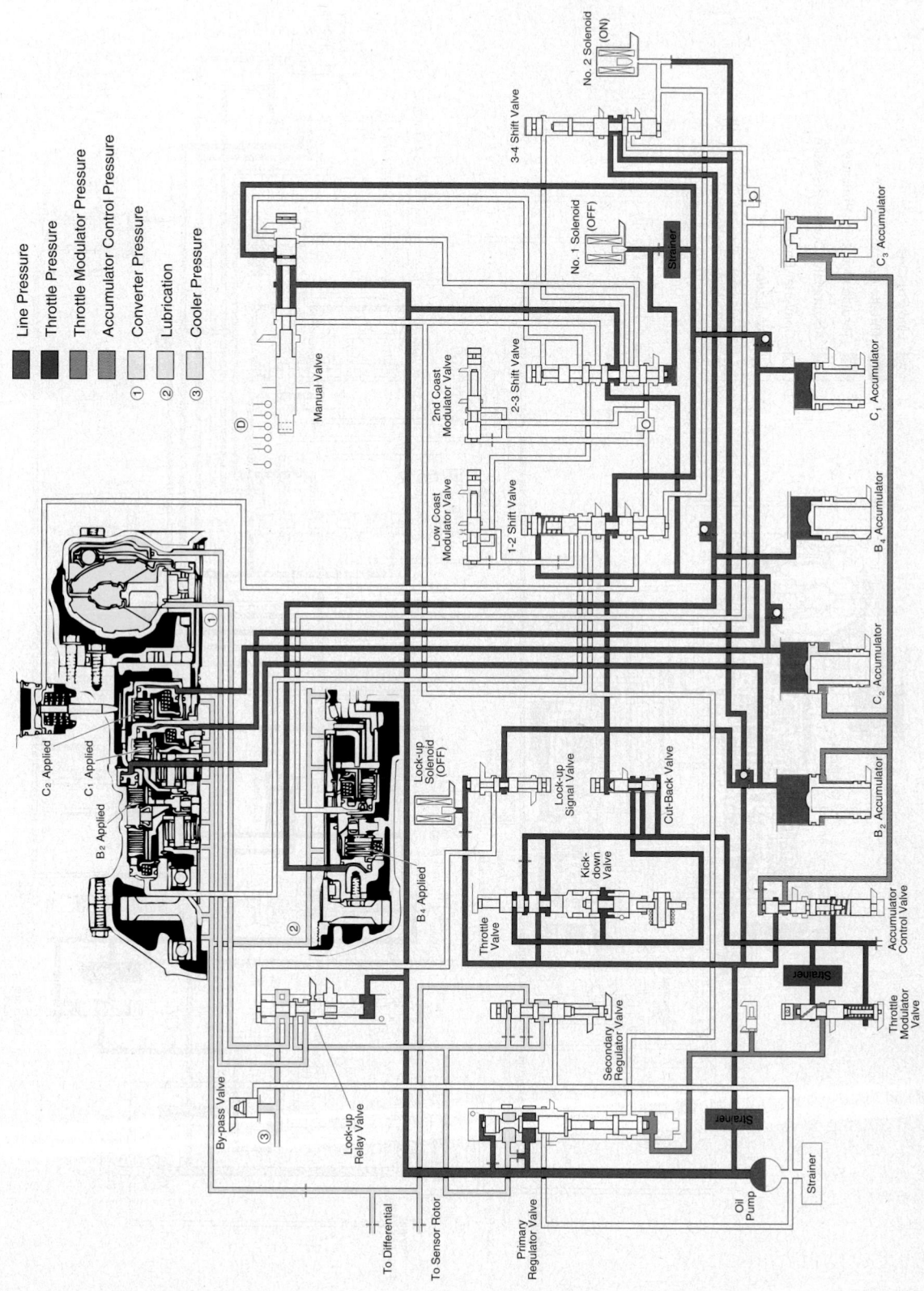

Fig. 4: "D" Position — 3rd Gear

Courtesy of Toyota Motor Sales, U.S.A., Inc.

OIL CIRCUIT DIAGRAMS
Toyota A-240E & A-241E (Cont.)

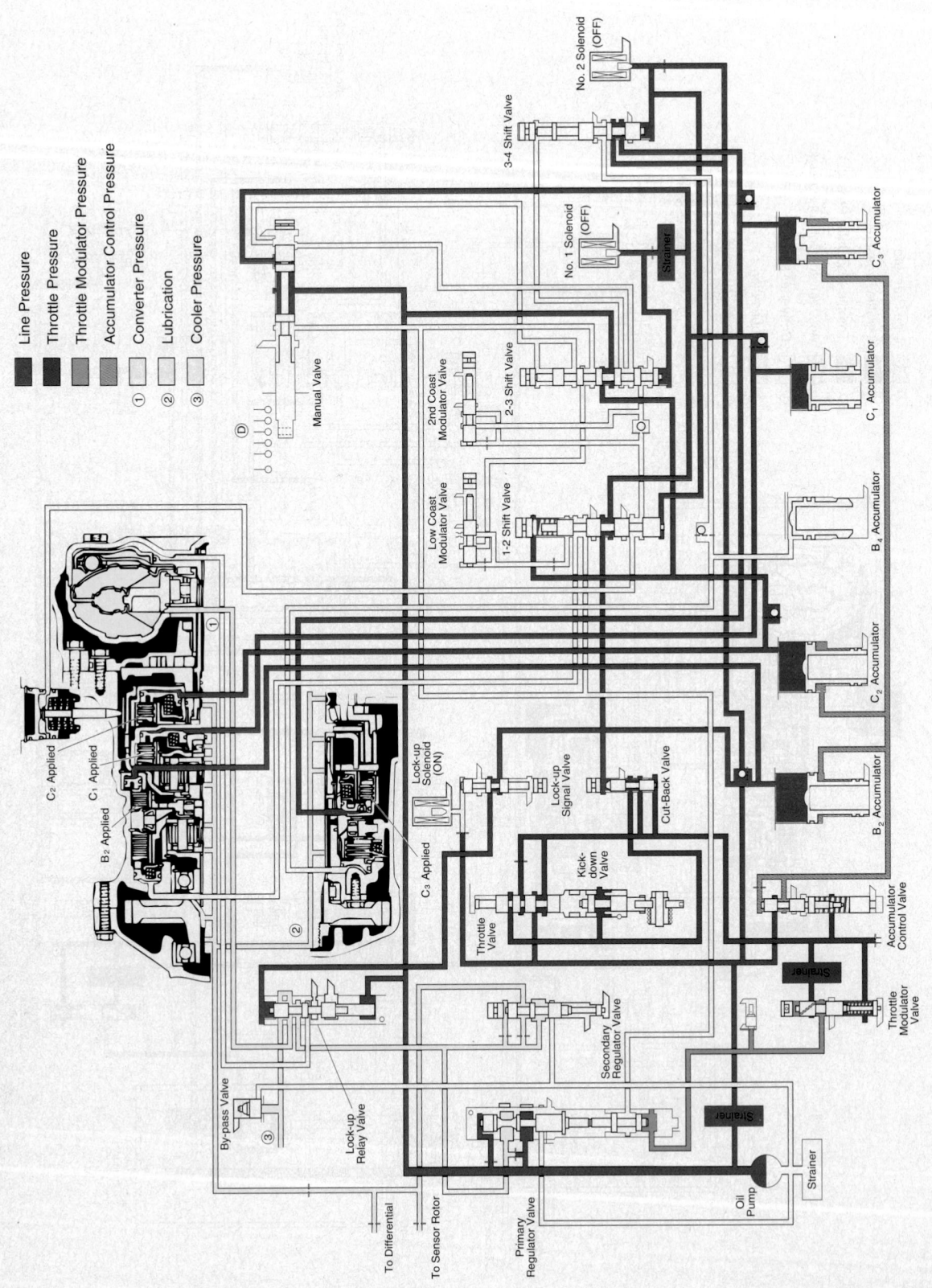

Fig. 5: "D" Position — OD Gear (Lock-Up ON)

Courtesy of Toyota Motor Sales, U.S.A., Inc.

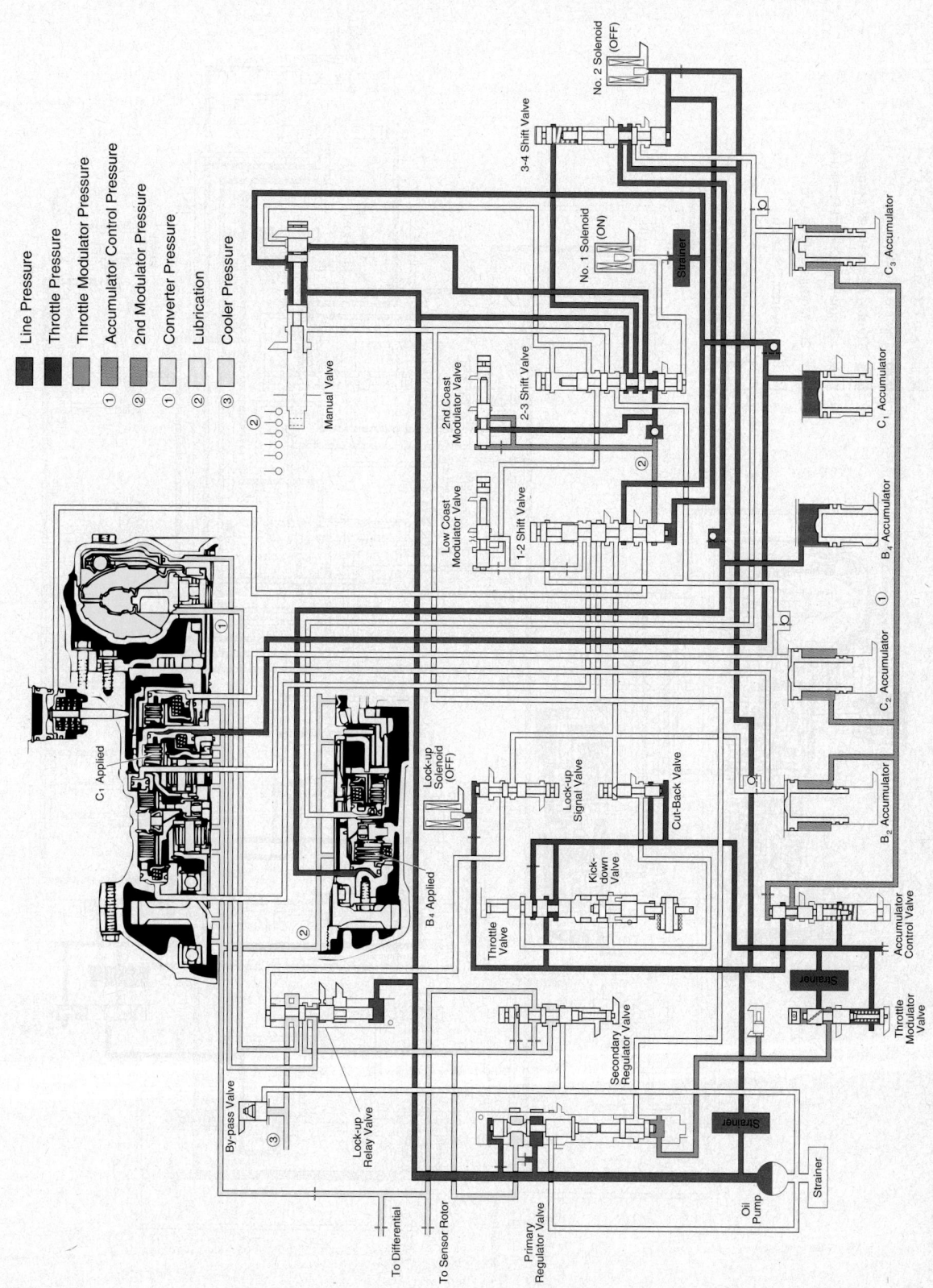

Line Pressure

Throttle Pressure

Throttle Modulator Pressure

Accumulator Control Pressure

2nd Modulator Pressure

Converter Pressure

Lubrication

Cooler Pressure

Fig. 6: "2" Position — 1st Gear

Courtesy of Toyota Motor Sales, U.S.A., Inc.

OIL CIRCUIT DIAGRAMS
Toyota A-240E & A-241E (Cont.)

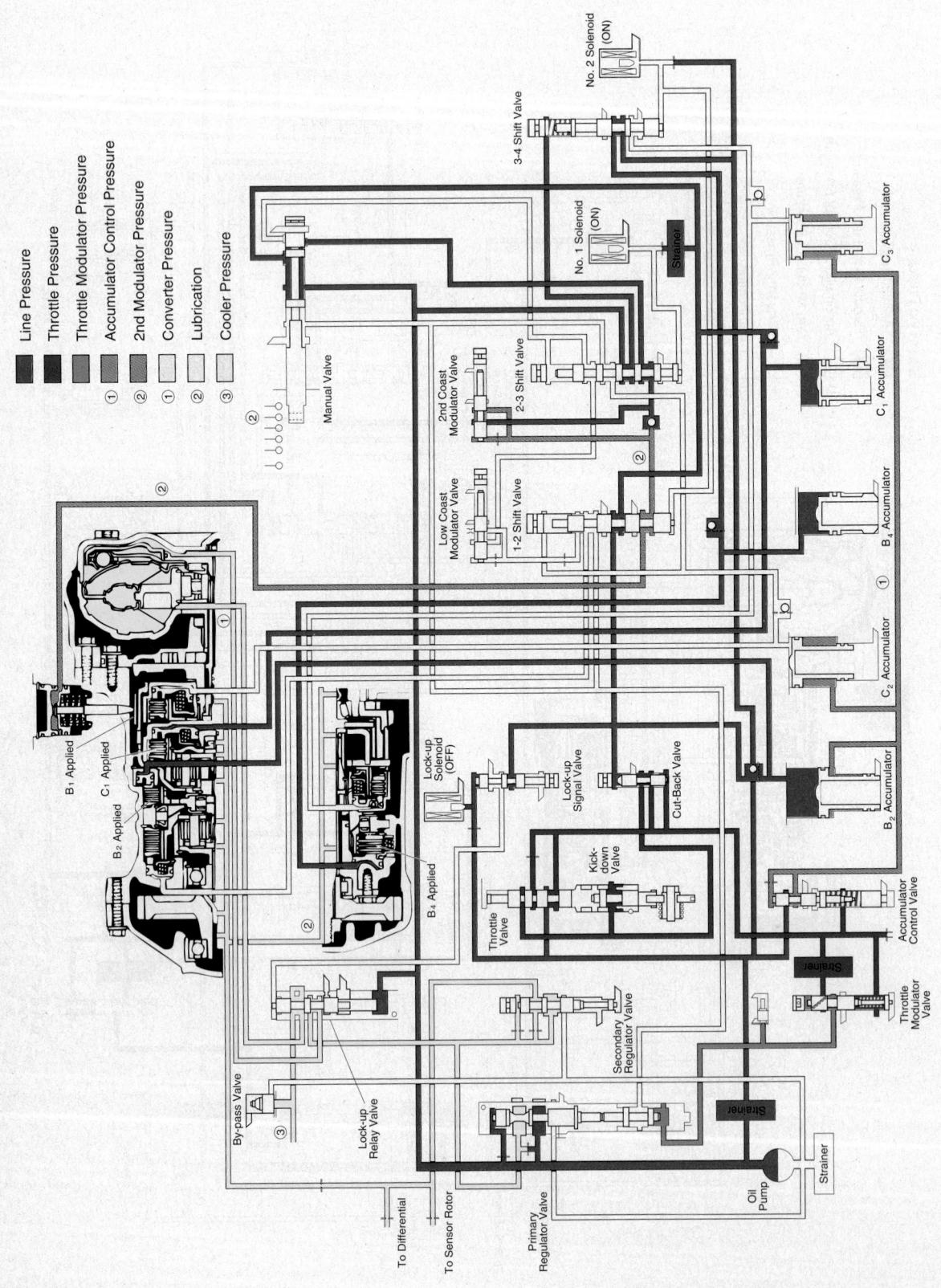

Line Pressure
Throttle Pressure
Throttle Modulator Pressure
Accumulator Control Pressure
2nd Modulator Pressure
Converter Pressure
Lubrication
Cooler Pressure

Fig. 7: "2" Position — 2nd Gear

Courtesy of Toyota Motor Sales, U.S.A., Inc.

OIL CIRCUIT DIAGRAMS
Toyota A-240E & A-241E (Cont.)

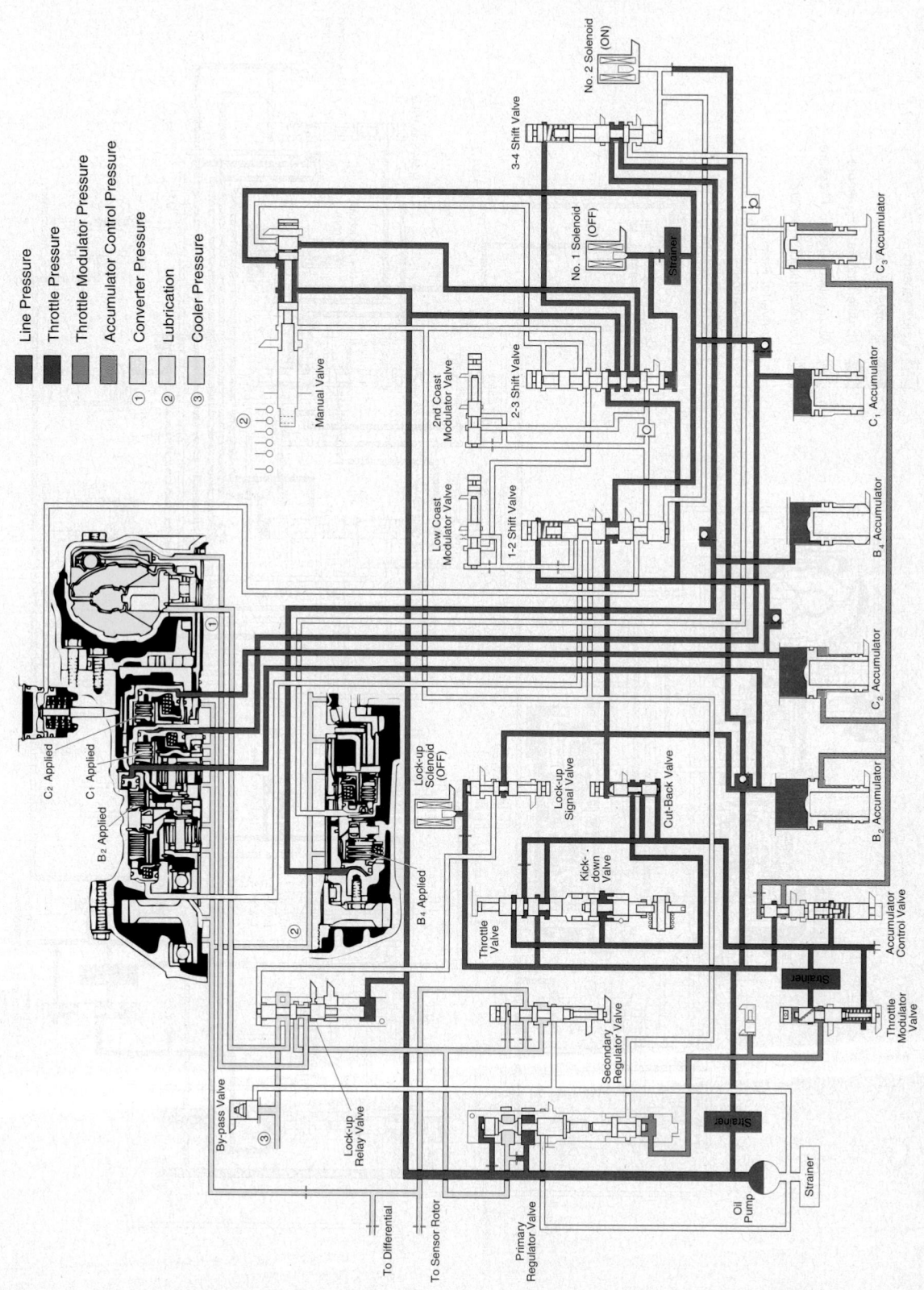

Fig. 8: "2" Position — 3rd Gear

Courtesy of Toyota Motor Sales, U.S.A., Inc.

OIL CIRCUIT DIAGRAMS
Toyota A-240E & A-241E (Cont.)

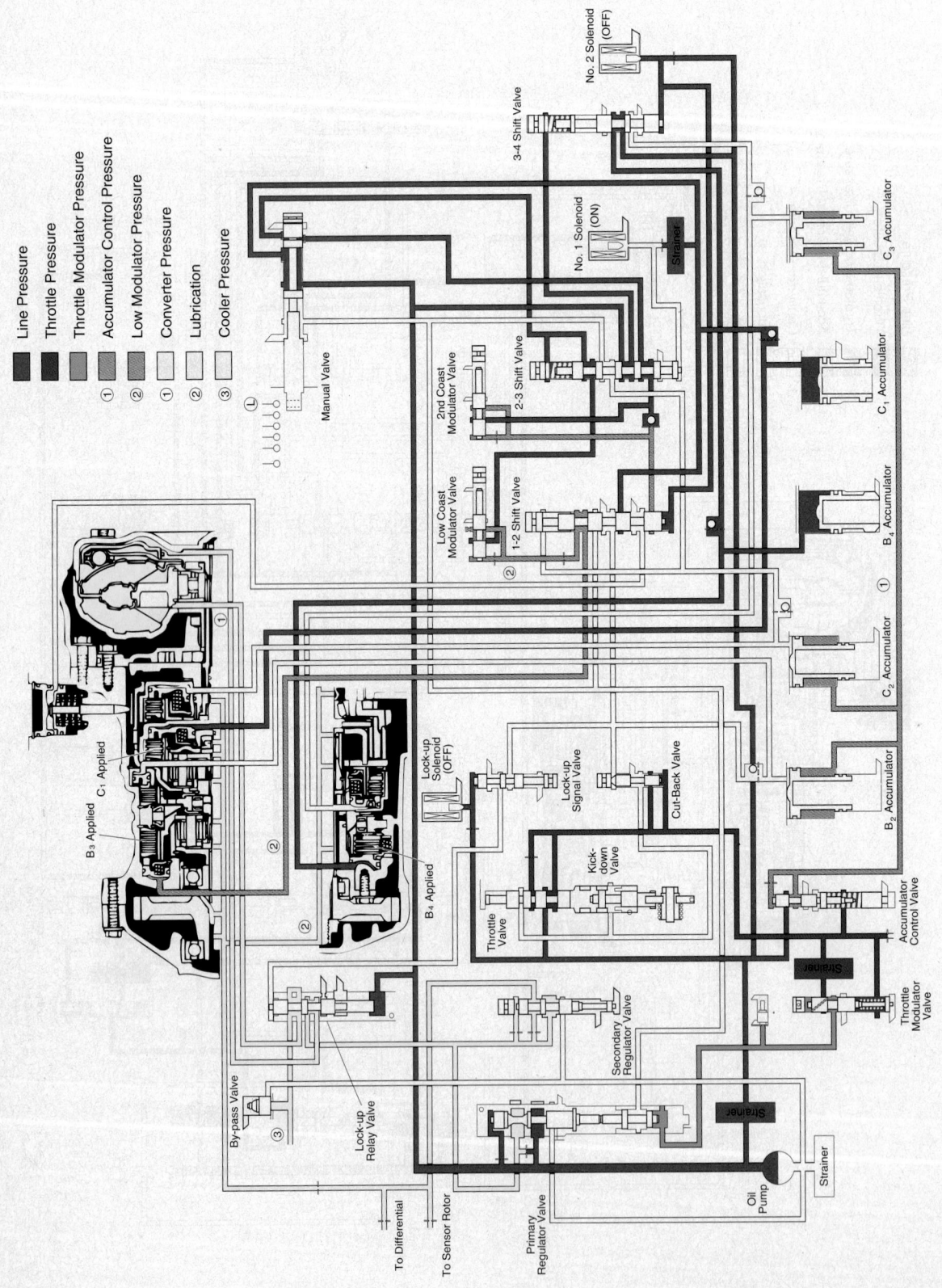

Fig. 9: "L" Position — 1st Gear

Courtesy of Toyota Motor Sales, U.S.A., Inc.

OIL CIRCUIT DIAGRAMS
Toyota A-340E & A-340H

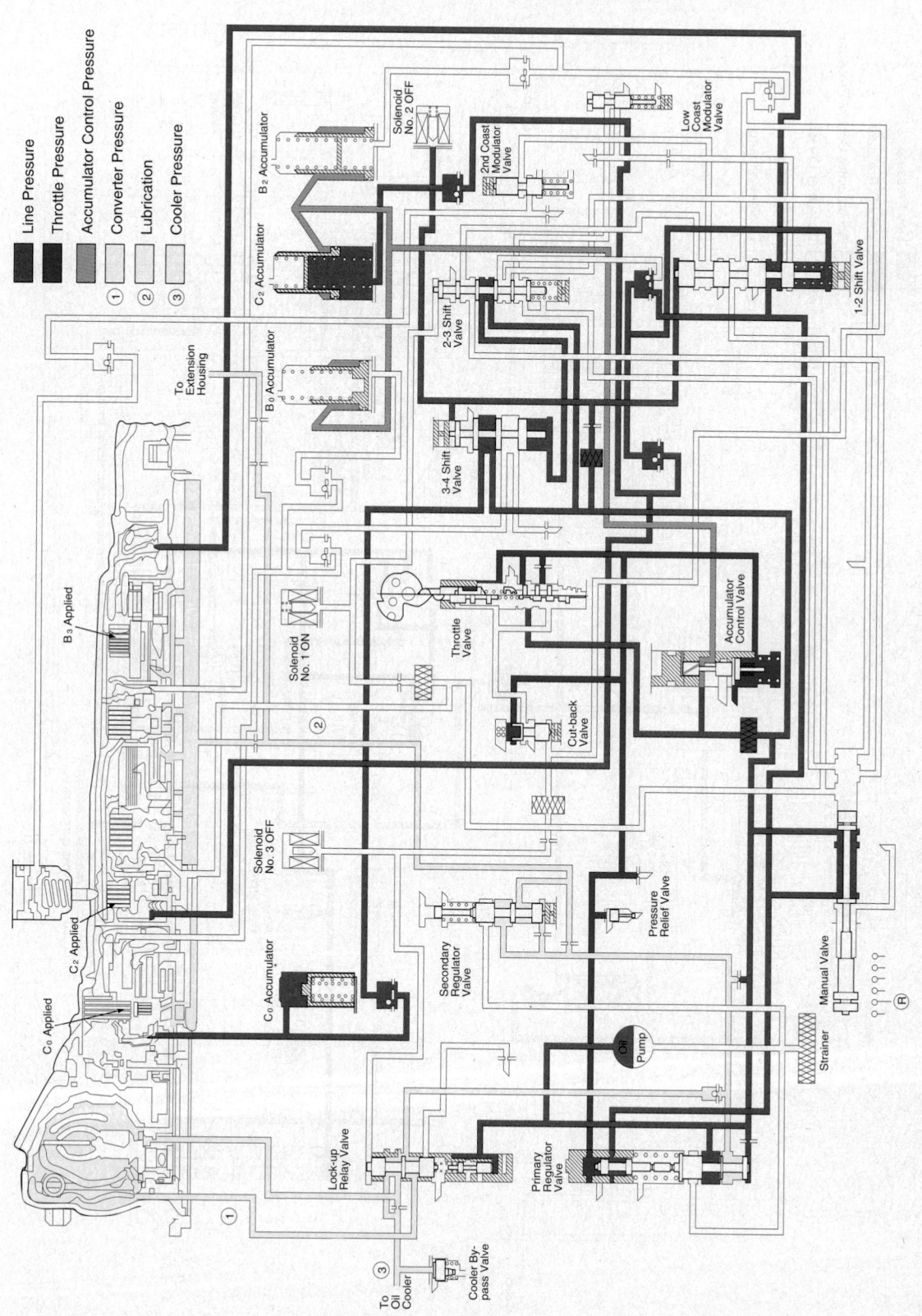

Fig. 1: "R" Position — Reverse

Courtesy of Toyota Motor Sales, U.S.A., Inc.

OIL CIRCUIT DIAGRAMS
Toyota A-340E & A-340H (Cont.)

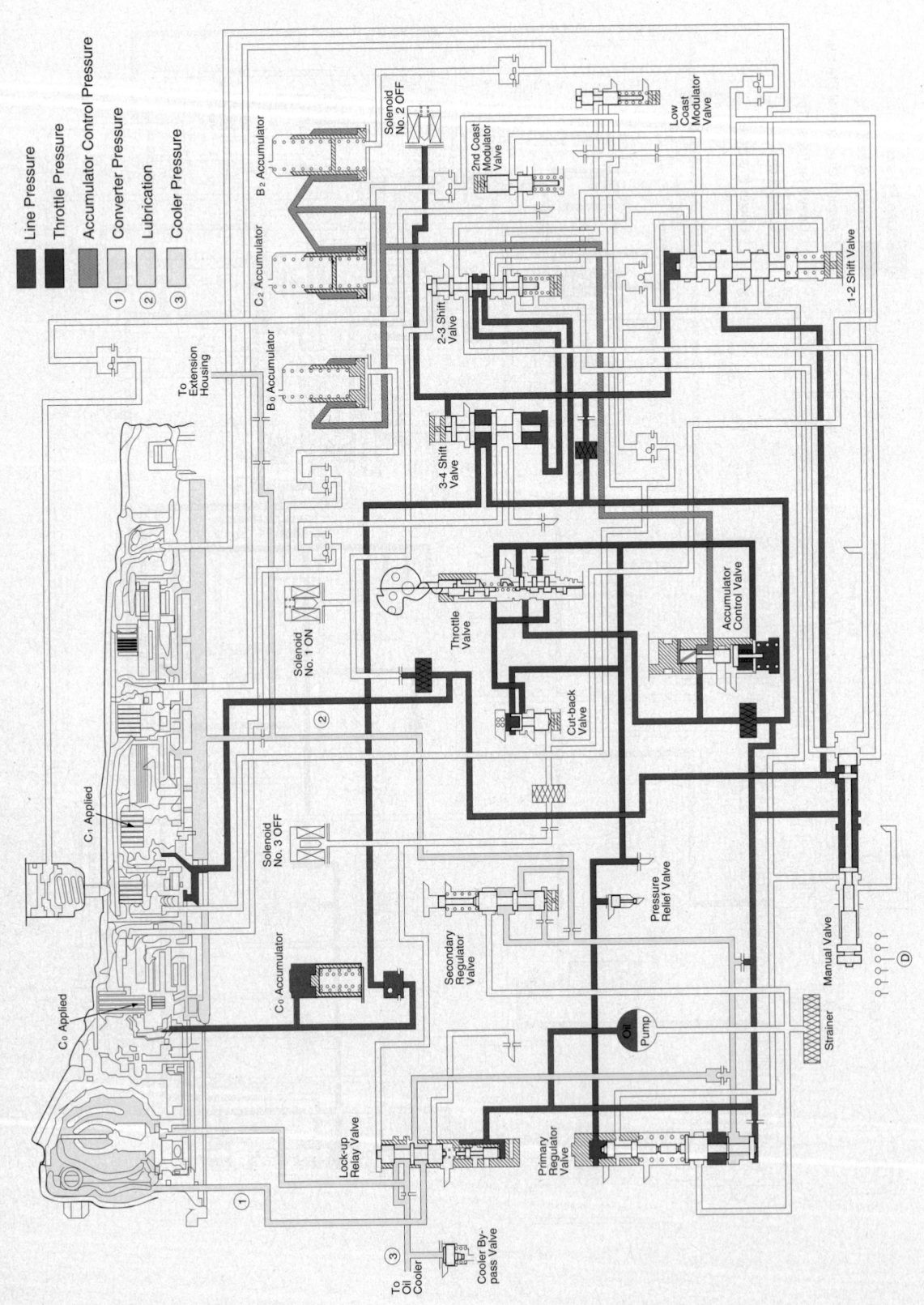

Fig. 2: "D" Position — 1st Gear

Courtesy of Toyota Motor Sales, U.S.A., Inc.

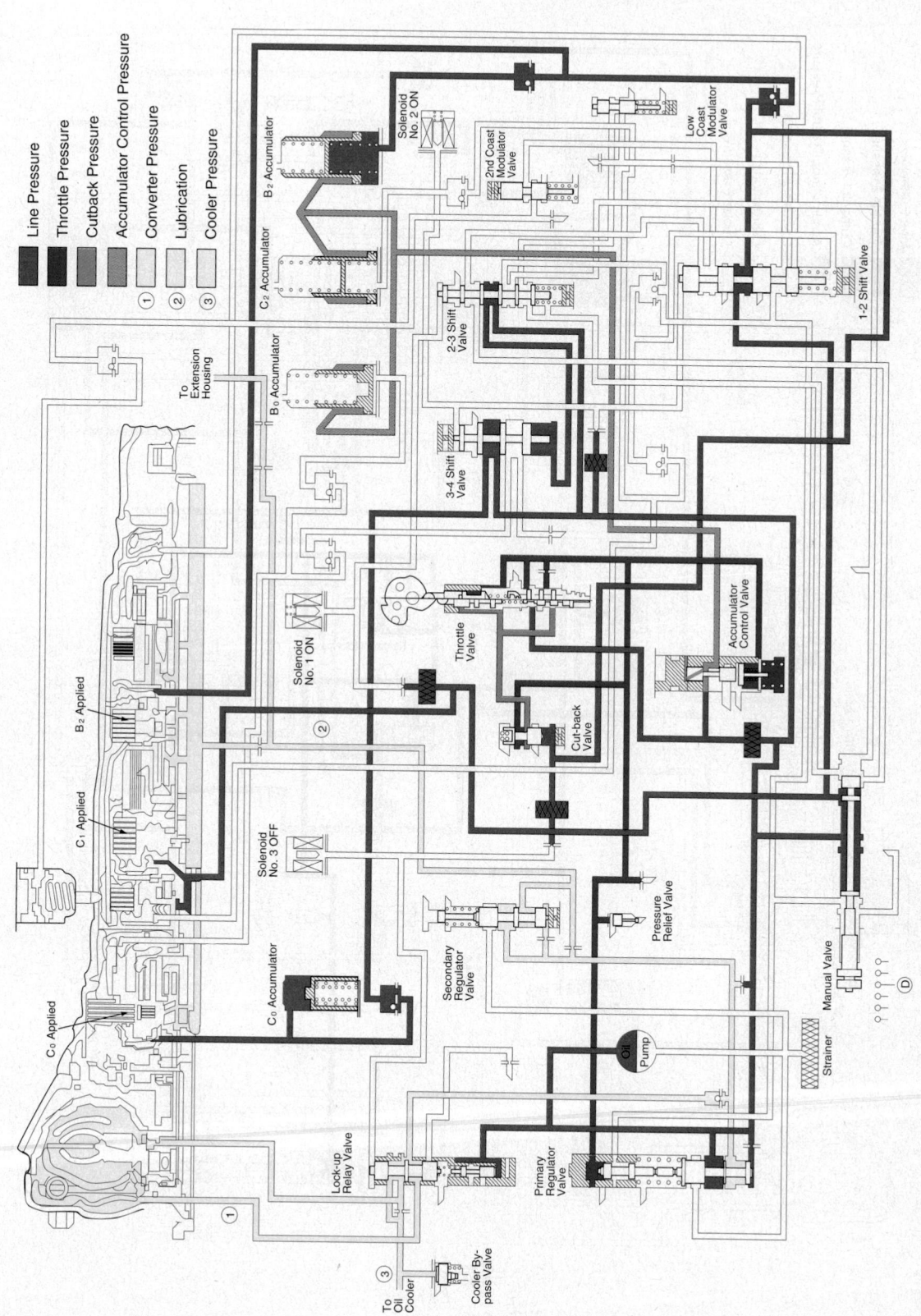

Fig. 3: "D" Position — 2nd Gear

Courtesy of Toyota Motor Sales, U.S.A., Inc.

OIL CIRCUIT DIAGRAMS
Toyota A-340E & A-340H (Cont.)

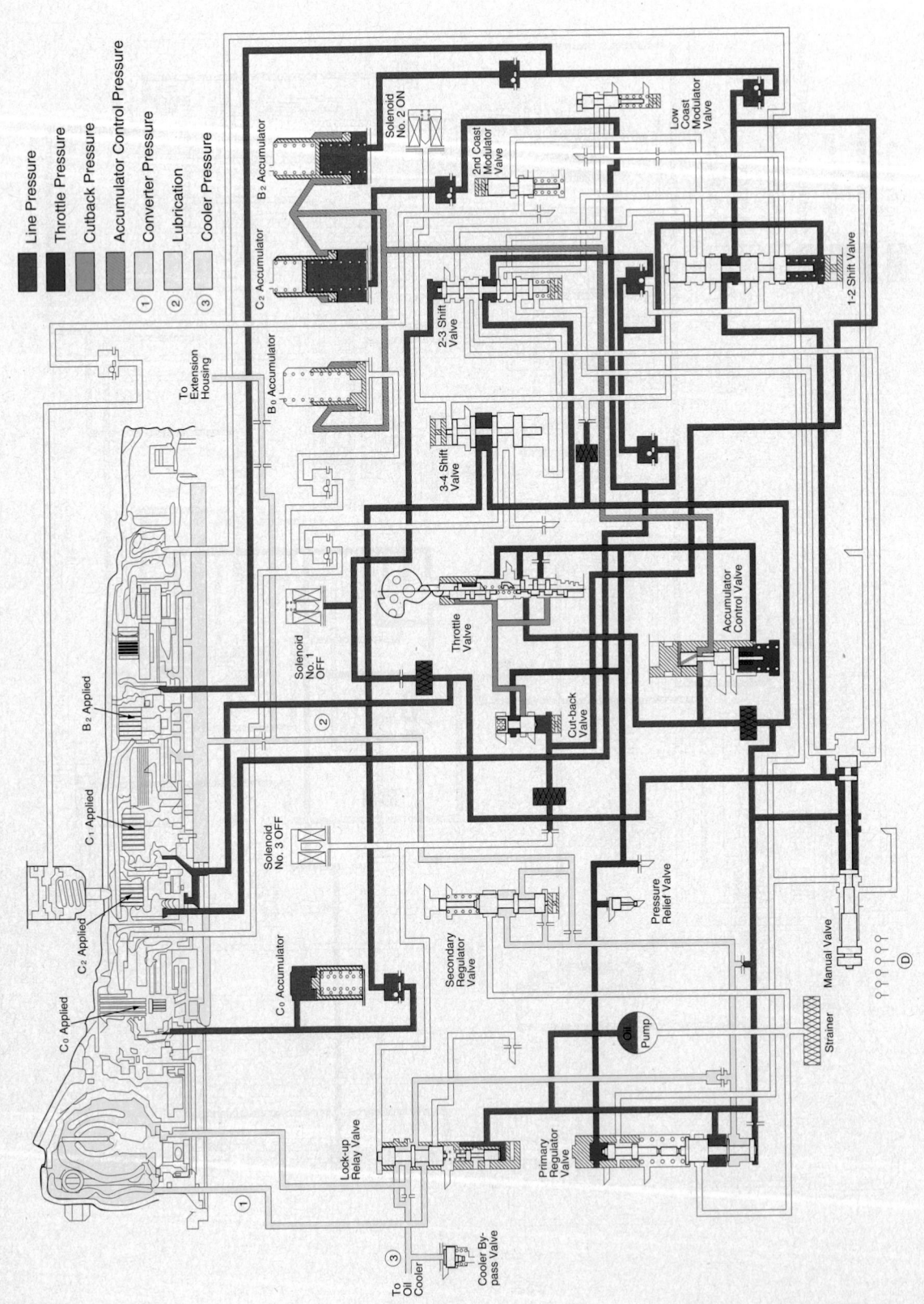

Line Pressure
Throttle Pressure
Cutback Pressure
Accumulator Control Pressure
Converter Pressure
Lubrication
Cooler Pressure

① ② ③

Solenoid No. 2 ON
2nd Coast Modulator Valve
Low Coast Modulator Valve
B₂ Accumulator
C₂ Accumulator
1-2 Shift Valve
2-3 Shift Valve
To Extension Housing
B₀ Accumulator
3-4 Shift Valve
Throttle Valve
Accumulator Control Valve
Solenoid No. 1 OFF
B₂ Applied
Cut-back Valve
C₁ Applied
Solenoid No. 3 OFF
C₂ Applied
Pressure Relief Valve
C₀ Applied
Secondary Regulator Valve
C₀ Accumulator
Manual Valve
Strainer
Oil Pump
Lock-up Relay Valve
Primary Regulator Valve
To Oil Cooler
Cooler By-pass Valve

Fig. 4: "D" Position — 3rd Gear

Courtesy of Toyota Motor Sales, U.S.A., Inc.

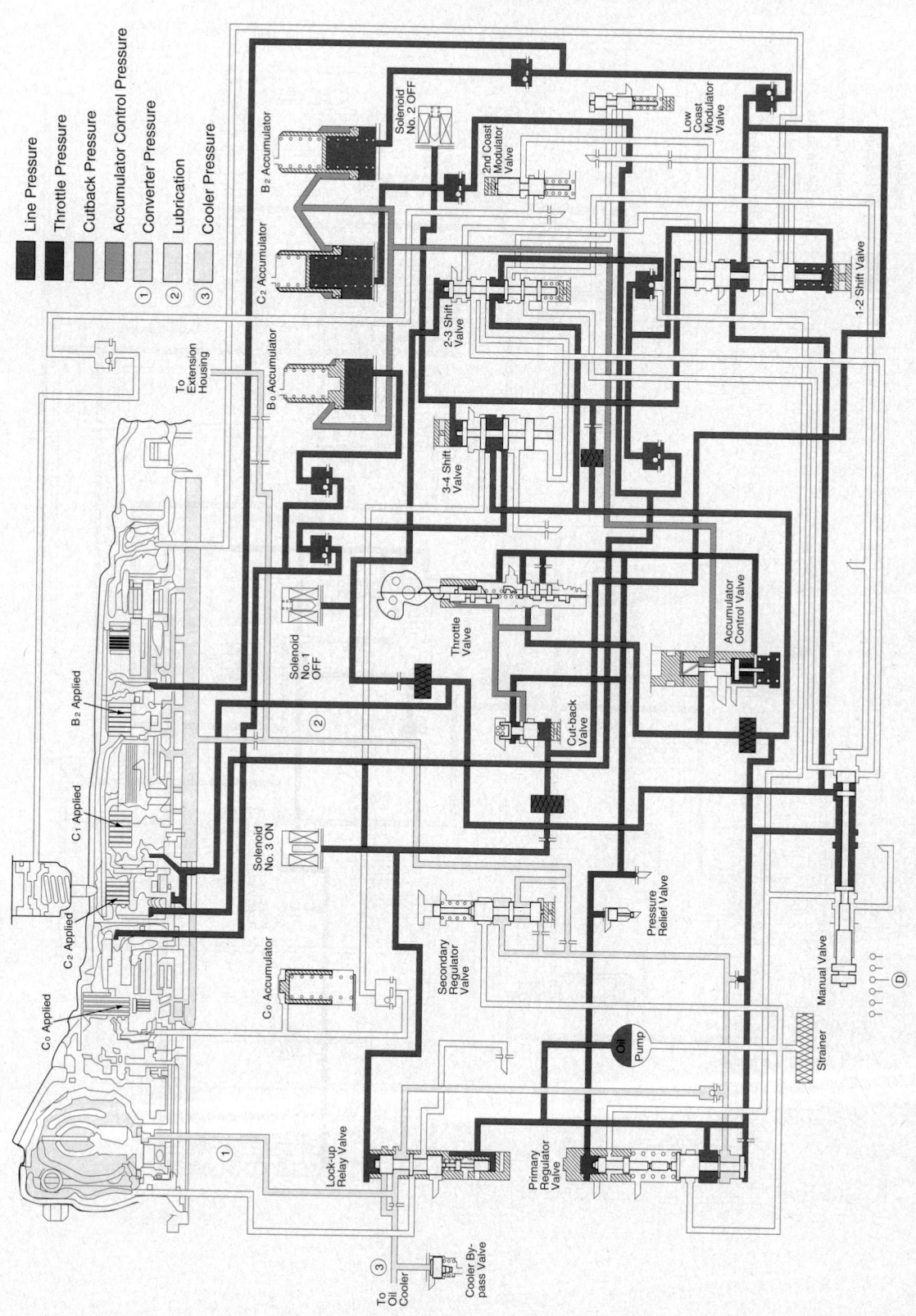

Fig. 5: "D" Position — OD Gear (Lock-Up ON)

Courtesy of Toyota Motor Sales, U.S.A., Inc.

OIL CIRCUIT DIAGRAMS
Toyota A-340E & A-340H (Cont.)

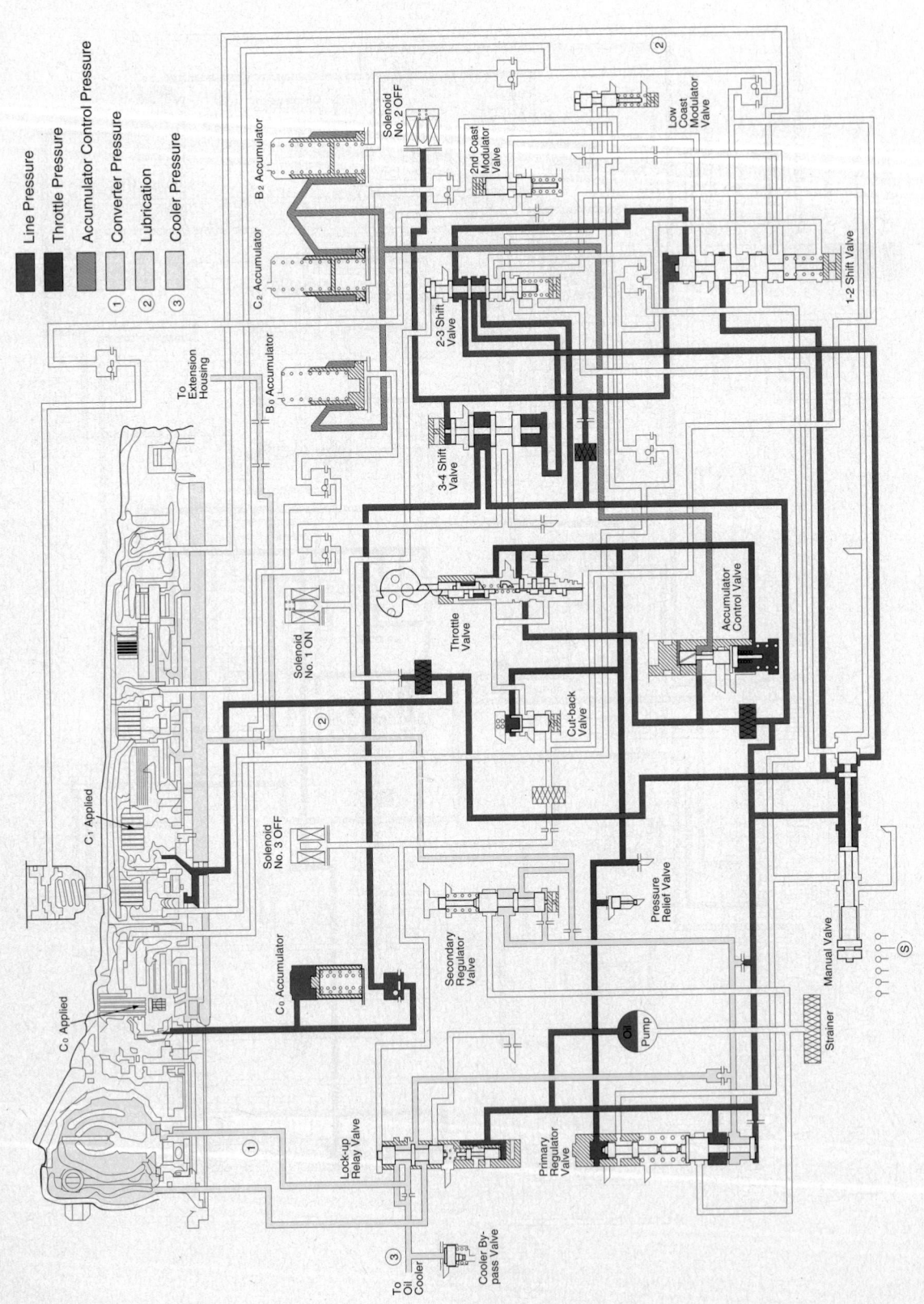

Fig. 6: "S" Or "2" Position — 1st Gear

Courtesy of Toyota Motor Sales, U.S.A., Inc.

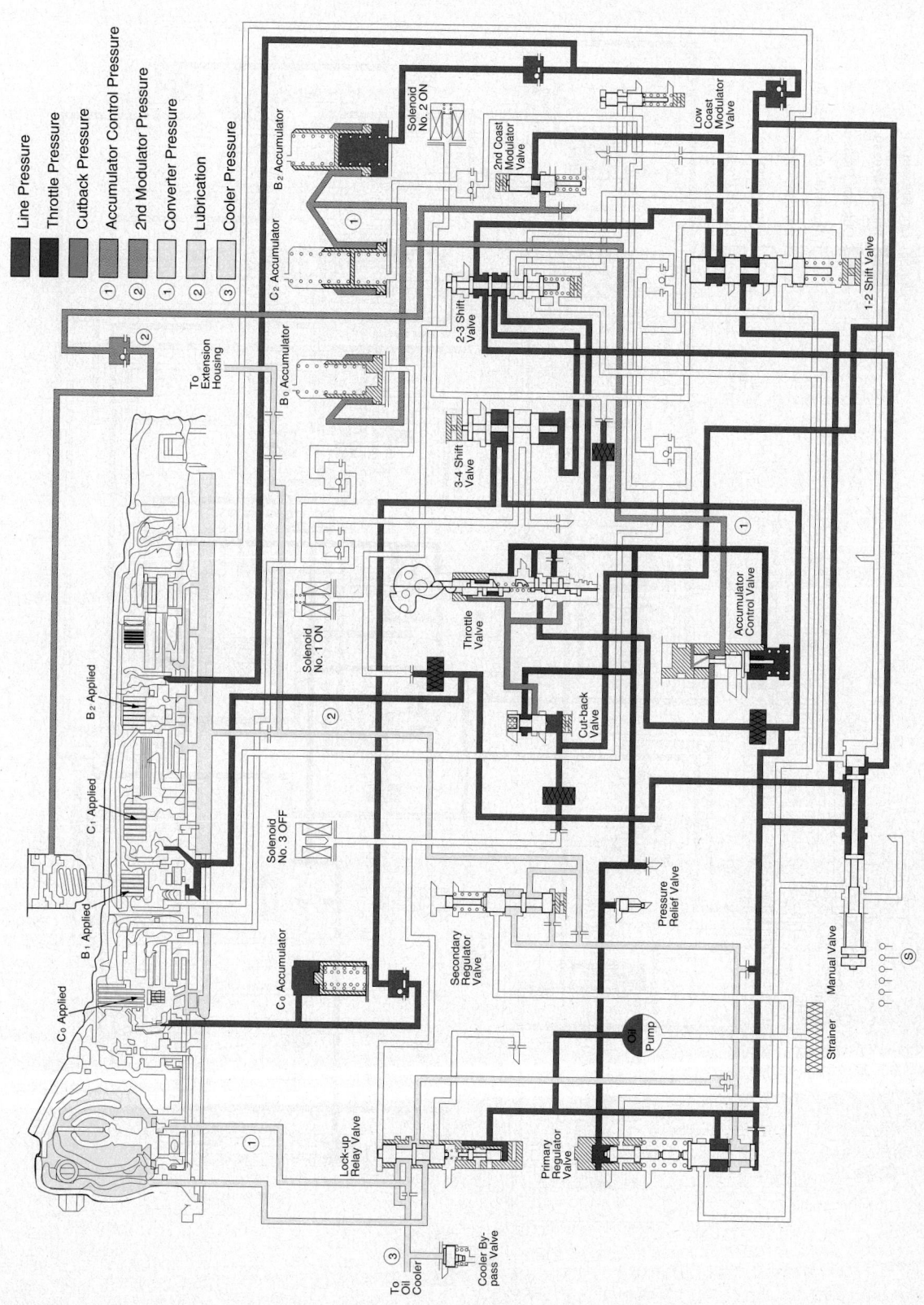

OIL CIRCUIT DIAGRAMS
Toyota A-340E & A-340H (Cont.)

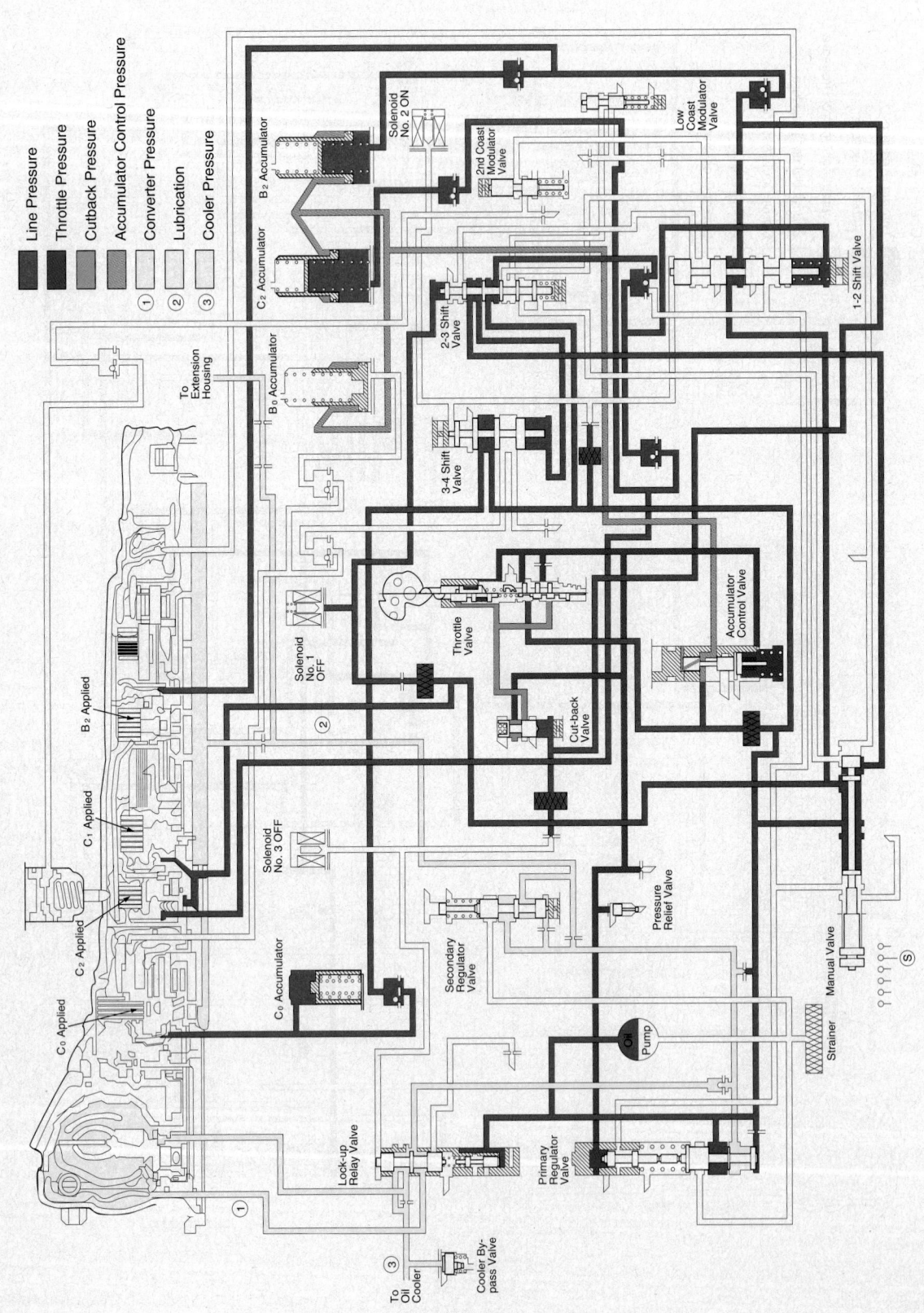

Line Pressure
Throttle Pressure
Cutback Pressure
Accumulator Control Pressure
Converter Pressure
Lubrication
Cooler Pressure

① ② ③

B₂ Accumulator

C₂ Accumulator

B₀ Accumulator

To Extension Housing

Solenoid No. 2 ON

2nd Coast Modulator Valve

Low Coast Modulator Valve

1-2 Shift Valve

2-3 Shift Valve

3-4 Shift Valve

Throttle Valve

Accumulator Control Valve

Solenoid No. 1 OFF

Cut-back Valve

②

B₂ Applied

C₁ Applied

Solenoid No. 3 OFF

Pressure Relief Valve

Secondary Regulator Valve

C₂ Applied

C₀ Accumulator

C₀ Applied

Manual Valve

Strainer

Ⓢ

Oil Pump

Lock-up Relay Valve

Primary Regulator Valve

①

To Oil Cooler

③

Cooler By-pass Valve

Fig. 8: **"S" Or "2" Position — 3rd Gear**

Courtesy of Toyota Motor Sales, U.S.A., Inc.

OIL CIRCUIT DIAGRAMS
Toyota A-340E & A-340H (Cont.)

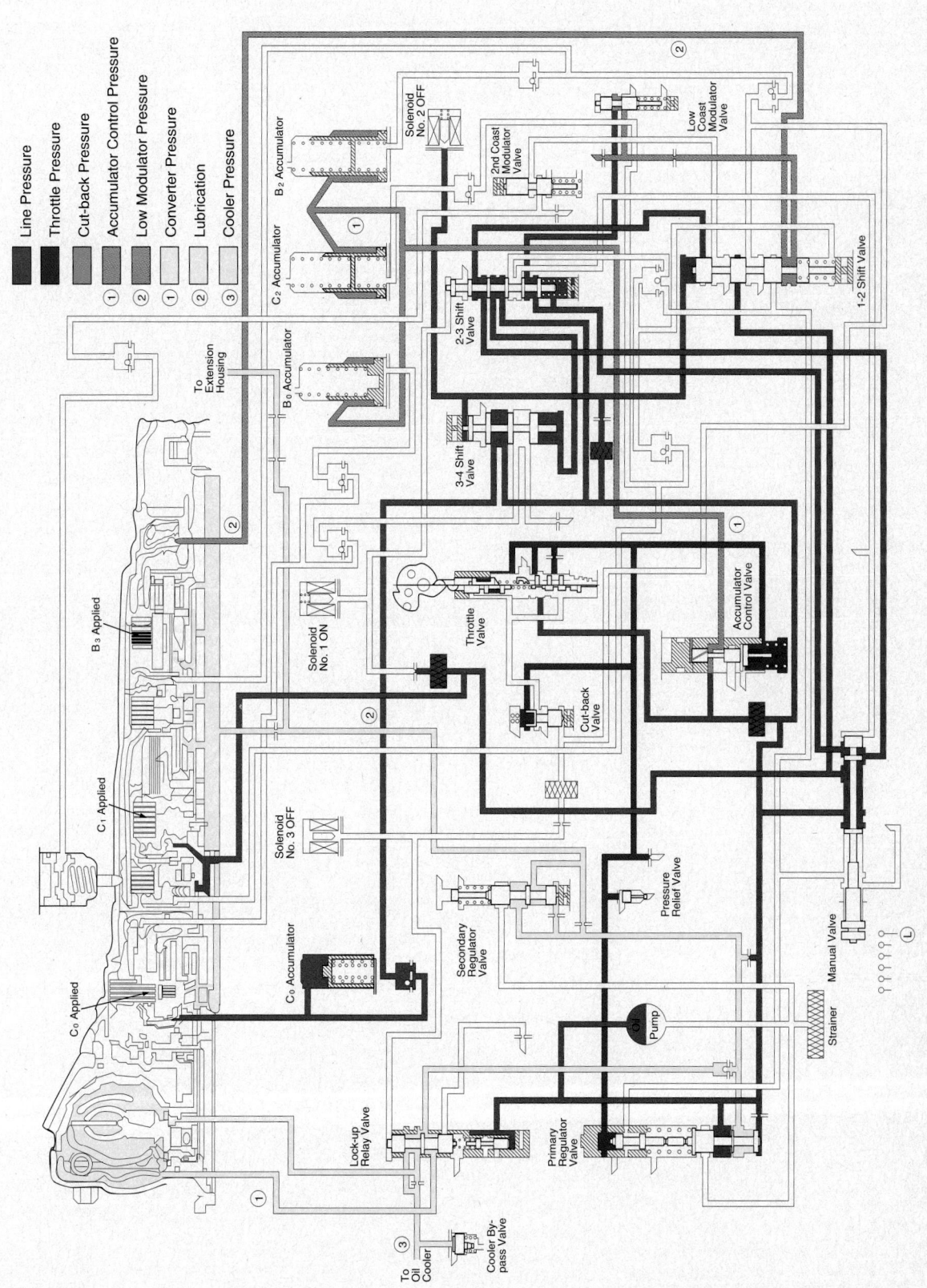

Line Pressure
Throttle Pressure
Cut-back Pressure
Accumulator Control Pressure ①
Low Modulator Pressure ②
Converter Pressure ①
Lubrication ②
Cooler Pressure ③

Fig. 9: "L" Position — 1st Gear

Courtesy of Toyota Motor Sales, U.S.A., Inc.

TRANSMISSION SERVICING

AUTOMATIC TRANSMISSION SERVICING	Page
Acura	2-2
Audi	2-5
BMW	2-6
Geo	2-7
Honda	2-12
Hyundai	2-13
Infiniti	2-15
Isuzu	2-17
Jaguar	2-19
Kia	2-22
Lexus	2-26
Mazda	2-27
Mercedes-Benz	2-33
Mitsubishi	2-36
Nissan	2-40
Porsche	2-43
Rover	2-45
Saab	2-51
Subaru	2-52
Suzuki	2-53
Toyota	2-57
Volkswagen	2-62
Volvo	2-63

AUTOMATIC TRANSMISSION REMOVAL	
Acura	2-66
Audi	2-69
BMW	2-70
Geo	2-71
Honda	2-73
Hyundai	2-75
Infiniti	2-77
Isuzu	2-79
Jaguar	2-80
Kia	2-81
Lexus	2-82
Mazda	2-83
Mercedes-Benz	2-87
Mitsubishi	2-88
Nissan	2-89
Porsche	2-93
Rover	2-94
Saab	2-95
Subaru	2-96
Suzuki	2-97
Toyota	2-98
Volkswagen	2-116
Volvo	2-117

MANUAL TRANSMISSION SERVICING	Page
Acura	2-119
Audi	2-119
BMW	2-121
Geo	2-121
Honda	2-122
Hyundai	2-123
Infiniti	2-123
Isuzu	2-124
Kia	2-125
Lexus	2-125
Mazda	2-126
Mitsubishi	2-127
Nissan	2-128
Porsche	2-129
Rover	2-129
Saab	2-130
Subaru	2-131
Suzuki	2-132
Toyota	2-133
Volkswagen	2-134
Volvo	2-135

MANUAL TRANSMISSION REMOVAL	
Acura	2-136
Audi	2-138
BMW	2-139
Geo	2-140
Honda	2-142
Hyundai	2-143
Infiniti	2-144
Isuzu	2-145
Kia	2-147
Lexus	2-147
Mazda	2-148
Mitsubishi	2-150
Nissan	2-152
Porsche	2-156
Rover	2-156
Saab	2-156
Subaru	2-158
Suzuki	2-158
Toyota	2-159
Volkswagen	2-166
Volvo	2-168

AUTOMATIC TRANSMISSION SERVICING
Acura

Integra, Legend, SLX, 2.5TL, 3.2TL, 3.5RL

APPLICATION & IDENTIFICATION
AUTOMATIC TRANSAXLE APPLICATIONS

Application	Trans. Model
Integra	
1995	SP7A
1996	MP7A
Legend (1995)	MPYA
SLX	4L30-E
2.5TL	M1WA
3.2TL	M5HA
3.5RL	M5DA

NOTE: For electronic shift interlock system iformation, see appropriate ELECTRONIC CONTROLS article in AUTOMATIC TRANSMISSIONS.

LUBRICATION

SERVICE INTERVALS

On Integra and Legend models, change fluid every 30,000 miles (1995 models), or every 90,000 miles (1996 Models). On SLX models, change fluid and filter at 20,000 miles only if vehicle is operated under extreme conditions. No service is required on normally operated vehicles. On 2.5TL, 3.2TL and 3.5RL models, change transaxle fluid at 90,000 mile intervals, and differential fluid at 30,000 mile intervals.

CHECKING FLUID LEVEL

All Models (Except SLX) – Start and run engine until it reaches normal operating temperature. Turn ignition off. Check fluid level with vehicle on level floor. Fluid level should be between upper and lower marks on dipstick. Add fluid if necessary.

SLX – Transmission is not equipped with a dipstick. Ensure vehicle is level, with engine running at idle and parking brake applied. Fluid temperature must be less than 86°F (30°C). Move gear selector through all gear positions, ending in Park. Let engine idle for 3 minutes and open OVERFILL screw on bottom of pan. Transmission is filled through OVERFILL screw. Fluid will seek correct level and excess should flow out from OVERFILL screw. See Fig. 1.

WARNING: On SLX models, DO NOT overfill transmission. DO NOT open OVERFILL screw with engine stopped. DO NOT check fluid level if fluid is HOT, allow transmission to cool for 30 minutes before checking.

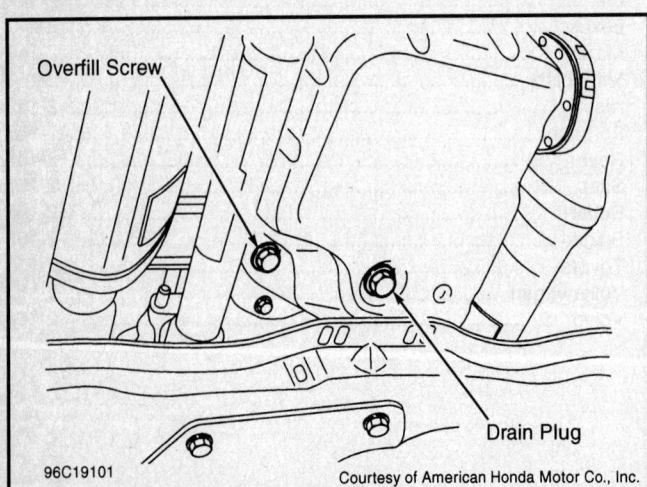

Overfill Screw

Drain Plug

96C19101

Courtesy of American Honda Motor Co., Inc.

Fig. 1: Identifying SLX Transmission Pan

RECOMMENDED FLUID

Transaxle (Integra, Legend, 2.5TL, 3.2TL & 3.5RL) – Use Honda Premium Formula Automatic Transmission Fluid (ATF) or equivalent Dexron-III ATF. Dexron-III should only be used if Honda fluid is unavailable.
Transmission (SLX) – Use Dexron-III ATF.
Transfer Case (SLX) – Use engine oil SAE 5W-30 for operational temperature range up to 95°F (35°C). Use SAE 15W-40, 20W-40 or 20W-50 for operational temperatures above 50°F (10°C).
Differential (Legend, 2.5TL, 3.2TL & 3.5RL) – A separate differential is attached to the transaxle. Use GL4 or GL5 hypoid gear oil, SAE 80W if operational temperatures are less than 0°F (-18°C) or SAE 90W for temperatures above 0°F (-18°C).

FLUID CAPACITIES
TRANSMISSION REFILL CAPACITIES

Application	Refill Qts. (L)	Dry Fill Qts. (L)
Integra	2.9 (2.7)	6.2 (5.9)
Legend	3.5 (3.3)	9.2 (8.7)
SLX	3.1 (2.9)	9.1 (8.6)
2.5TL	2.9 (2.7)	7.6 (7.2)
3.2TL	3.5 (3.3)	9.2 (8.7)
3.5RL	3.2 (3.0)	9.1 (8.6)

DIFFERENTIAL REFILL CAPACITIES

Application	Refill Qts. (L)	Dry Fill Qts. (L)
Legend [1]	1.1 (1.00)	1.2 (1.1)
2.5TL [1]	1.0 (.95)	1.1 (1.0)
3.2TL & 3.5RL	1.1 (1.05)	1.2 (1.1)

[1] – Use Hypoid SAE 90 fluid above 0°F (-18°C). Use SAE 80W-90 below 0°F (-18°C).

TRANSFER CASE REFILL CAPACITIES

Application	Qts. (L)
SLX [1]	1.53 (1.45)

[1] – Use engine oil SAE 5W-30 for operational temperature range up to 95°F (35°C). Use SAE 15W-40, 20W-40 or 20W-50 for operational temperatures above 50°F (10°C).

DRAINING & REFILLING

All Models (Except SLX) – Warm transaxle to normal operating temperature. Remove transaxle drain plug. Using new gasket, replace drain plug when fluid is drained. Tighten drain plug to specification. See TORQUE SPECIFICATIONS. Refill transaxle to upper mark on dipstick. Check and adjust fluid level as necessary, see CHECKING FLUID LEVEL.

SLX – Remove drain plug to drain transmission pan. Install and torque drain plug. Remove OVERFILL screw and fill transmission through OVERFILL screw opening. Adjust fluid level as necessary, see CHECKING FLUID LEVEL.

ADJUSTMENTS

WARNING: All models are equipped with a Supplemental Restraint System (SRS). All SRS wiring is color-coded Yellow. DO NOT use electrical test equipment on these circuits. Disconnect negative and positive battery cables before removing console. Wait at least 3 minutes after deactivating air bag system. System maintains voltage for about 3 minutes after battery is disconnected. Servicing air bag system within this 3 minute time period may cause accidental air bag deployment and possible personal injury.

CAUTION: Radio has a coded theft protection circuit. Before disconnecting battery cables, obtain radio anti-theft code number from customer. After reconnecting power, turn radio on. Word CODE will be displayed. Enter customer 5-digit code to restore radio operation.

BRAKE BAND

NOTE: Band adjustment is not considered a normal maintenance item. If band adjustment is required, use following procedure. Amigo and Pickup automatic transmission do not use bands.

SLX – 1) Remove oil pan, gasket, servo cover and gasket. Loosen lock nut. Slightly back off servo adjusting bolt. *See Fig. 2.* Using INCH-lb. torque wrench, tighten servo adjusting bolt to 40 INCH lbs. (4.5 N.m).

2) Back off servo adjusting bolt 5 turns. Hold servo adjusting bolt and tighten lock nut to specification. See TORQUE SPECIFICATIONS. Install servo cover and gasket. Tighten servo cover bolts to specification. Install gasket and oil pan. Tighten oil pan bolts to specification.

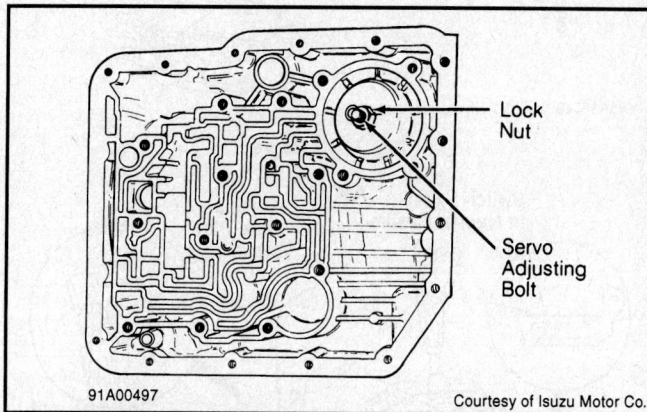

Fig. 2: Adjusting Brake Band (SLX)

SHIFT CONTROL CABLE

Integra – 1) Remove console and shift gear selector into "N" position. Remove lock pin from cable adjuster. Align hole in adjuster with hole in shift cable. *See Fig. 3.*

2) Two holes in end of shift cable are positioned at 90 degrees to allow cable adjustments in 1/4-turn increments. Loosen lock nut on shift cable, and adjust if necessary. *See Fig. 3.* Tighten lock nut. Install lock pin.

3) Lock pin should not bind as it is installed. If it binds, cable is still out of adjustment. Repeat adjustment procedure. Start engine, and check shift lever selection of all gears.

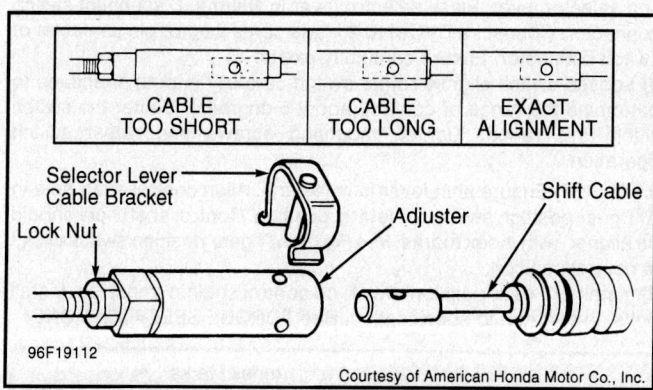

Fig. 3: Adjusting Shift Control Cable (Typical)

Legend, 2.5TL, 3.2TL & 3.5RL – 1) Remove center console and shift gear selector into "N" position. Remove lock pin from link adjuster. Insert a .16" (4.0 mm) pin into the shift lever bracket through the "N" position shift lever cutout. *See Fig. 4.*

2) Ensure transmission control lever is in "N" position. Turn ignition on and verify "N" indicator light in dash is on. Align hole in adjuster with hole in shift cable. *See Fig. 3.*

3) Two holes in end of shift cable are positioned at 90 degrees to allow cable adjustments in 1/4-turn increments. Loosen lock nut on shift cable, and adjust if necessary. *See Fig. 3.* Tighten lock nut. Install lock pin.

4) Lock pin should not bind as it is installed. If it binds, cable is still out of adjustment. Repeat adjustment procedure. Start engine, and check shift lever selection of all gears.

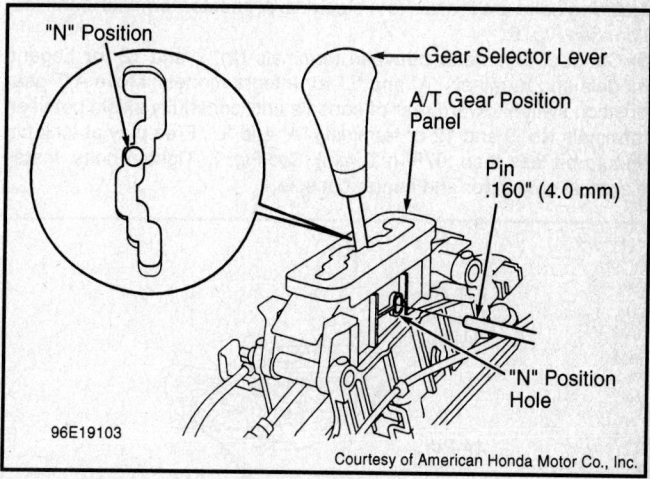

Fig. 4: Indexing "N" Selector Position

SLX – 1) Loosen transmission control rod lock nut at end of selector lever. Ensure transmission control lever is in Neutral. Select "N" position with gear selector lever.

2) Push gear selector lever forward so it is against the forward edge of the neutral detent. Hold gear selector lever in this position. Tighten control rod and ensure selector operates smoothly through all indicated positions. Readjust if necessary.

SHIFT INDICATOR PANEL

Integra – Shift gear selector into Neutral position. Index mark on shift indicator should align with "N" mark on shift indicator panel. *See Fig. 5.* If index mark is not aligned, remove center console. Remove shift indicator panel mounting screws, and adjust by moving panel.

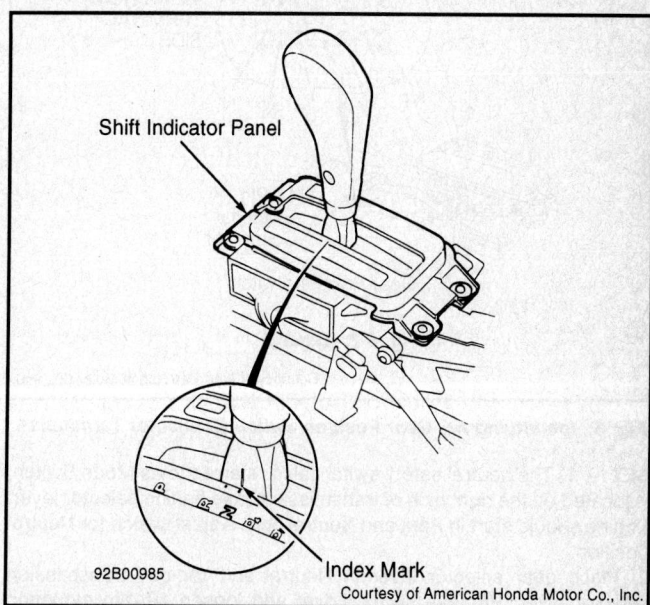

Fig. 5: Adjusting Shift Indicator Panel (Typical)

A/T GEAR POSITION SWITCH (MODE SWITCH)

Integra & Legend – 1) Ensure parking brake is applied. Place switch slider on A/T gear position switch in Neutral. Place shift lever in Neutral. Install A/T gear position switch and bolts. DO NOT tighten bolts before adjusting A/T gear position switch.

2) To adjust A/T gear position switch, place shift lever in Park. Ensure retaining bolts are loose. Note electrical connector terminal identification. See Fig. 6.

3) Connect ohmmeter between terminals No. 9 and 12 for Legend models and terminals "A" and "L" for Integra models. Move A/T gear position switch toward rear of console until continuity exists between terminals No. 9 and 12 or terminals "A" and "L". Free play at lock pin should be less than .079" (2.0 mm). See Fig. 7. Tighten bolts. Install electrical connector and center console.

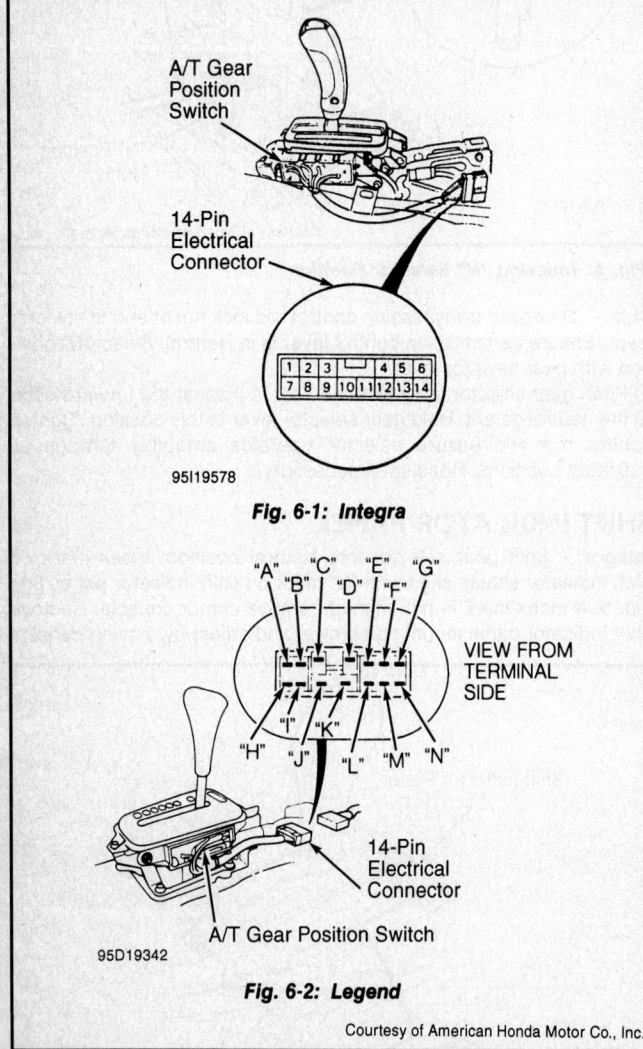

Fig. 6-1: Integra

Fig. 6-2: Legend

Courtesy of American Honda Motor Co., Inc.

Fig. 6: Identifying A/T Gear Position Switch Connector Terminals

SLX – 1) The neutral safety switch (also referred to as Mode Switch) is located on the right side of transmission case behind selector lever. Engine should start in Park and Neutral only. Adjust switch for Neutral position.

2) Place gear selector lever in Neutral and remove transmission selector lever. Remove switch cover and loosen 10 mm mounting screws. Rotate switch until slot in housing (around selector shaft) aligns with selector shaft. Insert a 3/32" (2.4 mm) drill bit or punch into slot.

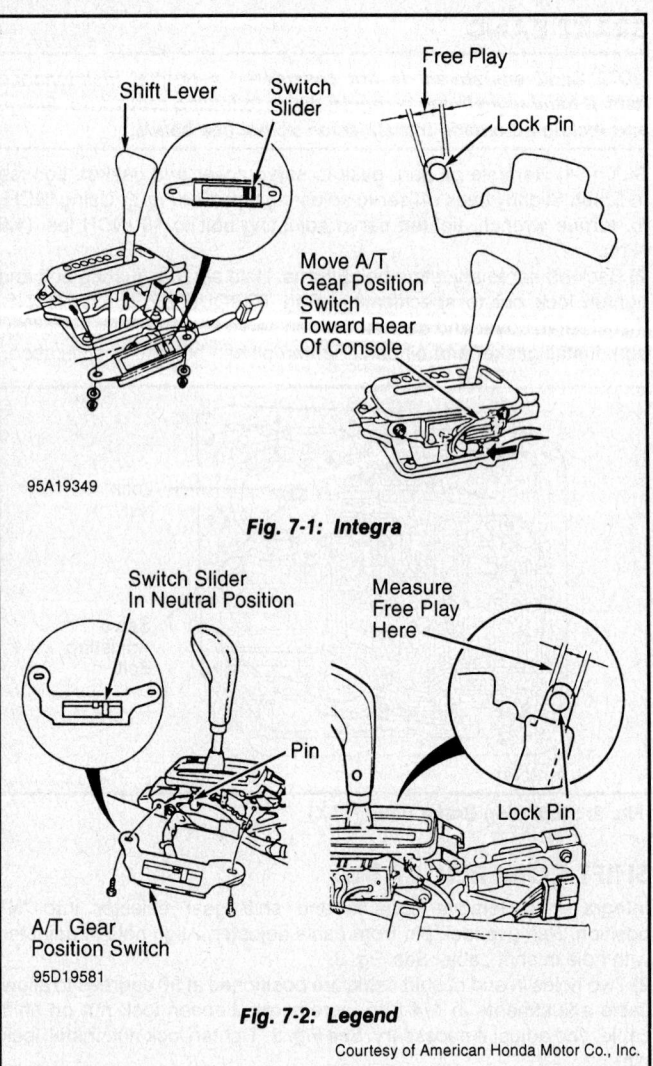

Fig. 7-1: Integra

Fig. 7-2: Legend

Courtesy of American Honda Motor Co., Inc.

Fig. 7: Installing A/T Gear Position Switch

3) Tighten mounting screws to 113 INCH lbs. (13 N.m). Replace cover and selector lever. Place selector lever in Neutral. Disconnect switch connector. Connect a DVOM to 2 blade contacts (not pin contacts) of switch connector. Ensure continuity exists.

4) Loosen switch slightly rotate switch carefully in both directions to determine the range of contact (about 5 degrees). Center the switch within this range. Tighten mounting screws and retest switch operation.

2.5TL – 1) Ensure shift lever is in Neutral. Align control shaft hole in A/T gear position switch to Neutral position. Control shaft hole should be aligned with index marks. See Fig. 8. A/T gear position switch clicks in neutral position.

2) Install A/T gear position switch on control shaft in transaxle. Install bolts and tighten to specification. See TORQUE SPECIFICATIONS.

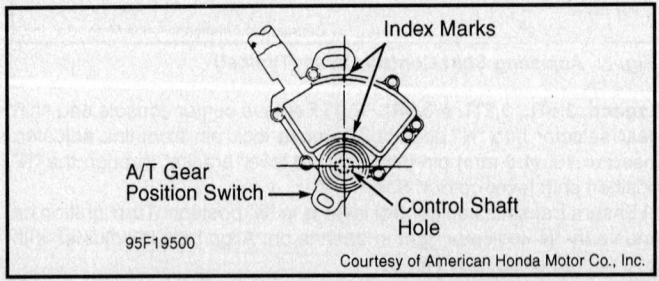

Courtesy of American Honda Motor Co., Inc.

Fig. 8: Installing A/T Gear Position Switch (2.5TL)

3) To check proper adjustment, check shift position sensor for correct continuity in all gears. See A/T GEAR POSITION SWITCH under COMPONENT TESTING in appropriate ELECTRONIC CONTROLS article.

4) If continuity is not as specified, loosen retaining bolts and slightly rotate A/T gear position switch until proper continuity exists. Install electrical connector and A/T gear position switch cover.

3.2TL & 3.5RL – **1)** Ensure parking brake is applied. Place A/T gear position switch in Neutral position. See Fig. 7-2. Place control shaft (transaxle) in Neutral.

2) Install A/T gear position switch and bolts. DO NOT tighten bolts before adjusting A/T gear position switch. Install NEW lock washer on A/T gear position switch, aligning projected tip with neutral mark on switch.

3) Install lock nut and tighten to specification while holding control shaft. See TORQUE SPECIFICATIONS. Bend lock tabs against lock nut. See Fig. 7-2. Tighten A/T gear position switch bolts.

4) Install control shaft. Connect electrical connector to A/T gear position switch. Install shift cable cover. Check A/T gear position switch for synchronization with indicator.

5) If A/T gear position switch is not synchronized with indicator, loosen bolts and adjust. After adjustment, start engine and verify proper operation:

- Shift lever cannot be moved from "N" to "R" position without pressing button.
- Engine will only start in "N" to "P" position.
- Back-up lights come on in "R" position.

TORQUE SPECIFICATIONS
TORQUE SPECIFICATIONS

Application	Ft. Lbs. (N.m)
Differential	
Drain Plug	
2.5TL	33 (44)
Legend, 3.2TL & 3.5RL	29 (39)
Filler Plug	33 (44)
Transmission Drain Plug	
Integra, 2.5TL, 3.2TL & 3.5RL	36 (49)
SLX	28 (38)
Transmission Overfill Plug	
SLX	28 (38)
Transfer Case	
Drain Plug	N/A
Filler Plug	N/A

	INCH Lbs. (N.m)
A/T Gear Position Switch Bolt (2.5TL, 3.2TL & 3.5RL)	106 (12)
Shift Cable Lock Nut	62 (7)

Audi

A4, A6, Cabriolet, 90

APPLICATION
AUTOMATIC TRANSAXLE APPLICATION

Vehicle Model	Transaxle Model Type
Cabriolet, 90 FWD	097 4-Speed
	01N 4-Speed
A6	
AWD	01F 4-Speed
FWD	01K 4-Speed
A4 (FWD & AWD)	01V 5-Speed

LUBRICATION

SERVICE INTERVALS

Check fluid level every 15,000 miles. Change transaxle fluid and filter every 30,000 miles under normal driving conditions.

CHECKING FLUID LEVEL

Final Drive (Differential) – Place vehicle on level surface. Fluid level must be to edge of fill hole on side of case. If level is too high, this may indicate a leaking seal between transaxle and final drive.

Transaxle – With transaxle at normal operating temperature, park vehicle on level surface. Place selector lever in "P" position. Apply parking brake. Allow engine to idle. Remove dipstick, wipe clean and insert. Remove dipstick and ensure fluid level is between marks on dipstick. On some Type 01K and all Type 01V transaxles, fluid level must be checked at fill hole (same as final drive).

NOTE: Late model Type 01F and 01K transaxles are not equipped with a dipstick. Transaxle uses filler tube as a vent. A breather cap has been installed in filler tube. Dipstick may be purchased from dealer, and can be used to check fluid level only. Always remove dipstick from filler tube and reinstall breather cap.

RECOMMENDED FLUID

Final Drive – Use API G50 (Synthetic), SAE 75W-90.
Transaxle – Use Audi ATF (G 052 162 A2-Yellow).

FLUID CAPACITIES
TRANSAXLE REFILL CAPACITIES

Application	Refill Qts. (L)	Dry Fill Qts. (L)
Final Drive	.7 (.75)	.7 (.75)
Transaxle	2.9 (2.7)	7.4 (7.0)

DRAINING & REFILLING

Remove oil pan and clean. Remove filter and allow oil to drain. Install NEW filter and install oil pan.

ADJUSTMENTS

NOTE: Information on throttle cable and neutral safety switch is not available

---

CAUTION: DO NOT move selector lever out of Park until brake pedal is pressed down.

AUTOMATIC SHIFT LOCK SOLENOID

1) Remove gear selector lever handle and console cover to access gear selector assembly. Place gear selector lever in Reverse.
2) Clearance between gear selector lever and solenoid switch valve should be .04" (1.0 mm). See Fig. 1. If clearance is not correct, loosen retaining screws and adjust.

SELECTOR LEVER CABLE

Remove center console. Place gear selector lever in Park. Loosen cable clamp nut. Place shifter lever on transaxle in Park. Tighten nut on clamp to specification. See TORQUE SPECIFICATIONS. Check all gearshift selector lever positions. Replace center console.

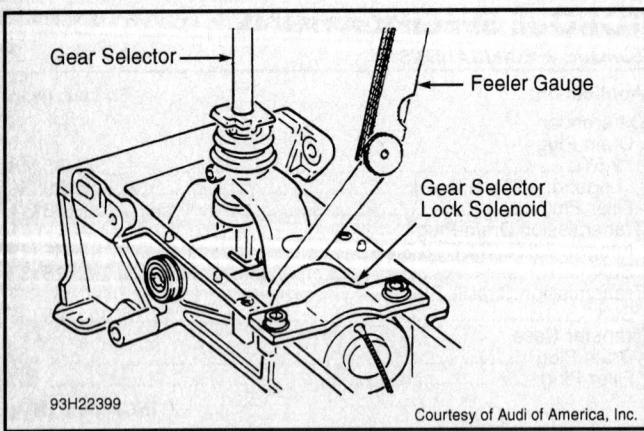

Fig. 1: Adjusting Automatic Shift Lock Solenoid (Typical)

STEERING COLUMN CABLE

Remove center console. Turn ignition switch to ON position. There should be .05-.07" (1.2-1.7 mm) gap between locking pin and lock flap. *See Fig. 2.* If gap is incorrect, loosen lock nut and adjust.

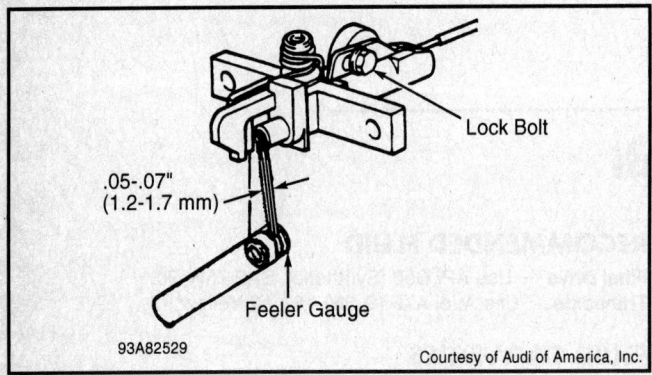

Fig. 2: Checking Steering Column Lock Pin Gap

THROTTLE CABLE

NOTE: Adjust accelerator controls so transmission throttle lever is at zero throttle position with throttle closed. If adjustment is incorrect, shift speeds and transmission main line pressure will also be incorrect.

1) Remove throttle control cover. Disconnect cruise control linkage (if equipped). Loosen throttle cable adjusting nuts and remove accelerator cable-top-mounting bracket retaining clip.

NOTE: Pressure point for full throttle position of accelerator pedal must be about 5/8-13/16" (16-20 mm) from pedal stop.

2) Turn throttle cable cam to full throttle position and hold. Insert a 11/16" shim between accelerator pedal and pedal stop. Push pedal until it touches spacer and hold pedal in this position.
3) Pull accelerator pedal cable housing until all slack is removed. Install locking clip. Lightly pull transmission throttle cable until spring pressure (resistance) of transmission kickdown is felt.
4) Turn adjusting nut (closest to transmission) against bracket and tighten other nut. Release throttle cable cam and accelerator pedal. Remove spacer and install throttle control covering.

TORQUE SPECIFICATIONS
TORQUE SPECIFICATIONS

Application	Ft. Lbs. (N.m)
Selector Lever Cable Clamp Lock Nut	15 (20)
Transaxle Protection Plate Bolts	18 (25)
	INCH Lbs. (N.m)
Oil Filter Bolts	44 (5)
Oil Pan Bolts	89 (10)
Throttle Rod Adjuster Lock Nut	71 (8)

BMW

Z3, 3-Series, 5-Series, 7-Series, 8-Series
IDENTIFICATION
TRANSMISSION APPLICATION

Vehicle Model	Transmission Model
1995	
M3, 530I, 530iT, 540i	5HP18
318i, 318iC, 318is, 318ti	
325i, 325iC, 325is, 525i, 525iT	4L30E
740i, 840Ci	5HP30
1996	
M3, Z3, 318i, 318is, 318ti, 328i, 328is	4L30E
740i, 840Ci	5HP30

LUBRICATION

NOTE: Transmissions are filled at factory for life of transmission. There is NO dipstick to check fluid level from engine compartment. If necessary, fluid level is checked from underneath vehicle. If any leaks are found, factory recommends replacing transmission.

SERVICE INTERVALS

Check fluid level during every oil service.

CHECKING FLUID LEVEL

NOTE: Check fluid with vehicle on level surface.

Checking Procedure – Ensure vehicle is level and transmission fluid is cold (68°-86°F, 20-30°C). Some transmission models have an oil fill plug located high on side of transmission oil pan. Oil from filler plug will leak out when it is removed. If oil continues to spill out from around raised area of oil pan, transmission is full. If oil does not continue to spill out, add oil. See SERVICE OR REFILL PROCEDURE. Tighten filler plug to 74 ft. lbs. (100 N.m).
Service Or Refill Procedure – If transmission has been repaired or oil level is low, fill with fluid through transmission filler plug until oil overflows. Start engine with selector lever in "P" position. Turn lights on. Top off transmission until it overflows. Install and tighten filler plug to 74 ft. lbs. (100 N.m). Place gear selector in "P" and start engine. Remove oil filler plug and recheck level as described in NORMAL CHECKING PROCEDURE.

RECOMMENDED FLUID

Use Dexron-II or other BMW approved transmission fluid.

FLUID CAPACITIES

TRANSMISSION REFILL CAPACITIES

Application	Refill Qts. (L)	Dry Qts. (L)
Except 540i, 740i & 740iL	3.2 (3.0)	8.0-10.0 (7.5-8.8)
540i, 740i & 740iL	[1]	5.8 (5.5)

[1] – Transmission refill capacity is not available.

ADJUSTMENTS

GEARSHIFT CABLE

1) Move gearshift lever to Park position. Loosen cable attaching nut on shift lever at transmission. Push transmission shift lever forward to Park position, and push cable rod rearward. See Fig. 1.

2) Tighten shift cable rod nut to 88-106 INCH lbs. (10-12 N.m). Check proper operation of shifter in each gear selection, and readjust cable if necessary.

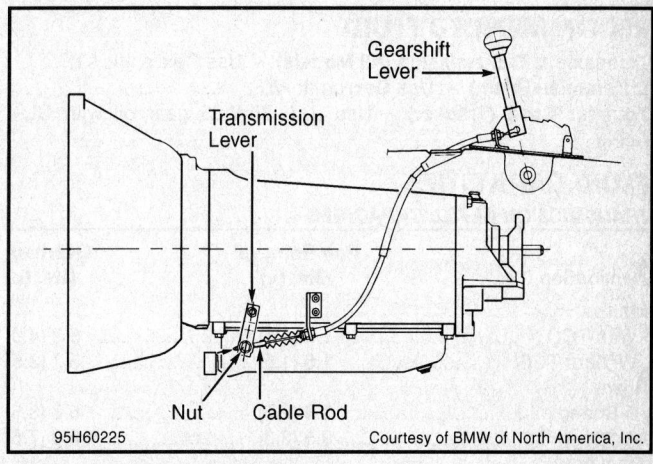

95H60225   Courtesy of BMW of North America, Inc.

Fig. 1: Adjusting Gearshift Cable

Geo

Metro, Prizm, Tracker

IDENTIFICATION

AUTOMATIC TRANSMISSION APPLICATIONS

Model	Transaxle/Transmission
Metro	ECC 3-Speed
Prizm	A-131L 3-Speed
Prizm LSi	A-245E Electronic 4-Speed
Tracker (1995-96)	[1] 3L30 3-Speed
Tracker (1996)	AW03-72LE Electronic 4-Speed

[1] – Also known as Turbo Hydra-Matic 180C.

LUBRICATION

SERVICE INTERVALS

Metro – Manufacturer recommends replacing transaxle oil cooler hoses at 45,000-mile intervals. Replace transaxle fluid and clean filter and pan magnet every 100,000 miles under normal driving conditions. Change fluid and clean filter and pan magnet every 15,000 miles under severe driving conditions.

Prizm – Replace transaxle fluid and clean filter and pan magnet every 100,000 miles under normal driving conditions. Also replace differential fluid if equipped with 3-speed transaxle. Replace transaxle fluid and clean filter and pan magnet every 15,000 miles or 15 months under severe driving conditions.

Tracker – 1) Manufacturer recommends replacing transmission oil cooler hoses at 45,000-mile intervals. Under normal driving conditions, replace transmission fluid and clean filter and pan magnet every 100,000 miles. Replace transfer case fluid initially at 7500 miles, then 30,000 miles or 30 month intervals thereafter.

2) Under severe driving conditions or if towing a trailer, replace transmission fluid and clean filter and pan magnet every 15,000 miles or 15 months. Replace transfer case fluid initially at 7500 miles, then 15,000 miles or 15 month intervals thereafter.

Severe Conditions (All Vehicles) – Severe driving conditions are when vehicle is operated under one or more of the following conditions:

- Most driving is done in stop-and-go traffic when outside temperatures are greater than 90°F (32°C).
- Delivery service, Taxi or Police vehicles.
- Trailer towing.
- In hilly or mountainous terrain.
- Most trips are less than 4 miles.
- Most trips are less than 10 miles, and outside temperatures remain below freezing.
- Driving in dusty areas.

CHECKING FLUID LEVEL

CAUTION: Check differential fluid level on Prizm (3-speed) and transfer case level on Tracker.

Transaxle & Transmission – 1) Engine must be at normal operating temperature. Park vehicle on level surface and apply parking brake. Place selector lever in Park.

2) Start engine and allow it to idle. Apply brakes, shift through all gears and return selector lever to Park.

3) Remove dipstick, wipe dipstick off and reinsert fully. Remove dipstick and read level. Fluid level should be in HOT or FULL HOT range. Add fluid (if necessary), and recheck level. DO NOT overfill.

Differential (Prizm – 3-Speed) – Differential ATF reservoir is separate from transaxle fluid reservoir. Remove differential fill plug from transaxle case. Ensure ATF is level with bottom of fill plug hole. See Fig. 1.

Transfer Case (Tracker) – Remove transfer case fill plug (upper plug) from rear of transfer case. Fill plug is located near speedometer gear housing. Fluid level must be at bottom of fill plug hole. Install fill plug and tighten to 17 ft. lbs. (23 N.m).

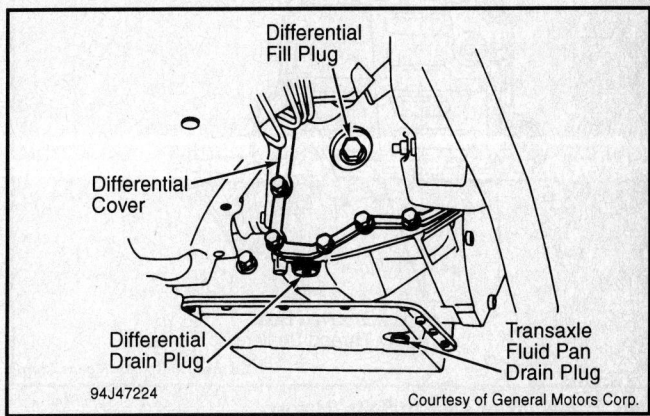

94J47224   Courtesy of General Motors Corp.

Fig. 1: Identifying Differential Fill & Drain Plugs (Prizm – 3-Speed)

RECOMMENDED FLUID

Transaxle & Transmission (All Models) – Use Dexron-III ATF.
Differential (Prizm) – Use Dexron-III ATF.
Transfer Case (Tracker) – Use SAE 75W-85 gear oil with GL-4 rating.

FLUID CAPACITIES

TRANSMISSION REFILL CAPACITIES

Application	Pan Removal Qts. (L)	Overhaul Qts. (L)
Metro		
With TCC [1]	1.6 (1.5)	5.2 (4.9)
Without TCC [1]	1.6 (1.5)	3.7 (3.5)
Prizm		
3-Speed	2.6 (2.5)	[2] 5.8 (5.5)
4-Speed	3.5 (3.3)	[2] 8.0 (7.6)
Tracker		
3-Speed	3.0 (2.8)	5.3 (5.0)
4-Speed	2.6 (2.5)	7.3 (6.9)

[1] – Torque Converter Clutch (TCC).
[2] – Does not include torque converter.

DIFFERENTIAL REFILL CAPACITIES

Application	Qts. (L)
Prizm (3-Speed)	1.5 (1.4)

TRANSFER CASE REFILL CAPACITIES

Application	Qts. (L)
Tracker	1.8 (1.7)

DRAINING & REFILLING

CAUTION: Manufacturer recommends flushing oil cooler whenever transmission or transaxle is removed.

Metro – **1)** Remove drain plug from bottom of transaxle oil pan and drain fluid. Remove 15 oil pan bolts, oil pan, oil pan guard, gasket and filter screen. Note position of 2 cross-grooved oil pan bolts. *See Fig. 2.* If oil pan is frozen to transaxle case, use a rubber mallet and a wood block to remove it. DO NOT pry oil pan away from transfer case.
2) Install clean filter screen and NEW gasket. Tighten retaining bolts to 53 INCH lbs. (6 N.m). Install oil pan and NEW gasket. Apply thread sealant to threads of 2 cross-grooved bolts. DO NOT apply thread sealant to other 13 bolts. Tighten oil pan bolts to 53 INCH lbs. (6 N.m). Tighten drain plug to 17 ft. lbs. (23 N.m).
3) Add 1.6 qts. (1.5L) of Dexron-III through dipstick tube. Check fluid level. See CHECKING FLUID LEVEL.

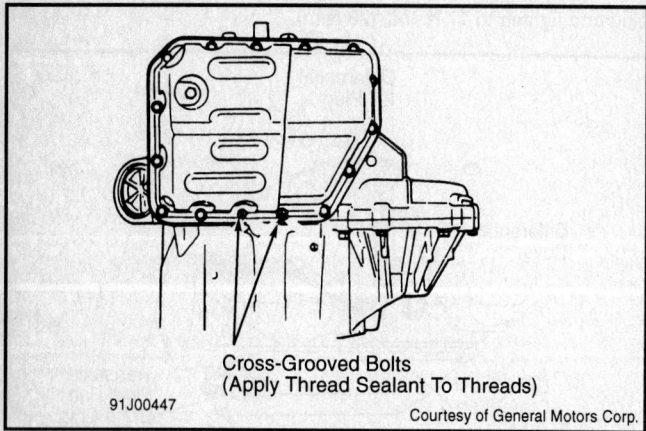

Cross-Grooved Bolts
(Apply Thread Sealant To Threads)

91J00447   Courtesy of General Motors Corp.

Fig. 2: Identifying Oil Pan Bolts (Metro)

Prizm (Transaxle – 3-Speed) – 1) Raise and support vehicle. Remove left splash shield. Remove drain plug and drain fluid. Remove oil pan bolts, oil pan and gasket. If oil pan is frozen to transaxle case, use a rubber mallet and a wood block to remove it. DO NOT pry oil pan away from transfer case. Remove filter screen bolts and filter screen, noting bolt length and position for reassembly reference.
2) Install clean filter screen and NEW gasket. Ensure bolts are installed in original locations. Tighten filter screen bolts to 89 INCH lbs. (10 N.m). Install oil pan using NEW gasket. Tighten bolts to 44 INCH lbs. (5 N.m). Install drain plug and tighten to 36 ft. lbs. (49 N.m). Install left splash shield and tighten bolts to 44 INCH lbs. (5 N.m).
3) Add correct amount of Dexron-III through dipstick tube. See TRANSMISSION REFILL CAPACITIES table. Check fluid level.

Prizm (Transaxle – 4-Speed) – 1) Raise and support vehicle. Remove left splash shield. Remove drain plug from oil pan and drain fluid. Remove 18 oil pan bolts, oil pan protector, oil pan and gasket. If oil pan is frozen to transaxle case, use a rubber mallet and a wood block to remove it. DO NOT pry oil pan away from transfer case. Remove filter screen and gasket.
2) Install clean filter screen and NEW gasket. Tighten filter screen bolts to 89 INCH lbs. (10 N.m). Install oil pan, NEW gasket and oil pan protector. Tighten oil pan bolts to 44 INCH lbs. (5 N.m). Tighten drain plug to 13 ft. lbs. (17 N.m). Install left splash shield and tighten bolts to 44 INCH lbs. (5 N.m).
3) Add correct amount of Dexron-III through dipstick tube. See TRANSMISSION REFILL CAPACITIES table. Check fluid level.

Prizm (Differential) – Remove drain plug in bottom of differential cover and drain fluid. *See Fig. 1.* Install drain plug and tighten to 29 ft. lbs. (39 N.m). Remove fill plug on side of differential cover. Fill with Dexron-III until fluid runs from fill hole. Install fill plug and tighten to 29 ft. lbs. (39 N.m).

Tracker (Transmission – 3-Speed) – 1) Raise and support vehicle. Place match marks on drive shaft and flange, then disconnect front drive shaft from front differential flange. Remove all transmission oil pan bolts except 3 bolts on rear of oil pan. Loosen remaining 3 bolts, allowing pan to tip downward so fluid will drain. Once fluid is drained, remove remaining oil pan bolts, oil pan and gasket. Remove filter screen and gasket.
2) Install clean filter screen and NEW gasket. Tighten filter screen bolts to 14 ft. lbs. (19 N.m.). Install oil pan using NEW gasket. Tighten oil pan bolts to 115 INCH lbs. (13 N.m). Install drive shaft and tighten flange bolts to 37 ft. lbs. (50 N.m). Fill transmission with 1.6 qts. (1.5L) of Dexron-III and check fluid level.

Tracker (Transmission – 4-Speed) – 1) Raise and support vehicle. Place match marks on drive shaft and flange, then disconnect front drive shaft from front differential flange. Remove transmission oil pan drain plug and drain fluid. Once fluid is drained, remove oil pan bolts, oil pan and gasket. Remove oil pipes (mark each pipe for installation), filter screen and gasket.
2) Install clean filter screen and NEW gasket. Tighten filter screen bolts to 44 INCH lbs. (5 N.m.). Install oil pipes. Install oil pan using NEW gasket. Tighten oil pan bolts to 44 INCH lbs. (5 N.m). Tighten oil pan drain plug to 13 ft. lbs. (17 N.m). Install drive shaft and tighten flange bolts to 37 ft. lbs. (50 N.m). Fill transmission with 1.6 qts. (1.5L) of Dexron-III and check fluid level.

Tracker (Transfer Case) – 1) Raise and support vehicle. Remove drain plug from back of transfer case, below speedometer gear housing. Drain fluid. Install drain plug and tighten to 21 ft. lbs. (28 N.m).
2) Remove transfer case fill plug (upper plug) from rear of transfer case. Fill plug is located near speedometer gear housing.
3) Fill transfer case with SAE 75W-85 gear oil with GL-4 rating until fluid level is at bottom of fill plug hole. Install fill plug and tighten to 17 ft. lbs. (23 N.m).

ADJUSTMENTS

BAND

Low Band Servo (Tracker) – 1) Raise and support vehicle. Remove transmission oil pan. Remove filter screen. Remove Torque Converter Clutch (TCC) pipes from valve body. Disconnect wires from TCC solenoid.

2) Remove 6 bolts securing reinforcement plate. Remove reinforcement plate. Remove 4 bolts and low band piston servo cover.

3) Hold servo piston with an open-end wrench. *See Fig. 3.* Loosen lock nut on adjusting sleeve. Using a torque wrench with a 5 mm Allen head socket, tighten servo piston adjusting screw to 18 ft. lbs. (24 N.m.).

4) Back off servo piston adjusting screw exactly 5 turns. Tighten lock nut to 14 ft. lbs. (19 N.m.). Ensure adjusting screw does not turn while tightening lock nut.

5) Replace servo piston cover gasket. Install servo piston cover and tighten to 18 ft. lbs. (24 N.m.). Install reinforcement plate and tighten to 14 ft. lbs. (19 N.m). To complete installation, reverse removal procedure. Tighten bolts to specification see TORQUE SPECIFICATIONS.

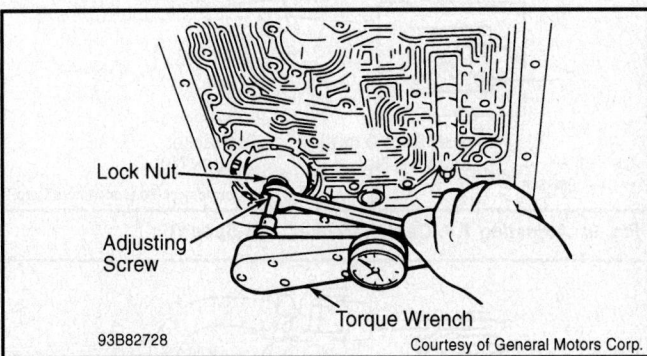

Fig. 3: Adjusting Low Band (Tracker)

INTERLOCK CABLE

NOTE: Interlock system will not allow gearshift to move from Park unless ignition is turned on. It also prevents ignition key removal unless gearshift is in Park. For diagnostic procedures, see GEO SHIFT LOCK SYSTEM article.

Metro & Tracker – **1)** Remove center console cover and manual selector cover. Place gearshift in Park. Loosen interlock cable bolt. Rotate key release plate and insert a small screwdriver into hole in lower key release plate. Retaining spring will move interlock cable bracket into position. Tighten interlock cable bolt to 115 INCH lbs. (13 N.m). *See Fig. 4.*

2) Ensure ignition switch operates from ACC to LOCK position, and ignition key can be removed when gearshift is in Park. Move transaxle gearshift lever to any other position. Ensure ignition switch cannot be turned from ACC to LOCK position. If ignition switch will turn, readjust interlock cable.

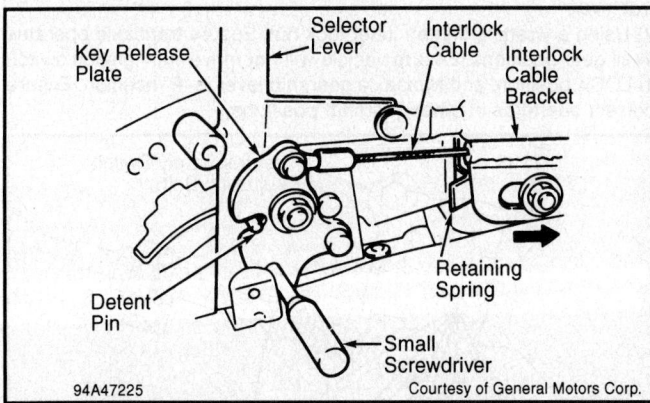

Fig. 4: Adjusting Interlock Cable (Metro Shown; Tracker Is Similar)

SHIFT LOCK SOLENOID

NOTE: Shift lock solenoid prevents gear selector lever from being moved from Park unless brake pedal is applied. For diagnostic procedures, see GEO SHIFT LOCK SYSTEM article.

Metro – **1)** Remove center console. Solenoid should be adjusted so that when ignition switch is in OFF position, solenoid is NOT operating (lock position). With ignition on and brake pedal depressed, solenoid is operating (unlock position). Ensure lock plate detent pin is in correct position. *See Fig. 5.*

2) If operation is not as specified, loosen solenoid mounting screws and reposition solenoid. With ignition off, gearshift should not shift from Park. If manual override is enabled with ignition off, gearshift should move from Park to any other gear position.

Prizm & Tracker – Shift lock solenoid requires no adjustment. For diagnostic procedures, see GEO SHIFT LOCK SYSTEM article.

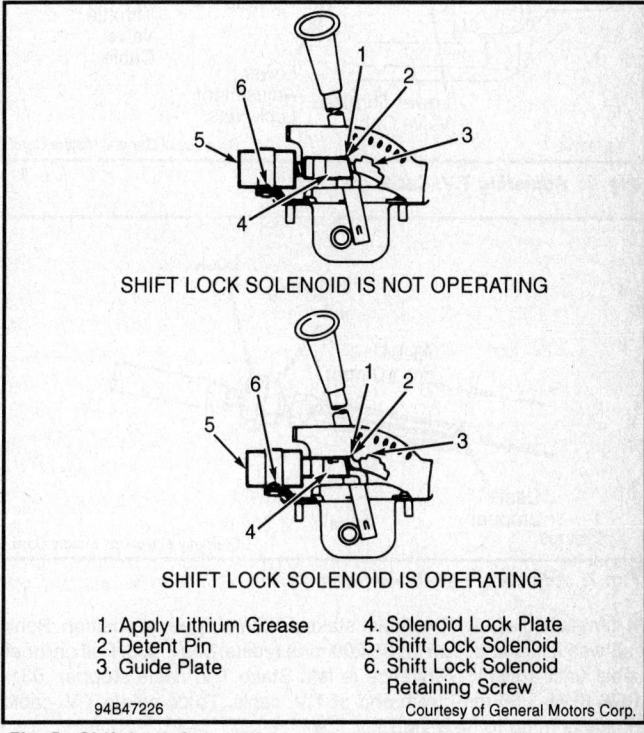

SHIFT LOCK SOLENOID IS NOT OPERATING

SHIFT LOCK SOLENOID IS OPERATING

1. Apply Lithium Grease
2. Detent Pin
3. Guide Plate
4. Solenoid Lock Plate
5. Shift Lock Solenoid
6. Shift Lock Solenoid Retaining Screw

Fig. 5: Shift Lock Solenoid Operation (Metro)

THROTTLE VALVE (T.V.) CABLE

Metro – **1)** Ensure accelerator cable is adjusted. Accelerator cable should have .394-.591" (10-15 mm) end play at throttle body with accelerator at idle position and engine off.

2) Warm engine to normal operating temperature. Ensure base idle speed (hot) is to specification. Turn engine off. Remove T.V. cable cover. Check boot-to-inner cable stopper clearance. *See Fig. 6.*

3) If clearance is greater than .020" (.5 mm), loosen lower adjustment lock nuts and adjust cable length. If lower adjustment lock nuts do not provide enough adjustment, use upper adjustment lock nuts to change cable length. *See Fig. 6.* Tighten all lock nuts.

Prizm – Ensure throttle valve is fully closed on 4-speed transaxle, and wide open throttle on 3-speed transaxle. Adjust T.V. cable housing so distance between end of outer cable boot and cable stopper is 0-.040" (0-1.0 mm). *See Fig. 7.* Tighten T.V. cable adjusting and lock nuts to 71 INCH lbs. (8 N.m).

NOTE: On Prizm, use the following procedure if installing a new T.V. cable.

Prizm (Cable Replacement) – **1)** Disconnect negative battery cable. Loosen T.V. cable adjusting and lock nuts. Remove T.V. cable from throttle valve linkage and T.V. cable bracket. Remove left splash shield. Remove neutral safety switch.

2) Drain transaxle fluid and remove oil pan. Remove T.V. cable from throttle valve cam at valve body assembly. Remove T.V. cable from transaxle. If installing a new T.V. cable, go to next step. If reinstalling old T.V. cable, go to step **4)**.

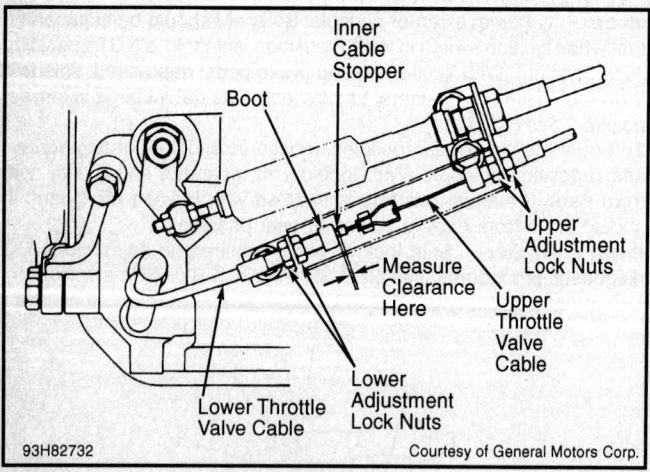

Fig. 6: Adjusting T.V. Cable (Metro)

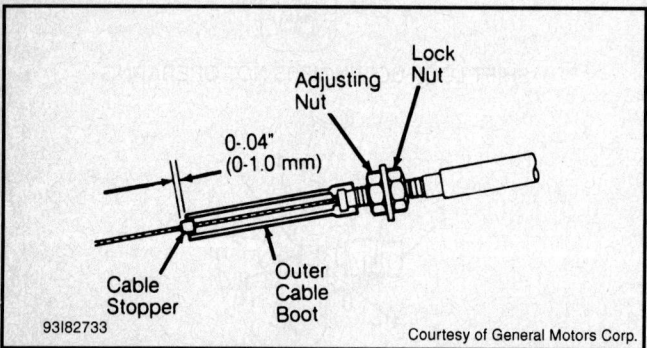

Fig. 7: Adjusting T.V. Cable (Prizm)

3) If installing a new T.V. cable, stake a NEW stopper in position. Bend cable so it has about a 7.870" (200 mm) radius. *See Fig. 8*. Pull on inner cable until a slight resistance is felt. Stake T.V. cable stopper .031-.059" (0.78-1.50 mm) from end of T.V. cable. To complete T.V. cable installation, go to next step.

4) Install T.V. cable into transaxle and tighten retaining bolt to 71 INCH lbs. (8 N.m). Install T.V. cable into throttle valve cam at valve body assembly. To complete installation reverse removal procedures. Adjust T.V. cable and refill transaxle.

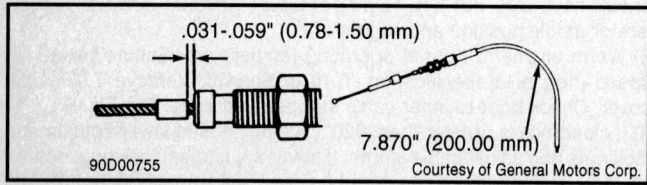

Fig. 8: Staking T.V. Cable Stopper (Prizm)

Tracker (3-Speed) – 1) Ensure accelerator cable is adjusted correctly. Loosen and back off T.V. cable lock nut and adjusting nut. *See Fig. 9*. Turn ignition switch to LOCK position. Have an assistant fully depress and hold accelerator pedal.

2) Pull T.V. cable casing in direction "A" until tight, and no cable deflection is present. *See Fig. 9*. Tighten lock nut to obtain a .039" (1.0 mm) lock nut-to-bracket clearance (dimension "B"). *See Fig. 9*. When adjusting clearance, ensure adjusting nut does not contact bracket.

3) Release accelerator pedal. Maintain lock nut-to-bracket clearance at .039" (1.0 mm). Rotate adjusting nut until it engages bracket. With adjusting nut even with bracket surface, tighten lock nut securely.

Tracker (4-Speed) – 1) Ensure accelerator cable is adjusted correctly. Loosen and back off T.V. cable lock nut and adjusting nut. *See Fig. 10*. Turn ignition key switch to LOCK position. Have an assistant fully depress and hold accelerator pedal.

2) Measure distance "A". *See Fig. 10*. Ensure distance is .031-.059" (.8-1.5 mm). Adjust as necessary. With T.V. cable pulled tight, tighten lock nut. Ensure distance "A" remains within specification.

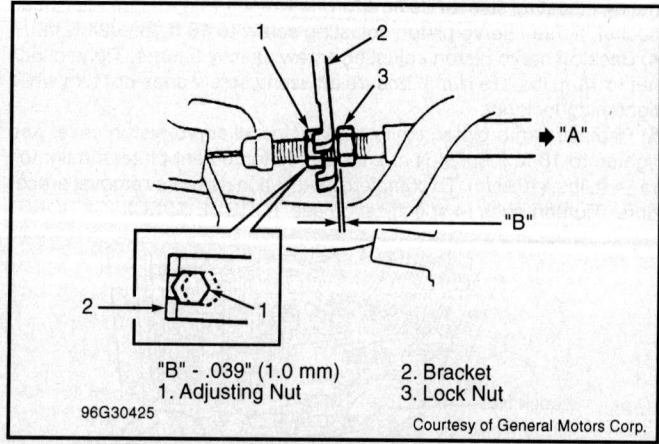

"B" - .039" (1.0 mm)   2. Bracket
1. Adjusting Nut   3. Lock Nut

Fig. 9: Adjusting T.V. Cable (Tracker – 3-Speed)

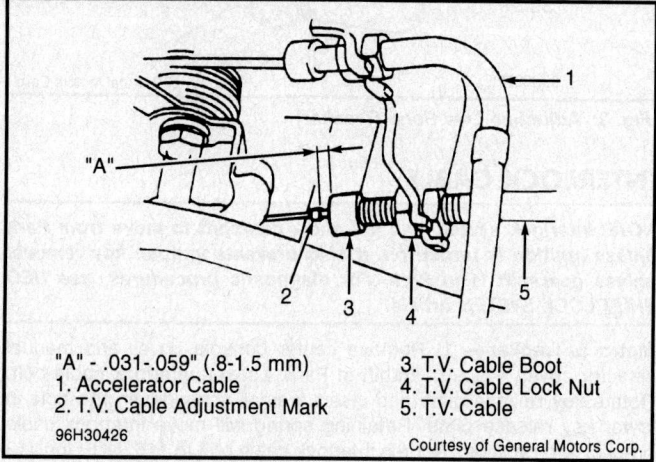

"A" - .031-.059" (.8-1.5 mm)   3. T.V. Cable Boot
1. Accelerator Cable   4. T.V. Cable Lock Nut
2. T.V. Cable Adjustment Mark   5. T.V. Cable

Fig. 10: Adjusting T.V. Cable (Tracker – 4-Speed)

SHIFT CONTROL CABLE

Metro – 1) Set parking brake. Move gearshift lever to Neutral. Loosen inner and outer lock nuts. *See Fig. 11*. Ensure transaxle control lever is in Neutral. Tighten outer lock nut by hand until it contacts control lever.

2) Using a wrench, tighten inner lock nut. Ensure transaxle operates in all gear positions. Ensure vehicle will not move with ignition switch in LOCK position, and transaxle gearshift lever in "P" position. Ensure correct operation in other gearshift positions.

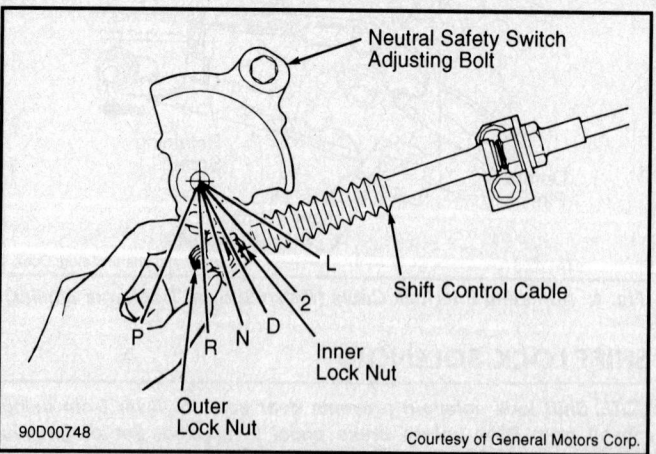

Fig. 11: Adjusting Shift Control Cable (Metro)

Prizm – 1) Set parking brake. Loosen adjusting nut on transaxle selector lever. Move selector lever on transaxle fully counterclockwise to PARK position.

2) Move shift selector lever clockwise 2 notches to "N" position. While holding selector lever, pull shift control cable tight. Tighten adjustment nut. Ensure vehicle will not move with ignition switch in LOCK position, and transaxle gearshift lever in "P" position. Ensure correct operation in other gearshift positions.

Tracker – 1) Remove center console covers. Place gearshift in Neutral. Loosen adjusting nut and lock nut. See Fig. 12.

2) Ensure shift lever on transmission is in "N" position. Pull shift control cable tight.

3) Tighten adjusting nut, then lock nut. Ensure gearshift operates properly in all gear ranges. Install console covers.

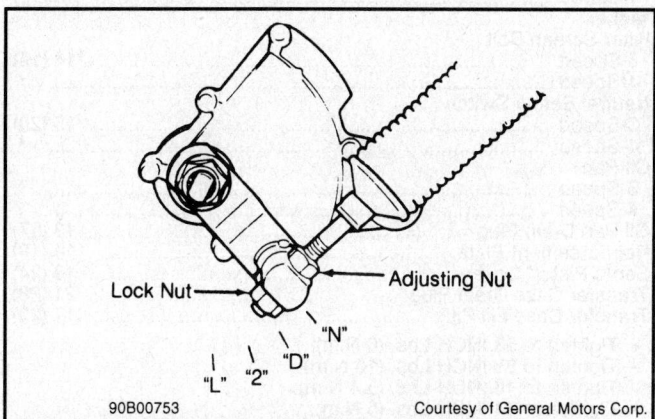

Fig. 12: Adjusting Shift Control Cable (Tracker)

NEUTRAL SAFETY SWITCH

NOTE: Neutral safety switch may also be known as Transmission Range (TR) switch.

Metro – 1) Remove neutral safety switch from vehicle. Place transaxle gear selector lever in "N" position.

2) Using a flat-blade screwdriver, turn slotted hole in either direction until a "click" sound is heard and switch is in position shown. See Fig. 13. Install switch to transaxle. Ensure gear selector lever is in "N" position. Tighten switch mounting bolt to 17 ft. lbs. (23 N.m). Set parking brake, block vehicle wheels and ensure starter operates with transaxle in neutral and park only.

Prizm – 1) Set parking brake. Place gearshift in "N" position. Loosen neutral safety switch adjusting bolt. See Fig. 14. Align neutral basic line scribed in switch body with groove in switch sleeve. See Fig. 14.

2) Hold switch at this position and tighten neutral witch adjusting bolt to 48 INCH lbs. (5.4 N.m). Ensure starter operates with transaxle in neutral and park only.

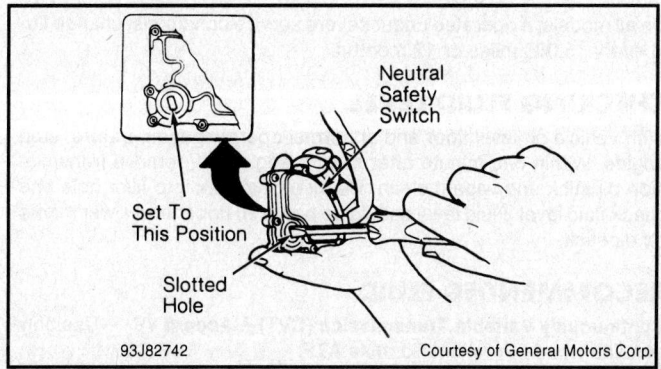

Fig. 13: Adjusting Neutral Safety Switch (Metro)

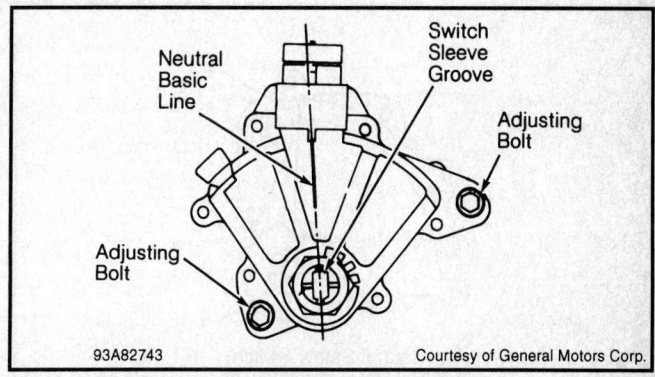

Fig. 14: Adjusting Neutral Safety Switch (Prizm)

Tracker (3-Speed) – 1) Disconnect negative battery cable. Ensure gearshift lever and transmission shift selector lever are in neutral. Loosen neutral safety switch retaining bolt. Disconnect neutral safety switch 2 wire connector. See Fig. 15.

2) Connect a DVOM to neutral safety switch connector terminals. Rotate neutral safety switch as far clockwise (downward) as possible.

3) Slowly rotate neutral safety switch counterclockwise (upward) until a "click" sound is heard and continuity is obtained on DVOM. Tighten switch retaining bolt to 15 ft. lbs. (20 N.m). Connect neutral safety switch connector and negative battery cable.

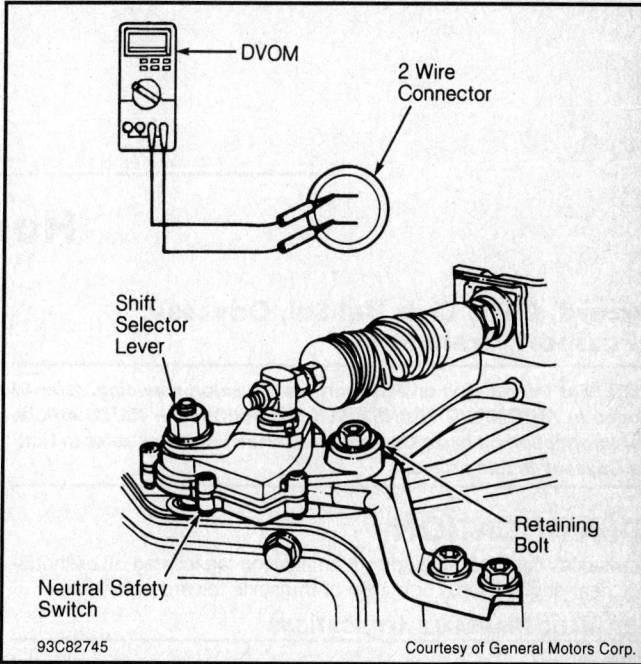

Fig. 15: Adjusting Neutral Safety Switch (Tracker – 3-Speed)

Tracker (4-Speed) – 1) Disconnect shift control cable from neutral safety switch. Loosen neutral safety switch retaining bolt. Move transmission shift lever rearward, then turn back 2 notches to obtain neutral position. Ensure gearshift lever is in "N" position. Remove shift lever.

2) Ensure neutral reference line and cut groove in neutral safety switch is aligned. Rotate switch as necessary. See Fig. 16. Tighten switch retaining bolt to 44 INCH lbs. (5 N.m). Install shift lever and tighten nut to 115 INCH lbs. (13 N.m). Install shift control cable. Ensure starter operates with transmission in neutral and park only.

VACUUM MODULATOR INSPECTION

Tracker (3-Speed) – 1) Raise and support vehicle. Remove vacuum hose from modulator. Using Modulator Wrench (J-23100), remove modulator from transmission.

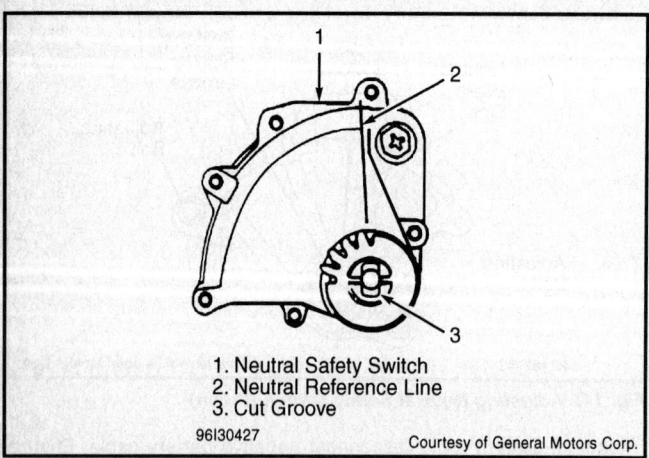

1. Neutral Safety Switch
2. Neutral Reference Line
3. Cut Groove

96I30427   Courtesy of General Motors Corp.

Fig. 16: Adjusting Neutral Safety Switch (Tracker – 4-Speed)

2) Inspect modulator for fluid leakage. Replace vacuum modulator if any transmission fluid drains from modulator. With diaphragm rod in place, test for vacuum leakage by attaching vacuum pump to fitting on vacuum modulator. Apply 20 in. Hg of vacuum to modulator. If vacuum gauge on pump indicates a vacuum loss, replace vacuum modulator. Inspect vacuum modulator "O" ring for cuts and other damage. To install components, reverse removal procedure.

TORQUE SPECIFICATIONS
TORQUE SPECIFICATIONS

Application	Ft. Lbs. (N.m)
Metro	
Drain Plug	17 (23)
Filter Screen	[1]
Neutral Safety Switch	17 (23)
Oil Pan	[1]
Prizm	
Differential Drain/Fill Plugs	29 (39)
Filter Screen	[2]
Neutral Safety Switch	[3]
Oil Pan	[4]
Transaxle Drain Plug	
3-Speed	36 (49)
4-Speed	13 (17)
Tracker	
Filter Screen Bolt	
3-Speed	14 (19)
4-Speed	[4]
Neutral Safety Switch	
3-Speed	15 (20)
4-Speed	[4]
Oil Pan	
3-Speed	[5]
4-Speed	[4]
Oil Pan Drain Plug	13 (17)
Reinforcement Plate	14 (19)
Servo Piston Cover	18 (24)
Transfer Case Drain Plug	21 (28)
Transfer Case Fill Plug	17 (23)

[1] – Tighten to 53 INCH Lbs. (6 N.m)
[2] – Tighten to 89 INCH Lbs. (10 N.m)
[3] – Tighten to 48 INCH Lbs. (5.4 N.m).
[4] – Tighten to 44 INCH Lbs. (5 N.m).
[5] – Tighten to 115 INCH Lbs. (13 N.m).

Honda

Accord, Civic, Civic Del Sol, Odyssey, Passport, Prelude

NOTE: For information on Passport transmission servicing, refer to Rodeo in AUTOMATIC TRANSMISSION SERVICING – ISUZU article. For information on Isuzu Oasis transmission servicing, refer to Honda Odyssey in this article.

IDENTIFICATION

Transaxles can be identified by identification tag located on bellhousing, near engine block, or on top of transaxle toward outer end.

AUTOMATIC TRANSAXLE APPLICATIONS

Vehicle	Model
Honda	
Accord	
4-Cylinder (Japan)	MPOA
4-Cylinder (U.S.A.)	AOYA
V6	MPZA
1995 Civic	A24A
1996 Civic	
4-Speed	AR4A
CVT	M4VA
Civic Del Sol	S24A
Odyssey	MPJA
Passport	THM 4L30E
Prelude	MP1A
Isuzu	
Oasis	MPJA

LUBRICATION

SERVICE INTERVALS

1995 Models – Change fluid every 30,000 miles or 24 months under normal driving conditions on 1995 models. If operated under severe service conditions, change fluid every 15,000 miles or 12 months.

1996 Models – On Honda Odyssey and Isuzu Oasis models, change fluid at 45,000 miles or 36 months and every 30,000 miles or 24 months there after under normal driving conditions.

On Civic CVT (M4VA), change fluid, transmission filter and strainer at 30,000 miles or 24 months and every 15,000 miles or 12 months there after under normal driving conditions.

On all other models, change fluid every 90,000 miles or 72 months under normal driving conditions.

On all models, if operated under severe service conditions, change fluid every 15,000 miles or 12 months.

CHECKING FLUID LEVEL

With vehicle on level floor and at normal operating temperature, stop engine. Within one minute after turning engine off, remove transmission dipstick and wipe it clean. Re-insert dipstick into filler hole and check fluid level. Fluid level should be between upper and lower marks on dipstick.

RECOMMENDED FLUID

Continuously Variable Transmission (CVT) & Accord V6 – Use only genuine Honda Premium Formula ATF.

Except CVT & Accord V6 – Dexron-II ATF is approved for all models, Dexron-III ATF is approved for use on Civic, Honda Odyssey and Isuzu Oasis.

FLUID CAPACITIES
TRANSAXLE REFILL CAPACITIES

Application	Refill Qts. (L)	Dry Fill Qts. (L)
Honda		
Accord		
AOYA & MPOA	2.5 (2.4)	6.3 (6.0)
MPZA	2.9 (2.7)	7.5 (7.1)
Civic		
4-Speed	3.2 (3.0)	6.2 (5.9)
CVT	3.4 (3.2)	6.7 (6.3)
Civic Del Sol	2.9 (2.7)	6.2 (5.9)
Odyssey	2.5 (2.4)	6.3 (6.0)
Prelude	2.5 (2.4)	6.3 (6.0)
Isuzu		
Oasis	2.5 (2.4)	6.3 (6.0)

DRAINING & REFILLING

1) Ensure transaxle is at normal operating temperature (cooling fan comes on). Remove transaxle drain plug to drain fluid. Install NEW plug gasket. Tighten drain plug to 37 ft. Lbs (50 N.m.).
2) Add fluid through dipstick hole. Start engine. Move gear selector lever through all selector positions 3 times. Ensure each gear engages. With selector lever in Neutral or Park, let transmission fluid warm to normal operating temperature. Shut off engine. Check fluid level. Add enough fluid to bring level to upper mark on dipstick.

FILTER REPLACEMENT

Civic CVT (M4VA) Transmission – 1) Raise and support vehicle. Remove drain plug to drain fluid. Disconnect transmission cooler hoses at cooler pipes.
2) Remove right/front motor mount bracket. Remove transmission cooler inlet bracket bolt. Remove transmission cooler outlet pipe.
3) Remove transmission pan bolts and pan. Remove cooler inlet pipe from transmission pan. Remove strainer bolts and strainer. Clean or replace filter and strainer as necessary.
4) Replace "O" rings, pan gasket and drain plug sealing washer. To install, reverse removal procedure. Tighten pan bolts to 104 INCH Lbs. (12 N.m.).

ADJUSTMENTS

SHIFT CONTROL CABLE

1) Start engine and move shift lever into Reverse. Verify transaxle engages in Reverse. On Honda Odyssey and Isuzu Oasis, remove steering column lower cover. On all models, remove center console. Move shift lever into Neutral. Remove lock pin from cable adjuster. Ensure adjuster and shift cable holes align perfectly. *See Fig. 1.*

2) Holes in end of adjuster are positioned to allow cable adjustments in 1/4 turn increments. Adjust shift cable if it is not perfectly aligned. Loosen lock nut and adjust cable as necessary. Tighten lock nut. Install lock pin into adjuster. *See Fig. 1.*
3) Lock pin should not bind during installation. Start engine and check shift lever in all gears. Vehicle should start only with shift lever in Park or Neutral. Adjust gear range switch (if necessary). Install center console.

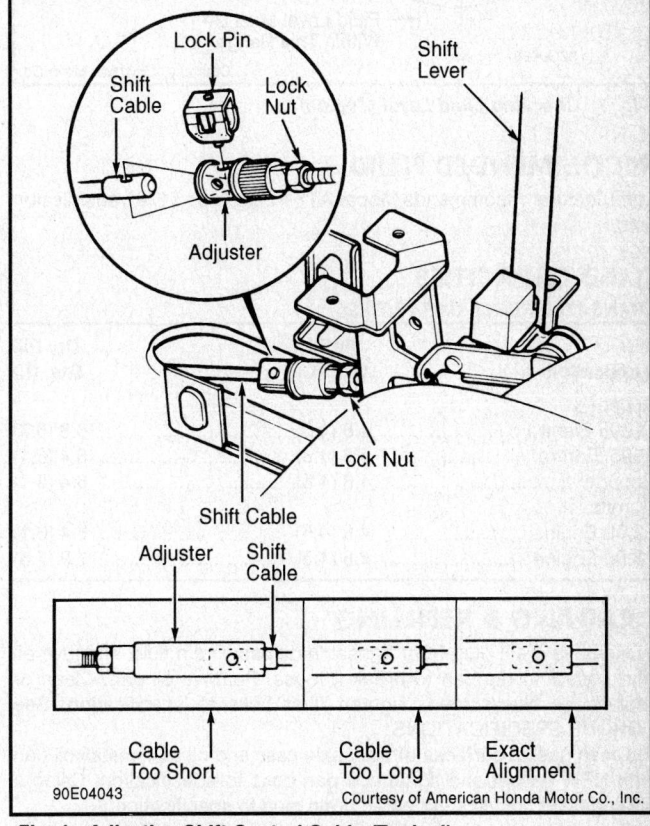

90E04043   Courtesy of American Honda Motor Co., Inc.

Fig. 1: Adjusting Shift Control Cable (Typical)

A/T GEAR POSITION SWITCH

NOTE: Switch may also be referred to as Gear Range Switch or Neutral Safety Switch. For adjustment procedures, see A/T GEAR POSITION SWITCH under REMOVAL & INSTALLATION in appropriate ELECTRONIC CONTROLS article.

Hyundai

Accent, Elantra, Scoupe, Sonata

IDENTIFICATION
TRANSAXLE APPLICATION

Vehicle	Trans. Model
Accent	A4AF2
Elantra	
1995	KM175
1996	A4BF1
Scoupe	A4AF1
Sonata	
2.0L Engine	KM175
3.0L Engine	F4A33

LUBRICATION

SERVICE INTERVALS

Check fluid at every engine oil change. Under normal conditions, replace fluid and oil screen every 30,000 miles. Under severe conditions, change oil and screen at 15,000 mile intervals.

CHECKING FLUID LEVEL

Vehicle must be level, with engine at normal operating temperature. Ensure gearshift lever is in the "P" position. Add enough ATF to bring fluid level to lower mark on dipstick. With engine idling (in "P" position) fluid level should be full, between upper and middle marks of dipstick (HOT range). *See Fig. 1.* Insert dipstick fully into tube to prevent dirt from entering transaxle.

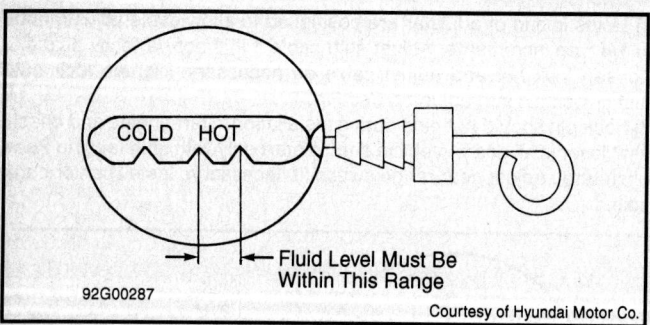

Fig. 1: Checking Fluid Level (Typical)

RECOMMENDED FLUID

Manufacturer recommends Mopar ATF PLUS Type 7176 transmission fluid.

FLUID CAPACITIES

TRANSAXLE REFILL CAPACITIES

Application	Refill Qts. (L)	Dry Fill Qts. (L)
Accent &		
1996 Elantra	4.8 (4.5)	6.8 (6.7)
1995 Elantra	4.8 (4.5)	6.4 (6.1)
Scoupe	4.8 (4.5)	6.4 (6.1)
Sonata		
2.0L Engine	4.8 (4.5)	6.4 (6.1)
3.0L Engine	4.8 (4.5)	7.9 (7.5)

DRAINING & REFILLING

1) Remove drain plug from transaxle oil pan. Drain fluid. Remove oil pan bolts and tap pan to break it loose. Remove oil pan. Clean or replace oil filter/screen. Tighten filter bolts to specification. See TORQUE SPECIFICATIONS.

2) Clean gasket surfaces of transaxle case and oil pan. Install oil pan with NEW gasket and tighten oil pan bolts to specification. Using a NEW gasket, install and tighten drain plug to specification.

3) Pour 4.2 qts. (4.0L) of ATF into case through dipstick hole. Unless torque converter was drained, dry fill amount is not necessary. Start engine and allow to idle for at least 2 minutes. With parking brake on, move gearshift lever slowly to each position and back to "P" position. Recheck fluid level on dipstick.

4) Add sufficient ATF to bring fluid level to lower mark. Recheck fluid level after transaxle is at normal operating temperature. Fluid level should be between marks of dipstick HOT range. See Fig. 1. Insert dipstick fully into tube to prevent dirt from entering transaxle.

ADJUSTMENTS

GEARSHIFT LEVER SLEEVE

1) If control cable has been replaced, or gearshift lever does not properly lock into each position, cable sleeve must be readjusted. Set parking brake. Place gearshift lever in "N" position. Remove set screws and lift off gearshift lever handle. Turn sleeve so that clearance between gearshift lever end and sleeve is .598-.625" (15.2-15.9 mm). See Fig. 2.

2) Apply grease to push button contact area and to slope of sleeve before reassembly. Ensure angled side faces push button side of handle when reassembled.

KICKDOWN SERVO

Elantra (1995) & Sonata – **1)** Clean dirt and other contaminants from servo switch and cover. Remove snap ring. Remove kickdown servo switch. Prevent servo piston from turning by using Holder (09454-33101A). See Fig. 3. Loosen adjusting screw lock nut.

2) Using Socket (09454-33101B) and INCH-lb. torque wrench, tighten adjustment screw to 89 INCH lbs. (10 N.m). Loosen adjustment screw and retighten 2 more times to specification.

3) Loosen screw again and tighten to 44 INCH lbs. (5 N.m). Finally, loosen screw 2-2 1/4 turns. Hold adjustment screw at that setting, and tighten lock nut to specification. See TORQUE SPECIFICATIONS.

4) Install "O" ring in groove and lightly lubricate it with ATF. Install servo cover to case and install snap ring. Install kickdown switch to cover.

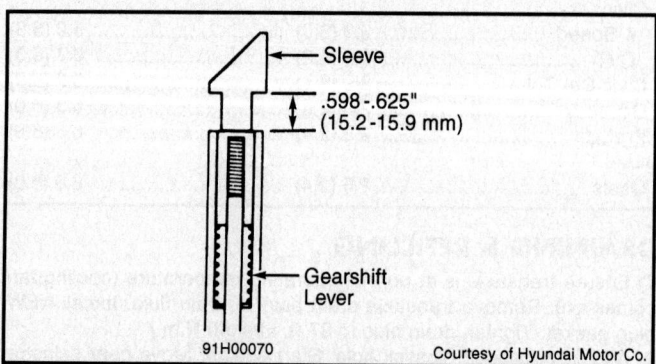

Fig. 2: Adjusting Gearshift Lever Sleeve

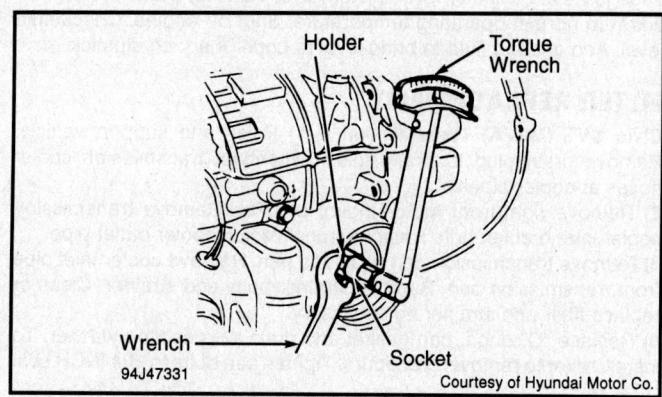

Fig. 3: Adjusting Kickdown Servo (1995 Elantra & Sonata)

Accent, 1996 Elantra & Scoupe – **1)** Clean dirt and other contaminants from servo switch and cover. Loosen adjusting screw lock nut. See Fig. 4.

2) Loosen and tighten adjusting screw twice to 44 INCH lbs. (5 N.m). After tightening screw the second time, loosen 3-3 1/3 turns. Tighten lock nut to 11-18 ft. lbs. (15-25 N.m).

NOTE: *Before assembly, apply sealant to center portion of the adjusting screw.*

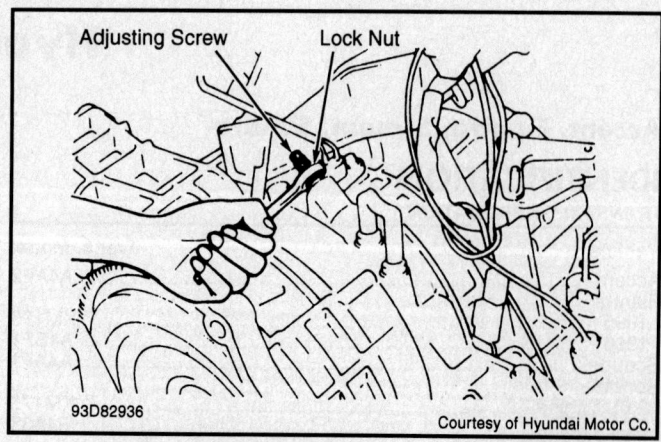

Fig. 4: Adjusting Kickdown Servo (Accent, 1996 Elantra & Scoupe)

NEUTRAL SAFETY SWITCH & CONTROL CABLE

1) Place gearshift lever in "N" position. Loosen control cable adjusting nuts at transaxle control lever, to allow slack in control cable. Loosen neutral safety switch bolts, and turn switch until .47" (12 mm) wide end of control lever aligns with .47" (12 mm) flange on switch body or until .20" (5 mm) diameter hole in lever and switch line up. See Fig. 5.

2) Tighten neutral safety switch bolts to specification. See TORQUE SPECIFICATIONS. Ensure transaxle control lever and gearshift lever handle are in Neutral and "N" positions. Adjust cable adjusting nuts to remove slack in control cable. Ensure gearshift lever operates smoothly. Drive vehicle to ensure transaxle shifts into each position selected.

TORQUE SPECIFICATIONS

TORQUE SPECIFICATIONS

Application	Ft. Lbs. (N.m)
Drain Plug	22-26 (30-35)
Kickdown Servo Lock Nut	18-24 (24-33)
	INCH Lbs. (N.m)
Neutral Safety Switch Bolts	89-106 (10-12)
Oil Pan Bolts	89-106 (10-12)
Oil Filter/Screen Bolts	44-62 (5-7)

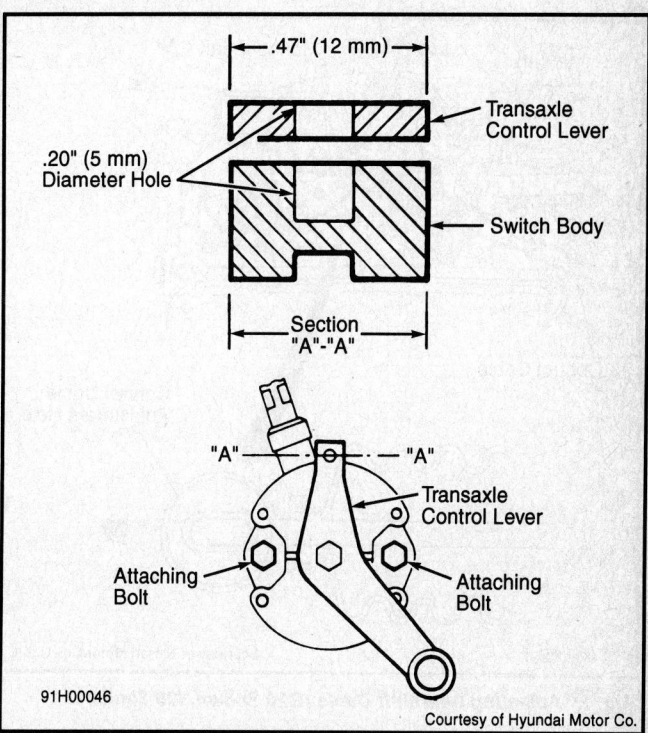

91H00046

Courtesy of Hyundai Motor Co.

Fig. 5: Adjusting Neutral Safety Switch (Sonata Shown, Others Are Similar)

Infiniti

G20, I30, J30, Q45

IDENTIFICATION

AUTOMATIC TRANSMISSION APPLICATIONS

Vehicle Model	Transmission Vehicle
G20	RE4F03A/V
I30	RE4F03A/V
J30	RE4R01A
Q45	RE4R03A

LUBRICATION

SERVICE INTERVALS

Check fluid at every engine oil change. Change at 60,000 miles or 48 months. Under severe conditions, change transmission fluid every 30,000 miles or 24 months.

CHECKING FLUID LEVEL

1) Park vehicle on level ground. Set parking brake. Start engine and move gear selector through each gear range, ending in "P". Check fluid with engine idling. Add fluid if necessary. DO NOT overfill.

2) Check for fluid contamination. If fluid is very dark, smells burned or contains frictional material (clutches, brake bands, etc.), change fluid and check transmission operation.

NOTE: Check fluid at HOT range on dipstick when fluid is 122-176°F (50-80°C). Use COLD range when fluid is 86-122°F (30-50°C) and recheck fluid level when hot.

RECOMMENDED FLUID

Use Dexron-III/Mercon ATF or equivalent.

FLUID CAPACITIES

TRANSMISSION REFILL CAPACITIES

Application	Qts. (L)
G20	7.4 (7.0)
I30	10 (9.4)
J30	8.8 (8.3)
Q45	11.2 (10.5)

DRAINING & REFILLING

Raise and support vehicle. On all models, drain fluid by removing drain plug. On J30 and Q45, remove oil screen. Clean oil pan, magnet and oil screen in clean solvent and dry. On G20 and I30, tighten drain plug to 21-29 ft. lbs. (29-39 N.m). On J30 and Q45, install and tighten pan bolts in a crisscross pattern to 62-80 INCH lbs. (7-9 N.m). On all models, add fluid and check level.

ADJUSTMENTS

NOTE: Most adjustments and transmission operations are computer controlled.

CONTROL CABLE

G20 & I30 – 1) Detents should be felt in each range as selector lever goes from "P" to "1". If detents cannot be felt or pointer is improperly aligned, adjust gearshift linkage.

2) Place selector lever in "P" range and loosen lock nuts on linkage. Place selector lever in Park. Ensure transaxle is fully engaged in Park. Loosen control cable lock nut and place manual shaft in "P" position. Pull cable with 1.5 lb. (6.9 N.m) in direction of arrow. Return cable in opposite direction .039" (1.0 mm). Tighten control cable lock nut. Move selector lever from "P" to "1" position. Ensure selector lever moves smoothly. Apply grease to contacting areas of selector lever and control cable. See Fig. 1.

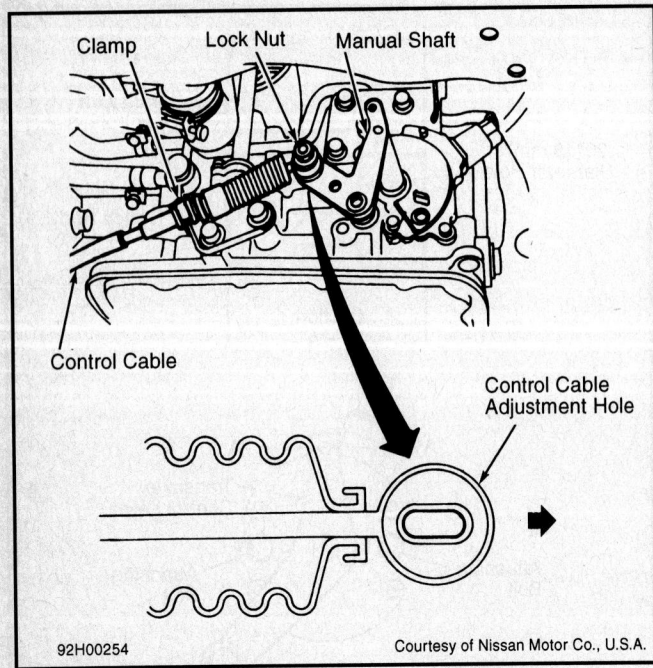

Fig. 1: *Adjusting Gearshift Cable (G20 Shown, I30 Similar)*

GEARSHIFT LINKAGE

J30 & Q45 – 1) Detents should be felt in each range as selector lever goes from "P" to "1". If detents cannot be felt or pointer is improperly aligned, adjust gearshift linkage. Place selector lever in "P" range and loosen lock nuts on linkage. *See Fig. 2.*

2) Tighten lock nut "X" until it touches trunnion, pulling selector lever toward "R" range side without pushing button. Back off lock nut "X" one turn and tighten lock nut "Y" to 97-133 INCH lbs. (11-15 N.m). Move selector lever from "P" range to "1" range. Ensure selector lever moves smoothly and pointer aligns properly.

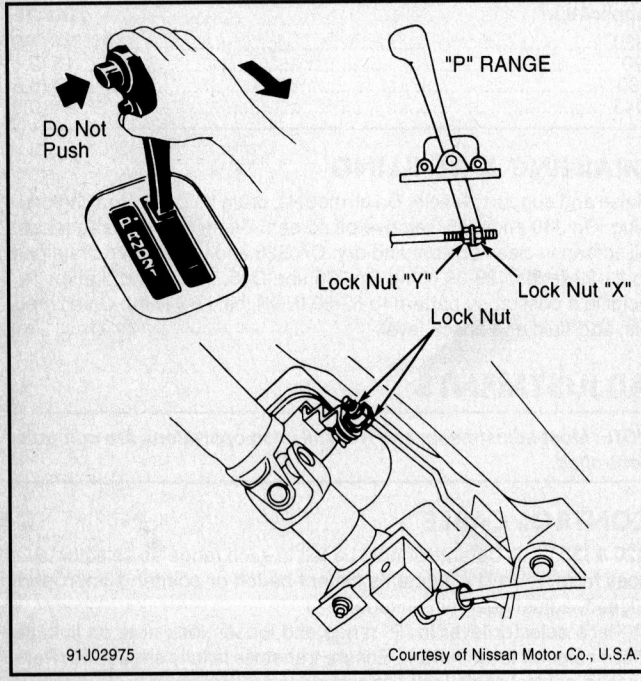

Fig. 2: *Adjusting Gearshift Linkage (J30 & Q45)*

KICKDOWN SWITCH (Q45)

Adjust clearance "C" between stopper rubber and end of kickdown switch thread while depressing accelerator pedal fully. Clearance "C" should be .012-.039" (.30-1.0). *See Fig. 3.*

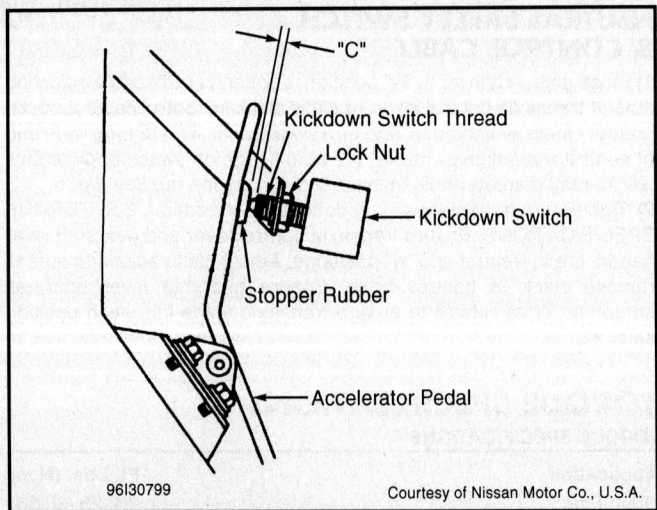

Fig. 3: *Adjusting Kickdown Switch*

INHIBITOR SWITCH

Inhibitor switch operates back-up lights and prevents starting except in Park and Neutral. To adjust, place transaxle in Neutral. Disconnect shift cable from transaxle shift shaft lever. Loosen inhibitor switch screws. *See Fig. 4.* Insert 0.16" (4 mm) pin into adjustment holes in both neutral safety switch and manual shaft. Tighten screws. Remove pin and install control linkage. Ensure vehicle starts in only "P" and "N" positions.

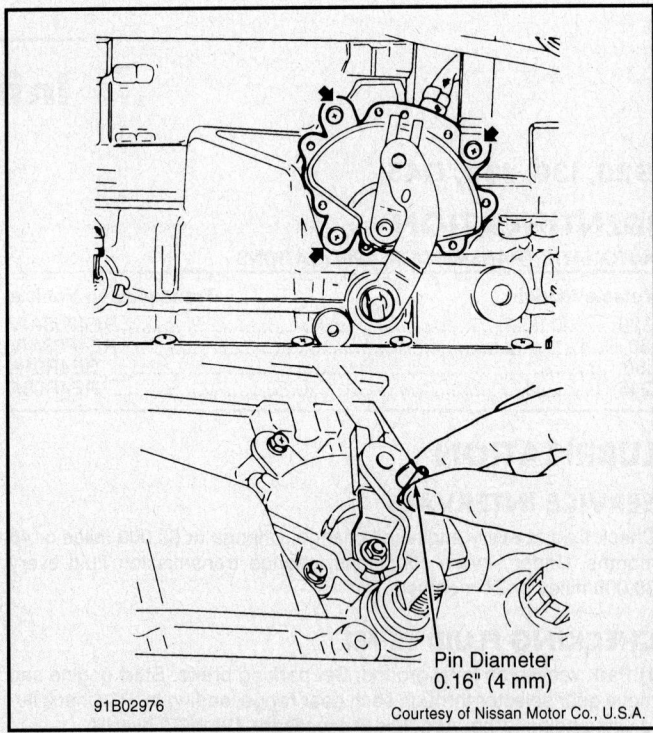

Fig. 4: *Adjusting Neutral Safety Switch (Typical)*

TORQUE SPECIFICATIONS
TORQUE SPECIFICATIONS

Application	Ft. Lbs. (N.m)
Drain Plug	21-29 (29-39)
Gear Shift Cable Lock Nut	13-18 (18-24)
	INCH Lbs. (N.m)
Oil Pan Bolts	62-80 (7-9)
Kickdown Switch Locknut	69-104 (8-12)

Oasis, Rodeo, Trooper

IDENTIFICATION

AUTOMATIC TRANSMISSION APPLICATIONS

Application	Transmission Model
1996 Oasis	Honda MPJA
1995-96 Rodeo & Trooper	Hydra-Matic 4L30-E

LUBRICATION

SERVICE INTERVALS

Transaxle (Oasis) – Under normal driving conditions, change fluid initially at 45,000 miles, then every 30,000 mile intervals thereafter. If vehicle is operated in severe service conditions, change fluid initially at 30,000 miles.

Transmission (Rodeo & Trooper) – Check fluid at every engine oil change. Under normal conditions, manufacturer does not recommend fluid change. Under severe conditions such as repeated short trips, rough roads or dusty conditions, change transmission fluid and screen at 20,000-mile intervals.

Transfer Case (Rodeo & Trooper) – Check lubricant level every 7500 miles. Replace lubricant after initial 15,000 and 30,000 miles, then every 30,000 mile intervals thereafter.

CHECKING FLUID LEVEL

Transaxle (Oasis) – 1) Park vehicle on level surface and apply parking brake. Ensure transmission fluid is at normal operating temperature. Place gear selector lever in Park with engine off.

2) Check fluid level on dipstick. Fluid level should be between upper and lower marks (crosshatched area). If fluid level is below lower mark, add fluid to bring level up to upper mark. DO NOT overfill.

Transmission (1995-95 1/2 Rodeo & 1995 Trooper) – 1) Park vehicle on level surface and apply parking brake. Place gear selector lever in Park. Start engine and allow it to reach normal operating temperature. Apply brake pedal and move gear selector lever through all gear positions, ending in Park.

2) Allow engine to idle for 3 minutes with all accessories off, then check fluid level on dipstick. Fluid level should be in "H" (Hot) range with engine at normal operating temperature. Add fluid if necessary. DO NOT overfill.

Transmission (1996 Rodeo & Trooper) – 1) Transmission is not equipped with a dipstick. Ensure vehicle is level, with engine running at idle and parking brake applied. Fluid temperature must be less than 86°F (30°C). Move gear selector lever through all gear positions, ending in Park.

2) Let engine idle for 3 minutes and open OVERFILL screw on bottom of transmission oil pan. Transmission is filled through OVERFILL screw. Fluid will seek correct level and excess should flow out from OVERFILL screw. See Fig. 1.

Transfer Case (Rodeo & Trooper) – Remove fill plug from right rear of transfer case. Fluid level should be even with fill plug hole. Add fluid if necessary. Install fill plug.

RECOMMENDED FLUID

Transmission – Use Dexron-III ATF on all applications.

Transaxle (Oasis) – Use Honda Premium Formula Automatic Transmission Fluid (ATF) or equivalent Dexron-II or Dexron-III ATF. Dexron should only be used if Honda ATF is unavailable.

Transfer Case – Use engine oil SAE 5W-30 for operational temperature range up to 95°F (35°C). Use SAE 15W-40, 20W-40 or 20W-50 for operational temperatures above 50°F (10°C).

FLUID CAPACITIES

TRANSAXLE/TRANSMISSION REFILL CAPACITIES

Application	Refill Qts. (L)	Dry Fill Qts. (L)
Oasis	2.5 (2.4)	6.3 (6.0)
Rodeo & Trooper	[1]	9.1 (8.6)

[1] – Information is not available from manufacturer.

TRANSFER CASE REFILL CAPACITIES

Application	Qts. (L)
Rodeo & Trooper	1.5 (1.4)

DRAINING & REFILLING

Oasis – Ensure vehicle is at normal operating temperature. Park vehicle on level ground and turn engine off. Remove transaxle drain plug. After draining fluid, install a NEW sealing washer on drain plug, install and torque to specification. See TORQUE SPECIFICATIONS. Fill transaxle to upper mark on dipstick. See CHECKING FLUID LEVEL.

1995-95 1/2 Rodeo & 1995 Trooper – 1) Remove all except 3 transmission oil pan bolts on rear of oil pan. Loosen remaining 3 bolts to allow transmission oil pan to tip downward so fluid will drain. Once fluid is drained, remove remaining bolts, transmission oil pan and gasket. If changing oil strainer, remove bolts and oil strainer.

2) Clean transmission oil pan. Install oil strainer. Torque bolts to specification. See TORQUE SPECIFICATIONS. Install gasket and transmission oil pan. Torque bolts to specification. Add Dexron-III through dipstick tube. Check fluid level. See CHECKING FLUID LEVEL.

1996 Rodeo & Trooper – Remove transmission oil pan drain plug. After draining fluid, install drain plug and torque to specification. See TORQUE SPECIFICATIONS. Remove OVERFILL screw and fill transmission through OVERFILL screw opening. Adjust fluid level as necessary. See CHECKING FLUID LEVEL.

Transfer Case (Rodeo & Trooper) – Remove drain plug from bottom of transfer case and drain fluid. Install drain plug. Remove fill plug. Fill transfer case until fluid is even with fill plug hole. Install fill plug.

ADJUSTMENTS

BRAKE BAND

NOTE: Band adjustment is not considered a normal maintenance item. If band adjustment is required, use the following procedure.

Rodeo & Trooper – 1) Remove oil pan, gasket, servo cover and gasket. Loosen lock nut. Slightly back off servo adjusting bolt. See Fig. 2. Using an INCH-lb. torque wrench, torque servo adjusting bolt to 40 INCH lbs. (4.5 N.m).

2) Back off servo adjusting bolt exactly 5 turns. Hold servo adjusting bolt and torque lock nut to specification. See TORQUE SPECIFICATIONS. Install servo cover and gasket. Torque servo cover bolts to specification. Install gasket and oil pan. Torque oil pan bolts to specification.

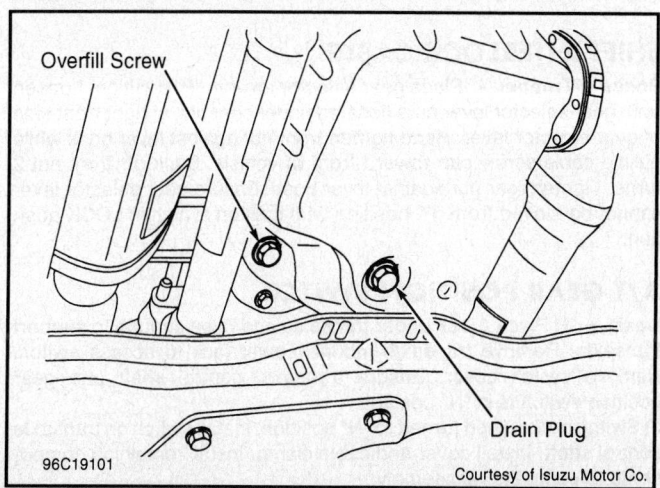

Overfill Screw

Drain Plug

96C19101

Courtesy of Isuzu Motor Co.

Fig. 1: Identifying Transmission Oil Pan (1996 Rodeo & Trooper)

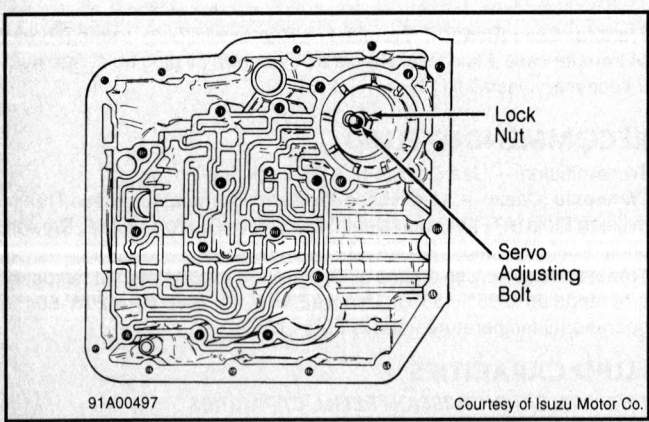

Fig. 2: Adjusting Brake Band (Rodeo & Trooper)

KICKDOWN SWITCH

Rodeo & Trooper – Turn kickdown switch so continuity is present only when depressing accelerator pedal to more than 7/8 of its travel.

THROTTLE VALVE (T.V.) CABLE

Oasis – **1)** Ensure idle speed and throttle cable adjustment is correct. Ensure T.V. cable is routed correctly and held in place by middle of protector tube in cable bracket. Ensure throttle linkage is in fully-closed position.
2) Loosen T.V. cable housing locknut at throttle lever bracket. *See Fig. 3*. Remove cable free play by adjusting locknut while pushing throttle control lever to the fully-closed position. Tighten locknuts. Check throttle lever movement.

NOTE: Oasis shift and lock-up characteristics may be adjusted by shortening the cable up to .078" (2.0 mm) shorter than the standard adjustment position.

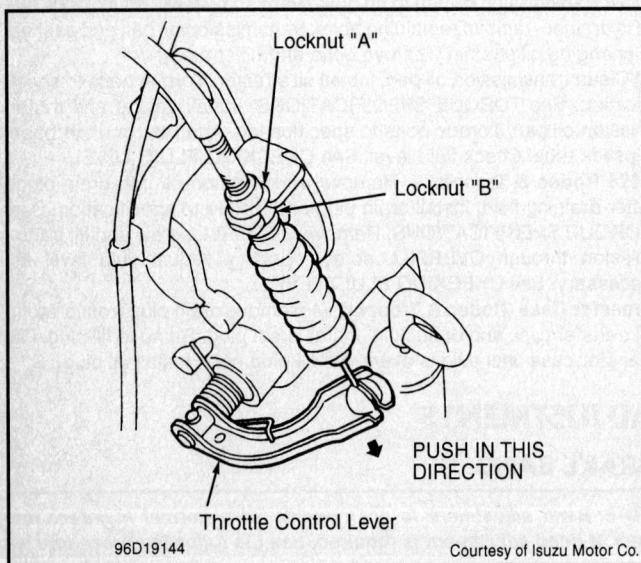

Fig. 3: Adjusting Throttle Valve (T.V.) Cable (Oasis)

GEAR SELECTOR LEVER & CONTROL ROD

Rodeo & Trooper – **1)** Ensure jam nuts on selector control rod are loose. Place selector lever in "N" position. Push selector lever forward against Neutral detent. Hold selector lever in this position.
2) Turn control rod forward jam nut until it comes in contact with boss. Tighten rear nut against selector lever boss. Install locking clip and tighten nut. Ensure gear selector operation is correct.

SHIFT CABLE

WARNING: *Some models are equipped with a Supplemental Restraint System (SRS). All SRS wiring is color-coded Yellow. DO NOT use electrical test equipment on these circuits. Disconnect negative and positive battery cables before removing console. Wait at least 3 minutes after deactivating air bag system. System maintains voltage for about 3 minutes after battery is disconnected. Servicing air bag system within this 3 minute time period may cause accidental air bag deployment and possible personal injury.*

Oasis – **1)** Remove access cover from lower steering column. Place gear selector lever in "N" position. Remove lock pin from cable adjuster. Align hole in adjuster with hole in shift cable. *See Fig. 4*.
2) Two holes in end of shift cable are positioned at 90 degrees to allow cable adjustments in 1/4-turn increments. Loosen lock nut on shift cable. Adjust if necessary. *See Fig. 4*. Tighten lock nut. Install lock pin.
3) Lock pin should not bind as it is installed. If it binds, cable is still out of adjustment. Repeat adjustment procedure. Start engine and check shift lever selection of all gears. Ensure shift lock lever is released when key is inserted into lock cylinder.

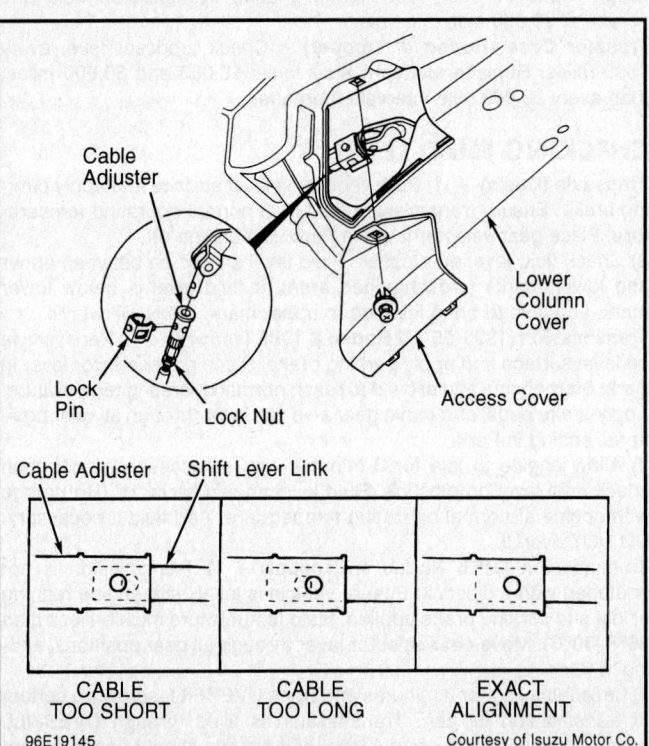

Fig. 4: Adjusting Shift Cable (Oasis)

SHIFT INTERLOCK CABLE

Rodeo & Trooper – Place gear selector lever in "P" position. Loosen both gear selector lever nuts (located under console, at right front side of gear selector lever. Hand tighten front nut against lever boss while pulling cable screw cap toward front of vehicle. Back off front nut 2 turns. Tighten rear nut against lever boss. Ensure gear selector lever cannot be moved from "P" position with ignition switch in LOCK position.

A/T GEAR POSITION SWITCH

Oasis – **1)** Place a jack under transaxle and raise enough to support transaxle. Remove transaxle mount. Lower jack to access switch. Remove switch cover. Ensure transaxle control shaft and gear position switch is in "N" position.
2) Switch clicks when turned to "N" position. Install switch on transaxle control shaft. Install cover and cable clamp. Install remaining components to complete reassembly.

MODE SWITCH

Rodeo & Trooper – 1) Place gear selector lever in "N" position. Remove cover from mode switch. Disconnect gear selector lever from mode switch. Loosen switch mounting bolts. Align slot in switch housing with slot in selector shaft bushing. *See Fig. 5.*

2) Insert a 3/32" diameter alignment pin into both ports and rotate switch body to feel for proper alignment. Torque switch mounting bolts to specification. See TORQUE SPECIFICATIONS. Remove alignment pins before moving gear selector lever.

TORQUE SPECIFICATIONS

TORQUE SPECIFICATIONS

Application	Ft. Lbs. (N.m)
Oasis	
Transaxle Drain Plug	36 (49)
Rodeo & Trooper	
Oil Strainer Bolt	15 (20)
Overfill Screw (1996)	28 (38)
Servo Cover Bolt	18 (24)
Servo Lock Nut	14 (19)
Transfer Case Drain Plug	1
Transfer Case Fill Plug	1
Transmission Drain Plug (1996)	28 (38)
	INCH Lbs. (N.m)
Rodeo & Trooper	
Mode Switch Bolt	113 (12.8)
Oil Pan Bolt	96 (10.8)

¹ – Information is not available.

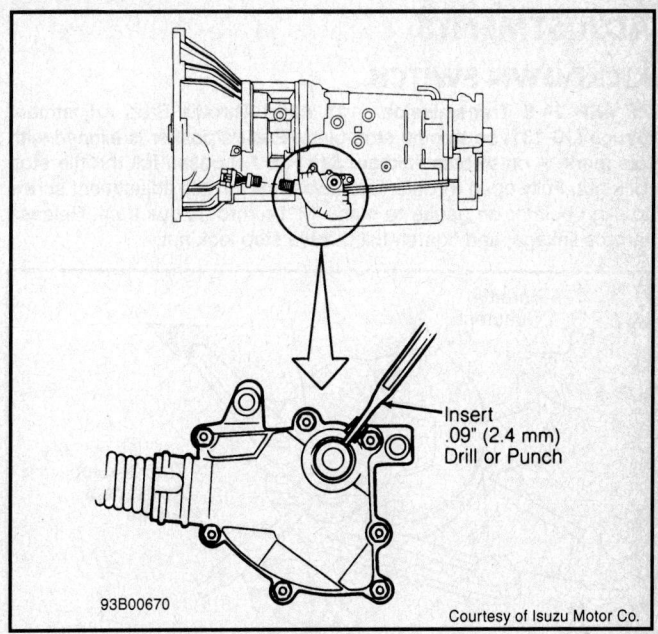

Insert .09" (2.4 mm) Drill or Punch

93B00670

Courtesy of Isuzu Motor Co.

Fig 5: Adjusting Mode Switch (Rodeo & Trooper)

Jaguar

XJR, XJS, XJ6, XJ12

IDENTIFICATION

AUTOMATIC TRANSMISSION APPLICATIONS

Model	Transmission
1995	
XJR & XJ12	4L80-E
XJS	
4.0L	ZF 4HP 24-E
6.0L	4L80-E
XJ6	ZF 4HP 24-E
1996	
XJR & XJ12	4L80-E
XJS & XJ6	ZF 4HP 24-E

LUBRICATION

SERVICE INTERVALS

Check fluid level at first 1000 miles and every 3000 miles thereafter. Change fluid and filter every 24,000 miles.

CHECKING FLUID LEVEL

1) Park vehicle on level ground. Apply parking brake, and run engine at 750 RPM for several minutes. Shift gear selector through all ranges and return to Park.

2) With engine idling, withdraw and wipe dipstick. Replace dipstick in filler tube, withdraw it and check fluid level. Fluid level should be between MAX and MIN marks on dipstick. Add fluid if necessary. DO NOT overfill.

RECOMMENDED FLUID

On 4L80-E transmissions, use Dexron-III Automatic Transmission Fluid (ATF). If Dexron-III ATF is not available, Dexron-IID or Dexron-IIE ATF may be used. On ZF 4HP 24-E transmissions, use Dexron-IID ATF.

FLUID CAPACITIES

TRANSMISSION REFILL CAPACITIES

Model	Refill Capacity Qts. (L)	Dry Fill Qts. (L)
1995		
XJR & XJ12	5.0 (4.7)	11.5 (10.9)
XJS		
4.0L	3.2 (3.0)	11 (10.2)
6.0L	5.0 (4.7)	11.5 (10.9)
XJ6	3.2 (3.0)	11 (10.2)
1996		
XJR & XJ12	5.0 (4.7)	11.5 (10.9)
XJS & XJ6	3.2 (3.0)	11 (10.2)

DRAINING & REFILLING

ZF 4HP 24-E Transmission – 1) Remove dipstick. Raise and support vehicle. Remove drain plug. Remove filler tube from transmission pan. Remove rotary switch guard. Remove oil pan bolts, and tap on pan to break seal loose. Remove oil pan and gasket. Remove filter. Clean and replace components as necessary.

2) Clean gasket mating services. Install new filter, gasket, oil pan, drain plug and filler tube. Tighten oil pan bolts, drain plug and filler tube to specification. See TORQUE SPECIFICATIONS. Fill transmission with Dexron-IID ATF. See TRANSMISSION REFILL CAPACITIES table.

4L80E Transmission – 1) Raise and support vehicle. Loosen intermediate exhaust pipe-to-muffler bolts. Disconnect intermediate exhaust pipe (both pipes on 6.0L) from downpipe. Remove oil pan bolts, and tap on pan to break seal loose. Remove oil pan and gasket. Remove filter. Clean and replace components as necessary.

2) Clean gasket mating surfaces. Install new filter, gasket and oil pan. Tighten oil pan bolts to specification. See TORQUE SPECIFICATIONS. Connect intermediate exhaust pipe(s). Fill transmission with Dexron-III ATF. See TRANSMISSION REFILL CAPACITIES table.

ADJUSTMENTS

KICKDOWN SWITCH

ZF 4HP 24-E Transmission – 1) Install Throttle Stop Adjustment Gauge (JD-131) on throttle stop plate. Ensure pointer is aligned with idle mark "I" on throttle linkage. *See Fig. 1*. Loosen full throttle stop lock nut. Fully open throttle, and adjust full throttle adjustment screw to align pointer on gauge to mark "M" on throttle quadrant. Release throttle linkage, and tighten full throttle stop lock nut.

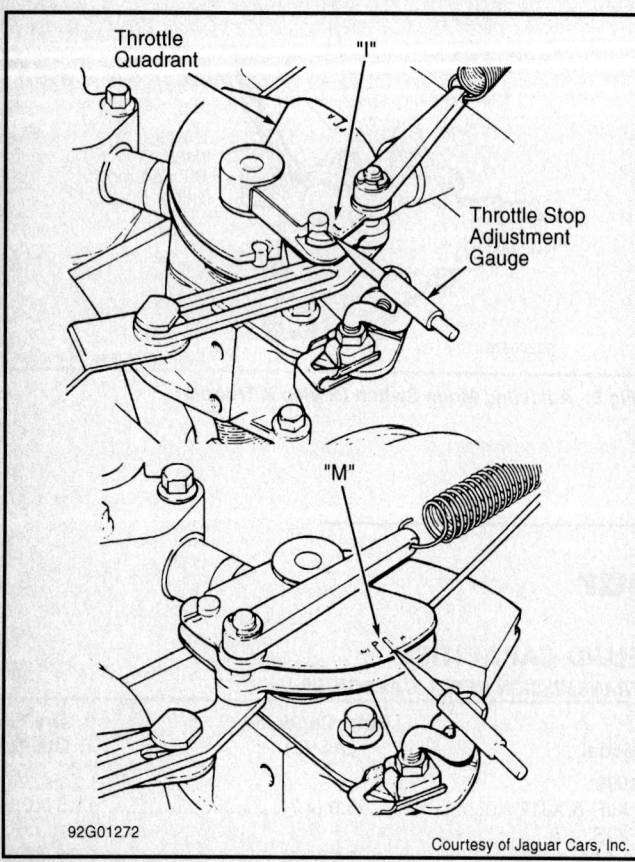

Fig. 1: *Adjusting Throttle Stops (ZF 4HP 24-E Transmission)*

2) Rotate throttle quadrant aside, and install Throttle Stop/Kickdown Setting Gauge (JD-162) onto throttle quadrant. *See Fig. 2*. Tighten Allen screw, and gently return throttle quadrant against its stop.
3) Move carpet away from kickdown switch. Cut and remove tie-wrap securing switch harness to side harness. Disconnect kickdown switch connector. Place a thin piece of paper over kickdown switch operating pad.
4) Press throttle pedal by hand until resistance is felt (about 90 percent of full throttle). *See Fig. 3*. Adjust kickdown switch (up/down) until paper can just be released from between pedal and pad with minimal resistance. Release throttle pedal, and remove paper.
5) Reconnect switch connector, and secure harness using new tie-wrap. Install carpet. Remove throttle stop/kickdown setting gauge and throttle stop adjustment gauge. Return throttle quadrant to stop.

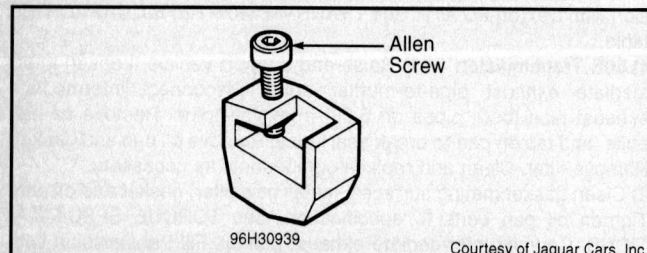

Fig. 2: *Identifying Throttle Stop/Kickdown Setting Gauge*

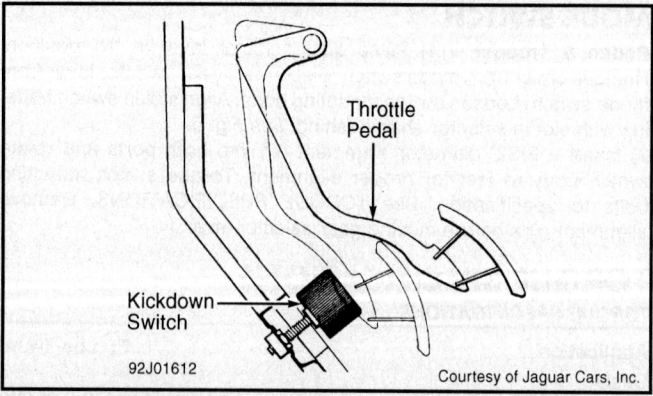

Fig. 3: *Adjusting Kickdown Switch (ZF 4HP 24-E Transmission)*

ROTARY SWITCH

ZF 4HP 24-E Transmission – 1) Rotary switch is located on left side of transmission case. Place shift selector in Neutral position. Raise and support vehicle. Remove rotary switch guard bolts and guard. Loosen switch-to-mounting bracket securing nuts. Remove rubber blanking plug from center of switch. Switch will now rotate to its limits.
2) Install Switch Adjuster (JD-161) to switch shaft and locating hole in switch body. *See Fig. 4*. Lightly tighten retaining nuts, and ensure adjuster can be withdrawn easily using a bar. *See Fig. 5*. Readjust switch if adjuster withdrawal is difficult.
3) When adjustment is correct, tighten retaining nuts. Remove adjuster, and install rubber blanking plug. Install switch guard, and tighten switch guard bolts to specification. See TORQUE SPECIFICATIONS. Lower vehicle.

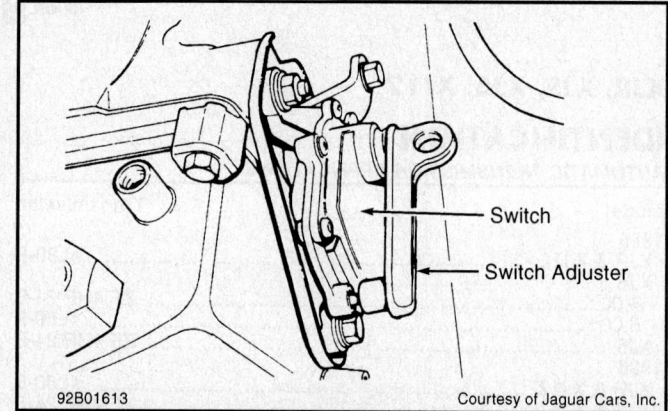

Fig. 4: *Adjusting Rotary Switch (ZF 4HP 24-E Transmission)*

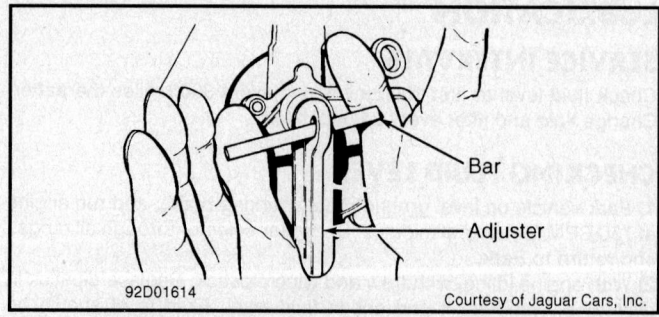

Fig. 5: *Checking Correct Rotary Switch Adjustment (ZF 4HP 24-E Transmission)*

SHIFT CABLE

1) Position vehicle over lift. Open center console, and remove ashtray. Disconnect sport mode switch from harness. Remove console panel and spacers. Position shift selector lever in Neutral. Loosen front and rear adjustment lock nuts to end of threads.

2) Raise and support vehicle. From below vehicle, remove selector cable ball pin-to-selector lever securing nut. Remove ball pin from selector lever. Ensuring selector is in Neutral, install ball pin to selector lever. Tighten selector lever nut to specification. See TORQUE SPECIFICATIONS.

3) Lower vehicle. Adjust selector cable nuts so selector lever freely engages Neutral position notch. Tighten front and rear lock nuts. Ensure washer tabs are engaged in bracket. Install console panel and spacers. Install selector. Connect harness to mode switch, and install switch. Install ashtray.

SHIFT INTERLOCK SYSTEM

All models are equipped with a shift interlock system. Transmission shift lever can only be moved from Park position if ignition is on (position II) and brake pedal is depressed. System testing is not available from manufacturer. If system does not function properly, check power and ground circuits. See WIRING DIAGRAMS. If no problem is found, check for open and short circuits. Repair as necessary.

WIRING DIAGRAMS

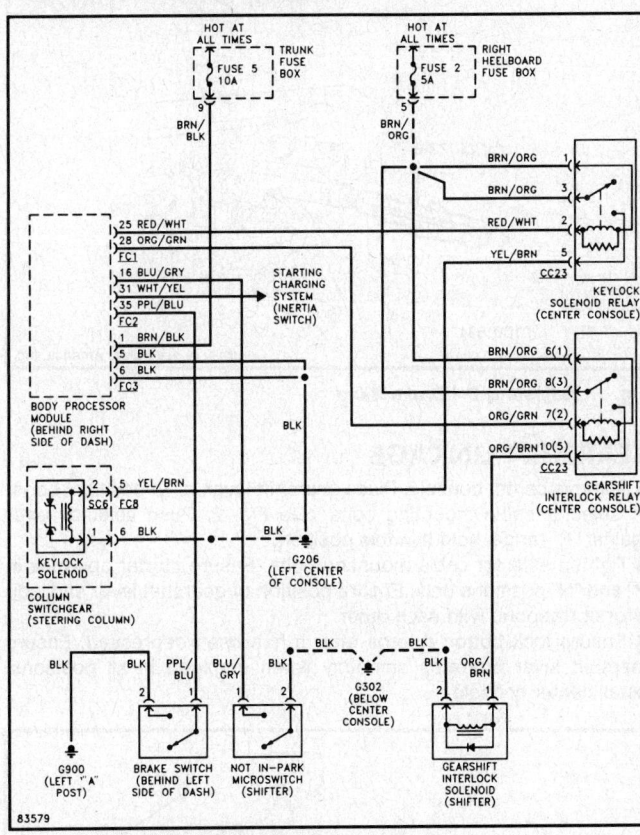

Fig. 6: Shift Interlock System Wiring Diagram (1995-96 XJR, XJ6 & XJ12)

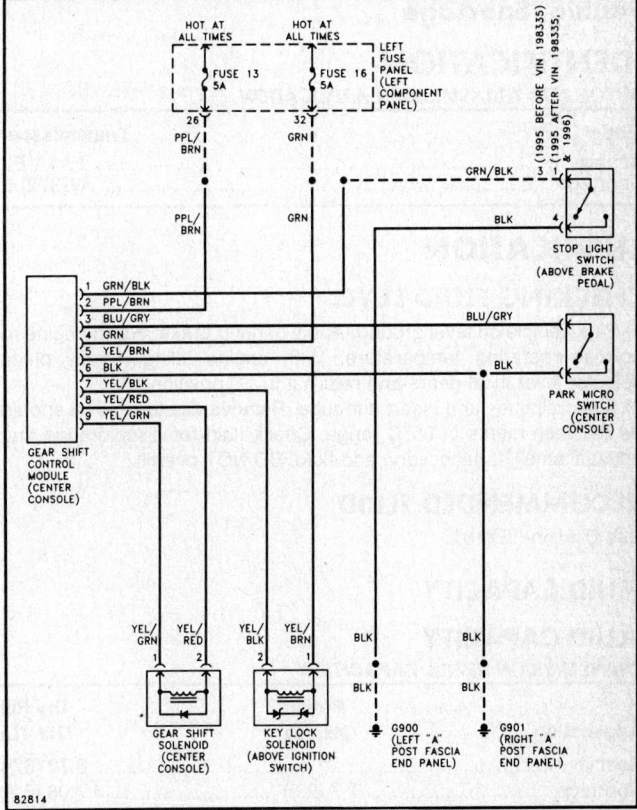

Fig. 7: Shift Interlock System Wiring Diagram (1995-96 XJS)

TORQUE SPECIFICATIONS
TORQUE SPECIFICATIONS

Application	Ft. Lbs. (N.m)
4L80-E	
Oil Pan Bolts	18 (24)
ZF 4HP 24-E	
Drain Plug	11 (15)
Filler Tube	66 (90)
Selector Lever Nut	30-37 (40-50)
Switch Guard-To-Sump Pan Bolts	11-13 (15-18)
Switch-To-Mounting Bracket Nuts	11-13 (15-18)
	INCH Lbs. (N.m)
Oil Pan Bolts (ZF 4HP 24-E)	71 (8)

Sephia, Sportage

IDENTIFICATION
AUTOMATIC TRANSMISSION APPLICATION

Model	Transmission
Sephia	FA4A-EL
Sportage	AW372LE

LUBRICATION

CHECKING FLUID LEVEL

1) Park vehicle on level ground. Apply parking brake. Warm engine to normal operating temperature. With engine idling, briefly place selector lever in all gears and return it to "P" position.

2) Clean dipstick and insert it in tube. Remove dipstick. Level should be between marks in 65°C range. Check fluid for discoloration and unusual smell. If necessary, add fluid. DO NOT overfill.

RECOMMENDED FLUID

Use Dexron-IIE fluid.

FLUID CAPACITY

FLUID CAPACITY
TRANSMISSION REFILL CAPACITIES

Application	Refill Qts. (L)	Dry Fill Qts. (L)
Sephia	¹	6.70 (6.3)
Sportage	2.7 (2.5)	² 7.08 (6.7)

¹ – Refill capacity is not available from manufacturer.
² – Excludes cooler lines.

DRAINING & REFILLING

Drain fluid into a suitable container. If oil pan is removed, discard old oil pan gasket. Clean oil pan, and install it using NEW gasket. Tighten bolts to specification. See TORQUE SPECIFICATIONS. Add fluid, and check level. DO NOT overfill.

ADJUSTMENTS

2-4 BRAKE BAND (SEPHIA)

1) Support engine. Raise and support vehicle. Drain transaxle fluid. Remove engine crossmember. Remove transaxle oil pan, gasket and valve body assembly. Remove snap ring and 2-4 band servo assembly. See Fig. 1.

2) Install servo piston onto Adapter (K94A-4206-AT for 1.6L) or (K94A-4204-AT for 1.8L). Remove "O" ring from servo retainer. Coat "O" ring with ATF, and install ring onto adapter. Install 2-4 band servo assembly into transaxle case and secure it using snap ring. Position dial indicator against piston stem. See Fig. 1.

3) Using a rubber-tipped air nozzle, apply compressed air through fluid passage and measure piston stem stroke. See Fig. 1. Piston stem stroke should be .040-.067" (1.00-1.70 mm) at 57 psi (4.0 kg/cm²). If piston stem stroke is not as specified, replace piston stem.

4) Nine different length piston stems are available in .02" (.5 mm) increments ranging from 3.74" (95.0 mm) to 3.90" (99.1 mm). Remove 2-4 band servo assembly and adapter. Install servo retainer using NEW "O" ring.

5) Install valve body assembly. Tighten bolts to specification. Install oil pan with NEW gasket. Tighten bolts to specification. See TORQUE SPECIFICATIONS. Install engine crossmember. Lower vehicle. Add fluid, and check level. DO NOT overfill.

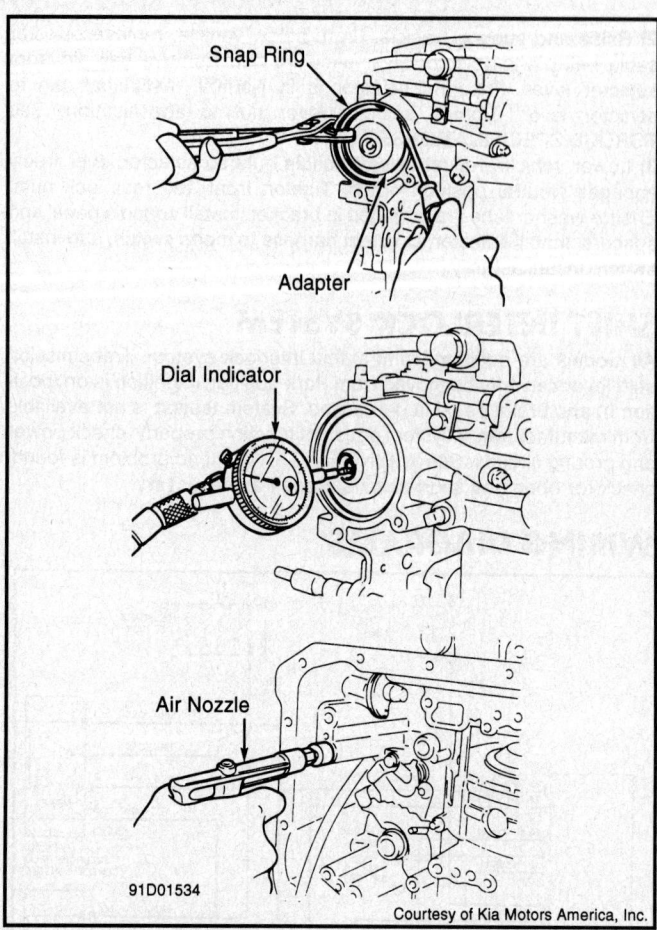

91D01534
Courtesy of Kia Motors America, Inc.

Fig. 1: Adjusting 2-4 Brake Band

GEARSHIFT LINKAGE

1) Remove center console. Place gearshift lever in "P" position. Loosen selector cable mounting bolts. See Fig. 2. Push selector lever against "P" range; hold it in this position.

2) Tighten selector cable mounting bolts. Ensure starter operates in "P" and "N" positions only. Ensure position of gearshift lever and indicator correspond with each other.

3) Ensure lock button returns after it has been depressed. Ensure gearshift lever operates smoothly when engaged in all positions. Install center console.

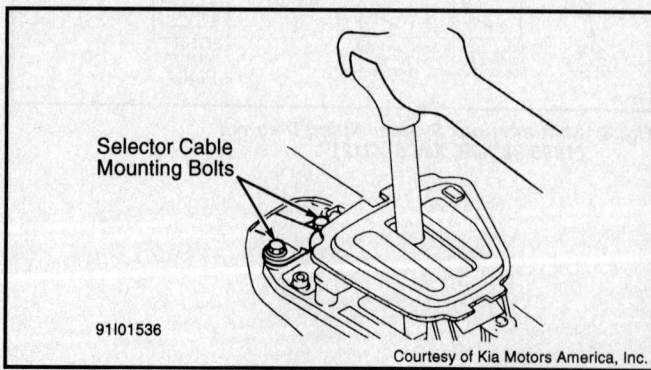

91I01536
Courtesy of Kia Motors America, Inc.

Fig. 2: Adjusting Gearshift Position

THROTTLE CABLE (T.V. CABLE)

NOTE: On Sephia, oil pressure gauge is needed to properly adjust throttle cable.

Sephia – 1) Remove left splash shield, near left front tire. Remove transaxle lower pressure port plug. Install oil pressure gauge to port. *See Fig. 3.* Move gearshift lever to "P" position. Start engine, and warm it to normal operating temperature.

2) Ensure engine is at normal idle speed. Check throttle pressure. See THROTTLE PRESSURE SPECIFICATIONS table. If pressure is not within specification, adjust throttle cable.

3) With engine running, loosen adjustment bolt No. 2. Adjust throttle cable until pressure reading is within specification. *See Fig. 4.* Tighten throttle cable adjustment bolt No. 2 to 61-87 INCH lbs. (6.9-9.8 N.m) when pressure is within specification.

4) Turn engine off. Remove oil pressure gauge. Install pressure port plug, and tighten it to 44-87 INCH lbs. (5.0-9.8 N.m).

THROTTLE PRESSURE SPECIFICATIONS

Gear Shift Lever Position	psi (kg/cm²)
"D", "2" Or "L"	62-81 (4.4-5.7)
"R"	110-120 (7.7-8.4)

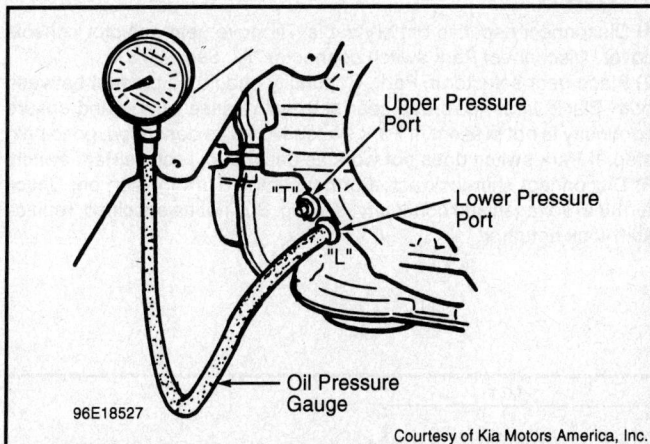

Fig. 3: Checking Throttle Pressure (Sephia)

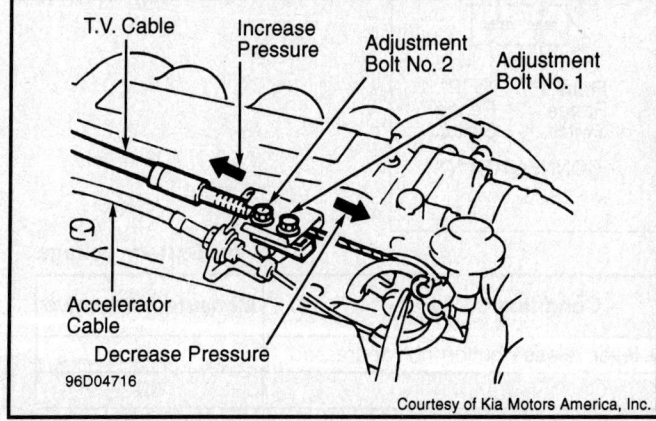

Fig. 4: Adjusting Throttle Valve (T.V.) Cable (Sephia)

Sportage – 1) Check throttle valve cable and housing for damage and replace as necessary. Depress accelerator pedal fully and ensure throttle body throttle valve is fully open. Adjust accelerator cable as necessary.

2) Slide throttle valve cable rubber boot down cable housing. Pull lightly on inner cable until slight resistance is felt. Measure distance between cable housing end and cable stop. Distance should be .031-.059" (.8-1.5 mm). *See Fig. 5.* Adjust cable housing as necessary to obtain specified distance.

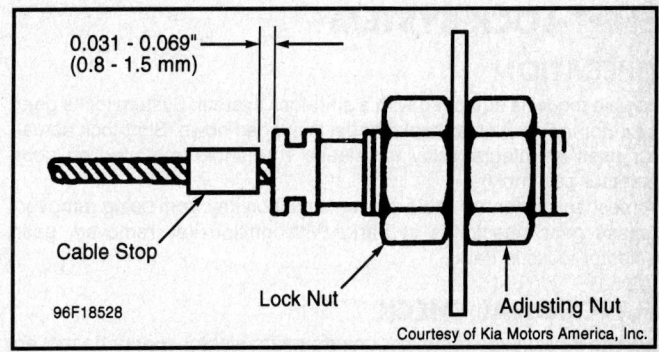

Fig. 5: Adjusting Throttle Valve (T.V.) Cable (Sportage)

TRANSMISSION RANGE SWITCH

Sephia – 1) Disconnect negative battery cable. Remove battery, air cleaner and battery tray. Disconnect shift selector cable. Rotate manual shaft to "N" position. Disconnect range switch connector. Loosen range switch mounting bolts at transmission.

2) Connect ohmmeter leads between switch terminals No. 5 and 7. *See Fig. 6.* Rotate switch until continuity exists. Tighten mounting bolts 71-97 INCH lbs. (8-11 N.m).

3) Reassemble in reverse order of disassembly. Vehicle should start only with gearshift in "P" or "N" position.

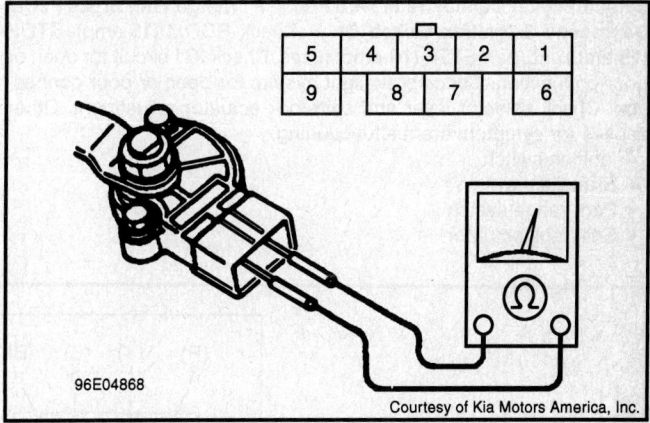

Fig. 6: Adjusting Transmission Range Switch (Sephia)

Sportage – Place gearshift lever in "N" position. Loosen transmission range switch attaching bolt. Align neutral base line groove on switch housing and groove on selector shaft. *See Fig. 7.* Tighten switch attaching bolt to 35-61 INCH lbs. (3.9-6.9 N.m). Ensure starter operates in "N" or "P" position.

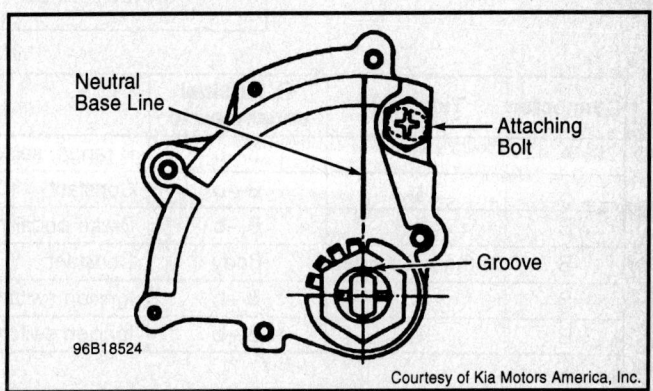

Fig. 7: Adjusting Transmission Range Switch (Sportage)

SHIFT-LOCK SYSTEM

OPERATION

Sephia model is equipped with a shift-lock system. System locks gear selector in Park unless brake pedal is pushed down. Shift-lock actuator uses an integral relay to release a solenoid (mounted on gear selector assembly).

A mechanical control cable prevents ignition key from being removed unless gear selector is in Park. With ignition key removed, gear selector locks in Park.

FUNCTIONAL CHECK

1) With ignition key removed, ensure gear selector connot be moved from Park. Insert key in ignition switch. Turn ignition on. Ensure gear selector can only be moved with brake pedal pressed down.

2) Ensure ignition key cannot be removed. Move gear selector to Park. Ensure it is now possible to remove ignition key. If shift-lock system does not operate as described, see TROUBLE SHOOTING.

3) Place gear selector in Park. Using a screwdriver, turn emergency override button on shifter console and verify gear selector can be moved from Park position. If gear selector cannot be moved out of Park, adjust or replace the shift-lock actuator. Shift-lock actuator is fixed. Adjust gearshift lever as needed. See GEARSHIFT LINKAGE under ADJUSTMENTS.

TROUBLE SHOOTING

Selector Lever Cannot Be Moved From "P" Range With Brake Pedal Depressed & Ignition Switch On – Check ROOM (15-amp), STOP (15-amp) and/or METER (15-amp) fuses. Check IG1 circuit for open or poor connection. Check brakelight system for open or poor connection. Check selector lever and shift-lock actuator adjustment. Other causes for symptom are malfunctioning;
- Ignition switch
- Brakelight switch
- Park range switch
- Shift lock actuator

Selector Lever Can Be Moved From "P" Range With Ignition Switch On, But Without Brake Pedal Depressed – Check ROOM (15-amp) fuse. Brakelight switch stays on. Check operation of shift-lock actuator. Check selector lever and shift-lock actuator adjustment.

Selector Lever Can Be Moved From "P" Range With Ignition Switch Off, & Brake Pedal Depressed – Check ROOM (15-amp) fuse. Inspect ignition switch operation. Check operation of shift-lock actuator. Check selector lever and shift-lock actuator adjustment.

Shift Lock Actuator Operation Difficult When Brake Pedal Is Depressed With Ignition Switch On & Selector Lever In Ranges Other Than "P" Range – Check if park range switch remains on. Check selector lever and shift-lock actuator adjustment.

Shifter Remains Locked When Emergency Override Button Is Operated – Ensure emergency override button is slid fully back. Check if emergency override button is broken. Indicator light panel is misadjusted.

Ignition Key Can Be Turned To LOCK Position With Selector Lever In Ranges Other Than "P" Range – Inspect interlock cable operation. Inspect key cylinder operation.

Ignition Key Can Be Turned To LOCK Position With Selector Lever In Ranges Other Than "P" Range – Inspect interlock cable operation. Inspect key cylinder operation.

TESTING

1) Disconnect negative battery cable. Remove gear selector console cover. Disconnect Park switch connector "A". *See Fig. 8.*

2) Place gear selector in Park. Continuity should be present between both Black wires. Depress gear selector release button and ensure continuity is not present. If Park switch works as described, go to next step. If Park switch does not work as described, replace Park switch.

3) Disconnect shift-lock actuator connector. Turn ignition on. Check terminal voltages and continuity. *See Fig. 8.* If not as specified, replace shift-lock actuator.

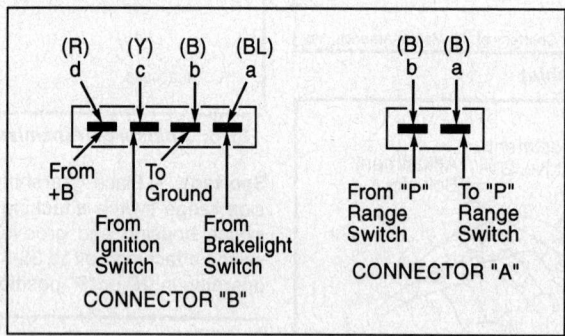

VB: Battery voltage

Connector	Terminal	⊖ terminal connected to	Condition	Measurement valve
A	a	B—b	P range, selector lever release button not depressed	0Ω
A	b	B—b	Constant	0Ω
B	a	B—b	Brake pedal released → depressed	0V → VB
B	b (harness side)	Body	Constant	0Ω
B	c	B—b	Ignition switch ON	VB
B	d	B—b	Ignition switch OFF	VB

96G04968

Courtesy of Mazda Motors Corp.

Fig. 8: Testing Shift Lock Actuator, Park Switch & Connectors

TORQUE SPECIFICATIONS

TORQUE SPECIFICATIONS

Application	Ft. Lbs.
Engine Crossmember	
Bolts	47-66 (64-89)
Nuts	28-38 (38-51)
Transfer Case Drain Plug	22 (30)
Transfer Case Side Mount Bolt/Nut	38 (51)
Wheel Lug Nuts	66-86 (89-117)
	INCH Lbs. (N.m)
Transmission Range Switch Mounting Bolt	
Sephia	71-97 (8-11)
Sportage	35-61 (3.9-6.9)
Pressure Port Plug	44-87 (5.0-9.8)
Transaxle Pan Bolt	71-97 (8-11)
Valve Body Bolt	71-97 (8-11)

WIRING DIAGRAMS

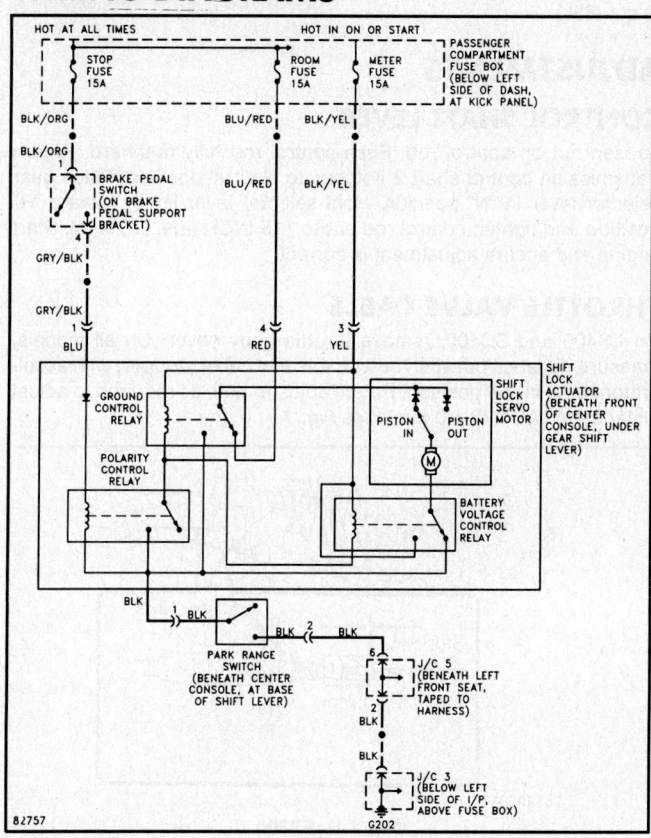

Fig. 9: Shift Interlock System Wiring Diagram (1995-96 Sephia)

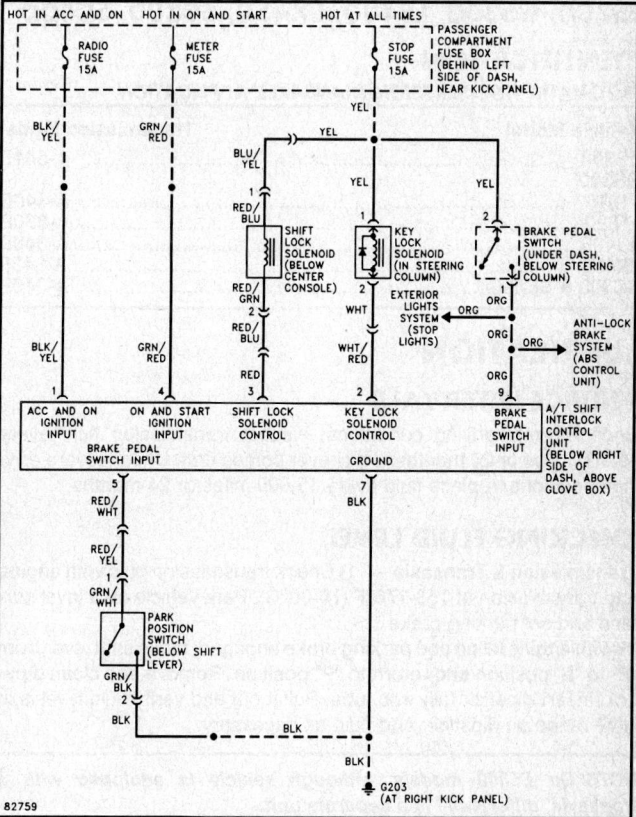

Fig. 10: Shift Interlock System Wiring Diagram (1995-96 Sportage)

ES300, GS300, LS400, LX450, SC300, SC400

IDENTIFICATION

AUTOMATIC TRANSMISSION/TRANSAXLE APPLICATION

Vehicle Model	Transmission Model
ES300	A-541E
GS300	
1995	A-340E
1996	A-350E
LS400	A-340E
LX450	A-343F
SC300 & SC400	A-340E

LUBRICATION

SERVICE INTERVALS

Under normal driving conditions, inspect transmission fluid every 15,000 miles or 24 months, whichever comes first. Under severe driving conditions, replace fluid every 15,000 miles or 24 months.

CHECKING FLUID LEVEL

Transmission & Transaxle – 1) Check transmission fluid with engine and transmission at 158-176°F (70-80°C). Park vehicle on a level surface and set parking brake.
2) With engine idling and parking brake engaged, move shift lever from "P" to "L" position and return to "P" position. Remove and clean dipstick. Insert dipstick fully into tube. Pull it out and verify fluid level is in HOT range on dipstick. Add fluid as necessary.

NOTE: On ES300 models, although vehicle is equipped with a transaxle, differential is a separate unit.

Differential (ES300) – Raise vehicle and check level with engine off. Remove 10-mm filler plug on front of differential housing. Add fluid until it runs out of filler hole or is at bottom edge of hole. Capacity is .9 qt. (.85L).

RECOMMENDED FLUID

ES300, LX450 and SC300 models use Dexron-II ATF. All other automatic transmissions use Lexus/Toyota Type T-II fluid.

FLUID CAPACITY

AUTOMATIC TRANSMISSION/TRANSAXLE REFILL CAPACITIES

Model	Qts. (L)
Dry Fill	
ES300 [1]	7.1 (6.7)
GS300	
1995	8.3 (7.9)
1996	8.0 (7.6)
LS400	8.8 (8.3)
LX450	12.4 (11.7)
SC300	7.6 (7.2)
SC400	8.7 (8.2)
Refill	
ES300 [1]	3.7 (3.5)
GS300, LS400, LX450 & SC400	2.0 (1.9)
SC300	1.7 (1.6)

[1] – DOES NOT include differential capacity. ES300 differential is filled separately. Differential capacity is .9 qt. (.85L). Use Dexron-II ATF.

DRAINING & REFILLING

CAUTION: On models equipped with air suspension, turn air suspension height control switch to OFF position BEFORE raising vehicle. If height control switch is in ON position when vehicle is raised, vehicle automatic height adjustment will operate, resulting in possible damage to vehicle. Air suspension height control switch is located inside tool storage on left side of trunk. When vehicle is lowered, air suspension HI indicator light will blink if height control is in OFF position.

NOTE: On ES300 models, although vehicle is equipped with a transaxle, differential is a separate unit.

Transmission – 1) On ES300, remove engine undercover. On all models, remove drain plug to drain fluid. If transmission oil filter is to be changed, remove oil pan. Remove oil filter and gasket.
2) Clean transmission oil pan and replace pan gasket. Install oil filter and gasket. Reinstall transmission oil pan. Tighten bolts. Install drain plug. With engine off, add new fluid through dipstick hole.
3) Start engine and shift gear selector into all positions. Shift gear selector back into "P" position. Check fluid level. Add fluid to bring level up to COOL mark on dipstick.
4) Recheck fluid level when engine and transmission reaches operating temperature of 158-176°F (70-80°C). Add fluid up to HOT mark. On ES300, install engine undercover.
Differential (ES300) – Raise vehicle and check level with engine off. Remove 10-mm filler plug on front of differential housing. Add fluid until it runs out of filler hole or is at bottom edge of hole. Capacity is .9 qt. (.85L).

ADJUSTMENTS

CONTROL SHAFT LEVER

Loosen nut on control rod. Push control rod fully rearward. Return transmission control shaft 2 notches to Neutral position. Place gear selector lever in "N" position. Hold selector lever lightly toward "R" position and tighten control rod nut to 115 INCH Lbs. (13 N.m). Start engine and ensure adjustment is correct.

THROTTLE VALVE CABLE

On LS400 and SC400, remove throttle body cover. On all models, measure distance between outer cable and cable stopper, with accelerator pedal in idle position. Rotate adjuster nuts as required to adjust distance to 0-.04" (0-1.0 mm). *See Fig. 1.*

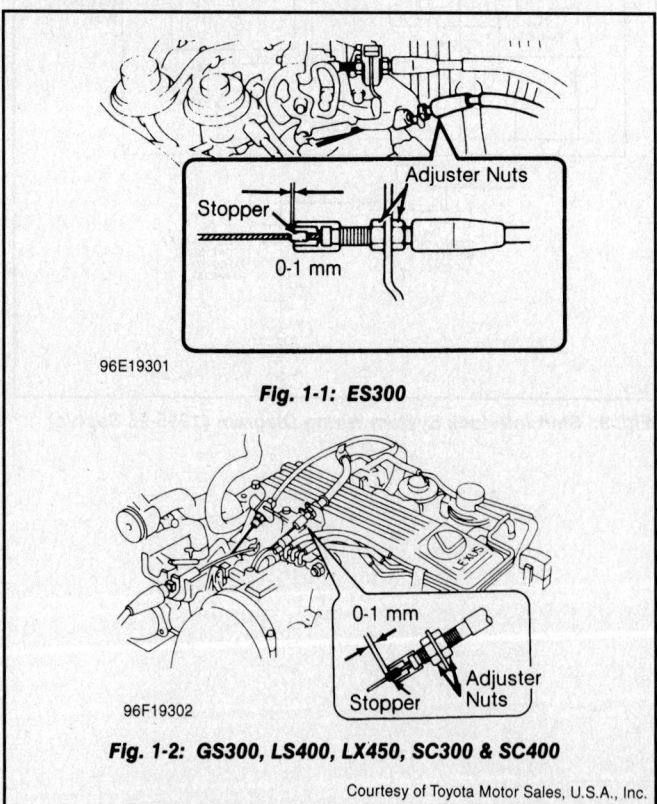

96E19301

Fig. 1-1: ES300

96F19302

Fig. 1-2: GS300, LS400, LX450, SC300 & SC400

Courtesy of Toyota Motor Sales, U.S.A., Inc.

Fig. 1: Adjusting Throttle Cable

SHIFT CABLE

ES300 – Loosen swivel nut on transaxle shift lever linkage under vehicle. Rotate shift lever on transaxle fully toward right side of vehicle. Return lever 2 notches to Neutral position. Set in-car gear selector to "N" position. With gear selector in "N" position, lightly hold lever toward "R" position. Tighten swivel nut on transaxle lever.

GS300, LS400, SC300 & SC400 – Loosen swivel nut on transmission shift lever linkage under vehicle. Rotate shift lever on transmission fully to rear. Return lever 2 notches to Neutral position. Set in-car gear selector to "N" position. With gear selector in "N" position, lightly hold lever toward "R" position and tighten swivel nut on transmission lever.

PARK/NEUTRAL POSITION (PNP) SWITCH

If vehicle starts in positions other than Neutral and Park, adjust PNP switch. Loosen park/neutral position switch bolt and set shift lever to "N" position. Align groove and neutral base line on park/neutral position switch. *See Fig. 2.* Hold switch in position and tighten bolt to 48 INCH lbs. (5.4 N.m) on ES300 and LS400, 106 INCH lbs. (12 N.m) on GS300 and SC400, or 115 INCH lbs. (13 N.m) on all other models.

TORQUE SPECIFICATIONS

NOTE: Torque specifications for all service items are not available.

TORQUE SPECIFICATIONS

Application	Ft. Lbs. (N.m)
GS300, LX450 & SC300	
Drain Plug	15 (20)
	INCH Lbs. (N.m)
ES300	
Drain Plug	43 (4.9)
Filter	97 (11)
GS300, LS400, LX450, SC300 & SC400	
Filter	89 (10)
Oil Pan	65 (7.4)

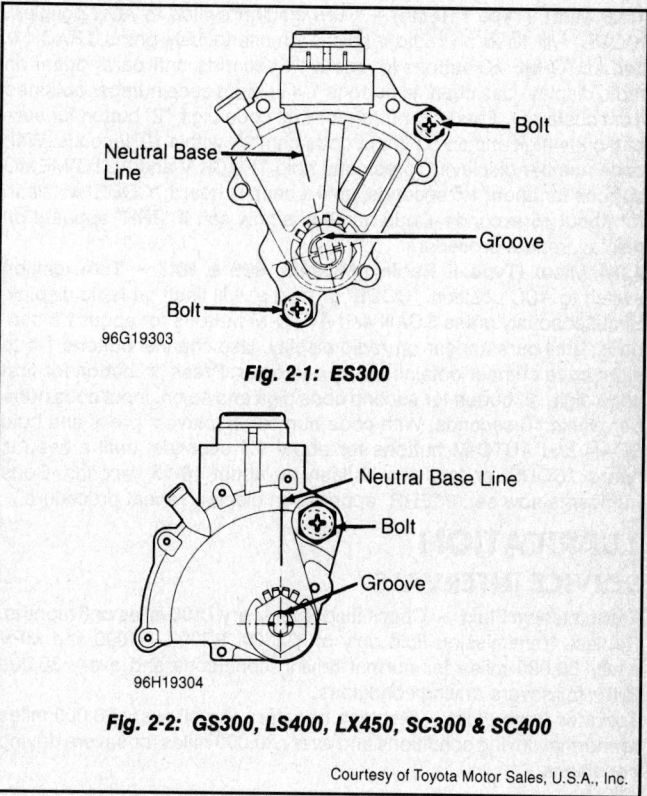

Neutral Base Line — Bolt — Groove — Bolt

96G19303

Fig. 2-1: ES300

Neutral Base Line — Bolt — Groove

96H19304

Fig. 2-2: GS300, LS400, LX450, SC300 & SC400

Courtesy of Toyota Motor Sales, U.S.A., Inc.

Fig. 2: Adjusting Park/Neutral Position Switch

Mazda

B2300, B3000, B4000 Miata, Millenia, MPV, MX-3, MX-6, Protege, RX7, 626, 929

CAUTION: Disconnecting battery on models equipped with anti-theft radio require cancelling of anti-theft operation. See CANCELLING ANTI-THEFT RADIO OPERATION.

APPLICATION

TRANSMISSION APPLICATION

Vehicle Application	Transmission Model
B2300 & B3000	4R44E
B4000	4R55E
Miata	NC4A-EL
Millenia	
2.3L	LJ4A-EL
2.5L	GF4A-EL
MPV	
2WD	RA4A-EL
4WD	RA4AX-EL
MX-3 & Protege	FA4A-EL
MX-6 & 626	
2.0L	LA4A-EL
2.5L	GF4A-EL
RX7	RB4A-EL
929	RA4A-EL

TRANSFER CASE APPLICATIONS

Model	Transfer Case
B2300, B3000 & B4000	BW13-54
MPV 4WD	RA4AX-EL

CANCELLING ANTI-THEFT RADIO OPERATION

On models with anti-theft radio system, obtain code number from customer to deactivate radio anti-theft system. Anti-theft system is activated if battery is disconnected, looses significant voltage or radio is disconnected.

1995 Miata – Turn ignition switch to ACC position. Press FF and REW buttons simultaneously until "cod e" is displayed on radio. Press FF and REW buttons again until 4 bars are displayed. Use channel buttons 1-4 to input code number obtained from customer. Press "1" button for first code digit, "2" button for second code digit and so on. Input code number within 10 seconds. Press FF and REW buttons for about 2 seconds until a beep is heard. After 5 seconds, flashing "cod e" will go away and radio will operate. If "ERR" appears on display, repeat procedure. If input errors occur 3 times, turn ignition to LOCK position and repeat procedure.

NOTE: Three consecutive programming errors, including turning off ignition switch and disconnecting radio will lock-out radio unit and render it completely inoperative, requiring repair by manufacturer.

1996 Miata (Type I Radio) – Turn ignition switch to ACC position. "CODE" will flash on radio display. Simultaneously press TRACK V and AUTO-MEMO buttons for about 1.5 seconds, until bars appear on radio display. Use channel buttons 1-4 to input code number obtained from customer. Press "1" button for first code digit, "2" button for second code digit and so on. Input code number within 10 seconds. With code number displayed, press and hold TRACK V and AUTO-MEMO buttons for about 1.5 seconds, until a beep is heard. "CODE" will flash for about 15 seconds. Code number is now set. If "ERR" appears on display, repeat procedure.

1996 Miata (Type II Radio), Millenia, 929 & RX7 – Turn ignition switch to ACC position. "CODE" or "cod e" will flash on radio display. Simultaneously press SCAN and AUTO-M buttons for about 1.5 seconds, until bars appear on radio display. Use channel buttons 1-4 to input code number obtained from customer. Press "1" button for first code digit, "2" button for second code digit and so on. Input code number within 10 seconds. With code number displayed, press and hold SCAN and AUTO-M buttons for about 1.5 seconds, until a beep is heard. "CODE" or "cod e" will flash for about 10-15 seconds. Code number is now set. If "ERR" appears on display, repeat procedure.

LUBRICATION

SERVICE INTERVALS

Transmission Fluid – Check fluid level every 7500 miles or 6 months. Replace transmission fluid only on B2300, B3000, B4000 and MPV every 60,000 miles for normal driving conditions and every 30,000 miles for severe driving conditions.

Transfer Case Fluid – Replace transfer case oil every 60,000 miles for normal driving conditions and every 30,000 miles for severe driving conditions.

CHECKING FLUID LEVEL

Transmission – Park vehicle on level ground. Apply parking brake. Warm engine to normal operating temperature. Briefly place selector lever in all gears and return it to "P" position. Clean dipstick and insert it in tube. Remove dipstick. Level should be between marks in HOT (65°C) range. On MX-6 and 626 fluid level should be in cross-hatch area of dipstick. Check fluid for discoloration and unusual smell. If necessary, add fluid. DO NOT overfill.

Transfer Case (B2300, B3000 & B4000) – Remove oil fill plug. If fluid drains out or is level with opening, install fill plug. If fluid is low, fill until fluid is level with fill plug opening. Install plug.

Transfer Case (MPV 4WD) – Remove level (lower) plug. If fluid drains out or is level with opening, install plug. If fluid is low, remove fill plug above and left of level plug opening. Fill until fluid is level with lower plug opening. Install plugs.

RECOMMENDED FLUID

Transmission – For B2300, B3000, B4000, MX-6 (2.0L) and 626 (2.0L), use Mercon ATF. For all other models, use Dexron-II or M-III ATF.

Transfer Case (MPV 4WD) – More than 50°F (10°C), use SAE 80W-90; less than 50°F (10°C), use SAE 75W-90.

Transfer Case (B2300, B3000 & B4000) – Use Mercon ATF.

FLUID CAPACITIES

TRANSMISSION REFILL CAPACITIES

Application	Refill Qts. (L)	Dry Fill Qts. (L)
B2300, B3000, B4000	N/A	10.0 (9.5)
Miata	4.2 (4.0)	7.7 (7.3)
Millenia		
2.3L	N/A	7.9 (7.5)
2.5L	N/A	7.8 (7.4)
MPV	4.2 (4.0)	9.1 (8.6)
MX-3	N/A	5.8 (6.1)
MX-6 & 626		
2.0	N/A	8.8 (8.3)
2.5	N/A	9.3 (8.8)
Protege	N/A	5.2 (4.9)
RX7 & 929	4.2 (4.0)	9.1 (8.6)

TRANSFER CASE REFILL CAPACITIES

Application	Refill Qts. (L)
B2300, B3000 & B4000	1.3 (1.2)
MPV 4WD	1.6 (1.5)

DRAINING & REFILLING

B2300, B3000, B4000, Miata, MPV, RX7 & 929 – Disconnect negative battery cable. Loosen oil pan bolts to drain fluid. Remove oil pan, and discard old gasket. Clean oil pan, and install it using NEW gasket. Tighten oil pan bolts to specification. See TORQUE SPECIFICATIONS. Connect negative battery cable. Add fluid, and check level. DO NOT overfill.

Millenia, MX-3, MX-6, Protege & 626 – Remove drain plug from oil pan or case (as applicable). If oil pan is removed, discard old oil pan gasket. Clean oil pan, and install with NEW gasket. Tighten bolts to specification. See TORQUE SPECIFICATIONS. Add fluid, and check level. DO NOT overfill.

ADJUSTMENTS

NOTE: Adjustment information for MX-6 and 626 with 2.0L engine is not available from manufacturer.

BRAKE BAND (2ND GEAR)

Miata – 1) Disconnect negative battery cable. Loosen oil pan, and drain fluid. Remove bracket, oil pan and gasket. Disconnect vacuum hose at vacuum diaphragm (modulator), and remove vacuum diaphragm.

2) Disconnect solenoid valve connector, and remove harness from bracket (if equipped). Remove valve body bolts and valve body assembly. Loosen lock nut on 2nd gear brake band while holding piston stem stationary. See Fig. 1.

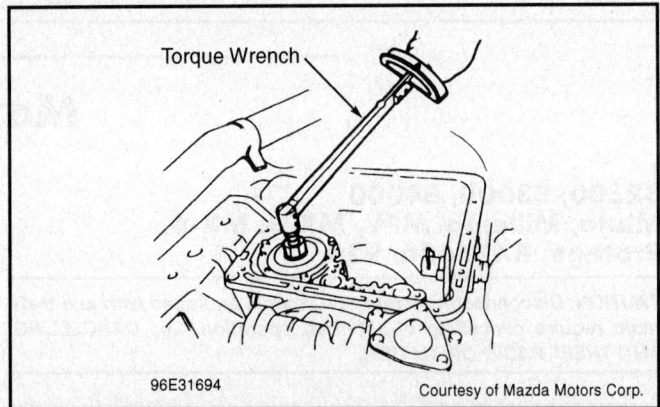

Torque Wrench

96E31694   Courtesy of Mazda Motors Corp.

Fig. 1: Adjusting 2nd Gear Brake Band (Miata)

3) Tighten piston stem to 106-130 INCH lbs. (12-15 N.m). Loosen piston stem 2 1/2 turns. Tighten lock nut to 11-29 ft. lbs. (15-39 N.m) while holding stem stationary. Install valve body assembly. Tighten bolts to specification. See TORQUE SPECIFICATIONS.

4) Connect solenoid valve connector, and install harness. Clean oil pan, and install it using NEW pan gasket. Tighten pan bolts to specification. See TORQUE SPECIFICATIONS. Install vacuum diaphragm, and connect vacuum hose. Connect negative battery cable. Add fluid, and check level. DO NOT overfill.

MPV, RX7 & 929 – Loosen lock nut on band adjusting bolt. See Fig. 2. Tighten bolt to 35-53 INCH lbs (4-6 N.m). Loosen band adjusting bolt 2 1/2 turns. Tighten lock nut to 24-31 ft. lbs. (32-42 N.m).

2-4 BRAKE BAND

MX-3, Protege & 323 – 1) Support engine. Raise and support vehicle. Remove drain plug, and drain transaxle. Remove engine mounting member. Remove oil pan, gasket and valve body assembly. Remove snap ring and 2-4 band servo assembly. See Fig. 3.

2) Install servo piston onto adapter. See 2-4 BAND ADJUSTMENT ADAPTER (MX-3, PROTEGE & 323) table. Remove "O" ring from servo retainer. Coat "O" ring with ATF, and install ring onto adapter. Install 2-4 band servo assembly into transaxle case and secure it using snap ring. Position dial indicator against piston stem. See Fig. 3.

2-4 BAND ADJUSTMENT ADAPTER (MX-3 & PROTEGE)

Application	Adapter No.
MX-3	49-B019-004
Protege	49-B019-004

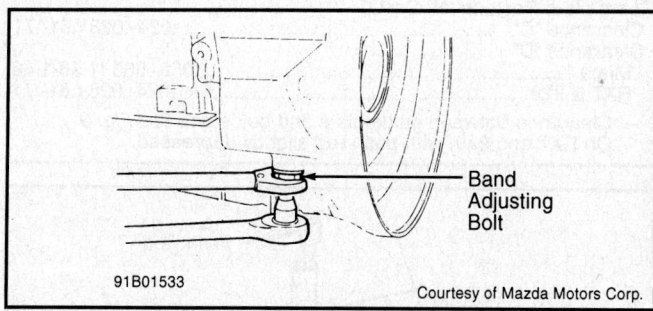

Fig. 2: Adjusting Brake Band (MPV, RX7 & 929)

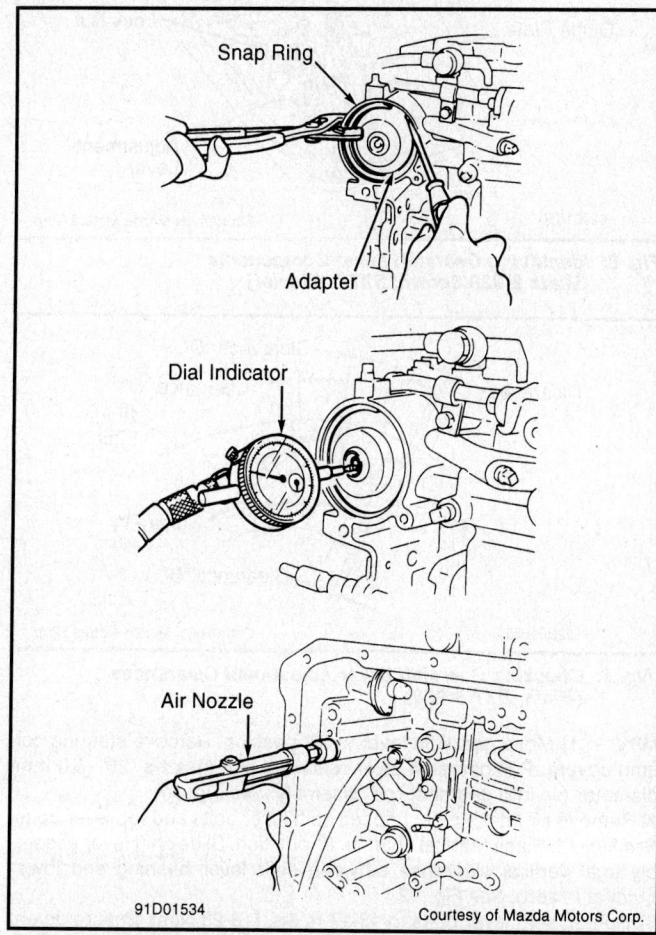

Fig. 3: Adjusting 2-4 Brake Band (MX-3 & Protege)

3) Using a rubber-tipped air nozzle, apply compressed air through fluid passage and measure piston stem stroke. See Fig. 3. Piston stem stroke should be .040-.067" (1.00-1.70 mm) at 57 psi (4.0 kg/cm²). If piston stem stroke is not as specified, replace piston stem.
4) Nine different length piston stems are available in .02" (.5 mm) increments ranging from 3.74" (95.0 mm) to 3.90" (99.1 mm). Remove 2-4 band servo assembly and adapter. Install servo retainer using NEW "O" ring.

5) Install valve body assembly. Tighten bolts to specification. Install oil pan with NEW gasket. Tighten bolts to specification. See TORQUE SPECIFICATIONS. Install engine mounting member. Lower vehicle. Add fluid, and check level. DO NOT overfill.
MX-6 & 626 – **1)** Remove drain plug, and drain transaxle. Remove oil pan and gasket. Loosen lock nut, and tighten piston stem to 78-95 INCH lbs. (9-11 N.m). See Fig. 4. Loosen piston stem 2 turns.
2) Hold piston stem and tighten lock nut to 18-29 ft. lbs. (24-39 N.m). Install oil pan using NEW gasket. Tighten oil pan bolts to specification. See TORQUE SPECIFICATIONS. Add fluid, and check level. DO NOT overfill.

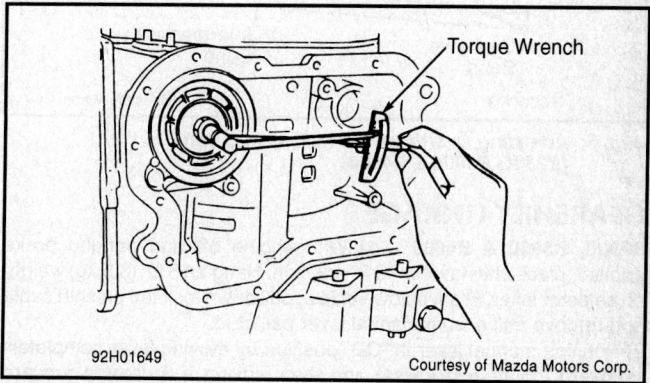

Fig. 4: Adjusting 2-4 Brake Band (Millenia, MX-6 & 626)

4TH GEAR BRAKE BAND

NOTE: Overdrive brake band is not adjustable on B2600i 4WD, MPV 3.0L, RX7 and 929.

Miata – **1)** Remove overdrive band servo cover and gasket. See Fig. 5. Loosen overdrive adjustment screw lock nut while holding piston stem stationary. Tighten piston stem to 106-130 INCH lbs. (12-15 N.m).
2) Back off piston stem 2 turns. While holding stem in this position, tighten lock nut to 11-30 ft. lbs. (15-40 N.m). Install overdrive band servo cover with NEW gasket. Tighten cover bolts to 44-62 INCH lbs. (5-7 N.m).

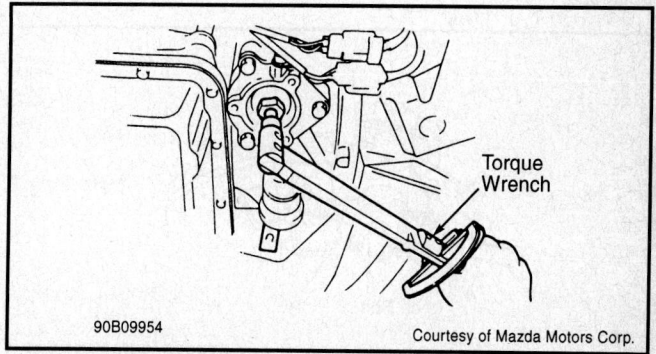

Fig. 5: Adjusting 4th Gear Brake Band (Miata)

NOTE: B2300, B3000 & B4000 overdrive band adjustment procedure can also be used for intermediate band adjustment. See Fig. 6.

B2300, B3000 & B4000 – Clean dirt from band adjusting screw area. Remove and discard adjusting screw lock nut. Install NEW lock nut. Tighten adjusting screw to 120 INCH lbs. (14 N.m). See Fig. 6. Back off adjusting screw 2 turns. Hold adjusting screw in position and tighten lock nut to 35-45 ft. lbs. (48-61 N.m).

INTERMEDIATE BAND

B2300, B3000 & B4000 – See OVERDRIVE BRAKE BAND.

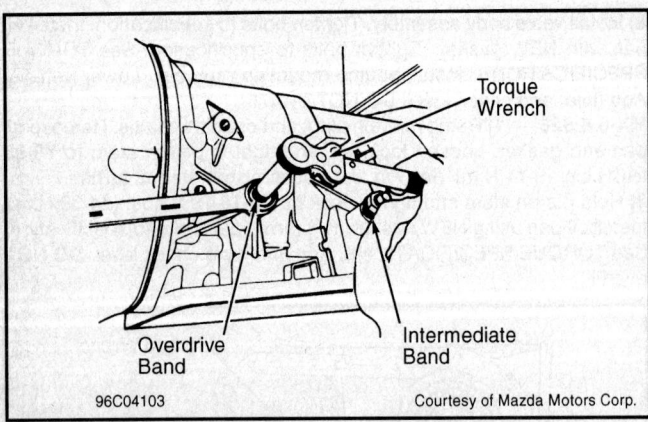

**Fig. 6: Adjusting Overdrive Or Intermediate Band
(B2300, B3000 & B4000)**

GEARSHIFT LINKAGE

B2300, B3000 & B4000 – 1) With engine off and parking brake applied, place shift lever in "OD" position. Hang an 8 lb. (3.6 kg) weight on selector lever. From below vehicle, pull down lock tab on shift cable and remove fitting from manual lever ball stud.

2) Position manual lever in "OD" position by moving lever completely rearward (counterclockwise) and then moving it 3 detents forward (clockwise). Connect cable end fitting to manual lever.

3) Push up on lock tab to lock cable in adjusted position. Remove weight from selector lever. Move lever through all positions, ensuring transmission is at full detent in each position.

MX-6 & 626 – 1) Remove center console. Loosen lock bolt and lock nuts "A" and "B" on gearshift assembly. See Fig. 7. Move gearshift lever to "P" position. Ensure transaxle lever is in "P" position. Tighten lock bolt to 71-97 INCH lbs. (8-11 N.m).

2) Turn lock nut "A" by hand until lock nut "A" touches spacer lightly. Tighten lock nut "B" to 71-97 INCH lbs. (8-11 N.m). Ensure a click is heard in each range when shifting from "P" through "L" positions. Ensure starter will only operate in "P" and "N" positions.

3) Ensure position of gearshift lever and indicator correspond with each other. Ensure lock button returns after it has been depressed. Ensure gearshift lever operates smoothly when engaged in all positions.

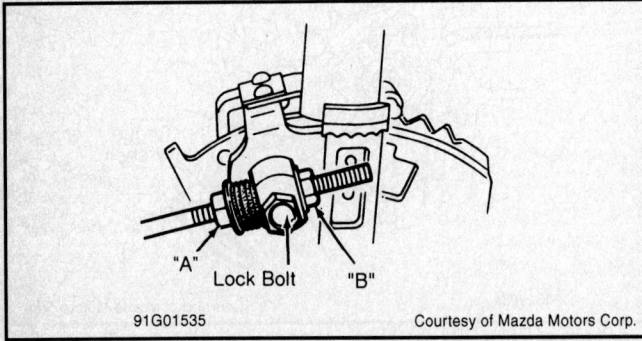

Fig. 7: Adjusting Gearshift Linkage (MX-6 & 626)

Miata, RX7 & 929 – 1) Disconnect negative battery cable. On Miata, remove upper panel, selector sleeve and indicator panel. On RX7 and 929, remove center console. On all models, remove boot plate. Place gearshift lever in "P" position. Loosen lock nut on side of gearshift lever. See Fig. 8. Move adjustment lever forward to set transmission in "P" position.

2) Adjust lever so clearance between guide plate and guide pin with lever in position "P" is as specified. See GEARSHIFT LEVER ADJUSTMENT SPECIFICATIONS (MIATA, RX7 & 929) table. See Fig. 9. Tighten rear lock nut to 14-21 ft. lbs. (19-28 N.m).

3) Place gearshift lever in "N" and "D" positions to ensure clearances are correct. See GEARSHIFT LEVER ADJUSTMENT SPECIFICATIONS (MIATA, RX7 & 929) table. See Fig. 9. Adjust lever if necessary. Install boot plate, center console, indicator panel, selector sleeve, selector knob and upper panel. Connect negative battery cable.

GEARSHIFT LEVER ADJUSTMENT SPECIFICATIONS (MIATA, RX7 & 929)

Application	[1] In. (mm)
Gearshift In Position "P"	
Clearance "A" [2]	.035-.039 (.89-.99)
Clearance "B" [2]	.020-.024 (.51-.61)
Gearshift In Position "N" Or "D"	
Clearance "C"	.024-.028 (.61-.71)
Clearance "D"	
Miata	.059-.063 (1.50-1.60)
RX7 & 929	.024-.028 (.61-.71)

[1] – Clearance between guide plate and guide pin. See Fig. 9.
[2] – On RX7 and 929, with push rod slightly depressed.

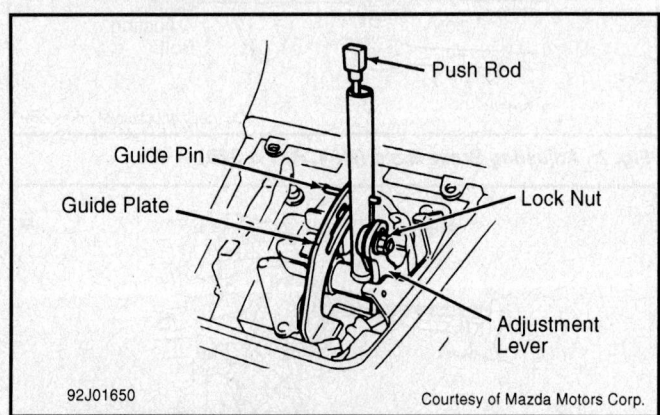

**Fig. 8: Identifying Gearshift Lever Components
(Miata & 929 Shown; RX7 Is Similar)**

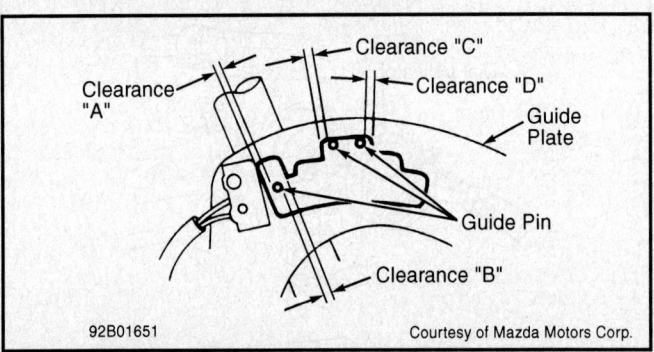

**Fig. 9: Checking Gearshift Lever Adjustment Clearances
(Miata, RX7 & 929)**

MPV – 1) Move gearshift lever to "P" position. Remove steering column covers. Pull gearshift lever rearward and insert a .20" (5.0 mm) diameter pin into gearshift rod assembly. See Fig. 10.

2) Remove air intake pipe. Loosen shift lever bolts and top lever bolts. See Fig. 11. Place manual shaft in "P" position. Slide shift lever assembly until vertical clearance between shift lever bushing and lower bracket is zero. See Fig. 12.

3) Tighten shift lever bolts to 12-17 ft. lbs. (16-23 N.m). Ensure detent ball is in center of "P" range detent. See Fig. 13. Loosen detent mounting bolts and rotate bracket to adjust detent ball placement. Tighten detent mounting bolts to 61-87 INCH lbs. (7-10 N.m).

4) Rotate top lever until horizontal clearance between rear of shift lever bushing and lower bracket is zero. See Fig. 12. Tighten top lever bolts to 12-17 ft. lbs. (16-23 N.m). Remove pin from gear shift assembly. Install column covers. Check gearshift selector lever operation.

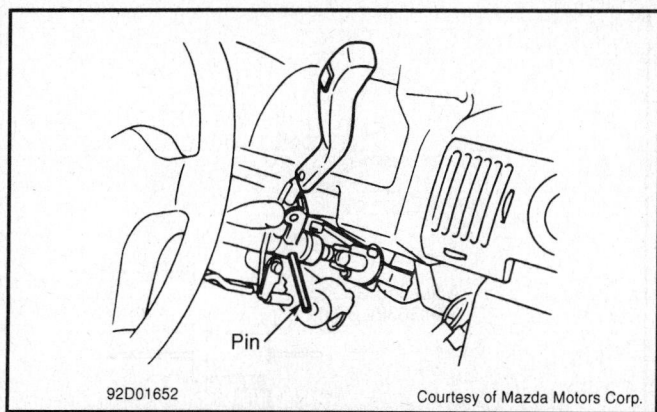

Fig. 10: Inserting Pin In Gearshift Rod Assembly (MPV)

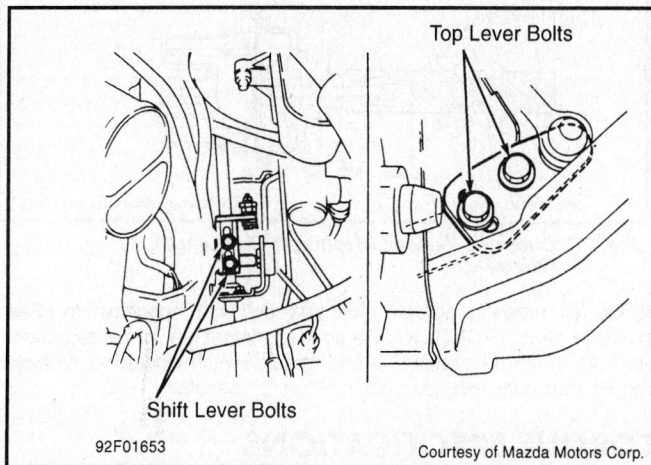

Fig. 11: Identifying Shift Lever Bolts & Top Lever Bolts (MPV)

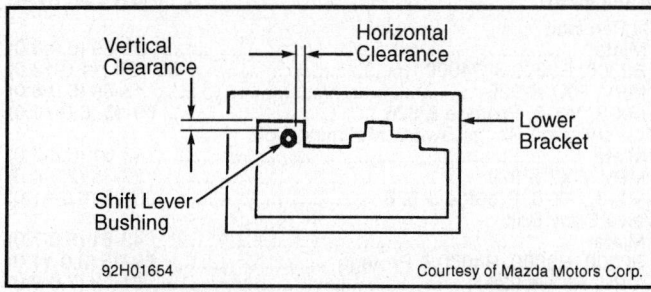

Fig. 12: Adjusting Shift Lever Bushing-To-Lower Bracket Clearances (MPV)

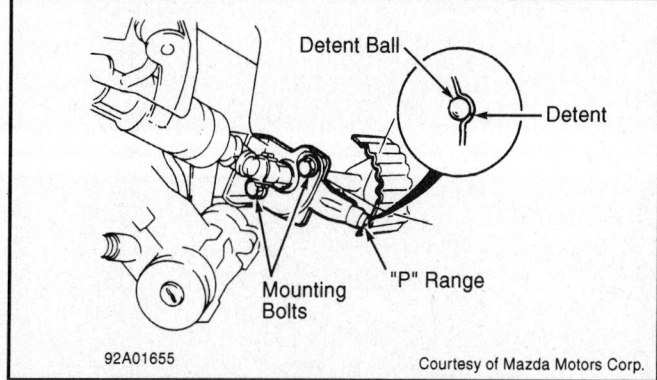

Fig. 13: Adjusting Shift Lever Detent Ball (MPV)

MX-3, Protege & 323 – 1) Remove center console. Place gearshift lever in "P" position. Loosen selector cable mounting bolts. *See Fig. 14*. Push selector lever against "P" range; hold it in this position.
2) Tighten selector cable mounting bolts. Ensure starter operates in "P" and "N" positions only. Ensure position of gearshift lever and indicator correspond with each other.
3) Ensure lock button returns after it has been depressed. Ensure gearshift lever operates smoothly when engaged in all positions. Install center console.

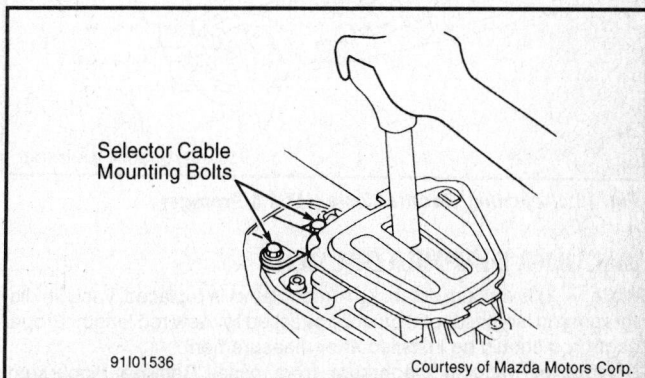

Fig. 14: Adjusting Gearshift Position (MX-3 & Protege)

THROTTLE CABLE

NOTE: Oil pressure gauge is needed to properly adjust throttle cable.

MX-3, MX-6, Protege & 626 – 1) Remove left splash shield, near left front tire. Remove lower pressure port plug. Install oil pressure gauge to port. *See Fig. 15*.

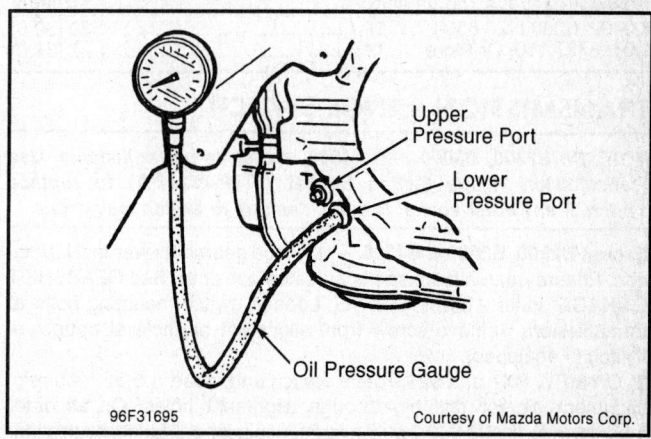

Fig. 15: Checking Throttle Pressure (MX-3 & Protege)

2) Move gearshift lever to "P" position. Start engine, and warm it to normal operating temperature. Ensure engine is at normal idle speed. Check throttle pressure. See THROTTLE PRESSURE SPECIFICATIONS table. If pressure is not within specification, adjust throttle cable.

THROTTLE PRESSURE SPECIFICATIONS

Application	psi (kg/cm²)
MX-3 & Protege	73-75 (5.1-5.3)

3) With engine running, loosen adjustment bolt/nut. Adjust throttle cable until pressure reading is within specification. *See Fig. 16*.
4) Tighten throttle cable adjustment bolt/nut when pressure is within specification. Turn engine off. Remove oil pressure gauge. Install pressure port plug, and tighten it to 44-89 INCH lbs. (5-10 N.m). Install left splash shield.

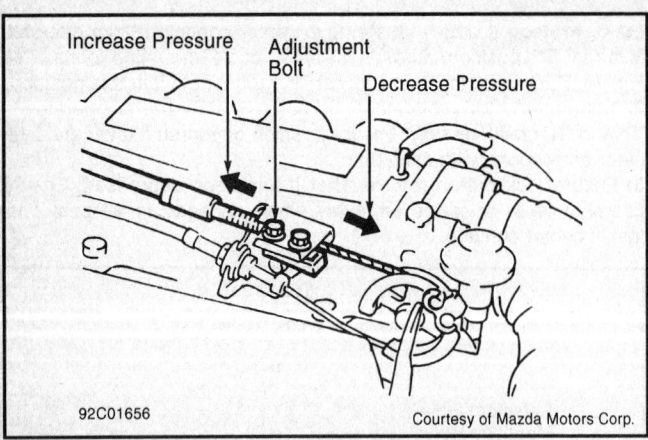

Fig. 16: Adjusting Throttle Cable (MX-3 & Protege)

VACUUM DIAPHRAGM ROD

Miata – 1) If vacuum diaphragm (modulator) is replaced, vacuum diaphragm rod length (depth) must be checked for new rod length. Proper length rod should be installed after measurement.

2) Unscrew vacuum diaphragm from case. Remove diaphragm, diaphragm rod and rubber "O" ring. Measure dimension "N" using Adjusting Gauge (49-G032-355). See Fig. 17. Use VACUUM DIAPHRAGM ROD SELECTION table to select proper length rod.

VACUUM DIAPHRAGM ROD SELECTION

Dimension "N" In. (mm)	Rod Length In. (mm)
1.0099 (25.650) Or Less	1.14 (29.0)
1.0099-1.0197 (25.650-25.900)	1.16 (29.5)
1.0197-1.0394 (25.900-26.400)	1.17 (29.7)
1.0394-1.0492 (26.400-26.650)	1.18 (30.0)
1.0492-1.0689 (26.650-27.150)	1.20 (30.5)
1.0689 (27.150) Or More	1.22 (31.0)

TRANSMISSION RANGE SWITCH

NOTE: On B2300, B3000 and B4000, switch is not adjustable. Use Transmission Range Switch Socket (T74P-77247-A) to replace switch. If any other socket is used, damage to switch may occur.

Except B2300, B3000 & B4000 – 1) Place gearshift lever in "N" position. Ensure gearshift linkage is adjusted correctly. See GEARSHIFT LINKAGE under ADJUSTMENTS. Loosen switch mounting bolts at transmission. Remove screw from alignment pin hole at bottom of switch (if equipped).

2) On MPV, RX7 and 929, rotate switch and insert a 5/32" (4.0 mm) alignment pin (or drill bit) through alignment holes. On all other models, insert a 5/64" (2.0 mm) alignment pin (or drill bit) through alignment holes.

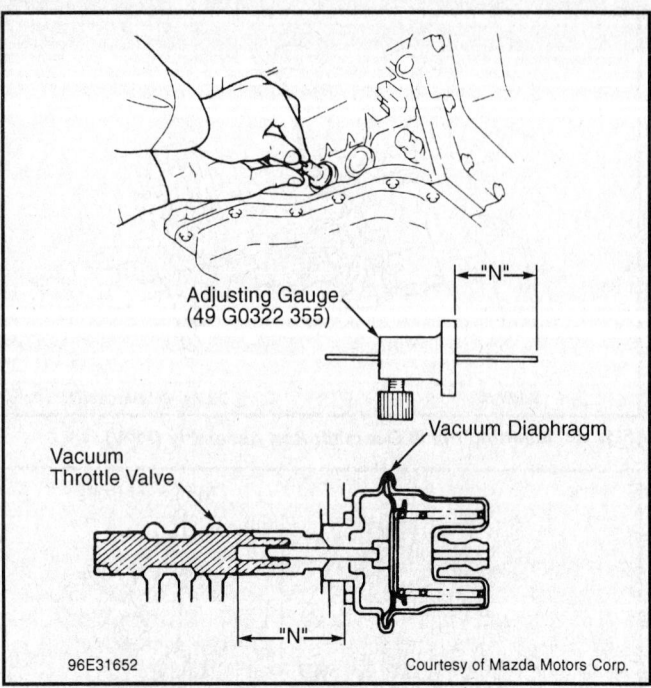

Fig. 17: Checking Vacuum Diaphragm Rod Length (Miata)

3) On all models, tighten mounting bolts to specification. See TORQUE SPECIFICATIONS. Remove alignment pin. Install alignment pin hole screw (if equipped), and check switch operation. Vehicle should start only with gearshift in "P" or "N" position.

TORQUE SPECIFICATIONS

TORQUE SPECIFICATIONS

Application	INCH Lbs. (N.m)
Oil Pan Bolt	
Miata	52-69 (6.0-8.0)
B2300, B3000 & B4000	95-120 (11.0-13.0)
MPV, RX7 & 929	43-69 (5.0-8.0)
MX-3, MX-6, Protege & 626	69-95 (8.0-11.0)
Transmission Range Switch Mounting Bolt	
Miata	43-61 (5.0-7.0)
MPV, RX7 & 929	22-35 (2.5-4.0)
MX-3, MX-6, Protege & 626	69-95 (8.0-11.0)
Valve Body Bolt	
Miata	43-61 (5.0-7.0)
B2300, B3000, B4000 & Protege	69-95 (8.0-11.0)
MPV, RX7 & 929	61-78 (7.0-9.0)
MX-6 & 626	95-130 (11.0-15.0)

1995
C220, C280, C36, E300D, E320, E420, S320, S350D, S420, S500, S600, SL320, SL500, SL600

1996
C220, C280, C36, E300D, E320, S320, S420, S500, S600, SL320, SL500, SL600

IDENTIFICATION
AUTOMATIC TRANSMISSION APPLICATIONS

Model	Body	Transmission
1995		
C220 2.2L	202.022	722.423
C280 2.8L	202.028	722.424
C36 3.6L	202.028	722.424
E300D 3.0L	124.131	722.435
E320 3.2L		
Cabriolet	124.066	722.369
Coupe	124.052	722.369
Sedan	124.032	722.369
Wagon	124.092	722.369
E420 4.2L	124.034	722.366
S320 3.2L		
Short Wheelbase	140.032	722.508
Long Wheelbase	140.033	722.508
S350D 3.5L	140.134	722.367
S420 4.2L	140.043	722.366
S500 5.0L		
Coupe	140.070	722.370
Sedan	140.051	722.370
S600 6.0L		
Coupe	140.076	722.362
Sedan	140.057	722.362
SL320 3.2L	129.063	722.507
SL500 5.0L	129.067	722.364
SL600 6.0L	129.076	722.362
1996		
C220 2.2L	202.022	722.423
C280 2.8L	202.028	722.424
C36 3.6L	202.028	722.424
E300D 3.0L	210.020	722.438
E320 3.2L	210.055	722.329
S320 3.2L		
Short Wheelbase	140.032	722.508
Long Wheelbase	140.033	722.508
S420 4.2L	140.043	722.622
S500 5.0L		
Coupe	140.070	722.620
Sedan	140.051	722.620
S600 6.0L		
Coupe	140.076	722.621
Sedan	140.057	722.621
SL320 3.2L	129.063	722.507
SL500 5.0L	129.067	722.620
SL600 6.0L	129.076	722.621

LUBRICATION

NOTE: On 1996 S420, S500, S600, SL500 & SL600 models, transmission fluid is not changed at regular intervals. Transmission is filled with lifetime transmission fluid. If transmission is leaking, repair leak and refill.

SERVICE INTERVALS

Check fluid level at first 800-1000 miles and every 15,000 miles afterward. Change fluid and filter every 30,000 miles. Under severe service conditions, change fluid every 15,000 miles.

CHECKING FLUID LEVEL

With transmission fluid at normal operating temperature of 176°F (80°C), park vehicle on level surface. Place selector lever in the "P" position and set parking brake. Allow engine to idle for 2 minutes. Measure fluid level with dipstick completely inserted and locking lever released.

RECOMMENDED FLUID

Use Dexron-II ATF.

FLUID CAPACITIES
TRANSMISSION REFILL CAPACITIES

Application	Refill Qts. (L)	Dry Fill Qts. (L)
1995		
C220 & C280	5.8 (5.5)	7.0 (6.6)
C36, E320 & S350D	6.6 (6.2)	7.7 (7.3)
E420, S420, S500, S600 SL500 & SL600	8.1 (7.7)	9.1 (8.6)
E300D, S320 & SL320	6.3 (6.0)	7.5 (7.1)
1996		
C220 & C280	5.8 (5.5)	7.0 (6.6)
E300D, S320 & SL320	6.3 (6.0)	7.5 (7.1)
C36, E320 & S320	6.6 (6.2)	7.7 (7.3)
S420, S500, S600, SL500 & SL600	[1]	9.9 (9.4)

[1] - Regular fluid changes are not required.

DRAINING & REFILLING

1) Disconnect filler tube from oil pan, and drain fluid. Rotate engine until torque converter drain plug is at bottom of torque converter housing. Remove plug and drain fluid. Install plug, using a new sealing ring. Remove oil pan and filter.

2) Install filter and oil pan, using a NEW gasket. Attach fill tube, using NEW sealing rings on hollow screw. Add about 3.2 qts. (3L) of automatic transmission fluid.

3) Apply parking brake and start engine. Place selector lever in the "P" position. Run engine at idle and gradually add fluid. Momentarily place selector lever in each gear, and then return to "P" position. Check fluid level and add if necessary. DO NOT overfill.

ADJUSTMENTS

NOTE: Adjustment information for 722.6 series transmission is not available.

SHIFT LINKAGE

All Models (Except 1996 E300D & E320) – Before adjusting shift linkage, ensure neutral safety switch is properly adjusted. See NEUTRAL SAFETY SWITCH. To adjust shift linkage, disconnect control rod from gear selector lever. Place transmission lever in "N" position. Loosen lock nut at end of control rod. Adjust rod length so clearance is .04" (1 mm) between gear selector lever and "N" position stop on gate plate. Connect control rod, and secure and tighten lock nut. See Fig. 1.

1996 E300D & E320 – Before adjusting shift linkage, ensure neutral safety switch is properly adjusted. See NEUTRAL SAFETY SWITCH. Park vehicle on level surface. Move selector lever to "N" position. Loosen set screw and adjust shift rod. See Fig. 2. Ensure tension does not exist in shift rod. Tighten set screw to 106 INCH lbs. (12 N.m).

CONTROL PRESSURE CABLE

E300D – Disconnect cable ball socket. Pull idle travel rod apart as far as the stop. Pull control pressure cable forward until a slight resistance is felt. Holding cable in this position, check if ball socket fits on ball with no tension. If tension is felt, adjust idle travel rod to connect ball socket onto ball with no tension. See Fig. 3.

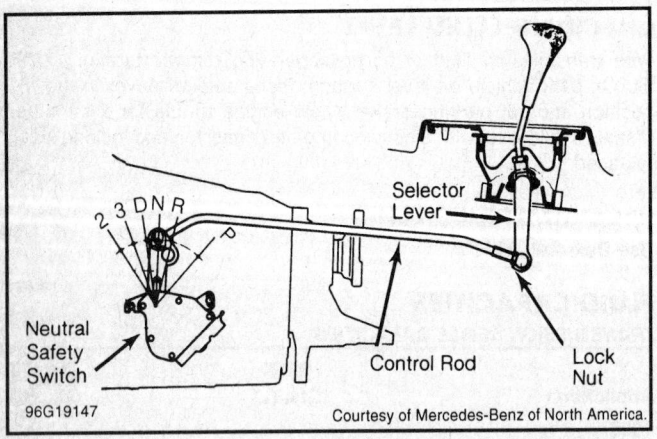

Fig. 1: Adjusting Shift Linkage (All Models, Except E300D & E320)

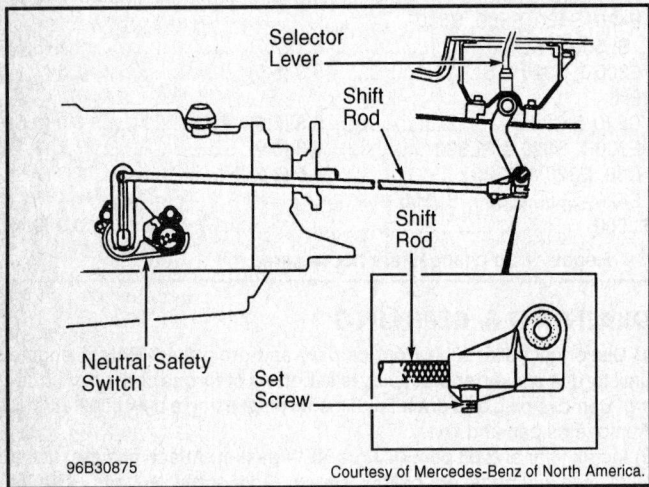

Fig. 2: Adjusting Shift Linkage (1996 E300D & E320)

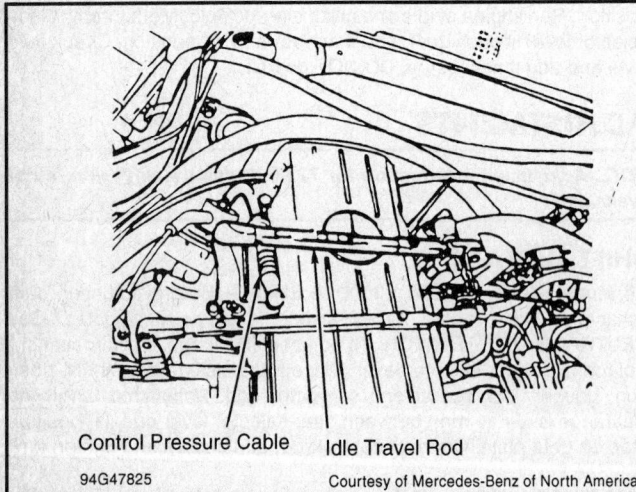

Fig. 3: Adjusting Control Pressure Cable (E300D)

S350D – Ensure throttle control cable is correctly adjusted. Disconnect cable ball socket. Pull control cable forward until slight resistance is felt. Holding cable in this position, check if ball socket fits on ball with no tension. If tension is felt, use adjusting nut to change cable length.

E320 & S320 – Remove air cleaner. Adjust control pressure cable by turning adjusting screw until tips of needles align. Install air cleaner. *See Fig. 4.*

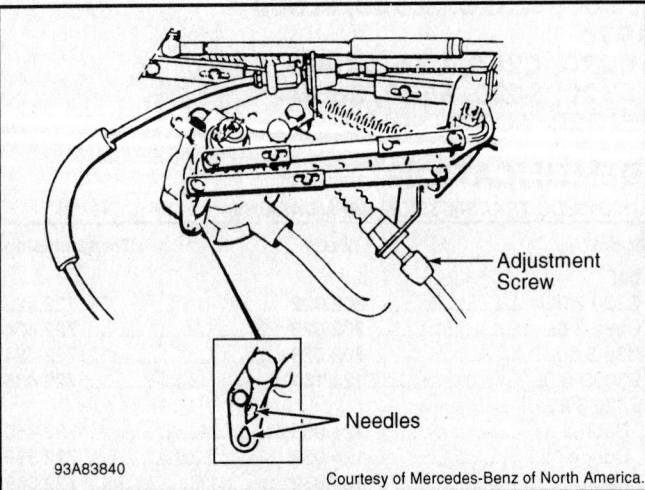

Fig. 4: Aligning Needles (E320 & S320)

E420, S420, S500 & SL500 – Remove air cleaner. Loosen 2 nuts on connecting rod. Turn connecting rod until tips of needles align. *See Fig. 5.* Tighten 2 nuts on connecting rod. Install air cleaner.

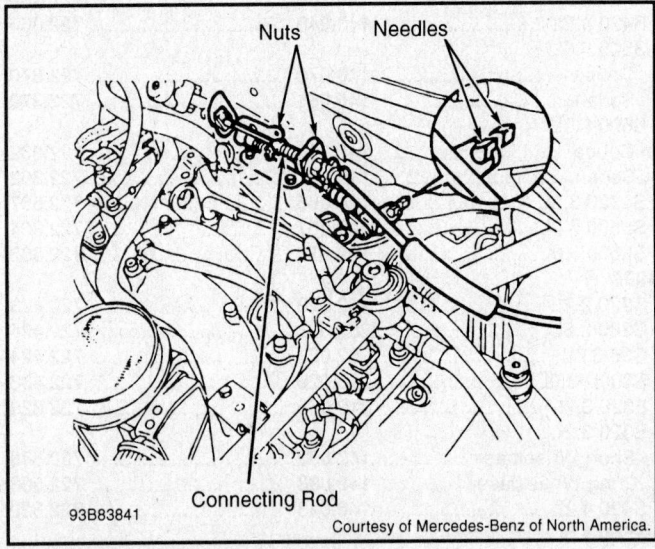

Fig. 5: Aligning Needles (V8 Engine)

CONTROL PRESSURE CABLE VACUUM ELEMENT

NOTE: Not all vehicles are equipped with a control pressure cable vacuum element. Only vehicles with dual shifting modes may have this option.

1) Ensure control pressure cable is properly adjusted. See CONTROL PRESSURE CABLE. Raise and support vehicle. Disconnect vacuum hose from control pressure cable vacuum element. *See Fig. 6.*
2) Connect a vacuum supply to vacuum element. Pull control pressure cable up to full load stop. Measure how far piston sticks out of vacuum element (distance "A"). *See Fig. 7.* See VACUUM ELEMENT PISTON PROTRUSION table. If vacuum element piston protrusion is not to specification, turn adjustment screw on control pressure cable vacuum element. *See Fig. 6.*

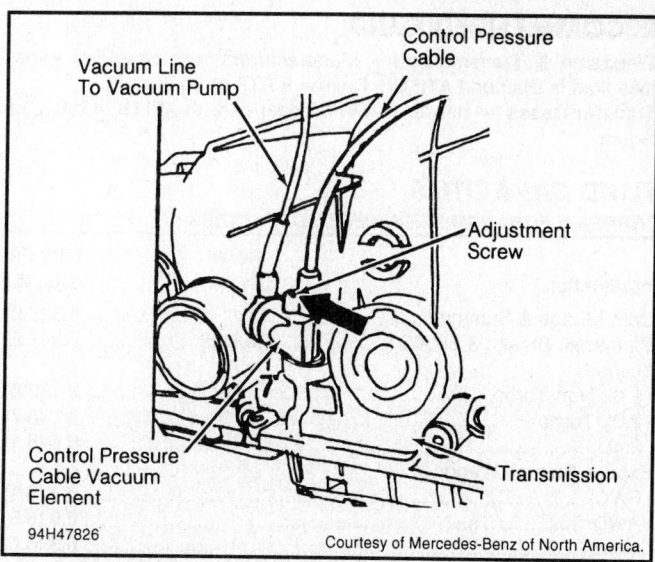

Fig. 6: Connecting Vacuum Hose To Control Pressure Cable Vacuum Element

VACUUM ELEMENT PISTON PROTRUSION

Application	In. (mm)
4-Cyl. Engine	.31 (8.0)
6-Cyl. Engine	
With 722.3 Transmission [1]	.28 (7.0)
With 722.4 Transmission [1]	.24 (6.0)
8-Cyl. Engine	.24 (6.0)

[1] – See IDENTIFICATION for transmission application.

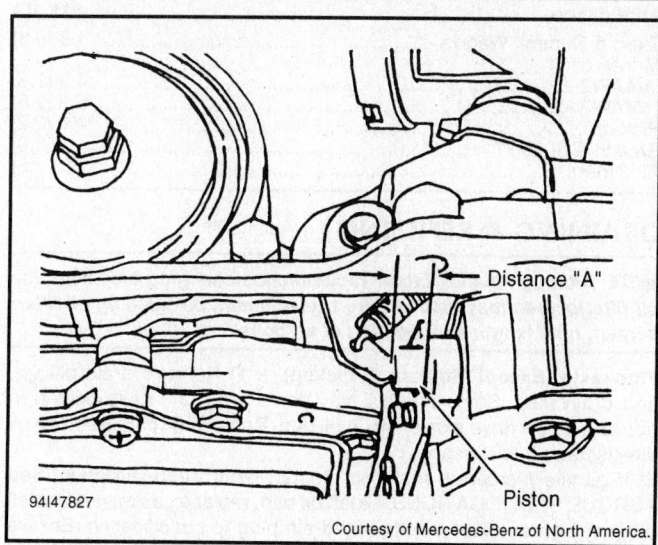

Fig. 7: Checking Vacuum Element Piston Protrusion

NEUTRAL SAFETY SWITCH

All Models – 1) Neutral safety switch is located behind transmission selector lever on transmission. Loosen neutral safety switch attaching screws. Ensure transmission selector lever is in "N" position.
2) Insert a 5/32" (4 mm) drill bit through select lever adjustment hole and into neutral safety switch housing. Tighten screws and remove drill bit. Ensure vehicle starts in "P" and "N" positions only. *See Fig. 1 or 2.*

SHIFT POINT RETARD UNIT

NOTE: Not all vehicles are equipped with shift point retard.

1) If shift point retard unit is being replaced, ensure distances "A" and "B" are transferred to replacement unit. *See Fig. 8.* To check shift point retard, drive vehicle in "D" range with light throttle pressure from a stop.
2) If shift point retard is functioning properly, vehicle will start moving in second gear and 2-3 shift will occur above 30 MPH. If vehicle starts in first gear, shift point retard is too high. To lower shift point retard, turn adjustment screw to the right.
3) If vehicle 2-3 shift occurs at less than 30 MPH, shift point retard is too low. To raise shift point retard, turn adjustment screw to the left.

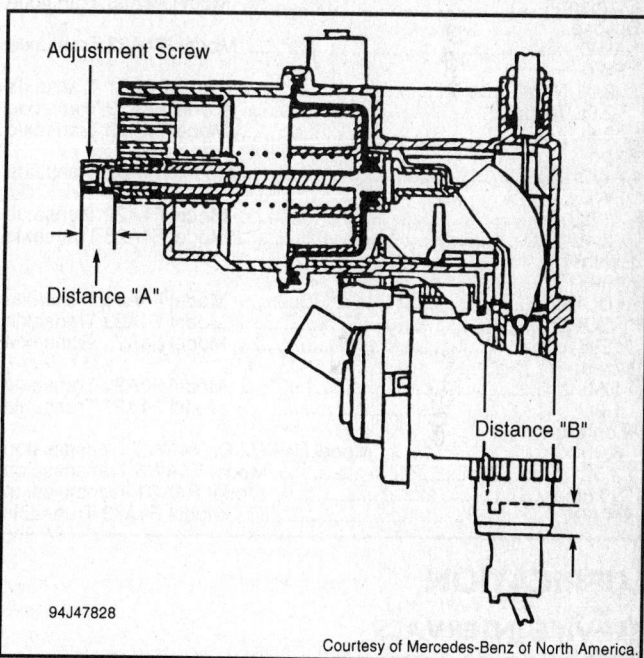

Fig. 8: Identifying Shift Point Retard Adjustment Screw

Chrysler Corp.: Colt, Colt Vista, Stealth Summit, Summit Wagon, Talon
Mitsubishi: Diamante, Eclipse, Expo, Galant Mirage, Montero, Pickup, 3000GT

IDENTIFICATION
AUTOMATIC TRANSMISSION/TRANSAXLE APPLICATIONS

Model	Transmission/Transaxle
Chrysler Corp.	
Colt & Summit	
1.5L	Model F3A21 Transaxle
1.8L	Model F4A22 Transaxle
Colt Vista & Summit Wagon	
AWD	Model W4A32 Transaxle
FWD	
1.8L	Model F4A22 Transaxle
2.4L	Model F4A23 Transaxle
Stealth	Model F4A33 Transaxle
Talon	
AWD	Model W4A33 Transaxle
FWD	
Non-Turbo	Model F4AC1 Transaxle
Turbo	Model F4A33 Transaxle
Mitsubishi	
Diamante	Model F4A33 Transaxle
Eclipse	
AWD	Model W4A33 Transaxle
FWD	
2.0L Non-Turbo	Model F4AC1 Transaxle
2.0L Turbo	Model F4A33 Transaxle
2.4L	Model F4A23 Transaxle
Expo	
AWD	Model W4A32 Transaxle
FWD	
1.8L	Model F4A22 Transaxle
2.4L	Model F4A23 Transaxle
Galant	
1995	
DOHC	Model F4A33 Transaxle
SOHC	Model F4A23 Transaxle
1996	Model F4A23 Transaxle
Mirage	
1.5L	Model F3A21 Transaxle
1.8L	Model F4A22 Transaxle
Montero	
3.0L	Model V4AW2 Or V4AW3 Transmission
3.5L	Model V4AW3 Transmission
Pickup	Model R4AC1 Transmission
3000GT	Model F4A33 Transaxle

LUBRICATION
SERVICE INTERVALS

Transaxle & Transmission – Check fluid level every 12 months or 15,000 miles. Change fluid and filter every 30,000 miles. If vehicle is operated under severe conditions, change fluid more often. If severe darkening of fluid and strong odor are noted, bands should also be adjusted (if equipped).
Transfer Case – On 4WD and AWD models, change transfer case fluid every 30,000 miles.

CHECKING FLUID LEVEL

CAUTION: If severe darkening of fluid and strong odor are noted, change fluid and filter, and adjust bands.

Transaxle & Transmission – 1) Park vehicle on level area. Ensure oil is at normal operating temperature, parking brake is engaged, and engine is at idle. Move gear selector through each position, stopping briefly at each selection.
2) Place gear selector in Neutral, and clean area around dipstick tube. Ensure fluid level is between lower and upper marks, but never over upper mark, in HOT range. Add or drain fluid if necessary.
Transfer Case – Lubricant level should be to bottom of fill hole on side of transfer case.

RECOMMENDED FLUID

Transaxle & Transmission – Manufacturers recommended transaxle fluid is Diamond ATF SP, Dexron II ATF or equivalent.
Transfer Cases – Use SAE 75W-85 gear oil with API GL-4 rating or higher.

FLUID CAPACITIES
TRANSAXLE/TRANSMISSION REFILL CAPACITIES

Application	Refill Qts. (L)	Dry Fill Qts. (L)
Colt, Mirage & Summit	[1]	6.3 (6.0)
Diamante, Stealth & 3000GT	4.8 (4.5)	7.9 (7.5)
Eclipse		
2.0L Non-Turbo	[1]	9.1 (8.6)
2.0L Turbo	[1]	7.1 (6.7)
2.4L	[1]	6.4 (6.1)
Expo & Summit Wagon		
FWD	[1]	6.4 (6.1)
AWD	[1]	6.9 (6.5)
Galant	[1]	6.3 (6.0)
Montero		
V4AW2	5.8 (5.5)	7.6 (7.2)
V4AW3	5.8 (5.5)	9.0 (8.5)
Pickup	[1]	7.4 (7.0)
Talon		
Non-Turbo	4.0 (3.8)	9.1 (8.6)
Turbo	[1]	7.1 (6.7)

[1] – Add fluid to "C" mark. Idle engine in Neutral, then add fluid to bring level to "H" mark.

TRANSFER CASE REFILL CAPACITIES

Application	Pts. (L)
Expo & Summit Wagon	1.3 (0.6)
Montero	
V4AW2	4.9 (2.3)
V4AW3	5.2 (2.5)
Pickup	4.6 (2.2)
Stealth & 3000GT	.6 (.3)
All Others	1.1 (.5)

DRAINING & REFILLING

NOTE: Although manufacturer recommends changing only fluid, the oil filter/screen may also require replacement. If replacing oil filter/screen, note length and location of all bolts.

Transaxle (Except Montero & Pickup) – 1) Remove drain plug(s), and drain fluid. Some models may contain a drain plug located in housing below drive axle shaft, in oil pan. Remove oil pan. Remove oil filter/screen if necessary.
2) If oil filter/screen is replaced, tighten bolts to specification. See TORQUE SPECIFICATIONS. Clean oil pan, replace gasket, and install oil pan. Tighten oil pan bolts and drain plug to specification. Ensure dipstick hole area is clean, and pour approximately 4.2 qts. (4.0L) of ATF into dipstick hole.
3) Operate engine at idle for 2 minutes. Shift transaxle to each position, ending in Neutral. Add sufficient fluid to reach lower mark. After reaching normal operating temperature, fluid should be between upper and lower marks of HOT range on dipstick.
Transmission (Montero & Pickup) – 1) Remove drain plug (if equipped) from transmission pan, and allow fluid to drain. On models without drain plug, oil pan must be removed to drain fluid. Remove oil filter/screen if necessary.
2) If oil filter/screen is replaced, tighten bolts to specification. See TORQUE SPECIFICATIONS. Clean oil pan, replace gasket, and install oil pan. Tighten oil pan bolts and drain plug to specification. Fill transmission, through filler tube, with 5.3 qts. (5.0L) of ATF on Montero, or 2.0 qts. (1.9L) on all others. Start engine, and allow to idle for 2 minutes.

3) Shift transmission into each position, ending in Neutral. Check fluid level with engine running at idle. If necessary, add sufficient fluid to bring level to lower mark on dipstick. Recheck fluid level after transmission is at normal operating temperature.

Transfer Case – Drain plug is located on bottom of transfer case. Change drain plug gasket whenever fluid is changed. Lubricant level should be at bottom of fill hole on side of transfer case.

ADJUSTMENTS

KICKDOWN BAND

Pickup – 1) Locate kickdown band adjusting screw on left side of transmission case. Loosen lock nut, and back off 5 turns. Ensure adjusting screw turns freely in transmission case.

2) Using torque wrench, tighten adjusting screw to 72 INCH lbs. (8 N.m). Back off adjusting screw 2 7/8 turns. Hold adjuster screw in this position, and tighten lock nut to 30 ft. lbs. (41 N.m).

LOW-REVERSE BAND

Pickup – 1) Raise vehicle, drain transmission, and remove oil pan. Loosen adjusting screw lock nut, and back off nut 5 turns. Ensure adjusting screw turns freely in lever.

2) Using torque wrench, tighten band adjusting screw to 30 INCH lbs. (3.5 N.m). Back off adjusting screw 6 turns. Hold adjusting screw in this position, and tighten lock nut to 25 ft. lbs. (34 N.m). Reinstall oil pan using new gasket. Tighten pan bolts to 150 INCH lbs. (17 N.m). Refill transmission with specified fluid.

KICKDOWN SERVO

Except Montero & Pickup – 1) Remove all dirt and grease around kickdown servo switch. Remove snap ring and kickdown servo switch.

2) To prevent servo piston from turning, install Adapter (MD998915) and Kickdown Servo Wrench (MD998918) so tab of wrench engages with notch of piston. *See Fig. 1.*

CAUTION: DO NOT push servo piston inward while installing adapter and servo wrench. Install adapter in brake pressure port by hand ONLY. DO NOT use wrench to tighten adapter.

---

3) Loosen lock nut to "V" channel of adjuster rod. *See Fig. 1.* Tighten inner section of Kickdown Service Adjustment Assembly (MD998916) until it contacts lock nut.

4) Install outer section of kickdown service adjustment assembly on lock nut. Rotate outer section to left and inner section to right to contact lock nut with inner section.

5) Using an INCH-lb. torque wrench on inner section, tighten inner section to 86 INCH lbs. (9.8 N.m), and then loosen inner section. Tighten inner section to 43 INCH lbs. (4.9 N.m).

CAUTION: Before tightening lock nut with torque wrench, tighten it by hand until it contacts piston. If torque wrench is used initially, lock nut and adjustment rod may rotate together.

---

6) Back off outer section 2 to 2 1/4 turns. Rotate outer section to right and inner section to left until inner section is free of lock nut. Tighten lock nut by hand until it contacts piston. Using torque wrench, tighten lock nut to 18-23 ft. lbs. (25-32 N.m).

7) Remove adapter and kickdown servo wrench. Install new "O" ring in groove around switch. Install switch and snap ring.

TRANSMISSION THROTTLE CONTROL

Mirage & Summit – 1) Ensure throttle lever is in curb idle position. Engine must be at normal operating temperature.

2) Raise cover "B" of throttle cable upward to expose nipple. *See Fig. 2.* Loosen lower cable bracket mounting bolt. Move lower cable bracket until distance between nipple and top of cover "A" on throttle cable is .02-.06" (.5-1.5 mm).

3) Tighten lower cable bracket mounting bolt to 113 INCH lbs. (13 N.m). With throttle lever in wide open throttle position, pull cable upward to ensure some cable free play exists.

CAUTION: On Pickup, always adjust throttle control cable whenever idle is adjusted.

Pickup – 1) Ensure engine idle is adjusted correctly. Ensure throttle lever and throttle cable bracket are not bent. Pull lightly on inner throttle cable.

2) While in closed throttle position, measure gap between inner cable stopper and outer cable housing. Adjust cable as necessary to obtain a gap of .031-.059" (.79-1.50 mm). *See STEP 1 in Fig. 3.*

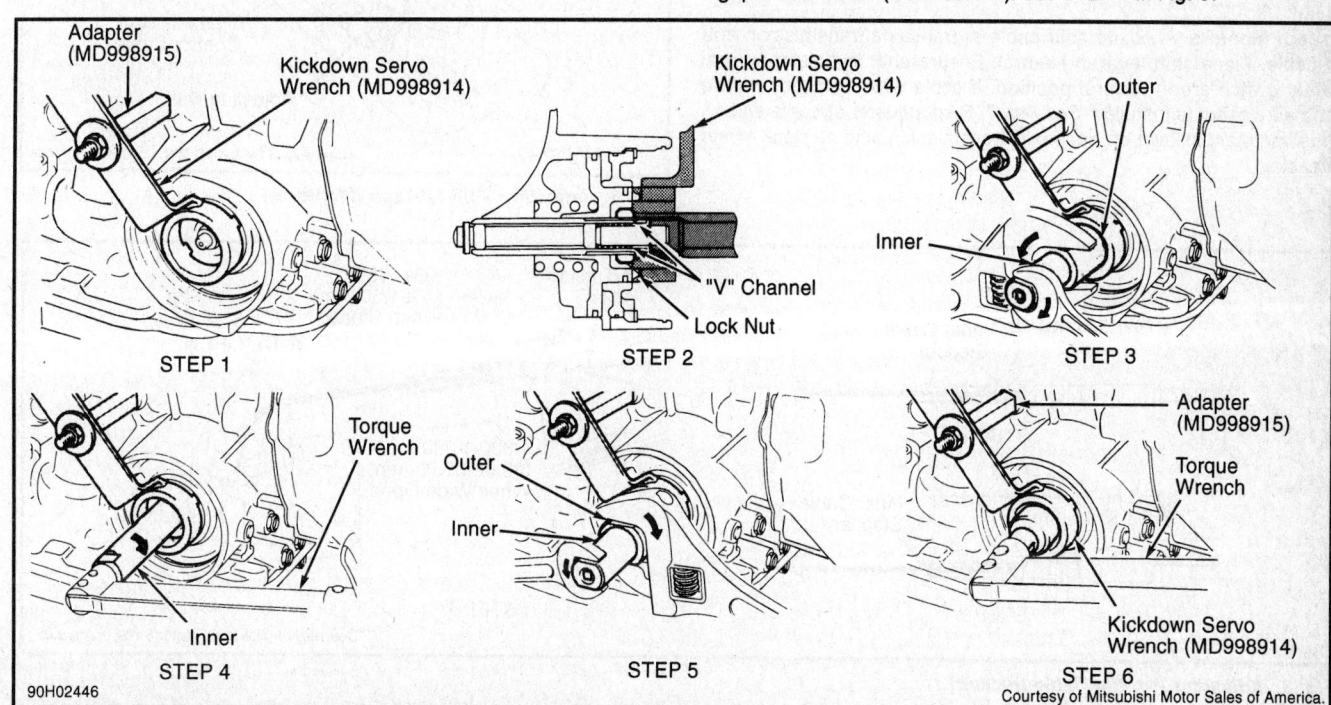

90H02446

Courtesy of Mitsubishi Motor Sales of America.

Fig. 1: Adjusting Kickdown Servo (Except Montero & Pickup)

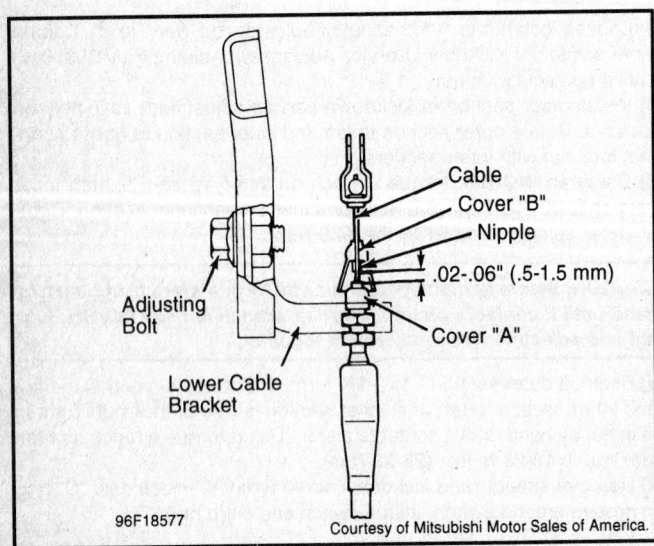

Fig. 2: Adjusting Throttle Cable (Mirage)

3) While holding throttle in wide open position, pull on inner throttle cable. Adjust bellcrank as necessary to obtain a gap of 1.46-1.50" (37.08-38.10 mm) between inner cable stopper and outer cable. *See STEP 2 in Fig. 3.*

4) With throttle fully closed, recheck gap between inner cable stopper and outer cable housing. Gap should be .031-.059" (.79-1.50 mm). *See STEP 3 in Fig. 3.* While holding throttle in wide open position, pull on inner throttle cable. Check for a gap of 1.30-1.38" (33.02-35.05 mm).

Montero – Ensure throttle lever and throttle cable bracket are not bent. On 3.0L engines, ensure distance between inner cable stopper end and outer cable end is 1.34-1.38" (34-35 mm) at WOT. *See Fig. 4.* On 3.5L engines, ensure distance between inner cable stopper end and dust cover is 0-.04" (0-1.0 mm). *See Fig. 5.*

SHIFT LINKAGE

Montero – Loosen swivel nut on transmission control rod. *See Fig. 6.* Ensure shift and transmission levers are both in Neutral. Tighten swivel nut.

Except Montero – Adjust shift cable at transaxle/transmission end of cable. Place shift lever in Neutral. Ensure shift lever and neutral safety switch are in Neutral position. If cable was replaced, ensure toothed washer is installed. *See Fig. 7.* Turn adjuster at cable end so it fits into manual lever on transaxle/transmission, and no slack exists in cable.

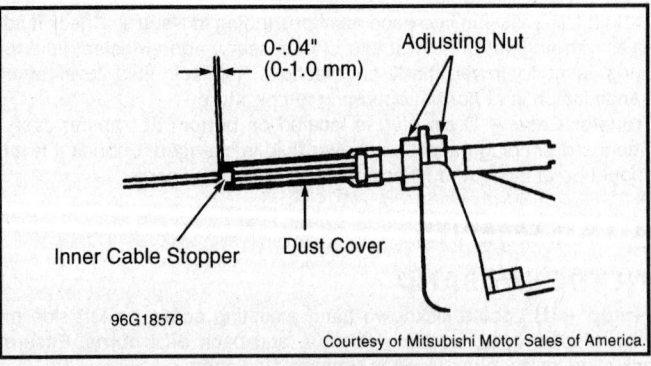

Fig. 4: Adjusting Throttle Cable (Montero 3.0L)

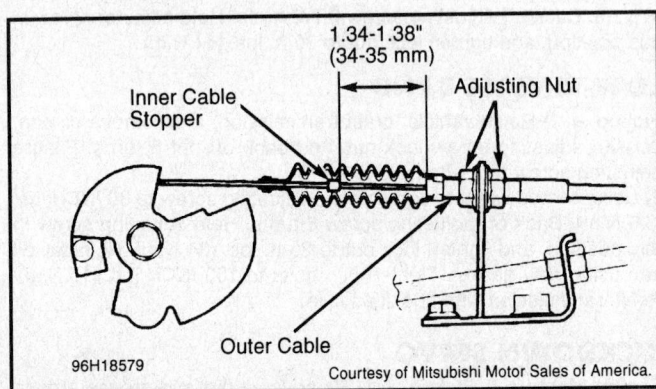

Fig. 5: Adjusting Throttle Cable (Montero 3.5L)

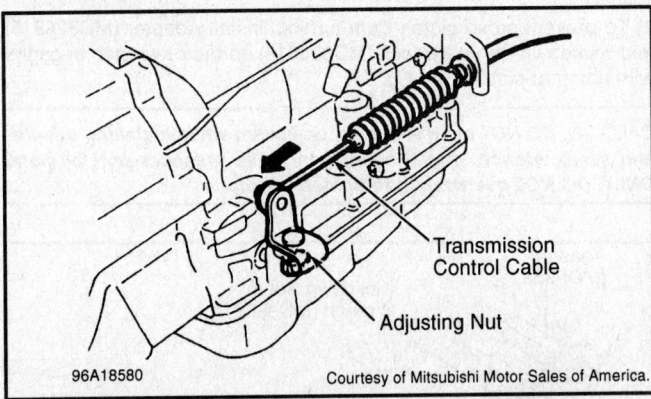

Fig. 6: Adjusting Shift Linkage (Montero)

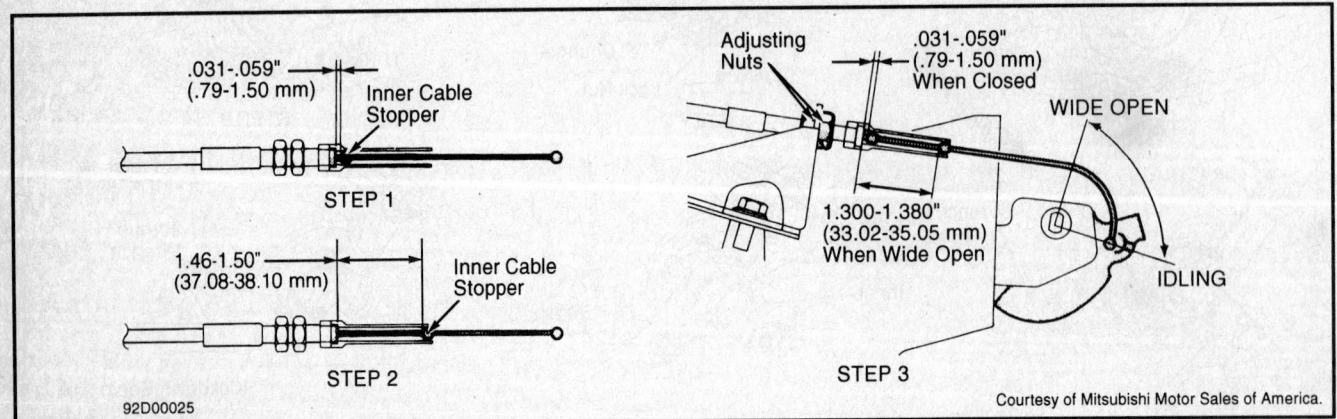

Fig. 3: Adjusting Throttle Cable (Pickup)

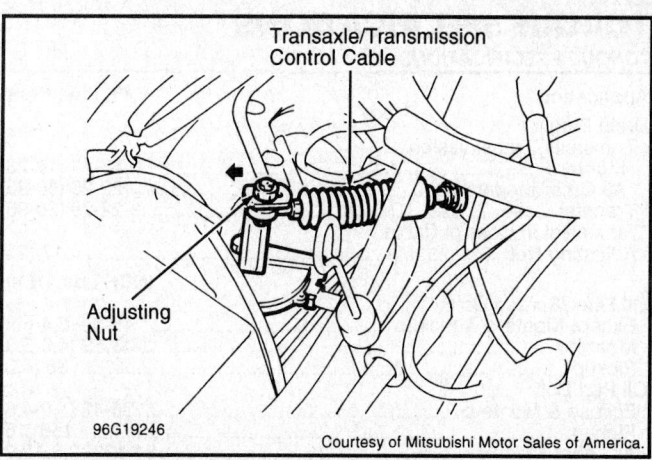

Fig. 7: Adjusting Shift Cable (Except Montero)

SHIFT LEVER SLEEVE

NOTE: Pickup does not have shift lever sleeve.

All Models Except Pickup – To adjust shift lever sleeve, remove shift handle on top of shift lever. With lever in Neutral, turn sleeve so distance between sleeve and lever end is within specification. See SHIFT LEVER SLEEVE CLEARANCE SPECIFICATION table. *See Fig. 8.* Ensure beveled side of sleeve faces toward push button (if equipped).

SHIFT LEVER SLEEVE CLEARANCE SPECIFICATION

Application	Clearance In. (mm)
Expo	.71-.75 (18-19)
Mirage	.45-.49 (11.5-12.5)
Montero	.72-.74 (18.2-18.9)
All Others	.60-.63 (15.2-16.0)

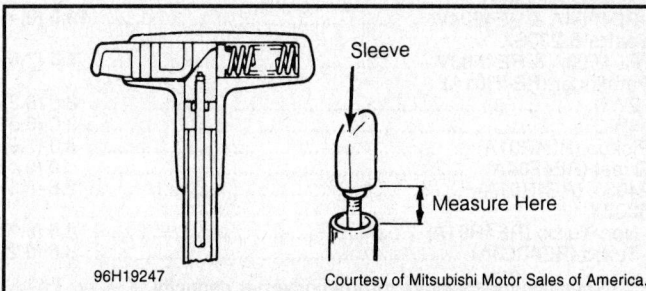

Fig. 8: Adjusting Shift Lever Sleeve (Except Pickup)

NEUTRAL SAFETY SWITCH

Except Montero & Pickup – 1) Place shift and manual control levers in Neutral. For adjustment, turn switch body in order to align small end of manual control lever with corresponding flange on switch body. Tighten switch mounting bolts to 84-108 INCH lbs. (10-12 N.m).
2) Loosen nut at end of transaxle control cable, and lightly pull in direction of switch. Tighten nut to 84-120 INCH lbs. (10-14 N.m). *See Fig. 9.* Ensure selector lever is in Neutral. Ensure lever functions correctly at transaxle, in range corresponding to that indicated by selector lever.

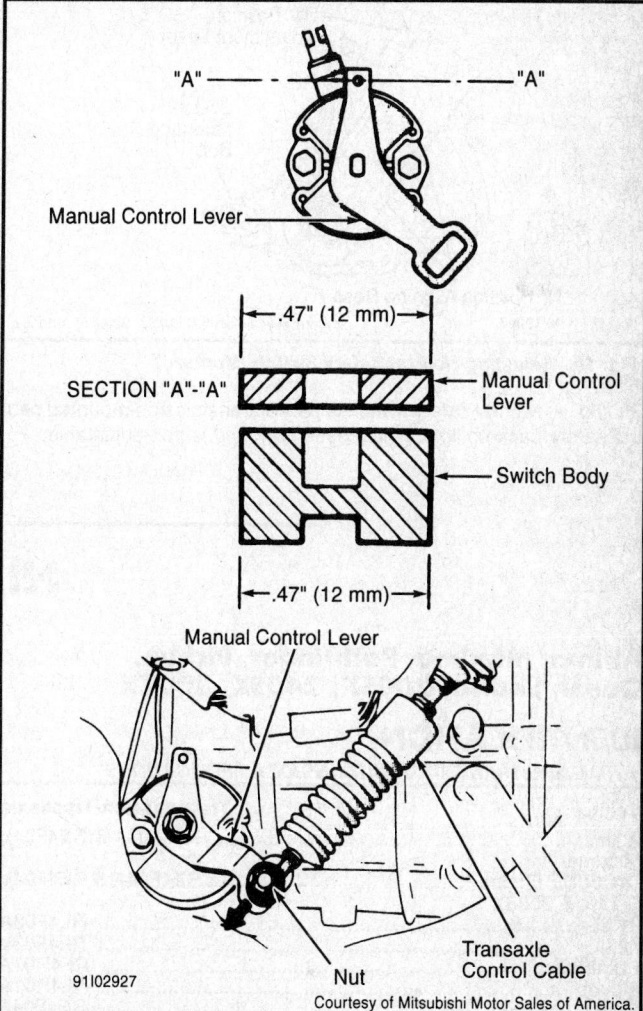

Fig. 9: Adjusting Inhibitor (Neutral Safety) Switch (Except Montero & Pickup)

Montero – 1) Move selector lever to "N" position. Loosen adjusting nut of control cable. *See Fig. 6.* Loosen park/neutral switch mounting bolt.
2) Adjust neutral safety switch by turning park/neutral switch so that the bosses for aligning "N" position on park/neutral switch are aligned with the "N" position adjustment lever. Tighten park/neutral switch mounting bolt to specification. See TORQUE SPECIFICATIONS.
3) Gently pull end of transmission control cable in direction of arrow. *See Fig. 10.* Tighten adjusting nut to specification. See TORQUE SPECIFICATIONS.
4) Ensure selector lever is in "N" position after adjustment. Ensure each range of the transmission functions correctly at appropriate position of the selector lever.

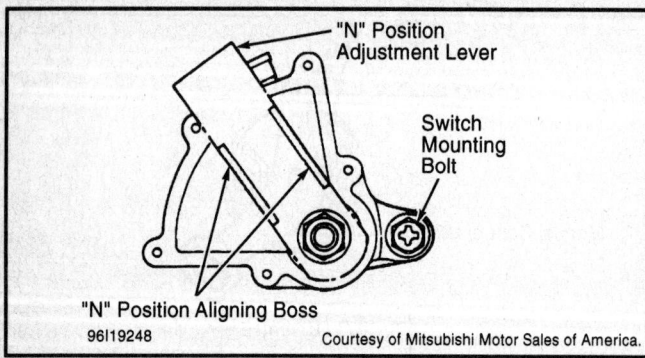

"N" Position Adjustment Lever

Switch Mounting Bolt

"N" Position Aligning Boss

96119248 Courtesy of Mitsubishi Motor Sales of America.

Fig. 10: Adjusting Neutral Safety Switch (Montero)

Pickup – Neutral safety switch is part of transmission-mounted neutral safety/back-up light switch assembly, and is non-adjustable.

TORQUE SPECIFICATIONS
TORQUE SPECIFICATIONS

Application	Ft. Lbs. (N.m)
Drain Plug	
Transaxle/Transmission	
Montero	13-17 (18-23)
All Other Models	22-25 (30-35)
Transfer Case	22-25 (30-35)
Transmission Control Cable	
Adjusting Nut	17 (24)
	INCH Lbs. (N.m)
Oil Filter/Screen Bolt	
Except Montero & Pickup	48-60 (5.4-6.8)
Montero	43-52 (4.9-5.9)
Pickup	36 (4.0)
Oil Pan Bolt	
Eclipse & Montero	36-42 (4.0-4.8)
Pickup	156 (18)
All Other Models	84-108 (9.5-12.2)
Park/Neutral Switch Mounting Bolt (Montero)	48 (5.4)

Nissan

Altima, Maxima, Pathfinder, Pickup, Quest, Sentra, 200SX, 240SX, 300ZX

IDENTIFICATION
AUTOMATIC TRANSMISSION/TRANSAXLE APPLICATIONS

Vehicle	Transmission/Transaxle
Altima	RE4F04A & RE4F04V
Maxima	
VQ30DE Engine	RE4F04A & RE4F04V
Sentra & 200SX	
1.6L	RL4F03A
2.0L	RE4F03V
Pathfinder	RE4R01A
Pickup	RL4R01A
Quest	RE4F04A
240SX	RE4R01A
300ZX	
Non-Turbo	RE4R01A
Turbo	RE4R03A

LUBRICATION

SERVICE INTERVAL

Inspect fluid level every 15,000 miles or 12 months. Change fluid as needed. Under severe operating conditions, change fluid every 30,000 miles or 24 months.

CHECKING FLUID LEVEL

Transaxle & Transmission – **1)** Check fluid with engine and transmission at normal operating temperature. With vehicle level and at idle, shift transmission/transaxle through all positions and return to Park.

2) Clean area around dipstick. Remove dipstick, wipe clean, insert and withdraw. Level should be between "H" and "L" marks. If level is not as indicated, add fluid as necessary.

3) Dipstick on some models may be marked with HOT and COLD ranges. Use COLD range if fluid is 86-122°F (30-50°C) and vehicle was not driven before checking level.

NOTE: Normal fluid should be clear with a Pink color and should not have a strong burnt odor.

Transfer Case – Oil level should be at bottom of fill hole.

RECOMMENDED FLUID

Transaxle & Transmission – All models use Genuine Nissan Matic "D", Dexron-III/Mercon ATF or equivalent.
Transfer Case (Pathfinder & Pickup) – Use Dexron II ATF.

CAUTION: Transfer case is factory-filled with Dexron-II ATF.

FLUID CAPACITIES
TRANSMISSION/TRANSAXLE CAPACITIES

Transmission/Transaxle	[1] Qts. (L)
Altima & Maxima	
RE4F04A & RE4F04V	10.0 (9.4)
Sentra & 200SX	
RL4F03A & RE4F03V	7.4 (7.0)
Pathfinder (RE4R01A)	
2WD	8.8 (8.3)
4WD	9.0 (8.5)
Pickup (RL4R01A)	8.3 (7.9)
Quest (RE4F04A)	10 (9.4)
240SX (RE4R01A)	8.8 (8.3)
300ZX	
Non-Turbo (RE4R01A)	8.8 (8.3)
Turbo (RE4R03A)	8.6 (8.2)

[1] – Specification includes torque converter capacity.

TRANSFER CASE CAPACITIES

Application	Qts. (L)
Pathfinder & Pickup	2.4 (2.3)

DRAINING & REFILLING

Transaxle (Except Pathfinder, Pickup, 240SX & 300ZX) – **1)** Remove drain plug, and allow fluid to drain. Reinstall drain plug. Tighten drain plug to specification. See TORQUE SPECIFICATIONS. Add fluid through fill tube.

2) Warm transaxle to normal operating temperature. Shift transaxle through all gears. Return to Park. Check fluid level. Add fluid as necessary.

Transmission (Pathfinder, Pickup, 240SX & 300ZX) – **1)** Loosen oil pan bolts. Allow ATF to drain. Remove pan. Thoroughly clean pan and screen. If replacing screen, tighten bolts to specification. See TORQUE SPECIFICATIONS.

2) Install pan using NEW gasket. Tighten pan bolts to specification. Add fluid through fill tube. Warm transmission to normal operating temperature. Shift transmission through all gears and return to Park. Check fluid level. Add fluid as necessary.

Transfer Case (Pathfinder & Pickup) – Remove drain plug, and allow fluid to drain. Reinstall drain plug. Tighten drain plug to specification. See TORQUE SPECIFICATIONS. Add fluid through fill hole until fluid level is at bottom of fill hole.

ADJUSTMENTS

NOTE: Band adjustments are not part of on-vehicle adjustment procedures. Band adjustments should only be performed during bench inspection or overhaul.

THROTTLE VALVE CABLE

Pickup 2.4L, Sentra & 200SX – 1) Press spring loaded lock plate on throttle cable at engine side bracket to release cable. *See Fig. 1.* Move adjusting tube toward engine side bracket to remove all play. Release lock plate.

2) Paint reference mark on throttle wire. Quickly move throttle drum from P_2 (idling position) to P_1. Measure throttle cable stroke "L" between full throttle and idle. If stroke "L" is not within specification, adjust cable. See THROTTLE VALVE CABLE STROKE SPECIFICATIONS table. While road testing vehicle, ensure kickdown point is correct.

THROTTLE VALVE CABLE STROKE SPECIFICATIONS

Model	Stroke – In. (mm)
Sentra & 200SX 1.6L (RL4F03A)	1.57-1.65 (40-42)
Pickup 2.4L (RL4R01A)	1.50-1.65 (38-42)

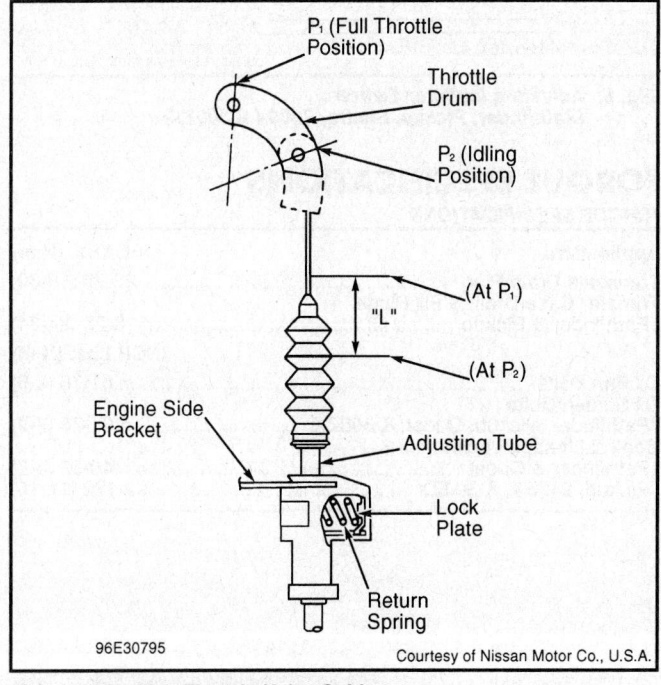

Fig. 1: Adjusting Throttle Valve Cable (Pickup 2.4L, Sentra & 200SX)

CONTROL CABLE ADJUSTMENT

NOTE: Move shift lever through all gear positions. If each detent cannot be felt and shift lever pointer does not align with each position indicator, adjust gearshift linkage.

Altima, Maxima (1995), Sentra & 200SX – Move shift lever to Park. Loosen lock nuts holding shift cable housing to bracket on transaxle. Ensure transaxle is fully engaged in Park. Tighten lock nut pulling selector lever toward "R" side. Ensure shift lever moves smoothly from "P" to "1" without sliding noise.

Maxima (1996) – Place selector lever in Park. Ensure transaxle is fully engaged in Park. Loosen control cable lock nut and place manual shaft in "P" position. Pull cable with 1.5 lbs. (6.9 N.) in direction of arrow. Return cable in opposite direction .0039" (1.0 mm). Tighten control cable lock nut. Move selector lever from "P" to "1" position. Ensure selector lever moves smoothly. Apply grease to contacting areas of selector lever and control cable. *See Fig. 2.*

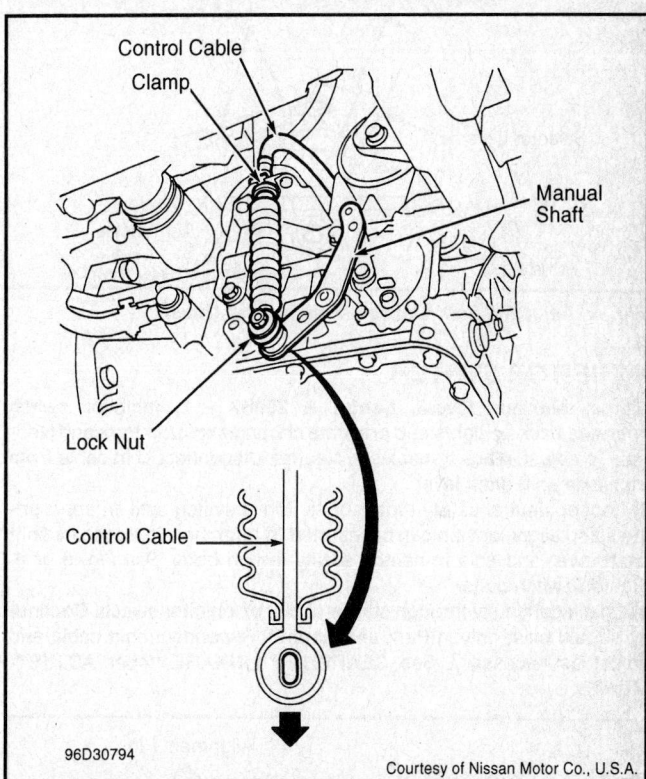

Fig. 2: Adjusting Shift Linkage (Maxima 1996)

MANUAL CONTROL LINKAGE

Pickup, 240SX & 300ZX – 1) Place shift lever in Park. Loosen lock nuts on rod. *See Fig. 3.* While pulling selector lever toward Reverse (without pushing shifter release button), tighten lock nut "X" until it touches trunnion.

2) Back off lock nut "X" one turn. Tighten lock nut "Y" to 97-132 INCH lbs. (11-15 N.m). Recheck shift lever positions, ensuring shift lever moves smoothly.

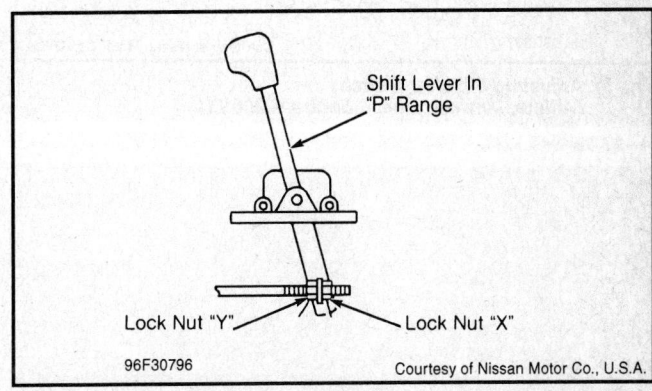

Fig. 3: Adjusting Control Cable (Pickup 2WD, 240SX & 300ZX)

Pathfinder & Quest – 1) Place selector lever in Park. Remove center console. Loosen lock nuts. *See Fig. 4.* Ensure transmission is in Park position.

2) While pulling selector lever toward Reverse (without pushing shift lever release button), tighten turnbuckle until slight cable tension is achieved. Back off turnbuckle one turn. Tighten lock nuts to 36-48 INCH lbs. (4-6 N.m). Ensure shift lever moves smoothly.

3) On Quest, ensure position indicator is accurate. If not, remove steering column cover. Turn position indicator adjusting screw.

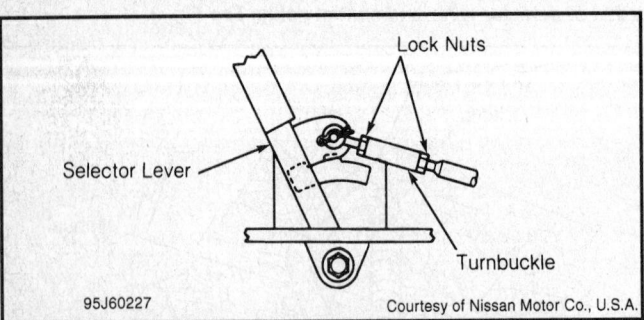

95J60227   Courtesy of Nissan Motor Co., U.S.A.

Fig. 4: Adjusting Shift Linkage (Pathfinder & Quest)

INHIBITOR SWITCH

Altima, Maxima, Quest, Sentra & 200SX – 1) Inhibitor switch operates back-up lights and prevents starting except in Park and Neutral. To adjust, place transaxle in Neutral. Disconnect shift cable from transaxle shift shaft lever.

2) Loosen neutral safety switch bolts. Move switch until an appropriate sized alignment pin can be inserted through hole in transaxle shift shaft lever and hole in neutral safety switch body. *See Fig. 5 or 6.* Tighten switch bolts.

3) Check continuity through starter circuit of inhibitor switch. Continuity should exist only in Park and Neutral. Reconnect shift cable and adjust as necessary. See GEARSHIFT LINKAGE under ADJUSTMENTS.

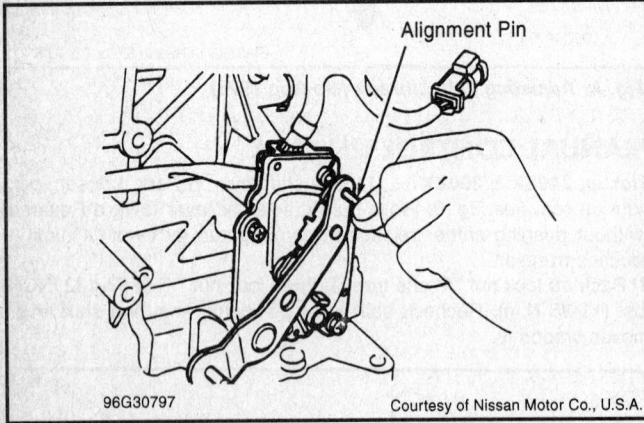

96G30797   Courtesy of Nissan Motor Co., U.S.A.

*Fig. 5: Adjusting Inhibitor Switch
(Altima, Maxima, Quest, Sentra & 200SX)*

Pathfinder, Pickup, 240SX & 300ZX – 1) Inhibitor switch operates back-up lights and prevents starting except in "P" and "N" positions. To adjust, place shift lever in "N" position. Ensure transaxle/transmission is in Neutral (transaxle/transmission shift shaft lever should be in vertical position). *See Fig. 6.*

2) Loosen inhibitor switch bolts. Rotate switch until correct size alignment pin can be inserted through shift shaft lever and switch arm. See INHIBITOR SWITCH ALIGNMENT PIN table. Tighten neutral safety switch bolts and remove pin. Check continuity through starter circuit of inhibitor switch. Continuity should exist only in Neutral and Park positions.

INHIBITOR SWITCH ALIGNMENT PIN

Application	Pin Diameter In. (mm)
All Models	.16 (4.0)

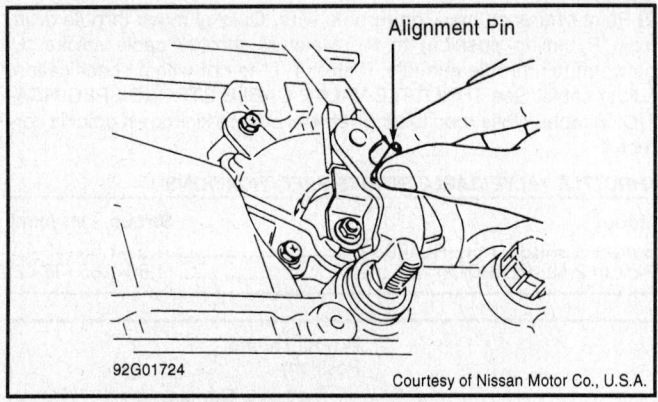

92G01724   Courtesy of Nissan Motor Co., U.S.A.

*Fig. 6: Adjusting Inhibitor Switch
(Pathfinder, Pickup, Sentra, 240SX & 300ZX)*

TORQUE SPECIFICATIONS
TORQUE SPECIFICATIONS

Application	Ft. Lbs. (N.m)
Transaxle Drain Plug	22-29 (30-39)
Transfer Case Drain & Fill Plugs	
Pathfinder & Pickup	18-25 (24-34)
	INCH Lbs. (N.m)
Oil Pan Bolts	61-78 (7-9)
Oil Screen Bolts	
Pathfinder, Pickup, Quest, & 300ZX	61-78 (7-9)
Control Linkage Locknut	
Pathfinder & Quest	40-52 (4-6)
Pickup, 240SX, & 300ZX	92-132 (11-15)

911 Carrera 2

IDENTIFICATION

AUTOMATIC TRANSMISSION APPLICATION

Model	Transmission
911 Carrera 2	A50/05

LUBRICATION

SERVICE INTERVALS

Check fluid level at every engine oil change. Replace fluid and oil screen every 30,000 miles. Under severe conditions, replace fluid and screen every 15,000 miles.

CHECKING FLUID LEVEL

Transmission – 1) Apply parking brake. Check fluid level with gear selector in Park and engine idling at normal operating temperature. Raise and support vehicle. Remove vehicle undercover. With vehicle level, observe fluid level at sight tube on right side of transmission.

2) Fluid level should be within 50°C range in sight tube. If level is not within specification, turn engine off. Add needed fluid at quick fill connector located next to sight tube. *See Fig. 1.* Recheck and ensure fluid level is filled to proper level.

Final Drive – Ensure engine is off. Remove filler plug. Check fluid level at filler plug. Fluid level is okay if fluid drains out or fluid is even with bottom of fill hole. Add fluid as needed.

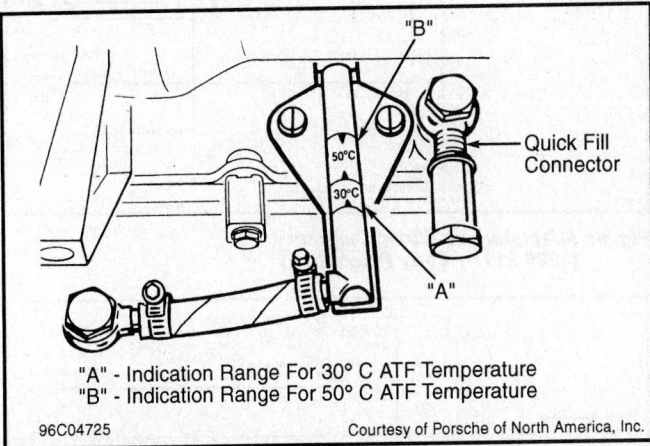

"A" - Indication Range For 30° C ATF Temperature
"B" - Indication Range For 50° C ATF Temperature

96C04725   Courtesy of Porsche of North America, Inc.

Fig. 1: Checking Transmission Fluid Level

RECOMMENDED FLUID

Transmission – Use Dexron-II ATF type fluid.
Final Drive – Use API GL-5 75W/90 gear oil.

FLUID CAPACITIES

TRANSMISSION REFILL CAPACITIES

Application	Refill Qts. (L)	Dry Fill Qts. (L)
911 Carrera 2	3.7 (3.5L)	10.0 (9.5L)

FINAL DRIVE REFILL CAPACITY

Application	Pts. (L)
911 Carrera 2	.95 (0.9L)

DRAINING & REFILLING

Draining – Raise and support vehicle. Remove drain plug and drain fluid. Remove oil pan. Remove oil screen. Clean oil pan, magnet (if equipped) and oil screen in clean solvent and air dry. Replace screen with new "O" ring. Install pan with new pan gasket.

NOTE: Normal tiptronic transmission filling procedure requires Porsche quick-fill device, however, an alternate method may be used.

Filling (Normal Procedure) – Connect hose from Porsche quick-fill device to quick-fill connector on transmission. *See Fig 1.* Add Dexron II ATF up to 30°C mark on transmission sight tube. Start engine and run with transmission in Park. Ensure fluid level remains at 30°C level in transmission sight tube. Add additional fluid if necessary. Remove quick-fill device and drive vehicle until engine is fully warm. Recheck fluid level. Fluid level should within 50°C range in sight tube. Adjust fluid level as needed.

Filling (Alternate Method) – With engine off, unscrew quick-fill connector fitting from transmission. *See Fig. 1.* Insert a rubber hose to threaded hole (where quick-fill connector was removed from). Add Dexron II ATF through rubber hose and check fluid level through sight tube. Fluid level on sight tube should be to 30°C mark with engine cold. Drive vehicle until engine is fully warm. Recheck fluid level. Fluid level should be within 50°C range in sight tube. Adjust fluid level as needed.

ADJUSTMENTS

MULTIFUNCTIONAL SWITCH

1) Move shift selector to "N" position. Remove transmission undercover. Remove left rear hot-air pipe. Disconnect selector lever cable from switch actuating lever. Remove actuator lever from multifunctional switch.

2) Place Alignment Tool (9326) on switch. *See Fig. 2.* Adjust switch until pin can be inserted into switch. Tighten adjustment bolt. Assemble remaining components in reverse order of disassembly.

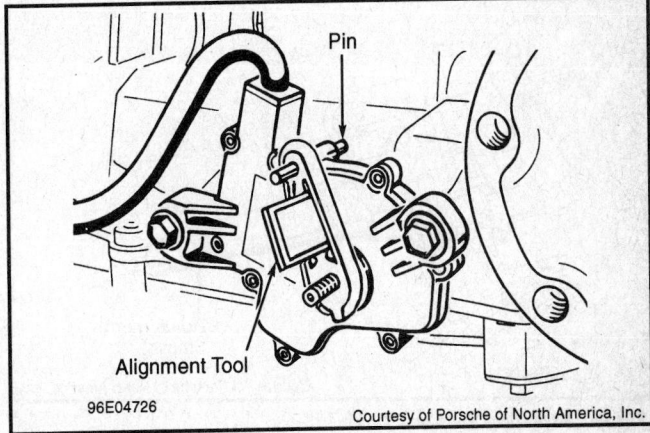

96E04726   Courtesy of Porsche of North America, Inc.

Fig. 2: Identifying Multifunctional Switch Alignment Tool

SHIFTER CABLE

1) Place gear selector in "P" position in automatic shifting gate. Raise and support vehicle. Remove transmission undercover. Disconnect fork head from multifunctional switch actuating lever. *See Fig. 3.* Move neutral safety switch to "P" position by pushing switch actuating lever to maximum rearward position. Push gearshift cable forward.

2) Adjust position of fork head until bore holes of fork head and switch actuating lever are aligned. Connect fork head to switch actuating lever. Lower vehicle.

3) Check gearshift cable adjustment by shifting through all gears and confirming that proper gear selection is displayed at speedometer. Shift gear selector from "D" selection in automatic shift gate to "M" position in manual selection gate. Shift should occur with one smooth and straight movement. *See Fig. 3.* Readjust gearshift cable if necessary. Attach transmission undercover.

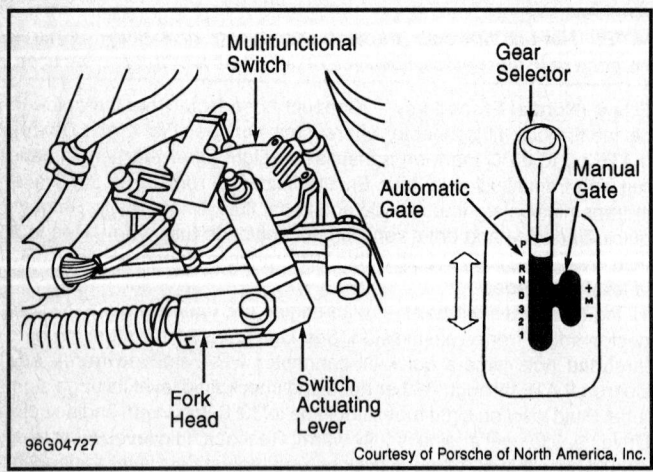

Fig. 3: Adjusting Gearshift Cable

SHIFT LOCK CABLE

Remove center console, knee guard and side vent. Remove central information system, leave wiring attached. Place transmission selector lever in Park and ignition lock to "O" position. Adjust shiftlock cable by turning adjustment sleeve until the lock slide protrudes .059-.098" (1.5-2.5 mm). *See Fig. 4.* Check operation of ignition lock and shiftlock. Install console assembly.

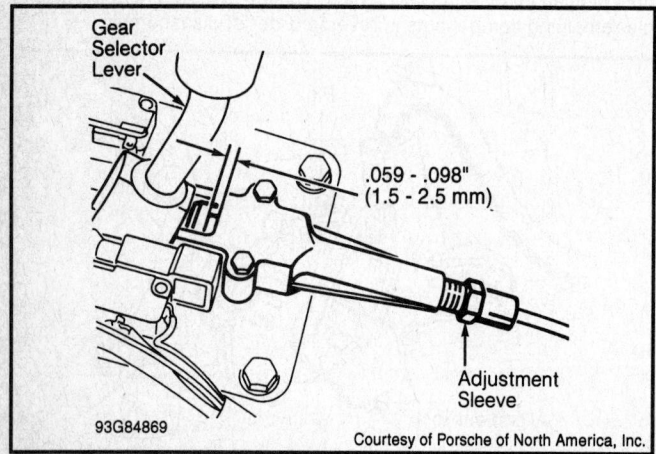

Fig. 4: Adjusting Shiftlock Cable

SHIFT LOCK SOLENOID

Remove center console and access gear selector assembly. Place gear selector lever in Park. Completely back off solenoid adjustment. Pull solenoid plunger and hold it completely extended. Slide solenoid with plunger extended until plunger contacts lock lever stop. *See Fig. 5.* Tighten solenoid screws to 24 INCH lbs. (2.5 N.m). Check operation of shift lock. Install center console assembly.

TORQUE SPECIFICATIONS

TORQUE SPECIFICATIONS

Application	Ft. Lbs. (N.m)
Gearshift Actuating Lever Nut	11 (15)

	INCH Lbs. (N.m)
Multifunctional Switch Bolt	89 (10)
Oil Screen Bolt	71 (8)
Transmission Pan Bolt	71 (8)

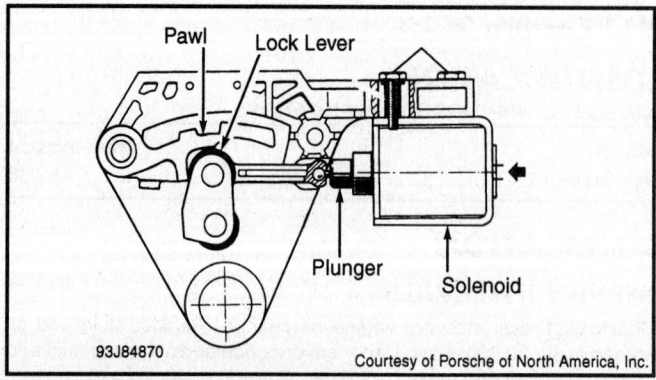

Fig. 5: Adjusting Shiftlock Solenoid.

WIRING DIAGRAMS

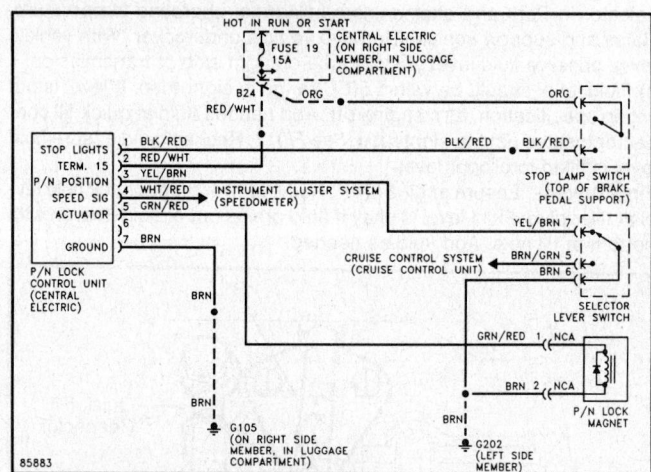

Fig. 6: Shift Interlock Wiring Diagram (1995 911 – Early Production)

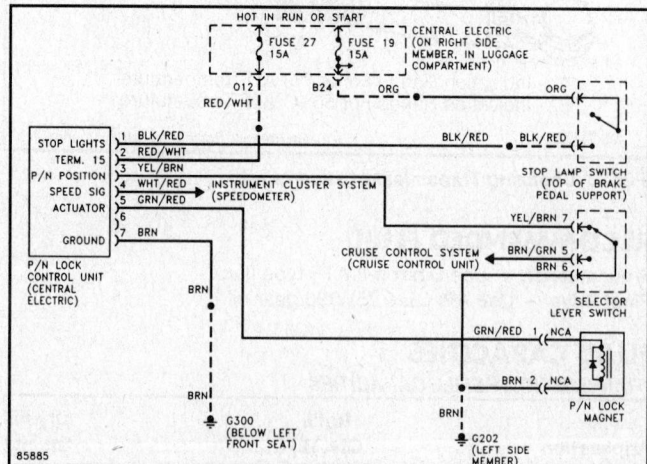

Fig. 7: Shift Interlock Wiring Diagram (1995 911 – Late Production)

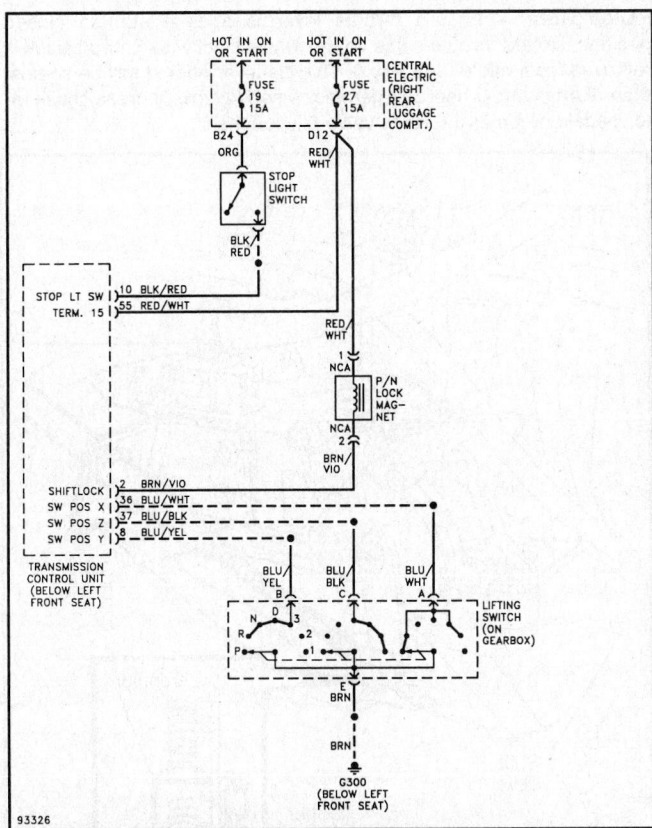

Fig. 8: Shift Interlock Wiring Diagram (1996 911)

Rover

Discovery, Range Rover

IDENTIFICATION

AUTOMATIC TRANSMISSION APPLICATIONS

Application	Transmission Model
Discovery	ZF4HP22
Range Rover	ZF4HP24

LUBRICATION

SERVICE INTERVALS

Inspect fluid level every 15,000 miles. Under severe operating conditions, change ATF and filter every 15,000 miles or 24 months.

CHECKING FLUID LEVEL

Transmission – Check fluid level with vehicle on level surface with engine cold. With engine idling and transmission in Neutral, check fluid level. Fluid level should be between minimum and maximum identification marks on dipstick. Top off fluid as necessary. See RECOMMENDED FLUID. DO NOT overfill.

Transfer Case – Raise and support vehicle. Place drain pan under transmission. Clean area around oil fill plug and remove plug. Lubricant level should be to bottom of fill hole. Top off fluid as necessary. See RECOMMENDED FLUID. Clean oil fill plug threads and apply Hylomar sealant. Reinstall fill plug and tighten to specification. See TORQUE SPECIFICATIONS.

RECOMMENDED FLUID

Transmission – All transmissions use Dexron automatic transmission fluid.

Transfer Case – On Discovery, use Hypoid SAE 80W-90 (API GL-4 or GL-5). On Range Rover, use Dexron automatic transmission fluid.

FLUID CAPACITIES

TRANSMISSION REFILL CAPACITIES

Application	Refill Qts. (L)	Dry-Fill [1] Qts. (L)
Discovery	[2]	9.6 (9.1)
Range Rover		
4.0L	[2]	10.3 (9.7)
4.6L	[2]	11.6 (11)

[1] – Specification is approximate.
[2] – Refill to maximum identification mark on transmission dipstick.

TRANSFER CASE FLUID & REFILL CAPACITIES

Application	Qts. (L)
Discovery [1]	2.4 (2.3)
Range Rover [2]	2.5 (2.4)

[1] – Use Hypoid SAE 80W-90 (API GL-4 or GL-5).
[2] – Use Dexron automatic transmission fluid.

DRAINING & REFILLING

Transmission – Raise and support vehicle. Remove dipstick to aid in oil drainage. Place drain pan under transmission. Remove drain plug and drain fluid. If replacing transmission filter, remove oil pan. Thoroughly clean transmission oil pan. Install filter and pan with NEW gasket. Add fluid. See FLUID CAPACITIES.

Transfer Case – Raise and support vehicle. Place drain pan under transfer case. Clean area around oil drain and fill plugs. Remove both plugs. Clean oil drain and fill plug threads. Apply Hylomar sealant to drain plug. Reinstall drain plug and tighten to specification. See TORQUE SPECIFICATIONS. Add fluid. See FLUID CAPACITIES. Apply Hylomar sealant to fill plug. Reinstall fill plug and tighten to specification.

ADJUSTMENTS

KICKDOWN CABLE

Discovery – **1)** Loosen kickdown cable lock nut. Ensure throttle valve is fully closed. Measure distance "A" between end of outer cable and crimped collar on inner cable. *See Fig. 1.* Distance should be .010-.050" (.25-1.25 mm). Adjust as necessary, tighten lock nut and recheck.

2) If installing a new kickdown cable, and collar on inner cable is loose, measure distance "B" on old cable. *See Fig. 1.* Crimp collar on new cable to distance measured and perform step 1).

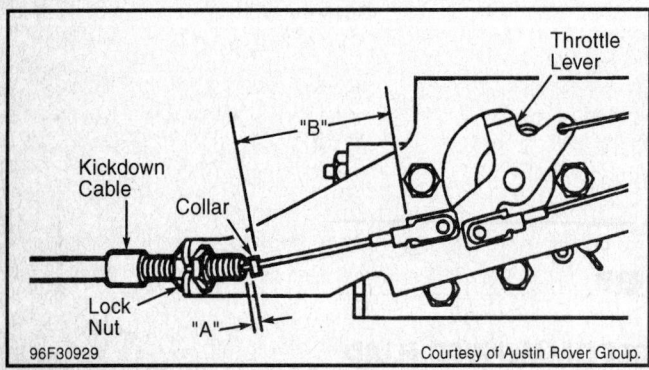

Fig. 1: Adjusting Kickdown Cable (Discovery)

SHIFT CABLE

Range Rover – **1)** Raise and support vehicle. Loosen shift cable trunnion lock nut. *See Fig. 2.* Remove cotter key and washer from trunnion. Separate trunnion from transmission shift lever. From inside of vehicle, place transmission shift lever in Park position.

2) Working underneath vehicle, set transmission shift lever in full forward position. Adjust cable until shift cable trunnion slides in transmission shift lever easily. Install washer and new cotter pin. Tighten lock nut.

PARK/NEUTRAL POSITION (PNP) SWITCH

Range Rover – **1)** Shift transmission into Park position. Raise and support vehicle. Rotate shift lever counterclockwise 2 detents to Neutral position. Remove nut securing shift lever to selector shaft. *See Fig. 3.* Loosen PNP switch retaining nut and bolt.

2) Install Switch Adjuster (LRT-44-011) to shift lever shaft. *See Fig. 4.* Position pin into switch adjuster. Rotate switch until pin engages hole in PNP switch. Tighten PNP switch retaining nut and bolt. Remove switch adjuster. Rotate shift lever clockwise 2 detents to Park position. Install shift selector and tighten shift lever nut.

THROTTLE CABLE

Discovery – Loosen throttle cable thumb-wheel. *See Fig. 5.* Hold throttle lever in fully closed position. Rotate thumb-wheel trntil inner cable free play is .062" (1.57 mm). Depress accelerator pedal and ensure throttle valve fully opens.

Range Rover – Ensure throttle lever is against stop in closed position. Rotate throttle cable thumb-wheel clockwise until all slack is removed from cable. *See Fig. 6.* Throttle lever should still be against stop. Turn thumb-wheel counterclockwise 1/4 turn. Depress accelerator pedal and ensure throttle valve fully opens.

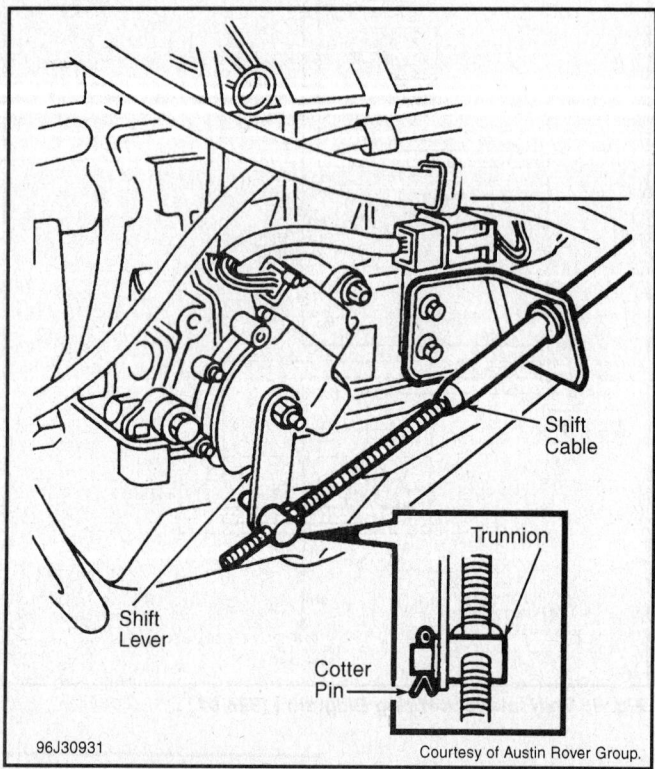

Fig. 2: Adjusting Shift Cable (Range Rover)

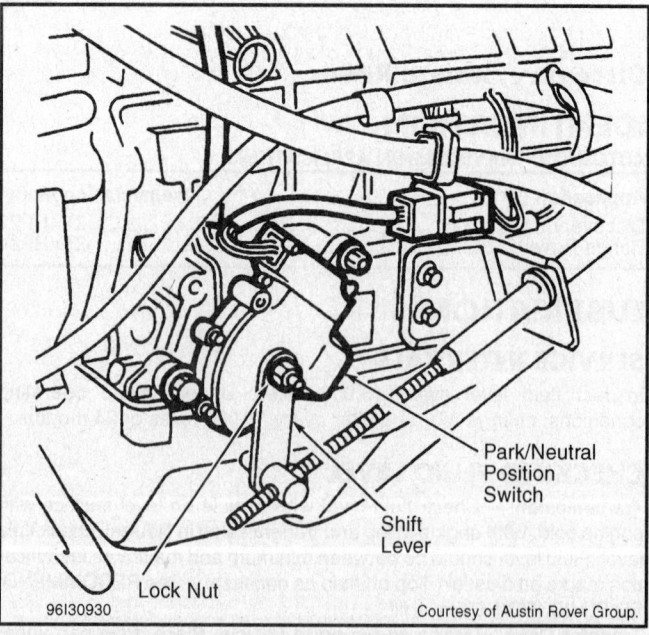

Fig. 3: Identifying Park/Neutral Position Switch (Range Rover)

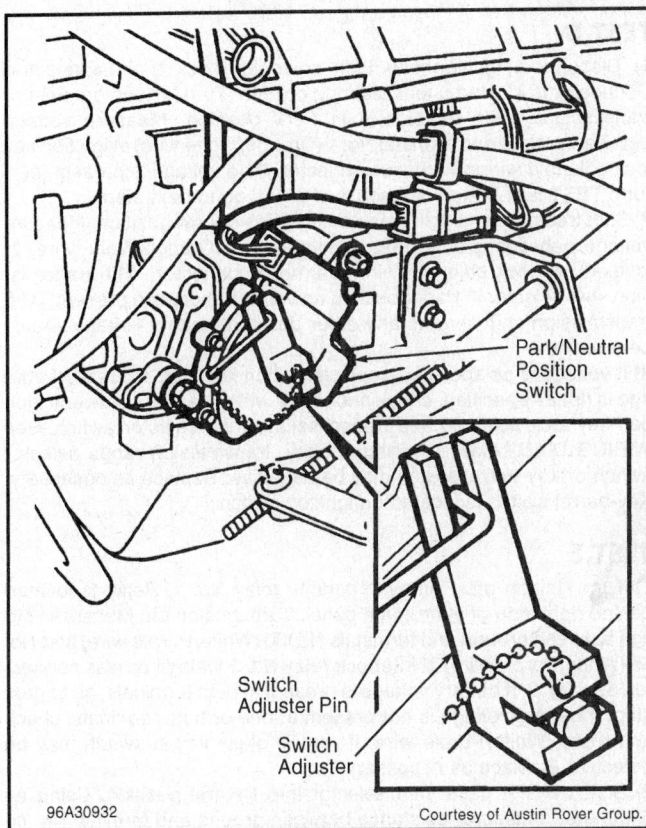

Fig. 4: Adjusting Park/Neutral Shift Position Switch (Range Rover)

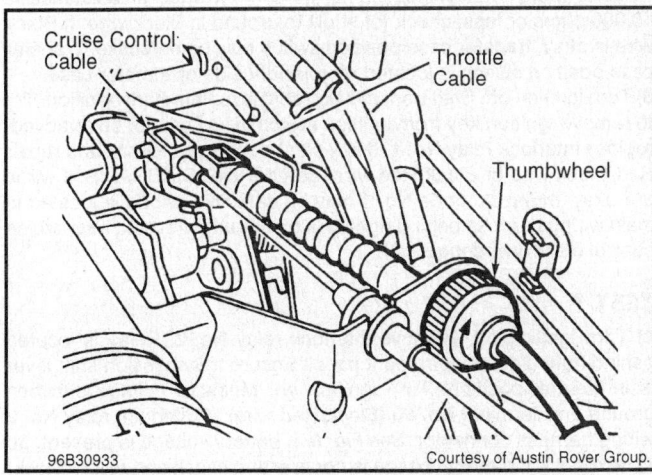

Fig. 5: Adjusting Throttle Cable (Discovery)

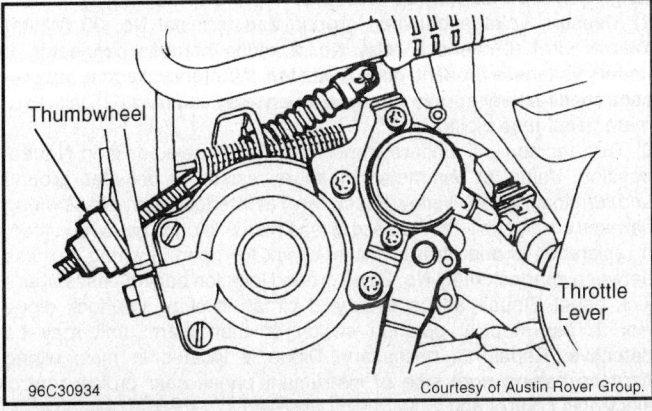

Fig. 6: Adjusting Throttle Cable (Range Rover)

TESTING SHIFT INTERLOCK SYSTEM (DISCOVERY)

Discovery – Identify symptom and perform appropriate test.
- If transmission shift lever cannot be shifted out of Park, perform TEST A.
- If ignition key cannot be removed with the transmission shift lever in Park and transfer case shifter in High or Low, perform TEST B.
- If transfer case can be shifted out of High or Low while in any gear except Neutral position, perform TEST C.
- If ignition key can be removed with transmission shift selector in any gear except Park or with transfer case in Neutral, perform TEST D.
- If transfer case cannot be shifted into Neutral, High or Low, with ignition key in ignition switch and transmission shift selector in Neutral, perform TEST F.

TEST A

1) Disconnect transmission range selector switch 6-pin connector, located under center console near shift lever. *See Fig. 7*. Turn ignition on. Measure voltage between ground and terminal No. 2 (Green/Purple wire) at transmission range selector switch wiring harness connector. *See Fig. 8*.
2) With brake pedal depressed, battery voltage should be present. With brake pedal released, zero volts should be present. If voltage is as specified, go to next step. If voltage is not as specified, locate and repair open or short in wiring harness between instrument panel fuse block and transmission range selector switch. See WIRING DIAGRAMS.
3) Turn ignition off. Using an ohmmeter, measure resistance between ground and terminal No. 3 (Black wire) at transmission range selector switch wiring harness connector. If resistance is less than one ohm, go to next step. If resistance is one ohm or more, repair open Black wire between transmission range selector switch and ground location behind passenger's kick panel.
4) Measure resistance of Pink/Gray wire between terminals No. 5 and 6 at transmission range selector wiring harness connector. If resistance is less than one ohm, go to next step. If resistance is one ohm or more, repair open in Pink/Gray wire.
5) Measure resistance between terminals No. 3 (Black/White wire) and No. 6 (Orange/Yellow wire) at transmission range selector switch connector. With shift lever in Park position, resistance should be less than one ohm. With shift lever in any other position, resistance should be more than 1000 ohms. If resistance is as specified, replace shift interlock solenoid. If resistance is not as specified, replace shift selector microswitch.

TEST B

1) Disconnect ignition key lock solenoid Black 2-pin connector. Connector is located under steering column. Turn ignition off. Ensure transmission shift selector is in Park and transfer case selector is in High or Low position. Measure voltage between ground and terminal No. 1 (Orange/White wire) at ignition key lock solenoid wiring harness connector. If no voltage is present, replace ignition key lock solenoid. If any voltage is present, go to next step.
2) Disconnect transmission range selector switch 6-pin connector, located under center console near shift lever. *See Fig. 7*. Place transmission shift selector in Park position. Using an ohmmeter, measure resistance between terminals No. 1 (Black/White wire) and No. 4 (Brown/White wire) at transmission range selector switch wiring harness connector. *See Fig. 8*. If resistance is more than 10,000 ohms, go to next step. If resistance is 10,000 ohms or less, replace transmission range selector switch.
3) Remove interlock relay No. 1. Relay is located behind right side of instrument panel. Measure voltage between terminals No. 86 (White/Purple wire) and No. 85 (Black wire) at interlock relay No. 1 wiring harness connector. *See Fig. 9*. If battery voltage is present, replace interlock relay No. 1. If battery voltage is not present, check and repair wiring harness between key-in switch and ground location behind driver's kick panel. See WIRING DIAGRAMS.

4) If wiring is okay, key-in switch or transfer case position switch may be defective. Replace as necessary. Key-in switch is located on ignition switch. Transfer case position switch is located on top right side of transfer case.

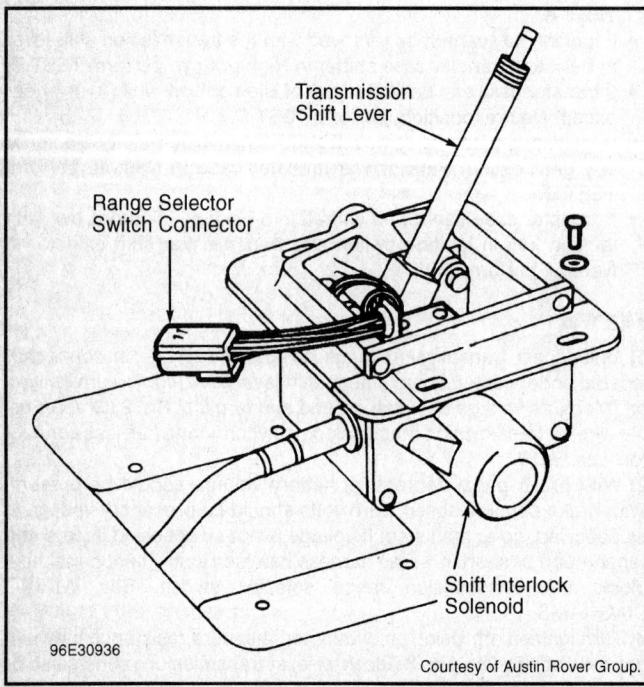

96E30936
Courtesy of Austin Rover Group.

Fig. 7: Locating Transmission Range Selector Connector

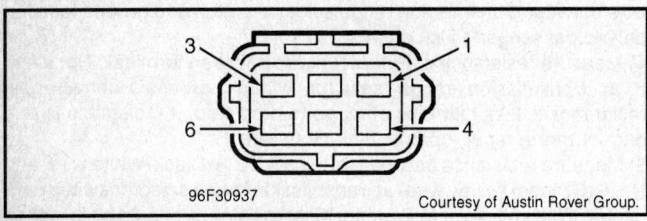

96F30937
Courtesy of Austin Rover Group.

Fig. 8: Identifying Transmission Range Selector Wiring Harness Connector

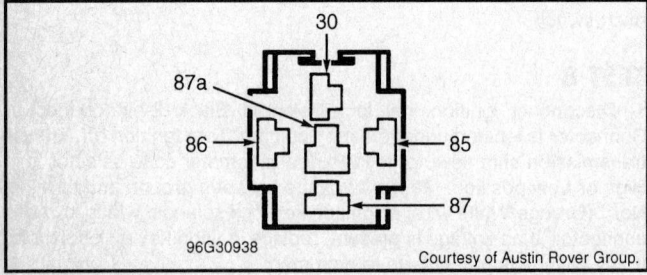

96G30938
Courtesy of Austin Rover Group.

Fig. 9: Identifying Relay No. 1 & No. 2 Wiring Harness Connector Terminals

TEST C

1) Turn ignition off. Remove interlock relay No. 2. Relay is located behind right side of instrument panel. Using an ohmmeter, measure resistance between terminals No. 30 and 87 at interlock relay No. 2 connector. *See Fig. 9.* If resistance is 10,000 ohms or less, replace interlock relay No. 2.

2) If resistance is more than 10,000 ohms, check and repair wiring harness between Park/Neutral Position (PNP) switch and interlock relay No. 2. See WIRING DIAGRAMS. If wiring is okay, transfer case solenoid or PNP switch may be defective. Replace as necessary. PNP switch is located on left side of transmission. Transfer case solenoid is located on top right side of transfer case.

TEST D

1) Disconnect ignition key lock solenoid Black 2-pin connector. Connector is located under steering column. Turn ignition on. Ensure transmission shift selector is in Park position. Measure voltage between ground and terminal No. 1 (Orange/White wire) at ignition key lock solenoid wiring harness connector. If no voltage is present, perform TEST E. If battery voltage is present, go to next step.

2) Shift transfer case shift selector into High or Low position. Measure voltage between ground and terminal No. 1 (Orange/White wire) at ignition key lock solenoid wiring harness connector. With transmission shift selector in Park position, no voltage should be present. With transmission shift lever is any other position, battery voltage should be present.

3) If voltage is as specified, replace ignition key lock solenoid. If voltage is not as specified, check and repair wiring harness between ignition key lock solenoid and transmission range selector switch. See WIRING DIAGRAMS. If wiring is okay, transmission range selector switch or key-barrel switch may be defective. Replace as necessary. Key-barrel switch is located on ignition switch.

TEST E

1) Turn ignition off. Remove interlock relay No. 1. Relay is located behind right side of instrument panel. Turn ignition on. Measure voltage between ground and terminals No. 30 (White/Purple wire) and No. 86 (White/Purple wire) at interlock relay No. 1 wiring harness connector. *See Fig. 9.* If battery voltage is present at both terminals, go to next step. If battery voltage is not present at one or both terminals, check and repair White/Purple wire. If wire is okay, key-in switch may be defective. Replace as necessary.

2) Shift transfer case shift selector into Neutral position. Using an ohmmeter, measure resistance between ground and terminal No. 85 (Black wire) at interlock relay No. 1 wiring harness connector. If resistance is more than 10,000 ohms, go to next step. If resistance is 10,000 ohms or less, check for short to ground in Black wire. If Black wire is okay, transfer case position switch may be defective. Transfer case position switch is located on top right side of transfer case.

3) Turn ignition off. Shift transmission shift lever into Park position. Try to remove ignition key from ignition switch. If key cannot be removed, replace interlock relay No. 1. If key can be removed, check and repair Red/Black wire or Black/Red wire. See WIRING DIAGRAMS. If wires are okay, interlock diode No. 1 may be defective. Diode is located in main wiring harness behind right side of instrument panel, near cruise control electronic control unit.

TEST F

1) Turn ignition off. Remove interlock relay No. 2. Relay is located behind right side of instrument panel. Ensure transmission shift lever is in Neutral position. Turn ignition on. Measure voltage between ground and terminal No. 86 (Black/Red wire) at interlock relay No. 2 wiring harness connector. *See Fig. 9.* If battery voltage is present, go to next step. If battery voltage is not present, check and repair Black/Red wire. See WIRING DIAGRAMS. If wire is okay, transmission range select switch may be defective. Replace as necessary.

2) Measure voltage between ground and terminal No. 30 (White/Yellow wire) at interlock relay No. 2 wiring harness connector. If battery voltage is present, go to next step. If battery voltage is not present, repair power supply circuit between relay and fuse F13 in instrument panel fuse block.

3) Turn ignition off. Ensure transmission shift selector is in Neutral position. Using an ohmmeter, measure resistance between ground and terminal No. 85 (Yellow/Black wire) at interlock relay No. 2 wiring harness connector. If resistance is less than one ohm, go to next step. If resistance is one ohm or more, check for open in wiring harness between interlock relay No. 2 and ground location behind passenger's kick panel. Repair as necessary. If circuit is okay, interlock diode No. 2, park/neutral position switch or theft alarm unit may be defective. Repair as necessary. Diode is located in main wiring harness behind right side of instrument panel, near cruise control electronic control unit.

4) Turn ignition on. Connect a fused jumper wire between terminals No. 30 (White/Yellow wire) and No. 87 (Gray/Black wire) at interlock relay No. 2 wiring harness connector. Attempt to shift transfer case shift lever into High or Low position. If transfer case shifts, replace interlock relay No. 2. If transfer case does not shift, check and repair ground circuit between interlock relay No. 2 and ground location behind driver's kick panel. If ground circuit is okay, transfer case solenoid may be defective. Replace as necessary. Solenoid is located on top right side of transfer case.

TESTING SHIFT INTERLOCK SYSTEM (RANGE ROVER)

PARK/NEUTRAL POSITION SWITCH

1) Park/Neutral Position (PNP) switch has 3 switches that are integral to switch. See WIRING DIAGRAMS. Disconnect PNP switch connector. Switch is located on left side of transmission. Using an ohmmeter, check for continuity between PNP switch terminal No. 6 and specified terminals. See CHECKING PNP SWITCH CONTINUITY table.

2) Continuity should only exist between terminals being checked. If continuity is not as specified, replace PNP switch. If switch is okay, and shift interlock system does not function properly, check for open and shorts in wiring harness. See WIRING DIAGRAMS. Repair as necessary.

CHECKING PNP SWITCH CONTINUITY

Transmission Shift Lever Position	Continuity Between Terminals
"P"	1 & 6
"R"	1 & 6; 2 & 6
"N"	1 & 6; 3 & 6
"D"	1 & 6
"D3"	[1]
"D2"	2 & 6
"D1"	1 & 6; 2 & 6

[1] – Continuity should not exist between terminal No. 6 and terminals No. 1, 2 or 3.

TORQUE SPECIFICATIONS

TORQUE SPECIFICATIONS

Application	Ft. Lbs. (N.m)
Transfer Case	
Drain & Fill Plugs	18 (25)
Transmission Oil Filler Tube	
Discovery	50 (68)
Range Rover	52 (70)
	INCH Lbs. (N.m)
Transmission Pan Bolts	71 (8)
Transmission Drain Plug	89 (10)

WIRING DIAGRAMS

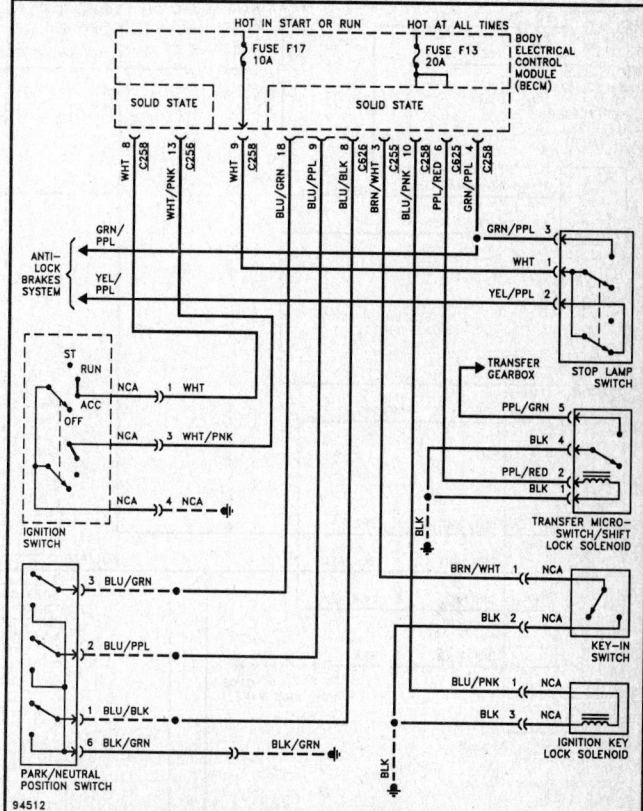

Fig. 10: Shift Interlock System Wiring Diagram (1995-96 Range Rover)

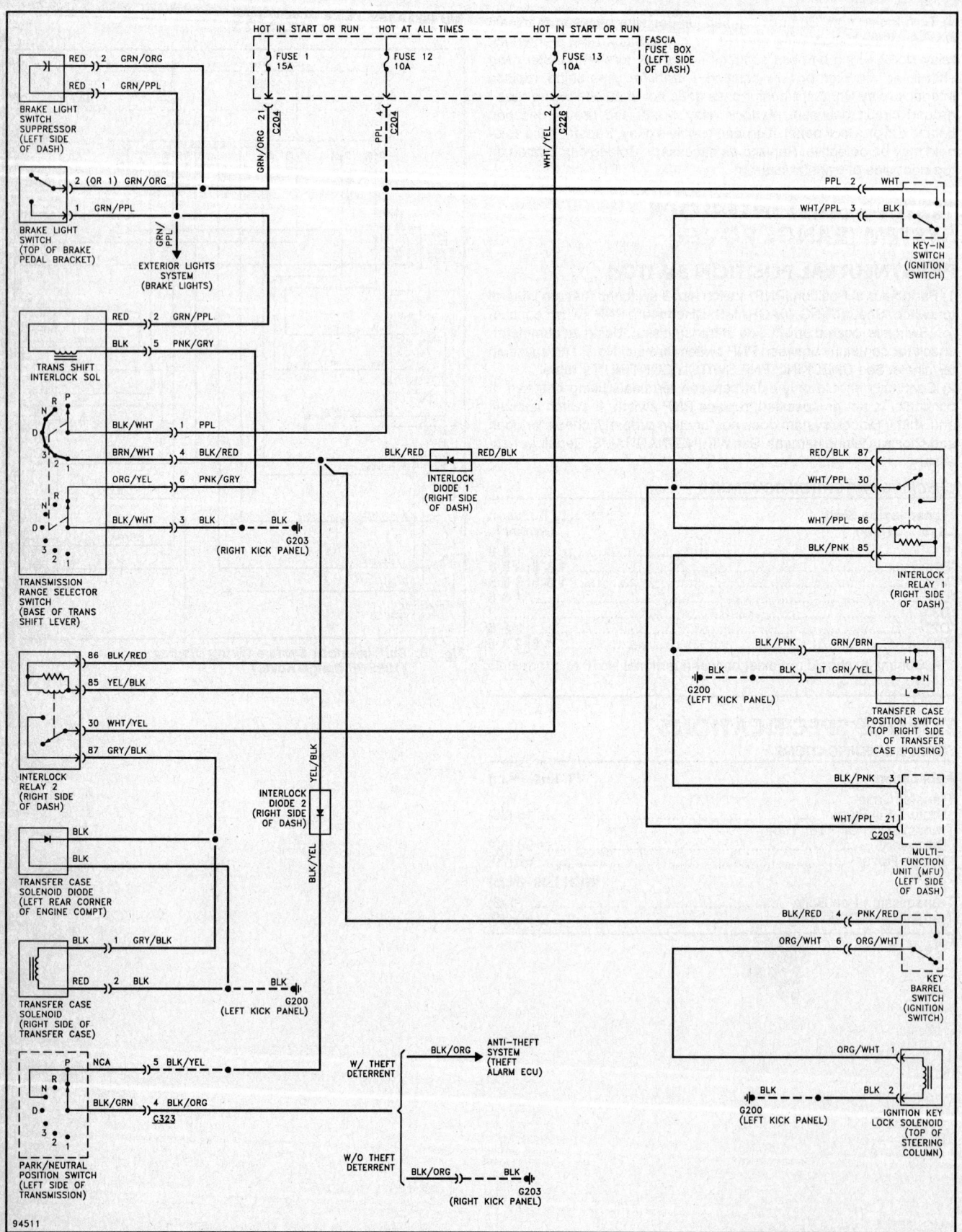

Fig. 11: *Shift Interlock System Wiring Diagram (1995-96 Discovery)*

900 Series, 9000 Series

IDENTIFICATION

Use illustrations for transaxle identification. *See Fig. 1, 2 or 3.*

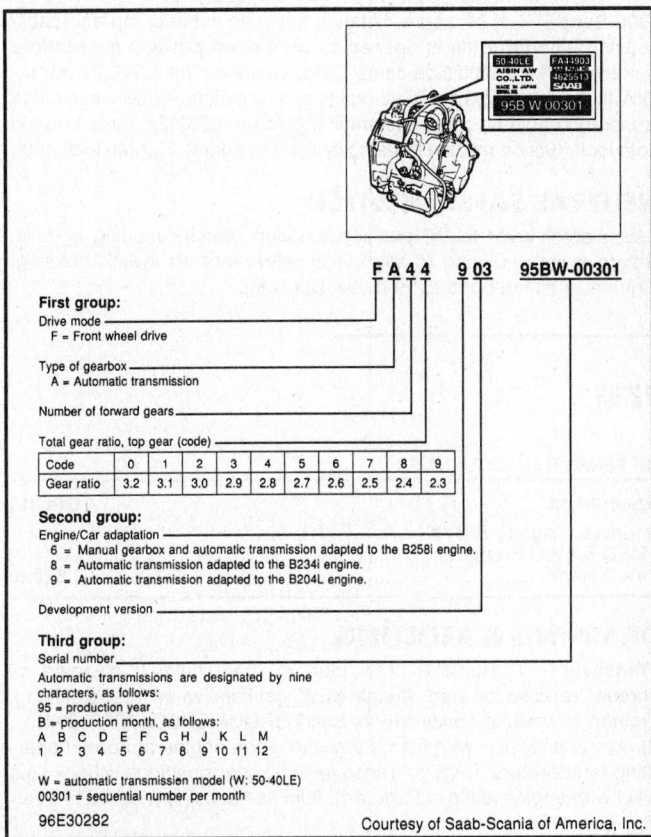

Fig. 1: Identifying Transaxle (900 Series)

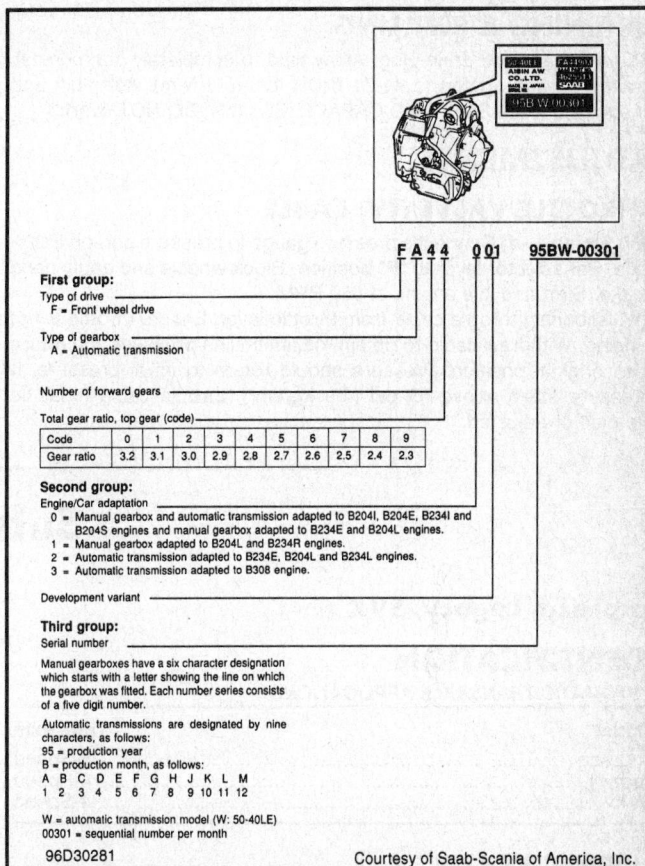

Fig. 2: Identifying Transaxle (9000 4 Cyl. Series)

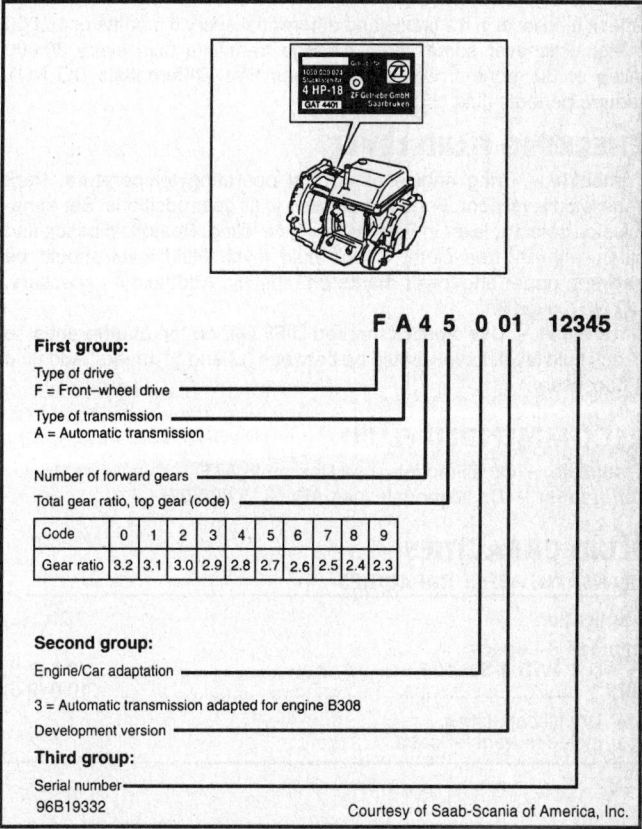

Fig. 3: Identifying Transaxle (9000 V6 Series)

LUBRICATION

SERVICE INTERVALS

On 900 Series, check fluid level every 15,000 miles, change fluid at 65,000 miles. On 9000 Series, change fluid at first 5000 miles, then every 30,000 miles.

CHECKING FLUID LEVEL

1) Park vehicle on level surface. Apply hand brake. Allow engine to idle at normal operating temperature. Place selector lever in each gear position for at least 15 seconds. Return to "P" position.

2) Check fluid level. Fluid level should be between the MIN and MAX marks on dipstick. Use hot or cold markings on dipstick, depending on transmission fluid temperature. Do not overfill.

RECOMMENDED FLUID

On all models, use Dexron-II automatic transmission fluid.

FLUID CAPACITIES

TRANSAXLE CAPACITIES

Application	Refill Qts. (L)	Dry Fill Qts. (L)
900 Series	3.4 (3.3)	7.6 (7.2)
9000 Series	3.1-3.7 (3.0-3.5)	8.7 (8.2)

DRAINING & REFILLING

Remove transaxle drain plug. Allow fluid to completely drain. Install drain plug and tighten to 44-71 INCH lbs. (5-8 N.m). Add fluid and check fluid level. See FLUID CAPACITIES table. DO NOT overfill.

ADJUSTMENTS

THROTTLE VALVE (TV) CABLE

900 Series – 1) Connect a pressure gauge to pressure port on transaxle. Set selector lever to "P" position. Block wheels and apply hand brake. Start and idle engine at 850 RPM.
2) Disconnect throttle cable from throttle lever. Ensure throttle is not binding. Withdraw cable to obtain maximum line pressure and return it to original position. Pressure should return to initial pressure. If pressure stays above 69 psi (4.9 kg/cm²), throttle cable must be cleaned or adjusted.

3) Connect throttle cable to throttle lever. Set selector lever to "D" position. Ensure cable is released to obtain lowest pressure. Increase pressure to 1.4 psi (0.1 kg/cm²) by adjusting throttle cable. Adjust cable at bracket in engine compartment. Set selector lever to "P" position. Pressure should be 59-69 psi (4.1-4.9 kg/cm²).
9000 Series – 1) Measure distance between cable crimp and cable housing when throttle is opened to wide open position (just before kickdown on transmission cam). Distance should be 1.54" (39 mm).
2) With throttle in idle position, again measure distance between cable crimp and cable housing. Distance should be .098" (2.5 mm). Loosen both lock nuts on throttle housing bracket to adjust. Tighten lock nuts.

NEUTRAL SAFETY SWITCH

Set selector lever to "N" position. Loosen switch retaining screws. Rotate switch housing to align lever with mark on switch housing. Tighten retaining bolts to 19 ft. lbs. (25 N.m).

Subaru

Impreza, Legacy, SVX

IDENTIFICATION
AUTOMATIC TRANSAXLE APPLICATIONS

Model	Transaxle
Impreza	4-Speed
Legacy	4-Speed
SVX	4-Speed

LUBRICATION

SERVICE INTERVALS

Check fluid level in transaxle and differential every 5 months or 15,000 miles, whichever comes first. Change transaxle fluid every 30,000 miles or 30 months, whichever comes first. Differentials DO NOT require periodic fluid change.

CHECKING FLUID LEVEL

Transaxle – Bring engine to normal operating temperature. Park vehicle on level floor. Engage transaxle in all gear positions. Set transmission selector lever in Park with engine idling. Remove dipstick and clean with lint-free cloth. Check fluid level. Fluid level should be between upper and lower marks on dipstick. Add fluid if necessary. DO NOT overfill.
Differential – Use dipstick marked DIFF OIL on top of differential to check fluid level. Level should be between "L" and "F" marks. Add fluid if necessary.

RECOMMENDED FLUID

Transaxle – On all models, use Dexron III ATF.
Differential – On all models, use API GL-5 80-90W.

FLUID CAPACITIES
TRANSAXLE REFILL CAPACITIES

Application	¹ Qts. (L)
Impreza & Legacy	
2WD & 4WD 4-Speed ²	8.4 (7.9)
SVX ²	10.0 (9.5)

¹ – Dry fill capacities.
² – Includes transfer case.

DIFFERENTIAL CAPACITIES

Application	Qts. (L)
Impreza, Legacy & SVX	
2WD & 4WD Front	1.3 (1.2)
4WD Rear	0.8 (0.8)

DRAINING & REFILLING

Transaxle – 1) Remove drain plug to drain fluid. If cleaning oil screen, remove oil pan. Install NEW gaskets when reassembling. Tighten all bolts to specification. See TORQUE SPECIFICATIONS.
2) Fill transmission with fluid. Start and warm engine to normal operating temperature. Engage transaxle in all gear positions. Check fluid level with engine idling in Park. Add fluid as necessary. DO NOT overfill.
Differential – Remove differential drain plug to drain fluid. Fill to bottom of filler hole.

ADJUSTMENTS

BAND

Impreza, Legacy, & SVX – Band adjustment screw is located on left side of transmission housing. Hold band adjustment screw, and loosen lock nut. Tighten adjustment screw to 80 INCH lbs (9 N.m), and back screw off 3 turns. Hold adjustment screw, and tighten lock nut to 18-21 ft. lbs. (25-28 N.m).

INHIBITOR SWITCH

Inhibitor switch allows back-up lights to turn on when select lever is in "R" position and allows starter motor to start when in "P" or "N" positions. It supplies input signal for each range and turns on corresponding range light on instrument panel.
Adjustment –)Loosen inhibitor switch mounting bolts. Move gear selector lever to Neutral. Insert Stopper Pin (499267300) as vertically as possible into holes in neutral safety switch lever and switch body. *See Fig. 1.* Tighten mounting bolts and recheck adjustment. Ensure engine will start only in selector positions "P" or "N" and back-up lights come on in "R" position.

SHIFT LINKAGE

Impreza, Legacy & SVX – 1) Move selector lever through all gear positions. Lever should go into each position with a corresponding click from transaxle when engaged. At each position, ensure selector needle indicates proper gear position.

2) If linkage is out of adjustment, move selector lever to Neutral. Loosen linkage adjuster nut at transaxle lever. With transaxle lever in Neutral position, adjust inner cable length. *See Fig. 2.*

3) Turn lock nut "A" until it contacts trunnion. Tighten lock nut "B" to 48-82 INCH lbs. (5.4-9.4 N.m). If indicator needle is not aligned with guide plate marking, loosen lock nut "B" adjust cable length as required. *See Fig. 2.*

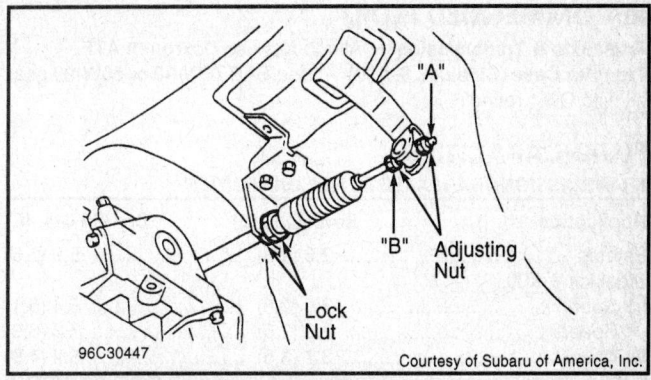

Fig. 2: *Adjusting Shift Cables (Typical)*

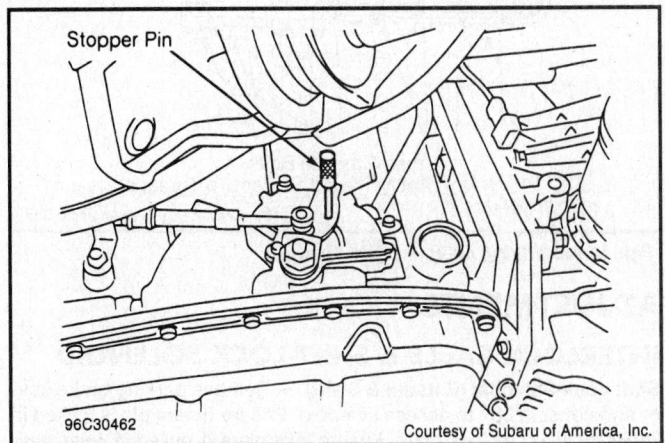

Fig. 1: *Adjusting Inhibitor Switch*

TORQUE SPECIFICATIONS
TORQUE SPECIFICATIONS

Application	Ft. Lbs. (N.m)
Band Adjustment Lock Nut	18-21 (25-28)
Drain Plug	17-20 (23-27)
	INCH Lbs. (N.m)
Oil Pan Bolt	38-48 (4.5-5.4)
Oil Screen Retaining Bolt	61-78 (7-9)
Shift Linkage Adjusting Nut "B"	48-82 (5.4-9.4)

Suzuki

Esteem, Sidekick, Swift, X-90

IDENTIFICATION
AUTOMATIC TRANSMISSION APPLICATIONS

Model	Transaxle/Transmission
Esteem (4-Speed)	[1] [2]
Sidekick	
3-Speed	[3] 3L30
4-Speed	[4] AW03-72LE
Swift (3-Speed)	ECC
X90 (4-Speed)	AW03-72LE

[1] – Transaxle code not available from manufacturer.
[2] – Electronically controlled 3-speed with overdrive.
[3] – Also known as Turbo Hydra-Matic 180C.
[4] – Transmission is an option on 4-door model.

LUBRICATION

SERVICE INTERVALS

Esteem – Manufacturer recommends replacing transaxle oil cooler hoses at 45,000 mile intervals. Replace transaxle fluid every 100,000 miles under normal driving conditions. Change fluid every 12,000 miles under severe operating conditions. Severe conditions are same as listed under SIDEKICK & X90.

Sidekick & X90 – **1)** Manufacturer recommends replacing transmission oil cooler hoses at 45,000 mile intervals. Under normal driving conditions, replace transmission fluid every 100,000 miles. Replace transfer case fluid at 30,000 mile intervals.

2) Under severe driving conditions, replace transmission fluid every 15,000 miles or 15 months (4-speed), or every 52,500 miles or 52 1/2 months (3-speed). Replace transfer case fluid at 7500 miles, then every 15,000 miles or 15 months thereafter. Severe driving conditions are any of the following:

- Driving Mostly In Stop-And-Go Traffic
- Delivery Service

- Towing
- Most Trips Are Less Than 4 Miles
- Most Trips Are Less Than 10 Miles With Outside Temperature Below Freezing
- Driving In Dusty Conditions

Swift – Manufacturer recommends replacing transaxle oil cooler hoses at 45,000 mile intervals. Replace transaxle fluid every 100,000 miles under normal driving conditions. Change fluid every 15,000 miles or 15 months under severe driving conditions. Severe conditions are same as listed under SIDEKICK & X90.

CHECKING FLUID LEVEL

NOTE: Check transfer case oil level on Sidekick & X90.

Transaxle & Transmission (Except Esteem) – **1)** Engine must be at normal operating temperature. Park vehicle on level surface and apply parking brake. Place selector lever in Park.

2) Start engine and allow it to idle. Apply brakes, shift through all gears and return selector lever to Park.

3) Remove dipstick. Fluid level should be in HOT or FULL HOT range. Add fluid (if necessary) and recheck. DO NOT overfill.

Transaxle (Esteem) – **1)** Engine must be at normal operating temperature. Park vehicle on level surface and apply parking brake. Place selector lever in Park.

2) Start engine and allow it to idle. Apply brakes, shift through all gears and return selector lever to Park.

3) Remove dipstick. Fluid level should be between FULL HOT and LOW HOT. If level is below LOW HOT add fluid until it is at FULL HOT level.

Transfer Case (Sidekick & X90) – Remove transfer case fill plug (upper plug) from rear of transfer case. Fill plug is located near speedometer gear housing. Fluid level must be at bottom of fill plug hole. Install fill plug and tighten to specification. See TORQUE SPECIFICATIONS.

RECOMMENDED FLUID

Transaxle & Transmission – All models use Dexron-III ATF.
Transfer Case (Sidekick & X90) – Use SAE 75W-90 or 80W-90 gear oil with GL-4 rating.

FLUID CAPACITIES

TRANSMISSION/TRANSAXLE REFILL CAPACITIES

Application	Refill Qts. (L)	Dry Fill Qts. (L)
Esteem	2.6 (2.5)	5.9 (5.6)
Sidekick & X90		
3-Speed	3.0 (2.8)	5.4 (5.1)
4-Speed	2.6 (2.5)	7.3 (6.9)
Swift	3.7 (3.5)	5.2 (4.9)

TRANSFER CASE REFILL CAPACITIES

Application	Pts. (L)
Sidekick & X90	3.6 (1.7)

DRAINING & REFILLING

CAUTION: Manufacturer recommends flushing oil cooler whenever transmission or transaxle is removed.

Esteem (Transaxle) – Raise vehicle. With engine cool, remove drain plug from oil pan and drain ATF. Install drain plug. Lower vehicle and fill with Dexron-III. Check fluid level. See CHECKING FLUID LEVEL under LUBRICATION.

Sidekick & X90 (Transmission) – **1)** On 3-speed model, raise and support vehicle. Disconnect front drive shaft from front differential flange. Remove all oil pan bolts except 3 bolts on rear of oil pan. Loosen remaining 3 bolts, allowing pan to tip downward so fluid will drain.

2) Once fluid is drained, remove remaining oil pan bolts, oil pan and gasket. Remove filter screen and gasket. Install NEW filter screen and gasket. Install oil pan gasket and oil pan. Tighten oil pan bolts to specification. See TORQUE SPECIFICATIONS.

3) Install drive shaft. Tighten drive shaft flange bolts to specification. See TORQUE SPECIFICATIONS. Fill transmission with 3 qts. (2.8L) of Dexron-III. Check fluid level. See CHECKING FLUID LEVEL under LUBRICATION.

4) On 4-speed model, raise and support vehicle. Ensure engine is cool and remove oil pan drain plug. Once fluid is drained, install drain plug and tighten to 13-20 ft. lbs. (18-27 N.m). Lower vehicle and fill transmission with 2.6 qts. (2.5L) of Dexron-III. Check fluid level. See CHECKING FLUID LEVEL under LUBRICATION.

Sidekick & X90 (Transfer Case) – **1)** Raise and support vehicle. Remove drain plug from back of transfer case, below speedometer gear housing and drain fluid. Install drain plug and tighten to specification. See TORQUE SPECIFICATIONS.

2) Remove transfer case fill plug (upper plug) from rear of transfer case. Fill plug is located near speedometer gear housing.

3) Fill transfer case with SAE 75W-90 or 80W-90 gear oil with GL-4 rating until fluid level is at bottom of fill plug hole. Install fill plug and tighten to specification. See TORQUE SPECIFICATIONS.

Swift (Transaxle) – **1)** Remove drain plug from bottom of oil pan and drain fluid. If removing filter screen, note position of cross-grooved oil pan bolts. *See Fig. 1.* Remove oil pan bolts, oil pan, gasket, filter screen bolts and filter screen.

2) Install filter screen. Install oil pan with NEW gasket. Apply thread sealant to threads of cross-grooved bolts. Tighten oil pan bolts to specification. Tighten drain plug to specification. See TORQUE SPECIFICATIONS.

3) Add 1.6 qts. (1.5L) of Dexron-III through dipstick tube. Check fluid level. See CHECKING FLUID LEVEL under LUBRICATION.

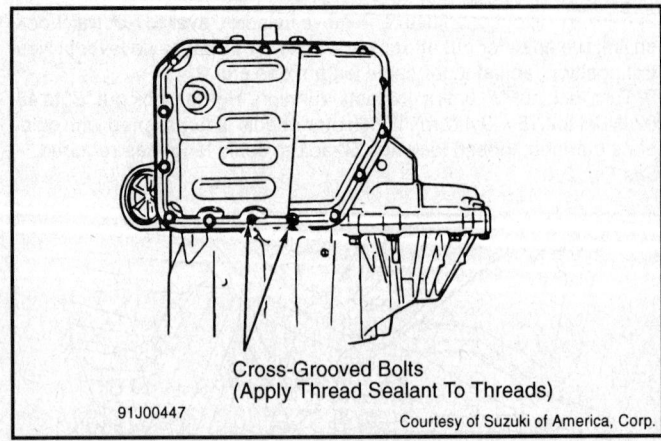

Cross-Grooved Bolts
(Apply Thread Sealant To Threads)

91J00447   Courtesy of Suzuki of America, Corp.

Fig. 1: Identifying Oil Pan Bolts (Swift)

ADJUSTMENTS

INTERLOCK CABLE & SHIFT LOCK SOLENOID

Shift Lock Solenoid (Esteem & Swift) – Remove parking brake cover and console box to access solenoid. Ensure detent pin is locked in PARK position by lock plate. Ensure lock plate is pulled in when ignition is turned to ON position and brake pedal is depressed. This allows detent pin to be pushed down.

Interlock Cable (Esteem & Swift) – **1)** Disconnect negative battery cable and disable air bag system. Remove covers to access upper steering column. Ensure interlock cable clamp screw is tight and cable is attached to release shaft.

2) Loosen cable bracket nut at gear selector cable. Place gear selector lever in Park and manually move solenoid lock plate towards front of vehicle, push gear selector lever lock knob. Insert Special Alignment Tool (09925-78210) into holes in gear selector key release cam and selector lever.

3) Ensure cable is connected to key release cam and tighten cable bracket nut to 114 INCH lbs. (13 N.m). Remove special tool. Manually hold solenoid shift lock plate toward front of vehicle and ensure key release cam moves smoothly when gear selector button is pushed.

4) With selector lever in Park, turn ignition key to ACC position. Ensure when knob is released, ignition key can be turned from ACC to LOCK position. Replace components removed for service.

NOTE: Shift Interlock system will not allow gearshift to move from Park unless ignition is on. It also prevents ignition key removal unless gearshift is in Park.

Shift Lock Solenoid (Sidekick & X90) – Remove parking brake cover and console box to access solenoid. Ensure detent pin is locked in PARK position by lock plate. Ensure lock plate is pulled in when ignition is turned to ON position and brake pedal is depressed (this allows voltage to energize solenoid). This allows detent pin to be pushed down.

Interlock Cable (Sidekick & X90) – **1)** Remove console covers. Cable is adjusted at bracket, located near gearshift. Place ignition in ACC position. Ensure cable is attached to key interlock lever.

2) Loosen cable bracket nut. *See Figs. 4 and 5.* Position release cam and insert Special Alignment Tool (09925-78210) into holes in gear selector key release cam and selector lever.

3) Ensure cable is connected to key release cam and tighten cable bracket nut to 114 INCH lbs. (13 N.m). Remove special tool. Ensure key release cam moves smoothly when gear selector button is pushed.

4) With selector lever in Park, turn ignition key to ACC position. Ensure when knob is released, ignition key can be turned from ACC to LOCK position. Replace components removed for service.

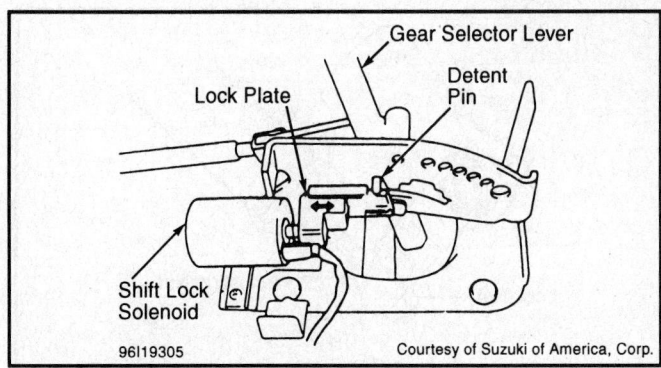

Fig. 2: Adjusting Shift Lock Solenoid (Swift Shown; Sidekick Is Similar)

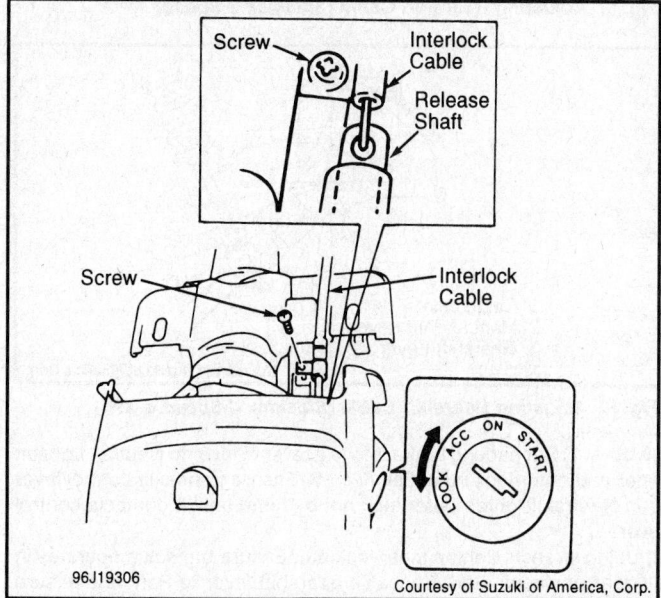

Fig. 3: Adjusting Shift Lock Cable (Swift Shown; Sidekick Is Similar)

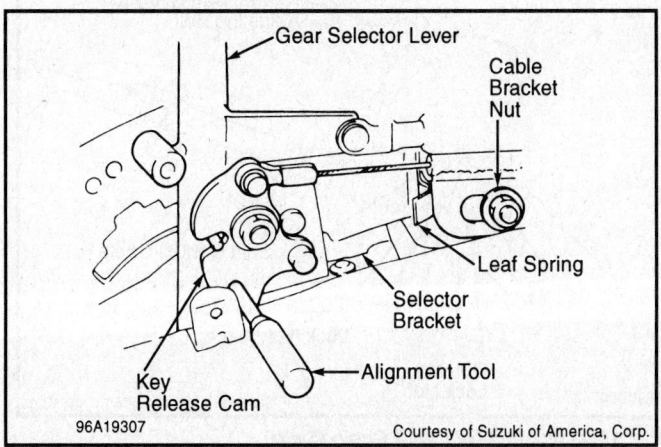

Fig. 4: Adjusting Interlock Cable Release Cam (Sidekick & X90)

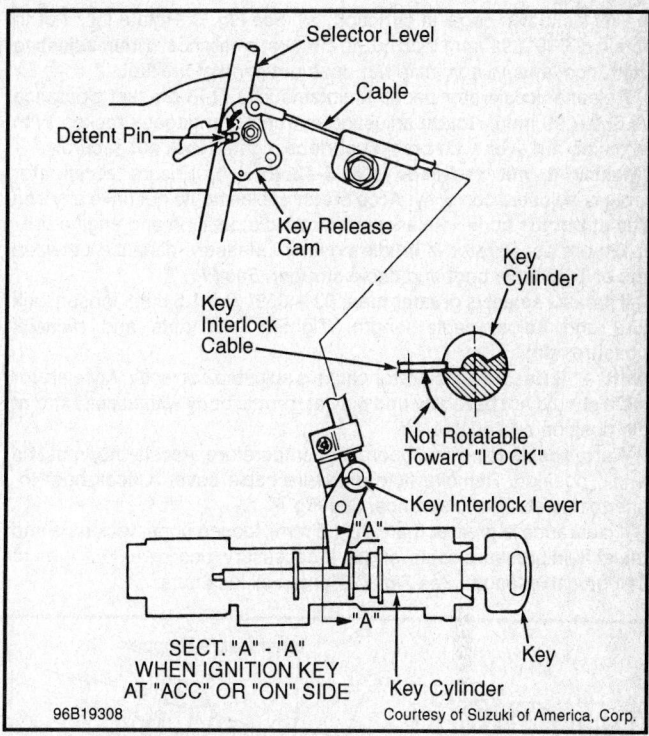

Fig. 5: Identifying Interlock System Components (Sidekick & X90)

KICKDOWN CABLE, THROTTLE VALVE (T.V.) CABLE

NOTE: Terminology differs between vehicle models. Sidekick equipped with 3-speed transmission uses a kickdown cable, Sidekick and X90 equipped with 4-speed transmission use a Throttle Valve (T.V.) cable, and Swift uses a fluid pressure control cable.

Sidekick (3-Speed 3L30) – 1) Ensure accelerator cable is adjusted correctly. Loosen kickdown cable lock nut and adjusting nut. See Fig. 6. Fully depress and hold accelerator pedal.

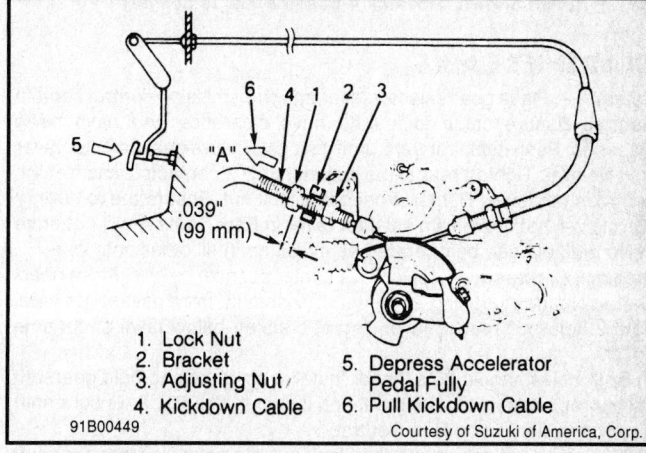

1. Lock Nut
2. Bracket
3. Adjusting Nut
4. Kickdown Cable
5. Depress Accelerator Pedal Fully
6. Pull Kickdown Cable

Fig. 6: Adjusting Kickdown Cable (Sidekick 3-Speed)

2) Pull kickdown cable in direction "A". *See Fig. 6.* Rotate lock nut to obtain a .039" (.99 mm) lock nut-to-bracket clearance. When adjusting clearance, ensure adjusting nut does not contact bracket.

3) Release accelerator pedal. Maintain lock nut-to-bracket clearance at .039" (.99 mm). Rotate adjusting nut until it engages bracket. With adjusting nut even with bracket surface, tighten lock nut securely.

Sidekick & X90 (4-Speed AW03-72LE) – 1) Ensure accelerator cable is adjusted correctly. Accelerator cable should not have any end play at throttle body with accelerator at idle position and engine off.

2) Ensure accelerator is in idle position. Measure distance between end of T.V. cable boot and cable stopper. *See Fig. 7.*

3) If measurement is greater than .031-.059" (0.8-1.5 mm), loosen lock nuts and adjust cable length. Tighten lock nuts and recheck measurement.

Swift – 1) Ensure accelerator cable is adjusted correctly. Accelerator cable should not have any end play at throttle body with accelerator at idle position and engine off.

2) Warm engine to normal operating temperature. Accelerator must be in idle position. Remove fluid pressure cable cover. Check boot-to-inner cable stopper clearance. *See Fig. 7.*

3) If clearance is greater than .02" (.5 mm), loosen upper lock nuts and adjust fluid pressure cable length. If necessary, use lower lock nuts to change cable length. *See Fig. 7.* Tighten all lock nuts.

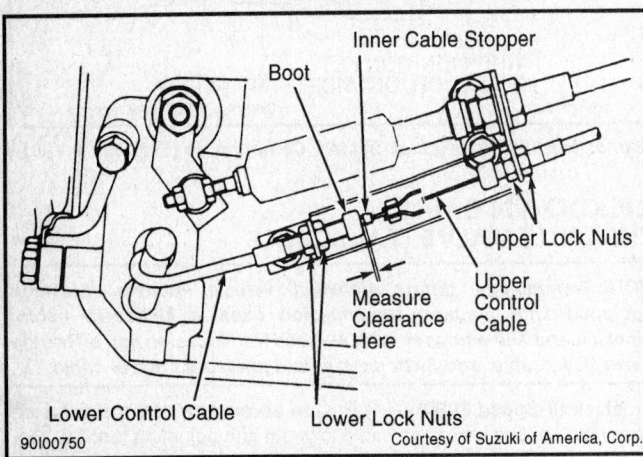

Fig. 7: *Adjusting T.V. Cable/Fluid Pressure Control Cable (Swift Shown; Sidekick 4-Speed & X90 Is Similar)*

GEARSHIFT CABLE

Esteem – Place gear selector lever and transmission control shaft in Neutral. Ensure cable lock nuts have clearance and have been loosened. Push cable forward until it stops. Ensure gear selector lever is in Neutral. Tighten rear cable lock nut until it contacts transmission control shaft lever. Tighten front cable lock nut. Ensure the following: vehicle will not move with selector lever in Park. Vehicle will not drive in Neutral, but can be operated as indicated in all other positions.

Sidekick (3-Speed) – 1) Remove center console covers. Place gearshift in Neutral. Looking at gearshift assembly from passenger side, note 2 holes on rear of lever detent bracket, below level of console cover.

2) Both holes should be aligned. Install a pin in hole to hold gearshift in Neutral. Loosen adjusting nut and lock nut. *See Fig. 8.* Ensure shift lever on transmission is in Neutral.

3) Tighten adjusting nut and then lock nut. Remove pin from gearshift assembly. Ensure gearshift operates properly in all gear ranges. Install console covers.

Sidekick (4-Speed) & X90 – 1) Place gearshift and manual shift levers in Neutral position. Loosen lock nuts at transmission end of cable. Ensure transmission shift lever is in Neutral. *See Fig 9.*

2) Turn adjusting nut "A" until it contacts cable joint, then tighten lock nut "B". After adjustment, ensure gearshift operates properly in all gear ranges.

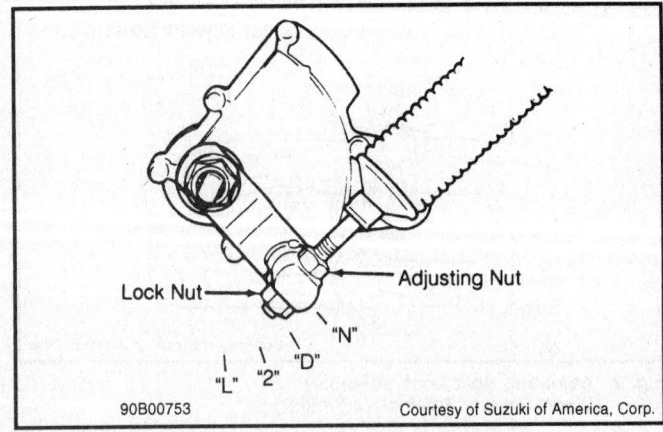

Fig. 8: *Adjusting Gearshift Cable (Sidekick 3-Speed)*

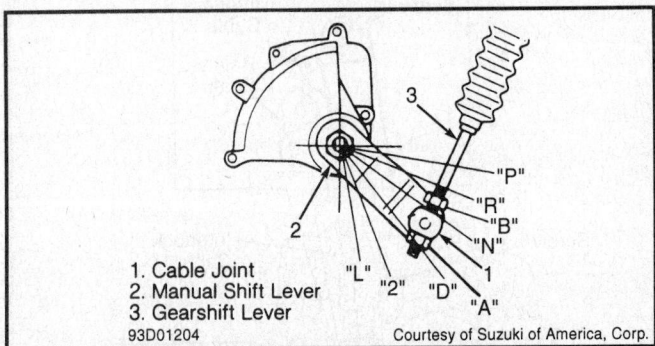

1. Cable Joint
2. Manual Shift Lever
3. Gearshift Lever

Fig. 9: *Adjusting Gearshift Cable (Sidekick 4-Speed & X90)*

Swift – 1) Set parking brake. Move gearshift lever to Neutral. Loosen inner and outer lock nuts. *See Fig. 10.* Ensure transaxle control lever is in Neutral. Tighten outer lock nut by hand until it contacts control lever.

2) Using wrench, tighten inner lock nut. Ensure transaxle operates in all gear positions. Shift transaxle gearshift lever to Park and ensure vehicle will not move.

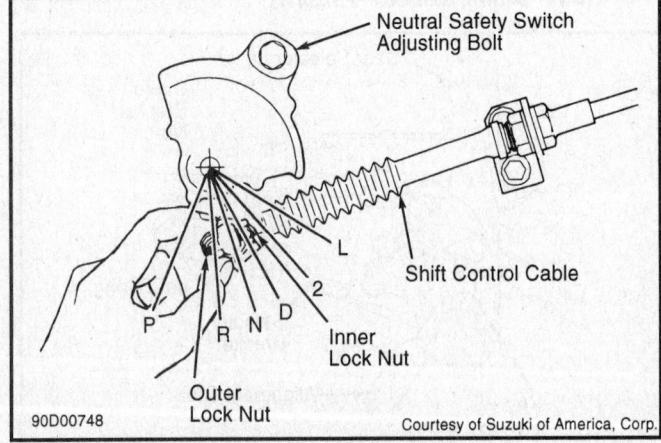

Fig. 10: *Adjusting Gearshift Cable (Swift)*

NEUTRAL SAFETY SWITCH, TRANSMISSION RANGE SWITCH

Esteem – Place gear selector lever in Neutral. Disconnect switch. Connect ohmmeter between the outside terminals (terminals No. 7 and 9 on 3-terminal side of connector). Continuity should be present when switch is in "N" position. Loosen and adjust switch as necessary.

Sidekick (3-Speed) – See SIDEKICK (3-SPEED) Under GEARSHIFT CABLE.

Sidekick (4-Speed) & X90 – **1)** Set parking brake. Place gearshift in Neutral. Loosen neutral safety switch adjusting bolt. Align groove on switch with match mark on manual shift lever shaft.

2) Hold switch at this position and tighten neutral switch adjusting bolt. Ensure starter operates with gearshift lever in Neutral and Park only.

Swift – **1)** Set parking brake. Place gearshift in Neutral. Loosen neutral safety switch adjusting bolt. *See Fig. 10.* Move neutral safety switch back and forth until a click is heard.

2) Hold switch at this position and tighten neutral switch adjusting bolt to specification. Ensure starter operates with gearshift lever in Neutral and Park only.

TORQUE SPECIFICATIONS
TORQUE SPECIFICATIONS

Application	Ft. Lbs. (N.m)
Esteem	
Drain Plug	29 (40)
Sidekick & X90	
Drain Plug(s)	13-20 (18-27)
Drive Shaft Flange Bolts	37-44 (50-60)
Fill Plug	13-20 (18-27)
Neutral Safety Switch Adjusting Bolt	[1]
Oil Filter Screen	14 (19)
Oil Pan Bolts	[1]
Transfer Case Fill Plug	17 (23)
Swift	
Drain Plug	13-17 (18-23)
Oil Pan Bolts	[2]
Neutral Safety Switch Adjusting Bolt	13-17 (18-23)

[1] – Tighten to 35-44 INCH lbs. (4-5 N.m).
[2] – Tighten to 35-53 INCH lbs. (4-6 N.m)

Toyota

Avalon, Camry, Celica, Corolla, Land Cruiser, MR2 (1995), Paseo, Pickup (1995), Previa, RAV4 (1996), Supra, Tacoma, Tercel, T100, 4Runner

APPLICATION
AUTOMATIC TRANSMISSION APPLICATIONS

Model	Transmission/Transaxle
Avalon	A541E
Camry	
2.2L 4-Cyl.	A140E
3.0L V6	A541E
Celica	
1.8L (7A-FE) 4-Cyl.	A246E
2.2L (5S-FE) 4-Cyl.	A140E
Corolla	
1.6L (4A-FE) 4-Cyl.	A131L
1.8L (7A-FE) 4-Cyl.	A245E
Land Cruiser	A343F
MR2	
1995 Models	
2.2L Non-Turbo	A241E
Paseo	A244E
Pickup	
1995 Models	
2WD	
2.4L 4-Cyl.	A43D
3.0L V6	A340E
4WD	
2.4L 4-Cyl.	A340F
3.0L V6	A340H
Previa	
1995 Models	
Non-Supercharged	
2WD	A46DE
All-Trac 4WD	A46DF
Supercharged	
2WD	A340E
All-Trac 4WD	A340F
1996 Models	
2WD	A340E
All-Trac 4WD	A340F
RAV4	
1996 Models	
2WD	A241E
4WD	A540H

AUTOMATIC TRANSMISSION APPLICATIONS (Cont.)

Model	Transmission/Transaxle
Supra	[1] A340E
Tacoma	
2WD	
2.4L (2RZ-FE) 4-Cyl.	A43D
3.4L (5VZ-FE) V6	A340E
4WD	
2.7L (3RZ-FE) 4-Cyl.	A340F
3.4L (5VZ-FE) V6	A340F
Tercel	
3-Speed	A132L
4-Speed	A242L
T100	
2WD	A340E
4WD	A340F
4Runner	
1995 Models	
2WD	
3.0L V6	A340E
4WD	
2.4L 4-Cyl. [2]	A340F
3.0L V6	A340H
1996 Models	
2WD	A340E
4WD	A340F

[1] – Transmission in turbo models contains a different electronic control system than the non-turbo models.
[2] – Applies only to Canada models.

LUBRICATION

SERVICE INTERVALS

Severe Service (All Models) – Under severe conditions such as trailer towing, police, taxi, local delivery service or operating under dusty conditions, replace transmission fluid and differential fluid every 15,000 miles or 12 months.

Avalon, Camry, Celica 2.2L 5S-FE, Corolla 1.6L 4A-FE & Tercel With 3-Speed – Check transmission fluid level and transmission/differential fluid level every 15,000 miles or 24 months. Transmission/differential fluid reservoir is independent from the transmission. Normal operating conditions service interval is not available.

Celica 1.8L 7A-FE, Corolla 1.8L 7A-FE, MR2, Paseo, RAV4 & Tercel With 4-Speed, Land Cruiser, Pickup, Previa, Supra, Tacoma, T100 & 4Runner – Check transmission fluid level every 15,000 miles or 24 months. Differential fluid reservoir is incorporated with the transmission. Normal operating conditions service interval is not available.

CHECKING FLUID LEVEL

NOTE: When checking fluid level for the transmission, if vehicle has been operating in heavy traffic, towing a trailer or at high speeds in hot weather, wait 30 minutes before checking the fluid level.

NOTE: Some models have a transmission/differential unit. On these models the differential lubrication is seperate from the transmission fluid. It must be checked and filled seperately.

Transmission – **1)** Drive vehicle until engine and transmission reach normal operating temperature. Park vehicle on level surface and apply parking brake. With engine idling and brakes applied, move gearshift from Park through Low and back to Park.
2) Check fluid level on transmission dipstick. Fluid level should be in HOT range marked on dipstick. Add proper type of fluid if necessary. See RECOMMENDED FLUID under LUBRICATION. DO NOT overfill transmission.

Transmission/Differential (Avalon, Camry, Celica 2.2L 5S-FE, Corolla 1.6L 4A-FE & Tercel 3-Speed) – Remove filler plug. *See Fig. 1.* Fluid should be level with bottom edge of filler plug hole. If fluid is low, fill with proper type fluid until fluid is level with filler plug opening. See RECOMMENDED FLUID under LUBRICATION. Reinstall filler plug.

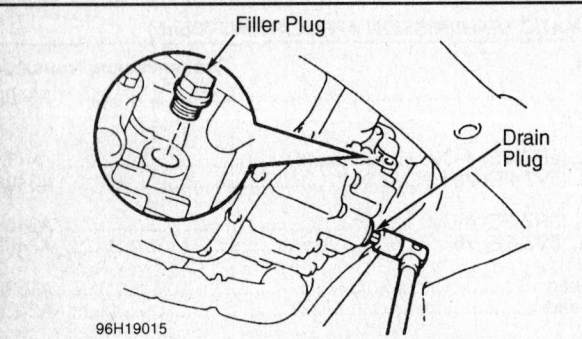

96H19015
Fig. 1-1: Avalon & Camry 3.0L V6

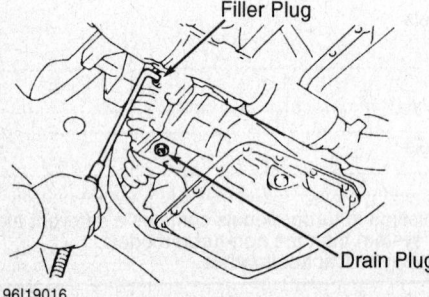

96I19016
Fig. 1-2: Camry 2.2L 4-Cyl. & Celica 2.2L (5S-FE)

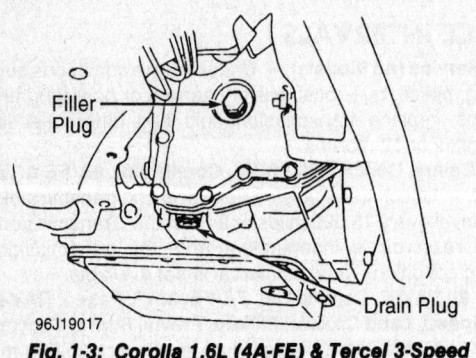

96J19017
Fig. 1-3: Corolla 1.6L (4A-FE) & Tercel 3-Speed

Courtesy of Toyota Motor Sales, U.S.A., Inc.

Fig. 1: Identifying Transmission/Differential Drain & Filler Plugs

Transfer Case (Land Cruiser, Pickup, Previa, Tacoma, T100 & 4Runner) – Remove filler plug located on rear of transfer case. Fluid should be level with bottom edge of filler plug hole. If fluid is low, fill with proper type fluid until fluid is level with filler plug opening. See RECOMMENDED FLUID under LUBRICATION. Reinstall filler plug.
Transfer Case (RAV4) – Park vehicle on level surface and apply parking brake. Check fluid level on transfer case dipstick. Fluid level should be in the LOW to HIGH range. Add proper type of fluid if necessary. See RECOMMENDED FLUID under LUBRICATION. DO NOT overfill transfer case.

RECOMMENDED FLUID

For recommend fluid and transmission refill capacity, see FLUID APPLICATION table. For fluid capacity, see TRANSMISSION REFILL CAPACITIES table under FLUID CAPACITIES.

FLUID APPLICATION

Application	Fluid Type
Transmission	
RAV4	
2WD	Dexron-II ATF
4WD	Toyota Type "T" ATF
Supra	
Non-Turbo	Dexron-II ATF
Turbo	Toyota Type "T"-II ATF
All Others	Dexron-II
Transmission/Differential	
Avalon, Camry, Celica 2.2L (5S-FE),	
Corolla 1.6L (4A-FE) & Tercel 3-Speed	Dexron-II
Transfer Case	
Land Cruiser	SAE 75W-90 GL-5 Gear Oil
Pickup	
2.4L 4-Cyl.	SAE 75W-90 GL-5 Gear Oil
3.0L V6	Dexron-II ATF
Previa, RAV4, Tacoma & T100	SAE 75W-90 GL-5 Gear Oil
4Runner	
1995 Models	
2.4L 4-Cyl.	SAE 75W-90 GL-5 Gear Oil
3.0L V6	Dexron-II ATF
1996 Models	SAE 75W-90 GL-5 Gear Oil

FLUID CAPACITIES

TRANSMISSION REFILL CAPACITIES [1]

Application	Refill Qts. (L)	Dry-Fill Qts. (L)
Avalon	3.7 (3.5)	7.1 (6.7)
Camry		
2.2L 4-Cyl.	2.6 (2.5)	5.9 (5.6)
3.0L V6	3.7 (3.5)	7.1 (6.7)
Celica		
1.8L (7A-FE)	3.3 (3.1)	8.0 (7.6)
2.2L (5S-FE)	2.6 (2.5)	5.9 (5.6)
Corolla		
1.6L (4A-FE)	2.6 (2.5)	5.8 (5.5)
1.8L (7A-FE)	3.3 (3.1)	8.0 (7.6)
Land Cruiser	2.0 (1.9)	11.6 (11.0)
MR2		
2.2L Non-Turbo	3.5 (3.3)	8.5 (8.0)
Paseo	3.3 (3.1)	7.6 (7.2)
Pickup		
2WD		
2.4L 4-Cyl.	2.5 (2.4)	6.9 (6.5)
3.0L V6	1.7 (1.6)	7.6 (7.2)
4WD		
2.4L 4-Cyl.	2.1 (2.0)	8.0 (7.6)
3.0L V6	4.8 (4.5)	10.9 (10.3)
Previa		
Non-Supercharged	2.5 (2.4)	6.0 (5.7)
Supercharged	1.7 (1.6)	7.6 (7.2)
RAV4		
2WD	3.5 (3.3)	8.5 (8.0)
4WD	3.5 (3.3)	7.4 (7.0)

[1] – Approximate capacity is listed.

TRANSMISSION REFILL CAPACITIES [1] (Cont.)

Application	Refill Qts. (L)	Dry-Fill Qts. (L)
Supra		
Non-Turbo	1.7 (1.6)	7.6 (7.2)
Turbo	2.0 (1.9)	8.7 (8.2)
Tacoma		
2WD		
2.4L 4-Cyl.	2.5 (2.4)	6.9 (6.5)
3.4L V6	1.7 (1.6)	7.6 (7.2)
4WD	2.1 (2.0)	10.5 (9.9)
Tercel		
3-Speed	2.6 (2.5)	5.8 (5.5)
4-Speed	3.3 (3.1)	7.6 (7.2)
T100		
2WD	1.7 (1.6)	7.6 (7.2)
4WD	2.1 (2.0)	8.0 (7.6)
4Runner		
1995		
2WD	1.7 (1.6)	7.6 (7.2)
4WD		
2.4L 4-Cyl.	2.1 (2.0)	8.0 (7.6)
3.0L V6	4.8 (4.5)	10.9 (10.3)
1996		
2WD	1.7 (1.6)	7.6 (7.2)
4WD	2.1 (2.0)	9.3 (8.8)

[1] – Approximate capacity is listed.

TRANSMISSION DIFFERENTIAL REFILL CAPACITIES [1]

Application	Qts. (L)
Avalon	1.0 (.9)
Camry	
2.2L 4-Cyl.	1.7 (1.6)
3.0L V6	1.0 (.9)
Celica	
2.2L (5S-FE)	1.7 (1.6)
Corolla	
1.6L (4A-FE)	1.5 (1.4)
Tercel	
3-Speed	1.5 (1.4)

[1] – Approximate capacity is listed.

TRANSFER CASE REFILL CAPACITIES [1]

Application	Qts. (L)
Land Cruiser	1.8 (1.7)
Pickup	
2.4L 4-Cyl.	1.2 (1.1)
3.0L V6	.8 (.7)
Previa	1.4 (1.3)
RAV4	.8 (.7)
Tacoma	1.1 (1.0)
T100	1.2 (1.1)
4Runner	
1995 Models	
2.4L 4-Cyl.	1.2 (1.1)
3.0L V6	.8 (.7)
1996 Models	1.1 (1.0)

[1] – Approximate capacity is listed.

DRAINING & REFILLING

NOTE: All transmissions contain a transmission oil strainer mounted on the valve body. Manufacturer does list transmission oil strainer replacement when servicing the transmission. If servicing transmission oil strainer, oil pan removal is required.

Transmission (Pickup 4WD With 3.0L V6 & 1995 4Runner 4WD With V6) – 1) Remove transmission oil pan drain plugs from transmission. *See Fig. 2.* Allow fluid to fully drain. If replacing transmission oil strainer, remove transmission oil pan and gasket.

CAUTION: When removing transmission oil strainer, note bolt size and length for reassembly reference.

2) Remove bolts, transmission oil strainer and gasket (if equipped). Thoroughly clean transmission oil pan. Using NEW gasket (if equipped), install transmission oil strainer. Install and tighten bolts to specification. See TORQUE SPECIFICATIONS.

3) Using NEW gasket, install transmission oil pan (if removed). Install and tighten bolts to specification See TORQUE SPECIFICATIONS. Fill transmission through dipstick tube to specified capacity using recommended fluid. See RECOMMENDED FLUID under LUBRICATION.

4) Ensure vehicle is on a level surface. Apply parking brake. Start engine and apply brakes. Move gearshift from Park through Low and back to Park.

5) Check fluid level on transmission dipstick. Add proper type fluid so fluid level is at the COOL range marked on the dipstick. Operate vehicle to normal operating temperature and recheck. See CHECKING FLUID LEVEL under LUBRICATION.

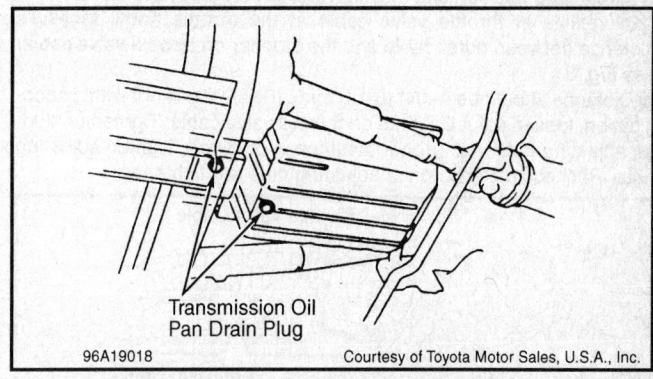

Transmission Oil Pan Drain Plug

96A19018   Courtesy of Toyota Motor Sales, U.S.A., Inc.

Fig. 2: Identifying Transmission Oil Pan Drain Plugs (Pickup 4WD With 3.0L V6 & 1995 4Runner 4WD With V6)

Transmission (All Others) – 1) Remove transmission oil pan drain plug from transmission oil pan. Allow fluid to fully drain. If replacing transmission oil strainer, remove transmission oil pan and gasket.

CAUTION: When removing transmission oil strainer, note bolt size and length for reassembly reference.

2) Remove bolts, transmission oil strainer and gasket (if equipped). Thoroughly clean transmission oil pan. Using NEW gasket (if equipped), install transmission oil strainer. Install and tighten bolts to specification. See TORQUE SPECIFICATIONS.

3) Using NEW gasket, install transmission oil pan (if removed). Install and tighten bolts to specification See TORQUE SPECIFICATIONS. Fill transmission through dipstick tube to specified capacity using recommended fluid. See RECOMMENDED FLUID under LUBRICATION.

4) Ensure vehicle is on a level surface. Apply parking brake. Start engine and apply brakes. Move gearshift from Park through Low and back to Park.

5) Check fluid level on transmission dipstick. Add proper type fluid so fluid level is at the COOL range marked on the dipstick. Operate vehicle to normal operating temperature and recheck. See CHECKING FLUID LEVEL under LUBRICATION.

Transmission Differential (Avalon, Camry, Celica 2.2L 5S-FE, Corolla 1.6L 4A-FE & Tercel 3-Speed) – 1) Remove oil filler and drain plugs from differential. *See Fig. 1.* Allow fluid to drain. Reinstall drain plug.

2) Fill differential through oil filler plug hole to specified capacity using recommended fluid. See RECOMMENDED FLUID under LUBRICATION. Ensure fluid is level with bottom edge of filler plug hole. Reinstall filler plug.

Transfer Case (Land Cruiser, Pickup, Previa, Tacoma, T100 & 4Runner) – 1) Remove filler plug located on rear of transfer case. Remove drain plug from bottom of transfer case. Allow fluid to drain. Reinstall drain plug.

2) Fill transfer case through oil filler plug hole to specified capacity using recommended fluid. See RECOMMENDED FLUID under LUBRICATION. Ensure fluid is level with bottom edge of filler plug hole. Reinstall filler plug.

Transfer Case (RAV4) – 1) Remove drain plug from bottom of transfer case. Allow fluid to drain. Reinstall drain plug. Fill transfer case through transfer case oil dipstick tube to specified capacity using recommended fluid. See RECOMMENDED FLUID under LUBRICATION.

2) Check fluid level on transfer case dipstick. Fluid level should be in the LOW to HIGH range. Add fluid if necessary. DO NOT overfill transfer case.

ADJUSTMENTS

THROTTLE VALVE CABLE

Avalon, Camry, Celica, Corolla 1.8L 7A-FE, Land Cruiser, MR2, Paseo, Previa Supercharged, RAV4, Supra Non-Turbo, Tacoma 2WD 3.4L V6 & 4WD, T100 & 1996 4Runner – 1) Ensure accelerator pedal is in released position and throttle valve is fully closed. Check that no slack exists in throttle valve cable at the throttle body. Measure distance between outer cable and the stopper on throttle valve cable. See Fig. 3.

2) Distance should be 0-.04" (0-1.0 mm). If distance is not within specification, loosen adjusting nuts on throttle valve cable. Tighten or loosen adjusting nuts until proper distance is obtained. Tighten adjusting nuts. Recheck distance once adjusting nuts are tightened.

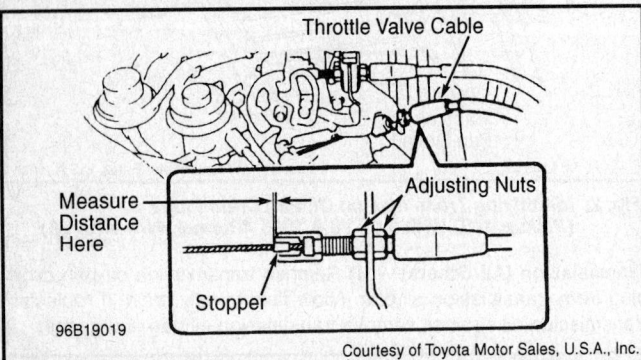

96B19019   Courtesy of Toyota Motor Sales, U.S.A., Inc.

Fig. 3: Measuring Distance On Typical Throttle Valve Cable (Avalon, Camry, Celica, Corolla 1.8L 7A-FE, Land Cruiser, MR2, Paseo, Previa Supercharged, RAV4, Supra Non-Turbo, Tacoma 2WD 3.4L V6 & 4WD, T100 & 1996 4Runner)

Corolla 1.6L 4A-FE, Pickup, Previa Non-Supercharged, Tacoma 2WD 2.4L 4-Cyl., Tercel & 1995 4Runner – 1) Fully depress accelerator pedal and ensure throttle valve is fully open. If throttle valve is fully open, go to step **2)**. If throttle valve is not fully open, adjust throttle linkage or cable so throttle valve is fully open and then go to step **2)**.

2) Ensure accelerator pedal is fully depressed. Loosen adjusting nuts on throttle valve cable. Adjust outer cable so distance between end of rubber boot and stopper on throttle valve cable is 0-.04" (0-1.0 mm). See Fig. 4. Tighten adjusting nuts. Recheck distance once adjusting nuts are tightened.

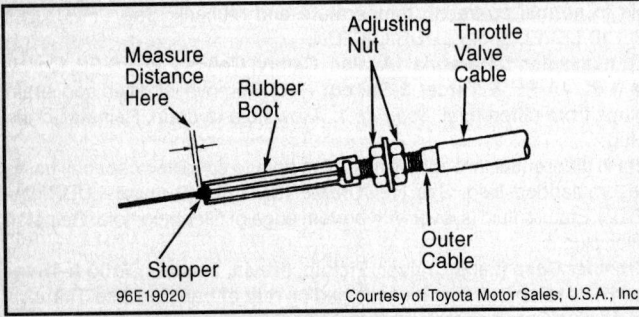

96E19020   Courtesy of Toyota Motor Sales, U.S.A., Inc.

Fig. 4: Measuring Distance On Throttle Valve Cable (Corolla 1.6L 4A-FE, Pickup, Previa Non-Supercharged, Tacoma 2WD 2.4L 4-Cyl., Tercel & 1995 4Runner)

GEARSHIFT LINKAGE

Land Cruiser – 1) Apply parking brake. Loosen control rod nut on control rod at control shaft lever on side of transmission. See Fig. 5. Rotate control shaft lever fully counterclockwise toward rear of vehicle to the Park position.

2) Rotate control shaft lever clockwise 2 notches to Neutral position. Ensure gearshift is in Neutral. While holding control shaft lever lightly counterclockwise back toward the Reverse position, tighten control rod nut.

3) Start engine. Ensure vehicle moves forward when shifting gearshift from Neutral to Drive, and in reverse when shifting to Reverse.

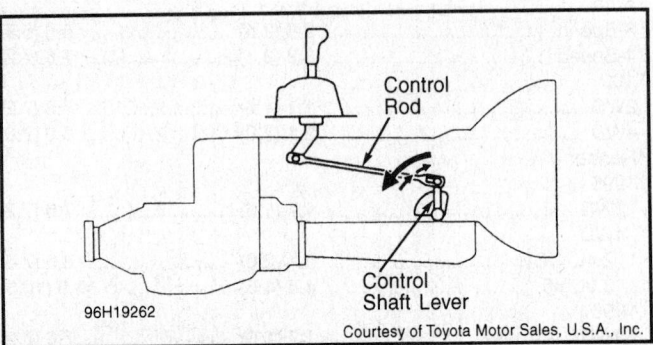

96H19262   Courtesy of Toyota Motor Sales, U.S.A., Inc.

Fig. 5: Adjusting Shift Linkage (Land Cruiser)

Pickup 2WD & Pickup 4WD With 2.4L 4-Cyl. – 1) Apply parking brake. On models with column shift, remove control rod nut from control rod at bottom of steering column. See Fig. 6. Push control rod fully downward to the Park position.

2) Pull control rod upward 2 notches to the Neutral position. While holding gearshift lightly toward the Reverse position, tighten control rod nut.

3) On models with floor shift, loosen nut for control rod at the gearshift. See Fig. 7. Pull control rod fully backward toward rear of vehicle to the Park position. Push control rod forward 2 notches to the Neutral position. Ensure gearshift is in Neutral. Tighten nut for control rod at gearshift.

4) On all models, start engine. Ensure vehicle moves forward when shifting gearshift from Neutral to Drive, and in reverse when shifting to Reverse.

Pickup 4WD With 3.0L V6 & 1995 4Runner 4WD With 3.0L V6 – 1) Apply parking brake. Loosen nut(s) for control rod at shift lever on driver's side of transmission. The control rod fits between shifting mechanism at rear of the transmission and the shift lever on side of transmission. The shifting mechanism has a rod which goes to the gearshift.

2) Pull control rod fully backward toward rear of vehicle to the Park position. Push control rod forward 2 notches to the Neutral position.

3) Ensure gearshift is in Neutral. While holding gearshift lightly toward the Reverse position, tighten nut(s) for control rod.

Supra, Tacoma With Floor Shift, 1995 4Runner 2WD & 4WD 2.4L 4-Cyl., & 1996 4Runner – 1) Apply parking brake. Loosen nut for control rod at the gearshift. See Fig. 7. Pull control rod fully backward toward rear of vehicle to the Park position.

2) Push control rod forward 2 notches to the Neutral position. Ensure gearshift is in Neutral. Tighten nut for control rod at gearshift.

3) Start engine. Ensure vehicle moves forward when shifting gearshift from Neutral to Drive, and in reverse when shifting to Reverse.

T100 – 1) Apply parking brake. Remove control rod nut from control rod at bottom of steering column. See Fig. 6. Push control rod fully downward to the Park position.

2) Pull control rod upward 2 notches to the Neutral position. While holding gearshift lightly toward the Reverse position, tighten control rod nut.

3) Start engine. Ensure vehicle moves forward when shifting gearshift from Neutral to Drive, and in reverse when shifting to Reverse.

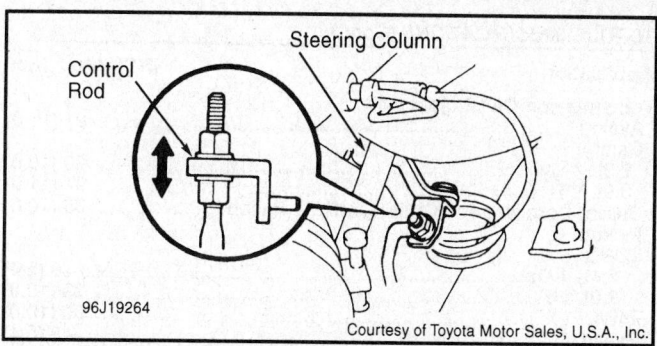

Fig. 6: *Adjusting Typical Shift Linkage For Column Shifts*

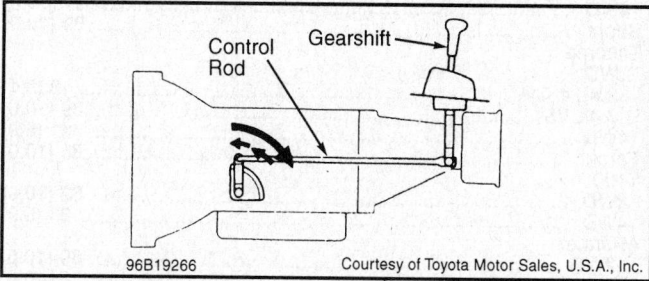

Fig. 7: *Adjusting Typical Shift Linkage For Floor Shifts*

GEARSHIFT CABLE

Avalon, Camry, Celica, Corolla, MR2, Paseo, Previa, RAV4, Tercel –
1) Apply parking brake. Loosen swivel nut on manual shift lever on side of transmission. *See Fig. 8.* Rotate manual shift lever counterclockwise (downward) toward the oil pan to the Park position.
2) Rotate manual shift lever clockwise (upward) 2 notches to Neutral position. Ensure gearshift is in Neutral. While holding manual shift lever slightly counterclockwise to Reverse position, tighten swivel nut.
3) Start engine. Ensure vehicle moves forward when shifting gearshift from Neutral to Drive, and moves in reverse when shifting to Reverse.

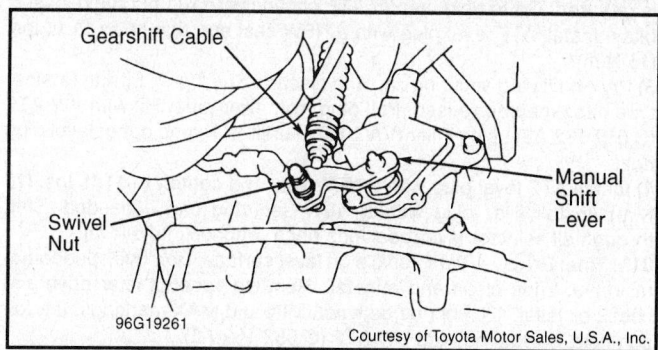

Fig. 8: *Adjusting Typical Gearshift Cable*

Tacoma With Column Shift – 1) Apply parking brake. Loosen swivel nut on manual shift lever on side of transmission. Rotate manual shift lever fully forward toward front of engine Park position.
2) Rotate manual shift lever back toward rear of vehicle 2 notches to Neutral position. Ensure gearshift is in Neutral. While holding manual shift lever lightly toward the Reverse position, tighten swivel nut.
3) Start engine. Ensure vehicle moves forward when shifting gearshift from Neutral to Drive, and moves in reverse when shifting to Reverse.

PARK/NEUTRAL SWITCH

NOTE: Park/neutral switch may also be referred to as Park/Neutral Position (PNP) switch.

1) Loosen park/neutral switch retaining bolt(s). Position gearshift in Neutral. Align neutral line on park/neutral switch with groove on the shaft. *See Fig. 9.*
2) Hold park/neutral switch in this position and tighten retaining bolt to specification. Ensure vehicle only starts with gearshift in Park or Neutral.

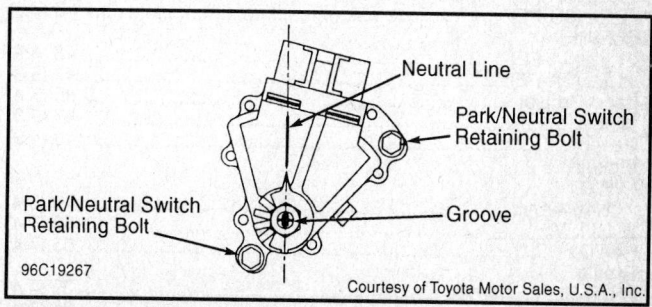

Fig. 9: *Adjusting Park/Neutral Switch (Typical)*

TRANSFER CASE SHIFT LINKAGE

Pickup & 1995 4Runner – 1) Loosen shift rod nut on cross shaft for transfer case. Cross shaft is located at rear of transfer case, just above the drive shaft flange. Push control shaft for transfer case shift linkage fully toward front of vehicle.
2) Pull control shaft toward rear of vehicle one notch to the "H4" position. Ensure transfer case gearshift is in "H4" position. While holding transfer case gearshift lightly toward "H4" position, tighten shift rod nut on cross shaft. Check transfer case operation.

TORQUE SPECIFICATIONS

TORQUE SPECIFICATIONS

Application	Ft. Lbs. (N.m)
Transmission Oil Pan Drain Plug	
Avalon & Camry	36 (49)
Celica	
1.8L (7A-FE)	13 (18)
2.2L (5S-FE)	36 (49)
Corolla	
1.6L (4A-FE)	36 (49)
1.8L (7A-FE)	13 (18)
Land Cruiser	15 (20)
MR2 & Paseo	13 (18)
Pickup & Previa	15 (20)
RAV4	
2WD	13 (18)
4WD	36 (49)
Supra	
Non-Turbo	15 (20)
Turbo	13 (18)
Tacoma	15 (20)
Tercel	
3-Speed	36 (49)
4-Speed	13 (18)
T100	15 (20)
4Runner	15 (20)

	INCH Lbs. (N.m)
Park/Neutral Switch Retaining Bolt	
Land Cruiser	115 (13.0)
Pickup	
2WD	
2.4L 4-Cyl.	48 (5.4)
All Others	115 (13.0)
Previa & Supra	115 (13.0)
Tacoma	
2WD 2.4L 4-Cyl.	48 (5.4)
All Others	115 (13.0)
T100 & 4Runner	115 (13.0)
All Others	48 (5.4)

TORQUE SPECIFICATIONS (Cont.)

Application	INCH Lbs. (N.m)
Transmission Oil Pan Bolt	
Avalon & Camry	43 (4.9)
Celica	
1.8L (7A-FE)	47 (5.3)
2.2L (5S-FE)	43 (4.9)
Corolla	
1.6L (4A-FE)	43 (4.9)
1.8L (7A-FE)	47 (5.3)
Land Cruiser	65 (7.4)
MR2	47 (5.3)
Paseo	43 (4.9)
Pickup	
2WD	
2.4L 4-Cyl.	48 (5.4)
3.0L V6	65 (7.4)
4WD	65 (7.4)
Previa	
Non-Supercharged	39 (4.4)
Supercharged	65 (7.4)
RAV4	43 (4.9)
Supra	65 (7.4)
Tacoma	
2WD	
2.4L 4-Cyl.	48 (5.4)
3.4L V6	65 (7.4)
4WD	65 (7.4)
Tercel	43 (4.9)
T100	65 (7.4)
4Runner	65 (7.4)

TORQUE SPECIFICATIONS (Cont.)

Application	INCH Lbs. (N.m)
Transmission Oil Strainer Bolt	
Avalon	97 (11.0)
Camry	
2.2L 4-Cyl.	89 (10.0)
3.0L V6	97 (11.0)
Celica, Corolla, Land Cruiser, MR2 & Paseo	89 (10.0)
Pickup	
2WD	
2.4L 4-Cyl.	48 (5.4)
3.0L V6	89 (10.0)
4WD	89 (10.0)
Previa	48 (5.4)
RAV4	
2WD	89 (10.0)
4WD	97 (11.0)
Supra	89 (10.0)
Tacoma	
2WD	
2.4L 4-Cyl.	48 (5.4)
3.4L V6	89 (10.0)
4WD	61 (6.9)
Tercel	89 (10.0)
T100	
2WD	89 (10.0)
4WD	61 (6.9)
4Runner	
2WD	89 (10.0)
4WD	61 (6.9)

Volkswagen

Cabrio, Golf, Golf III, GTI VR6
Jetta, Jetta III, Passat

IDENTIFICATION

AUTOMATIC TRANSAXLE APPLICATIONS

Vehicle Year & Model	Transaxle Model
1995	
Cabrio, Golf III, GTI VR6	
Jetta III & Passat	096
1996	
Cabrio, Golf, Jetta & Passat	01M

LUBRICATION

SERVICE INTERVALS

Check fluid level at each oil change. Change fluid every 30,000 miles under severe driving conditions. Replace filter if needed during fluid change.

CHECKING FLUID LEVEL

CAUTION: Fill 01M transaxle with VW ATF (G 052 162 A2) only. DO NOT use Dexron or Dexron-II type fluids.

096 Transaxle – 1) Park vehicle on level surface, with transaxle at normal operating temperature. Set selector lever to Park. Apply parking brake. Allow engine to idle. Remove dipstick, wipe clean, and reinsert. Shift through all selector lever positions once.

2) Remove dipstick. Fluid level should be between marks on dipstick. If additional fluid is required, use Dexron or Dexron-II type fluid only and add as needed. DO NOT use any lubricant additives.

096 Final Drive – Park vehicle on level surface. Remove speedometer drive. Wipe clean and reinstall. Remove speedometer drive and check oil level. Oil must be between MIN and MAX markings. If additional fluid is required, add Synthetic G 50, SAE 75W–90 (G 052 145 A2).

01M Transaxle – 1) Set selector lever to Park. Start engine and allow it to idle. Raise and support vehicle. With transaxle at normal operating temperature, remove ATF level plug from oil pan. Any ATF present in overflow tube (inside plug hole) will run out.

2) If only a small amount, or no ATF flows from overflow tube, filling is required. Go to next step. If ATF continues to run out, fluid level is okay. Install ATF level plug with a NEW seal and tighten to 11 ft. lbs. (15 N.m).

3) Pry off fill plug securing cap and discard. *See Fig. 1*. Spring retainer type caps may be reused. Pull plug from filler pipe. Fill with VW ATF (G 052 162 A2) using Filler (VAG 1924) until ATF runs out of level plug hole.

4) Install ATF level plug with a NEW seal and tighten to 11 ft. lbs. (15 N.m). Install filler plug with a NEW securing cap if needed. Shift through all selector lever positions once. Recheck fluid level.

01M Final Drive – Park vehicle on level surface. Remove speedometer drive. Wipe clean and reinstall. Remove speedometer drive and check oil level. Oil must be between MIN and MAX markings. If addition fluid is required, add VW ATF (G 052 162 A2).

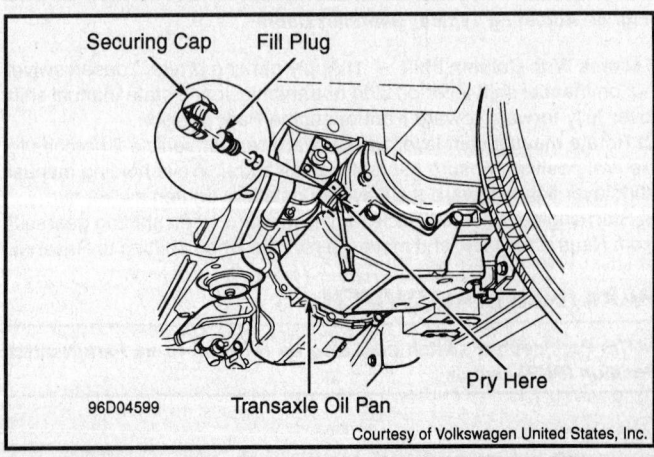

96D04599

Courtesy of Volkswagen United States, Inc.

Fig. 1: Removing Filler Plug Securing Cap (01M Transaxle)

RECOMMENDED FLUID
RECOMMENDED FLUID

Application	Fluid Type
Transaxle	
096	Dexron Or Dexron-II ATF
01M	VW ATF (G 052 162 A2)
Final Drive	
096	[1] G 50, SAE 75W–90 (G 052 145 A2)
01M	VW ATF (G 052 162 A2)

[1] – Synthetic oil.

FLUID CAPACITIES
TRANSAXLE REFILL CAPACITIES

Application	Refill Qts. (L)	Dry Fill Qts. (L)
096	3.2 (3.0)	5.9 (5.6)
01M	3.2 (3.0)	5.6 (5.3)

FINAL DRIVE REFILL CAPACITIES

Model	Qts. (L)
All Models	.8 (.75)

DRAINING & REFILLING

096 Transaxle – 1) Remove rear pan bolts. Loosen front pan bolts. Carefully lower pan to drain as much fluid as possible. Remove oil pan. Pour out remaining fluid.
2) Remove filter. Clean oil pan. Install NEW filter. Tighten filter retaining screws to 71 INCH lbs. (8 N.m). Install oil pan with NEW gasket. Tighten oil pan bolts to 108 INCH lbs. (12 N.m). Add 3.2 qts. (3.0L) ATF.
3) With engine running at normal operating temperature, shift through all selector lever positions once. Check fluid level. Add if necessary.
01M Transaxle – 1) Remove ATF level plug from oil pan. Remove overflow tube through plug hole. Drain ATF. Install overflow tube. Screw level plug in hand-tight.
2) Add 3.2 qts. (3.0L) ATF through filler pipe. See 01M TRANSAXLE under CHECKING FLUID LEVEL. With engine running at normal operating temperature, shift through all selector lever positions once. Check fluid level. Add if necessary. Tighten ATF level plug to 11 ft. lbs. (15 N.m).

ADJUSTMENTS
CONTROL CABLE

Loosen lock screw at gear selector lever on transaxle. Move gear selector in center console to "P" position. Ensure front wheels are locked. Tighten cable housing-to-gear selector lever lock screw.

SHIFT LOCK CABLE

1) Move gear selector to "1" position. Remove steering column covers. Turn ignition key to Start position and release. Check clearance between shift lock cable lever and ignition switch locking pin.
2) Clearance should be .028" (.70 mm). If clearance is not correct, loosen lock nut on shift lock cable sheath. Position shift lock cable lever to obtain correct clearance. Tighten lock nut. *See Fig. 2.* Tighten gear selector housing screws and install steering column covers.

SHIFT LOCK SOLENOID

Place gear selector in Neutral or Park. Loosen shift lock solenoid mounting screws. Insert a .019" (.30 mm) feeler gauge between shift lock solenoid push rod and shift lever. *See Fig. 3.* If necessary, move shift lock solenoid and tighten screws.

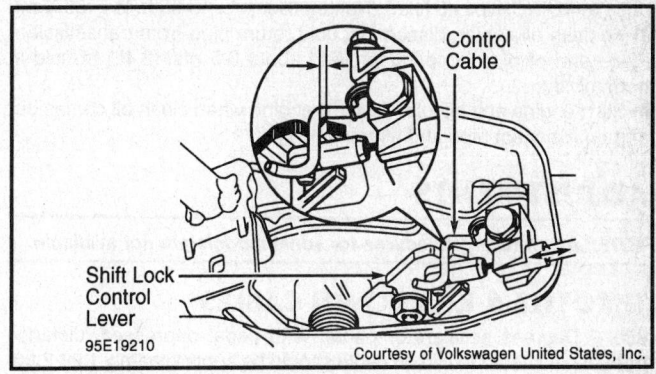

Fig. 2: Adjusting Shift Lock Cable

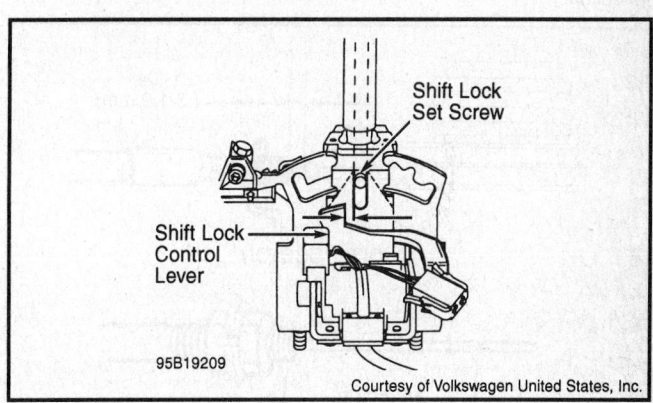

Fig. 3: Adjusting Shift Lock Solenoid

Volvo

850, 940, 960
APPLICATION
VOLVO AUTOMATIC TRANSMISSION APPLICATIONS

Vehicle Model	Transmission Model
850	AW50-42
940	AW-70
940 Turbo	AW-71
960	AW-40

LUBRICATION
SERVICE INTERVAL

Check fluid level every 10,000 miles.

CHECKING FLUID LEVEL

1) Ensure vehicle is level. Apply parking brake and gear selector lever to "P" position. Start and idle engine. Move gear selector lever through all gears, while pausing 4-5 seconds for engagement at each position.
2) Return gear selector lever to "P" position. Wait 2 minutes and check fluid level with engine idling. Level should be between MIN and MAX marks.

RECOMMENDED FLUID
FLUID SPECIFICATIONS

Application	ATF Type
850 (AW50-42)	Dexron IIE Or Mercon
940 (AW-70)	Type "F" Or "G"
940 Turbo (AW-71)	Type "F" Or "G"
960	Dexron IIE Or Mercon

FLUID CAPACITIES

TRANSAXLE REFILL CAPACITIES

Application	Refill Qts. (L)	Dry Fill Qts. (L)
850 (AW50-42)	N/A	8.1 (7.6)
940 (AW-70)	4.1 (3.9)	7.8 (7.4)
940 Turbo (AW-71)	4.1 (3.9)	7.8 (7.4)
960 (AW-40)	5.6L (5.2)	8.2 (7.7)

DRAINING & REFILLING

940 – 1) Remove drain plug and drain transmission. Disconnect filler tube and remove oil pan.

2) Remove and clean oil strainer. Install strainer. Tighten strainer bolts to 18-25 INCH lbs. (2-3 N.m). Install oil pan with new gasket. Tighten bolts to 42 INCH lbs. (5 N.m). Tighten filler tube to 65 ft. lbs. (88 N.m).

3) To flush oil cooler, disconnect fluid return pipe from transmission. Place end of pipe in container. Add about 3.5 qts. (3.4L) of fluid in transmission.

4) Start engine and let idle. Turn off engine when clean oil comes out of pipe. Connect pipe and fill transmission.

ADJUSTMENTS

NOTE: Adjustment procedures for some models are not available.

THROTTLE & KICKDOWN CABLES

850 – Depress accelerator pedal. With pedal depressed, distance from cable sheath to clip on cable should be approximately 1.98-2.06" (50.2-52.3 mm). *See Fig. 1.* Adjust distance on cable sheath if necessary.

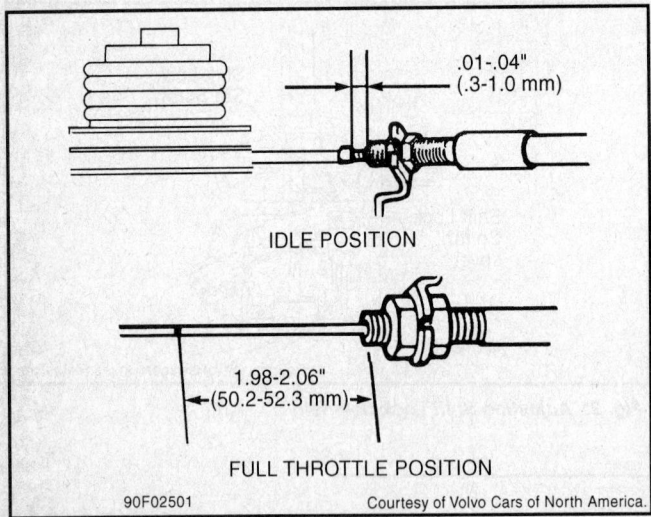

IDLE POSITION

.01-.04"
(.3-1.0 mm)

1.98-2.06"
(50.2-52.3 mm)

FULL THROTTLE POSITION

90F02501   Courtesy of Volvo Cars of North America.

Fig. 1: Checking Transmission Throttle Cable

GEARSHIFT CABLE

850 – 1) Shift gear selector lever to "R" position. Disconnect gearshift cable at transmission rod arm. Move transmission rod arm forward to "P" position. *See Fig. 2.*

NOTE: Do not move transmission cable to adjust selector lever position. Transmission cable position must not be altered.

2) Ensure vehicle is in Park by attempting to roll vehicle. Move transmission rod arm to "R" (next position). Apply a small amount of grease to rod arm pin. Carefully reinstall cable on transmission rod arm. Ensure gear selector does not move during installation.

3) Move gear selector lever to "N" position. Push lever forward, but do not touch lock button. Play should be felt. Move gear selector lever to "D" position. Push selector lever backward, but do not touch lock button. Play should be felt.

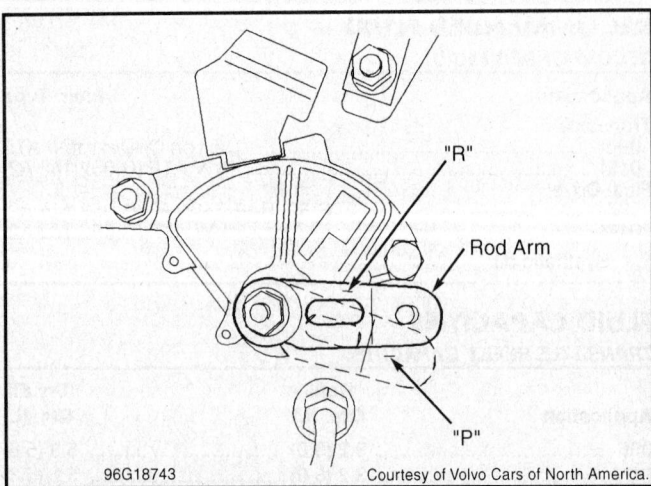

"R"

Rod Arm

"P"

96G18743   Courtesy of Volvo Cars of North America.

Fig. 2: Adjusting Rod Arm

GEARSHIFT LINKAGE

940 – 1) Engine should start in Neutral or Park only. Back-up lights should only operate in Reverse. Gear selector should be vertical in Park. If gear selector is not vertical, proceed to next step.

2) Place gear selector in Park. Loosen lock nuts for actuator and selector rods. *See Fig. 3.* Ensure transmission lever is in Park. Rotate output shaft on transmission until it locks.

3) Place gear selector in a vertical position, or slightly forward, and tighten lock nut. Push reaction lever lightly rearward until a slight resistance is felt. Tighten lock nut to 42 INCH lbs. (5 N.m).

4) Ensure free play between pin and stop in Drive and Neutral is less than or equal to play between pin and stop in "3" and "2" positions. If free play is correct, tighten lock nut to 12-17 ft. lbs. (17-23 N.m).

NOTE: If gear selector is stiff in "3" position, move reaction lever approximately 1/8" toward front and recheck operation.

5) After adjustment, ensure vehicle only starts in Neutral or Park and back-up lights come on only in Reverse.

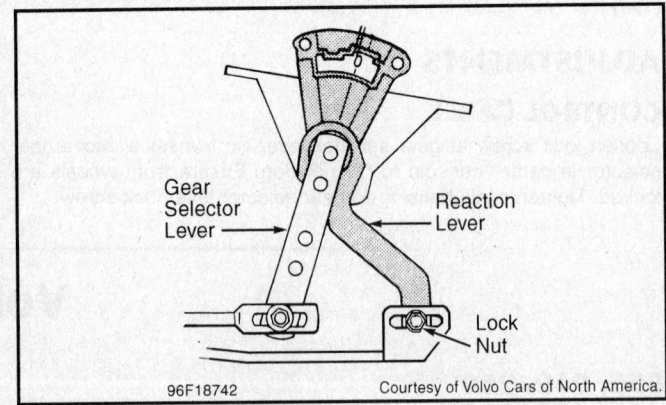

Gear
Selector
Lever

Reaction
Lever

Lock
Nut

96F18742   Courtesy of Volvo Cars of North America.

Fig. 3: Adjusting Shift Linkage (940)

NEUTRAL SAFETY SWITCH

Neutral safety switch is located at bottom of selector lever. No adjustment is necessary.

SHIFT INTERLOCK SYSTEM

Testing and adjustment information for shift interlock system is not available. See WIRING DIAGRAMS.

WIRING DIAGRAMS

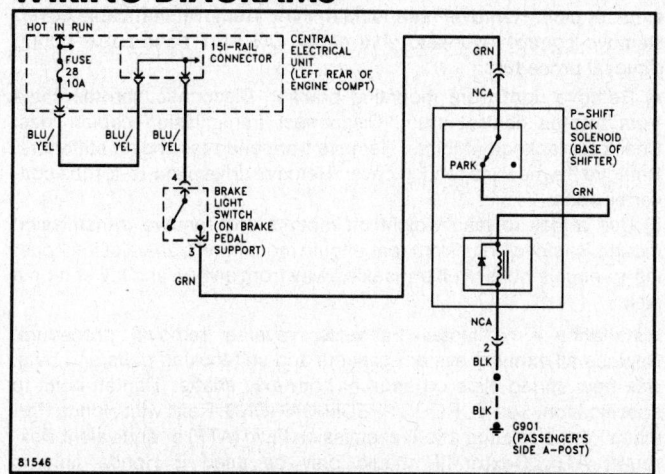

Fig. 4: Shift Interlock System Wiring Diagram (1995-96 850)

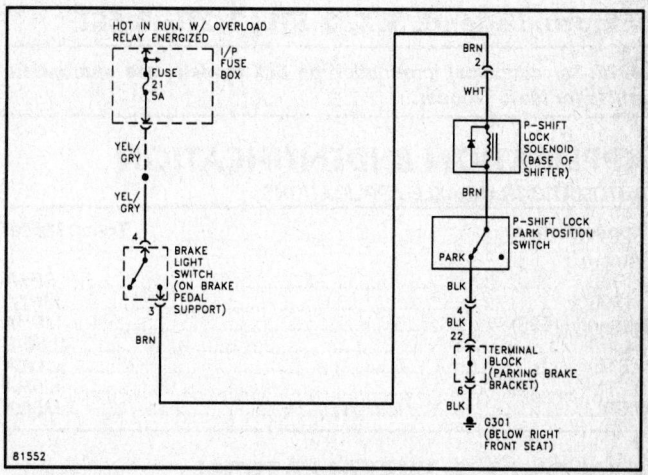

Fig. 6: Shift Interlock System Wiring Diagram (1995-96 960)

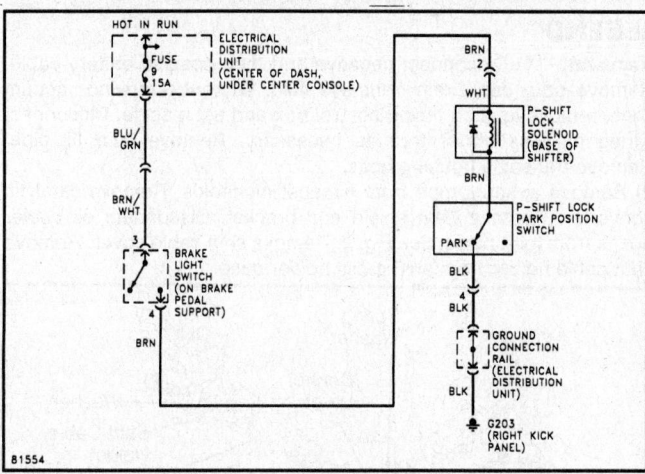

Fig. 5: Shift Interlock System Wiring Diagram (1995 940)

Integra, Legend, SLX, 2.5TL, 3.2TL, 3.5RL

NOTE: For additional information on SLX models, see appropriate article for Isuzu Trooper.

APPLICATION & IDENTIFICATION

AUTOMATIC TRANSAXLE APPLICATIONS

Application	Trans. Model
Integra	
1995	SP7A
1996	MP7A
Legend (1995)	MPYA
SLX [1]	4L30-E
2.5TL	M1WA
3.2TL	M5HA
3.5RL	M5DA

REMOVAL & INSTALLATION

WARNING: All models are equipped with Supplemental Restraint System (SRS). All SRS wiring is color-coded Yellow. Before performing any repairs, disable air bag system. See AIR BAG RESTRAINT SYSTEM article in ACCESSORIES & EQUIPMENT. Wait at least 3 minutes after deactivating air bag system. System maintains voltage for about 3 minutes after battery is disconnected. Servicing air bag system before 3 minutes may cause accidental air bag deployment and possible personal injury.

CAUTION: Radio has a coded theft protection circuit. Before disconnecting battery cables, obtain radio anti-theft code number from customer. After reconnecting power, turn radio on. Word CODE will be displayed. Enter customer 5-digit code to restore radio operation.

INTEGRA

Removal – 1) Disconnect negative and then positive battery cable. Remove battery. Remove air intake hose and battery base. Disconnect starter wiring. Remove starter retaining bolts and starter. Disconnect transaxle ground strap. Disconnect speed sensors and solenoid connectors.

2) Remove upper transaxle-to-engine mounting bolts. Drain transaxle fluid. Remove lower splash shield. Remove right shock strut fork and pinch bolt. Pry right side driveshaft from differential. Pry left side driveshaft from intermediate shaft. Protect drive shaft ends.

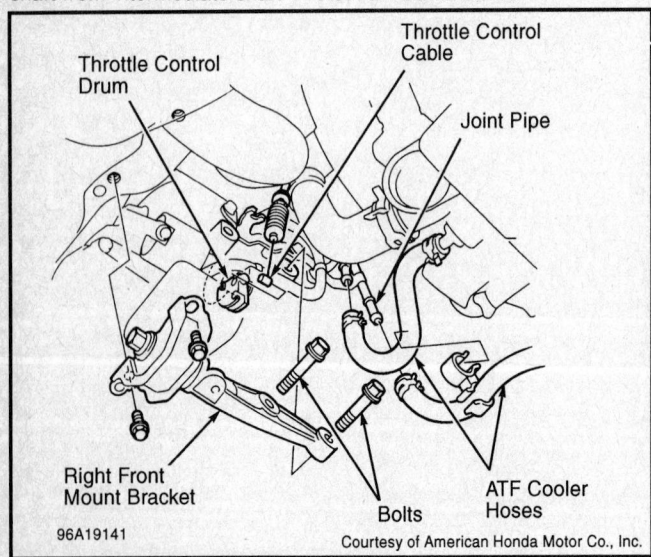

Fig. 1: Identifying Integra Components

3) Disconnect heated HO2S (oxygen sensor) connector. Remove exhaust pipe. Remove intermediate shaft. Remove shift cable cover. Remove control lever and shift cable. DO NOT bend cable during removal procedure.

4) Remove right front mounting bracket. Disconnect throttle cable from throttle control drum. Disconnect transmission cooler lines. Check for leakage at joints. Remove front and rear engine stiffeners. Remove flywheel inspection cover. Remove drive plate-to-torque converter bolts.

5) Use a jack to take weight off mounts and remove transmission mount. Remove bolts from rear engine mount and transmission housing-to-engine bolts. Pull transaxle away from engine and lower it on a jack.

Installation – To install transaxle, reverse removal procedure. Replace all exhaust system gaskets and self-locking bolts and nuts. Use new spring clips on ends of both axle shafts. Tighten bolts to specification. See TORQUE SPECIFICATIONS. Refill with Honda Premium Formula Automatic Transmission Fluid (ATF) or equivalent Dexron-III ATF. Dexron-III should only be used if Honda fluid is unavailable.

LEGEND

Removal – 1) Disconnect negative and then positive battery cable. Remove strut bar. Drain transaxle fluid. Without removing vacuum lines, remove ignition timing control box and set it aside. Disconnect wiring harness connectors as necessary. Remove fluid fill pipe. Remove transaxle housing bolts.

2) Remove exhaust pipe from exhaust manifolds. Remove catalytic converter. Remove heat shield and bracket. Disconnect oil cooler hoses from joint pipes. *See Fig. 2.* Remove shift cable cover. Remove shift cable holder from shift cable holder base.

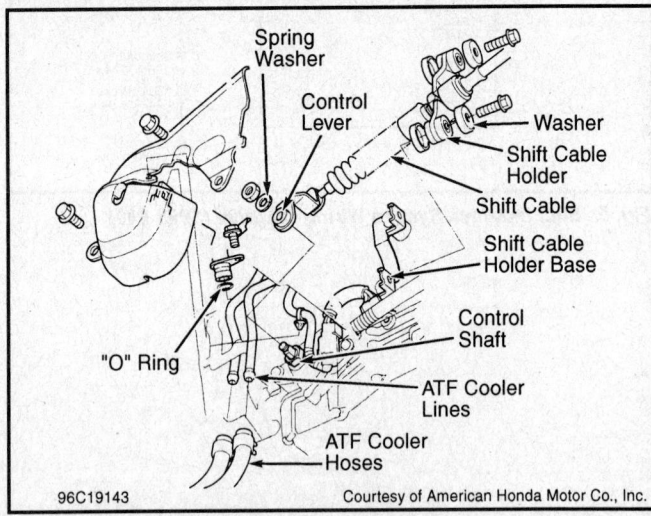

Fig. 2: Identifying Shift Cable & Components (3.2TL Shown, Legend & 3.5RL Similar)

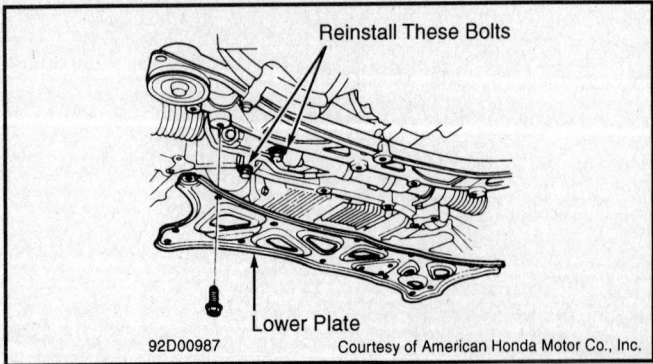

Fig. 3: Removing Lower Plate (Legend & 3.2TL Shown, 3.5RL Similar)

3) Remove control lever from control shaft. *See Fig. 1.* Remove lower plate, and reinstall steering gear assembly mounting bolts. *See Fig. 3.* Rotate control shaft and place transaxle in "P" position (Park).

4) Remove 36-mm sealing bolt from transaxle. *See Fig. 4.* Using Extension Shaft Puller (07LAC-PW50100), disconnect extension shaft from differential. Remove and discard set ring. Place jack under transaxle.

5) Raise transaxle high enough to take weight off middle transaxle mounts. Remove middle transaxle mounts. Remove shift cable guide from transaxle. Remove rear transaxle mount/mount bracket and exhaust pipe bracket. Remove engine stiffener. Remove flywheel inspection cover.

6) Remove drive plate bolts. Remove transaxle housing mounting bolts and 26-mm shim. *See Fig. 5.* Check for wires, hoses and other components that may still be attached. Pull transaxle away from engine until it clears dowel pins, and remove transaxle.

Installation – 1) Ensure both dowel pins are installed in torque converter housing. Apply Honda Grease (UM264) to extension shaft splines. Ensure secondary spring is positioned in differential side of extension housing. *See Fig. 6.*

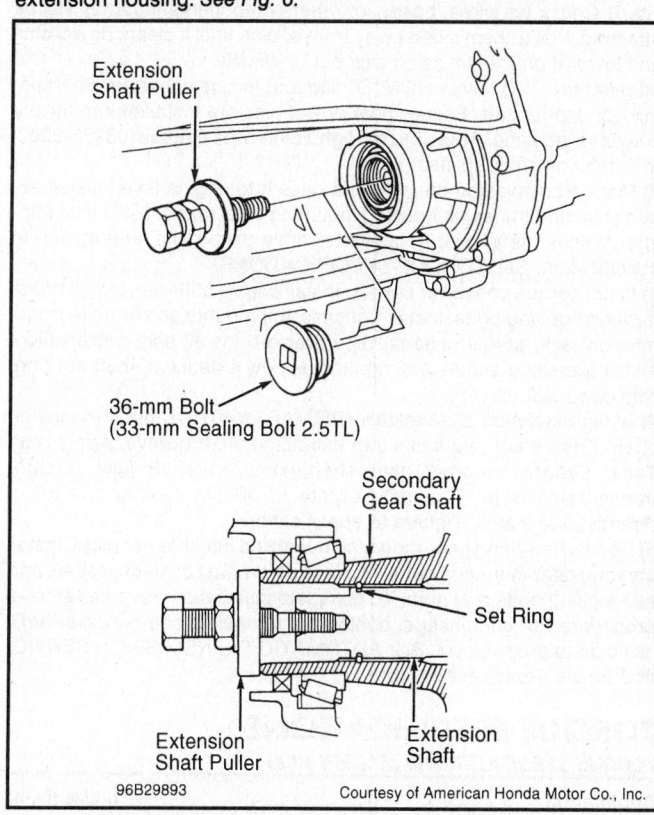

Fig. 4: *Identifying Differential Sealing Bolt (Typical)*

Labels: Extension Shaft Puller; 36-mm Bolt (33-mm Sealing Bolt 2.5TL); Secondary Gear Shaft; Set Ring; Extension Shaft Puller; Extension Shaft; 96B29893; Courtesy of American Honda Motor Co., Inc.

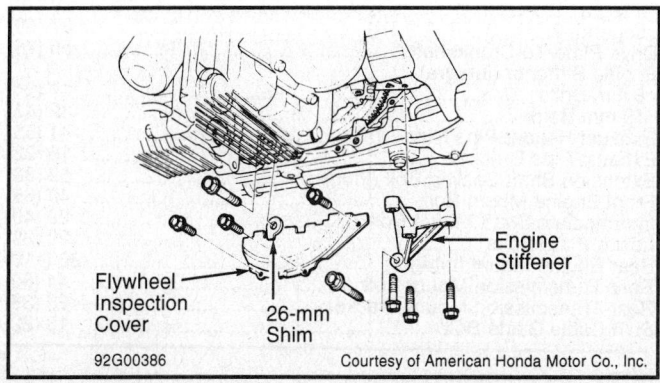

Fig. 5: *Identifying 26-mm Transaxle Mounting Bolt Shim (Legend)*

Labels: Flywheel Inspection Cover; 26-mm Shim; Engine Stiffener; 92G00386; Courtesy of American Honda Motor Co., Inc.

2) Place transaxle on transmission jack, and raise it to engine level. Install 26-mm shim and transaxle housing mounting bolt. Install remaining transaxle housing bolts. Install drive plate-to-torque converter bolts, and tighten bolts to specification. See TORQUE SPECIFICATIONS.

3) Install flywheel inspection cover. Install engine stiffener. Install rear transaxle mount bracket and exhaust pipe bracket. Install shift cable guide. Install transaxle middle mounts. Install new extension shaft set ring. Ensure open slot in set ring faces upward.

4) Using Extension Shaft Installer (07MAF-PY40100), install extension shaft. Ensure set ring locks into extension shaft groove. Apply Loctite to 36-mm sealing bolt threads, and install bolt. Tighten bolt to specification.

5) Remove steering gear mounting bolts, and install lower plate. Install steering gear mounting bolts. To complete installation, reverse removal procedure.

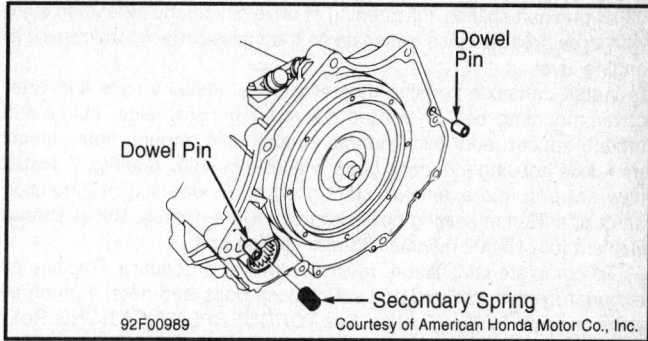

Fig. 6: *Identifying Secondary Spring (Legend)*

Labels: Dowel Pin; Dowel Pin; Secondary Spring; 92F00989; Courtesy of American Honda Motor Co., Inc.

SLX

Removal – 1) Remove hood and disconnect negative (–) battery cable. Remove transfer case control lever knob and disconnect wiring harness connectors at console. Disconnect shift control rod, cable and electrical connectors.

2) Disconnect transfer case control lever and electrical connectors. Remove lower shields, rear drive shaft. Support transmission and remove rear mount and crossmember. Disconnect front drive shaft.

3) Disconnect oxygen sensors and remove catalytic converters. Disconnect ATF cooler lines and loosen pipe clamps. Remove front crossmember, stiffener brace, heat shields and starter.

4) Remove flywheel cover. Remove 3 torque converter bolts. Using a chain hoist, raise engine. Identify engine-to-transmission bolts for reassembly reference. Remove engine-to-transmission bolts. Remove transmission assembly.

Installation – To install transmission, reverse removal procedures. Tighten bolts to specifications. See TORQUE SPECIFICATIONS.

2.5TL

Removal – 1) Disconnect negative and then positive battery cable. Remove battery and battery box. Disconnect coil wire and ground cable. Remove heat shield. Remove connector from control box. Without removing vacuum tubes, remove control box and lay it aside.

2) Remove torque converter cover. Remove drive plate bolts. Unplug transaxle sub-harness electrical connector. Remove transaxle ground cable. Remove transaxle housing mounting bolts and 26-mm shim. *See Fig. 7.*

3) Remove transaxle splash shield. Drain transaxle fluid. Reinstall drain plug using a new sealing washer. Remove transaxle mount and mount bracket. Disconnect ATF cooler hoses at joint pipes. Turn pipe ends up to avoid spilling fluid, then plug joint pipes.

4) Shift transaxle to "P" position (Park). Remove 33-mm sealing bolt. Remove extension shaft from differential with Puller (07LAC-PW50101). *See Fig. 4.* Remove bolts from exhaust pipe brackets. Remove exhaust pipe. Remove exhaust manifold brackets. Remove shift cable cover. Remove control lever from control shaft. Remove shift cable holder from transaxle housing.

CAUTION: Take care not to bend shift cable.

5) Disconnect gear position switch, and then remove harness bracket. Remove transaxle mid-mount nuts. Using a transmission jack, raise transaxle just enough to take weight from mounts. Remove mid-mounts and mid-mount spacer.

NOTE: DO NOT remove torque converter bolt on differential carrier side or torque converter cover.

6) Remove transaxle housing mounting bolts. Remove torque converter cover mounting bolt on torque converter housing side.

7) Pull transaxle away from engine until it clears dowel pins. Lower transaxle from vehicle to remove.

Installation – 1) Install dowel pins into torque converter housing. Install extension shaft with Super High Temp Urea Grease (08798-9002) on shaft splines. Fill opening of drive pinion and extension shaft with Urea grease. Place transaxle on transmission jack, and raise it to engine level.

2) Install transaxle housing mounting bolts. Install torque converter cover mounting bolt on torque converter housing side. Install mid mount spacer and mid mounts. Install mid mount nuts. Install transaxle housing mounting bolts and 26-mm shim. See Fig. 7. Install new set ring into extension shaft groove. Fill opening of extension shaft and 33-mm sealing bolt (plug) with Urea grease. Using Thread Sealant (08718-0001), install 33-mm sealing bolt.

3) To complete installation, reverse removal procedure. Replace all exhaust system gaskets and self-locking bolts and nuts. Tighten all bolts and nuts to specification. See TORQUE SPECIFICATIONS. Refill with Honda Premium Formula Automatic Transmission Fluid (ATF) or equivalent Dexron-III ATF. Dexron-III should only be used if Honda fluid is unavailable.

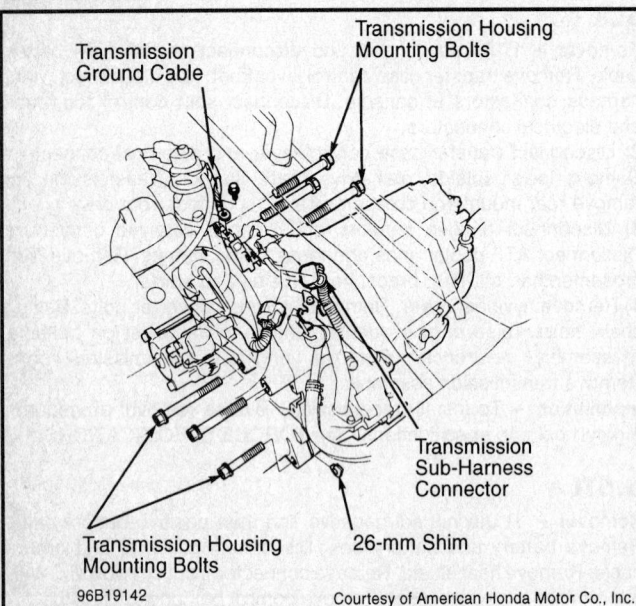

Transmission Ground Cable

Transmission Housing Mounting Bolts

Transmission Sub-Harness Connector

26-mm Shim

Transmission Housing Mounting Bolts

96B19142   Courtesy of American Honda Motor Co., Inc.

Fig. 7: Identifying 26-mm Transaxle Mounting Bolt Shim (2.5TL Shown, 3.2TL & 3.5RL Similar)

3.2TL & 3.5RL

Removal – 1) Disconnect negative and then positive battery cable. Shift transmission to "P" position. Disconnect electrical connectors and remove control box. DO NOT disconnect vacuum hoses from control box. Remove strut brace (if equipped). Drain transaxle fluid. Remove bolts (3) from dipstick tube. Remove transaxle upper housing bolts.

2) From inside vehicle, lift up carpet underneath passenger seat and disconnect secondary oxygen sensor connector. Push connector out from inside of vehicle. From underside of vehicle, remove harness cover. Remove 3-way catalytic converter. Remove heat shield and

exhaust Y-pipe. Remove exhaust pipe heat shields. Disconnect oil cooler hoses from cooler lines.

3) Remove shift cable cover. Remove gear position switch harness clamp and linear solenoid harness connector from shift cable cover. Remove shift cable cover from transmission housing. Remove shift cable and holder from cable base. See Fig. 7.

4) Remove control lever from control shaft. Remove dipstick pipe from torque converter housing. Remove lower plate, and reinstall steering rack assembly mounting bolts. See Fig. 4. Remove shift cable guide bracket from transmission support beam.

5) Remove transmission beam, rear transmission mounting bracket and exhaust pipe bracket. Ensure transmission control shaft is in "P" position.

6) Remove 36-mm sealing bolt from transaxle. See Fig. 4. Using Extension Shaft Puller (07LAC-PW50101), disconnect extension shaft from differential. Place jack under transaxle.

7) Raise transmission high enough to take weight from transaxle mounts. Remove engine/transmission stiffener. Remove torque converter covers and torque converter bolts.

8) Remove transaxle housing mounting bolts and 26-mm shim. See Fig. 7. Check for wires, hoses, or other components that may still be attached. Pull transmission away from engine until it clears dowel pins and lower it on transmission jack out of vehicle.

Installation – 1) Install NEW "O" ring and torque converter on transmission input shaft. Ensure both dowel pins are installed into torque converter housing. Apply Super High Temp Urea Grease (08798-9002) to extension shaft splines.

2) Place transmission on jack, and raise it to engine level. Install 26-mm shim and transaxle housing mounting bolts (except side with stiffener brace). Install torque converter drive plate bolts, and tighten to specification. See TORQUE SPECIFICATIONS.

3) Install torque converter covers. Install engine stiffener. Install transmission housing bolts. Install transmission mounts and remove transmission jack. Install exhaust pipe bracket. Install shift cable guide. Install transaxle middle mounts. Install new extension shaft set ring, with open slot upward.

4) Using Extension Shaft Installer (07MAF-PY40101), install extension shaft. Ensure set ring locks into extension shaft groove. Apply High Temp Grease to drive gear shaft/extension shaft joint. Ensure transmission is in "P". Apply Loctite to 36-mm sealing bolt (plug) threads, and install. Tighten to specification.

5) Remove steering gear mounting bolts, and install lower plate. Install steering gear mounting bolts. Replace all exhaust system gaskets and self-locking bolts and nuts. To complete installation, reverse removal procedure for shift linkage, cooler and remaining components. Refill all fluids to proper level. See AUTOMATIC TRANSMISSION SERVICING article. Road test vehicle.

TORQUE SPECIFICATIONS

TORQUE SPECIFICATIONS (EXCEPT SLX)

Application	Ft. Lbs (N.m)
Center Crossmember (Integra)	33 (45)
Drain Plug	
Integra	29 (40)
Legend, 2.5TL, 3.2TL & 3.5RL	37 (50)
Drive Plate-To-Crankshaft	55 (75)
Engine Stiffener (Integra)	
8 mm Bolts	17 (24)
10 mm Bolts	32 (43)
Exhaust Header Pipe Nuts	41 (55)
Exhaust Pipe Bracket	16 (22)
Extension Shaft Sealing Bolt (Plug)	59 (80)
Front Engine Mount Bolt	48 (65)
Intermediate Shaft Mount Bolt	29 (40)
Lower Plate Bolts	29 (39)
Rear Engine Mount (Integra)	86 (118)
Rear Transmission Mount Bolt	44 (60)
Rear Transmission Mount Bracket	28 (38)
Shift Cable Guide Bolt	16 (22)

TORQUE SPECIFICATIONS (EXCEPT SLX) – (Cont.)

Application	Ft. Lbs (N.m)
Starter-To-Housing Bolts [1]	33 (45)
2.5TL Lower Starter-To-Housing Bolt	47 (64)
Top Transmission Mount Bolt	47 (64)
Torque Converter Bolts	
Integra, Legend & 2.5TL	[2]
3.2TL	20 (27)
3.5RL	16 (22)
Transmission Housing-To-Engine Bolt	
Integra	43 (59)
Legend & 2.5TL	54 (74)
3.2TL, 3.5RL	47 (64)
Transmission Middle Mount-To-Engine Bolt	28 (38)
	INCH Lbs. (N.m)
Flywheel Inspection Cover Bolt	106 (12)
Shift Cable Housing Bolt	89 (10)

[1] – Except Legend and 2.5TL lower starter-to-housing bolt.
[2] – Tighten bolt to 106 INCH lbs. (12 N.m).

SLX TORQUE SPECIFICATIONS

Application	Ft. Lbs (N.m)
ATF Cooler Pipes	40 (54)
Crossmember	37 (50)
Exhaust Pipe-To-Manifold	49 (67)
Exhaust Pipe Flange	32 (43)
Flywheel-To-Torque Converter Bolts	40 (54)
Front Crossmember	58 (78)
Rear Drive Shaft	46 (63)
Starter	29 (40)
Stiffener	35 (48)
Transfer Case Protectors	27 (37)
	INCH Lbs.
Flywheel Undercover	52 (6)
Heat Shields	52 (6)

Audi

A4, A6, Cabriolet, 90

APPLICATION

APPLICATION

Vehicle	Transmission Model
Cabriolet FWD	097 (AZB)
90 FWD	097 (AZB)
A6 AWD	01F (CEZ)
A6 FWD	01K (CRC, CJE)
Cabriolet FWD	01N (CLR)
90 FWD	01N (CLR)
A4 FWD	01V (DCS, DDT)
A4 AWD	01V (CJP)

REMOVAL & INSTALLATION

Removal & Installation – 1) Obtain radio code for reassembly reference. Disconnect negative battery cable. Disconnect vehicle speed sensor from transaxle. Remove air intake duct and noise insulation shield.

2) On models with split ATF filler tube, remove upper tube and plug lower tube. On all models, remove upper engine-to-transaxle bolts. Using Engine Supports (10-222/A and 10-222/1), support engine from above.

3) Raise vehicle and remove drive shaft heat shields. On A4 (01V), remove front wheels. Remove lower engine cover and brackets. Remove body crossmember and/or exhaust pipe below catalysts. Remove exhaust. Disconnect axle shafts from transaxle. Wire axle shafts aside. Remove starter. On V6 models, alternator may need to be removed or subframe loosened to remove starter. Remove torque converter-to-drive plate nuts. See Fig. 1.

4) Remove shield from multi-function switch. Unhook transaxle cable holders. See Fig. 2. Disconnect electrical connectors. Remove selector lever cable holder and selector lever cable at transaxle lever. Detach lower accelerator cable from transaxle. Disconnect hoses from transaxle cooler lines. See Fig. 3.

5) Support transaxle using jack, and raise transaxle slightly. Remove lower transaxle mounting bolts and rear subframe bolts. Separate transaxle from engine. Secure torque converter to transaxle to prevent converter from falling out of transaxle. Lower transaxle from vehicle.

6) To install, reverse removal procedure. Ensure torque converter is fully seated on transaxle. Use NEW bolts and lock washers to secure torque converter. Clean driveshaft flanges of thread locking compound. Adjust accelerator and shift cables. Ensure radio is coded correctly (if necessary).

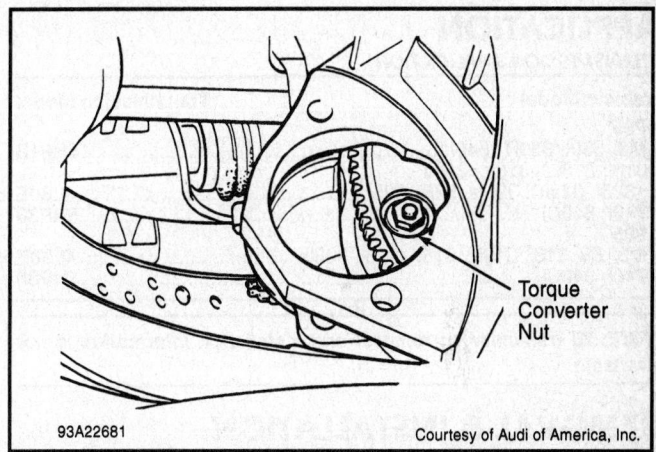

93A22681   Courtesy of Audi of America, Inc.

Fig. 1: Locating Torque Converter-To-Drive Plate Nuts

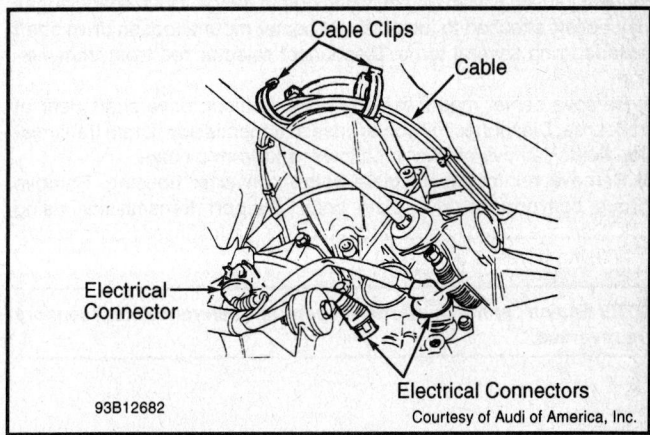

93B12682   Courtesy of Audi of America, Inc.

Fig. 2: Locating Transaxle Cable Holders

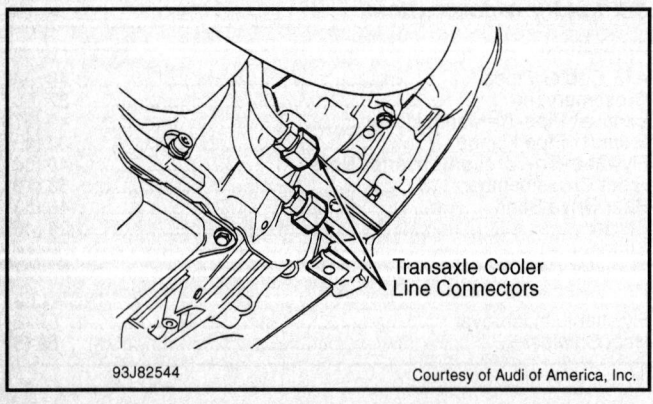

93J82544   Courtesy of Audi of America, Inc.

Fig. 3: Locating Transaxle Cooler Line Connectors (Typical)

TORQUE SPECIFICATIONS
TORQUE SPECIFICATIONS

Application	Ft. Lbs. (N.m)
Ball Joint Nut	48 (65)
CV Joint Bolt	59 (80)
Drive Shaft-To-Flange Bolt	59 (80)
Flexplate Bolt	[1] 44 (60)
Torque Converter-To-Drive Plate Nut	44 (60)
Transaxle Mount-To-Transaxle Bolt	29 (40)
Transaxle Mount-To-Subframe Bolt	
Series 01N	74 (110)
All Others	29 (40)
Transaxle-To-Engine Bolt	
10-mm Bolt	
097 Transaxle	44 (60)
All Others	33 (45)
12-mm Bolt	
097 Transaxle	41 (56)
All Others	48 (65)

[1] – Plus 1/4 turn (90 degrees).

BMW

Z3, 3-Series, 5-Series, 7-Series, 8-Series

APPLICATION
TRANSMISSION APPLICATION

Vehicle Model	Transmission Model
1995	
M3, 530I, 530iT, 540i	5HP18
318i, 318iC, 318is, 318ti	
325i, 325iC, 325is, 525i, 525iT	4L30E
740i, 840Ci	5HP30
1996	
M3, Z3, 318i, 318is, 318ti, 328i, 328is	4L30E
740i, 840Ci	5HP30

NOTE: Z3 transmission removal and installation information is not available.

REMOVAL & INSTALLATION

Removal & Installation – **1)** Disconnect negative battery cable. Raise and support vehicle. Remove exhaust assembly and heat shields. Disconnect joint disc from transmission output flange. Drive shaft flanges may be left attached to joint disc. At center mount, loosen drive shaft threaded ring several turns. Disconnect selector rod from transmission.

2) Remove center mount-to-body bolts. Position drive shaft clear of work area. Disconnect oil cooler lines at transmission. Drain transmission fluid. Remove oil filler tube lower end from oil pan.

3) Remove reinforcement plate below converter housing. Remove torque converter-to-drive plate bolts. Support transmission using jack. Remove speed sensor and reference mark sensor from converter housing bores (if equipped).

NOTE: Engine cannot be started if speed and reference mark sensors are reversed.

4) Disconnect wiring harness from transmission (if equipped). Remove transmission crossmember. Remove transmission-to-engine attaching bolts. Slide back and remove transmission.

5) To install, reverse removal procedure. Clean interior passages of all transmission oil cooler lines. Check for full engagement of torque converter. Adjust throttle cable and selector rod. If drive plate was removed, use NEW bolts, coating threads with Loctite No. 270. See TORQUE SPECIFICATIONS.

NOTE: BMW recommends replacing drive shaft flange nuts and bolts. To prevent stress in coupling, tighten nuts only. DO NOT tighten bolts.

TORQUE SPECIFICATIONS
TORQUE SPECIFICATIONS

Application	Ft. Lbs. (N.m)
Drive Plate-To-Engine (12-mm)	71-81 (98-112)
Drive Shaft Joint Disc-To-Transmission Flange	
10 x 8.8-mm	33 (46)
10 x 10.9-mm	52 (72)
12-mm (Except 7-Series)	89 (123)
12-mm (7-Series)	59 (81)
Drive Shaft Threaded Ring	15 (21)
Torque Converter-To-Drive Plate	
8-mm	18-20 (25-27)
10-mm [1]	34-37 (47-51)
Transmission-To-Engine Bolts	
Hex Head Bolts	
8-mm	17 (24)
10-mm	33 (46)
12-mm	56-62 (78-86)
Torx Bolts [2]	
8-mm	15 (21)
12-mm	46 (63)

[1] – Always use spring washers with 10 x 16-mm bolts.
[2] – Always use washers with Torx-type bolts.

Metro, Prizm, Tracker
APPLICATION

APPLICATION

Vehicle	Trans. Model
Metro	ECC 3-Speed
Prizm	A-131L 3-Speed
Prizm LSi	A-245E Electronic 4-Speed
Tracker (1995-96)	¹ 3L30 3-Speed
Tracker (1996)	03-72LE Electronic 4-Speed

¹ – Also known as Turbo Hydra-Matic 180C.

REMOVAL & INSTALLATION
METRO

Removal – 1) Disconnect negative battery cable. Remove Throttle Valve (T.V.) cable, shift select cable and accelerator cable from bracket located on top of transaxle. Remove engine harness bracket from rear of transaxle case. Disconnect Vehicle Speed Sensor (VSS), shift solenoid and Park/Neutral Position (PNP) switch harness connectors. Disconnect speedometer cable.

2) Disconnect oil cooler lines from transaxle and plug. Disconnect ground cable at transaxle. Remove starter motor. Disconnect rear transaxle mount. Remove 2 upper transaxle-to-engine bolts. Using Universal Support Fixture (J-28467-A) and Support Adapters (J-28467-89), support engine. Raise and support vehicle. Drain transaxle fluid. Remove 10 splash shield retaining clips and splash shields.

CAUTION: Overextending inner CV joint may result in separation of internal components and possible joint failure.

3) Separate ball joints from steering knuckles. Install Drive Axle Boot Protectors (J-28712) to drive axles. Remove front wheels. Unstake axle shaft nuts and remove nuts and washers. Using 2 large screwdrivers, pry axle shafts from transaxle case and remove differential side gear snap ring. Remove inner CV joint from transaxle case, then outer CV joint from steering knuckle.

4) Remove 3 bolts and rear engine torque rod from transaxle case. Remove lower cover from torque converter housing. Hold flexplate by engaging a screwdriver into ring gear through notch provided at underside of transaxle case. Remove 6 flexplate-to-torque converter bolts.

5) Remove muffler mounting from rear engine mount bracket exhaust hanger. Remove rear engine mount. Lower vehicle. Using engine support, lower engine slightly. Raise vehicle and support transaxle. Support transaxle with a jack. Disconnect transaxle mounts. Remove remaining lower transaxle-to-engine bolt. Remove transaxle assembly.

Installation – 1) To install transaxle, reverse removal procedure. Before installing, apply grease around pilot cup at center of torque converter.

2) Ensure torque converter is correctly installed. Distance from top of torque converter flange nuts to engine mating surface of transaxle housing should be at least .843" (21.4 mm).

3) Tighten all fasteners to specification. See TORQUE SPECIFICATIONS (METRO) table. Adjust all control cables. Fill and check fluid levels.

PRIZM

Removal – 1) Disconnect battery cables. Remove battery and tray. Disconnect Intake Air Temperature (IAT) sensor harness connector. Remove air cleaner assembly. Disconnect Park/Neutral Position (PNP) switch and solenoid wire harness connectors. Disconnect ground cable at transaxle.

2) Disconnect Throttle Valve (T.V.) cable at throttle body. Disconnect shift select cable from shift lever and transaxle. Disconnect T.V. cable guide bracket from transaxle case. Disconnect Vehicle Speed Sensor (VSS) harness connector from transaxle.

3) Remove 2 upper transaxle-to-engine bolts. Remove upper starter motor retaining bolt. Install Universal Support Fixture (J-28467-A).

Remove left-side brace connecting upper part of transaxle to transaxle mount.

4) Raise and support vehicle. Drain transaxle fluid. On 3-speed transaxle, remove drain plug from under differential cover and drain differential fluid. On all models, remove lower starter retaining bolt and remove starter motor. Disconnect and plug oil cooler lines from transaxle. Remove 12 splash shield bolts and remove splash shields. Remove front wheels.

CAUTION: Overextending inner CV joint may result in separation of internal components and possible joint failure. Use care not to damage ABS speed sensor ring on outer CV joint (if equipped).

5) Remove ABS sensor from steering knuckle (if equipped). Remove axle shaft nuts from both axle shafts. Remove tie rod nuts from steering knuckles. Separate tie rods from steering knuckles. Remove one bolt and 2 nuts from lower ball joint at lower control arm. Separate both lower control arms from ball joint and steering knuckles. Remove outer CV joint from steering knuckle. Gently pry inner CV joint from differential housing and remove axle shaft.

6) Remove exhaust pipe hanger-to-center crossmember bolts and remove exhaust pipe hanger. Disconnect exhaust pipe from three-way catalyst and exhaust manifold flange. Remove front exhaust pipe.

7) Remove plastic access cover from center crossmember. Remove 2 bolts from front transaxle mount and 3 nuts from rear transaxle mount. While supporting center crossmember with jack, remove 2 bolts from center crossmember and 10 bolts from front crossmember. Remove crossmembers. On 3-speed transaxle, remove 5 bolts and remove lower engine-to-transaxle brace.

8) Support transaxle with jack. Remove flexplate access cover from engine rear end plate. Remove 6 flexplate-to-torque converter bolts. Remove remaining transaxle-to-engine bolts. It may be necessary to lower engine slightly so transaxle can clear body.

Installation – 1) To install, reverse removal procedure. Before installing, apply grease around pilot at center of torque converter.

2) Ensure torque converter is correctly installed. Distance from torque converter drive lugs to engine mating surface of transaxle housing should be greater than .906" (23 mm).

3) Tighten all fasteners to specification. See TORQUE SPECIFICATIONS (PRIZM) table. Adjust all control cables. Fill and check fluid levels.

CAUTION: Differential portion of 3-speed transaxle is separate from transaxle and must be drained and refilled through separate drain and refill holes. Refill differential with 3 pts. (1.4 L) of Dexron-III automatic transmission fluid. Ensure fluid is level with bottom of differential filler plug hold.

TRACKER

Removal (2WD) – 1) Disconnect negative battery cable. Remove transmission dip stick. Remove vacuum modulator hose at intake manifold. On 3-speed models, disconnect Transmission Range (TR) switch under intake manifold.

2) On 4-speed models, disconnect Throttle Valve (T.V.) cable from throttle body. On all models, remove console box. Remove 4 bolts from shift lever. Position shift lever aside. On all models, raise and support vehicle.

3) Remove front exhaust pipe and catalytic converter. Put match marks on rear drive shaft and flange yoke. Remove rear drive shaft. Disconnect Vehicle Speed Sensor (VSS) harness connector. Disconnect Park/Neutral Position (PNP) switch (3-speed models), or TR switch (4-speed models) harness connector.

4) On 4-speed models, disconnect Torque Converter Clutch (TCC) harness connector. On 3-speed models, disconnect T.V. cable from valve body. On all models, remove 2 mounting bolts and starter motor. Remove 2 upper transmission-to-engine bolts. Disconnect shift select cable and bracket from transmission.

5) Drain transmission fluid. Support transmission with jack. Remove 2 bolts from rear transmission mount, and 4 bolts and rear crossmember. Remove one bolt and filler tube from transmission. Remove speedometer cable from gear case.

6) On 4-speed models, remove 4 bolts and both right and left-side case stiffeners. On all models, disconnect and plug transmission oil cooler hoses at transmission. Remove flexplate inspection cover.

7) Remove 2 bolts and flexplate inspection plug from converter housing. Remove 3 flexplate-to-converter bolts. Remove skid plate (if equipped). Remove 2 bolts, 2 nuts and exhaust pipe bracket from extension housing.

8) Place a wood block (1.8" x 5" x 8") between distributor gear housing and bulkhead to prevent damage to components when transmission is lowered. Using a jack, slowly lower transmission. On 3-speed models, disconnect vent hose from top of transmission. On all models, remove 2 lower transmission mounting nuts. Lower transmission and remove from vehicle.

Removal (4WD) – 1) Disconnect negative battery cable. Remove transmission dip stick. Remove vacuum modulator hose at intake manifold. On 3-speed models, disconnect Transmission Range (TR) switch under intake manifold.

2) On 4-speed models, disconnect Throttle Valve (T.V.) cable from throttle body. On all models, remove console box. Remove 4 bolts from shift lever. Position shift lever aside. Remove transfer case shift lever knob, boot, plate, bracket and case cover. Disconnect 4WD switch electrical connector from transfer case.

3) Raise and support vehicle. Remove front exhaust pipe and catalytic converter. Put match marks on both front and rear drive shafts and flange yokes. Remove both front and rear drive shafts. Remove transfer case. Disconnect Vehicle Speed Sensor (VSS) harness connector. Disconnect Park/Neutral Position (PNP) switch (3-speed models), or TR switch (4-speed models) harness connector.

4) On 4-speed models, disconnect Torque Converter Clutch (TCC) harness connector. On 3-speed models, disconnect T.V. cable from valve body. On all models, remove 2 mounting bolts and starter motor. Remove 2 upper transmission-to-engine bolts. Disconnect shift select cable and bracket from transmission.

5) Drain transmission fluid. Support transmission with jack. Remove 2 bolts from rear engine mount. Remove 2 bolts from rear engine mounting member and torque stopper member. Remove 4 bolts and rear engine mounting member. Remove one bolt and filler tube from transmission.

6) Remove speedometer cable from gear case. On 4-speed models, remove 4 bolts and both right and left-side case stiffeners. On all models, disconnect and plug transmission oil cooler hoses at transmission.

7) Remove flexplate inspection cover. Remove 2 bolts and flexplate inspection plug from converter housing. Remove 3 flexplate-to-converter bolts. Remove skid plate (if equipped).

8) Place a wood block (1.8" x 5" x 8") between distributor gear housing and bulkhead to prevent damage to components when transmission is lowered. Using a jack, slowly lower transmission. On 3-speed models, disconnect vent hose from top of transmission. On all models, remove 2 lower transmission mounting nuts. Lower transmission and remove from vehicle.

Installation – To install, reverse removal procedure. Tighten all fasteners to specification. See TORQUE SPECIFICATIONS (TRACKER) table. Ensure reference marks are aligned on drive shaft flanges and yokes. Adjust all control cables. Fill and check fluid levels.

TORQUE SPECIFICATIONS

TORQUE SPECIFICATIONS (METRO)

Application	Ft. Lbs. (N.m)
Axle Shaft Nut	129 (175)
Ball Joint Pinch Bolt & Nut	44 (60)
Flexplate Cover Bolts	[1]
Flexplate-To-Torque Converter Bolts	14 (19)
Rear Engine Torque Rod	40 (54)
Starter Mounting Bolts	17 (23)
Tie Rod End Lock Nuts	32 (43)
Torque Converter Bolt	14 (19)
Transaxle Drain Plug	17 (23)
Transaxle Mounting Bolts & Nuts	40 (54)
Wheel Lug Nuts	44 (60)

[1] – Tighten to 89 INCH lbs. (10 N.m).

TORQUE SPECIFICATIONS (PRIZM)

Application	Ft. Lbs. (N.m)
Axle Shaft Nut	159 (216)
Ball Joint-To-Lower Control Arm Bolts & Nuts	105 (142)
Center Crossmember Bolts	45 (61)
Differential Drain Plug (3-Speed)	29 (39)
Differential Filler Plug (3-Speed)	29 (39)
Exhaust Pipe Support Bolts & Nuts	14 (19)
Exhaust Pipe-To-Manifold Nuts	46 (62)
Exhaust Pipe-To-Catalytic Converter	32 (43)
Flexplate-To-Torque Converter Bolts	14 (19)
Front Crossmember-To-Body Bolts	152 (206)
Front Transaxle Mount Bolts	35 (48)
Front Transaxle Mount Through Bolt & Nut	64 (87)
Left Transaxle Mounting Bracket Bolts	41 (56)
Left Transaxle Mount Through Bolt	64 (87)
Left Transaxle Bracket Reinforcement Bolts	15 (20)
Lower Engine Reinforcement Brace Bolt (3-Speed)	47 (64)
Rear Transaxle Mount Nuts	42 (57)
Rear Transaxle Mount Through Bolt	64 (87)
Starter Mounting Bolts	29 (39)
Tie Rod End Nuts	36 (49)
Transaxle-To-Engine Bolts	47 (64)
Transaxle Drain Plug	
3-Speed	36 (49)
4-Speed	13 (18)
Wheel Lug Nuts	76 (103)

	INCH Lbs. (N.m)
Air Cleaner Bolts	106 (12)
ABS Speed Sensor Bolt	71 (8)
Ground Cable-To-Transaxle Case	115 (13)
Shift Select Cable Nut	106 (12)
Splash Shield Bolts	44 (5)
TV Cable Guide Bracket Bolt	71 (8)

TORQUE SPECIFICATIONS (TRACKER)

Application	Ft. Lbs. (N.m)
Drive Shaft Flange Bolts	37 (50)
Exhaust Pipe Bracket	
2WD	17 (23)
4WD	44 (60)
Exhaust-To-Catalytic Converter	37 (50)
Filler Tube Bracket Bolt	17 (23)
Flexplate-To-Torque Converter Bolts	
3-Speed	41 (55)
4-Speed	48 (65)
Front Locking Hub Bolt	18 (25)
Front Wheel Bearing Nut	155 (210)
Locking Hub Cover Bolts	18 (25)
Rear Transmission Crossmember-To-Body Bolts (2WD)	44 (60)
Rear Transmission Mounting Bolts (2WD)	44 (60)
Reinforcement Plate Bolts	14 (19)
Skid Plate Bolts	40 (54)
Starter Mounting Bolts	22 (30)
Torque Mount Bracket Bolts (4WD)	37 (50)
Transfer Adapter Case Bolts	23 (31)
Transfer Case-To-Crossmember Bolts	37 (50)
Transfer Case Drain Plug (4WD)	21 (28)
Transfer Case Fill Plug (4WD)	17 (23)
Transfer Case Mounting Bolts	37 (50)
Transfer Case-To-Transmission Bolts	21 (28)
Transmission Case Stiffener Bolts	44 (60)
Transmission-To-Engine Bolts	63 (85)
Wheel Lug Nuts	70 (95)

	INCH Lbs. (N.m)
Flexplate Inspection Cover Bolts	89 (10)
Speedometer Guide Bracket Bolt (2WD)	80 (9)
Speedometer Case Retaining Bolt (4WD)	89 (10)
Speedometer Cable Clip Bolt (4WD)	89 (10)
Transmission Oil Pan Bolts	
3-Speed	115 (13)
4-Speed	44 (5)

**Honda: Accord, Civic, Civic Del Sol,
Odyssey, Passport, Prelude
Isuzu: Oasis**

NOTE: For information on Passport transmission removal and installation, refer to Rodeo in AUTOMATIC TRANSMISSION REMOVAL – ISUZU article. For information on Isuzu Oasis transmission removal and installation, refer to Honda Odyssey in this article.

APPLICATIONS

AUTOMATIC TRANSAXLE APPLICATIONS

Vehicle Model	Transaxle Model
Honda	
Accord	
4-Cylinder (Japan)	MPOA
4-Cylinder (U.S.A.)	AOYA
V6	MPZA
1995 Civic	A24A
1996 Civic	
4-Speed	AR4A
CVT	M4VA
Civic Del Sol	S24A
Odyssey	MPJA
Passport	THM 4L30E
Prelude	MP1A
Isuzu	
Oasis	MPJA

NOTE: Before disconnecting negative battery cable or fuses, ensure radio anti-theft code is obtained from customer. Radio anti-theft code must be re-entered into radio for radio operation. When the word "CODE" is displayed on radio, re-enter anti-theft code by using the radio station preset buttons.

REMOVAL & INSTALLATION

ACCORD

Removal – 1) Disconnect negative and then positive battery cables, and remove battery. Remove battery base and battery base support. Remove air cleaner assembly. Disconnect Intake Air Resonator (IAR) control solenoid valve connector. *See Fig. 1.* Remove vacuum hoses and IAR.

2) Disconnect throttle cable from control lever. Disconnect transaxle-to-chassis ground cable. Disconnect mainshaft and countershaft speed sensor connectors. Remove starter and all upper transaxle housing bolts from transaxle.

3) Raise and support vehicle. Disconnect lock-up control solenoid valve and shift control solenoid valve wire connectors. Remove front wheels. Drain transaxle, and install drain plug and NEW washer.

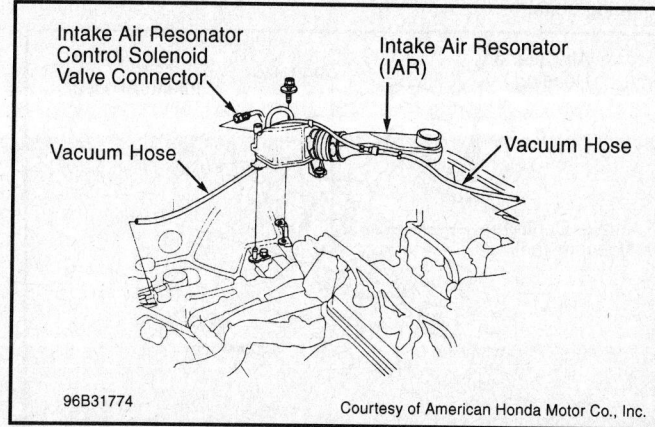

Fig. 1: **Removing Intake Air Resonator (IAR) Components (Accord)**

4) Remove Vehicle Speed Sensor (VSS). Disconnect transaxle cooler hoses at coolant pipes. Plug openings to prevent contamination. Remove transaxle housing mounting bolts. Remove front engine mount bracket bolts. Remove transaxle mount. Remove splash shield.

5) Remove center beam. Remove ball joint pinch bolt from right lower control arm. Use a puller to separate ball joint from knuckle. Remove shock strut damper fork bolt.

CAUTION: When removing CV joints and drive axle assemblies from transaxle, DO NOT pull on drive axle or knuckle. Inboard CV joint may separate. Pull on inboard joint.

6) Pry drive axle inboard CV joints out 1/2" using 2 large screwdrivers, and then remove joints completely from transaxle. Protect inner CV joint spline from contamination by covering drive axle end by covering it with a plastic bag. Support drive shafts to side.

7) Remove right radius rod. Remove control cable holder and torque converter cover plate. Remove shift control cable and control lever. Using wire, support cable aside.

8) Ensure control cable is not bent. Manually turn crankshaft pulley clockwise to access and remove 8 torque converter mounting bolts from torque converter drive plate. Remove intake manifold bracket.

9) Remove engine housing bolts from transaxle, and remove rear engine mount. Remove remaining mounting bolts. Place transaxle jack under transaxle. Pull transaxle away from engine just enough to clear 14-mm engine dowel pins. Lower transaxle on jack away from chassis. Ensure torque converter remains with transaxle assembly.

Installation – 1) To install transaxle, reverse removal procedure. Inspect drive plate for cracks, elongated holes and warpage. Replace drive plate if necessary. Replace 26-mm spring clips on end of each inner CV joint splined shaft. Tighten bolts to specification. See TORQUE SPECIFICATIONS.

2) Ensure speedometer cable is completely installed. Check shift control cable and throttle control cable. Adjust cables as necessary. See AUTOMATIC TRANSMISSION SERVICING – HONDA article.

CIVIC & CIVIC DEL SOL

Removal – 1) Disconnect negative and then positive battery cables, and remove battery. Remove complete air cleaner assembly with intake hose.

2) Remove transaxle ground cables. Remove starter cables and cable holder. Disconnect wire connector from lock-up control solenoid valve. Disconnect Vehicle Speed Sensor (VSS) connector. Remove transaxle housing mounting bolts and rear engine mounting bolt.

3) Remove transaxle drain plug and drain fluid (remove fill plug to speed draining). Install drain plug and NEW washer. Tighten plug to specification. See TORQUE SPECIFICATIONS. Remove splash shields from bottom of engine and from right wheelwell.

4) Remove front exhaust header pipe and bracket. Remove cotter pin and remove lower control arm ball joint nut. Separate ball joint from lower control arm. Remove shock strut damper fork bolt and separate strut damper from fork.

CAUTION: When removing CV joint and drive axle assembly from transaxle, DO NOT pull on drive axle or knuckle. Inboard CV joint may separate. Pull on inboard joint.

5) Using 2 large screwdrivers, pry inboard CV joints from transaxle. Remove or support shafts aside. Protect inner CV joint spline from contamination by covering drive axle end by covering it with a plastic bag. Remove header pipe bracket, torque converter cover and shift control cable holder. Remove header pipe. Remove stopper mount. *See Fig. 2.*

6) Disconnect cooler hoses at joint pipes. Using wire, support hoses aside. Remove shift control cable cover. Remove shift control cable and control lever. Using wire, support cable aside. Remove front and rear engine stiffeners. Only Civic Del Sol with D16Z6 engine uses a rear stiffener. Remove torque converter inspection cover plate. Manually turn crankshaft pulley clockwise to access and remove 8 torque

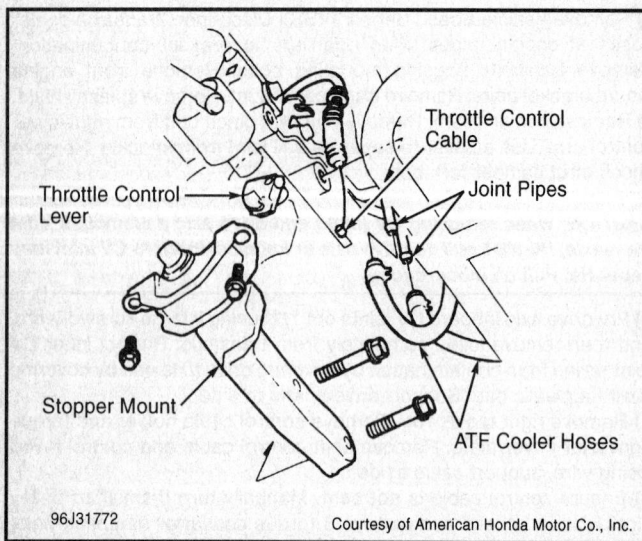

Fig. 2: Removing Stopper Mount & Cooler Hoses (Civic & Civic Del Sol)

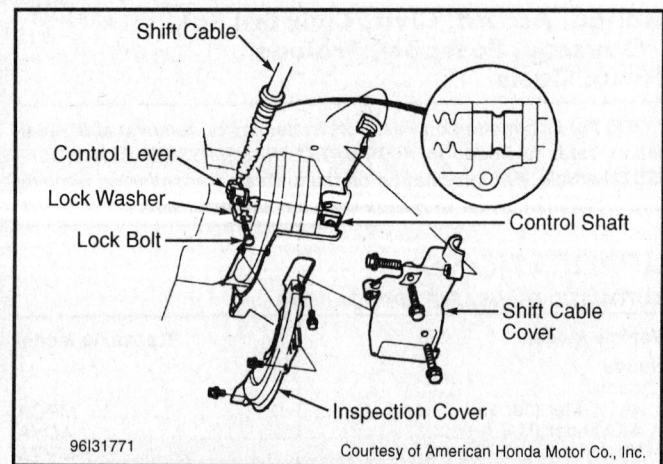

Fig. 3: Removing Shift Cable Cover & Inspection Cover (Honda Odyssey & Isuzu Oasis)

converter mounting bolts from torque converter drive plate. Remove distributor.

7) Using engine hoist or an appropriate engine support fixture, relieve weight of engine from mounts. Support transaxle using transaxle jack and raise it slightly. Remove front and side mount bolts. Remove engine mounting bolts.

8) Remove all transaxle mounting bolts. Pull transaxle away from engine until it clears 14-mm guide pins on engine. Lower transaxle assembly from vehicle. Ensure torque converter remains with transaxle.

Installation – 1) To install transaxle, reverse removal procedure. Inspect drive plate for cracks, elongated holes and warpage. Replace drive plate if necessary. Replace distributor "O" ring.

2) Replace 26-mm spring clips on end of each inboard CV joint splined shaft. Check shift control cable and throttle control cable operation. Adjust cables as necessary. See AUTOMATIC TRANSMISSION SERVICING – HONDA article.

HONDA ODYSSEY & ISUZU OASIS

Removal – 1) Disconnect negative battery cable. Disconnect positive battery cable. Remove battery hold down, base and bracket. Remove drain plug and drain transaxle fluid. Install drain plug with NEW washer and tighten plug to specification. See TORQUE SPECIFICATIONS.

2) Remove intake air duct. Remove ground cable from body and transaxle. Disconnect transaxle lock-up control solenoid and shift control solenoid wiring. Disconnect throttle cable from throttle control lever.

3) Disconnect mainshaft and countershaft speed sensor connectors. Remove cooler lines. Disconnect wiring for starter motor. Remove A/T gear position switch connector. Disconnect Vehicle Speed Sensor (VSS) connector.

4) Remove upper transaxle housing bolts. Loosen front engine mount bracket bolts. Remove splash shield. Remove center beam. Separate ball joints from lower control arms.

> **CAUTION: When removing CV joint and drive axle assemblies from transaxle, DO NOT pull on drive axle or knuckle. Inboard CV joint may separate. Pull on inboard joint.**

5) Pry on drive axles at differential and intermediate shaft to separate axles from differential case and bearing support. It may be necessary to tap on left inboard joint with a plastic to separate from bearing support. Remove or support shafts aside, swinging right drive shaft forward. Protect inner CV joint spline from contamination by covering drive axle end by covering it with a plastic bag.

6) Remove right damper fork. Remove right radius rod. Remove intermediate shaft. Remove inspection cover and shaft cable cover. See Fig. 3. Remove shift cable with control lever. Remove drive plate bolts.

7) Support transaxle using transaxle jack and raise it slightly. Remove transaxle mount. Remove intake manifold bracket. Remove remaining transaxle housing bolts. Pull transaxle away from engine until it clears 14-mm guide pins on engine. Lower transaxle assembly from vehicle.

Installation – 1) To install transaxle, reverse removal procedure. Inspect drive plate for cracks, elongated holes and warpage. Replace drive plate if necessary.

2) Replace 26-mm spring clips on end of each inboard CV joint splined shaft. Check shift control cable and throttle control cable operation. Adjust cables as necessary. See AUTOMATIC TRANSMISSION SERVICING – HONDA article.

PRELUDE

Removal – 1) Disconnect negative battery cable and ground strap at transaxle and body. Disconnect positive battery cable. Remove battery and battery base. Remove drain plug and drain transaxle fluid (remove fill plug to speed draining). Install drain plug with NEW washer and tighten plug to specification. See TORQUE SPECIFICATIONS.

2) Disconnect intake control vacuum tank connector. Remove intake control vacuum tank and bracket. See Fig. 4. Remove complete air cleaner case assembly. Disconnect wiring for transaxle lock-up control solenoid and shift control solenoid. Disconnect mainshaft speed sensor connector. Disconnect and remove throttle control cable at transaxle bracket.

3) Disconnect oil cooler hoses at joint pipes. Disconnect starter cables. Disconnect countershaft speed sensor connector. Plug and support hoses aside. Remove vehicle speed sensor from transaxle without removing power steering hoses. Remove 4 upper transaxle mounting bolts.

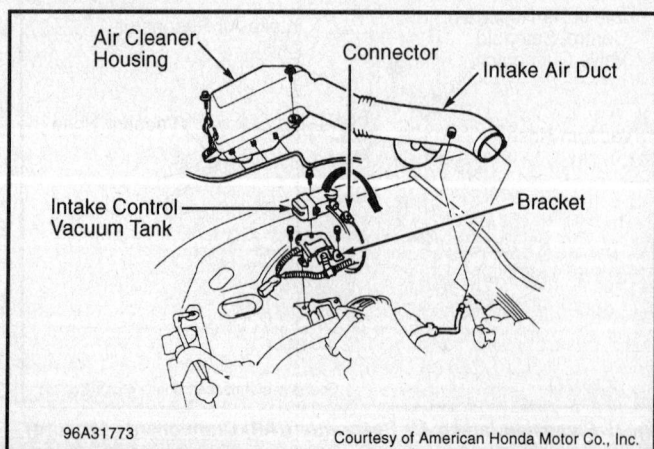

Fig. 4: Removing Intake Control Vacuum Tank (Prelude)

CAUTION: When removing CV joint and drive axle assembly from transaxle, DO NOT pull on drive axle or knuckle. Inboard CV joint may separate. Pull on inboard joint.

4) Loosen front engine mount bracket. Remove transaxle mount. Raise and support vehicle and remove front wheels. Remove engine splash shield. Remove center and rear crossmember bolts and remove crossmembers. Separate ball joints from lower control arms. Remove shock strut damper fork bolts and separate strut damper from fork.

5) While prying on inboard CV joints, remove both drive axles from transaxle. Remove or support shafts aside. Protect inner CV joint spline from contamination by covering drive axle end by covering it with a plastic bag. Remove right radius rod from control arm and frame.

6) Remove engine stiffener bracket from between lower transaxle and engine block. Remove torque converter inspection cover plate and shift cable cover. Remove shift control cable from transaxle. Using wire, hang cable aside. DO NOT bend cable.

7) Manually turn crankshaft pulley clockwise to access and remove 8 torque converter mounting bolts from torque converter drive plate. Support transaxle using transmission jack. Remove lower bolts from rear engine mount bracket. With jack in place, remove remaining transaxle mounting bolts.

8) Separate transaxle from engine block far enough to disengage both 14-mm dowel pins. Lower transaxle assembly.

Installation – 1) To install transaxle, reverse removal procedure. Inspect drive plate for cracks, elongated holes and warpage. Replace drive plate if necessary.

2) Replace 26-mm spring clips on end of each inner CV joint splined shaft. Check shift control cable and throttle control cable. Adjust cables as necessary. See AUTOMATIC TRANSMISSION SERVICING – HONDA article.

TORQUE SPECIFICATIONS

TORQUE SPECIFICATIONS

Application	Ft. Lbs. (N.m)
Ball Joint-To-Knuckle Bolt	40 (54)
Center Beam Stiffener Bolts	37 (50)
Control Cable Holder (Accord)	13 (18)
Drain Plug	37 (50)
Drive Plate-To-Crankshaft Bolts	55 (74)
Engine Stiffener Mounting Bolts	33 (45)
Intake Manifold Bracket Bolts	16 (22)
Starter Mounting Bolts	32 (44)
Stopper Mount (Civic & Civic Del Sol)	
10-mm Bolts	29 (39)
12-mm Bolts	48 (65)
Strut Damper Fork Bolt Lock Nut	
Accord	41 (55)
Civic, Civic Del Sol & Prelude	48 (65)
Odyssey	36-43 (49-59)
Strut Damper Pinch Bolt	32 (44)
Transaxle-To-Engine Mounting Bolts	
Accord, Odyssey & Prelude	47 (64)
Civic & Civic Del Sol	44 (60)
Wheel Lug Nuts	81 (110)

	INCH Lbs. (N.m)
Drive Plate-To-Torque Converter Bolts	108 (12)
Torque Converter Cover Bolts	108 (12)
Torque Converter Mounting Bolts	108 (12)

Hyundai

Accent, Elantra, Scoupe, Sonata

APPLICATION

TRANSAXLE APPLICATION

Vehicle	Trans. Model
Accent	A4AF2
Elantra	
1995	KM175
1996	A4BF1
Scoupe	A4AF1
Sonata	
2.0L Engine	KM175
3.0L Engine	F4A33

REMOVAL & INSTALLATION

SONATA 3.0L

Removal – 1) Remove drain plug and drain transaxle fluid. Remove air cleaner assembly. Remove battery. Disconnect fluid cooler hoses at top of transaxle and plug fittings and lines.

2) Remove control cable and speedometer cable. Remove upper transaxle-to-engine mounting bolts "C". See Fig. 1. Remove transaxle upper mounting bracket.

3) Disconnect all harness connectors from transaxle case. Remove starter. Ensure transaxle is in Neutral. Raise and support vehicle. Remove engine undercover panel. Remove both axle shaft assemblies, intermediate shaft and bearing bracket assembly. See appropriate AXLE SHAFTS article in AXLE SHAFTS & TRANSFER CASES section.

4) Support transaxle with jack. Remove transaxle lower brace behind starter. Remove lower bellhousing cover to access torque converter bolts. Remove torque converter bolts. Push torque converter into transaxle bellhousing, away from flywheel. Remove lower transaxle-to-engine mounting bolts. Remove transaxle from vehicle.

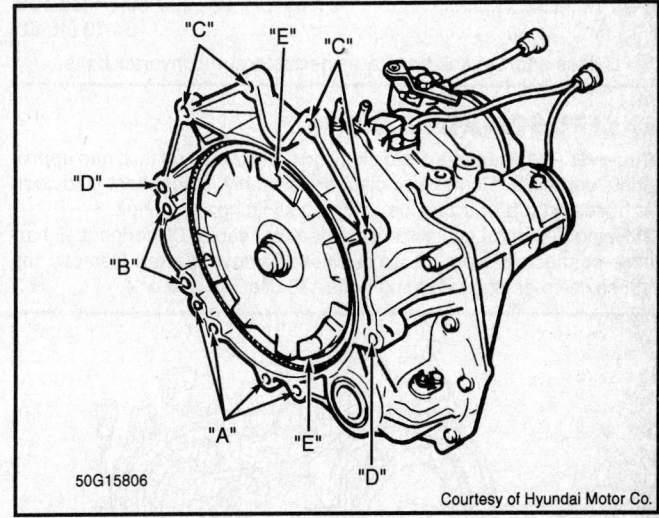

50G15806 — Courtesy of Hyundai Motor Co.

Fig. 1: Locating Transaxle-To-Engine Mounting Bolts (Sonata 3.0L)

Installation – 1) To install, reverse removal procedure. Before installing transaxle to engine, install torque converter into transaxle first, aligning torque converter to transaxle pump drive.

2) Install transaxle-to-engine mounting bolts are in correct locations. See Fig. 1. Tighten mounting bolts to specification. See TRANSAXLE MOUNTING BOLT TORQUE SPECIFICATIONS.

3) Tighten all other bolts to specification. See TORQUE SPECIFICATIONS. Refill transaxle fluid to specified level on dipstick. Adjust control cable.

4) Check neutral safety switch adjustment. See ADJUSTMENTS in AUTOMATIC TRANSMISSION SERVICING article in TRANSMISSION SERVICING. Recheck fluid level after engine is at operating temperature and before driving vehicle.

TRANSAXLE MOUNTING BOLT TORQUE SPECIFICATIONS

Location	Bolt Size (mm)	Ft. Lbs. (N.m)
Accent & 1996 Elantra		
"A"	12 x 40	43-58 (60-80)
"B"	10 x 70	33-38 (46-55)
"C"	10 x 55	20-25 (27-34)
"D"	6 x 10	6-7 (8-10)
"E"	[1]	33-38 (46-53)
1995 Elantra		
"A"	10 x 40	32-41 (43-55)
"B"	10 x 65	32-41 (43-55)
"C"	10 x 55	20-25 (27-34)
"D"	8 x 60	22-26 (30-35)
"E"	6 x 12	7-9 (10-12)
"F"	8 x 12	22-26 (30-35)
"G"	[1]	34-39 (46-53)
Scoupe		
"A"	12 x 40	32-41 (43-55)
"B"	10 x 70	32-41 (43-55)
"C"	10 x 55	20-25 (27-34)
"D"	10 x 60	22-26 (30-35)
"E"	6 x 12	6-7 (8-10)
"F"	[1]	17-20 (24-27)
Sonata 2.0L		
"A"	10 x 40	32-41 (43-55)
"B"	10 x 65	32-41 (43-55)
"C"	10 x 55	16-24 (22-32)
"D"	10 x 60	22-26 (30-35)
"E"	8 x 14	7-9 (10-12)
"F"	8 x 20	11-16 (15-22)
"G"	[1]	34-39 (46-53)
Sonata 3.0L		
"A"	10 x 55	22-31 (30-42)
"B"	10 x 55	20-25 (27-34)
"C"	12 x 40	48-63 (65-85)
"D"	12 x 55	59-74 (80-100)
"E"	[1]	34-39 (46-53)

[1] – These short shank bolts are special torque converter bolts.

EXCEPT SONATA 3.0L

Removal – **1)** Remove drain plug and drain transaxle fluid into appropriate container. Remove air cleaner assembly. Disconnect fluid cooler hoses on top of transaxle and plug all fittings and lines.

2) Remove control cable and speedometer cable. Disconnect all harness connectors from transaxle case. Remove starter. Remove top transaxle-to-engine mounting bolts "A". See Fig. 2, 3 or 4.

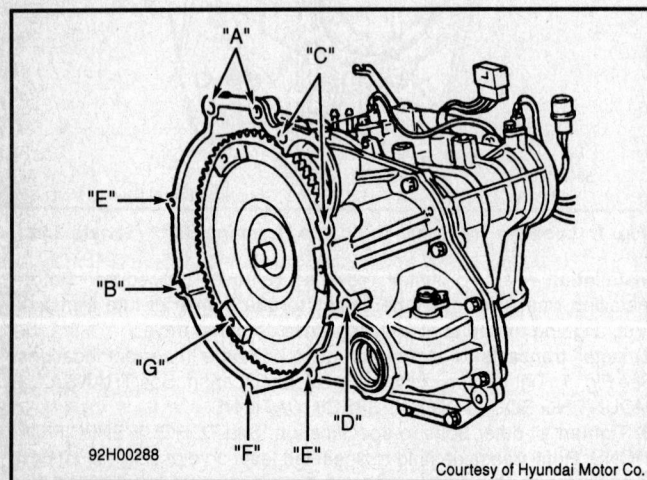

**Fig. 2: Locating Transaxle-To-Engine Mounting Bolts
(Elantra Shown; Sonata 2.0L Is Similar)**

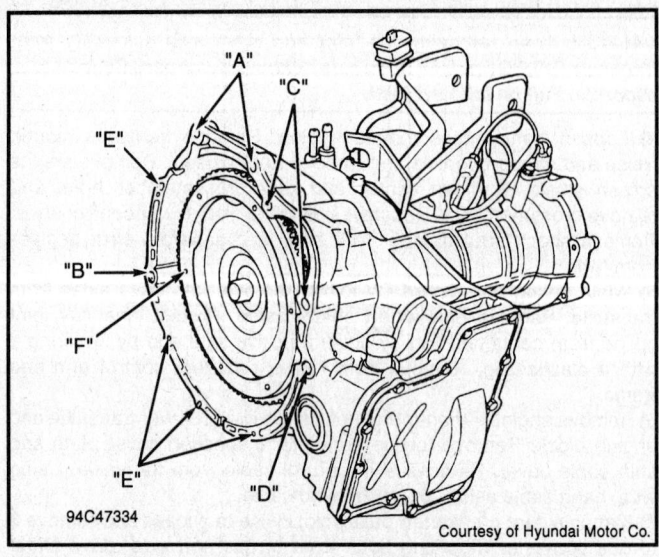

Fig. 3: Locating Transaxle-To-Engine Mounting Bolts (Scoupe)

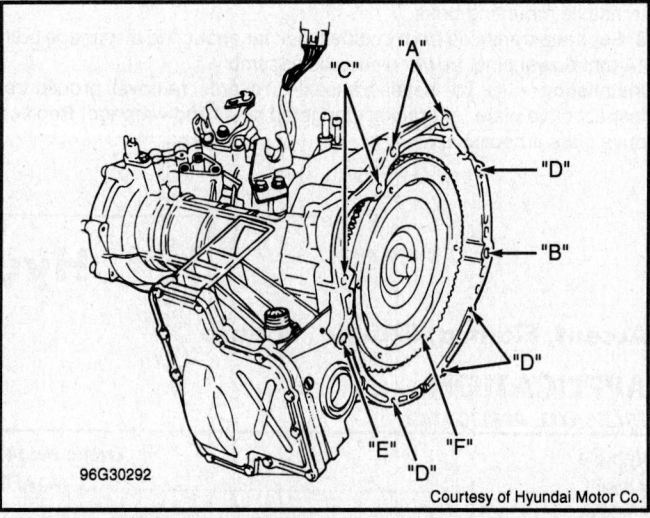

Fig. 4: Locating Transaxle-To-Engine Mounting Bolts (Accent)

3) On Accent, Elantra and Scoupe, remove transaxle top mounting bracket. On Sonata, remove bolt hole rubber covers inside fenderwell, and remove transaxle mounting bracket bolts. See Fig. 5. Ensure transaxle is in Neutral.

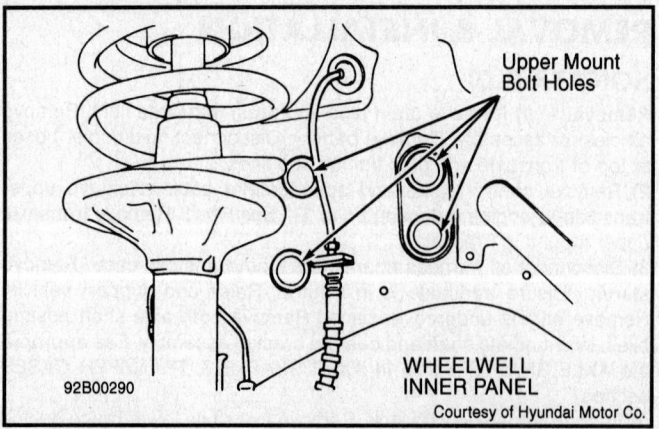

**Fig. 5: Locating Transaxle Top Mounting Bracket Bolt Holes
(Sonata 2.0L)**

4) On all models, support engine from top, or by suitable jack from bottom, using care not to damage engine oil pan. Remove undercover panel(s). Remove centermember support under engine. See Fig. 6. Remove lower bellhousing cover to access torque converter bolts.

5) Mark torque converter to flywheel/drive plate and remove special torque converter bolts. Push torque converter away from engine into transaxle. Reinstall centermember support under engine, but only hand-tighten bolts.

6) Remove both axle shaft assemblies. See appropriate AXLE SHAFTS article in AXLE SHAFTS & TRANSFER CASES section. Support transaxle with jack. Remove lower transaxle-to-engine mounting bolts. Remove transaxle from vehicle.

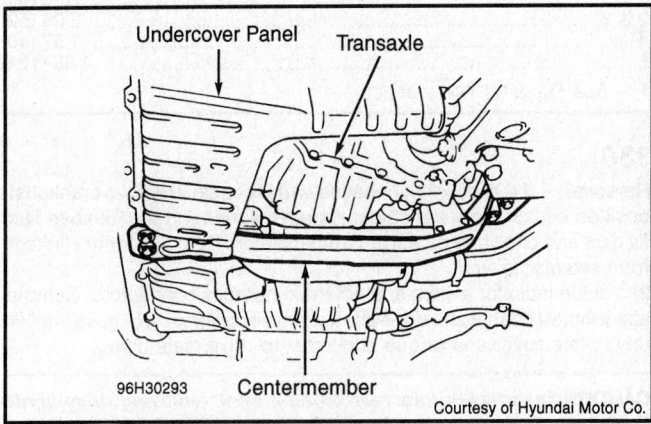

96H30293   Courtesy of Hyundai Motor Co.

***Fig. 6: Removing Center Crossmember
(Accent Shown; Elantra & Scoupe Are Similar)***

Installation – 1) To install, reverse removal procedure. Before installing transaxle to engine, be sure to install torque converter into transaxle first, aligning torque converter to transaxle pump drive.

2) Install transaxle-to-engine mounting bolts in correct locations. See Fig. 2, 3 or 4. Tighten to proper specification. See TRANSAXLE MOUNTING BOLT TORQUE SPECIFICATIONS table.

3) Tighten all bolts to specification. See TORQUE SPECIFICATIONS. Refill transaxle fluid to correct level on dipstick. Adjust control cable. Check neutral safety switch adjustment. See ADJUSTMENTS in appropriate AUTOMATIC TRANSMISSION SERVICING article in TRANSMISSION SERVICING. Recheck fluid level after engine is brought to operating temperature before driving vehicle.

TORQUE SPECIFICATIONS
TORQUE SPECIFICATIONS

Application	Ft. Lbs. (N.m)
Centermember End Mounting Bolt	44-59 (60-80)
Centermember-To-Front Engine Mount Bolt	22-30 (30-40)
Centermember-To-Rear Engine Mount Bolt	33-44 (45-60)
Drain Plug	22-26 (30-35)
Lower Ball Joint Nut	44-53 (60-72)
Starter Bolt	
Except Sonata 2.0L	20-25 (27-34)
Sonata 2.0L	16-24 (22-32)
Strut Bar Nut	55-66 (75-90)
Tie Rod End Nut	18-26 (24-35)
Transaxle Top Mounting	
Bracket-To-Transaxle Bolt	44-59 (60-80)
Bracket-To-Body Sidemember Bolt	22-30 (30-40)
Bracket Long Through Bolt	66-80 (90-108)
Transaxle Lower Brace (Sonata 3.0L) [1]	
Engine Side Bolt	48-63 (65-85)
Transaxle Side Bolt	22-31 (30-42)
	INCH Lbs. (N.m)
Air Cleaner Mounting Bolt	71-89 (8-10)
Neutral Safety Switch Bolts	89-106 (10-12)
Oil Pan Bolts	89-106 (10-12)
Speedometer Sleeve Locking Bolt	27-44 (3-5)

[1] – Brace is located behind starter.

Infiniti

G20, I30, J30, Q45
APPLICATION
TRANSMISSION APPLICATION

Vehicle Application	Transmission Model
G20	RE4F03A/V
I30	RE4F03A/V
J30	RE4R01A
Q45	RE4R03A

REMOVAL & INSTALLATION

G20 & I30

Removal – 1) Remove battery and bracket. Remove air duct. Disconnect transaxle solenoid and inhibitor switch harness connectors. Disconnect revolution harness connector. Disconnect and remove crankshaft position sensor from transaxle. On I30, remove left hand mounting bracket from transaxle and body.

2) Drain transaxle. Disconnect shift control cable. Disconnect and plug oil cooler hoses. Remove drive axles. See appropriate AXLE SHAFTS article in AXLE SHAFTS & TRANSFER CASES section. Remove front exhaust pipe.

3) Remove starter. Remove drive plate cover. Remove torque converter-to-drive plate bolts. Support engine with jack. Support transaxle with transmission jack. Remove transaxle mounts and centermember. Remove bellhousing bolts. Lower and remove transaxle from vehicle.

Inspection – Check drive plate runout using dial indicator. If drive plate runout is greater than .008" (0.2 mm), replace drive plate. To ensure correct assembly when connecting torque converter to transaxle, measure distance "A". See Fig. 1. On G20, distance "A" should be .63" (16 mm). On I30, distance "A" should be .55" (14 mm).

Installation – To install, reverse removal procedure. After connecting torque converter to drive plate, rotate crankshaft several turns to ensure transaxle rotates freely. Tighten bolts to specifications. See TORQUE SPECIFICATIONS. Install bolts to their proper location according to length. See TRANSAXLE BOLT LOCATION & LENGTH table. Check transaxle fluid. Move selector through all positions to ensure transaxle operates correctly. Perform road test.

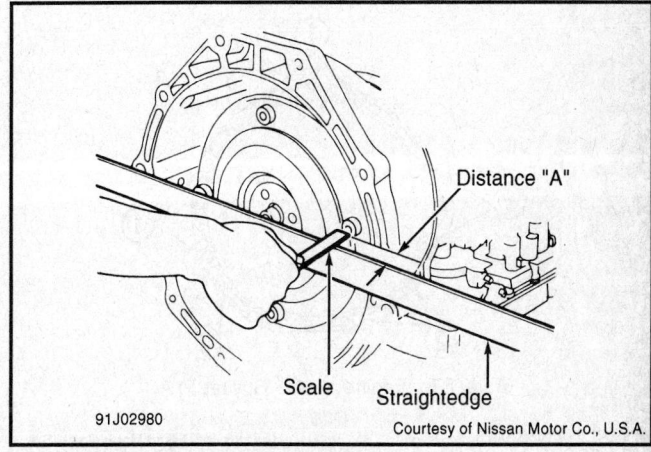

91J02980   Courtesy of Nissan Motor Co., U.S.A.

Fig. 1: Connecting Torque Converter

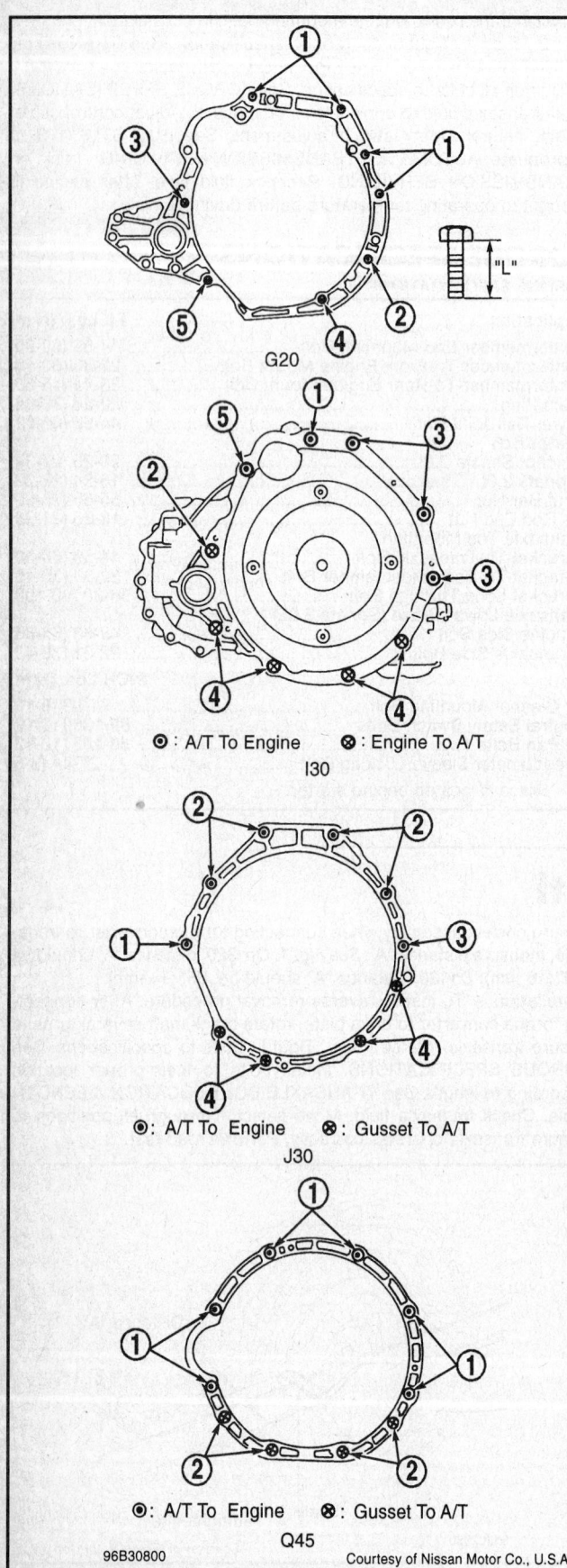

⊙ : A/T To Engine   ⊗ : Engine To A/T

I30

⊙ : A/T To Engine   ⊗ : Gusset To A/T

J30

⊙ : A/T To Engine   ⊗ : Gusset To A/T

Q45

96B30800   Courtesy of Nissan Motor Co., U.S.A.

Fig. 2: Locating Transaxle bolts

TRANSAXLE BOLT LOCATION ¹ & LENGTH (G20)

Bolt Number	Length In. (mm)
1	2.17 (55)
2	1.97 (50)
3	2.56 (65)
4	1.38 (35)
5	1.77 (45)

¹ – See Fig. 2 for bolt location.

TRANSAXLE BOLT LOCATION ¹ & LENGTH (I30)

Bolt Number	Length In. (mm)
1	2.56 (65)
2 & 3	2.06 (52)
4	1.57 (40)
5	4.88 (124)

¹ – See Fig. 2 for bolt location.

J30

Removal – 1) Disconnect negative battery cable. Remove crankshaft position sensor from transaxle. Remove exhaust pipe. Remove fluid fill pipe and oil cooler pipe from transmission. Remove control linkage from selector lever.

2) Unplug inhibitor switch and solenoid harness connectors. Remove speedometer cable and drive shaft. Plug all openings. Remove starter, drive plate cover and torque converter-to-drive plate bolts.

CAUTION: Insert plug into rear oil seal after removing drive shaft. Ensure no damage occurs to spline, sleeve yoke or rear seal when removing drive shaft.

3) Support engine/transmission with jack. Remove rear transmission mounting bracket. Remove bellhousing bolts. Lower and remove transmission assembly from vehicle.

Inspection – Check drive plate runout using dial indicator. If drive plate runout is greater than .060" (0.15 mm), replace drive plate. To ensure correct assembly when connecting torque converter to transmission, measure distance "A". See Fig. 1. Distance "A" should be 1.02" (26 mm).

Installation – To install, reverse removal procedure. Tighten bolts to specifications. See Fig. 2. Ensure bolts are installed in proper location according to length. See TRANSAXLE BOLT LOCATION & LENGTH table. After connecting torque converter to drive plate, rotate crankshaft several turns to ensure transmission rotates freely. Check transmission fluid. Move selector through all positions to ensure transmission operates correctly. Perform road test.

TRANSAXLE BOLT LOCATION ¹ & LENGTH (J30)

Bolt Number	Length In. (mm)
1	2.28 (58)
2 & 3	1.87 (47.5)
4	.98 (25)
Gusset to Engine	
Left Hand, Right Hand	.79 (20)
Left Hand	.98 (25)

¹ – See Fig. 2 for bolt location.

Q45

Removal – 1) Disconnect negative battery cable. Remove crankshaft position sensor from transaxle. Remove fill pipe, oil cooler pipe clamps and oil cooler pipe from transmission assembly. Remove exhaust pipes.

2) Unplug A/T harness and speed sensor connectors. Remove control linkage from selector lever. Plug all openings. Remove drive shaft.

CAUTION: Insert plug into rear oil seal after removing drive shaft. Ensure no damage occurs to spline, sleeve yoke or rear seal when removing drive shaft.

3) Remove starter, gusset securing engine to A/T assembly and torque converter-to-drive plate bolts. Support engine/transmission assembly with, jack and remove rear mounting bracket from body. Remove bellhousing bolts, and lower transmission assembly from vehicle.

Inspection – Check drive plate runout using dial indicator. If drive plate runout is greater than .008" (.20 mm), replace drive plate. To ensure correct assembly when connecting torque converter to transmission, measure distance "A". *See Fig. 1.* Distance "A" should be .866" (22 mm).

Installation – To install, reverse removal procedure. Tighten bolts to specifications. *See Fig. 2.* Ensure bolts are installed in proper location according to length. See TRANSAXLE BOLT LOCATION & LENGTH table. After torque converter is installed to drive plate, rotate crankshaft several turns to ensure transmission rotates freely. Check transmission fluid. Move selector through all positions to ensure transmission operates correctly. Perform road test.

TRANSAXLE BOLT LOCATION & LENGTH (Q45)

Bolt Number	Length In. (mm)
1	2.76 (70)
2 & Gusset to Engine	1.18 (30)

¹ – See Fig. 2 for bolt location.

TORQUE SPECIFICATIONS
TORQUE SPECIFICATIONS

Applications	Ft. Lbs. (N.m)
Bellhousing Bolts	
G20	
No. 1, 2 & 3	51-59 (70-79)
No. 4 & 5	12-15 (16-21)
I30	
No. 1-5	51-59 (70-79)
J30	
No. 1, 2 & 3	29-36 (39-49)
No. 4 & Gusset	22-29 (29-39)
Q45	
No. 1	80-87 (108-118)
No. 2 & Gusset	51-58 (69-78)
Drive Plate Cover Bolts	
G20 & I30	12-15 (16-20)
J30	22-29 (30-39)
Q45	51-58 (69-79)
Torque Converter-To-Drive Plate Bolts	33-43 (45-58)

Isuzu

Oasis, Rodeo, Trooper
APPLICATION
AUTOMATIC TRANSAXLE/TRANSMISSION APPLICATIONS

Application	Transaxle/Transmission Model
1996 Oasis	Honda MPJA
1995-96 Rodeo & Trooper	Hydra-Matic 4L30-E

REMOVAL & INSTALLATION
OASIS

CAUTION: When battery is disconnected, radio will go into anti-theft protection mode. Obtain radio anti-theft protection code from owner prior to servicing vehicle.

Removal – **1)** Disconnect and remove battery. Drain transaxle. Remove air intake duct. Remove cable holder from battery base. Disconnect ground cable from body. Remove battery base and bracket. Disconnect ground strap from transaxle. Disconnect solenoid, switch and sensor harness connectors.

2) Disconnect throttle control cable from throttle control lever. Disconnect and plug ATF cooler hoses. Disconnect starter cables. Remove transaxle housing mounting bolts. Loosen front engine mount bracket bolts. Remove lower splash shield. Remove lower center beam.

3) Disconnect lower strut bolt and lower control arm ball joint. Pry drive shafts from differential and intermediate shafts. Lubricate and protect driveshaft ends. Remove right-side damper pinch bolt. Separate damper fork from damper. Remove right-side radius rod. Pivot right-side drive shaft towards front of vehicle.

4) Remove intermediate shaft assembly from vehicle. Remove torque converter cover and shift cable cover. Disconnect control lever and cable from transaxle. Remove 8 drive plate bolts. Raise transaxle with jack enough to take weight off mount. Remove transaxle mount.

5) Remove intake manifold support bracket. Remove remaining transaxle housing bolts and rear engine mount bolts. Pull transaxle away from engine to clear dowel pins and lower from vehicle.

Installation – **1)** Flush ATF cooler. Install NEW mainshaft "O" ring. Install torque converter on mainshaft. Install starter onto transaxle housing. Ensure alignment dowels are in place on torque converter housing. Raise transaxle into position with jack.

2) To complete installation, reverse removal procedure. Torque all fasteners to specification. See TORQUE SPECIFICATIONS. Refill transaxle with ATF to proper level. Check throttle cable adjustment. Align front suspension. Road test vehicle. After road test, loosen front engine mount bolts and retighten to specification.

RODEO & TROOPER

Removal – **1)** Remove engine hood. Disconnect negative battery cable. Remove air cleaner assembly. Raise and support vehicle. Remove skid plates. Remove exhaust and transfer case protectors. Place reference marks on drive shaft flanges at transfer case (4WD), transmission and differential for reassembly reference. Remove drive shaft flange bolts. Remove drive shaft(s).

2) Disconnect exhaust pipes at exhaust manifolds and rear of catalytic converter. Remove exhaust pipe assembly with catalytic converter attached. Disconnect oxygen sensor harness connector.

3) Remove transfer case control lever knob. Remove front console box and PCM cover. Disconnect shift lock cable from selector lever assembly. Disconnect necessary harness connectors. Disconnect oil cooler lines, speedometer cables, hoses and shift linkage at transmission.

4) Remove transmission dipstick and tube. Remove starter. Remove flywheel cover. Remove torque converter-to-flywheel bolts. Support transmission with jack. Remove rear mount bolts. Raise transmission slightly and remove crossmember and rear mount. Support engine with hoist. Remove transmission-to-engine bolts and remove transmission.

Installation – **1)** To install, reverse removal procedure. Ensure reference marks on drive shaft flanges align. Torque all fasteners to specification. See TORQUE SPECIFICATIONS.

2) If transmission was drained, fill with Dexron-III ATF. If transfer case was drained, fill with SAE 5W-30 for operational temperature range up to 95°F (35°C). Use SAE 15W-40, 20W-40 or 20W-50 for operational temperatures above 50°F (10°C). Adjust shift linkage if necessary.

TORQUE SPECIFICATIONS

TORQUE SPECIFICATIONS

Application	Ft. Lbs. (N.m)
Oasis	
Battery Bracket Bolt	16 (22)
Center Beam Support Bolt	37 (50)
Front Damper Fork Bolt Lock Nut	47 (64)
Front Engine Mount Bolt	28 (38)
Intake Manifold Brace Bolt	16 (22)
Intermediate Shaft Bolt	28 (38)
Lower Ball Joint Castle Nut	36-43 (49-58)
Rear Engine Mount Bolt	40 (54)
Starter Bolt	33 (45)
Torque Converter Drive Plate Bolt	9 (12)
Transaxle Housing Bolt	47 (64)
Transaxle Mount Bolt	47 (64)
Transaxle Mount Nut	28 (38)
Rodeo & Trooper	
Drive Shaft-To-Differential Flange Bolt	46 (62)
Drive Shaft-To-Transfer Case Flange Bolt	46 (62)
Exhaust & Transfer Case Protector Bolt	27 (37)
Exhaust Pipe To Manifold Bolt	49 (67)
Oil Cooler Pipe Nut	40 (54)
Starter Bolt	30 (41)
Torque Converter Bolt	40 (54)
Transmission-To-Engine Bolt	56 (76)

Jaguar

XJR, XJS, XJ6, XJ12

APPLICATION

AUTOMATIC TRANSMISSION APPLICATIONS

Model	Transmission
1995	
XJR & XJ12	4L80-E
XJS	
4.0L	ZF 4HP 24-E
6.0L	4L80-E
XJ6	ZF 4HP 24-E
1996	
XJR & XJ12	4L80-E
XJS & XJ6	ZF 4HP 24-E

REMOVAL & INSTALLATION

NOTE: Transmission removal and installation procedures for XJR are not available from manufacturer.

XJS 6.0L & XJ12

Removal & Installation – 1) Disconnect negative battery cable. Remove air cleaner assemblies. Remove transmission dipstick. Remove upper dipstick tube. Remove engine bay bars from inner fenders. Attach Lifting Bracket (18G 1465) or equivalent to cylinder head. See Fig. 1. Attach Engine Support Bracket (MS 53B) or equivalent, and engage hook to lifting bracket.

2) Tighten hook to take weight of engine. Place transmission shifter in Neutral position with parking brake off. Raise and support vehicle. Separate intermediate exhaust pipes from exhaust downpipes, and remove exhaust seals. Remove intermediate and rear heat shields. Secure exhaust pipes aside. Remove front heat shields. Remove rear transmission mount center nut, bracket plate and spacer. Using a jack and a block of wood, support transmission.

3) Remove rear mount bolts and spacers. Lower jack and remove rear mount assembly. Remove jack supporting transmission. Disconnect drive shaft from transmission and secure shaft aside. Working in engine compartment from above, lower engine support slightly. From beneath vehicle, disconnect transmission wiring harness connectors as necessary. Disconnect shift cable from transmission.

4) Drain transmission fluid. Disconnect and plug transmission oil cooler lines at transmission. Remove bolt securing cooler lines to engine oil pan. Remove spacer. Remove access cover to torque converter. Remove drive plate-to-torque converter bolts. Remove heat shield from right side of steering rack. Remove right exhaust downpipe from exhaust manifold.

5) Remove all transmission-to-engine bolts except 2 lower left side bolts and lower starter bolt. Remove transmission fill tube, and plug oil pan. Place transmission jack under oil pan. Remove remaining transmission-to-engine bolts. Ensure all hoses and wiring harness connectors are out of way.

6) Lower transmission and remove from vehicle. To install, reverse removal procedure. Add transmission fluid. See AUTOMATIC TRANSMISSION SERVICING article.

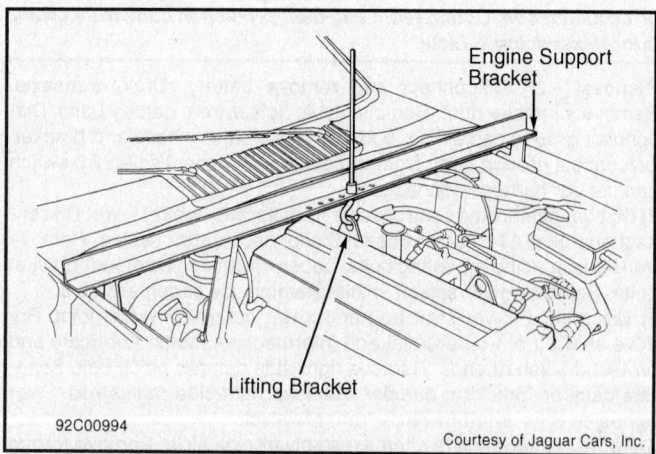

Fig. 1: Installing Engine Support Bracket (4.0L Shown)

XJ6 & XJS 4.0L

Removal & Installation – 1) Disconnect negative battery cable. Remove bolt securing dipstick tube to intake manifold. Attach Lifting Bracket (18G 1465) or equivalent to cylinder head. See Fig. 1. Attach Engine Support Bracket (MS 53B) or equivalent, and engage hook to lifting bracket.

2) Tighten hook to take weight of engine. Place transmission shifter in Neutral position with parking brake off. Raise and support vehicle. Drain transmission fluid. Remove front exhaust pipe. Support weight of transmission with a jack. Remove rear transmission mount assembly. Lower jack to access drive shaft bolts. Place mating marks on flanges, and remove drive shaft from transmission. Disconnect shift cable from transmission.

3) Remove rotary switch from left side of transmission. Remove fill tube from transmission pan. Plug oil pan. Remove and plug transmission oil cooler lines. Remove torque converter access plate. Remove torque converter-to-drive plate bolts. Lower engine/transmission, ensuring engine does not contact steering rack.

4) Remove transmission-to-engine bolts. Ensure all wires and hoses are clear and withdraw transmission from engine. Remove transmission from vehicle. To install, reverse removal procedure. Add transmission fluid. Ensure transmission rotary switch is adjusted properly. See AUTOMATIC TRANSMISSION SERVICING article.

TORQUE SPECIFICATIONS
TORQUE SPECIFICATIONS

Application	Ft. Lbs. (N.m)
XJ6 & XJS 4.0L	
Dipstick Tube-Intake Manifold Bolt	15 (20)
Down Pipe-To-Intermediate Pipe Bolts	11-13 (15-18)
Drain Plug	11 (15)
Drive Shaft Bolts	70-77 (95-105)
Drive Plate-To-Torque Converter Bolts	36-40 (49-54)
Filler Tube	66 (90)
Intermediate Pipe-To-Muffler	11-13 (15-18)
Oil Cooler Pipe Banjo Bolt	24-27 (32-36)
Rear Engine Mounting Bracket-To-Body	15-18 (20-25)
Transmission-To-Engine Bolts	36-40 (49-54)
XJS 6.0L & XJ12	
Down Pipe-To-Intermediate Pipe Bolts	11-13 (15-18)
Drive Shaft Bolts	28-32 (36-43)
Drive Plate-To-Torque Converter Bolts	36 (49)
Intermediate Pipe-To-Muffler	11-13 (15-18)
Transmission Mount Assembly Bolts	
5/16" Bolts	15-18 (20-25)
3/8" Bolts	26-32 (36-44)

Kia

Sephia, Sportage
APPLICATION
TRANSMISSION APPLICATION

Vehicle Application	Transmission Model
Sephia	FA4A-EL
Sportage	AW372LE

REMOVAL & INSTALLATION

NOTE: Any time battery cables are disconnected from battery and then reconnected, theft deterrent system will be activated (horn will sound and emergency lights will flash for about 3 minutes). To disarm theft deterrent system, insert ignition key and turn it to ACC position.

Sephia – 1) Raise and support vehicle. Drain transaxle. Remove wheels and splash shields. Disconnect air hose, and remove air cleaner and resonance chamber. Remove battery and battery tray. Disconnect speedometer cable and throttle cable assemblies from transaxle.

2) Disconnect range switch and solenoid valve connectors. Remove starter. Support engine from above using engine support assembly. Remove engine mounts, crossmember and front exhaust pipe. Remove oil pan stiffener-to-transaxle bolts. Disconnect tie rod ends from knuckles.

3) Remove stabilizer bar. Remove lower ball joint-to-steering knuckle pinch bolts. Separate lower control arm from steering knuckle. Separate left axle shaft from transaxle using pry bar inserted between axle shaft and case. DO NOT damage oil seal.

4) Install Differential Side Gear Holder (K94A-4208-AT) into differential side gear opening (to prevent side gears from becoming misaligned). Separate right axle shaft from transaxle. Disconnect and plug oil cooler lines. Support transaxle from below using transmission jack.

5) Remove front torque converter housing access plates and cover. Mark converter to drive plate for reassembly reference, and remove torque converter bolts. Slightly lower engine using engine support from above. Remove remaining transaxle-to-engine bolts, and lower transaxle assembly from vehicle.

6) To install transaxle, reverse removal procedure. Torque converter is seated properly when distance between engine mating service of converter housing and face of converter is .54" (14 mm).

7) Tighten bolts to specification. See TORQUE SPECIFICATIONS. Install NEW clips on axle ends before installing axle shafts. For more information on axle shafts, see appropriate AXLE SHAFTS article in AXLE SHAFTS & TRANSFER CASES section.

8) Tighten stabilizer bar nut until 9/32-7/16" of thread is exposed at top of bolt. Fill transaxle with required amount of fluid, and check for external leaks.

Sportage – 1) Disconnect negative battery cable. Loosen A/T control cable locknut and remove from mounting bracket. Remove cable from throttle body. Remove rear section of center console. Remove transfer case shift lever knob. Remove front section of center console. Disconnect POWER/ECONOMY switch harness connector when lifting up front section of console.

2) Move transfer case shift lever to 4L position. Remove 4 transfer shift lever cover plate bolts. Lift up and remove cover plate and boot. Remove 5 top retaining bolts. Lift shift lever straight out.

3) Shift transmission shift selector lever to Park. Remove 4 selector lever nuts. Raise and support vehicle. Drain transmission fluid. Disconnect shift rod at transmission. Lower vehicle. Disconnect connector from below selector lever assembly. Note that park position connector is hard wired.

4) Remove shift selector lever assembly. Pull upper dipstick tube free of lower dipstick tube. Raise and support vehicle. Disconnect all electrical harness connectors. Some harness connectors may not be accessed until transmission is slightly lowered.

5) Place matching marks on driveshaft and mating flange. Disconnect driveshafts from flanges. Disconnect cooler lines at transmission. Remove and support starter aside. Remove transfer case bolts from crossmember.

6) Support transmission assembly with appropriate transmission jack. Unbolt and remove crossmember. Remove bellhousing bolts attaching transmission to engine. Remove lower front splash guard. Remove converter inspection plate. Remove torque converter-to-drive plate nuts.

7) Move transmission backward and lower slightly. Remove crankshaft position sensor. Slowly lower transmission until remaining harness connectors become accessible. Disconnect harness connectors.

8) Fully lower transmission. Ensure all electrical connectors are disconnected and A/T control cable is free from engine compartment. To install, reverse disassembly procedure. Tighten all bolts to specifications. See TORQUE SPECIFICATIONS.

TORQUE SPECIFICATIONS

TORQUE SPECIFICATIONS

Application	Ft. Lbs. (N.m)
Sephia	
Crossmember Bolt	47-66 (64-89)
Exhaust Pipe Nut	23-34 (31-46)
Lower Control Arm Ball Joint-To-Knuckle Bolt	32-40 (43-54)
Starter Bolt	14-18 (19-25)
Transaxle-To-Engine Bolt	47-66 (64-89)
Transaxle-To-Oil Pan Stiffener Bolt	27-38 (37-52)
Wheel Lug Nut	65-87 (88-118)
Sportage	
Clutch Housing Bolts	
12 mm	51-65 (69-88)
10 mm	38-60 (57-81)
Crossmember-To-Frame Bolt	23-34 (31-46)
Crossmember-To-Mount Bolt	80 (108)
Differential Flange Bolt	20-22 (27-30)
Exhaust Bracket Bolt	20 (27)
Gusset Mounting Bolt	38-60 (57-81)
Oil Cooler Line Fitting	23-34 (31-46)
Shift Lever Mount Bolt	16-21 (22-28)
Starter Bolt	29 (39)
Torque Converter-To-Plate Nut	12-20 (16-27)
Transfer Case Flange Bolt	36-43 (49-59)
Transfer Case Side Mount Bolt	23-34 (31-46)
	INCH Lbs. (N.m)
Crankshaft Position Sensor Bolt	62 (7)
Dust Cover Plate Bolt	72-102 (8-12)
Inspection Plate Bolt	41-62 (5-7)
Splash Guard Bolt	41-62 (5-7)

Lexus

ES300, GS300, LS400, LX450, SC300, SC400
REMOVAL & INSTALLATION

CAUTION: To prevent accidental air bag deployment, wait at least 90 seconds after disconnecting negative battery cable.

TRANSAXLE

Removal & Installation (ES300) – 1) Remove battery. Remove air cleaner. Disconnect throttle cable. On models with cruise control, remove actuator cover and unplug actuator. Disconnect ground strap cables. Remove starter. Unplug both speed control sensors. Unplug park/neutral position switch connector.

2) Unplug solenoid connector at bracket. Disconnect shift control cable. Disconnect oil cooler hoses. Remove front transaxle mount bolts. Remove front engine mount bolts. Remove oil cooler clamp bolts from front frame. Remove 4 upper transaxle-to-engine bolts.

3) Install engine support fixture. Suspend steering gear from support fixture. Raise and support vehicle. Remove front wheels. Remove exhaust pipe. Drain differential. Remove splash shields. Remove axle shafts. See appropriate AXLE SHAFTS article in AXLE SHAFTS & TRANSFER CASES section. Remove front side engine mount nut. Remove rear side engine mount bolts.

4) Remove left side transaxle mount bolts. Remove steering gear housing. Remove 2 screws, 6 bolts, and 4 nuts which retain front frame. Remove front frame.

5) Support transaxle with appropriate jack. Remove rear inspection plate. Remove torque converter bolts. Remove remaining transaxle-to-engine bolts. Lower transaxle from vehicle. Remove torque converter.

6) To install, reverse removal procedure. Before installation, measure torque converter mounting depth. *See Fig. 1.* Measure distance between torque converter mounting surface and transmission/transaxle case front surface. See TORQUE CONVERTER MOUNTING DEPTH table. If distance is less than specified, reposition torque converter until fully seated.

TRANSMISSION

Removal (GS300, LS400, SC300 & SC400) – 1) Disconnect negative battery cable. Remove dipstick tube. Disconnect throttle cable. Disconnect oxygen sensor. Remove both tailpipes. Remove front and center exhaust pipes. Remove heat insulator. Remove center floor crossmember brace.

2) Disconnect shift control rod from shift lever. Unbolt and remove drive shaft. Disconnect both vehicle speed sensor harness connectors. Disconnect O/D direct clutch speed sensor harness connector. Disconnect solenoid harness connector. Disconnect park/neutral position switch harness connector. Unbolt all harness hold-down clamps.

3) Disconnect starter harness connections. Disconnect and remove oil cooler pipes. Remove torque converter inspection plate. Remove 6 bolts securing torque converter to flywheel. Using appropriate transmission jack, support transmission.

4) Support front and rear of engine. Remove transmission rear support. Unbolt and move starter forward. Remove transmission to engine securing bolts. Move transmission rearward and lower.

Installation – To install, reverse removal procedure. Before installation, measure torque converter mounting depth. *See Fig. 1.* Measure distance between torque converter mounting surface and transmission/transaxle case front surface. See TORQUE CONVERTER MOUNTING DEPTH table. If distance is less than specified, reposition torque converter until fully seated.

Removal (LX450) – 1) Remove battery and tray. Loosen cooling fan shroud. Disconnect throttle cable. Remove top starter bolt. Disconnect gear selector lever and transfer case lever from transmission. Remove knob and boot from transfer case lever.

2) Remove console box and disconnect electrical connectors. Remove shift lever assembly and transfer case shift lever. Disconnect transmission solenoid and sensor connectors. Disconnect transfer case bleed hose and remove drive shafts. Remove oil filler pipe.

3) Loosen ATF cooler fittings. Remove stabilizer bar bracket mounting bolts. Remove lower engine shield. Remove dust shield and torque converter clutch mounting bolts.

4) Remove front exhaust pipe assembly. Remove starter and crossmember. Lower transmission. Remove oil cooler pipes and disconnect any remaining wiring connectors. Remove transmission-to-engine mounting bolts. Remove transmission from vehicle.

Installation – 1) Install torque converter on transmission. Measure distance between torque converter mounting surface and transmission case front surface. See TORQUE CONVERTER MOUNTING DEPTH table.

2) To complete installation, reverse removal procedures. Adjust gear selector control rod and throttle cable. Check and refill fluid level as necessary. Road test vehicle.

TORQUE CONVERTER MOUNTING DEPTH [1]

Application	In. (mm)
ES300	.539 (13.7)
GS300	.004 (0.10)
LS400	.673 (17.1)
LX450	.618 (15.7)
SC300	1.039 (26.4)
SC400	.673 (17.1)

[1] – For measurement procedure, *see Fig. 1.*

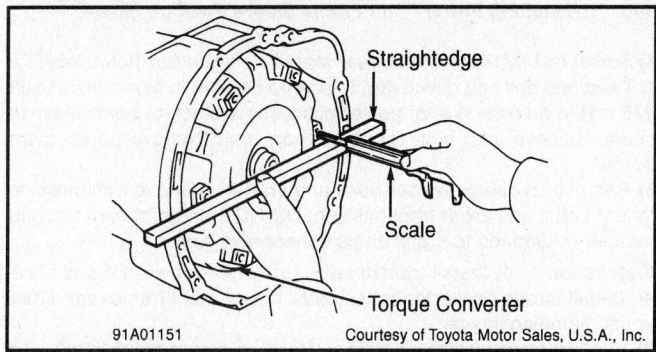

91A01151   Courtesy of Toyota Motor Sales, U.S.A., Inc.

Fig. 1: Measuring Torque Converter Mounting Depth (Typical)

TORQUE SPECIFICATIONS

TORQUE SPECIFICATIONS

Application	Ft. Lbs. (N.m)
ES300	
Exhaust Flange Nut	46 (62)
Flywheel-To-Crankshaft Bolt	61 (83)
Flywheel-To-Torque Converter Bolt	20 (27)
Front Frame Bolt	
12-mm Head	24 (33)
19-mm Head	134 (181)
Nut	27 (37)
Front Side Engine Mount Bolt	59 (80)

TORQUE SPECIFICATIONS (Cont.)

Application	Ft. Lbs. (N.m)
Front Side Transaxle Mount Bolt	59 (80)
Left Side Transaxle Mount Bolt	38 (52)
Lug Nut	76 (103)
Rear Inspection Plate Bolt	27 (37)
Rear Side Engine Mount Bolt	49 (66)
Starter Bolt	29 (39)
Steering Gear Bolt	134 (181)
Transaxle-To-Engine Bolt	
10-mm Head	34 (46)
12-mm Head	47 (64)
GS300, LS400 & SC400	
Catalytic Converter Bolt	46 (62)
Drive Shaft Center Bearing Bolt	27 (37)
Drive Shaft-To-Differential Nut	58 (79)
Drive Shaft-To-Transmission Nut	58 (79)
Exhaust Pipe Support Bracket Bolt	32 (44)
Flywheel-To-Crankshaft Bolt	61 (83)
Flywheel-To-Torque Converter Bolt	30 (41)
Oil Cooler Fitting	32 (44)
Oxygen Sensor	32 (44)
Rear Mount Bolt	18 (25)
Starter Bolt	27 (37)
Steering Damper Bolt	19 (26)
Transmission-To-Engine Bolt	
14-mm Head	27 (37)
17-mm Head	53 (72)
"U" Joint Nut	58 (79)
LX450	
Crossmember	
Bolt	45 (61)
Nut	55 (74)
Drive Plate Bolt	72 (98)
Drive Shaft Flange Nut	65 (88)
Dust Shield Bolt	21 (28)
Rear Engine Mount Bolt	44 (59)
Starter Bolt	29 (39)
Torque Converter Nut	41 (55)
Transmission-To-Engine Bolt	53 (72)
SC300	
Drive Shaft Center Bearing Bolt	27 (37)
Flywheel-To-Crankshaft Bolt	55 (74)
Flywheel-To-Torque Converter Bolt	24 (33)
Oil Cooler Fitting	25 (34)
Rear Mounting Bolt	18 (25)
Transmission-To-Engine Bolt	
14-mm Head	27 (37)
17-mm Head	53 (72)
"U" Joint Nut	69 (93)

Mazda

B2300, B3000, B4000, Miata, Millenia, MPV, MX-3, MX-6, Protege, RX7, 626, 929

APPLICATION

TRANSMISSION APPLICATION

Vehicle Application	Transmission Model
B2300 & B3000	4R44E
B4000	4R55E
Miata	NC4A-EL
Millenia	
2.3L	LJ4A-EL
2.5L	GF4A-EL
MPV	
3.0L	
2WD	RA4A-EL
4WD	RA4AX-EL
MX-3 & Protege	FA4A-EL
MX-6 & 626	
2.0L	LA4A-EL
2.5L	GF4A-EL
RX7	RB4A-EL
929	RA4A-EL

CAUTION: Disconnecting battery on models equipped with anti-theft radio require cancelling of anti-theft operation. See CANCELLING ANTI-THEFT RADIO OPERATION.

REMOVAL & INSTALLATION

CANCELLING ANTI-THEFT RADIO OPERATION

On models with anti-theft radio system, obtain code number from customer to deactivate radio anti-theft system. Anti-theft system is activated if battery is disconnected, looses significant voltage or radio is disconnected.

1995 Miata – Turn ignition switch to ACC position. Press FF and REW buttons simultaneously until "cod e" is displayed on radio. Press FF and REW buttons again until 4 bars are displayed. Use channel buttons 1-4 to input code number obtained from customer. Press "1" button for first code digit, "2" button for second code digit and so on. Input code number within 10 seconds. Press FF and REW buttons for about 2 seconds until a beep is heard. After 5 seconds, flashing "cod e" will go away and radio will operate. If "ERR" appears on display, repeat procedure. If input errors occur 3 times, turn ignition to LOCK position and repeat procedure.

NOTE: Three consecutive programming errors, including turning off ignition switch and disconnecting radio will lock-out radio unit and render it completely inoperative, requiring repair by manufacturer.

1996 Miata (Type I Radio) – Turn ignition switch to ACC position. "CODE" will flash on radio display. Simultaneously press TRACK V and AUTO-MEMO buttons for about 1.5 seconds, until bars appear on radio display. Use channel buttons 1-4 to input code number obtained from customer. Press "1" button for first code digit, "2" button for second code digit and so on. Input code number within 10 seconds. With code number displayed, press and hold TRACK V and AUTO-MEMO buttons for about 1.5 seconds, until a beep is heard. "CODE" will flash for about 15 seconds. Code number is now set. If "ERR" appears on display, repeat procedure.

1996 Miata (Type II Radio), Millenia, 929 & RX7 – Turn ignition switch to ACC position. "CODE" or "cod e" will flash on radio display. Simultaneously press SCAN and AUTO-M buttons for about 1.5 seconds, until bars appear on radio display. Use channel buttons 1-4 to input code number obtained from customer. Press "1" button for first code digit, "2" button for second code digit and so on. Input code number within 10 seconds. With code number displayed, press and hold SCAN and AUTO-M buttons for about 1.5 seconds, until a beep is heard. "CODE" or "cod e" will flash for about 10-15 seconds. Code number is now set. If "ERR" appears on display, repeat procedure.

B2300, B3000 & B4000

Removal – **1)** Disconnect negative battery cable. Raise and support vehicle. Drain transmission fluid. On 3.0L engines, remove lower converter cover. On other engines, remove starter. On all models, remove torque converter bolts. Mark drive shaft for reassembly reference, and remove drive shaft. Install plug in rear of transmission to prevent fluid leakage.

2) Disconnect speedometer cable, shift rod and kickdown cable from transmission. Depress tab on cable downshift retainer, and remove cable from bracket. Disconnect electrical connectors, vacuum hose and oil cooler lines.

3) Support transmission using jack. Remove crossmember. Lower transmission slightly. Using another jack, slightly raise front of engine to access upper engine-to-transmission bolts, but DO NOT remove bolts yet.

4) Remove lower converter housing-to-engine bolts. Remove dipstick tube. Remove upper converter housing-to-engine bolts. Slowly lower transmission.

Installation – **1)** To install transmission, reverse removal procedure. Adjust shift linkage. Ensure converter is fully seated before installing transmission. Torque converter is correctly seated when distance between engine mating surface of converter housing and face of converter drive lug is .43-.56" (10.9-14.2 mm).

2) Tighten torque converter bolts to specification. See TORQUE SPECIFICATIONS. Fill transmission with required amount of fluid, and check for external leaks.

MIATA

Removal – **1)** Disconnect negative battery cable. Raise and support vehicle. Drain transmission fluid. Remove shift rod and undercover. Remove front exhaust pipe. Mark drive shaft for reassembly reference, and remove drive shaft. Install plug in rear of transmission to prevent fluid leakage.

2) Disconnect speedometer cable, vacuum hose and electrical connectors from transmission. Remove dipstick tube. Disconnect oil cooler lines from transmission. Disconnect wire harness from power plant frame (beam connecting transmission to differential).

3) Support transmission using jack. Remove front and rear bolts from power plant frame, and pry out rear bolt spacer. Remove differential mounting spacer bolts, but leave spacers in place.

CAUTION: DO NOT remove spacers from top rear of power plant frame. If spacers are removed, replace entire power plant frame as an assembly.

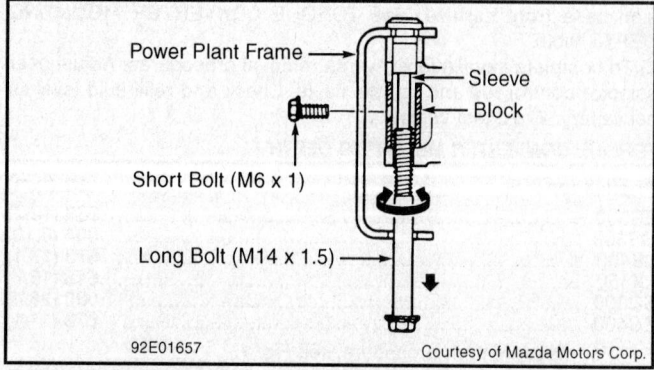

Fig. 1: Resetting Power Plant Frame Sleeve Position (Miata)

4) Screw bolt (M14 x 1.5) into rear sleeve (forward bolt hole). *See Fig. 1.* Twist and pull bolt downward to position sleeve in block. Install bolt (M6 x 1) in hole on side of power plant frame block to hold sleeve in place. Remove long bolt. Remove short bolt. Remove power plant frame.

5) Remove torque converter bolts and starter. Remove transmission mount bolts, and lower transmission. DO NOT shake transmission to remove or damage to crank angle sensor may result.

Installation – **1)** Install transmission, transmission mount and starter. Install torque converter bolts. Install power plant frame rear differential mounting spacer.

2) Support transmission until level. Position power plant frame, and hand-tighten transmission side bolts. Ensure sleeve is installed in block. *See Fig. 1.* Install spacer, and hand-tighten bolts. Ensure reamer bolt goes in forward hole.

3) Tighten front and then rear power plant frame bolts to specification. See TORQUE SPECIFICATIONS. Remove jack. Ensure clearance between bottom of power plant frame and lowest point of body frame is 2.0-2.4" (51-61 mm). *See Fig. 2.*

4) To install remaining components, reverse removal procedure. Tighten bolts to specification. See TORQUE SPECIFICATIONS. Fill transmission with required amount of fluid, and check for external leaks.

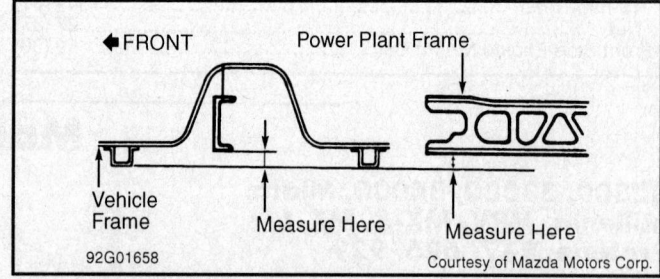

Fig. 2: Measuring Power Plant Frame Clearance (Miata)

MILLENIA

Removal – **1)** Disconnect negative, then positive battery cable. Remove battery tray. Remove air cleaner assembly (including intercooler duct, if applicable). Remove shift selector cable retaining clip. Disconnect shifter cable end at transaxle range switch lever.

2) Disconnect transaxle range switch, turbine/output speed sensor and shift solenoid harness connectors. Unbolt electrical harness bracket and selector cable bracket. Disconnect No. 1 engine mount strut. Remove starter.

3) Disconnect vehicle speed sensor harness connector. Remove intake plenum cover. Disconnect both O^2 sensor harness connectors (2.5L). Raise and support vehicle. Remove front wheels. Remove all plastic splash shields and undercover panel. Unbolt and remove exhaust pipe ("Y" pipe).

4) Disconnect and separate upper lateral link from left steering knuckle. Unbolt lower ball joints from lower control arms. Using a brass drift and hammer, drive off right side axle inner joint from joint shaft. Remove joint shaft. Insert differential side gear plug once joint axle is removed.

5) Install appropriate engine support and remove mount on rear of transaxle. Remove engine mount at bell housing of transaxle. Remove lower mount and crossmember. Remove oil cooler line banjo bolts at transaxle. Remove remaining undercover panels.

6) Remove lower access panel at bell housing. Rotate torque converter and remove torque converter nuts at flywheel. Separate left side axle from transaxle by prying with appropriate pry bar inserted between outer ring and transaxle case. Insert differential side gear plug once axle is removed. Remove bolts securing transaxle to engine. Support transaxle with appropriate jack and remove transaxle from vehicle.

Installation – 1) To install transaxle, reverse removal procedure. Tighten bolts to specification. See TORQUE SPECIFICATIONS. Fill transaxle with required amount of fluid, and check for external leaks.

MPV

Removal – 1) Disconnect negative battery cable. Raise and support vehicle. Drain transmission fluid. Disconnect speedometer cable and electrical connections. Remove front exhaust pipe and heat shield. Mark front (if equipped) and rear drive shafts for reassembly reference, and remove drive shaft(s). Install plug in rear of transmission to prevent fluid leakage. Remove shift linkage. Remove dipstick tube. Remove torque converter undercover and torque converter bolts. Remove starter.

2) Remove exhaust pipe bracket and engine-to-transmission gusset plates (if equipped). Disconnect transmission oil cooler lines. Remove vacuum pipe (if equipped). Support transmission using jack. Remove transmission mounting bolts, and slowly remove transmission.

Installation – 1) To install transmission, reverse removal procedure. Torque converter is correctly seated when distance between engine mating surface of converter housing and face of converter is 2.13" (54 mm) on 2.6L and 1.16" (30 mm) on 3.0L.

2) Tighten bolts to specification. See TORQUE SPECIFICATIONS. Fill transmission with required amount of fluid, and check for external leaks.

MX-3

Removal – 1) Remove battery cover, battery, and battery tray. Disconnect engine wiring harness as necessary. Raise and support vehicle. Drain transaxle. Remove front wheels and splash shields. Remove fresh air resonance duct and disconnect airflow meter. Remove air cleaner assembly.

2) Disconnect vehicle speed sensor connector and shift cable from transaxle. Disconnect range switch, shift solenoid and oxygen sensor (V/6) connectors. Remove front wiring harness bracket. Disconnect and remove throttle cable.

3) Disconnect oil cooler lines from transaxle. On V/6 models, remove fuel filter bracket from transaxle. Remove transverse crossmember. On all models, remove starter and support bracket. Disconnect exhaust pipe at manifold and converter.

4) Remove pinch bolts on steering knuckles. Pull lower control arms downward to separate ball joints from knuckles. DO NOT damage ball joint dust boots. Disconnect tie rod ends from knuckles. Disconnect stabilizer bar from lower control arms. Separate left axle shaft from transaxle using pry bar inserted between shaft and case. DO NOT damage oil seal.

5) Disconnect brake hoses from struts. Remove joint shaft bracket, and separate right axle shaft together with joint shaft in same manner. Install Differential Side Gear Holder (49-G030-455) into differential side gear opening (to prevent side gears from becoming misaligned).

6) Remove lower cover on converter housing. Remove torque converter nuts. Support transaxle using jack. Support engine from above using proper engine support assembly, and take up weight of engine. Disconnect and remove both engine mounts. Remove transaxle-to-engine bolts and crossmember. Slowly lower transaxle out of vehicle.

Installation – 1) To install transaxle, reverse removal procedure. Torque converter is correctly seated when distance between engine

mating surface of converter housing and face of converter is .54" (14 mm).

2) Tighten bolts to specification. See TORQUE SPECIFICATIONS. Install NEW clips on axle ends before installing axle shafts. Fill transaxle with proper amount of fluid, and check for external leaks.

MX-6 & 626

Removal – 1) Remove battery and battery tray. Remove fresh air duct. Disconnect airflow meter connector and remove air cleaner assembly. Disconnect shift selector cable.

2) Disconnect range switch, shift solenoid valve, turbine shaft speed sensor and vehicle speed sensor harness connectors from transaxle. Disconnect all ground cable connections from transaxle. Unbolt fuel filter and wire aside.

3) Raise and support vehicle. Remove front wheels, engine undercover and splash shields. Drain fluid, and disconnect oil cooler outlet and inlet lines. Disconnect tie rod ends from knuckles, and remove stabilizer bar control links.

4) Remove bolts and nuts at left and right lower control arm ball joints. Pull lower arms downward to separate from knuckles. DO NOT damage ball joint dust boots. Separate left axle shaft from transaxle using pry bar inserted between shaft and case. DO NOT damage oil seal.

5) Remove joint shaft bracket, and separate right axle shaft together with joint shaft in same manner. Install Differential Side Gear Holder (49-G030-455) into differential side gear opening (to prevent side gears from becoming misaligned).

6) Remove starter. Remove exhaust pipe hanger and stiffener plates from front of transaxle. Disconnect exhaust pipe from manifolds. Remove torque converter access cover, and torque converter nuts. Remove manifold bracket, and remove starter. Support engine from above using proper engine support assembly, and take up weight of engine.

7) Disconnect and remove 3 engine mounts. Remove transverse crossmember and crossmember. Lower engine assembly with above engine support. Support transaxle using transmission jack from below. Remove transaxle-to-engine mounting bolts, and remove transaxle from vehicle.

Installation – 1) To install transaxle, reverse removal procedure. Torque converter is correctly seated when distance between engine mating surface of converter housing and face of converter is .81" (21 mm).

2) Tighten bolts to specification. See TORQUE SPECIFICATIONS. Install NEW clips on axle ends before installing axle shafts. Fill transaxle with required amount of fluid, and check for external leaks.

PROTEGE

Removal – 1) Raise and support vehicle. Drain transaxle. Remove wheels and splash shields. Disconnect fresh air hose and remove air cleaner assembly. Remove battery and battery tray.

2) Disconnect vehicle speed sensor connector and shift cable from transaxle. Disconnect range switch and shift solenoid connectors. Disconnect and remove shift selector cable.

3) On DOHC models, remove transverse crossmember. On all models, remove starter and support bracket. Remove pinch bolts on steering knuckles. Pull lower control arms downward to separate ball joints from knuckles. DO NOT damage ball joint dust boots. Disconnect tie rod ends from knuckles. Disconnect stabilizer bar from lower control arms. Separate left axle shaft from transaxle using pry bar inserted between shaft and case. DO NOT damage oil seal.

4) Install Differential Side Gear Holder (49-G030-455) into differential side gear opening (to prevent side gears from becoming misaligned). Separate right axle shaft or intermediate shaft from transaxle. Support engine from above using engine support assembly. Remove engine mounts. Disconnect and plug oil cooler lines. Support transaxle from below using transmission jack.

5) Remove crossmember. Remove front torque converter housing access plates and cover. Mark converter to drive plate for reassembly reference, and remove torque converter bolts. Slightly lower engine using engine support from above. Remove transaxle-to-engine bolts, and lower transaxle assembly from vehicle.

Installation – 1) To install transaxle, reverse removal procedure. Torque converter is correctly seated when distance between engine mating surface of converter housing and face of converter is .54" (14 mm).
2) Tighten bolts to specification. See TORQUE SPECIFICATIONS. Install NEW clips on axle ends before installing axle shafts. Fill transaxle with required amount of fluid, and check for external leaks.

RX7

Removal – 1) Disconnect negative battery cable. Raise and support vehicle. Drain transmission fluid. Remove pipe and heat insulator. Mark drive shaft-to-differential assembly for reassembly reference.
2) Support engine from above. Remove shaft. Insert plug in rear of transmission to prevent leakage. Remove vacuum hose, shift rod, oil cooler lines and speedometer cable from transmission.
3) Remove starter and dipstick tube. Remove all wiring harness connectors from transmission. Remove lower cover from converter housing. Mark converter to drive plate for reassembly reference. Using Wrench (49 0877 435) remove torque converter-to-drive plate bolts.
4) Support transmission from below using transmission jack. Remove crossmember. Remove transaxle-to-engine bolts. Slowly lower transmission assembly out of vehicle.
Installation – To install transmission, reverse removal procedure. Tighten bolts to specification. See TORQUE SPECIFICATIONS. Fill transmission with required amount of fluid, and check for external leaks.

929

Removal – 1) Disconnect negative battery cable. Raise and support vehicle. Drain transmission fluid. Remove dipstick tube. Disconnect shift rod and 2 oxygen sensor connectors. Remove front exhaust pipe assembly from manifold flange to rear of muffler assembly.
2) Remove heat insulator shield. Mark drive shaft for reassembly reference, and remove drive shaft assembly. Install plug in rear of transmission to prevent fluid leakage. Disconnect speedometer cable. Remove starter. Disconnect neutral safety switch connector, 2 speed sensor connectors and solenoid valve connector. Disconnect pulse generator and knock sensor connectors.
3) Disconnect oil cooler lines at transmission. Disconnect vacuum hose, and remove torque converter access cover. Remove torque converter bolts. Support transmission using jack, and remove crossmember. Remove transmission mount, and lower transmission assembly.
Installation – 1) To install transmission, reverse removal procedure. Torque converter is correctly seated when distance between engine mating surface of converter housing and face of converter is at least 1.16" (30 mm).
2) Tighten bolts to specification. See TORQUE SPECIFICATIONS. Fill transmission with required amount of fluid, and check for external leaks.

TORQUE SPECIFICATIONS
TORQUE SPECIFICATIONS

Application	Ft. Lbs. (N.m)
B2300 & B4000	
Companion Flange "U" Bolt Nut	70-95 (95-129)
Crossmember Mounting Nut	20-30 (27-41)
Dipstick Stub Tube Mounting Bolt	28-38 (38-52)
Engine Support-To-Crossmember Nut	65-85 (88-115)
Starter Bolt	15-20 (20-27)
Torque Converter Bolt	20-34 (27-46)
Transmission-To-Engine Bolt	33-44 (44-60)
B3000	
Companion Flange "U" Bolt Nut	70-95 (95-129)
Crossmember Mounting Nut	20-30 (27-41)
Dipstick Stub Tube Mounting Bolt	28-38 (38-52)
Engine Support-To-Crossmember Nut	65-85 (88-115)
Starter Bolt	15-20 (20-27)
Torque Converter Bolt	20-34 (27-46)
Transmission-To-Engine Bolt	28-38 (38-52)
Miata	
Differential Mounting Spacer Bolt	27-38 (37-52)
Drive Shaft Flange Nut	20-22 (27-30)

TORQUE SPECIFICATIONS (Cont.)

Application	Ft. Lbs. (N.m)
Miata	
Exhaust Pipe Nut	23-34 (31-46)
Power Plant Frame Bolt	77-91 (104-123)
Starter Bolt	27-38 (37-52)
Torque Converter Bolt	27-40 (37-54)
Transmission-To-Engine Bolt	47-66 (63-89)
Millenia	
Crossmember-To-Frame Bolt	50-68 (67-93)
Crossmember Engine Mount Nut	55-77 (75-104)
Exhaust Pipe-To-Manifold Nut	15-20 (20-28)
Exhaust Pipe-To-Converter	48-65 (64-89)
Joint Shaft Bracket Bolt	32-45 (43-61)
Lower Ball Joint-To-Lower Arm Bolt	86-115 (116-156)
Shift Cable Nut	12-14 (16-19)
Starter Bolt	24-33 (32-46)
Torque Converter Bolt	28-44 (38-60)
Transaxle-To-Body Mount Nut	50-68 (67-93)
Transaxle-To-Engine Bolt	50-73 (68-99)
Undercover Bolt	32-44 (44-60)
Upper Lateral Link-To-Knuckle	41-59 (55-80)
Wheel Lug Nut	66-94 (89-127)
MPV	
Drive Shaft Center Support Bolt	27-39 (37-53)
Drive Shaft Flange Nut	36-43 (49-58)
Exhaust Pipe Nut	25-36 (34-49)
Starter Bolt	27-38 (37-52)
Torque Converter Bolt	27-40 (37-54)
Transmission Mount Bolt	32-45 (43-61)
Transmission-To-Engine Bolt	27-38 (37-52)
MX-3	
Crossmember-To-Frame Bolt	48-65 (64-89)
Crossmember-To-Mount	28-38 (38-51)
Exhaust Pipe-To-Manifold Nut	23-34 (31-46)
Exhaust Pipe-To-Converter Nut	48-65 (64-89)
Lower Control Arm Ball Joint-To-Knuckle Bolt	32-42 (43-57)
Stabilizer Bar Link Nut	48-65 (64-89)
Tie Rod Nut	31-42 (42-57)
Torque Converter Nut	25-36 (34-49)
Transaxle Mount Bolt	27-38 (37-52)
Transverse Crossmember Bolt	69-90 (92-122)
Transaxle-To-Engine Bolt	41-59 (56-80)
Wheel Lug Nut	65-87 (88-118)
MX-6 & 626	
Crossmember-To-Frame Bolt	48-65 (64-89)
Crossmember-To-Mount	55-77 (75-104)
Engine Mount Bolt	50-68 (67-93)
Exhaust Pipe-To-Manifold Nut	23-34 (31-46)
Lower Control Arm Ball Joint-To-Knuckle Bolt	27-40 (37-54)
Stabilizer Bar Link Nut	27-39 (37-53)
Starter Bolt	24-33 (32-46)
Tie Rod Nut	24-32 (32-44)
Torque Converter Nut	28-45 (33-61)
Transaxle-To-Engine Bolt	50-73 (68-99)
Transverse Crossmember Bolt	69-96 (92-131)
Wheel Lug Nut	65-87 (88-118)
Protege	
Crossmember-To-Frame Bolt	48-65 (64-89)
Crossmember-To-Mount	28-38 (38-51)
Engine Mount Bolt	50-68 (67-93)
Joint Axle Bracket Bolt	32-46 (42-62)
Lower Control Arm Ball Joint-To-Knuckle Bolt	32-40 (43-54)
Starter Bolt	27-38 (37-52)
Torque Converter Bolt	25-36 (34-49)
Transaxle-To-Engine Bolt	47-66 (63-89)
Transverse Crossmember Bolt	69-97 (94-131)
Wheel Lug Nut	65-87 (88-118)
RX7	
Companion Flange Bolt/Nut	37-43 (50-58)
Crossmember Mounting Nut	14-19 (18-26)
Dipstick Stub Tube Mounting Bolt	8 (11)
Starter Bolt	28-38 (38-51)
Torque Converter Bolt	26-36 (35-49)
Transmission-To-Engine Bolt	28-38 (38-52)
929	
Crossmember-To-Frame Bolt	32-45 (43-61)
Drive Shaft Center Support Bolt	27-38 (37-52)
Drive Shaft Flange Nut	36-43 (49-58)
Exhaust Pipe Nut	30-41 (41-56)
Starter Bolt	23-34 (31-46)
Torque Converter Bolt	25-36 (34-49)
Transmission-To-Engine Bolt	27-38 (37-52)
Transmission Mounting Bolt	40-56 (54-76)

1995
C220, C280, C36, E300D, E320, E420, S320, S350D, S420, S500, S600, SL320, SL500, SL600
1996
C220, C280, C36, E300D, E320, S320, S420, S500, S600, SL320, SL500, SL600

APPLICATION

TRANSMISSION APPLICATION

Vehicle Application	Transmission Model
1995	
C220 2.2L	722.423
C280 2.8L	722.424
C36 3.6L	722.424
E300D 3.0L	722.435
E320 3.2L	722.369
E420 4.2L	722.366
S320 3.2L	722.508
S350D 3.5L	722.367
S420 4.2L	722.366
S500 5.0L	722.370
S600 6.0L	722.362
SL320 3.2L	722.507
SL500 5.0L	722.364
SL600 6.0L	722.362
1996	
C220 2.2L	722.423
C280 2.8L	722.424
C36 3.6L	722.424
E300D 3.0L	722.438
E320 3.2L	722.329
S320 3.2L	722.508
S420 4.2L	722.622
S500 5.0L	722.620
S600 6.0L	722.621
SL320 3.2L	722.507
SL500 5.0L	722.620
SL600 6.0L	722.621

REMOVAL & INSTALLATION

CAUTION: If metal chips are present in transmission oil pan, torque converter must be replaced. Flushing will not remove all metal chips from a torque converter. Failure to replace torque converter may result in future transmission failure.

C220, C280, C36 & E300D

Removal – 1) Disconnect negative battery cable. On gasoline engines, use a screwdriver to press control pressure cable plastic ball socket apart. Remove circlip at fulcrum lever. Disconnect control pressure cable.

2) On diesel engines, push off ball socket. Remove retaining clip and disconnect control pressure cable. On all vehicles, remove engine compartment covering from under vehicle.

3) Remove transmission oil pan drain plug. Remove torque converter drain plug. Drain transmission fluid. Remove starter. Remove torque converter drive plate bolts (6 bolts) through starter opening. Remove crossmember with mount.

4) Remove exhaust support bracket bolts from transmission. Using a drift, unscrew flexible coupling (on driveshaft) from transmission joint flange. Disconnect exhaust system at rear mount.

5) Loosen large clamping nut on drive shaft. Clamping nut is located near center bearing. Remove drive shaft flange bolts. With clamping nut loosened, push drive shaft as far back from transmission as possible.

6) Disconnect kickdown solenoid valve electrical connector. Loosen speedometer shaft from transmission. Remove clip from speedometer shaft. Remove speedometer shaft. On vehicles equipped with an electronic speedometer, unscrew pulse generator. On all vehicles, disconnect shift rod from range selector lever.

7) Turn starter lockout switch locking element before disconnecting starter lockout switch connector. Using 2 screwdrivers, pry off starter lockout switch connector from transmission.

8) Disconnect White vacuum line from vacuum box. Disconnect Red vacuum line for selector program. Disconnect Black/Green vacuum line for shift point retard.

9) Remove transmission dipstick tube bolt from transmission and cylinder head. Remove transmission dipstick tube. Disconnect transmission oil cooler feed and return lines.

10) On diesel engines, install Retainer (201 589 00 40 00) through ventilation grill cutout into torque converter drain plug. On all vehicles, support transmission with a jack. Remove transmission mounting bolts except 2 bolts on either side of transmission. Using a transmission jack, lift transmission slightly. Remove 2 remaining transmission mounting bolts. Push transmission rearward and lower.

Installation – To install, reverse removal procedure. When installing torque converter to transmission, apply a light coat of grease to torque converter centering pin. Tighten bolts and nuts to specification. See TORQUE SPECIFICATIONS. Adjust control pressure cable and linkages as necessary. Fill transmission with fluid. See AUTOMATIC TRANSMISSION SERVICING article in TRANSMISSION SERVICING.

E320, E420, S420, S350D, S500, S600, SL500 & SL600 (1995 MODELS)

Removal – 1) Disconnect negative battery cable. Disconnect longitudinal engine throttle control shaft. Disconnect control pressure cable. Remove front crossmember assembly.

2) Remove transmission oil pan drain plug. Remove torque converter drain plug. Drain transmission fluid. Remove starter. Remove torque converter drive plate bolts through starter opening. Remove entire exhaust system assembly from exhaust manifold(s). Remove rear crossmember with mount.

3) Release cable strap and unscrew cable on kickdown solenoid valve. Unscrew retaining bolts for pulse generator. Remove pulse generator. On V8 engines, disconnect shift point retard connector located on right rear corner of engine.

4) On all models, loosen drive shaft center bearing bolts. Loosen large clamping nut on drive shaft. Clamping nut is located near center bearing. Remove drive shaft flange bolts. With clamping nut loosened, push drive shaft as far back from transmission as possible.

5) Turn starter lockout switch locking element before disconnecting starter lockout switch connector. Using 2 screwdrivers, pry off starter lockout switch connector from transmission.

6) Disconnect shift rod from range selector lever. Disconnect White vacuum line for vacuum box. Disconnect Red vacuum line for mode program. Disconnect Black/Green vacuum line for shift point retard.

7) Disconnect transmission oil cooler feed and return lines. Remove transmission dipstick tube bolt from transmission and cylinder head. Remove transmission dipstick tube.

8) On V8 engines, remove transmission mounting bolts except 2 nuts on either side of transmission. Using a transmission jack, lift transmission slightly. Remove 2 remaining transmission mounting nuts.

9) On 6-cylinder engines, remove transmission mounting bolts except 2 bolts on either side of transmission. Using a transmission jack, lift transmission slightly. Remove 2 remaining transmission mounting bolts. On all vehicles, push transmission rearward and lower. Ensure torque converter does not fall from transmission during removal.

Installation – To install, reverse removal procedure. Tighten bolts and nuts to specification. See TORQUE SPECIFICATIONS. Flush transmission cooler lines and cooler before reinstalling transmission. Use NEW transmission oil cooler feed and return line "O" rings. Adjust control pressure cable and linkages as necessary. Fill transmission with fluid. See AUTOMATIC TRANSMISSION SERVICING article in TRANSMISSION SERVICING.

S420, S500, S600, SL500 & SL600 (1996 MODELS)

Removal – 1) Disconnect negative battery cable. Remove transmission fluid filler pipe securing bolt. Remove fluid filler pipe. Remove transmission drain plug and drain fluid. Remove torque converter drain plug and drain fluid.

2) Remove heat shield and disconnect 13-pin transmission electrical connector. With transmission in "P" position, disconnect parking interlock cable. Remove transmission lower cover. Remove torque converter to drive plate bolts.

3) Disconnect and remove oil cooler lines. Remove shift rod securing clips and shift rod. Remove exhaust bracket. Disconnect exhaust pipes from exhaust manifolds. Disconnect front exhaust pipe section from rear exhaust section and secure rear exhaust aside with wire.

4) Install transmission jack. On vehicles with V8 engines, remove rear engine mount and bracket. Disconnect front drive shaft flange and allow drive shaft to hang free. Remove ground wire from transmission case. Unbolt transmission from engine and lower transmission ensuring torque converter does not fall from transmission during removal.

Installation – To install, reverse removal procedure. Tighten bolts and nuts to specification. See TORQUE SPECIFICATIONS. Flush transmission cooler lines and cooler before reinstalling transmission. Use NEW transmission oil cooler feed and return line "O" rings. Adjust control pressure cable and linkages as necessary. Fill transmission with fluid. See AUTOMATIC TRANSMISSION SERVICING article in TRANSMISSION SERVICING.

S320 & SL320

Removal – 1) Disconnect negative battery cable. Remove transmission dipstick tube bolt from transmission and cylinder head. Using pliers, squeeze plastic clip together and pull out control pressure cable.

2) Remove transmission oil pan drain plug. Remove torque converter drain plug. Drain transmission fluid. Remove plastic cover to access torque converter drive plate bolts. Remove torque converter drive plate bolts through opening.

3) Install transmission jack. Remove crossmember with mount. Remove drive shaft flange bolts. Disconnect oxygen sensor harness on tunnel and disconnect mounting clips. Remove exhaust support bracket bolts from transmission. Remove entire exhaust system assembly from exhaust manifold.

4) Remove speedometer shaft. On vehicles equipped with an electronic speedometer, unscrew pulse generator. On all vehicles, disconnect shift point increase solenoid valve connector. Disconnect transmission overload switch connector and pull off vacuum line.

5) Turn starter lockout switch locking element before disconnecting starter lockout switch connector. Using 2 screwdrivers, pry off starter lockout switch connector from transmission.

6) Disconnect shift rod from range selector lever. Disconnect transmission oil cooler feed and return lines. Remove transmission dipstick tube bolt from transmission. Remove transmission dipstick tube. Ensure all electrical connections are disconnected from transmission.

7) Install Retainer (126 589 01 62 00) through ventilation grill cutout into torque converter drain plug. Remove transmission mounting bolts except 2 bolts on either side of transmission. Using a transmission jack, lift transmission slightly. Remove 2 remaining transmission mounting bolts. Push transmission rearward and lower.

Installation – To install, reverse removal procedure. When installing torque converter to transmission, apply a light coat of grease to torque converter centering pin. Flush transmission cooler lines and cooler before reinstalling transmission. Tighten bolts and nuts to specification. See TORQUE SPECIFICATIONS. Adjust control pressure cable and linkages as necessary. Fill transmission with fluid. See AUTOMATIC TRANSMISSION SERVICING article in TRANSMISSION SERVICING.

TORQUE SPECIFICATIONS
TORQUE SPECIFICATIONS

Application	Ft. Lbs. (N.m)
Drive Plate Bolt	31 (42)
Front Crossmember Bolt [1]	33 (45)
Drive Shaft Clamping Nut	22-30 (30-40)
Transmission Mounting Bolt [2]	
10-mm	41 (55)
12-mm	48 (65)
Transmission Oil Pan Drain Plug	10 (14)
Torque Converter Drain Bolt	12 (16)

[1] – Replace self-locking bolts.
[2] – V8 engines use 2 nuts, one on each side of transmission.

Mitsubishi

Chrysler Corp.: Colt, Colt Vista, Stealth Summit, Summit Wagon, Talon
Mitsubishi: Diamante, Eclipse, Expo, Expo Mirage, Montero, Pickup, 3000GT

APPLICATION
AUTOMATIC TRANSMISSION/TRANSAXLE APPLICATIONS

Vehicle Application	Transmission/Transaxle Model
Chrysler Corp.	
Colt & Summit	
1.5L	F3A21
1.8L	F4A22
Colt Vista & Summit Wagon	
AWD	W4A32
FWD	
1.8L	F4A22
2.4L	F4A23
Stealth	F4A33
Talon	
AWD	W4A33
FWD	
Non-Turbo	F4AC1
Turbo	F4A33
Mitsubishi	
Diamante	F4A33
Eclipse	
AWD	W4A33
FWD	
2.0L Non-Turbo	F4AC1
2.0L Turbo	F4A33
2.4L	F4A23

AUTOMATIC TRANSMISSION/TRANSAXLE APPLICATIONS (Cont.)

Vehicle Application	Transmission/Transaxle Model
Expo	
AWD	W4A32
FWD	
1.8L	F4A22
2.4L	F4A23
Galant	
1995	
DOHC	F4A33
SOHC	F4A23
1996	F4A23
Mirage	
1.5L	F3A21
1.8L	F4A22
Montero	
3.0L	V4AW2 Or V4AW3
3.5L	V4AW3
Pickup	R4AC1
3000GT	F4A33

REMOVAL & INSTALLATION

FWD MODELS

Removal – 1) Remove battery and battery tray. On Diamante remove undercover and air compressor assembly. On turbo models, drain and remove intercooler. On all models, remove air cleaner and case. Disconnect control cables at transaxle.

2) On Mirage 1.8L, disconnect tension rod. On all models, disconnect neutral safety switch connector, oil cooler hoses and electrical

connectors from transaxle. Disconnect speedometer cable and throttle control cable (if equipped).

3) Remove starter motor and secure aside with wire. On all models, remove upper transaxle-to-engine bolts. Install engine support assembly. Raise and support vehicle. Remove wheels. Drain transaxle fluid. Disconnect front height sensor rod at lower control arm.

4) Remove engine undercover (if equipped). Remove tie-rod ends from knuckle. On all models, remove drive axle shafts. Separate lower control arms from struts for access to axle shafts (if necessary).

5) Remove front exhaust pipe (if necessary). On Eclipse AWD, Galant AWD and 3000GT, remove right member and gusset. On AWD models, separate transfer assembly from transaxle. Reference mark transfer assembly-to-drive shaft and remove transfer assembly.

6) On all models, remove transmission inspection (dust) cover. Place index mark on torque converter and drive plate for reassembly reference. Remove torque converter-to-drive plate bolts. Push torque converter away from engine into transaxle.

7) Support transaxle with jack. Remove transaxle mounts bolts, mounting brackets and remaining transaxle-to-engine bolts. Slide transaxle assembly to right and lower to remove.

CAUTION: Ensure torque converter is fully seated in transaxle before installation. Always install new snap rings on inner constant velocity joints.

Installation – 1) To install, reverse removal procedure. Tighten transaxle-to-engine bolts and torque converter-to-drive plate bolts to specification. See TORQUE SPECIFICATIONS.

2) Ensure reference marks on torque converter-to-drive plate and transfer assembly-to-drive shaft align. Tighten mounting bolts with weight of engine and transaxle on mounts. Refill transaxle fluid to specified level. Adjust all control cables.

RWD MODELS

Removal – 1) Disconnect battery negative cable. Remove front exhaust pipe. On Montero, remove transfer case shift lever knob, dust boot and retainer plate or console. Remove transfer case gearshift assembly.

2) On all models, raise and support vehicle. Remove undercarriage cover and/or skid plate(s). Drain transmission and transfer case (if applicable). Place reference mark on drive shaft(s) and remove. Disconnect all external solenoid and switch connections.

3) Disconnect speedometer cable and control cables at transmission. Remove starter and bellhousing cover. Place reference mark on torque converter and drive plate for reassembly reference. Remove torque converter bolts.

4) Disconnect transmission cooler lines. Remove oil filler tube. Secure transmission on a jack. Raise transmission slightly to take weight off mount. Remove crossmember-to-mount bolts and crossmember.

5) Remove transfer case mounting bracket and mount (if equipped). Remove transmission-to-engine mounting bolts. Carefully lower transmission from vehicle.

CAUTION: Ensure torque converter is fully seated in transmission before installation.

Installation – 1) To install, reverse removal procedure. Tighten transmission-to-engine bolts and torque converter-to-drive plate bolts to specification. See TORQUE SPECIFICATIONS. Tighten mount bolts with weight of engine and transmission on mounts. Ensure reference marks on drive shaft(s) and torque converter-to-drive plate align.

2) Apply sealant to transfer case gearshift assembly gasket before installation. Coat transmission oil filler tube "O" ring with transmission fluid before installation. Refill transmission fluid to specified level. Adjust all control cables.

TORQUE SPECIFICATIONS
TORQUE SPECIFICATIONS

Applications	Ft. Lbs. (N.m)
FWD Models	
Torque Converter-To-Drive Plate Bolt	34-38 (46-52)
Transaxle-To-Engine Block Bolt	
8-mm Bolt	[1]
10-mm Bolt	22-25 (30-34)
12-mm Bolt	31-40 (42-54)
Diamante & 3000GT	
Upper Coupling Bolts	54 (73)
Lower Coupling Bolts	65 (88)
RWD Models	
Torque Converter-To-Drive Plate Bolt	
Montero	25-30 (34-41)
Pickup	33-38 (45-52)
Transmission-To-Engine Block Bolt	
Montero	
10 x 40-mm Bolt	22-30 (30-41)
10 x 55-mm Bolt	18-26 (25-35)
12 x 40-mm Bolt	47-61 (64-83)
12 x 55-mm Bolt	58-72 (79-98)
Pickup	
10 x 16-mm Bolt	22-30 (30-41)
10 x 50-mm Bolt	31-40 (42-54)
10 x 70-mm Bolt	31-40 (42-54)

[1] – Tighten to 84-108 INCH lbs. (10-12 N.m).

Nissan

Altima, Maxima, Pathfinder, Pickup, Quest, Sentra, 200SX 240SX, 300ZX

APPLICATION
TRANSMISSION APPLICATION

Vehicle Application	Transmission Model
Altima & Maxima	RE4F04A/V
Sentra & 200SX	
1.6L	RL4F03A
2.0L	RE4F03V
Pathfinder	RE4R01A
Pickup	RL4R01A
Quest	RE4F04A
240SX	RE4R01A
300ZX	
Non-Turbo	RE4R01A
Turbo	RE4R03A

REMOVAL & INSTALLATION
FWD MODELS

Removal (Altima, Maxima, Quest, Sentra & 200SX) – 1) Remove battery and battery bracket. Remove air cleaner and airflow meter (Sentra) or resonator (Altima). Disconnect terminal cord assembly harness and inhibitor switch harness connectors. Remove starter. Disconnect electrical connectors, control cables, shift linkage and hoses as necessary for removal. Remove crankshaft position sensor from transaxle. On Sentra and 240SX (RL4F03A), disconnect throttle wire at engine side. Remove left mounting bracket from transaxle and body (Altima). Raise and support vehicle. Drain transaxle fluid.

2) Remove front axle shafts. See appropriate AXLE SHAFTS article in AXLE SHAFTS & TRANSFER CASES section. Remove oil cooler lines, center crossmember and rear plate cover (Maxima). Remove intake manifold support bracket, (Sentra and 200SX). Remove bolts securing front exhaust pipe brackets (if necessary). Remove dust cover. Index mark torque converter in reference to drive plate. Remove torque converter bolts.

3) Support engine. Set transaxle jack under transaxle. On Altima, remove left engine mounting bracket. On all models, remove transaxle mounts. Remove engine-to-transaxle bolts. Carefully lower transaxle.

Installation (All FWD Models) – 1) Before installing torque converter, measure drive plate runout with a dial indicator. If runout exceeds .006" (.15 mm), replace drive plate. Install torque converter into transaxle, aligning index marks made during removal.

2) Ensure torque converter is seated by measuring distance from drive plate mounting pad to engine mating surface of transaxle. If distance is not as specified, torque converter is not seated. See DRIVE PLATE MOUNTING PAD DEPTH table.

3) To complete installation, reverse removal procedure. Apply sealant to torque converter bolts before installing bolts. Rotate crankshaft several times to ensure torque converter moves freely without binding. Tighten nuts and bolts to specification. See TORQUE SPECIFICATIONS. See BOLT LENGTH SPECIFICATION tables for correct location.

BOLT LENGTH SPECIFICATION (ALTIMA)

Bolt Number [1]	Length In. (mm)
1 & 4	1.77 (45)
2	1.18 (30)
3	1.57 (40)
5	3.15 (80)
6	2.56 (65)

[1] – See Fig. 1 for location and tightening sequence.

BOLT LENGTH SPECIFICATION (MAXIMA)

Bolt Number [1]	Length In. (mm)
1	2.56 (65)
2 & 3	2.05 (52)
4	1.57 (40)
5	4.88 (124)

[1] – See Fig. 2 for location and tightening sequence.

BOLT LENGTH SPECIFICATION (QUEST)

Bolt Number [1]	Length In. (mm)
1	2.36 (60)
2 & 3	.98 (25)

[1] – See Fig. 3 for location and tightening sequence.

BOLT LENGTH SPECIFICATION (SENTRA & 200SX – RL4F03A WITH 1.6L)

Bolt Number [1]	Length In. (mm)
1	1.97 (50)
2	1.18 (30)
3	.98 (25)
Front Gusset To Engine	.79 (20)
Rear Gusset To Engine	.63 (16)

[1] – See Fig. 4 for location and tightening sequence.

BOLT LENGTH SPECIFICATION (SENTRA & 200SX – RE4F03V WITH 2.0L)

Bolt Number [1]	Length In. (mm)
1	2.17 (55)
2	1.97 (50)
3	2.56 (65)
4	1.38 (35)
5	1.77 (45)

[1] – See Fig. 5 for location and tightening sequence.

DRIVE PLATE MOUNTING PAD DEPTH

Application	In. (mm)
Altima	.75 (19)
Maxima	.55 (14)
Sentra & 200SX	
1.6L	.83 (21)
2.0L	.63 (16)
Quest	.55 (14)

RWD MODELS

Removal (240SX & 300ZX) – 1) Disconnect negative battery cable. Raise and support vehicle. Remove crankshaft position sensor. Disconnect A/T harness connector and clamps. Drain transmission fluid. Remove drive shaft. Insert plug into rear oil seal. Use caution not to damage splines. Disconnect starter wiring. Remove starter.

2) Remove exhaust support brackets attached to transmission. Disconnect exhaust pipe(s) from manifold(s). Disconnect electrical connectors, control cables, shift linkage and hoses as necessary for removal. Disconnect speedometer cable.

3) Remove transmission fluid filler tube and plug opening. Remove gussets and end plate. Mark torque converter in relation to drive plate for installation reference. Remove torque converter bolts.

4) Support transmission with transmission jack. Remove rear mount and crossmember mounting bolts. Remove engine-to-transmission bolts. Carefully remove transmission.

Removal (Pathfinder & Pickup) – 1) Remove front exhaust tubes. Remove rear exhaust tubes on 4WD models. Remove dipstick tube. Remove oil cooler pipe and plug opening. Disconnect electrical harness connectors, control cables, shift linkage and hoses as necessary for removal. Remove front (4WD) and rear drive shaft. Insert plug(s) using caution not to damage splines. Remove starter, gussets and rear plate cover.

CAUTION: Secure torque converter to prevent from dropping out.

2) On 4WD model, Mark torque converter in relation to drive plate for installation reference, remove torque converter bolts. Support A/T and transfer assembly with jack. Remove rear mounting bracket from body and A/T assembly. Remove A/T mounting bolts to engine. Lower transmission with transfer.

3) On 2WD model, Mark torque converter in relation to drive plate for installation reference, remove torque converter bolts. Support and secure A/T with jack. Remove rear mounting bracket from body and A/T assembly. Remove A/T mounting bolts to engine. Pull backwards and lower A/T assembly.

Installation (All RWD Models) – 1) Before installing torque converter, measure drive plate runout with a dial indicator. On Pathfinder, if runout exceeds .006" (.15 mm), replace drive plate. On Pickup, if runout exceeds .004" (0.1 mm) replace drive plate. Install torque converter into transaxle, aligning index marks made during removal.

2) Ensure torque converter is seated by measuring distance from drive plate mounting pad to engine mating surface of transaxle. If distance is not as specified, torque converter is not seated. See DRIVE PLATE MOUNTING PAD DEPTH table.

3) To complete installation, reverse removal procedure. Apply sealant to torque converter bolts before installing bolts. Rotate crankshaft several times to ensure torque converter moves freely without binding. Tighten nuts and bolts in sequence to specification. See BOLT LENGTH SPECIFICATION table. See TORQUE SPECIFICATIONS.

BOLT LENGTH SPECIFICATION (240SX)

Bolt Number [1]	Length In. (mm)
1	1.57 (40)
2	1.97 (50)
3	.98 (25)
Gusset To Engine	.79 (20)

[1] – See Fig. 6 for location and tightening sequence.

BOLT LENGTH SPECIFICATION (300ZX)

Bolt Number [1]	Length In. (mm)
RE4R01A	
1	1.87 (47.5)
2	2.28 (58)
3	.98 (25)
4	2.36 (60)
5	2.56 (65)
Gusset To Engine	.79 (20)

[1] – See Fig. 7 for location and tightening sequence.

BOLT LENGTH SPECIFICATION (300ZX)

Bolt Number [1]	Length In. (mm)
RE4R03A	
1	2.56 (65)
2	.98 (25)
3	2.28 (58)
4	2.44 (62)
5	3.94 (100)
Gusset To Engine	.79 (20)

[1] – See Fig. 7 for location and tightening sequence.

BOLT LENGTH SPECIFICATION (PATHFINDER)

Bolt Number [1]	Length In. (mm)
1	1.87 (47.5)
2	2.28 (58)
3	.98 (25)
Gusset To Engine	.79 (20)

[1] – See Fig. 8 for location and tightening sequence.

BOLT LENGTH SPECIFICATION (PICKUP)

Bolt Number [1]	Length In. (mm)
1	1.69 (43)
2 & 3	.63 (16)

[1] – See Fig. 9 for location and tightening sequence.

DRIVE PLATE MOUNTING PAD DEPTH

Application	In. (mm)
Pathfinder, Pickup & 240SX	1.02 (26)
300ZX	
Non-Turbo (RE4R01A)	1.02 (26)
Turbo (RE4R03A)	0.98 (25)

TORQUE SPECIFICATIONS

TORQUE SPECIFICATIONS

Application	Ft. Lbs. (N.m)
Altima	
Engine-To-Transaxle Bolt	
Bolt No. 1	[1] 29-36 (39-49)
Bolts No. 2, 3, 5 & 6	[1] 22-27 (30-36)
Bolt No. 4	[1] 55-61 (74-83)
Torque Converter Bolt	33-43 (45-58)
Wheel Bearing Lock Nut	174-231 (235-314)
Wheel Lug Nut	72-86 (98-117)
Maxima	
Engine-To-Transaxle Bolt (All)	51-59 (70-79)
Torque Converter Bolt	33-43 (45-58)
Wheel Bearing Lock Nut	174-231 (235-314)
Wheel Lug Nut	72-87 (98-118)
Pathfinder & Pickup	
Crossmember Mounting Bolt	
2WD	50-64 (68-87)
4WD	30-38 (41-52)
Drive Shaft Flange Bolt/Nut	
Except 1-Piece Rear Drive Shaft	41-48 (55-65)
1-Piece Rear Drive Shaft	51-58 (70-78)
Engine-To-Transmission Bolt	
Bolt No. 1 & 2	[8][9] 29-36 (39-49)
Bolt No. 3 & Gusset	[8][9] 22-29 (30-39)
Exhaust Pipe-To-Manifold Bolt (V6)	
Pathfinder	21-25 (28-34)
Pickup	20-27 (27-36)
Rear Transmission Mount Nut	30-38 (41-52)
Torque Converter Bolt	33-43 (45-58)

[1] – See Fig. 1.
[2] – See Fig. 2.
[3] – See Fig. 3.
[4] – See Fig. 4.
[5] – See Fig. 5.
[6] – See Fig. 6.
[7] – See Fig. 7.
[8] – See Fig. 8.
[9] – See Fig. 9.

TORQUE SPECIFICATIONS (Cont.)

Application	Ft. Lbs. (N.m)
Sentra & 200SX	
Brake Caliper Mount Bolt	40-47 (54-64)
Engine-To-Transaxle Bolt	
RL4F03A Transaxle	
Bolts No. 1 & 2	[4] 22-30 (30-41)
Bolt No. 3	[4] 12-15 (16-21)
Front Gusset To Engine	22-30 (30-41)
Rear Gusset To Engine	12-15 (16-21)
RE4F03V Transaxle	
Bolts No. 1, 2 & 3	[5] 51-59 (70-79)
Bolts No. 4 & 5	[5] 12-15 (16-21)
Knuckle-To-Strut Bolt/Nut	68-92 (92-111)
Lower Ball Joint-To-Knuckle Nut	43-54 (58-73)
Tie Rod Ball Joint Nut	22-29 (30-39)
Torque Converter Bolt	33-43 (45-58)
Wheel Bearing Lock Nut	145-203 (197-275)
Wheel Lug Nut	72-87 (98-118)
Quest	
Engine-To-Transaxle Bolt	
Bolts No. 1	[3] 29-36 (39-49)
Bolt No. 2 & 3	[3] 22-30 (30-41)
Torque Converter Bolt	33-43 (45-58)
Wheel Bearing Lock Nut	174-231 (235-314)
Wheel Lug Nut	72-87 (98-118)
240SX	
Crossmember Mounting Bolt	32-41 (43-55)
Drive Shaft Flange Bolt	41-48 (55-65)
Engine-To-Transmission Bolt	
Bolts No. 1 & 2	[6] 29-36 (39-49)
Bolt No. 3	[6] 22-29 (30-39)
Gusset To Engine	22-29 (30-39)
Rear Transmission Mount Nut	16-21 (22-28)
Torque Converter Bolt	33-43 (45-58)
Wheel Lug Nut	72-87 (98-118)
300ZX	
Crossmember Mounting Bolt	38-48 (52-65)
Drive Shaft Flange Bolt	41-48 (55-65)
Engine-To-Transmission Bolt	
RE4R01A	
Bolts No. 1 & 2	[7] 29-36 (39-49)
Bolts No. 3, 4, 5 & Gusset	[7] 22-29 (30-39)
RE4R03A	
Bolts No. 1 & 3	[7] 29-36 (39-49)
Bolts No. 2, 4, 5 & Gusset	[7] 22-29 (30-39)
Exhaust Pipe-To-Manifold Nut	33-37 (45-50)
Rear Transmission Mount Nut	43-55 (58-74)
Torque Converter Bolt	33-43 (45-58)

[1] – See Fig. 1.
[2] – See Fig. 2.
[3] – See Fig. 3.
[4] – See Fig. 4.
[5] – See Fig. 5.
[6] – See Fig. 6.
[7] – See Fig. 7.
[8] – See Fig. 8.
[9] – See Fig. 9.

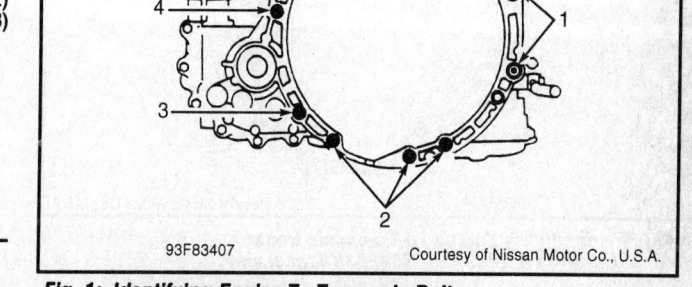

93F83407   Courtesy of Nissan Motor Co., U.S.A.

Fig. 1: Identifying Engine-To-Transaxle Bolts (Altima – RE4F04A/V Transaxles)

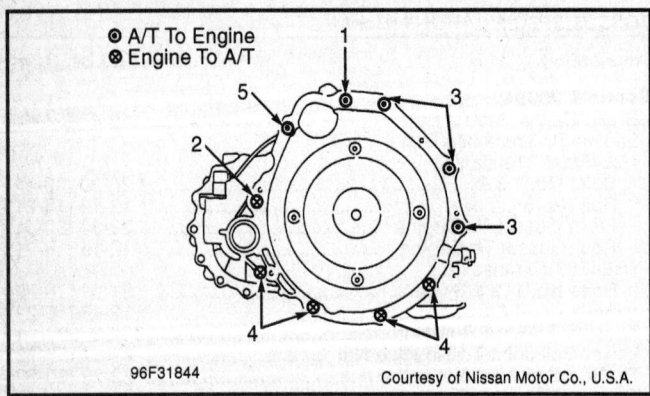

**Fig. 2: Identifying Engine-To-Transaxle Bolts
(Maxima RE4F04A/V Transaxle)**

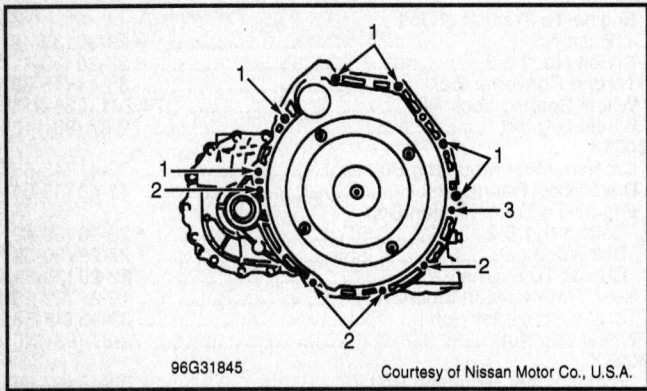

Fig. 3: Identifying Engine-To-Transaxle Bolts (Quest)

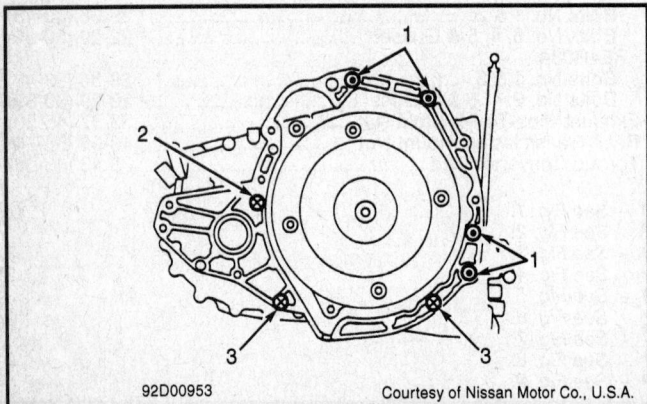

**Fig. 4: Identifying Engine-To-Transaxle Bolts
(Sentra & 200SX – RL4F03A Transaxle)**

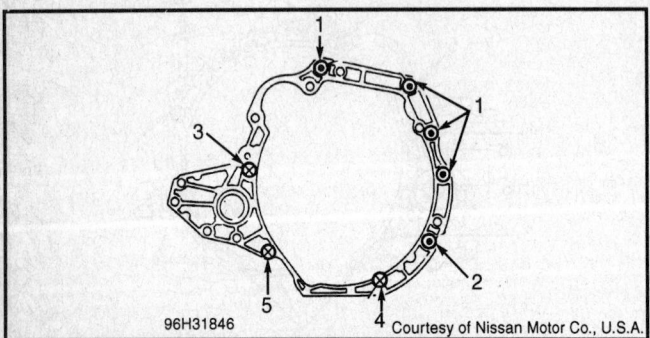

**Fig. 5: Identifying Engine-To-Transaxle Bolts
(Sentra & 200SX – RE4F03V Transaxle)**

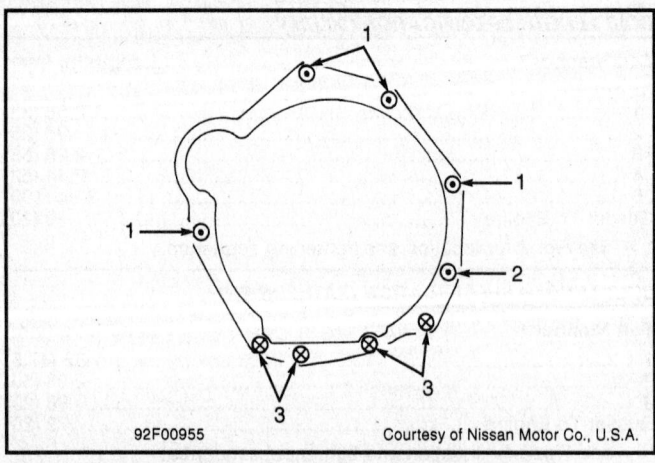

Fig. 6: Identifying Engine-To-Transmission Bolts (240SX)

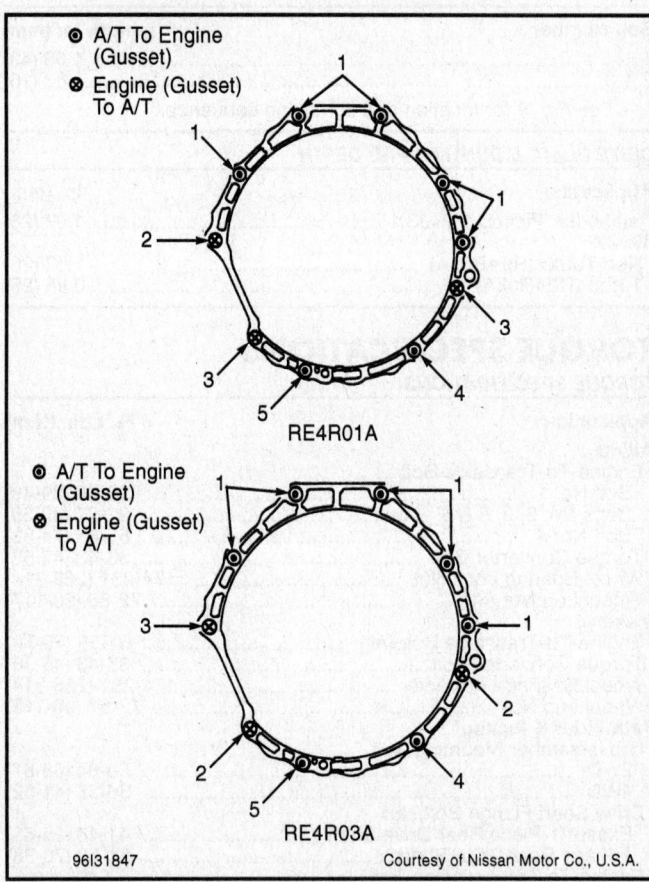

Fig. 7: Identifying Engine-To-Transmission Bolts (300ZX)

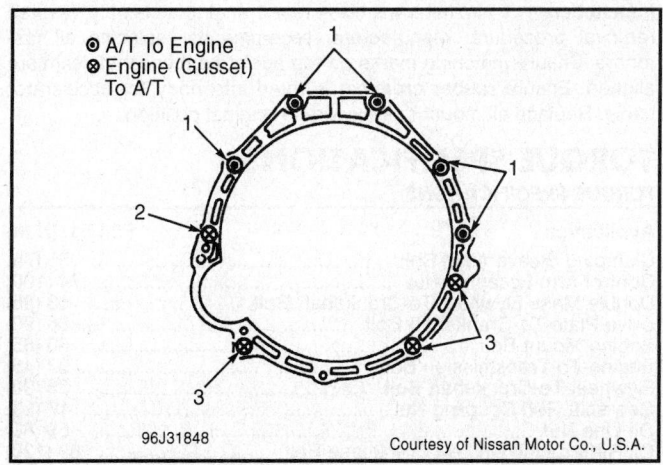

Fig. 8: Identifying Engine-To-Transmission Bolts (Pathfinder)

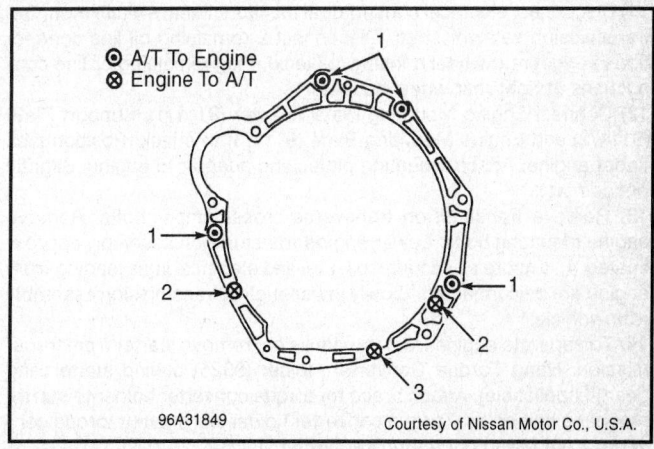

Fig. 9: Identifying Engine-To-Transmission Bolts (Pickup)

Porsche

911 Carrera 2

NOTE: For manual transaxle models, use applicable procedures in this article to remove engine/transaxle assembly.

APPLICATION

TRANSAXLE APPLICATION

Vehicle Application	Transaxle Model
911 Carrera 2 (Automatic)	A50/05
911 Carrera 2 (Manual)	G50/20

CAUTION: DO NOT start engine with ground strap between transmission and chassis disconnected, or Digital Motor Electronics (DME) control unit will be permanently damaged.

FUEL PRESSURE RELEASE

Turn ignition off. Access fuse panel in luggage compartment. Remove fuel pump/oxygen sensor fuse. Start engine. Allow engine to run until it stalls. Crank engine to ensure residual fuel pressure is released.

REMOVAL & INSTALLATION

NOTE: Engine and transmission are removed as an assembly from underneath vehicle.

Removal – 1) Release fuel pressure. See FUEL PRESSURE RELEASE. Disconnect negative battery cable. Raise and support vehicle. Position supports for vehicle so transmission supports can be removed later. Remove rear wheels.
2) On A/C-equipped vehicles, disconnect A/C compressor mounting bolts. Set A/C compressor aside with hoses attached. Remove hot air blower (electric fan) from engine. Remove air cleaner assembly. Disconnect crankcase/oil tank vent hoses.
3) Remove power steering fluid from power steering pump reservoir. Disconnect plug wires for cylinders No. 4 and 6. Remove top hose from power steering pump, and collect any remaining fluid. Remove lower hose from power steering pump, and collect any remaining fluid. Disconnect plug from intake rail.

NOTE: Place matching marks on electrical connectors for reassembly reference.

4) On left side of engine compartment, disconnect carbon canister hose, brake booster vacuum hose, knock sensor, temperature sensor, cruise control, reference mark sensor. See Fig. 1.

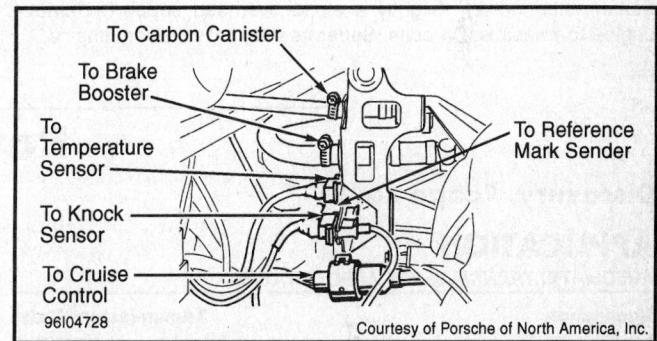

Fig. 1: Identifying Miscellaneous Under-Hood Connections

5) Disconnect 6 electrical connections at intake manifold assembly. Remove cover from engine electrics compartment. Disconnect multiple electrical connectors and remove harness. Remove right hand cover next to A/C compressor. Disconnect oxygen sensor connector.
6) Disconnect fuel supply and fuel return line. If fuel tank is full, connect an extra piece of fuel line to vehicle fuel return line. Pinch off extra fuel line connected to vehicle fuel return line to prevent fuel from leaking.
7) Disconnect throttle linkage. Raise vehicle. Remove engine and transmission covers from underside of vehicle. Remove tailpipes from mufflers. Remove both mufflers. Remove rear axle shafts. See RWD AXLE SHAFTS article.
8) Disconnect hexagon head screw and pull selector rod coupling off internal shift rod. Remove hot air hoses, pipes and hot air flaps. Remove transverse strut. Remove rear sway bar assembly. Place matching marks on toe adjustment eccentric cam for rear lower control arm (trailing).
9) Disconnect lower control arm at frame and allow arm to hang down. Outer mount may need to be loosened to prevent damage to bushing and dust boot. Remove rear crossmember. Disconnect fluid return line from transmission (if applicable). Drain engine oil at thermostat housing.
10) Using Line Wrench (9501), disconnect oil line at right rear wheel housing (oil tank). Disconnect oil line retaining clip. Disconnect and plug oil line. Disconnect ground strap at bottom starter mounting bolt. Disconnect starter cables. Disconnect throttle linkage at under floor assembly guide tube. Disconnect transmission selector lever cable at transmission.

11) Disconnect electrical connector at multifunctional switch, mounted transmission selector shaft. Disconnect 2 remaining oil line connections at right rear wheel housing (oil tank). Plug remaining oil line connections at right rear wheel housing.

12) Connect Engine Mounting Plate Adapter (9111/1), Support Plate (9111/2) and Engine Mounting Plate (9111/3) to a jack. Position jack under engine. Attach mounting plates and adapter to engine. Slightly preload jack.

13) Remove transmission transverse crossmember bolts. Remove engine mounting bolts. Lower engine/transmission assembly approximately 4". Ensure all vacuum, oil, fuel and electrical lines leading from engine are disconnected. Slowly lower engine/transmission assembly from vehicle.

14) To separate engine from transmission, remove starter from transmission. Hang Torque Converter Holder (9325) behind starter ring gear (if applicable). Attach brace for torque converter holder to starter mounting bolt holes. Torque converter holder will prevent torque converter from falling out during separation.

CAUTION: Ensure Torque Converter Holder (9325) is positioned properly. If holder is not positioned properly, torque converter may fall out when transmission is separated from engine.

---

15) Install Transmission Holder (9324) to transmission mounting bores on sides of transmission case. Attach an overhead support to transmission holder. Slightly preload overhead support. Remove engine-to-transmission bolts. Separate transmission from engine.

Installation – To install transmission and engine assembly, reverse removal procedure. Manufacturer recommends replacing all fasteners. Ensure matching marks on toe adjustment eccentric cam are aligned. Ensure rubber grommet is fitted into body for accelerator cable. Replace all mount dust covers in original position.

TORQUE SPECIFICATIONS
TORQUE SPECIFICATIONS

Application	Ft. Lbs. (N.m)
Clamping Sleeve Allen Bolt	55 (75)
Control Arm Eccentric Nut	74 (100)
Double Mass Flywheel-To-Crankshaft Bolt	63 (85)
Drive Plate-To-Crankshaft Bolt	66 (90)
Engine Mount Bolt	63 (85)
Engine-To-Transmission Bolts	32 (45)
Flywheel-To-Crankshaft Bolt	66 (90)
Gearshift Rod Coupling Nut	17 (23)
Oil Line Nut	[1] 59 (80)
Oil Return Line On Left Crankcase Half	89 (120)
Oil Supply Line On Right Crankcase Half	66 (90)
Stabilizer Bar Mounting Bolt	34 (46)
Torque Converter Housing-To-Transmission Bolts	34 (46)
Transmission Crossmember-To-Chassis Bolt	34 (46)
Transmission-To-Chassis Bolt	[2] 63 (85)

	INCH Lbs. (N.m)
Fuel Distribution Line Nut	106 (12)

[1] – Located in right rear wheelwell.
[2] – These 2 bolts are accessible through small opening from inside vehicle.

Rover

Discovery, Range Rover
APPLICATION
AUTOMATIC TRANSMISSION APPLICATIONS

Application	Transmission Model
Discovery	ZF4HP22
Range Rover	ZF4HP24

REMOVAL & INSTALLATION
DISCOVERY

) Disconnect negative battery cable. Remove fan shroud from radiator. Disconnect airflow hose from air intake chamber. Disconnect kickdown cable from throttle linkage. Disconnect 2 transmission breather pipes from right rear of cylinder head.

2) Remove transmission dipstick. Disconnect transfer case shift boot from console. Remove shift knob and shift boot. Raise and support vehicle. Drain fluid from transmission and transfer case. Remove exhaust pipe-to-exhaust manifold heat shield. Disconnect oxygen sensor connectors.

3) Remove catalytic converter assembly. Support engine/transmission and remove transmission crossmember. Secure transmission jack to transmission. Remove speedometer cable heat shield at transfer case. Disconnect speedometer cable from transfer case. Mark position of driveshafts for installation reference.

4) Disconnect front and rear driveshafts. Remove front and rear muffler brackets and secure muffler to one side. Disconnect oil cooler lines from transmission. Plug oil cooler lines and fittings. Disconnect oil cooler lines from engine oil pan. Secure oil cooler lines out of way.

5) Disconnect shift cable at transmission. Disconnect wiring harness connectors as necessary. Slightly raise transmission jack. Remove transfer case side mounts and mounting brackets. Slightly lower transmission. Disconnect parking brake cable from parking brake lever.

6) Disconnect breather pipes from harness. Remove drive plate inspection cover. Mark drive plate-to-converter for installation reference. Remove drive plate-to-torque converter bolts. Remove fluid fill tube at transmission. Remove transmission fill tube-to-bellhousing bolt. Remove bellhousing-to-engine bolts. Pull transmission jack rearwards. Secure torque converter in bellhousing. Remove transmission from vehicle.

7) To install, reverse removal procedure. Apply Loctite to drive plate-to-torque converter bolts. Tighten bolts to specification. See TORQUE SPECIFICATIONS. Fill transfer case and transmission. See appropriate TRANSMISSION SERVICING article.

RANGE ROVER

1) Disconnect negative battery cable. Remove transmission dip stick. Remove 2 screws securing power window switch panel to center console. Remove power window switch panel and disconnect connectors. Release parking brake. Disconnect parking brake cable from parking brake lever. Raise and support vehicle.

2) Drain transmission and transfer case. Remove front exhaust pipe. Support engine/transmission and remove transmission mount assembly. Secure transmission jack to transmission. Remove driveshaft safety bracket. Mark position of driveshafts for installation reference. Disconnect front and rear driveshafts and secure driveshafts out of way. Disconnect shift cable from transmission.

3) Disconnect wiring harness connectors as necessary. Remove bolt securing oil cooler lines to engine block. Disconnect oil cooler lines from transmission. Secure oil cooler lines out of way. Plug oil cooler lines and fittings. Remove fluid fill tube at transmission. Disconnect breather pipes from transmission and transfer case.

4) Remove inspection plate from bottom of bellhousing. Remove drive plate inspection cover. Mark drive plate-to-torque converter for installation reference. Remove drive plate-to-torque converter bolts. Remove bellhousing-to-engine bolts. Pull transmission jack rearwards. Secure torque converter in bellhousing. Remove transmission from vehicle.

5) To install, reverse removal procedure. Apply Loctite to drive plate-to-torque converter bolts. Tighten bolts to specification. See TORQUE SPECIFICATIONS. Fill transfer case and transmission. See appropriate TRANSMISSION SERVICING article.

TORQUE SPECIFICATIONS

TORQUE SPECIFICATIONS

Application	Ft. Lbs. (N.m)
Bellhousing Bolts	31 (42)
Drive Plate-To-Converter Bolts	
Discovery	[1] 29 (39)
Range Rover	33 (45)
Drive Shaft Bolts	35 (48)
Oil Cooler Pipes-To-Transmission	22 (30)
Transfer Case	
Drain & Fill Plugs	18 (25)
Transmission Mount Assembly	
Bolts (Range Rover)	33 (45)
Transmission Oil Filler Tube	
Discovery	50 (68)
Range Rover	52 (70)
	INCH Lbs. (N.m)
Drive Plate Inspection Cover Bolts	80 (9)
Transmission Drain Plug	89 (10)

[1] – Apply Loctite to bolts.

Saab

900 Series, 9000 Series

APPLICATION

TRANSAXLE APPLICATION

Vehicle Application	Transaxle Model
900 Series	AW 50-40LE
9000 4 Cyl. Series	AW 50-40LE
9000 V6 Series	ZF 4HP-18

REMOVAL & INSTALLATION

900 SERIES

Removal & Installation – 1) Remove battery. Remove negative battery cable. On 4-cylinder models, remove cable retaining clamp on dipstick. On all models, remove dipstick and plug hole. Remove vent hose.

2) Remove transmission selector lever arm. Disconnect and remove shift cable. Disconnect Gray and Black electrical connectors. Cut all plastic straps which hold wiring to transmission.

3) On 4-cylinder models, remove air filter housing. On all models, remove rubber bushings from lift brackets. Install Lifting Beam (83 948 50). On 6-cylinder models, install Holder (83 94 835) in 2 engine lifting brackets. Connect lifting beam to lifting sling and tighten. Disconnect 4 heated oxygen sensors connectors. On 4-cylinder models, disconnect 2 heated oxygen sensors connectors.

4) On all models, raise and support vehicle. Remove front wheels. Remove center and right spoiler sections. On 4-cylinder models, remove clip for oxygen sensor wire on front of engine. On all models, remove front section of exhaust pipe. Disconnect lower control arm ball joints.

5) Remove 2 subframe-to-engine bolts. Position a jack under subframe. Remove remaining 6 subframe bolts. Lower jack about 1". Release frame from pivots and remove subframe.

6) Place container under vehicle and remove transmission cooling lines. Plug all openings. Release left drive shaft from its splines and pull it straight out. Plug drive shaft inlet hole. Separate right drive shaft from intermediate shaft. Secure drive shafts to car body and hang aside. Remove intermediate shaft attachment on engine.

7) On 6-cylinder models, remove 2 retaining bolts in shaft attachment. Carefully knock shaft out of attachment. On 4-cylinder models, remove lower alternator bolt. Remove 3 intermediate shaft attachment bolts. Turn alternator upward. Force shaft attachment out to free 2 guide pins. Pull out intermediate shaft with attachment.

8) On all models, plug inlet hole. Remove actuator cover between engine and transmission. Remove 6 torque converter-to-flexplate bolts. Lock torque converter in position to avoid having it fall during transmission removal. Remove lower engine-to-transmission bolts. Remove front engine mount bolts.

9) Remove 3 upper rear engine-to-transmission bolts. Lower vehicle. Using lifting beam, lower engine and transmission so about a 4" gap is present between car body and transmission front mount. Gap can be seen from left front wheelhousing.

10) Secure Lifting Cable (87 92 251) to transmission rear bolt holes. Install other end to lifting beam. Remove slack from cable. Remove 2 remaining transmission-to-engine bolts. Remove transmission from engine. Unhook cable from lifting device, raise vehicle, and pull out transmission. Remove lifting cable from transmission. To install transmission, reverse removal procedure. Tighten bolts to specification. See TORQUE SPECIFICATIONS.

9000 SERIES

Removal – 1) Open hood. Remove battery and windshield washer fluid reservoir. Disconnect electrical cable from battery tray. Remove clamps for positive cable under the tray. Remove fuel filter. Remove battery tray.

2) Disconnect wiring from mass airflow meter. Remove mass airflow meter. Disconnect by-pass hose from turbocharger output duct (if equipped). Remove turbocharger outlet duct (if equipped).

3) Disconnect throttle cable from throttle body. Remove gear selector cable from transaxle lever. DO NOT separate ball joint. Disconnect oil cooler hose from top of transaxle.

4) Disconnect gear selector cable from transaxle. Disconnect oil cooler hose from front of transaxle. Remove turbocharger oil supply hose clamp (if equipped) from transaxle.

5) Remove negative battery cable. Disconnect speed sensor wiring from transaxle. Remove transaxle-to-engine bolts that are accessible from above. Remove upper starter retaining bolt. Disconnect starter brace.

6) Support engine from above. Raise and support vehicle. Remove left front wheel. Remove fender liner. Remove starter motor without disconnecting cables. Suspend starter motor from chassis.

7) Remove torque converter-to-flexplate bolts. Remove 2 ball joint- to-lower suspension arm bolts. Disconnect anti-roll bar from lower suspension arm. Remove front engine mount bolt. Remove bolts that retain subframe to front of vehicle. Loosen bolts that retain rear of subframe to vehicle. Carefully lower front of subframe.

8) Remove clamps around axle shaft universal joint boots. Withdraw axle shafts from transaxle. Support weight of transaxle with jack. Remove remaining transaxle-to-engine bolts. Separate transaxle from engine. Lower transaxle from vehicle.

Installation – To install transaxle, reverse removal procedure. Coat torque converter-to-flexplate bolts with thread sealant. Refill transaxle with fluid. Tighten bolts to specification. See TORQUE SPECIFICATIONS. Adjust throttle and gear selector cables.

TORQUE SPECIFICATIONS
TORQUE SPECIFICATIONS

Application	Ft. Lbs. (N.m)
Oil Cooler Bolt	16 (22)
Torque Converter-To-Flexplate Bolt	
900	
4-Cylinder	44 (60)
6-Cylinder	22 (30)
9000	24-29 (33-39)
Transmission-To-Engine Bolt	55 (75)
Wheel Lug Nut	
Steel Rims	74 (100)
Light Alloy Rims	89 (120)
Other Bolts	
5-mm	[1]
6-mm	[2]
8-mm	15 (20)
10-mm	30 (40)

[1] – Tighten to 44 INCH lbs. (5 N.m).
[2] – Tighten to 89 INCH lbs. (10 N.m).

Subaru

Impreza, Legacy, SVX
APPLICATION
TRANSAXLE APPLICATION

Vehicle Application	Transaxle Model
Impreza	4-Speed
Legacy	4-Speed
SVX	4-Speed

REMOVAL & INSTALLATION
IMPREZA

Removal – **1)** Fully open front hood. Disconnect battery. Remove air intake duct. Disconnect clutch cable, parking brake cable and harness connectors. Disconnect Oxygen sensor. Disconnect speedometer cable. Remove starter.

2) Remove service plug on transaxle bellhousing. Unbolt torque converter from drive plate. Remove transaxle dipstick. Remove harness connector mounting bracket. Remove torque rod and install Engine Support Bracket (41099AA000), in its place. Remove upper transaxle bellhousing bolts.

3) Lift and support vehicle. On FWD models, remove exhaust "Y" pipe assembly. On AWD models, also remove rear exhaust assembly. On all models, remove front differential drain plug and transaxle drain plug. Once fluid is drained, install drain plugs. Disconnect transaxle cooling hoses. On AWD models, disconnect drive shaft from differential companion flange. Place reference mark on both components for reassembly.

4) Unbolt drive shaft center support bracket and remove drive shaft. Place yoke plug in transaxle. Disconnect shift selector cable and bracket. Unbolt stabilizer mounting brackets from crossmember. Unbolt and separate ball joints from lower control arms.

5) Using punch pin and hammer, remove roll pins from inner CV joints at transaxle. Discard roll pins. Disconnect axles from transaxle. Remove remaining bellhousing mounting bolts. Support transaxle with appropriate jack. Remove rear crossmember. Move transaxle and torque converter as an assembly away from engine and remove.
Installation – To install transaxle, reverse removal procedure. Always use NEW roll pins when installing axle shafts. Tighten bolts to specification. See TORQUE SPECIFICATIONS.

LEGACY

Removal – **1)** Disconnect negative battery cable. Remove air intake duct. Disconnect front oxygen sensor connector, transmission harness connector, transmission ground terminal and vehicle speed sensor "2". Raise and support vehicle. Disconnect speedometer cable and vacuum hoses from transaxle.

2) Remove torque strut. In place of torque strut, install Engine Support (41099AA000). Remove starter harness and starter. Remove timing hole plug and 4 drive plate-to-converter bolts.

3) Raise and support vehicle. Disconnect front exhaust pipe from engine, leaving one nut in place to temporarily hold exhaust pipe. Disconnect front-to-rear exhaust pipe connection. Remove front exhaust pipe. Disconnect rear oxygen sensor connector.

4) Drain transaxle fluid. On 4WD models, remove rear drive shaft and rear exhaust pipe. Remove hanger bracket from right side of transmission. On all models, disconnect shift linkage from transaxle. Disconnect stabilizer bar and parking brake cables from lower control arms.

5) Remove bolts attaching lower control arms to crossmember. Drop lower control arms. Remove roll pins and separate both axles from transaxle. Discard roll pins.

6) Remove engine-to-transaxle mounting bolts. Disconnect and plug ATF cooler hoses. Place jack under transaxle. Remove rear transaxle mounting nuts and rear crossmember. Pull transaxle away from engine and lower from vehicle.
Installation – To install transaxle, reverse removal procedure. Always use NEW roll pins when installing axle shafts. Tighten bolts to specification. See TORQUE SPECIFICATIONS.

SVX

Removal – **1)** Open hood fully. Disconnect negative battery cable. Remove throttle body cover and air intake boot. Remove torque rod and bracket. Install Engine Support Assembly (927670000). Disconnect transmission air vent hoses from torque rod bracket and remove bracket from transmission case.

2) Disconnect PCV valve hose and hose from crankcase to collector. Disconnect transmission harness connectors. Disconnect transmission ground terminal connector. Disconnect vehicle speed sensor "2". Disconnect left and right oxygen sensors.

3) Raise and support vehicle. Remove lower starter nut. Lower vehicle. Disconnect starter wiring. Remove starter. Remove torque converter service hole plug. Remove torque converter-to-drive plate bolts. Rotate engine to bring bolts to service plug hole. Install Engine Support (927670000), in place of torque strut. Remove bolts holding right upper side of transmission to engine. Remove transmission and differential dipsticks.

4) Raise vehicle and remove engine undercover. Remove oxygen sensor harness from clip. Remove front exhaust pipes and rear catalytic converter. Remove front exhaust cover.

5) Remove drive shaft-to-companion flange bolts of rear differential. Remove bolts holding center bearing to body. Remove drive shaft from transmission. Plug opening in transmission after removal of drive shaft. Remove selector cable from selector lever assembly. Remove selector cable bracket from body.

6) Remove ball joint of lower arm from knuckle arm of housing. Remove stabilizer link from bracket. Remove brake hose and ABS sensor harness from starter bracket. Remove spring pin holding axle shaft into front differential drive shaft. Remove axle shaft from transmission.

7) Disconnect ATF cooler hoses from pipes and transmission side. Remove nuts holding lower side of transmission to engine. Support transmission with transmission jack. Remove bolts securing rear crossmember to body. Ensure torque converter stays with transmission, pull transmission away from engine and remove transmission from vehicle.

Installation – To install transaxle, reverse removal procedure. Always use NEW roll pins when installing axle shafts. Tighten bolts to specification. See TORQUE SPECIFICATIONS table.

TORQUE SPECIFICATIONS
TORQUE SPECIFICATIONS

Application	Ft. Lbs. (N.m)
Crossmember Bolts	40-61 (54-83)
Center Support Bearing Bracket	35-42 (47-57)
Center Exhaust Pipe To Rear Pipe	9-17 (13-23)
Engine Mount Bracket Bolts	27-49 (37-67)
Engine Mount-To-Body Bolts	27-49 (37-67)
Exhaust Pipe to Engine	15-26 (21-35)
Exhaust To Muffler (AWD)	32-40 (43-53)
Lower Control Arm-To-Crossmember Bolts	
Impreza	18-22 (25-29)
Legacy & SVX	61-83 (83-113)
Torque Rod	
Engine Side	33-40 (44-54)
Body Side	35-49 (47-67)
Shift Selector Cable Bracket	9-17 (13-23)
Stabilizer Clamp	15-21 (21-28)
Starter Bolts	34-40 (46-54)
Torque Converter-To-Drive Plate Bolts	17-20 (23-27)
Torque Strut Bolt	31-46 (42-62)
Transaxle-To-Engine Bolts	34-40 (46-54)
Transaxle Mount-To-Body Bolts	27-49 (37-67)
Transverse Link-To-Crossmember	54-69 (73-94)

Suzuki

Esteem, Sidekick, Swift, X90
AUTOMATIC TRANSMISSION APPLICATIONS

Model	Transaxle/Transmission
Esteem	
4-Speed	[1][2]
Sidekick	
3-Speed	[3] 3L30
4-Speed	[4] AW03-72LE
Swift	
3-Speed	ECC
X90	
4-Speed	AW03-72LE

[1] – Transaxle code not available from manufacturer.
[2] – Electronically controlled 3-speed with overdrive.
[3] – Also known as Turbo Hydra-Matic 180C.
[4] – Transmission is an option on 4-door model.

REMOVAL & INSTALLATION

ESTEEM

Removal – 1) Disconnect negative battery cable at transaxle and at battery. Disconnect transaxle wiring harness and clamps. Disconnect gear select cable from transaxle. Drain cooling system and remove water intake hose.

2) Remove transaxle-to-engine bolts. Remove starter. Remove exhaust manifold shield. Support engine. From underhood, remove or disconnect any other transaxle components that require underhood access.

3) Raise and support vehicle. Drain fluid. Remove engine dust shields. Disconnect oil cooler hoses. Remove mounts, engine-to-transaxle stiffener and exhaust pipe. Remove flywheel dust shield and drive plate bolts. Pry out drive shaft joints from differential. Disconnect lower suspension arms and pull drive shafts from differential.

4) Remove rear engine mount and bracket. Remove engine-to-transaxle bolts and nuts. Support engine with a transmission jack. Remove left-side engine mount. Remove transaxle and torque converter from engine compartment. Ensure torque converter does not fall off transaxle. Remove left-side engine mount from transaxle case.

Installation – 1) Install torque converter on transaxle. Measure distance from edge of transaxle case to torque converter mounting flange. Distance should be .929-1.002" (23.6-25.5 mm). If measured distance is less than specification, torque converter is not installed correctly.

2) To install transaxle, reverse removal procedures. Ensure oil seals are not damaged when drive shafts are installed. Push in drive shafts, DO NOT hit drive shafts with a hammer during installation. Tighten all fasteners to specification. See TORQUE SPECIFICATIONS. Check fluid level and adjust as necessary. Road test vehicle and check for leaks.

SIDEKICK & X90

NOTE: If vehicle is 2WD, disregard transfer case and 4WD component removal procedures in the following steps.

Removal – 1) Disconnect negative battery cable. Remove transfer case shift lever knob. Remove console box. Remove retaining screws, shift lever boot and bracket.

2) Remove clamp and small boot located on top of transfer case at shift lever opening. Push downward on case cover (center area around shift lever) and rotate counterclockwise. Remove transfer case shift lever.

3) Disconnect kickdown cable at throttle body. Remove battery, transmission dipstick, filler tube, and starter without disconnection harness. Using Engine Support Fixture (J-28467-A), support engine.

4) Disconnect electrical connections, breather hose and control cables from transmission. Disconnect speedometer cable from transfer case. Disconnect and plug oil cooler lines from transmission. Remove gearshift assembly, if necessary.

5) Raise and support vehicle. Remove transfer case skid plate. Mark drive shaft flange and yokes for reassembly reference. Remove front and rear drive shafts.

6) Remove E-ring and nut from end of gear select cable. Remove cable bracket. Remove exhaust pipe bracket at catalytic converter and transmission. Remove left case stiffener bracket. Disconnect oil cooler lines and plug ends to prevent leakage. Loosen left case stiffener and remove bracket bolts from transmission.

7) Remove torque converter dust shield. Use Gear Stopper (09927-56010) to hold drive plate stationary and remove torque converter-to-drive plate bolts. Support transmission with jack. DO NOT damage transmission oil pan.

8) Remove crossmember located below transmission and transfer case. Remove remaining transmission-to-engine bolts. Move transmission and transfer case away from engine. Disconnect wiring and hoses. Remove transmission from vehicle.

WARNING: *Transmission and transfer assemblies may tilt on jack. Torque converter could fall off causing injury or damage. Use an auxiliary arm of jack for additional support.*

Installation – To install, reverse removal procedure. Tighten all fasteners to specification. See TORQUE SPECIFICATIONS. Ensure reference marks are aligned on drive shaft flanges and yokes. Adjust all control cables. See ADJUSTMENTS in appropriate AUTOMATIC TRANSMISSION SERVICING article. Fill and check fluid levels.

SWIFT

NOTE: *Engine and transaxle are removed as a unit. For removal procedures not covered in this article, see appropriate article in ENGINES in appropriate MITCHELL® manual.*

Removal – **1)** Release fuel system pressure. Disconnect air intake tubing from air cleaner. Disconnect battery cables. Remove battery and tray. Disconnect ground cable at transaxle. Disconnect electrical connections, speedometer cable and control cables from engine and transaxle. Drain cooling system and remove radiator with cooling fan.
2) Remove starter. Raise and support vehicle. Drain engine and transaxle fluids. Disconnect and plug oil cooler lines from transaxle. Disconnect exhaust pipe from exhaust manifold.
3) Remove left axle shaft and disengage right axle shaft from differential. Remove left wheel. Remove staked area from left axle shaft nut at hub assembly. Remove nut and washer from left axle shaft.
4) Remove left ball joint-to-steering knuckle bolt. Separate ball joint from steering knuckle. Using 2 screwdrivers, pry axle shafts from transaxle case. Remove left axle shaft. Disconnect engine torque rod and bracket from transaxle. Lower vehicle and install engine hoist. Remove mounting nuts and bolts. Before raising engine and transaxle, ensure all hoses, wires and cables are disconnected. Remove engine and transaxle.
5) Support transaxle using a jack. Remove lower cover from torque converter housing. Disconnect transaxle mounts. Remove transaxle-to-engine bolts. Remove transaxle assembly. Remove drive plate-to-torque converter bolts. Drive plate can be held by engaging a screwdriver into drive plate gear through notch provided at underside of transaxle case.

CAUTION: *When removing transaxle from engine, keep it parallel to crankshaft using care not to stress drive plate and torque converter. Keep transaxle level or with torque converter pointed upward to keep it from falling off.*

Installation – **1)** To install transaxle, apply grease around cup at center of torque converter and reverse removal procedure.
2) Ensure torque converter is correctly installed. Distance from torque converter drive lugs to engine mating surface of transaxle housing should be at least .85" (21.6 mm). If distance to mating surface is less than specified, torque converter has been installed improperly. Remove and reinstall torque converter correctly. Tighten drive plate bolts to 13-14 ft. lbs. (18-19 N.m). Remount transaxle to engine. Install engine and transaxle into vehicle.
3) Tighten all fasteners to specification. See TORQUE SPECIFICATIONS. Install all hoses and wires. Adjust all cables. See ADJUSTMENTS in appropriate AUTOMATIC TRANSMISSION SERVICING article. Fill and check coolant, engine and transaxle fluid levels.

TORQUE SPECIFICATIONS
TORQUE SPECIFICATIONS

Application	Ft. Lbs. (N.m)
Esteem	
Engine-To-Transaxle	65 (90)
Engine Mounts	40 (55)
Exhaust Manifold	37 (50)
Lower Ball Joint Pinch-Bolt	44 (60)
Oil Cooler Fittings	26 (35)
Sway Bar Link	21 (28)
Support Brace	33 (45)
Torque Converter	14 (19)
Sidekick & X90	
Crossmember Bolt	62 (84)
Drive Shaft Flange Bolt	38 (51)
Torque Converter Bolt	41 (55)
Transfer Case Skid Plate	41 (55)
Transmission-To-Engine Bolt	62 (84)
Swift	
Drive Plate-To-Torque Converter Bolts	13-14 (18-19)
Transaxle-To-Engine Bolt	29-44 (39-60)
Wheel Lug Nut	44 (60)

Toyota

Avalon, Camry, Celica, Corolla, Land Cruiser, MR2 (1995), Paseo, Pickup (1995), Previa, RAV4 (1996), Supra, Tacoma, Tercel, T100, 4Runner

APPLICATION
AUTOMATIC TRANSMISSION APPLICATIONS

Application	Transmission Model
Avalon	A-541E
Camry	
4-Cyl.	A-140E
V6	A-541E
Celica	
1.8L (7A-FE)	A-246E
2.2L (5S-FE)	A-140E
Corolla	
1.6L (4A-FE)	A-131L
1.8L (7A-FE)	A-245E
Land Cruiser	A-343F
MR2 2.2L (5S-FE)	A-241E
Paseo	A-244E
Pickup	
2WD	
4-Cyl.	A-43D
V6	A-340E
4WD	
4-Cyl.	A-340F
V6	A-340H

AUTOMATIC TRANSMISSION APPLICATIONS (Cont.)

Application	Transmission Model
Previa	
Non-Supercharged	
AWD	A-46DF
2WD	A-46DE
Supercharged	
AWD	A-340F
2WD	A-340E
RAV4	
2WD	A-241E
4WD	A-540H
Supra	A-340E
Tacoma	
2WD	
2.4L (2RZ-FE)	A-43D
3.4L (5VZ-FE)	A-340E
4WD	
2.7L (3RZ-FE)	A-340E
3.4L (5VZ-FE)	A-340E
Tercel	
3-Speed	A-132L
4-Speed	A-242L
T100	
2WD	A-340E
4WD	A-340F

AUTOMATIC TRANSMISSION APPLICATIONS (Cont.)

Application	Transmission Model
4Runner	
1995	
2WD V6	A-340E
4WD 4-Cyl.	A-340F
4WD V6	A-340H
1996	
2WD	A-340E
4WD	A-340F

WARNING: On models equipped with a Supplemental Restraint System (SRS), SRS must be disabled before repairs are started. Turn ignition switch to LOCK position and disconnect negative battery cable and wait at least 90 seconds. Back-up power supply maintains SRS activation voltage for about 90 seconds after battery is disconnected.

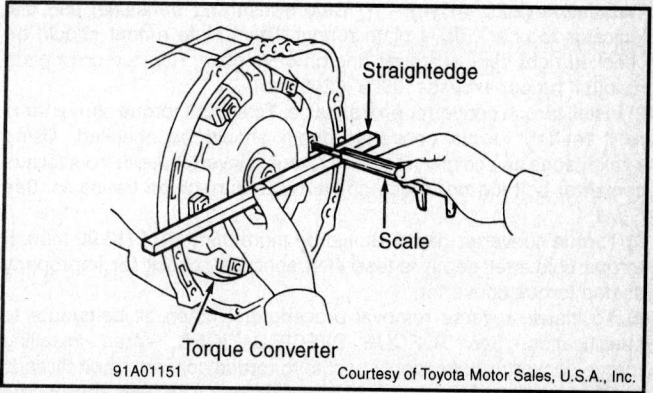

Fig. 1: Measuring Typical Torque Converter Depth

AVALON

Removal – 1) Disconnect negative battery cable. Remove battery, battery tray, air cleaner assembly and air cleaner case. Disconnect throttle valve cable from throttle body. Remove cruise control actuator with mounting bracket from body.

2) Raise and support vehicle. Disconnect necessary electrical connectors and ground cables for transaxle removal. Disconnect shift cable and oil cooler lines at transaxle. Remove shift cable clamp bracket from transaxle.

3) Remove front (radiator side) engine mount shock absorber-to-lower frame assembly bolts. Remove front (radiator side) engine mount-to-lower frame assembly bolts/nuts. Remove starter.

4) Remove front (radiator side) exhaust manifold brace from rear of exhaust manifolds. Brace fits between rear of exhaust manifold and front of transaxle.

5) Remove 4 upper transaxle-to-cylinder block bolts. Support engine with hoist. Steering gear assembly must be supported in place during transaxle removal. Secure steering gear assembly to engine hoist using an attaching strap placed at each end of steering gear assembly.

6) Remove front wheels. Remove front exhaust pipe located between exhaust manifolds and rear exhaust pipe. Drain transaxle fluid. Remove axle shafts from transaxle. See appropriate AXLE SHAFTS article in AXLE SHAFTS & TRANSFER CASES section.

7) Disconnect shift control cable from mounting bracket. Remove rear (firewall side) engine mount-to-lower frame assembly bolts/nuts. Remove transaxle mount-to-transaxle bolts at driver's side end of transaxle.

8) Remove stabilizer bar mount bracket-to-lower frame assembly bolts. Remove steering gear assembly-to-lower frame assembly bolts/nuts. Support lower frame assembly with floor jack. Lower frame assembly is located below engine and transaxle.

9) Disconnect power steering reservoir pipe mounting brackets from lower frame assembly. Remove bolts for each fender liner from lower frame assembly. Remove lower frame assembly mounting brackets. Lower frame assembly mounting brackets are located on front and rear of lower frame assembly and attach lower frame assembly to body. Remove lower frame assembly.

10) Support transaxle with transmission jack. Remove torque converter cover from front of transaxle. Remove torque converter bolts. Remove remaining exhaust manifold support brace. Remove remaining transaxle-to-cylinder block bolts. Lower transaxle from vehicle.

Installation – 1) Before installing transaxle, use dial indicator to check drive plate runout. Drive plate runout should be checked right next to starter ring on drive plate. Replace drive plate runout if runout exceeds .0079" (.200 mm).

2) Install torque converter on transaxle. To ensure torque converter is fully seated, torque converter depth should be checked. Using straightedge and caliper, measure torque converter depth from torque converter bolt lug on torque converter to surface on transaxle. See Fig. 1.

3) Torque converter depth should be more than .539" (13.70 mm). If torque converter depth is less than specified, check for improperly seated torque converter.

4) To install, reverse removal procedure. Tighten all bolts/nuts to specification. See TORQUE SPECIFICATIONS. When installing torque converter bolts, apply Loctite to torque converter bolt threads before installing. Ensure Dark Green-colored torque converter bolt is installed first before installing remaining torque converter bolts.

5) Use NEW gaskets and NEW nuts when installing front exhaust pipe. Adjust all cables and fill with ATF. See appropriate TRANSMISSION SERVICING article.

CAMRY

Removal (2.2L 4-Cyl.) – 1) Disconnect negative battery cable. Remove air cleaner assembly and air cleaner case. Disconnect throttle valve cable from throttle body. Remove cover from cruise control actuator (if equipped). Disconnect electrical connector at cruise control actuator.

2) Raise and support vehicle. Disconnect necessary electrical connectors and ground cables for transaxle removal. Disconnect shift cable and oil cooler lines at transaxle. Remove starter.

3) Remove front (radiator side) engine mount-to-lower frame assembly bolts/nuts. Remove bolts and separate power steering pipe from lower frame assembly.

4) Remove 3 upper transaxle-to-cylinder block bolts. Support engine with hoist. Steering gear assembly must be supported in place during transaxle removal. Secure steering gear assembly to engine hoist using an attaching strap placed at each end of steering gear assembly.

5) Remove front exhaust pipe located between exhaust manifold and rear exhaust pipe. Remove front wheels. Drain transaxle fluid. Remove axle shafts from transaxle. See appropriate AXLE SHAFTS article in AXLE SHAFTS & TRANSFER CASES section.

6) Remove rear (firewall side) engine mount-to-lower frame assembly nuts. Remove transaxle mount-to-transaxle bolts at driver's side end of transaxle.

7) Remove stabilizer bar mount bracket-to-lower frame assembly bolts. Remove steering gear assembly-to-lower frame assembly bolts/nuts. Support lower frame assembly with floor jack. Lower frame assembly is located below engine and transaxle.

8) Remove bolts for each fender liner from lower frame assembly. Remove lower frame assembly mounting brackets. Lower frame assembly mounting brackets are located on front and rear of lower frame assembly and attach lower frame assembly to body. Remove lower frame assembly.

9) Remove stiffener plates located on each side of cylinder block. Stiffener plate fits between side of cylinder block and front of transaxle. Support transaxle with transmission jack.

10) Remove torque converter cover from front of transaxle. Remove Dark Green-colored torque converter bolt first and then remaining torque converter bolts. Remove remaining transaxle-to-cylinder block bolts. Lower transaxle from vehicle.

Installation (2.2L 4-Cyl.) – 1) Before installing transaxle, use dial indicator to check drive plate runout. Drive plate runout should be checked right next to starter ring on drive plate. Replace drive plate runout if runout exceeds .0079" (.200 mm).

2) Install torque converter on transaxle. To ensure torque converter is fully seated, torque converter depth should be checked. Using straightedge and caliper, measure torque converter depth from torque converter bolt lug on torque converter to surface on transaxle. *See Fig. 1.*

3) Torque converter depth should be more than .510" (13.00 mm). If torque converter depth is less than specified, check for improperly seated torque converter.

4) To install, reverse removal procedure. Tighten all bolts/nuts to specification. See TORQUE SPECIFICATIONS. When installing torque converter bolts, apply Loctite to torque converter bolt threads before installing. Adjust all cables and fill with ATF. See appropriate TRANSMISSION SERVICING article.

Removal (3.0L V6) – 1) Disconnect negative battery cable. Remove battery, air cleaner assembly and air cleaner case. Disconnect throttle valve cable from throttle body. Remove cruise control actuator with mounting bracket from body.

2) Raise and support vehicle. Disconnect necessary electrical connectors and ground cables for transaxle removal. Disconnect shift cable and oil cooler lines at transaxle. Remove shift cable clamp bracket from transaxle.

3) Remove front (radiator side) engine mount shock absorber-to-lower frame assembly bolts. Remove front (radiator side) engine mount-to-lower frame assembly bolts/nuts. Remove starter.

4) Remove 4 upper transaxle-to-cylinder block bolts. Support engine with hoist. Steering gear assembly must be supported in place during transaxle removal. Secure steering gear assembly to engine hoist using an attaching strap placed at each end of steering gear assembly.

5) Remove front wheels. Remove front exhaust pipe located between exhaust manifolds and rear exhaust pipe. Drain transaxle fluid. Remove axle shafts from transaxle. See appropriate AXLE SHAFTS article in AXLE SHAFTS & TRANSFER CASES section.

6) Remove rear (firewall side) engine mount-to-lower frame assembly bolts/nuts. Remove transaxle mount-to-transaxle bolts at driver's side end of transaxle.

7) Remove stabilizer bar mount bracket-to-lower frame assembly bolts. Remove steering gear assembly-to-lower frame assembly bolts/nuts. Support lower frame assembly with floor jack. Lower frame assembly is located below engine and transaxle.

8) Remove bolts for each fender liner from lower frame assembly. Remove lower frame assembly mounting brackets. Lower frame assembly mounting brackets are located on front and rear of lower frame assembly and attach lower frame assembly to body. Remove lower frame assembly.

9) Support transaxle with transmission jack. Remove torque converter cover from front of transaxle. Remove torque converter bolts. Remove exhaust manifold support brace from rear of exhaust manifold. Remove remaining transaxle-to-cylinder block bolts. Lower transaxle from vehicle.

Installation (3.0L V6) – 1) Before installing transaxle, use dial indicator to check drive plate runout. Drive plate runout should be checked right next to starter ring on drive plate. Replace drive plate runout if runout exceeds .0079" (.200 mm).

2) Install torque converter on transaxle. To ensure torque converter is fully seated, torque converter depth should be checked. Using straightedge and caliper, measure torque converter depth from torque converter bolt lug on torque converter to surface on transaxle. *See Fig. 1.*

3) Torque converter depth should be more than .539" (13.70 mm). If torque converter depth is less than specified, check for improperly seated torque converter.

4) To install, reverse removal procedure. Tighten all bolts/nuts to specification. See TORQUE SPECIFICATIONS. When installing torque converter bolts, apply Loctite to torque converter bolt threads before installing. Ensure Dark Green-colored torque converter bolt is

installed first before installing remaining torque converter bolts.

5) Use NEW gaskets when installing front exhaust pipe. Adjust all cables and fill with ATF. See appropriate TRANSMISSION SERVICING article.

CELICA

Removal (1.8L 7A-FE) – 1) Disconnect negative battery cable. Remove transaxle oil dipstick and battery. Disconnect throttle cable valve from throttle body. Remover air cleaner assembly. Remove transaxle-to-mount nut from top of transaxle at driver's side end of transaxle.

2) Remove throttle valve cable mounting bracket and wiring harness clamp bolts from top of transaxle. Remove upper mounting bolt from starter. Remove 2 upper transaxle-to-cylinder block bolts located at top of transaxle.

3) Remove transaxle oil dipstick tube and "O" ring from transaxle. Raise and support vehicle. Remove lower engine covers. Disconnect necessary electrical connectors and ground cables for transaxle removal. Disconnect oil cooler lines for transaxle.

4) Support engine with hoist. Steering gear assembly must be supported in place during transaxle removal. Secure steering gear assembly to engine hoist using an attaching strap placed at each end of steering gear assembly.

5) Remove front wheels. Drain transaxle fluid. Remove axle shafts from transaxle. See appropriate AXLE SHAFTS article in AXLE SHAFTS & TRANSFER CASES section.

6) Support transaxle with transmission jack. Remove rear (firewall side) engine mount through-bolt. Remove front exhaust pipe-to-front exhaust pipe support bracket bolts. Front exhaust pipe is located between exhaust manifold and rear exhaust pipe. Remove front exhaust pipe support bracket located between front exhaust pipe and front suspension crossmember.

7) Remove steering gear assembly-to-suspension crossmember bolts. Remove front exhaust pipe. Remove shift cable brackets and A/C pipe from suspension crossmember. Suspension crossmember is located below engine and fits between both lower control arms. *See Fig. 2.*

8) Remove engine mount crossmember located below oil pan. Engine mount crossmember holds front and rear engine mounts, and is bolted to body and suspension crossmember.

9) Support suspension crossmember with floor jack. Remove suspension crossmember bolts. *See Fig. 2.* Remove suspension crossmember. Remove starter. Disconnect shift cable and electrical connectors at transaxle.

10) Remove torque converter cover from front of transaxle. Remove torque converter bolts. Remove transaxle-to-mount bolts from top of transaxle at driver's side end of transaxle. Remove 5 lower transaxle-to-cylinder block bolts. *See Fig. 3.* Lower transaxle from vehicle.

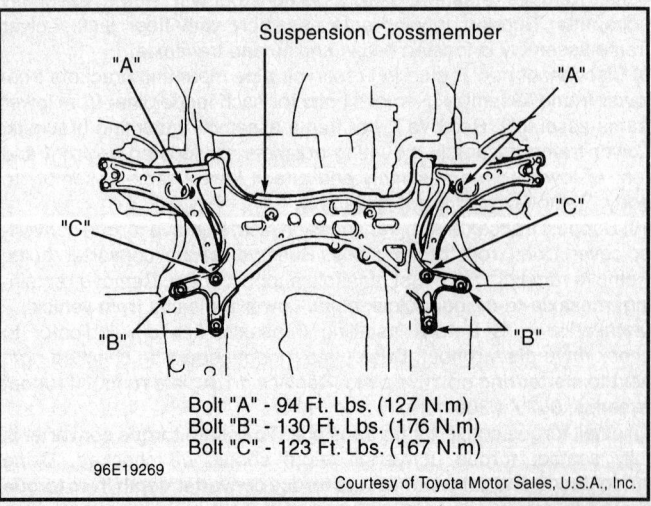

Suspension Crossmember

"A"   "A"

"C"   "C"

"B"   "B"

Bolt "A" - 94 Ft. Lbs. (127 N.m)
Bolt "B" - 130 Ft. Lbs. (176 N.m)
Bolt "C" - 123 Ft. Lbs. (167 N.m)

96E19269   Courtesy of Toyota Motor Sales, U.S.A., Inc.

Fig. 2: Identifying Suspension Crossmember, Bolt Locations & Bolt Tightening Specifications (Celica 1.8L 7A-FE)

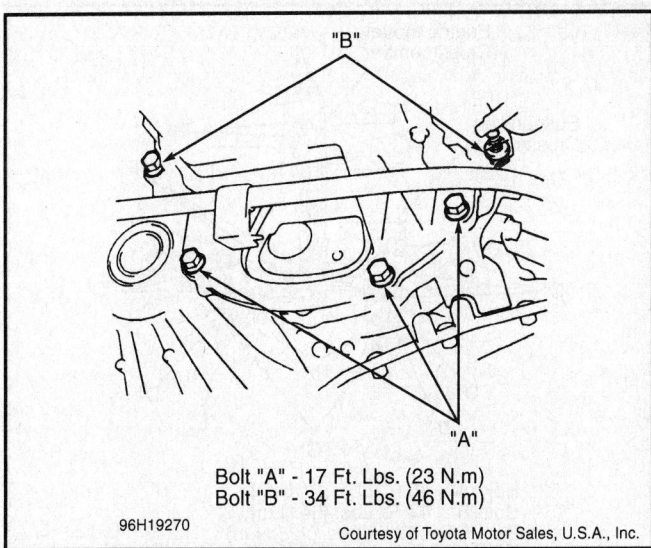

Bolt "A" - 17 Ft. Lbs. (23 N.m)
Bolt "B" - 34 Ft. Lbs. (46 N.m)

96H19270
Courtesy of Toyota Motor Sales, U.S.A., Inc.

Fig. 3: Identifying Lower Transaxle Bolts & Bolt Tightening Specifications (Celica 1.8L 7A-FE)

Installation (1.8L 7A-FE) – 1) Before installing transaxle, use dial indicator to check drive plate runout. Drive plate runout should be checked right next to starter ring on drive plate. Replace drive plate runout if runout exceeds .0079" (.200 mm).

2) Install torque converter on transaxle. To ensure torque converter is fully seated, torque converter depth should be checked. Using straightedge and caliper, measure torque converter depth from torque converter bolt lug on torque converter to surface on transaxle. See Fig. 1.

3) Torque converter depth should be more than .898" (22.80 mm). If torque converter depth is less than specified, check for improperly seated torque converter.

4) To install, reverse removal procedure. Tighten all bolts/nuts to specification. See TORQUE SPECIFICATIONS. Tighten lower transaxle bolts to specification. See Fig. 3.

5) When installing suspension crossmember, ensure all bolts and nuts are tightened to specification. See Fig. 2. When installing torque converter bolts, apply Loctite to torque converter bolt threads before installing. Ensure Gray-colored torque converter bolt is installed first before installing remaining torque converter bolts.

6) Use NEW gaskets and NEW nuts when installing front exhaust pipe. Adjust all cables and fill with ATF. See appropriate TRANSMISSION SERVICING article.

Removal (2.2L 5S-FE) – 1) Disconnect negative battery cable. Remove battery. Disconnect throttle valve cable from throttle body. Remove cruise control actuator (if equipped). Remover air cleaner assembly.

2) Remove transaxle-to-mount bolts/nuts from top of transaxle at driver's side end of transaxle. Remove starter. Disconnect necessary ground cables and electrical connectors at transaxle.

3) Remove 3 upper transaxle-to-cylinder block bolts located at top of transaxle. Disconnect oil cooler lines for transaxle. Raise and support vehicle. Remove lower engine covers.

4) Support engine with hoist. Steering gear assembly must be supported in place during transaxle removal. Secure steering gear assembly to engine hoist using an attaching strap placed at each end of steering gear assembly.

5) Remove front wheels. Drain transaxle fluid. Remove axle shafts from transaxle. See appropriate AXLE SHAFTS article in AXLE SHAFTS & TRANSFER CASES section.

6) Support transaxle with transmission jack. Disconnect shift cable at transaxle. Remove rear (firewall side) engine mount through-bolt. Remove front exhaust pipe-to-front exhaust pipe support bracket bolts. Front exhaust pipe is located between exhaust manifold and rear exhaust pipe.

7) Remove front exhaust pipe support bracket located between front exhaust pipe and front suspension crossmember. Remove front exhaust pipe.

8) Remove shift cable brackets and A/C pipe from suspension crossmember. Suspension crossmember is located below engine and fits between both lower control arms. See Fig. 4. Remove steering gear assembly-to-suspension crossmember bolts.

9) Support suspension crossmember with floor jack. Remove grommets, engine mount crossmember and suspension crossmember. See Fig. 4.

10) Remove intake manifold brace located at bottom of intake manifold and stiffener plate. Remove stiffener plate. Stiffener plate wraps around rear of oil pan and fits between sides of cylinder block and front of transaxle.

11) Remove torque converter bolts. Remove 3 lower transaxle-to-cylinder block bolts. Lower transaxle from vehicle.

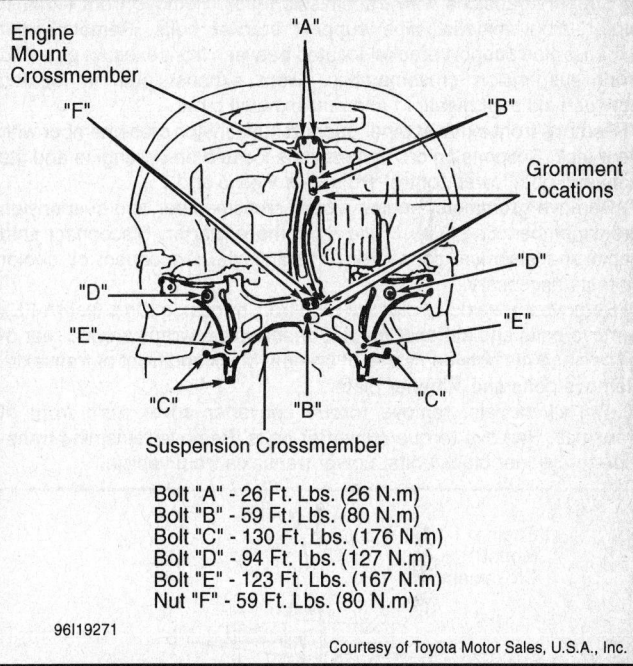

Bolt "A" - 26 Ft. Lbs. (26 N.m)
Bolt "B" - 59 Ft. Lbs. (80 N.m)
Bolt "C" - 130 Ft. Lbs. (176 N.m)
Bolt "D" - 94 Ft. Lbs. (127 N.m)
Bolt "E" - 123 Ft. Lbs. (167 N.m)
Nut "F" - 59 Ft. Lbs. (80 N.m)

96I19271
Courtesy of Toyota Motor Sales, U.S.A., Inc.

Fig. 4: Identifying Engine Mount Crossmember, Suspension Crossmember & Bolt Tightening Specifications (Celica 2.2L 5S-FE)

Installation (2.2L 5S-FE) – 1) Before installing transaxle, use dial indicator to check drive plate runout. Drive plate runout should be checked right next to starter ring on drive plate. Replace drive plate runout if runout exceeds .0079" (.200 mm).

2) Install torque converter on transaxle. To ensure torque converter is fully seated, torque converter depth should be checked. Using straightedge and caliper, measure torque converter depth from torque converter bolt lug on torque converter to surface on transaxle. See Fig. 1.

3) Torque converter depth should be more than .898" (22.80 mm) on 1995 models or .512" (13.00 mm) on 1996 models. If torque converter depth is less than specified, check for improperly seated torque converter.

4) To install, reverse removal procedure. Tighten all bolts/nuts to specification. See TORQUE SPECIFICATIONS. When installing torque converter bolts, apply Loctite to torque converter bolt threads before installing.

5) When installing suspension crossmember and engine mount crossmember, ensure all bolts and nuts are installed before tightening to specification. See Fig. 4.

6) Use NEW gaskets and NEW nuts when installing front exhaust pipe. Adjust all cables and fill with ATF. See appropriate TRANSMISSION SERVICING article.

AUTOMATIC TRANSMISSION REMOVAL
Toyota (Cont.)

COROLLA

Removal – **1)** Disconnect negative battery cable. Remove transaxle oil dipstick. Remove coolant reservoir tank for access to transaxle (if necessary). Disconnect throttle valve cable from throttle body. On 1.8L (7A-FE), remove air cleaner assembly.

2) On all models, remove transaxle mount assembly and brace located on top of transaxle at driver's side end of transaxle. Remove throttle valve cable mounting bracket and wiring harness clamp bolts from top of transaxle. Remove upper mounting bolt from starter. Remove 2 upper transaxle-to-cylinder block bolts located at top of transaxle.

3) Raise and support vehicle. Remove lower engine covers. Disconnect necessary electrical connectors and ground cables for transaxle removal.

4) Support engine with hoist. Remove front wheels. Drain transaxle fluid. Remove axle shafts from transaxle. See appropriate AXLE SHAFTS article in AXLE SHAFTS & TRANSFER CASES section.

5) Support transaxle with transmission jack. Remove front exhaust pipe-to-front exhaust pipe support bracket bolts. Remove front exhaust pipe support bracket located between front exhaust pipe and front suspension crossmember. Front exhaust pipe is located between exhaust manifold and rear exhaust pipe.

6) Remove front exhaust pipe. Support suspension crossmember with floor jack. Suspension crossmember is located below engine and fits between both lower control arms. *See Figs. 5 and 6.*

7) Remove grommets, engine mount crossmember and suspension crossmember. *See Figs. 5 and 6.* Remove starter. Disconnect shift cable and electrical connectors at transaxle. Disconnect oil cooler lines as necessary.

8) Remove transaxle oil dipstick tube from transaxle. On 1.6L (4A-FE), remove bolts and stiffener plate. Stiffener plate wraps around rear of oil pan and fits between sides of cylinder block and front of transaxle. Remove bolts and stiffener plate.

9) On all models, remove torque converter cover from front of transaxle. Remove torque converter bolts. Remove remaining transaxle-to-cylinder block bolts. Lower transaxle from vehicle.

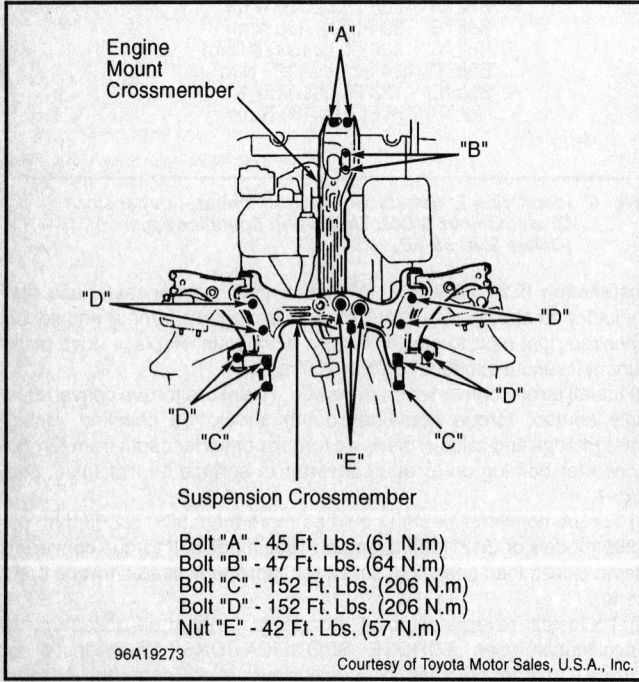

Bolt "A" - 45 Ft. Lbs. (61 N.m)
Bolt "B" - 47 Ft. Lbs. (64 N.m)
Bolt "C" - 152 Ft. Lbs. (206 N.m)
Bolt "D" - 152 Ft. Lbs. (206 N.m)
Nut "E" - 42 Ft. Lbs. (57 N.m)

96A19273   Courtesy of Toyota Motor Sales, U.S.A., Inc.

Fig. 5: Identifying Engine Mount Crossmember, Suspension Crossmember & Bolt Tightening Specifications (1995 Corolla)

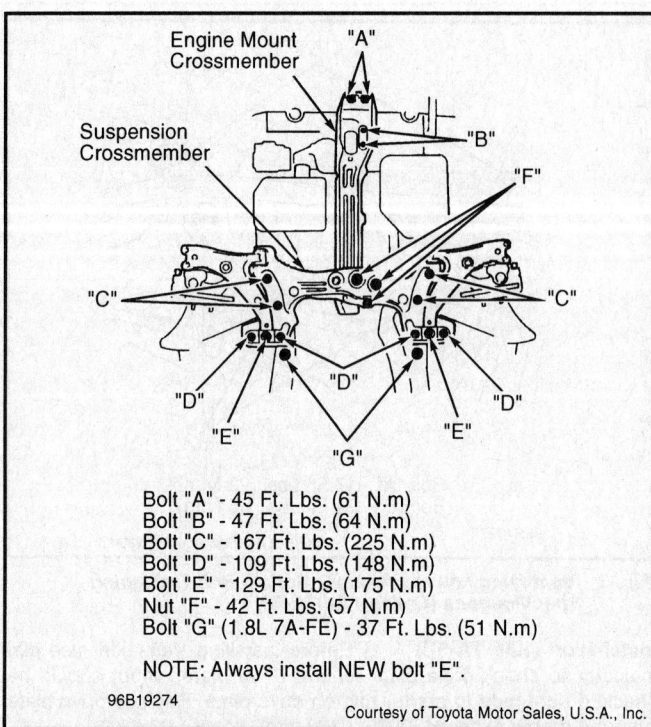

Bolt "A" - 45 Ft. Lbs. (61 N.m)
Bolt "B" - 47 Ft. Lbs. (64 N.m)
Bolt "C" - 167 Ft. Lbs. (225 N.m)
Bolt "D" - 109 Ft. Lbs. (148 N.m)
Bolt "E" - 129 Ft. Lbs. (175 N.m)
Nut "F" - 42 Ft. Lbs. (57 N.m)
Bolt "G" (1.8L 7A-FE) - 37 Ft. Lbs. (51 N.m)

NOTE: Always install NEW bolt "E".

96B19274   Courtesy of Toyota Motor Sales, U.S.A., Inc.

Fig. 6: Identifying Engine Mount Crossmember, Suspension Crossmember & Bolt Tightening Specifications (1996 Corolla)

Installation – **1)** Before installing transaxle, use dial indicator to check drive plate runout. Drive plate runout should be checked right next to starter ring on drive plate. Replace drive plate runout if runout exceeds .0079" (.200 mm).

2) Install torque converter on transaxle. To ensure torque converter is fully seated, torque converter depth should be checked. Using straightedge and caliper, measure torque converter depth from torque converter bolt lug on torque converter to surface on transaxle. *See Fig. 1.*

3) Torque converter depth should be more than .906" (23.00 mm) on 1.6L (4A-FE) or .898" (22.80 mm) on 1.8L (7A-FE). If torque converter depth is less than specified, check for improperly seated torque converter.

4) To install, reverse removal procedure. Tighten all bolts/nuts to specification. See TORQUE SPECIFICATIONS. On 1.8L (7A-FE), for transaxle-to-cylinder block bolt tightening specifications, *see Fig. 7.*

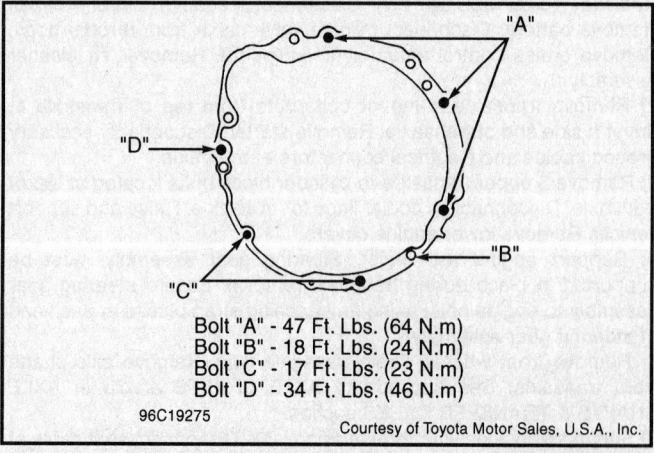

Bolt "A" - 47 Ft. Lbs. (64 N.m)
Bolt "B" - 18 Ft. Lbs. (24 N.m)
Bolt "C" - 17 Ft. Lbs. (23 N.m)
Bolt "D" - 34 Ft. Lbs. (46 N.m)

96C19275   Courtesy of Toyota Motor Sales, U.S.A., Inc.

Fig. 7: Identifying Transaxle-To-Cylinder Block Bolt Tightening Specifications (Corolla 1.8L 7A-FE)

5) On all models, when installing torque converter bolts, apply Loctite to torque converter bolt threads before installing. Use NEW gaskets and NEW nuts when installing front exhaust pipe. Adjust all cables and fill with ATF. See appropriate TRANSMISSION SERVICING article.

LAND CRUISER

Removal – 1) Disconnect negative battery cable. Remove battery and battery tray. Remove fan shroud bolts from top of radiator to prevent damage to cooling fan.

2) Remove throttle valve cable from mounting bracket and throttle linkage. Remove upper starter bolt. Disconnect transfer case shift linkage at transfer case. Disconnect transmission shift linkage at control rod on transmission. Remove knob from transfer case shift lever.

3) Remove screws from each side of center console located around transmission and transfer case shift levers. Remove center console. Remove shift boot from transfer case shift lever.

4) Remove bolts and center console box located between seats. Disconnect electrical connectors at transmission shift lever assembly for removal of transmission shift lever assembly.

5) Remove bolts and transmission shift lever assembly from top of transmission. Remove bolts, transfer case shift lever assembly and cushions. Cushions are located between transfer case shift lever assembly and transfer case.

6) Disconnect necessary electrical connectors and hoses for transmission and transfer case removal. Place reference marks on drive shaft flanges for reassembly reference. Remove bolts and all drive shafts.

7) Remove transmission oil dipstick, dipstick tube and "O" ring. Loosen oil cooler lines at side of transmission. Remove stabilizer bar-to-frame mounting bracket bolts at each end of stabilizer bar. Remove lower engine cover.

8) Remove plug on front of transmission for access to torque converter bolts. Remove torque converter bolts. Remove support brackets and front exhaust pipe with front catalytic converter and gasket. Front exhaust pipe fits between exhaust manifolds and rear catalytic converter and exhaust pipe.

CAUTION: When lowering rear of transmission, use care not to damage cooling fan, brake booster and brake line.

---

9) Remove starter. Support transmission with floor jack. Remove transmission crossmember located below transmission. Lower rear of transmission. Separate wiring harness from transmission and transfer case.

10) Remove oil cooler line mounting bolts from torque converter housing. Disconnect oil cooler lines from side of transmission. Remove transmission-to-cylinder block bolts. Lower transmission with transfer case from vehicle.

Installation – 1) Before installing transmission, use dial indicator to check drive plate runout. Drive plate runout should be checked right next to starter ring on drive plate. Replace drive plate runout if runout exceeds .0079" (.200 mm).

2) Install torque converter on transmission. To ensure torque converter is fully seated, torque converter depth should be checked. Using straightedge and caliper, measure torque converter depth from torque converter bolt lug on torque converter to surface on transmission. See Fig. 1.

3) Torque converter depth should be more than .618" (15.70 mm). If torque converter depth is less than specified, check for improperly seated torque converter.

4) To install, reverse removal procedure. Tighten all bolts/nuts to specification. See TORQUE SPECIFICATIONS. When installing torque converter bolts, apply Loctite to torque converter bolt threads before installing. Ensure Gray-colored torque converter bolt is installed first before installing remaining torque converter bolts.

5) Use NEW gaskets and NEW nuts when installing front exhaust pipe. Adjust all cables, shift linkages and fill with ATF. See appropriate TRANSMISSION SERVICING article.

MR2

Removal (2.2L Non-Turbo) – 1) Disconnect negative battery cable. Remove air cleaner assembly and air cleaner case. Remove transaxle oil dipstick. Disconnect throttle valve cable from throttle body.

2) Remove starter. Raise and support vehicle. Disconnect necessary electrical connectors for transaxle removal. Remove transaxle mount assembly and lateral control rod assembly from top of transaxle at driver's side end of transaxle. See Fig. 8.

3) Remove 3 upper transaxle-to-cylinder block bolts. Remove rear wheels. Remove lower engine covers. Drain transaxle fluid. Remove axle shafts from transaxle. See appropriate AXLE SHAFTS article in AXLE SHAFTS & TRANSFER CASES section.

4) Disconnect shift cable and oil cooler lines at transaxle. Remove front exhaust pipe located between exhaust manifold and rear tailpipe assembly.

5) Support engine with hoist. Remove through-bolts, front (exhaust manifold side) and rear (intake manifold side) engine mounts.

6) Suspension crossmember must be removed. Suspension crossmember is located below engine and transaxle. Lower control arms are attached to suspension crossmember.

7) Remove lower control arm-to-suspension crossmember bolt. Lower control arm fits between suspension crossmember and axle carrier for rear wheel bearings.

8) Remove suspension rod-to-axle carrier bolt/nut. Suspension rod fits between suspension crossmember and rear of axle carrier. Separate suspension rod from axle carrier. Disconnect wiring brackets from suspension crossmember.

9) Support suspension crossmember with floor jack. Remove suspension crossmember-to-body bolts. Lower suspension crossmember from vehicle. Support transaxle with transmission jack.

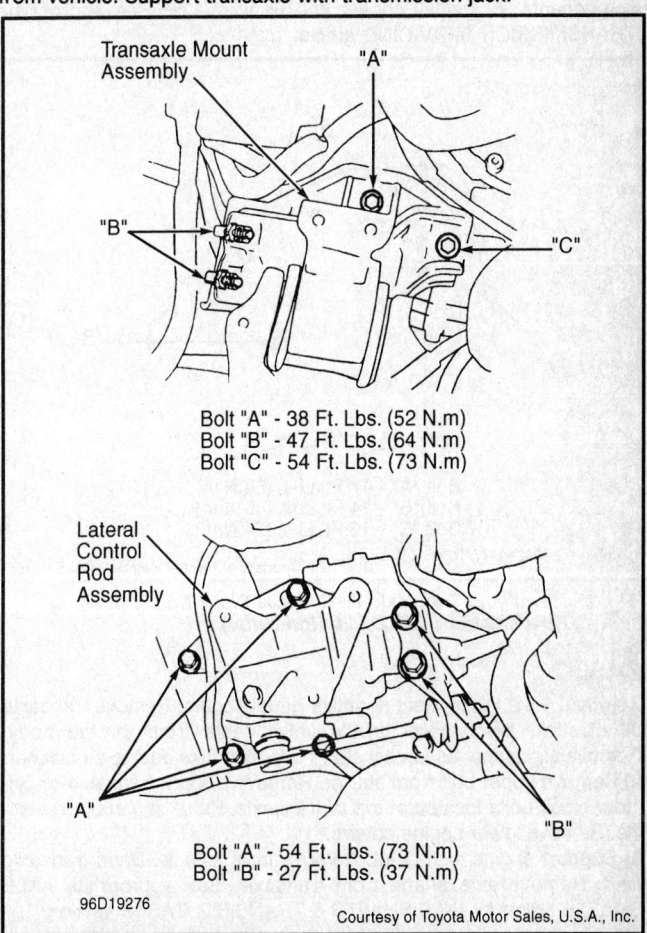

Bolt "A" - 38 Ft. Lbs. (52 N.m)
Bolt "B" - 47 Ft. Lbs. (64 N.m)
Bolt "C" - 54 Ft. Lbs. (73 N.m)

Bolt "A" - 54 Ft. Lbs. (73 N.m)
Bolt "B" - 27 Ft. Lbs. (37 N.m)

96D19276

Courtesy of Toyota Motor Sales, U.S.A., Inc.

Fig. 8: Identifying Transaxle Mount Assembly, Lateral Control Rod Assembly & Bolt Tightening Specifications (MR2 2.2L Non-Turbo)

10) Slightly raise transaxle. Remove transaxle mount assembly bracket from top of transaxle at driver's side end of transaxle. This is the bracket that transaxle mount assembly was mounted on.

11) Remove stiffener plate located on side of cylinder block and front of transaxle. Remove torque converter cover from front of transaxle. Remove torque converter bolts. Remove transaxle-to-cylinder block bolts. Lower transaxle from vehicle.

Installation – 1) Before installing transaxle, use dial indicator to check drive plate runout. Drive plate runout should be checked right next to starter ring on drive plate. Replace drive plate runout if runout exceeds .0079" (.200 mm).

2) Install torque converter on transaxle. To ensure torque converter is fully seated, torque converter depth should be checked. Using straightedge and caliper, measure torque converter depth from torque converter bolt lug on torque converter to surface on transaxle. See Fig. 1.

3) Torque converter depth should be more than .502" (12.75 mm). If torque converter depth is less than specified, check for improperly seated torque converter.

4) To install, reverse removal procedure. Tighten all bolts/nuts to specification. See TORQUE SPECIFICATIONS. Tighten transaxle-to-cylinder block bolts to specification as indicated, see Fig. 9.

5) Tighten transaxle mount assembly and later control rod assembly bolts to specification as indicated, see Fig. 8. When installing torque converter bolts, apply Loctite to torque converter bolt threads before installing. Ensure Gray-colored torque converter bolt is installed first before installing remaining torque converter bolts.

6) Use NEW gaskets nuts when installing front exhaust pipe. Tighten suspension rod-to-axle carrier bolt/nut to specification after vehicle is lowered to ground and bounced several times to stabilize suspension components. Adjust all cables and fill with ATF. See appropriate TRANSMISSION SERVICING article.

5) On 1996 models, remove intake manifold brace for access to starter. On all models, remove starter. Support transaxle with transmission jack.

6) Remove stabilizer bar and mounts for access to transaxle (if necessary). Remove transaxle bracket-to-rear (firewall side) transaxle mount assembly. Remove rear (firewall side) engine mount assembly (if necessary) for transaxle removal.

7) On all models, remove plug from front of transaxle for access to torque converter bolts. Remove torque converter bolts. Remove remaining transaxle-to-cylinder block bolts. Lower transaxle from vehicle.

Installation – 1) Before installing transaxle, use dial indicator to check drive plate runout. Drive plate runout should be checked right next to starter ring on drive plate. Replace drive plate runout if runout exceeds .0079" (.200 mm).

2) Install torque converter on transaxle. To ensure torque converter is fully seated, torque converter depth should be checked. Using straightedge and caliper, measure torque converter depth from torque converter bolt lug on torque converter to surface on transaxle. See Fig. 1.

3) Torque converter depth should be more than .528" (13.40 mm). If torque converter depth is less than specified, check for improperly seated torque converter.

4) To install, reverse removal procedure. Tighten all bolts/nuts to specification. See TORQUE SPECIFICATIONS. Tighten transaxle-to-cylinder block bolts to specification as indicated, see Fig. 10.

5) When installing torque converter bolts, apply Loctite to torque converter bolt threads before installing. Ensure Gray-colored torque converter bolt is installed first (if equipped) before installing remaining torque converter bolts. Adjust all cables and fill with ATF. See appropriate TRANSMISSION SERVICING article.

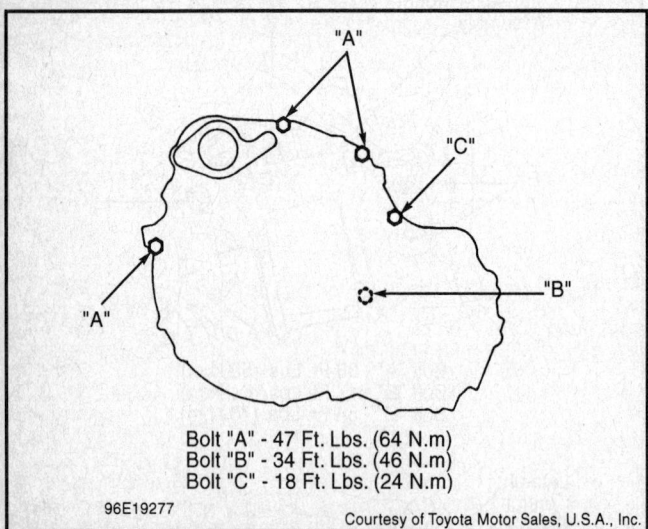

Bolt "A" - 47 Ft. Lbs. (64 N.m)
Bolt "B" - 34 Ft. Lbs. (46 N.m)
Bolt "C" - 18 Ft. Lbs. (24 N.m)

96E19277   Courtesy of Toyota Motor Sales, U.S.A., Inc.

Fig. 9: Identifying Transaxle-To-Cylinder Block Bolt Tightening Specifications (MR2 2.2L Non-Turbo)

PASEO

Removal – 1) Disconnect negative battery cable. Remove transaxle oil dipstick. Disconnect throttle valve cable from throttle body. Remove air cleaner assembly along with air intake duct to air cleaner.

2) Remove upper bolt from starter. Remove 2 upper transaxle-to-cylinder block bolts located at top of transaxle. Raise and support vehicle. Remove lower engine covers.

3) Support engine with hoist. Remove front wheels. Drain transaxle fluid. Remove axle shafts from transaxle. See appropriate AXLE SHAFTS article in AXLE SHAFTS & TRANSFER CASES section.

4) Disconnect necessary electrical connectors, ground cables, speedometer cable, control cables and oil cooler lines for transaxle removal. Remove 2 vertical bottom bolts from front (radiator side) transaxle mount.

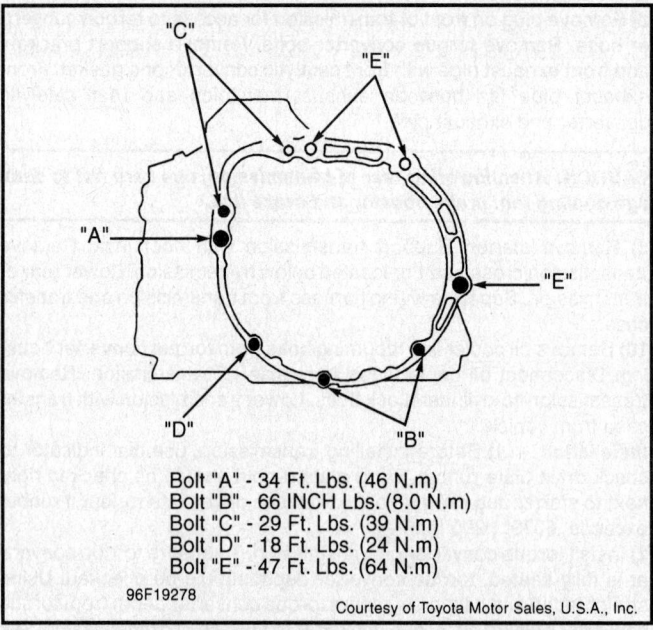

Bolt "A" - 34 Ft. Lbs. (46 N.m)
Bolt "B" - 66 INCH Lbs. (8.0 N.m)
Bolt "C" - 29 Ft. Lbs. (39 N.m)
Bolt "D" - 18 Ft. Lbs. (24 N.m)
Bolt "E" - 47 Ft. Lbs. (64 N.m)

96F19278   Courtesy of Toyota Motor Sales, U.S.A., Inc.

Fig. 10: Identifying Transaxle-To-Cylinder Block Bolt Tightening Specifications (Paseo)

PICKUP

Removal (2WD With 2.4L & 3.0L & 4WD With 2.4L) – 1) Disconnect negative battery cable. Remove transmission oil dipstick, dipstick tube and "O" ring. Disconnect throttle valve cable from throttle body.

2) Raise and support vehicle. Remove lower engine cover. Remove starter. Disconnect shift linkage at transmission. It may be necessary to remove shift linkage cross shaft assembly. On 4WD models, remove transfer case shift lever from transmission.

3) On 2WD 2.4L 4-cylinder models, disconnect front exhaust pipe at exhaust manifold. Remove front exhaust pipe support bracket. It may be necessary to remove front exhaust pipe.

4) On 2WD 3.0L V6 models, remove front exhaust pipe located between exhaust manifolds and catalytic converter on rear exhaust pipe. On all models, disconnect necessary electrical connectors for transmission removal. Remove transmission oil cooler pipes and brackets as necessary.

5) Support transmission with floor jack. On 2WD models, remove rear transmission mount from rear of transmission. Remove transmission mount bracket for rear transmission mount from crossmember. On 4WD models, remove transmission crossmember located below transmission and transfer case.

6) On all models, place reference marks on drive shaft flanges for reassembly reference. Remove drive shaft(s) as necessary. Remove lower crossmember for transmission removal.

7) On 2WD 3.0L V6 models, remove stabilizer bar. On all models, remove stiffener plates located on each side of cylinder block. Stiffener plate fits between side of cylinder block and front of transmission.

8) Remove plug or cover from front of transmission for access to torque converter bolts. Remove torque converter bolts. Remove transmission-to-cylinder block bolts. Lower transmission from vehicle.

Installation (2WD With 2.4L & 3.0L & 4WD With 2.4L) – **1)** Before installing transmission, use dial indicator to check drive plate runout. Drive plate runout should be checked right next to starter ring on drive plate. Replace drive plate runout if runout exceeds .0079" (.200 mm).

2) Install torque converter on transmission. To ensure torque converter is fully seated, torque converter depth should be checked. Using straightedge and caliper, measure torque converter depth from torque converter bolt lug on torque converter to surface on transmission. *See Fig. 1.*

3) Torque converter depth should be more than .787" (20.00 mm). If torque converter depth is less than specified, check for improperly seated torque converter.

4) To install, reverse removal procedure. Tighten all bolts/nuts to specification. See TORQUE SPECIFICATIONS. When installing torque converter bolts, apply Loctite to torque converter bolt threads before installing.

5) Use NEW gasket when installing front exhaust pipe. Adjust all cables, shift linkages and fill with ATF. See appropriate TRANSMISSION SERVICING article.

Removal (4WD With 3.0L) – **1)** Disconnect negative battery cable. Remove transmission oil dipstick, dipstick tube and "O" ring. Disconnect throttle valve cable from throttle body.

2) Raise and support vehicle. Remove lower engine cover. Disconnect shift linkage at transmission. Disconnect shift linkage for transfer case at transfer case shift linkage cross shaft located at rear of transfer case. Remove transfer case shift linkage cross shaft.

3) It may be necessary to remove front exhaust pipe located between exhaust manifolds and catalytic converter on rear exhaust pipe. Disconnect speedometer cable and necessary electrical connectors for transmission and transfer case removal. Remove transmission oil cooler hose, pipes and brackets as necessary.

4) It may be necessary to lower or remove front differential assembly for transmission removal. Support transmission with floor jack. Remove transmission crossmember located below transmission and transfer case. Place reference marks on drive shaft flanges for reassembly reference. Remove drive shafts.

5) Remove stabilizer bar. Remove stiffener plates located on each side of cylinder block. Stiffener plate fits between side of cylinder block and front of transmission.

6) Remove cover from front of transmission for access to torque converter bolts. Remove torque converter bolts. Remove transmission-to-cylinder block bolts. Lower transmission with transfer case from vehicle.

Installation (4WD With 3.0L) – **1)** Before installing transmission, use dial indicator to check drive plate runout. Drive plate runout should be checked right next to starter ring on drive plate. Replace drive plate runout if runout exceeds .0079" (.200 mm).

2) Install torque converter on transmission. To ensure torque converter is fully seated, torque converter depth should be checked. Using

straightedge and caliper, measure torque converter depth from torque converter bolt lug on torque converter to surface on transmission. *See Fig. 1.*

3) Torque converter depth should be more than .709" (18.00 mm). If torque converter depth is less than specified, check for improperly seated torque converter.

4) To install, reverse removal procedure. Tighten all bolts/nuts to specification. See TORQUE SPECIFICATIONS. When installing torque converter bolts, apply Loctite to torque converter bolt threads before installing.

5) Use NEW gasket when installing front exhaust pipe. Adjust all cables, shift linkages and fill with ATF. See appropriate TRANSMISSION SERVICING article.

PREVIA

Removal – **1)** Disconnect negative battery cable. Remove transmission oil dipstick. Disconnect throttle valve cable from throttle body. Raise and support vehicle.

2) Remove transmission oil dipstick tube and "O" ring. Place reference marks flanges on drive shaft(s) for reassembly reference. Remove drive shaft(s). Disconnect shift cable and necessary electrical connectors for transmission removal.

3) Remove starter. On 4WD models, remove front drive shaft bracket. This is the bracket that front drive shaft center bearing assembly was bolted on.

4) On 2WD models, remove lower stiffener plate located between side of cylinder block and front of transmission. On 4WD models, remove transmission-to-cylinder block through-bolt located near bottom of transmission.

5) On all models, remove upper stiffener plate located just above starter opening. Upper stiffener plate fits between cylinder block and front of transmission. Remove torque converter bolts.

6) Remove transmission oil cooler pipes and brackets as necessary. Remove exhaust pipe support bracket located between transmission and exhaust pipe. Support transmission with transmission jack. Remove bolts/nuts from rear transmission mount. Remove transmission-to-cylinder block bolts. Lower transmission from vehicle.

Installation – **1)** Before installing transmission, use dial indicator to check drive plate runout. Drive plate runout should be checked right next to starter ring on drive plate. Replace drive plate runout if runout exceeds .0079" (.200 mm).

2) Install torque converter on transmission. To ensure torque converter is fully seated, torque converter depth should be checked. Using straightedge and caliper, measure torque converter depth from torque converter bolt lug on torque converter to surface on transmission. *See Fig. 1.*

3) Torque converter depth should be more than 1.250" (31.75 mm). If torque converter depth is less than specified, check for improperly seated torque converter.

4) To install, reverse removal procedure. Tighten all bolts/nuts to specification. See TORQUE SPECIFICATIONS. When installing torque converter bolts, apply Loctite to torque converter bolt threads before installing. Adjust all cables and fill with ATF. See appropriate TRANSMISSION SERVICING article.

RAV4

Removal (2WD) – **1)** Disconnect negative battery cable. Disconnect throttle valve cable from throttle body. Remove coolant reservoir tank. Remover air cleaner assembly.

2) Remove starter. Remove 3 upper transaxle-to-cylinder block bolts located at top of transaxle. Raise and support vehicle. Remove lower engine covers.

3) Support engine with hoist. Steering gear assembly must be supported in place during transaxle removal. Secure steering gear assembly to engine hoist using an attaching strap placed at each end of steering gear assembly.

4) Remove transaxle-to-mount bolts/nuts from top of transaxle at driver's side end of transaxle. Remove front wheels. Drain transaxle fluid. Remove axle shafts from transaxle. See appropriate AXLE SHAFTS article in AXLE SHAFTS & TRANSFER CASES section.

5) Remove front exhaust pipe located between exhaust manifold and rear exhaust pipe. Support transaxle with transmission jack. Disconnect shift cable, necessary electrical connectors and oil cooler hoses at transaxle.

6) Remove shift cable brackets from suspension crossmember. Suspension crossmember is located below engine and fits between both lower control arms. *See Fig. 11.* Remove steering gear assembly-to-suspension crossmember bolts.

7) Support suspension crossmember with floor jack. Remove bolts/nuts, engine mount crossmember and suspension crossmember with stabilizer bar. *See Fig. 11.*

8) Remove bolts and stiffener plate. Stiffener plate fits between side of cylinder block and front of transaxle. Remove torque converter cover from front of transaxle. Remove torque converter bolts.

9) Remove 2 cylinder block-to-transaxle bolts. These bolts are located on cylinder block side and thread into transaxle. Lower transaxle from vehicle.

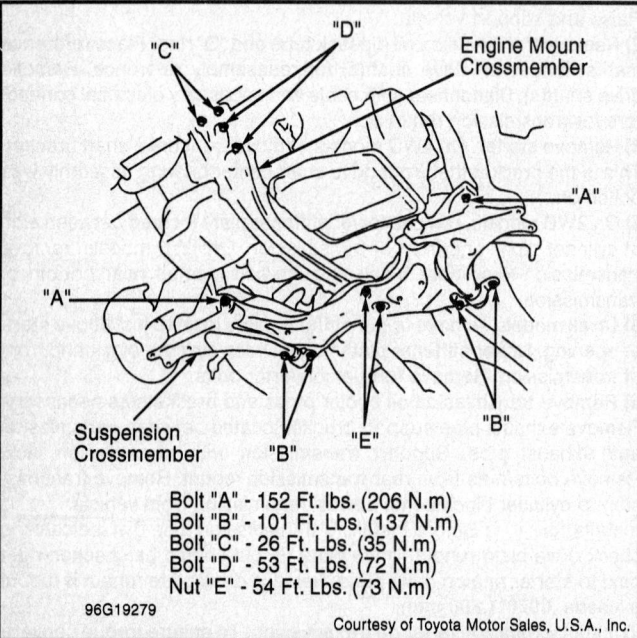

Bolt "A" - 152 Ft. lbs. (206 N.m)
Bolt "B" - 101 Ft. Lbs. (137 N.m)
Bolt "C" - 26 Ft. Lbs. (35 N.m)
Bolt "D" - 53 Ft. Lbs. (72 N.m)
Nut "E" - 54 Ft. Lbs. (73 N.m)

96G19279

Courtesy of Toyota Motor Sales, U.S.A., Inc.

Fig. 11: Identifying Engine Mount Crossmember, Suspension Crossmember & Bolt Tightening Specifications (RAV4 2WD)

Installation (2WD) – 1) Before installing transaxle, use dial indicator to check drive plate runout. Drive plate runout should be checked right next to starter ring on drive plate. Replace drive plate runout if runout exceeds .0079" (.200 mm).

2) Install torque converter on transaxle. To ensure torque converter is fully seated, torque converter depth should be checked. Using straightedge and caliper, measure torque converter depth from torque converter bolt lug on torque converter to surface on transaxle. *See Fig. 1.*

3) Torque converter depth should be more than .502" (12.75 mm). If torque converter depth is less than specified, check for improperly seated torque converter.

4) To install, reverse removal procedure. Tighten all bolts/nuts to specification. See TORQUE SPECIFICATIONS. When installing torque converter bolts, apply Loctite to torque converter bolt threads before installing. Ensure Gray-colored torque converter bolt is installed first before installing remaining torque converter bolts.

5) When installing suspension crossmember and engine mount crossmember, ensure all bolts and nuts are installed before tightening to specification. *See Fig. 11.*

6) Use NEW gaskets and NEW nuts when installing front exhaust pipe. Adjust all cables and fill with ATF. See appropriate TRANSMISSION SERVICING article.

Removal (4WD) – 1) Engine and transaxle are removed as an assembly from bottom of engine compartment. Release fuel pressure. Manufacturer recommends disconnecting electrical connector at electric fuel pump and operating engine until engine stalls before loosening fuel line connection. Remove driver's side rear seat and floor panel cover for access to electrical connector for electric fuel pump.

2) Disconnect electrical connector for electric fuel pump. Start engine and allow engine to idle until engine stalls. Turn ignition off. Reconnect electrical connector for electric fuel pump. Reinstall floor panel cover and driver's side rear seat.

3) Disconnect negative battery cable. Place an approved gasoline container under fuel line. Cover fuel line connection with shop towel. Slowly loosen fuel line connection to release fuel pressure. Once fuel pressure is released, fuel system components may be serviced. Remove hood, battery and battery tray. Drain cooling system and engine oil.

4) Disconnect control cables at throttle body. Remove air cleaner assembly and air cleaner case. Remove bolts and disconnect relay box from body. Relay box is located near driver's side strut tower. *See Fig. 12.*

5) Remove upper cover from relay box. Disconnect electrical connector from relay box. *See Fig. 12.* Remove nuts and disconnect engine wiring harness from relay box.

6) Remove charcoal canister. Remove accessory drive belt and generator. Disconnect upper and lower radiator hoses. Remove thermostat housing from front of engine.

7) Disconnect necessary electrical connectors, coolant hoses, vacuum hoses and fuel lines for engine removal. Remove A/C compressor with hoses attached and secure aside.

8) Remove scuff plate from passenger's side door opening and passenger's side kick panel. Remove center console trim panel from passenger's side of center console. *See Fig. 13.*

9) Disconnect 2 electrical connectors from Engine Control Module (ECM) and 2 electrical connectors on bracket. *See Fig. 13.* Disconnect electrical connector for relay box located behind passenger's side kick panel.

10) Disconnect engine wiring harness clamp located on engine wiring harness, near firewall. Pull engine wiring harness out through firewall.

11) Raise and support vehicle. Remove lower engine covers. Disconnect oil cooler lines at transaxle. Disconnect shift cable bracket from engine mount crossmember.

12) Disconnect control cables and electrical connectors at transaxle. Remove front exhaust pipe that fits between front catalytic converter on exhaust manifold and rear exhaust pipe.

13) On 4WD models, place reference marks on drive shaft flanges for reassembly reference. Remove drive shaft flange bolts/nuts at rear axle. Remove drive shaft center support bearing bolts. Pull drive shaft from transaxle. Remove drive shaft.

14) On all models, remove front wheels. Drain transaxle fluid. On models with Anti-Lock Brake System (ABS), remove bolt and pull ABS speed sensor from front of axle carrier.

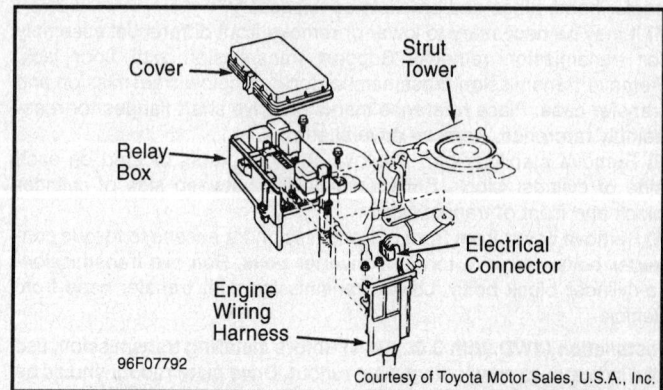

96F07792

Courtesy of Toyota Motor Sales, U.S.A., Inc.

Fig. 12: Identifying Relay Box, Electrical Connector & Engine Wiring Harness

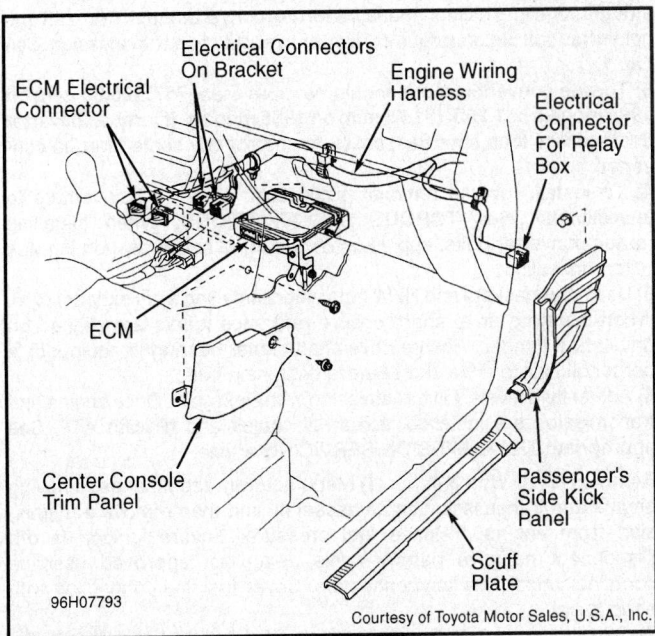

Fig. 13: Identifying ECM & Electrical Connectors

96H07793

Courtesy of Toyota Motor Sales, U.S.A., Inc.

15) On all models, remove cotter pin and retainer from end of axle shaft. Loosen axle shaft nut while applying brakes. Remove axle shaft nut. Remove nut and separate tie rod from steering knuckle. Disconnect stabilizer bar link from lower control arm. Remove ball joint-to-lower control arm bolts/nuts.

16) Remove axle shafts from transaxle. See appropriate AXLE SHAFTS article in AXLE SHAFTS & TRANSFER CASES section. Remove stabilizer bar-to-frame mount bolts. Remove stabilizer bar-to-frame mount bolts. Remove stabilizer bar with mounting brackets and insulators. Remove 2 steering gear assembly-to-front suspension crossmember bolts/nuts located at each end of steering gear assembly.

17) Support engine with hoist. Remove engine mount crossmember-to-front suspension crossmember nuts. Front suspension crossmember fits between both lower control arms.

18) Support front suspension crossmember with floor jack. Remove front suspension crossmember bolts and front suspension crossmember. Remove front (exhaust manifold side) engine mount-to-engine mount crossmember bolts. Remove engine mount crossmember-to-body bolts. Remove engine mount crossmember.

19) Remove power steering pump with hoses attached and secure aside. Remove left (transaxle side) engine mounting bracket-to-engine mount bolts/nuts. Remove right (timing belt side) engine mounting bracket-to-engine mount bolts/nuts. Lower engine from engine compartment. Remove transaxle from engine.

20) With engine and transaxle removed, remove starter. Remove bolts and stiffener plate. Stiffener plate fits between side of cylinder block and front of transaxle.

21) Remove torque converter cover from front of transaxle. Remove torque converter bolts. Remove bolts and center stiffener plate. Center stiffener plate fits between top of transaxle and cylinder block. Remove 2 transfer case-to-cylinder block bolts. Remove transaxle-to-cylinder block bolts. Separate transaxle from engine.

Installation (4WD) – 1) Before installing transaxle, use dial indicator to check drive plate runout. Drive plate runout should be checked right next to starter ring on drive plate. Replace drive plate runout if runout exceeds .0079" (.200 mm).

2) Install torque converter on transaxle. To ensure torque converter is fully seated, torque converter depth should be checked. Using straightedge and caliper, measure torque converter depth from torque converter bolt lug on torque converter to surface on transaxle. *See Fig. 1.*

3) Torque converter depth should be more than .539" (13.70 mm). If torque converter depth is less than specified, check for improperly seated torque converter.

4) Install transaxle to engine. Install engine in engine compartment. Loosely install right (timing belt side) engine mounting bracket-to-engine mount bolts/nuts.

5) Install and tighten left (transaxle side) engine mounting bracket-to-engine mount bolts/nuts to specification. See TORQUE SPECIFICATIONS. Tighten right (timing belt side) engine mounting bracket-to-engine mount bolts/nuts to specification.

6) Install power steering pump. Install and tighten bolts to specification. See TORQUE SPECIFICATIONS. Install engine mount crossmember with front (exhaust manifold side) engine mount-to-engine mount crossmember bolts and engine mount crossmember-to-body bolts loosely installed. DO NOT tighten bolts at this time.

7) Install front suspension crossmember on body with bolts loosely installed. Loosely install engine mount crossmember-to-front suspension crossmember nuts and steering gear assembly-to-front suspension crossmember bolts/nuts. DO NOT tighten bolts/nuts at this time.

8) Install and tighten front suspension crossmember bolts to specification. See TORQUE SPECIFICATIONS. Tighten steering gear assembly-to-front suspension crossmember bolts/nuts and then engine mount crossmember-to-front suspension crossmember nuts to specification. See TORQUE SPECIFICATIONS.

9) Tighten front (exhaust manifold side) engine mount-to-engine mount crossmember bolts and then engine mount crossmember-to-body bolts to specification. See TORQUE SPECIFICATIONS.

10) Install axle shafts. See appropriate AXLE SHAFTS article in AXLE SHAFTS & TRANSFER CASES section. To install remaining components, reverse removal procedure. On 4WD models, ensure reference marks on drive shaft flanges are aligned. Ensure mounting bracket on drive shaft center support bearing is straight and perpendicular to drive shaft before tightening bolts to specification.

11) On all models, use NEW gasket and NEW nuts when installing front exhaust pipe on catalytic converter. Ensure all bolts/nuts are loosely installed before tightening to specification.

12) To complete installation, reverse removal procedure. Tighten all bolts/nuts to specification. See TORQUE SPECIFICATIONS. When installing torque converter bolts, apply Loctite to torque converter bolt threads before installing. Ensure Dark Green-colored torque converter bolt is installed first before installing remaining torque converter bolts.

13) Once engine and transaxle are installed, adjust all cables and fill with ATF. See appropriate TRANSMISSION SERVICING article. On 2WD models with A/T, use Dexron-II ATF. On 4WD models with A/T, use Type "T" ATF.

SUPRA

Removal – 1) Disconnect negative battery cable. Remove transmission oil dipstick, dipstick tube and "O" ring. Disconnect throttle valve cable from throttle body.

2) Raise and support vehicle. Remove lower engine cover. Remove exhaust pipes and heat insulators as necessary for access to transmission. Remove floor crossmember brace located between each side of body and is directly below drive shaft.

CAUTION: When removing drive shaft, DO NOT remove bolts that hold drive shaft on flange. Remove only bolts that fastens flange on drive shaft to flange on rear differential.

3) Place reference marks drive shaft flanges for reassembly reference. Remove drive shaft. Disconnect necessary electrical connectors and oil cooler pipes for transmission removal. Remove shift control rod located between gearshift and shift lever on side of transmission.

4) Remove starter. On Turbo models, remove intercooler pipe located below radiator. On all models, support transmission with floor jack. Remove transmission crossmember located below transmission. Remove torque converter bolts. Remove transmission-to-cylinder block bolts. Lower transmission from vehicle.

Installation – 1) Before installing transmission, use dial indicator to check drive plate runout. Drive plate runout should be checked right next to starter ring on drive plate. Replace drive plate runout if runout exceeds .0079" (.200 mm).

2) Install torque converter on transaxle. To ensure torque converter is fully seated, place straightedge on torque converter bolt mounting lugs on torque converter with straightedge extending out over cylinder block mounting surface on transmission.

3) Using feeler gauge, measure distance between straightedge and cylinder block mounting surface on transmission. Distance should be less than .0040" (.100 mm). If distance is more than specified, check for improperly seated torque converter.

4) To install, reverse removal procedure. Tighten all bolts/nuts to specification. See TORQUE SPECIFICATIONS. When installing torque converter bolts, apply Loctite to torque converter bolt threads before installing. Adjust shift linkage and fill with ATF. See appropriate TRANSMISSION SERVICING article.

TACOMA

Removal (2WD With 2.4L) – 1) Manufacturer recommends removing engine and transmission as an assembly and then remove transmission from engine. Release fuel pressure. Ensure ignition is off. Disconnect negative battery cable. Place an approved gasoline container under fuel line connection. Cover fuel line connection with shop towel.

2) Slowly loosen fuel line connection, allowing fuel pressure to be released. Once fuel pressure is released, fuel system components may be serviced. Drain cooling system and engine oil. Drain transmission oil.

3) Remove hood, front grill, lower fan shroud and radiator. Remove accessory drive belts. Remove cooling fan, fan clutch and water pump. Remove air cleaner cap and airflow meter with air cleaner hose. Remove air cleaner case. Disconnect control cables at throttle body and cruise control actuator (if equipped). Remove intake air connector.

4) Remove A/C compressor with hoses attached and secure aside. Disconnect necessary electrical connectors, coolant hoses, vacuum hoses and fuel lines for engine removal.

5) Remove power steering pump drive belt. Remove nut and pulley from power steering pump. Remove power steering pump with hoses attached and secure aside. Remove glove compartment door and lower finish panel on instrument panel for access to Engine Control Module (ECM).

6) Disconnect electrical connectors from ECM. Disconnect remaining electrical connectors so engine wiring may be pulled out from passenger's corner on firewall. Remove retaining nuts and pull engine wiring out through firewall.

7) Raise and support vehicle. Remove lower engine cover. Place reference marks on drive shaft flange at rear axle. Remove drive shaft with drive shaft center bearing (if equipped). Disconnect speedometer cable and electrical connectors from transmission. DO NOT lose felt protector and washers when disconnecting speedometer cable.

8) Remove front exhaust pipe that fits between exhaust manifold and rear exhaust pipe. Disconnect shift linkage cross shaft. Support transmission with floor jack. Remove rear engine mount-to-crossmember bolts.

9) Support engine with hoist. Remove engine mount-to-frame bolts/nuts. Lift engine and transmission from vehicle. With engine and transmission removed, remove starter. Remove bolts and stiffener plates. Stiffener plate fits between each side of cylinder block and front of transmission.

10) Remove torque converter cover from front of transmission. Remove torque converter bolts. Remove transmission-to-cylinder block bolts. Separate transmission from engine.

Installation (2WD With 2.4L) – 1) Before installing transaxle, use dial indicator to check drive plate runout. Drive plate runout should be checked right next to starter ring on drive plate. Replace drive plate runout if runout exceeds .0079" (.200 mm).

2) Install torque converter on transmission. To ensure torque converter is fully seated, torque converter depth should be checked. Using

straightedge and caliper, measure torque converter depth from torque converter bolt lug on torque converter to surface on transmission. See Fig. 1.

3) Torque converter depth should be more than .787" (20.00 mm) on 1995 models or 1.250" (31.75 mm) on 1996 models. If torque converter depth is less than specified, check for improperly seated torque converter.

4) To install, reverse removal procedure. Tighten all bolts/nuts to specification. See TORQUE SPECIFICATIONS. When installing torque converter bolts, apply Loctite to torque converter bolt threads before installing.

5) Use NEW gaskets and NEW nuts when installing front exhaust pipe. When installing drive shaft, ensure reference marks are aligned on drive shaft flanges. Ensure drive shaft center bearing (if equipped) is perpendicular to drive shaft before tightening bolts.

6) Adjust fluid levels. Fill transmission with Dexron-II. Once engine and transmission are installed, adjust all cables and fill with ATF. See appropriate TRANSMISSION SERVICING article.

Removal (2WD With 3.4L) – 1) Manufacturer recommends removing engine and transmission as an assembly and then remove transmission from engine. Release fuel pressure. Ensure ignition is off. Disconnect negative battery cable. Place an approved gasoline container under fuel line connection. Cover fuel line connection with shop towel.

2) Slowly loosen fuel line connection, allowing fuel pressure to be released. Once fuel pressure is released, fuel system components may be serviced. Drain cooling system and engine oil. Drain transmission oil.

3) Remove hood. Remove radiator. Disconnect heater hoses. Disconnect cruise control and throttle cables. Remove drive belt and remove radiator fan with fan clutch and pulley. Remove air filter case. Disconnect brake booster hose, EVAP hose, fuel return and fuel inlet lines. Remove starter. Disconnect harness connector to generator. Disconnect igniter and ECM harness connectors. ECM is located behind glove compartment.

4) Remove shift control cable. If vehicle is equipped with A/C, remove compressor (do not disconnect hoses) and wire aside. Remove front exhaust pipe. Disconnect speedometer cable. Mark drive shaft for reference and remove drive shaft.

5) Position transmission jack under transmission. Remove transmission rear mounting bracket. Attach engine hoist chain to engine. Remove engine mounts. Lift engine and transmission out of vehicle. Ensure all wiring and hoses attached to engine are disconnected.

6) With engine and transmission removed, remove transmission oil dipstick, dipstick tube and "O" ring. Remove oil cooler pipes and brackets from engine and transmission. Disconnect necessary wiring connectors from transmission.

7) Remove torque converter cover from front of transmission. Remove torque converter bolts. Remove transmission-to-cylinder block bolts. Separate transmission from engine.

Installation (2WD With 3.4L) – 1) Before installing transaxle, use dial indicator to check drive plate runout. Drive plate runout should be checked right next to starter ring on drive plate. Replace drive plate runout if runout exceeds .0079" (.200 mm).

2) Install torque converter on transmission. To ensure torque converter is fully seated, torque converter depth should be checked. Using straightedge and caliper, measure torque converter depth from torque converter bolt lug on torque converter to surface on transmission. See Fig. 1.

3) Torque converter depth should be more than .707" (17.95 mm). If torque converter depth is less than specified, check for improperly seated torque converter.

4) To install, reverse removal procedure. Tighten all bolts/nuts to specification. See TORQUE SPECIFICATIONS. When installing torque converter bolts, apply Loctite to torque converter bolt threads before installing. Ensure Green-colored torque converter bolt is installed first before installing remaining torque converter bolts.

5) Once engine and transmission are installed, adjust all cables and fill with ATF. See appropriate TRANSMISSION SERVICING article.

Removal (4WD) – 1) Disconnect negative battery cable. Remove transmission oil dipstick. Disconnect throttle valve cable from throttle body.

2) Raise and support vehicle. Remove lower engine cover. Remove fan shroud from radiator. Remove rear console box located between seats. Remove screws from front console located near transfer case and transmission shift levers.

3) Remove front console with transfer case shift lever knob. Disconnect electrical connectors for removal of transmission shift lever assembly. Disconnect shift linkage at transmission shift lever assembly. Remove transmission shift lever assembly.

4) Remove snap ring and transfer case shift lever from transfer case. Remove transmission oil dipstick tube and "O" ring. Place reference marks on drive shaft flanges for reassembly reference. Remove drive shafts.

5) Remove exhaust pipes as necessary for access to transmission and transfer case. Disconnect speedometer cable and necessary electrical connectors for transmission and transfer case removal. Remove transmission oil cooler pipes and brackets as necessary.

6) Remove starter and stabilizer bar. Remove torque converter cover from front of transmission. Remove torque converter bolts. Front differential assembly rear mount must be removed for transmission removal. Rear mount is located on front differential assembly, just behind drive shaft flange.

7) Support front differential assembly with jack. Remove front differential assembly rear mount-to-crossmember nut. Slightly raise front differential assembly. Remove 2 front differential assembly rear mount bolts.

8) Support transmission with floor jack. Remove transmission mount-to-transmission crossmember bolts. Remove transmission crossmember located below transmission and transfer case. Remove transmission-to-cylinder block bolts. Lower transmission with transfer case from vehicle.

Installation (4WD) – 1) Before installing transmission, use dial indicator to check drive plate runout. Drive plate runout should be checked right next to starter ring on drive plate. Replace drive plate runout if runout exceeds .0079" (.200 mm).

2) Install torque converter on transmission. To ensure torque converter is fully seated, torque converter depth should be checked. Using straightedge and caliper, measure torque converter depth from torque converter bolt lug on torque converter to surface on transmission. See Fig. 1.

3) Torque converter depth should be more than 1.250" (31.75 mm) on 2.7L 4-cylinder or .707" (17.95 mm) on 3.4L V6. If torque converter depth is less than specified, check for improperly seated torque converter.

4) To install, reverse removal procedure. Tighten all bolts/nuts to specification. See TORQUE SPECIFICATIONS. When installing torque converter bolts, apply Loctite to torque converter bolt threads before installing. Ensure Green-colored torque converter bolt is installed first before installing remaining torque converter bolts.

5) Apply grease to transfer case shift lever before installing. Use NEW gasket when installing exhaust pipe. Adjust all cables, shift linkages and fill with ATF. See appropriate TRANSMISSION SERVICING article.

TERCEL

Removal – 1) Disconnect negative battery cable. Remove battery. Disconnect throttle valve cable from throttle body. Remove air cleaner assembly along with air intake duct to air cleaner.

2) Remove starter. Remove 2 upper transaxle-to-cylinder block bolts located at top of transaxle. Raise and support vehicle. Remove lower engine covers.

3) Support engine with hoist. Remove front wheels. Drain transaxle fluid. Remove axle shafts from transaxle. See appropriate AXLE SHAFTS article in AXLE SHAFTS & TRANSFER CASES section.

4) Disconnect necessary electrical connectors, ground cables, speedometer cable, control cables and oil cooler lines for transaxle removal.

Remove exhaust pipe as necessary for access to transaxle. Support transaxle with transmission jack. Remove 2 vertical bottom bolts from front (radiator side) transaxle mount.

5) Remove through-bolt and rear (firewall side) engine mount assembly for transaxle removal. Remove plug from front of transaxle for access to torque converter bolts. Remove torque converter bolts. Remove remaining transaxle-to-cylinder block bolts. Lower transaxle from vehicle.

Installation – 1) Before installing transaxle, use dial indicator to check drive plate runout. Drive plate runout should be checked right next to starter ring on drive plate. Replace drive plate runout if runout exceeds .0079" (.200 mm).

2) Install torque converter on transaxle. To ensure torque converter is fully seated, torque converter depth should be checked. Using straightedge and caliper, measure torque converter depth from torque converter bolt lug on torque converter to surface on transaxle. See Fig. 1.

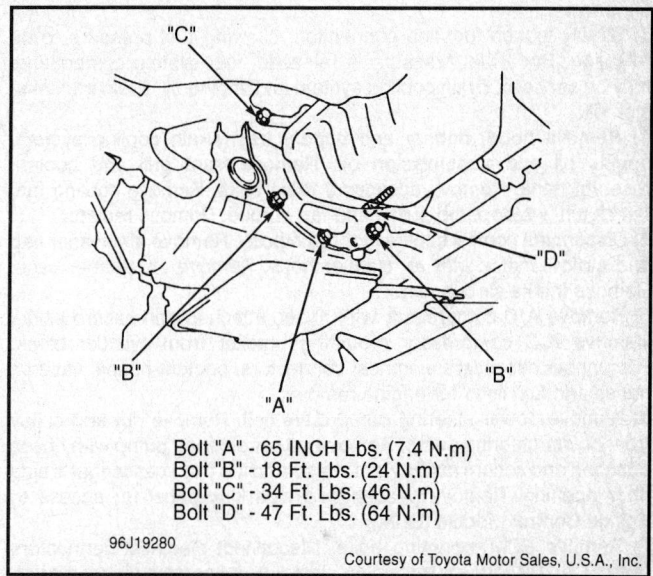

Bolt "A" - 65 INCH Lbs. (7.4 N.m)
Bolt "B" - 18 Ft. Lbs. (24 N.m)
Bolt "C" - 34 Ft. Lbs. (46 N.m)
Bolt "D" - 47 Ft. Lbs. (64 N.m)
96J19280

Courtesy of Toyota Motor Sales, U.S.A., Inc.

Fig. 14: Identifying Transaxle-To-Cylinder Block Bolt Tightening Specifications (Tercel 3-Speed)

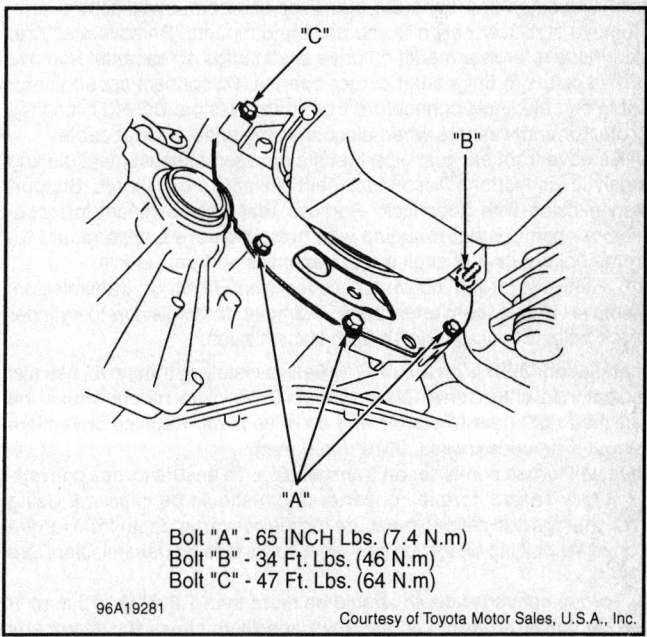

Bolt "A" - 65 INCH Lbs. (7.4 N.m)
Bolt "B" - 34 Ft. Lbs. (46 N.m)
Bolt "C" - 47 Ft. Lbs. (64 N.m)
96A19281

Courtesy of Toyota Motor Sales, U.S.A., Inc.

Fig. 15: Identifying Transaxle-To-Cylinder Block Bolt Tightening Specifications (Tercel 4-Speed)

3) Torque converter depth should be more than .512" (13.00 mm). If torque converter depth is less than specified, check for improperly seated torque converter.

4) To install, reverse removal procedure. Tighten all bolts/nuts to specification. See TORQUE SPECIFICATIONS. Tighten lower transaxle-to-cylinder block bolts to specification as indicated, *see Figs. 14 and 15.*

5) When installing torque converter bolts, apply Loctite to torque converter bolt threads before installing. Adjust all cables and fill with ATF. See appropriate TRANSMISSION SERVICING article.

T100

Removal (2WD With 2.7L) – **1)** Manufacturer recommends removing engine and transmission as an assembly and then remove transmission from engine. Release fuel pressure. Ensure ignition is off. Disconnect negative battery cable. Place an approved gasoline container under fuel line connection. Cover fuel line connection with shop towel.

2) Slowly loosen fuel line connection, allowing fuel pressure to be released. Once fuel pressure is released, fuel system components may be serviced. Drain cooling system and engine oil. Drain transmission oil.

3) Remove hood, battery and battery tray. Drain cooling system, engine oil and transmission oil. Remove front grill and coolant reservoir tank. Remove accessory drive belts. Remove cooling fan, fan clutch, water pump pulley and fan shroud. Remove radiator.

4) Disconnect control cables at throttle body. Remove air cleaner cap and airflow meter with air cleaner hose. Remove air cleaner case. Remove intake air connector.

5) Remove A/C compressor with hoses attached and secure aside. Remove A/C compressor mounting bracket from cylinder block. Disconnect necessary electrical connectors, coolant hoses, vacuum hoses and fuel lines for engine removal.

6) Remove power steering pump drive belt. Remove nut and pulley from power steering pump. Remove power steering pump with hoses attached and secure aside. Remove scuff plate from passenger's side door opening. Remove passenger's side kick panel for access to Engine Control Module (ECM).

7) Remove ECM mounting bolts. Disconnect electrical connectors from ECM. Disconnect remaining electrical connectors so engine wiring can be pulled out from passenger's corner on firewall.

8) Raise and support vehicle. Remove lower engine cover. Remove nuts, bushings and separate stabilizer bar from lower control arm. Remove stabilizer bar-to-frame bolts and mounts. Remove stabilizer bar. Place reference marks on drive shaft flange at rear axle. Remove drive shaft with drive shaft center bearing. Disconnect speedometer cable and electrical connectors from transmission. DO NOT lose felt protector and washers when disconnecting speedometer cable.

9) Remove front exhaust pipe that fits between exhaust manifold and catalytic converter. Disconnect shift linkage cross shaft. Support transmission with floor jack. Remove rear engine mount-to-crossmember bolts. Support engine with hoist. Remove engine mount-to-frame bolts/nuts. Lift engine and transmission from vehicle.

10) Remove torque converter cover from front of transmission. Remove torque converter bolts. Remove transmission-to-cylinder block bolts. Separate engine from transmission.

Installation (2WD With 2.7L) – **1)** Before installing transaxle, use dial indicator to check drive plate runout. Drive plate runout should be checked right next to starter ring on drive plate. Replace drive plate runout if runout exceeds .0079" (.200 mm).

2) Install torque converter on transmission. To ensure torque converter is fully seated, torque converter depth should be checked. Using straightedge and caliper, measure torque converter depth from torque converter bolt lug on torque converter to surface on transmission. *See Fig. 1.*

3) Torque converter depth should be more than 1.205" (31.75 mm). If torque converter depth is less than specified, check for improperly seated torque converter.

4) To install, reverse removal procedure. Tighten all bolts/nuts to specification. See TORQUE SPECIFICATIONS. When installing torque converter bolts, apply Loctite to torque converter bolt threads before installing. Once engine and transmission are installed, adjust all cables and fill with ATF. See appropriate TRANSMISSION SERVICING article.

Removal (2WD With 3.4L) – **1)** Manufacturer recommends removing engine and transmission as an assembly and then remove transmission from engine. Release fuel pressure. Ensure ignition is off. Disconnect negative battery cable. Place an approved gasoline container under fuel line connection. Cover fuel line connection with shop towel.

2) Slowly loosen fuel line connection, allowing fuel pressure to be released. Once fuel pressure is released, fuel system components may be serviced. Drain cooling system and engine oil. Drain transmission oil.

3) Remove hood. Remove radiator assembly. Disconnect heater hoses. Disconnect cruise control and throttle cables. Remove drive belt and remove radiator fan with fan clutch and pulley. Remove air filter case. Disconnect brake booster hose, EVAP hose, fuel return and fuel inlet lines. Remove starter. Disconnect harness connector to generator. Disconnect igniter and ECM harness connectors. ECM is located behind glove compartment.

4) Remove shift control cable. If vehicle is equipped with A/C, remove compressor (do not disconnect hoses) and wire aside. Remove front exhaust pipe. Disconnect speedometer cable. Mark drive shaft for reference and remove drive shaft.

5) Position transmission jack under transmission. Remove transmission rear mounting bracket. Attach engine hoist chain to engine. Remove engine mounts. Lift engine and transmission out of vehicle. Ensure all wiring and hoses attached to engine are disconnected.

6) With engine and transmission removed, remove transmission oil dipstick, dipstick tube and "O" ring. Remove starter if not previously removed. Remove oil cooler pipes and brackets from engine and transmission. Disconnect necessary wiring connectors from transmission.

7) Remove torque converter cover from front of transmission. Remove torque converter bolts. Remove transmission-to-cylinder block bolts. Separate transmission from engine.

Installation (2WD With 3.4L) – **1)** Before installing transaxle, use dial indicator to check drive plate runout. Drive plate runout should be checked right next to starter ring on drive plate. Replace drive plate runout if runout exceeds .0079" (.200 mm).

2) Install torque converter on transmission. To ensure torque converter is fully seated, torque converter depth should be checked. Using straightedge and caliper, measure torque converter depth from torque converter bolt lug on torque converter to surface on transmission. *See Fig. 1.*

3) Torque converter depth should be more than .707" (17.95 mm). If torque converter depth is less than specified, check for improperly seated torque converter.

4) To install, reverse removal procedure. Tighten all bolts/nuts to specification. See TORQUE SPECIFICATIONS. When installing torque converter bolts, apply Loctite to torque converter bolt threads before installing. Once engine and transmission are installed, adjust all cables and fill with ATF. See appropriate TRANSMISSION SERVICING article.

Removal (4WD) – **1)** Disconnect negative battery cable. Remove knob from transfer case shift lever. Remove screws and boot from transfer case shift lever. Remove snap ring and transfer case shift lever from transfer case.

2) Disconnect throttle valve cable from throttle body. Raise and support vehicle. Remove lower engine cover. Remove transmission oil dipstick, dipstick tube and "O" ring.

3) Place reference marks on drive shaft flanges for reassembly reference. Remove drive shafts. Remove front exhaust pipe located between exhaust manifold and catalytic converter.

4) Disconnect speedometer cable and necessary electrical connectors for transmission and transfer case removal. Disconnect shift linkage at side of transmission. Remove shift linkage cross shaft located between frame and shift lever on transmission.

5) Remove starter. Remove transmission oil cooler pipes and brackets as necessary. Remove stiffener plates located on each side of cylinder block. Stiffener plate fits between side of cylinder block and front of transmission.

6) Remove stabilizer bar. Support transmission with floor jack. Remove bolts and dynamic damper transmission crossmember. Dynamic damper is located on driver's side of transmission crossmember, next to transmission mount bolts and is fastened to bottom of transmission crossmember using 2 bolts.

7) Remove transmission mount-to-transmission crossmember bolts. Remove transmission crossmember located below transmission and transfer case.

8) Remove torque converter cover from front of transmission. Remove torque converter bolts. Remove transmission-to-cylinder block bolts. Lower transmission with transfer case from vehicle.

Installation (4WD) – 1) Before installing transmission, use dial indicator to check drive plate runout. Drive plate runout should be checked right next to starter ring on drive plate. Replace drive plate runout if runout exceeds .0079" (.200 mm).

2) Install torque converter on transmission. To ensure torque converter is fully seated, torque converter depth should be checked. Using straightedge and caliper, measure torque converter depth from torque converter bolt lug on torque converter to surface on transmission. See Fig. 1.

3) Torque converter depth should be more than .707" (17.95 mm). If torque converter depth is less than specified, check for improperly seated torque converter.

4) To install, reverse removal procedure. Tighten all bolts/nuts to specification. See TORQUE SPECIFICATIONS. When installing torque converter bolts, apply Loctite to torque converter bolt threads before installing.

5) Apply grease to transfer case shift lever before installing. Use NEW gasket when installing front exhaust pipe. Adjust all cables, shift linkages and fill with ATF. See appropriate TRANSMISSION SERVICING article.

4RUNNER

Removal (1995 2WD 3.0L V6 & 4WD 2.4L 4-Cyl.) – 1) Disconnect negative battery cable. Remove transmission oil dipstick, dipstick tube and "O" ring. Disconnect throttle valve cable from throttle body.

2) Raise and support vehicle. Remove lower engine cover. Remove starter. Disconnect shift linkage at transmission. On 4WD models, remove transfer case shift lever from transmission.

3) On 2WD models, disconnect front exhaust pipe at exhaust manifold. Remove front exhaust pipe support bracket. It may be necessary to remove front exhaust pipe.

4) On all models, disconnect necessary electrical connectors for transmission removal. Remove transmission oil cooler pipes and brackets as necessary.

5) Support transmission with floor jack. On 2WD models, remove rear transmission mount from rear of transmission. On all models, remove transmission crossmember located below transmission.

6) Place reference marks on drive shaft flanges for reassembly reference. Remove drive shaft(s) as necessary. On 2WD models, remove stabilizer bar.

7) On all models, remove stiffener plates located on each side of cylinder block. Stiffener plate fits between side of cylinder block and front of transmission.

8) Remove cover from front of transmission for access to torque converter bolts. Remove torque converter bolts. Remove transmission-to-cylinder block bolts. Lower transmission from vehicle.

Installation (1995 2WD 3.0L V6 & 4WD 2.4L 4-Cyl.) – 1) Before installing transmission, use dial indicator to check drive plate runout. Drive plate runout should be checked right next to starter ring on drive plate. Replace drive plate runout if runout exceeds .0079" (.200 mm).

2) Install torque converter on transmission. To ensure torque converter is fully seated, torque converter depth should be checked. Using straightedge and caliper, measure torque converter depth from torque converter bolt lug on torque converter to surface on transmission. See Fig. 1.

3) Torque converter depth should be more than .787" (20.00 mm). If torque converter depth is less than specified, check for improperly seated torque converter.

4) To install, reverse removal procedure. Tighten all bolts/nuts to specification. See TORQUE SPECIFICATIONS. When installing torque converter bolts, apply Loctite to torque converter bolt threads before installing.

5) Use NEW gasket when installing front exhaust pipe. Adjust all cables, shift linkages and fill with ATF. See appropriate TRANSMISSION SERVICING article.

Removal (1995 4WD 3.0L V6) – 1) Disconnect negative battery cable. Remove transmission oil dipstick, dipstick tube and "O" ring. Disconnect throttle valve cable from throttle body.

2) Raise and support vehicle. Remove lower engine cover. Disconnect shift linkage at transmission. Disconnect shift linkage for transfer case at transfer case shift linkage cross shaft located at rear of transfer case. Remove transfer case shift linkage cross shaft.

3) It may be necessary to remove front exhaust pipe located between exhaust manifolds and catalytic converter on rear exhaust pipe. Disconnect speedometer cable, necessary electrical connectors for transmission and transfer case removal. Remove transmission oil cooler hose, pipes and brackets as necessary.

4) It may be necessary to lower or remove front differential assembly for transmission removal. Support transmission with floor jack. Remove transmission crossmember located below transmission and transfer case. Place reference marks on drive shaft flanges for reassembly reference. Remove drive shafts.

5) Remove stabilizer bar. Remove stiffener plates located on each side of cylinder block. Stiffener plate fits between side of cylinder block and front of transmission.

6) Remove cover from front of transmission for access to torque converter bolts. Remove torque converter bolts. Remove transmission-to-cylinder block bolts. Lower transmission with transfer case from vehicle.

Installation (1995 4WD 3.0L V6) – 1) Before installing transmission, use dial indicator to check drive plate runout. Drive plate runout should be checked right next to starter ring on drive plate. Replace drive plate runout if runout exceeds .0079" (.200 mm).

2) Install torque converter on transmission. To ensure torque converter is fully seated, torque converter depth should be checked. Using straightedge and caliper, measure torque converter depth from torque converter bolt lug on torque converter to surface on transmission. See Fig. 1.

3) Torque converter depth should be more than .709" (18.00 mm). If torque converter depth is less than specified, check for improperly seated torque converter.

4) To install, reverse removal procedure. Tighten all bolts/nuts to specification. See TORQUE SPECIFICATIONS. When installing torque converter bolts, apply Loctite to torque converter bolt threads before installing.

5) Use NEW gasket when installing front exhaust pipe. Adjust all cables, shift linkages and fill with ATF. See appropriate TRANSMISSION SERVICING article.

Removal (1996 2WD) – 1) Disconnect negative battery cable. Remove transmission oil dipstick, dipstick tube and "O" ring. Disconnect throttle valve cable from throttle body.

2) Raise and support vehicle. Remove lower engine cover. Disconnect shift linkage for transmission at gearshift. Remove front exhaust pipe located between exhaust manifold and catalytic converter on rear exhaust pipe.

3) Place reference marks on drive shaft flange for reassembly reference. Remove drive shaft. Disconnect necessary electrical connectors for transmission removal. Remove transmission oil cooler pipes and brackets as necessary.

4) Support transmission with floor jack. Remove transmission crossmember located below transmission. Remove starter. Remove cover from front of transmission for access to torque converter bolts. Remove torque converter bolts. Remove transmission-to-cylinder block bolts. Lower transmission from vehicle.

Installation (1996 2WD) – 1) Before installing transmission, use dial indicator to check drive plate runout. Drive plate runout should be checked right next to starter ring on drive plate. Replace drive plate runout if runout exceeds .0079" (.200 mm).

2) Install torque converter on transmission. To ensure torque converter is fully seated, torque converter depth should be checked. Using straightedge and caliper, measure torque converter depth from torque converter bolt lug on torque converter to surface on transmission. See Fig. 1.

3) Torque converter depth should be more than 1.250" (31.75 mm) on 2.7L 4-cylinder or .707" (17.95 mm) on 3.4L V6. If torque converter depth is less than specified, check for improperly seated torque converter.

4) To install, reverse removal procedure. Tighten all bolts/nuts to specification. See TORQUE SPECIFICATIONS. When installing torque converter bolts, apply Loctite to torque converter bolt threads before installing. On 3.4L V6, ensure Green-colored torque converter bolt is installed first before installing remaining torque converter bolts.

5) Use NEW gasket when installing front exhaust pipe. Adjust all cables, shift linkages and fill with ATF. See appropriate TRANSMISSION SERVICING article.

Removal (1996 4WD) – 1) Disconnect negative battery cable. Remove rear console upper panel and disconnect electrical connectors. Rear console upper panel is located on top of console, near emergency brake lever.

2) Remove heater control knobs from instrument panel. Using screwdriver, pry heater control plate from center finish panel on instrument panel. Center finish panel is panel that fits around radio and air outlet ducts located at center of instrument panel.

3) Remove screws and disconnect electrical connectors from center finish panel from instrument panel. Remove center finish panel.

4) On models without 2-4 selector button on side of transfer case shift lever, unscrew knob from transfer case shift lever. On models with 2-4 selector button on side of transfer case shift lever, remove screw from knob on transfer case shift lever. Remove knob from transfer case shift lever and lay aside with wire attached.

5) On all models, remove upper console panel which contains boot for transfer case shift lever and is located on center console. On models with 2-4 selector button on side of transfer case shift lever, disconnect electrical connector for 2-4 selector button and remove knob on transfer case shift lever.

6) On all models, remove screws, clips and front console box located around transmission shift lever assembly and transfer case shift lever. Raise and support vehicle. Disconnect shift linkage at transmission shift lever.

7) Disconnect electrical connectors for removal of transmission shift lever assembly. Remove transmission shift lever assembly. Remove snap ring and transfer case shift lever.

8) Remove transmission oil dipstick, dipstick tube and "O" ring. Remove lower engine covers. Place reference marks on drive shaft flanges for reassembly reference. Remove drive shafts.

9) Remove front exhaust pipe located between exhaust manifold and catalytic converter on rear exhaust pipe. Disconnect and necessary electrical connectors for transmission and transfer case removal. Separate wiring harness from transmission and transfer case.

10) Remove starter. Remove transmission oil cooler pipes and brackets as necessary. On 3.4L V6, it may be necessary to remove stabilizer bar.

11) On all models, support transmission with floor jack. Remove rear transmission mount-to-transmission crossmember bolts. Remove transmission crossmember located below transmission and transfer case.

12) Remove torque converter cover from front of transmission. Remove torque converter bolts. Remove transmission-to-cylinder block bolts. Lower transmission with transfer case from vehicle.

Installation (1996 4WD) – 1) Before installing transmission, use dial indicator to check drive plate runout. Drive plate runout should be checked right next to starter ring on drive plate. Replace drive plate runout if runout exceeds .0079" (.200 mm).

2) Install torque converter on transmission. To ensure torque converter is fully seated, torque converter depth should be checked. Using straightedge and caliper, measure torque converter depth from torque converter bolt lug on torque converter to surface on transmission. See Fig. 1.

3) Torque converter depth should be more than 1.250" (31.75 mm) on 2.7L 4-cylinder or .707" (17.95 mm) on 3.4L V6. If torque converter depth is less than specified, check for improperly seated torque converter.

4) To install, reverse removal procedure. Tighten all bolts/nuts to specification. See TORQUE SPECIFICATIONS. When installing torque converter bolts, apply Loctite to torque converter bolt threads before installing. On 3.4L V6, ensure Green-colored torque converter bolt is installed first before installing remaining torque converter bolts.

5) Apply grease to transfer case shift lever before installing. Use NEW gasket when installing front exhaust pipe. Adjust all cables, shift linkages and fill with ATF. See appropriate TRANSMISSION SERVICING article.

TORQUE SPECIFICATIONS

TORQUE SPECIFICATIONS (AVALON)

Application	Ft. Lbs. (N.m)
Drive Plate-To-Crankshaft Bolt	61 (83)
Front Exhaust Pipe Support Bracket Bolt	14 (19)
Front Exhaust Pipe-To-Exhaust Manifold Nut	46 (62)
Front Exhaust Pipe-To-Rear Exhaust Pipe Bolt/Nut	41 (56)
Front (Radiator Side) Engine Mount Shock Absorber-To-Lower Frame Assembly Bolt	35 (47)
Front (Radiator Side) Engine Mount-To-Lower Frame Assembly Bolt/Nut	
1995	59 (80)
1996	48 (65)
Lower Frame Assembly Mounting Bracket-To-Body Bolt	
Large Bolt	134 (182)
Small Bolt	24 (33)
Nut	27 (37)
Rear (Firewall Side) Engine Mount-To-Lower Frame Assembly Bolt/Nut	49 (66)
Stabilizer Bar Mount Bracket-To-Lower Frame Assembly Bolt	14 (19)
Starter Bolt	29 (39)
Steering Gear Assembly-To-Lower Frame Assembly Bolt/Nut	134 (182)
Torque Converter Bolt	20 (27)
Transaxle Mount-To-Transaxle Bolt	47 (64)
Transaxle-To-Cylinder Block Bolt	
12-mm	34 (46)
17-mm	47 (64)
Wheel Lug Nut	76 (103)

TORQUE SPECIFICATIONS (CAMRY)

Application	Ft. Lbs. (N.m)
Drive Plate-To-Crankshaft Bolt	61 (83)
Front Exhaust Pipe Support Bracket Bolt (3.0L V6)	14 (19)
Front Exhaust Pipe-To-Exhaust Manifold Nut	46 (62)
Front Exhaust Pipe-To-Rear Exhaust Pipe Bolt/Nut	41 (56)
Front (Radiator Side) Engine Mount Shock Absorber-To-Lower Frame Assembly Bolt (3.0L V6)	35 (47)
Front (Radiator Side) Engine Mount-To-Lower Frame Assembly Bolt/Nut	
2.2L 4-Cyl.	59 (80)
3.0L V6	
1995	59 (80)
1996	
Toyota Motor Corporation	59 (80)
Toyota Motor Manufacturing	48 (65)
Lower Frame Assembly Bracket-To-Body Bolt/Nut	
Large Bolt	134 (182)
Small Bolt	24 (33)
Nut	27 (37)

TORQUE SPECIFICATIONS (CAMRY) (Cont.)

Application	Ft. Lbs. (N.m)
Rear (Firewall Side) Engine Mount-To-Lower Frame Assembly Bolt/Nut	49 (66)
Stabilizer Bar Mount Bracket-To-Lower Frame Assembly Bolt	14 (19)
Starter Bolt	29 (39)
Steering Gear Assembly-To-Lower Frame Assembly Bolt/Nut	134 (182)
Stiffener Plate Bolt	
2.2L 4-Cyl.	27 (37)
Torque Converter Bolt	20 (27)
Transaxle Mount-To-Transaxle Bolt	
2.2L 4-Cyl.	38 (52)
3.0L V6	47 (64)
Transaxle-To-Cylinder Block Bolt	
10-mm	34 (46)
12-mm	47 (64)
Wheel Lug Nut	76 (103)

TORQUE SPECIFICATIONS (CELICA)

Application	Ft. Lbs. (N.m)
Drive Plate-To-Crankshaft Bolt	47 (64)
Engine Mount Crossmember Bolt/Nut	
2.2L (5S-FE)	1
Engine Mount Crossmember-To-Body Bolt	
1.8L (7A-FE)	26 (35)
Front (Exhaust Manifold Side) Engine Mount-To-Suspension Crossmember Bolt/Nut	
1.8L (7A-FE)	59 (80)
Front Exhaust Pipe Support Bracket-To-Suspension Crossmember Bolt/Nut	14 (19)
Front Exhaust Pipe-To-Rear Exhaust Pipe Bolt/Nut	31 (42)
Front Exhaust Pipe-To-Exhaust Manifold Nut	46 (62)
Front Exhaust Pipe-To-Front Exhaust Pipe Support Bracket Bolt	18 (24)
Intake Manifold Brace Bolt/Nut	
2.2L (5S-FE)	
Bolt	15 (20)
Nut	32 (43)
Rear (Firewall Side) Engine Mount Through-Bolt	64 (87)
Rear (Firewall Side) Engine Mount-To-Suspension Crossmember Bolt/Nut	
1.8L (7A-FE)	59 (80)
Starter Bolt	29 (39)
Steering Gear Assembly-To-Suspension Crossmember Bolt	94 (127)
Stiffener Plate Bolt	
2.2L (5S-FE)	
12-mm	15 (20)
14-mm	32 (43)
Suspension Crossmember Bolt/Nut	
1.8L (7A-FE)	2
2.2L (5S-FE)	1
Torque Converter Bolt	18 (24)
Transaxle-To-Cylinder Block Bolt	
1.8L (7A-FE)	3
2.2L (5S-FE)	
10-mm	34 (46)
12-mm	47 (64)
Starter Bolt	29 (39)
Steering Gear Assembly-To-Suspension Crossmember Bolt	94 (127)
Stiffener Plate Bolt	
2.2L (5S-FE)	
12-mm	15 (20)
14-mm	32 (43)
Suspension Crossmember Bolt/Nut	
1.8L (7A-FE)	2
2.2L (5S-FE)	1
Torque Converter Bolt	18 (24)
Transaxle-To-Cylinder Block Bolt	
1.8L (7A-FE)	
2 Bolts At Top Of Transaxle	47 (64)
5 Bolts At Bottom Of Transaxle	3

[1] – For bolt/nut tightening specifications, *see Fig. 4.*
[2] – For bolt tightening specifications, *see Fig. 2.*
[3] – For bolt tightening specifications, *see Fig. 3.*

TORQUE SPECIFICATIONS (CELICA) (Cont.)

Application	Ft. Lbs. (N.m)
2.2L (5S-FE)	
3 Bolts At Top Of Transaxle	47 (64)
3 Bolts At Bottom Of Transaxle	
10-mm	34 (46)
12-mm	47 (64)
Transaxle-To-Mount Bolt/Nut	47 (64)
Wheel Lug Nut	76 (103)

[1] – For bolt/nut tightening specifications, *see Fig. 4.*
[2] – For bolt tightening specifications, *see Fig. 2.*
[3] – For bolt tightening specifications, *see Fig. 3.*

TORQUE SPECIFICATIONS (COROLLA)

Application	Ft. Lbs. (N.m)
Drive Plate-To-Crankshaft Bolt	47 (64)
Engine Mount Crossmember Bolt/Nut	1
Front Exhaust Pipe Support Bracket-To-Suspension Crossmember Bolt/Nut	14 (19)
Front Exhaust Pipe-To-Front Exhaust Pipe Support Bracket Bolt	14 (19)
Front Exhaust Pipe-To-Exhaust Manifold Nut	46 (62)
Front Exhaust Pipe-To-Rear Exhaust Pipe Bolt	32 (43)
Starter Bolt	29 (39)
Stiffener Plate Bolt	
1.6L (4A-FE)	17 (23)
Suspension Crossmember Bolt/Nut	1
Torque Converter Bolt	
1.6L (4A-FE)	13 (18)
1.8L (7A-FE)	18 (24)
Transaxle Mount Assembly Bolt	
1.6L (4A-FE)	47 (64)
1.8L (7A-FE)	41 (56)
Transaxle Mount Assembly Brace Bolt	15 (20)
Transaxle-To-Cylinder Block Bolt	
1.6L (4A-FE)	47 (64)
1.8L (7A-FE)	2
Wheel Lug Nut	76 (103)

[1] – For bolt/nut tightening specifications, *see Figs. 5 and 6.*
[2] – For bolt tightening specifications, *see Fig. 7.*

TORQUE SPECIFICATIONS (LAND CRUISER)

Application	Ft. Lbs. (N.m)
Drive Plate-To-Crankshaft Bolt	72 (98)
Drive Shaft Flange Bolt/Nut	
Front Drive Shaft	54 (73)
Rear Drive Shaft	65 (88)
Front Exhaust Pipe-To-Exhaust Manifold Nut	46 (62)
Front Exhaust Pipe-To-Rear Catalytic Converter Bolt/Nut	29 (39)
Front Exhaust Support Bracket Bolt	29 (39)
Stabilizer Bar-To-Frame Mounting Bracket Bolt	13 (18)
Starter Bolt	29 (39)
Torque Converter Bolt	40 (54)
Transfer Case Shift Lever Assembly Bolt	13 (18)
Transmission Crossmember Bolt/Nut	
Bolt	45 (61)
Nut	54 (73)
Transmission-To-Cylinder Block Bolt	53 (72)

	INCH Lbs. (N.m)
Transmission Shift Lever Assembly Bolt	48 (5.4)

TORQUE SPECIFICATIONS (MR2)

Application	Ft. Lbs. (N.m)
Drive Plate-To-Crankshaft Bolt	61 (83)
Front (Exhaust Manifold Side) Engine Mount Bolt/Nut	
Body Side	54 (73)
Transaxle Side	57 (77)
Through-Bolt	71 (96)
Front Exhaust Pipe Support Bracket Bolt	14 (19)
Front Exhaust Pipe-To-Exhaust Manifold Nut	46 (62)
Front Exhaust Pipe-To-Rear Tailpipe Assembly Bolt	32 (43)

[1] – For bolt tightening specifications, see Fig. 8.
[2] – For bolt tightening specifications, see Fig. 9.

TORQUE SPECIFICATIONS (MR2) – (Cont.)

Application	Ft. Lbs. (N.m)
Lateral Control Rod Assembly Bolt	1
Lower Control Arm-To-Suspension Crossmember Bolt	98 (133)
Rear (Intake Manifold Side) Engine Mount Bolt/Nut	
Transaxle Side	57 (77)
Through-Bolt	64 (87)
Suspension Crossmember Side	47 (64)
Starter Bolt	29 (39)
Stiffener Plate Bolt	27 (37)
Suspension Crossmember-To-Body Bolt	83 (113)
Suspension Rod-To-Axle Carrier Bolt/Nut	76 (103)
Torque Converter Bolt	20 (27)
Transaxle Mount Assembly Bolt	1
Transaxle Mount Assembly Bracket Bolt	47 (64)
Transaxle-To-Cylinder Block Bolt	2
Wheel Lug Nut	76 (103)

1 – For bolt tightening specifications, *see Fig. 8.*
2 – For bolt tightening specifications, *see Fig. 9.*

TORQUE SPECIFICATIONS (PASEO)

Application	Ft. Lbs. (N.m)
Drive Plate-To-Crankshaft Bolt	61 (83)
Front (Radiator Side) Transaxle Mount Bolt	35 (47)
Intake Manifold Brace Bolt/Nut	
1996 Models	15 (20)
Rear (Firewall) Engine Mount Assy.-To-Body Bolt	
Outside Small Bolts (2)	58 (79)
Center Large Bolts (3)	67 (91)
Stabilizer Bar Mounting Bracket-To-Frame Bolt	14 (19)
Stabilizer Bar-To-Lower Control Arm Bolt	13 (18)
Starter Bolt	29 (39)
Torque Converter Bolt	13 (18)
Transaxle Bracket-To-Rear (Firewall Side) Engine	
Mount Assembly Bolt	47 (64)
Transaxle-To-Cylinder Block Bolt	1
Wheel Lug Nut	76 (103)

1 – For bolt tightening specifications, *see Fig. 10.*

TORQUE SPECIFICATIONS (PICKUP)

Application	Ft. Lbs. (N.m)
Drive Plate-To-Crankshaft Bolt	61 (83)
Drive Shaft Center Bearing Assembly-To-Body Bolt	27 (37)
Drive Shaft Flange Bolt/Nut	54 (73)
Front Differential-To-Body Bolt	
4WD 3.0L V6	123 (167)
Front Differential-To-Front Mounting Bracket Bolt	
At Front Of Differential	
4WD 3.0L V6	108 (146)
Front Exhaust Pipe Support Bracket Bolt	
2WD 2.4L 4-Cyl.	14 (19)
2WD 3.0L V6 & 4WD 3.0L V6	29 (39)
Front Exhaust Pipe-To-Catalytic Converter Bolt/Nut	
2WD 3.0L V6 & 4WD 3.0L V6	29 (39)
Front Exhaust Pipe-To-Exhaust Manifold Nut	46 (62)
Lower Crossmember Bolt	70 (95)
Rear Transmission Mount-To-Transmission Bolt	
2WD 2.4L 4-Cyl.	29 (39)
2WD 3.0L V6	18 (24)
Stabilizer Bar Mounting Bracket-To-Frame Bolt	
2WD 3.0L V6 & 4WD 3.0L V6	22 (30)
Starter Bolt	29 (39)
Stiffener Plate Bolt	27 (37)
Torque Converter Bolt	
2WD 2.4L 4-Cyl.	20 (27)
All Others	30 (41)
Transmission Crossmember-To-Frame Bolt	
4WD 2.4L Cyl. & 4WD 3.0L V6	70 (95)
Transmission Mount Bracket-To-Crossmember Bolt	43 (58)
Transmission-To-Cylinder Block Bolt	1

	INCH Lbs. (N.m)
Rear Transmission Mount-To-Transmission	
Mount Bracket Bolt	115 (13.0)
Stabilizer Bar-To-Lower Control Arm Bolt/Nut	
2WD 3.0L V6 & 4WD 3.0L V6	115 (13.0)

1 – Information is not available from manufacturer.

TORQUE SPECIFICATIONS (PREVIA)

Application	Ft. Lbs. (N.m)
Drive Plate-To-Crankshaft Bolt	54 (73)
Drive Shaft Center Bearing Assembly-To-Body Bolt	
4WD Front Drive Shaft	27 (37)
Drive Shaft Flange Bolt/Nut	
2WD	54 (73)
4WD	
Front Drive Shaft	31 (42)
Rear Drive Shaft	54 (73)
Exhaust Pipe Support Bracket Bolt	
Exhaust Pipe Side	32 (43)
Transmission Side	38 (51)
Front Drive Shaft Bracket Bolt	
4WD	
Lower Bolt	41 (56)
Upper Bolt Nearest Starter	22 (30)
Lower Stiffener Plate Bolt	
2WD	27 (37)
Rear Transmission Mount Bolt/Nut	
Non-Supercharged	21 (29)
Supercharged	50 (68)
Torque Converter Bolt	30 (41)
Transmission-To-Cylinder Block Bolt	53 (72)
Upper Stiffener Plate Bolt	27 (37)

TORQUE SPECIFICATIONS (RAV4)

Application	Ft. Lbs. (N.m)
A/C Compressor Bolt/Nut	
Bolt	27 (37)
Nut	20 (27)
Stud Bolt	34 (46)
Ball Joint-To-Lower Control Arm Bolt/Nut	94 (127)
Cylinder Block-To-Transaxle Bolt (2WD)	
Lower Bolt (Large Bolt)	34 (46)
Upper Bolt (Small Bolt)	18 (24)
Drive Plate-To-Crankshaft Bolt	61 (83)
Drive Shaft Center Support Bearing Bolt (4WD)	27 (37)
Drive Shaft Flange Bolt/Nut (4WD)	54 (73)
Engine Mounts & Brackets	
Front (Exhaust Manifold Side) Engine Mount-To-Engine	
Mount Crossmember Bolt	59 (80)
Left (Transaxle Side) Engine Mounting	
Bracket-To-Engine Mount Bolt/Nut	47 (64)
Right (Timing Belt Side) Engine Mounting	
Bracket-To-Cylinder Block Bolt	38 (52)
Right (Timing Belt Side) Engine Mount-To-Body Bolt	47 (64)
Right (Timing Belt Side) Engine Mounting	
Bracket-To-Engine Mount Bolt/Nut	
Bolt	27 (37)
Nut	38 (52)
Engine Mount Crossmember Bolt/Nut (2WD)	1
Engine Mount Crossmember-To-Body Bolt	26 (35)
Engine Mount Crossmember-To-Front Suspension	
Crossmember Nut	82 (111)
Exhaust Manifold Nut	36 (49)
Flywheel/Drive Plate Bolt	61 (83)
Front Catalytic Converter Brace Bolt/Nut	31 (42)
Front Catalytic Converter-To-Exhaust Manifold Bolt/Nut	21 (29)
Front Exhaust Pipe-To-Front Catalytic Converter Nut	46 (62)
Front Exhaust Pipe-To-Rear Exhaust Pipe Bolt/Nut	35 (47)
Front Suspension Crossmember Bolt	
Bolt At Body	152 (206)
Bolt At Lower Control Arm	101 (137)
Fuel Line-To-Fuel Filter Union Bolt	21 (29)
Fuel Pipe-To-Delivery Pipe Union Bolt	25 (34)
Generator Adjusting Bracket Bolt	20 (27)
Generator Mounting Bracket Bolt	31 (42)
Power Steering Pump Bolt	32 (43)
Power Steering Pump Mounting Bracket-To-Cylinder	
Block Bolt	32 (43)
Stabilizer Bar Link-To-Lower Control Arm Nut	
3-Door Vehicles	47 (64)
5-Door Vehicles	83 (113)
Stabilizer Bar-To-Frame Mount Bolt	21 (29)
Starter Bolt	29 (39)
Steering Gear Assembly-To-Front Suspension	
Crossmember Bolt/Nut	83 (113)
Stiffener Plate Bolt	27 (37)

1 – For bolt/nut tightening specifications, see Fig. 11.

TORQUE SPECIFICATIONS (RAV4) (Cont.)

Application	Ft. Lbs. (N.m)
Suspension Crossmember Bolt/Nut	
2WD	[1]
Tie Rod Nut	36 (49)
Torque Converter Bolt	20 (27)
Transaxle-To-Cylinder Block Bolt	
2WD	47 (64)
4WD	
12-mm	34 (46)
14-mm	47 (64)
Transaxle-To-Mount Bolt/Nut (2WD)	47 (64)
Transfer Case-To-Cylinder Block Bolt (4WD)	27 (37)
Wheel Lug Nut	76 (103)

	INCH Lbs. (N.m)
ABS Speed Sensor Bolt	71 (8.0)
Fuel Delivery Pipe-To-Cylinder Head Bolt	115 (13.0)
Thermostat Housing Nut	78 (8.8)

[1] – For bolt/nut tightening specifications, *see Fig. 11.*

TORQUE SPECIFICATIONS (SUPRA)

Application	Ft. Lbs. (N.m)
Drive Plate-To-Crankshaft Bolt	
Non-Turbo	54 (73)
Turbo	47 (64)
Drive Shaft Center Bearing Assembly-To-Body Bolt	36 (49)
Drive Shaft Flange Bolt/Nut	57 (77)
Starter Bolt	27 (37)
Torque Converter Bolt	
Non-Turbo	
1995	25 (34)
1996	30 (41)
Turbo	
1995	25 (34)
1996	40 (54)
Transmission Crossmember Bolt	18 (24)
Transmission-To-Cylinder Block Bolt	
14-mm	27 (37)
17-mm	53 (72)

	INCH Lbs. (N.m)
Floor Crossmember Brace Bolt	115 (13.0)

TORQUE SPECIFICATIONS (TACOMA)

Application	Ft. Lbs. (N.m)
A/C Compressor Bolt (4-Cyl.)	18 (24)
A/C Compressor Mounting Bracket Bolt (4-Cyl.)	32 (43)
Accessory Drive Pulley Bolt (4-Cyl.)	18 (24)
Cooling Fan & Fan Clutch-To-Water Pump	
Nut (4-Cyl.)	15 (20)
Drive Plate-To-Crankshaft Bolt	
2.4L 4-Cyl. & 2.7L 4-Cyl.	54 (73)
3.4L V6	61 (83)
Drive Shaft Center Bearing Assembly-To-Crossmember	
Bolt (4WD)	27 (37)
Drive Shaft Flange Bolt/Nut (4WD)	54 (73)
Engine Mount Insulator	
Front (V6)	28 (38)
Rear (V6)	13 (18)
Engine Mount-To-Frame Bolt/Nut (4-Cyl.)	28 (38)
Exhaust Crossover Pipe Nut (V6)	33 (45)
Exhaust Manifold Nut (V6)	30 (40)
Front Differential Assembly Rear Mount Bolt (4WD)	80 (109)
Front Differential Assembly Rear Mount	
To-Crossmember Nut (4WD)	64 (87)
Front Exhaust Pipe-To-Catalytic Converter Bolt/Nut (4-Cyl.)	29 (39)
Front Exhaust Pipe-To-Exhaust Manifold Nut (4-Cyl.)	46 (52)
Power Steering Pump Bolt (4-Cyl.)	43 (58)
Power Steering Pump Bracket Bolt	15 (20)
Power Steering Pump Idler Pulley Bolt (4-Cyl.)	15 (20)
Power Steering Pump Pulley Nut (4-Cyl.)	32 (43)
Rear Engine Mount-To-Crossmember Bolt	
4-Cyl.	19 (26)
V6	43 (58)
Rear Engine Mount-To-Mounting Bracket Bolt (4-Cyl.)	13 (18)

TORQUE SPECIFICATIONS (TACOMA) (Cont.)

Application	Ft. Lbs. (N.m)
Rear Engine Mount-To-Mounting Bracket	
To Frame Bolt (V6)	13 (18)
To Insulator Bolt (V6)	43 (58)
Stabilizer Bar Link-To-Lower Control Arm Nut (4WD)	51 (69)
Stabilizer Bar Mounting Bracket-To-Frame Bolt (4WD)	19 (26)
Starter Bolt	29 (39)
Stiffener Plate Bolt	
2WD 2.4L 4-Cyl.	27 (37)
Transmission Crossmember Bolt/Nut (4WD)	48 (65)
Transmission-To-Cylinder Block Bolt	
4-Cyl.	53 (72)
V6	53 (65)
Transmission Mount-To-Transmission Crossmember	
Bolt (4WD)	14 (19)
Torque Converter Bolt	30 (41)

TORQUE SPECIFICATIONS (TERCEL)

Application	Ft. Lbs. (N.m)
Drive Plate-To-Crankshaft Bolt	65 (88)
Front (Radiator Side) Transaxle Mount Bolt	36 (49)
Rear (Firewall) Engine Mount Assy.-To-Body Bolt	
Outside Small Bolts (2)	59 (80)
Center Large Bolts (3)	68 (92)
Rear (Firewall) Engine Mount Through-Bolt	48 (65)
Starter Bolt	29 (39)
Torque Converter Bolt	20 (27)
Transaxle-To-Cylinder Block Bolt	
Upper Bolt	47 (64)
Lower Bolt	[1]
Wheel Lug Nut	76 (103)

[1] – For bolt tightening specifications, *see Figs. 14 and 15.*

TORQUE SPECIFICATIONS (T100)

Application	Ft. Lbs. (N.m)
A/C Compressor Bolt (4-Cyl.)	18 (24)
A/C Compressor Mounting Bracket Bolt (4-Cyl.)	32 (43)
Accessory Drive Pulley Bolt (4-Cyl.)	18 (24)
Cooling Fan & Fan Clutch-To-Water Pump	
Nut (4-Cyl.)	15 (20)
Drive Plate-To-Crankshaft Bolt	61 (83)
Drive Shaft Center Bearing Assembly	
To-Crossmember Bolt (4WD)	27 (37)
Drive Shaft Flange Bolt/Nut	
4WD	
Front Drive Shaft	54 (73)
Rear Drive Shaft	56 (76)
Engine Mount Insulator (V6)	
Front	28 (38)
Rear	13 (18)
Engine Mount-To-Frame Bolt/Nut (4-Cyl.)	28 (38)
Exhaust Crossover Pipe Nut (V6)	33 (45)
Exhaust Manifold Nut (V6)	30 (40)
Front Exhaust Pipe-To-Catalytic Converter	
Bolt/Nut (4-Cyl.)	29 (39)
Front Exhaust Pipe-To-Exhaust Manifold Nut (4-Cyl.)	46 (52)
Power Steering Pump Bolt (4-Cyl.)	43 (58)
Power Steering Pump Bracket Bolt	15 (20)
Power Steering Pump Idler Pulley Bolt (4-Cyl.)	15 (20)
Power Steering Pump Pulley Nut (4-Cyl.)	32 (43)
Rear Engine Mount-To-Crossmember Bolt	
4-Cyl.	19 (26)
V6	43 (58)
Rear Engine Mount-To-Mounting Bracket Bolt (4-Cyl.)	13 (18)
Rear Engine Mount-To-Mounting Bracket	
To Frame Bolt (V6)	13 (18)
To Insulator Bolt (V6)	43 (58)
Stabilizer Bar-To-Lower Control Bolt/Nut (4WD)	18 (25)
Stabilizer Bar Mounting Bracket-To-Frame	
Bolt (4WD)	22 (30)
Starter Bolt	29 (39)
Stiffener Plate Bolt	27 (37)
Transmission Crossmember Bolt	
4WD	70 (95)
Transmission-To-Cylinder Block Bolt	
4-Cyl.	53 (72)
V6	53 (65)

TORQUE SPECIFICATIONS (T100) (Cont.)

Application	Ft. Lbs. (N.m)
Transmission Mount-To-Transmission Crossmember Bolt (4WD)	13 (18)
Torque Converter Bolt	30 (41)

TORQUE SPECIFICATIONS (1995 4RUNNER)

Application	Ft. Lbs. (N.m)
Drive Plate-To-Crankshaft Bolt	61 (83)
Drive Shaft Center Bearing Assembly-To-Body Bolt	27 (37)
Drive Shaft Flange Bolt/Nut	54 (73)
Front Differential-To-Body Bolt (4WD)	123 (167)
Front Differential-To-Front Mounting Bracket Bolt At Front Of Differential (4WD)	67 (91)
Front Exhaust Pipe Support Bracket Bolt	29 (39)
Front Exhaust Pipe-To-Catalytic Converter Bolt/Nut	29 (39)
Front Exhaust Pipe-To-Exhaust Manifold Nut	46 (62)
Rear Transmission Mount-To-Transmission Bolt (2WD)	18 (24)
Stabilizer Bar Mounting Bracket-To-Frame Bolt (2WD)	22 (30)
Stabilizer Bar-To-Lower Control Arm Nut (2WD)	19 (26)
Stiffener Plate Bolt	27 (37)
Torque Converter Bolt	30 (41)
Transmission Crossmember-To-Frame Bolt	70 (95)
Transmission-To-Cylinder Block Bolt	1

	INCH Lbs. (N.m)
Rear Transmission Mount-To-Transmission Mount Bracket Bolt 2WD	115 (13.0)

1 – Information is not available from manufacturer.

TORQUE SPECIFICATIONS (1996 4RUNNER)

Application	Ft. Lbs. (N.m)
Drive Plate-To-Crankshaft Bolt	
2.7L 4-Cyl.	54 (73)
3.4L V6	61 (83)
Drive Shaft Flange Bolt/Nut	54 (73)
Front Exhaust Pipe-To-Exhaust Manifold Nut	46 (62)
Front Exhaust Pipe-To-Rear Exhaust Pipe Bolt/Nut	35 (47)
Rear Transmission Mount-To-Transmission Bolt	48 (65)
Rear Transmission Mount-To-Transmission Crossmember Bolt	14 (19)
Stabilizer Bar Mounting Bracket-To-Frame Bolt 3.4L V6	19 (26)
Stabilizer Bar-To-Lower Control Arm Nut 3.4L V6	51 (69)
Starter Bolt	29 (39)
Torque Converter Bolt	30 (41)
Transmission Crossmember-To-Frame Through-Bolt	48 (65)
Transmission-To-Cylinder Block Bolt	53 (72)

	INCH Lbs. (N.m)
Transmission Shift Lever Assembly Bolt (4WD)	52 (5.9)

Volkswagen

Cabrio, Golf, Golf III, GTI VR6
Jetta, Jetta III, Passat

APPLICATION

AUTOMATIC TRANSAXLE APPLICATIONS

Vehicle Year & Model	Transaxle Model
1995	
Cabrio, Golf III, GTI VR6 Jetta III & Passat	096
1996	
Cabrio, Golf, Jetta & Passat	01M

REMOVAL & INSTALLATION

CABRIO, GOLF, GTI & JETTA

Removal & Installation – 1) Obtain radio code. Disconnect negative battery cable. On models equipped with V6 engine, remove battery. On all models, disconnect speedometer cable from transaxle. Disconnect all harness connections at transaxle. Position harnesses aside.

2) On models equipped with V6 engine, remove multi-function Transaxle Range (TR) switch. On all models, move selector lever to Park position. Disconnect selector lever cable from lever/selector shaft. Remove selector lever cable anchor circlip and remove selector lever cable.

3) Using appropriate tool, clamp-off ATF cooler hoses. Disconnect hoses at ATF cooler. Support engine and transaxle assembly from top of vehicle with appropriate support fixture.

4) Remove starter. Remove power steering pressure hose bracket. On models equipped with V6 engine, disconnect cooling fan harness connector. On all models, remove front engine mount bolt and remove mount bracket.

5) Remove engine coolant recovery tank and set aside. Remove left engine mount assembly. Remove upper engine-to-transaxle bolts. Remove transaxle oil pan protective plate.

6) On models equipped with V6 engine, remove right-side drive belt cover and vibration dampening weight. On all models, remove torque converter cover plate and nuts from torque converter. Disconnect axle shafts at transaxle flanges.

7) Raise right-side axle shaft and secure. Remove left front wheel. Turn steering full-right to its lock. Mark position of ball joint bolts on left-side control arm for installation reference. On vehicles equipped with Plus Suspension option, remove both outer-most bolts. Loosen, but do not remove inner bolt. On models equipped with 4-cylinder engine, remove all bolts.

8) On all models, swing ball joint outward and secure left-side axle shaft aside (remove axle shaft if triple-roller type joint). Support transaxle with transmission jack.

9) Remove lower engine-to-transmission bolts. Tilt engine and transaxle forward. Separate transaxle from engine. Push torque converter up against pump. Lower engine, then transaxle slightly and guide power steering pressure line past transaxle.

10) Remove transaxle from vehicle. To install, reverse removal procedure. Adjust control cable. See ADJUSTMENTS in appropriate AUTOMATIC TRANSMISSION SERVICING article. Tighten bolts to specification. See TORQUE SPECIFICATIONS.

PASSAT

Removal & Installation – 1) Obtain radio code. Disconnect negative battery cable. On models equipped with V6 engine, remove battery. On all models, disconnect speedometer cable from transaxle. Disconnect all harness connections at transaxle. Position harnesses aside.

2) Remove multi-function Transaxle Range (TR) switch. Move selector lever to Park position. Disconnect selector lever cable from lever/selector shaft. Remove selector lever cable anchor circlip and remove selector lever cable.

3) Using appropriate tool, clamp-off ATF cooler hoses. Disconnect hoses at ATF cooler. Disconnect cooling fan harness connector. Remove upper engine-to-transaxle bolts.

4) Remove starter. Support engine and transaxle assembly from top of vehicle with appropriate support fixture. Remove front engine mount bolt and remove mount bracket.

5) Remove engine coolant recovery tank and set aside. Remove left engine mount assembly. On models equipped with V6 engine, remove drive belt cover. Disconnect axle shafts at transaxle flanges.

6) Remove left front wheel. Turn steering full-right to its lock. Raise right-side axle shaft and secure. Mark position of ball joint bolts on left-side control arm for installation reference.

7) On vehicles equipped with Plus Suspension option, remove both outer-most bolts. Loosen, but do not remove inner bolt. On models equipped with 4-cylinder engine, remove all bolts. On all models, swing ball joint outward and secure left-side axle shaft aside (remove axle shaft if triple-roller type joint).

8) Remove transaxle oil pan protective plate and vibration dampening weight. Remove power steering pressure hose bracket. Remove torque converter cover plate and nuts from torque converter.

9) Support transaxle with transmission jack. Remove lower engine-to-transmission bolts. Tilt engine and transaxle forward. Separate transaxle from engine. Push torque converter up against pump. Lower engine, then transaxle slightly and guide past wheelhousing.

10) Rotate transaxle and remove from vehicle. To install, reverse removal procedure. Adjust control cable. See ADJUSTMENTS in appropriate AUTOMATIC TRANSMISSION SERVICING article. Tighten bolts to specification. See TORQUE SPECIFICATIONS.

TORQUE SPECIFICATIONS
TORQUE SPECIFICATIONS

Application	Ft. Lbs. (N.m)
Axle Shaft-To-Flange Bolts	33 (45)
Axle-To-Hub Lock Nut	
Without Plus Suspension	195 (265)
With Plus Suspension	
Except Passat	[1]
Passat	[2]
Ball Joint-To-Control Arm Bolt	26 (35)
Cover Plate-To-Transaxle Bolt	11 (15)
Front Mount-To-Bracket Bolt	44 (60)
Left Mount-To-Bracket Bolt	44 (60)
Left Mount-To-Transaxle Bolt	18 (25)
Starter-To-Transaxle Bolt	44 (60)
Torque Converter-To-Drive Plate Bolts	44 (60)
Transaxle-To-Engine	
M10 Bolts	44 (60)
M12 Bolts	59 (80)

[1] – Tighten to 148 ft. lbs. (200 N.m), then back off one turn. Torque to 37 ft. lbs. (50 N.m) plus an additional 30 degrees.

[2] – Tighten to 66 ft. lbs. (90 N.m) plus an additional 45 degrees.

Volvo

850, 940, 960
APPLICATION
TRANSMISSION APPLICATION

Vehicle Application	Transaxle Model
1995	
850	AW50-42LE
940	AW-70L
940 Turbo	AW-71
960	AW-40
1996	
850	AW50-42LE
960	AW-40

REMOVAL & INSTALLATION

850

Removal – 1) Release steering wheel adjustment lever and move steering wheel up as far as possible. Put gear selector in "N" position. Remove battery, air cleaner, and air cleaner intake. Remove battery shelf.

2) Remove transmission cable from transmission. Disconnect electrical connector from transmission. Remove wiring harness and ground wire clamp on control system cover. Remove clamp from transmission ventilation hose.

3) Remove inlet hose from upper transmission cooler quick connector and return hose at transmission. Drain oil from transmission. Remove dipstick tube. Remove EGR hoses from EGR valve. Remove 5 transmission-to-engine and transmission-to-starter bolts. Disconnect ground wire from transmission. Lift radiator expansion tank from its mount and lay it to one side.

4) Disconnect torque rod arm at engine. Lift engine about 1/4" to relieve weight from engine mounts. Remove front wheels. Remove ABS sensor from left outboard shaft. DO NOT disconnect ABS electrical connector. Disconnect left and right brake lines and ABS cable brackets. Unhook brackets and allow them to hang free. Remove Torx screws and plastic nuts from left fender liner. Remove hub center nut locking clip. Remove hub center nut. Using a rubber or plastic mallet, knock in end of drive shaft about 1/2".

5) Remove front splash guard bolts. Push guard forward so locating pins on back come loose. Disconnect front of splash guard and remove. Remove splash guard under engine. Remove ball joint-to-link arm nuts on both sides. Disconnect link arms from ball joints. Disconnect and remove link arms from anti-roll bar.

6) Remove bolts connecting cable pipe on subframe and unhook pipe from frame. Disconnect charcoal canister from subframe and hang from body. Disconnect exhaust gas tie behind 3-way catalytic converter. Remove bolts holding pipe brackets to steering gear in subframe. Remove 2 bolts holding torque rod on transmission.

7) Remove bolts from front engine mounting subframe. Loosen bolts securing steering gear to engine mounting about one turn. Remove nuts holding steering gear to subframe. Disconnect subframe from vehicle by positioning Jack (998 5972) under left side of subframe. Tighten jack up gently against subframe. Remove bolts on both sides of subframe brackets. Loosen 2 right subframe-to-body bolts.

8) Lower subframe while ensuring steering gear bolts do not hang up. Ensure MacPherson strut disengages from right drive shaft bellows. Remove jack and allow subframe to hang free on right side. Secure end of right drive shaft onto back of oil pipes. Hang steering gear on left side using Hook (999 5045) in hole in frame member flange. Ensure lower steering wheel shaft section does not slip out of steering column.

9) Remove engine mount-to-subframe bolts and nut on top of engine mount. Remove engine mount. Disconnect HO2S cable terminals from cover. Disconnect speed sensor connector. Remove rear engine mount cover and rear mounting from gearbox.

10) Remove left drive shaft by twisting and pulling out MacPherson strut. Tap drive shaft end with plastic mallet and pull shaft from hub. Using Lever (999 5462), remove drive shaft from gearbox. Use care not to damage drive shaft seal or bellows. Install Plug (999 5488) to seal hole. Clean metal glue off hub drive shaft splines.

11) Use lifting hook and lower engine and transmission. DO NOT lower engine too much, as exhaust pipe may press on steering gear. Ensure no wiring or hoses are pinched or stretched, and that dipstick clears fan.

12) Install Universal Tool (999 5972) and Transmission Fixture (999 5463) to jack. Attach transmission fixture to gearbox using bolts from torque rod. At same time, position Support Plate (999 5463-1) on fixture. Raise engine. Remove lower plastic nut and fold out right fender liner. Turn crankshaft with a socket wrench. Remove 6 torque converter bolts and 7 engine-to-transmission bolts. Pull transmission straight out from engine, using care to ensure torque converter does not slip off shaft.

Installation – 1) Ensure torque converter is in transmission as far as possible. Distance between cover and mounting lip should be about .50" (13 mm). Install transmission to engine, adjusting height and angle with transmission jack. Install and tighten crosswise 7 engine-to-transmission bolts. See TORQUE SPECIFICATIONS. Remove jack.

2) Fit torque converter to flexplate. Install new torque converter bolts loosely. Tighten bolts so bolt heads are in contact with flexplate. Final tighten bolts to specification. See TORQUE SPECIFICATIONS. To install remaining components, reverse removal procedure.

940

Removal & Installation – 1) Place gearshift lever in "P" position. Detach kickdown cable from throttle pulley. Disconnect negative battery cable.

CAUTION: On vehicles with front rubber drive shaft flange, flange should only be disconnected from transmission. DO NOT disconnect flange from drive shaft or an imbalance may occur. On standard (non-rubber) drive shafts, always replace 4 retaining bolts and nuts.

2) Raise and support vehicle. Remove propeller shaft. Drain transmission fluid. Unscrew oil filler tube from transmission oil pan. Disconnect reaction rod and actuator rod from transmission shift levers. Disconnect solenoid lead on AW71. On all models, support transmission with jack. Remove rear transmission crossmember.

3) Remove starter motor bolts and cover plate. Remove torque converter-to-flexplate bolts. Disconnect oil cooler lines. Remove transmission-to-engine bolts. Slide transmission rearward and lower from vehicle. To install, reverse removal procedure. Tighten bolts to specification. See TORQUE SPECIFICATIONS. Adjust kickdown cable and gearshift linkage. Fill transmission with ATF fluid.

960

Removal & Installation – 1) Lift engine slightly to relieve weight on engine and transmission mounts. Remove splash guard under engine. Remove air preheater pipe. Disconnect oxygen sensor. Remove cable clip on torque converter housing. Open clips on transmission and remove 2 clips on transmission support member. Remove 3 connectors from bracket on torque converter housing. Remove front exhaust pipe. Disconnect drive shaft.

2) Remove heat shield. Disconnect fluid pipes from transmission. Plug pipe ends. Remove transmission support member. Lower rear of engine as far as possible. Use care so no hoses, wiring, or sensors are damaged. Remove torque converter bolts. Install jack under transmission. Remove torque converter housing bolts. Lower transmission.

3) To install, reverse removal procedure. Tighten bolts to specification. See TORQUE SPECIFICATIONS. Ensure torque converter is in transmission as far as possible. Distance between cover and mounting lip should be about .55" (14 mm).

TORQUE SPECIFICATIONS

TORQUE SPECIFICATIONS

Application	Ft. Lbs. (N.m)
850	
Control Arm-To-Ball Joint Nut (New)	[1] 13 (18)
Drive Shaft Nut	[2] 89 (120)
Engine-To-Transmission Bolt	37 (50)
Frame Bolt	[1] 77 (105)
Frame Bracket Bolt	37 (50)
Flexplate-To-Torque Converter Bolt	22 (30)
Rear Transmission/Engine Mount	37 (50)
Roll Bar Bearing Cap Bolt	37 (50)
Steering Gear Nut (New)	37 (50)
Torque Rod-To-Transmission Bolt	[3] 13 (18)
940	
Drive Shaft Flange Retaining Bolt (Non-Rubber)	
8-mm	26 (35)
10-mm	37 (50)
Drive Shaft Flange Retaining Bolt (Rubber)	52-65 (70-88)
Flexplate-To-Torque Converter Bolts	33 (45)
Lower Oil Filler Tube Nut	65 (88)
960	
Drive Shaft-To-Transmission Bolt	37 (50)
Flexplate-To-Torque Converter Bolt	22 (30)
Transmission-To-Engine Bolt	
Starter Bolts	30 (40)
Remaining Bolts	35 (48)

[1] – Tighten an additional 120 degrees.
[2] – Tighten an additional 60 degrees.
[3] – Tighten an additional 90 degrees.

Acura

Integra, Legend, SLX

IDENTIFICATION

MANUAL TRANSAXLE APPLICATIONS

Application	Trans. Model
Integra	
1995	Y80
1996	S80
Legend	
5-Speed	K4A6
6-Speed	K4F6
SLX	MUA5C

LUBRICATION

SERVICE INTERVALS

On Integra models, change fluid every 30,000 miles (1995 models), or every 90,000 miles (1996 Models). On Legend models, change fluid every 30,000 miles. On SLX models change transmission and transfer case fluid at 15,000 miles and then at every 30,000 mile interval.

CHECKING FLUID LEVEL

Ensure fluid level is at bottom of fill hole. Drain plug is located on bottom of case. Replace drain plug gasket whenever fluid is changed.

RECOMMENDED FLUID

Integra – Use Honda MTF. If Honda MTF is not available API SG or SH-rated SAE 10W-30 or 10W-40 engine oil may be used. Engine oil should be used on a temporary basis only as increased wear or harder shifting may result.

Legend – Use engine oil, API SF or SG-rated SAE 10W-30 or 10W-40.

SLX Transmission & Transfer Case – Use engine oil, API SG or SH-rated SAE 5W-30 (below 95°F/35°C), 10W-30 (41°F/5°C to 95°F/35°C) or 15W-40, 20W-40, 20W-50 (above 50°F/10°C).

FLUID CAPACITIES

TRANSAXLE REFILL CAPACITIES

Application	Fluid Change Qts. (L)	Overhaul Qts. (L)
Integra	2.3 (2.2)	2.4 (2.3)
Legend	2.4 (2.3)	2.7 (2.6)
SLX		
Transmission	3.1 (2.95)	N/A
Transfer Case	1.5 (1.45)	N/A

ADJUSTMENTS

LINKAGE

No external adjustments are required.

TORQUE SPECIFICATIONS

TORQUE SPECIFICATIONS

Application	Ft. Lbs. (N.m)
Except SLX	
Oil Drain Plug	30 (40)
Oil Filler Plug	33 (45)
SLX	[1]

Information not available from manufacture.

Audi

A4, A6, S6, 90

APPLICATION

MANUAL TRANSAXLE APPLICATION

Vehicle Model	Transaxle Model
1995 A6, 90	012 5-Speed
1996 A4	012 5-Speed
1995 A6, 90	01A 5-Speed
1996 A4	01A 5-Speed
1995 S6	01E 5-Speed

LUBRICATION

SERVICE INTERVALS

Check transaxle lubricant level when vehicle is serviced. Under normal operating conditions, manufacturer does not require periodic lubricant changes.

CHECKING FLUID LEVEL

Check fluid level at fill hole with vehicle level. Lubricant should be slightly below bottom of fill hole.

RECOMMENDED FLUID

Use G-50 synthetic gear oil (SAE 75W-90).

FLUID CAPACITY

TRANSAXLE REFILL CAPACITY

Application	[1] Qts. (L)
012	2.5 (2.4)
01A	3.0 (2.8)
01E	[2] 2.7 (2.6)

[1] – Includes differential.
[2] – Plus .1 qt (.1L) additive.

ADJUSTMENTS

MODEL 012 & 01A

Shifter – **1)** Place gearshift lever in Neutral. Remove shift knob, boot retaining screw and boot. Loosen shift rod retaining bolt on bottom of shift lever. See Fig. 1 or 2. Position gearshift lever as close to Neutral as possible.

2) Align shift lever so both lugs (left and right sides) on ball stop are same distance from ball housing. See Fig. 3. Ensure lever does not move and tighten bolt to specification. Check shifter for smooth travel into all gear positions.

3) Ensure reverse safety catch is effective. If reverse safety catch does not catch, loosen ball housing screws and turn ball housing slightly. Check reverse safety catch operation. Install boot and shift knob.

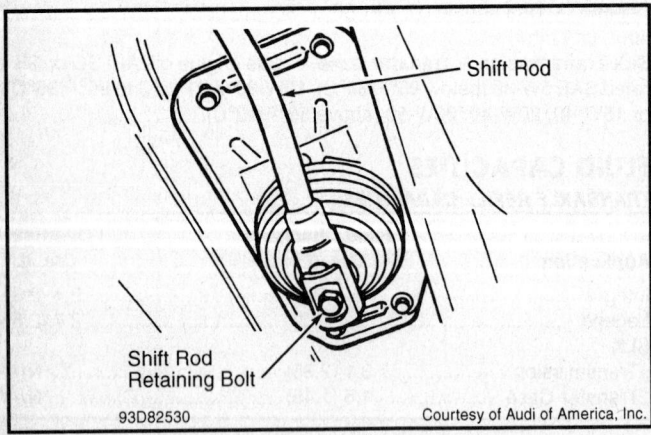

Fig. 1: Locating Shift Rod Retaining Bolt (012 & 01A)

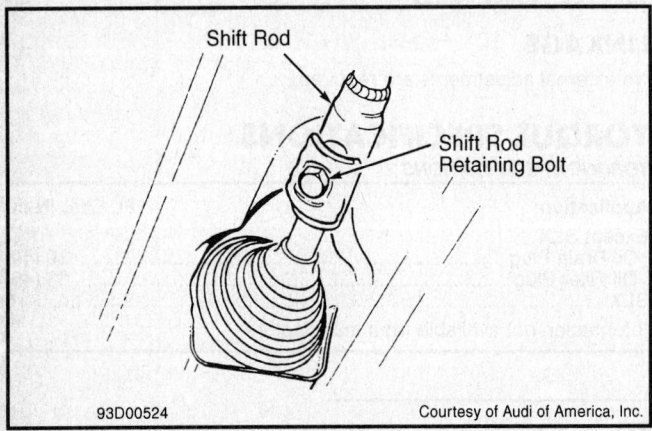

Fig. 2: Locating Shift Rod Retaining Bolt (012 & 01A)

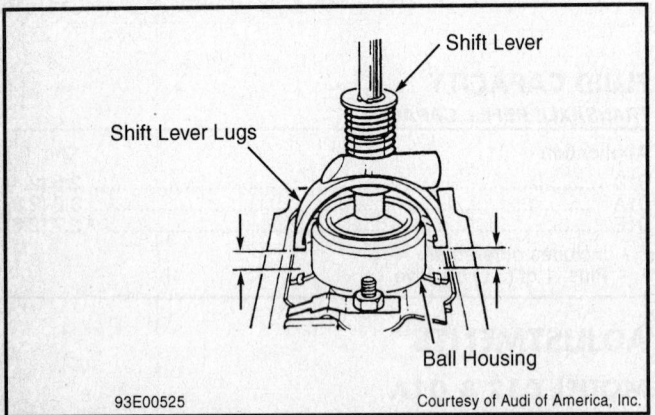

Fig. 3: Aligning Shift Lever Lugs With Ball Housing (012 & 01A)

4) Check adjustment by placing shifter in 2nd and holding shifter to the left. Allow shifter to spring back toward center. Travel should be .12-.35" (3-9 mm) at knob. Ensure shifter engages all gears. Ensure reverse lock out works. Ensure shifter will return to Neutral between 3rd and 4th from both ends of neutral plane. If return is not centered between 3rd and 4th, upper stop can be adjusted sideways in slots.

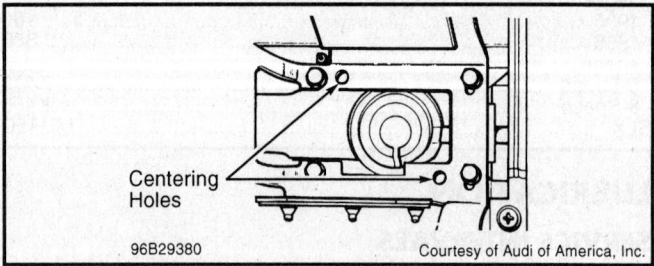

Fig. 4: Aligning Shifter Stop Holes (01E)

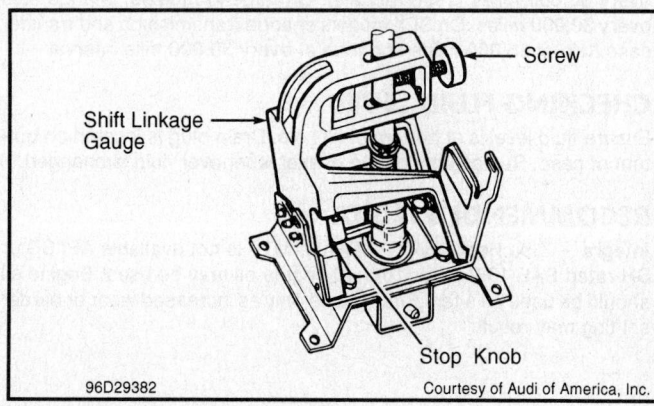

Fig. 5: Installing Shifter Gauge (01E)

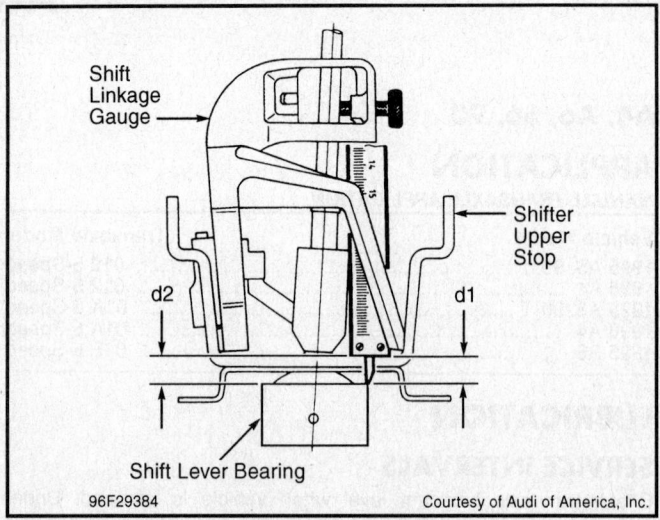

Fig. 6: Adjusting Rear Torque Rod (01E)

MODEL 01E

Shifter – 1) Adjust connecting rod length to 6.63" (168.5 mm) center-to-center with rod ends aligned. Remove shift knob and boot. Align centering holes on upper and lower sections of stop and tighten bolts to 7 ft. lbs. (10 Nm). See Fig. 4. Place shifter in Neutral between 3rd and 4th. Loosen clamp connection of shift and torque rods to allow free movement. Adjust shift lever, then rear torque rod.

2) To adjust shifter, install Shift Linkage Gauge (3286) on shift lever. See Fig. 5. Place left, then right side of gauge into holes of stop until seated. Carefully tighten knurled screw until stop knob is touching shift linkage gauge.

3) To adjust rear torque rod, check and adjust measurement "d1" and "d2" to within .04" (1 mm), aligning shift lever bearing "A" and upper stop "C". See Fig. 6. Tighten clamp connection of shift and torque rods. Loosen knurled screw and remove shift linkage gauge.

TORQUE SPECIFICATIONS
TORQUE SPECIFICATIONS

Application	Ft. Lbs. (N.m)
Shift Rod Retaining Bolt (012 & 01A)	18 (25)
Shift Rod Locking Bolts (01E)	52 (70)
Shifter Stop Bolts (012 & 01A)	7 (10)
Drain And Fill Plugs (012 & 01E)	26 (35)

Z3, 3-Series, 5-Series

IDENTIFICATION

TRANSMISSION APPLICATION

Vehicle Application	Transmission Model
1995	
M3	Getrag 310
318i, 318iC, 318is, 318ti	
325i, 325iC, 325is	Getrag 250
525i, 530i	S5-31
540i	Getrag 286
1996	
M3, 328i, 328is	S5-31
Z3, 318i, 318is, 318ti	Getrag 250

LUBRICATION

SERVICE INTERVALS

Inspect fluid level when vehicle is serviced. Change oil every 30,000 miles.

CHECKING FLUID LEVEL

Check fluid level at fill hole. Lubricant should be at bottom of filler plug hole.

RECOMMENDED FLUID

Use Dextron-II ATF.

FLUID CAPACITY

TRANSMISSION REFILL CAPACITY

Application	Pts. (L)
All Models	2.65 (1.25)

TORQUE SPECIFICATIONS

TORQUE SPECIFICATIONS

Application	Ft. Lbs. (N.m)
Drain Plug	30-44 (40-60)
Filler Plug	30-44 (40-60)

Geo

Metro, Prizm, Tracker

IDENTIFICATION

MANUAL TRANSMISSION APPLICATIONS

Model	Transaxle/Transmission
Metro	5-Speed Suzuki Transaxle
Prizm	5-Speed Toyota Transaxle
Tracker	5-Speed Suzuki Transmission

LUBRICATION

SERVICE INTERVALS

Metro – Replace transmission fluid every 30,000 miles under normal driving conditions. Under severe driving conditions, replace transmission fluid every 12,000 miles.

Prizm – Check fluid and add as required during normal periodic maintenance. Under severe driving conditions, replace transmission fluid every 15,000 miles.

Tracker – Replace transmission and transfer case fluid initially at 7500 miles, then every 30,000 miles or 30 months thereafter under normal driving conditions. Under severe driving conditions, replace transfer case and transmission fluid initially at 7500 miles, then every 15,000 miles or 15 months thereafter.

Severe Conditions (All Vehicles) – Severe driving conditions are when vehicle is operated under one or more of the following conditions:

* Most driving is done in stop-and-go traffic when outside temperatures are greater than 89°F (32°C).
* Delivery service, Taxi or Police vehicles.
* Trailer towing.
* In hilly or mountainous terrain.
* Most trips are less than 4 miles.
* Most trips are less than 10 miles, and outside temperatures remain below freezing.
* Driving in dusty areas.

CHECKING FLUID LEVEL

Metro & Prizm – Park vehicle on level surface. Remove filler plug on side of transaxle case. Fluid level should be level with bottom of filler plug hole. Add fluid if necessary. Install and tighten filler plug. See TORQUE SPECIFICATIONS.

NOTE: On Metro, if transaxle fluid is changed, clean drain plug and apply Sealant (1052080) to plug threads. Tighten drain plug to 15 ft. lbs. (20 N.m).

Tracker (Transmission & Transfer Case) – 1) Transmission and transfer case have separate drain and filler plugs. Park vehicle on level surface. To check transmission fluid level, remove transmission filler plug. Fluid should be level with bottom of filler plug hole. Add fluid if necessary. Install and tighten filler plug. See TORQUE SPECIFICATIONS.

2) To check transfer case fluid level, remove transfer case filler plug (upper plug) from rear of transfer case. Filler plug is located near speedometer gear housing. Ensure fluid is level with bottom of filler plug hole. Install and tighten filler plug. See TORQUE SPECIFICATIONS.

RECOMMENDED FLUID

Metro – Use SAE 75W-85 GL-4 Synthetic Gear Lubricant or GM Synchromesh Transmission Fluid SAE 75W-85.

Prizm – Use SAE 75W-85 GL-4 Synthetic Lubricant or GM Synchromesh Transmission Fluid SAE 75W-85.

Tracker (Transmission & Transfer Case) – Use SAE 75W-85 GL-4 Synthetic Lubricant or GM Synchromesh Transmission Fluid SAE 75W-85.

TORQUE SPECIFICATIONS

TORQUE SPECIFICATIONS

Application	Ft. Lbs. (N.m)
Metro	
Drain Plug	15 (20)
Filler Plug	15 (20)
Prizm	
Drain Plug	1
Filler Plug	1
Tracker	
Drain Plug	21 (28)
Filler Plug	21 (28)

1 – Tighten to 97 INCH Lbs. (11 N.m).

MANUAL TRANSMISSION SERVICING
Geo (Cont.)

FLUID CAPACITIES
TRANSMISSION REFILL CAPACITIES

Application	Pts. (L)
Metro	5.1 (2.4)
Prizm	5.5 (2.6)
Tracker	
2WD	4.0 (1.9)
4WD	3.2 (1.5)

TRANSFER CASE REFILL CAPACITY

Application	Pts. (L)
Tracker	3.6 (1.7)

ADJUSTMENTS
SHIFT CABLE

Prizm – Shift cables are not adjustable. If shift cables are out of adjustment, they must be replaced.

Honda

Accord, Civic, Civic Del Sol, Passport, Prelude

NOTE: For information on Passport manual transmission servicing, refer to Rodeo in MANUAL TRANSMISSION SERVICING – ISUZU article.

IDENTIFICATION
MANUAL TRANSAXLE APPLICATIONS

Model	Transaxle Code
Accord	
Sedan W/F22B2 Engine	P2A5
Sedan W/F22B1 Engine	P2U5
Station Wagon	P2A4
Civic	
1995 (All Models)	S20
1996 (Except VTEC)	S40
1996 (VTEC)	S4C
Civic Del Sol	
1995 D16A3 Engine	S21 Or Y21
1995 D15B7 Or D16Z6 Engine	S20
1996 D16A2 Engine	S21
1996 D16Y7 Or D16Y8 Engine	S8G
Prelude	
F22A1 Engine	M2F4
H22A2 Engine (VTEC)	M2L5
H23A1 Engine	M2S4

ADJUSTMENTS

NOTE: External linkage adjustments are not required. Inspect gearshift linkage components for wear or damage. Replace components as required.

LUBRICATION
SERVICE INTERVALS

On 1995 models, change lubricant every 30,000 miles or 24 months under normal driving conditions and 15,000 miles or 12 months under severe driving conditions. On 1996 models, change lubricant every 90,000 miles or 72 months under normal driving conditions and every 30,000 miles or 24 months under severe driving conditions.

CHECKING FLUID LEVEL

Check fluid level with transaxle at operating temperature. Ensure engine is off and vehicle is level. Remove fill plug on side of transaxle case. Fluid level should be at bottom of fill hole. Tighten oil filler plug to 33 ft. lbs. (45 N.m) and oil drain plug to 33 ft. lbs. (45 N.m).

RECOMMENDED FLUID

On 1995 models, use SAE 10W-30 or 10W-40 with a rating of SF or SG. Starting 1996 model year manufacturer recommends using genuine Honda Manual Transmission Fluid (MTF), however SAE 10W-30 or 10W-40 with a rating of SF or SG may be substituted temporarily.

FLUID CAPACITIES
TRANSAXLE REFILL CAPACITIES

Transaxle	After Draining Qts. (L)	After Overhaul Qts. (L)
M2F4, M2S4, M2L5, P2A4, P2A5, P2U5	2.0 (1.9)	2.1 (2.0)
A4RA, S40, S4C, S8G	1.9 (1.8)	2.0 (1.9)
S21, Y21	2.3 (2.2)	2.4 (2.3)

Accent, Elantra, Scoupe, Sonata

IDENTIFICATION
TRANSAXLE APPLICATION

Vehicle Application	Transaxle Model
Accent	M5AF3
Elantra	
1995	KM202
1996	M5BF1
Scoupe	M5AF
Sonata	
1995 [1]	KM202
1996	KM210

[1] – Sonata V6 is only available with automatic transaxle.

LUBRICATION

SERVICE INTERVALS
Inspect transaxle oil every 30,000 miles. Replace oil if it is noticeably dirty or is not of a suitable viscosity.

CHECKING FLUID LEVEL
Remove fill plug and ensure oil level is even with bottom of fill plug hole. Oil level should not be lower than .31" (8 mm) below bottom of fill plug hole.

RECOMMENDED FLUID
Manufacturer recommends SAE 75W-85W (API GL-4).

FLUID CAPACITY
TRANSAXLE REFILL CAPACITIES

Application	Qts. (L)
KM202 & KM210	1.9 (1.8)
M5AF, M5AF3 & M5BF1	2.3 (2.2)

DRAINING & REFILLING
With vehicle on level surface, remove drain plug and drain transaxle oil into suitable container. Replace drain plug. Fill transaxle with recommended type and amount of oil. Ensure oil level is level with bottom of fill plug hole.

ADJUSTMENTS

LINKAGE
No external adjustments are necessary.

Infiniti

G20, I30

IDENTIFICATION
AUTOMATIC TRANSMISSION APPLICATIONS

Vehicle	Transmission Model
G20	RS5F32A Or RS5F32V
I30	RS5F50A Or RS5F50V

LUBRICATION

SERVICE INTERVALS
Inspect fluid level every 15,000 miles or 12 months. If under severe usage, change every 30,000 miles or 24 months.

CHECKING FLUID LEVEL
Fill plug is located on side of transaxle case. Lubricant level should be to bottom of fill hole. Add fluid if necessary.

RECOMMENDED FLUID
Use API GL-4 gear oil.

FLUID CAPACITY
TRANSMISSION/TRANSAXLE REFILL CAPACITIES

Transmission/Transaxle	Pts. (L)
G20	7.9-8.3 pts. (3.7-3.9L)
I30	
RS5F50A	9.5-10.1 (4.5-4.8)
RS5F50V	9.1-9.5 (4.3-4.5)

ADJUSTMENTS

LINKAGE

NOTE: All models have direct shift mechanisms and require no adjustment.

TORQUE SPECIFICATIONS
TORQUE SPECIFICATIONS

Application	Ft. Lbs. (N.m)
Drain Plug	18-25 (25-34)
Filler Plug	7-14 (10-20)

Hombre, Pickup, Rodeo, Trooper

IDENTIFICATION
MANUAL TRANSMISSION APPLICATIONS

Model	Transmission
Hombre	New Venture Gear NV1500
Pickup	
2WD	MUA5C 5-Speed
4WD	MUA5CT 5-Speed
Rodeo	
2WD	
2.6L	MUA5C 5-Speed
3.2L	Borg-Warner T5R 5-Speed
4WD	MUA5CT 5-Speed
Trooper	MUA5CT 5-Speed

LUBRICATION

SERVICE INTERVALS

NOTE: Service intervals for Hombre are not available.

Transmission & Transfer Case – Check lubricant level every 7500 miles. Replace lubricant after initial 15,000 and 30,000 miles, then every 30,000 mile interval thereafter.

CHECKING FLUID LEVEL

Transmission (Hombre & Pickup 2WD) – Ensure vehicle is level. Remove fill plug from side of transmission case. Fluid level should be even with bottom of fill plug hole. Add fluid if necessary. Install fill plug and torque to specification. See TORQUE SPECIFICATIONS.

Transmission & Transfer Case (Pickup 4WD, Rodeo & Trooper) – To check transmission and transfer case, ensure vehicle is level. Remove both fill plugs from transmission case and transfer case. *See Fig. 1.* Fluid level should be even with bottom of fill plug hole. Add fluid if necessary. Install fill plugs and torque to specification. See TORQUE SPECIFICATIONS.

RECOMMENDED FLUID

Transmission – On Rodeo models equipped with Borg Warner (BW T5R) transmission, use Dexron-III automatic transmission fluid. On Hombre models, use GM Synchro-Mesh Transmission Fluid with 5% friction modifier. On all other transmissions, use SAE 5W-30 SF engine oil at ambient temperatures up to 95°F (35°C). Use SAE 15W-40, 20W-40 or 20W-50 for operational temperatures greater than 50°F (10°C).

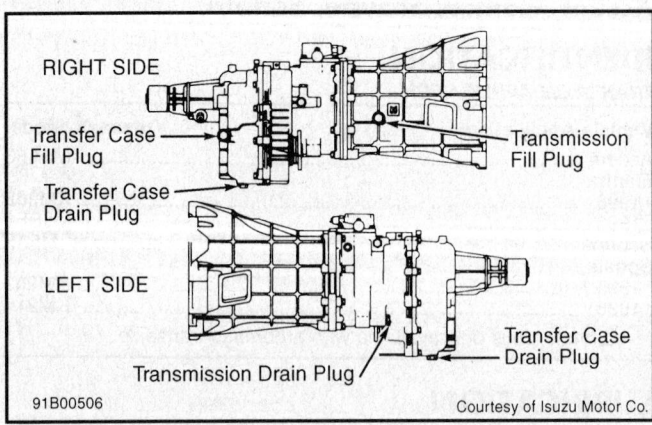

Fig. 1: Checking Manual Transmission & Transfer Case Fluid (4WD Models – Typical)

Transfer Case – Use engine oil SAE 5W-30 for operational temperature range up to 95°F (35°C). Use SAE 15W-40, 20W-40 or 20W-50 for operational temperatures greater than 50°F (10°C).

FLUID CAPACITIES
TRANSMISSION REFILL CAPACITIES

Application	Qts. (L)
Hombre	2.2 (2.1)
Pickup	
2.3L	1.6 (1.5)
2.6L	3.1 (2.9)
Rodeo	
BW T5R Transmission	2.3 (2.2)
MUA Transmission	3.1 (2.9)
Trooper	3.1 (2.9)

TRANSFER CASE REFILL CAPACITIES

Application	Qts. (L)
All Models	1.5 (1.4)

TORQUE SPECIFICATIONS
TORQUE SPECIFICATIONS

Application	Ft. Lbs. (N.m)
Drain Plug	28 (38)
Filler Plug	
Hombre	17 (23)
All Others	28 (38)

Sephia, Sportage

IDENTIFICATION
MANUAL TRANSMISSION APPLICATION

Model	Transmission
Sephia	
1995 1.6L SOHC	F5M-R
1995-96 1.6L DOHC	F25M-R
1995-96 1.8L DOHC	G25M-R
Sportage	Getrag 5-Speed

LUBRICATION

SERVICE INTERVALS

Transmission – Check transmission fluid at every engine oil change. Under normal conditions, replace fluid every 30,000 miles. Under severe conditions, replace fluid every 15,000 miles.

CHECKING FLUID LEVEL

Sephia – **1)** Disconnect speedometer at transaxle. Remove speedometer drive gear assembly hold-down bolt. Remove drive gear. Wipe speedometer drive gear and fully insert it into transaxle.
2) Ensure oil level is between middle and top of drive gear. *See Fig. 1.* If necessary, add oil through drive gear opening. Replace drive gear assembly "O" ring as necessary. Install drive gear and connect speedometer cable.

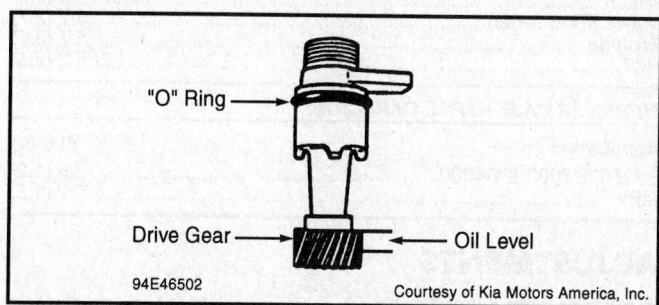

94E46502   Courtesy of Kia Motors America, Inc.

Fig. 1: Checking Transaxle Oil Level (Sephia)

Sportage – Raise and support vehicle in level position. Remove oil check/fill plug. Oil level should be even with bottom of oil check/fill plug hole. Add recommended fluid as necessary. See RECOMMENDED FLUID. Reinstall oil check/fill plug with new washer. Tighten oil check/fill plug to 22 ft. lbs. (30 N.m).

RECOMMENDED FLUID
Transmissions use SAE 75W-90/API GL-4 or GL-5 gear lube.

FLUID CAPACITY
TRANSMISSION REFILL CAPACITIES

Application	Qts. (L)
Sephia	
F5MR & F25M-R	2.83 (2.7)
G25M-R	3.55 (2.94)
Sportage	1.30 (1.25)

ADJUSTMENTS

GEARSHIFT LINKAGE
No external linkage adjustment is required.

TORQUE SPECIFICATIONS

Application	Ft. Lbs. (N.m)
Drain Plug	
Sephia	29-40 (39-54)
Sportage	22 (30)
Fill Plug	22 (30)
	INCH Lbs. (N.m)
Speedometer Drive Gear Bolt	71-97 (8-11)

Lexus

SC300

IDENTIFICATION
MANUAL TRANSAXLE APPLICATIONS

Model	Transaxle
SC300	W58

LUBRICATION

SERVICE INTERVALS

Under normal driving conditions, inspect transmission fluid every 15,000 miles or 24 months, whichever comes first. Under severe driving conditions, replace fluid every 15,000 miles or 24 months.

CHECKING FLUID LEVEL
Remove filler plug. Add fluid until it runs from filler hole.

RECOMMENDED FLUID
Use API GL-4 or GL-5 grade, SAE 75W-90 or 80W-90 transaxle oil.

FLUID CAPACITIES
TRANSAXLE REFILL CAPACITIES

Application	Qts. (L)
SC300	2.7 (2.6)

ADJUSTMENTS

GEARSHIFT LINKAGE

NOTE: SC300 has floor shift mechanism with internal linkage that requires no adjustment.

TORQUE SPECIFICATIONS
TORQUE SPECIFICATIONS

Application	Ft. Lbs. (N.m)
Drain & Filler Plug	27 (37)

MANUAL TRANSMISSION SERVICING
Mazda

B2300, B3000, B4000, Miata, MX-3, MX-6, Protege, RX7, 626

IDENTIFICATION
MANUAL TRANSMISSION/TRANSAXLE APPLICATIONS

Model	Transmission/Transaxle
B2300, B3000 & B4000	M-50D
Miata	M15M-D
MX-3	F25M-R
MX-6 & 626	G25M-R
Protege (1.5L)	F25M-R
Protege (1.8L)	G25M-R
RX-7	R15M-D

LUBRICATION
SERVICE INTERVALS

Check fluid level(s) at least once a year. Change transmission/transaxle and transfer case fluids every 60,000 miles for normal driving conditions and every 30,000 miles for severe driving conditions.

CHECKING FLUID LEVEL

Transaxle (FWD Models Except MX-3 DOHC) – Remove speedometer drive housing hold-down bolt and withdraw housing. Wipe speedometer driven gear and fully insert it back into transaxle. Use "L" and "F" marks on driven gear to determine fluid level. If necessary, add oil through driven gear opening.

Transmission (RWD Models & MX-3 DOHC) – Remove fill plug from transmission/transaxle. Fluid should be up to bottom of fill hole on side of case. B2600i, MPV and RX7 Turbo have 2 drain and 2 fill plugs in transmission case. Fluid level should be at bottom of rear fill hole on side of case.

Transfer Case (4WD Models) – Remove fill plug from transfer case. Fluid should be up to bottom of fill hole on side of transfer case.

RECOMMENDED FLUID
FLUID SPECIFICATIONS

Application	Recommended Fluid
Transmission/Transaxle Fluid	
Miata, MPV & RX7	
All-Season Usage	[1] SAE 75W-90
Temp. Greater Than 50°F (10°C)	[1] SAE 80W-90
B2300, B3000 & B4000	MERCON Or M-III ATF
MX-3	
All-Season Usage	[1] SAE 75W-90
Temp. Less Than 0°F (-18°C)	Dexron-II
Temp. Greater Than 0°F (-18°C)	[1] SAE 75W-90
MX-6 & 626	
All Season Usage	[1] SAE 75W-90
Temp. Greater Than 0°F (-18°C)	[1] SAE 80W-90
Protege	[1] SAE 75W-90
Transfer Case Fluid	
B2300, B3000, B4000	MERCON Or M-III ATF
MPV	
All-Season Usage	[1] SAE 75W-90
Temp. Greater Than 50°F (10°C)	[1] SAE 80W-90

[1] – API GL-4 or GL-5.

FLUID CAPACITIES
TRANSMISSION/TRANSAXLE REFILL CAPACITIES

Application	Pts. (L)
B2300, B3000 & B4000	5.6 (2.6)
Miata	4.2 (2.0)
MX-3, MX-6 & 626	5.7 (2.7)
Protege	5.7 (2.7)
RX7	5.2 (2.5)

TRANSFER CASE REFILL CAPACITIES

Application	Pts. (L)
B2300, B3000 & B4000	2.5 (1.2)
MPV	3.2 (1.5)

ADJUSTMENTS
GEARSHIFT LINKAGE

No external linkage adjustment is required.

TORQUE SPECIFICATIONS
TORQUE SPECIFICATIONS

Application	Ft. Lbs. (N.m)
Drain Plug	
Miata, MX-3, MX-6,	
Protege & 626	29-43 (39-58)
B2300, B3000 & B4000	
Drain Plug	32 (43)
Transfer Case Plug	14 (22)
MPV	
Forward Transmission Plug &	
Transfer Case Plug	29-43 (39-58)
Rearward Transmission Plug	18-29 (24-39)
RX7	
Forward Transmission Plug	29-43 (39-58)
Rearward Transmission Plug	15-23 (21-31)
Fill Plug	
Miata, MPV & RX7	18-29 (24-39)
B2300, B3000, B4000,	
MX-3, MX-6 & 626	29-43 (39-58)
	INCH Lbs. (N.m)
Speedometer Gear Bolt (FWD)	69-95 (8-11)

**Chrysler Corp.: Colt, Colt Vista, Stealth
Summit, Summit Wagon, Talon
Mitsubishi: Diamante, Eclipse, Expo, Galant
Mirage, Montero, Pickup, 3000GT**

IDENTIFICATION

MANUAL TRANSMISSION/TRANSAXLE APPLICATIONS

Model	Transmission/Transaxle (Model)
Chrysler Corp.	
Colt & Summit	
1.5L	5-Speed Transaxle (F5M21)
1.8L	5-Speed Transaxle (F5M22)
Colt Vista & Summit Wagon	
AWD	5-Speed Transaxle (W5M33)
FWD	
1.8L	5-Speed Transaxle (F5M22)
2.4L	5-Speed Transaxle (F5M31)
Stealth	
Non-Turbo	5-Speed Transaxle (F5M33)
Turbo	6-Speed Transaxle (W6MG1)
Talon	
AWD	5-Speed Transaxle (W5M33)
FWD	
Non-Turbo	5-Speed Transaxle (F5MC1)
Turbo	5-Speed Transaxle (F5M33)
Mitsubishi	
Eclipse	
AWD	5-Speed Transaxle (W5M33)
FWD	
2.0L Non-Turbo	5-Speed Transaxle (F5MC1)
2.0L Turbo	5-Speed Transaxle (F5M33)
2.4L	5-Speed Transaxle (F5M31)
Expo	
AWD	5-Speed Transaxle (W5M33)
FWD	
1.8L	5-Speed Transaxle (F5M22)
2.4L	5-Speed Transaxle (F5M31)
Galant	5-Speed Transaxle (F5M31)
Mirage	
1.5L	5-Speed Transaxle (F5M21)
1.8L	5-Speed Transaxle (F5M22)
Montero	5-Speed Transmission (V5MT1)
Pickup	
RWD	5-Speed Transmission (R5M21)
4WD	5-Speed Transmission (V5MT1)
3000GT	
AWD	6-Speed Transaxle (W6MG1)
FWD	5-Speed Transaxle (F5M33)

LUBRICATION

SERVICE INTERVALS

Check transaxle/transmission and transfer case fluid level every 30,000 miles. Change fluid at 30,000 miles if operated under severe conditions.

CHECKING FLUID LEVEL

Transaxle/Transmission – Check fluid level at fill hole on side of transaxle or transmission. Fill transaxle to bottom of fill hole.
Transfer Case (3000GT) – Transfer case contains separate drain and fill plugs. Fill transfer case to .5" (13 mm) from bottom of fill hole.
Transfer Case (Except 3000GT) – Transfer case contains separate drain and fill plugs. Fill transfer case to bottom of fill hole.

RECOMMENDED FLUID

Transaxle/Transmission – Use API classification GL-4 or higher SAE 75W-85W gear oil.
Transfer Case – Use API classification GL-4 or higher SAE 75W-85W gear oil.

FLUID CAPACITIES

TRANSMISSION REFILL CAPACITIES

Application	Pts. (L)
Colt, Mirage & Summit	3.8 (1.8)
Colt Vista, Expo & Summit Wagon	
FWD	
1.8L	3.8 (1.8)
2.4L	5.0 (2.4)
AWD	5.0 (2.4)
Eclipse	
2.0L	4.2 (2.0)
2.0L Turbo	4.9 (2.3)
2.4L	4.9 (2.3)
Galant	4.4 (2.1)
Montero	5.3 (2.5)
Pickup	4.9 (2.3)
Stealth & 3000GT	
FWD	4.2 (2.0)
AWD	5.0 (2.4)
Talon	
Non-Turbo	4.2 (2.0)
Turbo	4.9 (2.3)

TRANSFER CASE REFILL CAPACITIES

Application	Pts. (L)
Colt Vista, Expo & Summit Wagon	1.3 (0.6)
Eclipse & Talon	1.1 (0.5)
Montero & Pickup	4.9 (2.3)
Stealth & 3000GT	1.3 (0.6)

ADJUSTMENTS

SELECT CABLE

Place transaxle side shift lever in Neutral. This will also place transaxle side select lever in Neutral. See Fig. 1. Loosen selector cable adjuster nuts (inside of vehicle). See Fig. 2. With select lever in Neutral, adjust select cable end until eye fits easily over select lever pin. Tighten adjuster nuts.

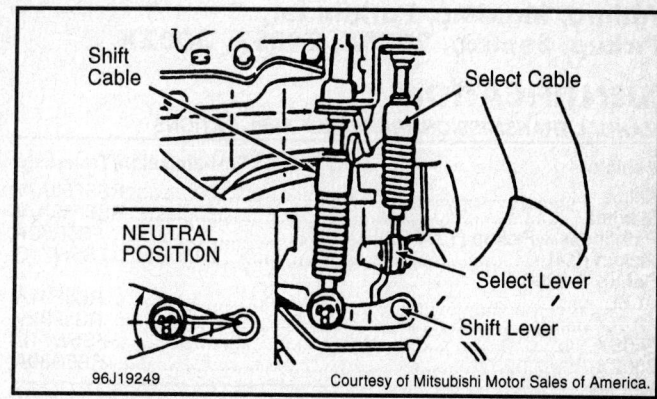

Fig. 1: Transaxle Control Cables (Typical)

SHIFT CABLE & GEARSHIFT LEVER

1) With transaxle select lever in Neutral, move gearshift lever into 4th gear. It may be necessary to depress clutch pedal. Loosen shift cable adjuster nuts (inside of vehicle).
2) Disconnect cable end from shift lever pin. Tilt gearshift lever into 4th gear position. Hold lever in this position, and adjust shift lever cable until it aligns with shift lever pin. Ensure cable bushing faces cotter pin.
3) Move shift lever between all gear positions. Ensure shift lever operates smoothly. Road test vehicle to ensure proper adjustment and smooth shifting.

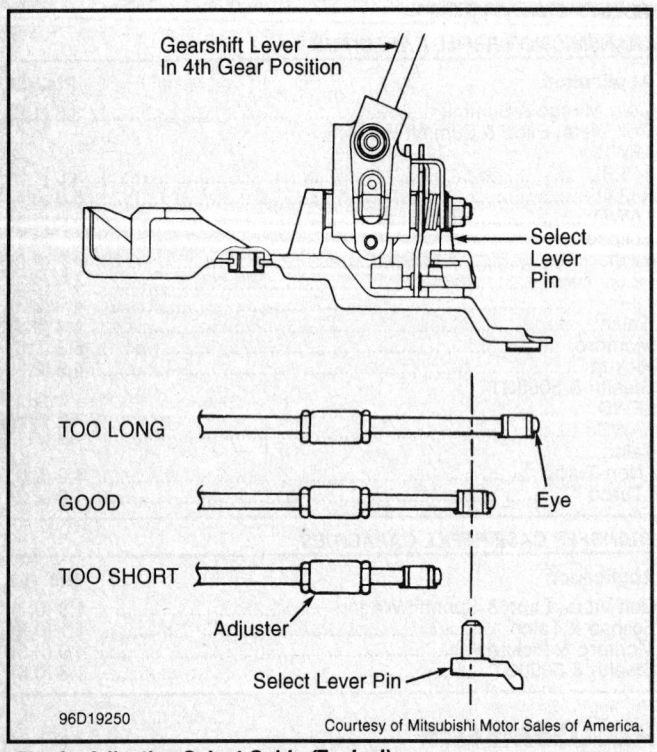

Fig. 2: Adjusting Select Cable (Typical)

TORQUE SPECIFICATIONS

TORQUE SPECIFICATIONS

Application	Ft. Lbs. (N.m)
Drain Plug & Filler Plug	
Except Montero	22-25 (30-34)
Montero	51 (69)

Nissan

Altima, Maxima, Pathfinder, Pickup, Sentra,, 200SX, 240SX, 300ZX

IDENTIFICATION

MANUAL TRANSMISSION/TRANSAXLE APPLICATIONS

Vehicle	Transmission/Transaxle
Altima	RS5F50A/V
Maxima	RS5F50A/V
Pathfinder & Pickup (1995 3.0L)	FS5R30A
Pickup (2.4L)	FS5W71C
Sentra & 200SX	
1.6L	RS5F31A
2.0L	RS5F32V
240SX	FS5W71C
300ZX	RS5R30A

LUBRICATION

SERVICE INTERVALS

Inspect fluid level every 15,000 miles or 12 months. If under severe usage, change fluid every 30,000 miles or 24 months.

CHECKING FLUID LEVEL

Transmission & Transaxle – Fill plug is located on side of transmission or transaxle case. Lubricant level should be to bottom of fill hole. Add fluid if necessary.
Transfer Case – Fill plug is located on side of transfer case. Lubricant level should be to bottom of fill hole. Add fluid if necessary.

RECOMMENDED FLUID

Use Hypoid SAE 75W-90 (API GL-4) gear oil for all transmissions, transaxles and transfer cases.

FLUID CAPACITIES

TRANSMISSION/TRANSAXLE REFILL CAPACITIES

Transmission/Transaxle	Pts. (L)
Altima & Maxima	
RS5F0A	10.0 (4.5)
RS5F0V	9.5 (4.3)
Sentra & 200SX	
RS5F31A	6.1-6.7 (2.9-3.2)
RS5F32V	7.0-7.9 (3.7-3.9)
Pathfinder & Pickup (3.0L)	
2WD	5.1 (2.4)
4WD	10.7 (5.1)
Pickup (2.4L)	
2WD	4.3 (2.0)
4WD	10.4 (4.9)
240SX	5.3 (2.5)
300ZX	5.9 (2.8)

TRANSFER CASE REFILL CAPACITIES

Application	Pts. (L)
Pathfinder & Pickup	4.6 (2.2)

ADJUSTMENTS

GEARSHIFT LINKAGE

NOTE: All models have floor shift mechanism with internal linkage that requires no adjustment.

TORQUE SPECIFICATIONS
TORQUE SPECIFICATIONS

Application	Ft. Lbs. (N.m)
Drain Plug	
Altima & Maxima	14-22 (19-30)
All Others	18-25 (24-34)
Filler Plug	
Sentra & 200SX	
RS5F31A	7-14 (10-20)
RS5F32V	7-14 (10-20)
All Others	18-25 (24-34)

Porsche

911 Carrera 2
IDENTIFICATION
MANUAL TRANSAXLE APPLICATIONS

Model	Transmission
911 Carrera 2	5-Speed – G50/20

LUBRICATION

SERVICE INTERVALS

Check fluid level every 15,000 miles. Replace fluid every 60,000 miles.

CHECKING FLUID LEVEL

Fluid should be level with bottom of fill hole on side of case.

RECOMMENDED FLUID

Use API GL-5 SAE 75W-90 gear oil.

FLUID CAPACITIES
TRANSMISSION REFILL CAPACITIES

Application	Qts. (L)
911 Carrera 2	3.8 (3.6)

ADJUSTMENTS

GEARSHIFT LINKAGE

Information is not available.

TORQUE SPECIFICATIONS
TORQUE SPECIFICATIONS

Application	Ft. Lbs. (N.m)
Drain Plug	22 (30)
Fill Plug	22 (30)

Rover

Defender 90, Discovery

NOTE: Defender 90 transmission servicing information is not available.

IDENTIFICATION
MANUAL TRANSMISSION APPLICATION

Vehicle Model	[1] Transmission/Series
Defender 90	R380/60A
Discovery	R380/53A

[1] – Transmission series (serial number prefix) is stamped on right side of transmission case.

LUBRICATION

SERVICE INTERVALS

Inspect fluid level every 15,000 miles or 12 months. If under severe usage, change fluid every 30,000 miles or 24 months.

CHECKING FLUID LEVEL

Transmission – Raise and support vehicle. Fill plug is located on side of transmission case. Lubricant level should be to bottom of fill hole. Add fluid if necessary. See RECOMMENDED FLUID. Install fill plug and tighten to specification. See TORQUE SPECIFICATIONS.

Transfer Case – Raise and support vehicle. Place drain pan under gearbox. Clean area around oil fill plug. Remove fill plug. Lubricant level should be to bottom of fill hole. Top off fluid as necessary. See RECOMMENDED FLUID. Clean oil fill plug threads and apply Hylomar sealant. Reinstall fill plug and tighten to specification. See TORQUE SPECIFICATIONS.

RECOMMENDED FLUID

Transmission – All transmissions use Dexron automatic transmission fluid.

Transfer Case – On Discovery, use Hypoid SAE 80W-90 (API GL-4 or GL-5). On Land Rover, use Dexron-II automatic transmission fluid.

FLUID CAPACITIES
TRANSMISSION/TRANSFER CASE REFILL CAPACITIES

Application	Qts. (L)
Transmission	[1] 2.9 (2.7)
Transfer Case	2.4 (2.3)

[1] – Specification is approximate.

ADJUSTMENTS

GEARSHIFT LINKAGE

NOTE: All models have floor shift mechanism with internal linkage that requires no adjustment.

DRAINING & REFILLING

Transmission – Raise and support vehicle. Place drain pan under transmission. Remove drain and fill plugs. Install drain plug and tighten to specification. See TORQUE SPECIFICATIONS. Add fluid. See FLUID CAPACITIES. Install fill plug and tighten to specification.
Transfer Case – Raise and support vehicle. Place drain pan under transfer case. Clean area around oil drain and fill plugs. Remove both plugs. Clean oil drain and fill plug threads. Apply Hylomar sealant to drain plug. Reinstall drain plug and tighten to specification. See TORQUE SPECIFICATIONS. Add fluid. See FLUID CAPACITIES. Apply Hylomar sealant to fill plug. Reinstall fill plug and tighten to specification.

TORQUE SPECIFICATIONS
TORQUE SPECIFICATIONS

Application	Ft. Lbs. (N.m)
Transfer Case	
Drain & Fill Plugs	18 (25)
Transmission	
Drain & Fill Plugs	18-26 (25-35)

Saab

900 Series, 9000 Series

IDENTIFICATION

For transaxle identification, *See Fig. 1.*

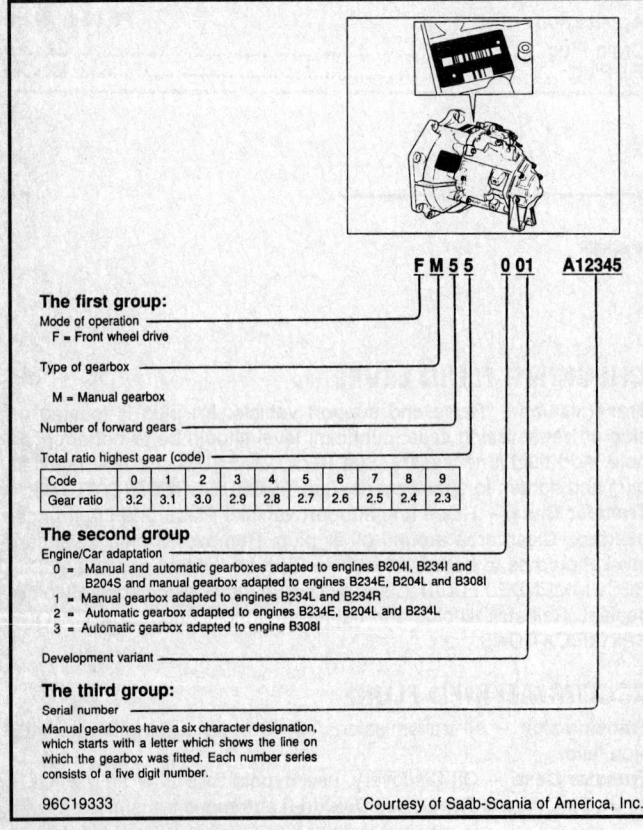

F M 5 5 0 01 A12345

The first group:
Mode of operation
F = Front wheel drive
Type of gearbox
M = Manual gearbox
Number of forward gears
Total ratio highest gear (code)

Code	0	1	2	3	4	5	6	7	8	9
Gear ratio	3.2	3.1	3.0	2.9	2.8	2.7	2.6	2.5	2.4	2.3

The second group:
Engine/Car adaptation
0 = Manual and automatic gearboxes adapted to engines B204I, B234I and B204S and manual gearbox adapted to engines B234E, B204L and B308I
1 = Manual gearbox adapted to engines B234L and B234R
2 = Automatic gearbox adapted to engines B234E, B204L and B234L
3 = Automatic gearbox adapted to engine B308I

Development variant

The third group:
Serial number
Manual gearboxes have a six character designation, which starts with a letter which shows the line on which the gearbox was fitted. Each number series consists of a five digit number.

96C19333   Courtesy of Saab-Scania of America, Inc.

Fig. 1: Identifying Manual Transaxle

LUBRICATION

SERVICE INTERVALS
Check fluid level every 10,000 miles.

CHECKING FLUID LEVEL
Remove oil level plug. Oil should be level with lower edge of oil level plug hole.

RECOMMENDED FLUID
Use SAE 10W-30 or 10W-40 engine oil. DO NOT use synthetic oil to lubricate transmission.

FLUID CAPACITIES
TRANSMISSION REFILL CAPACITIES

Application	Qts. (L)
900 Series	1.9 (1.8)
9000 Series	1.9 (1.8)

ADJUSTMENTS

GEARSHIFT LINKAGE

900 & 9000 Series – 1) Shift transmission into 4th gear. Remove plastic plug on transmission and secure shifter by inserting Locking Dowel (87 92 335). Ensure locking dowel ring is at top. Remove gear shift boot and check if locking dowel can be inserted into hole in gear lever housing. Ensure locking dowel ring is down in hole (900 Series), or at top (9000 Series). *See Fig. 2 or 3.* If locking dowel cannot be inserted, go to next step and adjust gear position. Remove locking dowels if no adjustment is necessary.
2) Remove clamp holding gear rod in transmission linkage. Ensure gear lever is in 4th gear. Position locking dowel in gear lever housing. Ensure locking dowel ring is down in hole (900 Series), or at top (9000 Series). Working from above, tighten nut on clamp joint to secure gear rod in transmission linkage.
3) Remove locking dowel from transmission and install NEW plastic plug. Remove locking dowel from gear lever housing and reinstall mounting frame and shift lever boot. Test by operating shift lever.

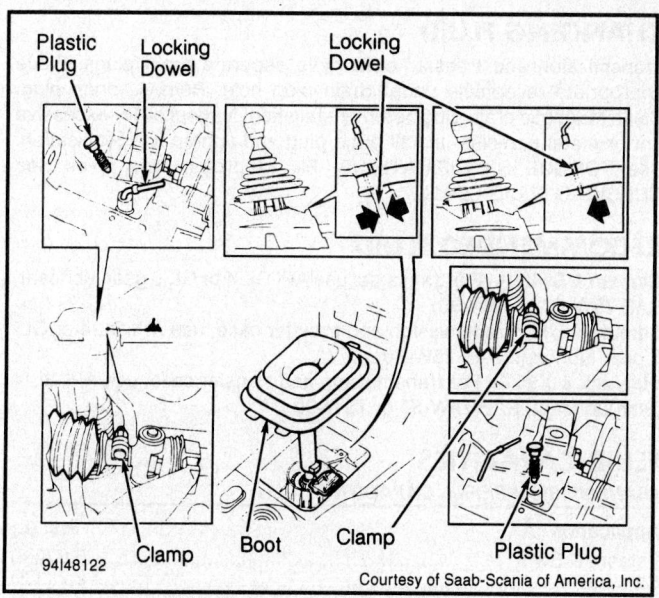

Fig. 2: Adjusting Gearshift Linkage (900 Series)

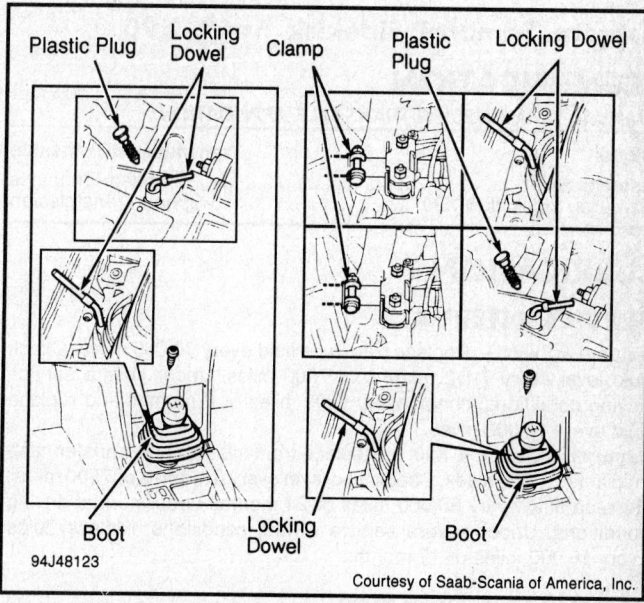

Fig. 3: Adjusting Gearshift Linkage (9000 Series)

TORQUE SPECIFICATIONS

TORQUE SPECIFICATIONS

Application	Ft. Lbs. (N.m)
Oil Drain Plug	30-44 (40-60)
Gear Rod Locking Nut	
900 Series	14-17 (19-23)
9000 Series	22-25.7 (30-35)

Subaru

Impreza, Legacy,

IDENTIFICATION

MANUAL TRANSAXLE APPLICATIONS

Model	Transaxle
Impreza	2WD & 4WD 5-Speed
Legacy	2WD & 4WD 5-Speed

LUBRICATION

SERVICE INTERVALS

Check fluid level every 15,000 miles. Replace fluid every 30,000 miles or 30 months when vehicle is operated under severe conditions.

CHECKING FLUID LEVEL

Check lubricant level at dipstick located in engine compartment. Transaxle and integral differential are lubricated through common oil supply.

RECOMMENDED FLUID

Use API GL-4, GL-5 or SAE 75W-90 gear oil.

FLUID CAPACITIES

TRANSMISSION REFILL CAPACITIES

Application	[1] Qts. (L)
Impreza	
2WD	3.5 (3.3)
4WD	4.2 (4.0)
Legacy	
2WD	3.5 (3.3)
4WD	4.2 (4.0)

[1] – Dry fill capacities.

MANUAL TRANSMISSION SERVICING
Suzuki

Esteem, Samurai, Sidekick, Swift, X90

IDENTIFICATION

MANUAL TRANSMISSION/TRANSAXLE APPLICATION

Model	Transmission/Transaxle
Esteem, Swift	5-Speed Transaxle
Samurai, Sidekick & X90	5-Speed Transmission

LUBRICATION

SERVICE INTERVALS

Esteem & Swift – Replace transaxle fluid every 30,000 miles. Check fluid level every 7 1/2 months or 7500 miles. Under severe service driving conditions, check every 6000 miles or 6 months and replace fluid every 12,000 miles.

Samurai, Sidekick & X90 – Replace transmission and transfer case fluid at first 7500 miles. Check fluid level every 6 months or 7500 miles. Replace fluid every 30,000 miles or 24 months under normal driving conditions. Under severe service driving conditions, replace fluids every 15,000 miles or 12 months.

CHECKING FLUID LEVEL

CAUTION: On Samurai, Sidekick and X90, DO NOT remove reverse idler gear bolt (hex head bolt) near right rear of main transmission case.

NOTE: Apply RTV sealant to threads of drain and filler plugs before installation.

Esteem & Swift (Transaxle) – Park vehicle on level surface. Inspect for leaks. Repair as necessary. Remove filler plug from side of transaxle case. Fluid should be level with bottom of filler plug hole. Fill if necessary. Install filler plug and tighten to specification. See TORQUE SPECIFICATIONS.

Samurai, Sidekick & X90 (Transmission & Transfer Case) – 1) Transmission and transfer case have separate drain and filler plugs. Park vehicle on level surface with engine off. Inspect for leaks. Repair as necessary. Remove transmission filler plug on right side of case. DO NOT remove reverse idler gear bolt (hex head bolt) near right rear of case. Fluid should be level with bottom of filler plug hole. Fill if necessary.

2) On transfer case, remove filler plug on rear side of transfer case. Fluid should be to level of filler plug hole. Fill if necessary.

CHANGING FLUID

Transmission and transfer case have separate drain plugs. Place appropriate receptacle under drain plug hole. Remove drain plug. Clean magnetic drain plug before installation. Inspect oil for excessive grit or metal particles. Install drain plug and tighten to specification. See TORQUE SPECIFICATIONS. Fill to proper fluid level. See CHECKING FLUID LEVEL.

RECOMMENDED FLUID

Esteem & Swift – For transaxle, use API GL-4 or GL-5 gear lubricant, SAE 75W-80 or 75W-90.

Samurai – For transmission and transfer case, use API GL-4 or GL-5 gear lubricant, SAE 75W-90.

Sidekick & X90 – For transmission and transfer case, use API GL-4 gear lubricant, SAE 75W-80 or 75W-90.

FLUID CAPACITIES

TRANSMISSION REFILL CAPACITIES

Application	Pts. (L)
Esteem & Swift	5.0 (2.4)
Samurai	2.7 (1.3)
Sidekick & X90	3.2 (1.5)

TRANSFER CASE REFILL CAPACITIES

Application	Pts. (L)
Samurai	1.7 (.8)
Sidekick & X90	3.6 (1.7)

ADJUSTMENTS

LINKAGE

No external adjustments are necessary.

TORQUE SPECIFICATIONS

TORQUE SPECIFICATIONS

Application	Ft. Lbs. (N.m)
Esteem	
Oil Drain Plug	15 (21)
Oil Filler/Inspection Plug	15 (21)
Swift	
Oil Drain Plug	14-17 (18-23)
Oil Filler/Inspection Plug	14-17 (18-23)
Samurai, Sidekick & X90	
Oil Drain Plug	17 (23)
Oil Filler/Inspection Plug	17 (23)

**Camry, Celica, Corolla, MR2 (1995),
Paseo, Pickup (1995), RAV4 (1996),
Supra, Tacoma, Tercel, T100, 4Runner**

APPLICATION

MANUAL TRANSMISSION/TRANSAXLE APPLICATIONS

Model	Transmission/Transaxle
Camry	
2.2L 4-Cyl.	5-Speed – S51
Celica	
1.8L (7A-FE)	5-Speed - C52
2.2L (5S-FE)	5-Speed - S54
Corolla	
1.6L (4A-FE)	5-Speed - C50
1.8L (7A-FE)	5-Speed - C52
MR2	
2.0L Turbo	5-Speed - E153
2.2L Non-Turbo	5-Speed - S54
Paseo	5-Speed - C150
Pickup	
2.4L 4-Cyl.	
2WD	5-Speed - W55
4WD	5-Speed - G58 Or W56
3.0L V6	
2WD	5-Speed - R150
4WD	5-Speed - R150F
RAV4	
2WD	5-Speed - E250
4WD	5-Speed - E250F
Supra	
3.0L Non-Turbo	5-Speed - W58
3.0L Turbo	6-Speed - V160
Tacoma	
2WD	
2.4L 4-Cyl.	5-Speed - W59
3.4L V6	5-Speed - R150
4WD	
2.7L 4-Cyl.	5-Speed - W59
3.4L V6	5-Speed - R150F
Tercel	4-Speed - C141 Or 5-Speed - C151
T100	
1995	
2WD	
2.7L 4-Cyl.	5-Speed - W56
3.4L V6	5-Speed - R150
4WD	5-Speed - R150F
1996	
2WD	
2.7L 4-Cyl.	5-Speed - W59
3.4L V6	5-Speed - R150
4WD	5-Speed - R150F
4Runner	
1995	
4WD	
2.4L 4-Cyl.	5-Speed - G58
3.0L V6	5-Speed - R150F
1996	
2WD	
2.7L 4-Cyl.	5-Speed - W59
4WD	
2.7L 4-Cyl.	5-Speed - W59
3.4L V6	5-Speed - R150F

LUBRICATION

SERVICE INTERVALS

Transmission – Check transmission fluid level every 15,000 miles or 24 months. Service interval is not available for vehicles operated under normal conditions. Under severe conditions such as trailer towing, police, taxi, local delivery service or operating under dusty conditions, replace transmission fluid every 15,000 miles or 24 months.

Transfer Case – Check transfer case fluid level every 15,000 miles or 24 months. Service interval is not available for vehicles operated under normal conditions. Under severe conditions such as trailer towing, police, taxi, local delivery service or operating under dusty conditions, replace transfer case fluid every 15,000 miles or 24 months.

CHECKING FLUID LEVEL

Transmission (All Models) – Remove filler plug from side of transmission. Fluid should be level with bottom edge of filler plug hole. If fluid is low, fill with proper type fluid until fluid is level with filler plug opening. See RECOMMENDED FLUID under LUBRICATION. Reinstall filler plug.

Transfer Case (Pickup, Tacoma, T100 & 4Runner) – Remove filler plug located on rear of transfer case. Fluid should be level with bottom edge of filler plug hole. If fluid is low, fill with proper type fluid until fluid is level with filler plug opening. See RECOMMENDED FLUID under LUBRICATION. Reinstall filler plug.

Transfer Case (RAV4) – Transfer case fluid level checking information is not available.

FLUID CAPACITIES

TRANSMISSION/TRANSAXLE REFILL CAPACITIES [1]

Application	Qts. (L)
Camry	2.7 (2.6)
Celica	
1.8L (7A-FE)	
1995	2.7 (2.6)
1996	2.0 (1.9)
2.2L (5S-FE)	2.7 (2.6)
Corolla	
1.6L (4A-FE) & 1.8L (7A-FE)	
1995	2.7 (2.6)
1996	2.0 (1.9)
MR2	
2.0L Turbo	
With Limited Slip Differential	4.1 (3.9)
Without Limited Slip Differential	4.4 (4.2)
2.2L Non-Turbo	2.7 (2.6)
Paseo	
1995	2.5 (2.4)
1996	2.0 (1.9)
Pickup	
2WD	2.7 (2.6)
4WD	
2.4L 4-Cyl.	
With G58 Trans.	4.1 (3.9)
With W56 Trans.	3.1 (2.9)
3.0L V6	2.3 (2.2)
RAV4	
2WD	4.1 (3.9)
4WD	5.3 (5.0)
Supra	
3.0L Non-Turbo	2.7 (2.6)
3.0L Turbo	1.9 (1.8)
Tacoma	
2WD	2.7 (2.6)
4WD	
2.7L 4-Cyl.	2.6 (2.5)
3.4L V6	2.3 (2.2)
Tercel	
1995	2.5 (2.4)
1996	2.0 (1.9)
T100	
2WD	2.7 (2.6)
4WD	2.3 (2.2)
4Runner	
1995	
2.4L 4-Cyl.	4.1 (3.9)
3.0L V6	2.3 (2.2)
1996	
2.7L 4-Cyl.	
2WD	2.7 (2.6)
4WD	2.6 (2.5)
3.4L V6	2.3 (2.2)

[1] – Approximate capacity is listed.

RECOMMENDED FLUID

For recommended fluid type, see FLUID APPLICATION table. For fluid capacity, see appropriate refill capacities table under FLUID CAPACITIES.

FLUID APPLICATION

Application	Fluid Type
Transmission	
Supra Turbo	ESSO ATF Dexron (D-21065) Or Toyota Gear Oil V160
All Others	SAE 75W-90/API GL-5 Gear Oil
Transfer Case	SAE 75W-90/API GL-5 Gear Oil

TRANSFER CASE REFILL CAPACITIES [1]

Application	Qts. (L)
Pickup	1.7 (1.6)
RAV4	[2]
Tacoma	1.1 (1.0)
T100	1.2 (1.1)
4Runner	1.2 (1.1)

[1] – Approximate capacity is listed.
[2] – Individual transfer case capacity is not available. Total capacity of transmission and transfer case are listed. See TRANSMISSION/TRANSAXLE REFILL CAPACITIES table.

ADJUSTMENTS

NOTE: Adjustments are not required during routine servicing and maintenance.

TORQUE SPECIFICATIONS
TORQUE SPECIFICATIONS

Application	Ft. Lbs. (N.m)
Transmission Drain & Filler Plugs	
Camry	36 (49)
Celica	
1.8L (7A-FE)	29 (39)
2.2L (5S-FE)	36 (49)
Corolla	29 (39)
MR2	
2.0L Turbo	[1]
2.2L Non-Turbo	36 (49)
Paseo	29 (39)
Pickup	27 (37)
RAV4	36 (49)
Supra	
3.0L Non-Turbo	29 (39)
3.0L Turbo	[1]
Tacoma	
2.4L 4-Cyl.	29 (39)
3.4L V6	27 (37)
Tercel	29 (39)
T100 & 4Runner	27 (37)

[1] – Information is not available.

Volkswagen

Cabrio, Golf, Golf III, GTI VR6, Jetta, Jetta III, Passat

IDENTIFICATION
MANUAL TRANSAXLE APPLICATIONS

Application	Model
1995	
Cabrio & Golf III	020
GTI VR6 & Passat	02A
Jetta III	
4-Cylinder	020
V6	02A
1996	
Cabrio	020
Golf & Jetta	
4-Cylinder	
Gas Engine	020
Turbo Diesel	02A
V6	02A
Passat	02A

LUBRICATION

SERVICE INTERVALS

No oil changes are required.

CHECKING FLUID LEVEL

Remove oil filler plug. Oil level should be up to lower edge of filler hole. Add if necessary. Install filler plug.

RECOMMENDED FLUID

Use API G50 75W-90 synthetic gear oil.

FLUID CAPACITIES
TRANSAXLE REFILL CAPACITIES

Transaxle	Qts. (L)
02A	2.1 (2.0)
020	2.0 (1.9)

ADJUSTMENTS

GEARSHIFT LINKAGE

02A Transaxle – 1) Place gear selector lever in Neutral position. Remove knob and boot. Remove balance weight. Loosen bolt "A" and nut "B" sufficiently so that operating cables move freely in centering holes. See Fig 1. Install Shift Linkage Gauge (3192). Loosen bolt "C". See Fig 2.

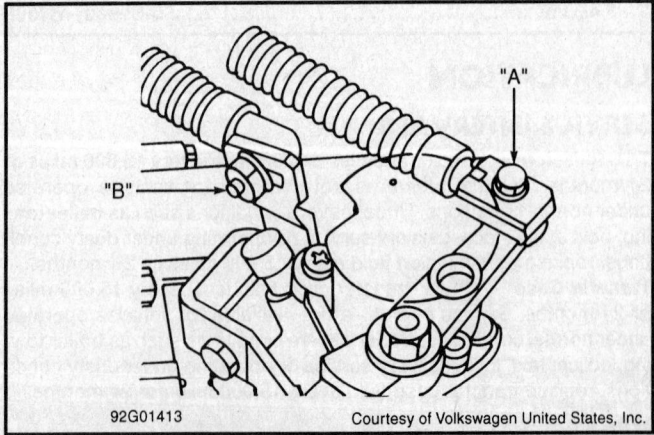

92G01413   Courtesy of Volkswagen United States, Inc.

Fig. 1: Identifying Centering Holes (02A Transaxle)

2) Pivot locating pin under bearing plate. Tighten nut "D". Place gearshift lever into left detent of slide. Move gearshift lever and slide together to left stop. Tighten slide with bolt "D". Move gearshift lever to right detent. Tighten bolt "E". Move gearshift lever to right detent. Tighten bolt "C".

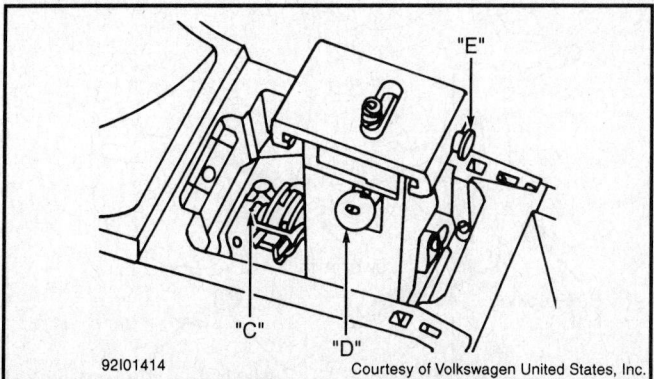

Fig. 2: **Installing Shift Linkage Gauge (02A Transaxle)**

020 Transaxle – 1) Place shift lever in Neutral position. Ensure transaxle is also in Neutral. Loosen lower shifter rod clamp. *See Fig. 3.* Selector lever must move freely on shifter rod.
2) Remove gearshift knob and boot. Position Adjustment Gauge (3104) over shift rod. *See Fig. 4.* With transaxle in Neutral, align shift rod with selector lever. Tighten shifter rod clamp to 19 ft. lbs. (26 N.m).
3) Move gearshift lever through all gear positions. Gears must engage smoothly and without jamming. Reinstall gearshift knob and boot.

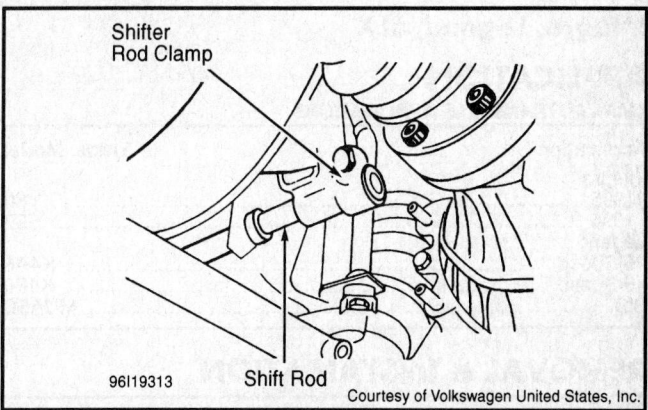

Fig. 3: **Loosening Shift Rod Clamp (020 Transaxle)**

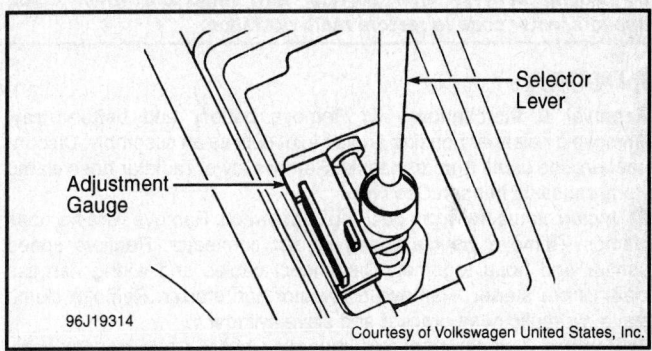

Fig. 4: **Locating Adjustment Gauge (020 Transaxle)**

Volvo

850

IDENTIFICATION

MANUAL TRANSMISSION APPLICATIONS

Vehicle Model	Transmission Model
850	M56L (5-Speed)

LUBRICATION

SERVICE INTERVALS

Check fluid every 7500 miles.

CHECKING FLUID LEVEL

Fluid level should be at bottom of fill hole. Use socket to remove plug. Clean strainer and magnet with solvent. Replace filter and tighten plug

RECOMMENDED FLUID

Use Type "F" ATF or Volvo Synthetic Oil (11614237).

FLUID CAPACITIES

TRANSMISSION REFILL CAPACITIES

Application	Qts. (L)
M56L	2.2 (2.1)

ADJUSTMENTS

LINKAGE

No external linkage adjustment is required.

Integra, Legend, SLX

APPLICATION

MANUAL TRANSAXLE APPLICATIONS

Application	Trans. Model
Integra	
1995	Y80
1996	S80
Legend	
5-Speed	K4A6
6-Speed	K4F6
SLX	MUA5C

REMOVAL & INSTALLATION

NOTE: If vehicle has anti-theft radio, obtain code number before disconnecting battery. After service, turn radio on. When CODE appears, enter code to restore radio operation.

INTEGRA

Removal & Installation – 1) Remove battery and battery tray. Remove air cleaner housing and air inlet duct as an assembly. Disconnect ground cable from transaxle. Remove lower radiator hose clamp from transaxle hanger. *See Fig. 1.*

2) Unplug connector from back-up light switch. Remove wire harness clamps. Remove vehicle speed sensor connector. Remove speed sensor and hose together. Disconnect cables and wiring harness clamp from starter. Remove distributor and starter. Remove clutch slave hydraulic hose bracket and slave cylinder.

3) Remove 3 upper transaxle mounting bolts. Drain transaxle oil. Remove engine splash shield. Unplug oxygen sensor connector. Remove exhaust pipe from manifold and catalytic converter. Separate lower ball joints from control arm. Remove right damper fork. *See Fig. 2.* Remove axle shafts and intermediate shafts. See appropriate AXLE SHAFTS article in AXLE SHAFTS & TRANSFER CASES.

4) Remove engine heat shield. Disconnect shift and extension rods from transaxle. *See Fig. 3.* Remove front and rear engine braces. Remove clutch housing cover. Remove right front transaxle mount/bracket. Place jack under transaxle. Support engine with jackstands. Remove transaxle mount.

5) Remove rear transaxle mount bracket and mount bolts from side of transaxle. Move transaxle away from engine until shaft clears clutch. Lower transaxle to remove from vehicle. To install, reverse removal procedure. When installing shift and extension rods, turn shift rod where hole is facing down. Install clip over spring pin as shown. *See Fig. 3.* Ensure shift rod boot is installed properly. Tighten nuts and bolts to specification. See TORQUE SPECIFICATIONS.

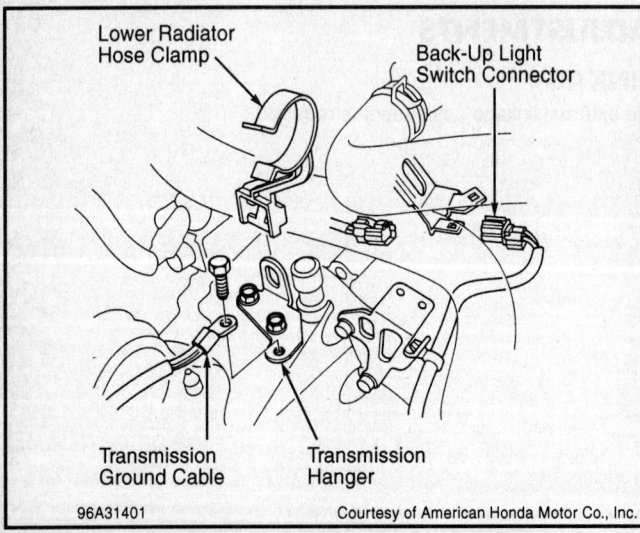

Fig. 1: Identifying Cable, Bracket & Connector (Integra)

96A31401   Courtesy of American Honda Motor Co., Inc.

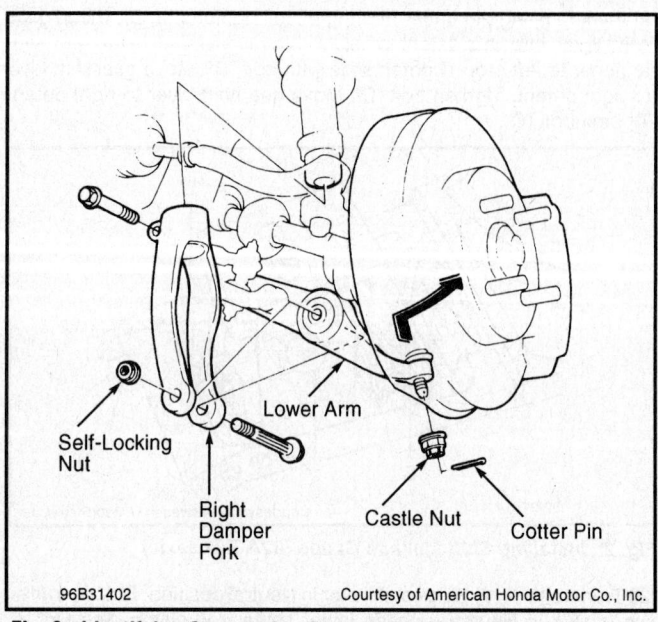

Fig. 2: Identifying Suspension Components (Integra)

96B31402   Courtesy of American Honda Motor Co., Inc.

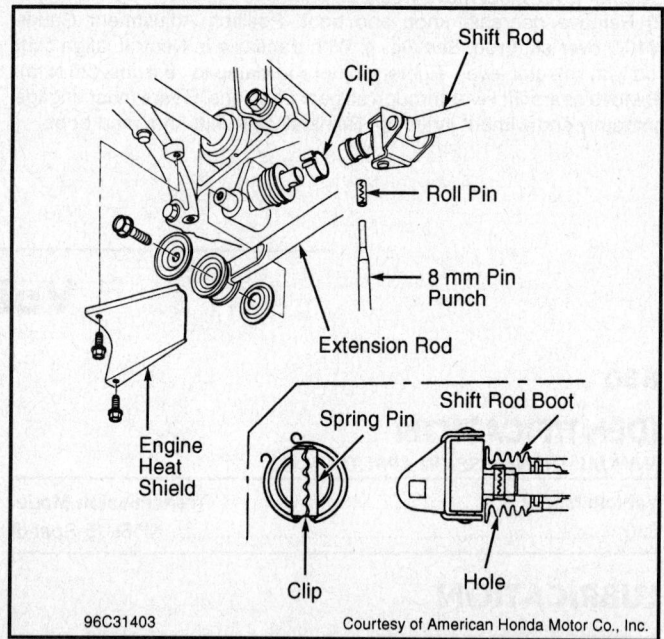

Fig. 3: Removing & Installing Shift & Extension Rods (Integra)

96C31403   Courtesy of American Honda Motor Co., Inc.

NOTE: Obtain radio anti-theft code number before disconnecting battery. After service, turn radio on. When CODE appears, enter code to restore radio operation.

LEGEND

Removal & Installation – 1) Disconnect battery cables. Remove strut bar. Drain transaxle fluid. Without removing vacuum lines, remove emission control box and set it aside. Unplug harness connectors (if necessary). Remove transaxle housing bolts.

2) Remove release cylinder hose bracket from rear engine hanger. Remove exhaust pipe and catalytic converter. Remove secondary cover and 36-mm sealing bolt. *See Fig. 4.* Remove heat shield and bracket. Shift transaxle into first gear to lock secondary gear. Using Puller (07LAC-PW50100), separate extension shaft from differential. *See Fig. 5.* Disconnect shift rod and torque rod from transaxle. Remove clutch release fork cover. Remove clutch release cylinder. Disconnect oil cooler hoses from oil pump pipes.

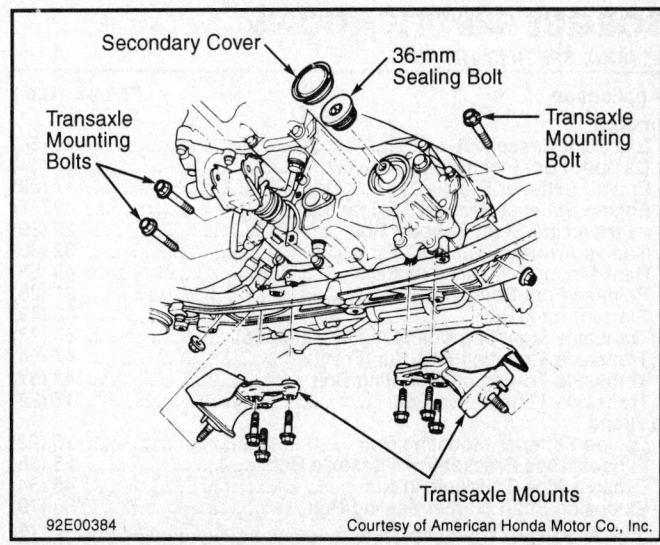

Fig. 4: Identifying Differential Secondary Cover & Sealing Bolt (Legend)

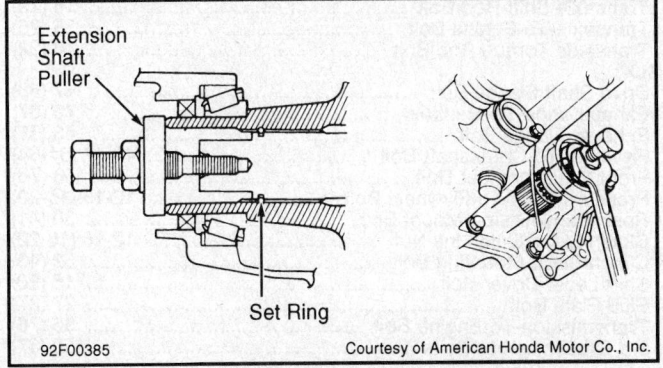

Fig. 5: Disconnecting Extension Shaft From Differential (Legend)

3) Remove lower engine shield. Temporarily reinstall steering gear bolts. Remove exhaust pipe bracket, transaxle mount, and transaxle bracket. Pull out release fork to disengage it from pivot and release bearing. Let fork hang from housing.

4) Place jack under transaxle. Remove transaxle mounts. Remove engine-to-transaxle bracket. Remove flywheel inspection cover. Remove transaxle housing mounting bolts and 26-mm shim. See Fig. 6. Check for wires, hoses, or any other components that may still be attached. Pull transaxle away from engine until clear. Lower transaxle to remove from vehicle. To install, reverse removal procedure. Tighten bolts and nuts to specification. See TORQUE SPECIFICATIONS.

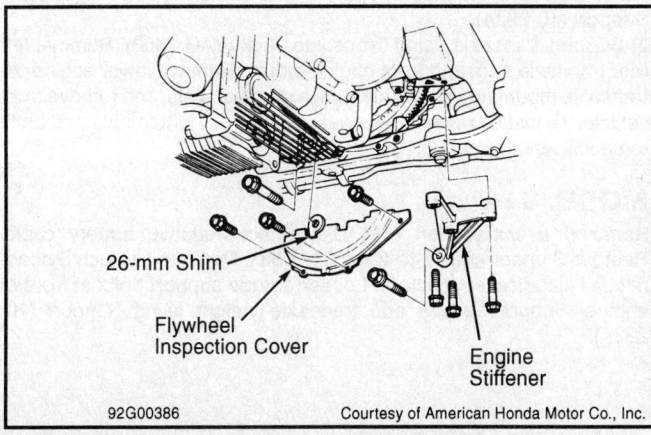

Fig. 6: Identifying 26-mm Transaxle Shim (Legend)

SLX

Removal & Installation – 1) Remove engine hood. Disconnect battery cables. Raise and support vehicle. Remove transfer case skid plate. Drain transmission and transfer case fluid. Disconnect 4 oxygen sensor connectors from transmission harness. Remove right front exhaust pipe and converter assembly. Remove transmission harness heat shield.

2) Remove slave cylinder with it's heat shield and dust covers. Mark rear drive shaft flanges for installation reference. Disconnect rear driveshaft at differential and remove driveshaft. Remove reverse light switch, and all transmission harness connectors at transmission. Disconnect harness from transmission.

3) Support transfer case and remove rear transmission mount bolts. See Fig. 7. Remove 3rd crossmember bolts. Remove rear transmission mount from transmission. Remove front crossmember. Mark front drive shaft for installation reference. Disconnect front driveshaft at differential and remove driveshaft.

4) Remove gear shift knob and front console assembly. Remove shift boot. Remove transmission and transfer case shift lever. Using transmission jack, support transmission and remove support from transfer case. Remove flywheel cover.

5) Pull shift fork toward transmission. To separate transmission from engine, clutch release bearing must be disengaged from pressure plate, using clutch release bearing remover or screwdriver. Pry between wedge collar and release bearing to separate release bearing from pressure plate. See Fig. 8.

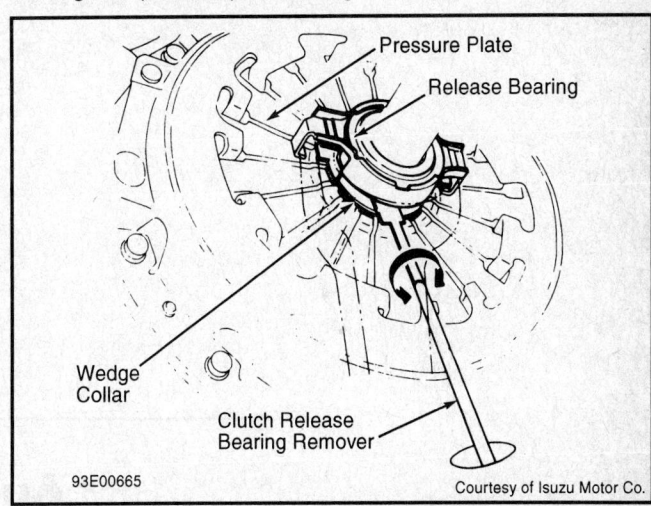

Fig. 7: Removing Rear Transmission Mount (SLX)

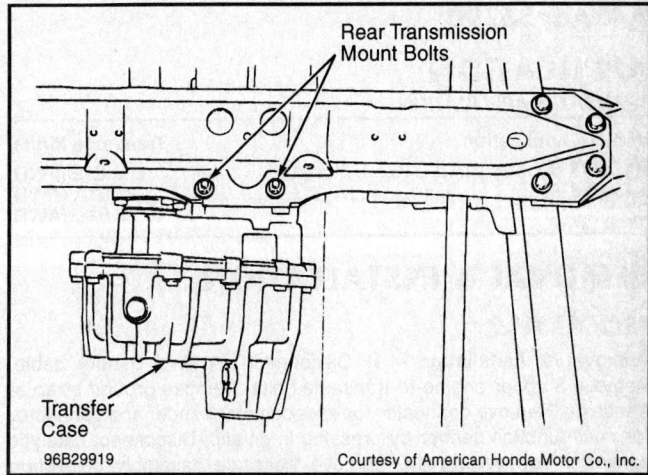

Fig. 8: Separating Clutch Release Bearing From Pressure Plate (SLX)

6) Remove transmission-to-engine retaining nuts and bolts. Tilt front of transmission downward and remove transmission from vehicle. Transmission and transfer case are removed as an assembly. For installation, reverse removal procedures. Apply grease on input shaft. Ensure transmission and engine angle are the same during installation.

7) Push shift fork toward transmission with a force of 13-18 lbs. (58-79 N). This will engage release bearing to pressure plate. A click sound should be heard as release bearing engages pressure plate. Tighten bolts and nuts to specification. See TORQUE SPECIFICATIONS.

TORQUE SPECIFICATIONS

TORQUE SPECIFICATIONS

Application	Ft. Lbs. (N.m)
Integra	
Ball Joint Castle Nut	40 (54)
Damper Fork Pinch Bolt	47 (64)
Engine Stiffener Bracket-To-Engine Bolt	17 (23)
Engine Stiffener Bracket-To-Transaxle Bolt	42 (57)
Intermediate Shaft Support Bolt	29 (39)
Radius Arm Nut	32 (43)
Rear Mount-To-Transaxle Bolt	43 (58)
Release Fork Bolt	21 (29)
Starter Motor Bolt	32 (43)
Transaxle Mounting Bolt/Nut (Firewall Side)	54 (73)
Transaxle Mounting Bolt/Nut (Front)	47 (64)
Transaxle-To-Engine Mounting Bolt	42 (57)
Transaxle Torque Rod Bolt	16 (22)
Legend	
Engine Stiffener Mounting Bolt	16 (22)
Exhaust Pipe Bracket-To-Transaxle Bolt	26 (35)
Exhaust Pipe-To-Manifold Nut	40 (54)
Extension Shaft 36-mm Sealing Bolt	58 (79)
Master Cylinder Mounting Bolt	10 (14)
Release Cylinder-To-Housing Bolt	16 (22)
Transaxle Mount Bolt	29 (39)
Transaxle Mount Nut	36 (49)
Transaxle Shift Rod Bolt	16 (22)
Transaxle-To-Engine Bolt	55 (75)
Transaxle Torque Rod Bolt	16 (22)
SLX	
Drive Shaft Flange Bolt	47 (63)
Exhaust Pipe-To-Manifold	49 (67)
Exhaust Flange Bolt	43 (32)
Flywheel-To-Crankshaft Bolt [1]	40-47 (54-64)
Front Crossmember Bolt	58 (78)
Pressure Plate-To-Flywheel Bolt [2]	12-15 (16-20)
Rear Transmission Mount Bolt	30 (41)
Clutch Slave Fluid Line Nut	12-16 (16-22)
Clutch Slave Mounting Bolt	32 (43)
Shift Lever Cover Bolt	15 (20)
Skid Plate Bolt	27 (37)
Transmission-To-Engine Bolt	56 (76)
3rd Crossmember Bolts	50 (37)

[1] – Install NEW bolts and apply Loctite (262) to bolt threads. Tighten bolts in a diagonal pattern.
[2] – Tighten bolts in a diagonal pattern.

Audi

A4, A6, S6, 90

APPLICATION

TRANSAXLE APPLICATION

Vehicle Application	Transaxle Model
A4, A6 & 90	012 (FWD)
A4, A6 & 90	01A (AWD)
S6	01E (AWD)

REMOVAL & INSTALLATION

MODEL 012

Removal & Installation – 1) Disconnect negative battery cable. Remove 3 upper engine-to-transaxle bolts. Remove ground strap at transaxle. Remove connector for speedometer sender and connector for multi-function sender by pressing in on clip. Disconnect catalytic converter connector pipe. Remove transaxle assembly protection plate. Remove front exhaust pipe from manifold. Remove engine torque arm, located near radiator.

2) Remove rear crossmember. Disconnect automatic seat belt tension cables at transaxle. Disconnect shift rod. Remove drive axle protection plate. Disconnect axle shafts at transaxle. Rotate steering to right lock, and support axle shafts using wire. Remove slave cylinder and steering bracket. Support engine and transaxle weight using Support (10-222A).

3) Support transaxle using Transaxle Jack (VAG 1383). Remove left rear transaxle strut and front engine mount. Remove lower engine-to-transaxle mounting bolts. Slide transaxle off dowels, and remove from vehicle. To install, reverse removal procedure. Tighten nuts and bolts to specification. See TORQUE SPECIFICATIONS.

MODEL 01A

Removal & Installation – 1) Disconnect negative battery cable. Remove 3 upper engine-to-transaxle bolts. Remove air duct. Disconnect all electrical connectors. Loosen torque support bolts at front of engine. Support engine and transaxle weight using Support (10-222A).

2) Remove crossmember. Remove exhaust. Remove shift rod from transaxle. Remove driveshaft. See DRIVESHAFT. Disconnect automatic seat belt tension cables at transaxle. Remove drive axle protection plate. Disconnect axle shafts at transaxle.

3) Remove starter. Unbolt clutch slave cylinder and secure out of the way. Support transaxle using Transaxle Jack (VAG 1383). Remove transaxle support and subframe. Remove lower engine-to-transaxle bolts. Remove transaxle. To install, reverse removal procedure. Tighten nuts and bolts to specification. See TORQUE SPECIFICATIONS.

MODEL 01E

Removal & Installation – 1) Disconnect negative battery cable. Remove 3 upper engine-to-transaxle bolts. Remove air duct. Disconnect all electrical connectors. Loosen torque support at front of engine. Support engine and transaxle weight using Support (10-222A).

2) Remove crossmember. Remove exhaust. Remove starter. Remove driveshaft. See DRIVESHAFT. Place shifter in 3rd gear and unbolt clamp for torque and select rods.

NOTE: The shift rod is separated by pulling shift lever back in direction of 4th gear.

3) Loosen torque support bolts at front of engine. Remove heat shields. Disconnect drive axles and secure out of the way. Support transaxle using Transaxle Jack (VAG 1383). Remove transaxle support and subframe. Disconnect automatic seat belt tension cables at transaxle. Remove lower engine-to-transaxle bolts. Remove transaxle. To install, reverse removal procedure. Tighten nuts and bolts to specification. See TORQUE SPECIFICATIONS.

DRIVESHAFT (AWD)

REMOVAL & INSTALLATION

1) Remove crossmembers, heat shields and exhaust, noting position. Mark front and rear flanges to index driveshaft location. Loosen flange and center bearing bolts. Install alignment fixture (3139) and tighten plastic nuts. Remove flange bolts. Support driveshaft and fixture and remove remaining bolts.

NOTE: Remove thread locking compound form threads in both flanges prior to installation. Always replace gaskets and self-locking bolts.

2) To install, reverse removal procedure and adjust driveshaft. Tighten nuts and bolts to specification. See TORQUE SPECIFICATIONS.

ADJUSTING

1) Remove components necessary to gain access to driveshaft. See Removal & Installation. Install alignment fixture (3139) and tighten plastic nuts. Remove center bearing bolts and shims. Measure gap between center bearing support and body. Ensure gap is equal on both sides. Determine shims required. See DRIVESHAFT SHIM TABLE.

DRIVESHAFT SHIM TABLE

Distance (mm)	Thickness (mm)	Part No.
0-3.0	-	-
3.1-5.0	2	857 521 143
5.1-7.0	4	857 521 143A
7.1-9.0	2	857 521 143B
9.1-11.0	2	857 521 143C
11.1-13.0	2	857 521 143D

2) Push alignment fixture and driveshaft forward and back, marking farthest travel of bearing support on body. Center bearing support between marks and install shims and bolts. Remove alignment fixture and reinstall components. Tighten nuts and bolts to specification. See TORQUE SPECIFICATIONS.

TORQUE SPECIFICATIONS

TORQUE SPECIFICATIONS

Application	Ft. Lbs. (N.m)
Engine-To-Transmission Bolt	
8-mm Bolt	18 (25)
10-mm Bolt	33 (45)
12-mm Bolt	48 (65)
Starter Bolt	40 (54)
Slave Cylinder To Transmission	18 (25)
Transmission Support To Subframe	33 (45)
Driveshaft Shield	18 (25)
Torque Support To Body	33 (45)
Driveshaft To Transmission	41 (55)
Driveshaft To Rear Differential	44 (55)
Driveshaft Center Bearing Support to Body	15 (20)
Shield To Transmission	18 (25)
Crossmember With Heat Shield	18 (25)
Converter To Front Pipe	18 (25)
Converter To Bracket	18 (25)
Crossmember To Body	18 (25)

BMW

Z3, 3-Series, 5-Series

APPLICATION

TRANSMISSION APPLICATION

Vehicle Application	Transmission Model
1995	
M3	Getrag 310
318i, 318iC, 318is, 318ti	
325i, 325iC, 325is	Getrag 250
525i, 530i	S5-31
540i	Getrag 286
1996	
M3, 328i, 328is	S5-31
Z3, 318i, 318is, 318ti	Getrag 250

NOTE: Z3 transmission removal and installation information is not available.

REMOVAL & INSTALLATION

Removal – 1) From inside engine compartment, remove upper clutch housing mount bolts and bracket. Remove control rod at transmission from gearshift lever.

2) Raise and support vehicle. Remove exhaust system components as necessary. Remove bolts and discard lock nuts holding drive shaft flange to transmission shaft flange. Remove heat shield.

3) Disconnect center support bearing and bracket. Remove drive shaft from front flange and position shaft out of way. Hold rear of engine with overhead support. Support transmission with jack. Remove rear transmission mount and crossmember from body.

4) Remove clutch slave cylinder from clutch housing. Remove engine position sensors from bellhousing (if equipped). Unplug electrical connectors from transmission. Remove transmission mount bolts. Slide transmission rearward and lower away from vehicle.

NOTE: On vehicles with speed and reference mark sensors, check component locations for proper installation reference. If sensors are reversed, engine will not start.

Installation – 1) Install clutch housing. Lightly apply molybdenum grease on contact surfaces of disc hub splines, release bearing, and release lever. Install slave cylinder with bleed screw at bottom. Install drive shaft.

2) To preload center bearing on models with slide on center mount, move bracket .16-.24" (4-6 mm) forward in slots. To preload center bearing on models without slide on center mount, move bracket .08-.16" (2-4 mm) forward in slots. Install and tighten NEW drive shaft flange lock nuts. To complete installation, reverse removal procedure. Tighten bolts to specification. See TORQUE SPECIFICATIONS.

TORQUE SPECIFICATIONS
TORQUE SPECIFICATIONS

Application	Ft. Lbs. (N.m)
Clutch Housing-To-Engine Bolt	
Hex Head Bolts	
8-mm Bolt	20 (27)
10-mm Bolt	38 (52)
12-mm Bolt	61 (83)
Torx Bolts	
8-mm Bolt	18 (24)
10-mm Bolt	35 (47)
12-mm Bolt	59 (80)
Drive Shaft Flange Bolt	72 (98)
Slave Cylinder-To-Clutch Housing	
Mount Bolt	18 (24)

Geo

Metro, Prizm, Tracker
APPLICATION
MANUAL TRANSMISSION APPLICATIONS

Model	Transaxle/Transmission
Metro	5-Speed Suzuki Transaxle
Prizm	5-Speed Toyota Transaxle
Tracker	5-Speed Suzuki Transmission

REMOVAL & INSTALLATION
METRO

Removal – 1) Disconnect negative battery cable at battery and transaxle. Disconnect back-up light switch harness connector. Loosen clutch release lever bolt and nut. Remove clutch release lever from shaft.

2) Remove 2 clutch cable bracket bolts and set bracket and cables aside. Remove 2 bolts from gear shift guide case and set engine wiring harness and bracket aside. Disconnect speedometer cable. Remove 2 upper right transaxle-to-engine bolts.

3) Using Universal Support Fixture (J-28467-A) and Support Adapters (J-28467-89), support engine. Raise and support vehicle. Drain transaxle fluid. Support transaxle with a jack. Install Drive Axle Boot Protectors (J-28712) to drive axles.

4) Remove both drive axles. See appropriate AXLE SHAFTS article in AXLE SHAFTS & TRANSFER CASES section. Remove 2 bolts and flywheel cover from transaxle. Remove gear shift control shaft bolt and nut. Disconnect control shaft from gear shift shaft.

5) Remove 4 gear shift control lever guide plate bolts. Separate extension rod from gear shift control lever guide plate. Remove one nut and 2 washers at extension rod mounting stud. Separate extension rod from transaxle. Remove starter motor.

6) Remove rear transaxle mount-through bolt and nut from rear transaxle mount. Remove 3 bolts from left-side transaxle mounting bracket. Remove 2 lower right-side transaxle-to-engine bolts.

7) To separate transaxle from engine, carefully move transaxle away from engine and toward left side of engine compartment until input shaft is clear of clutch pressure plate cover. Lower transaxle assembly and remove from vehicle.

Installation – To install, reverse removal procedure. Tighten nuts and bolts to specification. See TORQUE SPECIFICATIONS (METRO) table.

PRIZM

Removal – 1) Install Engine Support Fixture (J-28467-A). Remove battery, battery tray and air cleaner assembly. Disconnect back-up light switch electrical connector. Disconnect ground strap. Remove clutch slave cylinder and hydraulic line bracket. Disconnect shift control cables and remove brackets. Set aside.

2) Remove left-side transaxle mount cover, brace and mount-through bolt. Remove 2 upper transaxle-to-engine bolts. Remove upper starter motor bolt. Disconnect Vehicle Speed Sensor (VSS) 3-wire harness connector, located at rear of transaxle. Raise and support vehicle.

3) Remove splash shields. Drain transaxle fluid. Disconnect starter motor electrical connections. Remove bottom starter motor bolt and remove starter motor. Disconnect axle shafts from transaxle. See appropriate AXLE SHAFTS article in AXLE SHAFTS & TRANSFER CASES section.

4) Remove 2 center crossmember-to-radiator support bolts. Remove front mount bolt shield. Remove 2 front mount bolts, and 3 rear mount bolts. Disconnect exhaust hanger from transaxle.

WARNING: Hold center crossmember when lowering main crossmember to prevent center crossmember from falling and causing injury.

---

5) Support main crossmember. Remove 4 main crossmember-to-body bolts, and 6 lower control arm bracket-to-body bolts. Slowly lower main crossmember while holding center crossmember. Remove center crossmember.

6) Remove front mount-through bolt and mount. Remove front mount bracket from transaxle. Remove flywheel inspection cover. Remove lower transaxle bracket-to-mount bolts. Lower vehicle.

7) Remove remaining transaxle bracket-to-mount bolts. Lower Engine Support Fixture (J-28467-A) to gain clearance for transaxle removal. Remove transaxle mount. Raise and support vehicle. Support transaxle with a jack. Remove front and rear lower transaxle-to-engine bolts. Remove transaxle assembly from vehicle.

Installation – To install, reverse removal procedure. Tighten nuts and bolts to specification. See TORQUE SPECIFICATIONS (PRIZM) table.

TRACKER

Removal (2WD) – 1) Disconnect negative battery cable. Disconnect gear shift control lever from gear shift lever case. Remove 4 fan shroud-to-radiator bolts. Remove 2 upper transmission-to-engine bolts. Raise and support vehicle. Drain transmission fluid.

2) Disconnect back-up light switch and starter motor electrical connections. Remove starter motor. Place index marks on drive shaft and flange for installation reference. Remove drive shaft. Remove skid plate (if equipped). Disconnect speedometer cable.

3) Remove one bolt and ground wire from speedometer driven gear case. Temporarily install speedometer driven gear case retaining bolt. Remove Three-Way Catalytic Converter (TWC) and muffler/tail pipe assembly from vehicle. Support transmission with transmission jack.

4) Remove rear transmission mount and rear crossmember. Remove clutch release lever from clutch release shaft. Remove 2 bolts from flywheel inspection cover. Place a wood block (1.8" x 5" x 8") between distributor gear housing and bulkhead to prevent damage to components when transmission is lowered.

5) Slowly lower transmission. Disconnect breather hose from gear shift lever case. Disconnect all remaining electrical connectors. Remove flywheel inspection cover from left transmission-to-engine reinforcement brace. Remove right-side transmission-to-engine reinforcement brace. Remove 2 lower transmission-to-engine nuts. Lower and remove transmission assembly from vehicle.

Removal (4WD) – 1) Disconnect negative battery cable. Disconnect gear shift control lever from gear shift lever case. Remove bolt directly behind gearshift lever case. Remove transfer case gear shift control lever from transfer case. Remove 4 fan shroud-to-radiator bolts. Remove 2 upper transmission-to-engine bolts.

2) Remove front and rear console boxes from floor. Remove gearshift control lever knob, boot cover and boot from gear shift control lever. Remove case boot from gear shift lever case. Push down on gear shift control lever pivot and turn counterclockwise 90 degrees, then lift up to remove from gear shift lever case.

3) Disconnect 4WD switch harness connectors. Raise and support vehicle. Disconnect back-up light switch and starter motor electrical connections. Remove starter motor. Remove transfer case skid plate. Drain transmission and transfer case fluid. Place index marks on both front and rear drive shafts and flanges for installation reference. Remove drive shafts.

4) Disconnect speedometer cable. Remove one bolt and ground wire from speedometer driven gear case. Remove Three-Way Catalytic Converter (TWC) and muffler/tail pipe assembly from vehicle. Support transfer case with transmission jack. Remove 2 bolts from torque stopper bracket. Remove 6 bolts and transfer case crossmember.

5) Place a wood block (1.8" x 5" x 8") between distributor gear housing and bulkhead to prevent damage to components when transmission is lowered. Slowly lower transfer case. Remove breather hoses from gear shift lever case and cover. Remove gear shift lever case from rear of transmission case.

6) Remove 12 transmission-to-transfer case bolts. Slide transfer case off transmission output shaft. Lower and remove transfer case assembly from vehicle. Support transmission with transmission jack. Remove clutch release lever from clutch release shaft. Remove 2 bolts from flywheel inspection cover.

7) Slowly lower transmission. Disconnect all remaining electrical connectors. Remove flywheel inspection cover from left transmission-to-engine reinforcement brace. Remove right-side transmission-to-engine reinforcement brace. Remove 2 lower transmission-to-engine nuts. Lower and remove transmission assembly from vehicle.

Installation – To install, reverse removal procedure. Tighten nuts and bolts to specification. See TORQUE SPECIFICATIONS (TRACKER) table.

TORQUE SPECIFICATIONS

TORQUE SPECIFICATIONS (METRO)

Application	Ft. Lbs. (N.m)
Axle Shaft Nut	129 (175)
Ball Joint Stud Bolt	44 (60)
Clutch Cable Bracket Bolts	21 (28)
Clutch Release Lever Bolt & Nut	
1995	12 (16)
1996	15 (20)
Control Lever Guide Plate Bolts	24 (33)
Extension Rod Nuts	30 (40)
Flywheel Cover Bolts	15 (20)
Gearshift Control Shaft Bolts	15 (20)
Rear Transaxle Mount-Through Bolt	44 (60)
Starter Motor	21 (28)
Tie Rod End Nut	32 (43)
Transaxle Drain/Filler Plugs	15 (20)
Transaxle Mounting Bracket Bolts	44 (60)
Wheel Lug Nuts	44 (60)

TORQUE SPECIFICATIONS (METRO – Cont.)

Application	INCH Lbs. (N.m)
Gear Shift Guide Case Bolts	106 (12)
Transaxle Hanger Bolt	106 (12)

TORQUE SPECIFICATIONS (TRACKER)

Application	Ft. Lbs. (N.m)
Clutch Release Lever Bolt & Nut	18 (24)
Drive Shaft Bolts & Nuts	37 (50)
Gear Shift Lever Case Bolts	13 (17)
Lower Transmission-To-Engine Nuts	74 (100)
Rear Transmission Crossmember Bolts (4WD)	44 (60)
Rear Transmission Mount Bolts (2WD)	44 (60)
Skid Plate Bolts	40 (54)
Starter Motor Bolts & Nuts	22 (30)
Torque Mount Bracket Bolts	37 (50)
Torque Stopper Bushing Mount-Through Bolt & Nut	37 (50)
Torque Stopper Mounting Bolts	37 (50)
Transfer Case Crossmember Bolts	37 (50)
Transfer Case Drain Plug	21 (28)
Transfer Case Filler Plug	
1995	21 (28)
1996	17 (23)
Transfer Case Rear Mount Bolt	37 (50)
Transfer Case-To-Transmission Bolts	21 (28)
Transmission Drain/Filler Plugs	21 (28)
Transmission-To-Engine Reinforcement Brace Bolts	74 (100)
Upper Transmission-To-Engine Bolts	74 (100)

Application	INCH Lbs. (N.m)
Fan Shroud Bolts	89 (10)
Flywheel Inspection Cover Bolts	89 (10)
Speedometer Cable Clip Bolt	89 (10)
Speedometer Driven Gear Case Bolt	
Transfer Case	89 (10)
Transmission	106 (12)

TORQUE SPECIFICATIONS (PRIZM)

Application	Ft. Lbs. (N.m)
Axle Shaft Nut	159 (216)
Ball Joint Stud Bolt	87 (118)
Center Crossmember-To-Main Crossmember	45 (61)
Center Crossmember-To-Radiator Support Bolts	45 (61)
Center Mount-To-Transaxle Bolts	45 (61)
Center & Rear Mounting Nuts	45 (61)
Clutch Slave Cylinder & Bracket	15 (20)
Front, Left & Rear Mount-Through Bolts	64 (87)
Front Mount Bolts	45 (61)
Front Mount Bracket Bolts	45 (61)
Left Mount Bracket Bolts	45 (61)
Left Mount Cover Bolts	45 (61)
Lower Control Arm-To-Body Bolts	
1995	94 (127)
1996	
Center Bolt	161 (218)
Outer Bolt	108 (147)
Lower Mount Bolts	45 (61)
Main Crossmember-To-Body Bolts	152 (206)
Mount Cover Bolts	45 (61)
Rear Mount Nuts	45 (61)
Starter Bolts	29 (39)
Tie Rod End Nut	36 (49)
Transaxle-To-Engine Bolts	34 (46)
Upper Transaxle Mount Bolts	45 (61)
Wheel Lug Nuts	76 (103)

Application	INCH Lbs. (N.m)
Exhaust Support Bracket Bolts	115 (13)
Transaxle Drain/Filler Plugs	97 (11)

Accord, Civic, Civic Del Sol, Passport, Prelude

NOTE: For manual transmission removal procedure for Passport, refer to Rodeo MANUAL TRANSMISSION REMOVAL – ISUZU article.

APPLICATION
MANUAL TRANSAXLE APPLICATIONS

Model	Transaxle Code
Accord	
Sedan W/F22B2 Engine	P2A5
Sedan W/F22B1 Engine	P2U5
Station Wagon	P2A4
Civic	
1995 (All Models)	S20
1996 (Except VTEC)	S40
1996 (VTEC)	S4C
Civic Del Sol	
1995 D16A3 Engine	S21 Or Y21
1995 D15B7 Or D16Z6 Engine	S20
1996 D16A2 Engine	S21
1996 D16Y7 Or D16Y8 Engine	S8G
Prelude	
F22A1 Engine	M2F4
H22A2 Engine (VTEC)	M2L5
H23A1 Engine	M2S4

NOTE: Before disconnecting negative battery cable or fuses, ensure radio anti-theft code is obtained from customer. Radio anti-theft code must be re-entered into radio for radio operation. When the word "CODE" is displayed on radio, re-enter anti-theft code by using the radio station preset buttons.

REMOVAL & INSTALLATION
ACCORD & PRELUDE

Removal & Installation – 1) Remove positive and negative battery cables, and remove battery. Remove air intake hoses and battery base. On Accord models, remove intake air resonator. On all models, disconnect starter wiring, and remove starter. Disconnect transaxle ground cable. Disconnect back-up light switch connectors. Shift transaxle into Reverse. Remove shift cable stay and cables as an assembly. *See Fig. 1.*

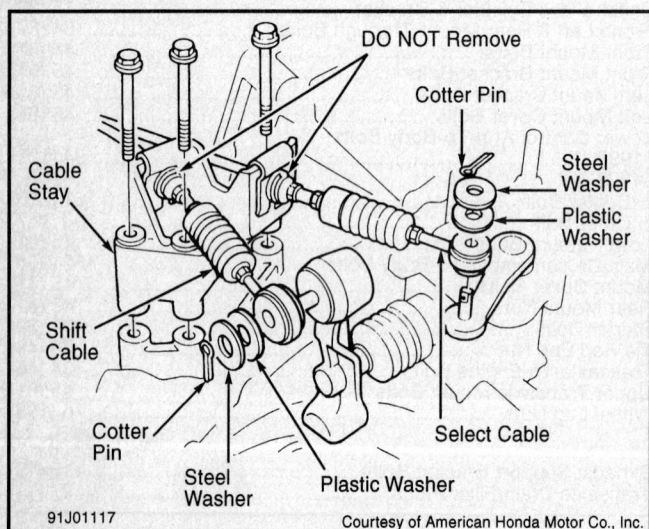

Fig. 1: Removing Shift Cable Assembly (Accord & Prelude)

91J01117   Courtesy of American Honda Motor Co., Inc.

2) Disconnect electrical connector, and remove Vehicle Speed Sensor (VSS). Remove both front wheels. On Accord models, remove undercarriage splash shield. On all models, drain transaxle fluid. Remove clutch slave cylinder, tubing and push rod. Remove clutch hose joint.

3) Remove clutch damper and support with wire bracket. Remove upper transaxle housing bolts. Separate left and right lower control arms from ball joints. Remove right damper fork bolt. Remove right radius rod. Pry axle shafts out of differential and intermediate shaft, and remove axle shafts. Lower bearing support, and remove intermediate shaft. Remove center beam.

4) On Prelude models, remove engine stiffener at inspection cover area. On all models, remove clutch inspection cover. Remove intake manifold bracket. On Prelude models, remove rear beam stiffener. On all models, remove rear engine mount bracket stay and bracket. Remove transaxle housing mount bolt from engine side.

5) Place a jack under transaxle, and slightly raise transaxle to take weight off mounts. Remove transaxle mount, and loosen mount bracket bolts. Remove remaining transaxle housing mount bolts. Lower transaxle from engine. To install, reverse removal procedure. Tighten nuts and bolts to specification. See TORQUE SPECIFICATIONS.

NOTE: New spring clips must be used on both axle shafts. Slide axles in until spring clips engage differential.

CIVIC & CIVIC DEL SOL

Removal – 1) Disconnect negative and positive battery cables. Remove battery base and air cleaner and tube assembly. Disconnect starter and transaxle ground cables. Remove engine harness clamp. Disconnect Vehicle Speed Sensor (VSS) connector. Disconnect back-up light switch.

2) Remove clutch pipe bracket and clutch slave cylinder. Drain transaxle fluid. Remove starter. Remove engine and right wheelwell splash shields. Remove header pipe. Separate lower control arms from ball joints. Remove right radius rod. Using 2 large screwdrivers, pry both axle shaft inner CV joints out of transaxle. Protect axle shaft ends.

3) Using drift punch, drive out shift rod roll pin. Remove shift and extension rods. *See Fig. 2.* Remove inspection cover and engine stiffener brackets. Install hoist at cylinder head attachment points of engine, and lift engine slightly to unload engine mounts. Remove splash guard and front stopper bracket.

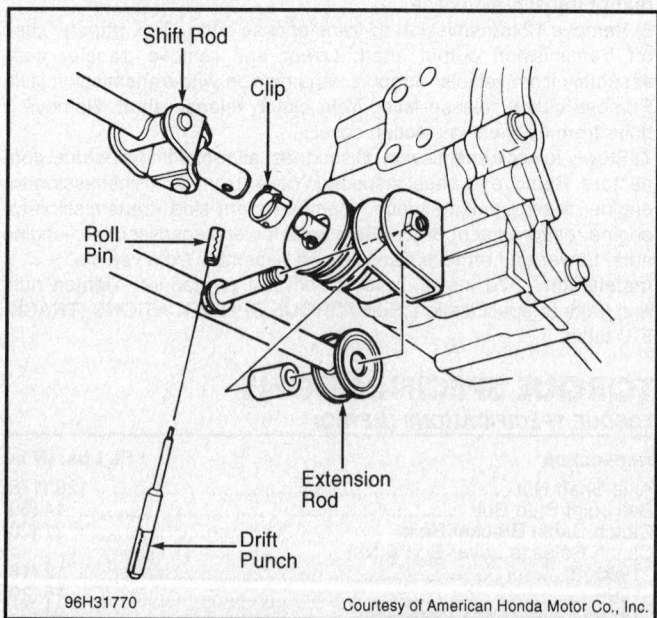

96H31770   Courtesy of American Honda Motor Co., Inc.

Fig. 2: Removing Shift & Extension Rods (Civic & Civic Del Sol)

4) Place a jack under transaxle, and slightly raise it to take weight off transaxle mounts. Remove front transaxle mount. Remove rear transaxle mount bracket. Remove side transaxle mount. Remove transaxle housing mount bolts. Pull transaxle away from engine, and remove transaxle.

Installation – Before installation, install NEW circlips on inboard side of axle shafts. Use NEW self-locking nuts on front end of radius rod and header pipe bracket. Use NEW through bolt on firewall side transaxle mount. To install transaxle, reverse removal procedure. Tighten nuts and bolts to specification. See TORQUE SPECIFICATIONS.

TORQUE SPECIFICATIONS
TORQUE SPECIFICATIONS

Application	Ft. Lbs. (N.m)
Battery Base Mounting Bolts	16 (22)
Extension Rod Bolt	16 (22)
Flywheel Housing-To-Engine Bolts	
Accord & Prelude	48 (65)
Civic & Civic Del Sol	44 (60)
Header Pipe	
At Manifold	41 (55)
At Flange	16 (22)
Intake Manifold Bracket Bolts	16 (22)
Intermediate Shaft Support Bolt	29 (39)
Rear Mount-To-Transmission Bolt	
Accord & Prelude	29 (39)
Civic & Civic Del Sol	41 (55)
Slave Cylinder-To-Housing	16 (22)
Starter Bolts	
Accord & Prelude	55 (75)
Civic & Civic Del Sol	33 (45)
Stiffener Bolt	33 (45)
VSS Mounting Bolts	14 (19)
Wheel Lug Nuts	80 (109)

Hyundai

Accent, Elantra, Scoupe, Sonata

APPLICATION
TRANSAXLE APPLICATION

Vehicle Application	Transaxle Model
Accent	M5AF3
Elantra	
1995	KM202
1996	M5BF1
Scoupe	M5AF
Sonata	
1995 [1]	KM202
1996	KM210

[1] – Sonata V6 is only available with automatic transaxle.

REMOVAL & INSTALLATION

Removal & Installation (Except 1996 Elantra) – 1) Disconnect negative battery cable. Remove air cleaner assembly. Remove clutch release cylinder (if equipped). Remove drain plug and drain transaxle fluid. Remove speedometer cable. Disconnect clutch cable (if equipped).

2) Disconnect back-up light switch connector. Remove starter. Disconnect stabilizer bar, tie rod end and lower ball joint. Remove axle shaft side cover and undercover. Remove axle shafts. See appropriate AXLE SHAFTS article in AXLE SHAFTS & TRANSFER CASES section.

3) Remove bellhousing cover. Remove transaxle-to-engine block mounting bolts. Remove transaxle mount bracket and transaxle. To install, reverse removal procedure. Tighten nuts and bolts to specifications. See TORQUE SPECIFICATIONS.

Removal & Installation (1996 Elantra) – 1) Disconnect negative battery cable. Remove air cleaner assembly. Disconnect back-up light switch connector. Remove clutch release cylinder. Remove speedometer cable.

2) Remove shifter cables. Remove starter. Remove upper transaxle-to-engine bolts. Install engine support. Remove transaxle mounting bracket. Lift and support vehicle. Remove front wheels. Remove axle shaft side cover and undercover.

3) Remove drain plug and drain transaxle fluid. Disconnect stabilizer bar, tie rod end and lower ball joint. Remove axle shafts. See appropriate AXLE SHAFTS article in AXLE SHAFTS & TRANSFER CASES section. Remove center cross member. Install transaxle support jack.

4) Remove transaxle rear mounting bracket. Remove bellhousing cover. Remove lower transaxle-to-engine block mounting bolts. Lower supporting jack and remove transaxle. To install, reverse removal procedure. Tighten nuts and bolts to specifications. See TORQUE SPECIFICATIONS.

TORQUE SPECIFICATIONS
TORQUE SPECIFICATIONS

Application	Ft. Lbs. (N.m)
Back-Up Light Switch	22-26 (30-35)
Release Cylinder Banjo Bolt	15-18 (20-25)
Release Cylinder Mounting Bolt	
Elantra & Sonata	15-20 (20-27)
Accent & Scoupe	11-16 (15-22)
Starter Bolt	
Accent, Elantra & Scoupe	20-25 (27-34)
Sonata	16-24 (22-32)
Transaxle Drain & Fill Plug	22-26 (30-35)
Transaxle Mount	
Bracket-To-Transaxle Bolts	43-58 (60-80)
Transaxle-To-Engine Bolt	
12-mm	32-41 (43-55)
10-mm	22-26 (30-35)

Application	INCH Lbs. (N.m)
Transaxle-To-Engine Bolt	
8-mm	71-89 (8-10)

G20, I30

APPLICATION
TRANSAXLE APPLICATION

Vehicle Application	Transaxle Model
G20	RS5F32A/V
I30	RS5F50A/V

REMOVAL & INSTALLATION

Removal & Installation – 1) Disconnect battery negative cable. Remove air duct. Remove crankshaft position sensor. Disconnect clutch cable at transaxle. Disconnect speedometer pinion, back-up light and neutral switch harness connectors. Disconnect ground harness connectors.

2) Raise and support vehicle. Remove starter. Disconnect shift control rod and support rod from transaxle. Drain transaxle lubricant. Remove front exhaust pipe. Remove axle shafts. See appropriate AXLE SHAFTS article in AXLE SHAFTS & TRANSFER CASES section.

3) Support engine with appropriate jack under oil pan. Remove rear and left-hand engine mounts. Raise jack for access to lower transaxle retaining bolts. *See Fig. 1.* Remove bolts and lower jack.

4) Support transaxle with appropriate jack. Remove remaining transaxle retaining bolts. Lower transaxle and remove from vehicle. To install, reverse removal procedure. Install transaxle-to-engine bolts in sequence. Ensure bolts are in proper location according to length. See TRANSAXLE BOLT LENGTH table. *See Fig. 1.* Tighten nuts and bolts to specification. See TORQUE SPECIFICATIONS.

TRANSAXLE BOLT LENGTH

Bolt Identification [1]	Length In. (mm)
G20	
1	2.57 (55)
2	2.56 (65)
3	1.38 (35)
4	1.77 (45)
I30	
1	2.05 (52)
2	2.56 (65)
3	4.88 (124)
4 & 5	1.57 (40)

[1] – See Fig. 1.

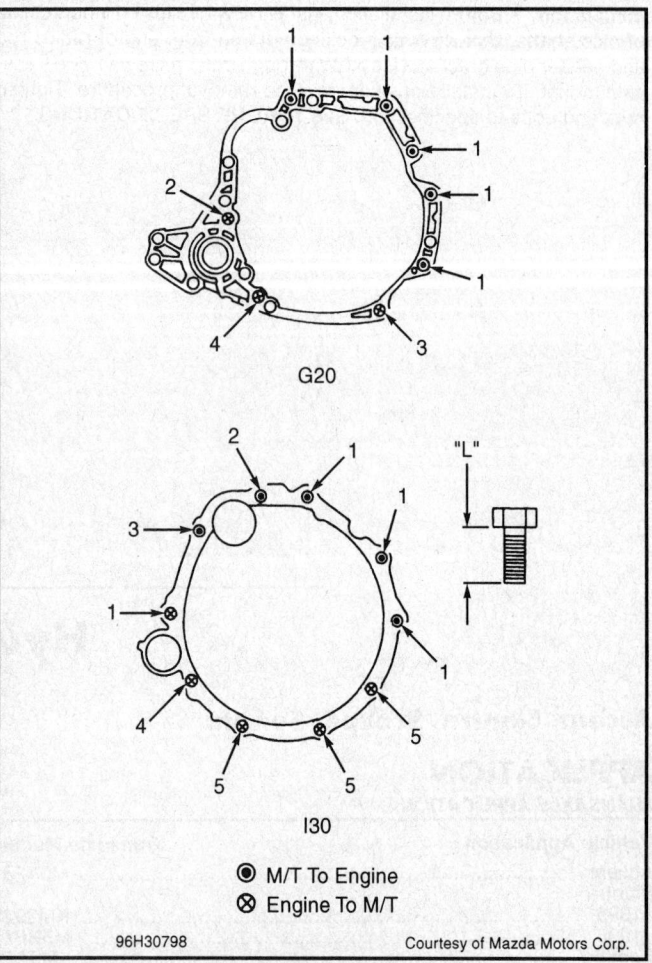

G20

I30

⊙ M/T To Engine
⊗ Engine To M/T

96H30798   Courtesy of Mazda Motors Corp.

Fig 1: Locating Transaxle-To-Engine Bolts

TORQUE SPECIFICATIONS
TORQUE SPECIFICATIONS

Application	Ft. Lbs. (N.m)
Clutch Cover Retaining Bolt	16-21 (22-29)
Exhaust Pipe-To-Manifold Nut	30-35 (41-48)
Transaxle-To-Engine Bolts[1]	
G20	
Bolt 1 & 2	51-59 (70-79)
Bolt 3 & 4	22-30 (30-40)
I30	
Bolt 1, 2 & 3	51-59 (70-79)
Bolt 4 & 5	26-35 (35-47)

[1] – See Fig. 1.

Hombre, Pickup, Rodeo, Trooper

APPLICATION

MANUAL TRANSMISSION APPLICATION

Model	Transmission
Hombre	New Venture Gear NV1500
Pickup	
2WD	MUA5C 5-Speed
4WD	MUA5CT 5-Speed
Rodeo	
2WD	
2.6L	MUA5C 5-Speed
3.2L	Borg-Warner T5R 5-Speed
4WD	MUA5CT 5-Speed
Trooper	MUA5CT 5-Speed

REMOVAL & INSTALLATION

HOMBRE

Removal & Installation – 1) Disconnect negative battery cable. Shift transmission into 3rd or 4th gear. Remove shift lever and housing. Raise and support vehicle.

2) Drain transmission oil. Disconnect parking brake cable and position aside. Mark drive shaft for installation reference. Remove drive shaft. Disconnect harness connectors from speed sensor and back-up light switch.

3) Detach wire harness from right side of transmission and position aside. Separate muffler from catalytic converter. Disconnect exhaust pipe from exhaust manifold. Remove catalytic converter and exhaust pipe.

4) Remove left and right-side transmission-to-engine braces. Disconnect clutch release cylinder hydraulic line quick-coupler. Remove clutch housing cover.

5) Detach fuel lines and wire harness from rear crossmember. Support transmission with jack. Remove rear crossmember. Remove transmission-to-engine bolts. Slide transmission rearward and remove from vehicle. To install, reverse removal procedure. Torque fasteners to specification. See TORQUE SPECIFICATIONS.

PICKUP

Removal & Installation (2WD) – 1) Disconnect and remove battery. Disconnect positive battery cable from starter, and negative battery cable from body. Remove engine hood. Place gearshift lever in Neutral. Remove front console and gearshift lever assembly.

2) Raise and support vehicle. Drain transmission oil. Mark drive shaft for installation reference. Remove drive shaft and starter. Disconnect exhaust pipe from manifold. Remove exhaust pipe bracket. Remove speedometer cable and clutch cable or release cylinder. Disconnect transmission harness connectors. Support engine and transmission. Remove rear transmission support from frame.

3) Remove transmission mount-to-transmission bolts. Using a jack, support transmission. Remove transmission mount-to-crossmember bolts and transmission mount. Lower transmission jack to gain access to upper bolts. Remove quadrant (shift linkage) box. Remove transmission-to-engine bolts and transmission. To install, reverse removal procedure. Torque fasteners to specification. See TORQUE SPECIFICATIONS.

Removal & Installation (4WD) – 1) Disconnect and remove battery. Place transmission gearshift lever in Neutral. Place transfer case gearshift lever in "H" position. Remove front console. Slide transmission and transfer case gearshift lever boots upward on levers. Remove gearshift and 4WD transfer case lever mounting bolts. Remove gearshift levers. Raise and support vehicle.

2) Drain transmission and transfer case. Remove transfer case skid plate. Mark drive shafts for installation reference. Remove front and rear drive shafts. Remove starter. Disconnect exhaust pipe from manifold. Remove exhaust hanger from transmission.

3) With engine supported, remove rear crossmember. Lower transmission. Remove engine-to-transmission mounting bolts and nuts. Disconnect speedometer cable and ground cable at transmission.

4) Pull transmission and transfer case rearward to clear clutch assembly and remove transmission and transfer case as an assembly. To install, reverse removal procedure. Torque fasteners to specification. See TORQUE SPECIFICATIONS.

RODEO (B-W T5R TRANSMISSION)

Removal & Installation – 1) Remove engine hood. Disconnect negative battery cable. Place gearshift lever in Neutral. Remove gearshift lever knob, console assembly and insulation. Pull gearshift lever grommet and dust cover up to expose gearshift lever cover bolts. Remove bolts.

2) Raise and support vehicle. Disconnect electrical connectors from starter. Remove starter. Remove slave cylinder assembly. Mark drive shaft flanges for installation reference. Remove drive shaft. Disconnect harness connectors from transmission. Remove flywheel dust cover.

3) Support engine with appropriate hoist or jack. Remove transmission mount bolts and nuts. Remove 8 center crossmember bolts. Remove center crossmember and transmission mount. Support transmission with jack. Remove transmission-to-engine bolts and exhaust pipe bracket. Lower transmission from vehicle. To install, reverse removal procedure. Torque fasteners to specification. See TORQUE SPECIFICATIONS.

RODEO & TROOPER
(MUA5 SERIES TRANSMISSION)

Removal & Installation – 1) Remove engine hood. Disconnect negative battery cable. Raise and support vehicle. On 4WD models, remove transfer case protector. On all models, drain transmission and transfer case fluid. Disconnect oxygen sensor harness connectors.

2) Remove right front exhaust pipe and catalytic converter assembly. Remove wiring harness heat protector. Remove slave cylinder heat protector, slave cylinder and both dust covers. Mark rear drive shaft flanges for installation reference. Remove rear drive shaft.

3) Disconnect transmission harness connectors. Using a transmission jack, support transmission (2WD), or transfer case (4WD). Remove 2 engine rear mount nuts. Remove 8 center crossmember bolts. Remove rear mount from transmission. Remove crossmember.

4) On 4WD models, remove 4 front crossmember bolts. Remove front crossmember from frame. Mark front drive shaft for installation reference. Remove front drive shaft.

5) On all models, remove gearshift lever knob, console assembly and grommet assembly. Remove gearshift lever(s). On 4WD models, support transmission and remove jack from transfer case. On all models, remove 3 flywheel undercover bolts.

6) To separate transmission from engine, clutch release bearing must be disengaged from pressure plate using Clutch Release Bearing Remover (J-39207). See Fig. 1. Pull clutch release lever rearward and insert bearing remover through access hole. Wedge bearing remover between release bearing and pressure plate and twist to disengage. See Fig. 2.

7) Remove transmission-to-engine retaining nuts and bolts. Tilt front of transmission downward and remove transmission from vehicle. On 4WD models, transmission and transfer case are removed as an assembly. To install, reverse removal procedure. Torque fasteners to specification. See TORQUE SPECIFICATIONS.

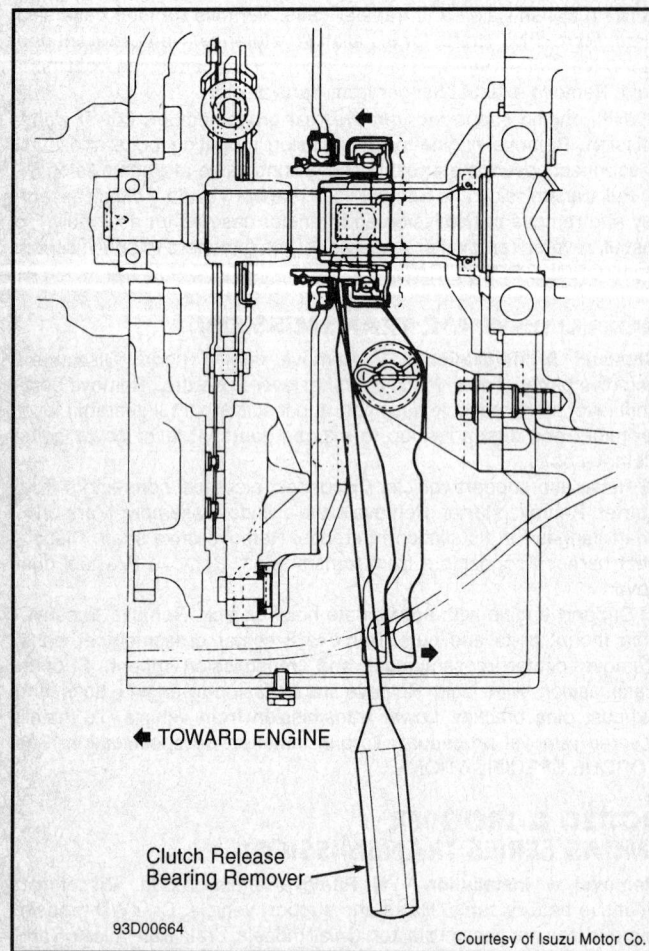

Fig. 1: Inserting Clutch Release Bearing Remover (Rodeo & Trooper – Pull-Type Clutch)

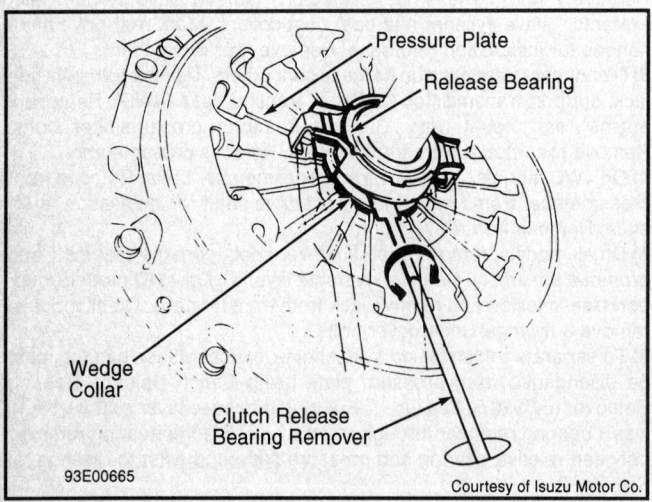

Fig. 2: Separating Clutch Release Bearing (Rodeo & Trooper – Pull-Type Clutch)

TORQUE SPECIFICATIONS

TORQUE SPECIFICATIONS

Application	Ft. Lbs. (N.m)
Hombre	
Clutch Housing Cover Bolt	1
Rear Crossmember Bolt	34 (46)
Transmission Mount Bolt	37 (50)
Transmission-To-Engine Brace	
Bolt	37 (50)
Stud	35 (47)
Transmission-To-Engine Bolt	66 (89)
Pickup	
Drive Shaft Center Bearing Bolt	43-46 (58-62)
Drive Shaft Flange Bolt	43-49 (58-66)
Engine Mount Nut	27-34 (37-46)
Gearshift Lever Cover Bolt	13-16 (18-22)
Rear Mount Bracket Bolt	20-34 (27-46)
Rear Transmission Mount Nut	58-65 (79-88)
Starter Bolt	47-80 (64-108)
Transmission-To-Engine Bolt	22-33 (30-45)
Rodeo (B-W T5R Transmission)	
Center Crossmember Bolt	56 (76)
Drive Shaft Center Bearing Bolt	45 (61)
Drive Shaft Flange Bolt	46 (62)
Gearshift Lever-To-Transmission	15 (20)
Slave Cylinder-To-Transmission Bolt	37 (50)
Starter Mounting Bolt	30 (41)
Transmission Mount-To-Crossmember Bolt	30 (41)
Transmission Mount-To-Transmission Bolt	30 (41)
Transmission-To-Engine Bolt	30 (41)
Rodeo & Trooper (MUA5 Series Transmission)	
Center Crossmember Bolt	37 (50)
Clutch Housing Dust Cover Bolts	2
Drive Shaft Flange Bolt	46 (62)
Exhaust Pipe Flange Bolt	32 (43)
Exhaust Pipe-To-Exhaust Manifold Bolt	49 (66)
Front Crossmember Bolt (4WD)	58 (79)
Rear Mount-To-Crossmember Nut	37 (50)
Rear Mount-To-Transmission Bolt	30 (41)
Slave Cylinder-To-Transmission	32 (43)
Starter Mounting Bolt	30 (41)
Transfer Case Protector Bolt	27 (37)
Transmission-To-Engine Bolt	56 (76)

1 – Tighten bolts to 62 INCH lbs. (7.0 N.m).
2 – Tighten bolts to 52 INCH lbs. (5.9 N.m).

Sephia, Sportage

APPLICATION

MANUAL TRANSMISSION APPLICATION

Model	Transmission
Sephia	
1995 1.6L SOHC	F5M-R
1995-96 1.6L DOHC	F25M-R
1995-96 1.8L DOHC	G25M-R
Sportage	Getrag 5-Speed

REMOVAL & INSTALLATION

Sephia – 1) Remove battery and tray. Mark and disconnect wiring harness connectors as necessary. Remove air cleaner hose, resonance chamber and air cleaner assembly. Raise and support vehicle.

2) Remove lower engine splash and side shields. Remove front wheels. Remove clutch release cylinder with hydraulic line attached and set aside. Disconnect speedometer cable from transaxle. Remove ground wire from transaxle.

3) Remove starter. Disconnect neutral switch connector. Remove top transaxle-to-engine bolts. Install appropriate engine support bar to support engine during transaxle removal. Drain transaxle fluid. Remove front stabilizer bar.

4) Remove castle nut and disconnect tie rod ends. Remove lower ball joint-to-spindle pinch bolt. Pry downward on lower control arm and separate lower ball joint from spindle.

5) Remove exhaust downpipe from manifold. Pry axle shafts out of transaxle. Remove and discard circlip from axle shafts. For further information on axle shafts, see appropriate AXLES SHAFTS article in AXLE SHAFTS & TRANSFER CASES section. Remove crossmember retaining bolts and crossmember. Remove shift control rod-to-transaxle bolt and nut, and slide control rod aside.

6) Remove shift extension bar mounting bracket bolt, and slide extension bar from bracket. Position transmission jack under transaxle. Disconnect engine mounts from clutch housing. Remove remaining clutch housing-to-engine bolts, and pull transaxle away from engine. To install, reverse removal procedure. Tighten nuts and bolts to specification. See TORQUE SPECIFICATIONS.

Sportage – 1) Disconnect negative batter cable. Remove center portion of center console. Remove shifter knobs (transmission and transfer case (if applicable). Remove front portion of center console.

2) Remove dust cover boots. Disconnect shift lever bracket from transmission housing. Tilt shift lever bracket back to allow access to shift linkage. Remove clip for one end of link pin attaching shift lever to control rod extension. Remove pin and remove shift lever.

3) Remove transfer case shift lever. Raise and support vehicle. Drain transmission oil if necessary. Drain transfer case oil (if applicable). Place matching marks on driveshaft and mating flange. Disconnect driveshafts from flanges. Disconnect electrical switch harness connector. Move harness aside.

4) Remove crankshaft position sensor. Unbolt clutch slave cylinder and position aside. Remove front exhaust pipe bracket. Remove 5 lower front clutch housing bolts. Remove transfer case side mount (if applicable). Support transmission with appropriate jack.

5) Remove transmission crossmember. Remove starter and support aside. Remove remaining clutch housing bolts and remove transmission. To install, reverse removal procedure. Tighten nuts and bolts to specification. See TORQUE SPECIFICATIONS. Check fluid level.

TORQUE SPECIFICATIONS

TORQUE SPECIFICATIONS

Application	Ft. Lbs. (N.m)
Sephia	
Axle Shaft Nut	155-206 (210-279)
Control Rod-To-Transaxle Bolt	12-17 (16-23)
Engine Mount Nut	49-69 (67-93)
Extension Bar-To-Bracket Bolt	23-34 (31-46)
Lower Ball Joint Pinch Bolt	32-43 (44-58)
Release Cylinder-To-Transaxle Bolt	12-17 (16-23)
Starter Bolt	14-18 (19-25)
Tie Rod End Lock Nut	31-42 (42-57)
Transaxle-To-Engine Bolt	47-66 (64-89)
Transaxle-To-Oil Pan Stiffener Bolt	27-38 (37-52)
Wheel Lug Nuts	65-87 (88-118)
Sportage	
Clutch Housing Bolts	
14 mm	80 (108)
10 mm	29 (39)
6 mm	5 (7)
Crossmember-To-Frame Bolt	32 (44)
Crossmember-To-Mount Bolt	80 (108)
Dust Cover Plate Bolt	15 (20)
Driveshaft Flange Bolt	27 (36)
Exhaust Bracket Bolt	20 (27)
Slave Cylinder Bolt	29 (39)
Shift Lever Mount Bolt	18 (24)
Starter Bolt	29 (39)
Transfer Case Side Mount Bolt	38 (52)
	INCH Lbs. (N.m)
Crankshaft Position Sensor Bolt	60 (7)

Lexus

SC300

APPLICATION

TRANSAXLE APPLICATION

Vehicle Application	Transaxle Model
SC300	W58

REMOVAL & INSTALLATION

SC300

Removal & Installation – 1) Disconnect negative battery cable from battery. Remove cup holder and shift lever knob. Using a screwdriver, pry out upper rear console panel. Remove 6 mounting screws. Using a screwdriver, pry out upper console panel. Remove 8 mounting bolts and shift lever boot and shift lever.

2) Raise and support vehicle. Drain transmission oil. Remove undercover. Remove exhaust front pipe and pipe support bracket. Remove exhaust center pipe.

3) Remove heat insulator. Remove crossmember brace. Place reference marks on differential companion flange and flexible coupling. Remove drive shaft. Remove 3 bolts from differential companion flange.

CAUTION: Bolts inserted into drive shaft companion flange should not be removed.

4) Separate flexible coupling from differential side. If flexible coupling can not be easily separated by hand, insert a screwdriver into bolt hole of flexible coupling and pry coupling outward.

5) Remove 2 center support bearing set bolts and adjusting washers if applicable. Support center support bearing by hand so that transmission and intermediate shaft, and drive shaft and differential, remain in a straight line. Remove drive shaft from transmission.

6) Remove clutch release cylinder and negative battery cable. Disconnect starter wire. Unbolt and move starter forward. Remove transmission lower side mounting bolt. Disconnect back-up light switch connector. Disconnect speed sensor connector.

7) Raise transmission enough to remove weight from rear support. Remove 4 nuts, 4 bolts and rear engine mounting member. Remove transmission. To install, reverse removal procedure. Tighten bolts to specification. See TORQUE SPECIFICATIONS.

TORQUE SPECIFICATIONS
TORQUE SPECIFICATIONS

Application	Ft. Lbs. (N.m)
Center Support Bolt	36 (49)
Drive Shaft-To-Differential Bolt	58 (79)
Exhaust Center Pipe Nut	14 (19)
Exhaust Front Pipe Nut	32 (43)
Pipe Support Bracket	27 (37)
Rear Engine Mounting Member	
Bolt	18 (25)
Nut	10 (14)
Starter Bolt	29 (39)
Transmission Shift Lever Bolt	14 (19)
Transmission-To-Engine Bolts	53 (72)

Mazda

B2300, B3000, B4000, Miata, MX-3, MX-6, Protege, RX7, 626

APPLICATION
MANUAL TRANSMISSION/TRANSAXLE APPLICATIONS

Model	Transmission/Transaxle
B2300, B3000 & B4000	M-50D
Miata	M15M-D
MX-3	F25M-R
MX-6 & 626	G25M-R
Protege (1.5L)	F25M-R
Protege (1.8L)	G25M-R
RX-7	R15M-D

REMOVAL & INSTALLATION

B2300, B3000 & B4000

Removal & Installation – **1)** Disconnect negative battery cable. Shift transmission into Neutral. Remove shift lever. Raise and support vehicle. Drain fluid. Disconnect hydraulic line at transmission with Disconnect Tool (T88T-70522-A). Disconnect speedometer cable. Disconnect wiring at transmission. Mark front and rear drive shafts as necessary for installation reference.

2) Disconnect drive shaft(s). Remove starter. Remove exhaust components as necessary for clearance. Remove transfer case (if equipped). Secure transmission jack under transmission. Remove bellhousing bolts. Remove transmission. To install, reverse removal procedure. Tighten bolts to specification. See TORQUE SPECIFICATIONS.

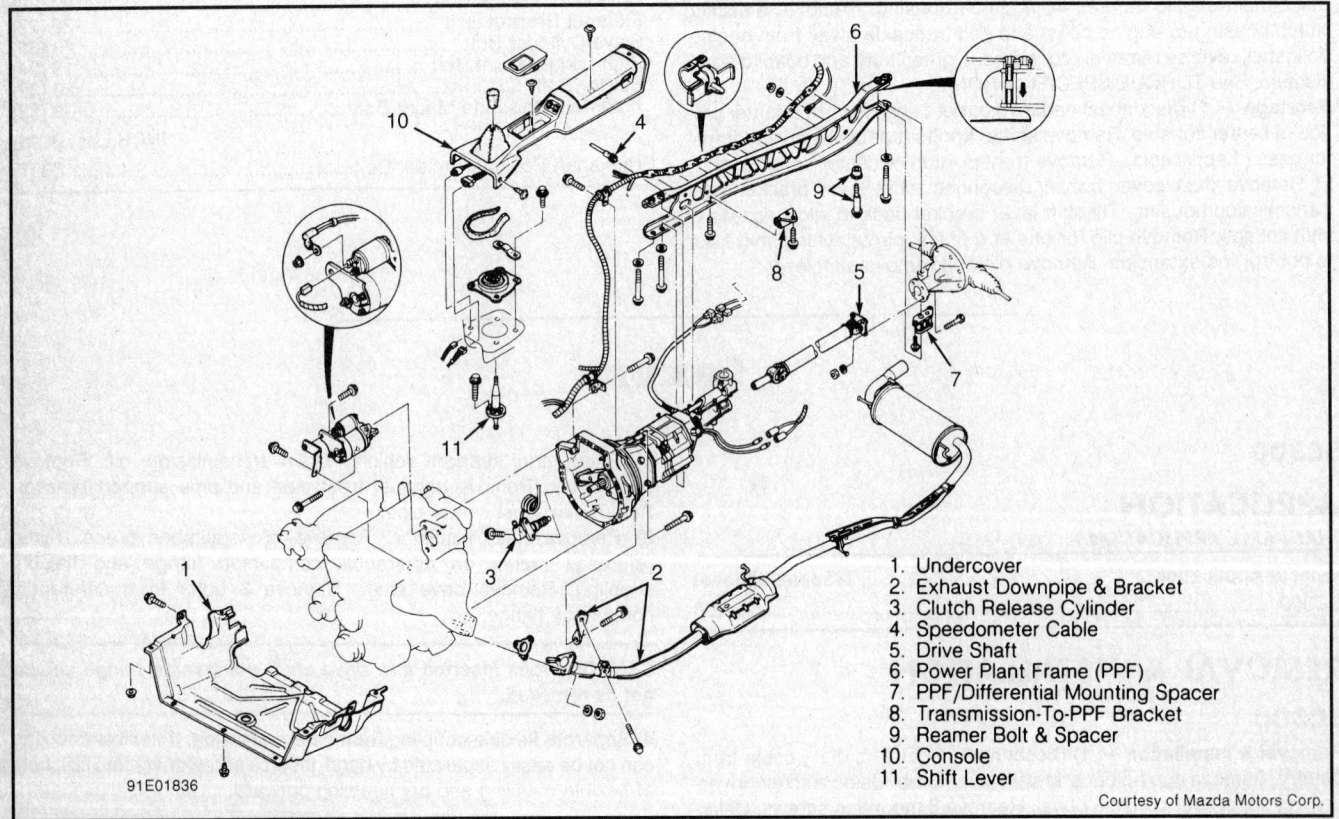

1. Undercover
2. Exhaust Downpipe & Bracket
3. Clutch Release Cylinder
4. Speedometer Cable
5. Drive Shaft
6. Power Plant Frame (PPF)
7. PPF/Differential Mounting Spacer
8. Transmission-To-PPF Bracket
9. Reamer Bolt & Spacer
10. Console
11. Shift Lever

91E01836

Courtesy of Mazda Motors Corp.

Fig. 1: Exploded View Of Drive Line (Miata)

MIATA

Removal – 1) Disconnect negative battery cable. Remove gearshift knob, console and shift lever. *See Fig. 1.* Raise and support vehicle. Remove engine undercover. Disconnect exhaust pipe from manifold. Mark position of drive shaft flanges, and remove drive shaft.

2) Remove clutch release cylinder. Remove starter. Disconnect speedometer cable from transmission. Note locations, and disconnect wiring harness from Power Plant Frame (PPF).

3) Remove PPF bracket from rear transmission extension housing. Remove PPF-to-differential side bolts, and pry out spacer. Remove PPF/differential mounting spacer. *See Fig. 2.*

4) Install metric bolt (M14 X 1.5) into sleeve. *See Fig. 3.* Twist bolt side-to-side while pulling it downward. Install a metric bolt (M6 X 1) into hole in housing block to hold sleeve, and remove long bolt (M14 X 1.5). Remove short bolt (M6 X 1).

NOTE: Do not remove spacers attached to top of power plant frame (PPF). If they are removed, replace PPF.

5) Remove PPF-to-transmission side bolts, and remove PPF. Remove clutch housing-to-engine bolts. Remove transmission from vehicle.

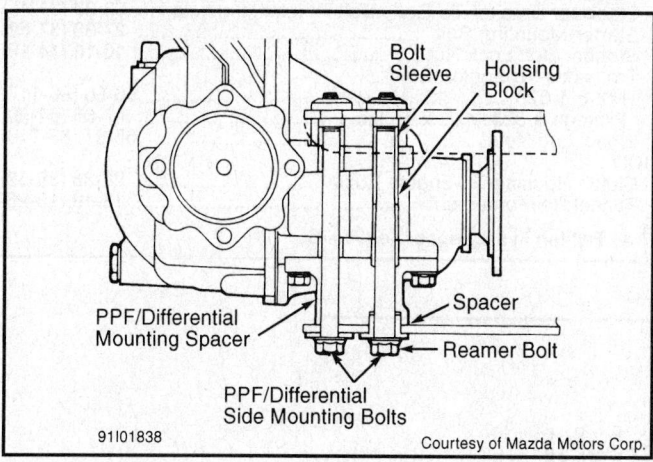

91l01838   Courtesy of Mazda Motors Corp.

Fig. 2: *Installing & Removing Power Plant Frame (Miata)*

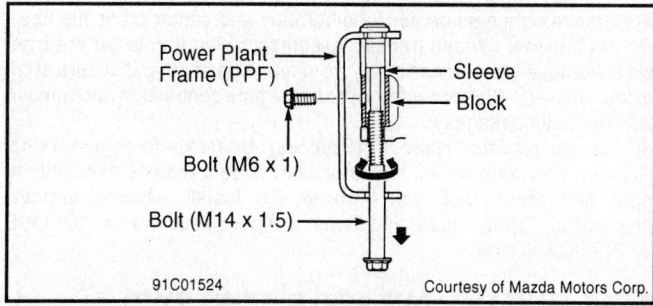

91C01524   Courtesy of Mazda Motors Corp.

Fig. 3: *Removing Reamer Bolt Sleeve (Miata)*

Installation – 1) Place jack (from front of engine) under transmission. Raise transmission until it is level with engine. Position Power Plant Frame (PPF) in place. Install PPF/differential mounting spacer, and tighten bolts to 27-38 ft. lbs. (37-52 N.m). Install and tighten PPF-to-transmission side mounting bolts.

NOTE: Front PPF-to-differential side mounting bolt is considered reamer bolt and is used to align frame.

2) Ensure sleeve is installed into PPF housing block. Install spacer and bolts. Ensure reamer bolt is installed into front hole, and tighten bolt. *See Fig. 2.*

3) Install transmission-to-PPF bracket. Install remaining PPF bolts, and tighten to specification. See TORQUE SPECIFICATIONS. To complete installation, reverse removal procedure.

MX-3, MX-6, Protege, 626

Removal & Installation – 1) Remove battery and tray. Mark and disconnect harness connectors as necessary. Remove air cleaner hose, resonance chamber and air cleaner assembly. Raise and support vehicle.

2) Remove lower engine splash and side shields. Remove front wheels. Remove clutch release cylinder with hydraulic line attached and set aside. Disconnect speedometer cable from transaxle. Remove ground wire from transaxle.

3) Remove surge tank bracket. Remove starter. Disconnect wiring connector for neutral switch and back-up light switch. Disconnect body electrical ground connector. Remove top transaxle-to-engine bolts.

4) Install appropriate engine support bar to support engine during transaxle removal. *See Fig. 4.* Drain transaxle fluid. Remove front stabilizer bar.

5) Remove castle nut and disconnect tie rod ends. Remove lower ball joint-to-spindle pinch bolt. Pry downward on lower control arm and separate lower ball joint from spindle.

6) Remove exhaust downpipe from manifold. Remove axle shafts. See appropriate AXLE SHAFTS article in AXLE SHAFTS & TRANSFER CASES section. Remove crossmember retaining bolts and crossmember. Remove shift control rod-to-transaxle bolt and nut, and slide control rod aside.

7) Remove shift extension bar mounting bracket bolt, and slide extension bar from bracket. Lower transaxle assembly using engine support bar. Position transmission jack under transaxle.

8) Disconnect engine mount, located beside exhaust pipe, from clutch housing. Remove remaining clutch housing-to-engine bolts, and pull transaxle away from engine. To install, reverse removal procedure. Tighten nuts and bolts to specification. See TORQUE SPECIFICATIONS.

RX7

Removal & Installation – 1) Disconnect negative battery cable. Remove console, gear shift knob, and insulator. Remove gear shift lever. Remove transmission cover.

2) Raise and support vehicle. Remove right and left under covers. Leave fluid pipe connected to clutch release cylinder. Remove clutch release cylinder from bell housing and secure aside with wire. Remove starter and center tunnel reinforcement. Remove secondary air injection pipe and catalytic converter. Remove front and rear tunnel reinforcement.

3) Mark drive shaft flange for reassembly reference. Remove drive shaft. Insert Main Shaft Holder (49-S120-440) into extension housing. Support engine and differential. Remove Power Plant Frame (PPF) from transmission and differential. Remove back up light switch from transmission.

4) Remove service access covers "A" and "B". *See Fig. 4.* Through service hole "A", swing clutch fork forward and hold release collar against pressure plate. Insert a screwdriver through service hole "B" into space between release collar and wedge collar. Pry and separate release from pressure plate.

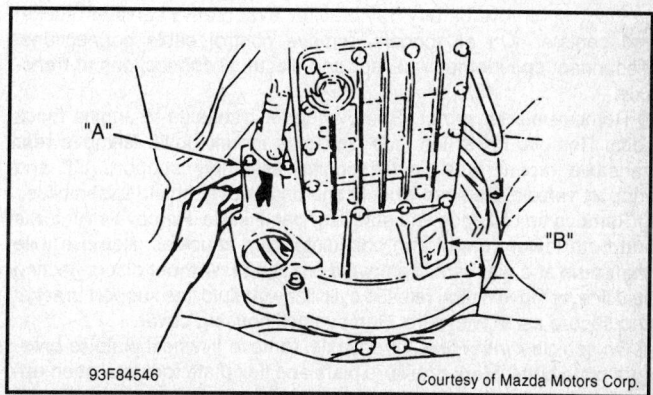

93F84546   Courtesy of Mazda Motors Corp.

Fig. 4: *Identifying Clutch Housing Service Access Holes (RX7)*

NOTE: *If release collar cannot be separated from clutch cover, remove cover-to-flywheel bolts through service hole "B". Remove clutch cover and disc with transmission.*

5) Secure transmission jack under transmission. Remove transmission bolts. Remove transmission. If clutch disc and clutch cover were removed with transmission, remove wire ring from release collar. Separate release collar from clutch cover. Remove clutch cover and disc.

6) To install, reverse removal procedure. Raise transmission into position. Install and tighten transmission bolts to specification. See TORQUE SPECIFICATIONS.

TORQUE SPECIFICATIONS
TORQUE SPECIFICATIONS

Application	Ft. Lbs. (N.m)
B2300, B3000 & B4000	
Clutch Housing-T0-Engine Bolts	28-38 (38-51)
Starter Bolts	15-20 (21-27)
Miata	
Clutch Housing-To-Engine Block Bolts	47-66 (64-90)
Drive Shaft Bolts	20-22 (27-30)
PPF-To-Differential Mounting	
Spacer Bolt (Short)	27-38 (37-52)
PPF-To-Differential	
Side Mounting Bolts (Long)	77-91 (104-123)
PPF-To-PPF Bracket Bolt	27-40 (37-54)
PPF-To-Transmission	
Side Mounting Bolts (Long)	77-91 (104-123)
Transmission-To-PPF Bracket Bolts	27-40 (37-54)
Starter Bolts	27-38 (37-52)
MX-3, MX-6, Protege & 626	
Axle Shaft Nut	174-235 (235-319)
Control Rod-To-Transaxle Bolt	12-17 (16-23)
Extension Bar-To-Bracket Bolt	23-34 (31-46)
Lower Ball Joint Pinch Bolt	32-43 (44-58)
Release Cylinder-To-Transaxle Bolt	12-17 (16-23)
Stabilizer Bracket-To-Body Bolt	23-33 (31-45)
Starter Mounting Bolt	27-38 (37-52)
Stopper Bolt Lock Nut	10-13 (14-18)
Transaxle-To-Engine Bolt	
MX-6 & 626	66-86 (90-117)
Protege & 323	47-66 (64-90)
Wheel Lug Nuts	65-87 (88-118)
RX7	
Clutch Housing-To-Engine Bolts	28-38 (38-52)
Tunnel Reinforcement	13-19 (18-26)

¹ – Tighten in sequence. *See Fig. 6.*

Mitsubishi

Chrysler Corp.: Colt, Colt Vista, Stealth
Summit, Summit Wagon, Talon
Mitsubishi: Diamante, Eclipse, Expo, Galant
Mirage, Montero, Pickup, 3000GT

REMOVAL & INSTALLATION

ECLIPSE, GALANT & TALON
(F5MC1, F5M31, F5M33 & W5M33)

Removal & Installation – 1) Drain transaxle. Remove air cleaner and air intake hoses. Remove battery and battery tray. On Eclipse and Talon models, remove battery tray bracket, evaporative canister bracket and canister. On all models, remove control cable connections. Disconnect speedometer sensor and electrical connections at transaxle.

2) Remove starter motor. Remove upper transaxle-to-engine block bolts. Remove lower left side transaxle mount bolts. Remove rear transaxle mount nuts. Install engine assembly support. Lift and support vehicle. Remove wheels and undercover shield assemblies.

3) Remove tie rod ends and stabilizer bar linkage. Remove strut forks and both lower control arm ball joints from knuckles. Remove axle shaft nuts and washers. Remove drive shafts. Without disconnecting fluid line, remove clutch release cylinder with fluid line support bracket and secure aside with wire. Remove bell housing cover.

4) On vehicles with F5MC1 transaxle, remove flywheel plate-to-pressure plate bolts. Mark pressure plate and flex plate for installation reference. On all models, install transaxle lifting hoist.

5) Remove right side center member stay and center cross member. On AWD models, move transfer assembly to left and lower the front side. Remove transfer assembly from rear axle shaft and secure shaft aside with wire. Disconnect front exhaust pipe connection and remove transfer case assembly.

6) On all models, remove remaining transaxle-to-engine bolts. Remove transaxle mount insulator bolt. Slide transaxle assembly to right and lower unit from vehicle. To install, reverse removal procedure. Tighten nuts and bolts to specification. See TORQUE SPECIFICATIONS.

COLT, SUMMIT, MIRAGE & EXPO 2WD
(F5M21 & F5M22)

Removal & Installation – 1) Remove air cleaner assembly. Drain transaxle oil. Disconnect control cables, speedometer cable and electrical connections at transaxle. Remove starter motor, with harness connected, and secure starter aside with wire.

2) Remove upper transaxle-to-engine bolts and transaxle mounting bracket bolt. Install engine assembly support. *See Fig. 1.* Lift and support vehicle. Remove undercover assemblies. Remove ball joints and tie rod ends.

3) Remove stabilizer bar connection. Disengage axle shafts and secure aside with wire. DO NOT damage oil seal. Plug shaft openings in transaxle. Remove lower transaxle brackets.

4) Remove clutch release cylinder with line connected and secure cylinder aside with wire. Remove bellhousing cover. Install transaxle lifting hoist. Remove remaining transaxle-to-engine bolts. Remove transaxle assembly. To install, reverse removal procedure. Tighten nuts and bolts to specification. See TORQUE SPECIFICATIONS.

IDENTIFICATION

MANUAL TRANSMISSION/TRANSAXLE APPLICATIONS

Model	Transmission/Transaxle Model
Chrysler Corp.	
Colt & Summit	
1.5L	F5M21
1.8L	F5M22
Colt Vista & Summit Wagon	
AWD	W5M33
FWD	
1.8L	F5M22
2.4L	F5M31
Stealth	
Non-Turbo	F5M33
Turbo	W6MG1
Talon	
AWD	W5M33
FWD	
Non-Turbo	F5MC1
Turbo	F5M33
Mitsubishi	
Eclipse	
AWD	W5M33
FWD	
2.0L Non-Turbo	F5MC1
2.0L Turbo	F5M33
2.4L	F5M31
Expo	
AWD	W5M33
FWD	
1.8L	F5M22
2.4L	F5M31
Galant	F5M31
Mirage	
1.5L	F5M21
1.8L	F5M22
Montero	V5MT1
Pickup	
RWD	R5M21
4WD	V5MT1
3000GT	
AWD	W6MG1
FWD	F5M33

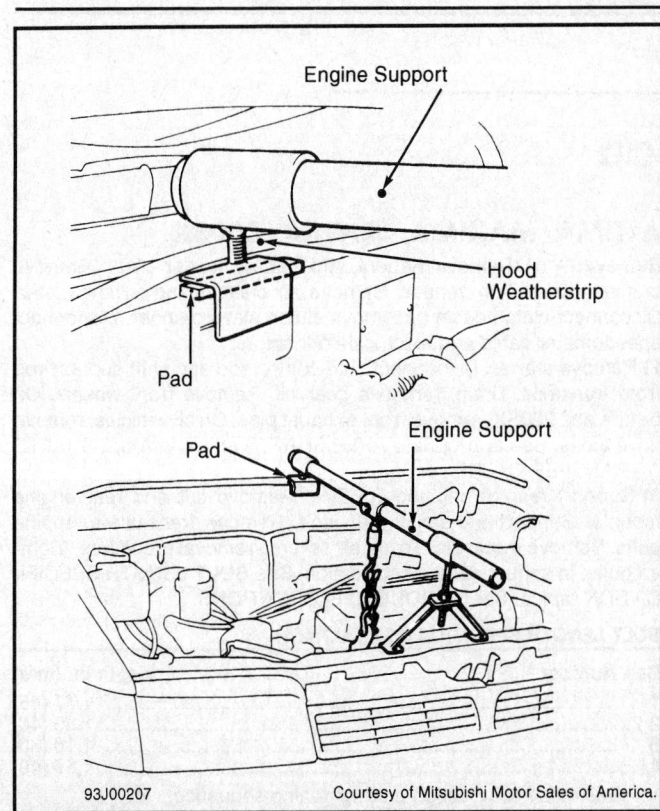

Engine Support

Hood Weatherstrip

Pad

Pad

Engine Support

93J00207   Courtesy of Mitsubishi Motor Sales of America.

Fig. 1: Supporting Engine For Transaxle Removal

COLT VISTA, EXPO, & SUMMIT WAGON AWD (W5M33)

Removal & Installation – 1) Remove air cleaner assembly. Drain transaxle oil. Disconnect control cables, speedometer cable and electrical connections at transaxle. Remove starter motor, with harness connected, and secure starter aside with wire.

2) Remove upper transaxle-to-engine bolts and transaxle mounting bracket bolt. Install engine assembly support. See Fig. 1. Lift and support vehicle. Remove undercover assemblies. Remove ball joints and tie rod ends.

3) Remove stabilizer bar connection. Remove axle shaft nuts and press out from front hub. Using pry bar, remove axle shafts from transaxle. Remove intermediate drive shaft. DO NOT damage oil seal. Plug shaft openings in transaxle.

4) Remove clutch release cylinder with line connected and secure cylinder aside with wire. Remove front exhaust pipe from vehicle. Remove transfer case assembly from transaxle. Remove center cross member. Remove bellhousing cover. Install transaxle lifting hoist. Remove remaining transaxle-to-engine bolts. Remove transaxle assembly. To install, reverse removal procedure. Tighten nuts and bolts to specification. See TORQUE SPECIFICATIONS.

PICKUP RWD (R5M21)

Removal & Installation – 1) Disconnect negative battery cable. Remove shift knob, dust cover retaining plate, gaskets, stopper plate and control lever assembly. Raise and support vehicle. Remove front exhaust pipe. drain transmission oil. Mark drive shaft flange for installation reference and remove drive shaft.

2) Disconnect back-up light switch connector, speedometer cable connection and exhaust pipe mounting bracket. Remove lower bellhousing cover. Disconnect clutch cable from clutch lever.

3) Support transmission with jack. Remove rear engine mount nuts and bolts from transmission. Remove crossmember with rear engine mount. Remove remaining bellhousing bolts, move transmission toward rear and lower from vehicle. To install, reverse removal procedure. Tighten nuts and bolts to specification. See TORQUE SPECIFICATIONS.

MONTERO & PICKUP 4WD (V5MT1)

Removal & Installation – 1) Remove switch panel from rear console. Remove suspension control switch or hole cover. Disconnect rear console harness connector. Remove side panel. Remove rear console assembly. Remove shift lever knob(s). Remove floor console harness connector. Remove front console assembly.

2) Move transmission lever to neutral position and transfer lever to 4H (4WD high range) position on Montero or 2H (RWD high range) on Pickup. Remove control lever boot retainer and boot. Remove transmission and transfer control lever assemblies. Remove control lever bushing (transmission), gaskets and stopper plates.

3) Raise and support vehicle. Remove skid plate and front exhaust pipe. Drain transmission and transfer case fluid. Mark front and rear drive shaft flanges for installation reference. Remove front and rear drive shafts.

4) Remove drive shaft dust seals. Disconnect HI/LO and 2WD/4WD detection switch connectors. Disconnect back-up light switch connector. Disconnect center differential lock detection switch connector. Disconnect center differential lock operation switch connector. Disconnect 4WD operation detection switch.

5) Disconnect speedometer cable. Remove clutch slave cylinder heat shield. Remove clutch slave cylinder (without disconnecting hydraulic line) and wire aside. Remove starter and starter cover. Remove heat shield and both transmission stays and then bellhousing lower cover.

6) Support transmission with transmission jack. Remove transfer case roll stopper and bracket. Remove crossmember and engine mounting rear insulator. Remove transfer case protector bracket and mass damper. Remove remaining bellhousing bolts. Pull toward rear of vehicle to free transmission input shaft from clutch.

7) Lower transmission/transfer case from vehicle. To install, reverse removal procedure. Tighten nuts and bolts to specification. See TORQUE SPECIFICATIONS.

STEALTH & 3000GT (F5M33 & W6MG1)

Removal & Installation – 1) Remove both inner fender splash shields. On AWD models, remove air cleaner cover, air hoses and vacuum pipe. On all models, remove air cleaner, intake hose, battery, battery tray and washer tank.

2) Disconnect transaxle control cables and speedometer cable. Remove clutch tube bracket and disconnect clutch release cylinder (including clutch damper assembly on FWD models) and wire aside.

3) Disconnect upper transaxle mount. Remove mount, bracket, plug and stoppers. Remove transaxle assembly upper coupling bolts. Disconnect tie rod ends and lower arm ball joints. Remove right support member, starter cover (if equipped) and starter.

4) Remove left side bearing bracket mounting bolts and pry left axle shaft from transaxle. Wire left axle shaft and inner shaft assembly aside. Pry right axle shaft from transaxle and wire aside.

5) Remove front bank side and rear bank side transaxle stays. Support transaxle assembly with a transmission jack. Remove transaxle assembly lower coupling bolts and lower transaxle from vehicle. To install, reverse removal procedure. Tighten nuts and bolts to specification. See TORQUE SPECIFICATIONS. Install mounting stoppers as shown in illustration. *See Fig. 2.*

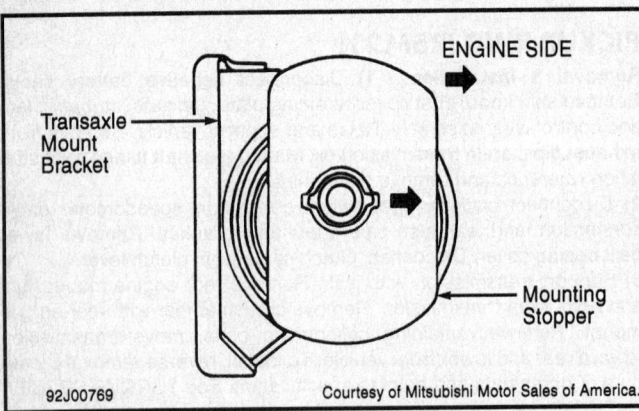

92J00769   Courtesy of Mitsubishi Motor Sales of America.

Fig. 2: Installing Transaxle Assembly Mounting Stopper (3000GT)

TORQUE SPECIFICATIONS
TORQUE SPECIFICATIONS

Application	Ft. Lbs. (N.m)
Eclipse, Expo, Galant, Precis & 3000GT	
Engine Mount-To-Transaxle	
Eclipse, Galant & Mirage	
8-mm Bolt	[1]
10-mm Bolt	22-25 (30-34)
12-mm Bolt	32-39 (43-53)
Expo	
2WD	32-39 (43-53)
AWD	
8-mm Bolt	22-25 (30-34)
10-mm Bolt	31-40 (42-54)
3000GT	
Upper Mounting Bolt	54 (73)
Lower Mounting Bolt	65 (88)
Transfer Case-To-Transaxle Bolt	
3000GT	64 (87)
All Others	40-43 (54-58)
Wheel Lug Nut	
Eclipse & 3000GT	89-103 (120-140)
Expo	
Aluminum Wheel	65-80 (88-109)
Steel Wheel	50-57 (68-77)
All Others	65-80 (88-109)
Montero & Pickup	
Flexhose-To-Release Cylinder Bolt	14-18 (19-24)
Gearshift-To-Transfer Case Bolt	11-15 (15-20)
Hydraulic Line-To-Master Cylinder	10-12 (14-16)
Release Cylinder-To-Transmission Bolt	22-30 (30-41)
Transmission-To-Engine Bolt	
2.4L Engines	
8 x 25 mm & 8 x 55 mm	15-20 (20-27)
10 x 40 mm & 10 x 65 mm	31-40 (42-54)
10 x 60 mm	20-25 (27-34)
3.0L Engines	
10 x 35 mm	24-36 (33-49)
10 x 40 mm	22-30 (30-41)
10 x 55 mm	20-25 (27-34)
12 x 35 mm, 12 x 40 mm & 12 x 50 mm	47-61 (64-83)
12 x 55 mm	58-72 (79-98)

[1] – Tighten to 84-108 INCH lbs. (9.5-12.2 N.m).

Nissan

Altima, Maxima, Pathfinder, Pickup, Sentra, 200SX, 240SX, 300SX

APPLICATION
TRANSMISSION & TRANSAXLE APPLICATION

Vehicle Model	Transmission/Transaxle
Altima	5-Speed RS5F50A/V
Maxima	RS5F50A/V
Pathfinder & Pickup (1995 3.0L)	FS5R30A
Pickup (2.4L)	FS5W71C
Sentra & 200SX	
1.6L	RS5F31A
2.0L	RS5F32V
240SX	FS5W71C
300ZX	RS5R30A

REMOVAL & INSTALLATION

CAUTION: When battery is disconnected, vehicle computer and memory systems may lose memory data. Driveability problems may exist until computer systems have completed a relearn cycle.

ALTIMA, MAXIMA, SENTRA, 200SX

Removal – 1) Remove battery and battery holder plate. Remove crankshaft position sensor. Remove air cleaner and airflow meter. Disconnect clutch cable or remove clutch slave cylinder. Disconnect speedometer cable and electrical connectors.

2) Remove starter. Disconnect shift control rod and shift support rod from transaxle. Drain transaxle gear oil. Remove front wheels. On Sentra and 200SX, remove front exhaust pipe. On all vehicles, remove drive axles. See appropriate AXLE SHAFTS article in AXLE SHAFTS & TRANSFER CASES section.

3) Support rear of engine with jack. Remove left and rear engine mounts. Support transaxle with jack. Remove transaxle-to-engine bolts. Remove transaxle. To install, reverse removal procedure. Tighten bolts, in sequence, to specification. See BOLT LENGTH SPECIFICATION tables. See TORQUE SPECIFICATIONS.

BOLT LENGTH SPECIFICATION (ALTIMA)

Bolt Number [1]	Length In. (mm)
1	1.77 (45)
2	1.89 (48)
3	1.18 (30)
4	1.57 (40)

[1] – See Fig. 1 for location and tightening sequence.

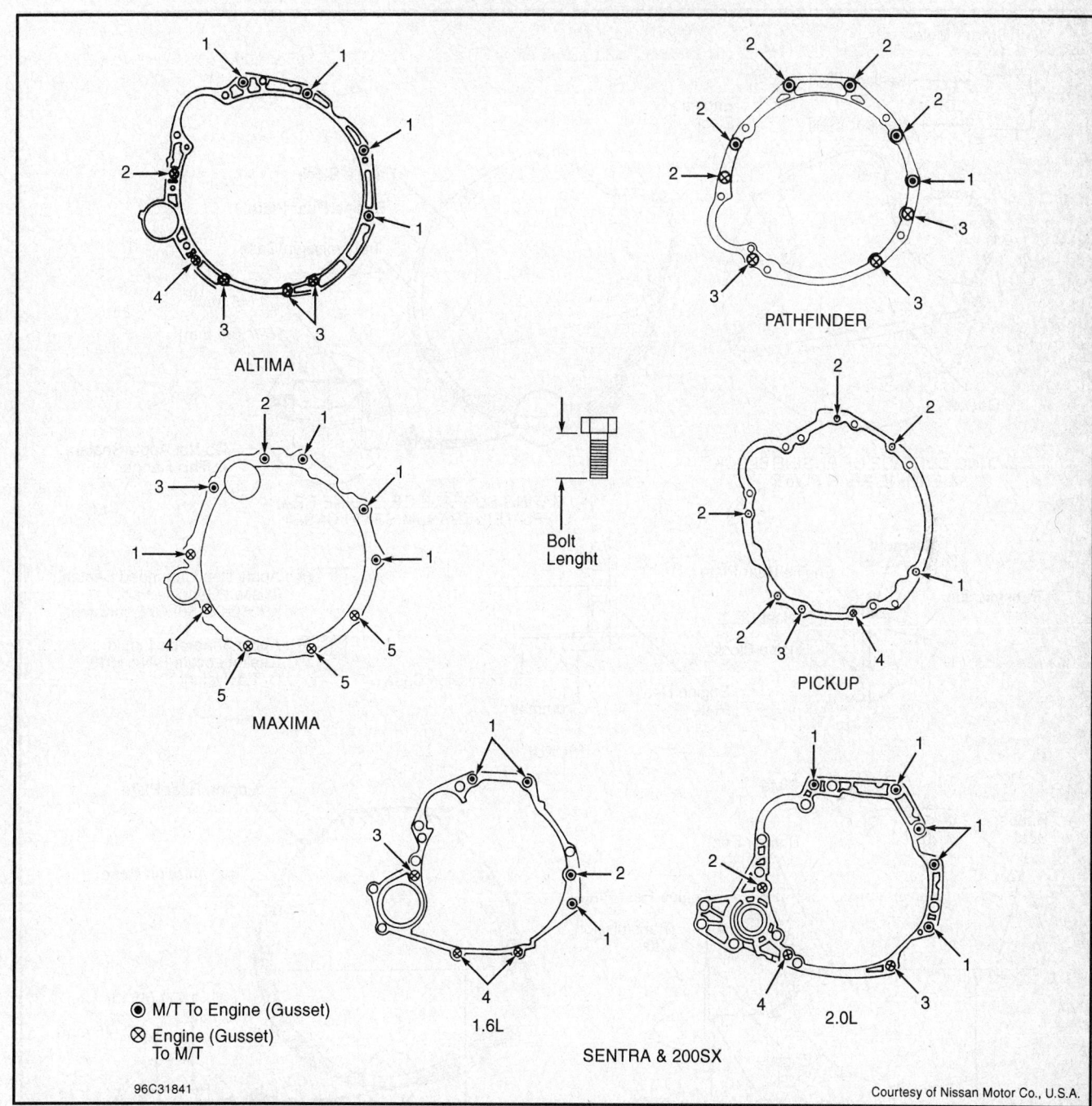

ALTIMA

PATHFINDER

MAXIMA

PICKUP

Bolt Lenght

⊙ M/T To Engine (Gusset)
⊗ Engine (Gusset) To M/T

1.6L

SENTRA & 200SX

2.0L

96C31841

Courtesy of Nissan Motor Co., U.S.A.

Fig. 1: Identifying Bolt Location & Tightening Sequence (Altima, Maxima, Sentra, 200SX, Pathfinder & Pickup)

BOLT LENGTH SPECIFICATION (MAXIMA)

Bolt Number [1]	Length In. (mm)
1	2.05 (52)
2	2.56 (65)
3	4.88 (124)
4 & 5	1.57 (40)

[1] – *See Fig. 1 for location and tightening sequence.*

BOLT LENGTH SPECIFICATION (SENTRA & 200SX)

Bolt Number [1]	Length In. (mm)
1.6L	
1	2.76 (70)
2	3.35 (85)
3	1.18 (30)
4	.98 (25)
Front Gusset-To-Engine	.79 (20)
Rear Gusset-To-Engine	.63 (16)
2.0L	
1	2.17 (55)
2	2.56 (65)
3	1.38 (35)
4	1.77 (45)

[1] – *See Fig. 1 for location and tightening sequence.*

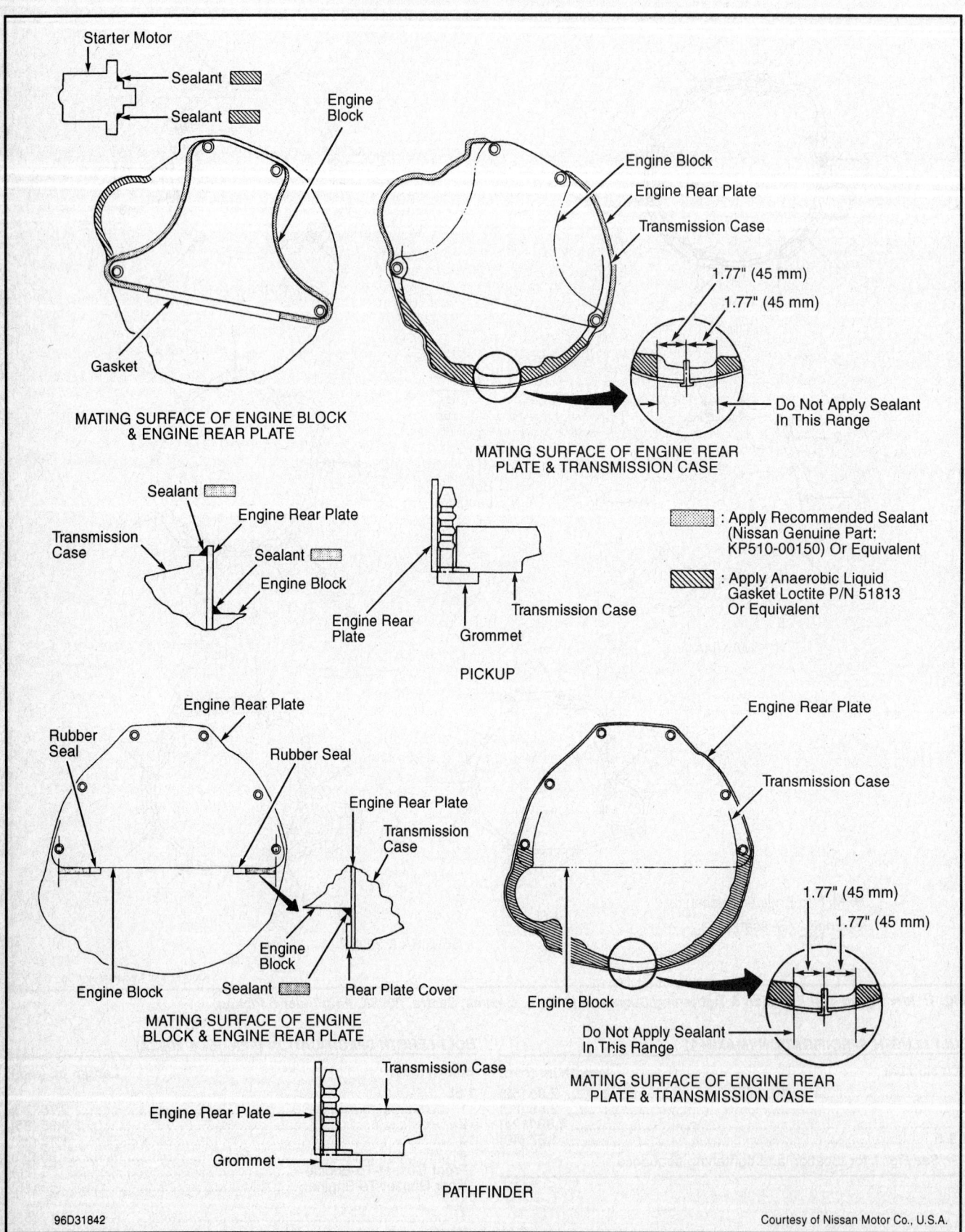

Fig. 2: *Identifying Sealant Location (Pathfinder & Pickup)*

PATHFINDER, PICKUP, 240SX, 300ZX

Removal & Installation – 1) Disconnect battery negative terminal and accelerator linkage. Place shift lever in Neutral. Remove shift lever boot, snap ring or nut, shift lever pin and shift lever. Raise and support vehicle.

2) Remove crankshaft position sensor. Disconnect exhaust pipe from manifold. Remove bolts mounting exhaust pipe bracket to extension housing or rear engine crossmember (if necessary). Remove exhaust pipe insulator. Disconnect all electrical connectors from transmission. Disconnect speedometer cable.

3) Mark drive shafts and companion flanges for installation reference. On 4WD vehicles, remove front and rear drive shafts. Remove front differential carrier crossmember and torsion bar springs.

4) On 2WD vehicles, separate center support bearing from crossmember. Remove drive shaft. On all vehicles, plug rear of transmission to prevent fluid loss. Remove slave cylinder. Support engine and transmission using jacks. Loosen rear engine mount attaching bolt.

5) Remove rear engine mount bracket. Support transmission. Remove starter and engine-to-transmission bolts. Slide transmission rearward and remove transmission. To install, reverse removal procedure. Apply Sealant (Nissan KP510-00150) or equivalent to mating surface of engine block and engine rear plate. Apply Sealant (Nissan KP610-00250) or equivalent to mating surface of engine rear plate and transmission case. See Fig. 2. Tighten bolts, in sequence, to specification. See BOLT LENGTH SPECIFICATION tables. See Fig. 3. See TORQUE SPECIFICATIONS.

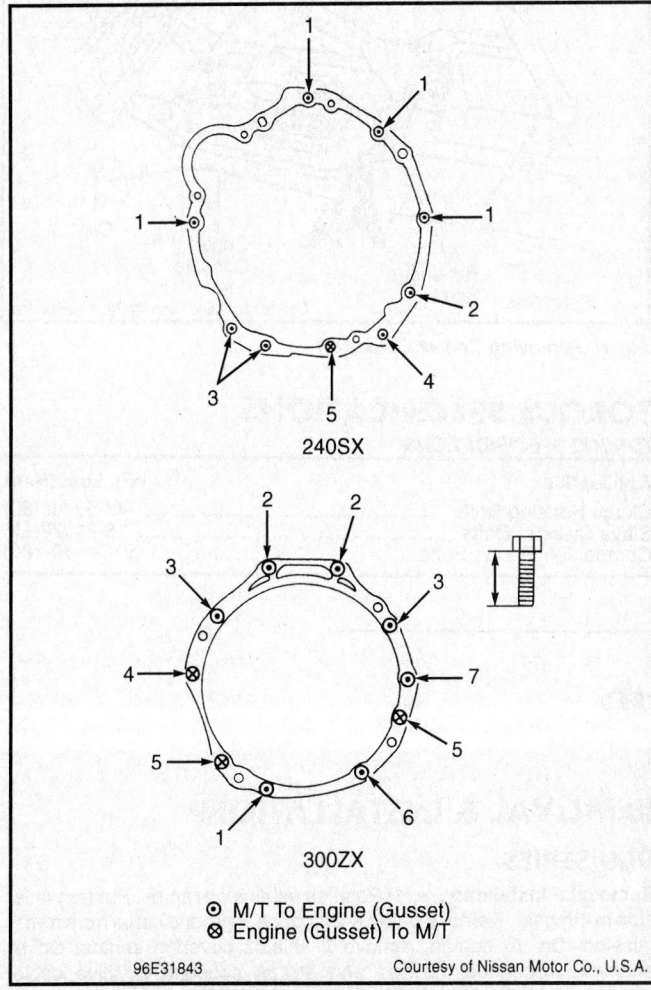

Fig. 3: Identifying Bolt Location & Tightening Sequence (240sx & 300ZX)

96E31843   Courtesy of Nissan Motor Co., U.S.A.

⊙ M/T To Engine (Gusset)
⊗ Engine (Gusset) To M/T

BOLT LENGTH SPECIFICATION (PATHFINDER & PICKUP)

Bolt Number [1]	Length In. (mm)
1	2.56 (65)
2	2.28 (58)
3 [2]	.98 (25)
4 (Pickup)	.63 (16)
Gusset To Engine (Pathfinder)	.79 (20)

[1] – See Fig. 3 for location and tightening sequence.
[2] – With nut on Pickup.

BOLT LENGTH SPECIFICATION (240SX)

Bolt Number [1]	Length In. (mm)
1	2.36 (60)
2	2.76 (70)
3 [2]	1.38 (35)
4 [2]	2.56 (65)
5	.98 (25)
Gusset To Engine	.79 (20)

[1] – See Fig. 3 for location and tightening sequence.
[2] – With nut.

BOLT LENGTH SPECIFICATION (300ZX)

Bolt Number [1]	Length In. (mm)
1	3.94 (100)
2	2.17 (55)
3	2.36 (60)
4	2.17 (55)
5	.98 (25)
6	2.36 (60)
7	2.56 (65)

[1] – See Fig. 3 for location and tightening sequence.

TORQUE SPECIFICATIONS
TORQUE SPECIFICATIONS

Application	Ft. Lbs. (N.m)
Starter-To-Transaxle	
Altima	22-30 (30-40)
Sentra & 200SX	30-38 (40-52)
Maxima	
Long Bolt	57-72 (78-98)
Short Bolt	22-30 (30-40)
Slave Cylinder Mounting Bolts	22-30 (30-40)
Transaxle-To-Engine Bolt	
Altima	
Bolt No. 1 & 2	29-36 (39-49)
Bolt No. 3 & 4	22-30 (30-40)
Maxima	
Bolt No. 1, 2 & 3	51-59 (70-79)
Bolt No. 4 & 5	26-35 (35-47)
Sentra & 200SX	
1.6L	
Bolt No. 1, 2, 3 &	
Front Gusset	22-30 (30-40)
Bolt No. 4 & Rear Gusset	12-15 (16-21)
2.0L	
Bolt No. 1 & 2	51-59 (70-79)
Bolt No. 3 & 4	22-30 (30-40)
Transmission-To-Engine Bolt	
Pathfinder	
Bolt No. 1 & 2	29-36 (39-49)
Bolt No. 3 & Gusset	22-29 (30-39)
Pickup	
Bolt No. 1 & 2	29-36 (39-49)
Bolt No. 3 & 4	12-16 (16-22)
240SX	
Bolt No. 1 & 2	29-36 (39-49)
Bolt No. 3, 4, 5 & Gusset	22-29 (30-39)
300ZX	
Bolt No. 1, 2, 3, 5 & 7	29-36 (39-49)
Bolt No. 4 & 6	22-29 (30-39)

MANUAL TRANSMISSION REMOVAL
Porsche

911 Carrera 2
APPLICATION
TRANSAXLE APPLICATION

Vehicle Application	Transaxle Model
911 Carrera 2	G50/20

NOTE: *Engine and transaxle assembly are removed from beneath vehicle as a complete unit. Refer to AUTOMATIC TRANSMISSION REMOVAL article and use appropriate procedures.*

Rover

Defender 90, Discovery

NOTE: *Defender 90 transmission removal and installation information is not available from manufacturer.*

APPLICATION
MANUAL TRANSMISSION APPLICATIONS

Model	[1] Transmission
Discovery	R380/53A

[1] – Transmission series (serial number prefix) is stamped on right side of transmission case.

REMOVAL & INSTALLATION

Removal & Installation – 1) Disconnect negative battery cable. Open center console door. *See Fig. 1.* Remove center console retaining screws. Release 2 clips securing front of center console. Disconnect parking brake cable from parking brake lever. Pull parking brake lever to full on position.

2) Lift center console and disconnect wiring harness connectors as necessary. Remove center console from vehicle. Remove insulation from top of transmission tunnel. Remove pinch bolt and upper shift lever. Shift transfer case into low range. Remove bolt securing transmission breather pipe to cylinder block.

3) Remove fan shroud from radiator and place shroud over fan blades. Raise and support vehicle. Remove front exhaust pipes. Remove clutch slave cylinder, leaving hydraulic line attached. Mark drive shaft position for installation reference and disconnect front and rear drive shafts from transmission.

4) Secure drive shafts out of way. Disconnect speedometer from transmission. Disconnect parking brake cable from transmission tunnel. Support transmission and remove transmission crossmember.

Lower transmission until transfer case shift lever clears transmission tunnel. Disconnect transmission wiring harness connectors as necessary.

5) Remove clips securing transmission breather pipe to harness. Using a block of wood and a jack, support engine underneath oil pan. Remove clutch housing-to-engine block bolts. Remove transmission from vehicle. To install, reverse removal procedure. Tighten bolts to specification. See TORQUE SPECIFICATIONS.

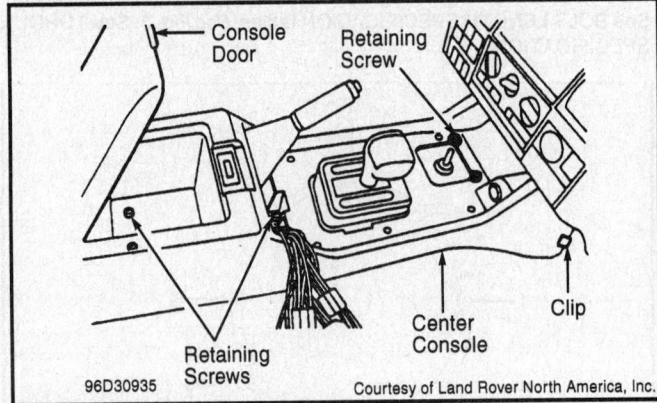

Fig 1: Removing Center Console

TORQUE SPECIFICATIONS
TORQUE SPECIFICATIONS

Application	Ft. Lbs. (N.m)
Clutch Housing Bolts	48-59 (65-80)
Slave Cylinder Bolts	16-21 (22-28)
Companion Flange Bolts	59-74 (80-100)

Saab

900 Series, 9000 Series
APPLICATION
TRANSAXLE APPLICATION

Vehicle Application	Transaxle Model
900	FM5 Series
9000	FM5 Series

REMOVAL & INSTALLATION

900 SERIES

Removal & Installation – 1) Position vehicle on ramps. Put transmission in 4th gear. Remove battery. Disconnect ground cable from transmission. On V6 engine, remove 2 shields covering engine. On all engines, disconnect clamps and straps securing positive cable. Disconnect back-up light switch connector.

2) Disconnect clutch cable from clutch lever. Release cable rubber damper from retaining clip on transmission. Disconnect oxygen sensor connectors. On 4-cylinder engine, remove resonator along with mass airflow sensor.

3) On all engines, install Holder (83 94 835) in engine lift brackets. On 4-cylinder engine, push out rubber bushing from left lift bracket. On all engines, place Yoke (83 93 850) on wheelhousings. Ensure yoke is in close contact with edges of fenders. Remove load from engine and transmission.

4) Remove plastic plug on transmission. Install Locking Pin (87 92 335), with ring facing upward, to secure gear position. Disconnect gear rod linkage clamp. Engage 3rd gear so gear rod is released from linkage. Install locking pin with ring in hole.

5) Raise and support front of vehicle. Remove front wheels. Remove front exhaust pipe. Remove left and right spoilers under bumper. Remove plastic seal at bottom of right inner fender. Disconnect both ball joints. Place Mobile Jack (83 94 793) with Fixture (83 94 801) under vehicle. Place Front Holder (83 94 819) on fixture and install guide pins. Place Rear Holders (83 94 827) on fixture and fit small bosses. Install mobile jack up against carrying frame.

6) Remove 2 rear engine support nuts. Remove carrying frame bolts, using care not to lose washers. Lower mobile jack and remove carrying frame. Drain oil from transmission. Using Remover (89 96 654 or 87 92 326), pull out left drive shaft. Suspend shaft with wire and install Cover (87 92 244) on transmission. Using Remover (89 96 654), pull out right drive shaft from intermediate shaft. Suspend shaft with wire.

7) Remove 2 intermediate shaft bearing bolts located in bearing bracket. On V6 engine, pull out shaft. On 4-cylinder engine, remove intermediate shaft with bearing bracket. On all engines, install Sealing Cover (87 92 244) on transmission. Remove splash plate behind flywheel. Remove 2 engine bracket-to-body bolts. Remove 3 transmission bracket bolts.

8) Remove all engine-to-transmission bolts that can be accessed from under vehicle. On 4-cylinder engine, remove bottom starter motor nut. Lower vehicle. Remove 2 outer transmission-to-engine bolts leaving one remaining bolt still attached. Install Lifting Bracket (87 92 368) with attaching cable to transmission.

9) Connect engine hoist to lifting bracket. Remove last transmission-to-engine bolt. Disconnect and lower transmission. To install, reverse removal procedure. Tighten nuts and bolts to specification. See TORQUE SPECIFICATIONS.

9000 SERIES

Removal & Installation – 1) Place vehicle on ramp and engage 4th gear. Remove battery. Disconnect accelerator cable. Remove positive cable from hose (TCS vehicles only). Disconnect front fuse box and set aside. Remove 2 clamps securing positive cable to battery shelf. Disconnect ABS control module connector. Remove battery shelf. Remove by-pass valve from turbo pressure pipe. Disconnect temperature sensor from turbo pressure pipe. Remove hose clips and turbo pressure pipe.

2) Disconnect speedometer sensor cable connector. Disconnect back-up light switch connector. Clamp off clutch slave cylinder hydraulic line and disconnect slave cylinder from hydraulic line. Remove clamp on oil pressure pipe. Remove engine-to-transmission bolts accessible from top of vehicle, except for center bolt.

3) Place Lifting Beam (83 93 977) on wheel housing, ensuring beam rests against inside edge of fender. Insert hook into engine lifting hook and tighten slightly, using wing nut on lifting beam.

4) Raise and support vehicle. Remove left front wheel. Remove wheel-housing molding. Remove front inner fender section. Remove left and middle spoiler assemblies.

5) Remove battery ground cable from transmission. Remove 2 nuts on transmission universal joint and separate gear lever. Disconnect ball joint and anti-roll bar from control arm. Remove anti-roll bar bearing bolts. Remove front engine mounting nut. Remove front link subframe bolt. Remove 2 front link bolts. Remove subframe rear link bolt. Remove remaining 2 front link bolts. Remove 2 bolts in front corners of subframe. Remove 4 bolts in rear corner of subframe.

6) Carefully fold down subframe. Ensure plate located between subframe and chassis is stored in a safe location. Remove bolts in 2 links and remove subframe. Remove universal joint boot clamps. Pull universal joint apart and allow shaft to hang. Protect universal joint and boot from damage by covering them with a shop rag. Remove remaining engine-to-transmission bolts accessible from under vehicle.

7) Remove transmission protection plate. Lower vehicle. Install cable hook on transmission. Hook cable on a hoist and tighten. Remove last engine-to-transmission bolt. Lower transmission from vehicle. To install, reverse removal procedure. Tighten nuts and bolts to specification. See TORQUE SPECIFICATIONS.

TORQUE SPECIFICATIONS
TORQUE SPECIFICATIONS

Applications	Ft. Lbs. (N.m)
900 Series	
Clutch Fork Bolt	18 (25)
Ball Joint/Link Arm Bolt	55 (75)
Carrying Frame Bolts & Nuts	
Front	85 (115)
Middle	140 (190)
Rear	[1] 81 (110)
Gear Lever Linkage Clamp Nut	14-17 (19-23)
Transmission Bracket Bolts	21-39 (28-52)
Transmission-To-Engine Bolts	35-65 (50-90)
9000 Series	
Anti-Roll Bar Clamp Bolt	30-40 (40-54)
Ball Joint/Link Arm Bolt	55 (75)
Carrying Frame Bolts & Nuts	
Front	32-42 (43-57)
Rear	35-47 (47-63)
Gear Lever Linkage Clamp Nut	14-17 (19-23)
Suspension Arm-To-Ball Joint Nut	19-25 (26-34)
Transmission Bracket Bolts	21-39 (28-52)
Transmission-To-Engine Bolts	35-65 (50-90)

[1] – Tighten an additional 75 degrees.

Impreza, Legacy

APPLICATION

TRANSAXLE APPLICATION

Vehicle Application	Transmission Model
Impreza	5-Speed
Legacy	5-Speed

REMOVAL & INSTALLATION

IMPREZA & LEGACY

Removal & Installation – 1) Disconnect negative battery cable. Remove clutch cable. Remove clutch cable return spring, lock nut, adjusting nut and clips. Disconnect neutral position sensor and back up light switch.

2) Remove speedometer cable and clip. Label and disconnect wiring and hoses connected to transaxle. Disconnect oxygen sensor wire connector. Remove air cleaner. Remove torque strut from engine and vehicle body. Install Engine Supporter (926610000) between engine and vehicle body.

3) Remove starter. Remove torque rod. Raise vehicle. Remove front and rear exhaust pipe. Remove front crossmember (if equipped). On AWD vehicles, mark drive shaft for installation reference and remove drive shaft.

4) Plug opening at rear of extension housing. Remove select rod and stay from transmission. Remove clutch release cylinder from transaxle and wire out of way. On all vehicles, disconnect spring, gearshift rod and brace from transaxle.

5) Using a pin punch, drive out each axle shaft roll pin. Remove stabilizer bar from transverse link. Remove hand brake cable bracket from transverse link. Remove transverse link bolt at ball joint and lower transverse link. Separate axle shafts from transaxle.

6) Remove engine-to-transaxle mounting bolts and nuts. Support transaxle with transmission jack. Remove rear cushion mounting nuts and remove rear crossmember. Separate transaxle from engine. Remove transaxle from vehicle.

7) To install, reverse removal procedure. Ensure NEW roll pins are installed in axle shafts. Tighten nuts and bolts to specification. See TORQUE SPECIFICATIONS.

TORQUE SPECIFICATIONS

TORQUE SPECIFICATIONS

Application	Ft. Lbs. (N.m)
Clutch Hose Bolt	11-15 (15-20)
Clutch Master Cylinder Nut	9-17 (12-23)
Clutch Release Cylinder Bolt	25-30 (34-40)
Drive Shaft Center Bearing Support Bolt	35-42 (47-57)
Drive Shaft-To-Differential Nut	17-29 (24-39)
Exhaust Pipe Support Bracket Bolt	18-26 (25-35)
Exhaust Pipe-To-Engine Nut	18-26 (25-35)
Exhaust Pipe To Muffler	32-40 (43-53)
Front Crossmember Bolt	35-63 (47-86)
Pitching Stopper	
To Transmission	33-40 (44-54)
To Body	35-49 (47-67)
Rear Crossmember Cushion Nut	17-20 (23-26)
Rear Crossmember Bolt To Body	40-61 (54-83)
Rear Crossmember Bolt To Mount	20-35 (27-47)
Stabilizer Bar-To-Transverse Link Bolt	15-21 (21-28)
Starter Bolt	34-40 (46-54)
Transaxle-To-Engine Bolt/Nut	34-40 (46-54)
Transverse Link-To-Ball Joint Nut	18-22 (25-29)

Suzuki

Esteem, Samurai, Sidekick, Swift, X90

APPLICATION

MANUAL TRANSMISSION/TRANSAXLE APPLICATION

Model	Transmission/Transaxle
Esteem, Swift	5-Speed Transaxle
Samurai, Sidekick & X90	5-Speed Transmission

REMOVAL & INSTALLATION

Esteem – 1) Disconnect negative battery cable. Disconnect clutch cable and bracket from transaxle. Disconnect wiring harness clamps and connectors. Remove transaxle-to-engine mounting bolts. Disconnect speedometer cable from transaxle. Remove starter and mounting plate.

2) Remove exhaust manifold cover. Disconnect exhaust pipe from manifold. Raise and support vehicle. Drain transaxle fluid. Remove left inner fender panel. Remove front section of exhaust pipe. Disconnect shift rod, bushings, and control shaft from transaxle. Remove lower plate/dust shield from clutch housing.

3) Disconnect lower ball studs and suspension control arms. Disconnect left drive axle from transaxle, using a screwdriver to pry drive axle from differential. Remove drive axle center support bearing and pull center shaft assembly from differential. Remove transaxle brace. Remove remaining engine-to-transaxle mounting bolts. Remove rear engine mount bolts.

4) Lower vehicle, and support engine using hoist. Support transaxle using a jack. Remove left-side engine mount and brace. Remove any remaining components attached to transaxle assembly. Remove transaxle from vehicle. To install, reverse removal procedure. Tighten bolts to specification. See TORQUE SPECIFICATIONS.

Samurai – 1) Disconnect negative battery cable. Remove shift lever boot. Remove shift lever case cover bolts, and remove shift lever. Disconnect back-up light and 5th gear switch. Disconnect starter motor wiring, and remove starter. Remove clamps attaching fuel hoses to transmission case. Drain transmission fluid.

2) Disconnect clutch cable from clutch release lever. Remove both drive shafts. Remove clutch inspection plate. Remove engine-to-transmission bolts and nuts. Remove crossmember and transmission rear mounting bracket. Remove center exhaust pipe. Lower transmission from vehicle. To install, reverse removal procedure. Tighten bolts to specification. See TORQUE SPECIFICATIONS.

Sidekick & X90 – 1) Disconnect negative battery cable. Remove transmission and transfer case shift levers. Remove breather hose from clamp at rear of cylinder head. Release clamp at rear of intake manifold to free wiring harness. Disconnect harness connector. Remove starter motor. Remove transmission mounting bolts.

NOTE: If vehicle is 2WD, disregard transfer case and 4WD component removal procedures in the following steps.

2) Raise vehicle and drain fluid from transfer case. Remove front and rear drive shafts. Disconnect clutch cable. Remove clutch housing lower plate. Remove center exhaust pipe. Remove engine-to-transmission mounting nuts. Disconnect speedometer cable.

3) Support transmission/transfer case assembly with floor jack. Remove rear engine mount crossmember. Move transmission/transfer case assembly to rear and lower. To install, reverse removal procedure. Tighten bolts to specification. See TORQUE SPECIFICATIONS.

Swift – 1) Disconnect negative battery cable. On models equipped with 1.3L engine, remove battery and tray. On all models, disconnect clutch cable and bracket from transaxle. Disconnect wiring harness clamps and connectors. Disconnect speedometer cable from transaxle. Remove transaxle-to-engine mounting bolts. Remove starter and mounting plate.

2) Raise and support vehicle. Drain transaxle fluid. Remove left inner fender panel. Remove front section of exhaust pipe. Disconnect shift rod, bushings, and control shaft from transaxle. Remove lower plate/dust shield from clutch housing.

3) Disconnect lower ball studs and suspension control arms. Disconnect left drive axle from transaxle, using a screwdriver to pry drive axle from differential. Remove drive axle center support bearing and pull center shaft assembly from differential. Remove transaxle brace. Remove remaining engine-to-transaxle mounting bolts. Remove rear engine mount bolts.

4) Lower vehicle, and support engine using hoist. Support transaxle using a jack. Remove left engine mount and brace. Remove any remaining components attached to transaxle assembly. Remove transaxle from vehicle. To install, reverse removal procedure. Tighten bolts to specification. See TORQUE SPECIFICATIONS.

TORQUE SPECIFICATIONS
TORQUE SPECIFICATIONS

Application	Ft. Lbs. (N.m)
Esteem	
Ball Joint Nut	37 (50)
Center Bearing Support Bolts	37 (50)
Exhaust Pipe-To-Manifold Nuts	37 (50)
Gear Shift Control Shaft	13 (18)
Gear Shift Extension Rod Nut	24 (33)
Rear Engine Mount Bracket Bolts	37 (50)
Starter Bolts	13-21 (18-28)
Transaxle-To-Engine Bolts	66 (90)
Samurai	
Center Exhaust Pipe Bolts	44 (60)
Starter Bolts	16-23 (22-31)
Transmission-To-Engine Bolts	32-39 (43-53)
Sidekick & X90	
Center Exhaust Pipe Bolts	37 (50)
Rear Engine Mounts	37 (50)
Starter Bolts	16-23 (22-31)
Transmission Filler Plugs	17 (23)
Transmission-To-Engine Bolts	63 (85)
"U" Joint Companion Flange	41 (55)
Swift	
Ball Joint Nut	37-44 (50-60)
Center Bearing Support Bolts	30-44 (40-60)
Engine Mount Brackets	
Bolts	30-44 (40-60)
Nuts	37-44 (50-60)
Exhaust Pipe-To-Manifold Nuts	26-37 (35-50)
Gear Shift Control Shaft	11-15 (15-20)
Gear Shift Extension Rod Nut	18-30 (25-40)
Starter Bolts	13-21 (18-28)
Transaxle-To-Engine Bolts	30-44 (40-60)

Toyota

Camry, Celica, Corolla, MR2 (1995), Paseo, Pickup (1995), RAV4 (1996), Supra, Tacoma, Tercel, T100, 4Runner

APPLICATION
MANUAL TRANSMISSION/TRANSAXLE APPLICATIONS

Application	Transmission/Transaxle
Camry	
2.2L 4-Cyl.	5-Speed - S51
Celica	
1.8L (7A-FE)	5-Speed - C52
2.2L (5S-FE)	5-Speed - S54
Corolla	
1.6L (4A-FE)	5-Speed - C50
1.8L (7A-FE)	5-Speed - C52
MR2	
2.0L Turbo	5-Speed - E153
2.2L Non-Turbo	5-Speed - S54
Paseo	5-Speed - C150
Pickup	
2.4L 4-Cyl.	
2WD	5-Speed - W55
4WD	5-Speed - G58 Or W56
3.0L V6	
2WD	5-Speed - R150
4WD	5-Speed - R150F
RAV4	
2WD	5-Speed - E250
4WD	5-Speed - E250F
Supra	
3.0L Non-Turbo	5-Speed - W58
3.0L Turbo	6-Speed - V160
Tacoma	
2WD	
2.4L 4-Cyl.	5-Speed - W59
3.4L V6	5-Speed - R150

MANUAL TRANSMISSION/TRANSAXLE APPLICATIONS (Cont.)

Application	Transmission/Transaxle
Tacoma (Cont.)	
4WD	
2.7L 4-Cyl.	5-Speed - W59
3.4L V6	5-Speed - R150F
Tercel	4-Speed - C141 Or 5-Speed - C151
T100	
1995	
2WD	
2.7L 4-Cyl.	5-Speed - W56
3.4L V6	5-Speed - R150
4WD	5-Speed - R150F
1996	
2WD	
2.7L 4-Cyl.	5-Speed - W59
3.4L V6	5-Speed - R150
4WD	5-Speed - R150F
4Runner	
1995	
4WD	
2.4L 4-Cyl.	5-Speed - G58
3.0L V6	5-Speed - R150F
1996	
2WD	
2.7L 4-Cyl.	5-Speed - W59
4WD	
2.7L 4-Cyl.	5-Speed - W59
3.4L V6	5-Speed - R150F

REMOVAL & INSTALLATION

WARNING: To prevent air bag deployment, disconnect negative battery cable and wait at least 90 seconds before working on vehicle.

CAMRY

Removal & Installation – 1) Disconnect negative battery cable. Remove air cleaner case with air intake hose. Remove cruise control actuator. Remove clutch release cylinder with hose attached and secure aside.

2) Remove starter. Disconnect necessary ground straps, electrical connections and control cables from transaxle. Remove upper transaxle mounting bolts from cylinder block.

3) Raise and support vehicle. Remove front wheels. Remove lower engine covers. Drain transaxle fluid. Remove axle shafts from transaxle. See appropriate AXLE SHAFTS article in AXLE SHAFTS & TRANSFER CASES section. Remove stabilizer bar mount and bushing from crossmember.

4) Support steering gear so steering gear remains in place. Remove steering gear-to-crossmember bolts and nuts. Remove front exhaust pipe, located below oil pan. Remove stiffener plates, located between cylinder block and transaxle, at rear of oil pan.

5) Support engine with hoist. Remove front (exhaust manifold side) engine mount-to-crossmember bolts and nuts. Remove rear (intake manifold side) engine mount-to-crossmember nuts.

6) Using transmission jack, slightly raise transaxle to remove weight from engine mounts. Remove transaxle mount-to-transaxle bolts and transaxle mount-to-crossmember nuts. Disconnect necessary pipes and clamps from crossmember. Remove bolts, nuts and crossmember, located below engine and transaxle.

7) Support transaxle with transmission jack. Remove remaining transaxle mounting bolts. Slightly lower engine and remove transaxle. To install, reverse removal procedure. Tighten nuts and bolts to specification. See TORQUE SPECIFICATIONS.

WARNING: To prevent air bag deployment, disconnect negative battery cable and wait at least 90 seconds before working on vehicle.

CELICA

Removal & Installation – 1) Disconnect negative battery cable. On 2.2L (5S-FE) models, remove battery and cruise control actuator. On all models, remove air cleaner case with air intake hose. Remove clutch release cylinder with hose attached and secure aside.

2) Remove starter. Disconnect necessary ground straps, electrical connections and control cables from transaxle. Remove upper transaxle mounting bolts from cylinder block.

3) Raise and support vehicle. Remove front wheels. Remove lower engine covers. Drain transaxle fluid. Remove axle shafts from transaxle. See AXLE SHAFTS article in AXLE SHAFTS & TRANSFER CASES section.

4) Remove front exhaust pipe, located below oil pan. Remove front exhaust pipe support bracket. On 2.2L (5S-FE), remove stiffener plate, located between cylinder block and transaxle, at rear of oil pan.

5) On all models, support engine with hoist. Using transmission jack, slightly raise transaxle to remove weight from engine mounts. Remove front (exhaust manifold side) engine mount-to-crossmember bolts and nuts. Remove rear (intake manifold side) engine mount-to-crossmember bolts and nuts.

6) Remove front (exhaust manifold side) engine mount and rear (intake manifold side) engine mount brackets from cylinder block. Remove bolts and crossmember, located below engine and transaxle. Remove transaxle mount bolts.

7) Remove remaining transaxle mounting bolts. Slightly lower engine and remove transaxle. To install, reverse removal procedure. Tighten nuts and bolts to specification. See TORQUE SPECIFICATIONS.

WARNING: To prevent air bag deployment, disconnect negative battery cable and wait at least 90 seconds before working on vehicle.

COROLLA

Removal & Installation – 1) Disconnect negative battery cable. Remove air cleaner case with air intake hose. Remove coolant reservoir tank. Remove clutch release cylinder with hose attached and secure aside.

2) Disconnect necessary ground straps, electrical connections and control cables from transaxle. Remove upper transaxle mounting bolts from cylinder block.

3) Raise and support vehicle. Remove front wheels. Remove lower engine covers. Drain transaxle fluid. Remove axle shafts from transaxle. See appropriate AXLE SHAFTS article in AXLE SHAFTS & TRANSFER CASES section.

4) Remove front exhaust pipe, located below oil pan. Remove exhaust pipe support bracket. Support engine with hoist. Remove bracket and bolts from top of transaxle mount. Using transmission jack, slightly raise transaxle to remove weight from engine mounts.

5) Remove front (exhaust manifold side) engine mount-to-crossmember bolts. Remove rear (intake manifold side) engine mount-to-crossmember nuts. Remove bolts and crossmember, located below engine and transaxle and between lower suspension arms. Remove starter. On 1.6L (4A-FE), remove stiffener plate, located between cylinder block and transaxle, at rear of oil pan. *See Fig. 1.*

6) On 1996 models, remove sub-frame and lower suspension arm. *See Fig. 2.* On all models, remove remaining transaxle mount bolts. On 1.8L (7A-FE), remove No. 1 oil pan-to-transaxle bolts, located at rear of No. 1 oil pan. On all models, remove remaining transaxle mounting bolts. Slightly lower engine and remove transaxle.

7) To install, reverse removal procedure. Tighten nuts and bolts to specification. On 1.6L (4A-FE), install and tighten stiffener plate bolts

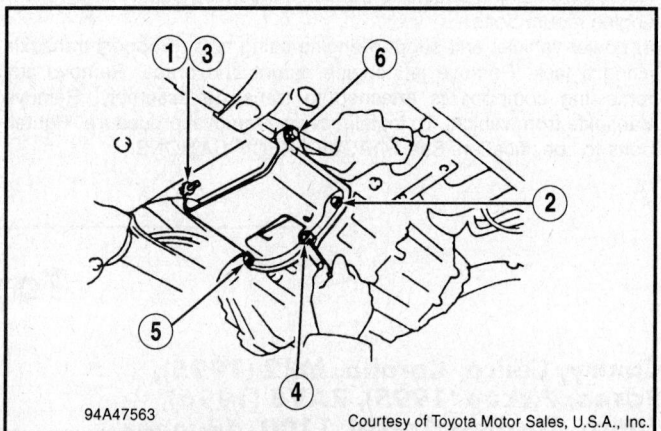

Fig. 1: Stiffener Plate Bolt Installation Sequence (Corolla 1.6L 4A-FE)

94A47563   Courtesy of Toyota Motor Sales, U.S.A., Inc.

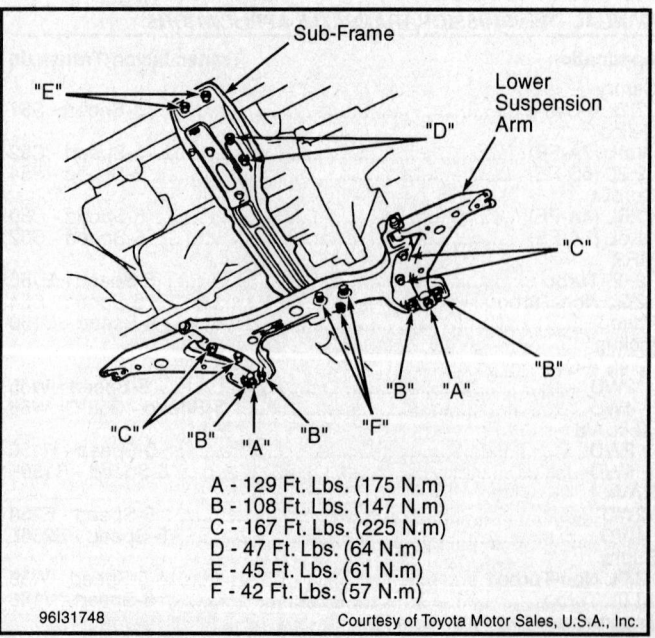

A - 129 Ft. Lbs. (175 N.m)
B - 108 Ft. Lbs. (147 N.m)
C - 167 Ft. Lbs. (225 N.m)
D - 47 Ft. Lbs. (64 N.m)
E - 45 Ft. Lbs. (61 N.m)
F - 42 Ft. Lbs. (57 N.m)

96I31748   Courtesy of Toyota Motor Sales, U.S.A., Inc.

Fig. 2: Tightening Sub-Frame & Lower Suspension Arm (1996 Corolla)

to specification in sequence. *See Fig. 1.* On 1996 models, tighten subframe and lower suspension arm bolts and nuts to specification. *See Fig. 2.* See TORQUE SPECIFICATIONS.

WARNING: To prevent air bag deployment, disconnect negative battery cable and wait at least 90 seconds before working on vehicle.

MR2

Removal & Installation – 1) Disconnect negative battery cable. Remove air cleaner assembly with air intake hose. Remove strut tower-to-firewall braces (if equipped).

2) Remove starter. Disconnect necessary ground straps, electrical connections and control cables from transaxle. Remove upper transaxle mounting bolts from cylinder block.

3) Raise and support vehicle. Remove rear wheels. Remove lower engine covers. Drain transaxle fluid. Remove axle shafts from transaxle. See appropriate AXLE SHAFTS article in AXLE SHAFTS & TRANSFER CASES section. Remove front exhaust pipe.

4) Remove brace from top of left transaxle mount. Support engine with hoist. Remove front engine mount. Remove clutch release cylinder with hose attached and secure aside. Remove rear engine mount.

5) Remove suspension arm-to-axle carrier bolt, located on rear of axle carrier, near brake backing plate. Disconnect speed sensor bracket from suspension crossmember, located below engine. Disconnect lower control arms from suspension crossmember. Remove bolts and suspension crossmember.

6) Using transmission jack, slightly raise transaxle to remove weight from engine mounts. Remove left transaxle mount bolts. Remove bolts and stiffener plates, located between rear of cylinder block and transaxle.

7) Remove rear plate, located at front of transaxle, just below oil pan. Remove remaining transaxle mounting bolts. Slightly lower engine and remove transaxle. To install, reverse removal procedure. Tighten nuts and bolts to specification. See TORQUE SPECIFICATIONS.

WARNING: To prevent air bag deployment, disconnect negative battery cable and wait at least 90 seconds before working on vehicle.

PASEO & TERCEL

Removal & Installation – 1) Disconnect negative battery cable. Remove air cleaner case with air intake hose. Remove battery. Remove clutch release cylinder with hose attached and secure aside.

2) Disconnect necessary ground straps, electrical connections, control cables and speedometer cable from transaxle. Remove upper transaxle mounting bolts from cylinder block.

3) Raise and support vehicle. Remove front wheels. Remove lower engine covers. Drain transaxle fluid. Remove axle shafts from transaxle. See appropriate AXLE SHAFTS article in AXLE SHAFTS & TRANSFER CASES section.

4) Support engine with hoist. Using transmission jack, slightly raise transaxle to remove weight from engine mounts. Remove front (exhaust manifold side) engine mount-to-body bolts. Remove rear (intake manifold side) engine mount-to-body bolts. Remove front exhaust pipe.

5) Remove starter. Remove remaining transaxle mounting bolts. Slightly lower engine and remove transaxle. To install, reverse removal procedure. Tighten nuts and bolts to specification. See TORQUE SPECIFICATIONS.

WARNING: To prevent air bag deployment, disconnect negative battery cable and wait at least 90 seconds before working on vehicle.

PICKUP & 4RUNNER

Removal & Installation – 1) Disconnect negative battery cable. Remove fan shroud bolts. Remove transmission shift lever boot retainer.

2) Pull transmission shift lever boot upward. Place shop towel on shift lever cap, located at top of transmission on transmission shift lever. Press shift lever cap downward and rotate counterclockwise to remove from transmission. Remove transmission shift lever with shift lever cap from transmission.

3) On 4WD models, remove snap ring and transfer case shift lever. On all models, raise and support vehicle. Drain transmission and transfer case fluid (if equipped).

4) Remove drive shaft dust cover (if equipped). Place reference mark on drive shaft flanges for reassembly reference. Remove drive shaft(s) as required. Disconnect necessary electrical connectors at transmission and transfer case (if equipped).

5) Remove necessary exhaust pipe components for removal of transmission and transfer case (if equipped). Remove clutch release cylinder with hose attached and secure aside.

6) On 4WD V6 models, support front differential with transmission jack. Remove front differential mounting bolts. On all models, remove stabilizer bar bracket-to-frame bolts.

7) Support transmission with transmission jack. Remove necessary crossmembers for removal of transmission and transfer case (if equipped). Place wooden block between oil pan and front crossmember or front differential. Slightly lower transmission.

8) Remove starter and exhaust pipe bracket. Remove stiffener plates, located between rear of cylinder block and transmission. Remove transmission mounting bolts.

9) Slowly pull transmission and transfer case (if equipped) rearward. On some models, it may be necessary to rotate transmission approximately 45 degrees for transmission removal. To install, reverse removal procedure. Tighten bolts to specification. See TORQUE SPECIFICATIONS.

WARNING: To prevent air bag deployment, disconnect negative battery cable and wait at least 90 seconds before working on vehicle.

RAV4 2WD

Removal & Installation – 1) Disconnect negative battery cable. Remove air cleaner case with air intake hose. Remove engine coolant reservoir tank. Remove clutch release cylinder with hose attached and secure aside.

2) Disconnect necessary ground straps, electrical connections, control cables and speedometer cable from transaxle. Remove 4 upper transaxle mounting bolts from cylinder block.

3) Raise and support vehicle. Remove front wheels. Remove lower engine covers. Drain transaxle fluid. Remove axle shafts from transaxle. See appropriate AXLE SHAFTS article in AXLE SHAFTS & TRANSFER CASES section. Remove front exhaust pipe.

4) Remove front suspension crossmember and stabilizer bar. Support engine with hoist. Using a transmission jack, slightly raise transaxle to remove weight from engine mounts.

5) Remove front (exhaust manifold side) engine mount-to-body bolts. Remove rear (intake manifold side) engine mount-to-body bolts.

6) Remove starter. Remove remaining transaxle mounting bolts. Slightly lower engine and remove transaxle. To install, reverse removal procedure. Tighten bolt/nuts to specification. See TORQUE SPECIFICATIONS. Fill transaxle with 75W-90 gear oil with API GL-4 or GL-5 rating.

WARNING: To prevent air bag deployment, disconnect negative battery cable and wait at least 90 seconds before working on vehicle.

RAV4 4WD

NOTE: Engine and transaxle are removed as an assembly from bottom of engine compartment. For reassembly reference, label all electrical connectors, vacuum hoses and fuel lines before removal. Also place mating marks on engine hood and other major assemblies before removal.

Removal – 1) Release fuel pressure. Manufacturer recommends disconnecting electrical connector at electric fuel pump and operating engine until engine stalls before loosening fuel line connection. Remove driver's side rear seat and floor panel cover for access to electrical connector for electric fuel pump.

2) Disconnect electrical connector for electric fuel pump. Start engine and allow engine to idle until engine stalls. Turn ignition off. Reconnect electrical connector for electric fuel pump. Reinstall floor panel cover and driver's side rear seat.

3) Disconnect negative battery cable. Place an approved gasoline container under fuel line. Cover fuel line connection with shop towel. Slowly loosen fuel line connection to release fuel pressure. Once fuel pressure is released, fuel system components may be serviced. Remove hood, battery and battery tray. Drain cooling system and engine oil.

4) Disconnect control cables at throttle body. Remove air cleaner assembly and air cleaner case. Remove bolts and disconnect relay box from body. Relay box is located near driver's side strut tower. See Fig. 3.

5) Remove upper cover from relay box. Disconnect electrical connector from relay box. See Fig. 4. Remove nuts and disconnect engine wiring harness from relay box.

6) Remove charcoal canister. Remove accessory drive belt and generator. Disconnect upper and lower radiator hoses. Remove thermostat housing from front of engine.

7) Disconnect necessary electrical connectors, coolant hoses, vacuum hoses and fuel lines for engine removal. Remove A/C compressor with hoses attached and secure aside.

8) Remove scuff plate from passenger's side door opening and passenger's side kick panel. Remove center console trim panel from passenger's side of center console. See Fig. 4.

9) Disconnect 2 electrical connectors from Engine Control Module (ECM) and 2 electrical connectors on bracket. Disconnect electrical connector for relay box located behind passenger's side kick panel.

10) Disconnect engine wiring harness clamp located on engine wiring harness, near firewall. Pull engine wiring harness out through firewall.

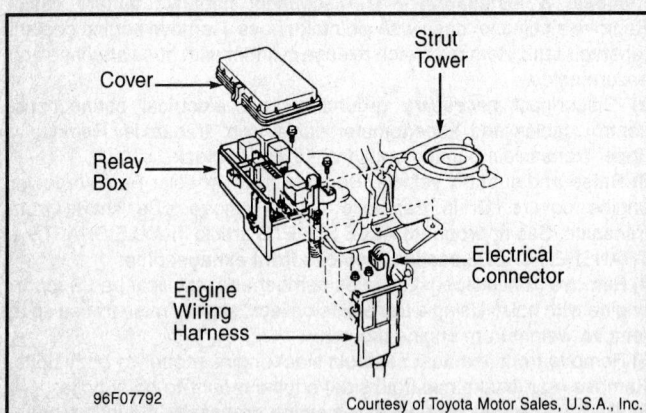

Fig. 3: Identifying Relay Box, Electrical Connector & Engine Wiring Harness

11) Raise and support vehicle. Remove lower engine covers. Remove clutch release cylinder with hose attached and secure aside. Remove starter. Disconnect control cables and electrical connectors at transaxle. Remove front exhaust pipe that fits between front catalytic converter on exhaust manifold and rear exhaust pipe.

12) Place reference marks on drive shaft flanges for reassembly reference. Remove drive shaft flange bolts/nuts at rear axle. Remove drive shaft center support bearing bolts. Pull drive shaft from transaxle. Remove drive shaft.

13) On all models, remove front wheels. Drain transaxle fluid. On models with Anti-Lock Brake System (ABS), remove bolt and pull ABS speed sensor from front of axle carrier.

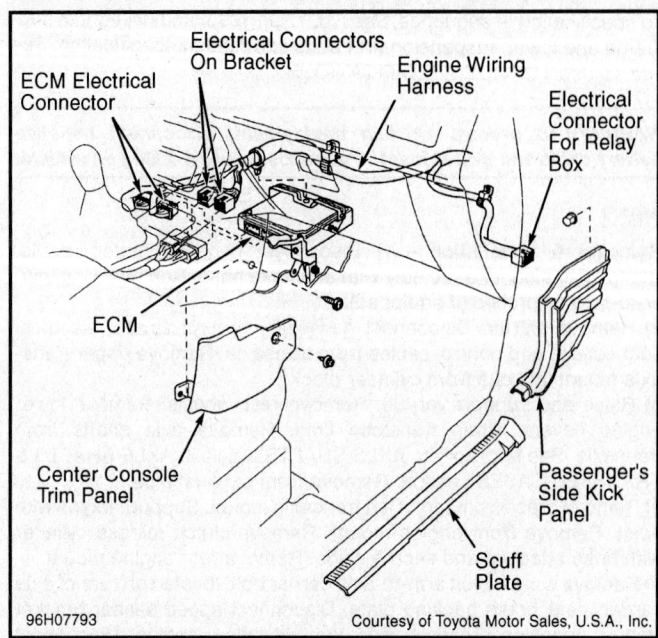

Fig. 4: Identifying ECM & Electrical Connectors

14) On all models, remove cotter pin and retainer from end of axle shaft. Loosen axle shaft nut while applying brakes. Remove axle shaft nut. Remove nut and separate tie rod from steering knuckle. Disconnect stabilizer bar link from lower control arm. Remove ball joint-to-lower control arm bolts/nuts.

15) Remove axle shafts from transaxle. See appropriate AXLE SHAFTS article in AXLE SHAFTS & TRANSFER CASES section. Remove stabilizer bar-to-frame mount bolts. Remove stabilizer bar with mounting brackets and insulators. Remove 2 steering gear assembly-to-front suspension crossmember bolts/nuts located at each end of steering gear assembly.

16) Support engine with hoist. Remove engine mount crossmember-to-front suspension crossmember nuts. Front suspension crossmember fits between both lower control arms.

17) Support front suspension crossmember with floor jack. Remove front suspension crossmember bolts and front suspension crossmember. Remove front (exhaust manifold side) engine mount-to-engine mount crossmember bolts. Remove engine mount crossmember-to-body bolts. Remove engine mount crossmember.

18) Remove power steering pump with hoses attached and secure aside. Remove left (transaxle side) engine mounting bracket-to-engine mount bolts/nuts. Remove right (timing belt side) engine mounting bracket-to-engine mount bolts/nuts. Lower engine from engine compartment.

19) Remove transaxle case protector. Disconnect remaining wire harnesses from transaxle. Label vacuum hoses and remove transfer vacuum actuator assembly. Remove stiffener plates between engine and transaxle. Remove 9 transaxle-to-engine bolts. Separate transaxle from engine.

Installation – 1) Install transaxle to engine. Install engine in engine compartment. Loosely install right (timing belt side) engine mounting bracket-to-engine mount bolts/nuts.

2) Install and tighten left (transaxle side) engine mounting bracket-to-engine mount bolts/nuts to specification. See TORQUE SPECIFICATIONS. Tighten right (timing belt side) engine mounting bracket-to-engine mount bolts/nuts to specification.

3) Install power steering pump. Install and tighten bolts to specification. See TORQUE SPECIFICATIONS. Install engine mount crossmember with front (exhaust manifold side) engine mount-to-engine mount crossmember bolts and engine mount crossmember-to-body bolts loosely installed. DO NOT tighten bolts at this time.

4) Install front suspension crossmember on body with bolts loosely installed. Loosely install engine mount crossmember-to-front suspension crossmember nuts and steering gear assembly-to-front suspension crossmember bolts/nuts. DO NOT tighten bolts/nuts at this time.
5) Install and tighten front suspension crossmember bolts to specification. See TORQUE SPECIFICATIONS. Tighten steering gear assembly-to-front suspension crossmember bolts/nuts and then engine mount crossmember-to-front suspension crossmember nuts to specification. See TORQUE SPECIFICATIONS.
6) Tighten front (exhaust manifold side) engine mount-to-engine mount crossmember bolts and then engine mount crossmember-to-body bolts to specification. See TORQUE SPECIFICATIONS.
7) Install axle shafts. See appropriate AXLE SHAFTS article in AXLE SHAFTS & TRANSFER CASES section. To install remaining components, reverse removal procedure. On 4WD models, ensure reference marks on drive shaft flanges are aligned. Ensure mounting bracket on drive shaft center support bearing is straight and perpendicular to drive shaft before tightening bolts to specification.
8) On all models, use NEW gasket and NEW nuts when installing front exhaust pipe on catalytic converter. Ensure all bolts/nuts are loosely installed before tightening to specification. Adjust fluid levels and control cables. Use SAE 75-90 GL-5 gear oil.

WARNING: To prevent air bag deployment, disconnect negative battery cable and wait at least 90 seconds before working on vehicle.

SUPRA

Removal & Installation – **1)** Disconnect negative battery cable. Remove shift knob from shift lever. Using screwdriver, pry upper console panel upward for access to shift lever bolts.
Upper console panel is located on top of console, near shift lever.
2) Remove bolts and shift lever boots. Remove shift lever bolts. On non-turbo models, remove upper shroud bolts from radiator. On all models, raise and support vehicle. Drain transmission fluid. Remove lower engine cover. Remove front exhaust pipe and support bracket.
3) Remove center exhaust pipe that fits between front exhaust pipe and tailpipe with muffler assembly. Remove heat insulator from body for access to drive shaft.
4) Remove crossmember brace bolted to body, below drive shaft. Place reference mark on drive shaft flanges for reassembly reference. Remove drive shaft flange-to-differential flange bolts. DO NOT remove drive shaft-to-drive shaft flange bolts. Support drive shaft and remove drive shaft center bearing bolts. Remove adjusting washers that fit between drive shaft center bearing and body (if equipped).
5) On turbo models, remove drive shaft flange-to-transmission flange nuts. On all models, slide drive shaft assembly forward to disengage drive shaft from centering pin on differential flange. Remove drive shaft.
6) Remove shift lever-to-shift linkage bolt at rear of transmission. Remove shift lever. Remove clutch release cylinder with hose attached and secure aside. Disconnect necessary electrical connectors at transmission. Remove starter.

NOTE: On turbo models, clutch cover bolts must be removed before transmission can be removed.

---

7) On turbo models, remove cover on driver's side of transmission for access to clutch cover bolts. Place reference mark on clutch cover and flywheel for reassembly reference. Remove 6 clutch cover bolts from flywheel. *See Fig. 5.*
8) On all models, support engine with hoist. Using transmission jack, slightly raise transmission to remove weight from mount. Remove bolts and nuts, and crossmember located at rear of transmission. Slightly lower engine. Remove transmission mounting bolts and transmission. To install, reverse removal procedure. Tighten nuts and bolts to specification. See TORQUE SPECIFICATIONS.

NOTE: On turbo models, clutch cover and clutch disc will be removed with transmission.

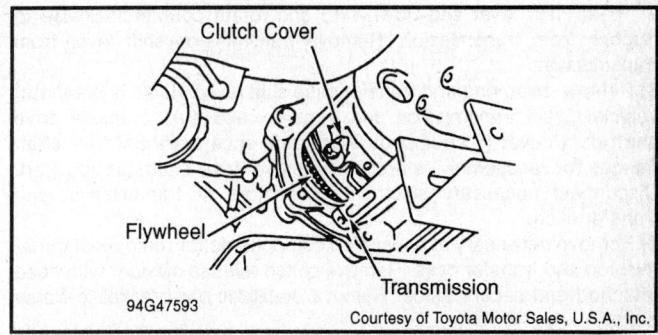

Fig. 5: Removing Clutch Cover Bolts (Supra Turbo)

WARNING: To prevent air bag deployment, disconnect negative battery cable and wait at least 90 seconds before working on vehicle.

TACOMA & T100 2WD

NOTE: Engine and transmission must be removed as an assembly because the rear crossmember is welded to chassis. For reassembly reference, label all electrical connectors, vacuum hoses and fuel lines before removal. Also place mating marks on engine hood and other major assemblies before removal.

Removal & Installation – **1)** Release fuel pressure. With ignition off, disconnect negative battery cable. Place suitable container under fuel line. Cover fuel line connection using shop towel. Slowly loosen fuel line connection to release fuel pressure.
2) Once fuel pressure is released, fuel system components can be removed. Remove hood, battery and lower engine covers. Drain cooling system and engine oil. Remove air cleaner case and hose.
3) Remove radiator, accessory drive belts and fan. Disconnect necessary electrical connections, vacuum hoses, coolant hoses and fuel lines. Disconnect control cables at throttle body. Disconnect cruise control cable (if equipped). Disconnect necessary ground straps. Remove power steering pump and A/C compressor with hoses attached and secure aside (if equipped).
4) Place reference mark on drive shaft flanges for reassembly reference. Remove bolts and all drive shaft(s). Remove shift lever(s) from inside vehicle. Remove clutch release cylinder with hoses attached and secure aside. Disconnect necessary shift linkages, hoses and electrical connections at transmission and transfer case (if equipped). Disconnect speedometer cable.

NOTE: DO NOT lose felt dust protector and washers from speedometer cable.

---

5) Disconnect oxygen sensor connector. Remove front exhaust pipe located between exhaust manifold and catalytic converter. Support transmission. Remove rear engine mount and bracket.
6) Support engine with hoist. Remove engine mount-to-frame bolts. Lift engine and transmission assembly from vehicle. To install, reverse removal procedure. Ensure reference marks on drive shaft flanges are aligned.
7) Use NEW nuts when installing front exhaust pipe on exhaust manifold. Tighten nuts and bolts to specification. See TORQUE SPECIFICATIONS. Adjust all fluid levels, control cables and shift linkages.

WARNING: To prevent air bag deployment, disconnect negative battery cable and wait at least 90 seconds before working on vehicle.

TACOMA & T100 4WD

Removal & Installation – **1)** Disconnect negative battery cable. Remove transmission shift lever boot retainer. Pull transmission shift lever boot upward. Place shop towel on shift lever cap, located at top of transmission on transmission shift lever.

2) Press shift lever cap downward and rotate counterclockwise to remove from transmission. Remove transmission shift lever from transmission.

3) Remove snap ring and transfer case shift lever. Raise and support vehicle. Drain transmission and transfer case fluid. Remove drive shaft dust cover (if equipped). Place reference mark on drive shaft flanges for reassembly reference. Remove drive shafts as required. Disconnect necessary electrical connectors at transmission and transfer case.

4) Remove necessary exhaust pipe components for removal of transmission and transfer case. Remove clutch release cylinder with hose attached and secure aside. Remove stabilizer bar bracket-to-frame bolts.

5) Support engine with hoist. Support transmission with transmission jack. Remove necessary crossmember for removal of transmission and transfer case. Remove starter. Remove stiffener plates, located between rear of cylinder block and transmission.

6) Remove transmission mounting bolts. Remove transmission. To install, reverse removal procedure. Tighten nuts and bolts to specification. See TORQUE SPECIFICATIONS.

TORQUE SPECIFICATIONS

TORQUE SPECIFICATIONS

Application	Ft. Lbs. (N.m)
Camry	
Clutch Cover Bolt	14 (19)
Crossmember-To-Body	
Large Bolt	134 (182)
Small Bolt	24 (33)
Small Nut	27 (37)
Front (Exhaust Manifold Side) Engine	
Mount-To-Crossmember Bolt/Nut	59 (80)
Pivot Stud-To-Transaxle	29 (39)
Rear (Intake Manifold Side) Engine	
Mount-To-Crossmember Nut	59 (80)
Stabilizer Bar Mount-To-Crossmember Bolt	14 (19)
Starter Bolt	29 (39)
Steering Gear-To-Crossmember Bolt/Nut	134 (182)
Stiffener Plate Bolt	27 (37)
Transaxle Mount-To-Crossmember Nut	59 (80)
Transaxle Mount-To-Transaxle Bolt	38 (52)
Transaxle Mounting Bolt	
10-mm Bolt	34 (46)
12-mm Bolt	47 (64)
Wheel Lug Nut	76 (103)
Celica	
Clutch Cover Bolt	14 (19)
Crossmember Bolt	
1.8L (7A-FE)	26 (35)
2.2L (5S-FE)	38 (52)
Exhaust Pipe Support Bracket Bolt/Nut	14 (19)
Front (Exhaust Manifold Side) Engine	
Mount Bracket-To-Cylinder Block Bolt	57 (77)
Front (Exhaust Manifold Side) Engine	
Mount-To-Crossmember Bolt/Nut	
1.8L (7A-FE)	59 (80)
2.2L (5S-FE)	47 (64)
Front (Exhaust Manifold Side) Engine	
Mount Through-Bolt	64 (87)
Pivot Stud-To-Transaxle	
1.8L (7A-FE)	27 (37)
2.2L (5S-FE)	29 (39)
Rear (Intake Manifold Side) Engine	
Mount Bracket-To-Cylinder Block Bolt	57 (77)
Rear (Intake Manifold Side) Engine	
Mount Through-Bolt	64 (87)
Rear (Intake Manifold Side) Engine	
Mount-To-Crossmember Bolt/Nut	
1.8L (7A-FE)	59 (80)
2.2L (5S-FE)	47 (64)
Starter Bolt	29 (39)
Stiffener Plate Bolt	
2.2L (5S-FE)	
Cylinder Block Side	32 (43)
Transaxle Side	15 (20)
Transaxle Mounting Bolt	
10-mm Bolt	34 (46)
12-mm Bolt	47 (64)

TORQUE SPECIFICATIONS (Cont.)

Application	Ft. Lbs. (N.m)
Transaxle-To-Mount Bolt	47 (64)
Wheel Lug Nut	76 (103)
Corolla	
Clutch Cover Bolt	14 (19)
Crossmember Bolt	
10-mm Bolt	45 (61)
14-mm Bolt	152 (206)
Exhaust Pipe Support Bracket Bolt/Nut	14 (19)
Front (Exhaust Manifold Side) Engine	
Mount-To-Crossmember Bolt	47 (64)
No. 1 Oil Pan-To-Transaxle Bolt (1.8L 7A-FE)	17 (23)
Pivot Stud-To-Transaxle	27 (37)
Rear (Intake Manifold Side) Engine	
Mount-To-Crossmember Nut	35 (47)
Starter Bolt	29 (39)
Stiffener Plate Bolt (1.6L 4A-FE) [1]	17 (23)
Sub-Frame & Lower Suspension Arm	[2]
Transaxle Mounting Bolt	
10-mm Bolt	34 (46)
12-mm Bolt	47 (64)
Transaxle-To-Mount Bolt	41 (56)
Wheel Lug Nut	76 (103)
MR2	
Brace-To-Left Transaxle Mount Bolt	
Body Side Bolt	54 (73)
Transaxle Side Bolt	18 (24)
Clutch Cover Bolt	14 (19)
Front Engine Mount Bolt	
Body Side Bolt	54 (73)
Mount Through-Bolt	71 (96)
Transaxle Side Bolt	57 (77)
Left Transaxle Mount Bolt	47 (64)
Lower Control Arm-To-Suspension	
Crossmember Bolt	98 (133)
Pivot Stud-To-Transaxle	35 (47)
Rear Engine Mount Bolt	
Crossmember Side Bolt	47 (64)
Mount Through-Bolt	64 (87)
Transaxle Side Bolt	57 (77)
Starter Bolt	29 (39)
Stiffener Plate Bolt	27 (37)
Strut Tower-To-Firewall Brace Bolt/Nut	
Bolt	54 (73)
Nut	47 (64)
Suspension Arm-To-Axle Carrier Bolt	76 (103)
Suspension Crossmember Bolt	83 (113)
Transaxle Mounting Bolt	
10-mm Bolt	34 (46)
12-mm Bolt	47 (64)
Wheel Lug Nut	76 (103)
Paseo & Tercel	
Clutch Cover Bolt	14 (19)
Front (Exhaust Manifold Side) Engine	
Mount-To-Body Bolt	35 (47)
Pivot Stud-To-Transaxle	27 (37)
Rear (Intake Manifold Side) Engine	
Mount-To-Body Bolt	58 (79)
Starter Bolt	29 (39)
Transaxle Mounting Bolt	
10-mm Bolt	34 (46)
12-mm Bolt	47 (64)
Wheel Lug Nut	76 (103)
Pickup & 4Runner	
Clutch Cover Bolt	14 (19)
Crossmember-To-Frame Bolt	70 (95)
Drive Shaft Center Bearing Bolt	27 (37)
Drive Shaft Flange Bolt	54 (73)
Front Differential Mounting Bolt (4WD V6 Models)	
Differential Carrier Cover-To-Frame Bolt	108 (146)
All Others	123 (167)
Pivot Stud-To-Transmission	
4-Cylinder	29 (39)
V6	35 (47)
Stabilizer Bar Bracket-To-Frame Bolt	21 (29)
Starter Bolt	29 (39)
Stiffener Plate Bolt	27 (37)
Transmission Mounting Bolt	53 (72)

[1] – Tighten bolts to specification in sequence. See Fig. 1.
[2] – Tighten bolts and nuts to specification. See Fig. 2.

TORQUE SPECIFICATIONS

Application	Ft. Lbs. (N.m)
RAV4	
A/C Compressor Bolt/Nut	
Bolt	27 (37)
Nut	20 (27)
Stud Bolt	34 (46)
Ball Joint-To-Lower Control Arm Bolt/Nut	94 (127)
Brake Line-To-ABS Actuator Nut	11 (15)
Clutch Cover Bolt	14 (19)
Crossmember-To-Body (2WD)	152 (206)
Drive Shaft Center Support Bearing Bolt (4WD)	27 (37)
Drive Shaft Flange Bolt/Nut (4WD)	54 (73)
Engine Left Mount	
Insulator-To-Bracket (2WD)	9 (12)
Engine Mounts & Brackets	
Front (Exhaust Manifold Side) Engine Mount-To-Engine Mount Crossmember Bolt	59 (80)
Left (Transaxle Side) Engine Mounting Bracket-To-Engine Mount Bolt/Nut	47 (64)
Right (Timing Belt Side) Engine Mounting Bracket-To-Cylinder Block Bolt	38 (52)
Right (Timing Belt Side) Engine Mount-To-Body Bolt	47 (64)
Right (Timing Belt Side) Engine Mounting Bracket-To-Engine Mount Bolt/Nut	
Bolt	27 (37)
Nut	38 (52)
Engine Mount Crossmember-To-Body Bolt	26 (35)
Engine Mount Crossmember-To-Front Suspension Crossmember Nut	82 (111)
Exhaust Manifold Nut	36 (49)
Front (Exhaust Manifold Side) Engine Mount-To-Crossmember (2WD)	59 (80)
Flywheel/Drive Plate Bolt	65 (88)
Front Catalytic Converter Brace Bolt/Nut	31 (42)
Front Catalytic Converter-To-Exhaust Manifold Bolt/Nut	21 (29)
Front Exhaust Pipe-To-Front Catalytic Converter Nut	46 (62)
Front Exhaust Pipe-To-Rear Exhaust Pipe Bolt/Nut	35 (47)
Front Suspension Crossmember Bolt	
Bolt At Body	152 (206)
Bolt At Lower Control Arm	101 (137)
Fuel Line-To-Fuel Filter Union Bolt	21 (29)
Fuel Pipe-To-Delivery Pipe Union Bolt	25 (34)
Generator Adjusting Bracket Bolt	20 (27)
Generator Mounting Bracket Bolt	31 (42)
Pivot Stud-To-Transaxle	35 (47)
Power Steering Pump Bolt	32 (43)
Power Steering Pump Mounting Bracket-To-Cylinder Block Bolt	32 (43)
P/S Gear-To-Crossmember (2WD)	83 (113)
Rear (Intake Manifold Side) Engine Mount-To-Crossmember (2WD)	82 (112)
Stabilizer Bar Link-To-Lower Control Arm Nut	
3-Door Vehicles	47 (64)
5-Door Vehicles	83 (113)
Stabilizer Bar-To-Frame Mount Bolt	21 (29)
Starter Bolt	29 (39)
Steering Gear Assembly-To-Front Suspension Crossmember Bolt/Nut	83 (113)
Stiffener Plate Bolt	27 (37)
Tie Rod Nut	36 (49)
Transaxle Case Protector	18 (25)
Transaxle Mounting Bolt	
10-mm Bolt	34 (46)
12-mm Bolt	47 (64)
Vacuum Actuator Assembly (4WD)	27 (37)
Wheel Lug Nut	76 (103)

Application	INCH Lbs. (N.m)
ABS Speed Sensor Bolt	71 (8.0)
Clutch Release Cylinder Bolt	106 (12.0)
Fuel Delivery Pipe-To-Cylinder Head Bolt	115 (13.0)
Thermostat Housing Nut	78 (8.8)

TORQUE SPECIFICATIONS (Cont.)

Application	Ft. Lbs. (N.m)
Supra	
Clutch Cover Bolt	14 (19)
Clutch Release Fork Support Bolt (Turbo Models)	18 (24)
Crossmember Bolt/Nut	
Bolt	19 (26)
Nut	[3]
Crossmember Brace Bolt	[3]
Drive Shaft Center Bearing Bolt	36 (49)
Drive Shaft Flange-To-Differential Flange Bolt	58 (79)
Drive Shaft Flange-To-Transmission Flange Nut	41 (56)
Shift Lever-To-Shift Linkage Bolt	14 (19)
Starter Bolt	29 (39)
Transmission Mounting Bolt	53 (72)
Tacoma & T100 2WD	
Air Intake Chamber Bolt/Nut	13 (18)
Alternator Bracket-To-Cylinder Head Bolt	27 (37)
Cold Start Injector Fuel Pipe Union Bolt	11 (15)
Coolant By-Pass Outlet Bolt	13 (18)
Coolant Inlet Nut	15 (20)
Coolant Outlet Nut	11 (15)
Crossover Pipe Nut	29 (39)
Drive Axle-To-Side Gear Flange Nut	61 (83)
Drive Shaft Flange Bolt	55 (75)
Engine Mount-To-Frame Bolt	27 (37)
Exhaust Manifold Nut	29 (39)
Fan Bracket Bolt/Nut	30 (41)
Front Differential Crossmember Bolt	93 (126)
Front Differential Mount Bolts	
Differential Cover Mount Bolt	108 (146)
Left & Right Mount Bolt	123 (167)
Front Exhaust Pipe-To-Catalytic Converter Bolt	29 (39)
Front Exhaust Pipe-To-Exhaust Manifold Nut	46 (62)
Fuel Pipe Bolt	
No. 2 & No. 3 Fuel Pipes	25 (34)
Idler Pulley Bolt	
No. 1 Pulley	25 (34)
No. 2 Pulley	13 (18)
Stabilizer Bar-To-Frame Mount Bolt	21 (29)
Stabilizer Bar-To-Lower Control Arm Bolt	19 (26)
Transmission Crossmember-To-Frame Bolt	70 (95)
Tacoma & T100 4WD	
Clutch Cover Bolt	14 (19)
Crossmember-To-Frame Bolt	70 (95)
Drive Shaft Center Bearing Bolt	27 (37)
Drive Shaft Flange Bolt	54 (73)
Pivot Stud-To-Transmission	
4-Cylinder	29 (39)
V6	35 (47)
Stabilizer Bar Bracket-To-Frame Bolt	21 (29)
Starter Bolt	29 (39)
Stiffener Plate Bolt	27 (37)
Transmission Mounting Bolt	53 (72)

[3] – Tighten to 115 INCH lbs. (13.0 N.m).

MANUAL TRANSMISSION REMOVAL
Volkswagen

Cabrio, Golf, Golf III, GTI VR6, Jetta, Jetta III, Passat

APPLICATION

MANUAL TRANSAXLE APPLICATIONS

Application	Model
1995	
Cabrio & Golf III	020
GTI VR6 & Passat	02A
Jetta III	
4-Cylinder	020
V6	02A
1996	
Cabrio	020
Golf & Jetta	
4-Cylinder	
Gas Engine	020
Turbo Diesel	02A
V6	02A
Passat	02A

REMOVAL & INSTALLATION

NOTE: Transaxle may be lowered out of vehicle without removing engine.

CAUTION: On models with theft protection system, obtain stereo security code from vehicle owner before disconnecting battery cable.

CABRIO, GOLF, GTI & JETTA (02A TRANSAXLE)

Removal & Installation – 1) Disconnect battery cables and remove battery. Remove power steering fluid reservoir. Remove battery bracket. Disconnect all electrical connections to transaxle and position harness aside.

2) Remove bolt from right-side engine mount. Remove wire harness bracket located next to engine mount if necessary. Remove balance weight located near gear selector cable.

3) Disconnect gear selector cable from gear selector lever. Disconnect gate selector cable at actuating arm/relay lever. Remove cable bracket-to-transmission bolts. Remove clutch slave cylinder (DO NOT open hydraulic system) and position aside.

4) Remove bolt from left-side transaxle mount. Remove transaxle support (if equipped). Remove connector attachment from front transaxle bracket. Support engine and transaxle with Support Bridge (10-222A) and Adapter Spindles (10-222A3). Slightly lift engine with support.

5) Remove engine undercover. Remove starter. Disconnect both axle shafts from flanges. Turn steering wheel to full-left lock. Tie axle shafts out of way. Remove lower support between engine and transaxle (if equipped).

6) Remove small clutch cover plate. Push engine/transaxle assembly as far right as possible. Remove transaxle mount. Push engine/transaxle assembly rearward, towards bulkhead. Remove lower mounting bolt.

7) Lower engine/transaxle assembly to previous position. Remove clutch cover plate. Remove bolt from transaxle mount above right-side axle flange. Place transmission jack under transaxle.

8) Remove lower engine-to-transaxle bolt. Separate transaxle from engine and remove from vehicle. To install, reverse removal procedure. Ensure engine/transaxle mounts are free of stress when tightening. Tighten bolts to specification. See TORQUE SPECIFICATIONS.

CABRIO, GOLF, GTI & JETTA (020 TRANSAXLE)

Removal & Installation – 1) Disconnect negative battery cable. Disconnect all electrical connectors from transaxle and position harness aside. Remove upper transaxle-to-engine bolts.

2) Remove right-side engine support bracket bolt. Remove connector support plate (if equipped). On Cabrio, remove front engine-to-body support. On all models, disconnect both selector rods from selector lever.

3) Remove long selector rod from relay lever. Remove 2 upper bolts from transaxle bracket at left side of transaxle. On Cabrio, remove transaxle-to-body support.

4) On all models, remove front bracket-to-engine mount bolt. Attach Engine Support (10-222A) and Adaptor Spindles (10-222 A/1). Slightly lift engine/transaxle assembly. Remove engine undercover.

5) Remove starter. Remove front bracket. Remove engine mount attaching bolts and large clutch shield. Remove small clutch shield from behind right-side axle shaft flange.

6) Remove left-side transaxle bracket. Using left-side adapter spindle, lower left side of transaxle. Remove left-side transaxle support if equipped. Disconnect both axle shafts from transaxle. If necessary, remove heat shield from inner Constant Velocity (CV) joint.

7) Turn steering wheel to full-left lock. Suspend both axle shafts as high as possible. Push engine/transaxle assembly toward front of vehicle. Place transmission jack under transaxle.

8) Remove lower transaxle-to-engine bolt. Separate transaxle from engine. Carefully lower and remove transaxle from vehicle. To install, reverse removal procedure. Ensure engine/transaxle mounts are free of stress when tightening. Tighten bolts to specification. See TORQUE SPECIFICATIONS.

PASSAT (4-CYLINDER ENGINE)

Removal – 1) Disconnect battery cables and remove battery. Remove radiator cover. Disconnect all electrical connections to transaxle and position harness aside.

2) Remove balance weight and disconnect gear selector cable from gear selector lever. Remove bolt with threaded sleeve from shift lever. Remove gear selector cable along with washer and square self-locking nut.

3) Disconnect gate selector cable from actuating arm/relay lever. Remove cable bracket support. Remove clutch slave cylinder (DO NOT open hydraulic system) and position aside.

4) Remove air intake duct between air cleaner and intake air elbow. Remove 3 bolts from right-side engine mount. Remove ground strap from upper transaxle-to-engine bolt. Remove upper rear transaxle-to-engine bolts. Loosen, but DO NOT remove front transaxle-to-engine bolts.

5) Remove bolt from left-side transaxle mount, and nut from front mount bracket. Support engine/transaxle assembly with Support Bridge (10-222A) and Adapter Spindles (10-222 A/1). Slightly raise engine. Remove engine undercover.

6) Remove starter. Remove power steering bracket from transaxle. Remove front mounting bracket and engine mount. Mark balance weight at subframe for installation reference.

7) Disconnect exhaust system in front of Three-Way Catalytic Converter (TWC). Remove right-side inner Constant Velocity (CV) joint protective cover from engine. Remove left-side air deflector from lower control arm.

8) Disconnect both axle shafts from flanges. Turn steering wheel to full-left lock. Push engine/transaxle assembly as far forward as possible. Tie axle shafts out of way.

9) Remove transaxle-to-mount bracket. Remove adapter spindles and lift engine/transaxle assembly until exhaust system contacts heat shield. Push engine/transaxle assembly forward and remove lower transaxle bracket mounting bolt.

10) Remove small clutch cover from behind right-side axle flange. Remove large clutch cover plate. Lower engine to previous position, then push as far as possible toward right side and lower engine using left-side adapter spindle.

11) Remove lower transaxle-to-engine bolt. Push engine/transaxle assembly forward from underneath vehicle using Set-Up Press (3300A). Place transmission jack under transaxle. Remove forward bolt from upper engine/transaxle support. Separate transaxle from engine. Lower transaxle and remove from vehicle.

Installation – 1) To install, reverse removal procedure. Plug transaxle openings to prevent contamination or fluid loss. Push clutch release lever rearward and temporarily install mounting pin or an 8 x 35 mm bolt through pivot arm. Remove pin or bolt after installation is complete.

2) Ensure engine/transaxle mounts are free of stress when tightening. Tighten bolts and nuts to specification. See TORQUE SPECIFICATIONS.

PASSAT (V6 ENGINE)

Removal – 1) Disconnect battery cables and remove battery. Remove upper section of air cleaner housing. Remove radiator cover. Remove right-side bracket-to-engine mount bolt and bracket. Disconnect all electrical connections to transaxle and position harness aside.

2) Remove balance weight and disconnect gear selector cable from gear selector lever. Disconnect gate selector cable from actuating arm/relay lever. Unclip clutch slave cylinder hose at cable support bracket. Remove cable support bracket.

3) Remove clutch slave cylinder (DO NOT open hydraulic system) and position aside. Remove upper transaxle-to-engine bolts. Remove cooling system recovery tank and position aside.

4) Remove left-side transaxle mount bolt. Remove bracket and mount. Install Engine Support (10-222A) and Adaptor Spindles (10-222 A/1 and 10-222 A/3). Slightly lift engine/transaxle assembly.

5) Remove lower belt guard and engine undercover. Remove starter. Remove balance weight from subframe. Disconnect exhaust system in front of Three-Way Catalytic Converter (TWC).

6) Disconnect both axle shafts from flanges. Turn steering wheel to full-left lock. Tie both axle shafts aside, as high as possible. Push engine/transaxle assembly as far right as possible.

7) Remove accessible transaxle mount-to-bracket bolts. Using adapter spindles, lift engine/transaxle assembly until exhaust system contacts heat shield. Remove remaining bolts and transaxle bracket (push engine/transaxle assembly rearward, toward bulkhead as needed).

8) Lower engine/transaxle assembly to previous position. Using left-side adapter spindle, tilt engine. Remove clutch cover plate. Remove transaxle-to-engine bolts above right-side axle flange.

9) Place transmission jack under transaxle. Remove lower transaxle-to-engine mounting bolt. Separate transaxle from engine. Using Engine Support (3300), push engine forward until it contacts subframe. Lower transaxle and remove from vehicle.

Installation – 1) To install, reverse removal procedure. Plug transaxle openings to prevent contamination or fluid loss. Push clutch release lever rearward and temporarily install mounting pin or an 8 x 35 mm bolt through pivot arm. Remove pin or bolt after installation is complete.

2) Ensure engine/transaxle mounts are free of stress when tightening. Tighten bolts and nuts to specification. See TORQUE SPECIFICATIONS.

TORQUE SPECIFICATIONS
TORQUE SPECIFICATIONS

Application	Ft. Lbs. (N.m)
Cabriolet, Golf, GTI, & Jetta	
02A Transaxle	
Axle Shaft-To-Flange Bolts	33 (45)
Left-Side Bracket-To-Engine Bolt	18 (25)
Lower Starter Bolt	44 (60)
Lower Transaxle Support Bolts	33 (45)
Right-Side Bracket-To-Subframe Bolt	44 (60)
Selector Cable Support Bracket Bolts	18 (25)
Selector Cable-To-Selector Lever Bolt	18 (25)
Transaxle Mounting Bolts	
M10 X 30 Bolt	37 (50)
M10 X 45 Bolt	37 (50)
M10 X 62 Bolt	33 (45)
Transaxle-To-Engine Bolts	
M7 Bolt	7 (10)
M10 Bolt	44 (60)
M12 Bolt	59 (80)
020 Transaxle	
Axle Shaft-To-Flange Bolts	33 (45)
Engine Mount-To-Subframe Bolt	37 (50)
Engine Support-To-Body [1]	
Bolts	37 (50)
Nuts	37 (50)
Left-Side Bracket-To-Transaxle Bolt	26 (35)
Right-Side Bracket-To-Subframe Bolt	44 (60)
Slave Cylinder-To-Engine Bolt	22 (30)
Transaxle Mounting Bolts	
M10 Nut	7 (10)
M10 X 30 Bolt	44 (60)
M10 X 45 Bolt	44 (60)
M10 X 60 Bolt	33 (45)
Transaxle Support-To-Body Bolts [1]	37 (50)
Transaxle-To-Engine Bolts	
M6 X 8 Bolt	59 (80)
M7 X 12 Bolt	7 (10)
M10 X 140 Bolt	44 (60)
M12 X 55 Bolt	59 (80)
M12 X 64 Bolt	59 (80)
Passat	
Axle Shaft-To-Flange Bolts	33 (45)
Balance Weight-To-Assembly Carrier	22 (30)
Balance Weight-To-Selector Lever Bolt	18 (25)
Left-Side Bracket-To-Engine	18 (25)
Lower Starter Bolt	44 (60)
Lower Transaxle Support Bolts	33 (45)
Right-Side Bracket-To-Subframe	44 (60)
Selector Cable Support Bracket Bolts	18 (25)
Selector Cable-To-Selector Lever Bolt	18 (25)
Transaxle Mounting Bolts	
M10 X 30 Bolt	37 (50)
M10 X 45 Bolt	37 (50)
Transaxle-To-Engine Bolts	
M7 Bolt	7 (10)
M10 Bolt	44 (60)
M12 Bolt	59 (80)

[1] – Cabrio only.

850

APPLICATION

TRANSMISSION APPLICATION

Vehicle Application	Transmission Model
850	M56L

REMOVAL & INSTALLATION

Removal – 1) Release steering wheel adjustment lever. Push steering wheel as far forward and upward as possible. Lock steering wheel with lever. Put shift lever in Neutral.

2) Remove battery, air cleaner, air intake, battery shelf and air cleaner bracket retaining screws. Remove transmission selector cables from bracket and levers. Tap out pin and remove selector link plate. Disconnect back-up light switch connector.

3) Remove cable tie from engine cable harness. Remove ground wire from gearbox. Remove circlip and clutch slave cylinder from gearbox. Leave bellows on cylinder. Loosen nut on rear engine mount/splash guard. Remove 5 bolts securing starter motor and gearbox. Remove cover over high tension wiring. Lift coolant expansion tank off bracket and allow it to hang free.

4) Remove bolt securing torque arm to engine. Disconnect ground lead next to torque arm. Using 2 bolts from torque arm, install Lifting Lug (999 5459) to valve cover. Install Lifting Lug (999 5464) to manifold heat guard. Install and adjust Lifting Yoke (999 5428) to lifting lugs.

5) Install Supports (999 5033) on fenders. Install Lifting Beam (999 5006) on supports. Install lifting beam directly above lugs on lifting yoke. Install Lifting Hook (999 5460). Lift hook about .20" (5 mm) to relieve weight on engine mountings. Measure and record height of lifting hook above engine.

6) Remove front wheels. Remove ABS sensor from left outboard shaft. DO NOT disconnect ABS electrical connector. Disconnect left and right brake lines and ABS cable brackets. Unhook brackets and allow them to hang free. Remove front plastic nuts from left fender liner and any Torx screws. Remove left hub center nut. Remove hub center nut locking clip. Remove hub center nut.

7) Remove front splash guard bolts. Push guard forward so locating pins on back come loose. Disconnect front of splash guard and remove. Remove splash guard under engine. Remove ball joint-to-link arm nuts on both sides. Disconnect link arms from ball joints. Disconnect and remove link arms from anti-roll bar.

8) Remove bolts connecting cable pipe on subframe and unhook pipe from frame. Disconnect charcoal canister from subframe and hang from body. Disconnect exhaust gas tie behind 3-way catalytic converter. Remove bolts holding pipe brackets to steering gear in subframe. Remove 2 bolts holding steady-bar bracket to gearbox.

9) Remove bolts from front engine mounting subframe. Loosen bolts securing steering gear to engine mounting about one turn. Remove nuts holding steering gear to subframe. Disconnect subframe from vehicle by positioning Jack (998 5972-0) under left side of subframe. Tighten jack up gently against subframe. Remove bolts on both sides of subframe brackets. Loosen 2 right subframe-to-body bolts.

10) Lower subframe while ensuring steering gear bolts do not hang up. Ensure MacPherson strut disengages from right axle shaft bellows. Remove jack and allow subframe to hang free on right side. Hang steering gear on left side using Hook (999 5045) in hole in frame member flange. Ensure lower steering wheel shaft section does not slip out of steering column.

11) Remove engine mount-to-subframe bolts and nut on top of engine mount. Remove engine mount. Disconnect HO2S cable terminals from cover. Disconnect speedometer connector and cable. Remove rear engine mount cover and rear mounting from gearbox.

12) Remove left axle shaft by twisting and pulling out MacPherson strut. Tap axle shaft end with plastic mallet and pull shaft from hub. Using Lever (999 5462), remove axle shaft from gearbox. Use care not to damage axle shaft seal or bellows. Install Plug (999 5488) to seal hole. Clean metal glue off hub axle shaft splines.

13) Use lifting hook and lower engine and gearbox until about 5" (130 mm) of hook thread is clear. DO NOT lower engine too much, as exhaust pipe may press on steering gear. Ensure no wiring or hoses are pinched or stretched, and that dipstick clears fan.

14) Install Universal Tool (999 5972) and Gearbox Fixture (999 5463) to jack. Attach gearbox fixture to gearbox using bolts from steady-bar bracket. At same time, position Support Plate (5463-2) on fixture. Raise engine. Remove remaining bolts securing gearbox to engine. Pull gearbox straight out from engine without any breaks in clutch plate center.

Installation – 1) Ensure mating flanges on gearbox and engine are clean and engine locating sleeves are in place. Install gearbox to engine using jack and gearbox fixture. Ensure gearbox lines up straight with engine without any breaks in clutch plate center. Install 7 engine-to-gearbox bolts and tighten in rotation to 37 ft. lbs. (50 N.m). Remove gearbox fixture and jack from gearbox.

2) Raise Lifting Hook (999 5460) to level previously recorded in step **5)** under REMOVAL. Ensure no cables, wiring, or hoses are pinched or trapped. Install 3 rear engine mount-to-gearbox bolts. Tighten 2 rear bolts to 37 ft. lbs. (50 N.m). Remove front bolt. Engage cover with engine mount and tighten bolt to 37 ft. lbs. (50 N.m).

3) Install engine mounting locating pin in cover and install, but do not tighten, NEW nut. Install, but do not tighten, engine mounting gear bolt. Disconnect support hook. Install HO2S cable and clips in cover. Install speedometer connector and cable.

4) Start with left side and raise subframe. Install 4 NEW bolts with greased threads. Install bolts to subframe and support plate. Tighten frame bolts to 77 ft. lbs. (105 N.m), then tighten another 120 degrees. Move jack to right side, remove existing bolts, and repeat procedure.

5) Remove lifting hook, lifting beam, hooks, supports and lifting lug. Remove lifting lug on rear of engine. Tighten manifold heat guard bolts. Install rear engine mounting splash guard nuts and tighten to 37 ft. lbs. (50 N.m). Install 5 NEW steering gear nuts and tighten to 37 ft. lbs. (50 N.m).

6) Install NEW steady bar bracket-to-gearbox bolts and tighten to 13 ft. lbs. (18 N.m), plus an additional 90 degrees (earlier version), or tighten to 26 ft. lbs. (35 N.m), plus an additional 60 degrees (later version). Install bolts holding pipe brackets to steering gear and tighten to 18 ft. lbs. (25 N.m). Tighten exhaust clamp.

7) Use care not to damage drive shaft seal or bellows and install right axle shaft to gear box. Install bearing cap and tighten to 18 ft. lbs. (25 N.m). Ensure ABS sensor gear well area is free of dirt and install left axle shaft. Push in axle shaft so it engages with differential. Ensure axle shaft circlip snaps into place. Use care not to damage axle shaft seal or bellows.

8) Apply Metal Glue (1161370-0) to axle shaft splines. Use a socket wrench to hold suspension arm down and twist MacPherson strut clear and insert axle shaft in hub. Oil nut threads and flange and hand-tighten NEW axle shaft nut.

9) Ensure ball joint seating in suspension arm is clean and free of grease. Tighten inside and outside nuts to 13 ft. lbs. (18 N.m), plus an additional 120 degrees. Apply Rustproofing Material (1161432-8) to area between ball joint, suspension arm and nuts. Use NEW nuts and install link arm to anti-roll bar. Tighten nuts to 37 ft. lbs. (50 N.m).

10) Tighten left hub center nut to 89 ft. lbs. (120 N.m), plus an additional 60 degrees. Use a chisel and tap locking flange onto axle shaft slot. Install brake lines and ABS cable brackets on both sides.

NOTE: Ensure ABS sensor seat is perfectly clean.

11) Install ABS sensor on wheel spindle and tighten to 7 ft. lbs. (10 N.m). Install plastic nuts and Torx screws to inner shield on left side. Install cable pipe on subframe, charcoal canister, and subframe under engine.

12) Install cover under engine and push it toward front of vehicle. Push up at back so cover locating pins fall in place. Install bolts. Install wheels. Ensure brake disc pad contact surfaces are clean. Grease hub center locating pin in front of pad using Rustproofing Agent (1161038-3). Install bolts and tighten in pairs to 81 ft. lbs. (110 N.m).

13) Install 5 gearbox-to-engine and gearbox-to-starter bolts. Tighten gearbox-to-engine bolts to 37 ft. lbs. (50 N.m). Tighten gearbox-to-starter bolts to 30 ft. lbs. (40 N.m). Install clutch slave cylinder and clip. Without moving fork, remove temporary strap from throw-out bearing fork. Install ground wire and lead tie. Install back-up light switch connector. Install shift lever link plate and locking pin. Install selector cables in brackets.

NOTE: Outside bracket and selector cables have Yellow markings.

---

14) Lubricate selector levers with Grease (1161241-3). Install selector cables to levers. Install 2 washers and clips. Install high tension wire cover, expansion tank, air cleaner-to-bracket bolts, spark plug cover, battery shelf, air cleaner and battery.

TORQUE SPECIFICATIONS
TORQUE SPECIFICATIONS

Application	Ft. Lbs. (N.m)
ABS Sensor Bolt	7 (10)
Bearing Cap Bolts	18 (25)
Engine Mount-To-Gearbox Bolts	37 (50)
Engine-To-Gearbox Bolts	37 (50)
Gearbox-To-Engine Bolts	37 (50)
Gearbox-To-Starter Bolt	30 (40)
Hub Center Nut	[1] 89 (120)
Knee Guard Bolts	15 (20)
Link Arm-To-Anti-Roll Bar Nuts	37 (50)
Lug Nuts	81 (110)
Pipe Brackets-To-Steering Gear Bolts	18 (25)
Rear Splash Guard Nuts	37 (50)
Steady Bar Bracket-To-Gearbox Bolts	
Early Version	[2] 13 (18)
Later Version	[3] 26 (35)
Steering Gear Nuts	37 (50)
Subframe & Support Plate Bolts	[4] 77 (105)
Suspension Arm-To-Ball Joint Nuts	[5] 13 (18)

[1] – Tighten nut an additional 60 degrees.
[2] – Tighten bolts another 90 degrees (early version).
[3] – Tighten bolts another 60 degrees (late version).
[4] – Tighten bolts another 120 degrees.
[5] – Tighten nuts an additional 120 degrees.

AUTOMATIC TRANSMISSIONS

TRANSMISSION MODEL	Page
Acura MPYA, M5DA & M5HA	3-2
Acura MPYA, M5DA & M5HA Electronic Controls	3-32
Acura M1WA	3-76
Acura M1WA Electronic Controls	3-104
Acura SP7A & SX4A	3-135
Acura SP7A Electronic Controls	3-157
Acura SX4A Electronic Controls	3-183
Aisin Warner AW03-72LE 4-Speed	3-202
AW03-72LE Electronic Controls (Except OBD-II)	3-217
AW03-72LE Electronic Controls (With OBD-II)	3-222
Audi Type 01N & 097	3-235
Audi Type 01V	3-271
Geo Shift Interlock Systems	3-280
Honda AOYA, MPJA & MPOA	3-286
Honda AOYA, MPJA & MPOA Electronic Controls	3-308
Honda A4RA	3-339
Honda A4RA Electronic Controls	3-360
Honda A24A & S24A	3-377
Honda A24A & S24A Electronic Controls	3-401
Honda MP1A	3-414
Honda MP1A Electronic Controls	3-436
Honda MPZA	3-466
Honda MPZA Electronic Controls	3-490
Honda M4VA CVT	3-508
Honda M4VA CVT Electronic Controls	3-524
Hydra-Matic 3L30	3-541
Hydra-Matic 4L30-E	3-552
Hydra-Matic 4L30-E 1995 Electronic Controls	3-571
Hydra-Matic 4L30-E 1996 Electronic Controls Acura SLX & Isuzu Trooper	3-676
Hydra-Matic 4L30-E 1996 Electronic Controls Honda Passport & Isuzu Rodeo	3-694
Hyundai A4AF & A4BF Series	3-713
Hyundai A4AF & A4BF Electronic Controls	3-732
Hyundai KM175	3-752
Hyundai KM175 Electronic Controls	3-771
Jaguar ZF 4HP 24-E Electronic Controls	3-785
Jaguar Hydra-Matic 4L80-E Electronic Controls	3-790
Kia AW372LE Electronic Controls	3-795
Kia FA4A-EL Electronic Controls	3-802
Lexus A-350E Electronic Controls	3-820
Mazda FA4A-EL & GF4A-EL	3-830
Mazda FA4A-EL & GF4A-EL Electronic Controls	3-863
Mazda LA4A-EL	3-908
Mazda LJ4A-EL	3-911
Mazda LJ4A-EL Electronic Controls	3-930
Mazda NC4A-EL	3-944
Mazda NC4A-EL Electronic Controls	3-960
Mazda RA4A-EL, RA4AX-EL & RB4A-EL	3-973
Mazda R4A-EL Series Electronic Controls	3-998
Mazda 4R44E & 4R55E	3-1031
Mazda Shift Lock System	3-1033

TRANSMISSION MODEL	Page
Mercedes-Benz 722 Series	3-1040
Mitsubishi F3A20 & F4A20 Series	3-1065
Mitsubishi F4AC1 Electronic Controls	3-1086
Mitsubishi F4A33, W4A32 & W4A33	3-1103
Mitsubishi F4A20, F4A30 & W4A30 Series Electronic Controls	3-1128
Mitsubishi V4AW2	3-1147
Mitsubishi V4AW3	3-1164
Mitsubishi V4AW3 Electronic Controls	3-1181
Nissan RE4F03A/V	3-1192
Nissan RE4F03A/V Electronic Controls	3-1214
Nissan RE4F04A & RE4F04V	3-1223
Nissan RE4F04A/V Electronic Controls	3-1246
Nissan RE4R01A, RE4R03A & RL4R01A	3-1261
Nissan RE4R01A, RE4R03A & RL4R01A Electronic Controls	3-1283
Nissan RL4F03A/V	3-1303
Porsche A50/05 Tiptronic	3-1325
Porsche A50/05 Tiptronic 1995 Electronic Controls	3-1345
Saab AW50-40LE Electronic Controls	3-1360
Saab ZF 4HP 18	3-1369
Subaru 4-Speed	3-1380
Subaru 4-Speed Electronic Controls	3-1397
Suzuki ECC 3-Speed	3-1417
Suzuki ECC 3-Speed 1995 Electronic Controls (Except OBD-II)	3-1429
Suzuki ECC 3-Speed 1996 Electronic Controls (OBD-II)	3-1437
Suzuki Esteem 4-Speed	3-1443
Suzuki Esteem 4-Speed 1995 Electronic Controls	3-1460
Suzuki Esteem 4-Speed 1996 Electronic Controls	3-1468
Toyota A-43D, A-46DE & A-46DF	3-1477
Toyota A-43D Electronic Controls	3-1497
Toyota A-46DE & A-46DF Electronic Controls	3-1500
Toyota A-131L & A-132L	3-1509
Toyota A-140E	3-1527
Toyota A-140E Electronic Controls	3-1547
Toyota A-240 "E" & "L" Series	3-1560
Toyota A-240 "E" Series Electronic Controls	3-1592
Toyota A-242L Electronic Controls	3-1614
Toyota A-340 & A-350 Series	3-1615
Toyota A-340 Series Elect. Controls (Except OBD-II)	3-1657
Toyota A-340 Series Elect. Controls (With OBD-II)	3-1682
Toyota Previa A-340E & A-340F Electronic Controls	3-1717
Toyota A-343F Electronic Controls	3-1727
Toyota A-540H & A-541E	3-1737
Toyota A-540H Electronic Controls	3-1765
Toyota A-541E Electronic Controls	3-1774
Toyota Shift Lock System	3-1787
Volkswagen Model 096	3-1796
Volkswagen Type 01M	3-1827
Volvo AW40 Series Electronic Controls	3-1858
Volvo AW50-42LE Electronic Controls	3-1875
Volvo AW-71	3-1897
ZF 5HP18 & ZF 5HP30	3-1914

AUTOMATIC TRANSMISSIONS
Acura MPYA, M5DA & M5HA

Legend (1995), 3.2TL, 3.5RL

APPLICATION & LABOR TIMES

APPLICATION & LABOR TIMES

Vehicle Application	Labor Times [1] R & I	[2] Overhaul	Trans. Model
Legend (1995)	6.0	8.9	MPYA
3.2TL	5.1	8.9	M5HA
3.5RL	6.0	8.9	M5DA

[1] – Removal and installation of transmission from vehicle chassis.
[2] – Bench overhaul time for transmission and differential. DOES NOT include removal and installation.

IDENTIFICATION

Transaxle model and serial number are stamped on the transaxle. See Fig. 1. Model and serial number may be required when ordering replacement components.

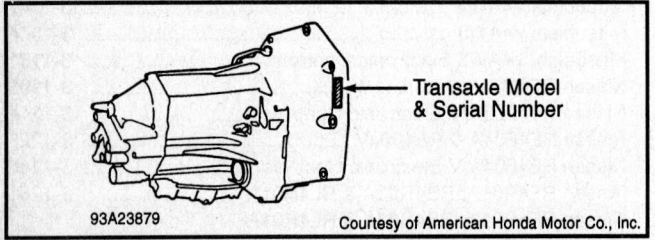

Transaxle Model & Serial Number

93A23879   Courtesy of American Honda Motor Co., Inc.

Fig. 1: Identifying Transaxle Model & Serial Number Location

DESCRIPTION

Automatic transaxle is electronically controlled with 4 forward speeds and one reverse speed. Transaxle consists of clutches, mainshaft, countershaft, shift control solenoid valves, lock-up control solenoid valves, linear solenoid and lock-up torque converter. Transaxle has a differential assembly bolted to the transaxle. Power is delivered from transaxle to the differential assembly by the extension shaft. See Fig. 2.

Lower valve body assembly consists of main valve body, secondary valve body, throttle valve body, linear solenoid, shift control solenoid valves and oil pass body. Lower valve body is bolted to transaxle housing. Other valve bodies used are regulator valve body, oil pump body and accumulator body. These valve bodies are bolted to torque converter housing.

Transaxle shifting and torque converter lock-up are controlled by the Powertrain Control Module (PCM). Transaxle shifting is related to engine torque through the linear solenoid used to operate the throttle valve. The PCM controls the linear solenoid located on the throttle valve body. The PCM determines appropriate shift point and activates proper shift control solenoid valve for transaxle shifting.

OPERATION

Shift lever has 7 positions. When shift lever is moved, manual valve on main valve body is moved by the shift cable. Shift lever also changes position of A/T gear position switch, mounted on the shift lever. The A/T gear position switch delivers an input signal to the PCM to indicate shift lever position. The PCM uses this input signal to control shift control solenoid valves. The PCM determines appropriate shift point and activates proper shift control solenoid valve for transaxle shifting.

When transaxle gear combinations are engaged by clutches, power is transmitted from mainshaft to countershaft to provide different gears. Shift lever positions operate as follows:

- **"P" (Park)** – Front wheels lock as parking pawl engages with parking gear on countershaft. All clutches are released. Neutral position switch, incorporated in A/T gear position switch, allows engine starting in this position.
- **"R" (Reverse)** – Reverse clutch is engaged. Back-up light switch, incorporated in A/T gear position switch, allows back-up lights to operate.
- **"N" (Neutral)** – All clutches are released. Neutral safety switch, incorporated in A/T gear position switch, allows engine starting in this position.
- **"D₄" (Drive)** – Transaxle starts in 1st gear and upshifts automatically to 2nd, 3rd and then 4th gear. Transaxle will downshift through 3rd, 2nd and 1st gears until vehicle stops. When in 2nd, 3rd or 4th gear in this range, PCM sends a signal to operate torque converter lock-up.
- **"D₃" (Drive)** – Transaxle starts off in 1st gear and upshifts automatically to 2nd gear and then 3rd gear. Transaxle will downshift through all gears on deceleration.
- **"2" (Second)** – Transaxle starts off and remains in 2nd gear for engine braking and better traction.
- **"1" (First)** – Transaxle starts off and remains in 1st gear for engine braking.

When in "D₄", 2nd, 3rd and 4th gears, torque converter lock-up exists and transaxle mainshaft rotates at same speed as engine crankshaft. Under certain conditions, torque converter lock-up clutch is applied during deceleration in 3rd and 4th gears. Torque converter lock-up is controlled by the PCM. The PCM receives various input signals and operates lock-up control solenoid valves. Operation of lock-up control solenoid valves controls the modulator pressure.

The PCM contains a self-diagnostic system, which stores a fault code if failure or problem exists in transaxle electronic control system. Fault code can be retrieved to determine transaxle problem area. For information on electronic transaxle components, see ACURA MPYA, M5DA & M5HA ELECTRONIC CONTROLS article.

Transaxle is equipped with shift and key interlock systems. Shift interlock system prevents shift lever from being moved from "P" position unless brake pedal is depressed and accelerator pedal is in idle position. In case of a malfunction, shift lever can be released by placing ignition key in release slot near shift lever. Key interlock system prevents ignition key from being removed from ignition switch unless shift lever is in "P" position. For additional information on shift and key interlock systems, see ACURA MPYA, M5DA & M5HA ELECTRONIC CONTROLS article.

The A/T gear position indicator on instrument panel contains lights to indicate which position A/T gear position switch on shift lever is in. For information and testing of A/T gear position indicator, see ACURA MPYA, M5DA & M5HA ELECTRONIC CONTROLS article.

LUBRICATION & ADJUSTMENTS

See appropriate AUTOMATIC TRANSMISSION SERVICING article in TRANSMISSION SERVICING section.

TROUBLE SHOOTING

Transaxle malfunctions may be caused by poor engine performance, improper adjustments or failure of hydraulic, mechanical or electronic components. Always begin by checking fluid level, fluid condition and cable adjustments. Perform road test to determine if problem has been corrected. If problem still exists, several tests must be performed on transaxle. See TESTING.

SYMPTOM DIAGNOSIS

Excessive Drag In Transaxle
- Binding Oil Pump

Excessive Idle Vibration
- Defective Torque Converter Or Oil Pump
- Incorrect Idle RPM
- Lock-Up Shift Valve Stuck

Excessive Vibration (RPM Related)
- Torque Converter Not Fully Seated In Oil Pump

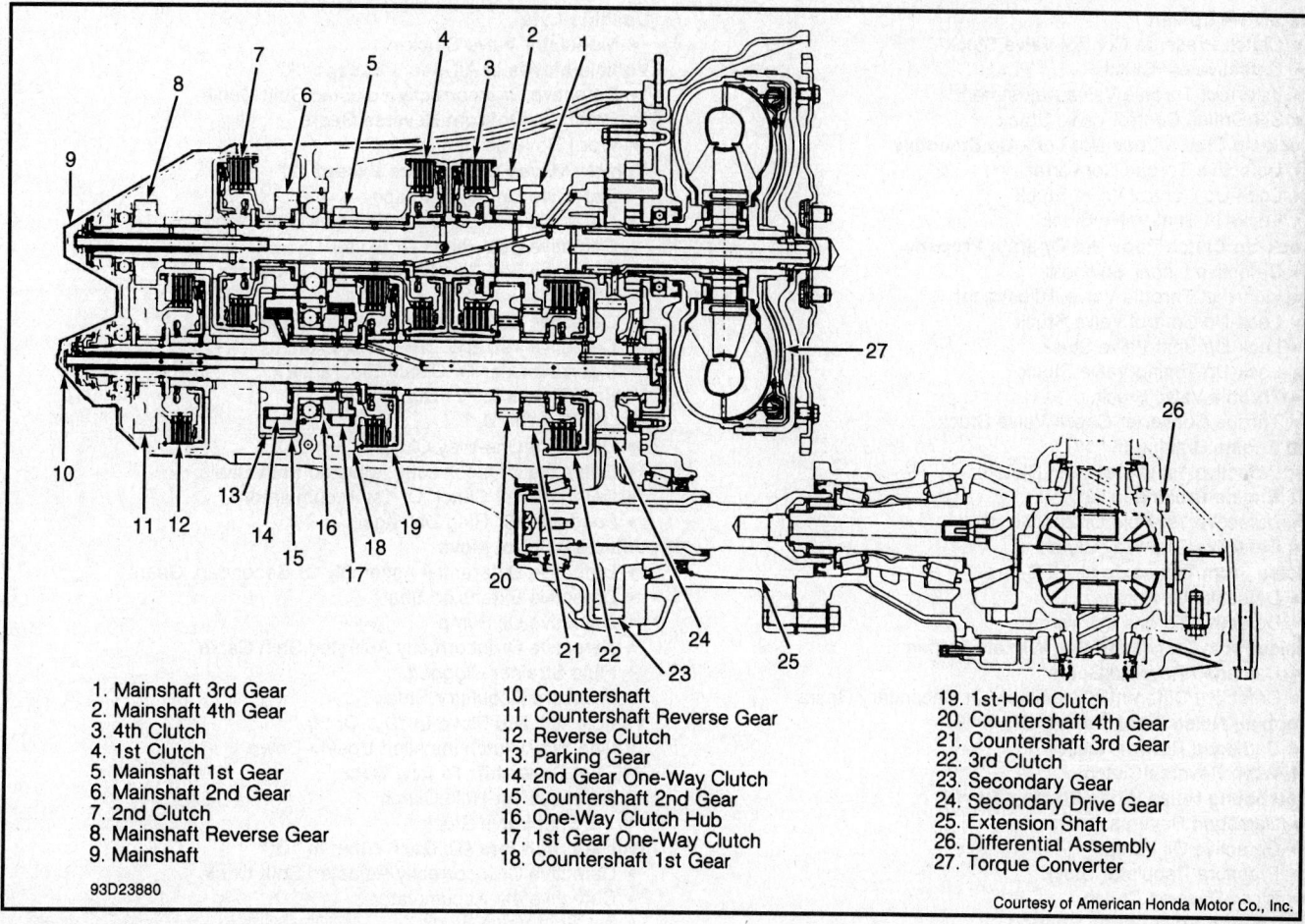

1. Mainshaft 3rd Gear
2. Mainshaft 4th Gear
3. 4th Clutch
4. 1st Clutch
5. Mainshaft 1st Gear
6. Mainshaft 2nd Gear
7. 2nd Clutch
8. Mainshaft Reverse Gear
9. Mainshaft
10. Countershaft
11. Countershaft Reverse Gear
12. Reverse Clutch
13. Parking Gear
14. 2nd Gear One-Way Clutch
15. Countershaft 2nd Gear
16. One-Way Clutch Hub
17. 1st Gear One-Way Clutch
18. Countershaft 1st Gear
19. 1st-Hold Clutch
20. Countershaft 4th Gear
21. Countershaft 3rd Gear
22. 3rd Clutch
23. Secondary Gear
24. Secondary Drive Gear
25. Extension Shaft
26. Differential Assembly
27. Torque Converter

93D23880

Courtesy of American Honda Motor Co., Inc.

Fig. 2: Identifying Transaxle Components

Flares On 1-2 Upshift
- Defective Linear Solenoid
- Defective One-Way Clutch
- Defective 2nd Accumulator
- Incorrect Throttle Valve Adjustment
- Throttle Valve Stuck
- 1-2 Shift Valve Stuck

Flares On 2-3 Upshift
- Defective Linear Solenoid
- Defective One-Way Clutch
- Defective 3rd Accumulator
- Feedpipe "O" Ring Damaged
- Incorrect Throttle Valve Adjustment
- Throttle Valve Stuck
- 2-3 Shift Valve Stuck

Flares On 3-4 Upshift
- Defective Linear Solenoid
- Defective 4th Accumulator
- Feedpipe "O" Ring Damaged
- Incorrect Throttle Valve Adjustment
- Throttle Valve Stuck
- 3-4 Orifice Control Valve Stuck
- 3-4 Shift Valve Stuck

Gear Whine That Changes With Shifts
- Defective 1st Clutch
- Defective 3rd Gears

Gear Whine That Changes With Speed
- Defective Differential Assembly Or Secondary Gears

Harsh Downshift At Closed Throttle
- Throttle Valve Stuck

Harsh Kickdown Shifts
- Clutch Pressure Control Valve Stuck
- Defective Linear Solenoid
- Incorrect Throttle Valve Adjustment
- 4-3 Kickdown Valve Stuck
- 4-3 Shift Timing Valve Stuck

Harsh Shift When Manually Shifting To "1"
- Defective 1st-Hold Accumulator

Harsh Upshifts & Downshifts
- Check Balls Missing
- Clutch Pressure Control Valve Stuck
- Defective Linear Solenoid
- Incorrect Throttle Valve Adjustment
- Incorrect ATF Type
- Incorrect Clutch Clearance
- 4-3 Kickdown Valve Stuck
- 4-3 Shift Timing Valve Stuck
- Throttle Valve Stuck

Harsh 1-2 Upshift
- Defective 2nd Clutch
- Incorrect Throttle Valve Adjustment

Harsh 2-1 Kickdown Shift
- Defective One-Way Clutch
- Defective 1st Clutch
- 3-4 Orifice Control Valve Stuck

Harsh 2-3 Upshift
- Clutch Pressure Control Valve Stuck
- Defective 3rd Clutch
- Incorrect Throttle Valve Adjustment
- 4-3 Shift Timing Valve Stuck

Harsh 3-4 Upshift
- Clutch Pressure Control Valve Stuck
- Defective 4th Clutch
- Incorrect Throttle Valve Adjustment
- 3-4 Orifice Control Valve Stuck

Lock-Up Clutch Does Not Lock Up Smoothly
- Defective Torque Converter
- Lock-Up Control Valve Stuck
- Lock-Up Shift Valve Stuck

Lock-Up Clutch Does Not Operate Properly
- Defective Linear Solenoid
- Incorrect Throttle Valve Adjustment
- Lock-Up Control Valve Stuck
- Lock-Up Shift Valve Stuck
- Lock-Up Timing Valve Stuck
- Throttle Valve Stuck
- Torque Converter Check Valve Stuck

No Engine Braking In "1"
- Defective 1st Or 1st-Hold Clutch

No Engine Braking In "2"
- Defective 1st-Hold Or 2nd Clutch
- Defective One-Way Clutch

Noise From Transaxle In All Gears
- Defective Oil Pump
- Defective Torque Converter

Noise From Transaxle With Wheels Rolling
- Damaged Reverse Gears
- Defective Differential Assembly Or Secondary Gears

Popping Noise When Taking Off In "R"
- Damaged Reverse Gears
- Worn Reverse Clutch

Ratcheting Noise When Shifting To "R"
- Damaged Reverse Gears
- Defective Oil Pump
- Pressure Regulator Stuck
- Worn Reverse Clutch

Ratcheting Noise When Shifting
From "R" To "P" Or "N"
- Damaged Reverse Gears
- Worn Reverse Clutch

Shifts Erratically
- Incorrectly Installed Springs Or Valves
- Modulator Valve Stuck
- 4-3 Shift Timing Valve Stuck

Slips In All Gears
- Defective Oil Pump
- Fluid Strainer Clogged
- Pressure Regulator Stuck

Slips In Reverse
- Defective Reverse Accumulator
- Defective Reverse Clutch
- Worn Reverse Gears

Slips In 1st Gear
- Defective One-Way Clutch
- Defective 1st Clutch Or 1st Accumulator
- Feedpipe "O" Ring Damaged

Slips In 2nd Gear
- Clutch Pressure Control Valve Stuck
- Defective One-Way Clutch
- Defective Seal Rings Or Guide
- Defective 2nd Clutch Or 2nd Accumulator
- 2-3 Shift Valve Stuck

Slips In 3rd Gear
- Clutch Pressure Control Valve Stuck
- Defective 3rd Clutch Or 3rd Accumulator
- Feedpipe "O" Ring Damaged
- 3-4 Shift Valve Stuck

Slips In 4th Gear
- Clutch Pressure Control Valve Stuck
- Defective 4th Clutch Or 4th Accumulator

Upshifts Late
- Modulator Valve Stuck

Vehicle Moves In All Gears Except "R"
- Defective Or Incorrectly Adjusted Shift Cable
- Defective Or Worn Reverse Gears
- Worn Reverse Clutch

Vehicle Moves In All Gears Except "2"
- Defective One-Way Clutch
- Defective Or Incorrectly Adjusted Shift Cable
- Defective Seal Rings Or Guide
- Defective 2nd Clutch Or 2nd Accumulator

Vehicle Moves In "N"
- Defective Or Incorrectly Adjusted Shift Cable
- Defective 1st, 2nd, 3rd Or 4th Clutch
- Incorrect Gear Or Clutch Clearance

Vehicle Moves In "2" But
Not In "D₃" Or "D₄"
- Defective One-Way Clutch
- Defective Or Incorrectly Adjusted Shift Cable
- Defective 1st Clutch Or 1st Accumulator
- Feedpipe "O" Ring Damaged

Vehicle Will Not Move
- Defective Differential Assembly Or Secondary Gears
- Defective Extension Shaft
- Defective Oil Pump
- Defective Or Incorrectly Adjusted Shift Cable
- Fluid Strainer Clogged
- Pressure Regulator Stuck

Vehicle Will Not Move In "D₃" Or "D₄"
- One-Way Clutch Installed Upside-Down

Will Not Downshift To Low Gear
- Defective 1st-Hold Clutch
- 1-2 Shift Valve Stuck

Will Not Shift Into 4th Gear When In "D₄"
- Defective Or Incorrectly Adjusted Shift Cable
- Defective 4th Accumulator
- 3-4 Shift Valve Stuck
- 3-4 Orifice Control Valve Stuck

Will Not Upshift (Stays In Low Gear)
- Clutch Pressure Control Valve Stuck
- Modulator Valve Stuck
- 1-2 Shift Valve Stuck

TESTING

ROAD TEST

NOTE: If shift lever cannot be moved from "P" position with brake pedal depressed and accelerator pedal at idle position, check shift interlock system. See ACURA MPYA, M5DA & M5HA ELECTRONIC CONTROLS article.

1) Warm engine to normal operating temperature. Apply parking brake and block wheels. Start engine. Move shift lever to "D₄" position while depressing brake pedal. Depress accelerator pedal and release it suddenly. Engine should not stall.

2) Repeat step 1) with shift lever in "D₃" position. Ensure engine does not stall. Manufacturer recommends monitoring of Throttle Position (TP) sensor voltage when performing road test to ensure proper throttle opening for verifying shift points and lock-up of torque converter.

3) Remove door sill molding and lower dash panel on passenger's side and remove small cover on passenger's side kick panel. Pull carpet back for access to the Powertrain Control Module (PCM), located on passenger's side, below carpet. *See Fig. 3.*

4) Remove PCM cover located above PCM. Ensure ignition is off. On Legend models, install Test Harness (07LAJ-PT3010A) between PCM and PCM electrical connectors. Install Digital Volt-Ohmmeter (DVOM) on test harness with positive lead at terminal D11 and negative lead at terminal D22 to monitor throttle position sensor voltage. Terminal numbers are on top of test harness. *See Fig. 3.*

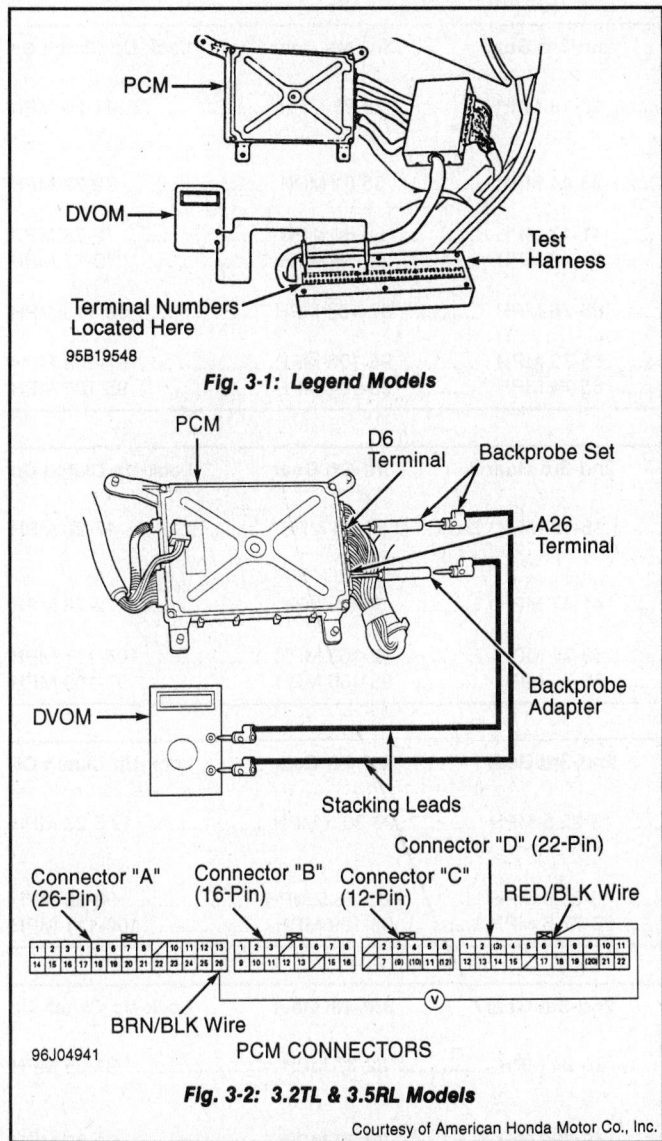

Fig. 3-1: Legend Models

95B19548

Fig. 3-1: Legend Models

PCM — D6 Terminal — Backprobe Set — A26 Terminal — Backprobe Adapter — DVOM — Stacking Leads

Connector "A" (26-Pin) — Connector "B" (16-Pin) — Connector "C" (12-Pin) — Connector "D" (22-Pin) — RED/BLK Wire

BRN/BLK Wire
PCM CONNECTORS
96J04941

Fig. 3-2: 3.2TL & 3.5RL Models

Courtesy of American Honda Motor Co., Inc.

Fig. 3: Measuring TP Sensor Voltage

5) On 3.2TL and 3.5RL models, install Backprobe Test Set (07SAZ-001000A) or equivalent between PCM and DVOM leads. *See Fig. 3.* Using DVOM, with positive lead at terminal D6 and negative lead at terminal A26. *See Fig. 3.* Ensure digital volt-ohmmeter is set for measuring voltage.

6) On all models, road test vehicle and check for abnormal noise and clutch slippage. See CLUTCH APPLICATION table for clutch engagement.

7) Ensure upshift and downshift points and torque converter lock-up are correct in relation to throttle position sensor voltage or throttle opening and vehicle speed with shift lever in "D₄" position. See appropriate TRANSAXLE UPSHIFT SPECIFICATIONS and TRANSAXLE DOWNSHIFT SPECIFICATIONS tables.

8) With shift lever in "D₄" position, accelerate to about 35 MPH so transaxle is in 4th gear. Move shift lever to "2" position. Ensure engine braking occurs.

CAUTION: DO NOT shift from "D₄" to "2" at speeds over 62 MPH or transaxle may be damaged.

9) Place shift lever in "1" position. Accelerate from a stop at full throttle. Check for abnormal noise or clutch slippage. Upshifts and downshifts should not occur in this shift lever position.

10) Place shift lever in "2" position. Accelerate from a stop at full throttle. Check for abnormal noise or clutch slippage. Upshifts and downshifts should not occur in this shift lever position.

11) Place shift lever in "R" position. Accelerate from a stop at full throttle. Check for abnormal noise or clutch slippage.

12) Park vehicle on a slope. Apply parking brake. Place shift lever in "P" position. Release parking brake. Ensure vehicle does not move. If vehicle moves, check for defective shift cable or parking components.

13) Ensure ignition is off. Remove test harness and reinstall electrical connectors, PCM cover, carpet and door sill molding.

CLUTCH APPLICATION

Shift Lever Position	Elements In Use
"P" & "N"	No Clutches Applied
"R"	Reverse Clutch
"D₄"	
1st Gear	1st Clutch
2nd Gear	[1] 2nd Clutch
3rd Gear	[2] 3rd Clutch
4th Gear	[2] 4th Clutch
"D₃"	
1st Gear	1st Clutch
2nd Gear	[1] 2nd Clutch
3rd Gear	[2] 3rd Clutch
"2"	1st-Hold Clutch, 2nd Clutch
"1"	1st-Hold Clutch, 1st Clutch

[1] – The 1st clutch engages, but driving power is not transmitted, as 1st gear one-way clutch slips.
[2] – The 1st and 2nd clutches engage, but driving power is not transmitted, as 2nd gear one-way clutch slips.

TORQUE CONVERTER STALL SPEED TEST

CAUTION: DO NOT perform torque converter stall speed test for more than 10 seconds or transaxle may be damaged. DO NOT move shift lever while increasing engine speed.

1) Apply parking brake and block all wheels. Connect tachometer and start engine. Ensure A/C is off. Warm engine to normal operating temperature. Place shift lever in "2" position.

2) Fully depress brake pedal. Fully depress accelerator for 6-8 seconds and note engine speed. This is torque converter stall speed.

3) Allow transaxle to cool for 2 minutes. Repeat test procedure in "D₄", "1" and "R" positions.

4) Torque converter stall speed should be the same in "D₄", "2", "1" and "R" positions. Torque converter stall speed should be 1850-2150 RPM on Legend, Legend Coupe and 3.2TL and 2100-2400 on 3.5RL. If torque converter stall speed is not within specification, see TORQUE CONVERTER STALL SPEED TROUBLE SHOOTING table for possible causes.

TORQUE CONVERTER STALL SPEED TROUBLE SHOOTING

Torque Converter Stall Speed Test Results	Probable Cause
Stall Speed RPM High In "D₄", "2", "1" & "R"	Low Fluid Level, Low Oil Pump Output, Clogged Fluid Strainer, Pressure Regulator Valve Stuck Closed, Slipping Clutch
Stall Speed RPM High In "R"	Slipping Reverse Clutch
Stall Speed RPM High In "D₄"	Slipping 1st Or 2nd Clutch, Defective 1st Gear Or 2nd Gear One-Way Clutch
Stall Speed RPM High In "2"	Slipping 1st-Hold Or 2nd Clutch, Defective 2nd Gear One-Way Clutch
Stall Speed RPM High In "1"	Slipping 1st Or 1st-Hold Clutch, Defective 1st Gear One-Way Clutch
Stall Speed RPM Low In "D₄", "2", "1" & "R"	Engine Output Low, Torque Converter One-Way Clutch Slipping

TRANSAXLE UPSHIFT SPECIFICATIONS (LEGEND)

"D₄" Position & Condition	1st-2nd Gear	2nd-3rd Gear	3rd-4th Gear	Lock-Up Clutch On
Throttle Position Sensor Voltage Is .822-.878 Volt & Coasting Downhill From Stop	9-12 MPH	16-19 MPH	23-28 MPH	17-20 MPH
Throttle Position Sensor Voltage Is 2.175-2.325 Volts & Accelerating From Stop				
Canadian Models	21-25 MPH	38-44 MPH	55-61 MPH	72-77 MPH
U.S Models				
"GS" Model	24-28 MPH	41-47 MPH	58-64 MPH	72-78 MPH
"L" & "LS" Models	20-24 MPH	37-42 MPH	52-58 MPH	72-77 MPH
Full Throttle & Accelerating From Stop				
Canadian Models	38-44 MPH	68-76 MPH	97-108 MPH	99-110 MPH
U.S Models				
"GS" Model	36-41 MPH	65-73 MPH	95-106 MPH	97-108 MPH
"L" & "LS" Models	37-42 MPH	65-74 MPH	93-104 MPH	95-106 MPH

TRANSAXLE UPSHIFT SPECIFICATIONS (LEGEND COUPE)

"D₄" Position & Condition	1st-2nd Gear	2nd-3rd Gear	3rd-4th Gear	Lock-Up Clutch On
Throttle Position Sensor Voltage Is .822-.878 Volt & Coasting Downhill From Stop	9-12 MPH	16-19 MPH	23-28 MPH	17-20 MPH
Throttle Position Sensor Voltage Is 2.175-2.325 Volts & Accelerating From Stop	24-28 MPH	41-47 MPH	58-64 MPH	72-78 MPH
Full Throttle & Accelerating From Stop				
"L" Model	35-40 MPH	63-71 MPH	92-103 MPH	106-117 MPH
"LS" Model	36-41 MPH	65-73 MPH	95-106 MPH	97-108 MPH

TRANSAXLE UPSHIFT SPECIFICATIONS (3.2TL)

"D₄" Position & Condition	1st-2nd Gear	2nd-3rd Gear	3rd-4th Gear	Lock-Up Clutch On
Throttle Position Sensor Voltage Is .702-.798 Volt & Coasting Downhill From Stop	9.5-12.5 MPH	19-22.5 MPH	26-30.5 MPH	19.5-23 MPH
Throttle Position Sensor Voltage Is 2.167-2.333 Volts & Accelerating From Stop	24-28 MPH	48-53.5 MPH	72.5-78.5 MPH	90-96 MPH
Full Throttle & Accelerating From Stop	39-44.5 MPH	69-77.5 MPH	98-109 MPH	100-111 MPH

TRANSAXLE UPSHIFT SPECIFICATIONS (3.5RL)

"D₄" Position & Condition	1st-2nd Gear	2nd-3rd Gear	3rd-4th Gear	Lock-Up Clutch On
Throttle Position Sensor Voltage Is .822-.878 Volt & Coasting Downhill From Stop	10-13 MPH	21-24 MPH	32-37 MPH	21-25 MPH
Throttle Position Sensor Voltage Is 2.175-2.325 Volts & Accelerating From Stop	25-29 MPH	48-53 MPH	73-79 MPH	91-97 MPH
Full Throttle & Accelerating From Stop	38-44 MPH	70-78 MPH	103-114 MPH	95-106 MPH

TRANSAXLE DOWNSHIFT SPECIFICATIONS (LEGEND)

"D₄" Position & Condition	Lock-Up Clutch Off	4th-3rd Gear	3rd-2nd Gear	2nd-1st Gear
Throttle Position Sensor Voltage Is .822-.878 Volt & Coasting Or Braking To A Stop	16-19 MPH	18-21 MPH	¹	6-9 MPH
Throttle Position Sensor Voltage Is 2.175-2.325 Volts & Vehicle Slowing By Grade Or Load				
Canadian Models	59-64 MPH	¹	¹	¹
U.S. Models				
"GS" Model	57-63 MPH	¹	¹	¹
"L" & "LS" Models	59-64 MPH	¹	¹	¹
Full Throttle & Vehicle Slowing By Grade Or Load				
Canadian Models	94-105 MPH	89-99 MPH	57-64 MPH	26-32 MPH
U.S. Models				
"GS" Models	92-103 MPH	87-97 MPH	55-62 MPH	25-30 MPH
"L" & "LS" Models	90-101 MPH	85-96 MPH	54-61 MPH	25-30 MPH

¹ – Specification not available from manufacturer.

TRANSAXLE DOWNSHIFT SPECIFICATIONS (LEGEND COUPE)

"D₄" Position & Condition	Lock-Up Clutch Off	4th-3rd Gear	3rd-2nd Gear	2nd-1st Gear
Throttle Position Sensor Voltage Is .822-.878 Volt & Coasting Or Braking To A Stop	16-19 MPH	18-21 MPH	[1]	6-9 MPH
Throttle Position Sensor Voltage Is 2.175-2.325 Volts & Vehicle Slowing By Grade Or Load				
"L" Model	59-64 MPH	[1]	[1]	[1]
"LS" Model	57-63 MPH	[1]	[1]	[1]
Full Throttle & Vehicle Slowing By Grade Or Load				
"L" Model	101-112 MPH	85-96 MPH	54-61 MPH	25-30 MPH
"LS" Model	92-103 MPH	87-97 MPH	55-62 MPH	25-30 MPH

[1] – Specification not available from manufacturer.

TRANSAXLE DOWNSHIFT SPECIFICATIONS (3.2TL)

"D₄" Position & Condition	Lock-Up Clutch Off	4th-3rd Gear	3rd-2nd Gear	2nd-1st Gear
Throttle Position Sensor Voltage Is .702-.798 Volt & Coasting Or Braking To A Stop	17-20.5 MPH	17.5-21 MPH	[1]	5.5-9 MPH
Throttle Position Sensor Voltage Is 2.167-2.333 Volts & Vehicle Slowing By Grade Or Load	71-76.56 MPH	[1]	[1]	[1]
Full Throttle & Vehicle Slowing By Grade Or Load	95.5-106 MPH	90.5-101 MPH	57.5-64.5 MPH	26-31.5 MPH

[1] – Specification not available from manufacturer.

TRANSAXLE DOWNSHIFT SPECIFICATIONS (3.5RL)

"D₄" Position & Condition	Lock-Up Clutch Off	4th-3rd Gear	3rd-2nd Gear	2nd-1st Gear
Throttle Position Sensor Voltage Is .822-.878 Volt & Coasting Or Braking To A Stop	21-25 MPH [1]	[2]	16-19 MPH	6-9 MPH
Throttle Position Sensor Voltage Is 2.175-2.325 Volts & Vehicle Slowing By Grade Or Load	72-78 MPH	[2]	[2]	[2]
Full Throttle & Vehicle Slowing By Grade Or Load	93-104 MPH	92-103 MPH	59-66 MPH	28-33 MPH

[1] – Throttle Position Sensor Voltage Is .725-.775 for lock-up off speeds.
[2] – Specification not available from manufacturer.

HYDRAULIC PRESSURE TEST

Pressure Test Preparation – Ensure transaxle fluid level is correct. Warm engine to normal operating temperature. Apply parking brake. Block rear wheels. Raise and support vehicle so front wheels can rotate.

Line Pressure Test – 1) With engine off, remove pressure tap plug from line pressure tap on transaxle. *See Fig. 4.* Attach pressure gauge to line pressure tap using NEW sealing washer. Tighten hose fitting to 13 ft. lbs. (18 N.m).

2) On 3.5RL models, disconnect transaxle sub-harness 14-pin connector, located near top of transaxle on driver's side. *See Fig. 5.* On all models, with shift lever in "P" position, start and operate engine at 2000 RPM. Note line pressure. Place shift lever in "N" position and note line pressure.

3) Line pressure should be within specification. See appropriate HYDRAULIC PRESSURE TEST SPECIFICATIONS table. If line pressure is not within specification, see HYDRAULIC PRESSURE TEST TROUBLE SHOOTING table.

4) On 3.5RL models, allow engine to idle. Connect positive battery terminal to Red wire and negative battery terminal to White wire of transaxle sub-harness connector. *See Fig. 5.* This will energize the linear solenoid.

5) Note fully closed throttle line pressure with sub-harness disconnected and voltage applied. Line pressure should be within specification. See HYDRAULIC PRESSURE TEST SPECIFICATIONS (3.5RL) table. If Line pressure is not within specification, see HYDRAULIC PRESSURE TEST TROUBLE SHOOTING table. On all models, shut engine off. Reconnect transaxle sub-harness 14-pin connector, if disconnected. Remove pressure gauge set.

6) Using NEW sealing washer, install and tighten pressure tap plug to specification. See TORQUE SPECIFICATIONS.

NOTE: Clutch pressure should be checked at each clutch pressure tap on transaxle. See Fig. 4.

Clutch Pressure Test – 1) With engine off, remove pressure tap plug from appropriate clutch pressure tap on transaxle. *See Fig. 4.* Attach pressure gauge to appropriate pressure tap using NEW sealing washer. Tighten hose fitting to 13 ft. lbs. (18 N.m).

NOTE: Clutch pressure on some applications may vary with position of the throttle. Clutch pressure may be need to be checked with throttle closed or with engine at 2000 RPM. Ensure shift lever is in proper position when checking clutch pressures.

2) Start engine. Note clutch pressure in relation to throttle setting or engine RPM with shift lever in proper location to check appropriate clutch. See appropriate HYDRAULIC PRESSURE TEST SPECIFICATIONS table.

3) Clutch pressure should be within specification. See appropriate HYDRAULIC PRESSURE TEST SPECIFICATIONS table. If clutch pressure is not within specification, see HYDRAULIC PRESSURE TEST TROUBLE SHOOTING table. Shut engine off. Remove pressure gauge set.

4) Using NEW sealing washer, install and tighten pressure tap plug to specification. See TORQUE SPECIFICATIONS.

Clutch Low-High Pressure Test – 1) Clutch low-high pressure is tested at 2nd, 3rd and 4th clutch pressure taps on transaxle. See Fig. 4.

2) With engine off, remove pressure tap plug from appropriate clutch pressure tap on transaxle. Attach pressure gauge to appropriate pressure tap using NEW sealing washer. Tighten hose fitting to 13 ft. lbs. (18 N.m).

3) Start engine and allow to idle. Place shift lever in "D₄". Slowly increase engine speed until pressure is indicated on pressure gauge. Release throttle, allowing engine to idle and note low pressure reading. This is the clutch low pressure.

4) With engine idling, gradually increase engine speed and note highest pressure reading. This is clutch high pressure.

5) Repeat procedure on remaining clutches. Ensure clutch low-high pressure is within specification. See appropriate HYDRAULIC PRESSURE TEST SPECIFICATIONS table.

6) If clutch pressure is not within specification, see HYDRAULIC PRESSURE TEST TROUBLE SHOOTING table. Shut engine off. Remove pressure gauge set.

7) Using NEW sealing washer, install and tighten pressure tap plug to specification. See TORQUE SPECIFICATIONS.

Throttle "B" Pressure Test – 1) With engine off, remove pressure plug from throttle "B" pressure tap on transaxle. See Fig. 4.

2) Attach pressure gauge to throttle "B" pressure tap using NEW sealing washer. Tighten hose fitting to 13 ft. lbs. (18 N.m).

HYDRAULIC PRESSURE TEST SPECIFICATIONS (LEGEND & 3.2TL)

Application	Shift Lever Position	psi. (kPa)
Line Pressure		
With Engine At 2000 RPM	"P" Or "N"	107-122 (740-840)
Clutch Pressure		
Reverse Clutch		
With Engine At 2000 RPM	"R"	164-181 (1130-1250)
1st Clutch		
With Engine At 2000 RPM	"1", "D₄" Or "D₃"	107-122 (740-840)
1st-Hold Clutch		
With Engine At 2000 RPM	"1" Or "2"	107-122 (740-840)
2nd Clutch		
With Engine At 2000 RPM	"2"	107-122 (740-840)
With Throttle Closed	"D₄"	54-57 (370-390)
With More Than 1/4 Throttle Opening	"D₄"	107-122 (740-840)
3rd Clutch		
With Throttle Closed	"D₄"	54-57 (370-390)
With More Than 1/4 Throttle Opening	"D₄"	107-122 (740-840)
4th Clutch		
With Throttle Closed	"D₄"	54-57 (370-390)
With More Than 1/4 Throttle Opening	"D₄"	107-122 (740-840)
Clutch Low Pressure		
2nd, 3rd Or 4th Clutch	"D₄"	54-57 (379-390)
Clutch High Pressure		
2nd, 3rd Or 4th Clutch	"D₄"	107-122 (740-840)
Throttle "B" Pressure		
With Transaxle Sub-Harness Disconnected & No Voltage Applied To Harness		
With Fully Opened Throttle	"D₄"	78-91 (540-630)
& Voltage Applied To Harness		
With Throttle Closed	"D₄"	0-2 (0-15)

HYDRAULIC PRESSURE TEST SPECIFICATIONS (3.5RL)

Application	Shift Lever Position	psi. (kPa)
Line Pressure		
With Engine At 2000 RPM	"P" Or "N"	116-132 (800-910)
With Throttle Closed	"D₄"	71-75 (490-520)
Clutch Pressure		
1st Clutch		
With Throttle Closed	"1", "D₃" Or "D₄"	74-86 (510-590)
1st-Hold Clutch		
With Throttle Closed	"1" Or "2"	74-86 (510-590)
2nd Clutch		
With Throttle Closed	"2"	74-86 (510-590)
3rd Clutch		
With Throttle Closed	"D₃"	74-86 (510-590)
4th Clutch		
With Throttle Closed	"D₄"	74-86 (510-590)
Reverse Clutch		
With Throttle Closed	"R"	107-123 (740-850)
Throttle "B" Pressure		
With Transaxle Sub-Harness Disconnected & No Voltage Applied To Harness At 2000 RPM	"D₄"	74-86 (510-590)
With Transaxle Sub-Harness Disconnected & Voltage Applied To Harness & Throttle Closed	"D₄"	0-2 (0-15)

NOTE: Throttle "B" pressure will be checked with transaxle sub-harness connector disconnected and again with battery voltage applied to linear solenoid.

3) Disconnect transaxle sub-harness connector, located near top of transaxle on driver's side. *See Fig. 5.*

4) Start and operate engine at 1000 RPM. Place shift lever in "D₄" position. Note fully opened throttle "B" pressure with sub-harness disconnected and no voltage applied.

5) Throttle "B" pressure should be within specification. See appropriate HYDRAULIC PRESSURE TEST SPECIFICATIONS table. If throttle "B" pressure is not within specification, see HYDRAULIC PRESSURE TEST TROUBLE SHOOTING table.

6) Allow engine to idle. Connect positive battery terminal to Red wire and negative battery terminal to White wire of transaxle sub-harness connector. *See Fig. 5.* This will energize the linear solenoid.

7) Increase engine speed to 1000 RPM with shift lever in "D₄" position. Note fully closed throttle "B" pressure with sub-harness disconnected and voltage applied.

8) Throttle "B" pressure should be within specification. See appropriate HYDRAULIC PRESSURE TEST SPECIFICATIONS table. If throttle "B" pressure is not within specification, see HYDRAULIC PRESSURE TEST TROUBLE SHOOTING table. Shut engine off. Remove pressure gauge set.

9) Using NEW sealing washer, install and tighten pressure tap plug to specification. See TORQUE SPECIFICATIONS. Reconnect transaxle sub-harness connector.

HYDRAULIC PRESSURE TEST TROUBLE SHOOTING

Application	Probable Cause
Line Pressure	
Low Or No Line Pressure	Defective Torque Converter, Defective Torque Converter Check Valve, Defective Pressure Regulator, Defective Oil Pump
Clutch Pressure	
Low Or No Reverse Clutch Pressure	Defective Reverse Clutch
Low Or No 1st Clutch Pressure	Defective 1st Clutch
Low Or No 1st-Hold Clutch Pressure	Defective 1st-Hold Clutch
Low Or No 2nd Clutch Pressure	Defective 2nd Clutch
Low Or No 3rd Clutch Pressure	Defective 3rd Clutch
Low Or No 4th Clutch Pressure	Defective 4th Clutch
Clutch Low-High Pressure	
Low Or No 2nd Clutch Pressure	Defective 2nd Clutch
Low Or No 3rd Clutch Pressure	Defective 3rd Clutch
Low Or No 4th Clutch Pressure	Defective 4th Clutch
Throttle "B" Pressure	
Low Or No Throttle "B" Pressure With No Voltage Applied	Defective Throttle Valve Body
High Throttle "B" Pressure With Voltage Applied	Defective Throttle Valve Body

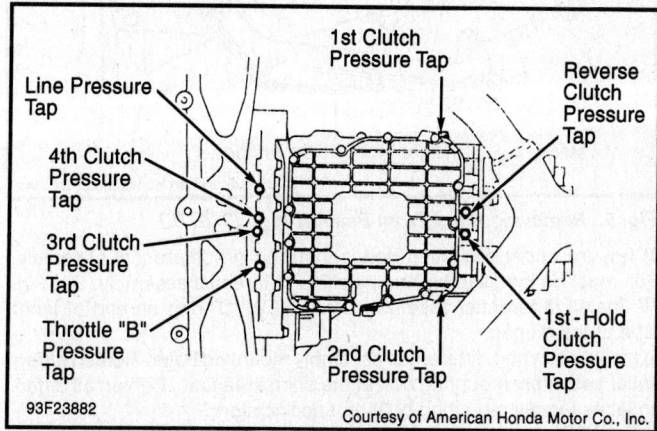

Fig. 4: Identifying Transaxle Pressure Taps

1st Clutch Pressure Tap

Line Pressure Tap

Reverse Clutch Pressure Tap

4th Clutch Pressure Tap

3rd Clutch Pressure Tap

Throttle "B" Pressure Tap

2nd Clutch Pressure Tap

1st-Hold Clutch Pressure Tap

93F23882

Courtesy of American Honda Motor Co., Inc.

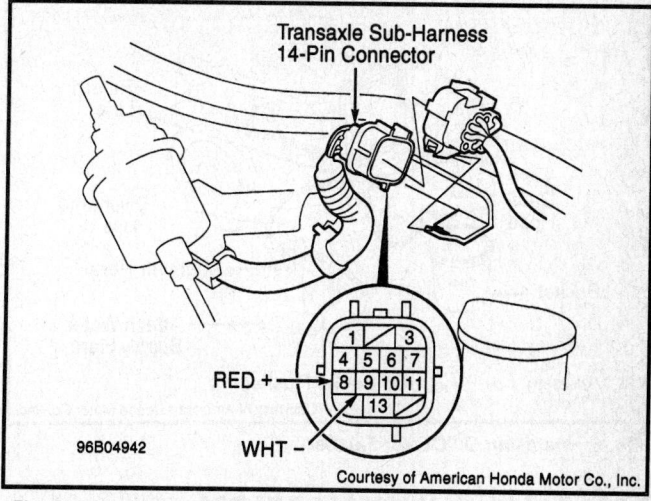

Transaxle Sub-Harness 14-Pin Connector

RED +

WHT –

96B04942

Courtesy of American Honda Motor Co., Inc.

Fig. 5: Identifying Transaxle Sub-Harness Connector

ON-VEHICLE SERVICE

AXLE SHAFTS

See appropriate article in AXLE SHAFTS & TRANSFER CASES section.

DIFFERENTIAL ASSEMBLY

Differential assembly may be removed from vehicle with transaxle in the vehicle. See DIFFERENTIAL ASSEMBLY under REMOVAL & INSTALLATION.

LOWER VALVE BODY ASSEMBLY

Lower valve body assembly consists of main valve body, secondary valve body, throttle valve body, linear solenoid, shift control solenoid valves and oil pass body. See LOWER VALVE BODY ASSEMBLY under REMOVAL & INSTALLATION.

OIL COOLER FLUSHING

1) Attach Oil Cooler Flusher (J38405-A) to oil cooler lines. *See Fig. 6.* Fill oil cooler flusher tank 2/3 full with Flushing Fluid (J35944-20). DO NOT use any other flushing fluid.

2) Ensure water and air valves on oil cooler flusher are off. Apply 80-120 psi (550-829 kPa) air pressure to oil cooler flusher. Turn oil cooler flusher water valve on so water flows through oil cooler for 10 seconds. Replace oil cooler if water will not flow through oil cooler. Shut water valve off.

3) Depress and hold mixing trigger on oil cooler flusher downward. Turn water valve on and flush oil cooler for 2 minutes. Turn air valve on for 5 seconds every 15-20 seconds to create a surging action.

4) Turn water valve off. Release mixing trigger. Disconnect oil cooler flusher and reverse hoses so oil cooler can be flushed in opposite direction.

5) Repeat steps **2)** and **3)**. Turn water valve off. Release mixing trigger. Turn water valve on and rinse oil cooler for at least one minute. Once oil cooler is flushed in both directions, turn water off. Turn air valve on until no moisture is visible from drain hose.

CAUTION: Ensure no moisture exists in oil cooler, as it can damage transaxle.

6) Turn air off. Disconnect oil cooler flusher. Reconnect inlet line on oil cooler. Once transaxle is installed, attach drain hose on return line and place in oil container. Ensure transaxle is in "P" position. Fill transaxle with Dexron-II ATF.

7) Start engine and operate for approximately 30 seconds or until one quart (.9L) of ATF is discharged from return line. Shut engine off. Remove drain hose. Reinstall return line. Fill transaxle to proper level.

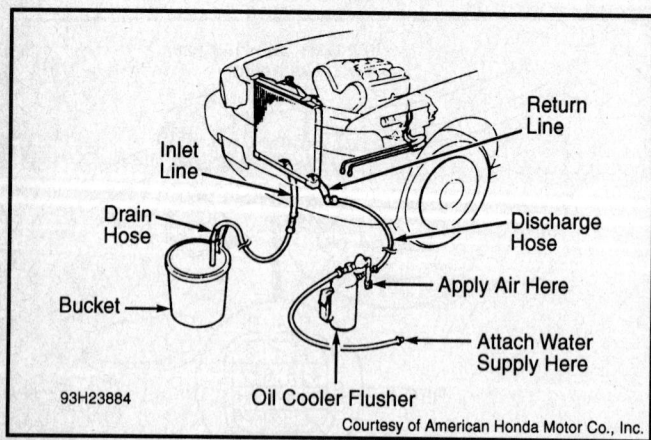

Fig. 6: Installing Oil Cooler Flusher

REMOVAL & INSTALLATION

DIFFERENTIAL ASSEMBLY

NOTE: Before disconnecting negative battery cable, ensure radio anti-theft code is obtained from customer. Radio anti-theft code must be re-entered into radio for radio operation.

Removal – 1) Obtain radio anti-theft code from customer. Disconnect negative battery cable. Raise and support vehicle. Drain differential assembly gear oil. Drain cooling system.

2) Remove axle shafts and intermediate shaft. See appropriate article in AXLE SHAFTS & TRANSFER CASES section. Remove extension shaft sealing bolt. Place shift lever in "P" to lock secondary gear. Using Puller (07LAC-PW50100 or 101), disconnect extension shaft. *See Fig. 7.*

3) Remove splash shield. Remove bolts and lower plate, located below differential assembly. *See Fig. 8.* Reinstall bolts to hold steering gear in place, as bolts must be removed for lower plate removal. On 3.2L TL models, remove right front beam bridge. *See Fig. 9.*

4) On all models, disconnect Vehicle Speed Sensor (VSS) connector, remove bolt, speed sensor assembly and "O" ring from differential assembly. Speed sensor assembly contains the VSS and power steering speed sensor. DO NOT disconnect the 2 hoses for the power steering at speed sensor assembly.

5) On Legend models, disconnect oil cooler hoses at pipes on differential assembly. *See Fig. 10.* On 3.5RL models, remove air cleaner housing. Remove power steering pump leaving hoses attached. Disconnect breather tube from clamp and remove right exhaust manifold cover.

6) Remove 2 lower engine stop mount bolts. Support engine with chain hoist. Remove right and left upper engine mount brackets.

7) On all models, remove differential assembly mounting bolts, shim and differential assembly. *See Fig. 10.*

NOTE: Differential shim must be checked and adjusted if differential is replaced. See Fig. 10. If differential case has not been replaced, start installation procedure with step 4).

Installation – 1) Install differential assembly. Ensure upper mounting bolt is installed on differential assembly, as bolt must be installed before installing differential assembly. *See Fig. 10.* Install and tighten differential assembly mounting bolts to specification. See TORQUE SPECIFICATIONS.

2) Using feeler gauge, measure clearance between differential case and torque converter housing at shim location. *See Fig. 11.*

3) Select a shim equal to measured dimension. Shims are available in .1 mm increments ranging from 1.9 mm to 3.0 mm. Remove differential assembly.

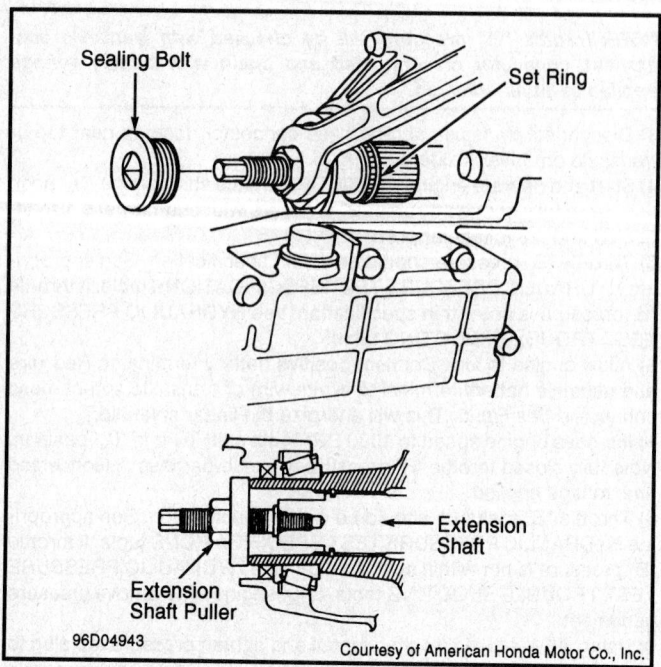

Fig. 7: Removing Extension Shaft

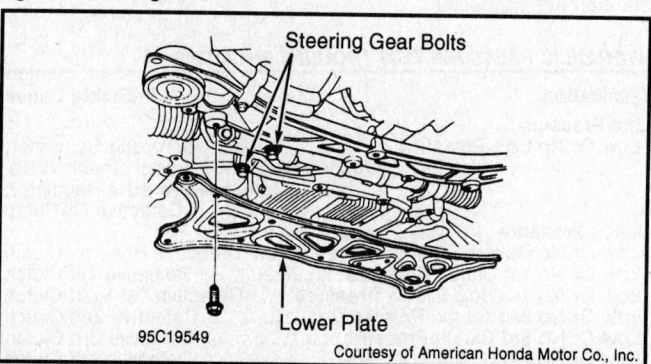

Fig. 8: Identifying Lower Plate

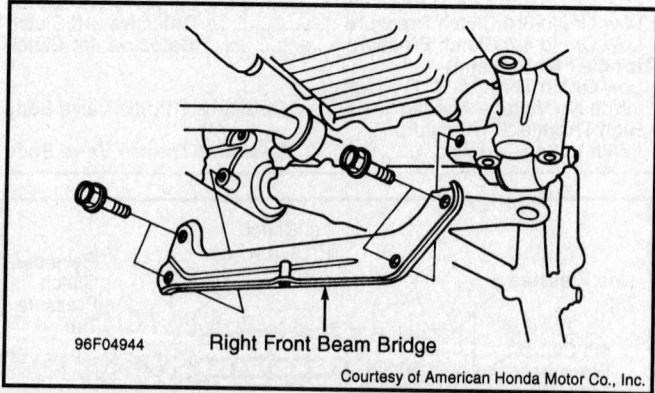

Fig. 9: Removing Right Front Beam Bridge (3.2L TL)

4) Ensure upper mounting bolt is installed on differential assembly. Bolt must be installed before installing differential assembly. *See Fig. 10.* Install differential assembly using NEW "O" ring on end of inner tube at the oil pan.

5) Install shim and differential assembly mounting bolts. Tighten differential assembly mounting bolt at the shim area first. Tighten all differential assembly mounting bolts to specification.

6) On 3.5RL models, install mount brackets and remove chain hoist. Install lower engine mount stop bolts. On all models, apply high-temperature grease on splines on extension shaft. Install NEW set ring on end of extension shaft so ends of set ring are at 12 o'clock position.

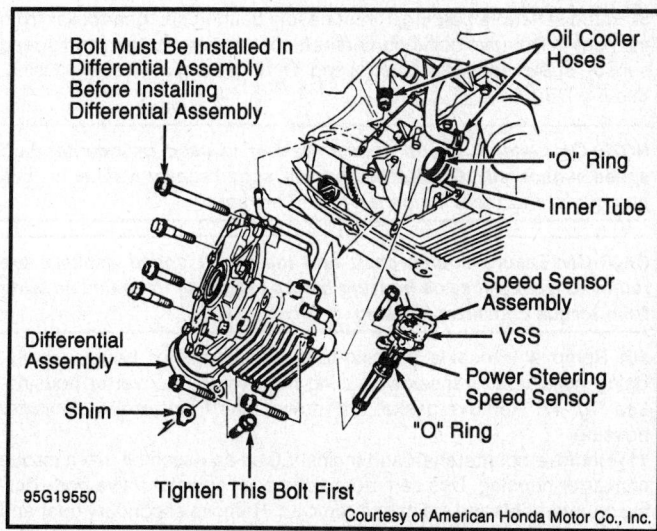

Fig. 10: *Identifying Differential Assembly, Oil Cooler Hoses & Speed Sensor Assembly (Legend, Others Are Similar)*

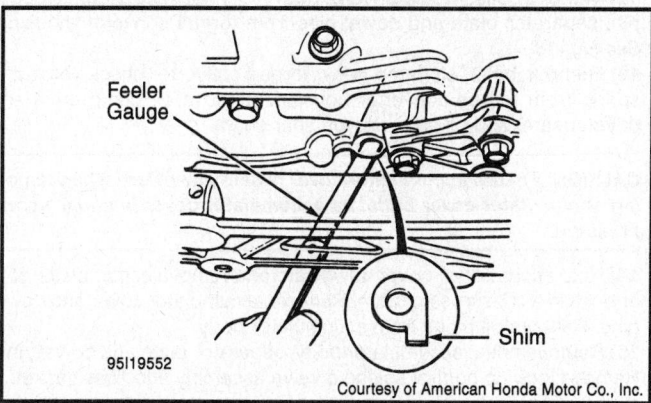

Fig. 11: *Determining Shim Thickness*

7) Using Extension Shaft Installer (07MAF-PY40100), install extension shaft. *See Fig. 12.* Ensure extension shaft locks into the secondary gear. Fill cavity on secondary gear around extension shaft with high-temperature grease.

8) Apply thread sealant on threads of sealing bolt. Install and tighten sealing bolt to specification. Install secondary cover.

9) On 3.5RL models, install breather tube in clamp and install right exhaust manifold cover. Install power steering pump. Install air cleaner housing. On all models, using NEW "O" ring, install speed sensor assembly. Install and tighten speed sensor assembly bolt to specification. Reconnect speed sensor assembly connector.

10) On 3.2TL models, install right front beam bridge. *See Fig. 9.* On all models, install lower plate. Install and tighten lower plate and steering gear bolts to specification. On Legend models, reconnect oil cooler coolant hoses.

11) On all models, install axle shafts and intermediate shaft using proper procedure. See appropriate article in AXLE SHAFTS & TRANSFER CASES section.

12) Fill differential assembly with 80W-90 (API GL5) hypoid gear oil. Use NEW seal washer when installing differential assembly oil filler plug. Tighten differential assembly oil filler plug to specification.

13) On Legend models, when refilling cooling system, open air bleeder bolt, located on upper radiator hosing housing on the engine. Fill cooling system until coolant flows from air bleeder bolt. Tighten air bleeder bolt to specification. Finish filling cooling system.

14) On all models, reconnect negative battery cable. To enter radio anti-theft code, turn radio on. When "CODE" is displayed on radio, re-enter anti-theft code by using the radio station preset buttons.

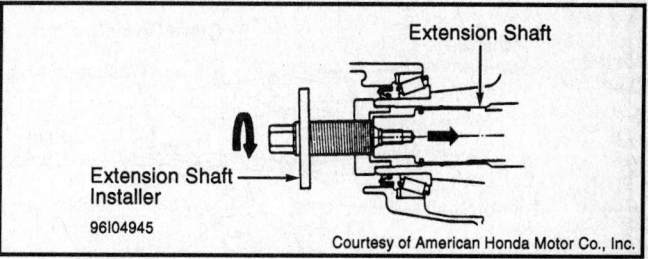

Fig. 12: *Installing Extension Shaft*

ELECTRICAL COMPONENTS

See ACURA MPYA, M5DA & M5HA ELECTRONIC CONTROLS article.

TRANSAXLE ASSEMBLY

See appropriate AUTOMATIC TRANSMISSION REMOVAL article in TRANSMISSION SERVICING section.

LOWER VALVE BODY ASSEMBLY

NOTE: *Lower valve body assembly consists of main valve body, secondary valve body, throttle valve body, linear solenoid, shift control solenoid valves and oil pass body.*

Removal – 1) Raise and support vehicle. Drain fluid by removing drain plug and seal washer from rear of transaxle. *See Fig. 13.*
2) Remove cable cover. Remove control lever from control shaft. Remove bolt and connector stopper. Disconnect electrical connector from transaxle sub-harness.
3) Remove bolts, oil pan, gasket, fluid strainer and "O" ring. Remove lower valve body assembly-to-transaxle case bolts. Remove lower valve body assembly.

NOTE: *If necessary to disassemble lower valve body assembly, see LOWER VALVE BODY ASSEMBLY under COMPONENT DISASSEMBLY & REASSEMBLY.*

Installation – 1) To install, reverse removal procedure using NEW "O" ring, gasket and bolt lock. Ensure manual valve engages with control shaft.
2) Tighten all bolts to specification. See TORQUE SPECIFICATIONS. Bend tabs over on bolt lock on control lever. Install NEW seal washer on drain plug. Tighten drain plug to specification.

TORQUE CONVERTER

Torque converter consists of pump, turbine and stator assembled as a unit. Torque converter cannot be serviced and must be replaced if defective.

NOTE: *For torque converter stall speed test, see TORQUE CONVERTER STALL SPEED TEST under TESTING.*

TRANSAXLE DISASSEMBLY

VALVE BODIES & INTERNAL COMPONENTS

1) Disconnect electrical connector from transaxle sub-harness. Remove control lever from control shaft. Remove bolt and connector stopper. *See Fig. 13.*
2) Remove bolts, oil pan, gasket, fluid strainer and "O" ring. Remove bolts and lower valve body assembly. Remove transaxle sub-harness, joint bolts, seal washer and cooler pipes. *See Fig. 15.*
3) Remove sealing bolt from rear cover. Remove snap ring from ball bearing on end of countershaft.

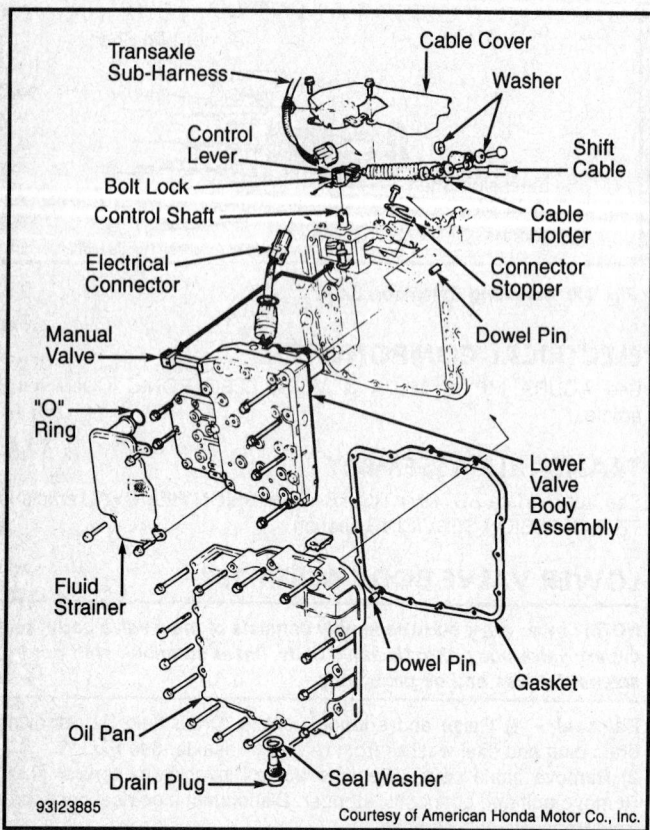

Fig. 13: Identifying Lower Valve Body Assembly & Components

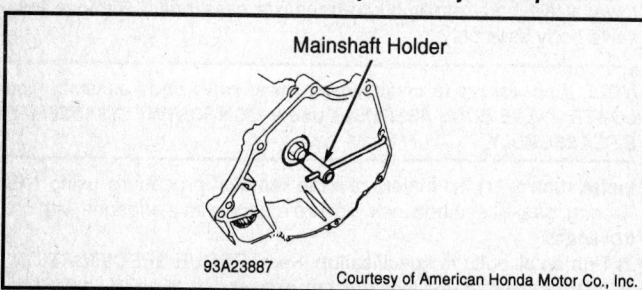

Fig. 14: Installing Mainshaft Holder

4) Remove rear cover, oil pipes, "O" rings and gasket. Install Mainshaft Holder (07924-PJ4010A) on mainshaft to secure mainshaft. *See Fig. 14.* Engage parking pawl with parking gear.

5) Using hammer and chisel, cut lock tabs on countershaft and mainshaft lock nuts and pry lock tab upward. Remove countershaft and mainshaft lock nuts and washers.

NOTE: Countershaft lock nut has left-hand thread.

6) Remove mainshaft holder. Remove washer, ball bearing, mainshaft reverse gear, distance collar, disc spring from mainshaft. Remove washer, ball bearing, thrust washer, thrust needle bearing and countershaft reverse gear from countershaft. Remove thrust needle bearing, needle bearing, gear collar, reverse clutch, disc spring and distance collar from countershaft. *See Fig. 15.*

7) Remove 2nd clutch assembly from mainshaft. Remove parking pawl shaft sleeve, parking pawl, parking pawl spring and parking pawl shaft. Remove parking gear from countershaft.

8) Remove thrust washer, thrust needle bearing and mainshaft 2nd gear as an assembly from mainshaft. *See Fig. 15.* Remove thrust needle bearing, thrust washer, 2nd gear one-way clutch and countershaft 2nd gear as an assembly from countershaft.

9) Remove needle bearing, thrust needle bearing and gear collar from mainshaft. Remove bolt, countershaft speed sensor, mainshaft speed sensor, speed sensor washer(s) and "O" rings from transaxle housing. *See Fig. 16.*

NOTE: On Legend, speed sensor washer is used on countershaft speed sensor only. On all other models, speed sensor washer is used on countershaft and mainshaft speed sensors.

CAUTION: Ensure countershaft and mainshaft speed sensors are removed from transaxle housing before removing transaxle housing from torque converter housing.

10) Remove transaxle housing-to-torque converter housing bolts. Using puller, pull transaxle housing from torque converter housing. *See Fig. 17.* Remove gasket and dowel pins from torque converter housing.

11) Remove countershaft and mainshaft as an assembly from torque converter housing. Use care not to damage regulator valve body during countershaft and mainshaft removal. Remove secondary gear and extension shaft as an assembly from torque converter housing. *See Fig. 16.*

12) Remove bolts, regulator valve body, "O" ring, stator shaft, stopper pin, separator plate and dowel pins from torque converter housing. *See Fig. 18.*

13) Remove bolts, oil pump body, torque converter check valve and spring from torque converter housing. Remove oil pump drive and driven gears, and oil pump driven gear shaft.

CAUTION: Ensure accumulator cover is held downward when removing accumulator cover bolts, as accumulator cover is under spring pressure.

14) Hold accumulator cover downward and remove accumulator cover bolts in a crisscross pattern. Remove accumulator cover and dowel pins. Remove oil pipes from accumulator body.

15) Remove bolts, accumulator body, separator plate and dowel pins. Remove lock-up control solenoid valve assembly and filter-gasket.

COMPONENT DISASSEMBLY & REASSEMBLY

LOWER VALVE BODY ASSEMBLY

Disassembly – 1) Remove flange nuts and disconnect wiring harness from linear solenoid. Remove throttle valve body with linear solenoid, separator plate, dowel pins and filter. *See Fig. 19.*

2) Remove wiring harness clamp. Remove shift control solenoid valves and "O" rings. Remove 1st and 2nd accumulator covers, "O" rings and springs. Mark spring location for reassembly reference.

3) Remove secondary valve body, filters, separator plate and dowel pins from main valve body. Use care not to lose check balls from main valve body. Remove oil pass body, separator plate and dowel pins from main valve body.

Cleaning & Inspection – Clean components with solvent and dry with compressed air. Inspect components for damage. Replace components if necessary. For testing of linear solenoid, see THROTTLE VALVE BODY under COMPONENT DISASSEMBLY & REASSEMBLY. For testing of shift control solenoid valves, see ACURA MPYA, M5DA & M5HA ELECTRONIC CONTROLS article.

Reassembly – 1) Coat all components with Dexron-II ATF. To reassemble, reverse disassembly procedure using NEW filters and NEW "O" rings.

2) Ensure check balls are installed in proper areas of main valve body. *See Fig. 19.* Ensure all filters are installed in proper direction.

3) Ensure proper length bolts are installed in designated areas. *See Fig. 20.* Tighten all bolts and flange nuts to specification. See TORQUE SPECIFICATIONS.

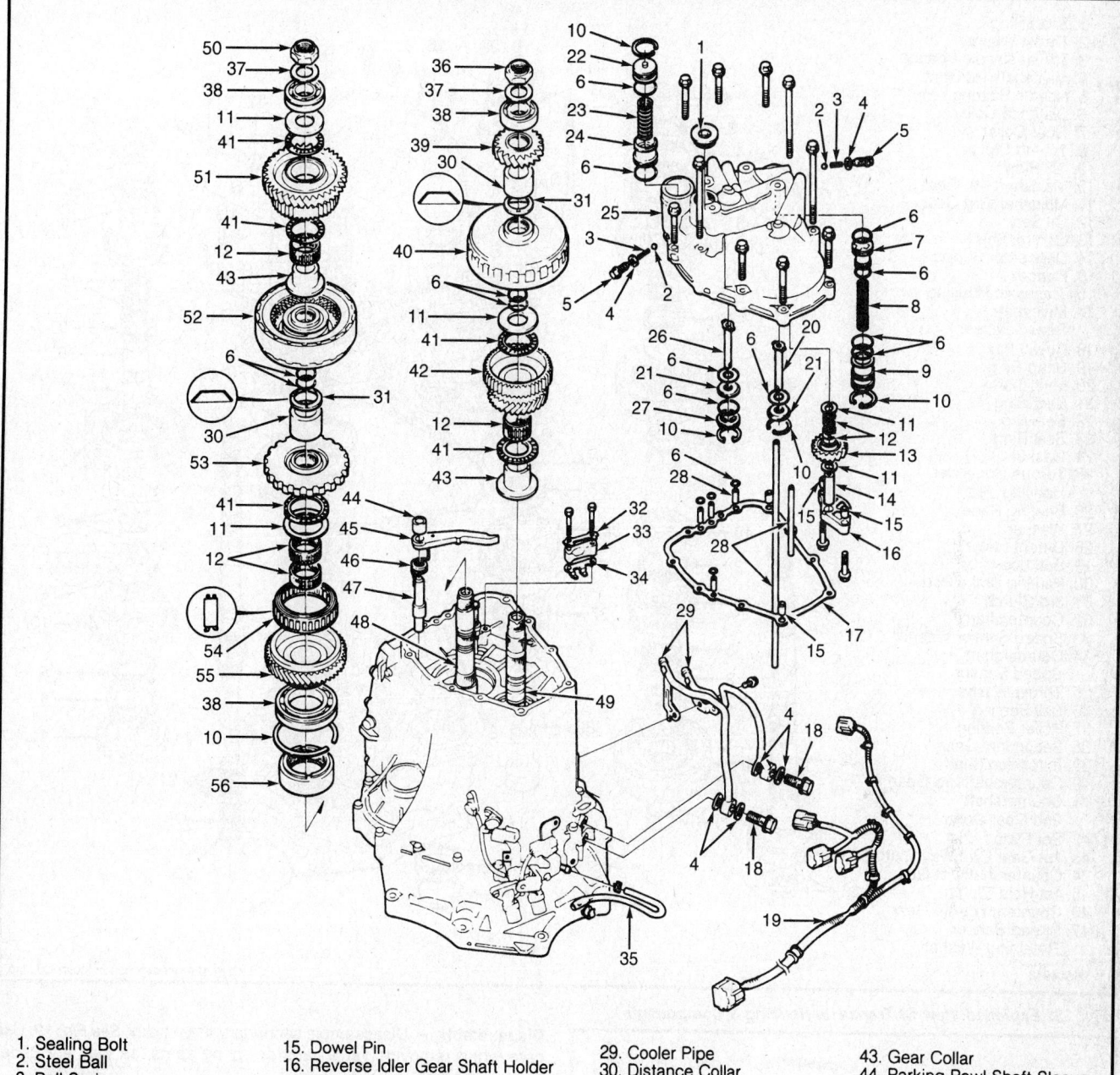

1. Sealing Bolt
2. Steel Ball
3. Ball Spring
4. Seal Washer
5. Ball Retaining Bolt
6. "O" Ring
7. Reverse Accumulator Piston
8. Reverse Accumulator Spring
9. Reverse Accumulator Sleeve
10. Snap Ring
11. Thrust Washer
12. Needle Bearing
13. Reverse Idler Gear
14. Reverse Idler Gear Shaft

15. Dowel Pin
16. Reverse Idler Gear Shaft Holder
17. Gasket
18. Joint Bolt
19. Transaxle Sub-Harness
20. 2nd Clutch Feedpipe
21. Feedpipe Guide
22. 1st-Hold Accumulator Sleeve
23. 1st-Hold Accumulator Spring
24. 1st-Hold Accumulator Piston
25. Rear Cover
26. Reverse Clutch Feedpipe
27. Oil Feed Guide
28. Oil Pipe

29. Cooler Pipe
30. Distance Collar
31. Disc Spring
32. Lock Plate
33. Parking Brake Rod Holder
34. Parking Brake Rod Guide
35. Breather Pipe
36. Mainshaft Lock Nut
37. Washer
38. Ball Bearing
39. Mainshaft Reverse Gear
40. 2nd Clutch
41. Thrust Needle Bearing
42. Mainshaft 2nd Gear

43. Gear Collar
44. Parking Pawl Shaft Sleeve
45. Parking Pawl
46. Parking Pawl Spring
47. Parking Pawl Shaft
48. Countershaft
49. Mainshaft
50. Countershaft Lock Nut
51. Countershaft Reverse Gear
52. Reverse Clutch
53. Parking Gear
54. 2nd Gear One-Way Clutch
55. Countershaft 2nd Gear
56. One-Way Clutch Hub

95J19553

Courtesy of American Honda Motor Co., Inc.

Fig. 15: *Exploded View Of Rear Cover & Components*

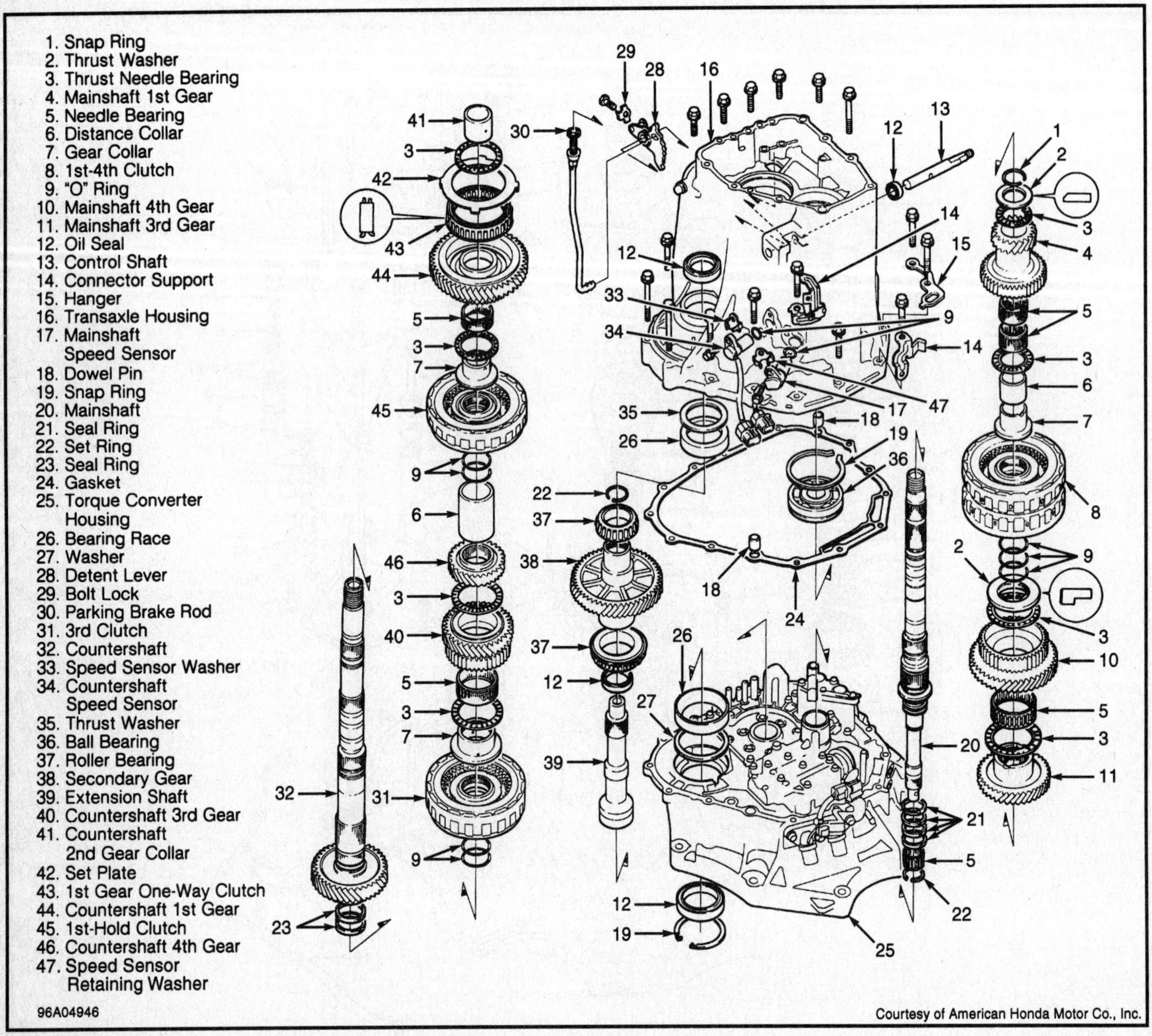

AUTOMATIC TRANSMISSIONS
Acura MPYA, M5DA & M5HA (Cont.)

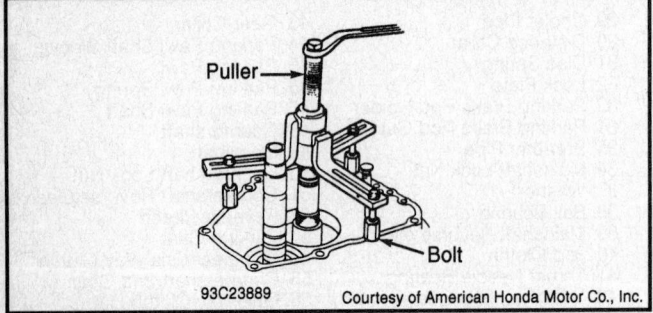

1. Snap Ring
2. Thrust Washer
3. Thrust Needle Bearing
4. Mainshaft 1st Gear
5. Needle Bearing
6. Distance Collar
7. Gear Collar
8. 1st-4th Clutch
9. "O" Ring
10. Mainshaft 4th Gear
11. Mainshaft 3rd Gear
12. Oil Seal
13. Control Shaft
14. Connector Support
15. Hanger
16. Transaxle Housing
17. Mainshaft
    Speed Sensor
18. Dowel Pin
19. Snap Ring
20. Mainshaft
21. Seal Ring
22. Set Ring
23. Seal Ring
24. Gasket
25. Torque Converter
    Housing
26. Bearing Race
27. Washer
28. Detent Lever
29. Bolt Lock
30. Parking Brake Rod
31. 3rd Clutch
32. Countershaft
33. Speed Sensor Washer
34. Countershaft
    Speed Sensor
35. Thrust Washer
36. Ball Bearing
37. Roller Bearing
38. Secondary Gear
39. Extension Shaft
40. Countershaft 3rd Gear
41. Countershaft
    2nd Gear Collar
42. Set Plate
43. 1st Gear One-Way Clutch
44. Countershaft 1st Gear
45. 1st-Hold Clutch
46. Countershaft 4th Gear
47. Speed Sensor
    Retaining Washer

96A04946

Courtesy of American Honda Motor Co., Inc.

Fig. 16: *Exploded View Of Transaxle Housing & Components*

93C23889   Courtesy of American Honda Motor Co., Inc.

Fig. 17: *Removing Transaxle Housing*

SECONDARY VALVE BODY

CAUTION: *When disassembling secondary valve body, place valve body components in order and mark spring locations for reassembly reference. DO NOT use force to remove components. Note direction of valve cap installation before removing valve cap from secondary valve body.*

Disassembly – Disassemble secondary valve body. *See Fig. 19.* Use care when removing valve caps or spring seats, as they are under spring pressure.

Cleaning & Inspection – **1)** Clean components with solvent and dry with compressed air. Replace secondary valve body if any parts are worn or damaged.

2) Ensure all valves slide freely in bores. If valves do not slide freely, polish burrs or rough areas using No. 600 sandpaper soaked in ATF. Thoroughly clean secondary valve body and components if polishing was needed.

3) Ensure spring free length is within specification. See SPRING SPECIFICATIONS table. Replace springs if not within specification.

Reassembly – Coat all components and bores with Dexron-II ATF. To reassemble, reverse disassembly procedure using NEW "O" rings and NEW filters. Ensure all components are installed in correct location and filters are installed in proper direction. *See Fig. 21.*

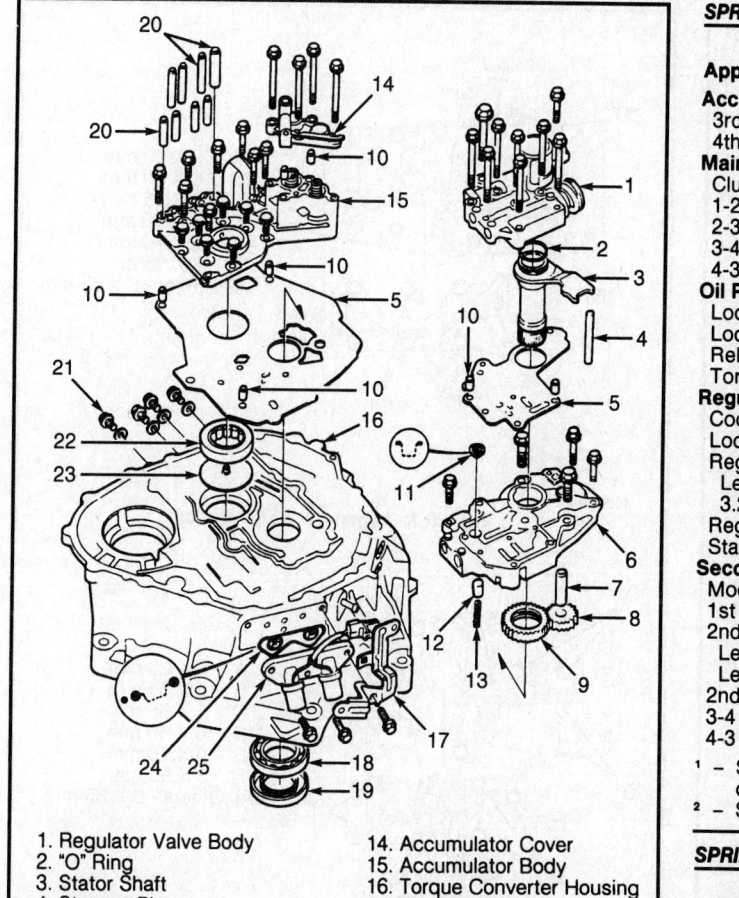

1. Regulator Valve Body
2. "O" Ring
3. Stator Shaft
4. Stopper Pin
5. Separator Plate
6. Oil Pump Body
7. Oil Pump Driven Gear Shaft
8. Oil Pump Driven Gear
9. Oil Pump Drive Gear
10. Dowel Pin
11. Filter
12. Torque Converter Check Valve
13. Torque Converter Check Valve Spring
14. Accumulator Cover
15. Accumulator Body
16. Torque Converter Housing
17. Connector Holder
18. Ball Bearing
19. Oil Seal
20. Oil Pipe
21. Pressure Tap Plug & Seal Washer
22. Needle Bearing
23. Oil Guide Plate
24. Filter-Gasket
25. Lock-Up Control Solenoid Valve Assembly

95B19555

Courtesy of American Honda Motor Co., Inc.

Fig. 18: Exploded View Of Torque Converter Housing & Components

MAIN VALVE BODY

CAUTION: When disassembling main valve body, place valve body components in order and mark spring locations for reassembly reference. DO NOT use force to remove components. DO NOT use magnet to remove check balls, as check balls may become magnetized. Note direction of valve cap installation before removing valve cap from main valve body.

Disassembly – Disassemble main valve body. *See Fig. 22.* Use care when removing valve caps or spring seats, as they are under spring pressure.

Cleaning & Inspection – 1) Clean components with solvent and dry with compressed air. Replace main valve body if any parts are worn or damaged.

2) Ensure all valves slide freely in bores. If valves do not slide freely, polish burrs or rough areas using No. 600 sandpaper soaked in ATF. Thoroughly clean main valve body and components if polishing was needed.

3) Ensure spring free length is within specification. See SPRING SPECIFICATIONS table. Replace springs if not within specification.

SPRING SPECIFICATIONS (LEGEND & 3.2TL)

Application	Free Length In. (mm)
Accumulator Body	
3rd Accumulator Spring	3.087 (78.40)
4th Accumulator Spring	3.181 (80.80)
Main Valve Body	
Clutch Pressure Control Valve Spring	1.350 (34.30)
1-2 Shift Valve Spring	2.185 (55.50)
2-3 Shift Valve Spring	1.657 (42.10)
3-4 Shift Valve Spring	1.657 (42.10)
4-3 Kickdown Valve Spring	2.020 (51.30)
Oil Pump Body	
Lock-Up Control Valve Spring	[1]
Lock-Up Timing Valve Spring	2.409 (61.20)
Relief Valve Spring	2.224 (56.50)
Torque Converter Check Valve Spring	1.646 (41.80)
Regulator Valve Body	
Cooler Relief Valve Spring	1.843 (46.80)
Lock-Up Shift Valve Spring	2.902 (73.70)
Regulator Valve Spring "A"	
Legend	3.406 (86.50)
3.2L TL	3.362 (85.40)
Regulator Valve Spring "B"	1.693 (43.00)
Stator Reaction Spring	1.193 (30.30)
Secondary Valve Body	
Modulator Valve Spring	[2]
1st Accumulator Spring	2.972 (75.50)
2nd Accumulator Spring "A"	
Legend & 3.2L TL	3.807 (96.70)
Legend Coupe	3.689 (93.70)
2nd Accumulator Spring "B"	3.150 (80.00)
3-4 Orifice Control Valve Spring	1.953 (49.60)
4-3 Shift Timing Valve Spring	1.378 (35.00)

[1] – Spring free length may be 1.429" (36.30 mm), 1.476" (37.50 mm) or 1.516" (38.50 mm).
[2] – Spring free length may be 1.205" (30.60 mm) or 1.299" (33.00 mm).

SPRING SPECIFICATIONS (3.5RL)

Application	Free Length In. (mm)
Accumulator Body	
3rd Accumulator Spring	2.854 (72.50)
4th Accumulator Spring	2.661 (67.60)
Main Valve Body	
Main Orifice Control Valve Spring	1.681 (42.70)
1-2 Shift Valve Spring	2.185 (55.50)
2-3 Shift Valve Spring	1.657 (42.10)
3-4 Shift Valve Spring	1.657 (42.10)
4-3 Kickdown Valve Spring	1.756 (44.60)
Oil Pump Body	
Lock-Up Control Valve Spring	[1]
Lock-Up Timing Valve Spring	2.409 (61.20)
Relief Valve Spring	2.224 (56.50)
Torque Converter Check Valve Spring	1.406 (35.70)
Regulator Valve Body	
Cooler Relief Valve Spring	1.331 (33.80)
Lock-Up Shift Valve Spring	2.902 (73.70)
Regulator Valve Spring "A"	3.224 (81.90)
Regulator Valve Spring "B"	1.693 (43.00)
Stator Reaction Spring	1.193 (30.30)
Secondary Valve Body	
Line Pressure Control Valve Spring	.949 (24.10)
Modulator Valve Spring	1.087 (27.60)
1st Accumulator Spring	3.280 (83.30)
2nd Accumulator Spring "A"	3.441 (87.40)
3-4 Orifice Control Valve Spring	1.878 (47.70)
4-3 Shift Timing Valve Spring	1.378 (35.00)

[1] – Spring free length may be 1.520" (38.60 mm), 1.547" (39.30 mm) or 1.575" (40.00 mm).

NOTE: On 3.5RL models the clutch pressure control valve is referred to as the main orifice control valve. The main orifice control valve uses a spring seat instead of a valve cap.

Reassembly – Coat all components and bores with Dexron-II ATF. To reassemble, reverse disassembly procedure using NEW filters. Ensure all components are installed in correct location and filters are installed in proper direction. *See Fig. 22.*

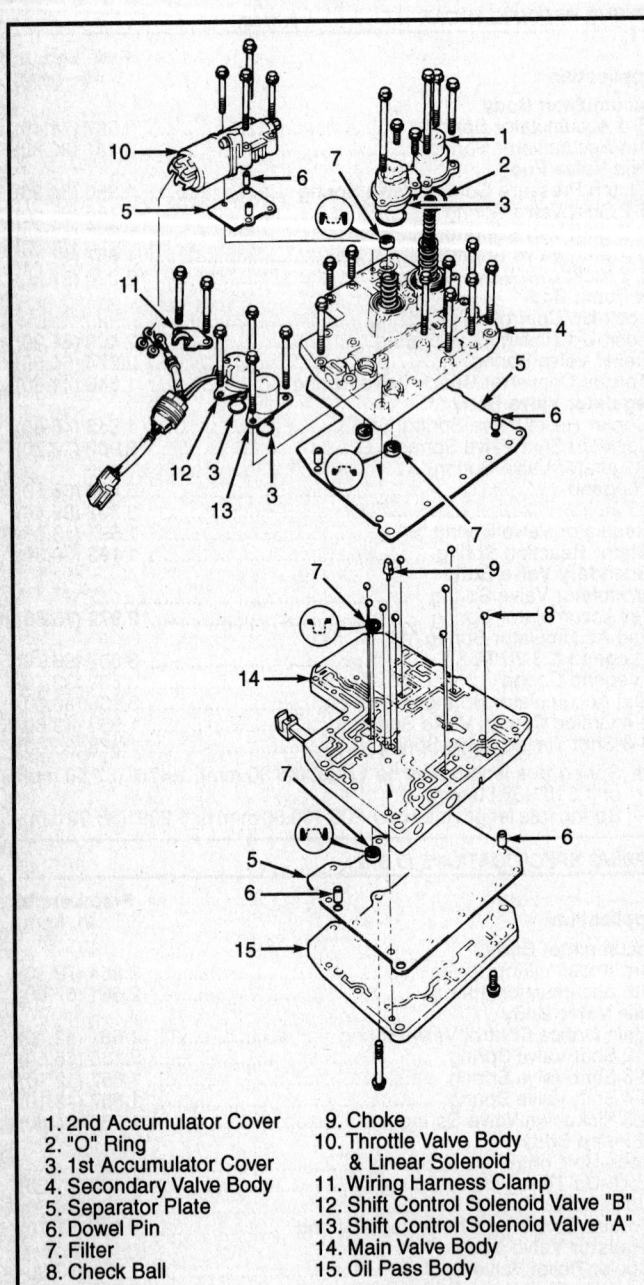

1. 2nd Accumulator Cover
2. "O" Ring
3. 1st Accumulator Cover
4. Secondary Valve Body
5. Separator Plate
6. Dowel Pin
7. Filter
8. Check Ball
9. Choke
10. Throttle Valve Body & Linear Solenoid
11. Wiring Harness Clamp
12. Shift Control Solenoid Valve "B"
13. Shift Control Solenoid Valve "A"
14. Main Valve Body
15. Oil Pass Body

95C19556   Courtesy of American Honda Motor Co., Inc.

Fig. 19: Exploded View Of Lower Valve Body Assembly

REGULATOR VALVE BODY

CAUTION: *Regulator spring cap is under spring pressure. Ensure regulator spring cap is held downward when removing regulator valve body lock bolt.*

Disassembly – Hold regulator spring cap downward. Remove regulator valve body lock bolt. Slowly remove regulator spring cap and components from regulator valve body. See Fig. 23.
Cleaning & Inspection – 1) Clean components with solvent and dry with compressed air. Replace regulator valve body if any parts are worn or damaged.
2) Ensure all valves slide freely in bores. If valves do not slide freely, polish burrs or rough areas using No. 600 sandpaper soaked in ATF. Thoroughly clean regulator valve body and components if polishing was needed.

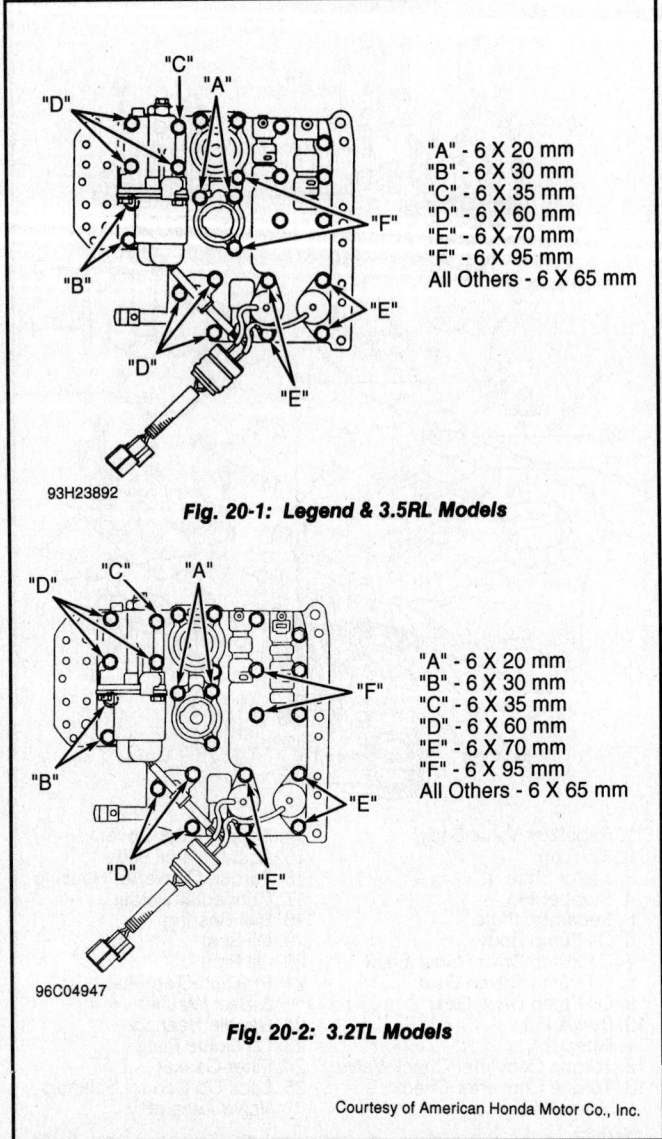

"A" - 6 X 20 mm
"B" - 6 X 30 mm
"C" - 6 X 35 mm
"D" - 6 X 60 mm
"E" - 6 X 70 mm
"F" - 6 X 95 mm
All Others - 6 X 65 mm

93H23892

Fig. 20-1: Legend & 3.5RL Models

"A" - 6 X 20 mm
"B" - 6 X 30 mm
"C" - 6 X 35 mm
"D" - 6 X 60 mm
"E" - 6 X 70 mm
"F" - 6 X 95 mm
All Others - 6 X 65 mm

96C04947

Fig. 20-2: 3.2TL Models

Courtesy of American Honda Motor Co., Inc.

Fig. 20: Identifying Lower Valve Body Assembly Bolts

3) Ensure spring free length is within specification. See SPRING SPECIFICATIONS table. Replace springs if not within specification.
Reassembly – 1) Coat all components and bores with Dexron-II ATF. To reassemble, reverse disassembly procedure. Ensure all components are installed in correct location. See Fig. 23.
2) Ensure hole in regulator spring cap aligns with hole for regulator valve body lock bolt before tightening lock bolt. Tighten regulator valve body lock bolt to specification. See TORQUE SPECIFICATIONS.

ACCUMULATOR BODY

NOTE: *3rd and 4th accumulator have the same diameter pistons. On 3.5RL models, 3rd accumulator piston has a spring in bottom of piston.*

Disassembly – Disassemble accumulator body. See Fig. 24.
Cleaning & Inspection – 1) Clean components with solvent and dry with compressed air. Replace accumulator body if any parts are worn or damaged.
2) Ensure spring free length is within specification. See SPRING SPECIFICATIONS table. Replace springs if not within specification.
Reassembly – Coat all components and bores with ATF. To reassemble, reverse disassembly procedure using NEW "O" rings.

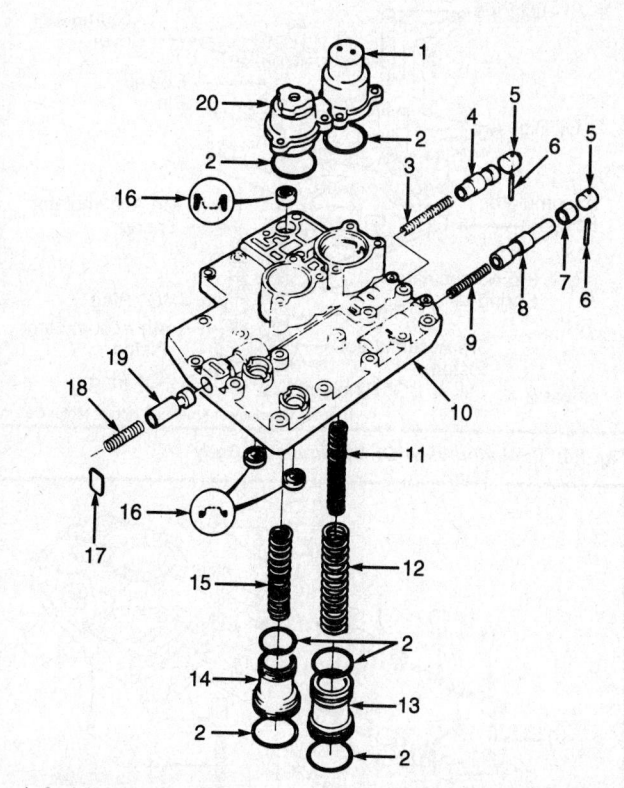

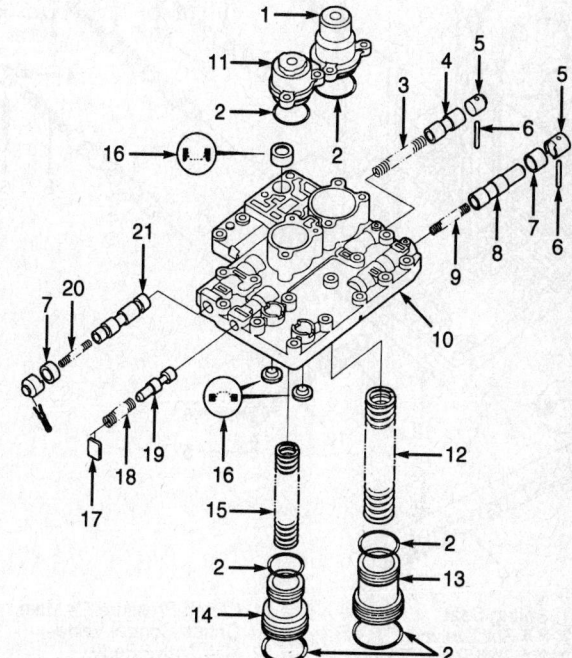

1. 2nd Accumulator Cover
2. "O" Ring
3. 3-4 Orifice Control Valve Spring
4. 3-4 Orifice Control Valve
5. Valve Cap
6. Roller
7. Valve Sleeve
8. 4-3 Shift Timing Valve
9. 4-3 Shift Timing Valve Spring
10. Secondary Valve Body

11. 2nd Accumulator Spring "B"
12. 2nd Accumulator Spring "A"
13. 2nd Accumulator Piston
14. 1st Accumulator Piston
15. 1st Accumulator Spring
16. Filter
17. Spring Seat
18. Modulator Valve Spring
19. Modulator Valve
20. 1st Accumulator Cover

95D19557

Fig. 21-1: Legend & 3.2TL Models

1. 2nd Accumulator Cover
2. "O" Ring
3. 3-4 Orifice Control Valve Spring
4. 3-4 Orifice Control Valve
5. Valve Cap
6. Roller
7. Valve Sleeve
8. 4-3 Shift Timing Valve
9. 4-3 Shift Timing Valve Spring
10. Secondary Valve Body
11. 1st Accumulator Cover

12. 2nd Accumulator Spring "A"
13. 2nd Accumulator Piston
14. 1st Accumulator Piston
15. 1st Accumulator Spring
16. Filter
17. Spring Seat
18. Modulator Valve Spring
19. Modulator Valve
20. Line Pressure Control Valve Spring
21. Line Pressure Control Valve

96E04948

Fig. 21-2: 3.5RL Models

Courtesy of American Honda Motor Co., Inc.

Fig. 21: Exploded View Of Secondary Valve Body

OIL PUMP BODY

CAUTION: When disassembling oil pump body, place components in order and mark spring locations for reassembly reference. DO NOT use force to remove components. Note direction of valve cap installation before removing valve cap from oil pump body.

Disassembly – Disassemble oil pump body. *See Fig. 25.* Use care when removing valve caps or spring seats, as they are under spring pressure.

Cleaning & Inspection – **1)** Clean components with solvent and dry with compressed air. Replace oil pump body if any parts are worn or damaged.

2) Ensure all valves slide freely in bores. If valves do not slide freely, polish burrs or rough areas using No. 600 sandpaper soaked in ATF. Thoroughly clean oil pump body and components if polishing was needed.

3) Ensure spring free length is within specification. See SPRING SPECIFICATIONS table. Replace springs if not within specification.

4) Install oil pump gears and oil pump driven gear shaft in oil pump body. Ensure chamfered and grooved side of oil pump driven gear is facing upward (toward separator plate side of oil pump body).

5) Using feeler gauge, measure side clearance of both gears between tip of gear teeth and oil pump valve body. *See Fig. 26.* Replace oil pump gears and/or oil pump body if side clearance is not within specification. See OIL PUMP SPECIFICATIONS table.

6) Remove oil pump driven gear shaft. Place straightedge across oil pump body surface. Using feeler gauge, measure thrust clearance between oil pump gear and straightedge. Replace oil pump gears and/or oil pump body if thrust clearance is not within specification. See OIL PUMP SPECIFICATIONS table.

OIL PUMP SPECIFICATIONS

Application	In. (mm)
Side Clearance	
Oil Pump Drive Gear	.0083-.0104 (.210-.265)
Oil Pump Driven Gear	.0028-.0049 (.070-.125)
Thrust Clearance	
Standard	.001-.002 (.03-.05)
Wear Limit	.0028 (.070)

Reassembly – Coat components with Dexron-II ATF. To reassemble, reverse disassembly procedure using NEW filter. Ensure chamfered and grooved side of oil pump driven gear faces upward (toward separator plate side of oil pump body). Ensure filter is installed in proper direction. *See Fig. 25.*

AUTOMATIC TRANSMISSIONS
Acura MPYA, M5DA & M5HA (Cont.)

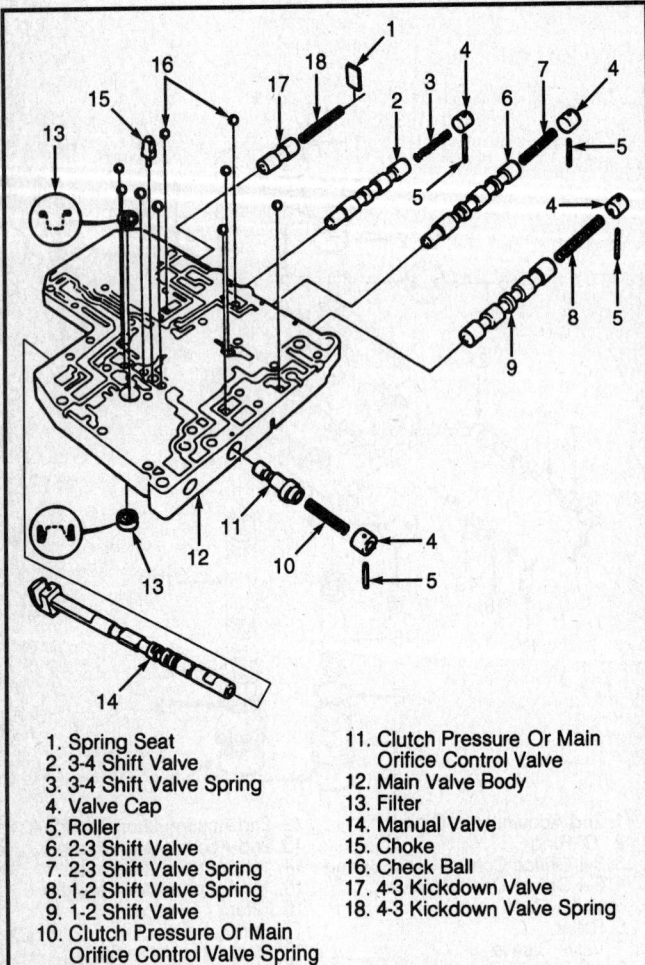

1. Spring Seat
2. 3-4 Shift Valve
3. 3-4 Shift Valve Spring
4. Valve Cap
5. Roller
6. 2-3 Shift Valve
7. 2-3 Shift Valve Spring
8. 1-2 Shift Valve Spring
9. 1-2 Shift Valve
10. Clutch Pressure Or Main Orifice Control Valve Spring
11. Clutch Pressure Or Main Orifice Control Valve
12. Main Valve Body
13. Filter
14. Manual Valve
15. Choke
16. Check Ball
17. 4-3 Kickdown Valve
18. 4-3 Kickdown Valve Spring

95E19558   Courtesy of American Honda Motor Co., Inc.

Fig. 22: Exploded View Of Main Valve Body

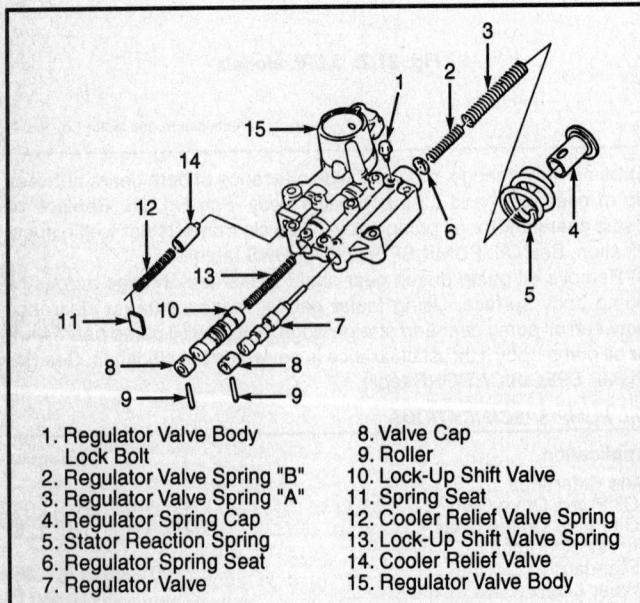

1. Regulator Valve Body Lock Bolt
2. Regulator Valve Spring "B"
3. Regulator Valve Spring "A"
4. Regulator Spring Cap
5. Stator Reaction Spring
6. Regulator Spring Seat
7. Regulator Valve
8. Valve Cap
9. Roller
10. Lock-Up Shift Valve
11. Spring Seat
12. Cooler Relief Valve Spring
13. Lock-Up Shift Valve Spring
14. Cooler Relief Valve
15. Regulator Valve Body

95F19559   Courtesy of American Honda Motor Co., Inc.

Fig. 23: Exploded View Of Regulator Valve Body

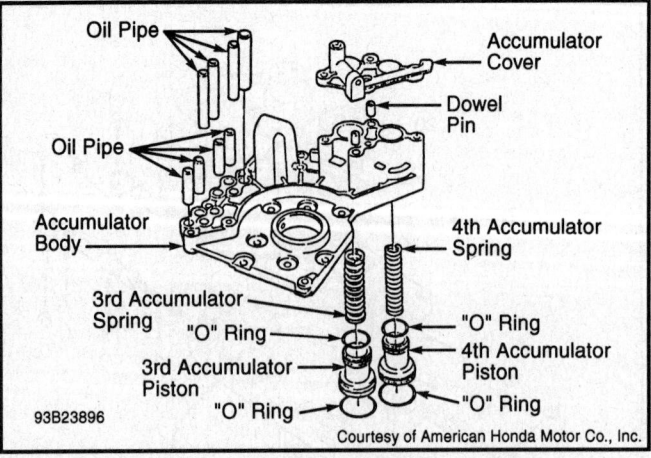

93B23896   Courtesy of American Honda Motor Co., Inc.

Fig. 24: Exploded View Of Accumulator Body

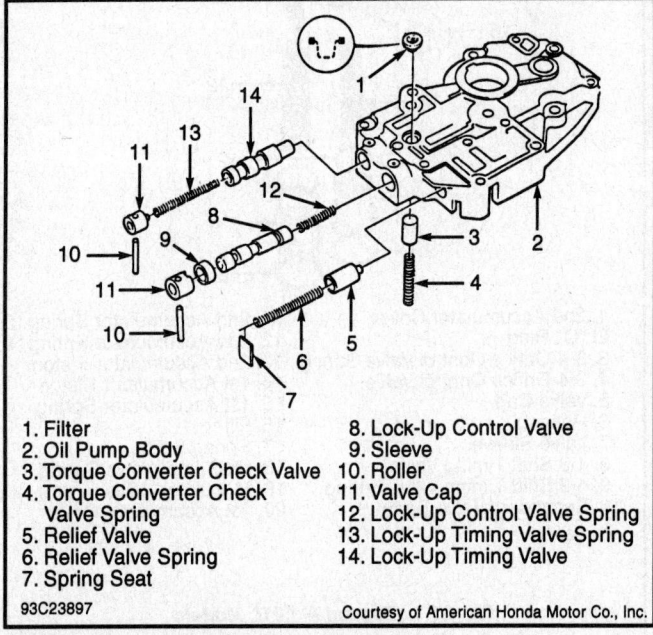

1. Filter
2. Oil Pump Body
3. Torque Converter Check Valve
4. Torque Converter Check Valve Spring
5. Relief Valve
6. Relief Valve Spring
7. Spring Seat
8. Lock-Up Control Valve
9. Sleeve
10. Roller
11. Valve Cap
12. Lock-Up Control Valve Spring
13. Lock-Up Timing Valve Spring
14. Lock-Up Timing Valve

93C23897   Courtesy of American Honda Motor Co., Inc.

Fig. 25: Exploded View Of Oil Pump Body

REVERSE & 1ST-HOLD ACCUMULATOR

Disassembly – 1) Remove snap ring, accumulator sleeve and accumulator spring from appropriate accumulator. See Fig. 27.
2) On Legend and 3.2TL models, remove ball retaining bolt, seal washer and spring near the accumulator from side of rear cover. DO NOT remove steel ball.

CAUTION: DO NOT place fingers over accumulator piston during removal. DO NOT apply more than 30 psi.

3) Place shop towel over accumulator piston. Apply light air pressure to oil passage in rear cover to force accumulator piston from rear cover.
Cleaning & Inspection – 1) Clean components with solvent and dry with compressed air. Replace components if worn or damaged.
2) Ensure spring free length is within specification. See REVERSE & 1ST-HOLD ACCUMULATOR SPRING SPECIFICATIONS table. Replace springs if not within specification.
Reassembly – Coat components with ATF. To reassemble, reverse disassembly procedure using NEW "O" rings and NEW seal washer. See Fig. 27. Tighten ball retaining bolts to specification. See TORQUE SPECIFICATIONS.

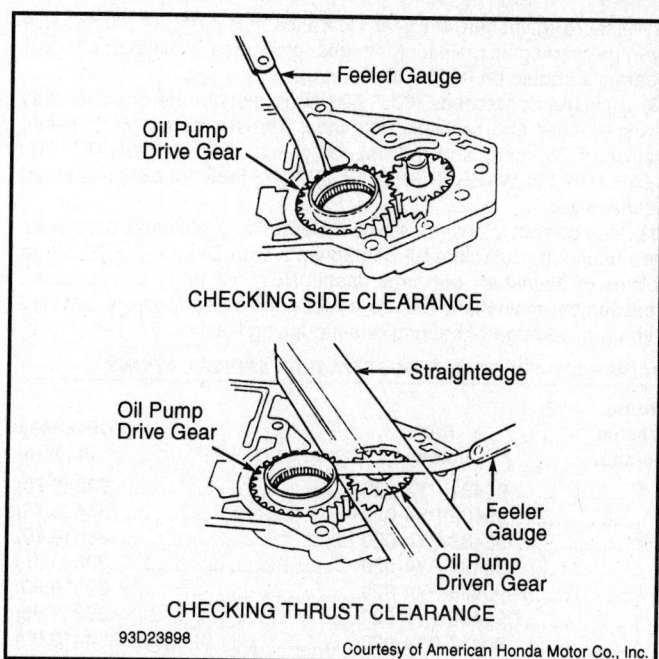

Fig. 26: Checking Oil Pump Clearances

REVERSE & 1ST-HOLD ACCUMULATOR SPRING SPECIFICATIONS

Application	Free Length In. (mm)
Reverse Accumulator Spring	
Legend & 3.2TL	4.547 (115.50)
3.5RL	4.823 (122.50)
1st-hold Accumulator Spring	
Legend & 3.2L TL	2.693 (68.40)
3.5RL	2.693 (68.40)
Ball Spring	.551 (14.00)

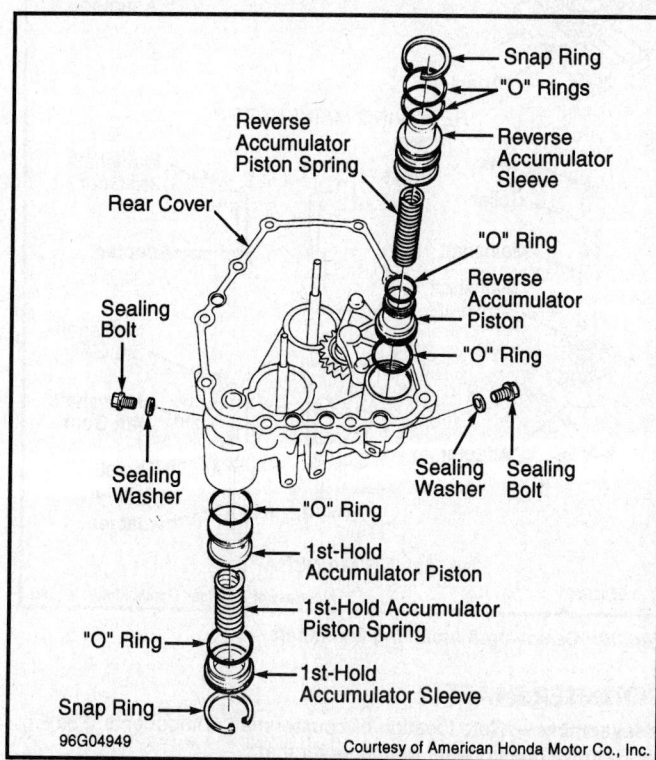

Fig. 27: Exploded View Reverse & 1st Hold Accumulator

REAR COVER

NOTE: Rear cover contains 2nd and reverse clutch feedpipes and reverse idler gear. See Fig. 15.

Disassembly – 1) To remove 2nd clutch feedpipe, remove snap ring, feedpipe guide, "O" rings and 2nd clutch feedpipe. See Fig. 15.
2) To remove reverse clutch feedpipe, remove snap ring, oil feed guide, "O" rings, feedpipe guide and reverse clutch feedpipe.
3) To remove reverse idler gear, remove bolts, reverse idle gear shaft holder and dowel pins. Remove reverse idler gear shaft, thrust washer, reverse idle gear, needle bearings and thrust washer.
Cleaning & Inspection – Clean components with solvent and dry with compressed air. Inspect components for damage. Inspect needle bearings for galling or rough movement.
Reassembly – 1) To reassemble reverse idler gear, coat components with Dexron-II ATF. Install thrust washers, needle bearings, reverse idler gear and reverse idler gear shaft. Ensure reverse idler gear is installed with offset area in correct direction. See Fig. 28.
2) Install reverse idler gear shaft holder. Install and tighten bolts to specification. See TORQUE SPECIFICATIONS.
3) To reassemble reverse and 2nd clutch feedpipes, reverse disassembly procedure using NEW "O" rings. Coat components with Dexron-II ATF before reassembly.

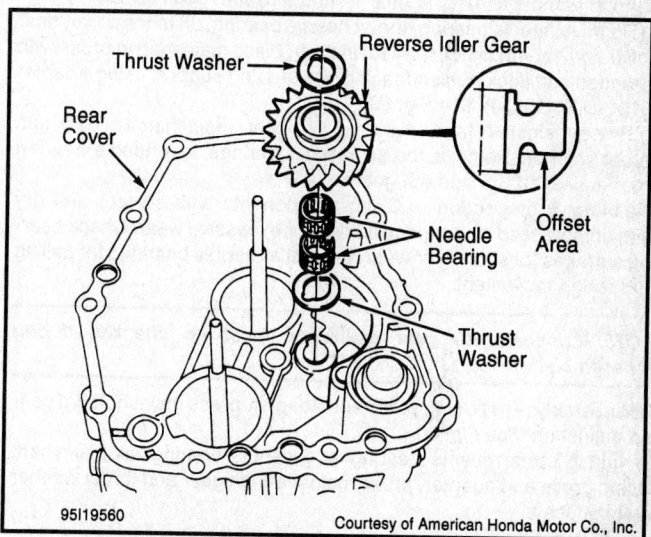

Fig. 28: Installing Reverse Idler Gear

THROTTLE VALVE BODY

NOTE: Throttle valve body cannot be disassembled. Only linear solenoid operation may be checked. Throttle valve body and linear solenoid must be replaced as an assembly.

1) To check linear solenoid operation, connect wiring harness to linear solenoid. Tighten flange nuts to specification. See TORQUE SPECIFICATIONS.
2) Connect positive battery terminal to Red wire and negative battery terminal to White wire of wiring harness. See Fig. 29.
3) Ensure throttle valve moves downward in throttle valve body by looking through passage on throttle valve body. If throttle valve moves downward with battery connected, linear solenoid is operating.
4) If throttle valve does not move, disconnect wiring harness at linear solenoid. Connect battery directly to linear solenoid.
5) If throttle valve now moves, replace wiring harness for linear solenoid. If linear solenoid still does not operate, replace linear solenoid and throttle valve body as an assembly.

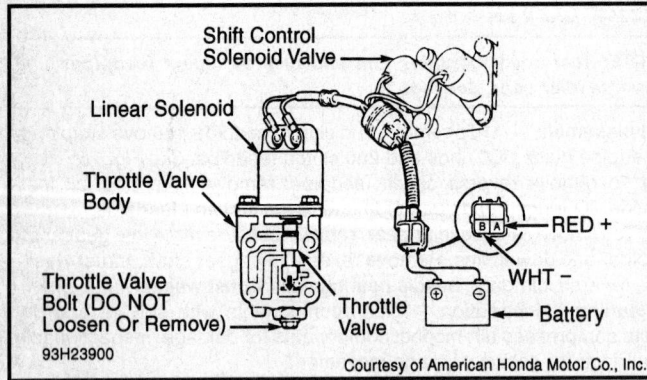

Fig. 29: Checking Linear Solenoid Operation

MAINSHAFT

NOTE: Mainshaft 3rd and 4th gears and thrust washer are a press-fit on the mainshaft and must be pressed from mainshaft.

Disassembly – 1) Remove snap ring, thrust washer, thrust needle bearing and mainshaft 1st gear from mainshaft. See Fig. 16.
2) Remove needle bearing, thrust needle bearing, distance collar, gear collar and 1st-4th clutch from mainshaft. Place mainshaft in press with threaded end (lock nut) end facing upward and support using Adapter (07MAD-PR90100). See Fig. 30.
3) Press mainshaft from mainshaft 3rd gear, mainshaft 4th gear and thrust washer. Remove thrust needle bearings and needle bearing from mainshaft 3rd and 4th gears.
Cleaning & Inspection – Clean components with solvent and dry with compressed air. Inspect splines for excessive wear. Check bearing surfaces for scoring or wear. Inspect all needle bearings for galling and rough movement.

NOTE: Mainshaft 4th gear clearance must be checked during reassembly.

Reassembly – 1) Using press and adapter, press mainshaft 3rd gear on mainshaft. See Fig. 30.
2) Install thrust needle bearing and needle bearing on mainshaft. Using press and adapter, press mainshaft 4th gear and thrust washer on mainshaft.

NOTE: Replace thrust washer if washer can be installed on mainshaft by-hand.

3) Remove mainshaft from press. Ensure mainshaft 4th gear rotates freely on mainshaft.
4) Install 1st-4th clutch, gear collar, distance collar, thrust washer and snap ring on mainshaft.

NOTE: DO NOT install thrust needle bearing, needle bearings, mainshaft 1st gear and thrust needle bearing on mainshaft at this time.

5) Remove ball bearing for mainshaft from transaxle housing. Install ball bearing on mainshaft.
6) Install gear collar, thrust washer and 2nd clutch on mainshaft. See Fig. 15. DO NOT install thrust needle bearings, needle bearings and mainshaft 2nd gear at this time.
7) Install disc spring, distance collar, mainshaft reverse gear, ball bearing, washer and used lock nut on mainshaft. Ensure disc spring is installed with largest side against 2nd clutch. Tighten lock nut to 22 ft. lbs. (30 N.m).
8) Move 1st-4th clutch against 4th clutch collar. Using feeler gauge, measure mainshaft 4th gear clearance between gear collar and 1st-4th clutch guide. See Fig. 31.

9) Measure mainshaft 4th gear clearance in 3 different places. Use average reading as mainshaft 4th gear clearance. Mainshaft 4th gear clearance should be 0-.003" (0-.08 mm).
10) If clearance exceeds .003" (.08 mm), install different thickness thrust washer and recheck clearance. Thrust washer fits between mainshaft 4th gear and the 1st-4th clutch. See MAINSHAFT 4TH GEAR THRUST WASHER SPECIFICATIONS table for available thrust washer sizes.
11) Once correct mainshaft 4th gear clearance is obtained, disassemble mainshaft. Lubricate all components with Dexron-II ATF. Wrap splines of mainshaft with tape. Install NEW "O" rings on mainshaft. Reassemble mainshaft. Ensure thrust needle bearings are installed with unrolled edge of bearing retainer facing washer.

MAINSHAFT 4TH GEAR THRUST WASHER SPECIFICATIONS

Thrust Washer Number	Part Number	Thickness In. (mm)
1	90431-PY4-020	.382 (9.70)
2	90432-PY4-020	.384 (9.75)
3	90433-PY4-020	.386 (9.80)
4	90434-PY4-020	.388 (9.85)
5	90435-PY4-020	.390 (9.90)
6	90436-PY4-020	.392 (9.95)
7	90437-PY4-020	.394 (10.00)

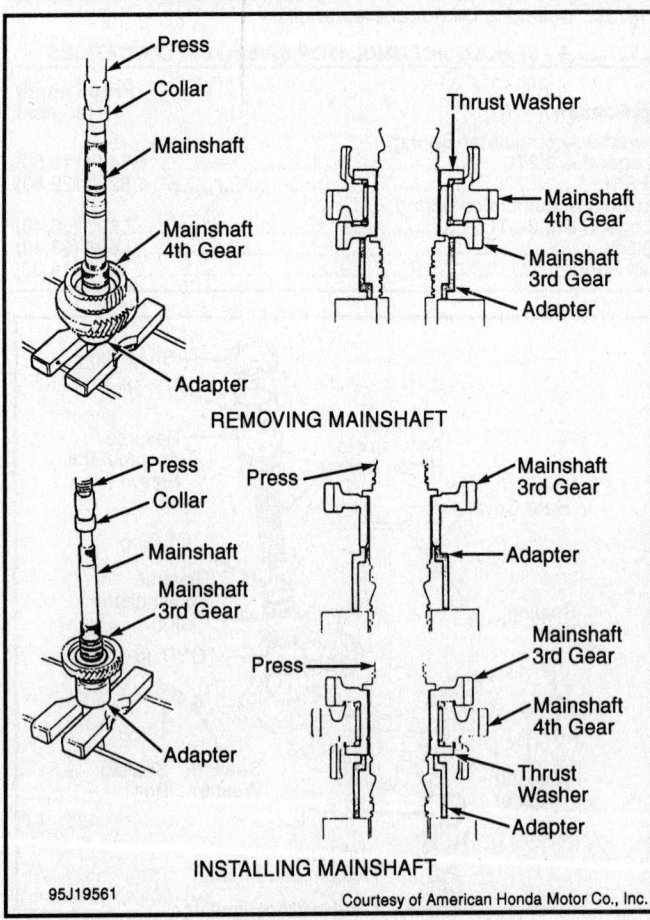

Fig. 30: Removing & Installing Mainshaft

COUNTERSHAFT

Disassembly – Note location of countershaft components. See Fig. 16. Remove components from countershaft.
Cleaning & Inspection – Clean components with solvent and dry with compressed air. Inspect splines for excessive wear. Check bear-

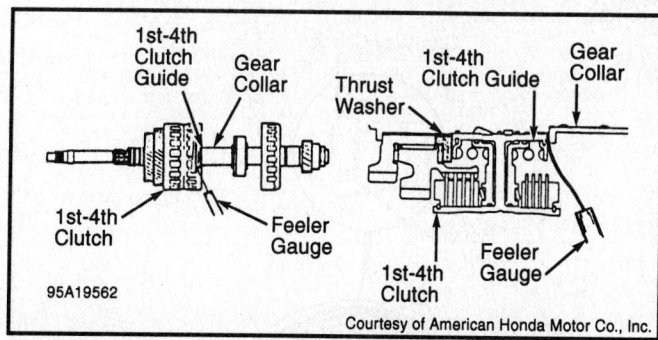

Fig. 31: Measuring Mainshaft 4th Gear Clearance

ing surfaces for scoring or wear. Inspect all needle bearings for galling and rough movement.

NOTE: Countershaft 2nd gear and 4th gear clearance must be checked during reassembly.

Reassembly – 1) Install components on countershaft without installing "O" rings on countershaft. See Figs. 15 and 16.
2) Install used lock nut on countershaft. Tighten lock nut to 22 ft. lbs. (30 N.m). To check countershaft 4th gear clearance, hold 1st-hold clutch against reverse clutch.
3) Using feeler gauge, measure countershaft 4th gear clearance between 1st-hold clutch and 1st-hold clutch distance collar (selective fit). See Fig. 32.
4) Countershaft 4th gear clearance should be 0-.003" (0-.08 mm). If countershaft 4th gear clearance exceeds .003" (.08 mm), install different thickness 1st-hold clutch distance collar and recheck clearance. See COUNTERSHAFT 1ST-HOLD CLUTCH DISTANCE COLLAR SPECIFICATIONS table for available distance collar sizes.

COUNTERSHAFT 1ST-HOLD CLUTCH DISTANCE COLLAR SPECIFICATIONS

Thrust Washer Number	Part Number	Thickness In. (mm)
1	90451-PY4-000	2.835 (72.00)
2	90452-PY4-000	2.837 (72.05)
3	90453-PY4-000	2.839 (72.10)
4	90454-PY4-000	2.841 (72.15)
5	90455-PY4-000	2.843 (72.20)
6	90456-PY4-000	2.844 (72.25)
7	90457-PY4-000	2.846 (72.30)
8	90458-PY4-000	2.848 (72.35)
9	90459-PY4-000	2.850 (72.40)
10	90460-PY4-000	2.852 (72.45)
11	90461-PY4-000	2.854 (72.50)

5) To check countershaft 2nd gear clearance, install dial indicator on countershaft so stem of dial indicator is resting against countershaft 2nd gear.
6) Measure countershaft 2nd gear clearance while holding countershaft 1st gear toward reverse clutch. Measure countershaft 2nd gear clearance in 3 different places.
7) Use average reading as countershaft 2nd gear clearance. Countershaft 2nd gear clearance should be .002-.005" (.05-.13 mm).
8) If countershaft 2nd gear clearance is not within specification, install different thickness thrust washer between countershaft 2nd gear and parking gear. Recheck countershaft 2nd gear clearance. See COUNTERSHAFT 2ND GEAR THRUST WASHER SPECIFICATIONS table for available thrust washer sizes.
9) Once correct gear clearances are obtained, disassemble countershaft. Lubricate all components with Dexron-II ATF. Wrap splines

of countershaft with tape. Install NEW "O" rings on countershaft. Reassemble countershaft. Ensure thrust needle bearings are installed with unrolled edge of bearing retainer facing washer.

COUNTERSHAFT 2ND GEAR THRUST WASHER SPECIFICATIONS

Thrust Washer Number	Part Number	Thickness In. (mm)
1	90411-PY4-000	.051 (1.30)
2	90412-PY4-000	.053 (1.35)
3	90413-PY4-000	.055 (1.40)
4	90414-PY4-000	.057 (1.45)
5	90415-PY4-000	.059 (1.50)
6	90416-PY4-000	.061 (1.55)
7	90417-PY4-000	.063 (1.60)
8	90418-PY4-000	.065 (1.65)
9	90419-PY4-000	.067 (1.70)
10	90420-PY4-000	.069 (1.75)
11	90421-PY4-000	.071 (1.80)
12	90422-PY4-000	.073 (1.85)
13	90423-PY4-000	.075 (1.90)

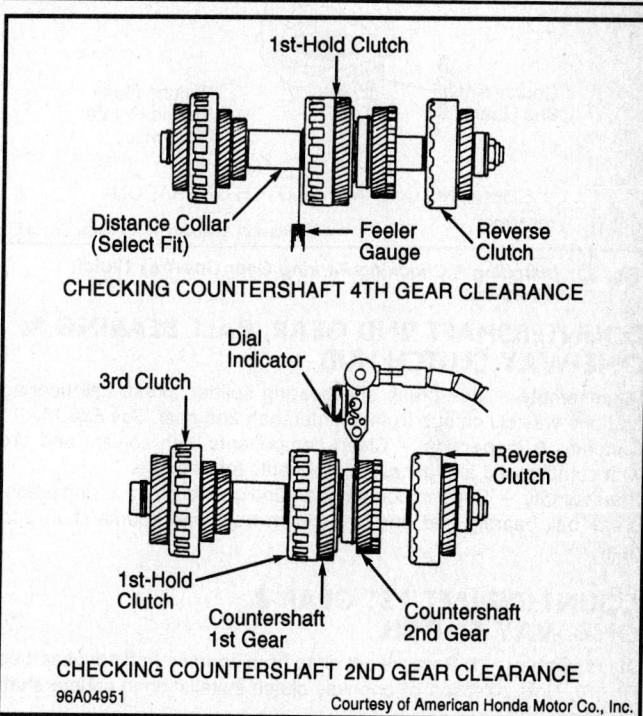

CHECKING COUNTERSHAFT 4TH GEAR CLEARANCE

CHECKING COUNTERSHAFT 2ND GEAR CLEARANCE

Fig. 32: Measuring Countershaft 2nd & 4th Gear Clearances

PARKING GEAR & ONE-WAY CLUTCH

Disassembly –1) Separate countershaft 2nd gear from parking gear by rotating parking gear clockwise while holding countershaft 2nd gear. Remove parking gear, thrust needle bearing, thrust washer and needle bearings. See Fig. 15.
2) Note direction of one-way clutch installation in countershaft 2nd gear. Using screwdriver, gently pry one-way clutch from countershaft 2nd gear.
Cleaning & Inspection – Clean components with solvent and dry with compressed air. Inspect components for damage.
Reassembly – Lubricate all components with Dexron-II ATF. Install one-way clutch with retainer tab toward countershaft 2nd gear. See Fig. 33. Install thrust needle bearing, thrust washer, needle bearings and parking gear. Ensure parking gear rotates clockwise when holding countershaft 2nd gear. See Fig. 33.

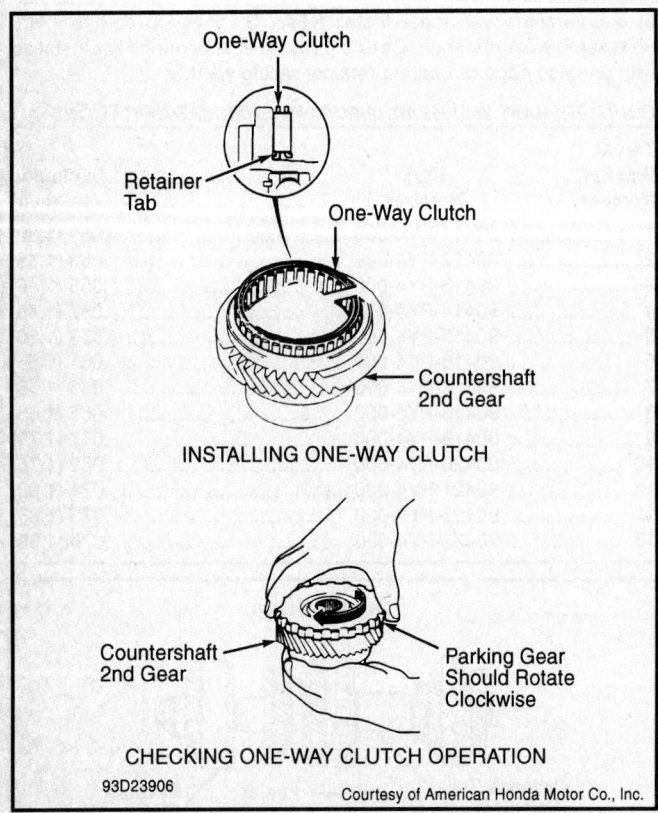

Fig. 33: *Installing & Checking Parking Gear One-Way Clutch Operation*

COUNTERSHAFT 2ND GEAR, BALL BEARING & ONE-WAY CLUTCH HUB

Disassembly – Use press and bearing splitter, press ball bearing and one-way clutch hub from countershaft 2nd gear. *See Fig. 15.*

Cleaning & Inspection – Clean components with solvent and dry with compressed air. Inspect components for damage.

Reassembly – Support countershaft 2nd gear in press. Using press, press ball bearing and one-way clutch hub onto countershaft 2nd gear.

COUNTERSHAFT 1ST GEAR & ONE-WAY CLUTCH

Disassembly – 1) Remove set plate from countershaft 1st gear. *See Fig. 16.* Note direction of one-way clutch installation in countershaft 1st gear.

2) Using screwdriver, gently pry one-way clutch from countershaft 1st gear. Remove thrust needle bearing from countershaft 1st gear.

Cleaning & Inspection – Clean components with solvent and dry with compressed air. Inspect components for damage.

Reassembly – 1) Lubricate all components with Dexron-II ATF. Install one-way clutch with retainer tab toward countershaft 1st gear. Install thrust needle bearing and set plate. *See Fig. 34.*

2) Install countershaft 2nd gear into one-way clutch. Ensure countershaft 2nd gear rotates clockwise when holding countershaft 1st gear.

SECONDARY GEAR & EXTENSION SHAFT

NOTE: *If secondary gear, roller bearings, bearing races, thrust washer, washer, transaxle housing or torque converter housing are replaced, secondary gear bearing preload must be checked before installing secondary gear oil seal. See SECONDARY GEAR BEARING PRELOAD under TRANSAXLE REASSEMBLY.*

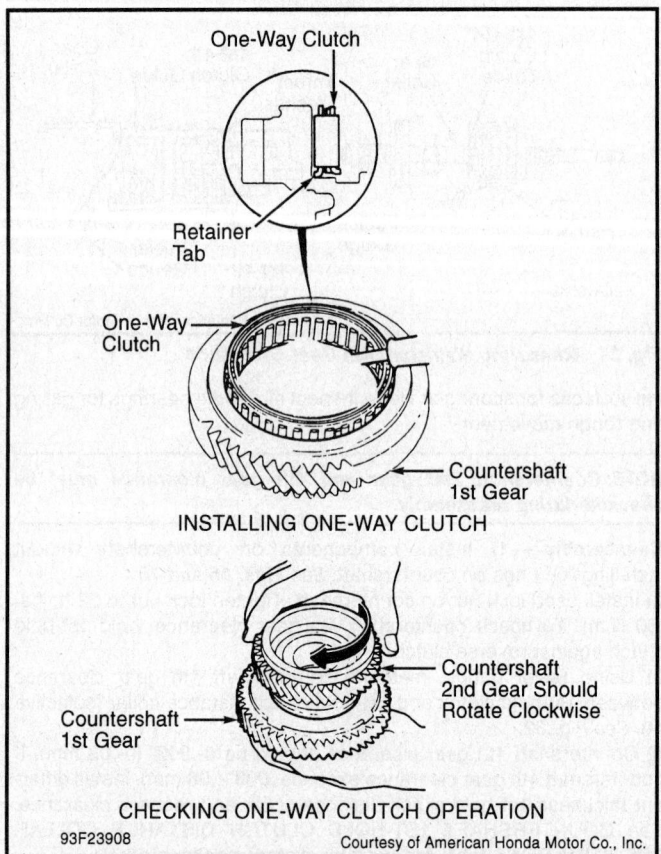

Fig. 34: *Installing & Checking Countershaft 1st Gear One-Way Clutch Operation*

Disassembly – 1) Remove set ring and extension shaft from secondary gear. *See Fig. 16.* Using screwdriver, pry oil seal for extension shaft from secondary gear.

2) If removing roller bearing from secondary gear, support secondary gear in press using bearing remover and remove secondary gear from roller bearing.

CAUTION: DO NOT heat torque converter housing or transaxle housing to more than 212°F (100°C) or housing may be damaged.

3) If removing bearing races for secondary gear from torque converter or transaxle housing, use heat gun to heat area around bearing race to 212°F (100°C). Tap bearing race from housing.

CAUTION: When removing bearing race from housing, use care not to damage thrust washer (transaxle housing) or washer (torque converter housing) located below bearing race. See Fig. 16.

Cleaning & Inspection – Clean components with solvent and dry with compressed air. Inspect splines for excessive wear. Check bearing surfaces for scoring or wear. Inspect secondary gear for damage.

Reassembly – 1) To reassemble extension shaft, use hammer and oil seal installer, install NEW oil seal in secondary gear. Using press, press roller bearings onto secondary gear. Ensure roller bearing fully bottoms on secondary gear.

NOTE: Adapter contains 2 different sizes for roller bearing installation. Ensure 45-mm side of adapter is used for bearing on transaxle housing side and 55-mm side is used on torque converter housing side.

---

2) Install extension shaft in secondary gear. Install NEW set ring wire circlip on end of extension shaft.

3) If installing bearing race for secondary gear in transaxle housing, install thrust washer in transaxle housing. Using hammer and bearing race installer, tap bearing race into transaxle housing.

4) If installing bearing race for secondary gear in torque converter housing, install washer. Using hammer and bearing race installer, tap bearing race into transaxle housing.

NOTE: *If secondary gear, roller bearings, bearing races, thrust washer, washer, transaxle housing or torque converter housing are replaced, secondary gear bearing preload must be checked. See SECONDARY GEAR BEARING PRELOAD under TRANSAXLE REASSEMBLY.*

CLUTCH ASSEMBLIES

Disassembly – 1) Remove snap ring, clutch end plate, clutch discs and clutch plates. *See Fig. 35.* On 1st-hold, 2nd, 3rd and 4th clutches, note direction of disc spring installation. Remove disc spring.

2) On all clutches, using spring compressor, compress return spring. Remove circlip. Release and remove spring compressor. Remove spring retainer and return spring.

3) Wrap shop towel around clutch drum. Apply light air pressure to oil passage on clutch drum to remove clutch piston. Remove "O" rings.

Cleaning & Inspection – 1) Clean metal components with solvent and dry with compressed air. Ensure check valve on rear of clutch piston is thoroughly cleaned.

2) Inspect components for damage and replace if necessary. Ensure no rough edges exist on "O" ring sealing areas. On 1st and reverse clutches, ensure disc spring is securely staked to clutch piston. On all clutches, inspect for loose check valve on rear of clutch piston.

Reassembly – 1) Lubricate all components with Dexron-II ATF. Install NEW "O" rings. Install clutch piston in clutch drum. Slightly rotate clutch piston back and forth during installation to prevent damaging "O" rings.

CAUTION: *DO NOT apply excessive force on clutch piston or "O" rings will be damaged.*

---

2) Install return spring and spring retainer in clutch drum. Place circlip on spring retainer. Using spring compressor, compress return spring. Install circlip and remove spring compressor.

3) Install disc spring on 1st-hold, 2nd, 3rd and 4th clutches. Ensure disc spring is installed in proper direction. *See Fig. 35.*

CAUTION: *Ensure clutch discs are soaked in Dexron-II ATF for at least 30 minutes before installing.*

---

4) Alternately install clutch plates and clutch discs starting with clutch plate. Install clutch end plate with flat side toward clutch disc. Install snap ring. Momentarily apply air to oil passage on clutch drum and ensure clutch piston moves and clutch engages.

5) Using dial indicator, measure clutch clearance between clutch end plate and top clutch disc. *See Fig. 36.* Zero dial indicator with clutch end plate lowered and then lift clutch end plate upward against snap ring. Distance measured is clutch clearance.

6) Measure clutch clearance at 3 different locations. Ensure clutch clearance is within specification. See CLUTCH CLEARANCE SPECIFICATIONS table.

7) If clutch clearance is not within specification, install different thickness clutch end plate. See CLUTCH END PLATE SPECIFICATIONS table.

NOTE: *If thickest clutch end plate is installed and clutch clearance still exceeds specification, replace clutch discs and clutch plates.*

CLUTCH CLEARANCE SPECIFICATIONS

Application	In. (mm)
Reverse Clutch	.030-.037 (.75-.95)
1st Clutch	.026-.033 (.65-.85)
1st-Hold Clutch	.028-.035 (.70-.90)
2nd & 3rd Clutches	.024-.031 (.60-.80)
4th Clutch	.020-.028 (.50-.70)

CLUTCH END PLATE SPECIFICATIONS

Plate Number	Part Number	Thickness In. (mm)
Reverse Clutch		
R1	22451-PY4-003	.161 (4.10)
R2	22452-PY4-003	.165 (4.20)
R3	22453-PY4-003	.169 (4.30)
R4	22454-PY4-003	.173 (4.40)
R5	22455-PY4-003	.177 (4.50)
R6	22456-PY4-003	.181 (4.60)
R7	22457-PY4-003	.185 (4.70)
R8	22458-PY4-003	.189 (4.80)
R9	22459-PY4-003	.193 (4.90)
1st, 2nd, 3rd & 4th Clutches		
1	22551-PY4-003	.083 (2.10)
2	22552-PY4-003	.087 (2.20)
3	22553-PY4-003	.091 (2.30)
4	22554-PY4-003	.094 (2.40)
5	22555-PY4-003	.098 (2.50)
6	22556-PY4-003	.102 (2.60)
7	22557-PY4-003	.106 (2.70)
8	22558-PY4-003	.110 (2.80)
9	22559-PY4-003	.114 (2.90)
1st-Hold Clutch		
L1	22351-PY4-003	.083 (2.10)
L2	22352-PY4-003	.087 (2.20)
L3	22353-PY4-003	.091 (2.30)
L4	22354-PY4-003	.094 (2.40)
L5	22355-PY4-003	.098 (2.50)
L6	22356-PY4-003	.102 (2.60)
L7	22357-PY4-003	.106 (2.70)
L8	22358-PY4-003	.110 (2.80)
L9	22359-PY4-003	.114 (2.90)

TORQUE CONVERTER HOUSING

Disassembly – 1) Remove countershaft needle bearing from torque converter housing, using slide hammer puller. Remove oil guide plate. *See Fig. 18.*

2) Using hammer and bearing driver, remove mainshaft ball bearing and oil seal from torque converter housing. Remove snap ring retaining secondary gear oil seal in torque converter housing. Using hammer and drift, tap secondary gear oil seal from torque converter housing.

Cleaning & Inspection – Clean components with solvent and dry with compressed air. Inspect torque converter housing for cracks and damage in bearing areas. Replace torque converter housing if damaged.

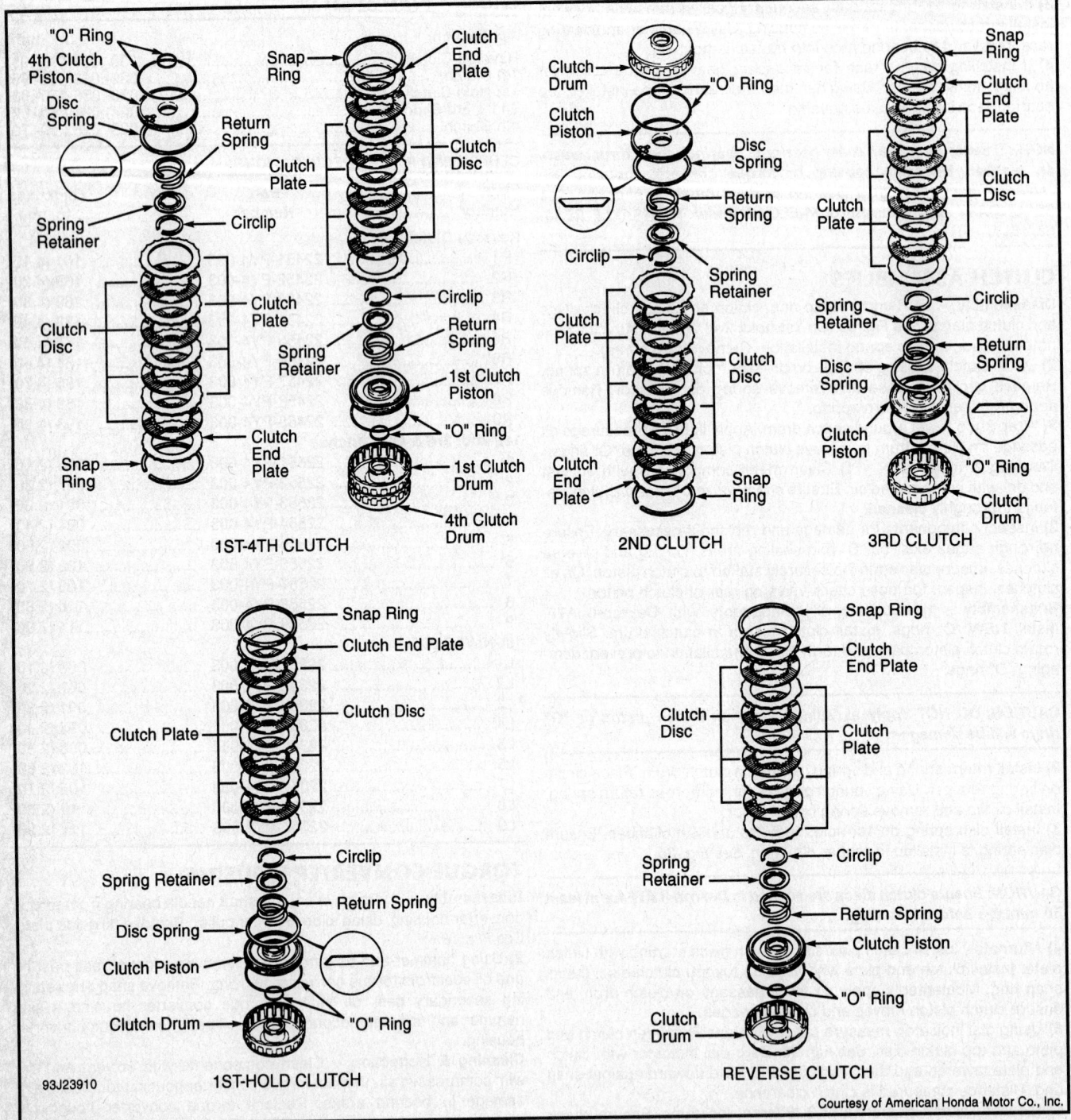

Courtesy of American Honda Motor Co., Inc.

Fig. 35: Exploded View Of Clutch Assemblies

Reassembly – 1) To install mainshaft ball bearing, using hammer and bearing driver, install ball bearing until bearing bottoms in torque converter housing.

2) Using hammer and oil seal installer, install NEW mainshaft oil seal in torque converter housing. Oil seal should be even with torque converter housing surface.

3) To install countershaft needle bearing, install NEW oil guide plate in countershaft bearing bore of torque converter housing. Ensure oil guide plate is installed so tab at center of oil guide plate faces upward (away from torque converter housing surface). *See Fig. 18.* Using hammer and bearing driver, drive countershaft needle bearing into torque converter housing.

NOTE: If secondary gear, roller bearings, bearing races, thrust washer, washer, transaxle housing or torque converter housing are replaced, secondary gear bearing preload must be checked before installing secondary gear oil seal. See SECONDARY GEAR BEARING PRELOAD under TRANSAXLE REASSEMBLY.

4) Install NEW secondary gear oil seal in torque converter housing. Install snap ring in torque converter housing.

TRANSAXLE HOUSING

Disassembly – Expand snap ring and press mainshaft ball bearing from transaxle housing. Using hammer and drift, tap secondary gear oil seal from transaxle housing.

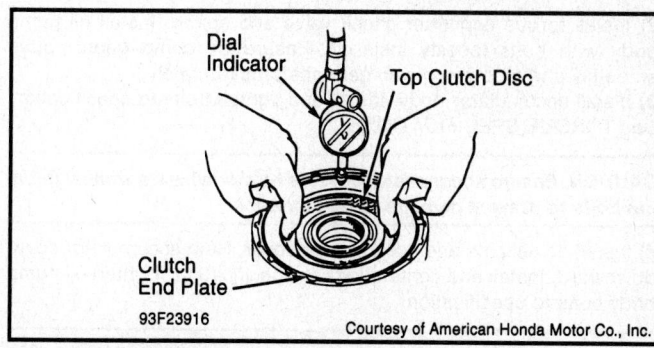

Fig. 36: Measuring Clutch Clearance

Cleaning & Inspection – Clean components with solvent and dry with compressed air. Inspect transaxle housing for cracks and damage in bearing areas. Replace transaxle housing if damaged.

Reassembly – **1)** Expand snap ring and install mainshaft ball bearing part way into transaxle housing. Release snap ring. Press mainshaft ball bearing into transaxle housing until snap ring engages with groove in ball bearing.

2) Using hammer and oil seal installer, install NEW secondary gear oil seal in transaxle housing.

CAUTION: Ensure mainshaft ball bearing is installed with groove of ball bearing facing inside of transaxle housing so snap ring engages in ball bearing when ball bearing is fully installed. Ensure snap ring fully engages in ball bearing.

NOTE: If secondary gear, roller bearings, bearing races, thrust washer, washer, transaxle housing or torque converter housing are replaced, secondary gear bearing preload must be checked before installing secondary gear oil seal. See SECONDARY GEAR BEARING PRELOAD under TRANSAXLE REASSEMBLY.

PARKING BRAKE MECHANISM

Disassembly – **1)** Remove parking pawl shaft sleeve, parking pawl spring and parking pawl. *See Fig. 15.*

2) Remove bolt and bolt lock from detent lever. *See Fig. 16.* Remove control shaft. Remove detent lever and parking brake rod.

Cleaning & Inspection – Clean components with solvent and dry with compressed air. Inspect components for damage.

Reassembly – To reassemble, reverse disassembly procedure using NEW bolt locks. Tighten bolts to specification. See TORQUE SPECIFICATIONS. Bend over tabs on bolt locks.

TRANSAXLE REASSEMBLY

SECONDARY GEAR BEARING PRELOAD

NOTE: If secondary gear, roller bearings, bearing races, thrust washer, washer, transaxle housing or torque converter housing are replaced, secondary gear bearing preload must be checked.

1) Oil seals must be removed from torque converter housing and transaxle housing before checking secondary gear bearing preload. Remove snap ring retaining secondary gear oil seal in torque converter housing.

2) Using hammer and drift, tap oil seal from torque converter housing and transaxle housing. Remove set ring and extension shaft from secondary gear. *See Fig. 16.*

3) Install sealing bolt in secondary gear. *See Fig. 37.* Tighten sealing bolt to 15 ft. lbs. (20 N.m). Install secondary gear in torque converter housing. DO NOT install mainshaft and countershaft in torque converter housing.

4) Install dowel pins and gasket on torque converter housing. Install transaxle housing on torque converter housing. Install and tighten transaxle housing bolts to specification in sequence. *See Fig. 38.* See TORQUE SPECIFICATIONS.

5) Rotate secondary gear in both directions to fully seat roller bearings on secondary gear. Secondary gear bearing preload is determined by measuring starting torque required to rotate secondary gear in both directions.

6) Using INCH-lb torque wrench, measure starting torque required to rotate secondary gear in both directions. *See Fig. 37.* The starting torque should be 31-40 INCH lbs. (3.5-4.5 N.m) at room temperature.

7) If starting torque is not within specification, install different thickness thrust washer below bearing race in transaxle housing. *See Fig. 16.* See THRUST WASHER SPECIFICATIONS table.

THRUST WASHER SPECIFICATIONS

Thrust Washer I.D. Letter	Part Number [1]	Thickness In. (mm)
A	23941-PY5-000	.061 (1.56)
B	23942-PY5-000	.063 (1.59)
C	23943-PY5-000	.064 (1.62)
D	23944-PY5-000	.065 (1.65)
E	23945-PY5-000	.066 (1.68)
F	23946-PY5-000	.067 (1.71)
G	23947-PY5-000	.069 (1.74)
H	23948-PY5-000	.070 (1.77)
I	23949-PY5-000	.071 (1.80)
J	23950-PY5-000	.072 (1.83)
K	23951-PY5-000	.073 (1.86)
L	23952-PY5-000	.074 (1.89)
M	23953-PY5-000	.076 (1.92)
N	23954-PY5-000	.077 (1.95)
O	23955-PY5-000	.078 (1.98)
P	23956-PY5-000	.079 (2.01)
Q	23957-PY5-000	.080 (2.04)
R	23958-PY5-000	.081 (2.07)
S	23959-PY5-000	.083 (2.10)
T	23960-PY5-000	.084 (2.13)
U	23961-PY5-000	.085 (2.16)
V	23962-PY5-000	.086 (2.19)
W	23963-PY5-000	.087 (2.22)
X	23964-PY5-000	.089 (2.25)
Y	23965-PY5-000	.090 (2.28)
Z	23966-PY5-000	.091 (2.31)
AA	23967-PY5-000	.092 (2.34)
AB	23968-PY5-000	.093 (2.37)
AC	23969-PY5-000	.094 (2.40)
AD	23970-PY5-000	.096 (2.43)

[1] – Part numbers are for Legend and 3.2TL models, for 3.5RL models replace PY5 with P5D in part number.

8) If changing thrust washer, remove transaxle housing from torque converter housing. Using heat gun, heat area around bearing race in transaxle housing to 212°F (100°C). Tap bearing race from transaxle housing. Remove thrust washer.

CAUTION: DO NOT heat transaxle housing to more than 212°F (100°C) or housing may be damaged.

9) Install thrust washer in transaxle housing. Using hammer and bearing race installer, tap bearing race into transaxle housing. Recheck secondary gear bearing preload.

10) Once correct secondary gear bearing preload is obtained, remove transaxle housing and secondary gear from torque converter housing. Using hammer and oil seal installer, install NEW secondary gear oil seal in torque converter housing. Install snap ring in torque converter housing.

11) Using hammer and oil seal installer, install NEW secondary gear oil seal in transaxle housing. Install extension shaft in secondary gear. Install NEW set ring on end of extension shaft.

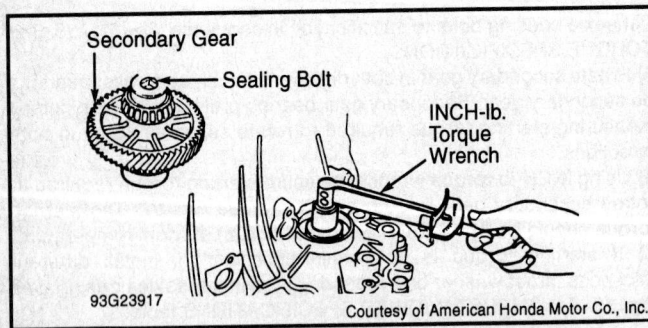

Fig. 37: Installing Sealing Bolt & Checking Starting Torque

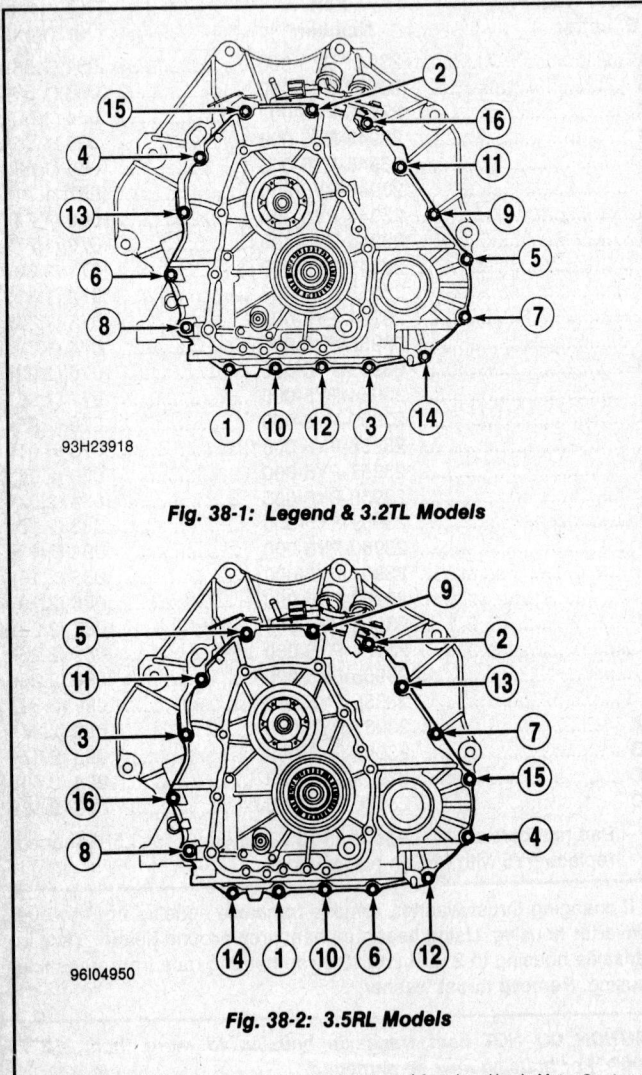

Fig. 38-1: Legend & 3.2TL Models

Fig. 38-2: 3.5RL Models

Courtesy of American Honda Motor Co., Inc.

Fig. 38: Transaxle Housing Bolt Tightening Sequence

VALVE BODIES & INTERNAL COMPONENTS

NOTE: Coat all components with ATF before reassembly.

1) Install separator plate and dowel pins on torque converter housing. *See Fig. 18.* Install oil pump drive gear, oil pump driven gear and oil pump driven gear shaft.

CAUTION: Ensure oil pump driven gear is installed with chamfered and grooved side facing downward (toward separator plate).

2) Install torque converter check valve and spring. Install oil pump body with bolts loosely installed. Ensure oil pump gears rotate smoothly and oil pump driven gear shaft moves freely.
3) Install accumulator body. Install and tighten bolts to specification. See TORQUE SPECIFICATIONS.

CAUTION: Ensure accumulator cover is held downward while tightening bolts to prevent damage to bolt threads.

4) Install dowel pins and accumulator cover. Hold accumulator cover downward. Install and tighten bolts to specification. Tighten oil pump body bolts to specification.

CAUTION: Ensure oil pump gears rotate smoothly and oil pump driven gear shaft moves freely once oil pump body is installed. If components do not operate correctly, loosen oil pump body bolts and accumulator body bolts and realign oil pump gears and oil pump driven gear shaft. Failure to align oil pump driven gear shaft may result in seized oil pump gears or shaft.

5) Install NEW filter in oil pump body. Ensure filter is installed in proper direction. *See Fig. 18.*
6) Install dowel pins and separator plate on oil pump body. Install stator shaft, NEW "O" ring and stopper pin.
7) Install regulator valve body. Install and tighten bolts to specification. Install all oil pipes in accumulator body.
8) Install parking brake rod, detent lever and control shaft (if removed). *See Fig. 16.* Install bolt and NEW bolt lock on detent lever. Tighten detent lever bolt to specification. Bend over tabs on bolt lock.
9) Install secondary gear and extension shaft assembly in torque converter housing. Install mainshaft and countershaft as an assembly in torque converter housing. Install dowel pins and NEW gasket on torque converter housing.

CAUTION: Ensure countershaft and mainshaft speed sensors are not installed in transaxle housing when installing transaxle housing on torque converter housing.

10) Install transaxle housing on torque converter housing. Install and tighten transaxle housing bolts to specification in sequence using 3 steps. *See Fig. 38.*

NOTE: On Legend, speed sensor washer is used on countershaft speed sensor only. On all other models, speed sensor washer is used on countershaft and mainshaft speed sensors.

CAUTION: Ensure speed sensor washer is installed on countershaft speed sensor and mainshaft speed sensor during installation, if equipped. See Fig. 16. The .08" (2.1 mm) thick speed sensor washer fits on mainshaft speed sensor, (if equipped) and .02" (.5 mm) thick speed sensor washer fits on countershaft speed sensor on all models.

11) Install NEW "O" rings on countershaft and mainshaft speed sensors. Install .08" (2.1 mm) thick speed sensor washer on mainshaft speed sensor and .02" (.5 mm) thick speed sensor washer on countershaft speed sensor.
12) Install countershaft and mainshaft speed sensors on transaxle housing. Install and tighten bolts to specification.
13) Install countershaft 2nd gear with one-way clutch, needle bearings, thrust washer and thrust needle bearing on countershaft. *See Fig. 15.*
14) Install gear collar, thrust needle bearing and needle bearing on mainshaft. Engage mainshaft 2nd gear with teeth on parking gear. Install mainshaft 2nd gear and parking gear as an assembly onto mainshaft and countershaft.
15) Using hammer and Driver (07746-0030100), tap parking gear onto countershaft. Install parking pawl shaft, parking pawl spring, parking pawl and parking pawl shaft sleeve.

16) Install oil pipe in accumulator cover. Install distance collar and NEW disc spring on countershaft. Ensure disc spring is installed with large area toward distance collar. *See Fig. 15.* Install thrust needle bearing and thrust washer on mainshaft.

17) Wrap splines of countershaft and mainshaft with tape. Install NEW "O" rings on countershaft and mainshaft. Remove tape. Install 2nd clutch on mainshaft.

18) Install reverse clutch, gear collar, needle bearing, thrust needle bearing and countershaft reverse gear on countershaft. Install thrust needle bearing, thrust washer, ball bearing, NEW washer and NEW countershaft lock nut.

19) Install NEW disc spring on mainshaft. Ensure disc spring is installed with large area toward 2nd clutch. *See Fig. 15.* Install distance collar, mainshaft reverse gear, ball bearing, NEW washer and NEW mainshaft lock nut.

20) Install Mainshaft Holder (07924-PJ4010A) on mainshaft to secure mainshaft. *See Fig. 14.* Engage parking pawl with parking gear. Tighten mainshaft and countershaft lock nuts to specification. Stake lock nuts against the shaft.

NOTE: Ensure mainshaft and countershaft lock nuts are securely staked against the shaft.

21) Remove mainshaft holder. Install dowel pins, oil pipes, NEW "O" rings and NEW gasket for rear cover on transaxle housing.

22) Install rear cover and engage reverse gears with reverse idler gear while rotating mainshaft. Install snap ring in groove of ball bearing on end of countershaft.

NOTE: Ensure snap ring fully engages groove on ball bearing. It may be necessary to raise countershaft upward so snap ring will fully engage with ball bearing.

23) Install and tighten rear cover bolts to specification. Apply thread sealant on threads of sealing bolt for rear cover. Install sealing bolt on rear cover and tighten to specification.

24) Install dowel pins for lower valve body assembly in transaxle housing. Position electrical connector on lower valve body assembly through opening on transaxle housing.

25) Install lower valve body assembly. Ensure manual valve engages with detent lever. Install and tighten lower valve body assembly-to-transaxle housing bolts to specification.

26) Install fluid strainer using NEW "O" ring. Tighten bolts to specification. Install connector stopper on electrical connector. *See Fig. 13.* Tighten connector stopper bolt to specification.

27) Install dowel pins, NEW gasket and oil pan. Install and tighten bolts to specification. Install NEW seal washer on drain plug. Tighten drain plug to specification.

28) Using NEW seal washers, install cooler pipes and joint bolts. Tighten joint bolts to specification. Reconnect electrical connector to transaxle sub-harness.

NOTE: If transaxle failure existed, flush oil cooler. See OIL COOLER FLUSHING under ON-VEHICLE SERVICE.

DIFFERENTIAL ASSEMBLY

OVERHAUL

NOTE: Pre-disassembly inspection should be performed before disassembly of differential assembly. This will indicate if proper thrust shims and thrust washers are used.

Pre-Disassembly Inspection – 1) Ring gear backlash, total bearing preload and gear tooth contact pattern should be checked before disassembling differential assembly. Record measurements for reassembly reference.

2) To check ring gear backlash, mount differential assembly in soft-jawed vice. Remove oil filler plug and seal washer from differential case cover. Remove oil seal from differential case cover. Align inspec-

tion hole on differential carrier with oil filler plug hole.

3) Install Wrench (07HAA-SF10100) in differential assembly. *See Fig. 39.* Mount dial indicator on differential case.

4) Measure ring gear backlash on differential carrier. Ring gear backlash should be .002-.006" (.06-.14 mm).

5) If ring gear backlash is within specification, proper thickness thrust shims are installed behind bearing races for differential carrier bearings. Provided no components are changed, shim is okay. If ring gear backlash is not within specification, different thickness thrust shim must be installed during reassembly.

6) To measure total bearing preload, install a dial-type INCH-lb. torque wrench on end of drive pinion. Rotate drive pinion and note total bearing preload. Total bearing preload, with used bearings, should be 21-26 INCH-lbs. (2.4-3.0 N.m).

NOTE: If total bearing preload is not within specification, different thickness shim must be installed behind bearing race for differential carrier bearings.

7) To check gear tooth contact pattern, remove differential case cover bolts in a crisscross pattern. Remove differential case cover. *See Fig. 40.* Clean and paint both sides of ring gear teeth with Prussian Blue.

8) Install differential case cover. Install and tighten bolts in a crisscross pattern to 33 ft.lbs. (45 N.m). Install Wrench (07HAA-SF10100) in differential assembly. *See Fig. 39.*

9) Rotate ring gear both directions while applying resistance on drive pinion. Remove differential case cover and inspect ring gear tooth contact pattern. Correct gear tooth contact should be centered on the ring gear. See GEAR TOOTH CONTACT PATTERNS article in APPLICATIONS & IDENTIFICATION section.

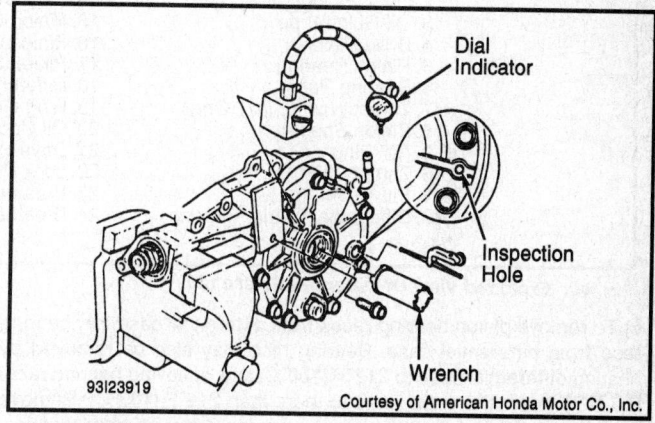

Dial Indicator

Inspection Hole

Wrench

93123919

Courtesy of American Honda Motor Co., Inc.

Fig. 39: Rotating Ring Gear & Checking Ring Gear Backlash

Disassembly – 1) Remove bolts, speed sensor assembly and "O" ring. Remove differential case cover bolts in a crisscross pattern. Remove differential case cover. Remove breather plate from differential case cover (if necessary). *See Fig. 40.*

2) Remove differential carrier assembly from differential case. On Legend models, remove coolant pipe joint bolts, seal washers and coolant pipes. On all models, remove oil cooler nuts, oil cooler, "O" rings and oil guide pipe.

3) Using hammer and chisel, cut lock nut tab and pry away from drive pinion. Insert 32-mm hex bit socket into gear end of drive pinion.

4) Remove lock nut, thrust washer and drive pinion hub. Remove oil seal and thrust washer. Using soft-faced hammer, tap drive pinion from pinion bearing on front of drive pinion. Remove drive pinion, pinion spacer and thrust washers.

5) Inspect pinion bearings. If replacing pinion bearing on drive pinion, use press and bearing remover to press bearing from drive pinion. Remove drive pinion thrust shim from drive pinion.

NOTE: If pinion bearings are replaced, bearing races must also be replaced.

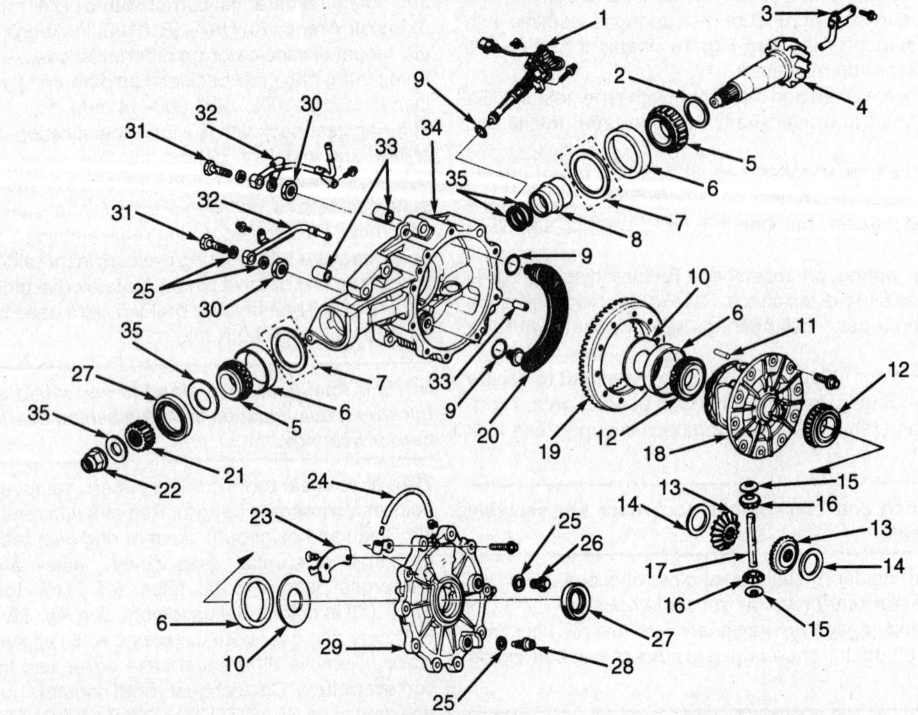

1. Speed Sensor Assembly
2. Drive Pinion Thrust Shim
3. Oil Guide Pipe
4. Drive Pinion
5. Pinion Bearing
6. Bearing Race
7. Thrust Washer (A/T Only)
8. Pinion Spacer
9. "O" Ring
10. Thrust Shim
11. Pin
12. Differential Carrier Bearing

13. Side Gear
14. Side Gear Thrust Washer
15. Pinion Gear Thrust Washer
16. Pinion Gear
17. Pinion Shaft
18. Differential Carrier
19. Ring Gear
20. Oil Cooler
21. Drive Pinion Hub
22. Lock Nut
23. Breather Plate
24. Breather Tube

25. Seal Washer
26. Oil Filler Plug
27. Oil Seal
28. Drain Plug
29. Differential Case Cover
30. Oil Cooler Nut
31. Coolant Pipe Joint Bolt
32. Coolant Pipe
33. Dowel Pin
34. Differential Case
35. Thrust Washer

95C19564

Courtesy of American Honda Motor Co., Inc.

Fig. 40: Exploded View Of Differential Assembly

6) To remove pinion bearing races from differential case, pry bearing race from differential case. Bearing race may also be removed by heating differential case to 212°F (100°C) and removing bearing race. DO NOT heat differential case to more than 212°F (100°C). Remove thrust washers, located below bearing races, from differential case.

7) Inspect differential carrier bearings. If replacing differential carrier bearings, use press and bearing remover to press bearing from differential carrier.

NOTE: If differential carrier bearings are replaced, bearing races must also be replaced.

8) To remove differential carrier bearing races, pry bearing race from differential case or differential case cover. Bearing race may also be removed by heating differential case or differential case cover to 212°F (100°C) and removing bearing race. DO NOT heat differential case or differential case cover to more than 212°F (100°C). Remove thrust shim(s), located below bearing races, from differential case or differential case cover.

NOTE: Thrust shim must be replaced if bearing race was removed from differential case or differential case cover.

NOTE: Pinion gear backlash must be checked to determine if differential carrier assembly must be replaced. Differential carrier bearings must be removed from differential carrier to measure pinion gear backlash.

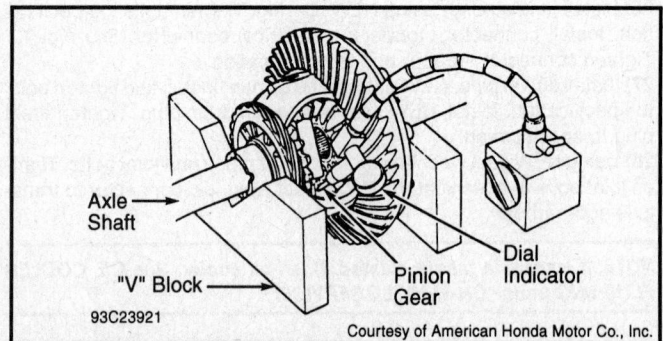

Courtesy of American Honda Motor Co., Inc.

Fig. 41: Checking Pinion Gear Backlash

9) Mount differential carrier in "V" blocks with axle shaft and intermediate shaft inserted into side gears. See Fig. 41. Using dial indicator, check pinion gear backlash. Pinion gear backlash should be .002-.012" (.05-.30 mm).

10) Replace differential carrier assembly if pinion gear backlash is not within specification. Remove ring gear (if necessary).

Cleaning & Inspection – Clean components with solvent and dry with compressed air. Inspect components for damage. Replace components if damaged.

Reassembly – 1) Install ring gear. Install and tighten ring gear bolts to specification in a crisscross pattern. See TORQUE SPECIFICATIONS. Using press, install differential carrier bearings on differential carrier (if removed).

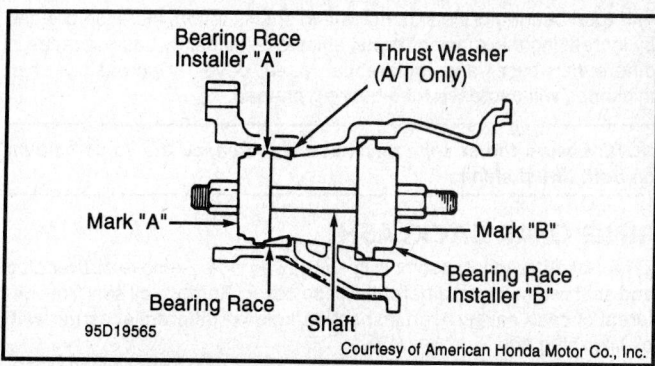

Fig. 42: Installing Bearing Race For Drive Pinion (Outer Bearing Shown; Inner Bearing Race Is Similar)

2) If installing bearing races for the drive pinion in differential case, install thrust washer in differential case. Thrust washer is located behind bearing race in the differential case. See Fig. 40.

3) Install bearing races. See Fig. 42. Install drive pinion bearing races in differential case starting with outer bearing race (lock nut side) and then inner bearing race.

4) If installing bearing races for differential carrier bearings, install NEW thrust shim(s) in differential case or differential case cover. Ensure thrust shim is the same thickness as thrust shim that was removed. Using hammer and bearing race installer, drive bearing race into differential case and differential case cover.

5) If original drive pinion and ring gear are being installed, install original thickness drive pinion thrust shim on drive pinion (if removed). If NEW drive pinion and ring gear are being installed, proper thickness drive pinion thrust shim must be determined to obtain correct drive pinion height. See DRIVE PINION HEIGHT under ADJUSTMENTS.

6) If installing pinion bearing on drive pinion, use press, old pinion spacer and bearing installer to press pinion bearing onto drive pinion. Lubricate all pinion bearings and threads on drive pinion with oil.

7) Install drive pinion in differential case. DO NOT install pinion spacer and thrust washers at this time. Install pinion bearing on drive pinion.

8) Using hammer and bearing installer, drive outer pinion bearing onto drive pinion while supporting drive pinion. Install thrust washer, drive pinion hub, thrust washer and lock nut.

9) Tighten lock nut to 15 ft. lbs. (20 N.m). DO NOT overtighten lock nut or pinion bearings may be damaged, as pinion spacer and thrust washers are not installed.

10) Clean drive pinion and ring teeth and coat with Prussian Blue. Lubricate differential carrier bearings with oil.

11) Install differential carrier into differential case. Install differential case cover. Install and tighten differential case cover bolts in a crisscross pattern to 33 ft.lbs. (45 N.m).

12) Install Wrench (07HAA-SF10100) in differential assembly. See Fig. 39. Rotate ring gear on full revolution in both directions while applying resistance on drive pinion.

13) Remove differential cover and inspect ring gear tooth contact pattern. Correct gear tooth contact should be centered on the ring gear. See GEAR TOOTH CONTACT PATTERNS article in APPLICATIONS & IDENTIFICATION section.

14) If gear tooth contact pattern is incorrect, drive pinion height must be changed to correct gear tooth contact pattern. Change drive pinion thrust shim located below bearing on drive pinion to adjust drive pinion height.

15) If gear tooth contact pattern is correct, remove components from drive pinion for installation of pinion spacer. Install NEW pinion spacer and thrust washers on drive pinion.

16) Install outer pinion bearing on drive pinion. Using hammer and bearing installer, drive outer pinion bearing onto drive pinion while supporting drive pinion.

17) Install thrust washer, drive pinion hub, thrust washer and NEW lock nut on drive pinion. Check pinion bearing preload. See PINION BEARING PRELOAD under ADJUSTMENTS.

18) Once correct pinion bearing preload is obtained, stake lock nut against drive pinion. Clean drive pinion and ring gear teeth and coat with Prussian Blue. Lubricate differential carrier bearings with oil.

19) Install differential carrier into differential case. Install differential case cover. Install and tighten differential case cover bolts in a crisscross pattern to 33 ft.lbs. (45 N.m).

20) Check TOTAL BEARING PRELOAD. See TOTAL BEARING PRELOAD under ADJUSTMENTS. Once correct total bearing preload is correct, check ring gear backlash. See RING GEAR BACKLASH under ADJUSTMENTS.

21) Once correct ring gear backlash is obtained, remove differential case cover and differential assembly. Check gear tooth contact pattern. Correct gear tooth contact should be centered on the ring gear. See GEAR TOOTH CONTACT PATTERNS article in APPLICATIONS & IDENTIFICATION section.

22) Install breather plate on differential case cover (if removed). Install breather plate bolts and tighten to specification. Stake heads of breather plate bolts against differential case cover.

23) Install oil guide pipe, oil cooler and NEW "O" rings. Tighten oil guide pipe bolt and oil cooler nuts to specification. Using NEW seal washers, install coolant pipes and coolant pipe joint bolts. Tighten coolant pipe joint bolts to specification.

24) Install differential assembly. Apply Liquid Gasket (08718-0001) on sealing surface of differential case cover. Install differential case cover. Install and tighten bolts to specification in a crisscross pattern.

25) Using hammer and oil seal installer, install NEW oil seal in differential case cover. Using hammer and oil seal installer, install NEW oil seal for drive pinion.

26) Oil seal must be installed so seal is below surface of differential case .61-.63" (15.5-16.0 mm). See Fig. 43. Using NEW "O" ring, install speed sensor assembly. Install and tighten bolt to specification.

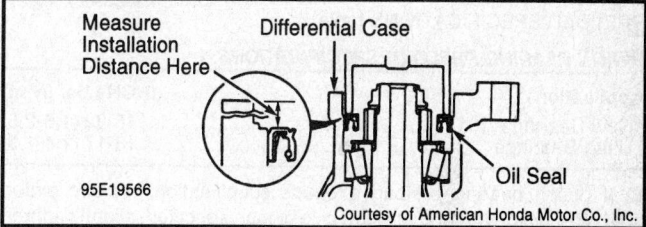

Fig. 43: Measuring Drive Pinion Oil Seal Installation Distance

ADJUSTMENTS

DRIVE PINION HEIGHT

NOTE: If drive pinion and ring gear are replaced, drive pinion height must be set. Drive pinion height may also need to be set if incorrect gear tooth contact pattern exists.

1) Drive pinion height is controlled by thickness of drive pinion thrust shim located between pinion bearing and drive pinion shaft. When installing used drive pinion and ring gear and gear tooth contact pattern is incorrect, see GEAR TOOTH CONTACT PATTERN article in APPLICATIONS & IDENTIFICATION section to determine if thrust shim should be thicker or thinner.

2) When installing NEW drive pinion and ring gear, calculate drive pinion thrust shim thickness by noting etched mark located on side of drive pinion. See Fig. 44.

3) Etched mark is a positive (+) or negative (-) mark along with a numerical digit indicating drive pinion size. Etched mark is positive or negative in thousandths of a millimeter.

NOTE: Etched mark is indicated in thousandths of a millimeter. If etched mark is -20, this is a negative .02 mm.

4) If etched mark on old drive pinion is positive (+), add it to the old drive pinion thrust shim thickness. If etched mark on old drive pinion is negative (–), subtract it from the old drive pinion thrust shim thickness.

5) If etched mark on NEW drive pinion is positive (+), subtract it from drive pinion thrust shim thickness obtained in step 4). If etched mark on NEW drive pinion is negative (–), add it to drive pinion thrust shim thickness obtained in step 4).

6) For example, if old drive pinion thrust shim thickness is 2.00 mm and old drive pinion etched mark is +20 (.02 mm) and NEW drive pinion etched mark is –10 (.01 mm), replacement drive pinion thrust shim thickness should be 2.03 mm.

7) Select drive pinion thrust shim that is closest to but not more than the determined drive pinion thrust shim thickness. Drive pinion thrust shims are available in thicknesses of .064-.089" (1.64-2.27 mm) in .001" (.03 mm) increments. Part numbers are 41410-PY4-000 to 41431-PY4-000 in numerical sequence.

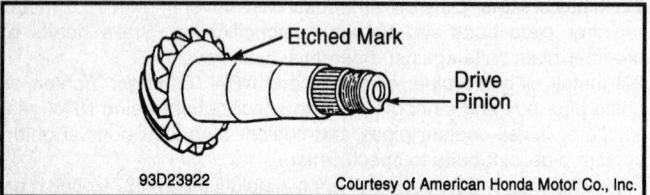

93D23922   Courtesy of American Honda Motor Co., Inc.

Fig. 44: Identifying Drive Pinion Etched Mark Location

PINION BEARING PRELOAD

1) Tighten drive pinion lock nut to 162 ft. lbs. (220 N.m). Rotate drive pinion several revolutions to seat bearings.

2) Install a dial-type INCH-lb. torque wrench on end of drive pinion. Rotate drive pinion and note pinion bearing preload. Pinion bearing preload should be within specification. See PINION BEARING PRELOAD SPECIFICATIONS table.

PINION BEARING PRELOAD SPECIFICATIONS

Application	INCH Lbs. (N.m)
New Bearings	16-22 (1.8-2.5)
Used Bearings	13-17 (1.4-1.9)

3) If pinion bearing preload exceeds specification, replace pinion spacer. If pinion bearing preload is less than specified, slightly tighten lock nut until correct pinion bearing preload is obtained.

CAUTION: DO NOT tighten lock nut to more than 236 ft. lbs. (320 N.m). If pinion bearing preload is still less than specified with lock nut tightened to 236 ft. lbs. (320 N.m), replace pinion spacer.

TOTAL BEARING PRELOAD

1) With differential fully assembled, without oil seals, install Wrench (07HAA-SF10100) in differential assembly. See Fig. 39.

2) Rotate ring gear one full revolution in both directions while applying resistance on drive pinion. Remove wrench from differential assembly.

3) Install a dial-type INCH-lb. torque wrench on end of drive pinion. Rotate drive pinion several times and note total bearing preload. Total bearing preload should be within specification. See TOTAL BEARING PRELOAD SPECIFICATIONS table.

TOTAL BEARING PRELOAD SPECIFICATIONS

Application	INCH Lbs. (N.m)
New Bearings	
All New Bearings	25-33 (2.9-3.8)
Differential Carrier Bearings Only	
Outer Bearing (Ring Gear Side) Only	22-28 (2.5-3.2)
Inner Bearing (Drive Pinion Side) Only	25-32 (2.8-3.6)
Used Bearings	21-26 (2.4-3.0)

4) If total bearing preload is not within specification, increase preload by increasing thickness of thrust shim located below bearing races in differential case and differential case cover. Decreasing shim thickness will decrease total bearing preload.

NOTE: Ensure thrust shim thickness is increased the same amount on both thrust shims.

RING GEAR BACKLASH

1) Mount differential assembly in soft-jawed vice. Remove oil filler plug and seal washer from differential case cover. Remove oil seal from differential case cover. Align inspection hole on differential carrier with oil filler plug hole.

2) Install Wrench (07HAA-SF10100) in differential assembly. See Fig. 39. Mount dial indicator on differential case cover.

3) Measure ring gear backlash on differential carrier. Ring gear backlash should be .002-.006" (.06-.14 mm).

4) If ring gear backlash is within specification, proper thickness thrust shims are installed behind bearing races for differential carrier bearings, provided no components are changed.

5) If ring gear backlash exceeds specification, decrease thickness of thrust shim located behind bearing race in differential case. Increase thickness of thrust shim in differential case cover the same amount.

6) If ring gear backlash is less than specified, increase thickness of thrust shim located behind bearing race in differential case. Decrease thickness of thrust shim in differential case cover the same amount.

7) Thrust shims are available in thicknesses of .0461-.0720" (1.170-1.830 mm) in .001" (.03 mm) increments. Part numbers are 41461-PY4-000 to 41483-PY4-000. One thrust shim is available at .0260" (.660 mm) and part number is 41460-PY4-000.

TRANSAXLE SPECIFICATIONS
TRANSAXLE SPECIFICATIONS

Application	Specification In. (mm)
Clutch Clearance	
Reverse Clutch	.030-.037 (.75-.95)
1st Clutch	.026-.033 (.65-.85)
1st-Hold Clutch	.028-.035 (.70-.90)
2nd & 3rd Clutches	.024-.031 (.60-.80)
4th Clutch	.020-.028 (.50-.70)
Differential Ring Gear Backlash	.002-.006 (.06-.14)
Gear Clearances	
Countershaft 2nd Gear Clearance	.003-.006 (.07-.15)
Countershaft 4th Gear Clearance	0-.003 (0-.08)
Mainshaft 4th Gear Clearance	0-.003 (0-.08)
Oil Pump Clearances	
Side Clearance	
Oil Pump Drive Gear	.0083-.0104 (.210-.265)
Oil Pump Driven Gear	.0028-.0049 (.070-.125)
Thrust Clearance	
Standard	.001-.002 (.03-.05)
Wear Limit	.0028 (.070)
Pinion Gear Backlash	.002-.012 (.05-.30)

Application	INCH Lb. (N.m)
Secondary Gear Bearing Preload [1]	31-40 (3.5-4.5)

[1] – This is the starting torque required to rotate secondary gear in both directions.

TORQUE SPECIFICATIONS

TORQUE SPECIFICATIONS

Application	Ft. Lbs. (N.m)
Accumulator Body Bolt	
6-mm Bolt	1
8-mm Bolt	13 (18)
Ball Retaining Bolt	13 (18)
Coolant Pipe Joint Bolt	21 (29)
Countershaft Lock Nut	96 (130)
Differential Assembly Mounting Bolt	47 (64)
Differential Assembly Oil Filler Plug	33 (45)
Differential Case Cover Bolt	33 (45)
Drive Pinion Lock Nut	2
Joint Bolt	29 (39)
Lower Plate Bolt	29 (39)
Mainshaft Lock Nut	96 (130)
Oil Cooler Nut	55 (75)
Oil Pump Body Bolt	
6-mm Bolt	1
8-mm Bolt	13 (18)
Pressure Tap Plug	13 (18)
Rear Cover Bolt	20 (27)
Rear Cover Sealing Bolt	59 (80)
Regulator Valve Body Bolt	
6-mm Bolt	1
8-mm Bolt	13 (18)
Reverse Idler Gear Shaft Holder Bolt	20 (27)
Ring Gear Bolt	88 (119)
Sealing Bolt	58 (79)
Steering Gear Bolt	44 (60)
Transaxle Drain Plug	36 (49)
Transaxle Housing Bolt [3]	25 (34)

Application	INCH Lbs. (N.m)
Accumulator Cover Bolt	106 (12.0)
Air Bleeder Bolt	89 (10.0)
Breather Plate Bolt	106 (12.0)
Cable Cover Bolt	106 (12.0)
Cable Holder Bolt	106 (12.0)
Connector Stopper Bolt	106 (12.0)
Control Lever Bolt	124 (14.0)
Countershaft Speed Sensor Bolt	106 (12.0)
Detent Lever Bolt	124 (14.0)
Detent Spring Plate Bolt	106 (12.0)
Flange Nut	53 (6.0)
Fluid Strainer Bolt	106 (12.0)
Lock-Up Control Solenoid Valve Bolt	106 (12.0)
Lower Valve Body Assembly Bolt	106 (12.0)
Lower Valve Body Assembly-To-Transaxle	
Housing Bolt	106 (12.0)
Mainshaft Speed Sensor Bolt	106 (12.0)
Oil Guide Pipe Bolt	106 (12.0)
Oil Pan Bolt	106 (12.0)
Oil Pass Body Bolt	106 (12.0)
Regulator Valve Body Lock Bolt	106 (12.0)
Secondary Valve Body Bolt	106 (12.0)
Shift Control Solenoid Valve Bolt	106 (12.0)
Speed Sensor Assembly Bolt	106 (12.0)
Throttle Valve Body Bolt	106 (12.0)
Wiring Harness Clamp Bolt	106 (12.0)
1st & 2nd Accumulator Cover Bolt	106 (12.0)

[1] – Tighten bolt to 106 INCH lbs. (12.0 N.m).

[2] – Pinion bearing preload is adjusted when tightening lock nut. See PINION BEARING PRELOAD under ADJUSTMENTS for adjusting procedure.

[3] – Tighten bolts to specification in sequence. *See Fig. 38.*

AUTOMATIC TRANSMISSIONS
Acura MPYA, M5DA & M5HA Electronic Controls

Legend, 3.2TL, 3.5RL

APPLICATION

APPLICATION

Vehicle	Transaxle Model
Legend (1995)	MPYA
3.2TL (1996)	M5HA
3.5RL (1996)	M5DA

CAUTION: Vehicle is equipped with a Supplemental Restraint System (SRS). When servicing vehicle, use care not to cause accidental air bag deployment. All SRS electrical connections and wiring harness are covered with Yellow insulation. Related components are located in steering column, center console, instrument panel and lower panel on instrument panel. DO NOT use electrical test equipment on these circuits. It may be necessary to deactivate SRS before servicing components. See AIR BAG SERVICING article in APPLICATIONS & IDENTIFICATION.

NOTE: Obtain radio anti-theft code from customer before disconnecting negative battery cable. Radio anti-theft code must be re-entered into radio once negative battery cable is reconnected. To re-enter radio anti-theft code, turn ignition and radio on. When the word "CODE" is displayed on radio, re-enter radio anti-theft code by using the radio station preset buttons.

DESCRIPTION

Automatic transaxle is electronically controlled. Transaxle shifting and torque converter lock-up are controlled by the Powertrain Control Module (PCM). The PCM receives information from various input devices and uses this information to control linear solenoid along with shift and lock-up control solenoid valves.

Transaxle is equipped with shift and key interlock systems. Shift interlock system prevents shift lever from being moved from Park unless brake pedal is depressed and accelerator pedal is in idle position. In case of a malfunction, shift lever can be released by placing ignition key in key release slot near shift lever. Key interlock system prevents ignition key from being removed from ignition lock assembly unless shift lever is in Park.

The A/T gear position indicator on instrument panel contains lights to indicate which position A/T gear position switch on shift lever is in.

OPERATION

A/T GEAR POSITION INDICATOR

With ignition in RUN or START position, voltage is supplied to A/T gear position indicator, located on instrument panel. *See Fig. 1.* When shift lever is moved to designated gear position, A/T gear position switch completes the ground circuit for A/T gear position indicator on instrument panel. The light on A/T gear position indicator will be illuminated to indicate shift lever gear position. The PCM controls operation of the "D₄" light on A/T gear position indicator on instrument panel. On Legend models, A/T gear position switch is mounted on driver's side of shift lever. *See Fig. 2.* On 3.2TL and 3.5RL models, A/T gear position switch is mounted on driver's side of transaxle.

When headlights are turned on, voltage is supplied on Red/Black wire terminal on A/T gear position indicator. This changes light illumination from fixed illumination to being controlled by the dash light dimmer input on the Red wire.

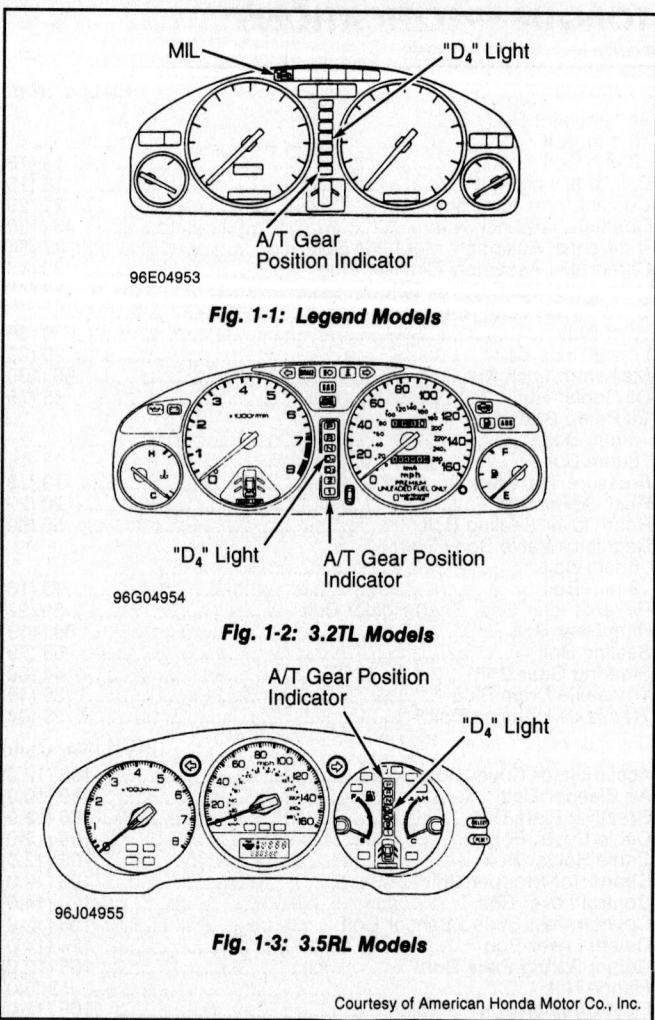

Fig. 1-1: Legend Models

96E04953

Fig. 1-2: 3.2TL Models

96G04954

Fig. 1-3: 3.5RL Models

96J04955

Courtesy of American Honda Motor Co., Inc.

Fig. 1: Identifying A/T Gear Position Indicator, "D₄" Light & MIL Light

SHIFT & KEY INTERLOCK SYSTEMS

Shift Interlock System – Shift interlock system prevents shift lever from being moved from Park unless brake pedal is depressed and accelerator pedal is in idle position. In case of a malfunction, shift lever can be released by placing ignition key in key release slot near shift lever and pushing down. Voltage is provided to shift lock solenoid when ignition is on.

When brake pedal is depressed, battery voltage is applied to the PCM from brakelight switch. With accelerator pedal in idle position, a low voltage is applied to the PCM from the throttle position sensor. The PCM then supplies voltage to shift lock circuit in the interlock control unit. When A/T gear position switch is in Park position, interlock control unit then operates shift lock solenoid by controlling the ground circuit. When shift lock solenoid is energized, shift lever is released and can be moved.

Shift lock solenoid is located on side of shift lever. *See Fig. 2.* Interlock control unit is located behind driver's side of instrument panel, left of steering column and contains an 8-pin electrical connector. *See Fig. 2.* The A/T gear position switch is mounted on driver's side of shift lever on Legend models and left side of transaxle on control shaft on 3.5RL models. *See Fig. 2.*

Key Interlock System – Key interlock system prevents ignition key from being removed from ignition lock assembly on steering column unless shift lever is in Park. Voltage is provided to key interlock switch from No. 39 (20-amp on Legend and 15-amp on 3.5RL) fuse in engine compartment fuse box, near battery. When ignition key is in ignition lock assembly, key interlock switch closes, providing voltage to key interlock solenoid and interlock control unit.

If shift lever is not in Park, interlock control unit energizes key interlock solenoid by completing ground circuit. When key interlock solenoid is energized, ignition key cannot be removed from ignition lock assembly. Key interlock switch and solenoid are located on ignition lock assembly. See Fig. 2. Interlock control unit is located behind driver's side of instrument panel, left of steering column and contains an 8-pin electrical connector. See Fig. 2.

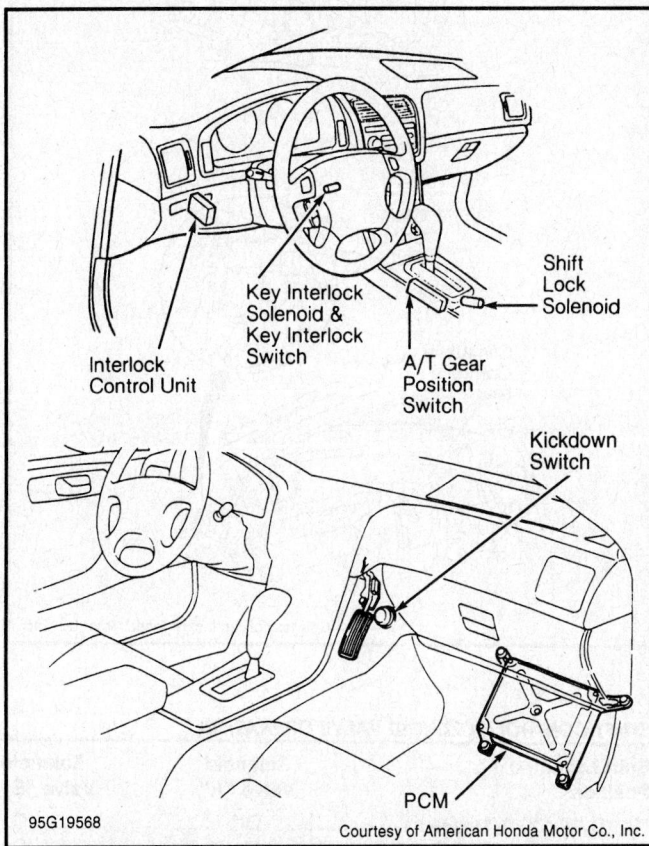

Fig. 2: Identifying Interlock Control Unit, Shift Lock Solenoid, Key Interlock Solenoid & Switch, Kickdown Switch & PCM (Legend, 3.5RL Is Similar)

POWERTRAIN CONTROL MODULE (PCM)

The Powertrain Control Module (PCM) receives information from various input devices and uses this information to control linear solenoid along with shift and lock-up control solenoid valves. See Fig. 3. The PCM contains a self-diagnostic system which stores Diagnostic Trouble Code (DTC) information if a failure or problem exists in the transaxle electronic control or the fuel injection system. DTC or Flash Code can be retrieved to determine transaxle problem area. For information on self-diagnostic system, see SELF-DIAGNOSTIC SYSTEM. The PCM is located below the carpet on passenger's side of instrument panel. See Fig. 2.

PCM INPUT DEVICES

NOTE: The following components send input signals to the PCM.

Brake Switch – Brakelight switch delivers input signal to PCM, indicating vehicle braking. Brakelight switch is located on brake pedal support.

Countershaft Speed Sensor – Countershaft speed sensor delivers a countershaft speed signal to the PCM. Countershaft speed sensor is located on the transaxle. See Fig. 4.

Engine Coolant Temperature (ECT) Sensor – ECT sensor delivers input signal to PCM, indicating engine coolant temperature. ECT sensor is located in coolant pipe, near throttle body and contains a Red/White wire and Green/White wire in the electrical connector. See Fig. 4.

Engine RPM – Engine RPM is determined by engine RPM signal delivered to the PCM.

Gear Position Sensor – Gear position signal is sent to PCM by A/T gear position switch to indicate shift lever position. The A/T gear position switch is mounted on driver's side of shift lever on Legend models and on driver's side of transaxle on 3.2TL and 3.5RL models. See Fig. 2.

Kickdown Switch (Legend) – Kickdown switch delivers an input signal to PCM to indicate when accelerator pedal is fully depressed. Kickdown switch is located below accelerator pedal. See Fig. 2.

Mainshaft Speed Sensor – Mainshaft speed sensor delivers a mainshaft speed signal to the PCM. Mainshaft speed sensor is located on the transaxle. See Fig. 4.

Service Check Connector – Service check connector is used when retrieving Flash Codes for transaxle electronic control system diagnosis. When jumper wire is installed between service check connector terminals, an input is delivered to the PCM to display Flash Codes on the "D₄" light on A/T gear position indicator on instrument panel. See Fig. 1. Service check connector is a Gray 2-pin connector located on the PCM cover, below passenger's side of instrument panel. See Fig. 5.

Throttle Position (TP) Sensor – TP sensor delivers input signal to PCM to indicate throttle position. TP sensor is mounted on throttle body. See Fig. 4.

Vehicle Speed Sensor (VSS) – VSS delivers input signal to PCM to indicate vehicle speed. Sensor is located on top of differential assembly. See Fig. 4.

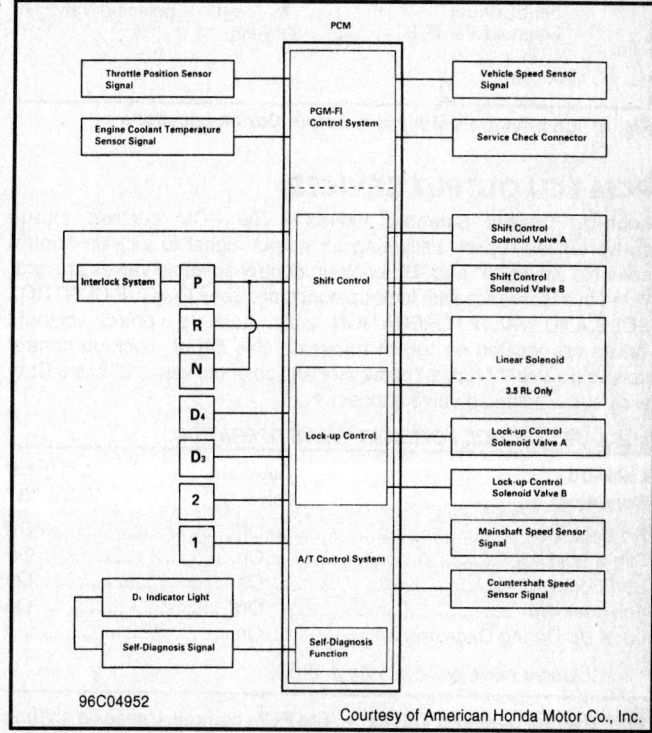

Fig. 3: Identifying Input & Output Devices

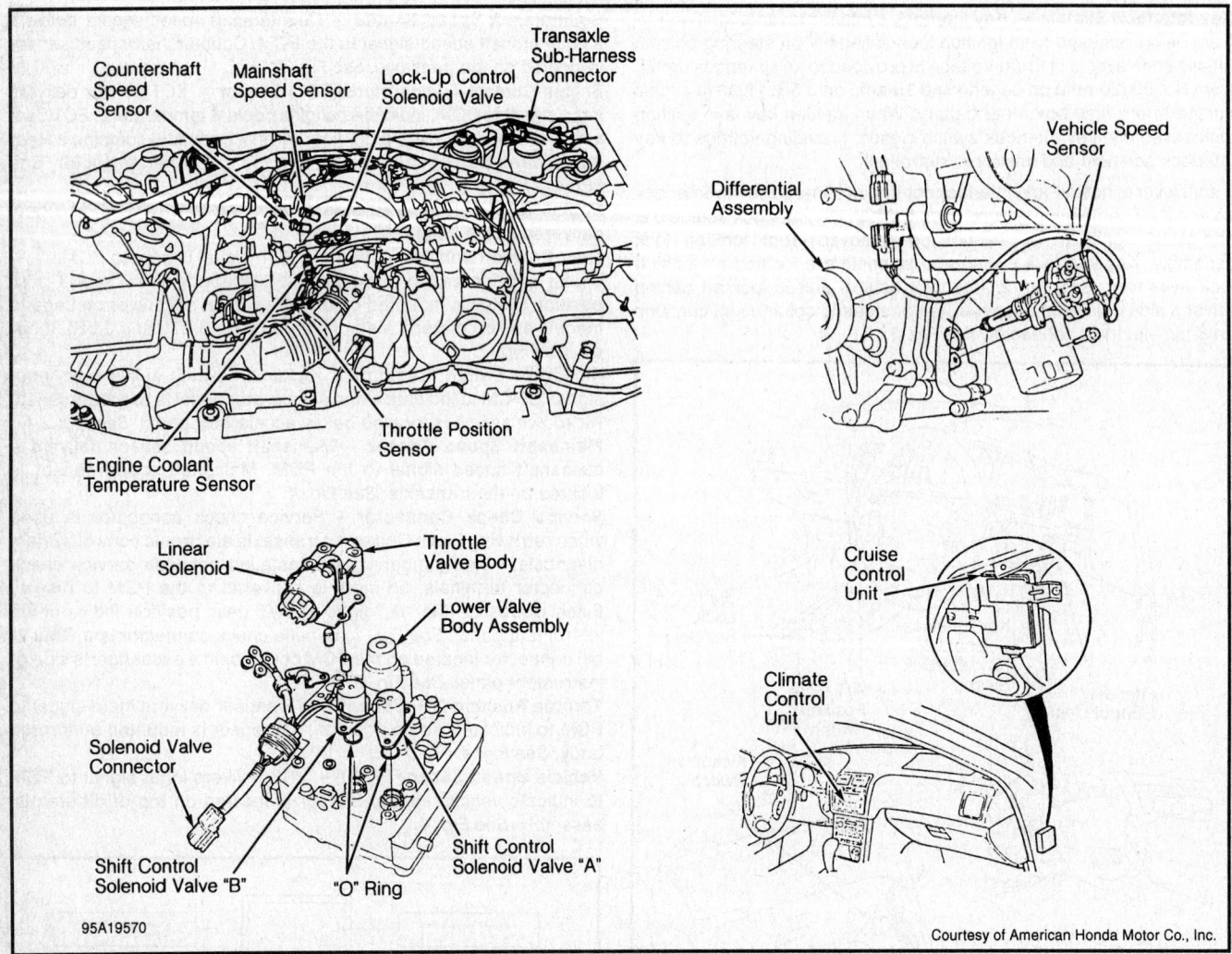

95A19570   Courtesy of American Honda Motor Co., Inc.

Fig. 4: Identifying PCM Input & Output Device Locations

PCM ECU OUTPUT DEVICES

Lock-Up Control Solenoid Valves – The PCM controls torque converter lock-up by delivering an output signal to lock-up control solenoid valves "A" and "B". Lock-up control solenoid valves are activated in accordance with lock-up condition. See LOCK-UP CONTROL SOLENOID VALVE OPERATION table. Lock-up control solenoid valves are located on top of transaxle. See Fig. 4. Lock-up control solenoid valve "A" has a Yellow wire and solenoid valve "B" has a Gray wire at the solenoid valve connector.

LOCK-UP CONTROL SOLENOID VALVE OPERATION

Lock-Up Condition	Solenoid Valve "A"	Solenoid Valve "B"
No Lock-Up	Off	Off
Slight Lock-Up	On	Off
Half Lock-Up	On	On
Full Lock-Up	On	On
Lock-Up During Deceleration	On	1

1 – Solenoid valve will cycle on and off.

Shift Control Solenoid Valves – The PCM controls transaxle shifting by delivering an output signal to shift control solenoid valves "A" and "B". Solenoid valves are operated in accordance with gear position. See SHIFT CONTROL SOLENOID VALVE OPERATION table. Shift control solenoid valves are located on lower valve body assembly. See Fig. 4. Shift control solenoid valve "A" has a Blue wire and solenoid valve "B" has a Green wire at the solenoid valve connector.

SHIFT CONTROL SOLENOID VALVE OPERATION

Shift Lever Position	Solenoid Valve "A"	Solenoid Valve "B"
"1", "D₄" Or "D₃" (1st Gear)	Off	On
"2", "D₄" Or "D₃" (2nd Gear)	On	On
"D₄" Or "D₃" (3rd Gear)	On	Off
"D₄" (4th Gear)	Off	Off
"R" (Reverse)	On	Off

Interlock Control Unit – When A/T gear position switch is in Park position, PCM provides voltage to shift lock circuit in the interlock control unit, provided brake pedal is depressed and accelerator pedal is in idle position. Interlock control unit then operates shift lock solenoid by controlling the ground circuit. When shift lock solenoid is energized, shift lever is released and can be moved.

Linear Solenoid – The PCM controls transaxle shifting related to engine torque by delivering an output signal to operate linear solenoid. Linear solenoid operates throttle valve on throttle valve body. Linear solenoid is located on throttle valve body. See Fig. 4.

Self-Diagnosis Indicator – If an abnormality exists in transaxle electronic control system and DTC is stored, PCM will deliver an output signal (Flash Code) to turn on and blink "D₄" light. The "D₄" light is located on the A/T gear position indicator on instrument panel. See Fig. 1. Flash Code can be retrieved to identify problem area by installing jumper wire between service check connector terminals. Flash Codes will be displayed by blinking "D₄" light.

SELF-DIAGNOSTIC SYSTEM

SYSTEM DIAGNOSIS

The PCM monitors transaxle operation. PCM contains a self-diagnostic system which stores a DTC if a transaxle electronic control system failure or problem exists. If DTC is stored, PCM will turn on and blink "D₄" light on A/T gear position indicator on instrument panel. If a transaxle electronic control system failure or problem is suspected and "D₄" light on A/T gear position indicator does not flash, perform diagnostic circuit check to ensure proper operation of "D₄" light. See DIAGNOSTIC CHARTS. Flash Codes can be retrieved on all years/models but are the only codes available on 1995 models. DTC can be retrieved using scan tool at Data Link Connector (DLC) located behind ashtray. Flash Code may also be retrieved for diagnosing transaxle electronic control system.

RETRIEVING DTCS & FLASH CODES

NOTE: Manufacturer does not provide scan tool information for Legend models. See RETRIEVING FLASH CODES USING "D₄" LIGHT.

NOTE: During diagnostics, ensure "D₄" indicator light on A/T gear position indicator on instrument panel is not turned on by a fault in the PGM-FI system. The PGM-FI system controls the fuel injection system. To repair PGM-FI system, see appropriate SELF-DIAGNOSTICS article in ENGINE PERFORMANCE in appropriate MITCHELL® manual.

NOTE: Before any diagnostic procedure, obtain radio anti-theft code from customer. Note radio preset stations, as radio stations and clock setting will be cleared and must be reset. Radio anti-theft code must be re-entered for radio operation.

Retrieving DTCs Using Scan Tool – 1) If fault code exists, "D₄" light on A/T gear position on instrument panel will blink when ignition is turned on. To retrieve DTC using scan tool, turn ignition off.

2) Connect scan tool to 16-pin Data Link Connector (DLC) located behind ashtray. Turn ignition on. Scan tool will indicate DTCs. Follow scan tool manufacturers instructions.

3) Once DTC is obtained, turn ignition off. Determine probable cause and symptom. See DTC/FLASH CODE IDENTIFICATION table. If any other fault codes except those listed are displayed, see appropriate SELF-DIAGNOSTICS article in ENGINE PERFORMANCE in appropriate MITCHELL® manual. For trouble shooting of fault codes, see DIAGNOSTIC CHARTS. If "D₄" light does not flash or stays on, see appropriate "D₄" light flow chart.

NOTE: Flash Codes can be retrieved on all years/models but are the only codes available on 1995 models.

Retrieving Flash Codes Using "D₄" Light – 1) If fault code exists, "D₄" light on A/T gear position on instrument panel will blink when ignition is turned on. To retrieve fault code, turn ignition off.

2) Install jumper wire between service check connector terminals. Service check connector is a Gray 2-pin connector located on the PCM cover, below passenger's side of instrument panel. *See Fig. 5.*

3) Turn ignition on. Fault codes with be displayed by blinking "D₄" light on A/T gear position indicator on instrument panel.

NOTE: If Malfunction Indicator Light (MIL) on instrument panel also starts blinking, PGM-FI system must be checked. See appropriate SELF-DIAGNOSTICS article in ENGINE PERFORMANCE in appropriate MITCHELL® manual.

4) Note number of blinks from "D₄" light. A short blink indicates a single digit Flash Code. A long blink equals 10 short blinks. For example, if "D₄" light blinks once, this is a Flash Code No. 1. If "D₄" light blinks one long blink and then 4 short blinks, this is a Flash Code No. 14. *See Fig. 6.*

5) Once Flash Code is obtained, turn ignition off. Remove jumper wire from service check connector. Determine probable cause and symptom. See DTC/FLASH CODE IDENTIFICATION table. If any other Flash Codes except those listed are displayed, PCM is defective. For trouble shooting of Flash Codes, see DIAGNOSTIC CHARTS.

6) On Legend models, if Flash Code No. 1, 2, 3, 7, 8 or 16 exists, check specified fuses. See FUSE IDENTIFICATION table. If any fuses are defective, replace fuses. On all models, clear DTCs, see CLEARING DTCS under SELF-DIAGNOSTIC SYSTEM and then recheck system operation. If customer describes symptoms listed DTC/FLASH CODE IDENTIFICATION table and "D₄" indicator light is off, it may be necessary to test drive vehicle to recreate the symptom and then check for Flash Code with ignition still on.

FUSE IDENTIFICATION

Fuse Number	Fuse Location
No. 5 (20-Amp), No. 22 (20-Amp) & No. 25 (30-Amp)	Fuse-Relay Box Behind Driver's Side Kick Panel
No. 31 (120-Amp) & 35 (50 Amp)	Engine Compartment Fuse Box, Near Battery

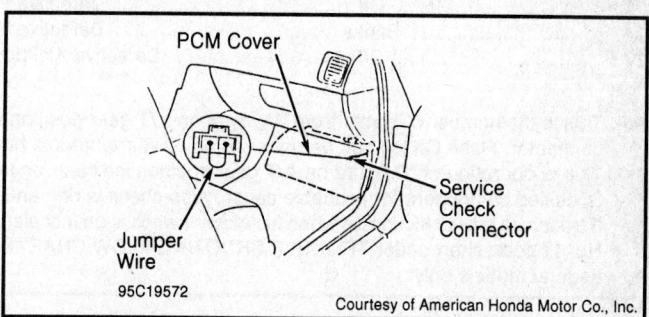

95C19572

Courtesy of American Honda Motor Co., Inc.

Fig. 5: Identifying Service Check Connector & Installing Jumper Wire

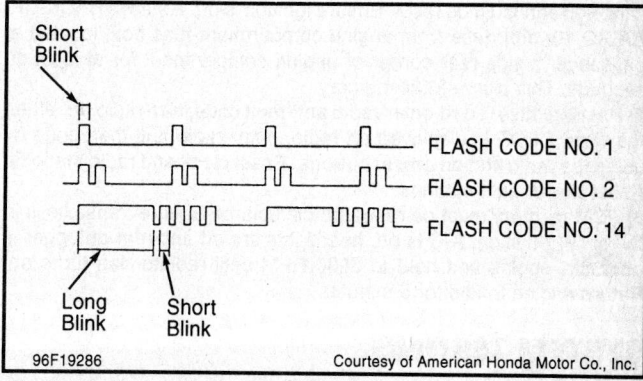

96F19286

Courtesy of American Honda Motor Co., Inc.

Fig. 6: Identifying Flash Code Displays

DTC/FLASH CODE IDENTIFICATION

DTC/Flash Code [1] Number	Indicator Light [2] Condition	Probable [3] Cause	[4] Symptom
P0715/15	Off	Defective Mainshaft Speed Sensor	Transaxle Jerks Hard When Shifting
P0720/9	Blinks	Defective Countershaft Speed Sensor	Lock-Up Clutch Does Not Engage
P0730/41	Off	Defective Shift Control System	Fails To Shift, Stuck In 1st Or 4th Gears
P0740/40	Off	Defective Lock-Up Control System	Lock-Up Clutch Does Not Engage Or Remains Engaged, Unstable Engine Idle
P0753/7	Blinks	Defective Shift Control Solenoid "A"	Remains In 4th Gear, Fails To Shift Other Than 1st-4th, 2nd-4th Or 2nd-3rd Gears
P0758/8	Blinks	Defective Shift Control Solenoid "B"	Remains In 1st Or 4th Gear
P1705/5	Blinks	Defective A/T Gear Position Switch	Lock-Up Clutch Does Not Engage, Fails To Shift Other Than 2nd-4th Gears
P1706/6	Off	Defective A/T Gear Position Switch	Lock-Up Clutch Does Not Engage, Lock-Up Clutch Engages & Disengages, Fails To Shift Other Than 2nd-4th Gears
P1753/1	Blinks	Defective Lock-Up Control Solenoid "A"	Lock-Up Clutch Does Not Engage Or Remains Engaged, Unstable Engine Idle
P1758/2	Blinks	Defective Lock-Up Control Solenoid "B"	Lock-Up Clutch Does Not Engage
P1768/16	Blinks	Defective Linear Solenoid	Transaxle Jerks Hard When Shifting Lock-Up Clutch Does Not Engage
P1791/4	Blinks	Defective Vehicle Speed Sensor	Lock-Up Clutch Does Not Engage
3 [5]	Blinks Or Remains Off	Defective Throttle Position Sensor	Lock-Up Clutch Does Not Engage
10 [5]	Blinks	Defective Engine Coolant Temp. Sensor	Lock-Up Clutch Does Not Engage
11 [5]	Off	Defective PCM	Lock-Up Clutch Does Not Engage
14 [5]	Blinks	Defective PCM	Transaxle Jerks Hard When Shifting
17 [5]	Off	Defective Kickdown Switch	4th-2nd Gear Kickdown Speed Is Low Or Does Not Exist

[1] – This is the number of blinks from "D4" light on A/T gear position indicator on instrument panel with jumper wire installed in service check connector. Flash Codes can be retrieved on all years/models but are the only codes available on 1995 models.

[2] – This is operation of "D4" light on A/T gear position indicator on instrument panel.

[3] – Specified component for probable cause. Also check wiring and connections for the specified component.

[4] – If transaxle fails to kickdown when kickdown switch is on (accelerator pedal fully depressed), check kickdown switch signal. See Fault Code No. 17 code chart under TROUBLE SHOOTING FLOW CHARTS.

[5] – Legend models only.

CLEARING FAULT CODES

1) Once repairs have been performed, fault codes must be cleared from PCM memory. Note power seat setting, as setting will be canceled and must be reset. Ensure ignition is off. Remove BACK-UP, RADIO 10- amp fuse from engine compartment fuse box, located at passenger's side rear corner of engine compartment for at least 10 seconds. This clears PCM memory.

2) Reinstall fuse. To re-enter radio anti-theft code, turn radio on. When the word CODE is displayed on radio, enter radio anti-theft code by using the radio station preset buttons. Reset clock and radio stations. Reset power seat settings.

3) PCM memory must be reset for idle control. Ensure transaxle is in "N" or "P" position, A/C is off, headlights are off and rear defogger is off. Start engine and hold to 3000 RPM until radiator fan turns on. Return engine to idle for 5 minutes.

SYSTEM TESTING

A/T GEAR POSITION INDICATOR

NOTE: Information for testing 3.2TL models is not provided by manufacture. If necessary, refer to wiring schematic when checking component wiring. See WIRING DIAGRAMS.

Legend – 1) Remove instrument panel gauge assembly from instrument panel. Disconnect 22-pin electrical connector from rear of instrument panel gauge assembly.

2) Check for voltage and continuity at electrical connectors as specified. See Fig. 7. Follow tests in number order. If necessary to check ground connections, G301, G302, G303 or G501, See Fig. 8. Ground connection G301 is located behind driver's side kick panel

area. Ground connection G302 is located on passenger's side front strut tower. Ground connection G303 is located behind passenger's side kick panel area. Ground connection G501 is located at center console area, just below the stereo.

3) If necessary to check No. 13 fuse (7.5-amp), fuse is located in fuse-relay box, located behind kick panel on driver's side. If necessary to access PCM, PCM is located below the carpet on passenger's side of instrument panel. See Fig. 2.

4) If necessary to access A/T gear position switch, A/T gear position switch is mounted on driver's side of shift lever. See Fig. 2.

3.5RL – 1) Remove instrument panel gauge assembly from instrument panel. Disconnect 22-pin and 30-pin connectors from rear of instrument panel gauge assembly.

2) Inspect and repair as necessary any loose, corroded or bent terminals. Check for voltage and continuity at electrical connectors as specified. See Fig. 9.

3) Repair any circuit were specifications are outside desired result. If all tests are okay and A/T gear position indicator is defective, replace printed circuit board.

NOTE: 3.2TL interlock systems diagnosis information is not available, refer to wiring schematic for diagnosis. See Fig. 11. For 3.5RL interlock system testing, see DIAGNOSTIC CHARTS and wiring schematic. See Fig. 12.

NO.	WIRE	TEST CONDITION	TEST: DESIRED RESULT	POSSIBLE CAUSE
1	BLK	Under all conditons	Check for continuity to ground: There should be continuity.	• Poor ground (G301, G302, G303) • An open in the wire
2	YEL	Ignition switch ON (II)	Check for voltage to ground: There should be battery voltage.	• Blown No.13 (7.5 A) fuse • An open in the wire
3	GRN/WHT	Shift lever in [P] NOTE: Don't push the brake pedal.	Check for continuity to ground: There should be continuity. There should be no continuity in any other position.	• Faulty A/T gear position switch • Poor ground (G501) • An open in the wire
	GRN/RED	Shift lever in [R]		
	GRN	Shift lever in [N]		
	GRN/BLU	Shift lever in [D₃]		
	GRN/YEL	Shift lever in [2]		
	GRN/ORN	Shift lever in [1]		
4	YEL/RED	Ignition switch ON (II) and shift lever in [D₄]	Check for voltage to ground: There should be battery voltage.	• Faulty A/T gear position switch • Faulty PCM • Poor ground (G501) • An open in the wire
5	RED/BLK and RED	Combination light switch ON and dash lights brightness control dial on full bright	Check for voltage between RED/BLK and RED terminals: There should be battery voltage.	• Faulty dash lights brightness control system • An open in the wire
6	YEL/RED	Ignition switch ON (II) and shift lever in any position except [D₄]	Check for voltage to ground: There should be battery voltage for two seconds after the ignition switch is turned ON (II), and less than 1 V two seconds later.	• Faulty PCM • Faulty A/T gear position switch • An open in the wire
7	NOT USED			
8	LT GRN	Ignition switch ON (II)	Check for voltage to ground: There should be more than 11 V.	• Faulty PCM • An open in the wire

96G19287

Courtesy of American Honda Motor Co., Inc.

Fig. 7: Testing A/T Gear Position Indicator (Legend)

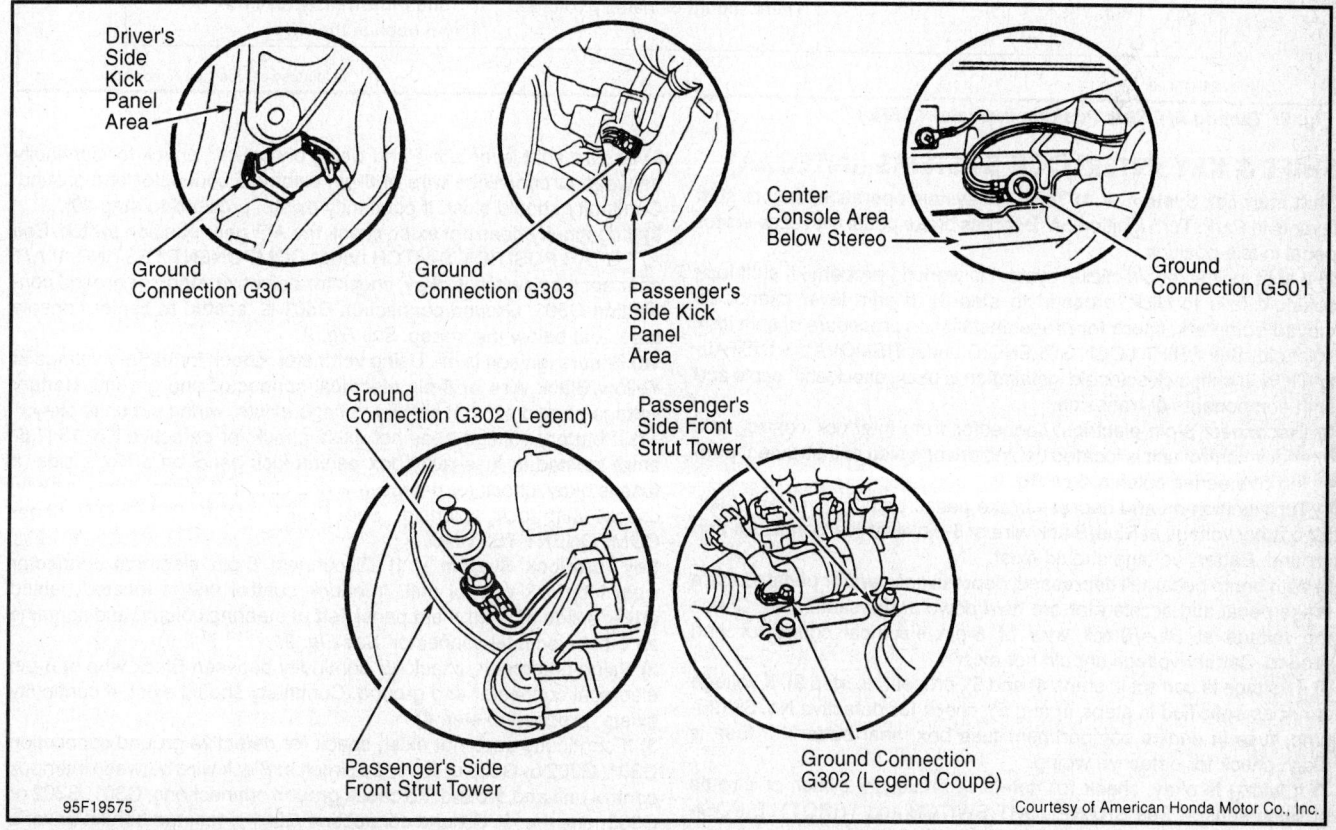

Driver's Side Kick Panel Area

Ground Connection G301

Ground Connection G303

Passenger's Side Kick Panel Area

Center Console Area Below Stereo

Ground Connection G501

Ground Connection G302 (Legend)

Passenger's Side Front Strut Tower

Passenger's Side Front Strut Tower

Ground Connection G302 (Legend Coupe)

95F19575

Courtesy of American Honda Motor Co., Inc.

Fig. 8: Identifying Ground Connections

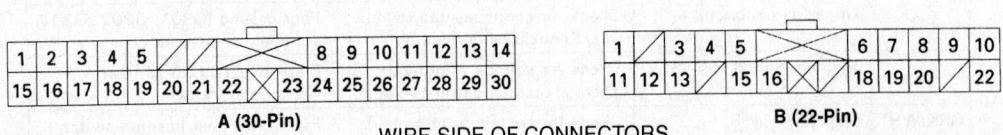

WIRE SIDE OF CONNECTORS

Terminal Number	Wire Color	Test Condition	Test: Desired Result	Posible Cause (If result is not obtained)
A23	LT GRN	Ignition switch ON (II)	Check for voltage to ground: There should be battery voltage.	• Faulty PCM • An open in the wire
A24	BLK/BLU	Shift lever in P NOTE: Do not push the brake pedal.	Check for continuity to ground: There should be continuity. NOTE: There should be no continuity in any other shift lever position.	• Faulty A/T gear position switch • An open in the wire
A25	WHT	Shift lever in R		
A26	RED	Shift lever in N		
A27	BRN/YEL	Ignition switch ON (II) and shift lever in any position except D4	Check for voltage to ground: There should be battery voltage for two seconds after the ignition switch is turned ON (II), and less than 1 V two seconds later.	• Faulty PCM • An open in the wire
A28	GRN	Shift lever in D3	Check for continuity to ground: There should be continuity. NOTE: There should be no continuity in any other shift lever position.	• Faulty A/T gear position switch • An open in the wire
A29	BLU	Shift lever in 2		
A30	BRN	Shift lever in 1		
B9	BLK	Under all conditions	Check for continuity to ground: There should be continuity.	• Poor ground (G401) • An open in the wire
B11	BLK/YEL	Ignition switch ON (II)	Check for voltage to ground: There should be battery voltage.	• Blown No. 20 (7.5 A) fuse in the under-dash fuse/relay box • An open in the wire

96H19288

Courtesy of American Honda Motor Co., Inc.

Fig. 9: Testing A/T Gear Position Indicator (3.5RL)

SHIFT & KEY INTERLOCK SYSTEMS (INTEGRA)

Shift Interlock System – 1) To check system operation, ensure shift lever is in Park. Turn ignition on. Depress brake pedal with accelerator pedal in idle position.

2) If shift lock solenoid clicks, system is working properly. If shift lock solenoid fails to click, proceed to step 3). If shift lever cannot be moved from Park, check for proper installation procedure of shift lock solenoid. See SHIFT LOCK SOLENOID under REMOVAL & INSTALLATION. If shift lock solenoid installation is okay, check shift cable and shift components at transaxle.

3) Disconnect 8-pin electrical connector from interlock control unit. Interlock control unit is located behind driver's side of instrument panel, left of steering column. See Fig. 2.

4) Turn ignition on and depress brake pedal. Using voltmeter, check for battery voltage at Blue/Black wire of 8-pin electrical connector and ground. Battery voltage should exist.

5) With brake pedal still depressed, depress accelerator pedal. Ensure brake pedal and accelerator are held down at the same time. Check for voltage at Blue/Black wire of 8-pin electrical connector and ground. Battery voltage should not exist.

6) If voltage is correct in steps 4) and 5), proceed to step 8). If voltage is not as specified in steps 4) and 5), check for defective No. 39 (20-amp) fuse in engine compartment fuse box, near battery. If fuse is okay, check for defective wiring.

7) If wiring is okay, check for defective brakelight switch or throttle position sensor. See BRAKELIGHT SWITCH and THROTTLE POSITION SENSOR under COMPONENT TESTING. If all components are okay, substitute PCM and recheck operation.

8) Ensure shift lever is in Park. Using ohmmeter, check for continuity between Green/White wire of 8-pin electrical connector and ground. Continuity should exist. If continuity exists, proceed to step 10).

9) If continuity does not exist, check the A/T gear position switch. See A/T GEAR POSITION SWITCH under COMPONENT TESTING. If A/T gear position switch is okay, check for defective wiring or ground connection G501. Ground connection G501 is located at center console area, just below the stereo. See Fig. 9.

10) Ensure ignition is on. Using voltmeter, check for battery voltage at Yellow/Black wire of 8-pin electrical connector and ground. Battery voltage should exist. If battery voltage exists, wiring circuit is okay.

11) If battery voltage does not exist, check for defective No. 13 (7.5-amp) located in fuse-relay box behind kick panel on driver's side. If fuse is okay, check for defective wiring circuit. If wiring circuit is okay, check shift lock solenoid. See SHIFT LOCK SOLENOID under COMPONENT TESTING.

Key Interlock System – 1) Disconnect 8-pin electrical connector from interlock control unit. Interlock control unit is located behind driver's side of instrument panel, left of steering column and contains an 8-pin electrical connector. See Fig. 2.

2) Using ohmmeter, check for continuity between Black wire of 8-pin electrical connector and ground. Continuity should exist. If continuity exists, proceed to step 4).

3) If continuity does not exist, check for defective ground connection G301, G302 or G303 or for open circuit in Black wire between interlock control unit and ground. To check ground connections, G301, G302 or G303, See Fig. 9. Ground connection G301 is located behind driver's side kick panel area. Ground connection G302 is located on passenger's side front strut tower. Ground connection G303 is located behind passenger's side kick panel area.

4) Ensure shift lever is in Park. Using ohmmeter, check for continuity between Green/White wire of 8-pin electrical connector and ground. Continuity should exist. If continuity exists, proceed to step 7).

5) If continuity does not exist, check for open circuit in Green/White wire between interlock control unit and A/T gear position switch. The A/T gear position switch is mounted on driver's side of shift lever. *See Fig. 2.* If Green/White wire is okay, proceed to step 6).

6) Check for open circuit in Black wire between A/T gear position switch and ground connection G501 or for defective ground connection G501. Ground connection G501 is located at center console area, just below the stereo. *See Fig. 9.* If ground connection G501 and wiring are okay, check A/T gear position switch. See A/T GEAR POSITION SWITCH under COMPONENT TESTING.

7) Turn ignition lock assembly to ACC position. Using voltmeter, check for battery voltage at White/Red and Black/Red wires of 8-pin electrical connector and ground. Battery voltage should exist. If battery voltage exists, wiring circuit is okay.

8) If battery voltage does not exist, check for defective No. 39 (20-amp) fuse in engine compartment fuse box, near battery. If fuse is okay, check for open circuit in White/Green wire between No. 39 fuse and key interlock switch and key interlock solenoid. Key interlock switch and key interlock solenoid are located on ignition lock assembly. *See Fig. 2.*

9) If White/Green wire is okay, check key interlock solenoid. See KEY INTERLOCK SOLENOID under COMPONENT TESTING. If key interlock solenoid is okay, check for open circuit in White/Red and Black/Red wires between key interlock solenoid and interlock control unit. Repair wiring as necessary.

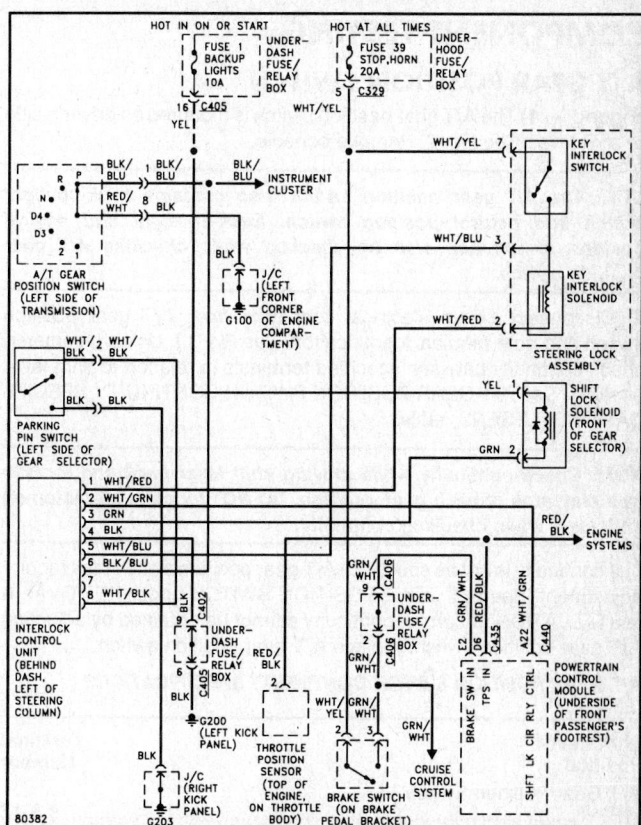

Fig. 11: Shift & Key Interlock System Wiring Schematic (3.2TL)

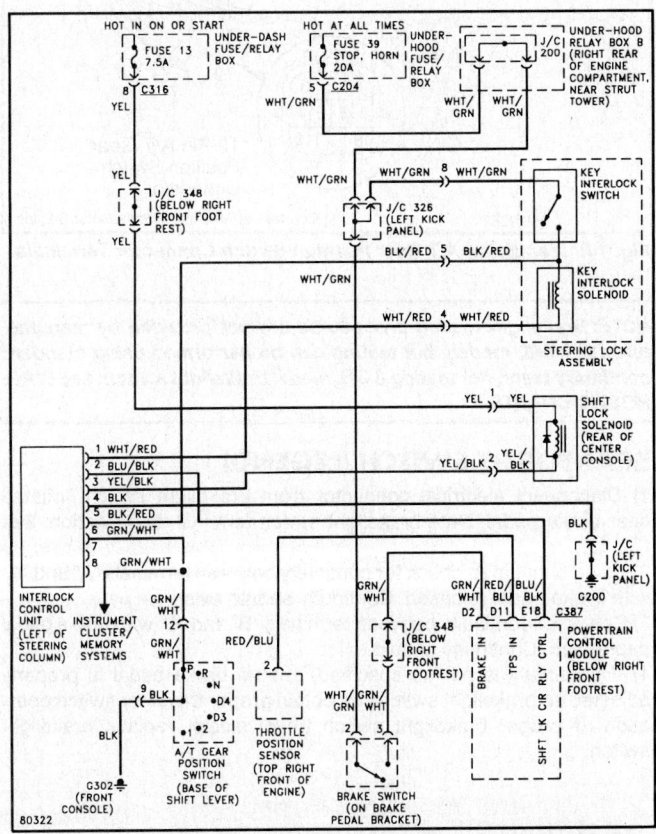

Fig. 10: Shift & Key Interlock System Wiring Schematic (Legend)

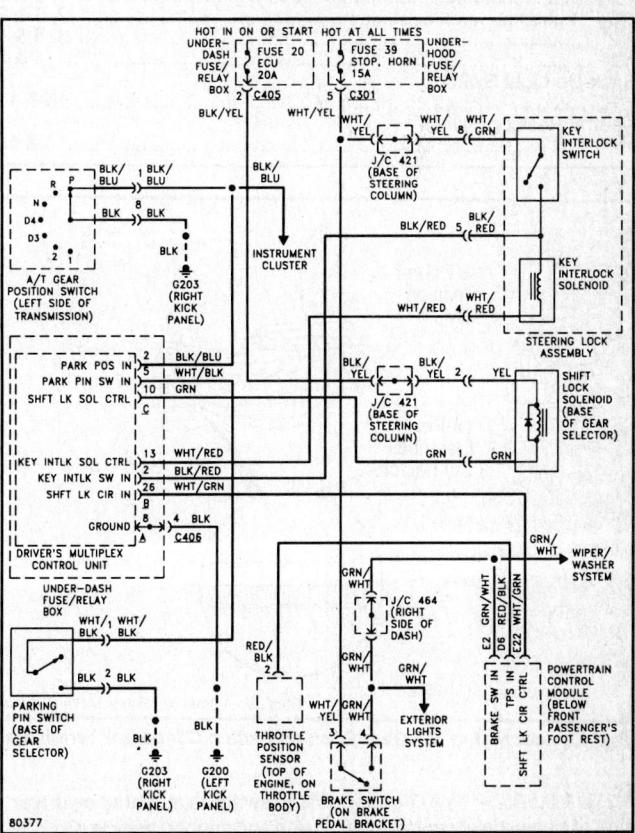

Fig. 12: Shift & Key Interlock System Wiring Schematic (3.5RL)

COMPONENT TESTING

A/T GEAR POSITION SWITCH

Legend – 1) The A/T gear position switch is mounted on driver's side of shift lever. *See Fig. 2.* Remove console.

NOTE: The A/T gear position switch also contains back-up light switch and neutral position switch. Back-up light and neutral position switch can also be checked when checking A/T gear position switch.

2) Disconnect 14-pin electrical connector from A/T gear position switch and note terminal identification. *See Fig. 13.* Using ohmmeter, check continuity between specified terminals in relation to shift lever position. See A/T GEAR POSITION SWITCH CONTINUITY SPECIFI-CATIONS (LEGEND) table.

NOTE: Check continuity while moving shift lever back and forth in free play area of each gear position. DO NOT touch push button on shift lever when checking continuity.

3) If continuity is not as specified, A/T gear position switch may require adjustment. See A/T GEAR POSITION SWITCH under REMOVAL & INSTALLATION. If correct continuity cannot be obtained by adjusting A/T gear position switch, replace A/T gear position switch.

A/T GEAR POSITION SWITCH CONTINUITY SPECIFICATIONS (LEGEND)

Shift Lever Position	Terminal Number
A/T Gear Position Switch	
"P"	9 & 12
"R"	8 & 9
"N"	7 & 9
"D₄"	1, 5 & 9
"D₃"	2, 5 & 9
"2"	3, 5 & 9
"1"	4 & 9
Back-Up Light Switch	
"R"	10 & 11
Neutral Position Switch	
"P" & "N"	6 & 14

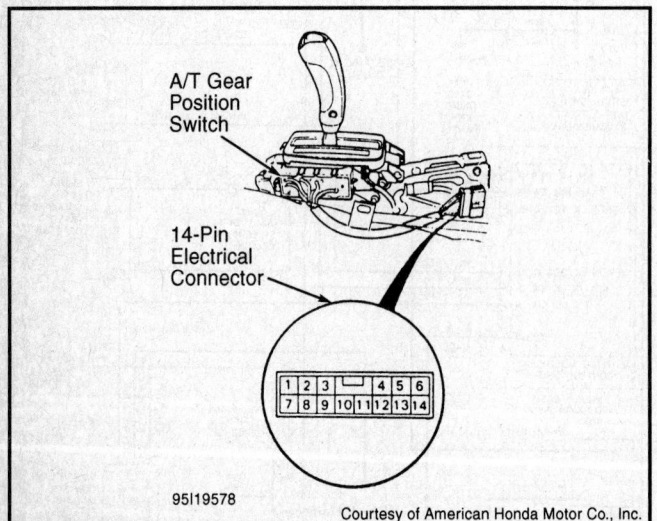

Fig. 13: Identifying A/T Gear Position Switch Connector Terminals

A/T Gear Position Switch

14-Pin Electrical Connector

95I19578

Courtesy of American Honda Motor Co., Inc.

3.2TL & 3.5RL – 1) A/T gear position switch is mounted on driver's side of transaxle at control shaft. Raise and support vehicle. On 3.5RL model, remove exhaust pipe and catalytic converter.
2) On both models, disconnect 10-pin connector and note terminal identification. *See Fig. 14.* Using ohmmeter, check continuity between specified terminals in relation to shift lever position. See A/T GEAR POSITION SWITCH CONTINUITY SPECIFICATIONS (3.2TL & 3.5RL) table.

NOTE: Check continuity while moving shift lever back and forth in free play area of each gear position. DO NOT touch push button on shift lever when checking continuity.

3) If continuity is not as specified, A/T gear position switch may require adjustment. See A/T GEAR POSITION SWITCH under REMOVAL & INSTALLATION. If correct continuity cannot be obtained by adjusting A/T gear position switch, replace A/T gear position switch.

A/T GEAR POSITION SWITCH CONTINUITY SPECIFICATIONS (3.2TL & 3.5RL)

Shift Lever Position	Terminal Number
A/T Gear Position Switch	
"P"	1 & 8
"R"	2 & 8
"N"	3 & 8
"D₄"	4, 8 & 9
"D₃"	5, 8 & 9
"2"	6, 8 & 9
"1"	7 & 8
Neutral Position Switch	
"P" & "N"	8 & 10

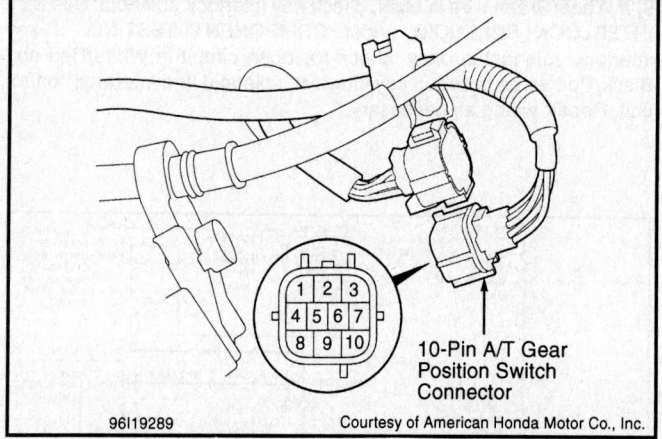

10-Pin A/T Gear Position Switch Connector

96I19289

Courtesy of American Honda Motor Co., Inc.

Fig. 14: Identifying A/T Gear Position Switch Connector Terminals

NOTE: Brakelight testing procedures are not provided by manufacture for 3.5RL models but testing can be performed using standard continuity tests. For testing 3.2TL model brakelight switch, see DIAGNOSTIC CHARTS.

BRAKELIGHT SWITCH (LEGEND)

1) Disconnect electrical connector from brakelight switch, located near brake pedal. Note brakelight switch terminal identification. *See Fig. 15.*
2) Using ohmmeter, check for continuity between terminals "A" and "D" with brake pedal released. Continuity should exist.
3) Check for continuity between terminals "B" and "C" with brake pedal depressed. Continuity should exist.
4) If continuity is not as specified, ensure brake pedal is properly adjusted so brakelight switch can obtain proper travel for switch operation. If proper brakelight switch travel exists, replace brakelight switch.

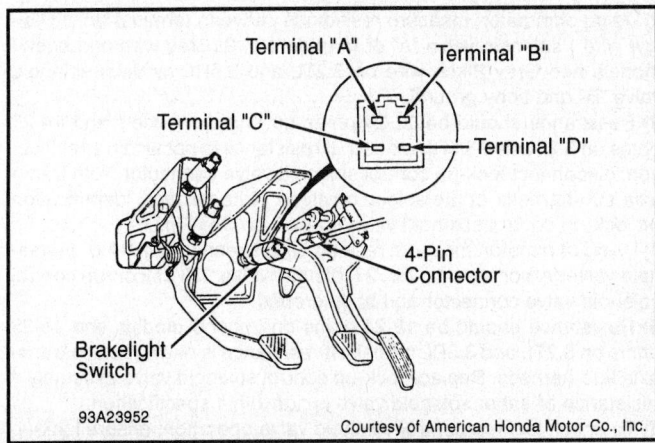

Fig. 15: Identifying Brakelight Switch Terminals

COUNTERSHAFT SPEED SENSOR

1) Countershaft speed sensor is located on the transaxle. See Fig. 4. Disconnect electrical connector for countershaft shaft speed sensor from transaxle sub-harness.

2) Using ohmmeter, check resistance between terminals of countershaft speed sensor electrical connector. Replace countershaft speed sensor if resistance is not 400-600 ohms at 70°F (20°C).

ENGINE COOLANT TEMPERATURE (ECT) SENSOR

1) Engine coolant temperature sensor is located in coolant pipe, near throttle body and contains a Red/White wire and Green/White wire in the electrical connector. See Fig. 4.

2) Disconnect electrical connector from engine coolant temperature sensor. Using ohmmeter, check engine coolant temperature sensor resistance in accordance with engine coolant temperature. See ENGINE COOLANT TEMPERATURE (ECT) SENSOR RESISTANCE table. Replace engine coolant temperature sensor if resistance is not as specified.

ENGINE COOLANT TEMPERATURE (ECT) SENSOR RESISTANCE

Temperature °F (°C)	Resistance [1] In Ohms
-4 (-20)	15,000-18,000
68 (20)	2500-3500
175 (80)	400-600
212 (100)	250-350

[1] – Measure resistance across sensor terminals.

KEY INTERLOCK SOLENOID

Legend – 1) Remove lower panel from instrument panel. Disconnect 8-pin electrical connector from main wiring harness and note terminal identification. See Fig. 16.

2) Using ohmmeter, check for continuity between designated terminals with ignition lock assembly in ACC position in relation to installation of ignition key. See KEY INTERLOCK SOLENOID CONTINUITY SPECIFICATIONS table.

3) Replace ignition lock assembly if continuity is not as specified, as key interlock solenoid cannot be serviced separately.

KEY INTERLOCK SOLENOID CONTINUITY SPECIFICATIONS

Ignition Key Position	Continuity Between Terminals
Key Installed	A & C, B & C
Key Removed	A & B

4) Connect battery voltage and ground to terminals "A" and "C". Ensure ignition key cannot be removed with battery voltage applied.

5) If ignition key cannot be removed, key interlock solenoid is okay. If ignition key can be removed, replace ignition lock assembly, as key interlock solenoid cannot be serviced separately.

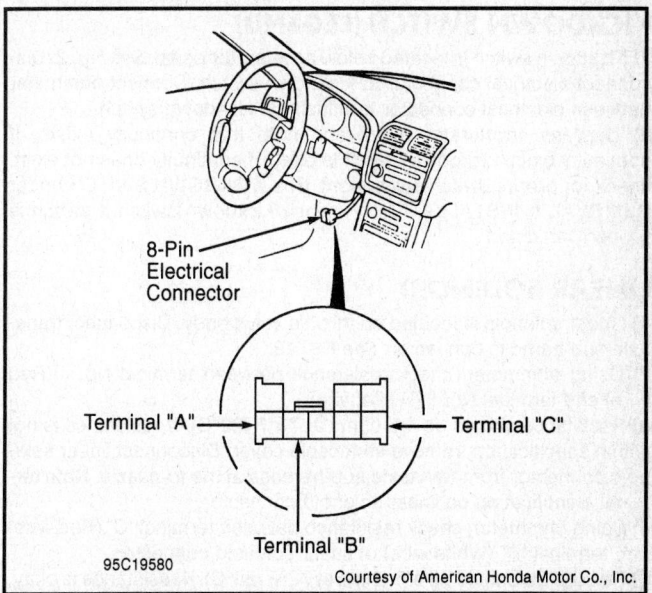

Fig. 16: Identifying Key Interlock Solenoid Electrical Connector & Terminals

3.2TL & 3.5RL – Remove instrument panel lower cover and knee bolster. Disconnect ignition switch Gray 8-pin connector from main wiring harness, located left of steering column. See Fig. 17. Using an ohmmeter, check for continuity between ignition switch Gray 8-pin connector terminal No. 2 (Black wire) and terminal No. 7 (Blue/White wire). Continuity should exist with key inserted into ignition switch. Continuity should not exist when key is removed from ignition switch. If continuity is not as specified, replace hood switch.

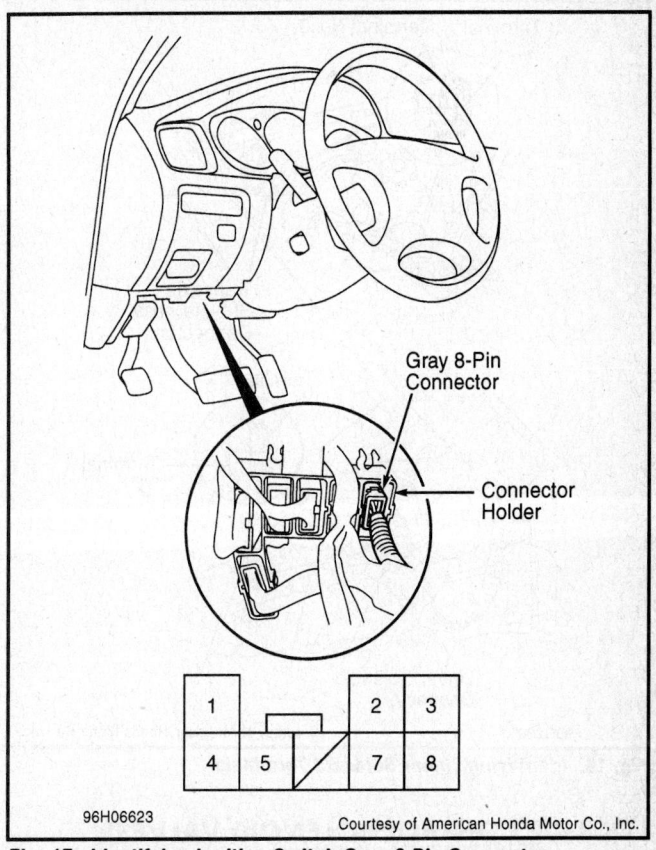

Fig. 17: Identifying Ignition Switch Gray 8-Pin Connector Terminals

KICKDOWN SWITCH (LEGEND)

1) Kickdown switch is located below accelerator pedal. *See Fig. 2.* Disconnect electrical connector at kickdown switch. Connect ohmmeter between electrical connector terminals on kickdown switch.

2) Depress accelerator pedal and note that continuity exists. If continuity exits, kickdown switch is okay. If continuity does not exist, check for proper switch adjustment. See KICKDOWN SWITCH under REMOVAL & INSTALLATION. Replace kickdown switch if switch is properly adjusted.

LINEAR SOLENOID

1) Linear solenoid is located on throttle valve body. Disconnect transaxle sub-harness connector. *See Fig. 18.*

2) Using ohmmeter, check resistance between terminal No. 7 (Red wire) and terminal No. 8 (White wire).

3) Resistance should be 4-6 ohms at 70°F (20°C). If resistance is not within specification, remove shift cable cover. Disconnect linear solenoid connector from transaxle sub-harness at the transaxle. Note terminal identification on linear solenoid connector.

4) Using ohmmeter, check resistance between terminal "C" (Red wire) and terminal "D" (White wire) of linear solenoid connector.

5) Resistance should be 4-6 ohms at 70°F (20°C). If resistance is okay, replace transaxle sub-harness. Replace linear solenoid if resistance is not within specification.

6) To check linear solenoid operation, connect positive battery terminal to terminal "C" and negative battery terminal to terminal "D" of linear solenoid connector.

7) Clicking sound should be heard, indicating linear solenoid operation. Replace linear solenoid if solenoid fails to operate.

NOTE: Linear solenoid and throttle valve body must be replaced as an assembly.

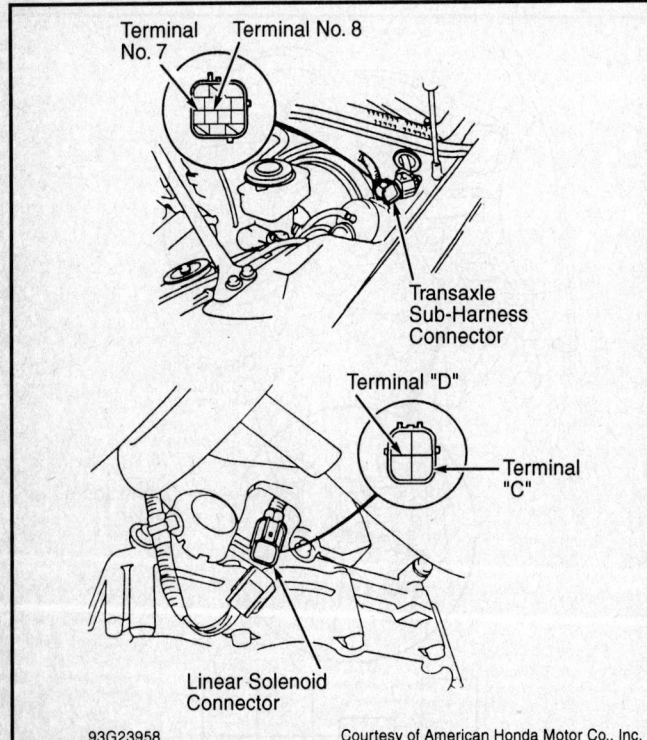

Fig. 18: Identifying Linear Solenoid Terminals

LOCK-UP CONTROL SOLENOID VALVES

1) Lock-up control solenoid valves are located on top of transaxle. *See Fig. 4.* Disconnect transaxle sub-harness connector. *See Fig. 19.*

2) Using ohmmeter, measure resistance between terminal No. 1 (Yellow wire) solenoid valve "A" or terminal No. 2 (Gray wire on Legend models and Gray/Black wire on 3.2TL and 3.5RL models) solenoid valve "B" and body ground.

3) Resistance should be 12-24 ohms on Legend models and 14-25 ohms on 3.2TL and 3.5RL models. If resistance is not within specification, disconnect lock-up control solenoid valve connector from transaxle sub-harness at the solenoid valves. Note terminal identification on lock-up control solenoid valve connector. *See Fig. 19.*

4) Using ohmmeter, measure resistance between terminal No. 1 (solenoid valve "A") or terminal No. 2 (solenoid valve "B") of lock-up control solenoid valve connector and body ground.

5) Resistance should be 12-24 ohms on Legend models and 14-25 ohms on 3.2TL and 3.5RL models. If resistance is okay, replace transaxle sub-harness. Replace lock-up control solenoid valve assembly if resistance of either solenoid valve is not within specification.

6) To check lock-up control solenoid valve operation, ensure lock-up control solenoid valve body is grounded. Connect battery voltage to terminal No. 1 (solenoid valve "A") or terminal No. 2 (solenoid valve "B") of lock-up control solenoid valve connector.

7) Clicking sound should be heard, indicating solenoid valve operation. Replace lock-up control solenoid valve assembly if either solenoid valve fails to operate.

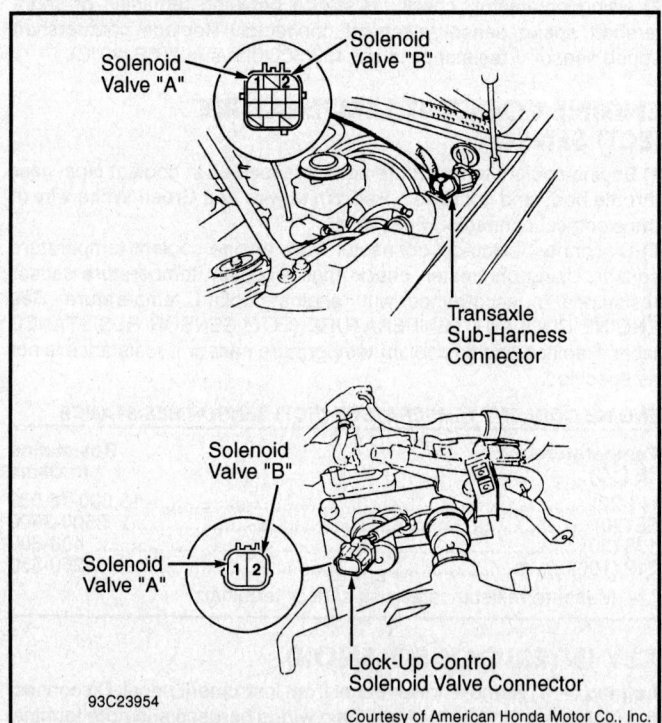

Fig. 19: Identifying Lock-Up Control Solenoid Valve Terminals

MAINSHAFT SPEED SENSOR

1) Mainshaft speed sensor is located on the transaxle. *See Fig. 4.* Disconnect electrical connector for mainshaft shaft speed sensor from transaxle sub-harness.

2) Using ohmmeter, check resistance between terminals of mainshaft speed sensor electrical connector. Replace mainshaft speed sensor if resistance is not 400-600 ohms at 70°F (20°C).

SHIFT CONTROL SOLENOID VALVES

1) Shift control solenoid valves are located on lower valve body assembly. *See Fig. 4.* Shift control solenoid valve "A" has a Blue wire and solenoid valve "B" has a Light Green wire on Legend models and Green wire on 3.2TL and 3.5RL models.

2) Disconnect transaxle sub-harness connector. *See Fig. 20.* Using ohmmeter, measure resistance between terminal No. 3 (Light Green wire) or terminal No. 4 (Blue wire) and body ground.

3) Resistance should be 12-24 ohms on Legend models and 14-25 ohms on 3.2TL and 3.5RL models. If resistance is not within specification, disconnect shift control solenoid valve connector from transaxle sub-harness at the transaxle. Note terminal identification on shift control solenoid valve connector.

4) Using ohmmeter, measure resistance between terminal "A" (Blue wire) and body ground. Measure resistance between terminal "B" (Light Green wire on Legend models and Green wire on 3.2TL and 3.5RL models) and body ground.

5) Resistance should be 12-24 ohms on Legend models and 14-25 ohms on 3.2TL and 3.5RL models. If resistance is okay, replace transaxle sub-harness. Replace shift control solenoid valve assembly if resistance of either solenoid valve is not within specification.

6) To check shift control solenoid valve operation, ensure shift control solenoid valve body is grounded. Apply battery voltage to terminal "A" (Blue wire) and then terminal "B" (Light Green wire) of shift control solenoid valve connector.

7) Clicking sound should be heard, indicating solenoid valve operation. Replace shift control solenoid valve assembly if either solenoid valve fails to operate.

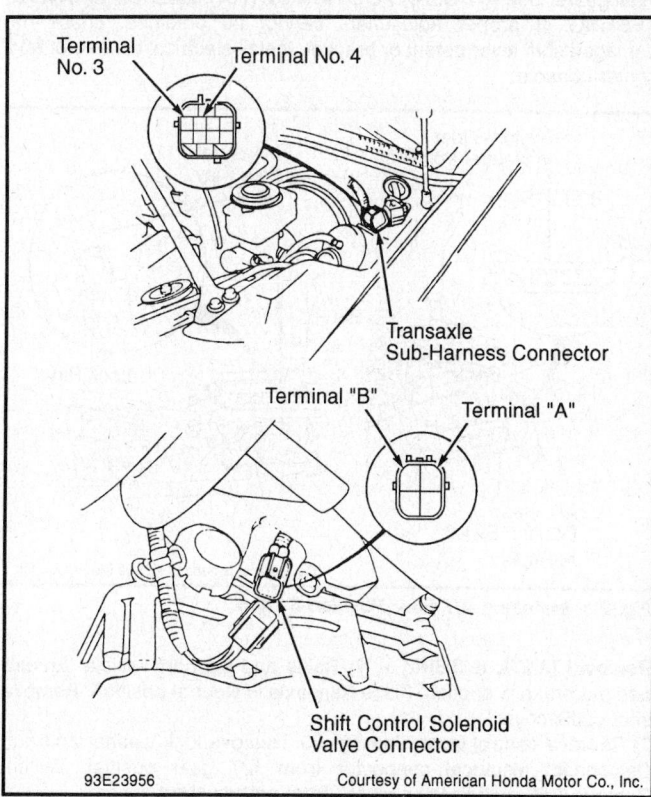

Fig. 20: Identifying Shift Control Solenoid Valve Terminals

SHIFT LOCK SOLENOID

NOTE: Information for testing shift lock system on 3.2TL models is not available from manufacturer.

Legend – 1) Remove center console. Disconnect electrical connector from main wiring harness and note terminal identification. *See Fig. 21.*

CAUTION: Battery voltage must be applied to correct shift lock solenoid terminals or diode inside shift lock solenoid will be damaged.

2) Momentarily connect positive battery voltage to terminal "A" and negative battery terminal to terminal "B". *See Fig. 21.* Note that shift lock solenoid operates with battery voltage applied. Replace shift lock solenoid if solenoid does not operate.

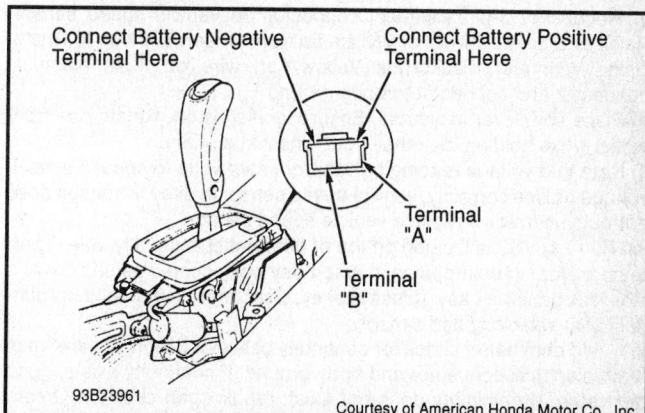

Fig. 21: Identifying Shift Lock Solenoid Connector Terminals

3.5RL – 1) Remove center console. Disconnect electrical connector from main wiring harness and note wire colors. *See Fig. 21.*

CAUTION: Battery voltage must be applied to correct shift lock solenoid terminals or diode inside shift lock solenoid will be damaged.

2) Momentarily connect positive battery voltage to Black/Yellow wire terminal and negative battery terminal to Green wire terminal. Note that shift lock solenoid operates with battery voltage applied. Replace shift lock solenoid if solenoid does not operate.

THROTTLE POSITION (TP) SENSOR

NOTE: If problem in TP sensor exists, TP sensor may set DTC P0122 or P0123 in PCM. See appropriate SELF-DIAGNOSTICS article in ENGINE PERFORMANCE in appropriate MITCHELL® manual.

TP sensor should input a .5-volt reference signal to PCM at closed throttle, 2.3-2.7 volts at half throttle and approximately 4.5 volts at full throttle. Voltage should change smoothly as throttle valve is opened and closed. If voltage is not correct, check TP sensor wiring circuit. See WIRING DIAGRAMS. Individual component testing of TP sensor is not available.

VEHICLE SPEED SENSOR (VSS)

Legend – 1) Vehicle speed sensor is located on top of differential assembly. *See Fig. 4.* Ensure No. 22 (20-amp) fuse in fuse-relay box, located behind driver's side kick panel, is okay. If fuse is okay, disconnect 3-pin electrical connector at vehicle speed sensor.

2) Turn ignition on. Using voltmeter, measure voltage between the Black/Yellow wire of 3-pin electrical connector and body ground. If battery voltage exists, go to step **5)**. If battery voltage does not exist, go next to step.

3) Using ohmmeter, check for continuity between Green/White wire of 3-pin electrical connector and body ground. If continuity exists, repair open circuit in Black/Yellow wire between 3-pin electrical connector and No. 22 (20-amp) fuse in fuse-relay box, located behind driver's side kick panel.

4) If continuity does not exist, check for open circuit in Green/White between 3-pin electrical connector and ground connection. See WIRING DIAGRAMS. Ground connection is located on mounting bolt for throttle body.

NOTE: Vehicle speed sensor is grounded through the PCM to ground connection on mounting bolt for throttle body.

5) Using voltmeter, measure voltage between Yellow/Red wire and Green/White wire of 3-pin electrical connector. If about 5 volts exist, go to next step. If about 5 volts does not exist, repair open circuit or short circuit to ground in Yellow/Red wire. The Yellow/Red wire goes to gauge assembly, PCM, cruise control unit, climate control unit or driving position memory system control unit.

6) Reconnect 3-pin electrical connector on vehicle speed sensor. Raise and support front of vehicle so front wheels are free to rotate. Using voltmeter, backprobe Yellow/Red wire on 3-pin electrical connector and connect it to body ground.

7) Place shift lever in Neutral. Ensure ignition is on. Rotate one front wheel while holding the other front wheel stationary.

8) Note that voltage reading pulses from zero volts to about 5 volts. If voltage pulses correctly, vehicle speed sensor is okay. If voltage does not pulse correctly, replace vehicle speed sensor.

3.2TL – 1) VSS is located on top of differential assembly. *See Fig. 4.* Ensure No. 1 (10-amp) fuse in fuse-relay box, located behind driver's side kick panel, is okay. If fuse is okay, disconnect 3-pin electrical connector at vehicle speed sensor.

2) Using ohmmeter, check for continuity between Green/White wire of 3-pin electrical connector and body ground. If continuity exists, go to next step. If continuity does not exist, repair open circuit in Green/White wire between 3-pin electrical connector and ground.

3) Turn ignition on. Using voltmeter, measure voltage between Yellow wire of 3-pin electrical connector and body ground. If battery voltage exists, go to next step. If battery voltage does not exist, repair open Yellow wire.

4) Measure voltage on Orange wire between 3-pin electrical connector and body ground. If voltage is 5 volts or more, go to next step. If voltage is less than 5 volts, repair open circuit or short circuit to ground in Orange wire. The Blue/White wire goes from VSS to PCM or cruise control unit.

5) Turn ignition off. Raise and support vehicle. Place shifter in Neutral and turn ignition on. Rotate one front wheel while holding the other front wheel stationary. If voltage pulses from zero volts to about 5 volts, go to next step. If voltage does not pulse correctly, replace vehicle speed sensor.

6) Disconnect instrument cluster 16-pin connector. Measure voltage on Orange wire between instrument cluster 16-pin connector and ground while rotating one front wheel and holding other front wheel stationary. If voltage pulses from zero volts to about 5 volts, replace speedometer. If voltage does not pulse correctly, repair open Orange wire between VSS connector and speedometer.

3.5RL – 1) VSS is located on top of differential assembly. *See Fig. 4.* Ensure No. 13 (7.5 amp) fuse in fuse-relay box, located behind driver's side kick panel, is okay. If fuse is okay, disconnect 3-pin electrical connector at vehicle speed sensor.

2) Turn ignition on. Using voltmeter, measure voltage between Yellow wire of 3-pin electrical connector and body ground. If battery voltage exists, go to next step. If battery voltage does not exist, repair open Yellow wire.

3) Measure voltage of Blue/White wire between 3-pin electrical connector and body ground. If voltage is 5 volts or more, go to next step. If voltage is less than 5 volts, repair open circuit or short circuit to ground in Blue/White wire. The Blue/White wire goes from VSS to PCM, cruise control unit, driver's multiplex control unit or navigation control unit.

4) Turn ignition off. Disconnect PCM 22-pin connector. PCM is located below passenger's side of instrument panel below carpet. Using ohmmeter, check continuity of Green/Blue wire between VSS 3-pin electrical connector and PCM 22-pin connector terminal No. 22. If continuity exists, go to next step. If continuity does not exist, repair open Green/Blue wire between VSS connector and PCM.

5) Raise and support vehicle. Place shifter in Neutral and turn ignition on. Rotate one front wheel while holding the other front wheel stationary. If voltage pulses from zero volts to about 5 volts, go to next step. If voltage does not pulse correctly, replace vehicle speed sensor.

6) Disconnect instrument cluster 30-pin connector. Measure voltage of Blue/White wire between instrument cluster 30-pin connector and ground while rotating one front wheel and holding other front wheel stationary. If voltage pulses from zero volts to about 5 volts, replace speedometer. If voltage does not pulse correctly, repair open Blue/White wire between VSS connector and speedometer.

REMOVAL & INSTALLATION

A/T GEAR POSITION SWITCH

Removal (Legend) – Remove center console. Disconnect electrical connector from A/T gear position switch. Remove bolts and A/T gear position switch.

Installation – 1) Ensure parking brake is applied. Place switch slider on A/T gear position switch in Neutral position. *See Fig. 22.* Place shift lever in Neutral.

2) Install A/T gear position switch and bolts. DO NOT tighten bolts before adjusting A/T gear position switch.

3) To adjust A/T gear position switch, place shift lever in Park. Ensure retaining bolts are loose. Note electrical connector terminal identification. *See Fig. 13.*

4) Connect ohmmeter between terminals No. 9 and 12. Move A/T gear position switch toward rear of console until continuity exists between terminals No. 9 and 12. Free play at lock pin should be less than .079" (2.0 mm). *See Fig. 22.*

5) Tighten bolts. Check A/T gear position switch for correct continuity in all gears. See A/T GEAR POSITION SWITCH under COMPONENT TESTING. If proper adjustment cannot be obtained, check for damaged shift lever detent or bracket. Install electrical connector and center console.

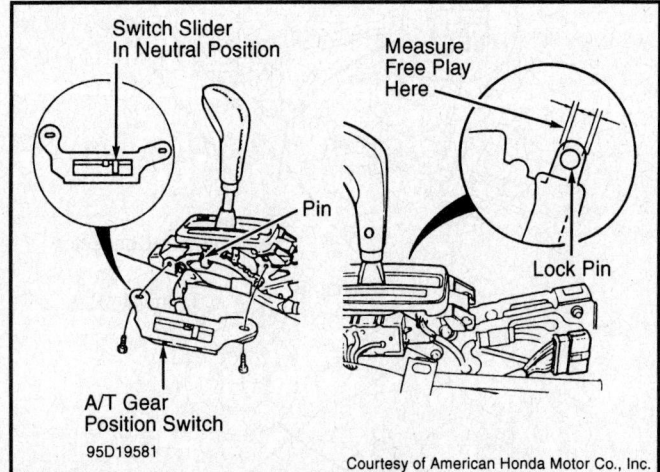

Switch Slider In Neutral Position

Measure Free Play Here

Pin

Lock Pin

A/T Gear Position Switch

95D19581

Courtesy of American Honda Motor Co., Inc.

Fig. 22: Installing A/T Gear Position Switch

Removal (3.2TL & 3.5RL) – 1) Raise and support vehicle. Ensure parking brake is applied. Place transaxle in Neutral position. Remove shift cable cover.

2) Remove control lever. *See Fig. 23.* Remove lock washer and nut. Disconnect electrical connector from A/T gear position switch. Remove A/T gear position switch from control shaft.

Installation – 1) Ensure parking brake is applied. Place A/T gear position switch in Neutral position. *See Fig. 24.* Place control shaft (transaxle) in Neutral.

2) Install A/T gear position switch and bolts. DO NOT tighten bolts before adjusting A/T gear position switch. Install NEW lock washer on A/T gear position switch, aligning projected tip with neutral mark on switch.

3) Install lock nut and tighten to specification while holding control shaft. See TORQUE SPECIFICATIONS. Bend lock tabs against lock nut. *See Fig. 24.* Tighten A/T gear position switch bolts to specification.

4) Install control shaft. Connect electrical connector to A/T gear position switch. Install shift cable cover. Check A/T gear position switch for synchronization with indicator.

5) If A/T gear position switch is not synchronized with indicator, loosen bolts and adjust. After adjustment, start engine and verify proper operation:

- Shift lever cannot be moved from "N" to "R" position without pressing button.
- Engine will only start in "N" to "P" position.
- Back-up lights come on in "R" position.

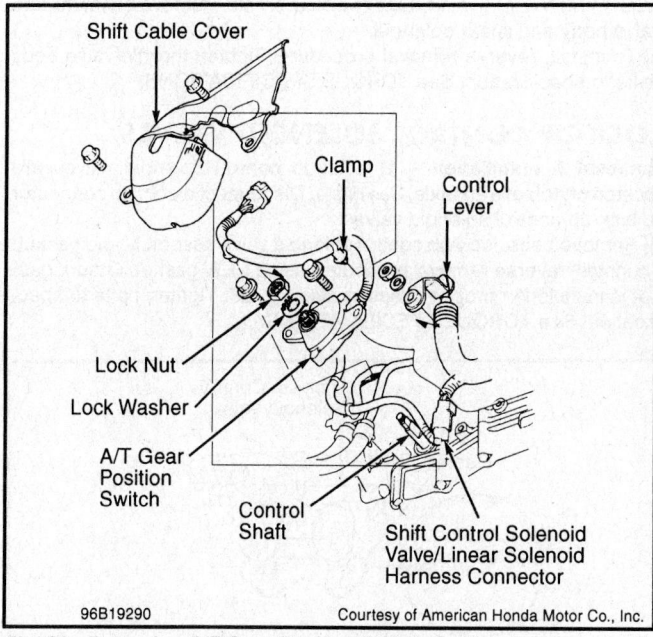

Fig. 23: Removing A/T Gear Position Switch Control Lever

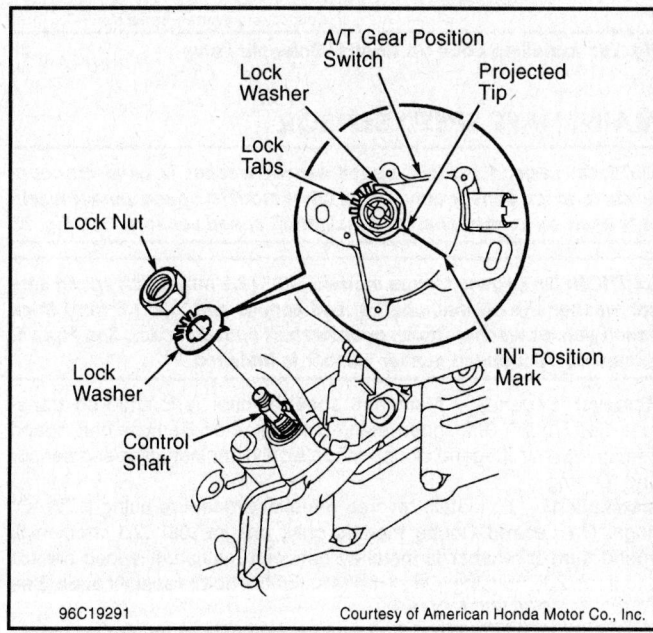

Fig. 24: Installing & Adjusting A/T Gear Position Switch

BRAKELIGHT SWITCH

Removal & Installation – 1) Disconnect electrical connector from brakelight switch. Remove lock nut and unscrew brakelight switch. To install, screw brakelight switch inward until brakelight plunger is fully depressed.

2) Back off brakelight switch 1/2 turn. Install and tighten lock nut. Install electrical connector. Ensure brakelights and cruise control operate properly.

COUNTERSHAFT SPEED SENSOR

NOTE: On Legend models, speed sensor washer is used on countershaft speed sensor only. On all other models, speed sensor washer is used on countershaft and mainshaft speed sensors. See Fig. 25

CAUTION: On Legend Coupe models, .08" (2.1 mm) thick speed sensor washer fits on mainshaft speed sensor and .02" (.5 mm) thick speed sensor washer fits on countershaft speed sensor. See Fig. 21. Ensure correct speed sensor washer is installed.

Removal (Legend) – Countershaft speed sensor is located on transaxle. See Fig. 25. Disconnect electrical connector. Remove bolt, speed sensor washer, countershaft speed sensor and "O" ring.

Installation – To install, reverse removal procedure using NEW "O" rings. Ensure speed sensor washer is installed between countershaft speed sensor and transaxle housing. Tighten bolt to specification. See TORQUE SPECIFICATIONS.

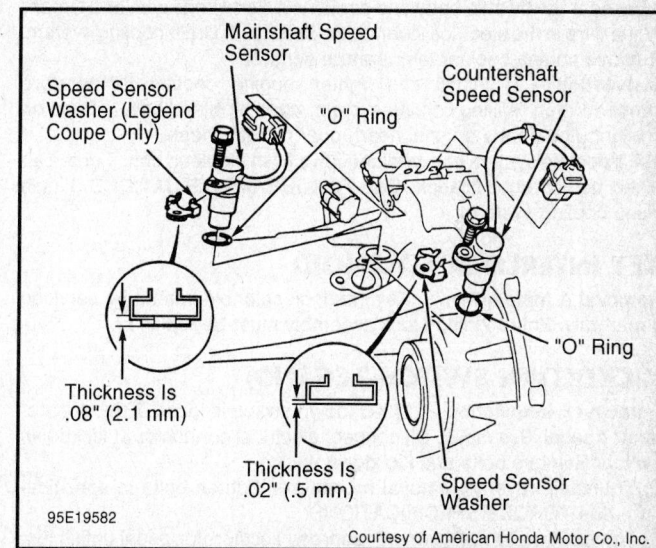

Fig. 25: Identifying Countershaft & Mainshaft Speed Sensors

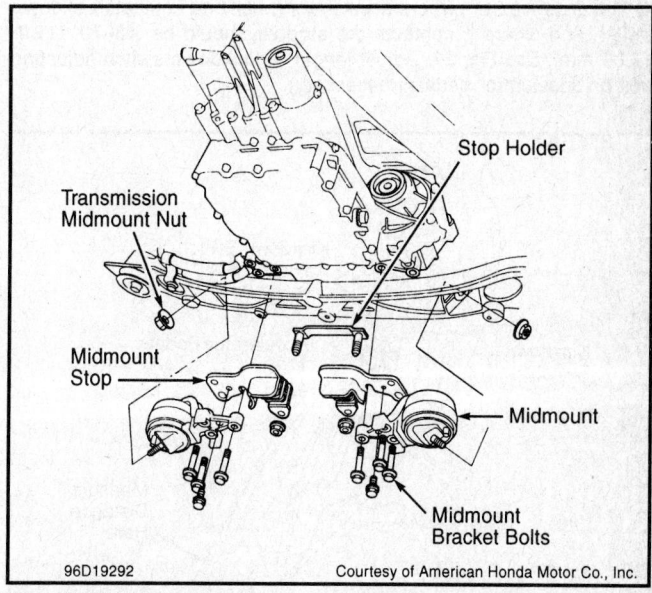

Fig. 26: Removing Mounts & Lowering Transaxle (3.2L TL)

Removal (3.2TL & 3.5RL) – 1) Mainshaft speed sensor is located on transaxle. See Fig. 25. Pull carpet back on passenger side. Disconnect secondary HO²S electrical connector and push through to outside. Secondary HO²S connector is located under passenger seat.

2) Remove exhaust pipe and catalytic converter. Remove heat shields. Place jack under transaxle and take weight off mounts and beam. Remove shift cable bracket and transaxle beam.

3) On 3.2TL models, remove stop holder, mid mount stops and mid mounts. See Fig. 26. On all models, lower transaxle with jack. Remove bolt, speed sensor washer, mainshaft speed sensor and "O" ring.

Installation – To install, reverse removal procedure using NEW "O" rings. Ensure speed sensor washer is installed between countershaft speed sensor and transaxle housing. Tighten bolt to specification. See TORQUE SPECIFICATIONS.

ENGINE COOLANT TEMPERATURE (ECT) SENSOR

Removal – Engine coolant temperature sensor is located in coolant pipe, near the throttle body and contains a Red/White wire and Green/White wire in the electrical connector. See Fig. 4. Drain cooling system. Remove engine coolant temperature sensor.

Installation – 1) Install and tighten engine coolant temperature sensor. When refilling cooling system, open air bleed bolt, located on coolant pipe on the engine, near upper radiator hose.

2) Fill cooling system until coolant flows from air bleed bolt. Tighten air bleed bolt to specification. See TORQUE SPECIFICATIONS. Finish filling cooling system.

KEY INTERLOCK SOLENOID

Removal & Installation – Key interlock solenoid cannot be serviced separately. Entire ignition lock assembly must be replaced.

KICKDOWN SWITCH (LEGEND)

Removal & Installation – 1) Kickdown switch is located below accelerator pedal. See Fig. 2. Disconnect electrical connector at kickdown switch. Remove bolts and kickdown switch.

2) To install, reverse removal procedure. Tighten bolts to specification. See TORQUE SPECIFICATIONS.

3) To check switch adjustment, depress accelerator pedal until it just contacts the kickdown switch. Continue depressing accelerator pedal until it contacts stopper on the floor panel. See Fig. 27.

4) The distance from where accelerator pedal first contacts kickdown switch and where it contacts the stopper should be .43-.70" (11.0-17.00 mm). See Fig. 27. Adjust length of kickdown switch adjusting bolt on accelerator pedal (if necessary).

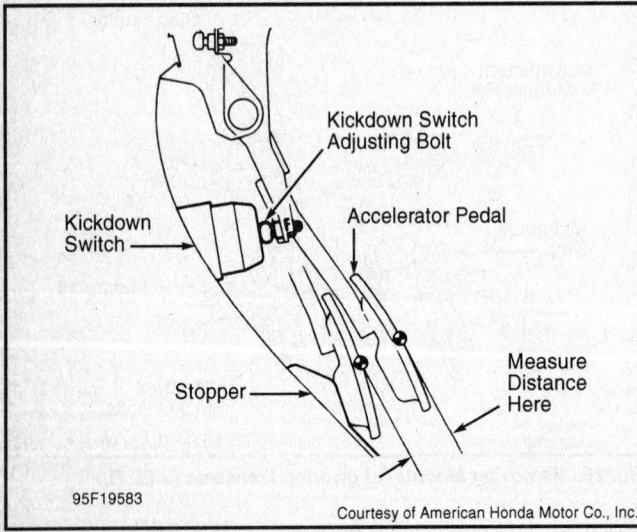

Fig. 27: Checking & Adjusting Kickdown Switch

LINEAR SOLENOID

NOTE: Linear solenoid and throttle valve body must be replaced as an assembly.

Removal & Installation – 1) Linear solenoid is located on throttle valve body. See Fig. 4. Remove lower valve body assembly. See LOWER VALVE BODY ASSEMBLY under REMOVAL & INSTALLATION in ACURA MPYA, M5HA & M5DA overhaul article. Remove bolts, throttle valve body and linear solenoid.

2) To install, reverse removal procedure. Tighten throttle valve body bolts to specification. See TORQUE SPECIFICATIONS.

LOCK-UP CONTROL SOLENOID VALVES

Removal & Installation – 1) Lock-up control solenoid valves are located on top of transaxle. See Fig. 4. Disconnect electrical connector at lock-up control solenoid valves.

2) Remove bolts, lock-up control solenoid valve assembly and gasket. To install, reverse removal procedure using NEW gasket. Ensure gasket is installed in proper direction. See Fig. 28. Tighten bolts to specification. See TORQUE SPECIFICATIONS.

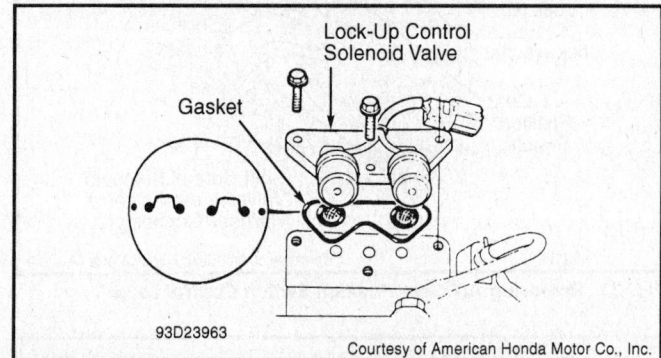

Fig. 28: Installing Lock-Up Control Solenoid Valve

MAINSHAFT SPEED SENSOR

NOTE: On Legend models, speed sensor washer is used on countershaft speed sensor only. On all other models, speed sensor washer is used on countershaft and mainshaft speed sensors. See Fig. 25

CAUTION: On Legend Coupe models, .08" (2.1 mm) thick speed sensor washer fits on mainshaft speed sensor and .02" (.5 mm) thick speed sensor washer fits on countershaft speed sensor. See Fig. 25. Ensure correct speed sensor washer is installed.

Removal (Legend) – Mainshaft speed sensor is located on transaxle. See Fig. 25. Disconnect electrical connector. Remove bolt, speed sensor washer (Legend Coupe models only), mainshaft speed sensor and "O" ring.

Installation – To install, reverse removal procedure using NEW "O" rings. On Legend Coupe models only, ensure .08" (2.1 mm) thick speed sensor washer is installed between mainshaft speed sensor and transaxle housing. On all models, tighten bolt to specification. See TORQUE SPECIFICATIONS.

Removal (3.2TL & 3.5RL) – 1) Countershaft speed sensor is located on transaxle. See Fig. 25. Pull carpet back on passenger side. Disconnect secondary HO2S electrical connector and push through to outside. Secondary HO2S connector is located under passenger seat.

2) Remove exhaust pipe and catalytic converter. Remove heat shields. Place jack under transaxle and take weight off mounts and beam. Remove shift cable bracket and transaxle beam.

3) On 3.2TL models, remove stop holder, mid mount stops and mid mounts. See Fig. 26. On all models, lower transaxle with jack. Remove bolt, speed sensor washer, countershaft speed sensor and "O" ring.

Installation – To install, reverse removal procedure using NEW "O" rings. Ensure speed sensor washer is installed between mainshaft speed sensor and transaxle housing. Tighten bolt to specification. See TORQUE SPECIFICATIONS.

POWERTRAIN CONTROL MODULE (PCM)

Removal & Installation – The PCM is located below the carpet on passenger's side of instrument panel. *See Fig. 2.* Replacement information not available from manufacturer.

SHIFT CONTROL SOLENOID VALVES

Removal – 1) Shift control solenoid valves are located on top of lower valve body assembly in transaxle. *See Fig. 4.*

2) Remove lower valve body assembly. See LOWER VALVE BODY ASSEMBLY under REMOVAL & INSTALLATION in ACURA MPYA, M5HA & M5DA overhaul article. Remove bolts, shift control solenoid valves and "O" rings.

Installation – To install, reverse removal procedure using NEW "O" rings. Tighten bolts to specification. See TORQUE SPECIFICATIONS.

SHIFT LOCK SOLENOID

NOTE: Information for repairing shift lock system on 3.2TL models is not provided by manufacturer.

Removal (Legend) – Remove center console. Shift lock solenoid is located on side of shift lever. *See Fig. 2.* Disconnect electrical connector. Remove clip and pin from shift lock solenoid. Remove nuts and shift lock solenoid.

Installation – 1) Install shift lock solenoid with NEW nuts snugly installed. Install pin, clip and electrical connector.

2) Turn ignition on. With solenoid energized, ensure clearance between top of shift lock lever and side of lock pin is .078-.118" (2.0-3.0 mm). *See Fig. 29.*

3) If clearance is not as specified, loosen nuts and reposition shift lock solenoid until correct clearance is obtained. Once correct clearance is obtained, tighten nuts to specification. See TORQUE SPECIFICATIONS.

4) Turn ignition off. With solenoid de-energized, ensure lock pin is blocked by shift lock lever. Check solenoid operation several times.

Removal (3.5RL) – 1) Remove center console. Shift lock solenoid is located on side of shift lever. Disconnect electrical connectors from shift lock solenoid and park pin switch.

2) Remove lock nuts and through bolts. Remove A/T gear position panel. *See Fig. 30.* Remove shift lock solenoid.

Installation – To install, reverse removal procedure. Ensure clearance exists between stop pin and base bracket. *See Fig. 31.*

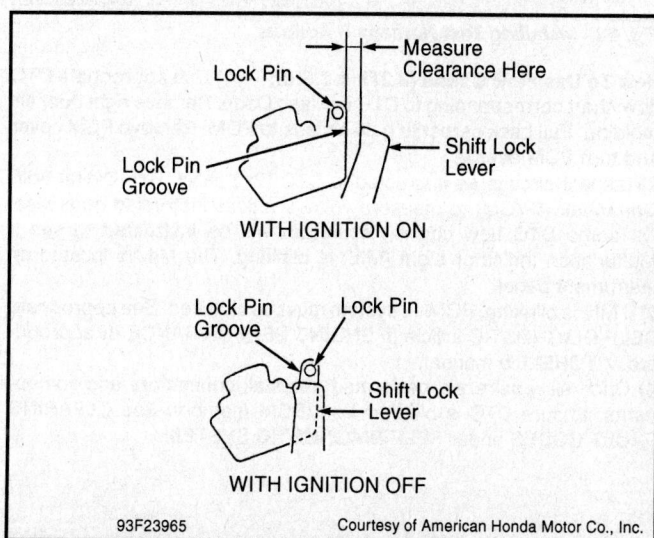

WITH IGNITION ON

WITH IGNITION OFF

93F23965   Courtesy of American Honda Motor Co., Inc.

Fig. 29: Checking Shift Lock Solenoid Operation (Legend)

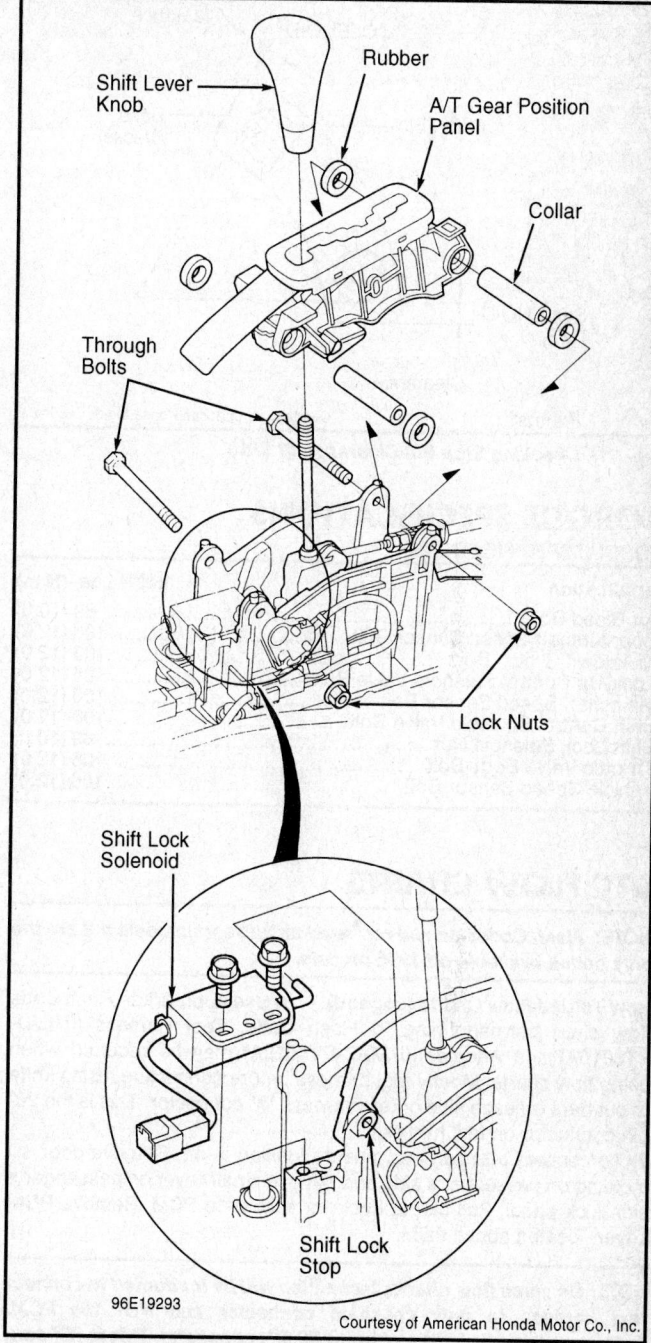

96E19293   Courtesy of American Honda Motor Co., Inc.

Fig. 30: Removing Shift Lock Solenoid (3.5RL)

THROTTLE POSITION (TP) SENSOR

Removal & Installation – TP sensor is mounted on side of throttle body. Replacement information is not available from manufacturer.

VEHICLE SPEED SENSOR (VSS)

Removal & Installation – 1) Vehicle speed sensor is located on top of differential assembly. *See Fig. 4.* Disconnect 3-pin electrical connector from vehicle speed sensor. Remove bolts, vehicle speed senor and "O" ring.

2) To install, reverse removal procedure using NEW "O" ring. Install and tighten bolt to specification. See TORQUE SPECIFICATIONS.

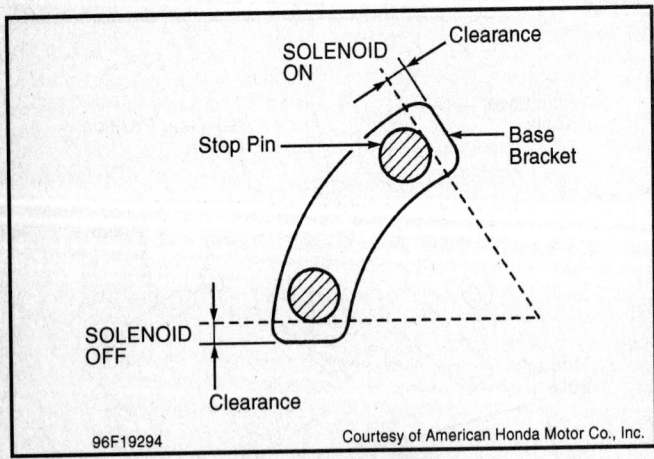

Fig. 31: Checking Stop Pin Clearance (3.5RL)

Courtesy of American Honda Motor Co., Inc.

TORQUE SPECIFICATIONS

TORQUE SPECIFICATIONS

Application	INCH Lbs. (N.m)
Air Bleed Bolt	89 (10.0)
Countershaft Speed Sensor Bolt	106 (12.0)
Kickdown Switch Bolt	106 (12.0)
Lock-Up Control Solenoid Valve Bolt	106 (12.0)
Mainshaft Speed Sensor Bolt	106 (12.0)
Shift Control Solenoid Valve Bolt	106 (12.0)
Shift Lock Solenoid Nut	89 (10.0)
Throttle Valve Body Bolt	106 (12.0)
Vehicle Speed Sensor Bolt	106 (12.0)

DTC FLOW CHARTS

NOTE: Flash Codes can be retrieved on all years/models but are the only codes available on 1995 models.

How To Use Flow Charts (Legend) – 1) Use appropriate Flash Code flow chart corresponding to Flash Code. Test Harness (07LAJ-PT3010A) and Adapter (07MAZ-PY4010A) may be required when using flow charts. Modify test harness before connecting, using knife to cut bars off each side of test harness "A" connector. This is the 26-pin connector on test harness.

2) To connect test harness, ensure ignition is off. Remove door sill molding on passenger's side and remove small cover on passenger's side kick panel. Pull carpet back for access to PCM. Remove PCM cover, located above PCM.

NOTE: On some flow charts, technician will be instructed to connect test harness to only specified connector and NOT the PCM. Reference is made in flow chart to E(26P) connector. This is "E" connector on left side of PCM. See Fig. 32.

3) If connecting to PCM, disconnect "E" connector from left side of PCM. See Fig. 32. This is 26-pin connector used for transaxle control.
4) Connect test harness "A" connector to "E" connector opening on left side of PCM. Install adapter between test harness and "E" connector on wiring harness. See Fig. 33. Disconnect necessary wiring connectors on right side of PCM and connect to test harness.
5) Use Digital Volt-Ohmmeter (DVOM) to measure voltage unless instructed otherwise. Terminal numbers are located on top of test harness. Test harness is divided into different sections.

NOTE: The "A" section of test harness and cable adapter corresponds to "E" 26-pin connector on PCM.

6) On some DTC flow charts, technician will be instructed to see if Malfunction Indicator Light (MIL) is blinking. The MIL is located on instrument panel. See Fig. 1.
7) If MIL is blinking, PGM-FI system must be checked. See appropriate ENGINE PERFORMANCE article in ENGINE PERFORMANCE of appropriate MITCHELL® manual.
8) Once all repairs are performed, remove test harness and adapter and reinstall components. Ensure DTC is cleared from PCM memory. See CLEARING FAULT CODES under SELF-DIAGNOSTIC SYSTEM.

NOTE: The following DTC flow charts and illustrations are courtesy of American Honda Motor Co., Inc.

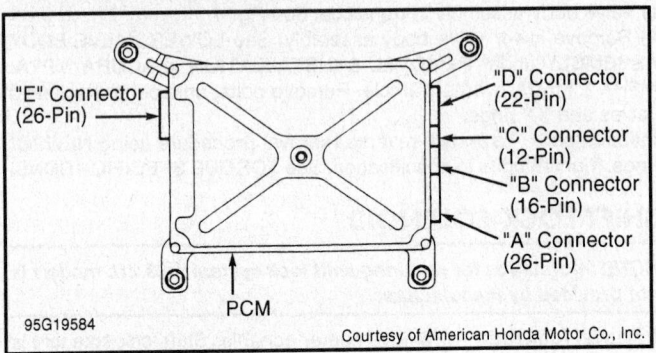

Fig. 32: Identifying PCM Connectors

Courtesy of American Honda Motor Co., Inc.

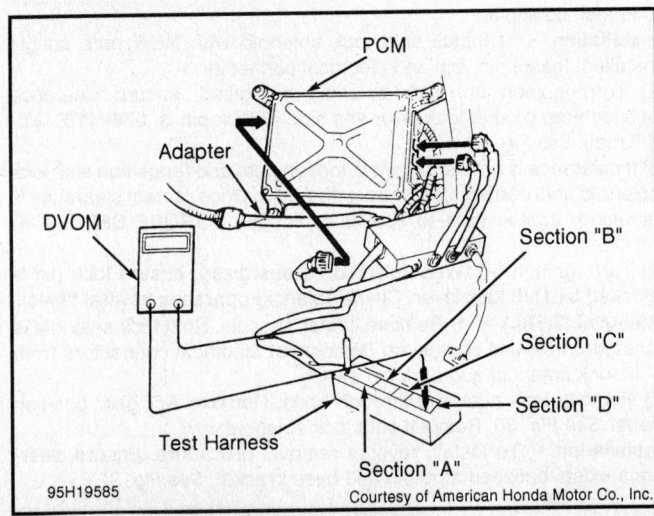

Fig. 33: Installing Test Harness & Adapter

Courtesy of American Honda Motor Co., Inc.

How To Use Flow Charts (3.2TL & 3.5RL) – 1) Use appropriate DTC flow chart corresponding to DTC or Flash Code. Remove right door sill molding. Pull back carpet to gain access to PCM. Remove PCM cover and turn PCM over.
2) Inspect circuits as instructed in DTC flow chart. Use Digital Volt-Ohmmeter (DVOM) to measure voltage unless instructed otherwise. On some DTC flow charts, technician will be instructed to see if Malfunction Indicator Light (MIL) is blinking. The MIL is located on instrument panel.
3) If MIL is blinking, PGM-FI system must be checked. See appropriate SELF-DIAGNOSTIC article in ENGINE PERFORMANCE of appropriate MITCHELL® manual.
4) Once all repairs are performed, reinstall connectors and components. Ensure DTC is cleared from PCM memory. See CLEARING FAULT CODES under SELF-DIAGNOSTIC SYSTEM.

WIRING DIAGRAMS

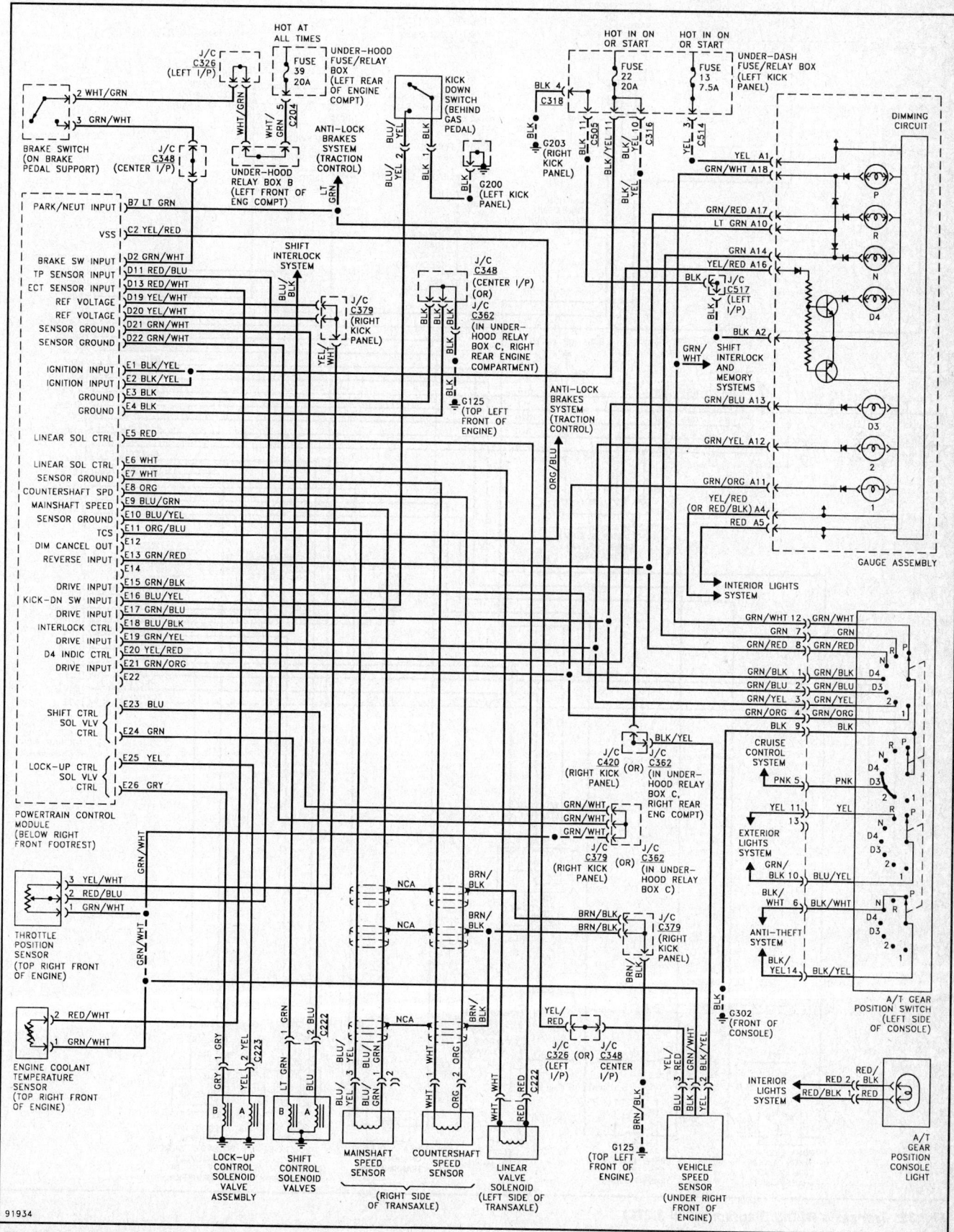

Fig. 34: Transaxle Wiring Diagram (1995 Legend & Legend Coupe)

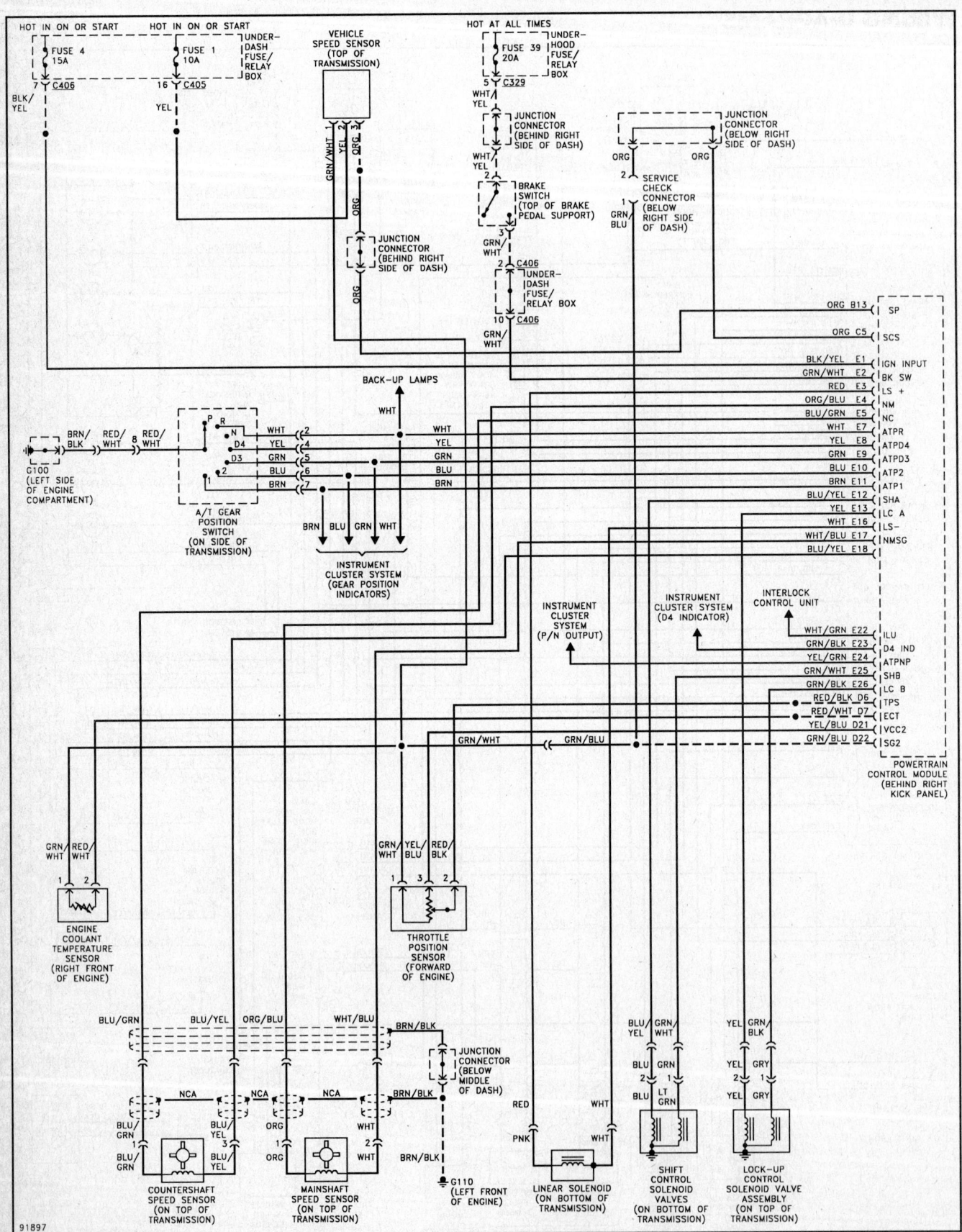

Fig. 35: Transaxle Wiring Diagram (1996 3.2TL)

91897

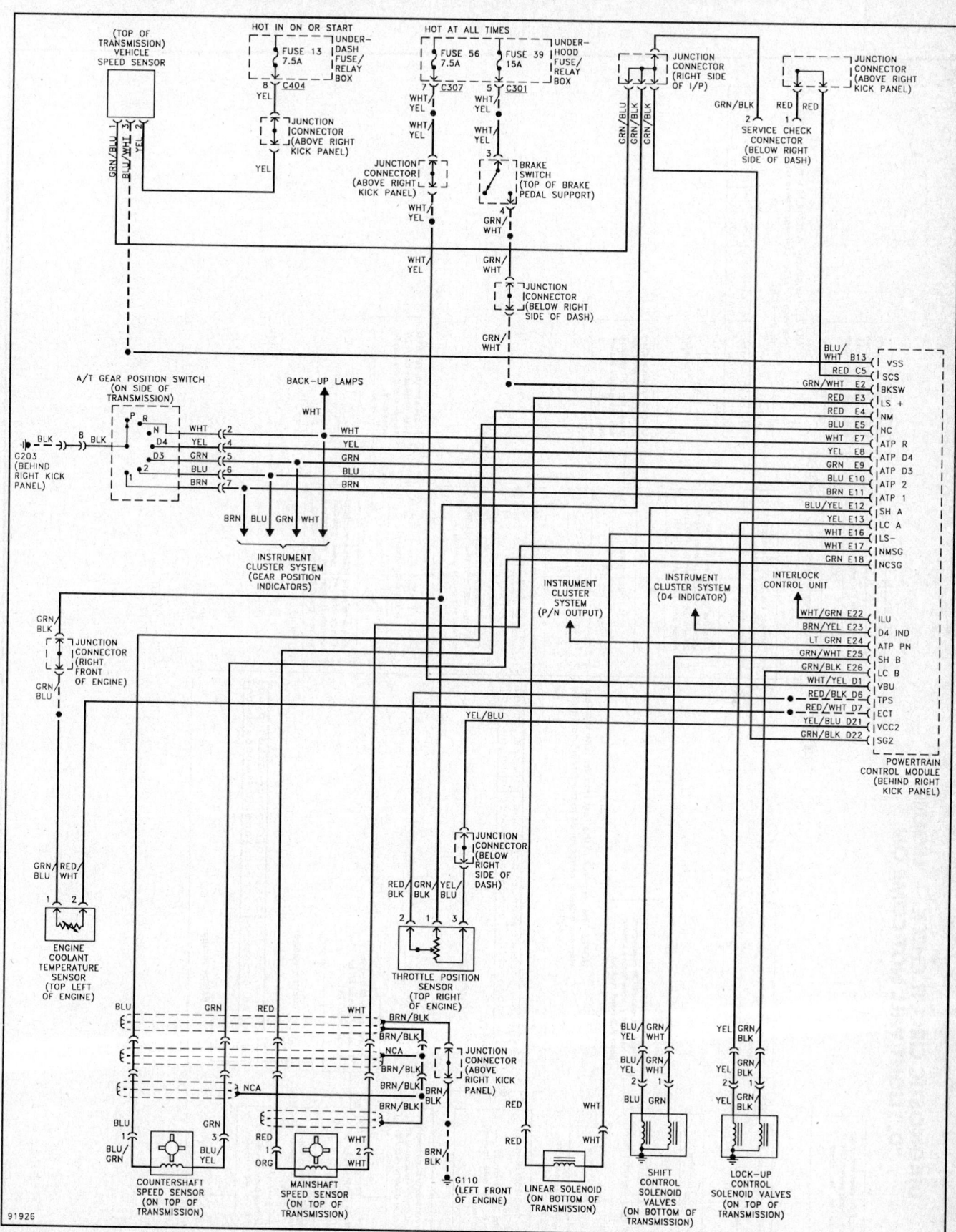

Fig. 36: Transaxle Wiring Diagram (1996 3.5RL)

91926

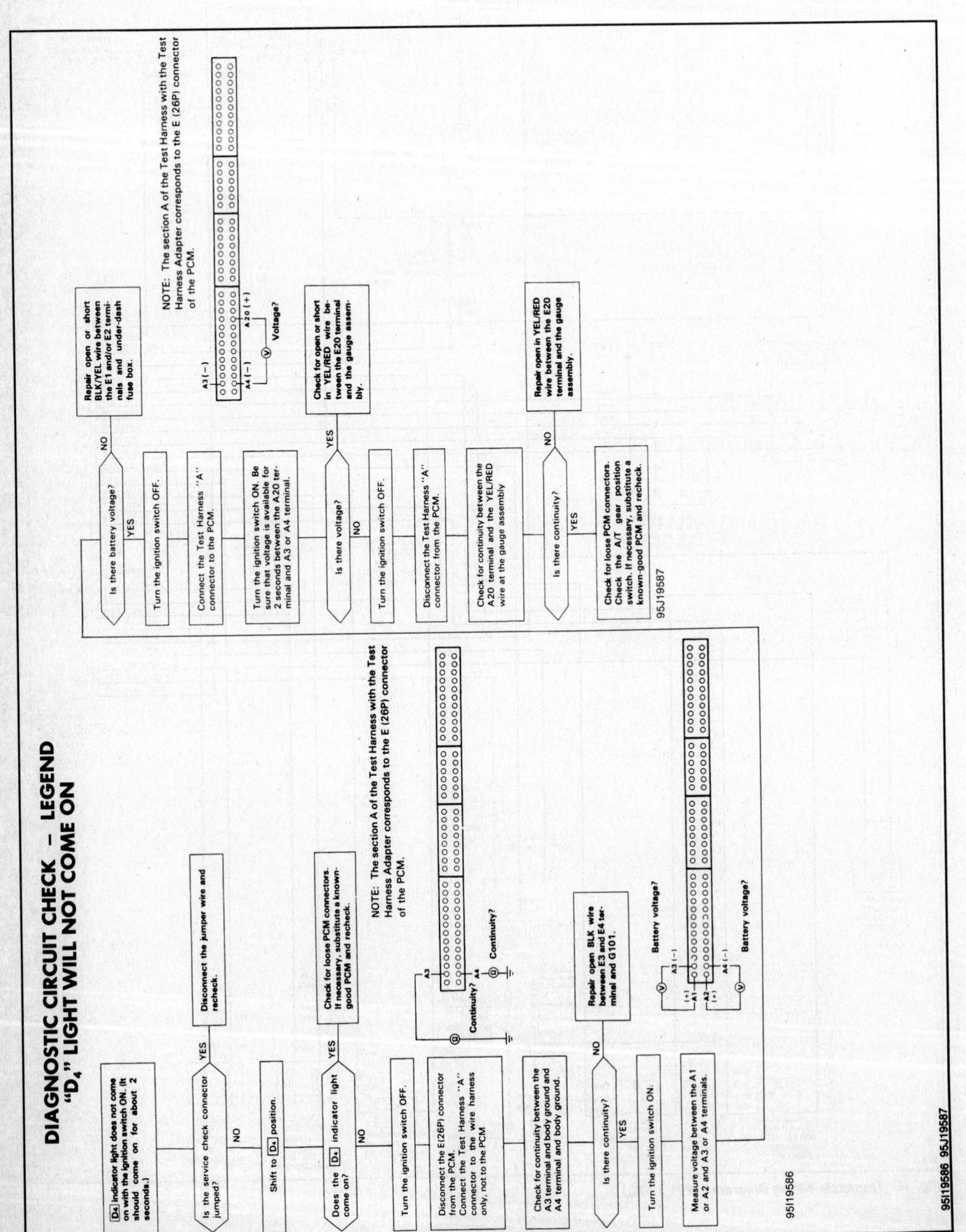

DIAGNOSTIC CIRCUIT CHECK — LEGEND
"D₄" LIGHT WILL NOT COME ON

NOTE: The section A of the Test Harness Adapter corresponds to the E (26P) connector of the PCM.

95J19586

95J19586 95J19587

95J19587

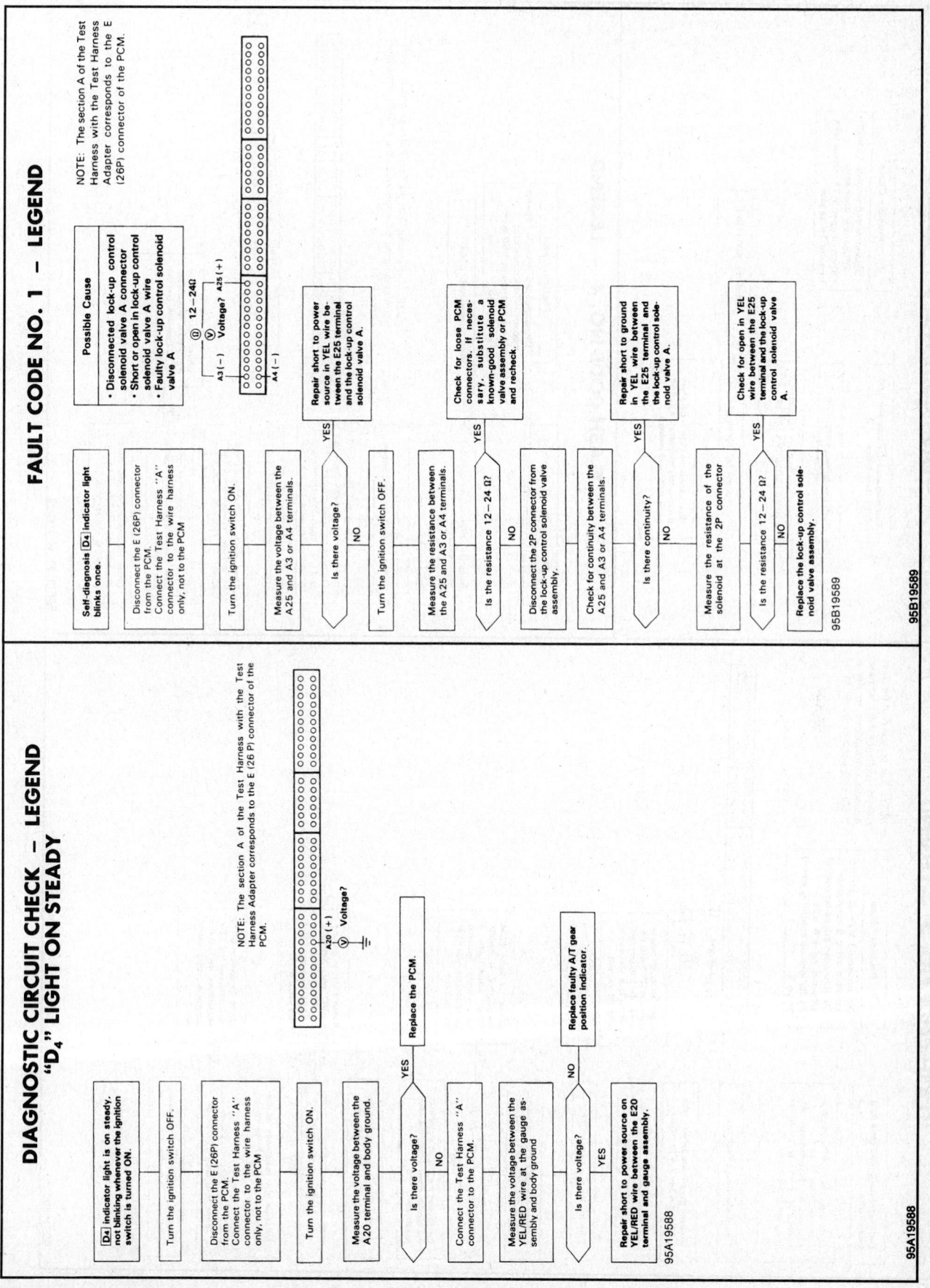

FAULT CODE NO. 1 – LEGEND

Possible Cause
- Disconnected lock-up control solenoid valve A connector
- Short or open in lock-up control solenoid valve A wire
- Faulty lock-up control solenoid valve A

NOTE: The section A of the Test Harness with the Test Harness Adapter corresponds to the E (26P) connector of the PCM.

Self-diagnosis D₄ indicator light blinks once.

Disconnect the E (26P) connector from the PCM. Connect the Test Harness "A" connector to the wire harness only, not to the PCM

Turn the ignition switch ON.

Measure the voltage between the A25 and A3 or A4 terminals.

Is there voltage? — YES → Repair short to power source in YEL wire between the E25 terminal and the lock-up control solenoid valve A.

NO

Turn the ignition switch OFF.

Measure the resistance between the A25 and A3 or A4 terminals.

Is the resistance 12 – 24 Ω? — YES → Check for loose PCM connectors. If necessary, substitute a known-good solenoid valve assembly or PCM and recheck.

NO

Disconnect the 2P connector from the lock-up control solenoid valve assembly.

Check for continuity between the A25 and A3 or A4 terminals.

Is there continuity? — YES → Repair short to ground in YEL wire between the E25 terminal and the lock-up control solenoid valve A.

NO

Measure the resistance of the solenoid at the 2P connector

Is the resistance 12 – 24 Ω? — YES → Check for open in YEL wire between the E25 terminal and the lock-up control solenoid valve A.

NO

Replace the lock-up control solenoid valve assembly.

95B19589

DIAGNOSTIC CIRCUIT CHECK – LEGEND
"D₄" LIGHT ON STEADY

D₄ indicator light is on steady, not blinking whenever the ignition switch is turned ON.

Turn the ignition switch OFF.

Disconnect the E (26P) connector from the PCM. Connect the Test Harness "A" connector to the wire harness only, not to the PCM

Turn the ignition switch ON.

Measure the voltage between the A20 terminal and body ground.

Is there voltage? — YES → Replace the PCM.

NO

Connect the Test Harness "A" connector to the PCM.

Measure the voltage between the YEL/RED wire at the gauge assembly and body ground

Is there voltage? — NO → Replace faulty A/T gear position indicator.

YES

Repair short to power source on YEL/RED wire between the E20 terminal and gauge assembly.

95A19588

NOTE: The section A of the Test Harness with the Test Harness Adapter corresponds to the E (26 P) connector of the PCM.

95A19588

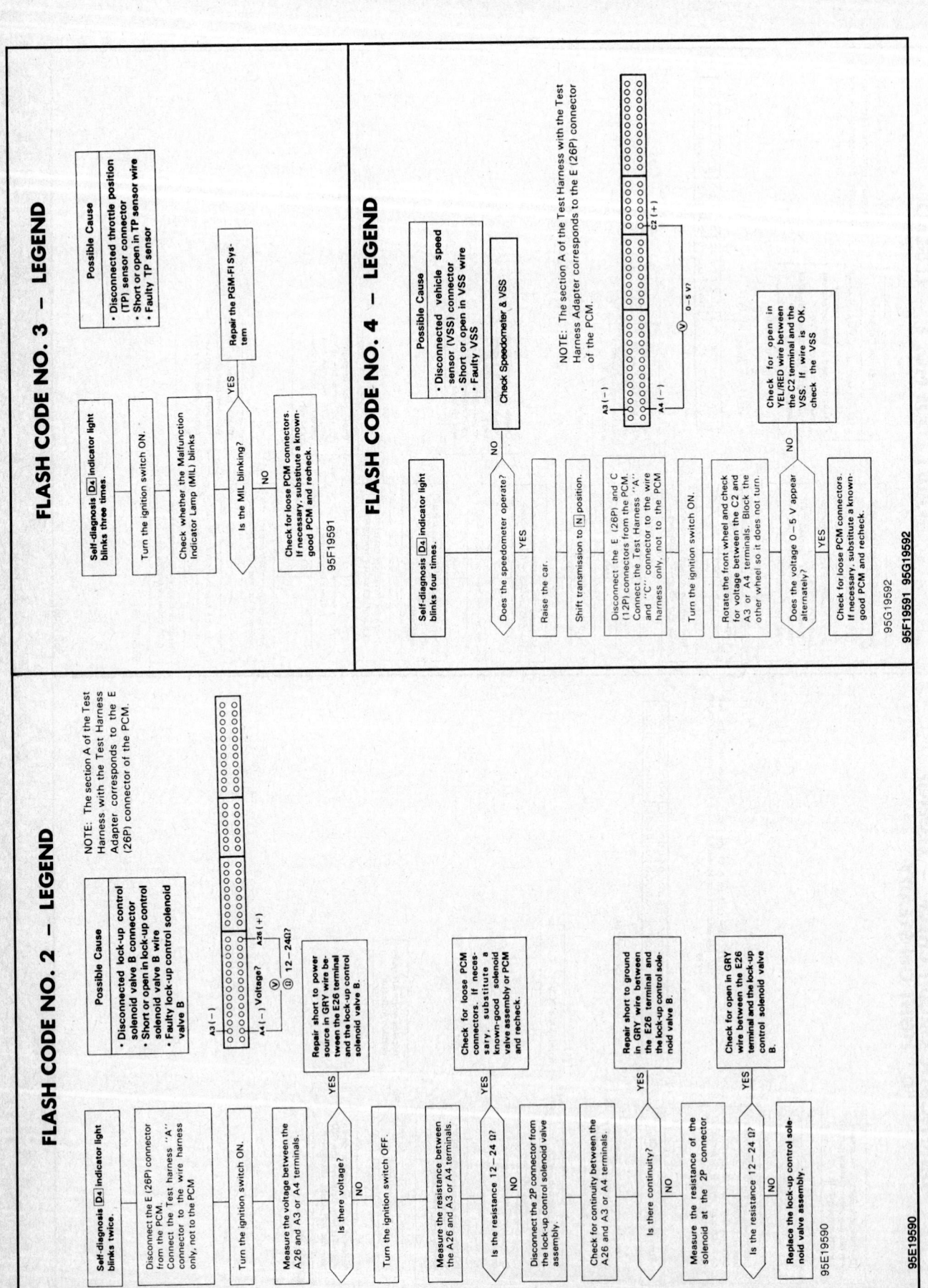

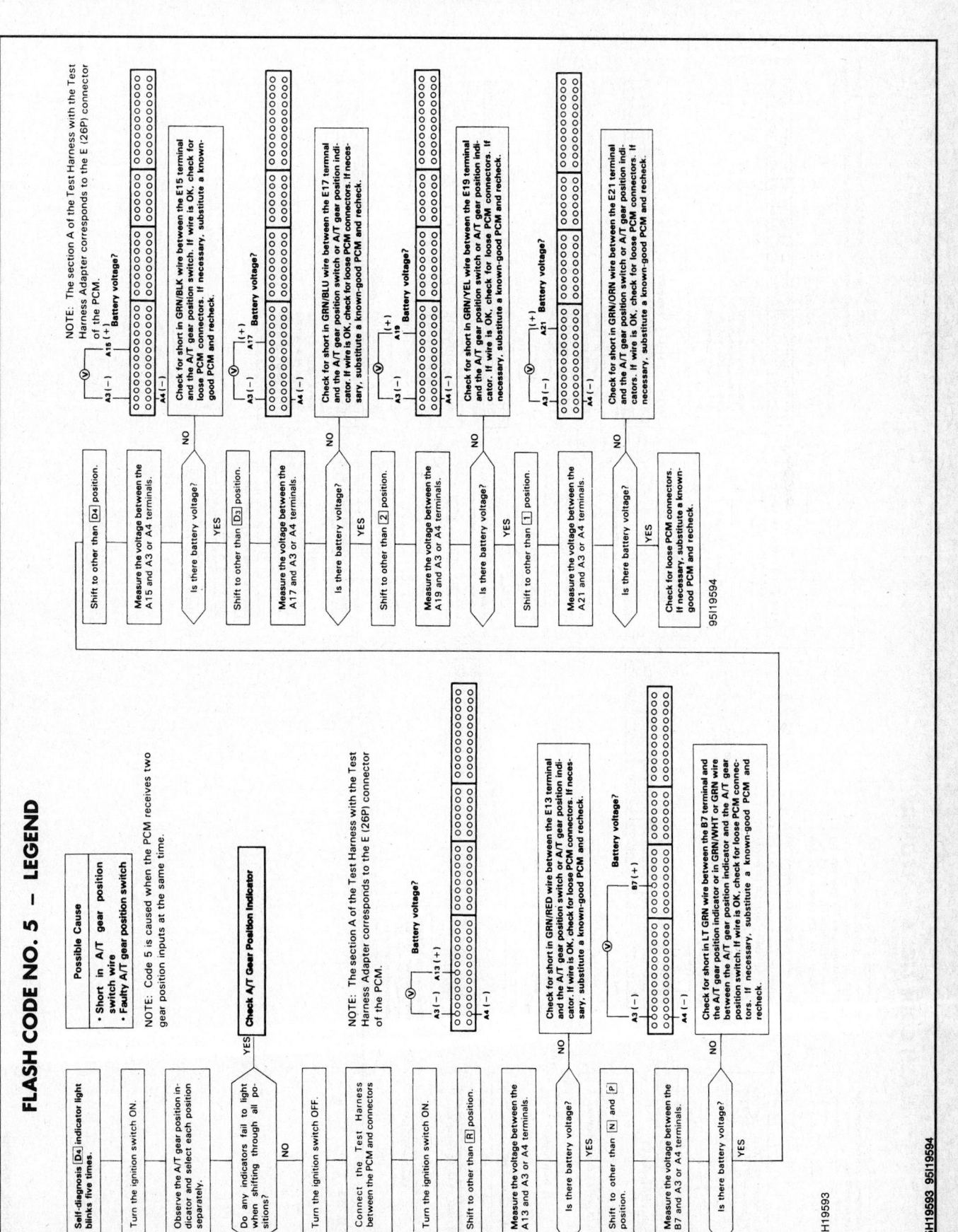

FLASH CODE NO. 5 – LEGEND

95H19593

95H19593 95I19594

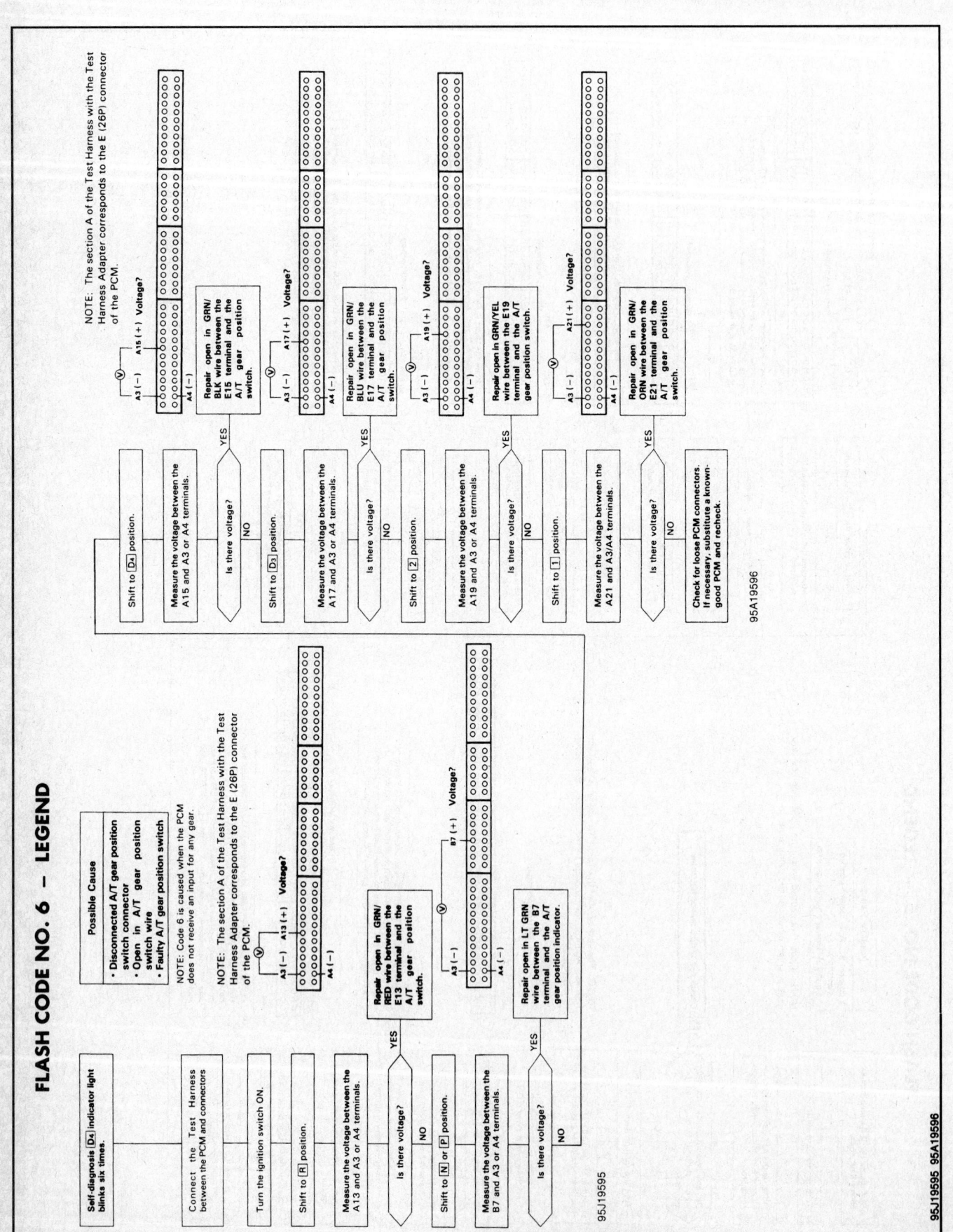

FLASH CODE NO. 6 - LEGEND

Possible Cause
- Disconnected A/T gear position switch connector
- Open in A/T gear position switch wire
- Faulty A/T gear position switch

NOTE: Code 6 is caused when the PCM does not receive an input for any gear.

NOTE: The section A of the Test Harness with the Test Harness Adapter corresponds to the E (26P) connector of the PCM.

NOTE: The section A of the Test Harness with the Test Harness Adapter corresponds to the E (26P) connector of the PCM.

Self-diagnosis [D4] indicator light blinks six times.

Connect the Test Harness between the PCM and connectors

Turn the ignition switch ON.

Shift to [R] position.

Measure the voltage between the A13 and A3 or A4 terminals.

Is there voltage?

Shift to [N] or [P] position.

Measure the voltage between the B7 and A3 or A4 terminals.

Is there voltage?

A3 (−)   A13 (+)   Voltage?
A4 (−)

Repair open in GRN/RED wire between the E13 terminal and the A/T gear position switch.

B7 (+)   Voltage?
A3 (−)
A4 (−)

Repair open in LT GRN wire between the B7 terminal and the A/T gear position indicator.

Shift to [D4] position.

Measure the voltage between the A15 and A3 or A4 terminals.

Is there voltage?

Shift to [D3] position.

Measure the voltage between the A17 and A3 or A4 terminals.

Is there voltage?

Shift to [2] position.

Measure the voltage between the A19 and A3 or A4 terminals.

Is there voltage?

Shift to [1] position.

Measure the voltage between the A21 and A3/A4 terminals.

Is there voltage?

Check for loose PCM connectors. If necessary, substitute a known-good PCM and recheck.

A3 (−)   A15 (+)   Voltage?
A4 (−)

Repair open in GRN/BLK wire between the E15 terminal and the A/T gear position switch.

A3 (−)   A17 (+)   Voltage?
A4 (−)

Repair open in GRN/BLU wire between the E17 terminal and the A/T gear position switch.

A3 (−)   A19 (+)   Voltage?
A4 (−)

Repair open in GRN/YEL wire between the E19 terminal and the A/T gear position switch.

A3 (−)   A21 (+)   Voltage?
A4 (−)

Repair open in GRN/ORN wire between the E21 terminal and the A/T gear position switch.

YES — NO

95J19595

95A19596

95J19595 95A19596

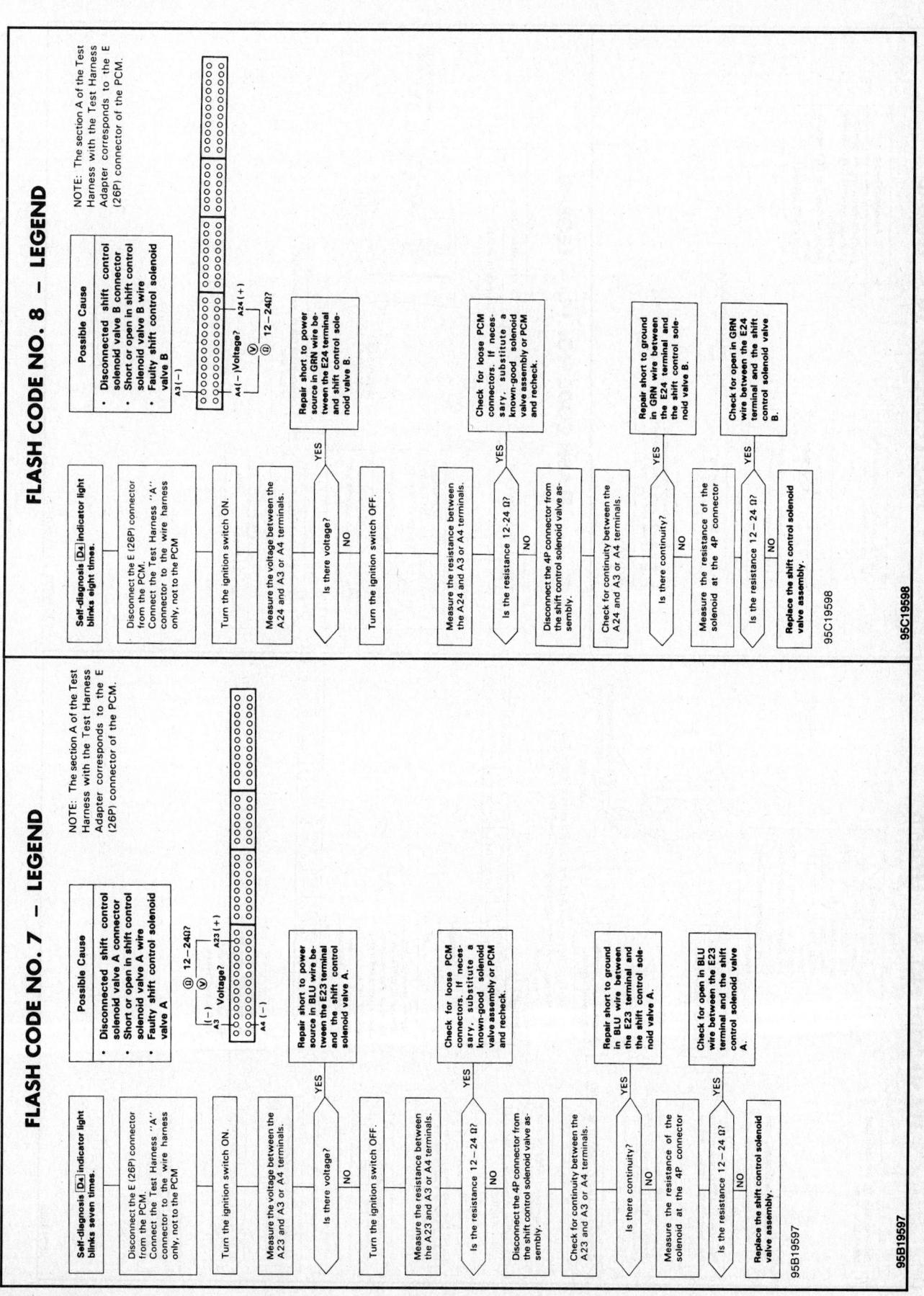

FLASH CODE NO. 7 – LEGEND

NOTE: The section A of the Test Harness with the Test Harness Adapter corresponds to the E (26P) connector of the PCM.

	Possible Cause
•	Disconnected shift control solenoid valve A connector
•	Short or open in shift control solenoid valve A wire
•	Faulty shift control solenoid valve A

Self-diagnosis D4 indicator light blinks seven times.

Disconnect the E (26P) connector from the PCM. Connect the Test Harness "A" connector to the wire harness only, not to the PCM.

Turn the ignition switch ON.

Measure the voltage between the A23 and A3 or A4 terminals.

Is there voltage?

YES → Repair short to power source in BLU wire between the E23 terminal and the shift control solenoid valve A.

NO → Turn the ignition switch OFF.

Measure the resistance between the A23 and A3 or A4 terminals.

Is the resistance 12–24 Ω?

YES → Check for loose PCM connectors. If necessary, substitute a known-good solenoid valve assembly or PCM and recheck.

NO → Disconnect the 4P connector from the shift control solenoid valve assembly.

Check for continuity between the A23 and A3 or A4 terminals.

Is there continuity?

YES → Repair short to ground in BLU wire between the E23 terminal and the shift control solenoid valve A.

NO → Measure the resistance of the solenoid at the 4P connector

Is the resistance 12–24 Ω?

YES → Check for open in BLU wire between the E23 terminal and the shift control solenoid valve A.

NO → Replace the shift control solenoid valve assembly.

95B19597

FLASH CODE NO. 8 – LEGEND

NOTE: The section A of the Test Harness with the Test Harness Adapter corresponds to the E (26P) connector of the PCM.

	Possible Cause
•	Disconnected shift control solenoid valve B connector
•	Short or open in shift control solenoid valve B wire
•	Faulty shift control solenoid valve B

Self-diagnosis D4 indicator light blinks eight times.

Disconnect the E (26P) connector from the PCM. Connect the Test Harness "A" connector to the wire harness only, not to the PCM.

Turn the ignition switch ON.

Measure the voltage between the A24 and A3 or A4 terminals.

Is there voltage?

YES → Repair short to power source in GRN wire between the E24 terminal and shift control solenoid valve B.

NO → Turn the ignition switch OFF.

Measure the resistance between the A24 and A3 or A4 terminals.

Is the resistance 12-24 Ω?

YES → Check for loose PCM connectors. If necessary, substitute a known-good solenoid valve assembly or PCM and recheck.

NO → Disconnect the 4P connector from the shift control solenoid valve assembly.

Check for continuity between the A24 and A3 or A4 terminals.

Is there continuity?

YES → Repair short to ground in GRN wire between the E24 terminal and the shift control solenoid valve B.

NO → Measure the resistance of the solenoid at the 4P connector

Is the resistance 12 – 24 Ω?

YES → Check for open in GRN wire between the E24 terminal and the shift control solenoid valve B.

NO → Replace the shift control solenoid valve assembly.

95C19598

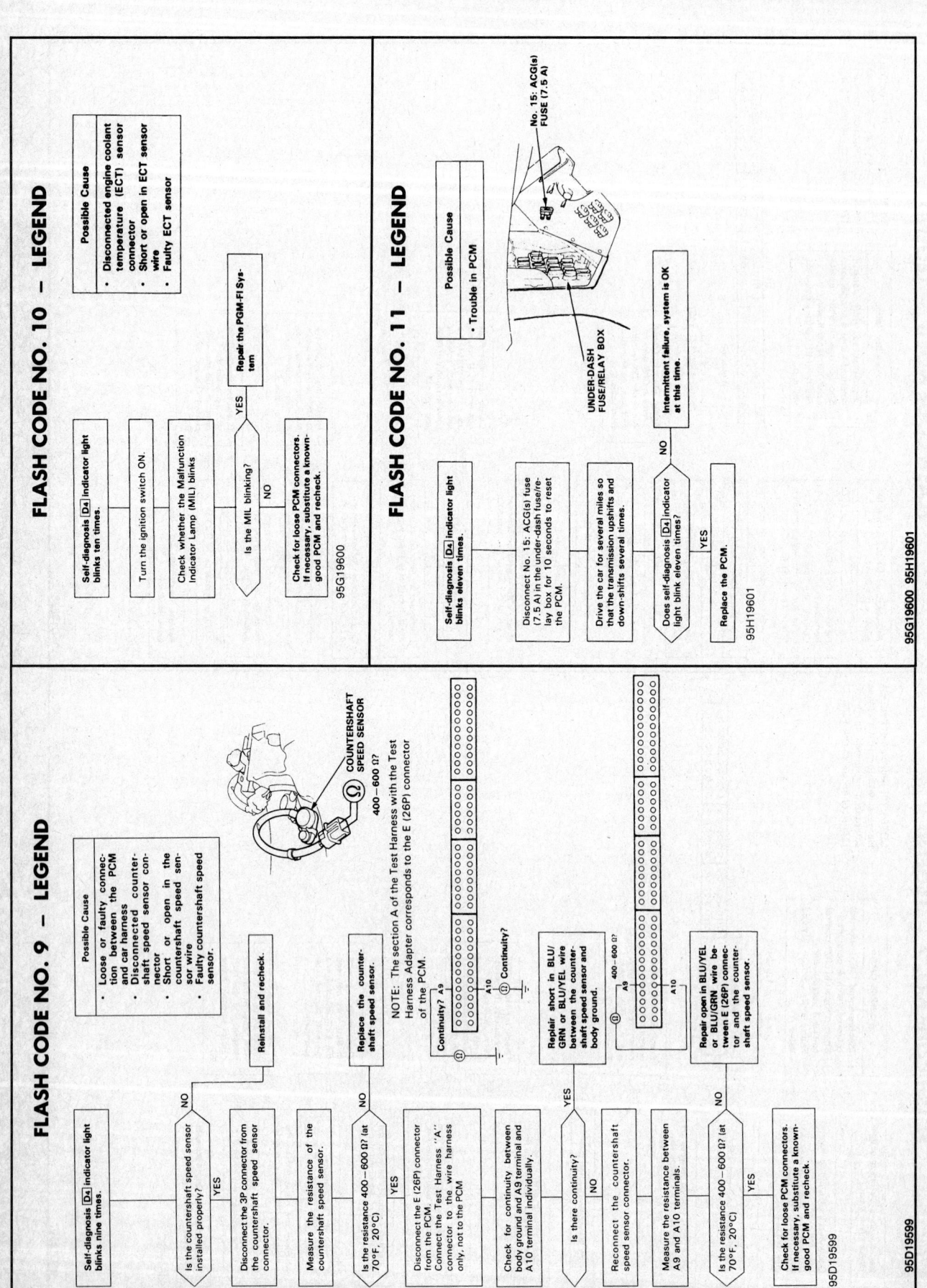

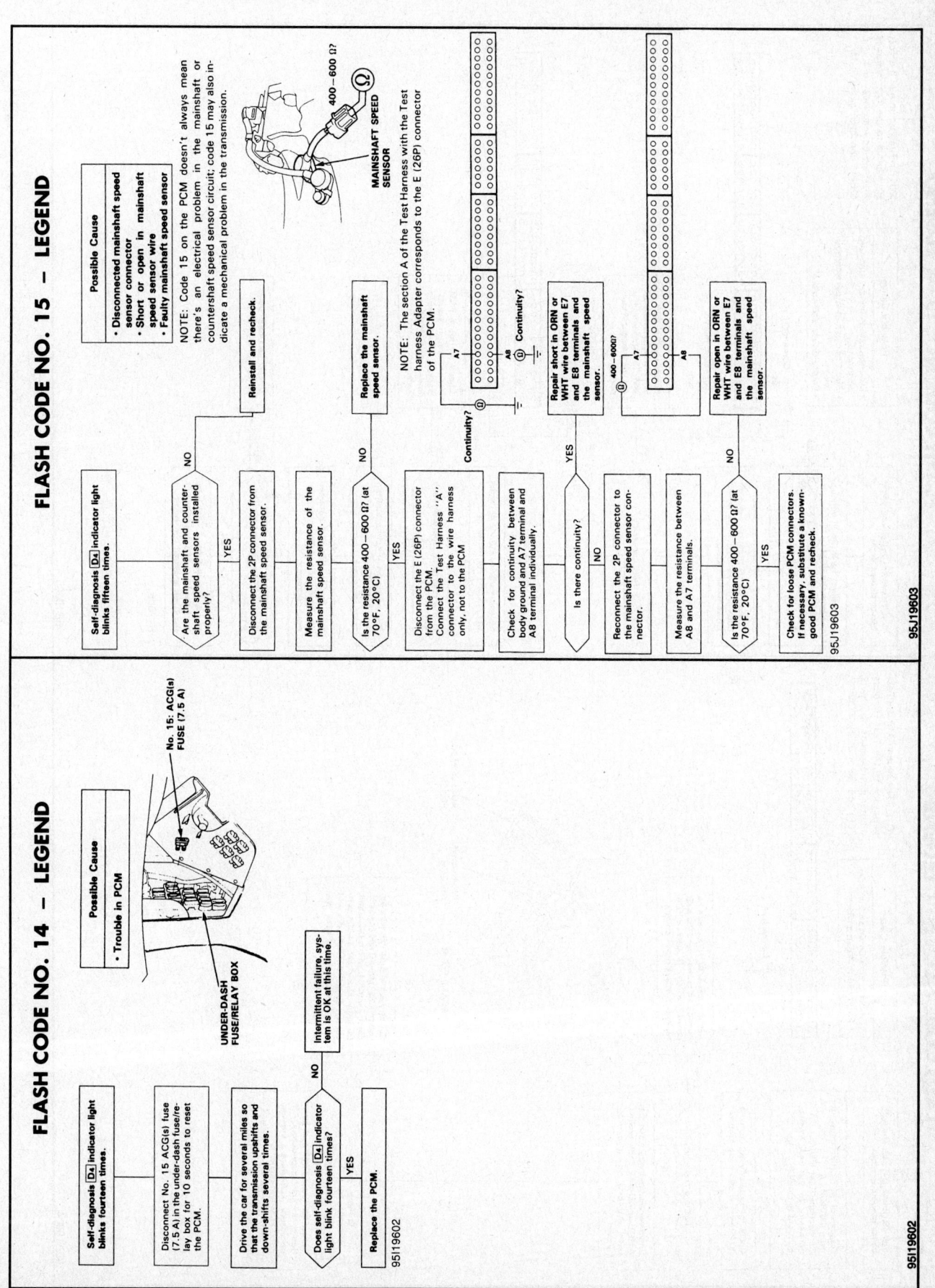

FLASH CODE NO. 14 – LEGEND

Possible Cause
- Trouble in PCM

Self-diagnosis D₄ indicator light blink fourteen times.

Disconnect No. 15 ACG(s) fuse (7.5 A) in the under-dash fuse/relay box for 10 seconds to reset the PCM.

Drive the car for several miles so that the transmission upshifts and down-shifts several times.

Does self-diagnosis D₄ indicator light blink fourteen times?

NO → Intermittent failure, system is OK at this time.

YES → Replace the PCM.

No. 15: ACG(s) FUSE (7.5 A)

UNDER-DASH FUSE/RELAY BOX

95J19602

FLASH CODE NO. 15 – LEGEND

Possible Cause
- Disconnected mainshaft speed sensor connector
- Short or open in mainshaft speed sensor wire
- Faulty mainshaft speed sensor

NOTE: Code 15 on the PCM doesn't always mean there's an electrical problem in the mainshaft or countershaft speed sensor circuit; code 15 may also indicate a mechanical problem in the transmission.

Self-diagnosis D₄ indicator light blinks fifteen times.

Are the mainshaft and countershaft speed sensors installed properly?

NO → Reinstall and recheck.

YES → Disconnect the 2P connector from the mainshaft speed sensor.

Measure the resistance of the mainshaft speed sensor.

Is the resistance 400–600 Ω? (at 70°F, 20°C)

NO → Replace the mainshaft speed sensor.

YES → Disconnect the E (26P) connector from the PCM. Connect the Test Harness "A" connector to the wire harness only, not to the PCM.

Check for continuity between body ground and A7 terminal and A8 terminal individually.

Continuity? → Repair short in ORN or WHT wire between E7 and E8 terminals and the mainshaft speed sensor.

Is there continuity?

YES → Reconnect the 2P connector to the mainshaft speed sensor connector.

Measure the resistance between A8 and A7 terminals.

Is the resistance 400–600 Ω? (at 70°F, 20°C)

NO → Repair open in ORN or WHT wire between E7 and E8 terminals and the mainshaft speed sensor.

YES → Check for loose PCM connectors. If necessary, substitute a known-good PCM and recheck.

MAINSHAFT SPEED SENSOR

400–600 Ω?

NOTE: The section A of the Test Harness with the Test harness Adapter corresponds to the E (26P) connector of the PCM.

95J19603

95J19603

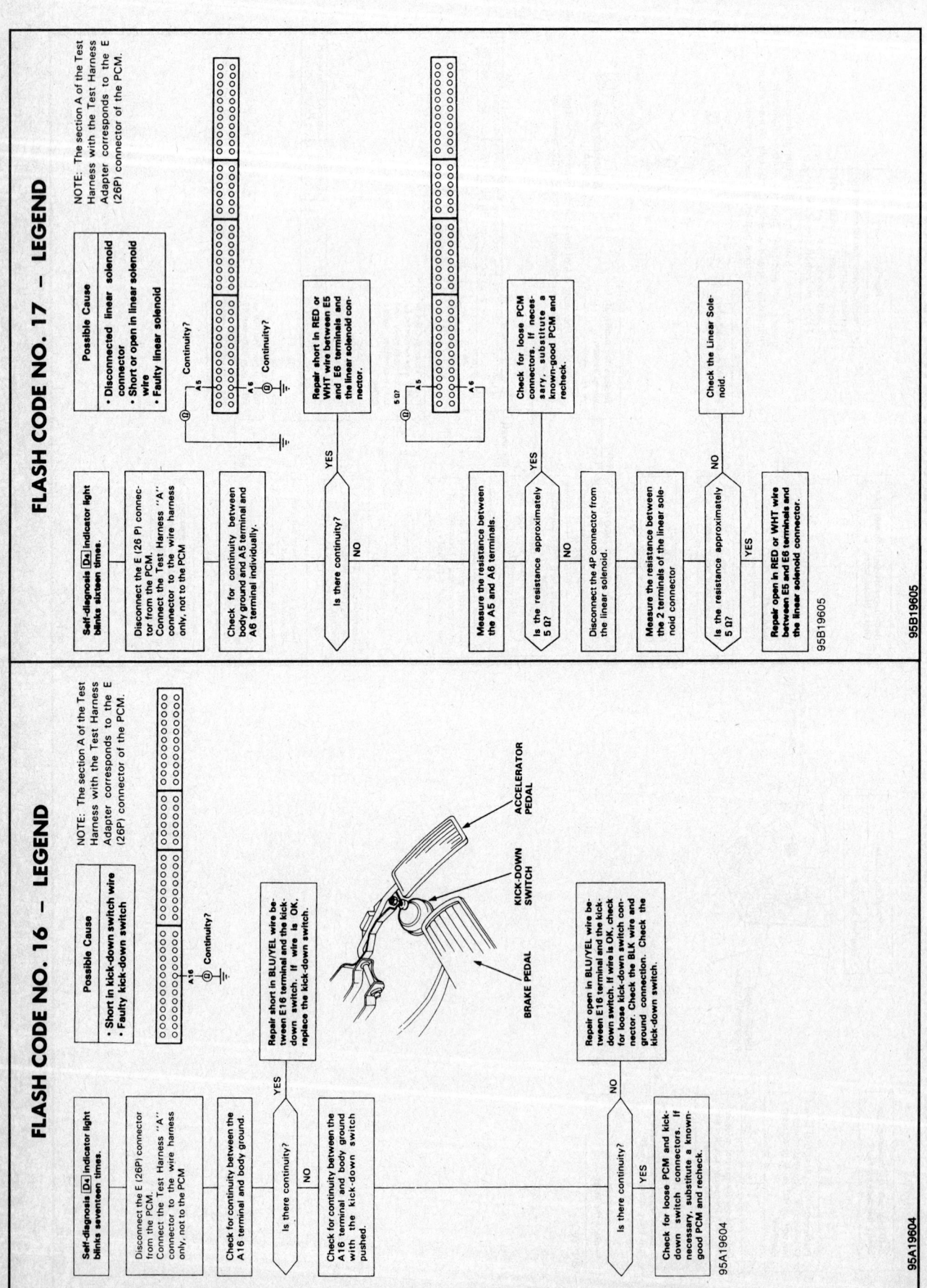

FLASH CODE NO. 16 — LEGEND

NOTE: The section A of the Test Harness with the Test Harness Adapter corresponds to the E (26P) connector of the PCM.

Possible Cause
• Short in kick-down switch wire
• Faulty kick-down switch

Self-diagnosis D4 indicator light blinks seventeen times.

Disconnect the E (26P) connector from the PCM. Connect the Test Harness "A" connector to the wire harness only, not to the PCM

Check for continuity between the A16 terminal and body ground.

Is there continuity?

YES — Repair short in BLU/YEL wire between E16 terminal and the kick-down switch. If wire is OK, replace the kick-down switch.

NO — Check for continuity between the A16 terminal and body ground with the kick-down switch pushed.

Is there continuity?

NO — Repair open in BLU/YEL wire between E16 terminal and the kick-down switch. If wire is OK, check for loose kick-down switch connector. Check the BLK wire and ground connection. Check the kick-down switch.

YES — Check for loose PCM and kick-down switch connectors. If necessary, substitute a known-good PCM and recheck.

ACCELERATOR PEDAL
KICK-DOWN SWITCH
BRAKE PEDAL

95A19604

FLASH CODE NO. 17 — LEGEND

NOTE: The section A of the Test Harness with the Test Harness Adapter corresponds to the E (26P) connector of the PCM.

Possible Cause
• Disconnected linear solenoid connector
• Short or open in linear solenoid wire
• Faulty linear solenoid

Self-diagnosis D4 indicator light blinks sixteen times.

Disconnect the E (26 P) connector from the PCM. Connect the Test Harness "A" connector to the wire harness only, not to the PCM

Check for continuity between body ground and A5 terminal and A6 terminal individually.

Is there continuity?

YES — Repair short in RED or WHT wire between E5 and E6 terminals and the linear solenoid connector.

NO — Measure the resistance between the A5 and A6 terminals.

Is the resistance approximately 5 Ω?

YES — Check for loose PCM connectors. If necessary, substitute a known-good PCM and recheck.

NO — Disconnect the 4P connector from the linear solenoid.

Measure the resistance between the 2 terminals of the linear solenoid connector

Is the resistance approximately 5 Ω?

NO — Check the Linear Solenoid.

YES — Repair open in RED or WHT wire between E5 and E6 terminals and the linear solenoid connector.

95B19605

95B19605

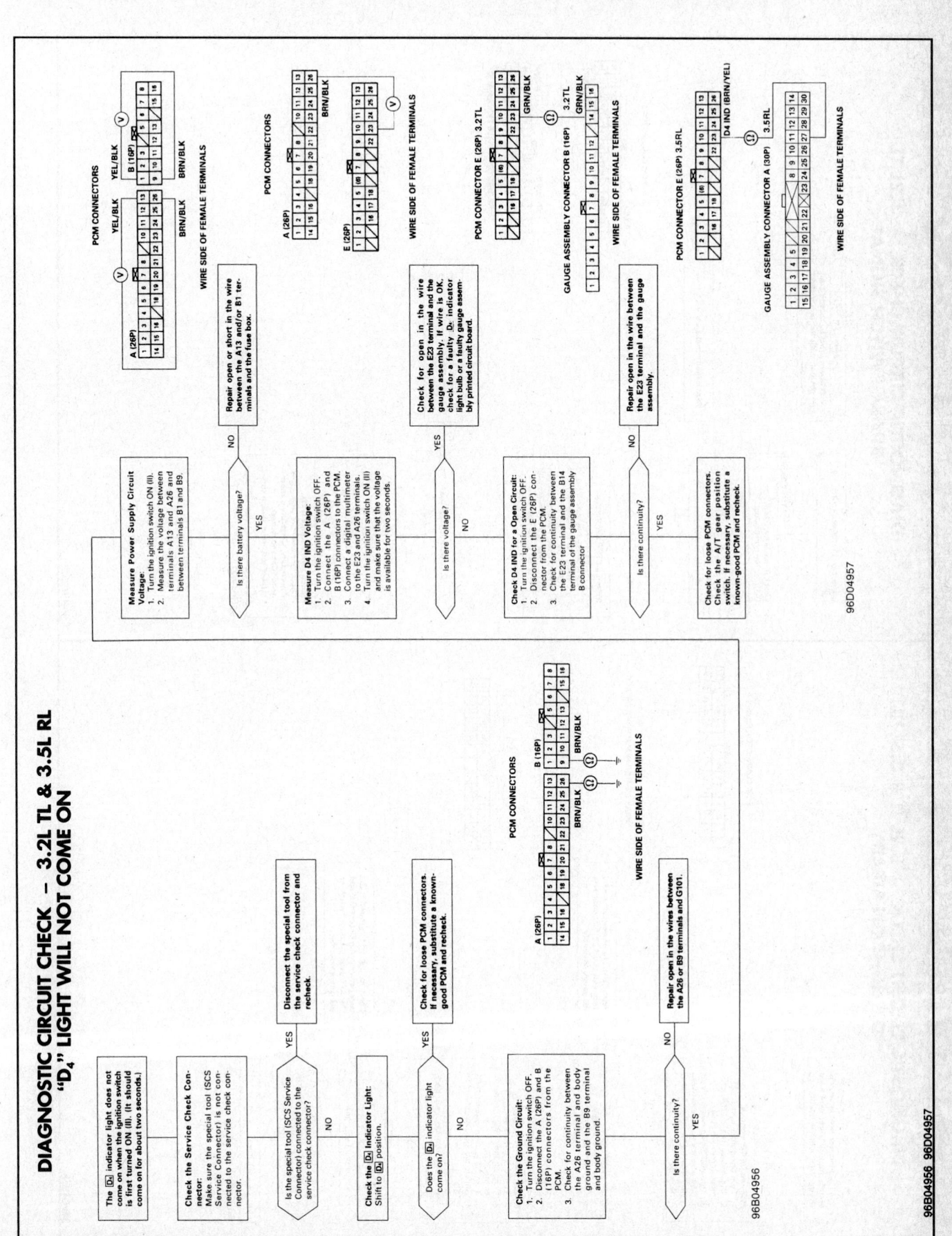

DIAGNOSTIC CIRCUIT CHECK – 3.2L TL & 3.5L RL
"D4" LIGHT WILL NOT COME ON

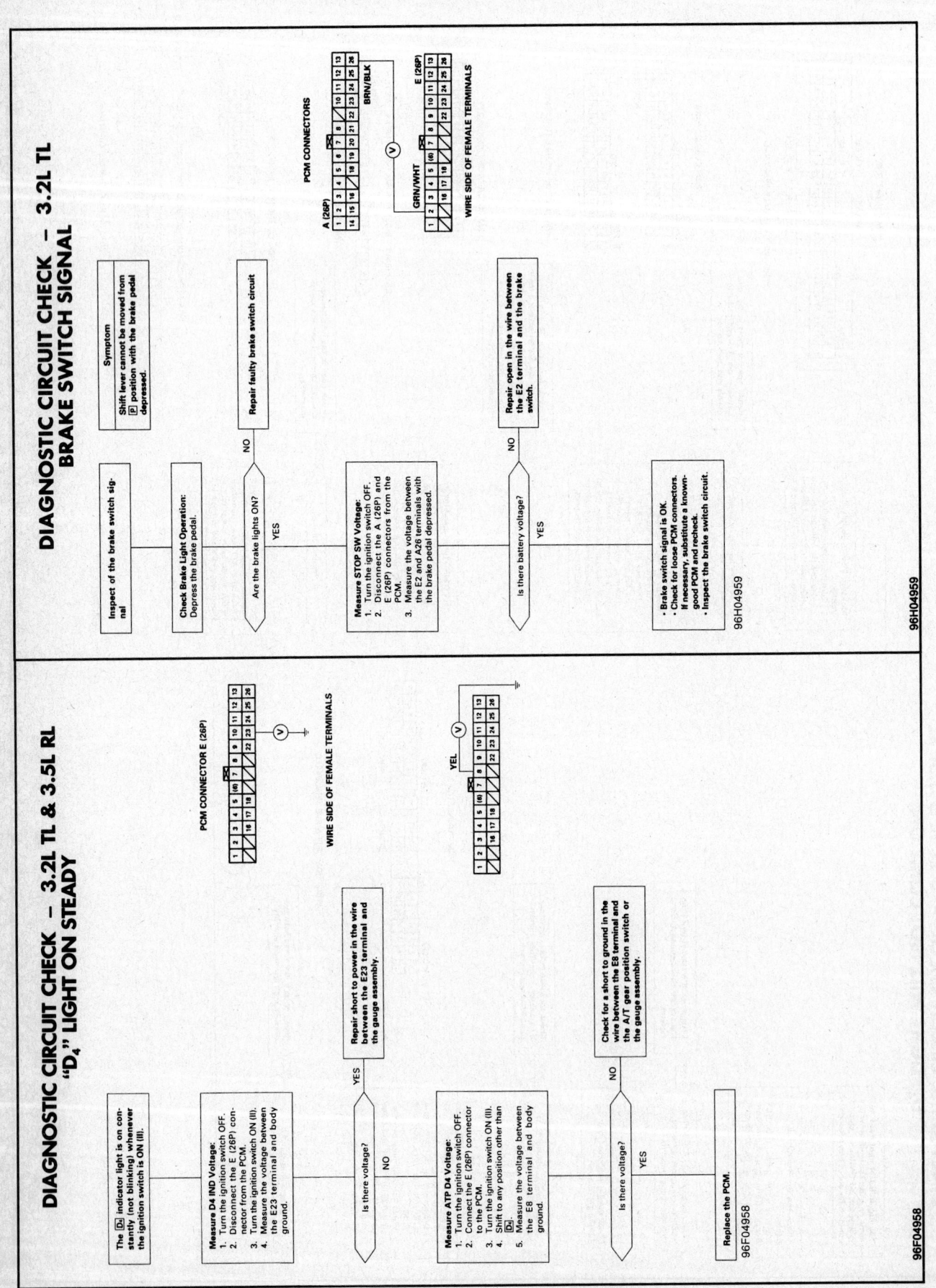

DIAGNOSTIC CIRCUIT CHECK — 3.2L TL BRAKE SWITCH SIGNAL

Inspect of the brake switch signal

Check Brake Light Operation: Depress the brake pedal.

Are the brake lights ON? — NO → Repair faulty brake switch circuit.

YES

Measure STOP SW Voltage:
1. Turn the ignition switch OFF.
2. Disconnect the A (26P) and E (26P) connectors from the PCM.
3. Measure the voltage between the E2 and A26 terminals with the brake pedal depressed.

Is there battery voltage? — NO → Repair open in the wire between the E2 terminal and the brake switch.

YES

- Brake switch signal is OK.
- Check for loose PCM connectors. If necessary, substitute a known-good PCM and recheck.
- Inspect the brake switch circuit.

96H04959

96H04959

DIAGNOSTIC CIRCUIT CHECK — 3.2L TL & 3.5L RL "D4" LIGHT ON STEADY

The D4 indicator light is on constantly (not blinking) whenever the ignition switch is ON (II).

Measure D4 IND Voltage:
1. Turn the ignition switch OFF.
2. Disconnect the E (26P) connector from the PCM.
3. Turn the ignition switch ON (II).
4. Measure the voltage between the E23 terminal and body ground.

Is there voltage? — YES → Repair short to power in the wire between the E23 terminal and the gauge assembly.

NO

Measure ATP D4 Voltage:
1. Turn the ignition switch OFF.
2. Connect the E (26P) connector to the PCM.
3. Turn the ignition switch ON (II).
4. Shift to any position other than D4.
5. Measure the voltage between the E8 terminal and body ground.

Is there voltage? — NO → Check for a short to ground in the wire between the E8 terminal and the A/T gear position switch or the gauge assembly.

YES

Replace the PCM.

96F04958

96F04958

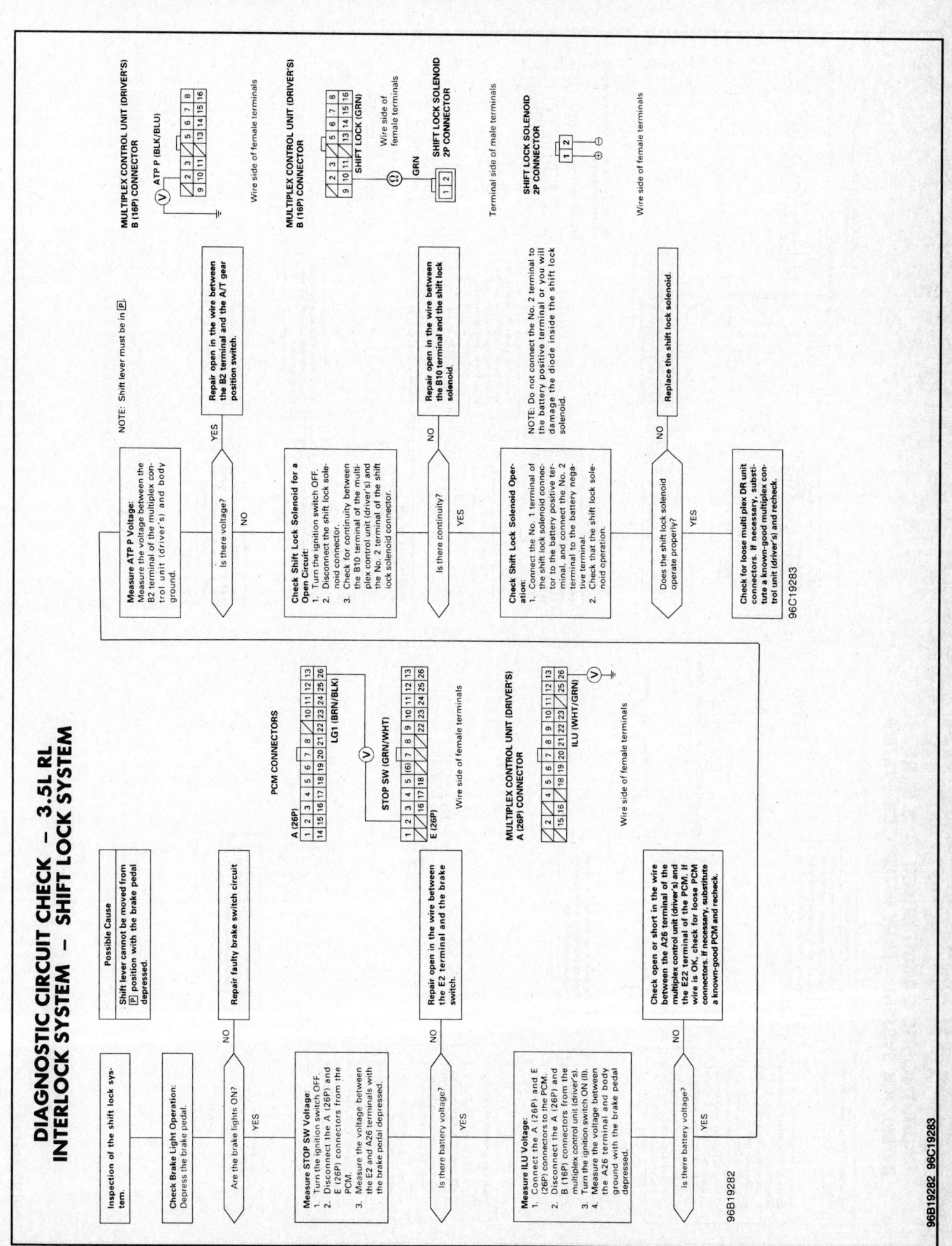

DIAGNOSTIC CIRCUIT CHECK – 3.5L RL INTERLOCK SYSTEM – SHIFT LOCK SYSTEM

96B19282 96C19283

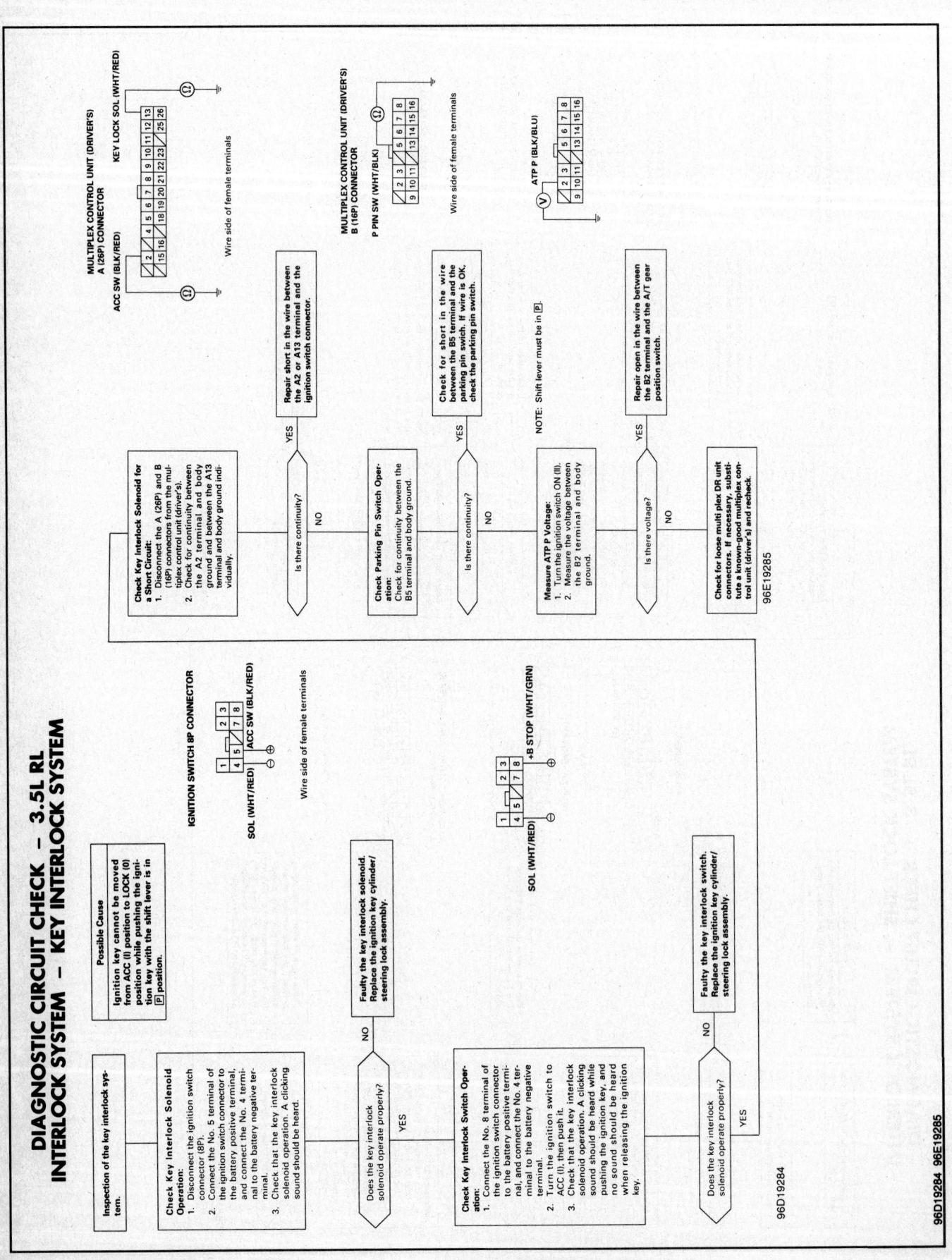

DIAGNOSTIC CIRCUIT CHECK – 3.5L RL
INTERLOCK SYSTEM – KEY INTERLOCK SYSTEM

96D19284   96E19285

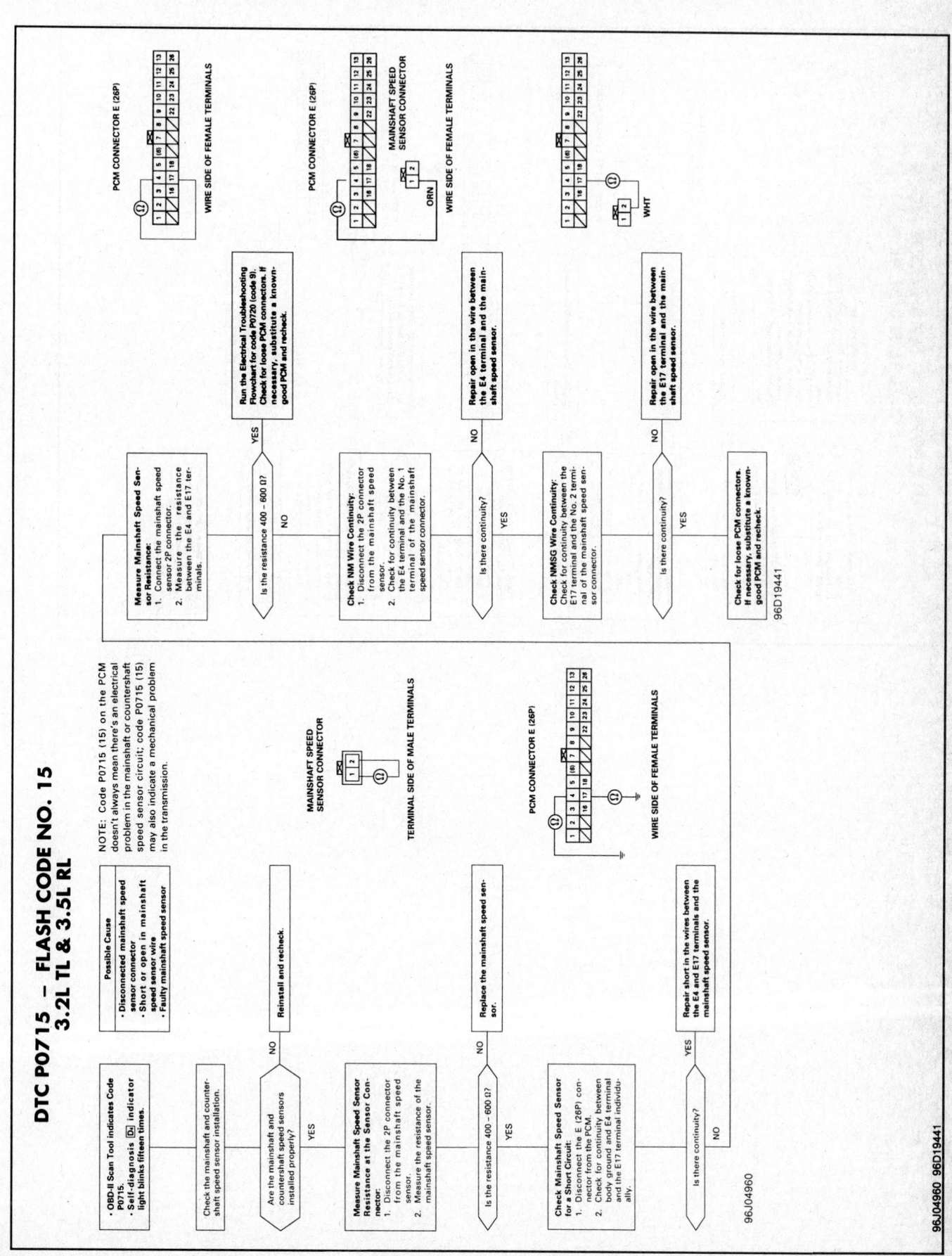

DTC P0715 – FLASH CODE NO. 15
3.2L TL & 3.5L RL

Possible Cause
- Disconnected mainshaft speed sensor connector
- Short or open in mainshaft speed sensor wire
- Faulty mainshaft speed sensor

NOTE: Code P0715 (15) on the PCM doesn't always mean there's an electrical problem in the mainshaft or countershaft speed sensor circuit; code P0715 (15) may also indicate a mechanical problem in the transmission.

96J04960 96D19441

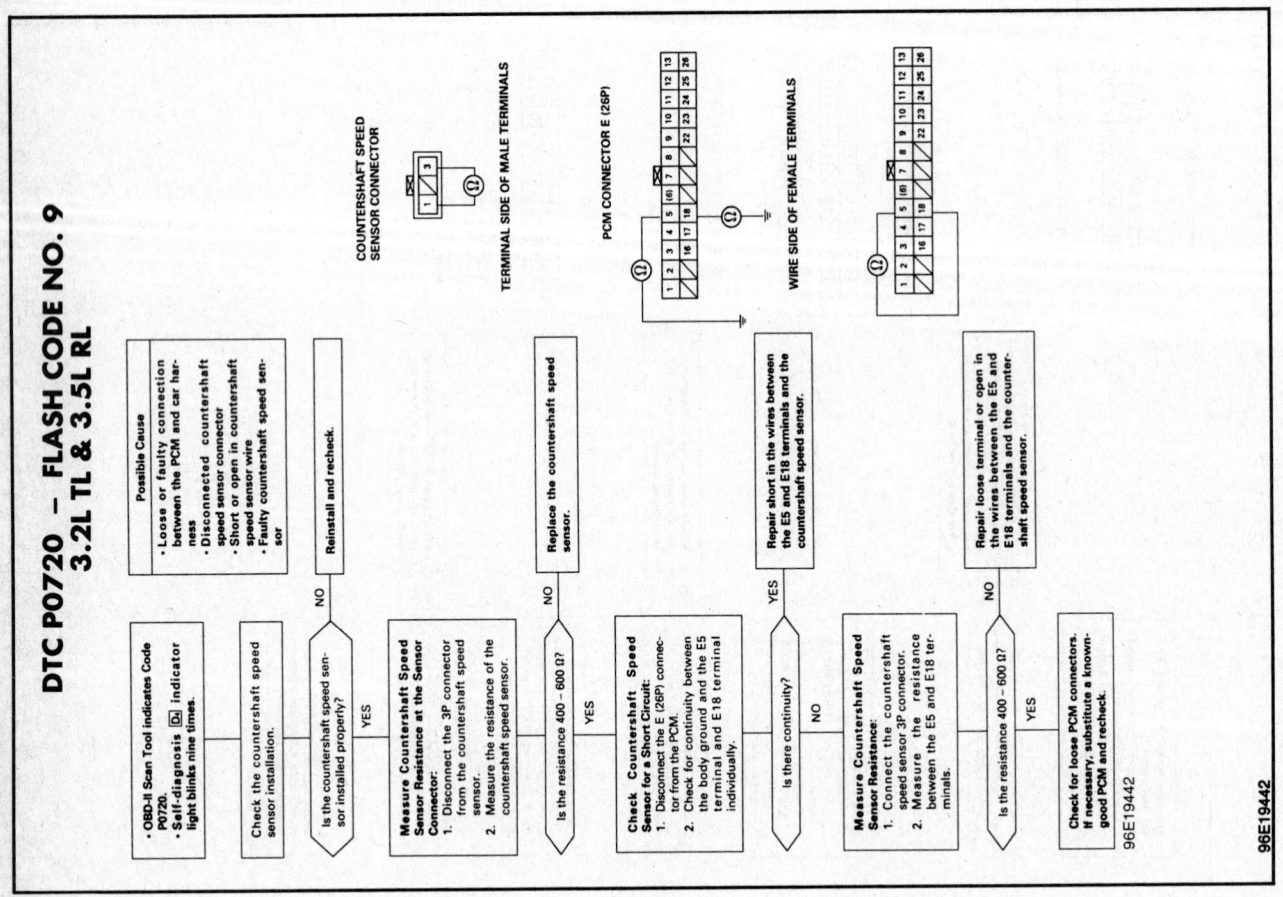

DTC P0720 – FLASH CODE NO. 9
3.2L TL & 3.5L RL

Possible Cause
- Loose or faulty connection between the PCM and car harness
- Disconnected countershaft speed sensor connector
- Short or open in countershaft speed sensor wire
- Faulty countershaft speed sensor

- OBD-II Scan Tool indicates Code P0720.
- Self-diagnosis D indicator light blinks nine times.

Check the countershaft speed sensor installation.

Is the countershaft speed sensor installed properly?

NO → Reinstall and recheck.

YES

Measure Countershaft Speed Sensor Resistance at the Sensor Connector:
1. Disconnect the 3P connector from the countershaft speed sensor.
2. Measure the resistance of the countershaft speed sensor.

Is the resistance 400 – 600 Ω?

NO → Replace the countershaft speed sensor.

YES

Check Countershaft Speed Sensor for a Short Circuit:
1. Disconnect the E (26P) connector from the PCM.
2. Check for continuity between the body ground and the E5 terminal and E18 terminal individually.

Is there continuity?

YES → Repair short in the wires between the E5 and E18 terminals and the countershaft speed sensor.

NO

Measure Countershaft Speed Sensor Resistance:
1. Connect the countershaft speed sensor 3P connector.
2. Measure the resistance between the E5 and E18 terminals.

Is the resistance 400 – 600 Ω?

NO → Repair loose terminal or open in the wires between the E5 and E18 terminals and the countershaft speed sensor.

YES

Check for loose PCM connectors. If necessary, substitute a known-good PCM and recheck.

COUNTERSHAFT SPEED SENSOR CONNECTOR

TERMINAL SIDE OF MALE TERMINALS

PCM CONNECTOR E (26P)

WIRE SIDE OF FEMALE TERMINALS

96E19442

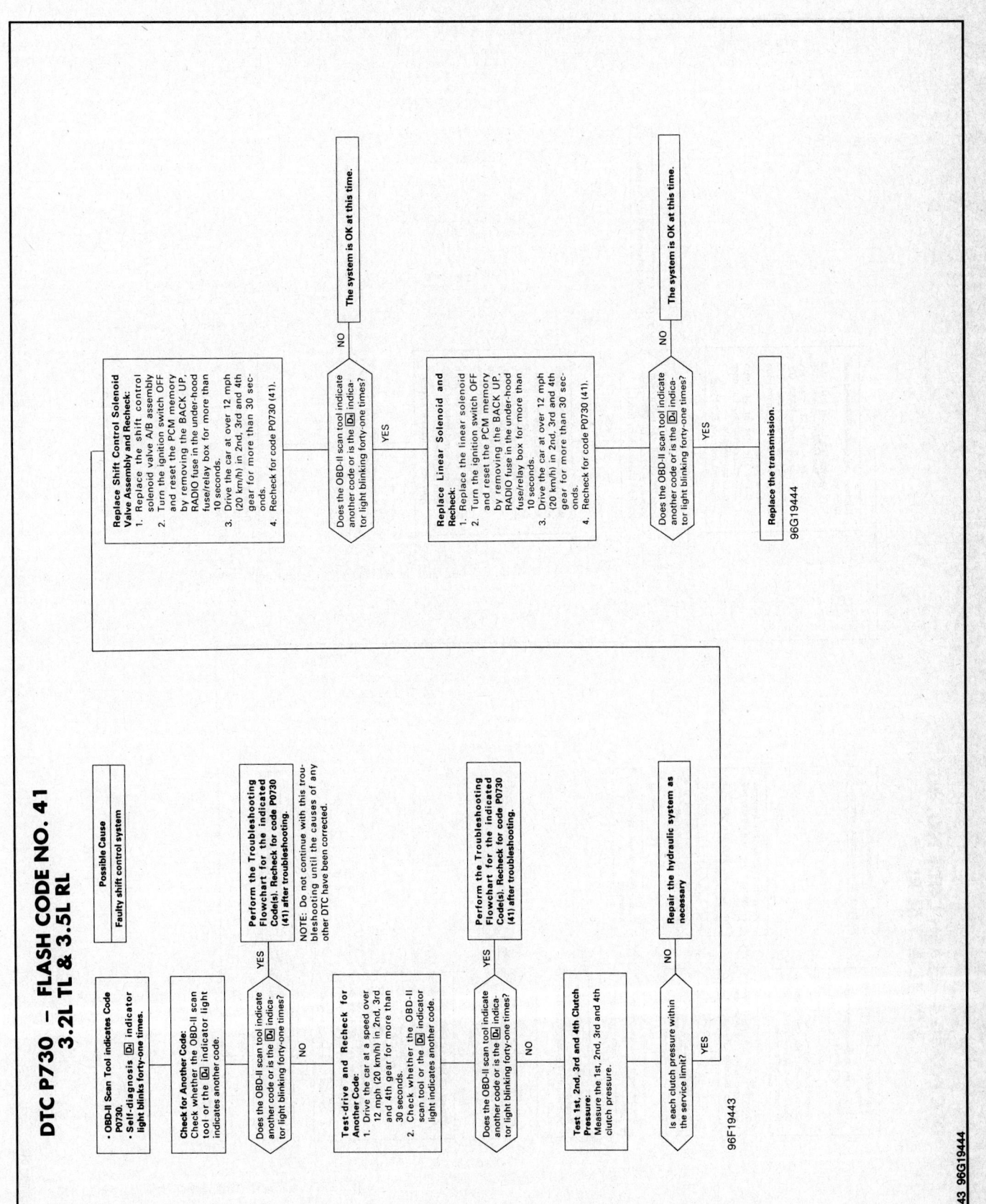

DTC P730 – FLASH CODE NO. 41
3.2L TL & 3.5L RL

Possible Cause
Faulty shift control system

- OBD-II Scan Tool indicates Code P0730.
- Self-diagnosis [D₄] indicator light blinks forty-one times.

Check for Another Code:
Check whether the OBD-II scan tool or the [D₄] indicator light indicates another code.

Does the OBD-II scan tool indicate another code or is the [D₄] indicator light blinking forty-one times?

NO →

Test-drive and Recheck for Another Code:
1. Drive the car at a speed over 12 mph (20 km/h) in 2nd, 3rd and 4th gear for more than 30 seconds.
2. Check whether the OBD-II scan tool or the [D₄] indicator light indicates another code.

Does the OBD-II scan tool indicate another code or is the [D₄] indicator light blinking forty-one times?

NO →

Test 1st, 2nd, 3rd and 4th Clutch Pressure:
Measure the 1st, 2nd, 3rd and 4th clutch pressure.

Is each clutch pressure within the service limit?

NO →

YES ↑ (from first decision) → **Perform the Troubleshooting Flowchart for the indicated Code(s). Recheck for code P0730 (41) after troubleshooting.**

NOTE: Do not continue with this troubleshooting until the causes of any other DTC have been corrected.

YES ↑ (from second decision) → **Perform the Troubleshooting Flowchart for the indicated Code(s). Recheck for code P0730 (41) after troubleshooting.**

YES (from clutch pressure decision) → **Repair the hydraulic system as necessary**

96F19443

Replace Shift Control Solenoid Valve Assembly and Recheck:
1. Replace the shift control solenoid valve A/B assembly.
2. Turn the ignition switch OFF and reset the PCM memory by removing the BACK UP, RADIO fuse in the under-hood fuse/relay box for more than 10 seconds.
3. Drive the car at over 12 mph (20 km/h) in 2nd, 3rd and 4th gear for more than 30 seconds.
4. Recheck for code P0730 (41).

Does the OBD-II scan tool indicate another code or is the [D₄] indicator light blinking forty-one times?

NO → **The system is OK at this time.**

YES →

Replace Linear Solenoid and Recheck:
1. Replace the linear solenoid.
2. Turn the ignition switch OFF and reset the PCM memory by removing the BACK UP, RADIO fuse in the under-hood fuse/relay box for more than 10 seconds.
3. Drive the car at over 12 mph (20 km/h) in 2nd, 3rd and 4th gear for more than 30 seconds.
4. Recheck for code P0730 (41).

Does the OBD-II scan tool indicate another code or is the [D₄] indicator light blinking forty-one times?

NO → **The system is OK at this time.**

YES → **Replace the transmission.**

96G19444

96F19443 96G19444

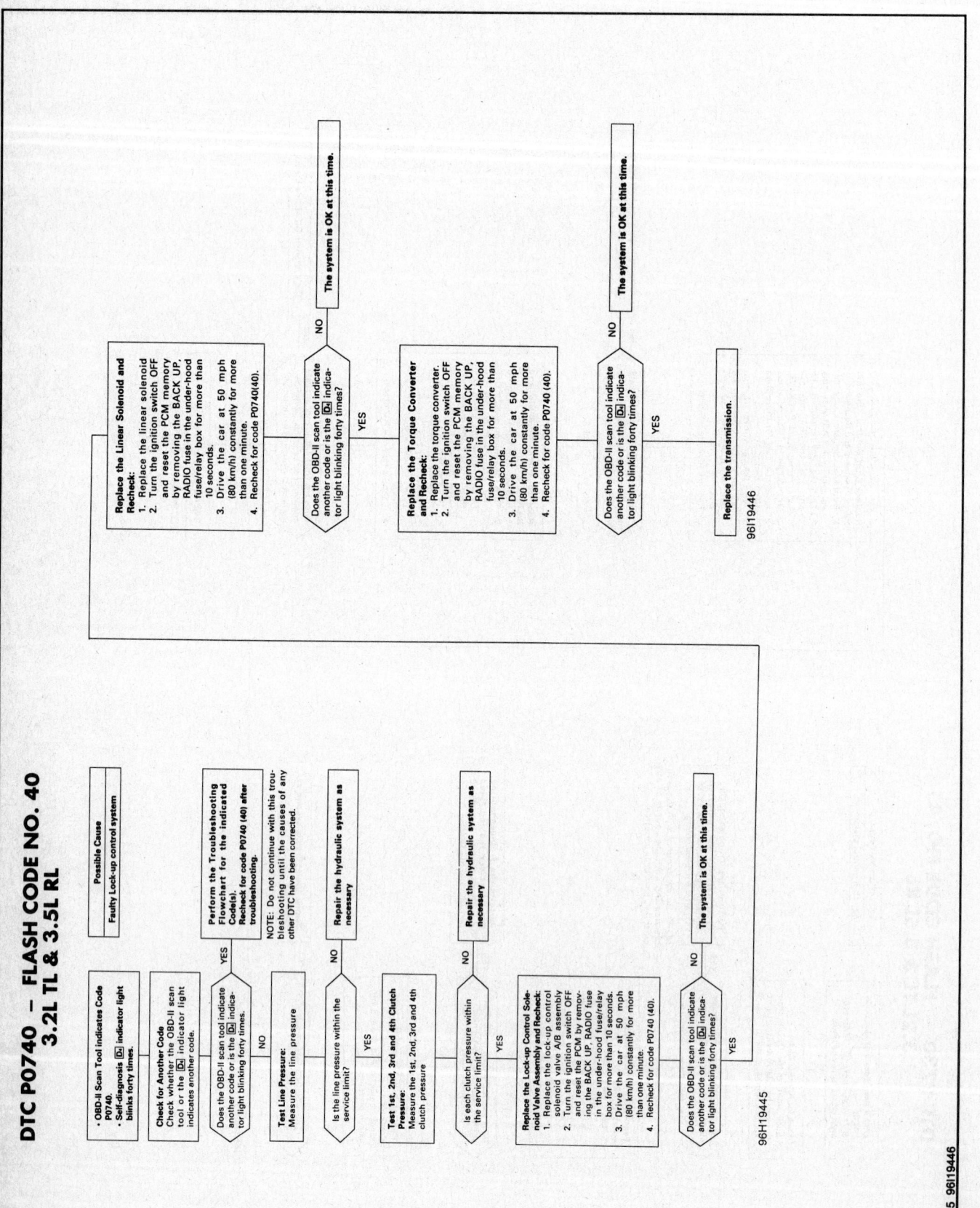

DTC P0740 – FLASH CODE NO. 40
3.2L TL & 3.5L RL

- OBD-II Scan Tool indicates Code P0740.
- Self-diagnosis [D4] indicator light blinks forty times.

Possible Cause

Faulty Lock-up control system

Check for Another Code
Check whether the OBD-II scan tool or the [D4] indicator light indicates another code.

Does the OBD-II scan tool indicate another code or is the [D4] indicator light blinking forty times?

YES →

Perform the Troubleshooting Flowchart for the indicated Code(s).
Recheck for code P0740 (40) after troubleshooting.

NOTE: Do not continue with this troubleshooting until the causes of any other DTC have been corrected.

NO ↓

Test Line Pressure:
Measure the line pressure

Is the line pressure within the service limit?

NO → **Repair the hydraulic system as necessary**

YES ↓

Test 1st, 2nd, 3rd and 4th Clutch Pressure:
Measure the 1st, 2nd, 3rd and 4th clutch pressure

Is each clutch pressure within the service limit?

NO → **Repair the hydraulic system as necessary**

YES ↓

Replace the Lock-up Control Solenoid Valve Assembly and Recheck:
1. Replace the lock-up control solenoid valve A/B assembly
2. Turn the ignition switch OFF and reset the PCM by removing the BACK UP, RADIO fuse in the under-hood fuse/relay box for more than 10 seconds.
3. Drive the car at 50 mph (80 km/h) constantly for more than one minute.
4. Recheck for code P0740 (40).

Does the OBD-II scan tool indicate another code or is the [D4] indicator light blinking forty times?

NO → **The system is OK at this time.**

YES ↓

96H19445

Replace the Linear Solenoid and Recheck:
1. Replace the linear solenoid and reset the PCM memory by removing the BACK UP, RADIO fuse in the under-hood fuse/relay box for more than 10 seconds.
2. Turn the ignition switch OFF and reset the PCM memory by removing the BACK UP, RADIO fuse in the under-hood fuse/relay box for more than 10 seconds.
3. Drive the car at 50 mph (80 km/h) constantly for more than one minute.
4. Recheck for code P0740 (40).

Does the OBD-II scan tool indicate another code or is the [D4] indicator light blinking forty times?

NO → **The system is OK at this time.**

YES ↓

Replace the Torque Converter and Recheck:
1. Replace the torque converter.
2. Turn the ignition switch OFF and reset the PCM memory by removing the BACK UP, RADIO fuse in the under-hood fuse/relay box for more than 10 seconds.
3. Drive the car at 50 mph (80 km/h) constantly for more than one minute.
4. Recheck for code P0740 (40).

Does the OBD-II scan tool indicate another code or is the [D4] indicator light blinking forty times?

NO → **The system is OK at this time.**

YES ↓

Replace the transmission.

96H19446

96H19445 96H19446

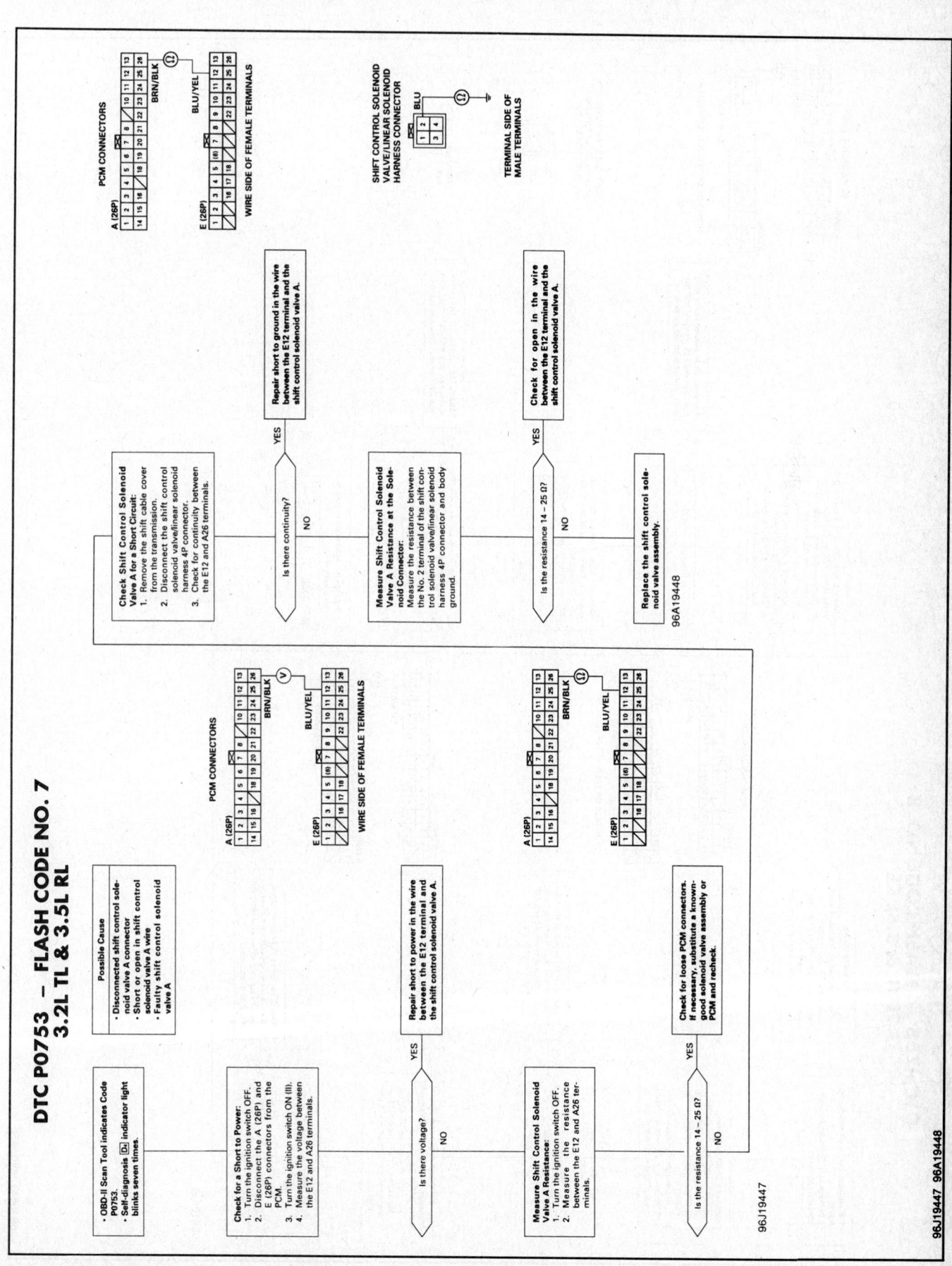

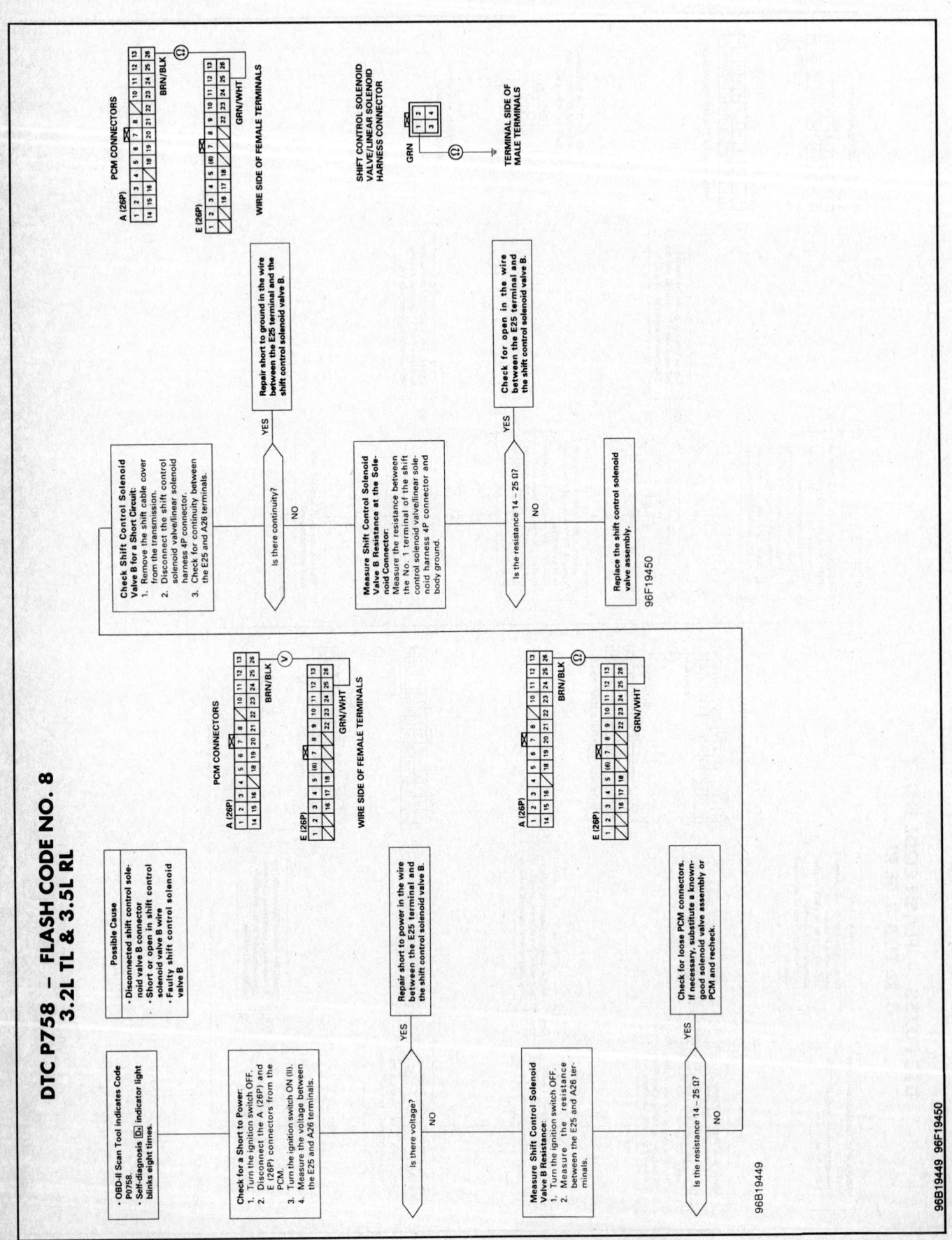

DTC P758 – FLASH CODE NO. 8
3.2L TL & 3.5L RL

- OBD-II Scan Tool indicates Code P0758.
- Self-diagnosis [D4] indicator light blinks eight times.

Possible Cause
- Disconnected shift control solenoid valve B connector
- Short or open in shift control solenoid valve B wire
- Faulty shift control solenoid valve B

Check for a Short to Power:
1. Turn the ignition switch OFF.
2. Disconnect the A (26P) and E (26P) connectors from the PCM.
3. Turn the ignition switch ON (II).
4. Measure the voltage between the E25 and A26 terminals.

Is there voltage? — YES → Repair short to power in the wire between the E25 terminal and the shift control solenoid valve B.

NO ↓

Measure Shift Control Solenoid Valve B Resistance:
1. Turn the ignition switch OFF.
2. Measure the resistance between the E25 and A26 terminals.

Is the resistance 14 – 25 Ω? — YES → Check for loose PCM connectors. If necessary, substitute a known-good solenoid valve assembly or PCM and recheck.

Check Shift Control Solenoid Valve B for a Short Circuit:
1. Remove the shift cable cover from the transmission.
2. Disconnect the shift control solenoid valve/linear solenoid harness 4P connector.
3. Check for continuity between the E25 and A26 terminals.

Is there continuity? — YES → Repair short to ground in the wire between the E25 terminal and the shift control solenoid valve B.

NO ↓

Measure Shift Control Solenoid Valve B Resistance at the Solenoid Connector:
Measure the resistance between the No. 1 terminal of the shift control solenoid valve/linear solenoid harness 4P connector and body ground.

Is the resistance 14 – 25 Ω? — YES → Check for open in the wire between the E25 terminal and the shift control solenoid valve B.

NO ↓

Replace the shift control solenoid valve assembly.

96F19450

PCM CONNECTORS

A (26P)
E (26P)

BRN/BLK
GRN/WHT

WIRE SIDE OF FEMALE TERMINALS

SHIFT CONTROL SOLENOID VALVE/LINEAR SOLENOID HARNESS CONNECTOR

GRN

TERMINAL SIDE OF MALE TERMINALS

96B19449 96F19450

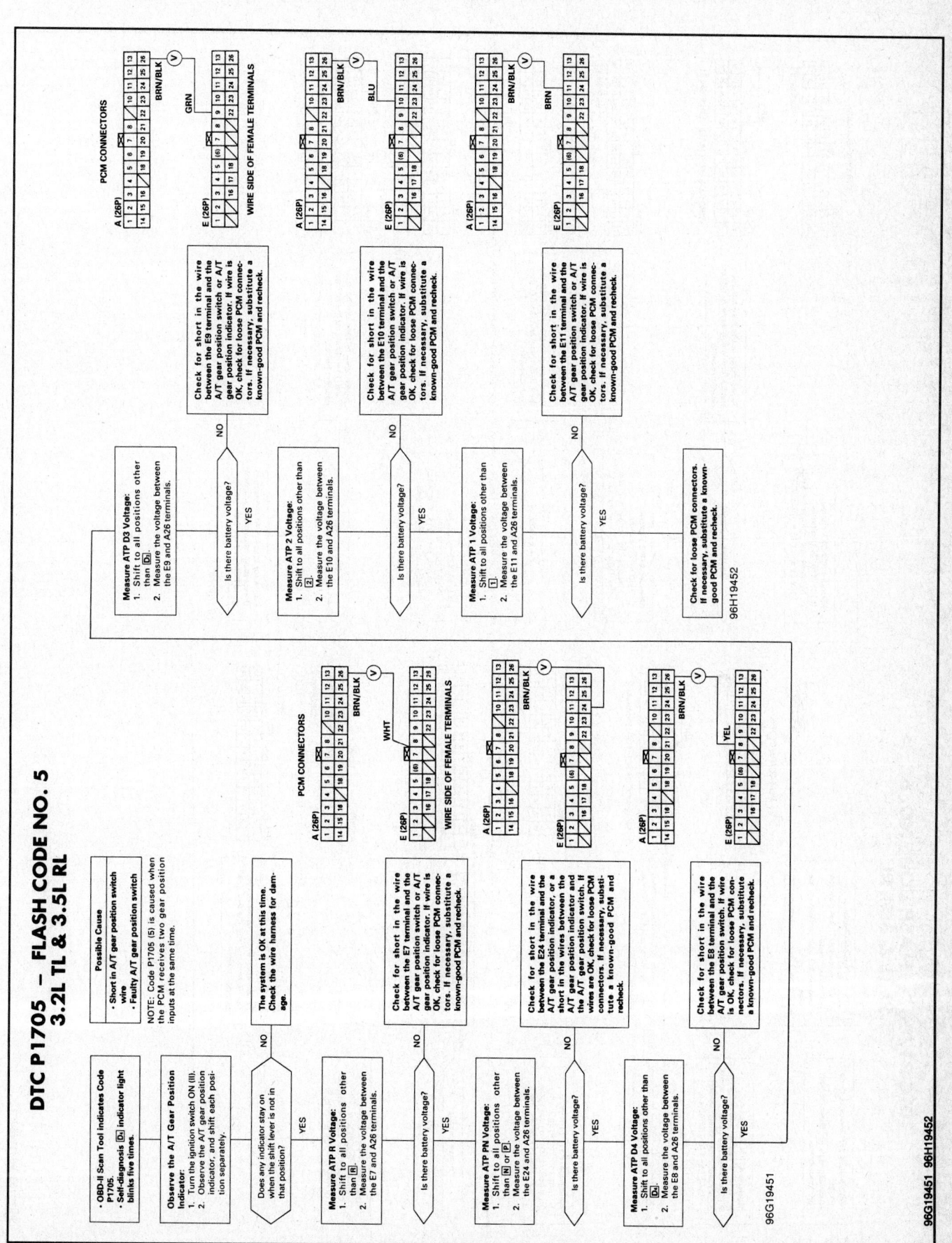

DTC P1705 – FLASH CODE NO. 5
3.2L TL & 3.5L RL

96G19451 96H19452

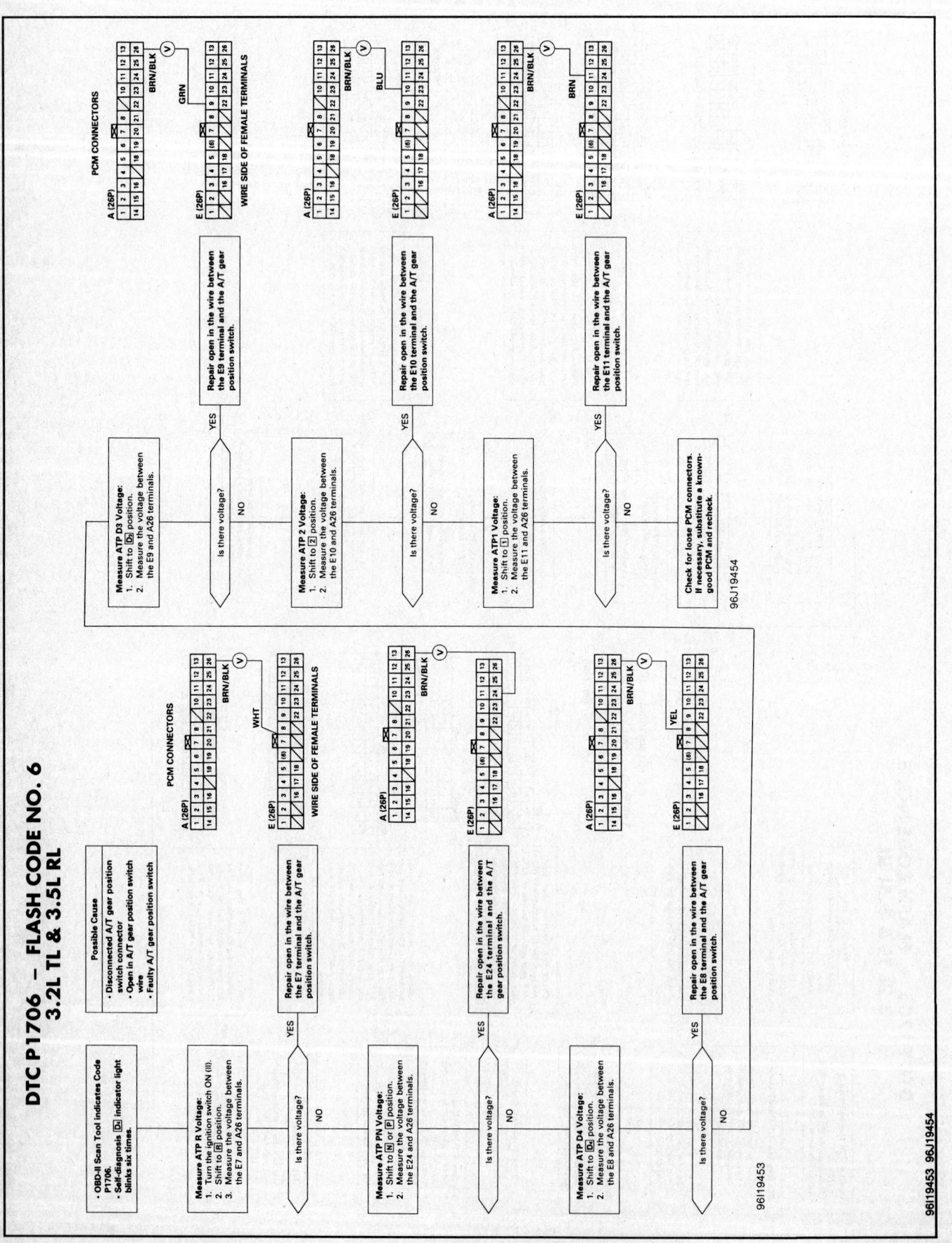

DTC P1706 – FLASH CODE NO. 6
3.2L TL & 3.5L RL

96J19453 96J19454

96J19454

96J19453

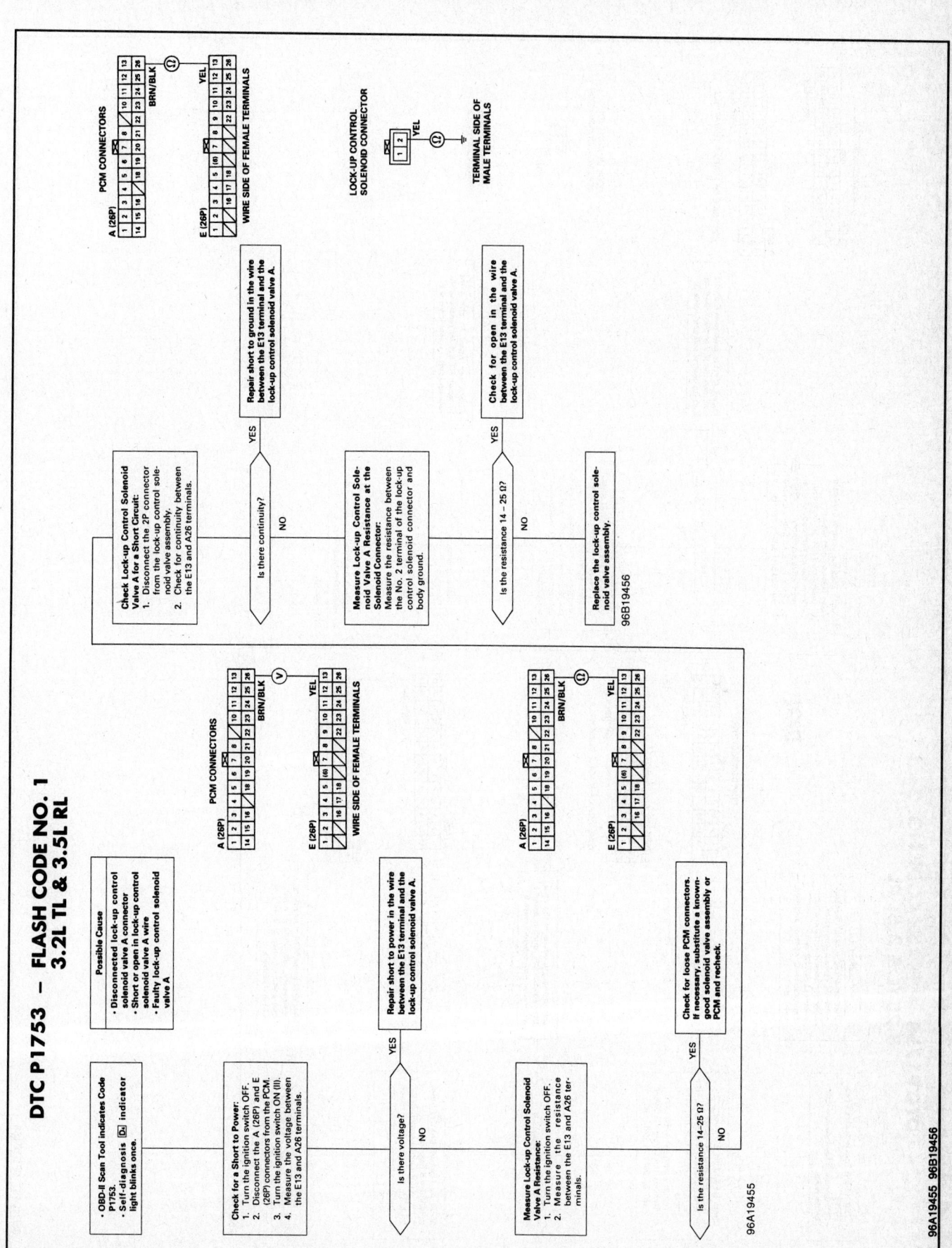

DTC P1753 – FLASH CODE NO. 1
3.2L TL & 3.5L RL

96A19455   96B19456

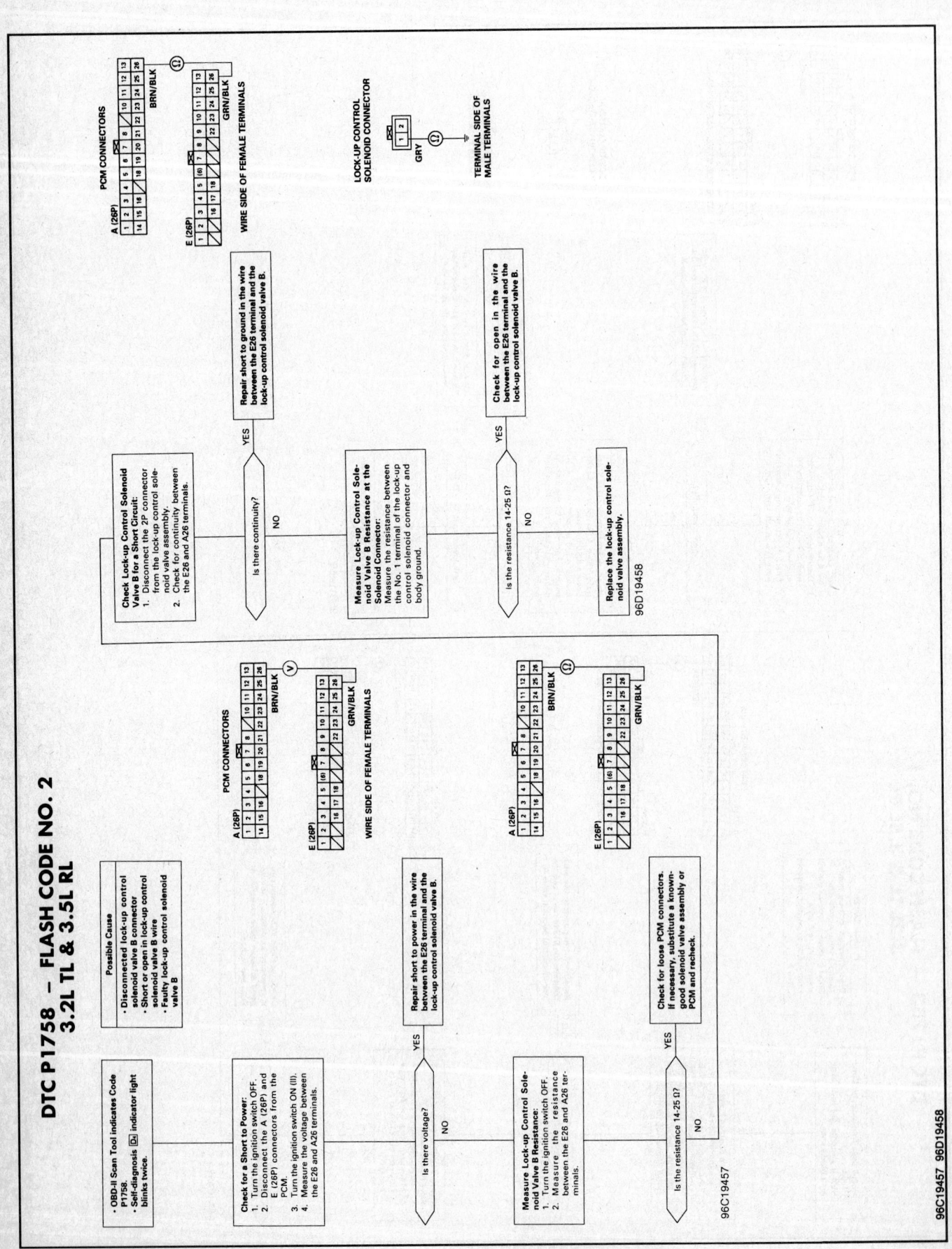

DTC P1758 – FLASH CODE NO. 2
3.2L TL & 3.5L RL

Possible Cause
- Disconnected lock-up control solenoid valve B connector.
- Short or open in lock-up control solenoid valve B wire.
- Faulty lock-up control solenoid valve B

- OBD-II Scan Tool indicates Code P1758.
- Self-diagnosis [D] indicator light blinks twice.

Check for a Short to Power:
1. Turn the ignition switch OFF.
2. Disconnect the A (26P) and E (26P) connectors from the PCM.
3. Turn the ignition switch ON (II).
4. Measure the voltage between the E26 and A26 terminals.

Is there voltage?

YES — Repair short to power in the wire between the E26 terminal and the lock-up control solenoid valve B.

NO

Measure Lock-up Control Solenoid Valve B Resistance:
1. Turn the ignition switch OFF.
2. Measure the resistance between the E26 and A26 terminals.

Is the resistance 14-25 Ω?

YES — Check for loose PCM connectors. If necessary, substitute a known-good solenoid valve assembly or PCM and recheck.

NO

96C19457

Check Lock-up Control Solenoid Valve B for a Short Circuit:
1. Disconnect the 2P connector from the lock-up control solenoid valve assembly.
2. Check for continuity between the E26 and A26 terminals.

Is there continuity?

YES — Repair short to ground in the wire between the E26 terminal and the lock-up control solenoid valve B.

NO

Measure Lock-up Control Solenoid Valve B Resistance at the Solenoid Connector:
Measure the resistance between the No. 1 terminal of the lock-up control solenoid connector and body ground.

Is the resistance 14-25 Ω?

YES — Check for open in the wire between the E26 terminal and the lock-up control solenoid valve B.

NO — Replace the lock-up control solenoid valve assembly.

96D19458

PCM CONNECTORS

A (26P)
BRN/BLK

E (26P)
GRN/BLK

WIRE SIDE OF FEMALE TERMINALS

LOCK-UP CONTROL SOLENOID CONNECTOR
GRY

TERMINAL SIDE OF MALE TERMINALS

96C19457 96D19458

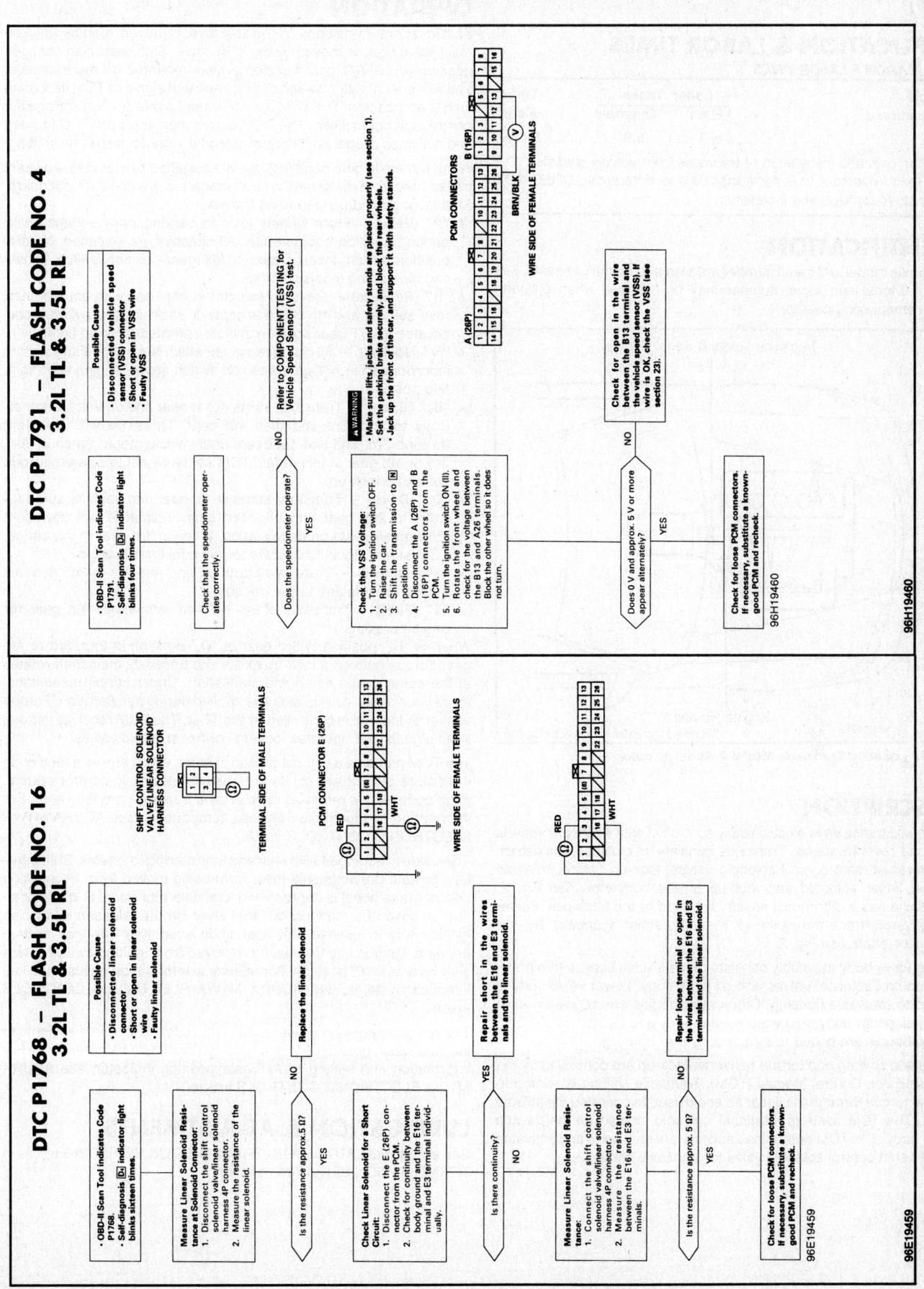

DTC P1791 – FLASH CODE NO. 4
3.2L TL & 3.5L RL

- OBD-II Scan Tool indicates Code P1791.
- Self-diagnosis D₄ indicator light blinks four times.

Possible Cause
- Disconnected vehicle speed sensor (VSS) connector
- Short or open in VSS wire
- Faulty VSS

Check that the speedometer operates correctly.

Does the speedometer operate?

NO → Refer to COMPONENT TESTING for Vehicle Speed Sensor (VSS) test.

YES

Check the VSS Voltage:
1. Turn the ignition switch OFF.
2. Raise the car.
3. Shift the transmission to N position.
4. Disconnect the A (26P) and B (16P) connectors from the PCM.
5. Turn the ignition switch ON (II).
6. Rotate the front wheel and check for the voltage between the B13 and A26 terminals. Block the other wheel so it does not turn.

⚠ WARNING
- Make sure lifts, jacks and safety stands are placed properly (see section 1).
- Set the parking brake securely, and block the rear wheels.
- Jack up the front of the car, and support it with safety stands.

Does 0 V and approx. 5 V or more appear alternately?

NO → Check for open in the wire between the B13 terminal and the vehicle speed sensor (VSS). If wire is OK, check the VSS (see section 23).

YES

Check for loose PCM connectors. If necessary, substitute a known-good PCM and recheck.

PCM CONNECTORS

B (16P)

BRN/BLK

WIRE SIDE OF FEMALE TERMINALS

A (26P)

96H19460

96H19460

DTC P1768 – FLASH CODE NO. 16
3.2L TL & 3.5L RL

- OBD-II Scan Tool indicates Code P1768.
- Self-diagnosis D₄ indicator light blinks sixteen times.

Possible Cause
- Disconnected linear solenoid connector
- Short or open in linear solenoid wire
- Faulty linear solenoid

Measure Linear Solenoid Resistance at Solenoid Connector:
1. Disconnect the shift control solenoid valve/linear solenoid harness 4P connector.
2. Measure the resistance of the linear solenoid.

Is the resistance approx. 5 Ω?

NO → Replace the linear solenoid

YES

Check Linear Solenoid for a Short Circuit:
1. Disconnect the E (26P) connector from the PCM.
2. Check for continuity between body ground and the E16 terminal and E3 terminal individually.

Is there continuity?

YES → Repair short in the wires between the E16 and E3 terminals and the linear solenoid.

NO

Measure Linear Solenoid Resistance:
1. Connect the shift control solenoid valve/linear solenoid harness 4P connector.
2. Measure the resistance between the E16 and E3 terminals.

Is the resistance approx. 5 Ω?

NO → Repair loose PCM terminal or open in the wires between the E16 and E3 terminals and the linear solenoid.

YES

Check for loose PCM connectors. If necessary, substitute a known-good PCM and recheck.

SHIFT CONTROL SOLENOID VALVE/LINEAR SOLENOID HARNESS CONNECTOR

TERMINAL SIDE OF MALE TERMINALS

PCM CONNECTOR E (26P)

RED

WHT

WIRE SIDE OF FEMALE TERMINALS

RED

WHT

96E19459

96E19459

2.5TL

APPLICATION & LABOR TIMES

APPLICATION & LABOR TIMES

Vehicle Application	Labor Times		Trans. Model
	[1] R & I	[2] Overhaul	
2.5TL	5.1	8.9	M1WA

[1] – Removal and installation of transaxle from vehicle chassis.

[2] – Bench overhaul time for transaxle and differential. DOES NOT include removal and installation.

IDENTIFICATION

Transaxle model and serial number are stamped on the transaxle. *See Fig. 1.* Model and serial number may be required when ordering replacement components.

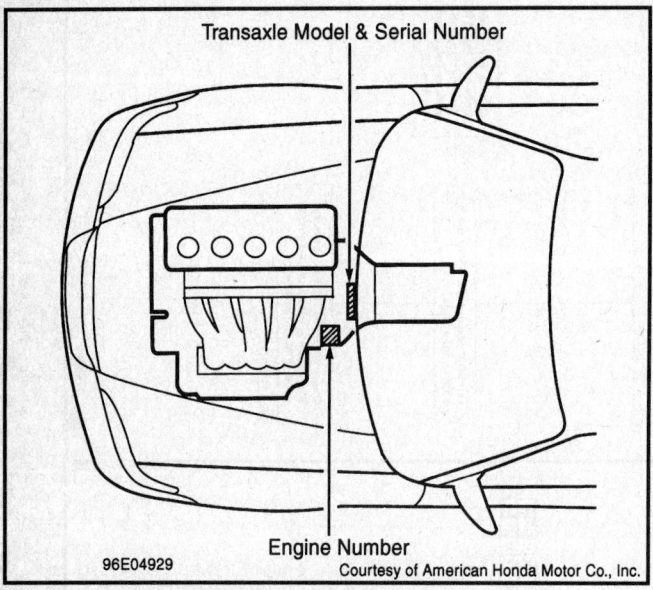

Transaxle Model & Serial Number

Engine Number

96E04929   Courtesy of American Honda Motor Co., Inc.

Fig. 1: Locating Transaxle Model & Serial Number

DESCRIPTION

Automatic transaxle is electronically controlled with 4 forward speeds and one reverse speed. Transaxle consists of clutches, mainshaft, countershaft, shift control solenoid valves, lock-up control solenoid valves, linear solenoid and lock-up torque converter. *See Fig. 2.* Transaxle has a differential assembly bolted to the transaxle. Power is delivered from transaxle to the differential assembly by the extension shaft. *See Fig. 2.*

Lower valve body assembly consists of main valve body, servo body, shift control solenoid valves and oil pass body. Lower valve body is bolted to transaxle housing. Other valve bodies are, regulator valve body, oil pump body, 2nd accumulator body and throttle valve body. These bodies are bolted to torque converter housing.

Transaxle shifting and torque converter lock-up are controlled by the Transmission Control Module (TCM). Transaxle shifting is related to engine torque through the linear solenoid used to operated the throttle valve. The TCM controls the linear solenoid located on the throttle valve body. The TCM determines appropriate shift point and activates proper shift control solenoid valve for transaxle shifting.

OPERATION

Shift lever has 7 positions. When shift lever is moved, manual valve on main valve body is moved by the shift cable. Shift lever also changes position of the A/T gear position switch, mounted on the transaxle. The A/T gear position switch delivers an input signal to TCM indicating shift lever position. The TCM uses this input signal for controlling shift control solenoid valves. The TCM determines appropriate shift point and activates proper shift control solenoid valve for transaxle shifting.

When transaxle gear combinations are engaged by clutches, power is transmitted from mainshaft to countershaft to provide different gears. Shift lever positions operate as follows:

- **"P" (Park)** – Front wheels lock as parking pawl engages with parking gear on countershaft. All clutches are released. Neutral position switch, incorporated in A/T gear position switch, allows engine starting in this position.
- **"R" (Reverse)** – Reverse selector is engaged with countershaft reverse gear and 4th clutch is applied. Back-up light switch, incorporated in A/T gear position switch, operates back-up lights.
- **"N" (Neutral)** – All clutches are released. Neutral position switch, incorporated in A/T gear position switch allows engine starting in this position.
- **"D_4" (Drive)** – Transaxle starts in 1st gear and upshifts automatically to 2nd, 3rd and then 4th gear. Transaxle will downshift through 3rd, 2nd and 1st gears until vehicle stops. When in 2nd, 3rd or 4th gear in this range, TCM sends signal to operate torque converter lock-up.
- **"D_3" (Drive)** – Transaxle starts in 1st gear and upshifts automatically to 2nd gear and then 3rd gear. Transaxle will downshift through all gears on deceleration. When in 3rd gear in this range, TCM sends signal to operate torque converter lock-up.
- **"2" (Second)** – Transaxle starts off and remains in 2nd gear for engine braking and better traction.
- **"1" (First)** – Transaxle starts off and remains in 1st gear for engine braking.

When in "D_3" position in 3rd gear or "D_4" position in 2nd, 3rd or 4th gear, torque converter lock-up exists and transaxle mainshaft rotates at the same speed as engine crankshaft. Under certain conditions, torque converter lock-up clutch is applied during deceleration. Torque converter lock-up is controlled by the TCM. The TCM receives various input signals and operates lock-up control solenoid valves.

The TCM contains a self-diagnostic system, which stores a fault code if a failure or problem exists in transaxle electronic control system. Fault code can be retrieved to determine transaxle problem area. For information on electronic transaxle components, see ACURA M1WA ELECTRONIC CONTROLS article.

Transaxle is equipped with shift and key interlock systems. Shift interlock system prevents shift lever from being moved from "P" position unless brake pedal is depressed and accelerator pedal is in idle position. In case of a malfunction, shift lever can be released by placing ignition key in release slot near shift lever. Key interlock system prevents ignition key from being removed from ignition switch unless shift lever is in "P" position. For additional information on shift and key interlock systems, see ACURA M1WA ELECTRONIC CONTROLS article.

The A/T gear position indicator on instrument panel contains lights to indicate which position A/T gear position switch on shift lever is in. For information and testing of A/T gear position indicator, see ACURA M1WA ELECTRONIC CONTROLS article.

LUBRICATION & ADJUSTMENTS

See appropriate AUTOMATIC TRANSMISSION SERVICING article in TRANSMISSION SERVICING section.

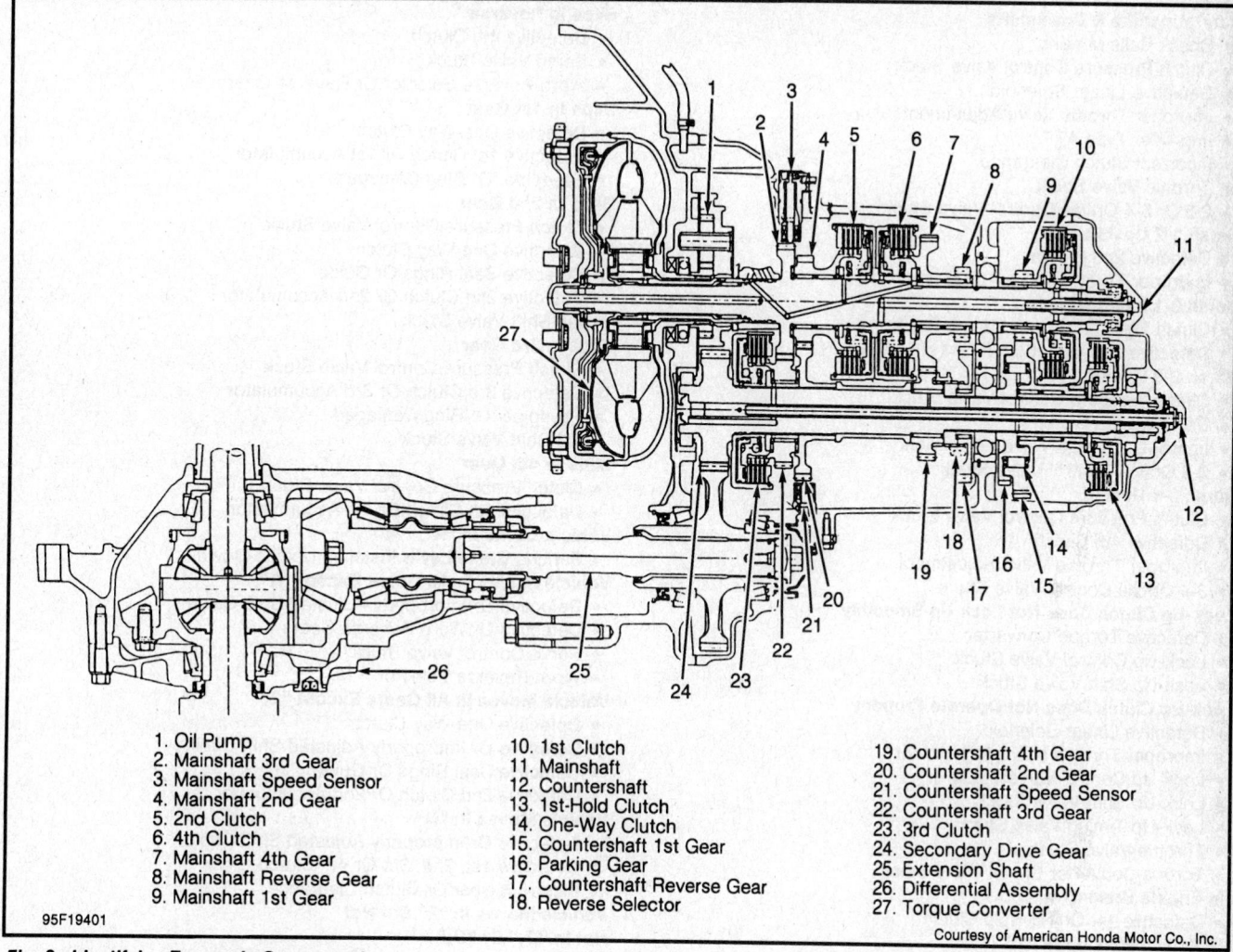

1. Oil Pump
2. Mainshaft 3rd Gear
3. Mainshaft Speed Sensor
4. Mainshaft 2nd Gear
5. 2nd Clutch
6. 4th Clutch
7. Mainshaft 4th Gear
8. Mainshaft Reverse Gear
9. Mainshaft 1st Gear
10. 1st Clutch
11. Mainshaft
12. Countershaft
13. 1st-Hold Clutch
14. One-Way Clutch
15. Countershaft 1st Gear
16. Parking Gear
17. Countershaft Reverse Gear
18. Reverse Selector
19. Countershaft 4th Gear
20. Countershaft 2nd Gear
21. Countershaft Speed Sensor
22. Countershaft 3rd Gear
23. 3rd Clutch
24. Secondary Drive Gear
25. Extension Shaft
26. Differential Assembly
27. Torque Converter

95F19401

Courtesy of American Honda Motor Co., Inc.

Fig. 2: Identifying Transaxle Components

TROUBLE SHOOTING

Transaxle malfunctions may be caused by poor engine performance, improper adjustments or failure of hydraulic, mechanical or electronic components. Always begin by checking fluid level, fluid condition and cable adjustments. Perform road test to determine if problem has been corrected. If problem still exists, several tests must be performed on transaxle. See TESTING in this article. Refer to the following symptoms and check the specified components:

Excessive Drag In Transaxle
• Binding Oil Pump

Excessive Idle Vibration
• Defective Torque Converter Or Oil Pump
• Incorrect Idle RPM
• Lock-Up Shift Valve Stuck

Excessive Vibration (RPM Related)
• Torque Converter Not Fully Seated In Oil Pump

Flares On 1-2 Upshift
• Defective Linear Solenoid
• Defective One-Way Clutch
• Defective 2nd Accumulator
• Improper Throttle Valve Adjustment
• Throttle Valve Stuck
• 1-2 Shift Valve Stuck

Flares On 2-3 Upshift
• Defective Linear Solenoid
• Defective One-Way Clutch
• Defective 3rd Accumulator

• Feedpipe "O" Ring Damaged
• Improper Throttle Valve Adjustment
• Throttle Valve Stuck
• 2-3 Shift Valve Stuck

Flares On 3-4 Upshift
• Defective Linear Solenoid
• Defective 4th Accumulator
• Feedpipe "O" Ring Damaged
• Improper Throttle Valve Adjustment
• Throttle Valve Stuck
• 3-4 Orifice Control Valve Stuck
• 3-4 Shift Valve Stuck

Gear Whine That Changes With Shifts
• Defective 1st Clutch
• Defective 3rd Gears

Gear Whine That Changes With Speed
• Defective Differential Gears

Harsh Downshift At Closed Throttle
• Throttle Valve Stuck

Harsh Kickdown Shifts
• Clutch Pressure Control Valve Stuck
• Defective Linear Solenoid
• Improper Throttle Valve Adjustment
• 3rd Or 4th Kickdown Valve Stuck

Harsh Shift When Manually Shifting To "1"
• Defective 1st-Hold Accumulator

Harsh Upshifts & Downshifts
- Check Balls Missing
- Clutch Pressure Control Valve Stuck
- Defective Linear Solenoid
- Improper Throttle Valve Adjustment
- Improper Type ATF
- Incorrect Clutch Clearance
- Throttle Valve Stuck
- 2-3 Or 3-4 Orifice Control Valve Stuck

Harsh 1-2 Upshift
- Defective 2nd Clutch
- Improper Throttle Valve Adjustment

Harsh 2-1 Kickdown Shift
- Clutch Pressure Control Valve Stuck
- Defective One-Way Clutch Or 1st Clutch

Harsh 2-3 Upshift
- Clutch Pressure Control Valve Stuck
- Defective 3rd Clutch
- Improper Throttle Valve Adjustment
- 2-3 Orifice Control Valve Stuck

Harsh 3-4 Upshift
- Clutch Pressure Control Valve Stuck
- Defective 4th Clutch
- Improper Throttle Valve Adjustment
- 3-4 Orifice Control Valve Stuck

Lock-Up Clutch Does Not Lock Up Smoothly
- Defective Torque Converter
- Lock-Up Control Valve Stuck
- Lock-Up Shift Valve Stuck

Lock-Up Clutch Does Not Operate Properly
- Defective Linear Solenoid
- Improper Throttle Valve Adjustment
- Lock-Up Control Valve Stuck
- Lock-Up Shift Valve Stuck
- Lock-Up Timing Valve Stuck
- Throttle Valve Stuck
- Torque Converter Check Valve Stuck

No Engine Braking In "1"
- Defective 1st Or 1st-Hold Clutch

No Engine Braking In "2"
- Defective 2nd Clutch
- Defective One-Way Clutch

Noise From Transaxle In All Gears
- Defective Oil Pump
- Defective Torque Converter

Noise From Transaxle With Wheels Rolling
- Damaged Reverse Gears
- Defective Differential Assembly Or Secondary Gears

Popping Noise When Taking Off In "R"
- Damaged Reverse Gears
- Worn Reverse Selector

Ratcheting Noise When Shifting To "R"
- Damaged Reverse Gears
- Defective Oil Pump
- Pressure Regulator Stuck
- Worn Reverse Selector

Ratcheting Noise When Shifting From "R" To "P" Or "N"
- Damaged Reverse Gears
- Damaged 4th Gears
- Shift Fork Bent
- Worn Reverse Selector

Shifts Erratically
- Improperly Installed Springs Or Valves
- 3rd Kickdown Valve Stuck

Slips In All Gears
- Defective Oil Pump
- Fluid Strainer Clogged
- Pressure Regulator Stuck

Slips In Reverse
- Defective 4th Clutch
- Servo Valve Stuck
- Worn Reverse Selector Or Reverse Gears

Slips In 1st Gear
- Defective One-Way Clutch
- Defective 1st Clutch Or 1st Accumulator
- Feedpipe "O" Ring Damaged

Slips In 2nd Gear
- Clutch Pressure Control Valve Stuck
- Defective One-Way Clutch
- Defective Seal Rings Or Guide
- Defective 2nd Clutch Or 2nd Accumulator
- 2-3 Shift Valve Stuck

Slips In 3rd Gear
- Clutch Pressure Control Valve Stuck
- Defective 3rd Clutch Or 3rd Accumulator
- Feedpipe "O" Ring Damaged
- 3-4 Shift Valve Stuck

Slips In 4th Gear
- Clutch Pressure Control Valve Stuck
- Defective 4th Clutch Or 4th Accumulator

Vehicle Locks In "R"
- Parking Brake Lever Installed Upside-Down

Vehicle Moves In All Gears Except "R"
- Defective Or Improperly Adjusted Shift Cable
- Defective Or Worn Reverse Gears
- Servo Control Valve Stuck
- Worn Reverse Selector

Vehicle Moves In All Gears Except "2"
- Defective One-Way Clutch
- Defective Or Improperly Adjusted Shift Cable
- Defective Seal Rings Or Guide
- Defective 2nd Clutch Or 2nd Accumulator

Vehicle Moves In "N"
- Defective Or Improperly Adjusted Shift Cable
- Defective 1st, 2nd, 3rd Or 4th Clutch
- Incorrect Gear Or Clutch Clearance

Vehicle Moves In "2" But Not Not In "D₃" Or "D₄"
- Defective One-Way Clutch
- Defective Or Improperly Adjusted Shift Cable
- Defective 1st Clutch Or 1st Accumulator
- Feedpipe "O" Ring Damaged

Vehicle Will Not Move
- Defective Differential Assembly
- Defective Extension Shaft
- Defective Oil Pump
- Defective Or Improperly Adjusted Shift Cable
- Fluid Strainer Clogged
- Pressure Regulator Stuck

Vehicle Will Not Move In "D₃" Or "D₄"
- One-Way Clutch Installed Upside-Down

Will Not Downshift To Low Gear
- Defective 1st-Hold Clutch
- 1-2 Shift Valve Stuck

Will Not Shift Into 4th Gear When In "D₄"
- Defective Or Improperly Adjusted Shift Cable
- Defective 4th Accumulator
- 3-4 Shift Valve Stuck
- 3-4 Orifice Control Valve Stuck

Will Not Upshift (Stays In Low Gear)
- Clutch Pressure Control Valve Stuck
- 1-2 Shift Valve Stuck

TESTING

ROAD TEST

NOTE: If shift lever cannot be moved from "P" position with brake pedal depressed and accelerator pedal at idle position, check shift interlock system. See ACURA M1WA ELECTRONIC CONTROLS article.

CAUTION: Vehicle is equipped with an air bag system (Supplemental Restraint System (SRS). All wires have Yellow insulation and are located underdash or in instrument panel area. To avoid injury from accidental deployment, read and carefully follow all SERVICE PRECAUTIONS and DISABLING & ACTIVATING AIR BAG SYSTEM procedures in APPLICATIONS & IDENTIFICATIONS.

1) Warm engine to normal operating temperature. Apply parking brake and block wheels. Start engine. Move shift lever to "D_4" position while depressing brake pedal. Depress accelerator pedal and release it suddenly. Engine should not stall.

2) Repeat step 1) in "D_3" position. Ensure engine does not stall. Manufacturer recommends monitoring of throttle position sensor voltage when performing road test to ensure proper throttle opening for verifying shift points.

3) Ensure ignition is off. Remove glove box. Remove ABS control unit mounting bolts and turn control unit over. Disconnect radiator fan control module connector on left side. Do not disconnect ABS control unit connectors.

4) Remove TCM bracket and remove TCM from bracket. Install Backprobe Test Set (07SAZ-001000A) or equivalent between TCM and Digital Volt-Ohmmeter (DVOM) leads. *See Fig. 3.*

5) Using DVOM, with positive lead at terminal B4 and negative lead at terminal A13 or A26. *See Fig. 3.* Ensure digital volt-ohmmeter is set for measuring voltage.

6) Road test vehicle and check for abnormal noise and clutch slippage. Specified clutch is applied in designated gears. See CLUTCH APPLICATION table.

7) Note that shift points and lock-up clutch operation are within specification in accordance with throttle position sensor voltage. See TRANSAXLE UPSHIFT SPECIFICATIONS and TRANSAXLE DOWNSHIFT SPECIFICATIONS tables.

8) With shift lever in "D_4" position, accelerate to about 35 MPH so transaxle is in 4th gear. Move shift lever to "2" position. Ensure engine braking occurs.

CAUTION: DO NOT shift from "D_4" to "2" at speeds greater than 62 MPH or transaxle may be damaged.

9) Place shift lever in "1" position. Accelerate from a stop at full throttle. Check for abnormal noise or clutch slippage. Upshifts and downshifts should not occur in this range.

10) Place shift lever in "2" position. Accelerate from a stop at full throttle. Check for abnormal noise or clutch slippage. Upshifts and downshifts should not occur in this range.

11) Place shift lever in "R" position. Accelerate from a stop at full throttle. Check for abnormal noise or clutch slippage.

12) Park vehicle on a slope. Apply parking brake and place shift lever in "P" position. Release parking brake. Ensure vehicle does not move. If vehicle moves, check for defective shift cable or parking components.

13) Ensure ignition is off. Remove test harness. Reinstall electrical connectors, ABS control unit, TCM bracket and TCM.

CLUTCH APPLICATION

Shift Lever Position	Elements In Use
"P" & "N"	No Clutches Are Applied
"R"	4th Clutch
"D_4"	
1st Gear	1st Clutch
2nd Gear	[1] 2nd Clutch
3rd Gear	[1] 3rd Clutch
4th Gear	[1] 4th Clutch
"D_3"	
1st Gear	1st Clutch
2nd Gear	[1] 2nd Clutch
3rd Gear	[1] 3rd Clutch
"2"	[1] 2nd Clutch
"1"	1st-Hold Clutch, 1st Clutch

[1] – The 1st clutch engages, but driving power is not transmitted, as one-way clutch slips.

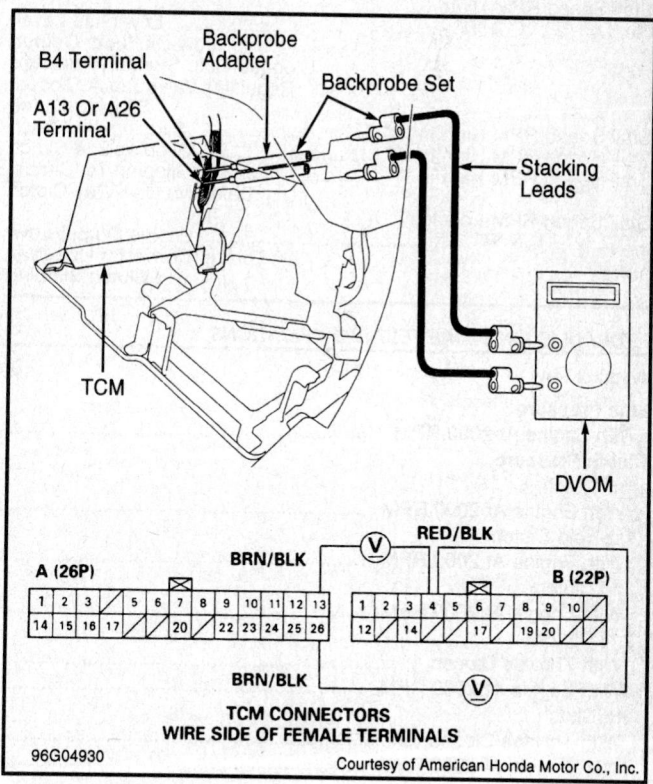

Fig. 3: Installing Backprobe Test Set

TRANSAXLE UPSHIFT SPECIFICATIONS

"D_4" Position & Condition	1st-2nd Gear	2nd-3rd Gear	3rd-4th Gear	Lock-Up Clutch On
TPS Voltage .75 Volt	10-13 MPH	17.5-20 MPH	28-33.5 MPH	20.5-24 MPH
TPS Voltage 2.25 Volts	19-23 MPH	34-40.5 MPH	55-61 MPH	65-71 MPH
TPS Voltage 4.5 Volts (Full Throttle)	35-40.5 MPH	63-72 MPH	100-111 MPH	92-103 MPH

TRANSAXLE DOWNSHIFT SPECIFICATIONS

"D_4" Position & Condition	Lock-Up Clutch Off	4th-3rd Gear	3rd-2nd Gear	2nd-1st Gear
TPS Voltage .75 Volt	15.5-19 MPH	19-22 MPH	7.5-11 MPH	7.5-11 MPH
TPS Voltage 2.25 Volts	48-54 MPH	[1]	[1]	[1]
TPS Voltage 4.5 Volts (Full Throttle)	90-101 MPH	86-96.5 MPH	53-60 MPH	26-32 MPH

[1] – Specification not available from manufacturer.

TORQUE CONVERTER STALL SPEED TEST

CAUTION: DO NOT perform torque converter stall speed test for more than 10 seconds or transaxle may be damaged. DO NOT move shift lever while increasing engine speed.

1) Apply parking brake and block all wheels. Connect tachometer. Start engine. Ensure A/C is off. Warm engine to normal operating temperature. Place shift lever in "2" position.

2) Fully depress brake pedal. Fully depress accelerator for 6-8 seconds and note engine speed. This is the torque converter stall speed.

3) Allow transaxle to cool for 2 minutes at idle in "N" or "P". Repeat test procedure in "D₄", "1" and "R" positions.

4) Torque converter stall speed should be the same in "D₄", "2", "1" and "R" positions. Torque converter stall speed should be 2200-2500 RPM. If torque converter stall speed is not within specification, see TORQUE CONVERTER STALL SPEED TROUBLE SHOOTING table for possible causes.

TORQUE CONVERTER STALL SPEED TROUBLE SHOOTING

Torque Converter Stall Speed Test Results	Probable Cause
Stall Speed RPM High In "D₄", "2", "1" & "R"	Low Fluid Level, Low Oil Pump Output, Clogged Fluid Strainer, Pressure Regulator Valve Stuck Closed, Slipping Clutch
Stall Speed RPM High In "R"	Slipping 4th Clutch
Stall Speed RPM High In "2"	Slipping 2nd Clutch
Stall Speed RPM High In "1"	Slipping 1st Clutch, Defective One-Way Clutch
Stall Speed RPM Low In "D₄", "2", "1" & "R"	Engine Output Low, Torque Converter One-Way Clutch Slipping

HYDRAULIC PRESSURE TEST

Test Preparation – Ensure transaxle fluid level is correct. Warm engine to normal operating temperature. Apply parking brake and block rear wheels. Raise and support vehicle so front wheels can rotate. Attach tachometer.

Pressure Testing – 1) With engine off, remove pressure tap plug from appropriate pressure tap on transaxle. *See Fig. 4.* Attach pressure gauge to appropriate pressure tap using NEW washer. Tighten hose fitting to 13 ft. lbs. (18 N.m).

2) Disconnect linear solenoid 2-pin connector at transaxle. *See Fig. 5.* Start and operate engine at 2000 RPM for line and clutch pressure tests or 1000 RPM for throttle "B" pressure measurement. With shift lever in appropriate position, measure each line pressure at full throttle.

3) Line pressure should be within specification. See HYDRAULIC PRESSURE TEST SPECIFICATIONS table. If line pressure is not within specification, see HYDRAULIC PRESSURE TEST TROUBLE SHOOTING table.

4) Apply battery voltage to linear solenoid connector terminals. With shift lever in appropriate position, measure each line pressure at closed throttle. Line pressure should be within specification. See HYDRAULIC PRESSURE TEST SPECIFICATIONS table. If line pressure is not within specification, see HYDRAULIC PRESSURE TEST TROUBLE SHOOTING table. Shut engine off.

5) Remove pressure gauge set. Using NEW seal washer, install and tighten pressure tap plug to specification. See TORQUE SPECIFICATIONS.

HYDRAULIC PRESSURE TEST SPECIFICATIONS

Application	Shift Lever Position	psi. (kPa)
Line Pressure		
With Engine At 2000 RPM	"P" Or "N"	120-128 (830-880)
Clutch Pressure		
1st Clutch		
With Engine At 2000 RPM	"1" Or "D₄"	120-128 (830-880)
1st-Hold Clutch		
With Engine At 2000 RPM	"1"	120-128 (830-880)
2nd Clutch		
With Engine At 2000 RPM	"2"	120-128 (830-880)
2nd Clutch		
With Throttle Closed	"D₄"	78-86 (540-590)
With Engine At 2000 RPM	"D₄"	120-128 (830-880)
3rd Clutch		
With Throttle Closed	"D₄"	78-86 (540-590)
With Engine At 2000 RPM	"D₄"	120-128 (830-880)
4th Clutch		
With Throttle Closed	"D₄"	78-86 (540-590)
With Engine At 2000 RPM	"D₄"	120-128 (830-880)
4th Clutch		
With Engine At 2000 RPM	"R"	120-128 (830-880)
Clutch Low Pressure		
2nd, 3rd Or 4th Clutch	"D₄"	78-86 (540-590)
Clutch High Pressure		
2nd, 3rd Or 4th Clutch	"D₄"	120-128 (830-880)
Throttle "B" Pressure		
With Transaxle Sub-Harness Disconnected & No Voltage Applied To Harness	"D₄"	81-87 (560-600)
With Transaxle Sub-Harness Disconnected & Voltage Applied To Harness	"D₄"	0-2.2 (0-15)

HYDRAULIC PRESSURE TEST TROUBLE SHOOTING

Application	Probable Cause
Line Pressure	
Low Or No Line Pressure	Defective Torque Converter, Defective Torque Converter Check Valve, Defective Oil Pump Pressure Regulator, Defective Oil Pump
Clutch Pressure	
Low Or No 1st Clutch Pressure	Defective 1st Clutch
Low Or No 1st-Hold Clutch Pressure	Defective 1st-Hold Clutch
Low Or No 2nd Clutch Pressure	Defective 2nd Clutch
Low Or No 3rd Clutch Pressure	Defective 3rd Clutch
Low Or No 4th Clutch Pressure	Defective 4th Clutch, Defective Servo Valve
Clutch Low-High Pressure	
Low Or No 2nd Clutch Pressure	Defective 2nd Clutch
Low Or No 3rd Clutch Pressure	Defective 3rd Clutch
Low Or No 4th Clutch Pressure	Defective 4th Clutch
Throttle "B" Pressure	
Low Or No Throttle "B" Pressure With No Voltage Applied	Linear Solenoid Or Defective Throttle Valve Body
High Throttle "B" Pressure With Voltage Applied	Linear Solenoid Or Defective Throttle Valve Body

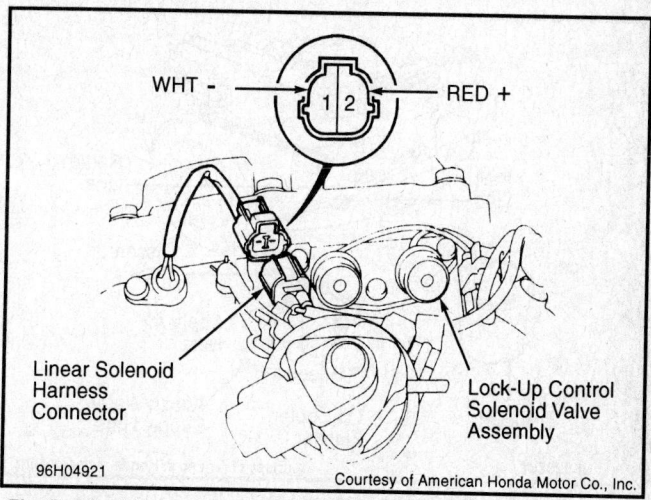

96H04921   Courtesy of American Honda Motor Co., Inc.

Fig. 5: Identifying linear solenoid 2-pin Connector

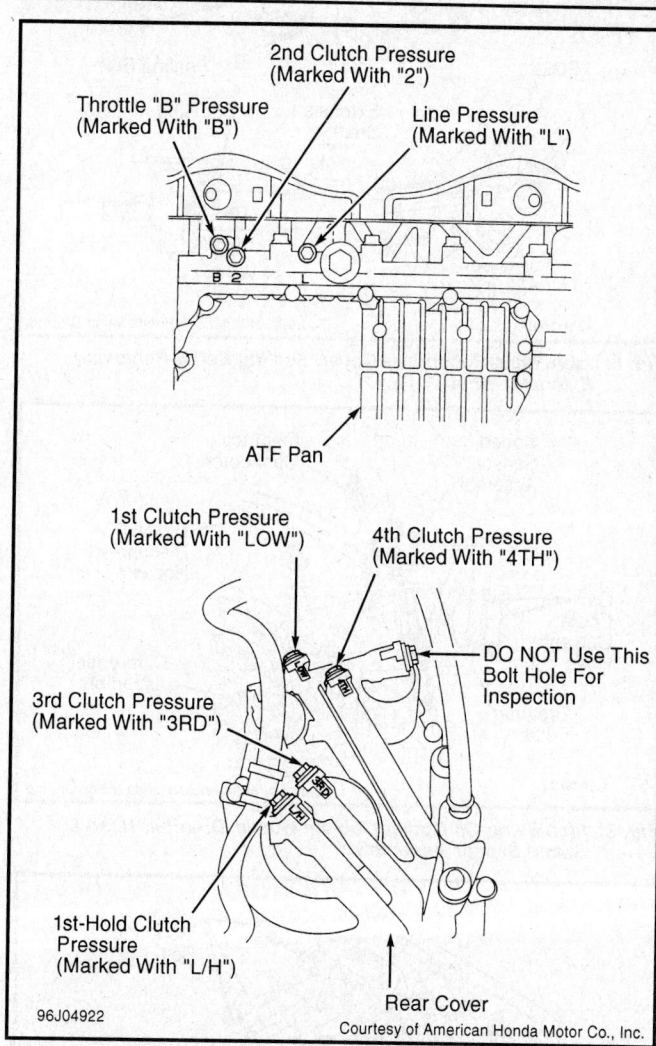

96J04922   Courtesy of American Honda Motor Co., Inc.

Fig. 4: Identifying Transaxle Pressure Taps

ON-VEHICLE SERVICE

AXLE SHAFTS

See appropriate article in AXLE SHAFTS & TRANSFER CASES section.

DIFFERENTIAL ASSEMBLY

Differential assembly may be removed from vehicle with transaxle in the vehicle. See DIFFERENTIAL ASSEMBLY under REMOVAL & INSTALLATION.

LOWER VALVE BODY ASSEMBLY

Lower valve body assembly consists of main valve body, servo body, shift control solenoid valves and oil pass body. See LOWER VALVE BODY ASSEMBLY under REMOVAL & INSTALLATION.

OIL COOLER FLUSHING

1) Attach Oil Cooler Flusher (J38405-A) to oil cooler lines. *See Fig. 6.* Fill oil cooler flusher tank 2/3 full with Flushing Fluid (J35944-20). DO NOT use any other flushing fluid.

2) Ensure water and air valves on oil cooler flusher are turned off. Apply 80-120 psi (550-829 kPa) air pressure to oil cooler flusher. Turn oil cooler flusher water valve on so water will flow through oil cooler for 10 seconds. Shut water valve off. Replace oil cooler if water will not flow through oil cooler.

3) Depress and hold mixing trigger on oil cooler flusher downward. Turn water valve on and flush oil cooler for 2 minutes. Turn air valve on for 5 seconds every 15-20 seconds to create a surging action.

4) Turn water valve off. Release mixing trigger. Disconnect oil cooler flusher and reverse hoses so oil cooler can be flushed in the opposite direction.

5) Repeat steps 2) and 3). Turn water valve off. Release mixing trigger. Turn water valve on and rinse oil cooler for at least one minute. Once oil cooler is flushed in both directions, turn water off. Turn air valve on for 2 minutes or until no moisture is visible from drain hose.

CAUTION: *Ensure no moisture exists in oil cooler, as it can damage transaxle.*

6) Turn air off. Disconnect oil cooler flusher. Reconnect inlet line on oil cooler. Once transaxle is installed, attach drain hose on return line and place in oil container. Ensure transaxle is in "P" position. Fill transaxle with Dexron-II ATF.

7) Start engine and operate for approximately 30 seconds or until one quart (.9L) of ATF is discharged from return line. Shut engine off. Remove drain hose. Reinstall return line. Fill transaxle to proper level.

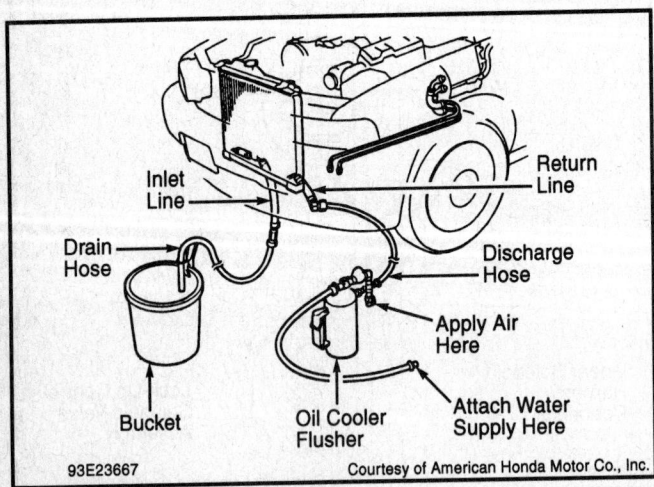

Fig. 6: Installing Oil Cooler Flusher

REMOVAL & INSTALLATION

DIFFERENTIAL ASSEMBLY

NOTE: Before disconnecting negative battery cable, ensure radio anti-theft code is obtained from customer. Radio anti-theft code must be re-entered into radio for radio operation.

CAUTION: When battery is disconnected, vehicle computer and memory systems may lose memory data. Driveability problems may exist until computer systems have completed a relearn cycle. See COMPUTER RELEARN PROCEDURES article in GENERAL INFORMATION before disconnecting battery.

Removal – 1) Obtain radio anti-theft code from customer. Disconnect negative battery cable. Remove air cleaner assembly. Raise and support vehicle. Drain differential assembly gear oil.
2) Remove axle shafts and intermediate shaft. See appropriate AXLE SHAFTS article. Remove splash guard. Support engine with hoist. Slightly raise engine to remove pressure from engine mounts.
3) Remove left front engine mount and brackets to access differential assembly. Remove transaxle mount and bracket. See Fig. 7. Remove secondary cover and sealing bolt from transaxle. See Fig. 8.

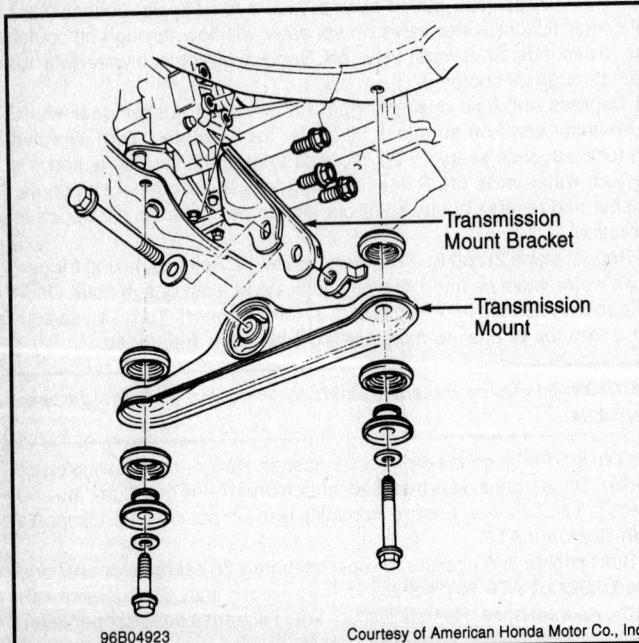

Fig. 7: Identifying Drain Plug, Mount Bracket & Transaxle Mount

4) Place gear selector lever in "P". Using puller, remove extension shaft from differential assembly. See Fig. 8.
5) Disconnect and plug oil cooler coolant hoses from differential assembly. See Fig. 9. Disconnect breather hose from differential assembly. DO NOT disconnect the 2 hoses for the power steering.
6) Remove speed sensor assembly from differential assembly. See Fig. 9. Speed sensor assembly contains the Vehicle Speed Sensor (VSS) and power steering speed sensor.
7) Remove differential assembly upper mounting bolts and shim. See Fig. 10. Remove lower mounting bolts and differential assembly.

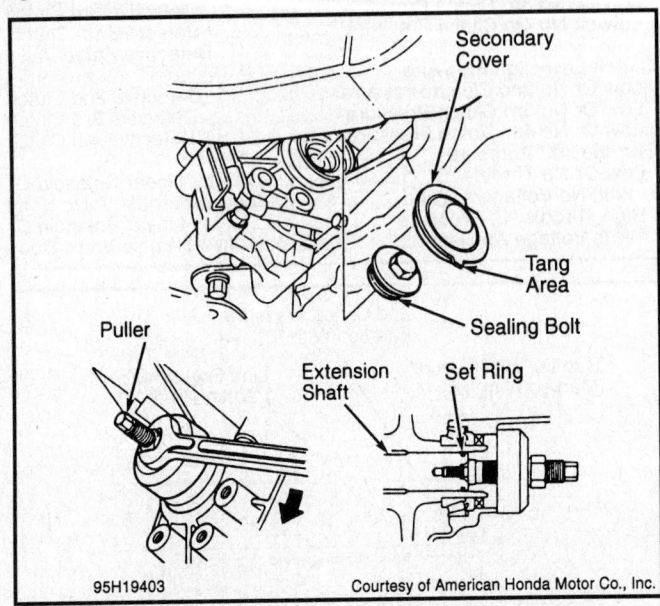

Fig. 8: Identifying Secondary Cover, Sealing Bolt & Removing Extension Shaft

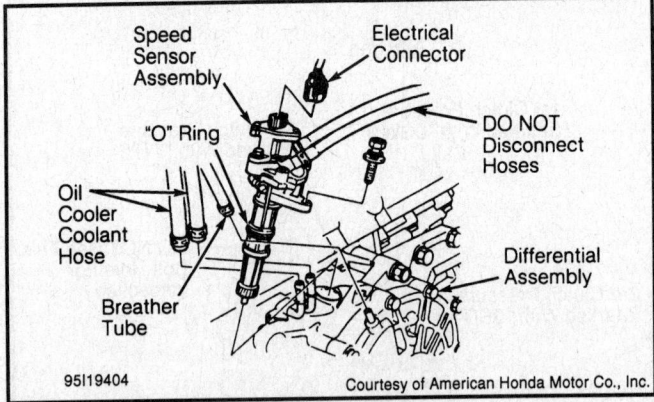

Fig. 9: Identifying Oil Cooler Coolant Hoses, Breather Hose & Speed Sensor Assembly

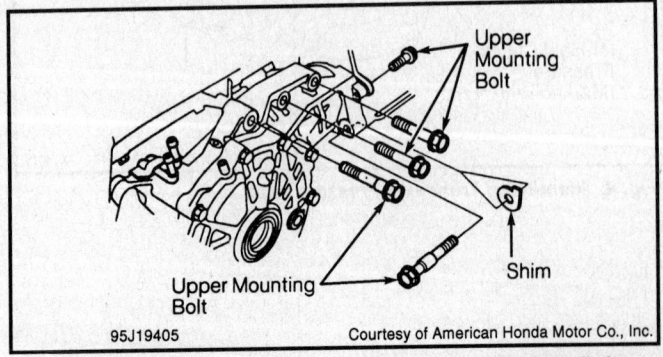

Fig. 10: Identifying Differential Assembly Upper Mounting Bolts & Shim

Installation – 1) If differential case was not replaced, proceed to step 4). If differential case was replaced, thickness of shim must be determined. Install differential assembly. Tighten all mounting bolts to specification. See TORQUE SPECIFICATIONS.

2) Using feeler gauge, measure clearance between differential case and clutch housing where the shim fits. *See Fig. 11.*

NOTE: The clutch housing is the surface on torque converter housing.

3) Select proper thickness shim. Shims are available in .1 mm increments ranging from 1.9 mm to 3.0 mm. Remove differential assembly.

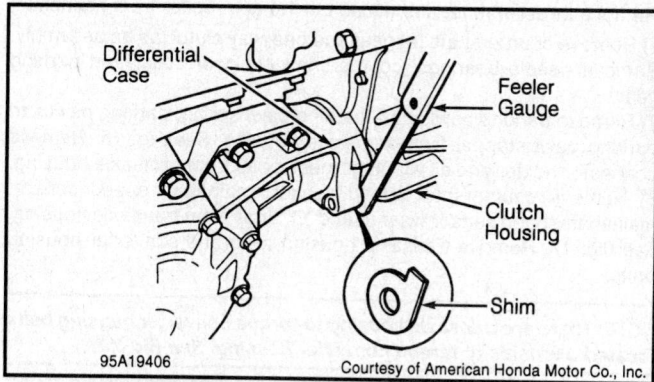

95A19406   Courtesy of American Honda Motor Co., Inc.

Fig. 11: Determining Shim Thickness

4) Fill cavity on end of extension shaft and drive pinion and splines on extension shaft with high-temperature grease. Ensure 2 dowel pins are installed on rear side of differential assembly.

5) Install differential assembly. Install lower mounting bolts, upper mounting bolts and shim. Tighten mounting bolts to specification. See TORQUE SPECIFICATIONS.

6) Using NEW "O" ring, install speed sensor assembly. Tighten bolt to specification. Reconnect oil cooler coolant hoses, breather hose and electrical connector on speed sensor assembly.

7) Install left front engine mount and brackets. Install NEW set ring on end of extension shaft. Install extension shaft. Place gear selector lever "P".

8) Apply thread sealant on threads of sealing bolt. Install and tighten sealing bolt to specification. Install secondary cover so tang area on secondary cover is facing downward. *See Fig. 8.*

9) Install transaxle mount and mount bracket. Install and tighten transaxle mount and mount bracket bolts to specification.

10) Install axle shafts and intermediate shaft using proper procedure. See appropriate article AXLE SHAFTS article.

11) Fill differential assembly with 80W-90 hypoid gear oil with API GL5 rating. Use NEW seal washer when installing differential assembly oil filler plug. Tighten differential assembly oil filler plug to specification.

12) Refill cooling system. Install air cleaner assembly. Reconnect negative battery cable. To re-enter radio anti-theft code, turn radio on. When the word "CODE" is displayed on radio enter anti-theft code by using the radio station preset buttons.

ELECTRICAL COMPONENTS

See ACURA M1WA ELECTRONIC CONTROLS article.

TRANSAXLE

See appropriate AUTOMATIC TRANSMISSION REMOVAL article in TRANSMISSION SERVICING section.

LOWER VALVE BODY ASSEMBLY

NOTE: Lower valve body assembly consists of main valve body, servo body, servo detent base, shift control solenoid valves and oil pass body.

Removal – 1) Raise and support vehicle. Drain fluid by removing drain plug and seal washer from rear of transaxle. See Fig. 7. Support transaxle with floor jack.

2) Remove transaxle mount and mount bracket. Disconnect shift control solenoid valve harness from transaxle sub-harness. See Fig. 12. Remove gear position switch cover, transaxle pan and gasket.

3) Remove shift control solenoid valve 2-pin connector from holder and disconnect. Remove fluid strainer and main valve body cover plate. Remove harness cover. Remove shift control solenoid valve harness connector from case then pull harness out through transaxle housing.

4) Push shift fork into Drive position (toward lower valve body assembly). See Fig. 12. Ensure shift lever is in Park. Remove proper bolts for lower valve body assembly. See Fig. 13. Remove lower valve body assembly.

NOTE: To disassemble lower valve body assembly, see LOWER VALVE BODY ASSEMBLY under COMPONENT DISASSEMBLY & REASSEMBLY.

Installation – 1) Ensure shift lever is in Park. Push shift fork into Drive position (toward lower valve body assembly). See Fig. 12. Install lower valve body assembly while engaging manual valve on valve body with detent lever and engaging shift fork with reverse selector.

2) Install main valve body cover plate. Pass shift control solenoid valve harness through transaxle housing and install connector bolt. Install harness cover. Install fluid strainer and all bolts. Ensure proper length bolts are installed in correct location on lower valve body assembly and fluid strainer. See Fig. 13.

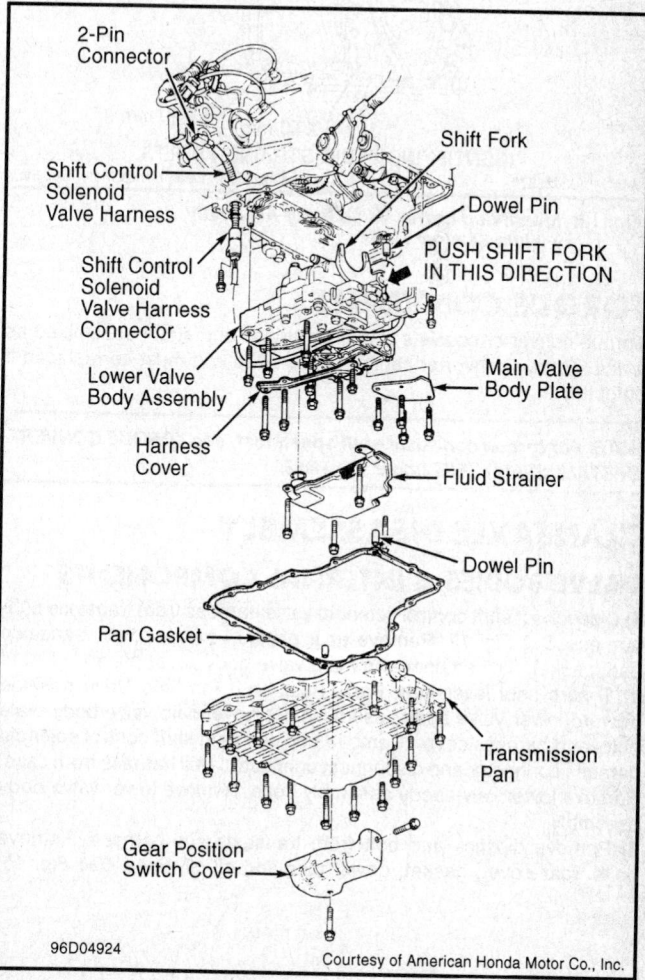

96D04924   Courtesy of American Honda Motor Co., Inc.

Fig. 12: Identifying Lower Valve Body Assembly

3) Tighten all bolts to specification. See TORQUE SPECIFICATIONS. Using NEW gasket, install transaxle pan and gear position switch cover. Install and tighten bolts to specification.

4) Install NEW seal washer on drain plug. Install and tighten drain plug for transaxle to specification. For remainder of installation, reverse removal procedure.

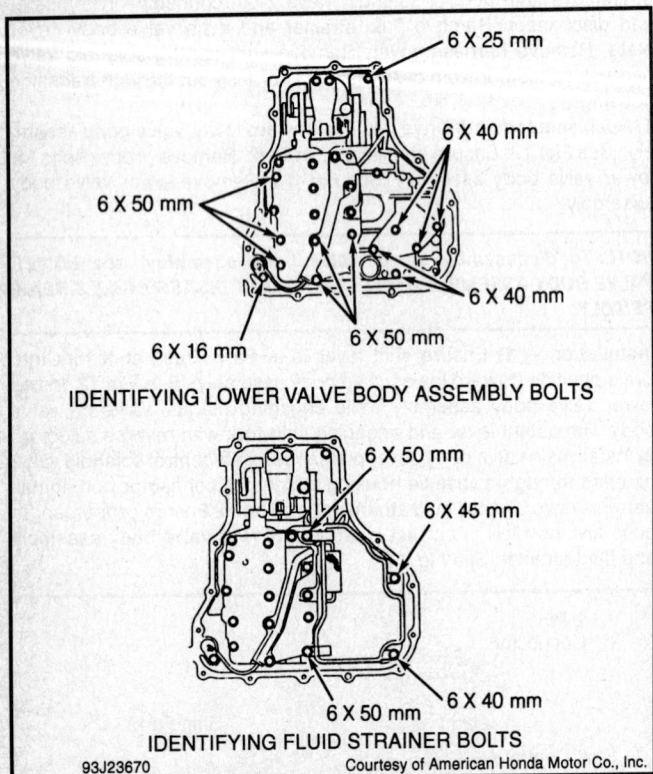

IDENTIFYING LOWER VALVE BODY ASSEMBLY BOLTS

IDENTIFYING FLUID STRAINER BOLTS

93J23670   Courtesy of American Honda Motor Co., Inc.

Fig. 13: Identifying Lower Valve Body Assembly & Fluid Strainer Bolts

TORQUE CONVERTER

Torque converter consists of pump, turbine and stator assembled as a unit. Torque converter cannot be serviced and must be replaced if defective.

NOTE: For torque converter stall speed test, see TORQUE CONVERTER STALL SPEED TEST under TESTING.

TRANSAXLE DISASSEMBLY

VALVE BODIES & INTERNAL COMPONENTS

1) Disconnect shift control solenoid valve harness from transaxle sub-harness. See Fig. 12. Remove gear position switch cover, transaxle pan, gasket, fluid strainer and main valve body cover plate.

2) Ensure shift lever is in Park. Push shift fork into Drive position (toward lower valve body assembly). Remove main valve body plate bolts and harness cover. Remove bolt securing shift control solenoid harness connector and disconnect connector. Pull harness from case. Remove lower valve body assembly bolts. Remove lower valve body assembly.

3) Remove dipstick and bolt from transaxle sub-harness. Remove bolts, rear cover, gasket, dowel pins and all oil pipes. See Fig. 15.

Install Mainshaft Holder (07GAB-PF50100) onto mainshaft to secure mainshaft. See Fig. 16.

NOTE: Mainshaft lock nut has left-hand threads.

4) Engage parking pawl with parking gear. Using hammer and chisel, cut lock tabs on countershaft and mainshaft lock nuts and pry upward. Remove countershaft and mainshaft lock nuts and disc springs. See Fig. 15.

5) Remove mainshaft holder. Remove 1st-hold clutch and bearing, thrust washer, thrust needle bearing and 1st-hold clutch hub from countershaft. See Fig. 15. Remove 1st clutch, thrust washer, thrust needle bearing, needle bearing and mainshaft 1st gear. See Fig. 15. Remove thrust washer and mainshaft 1st gear collar from mainshaft.

6) Remove countershaft 1st gear and one-way clutch as an assembly. Remove needle bearings, countershaft 1st gear collar and parking gear.

7) Remove parking pawl shaft, parking pawl spring, parking pawl and parking pawl stopper from transaxle housing. See Fig. 15. Remove connector holder and all wiring harness bolts from transaxle housing.

8) Remove countershaft speed sensor, mainshaft speed sensor, mainshaft speed sensor washer and "O" rings from transaxle housing. See Fig. 17. Remove transaxle housing-to-torque converter housing bolts.

NOTE: There are transaxle housing-to-torque converter housing bolts located on inside of torque converter housing. See Fig. 17.

CAUTION: Ensure countershaft and mainshaft speed sensors are removed from transaxle housing before removing transaxle housing from torque converter housing.

9) Using Puller (07HAC-PK4010A), pull transaxle housing from torque converter housing. See Fig. 18. Remove gasket and dowel pins from torque converter housing.

10) Remove countershaft and mainshaft subassemblies from torque converter housing as one unit. Remove secondary gear and extension shaft as an assembly from torque converter housing. See Fig. 17.

11) If removing reverse idler gear from transaxle housing, remove bolts and reverse idler gear shaft holder. Remove reverse idler gear from transaxle housing.

CAUTION: Use care when removing reverse idler gear shaft holder from reverse idler gear, as steel ball and spring are located behind needle bearing at bottom of shaft. See Fig. 17.

12) Remove oil feedpipes from oil pump body and torque converter housing. See Fig. 19. Remove flange nuts and disconnect wiring harness at linear solenoid.

13) Remove regulator valve body, "O" ring, stopper shaft, stator shaft, separator plate and dowel pins. Remove 2nd accumulator body along with throttle valve body. Remove 2nd accumulator piston and 2nd accumulator spring.

14) Remove bolts, harness clamp, throttle valve body and separator plate from 2nd accumulator body (if necessary). Remove oil pump body, oil pump drive and driven gears and oil pump driven gear shaft.

15) Remove torque converter check valve and spring. Remove dowel pins and separator plate.

NOTE: If necessary to disassemble lower valve body assembly, see LOWER VALVE BODY ASSEMBLY under COMPONENT DISASSEMBLY & REASSEMBLY.

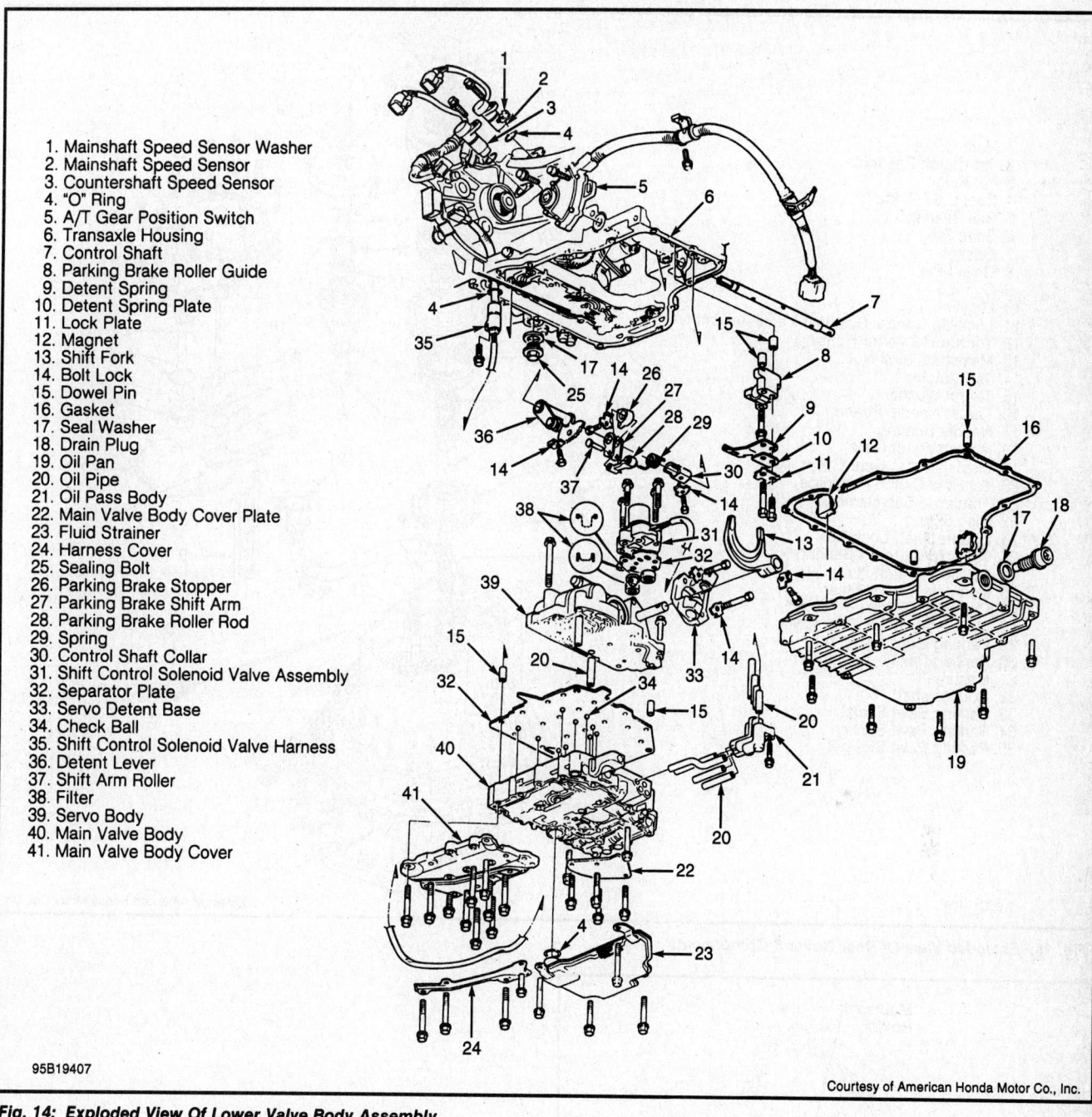

1. Mainshaft Speed Sensor Washer
2. Mainshaft Speed Sensor
3. Countershaft Speed Sensor
4. "O" Ring
5. A/T Gear Position Switch
6. Transaxle Housing
7. Control Shaft
8. Parking Brake Roller Guide
9. Detent Spring
10. Detent Spring Plate
11. Lock Plate
12. Magnet
13. Shift Fork
14. Bolt Lock
15. Dowel Pin
16. Gasket
17. Seal Washer
18. Drain Plug
19. Oil Pan
20. Oil Pipe
21. Oil Pass Body
22. Main Valve Body Cover Plate
23. Fluid Strainer
24. Harness Cover
25. Sealing Bolt
26. Parking Brake Stopper
27. Parking Brake Shift Arm
28. Parking Brake Roller Rod
29. Spring
30. Control Shaft Collar
31. Shift Control Solenoid Valve Assembly
32. Separator Plate
33. Servo Detent Base
34. Check Ball
35. Shift Control Solenoid Valve Harness
36. Detent Lever
37. Shift Arm Roller
38. Filter
39. Servo Body
40. Main Valve Body
41. Main Valve Body Cover

95B19407

Courtesy of American Honda Motor Co., Inc.

Fig. 14: Exploded View Of Lower Valve Body Assembly

1. Rear Cover
2. 1st Clutch Feedpipe
3. "O" Ring
4. Feedpipe Guide
5. Ball Bearing
6. Snap Ring
7. Gasket
8. Dowel Pin
9. Oil Pipe
10. Dipstick
11. Lock-Up Control Solenoid Valve Assembly
12. Torque Converter Housing
13. Mainshaft Lock Nut
14. 1st Clutch
15. Thrust Washer
16. Thrust Needle Bearing
17. Needle Bearing
18. Mainshaft 1st Gear
19. Mainshaft 1st Gear Collar
20. 1st-Hold Clutch Feedpipe
21. Transaxle Sub-Harness
22. Disc Spring
23. Countershaft Lock Nut
24. 1st-Hold Clutch & Bearing
25. 1st-Hold Clutch Hub
26. Countershaft 1st Gear
27. One-Way Clutch
28. Countershaft 1st Gear Collar
29. Parking Gear
30. Parking Pawl
31. Mainshaft
32. Countershaft
33. Parking Pawl Shaft
34. Parking Pawl Spring
35. Parking Pawl Stopper

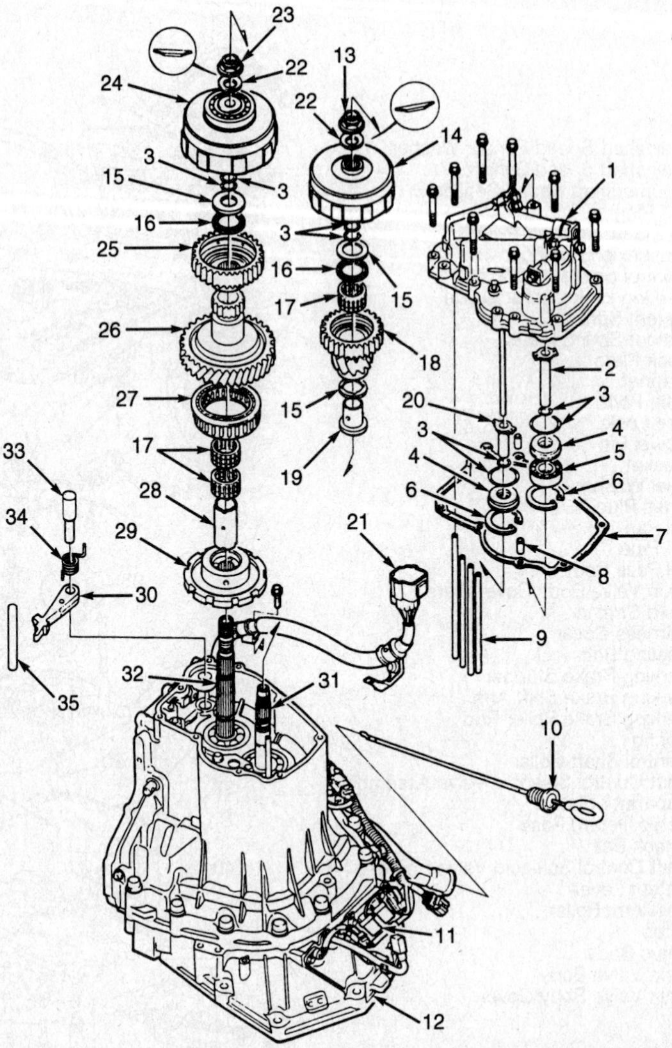

95C19408

Courtesy of American Honda Motor Co., Inc.

Fig. 15: Exploded View Of Rear Cover & Components

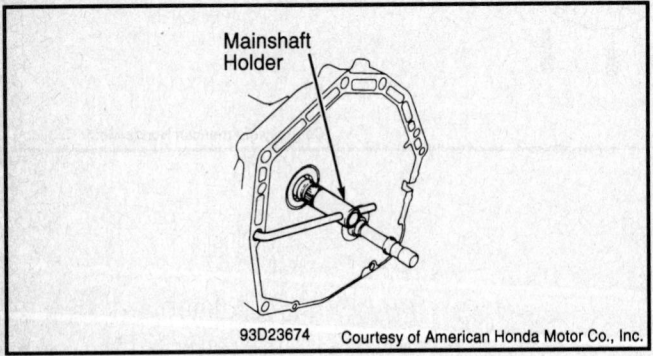

Mainshaft Holder

93D23674   Courtesy of American Honda Motor Co., Inc.

Fig. 16: Installing Mainshaft Holder

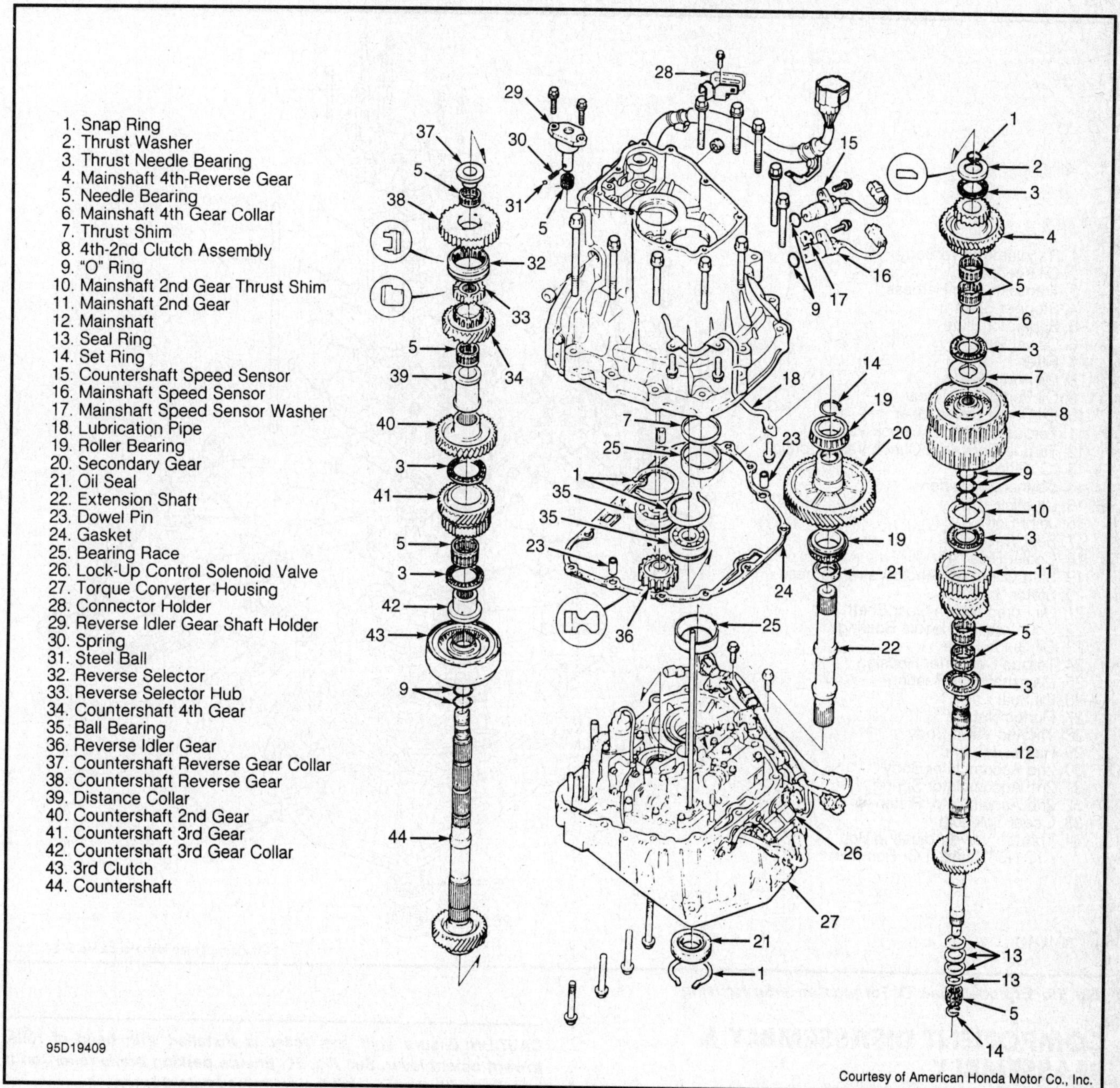

1. Snap Ring
2. Thrust Washer
3. Thrust Needle Bearing
4. Mainshaft 4th-Reverse Gear
5. Needle Bearing
6. Mainshaft 4th Gear Collar
7. Thrust Shim
8. 4th-2nd Clutch Assembly
9. "O" Ring
10. Mainshaft 2nd Gear Thrust Shim
11. Mainshaft 2nd Gear
12. Mainshaft
13. Seal Ring
14. Set Ring
15. Countershaft Speed Sensor
16. Mainshaft Speed Sensor
17. Mainshaft Speed Sensor Washer
18. Lubrication Pipe
19. Roller Bearing
20. Secondary Gear
21. Oil Seal
22. Extension Shaft
23. Dowel Pin
24. Gasket
25. Bearing Race
26. Lock-Up Control Solenoid Valve
27. Torque Converter Housing
28. Connector Holder
29. Reverse Idler Gear Shaft Holder
30. Spring
31. Steel Ball
32. Reverse Selector
33. Reverse Selector Hub
34. Countershaft 4th Gear
35. Ball Bearing
36. Reverse Idler Gear
37. Countershaft Reverse Gear Collar
38. Countershaft Reverse Gear
39. Distance Collar
40. Countershaft 2nd Gear
41. Countershaft 3rd Gear
42. Countershaft 3rd Gear Collar
43. 3rd Clutch
44. Countershaft

95D19409

Courtesy of American Honda Motor Co., Inc.

Fig. 17: Exploded View Of Transaxle Housing & Components

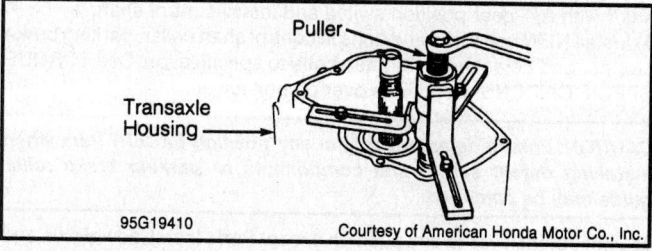

95G19410

Courtesy of American Honda Motor Co., Inc.

Fig. 18: Removing Transaxle Housing

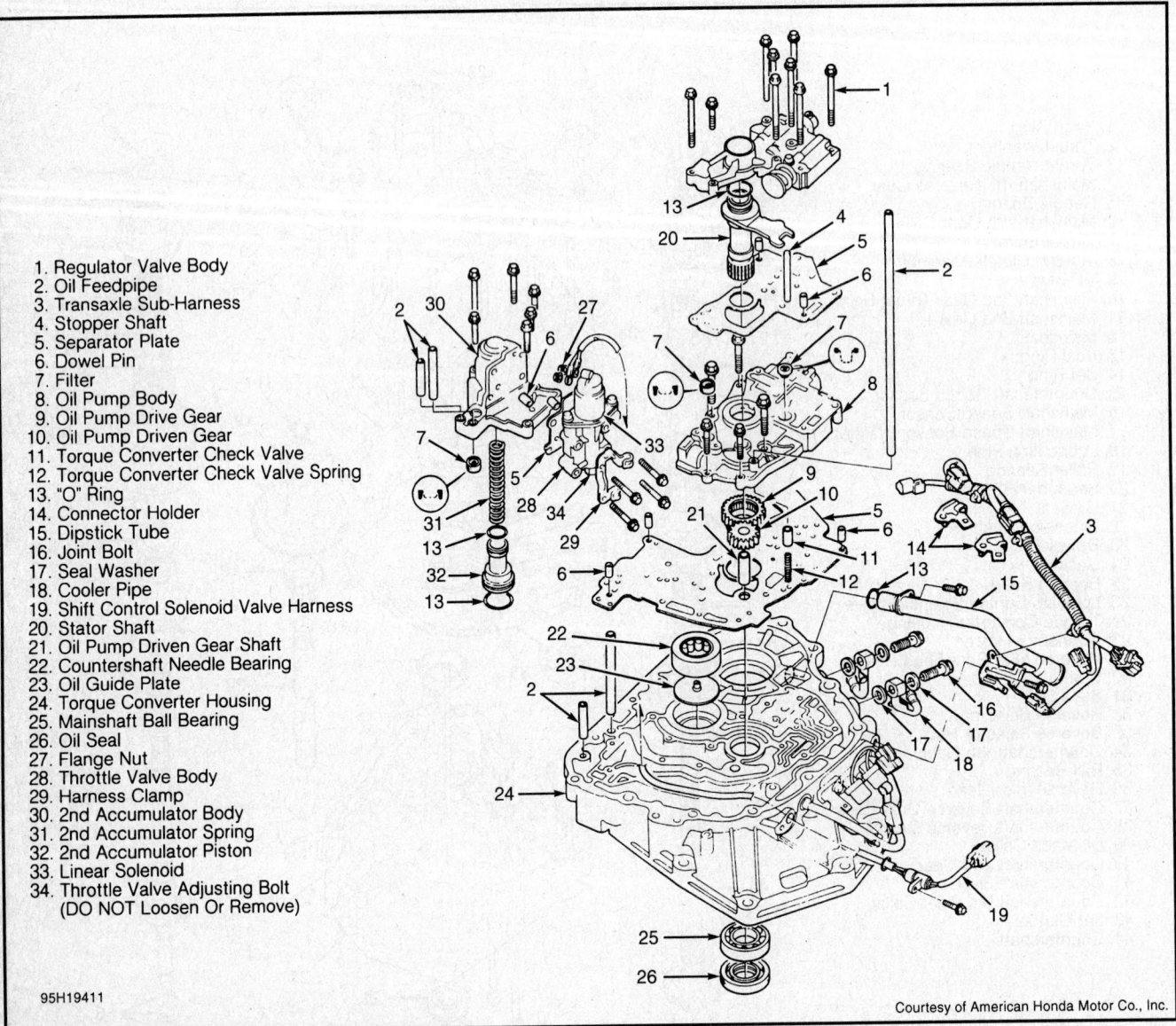

1. Regulator Valve Body
2. Oil Feedpipe
3. Transaxle Sub-Harness
4. Stopper Shaft
5. Separator Plate
6. Dowel Pin
7. Filter
8. Oil Pump Body
9. Oil Pump Drive Gear
10. Oil Pump Driven Gear
11. Torque Converter Check Valve
12. Torque Converter Check Valve Spring
13. "O" Ring
14. Connector Holder
15. Dipstick Tube
16. Joint Bolt
17. Seal Washer
18. Cooler Pipe
19. Shift Control Solenoid Valve Harness
20. Stator Shaft
21. Oil Pump Driven Gear Shaft
22. Countershaft Needle Bearing
23. Oil Guide Plate
24. Torque Converter Housing
25. Mainshaft Ball Bearing
26. Oil Seal
27. Flange Nut
28. Throttle Valve Body
29. Harness Clamp
30. 2nd Accumulator Body
31. 2nd Accumulator Spring
32. 2nd Accumulator Piston
33. Linear Solenoid
34. Throttle Valve Adjusting Bolt
    (DO NOT Loosen Or Remove)

95H19411

Courtesy of American Honda Motor Co., Inc.

Fig. 19: Exploded View Of Torque Converter Housing

COMPONENT DISASSEMBLY & REASSEMBLY

CONTROL SHAFT & COMPONENTS

Removal – 1) Remove bolts, lock plate, detent spring plate and detent spring. *See Fig. 20.* Remove bolt, parking brake roller guide and dowel pins from transaxle housing.
2) Remove bolt and bolt lock from detent lever, parking brake stopper and control shaft collar. Remove control shaft, control shaft collar, spring, parking brake shift arm and detent lever.
Installation – 1) Coat components with Dexron-II ATF. Install control shaft into transaxle housing. Install control shaft collar and spring on control shaft.
2) Install parking brake stopper and parking brake shift arm on control shaft. Install parking brake roller rod and shift arm roller on parking brake shift arm.

CAUTION: Ensure shift arm roller is installed with head of roller toward detent lever. See Fig. 20. Ensure parking brake roller rod is installed with rivets in rod facing toward detent lever.

3) Install detent lever on control shaft. Align cutout area on control shaft with A/T gear position switch and install control shaft.
4) Install NEW bolt locks and bolts in control shaft collar, parking brake stopper and detent lever. Tighten bolts to specification. See TORQUE SPECIFICATIONS. Bend tabs over on bolt locks.

CAUTION: Ensure detent lever is in any position EXCEPT Park when installing detent spring and components or parking brake roller guide may be damaged.

5) Shift detent lever to any position except Park. Install dowel pins and parking brake roller guide. *See Fig. 20.*
6) Install detent spring, detent spring plate, NEW lock plate and bolts. Tighten parking brake roller guide bolts to specification.

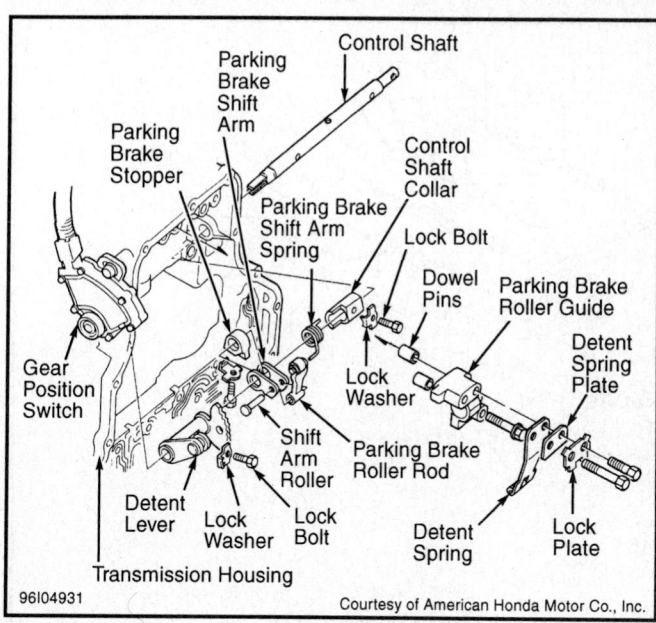

Fig. 20: Identifying Control Shaft & Components

LOWER VALVE BODY ASSEMBLY

Disassembly – 1) Remove harness cover and main valve body cover. *See Fig. 14.* Remove oil pass body and oil pipes from main valve body.

2) Remove shift control solenoid valve assembly, separator plate and filters. Remove bolt, bolt lock and shift fork. Remove servo detent base from servo body.

3) Remove servo body, separator plate and dowel pins from main valve body. Use care not to loose check balls in main valve body. Remove check balls from main valve body (if necessary).

CAUTION: DO NOT use magnet to remove check balls, as check balls may become magnetized.

Cleaning & Inspection – Clean components with solvent and dry with compressed air. Inspect components for damage. Replace components if necessary.

Reassembly – 1) Coat all components with Dexron-II ATF. To reassemble, reverse disassembly procedure.

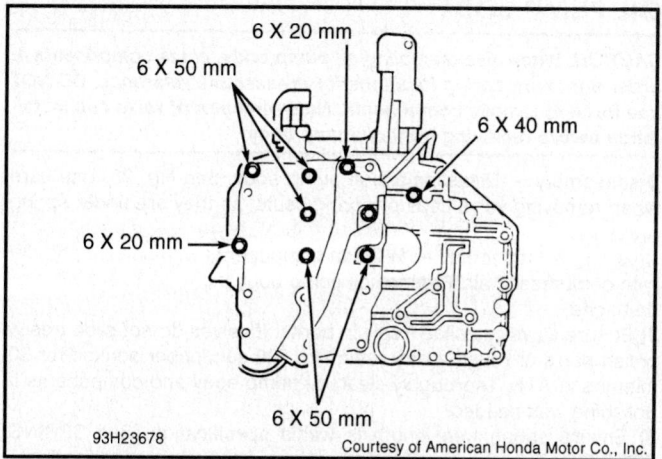

Fig. 21 Identifying Main Valve Body Cover Bolts

2) Ensure check balls are installed in proper areas of main valve body. *See Fig. 22.* Install NEW filters and NEW bolt locks. Ensure all filters are installed in proper direction. *See Fig. 14.*

3) When installing shift fork, rotate shift fork shaft in servo body so large chamfered hole in shaft aligns with bolt hole in shift fork. Install bolt and tighten to specification. See TORQUE SPECIFICATIONS. Bend tabs over on bolt locks.

4) Ensure proper length main valve body cover bolts are installed in specified location. *See Fig. 21.* Tighten all bolts to specification.

MAIN VALVE BODY

CAUTION: When disassembling main valve body, place main valve body components in order removed and mark spring locations for reassembly reference. DO NOT use force to remove components. DO NOT use magnet to remove check balls, as check balls may become magnetized. Note direction of valve cap installation before removing from main valve body.

Disassembly – Disassemble main valve body. *See Fig. 22.* Use care when removing valve caps or spring seats, as they are under spring pressure.

Cleaning & Inspection – 1) Clean components with solvent and dry with compressed air. Replace main valve body if any parts are worn or damaged.

2) Ensure all valves slide freely in bores. If valves do not slide freely, polish burrs or rough areas using No. 600 sandpaper soaked for 30 minutes in ATF. Thoroughly clean main valve body and components if polishing was needed.

3) Ensure spring free length is within specification. See SPRING SPECIFICATIONS table. Replace springs if not within specification.

Reassembly – Coat all components and bores with Dexron-II ATF. To reassemble, reverse disassembly procedure. Ensure all components are installed in correct location. *See Fig. 22.*

SPRING SPECIFICATIONS

Application	Free Length In. (mm)
Main Valve Body	
Main Orifice Control Valve Spring	1.382 (35.10)
Servo Control Valve Spring	2.051 (52.10)
1-2 Shift Valve Spring	1.591 (40.40)
2-3 Orifice Control Valve Spring	1.331 (33.80)
2-3 Shift Valve Spring	1.693 (43.00)
3-4 Orifice Control Valve Spring	1.370 (34.80)
3-4 Shift Valve Spring	1.693 (43.00)
4th Exhaust Valve Spring	1.933 (49.10)
4th Kickdown Valve Spring	1.898 (48.20)
Oil Pump Body	
Lock-Up Control Valve Spring	1.496 (38.00)
Lock-Up Timing Valve Spring	2.394 (60.80)
Modulator Valve Spring	1.087 (27.60)
Relief Valve Spring	1.500 (38.10)
Torque Converter Check Valve Spring	1.646 (41.80)
Regulator Valve Body	
Cooler Relief Valve Spring	1.539 (39.10)
Lock-Up Shift Valve Spring	2.902 (73.70)
Regulator Valve Spring "A"	3.055 (77.60)
Regulator Valve Spring "B"	1.732 (44.00)
Stator Reaction Spring	1.193 (30.30)
Servo Body	
3rd Accumulator Spring "A"	3.571 (90.70)
3rd Accumulator Spring "B"	2.441 (62.00)
4th Accumulator Spring "A"	2.878 (73.10)
4th Accumulator Spring "B"	1.929 (49.00)
1st & 1st-Hold Accumulator	
1st Accumulator Spring "A"	3.197 (81.20)
1st Accumulator Spring "B"	1.890 (48.60)
1st-Hold Accumulator Spring "A"	2.201 (55.90)
1st-Hold Accumulator Spring "B"	2.102 (53.40)
2nd Accumulator	
2nd Accumulator Spring	3.764 (95.6)

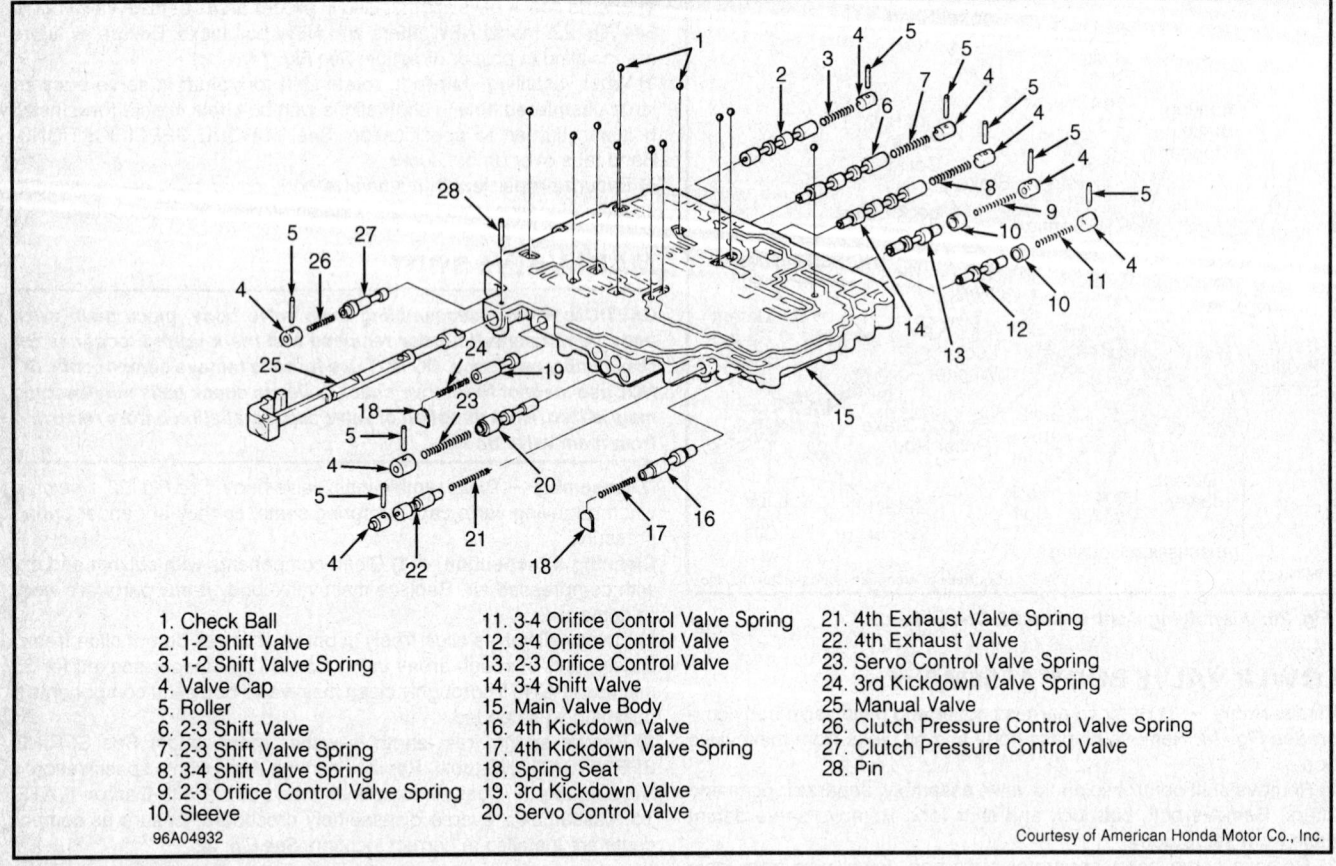

1. Check Ball	11. 3-4 Orifice Control Valve Spring	21. 4th Exhaust Valve Spring
2. 1-2 Shift Valve	12. 3-4 Orifice Control Valve	22. 4th Exhaust Valve
3. 1-2 Shift Valve Spring	13. 2-3 Orifice Control Valve	23. Servo Control Valve Spring
4. Valve Cap	14. 3-4 Shift Valve	24. 3rd Kickdown Valve Spring
5. Roller	15. Main Valve Body	25. Manual Valve
6. 2-3 Shift Valve	16. 4th Kickdown Valve	26. Clutch Pressure Control Valve Spring
7. 2-3 Shift Valve Spring	17. 4th Kickdown Valve Spring	27. Clutch Pressure Control Valve
8. 3-4 Shift Valve Spring	18. Spring Seat	28. Pin
9. 2-3 Orifice Control Valve Spring	19. 3rd Kickdown Valve	
10. Sleeve	20. Servo Control Valve	

96A04932   Courtesy of American Honda Motor Co., Inc.

Fig. 22: Exploded View Of Main Valve Body

SERVO BODY

Disassembly – Disassemble servo body. *See Fig. 23.* Use care when removing accumulator covers, as they are under spring pressure.

Cleaning & Inspection – 1) Clean components with solvent and dry with compressed air. Replace servo body if any parts are worn or damaged.

2) Ensure spring free length is within specification. See SPRING SPECIFICATIONS table. Replace springs if not within specification.

Reassembly – Coat all components and bores with Dexron-II ATF. To reassemble, reverse disassembly procedure using NEW filters and NEW "O" rings. Ensure filters are installed in proper direction. *See Fig. 23.*

REGULATOR VALVE BODY

CAUTION: Regulator spring cap is under spring pressure. Ensure regulator spring cap is held downward when removing lock bolt. Note direction of valve cap installation before removing from regulator valve body.

Disassembly – Hold regulator spring cap downward and remove lock bolt. Slowly remove regulator spring cap and components from regulator valve body. *See Fig. 24.*

Cleaning & Inspection – 1) Clean components with solvent and dry with compressed air. Replace regulator valve body if any parts are worn or damaged.

2) Ensure all valves slide freely in bores. If valves do not slide freely, polish burrs or rough areas using No. 600 sandpaper soaked for 30 minutes in ATF. Thoroughly clean regulator valve body and components if polishing was needed.

3) Ensure spring free length is within specification. See SPRING SPECIFICATIONS table. Replace springs if not within specification.

Reassembly – 1) Coat all components and bores with Dexron-II ATF. To reassemble, reverse disassembly procedure. Ensure all components are installed in correct location. *See Fig. 24.*

2) Ensure hole in regulator spring cap aligns with hole for lock bolt in valve body before tightening lock bolt. Tighten lock bolt to specification. See TORQUE SPECIFICATIONS.

OIL PUMP BODY

CAUTION: When disassembling oil pump body, place components in order and mark spring locations for reassembly reference. DO NOT use force to remove components. Note direction of valve cap installation before removing from oil pump body.

Disassembly – Disassemble oil pump body. *See Fig. 25.* Use care when removing valve caps or spring seats, as they are under spring pressure.

Cleaning & Inspection – 1) Clean components with solvent and dry with compressed air. Replace oil pump body if any parts are worn or damaged.

2) Ensure all valves slide freely in bores. If valves do not slide freely, polish burrs or rough areas using No. 600 sandpaper soaked for 30 minutes in ATF. Thoroughly clean oil pump body and components if polishing was needed.

3) Ensure spring free length is within specification. See SPRING SPECIFICATIONS table. Replace springs if not within specification.

4) Install oil pump gears and oil pump driven gear shaft in oil pump body. Ensure chamfered and grooved side of oil pump driven gear is facing upward (toward separator plate side of oil pump body).

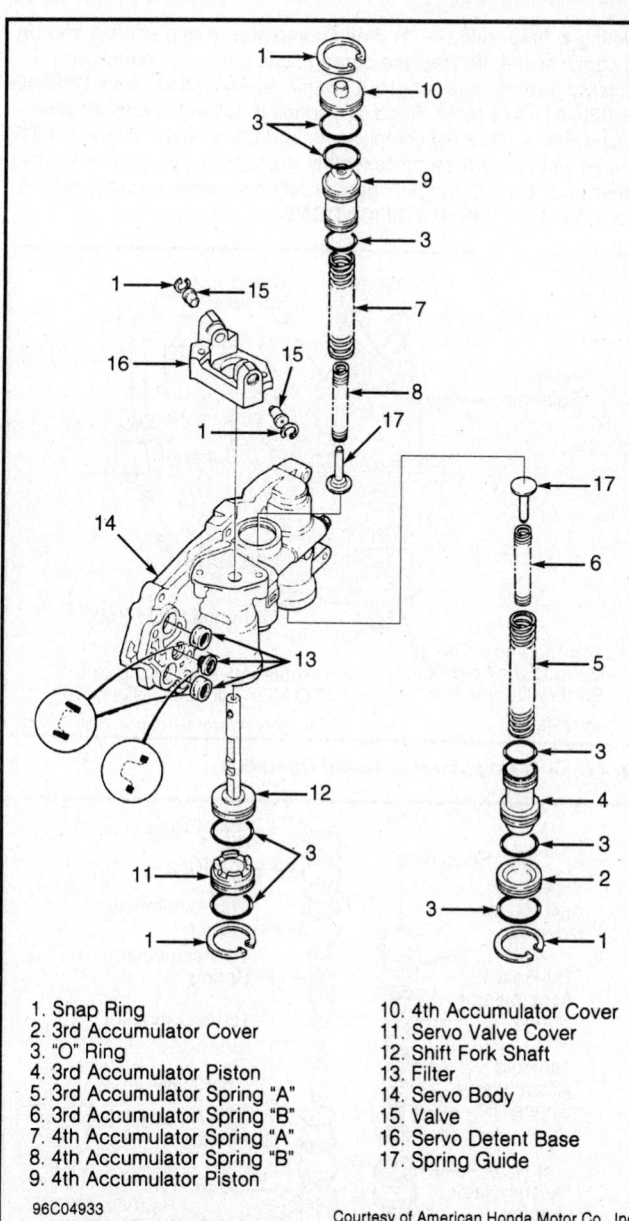

1. Snap Ring
2. 3rd Accumulator Cover
3. "O" Ring
4. 3rd Accumulator Piston
5. 3rd Accumulator Spring "A"
6. 3rd Accumulator Spring "B"
7. 4th Accumulator Spring "A"
8. 4th Accumulator Spring "B"
9. 4th Accumulator Piston
10. 4th Accumulator Cover
11. Servo Valve Cover
12. Shift Fork Shaft
13. Filter
14. Servo Body
15. Valve
16. Servo Detent Base
17. Spring Guide

96C04933

Courtesy of American Honda Motor Co., Inc.

Fig. 23: Exploded View Of Servo Body

5) Using feeler gauge, measure side clearance of both gears between tip of gear teeth and oil pump valve body. *See Fig. 26.* Replace oil pump gears and/or oil pump body if side clearance is not within specification. See OIL PUMP SPECIFICATIONS table.

6) Remove oil pump driven gear shaft. Place straightedge across oil pump body surface. Using feeler gauge, measure thrust clearance between oil pump driven gear and straightedge. *See Fig. 26.* Replace oil pump gears and/or oil pump body if thrust clearance is not within specification. See OIL PUMP SPECIFICATIONS table.

OIL PUMP SPECIFICATIONS

Application	In. (mm)
Side Clearance	
Oil Pump Drive Gear	.0083-.0104 (.210-.265)
Oil Pump Driven Gear	.0028-.0049 (.070-.125)
Thrust Clearance	
Standard	.001-.002 (.03-.05)
Wear Limit	.0028 (.070)

Reassembly – Coat components with Dexron-II ATF. To reassemble, reverse disassembly procedure using NEW filters. Ensure cham-

fered and grooved side of oil pump driven gear faces upward (toward separator plate side of oil pump body). Ensure filters are installed in proper direction. *See Fig. 25.*

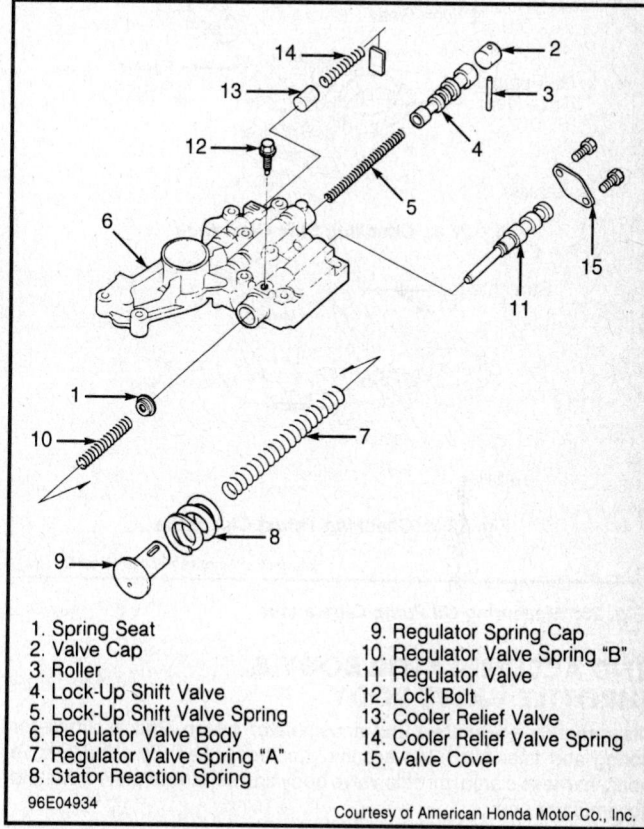

1. Spring Seat
2. Valve Cap
3. Roller
4. Lock-Up Shift Valve
5. Lock-Up Shift Valve Spring
6. Regulator Valve Body
7. Regulator Valve Spring "A"
8. Stator Reaction Spring
9. Regulator Spring Cap
10. Regulator Valve Spring "B"
11. Regulator Valve
12. Lock Bolt
13. Cooler Relief Valve
14. Cooler Relief Valve Spring
15. Valve Cover

96E04934

Courtesy of American Honda Motor Co., Inc.

Fig. 24: Exploded View Of Regulator Valve Body

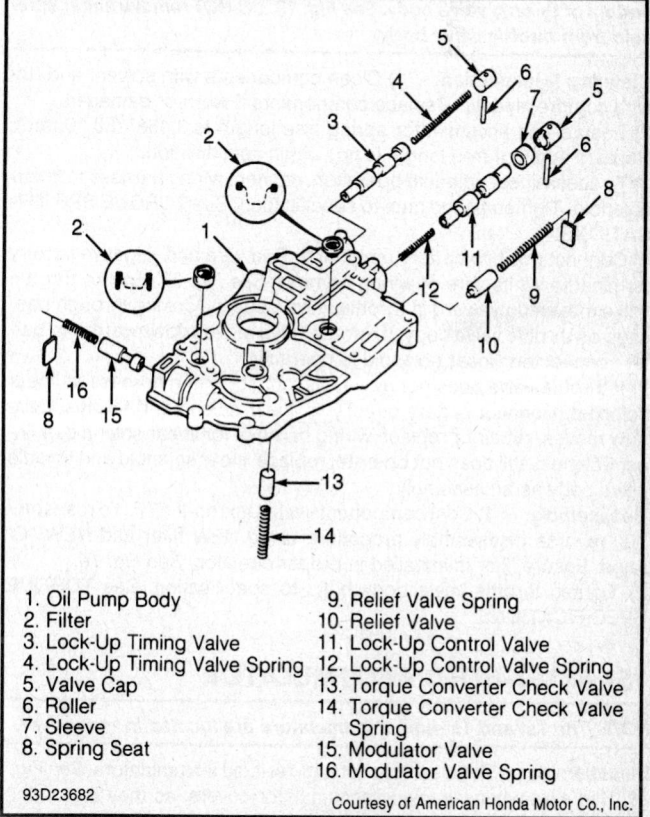

1. Oil Pump Body
2. Filter
3. Lock-Up Timing Valve
4. Lock-Up Timing Valve Spring
5. Valve Cap
6. Roller
7. Sleeve
8. Spring Seat
9. Relief Valve Spring
10. Relief Valve
11. Lock-Up Control Valve
12. Lock-Up Control Valve Spring
13. Torque Converter Check Valve
14. Torque Converter Check Valve Spring
15. Modulator Valve
16. Modulator Valve Spring

93D23682

Courtesy of American Honda Motor Co., Inc.

Fig. 25: Exploded View Of Oil Pump Body

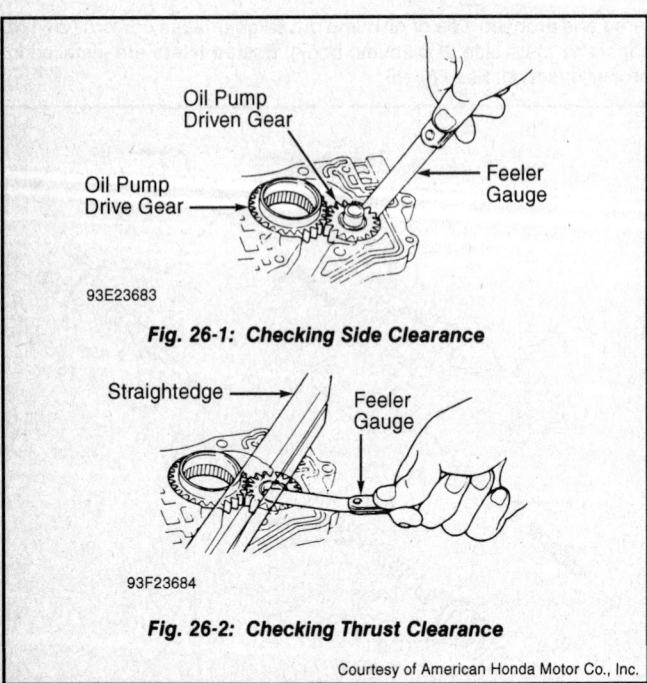

Fig. 26-1: Checking Side Clearance

93E23683

Fig. 26-2: Checking Thrust Clearance

93F23684

Courtesy of American Honda Motor Co., Inc.

Fig. 26: Measuring Oil Pump Clearances

2ND ACCUMULATOR BODY & THROTTLE VALVE BODY

Disassembly – Remove 2nd accumulator piston, 2nd accumulator spring and filter from 2nd accumulator body. *See Fig. 19.* Remove bolts, harness clamp, throttle valve body and separator plate from 2nd accumulator body.

CAUTION: DO NOT loosen or remove throttle valve adjusting bolt on bottom of throttle valve body. See Fig. 19. DO NOT remove linear solenoid from throttle valve body.

Cleaning & Inspection – 1) Clean components with solvent and dry with compressed air. Replace components if worn or damaged.
2) Ensure 2nd accumulator spring free length is 3.468" (88.10 mm). Replace spring if free length is not within specification.
3) To check linear solenoid operation, connect wiring harness to linear solenoid. Tighten flange nuts to specification. See TORQUE SPECIFICATIONS.
4) Connect positive battery terminal to Red wire and negative battery terminal to White wire of wiring harness. *See Fig. 27.* Ensure throttle valve moves downward in throttle valve body by looking through passage on throttle valve body. If throttle valve moves downward with battery connected, linear solenoid is operating.
5) If throttle valve does not move, disconnect wiring harness at linear solenoid. Connect battery directly to linear solenoid. If throttle valve now moves, repair or replace wiring harness for linear solenoid. If linear solenoid still does not operate, replace linear solenoid and throttle valve body as an assembly.

Reassembly – 1) Coat components with Dexron-II ATF. To reassemble, reverse disassembly procedure using NEW filter and NEW "O" rings. Ensure filter is installed in proper direction. *See Fig. 19.*
2) Tighten throttle valve body bolts to specification. See TORQUE SPECIFICATIONS.

1ST & 1ST-HOLD ACCUMULATOR

NOTE: The 1st and 1st-hold accumulators are located in rear cover.

Disassembly – Disassemble 1st and 1st-hold accumulators. *See Fig. 28.* Use care when removing accumulator covers, as they are under spring pressure.

Cleaning & Inspection – 1) Clean components with solvent and dry with compressed air. Replace components if worn or damaged.
2) Ensure spring free length is within specification. See SPRING SPECIFICATIONS table. Replace springs if not within specification.
Reassembly – Coat all components and bores with Dexron-II ATF. To reassemble, reverse disassembly procedure using NEW sealing washer and NEW "O" rings. Tighten rear cover sealing bolt to specification. See TORQUE SPECIFICATIONS.

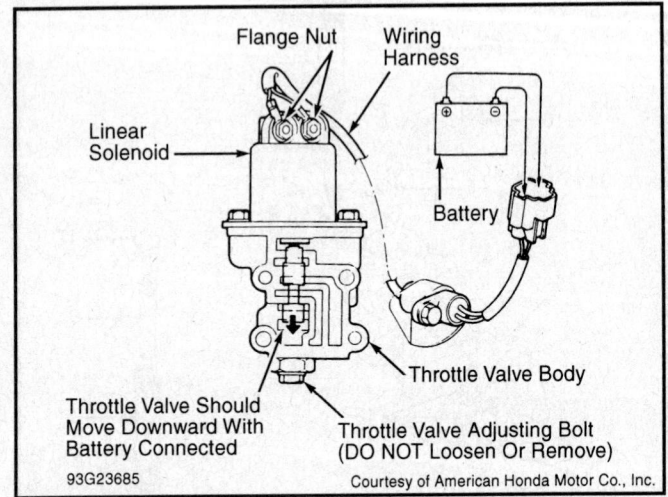

Fig. 27: Checking Linear Solenoid Operation

93G23685

Courtesy of American Honda Motor Co., Inc.

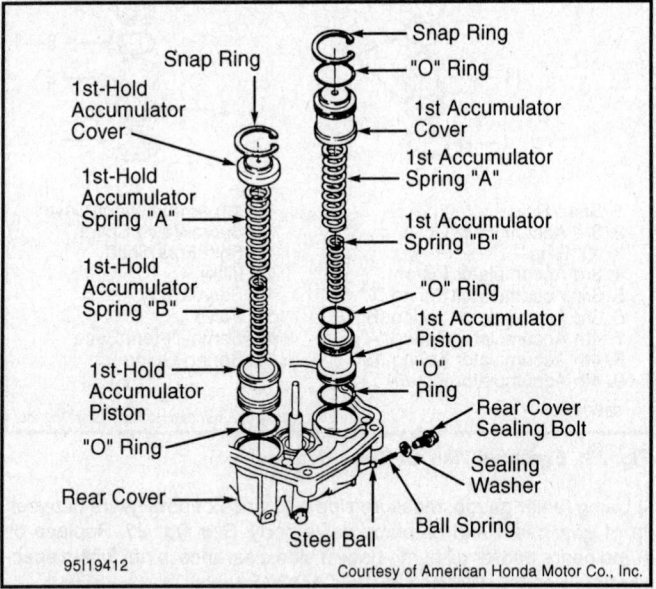

Fig. 28: Exploded View Of 1st & 1st-Hold Accumulators

95I19412

Courtesy of American Honda Motor Co., Inc.

MAINSHAFT

Disassembly – Note location of mainshaft components. *See Fig. 17.* Remove components from mainshaft.
Cleaning & Inspection – Clean components with solvent and dry with compressed air. Inspect splines for excessive wear. Check bearing surfaces for scoring or wear. Inspect all needle bearings for galling and rough movement.

NOTE: Mainshaft 2nd gear clearance must be checked during reassembly.

Reassembly – 1) Install all components on mainshaft except mainshaft 4th-reverse gear and needle bearings without installing "O" rings on mainshaft. *See Fig. 17.* Remove ball bearing for mainshaft from transaxle housing. Install ball bearing on mainshaft.

2) Install mainshaft 1st gear collar, thrust washer and 1st clutch on mainshaft. DO NOT install mainshaft 1st gear and needle bearings at this time. *See Fig. 15.*

3) Install disc spring and used mainshaft lock nut on mainshaft. Ensure disc spring is installed with largest side against lock nut. *See Fig. 15.* Tighten mainshaft lock nut to 22 ft. lbs. (30 N.m).

NOTE: Mainshaft lock nut has left-hand threads.

---

4) Install dial indicator on mainshaft so stem of dial indicator is resting against mainshaft 2nd gear. *See Fig. 29.* Move 4th-2nd clutch toward 1st clutch and note reading on dial indicator. This is the mainshaft 2nd gear clearance.

5) Measure mainshaft 2nd gear clearance in 3 different places. Use average reading as mainshaft 2nd gear clearance. Mainshaft 2nd gear clearance should be .003-.006" (.07-.15 mm).

6) Install different thickness mainshaft 2nd gear thrust shim and recheck clearance if mainshaft 2nd gear clearance is not within specification. Mainshaft 2nd gear thrust washers are available in .02" (.05 mm) increments. See MAINSHAFT 2ND GEAR THRUST SHIM SPECIFICATIONS table.

MAINSHAFT 2ND GEAR THRUST SHIM SPECIFICATIONS

Thrust Shim Number	Part Number	Thickness In. (mm)
1	90441-PW4-000	.157 (4.00)
2	90442-PW4-000	.159 (4.05)
3	90443-PW4-000	.161 (4.10)
4	90444-PW4-000	.163 (4.15)
5	90445-PW4-000	.165 (4.20)
6	90446-PW4-000	.167 (4.25)
7	90447-PW4-000	.169 (4.30)
8	90448-PW4-000	.171 (4.35)
9	90449-PW4-000	.173 (4.40)
10	90450-PW4-000	.175 (4.45)
11	90451-PW4-000	.177 (4.50)

7) Once correct mainshaft 2nd gear thrust shim is obtained, disassemble mainshaft. Lubricate all components with Dexron-II ATF. Wrap splines of mainshaft with tape.

8) Install NEW "O" rings on mainshaft. Reassemble mainshaft. Ensure thrust needle bearings are installed with unrolled edge of bearing retainer facing washer.

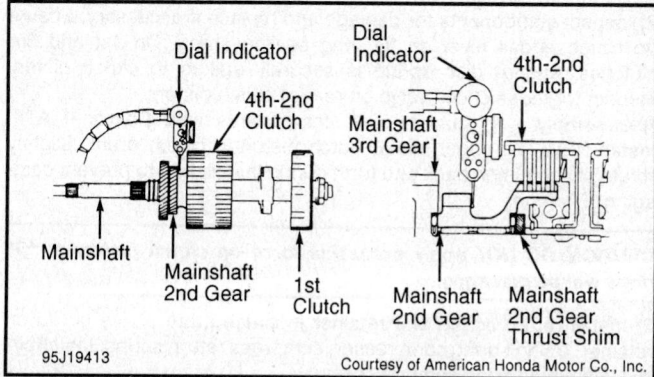

95J19413

Courtesy of American Honda Motor Co., Inc.

Fig. 29: Checking Mainshaft 2nd Gear Clearance

COUNTERSHAFT

Disassembly – Note location of countershaft components. *See Fig. 17.* Remove components from countershaft.

Cleaning & Inspection – Clean components with solvent and dry with compressed air. Inspect splines for excessive wear. Check bearing surfaces for scoring or wear. Inspect all needle bearings for galling and rough movement.

NOTE: Countershaft 4th gear clearance must be checked during reassembly.

Reassembly – 1) Install components on countershaft without installing "O" rings on countershaft. *See Fig. 30.*

2) Install disc spring and used countershaft lock nut on countershaft. Ensure disc spring is installed with largest side against countershaft lock nut. *See Fig. 15.*

3) Tighten countershaft lock nut to 22 ft. lbs. (30 N.m). Hold countershaft 4th gear against distance collar. Using feeler gauge, measure countershaft 4th gear clearance between countershaft 4th gear and reverse selector hub. *See Fig. 31.*

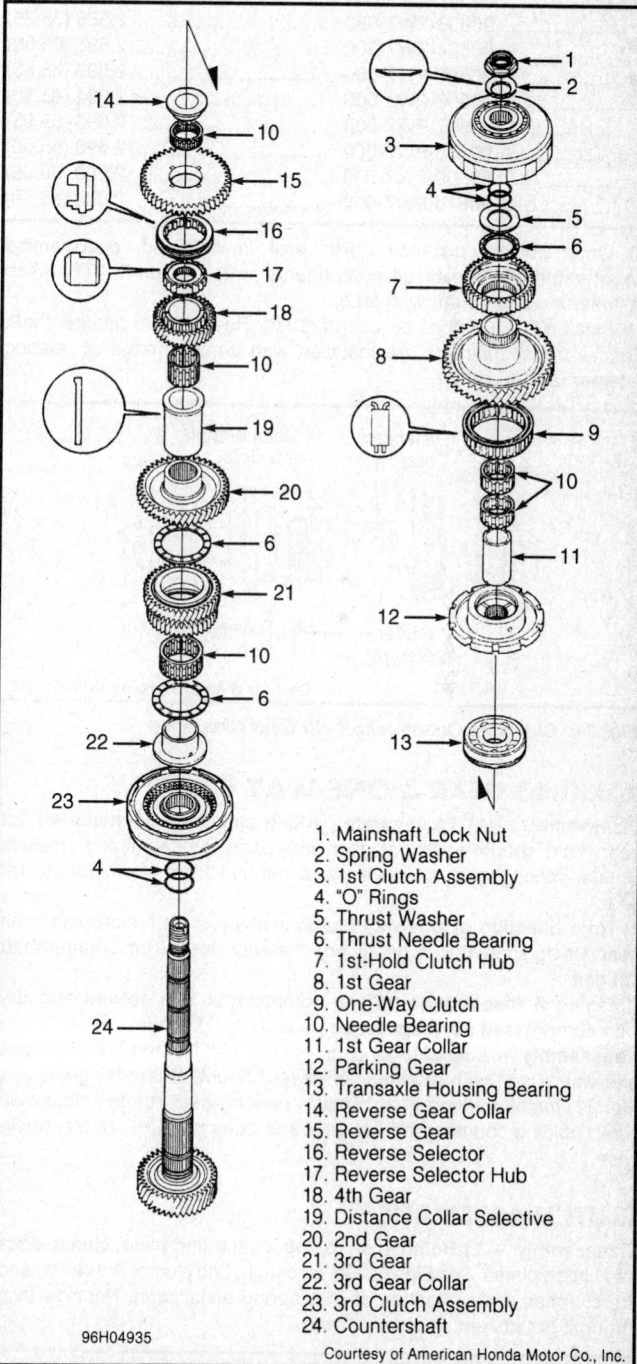

1. Mainshaft Lock Nut
2. Spring Washer
3. 1st Clutch Assembly
4. "O" Rings
5. Thrust Washer
6. Thrust Needle Bearing
7. 1st-Hold Clutch Hub
8. 1st Gear
9. One-Way Clutch
10. Needle Bearing
11. 1st Gear Collar
12. Parking Gear
13. Transaxle Housing Bearing
14. Reverse Gear Collar
15. Reverse Gear
16. Reverse Selector
17. Reverse Selector Hub
18. 4th Gear
19. Distance Collar Selective
20. 2nd Gear
21. 3rd Gear
22. 3rd Gear Collar
23. 3rd Clutch Assembly
24. Countershaft

96H04935

Courtesy of American Honda Motor Co., Inc.

Fig. 30: Assembling Countershaft For Checking Countershaft 4th Gear Clearance

4) Measure countershaft 4th gear clearance in 3 different places. Use average reading as countershaft 4th gear clearance. Countershaft 4th gear clearance should be .003-.006" (.07-.15 mm).

5) Install different length distance collar and recheck clearance if countershaft 4th gear clearance is not within specification. Countershaft distance collars are available in .02" (.05 mm) increments. See DISTANCE COLLAR SPECIFICATIONS table.

DISTANCE COLLAR SPECIFICATIONS

Collar Number	Part Number	Length In. (mm)
1	90501-PW7-000	2.585 (65.65)
2	90502-PW7-000	2.587 (65.70)
3	90503-PW7-000	2.589 (65.75)
4	90504-PW7-000	2.591 (65.80)
5	90505-PW7-000	2.593 (65.85)
6	90506-PW7-000	2.594 (65.90)
7	90507-PW7-000	2.596 (65.95)
8	90508-PW7-000	2.598 (66.00)
9	90509-PW7-000	2.600 (66.05)
10	90510-PW7-000	2.602 (66.10)

6) Once correct distance collar size is obtained, disassemble countershaft. Lubricate all components with Dexron-II ATF. Wrap splines of countershaft with tape.

7) Install NEW "O" rings on countershaft. Reassemble countershaft. Ensure thrust bearings are installed with unrolled edge of bearing retainer facing washer.

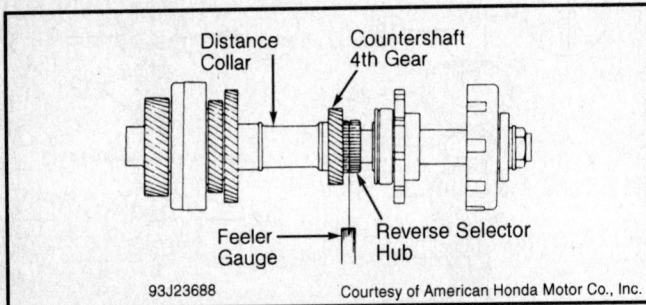

Fig. 31: Checking Countershaft 4th Gear Clearance

PARKING GEAR & ONE-WAY CLUTCH

Disassembly – 1) To separate parking gear from countershaft 1st gear, hold countershaft 1st gear with parking gear facing upward. Rotate parking gear clockwise and remove from countershaft 1st gear.

2) Note direction of one-way clutch installation in countershaft 1st gear. Using screwdriver, gently pry one-way clutch from countershaft 1st gear.

Cleaning & Inspection – Clean components with solvent and dry with compressed air. Inspect components for damage.

Reassembly – Lubricate all components with Dexron-II ATF. Install one-way clutch with retainer tab toward countershaft 1st gear. See Fig. 32. Install parking gear. Ensure parking gear rotates clockwise when holding countershaft 1st gear and does not turn counterclockwise.

CLUTCH ASSEMBLIES

Disassembly – 1) Remove snap ring, clutch end plate, clutch discs and clutch plates. See Fig. 33. On 1st clutch, 2nd clutch, 3rd clutch and 4th clutches, note direction of disc spring installation. Remove disc spring if not staked on clutch piston.

NOTE: Disc spring is not used on 1st-hold clutch. On all other clutch assemblies disc spring may be staked on clutch piston.

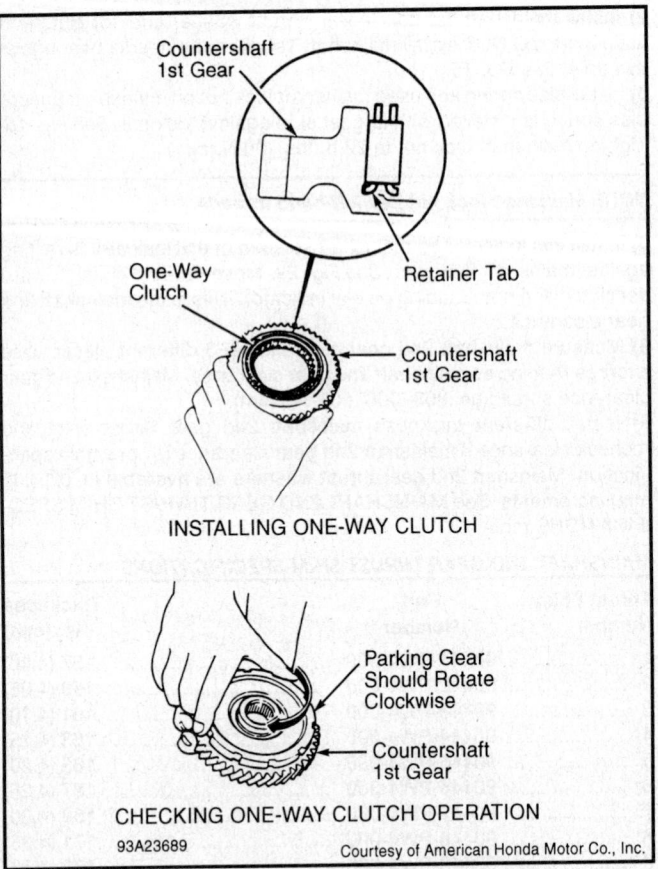

INSTALLING ONE-WAY CLUTCH

CHECKING ONE-WAY CLUTCH OPERATION

93A23689   Courtesy of American Honda Motor Co., Inc.

Fig. 32: Installing & Checking One-Way Clutch Operation

2) Using spring compressor, compress return spring. Remove circlip. Release and remove spring compressor. Remove retainer and return spring.

3) Wrap shop towel around clutch drum. Apply light air pressure to oil passage on clutch drum to remove clutch piston. Remove "O" rings.

Cleaning & Inspection – 1) Clean metal components with solvent and dry with compressed air. Ensure check valve on rear of clutch piston is thoroughly cleaned.

2) Inspect components for damage and replace if necessary. Ensure no rough edges exist on "O" ring sealing areas. On 1st and 3rd clutches, ensure disc spring is securely staked to clutch piston. Inspect for loose check valve on rear of clutch piston.

Reassembly – 1) Lubricate all components with Dexron-II ATF. Install NEW "O" rings. Install clutch piston in clutch drum. Slightly rotate clutch piston back and forth during installation to prevent damaging "O" rings.

CAUTION: DO NOT apply excessive force on clutch piston or "O" rings will be damaged.

2) Install return spring and retainer in clutch drum. Place circlip on retainer. Using spring compressor, compress return spring. Install circlip. Remove spring compressor.

3) Install disc spring if not staked on clutch piston. Ensure disc spring is installed in proper direction. See Fig. 33.

CAUTION: Ensure clutch discs are soaked in Dexron-II ATF for at least 30 minutes before installing.

4) Alternately install clutch plates and clutch discs starting with clutch plate. Install clutch end plate with flat side toward clutch disc. Install snap ring. Momentarily apply air to oil passage on clutch drum and note that the clutch piston moves and clutch engages.

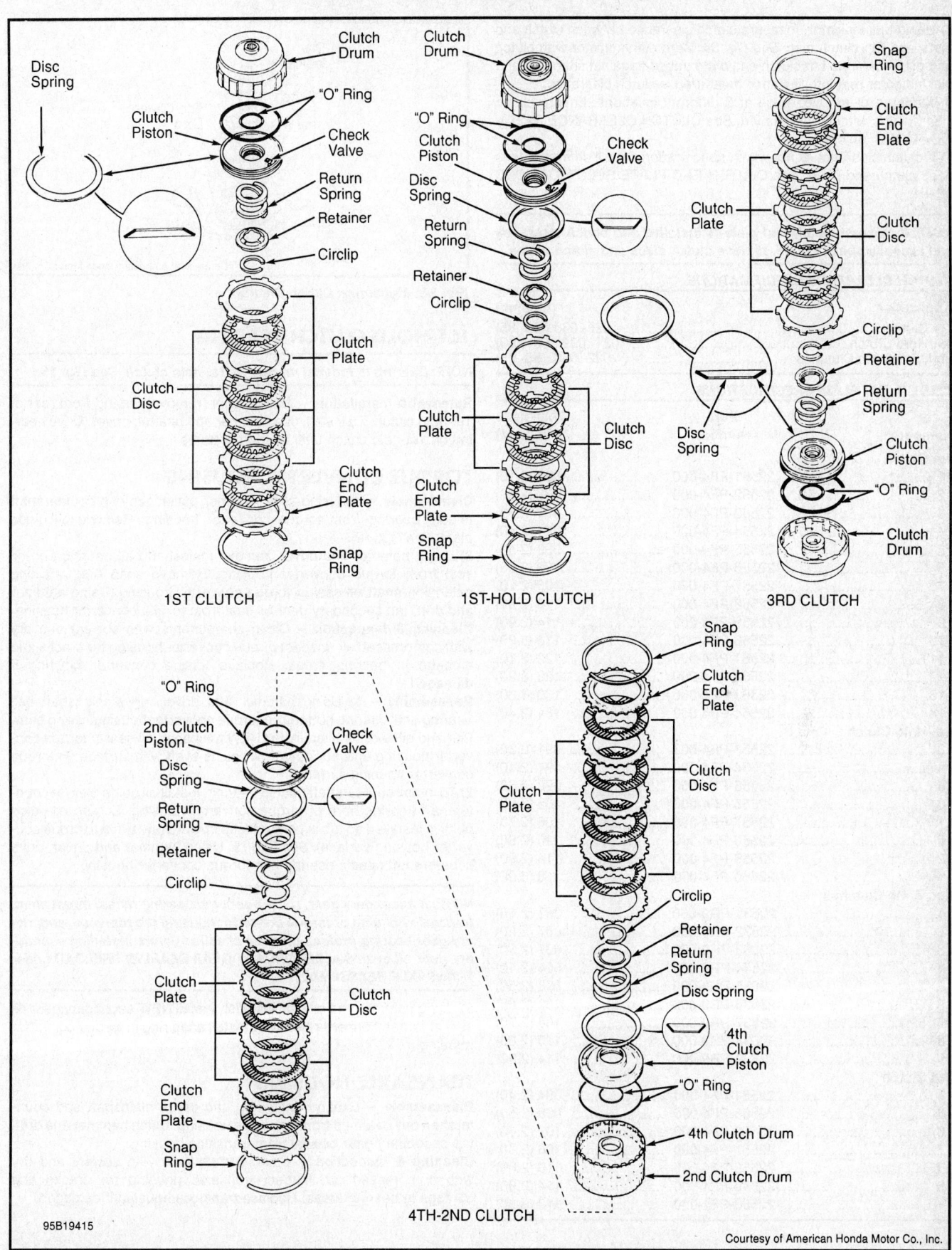

95B19415

Courtesy of American Honda Motor Co., Inc.

Fig. 33: Exploded View Of Clutch Assemblies

5) Using dial indicator, measure clutch clearance between clutch end plate and top clutch disc. *See Fig. 34.* Zero dial indicator with clutch end plate lowered. Lift clutch end plate upward against snap ring and dial indicator reading. Distance measured is clutch clearance.

6) Measure clutch clearance at 3 different locations. Ensure clutch clearance is within specification. See CLUTCH CLEARANCE SPECIFICATIONS table.

7) If clutch clearance is not within specification, install different thickness clutch end plate. See CLUTCH END PLATE SPECIFICATIONS table.

NOTE: If thickest clutch end plate is installed and clutch clearance still exceeds specification, replace clutch discs and clutch plates.

CLUTCH CLEARANCE SPECIFICATIONS

Application	In. (mm)
1st Clutch	.026-.033 (.65-.85)
1st-Hold Clutch	.031-.039 (.80-1.00)
2nd, 3rd & 4th Clutches	.022-.030 (.55-.75)

CLUTCH END PLATE SPECIFICATIONS

Plate Number	Part Number	Thickness In. (mm)
1st Clutch		
1	22551-PF4-000	.083 (2.10)
2	22552-PF4-000	.087 (2.20)
3	22553-PF4-000	.091 (2.30)
4	22554-PF4-000	.094 (2.40)
5	22555-PF4-000	.098 (2.50)
6	22556-PF4-000	.102 (2.60)
7	22557-PF4-000	.106 (2.70)
8	22558-PF4-000	.110 (2.80)
9	22559-PF4-000	.114 (2.90)
10	22560-PF4-000	.118 (3.00)
11	22561-PF4-000	.122 (3.10)
12	22562-PF4-000	.126 (3.20)
13	22563-PF4-000	.130 (3.30)
14	22564-PF4-000	.134 (3.40)
1st-Hold Clutch		
3	22553-PF4-000	.091 (2.30)
4	22554-PF4-000	.094 (2.40)
5	22555-PF4-000	.098 (2.50)
6	22556-PF4-000	.102 (2.60)
7	22557-PF4-000	.106 (2.70)
8	22558-PF4-000	.110 (2.80)
9	22559-PF4-000	.114 (2.90)
10	22560-PF4-000	.118 (3.00)
2nd & 4th Clutches		
1	22631-PR9-000	.083 (2.10)
2	22632-PR9-000	.087 (2.20)
3	22633-PR9-000	.091 (2.30)
4	22634-PR9-000	.094 (2.40)
5	22635-PR9-000	.098 (2.50)
6	22636-PR9-000	.102 (2.60)
7	22637-PR9-000	.106 (2.70)
8	22638-PR9-000	.110 (2.80)
9	22639-PR9-000	.114 (2.90)
3rd Clutch		
4	22554-PF4-000	.094 (2.40)
5	22555-PF4-000	.098 (2.50)
6	22556-PF4-000	.102 (2.60)
7	22557-PF4-000	.106 (2.70)
8	22558-PF4-000	.110 (2.80)
9	22559-PF4-000	.114 (2.90)
10	22560-PF4-000	.118 (3.00)

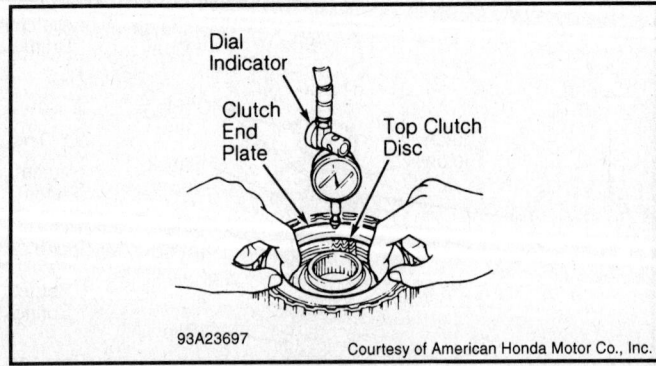

93A23697
Courtesy of American Honda Motor Co., Inc.

Fig. 34: Measuring Clutch Clearance

1ST-HOLD CLUTCH BEARING

NOTE: Bearing is located on rear of 1st-hold clutch. See Fig. 15.

Removal & Installation – Using puller, remove bearing from rear of 1st-hold clutch. To install, use hammer and bearing driver. Drive bearing on 1st-hold clutch until bearing bottoms.

TORQUE CONVERTER HOUSING

Disassembly – **1)** Using slide hammer puller, remove countershaft needle bearing from torque converter housing. Remove oil guide plate. *See Fig. 19.*

2) Using hammer and driver, remove mainshaft ball bearing and oil seal from torque converter housing. Remove snap ring retaining extension shaft oil seal in torque converter housing. Using hammer and drift, tap secondary gear oil seal from torque converter housing.

Cleaning & Inspection – Clean components with solvent and dry with compressed air. Inspect torque converter housing for cracks and damage in bearing areas. Replace torque converter housing if damaged.

Reassembly – **1)** Using hammer and driver, drive mainshaft ball bearing until bearing bottoms in torque converter housing. Using hammer and oil seal installer, install NEW mainshaft oil seal in torque converter housing until surface of oil seal is even with surface on torque converter housing surface.

2) To install countershaft needle bearing, install oil guide plate in countershaft bearing bore of torque converter housing. Ensure oil guide plate is installed so tab in center faces upward (away from torque converter housing surface). *See Fig. 19.* Using hammer and driver, drive countershaft needle bearing into torque converter housing.

NOTE: If secondary gear, roller bearings, bearing races, thrust shim, transaxle housing or torque converter housing are replaced, secondary gear bearing preload must be checked before installing secondary gear oil seal. See SECONDARY GEAR BEARING PRELOAD under TRANSAXLE REASSEMBLY.

3) Using hammer and oil seal installer, install NEW secondary gear oil seal in torque converter housing. Install snap ring in torque converter housing.

TRANSAXLE HOUSING

Disassembly – Expand snap ring and press mainshaft and countershaft ball bearings from transaxle housing. Using hammer and drift, tap secondary gear oil seal from transaxle housing.

Cleaning & Inspection – Clean components with solvent and dry with compressed air. Inspect transaxle housing for cracks and damage in bearing areas. Replace transaxle housing if damaged.

Reassembly – 1) Expand snap ring and install ball bearing part way into transaxle housing. Release snap ring. Press ball bearing into transaxle housing until snap ring engages with groove in ball bearing.

CAUTION: Ensure ball bearings are installed with groove of ball bearing facing inside of transaxle housing so snap ring engages in ball bearing when ball bearing is fully installed. Ensure snap ring fully engages in ball bearing.

NOTE: If secondary gear, roller bearings, bearing races, thrust shim, transaxle housing or torque converter housing are replaced, secondary gear bearing preload must be checked before installing secondary gear oil seal. See SECONDARY GEAR BEARING PRELOAD under TRANSAXLE REASSEMBLY.

2) Using hammer and oil seal installer, install NEW secondary gear oil seal into transaxle housing.

SECONDARY GEAR & EXTENSION SHAFT

NOTE: If secondary gear, roller bearings, bearing races, thrust shim, transaxle housing or torque converter housing are replaced, secondary gear bearing preload must be checked before installing secondary gear oil seal. See SECONDARY GEAR BEARING PRELOAD under TRANSAXLE REASSEMBLY.

Disassembly – 1) Remove set ring and extension shaft from secondary gear. *See Fig. 17.* Using screwdriver, pry oil seal for extension shaft from secondary gear.
2) If removing roller bearing from secondary gear, support secondary gear in press using bearing remover. Using press, press secondary gear from roller bearing.

CAUTION: DO NOT heat torque converter housing or transaxle housing to more than 212°F (100°C) or housing may be damaged.

3) If removing bearing races for secondary gear from torque converter or transaxle housing, use heat gun to heat area around bearing race to 212°F (100°C). Tap bearing race from housing.

CAUTION: When removing bearing race from transaxle housing, use care not to damage thrust shim located below bearing race. See Fig. 17.

Cleaning & Inspection – Clean components with solvent and dry with compressed air. Inspect splines for excessive wear. Check bearing surfaces for scoring or wear. Inspect secondary gear for damage.
Reassembly – 1) To reassemble extension shaft, use hammer and oil seal installer, install NEW oil seal in secondary gear. If installing roller bearings on secondary gear, use press to press roller bearings on secondary gear. Ensure roller bearing fully bottoms on secondary gear.
2) Install extension shaft in secondary gear. Install NEW set ring on end of extension shaft.
3) If installing bearing race for secondary gear in transaxle housing, install thrust shim in transaxle housing. Using hammer and driver, tap bearing race into transaxle housing.
4) If installing bearing race for secondary gear in torque converter housing, use hammer and driver, tap bearing race into transaxle housing.

NOTE: If secondary gear, roller bearings, bearing races, thrust shim, transaxle housing or torque converter housing are replaced, secondary gear bearing preload must be checked before installing secondary gear oil seal. See SECONDARY GEAR BEARING PRELOAD under TRANSAXLE REASSEMBLY.

TRANSAXLE REASSEMBLY

SECONDARY GEAR BEARING PRELOAD

1) Oil seals must be removed from torque converter housing and transaxle housing before checking secondary gear bearing preload. Remove snap ring retaining extension shaft oil seal in torque converter housing.
2) Using hammer and drift, tap extension shaft oil seal from torque converter housing and transaxle housing. Remove set ring and extension shaft from secondary gear. *See Fig. 17.*
3) Install sealing bolt in secondary gear. *See Fig. 35.* Tighten sealing bolt to 15 ft. lbs. (20 N.m). Install secondary gear in torque converter housing. DO NOT install mainshaft and countershaft in torque converter housing.
4) Install dowel pins and gasket on torque converter housing. Install transaxle housing on torque converter housing. Install and tighten transaxle housing bolts to specification in sequence. *See Fig. 36.* See TORQUE SPECIFICATIONS.

CAUTION: Ensure transaxle housing bolts are also installed on inside of torque converter housing. See Fig. 17.

5) Rotate secondary gear in both directions to fully seat roller bearings on secondary gear. Secondary gear bearing preload is determined by measuring starting torque required to rotate secondary gear in both directions.
6) Using INCH-lb. torque wrench, measure starting torque required to rotate secondary gear in both directions at room temperature. *See Fig. 35.* The starting torque should be 20-29 INCH lbs. (2.3-3.3 N.m).
7) If starting torque is not within specification, install different thickness thrust shim below bearing race in transaxle housing. *See Fig. 17.* See THRUST SHIM SPECIFICATIONS table. Changing thrust shim to next thickness will increase or decrease starting torque approximately 3 INCH lbs. (3-4 N.m).

THRUST SHIM SPECIFICATIONS

Thrust Shim I.D. Letter	Part Number	Thickness In. (mm)
A	23941-PW5-000	.061 (1.56)
B	23942-PW5-000	.063 (1.59)
C	23943-PW5-000	.064 (1.62)
D	23944-PW5-000	.065 (1.65)
E	23945-PW5-000	.066 (1.68)
F	23946-PW5-000	.067 (1.71)
G	23947-PW5-000	.069 (1.74)
H	23948-PW5-000	.070 (1.77)
I	23949-PW5-000	.071 (1.80)
J	23950-PW5-000	.072 (1.83)
K	23951-PW5-000	.073 (1.86)
L	23952-PW5-000	.074 (1.89)
M	23953-PW5-000	.076 (1.92)
N	23954-PW5-000	.077 (1.95)
O	23955-PW5-000	.078 (1.98)
P	23956-PW5-000	.079 (2.01)
Q	23957-PW5-000	.080 (2.04)
R	23958-PW5-000	.081 (2.07)
S	23959-PW5-000	.083 (2.10)
T	23960-PW5-000	.084 (2.13)
U	23961-PW5-000	.085 (2.16)
V	23962-PW5-000	.086 (2.19)
W	23963-PW5-000	.087 (2.22)
X	23964-PW5-000	.089 (2.25)
Y	23965-PW5-000	.090 (2.28)
Z	23966-PW5-000	.091 (2.31)
AA	23967-PW5-000	.092 (2.34)
AB	23968-PW5-000	.093 (2.37)
AC	23969-PW5-000	.094 (2.40)
AD	23970-PW5-000	.096 (2.43)

8) If changing thrust shim, remove transaxle housing from torque converter housing. Using heat gun, heat area around bearing race in transaxle housing to 212°F (100°C). Tap bearing race from transaxle housing. Remove thrust shim.

CAUTION: DO NOT heat transaxle housing to more than 212°F (100°C) or housing may be damaged.

9) Install thrust shim in transaxle housing. Using hammer and driver, tap bearing race into transaxle housing. Recheck secondary gear bearing preload.

10) Once correct secondary gear bearing preload is obtained, remove transaxle housing and secondary gear from torque converter housing. Using hammer and oil seal installer, install NEW secondary gear oil seal in torque converter housing. Install snap ring in torque converter housing.

11) Using hammer and oil seal installer, install NEW secondary gear oil seal into transaxle housing. Install extension shaft in secondary gear. Install NEW set ring on end of extension shaft.

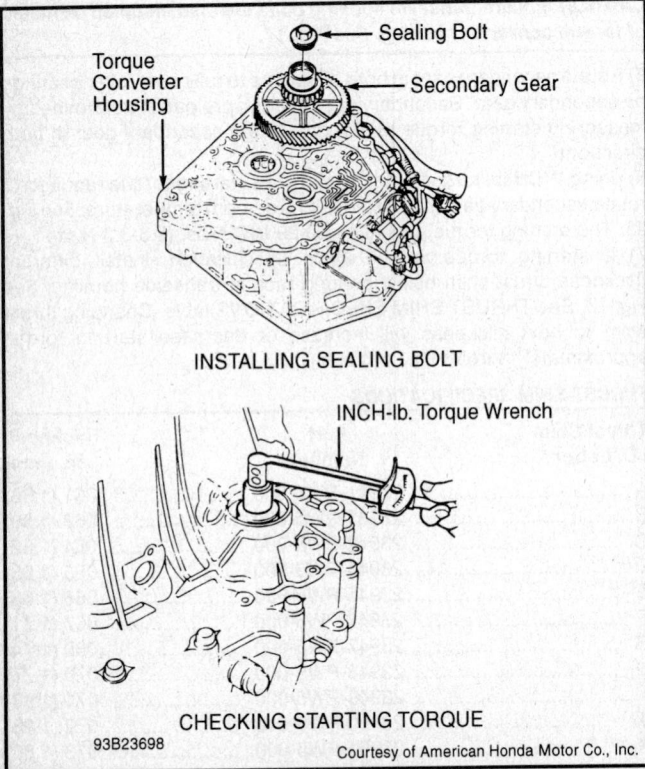

Fig. 35: *Installing Sealing Bolt & Checking Starting Torque*

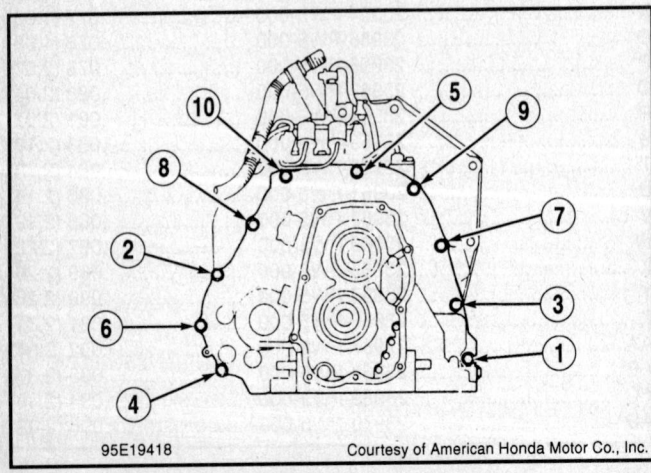

Fig. 36: *Transaxle Housing Bolt Tightening Sequence*

VALVE BODIES & INTERNAL COMPONENTS

CAUTION: If secondary gear, roller bearings, bearing races, thrust shim, transaxle housing or torque converter housing are replaced, secondary gear bearing preload must be checked before installing secondary gear oil seal. See SECONDARY GEAR BEARING PRELOAD under TRANSAXLE REASSEMBLY.

NOTE: Coat all components with Dexron-II ATF during reassembly.

1) If installing reverse idler gear in transaxle housing, install spring and steel ball in reverse idler gear shaft holder. Install needle bearing on end of reverse idler gear shaft holder. Ensure needle bearing retains steel ball and spring in reverse idler gear shaft holder.

2) Install reverse idler gear in transaxle housing. *See Fig. 17.* Install reverse idler gear shaft holder on transaxle housing. Install and tighten reverse idler gear shaft holder bolts to specification. See TORQUE SPECIFICATIONS.

3) Install shift control solenoid valve harness in torque converter housing. *See Fig. 19.* Install and tighten solenoid valve harness bolt to specification. Install dowel pins and separator plate on torque converter housing.

CAUTION: Ensure oil pump driven gear is installed with groove and chamfered side facing downward (toward separator plate on torque converter housing).

4) Install oil pump drive gear, oil pump driven gear and oil pump driven gear shaft. Install torque converter check valve and spring.

5) Install oil pump body. Install and tighten oil pump body bolts to specification.

CAUTION: Ensure oil pump gears rotate smoothly and oil pump driven gear shaft moves freely once oil pump body is installed. If components do not operate correctly, loosen bolts and realign oil pump gears and oil pump driven gear shaft. Failure to align oil pump driven gear shaft may result in seized oil pump gears or shaft.

6) Install NEW filters in oil pump body. Ensure filters are installed in proper direction. *See Fig. 19.*

7) Install dowel pins, separator plate, throttle valve body/linear solenoid and harness clamp on 2nd accumulator body. Install and tighten throttle valve body bolts to specification.

8) Install NEW "O" rings on 2nd accumulator piston. Install 2nd accumulator spring and 2nd accumulator piston in 2nd accumulator body. Install NEW filter in 2nd accumulator body. Ensure filter is installed in proper direction.

9) Install 2nd accumulator body. Install and tighten 2nd accumulator body bolts to specification. Install oil feedpipes in 2nd accumulator body. Install dowel pin and separator plate for regulator valve body.

10) Install stator shaft, NEW "O" ring and stopper shaft. Install regulator valve body. Install and tighten regulator valve body bolts to specification.

11) Connect shift control solenoid harness connector to linear solenoid terminal. Install flange nuts and harness connector bolt. Install oil feedpipes in oil pump body, torque converter housing and 2nd accumulator housing. *See Fig. 19.* Install wiring harness on linear solenoid. Tighten flange nuts on linear solenoid to specification.

12) Install NEW "O" ring and dipstick tube. Install and tighten bolt to specification. Using NEW seal washers, install cooler pipes and joint bolts. Tighten joint bolts to specification.

13) Install reverse idler gear and reverse idler gear shaft assembly in torque converter housing. Install extension shaft and secondary gear in torque converter housing. Install countershaft and mainshaft as an assembly in torque converter housing. Install dowel pins and NEW gasket on torque converter housing.

CAUTION: Ensure mainshaft and countershaft speed sensors ARE NOT installed in transaxle housing when installing transaxle housing on torque converter housing.

14) Install transaxle housing on torque converter housing. Install and tighten transaxle housing bolts to specification in sequence. *See Fig. 36.*

15) Ensure transaxle housing-to-torque converter housing bolts are installed on inside of torque converter housing. *See Fig. 17.* Tighten bolts to specification.

16) Install NEW "O" rings on mainshaft and countershaft speed sensors. Install countershaft speed sensor. Install mainshaft speed sensor washer and mainshaft speed sensor. *See Fig. 17.* Install and tighten speed sensor bolts to specification.

CAUTION: Ensure mainshaft speed sensor washer is installed when installing mainshaft speed sensor. Countershaft speed sensor does not use a washer.

---

17) Install parking pawl, parking pawl spring, parking pawl shaft and parking pawl stopper. Turn control shaft or detent lever to shift into any gear except park. Install mainshaft 1st gear collar and thrust washer on mainshaft.

18) Install parking gear, countershaft 1st gear collar and needle bearings on countershaft. *See Fig. 15.* Install one-way clutch and countershaft 1st gear as an assembly on countershaft.

19) Wrap splines of countershaft and mainshaft with tape. Install NEW "O" rings on countershaft and mainshaft. Remove tape from countershaft and mainshaft.

20) Install mainshaft 1st gear, needle bearing, thrust needle bearing, thrust washer and 1st clutch on mainshaft. Install 1st-hold clutch hub, thrust needle bearing, thrust washer and 1st-hold clutch on countershaft.

21) Coat NEW disc springs and NEW lock nuts with Dexron-II ATF. Install disc spring on mainshaft and countershaft. Ensure disc spring is installed with largest side against lock nut.

22) Install mainshaft and countershaft lock nuts. Install Mainshaft Holder (07GAB-PF50100) on mainshaft to secure mainshaft. *See Fig. 16.*

23) Engage parking pawl with parking gear. Tighten mainshaft and countershaft lock nuts to specification. Remove mainshaft holder. Stake lock nuts against the shaft.

CAUTION: Ensure mainshaft and countershaft lock nuts are securely staked.

---

24) Position control shaft in Park position. Push shift fork into Drive position (toward lower valve body assembly). *See Fig. 12.* Install lower valve body assembly while engaging manual valve on valve body with detent lever and engaging shift fork with reverse selector.

25) Install main valve body cover plate. Pass shift control solenoid valve harness through transaxle housing. Install harness connector bolt. Install harness cover. *See Fig. 12.* Install fluid strainer ensuring proper length bolts are installed in correct location on lower valve body assembly and fluid strainer. *See Fig. 13.*

26) Ensure wiring harness is not pinched. Tighten all bolts to specification. Install dowel pins, NEW gasket and oil pan. Install and tighten oil pan bolts to specification. Install NEW seal washer on drain plug. Tighten drain plug to specification.

27) Install oil pipes, dowel pins, NEW gasket and rear cover. Install and tighten rear cover bolts to specification. Reconnect shift control solenoid valve harness to transaxle sub-harness. Install gear position switch cover. *See Fig. 37.* Tighten bolt on transaxle pan side first hand tight, then tighten side cover side bolt to specification. Tighten transaxle pan side bolt to specification.

CAUTION: If transaxle failure existed, flush oil cooler. See OIL COOLER FLUSHING under ON-VEHICLE SERVICE.

DIFFERENTIAL ASSEMBLY
OVERHAUL

NOTE: Pre-disassembly inspection should be performed before disassembly of differential assembly. This will indicate if proper thrust shims and thrust washers are used.

Pre-Disassembly Inspection – Ring Gear Backlash – 1) Check ring gear backlash, total bearing preload and gear tooth contact pattern before disassembling differential assembly. Record measurements for use during reassembly.

2) To check ring gear backlash, mount differential assembly in soft-jawed vice. Remove side plug and seal washer from differential case cover. *See Fig. 40.* Remove oil seal from differential case cover. Align differential carrier rib with side plug hole.

3) Install Shaft (07HAJ-PK40201) in differential assembly. *See Fig. 38.* Mount dial indicator on differential case cover.

4) Measure ring gear backlash in 3 different locations on differential carrier. Ring gear backlash should be .002-.004" (.04-.10 mm) and maximum variation in ring gear backlash readings should not exceed .0016" (.040 mm).

5) If ring gear backlash is within specification, proper thickness thrust shims are installed behind bearing races for differential carrier bearings provided no components are changed. If ring gear backlash is not within specification, different thickness thrust shim must be installed during reassembly.

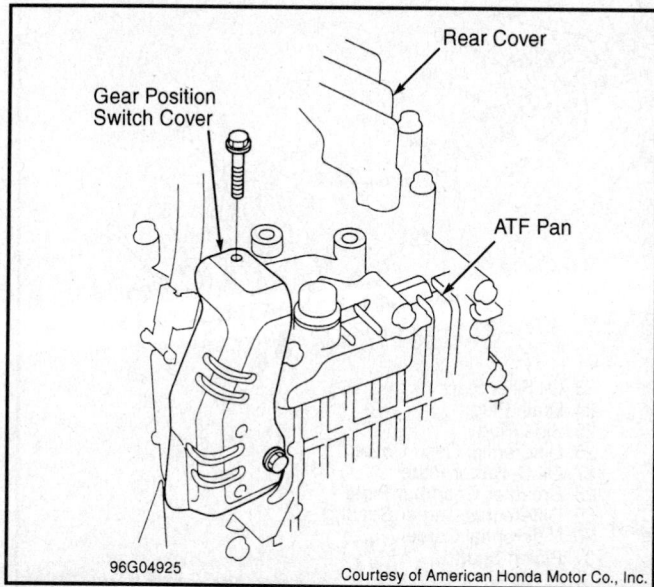

Fig. 37: Installing Gear Position Switch Cover

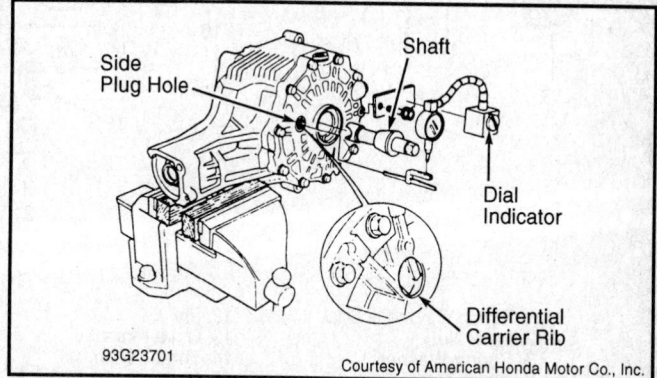

Fig. 38: Checking Differential Assembly Ring Gear Backlash

Bearing Preload – 1) Punch 2 holes on opposite sides in surface of pinion collar seal. Using wood block, screwdriver and 2 holes, pry pinion collar oil seal from differential case. *See Fig. 39.*

2) Remove differential case cover and differential carrier. To measure pinion preload, install a dial-type INCH-lb. torque wrench on end of drive pinion. Rotate drive pinion and note pinion preload. Pinion preload should be 5.6-9.1 INCH lbs. (.64-1.03 N.m).

3) Reinstall differential carrier and differential case cover. To measure total bearing preload, install a dial-type INCH-lb. torque wrench on end of drive pinion. Rotate drive pinion and note total bearing preload. Total bearing preload should be 13.50-19.08 INCH lbs. (1.536-2.16 N.m) with used bearings.

NOTE: If total bearing preload is not within specification, different thickness shim must be installed behind bearing race for differential carrier bearings.

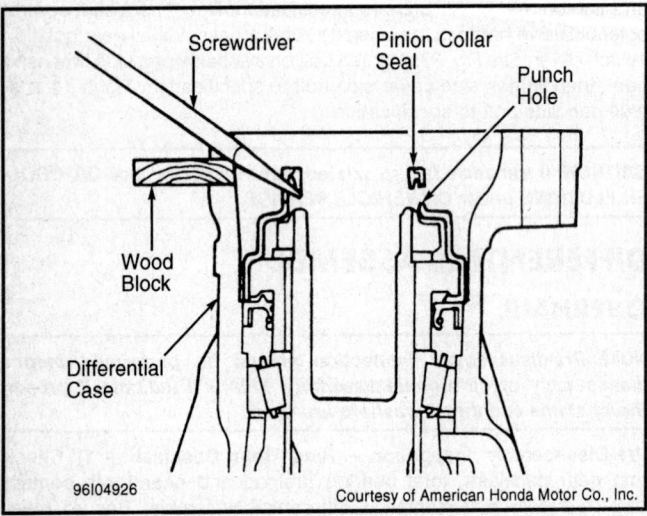

96I04926   Courtesy of American Honda Motor Co., Inc.

Fig. 39: Removing Pinion Collar Seal

Gear Tooth Contact – 1) To check gear tooth contact pattern, remove differential case cover bolts in a crisscross pattern. Remove differential case cover. *See Fig. 40.* Clean and paint both sides of ring gear teeth with Prussian Blue.

2) Install differential case cover. Install and tighten bolts in a crisscross pattern to 35 ft.lbs. (47 N.m). Install Shaft (07HAJ-PK40201) in differential assembly.

3) Rotate ring gear one full turn in both directions while applying resistance on pinion shaft. Remove differential case cover and inspect ring gear tooth contact pattern. Correct gear tooth contact should be centered on the ring gear. See GEAR TOOTH CONTACT PATTERN article in APPLICATIONS & IDENTIFICATION section.

Disassembly – 1) Remove differential case cover bolts in a crisscross pattern. Remove differential case cover. Remove oil collector plate and breather chamber plate from differential case cover (if necessary). *See Fig. 40.*

2) Remove differential carrier with ring gear from differential case. Remove bolts, oil cooler and "O" ring. Punch 2 small holes in pinion collar seal 180 degrees apart from each other. *See Fig. 39.*

3) Place wooden block on differential case to protect case when prying pinion collar seal from differential case. Place screwdriver in small holes and pry pinion collar seal from differential case.

4) Using hammer and chisel, cut lock nut tab and pry away from drive pinion. Insert Allen wrench or hex socket into gear end of drive pinion.

NOTE: Lock nut on drive pinion contains left-hand threads.

5) Secure long end of 1 1/4" (32 mm) Allen wrench in vise or hold hex socket. Remove lock nut and spring washer from drive pinion.

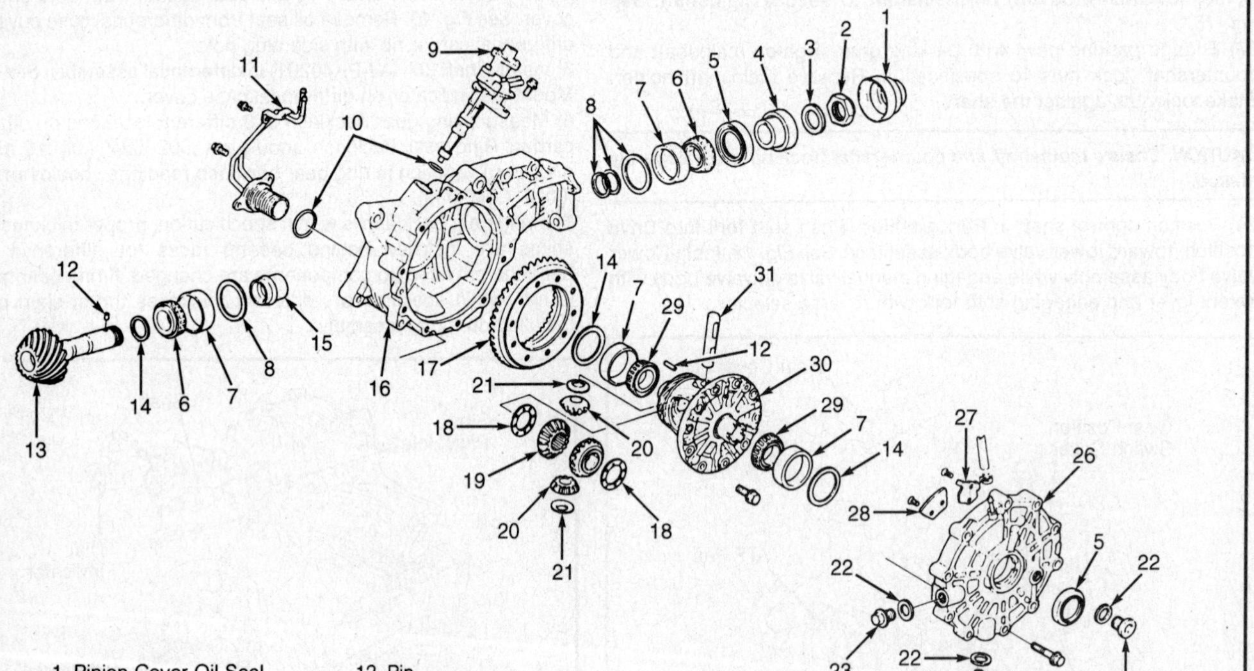

1. Pinion Cover Oil Seal
2. Lock Nut
3. Spring Washer
4. Pinion Collar
5. Oil Seal
6. Pinion Bearing
7. Bearing Race
8. Thrust Washer
9. Speed Sensor Assembly
10. "O" Ring
11. Oil Cooler
12. Pin
13. Drive Pinion
14. Thrust Shim
15. Pinion Spacer
16. Differential Case
17. Ring Gear
18. Side Gear Thrust Washer
19. Side Gear
20. Pinion Gear
21. Pinion Gear Thrust Trasher
22. Seal Washer
23. Oil Filler Plug
24. Drain Plug
25. Side Plug
26. Differential Case Cover
27. Oil Collector Plate
28. Breather Chamber Plate
29. Differential Carrier Bearing
30. Differential Carrier
31. Pinion Shaft

95F19419   Courtesy of American Honda Motor Co., Inc.

Fig. 40: Exploded View Of Differential Assembly

6) Remove pinion collar and oil seal. Remove pin from end of drive pinion. Tap drive pinion out of the front pinion bearing. Remove drive pinion, pinion spacer and thrust washers. See Fig. 40.

7) Inspect pinion bearings. If replacing pinion bearing on drive pinion, use press and bearing remover to press bearing from drive pinion. Remove thrust shim from drive pinion.

NOTE: If pinion bearings are replaced, bearing races must also be replaced.

8) Use a hammer and drift to remove pinion bearing races from differential case. Remove thrust washer, located below bearing race, from differential case. See Fig. 40.

9) Inspect differential carrier bearings. If replacing differential carrier bearings, use press and bearing remover to press bearing from differential carrier.

NOTE: If differential carrier bearings are replaced, bearing races must also be replaced.

10) Use a hammer and drift to remove differential carrier bearing races. Remove thrust shim, located below bearing race, from differential case or differential case cover. See Fig. 40.

NOTE: Thrust shim must be replaced if bearing race was removed from differential case or differential case cover.

NOTE: Pinion gear backlash must be checked. Differential carrier bearings must be removed from differential carrier to measure pinion gear backlash.

11) Mount differential carrier in "V" blocks with axle shaft and intermediate shaft inserted into side gears. See Fig. 41. Using dial indicator, check pinion gear backlash. Pinion gear backlash should be .002-.012" (.05-.30 mm).

12) If pinion gear backlash is not within specification, replace differential carrier as an assembly. Remove bolts and ring gear from differential carrier in crisscross pattern.

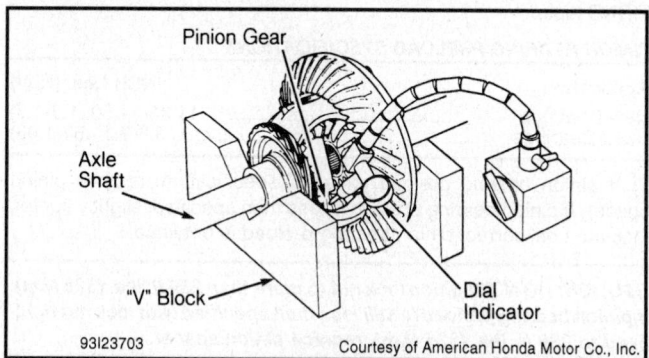

Fig. 41: Checking Pinion Gear Backlash

Cleaning & Inspection – Clean components with solvent and dry with compressed air. Inspect components for damage. Replace components if damaged.

Reassembly – 1) Install ring gear on differential carrier. Install and tighten ring gear bolts to specification in a crisscross pattern. See TORQUE SPECIFICATIONS. Using press, press NEW differential carrier bearings on differential carrier (if removed).

2) If installing bearing races for drive pinion in differential case, install thrust washer, located behind bearing race, in differential case. Use Shaft (07MAF-SP0013A) and Bearing Race Installer "A" (07MAF-SP0011A) and "B" (07MAF-SP0012A) to install bearing races. See Fig. 42.

3) Install bearing races for drive pinion in differential case, starting with outer bearing race (lock nut side) and then the inner bearing race.

CAUTION: Heating differential case to 212°F (100°C) will assist in bearing race installation. DO NOT exceed 212°F (100°C) or differential case may be damaged.

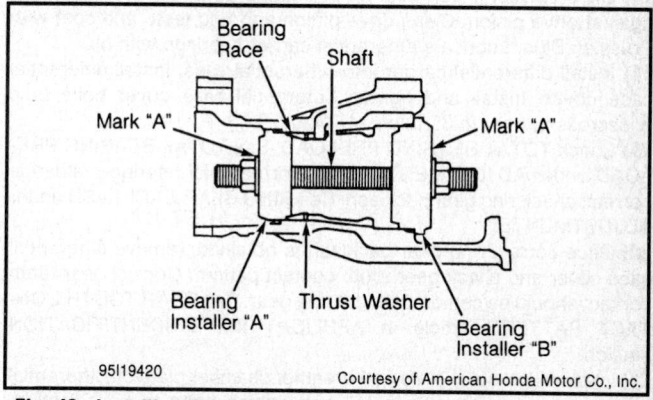

Fig. 42: Installing Bearing Race
(Outer Race Shown; Inner Race Is Similar)

4) If installing bearing races for differential carrier bearings, install NEW thrust shim in differential case or differential case cover. Ensure thrust shim is the same thickness as thrust shim that was removed. Using hammer and bearing race installer, drive bearing race into differential case and differential case cover.

5) If original drive pinion and ring gear are being installed, install original thickness thrust shim on drive pinion (if removed). If NEW drive pinion and ring gear are being installed, proper thickness thrust shim must be determined to obtain correct drive pinion height. See DRIVE PINION HEIGHT under ADJUSTMENTS.

6) If installing pinion bearing on drive pinion, ensure thrust shim is installed on drive pinion. Using press, old pinion spacer and bearing installer, press pinion bearing onto drive pinion. Lubricate all pinion bearings with oil.

7) Install drive pinion in differential case. DO NOT install pinion spacer and thrust washers at this time. Install pinion bearing on drive pinion.

8) Using hammer and bearing installer, drive outer pinion bearing onto drive pinion while supporting drive pinion. Install pin in drive pinion. Install pinion collar. Ensure groove in pinion collar aligns with pin in drive pinion.

9) Apply light coat of hypoid gear oil on threads on drive pinion. Install spring washer and lock nut on drive pinion. Tighten lock nut to 15 ft. lbs. (20 N.m). DO NOT overtighten lock nut or pinion bearings may be damaged. Clean drive pinion and ring teeth and coat with Prussian Blue.

10) Lubricate differential carrier bearings with oil. Install differential carrier into differential case. Install differential case cover. Install and tighten differential case cover bolts in a crisscross pattern to 35 ft.lbs. (47 N.m).

11) Install Shaft (07HAJ-PK40201) in differential assembly. Rotate ring gear one full revolution in both directions while applying resistance on pinion shaft.

12) Remove differential cover and inspect ring gear tooth contact pattern. Correct gear tooth contact pattern should be centered on the ring gear. See GEAR TOOTH CONTACT PATTERN article in APPLICATIONS & IDENTIFICATION section.

13) If gear tooth contact pattern is incorrect, drive pinion height must be changed to correct gear tooth contact pattern. Change thrust shim located below bearing on drive pinion to adjust drive pinion height.

14) If gear tooth contact pattern is correct, remove components from drive pinion for installation of pinion spacer. Install NEW pinion spacer and thrust washers on drive pinion.

15) Install outer pinion bearing on drive pinion. Using hammer and bearing installer, drive outer pinion bearing onto drive pinion while supporting drive pinion. Using hammer and oil seal installer, install NEW oil seal for drive pinion.

16) Install pin in drive pinion. Install pinion collar. Install NEW spring washer and NEW lock nut. Ensure spring washer is installed with raised area toward the lock nut. Check pinion bearing preload. See PINION BEARING PRELOAD under ADJUSTMENTS.

17) Once correct pinion bearing preload is obtained, stake lock nut against drive pinion. Clean drive pinion and ring teeth and coat with Prussian Blue. Lubricate differential carrier bearings with oil.

18) Install differential carrier into differential case. Install differential case cover. Install and tighten differential case cover bolts in a crisscross pattern to 35 ft.lbs. (47 N.m).

19) Check TOTAL BEARING PRELOAD. See TOTAL BEARING PRELOAD under ADJUSTMENTS. Once correct total bearing preload is correct, check ring gear backlash. See RING GEAR BACKLASH under ADJUSTMENTS.

20) Once correct ring gear backlash is obtained, remove differential case cover and check gear tooth contact pattern. Correct gear tooth contact should be centered on the ring gear. See GEAR TOOTH CONTACT PATTERN article in APPLICATIONS & IDENTIFICATION section.

21) Install oil collector plate and breather chamber plate on differential case cover (if removed). Install and tighten bolts to specification. Stake heads of bolts against differential case cover.

22) Apply Liquid Gasket (08718-0001) on differential case cover-to-differential case sealing surfaces. Install differential case cover. Install and tighten bolts to specification in a crisscross pattern.

23) Using hammer and oil seal installer, install NEW oil seal in differential case and differential case cover. Install oil cooler and NEW "O" ring. Install and tighten bolts to specification. Using hammer and oil seal installer, install NEW pinion collar seal.

ADJUSTMENTS

DRIVE PINION HEIGHT

NOTE: If drive pinion and ring gear are replaced, drive pinion height must be set. Drive pinion height may also need to be set if incorrect gear tooth contact pattern exists.

1) Drive pinion height is controlled by thickness of thrust shim located between rear pinion bearing and drive pinion. When installing used drive pinion and ring gear and gear tooth contact pattern is incorrect, see GEAR TOOTH CONTACT PATTERN article in APPLICATIONS & IDENTIFICATION section to determine if thrust shim should be thicker or thinner.

2) When installing NEW drive pinion and ring gear, calculate thrust shim thickness by noting etched mark located on side of drive pinion. *See Fig. 43.*

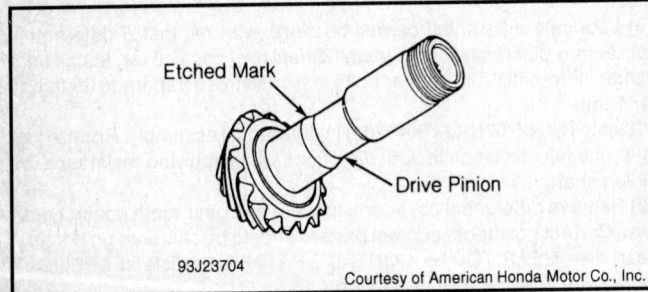

93J23704 — Courtesy of American Honda Motor Co., Inc.

Fig. 43: Identifying Drive Pinion Markings

3) Etched mark indicate with a (+) positive or (-) negative mark along with a numerical digit to indicate drive pinion size. Etched mark is positive or negative in thousandths of a millimeter.

NOTE: Etched mark is indicated in thousandths of a millimeter. If etched mark is -20, this would be a negative .02 mm.

4) If etched mark on old drive pinion is positive, add it to the old thrust shim thickness. If etched mark on old drive pinion is negative, subtract it from the old thrust shim thickness.

5) If etched mark on NEW drive pinion is positive, subtract it from thrust shim thickness obtained in step **4)**. If etched mark on NEW drive pinion is negative, add it to thrust shim thickness obtained in step **4)**.

6) For example; if old thrust shim thickness is 1.30 mm and old drive pinion etched mark is +20 (.02 mm) and NEW drive pinion etched mark is -20 (.02mm), replacement thrust shim thickness should be 1.34 mm.

7) Select thrust shim that is closest to, but not more than, the determined thrust shim thickness. Thrust shims are available in thickness from .047-.064" (1.18-1.63 mm) in .001" (.03 mm) increments. Part numbers are 41381-PW5-000 to 41396-PW5-000. See DRIVE PINION THRUST SHIMS table.

DRIVE PINION THRUST SHIMS

Thrust Shim I.D. Letter	Part Number	Thickness In. (mm)
A	41381-PW5-000	1.18 (.047)
B	41382-PW5-000	1.21 (.048)
C	41383-PW5-000	1.24 (.049)
D	41384-PW5-000	1.27 (.050)
E	41385-PW5-000	1.30 (.051)
F	41386-PW5-000	1.33 (.052)
G	41387-PW5-000	1.36 (.054)
H	41388-PW5-000	1.39 (.055)
I	41389-PW5-000	1.42 (.056)
J	41390-PW5-000	1.45 (.057)
K	41391-PW5-000	1.48 (.058)
L	41392-PW5-000	1.51 (.059)
M	41393-PW5-000	1.54 (.061)
N	41394-PW5-000	1.57 (.062)
O	41395-PW5-000	1.60 (.063)
P	41396-PW5-000	1.63 (.064)

PINION BEARING PRELOAD

1) Tighten drive pinion lock nut to 188 ft. lbs. (255 N.m). Install a dial-type INCH-lb. torque wrench on end of drive pinion. Rotate drive pinion and note pinion bearing preload. Pinion bearing preload should be within specification. See PINION BEARING PRELOAD SPECIFICATIONS table.

PINION BEARING PRELOAD SPECIFICATIONS

Application	INCH Lbs. (N.m)
New Bearings	11.30-14.80 (1.3-1.7)
Used Bearings	5.6-9.1 (.64-1.03)

2) If pinion bearing preload exceeds specification, replace pinion spacer. If pinion bearing preload is less than specified, slightly tighten lock nut until correct pinion bearing preload is obtained.

CAUTION: DO NOT tighten lock nut to more than 239 ft. lbs. (325 N.m). If pinion bearing preload is still less than specified with lock nut tightened to 239 ft. lbs. (325 N.m), replace pinion spacer.

TOTAL BEARING PRELOAD

1) With differential fully assembled, install Shaft (07HAJ-PK40201) in differential assembly. Rotate ring gear one full revolution in both directions while applying resistance on drive pinion. Remove shaft from differential assembly.

2) Install a dial-type INCH-lb. torque wrench on end of drive pinion. Rotate drive pinion and note total bearing preload. Total bearing preload should be within specification. See TOTAL BEARING PRELOAD SPECIFICATIONS table.

TOTAL BEARING PRELOAD SPECIFICATIONS

Application	INCH Lbs. (N.m)
New Bearings	
All New Bearings	22.40-28.63 (2.58-3.30)
Differential Carrier Bearings Only	
Outer Bearing (Ring Gear Side) Only	16.80-23.00 (1.93-2.65)
Inner Bearing (Drive Pinion Side) Only	19.20-24.72 (2.21-2.85)
Used Bearings	13.53-19.10 (1.56-2.20)

3) If total bearing preload is not within specification, increase preload by increasing thickness of thrust shim located below bearing races in differential case and differential case cover.

CAUTION: Ensure thrust shim thickness is increased the same amount on both thrust shims.

RING GEAR BACKLASH

1) Mount differential assembly in soft-jawed vice. Remove side plug and seal washer from differential case cover. *See Fig. 40.* Remove oil seal from differential case cover. Align differential carrier rib with side plug hole.

2) Install Shaft (07HAJ-PK40201) in differential assembly. *See Fig. 38.* Mount dial indicator on differential case cover.

3) Measure ring gear backlash in 3 different locations on differential carrier. Ring gear backlash should be .002-.004" (.04-.10 mm) and maximum variation in ring gear backlash readings should not exceed .0015" (.040 mm).

4) If ring gear backlash is within specification, proper thickness thrust shims are installed behind bearing races for differential carrier bearings provided no components are changed.

5) If ring gear backlash exceeds specification, decrease thrust shim thickness on thrust shim located behind bearing race in differential case. Increase thickness of thrust shim in differential case cover the same amount.

6) If ring gear backlash is less than specified, increase thrust shim thickness on thrust shim located behind bearing race in differential case. Decrease thickness of thrust shim in differential case cover the same amount.

7) Thrust shims are available in thickness from .0657-.0941" (1.67-2.39 mm) in .0012" (.03 mm) increments. Part numbers are 41402-PW8-010 to 41426-PW8-010. One shim is available at .0260" (.660 mm), part number is 41401-PW8-010.

TORQUE SPECIFICATIONS

TORQUE SPECIFICATIONS

Application	Ft. Lbs. (N.m)
Control Shaft Lock Bolts	10 (14)
Countershaft Lock Nut	101 (137)
Differential Assembly Drain Plug	33 (44)
Differential Assembly Mounting Bolt	
Lower 12-mm Mounting Bolt	55 (75)
Upper Mounting Bolt	
6-mm Bolt	[1]
12-mm Bolt	55 (75)
Differential Assembly Oil Filler Plug	33 (44)
Differential Case Cover Bolt	35 (47)
Drive Pinion Lock Nut [2]	188-239 (255-325)
Joint Bolt	21 (28)
Mainshaft Lock Nut	101 (137)
Mount Bracket Bolt	40 (54)
Oil Cooler Bolt	
6-mm Bolt	[1]
8-mm Bolt	20 (27)
Oil Pump Body Bolt	
6-mm Bolt	[1]
8-mm Bolt	13 (18)
Parking Brake Roller Guide Bolt	22 (29)
Pressure Tap Plug	13 (18)
Rear Cover Sealing Bolt	15 (20)
Ring Gear Bolt	100 (135)
Sealing Bolt	59 (80)
Secondary Driven Gear Sealing Bolt	20 (15)
Side Plug	33 (44)
Transaxle Drain Plug	36 (49)
Transaxle Housing Bolt [3]	
8-mm Bolt	24 (33)
10-mm Bolt	33 (44)
Transaxle Mount Bolt	47 (64)
Wheel Lug Nut	80 (109)

[1] – Tighten bolt to 106 INCH lbs. (12.0 N.m).
[2] – Pinion bearing preload is adjusted when tightening lock nut. See PINION BEARING PRELOAD under ADJUSTMENTS for adjusting procedure.
[3] – Tighten bolts to specification in sequence. *See Fig. 36.*

TORQUE SPECIFICATIONS (Cont.)

Application	INCH Lbs. (N.m)
A/T Gear Position Switch Bolt	106 (12.0)
Breather Chamber Plate Bolt	106 (12.0)
Control Shaft Collar Bolt	124 (14.0)
Countershaft Speed Sensor Bolt	106 (12.0)
Detent Lever Bolt	124 (14.0)
Dipstick Tube Bolt	106 (12.0)
Flange Nut	53 (6.0)
Fluid Strainer Bolt	106 (12.0)
Harness Cover Bolt	106 (12.0)
Linear Solenoid Assembly Flange Nuts	53 (6)
Lower Valve Body Assembly Bolt	106 (12.0)
Main Valve Body Cover Bolt	106 (12.0)
Main Valve Body Cover Plate Bolt	106 (12.0)
Mainshaft Speed Sensor Bolt	106 (12.0)
Oil Collector Plate Bolt	106 (12.0)
Oil Pan Bolt	106 (12.0)
Oil Pass Body Bolt	106 (12.0)
Parking Brake Stopper Bolt	124 (14.0)
Rear Cover Bolt	106 (12.0)
Regulator Valve Body Valve Cover Bolt	71 (8)
Regulator Valve Body Bolt	106 (12.0)
Regulator Valve Body Lock Bolt	106 (12.0)
Reverse Idler Gear Shaft Holder Bolt	106 (12.0)
Servo Body Bolt	106 (12.0)
Servo Detent Base Bolt	106 (12.0)
Shift Control Solenoid Valve Assembly Bolt	106 (12.0)
Shift Control Solenoid Valve Harness Bolt	106 (12.0)
Shift Fork Bolt	124 (14.0)
Throttle Valve Body Bolt	106 (12.0)
Transaxle Sub-Harness Bolt	106 (12.0)
VSS/Power Steering Sensor Bolt	106 (12.0)
2nd Accumulator Body Bolt	106 (12.0)

[1] – Tighten bolt to 106 INCH lbs. (12.0 N.m).
[2] – Pinion bearing preload is adjusted when tightening lock nut. See PINION BEARING PRELOAD under ADJUSTMENTS for adjusting procedure.
[3] – Tighten bolts to specification in sequence. *See Fig. 36.*

TRANSAXLE SPECIFICATIONS

TRANSAXLE SPECIFICATIONS

Application	Specification
Clutch Clearance	
1st Clutch	.026-.033" (.65-.85 mm)
1st-Hold Clutch	.031-.039" (.80-1.00 mm)
2nd, 3rd & 4th Clutches	.022-.030" (.55-.75 mm)
Differential Assembly Ring	
Gear Backlash	.002-.004" (.04-.10 mm)
Gear Clearance	
Countershaft 4th Gear Clearance	.003-.006" (.07-.15 mm)
Mainshaft 2nd Gear Clearance	.003-.006" (.07-.15 mm)
Oil Pump Clearance	
Side Clearance	
Oil Pump Drive Gear	.0083-.0104" (.210-.265 mm)
Oil Pump Driven Gear	.0028-.0049" (.070-.125 mm)
Thrust Clearance	
Standard	.001-.002" (.03-.05 mm)
Wear Limit	.0028" (.070 mm)
Pinion Gear Backlash	.002-.012" (.05-.30 mm)
Secondary Gear	
Bearing Preload [1]	20-29 INCH lbs. (2.3-3.3 N.m)

[1] – This is the starting torque required to rotate secondary gear in both directions.

WIRING DIAGRAMS

For appropriate wiring diagram, see ACURA M1WA ELECTRONIC CONTROLS article.

2.5TL

APPLICATION

APPLICATION

Vehicle	Transaxle Model
1995-96 2.5TL	M1WA

CAUTION: Vehicle is equipped with a Supplemental Restraint System (SRS). When servicing vehicle, use care not to cause accidental air bag deployment. All SRS electrical connections and wiring harness have Yellow insulation. Related components are located in steering column, center console, instrument panel and lower panel on instrument panel. DO NOT use electrical test equipment on these circuits. It may be necessary to deactivate SRS before servicing components. See AIR BAG SERVICING article in APPLICATIONS & IDENTIFICATIONS

NOTE: If negative battery cable is to be disconnected, obtain radio anti-theft code from customer. Radio anti-theft code must be reset into radio once negative battery cable is reconnected. To reset radio anti-theft code, turn radio on. When the word "CODE" is displayed on radio, enter code by using the radio station preset buttons.

DESCRIPTION

Automatic transaxle is electronically controlled. Transaxle shifting and torque converter lock-up are controlled by Transmission Control Module (TCM). The TCM receives information from various input devices and uses this information to control linear solenoid along with shift and lock-up control solenoid valves.

Transaxle is equipped with shift and key interlock systems. Shift interlock system prevents shift lever from being moved from Park unless brake pedal is depressed and accelerator pedal is in idle position. In case of a malfunction, shift lever can be released by placing ignition key in key release slot near shift lever. Key interlock system prevents ignition key from being removed from ignition lock assembly unless shift lever is in Park.

The A/T gear position indicator on instrument panel contains lights to indicate position A/T gear position switch, on shift lever, is in.

OPERATION

A/T GEAR POSITION INDICATOR

With ignition in RUN or START position, voltage is supplied to A/T gear position indicator, located on instrument panel. *See Fig. 1.* When shift lever is moved to designated gear position, A/T gear position switch completes the ground circuit for A/T gear position indicator on instrument panel. The light on A/T gear position indicator will be illuminated to indicate shift lever gear position. The A/T gear position switch is mounted on side of transaxle. *See Fig. 5.*

When headlights are turned on, voltage is supplied on Red/Black wire terminal on A/T gear position indicator. This changes light illumination from fixed illumination to being controlled by the dash light dimmer input on the Red wire.

SHIFT & KEY INTERLOCK SYSTEMS

Shift Interlock System – Shift interlock system prevents shift lever from being moved from Park unless brake pedal is depressed and accelerator pedal is in idle position. Shift lever cannot be moved from Park if brake and accelerator pedal are depressed at the same time. In case of a malfunction, shift lever can be released by placing ignition key in key release slot near shift lever.

Voltage is supplied to shift lock solenoid when ignition is in RUN or START position. When brake pedal is depressed, brakelight switch supplies voltage to TCM, provided accelerator pedal is in idle position. With accelerator pedal in idle position, a voltage signal is delivered

between Throttle Position (TP) sensor and TCM. TCM then provides voltage to shift lock circuit in the interlock control unit. When A/T gear position switch is in Park, interlock control unit then operates shift lock solenoid by controlling the ground circuit. When shift lock solenoid is energized, shift lever is released and can be moved. If a shift interlock system malfunction occurs, shift lever can be released by placing ignition key in key release slot near shift lever and pushing down.

Shift lock solenoid is located on driver's side of shift lever. *See Fig. 2.* Interlock control unit is located behind passenger's side of instrument panel and contains an 8-pin electrical connector. *See Fig. 3.* The A/T gear position switch is mounted on side of transaxle. *See Fig. 5.*

Key Interlock System – Key interlock system prevents ignition key from being removed from ignition lock assembly on steering column unless shift lever is in Park. Voltage is provided to key interlock switch from No. 30 (20-amp) fuse in engine compartment fuse box, located at passenger's front corner of engine compartment. When ignition key is in ignition lock assembly, key interlock switch closes, providing voltage to key interlock solenoid and interlock control unit.

If shift lever is not in Park, interlock control unit energizes key interlock solenoid by completing ground circuit. When key interlock solenoid is energized, ignition key cannot be removed from ignition lock assembly. Key interlock switch and solenoid are located on ignition lock assembly. *See Fig. 2.* Interlock control unit is located behind driver's side of instrument panel and contains an 8-pin electrical connector. *See Fig. 3.*

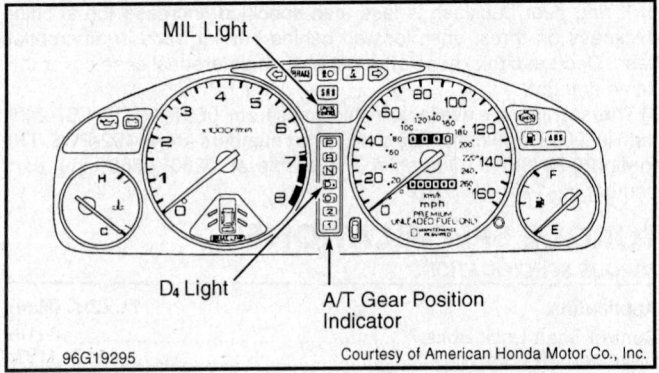

Fig. 1: Identifying A/T Gear Position Indicator & MIL Light

96G19295   Courtesy of American Honda Motor Co., Inc.

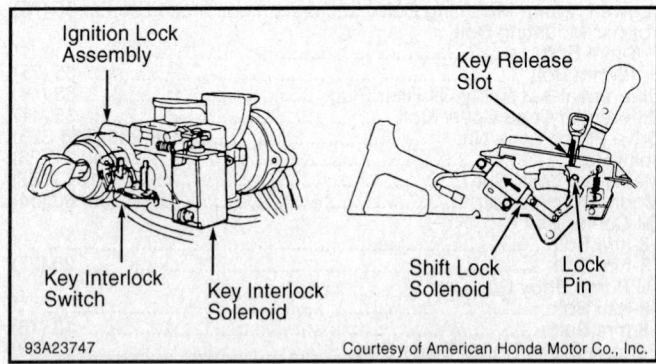

Fig. 2: Identifying Key Interlock Solenoid & Shift Lock Solenoid

93A23747   Courtesy of American Honda Motor Co., Inc.

TRANSMISSION CONTROL MODULE

The Transmission Control Module (TCM) receives information from various input devices and uses this information to control linear solenoid, shift and lock-up control solenoid valves. *See Fig. 4.* The TCM contains self-diagnostic system, which stores fault code if failure or problem exists in transaxle electronic control system. Fault code may also be referred to as Diagnostic Trouble Code (DTC) or flash code. DTC or flash code may be retrieved to determine transaxle problem area. See SELF-DIAGNOSTIC SYSTEM. The TCM is located behind glove box and contains 26-pin and 22-pin Gray electrical connectors. *See Fig. 3.*

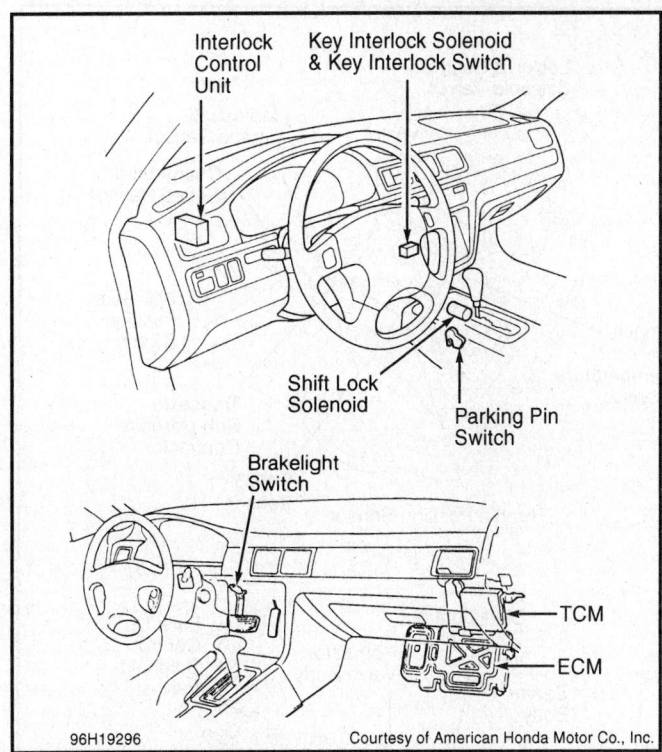

Fig. 3: Identifying Interlock Control Unit, TCM & ECM

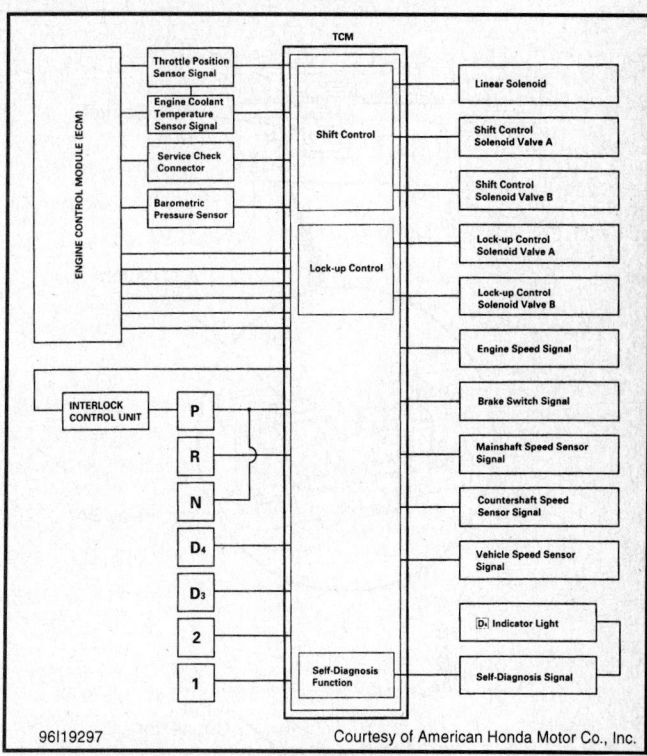

Fig. 4: Identifying Input & Output Devices

TCM INPUT DEVICES

Barometric Pressure Sensor (Baro) Signal – The Baro sensor delivers input signal to TCM to indicate manifold pressure. The Baro sensor is located in driver's side front corner of engine compartment. *See Fig. 5.*

Brakelight Switch Signal – Brakelight switch delivers input signal to TCM, indicating vehicle braking. Brakelight switch is located on brake pedal support. *See Fig. 3.*

Engine Coolant Temperature (ECT) Sensor Signal – ECT sensor delivers input signal to TCM, indicating engine coolant temperature. Engine coolant temperature sensor is located in thermostat housing and contains a Yellow/Green wire and Green/White wire in the electrical connector. *See Fig. 5.*

Countershaft Speed Signal – Countershaft speed sensor delivers a countershaft speed signal to the TCM. Countershaft speed sensor is the lower sensor located on the transaxle. *See Fig. 5.*

Engine RPM – Engine RPM signal is delivered to TCM from ignition coil.

Mainshaft Speed Signal – Mainshaft speed sensor delivers a mainshaft speed signal to the TCM. Mainshaft speed sensor is the upper sensor located on the transaxle. *See Fig. 5.*

Engine Control Module (ECM) – An upshift and downshift comparative signal and shift acknowledge signal is delivered between ECM and TCM. A 5-volt reference signal is delivered between ECM and TCM. The ECM is located below carpet on passenger's side, near the kick panel. *See Fig. 3.*

Service Check Connector – Service check connector is used when retrieving flash codes for transaxle electronic control system diagnosis. When jumper wire is installed between service check connector electrical terminals, an input is delivered to the TCM to display flash codes on the "D₄" indicator light on A/T gear position indicator on instrument panel. Service check connector is a 2-pin Blue colored electrical connector, located under passenger's side of instrument panel. *See Fig. 6.*

Gear Shift Position Signal – Gear Shift position signal is delivered to TCM by the A/T gear position switch, mounted on side of transaxle. *See Fig. 5.*

Throttle Position (TP) Sensor – Throttle Position (TP) Sensor delivers input signal to TCM to indicate throttle plate angle. TP sensor is mounted on throttle body. *See Fig. 5.*

Vehicle Speed Signal (VSS) – Vehicle speed signal is delivered to TCM by Vehicle Speed Sensor (VSS). The VSS is located on the transaxle. *See Fig. 5.*

TCM OUTPUT DEVICES

Shift Control Solenoid Valves – The TCM controls transaxle shifting by delivering an output signal to shift control solenoid valves "A" and "B". Solenoid valves are operated in accordance with gear position. See SHIFT CONTROL SOLENOID VALVE OPERATION table. Shift control solenoid valves are located on top of lower valve body assembly in the transaxle. *See Fig. 5.* Shift control solenoid valve "A" has a Pink wire and solenoid valve "B" has a Yellow wire at the solenoid valve electrical connector.

SHIFT CONTROL SOLENOID VALVE OPERATION

Shift Lever Position	Solenoid Valve "A"	Solenoid Valve "B"
"1" (1st Gear)	On	Off
"2" (2nd Gear)	On	On
"D₄" Or "D₃" (1st Gear)	Off	On
"D₄" Or "D₃" (2nd Gear)	On	On
"D₄" Or "D₃" (3rd Gear)	On	Off
"D₄" (4th Gear)	Off	Off
"R" (Reverse)	On	Off

Lock-Up Control Solenoid Valves – The TCM controls torque converter lock-up by delivering an output signal to lock-up control solenoid valves "A" and "B". Lock-up control solenoid valves are activated in accordance with lock-up condition. See LOCK-UP CONTROL SOLENOID VALVE OPERATION table. Lock-up solenoid valves are located on top of transaxle. *See Fig. 5.* Lock-up control solenoid valve "A" has a Brown wire and solenoid valve "B" has a Gray wire at the solenoid valve electrical connector.

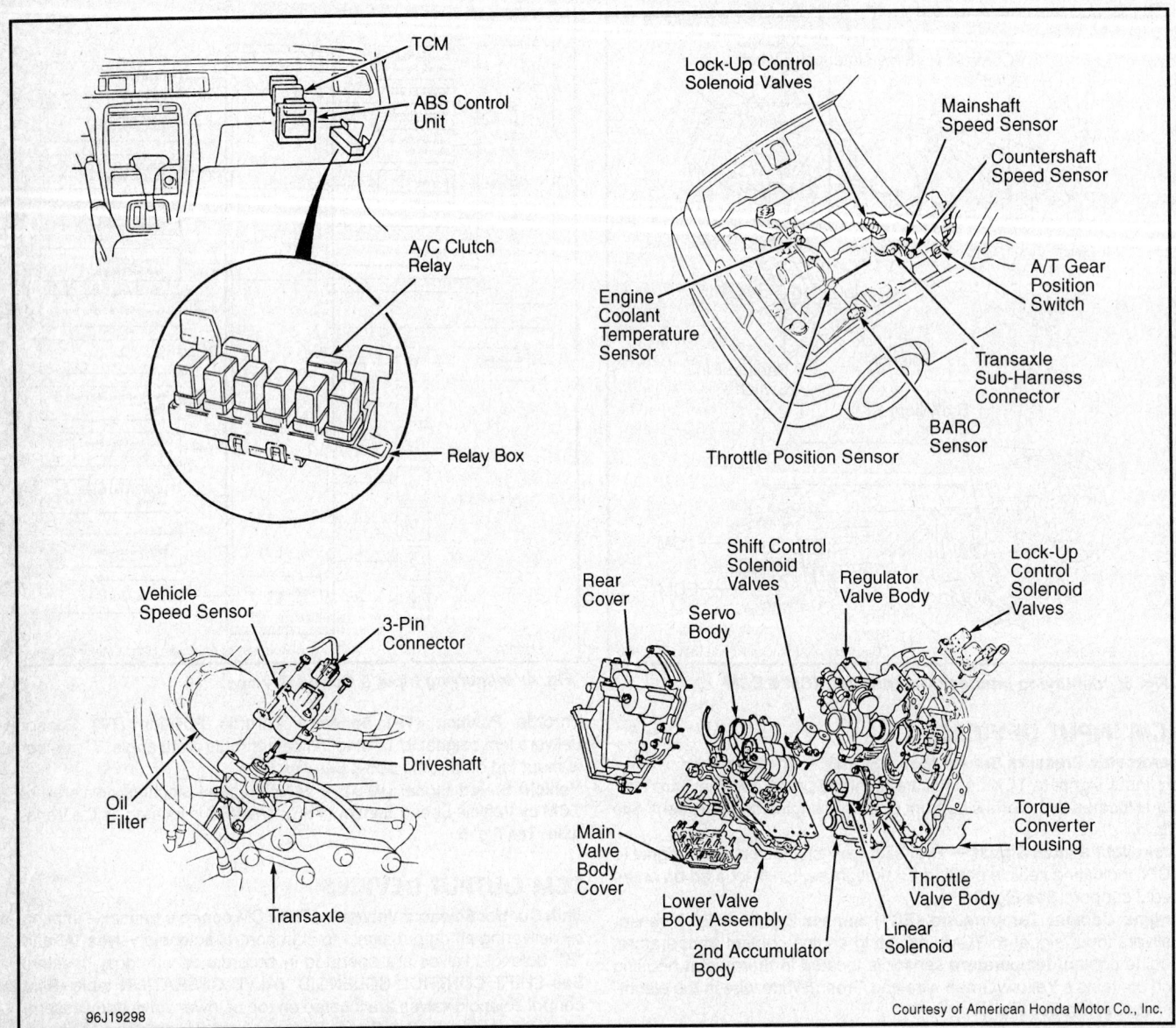

96J19298

Courtesy of American Honda Motor Co., Inc.

Fig. 5: Identifying TCM Input & Output Device Locations

LOCK-UP CONTROL SOLENOID VALVE OPERATION

Lock-Up Condition	Solenoid Valve "A"	Solenoid Valve "B"
No Lock-Up	Off	Off
Slight Lock-Up	On	Off
Half Lock-Up	On	On
Full Lock-Up	On	On
Lock-Up During Deceleration	On	[1]

[1] – Solenoid valve will cycle on and off.

Interlock Control Unit – When A/T gear position switch is in Park, TCM provides voltage to shift lock circuit in the interlock control unit, provided brake pedal is depressed and accelerator pedal is in idle position. Interlock control unit is located under left side of instrument panel. Interlock control unit then operates shift lock solenoid by controlling the ground circuit. When shift lock solenoid is energized, shift lever is released and can be moved.

Linear Solenoid – The TCM controls transaxle shifting related to engine torque by delivering an output signal to operate linear solenoid. Linear solenoid operates throttle valve on throttle valve body. Linear solenoid is located on throttle valve body. See Fig. 5. Linear solenoid

is connected to transaxle sub-harness located on side of transaxle. Linear solenoid has a Red and White wire at transaxle sub-harness electrical connector.

Self-Diagnosis Indicator – If an abnormality exists in transaxle electronic control system and DTC is stored, PCM will deliver an output signal (flash code) to turn on and blink "D₄" light. The "D₄" light is located on the A/T gear position indicator on instrument panel. See Fig. 1. Flash code can be retrieved to identify problem area by installing jumper wire between service check connector terminals. DTC "P" code can be retrieved to identify problem area using scan tool. Flash codes will be displayed by blinking "D₄" light.

SELF-DIAGNOSTIC SYSTEM

NOTE: Flash Codes can be retrieved on all years/models but are the only codes available on 1995 models.

SYSTEM DIAGNOSIS

TCM monitors transaxle operation. TCM contains a self-diagnostic system which stores a DTC if a transaxle electronic control system failure or problem exists. If DTC is stored, TCM will turn on and blink "D₄" light on A/T gear position indicator on instrument panel. If a transaxle electronic control system failure or problem is suspected and "D₄" light on A/T gear position indicator does not flash, perform diagnostic circuit check to ensure proper operation of "D₄" light. See DIAGNOS- TIC CHARTS. DTC can be retrieved using scan tool at Data Link Con- nector (DLC) located behind ashtray. Flash code may also be retrieved for diagnosing transaxle electronic control system.

RETRIEVING DTCS & FLASH CODES

NOTE: During diagnostics, ensure "D₄" indicator light on A/T gear position indicator on instrument panel is not turned on by a fault in the PGM-FI system. The PGM-FI system controls the fuel injection system. To repair PGM-FI system, see appropriate SELF-DIAGNOS- TICS article in ENGINE PERFORMANCE in appropriate MITCHELL® manual.

NOTE: Before clearing codes, obtain radio anti-theft code from customer. Note radio preset stations, as radio stations and clock set- ting will be cleared and must be reset. Radio anti-theft code must be reset for radio operation.

Retrieving DTCs Using Scan Tool – 1) If DTC exists, "D₄" light on A/T gear position on instrument panel will blink when ignition is turned on. To retrieve DTC using scan tool, turn ignition off.
2) Connect scan tool to 16-pin Data Link Connector (DLC) located behind ashtray. Turn ignition on. Scan tool will indicate DTCs. Follow scan tool manufactures instructions.
3) Once DTC is obtained, turn ignition off. Determine probable cause and symptom. See DTC/FLASH CODE IDENTIFICATION table. If any other DTCs except those listed are displayed, see appropriate SELF- DIAGNOSTICS article in ENGINE PERFORMANCE in appropriate MITCHELL® manual. For trouble shooting of DTCs, see DIAGNOSTIC CHARTS. If "D₄" light does not flash or stays on, see appropriate "D₄" light diagnostic chart.
Retrieving Flash Codes Using "D₄" Light – 1) If flash code exists, "D₄" light on A/T gear position indicator on instrument panel will blink when ignition is turned on. To retrieve flash code, turn ignition off.
2) Install jumper wire between service check connector electrical ter- minals. Service check connector is a 2-pin Blue colored electrical con- nector, located under passenger's side of instrument panel. See Fig. 6.
3) Turn ignition on. Flash codes will be displayed by short and long blinks of "D₄" light on A/T gear position indicator on instrument panel. If the Malfunction Indicator Light (MIL) is also flashing, see appropri- ate SELF-DIAGNOSTICS article in ENGINE PERFORMANCE in appropriate MITCHELL® manual. Repair MIL light codes first.
4) A short blink indicates a single digit flash code. A long blink equals 10 short blinks. For example, if "D₄" light blinks once, this is a Flash Code No. 1. If "D₄" light blinks one long blink and then 4 short blinks, this is a Flash Code No. 14. See Fig. 7.

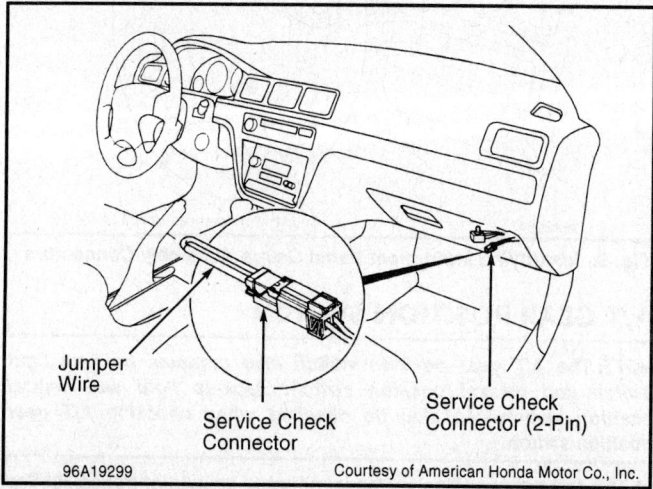

96A19299   Courtesy of American Honda Motor Co., Inc.

Fig. 6: Identifying Service Check Connector & Installing Jumper Wire

5) Once flash code is obtained, turn ignition off. Remove jumper wire from service check connector. Determine probable cause and symptom. See DTC/FLASH CODE IDENTIFICATION table. If any oth- er flash codes except those listed are displayed, TCM is defective. For trouble shooting of flash codes, see DIAGNOSTIC CHARTS.

NOTE: If customer describes symptoms for DTC P01790/Flash Code No. 3 and "D₄" indicator light is off or DTC P01706/Flash Code No. 6 or DTC P0725/Flash Code No. 11, it may be necessary to test drive vehicle to recreate the symptom and then check for trouble code with ignition still on.

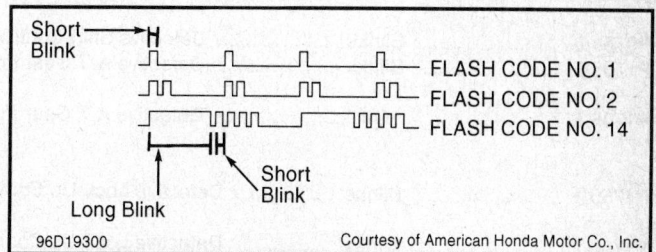

96D19300   Courtesy of American Honda Motor Co., Inc.

Fig. 7: Identifying Fault Code Displays

CLEARING FAULT CODES

NOTE: TCM memory can NOT be cleared using scan tool, the follow- ing procedure must be used. Before clearing fault codes, obtain radio anti-theft code from customer. Note radio preset stations, as radio stations and clock setting will be cleared and must be reset. Radio anti-theft code must be reset for radio operation.

1) Once repairs have been performed, DTC/flash codes must be cleared from TCM memory. Ensure ignition is off. Remove BACK UP RADIO (10-amp) fuse in engine compartment fuse box for 10 seconds. *See Fig. 8.* Engine compartment fuse box is located at passenger's front corner of engine compartment. This clears the TCM memory.
2) Reinstall fuse. To reset radio anti-theft code, turn ignition and radio on. When the word "CODE" is displayed on radio, reset radio anti-theft code by using the radio station preset buttons. Reset clock and radio stations.
3) TCM memory must be reset for idle control. Drive vehicle for several minutes over 30 MPH. Recheck for DTCs.

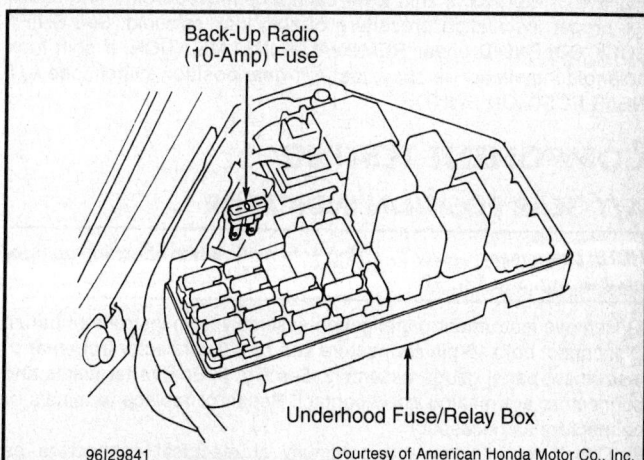

96I29841   Courtesy of American Honda Motor Co., Inc.

Fig. 8: Locating Back-Up Radio Fuse

SYSTEM TESTING

SHIFT & KEY INTERLOCK SYSTEMS

NOTE: For system testing, refer to wiring schematic when checking component wiring. See Fig. 15. To check individual components, see COMPONENT TESTING.

DTC/FLASH CODE IDENTIFICATION

DTC/Flash Code [1] Number	Indicator Light [2] Condition	Probable [3] Cause	Symptom
P0715/15	Off	Defective Mainshaft Speed Sensor	Transaxle Jerks Hard When Shifting
P0720/9	Blinks	Defective Countershaft Speed Sensor	Lock-Up Clutch Does Not Engage
P0725/11	Off	Defective Ignition Coil	Lock-Up Clutch Does Not Engage
P0730	Off	Defective Shift Control System	Fails To Shift, Stuck In 1st Or 4th Gears
P0740	Off	Defective Lock-Up Control System	Lock-Up Clutch Does Not Engage Or Remains Engaged, Unstable Engine Idle
P0753/7	Blinks	Defective Shift Control Solenoid "A"	Remains In 4th Gear, Fails To Shift Other Than 1st-4th, 2nd-4th Or 2nd-3rd Gears
P0758/8	Blinks	Defective Shift Control Solenoid "B"	Remains In 1st Or 4th Gear
P1705/5	Blinks	Defective A/T Gear Position Switch	Lock-Up Clutch Does Not Engage, Fails To Shift Other Than 2nd-4th Gears
P1706/6	Off	Defective A/T Gear Position Switch	Lock-Up Clutch Does Not Engage, Lock-Up Clutch Engages & Disengages, Fails To Shift Other Than 2nd-4th Gears
P1753/1	Blinks	Defective Lock-Up Control Solenoid "A"	Lock-Up Clutch Does Not Engage Or Remains Engaged, Unstable Engine Idle
P1758/2	Blinks	Defective Lock-Up Control Solenoid "B"	Lock-Up Clutch Does Not Engage
P1768/16	Blinks	Defective Linear Solenoid	Transaxle Jerks Hard When Shifting Lock-Up Clutch Does Not Engage
P1786/14	Off	Shorted Or Open FAS Wire (PNK) Between TCM Terminal B19 & ECM, Defective ECM	Transaxle Jerks Hard When Shifting
P1787/18	Off	Shorted Or Open FFS (RED/GRN) Wire Between TCM Terminal A24 & ECM	Lock-Up Clutch Has No Duty Operation
P1790/3	Blinks Or Remains Off	Defective Throttle Position Sensor	Lock-Up Clutch Does Not Engage
P1791/4	Blinks	Defective Vehicle Speed Sensor	Lock-Up Clutch Does Not Engage
P1792/10	Blinks	Defective Engine Coolant Temp. Sensor	Lock-Up Clutch Does Not Engage
P1794/13	Off	Defective Baro Sensor	No Specific Symptoms

[1] – This is the number of blinks from "D₄" light on A/T gear position indicator on instrument panel with jumper wire installed in service check connector. Flash codes can be retrieved on all years/models but are the only codes available on 1995 models.

[2] – This is operation of "D₄" light on A/T gear position indicator on instrument panel.

[3] – Specified component for probable cause. Check wiring and connections for the specified component.

1) To check system operation, ensure shift lever is in Park. Turn ignition on. Depress brake pedal with accelerator pedal in idle position.
2) If shift lock solenoid clicks, system is working properly. If shift lock solenoid fails to click, see INTERLOCK CONTROL UNIT under COMPONENT TESTING. If shift lever cannot be moved from Park, check for proper installation procedure of shift lock solenoid. See SHIFT LOCK SOLENOID under REMOVAL & INSTALLATION. If shift lock solenoid installation is okay, test A/T gear position switch, see A/T GEAR POSITION SWITCH.

COMPONENT TESTING

A/T GEAR POSITION INDICATOR

NOTE: *If necessary, refer to wiring schematic when checking component wiring. See Fig. 12.*

1) Remove instrument panel gauge assembly from instrument panel. Disconnect both 16-pin connectors and 13-pin connector from rear of instrument panel gauge assembly. See Fig. 9. Ensure terminals and connectors are making good contact. Repair or replace terminals or connectors as necessary.
2) Check for voltage and continuity at electrical connectors as specified. See Fig. 10. If necessary to check ground connections G401 or G404, ground connection G401 is located behind driver's side kick panel area, just above hood opening lever. Ground connection G404 is located behind passenger's side kick panel area. See Fig. 11.
3) If necessary to check No. 1 fuse (10-amp) or No. 21 fuse (15-amp), fuses are located in the fuse/relay box behind driver's side kick panel. If necessary to access TCM, the TCM is located behind glove box and contains Gray electrical connectors (26-pin and 22-pin). See Fig. 3.
4) If necessary to access ECM, the ECM is located below carpet on passenger's side, near the kick panel. See Fig. 3.

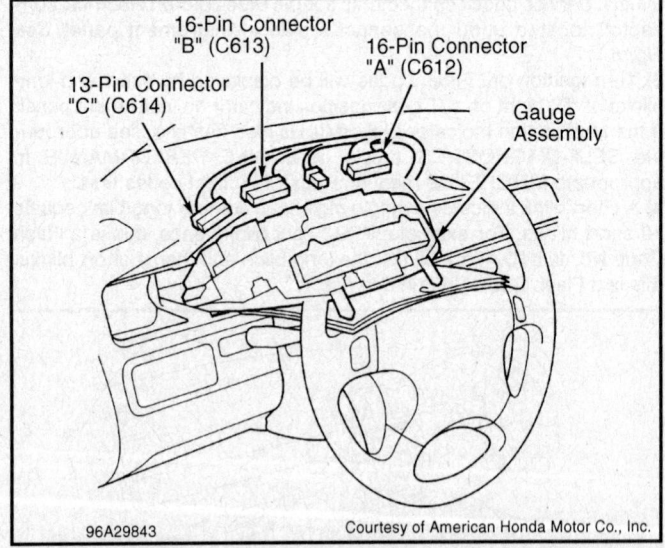

96A29843   Courtesy of American Honda Motor Co., Inc.

Fig. 9: Identifying Instrument Panel Gauge Assembly Connectors

A/T GEAR POSITION SWITCH

NOTE: *The A/T gear position switch also contains back-up light switch and neutral position switch. Back-up light and neutral position switch can also be checked when checking A/T gear position switch.*

1) The A/T gear position switch is mounted on side of transaxle. See Fig. 5. Raise and support vehicle. Remove splash shield located below transaxle.

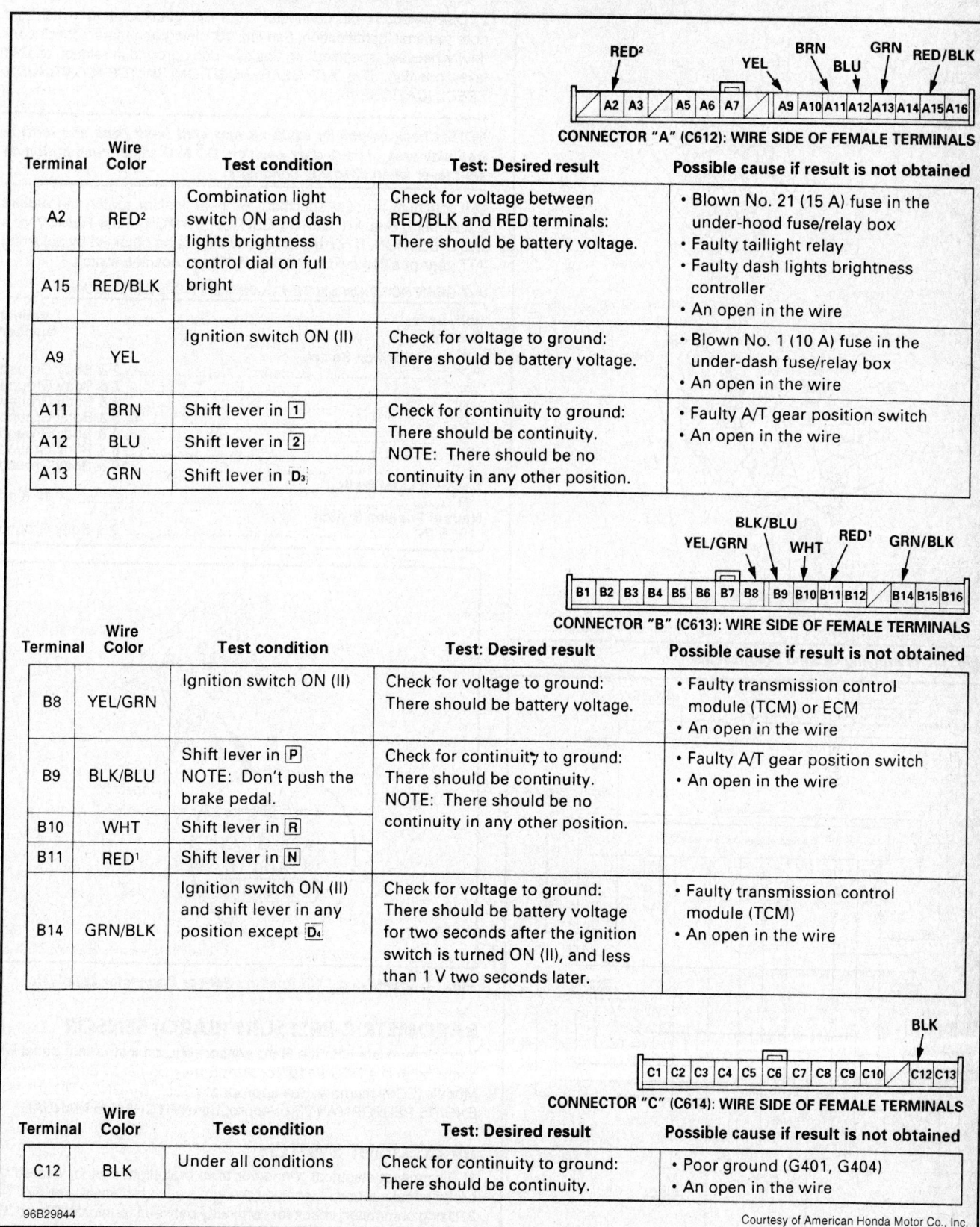

CONNECTOR "A" (C612): WIRE SIDE OF FEMALE TERMINALS

Terminal	Wire Color	Test condition	Test: Desired result	Possible cause if result is not obtained
A2	RED²	Combination light switch ON and dash lights brightness control dial on full bright	Check for voltage between RED/BLK and RED terminals: There should be battery voltage.	• Blown No. 21 (15 A) fuse in the under-hood fuse/relay box • Faulty taillight relay • Faulty dash lights brightness controller • An open in the wire
A15	RED/BLK			
A9	YEL	Ignition switch ON (II)	Check for voltage to ground: There should be battery voltage.	• Blown No. 1 (10 A) fuse in the under-dash fuse/relay box • An open in the wire
A11	BRN	Shift lever in 1	Check for continuity to ground: There should be continuity. NOTE: There should be no continuity in any other position.	• Faulty A/T gear position switch • An open in the wire
A12	BLU	Shift lever in 2		
A13	GRN	Shift lever in D₃		

CONNECTOR "B" (C613): WIRE SIDE OF FEMALE TERMINALS

Terminal	Wire Color	Test condition	Test: Desired result	Possible cause if result is not obtained
B8	YEL/GRN	Ignition switch ON (II)	Check for voltage to ground: There should be battery voltage.	• Faulty transmission control module (TCM) or ECM • An open in the wire
B9	BLK/BLU	Shift lever in P NOTE: Don't push the brake pedal.	Check for continuity to ground: There should be continuity. NOTE: There should be no continuity in any other position.	• Faulty A/T gear position switch • An open in the wire
B10	WHT	Shift lever in R		
B11	RED¹	Shift lever in N		
B14	GRN/BLK	Ignition switch ON (II) and shift lever in any position except D₄	Check for voltage to ground: There should be battery voltage for two seconds after the ignition switch is turned ON (II), and less than 1 V two seconds later.	• Faulty transmission control module (TCM) • An open in the wire

CONNECTOR "C" (C614): WIRE SIDE OF FEMALE TERMINALS

Terminal	Wire Color	Test condition	Test: Desired result	Possible cause if result is not obtained
C12	BLK	Under all conditions	Check for continuity to ground: There should be continuity.	• Poor ground (G401, G404) • An open in the wire

96B29844

Courtesy of American Honda Motor Co., Inc.

Fig. 10: Testing A/T Gear Position Indicator

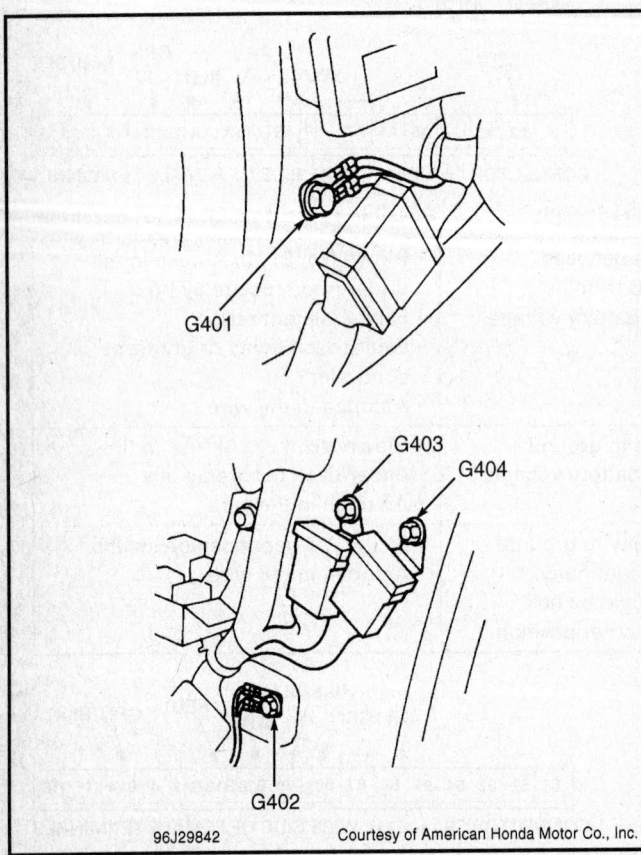

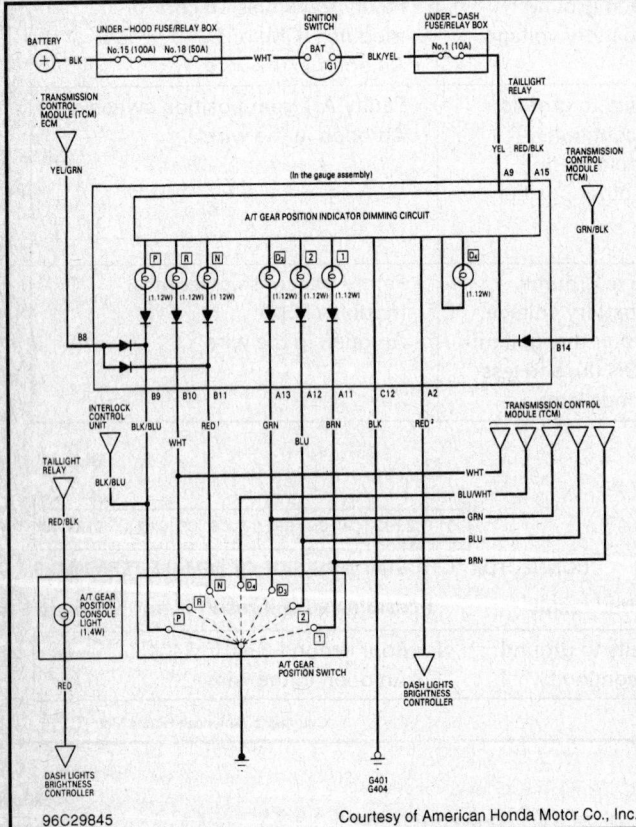

Fig. 11: Identifying Ground Connections

Fig. 12: A/T Gear Position Indicator Wiring Schematic

2) Disconnect 14-pin connector from A/T gear position switch and note terminal identification. *See Fig. 13.* Using ohmmeter, check continuity between specified terminals or body ground in relation to shift lever position. See A/T GEAR POSITION SWITCH CONTINUITY SPECIFICATIONS table.

NOTE: Check continuity while moving shift lever back and forth in free play area of each gear position. DO NOT touch push button on shift lever when checking continuity.

3) If continuity is not as specified, A/T gear position switch may require adjustment. See A/T GEAR POSITION SWITCH under REMOVAL & INSTALLATION. If correct continuity cannot be obtained by adjusting A/T gear position switch, replace A/T gear position switch.

A/T GEAR POSITION SWITCH CONTINUITY SPECIFICATIONS

Shift Lever Position	Terminal Number
A/T Gear Position Switch	
"P"	2 & Body Ground
"R"	7 & Body Ground
"N"	6 & Body Ground
"D$_4$"	8, 5 & Body Ground
"D$_3$"	8, 4 & Body Ground
"2"	11, 8 & Body Ground
"1"	10 & Body Ground
Back-Up Light Switch	
"R"	12 & 14
Neutral Position Switch	
"P" & "N"	9 & Body Ground

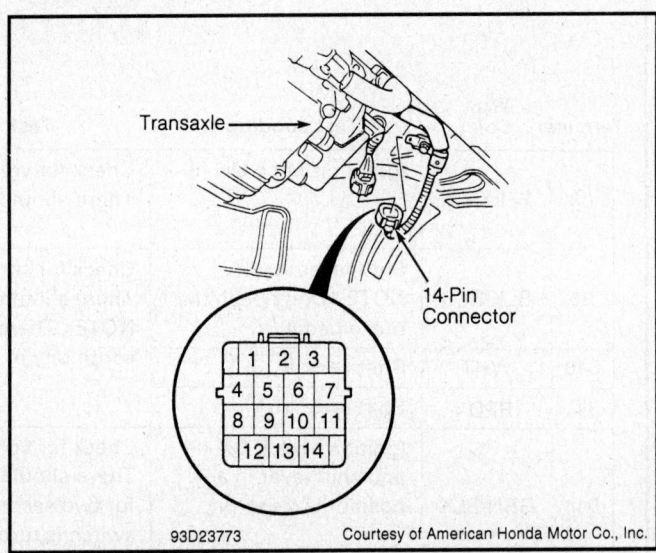

Fig. 13: Identifying Shift Position Sensor Connector Terminals

BAROMETRIC PRESSURE (BARO) SENSOR

If problem exists with the Baro sensor, MIL on instrument panel will come on and a DTC P1107 or P1108 may be set in Engine Control Module (ECM) memory. See appropriate SELF-DIAGNOSTIC article in ENGINE PERFORMANCE of appropriate MITCHELL® MANUAL.

BRAKELIGHT SWITCH

1) Disconnect electrical connector from brakelight switch, located on brake pedal support. Identify brakelight switch terminals. *See Fig. 14.*
2) Using ohmmeter, check for continuity between terminals "B" and "C" with brake pedal depressed. Continuity should exist. Ensure no continuity exists with brake pedal released.
3) If continuity is not as specified, ensure brake pedal is properly adjusted so brakelight switch can obtain proper travel for switch operation. If proper brakelight switch adjustment exists, replace brakelight switch.

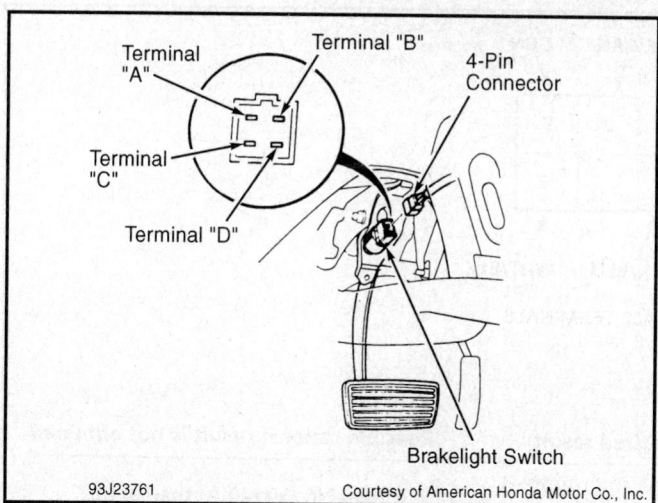

Fig. 14: Identifying Brakelight Switch Terminals

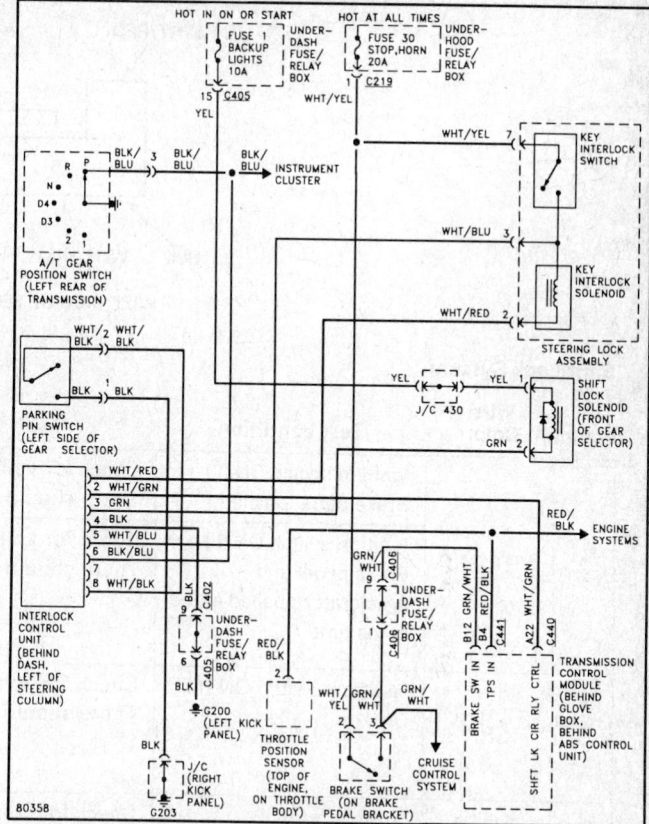

Fig. 15: Shift & Key Interlock System Wiring Schematic

COUNTERSHAFT SPEED SENSOR

Disconnect electrical connector from countershaft speed sensor located on transaxle. See Fig. 5. Using ohmmeter, measure resistance between terminals on electrical connector. Replace countershaft speed sensor if resistance is not 400-600 ohms at 70°F (20°C).

ENGINE COOLANT TEMPERATURE (ECT) SENSOR

1) ECT sensor is located in thermostat housing and contains a Yellow/Green wire in electrical connector. See Fig. 5.
2) Disconnect electrical connector from ECT sensor. Using ohmmeter, check sensor resistance between Yellow/Green wire and ground. Ensure resistance is within specification. See ECT SENSOR RESISTANCE table. Replace ECT sensor if resistance is not as specified.

ECT SENSOR RESISTANCE

Temperature °F (°C)	Resistance (Ohms)
133 (56)	137
185-212 (85-100)	46-30

INTERLOCK CONTROL UNIT

NOTE: It may be necessary to consult wiring schematic when checking any interlock system component wiring. See Fig. 15.

1) Remove lower panel from instrument panel. Disconnect 8-pin connector from interlock control unit. Interlock control unit is located under left side of instrument panel. See Fig. 3. Inspect terminals for corrosion or bending, repair as necessary.
2) Using DVOM, check for continuity or voltage between specified terminals or body ground. See Fig. 16. If necessary to check ground connections G401 or G404, ground connection G401 is located behind driver's side kick panel area, just above hood opening lever. Ground connection G404 is located behind passenger's side kick panel area. See Fig. 11.
3) If necessary to check No. 1 fuse (10-amp), fuse is located in the fuse/relay box behind driver's side kick panel. Fuse No. 30 (20-amp), is located in the fuse/relay box in engine compartment. If necessary to access TCM, the TCM is located behind glove box and contains Gray 26-pin and 22-pin colored electrical connectors. See Fig. 3.

KEY INTERLOCK SOLENOID

1) Remove lower panel from instrument panel. Disconnect 8-pin connector from main wiring harness and note terminal identification. See Fig. 17.

2) Using ohmmeter, check for continuity between designated terminals with ignition lock assembly in ACC position. See KEY INTERLOCK SOLENOID CONTINUITY SPECIFICATIONS table.
3) Replace ignition lock assembly if continuity is not as specified, as key interlock solenoid cannot be serviced separately.

KEY INTERLOCK SOLENOID CONTINUITY SPECIFICATIONS

Ignition Key Position	Continuity Between Terminals
Key Installed	5, 6 & 8
Key Removed	5 & 6

4) Connect battery voltage and ground to terminals "5" and "6". Ensure ignition key cannot be removed with battery voltage applied.
5) If ignition key cannot be removed, key interlock solenoid is okay. If ignition key can be removed, replace ignition lock assembly, as key interlock solenoid cannot be serviced separately.

LINEAR SOLENOID

1) Linear solenoid is located on throttle valve body. Disconnect transaxle sub-harness connector. See Fig. 5.
2) Using ohmmeter, check resistance between Red wire (terminal No. 7) and White wire (terminal No. 8). See Fig. 18.
3) Resistance should be 5.0-5.6 ohms at 70°F (20°C). If resistance is not within specification, disconnect linear solenoid connector from transaxle sub-harness at the transaxle. Note terminal identification on linear solenoid connector.
4) Using ohmmeter, check resistance between terminal "A" (Red wire) and terminal "B" (White wire) of linear solenoid connector. See Fig. 18.
5) Resistance should be 5.0-5.6 ohms at 70°F (20°C). If resistance is okay, replace transaxle sub-harness. Replace linear solenoid if resistance is not within specification.
6) Check linear solenoid operation. Apply positive battery voltage to Red wire terminal and negative battery to White wire terminal of linear solenoid connector.

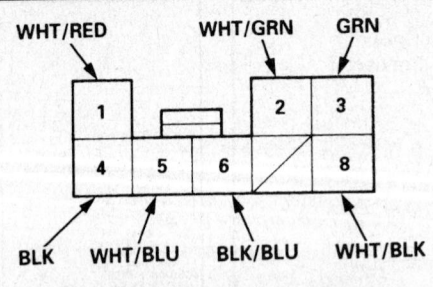

WIRE SIDE OF FEMALE TERMINALS

Shift Lock System

Terminal	Wire Color	Test condition	Test: Desired result	Possible cause if result is not obtained
2	WHT/GRN	Ignition switch ON (II) Brake pedal pushed	Check for voltage to ground: There should be about 12 V.	• Blown No. 30 (20 A) fuse in the under-hood fuse/relay box • Faulty TCM • Faulty brake switch • Faulty throttle position (TP) sensor • An open in the wire
		Ignition switch ON (II) Brake pedal and accelerator pushed at the same time	Check for voltage to ground: There should be 1 V or less.	
3	GRN	Ignition switch ON (II)	Check for voltage to ground: There should be battery voltage.	• Blown No. 1 (10 A) fuse in the under-dash fuse/relay box • Faulty shift lock solenoid • An open in the wire
6	BLK/BLU	Shift lever in P	Check for continuity to ground: There should be continuity.	• Faulty A/T gear position switch • Poor ground • An open in the wire

Key Interlock System

Terminal	Wire Color	Test condition	Test: Desired result	Possible cause if result is not obtained
1	WHT/RED	Ignition switch turned to ACC (I) and key pushed in	Check for voltage to ground: There should be battery voltage.	• Blown No. 30 (20 A) fuse in the under-hood fuse/relay box • Faulty steering lock assembly (key interlock solenoid) • An open in the wire
5	WHT/BLU			
4	BLK	Under all conditions	Check for continuity to ground: There should be continuity.	• Poor ground (G401, G404) • An open in the wire
6	BLK/BLU	Shift lever in P	Check for continuity to ground: There should be continuity.	• Faulty A/T gear position switch • Poor ground • An open in the wire
8	WHT/BLK	Shift lever in P and pushed to the right	Check for continuity to ground: There should be continuity.	• Faulty parking pin switch • Poor ground (G401, G404) • An open in the wire
		Shift lever in P and released	Check for continuity to ground: There should be no continuity.	• Faulty parking pin switch • Short to ground

Courtesy of American Honda Motor Co., Inc.

96C29878

Fig. 16: Testing Interlock Control Unit

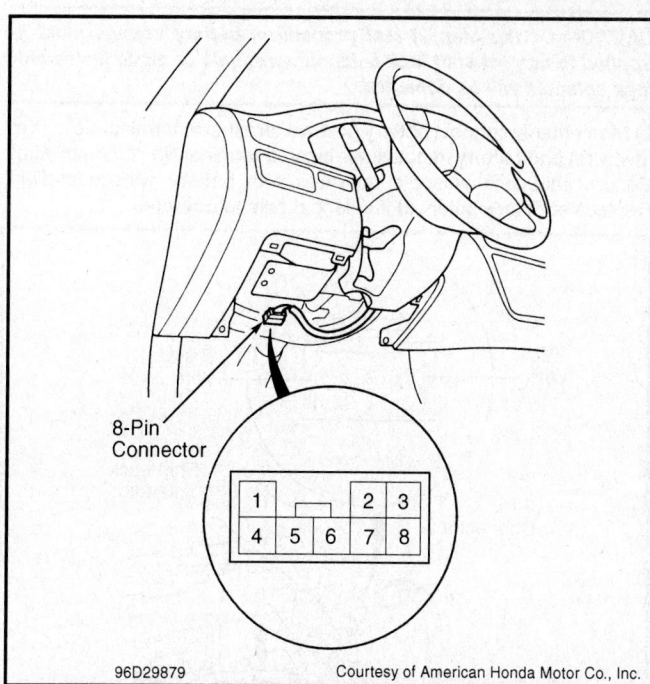

8-Pin Connector

1			2	3
4	5	6	7	8

96D29879   Courtesy of American Honda Motor Co., Inc.

Fig. 17: Identifying Key Interlock Solenoid Connector & Terminals

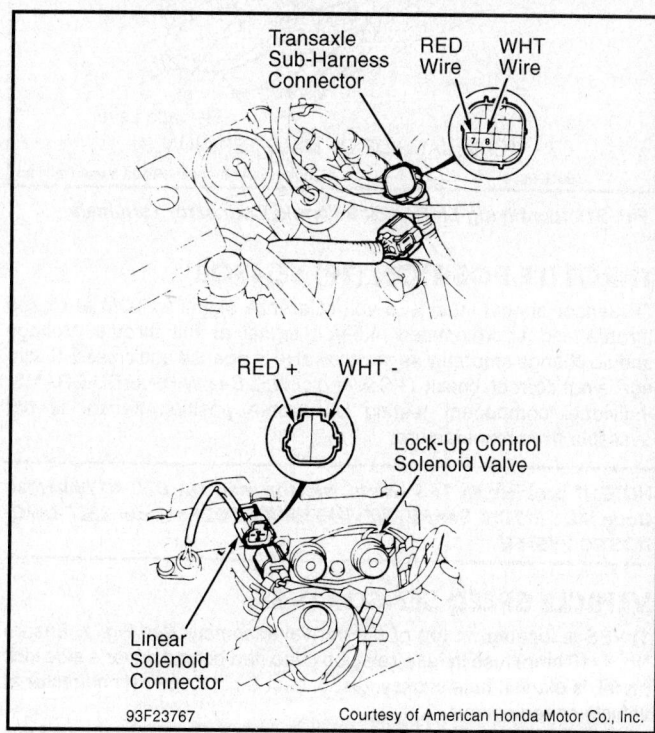

Transaxle Sub-Harness Connector — RED Wire — WHT Wire

RED +   WHT -

Lock-Up Control Solenoid Valve

Linear Solenoid Connector

93F23767   Courtesy of American Honda Motor Co., Inc.

Fig. 18: Identifying Linear Solenoid Terminals

7) Clicking sound should be heard, indicating linear solenoid operation. Replace linear solenoid if solenoid fails to operate.

NOTE: Linear solenoid and throttle valve body must be replaced as an assembly.

LOCK-UP CONTROL SOLENOID VALVES

1) Lock-up control solenoid valves are located on top of transaxle. Disconnect transaxle sub-harness connector. See Fig. 5.

2) Using ohmmeter, check resistance between Brown wire (terminal No. 1) solenoid valve "A" or Gray wire (terminal No. 2) solenoid valve "B" and body ground. See Fig. 19.

3) Resistance should be 14-25 ohms. If resistance is not within specification, disconnect lock-up control solenoid valve connector from transaxle sub-harness at the solenoid valves. Note terminal identification on lock-up control solenoid valve connector.

4) Using ohmmeter, check resistance between terminal No. 1 (solenoid valve "A") or terminal No. 2 (solenoid valve "B") of lock-up control solenoid valve connector and body ground.

5) Resistance should be 14-25 ohms. If resistance is okay, replace transaxle sub-harness. Replace lock-up control solenoid valve assembly if resistance of either solenoid valve is not within specification.

6) Check lock-up control solenoid valve operation. Ensure solenoid valve body is grounded. Apply battery voltage to terminal No. 1 (solenoid valve "A") or terminal No. 2 (solenoid valve "B") of lock-up control solenoid valve connector.

7) Clicking sound should be heard, indicating solenoid valve operation. Replace lock-up control solenoid valve assembly if either solenoid valve fails to operate.

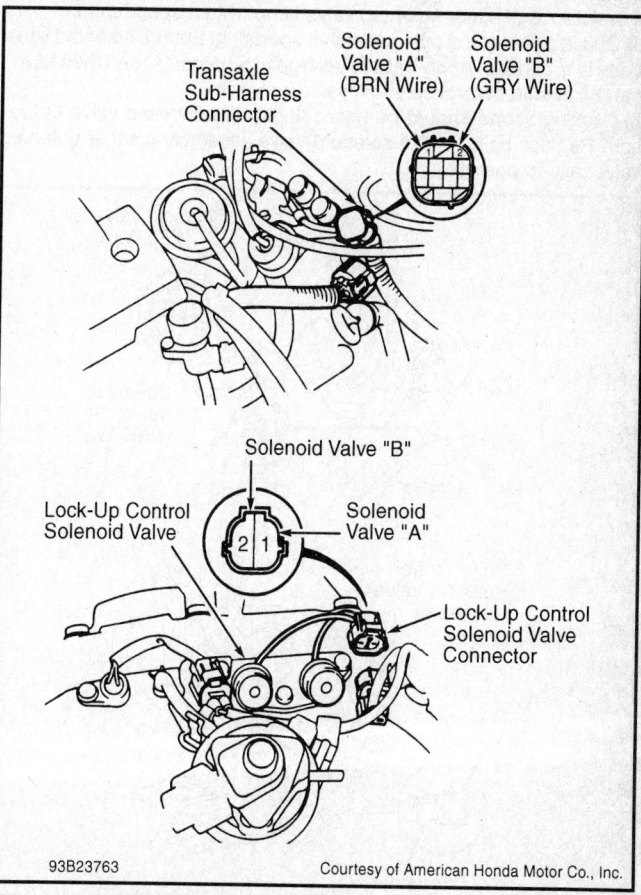

Transaxle Sub-Harness Connector

Solenoid Valve "A" (BRN Wire) — Solenoid Valve "B" (GRY Wire)

Solenoid Valve "B"

Lock-Up Control Solenoid Valve

| 2 | 1 |

Solenoid Valve "A"

Lock-Up Control Solenoid Valve Connector

93B23763   Courtesy of American Honda Motor Co., Inc.

Fig. 19: Identifying Lock-Up Control Solenoid Valve Terminals

MAINSHAFT SPEED SENSOR

Disconnect electrical connector from mainshaft speed sensor located on transaxle. See Fig. 5. Using ohmmeter, measure resistance between terminals on electrical connector. Replace mainshaft speed sensor if resistance is not 400-600 ohms at 70°F (20°C).

PARKING PIN SWITCH

1) Remove center console. Disconnect parking pin switch 2-pin connector. Parking pin switch is located on left side of shifter assembly.

2) Using an ohmmeter, check continuity between parking pin switch terminals. Continuity should exist when shift lever is pushed to right. Continuity should not exist with shift lever in stationary position. If continuity is not as described, replace parking pin switch.

SHIFT CONTROL SOLENOID VALVES

1) Shift control solenoid valves are located on top of lower valve body assembly in transaxle. Disconnect transaxle sub-harness connector. See Fig. 5.

2) Using ohmmeter, check resistance between Yellow wire (terminal No. 3) solenoid valve "B" or Pink wire (terminal No. 4) solenoid valve "A" and body ground. See Fig. 20.

3) Resistance should be 14-25 ohms. If resistance is not within specification, disconnect shift control solenoid valve connector from transaxle sub-harness at the transaxle. Note terminal identification on shift control solenoid valve connector.

4) Using ohmmeter, check resistance between terminal "A" and body ground. Check resistance between terminal "B" and body ground.

5) Resistance should be 14-25 ohms. If resistance is okay, replace transaxle sub-harness. Replace shift control solenoid valve assembly if resistance of either solenoid valve is not within specification.

6) Check shift control solenoid valve operation. Ensure solenoid valve body is grounded. Apply battery voltage to terminal "A" and then terminal "B" of shift control solenoid valve connector.

7) Clicking sound should be heard, indicating solenoid valve operation. Replace shift control solenoid valve assembly if either solenoid valve fails to operate.

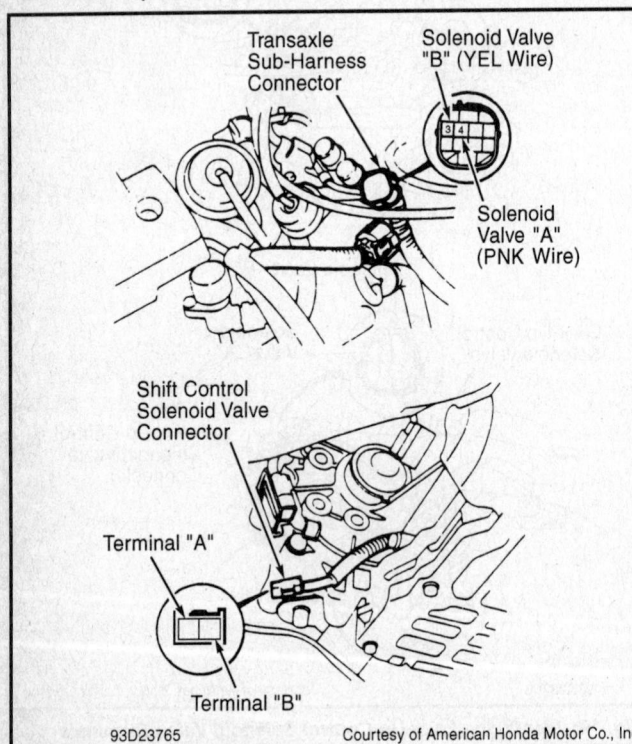

Fig. 20: Identifying Shift Control Solenoid Valve Terminals

SHIFT LOCK SOLENOID

1) Remove center console. Disconnect 2-pin connector at front of shifter assembly from main wiring harness and note terminal identification. See Fig. 21.

CAUTION: *During step 2) test procedure, battery voltage must be applied to correct shift lock solenoid terminals or diode inside shift lock solenoid will be damaged.*

2) Momentarily connect battery positive terminal to terminal No. 1 (Yellow wire) and battery negative terminal to terminal No. 2 (Green wire). Ensure shift lock solenoid operates with battery voltage applied. Replace shift lock solenoid if solenoid fails to operate.

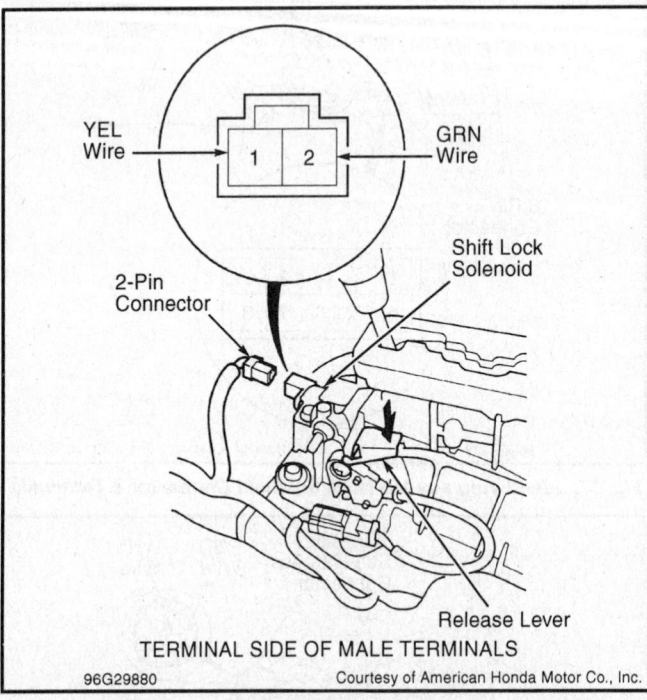

Fig. 21: Identifying Shift Lock Solenoid Connector Terminals

THROTTLE POSITION (TP) SENSOR

TP sensor should input a .5-volt reference signal to TCM at closed throttle and approximately 4.5-volt signal at full throttle. Voltage should change smoothly as throttle valve is opened and closed. If voltage is not correct, check TPS wiring circuit. See WIRING DIAGRAMS. Individual component testing of throttle position sensor is not available from manufacturer.

NOTE: *If problem in TPS exists, sensor may set DTC P1790/Flash Code No. 3 in TCM. See RETRIEVING FAULT CODES under SELF-DIAGNOSTIC SYSTEM.*

VEHICLE SPEED SENSOR (VSS)

1) VSS is located on top of differential assembly. See Fig. 4. Ensure No. 1 (10 amp) fuse in fuse-relay box, located behind driver's side kick panel, is okay. If fuse is okay, disconnect 3-pin electrical connector at vehicle speed sensor.

2) Using ohmmeter, check for continuity between Black wire of 3-pin electrical connector and body ground G101. If continuity exists, go to next step. If continuity does not exist, repair open circuit in Black wire between 3-pin electrical connector and ground G101. Ground connection G101 is located on side of intake manifold chamber. See Fig. 22.

3) Turn ignition on. Using voltmeter, measure voltage between Yellow wire of 3-pin electrical connector and body ground. If battery voltage exists, go to next step. If battery voltage does not exist, repair open Yellow wire.

4) Measure voltage of Orange wire between 3-pin electrical connector and body ground. If voltage is 5 volts or more, go to next step. If voltage is less than 5 volts, repair open circuit or short circuit to ground in Orange wire. The Orange wire goes from VSS to PCM or cruise control unit.

NOTE: Cruise control unit is located below instrument panel on driver's side. See Fig. 23.

5) Turn ignition off. Raise and support vehicle. Place shifter in neutral and turn ignition on. Rotate one front wheel while holding the other front wheel stationary. If voltage pulses from zero volts to about 5 volts, go to next step. If voltage does not pulse correctly, replace vehicle speed sensor.

6) Disconnect instrument cluster 16-pin connector. Measure voltage of Orange wire between instrument cluster 16-pin connector and ground while rotating one front wheel and holding other front wheel stationary. If voltage pulses from zero volts to about 5 volts, replace speedometer. If voltage does not pulse correctly, repair open Orange wire between VSS connector and speedometer.

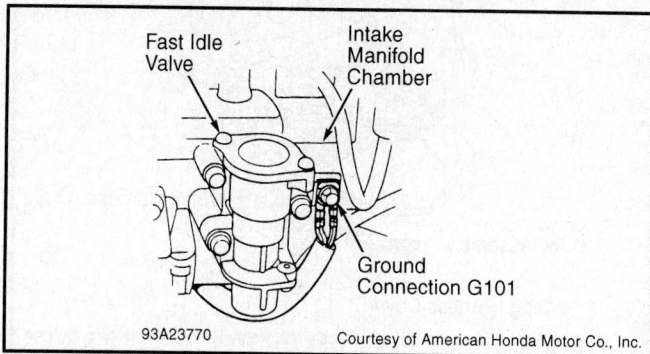

Fig. 22: Identifying Ground Connection

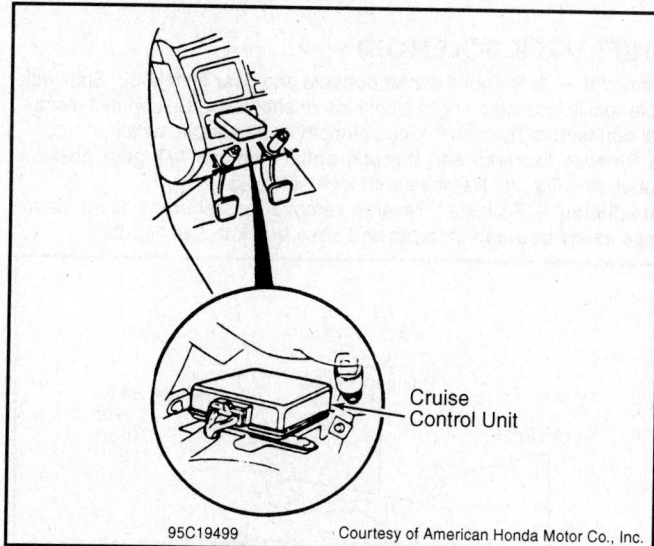

Fig. 23: Identifying Cruise Control Unit

REMOVAL & INSTALLATION

A/T GEAR POSITION SWITCH

Removal – 1) The A/T gear position switch is mounted on driver's side of transaxle. See Fig. 5. Raise and support vehicle. Apply parking brake. Place shift lever in Neutral. Remove A/T gear position switch cover located below transaxle.

2) Disconnect 14-pin electrical connector from A/T gear position switch. Remove bolt retaining wiring harness to rear of transaxle. Remove A/T gear position switch from control shaft on transaxle.

Installation – 1) Ensure shift lever is in Neutral. Align control shaft hole in A/T gear position switch to Neutral position. Control shaft hole should be aligned with index marks. See Fig. 24. A/T gear position switch clicks in "N" position.

2) Install A/T gear position switch on control shaft in transaxle. Install bolts and tighten to specification. See TORQUE SPECIFICATIONS.

3) To check proper adjustment, check shift position sensor for correct continuity in all gears. See A/T GEAR POSITION SWITCH under COMPONENT TESTING.

4) If continuity is not as specified, loosen retaining bolts and slightly rotate A/T gear position switch until proper continuity exists. Install electrical connector and A/T gear position switch cover.

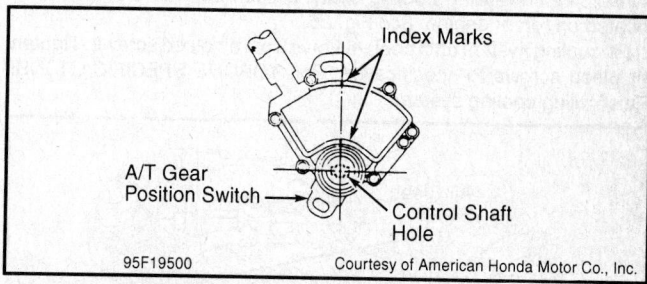

Fig. 24: Installing A/T Gear Position Switch

BAROMETRIC PRESSURE (BARO) SENSOR

Removal & Installation – The Baro sensor is located in driver's side front corner of engine compartment. See Fig. 5. Replacement information not available from manufacturer.

BRAKELIGHT SWITCH

Removal & Installation – 1) Disconnect electrical connector from brakelight switch located on brake pedal support. See Fig. 3. Remove lock nut. Unscrew brakelight switch from brake pedal support.

2) To install, screw brakelight switch inward until brakelight plunger is fully depressed. Back off brakelight switch 1/2 turn. Install and tighten lock nut. Install electrical connector. Ensure brakelights and cruise control operate properly.

COUNTERSHAFT SPEED SENSOR

Removal – 1) Countershaft speed sensor is located on transaxle. See Fig. 25. Raise and support vehicle.

2) Support transaxle with floor jack. Remove transaxle mount and transaxle mount crossmember. Disconnect countershaft speed sensor electrical connector. Remove bolt, countershaft speed sensor and "O" ring.

Installation – To install, reverse removal procedure using NEW "O" ring. Install and tighten bolts to specification. See TORQUE SPECIFICATIONS.

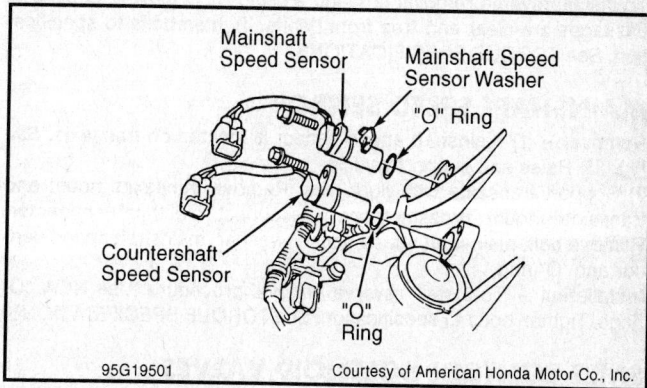

Fig. 25: Identifying Countershaft & Mainshaft Speed Sensors

ENGINE COOLANT TEMPERATURE (ECT) SENSOR

Removal – Engine coolant temperature sensor is located in thermostat housing and contains a Yellow/Green wire and Green/White wire in the electrical connector. *See Fig. 5.* Drain cooling system. Remove sensor.

Installation – 1) Install and tighten engine coolant temperature sensor. When refilling cooling system, open both air bleed screws, located on top of engine. *See Fig. 26.*

2) Fill cooling system until coolant flows from air bleed screws. Tighten air bleed screws to specification. See TORQUE SPECIFICATIONS. Finish filling cooling system.

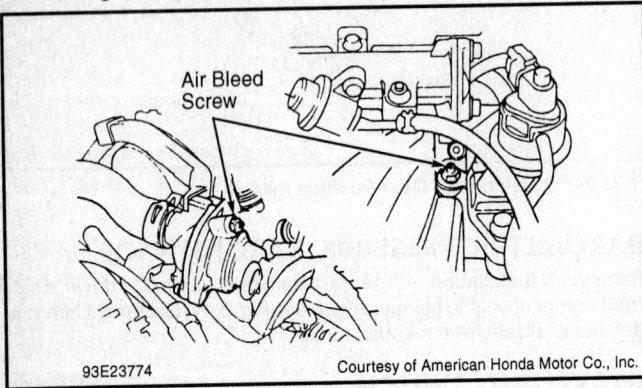

93E23774   Courtesy of American Honda Motor Co., Inc.

Fig. 26: Identifying Air Bleed Screws

KEY INTERLOCK SOLENOID

Removal & Installation – Key interlock solenoid cannot be serviced separately, as entire ignition lock assembly must be replaced.

LINEAR SOLENOID

Removal & Installation – Linear solenoid is located on throttle valve body. *See Fig. 5.* Linear solenoid and throttle valve body must be replaced as an assembly. Transaxle must be disassembled for linear solenoid replacement. See ACURA M1WA overhaul article.

LOCK-UP CONTROL SOLENOID VALVES

Removal & Installation – 1) Lock-up solenoid valves are located on top of transaxle. *See Fig. 5.* Disconnect electrical connector at lock-up control solenoid valves.

2) Remove bolts, lock-up control solenoid valve assembly and gasket. To install, reverse removal procedure using NEW gasket. Ensure oil passages are clear and free from debris. Tighten bolts to specification. See TORQUE SPECIFICATIONS.

MAINSHAFT SPEED SENSOR

Removal – 1) Mainshaft speed sensor is located on transaxle. *See Fig. 25.* Raise and support vehicle.

2) Support transaxle with floor jack. Remove transaxle mount and transaxle mount crossmember. Disconnect electrical connector. Remove bolt, mainshaft speed sensor washer, mainshaft speed sensor and "O" ring.

Installation – To install, reverse removal procedure. Use NEW "O" rings. Tighten bolts to specification. See TORQUE SPECIFICATIONS.

SHIFT CONTROL SOLENOID VALVES

Removal – 1) Shift control solenoid valves are located on top of lower valve body assembly in the transaxle. *See Fig. 27.*

2) Remove lower valve body assembly. See LOWER VALVE BODY ASSEMBLY under REMOVAL & INSTALLATION in ACURA M1WA overhaul article. Remove bolts and wiring harness cover from bottom of lower valve body. Remove bolts, shift control solenoid valve assembly, gasket and filters.

Installation – To install, reverse removal procedure using NEW filters. Ensure filters are installed in proper direction. Ensure oil passages are clear and free from debris. Tighten all bolts to specification. See TORQUE SPECIFICATIONS.

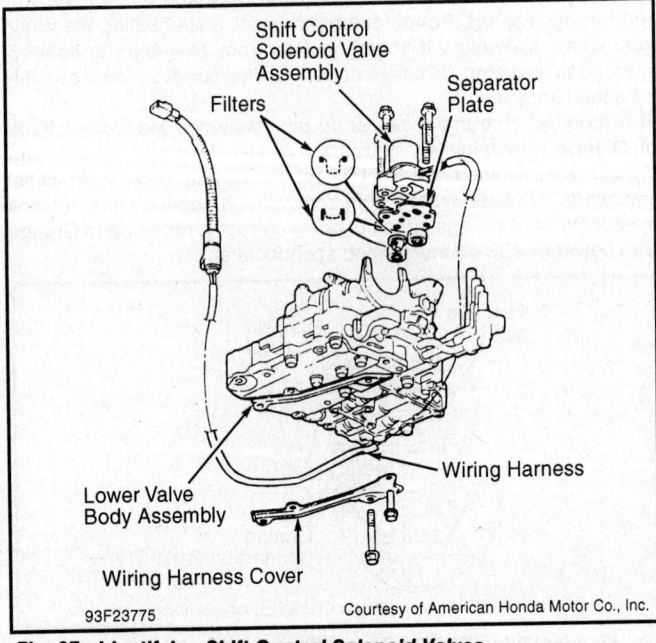

93F23775   Courtesy of American Honda Motor Co., Inc.

Fig. 27: Identifying Shift Control Solenoid Valves

SHIFT LOCK SOLENOID

Removal – 1) Remove center console and gear shift knob. Shift lock solenoid is located on right front side of shift lever. Disconnect electrical connectors from shift lock solenoid and park pin switch.

2) Remove locknuts and through bolts. Remove A/T gear position panel. *See Fig. 28.* Remove shift lock solenoid.

Installation – To install, reverse removal procedure. Ensure clearance exists between stop pin and base bracket. *See Fig. 29.*

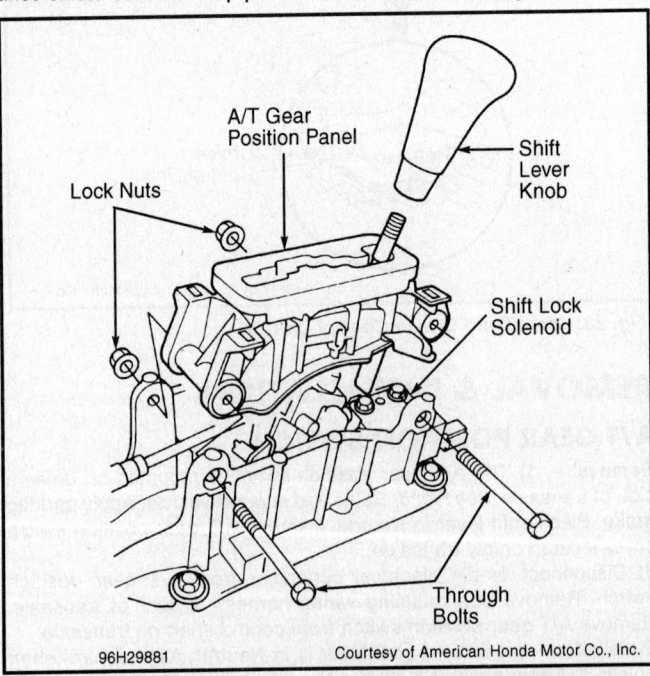

96H29881   Courtesy of American Honda Motor Co., Inc.

Fig. 28: Disassembling Shifter Assembly & Removing Shift Lock Solenoid

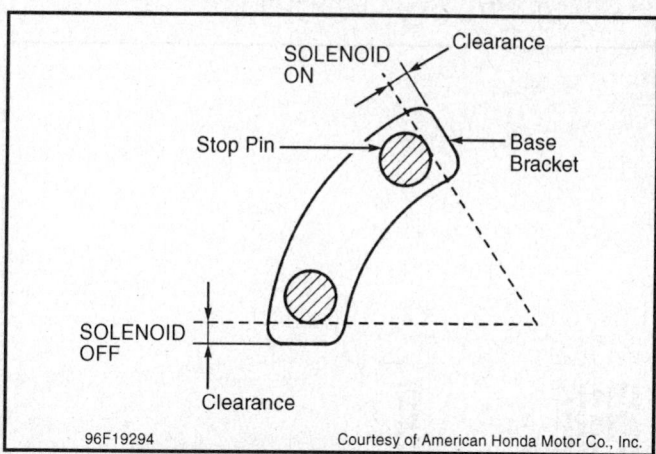

Fig. 29: Checking Stop Pin Clearance

THROTTLE POSITION (TP) SENSOR

Removal & Installation – Throttle position sensor is mounted on side of throttle body. Replacement information is not available from manufacturer.

TRANSMISSION CONTROL MODULE (TCM)

Removal & Installation – 1) The TCM is located behind glove box and contain Gray electrical connectors (26-pin and 22-pin). *See Fig. 3.* Ensure ignition is off. Remove glove box.

2) Remove ABS control unit mounting bolts and turn control unit over. Disconnect radiator fan control module connector on left side. Do not disconnect ABS control unit connectors.

3) Remove TCM bracket and remove TCM from bracket. *See Fig. 5.* To install, reverse removal procedure.

VEHICLE SPEED SENSOR (VSS)

Removal & Installation – 1) Vehicle speed sensor is located on transaxle. *See Fig. 5.* Disconnect 3-pin electrical connector from vehicle speed sensor. Remove bolts and vehicle speed senor.

CAUTION: DO NOT lose driveshaft located below vehicle speed sensor.

---

2) To install, reverse removal procedure. Ensure driveshaft fully engages vehicle speed sensor.

TORQUE SPECIFICATIONS

TORQUE SPECIFICATIONS

Application	Ft. Lbs. (N.m)
Transaxle Mount Bolt	40 (54)
Transaxle Mount Crossmember Bolt	47 (64)

	INCH Lbs. (N.m)
Air Bleed Screw	89 (10.0)
A/T Gear Position Switch Bolt	106 (12.0)
Countershaft Speed Sensor Bolt	106 (12.0)
Lock-Up Control Solenoid Valve Bolt	106 (12.0)
Mainshaft Speed Sensor Bolt	106 (12.0)
Shift Control Solenoid Valve Bolt	106 (12.0)
Shift Lock Solenoid Nut	89 (10.0)
Wiring Harness Cover Bolt	106 (12.0)

DIAGNOSTIC FLOW CHARTS

NOTE: Flash Codes can be retrieved on all years/models but are the only codes available on 1995 models. Diagnostic flow charts are set-up with DTC "P" code, followed by Flash Code number.

How To Use Flow Charts – 1) Use appropriate DTC flow chart corresponding to DTC or flash code. Remove TCM. The TCM is located behind glove box and contain Gray electrical connectors (26-pin and 22-pin). See TRANSMISSION CONTROL MODULE (TCM) under REMOVAL & INSTALLATION. Ensure ignition is off before disconnecting electrical connectors from TCM. *See Fig. 3.*

2) Connectors are referenced as connector 26P and 22P in trouble shooting flow charts. Inspect circuits as instructed in DTC flow chart. Use Digital Volt-Ohmmeter (DVOM) to measure voltage unless instructed otherwise. On some DTC flow charts, technician will be instructed to see if Malfunction Indicator Light (MIL) is blinking. The MIL is located on instrument panel. *See Fig. 1.*

3) If MIL is blinking, PGM-FI system must be checked. See appropriate SELF-DIAGNOSTIC article in ENGINE PERFORMANCE of appropriate MITCHELL® manual.

4) On some fault code charts, technician will be instructed to check A/T gear position indicator. See A/T GEAR POSITION INDICATOR under SYSTEM TESTING.

5) Once all repairs are performed, reinstall connectors and components. Ensure DTC is cleared from TCM memory. See CLEARING FAULT CODES under SELF-DIAGNOSTIC SYSTEM.

NOTE: The following trouble shooting flow charts and illustrations are courtesy of American Honda Motor Co., Inc.

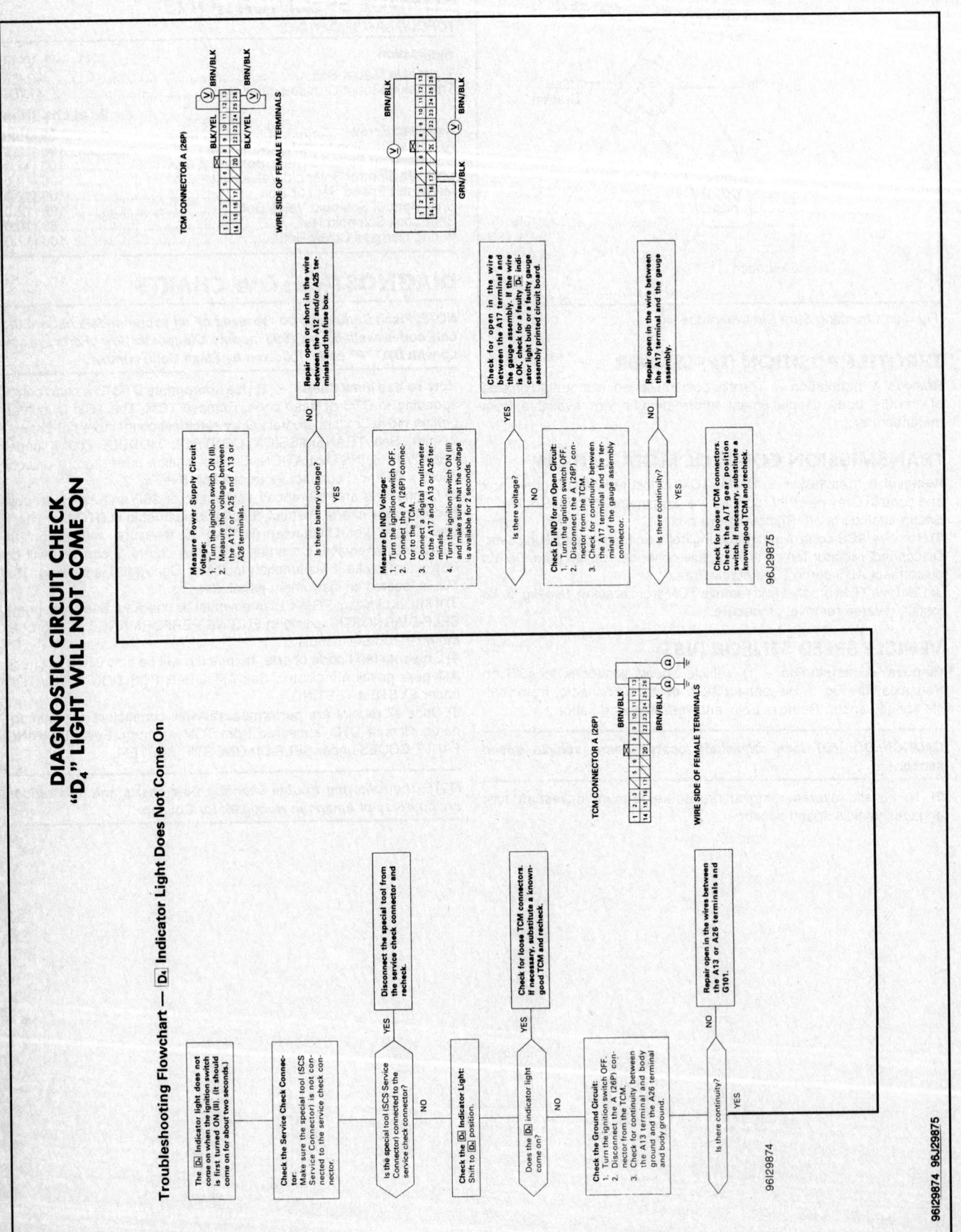

DIAGNOSTIC CIRCUIT CHECK
"D₄" LIGHT WILL NOT COME ON

96J29874   96J29875

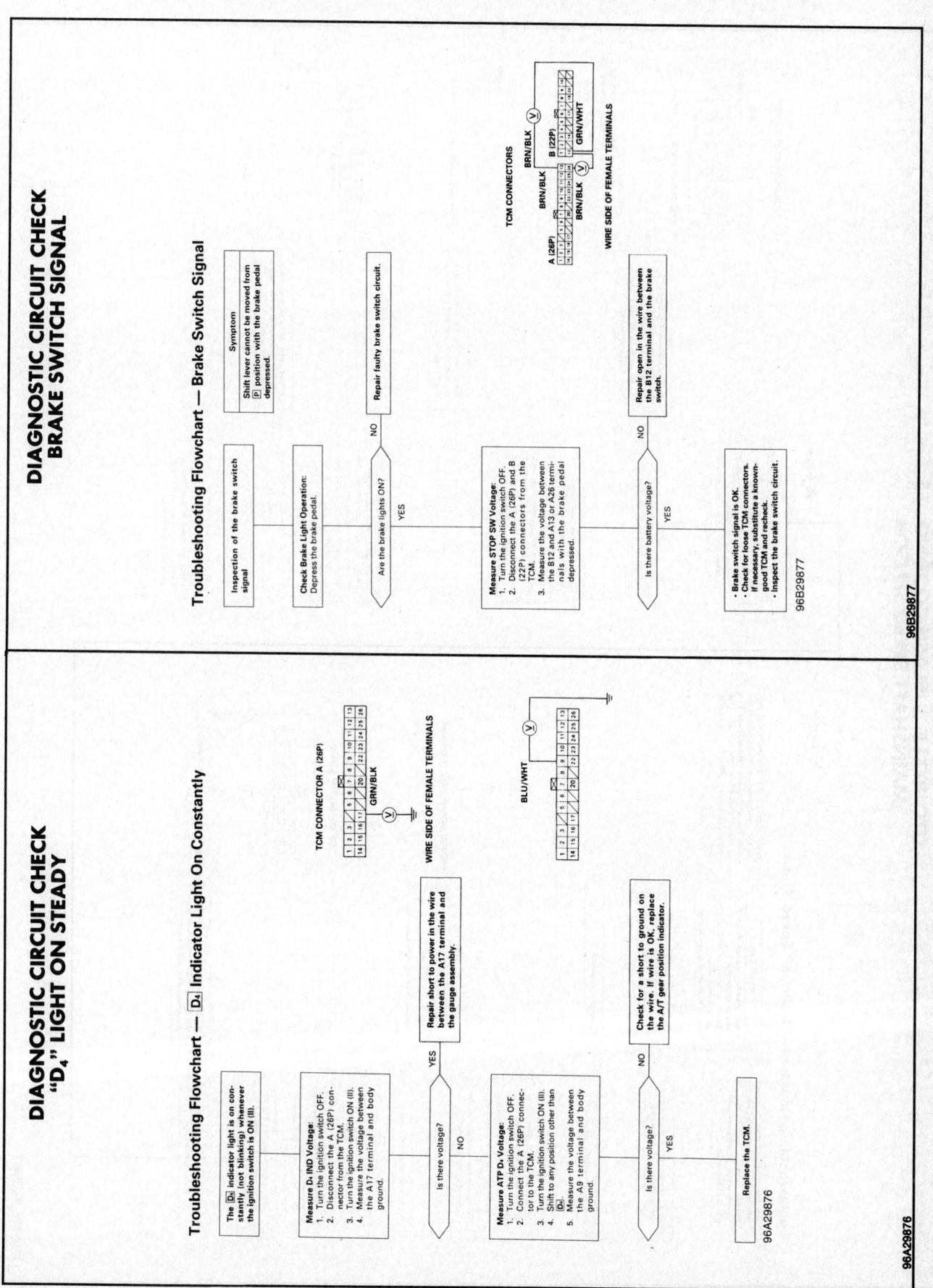

DIAGNOSTIC CIRCUIT CHECK "D₄" LIGHT ON STEADY

Troubleshooting Flowchart — D₄ Indicator Light On Constantly

The D₄ indicator light is on constantly (not blinking) whenever the ignition switch is ON (II).

Measure D₄ IND Voltage:
1. Turn the ignition switch OFF.
2. Disconnect the A (26P) connector from the TCM.
3. Turn the ignition switch ON (II).
4. Measure the voltage between the A17 terminal and body ground.

TCM CONNECTOR A (26P)

GRN/BLK

WIRE SIDE OF FEMALE TERMINALS

Is there voltage?

YES → Repair short to power in the wire between the A17 terminal and the gauge assembly.

NO ↓

Measure ATP D₄ Voltage:
1. Turn the ignition switch OFF.
2. Connect the A (26P) connector to the TCM.
3. Turn the ignition switch ON (II).
4. Shift to any position other than D₄.
5. Measure the voltage between the A9 terminal and body ground.

BLU/WHT

Is there voltage?

NO → Check for a short to ground on the wire. If wire is OK, replace the A/T gear position indicator.

YES ↓

Replace the TCM.

96A29876

DIAGNOSTIC CIRCUIT CHECK BRAKE SWITCH SIGNAL

Troubleshooting Flowchart — Brake Switch Signal

Symptom
Shift lever cannot be moved from P position with the brake pedal depressed.

Inspection of the brake switch signal

Check Brake Light Operation: Depress the brake pedal.

Are the brake lights ON?

NO → Repair faulty brake switch circuit.

YES ↓

Measure STOP SW Voltage:
1. Turn the ignition switch OFF.
2. Disconnect the A (26P) and B (22P) connectors from the TCM.
3. Measure the voltage between the B12 and A13 or A26 terminals with the brake pedal depressed.

TCM CONNECTORS

A (26P)   B (22P)

BRN/BLK   BRN/BLK   GRN/WHT

WIRE SIDE OF FEMALE TERMINALS

Is there battery voltage?

NO → Repair open in the wire between the B12 terminal and the brake switch.

YES ↓

- Brake switch signal is OK.
- Check for loose TCM connectors. If necessary, substitute a known-good TCM and recheck.
- Inspect the brake switch circuit.

96B29877

96B29877

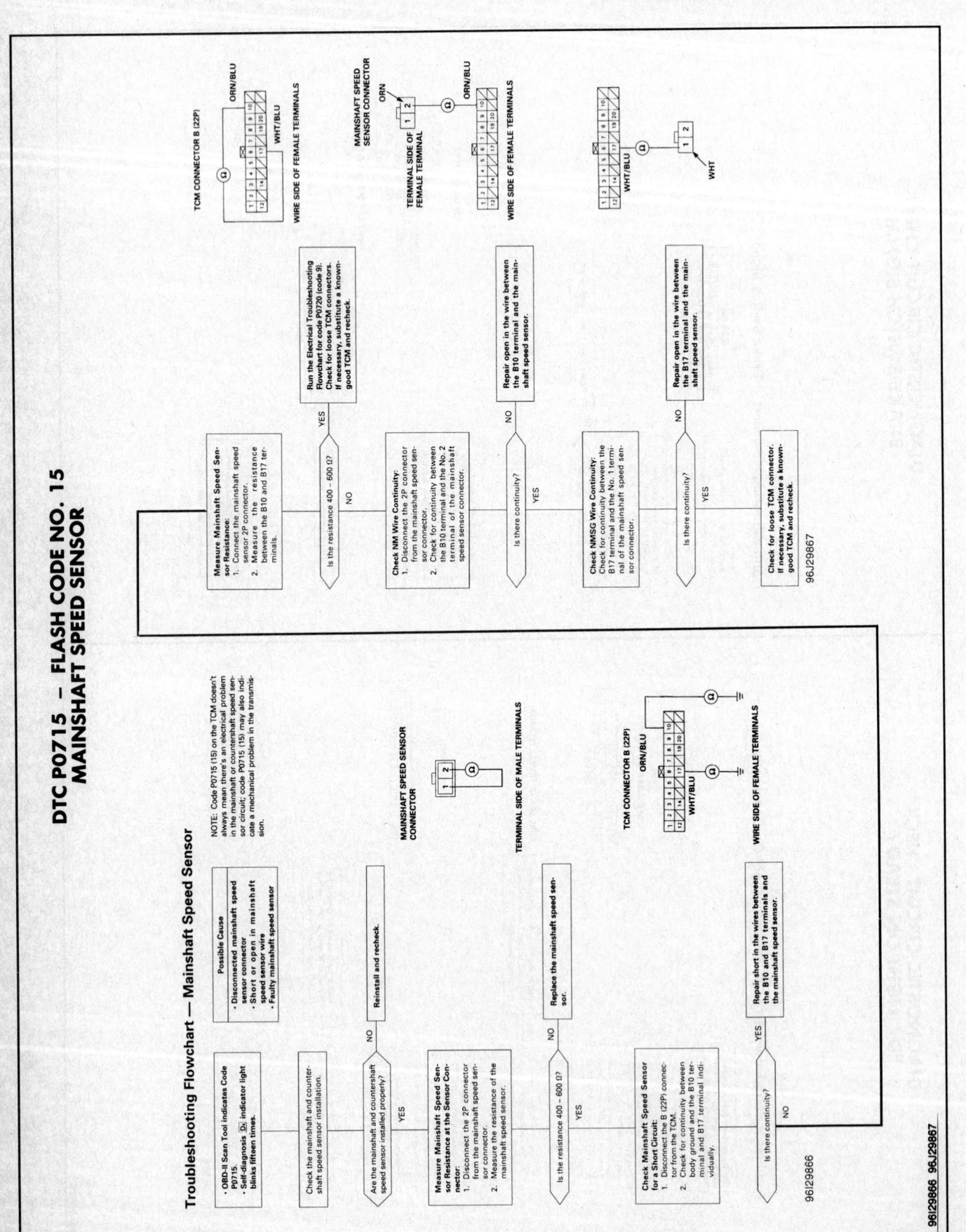

DTC P0715 – FLASH CODE NO. 15
MAINSHAFT SPEED SENSOR

Troubleshooting Flowchart — Mainshaft Speed Sensor

Possible Cause
- Disconnected mainshaft speed sensor connector
- Short or open in mainshaft speed sensor wire
- Faulty mainshaft speed sensor

NOTE: Code P0715 (15) on the TCM doesn't always mean there's an electrical problem in the mainshaft or countershaft speed sensor circuit; code P0715 (15) may also indicate a mechanical problem in the transmission.

- OBD-II Scan Tool indicates Code P0715.
- Self-diagnosis 🔲 indicator light blinks fifteen times.

Check the mainshaft and countershaft speed sensor installation.

Are the mainshaft and countershaft speed sensor installed properly?

YES

NO → Reinstall and recheck.

Measure Mainshaft Speed Sensor Resistance at the Sensor Connector:
1. Disconnect the 2P connector from the mainshaft speed sensor connector.
2. Measure the resistance of the mainshaft speed sensor.

Is the resistance 400 – 600 Ω?

NO → Replace the mainshaft speed sensor.

YES

Check Mainshaft Speed Sensor for a Short Circuit:
1. Disconnect the B (22P) connector from the TCM.
2. Check for continuity between body ground and the B10 terminal and B17 terminal individually.

Is there continuity?

YES → Repair short in the wires between the B10 and B17 terminals and the mainshaft speed sensor.

NO

MAINSHAFT SPEED SENSOR CONNECTOR

TERMINAL SIDE OF MALE TERMINALS

TCM CONNECTOR B (22P)

ORN/BLU

WHT/BLU

WIRE SIDE OF FEMALE TERMINALS

96J29866   96J29867

TCM CONNECTOR B (22P)

ORN/BLU

WHT/BLU

WIRE SIDE OF FEMALE TERMINALS

Measure Mainshaft Speed Sensor Resistance:
1. Connect the mainshaft speed sensor 2P connector.
2. Measure the resistance between the B10 and B17 terminals.

Is the resistance 400 – 600 Ω?

YES → Run the Electrical Troubleshooting Flowchart for code P0720 (code 9). Check for loose TCM connectors. If necessary, substitute a known-good TCM and recheck.

NO

Check NM Wire Continuity:
1. Disconnect the 2P connector from the mainshaft speed sensor connector.
2. Check for continuity between the B10 terminal and the No. 2 terminal of the mainshaft speed sensor connector.

Is there continuity?

NO → Repair open in the wire between the B10 terminal and the mainshaft speed sensor.

YES

Check NMSG Wire Continuity:
Check for continuity between the B17 terminal and the No. 1 terminal of the mainshaft speed sensor connector.

Is there continuity?

NO → Repair open in the wire between the B17 terminal and the mainshaft speed sensor.

YES

Check for loose TCM connector. If necessary, substitute a known-good TCM and recheck.

96J29867

MAINSHAFT SPEED SENSOR CONNECTOR

ORN

ORN/BLU

TERMINAL SIDE OF FEMALE TERMINAL

WIRE SIDE OF FEMALE TERMINALS

WHT/BLU

WHT

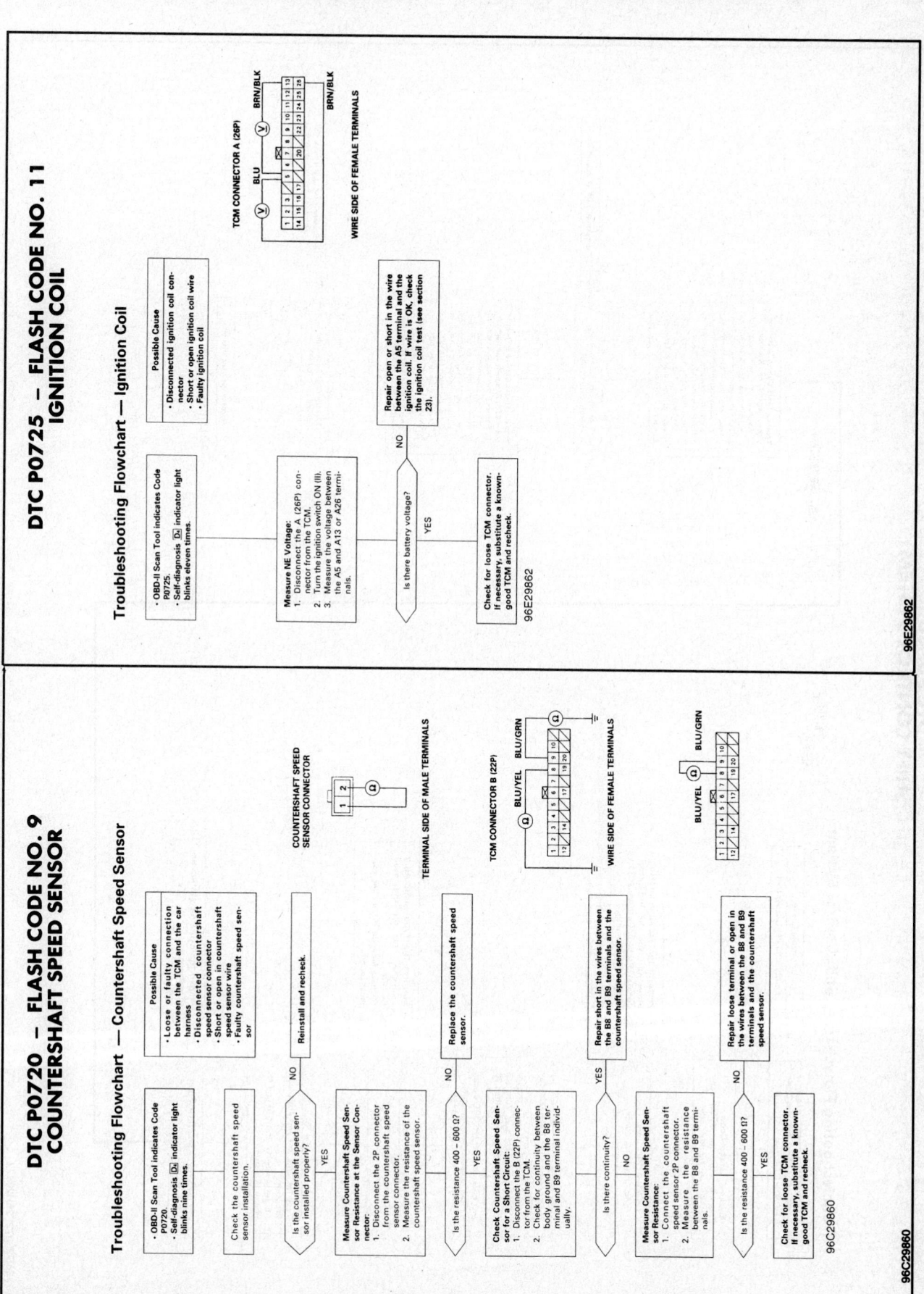

DTC P0725 – FLASH CODE NO. 11 IGNITION COIL

Troubleshooting Flowchart — Ignition Coil

- OBD-II Scan Tool indicates Code P0725.
- Self-diagnosis [D₄] indicator light blinks eleven times.

Possible Cause
- Disconnected ignition coil connector
- Short or open ignition coil wire
- Faulty ignition coil

Measure NE Voltage:
1. Disconnect the A (26P) connector from the TCM.
2. Turn the ignition switch ON (II).
3. Measure the voltage between the A5 and A13 or A26 terminals.

Is there battery voltage?

NO → Repair open or short in the wire between the A5 terminal and the ignition coil. If wire is OK, check the ignition coil test (see section 23).

YES →

Check for loose TCM connector. If necessary, substitute a known-good TCM and recheck.

TCM CONNECTOR A (26P)

BLU   BRN/BLK

BRN/BLK

WIRE SIDE OF FEMALE TERMINALS

96E29862

DTC P0720 – FLASH CODE NO. 9 COUNTERSHAFT SPEED SENSOR

Troubleshooting Flowchart — Countershaft Speed Sensor

- OBD-II Scan Tool indicates Code P0720.
- Self-diagnosis [D₄] indicator light blinks nine times.

Possible Cause
- Loose or faulty connection between the TCM and the car harness
- Disconnected countershaft speed sensor connector
- Short or open in countershaft speed sensor wire
- Faulty countershaft speed sensor

Check the countershaft speed sensor installation.

Is the countershaft speed sensor installed properly?

NO → Reinstall and recheck.

YES →

Measure Countershaft Speed Sensor Resistance at the Sensor Connector:
1. Disconnect the 2P connector from the countershaft speed sensor connector.
2. Measure the resistance of the countershaft speed sensor.

Is the resistance 400 – 600 Ω?

NO → Replace the countershaft speed sensor.

YES →

Check Countershaft Speed Sensor for a Short Circuit:
1. Disconnect the B (22P) connector from the TCM.
2. Check for continuity between body ground and the B8 terminal and B9 terminal individually.

Is there continuity?

YES → Repair short in the wires between the B8 and B9 terminals and the countershaft speed sensor.

NO →

Measure Countershaft Speed Sensor Resistance:
1. Connect the countershaft speed sensor 2P connector.
2. Measure the resistance between the B8 and B9 terminals.

Is the resistance 400 – 600 Ω?

NO → Repair loose terminal or open in the wires between the B8 and B9 terminals and the countershaft speed sensor.

YES →

Check for loose TCM connector. If necessary, substitute a known-good TCM and recheck.

COUNTERSHAFT SPEED SENSOR CONNECTOR

TERMINAL SIDE OF MALE TERMINALS

TCM CONNECTOR B (22P)

BLU/YEL   BLU/GRN

BLU/YEL   BLU/GRN

WIRE SIDE OF FEMALE TERMINALS

96C29860

DTC P0730
SHIFT CONTROL SYSTEM

Troubleshooting Flowchart — Shift Control System

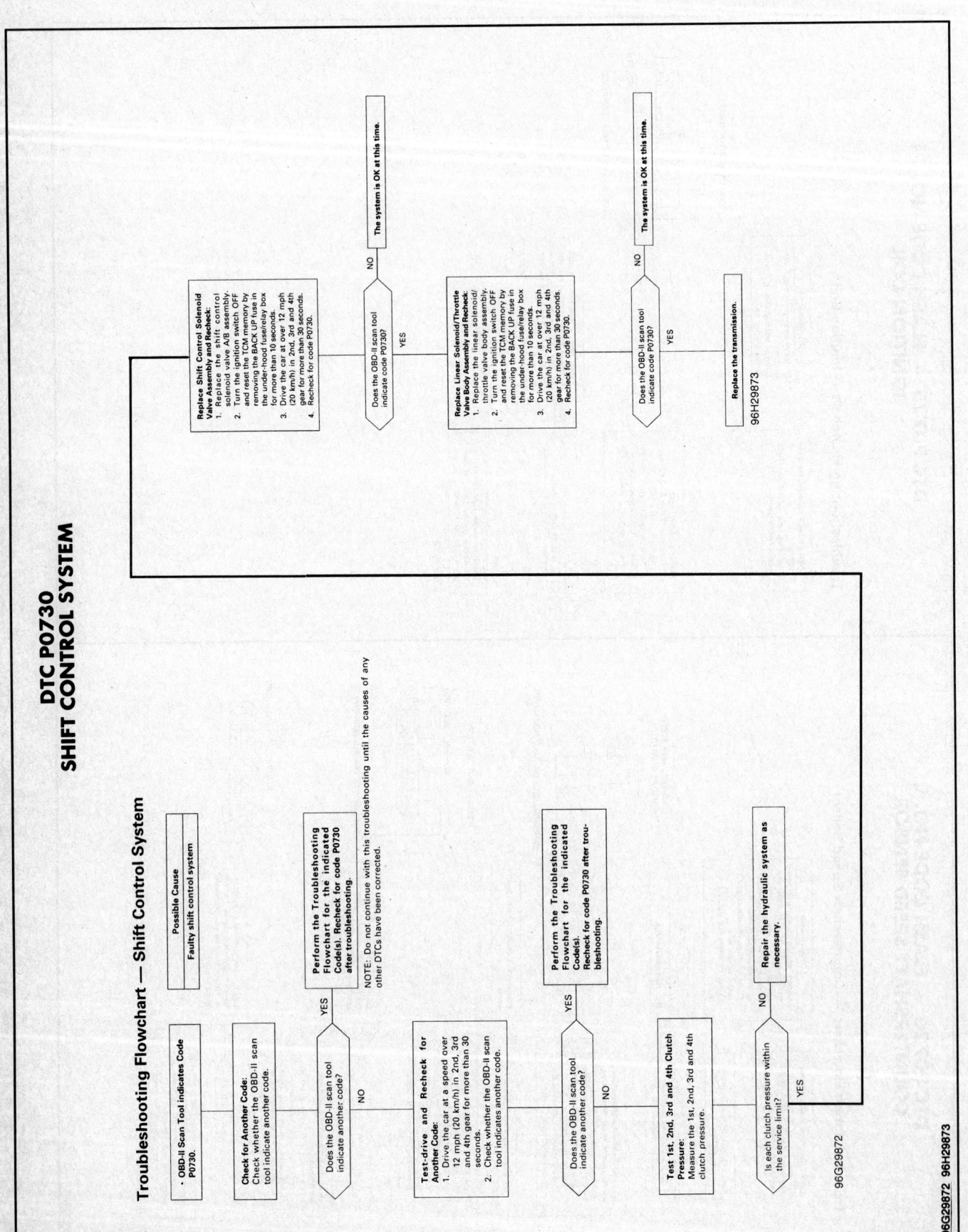

- OBD-II Scan Tool indicates Code P0730.

Possible Cause
Faulty shift control system

Check for Another Code:
Check whether the OBD-II scan tool indicate another code.

Does the OBD-II scan tool indicate another code?

YES → **Perform the Troubleshooting Flowchart for the indicated Code(s). Recheck for code P0730 after troubleshooting.**

NOTE: Do not continue with this troubleshooting until the causes of any other DTCs have been corrected.

NO

Test-drive and Recheck for Another Code:
1. Drive the car at a speed over 12 mph (20 km/h) in 2nd, 3rd and 4th gear for more than 30 seconds.
2. Check whether the OBD-II scan tool indicates another code.

Does the OBD-II scan tool indicate another code?

YES → **Perform the Troubleshooting Flowchart for the indicated Code(s). Recheck for code P0730 after troubleshooting.**

NO

Test 1st, 2nd, 3rd and 4th Clutch Pressure:
Measure the 1st, 2nd, 3rd and 4th clutch pressure.

Is each clutch pressure within the service limit?

NO → **Repair the hydraulic system as necessary.**

YES

Replace Shift Control Solenoid Valve Assembly and Recheck:
1. Replace the shift control solenoid valve A/B assembly.
2. Turn the ignition switch OFF and reset the TCM memory by removing the BACK UP fuse in the under-hood fuse/relay box for more than 10 seconds.
3. Drive the car at over 12 mph (20 km/h) in 2nd, 3rd and 4th gear for more than 30 seconds.
4. Recheck for code P0730.

Does the OBD-II scan tool indicate code P0730?

NO → **The system is OK at this time.**

YES

Replace Linear Solenoid/Throttle Valve Body Assembly and Recheck:
1. Replace the linear solenoid/throttle valve body assembly.
2. Turn the ignition switch OFF and reset the TCM memory by removing the BACK UP fuse in the under-hood fuse/relay box for more than 10 seconds.
3. Drive the car at over 12 mph (20 km/h) in 2nd, 3rd and 4th gear for more than 30 seconds.
4. Recheck for code P0730.

Does the OBD-II scan tool indicate code P0730?

NO → **The system is OK at this time.**

YES

Replace the transmission.

96H29873

96G29872

96G29872 96H29873

DTC P0740
LOCK-UP CONTROL SYSTEM

Troubleshooting Flowchart — Lock-up Control System

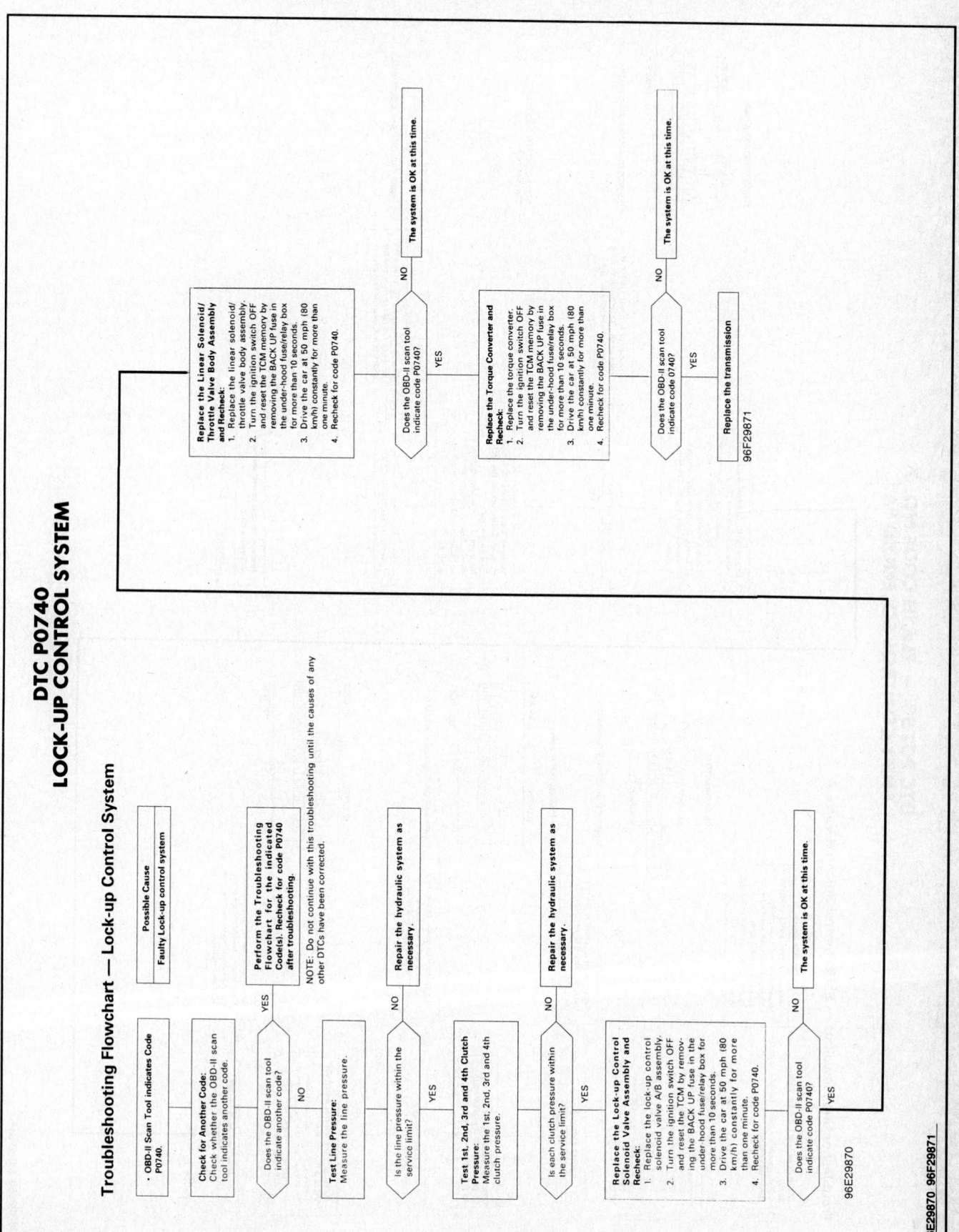

OBD-II Scan Tool indicates Code P0740.
- OBD-II Scan Tool indicates Code P0740.

Possible Cause

Faulty Lock-up control system

Check for Another Code:
Check whether the OBD-II scan tool indicates another code.

Does the OBD-II scan tool indicate another code?

YES → **Perform the Troubleshooting Flowchart for the indicated Code(s). Recheck for code P0740 after troubleshooting.**

NOTE: Do not continue with this troubleshooting until the causes of any other DTCs have been corrected.

NO ↓

Test Line Pressure:
Measure the line pressure.

Is the line pressure within the service limit?

NO → Repair the hydraulic system as necessary.

YES ↓

Test 1st, 2nd, 3rd and 4th Clutch Pressure:
Measure the 1st, 2nd, 3rd and 4th clutch pressure.

Is each clutch pressure within the service limit?

NO → Repair the hydraulic system as necessary.

YES ↓

Replace the Lock-up Control Solenoid Valve Assembly and Recheck:
1. Replace the lock-up control solenoid valve A/B assembly.
2. Turn the ignition switch OFF and reset the TCM by removing the BACK UP fuse in the under-hood fuse/relay box for more than 10 seconds.
3. Drive the car at 50 mph (80 km/h) constantly for more than one minute.
4. Recheck for code P0740.

Does the OBD-II scan tool indicate code 07407?

NO → The system is OK at this time.

YES ↓

Replace the Linear Solenoid/Throttle Valve Body Assembly and Recheck:
1. Replace the linear solenoid/throttle valve body assembly.
2. Turn the ignition switch OFF and reset the TCM memory by removing the BACK UP fuse in the under-hood fuse/relay box for more than 10 seconds.
3. Drive the car at 50 mph (80 km/h) constantly for more than one minute.
4. Recheck for code P0740.

Does the OBD-II scan tool indicate code P0740?

NO → The system is OK at this time.

YES ↓

Replace the Torque Converter and Recheck:
1. Replace the torque converter.
2. Turn the ignition switch OFF and reset the TCM memory by removing the BACK UP fuse in the under-hood fuse/relay box for more than 10 seconds.
3. Drive the car at 50 mph (80 km/h) constantly for more than one minute.
4. Recheck for code P0740.

Does the OBD-II scan tool indicate code 07407?

NO → The system is OK at this time.

YES ↓

Replace the transmission

96E29870

96F29871

96E29870 96F29871

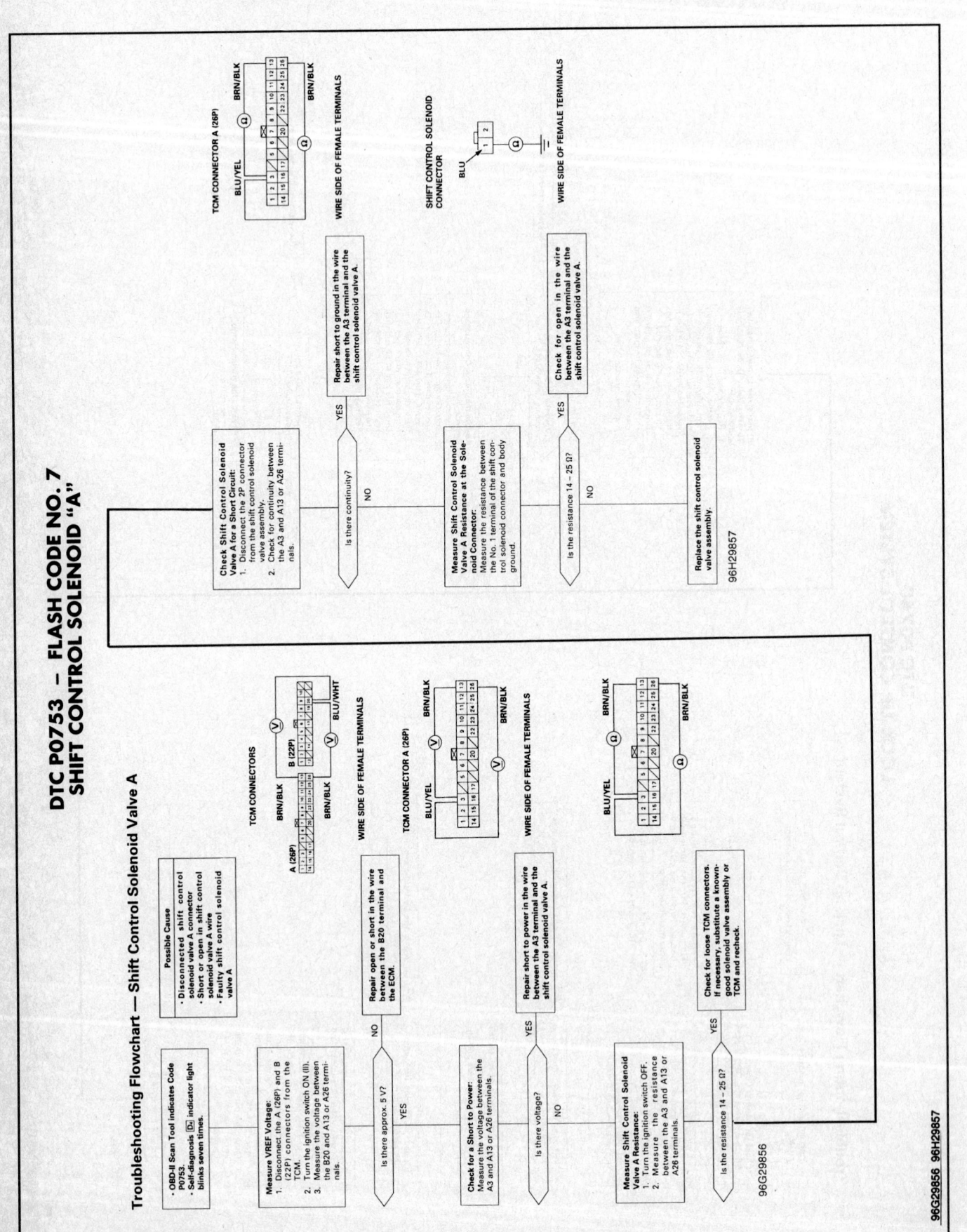

DTC P0753 – FLASH CODE NO. 7 SHIFT CONTROL SOLENOID "A"

Troubleshooting Flowchart — Shift Control Solenoid Valve A

OBD-II Scan Tool indicates Code P0753.
- Self-diagnosis D4 indicator light blinks seven times.

Possible Cause
- Disconnected shift control solenoid valve A connector
- Short or open in shift control solenoid valve A wire
- Faulty shift control solenoid valve A

Measure VREF Voltage:
1. Disconnect the A (26P) and B (22P) connectors from the TCM.
2. Turn the ignition switch ON (II).
3. Measure the voltage between the B20 and A13 or A26 terminals.

Is there approx. 5 V?

NO → Repair open or short in the wire between the B20 terminal and the ECM.

YES

Check for a Short to Power:
Measure the voltage between the A3 and A13 or A26 terminals.

Is there voltage?

YES → Repair short to power in the wire between the A3 terminal and the shift control solenoid valve A.

NO

Measure Shift Control Solenoid Valve A Resistance:
1. Turn the ignition switch OFF.
2. Measure the resistance between the A3 and A13 or A26 terminals.

Is the resistance 14 – 25 Ω?

YES → Check for loose TCM connectors. If necessary, substitute a known-good solenoid valve assembly or TCM and recheck.

NO

Check Shift Control Solenoid Valve A for a Short Circuit:
1. Disconnect the 2P connector from the shift control solenoid valve assembly.
2. Check for continuity between the A3 and A13 or A26 terminals.

Is there continuity?

YES → Repair short to ground in the wire between the A3 terminal and the shift control solenoid valve A.

NO

Measure Shift Control Solenoid Valve A Resistance at the Solenoid Connector:
Measure the resistance between the No. 1 terminal of the shift control solenoid connector and body ground.

Is the resistance 14 – 25 Ω?

YES → Check for open in the wire between the A3 terminal and the shift control solenoid valve A.

NO

Replace the shift control solenoid valve assembly.

96G29856

96H29857

96G29856 96H29857

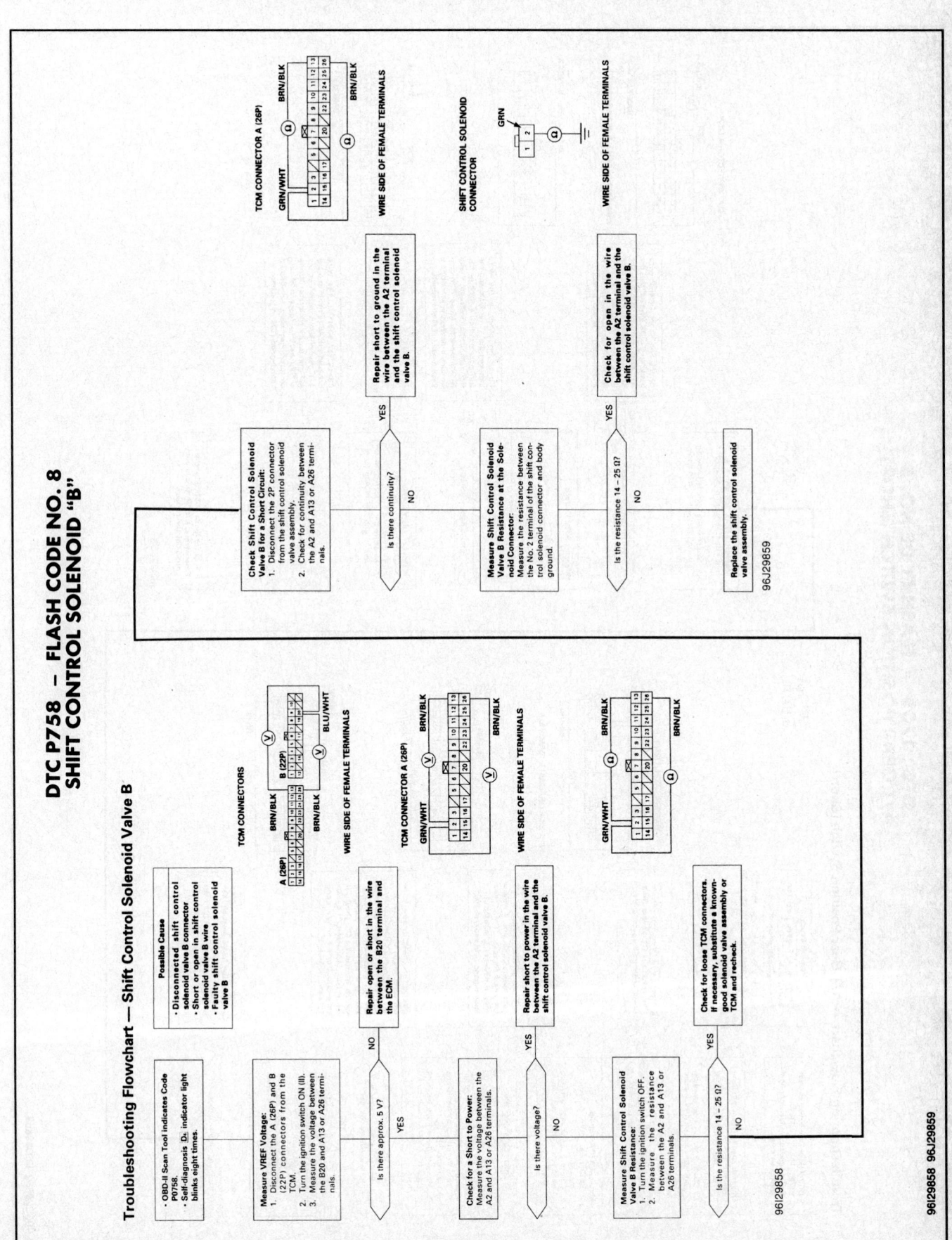

DTC P758 – FLASH CODE NO. 8
SHIFT CONTROL SOLENOID "B"

Troubleshooting Flowchart — Shift Control Solenoid Valve B

96I29858 96J29859

DTC P1705 — FLASH CODE NO. 5
A/T GEAR POSITION SWITCH (SHORT)

Troubleshooting Flowchart — A/T Gear Position Switch (Short)

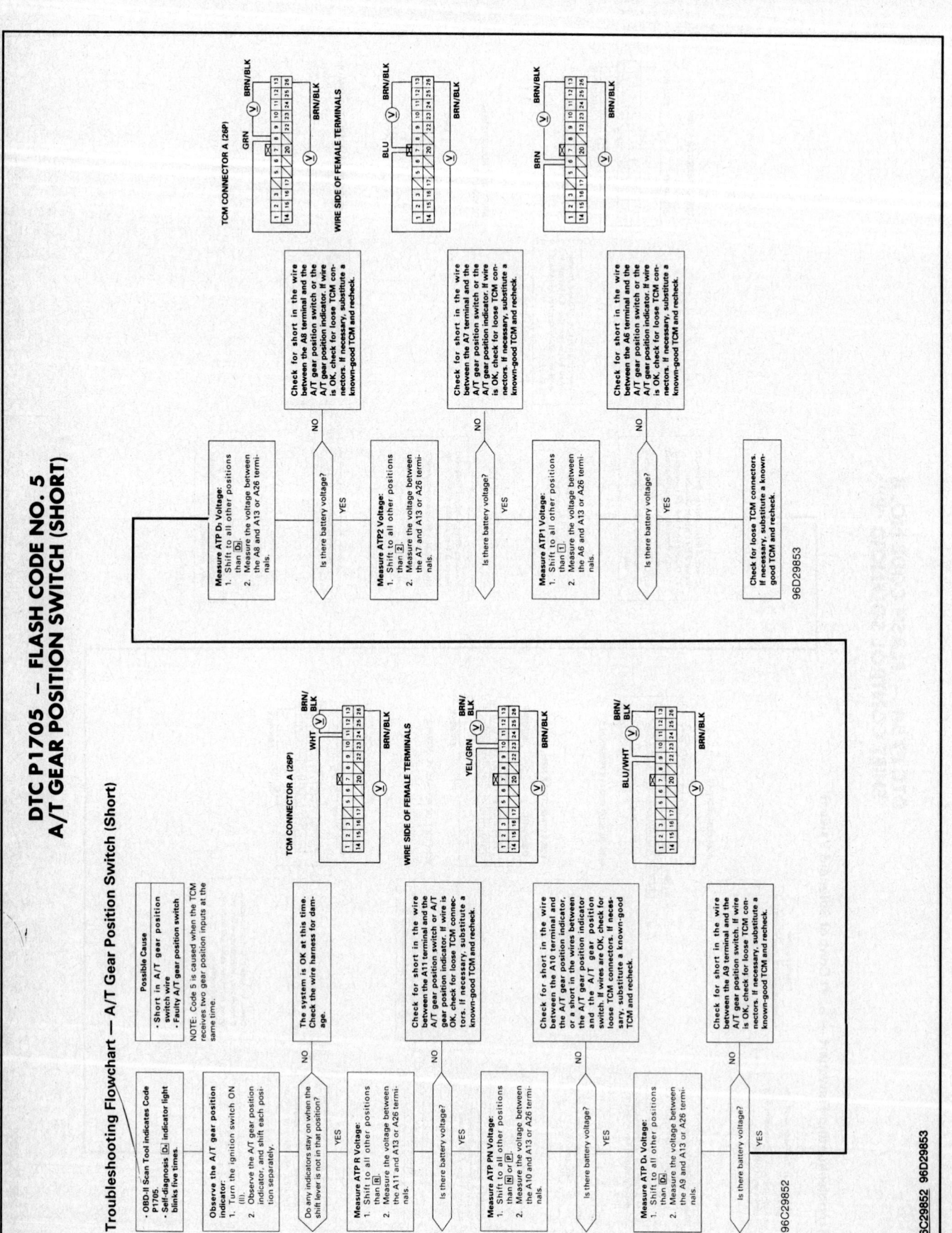

- OBD-II Scan Tool indicates Code P1705.
- Self-diagnosis [D4] indicator light blinks five times.

Possible Cause
- Short in A/T gear position switch wire
- Faulty A/T gear position switch

NOTE: Code 5 is caused when the TCM receives two gear position inputs at the same time.

Observe the A/T gear position indicator:
1. Turn the ignition switch ON.
2. Observe the A/T gear position indicator, and shift each position separately.

Do any indicators stay on when the shift lever is not in that position?

NO → The system is OK at this time. Check the wire harness for damage.

YES →

Measure ATP R Voltage:
1. Shift to all other positions than [R].
2. Measure the voltage between the A11 and A13 or A26 terminals.

Is there battery voltage?

NO → Check for short in the wire between the A11 terminal and the A/T gear position indicator. If wire is OK, check for loose TCM connectors. If necessary, substitute a known-good TCM and recheck.

YES →

Measure ATP PN Voltage:
1. Shift to all other positions than [N] or [P].
2. Measure the voltage between the A10 and A13 or A26 terminals.

Is there battery voltage?

NO → Check for short in the wire between the A10 terminal and the A/T gear position indicator, or a short in the wires between the A6 and the A/T gear position switch. If wires are OK, check for loose TCM connectors. If necessary, substitute a known-good TCM and recheck.

YES →

Measure ATP D4 Voltage:
1. Shift to all other positions than [D4].
2. Measure the voltage between the A9 and A13 or A26 terminals.

Is there battery voltage?

NO → Check for short in the wire between the A9 terminal and the A/T gear position switch. If wire is OK, check for loose TCM connectors. If necessary, substitute a known-good TCM and recheck.

YES →

Measure ATP D3 Voltage:
1. Shift to all other positions than [D3].
2. Measure the voltage between the A8 and A13 or A26 terminals.

Is there battery voltage?

NO → Check for short in the wire between the A8 terminal and the A/T gear position switch or the A/T gear position indicator. If wire is OK, check for loose TCM connectors. If necessary, substitute a known-good TCM and recheck.

YES →

Measure ATP2 Voltage:
1. Shift to all other positions than [2].
2. Measure the voltage between the A7 and A13 or A26 terminals.

Is there battery voltage?

NO → Check for short in the wire between the A7 terminal and the A/T gear position switch or the A/T gear position indicator. If wire is OK, check for loose TCM connectors. If necessary, substitute a known-good TCM and recheck.

YES →

Measure ATP1 Voltage:
1. Shift to all other positions than [1].
2. Measure the voltage between the A6 and A13 or A26 terminals.

Is there battery voltage?

NO → Check for short in the wire between the A6 terminal and the A/T gear position switch or the A/T gear position indicator. If wire is OK, check for loose TCM connectors. If necessary, substitute a known-good TCM and recheck.

YES → Check for loose TCM connectors. If necessary, substitute a known-good TCM and recheck.

TCM CONNECTOR A (26P)

WIRE SIDE OF FEMALE TERMINALS

96C29852   96D29853

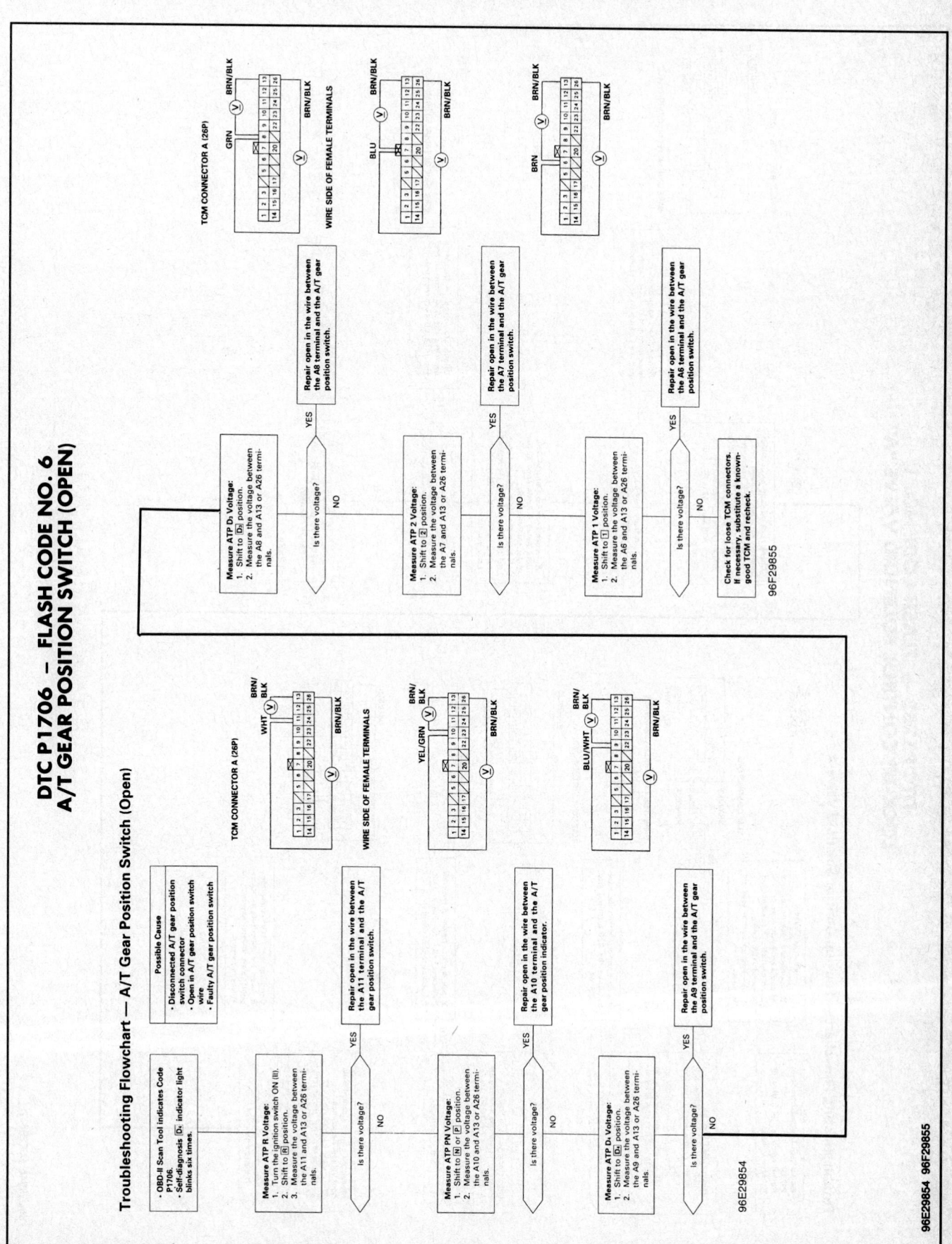

DTC P1706 – FLASH CODE NO. 6
A/T GEAR POSITION SWITCH (OPEN)

Troubleshooting Flowchart — A/T Gear Position Switch (Open)

96E29854 96F29855

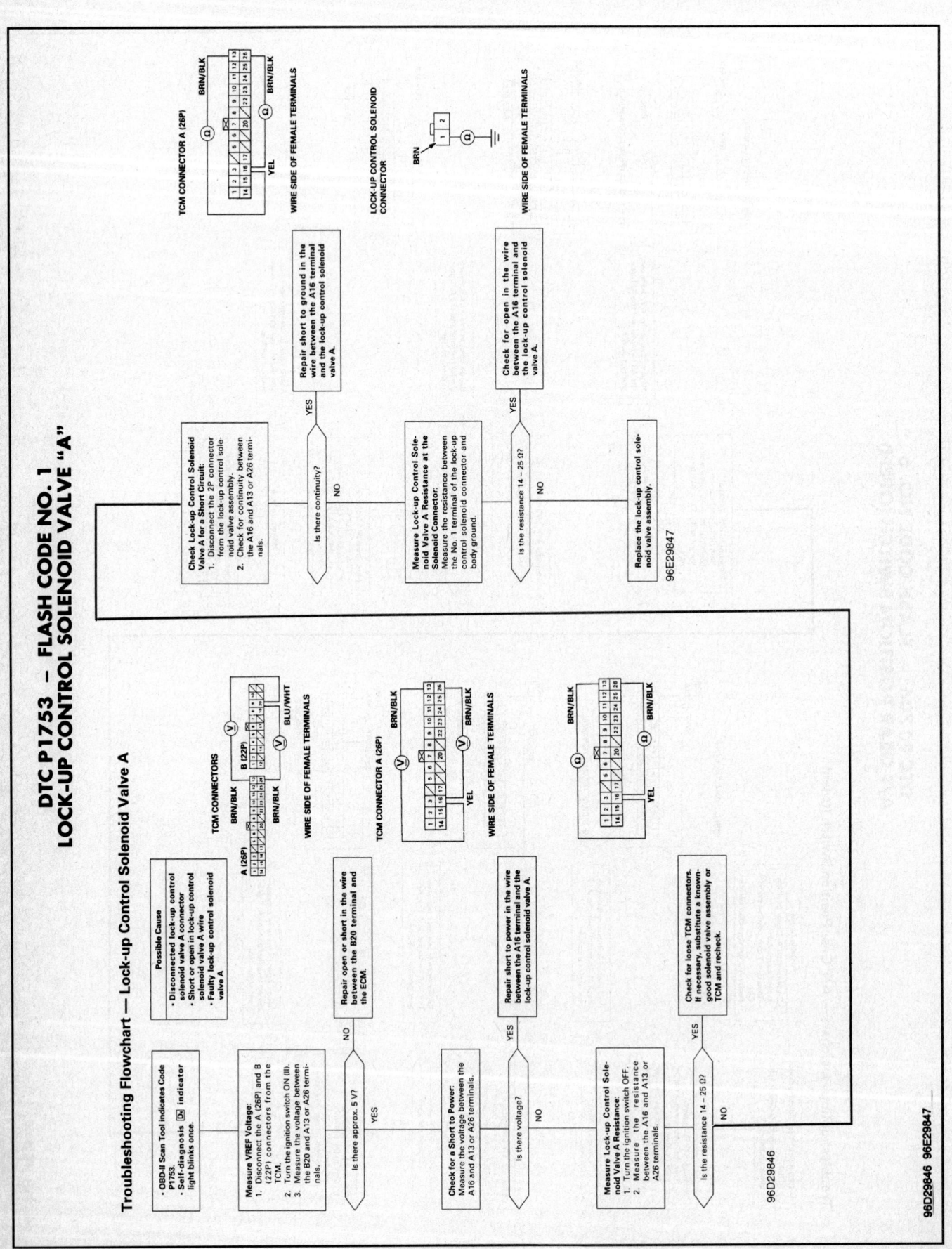

DTC P1753 – FLASH CODE NO. 1 LOCK-UP CONTROL SOLENOID VALVE "A"

Troubleshooting Flowchart — Lock-up Control Solenoid Valve A

96D29846   96E29847

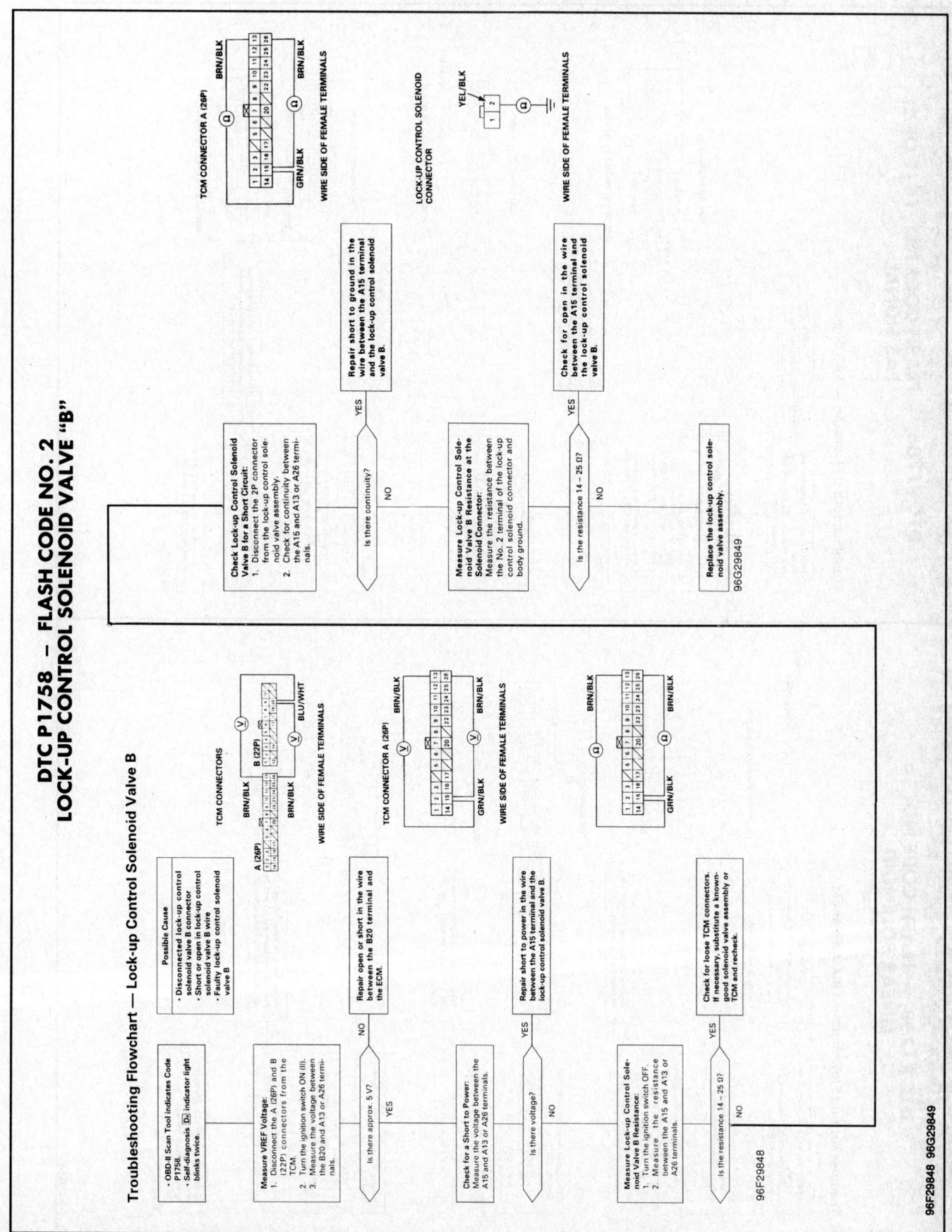

DTC P1758 — FLASH CODE NO. 2 LOCK-UP CONTROL SOLENOID VALVE "B"

Troubleshooting Flowchart — Lock-up Control Solenoid Valve B

- OBD-II Scan Tool indicates Code P1758.
- Self-diagnosis [D] indicator light blinks twice.

Possible Cause
- Disconnected lock-up control solenoid valve B connector
- Short or open in lock-up control solenoid valve B wire
- Faulty lock-up control solenoid valve B

Measure VREF Voltage:
1. Disconnect the A (26P) and B (22P) connectors from the TCM.
2. Turn the ignition switch ON (II).
3. Measure the voltage between the B20 and A13 or A26 terminals.

Is there approx. 5 V? — YES → Repair open or short in the wire between the B20 terminal and the ECM.

NO →

Check for a Short to Power: Measure the voltage between the A15 and A13 or A26 terminals.

Is there voltage? — YES → Repair short to power in the wire between the A15 terminal and the lock-up control solenoid valve B.

NO →

Measure Lock-up Control Solenoid Valve B Resistance:
1. Turn the ignition switch OFF.
2. Measure the resistance between the A15 and A13 or A26 terminals.

Is the resistance 14 – 25 Ω? — YES → Check for loose TCM connectors. If necessary, substitute a known-good solenoid valve assembly or TCM and recheck.

NO →

Check Lock-up Control Solenoid Valve B for a Short Circuit:
1. Disconnect the 2P connector from the lock-up control solenoid valve assembly.
2. Check for continuity between the A15 and A13 or A26 terminals.

Is there continuity? — YES → Repair short to ground in the wire between the A15 terminal and the lock-up control solenoid valve B.

NO →

Measure Lock-up Control Solenoid Valve B Resistance at the Solenoid Connector: Measure the resistance between the No. 2 terminal of the lock-up control solenoid connector and body ground.

Is the resistance 14 – 25 Ω? — YES → Check for open in the wire between the A15 terminal and the lock-up control solenoid valve B.

NO →

Replace the lock-up control solenoid valve assembly.

96G29849

96F29848 96G29849

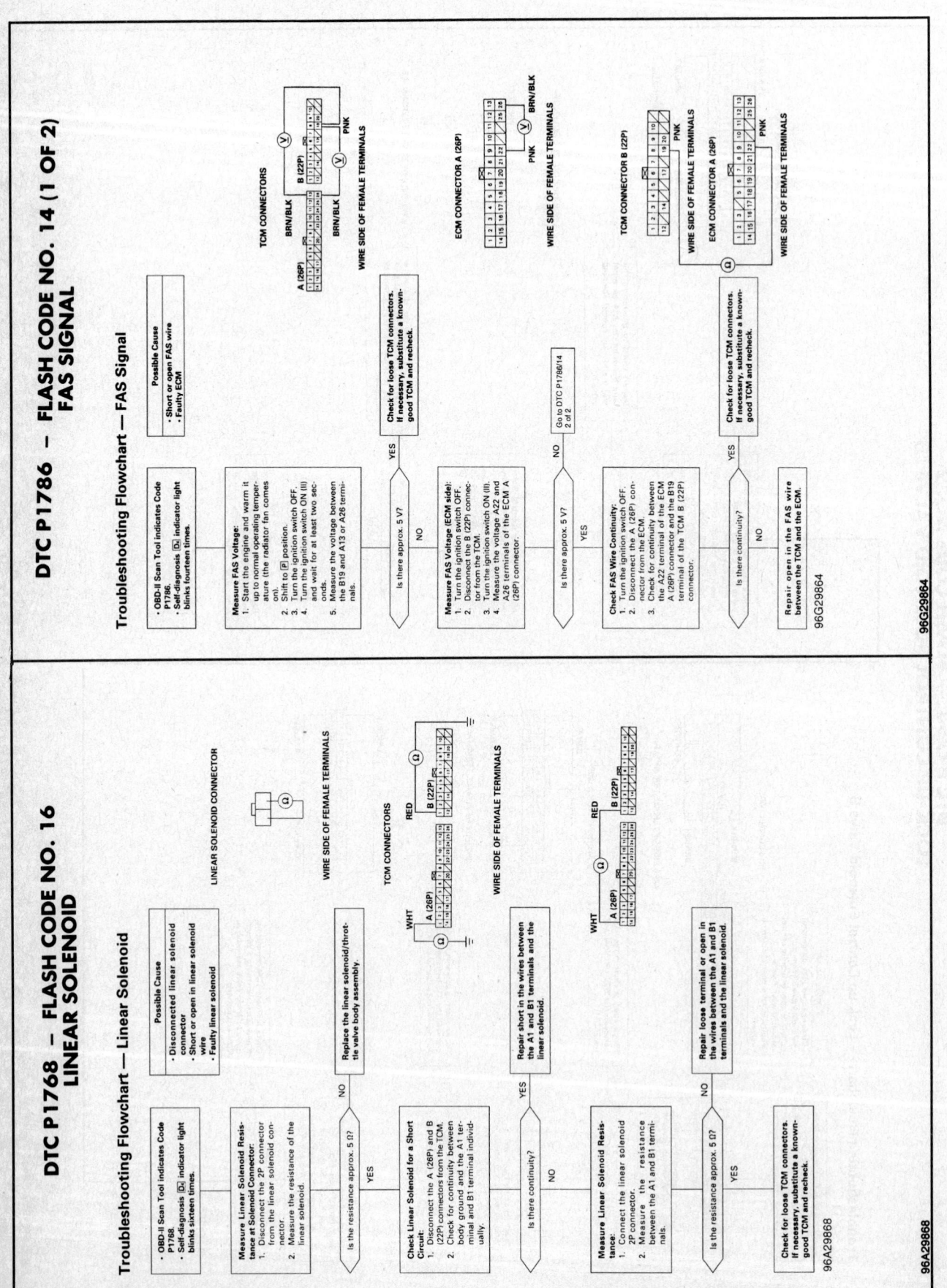

DTC P1768 – FLASH CODE NO. 16 LINEAR SOLENOID

Troubleshooting Flowchart — Linear Solenoid

- OBD-II Scan Tool indicates Code P1768.
- Self-diagnosis [D4] indicator light blinks sixteen times.

Possible Cause
- Disconnected linear solenoid connector
- Short or open in linear solenoid wire
- Faulty linear solenoid

Measure Linear Solenoid Resistance at Solenoid Connector:
1. Disconnect the 2P connector from the linear solenoid connector.
2. Measure the resistance of the linear solenoid.

Is the resistance approx. 5 Ω?

NO → Replace the linear solenoid/throttle valve body assembly.

YES → **Check Linear Solenoid for a Short Circuit:**
1. Disconnect the A (26P) and B (22P) connectors from the TCM.
2. Check for continuity between body ground and the A1 terminal and B1 terminal individually.

Is there continuity?

YES → Repair short in the wires between the A1 and B1 terminals and the linear solenoid.

NO → **Measure Linear Solenoid Resistance:**
1. Connect the linear solenoid 2P connector.
2. Measure the resistance between the A1 and B1 terminals.

Is the resistance approx. 5 Ω?

NO → Repair loose terminal or open in the wires between the A1 and B1 terminals and the linear solenoid.

YES → Check for loose TCM connectors. If necessary, substitute a known-good TCM and recheck.

LINEAR SOLENOID CONNECTOR
WIRE SIDE OF FEMALE TERMINALS

TCM CONNECTORS
A (26P) WHT — B (22P) RED
WIRE SIDE OF FEMALE TERMINALS

96A29868

DTC P1786 – FLASH CODE NO. 14 (1 OF 2) FAS SIGNAL

Troubleshooting Flowchart — FAS Signal

- OBD-II Scan Tool indicates Code P1786.
- Self-diagnosis [D4] indicator light blinks fourteen times.

Possible Cause
- Short or open FAS wire
- Faulty ECM

Measure FAS Voltage:
1. Start the engine and warm it up to normal operating temperature (the radiator fan comes on).
2. Shift to [P] position.
3. Turn the ignition switch OFF.
4. Turn the ignition switch ON (II) and wait for at least two seconds.
5. Measure the voltage between the B19 and A13 or A25 terminals.

Is there approx. 5 V?

YES → Check for loose TCM connectors. If necessary, substitute a known-good TCM and recheck.

NO → **Measure FAS Voltage (ECM side):**
1. Turn the ignition switch OFF.
2. Disconnect the B (22P) connector from the TCM.
3. Turn the ignition switch ON (II).
4. Measure the voltage A22 and A26 terminals of the ECM A (26P) connector.

Is there approx. 5 V?

YES → Go to DTC P1786/14 2 of 2

NO → **Check FAS Wire Continuity:**
1. Turn the ignition switch OFF.
2. Disconnect the A (26P) connector from the ECM.
3. Check for continuity between the A22 terminal of the ECM A (26P) connector and the B19 terminal of the TCM B (22P) connector.

Is there continuity?

YES → Check for loose TCM connectors. If necessary, substitute a known-good TCM and recheck.

NO → Repair open in the FAS wire between the TCM and the ECM.

TCM CONNECTORS
B (22P) BRN/BLK PNK
A (26P) BRN/BLK PNK
WIRE SIDE OF FEMALE TERMINALS

ECM CONNECTOR A (26P)
PNK   BRN/BLK
WIRE SIDE OF FEMALE TERMINALS

TCM CONNECTOR B (22P) PNK
ECM CONNECTOR A (26P) PNK
WIRE SIDE OF FEMALE TERMINALS

96G29864

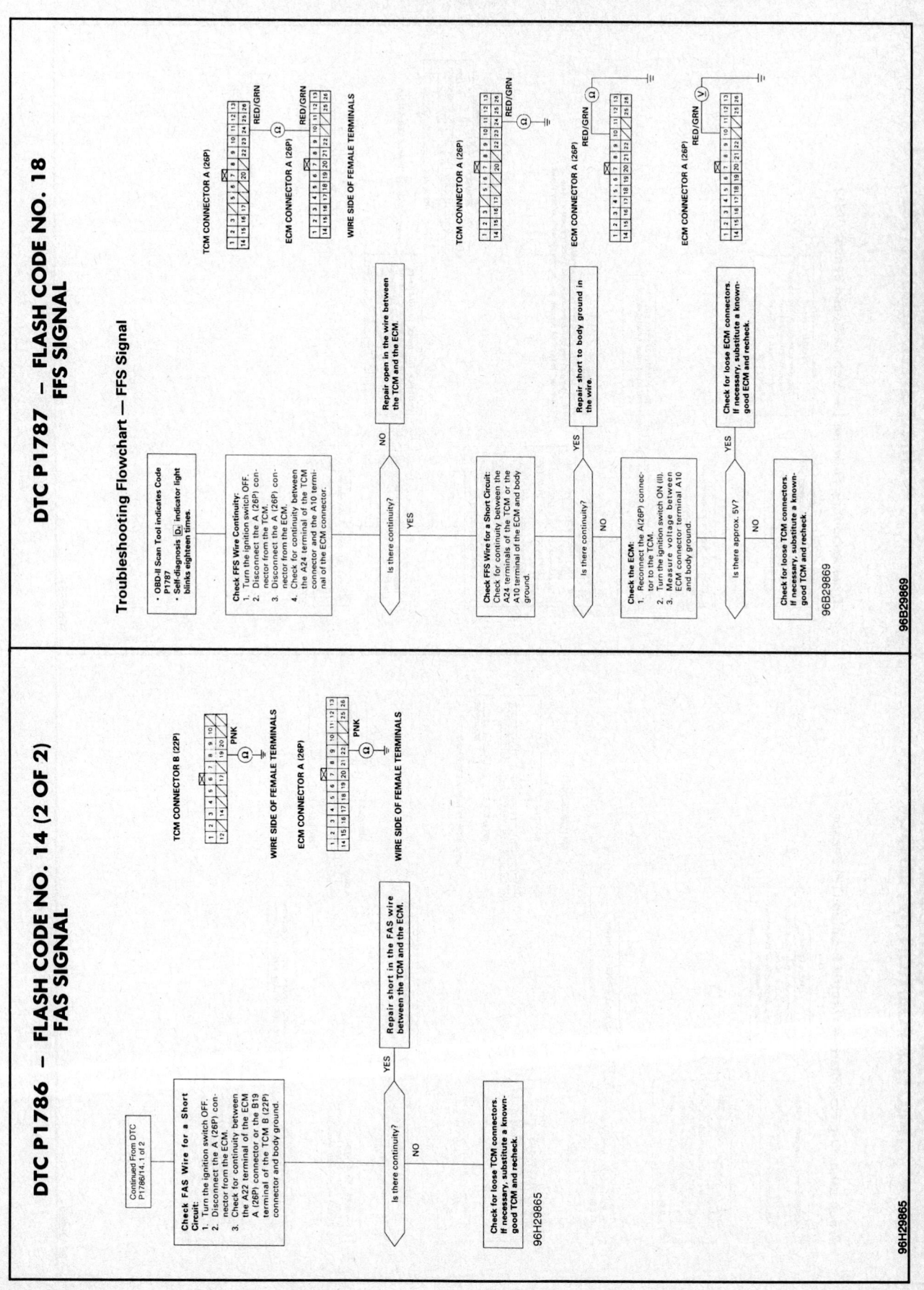

DTC P1786 – FLASH CODE NO. 14 (2 OF 2) FAS SIGNAL

Continued From DTC P1786/14, 1 of 2

Check FAS Wire for a Short Circuit:
1. Turn the ignition switch OFF.
2. Disconnect the A (26P) connector from the ECM.
3. Check for continuity between the A22 terminal of the ECM A (26P) connector or the B19 terminal of the TCM B (22P) connector and body ground.

Is there continuity?

YES — Repair short in the FAS wire between the TCM and the ECM.

NO — Check for loose TCM connectors. If necessary, substitute a known-good TCM and recheck.

TCM CONNECTOR B (22P)

PNK

WIRE SIDE OF FEMALE TERMINALS

ECM CONNECTOR A (26P)

PNK

WIRE SIDE OF FEMALE TERMINALS

96H29865

DTC P1787 – FLASH CODE NO. 18 FFS SIGNAL

Troubleshooting Flowchart — FFS Signal

- OBD-II Scan Tool indicates Code P1787
- Self-diagnosis [D] indicator light blinks eighteen times.

Check FFS Wire Continuity:
1. Turn the ignition switch OFF.
2. Disconnect the A (26P) connector from the TCM.
3. Disconnect the A (26P) connector from the ECM.
4. Check for continuity between the A24 terminal of the TCM connector and the A10 terminal of the ECM connector.

Is there continuity?

NO — Repair open in the wire between the TCM and the ECM.

YES — **Check FFS Wire for a Short Circuit:** Check for continuity between the A24 terminals of the TCM or the A10 terminal of the ECM and body ground.

Is there continuity?

YES — Repair short to body ground in the wire.

NO — **Check the ECM:**
1. Reconnect the A (26P) connector to the TCM.
2. Turn the ignition switch ON (II).
3. Measure voltage between ECM connector terminal A10 and body ground.

Is there approx. 5V?

YES — Check for loose ECM connectors. If necessary, substitute a known-good ECM and recheck.

NO — Check for loose TCM connectors. If necessary, substitute a known-good TCM and recheck.

TCM CONNECTOR A (26P)

RED/GRN

ECM CONNECTOR A (26P)

RED/GRN

WIRE SIDE OF FEMALE TERMINALS

TCM CONNECTOR A (26P)

RED/GRN

ECM CONNECTOR A (26P)

RED/GRN

ECM CONNECTOR A (26P)

RED/GRN

96B29869

96B29869

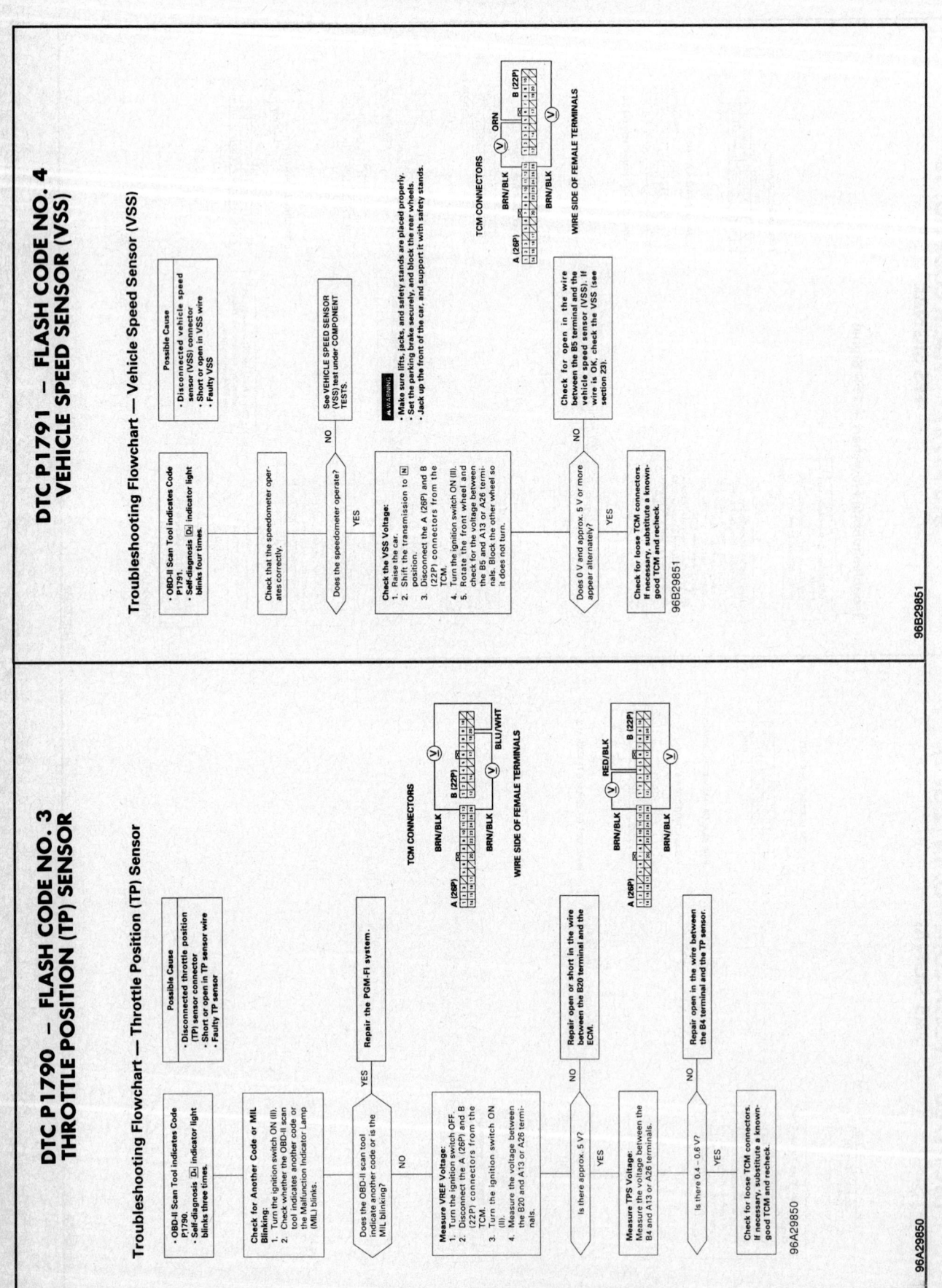

DTC P1791 – FLASH CODE NO. 4
VEHICLE SPEED SENSOR (VSS)

Troubleshooting Flowchart — Vehicle Speed Sensor (VSS)

- OBD-II Scan Tool indicates Code P1791.
- Self-diagnosis D4 indicator light blinks four times.

Possible Cause
- Disconnected vehicle speed sensor (VSS) connector
- Short or open in VSS wire
- Faulty VSS

Check that the speedometer operates correctly.

Does the speedometer operate?

NO → See VEHICLE SPEED SENSOR (VSS) test under COMPONENT TESTS.

YES

Check the VSS Voltage:
1. Raise the car.
2. Shift the transmission to N position.
3. Disconnect the A (26P) and B (22P) connectors from the TCM.
4. Turn the ignition switch ON (II).
5. Rotate the front wheel and check for the voltage between the B5 and A13 or A26 terminals. Block the other wheel so it does not turn.

⚠ WARNING
- Make sure lifts, jacks, and safety stands are placed properly.
- Set the parking brake securely, and block the rear wheels.
- Jack up the front of the car, and support it with safety stands.

Does 0 V and approx. 5 V or more appear alternately?

NO → Check for open in the wire between the B5 terminal and the vehicle speed sensor (VSS). If wire is OK, check the VSS (see section 23).

YES

Check for loose TCM connectors. If necessary, substitute a known-good TCM and recheck.

TCM CONNECTORS

A (26P)   B (22P)

ORN

BRN/BLK

BRN/BLK

WIRE SIDE OF FEMALE TERMINALS

96B29851

96B29851

DTC P1790 – FLASH CODE NO. 3
THROTTLE POSITION (TP) SENSOR

Troubleshooting Flowchart — Throttle Position (TP) Sensor

- OBD-II Scan Tool indicates Code P1790.
- Self-diagnosis D4 indicator light blinks three times.

Possible Cause
- Disconnected throttle position (TP) sensor connector
- Short or open in TP sensor wire
- Faulty TP sensor

Check for Another Code or MIL Blinking:
1. Turn the ignition switch ON (II).
2. Check whether the OBD-II scan tool indicates another code or the Malfunction Indicator Lamp (MIL) blinks.

Does the OBD-II scan tool indicate another code or is the MIL blinking?

YES → Repair the PGM-FI system.

NO

Measure VREF Voltage:
1. Turn the ignition switch OFF.
2. Disconnect the A (26P) and B (22P) connectors from the TCM.
3. Turn the ignition switch ON (II).
4. Measure the voltage between the B20 and A13 or A26 terminals.

Is there approx. 5 V?

NO → Repair open or short in the wire between the B20 terminal and the ECM.

YES

Measure TPS Voltage:
Measure the voltage between the B4 and A13 or A26 terminals.

Is there 0.4 – 0.6 V?

NO → Repair open in the wire between the B4 terminal and the TP sensor.

YES

Check for loose TCM connectors. If necessary, substitute a known-good TCM and recheck.

TCM CONNECTORS

A (26P)   B (22P)

BLU/WHT

BRN/BLK

BRN/BLK

RED/BLK

B (22P)

BRN/BLK

WIRE SIDE OF FEMALE TERMINALS

96A29850

96A29850

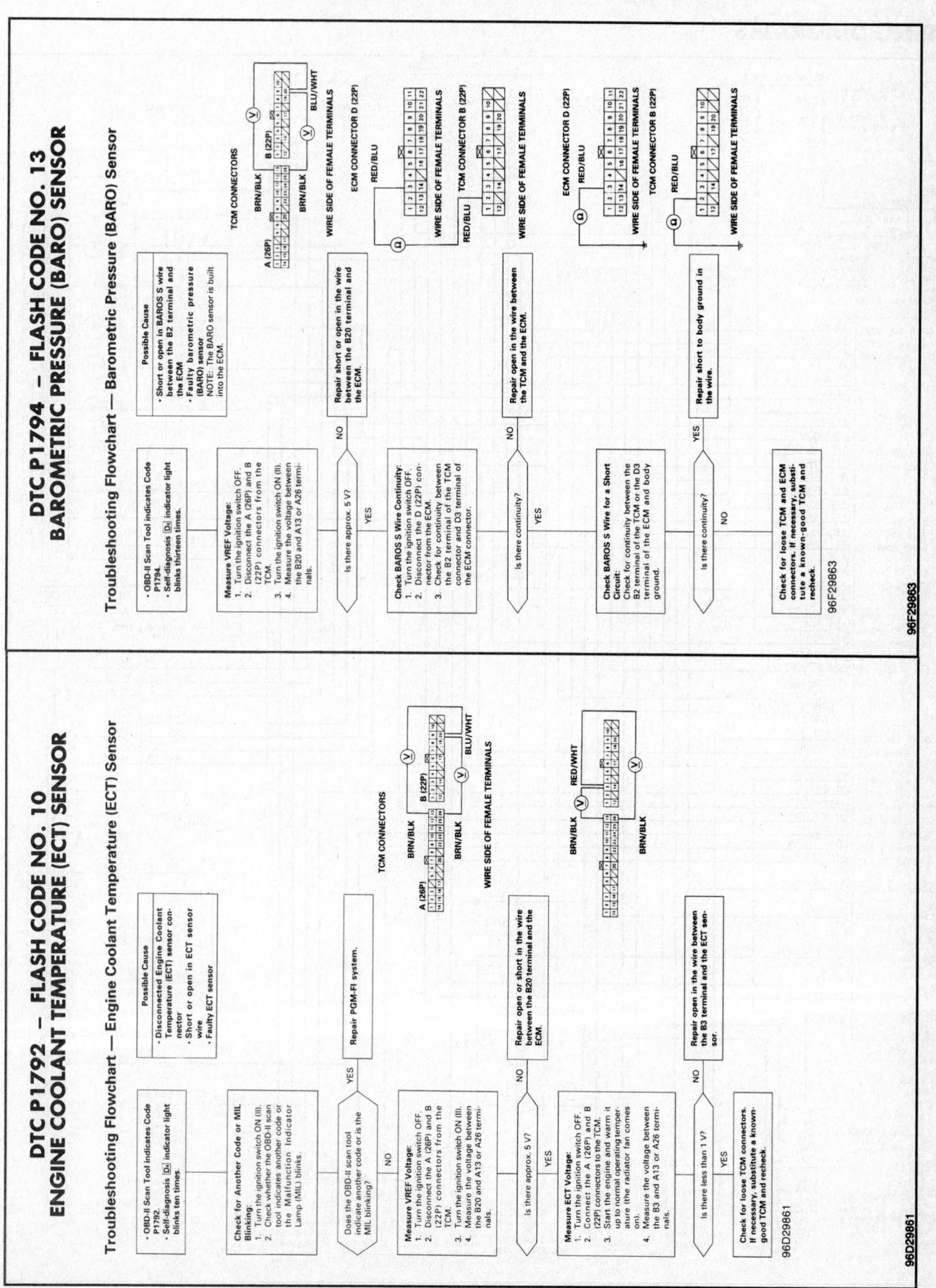

DTC P1792 – FLASH CODE NO. 10 ENGINE COOLANT TEMPERATURE (ECT) SENSOR

Troubleshooting Flowchart — Engine Coolant Temperature (ECT) Sensor

DTC P1794 – FLASH CODE NO. 13 BAROMETRIC PRESSURE (BARO) SENSOR

Troubleshooting Flowchart — Barometric Pressure (BARO) Sensor

WIRING DIAGRAMS

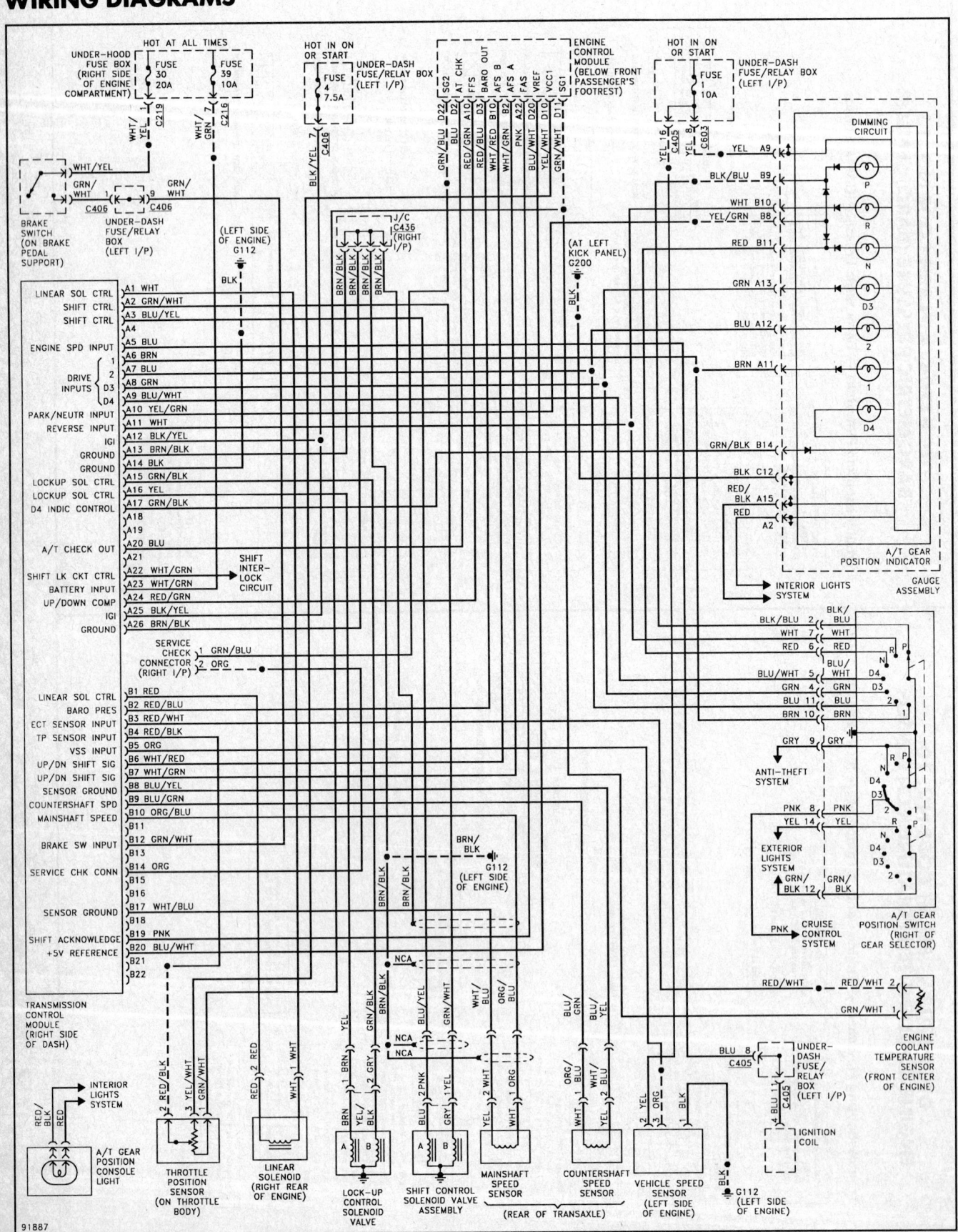

Fig. 30: Transaxle Wiring Diagram (1995-96 2.5TL)

91887

Integra

APPLICATION & LABOR TIMES

APPLICATION & LABOR TIMES

Vehicle Application	Labor Times		Trans. Model
	¹ R & I	² Overhaul	
Integra			
1995	4.6	8.9	SP7A
1996	4.6	8.9	SX4A

¹ – Removal and installation of transmission from vehicle chassis.

² – Bench overhaul time for transmission and differential. DOES NOT include removal and installation.

IDENTIFICATION

Transaxle model and serial number are stamped on the transaxle. *See Fig. 1.* Model and serial number may be required when ordering replacement components.

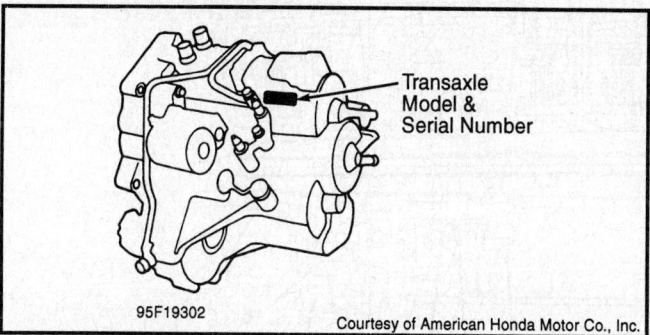

95F19302   Courtesy of American Honda Motor Co., Inc.

Fig. 1: Identifying Transaxle Model & Serial Number Location

DESCRIPTION

Automatic transaxle provides 4 forward speeds and one reverse. Transaxle consists of clutches, mainshaft, countershaft, sub-shaft, shift control solenoid valves, lock-up control solenoid valves and lock-up torque converter. *See Fig. 2.*

Valve bodies consists of main valve body, secondary valve body, servo body, lock-up valve body and regulator valve body. Valve bodies are attached to torque converter housing. Transaxle shifting and torque converter lock-up are controlled by the Transmission Control Module (TCM).

OPERATION

Shift lever has 7 positions. When shift lever is moved, manual valve on main valve body is moved by the shift cable. When certain transaxle gear combinations are engaged by clutches, power is transmitted from the mainshaft to the countershaft through the sub-shaft shaft to provide different gears. Shift lever positions operate as follows:

- **"P" (Park)** – Front wheels locked as parking pawl engages with parking gear on countershaft. All clutches are released. Neutral position switch, incorporated in A/T gear position switch, allows engine starting in this position.
- **"R" (Reverse)** – Reverse selector engages with countershaft reverse gear and 4th gear clutch is applied. Backup light switch, incorporated in A/T gear position switch, allows back-up lights to operate.
- **"N" (Neutral)** – All clutches are released. Neutral position switch, incorporated in A/T gear position switch, allows engine starting in this position.
- **"D₄" (Drive/4th)** – Transaxle starts in 1st gear and upshifts automatically to 2nd, 3rd and 4th gears. Transaxle will downshift through 3rd, 2nd and 1st gears until vehicle stops. When in 2nd, 3rd or 4th gear in "D₄" position, TCM sends signal to operate torque converter lock-up.
- **"D₃" (Drive/3rd)** – Transaxle starts off in 1st gear and upshifts automatically to 2nd gear and 3rd gear. On deceleration, transaxle

will downshift through 2nd gear to 1st gear. When in 3rd gear in "D₃" position, TCM sends signal to operate torque converter lock-up.

- **"2" (Second)** – Transaxle starts off and remains in 2nd gear for engine braking and better traction.
- **"1" (First)** – Transaxle starts off and remains in 1st gear for engine braking.

When in "D₃" position in 3rd gear or "D₄" position in 2nd, 3rd or 4th gear, torque converter lock-up exists and transaxle mainshaft rotates at the same speed as engine crankshaft. Under certain conditions, torque converter lock-up clutch is applied during deceleration when in 3rd and 4th gears. Torque converter lock-up is controlled by the TCM. The TCM receives various input signals and operates lock-up control solenoid valves. Operation of lock-up control solenoid valves controls the modulator pressure.

The TCM contains a grade logic control system which controls transaxle shifting while vehicle is ascending or descending on a slope or reducing vehicle speed. For more information on grade logic control system, see ACURA SP7A or SX4A ELECTRONIC CONTROLS article.

The TCM contains self-diagnostic system, which stores Diagnostic Trouble Code (DTC) if failure or problem exists in transaxle electronic control system. The DTC code can be retrieved to determine transaxle problem area. For information on electronic transaxle components, see ACURA SP7A or SX4A ELECTRONIC CONTROLS article.

Transaxle is equipped with shift and key interlock systems. Shift interlock system prevents shift lever from being moved from "P" position unless brake pedal is depressed and accelerator pedal is in idle position. In case of a malfunction, shift lever can be released by placing ignition key in release slot near shift lever. Key interlock system prevents ignition key from being removed from ignition switch unless shift lever is in "P" position. For additional information on interlock systems, see ACURA SP7A or SX4A ELECTRONIC CONTROLS article.

The A/T gear position indicator on instrument panel contains lights to indicate which position A/T gear position switch on shift lever is in. For information and testing of A/T gear position indicator, see ACURA SP7A or SX4A ELECTRONIC CONTROLS article.

LUBRICATION & ADJUSTMENTS

See appropriate AUTOMATIC TRANSMISSION SERVICING article in TRANSMISSION SERVICING section.

TROUBLE SHOOTING

Transaxle malfunctions may be caused by poor engine performance, improper adjustments, or failure of hydraulic, mechanical or electronic components. Always begin by checking fluid level, fluid condition and cable adjustments. Perform road test to determine if problem has been corrected. If problem still exists, several tests must be performed on transaxle. See TESTING.

Excessive Drag In Transaxle
- Binding Oil Pump

Excessive Idle Vibration
- Defective Torque Converter
- Incorrect Idle RPM

Excessive Vibration (RPM Related)
- Torque Converter Not Fully Seated In Oil Pump

Flares On 1-2 Upshift
- Clutch Pressure Control Valve Stuck
- Throttle Valve "B" Stuck
- Throttle Valve (T.V.) Cable Adjusted Too Long

Flares On 2-3 Upshift
- Clutch Pressure Control Valve Stuck
- Defective Seal Rings Or Guide
- Throttle Valve "B" Stuck
- Throttle Valve (T.V.) Cable Adjusted Too Long
- 2-3 Orifice Control Valve Stuck

Flares On 3-4 Upshift
- Clutch Pressure Control Valve Stuck

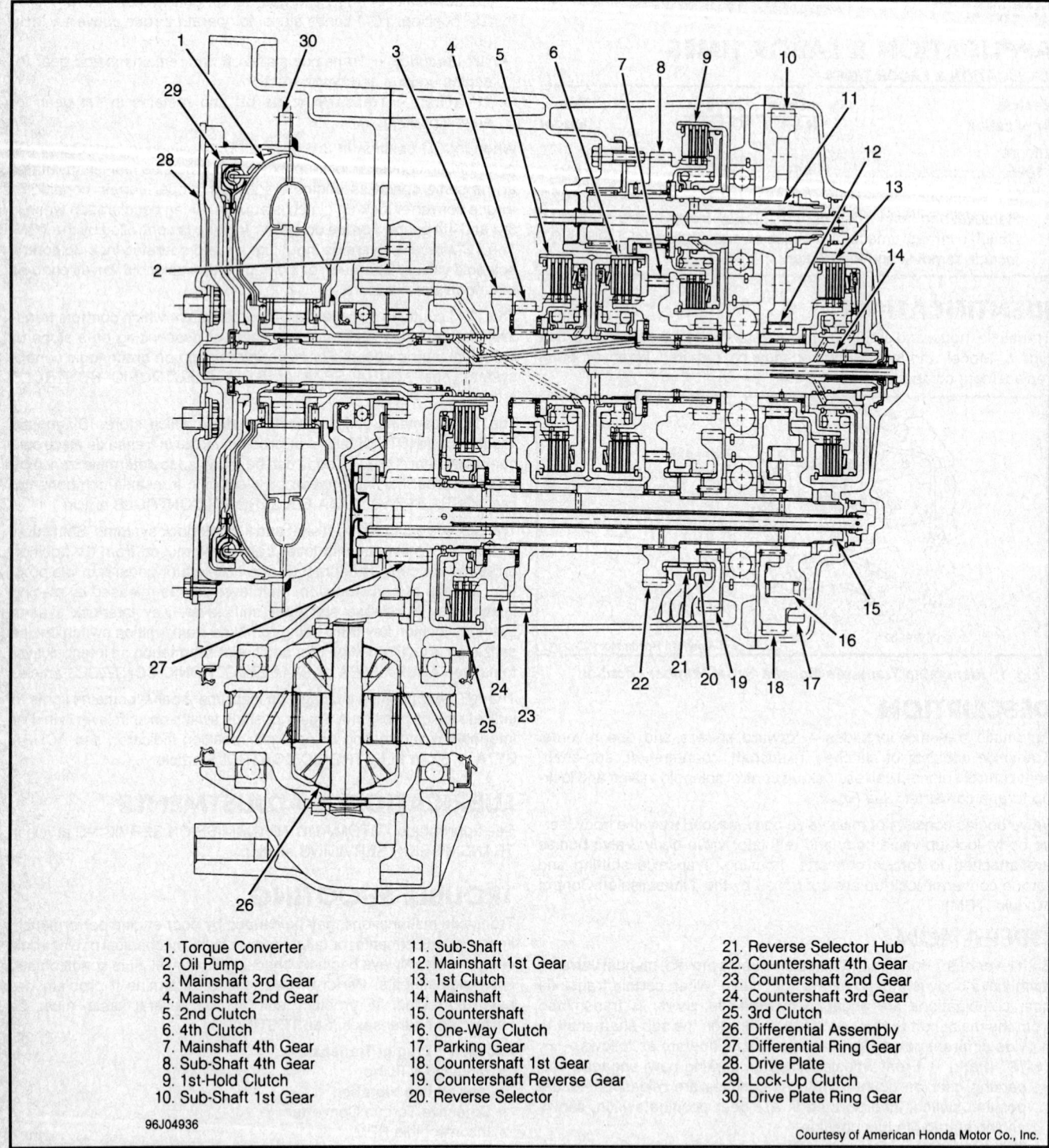

1. Torque Converter
2. Oil Pump
3. Mainshaft 3rd Gear
4. Mainshaft 2nd Gear
5. 2nd Clutch
6. 4th Clutch
7. Mainshaft 4th Gear
8. Sub-Shaft 4th Gear
9. 1st-Hold Clutch
10. Sub-Shaft 1st Gear
11. Sub-Shaft
12. Mainshaft 1st Gear
13. 1st Clutch
14. Mainshaft
15. Countershaft
16. One-Way Clutch
17. Parking Gear
18. Countershaft 1st Gear
19. Countershaft Reverse Gear
20. Reverse Selector
21. Reverse Selector Hub
22. Countershaft 4th Gear
23. Countershaft 2nd Gear
24. Countershaft 3rd Gear
25. 3rd Clutch
26. Differential Assembly
27. Differential Ring Gear
28. Drive Plate
29. Lock-Up Clutch
30. Drive Plate Ring Gear

96J04936

Courtesy of American Honda Motor Co., Inc.

Fig. 2: Identifying Transaxle Components

- Defective Seal Rings Or Guide
- Orifice Control Valve Stuck
- Throttle Valve "B" Stuck
- Throttle Valve (T.V.) Cable Adjusted Too Long

Gear Whine That Changes With Shifts
- Defective 1st Clutch
- Defective 3rd Gears
- Mainshaft Worn Or Damaged

Gear Whine That Changes With Speed
- Defective Differential Gears
- Shift Fork Bent

Harsh Downshift At Closed Throttle
- Clutch Pressure Control Valve Stuck
- Throttle Valve "B" Stuck
- Throttle Valve (T.V.) Cable Adjusted Too Short

Harsh Kickdown Shifts
- Clutch Pressure Control Valve Stuck
- Throttle Valve "B" Stuck
- Throttle Valve (T.V.) Cable Adjusted Too Short
- 3-2 Kickdown Valve Stuck
- 4-3 Kickdown Valve Stuck
- 4th Exhaust Valve Stuck

Harsh Shift When Manually Shifting To "1"
- Defective 1st-Hold Accumulator

Harsh Upshifts & Downshifts
- Check Balls Missing
- Clutch Pressure Control Valve Stuck
- Improper Type ATF
- Incorrect Clutch Clearance
- Orifice Control Valve Stuck
- Throttle Valve "B" Stuck
- Throttle Valve (T.V.) Cable Adjusted Too Short
- 2-3 Orifice Control Valve Stuck
- 3-2 Kickdown Valve Stuck
- 4-3 Kickdown Valve Stuck

Harsh 1-2 Upshift
- Clutch Pressure Control Valve Stuck
- Defective 2nd Clutch
- Throttle Valve "B" Stuck
- Throttle Valve (T.V.) Cable Adjusted Too Short

Harsh 2-1 Kickdown Shift
- Defective One-Way Clutch

Harsh 2-3 Upshift
- Clutch Pressure Control Valve Stuck
- Defective 3rd Clutch
- Throttle Valve "B" Stuck
- Throttle Valve (T.V.) Cable Adjusted Too Short
- 2-3 Orifice Control Valve Stuck

Harsh 3-4 Upshift
- Clutch Pressure Control Valve Stuck
- Defective 4th Clutch
- Orifice Control Valve Stuck
- Throttle Valve "B" Stuck
- Throttle Valve (T.V.) Cable Adjusted Too Short

Lock-Up Clutch Does Not Lock-Up Smoothly
- Defective Torque Converter
- Lock-Up Control Valve Stuck
- Lock-Up Shift Valve Stuck

Lock-Up Clutch Does Not Operate Properly
- Improperly Adjusted Throttle Valve (T.V.) Cable
- Lock-Up Control Valve Stuck
- Lock-Up Shift Valve Stuck
- Lock-Up Timing Valve "B" Stuck
- Modulator Valve Stuck
- Throttle Valve "B" Stuck
- Torque Converter Check Valve Stuck

No Engine Braking In "1"
- Defective 1st-Hold Clutch

Noise From Transaxle In All Gears
- Defective Oil Pump
- Defective Torque Converter

Noise From Transaxle With Wheels Rolling
- Damaged Reverse Gears
- Defective Differential Gears
- Reverse Selector Hub Installed Upside Down

Popping Noise When Taking Off In "R"
- Damaged Reverse Gears
- Shift Fork Bent
- Worn Reverse Selector

Ratcheting Noise When Shifting To "R"
- Damaged Reverse Gears
- Defective Oil Pump
- Pressure Regulator Stuck
- Shift Fork Bent
- Worn Reverse Selector

Ratcheting Noise When Shifting From "R" To "P" Or "N"
- Damaged Reverse Gears
- Damaged 4th Gears
- Shift Fork Bent
- Worn Reverse Selector

Shifts Erratically
- Modulator Valve Stuck
- Throttle Valve (T.V.) Cable Adjusted Too Short
- 3-2 Kickdown Valve Stuck

Slips In All Gears
- Defective Oil Pump
- Fluid Strainer Clogged
- Pressure Regulator Stuck

Slips In 1st Gear
- Defective One-Way Clutch
- Defective 1st Clutch Or 1st Accumulator
- Feedpipe "O" Ring Damaged

Slips In Reverse
- Defective 4th Clutch Or 4th Accumulator
- Feedpipe "O" Ring Damaged
- Servo Valve Stuck

Slips In 2nd Gear
- Clutch Pressure Control Valve Stuck
- Defective Seal Rings Or Guide
- Defective 2nd Clutch Or 2nd Accumulator
- 2-3 Shift Valve Stuck

Slips In 3rd Gear
- Clutch Pressure Control Valve Stuck
- Defective Seal Rings Or Guide
- Defective 3rd Clutch Or 3rd Accumulator
- 3-4 Shift Valve Stuck

Slips In 4th Gear
- Clutch Pressure Control Valve Stuck
- Defective 4th Clutch Or 4th Accumulator
- Feedpipe "O" Ring Damaged

Upshifts Late
- Modulator Valve Stuck

Vehicle Locks In "R"
- Parking Brake Lever Installed Upside Down
- Shift Fork Retaining Bolt Not Installed

Vehicle Moves In All Gears Except "R"
- Defective Or Improperly Adjusted Shift Cable
- Defective Or Worn Reverse Gears
- Defective 4th Clutch
- Servo Control Valve Stuck
- Servo Valve Stuck
- Shift Fork Bent
- Worn Reverse Selector

Vehicle Moves In All Gears Except "2"
- Defective Seal Rings Or Guide
- Defective 2nd Clutch Or 2nd Accumulator

Vehicle Moves In "N"
- Defective Or Improperly Adjusted Shift Cable
- Defective 1st, 2nd, 3rd Or 4th Clutch
- Incorrect Gear Or Clutch Clearance

Vehicle Moves In "R" & "2" Only
- Defective One-Way Clutch
- Defective 1st Clutch Or 1st Accumulator
- Feedpipe "O" Ring Damaged

Vehicle Will Not Move
- Defective Oil Pump
- Defective Or Improperly Adjusted Shift Cable
- Fluid Strainer Clogged
- Pressure Regulator Stuck

Vehicle Will Not Move In "D₃" Or "D₄"
- One-Way Clutch Installed Upside Down

Will Not Downshift To 1st Gear
- Defective 1st-Hold Clutch
- 1-2 Shift Valve Stuck

Will Not Shift Into 4th Gear When In "D₄"
- Defective Or Improperly Adjusted Shift Cable
- 3-4 Shift Valve Stuck
- 4th Accumulator Stuck
- 4th Exhaust Valve Stuck

Will Not Upshift (Stays In 1st Gear)
- Clutch Pressure Control Valve Stuck
- Modulator Valve Stuck
- 1-2 Shift Valve Stuck

TESTING

CAUTION: Vehicle is equipped with an air bag system (Supplemental Restraint System (SRS). All wires have Yellow insulation and are located underdash or in instrument panel area. To avoid injury from accidental deployment, read and carefully follow all SERVICE PRECAUTIONS and DISABLING & ACTIVATING AIR BAG SYSTEM procedures in APPLICATIONS & IDENTIFICATIONS.

ROAD TEST

NOTE: If shift lever cannot be moved from "P" position with brake pedal depressed and accelerator at idle position, check shift interlock system. See ACURA SP7A or SX4A ELECTRONIC CONTROLS article.

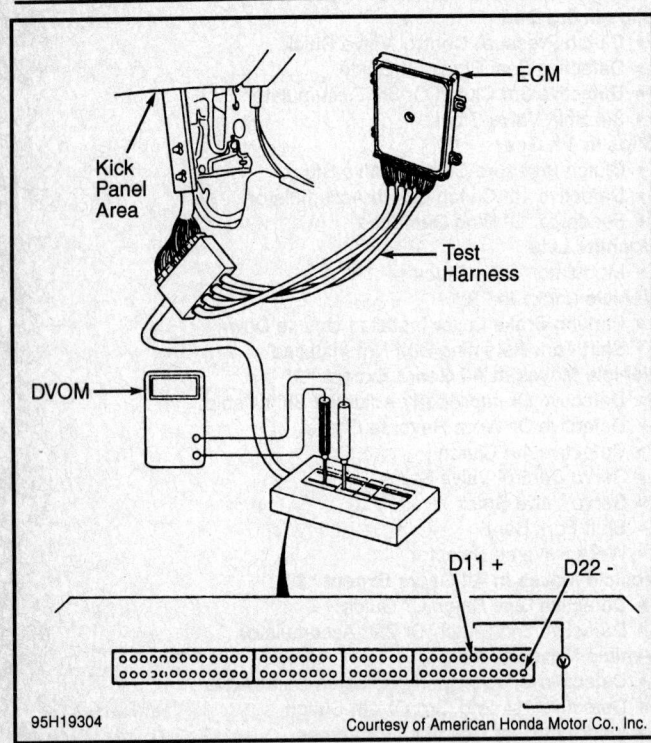

95H19304   Courtesy of American Honda Motor Co., Inc.

Fig. 3: Identifying ECM & Installing Test Harness

1) Warm engine to normal operating temperature. Apply parking brake, and block wheels. Start engine. Move shift lever to "D₄" position while depressing brake pedal. Depress accelerator pedal and release it suddenly. Engine should not stall.

2) Repeat step 1) with shift lever in "D₃" position. Ensure engine does not stall. Manufacturer recommends monitoring of throttle position sensor voltage when performing road test to ensure proper throttle opening for verifying shift points and lock-up of torque converter.

3) On 1995 models, remove door scuff plate from passenger's side door opening and passenger's side kick panel for access to Engine Control Module (ECM), mounted on kick panel area. *See Fig. 3.* Remove ECM cover, located above ECM.

4) Ensure ignition is off. Disconnect electrical connectors from ECM and install Test Harness (07LAJ-PT3010A) between electrical connectors and ECM. *See Fig. 3.*

5) Connect Digital Volt-Ohmmeter (DVOM) to terminals D11 (+) and D22 (−) on test harness for monitoring of throttle position sensor voltage. *See Fig. 3.*

CLUTCH APPLICATION

Shift Lever Position	Elements In Use
"P" Or "N"	No Clutches Are Applied
"R"	4th Clutch
"D₄"	
1st Gear	¹1st Clutch
2nd Gear	² 2nd Clutch
3rd Gear	² 3rd Clutch
4th Gear	² 4th Clutch
"D₃"	
1st Gear	1st Clutch
2nd Gear	² 2nd Clutch
3rd Gear	² 3rd Clutch
"2"	² 2nd Clutch
"1"	1st-Hold Clutch & 1st Clutch

¹ – One-way clutch engages on acceleration and slips on deceleration, no engine braking.
² – The 1st clutch engages, but driving power is not transmitted, as one-way clutch slips.

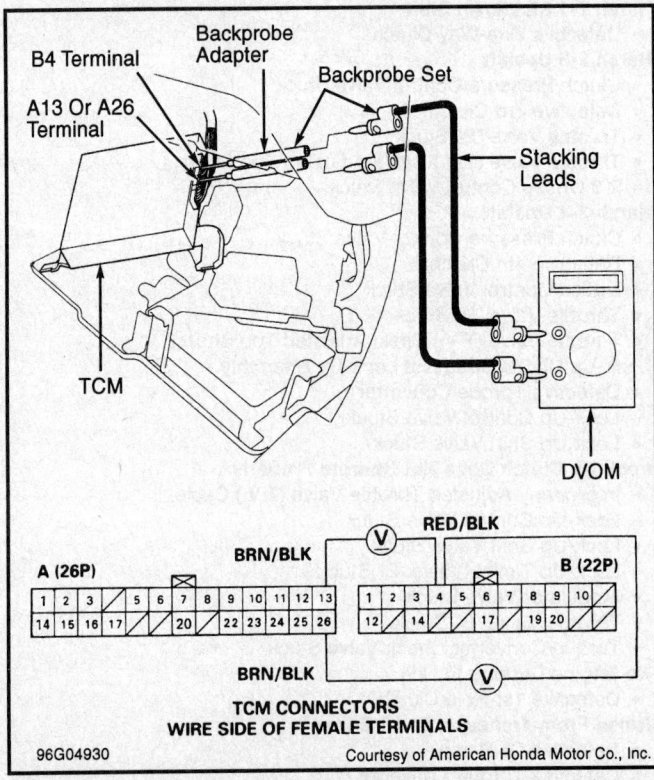

96G04930   Courtesy of American Honda Motor Co., Inc.

Fig. 4: Installing Backprobe Set At TCM

6) On 1996 models, remove left kick panel. Remove Transmission Control Module (TCM) and turn over to gain access to connectors. Install Backprobe Test Set (07SAZ-001000A) or equivalent between TCM and DVOM leads. *See Fig. 4.*

7) Using DVOM, with positive lead at terminal B4 and negative lead at terminal A13 or A26. *See Fig. 4.* Ensure digital volt-ohmmeter is set for measuring voltage.

8) On all models, road test vehicle and check for abnormal noise and clutch slippage. See CLUTCH APPLICATION table for clutch engagement.

9) Ensure upshift and downshift points and lock-up of torque converter are correct in relation to throttle position sensor voltage or throttle opening and vehicle speed. *See Fig. 5 or 6.*

10) With shift lever in "D₄" position, accelerate to about 35 MPH so transaxle is in 4th gear. Move shift lever to "2" position. Ensure engine braking occurs.

11) Place shift lever in "1" position. Accelerate from a stop at full throttle. Check for abnormal noise or clutch slippage. Upshifts and downshifts should not occur in this shift lever position.

"D₄" Or "D₃" Position

- Upshift

Throttle Opening	Unit of speed	1st→2nd	2nd→3rd	3rd→4th
Throttle position sensor voltage: 0.75 V	mph	11—12	20—22	27—30
	Km/h	17.0—19.0	32.5—35.5	43.5—48.5
Throttle position sensor voltage: 2.5 V	mph	21—23	35—39	55—59
	Km/h	33.5—36.5	57.0—63.0	89.0—95.0
Full-opened throttle	mph	30—34	62—65	98—101
	Km/h	49.0—55.0	99.0—105.0	157.0—163.0

- Downshift

Throttle Opening	Unit of speed	4th→3rd	3rd→2nd	2nd→1st
Full-closed throttle	mph	18—21	6—9 (3rd→1st)	——
	Km/h	29.0—33.0	10—14 (3rd→1st)	——
Full-opened throttle	mph	85—89	54—58	23—27
	Km/h	137.0—143.0	87.0—93.0	37.0—43.0

- Lock-up

Throttle Opening	Unit of speed	D₄ Position	
		Lock-up control solenoid valve A ON	Lock-up control solenoid valve B ON
Throttle position sensor voltage: 2.5 V	mph	13—16	17—20
	km/h	21.0—25.0	28.0—32.0
Full-opened throttle	mph	92—96	92—96
	km/h	148.0—154.0	148.0—154.0

Throttle Opening	Unit of speed	D₃ Position	
		Lock-up control solenoid valve A ON	Lock-up control solenoid valve B ON
Throttle position sensor voltage: 1.0 V	mph	61—63	61—63
	km/h	98—102	98—102
Full-opened throttle	mph	85—89	85—89
	km/h	137—143	137—143

95I19305

Courtesy of American Honda Motor Co., Inc.

Fig. 5: 1995 Upshift & Downshift Specifications

12) Place shift lever in "2" position. Accelerate from a stop at full throttle. Check for abnormal noise or clutch slippage. Upshifts and downshifts should not occur in this shift lever position.

13) Place shift lever in "R" position. Accelerate from a stop at full throttle. Check for abnormal noise or clutch slippage.

14) Park vehicle on a slope. Apply parking brake. Place shift lever in "P" position. Release parking brake. Ensure vehicle does not move. If vehicle moves, check for defective shift cable or parking components.

15) Ensure ignition is off. Remove test harness and reinstall ECM cover, carpet and door scuff plate.

TORQUE CONVERTER STALL SPEED TEST

CAUTION: DO NOT perform torque converter stall speed test for more than 10 seconds or transaxle may be damaged. DO NOT move shift lever while increasing engine speed.

1) Apply parking brake and block all wheels. Connect tachometer. Start engine. Ensure A/C is off. Warm engine to normal operating temperature. Place shift lever in "2" position.

2) Fully depress brake pedal. Fully depress accelerator for 6-8 seconds and note engine speed. This is torque converter stall speed.

3) Allow transaxle to cool for 2 minutes. Repeat test procedure with shift lever in "D₄", "1" and "R" positions.

4) Torque converter stall speed should be the same in "D₄", "2", "1" and "R" positions and within specification. See TORQUE CONVERTER STALL SPEED SPECIFICATIONS table. If torque converter stall speed is not within specification, see TORQUE CONVERTER STALL SPEED TROUBLE SHOOTING table for possible problem areas.

TORQUE CONVERTER STALL SPEED SPECIFICATIONS

Application	Engine RPM
Standard	2400
Service Limit	2200-2600

TORQUE CONVERTER STALL SPEED TROUBLE SHOOTING

Torque Converter Stall Speed Test Results	Probable Cause
Stall Speed RPM High In "D₄", "2", "1" & "R"	Low Fluid Level, Low Oil Pump Output, Clogged Fluid Strainer, Pressure Regulator Valve Stuck Closed, Slipping Clutch
Stall Speed RPM High In "R"	Slipping 4th Clutch
Stall Speed RPM High In "D₄"	Slipping 1st Clutch, Defective One-Way Clutch
Stall Speed RPM High In "2"	Slipping 2nd Clutch
Stall Speed RPM High In "1"	Slipping 1st-Hold Or 1st Clutch, Defective One-Way Clutch
Stall Speed RPM Low In "D₄", "2", "1" & "R"	Engine Output Low, Torque Converter One-Way Clutch Slipping

HYDRAULIC PRESSURE TEST

Pressure Test Preparation – Ensure transaxle fluid level is correct. Warm engine to normal operating temperature. Apply parking brake, and block rear wheels. Raise and support vehicle so front wheels can rotate.

Line Pressure Test – 1) With engine off, remove pressure tap plug from line pressure tap on transaxle. *See Fig. 7.* Attach Pressure Gauge Set (07406-0020400) to line pressure tap using NEW seal washer. Tighten hose fitting to 13 ft. lbs. (18 N.m).

2) With shift lever in "P" or "N" position, start and operate engine at 2000 RPM. Note line pressure. Line pressure should be within specification. See HYDRAULIC PRESSURE TEST SPECIFICATIONS table.

3) If line pressure is not within specification, see HYDRAULIC PRESSURE TROUBLE SHOOTING table. Shut engine off.

4) Using NEW seal washer, install and tighten pressure tap plug to specification. See TORQUE SPECIFICATIONS.

Clutch Pressure Test – 1) Clutch pressure should be checked at each clutch pressure tap on transaxle. *See Fig. 7.*

AUTOMATIC TRANSMISSIONS
Acura SP7A & SX4A (Cont.)

- Upshift: "D₄" & "D₃" Position

Throttle Opening	Unit of speed	1st → 2nd	2nd → 3rd	3rd → 4th
Throttle position sensor voltage: 1.0 V	mph	8.0 – 10.0	20.0 – 23.0	27.0 – 31.0
	km/h	13.5 – 16.1	32.2 – 37.0	43.5 – 49.9
Throttle position sensor voltage: 2.5 V	mph	21.0 – 25.0	38.0 – 43.0	58.0 – 64.0
	km/h	33.8 – 40.2	61.2 – 69.2	93.3 – 103.0
Fully-opened throttle	mph	31.0 – 36.0	63.0 – 71.0	97.0 – 108.0
	km/h	49.9 – 57.9	101.4 – 114.3	156.1 – 173.8

- Downshift: "D₄" & "D₃" Position

Throttle Opening	Unit of speed	4th → 3rd	3rd → 2nd	2nd → 1st
Throttle position sensor voltage: 0.5 V	mph	17.5 – 20.5	6.0 – 9.0 (3rd→1st)	——
	km/h	28.2 – 33.0	9.7 – 14.5 (3rd→1st)	——
Fully-opened throttle	mph	85.0 – 95.0	54.0 – 61.0	23.0 – 28.0
	km/h	137.0 – 152.9	86.9 – 98.2	37.0 – 45.1

- Lock-Up: "D₄" Position

Throttle Opening	Unit of speed	Lock-up control solenoid valve A: ON	Lock-up control solenoid valve B: ON
Throttle position sensor voltage: 1.0 V	mph	14.0 – 17.0	17.0 – 20.0
	km/h	22.5 – 27.4	27.4 – 32.2
Fully-opened throttle	mph	92.0 – 96.0	92.0 – 96.0
	km/h	148.1 – 154.5	148.1 – 154.5

- Lock-Up: "D₃" Position

Throttle Opening	Unit of speed	Lock-up control solenoid valve A: ON	Lock-up control solenoid valve B: ON
Throttle position sensor voltage: 1.0 V	mph	61.0 – 68.0	60.0 – 67.0
	km/h	98.2 – 109.4	96.6 – 107.8
Fully-opened throttle	mph	85.0 – 94.0	85.0 – 94.0
	km/h	136.8 – 151.3	136.8 – 151.3

96B04937

Courtesy of American Honda Motor Co., Inc.

Fig. 6: 1996 Upshift & Downshift Specifications

2) With engine off, remove pressure plug from appropriate clutch pressure tap on transaxle. *See Fig. 7.* Attach Pressure Gauge Set (07406-0020400) to appropriate pressure tap using NEW seal washer. Tighten hose fitting to 13 ft. lbs. (18 N.m).

NOTE: On some applications clutch pressure may vary with position of throttle control lever on transaxle. The Throttle Valve (T.V.) cable is connected to throttle control lever on transaxle. The T.V. cable may need to be disconnected from throttle control lever for some tests. Ensure shift lever is in proper position when checking clutch pressures.

3) Start and operate engine at 2000 RPM. Note clutch pressure reading with shift lever in proper location. See HYDRAULIC PRESSURE TEST SPECIFICATIONS table.

4) Clutch pressure should be within specification. If clutch pressure is not within specification, see HYDRAULIC PRESSURE TROUBLE SHOOTING table. Shut engine off.

5) Using NEW seal washer, install and tighten pressure tap plug to specification. See TORQUE SPECIFICATIONS.

Clutch Low/High Pressure Test – 1) Clutch low/high pressure is tested at 2nd, 3rd and 4th clutch pressure taps on transaxle. *See Fig. 7.* Disconnect Throttle Valve (T.V.) cable from throttle control lever on transaxle.

NOTE: When disconnecting T.V. cable, unhook cable from throttle control lever. DO NOT loosen lock nuts used for cable adjustment.

2) With engine off, remove pressure tap plug from appropriate clutch pressure tap on transaxle. Attach Pressure Gauge Set (07406-0020400) to appropriate pressure tap using NEW seal washer. Tighten hose fitting to 13 ft. lbs. (18 N.m).

3) Start engine and allow to idle. Move shift lever to "D₄" position. Slowly increase engine speed until pressure is indicated on pressure gauge. Release throttle. Allow engine to idle and note clutch low pressure reading.

4) With engine idling, lift throttle control lever on transaxle upward approximately 1/2 the distance of throttle control lever travel. Increase engine speed and note highest pressure reading. This is the clutch high pressure.

5) Repeat procedure on remaining clutches. The clutch low/high pressure should be within specification. See HYDRAULIC PRESSURE TEST SPECIFICATIONS table. If clutch low/high pressure is not within specification, see HYDRAULIC PRESSURE TROUBLE SHOOTING table.

6) Shut engine off. Remove pressure gauge set. Using NEW seal washer, install and tighten pressure tap plug to specification. See TORQUE SPECIFICATIONS. Reconnect T.V. cable.

Throttle "B" Pressure Test – 1) Disconnect Throttle Valve (T.V.) cable from throttle control lever on transaxle.

NOTE: When disconnecting T.V. cable, unhook cable from throttle control lever. DO NOT loosen lock nuts used for cable adjustment.

2) With engine off, remove pressure tap plug from throttle "B" pressure tap on transaxle. *See Fig. 7.*

3) Attach Pressure Gauge Set (07406-0020400) to throttle "B" pressure tap using NEW seal washer. Tighten hose fitting to 13 ft. lbs. (18 N.m).

4) Start and operate engine at 1000 RPM with shift lever in "D₃" or "D₄" position. Note pressure with throttle control lever closed (released position). Throttle "B" pressure should be within specification. See HYDRAULIC PRESSURE TEST SPECIFICATIONS table.

HYDRAULIC PRESSURE TEST SPECIFICATIONS

Application	Shift Lever Position	Pressure psi (kPa)
Line Pressure		
Engine Speed At 2000 RPM	"P" Or "N"	113-130 (780-880)
Clutch Pressure		
1st Clutch		
Engine Speed At 2000 RPM	"1" Or "D₄"	113-130 (780-880)
1st-Hold Clutch		
Engine Speed At 2000 RPM	"1"	113-130 (780-880)
2nd Clutch		
Engine Speed At 2000 RPM	"2"	113-130 (780-880)
Throttle Control Lever Fully Closed [1]	"D₄"	58-70 (400-480)
Throttle Control Lever Open More Than 3/16 [2]	"D₄"	113-130 (780-880)
3rd Clutch		
Throttle Control Lever Fully Closed [1]	"D₄"	58-70 (400-480)
Throttle Control Lever Open More Than 3/16 [2]	"D₄"	113-130 (780-880)
4th Clutch		
Engine Speed At 2000 RPM	"R"	113-130 (780-880)
Throttle Control Lever Fully Closed [1]	"D₄"	58-70 (400-480)
Throttle Control Lever Open More Than 3/16 [2]	"D₄"	113-130 (780-880)
Clutch Low Pressure		
Throttle Control Lever Fully Closed [1]		
2nd, 3rd Or 4th Clutch	"D₄"	58-70 (400-480)
Clutch High Pressure		
Throttle Control Lever Lifted Upward		
1/2 Distance Of Throttle Control Lever Travel		
2nd, 3rd Or 4th Clutch	"D₄"	113-130 (780-880)
Throttle "B" Pressure		
Throttle Control Lever Fully Closed [3]	"D₃" Or "D₄"	0-2.2 (0-15)
Throttle Control Lever Fully Open [3]	"D₃" Or "D₄"	113-130 (780-880)

[1] – Check pressure with engine speed at 2000 RPM. Fully closed position is with throttle control lever on transaxle in released position and not being pulled upward by T.V. cable.

[2] – Check pressure with engine speed at 2000 RPM. Open position is with transaxle T.V. lever being pulled upward 3/16 the distance of throttle control lever travel on 1995 models and 3/8 the distance of throttle control lever travel on 1996 models.

[3] – Check pressure with engine speed at 1000 RPM.

HYDRAULIC PRESSURE TROUBLE SHOOTING

Application	Probable Cause
Line Pressure	
Low Or No Pressure	Defective Torque Converter, Defective Torque Converter Check Valve, Defective Oil Pump Defective Pressure Regulator,
Clutch Pressure	
Low Or No 1st Clutch Pressure	Defective 1st Clutch
Low Or No 1st-Hold Clutch Pressure	Defective 1st-Hold Clutch
Low Or No 2nd Clutch Pressure	Defective 2nd Clutch
Low Or No 3rd Clutch Pressure	Defective 3rd Clutch
Low Or No 4th Clutch Pressure	Defective 4th Clutch, Defective Servo Valve On 4th Clutch
Clutch Low/High Pressure	
Low Or No 2nd Clutch Pressure	Defective 2nd Clutch
Low Or No 3rd Clutch Pressure	Defective 3rd Clutch
Low Or No 4th Clutch Pressure	Defective 4th Clutch
Throttle "B" Pressure	
High, Low Or No Throttle "B" Pressure	Defective Throttle Valve "B"

5) Lift throttle control lever on transaxle to fully open position with engine at 1000 RPM. Note throttle "B" pressure reading.

6) Throttle "B" pressure should be within specification. See HYDRAULIC PRESSURE TEST SPECIFICATIONS table. If pressure is not within specification, see HYDRAULIC PRESSURE TROUBLE SHOOTING table. Shut engine off. Remove pressure gauge set.

7) Using NEW seal washer, install and tighten pressure tap plug to specification. See TORQUE SPECIFICATIONS. Reconnect T.V. cable.

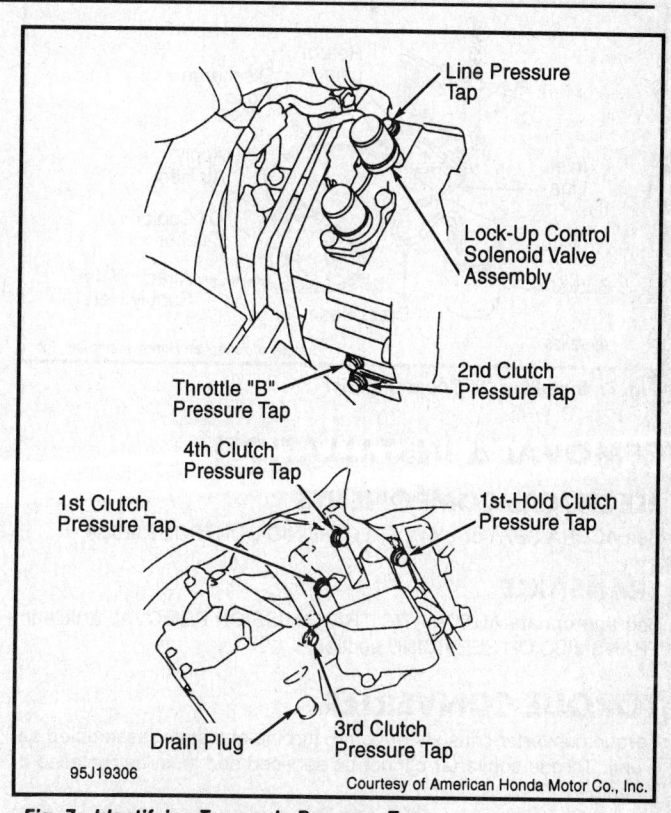

95J19306

Courtesy of American Honda Motor Co., Inc.

Fig. 7: Identifying Transaxle Pressure Taps

ON-VEHICLE SERVICE

AXLE SHAFTS

See appropriate article in AXLE SHAFTS & TRANSFER CASES section.

OIL COOLER FLUSHING

1) Attach Oil Cooler Flusher (J38405-A) to oil cooler lines. *See Fig. 8.* Fill oil cooler flusher tank 2/3 full with Flushing Fluid (J35944-20). DO NOT use any other flushing fluid.

2) Ensure water and air valves on oil cooler flusher are off. Apply 80-120 psi (550-829 kPa) air pressure to oil cooler flusher. Turn oil cooler flusher water valve on so water will flow through oil cooler for 10 seconds. Shut water valve off. Replace oil cooler if water will not flow through oil cooler.

3) Depress and hold mixing trigger on oil cooler flusher downward. Turn water valve on and flush oil cooler for 2 minutes. Turn air valve on for 5 seconds every 15-20 seconds to create a surging action.

4) Turn water valve off. Release mixing trigger. Disconnect oil cooler flusher and reverse hoses so oil cooler can be flushed in the opposite direction.

5) Repeat steps **2)** and **3)**. Turn water valve off. Release mixing trigger. Turn water valve on and rinse oil cooler for at least one minute. Once oil cooler is flushed in both directions, turn water off. Turn air valve on for 2 minutes or until no moisture is visible from drain hose.

CAUTION: Ensure no moisture exists in oil cooler, as it can damage transaxle.

6) Turn air off. Disconnect oil cooler flusher. Reconnect inlet line on oil cooler. Once transaxle is installed, attach drain hose on return line and place in oil container. Ensure transaxle is in "P" position. Fill transaxle with Dexron-II ATF.

7) Start engine and operate for approximately 30 seconds or until one quart (.9L) of ATF is discharged from return line. Shut engine off. Remove drain hose. Reinstall return line. Fill transaxle to proper level.

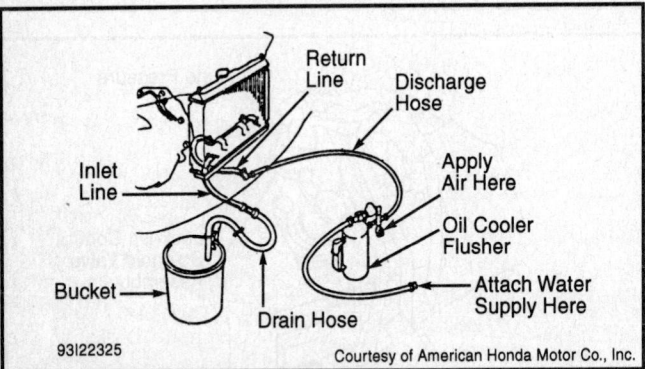

Fig. 8: Installing Oil Cooler Flusher

REMOVAL & INSTALLATION

ELECTRICAL COMPONENTS

See ACURA SP7A or SX4A ELECTRONIC CONTROLS article.

TRANSAXLE

See appropriate AUTOMATIC TRANSMISSION REMOVAL article in TRANSMISSION SERVICING section.

TORQUE CONVERTER

Torque converter consists of pump, turbine and stator assembled as a unit. Torque converter cannot be serviced and must be replaced if defective.

NOTE: For torque converter stall speed test, see TORQUE CONVERTER STALL SPEED TEST under TESTING.

TRANSAXLE DISASSEMBLY

VALVE BODIES & INTERNAL COMPONENTS

1) Remove bolts, right side cover protector, right side cover and gasket. *See Fig. 9.* Install Mainshaft Holder (07GAB-PF50101) on mainshaft to secure mainshaft. *See Fig. 10.*

2) Engage parking pawl with parking gear. Align hole in sub-shaft 1st gear with hole in transaxle housing. Install pin in sub-shaft 1st gear and transaxle housing to prevent sub-shaft 1st gear from rotating. *See Fig. 11.*

3) Using hammer and chisel, cut lock tabs on countershaft and sub-shaft lock nuts. Pry lock tabs on mainshaft lock nut upward. Remove all lock nuts and spring washers from countershaft, mainshaft and sub-shaft. *See Fig. 11.*

NOTE: Mainshaft and countershaft lock nuts contain left-hand threads.

4) Remove mainshaft holder once all lock nuts are removed. Remove pin securing sub-shaft 1st gear. Remove 1st clutch assembly, mainshaft 1st gear, thrust washer and mainshaft 1st gear collar from mainshaft. *See Fig. 9.*

5) Remove sub-shaft 1st gear. Remove parking pawl. Using puller, remove parking gear, one-way clutch and countershaft 1st gear from countershaft. Remove needle bearing and countershaft 1st gear collar from countershaft. *See Fig. 9.*

6) Remove parking brake lever and parking brake lever spring from control shaft. Remove throttle control lever and throttle control lever spring from throttle control shaft. *See Fig. 9.*

7) Remove dipstick, vehicle speed sensor, joint bolts and cooler pipes. Remove mount bracket from transaxle housing. *See Fig. 13.* Remove transaxle housing bolts and transaxle hanger.

8) Align spring pin on control shaft with groove in transaxle housing by rotating control shaft. Using Puller (07HAC-PK4010A), remove transaxle housing. *See Fig. 12.* Remove gasket for transaxle housing.

9) Remove countershaft reverse gear collar, needle bearing and countershaft reverse gear from countershaft. *See Fig. 13.* Remove bolt and bolt lock from reverse shift fork. Remove reverse shift fork with reverse selector from countershaft.

10) Remove countershaft and mainshaft together from torque converter housing. Remove differential assembly. Remove bolts, reverse idler gear shaft holder, reverse idler gear and needle bearing from transaxle housing (if necessary).

11) Remove oil feedpipes from servo body, servo detent base, accumulator cover, lock-up valve body and main valve body. *See Fig. 14.* Remove bolts and accumulator cover. Remove bolts, fluid strainer and servo detent base.

12) Remove bolts, servo body and separator plate. *See Fig. 14.* Remove bolt, secondary valve body and separator plate. DO NOT lose check balls in secondary valve body.

13) Remove bolts, lubrication plate, lock-up valve body and separator plate. Remove regulator valve body. Remove stopper shaft and stator shaft. Remove detent spring from detent arm. Remove control shaft from torque converter housing.

14) Remove detent arm shaft and detent arm from main valve body. Remove bolts and main valve body. DO NOT lose check balls in main valve body. *See Fig. 14.*

15) Remove oil pump driven gear shaft and oil pump gears. *See Fig. 14.* Remove separator plate for main valve body and dowel pins. Remove magnet. Remove lock-up control solenoid valve assembly (if necessary).

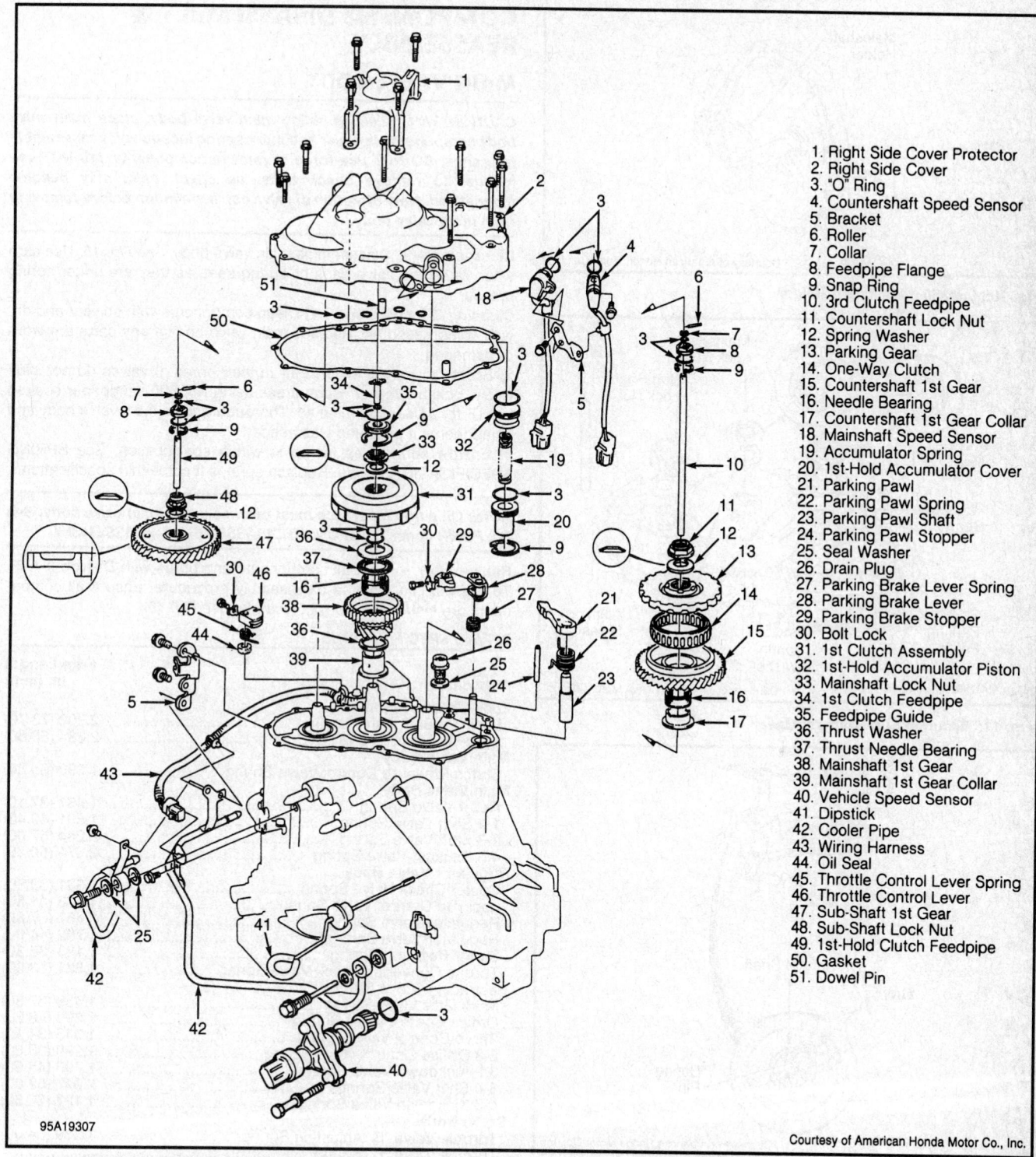

1. Right Side Cover Protector
2. Right Side Cover
3. "O" Ring
4. Countershaft Speed Sensor
5. Bracket
6. Roller
7. Collar
8. Feedpipe Flange
9. Snap Ring
10. 3rd Clutch Feedpipe
11. Countershaft Lock Nut
12. Spring Washer
13. Parking Gear
14. One-Way Clutch
15. Countershaft 1st Gear
16. Needle Bearing
17. Countershaft 1st Gear Collar
18. Mainshaft Speed Sensor
19. Accumulator Spring
20. 1st-Hold Accumulator Cover
21. Parking Pawl
22. Parking Pawl Spring
23. Parking Pawl Shaft
24. Parking Pawl Stopper
25. Seal Washer
26. Drain Plug
27. Parking Brake Lever Spring
28. Parking Brake Lever
29. Parking Brake Stopper
30. Bolt Lock
31. 1st Clutch Assembly
32. 1st-Hold Accumulator Piston
33. Mainshaft Lock Nut
34. 1st Clutch Feedpipe
35. Feedpipe Guide
36. Thrust Washer
37. Thrust Needle Bearing
38. Mainshaft 1st Gear
39. Mainshaft 1st Gear Collar
40. Vehicle Speed Sensor
41. Dipstick
42. Cooler Pipe
43. Wiring Harness
44. Oil Seal
45. Throttle Control Lever Spring
46. Throttle Control Lever
47. Sub-Shaft 1st Gear
48. Sub-Shaft Lock Nut
49. 1st-Hold Clutch Feedpipe
50. Gasket
51. Dowel Pin

95A19307

Courtesy of American Honda Motor Co., Inc.

Fig. 9: Exploded View Of Right Side Cover & Components

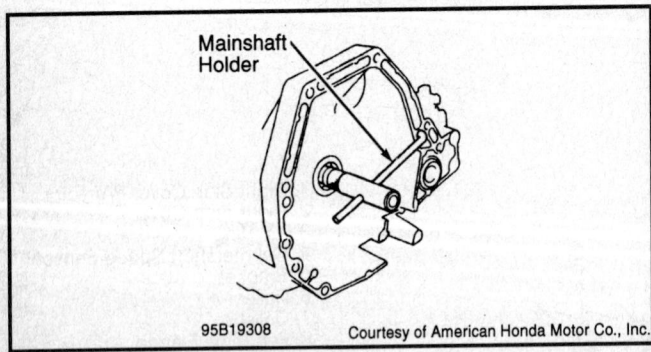

Fig. 10: Installing Mainshaft Holder

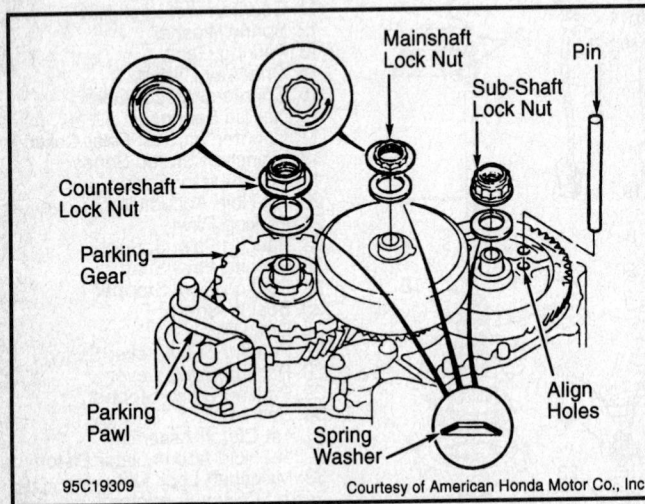

Fig. 11: Securing Sub-Shaft 1st Gear

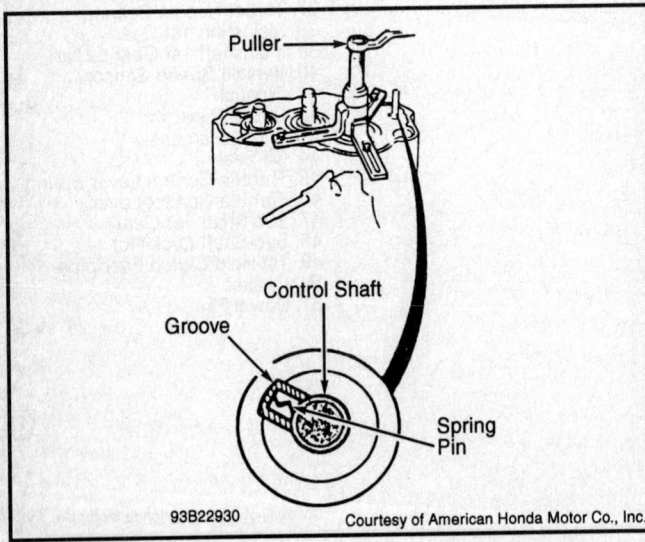

Fig. 12: Aligning Spring Pin & Removing Transaxle Housing

COMPONENT DISASSEMBLY & REASSEMBLY

MAIN VALVE BODY

CAUTION: When disassembling main valve body, place main valve body components in order and mark spring locations for reassembly reference. DO NOT use force to remove components. DO NOT use magnet to remove check balls, as check balls may become magnetized. Note direction of valve cap installation before removing from main valve body.

Disassembly – Disassemble main valve body. See Fig. 15. Use care when removing valve caps or spring seat, as they are under spring pressure.

Cleaning & Inspection – 1) Clean components with solvent and dry with compressed air. Replace main valve body if any parts are worn or damaged.

2) Ensure all valves slide freely in their bores. If valves do not slide freely, polish burrs or rough areas using No. 600 sandpaper soaked in ATF for at least 30 minutes. Thoroughly clean main valve body and components if polishing was needed.

3) Ensure spring free length is within specification. See SPRING SPECIFICATIONS table. Replace springs if not within specification.

NOTE: Oil pump clearance must be checked in main valve body. See OIL PUMP under COMPONENT DISASSEMBLY & REASSEMBLY.

Reassembly – Coat all components and bores with Dexron-II ATF. To reassemble, reverse disassembly procedure. Ensure all components are installed in correct location. See Fig. 15.

SPRING SPECIFICATIONS

Application	Free Length In. (mm)
Lock-Up Valve Body	
Lock-Up Shift Valve Spring	2.902 (73.70)
Lock-Up Timing Valve "B" Spring	2.394 (60.80)
Main Valve Body	
Clutch Pressure Control Valve Spring	1.390 (35.30)
Main Valve Body	
Relief Valve Spring	1.461 (37.10)
1-2 Shift Valve Spring	1.591 (40.40)
2-3 Shift Valve Spring	2.244 (57.00)
4th Exhaust Valve Spring	2.374 (60.30)
Regulator Valve Body	
Cooler Check Valve Spring	1.331 (33.80)
Lock-Up Control Valve Spring	1.638 (41.60)
Regulator Valve Spring "A"	3.457 (87.80)
Regulator Valve Spring "B"	1.732 (44.00)
Stator Reaction Spring	1.193 (30.30)
Torque Converter Check Valve Spring	1.331 (33.80)
Secondary Valve Body	
Modulator Valve Spring	1.469 (37.30)
Orifice Control Valve Spring	1.898 (48.20)
Servo Control Valve Spring	1.343 (34.10)
2-3 Orifice Control Valve Spring	1.299 (33.00)
3-2 Kickdown Valve Spring	1.795 (45.60)
3-4 Shift Valve Spring	2.047 (52.00)
4-3 Kickdown Valve Spring	1.122 (28.50)
Servo Body	
Throttle Valve "B" Adjusting Spring	1.339 (34.00)
Throttle Valve "B" Spring	[1]
1st Accumulator Spring	4.150 (105.40)
2nd Accumulator Spring	4.287 (108.90)
3rd Accumulator Spring	4.142 (105.20)
4th Accumulator Spring	4.067 (103.30)

[1] – Spring free length may be 1.634" (41.50 mm) or 1.638" (41.60 mm).

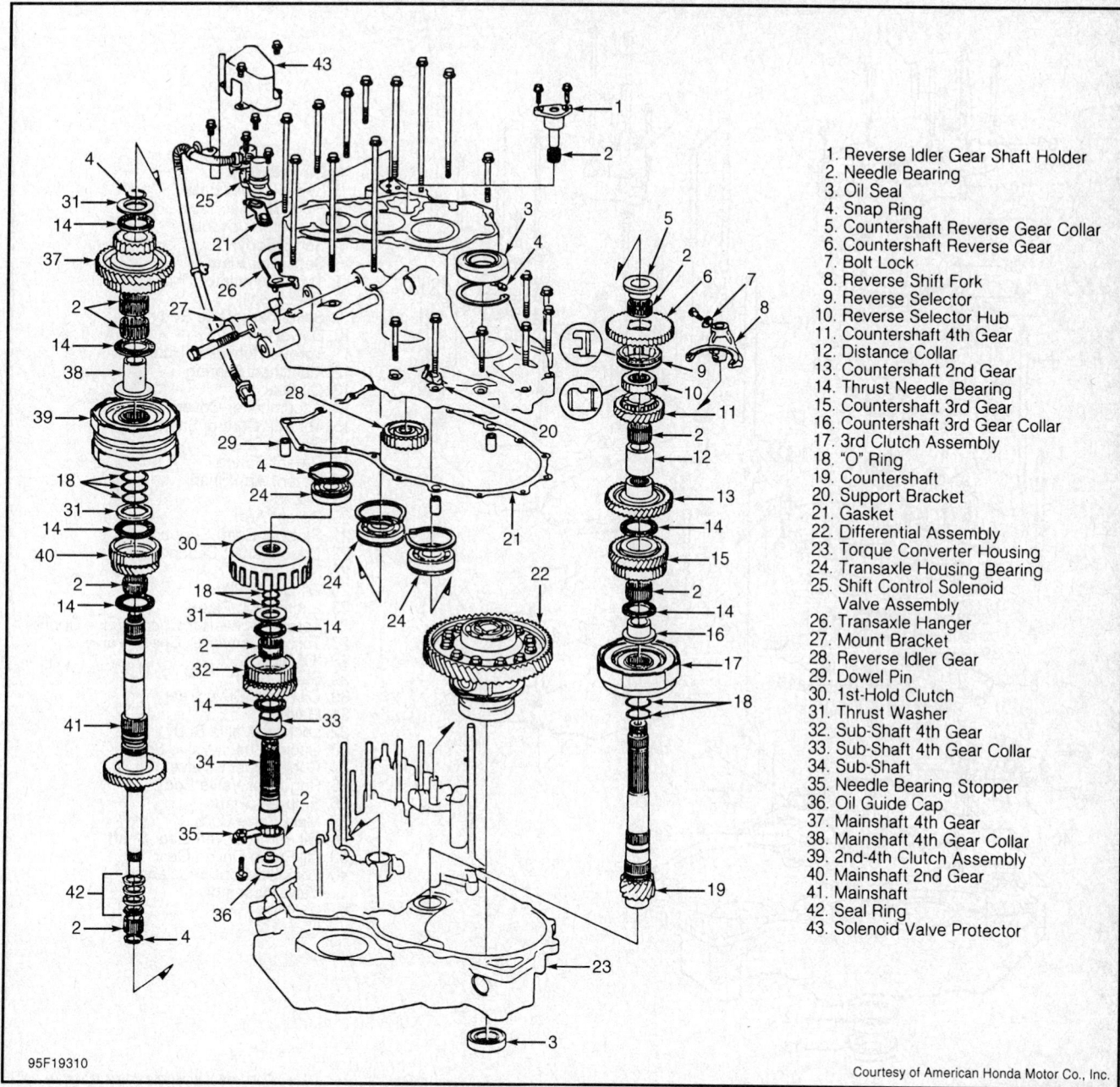

1. Reverse Idler Gear Shaft Holder
2. Needle Bearing
3. Oil Seal
4. Snap Ring
5. Countershaft Reverse Gear Collar
6. Countershaft Reverse Gear
7. Bolt Lock
8. Reverse Shift Fork
9. Reverse Selector
10. Reverse Selector Hub
11. Countershaft 4th Gear
12. Distance Collar
13. Countershaft 2nd Gear
14. Thrust Needle Bearing
15. Countershaft 3rd Gear
16. Countershaft 3rd Gear Collar
17. 3rd Clutch Assembly
18. "O" Ring
19. Countershaft
20. Support Bracket
21. Gasket
22. Differential Assembly
23. Torque Converter Housing
24. Transaxle Housing Bearing
25. Shift Control Solenoid Valve Assembly
26. Transaxle Hanger
27. Mount Bracket
28. Reverse Idler Gear
29. Dowel Pin
30. 1st-Hold Clutch
31. Thrust Washer
32. Sub-Shaft 4th Gear
33. Sub-Shaft 4th Gear Collar
34. Sub-Shaft
35. Needle Bearing Stopper
36. Oil Guide Cap
37. Mainshaft 4th Gear
38. Mainshaft 4th Gear Collar
39. 2nd-4th Clutch Assembly
40. Mainshaft 2nd Gear
41. Mainshaft
42. Seal Ring
43. Solenoid Valve Protector

95F19310

Courtesy of American Honda Motor Co., Inc.

Fig. 13: Exploded View Of Transaxle Housing & Components

OIL PUMP

Disassembly – Note direction of oil pump gear installation in main valve body. Remove oil pump driven gear shaft and oil pump gears from main valve body (if not previously removed).

Cleaning & Inspection – **1)** Clean components with solvent and dry with compressed air. Inspect components and replace if damaged.

2) Install oil pump gears in main valve body. Ensure chamfered and grooved side of oil pump driven gear is facing upward (toward separator plate side of main valve body).

3) Place straightedge across main valve body surface. Using feeler gauge, measure thrust clearance between oil pump driven gear and straightedge. See Fig. 16. Replace oil pump gears and/or main valve body if thrust clearance is not within specification. See OIL PUMP SPECIFICATIONS table.

4) Install oil pump driven gear shaft in oil pump driven gear. Using feeler gauge, measure side clearance of both gears between tip of gear

teeth and main valve body. See Fig. 16. Replace oil pump gears and/or main valve body if side clearance is not within specification. See OIL PUMP SPECIFICATIONS table.

OIL PUMP SPECIFICATIONS

Application	In. (mm)
Side Clearance	
Oil Pump Drive Gear	.0083-.0104 (.210-.265)
Oil Pump Driven Gear	.0028-.0049 (.070-.125)
Thrust Clearance	
Standard	.0010-.0020 (.030-.050)
Wear Limit	.0028 (.070)

Reassembly – Coat components with Dexron-II ATF. To reassemble, reverse disassembly procedure. Ensure chamfered and grooved side of oil pump driven gear is facing of oil pump driven gear faces upward (toward separator plate side of main valve body).

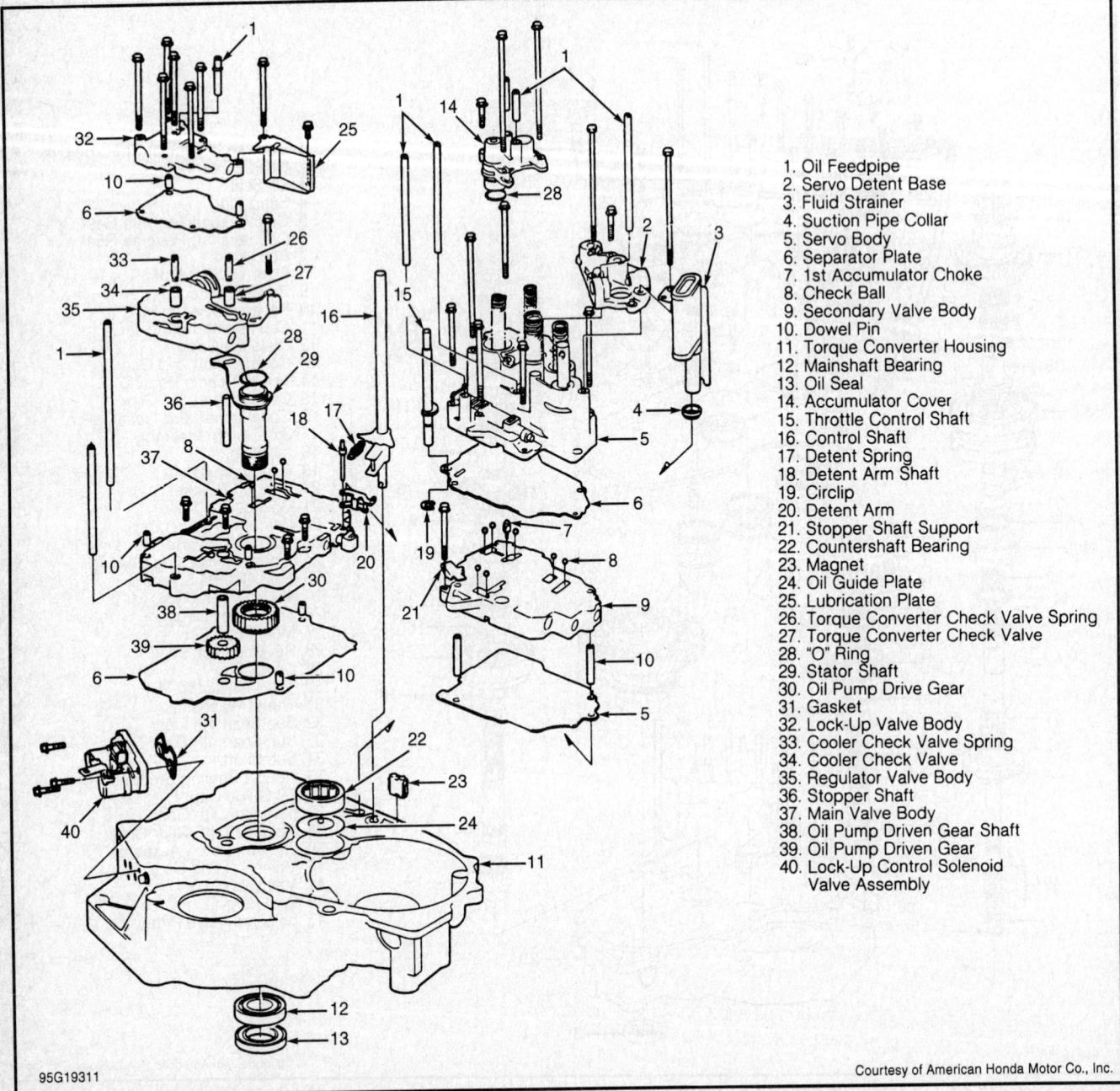

1. Oil Feedpipe
2. Servo Detent Base
3. Fluid Strainer
4. Suction Pipe Collar
5. Servo Body
6. Separator Plate
7. 1st Accumulator Choke
8. Check Ball
9. Secondary Valve Body
10. Dowel Pin
11. Torque Converter Housing
12. Mainshaft Bearing
13. Oil Seal
14. Accumulator Cover
15. Throttle Control Shaft
16. Control Shaft
17. Detent Spring
18. Detent Arm Shaft
19. Circlip
20. Detent Arm
21. Stopper Shaft Support
22. Countershaft Bearing
23. Magnet
24. Oil Guide Plate
25. Lubrication Plate
26. Torque Converter Check Valve Spring
27. Torque Converter Check Valve
28. "O" Ring
29. Stator Shaft
30. Oil Pump Drive Gear
31. Gasket
32. Lock-Up Valve Body
33. Cooler Check Valve Spring
34. Cooler Check Valve
35. Regulator Valve Body
36. Stopper Shaft
37. Main Valve Body
38. Oil Pump Driven Gear Shaft
39. Oil Pump Driven Gear
40. Lock-Up Control Solenoid
    Valve Assembly

95G19311

Courtesy of American Honda Motor Co., Inc.

Fig. 14: Exploded View Of Torque Converter Housing & Components

REGULATOR VALVE BODY

CAUTION: Regulator spring cap is under spring pressure. Ensure regulator spring cap is held down when removing stopper bolt. Use care when removing valve cap, as valve cap is under spring pressure.

Disassembly – Note direction of valve cap installation before removing from regulator valve body. Hold regulator spring cap down, and remove stopper bolt. Slowly remove regulator spring cap and components from regulator valve body. *See Fig. 17.*

Cleaning & Inspection – **1)** Clean components with solvent and dry with compressed air. Replace regulator valve body assembly if any parts are worn or damaged.

2) Ensure all valves slide freely in their bores. If valves do not slide freely, polish burrs or rough areas using No. 600 sandpaper soaked in ATF for at least 30 minutes. Thoroughly clean regulator valve body and components if polishing was needed.

3) Ensure spring free length is within specification. See SPRING SPECIFICATIONS table. Replace springs if not within specification.

Reassembly – Coat all components and bores with Dexron-II ATF. To reassemble, reverse disassembly procedure. Ensure all components are installed in correct location. *See Fig. 17.* Tighten stopper bolt to specification. See TORQUE SPECIFICATIONS.

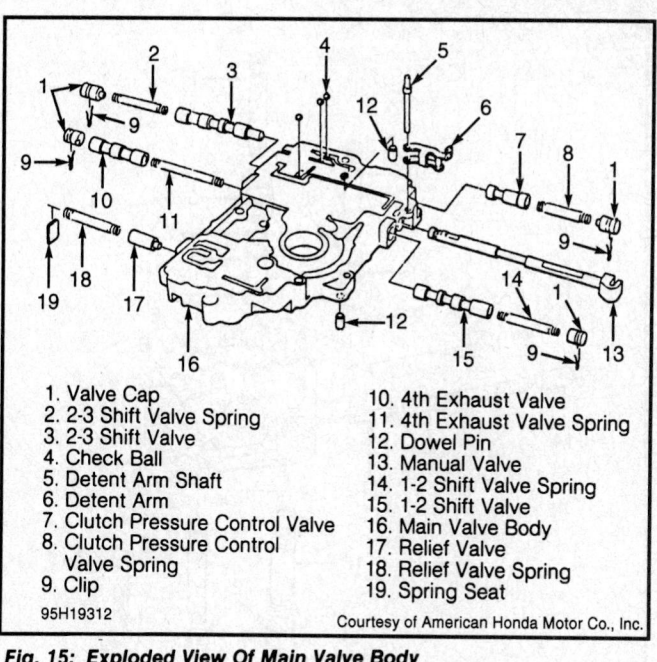

1. Valve Cap
2. 2-3 Shift Valve Spring
3. 2-3 Shift Valve
4. Check Ball
5. Detent Arm Shaft
6. Detent Arm
7. Clutch Pressure Control Valve
8. Clutch Pressure Control Valve Spring
9. Clip
10. 4th Exhaust Valve
11. 4th Exhaust Valve Spring
12. Dowel Pin
13. Manual Valve
14. 1-2 Shift Valve Spring
15. 1-2 Shift Valve
16. Main Valve Body
17. Relief Valve
18. Relief Valve Spring
19. Spring Seat

95H19312

Courtesy of American Honda Motor Co., Inc.

Fig. 15: Exploded View Of Main Valve Body

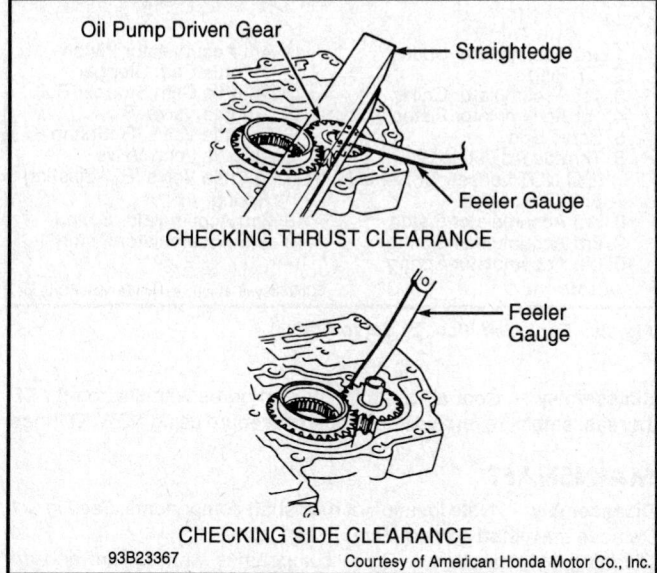

CHECKING THRUST CLEARANCE

CHECKING SIDE CLEARANCE

93B23367   Courtesy of American Honda Motor Co., Inc.

Fig. 16: Checking Oil Pump Clearances

LOCK-UP VALVE BODY

Disassembly – Note direction of valve cap installation before removing from lock-up valve body. Disassemble lock-up valve body. See Fig. 18. Use care when removing valve caps, as they are under spring pressure.

Cleaning & Inspection – 1) Clean components with solvent and dry with compressed air. Replace lock-up valve body assembly if any parts are worn or damaged.

2) Ensure all valves slide freely in their bores. If valves do not slide freely, polish burrs or rough areas using No. 600 sandpaper soaked for 30 minutes in ATF. Thoroughly clean lock-up valve body and components if polishing was needed.

3) Ensure spring free length is within specification. See SPRING SPECIFICATIONS table. Replace springs if not within specification.

Reassembly – Coat all components and bores with Dexron-II ATF. To reassemble, reverse disassembly procedure. See Fig. 18.

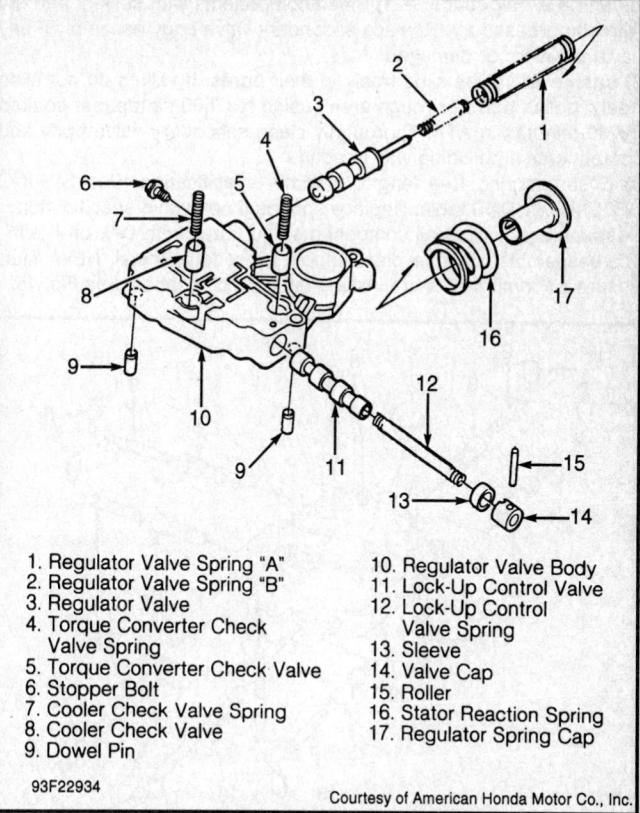

1. Regulator Valve Spring "A"
2. Regulator Valve Spring "B"
3. Regulator Valve
4. Torque Converter Check Valve Spring
5. Torque Converter Check Valve
6. Stopper Bolt
7. Cooler Check Valve Spring
8. Cooler Check Valve
9. Dowel Pin
10. Regulator Valve Body
11. Lock-Up Control Valve
12. Lock-Up Control Valve Spring
13. Sleeve
14. Valve Cap
15. Roller
16. Stator Reaction Spring
17. Regulator Spring Cap

93F22934   Courtesy of American Honda Motor Co., Inc.

Fig. 17: Exploded View Of Regulator Valve Body

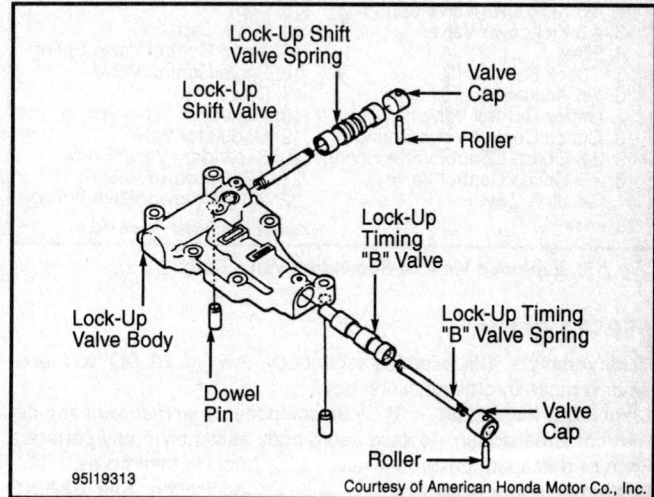

Lock-Up Shift Valve Spring
Lock-Up Shift Valve
Valve Cap
Roller
Lock-Up Timing "B" Valve
Lock-Up Valve Body
Lock-Up Timing "B" Valve Spring
Dowel Pin
Valve Cap
Roller

95I19313   Courtesy of American Honda Motor Co., Inc.

Fig. 18: Exploded View Of Lock-Up Valve Body

SECONDARY VALVE BODY

CAUTION: When disassembling secondary valve body, place secondary valve body components in order and mark spring locations for reassembly reference. DO NOT use force to remove components. DO NOT use magnet to remove check balls, as check balls may become magnetized. Note direction of valve cap installation before removing from secondary valve body.

Disassembly – Disassemble secondary valve body. See Fig. 19. Use care when removing valve caps or spring seats, as they are under spring pressure.

Cleaning & Inspection – 1) Clean components with solvent and dry with compressed air. Replace secondary valve body assembly if any parts are worn or damaged.

2) Ensure all valves slide freely in their bores. If valves do not slide freely, polish burrs or rough areas using No. 600 sandpaper soaked for 30 minutes in ATF. Thoroughly clean secondary valve body and components if polishing was needed.

3) Ensure spring free length is within specification. See SPRING SPECIFICATIONS table. Replace springs if not within specification.

Reassembly – Coat all components and bores with Dexron-II ATF. To reassemble, reverse disassembly procedure. Install NEW filter. Ensure all components are installed in correct location. See Fig. 19.

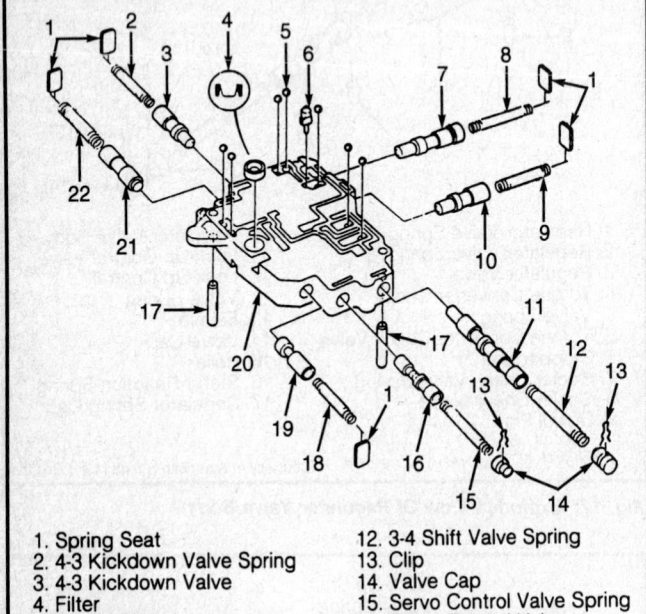

1. Spring Seat	12. 3-4 Shift Valve Spring
2. 4-3 Kickdown Valve Spring	13. Clip
3. 4-3 Kickdown Valve	14. Valve Cap
4. Filter	15. Servo Control Valve Spring
5. Check Ball	16. Servo Control Valve
6. 1st Accumulator Choke	17. Dowel Pin
7. Orifice Control Valve	18. Modulator Valve Spring
8. Orifice Control Valve Spring	19. Modulator Valve
9. 2-3 Orifice Control Valve Spring	20. Secondary Valve Body
10. 2-3 Orifice Control Valve	21. 3-2 Kickdown Valve
11. 3-4 Shift Valve	22. 3-2 Kickdown Valve Spring

95J19314   Courtesy of American Honda Motor Co., Inc.

Fig. 19: Exploded View Of Secondary Valve Body

SERVO BODY

Disassembly – Disassemble servo body. See Fig. 20. DO NOT loosen or remove throttle adjusting bolt.

Cleaning & Inspection – 1) Clean components with solvent and dry with compressed air. Replace servo body assembly if any parts are worn or damaged. Ensure all valves slide freely in their bores.

2) Ensure spring free length is within specification. See SPRING SPECIFICATIONS table. Replace springs if not within specification.

Reassembly – Coat all components and bores with Dexron-II ATF. To reassemble, reverse disassembly procedure using NEW "O" rings. Tighten throttle cam stopper bolt to specification. See TORQUE SPECIFICATIONS.

1st-HOLD ACCUMULATOR

Disassembly – Remove snap ring, 1st-hold accumulator cover, "O" ring, accumulator spring and 1st-hold accumulator piston from right side cover. See Fig. 9.

Cleaning & Inspection – Clean components with solvent and dry with compressed air. Replace components if worn or damaged. Ensure accumulator spring free length 2.823" (71.70 mm). Replace accumulator spring if not within specification.

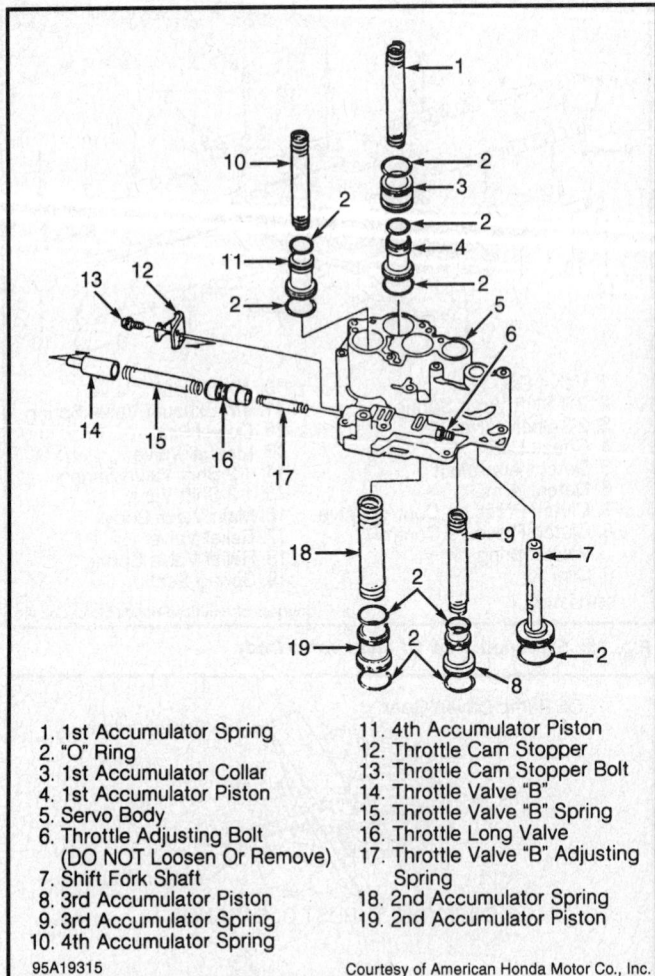

1. 1st Accumulator Spring	11. 4th Accumulator Piston
2. "O" Ring	12. Throttle Cam Stopper
3. 1st Accumulator Collar	13. Throttle Cam Stopper Bolt
4. 1st Accumulator Piston	14. Throttle Valve "B"
5. Servo Body	15. Throttle Valve "B" Spring
6. Throttle Adjusting Bolt	16. Throttle Long Valve
(DO NOT Loosen Or Remove)	17. Throttle Valve "B" Adjusting
7. Shift Fork Shaft	Spring
8. 3rd Accumulator Piston	18. 2nd Accumulator Spring
9. 3rd Accumulator Spring	19. 2nd Accumulator Piston
10. 4th Accumulator Spring	

95A19315   Courtesy of American Honda Motor Co., Inc.

Fig. 20: Exploded View Of Servo Body

Reassembly – Coat all components and bores with Dexron-II ATF. To reassemble, reverse disassembly procedure using NEW "O" rings.

MAINSHAFT

Disassembly – Note location of mainshaft components. See Fig. 21. Remove mainshaft components.

Cleaning & Inspection – Clean components with solvent and dry with compressed air. Inspect splines for excessive wear and bearing surfaces for scoring or wear. Inspect all bearings for galling and rough movement.

NOTE: Mainshaft 2nd gear-to-3rd gear clearance must be checked during reassembly.

Reassembly – 1) To check mainshaft 2nd gear-to-3rd gear clearance, install proper components, except "O" rings and mainshaft 4th gear on mainshaft. See Fig. 22.

2) Install used mainshaft lock nut on mainshaft. Tighten mainshaft lock nut to 22 ft. lbs. (30 N.m). Hold mainshaft 2nd gear against 2nd clutch.

3) Using feeler gauge, measure clearance between mainshaft 2nd gear and mainshaft 3rd gear. See Fig. 23. If mainshaft 2nd gear-to-3rd gear clearance is not .002-.005" (.05-.13 mm), replace thrust washer, located between mainshaft 2nd gear and 2nd clutch. Different thickness thrust washers are available. See THRUST WASHER SPECIFICATIONS table. Replace thrust washer and recheck mainshaft 2nd gear-to-3rd gear clearance.

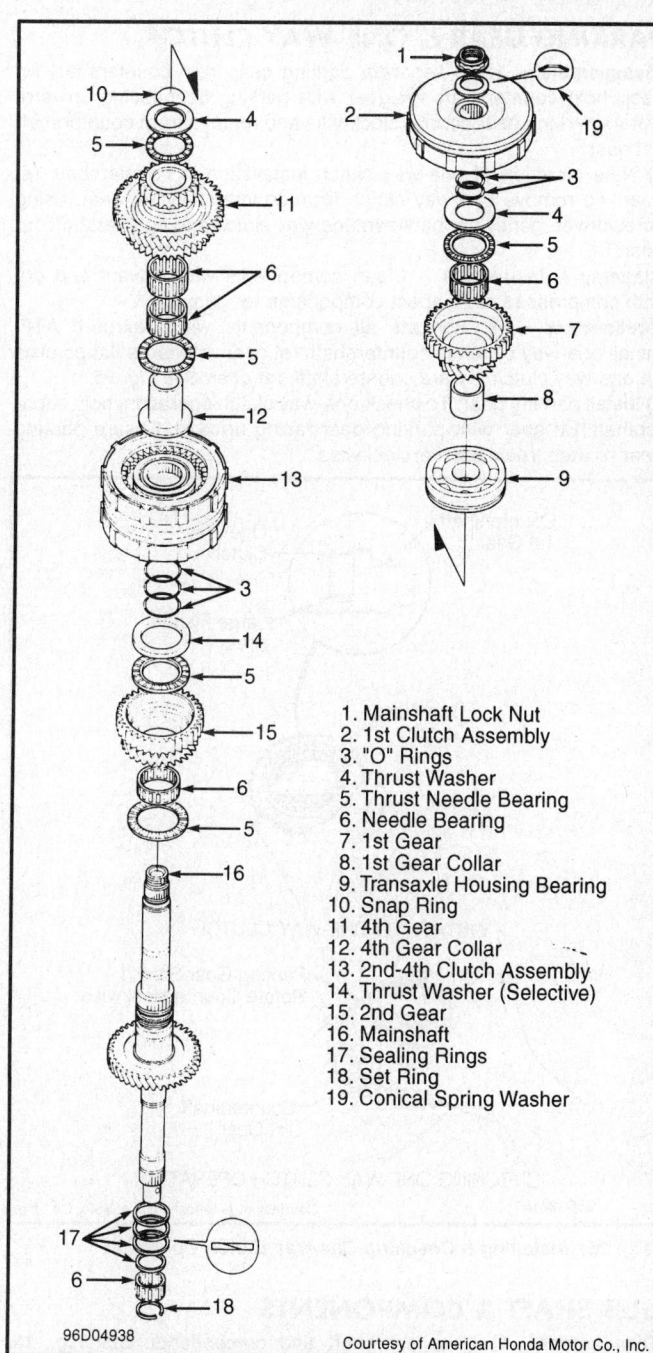

Fig. 21: Exploded View Of Mainshaft Assembly

1. Mainshaft Lock Nut
2. 1st Clutch Assembly
3. "O" Rings
4. Thrust Washer
5. Thrust Needle Bearing
6. Needle Bearing
7. 1st Gear
8. 1st Gear Collar
9. Transaxle Housing Bearing
10. Snap Ring
11. 4th Gear
12. 4th Gear Collar
13. 2nd-4th Clutch Assembly
14. Thrust Washer (Selective)
15. 2nd Gear
16. Mainshaft
17. Sealing Rings
18. Set Ring
19. Conical Spring Washer

96D04938

Courtesy of American Honda Motor Co., Inc.

THRUST WASHER SPECIFICATIONS

Washer Number	Part Number	Thickness In. (mm)
1	90441-PG4-010	.157 (4.00)
2	90442-PG4-010	.159 (4.05)
3	90443-PG4-010	.161 (4.10)
4	90444-PG4-010	.163 (4.15)
5	90445-PG4-010	.165 (4.20)
6	90446-PG4-010	.167 (4.25)
7	90447-PG4-010	.169 (4.30)
8	90448-PG4-010	.171 (4.35)
9	90449-PG4-010	.173 (4.40)
10	190450-PG4-000	.175 (4.45)

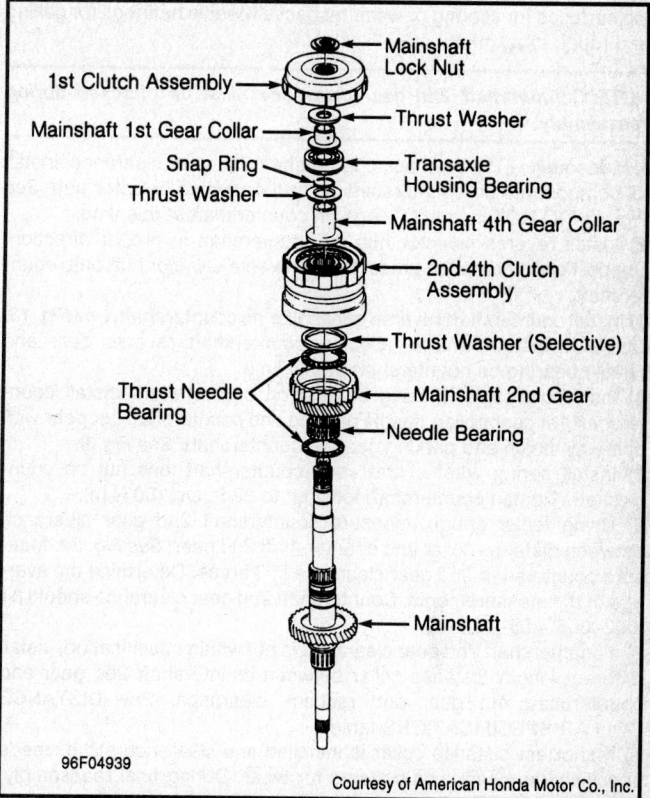

96F04939

Courtesy of American Honda Motor Co., Inc.

Fig. 22: Assembling Mainshaft To Measure 2nd Gear-To-3rd Gear Clearance

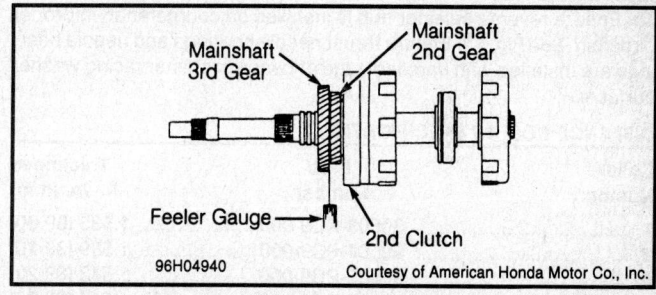

96H04940

Courtesy of American Honda Motor Co., Inc.

Fig. 23: Measuring Mainshaft 2nd Gear-To-3rd Gear Clearance

4) Once correct thickness thrust washer is obtained, lubricate all components with Dexron-II ATF. Reassemble mainshaft.

5) Ensure thrust needle bearings are installed with unrolled edge of bearing retainer facing washer. See Fig. 21. Before installing NEW "O" rings on mainshaft, wrap splines with tape.

COUNTERSHAFT

NOTE: Reverse selector hub is press-fit on countershaft. Countershaft must be pressed from reverse selector hub.

Disassembly – 1) Note location of countershaft components. See Fig. 13. Remove all components from countershaft down to the reverse selector hub.

2) Place countershaft in hydraulic press while supporting countershaft 4th gear. Threaded end of countershaft must be facing upward (toward ram of press). Place a protective cap between hydraulic press and countershaft to prevent damage to countershaft.

3) Press countershaft from reverse selector hub and countershaft 4th gear. Separate remaining components from countershaft. See Fig. 13.

Cleaning & Inspection – Clean components with solvent and dry with compressed air. Inspect splines for excessive wear. Check bearing surfaces for scoring or wear. Inspect all needle bearings for galling and rough movement.

NOTE: Countershaft 2nd gear clearance must be checked during reassembly.

Reassembly – 1) To check countershaft 2nd gear clearance, install all components on countershaft up to the reverse selector hub. *See Fig. 13.* DO NOT install "O" rings on countershaft at this time.

2) Install reverse selector hub on countershaft in proper direction. Support countershaft in press. Press reverse selector hub onto countershaft.

3) Install countershaft reverse gear collar on countershaft. *See Fig. 13.* DO NOT install reverse selector, countershaft reverse gear and needle bearing on countershaft at this time.

4) Install transaxle housing bearing on countershaft. Install countershaft 1st gear collar, needle bearing and countershaft 1st gear with one-way clutch and parking gear on countershaft. *See Fig. 9.*

5) Install spring washer and used countershaft lock nut on countershaft. Tighten countershaft lock nut to 22 ft. lbs. (30 N.m).

6) Using feeler gauge, measure countershaft 2nd gear clearance between distance collar and countershaft 2nd gear. *See Fig. 24.* Measure countershaft 2nd gear clearance in 3 areas. Determine the average of the measurements. Countershaft 2nd gear clearance should be .002-.005" (.05-.13 mm).

7) If countershaft 2nd gear clearance is not within specification, install different length distance collar between countershaft 2nd gear and countershaft 4th gear and recheck clearance. See DISTANCE COLLAR SPECIFICATIONS table.

8) If shortest distance collar is installed and clearance still exceeds specification, check components for wear. During final reassembly, lubricate all components with Dexron-II ATF.

9) Before installing NEW "O" rings on countershaft, wrap splines with tape. Ensure NEW "O" rings are installed on countershaft.

10) Ensure reverse selector hub is installed on countershaft in proper direction. *See Fig. 13.* Ensure thrust needle bearings and needle bearings are installed with unrolled edge of bearing retainer facing washer surface.

DISTANCE COLLAR SPECIFICATIONS

Collar Number	Part Number	Thickness In. (mm)
1	90503-PC9-000	1.535 (39.00)
2	90504-PC9-000	1.539 (39.10)
3	90505-PC9-000	1.543 (39.20)
4	90507-PC9-000	1.547 (39.30)
5	90508-PC9-000	1.537 (39.05)
6	90509-PC9-000	1.541 (39.15)
7	90510-PC9-000	1.545 (39.25)
8	90511-PC9-000	1.531 (38.90)
9	90512-PC9-000	1.533 (38.95)

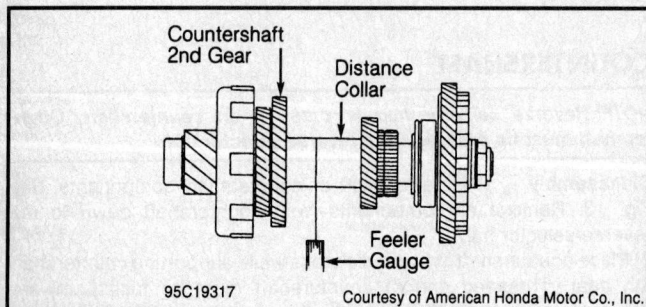

95C19317

Courtesy of American Honda Motor Co., Inc.

Fig. 24: Checking Countershaft 2nd Gear Clearance

PARKING GEAR & ONE-WAY CLUTCH

Disassembly – 1) To separate parking gear from countershaft 1st gear, hold countershaft 1st gear with parking gear facing upward. Rotate parking gear counterclockwise and remove from countershaft 1st gear.

2) Note direction of one-way clutch installation in countershaft 1st gear. To remove one-way clutch from countershaft 1st gear, using screwdriver, gently pry between one-way clutch and countershaft 1st gear.

Cleaning & Inspection – Clean components with solvent and dry with compressed air. Inspect components for damage.

Reassembly – 1) Lubricate all components with Dexron-II ATF. Install one-way clutch in countershaft 1st gear with large flange area on one-way clutch toward countershaft 1st gear. *See Fig. 25.*

2) Install parking gear. To check one-way clutch operation, hold countershaft 1st gear with parking gear facing upward. Ensure parking gear rotates freely counterclockwise.

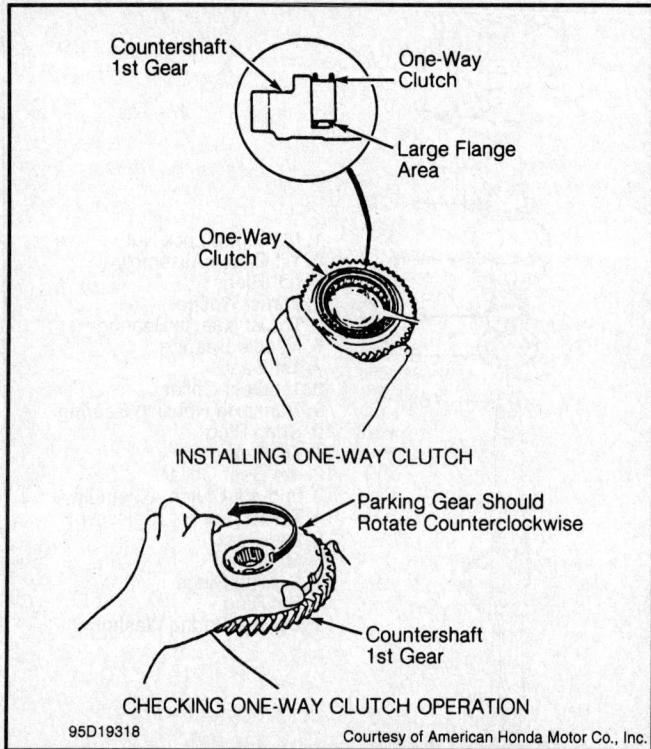

95D19318

Courtesy of American Honda Motor Co., Inc.

Fig. 25: Installing & Checking One-Way Clutch Operation

SUB-SHAFT & COMPONENTS

Disassembly –1) Note sub-shaft and components. *See Fig. 13.* Remove oil guide cap from transaxle housing by using hammer and driver and tapping on end of sub-shaft. Remove sub-shaft, sub-shaft 4th gear, 1st-hold clutch and components.

2) If removing needle bearing from transaxle housing, remove needle bearing stopper bolt and needle bearing stopper. Using hammer and drift, tap needle bearing from transaxle housing.

3) If removing transaxle housing bearing, expand snap ring. Using press, press bearing from transaxle housing. Remove snap ring (if necessary).

Cleaning & Inspection – 1) Clean components with solvent and dry with compressed air. Inspect splines on sub-shaft for excessive wear and bearing surfaces for scoring or wear.

2) Inspect all needle bearings for galling and rough movement. Inspect sub-shaft 4th gear for damage.

Reassembly – 1) Lubricate all components with Dexron-II ATF. If installing needle bearing in transaxle housing, use press, press needle bearing into transaxle housing.

2) Install needle bearing stopper. Tighten needle bearing stopper bolt to specification. See TORQUE SPECIFICATIONS.

3) If installing transaxle housing bearing in transaxle housing, expand snap ring. Using press, press bearing part way into transaxle housing.

CAUTION: Ensure transaxle housing bearing is installed with groove facing toward outside of transaxle housing so snap ring will engage with bearing.

4) Release snap ring. Continue pressing bearing into transaxle housing until snap ring engages in bearing. Ensure snap ring is fully seated.

5) Before installing "O" rings on sub-shaft, wrap splines with tape. Use NEW "O" rings on sub-shaft. Reassemble sub-shaft.

6) Ensure thrust needle bearings are installed with unrolled edge of bearing retainer facing washer. Install NEW oil guide cap.

CLUTCH ASSEMBLIES

Disassembly – 1) Remove snap ring, clutch end plate, clutch discs and clutch plates. *See Fig. 26.* Note direction of disc spring installation. Remove disc spring.

2) Using spring compressor, compress return spring. Remove snap ring. Release and remove spring compressor. Remove spring retainer and return spring.

3) Wrap shop towel around clutch drum. Apply light air pressure to oil passage on clutch drum to remove clutch piston. Remove "O" rings.

Cleaning & Inspection – 1) Clean metal components with solvent and dry with compressed air. Ensure check valve on rear of clutch piston (except 1st-hold clutch) is thoroughly cleaned and secured tightly on clutch piston.

2) Inspect components for damage. Replace as necessary. Ensure no rough edges exist on "O" ring sealing areas.

Reassembly – 1) Lubricate all components with Dexron-II ATF. Install NEW "O" rings. Install clutch piston in clutch drum. Slightly rotate clutch piston back and forth during installation to prevent damaging "O" rings.

CAUTION: DO NOT apply excessive force on clutch piston or "O" rings will be damaged.

2) Install return spring and spring retainer in clutch drum. Place snap ring on spring retainer. Using spring compressor, compress return spring. Install snap ring. Remove spring compressor.

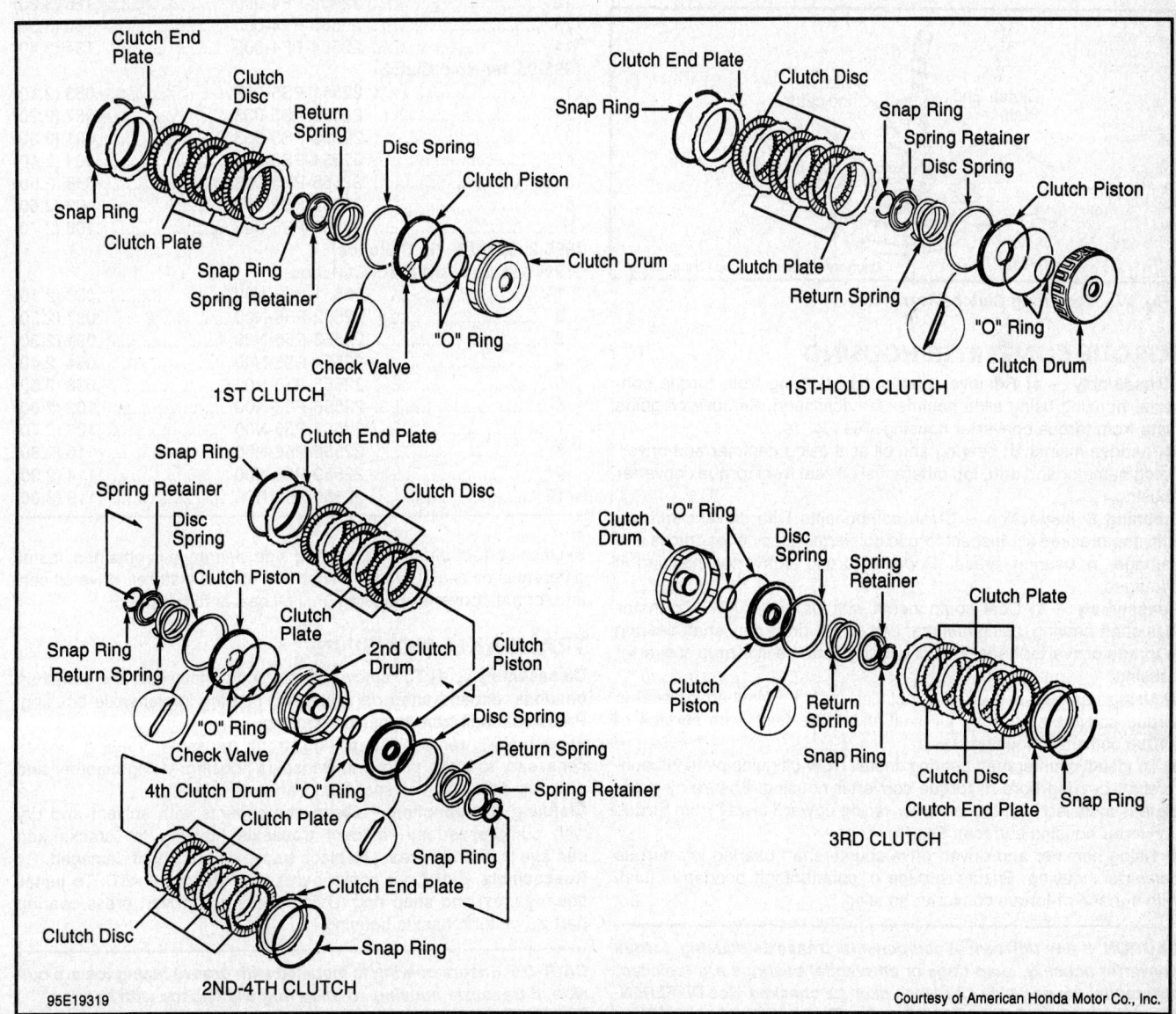

95E19319

Courtesy of American Honda Motor Co., Inc.

Fig. 26: *Exploded View Of Clutch Assemblies*

CAUTION: *Disc spring on 2nd clutch is opposite all other clutch assemblies. Ensure clutch discs are soaked in Dexron-II ATF for at least 30 minutes before installing.*

3) Install disc spring. Ensure disc spring is installed in proper direction. *See Fig. 26.*

4) Alternately install clutch plates and clutch discs starting with clutch plate. Install clutch end plate with flat side toward clutch disc. Install snap ring.

5) Using dial indicator, measure clutch clearance between clutch end plate and top clutch disc. *See Fig. 27.* Zero dial indicator with clutch end plate lowered. Lift clutch end plate upward against snap ring. Distance measured is clutch clearance.

6) Measure clutch clearance at 3 different locations. Clutch clearance should be within specification. See CLUTCH CLEARANCE SPECIFICATIONS table.

7) If clutch clearance is not within specification, install different thickness clutch end plate. See CLUTCH END PLATE SPECIFICATIONS table.

NOTE: *If thickest clutch end plate is installed and clutch clearance still exceeds specification, replace clutch discs and clutch plates.*

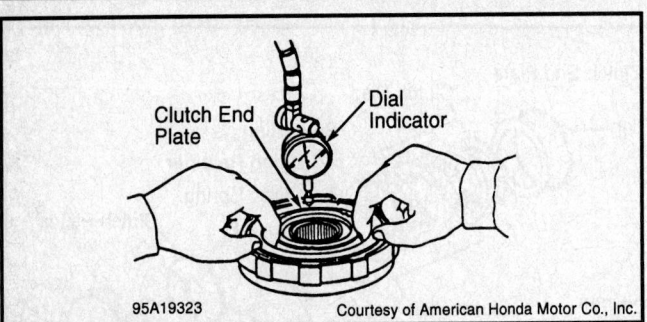

95A19323   Courtesy of American Honda Motor Co., Inc.

Fig. 27: Measuring Clutch Clearance

TORQUE CONVERTER HOUSING

Disassembly – 1) Remove countershaft bearing from torque converter housing using slide hammer (if necessary). Remove oil guide plate from torque converter housing. *See Fig. 14.*

2) Remove mainshaft bearing and oil seal using hammer and driver. Using hammer and drift, tap differential oil seal from torque converter housing.

Cleaning & Inspection – Clean components with solvent and dry with compressed air. Inspect torque converter housing for cracks and damage in bearing areas. Replace torque converter housing if damaged.

Reassembly – 1) Coat components with Dexron-II ATF. To install mainshaft bearing, using hammer and driver, drive mainshaft bearing in torque converter housing until bearing bottoms in torque converter housing.

2) Using hammer and oil seal installer, install mainshaft oil seal in torque converter housing. Oil seal should be flush with surface of torque converter housing.

3) To install countershaft bearing, install NEW oil guide plate in countershaft bearing bore of torque converter housing. Ensure oil guide plate is installed with tab in center facing upward (away from torque converter housing surface). *See Fig. 14.*

4) Using hammer and driver, drive countershaft bearing into torque converter housing. Ensure surface of countershaft bearing is flush with surface of torque converter housing.

CAUTION: *If any differential components, transaxle housing, torque converter housing, snap rings or differential bearings are replaced, differential bearing side clearance must be checked. See DIFFERENTIAL BEARING SIDE CLEARANCE under TRANSAXLE REASSEMBLY.*

CLUTCH CLEARANCE SPECIFICATIONS

Application	Clutch Clearance In. (mm)
1st & 2nd Clutches	.026-.033 (.65-.85)
1st-Hold Clutch	.020-.031 (.50-.80)
3rd & 4th Clutches	.016-.024 (.40-.60)

CLUTCH END PLATE SPECIFICATIONS

Plate Number	Part Number	Thickness In. (mm)
1995 1st Clutch		
1	22551-PF4-000	.083 (2.10)
2	22552-PF4-000	.087 (2.20)
3	22553-PF4-000	.091 (2.30)
4	22554-PF4-000	.094 (2.40)
5	22555-PF4-000	.098 (2.50)
6	22556-PF4-000	.102 (2.60)
7	22557-PF4-000	.106 (2.70)
8	22558-PF4-000	.110 (2.80)
9	22559-PF4-000	.114 (2.90)
10	22560-PF4-000	.118 (3.00)
11	22561-PF4-000	.122 (3.10)
12	22562-PF4-000	.126 (3.20)
13	22563-PF4-000	.130 (3.30)
14	22564-PF4-000	.134 (3.40)
1995-96 1st-Hold Clutch		
1	22551-PS5-003	.083 (2.10)
2	22552-PS5-003	.087 (2.20)
3	22553-PS5-003	.091 (2.30)
4	22554-PS5-003	.094 (2.40)
5 (No Mark)	22555-PS5-003	.098 (2.50)
6	22556-PS5-003	.102 (2.60)
7	22557-PS5-003	.106 (2.70)
1995 2nd, 3rd & 4th Clutches		
1996 1st, 2nd, 3rd & 4th Clutches		
1	22551-P56-N00	.083 (2.10)
2	22552-P56-N00	.087 (2.20)
3	22553-P56-N00	.091 (2.30)
4	22554-P56-N00	.094 (2.40)
5	22555-P56-N00	.098 (2.50)
6	22556-P56-N00	.102 (2.60)
7	22557-P56-N00	.106 (2.70)
8	22558-P56-N00	.110 (2.80)
9	22559-P56-N00	.114 (2.90)
10	22560-P56-N00	.118 (3.00)

5) Once correct differential bearing side clearance is obtained, install differential oil seal. Using hammer and oil seal installer, drive oil seal into torque converter housing until oil seal is fully seated.

TRANSAXLE HOUSING

Disassembly – 1) To remove countershaft, mainshaft and sub-shaft bearings, expand snap ring retaining bearing in transaxle housing. Press bearings from transaxle housing.

2) DO NOT remove snap ring from transaxle housing unless necessary to clean groove in transaxle housing. Using hammer and drift, tap differential oil seal from transaxle housing.

Cleaning & Inspection – Clean components with solvent and dry with compressed air. Inspect transaxle housing for cracks and damage in bearing areas. Replace transaxle housing if damaged.

Reassembly – 1) Coat components with Dexron-II ATF. To install bearings, expand snap ring. Using press and driver, press bearing part way into transaxle housing.

CAUTION: *Ensure bearing is installed with groove facing toward outside of transaxle housing so snap ring will engage with bearing.*

2) Release snap ring. Continue pressing bearing into transaxle housing until snap ring engages in bearing. Ensure snap ring is fully seated.

CAUTION: If differential carrier, differential bearings, transaxle housing, torque converter housing or snap rings are replaced, differential bearing side clearance must be checked. See DIFFERENTIAL BEARING SIDE CLEARANCE under TRANSAXLE REASSEMBLY.

3) Once correct differential bearing side clearance is obtained, install differential oil seal using hammer and oil seal installer until oil seal is fully seated.

DIFFERENTIAL ASSEMBLY

Disassembly – 1) Before disassembling differential assembly, check side gear backlash. Place differential assembly on "V" blocks with both axle shafts installed.
2) Install dial indicator with stem resting against pinion gear. *See Fig. 28.* Check side gear backlash. Side gear backlash should be .003-.006" (.08-.15 mm). If side gear backlash is not within specification, replace differential carrier.
3) If replacing differential bearings, use bearing puller to remove differential bearings from differential carrier. Remove bolts and ring gear.

NOTE: Ring gear bolts have left-hand threads.

4) If removing speedometer drive gear, remove snap ring, speedometer drive gear and roller. *See Fig. 29.*
Cleaning & Inspection – Clean components with solvent and dry with compressed air. Inspect components for wear and damage. Replace components as necessary.
Reassembly – 1) Install roller for speedometer drive gear in differential carrier. Install speedometer drive gear with chamfered side on inside of gear toward differential carrier. *See Fig. 29.* Ensure cutout area on speedometer drive gear is aligned with roller.

CAUTION: Ensure speedometer drive gear is installed with chamfered side on inside of gear toward differential carrier.

2) Aligned hooked end of snap ring with pinion shaft on differential carrier and install snap ring. *See Fig. 30.* Ensure snap ring is installed so hooked end of snap ring is facing in proper direction. *See Fig. 30.*

CAUTION: Ensure ring gear is installed with chamfered side on inside of ring gear toward differential carrier.

3) Install ring gear on differential carrier with chamfered side on inside of ring gear toward differential carrier. *See Fig. 29.* Install and tighten ring gear bolts to specification. See TORQUE SPECIFICATIONS. Using press, install NEW differential bearings on differential carrier (if removed).

CAUTION: If differential carrier, differential bearings, transaxle housing, torque converter housing or snap rings are replaced, differential bearing side clearance must be checked. See DIFFERENTIAL BEARING SIDE CLEARANCE under TRANSAXLE REASSEMBLY.

TRANSAXLE REASSEMBLY

DIFFERENTIAL BEARING SIDE CLEARANCE

CAUTION: If differential carrier, differential bearings, transaxle housing, torque converter housing or snap rings are replaced, differential bearing side clearance must be checked.

1) Install .098" (2.50 mm) thick snap ring in transaxle housing. This is the snap ring that differential bearing seats against. Ensure snap ring is fully seated.
2) Tap differential assembly into torque converter housing using Driver (07746-0030100). Perform STEP 1. *See Fig. 31.* Ensure

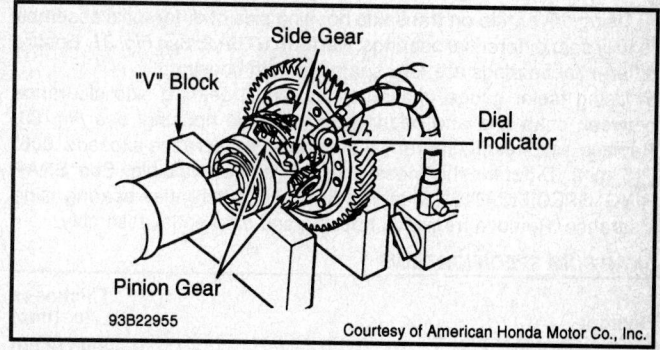

Fig. 28: Checking Side Gear Backlash

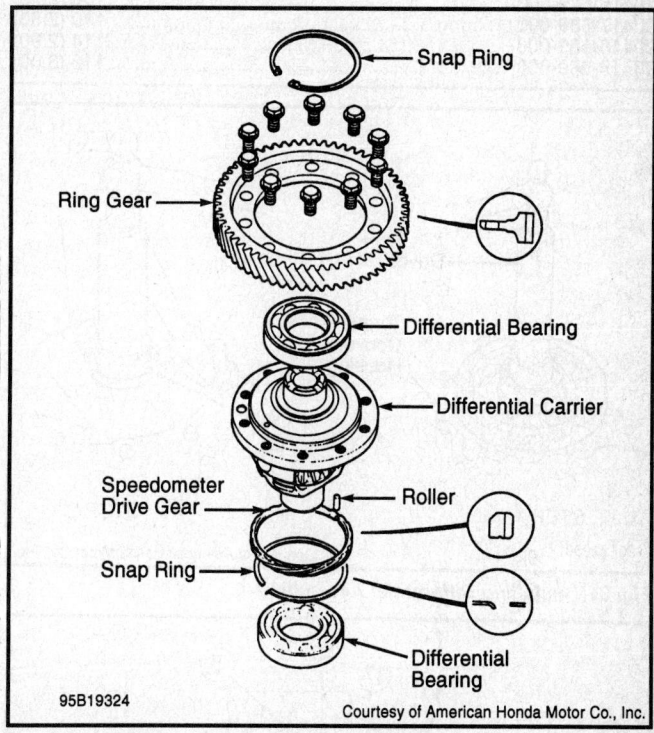

Fig. 29: Exploded View Of Differential Assembly

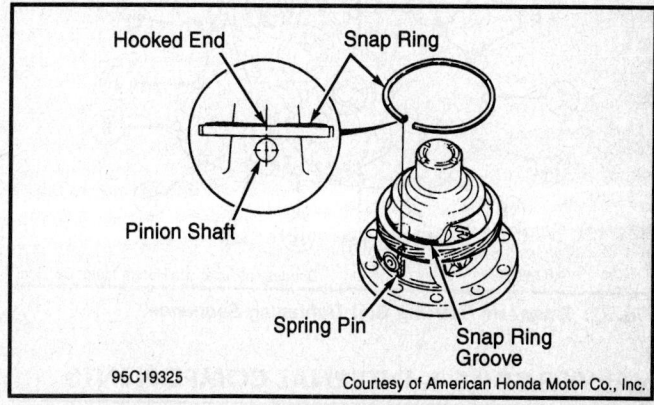

Fig. 30: Installing Speedometer Drive Gear Retaining Snap Ring

differential bearing on differential carrier is fully seated on torque converter housing.
3) Install gasket and transaxle housing on torque converter housing. Install and tighten transaxle housing bolts to 33 ft. lbs. (45 N.m) in 2 steps using proper sequence. *See Fig. 32.*

4) Using driver, tap on transaxle housing side of differential assembly to fully seat differential bearings. Perform STEP 2. *See Fig. 31.* Ensure differential bearings are fully seated in both housing.

5) Using feeler gauge, measure differential bearing side clearance between snap ring and bearing on transaxle housing. *See Fig. 33.* Replace snap ring if differential bearing side clearance exceeds .006" (.15 mm). Different thickness snap rings are available. See SNAP RING SPECIFICATIONS table. Recheck differential bearing side clearance. Remove transaxle housing and differential assembly.

SNAP RING SPECIFICATIONS

Part Number	Thickness In. (mm)
90414-689-000	.098 (2.50)
90415-689-000	.102 (2.60)
90416-689-000	.106 (2.70)
90417-689-000	.110 (2.80)
90418-689-000	.114 (2.90)
90419-689-000	.118 (3.00)

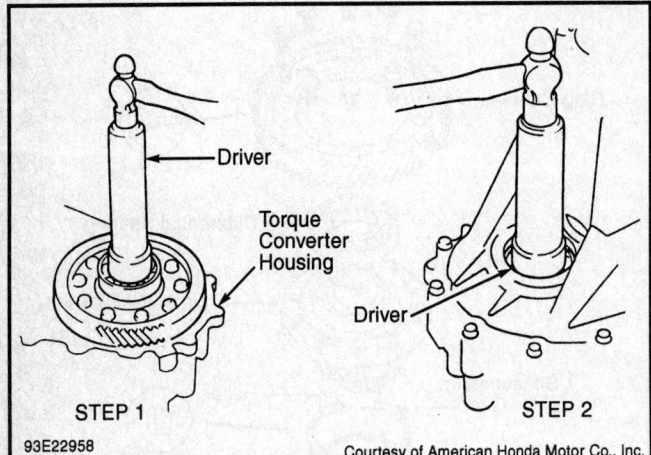

STEP 1   STEP 2

93E22958   Courtesy of American Honda Motor Co., Inc.

Fig. 31: Installing Differential Assembly

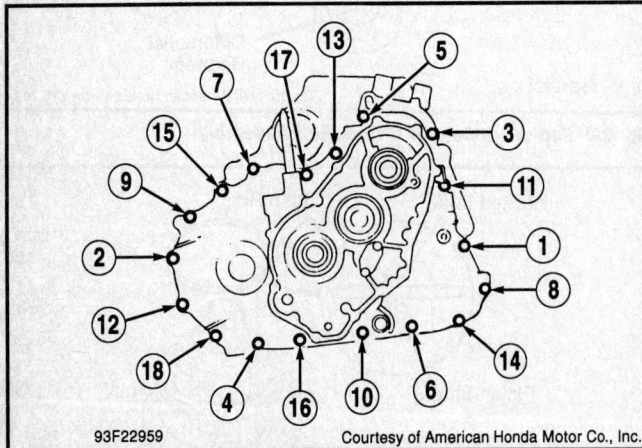

93F22959   Courtesy of American Honda Motor Co., Inc.

Fig. 32: Transaxle Housing Bolt Tightening Sequence

VALVE BODIES & INTERNAL COMPONENTS

CAUTION: If differential carrier, differential bearings, transaxle housing, torque converter housing or snap rings are replaced, differential bearing side clearance must be checked. See DIFFERENTIAL BEARING SIDE CLEARANCE.

NOTE: Coat all components with Dexron-II ATF before reassembly.

1) Install needle bearing on end of reverse idler gear shaft holder. Install reverse idler gear in transaxle housing (if removed). Install

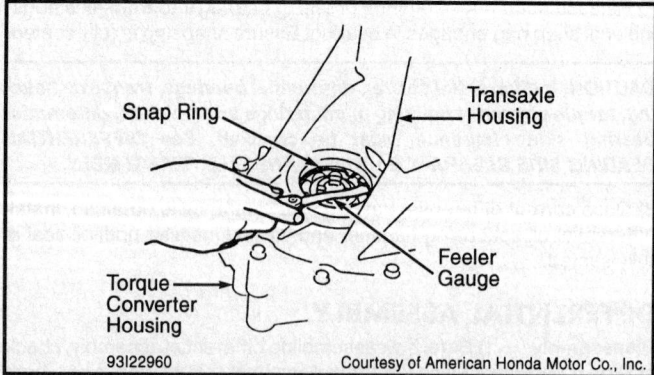

93I22960   Courtesy of American Honda Motor Co., Inc.

Fig. 33: Checking Differential Bearing Side Clearance

reverse idler gear shaft holder on transaxle housing. Install and tighten reverse idler gear shaft holder bolts to specification. See TORQUE SPECIFICATIONS.

2) Install magnet and suction pipe collar on torque converter housing. *See Fig. 14.* Install dowel pins and separator plate for main valve on torque converter housing.

CAUTION: Ensure oil pump driven gear is installed with groove and chamfered side facing downward (toward main separator plate).

3) Install oil pump drive gear, oil pump driven gear and oil pump driven gear shaft. Install main valve body. Install and tighten main valve body bolts to specification.

CAUTION: Ensure oil pump gears rotate smoothly and oil pump driven gear shaft moves freely once main valve body is installed. If components do not operate correctly, loosen bolts, and realign oil pump gears and oil pump driven gear shaft. Failure to align oil pump driven gear shaft may result in seized oil pump gears or shaft.

4) Ensure check balls are installed in main valve body. *See Fig. 15.* Install separator plate, dowel pins and secondary valve body on main valve body. Install and tighten bolts to specification. Ensure check balls and 1st accumulator choke are installed in secondary valve body. *See Fig. 19.*

5) Install control shaft on torque converter housing so control shaft engages manual valve on main valve body. Install detent arm and detent arm shaft on main valve body. Hook detent spring on detent arm.

6) Install separator plate and servo body. Install and tighten bolts to specification. Using NEW "O" ring, install accumulator cover. Install and tighten bolts to specification.

7) Install servo detent base and fluid strainer. Install NEW bolt locks on servo detent base bolts. Install and tighten bolts to specification. Bend over tabs on bolt locks.

8) Install stator shaft, NEW "O" ring and stopper shaft. Install stopper shaft support on secondary valve body. Install regulator valve body. Install and tighten bolt to specification.

9) Install cooler check valve and torque converter check valve and springs on regulator valve body. *See Fig. 17.* Install separator plate, dowel pins, lock-up valve body and lubrication plate on regulator valve body. Install and tighten bolts to specification.

10) Install oil feedpipes in accumulator cover, servo detent base, servo body, lock-up valve body and main valve body. *See Fig. 14.*

11) Install sub-shaft and components in transaxle housing (if removed). See SUB-SHAFT & COMPONENTS under COMPONENT DISASSEMBLY & REASSEMBLY.

12) Install differential assembly in torque converter housing. Using Driver (07746-0030100), tap differential assembly into torque converter housing. Perform STEP 1. *See Fig. 31.* Ensure differential bearing on differential carrier is fully seated on torque converter housing.

13) Install mainshaft and countershaft as an assembly on torque converter housing. Rotate shift fork shaft on servo body so large chamfered hole aligns with hole in reverse shift fork.

14) Install reverse shift fork and reverse selector. *See Fig. 13.* Install reverse shift fork bolt and NEW bolt lock. Tighten bolt to specification. Bend over tabs on bolt lock.

15) Install countershaft reverse gear, needle bearing and countershaft reverse gear collar on countershaft. *See Fig. 13.* Install dowel pins and NEW gasket on torque converter housing.

16) Align spring pin on control shaft with groove on transaxle housing by rotating control shaft. *See Fig. 12.*

17) Install transaxle housing on torque converter housing. Install and tighten transaxle housing bolts to specification in 2 steps using proper sequence. *See Fig. 32.*

18) Install mount bracket on transaxle housing. *See Fig. 13.* Install and tighten mount bracket bolts to specification.

19) Install mainshaft holder on mainshaft. *See Fig. 10.* Install parking brake lever with parking brake stopper and parking brake lever spring on control shaft. *See Fig. 9.*

20) Install mainshaft 1st gear collar and thrust washer on mainshaft. Install countershaft 1st gear collar, needle bearing and countershaft 1st gear with one-way clutch and parking gear on countershaft.

21) Install parking pawl stopper, parking pawl shaft, parking pawl spring and parking pawl on transaxle housing.

22) Engage parking pawl with parking gear. Install old spring washer and lock nut on countershaft. Tighten nut to 76 ft. lbs. (103 N.m) to seat parking gear and countershaft 1st gear on countershaft. Remove old lock nut and spring washer from countershaft.

23) Install sub-shaft 1st gear on sub-shaft. Wrap splines on mainshaft with tape. Install NEW "O" rings on mainshaft. Install mainshaft 1st gear on mainshaft. *See Fig. 9.* Install needle bearing, thrust needle bearing, thrust washer and 1st clutch assembly on mainshaft.

24) Align hole in sub-shaft 1st gear with hole in transaxle housing. Install pin in sub-shaft 1st gear and transaxle housing to prevent sub-shaft 1st gear from rotating. *See Fig. 11.*

CAUTION: Ensure spring washers are installed in correct direction. See Fig. 11.

25) Install NEW spring washers and NEW lock nuts on mainshaft, countershaft and sub-shaft. Ensure spring washers are installed with large area against the gear. *See Fig. 11.*

NOTE: Mainshaft and countershaft contain left-hand threads.

26) Tighten lock nuts on mainshaft, countershaft and sub-shaft to specification. Remove pin from sub-shaft 1st gear. Remove mainshaft holder.

27) Stake flange area of mainshaft lock nut against 1st clutch assembly. Stake thread area of countershaft lock nut against threads on countershaft. Stake thread area of sub-shaft lock nut against threads of sub-shaft.

CAUTION: Ensure all lock nuts are securely staked.

28) Place parking brake lever in "P" position. Ensure parking pawl engages parking gear. Measure parking brake stopper distance between parking pawl shaft and pin on parking brake lever. *See Fig. 34.*

29) Parking brake stopper distance should be 2.87-2.91" (72.9-73.9 mm). If parking brake stopper distance is not within specification install different size parking brake stopper, and recheck parking brake stopper distance. Parking brake stopper is available in 3 different sizes. Consult parts department for parking brake stopper sizes.

30) Once correct parking brake stopper distance is obtained, install NEW bolt lock on bolt for parking brake stopper. Tighten parking brake stopper bolt to specification. Bend over tabs on bolt lock.

31) Using NEW gasket, install right side cover and right side cover protector. Install and tighten bolts to specification. Install throttle control lever with spring on throttle control shaft. Install and tighten bolt to specification.

32) To install remaining components, reverse removal procedure. Use NEW seal washers when installing joint bolts for cooler pipes. Use NEW "O" ring when installing mainshaft or countershaft speed sensors. Tighten all fasteners to specification.

CAUTION: If transaxle failure existed, flush oil cooler. See OIL COOLER FLUSHING under ON-VEHICLE SERVICE.

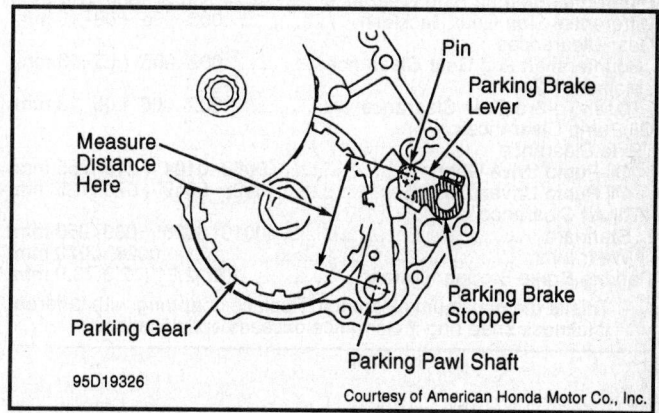

95D19326 — Courtesy of American Honda Motor Co., Inc.

Fig. 34: Measuring Parking Brake Stopper Distance

TORQUE SPECIFICATIONS
TORQUE SPECIFICATIONS

Application	Ft. Lbs. (N.m)
Countershaft Lock Nut	76 (103)
Drain Plug	36 (49)
Joint Bolt	21 (29)
Mainshaft Lock Nut	58 (78)
Mount Bracket Bolt	47 (64)
Parking Brake Stopper Bolt	10 (14)
Pressure Tap Plug	13 (18)
Reverse Shift Fork Bolt	10 (14)
Ring Gear Bolt	74 (100)
Sub-Shaft Lock Nut	69 (94)
Transaxle Housing Bolt [1]	33 (45)
Vehicle Speed Sensor Bolt	16 (22)

Application	INCH Lbs. (N.m)
Accumulator Cover Bolt	106 (12.0)
Countershaft Speed Sensor Bolt	106 (12.0)
Lock-Up Control Solenoid Valve Assembly Bolt	106 (12.0)
Lock-Up Valve Body Bolt	106 (12.0)
Mainshaft Speed Sensor Bolt	106 (12.0)
Main Valve Body Bolt	106 (12.0)
Needle Bearing Stopper Bolt	106 (12.0)
Regulator Valve Body Bolt	106 (12.0)
Reverse Idler Gear Shaft Holder Bolt	106 (12.0)
Right Side Cover Bolt	106 (12.0)
Secondary Valve Body Bolt	106 (12.0)
Servo Body Bolt	106 (12.0)
Servo Detent Base Bolt	106 (12.0)
Shift Control Solenoid Valve Assembly Bolt	106 (12.0)
Stopper Bolt	106 (12.0)
Throttle Cam Stopper Bolt	106 (12.0)
Throttle Control Lever Bolt	69 (7.8)

[1] – Tighten bolts to specification in sequence. *See Fig. 32.*

TRANSAXLE SPECIFICATIONS

TRANSAXLE SPECIFICATIONS

Application	Specification
Clutch Clearance	
1st & 2nd Clutches	.026-.033" (.65-.85 mm)
1st-Hold Clutch	.020-.031" (.50-.80 mm)
3rd & 4th Clutches	.016-.024" (.40-.60 mm)
Differential Bearing Side Clearance	[1] .006" (.15 mm)
Differential Side Gear Backlash	.003-.006" (.08-.15 mm)
Gear Clearances	
Countershaft 2nd Gear Clearance	.002-.005" (.05-.13 mm)
Mainshaft 2nd	
Gear-To-3rd Gear Clearance	.002-.005" (.05-.13 mm)
Oil Pump Clearances	
Side Clearance	
Oil Pump Drive Gear	.0083-.0104" (.210-.265 mm)
Oil Pump Driven Gear	.0028-.0049" (.070-.125 mm)
Thrust Clearance	
Standard	.0010-.0020" (.030-.050 mm)
Wear Limit	.0028" (.070 mm)
Parking Brake Stopper Distance	2.87-2.91" (72.9-73.9 mm)

[1] – This is the maximum clearance. Replace snap ring with different thickness snap ring if clearance exceeds specification.

WIRING DIAGRAMS

For appropriate wiring diagram, see ACURA SP7A or SX4A ELECTRONIC CONTROLS article.

Integra

APPLICATION

APPLICATION

Vehicle	Transaxle Model
1995 Integra	SP7A

CAUTION: Vehicle is equipped with a Supplemental Restraint System (SRS). When servicing vehicle, use care to avoid accidental air bag deployment. All SRS electrical connections and wiring harness are covered with Yellow insulation. SRS-related components are located in steering column, center console, instrument panel and lower panel on instrument panel. DO NOT use electrical test equipment on these circuits. It may be necessary to deactivate SRS before servicing components. See AIR BAG SERVICING article in APPLICATIONS & IDENTIFICATIONS.

NOTE: Obtain radio anti-theft code from customer before disconnecting negative battery cable. Radio anti-theft code must be re-entered into radio once negative battery cable is reconnected. To re-enter radio anti-theft code, turn ignition and radio on. When the word "CODE" is displayed on radio, re-enter radio anti-theft code by using the radio station preset buttons.

DESCRIPTION

Automatic transaxle is electronically controlled. Transaxle shifting and torque converter lock-up are controlled by Transmission Control Module (TCM). The TCM receives information from various input devices and uses this information to control shift and lock-up control solenoid valves.

The TCM contains a grade logic control system which controls transaxle shifting while vehicle is ascending or descending a slope or reducing vehicle speed. Transaxle is equipped with shift and key interlock systems. Shift interlock system prevents shift lever from being moved from Park unless brake pedal is depressed and accelerator pedal is in idle position. In case of a malfunction, shift lever can be released by placing ignition key in key release slot near shift lever. Key interlock system prevents ignition key from being removed from ignition lock assembly unless shift lever is in Park.

The A/T gear position indicator on instrument panel contains lights to indicate which position A/T gear position switch on shift lever is in.

OPERATION

A/T GEAR POSITION INDICATOR

With ignition in RUN or START position, voltage is supplied to A/T gear position indicator, located on instrument panel. *See Fig. 1.* When shift lever is moved to designated gear position, A/T gear position switch completes the ground circuit for A/T gear position indicator on instrument panel. The light on A/T gear position indicator will be illuminated to indicate the shift lever gear position. The A/T gear position switch is located on passenger's side of shift lever. *See Fig. 6.*

When headlights are turned on, voltage is supplied to Red/Black wire at A/T gear position indicator. This changes brightness control from fixed setting to control by the dash light dimmer input on the Red wire.

GRADE LOGIC CONTROL SYSTEM

The TCM compares actual driving conditions with driving conditions memorized in the TCM, based on input signals from Vehicle Speed Sensor (VSS), Throttle Position (TP) sensor, engine coolant temperature sensor, brakelight switch signal and A/T gear position switch. The TCM uses these input signals to control shifting while vehicle is ascending or descending a slope or during deceleration.

When TCM determines vehicle is ascending a slope with shift lever in "D₄" position, the TCM extends engagement of 3rd gear to prevent transaxle from frequently shifting between 3rd and 4th gears to provide smooth vehicle operation. Shift points between 3rd and 4th gear are stored in TCM which allows the most suitable gear selection depending on conditions.

When TCM determines vehicle is descending a slope with shift lever in "D₄" position, the TCM changes upshift speed from 3rd to 4th gear when throttle is fully closed. This widens the 3rd gear operating range from that programmed for level surface operation and, in conjunction with engine braking from torque converter lock-up, provides smooth vehicle operation. When vehicle is decelerating on a gradual hill in 4th gear, or when applying brakes on a steep hill, the transaxle will downshift to 3rd gear. When vehicle accelerates, transaxle will shift into 4th gear.

When vehicle decelerates from speeds greater than 27 MPH (such as entering a corner), TCM shifts transaxle from 4th gear to 3rd gear earlier than normal to reduce the number of times the transaxle shifts. This allows smoother acceleration and vehicle operation.

SHIFT & KEY INTERLOCK SYSTEMS

Shift Interlock System – Shift interlock system prevents shift lever from being moved from Park unless brake pedal is depressed and accelerator pedal is in idle position. Shift lever cannot be moved from Park if brake and accelerator pedal are depressed at the same time. In case of a malfunction, shift lever can be released by placing ignition key in key release slot near shift lever.

Voltage is provided to shift lock solenoid when ignition is in RUN or START position. When brake pedal is depressed, brakelight switch provides voltage to TCM, provided accelerator pedal is in idle position. With accelerator pedal in idle position, a voltage signal is delivered between Throttle Position (TP) sensor and the TCM. The TCM then provides voltage to shift lock circuit in the interlock control unit. When A/T gear position switch is in Park, interlock control unit then operates shift lock solenoid by controlling the ground circuit. When shift lock solenoid is energized, shift lever is released and can be moved.

The A/T gear position switch is located on passenger's side of shift lever. *See Fig. 6.* Shift lock solenoid is located on driver's side of shift lever. *See Fig. 2.* Interlock control unit is located behind driver's side of instrument panel and contains an 8-pin electrical connector. *See Fig. 4.*

Key Interlock System – Key interlock system prevents ignition key from being removed from ignition lock assembly unless shift lever is in Park. Voltage is provided to key interlock switch from No. 42 fuse (20-amp) in engine compartment fuse box, located at passenger's side rear corner of engine compartment. When ignition key is in ignition lock assembly, key interlock switch closes, providing voltage to key interlock solenoid and interlock control unit.

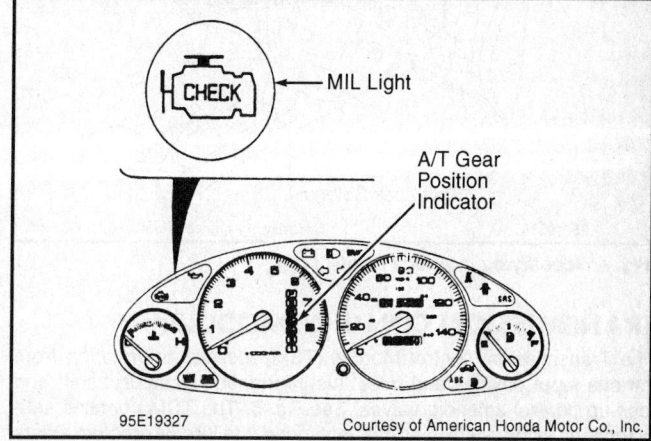

95E19327   Courtesy of American Honda Motor Co., Inc.

Fig. 1: Identifying A/T Gear Position Indicator & MIL Light

If shift lever is not in Park, interlock control unit energizes key interlock solenoid by completing ground circuit. When key interlock solenoid is energized, ignition key cannot be removed from ignition lock assembly. Key interlock switch and key interlock solenoid are located on ignition lock assembly. See Fig. 3. Interlock control unit is located behind driver's side of instrument panel and contains an 8-pin electrical connector. See Fig. 4.

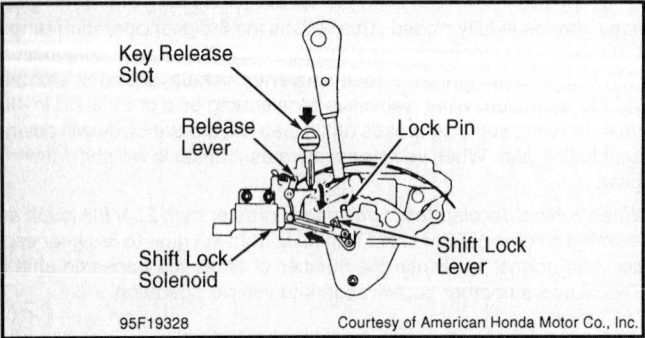

95F19328   Courtesy of American Honda Motor Co., Inc.

Fig. 2: Identifying Key Release Slot & Shift Lock Solenoid

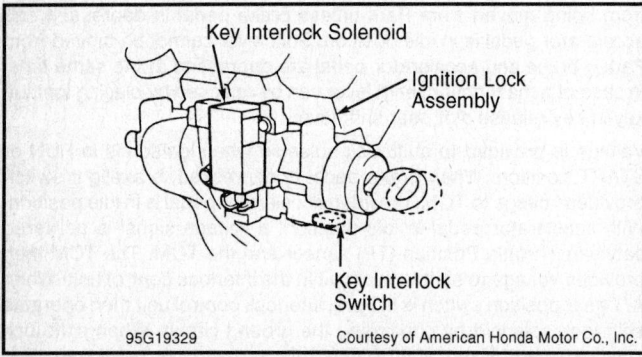

95G19329   Courtesy of American Honda Motor Co., Inc.

Fig. 3: Identifying Key Interlock Solenoid & Key Interlock Switch

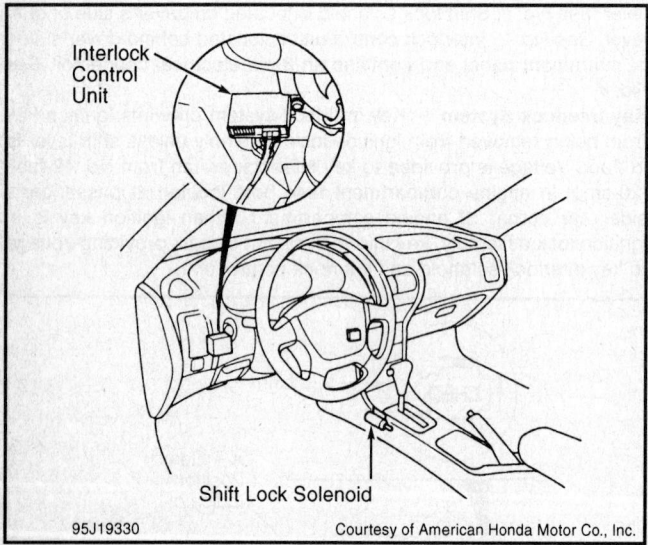

95J19330   Courtesy of American Honda Motor Co., Inc.

Fig. 4: Identifying Interlock Control Unit

TRANSMISSION CONTROL MODULE

The Transmission Control Module (TCM) receives information from various input devices and uses this information to control shift and lock-up control solenoid valves. See Fig. 5. The TCM contains self-diagnostic system which stores fault code if failure or problem exists in transaxle electronic control system. The fault code may be retrieved to determine transaxle problem area. See SELF-DIAGNOSTIC

SYSTEM. Fault code may also be referred to as Diagnostic Trouble Code (DTC). The TCM is located behind driver's side kick panel. See Fig. 6.

TCM INPUT DEVICES

Air Conditioning Signal – The A/C clutch relay delivers input signal to TCM, indicating A/C operation. The A/C clutch relay is located at front corner of engine compartment, near radiator. See Fig. 7.

Barometric Pressure Signal – Barometric pressure signal is delivered between Engine Control Module (ECM) and the TCM. The ECM contains a built-in barometric pressure sensor to determine atmospheric pressure. The ECM is located behind passenger's side kick panel, below instrument panel.

Brake Switch Signal – Brakelight switch delivers input signal to TCM, indicating vehicle braking. Brakelight switch is located on brake pedal support. See Fig. 6.

Engine Coolant Temperature Signal – Engine Coolant Temperature (ECT) sensor delivers input signal to TCM, indicating engine coolant temperature. The ECT sensor is located on cylinder head, below distributor and contains a Red/White wire and Green/Blue wire in the electrical connector. See Fig. 7.

Engine Speed – Engine speed signal is delivered to TCM from ignition control module in distributor assembly.

Engine Control Module (ECM) – An upshift and downshift signal and a shift acknowledgment signal is delivered between the ECM and TCM. A 5-volt reference signal exists between ECM and TCM. The ECM is located behind passenger's side kick panel, below instrument panel.

Mainshaft & Countershaft Speed Signal – Mainshaft speed signal is delivered to TCM, indicating speed of mainshaft in transaxle. Mainshaft speed sensor is located on top of transaxle. See Fig. 7. Countershaft speed signal is delivered to TCM, indicating speed of countershaft in transaxle. Countershaft speed sensor is located on top of transaxle.

Service Check Connector – Service check connector is used when retrieving fault codes for transaxle electronic control system diagnosis. When SCS short connector is installed between electrical terminals of service check connector, an input is delivered to TCM to display fault codes on "D₄" indicator light. Service check connector is a 2-pin Blue colored electrical connector located at passenger's corner of instrument panel. See Fig. 8.

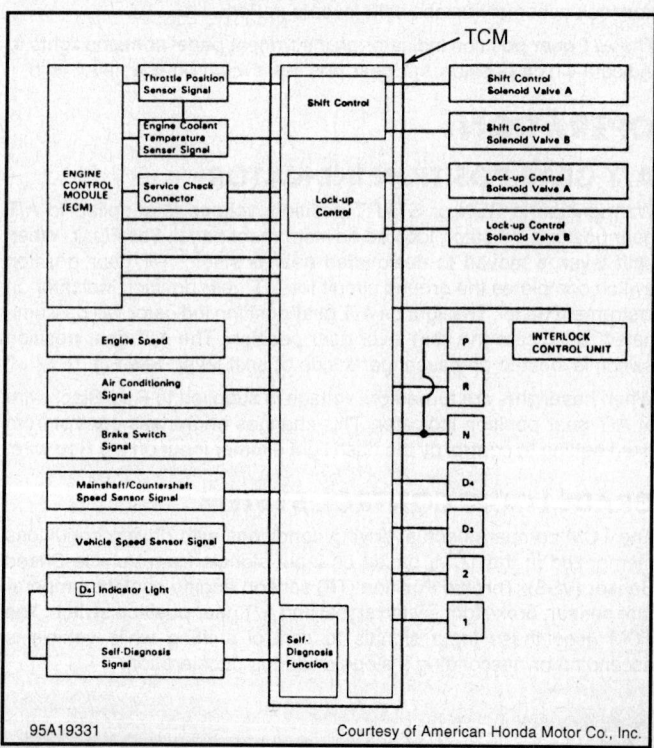

95A19331   Courtesy of American Honda Motor Co., Inc.

Fig. 5: Identifying Input & Output Devices

Shift Position Signal – Shift position signal is delivered to TCM by the A/T gear position switch, located on passenger's side of shift lever. *See Fig. 6.*

Throttle Position (TP) Sensor Signal – Throttle Position (TP) sensor delivers input signal to TCM to indicate throttle position. The TP sensor is mounted on throttle body. *See Fig. 7.*

Vehicle Speed Sensor Signal – Vehicle speed Sensor (VSS) delivers input signal to TCM to indicate vehicle speed. The VSS is located on top of transaxle. *See Fig. 7.*

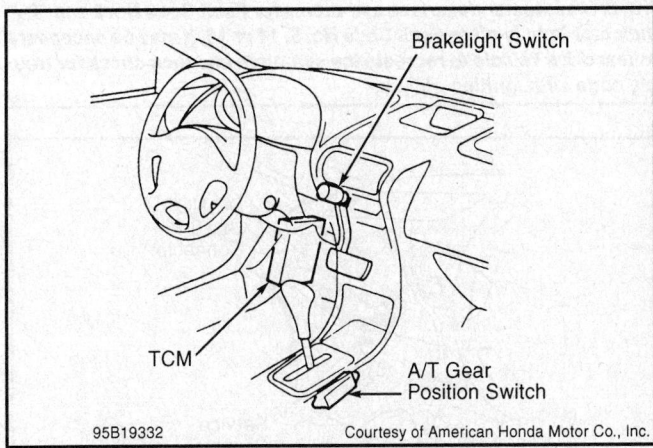

Fig. 6: Identifying TCM, Brakelight Switch & A/T Gear Position Switch

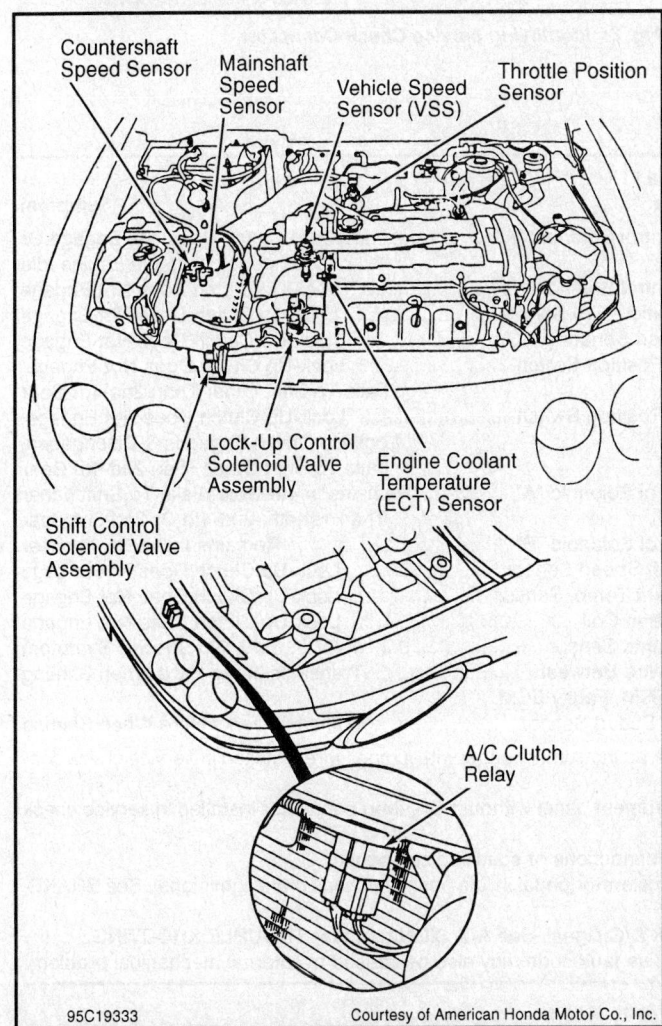

Fig. 7: Identifying Input & Output Device Locations

TCM OUTPUT DEVICES

Shift Control Solenoid Valves – The TCM controls transaxle shifting by delivering an output signal to shift control solenoid valves "A" and "B" on shift control solenoid valve assembly. Solenoid valves are operated in accordance with gear position. See SHIFT CONTROL SOLENOID VALVE OPERATION table. Shift control solenoid valve assembly is located on transaxle. *See Fig. 7.* Shift control solenoid valve "A" has a Blue/Yellow wire and solenoid valve "B" has a Green/White wire.

SHIFT CONTROL SOLENOID VALVE OPERATION

Shift Lever Position	Solenoid Valve "A"	Solenoid Valve "B"
"D₃" Or "D₄" (1st Gear)	Off	On
"D₃" Or "D₄" (2nd Gear)	On	On
"D₃" Or "D₄" (3rd Gear)	On	Off
"D₄" (4th)	Off	Off
"2" (2nd Gear)	On	On
"1" (1st Gear)	On	Off
"R" (Reverse)	On	Off

Lock-Up Control Solenoid Valves – The TCM controls torque converter lock-up by delivering an output signal to lock-up control solenoid valves "A" and "B" on lock-up control solenoid valve assembly. Lock-up control solenoid valves are activated in accordance with lock-up condition. See LOCK-UP CONTROL SOLENOID VALVE OPERATION table. Lock-up control solenoid valve assembly is located on transaxle. *See Fig. 7.* Lock-up control solenoid valve "A" has a Yellow wire and solenoid valve "B" has a Green/Black wire.

LOCK-UP CONTROL SOLENOID VALVE OPERATION

Lock-Up Condition	Solenoid Valve "A"	Solenoid Valve "B"
No Lock-Up	Off	Off
Slight Lock-Up	On	Off
Half Lock-Up	On	On
Full Lock-Up	On	On
Lock-Up During Deceleration	On	[1]

[1] – Solenoid valve will cycle on and off.

"D₄" Indicator Light – The "D₄" indicator light is located on A/T gear position indicator on instrument panel. *See Fig. 1.* When ignition is first turned on, "D₄" indicator light should come on for about 2 seconds and then go off, indicating light circuit is functioning properly. If a fault exists in transaxle electronic control system and fault code is stored, TCM delivers an output signal to blink "D₄" indicator light.

Interlock Control Unit – When A/T gear position switch is in Park, the TCM provides voltage to shift lock circuit in the interlock control unit, provided brake pedal is depressed and accelerator pedal is in idle position. Interlock control unit then operates shift lock solenoid by controlling the ground circuit. When shift lock solenoid is energized, shift lever is released and can be moved.

Self-Diagnosis Indicator – If a fault exists in transaxle electronic control system and fault code is stored, TCM will deliver an output signal to blink "D₄" indicator light. Fault code may be referred to as Diagnostic Trouble Code (DTC).

SELF-DIAGNOSTIC SYSTEM

SYSTEM DIAGNOSIS

TCM monitors transaxle operation. TCM contains a self-diagnostic system which stores a fault code if transaxle electronic control system failure or problem exists. If fault code is stored, TCM will blink "D₄" indicator light on A/T gear position indicator on instrument panel. *See Fig. 1.* Fault code may also be referred to as Diagnostic Trouble Code (DTC).

RETRIEVING FAULT CODES

NOTE: During diagnostics, ensure "D₄" indicator light on A/T gear position indicator on instrument panel is not turned on by a fault in the PGM-FI system. The PGM-FI system controls the fuel injection system. To repair PGM-FI system, see appropriate SELF-DIAGNOSTICS article in ENGINE PERFORMANCE in appropriate MITCHELL® manual. After PGM-FI system as been repaired, clear fault codes. See CLEARING FAULT CODES. After fault codes have been cleared, road test vehicle for several minutes at over 30 MPH and recheck fault codes.

NOTE: Before any diagnostic procedure, obtain radio anti-theft code from customer. Note radio preset stations, as radio stations and clock setting will be cleared and must be reset. Radio anti-theft code must be re-entered for radio operation.

Diagnostic Circuit Check – 1) With shift lever in Park, turn ignition on. The "D₄" indicator light on A/T gear position indicator on instrument panel should come on for about 2 seconds and then go off, indicating light circuit is operating properly. *See Fig. 1.* If indicator light functions as described, fault codes may be retrieved. See TCM FAULT CODES.

2) If "D₄" indicator light does not come on as described or remains on steady, proceed to appropriate diagnostic chart. See TROUBLE SHOOTING FLOW CHARTS.

TCM Fault Codes – 1) With ignition off, install jumper wire between terminals of service check connector, located at passenger's corner of instrument panel. *See Fig. 8.* Service check connector is a Blue 2-pin connector.

2) Turn ignition on. Fault codes will be displayed by blinking "D₄" indicator light on A/T gear position indicator on instrument panel. *See Fig. 1.*

3) Fault codes will by displayed by short and long blinks. One long blink equals 10 short blinks. For example, if a long blink is followed by 4 short blinks, this indicates Fault Code No. 14. *See Fig. 9.*

4) Once fault code is obtained, determine probable cause and symptom. See FAULT CODE IDENTIFICATION table. If any other fault codes except those listed are displayed, TCM is defective. For trouble shooting of fault codes, see TROUBLE SHOOTING FLOW CHARTS. Turn ignition off. Remove jumper wire from service check connector.

NOTE: If customer describes symptoms for Fault Code No. 3 and "D₄" indicator light is off or Fault Code No. 6, 11 or 15, it may be necessary to test drive vehicle to recreate the symptom and then check for trouble code with ignition still on.

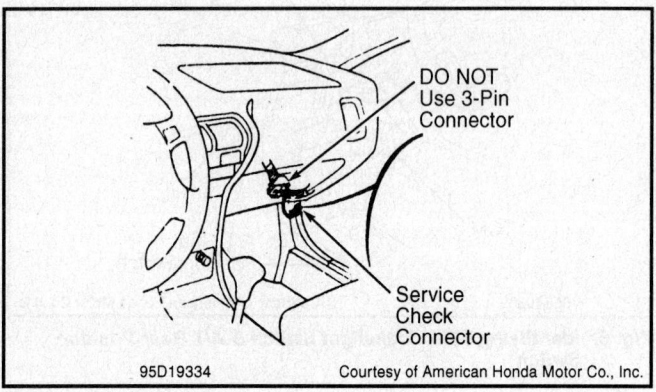

95D19334   Courtesy of American Honda Motor Co., Inc.

Fig. 8: Identifying Service Check Connector

FAULT CODE IDENTIFICATION

Fault Code [1] Number	Indicator Light [2] Condition	Probable [3] Cause	[4] [5] Symptom
1	Blinks	Defective Lock-Up Control Solenoid "A"	Lock-Up Clutch Does Not Engage Or Disengage, Unstable Engine Idle
2	Blinks	Defective Lock-Up Control Solenoid "B"	Lock-Up Clutch Does Not Engage
3	Blinks Or Remains Off	Defective Throttle Position (TP) Sensor	Lock-Up Clutch Does Not Engage
4	Blinks	Defective Vehicle Speed Sensor (VSS)	Lock-Up Clutch Does Not Engage
5	Blinks	Defective A/T Gear Position Switch	Lock-Up Clutch Does Not Engage, Fails To Shift Other Than 2nd-4th Gear
6	Off	Defective A/T Gear Position Switch	Lock-Up Clutch Does Not Engage, Lock-Up Clutch Engages & Disengages, Fails To Shift Other Than 2nd-4th Gear
7	Blinks	Defective Shift Control Solenoid "A"	Remains In 4th Gear, Fails To Shift Other Than 1st-4th, 2nd-4th Or 2nd-3rd Gear
8	Blinks	Defective Shift Control Solenoid "B"	Remains In 1st Or 4th Gear
9	Blinks	Defective Countershaft Speed Sensor	Lock-Up Clutch Does Not Engage
10	Blinks	Defective Engine Coolant Temp. Sensor	Lock-Up Clutch Does Not Engage
11	Off	Defective Ignition Coil	Lock-Up Clutch Does Not Engage
13	Blinks	Defective Barometric Sensor	No Specific Symptom
14	Blinks	Shorted Or Open Wire Between TCM Terminal D16 & ECM, Faulty ECM	Transaxle Jerks Hard When Shifting
15 [6]	Off	Defective Mainshaft Speed Sensor	Transaxle Jerks Hard When Shifting

[1] – Number of blinks from "D₄" indicator light on A/T gear position indicator on instrument panel with jumper wire installed in service check connector.

[2] – Operation of "D₄" indicator light on A/T gear position indicator on instrument panel without SCS short connector installed in service check connector.

[3] – Check listed component for probable cause. Also check wiring and connections of specified component.

[4] – If transaxle fails to shift from Park with brake pedal depressed and accelerator pedal in idle position, check brakelight signal. See BRAKELIGHT SIGNAL under TROUBLE SHOOTING.

[5] – If lock-up clutch does not engage or does not cycle on and off, check A/C signal. See A/C SIGNAL under TROUBLE SHOOTING.

[6] – Fault Code No. 15 does not necessary indicate an electrical problem, as fault code may also be caused by internal mechanical problem.

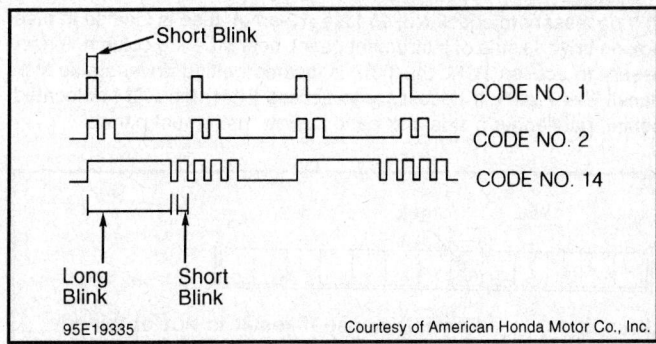

Fig. 9: Identifying Fault Code Displays

CLEARING FAULT CODES

NOTE: Before clearing fault codes, obtain radio anti-theft code from customer. Note radio preset stations, as radio stations and clock setting will be cleared and must be reset. Radio anti-theft code must be re-entered for radio operation.

1) Once repairs have been performed, fault codes must be cleared from TCM memory. Remove fuse No. 32 (BACK-UP, 7.5 amp fuse) from engine compartment fuse box, located at passenger's side rear corner of engine compartment for at least 10 seconds. This will clear TCM and ECM memories.

2) Reinstall fuse. To re-enter radio anti-theft code, turn radio on. When the word "CODE" is displayed on radio, re-enter radio anti-theft code by using the radio station preset buttons. Reset clock and radio stations.

TROUBLE SHOOTING

A/C SIGNAL

NOTE: If no A/C signal exists, torque converter lock-up clutch may not engage or cycle on and off.

1) Start engine. Turn blower switch and A/C switch to the ON position. Check if A/C compressor clutch engages.

2) If A/C compressor clutch does not engage, check A/C compressor clutch and wiring. See appropriate AUTOMATIC or MANUAL A/C-HEATER SYSTEMS article in appropriate MITCHELL® AIR CONDITIONING & HEATING SERVICE & REPAIR manual. If A/C compressor clutch engages, turn engine off. Disconnect 26-pin electrical connector from TCM, located behind driver's side kick panel. *See Fig. 6.*

3) Connect voltmeter between terminal A22 (Black/Red wire) and terminal A25 (Brown/Black wire). Start engine. Note voltage with A/C compressor off.

4) If battery voltage does not exist, go to next step. If battery voltage exists, A/C signal is okay. Check for loose TCM electrical connections. If electrical connections are okay, substitute TCM with a known good unit and recheck operation.

5) If battery voltage does not exist, check for open circuit in Black/Red wire between terminal A22 on 26-pin electrical connector and A/C clutch relay. The A/C clutch relay is located at front corner of engine compartment, near radiator. *See Fig. 7.*

BRAKELIGHT SIGNAL

NOTE: If no brakelight signal exists, transaxle may fail to shift from Park with brake pedal depressed and accelerator pedal in idle position.

1) Ensure brakelights come on when brake pedal is depressed. If brakelights come on, go to next step. If brakelights do not come on, check No. 42 fuse (20-amp) in engine compartment fuse box, located at passenger's side rear corner of engine compartment. If fuse is okay, repair brakelight signal circuit.

2) Ensure ignition is off. Disconnect the 26-pin and 22-pin electrical connectors from TCM, located behind driver's side kick panel. *See Fig. 6.*

3) Connect Test Harness (07LAJ-PT3010A) to 26-pin and 22-pin electrical connectors. *See Fig. 10.* DO NOT connect test harness to TCM.

4) Using Digital Volt-Ohmmeter (DVOM), measure voltage between terminals D2 and A25 or A26 on test harness with brake pedal depressed. Terminal numbers are located on test harness.

5) If battery voltage exists, brakelight signal to TCM is okay. Check for loose TCM electrical connections. If electrical connections are okay, substitute TCM with a known good unit and recheck operation.

6) If battery voltage does not exist, check for open circuit in the Green/White wire between terminal D2 and brakelight switch. Brakelight switch is located on brake pedal support. *See Fig. 6.*

7) Ensure ignition is off. Remove test harness. Reinstall electrical connectors on TCM.

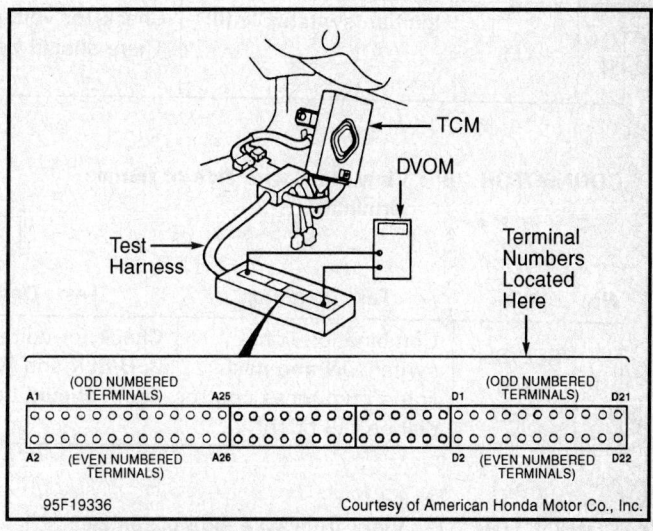

Fig. 10: Installing Test Harness

SYSTEM TESTING

A/T GEAR POSITION INDICATOR

NOTE: If necessary, refer to wiring schematic when checking component wiring. See Fig. 14.

1) Remove instrument panel gauge assembly from instrument panel. Disconnect electrical connectors "B" "C" and "D" from rear of instrument panel gauge assembly. *See Fig. 11.*

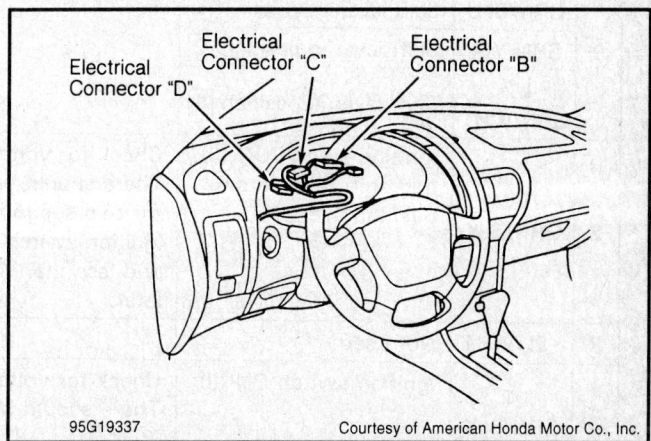

Fig. 11: Identifying Instrument Panel Gauge Assembly Electrical Connectors

2) Check for voltage and continuity at electrical connectors as specified. *See Fig. 12.* If necessary to check ground connections G201 or G401, ground connection G201 is located at passenger's side front corner of engine compartment, on inner fender panel. Ground connection G401 is located behind driver's side of instrument panel, above kick panel. *See Fig. 13.*

3) If necessary to check No. 15 fuse (10-amp), fuse is located in fuse box on driver's side of instrument panel, near steering column. If necessary to access TCM, the TCM is located behind driver's side kick panel. *See Fig. 6.* If necessary to access ECM, the ECM is located behind passenger's side kick panel, below instrument panel.

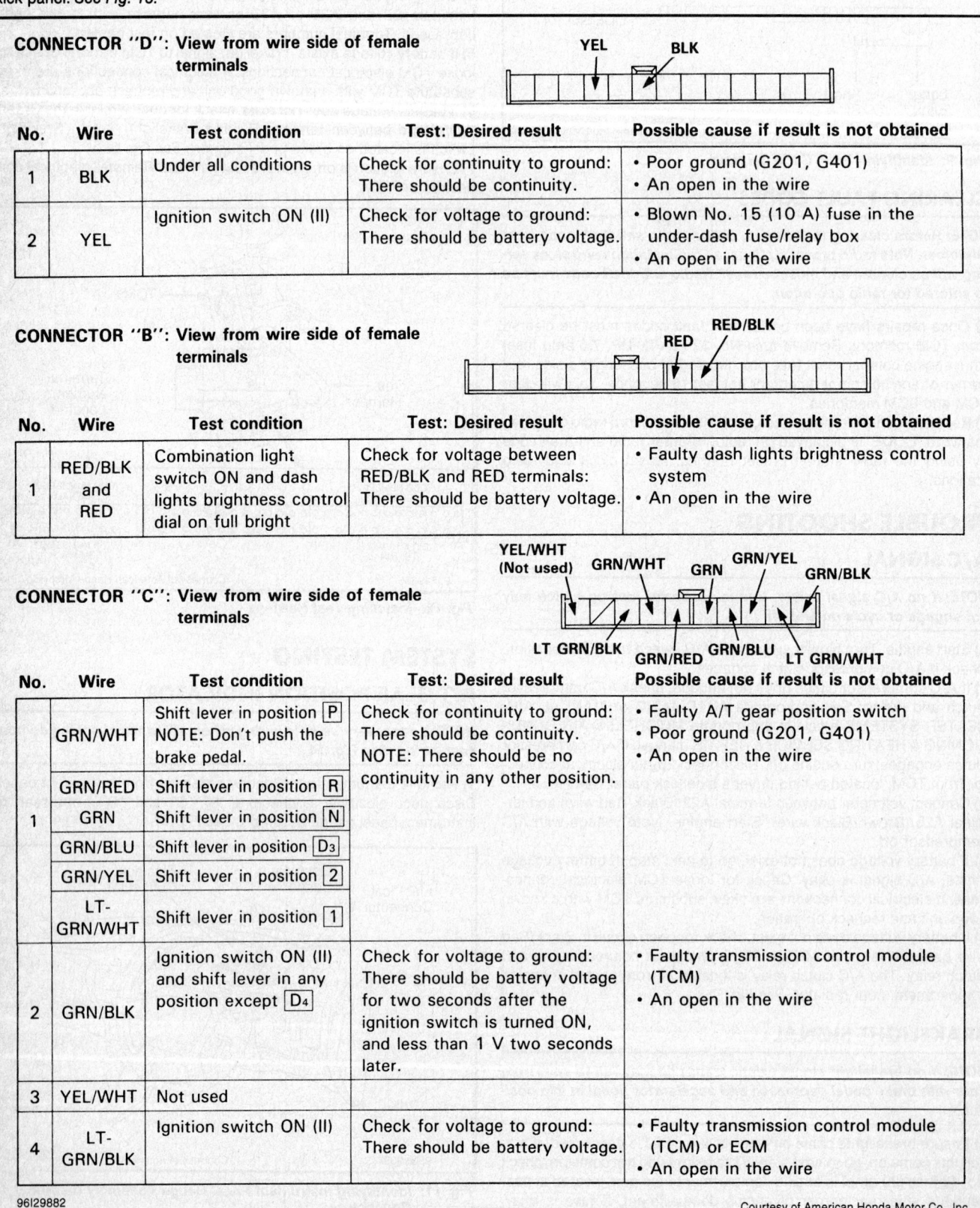

CONNECTOR "D": View from wire side of female terminals

No.	Wire	Test condition	Test: Desired result	Possible cause if result is not obtained
1	BLK	Under all conditions	Check for continuity to ground: There should be continuity.	• Poor ground (G201, G401) • An open in the wire
2	YEL	Ignition switch ON (II)	Check for voltage to ground: There should be battery voltage.	• Blown No. 15 (10 A) fuse in the under-dash fuse/relay box • An open in the wire

CONNECTOR "B": View from wire side of female terminals

No.	Wire	Test condition	Test: Desired result	Possible cause if result is not obtained
1	RED/BLK and RED	Combination light switch ON and dash lights brightness control dial on full bright	Check for voltage between RED/BLK and RED terminals: There should be battery voltage.	• Faulty dash lights brightness control system • An open in the wire

CONNECTOR "C": View from wire side of female terminals

No.	Wire	Test condition	Test: Desired result	Possible cause if result is not obtained
1	GRN/WHT	Shift lever in position P NOTE: Don't push the brake pedal.	Check for continuity to ground: There should be continuity. NOTE: There should be no continuity in any other position.	• Faulty A/T gear position switch • Poor ground (G201, G401) • An open in the wire
	GRN/RED	Shift lever in position R		
	GRN	Shift lever in position N		
	GRN/BLU	Shift lever in position D3		
	GRN/YEL	Shift lever in position 2		
	LT-GRN/WHT	Shift lever in position 1		
2	GRN/BLK	Ignition switch ON (II) and shift lever in any position except D4	Check for voltage to ground: There should be battery voltage for two seconds after the ignition switch is turned ON, and less than 1 V two seconds later.	• Faulty transmission control module (TCM) • An open in the wire
3	YEL/WHT	Not used		
4	LT-GRN/BLK	Ignition switch ON (II)	Check for voltage to ground: There should be battery voltage.	• Faulty transmission control module (TCM) or ECM • An open in the wire

96129882

Courtesy of American Honda Motor Co., Inc.

Fig. 12: Testing A/T Gear Position Indicator

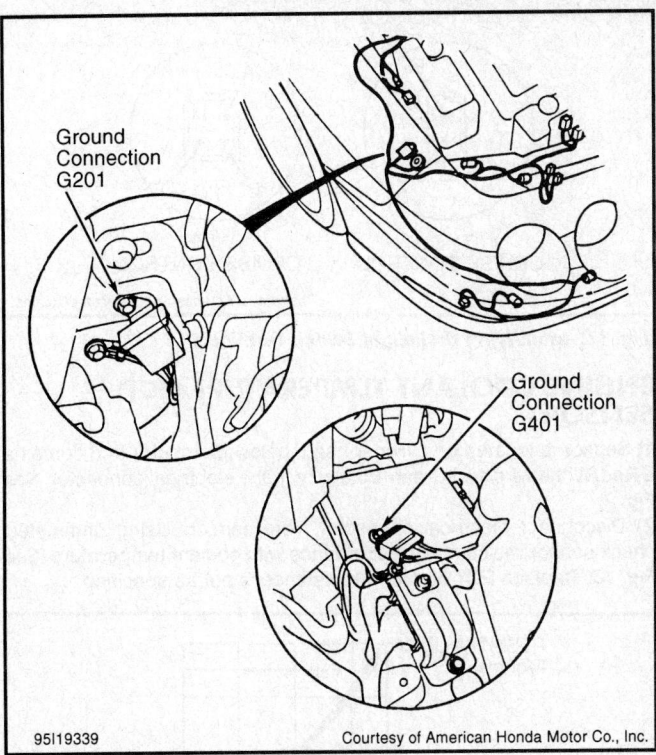

Fig. 13: Identifying Ground Connections

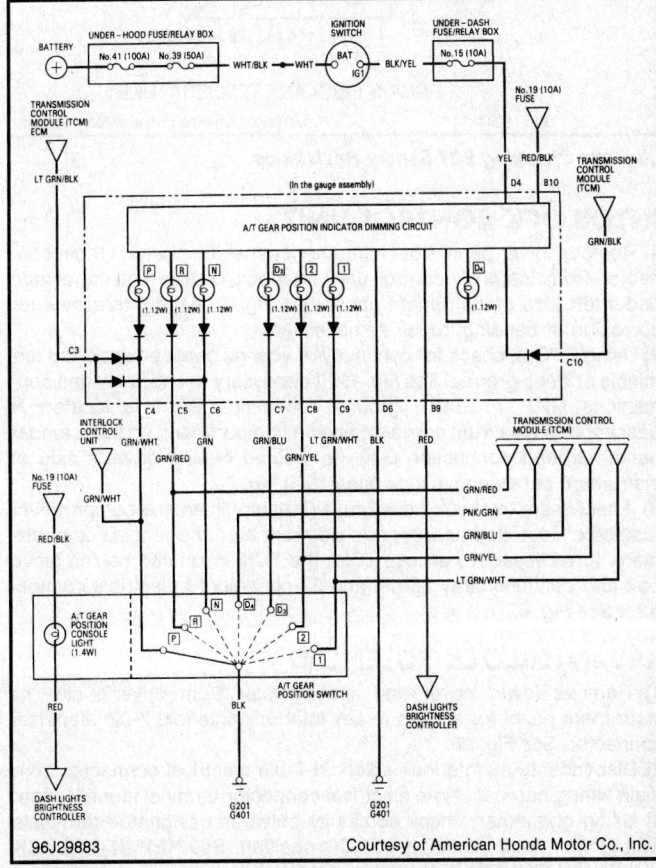

Fig. 14: A/T Gear Position Indicator Wiring Schematic

SHIFT & KEY INTERLOCK SYSTEMS

NOTE: *For system testing, refer to wiring schematic when checking component wiring. See Fig. 15. To check individual components, see COMPONENT TESTING.*

1) To check system operation, ensure shift lever is in Park. Turn ignition on. Depress brake pedal with accelerator pedal in idle position.

2) If shift lock solenoid clicks, system is working properly. If shift lock solenoid fails to click, see INTERLOCK CONTROL UNIT under COMPONENT TESTING. If shift lever cannot be moved from Park, check for proper installation procedure of shift lock solenoid. See SHIFT LOCK SOLENOID under REMOVAL & INSTALLATION. If shift lock solenoid installation is okay, test A/T gear position switch, see A/T GEAR POSITION SWITCH.

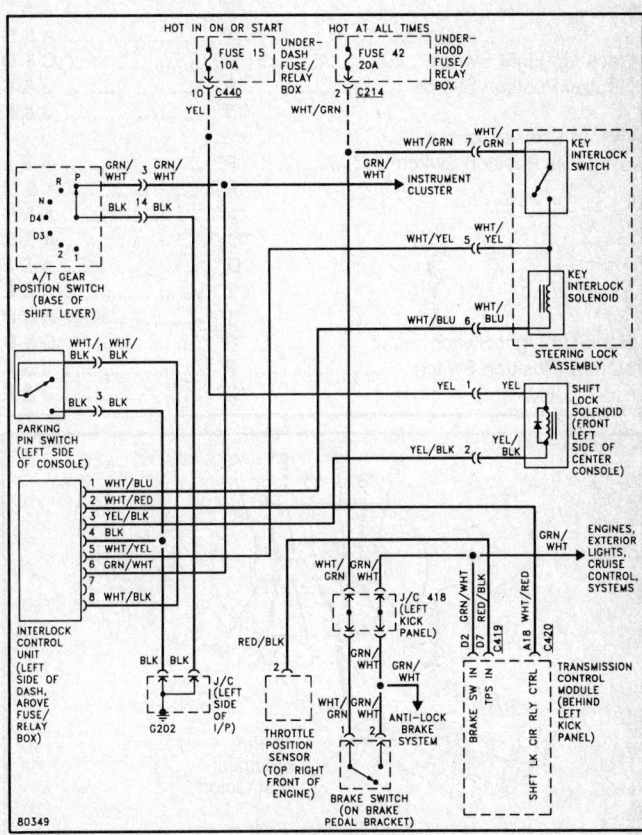

Fig. 15: Shift & Key Interlock System Wiring Schematic

COMPONENT TESTING

A/T GEAR POSITION SWITCH

NOTE: *The A/T gear position switch also contains back-up light switch and neutral position switch. Back-up light switch and neutral position switch can also be checked when checking A/T gear position switch.*

1) Remove center console. Disconnect 14-pin electrical connector from A/T gear position switch. Note electrical connector terminal identification. *See Fig. 16.*

2) Using ohmmeter, check continuity between specified terminal(s) with shift lever in indicated positions. See A/T GEAR POSITION SWITCH CONTINUITY table.

NOTE: *Check continuity while moving shift lever back and forth in free play area of each gear position. DO NOT touch push button on shift lever when checking continuity.*

3) If continuity is not as specified, A/T gear position switch may require adjustment. See A/T GEAR POSITION SWITCH under REMOVAL & INSTALLATION. If correct continuity cannot be obtained by adjusting A/T gear position switch, replace switch assembly.

A/T GEAR POSITION SWITCH CONTINUITY

Application	Shift Lever Position	Continuity Between Terminals
With Cruise Control		
A/T Gear Position Switch	"P"	A & L
	"R"	A & M
	"N"	A & N
	"D₄"	I, A & G
	"D₃"	I, A & F
	"2"	I, A & E
	"1"	A & B
Back-Up Light Switch	"R"	C & D
Neutral Position Switch	"P"	J & K
	"N"	J & K
Without Cruise Control		
A/T Gear Position Switch	"P"	A & L
	"R"	A & M
	"N"	A & N
	"D₄"	A & G
	"D₃"	A & F
	"2"	A & E
	"1"	A & B
Back-Up Light Switch	"R"	C & D
Neutral Position Switch	"P"	J & K
	"N"	J & K

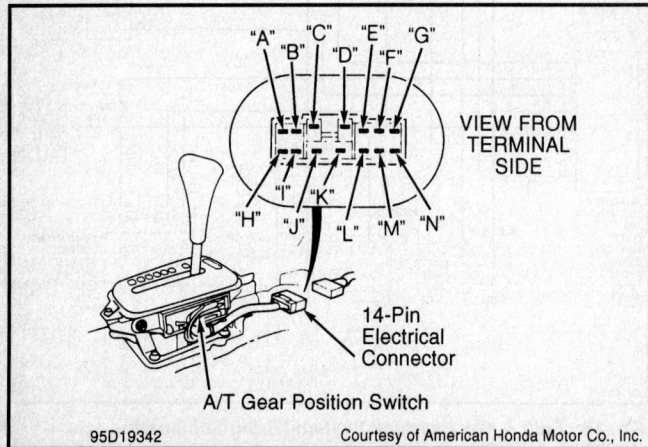

Fig. 16: Identifying A/T Gear Position Switch Electrical Connector Terminals

BRAKELIGHT SWITCH

1) Disconnect electrical connector from brakelight switch, located on brake pedal support. See Fig. 6. Note brakelight switch terminal identification. See Fig. 17.

2) On models with cruise control, using ohmmeter, check for continuity between terminals "A" and "D" with brake pedal released. Continuity should exist.

3) On all models, using ohmmeter, check continuity between terminals "B" and "C" with brake pedal depressed. Continuity should exist.

4) If continuity is not as specified, ensure brake pedal is properly adjusted so brakelight switch has proper travel for switch operation. If proper brakelight switch travel exists, replace brakelight switch.

COUNTERSHAFT SPEED SENSOR

Disconnect electrical connector from countershaft speed sensor located on top of transaxle. See Fig. 7. Using ohmmeter, measure resistance between terminals on electrical connector. Replace countershaft speed sensor if resistance is not 400-600 ohms.

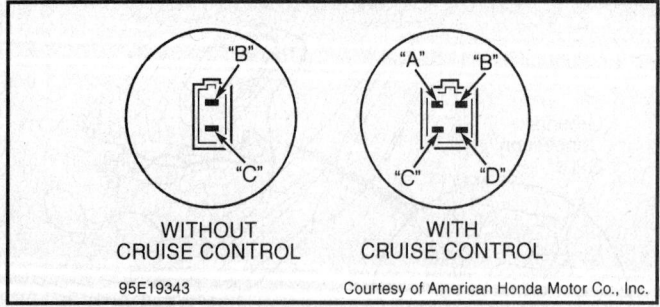

Fig. 17: Identifying Brakelight Switch Terminals

ENGINE COOLANT TEMPERATURE (ECT) SENSOR

1) Sensor is located on cylinder head, below distributor and contains a Red/White wire and Green/Blue wire in the electrical connector. See Fig. 7.

2) Disconnect electrical connector from sensor. Using ohmmeter, check sensor resistance in accordance with coolant temperature. See Fig. 18. Replace ECT sensor if resistance is not as specified.

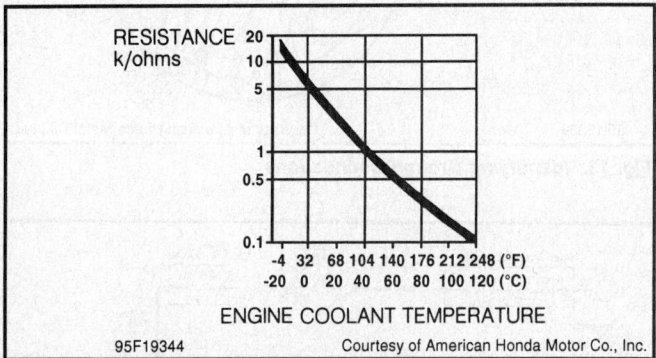

Fig. 18: Checking ECT Sensor Resistance

INTERLOCK CONTROL UNIT

1) Remove lower panel from instrument panel. Disconnect 8-pin connector from interlock control unit. Interlock control unit is located under left side of instrument panel. See Fig. 4. Inspect terminals for corrosion or bending, repair as necessary.

2) Using DVOM, check for continuity or voltage between specified terminals or body ground. See Fig. 19. If necessary to check ground connections G201 or G401, ground connection G201 is located at passenger's side front corner of engine compartment, on inner fender panel. Ground connection G401 is located behind driver's side of instrument panel, above kick panel. See Fig. 13.

3) If necessary to check No. 42 fuse (20-amp) in engine compartment fuse box, located at passenger's side rear corner of engine compartment. If necessary to access TCM, the TCM is located behind glove box and contains Gray 26-pin and 22-pin colored electrical connectors. See Fig. 6.

KEY INTERLOCK SOLENOID

1) Remove lower cover and knee bolster from driver's side of instrument panel for access to key interlock solenoid 7-pin electrical connector. See Fig. 20.

2) Disconnect key interlock solenoid 7-pin electrical connector from main wiring harness. Note electrical connector terminal identification.

3) Using ohmmeter, check continuity between designated terminals with ignition lock assembly in ACC position. See KEY INTERLOCK SOLENOID CONTINUITY SPECIFICATIONS table.

4) If continuity is as specified, proceed to next step. Replace ignition lock assembly if continuity is not as specified. Key interlock solenoid cannot be serviced separately.

5) Connect battery voltage and ground to terminals No. 6 and 7. Ensure ignition key cannot be removed with battery voltage applied.

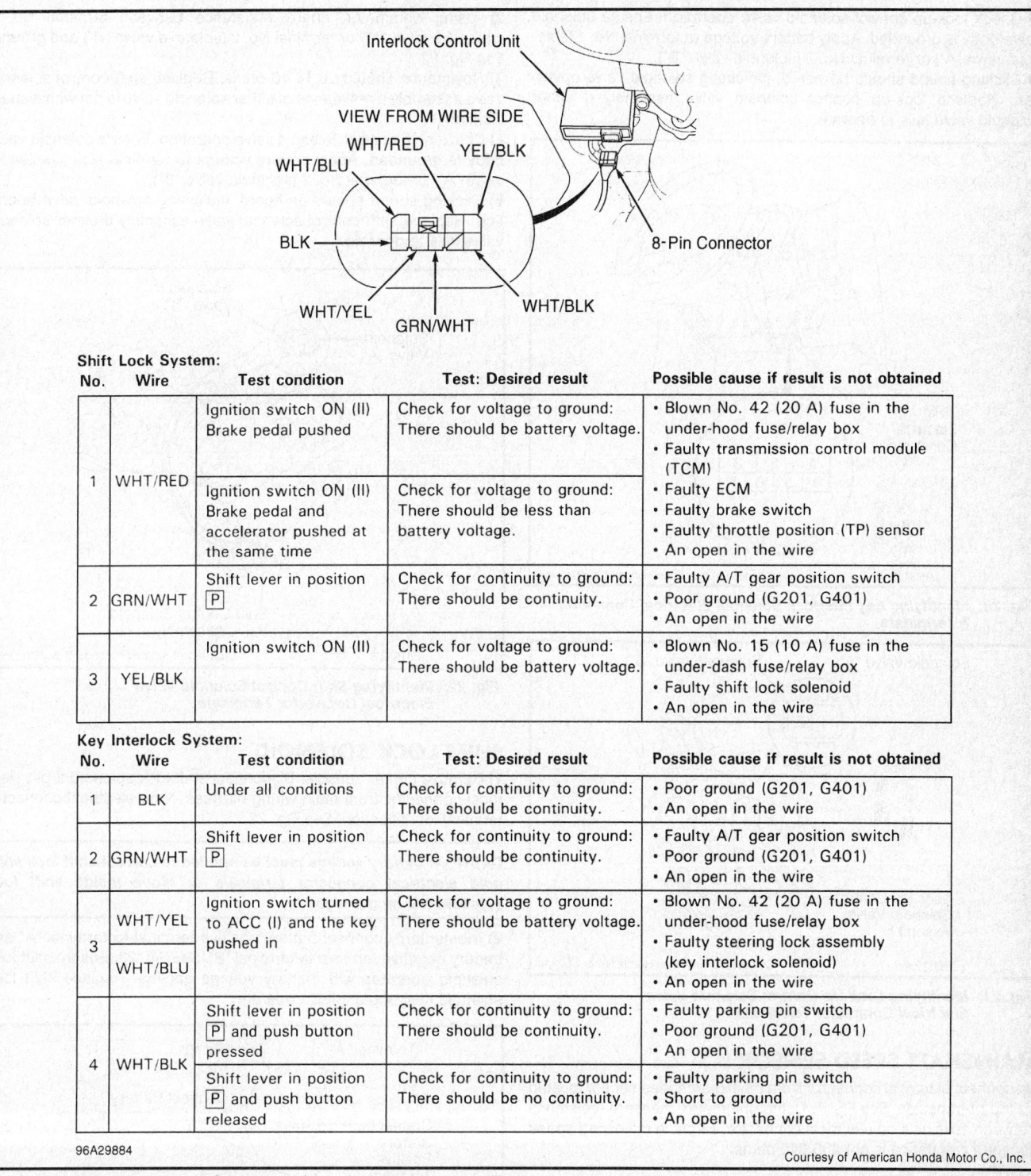

Shift Lock System:

No.	Wire	Test condition	Test: Desired result	Possible cause if result is not obtained
1	WHT/RED	Ignition switch ON (II) Brake pedal pushed	Check for voltage to ground: There should be battery voltage.	• Blown No. 42 (20 A) fuse in the under-hood fuse/relay box • Faulty transmission control module (TCM) • Faulty ECM • Faulty brake switch • Faulty throttle position (TP) sensor • An open in the wire
		Ignition switch ON (II) Brake pedal and accelerator pushed at the same time	Check for voltage to ground: There should be less than battery voltage.	
2	GRN/WHT	Shift lever in position P	Check for continuity to ground: There should be continuity.	• Faulty A/T gear position switch • Poor ground (G201, G401) • An open in the wire
3	YEL/BLK	Ignition switch ON (II)	Check for voltage to ground: There should be battery voltage.	• Blown No. 15 (10 A) fuse in the under-dash fuse/relay box • Faulty shift lock solenoid • An open in the wire

Key Interlock System:

No.	Wire	Test condition	Test: Desired result	Possible cause if result is not obtained
1	BLK	Under all conditions	Check for continuity to ground: There should be continuity.	• Poor ground (G201, G401) • An open in the wire
2	GRN/WHT	Shift lever in position P	Check for continuity to ground: There should be continuity.	• Faulty A/T gear position switch • Poor ground (G201, G401) • An open in the wire
3	WHT/YEL WHT/BLU	Ignition switch turned to ACC (I) and the key pushed in	Check for voltage to ground: There should be battery voltage.	• Blown No. 42 (20 A) fuse in the under-hood fuse/relay box • Faulty steering lock assembly (key interlock solenoid) • An open in the wire
4	WHT/BLK	Shift lever in position P and push button pressed	Check for continuity to ground: There should be continuity.	• Faulty parking pin switch • Poor ground (G201, G401) • An open in the wire
		Shift lever in position P and push button released	Check for continuity to ground: There should be no continuity.	• Faulty parking pin switch • Short to ground • An open in the wire

96A29884

Courtesy of American Honda Motor Co., Inc.

Fig. 19: Testing Interlock Control Unit

6) If ignition key cannot be removed, key interlock solenoid is okay. If ignition key can be removed, replace ignition lock assembly. Key interlock solenoid cannot be serviced separately.

KEY INTERLOCK SOLENOID CONTINUITY SPECIFICATIONS

Ignition Key Position	Continuity Between Terminals
Key Installed	5, 6 & 7
Key Removed	5 & 6

LOCK-UP CONTROL SOLENOID VALVES

1) Lock-up control solenoid valves are located on transaxle. See Fig. 7. Disconnect electrical connector at lock-up control solenoid valves.
2) Using ohmmeter, check resistance between terminal No. 1 (solenoid valve "A") or terminal No. 2 (solenoid valve "B") and body ground. See Fig. 21.
3) Resistance should be 14-16 ohms. Replace lock-up control solenoid valve assembly if resistance of either solenoid valve is not within specification.

4) Check lock-up control solenoid valve operation. Ensure solenoid valve body is grounded. Apply battery voltage to terminal No. 1 (solenoid valve "A") or terminal No. 2 (solenoid valve "B").

5) Clicking sound should be heard, indicating solenoid valve operation. Replace lock-up control solenoid valve assembly if either solenoid valve fails to operate.

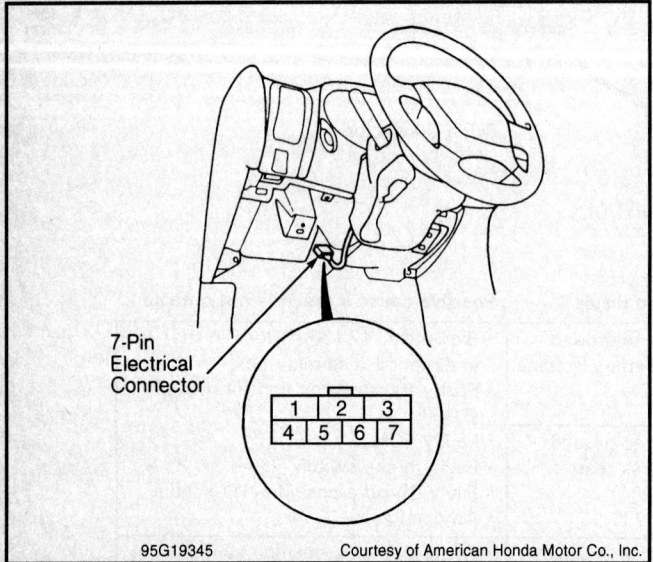

Fig. 20: Identifying Key Interlock Solenoid Electrical Connector & Terminals

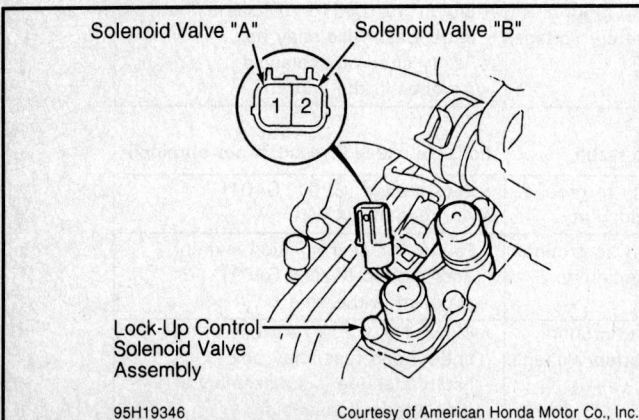

Fig. 21: Identifying Lock-Up Control Solenoid Valve Electrical Connector Terminals

MAINSHAFT SPEED SENSOR

Disconnect electrical connector from mainshaft speed sensor located on top of transaxle. See Fig. 7. Using ohmmeter, measure resistance between terminals on electrical connector. Replace mainshaft speed sensor if resistance is not 400-600 ohms.

PARKING PIN SWITCH

1) Remove center console. Disconnect parking pin switch 2-pin connector. Parking pin switch is located on left side of shifter assembly.

2) Using an ohmmeter, check continuity between parking pin switch terminals. Continuity should exist when shift lever button is depressed. Continuity should not exist with shift lever button is released. If continuity is not as described, replace parking pin switch.

SHIFT CONTROL SOLENOID VALVES

1) Shift control solenoid valves are located on transaxle. See Fig. 7. Disconnect electrical connector at shift control solenoid valves.

2) Using ohmmeter, check resistance between terminal No. 1 (solenoid valve "A") or terminal No. 2 (solenoid valve "B") and ground. See Fig. 22.

3) Resistance should be 14-16 ohms. Replace shift control solenoid valve assembly if resistance of either solenoid valve is not within specification.

4) Check shift control solenoid valve operation. Ensure solenoid valve body is grounded. Apply battery voltage to terminal No. 1 (solenoid valve "A") or terminal No. 2 (solenoid valve "B").

5) Clicking sound should be heard, indicating solenoid valve operation. Replace shift control solenoid valve assembly if either solenoid valve fails to operate.

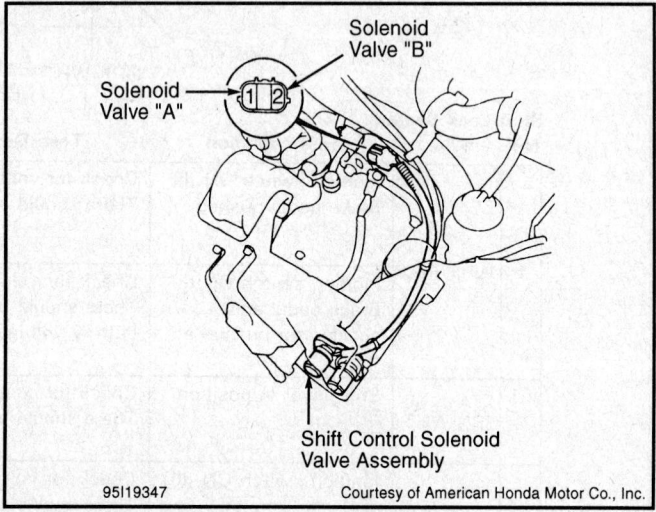

Fig. 22: Identifying Shift Control Solenoid Valve Electrical Connector Terminals

SHIFT LOCK SOLENOID

1) Remove center console. Disconnect shift lock solenoid 2-pin electrical connector from main wiring harness. Note electrical connector terminal identification. See Fig. 23.

CAUTION: Battery voltage must be applied to correct shift lock solenoid electrical connector terminals or diode inside shift lock solenoid will be damaged.

---

2) Momentarily connect battery positive terminal to terminal "A" and battery negative terminal to terminal "B". See Fig. 23. Ensure shift lock solenoid operates with battery voltage applied. Replace shift lock solenoid if solenoid fails to operate.

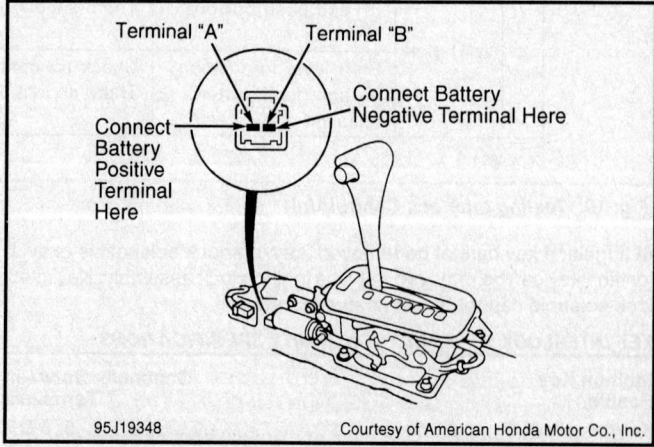

Fig. 23: Identifying Shift Lock Solenoid Electrical Connector Terminals

THROTTLE POSITION (TP) SENSOR

TP sensor should input a .5-volt reference signal to TCM at closed throttle. At full throttle, signal should be approximately 4 volts. Voltage should change smoothly as throttle valve is opened and closed. If voltage is not as specified, check throttle position sensor wiring circuit. See WIRING DIAGRAMS. Individual component testing of TP sensor is not available from manufacturer.

NOTE: If problem in TP sensor exists, TP sensor may set fault code No. 3 in TCM. See FAULT CODE NO. 3 trouble shooting flow chart under TROUBLE SHOOTING FLOW CHARTS.

VEHICLE SPEED SENSOR (VSS)

1) Ensure fuse No. 24 fuse (15-amp or 20-amp) in fuse box on driver's side of instrument panel, near steering column is okay. Replace fuse if necessary.
2) Disconnect 3-pin electrical connector from Vehicle Speed Sensor (VSS). The VSS is located on top of transaxle. See Fig. 7.
3) Check continuity between Black wire of 3-pin electrical connector and ground. If continuity exists, proceed to next step. If continuity does not exists, check for open circuit in Black wire and ground. Ground is located on coolant hose housing, just below distributor.
4) Turn ignition on. Measure voltage between Black wire and the Black/Yellow wire on harness side of 3-pin electrical connector. If battery voltage exists, proceed to next step. If battery voltage does not exist, check for open circuit in Black/Yellow wire between 3-pin electrical connector and fuse No. 24 in fuse box on driver's side of instrument panel.
5) Measure voltage between Orange wire and Black wire of 3-pin electrical connector. Voltage should be about 5 volts. If voltage is correct, proceed to next step. If voltage is not about 5 volts, check for open circuit or short to ground in Orange wire.
6) Reinstall 3-pin electrical connector on VSS. Raise and support vehicle so front wheels can rotate. Connect voltmeter to Orange wire on 3-pin electrical connector and ground.
7) Turn ignition on. Place shift lever in Neutral. Slowly rotate one front wheel while holding remaining front wheel from rotating and note voltage reading.
8) Ensure voltage pulses from zero volts to about 5 volts. If voltage pulses correctly, vehicle speed sensor is okay. If voltage does not pulse correctly, replace vehicle speed sensor. See VEHICLE SPEED SENSOR under REMOVAL & INSTALLATION. Turn ignition off. Remove voltmeter.

REMOVAL & INSTALLATION

A/T GEAR POSITION SWITCH

Removal – Remove center console. Disconnect 14-pin electrical connector from A/T gear position switch. Remove nuts and A/T gear position switch.
Installation – 1) Ensure parking brake is applied. Place switch slider on A/T gear position switch in neutral position. See Fig. 24. Place shift lever in Neutral.
2) Install A/T gear position switch and nuts. DO NOT tighten nuts at this time. The A/T gear position switch must be adjusted.
3) To adjust A/T gear position switch, place shift lever in Park. Ensure retaining nuts are loose. Note 14-pin electrical connector terminal identification. See Fig. 16.
4) Connect ohmmeter between terminals "A" and "L". Move A/T gear position switch toward rear of console until continuity exists between terminals "A" and "L". Free play at lock pin should be .079" (2.0 mm). See Fig. 24.
5) Tighten nuts. Check A/T gear position switch for correct continuity in all gears. See A/T GEAR POSITION SWITCH under COMPONENT TESTING. If proper adjustment cannot be obtained, check for damaged shift lever detent or bracket. Install electrical connector and center console.

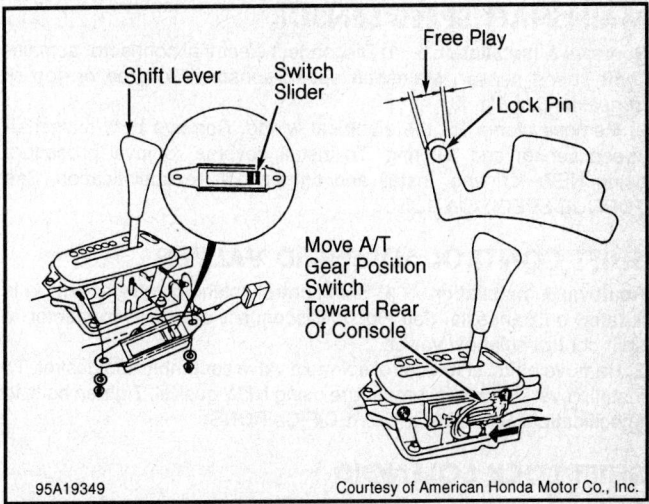

95A19349   Courtesy of American Honda Motor Co., Inc.

Fig. 24: Installing A/T Gear Position Switch

BRAKELIGHT SWITCH

Removal & Installation – 1) Disconnect electrical connector from brakelight switch. Remove lock nut from brakelight switch. Unscrew brakelight switch and remove. To install, screw brakelight switch inward until brakelight plunger is fully depressed.
2) Back off brakelight switch 1/4 turn. Ensure .010" (.30 mm) clearance exists between threaded end of brakelight switch and pad area on brake pedal. Install and tighten lock nut. Install electrical connector. Ensure brakelights and cruise control operate properly.

COUNTERSHAFT SPEED SENSOR

Removal & Installation – 1) Disconnect electrical connector at countershaft speed sensor. Countershaft speed sensor is located on top of transaxle. See Fig. 7.
2) Remove clamp for the electrical wiring. Remove bolt, countershaft speed sensor and "O" ring. To install, reverse removal procedure using NEW "O" ring. Install and tighten bolt to specification. See TORQUE SPECIFICATIONS.

ENGINE COOLANT TEMPERATURE (ECT) SENSOR

Removal – The ECT sensor is located on cylinder head, below distributor and contains a Red/White wire and Green/Blue wire in the electrical connector. See Fig. 7. Drain cooling system. Remove engine coolant temperature sensor.
Installation – 1) Install and tighten engine coolant temperature sensor. When refilling cooling system, open air bleeder bolt on coolant housing for upper radiator hose.
2) Fill cooling system until coolant flows from air bleeder bolt. Tighten air bleeder bolt to specification. See TORQUE SPECIFICATIONS. Finish filling cooling system.

KEY INTERLOCK SOLENOID

Removal & Installation – Key interlock solenoid cannot be serviced separately, as entire ignition lock assembly must be replaced.

LOCK-UP CONTROL SOLENOID VALVES

Removal & Installation – 1) Lock-up control solenoid valve assembly is located on transaxle. See Fig. 7. Disconnect electrical connector at lock-up control solenoid valves.
2) Remove bolts, lock-up control solenoid valve assembly and gasket. To install, reverse removal procedure using NEW gasket. Tighten bolts to specification. See TORQUE SPECIFICATIONS.

MAINSHAFT SPEED SENSOR

Removal & Installation – 1) Disconnect electrical connector at mainshaft speed sensor. Mainshaft speed sensor is located on top of transaxle. *See Fig. 7.*

2) Remove clamp for the electrical wiring. Remove bolt, mainshaft speed sensor and "O" ring. To install, reverse removal procedure using NEW "O" ring. Install and tighten bolt to specification. See TORQUE SPECIFICATIONS.

SHIFT CONTROL SOLENOID VALVES

Removal & Installation – 1) Shift control solenoid valve assembly is located on transaxle. *See Fig. 7.* Disconnect electrical connector at shift control solenoid valves.

2) Remove bolts, shift control solenoid valve assembly and gasket. To install, reverse removal procedure using NEW gasket. Tighten bolts to specification. See TORQUE SPECIFICATIONS.

SHIFT LOCK SOLENOID

Removal – Remove center console. Disconnect electrical connector at shift lock solenoid. Remove collar and pin from shift lock solenoid. Remove nuts and shift lock solenoid.

Installation – 1) Install shift lock solenoid with NEW nuts snugly installed. Install pin, collar and electrical connector.

2) Turn ignition on. With shift lock solenoid energized (ON position), ensure clearance between top of shift lock lever and lock pin groove is .079-.118" (2.0-3.0 mm). *See Fig. 25.*

3) If clearance is not as specified, loosen nuts and reposition shift lock solenoid until correct clearance is obtained. Once correct clearance is obtained, tighten nuts to specification. See TORQUE SPECIFICATIONS.

4) Turn ignition off. With shift lock solenoid de-energized (OFF position), ensure lock pin is blocked by shift lock lever. *See Fig. 24.* Check solenoid operation several times to ensure proper operation.

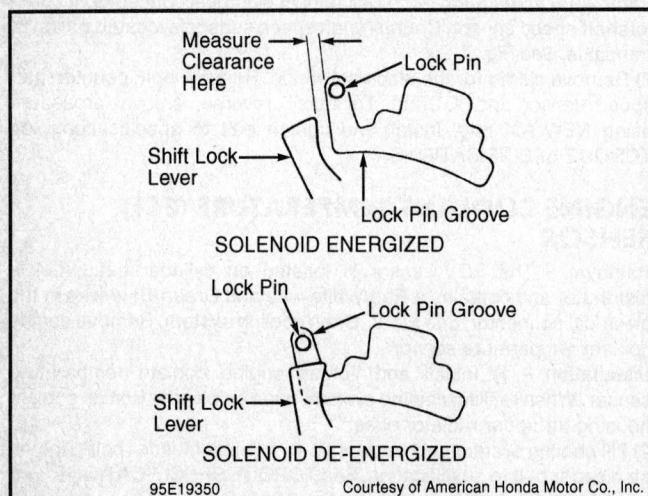

Fig. 25: *Checking Shift Lock Solenoid Operation*

THROTTLE POSITION (TP) SENSOR

Removal & Installation – TP sensor is mounted on side of throttle body. Replacement information is not available from manufacturer.

VEHICLE SPEED SENSOR (VSS)

Removal & Installation – 1) Disconnect electrical connector from vehicle speed sensor, located on top of transaxle. *See Fig. 7.*

2) Remove bolts and vehicle speed sensor. DO NOT lose small drive link, located between vehicle speed sensor and adapter body on transaxle. To install, reverse removal procedure. Install and tighten bolts to specification. See TORQUE SPECIFICATIONS.

TORQUE SPECIFICATIONS
TORQUE SPECIFICATIONS

Application	INCH Lbs. (N.m)
Air Bleeder Bolt	87 (9.8)
Countershaft Speed Sensor Bolt	106 (12.0)
Lock-Up Control Solenoid Valve Assembly Bolt	106 (12.0)
Mainshaft Speed Sensor Bolt	106 (12.0)
Shift Control Solenoid Valve Assembly Bolt	106 (12.0)
Shift Lock Solenoid Nut	87 (9.8)
Vehicle Speed Sensor Bolt	87 (9.8)

TROUBLE SHOOTING FLOW CHARTS

FLOW CHART USAGE

1) Use appropriate trouble shooting flow chart corresponding to fault code. Ensure ignition is off before disconnecting electrical connectors from TCM. The TCM is located behind driver's side kick panel. *See Fig. 6.*

2) The TCM has a 26-pin and 22-pin electrical connectors. These are referenced as connectors 26P and 22P in trouble shooting flow charts.

3) Test Harness (07LAJ-PT3010A) may be required for use with trouble shooting flow chart. To install test harness, ensure ignition is off.

4) Disconnect 26-pin and 22-pin electrical connectors from TCM, located behind driver's side kick panel. *See Fig. 6.*

5) Connect test harness to 26-pin and 22-pin electrical connectors or TCM as instructed in trouble shooting flow chart. *See Fig. 10.*

6) Perform all tests using Digital Volt-Ohmmeter (DVOM). Perform measurements at designated terminals on test harness as instructed in trouble shooting flow chart. Terminal numbers are located on test harness.

7) On some fault code trouble shooting flow charts, technician will be instructed to see if Malfunction Indicator Light (MIL) is blinking. The MIL is located on instrument panel. *See Fig. 1.*

8) If MIL is blinking, PGM-FI system must be checked. See appropriate SELF-DIAGNOSTIC article in ENGINE PERFORMANCE of appropriate MITCHELL® manual.

9) On some fault code trouble shooting flow charts, technician will be instructed to check wiring between ECM and TCM. The ECM is located behind passenger's side kick panel, below instrument panel.

10) On some fault code trouble shooting flow charts, technician will be instructed to clear fault codes. See CLEARING FAULT CODES under SELF-DIAGNOSTIC SYSTEM.

11) Once all repairs are performed, ensure fault code is cleared from TCM memory. See CLEARING FAULT CODES under SELF-DIAGNOSTIC SYSTEM.

NOTE: *The following trouble shooting flow charts and illustrations are courtesy of American Honda Motor Co., Inc.*

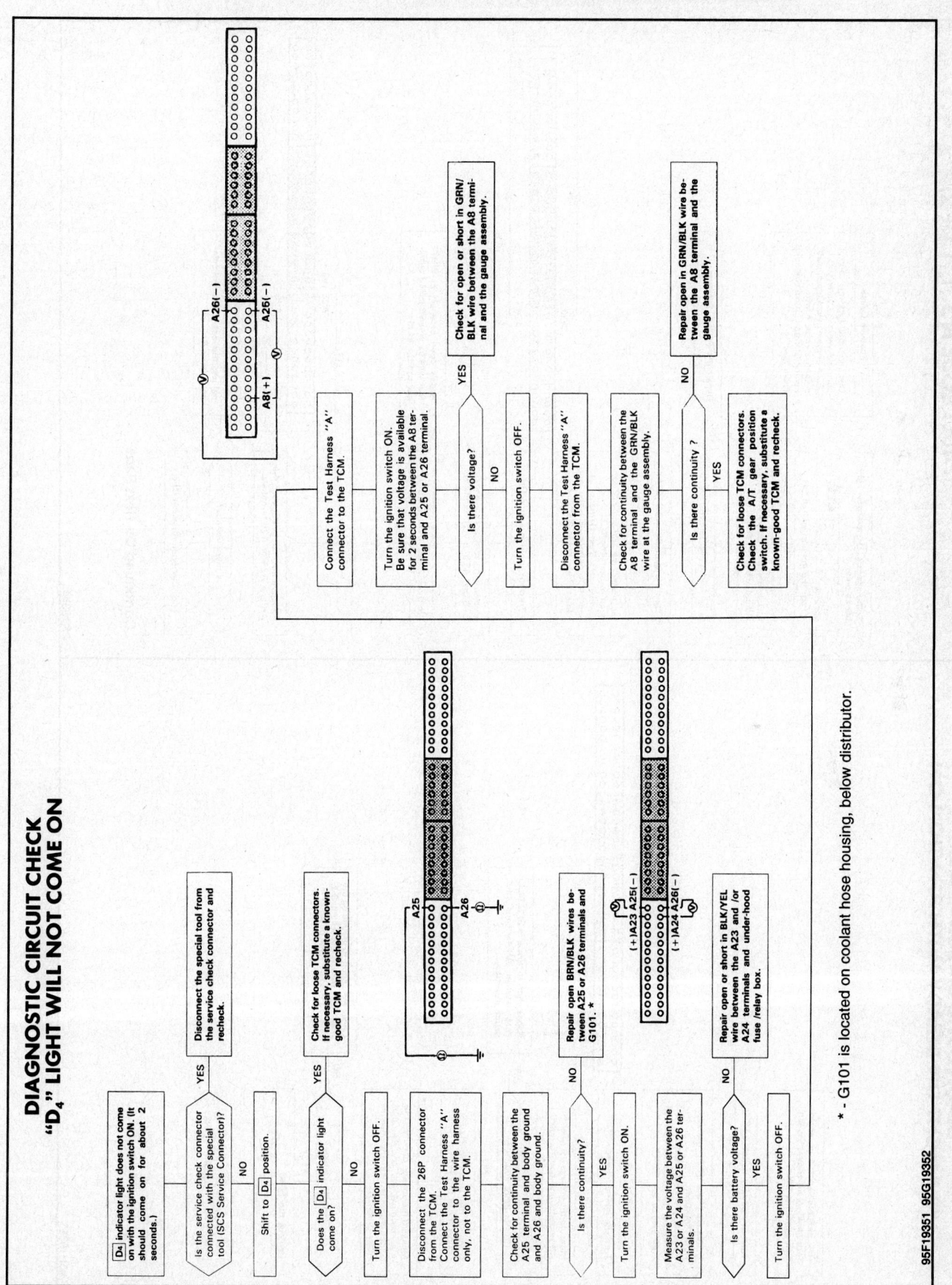

DIAGNOSTIC CIRCUIT CHECK
"D₄" LIGHT WILL NOT COME ON

95F19351 95G19352

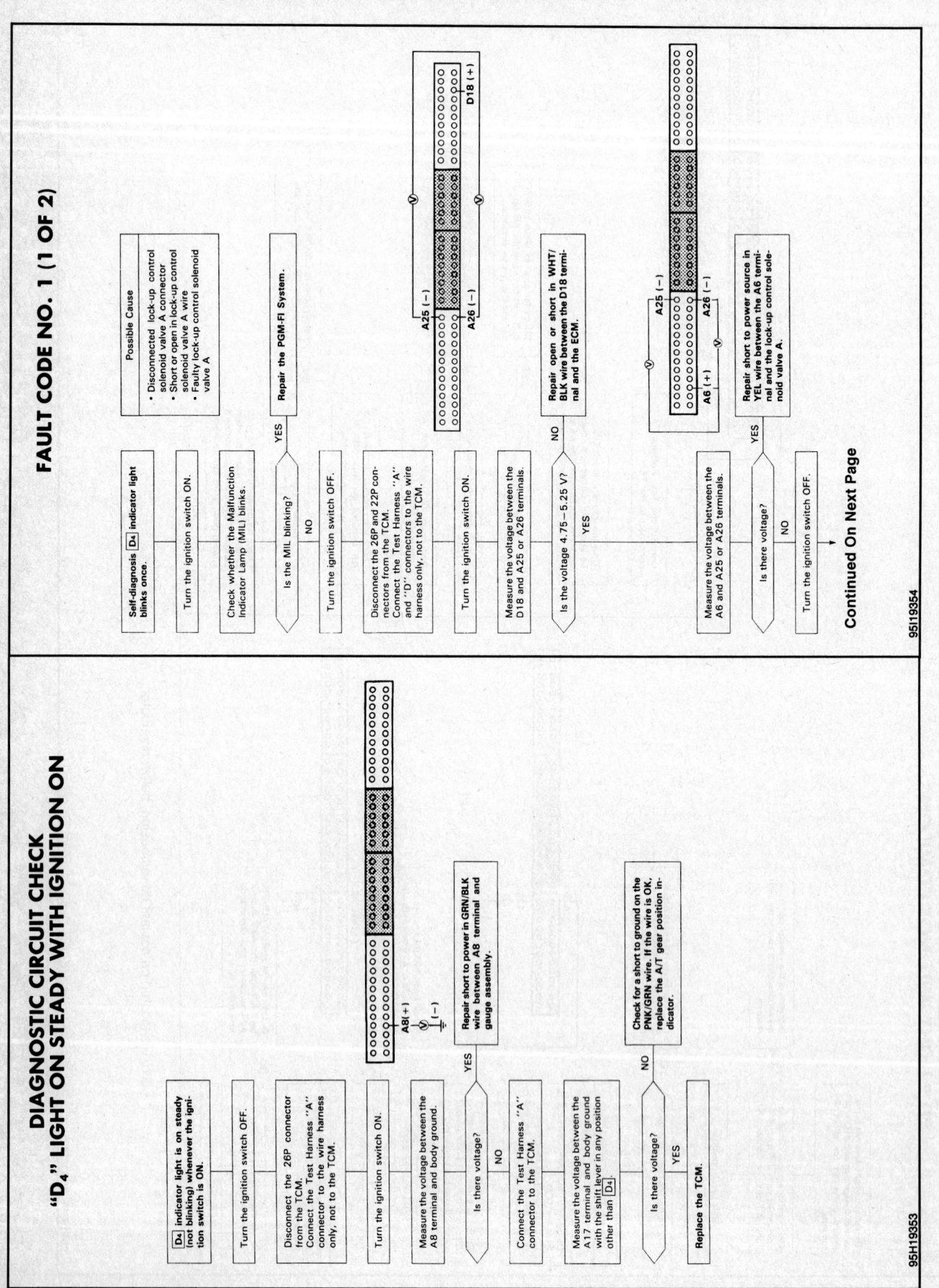

FAULT CODE NO. 1 (1 OF 2)

Self-diagnosis D4 indicator light blinks once.

Turn the ignition switch ON.

Check whether the Malfunction Indicator Lamp (MIL) blinks.

Is the MIL blinking? — YES → Repair the PGM-FI System.

NO

Turn the ignition switch OFF.

Disconnect the 26P and 22P connectors from the TCM. Connect the Test Harness "A" and "D" connectors to the wire harness only, not to the TCM.

Turn the ignition switch ON.

Measure the voltage between the D18 and A25 or A26 terminals.

A25 (−)   A26 (−)   D18 (+)

Is the voltage 4.75 — 5.25 V? — NO → Repair open or short in WHT/BLK wire between the D18 terminal and the ECM.

YES

Measure the voltage between the A6 and A25 or A26 terminals.

A25 (−)   A26 (−)   A6 (+)

Is there voltage? — YES → Repair short to power source in YEL wire between the A6 terminal and the lock-up control solenoid valve A.

NO

Turn the ignition switch OFF.

Continued On Next Page

Possible Cause
- Disconnected lock-up control solenoid valve A connector
- Short or open in lock-up control solenoid valve A wire
- Faulty lock-up control solenoid valve A

95119354

DIAGNOSTIC CIRCUIT CHECK
"D4" LIGHT ON STEADY WITH IGNITION ON

D4 indicator light is on steady (not blinking) whenever the ignition switch is ON.

Turn the ignition switch OFF.

Disconnect the 26P connector from the TCM. Connect the Test Harness "A" connector to the wire harness only, not to the TCM.

Turn the ignition switch ON.

Measure the voltage between the A8 terminal and body ground.

A8 (+)   (−)

Is there voltage? — YES → Repair short to power in GRN/BLK wire between A8 terminal and gauge assembly.

NO

Connect the Test Harness "A" connector to the TCM.

Measure the voltage between the A17 terminal and body ground with the shift lever in any position other than D4.

Is there voltage? — NO → Check for a short to ground on the PNK/GRN wire. If the wire is OK, replace the A/T gear position indicator.

YES

Replace the TCM.

95H19353

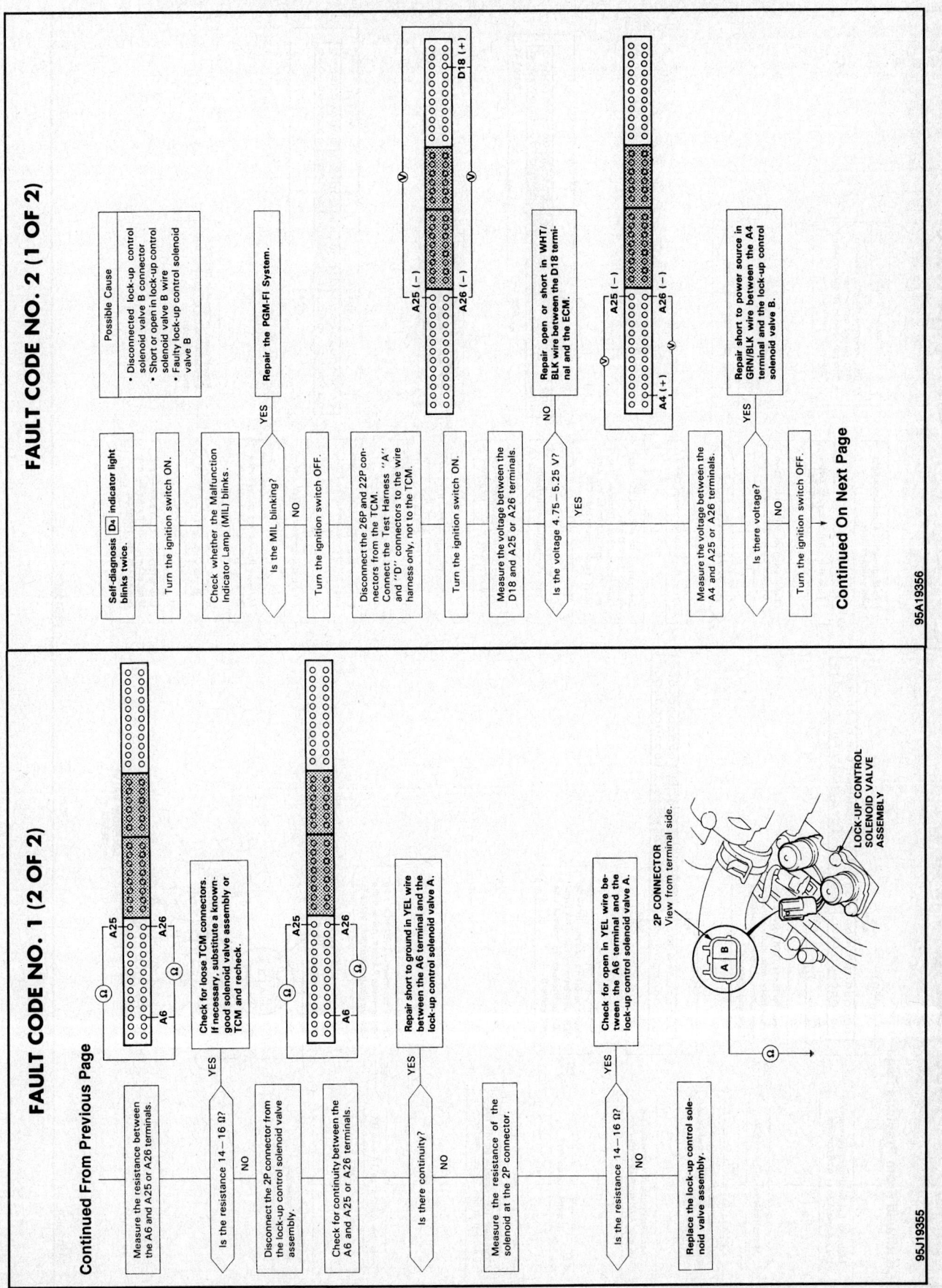

FAULT CODE NO. 2 (1 OF 2)

Possible Cause
- Disconnected lock-up control solenoid valve B connector
- Short or open in lock-up control solenoid valve B wire
- Faulty lock-up control solenoid valve B

Self-diagnosis D4 indicator light blinks twice.

Turn the ignition switch ON.

Check whether the Malfunction Indicator Lamp (MIL) blinks.

Is the MIL blinking? — YES → **Repair the PGM-FI System.**

NO

Turn the ignition switch OFF.

Disconnect the 26P and 22P connectors from the TCM. Connect the Test Harness "A" and "D" connectors to the wire harness only, not to the TCM.

Turn the ignition switch ON.

Measure the voltage between the D18 and A25 or A26 terminals.

D18 (+)
A25 (−)
A26 (−)

Is the voltage 4.75 — 5.25 V? — NO → **Repair open or short in WHT/BLK wire between the D18 terminal and the ECM.**

YES

Measure the voltage between the A4 and A25 or A26 terminals.

A25 (−)
A26 (−)
A4 (+)

Is there voltage? — YES → **Repair short to power source in GRN/BLK wire between the A4 terminal and the lock-up control solenoid valve B.**

NO

Turn the ignition switch OFF.

Continued On Next Page

95A19356

FAULT CODE NO. 1 (2 OF 2)

Continued From Previous Page

Measure the resistance between the A6 and A25 or A26 terminals.

A25
A26
A6

Is the resistance 14 — 16 Ω? — YES → **Check for loose TCM connectors. If necessary, substitute a known-good solenoid valve assembly or TCM and recheck.**

NO

Disconnect the 2P connector from the lock-up control solenoid valve.

Check for continuity between the A6 and A25 or A26 terminals.

A25
A26
A6

Is there continuity? — YES → **Repair short to ground in YEL wire between the A6 terminal and the lock-up control solenoid valve A.**

NO

Measure the resistance of the solenoid at the 2P connector.

Is the resistance 14 — 16 Ω? — YES → **Check for open in YEL wire between the A6 terminal and the lock-up control solenoid valve A.**

NO

Replace the lock-up control solenoid valve assembly.

2P CONNECTOR
View from terminal side.

A B

LOCK-UP CONTROL SOLENOID VALVE ASSEMBLY

95J19355

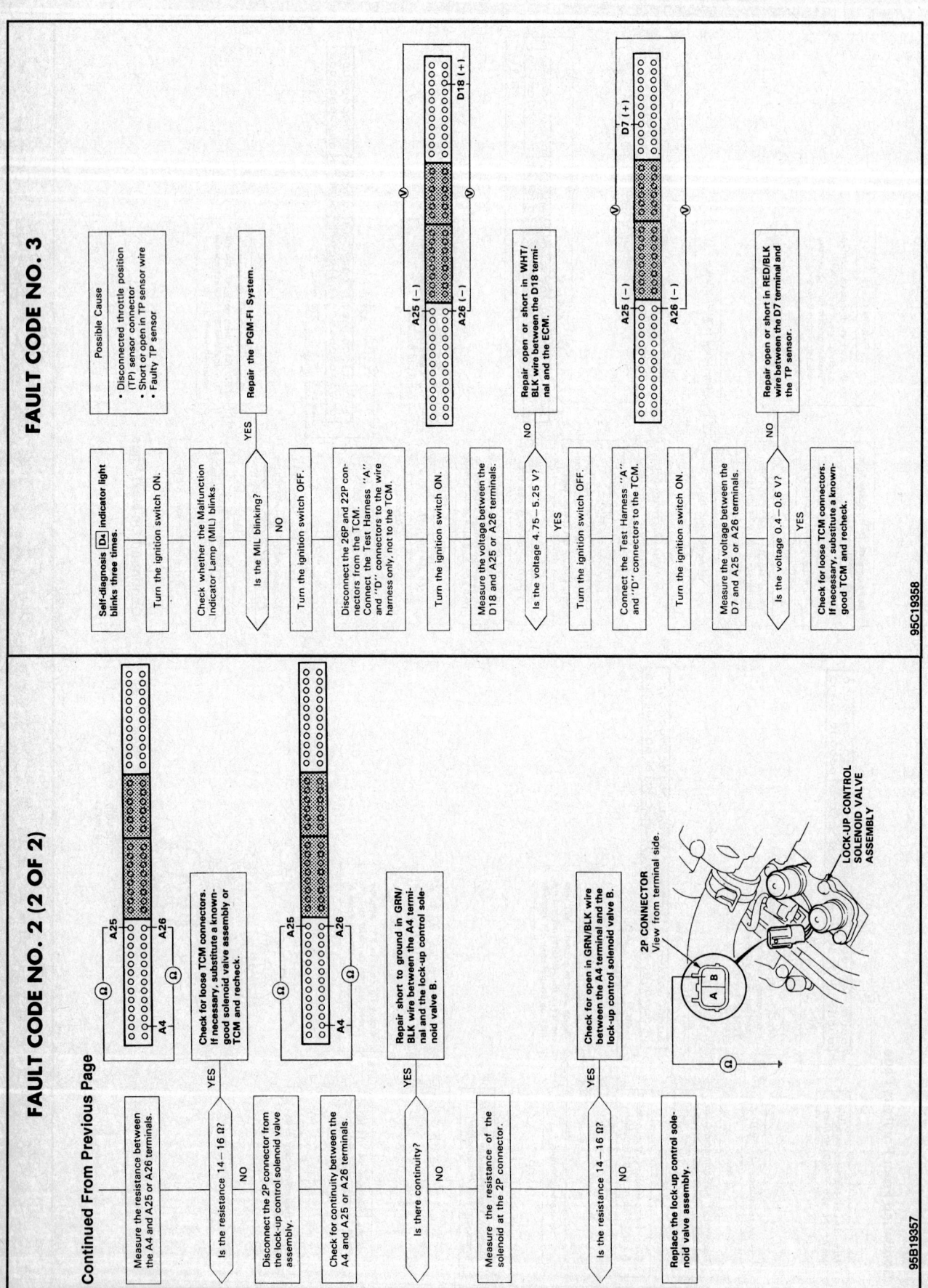

FAULT CODE NO. 3

Possible Cause
- Disconnected throttle position (TP) sensor connector
- Short or open in TP sensor wire
- Faulty TP sensor

Self-diagnosis D4 indicator light blinks three times.

Turn the ignition switch ON.

Check whether the Malfunction Indicator Lamp (MIL) blinks.

Is the MIL blinking?
— YES → Repair the PGM-FI System.
— NO

Turn the ignition switch OFF.

Disconnect the 26P and 22P connectors from the TCM. Connect the Test Harness "A" and "D" connectors to the wire harness only, not to the TCM.

Turn the ignition switch ON.

Measure the voltage between the D18 and A25 or A26 terminals.

Is the voltage 4.75 — 5.25 V?
— NO → Repair open or short in WHT/BLK wire between the D18 terminal and the ECM.
— YES

Turn the ignition switch OFF.

Connect the Test Harness "A" and "D" connectors to the TCM.

Turn the ignition switch ON.

Measure the voltage between the D7 and A25 or A26 terminals.

Is the voltage 0.4 — 0.6 V?
— NO → Repair open or short in RED/BLK wire between the D7 terminal and the TP sensor.
— YES

Check for loose TCM connectors. If necessary, substitute a known-good TCM and recheck.

D18 (+)
A25 (—)
A26 (—)

D7 (+)
A25 (—)
A26 (—)

95C19358

FAULT CODE NO. 2 (2 OF 2)

Continued From Previous Page

Measure the resistance between the A4 and A25 or A26 terminals.

Is the resistance 14 — 16 Ω?
— YES → Check for loose TCM connectors. If necessary, substitute a known-good solenoid valve assembly or TCM and recheck.
— NO

Disconnect the 2P connector from the lock-up control solenoid valve assembly.

Check for continuity between the A4 and A25 or A26 terminals.

Is there continuity?
— YES → Repair short to ground in GRN/BLK wire between the A4 terminal and the lock-up control solenoid valve B.
— NO

Measure the resistance of the solenoid at the 2P connector.

Is the resistance 14 — 16 Ω?
— YES → Check for open in GRN/BLK wire between the A4 terminal and the lock-up control solenoid valve B.
— NO

Replace the lock-up control solenoid valve assembly.

A25
A26
A4

A25
A26
A4

2P CONNECTOR
View from terminal side.

A B

LOCK-UP CONTROL SOLENOID VALVE ASSEMBLY

95B19357

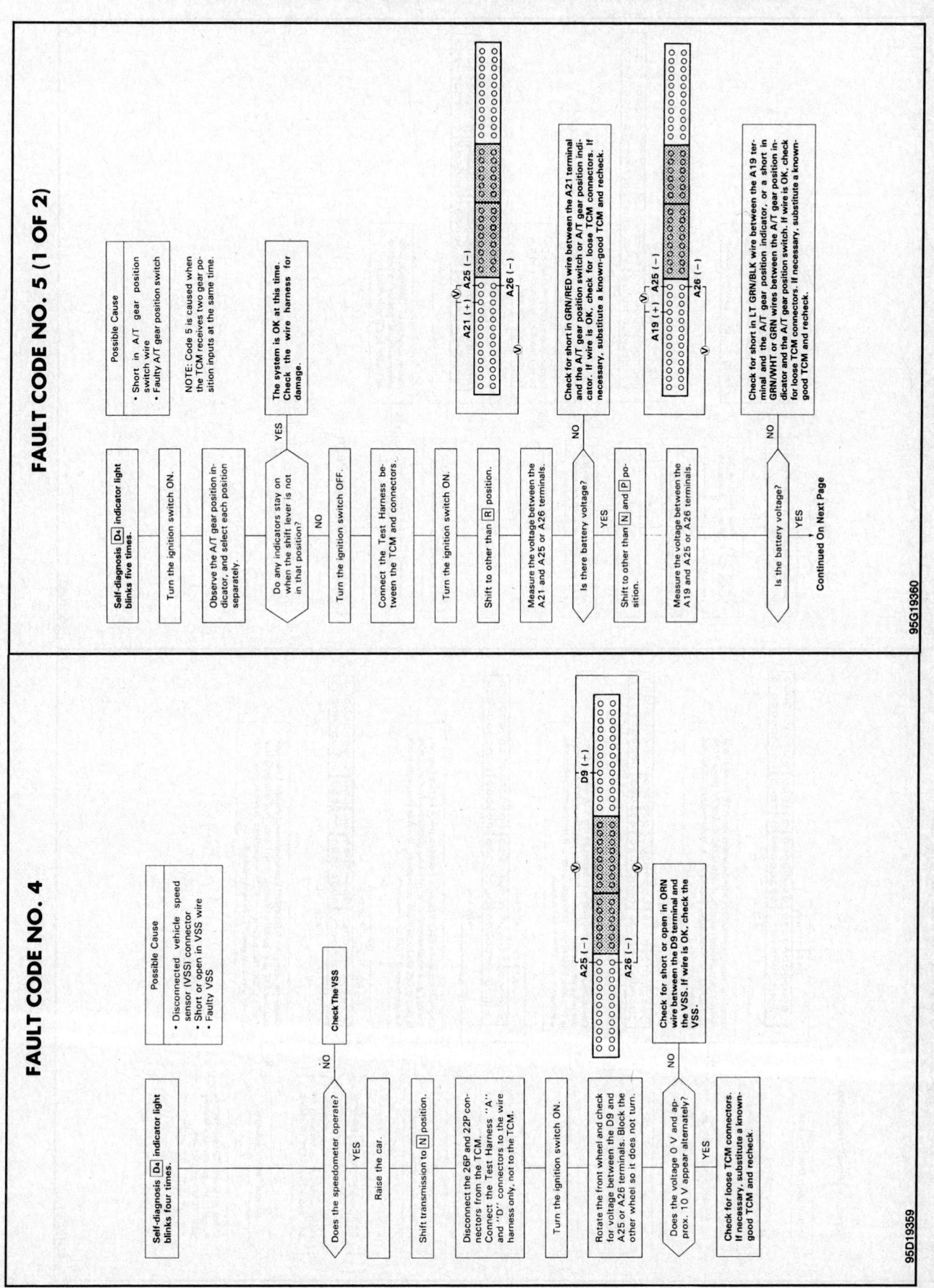

FAULT CODE NO. 5 (1 OF 2)

Possible Cause
- Short in A/T gear position switch wire
- Faulty A/T gear position switch

NOTE: Code 5 is caused when the TCM receives two gear position inputs at the same time.

Self-diagnosis [D₄] indicator light blinks five times.

Turn the ignition switch ON.

Observe the A/T gear position indicator, and select each position separately.

Do any indicators stay on when the shift lever is not in that position? — YES → The system is OK at this time. Check the wire harness for damage.

NO

Turn the ignition switch OFF.

Connect the Test Harness between the TCM and connectors.

Turn the ignition switch ON.

Shift to other than [R] position.

Measure the voltage between the A21 and A25 or A26 terminals.

A21 (+) A25 (−)
A26 (−)

Is there battery voltage? — NO → Check for short in GRN/RED wire between the A21 terminal and the A/T gear position switch or A/T gear position indicator. If wire is OK, check for loose TCM connectors. If necessary, substitute a known-good TCM and recheck.

YES

Shift to other than [N] and [P] position.

Measure the voltage between the A19 and A25 or A26 terminals.

A19 (+) A25 (−)
A26 (−)

Is the battery voltage? — NO → Check for short in LT GRN/BLK wire between the A19 terminal and the A/T gear position indicator, or a short in GRN/WHT or GRN wires between the A/T gear position indicator and the A/T gear position switch. If wire is OK, check for loose TCM connectors. If necessary, substitute a known-good TCM and recheck.

YES

Continued On Next Page

95G19360

FAULT CODE NO. 4

Possible Cause
- Disconnected vehicle speed sensor (VSS) connector
- Short or open in VSS wire
- Faulty VSS

Self-diagnosis [D₄] indicator light blinks four times.

Does the speedometer operate? — NO → Check The VSS

YES

Raise the car.

Shift transmission to [N] position.

Disconnect the 26P and 22P connectors from the TCM. Connect the Test Harness "A" and "D" connectors to the wire harness only, not to the TCM.

Turn the ignition switch ON.

Rotate the front wheel and check for voltage between the D9 and A25 or A26 terminals. Block the other wheel so it does not turn.

D9 (+)

A25 (−)
A26 (−)

Does the voltage 0 V and approx. 10 V appear alternately? — NO → Check for short or open in ORN wire between the D9 terminal and the VSS. If wire is OK, check the VSS.

YES

Check for loose TCM connectors. If necessary, substitute a known-good TCM and recheck.

95D19359

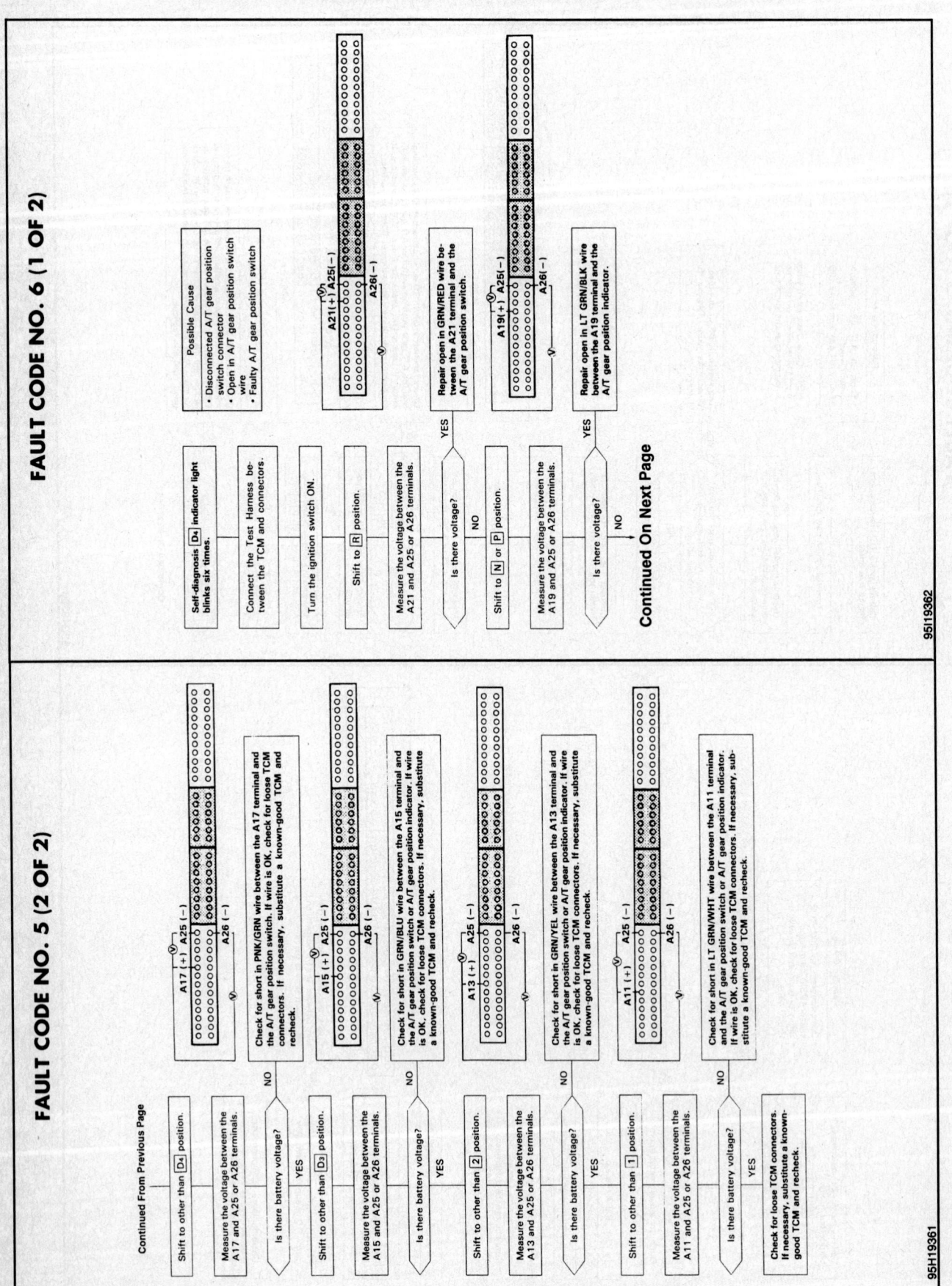

FAULT CODE NO. 6 (1 OF 2)

Possible Cause
- Disconnected A/T gear position switch connector
- Open in A/T gear position switch wire
- Faulty A/T gear position switch

Self-diagnosis D₄ indicator light blinks six times.

Connect the Test Harness between the TCM and connectors.

Turn the ignition switch ON.

Shift to R position.

Measure the voltage between the A21 and A25 or A26 terminals.

A21(+) A25(−)

A26(−)

Is there voltage? — YES → Repair open in GRN/RED wire between the A21 terminal and the A/T gear position switch.

NO

Shift to N or P position.

Measure the voltage between the A19 and A25 or A26 terminals.

A19(+) A25(−)

A26(−)

Is there voltage? — YES → Repair open in LT GRN/BLK wire between the A19 terminal and the A/T gear position indicator.

NO

Continued On Next Page

95H19362

FAULT CODE NO. 5 (2 OF 2)

Continued From Previous Page

Shift to other than D₄ position.

Measure the voltage between the A17 and A25 or A26 terminals.

A17 (+) A25 (−)

A26 (−)

Is there battery voltage? — NO → Check for short in PNK/GRN wire between the A17 terminal and the A/T gear position switch. If wire is OK, check for loose TCM connectors. If necessary, substitute a known-good TCM and recheck.

YES

Shift to other than D₃ position.

Measure the voltage between the A15 and A25 or A26 terminals.

A15 (+) A25 (−)

A26 (−)

Is there battery voltage? — NO → Check for short in GRN/BLU wire between the A15 terminal and the A/T gear position switch or A/T gear position indicator. If wire is OK, check for loose TCM connectors. If necessary, substitute a known-good TCM and recheck.

YES

Shift to other than 2 position.

Measure the voltage between the A13 and A25 or A26 terminals.

A13 (+) A25 (−)

A26 (−)

Is there battery voltage? — NO → Check for short in GRN/YEL wire between the A13 terminal and the A/T gear position switch or A/T gear position indicator. If wire is OK, check for loose TCM connectors. If necessary, substitute a known-good TCM and recheck.

YES

Shift to other than 1 position.

Measure the voltage between the A11 and A25 or A26 terminals.

A11 (+) A25 (−)

A26 (−)

Is there battery voltage? — NO → Check for short in LT GRN/WHT wire between the A11 terminal and the A/T gear position switch or A/T gear position indicator. If wire is OK, check for loose TCM connectors. If necessary, substitute a known-good TCM and recheck.

YES

Check for loose TCM connectors. If necessary, substitute a known-good TCM and recheck.

95H19361

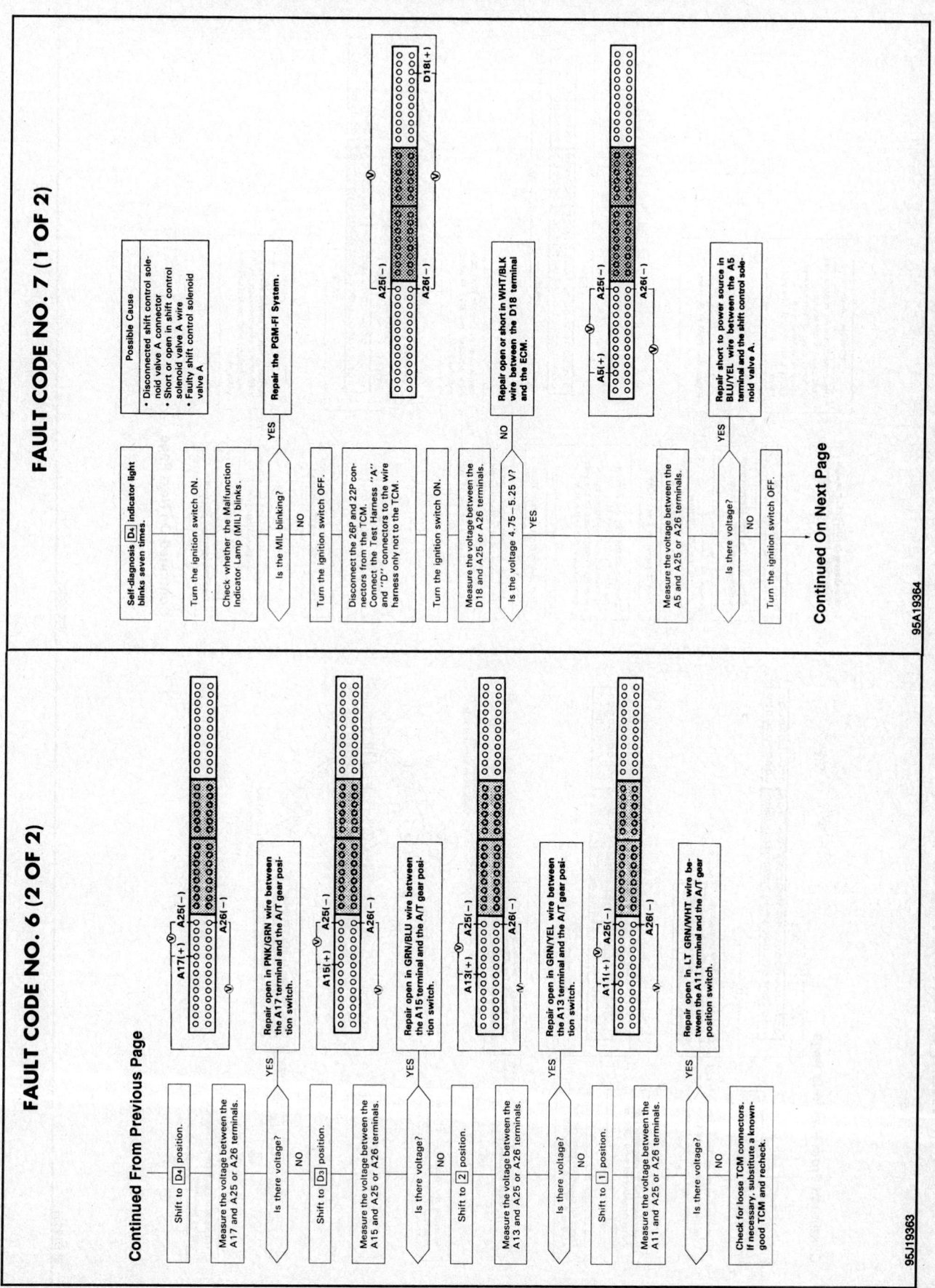

FAULT CODE NO. 7 (1 OF 2)

Possible Cause
- Disconnected shift control solenoid valve A connector
- Short or open in shift control solenoid valve A wire
- Faulty shift control solenoid valve A

Self-diagnosis D4 indicator light blinks seven times.

Turn the ignition switch ON.

Check whether the Malfunction Indicator Lamp (MIL) blinks.

Is the MIL blinking? — YES → Repair the PGM-FI System.

NO

Turn the ignition switch OFF.

Disconnect the 26P and 22P connectors from the TCM. Connect the Test Harness "A" and "D" connectors to the wire harness only not to the TCM.

Turn the ignition switch ON.

Measure the voltage between the D18 and A25 or A26 terminals.

D18(+)

A25(−)

A26(−)

Is the voltage 4.75 — 5.25 V? — NO → Repair open or short in WHT/BLK wire between the D18 terminal and the ECM.

YES

Measure the voltage between the A5 and A25 or A26 terminals.

A5(+)   A25(−)

A26(−)

Is there voltage? — YES → Repair short to power source in BLU/YEL wire between the A5 terminal and the shift control solenoid valve A.

NO

Turn the ignition switch OFF.

Continued On Next Page

95A19364

FAULT CODE NO. 6 (2 OF 2)

Continued From Previous Page

Shift to D4 position.

Measure the voltage between the A17 and A25 or A26 terminals.

A17(+)   A25(−)

A26(−)

Is there voltage? — YES → Repair open in PNK/GRN wire between the A17 terminal and the A/T gear position switch.

NO

Shift to D3 position.

Measure the voltage between the A15 and A25 or A26 terminals.

A15(+)   A25(−)

A26(−)

Is there voltage? — YES → Repair open in GRN/BLU wire between the A15 terminal and the A/T gear position switch.

NO

Shift to 2 position.

Measure the voltage between the A13 and A25 or A26 terminals.

A13(+)   A25(−)

A26(−)

Is there voltage? — YES → Repair open in GRN/YEL wire between the A13 terminal and the A/T gear position switch.

NO

Shift to 1 position.

Measure the voltage between the A11 and A25 or A26 terminals.

A11(+)   A25(−)

A26(−)

Is there voltage? — YES → Repair open in LT GRN/WHT wire between the A11 terminal and the A/T gear position switch.

NO

Check for loose TCM connectors. If necessary, substitute a known-good TCM and recheck.

95J19363

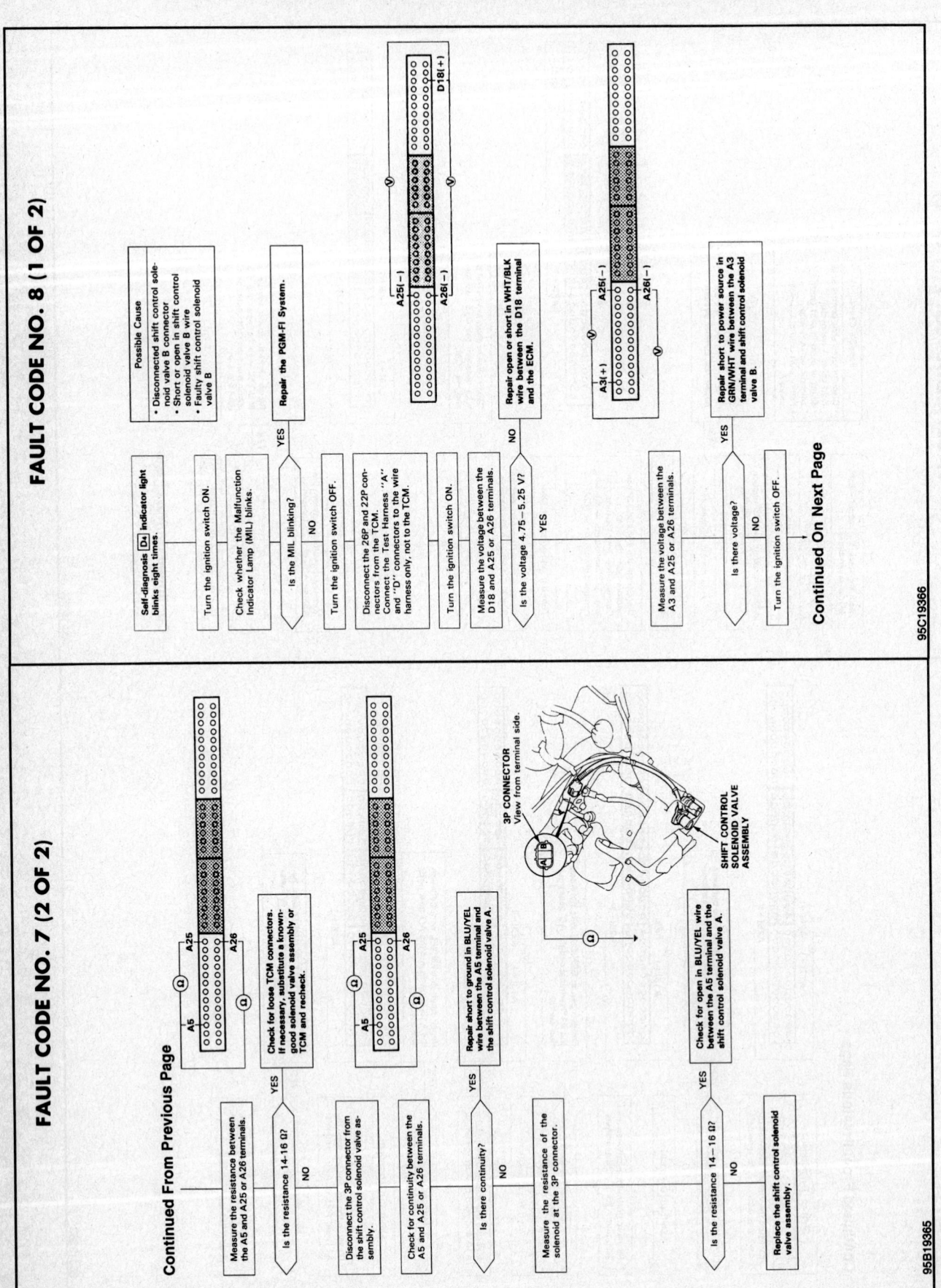

FAULT CODE NO. 8 (1 OF 2)

Possible Cause
- Disconnected shift control solenoid valve B connector
- Short or open in shift control solenoid valve B wire
- Faulty shift control solenoid valve B

Self-diagnosis [D₄] indicator light blinks eight times.

Turn the ignition switch ON.

Check whether the Malfunction Indicator Lamp (MIL) blinks.

Is the MIL blinking? — YES → Repair the PGM-FI System.

NO

Turn the ignition switch OFF.

Disconnect the 26P and 22P connectors from the TCM. Connect the Test Harness "A" and "D" connectors to the wire harness only, not to the TCM.

Turn the ignition switch ON.

Measure the voltage between the D18 and A25 or A26 terminals.

Is the voltage 4.75 — 5.25 V? — NO → Repair open or short in WHT/BLK wire between the D18 terminal and the ECM.

YES

Measure the voltage between the A3 and A25 or A26 terminals.

Is there voltage? — YES → Repair short to power source in GRN/WHT wire between the A3 terminal and shift control solenoid valve B.

NO

Turn the ignition switch OFF.

Continued On Next Page

D18(+)
A25(–)
A26(–)

A25(–)
A26(–)
A3(+)

95C19366

FAULT CODE NO. 7 (2 OF 2)

Continued From Previous Page

Measure the resistance between the A5 and A25 or A26 terminals.

Is the resistance 14–16 Ω? — YES → Check for loose TCM connectors. If necessary, substitute a known-good solenoid valve assembly or TCM and recheck.

NO

Disconnect the 3P connector from the shift control solenoid valve assembly.

Check for continuity between the A5 and A25 or A26 terminals.

Is there continuity? — YES → Repair short to ground in BLU/YEL wire between the A5 terminal and the shift control solenoid valve A.

NO

Measure the resistance of the solenoid at the 3P connector.

Is the resistance 14–16 Ω? — YES → Check for open in BLU/YEL wire between the A5 terminal and the shift control solenoid valve A.

NO

Replace the shift control solenoid valve assembly.

A5
A25
A26

A5
A25
A26

3P CONNECTOR
View from terminal side.

SHIFT CONTROL SOLENOID VALVE ASSEMBLY

95B19365

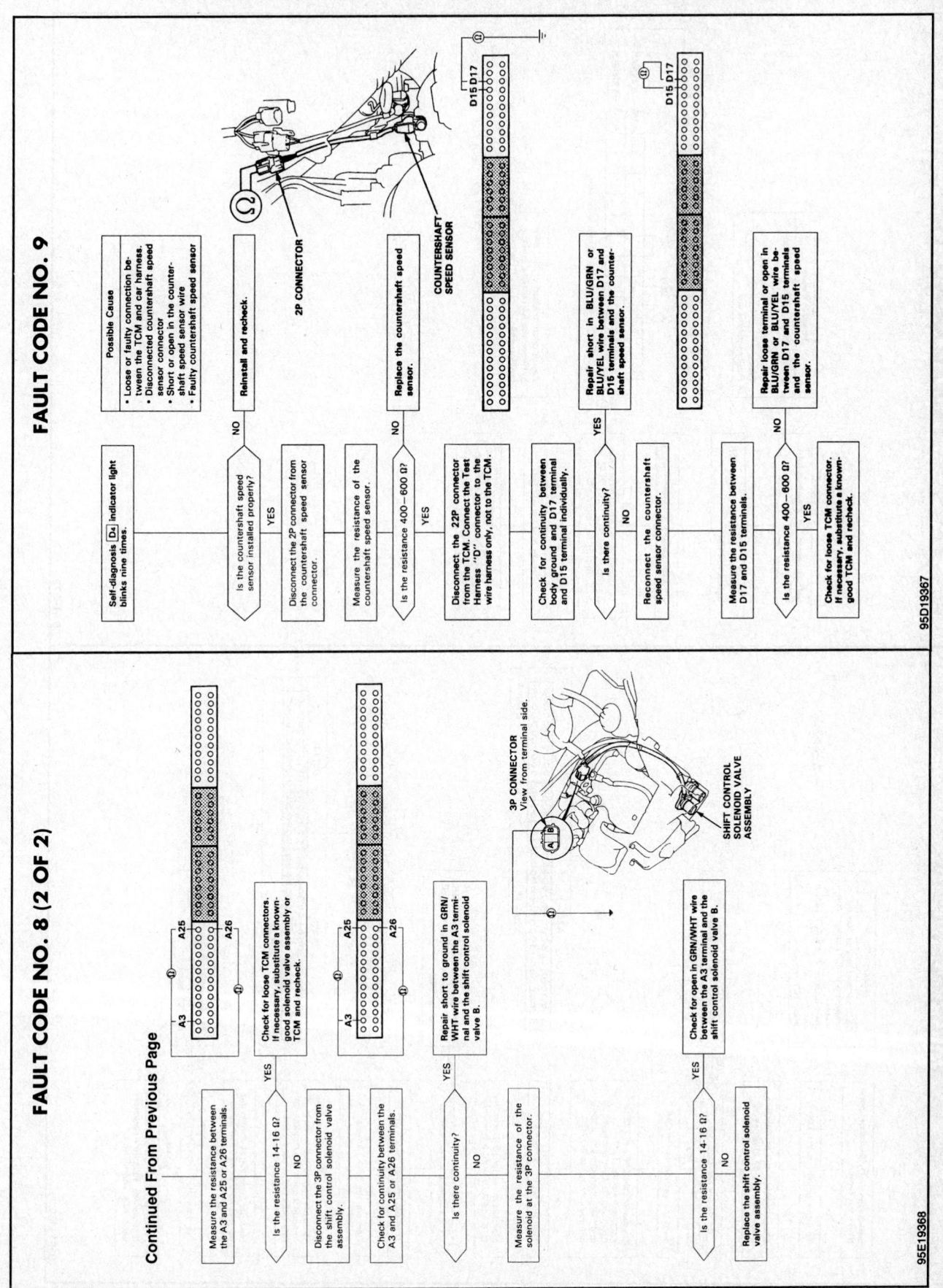

FAULT CODE NO. 9

Possible Cause
- Loose or faulty connection between the TCM and car harness.
- Disconnected countershaft speed sensor connector.
- Short or open in the countershaft speed sensor wire
- Faulty countershaft speed sensor

Self-diagnosis $\boxed{D_4}$ indicator light blinks nine times.

Is the countershaft speed sensor installed properly? — NO → Reinstall and recheck.

YES

Disconnect the 2P connector from the countershaft speed sensor connector.

Measure the resistance of the countershaft speed sensor.

Is the resistance 400 – 600 Ω? — NO → Replace the countershaft speed sensor.

YES

Disconnect the 22P connector from the TCM. Connect the Test Harness "D" connector to the wire harness only, not to the TCM.

Check for continuity between body ground and D17 terminal and D15 terminal individually.

Is there continuity? — YES → Repair short in BLU/GRN or BLU/YEL wire between D17 and D15 terminals and the countershaft speed sensor.

NO

Reconnect the countershaft speed sensor connector.

Measure the resistance between D17 and D15 terminals.

Is the resistance 400 – 600 Ω? — NO → Repair loose terminal or open in BLU/GRN or BLU/YEL wire between D17 and D15 terminals and the countershaft speed sensor.

YES

Check for loose TCM connector. If necessary, substitute a known-good TCM and recheck.

2P CONNECTOR

D15 D17

D15 D17

COUNTERSHAFT SPEED SENSOR

95D19367

FAULT CODE NO. 8 (2 OF 2)

Continued From Previous Page

Measure the resistance between the A3 and A25 or A26 terminals.

Is the resistance 14-16 Ω? — YES → Check for loose TCM connectors. If necessary, substitute a known-good solenoid valve assembly or TCM and recheck.

NO

Disconnect the 3P connector from the shift control solenoid valve assembly.

Check for continuity between the A3 and A25 or A26 terminals.

Is there continuity? — YES → Repair short to ground in GRN/WHT wire between the A3 terminal and the shift control solenoid valve B.

NO

Measure the resistance of the solenoid at the 3P connector.

Is the resistance 14-16 Ω? — YES → Check for open in GRN/WHT wire between the A3 terminal and the shift control solenoid valve B.

NO

Replace the shift control solenoid valve assembly.

A3 A25
A26

A3 A25
A26

3P CONNECTOR
View from terminal side.

SHIFT CONTROL SOLENOID VALVE ASSEMBLY

95E19368

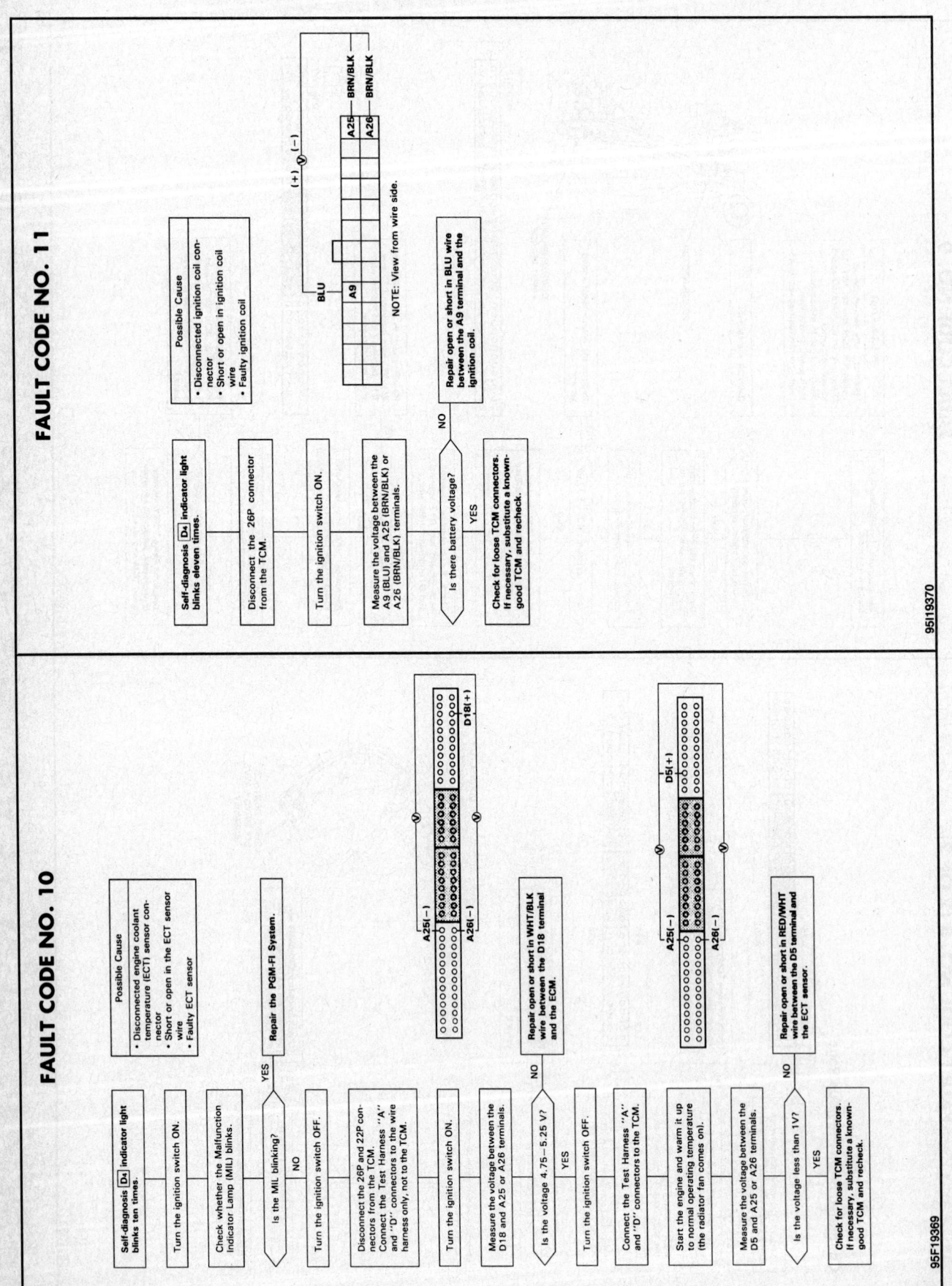

FAULT CODE NO. 11

Self-diagnosis D4 indicator light blinks eleven times.

↓

Disconnect the 26P connector from the TCM.

↓

Turn the ignition switch ON.

↓

Measure the voltage between the A9 (BLU) and A25 (BRN/BLK) or A26 (BRN/BLK) terminals.

↓

Is there battery voltage? — NO → Repair open or short in BLU wire between the A9 terminal and the ignition coil.

YES

↓

Check for loose TCM connectors. If necessary, substitute a known-good TCM and recheck.

Possible Cause
- Disconnected ignition coil connector
- Short or open in ignition coil wire
- Faulty ignition coil

BLU — A9
A25 — BRN/BLK
A26 — BRN/BLK
(+) (−)

NOTE: View from wire side.

95119370

FAULT CODE NO. 10

Self-diagnosis D4 indicator light blinks ten times.

↓

Turn the ignition switch ON.

↓

Check whether the Malfunction Indicator Lamp (MIL) blinks.

↓

Is the MIL blinking? — YES → Repair the PGM-FI System.

NO

↓

Turn the ignition switch OFF.

↓

Disconnect the 26P and 22P connectors from the TCM. Connect the Test Harness "A" and "D" connectors to the wire harness only, not to the TCM.

↓

Turn the ignition switch ON.

↓

Measure the voltage between the D18 and A25 or A26 terminals.

↓

Is the voltage 4.75—5.25 V? — NO → Repair open or short in WHT/BLK wire between the D18 terminal and the ECM.

YES

↓

Turn the ignition switch OFF.

↓

Connect the Test Harness "A" and "D" connectors to the TCM.

↓

Start the engine and warm it up to normal operating temperature (the radiator fan comes on).

↓

Measure the voltage between the D5 and A25 or A26 terminals.

↓

Is the voltage less than 1V? — NO → Repair open or short in RED/WHT wire between the D5 terminal and the ECT sensor.

YES

↓

Check for loose TCM connectors. If necessary, substitute a known-good TCM and recheck.

Possible Cause
- Disconnected engine coolant temperature (ECT) sensor connector
- Short or open in the ECT sensor wire
- Faulty ECT sensor

A25(−)   A26(−)   D18(+)

A25(−)   A26(−)   D5(+)

95F19369

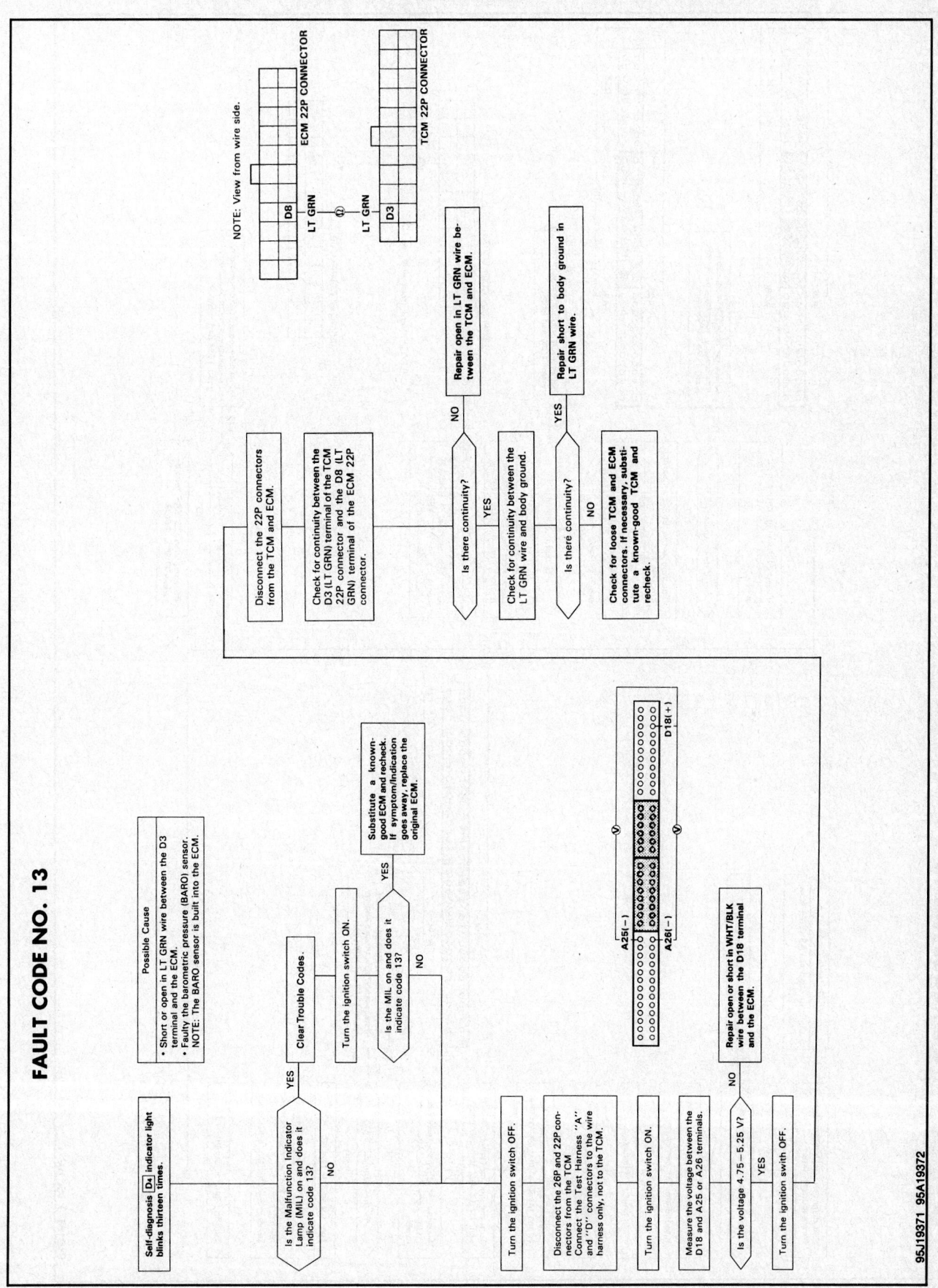

FAULT CODE NO. 13

Possible Cause

• Short or open in LT GRN wire between the D3 terminal and the ECM.
• Faulty the barometric pressure (BARO) sensor.
NOTE: The BARO sensor is built into the ECM.

Self-diagnosis Dᴅ indicator light blinks thirteen times.

Is the Malfunction Indicator Lamp (MIL) on and does it indicate code 13?

YES → Clear Trouble Codes.

Turn the ignition switch ON.

Is the MIL on and does it indicate code 13?

YES → Substitute a known-good ECM and recheck. If symptom/indication goes away, replace the original ECM.

NO ↓

NO ↓

Turn the ignition switch OFF.

Disconnect the 26P and 22P connectors from the TCM. Connect the Test Harness "A" and "D" connectors to the wire harness only, not to the TCM.

Turn the ignition switch ON.

Measure the voltage between the D18 and A25 or A26 terminals.

Is the voltage 4.75 – 5.25 V?

NO → Repair open or short in WHT/BLK wire between the D18 terminal and the ECM.

YES ↓

Turn the ignition switch OFF.

A25(−)   A26(−)   D18(+)

NOTE: View from wire side.

D8 —— ECM 22P CONNECTOR
LT GRN
LT GRN
D3 —— TCM 22P CONNECTOR

Disconnect the 22P connectors from the TCM and ECM.

Check for continuity between the D3 (LT GRN) terminal of the TCM 22P connector and the D8 (LT GRN) terminal of the ECM 22P connector.

Is there continuity?

NO → Repair open in LT GRN wire between the TCM and ECM.

YES ↓

Check for continuity between the LT GRN wire and body ground.

Is there continuity?

YES → Repair short to body ground in LT GRN wire.

NO ↓

Check for loose TCM and ECM connectors. If necessary, substitute a known-good TCM and recheck.

95J19371 95A19372

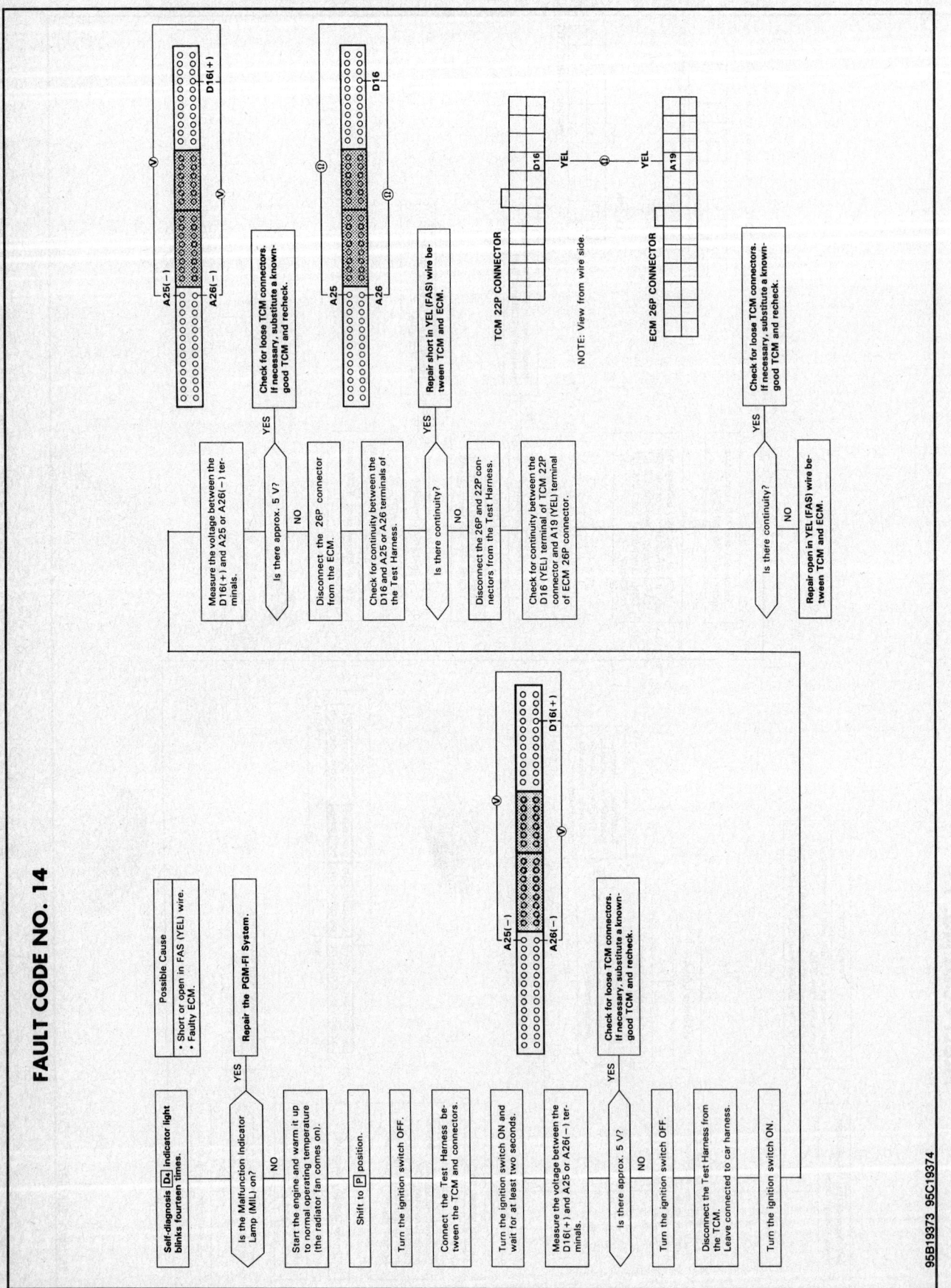

FAULT CODE NO. 14

Possible Cause
- Short or open in FAS (YEL) wire.
- Faulty ECM.

TCM 22P CONNECTOR

ECM 26P CONNECTOR

NOTE: View from wire side.

Self-diagnosis D4 indicator light blinks fourteen times.

Is the Malfunction Indicator Lamp (MIL) on?

YES → Repair the PGM-FI System.

NO

Start the engine and warm it up to normal operating temperature (the radiator fan comes on).

Shift to P position.

Turn the ignition switch OFF.

Connect the Test Harness between the TCM and connectors.

Turn the ignition switch ON and wait for at least two seconds.

Measure the voltage between the D16(+) and A25 or A26(−) terminals.

Is there approx. 5 V?

YES → Check for loose TCM connectors. If necessary, substitute a known-good TCM and recheck.

NO

Turn the ignition switch OFF.

Disconnect the Test Harness from the TCM. Leave connected to car harness.

Turn the ignition switch ON.

Measure the voltage between the D16(+) and A25 or A26(−) terminals.

Is there approx. 5 V?

YES → Check for loose TCM connectors. If necessary, substitute a known-good TCM and recheck.

NO

Disconnect the 26P connector from the ECM.

Check for continuity between the D16 and A25 or A26 terminals of the Test Harness.

Is there continuity?

YES → Repair short in YEL (FAS) wire between TCM and ECM.

NO

Disconnect the 26P and 22P connectors from the Test Harness.

Check for continuity between the D16 (YEL) terminal of TCM 22P connector and A19 (YEL) terminal of ECM 26P connector.

Is there continuity?

YES → Check for loose TCM connectors. If necessary, substitute a known-good TCM and recheck.

NO

Repair open in YEL (FAS) wire between TCM and ECM.

95B19373 95C19374

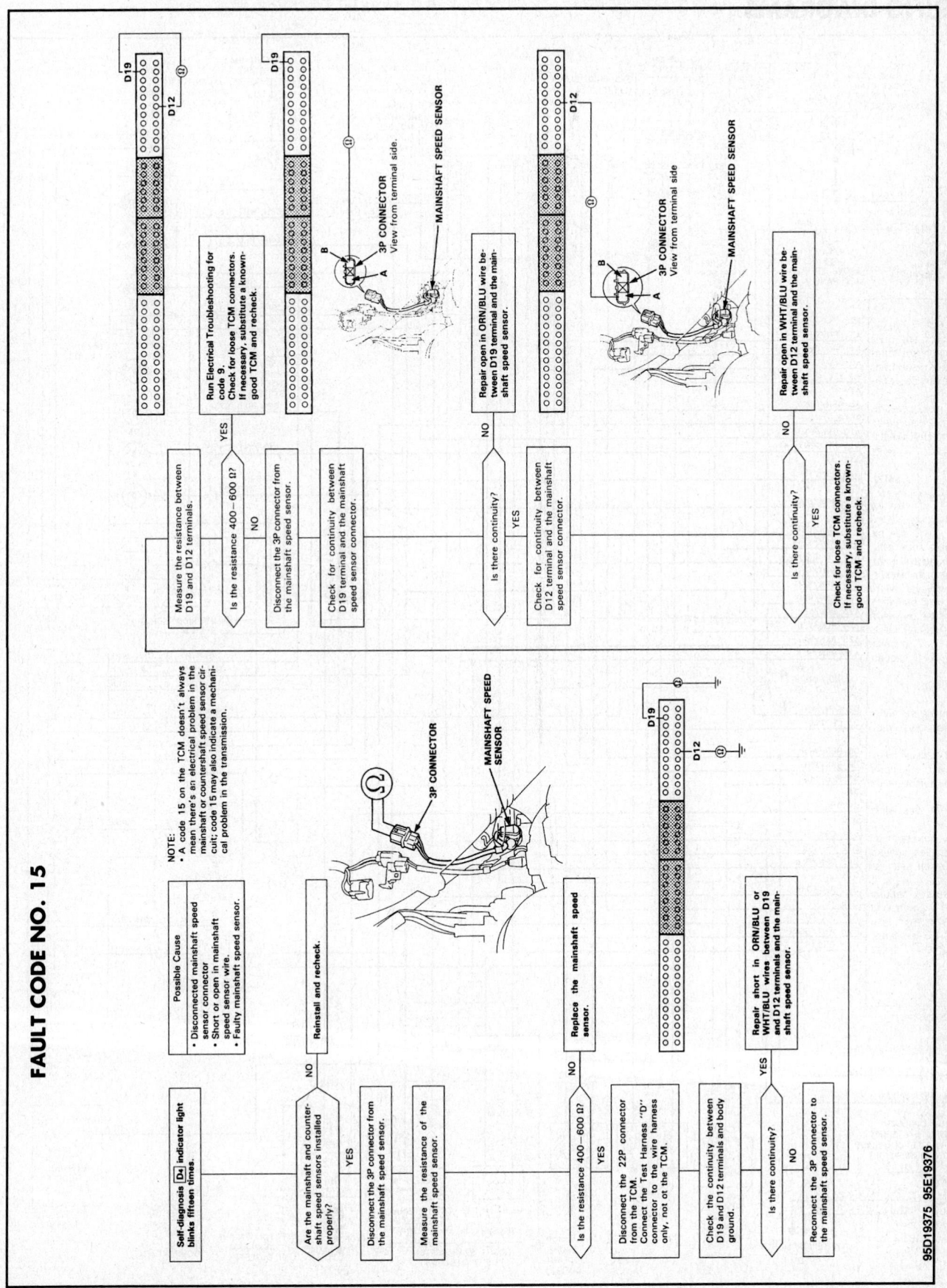

FAULT CODE NO. 15

Self-diagnosis [D₄] indicator light blinks fifteen times.

Possible Cause
- Disconnected mainshaft speed sensor connector
- Short or open in mainshaft speed sensor wire.
- Faulty mainshaft speed sensor.

NOTE:
• A code 15 on the TCM doesn't always mean there's an electrical problem in the mainshaft or countershaft speed sensor circuit; code 15 may also indicate a mechanical problem in the transmission.

Are the mainshaft and countershaft speed sensors installed properly? — NO → Reinstall and recheck.

YES

Disconnect the 3P connector from the mainshaft speed sensor.

Measure the resistance of the mainshaft speed sensor.

Is the resistance 400 – 600 Ω? — NO → Replace the mainshaft speed sensor.

YES

Disconnect the 22P connector from the TCM. Connect the Test Harness "D" connector to the wire harness only, not at the TCM.

Check the continuity between D19 and D12 terminals and body ground.

Is there continuity? — YES → Repair short in ORN/BLU or WHT/BLU wires between D19 and D12 terminals and the mainshaft speed sensor.

NO

Reconnect the 3P connector to the mainshaft speed sensor.

Measure the resistance between D19 and D12 terminals.

Is the resistance 400 – 600 Ω? — YES → Run Electrical Troubleshooting for code 9. Check for loose TCM connectors. If necessary, substitute a known-good TCM and recheck.

NO

Disconnect the 3P connector from the mainshaft speed sensor.

Check for continuity between D19 terminal and the mainshaft speed sensor connector.

Is there continuity? — NO → Repair open in ORN/BLU wire between D19 terminal and the mainshaft speed sensor.

YES

Check for continuity between D12 terminal and the mainshaft speed sensor connector.

Is there continuity? — NO → Repair open in WHT/BLU wire between D12 terminal and the mainshaft speed sensor.

YES

Check for loose TCM connectors. If necessary, substitute a known-good TCM and recheck.

95D19375 95E19376

WIRING DIAGRAMS

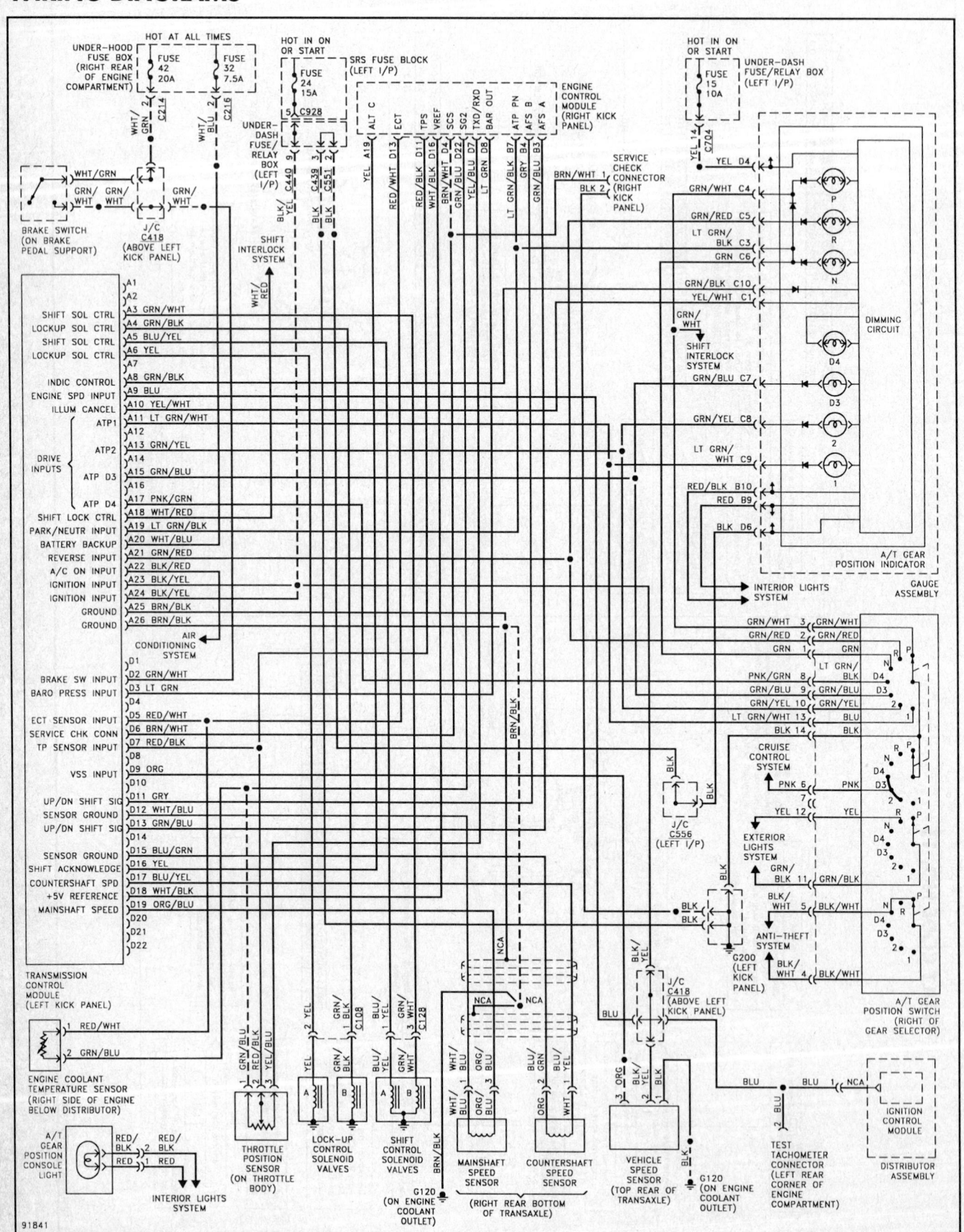

Fig. 26: Transaxle Wiring Diagram (1995 Integra)

Integra

APPLICATION

APPLICATION

Vehicle	Transaxle Model
1996 Integra	SX4A

CAUTION: Vehicle is equipped with a Supplemental Restraint System (SRS). When servicing vehicle, use care to avoid accidental air bag deployment. All SRS electrical connections and wiring harness are covered with Yellow insulation. SRS-related components are located in steering column, center console, instrument panel and lower panel on instrument panel. DO NOT use electrical test equipment on these circuits. It may be necessary to deactivate SRS before servicing components. See AIR BAG SERVICING article in APPLICATIONS & IDENTIFICATIONS.

NOTE: Obtain radio anti-theft code from customer before disconnecting negative battery cable. Radio anti-theft code must be re-entered into radio once negative battery cable is reconnected. To re-enter radio anti-theft code, turn ignition and radio on. When the word CODE is displayed on radio, re-enter radio anti-theft code by using the radio station preset buttons.

DESCRIPTION

Automatic transaxle is electronically controlled. Transaxle shifting and torque converter lock-up are controlled by Transmission Control Module (TCM). TCM is located below instrument panel behind left kick panel. TCM receives information from various input devices and uses this information to control shift and lock-up control solenoid valves.

The TCM contains a grade logic control system which controls transaxle shifting while vehicle is ascending or descending a slope or reducing vehicle speed. Transaxle is equipped with shift and key interlock systems. Shift interlock system prevents shift lever from being moved from Park unless brake pedal is depressed and accelerator pedal is in idle position. In case of a malfunction, shift lever can be released by placing ignition key in key release slot near shift lever. Key interlock system prevents ignition key from being removed from ignition lock assembly unless shift lever is in Park.

The A/T gear position indicator on instrument panel contains lights to indicate which position A/T gear position switch on shift lever is in.

OPERATION

A/T GEAR POSITION INDICATOR

With ignition in RUN or START position, voltage is supplied to A/T gear position indicator, located on instrument panel. *See Fig. 1.* When shift lever is moved to designated gear position, A/T gear position switch completes the ground circuit for A/T gear position indicator on instrument panel. The light on A/T gear position indicator will be illuminated to indicate the shift lever gear position. The A/T gear position switch is located on passenger's side of shift lever. *See Fig. 6.*

When headlights are turned on, voltage is supplied to Red/Black wire through fuse No. 19 (10-amp) at A/T gear position indicator. This changes brightness control from fixed setting to control by the dash light dimmer input on the Red wire.

GRADE LOGIC CONTROL SYSTEM

The TCM compares actual driving conditions with driving conditions memorized in the TCM, based on input signals from Vehicle Speed Sensor (VSS), Throttle Position (TP) sensor, Engine Coolant Temperature (ECT) sensor, Barometric Pressure (Baro) sensor, brakelight switch signal and A/T gear position switch. The TCM uses these input signals to control shifting while vehicle is ascending or descending a slope or during deceleration.

When TCM determines vehicle is ascending a slope with shift lever in "D₄" position, TCM extends engagement of 3rd gear to prevent transaxle from frequently shifting between 3rd and 4th gears. Shift points between 3rd and 4th gear are stored in TCM which allows the most suitable gear selection depending on conditions.

When TCM determines vehicle is descending a slope with shift lever in "D₄" position, TCM changes upshift speed from 3rd to 4th gear when throttle is fully closed. This widens the 3rd gear operating range from that programmed for level surface operation and, in conjunction with engine braking from torque converter lock-up, provides smooth vehicle operation. When vehicle is decelerating on a gradual hill in 4th gear, or when applying brakes on a steep hill, the transaxle will downshift to 3rd gear. When vehicle accelerates, transaxle will upshift into 4th gear.

When vehicle decelerates from speeds greater than 30 MPH, TCM shifts transaxle from 4th gear to 2nd gear earlier than normal to reduce the number of times the transaxle shifts. This allows smoother acceleration and vehicle operation.

SHIFT & KEY INTERLOCK SYSTEMS

Shift Interlock System – Shift interlock system prevents shift lever from being moved from Park unless brake pedal is depressed and accelerator pedal is in idle position. Shift lever cannot be moved from Park if brake and accelerator pedal are depressed at the same time. In case of a malfunction, shift lever can be released by placing ignition key in key release slot near shift lever.

Voltage is provided to shift lock solenoid when ignition is in RUN or START position. When brake pedal is depressed, brakelight switch provides voltage to TCM, provided accelerator pedal is in idle position. With accelerator pedal in idle position, a voltage signal is delivered between Throttle Position (TP) sensor and the TCM. The TCM then provides voltage to shift lock circuit in the interlock control unit. When A/T gear position switch is in Park, interlock control unit then operates shift lock solenoid by controlling the ground circuit. When shift lock solenoid is energized, shift lever is released and can be moved.

The A/T gear position switch is located on passenger's side of shift lever. *See Fig. 6.* Shift lock solenoid is located on driver's side of shift lever. *See Fig. 2.* Interlock control unit is located behind driver's side of instrument panel and contains an 8-pin electrical connector. *See Fig. 4.*

Key Interlock System – Key interlock system prevents ignition key from being removed from ignition lock assembly unless shift lever is in Park. Voltage is provided to key interlock switch from No. 42 fuse (20-amp) in engine compartment fuse box, located at passenger's side rear corner of engine compartment. When ignition key is in ignition lock assembly, key interlock switch closes, providing voltage to key interlock solenoid and interlock control unit.

If shift lever is not in Park (parking pin switch on), interlock control unit energizes key interlock solenoid by completing ground circuit. When key interlock solenoid is energized, ignition key cannot be removed from ignition lock assembly. Key interlock switch and key interlock solenoid are located on ignition lock assembly. *See Fig. 3.* Parking pin switch is located on driver's side of shift lever. Interlock control unit is located behind driver's side of instrument panel and contains an 8-pin electrical connector. *See Fig. 4.*

TRANSMISSION CONTROL MODULE

The Transmission Control Module (TCM) receives information from various input devices and uses this information to control shift and lock-up control solenoid valves. *See Fig. 5.* The TCM contains self-diagnostic system which stores fault code if failure or problem exists in transaxle electronic control system. Fault code may also be referred to as Diagnostic Trouble Code (DTC) or flash code. DTC or flash code may be retrieved to determine transaxle problem area. See SELF-DIAGNOSTIC SYSTEM. The TCM is located behind driver's side kick panel. *See Fig. 6.*

AUTOMATIC TRANSMISSIONS
Acura SX4A Electronic Controls (Cont.)

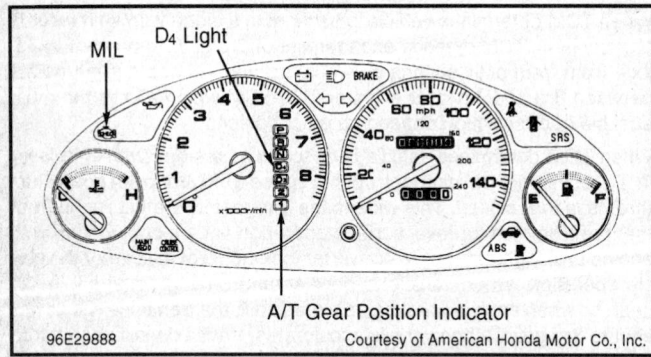

Fig. 1: Identifying A/T Gear Position Indicator & MIL Light

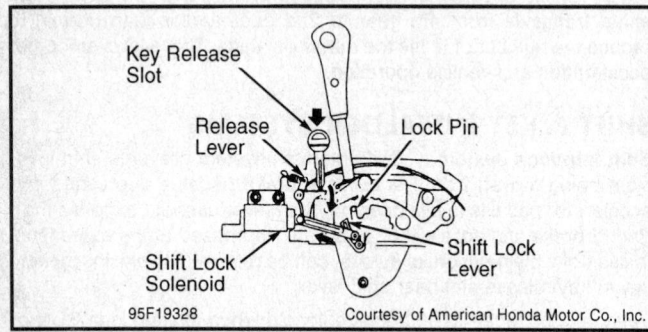

Fig. 2: Identifying Key Release Slot & Shift Lock Solenoid

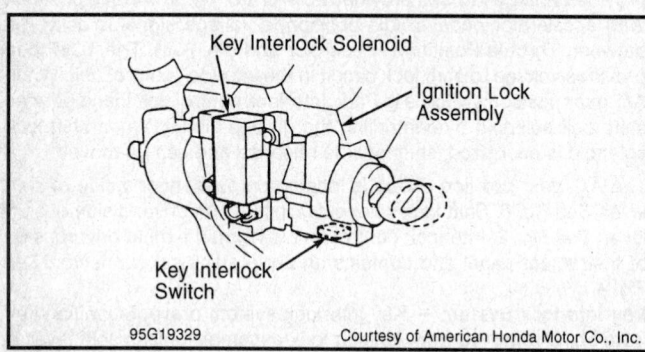

Fig. 3: Identifying Key Interlock Solenoid & Key Interlock Switch

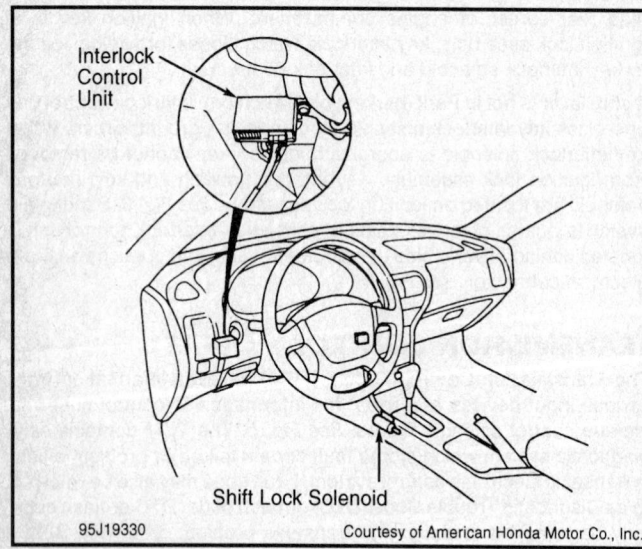

Fig. 4: Identifying Interlock Control Unit

TCM INPUT DEVICES

Air Conditioning Signal – The A/C clutch relay delivers input signal to TCM, indicating A/C operation. The A/C clutch relay is located at front corner of engine compartment, near radiator. See Fig. 7.

Barometric Pressure Signal – Barometric pressure signal is delivered between Engine Control Module (ECM) and the TCM. The ECM contains a built-in barometric pressure sensor to determine atmospheric pressure. The ECM is located behind passenger's side kick panel, below instrument panel.

Brake Switch Signal – Brakelight switch delivers input signal to TCM, indicating vehicle braking. Brakelight switch is also used in determining grade logic control. Brakelight switch is located on brake pedal support. See Fig. 6.

Engine Coolant Temperature (ECT) Signal – Engine Coolant Temperature (ECT) sensor delivers input signal to TCM, indicating engine coolant temperature. The ECT sensor is located on cylinder head, below distributor and contains a Red/White wire and Green/Blue wire in the electrical connector. See Fig. 7.

Engine Speed – Engine speed signal (RPM) is delivered to TCM from ignition control module in distributor assembly.

Engine Control Module (ECM) – An upshift and downshift signal and a shift acknowledgment signal is delivered between the ECM and TCM. A 5-volt reference signal exists between ECM and TCM. The ECM is located behind passenger's side kick panel, below instrument panel.

Mainshaft & Countershaft Speed Signal – Mainshaft speed signal is delivered to TCM. Mainshaft speed sensor is located on top of transaxle. See Fig. 7. Countershaft speed signal is delivered to TCM. Countershaft speed sensor is located on top of transaxle.

Service Check Connector – Service check connector is used when retrieving flash codes for transaxle electronic control system diagnosis. When jumper wire is installed between electrical terminals of service check connector, an input is delivered to TCM to display flash codes on "D₄" indicator light. Service check connector is a 2-pin Blue colored electrical connector located at passenger's corner of instrument panel. See Fig. 8.

Shift Position Signal – Shift position signal is delivered to TCM by the A/T gear position switch, located on passenger's side of shift lever. See Fig. 6.

Throttle Position (TP) Sensor Signal – Throttle Position (TP) sensor delivers input signal to TCM to indicate throttle position. The TP sensor is mounted on throttle body. See Fig. 7.

Vehicle Speed Sensor Signal – Vehicle speed Sensor (VSS) delivers input signal to TCM to indicate vehicle speed. The VSS is located on top of transaxle. See Fig. 7.

TCM OUTPUT DEVICES

Shift Control Solenoid Valves – The TCM controls transaxle shifting by delivering an output signal to shift control solenoid valves "A" and "B" on shift control solenoid valve assembly. Solenoid valves are operated in accordance with gear position. See SHIFT CONTROL SOLENOID VALVE OPERATION table. Shift control solenoid valve assembly is located on transaxle. See Fig. 7. Shift control solenoid valve "A" has a Blue/Yellow wire and solenoid valve "B" has a Green/White wire.

SHIFT CONTROL SOLENOID VALVE OPERATION

Shift Lever Position	Solenoid Valve "A"	Solenoid Valve "B"
"D₃" Or "D₄" (1st Gear)	Off	On
"D₃" Or "D₄" (2nd Gear)	On	On
"D₃" Or "D₄" (3rd Gear)	On	Off
"D₄" (4th)	Off	Off
"2" (2nd Gear)	On	On
"1" (1st Gear)	On	Off
"R" (Reverse)	On	Off

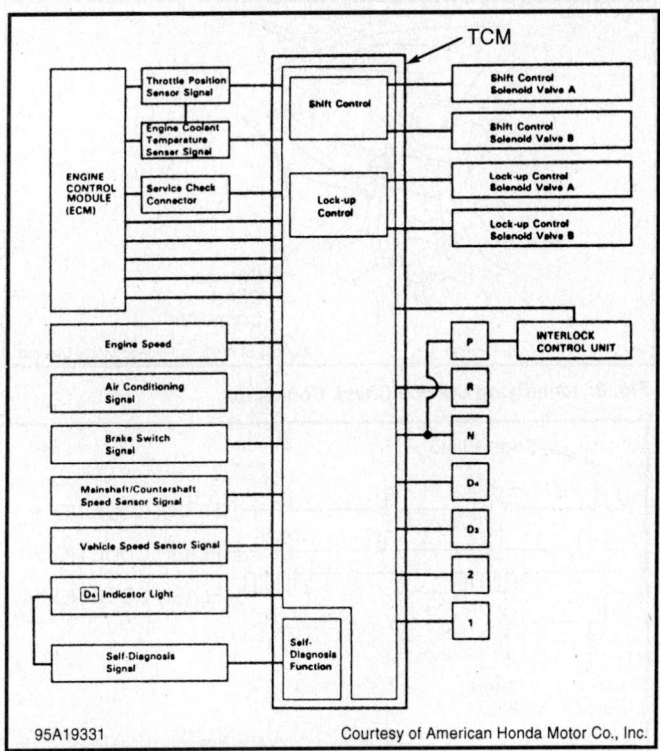

Fig. 5: Identifying Input & Output Devices

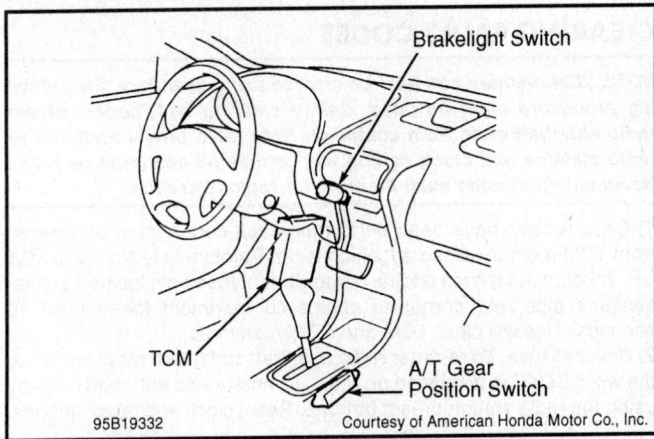

Fig. 6: Identifying TCM, Brakelight Switch & A/T Gear Position Switch

Lock-Up Control Solenoid Valves – The TCM controls torque converter lock-up by delivering an output signal to lock-up control solenoid valves "A" and "B" on lock-up control solenoid valve assembly. Lock-up control solenoid valves are activated in accordance with lock-up condition. See LOCK-UP CONTROL SOLENOID VALVE OPERATION table. Lock-up control solenoid valve assembly is located on transaxle. See Fig. 7. Lock-up control solenoid valve "A" has a Yellow wire and solenoid valve "B" has a Green/Black wire.

LOCK-UP CONTROL SOLENOID VALVE OPERATION

Lock-Up Condition	Solenoid Valve "A"	Solenoid Valve "B"
No Lock-Up	Off	Off
Slight Lock-Up	On	Off
Half Lock-Up	On	On
Full Lock-Up	On	On
Lock-Up During Deceleration	On	1

1 – Solenoid valve will cycle on and off.

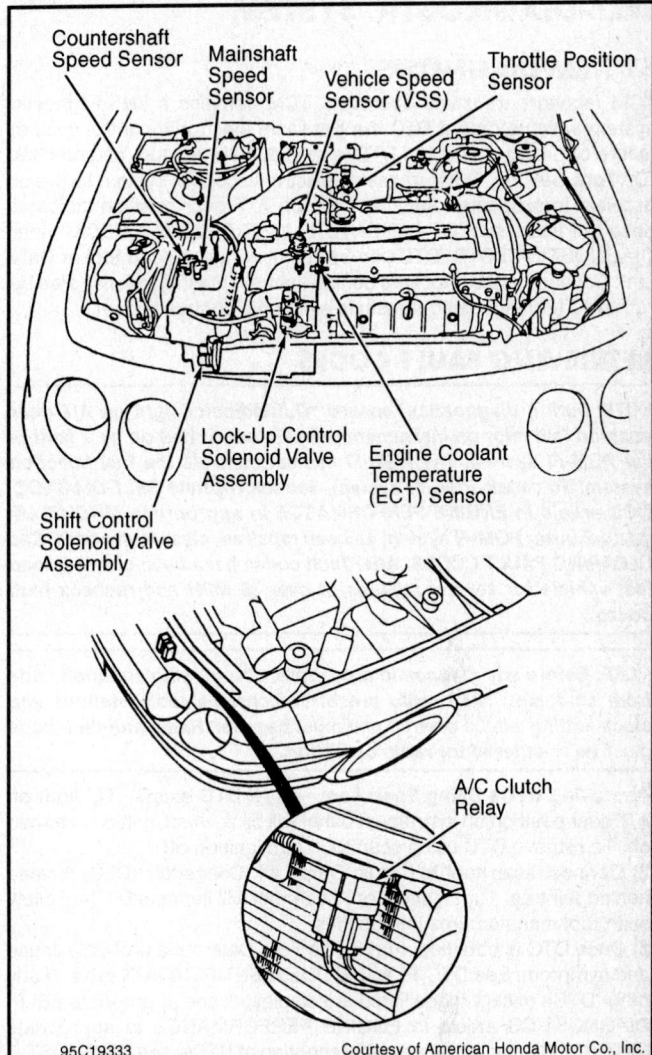

Fig. 7: Identifying Input & Output Device Locations

"D₄" Indicator Light – The "D₄" indicator light is located on A/T gear position indicator on instrument panel. See Fig. 1. When ignition is first turned on, "D₄" indicator light should come on for about 2 seconds and then go off, indicating light circuit is functioning properly. If a fault exists in transaxle electronic control system and fault code is stored, TCM delivers an output signal to blink "D₄" indicator light.

Interlock Control Unit – When A/T gear position switch is in Park, the TCM provides voltage to shift lock circuit in the interlock control unit, provided brake pedal is depressed and accelerator pedal is in idle position. Interlock control unit then operates shift lock solenoid by controlling the ground circuit. When shift lock solenoid is energized, shift lever is released and can be moved.

Self-Diagnosis Indicator – If an abnormality exists in transaxle electronic control system and DTC is stored, PCM will deliver an output signal (flash code) to turn on and blink "D₄" light. The "D₄" light is located on the A/T gear position indicator on instrument panel. See Fig. 1. Flash code can be retrieved to identify problem area by installing jumper wire between service check connector terminals. DTC "P" code can be retrieved to identify problem area using scan tool. Flash codes will be displayed by blinking "D₄" light.

AUTOMATIC TRANSMISSIONS
Acura SX4A Electronic Controls (Cont.)

SELF-DIAGNOSTIC SYSTEM

SYSTEM DIAGNOSIS

TCM monitors transaxle operation. TCM contains a self-diagnostic system which stores a DTC if a transaxle electronic control system failure or problem exists. If DTC is stored, TCM will turn on and blink "D₄" light. *See Fig. 1.* If a transaxle electronic control system failure or problem is suspected and "D₄" light on A/T gear position indicator does not flash, see "D₄" INDICATOR LIGHT CIRCUIT CHECK under DIAGNOSTIC TESTS. DTC can be retrieved using scan tool at Data Link Connector (DLC) located behind ashtray. Flash code may also be retrieved for diagnosing transaxle electronic control system.

RETRIEVING FAULT CODES

NOTE: During diagnostics, ensure "D₄" indicator light on A/T gear position indicator on instrument panel is not turned on by a fault in the PGM-FI system. The PGM-FI system controls the fuel injection system. To repair PGM-FI system, see appropriate SELF-DIAGNOSTICS article in ENGINE PERFORMANCE in appropriate MITCHELL® manual. After PGM-FI system as been repaired, clear fault codes. See CLEARING FAULT CODES. After fault codes have been cleared, road test vehicle for several minutes at over 30 MPH and recheck fault codes.

NOTE: Before any diagnostic procedure, obtain radio anti-theft code from customer. Note radio preset stations, as radio stations and clock setting will be cleared and must be reset. Radio anti-theft code must be re-entered for radio operation.

Retrieving DTCs Using Scan Tool – 1) If DTC exists, "D₄" light on A/T gear position on instrument panel will blink when ignition is turned on. To retrieve DTC using scan tool, turn ignition off.
2) Connect scan tool to 16-pin Data Link Connector (DLC) located behind ashtray. Turn ignition on. Scan tool will indicate DTCs. Follow scan tool manufactures instructions.
3) Once DTC is obtained, turn ignition off. Determine probable cause and symptom. See DTC/FLASH CODE IDENTIFICATION table. If any other DTCs except those listed are displayed, see appropriate SELF-DIAGNOSTICS article in ENGINE PERFORMANCE in appropriate MITCHELL® manual. For trouble shooting of DTCs, see DIAGNOSTIC TESTS. If "D₄" light does not flash or stays on, see "D₄" INDICATOR LIGHT CIRCUIT CHECK under DIAGNOSTIC TESTS.

Retrieving Flash Codes Using "D₄" Light – 1) If flash code exists, "D₄" light on A/T gear position indicator on instrument panel will blink when ignition is turned on. To retrieve flash code, turn ignition off.
2) Install jumper wire between service check connector electrical terminals. Service check connector is a Blue 2-pin electrical connector, located under passenger's side of instrument panel. *See Fig. 6.*
3) Turn ignition on. Flash codes will be displayed by short and long blinks of "D₄" light on A/T gear position indicator on instrument panel. If the Malfunction Indicator Light (MIL) is also flashing, see appropriate SELF-DIAGNOSTICS article in ENGINE PERFORMANCE in appropriate MITCHELL® manual. Repair MIL light codes first.
4) A short blink indicates a single digit flash code. A long blink equals 10 short blinks. For example, if "D₄" light blinks once, this is a Flash Code No. 1. If "D₄" light blinks one long blink and then 4 short blinks, this is a Flash Code No. 14. *See Fig. 9.*
5) Once flash code is obtained, turn ignition off. Remove jumper wire from service check connector. Determine probable cause and symptom. See DTC/FLASH CODE IDENTIFICATION table. If any other flash codes except those listed are displayed, TCM is defective. For trouble shooting of flash codes, see DIAGNOSTIC TESTS.

NOTE: If customer describes symptoms for DTC P0715/Flash Code 15, DTC P0725/Flash Code No. 11 DTC or P01706/Flash Code No. 6, it may be necessary to test drive vehicle to recreate the symptom and then check for trouble code with ignition still on.

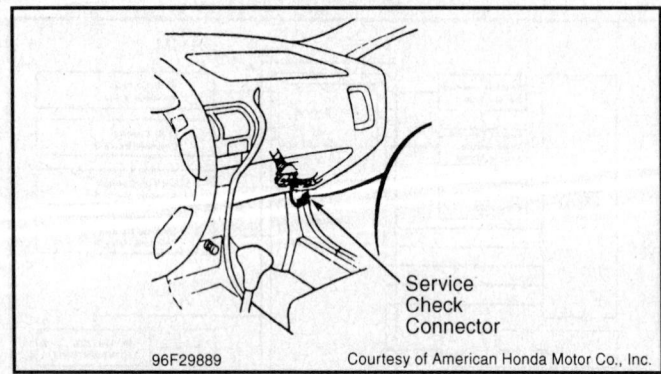

Fig. 8: Identifying Service Check Connector

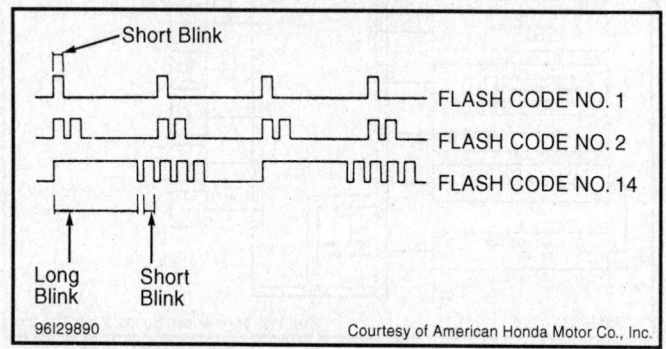

Fig. 9: Identifying Flash Code Displays

CLEARING FAULT CODES

NOTE: TCM memory can NOT be cleared using scan tool, the following procedure must be used. Before clearing fault codes, obtain radio anti-theft code from customer. Note radio preset stations, as radio stations and clock setting will be cleared and must be reset. Radio anti-theft code must be reset for radio operation.

1) Once repairs have been performed, fault codes must be cleared from TCM memory. Ensure ignition is off. Remove fuse No. 32 (BACK UP, 7.5 amp fuse) from engine compartment fuse box, located at passenger's side rear corner of engine compartment for at least 10 seconds. This will clear TCM and ECM memories.
2) Reinstall fuse. To re-enter radio anti-theft code, turn radio on. When the word CODE is displayed on radio, re-enter radio anti-theft code by using the radio station preset buttons. Reset clock and radio stations.

DIAGNOSTIC TESTS

NOTE: Terminal identification, circuit description and terminal voltage is included in PIN VOLTAGE CHARTS. See Figs. 11 and 12.

DTC P0715 (FLASH CODE 15): MAINSHAFT SPEED SENSOR

NOTE: DTC P0715 (FLASH CODE 15) doesn't always mean an electrical problem in mainshaft speed sensor or circuit, this DTC can also be caused by a mechanical problem in transaxle.

1) Ensure mainshaft and countershaft speed sensors are installed properly. See COUNTERSHAFT or MAINSHAFT SPEED SENSOR under REMOVAL & INSTALLATION. Disconnect mainshaft speed sensor connector and measure resistance between sensor connector terminals. See MAINSHAFT SPEED SENSOR under COMPONENT TESTING.
2) If resistance is not 400-600 ohms, replace mainshaft speed sensor. If resistance is 400-600 ohms, disconnect TCM 22-pin connector "B". Check continuity between ground and TCM 22-pin connector "B" terminals No. 10 (Red wire) and No. 17 (White wire). *See Figs. 11 and 12.*

DTC/FLASH CODE IDENTIFICATION

DTC/Flash Code [1] Number	Indicator Light [2] Condition	Probable [3] Cause	[4] [5] Symptom
P0715/15	Off	Defective Mainshaft Speed Sensor	Transaxle Jerks Hard When Shifting
P0720/9	Blinks	Defective Countershaft Speed Sensor	Lock-Up Clutch Does Not Engage
P0725/11	Off	Defective Ignition Coil	Lock-Up Clutch Does Not Engage
P0730	Off	Defective Shift Control System	Fails To Shift, Stuck In 1st Or 4th Gears
P0740	Off	Defective Lock-Up Control System	Lock-Up Clutch Does Not Engage Or Remains Engaged, Unstable Engine Idle
P0753/7	Blinks	Defective Shift Control Solenoid "A"	Remains In 4th Gear, Fails To Shift Other Than 1st-4th, 2nd-4th Or 2nd-3rd Gears
P0758/8	Blinks	Defective Shift Control Solenoid "B"	Remains In 1st Or 4th Gear
P1705/5	Blinks	Defective A/T Gear Position Switch	Lock-Up Clutch Does Not Engage, Fails To Shift Other Than 2nd-4th Gears
P1706/6	Off	Defective A/T Gear Position Switch	Lock-Up Clutch Does Not Engage, Lock-Up Clutch Engages & Disengages, Fails To Shift Other Than 2nd-4th Gears
P1753/1	Blinks	Defective Lock-Up Control Solenoid "A"	Lock-Up Clutch Does Not Engage Or Remains Engaged, Unstable Engine Idle
P1758/2	Blinks	Defective Lock-Up Control Solenoid "B"	Lock-Up Clutch Does Not Engage
P1786/14	Off	Shorted Or Open FAS Wire (PNK) Between TCM Terminal B19 & ECM, Defective ECM	Transaxle Jerks Hard When Shifting
P1790/3	Blinks Or Remains Off	Defective Throttle Position Sensor	Lock-Up Clutch Does Not Engage
P1791/4	Blinks	Defective Vehicle Speed Sensor	Lock-Up Clutch Does Not Engage
P1792/10	Blinks	Defective Engine Coolant Temp. Sensor	Lock-Up Clutch Does Not Engage
P1794/13	Off	Defective Baro Sensor	No Specific Symptoms

[1] – This is the number of blinks from "D₄" light on A/T gear position indicator on instrument panel with jumper wire installed in service check connector.

[2] – This is operation of "D₄" light on A/T gear position indicator on instrument panel.

[3] – Specified component for probable cause. Also check wiring and connections for the specified component.

[4] – If transaxle fails to shift from Park with brake pedal depressed and accelerator pedal in idle position, check brakelight signal. See BRAKE-LIGHT SIGNAL under TROUBLE SHOOTING.

[5] – If lock-up clutch does not engage or does not cycle on and off, check A/C signal. See A/C SIGNAL under TROUBLE SHOOTING.

3) If continuity exists, repair short to ground in Red or White wires between TCM and mainshaft speed sensor. If continuity does not exist, reconnect mainshaft speed sensor connector. Measure resistance between TCM 22-pin connector "B" terminals No. 10 (Red wire) and No. 17 (White wire).

4) If resistance is not 400-600 ohms, go to next step. If resistance is 400-600 ohms, perform DTC P0720 (flash code 9) diagnostic, check for loose TCM connectors and replace TCM with known good part, as necessary.

5) Disconnect mainshaft speed sensor connector. Check continuity of Red wire between TCM 22-pin connector "B" terminal No. 10 and mainshaft speed sensor connector. If continuity exists, go to next step. If continuity does not exist, repair open Red wire between TCM 22-pin connector and mainshaft speed sensor connector.

6) Check continuity of White wire between TCM 22-pin connector "B" terminal No. 17 and mainshaft speed sensor connector. If continuity exists, check for loose TCM connectors and replace TCM with known good part, as necessary. If continuity does not exist, repair open White wire between TCM 22-pin connector and mainshaft speed sensor connector.

DTC P0720 (FLASH CODE 9): COUNTERSHAFT SPEED SENSOR

1) Ensure countershaft speed sensor is installed properly. See COUNTERSHAFT SPEED SENSOR under REMOVAL & INSTALLATION. Disconnect countershaft speed sensor connector and measure resistance between sensor connector terminals. See COUNTERSHAFT SPEED SENSOR under COMPONENT TESTING.

2) If resistance is not 400-600 ohms, replace countershaft speed sensor. If resistance is 400-600 ohms, disconnect TCM 22-pin connector "B". Check continuity between ground and TCM 22-pin connector "B" terminals No. 8 (Green wire) and No. 9 (Blue wire). See Figs. 11 and 12.

3) If continuity exists, repair short to ground in Green or Blue wires between TCM and countershaft speed sensor. If continuity does not exist, reconnect countershaft speed sensor connector. Measure resistance between TCM 22-pin connector "B" terminals No. 8 (Green wire) and No. 9 (Blue wire).

4) If resistance is not 400-600 ohms, check for loose TCM connectors and replace TCM with known good part, as necessary. If resistance is 400-600 ohms, repair open Green or Blue wires between TCM 22-pin connector and countershaft speed sensor connector.

DTC P0725 (FLASH CODE 11): IGNITION COIL

1) Disconnect TCM 26-pin connector "A". Start engine. Using DVOM, measure voltage between TCM 26-pin connector "A" terminals No. 5 (Blue wire) and No. 13 (Brown/Black wire) or No. 26 (Brown/Black wire). See Figs. 11 and 12..

2) If battery voltage is present, check for loose TCM connectors and replace TCM with known good part, as necessary. If battery voltage is not present, repair open or short in Blue wire between ignition coil and TCM 26-pin connector "A".

DTC P0730: SHIFT CONTROL SYSTEM

NOTE: Do NOT perform this DTC test until all other DTCs have been repaired first.

1) Road test vehicle at over 12 MPH for more than 30 seconds in 2nd, 3rd and 4th gear. Using scan tool, check for any other DTCs. If any other DTCs exist, repair those DTCs first, then recheck for DTC P0730. If no other DTCs exist, go to next step.

2) Test clutch pressure. See HYDRAULIC PRESSURE TEST under TESTING in ACURA SP7A & SX4A overhaul article. If clutch pressure is within specification, go to next step. If clutch pressure is not within specification, repair hydraulic system as necessary. See HYDRAULIC

PRESSURE TROUBLE SHOOTING table under HYDRAULIC PRESSURE TEST in ACURA SP7A & SX4A overhaul article.

3) Replace shift control solenoid valve assembly. See SHIFT CONTROL SOLENOID VALVES under REMOVAL & INSTALLATION. Turn ignition off and clear codes. See CLEARING FAULT CODES. Road test vehicle at over 12 MPH for more than 30 seconds in 2nd, 3rd and 4th gear. Recheck DTCs. If P0730 returns, repair internal components as necessary. If P0730 does not return, system is okay.

DTC P0740: LOCK-UP CONTROL SYSTEM

NOTE: Do NOT perform this DTC test until all other DTCs have been repaired first.

1) Using scan tool, check for any other DTCs. If any other DTCs exist, repair those DTCs first, then recheck for DTC P0740. If no other DTCs exist, go to next step.
2) Test line pressure. See HYDRAULIC PRESSURE TEST under TESTING in AUTOMATIC TRANSMISSIONS ACURA SP7A & SX4A overhaul article. If clutch pressure is within specification, go to next step. If line pressure is not within specification, repair hydraulic system as necessary. See HYDRAULIC PRESSURE TROUBLE SHOOTING table under HYDRAULIC PRESSURE TEST in ACURA SP7A & SX4A overhaul article.
3) Test clutch pressure. If clutch pressure is within specification, go to next step. If clutch pressure is not within specification, repair hydraulic system as necessary. See HYDRAULIC PRESSURE TROUBLE SHOOTING table under HYDRAULIC PRESSURE TEST in ACURA SP7A & SX4A overhaul article.
4) Replace lock-up control solenoid valve assembly. See LOCK-UP CONTROL SOLENOID VALVES under REMOVAL & INSTALLATION. Turn ignition off and clear codes. See CLEARING FAULT CODES. Road test vehicle at over 50 MPH for more than one minute. Recheck DTCs. If P0740 returns, go to next step. If P0740 does not return, system is okay.
5) Replace torque converter. Turn ignition off and clear codes. See CLEARING FAULT CODES. Road test vehicle at over 50 MPH for more than one minute. Recheck DTCs. If P0740 returns, replace transaxle. If P0740 does not return, system is okay.

DTC P0753 (FLASH CODE 7):
SHIFT CONTROL SOLENOID VALVE "A"

1) Disconnect TCM 26-pin connector "A" and TCM 22-pin connector "B". Turn ignition on. Using DVOM, measure voltage between TCM 22-pin connector "B" terminal No. 20 (White/Black wire) and TCM 26-pin connector "A" terminals No. 13 or No. 26 (Brown/Black wires). See Figs. 11 and 12. If voltage is approximately 5 volts, go to next step. If voltage is not approximately 5 volts, repair open or short in White/Black wire between TCM 22-pin connector "B" and ECM.
2) Measure voltage between TCM 26-pin connector "A" terminals No. 13 or No. 26 (Brown/Black wires) and No. 3 (Blue/Yellow wire). If voltage is not present, go to next step. If voltage is present, repair short to voltage in Blue/Yellow wire.
3) Turn ignition off. Measure shift control solenoid valve "A" resistance at TCM. See SHIFT CONTROL SOLENOID VALVE under COMPONENT TESTING. If resistance is not 14-25 ohms, go to next step. If resistance is 14-25 ohms, check for loose TCM connectors and replace TCM with known good part, as necessary.
4) Disconnect shift control solenoid valve connector. Check for continuity between TCM 26-pin connector "A" terminals No. 13 or No. 26 (Brown/Black wires) and No. 3 (Blue/Yellow wire). If continuity does not exist, go to next step. If continuity exists, repair short to ground in Blue/Yellow wire between TCM 26-pin connector "A" and shift control solenoid valve.
5) Measure resistance between shift control solenoid valve connector (solenoid side) Blue/Yellow wire and ground. If resistance is not 14-25 ohms, replace shift control solenoid valve assembly. If resistance is 14-25 ohms, check and repair open Blue/Yellow wire between shift control solenoid valve connector and shift control solenoid valve.

DTC P0758 (FLASH CODE 8):
SHIFT CONTROL SOLENOID VALVE "B"

1) Disconnect TCM 26-pin connector "A" and TCM 22-pin connector "B". Turn ignition on. Using DVOM, measure voltage between TCM 22-pin connector "B" terminal No. 20 (White/Black wire) and TCM 26-pin connector "A" terminals No. 13 or No. 26 (Brown/Black wires). See Figs. 11 and 12. If voltage is approximately 5 volts, go to next step. If voltage is not approximately 5 volts, repair open White/Black wire between TCM 22-pin connector "B" and ECM.
2) Measure voltage between TCM 26-pin connector "A" terminals No. 13 or No. 26 (Brown/Black wires) and No. 2 (Green/White wire). If voltage is not present, go to next step. If voltage is present, repair short to voltage in Green/White wire.
3) Turn ignition off. Measure shift control solenoid valve "B" resistance at TCM. See SHIFT CONTROL SOLENOID VALVE under COMPONENT TESTING. If resistance is not 14-25 ohms, go to next step. If resistance is 14-25 ohms, check for loose TCM connectors and replace TCM with known good part, as necessary.
4) Disconnect shift control solenoid valve connector. Check for continuity between TCM 26-pin connector "A" terminals No. 13 or No. 26 (Brown/Black wires) and No. 2 (Green/White wire). If continuity does not exist, go to next step. If continuity exists, repair short to ground in Green/White wire between TCM 26-pin connector "A" and shift control solenoid valve.
5) Measure resistance between shift control solenoid valve connector (solenoid side) Green/White wire and ground. If resistance is not 14-25 ohms, replace shift control solenoid valve assembly. If resistance is 14-25 ohms, check and repair open Green/White wire between shift control solenoid valve connector and shift control solenoid valve.

DTC P1705 (FLASH CODE 5):
A/T GEAR POSITION SWITCH (SHORT)

NOTE: DTC P1705 is set when TCM receives 2 gear position signals at same time.

1) Turn ignition on. If any A/T gear position indicator light stays on when gear selector is moved from that gear, go to next step. If all A/T gear position indicator lights go off when gear selector is moved from that gear, system is okay at this time.
2) Shift to all gear positions except reverse. Using DVOM, measure voltage between TCM 26-pin connector "A" terminals No. 13 or No. 26 (Brown/Black wires) and No. 11 (Green/Red wire). See Figs. 11 and 12. If battery voltage is present, go to next step. If battery voltage is not present, check and repair short in Green/Red wire between TCM 26-pin connector "A" and A/T gear position indicator or A/T gear position switch. If Green/Red wire is okay, check for loose TCM connectors and replace TCM with known good part, as necessary.
3) Shift to all gear positions except Neutral and Park. Measure voltage between TCM 26-pin connector "A" terminals No. 13 or No. 26 (Brown/Black wires) and No. 10 (Light Green/Black wire). If battery voltage is present, go to next step. If battery voltage is not present, check and repair short in Light Green/Black wire between TCM 26-pin connector "A" and A/T gear position indicator or A/T gear position switch. If Green/Red wire is okay, check for loose TCM connectors and replace TCM with known good part, as necessary.
4) Shift to all gear positions except "D⁴". Measure voltage between TCM 26-pin connector "A" terminals No. 13 or No. 26 (Brown/Black wires) and No. 9 (Pink/Green wire). If battery voltage is present, go to next step. If battery voltage is not present, check and repair short in Pink/Green wire between TCM 26-pin connector "A" and A/T gear position switch. If Pink/Green wire is okay, check for loose TCM connectors and replace TCM with known good part, as necessary.
5) Shift to all gear positions except "D³". Measure voltage between TCM 26-pin connector "A" terminals No. 13 or No. 26 (Brown/Black wires) and No. 8 (Green/Blue wire). If battery voltage is present, go to next step. If battery voltage is not present, check and repair short in Green/Blue wire between TCM 26-pin connector "A" and A/T gear position indicator or A/T gear position switch. If Green/Blue wire is okay, check for loose TCM connectors and replace TCM with known good part, as necessary.

6) Shift to all gear positions except "2". Measure voltage between TCM 26-pin connector "A" terminals No. 13 or No. 26 (Brown/Black wires) and No. 7 (Green/Yellow wire). If battery voltage is present, go to next step. If battery voltage is not present, check and repair short in Green/Yellow wire between TCM 26-pin connector "A" and A/T gear position indicator or A/T gear position switch. If Green/Yellow wire is okay, check for loose TCM connectors and replace TCM with known good part, as necessary.

7) Shift to all gear positions except "1". Measure voltage between TCM 26-pin connector "A" terminals No. 13 or No. 26 (Brown/Black wires) and No. 6 (Light Green/White wire). If battery voltage is present, check for loose TCM connectors and replace TCM with known good part, as necessary. If battery voltage is not present, check and repair short in Light Green/White wire between TCM 26-pin connector "A" and A/T gear position indicator or A/T gear position switch. If Light Green/White wire is okay, check for loose TCM connectors and replace TCM with known good part, as necessary.

DTC P1706 (FLASH CODE 6): A/T GEAR POSITION SWITCH (OPEN)

1) Turn ignition on. If any A/T gear position indicator light stays on when gear selector is moved from that gear, go to next step. If all A/T gear position indicator lights go off when gear selector is moved from that gear, system is okay at this time.

2) Shift to Reverse. Using DVOM, measure voltage between TCM 26-pin connector "A" terminals No. 13 or No. 26 (Brown/Black wires) and No. 11 (Green/Red wire). See Figs. 11 and 12. If voltage is not present, go to next step. If voltage is present, check and repair open in Green/Red wire between TCM 26-pin connector "A" and A/T gear position switch.

3) Shift to Neutral or Park. Measure voltage between TCM 26-pin connector "A" terminals No. 13 or No. 26 (Brown/Black wires) and No. 10 (Light Green/Black wire). If voltage is not present, go to next step. If voltage is present, check and repair open in Light Green/Black wire between TCM 26-pin connector "A" and A/T gear position indicator.

4) Shift to "D⁴" position. Measure voltage between TCM 26-pin connector "A" terminals No. 13 or No. 26 (Brown/Black wires) and No. 9 (Pink/Green wire). If voltage is not present, go to next step. If voltage is present, check and repair open in Pink/Green wire between TCM 26-pin connector "A" and A/T gear position switch.

5) Shift to "D³" position. Measure voltage between TCM 26-pin connector "A" terminals No. 13 or No. 26 (Brown/Black wires) and No. 8 (Green/Blue wire). If voltage is not present, go to next step. If voltage is present, check and repair open in Green/Blue wire between TCM 26-pin connector "A" and A/T gear position switch.

6) Shift to "2" position. Measure voltage between TCM 26-pin connector "A" terminals No. 13 or No. 26 (Brown/Black wires) and No. 7 (Green/Yellow wire). If voltage is not present, go to next step. If voltage is present, check and repair open in Green/Yellow wire between TCM 26-pin connector "A" and A/T gear position switch.

7) Shift to "1" position. Measure voltage between TCM 26-pin connector "A" terminals No. 13 or No. 26 (Brown/Black wires) and No. 6 (Light Green/White wire). If voltage is not present, check for loose TCM connectors and replace TCM with known good part, as necessary. If voltage is present, check and repair open in Light Green/White wire between TCM 26-pin connector "A" and A/T gear position switch.

DTC P1753 (FLASH CODE 1): LOCK-UP CONTROL SOLENOID VALVE "A"

1) Disconnect TCM 26-pin connector "A" and TCM 22-pin connector "B". Turn ignition on. Using DVOM, measure voltage between TCM 22-pin connector "B" terminal No. 20 (White/Black wire) and TCM 26-pin connector "A" terminals No. 13 or No. 26 (Brown/Black wires). See Figs. 11 and 12. If voltage is approximately 5 volts, go to next step. If voltage is not approximately 5 volts, repair open or short in White/Black wire between TCM 22-pin connector "B" and ECM.

2) Measure voltage between TCM 26-pin connector "A" terminals No. 13 or No. 26 (Brown/Black wires) and No. 16 (Yellow wire). If voltage is not present, go to next step. If voltage is present, repair short to voltage in Yellow wire.

3) Turn ignition off. Measure lock-up control solenoid valve "A" resistance at TCM. See LOCK-UP CONTROL SOLENOID VALVE under COMPONENT TESTING. If resistance is not 14-25 ohms, go to next step. If resistance is 14-25 ohms, check for loose TCM connectors and replace TCM with known good part, as necessary.

4) Disconnect lock-up control solenoid valve connector. Check for continuity between TCM 26-pin connector "A" terminals No. 13 or No. 26 (Brown/Black wires) and No. 16 (Yellow wire). If continuity does not exist, go to next step. If continuity exists, repair short to ground in Yellow wire between TCM 26-pin connector "A" and lock-up control solenoid valve.

5) Measure resistance between lock-up control solenoid valve connector (solenoid side) Yellow wire and ground. If resistance is not 14-25 ohms, replace lock-up control solenoid valve assembly. If resistance is 14-25 ohms, check and repair open Yellow wire between lock-up control solenoid valve connector and lock-up control solenoid valve.

DTC P1758 (FLASH CODE 2): LOCK-UP CONTROL SOLENOID VALVE "B"

1) Disconnect TCM 26-pin connector "A" and TCM 22-pin connector "B". Turn ignition on. Using DVOM, measure voltage between TCM 22-pin connector "B" terminal No. 20 (White/Black wire) and TCM 26-pin connector "A" terminals No. 13 or No. 26 (Brown/Black wires). See Figs. 11 and 12. If voltage is approximately 5 volts, go to next step. If voltage is not approximately 5 volts, repair open or short in White/Black wire between TCM 22-pin connector "B" and ECM.

2) Measure voltage between TCM 26-pin connector "A" terminals No. 13 or No. 26 (Brown/Black wires) and No. 15 (Green/Black wire). If voltage is not present, go to next step. If voltage is present, repair short to voltage in Green/Black wire.

3) Turn ignition off. Measure lock-up control solenoid valve "B" resistance at TCM. See LOCK-UP CONTROL SOLENOID VALVE under COMPONENT TESTING. If resistance is not 14-25 ohms, go to next step. If resistance is 14-25 ohms, check for loose TCM connectors and replace TCM with known good part, as necessary.

4) Disconnect lock-up control solenoid valve connector. Check for continuity between TCM 26-pin connector "A" terminals No. 13 or No. 26 (Brown/Black wires) and No. 15 (Green/Black wire). If continuity does not exist, go to next step. If continuity exists, repair short to ground in Green/Black between TCM 26-pin connector "A" and lock-up control solenoid valve.

5) Measure resistance between lock-up control solenoid valve connector (solenoid side) Green/Black wire and ground. If resistance is not 14-25 ohms, replace lock-up control solenoid valve assembly. If resistance is 14-25 ohms, check and repair open Green/Black wire between lock-up control solenoid valve connector and lock-up control solenoid valve.

DTC P1786 (FLASH CODE 14): FAS SIGNAL

1) Start engine and warm to normal operating temperature. Shift to park. Cycle key off and on and wait for 2 seconds. Using DVOM, measure voltage between TCM 22-pin connector "B" terminal No. 19 (Yellow wire) TCM 26-pin connector "A" terminals No. 13 (Brown/Black wire) or No. 26 (Brown/Black wire). See Figs. 11 and 12.. If voltage is approximately 5 volts, check for loose TCM connectors and replace TCM with known good part, as necessary. If voltage is not approximately 5 volts, go to next step.

2) Turn ignition off. Disconnect TCM 22-pin connector "B". Turn ignition on. Measure voltage between ECM 31-pin connector "C" terminal No. 9 (Yellow wire) and ECM 32-pin connector "A" terminal No. 9 (Brown/Black wire). See Fig. 10. If voltage is approximately 5 volts, go to step 4). If voltage is not approximately 5 volts, go to next step.

3) Turn ignition off. Disconnect ECM 31-pin connector "C". Check for continuity of Yellow wire between ECM 31-pin connector "C" terminal No. 9 and TCM 22-pin connector "B" terminal No. 19. If continuity does not exist, repair open Yellow wire between TCM and ECM. If continuity exists, check for loose TCM connectors and replace TCM with known good part, as necessary.

4) Turn ignition off. Disconnect ECM 31-pin connector "C". Check for continuity between ECM 31-pin connector "C" terminal No. 9 and ground or TCM 22-pin connector "B" terminal No. 19 and ground. If continuity does not exist, check for loose TCM connectors and replace TCM with known good part, as necessary. If continuity exists, repair short in Yellow wire between TCM and ECM.

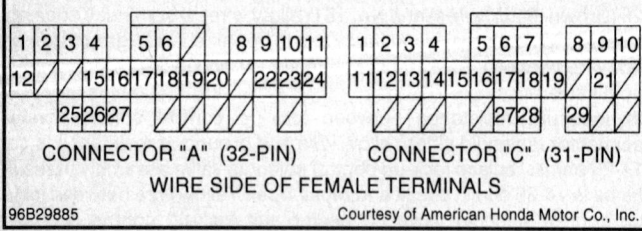

CONNECTOR "A" (32-PIN)   CONNECTOR "C" (31-PIN)
WIRE SIDE OF FEMALE TERMINALS

96B29885   Courtesy of American Honda Motor Co., Inc.

Fig. 10: Identifying ECM Connector Terminals

DTC P1790 (FLASH CODE 3):
THROTTLE POSITION (TP) SENSOR

1) Turn ignition on. Using scan tool, check for any other DTCs or check for Malfunction Indicator Light (MIL) flashing. If any other DTCs exist or MIL is flashing, repair those DTCs first, then recheck for DTC P1790. If no other DTCs exist and MIL is not flashing, go to next step.
2) Turn ignition off. Disconnect TCM 22-pin connector "B" and TCM 26-pin connector "A". Turn ignition on. Measure voltage between TCM 22-pin connector "B" terminal No. 20 (White/Black wire) and TCM 26-pin connector "A" terminals No. 13 or No. 26 (Brown/Black wires). See Figs. 11 and 12. If voltage is approximately 5 volts, go to next step. If voltage is not approximately 5 volts, repair open or short in White/Black wire between TCM 22-pin connector "B" and ECM.
3) Measure voltage between TCM 22-pin connector "B" terminal No. 4 (Red/Black wire) and TCM 26-pin connector "A" terminals No. 13 or No. 26 (Brown/Black wires). If voltage is .4-.6 volts, check for loose TCM connectors and replace TCM with known good part, as necessary. If voltage is not .4-.6 volts, repair open or short in Red/Black wire between TCM and TP sensor.

DTC P1791 (FLASH CODE 4):
VEHICLE SPEED SENSOR (VSS)

1) Ensure speedometer operates correctly. If speedometer operates properly, go to next step. If speedometer does not operate properly, see VEHICLE SPEED SENSOR (VSS) under COMPONENT TESTING.
2) Raise and support vehicle. Block one front wheel. Place gear selector in Neutral. Turn ignition off. Disconnect TCM 22-pin connector "B" and TCM 26-pin connector "A". Turn ignition on. While rotating unblocked front wheel, measure voltage between TCM 22-pin connector "B" terminal No. 5 (Orange wire) and TCM 26-pin connector "A" terminals No. 13 or No. 26 (Brown/Black wires). See Figs. 11 and 12.
3) If voltage alternates from zero to 5 volts, check for loose TCM connectors and replace TCM with known good part, as necessary. If voltage does not alternate from zero to 5 volts, check and repair short or open in Orange wire between TCM and VSS. If wire is okay, see VEHICLE SPEED SENSOR (VSS) under COMPONENT TESTING.

DTC P1792 (FLASH CODE 10):
ENGINE COOLANT TEMPERATURE (ECT) SENSOR

1) Turn ignition on. Using scan tool, check for any other DTCs or check for Malfunction Indicator Light (MIL) flashing. If any other DTCs exists or MIL is flashing, repair those DTCs first, then recheck for DTC P1792. If no other DTCs exist and MIL is not flashing, go to next step.
2) Turn ignition off. Disconnect TCM 22-pin connector "B" and TCM 26-pin connector "A". Turn ignition on. Measure voltage between TCM 22-pin connector "B" terminal No. 20 (White/Black wire) and TCM 26-pin connector "A" terminals No. 13 or No. 26 (Brown/Black wires). See Figs. 11 and 12. If voltage is approximately 5 volts, go to next step. If voltage is not approximately 5 volts, repair open or short in White/Black wire between TCM 22-pin connector "B" and ECM.

3) Measure voltage between TCM 22-pin connector "B" terminal No. 3 (Red/White wire) and TCM 26-pin connector "A" terminals No. 13 or No. 26 (Brown/Black wires). If voltage is less than one volt, check for loose TCM connectors and replace TCM with known good part, as necessary. If voltage is equal to or greater than one volt, repair open Red/White wire between TCM and ECT sensor.

DTC P1794 (FLASH CODE 13):
BAROMETRIC PRESSURE (BARO) SENSOR

NOTE: Baro sensor is built into ECM.

1) Turn ignition off. Disconnect TCM 22-pin connector "B" and TCM 26-pin connector "A". Turn ignition on. Measure voltage between TCM 22-pin connector "B" terminal No. 20 (White/Black wire) and TCM 26-pin connector "A" terminals No. 13 or No. 26 (Brown/Black wires). See Figs. 11 and 12. If voltage is approximately 5 volts, go to next step. If voltage is not approximately 5 volts, repair open or short in White/Black wire between TCM 22-pin connector "B" and ECM.
2) Disconnect TCM 22-pin connector "B". Check for continuity of Light Green wire between ECM 31-pin connector "C" terminal No. 21 and TCM 22-pin connector "B" terminal No. 2. See Fig. 10. If continuity exists, go to next step. If continuity does not exist, repair open Light Green wire between ECM and TCM.
3) Check for continuity between ECM 31-pin connector "C" terminal No. 21 (Light Green wire) and ground or TCM 22-pin connector "B" terminal No. 19 (Light Green wire) and ground. If continuity does not exist, check for loose TCM connectors and replace TCM with known good part, as necessary. If continuity exists, repair short to ground in Light Green wire.

"D₄" INDICATOR LIGHT CIRCUIT CHECK

"D₄" Indicator Light Does Not Come On – 1) Turn ignition on. Ensure SCS service connector is not connected to service check connector. Shift to "D₄" position. If "D₄" indicator light does not come on, go to next step. If "D₄" indicator light comes on, check for loose TCM connectors and replace TCM with known good part as necessary and retest.
2) Turn ignition off. Disconnect TCM 26-pin connector "A". Using a DVOM, check for continuity between ground and TCM 26-pin connector "A" terminals No. 13 and No. 26 (Black/Brown wires). If continuity is present, go to next step. If continuity is not present, check and repair open or poor connection in appropriate Black/Brown wire.
3) Turn ignition on. Measure voltage at TCM 26-pin connector "A", between terminals No. 12 (Yellow wire) and No. 13 (Black/Brown wire), then between terminals No. 25 (Yellow wire) and No. 26 (Black/Brown wire). If battery voltage is not present, go to next step. If battery voltage is present, check and repair open or short in appropriate wire between TCM and fuse/relay box on driver's side of instrument panel, near steering column. See WIRING DIAGRAMS.
4) Turn ignition off. Reconnect TCM 26-pin connector "A". Using a DVOM, measure voltage (backprobe) between TCM 26-pin connector "A" terminal No. 17 (Green/Black wire) and terminals No. 13 or No. 26 (Black/Brown wires). Turn ignition on. Voltage should be present for 2 seconds. If DVOM indicates voltage as specified, go to next step. If no voltage was indicated, go to step 6).
5) Check for an open or short in Green/Black wire between TCM and gauge assembly. Repair as necessary. If wire is okay, repair faulty "D₄" indicator bulb or gauge assembly printed circuit board.
6) Turn ignition off. Disconnect TCM 26-pin connector "A". Check for continuity between TCM 26-pin connector "A" terminal No. 17 (Green/Black wire) and gauge assembly connector "C" terminal No. 10 (Green/Black wire). If continuity is present, go to next step. If continuity is not present, check and repair Green/Black wire between TCM 26-pin connector "A" and gauge assembly.
7) Check for loose TCM connectors or faulty A/T gear position switch. Repair as necessary. If no problem is found, replace TCM with a known good part and retest.
"D₄" Indicator Light Remains On Constantly (Not Flashing) – 1) Turn ignition off. Disconnect TCM 26-pin connector "A". Turn ignition on. Using a DVOM, measure voltage between ground and TCM 26-pin

PIN VOLTAGE CHARTS

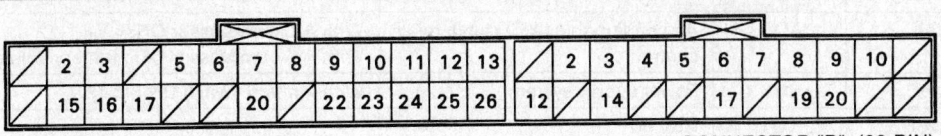

CONNECTOR "A" (26-PIN)   CONNECTOR "B" (22-PIN)

TCM TERMINAL LOCATIONS

Terminal Number	Signal	Description	Measuring Conditions/Terminal Voltage
A1	——	Not used	
A2	SHB	Shift control solenoid valve B control	In 1st and 2nd gear in D₃ and D₄ positions and 2 position: Battery voltage In 1 position, 3rd and 4th gear in D₃ and D₄ positions: 0 V
A3	SHA	Shift control solenoid valve A control	In 1, 2 positions, 2nd and 3rd gear in D₃ and D₄ positions: Battery voltage In 1st gear in D₃ and D₄ positons and 4th gear in D₄ position: 0 V
A4	——	Not used	
A5	NE	Engine speed signal input	When engine is rotating: Pulsing signal
A6	ATP1	A/T gear position switch 1 position input	In 1 position: 0 V In other than 1 position: Battery voltage
A7	ATP2	A/T gear position switch 2 position input	In 2 position: 0 V In other than 2 position: Battery voltage
A8	ATP D3	A/T gear position switch D₃ position input	In D₃ position: 0 V In other than D₃ position: Battery voltage
A9	ATP D4	A/T gear position switch D₄ position input	In D₄ position: 0 V In other than D₄ position: Battery voltage
A10	ATP PN	A/T gear position switch P and N positions input	In P or N positions: 0 V In other than P or N position: Battery voltage
A11	ATP R	A/T gear position switch R position input	In R position: 0 V In other than R position: Battery voltage
A12	IG1	Power supply system	With ignition switch ON (II): Battery voltage
A13	LG1	Ground	
A14	——	Not used	
A15	LCB	Lock-up control solenoid valve B control	During half and full lock-up and during deceleration: Battery voltage During no lock-up: 0 V
A16	LCA	Lock-up control solenoid valve A control	When lock-up is ON: Battery voltage With no lock-up: 0 V
A17	D4 IND	D4 Indicator light control	When ignition switch is first turned ON (II): Battery voltage for two seconds In D₄ position: Battery voltage
A18	——	Not used	
A19	——	Not used	
A20	AT CHK	Upshift/downshift comparative signal output	With ignition switch ON (II): Pulsing signal
A21	——	Not used	
A22	ILU	Interlock control	When ignition switch is ON (II), brake pedal depressed and accelerator pedal released: Battery voltage
A23	VBU	Back-up power system	Always Battery voltage

96C29886   Courtesy of American Honda Motor Co., Inc.

Fig. 11: Pin Voltage Chart & Terminal Identification (1 Of 2)

AUTOMATIC TRANSMISSIONS
Acura SX4A Electronic Controls (Cont.)

Terminal Number	Signal	Description	Measuring Conditions/Terminal Voltage
A24	ACCL	Air conditioning (A/C) clutch relay control	With A/C compressor ON: 0 V With A/C compressor OFF: Battery voltage
A25	IG1	Power supply system	With ignition switch ON (II): 12 V
A26	LG1	Ground	
B1	—	Not used	
B2	BAROS S	Barometric pressure sensor signal input	With ignition switch ON (II) and depending on barometric pressure: Approx. 3 V
B3	ECT	Engine coolant temperature sensor signal input	With ignition switch ON (II) and depending on engine coolant temperature: Approx. 0.1 – 4.8 V
B4	TPS	Throttle position sensor signal input	With ignition switch ON (II) and throttle fully open: 4.14 – 4.82 V With ignition switch ON (II) and throttle fully closed: 0.44 – 0.56 V
B5	VSS	Vehicle speed sensor signal input	With ignition switch ON (II) and front wheels rotating: Pulsing signal
B6	AFSB	Upshift/downshift comparative signal output	With engine idling: 0 V At upshift or downshift: 5 V for an instant
B7	AFSA	Upshift/downshift comparative signal output	With engine idling: 0 V At upshift or downshift: 5 V for an instant
B8	NCSG	Countershaft speed sensor signal ground	Always: 0 V
B9	NC	Countershaft speed sensor signal input	Depending on vehicle speed: Pulsing signal When vehicle is stopped: 0 V
B10	NM	Mainshaft speed sensor signal input	Depending on vehicle speed: Pulsing signal When vehicle is stopped: 0 V
B11	—	Not used	
B12	STOP SW	Brake switch signal input	With ignition switch ON (II) and brake pedal depressed: Battery voltage With ignition switch ON (II) and brake pedal released: 0 V
B13	—	Not used	
B14	SCS	Timing adjustment service check signal	With ignition switch ON (II) and service check connector open: 5 V With ignition switch ON (II) and service check connector connected with special tool: 0 V
B15	—	Not used	
B16	—	Not used	
B17	NMSG	Mainshaft speed sensor signal ground	Always: 0 V
B18	—	Not used	
B19	FAS	Shift acknowledge input	With engine idling: 5 V At upshift or downshift: 0 V for an instant
B20	VREF	+5 V reference	With ignition switch ON (II): Approx. 5 V
B21	—	Not used	
B22	—	Not used	

96D29887

Courtesy of American Honda Motor Co., Inc.

Fig. 12: Pin Voltage Chart (2 Of 2)

connector "A" terminal No. 17 (Green/Black wire). If no voltage is present, go to next step. If voltage is present, check and repair Green/Black wire for a short to power between TCM and gauge assembly.

2) Turn ignition off. Reconnect TCM 26-pin connector "A". Turn ignition on. Shift to any position except "D₄". Measure voltage (backprobe) between ground and TCM 26-pin connector "A" terminal No. 9 (Pink/Green wire). If voltage is present, replace TCM. If no voltage is present, check and repair Pink/Green wire for a short to ground. Repair as necessary. If wire is okay, replace A/T gear position indicator.

TROUBLE SHOOTING

A/C SIGNAL

NOTE: If no A/C signal exists, torque converter lock-up clutch may not engage or cycle on and off.

1) Start engine. Turn blower switch and A/C switch to the ON position. Check if A/C compressor clutch engages.

2) If A/C compressor clutch does not engage, check A/C compressor clutch and wiring. See appropriate AUTOMATIC or MANUAL A/C-HEATER SYSTEMS article in appropriate MITCHELL® AIR CONDITIONING & HEATING SERVICE & REPAIR manual. If A/C compressor clutch engages, turn engine off. Disconnect 26-pin electrical connector from TCM, located behind driver's side kick panel. *See Fig. 6.*

3) Connect voltmeter between terminal A24 (Black/Red wire) and terminal A13 (Brown/Black wire) or A26 (Brown/Black wire). Start engine. Note voltage with A/C compressor off.

4) If battery voltage does not exist, go to next step. If battery voltage exists, A/C signal is okay. Check for loose TCM electrical connections. If electrical connections are okay, substitute TCM with a known good unit and recheck operation.

5) If battery voltage does not exist, check for open circuit in Black/Red wire between terminal A24 on 26-pin electrical connector and A/C clutch relay. The A/C clutch relay is located at front corner of engine compartment, near radiator. *See Fig. 7.*

BRAKELIGHT SIGNAL

NOTE: If no brakelight signal exists, transaxle may fail to shift from Park with brake pedal depressed and accelerator pedal in idle position.

1) Ensure brakelights come on when brake pedal is depressed. If brakelights come on, go to next step. If brakelights do not come on, check No. 42 fuse (20-amp) in engine compartment fuse box, located at passenger's side rear corner of engine compartment. If fuse is okay, repair brakelight signal circuit.

2) Ensure ignition is off. Disconnect the 26-pin and 22-pin electrical connectors from TCM, located behind driver's side kick panel. *See Fig. 6.*

3) Using Digital Volt-Ohmmeter (DVOM), measure voltage between terminals B12 and A13 or A26 with brake pedal depressed. If battery voltage exists, brakelight signal to TCM is okay. Check for loose TCM electrical connections. If electrical connections are okay, substitute TCM with a known good unit and recheck operation.

4) If battery voltage does not exist, check for open circuit in the Green/White wire between terminal B12 and brakelight switch. Brakelight switch is located on brake pedal support. *See Fig. 6.*

SYSTEM TESTING

A/T GEAR POSITION INDICATOR

NOTE: If necessary, refer to wiring schematic when checking component wiring. See Fig. 14.

1) Remove instrument panel gauge assembly from instrument panel. Disconnect electrical connectors "B", "C" and "D" from rear of instrument panel gauge assembly. *See Fig. 13.*

2) Check for voltage and continuity at electrical connectors as specified. *See Fig. 14.* If necessary, check ground connections G201 or G401, ground connection G201 is located at passenger's side front corner of engine compartment, on inner fender panel. Ground connection G401 is located behind driver's side of instrument panel, above kick panel. *See Fig. 15.*

3) If necessary, check No. 15 fuse (10-amp), fuse is located in fuse box on driver's side of instrument panel, near steering column. If necessary, access TCM, the TCM is located behind driver's side kick panel. *See Fig. 6.* If necessary to access ECM, the ECM is located behind passenger's side kick panel, below instrument panel.

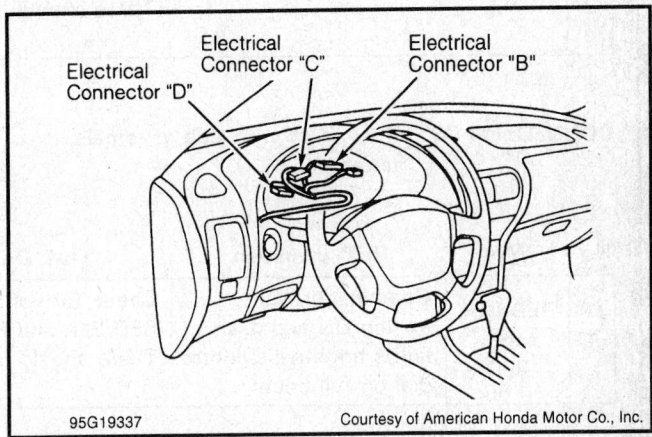

95G19337   Courtesy of American Honda Motor Co., Inc.

Fig. 13: Identifying Instrument Panel Gauge Assembly Electrical Connectors

SHIFT & KEY INTERLOCK SYSTEMS

NOTE: For system testing, refer to wiring schematic when checking component wiring. See Fig. 17. To check individual components, see COMPONENT TESTING.

1) To check system operation, ensure shift lever is in Park. Turn ignition on. Depress brake pedal with accelerator pedal in idle position.

2) If shift lock solenoid clicks, system is working properly. If shift lock solenoid fails to click, see INTERLOCK CONTROL UNIT under COMPONENT TESTING. If shift lever cannot be moved from Park, check for proper installation procedure of shift lock solenoid. See SHIFT LOCK SOLENOID under REMOVAL & INSTALLATION. If shift lock solenoid installation is okay, test A/T gear position switch, see A/T GEAR POSITION SWITCH.

COMPONENT TESTING

A/T GEAR POSITION SWITCH

NOTE: The A/T gear position switch also contains back-up light switch and neutral position switch. Back-up light switch and neutral position switch can also be checked when checking A/T gear position switch.

1) Remove center console. Disconnect 14-pin electrical connector from A/T gear position switch. Note electrical connector terminal identification. *See Fig. 18.*

2) Using ohmmeter, check continuity between specified terminal(s) with shift lever in indicated positions. See A/T GEAR POSITION SWITCH CONTINUITY table.

NOTE: Check continuity while moving shift lever back and forth in free play area of each gear position. DO NOT touch push button on shift lever when checking continuity.

3) If continuity is not as specified, A/T gear position switch may require adjustment. See A/T GEAR POSITION SWITCH under REMOVAL & INSTALLATION. If correct continuity cannot be obtained by adjusting A/T gear position switch, replace switch assembly.

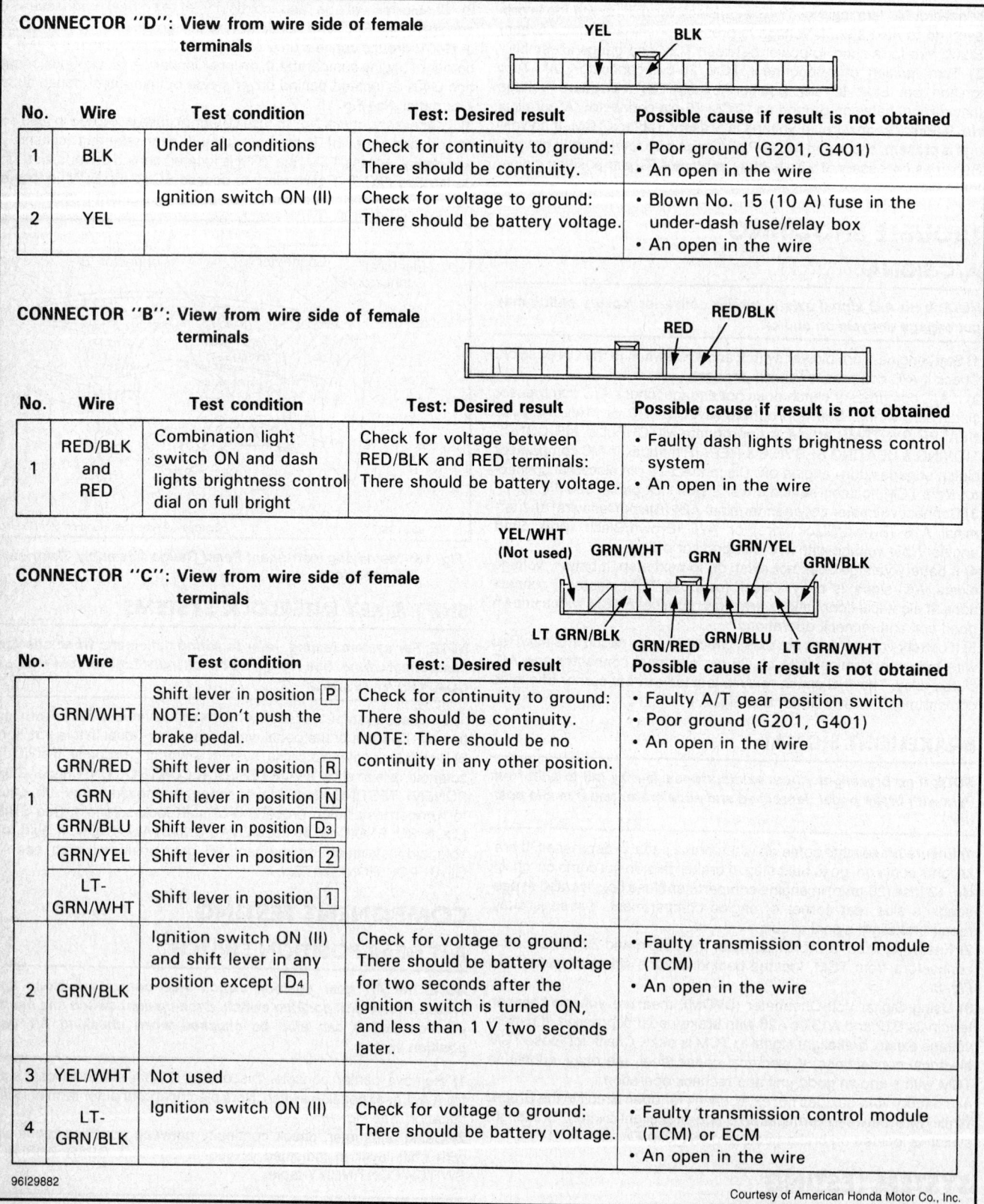

CONNECTOR "D": View from wire side of female terminals

No.	Wire	Test condition	Test: Desired result	Possible cause if result is not obtained
1	BLK	Under all conditions	Check for continuity to ground: There should be continuity.	• Poor ground (G201, G401) • An open in the wire
2	YEL	Ignition switch ON (II)	Check for voltage to ground: There should be battery voltage.	• Blown No. 15 (10 A) fuse in the under-dash fuse/relay box • An open in the wire

CONNECTOR "B": View from wire side of female terminals

No.	Wire	Test condition	Test: Desired result	Possible cause if result is not obtained
1	RED/BLK and RED	Combination light switch ON and dash lights brightness control dial on full bright	Check for voltage between RED/BLK and RED terminals: There should be battery voltage.	• Faulty dash lights brightness control system • An open in the wire

CONNECTOR "C": View from wire side of female terminals

No.	Wire	Test condition	Test: Desired result	Possible cause if result is not obtained
1	GRN/WHT	Shift lever in position [P] NOTE: Don't push the brake pedal.	Check for continuity to ground: There should be continuity. NOTE: There should be no continuity in any other position.	• Faulty A/T gear position switch • Poor ground (G201, G401) • An open in the wire
	GRN/RED	Shift lever in position [R]		
	GRN	Shift lever in position [N]		
	GRN/BLU	Shift lever in position [D₃]		
	GRN/YEL	Shift lever in position [2]		
	LT-GRN/WHT	Shift lever in position [1]		
2	GRN/BLK	Ignition switch ON (II) and shift lever in any position except [D₄]	Check for voltage to ground: There should be battery voltage for two seconds after the ignition switch is turned ON, and less than 1 V two seconds later.	• Faulty transmission control module (TCM) • An open in the wire
3	YEL/WHT	Not used		
4	LT-GRN/BLK	Ignition switch ON (II)	Check for voltage to ground: There should be battery voltage.	• Faulty transmission control module (TCM) or ECM • An open in the wire

96I29882

Courtesy of American Honda Motor Co., Inc.

Fig. 14: Testing A/T Gear Position Indicator

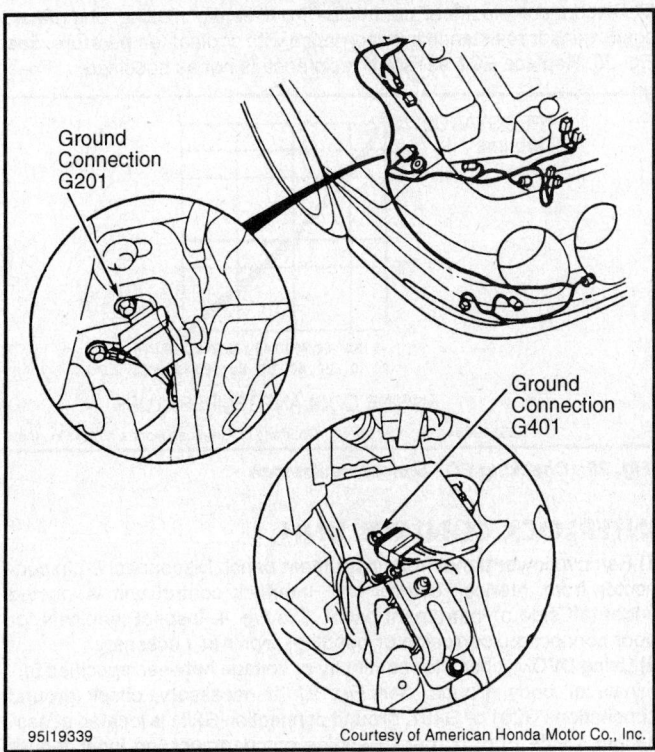

Fig. 15: Identifying Ground Connections

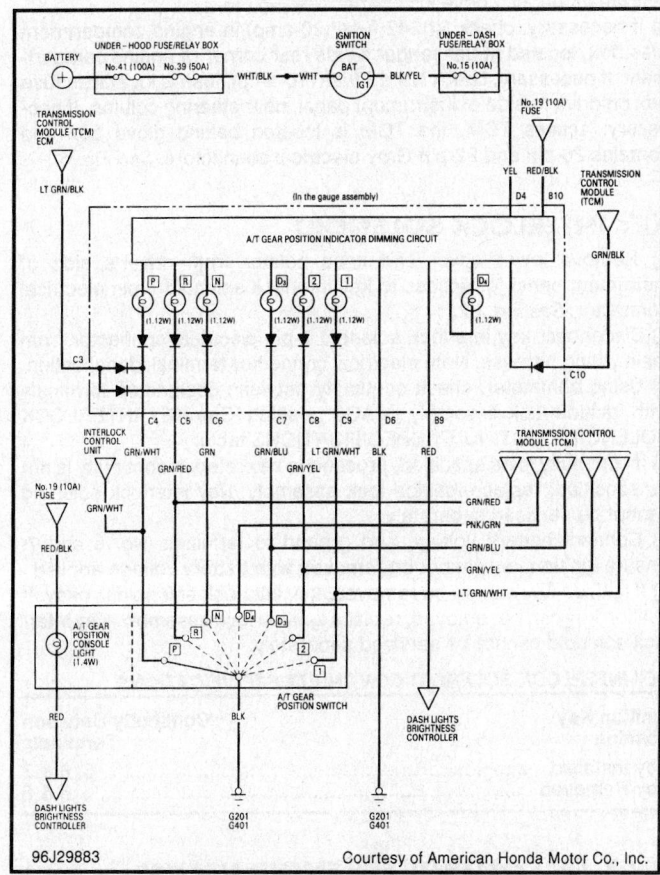

Fig. 16: A/T Gear Position Indicator Wiring Schematic

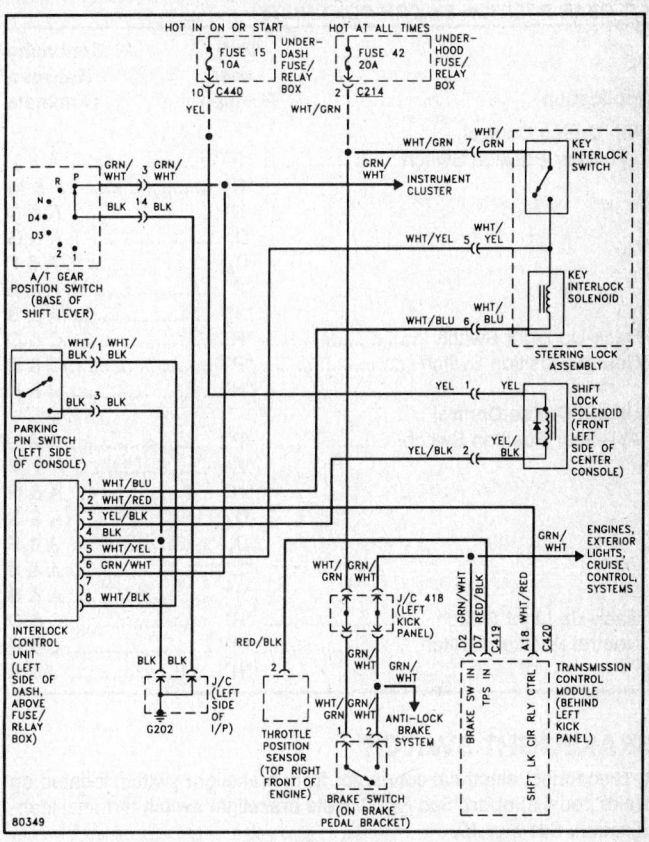

Fig. 17: Shift & Key Interlock System Wiring Schematic

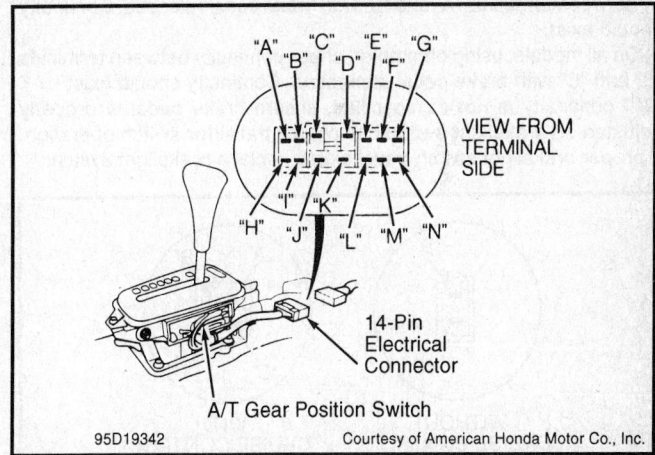

Fig. 18: Identifying A/T Gear Position Switch Electrical Connector Terminals

A/T GEAR POSITION SWITCH CONTINUITY

Application	Shift Lever Position	Continuity Between Terminals
With Cruise Control		
A/T Gear Position Switch	"P"	A & L
	"R"	A & M
	"N"	A & N
	D₄	I, A & G
	D₃	I, A & F
	"2"	I, A & E
	"1"	A & B
Back-Up Light Switch	"R"	C & D
Neutral Position Switch	"P"	J & K
	"N"	J & K
Without Cruise Control		
A/T Gear Position Switch	"P"	A & L
	"R"	A & M
	"N"	A & N
	D₄	A & G
	D₃	A & F
	"2"	A & E
	"1"	A & B
Back-Up Light Switch	"R"	C & D
Neutral Position Switch	"P"	J & K
	"N"	J & K

BRAKELIGHT SWITCH

1) Disconnect electrical connector from brakelight switch, located on brake pedal support. See Fig. 6. Note brakelight switch terminal identification. See Fig. 19.

2) On models with cruise control, using ohmmeter, check for continuity between terminals "A" and "D" with brake pedal released. Continuity should exist.

3) On all models, using ohmmeter, check continuity between terminals "B" and "C" with brake pedal depressed. Continuity should exist.

4) If continuity is not as specified, ensure brake pedal is properly adjusted so brakelight switch has proper travel for switch operation. If proper brakelight switch travel exists, replace brakelight switch.

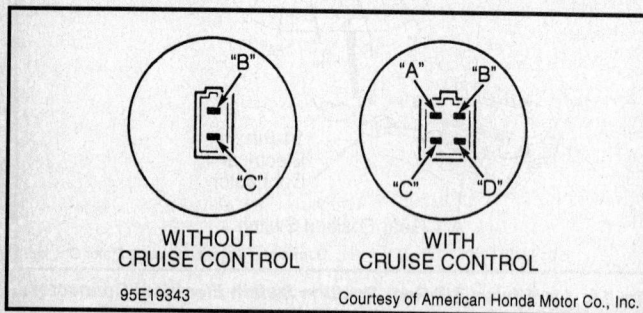

95E19343   Courtesy of American Honda Motor Co., Inc.

Fig. 19: Identifying Brakelight Switch Terminals

COUNTERSHAFT SPEED SENSOR

Disconnect electrical connector from countershaft speed sensor located on top of transaxle. See Fig. 7. Using ohmmeter, measure resistance between terminals of electrical connector. Replace countershaft speed sensor if resistance is not 400-600 ohms.

ENGINE COOLANT TEMPERATURE (ECT) SENSOR

1) Sensor is located on cylinder head, below distributor and contains a Red/White wire and Green/Blue wire in the electrical connector. See Fig. 7.

2) Disconnect electrical connector from sensor. Using ohmmeter, check sensor resistance in accordance with coolant temperature. See Fig. 20. Replace ECT sensor if resistance is not as specified.

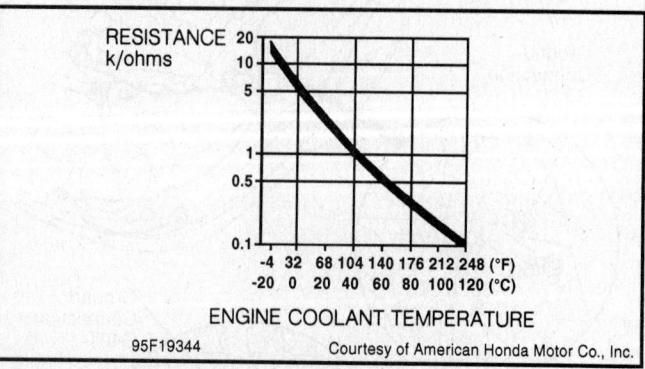

95F19344   Courtesy of American Honda Motor Co., Inc.

Fig. 20: Checking ECT Sensor Resistance

INTERLOCK CONTROL UNIT

1) Remove lower panel from instrument panel. Disconnect 8-pin connector from interlock control unit. Interlock control unit is located under left side of instrument panel. See Fig. 4. Inspect terminals for poor connection, corrosion or bending, repair as necessary.

2) Using DVOM, check for continuity or voltage between specified terminals or body ground. See Fig. 21. If necessary, check ground connections G201 or G401, ground connection G201 is located at passenger's side front corner of engine compartment, on inner fender panel. Ground connection G401 is located behind driver's side of instrument panel, above kick panel. See Fig. 15.

3) If necessary, check No. 42 fuse (20-amp) in engine compartment fuse box, located at passenger's side rear corner of engine compartment. If necessary, check No. 15 fuse (10-amp), fuse is located in fuse box on driver's side of instrument panel, near steering column. If necessary, access TCM, the TCM is located behind glove box and contains 26-pin and 22-pin Gray electrical connectors. See Fig. 6.

KEY INTERLOCK SOLENOID

1) Remove lower cover and knee bolster from driver's side of instrument panel for access to key interlock solenoid 7-pin electrical connector. See Fig. 22.

2) Disconnect key interlock solenoid 7-pin electrical connector from main wiring harness. Note electrical connector terminal identification.

3) Using ohmmeter, check continuity between designated terminals with ignition lock assembly in ACC position. See KEY INTERLOCK SOLENOID CONTINUITY SPECIFICATIONS table.

4) If continuity is as specified, proceed to next step. If continuity is not as specified, replace ignition lock assembly. Key interlock solenoid cannot be serviced separately.

5) Connect battery voltage and ground to terminals No. 6 and 7. Ensure ignition key cannot be removed with battery voltage applied.

6) If ignition key cannot be removed, key interlock solenoid is okay. If ignition key can be removed, replace ignition lock assembly. Key interlock solenoid cannot be serviced separately.

KEY INTERLOCK SOLENOID CONTINUITY SPECIFICATIONS

Ignition Key Position	Continuity Between Terminals
Key Installed	5, 6 & 7
Key Removed	5 & 6

LOCK-UP CONTROL SOLENOID VALVES

1) Lock-up control solenoid valves are located on transaxle. See Fig. 7. Disconnect electrical connector at lock-up control solenoid valves.

2) Using ohmmeter, check resistance between terminal No. 1 (solenoid valve "B") or terminal No. 2 (solenoid valve "A") and body ground. See Fig. 23.

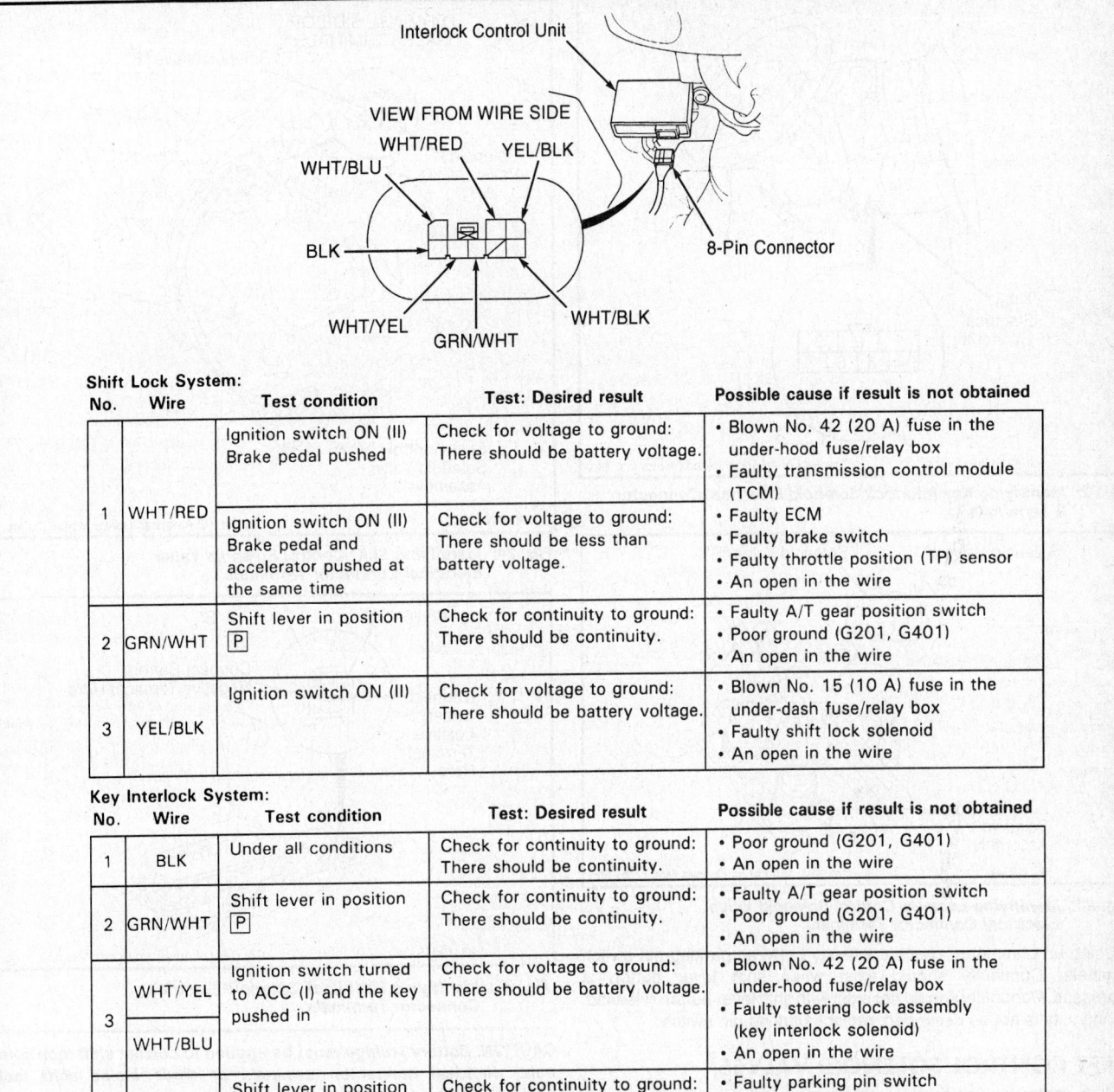

Shift Lock System:

No.	Wire	Test condition	Test: Desired result	Possible cause if result is not obtained
1	WHT/RED	Ignition switch ON (II) Brake pedal pushed	Check for voltage to ground: There should be battery voltage.	• Blown No. 42 (20 A) fuse in the under-hood fuse/relay box • Faulty transmission control module (TCM) • Faulty ECM • Faulty brake switch • Faulty throttle position (TP) sensor • An open in the wire
		Ignition switch ON (II) Brake pedal and accelerator pushed at the same time	Check for voltage to ground: There should be less than battery voltage.	
2	GRN/WHT	Shift lever in position ⓟ	Check for continuity to ground: There should be continuity.	• Faulty A/T gear position switch • Poor ground (G201, G401) • An open in the wire
3	YEL/BLK	Ignition switch ON (II)	Check for voltage to ground: There should be battery voltage.	• Blown No. 15 (10 A) fuse in the under-dash fuse/relay box • Faulty shift lock solenoid • An open in the wire

Key Interlock System:

No.	Wire	Test condition	Test: Desired result	Possible cause if result is not obtained
1	BLK	Under all conditions	Check for continuity to ground: There should be continuity.	• Poor ground (G201, G401) • An open in the wire
2	GRN/WHT	Shift lever in position ⓟ	Check for continuity to ground: There should be continuity.	• Faulty A/T gear position switch • Poor ground (G201, G401) • An open in the wire
3	WHT/YEL WHT/BLU	Ignition switch turned to ACC (I) and the key pushed in	Check for voltage to ground: There should be battery voltage.	• Blown No. 42 (20 A) fuse in the under-hood fuse/relay box • Faulty steering lock assembly (key interlock solenoid) • An open in the wire
4	WHT/BLK	Shift lever in position ⓟ and push button pressed	Check for continuity to ground: There should be continuity.	• Faulty parking pin switch • Poor ground (G201, G401) • An open in the wire
		Shift lever in position ⓟ and push button released	Check for continuity to ground: There should be no continuity.	• Faulty parking pin switch • Short to ground • An open in the wire

96A29884   Courtesy of American Honda Motor Co., Inc.

Fig. 21: Testing Interlock Control Unit

3) Resistance should be 14-25 ohms. Replace lock-up control solenoid valve assembly if resistance of either solenoid valve is not within specification.

4) Check lock-up control solenoid valve operation. Ensure solenoid valve body is grounded. Apply battery voltage to terminal No. 1 (solenoid valve "B") or terminal No. 2 (solenoid valve "A").

5) Clicking sound should be heard, indicating solenoid valve operation. Replace lock-up control solenoid valve assembly if either solenoid valve fails to operate.

MAINSHAFT SPEED SENSOR

Disconnect electrical connector from mainshaft speed sensor located on top of transaxle. *See Fig. 7.* Using ohmmeter, measure resistance between terminals on electrical connector. Replace mainshaft speed sensor if resistance is not 400-600 ohms.

PARKING PIN SWITCH

1) Remove center console. Disconnect parking pin switch 2-pin connector. Parking pin switch is located on left side of shifter assembly.

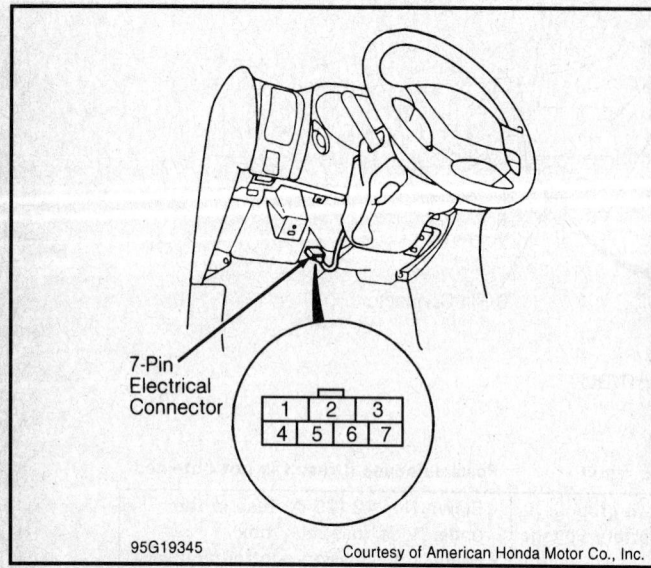

Fig. 22: Identifying Key Interlock Solenoid Electrical Connector & Terminals

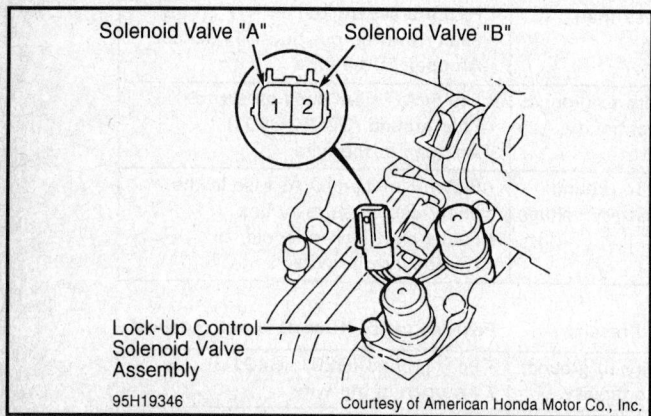

Fig. 23: Identifying Lock-Up Control Solenoid Valve Electrical Connector Terminals

2) Using an ohmmeter, check continuity between parking pin switch terminals. Continuity should exist when shift lever button is depressed. Continuity should not exist with shift lever button released. If continuity is not as described, replace parking pin switch.

SHIFT CONTROL SOLENOID VALVES

1) Shift control solenoid valves are located on transaxle. *See Fig. 7.* Disconnect electrical connector at shift control solenoid valves.

2) Using ohmmeter, check resistance between terminal No. 1 (solenoid valve "A") or terminal No. 3 (solenoid valve "B") and ground. *See Fig. 24.*

3) Resistance should be 14-25 ohms. Replace shift control solenoid valve assembly if resistance of either solenoid valve is not within specification.

4) Check shift control solenoid valve operation. Ensure solenoid valve body is grounded. Apply battery voltage to terminal No. 1 (solenoid valve "A") or terminal No. 3 (solenoid valve "B").

5) Clicking sound should be heard, indicating solenoid valve operation. Replace shift control solenoid valve assembly if either solenoid valve fails to operate.

SHIFT LOCK SOLENOID

1) Remove center console. Disconnect shift lock solenoid 2-pin electrical connector from main wiring harness. Note electrical connector terminal identification. *See Fig. 23.*

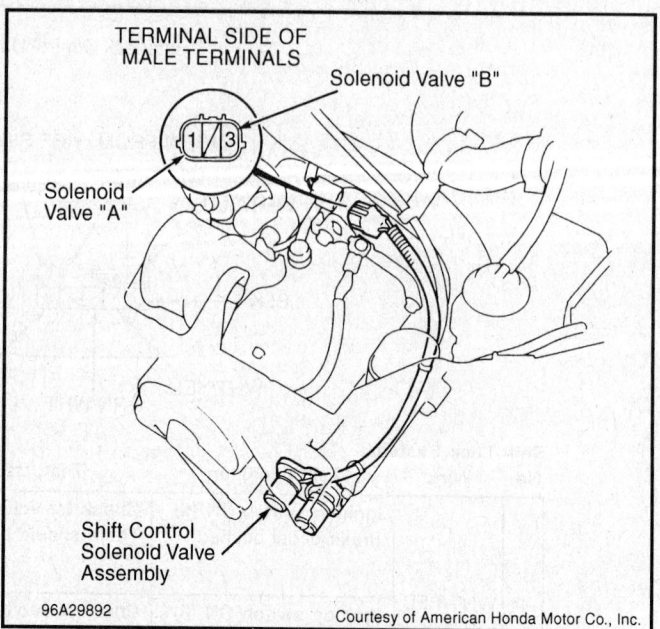

Fig. 24: Identifying Shift Control Solenoid Valve Electrical Connector Terminals

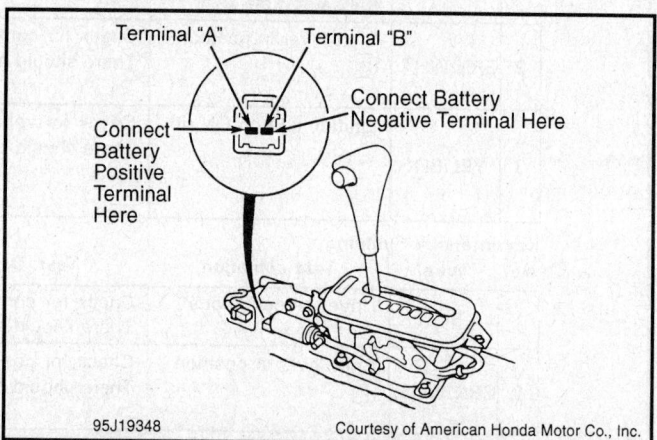

Fig. 25: Identifying Shift Lock Solenoid Electrical Connector Terminals

CAUTION: Battery voltage must be applied to correct shift lock solenoid electrical connector terminals or diode inside shift lock solenoid will be damaged.

2) Momentarily connect battery positive terminal to terminal "A" and battery negative terminal to terminal "B". *See Fig. 25.* Ensure shift lock solenoid operates with battery voltage applied. Replace shift lock solenoid if solenoid fails to operate.

THROTTLE POSITION (TP) SENSOR

TP sensor should input a .5-volt signal to TCM at closed throttle. At full throttle, signal should be approximately 4.5 volts. Voltage should change smoothly as throttle valve is opened and closed. If voltage is not as specified, check throttle position sensor wiring circuit. See WIRING DIAGRAMS.

NOTE: If problem in TP sensor exists, sensor may set DTC P1790 (FLASH CODE NO. 3) in TCM. See RETRIEVING FAULT CODES under SELF-DIAGNOSTIC SYSTEM.

VEHICLE SPEED SENSOR (VSS)

1) Ensure fuse No. 24 fuse (15-amp) in fuse box on driver's side of instrument panel, near steering column is okay. Replace fuse if necessary.

2) Disconnect 3-pin electrical connector from Vehicle Speed Sensor (VSS). The VSS is located on top of transaxle. *See Fig. 7.*

3) Turn ignition on. Measure voltage between Black wire and the Black/Yellow wire on harness side of 3-pin electrical connector. If battery voltage exists, go to step **5)**. If battery voltage does not exist, check continuity between Black wire of 3-pin electrical connector and ground.

4) If continuity exists, check and repair open circuit in Black/Yellow wire between 3-pin electrical connector and fuse No. 24 in fuse box on driver's side of instrument panel. If continuity does not exist, check for open circuit in Black wire to ground. Ground is located on coolant hose housing, just below distributor.

5) Measure voltage between Blue/White wire and Black wire of 3-pin electrical connector. Voltage should be about 5 volts. If voltage is correct, go to next step. If voltage is not about 5 volts, check for open circuit or short to ground in Blue/White wire.

6) Reinstall 3-pin electrical connector on VSS. Raise and support vehicle so front wheels can rotate. Connect voltmeter to Blue/White wire on 3-pin electrical connector and ground.

7) Turn ignition on. Place shift lever in Neutral. Slowly rotate one front wheel while holding remaining front wheel from rotating and note voltage reading.

8) Ensure voltage pulses from zero volts to about 5 volts. If voltage pulses correctly, vehicle speed sensor is okay. If voltage does not pulse correctly, replace vehicle speed sensor. See VEHICLE SPEED SENSOR under REMOVAL & INSTALLATION. Turn ignition off. Remove voltmeter.

REMOVAL & INSTALLATION

A/T GEAR POSITION SWITCH

Removal – Remove center console. Disconnect 14-pin electrical connector from A/T gear position switch. Remove nuts and A/T gear position switch.

Installation – 1) Ensure parking brake is applied. Place switch slider on A/T gear position switch in Neutral position. *See Fig. 26.* Place shift lever in Neutral.

2) Install A/T gear position switch and nuts. DO NOT tighten nuts at this time. The A/T gear position switch must be adjusted.

3) To adjust A/T gear position switch, place shift lever in Park. Ensure retaining nuts are loose. Note 14-pin electrical connector terminal identification. *See Fig. 18.*

4) Connect ohmmeter between terminals "A" and "L". Move A/T gear position switch toward rear of console until continuity exists between

terminals "A" and "L". Free play at lock pin should be .079" (2.0 mm). *See Fig. 26.*

5) Tighten nuts. Check A/T gear position switch for correct continuity in all gears. See A/T GEAR POSITION SWITCH under COMPONENT TESTING. If proper adjustment cannot be obtained, check for damaged shift lever detent or bracket. Install electrical connector and center console.

BRAKELIGHT SWITCH

Removal & Installation – 1) Disconnect electrical connector from brakelight switch. Remove lock nut from brakelight switch. Unscrew brakelight switch and remove. To install, screw brakelight switch inward until brakelight plunger is fully depressed.

2) Back off brakelight switch 1/4 turn. Ensure .010" (.30 mm) clearance exists between threaded end of brakelight switch and pad area on brake pedal. Install and tighten lock nut. Install electrical connector. Ensure brakelights and cruise control operate properly.

COUNTERSHAFT SPEED SENSOR

Removal & Installation – **1)** Disconnect electrical connector at countershaft speed sensor. Countershaft speed sensor is located on top of transaxle. *See Fig. 7.*

2) Remove clamp for the electrical wiring. Remove bolt, countershaft speed sensor and "O" ring. To install, reverse removal procedure using NEW "O" ring. Install and tighten bolt to specification. See TORQUE SPECIFICATIONS.

ENGINE COOLANT TEMPERATURE (ECT) SENSOR

Removal – The ECT sensor is located on cylinder head, below distributor and contains a Red/White wire and Green/Blue wire in the electrical connector. *See Fig. 7.* Drain cooling system. Remove engine coolant temperature sensor.

Installation – Install and tighten engine coolant temperature sensor. Fill cooling system to top of radiator neck. Warm engine until cooling fan turns on and off twice. Finish filling cooling system.

KEY INTERLOCK SOLENOID

Removal & Installation – Key interlock solenoid cannot be serviced separately, as entire ignition lock assembly must be replaced.

LOCK-UP CONTROL SOLENOID VALVES

Removal & Installation – **1)** Lock-up control solenoid valve assembly is located on transaxle. *See Fig. 7.* Disconnect electrical connector at lock-up control solenoid valves.

2) Remove bolts, lock-up control solenoid valve assembly and gasket. To install, reverse removal procedure using NEW gasket. Tighten bolts to specification. See TORQUE SPECIFICATIONS.

MAINSHAFT SPEED SENSOR

Removal & Installation – **1)** Disconnect electrical connector at mainshaft speed sensor. Mainshaft speed sensor is located on top of transaxle. *See Fig. 7.*

2) Remove clamp for the electrical wiring. Remove bolt, mainshaft speed sensor and "O" ring. To install, reverse removal procedure using NEW "O" ring. Install and tighten bolt to specification. See TORQUE SPECIFICATIONS.

SHIFT CONTROL SOLENOID VALVES

Removal & Installation – **1)** Shift control solenoid valve assembly is located on transaxle. *See Fig. 7.* Disconnect electrical connector at shift control solenoid valves.

2) Remove bolts, shift control solenoid valve assembly and gasket. To install, reverse removal procedure using NEW gasket. Tighten bolts to specification. See TORQUE SPECIFICATIONS.

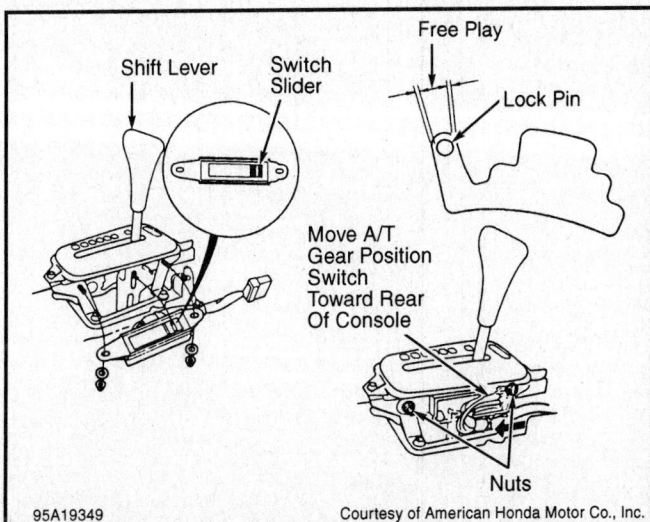

95A19349   Courtesy of American Honda Motor Co., Inc.

Fig. 26: Installing A/T Gear Position Switch

SHIFT LOCK SOLENOID

Removal – Remove center console. Disconnect electrical connector at shift lock solenoid. Remove collar and pin from shift lock solenoid. Remove nuts and shift lock solenoid.

Installation – **1)** Install shift lock solenoid with NEW nuts snugly installed. Install pin, collar and electrical connector.

2) Turn ignition on. With shift lock solenoid energized (ON position), ensure clearance between top of shift lock lever and lock pin groove is .079-.118" (2.0-3.0 mm). See Fig. 27.

3) If clearance is not as specified, loosen nuts and reposition shift lock solenoid until correct clearance is obtained. Once correct clearance is obtained, tighten nuts to specification. See TORQUE SPECIFICATIONS.

4) Turn ignition off. With shift lock solenoid de-energized (OFF position), ensure lock pin is blocked by shift lock lever. See Fig. 26. Check solenoid operation several times to ensure proper operation.

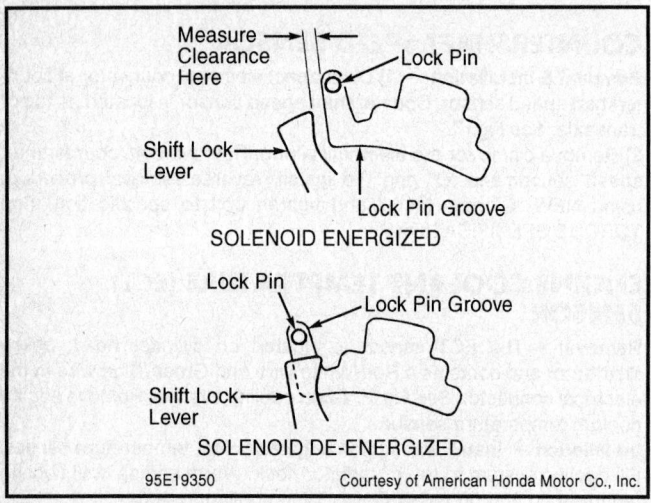

Fig. 27: Checking Shift Lock Solenoid Operation

THROTTLE POSITION (TP) SENSOR

Removal & Installation – TP sensor is mounted on side of throttle body. Replacement information is not available.

VEHICLE SPEED SENSOR (VSS)

Removal & Installation – **1)** Disconnect electrical connector from vehicle speed sensor, located on top of transaxle. See Fig. 7.

2) Remove bolts and vehicle speed sensor. DO NOT lose small drive link, located between vehicle speed sensor and adapter body on transaxle. To install, reverse removal procedure. Install and tighten bolts to specification. See TORQUE SPECIFICATIONS.

TORQUE SPECIFICATIONS

TORQUE SPECIFICATIONS

Application	INCH Lbs. (N.m)
Air Bleeder Bolt	87 (9.8)
Countershaft Speed Sensor Bolt	106 (12.0)
Lock-Up Control Solenoid Valve Assembly Bolt	106 (12.0)
Mainshaft Speed Sensor Bolt	106 (12.0)
Shift Control Solenoid Valve Assembly Bolt	106 (12.0)
Shift Lock Solenoid Nut	87 (9.8)
Vehicle Speed Sensor Bolt	87 (9.8)

WIRING DIAGRAMS

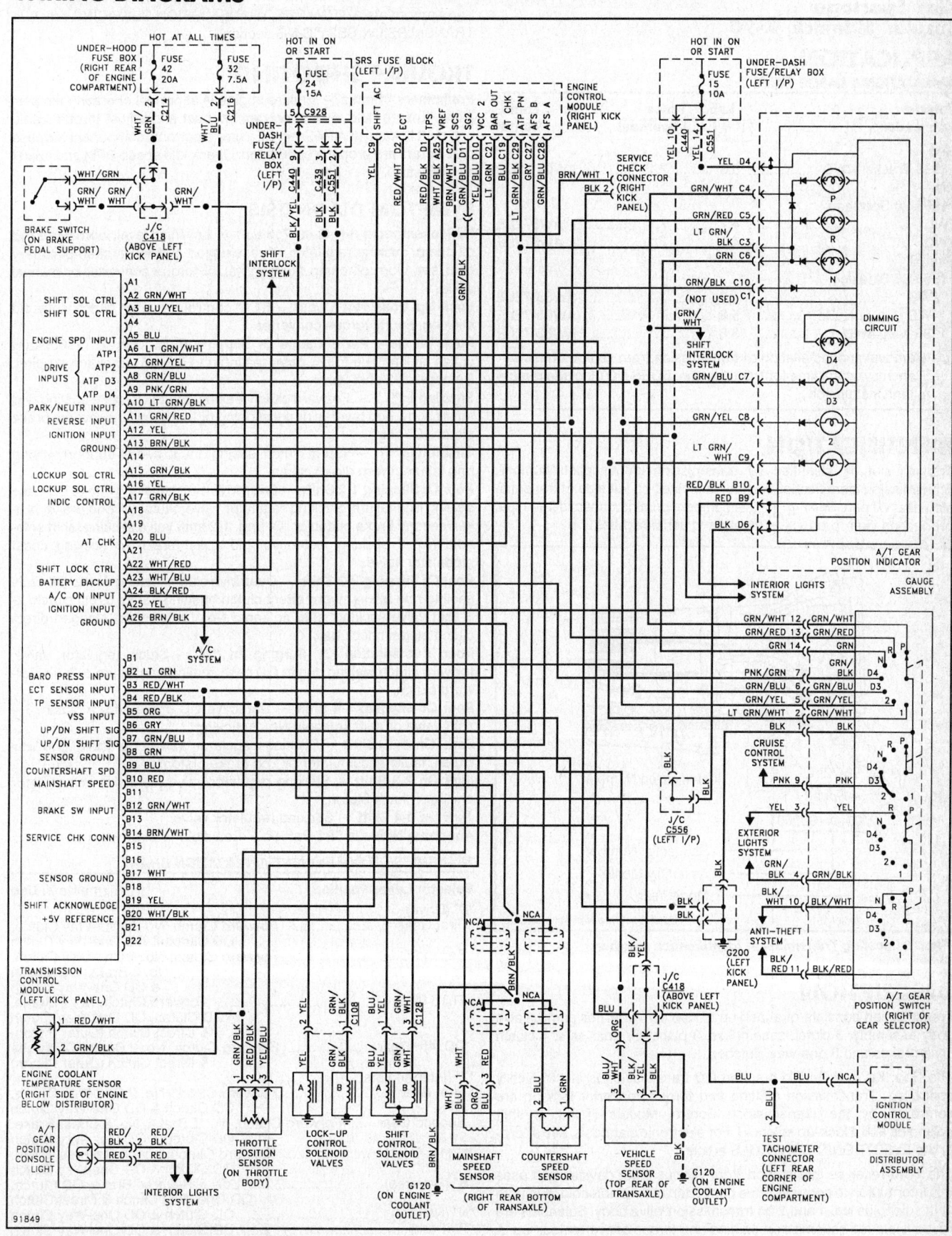

Fig. 28: *Transaxle Wiring Diagram (1996 Acura Integra)*

91849

AUTOMATIC TRANSMISSIONS
Aisin Warner AW03-72LE 4-Speed

Geo: Tracker
Kia: Sportage
Suzuki: Sidekick, X-90

APPLICATION

APPLICATION & LABOR TIMES

Vehicle Application	Labor Times [1] R & I	[2] Overhaul	Trans. Model
Geo			
1996 Tracker 4WD	5.8	7.1	AW03-72LE
Kia			
1995-96 Sportage			
2WD	4.7	7.1	AW372LE
4WD	4.7	7.1	AW372LE
Suzuki			
1995-96 Sidekick			
2WD	4.8	7.1	AW03-72LE
4WD	5.8	7.1	AW03-72LE
1996 X-90 4WD	5.8	7.1	AW03-72LE

[1] – Removal and installation of transmission from vehicle chassis.
[2] – Bench overhaul time for transmission. DOES NOT include removal and installation.

IDENTIFICATION

Transmission is identified by transmission identification number. Transmission identification number is located on left side of transmission near oil pan. *See Fig. 1.* This number contains transmission type, production year, production month and serial number.

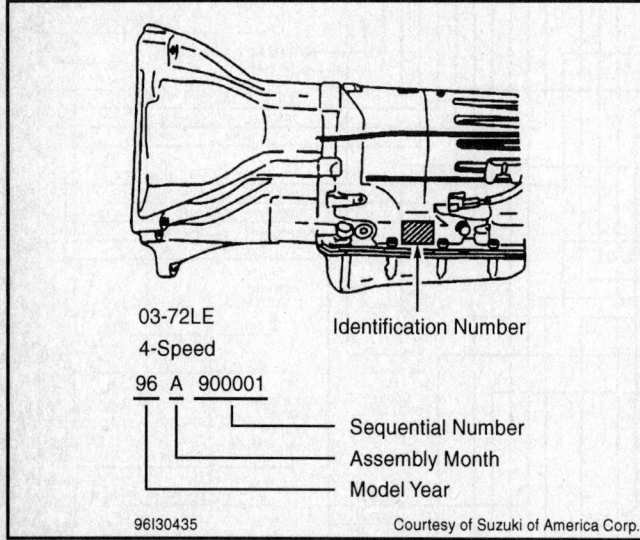

03-72LE
4-Speed

96 A 900001

Identification Number

Sequential Number
Assembly Month
Model Year

96I30435   Courtesy of Suzuki of America Corp.

Fig. 1: Locating Transmission Identification Number

DESCRIPTION

Transmission consists of a lock-up torque converter, oil pump, valve body assembly, 3 clutch assemblies, 3 planetary gear sets, 4 clutch style brakes and 3 one-way clutches.

The Geo, Kia and Suzuki 4-speed OD transmission is electronically controlled. Transmission shifting and torque converter lock-up are controlled by the Transmission Control Module (TCM), 2 shift solenoids and a lock-up solenoid. For electronic diagnosis, see appropriate ELECTRONIC CONTROLS article.

The TCM receives information from various input devices and uses this information to control torque converter lock-up solenoid, and both shift solenoids No. 1 and 2 on transmission valve body. Solenoids are responsible for transmission shifting and torque converter lock-up. A mode switch is mounted on console and is used to change TCM shift program from Economy to Power.

LUBRICATION & ADJUSTMENTS

See appropriate AUTOMATIC TRANSMISSION SERVICING article in TRANSMISSION SERVICING section.

TROUBLE SHOOTING

Preliminary Checks – Ensure engine is at normal operating temperature. Ensure fluid level is correct. Inspect and adjust throttle cable and shift linkage (if necessary). Ensure electronic component harness connectors are properly connected. Check idle speed RPM and adjust if necessary.

SYMPTOM DIAGNOSIS

No Movement In Any Gear Position – Low fluid level, worn or seized oil pump, sticking regulator valve, clogged oil filter, broken planetary gear set, worn oil pump bushing, faulty torque converter or manual valve.

Lock-Up Does Not Occur – TCC control valve or clutch solenoid sticking. Faulty torque converter.

Poor 1st Gear Performance Or Slipping In "D" Or "2" – Forward clutch leaking due to OD case sealing ring failure. OD clutch slipping. Defective 1-2 shift valve.

Slipping In "L" – Forward clutch leaking due to OD case sealing ring failure. Low and reverse brake slipping or faulty low and reverse brake piston "O" ring.

Slipping In "R" – Direct clutch leaking due to center support sealing ring failure. Worn direct clutch.

Poor Or Slipping 1-2 Shift – Overdrive clutch leaking due to OD case sealing ring failure. Sticking regulator valve, faulty second brake, broken second brake piston or "O" ring, 1-2 shift valve sticking, shift solenoid No. 2 sticking, defective 2nd coast brake or sticking coast modulator valve.

Poor Or Slipping 2-3 Shift – Overdrive clutch leaking due to OD case sealing ring failure, worn direct clutch bushing, faulty direct clutch, 2-3 shift valve sticking, shift solenoid No. 1 sticking or clogged direct clutch piston check ball.

Poor Acceleration Or Surging In "D" – Stuck regulator valve, forward clutch leaking due to OD case sealing ring failure or faulty forward clutch.

Poor Or Slipping 3-4 Shift – Defective OD brake and/or clutch. 3-4 shift valve or shift solenoid No. 2 sticking.

Jerk On 1-2 Shift – Sticking regulator valve, defective one-way clutch, faulty accumulator or 2nd brake piston.

Jerk On 2-3 Shift – Sticking regulator valve, defective accumulator or direct clutch piston.

Jerk On 3-4 Shift – Sticking regulator valve.

Abnormal Noise in "P" Or "N" – Low fluid level or worn oil pump.

TRANSMISSION COMPONENT APPLICATION CHART

Selector Lever Position	Elements In Use
"D" (Drive)	
First Gear	Forward Clutch, No. 2 One-Way Clutch, OD Clutch & OD One-Way Clutch
Second Gear	Forward Clutch, No. 1 One-Way Clutch, No. 2 Brake, OD Clutch & OD One-Way Clutch
Third Gear	Forward Clutch, No. 2 Brake, OD Clutch, OD One-Way Clutch & Direct Clutch (Outer Piston)
OD (4th Gear)	Forward Clutch, No. 2 Brake, OD Brake & Direct Clutch (Outer Piston)
"2" (Intermediate)	
First Gear	Forward Clutch, No. 2 One-Way Clutch, OD Clutch & OD One-Way Clutch
Second Gear	Forward Clutch, No. 2 Brake, No. 2 Coast Brake, OD Clutch & OD One-Way Clutch
"L" (1st Gear)	Forward Clutch, Low & Reverse Brake, OD Clutch & OD One-Way Clutch
"R" (Reverse)	Low & Reverse Brake, OD Clutch, OD One-Way Clutch & Direct Clutch
"N" (Neutral)	OD Clutch & OD One-Way Clutch
"P" (Park)	OD Clutch & OD One-Way Clutch

TESTING

NOTE: For electronic diagnosis and component testing of Aisin Warner AW03-72LE 4-speed transmission, see appropriate ELECTRONIC CONTROLS article.

PRELIMINARY CHECKS

1) Before testing transmission, ensure fluid level is correct and selector lever, throttle cable and idle speed are adjusted correctly. Battery must be fully charged for accurate testing.

2) To aid in transmission fault diagnosis, determine if fault is hydraulic, electronic or a combination of both. Electronic control transmissions are capable of storing self-diagnostic codes. To determine if a fault is electrical, retrieve any stored diagnostic trouble codes. See appropriate ELECTRONIC CONTROLS article for electronic diagnosis.

TIME LAG TEST

1) Engine and transmission must be at normal operating temperature. Start engine and ensure idle RPM is within specification with A/C off. Apply service and parking brakes. Block all 4 wheels. Using stop watch, measure amount of time until engagement shock is felt when selector lever is shifted from "N" to "D" position.

2) Allow one minute intervals between tests. Perform time measurements 2 more times and calculate average value. Time should be less than 1.2 seconds. Repeat test procedure to test time lag when selector lever is shifted from "N" to "R" position. Time lag should be less than 1.5 seconds.

Time Lag Test Results

- **"N" To "D" Position Time Lag Is Greater Than Specified:** Low line pressure, worn forward clutch or improper OD one-way clutch operation.
- **"N" To "R" Position Time Lag Is Greater Than Specified:** Low line pressure, worn direct clutch or low and reverse brake slipping.

ROAD TEST

"D" Position Test – 1) Engine and transmission must be at normal operating temperature. Shift transmission into "D" position. Accelerate vehicle by depressing accelerator pedal gradually. Ensure all upshifts and downshifts occur at specified points. Refer to appropriate SHIFT SPEED SPECIFICATIONS table.

2) Ensure lock-up occurs at appropriate speeds. See appropriate LOCK-UP SPEED SPECIFICATIONS table. Lightly depress accelerator pedal. If excessive increase in engine RPM is present, lock-up will not occur.

3) Check for shock and slippage at all upshifts. Check for abnormal noise and vibration. While driving in "D", "2" and "L" gear positions, ensure speeds at 2-1, 3-2 and OD-3 kickdown are within specification. Check for shock and slippage at kickdown.

"D" Position Test Results

- **No 1-2 Upshift:** Stuck 1-2 shift valve or stuck shift solenoid No. 2.
- **No 2-3 Upshift:** Stuck 2-3 shift valve or stuck shift solenoid No. 1.
- **No 3-OD Upshift:** Stuck 3-OD shift valve or stuck shift solenoids No. 1 or 2.
- **Incorrect Shift Point:** Check for misadjusted throttle cable or stuck shift valves.

"2" Position Test – Shift transmission to "2" position. Accelerate vehicle and verify 1-2 upshift is obtained at specified throttle positions. See appropriate SHIFT SPEED SPECIFICATIONS table. While driving vehicle in 2nd gear, release accelerator and check engine braking effect. If engine braking is not present, No. 1 brake is faulty.

"L" Position Test – While driving vehicle in "L" position, verify no upshift occurs to 2nd gear. Check engine braking effect when accelerator is released. If engine braking is not present, low and reverse brake is defective.

"R" Position Test – Shift vehicle to "R" position. Accelerate vehicle and check for transmission slippage.

"P" Position Test – Stop vehicle on incline. Shift vehicle to "P" position and release parking brake. Ensure parking lock pawl prevents vehicle from moving.

SHIFT SPEED SPECIFICATIONS (GEO & SUZUKI)

Application In "D" Position	Full Throttle MPH	Closed Throttle MPH
Power Mode		
1st-2nd	31	11
2nd-3rd	59	23
3rd-OD	83	30
OD-3rd	75	22
3rd-2nd	53	18
2nd-1st	26	4
Economy Mode		
1st-2nd	28	10
2nd-3rd	52	20
3rd-OD	75	28
OD-3rd	70	22
3rd-2nd	46	18
2nd-1st	24	4

SHIFT SPEED SPECIFICATIONS (KIA)

Application In "D" Position	Full Throttle MPH	Closed Throttle MPH
Power Mode		
1st-2nd	34	11
2nd-3rd	61	19
3rd-OD	93	27
OD-3rd	84	24
3rd-2nd	56	14
2nd-1st	28	6
Economy Mode		
1st-2nd	32	9
2nd-3rd	60	15
3rd-OD	88	24
OD-3rd	78	19
3rd-2nd	56	12
2nd-1st	28	8

LOCK-UP SPEED SPECIFICATIONS (GEO & SUZUKI) [1]

Application	MPH
Lock-Up ON	
3rd	29
OD	36
Lock-Up OFF	
3rd	23
OD	32

[1] – With vehicle in "D"' position and throttle angle at 5 percent.

LOCK-UP SPEED SPECIFICATIONS (KIA) [1]

Application	MPH
Lock-Up ON	
3rd	[2]
OD	47
Lock-Up OFF	
OD	39

[1] – With vehicle in "D"' position and throttle angle at 5 percent.
[2] – Lock-up does not occur in 3rd gear.

STALL SPEED TEST

1) Ensure engine and transmission are at normal operating temperature. Check fluid level and add if necessary. Connect tachometer to vehicle and ensure it is visible to driver. Apply parking brake and block all 4 wheels.

CAUTION: DO NOT maintain stall speed RPM for more than 5 seconds. Ensure at least a 30 second pause at idle between tests.

2) Start engine, apply brakes and place transmission in "D" position. Depress accelerator to full throttle and note maximum RPM obtained. Repeat test in "L" and "R" positions. Stall speed should be 2300-2600 RPM (Geo & Suzuki), or 2000-2300 RPM (Kia).

Stall Speed Test Results
- **Stall Speed Is Same In All Positions, But Less Than Specified:** Engine output may be insufficient or defective torque converter.
- **Stall Speed High In "D" Position:** Low line pressure, slipping forward clutch, slipping OD clutch, defective OD one-way clutch or OD one-way clutch No. 2.
- **Stall Speed High In "L" Position:** Low line pressure or slipping low and reverse brake.
- **Stall Speed High In "R" Position:** Low line pressure, slipping direct clutch, OD clutch, low and reverse brake or defective OD one-way clutch.

HYDRAULIC PRESSURE TESTS

NOTE: Hydraulic pressure tests should be performed with transmission fluid temperature at normal operating temperature of 158-176°F (70-80°C).

Line Pressure Test – 1) Ensure transmission fluid is at normal operating temperature. Check fluid level and add if necessary. Connect appropriate pressure gauge to line pressure test port on transmission with a 90 degree fitting to clear exhaust. *See Fig. 2.*
2) Connect tachometer to vehicle and ensure it is visible to driver. Block all 4 wheels and fully apply parking brake. Start engine and ensure idle speed is adjusted to specification.

CAUTION: DO NOT maintain stall speed RPM for more than 5 seconds. Ensure at least a one minute pause at idle between tests.

3) Apply service brake and shift transmission to "D" position. Check line pressure at idle and record pressure reading. Accelerate vehicle to stall speed and record line pressure reading.
4) Repeat test procedure in "L" and "R" positions. If line pressures are not as specified, check throttle cable adjustment. Adjust throttle cable (if necessary), and repeat test procedure and record pressure readings. Compare all readings to specification. See LINE PRESSURE SPECIFICATIONS table.

LINE PRESSURE SPECIFICATIONS

Engine Speed	"D" & "L" Positions psi (kg/cm²)	"R" Position psi (kg/cm²)
Idle Speed	53-58 (3.7-4.1)	79-86 (5.6-6.0)
Stall Speed	136-156 (9.6-11.0)	188-233 (13.2-16.4)

Line Pressure Test Results
- **Line Pressure High In Both Positions:** Defective regulator valve or throttle valve, or throttle cable out of adjustment.
- **Line Pressure Low In Both Positions:** Defective oil pump, regulator valve, throttle valve or OD clutch, or throttle cable out of adjustment.
- **Line Pressure Low In "D" Position Only:** Defective forward or OD clutch or fluid leak in "D" position circuit.
- **Line Pressure Low In "R" Position Only:** Defective direct clutch, OD clutch, reverse brake or fluid leak in "R" position circuit.

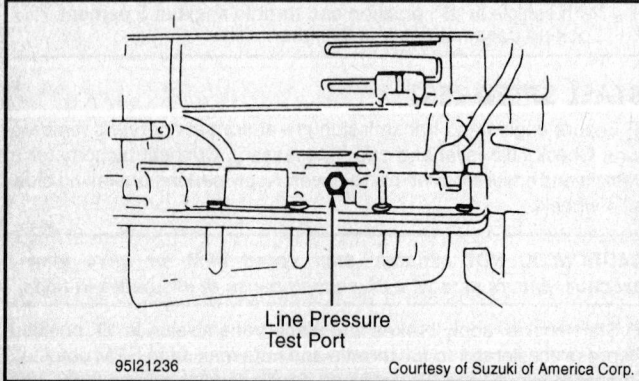

Line Pressure
Test Port

95I21236   Courtesy of Suzuki of America Corp.

Fig. 2: Identifying Transmission Hydraulic Pressure Test Ports

ON-VEHICLE SERVICE
VALVE BODY ASSEMBLY

Removal – Remove drain plug and drain ATF. Remove oil pan and gasket. Remove magnets from oil pan. Note location of oil tubes. *See Fig. 7.* Using screwdrivers, carefully pry at both ends of oil tubes and remove oil tubes. Disconnect solenoid wiring. Remove oil strainer (filter) and gasket. Remove valve body assembly retaining bolts. Note bolt location and length. *See Fig. 3.* Slightly lower valve body assembly. Disconnect throttle cable from valve assembly cam. Remove control valve assembly.
Installation – 1) To install, reverse removal procedure. Ensure manual shift lever in transmission case aligns with manual valve of valve body assembly. Connect throttle cable to cam.
2) Loosely install appropriate bolts in correct positions. *See Fig. 3.* Install valve assembly and torque to specification. See TORQUE SPECIFICATIONS. Install oil tubes in proper order. *See Fig. 7.* Install oil strainer and torque to specification. Ensure magnets are installed in oil pan. Install oil pan and torque to specification. Fill transmission with ATF to proper level.

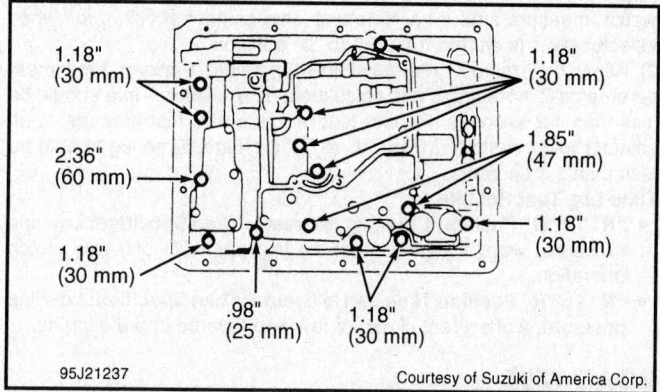

95J21237   Courtesy of Suzuki of America Corp.

Fig. 3: Identifying Valve Body Bolt Length & Locations

PARK/NEUTRAL POSITION (PNP) SWITCH

NOTE: PNP switch may also be known as Transmission Range (TR) switch.

For PNP switch adjustment, see appropriate AUTOMATIC TRANSMISSION SERVICING article in TRANSMISSION SERVICING section.

SHIFT LINKAGE

For shift linkage adjustment, see appropriate AUTOMATIC TRANSMISSION SERVICING article in TRANSMISSION SERVICING section.

THROTTLE CABLE

For throttle cable adjustment, see appropriate AUTOMATIC TRANSMISSION SERVICING article in TRANSMISSION SERVICING section.

REMOVAL & INSTALLATION

For transmission removal and installation procedure, see appropriate AUTOMATIC TRANSMISSION REMOVAL article in TRANSMISSION SERVICING section.

TORQUE CONVERTER

NOTE: Torque converter is a sealed unit and must be serviced as a complete assembly. Perform the following tests to check torque converter condition. Torque converter and transmission oil cooler must be thoroughly cleaned and flushed if transmission fluid is contaminated.

ONE-WAY CLUTCH TEST

1) Install turner and stopper of one-way clutch tester in torque converter. *See Fig. 4.* Turner fits in inner race of one-way clutch. Stopper fits in notch of converter hub and outer race of one-way clutch.
2) Clutch should lock when rotated counterclockwise, and turn freely when rotated clockwise. If necessary, clean torque converter and retest clutch. Replace torque converter if clutch fails test.

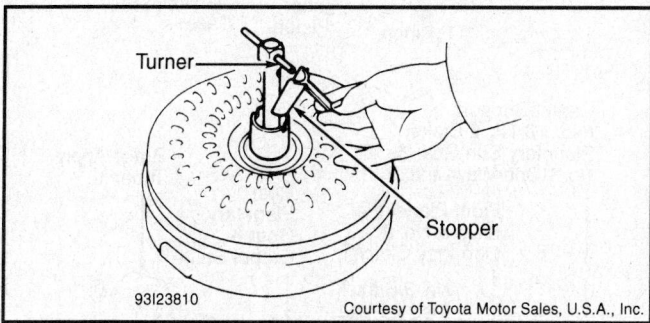

93I23810   Courtesy of Toyota Motor Sales, U.S.A., Inc.

Fig. 4: Checking Torque Converter One-Way Clutch

DRIVE PLATE RUNOUT TEST

Measure drive plate runout. *See Fig. 5.* If runout exceeds .008" (.20 mm), or if ring gear is damaged, replace drive plate. If installing a new drive plate, note position of spacers. Torque to specification. See TORQUE SPECIFICATIONS.

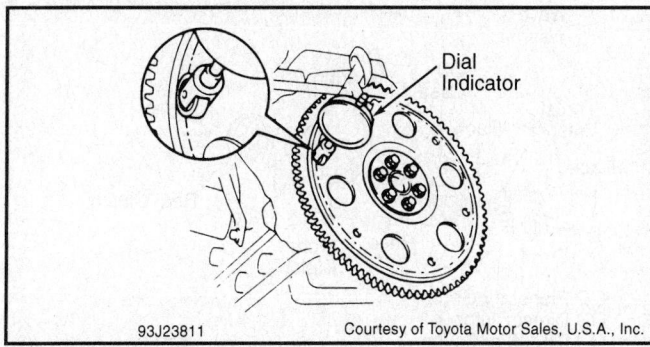

93J23811   Courtesy of Toyota Motor Sales, U.S.A., Inc.

Fig. 5: Checking Drive Plate Runout

CONVERTER SLEEVE RUNOUT TEST

1) Temporarily mount torque converter to drive plate. Mount a dial indicator with needle resting on torque converter sleeve. *See Fig. 6.* Rotate torque converter. If runout exceeds .012" (.30 mm), ensure torque converter is properly mounted to drive plate, and drive plate is not bent or broken.
2) If torque converter is properly mounted and runout exceeds specification, replace torque converter. Mark position of torque converter to ensure correct installation. Remove torque converter from drive plate.

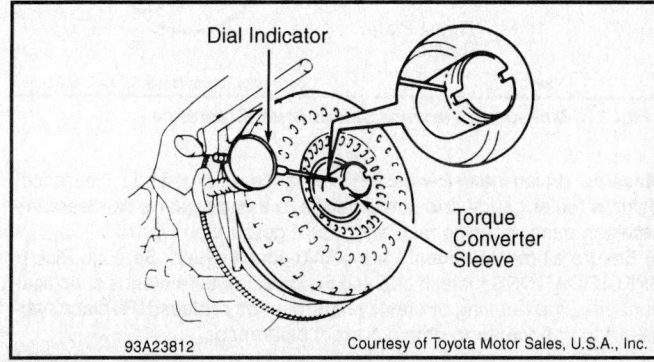

93A23812   Courtesy of Toyota Motor Sales, U.S.A., Inc.

Fig. 6: Checking Torque Converter Sleeve Runout

TRANSMISSION DISASSEMBLY

1) Remove torque converter. Remove oil filler tube. Remove vent hose and speed sensor. Unbolt and remove transfer case-to-transmission adapter or extension housing. Remove snap ring from output shaft and remove speed sensor rotor.
2) Remove manual lever from manual shaft. Remove lock plate from Park/Neutral Position (PNP) switch. Remove PNP switch. Remove oil pump bolts. Using appropriate 2-jaw puller, remove oil pump from transmission case. Remove bearing and race from rear of oil pump. Remove torque converter housing bolts. Note length and bolt location. While holding OD input shaft, remove torque converter housing. Remove "O" ring from transmission case.
3) Remove oil pan and gasket. Remove magnets from oil pan. Inspect magnets and pan for metal or brass particles. Remove oil tubes by carefully prying both ends of tube with screwdriver. *See Fig. 7.* Remove solenoid wiring harness from transmission case. Remove oil strainer (filter) and gasket. Remove valve body assembly. See VALVE BODY ASSEMBLY under ON-VEHICLE SERVICE.

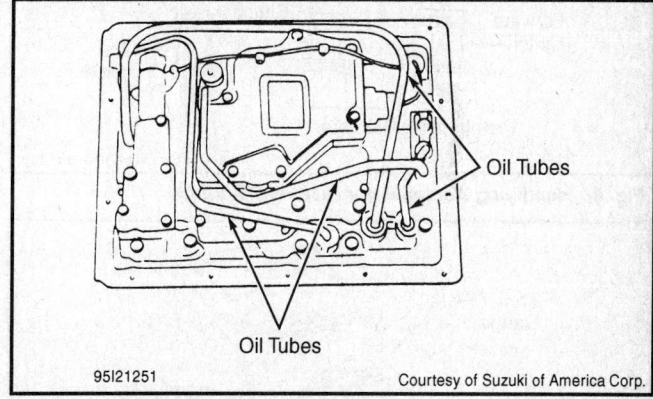

95I21251   Courtesy of Suzuki of America Corp.

Fig. 7: Identifying Oil Tube Locations

4) Remove throttle cable and "O" ring. Place a clean shop cloth over accumulator pistons. Apply compressed air to oil passages of transmission case to remove accumulator pistons and springs. Air passages are at base of accumulator bores. *See Fig. 8.* Note spring and piston locations.
5) Remove parking lock rod bracket and rod. Remove parking lock pawl, pivot pin and spring. If manual valve lever shaft requires removal, use a hammer and chisel to cut spacer and slide spacer toward lever to obtain clearance to shaft pin. Drive out roll pin. Remove shaft and spacer. Remove oil seals.
6) Position transmission case with front of case facing upward. Push input shaft and drum toward rear of transmission case to ensure OD direct clutch is installed correctly. Using calipers and appropriate thrust plate gauge (straightedge), measure distance between top of case and OD direct clutch drum. *See Fig. 9.*
7) Record measurement for reassembly reference. Remove OD planetary gear with OD direct clutch and one-way clutch from OD case. Note location of thrust washer and race on clutch assembly. Hold both sides of OD case and remove from transmission case. Note location of bearing and race. *See Fig. 10.*
8) Push input shaft and drum toward rear of transmission case. Ensure forward clutch is installed correctly. Using calipers and thrust plate gauge (straightedge) measure distance between top of case and forward clutch drum. *See Fig. 11.* Record measurement for reassembly reference.
9) Remove forward clutch assembly from transmission case. Note location of bearings and race. Remove direct clutch assembly. Remove center support-to-case retaining bolts. Bolts are located at valve body side of case.
10) Remove center support and sun gear assembly from transmission case. Note direction of bearing race on end of sun gear. Using 2 screwdrivers, remove front planetary gear snap ring. Remove snap ring. Insert 2 wires into planetary gear and remove gear. Using calipers, measure pack clearance of reverse brake between disc and

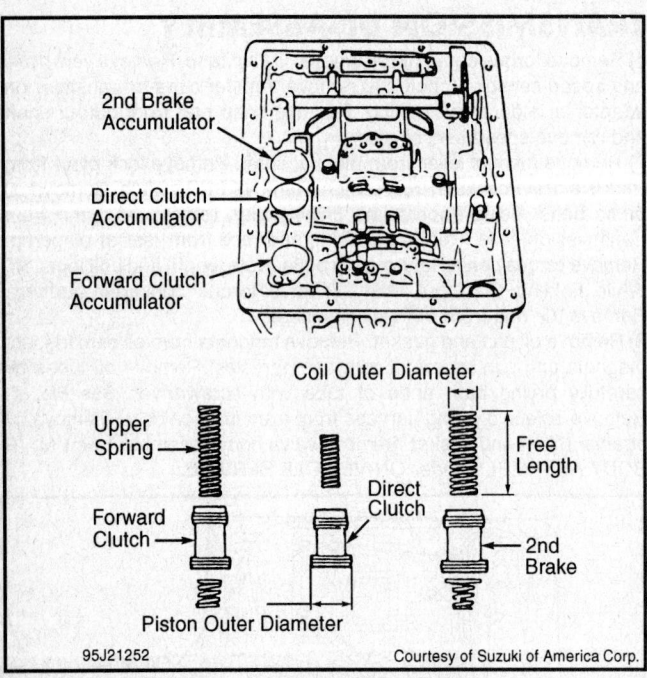

Fig. 8: Identifying Accumulator Pistons & Springs

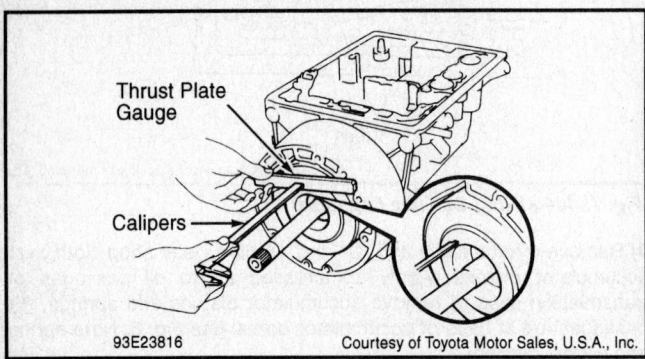

Fig. 9: Measuring OD Direct Clutch Drum Clearance

transmission case. See Fig. 12. Pack clearance should be .029-.098" (.74-2.50 mm). If clearance is not as specified, inspect brake discs.

11) Remove reverse brake pack and pressure plate. Remove rear planetary gear, output shaft and 2 bearings. Remove brake applying cover. See Fig. 13. Remove race from transmission case. Ensure reverse brake pistons move smoothly when applying compressed air into transmission case. See Fig. 14.

12) Using appropriate spring compressor, compress 1st and reverse brake return spring. Remove snap ring. Remove piston return spring. Hold outer piston with hand, apply compressed air to case and remove outer piston. Gradually lift reaction sleeve out of transmission case. Lift piston out of transmission case. See Fig. 10.

COMPONENT DISASSEMBLY & REASSEMBLY

OIL PUMP

Disassembly – Place oil pump assembly on torque converter. Remove sealing rings from stator shaft. Remove stator shaft from oil pump housing. Place reference mark on drive and driven gears and remove from pump housing. If oil seal requires replacement, pry seal from housing with a screwdriver. See Fig. 15.

Inspection – 1) Clean all components in solvent. Dry with compressed air. Inspect all components for damage or wear. Measure inside diameter of oil pump housing and stator shaft bushings.

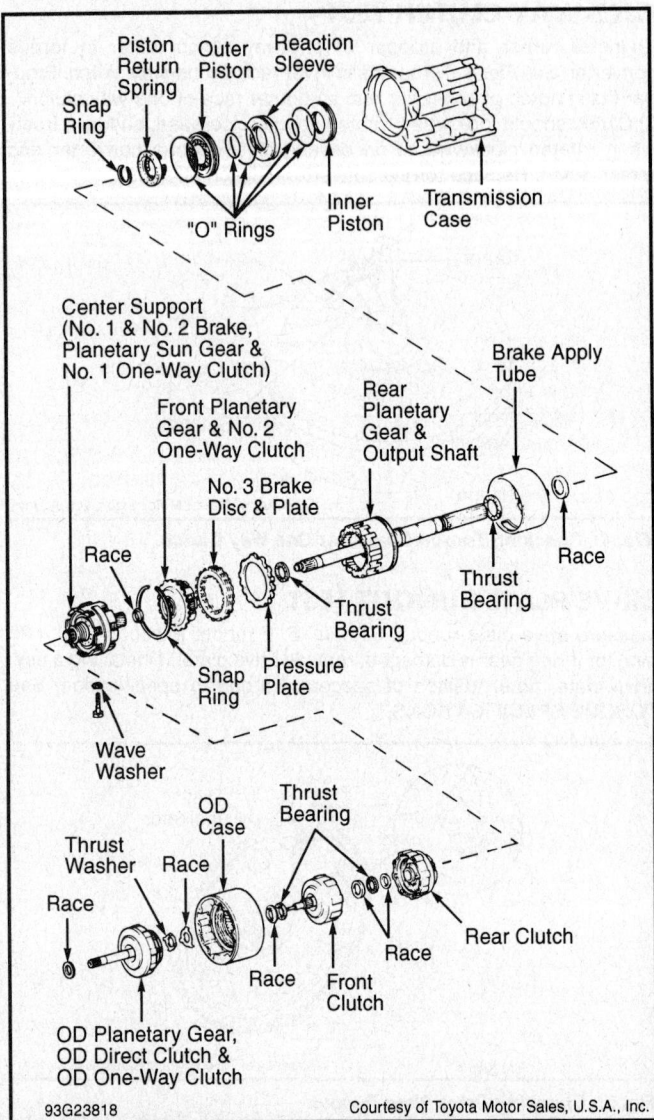

Fig. 10: Identifying Transmission Case Internal Components

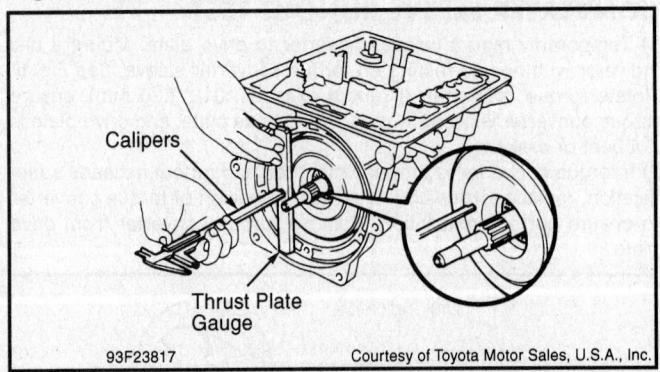

Fig. 11: Measuring Forward Clutch Drum Clearance

Measure driven gear-to-housing clearance and gear tip clearance. Using a feeler gauge and straightedge, measure gear side clearance between pump housing face and top of gears. See Fig. 16.

2) Ensure all measurements are within specification. See OIL PUMP SPECIFICATIONS table. If bushing inside diameter exceeds specification, oil pump housing or stator shaft must be replaced. Replace necessary components to obtain correct clearances.

OIL PUMP SPECIFICATIONS

Application	Standard In. (mm)	Maximum In. (mm)
Gear Side Clearance	.0028-.0059 (.07-.15)	.0118 (.30)
Gear Tip Clearance	.0043-.0055 (.11-.14)	.0118 (.30)
Gear-To-Housing	.0008-.0019 (.02-.05)	.0039 (.10)

Reassembly – 1) Place oil pump housing on torque converter. Coat all components with ATF. Align reference marks on driven and drive gears during installation. Align bolt holes and place stator shaft onto pump housing. Install but do not tighten attaching bolts. Install an oil pump aligning tool around outside of pump assembly to align pump housing and stator shaft. See Fig. 17.

2) Torque oil pump bolts to specification. See TORQUE SPECIFICATIONS. Remove aligning tool. Install oil sealing rings. DO NOT spread ring ends more than necessary for installation. Ensure sealing rings move smoothly after installation. Ensure pump drive gear rotates smoothly. Lubricate and install "O" ring on oil pump assembly.

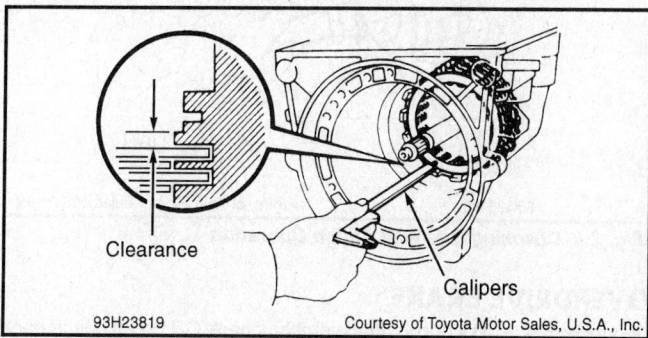

Fig. 12: Measuring Reverse Brake Pack Clearance

Fig. 13: Locating Brake Applying Cover

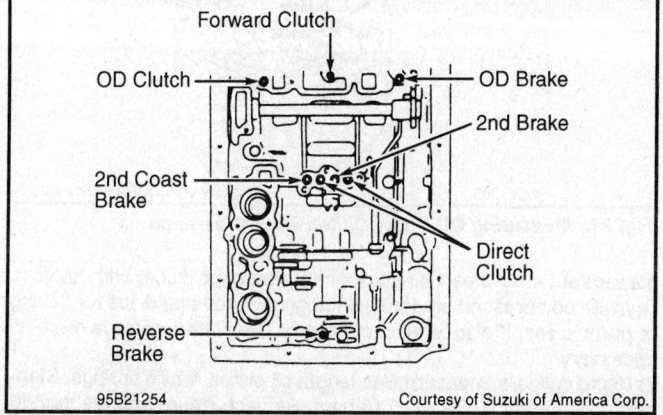

Fig. 14: Identifying Oil Supply Ports

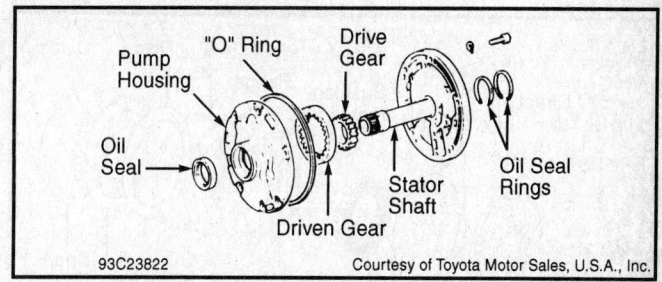

Fig. 15: Exploded View Of Oil Pump Assembly

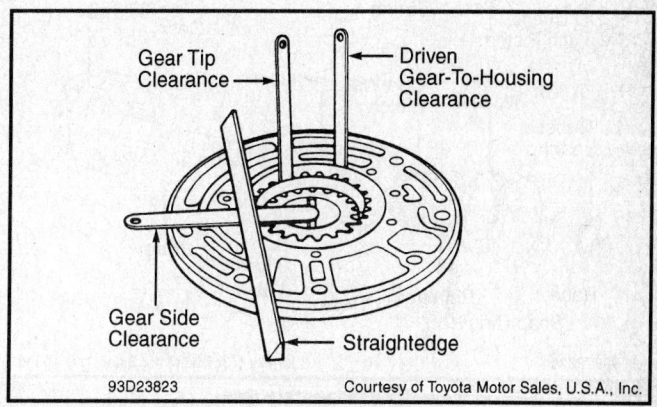

Fig. 16: Measuring Oil Pump Gear Clearances

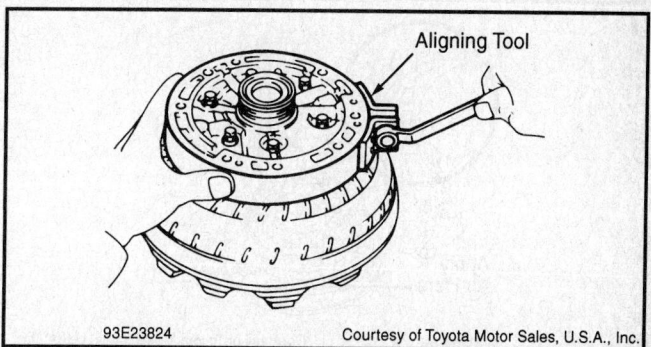

Fig. 17: Aligning Oil Pump Housing & Stator Shaft

OD PLANETARY GEAR, OD DIRECT CLUTCH & OD ONE-WAY CLUTCH

Disassembly – 1) Remove OD direct clutch drum from OD planetary gear. Remove thrust bearing and race (if equipped) from planetary gear. See Fig. 18. Place OD direct clutch assembly on oil pump assembly. Using a dial indicator, measure OD direct clutch piston stroke, while applying 57-114 psi (4-8 kg/cm²) to oil pump port. See Fig. 19.

2) Piston stroke should be .058-.089" (1.47-2.26 mm). If dial indicator reading is not within specified range, inspect discs for wear or damage. Remove OD direct clutch assembly from oil pump assembly. Remove OD brake hub snap ring and hub. Remove disc, snap ring, flange and cushion plate.

3) Using appropriate spring compressor, compress piston return spring and remove snap ring. Remove piston return spring. Install OD direct clutch drum on oil pump assembly. Hold OD direct clutch piston and apply compressed air to oil pump to remove OD direct clutch piston. See Fig. 19. Remove 2 "O" rings from piston.

4) Remove snap ring and thrust washer. Remove one-way clutch assembly. Disassemble one-way clutch. Remove 2 retainers from both sides of one-way clutch. Remove one-way clutch from outer race. See Fig. 18. Note direction of one-way clutch installation. Remove thrust washer. Using a magnet, remove 4 plugs (if applicable). DO NOT lose plugs.

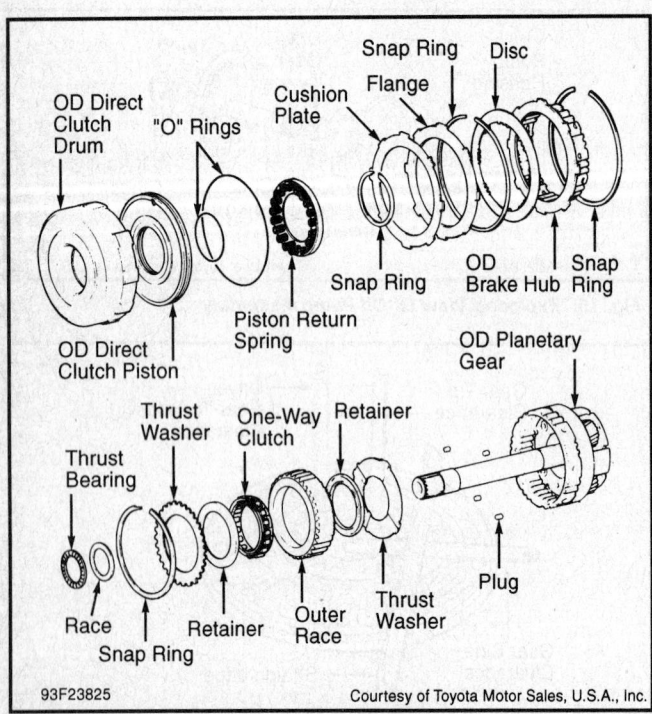

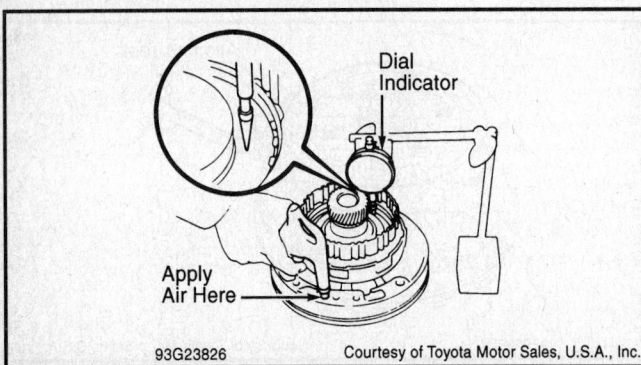

Fig. 18: Exploded View Of OD Planetary Gear, Direct Clutch & One-Way Clutch

Fig. 19: Measuring OD Direct Clutch Piston Stroke

Inspection – 1) Inspect disc and flange for flaking or burnt areas. If disc lining is peeling or discolored, replace disc. Inspect piston return springs for wear, damage and collapsed coils. Clean all components (except disc) with solvent. Dry with compressed air. Ensure check ball is free in direct clutch piston. Apply compressed air to check ball area. Ensure check ball does not allow air to bleed through piston.

2) Using a feeler gauge, measure clearance between planetary pinion gear and OD planetary gear housing. Standard clearance should be .008-.020" (.20-.51 mm). If clearance is not as specified, inspect planetary gear thrust washer. Replace planetary gear assembly (if necessary).

3) Using callipers, measure free length of each piston return spring. Standard free length is .594" (15.1 mm). Replace return springs that do not measure as specified.

CAUTION: Clutch discs should be soaked in ATF for 15 minutes prior to installation. Lubricate all parts with ATF. Coat thrust bearings and races with petroleum jelly.

Reassembly – 1) Install 4 plugs in planetary gear holes (if applicable). Install thrust washer to OD planetary gear with grooved side facing upward. Install one-way clutch in outer race with open end of retainers facing upward. Install retainer on both sides of one-way clutch. Install one-way clutch assembly. Install thrust washer and snap ring.

2) Coat NEW "O" rings with ATF and install on OD direct clutch piston. Carefully press direct clutch piston into clutch drum. Using spring compressor, compress piston return spring and install snap ring. Ensure end gap of snap ring is not aligned with spring seat claw.

3) Install cushion plate. Install flange with rounded edge facing upward. Install snap ring. Ensure end gap of snap ring is not aligned with cutout portion of clutch drum. Install disc, OD brake hub and snap ring. Ensure end gap of snap ring is not aligned with cutout portion of drum.

4) Recheck piston stroke of OD direct clutch. If piston stroke is less than specified, check for incorrect reassembly of components. Install race and thrust bearing on OD planetary gear. Install direct clutch assembly on OD planetary gear.

5) Rotate and push OD planetary gear to mesh splines of planetary gear with flukes of disc. Check one-way clutch operation. Hold OD direct clutch drum and rotate input shaft. Input shaft should rotate freely in clockwise direction and lock in counterclockwise direction. See Fig. 20.

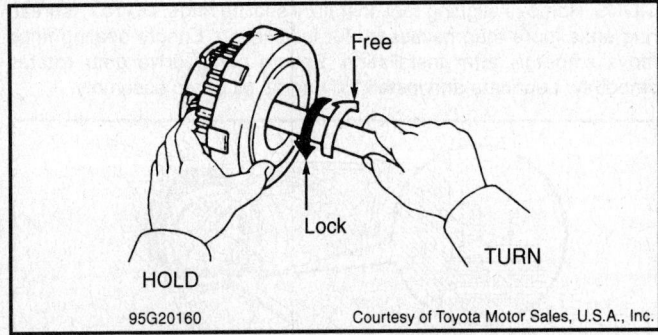

Fig. 20: Checking One-Way Clutch Operation

OVERDRIVE BRAKE

Disassembly – 1) Prior to disassembly, check OD brake clutch pack clearance. Using a feeler gauge, measure clearance between snap ring and flange. See Fig. 21. Clearance should be .014-.075" (.36-1.91 mm). If clearance is not as specified, inspect discs. Remove snap ring from OD case. Remove flange, discs, plates and cushion plate. Note location and number of components. See Fig. 22.

2) Remove OD planetary ring gear, thrust bearing and races from OD case. Remove snap ring, spring seat and piston return spring. Remove brake piston by applying air pressure to OD case. Remove oil seal rings from case and "O" rings from piston.

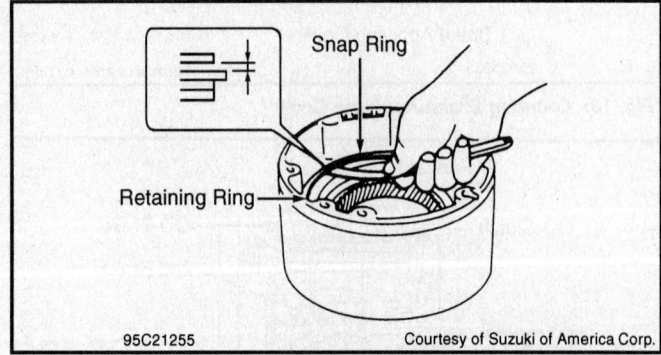

Fig. 21: Measuring OD Brake Clutch Pack Clearance

Inspection – 1) Clean all components (except discs) with solvent. Dry with compressed air. Inspect flanges, plates and discs for flaking or burnt areas. If disc lining is peeling or discolored, replace discs as necessary.

2) Using calipers, measure free length of piston return springs. Standard free length is .594" (15.10 mm). Replace return springs that do not measure as specified.

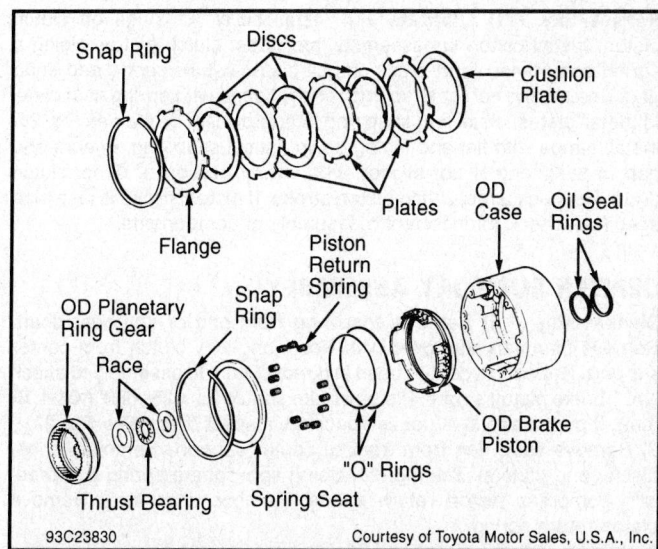

Fig. 22: Exploded View Of OD Brake Components

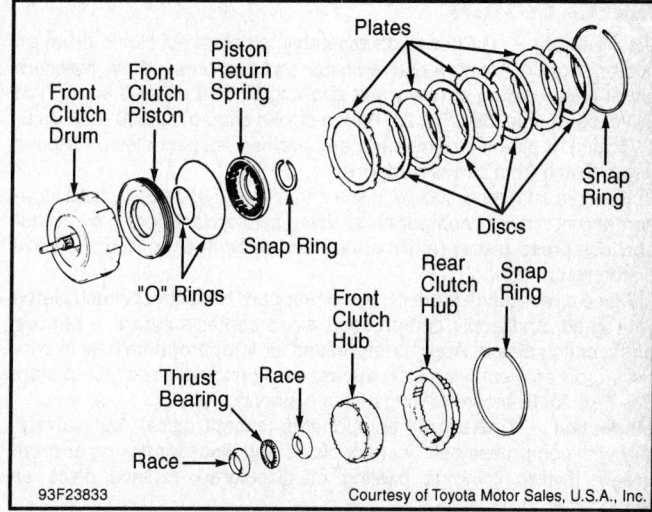

Fig. 23: Exploded View Of Forward Clutch Components

CAUTION: Clutch discs should be soaked in ATF for 15 minutes prior to installation. Lubricate all parts with ATF. Coat thrust bearings and races with petroleum jelly.

Reassembly – 1) Lubricate and install oil sealing rings on OD case. Ensure rings rotate smoothly after installation. Install NEW "O" rings on OD brake piston. Using hand pressure, carefully install brake piston into OD case with cup side upward.

2) Install piston return springs into OD case in appropriate locations. See Fig. 22. Install spring seat and snap ring. Ensure end gap of snap ring is not aligned with cutout portion of OD case. Ensure snap ring is inserted in its groove.

3) Install rear bearing race, thrust bearing and front bearing race on OD planetary ring gear. Install OD planetary ring gear assembly into OD case.

4) Install cushion plate into OD case with rounded side inward. Install plates and discs in appropriate order. Install flange with rounded edge facing upward. Install snap ring.

5) Ensure end gap of snap ring is not aligned with cutout portion of OD case. Recheck OD brake piston stroke or clearance. If measurement is not as specified, check for incorrect reassembly of components.

FORWARD CLUTCH

Disassembly – 1) Install forward clutch assembly to OD case. Remove snap ring. Remove front and direct clutch hubs. Remove thrust bearing and races from clutch drum, noting component direction prior to removal. See Fig. 23.

2) Check forward clutch piston stroke. Install direct clutch hub and snap ring. Using a dial indicator, measure forward clutch piston stroke while applying 57-114 psi (4-8 kg/cm²) to OD case oil hole. See Fig. 24. Piston stroke should be .055-.088" (1.40-2.24 mm). If piston stroke is not as specified, inspect discs. Remove snap ring and direct clutch hub.

3) Remove snap ring, discs and plates. Note location and number of components. Using appropriate spring compressor, compress piston return spring. Remove snap ring and piston return spring. Place clutch drum on OD case. Carefully apply air pressure to case oil hole to remove piston. See Fig. 24. Remove "O" rings from clutch piston.

Inspection – 1) Clean all components (except discs) with solvent. Dry with compressed air. Inspect plates and discs for flaking or burnt areas. If disc lining is peeling or discolored, replace discs as necessary.

2) Ensure check ball is free in clutch piston. Apply air pressure to check ball area. Ensure check ball does not allow air to bleed through piston.

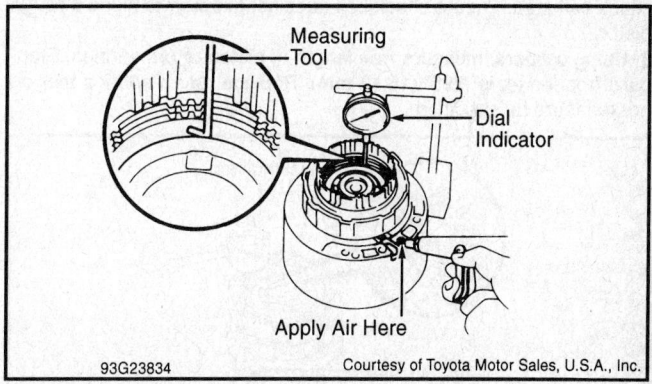

Fig. 24: Measuring Forward Clutch Piston Stroke

3) Using calipers, measure free length of piston return springs. Standard free length is .594" (15.10 mm). Replace return springs that do not measure as specified.

CAUTION: Clutch discs should be soaked in ATF for 15 minutes prior to installation. Lubricate all parts with ATF. Coat thrust bearings and races with petroleum jelly.

Reassembly – 1) Lubricate and install NEW "O" rings onto clutch piston. Carefully install forward clutch piston into clutch drum. Install piston return spring. Using a spring compressor and appropriate press, compress return spring and install snap ring. Ensure end gap of snap ring is not aligned with claw area on spring seat.

2) Install plates, discs and snap ring in appropriate order. See Fig. 27. Ensure end gap of snap ring is not aligned with cutout portion of forward clutch drum. Install direct clutch hub and snap ring. Recheck forward clutch piston stroke.

3) If piston stroke is less than specified, check for incorrect reassembly of components. If piston stroke is greater than specified, select a new plate. Plates are available in thicknesses of .071" (1.80 mm) and .079" (2.00 mm). Remove snap ring and direct clutch hub. Install bearing races and thrust bearing into forward clutch drum with flat surface of races facing away from clutch drum.

4) Rotate and push forward clutch hub to mesh splines of forward clutch hub with flukes of discs. Install forward clutch hub into forward clutch drum. Install direct clutch hub and snap ring. Ensure end gap of snap ring is not aligned with cutout portion of clutch drum.

DIRECT CLUTCH

Disassembly – 1) Prior to disassembly, place direct clutch drum on center support. Using a dial indicator and compressed air, measure direct clutch piston stroke while applying 57-114 psi (4-8 kg/cm²) to OD case oil hole. *See Fig. 25.* Piston stroke should be .008-.069" (.20-1.75 mm). If piston stroke is not as specified, inspect discs. Remove direct clutch from center support.

2) Remove snap ring, flange, discs and plates. *See Fig. 26.* Note location and number of components. Using appropriate spring compressor, compress piston return spring and remove snap ring. Remove piston return spring.

3) Place direct clutch drum on center support. Hold direct clutch piston with hand, and apply compressed air to center support to remove direct clutch piston. Apply compressed air to appropriate hole in center support to remove piston subassembly from direct clutch piston. *See Fig. 25.* Remove "O" rings from piston(s).

Inspection – 1) Clean all components (except discs) with solvent. Dry with compressed air. Inspect plates and discs for flaking or burnt areas. If disc lining is peeling or discolored, replace discs as necessary.

2) Ensure check ball is free in clutch piston. Apply air pressure to check ball area. Ensure check ball does not allow air to bleed through piston.

3) Using calipers, measure free length of piston return springs. Standard free length is .596" (15.13 mm). Replace return springs that do not measure as specified.

Reassembly – 1) Lubricate and install NEW "O" rings on clutch piston. Install piston subassembly into direct clutch piston. Using a spring compressor and press, install piston return spring and snap ring. Ensure end gap of snap ring is not aligned with spring seat claw.

2) Install plates, discs and snap ring in appropriate order. *See Fig. 26.* Install flange with flat end facing down. Install snap ring. Ensure end gap of snap ring is not aligned with cutout portion of direct clutch drum. Recheck direct clutch piston stroke. If piston stroke is less than specified, check for incorrect reassembly of components.

CENTER SUPPORT ASSEMBLY

Disassembly – 1) Remove snap ring from end of sun gear shaft. Remove planetary sun gear with No. 1 one-way clutch from center support. Repeat procedure used in direct clutch disassembly to check No. 1 brake piston stroke. Piston stroke should be .025-.068" (.64-1.73 mm). If piston stroke is not as specified, inspect discs. *See Fig. 27.*

2) Remove snap ring from front of center support. Remove flange, disc(s) and plate(s). *See Fig. 28.* Using appropriate spring compressor, compress piston return spring. Remove snap ring. Remove piston return spring.

3) Hold No. 1 brake piston and apply air pressure to center support oil hole to remove No. 1 brake piston. *See Fig. 27.* Remove "O" rings and oil sealing rings. Turn center support over.

4) Check No. 2 brake piston stroke. Repeat test procedure used previously for checking piston stroke on No. 1 brake piston. *See Fig. 29.* Piston stroke should be .040-.089" (1.02-2.26 mm). If piston stroke is not as specified, inspect discs. Remove rear snap ring, flange, discs and plates. Note location and number of components. *See Fig. 30.*

5) Using appropriate spring compressor and press, compress piston return spring. Remove snap ring. Remove piston return spring. Hold No. 2 brake piston and apply air pressure to center support oil hole to remove No. 2 brake piston. *See Fig. 29.* Remove "O" rings.

6) Hold No. 1 one-way clutch and rotate planetary gear. Sun gear should rotate freely in counterclockwise direction and lock in clockwise direction. *See Fig. 31.* If component does not test as described, one-way clutch requires replacement. Loosen staked part of rear side retainer. Remove No. 1 one-way clutch and 2 retainers from outer race. *See Fig. 32.* Using a pin punch and hammer, remove front side retainer. Remove oil sealing rings from sun gear.

7) Remove thrust washer from front planetary gear. Hold one-way clutch inner race and rotate planetary gear. Planetary gear should rotate freely in counterclockwise direction and lock in clockwise direction. *See Fig. 33.* Remove one-way clutch inner race. Remove snap ring, one-way clutch and 2 retainers. *See Fig. 34.*

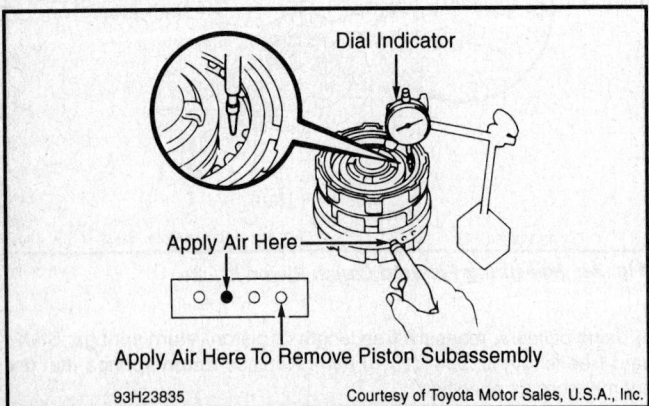

Fig. 25: Measuring Direct Clutch Piston Stroke & Removing Piston Subassembly

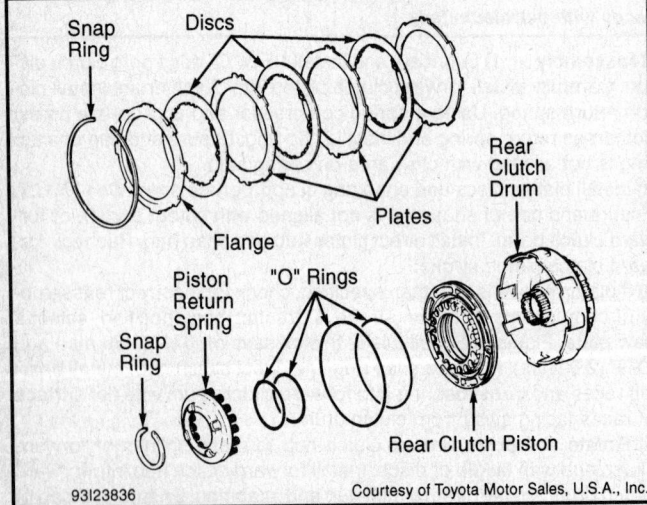

Fig. 26: Exploded View Of Rear Clutch Components

CAUTION: Clutch discs should be soaked in ATF for 15 minutes prior to installation. Lubricate all parts with ATF.

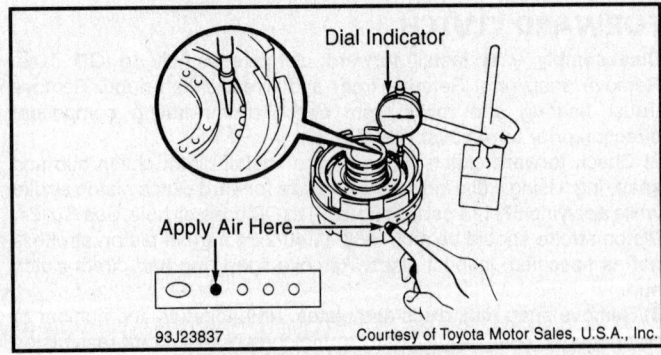

Fig. 27: Measuring No. 1 Brake Piston Stroke

Inspection – 1) Clean all components (except discs) with solvent. Dry with compressed air. Inspect plates and discs for flaking or burnt areas. If disc lining is peeling or discolored, replace disc as necessary. Inspect piston return springs for wear, damage or collapsed coils.

2) Using a feeler gauge, measure clearance between planetary pinion gear and planetary gear case. Standard clearance is .008-.020" (.20-.51 mm). If clearance is not as specified, replace planetary gear assembly.

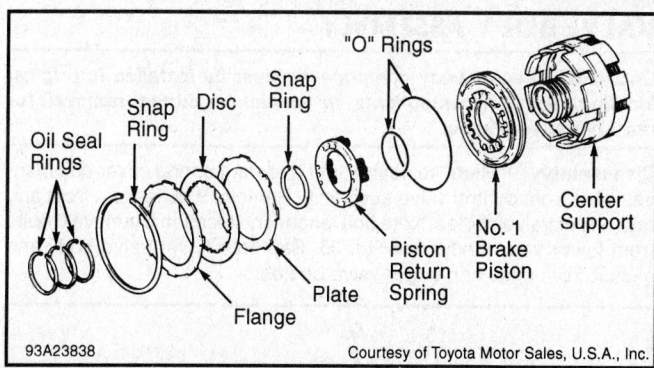

Fig. 28: Exploded View Of No. 1 Brake Components

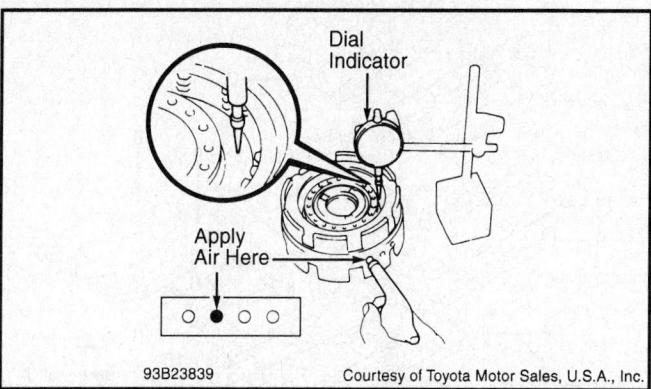

Fig. 29: Measuring No. 2 Brake Piston Stroke

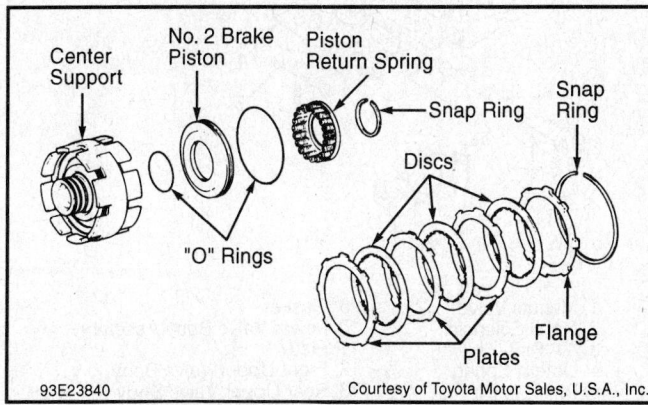

Fig. 30: Exploded View Of No. 2 Brake Components

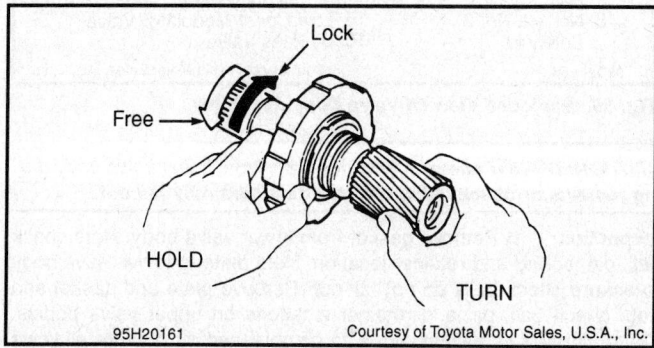

Fig. 31: Checking No. 1 One-Way Clutch Operation

CAUTION: *Clutch discs should be soaked in ATF for 15 minutes prior to installation. Lubricate all parts with ATF.*

Reassembly – 1) Lubricate "O" rings with ATF. To reassemble, reverse disassembly procedure. Ensure end gap of snap ring does not align with claw area on spring seat of piston return spring. Install plates and discs in appropriate order. *See Figs. 28 and 30.*

2) Install No. 1 brake flange with rounded side facing down. Install No. 2 brake flange with flat side facing down. Install all snap rings. Ensure ends of snap rings do not align with cutout areas of center support.

3) Recheck No. 1 and No. 2 brake piston stroke. *See Figs. 27 and 29.* If piston stroke is not as specified, check for incorrect reassembly of components. Reassemble sun gear and No. 1 one-way clutch. *See Fig. 32.* While turning one-way clutch, install sun gear into center support. Install snap ring on end of sun gear. Ensure sun gear rotates in counterclockwise direction only.

4) Reassembly front planetary gear and No. 2 one-way clutch. *See Fig. 34.* Ensure lug shaped cutout on thrust washer for No. 2 one-way clutch is aligned with lug shaped cutout on front planetary gear. Ensure front planetary gear rotates in counterclockwise direction only.

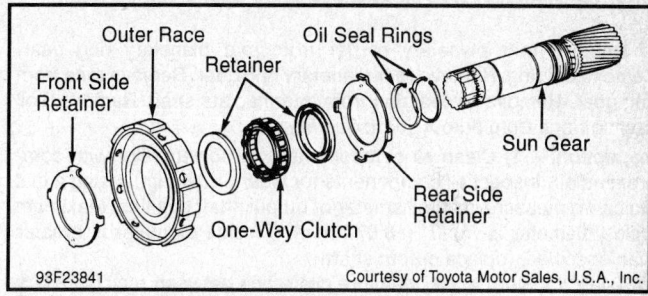

Fig. 32: Exploded View Of Planetary Sun Gear & No. 1 One-Way Clutch

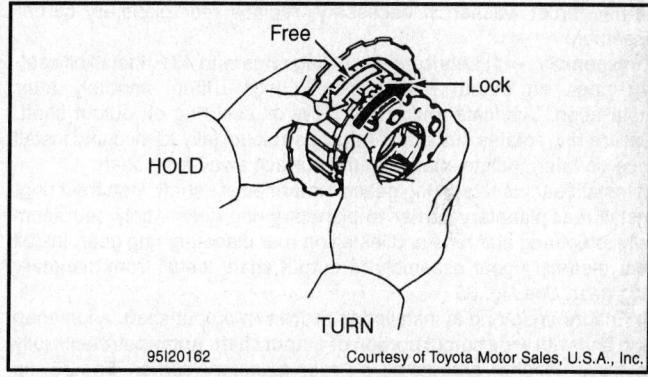

Fig. 33: Checking No. 2 One-Way Clutch Operation

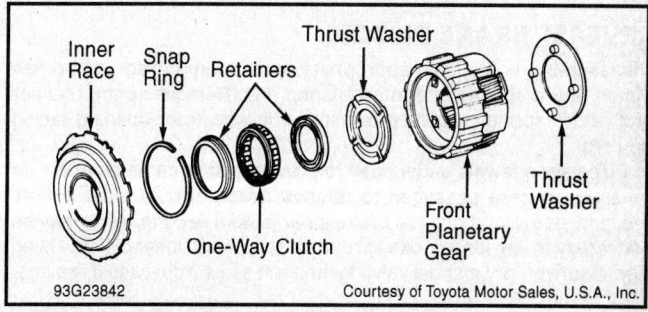

Fig. 34: Exploded View Of Front Planetary Gear & No. 2 One-Way Clutch

REAR PLANETARY GEAR & OUTPUT SHAFT

Disassembly – 1) Remove thrust washer from front planetary ring gear. Compress snap ring and remove front planetary ring gear. Remove snap ring from ring gear. Remove rear planetary gear assembly from output shaft. Remove bearing and race.

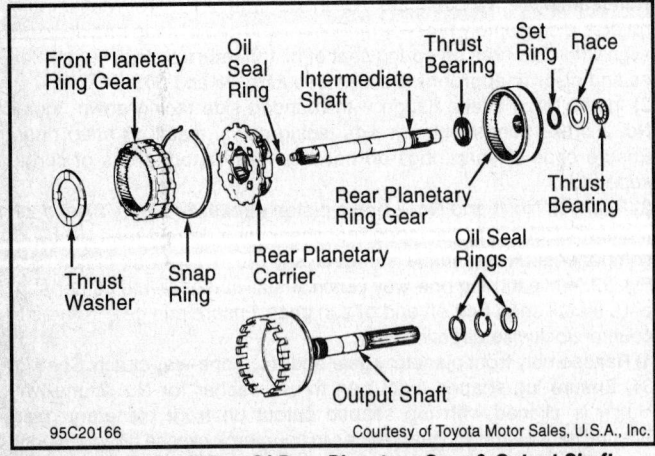

Fig. 35: Exploded View Of Rear Planetary Gear & Output Shaft

2) Remove rear planetary carrier from rear planetary ring gear. Remove set ring. Remove rear planetary ring gear. Remove race from ring gear. Remove oil seal ring from intermediate shaft. Remove 3 oil sealing rings from output shaft. *See Fig. 35.*

Inspection – 1) Clean all components with solvent. Dry with compressed air. Inspect all components for wear or damage. Using a dial indicator, measure inside diameter of output shaft bushing. Maximum inside diameter is .7117" (18.077 mm). If inside diameter is greater than specified, replace output shaft.

2) Using a feeler gauge, measure clearance between rear planetary carrier pinion gear and carrier case. Clearance should be .008-.020" (.20-.51 mm). If clearance is not as specified, inspect rear planetary carrier thrust washer. If necessary, replace rear planetary carrier assembly.

Reassembly – 1) Lubricate oil sealing rings with ATF. Install oil sealing rings on output shaft. Ensure rings rotate smoothly after installation. Lubricate and install NEW oil seal ring on output shaft. Ensure ring rotates smoothly. Apply petroleum jelly to race and install race on intermediate shaft with flat surface away from shaft.

2) Install rear planetary ring gear on intermediate shaft. Install set ring. Install rear planetary carrier to planetary ring gear. Apply petroleum jelly to bearing and race and install on rear planetary ring gear. Install rear planetary gear assembly to output shaft. Install front planetary ring gear. *See Fig. 35.*

3) Ensure snap ring is installed in groove of output shaft. Align snap ring end with wide cutout portion of output shaft. Apply petroleum jelly to thrust washer and install on rear planetary carrier. Ensure lug shapes match cutout portions on rear planetary carrier.

REVERSE BRAKE PISTON

Disassembly – 1) Using appropriate spring compressor, compress piston return springs and remove snap ring. Remove spring retainer and return springs. Position transmission with front opening facing upward.

2) Place shop towels under case to prevent piston damage. Apply air pressure to case passages to remove reverse brake outer piston, reaction sleeve and reverse brake inner piston. *See Fig. 14.* It may be necessary to use long hooks to remove sleeve and inner piston. Using a screwdriver, pry manual valve lever shaft seals from case if replacement is required.

Inspection – Clean all parts (except discs) in solvent. Dry with compressed air. Inspect pistons and sleeve for scoring, wear or damage. Check return springs for cracked or broken coils. If disc lining is peeled or discolored, replace discs as necessary. Replace damaged components as necessary.

Reassembly – Install manual valve lever shaft seals if removed. Lubricate and install all NEW "O" rings. Thin "O" ring goes on outside of reaction sleeve. Soak discs in ATF for 15 minutes prior to installation. To complete reassembly, reverse disassembly procedure. Check reverse brake operation. *See Fig. 14.*

VALVE BODY ASSEMBLY

CAUTION: All valve body components must be installed in original location. Lay all components in sequence during removal for reassembly reference.

Disassembly – Remove detent spring, detent spring cover and manual valve from control valve assembly. Remove 9 bolts from front and rear upper valve bodies. Note bolt length and location. Remove 6 bolts from lower valve body. *See Fig. 36.* Separate lower valve body and gasket from plate and upper valve bodies.

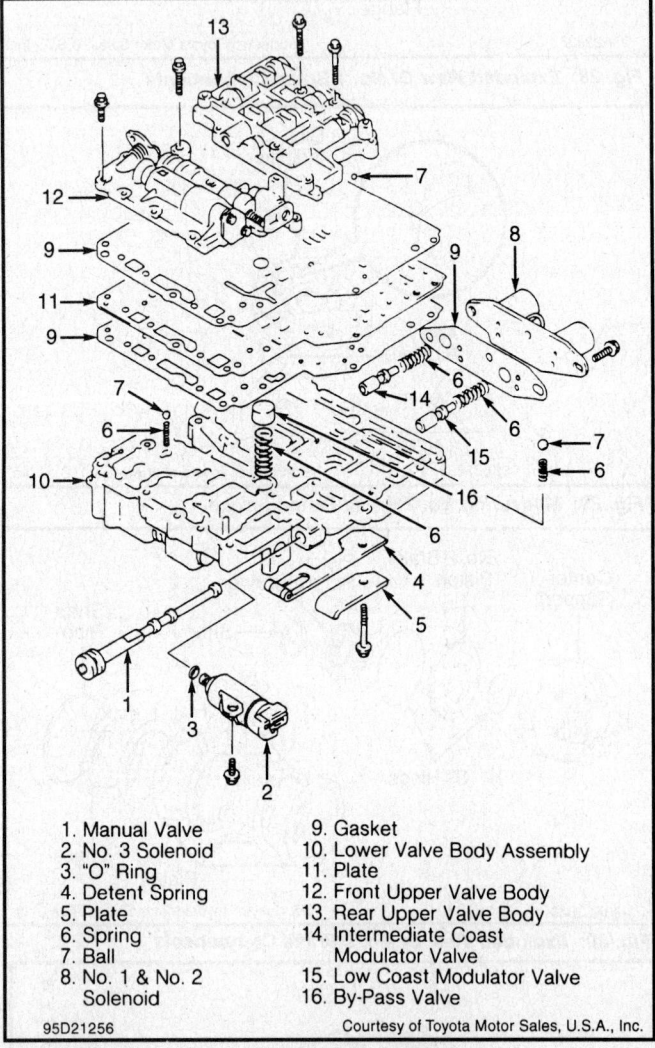

1. Manual Valve	9. Gasket
2. No. 3 Solenoid	10. Lower Valve Body Assembly
3. "O" Ring	11. Plate
4. Detent Spring	12. Front Upper Valve Body
5. Plate	13. Rear Upper Valve Body
6. Spring	14. Intermediate Coast
7. Ball	Modulator Valve
8. No. 1 & No. 2	15. Low Coast Modulator Valve
Solenoid	16. By-Pass Valve

95D21256   Courtesy of Toyota Motor Sales, U.S.A., Inc.

Fig. 36: Exploded View Of Valve Body Assembly

CAUTION: DO NOT allow plate to separate from lower valve body during removal or check balls, pins and retainers may fall out.

Inspection – 1) Remove gasket from lower valve body. Note check ball, pin, spring and retainer location. Hold plate to lower valve body to ensure check balls do not fall out. Remove plate and gasket and note check ball, pin and retainer locations on upper valve bodies. Clean all parts in solvent. Dry with compressed air. Ensure all valve body passages are clear.

2) Inspect valves for scoring or roughness. Ensure valves slide freely in bores. Inspect valve springs for damage, squareness and collapsed coils. Measure spring free length and outer diameter. Replace spring if not within specification. See appropriate VALVE BODY SPRING SPECIFICATIONS table. *See Figs. 36-40.*

LOWER VALVE BODY SPRING SPECIFICATIONS

Spring No.	Diameter In. (mm)	Free Length In. (mm)
1	.677 (17.20)	2.216 (56.29)
2	.394 (10.01)	1.395 (35.42)
3	.394 (10.01)	1.667 (42.34)
4	.445 (11.30)	1.362 (34.59)
5	.517 (13.13)	1.501 (38.13)
6	.437 (11.10)	1.265 (32.13)

FRONT UPPER VALVE BODY SPRING SPECIFICATIONS

Spring No.	Diameter In. (mm)	Free Length In. (mm)
1	.686 (17.42)	2.804 (71.22)
2	.338 (8.59)	.757 (19.23)
3	.429 (10.90)	1.557 (39.55)
4	.270 (6.86)	.906 (23.01)

REAR UPPER VALVE BODY SPRING SPECIFICATIONS

Spring No.	Diameter In. (mm)	Free Length In. (mm)
1-3	.350 (8.90)	1.148 (29.16)
4	.362 (9.19)	1.478 (37.54)

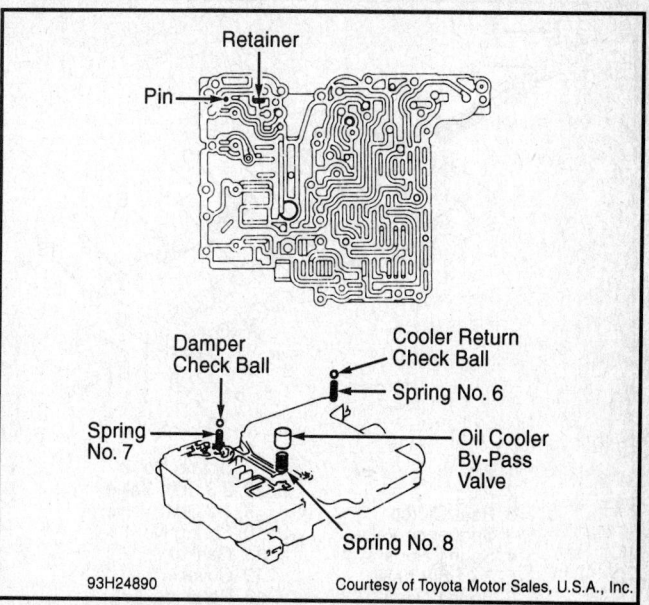

93H24890   Courtesy of Toyota Motor Sales, U.S.A., Inc.

Fig. 38: Identifying Lower Valve Body Check Ball Pin, Spring & Retainer Locations

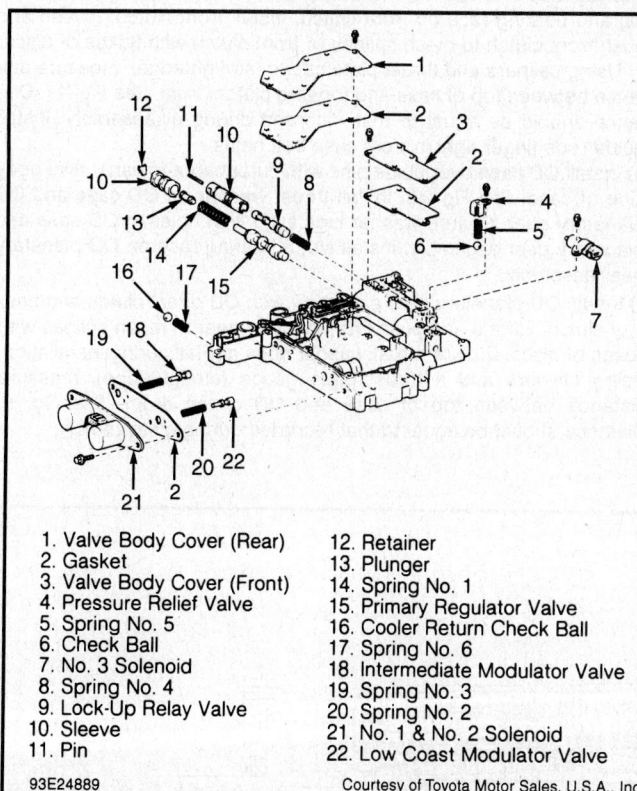

1. Valve Body Cover (Rear)
2. Gasket
3. Valve Body Cover (Front)
4. Pressure Relief Valve
5. Spring No. 5
6. Check Ball
7. No. 3 Solenoid
8. Spring No. 4
9. Lock-Up Relay Valve
10. Sleeve
11. Pin
12. Retainer
13. Plunger
14. Spring No. 1
15. Primary Regulator Valve
16. Cooler Return Check Ball
17. Spring No. 6
18. Intermediate Modulator Valve
19. Spring No. 3
20. Spring No. 2
21. No. 1 & No. 2 Solenoid
22. Low Coast Modulator Valve

93E24889   Courtesy of Toyota Motor Sales, U.S.A., Inc.

Fig. 37: Exploded View Of Lower Valve Body

Reassembly – 1) Position new gasket on upper rear valve body. Place lower valve body with separator plate and gaskets on top of upper rear valve body.

2) Install and finger tighten 3 bolts. Turn assembly over and install 4 bolts in upper rear valve body. Place assembly on top of upper front valve body. Install and finger tighten 3 bolts. Turn assembly over and install 5 bolts. Torque bolts to specification. See TORQUE SPECIFICATIONS.

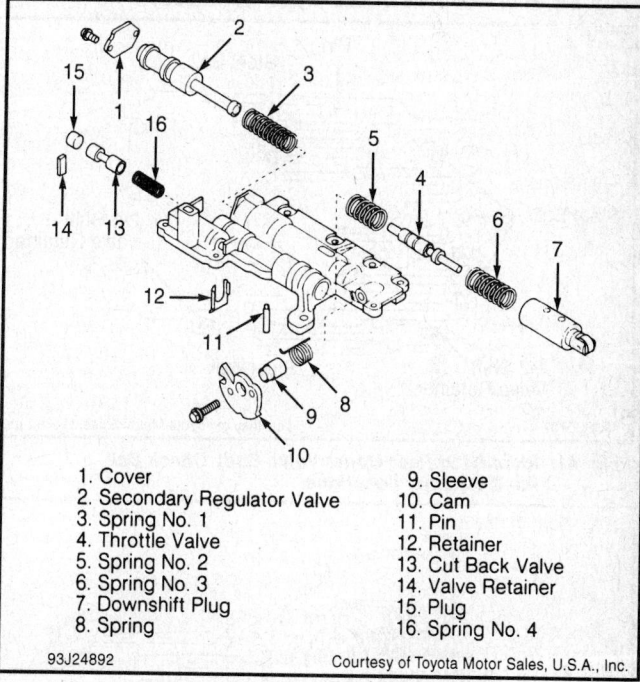

1. Cover
2. Secondary Regulator Valve
3. Spring No. 1
4. Throttle Valve
5. Spring No. 2
6. Spring No. 3
7. Downshift Plug
8. Spring
9. Sleeve
10. Cam
11. Pin
12. Retainer
13. Cut Back Valve
14. Valve Retainer
15. Plug
16. Spring No. 4

93J24892   Courtesy of Toyota Motor Sales, U.S.A., Inc.

Fig. 39: Exploded View Of Front Upper Valve Body

TRANSMISSION REASSEMBLY

NOTE: See illustration for bearing race and thrust bearing locations. See Fig. 42.

CAUTION: Lubricate all components with ATF. Clutch discs should be soaked in ATF for 15 minutes prior to installation. Coat thrust bearings and races with petroleum jelly. Ensure ends of snap rings are not aligned with cutout area of case.

1) Position transmission case with front facing upward. Assemble reverse brake inner piston, reaction sleeve and outer piston. Press assembled pistons into case with hand pressure. Using appropriate

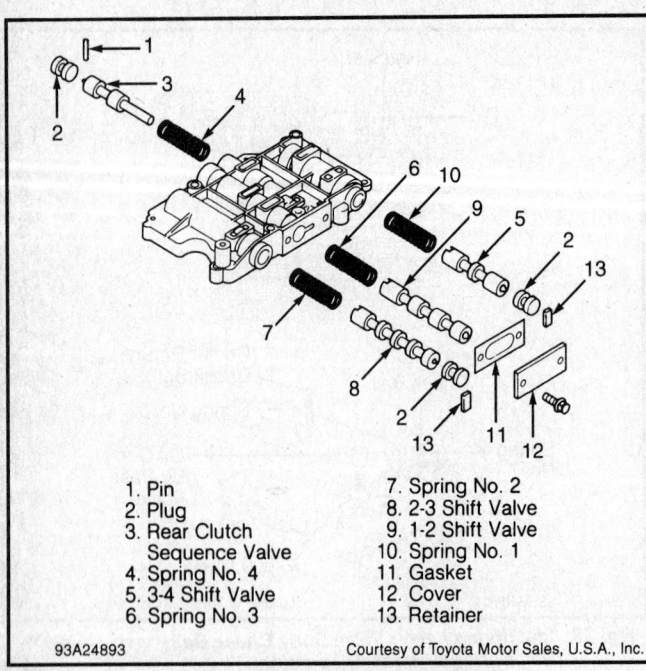

1. Pin
2. Plug
3. Rear Clutch Sequence Valve
4. Spring No. 4
5. 3-4 Shift Valve
6. Spring No. 3
7. Spring No. 2
8. 2-3 Shift Valve
9. 1-2 Shift Valve
10. Spring No. 1
11. Gasket
12. Cover
13. Retainer

93A24893   Courtesy of Toyota Motor Sales, U.S.A., Inc.

Fig. 40: Exploded View Of Rear Upper Valve Body

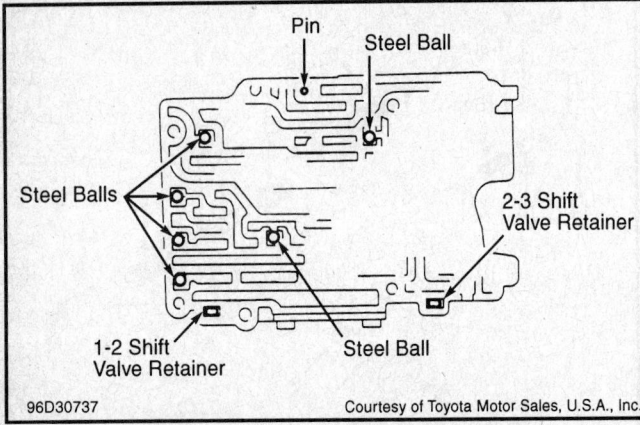

96D30737   Courtesy of Toyota Motor Sales, U.S.A., Inc.

Fig. 41: Identifying Rear Upper Valve Body Check Ball Pin & Retainer Locations

spring compressor, install piston return spring on outer piston. Install snap ring. Ensure reverse brake piston moves smoothly when compressed air is applied. See Fig. 14.

2) Install No. 1 bearing race. Install brake apply tube into transmission case, aligning locking tab with cutout in valve body side of transmission case. Ensure lips of tube end are completely inserted onto outer piston. Install output shaft No. 1 thrust bearing into case. Install rear planetary gear and output shaft into case. Install No. 2 thrust bearing. See Fig. 35.

3) Install pressure plate, with flat surface facing forward. Install 5 discs and 4 plates, starting with a disc and alternating each component. Measure reverse brake clutch pack clearance. See Fig. 12. Clearance should be .029-.098" (.74-2.49 mm).

4) Remove one-way clutch inner race from planetary gear assembly. Install front planetary gear. Mesh splines of planetary gear with flukes of discs by rotating and pushing planetary gear. Position inner race with notched tooth toward valve body side of case. Push plate into place. Install snap ring. Ensure snap ring is fully seated.

5) Align oil hole and bolt hole of center support toward valve body side. Align center support bolt holes with case holes and install. Install bolts with wave washers. Tighten bolt on accumulator piston side first to 19 ft. lbs. (26 N.m). Install direct clutch assembly while rotating to align with center support.

6) If fully installed, splined center of clutch will be even with end of sun gear shaft. Install No. 3 rear bearing race, thrust bearing and front bearing race over splined end of direct clutch. Install No. 4 thrust bearing and bearing race on front clutch. Install front clutch. Rotate and push front clutch to mesh splines of front clutch with flukes of discs.

7) Using calipers and thrust plate gauge (straightedge), measure distance between top of case and forward clutch drum. See Fig. 11. Distance should be equal to that recorded during disassembly. Install guide rods finger tight in front case bolt holes.

8) Install OD case over guide pins with cutout area toward valve body side of case. See Fig. 43. Install thrust washer on OD case and OD planetary gear. Ensure washer lugs align with holes in OD case and planetary gear assembly. Install No. 5 bearing race on OD planetary gear assembly.

9) Install OD planetary gear assembly with OD direct clutch and one-way clutch. Rotate and push OD planetary gear to mesh splines with flukes of discs. Ensure thrust washer does not fall during installation. Using calipers and a thrust plate gauge (straightedge), measure distance between top of case and OD clutch drum. See Fig. 9. Distance should be equal to that recorded during disassembly.

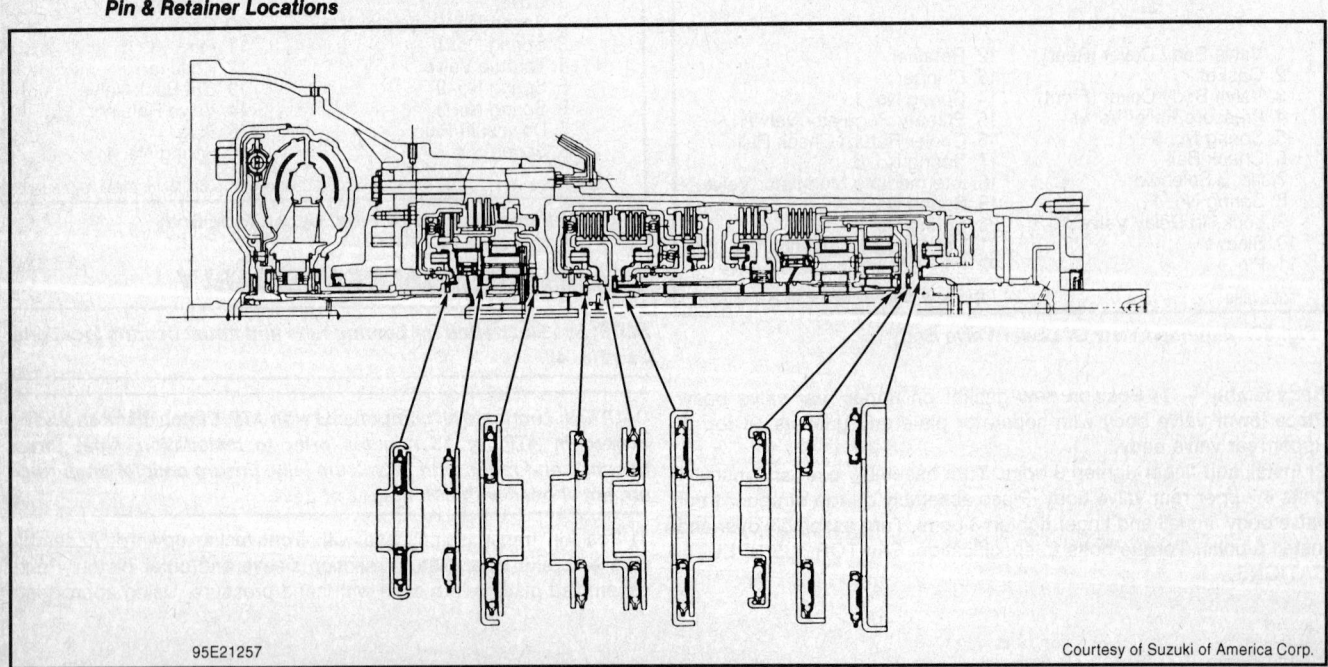

95E21257   Courtesy of Suzuki of America Corp.

Fig. 42: Identifying Bearing Race & Thrust Bearing Locations

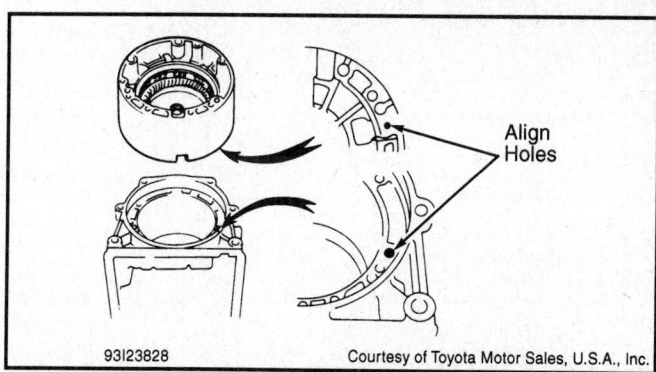

Fig. 43: Aligning OD Case & Transmission Case Oil Holes

10) Install "O" ring on OD case. Install torque converter housing to transmission case. Tighten 10-mm bolts to 25 ft. lbs. (34 N.m) and 12 mm bolts to 42 ft. lbs. (57 N.m). Install No. 5 thrust bearing on rear of oil pump. Ensure oil seal rings and "O" ring are installed on oil pump.

11) Install oil pump over guide studs and into transmission case. Ensure thrust bearing does not fall off oil pump. Coat oil pump retaining bolts below bolt heads with thread sealer. Remove guide studs. Install bolts and tighten to 15 ft. lbs. (21 N.m). Ensure input shaft turns freely. Using a dial indicator, check output shaft end play. Position dial indicator against end of output shaft. End play should be .012-.035" (.30-.89 mm).

12) Apply air pressure to specified oil passages to check appropriate operating components. See Fig. 14. Component application should be heard while applying air. Install NEW oil seals in transmission case. Lubricate oil seal lips prior to installation. Install NEW spacer on manual valve lever. Install manual valve lever shaft into case and through manual valve lever. Install NEW pin with slot at right angle to shaft.

13) Align spacer hole to hollow area of lever. Stake spacer to lever. Ensure manual valve lever shaft turns smoothly. Install parking lock pawl, pivot pin and spring in case. Install lock rod on manual valve lever and install parking lock pawl. Install parking pawl bracket on case. Ensure collar on control rod is toward front of transmission. Tighten bracket bolts to 66 INCH lbs. (7.5 N.m).

14) Check operation of park lock pawl. Ensure output shaft is locked when manual valve lever is in "P" position. Determine proper accumulator piston locations. See Fig. 8. Ensure accumulator piston is proper diameter. See ACCUMULATOR PISTON DIAMETER table. Determine proper spring free length and outer diameter for accumulator piston application. See ACCUMULATOR SPRING SPECIFICATIONS table.

ACCUMULATOR PISTON DIAMETER [1]

Application	In. (mm)
Front & Direct Clutch	1.252-1.254 (31.80-31.85)
No. 2 Brake	1.370-1.372 (34.80-34.85)

[1] – See illustration for accumulator piston locations. See Fig. 8.

ACCUMULATOR SPRING SPECIFICATIONS [1]

Application	Free Length In. (mm)
Forward Clutch Spring	
Upper	2.251 (57.18)
Lower	1.161 (29.49)
No. 2 Brake Spring	
Upper	2.172 (55.17)
Lower	1.383 (35.13)
Direct Clutch Spring	2.172 (55.17)

[1] – See illustration for accumulator piston locations. See Fig. 8.

15) Install accumulator pistons and springs. Ensure accumulator pistons are pressed fully into bore. Install NEW "O" rings on throttle cable fitting. Install throttle cable. Align manual valve with pin on manual valve lever. Connect throttle cable to cam. Install valve body assembly and tighten bolts to 89 INCH lbs. (10 N.m). See Fig. 3.

16) Install gasket and oil strainer. Tighten bolts to 49 INCH lbs. (5.5 N.m). Using a plastic hammer, install oil tubes. See Fig. 7. Do not bend or damage oil tubes. Install magnets in oil pan. Ensure magnets do not interfere with oil tubes. Install NEW gasket to transmission case. Align cut part of gasket and transmission case. Install oil pan bolts and tighten to 40 INCH lbs. (4.5 N.m).

17) Install speed sensor rotor and snap ring. Install oil supply tube and extension housing with NEW gasket. Clean all bolt threads. Apply thread sealer to top 4 extension housing bolts prior to installation. Install short bolts to bottom of extension housing. Tighten bolts to 26 ft. lbs. (35 N.m).

18) Lubricate and install new "O" rings on unions. Install unions and tighten to 26 ft. lbs. (35 N.m). Lubricate and install "O" ring to sleeve. Insert speedometer driven gear into sleeve. Install sleeve to extension housing. Install lock plate and bolt. Using control shaft lever, fully turn manual valve lever shaft forward and return 2 notches.

19) Insert park/neutral position switch on manual valve lever shaft and temporarily tighten adjusting bolt. Install lock washer and set nut. Torque set nut to 44 INCH lbs. (5 N.m). Bend over at least 2 washer tabs.

20) With neutral reference line and cut-out on park/neutral position switch aligned, torque switch retaining bolt to 44 INCH lbs. (5 N.m).

21) Install control shaft lever with spring washer and nut. Tighten nut to 115 INCH lbs. (13 N.m). Install wire harness and throttle cable clamp. Install torque converter. Ensure torque converter is installed correctly. Using a straightedge and calipers, measure torque converter depth. Distance at dimension "A" should be .669" (16.99 mm). See Fig. 44.

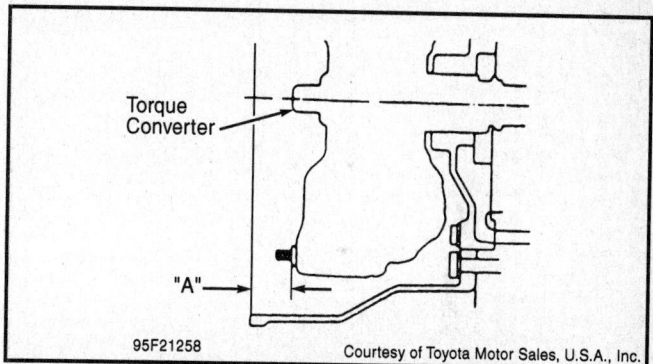

Fig. 44: Measuring Torque Converter Installed Depth

TRANSMISSION SPECIFICATIONS
TRANSMISSION SPECIFICATIONS

Application	In. (mm)
Converter Sleeve Runout (Maximum)	.0118 (.30)
Drive Plate Runout (Maximum)	.008 (.20)
Piston Stroke	
Forward Clutch	.055-.088 (1.40-2.24)
OD Direct Clutch	.058-.089 (1.47-2.26)
No. 1 Brake	.025-.068" (.64-1.73 mm)
No. 2 Brake	.040-.089 (1.02-2.26)
Direct Clutch	.008-.069 (.20-1.75)
Reverse Brake Pack Clearance	.029-.098 (.74-2.49)
OD Brake Snap Ring-To-Flange	
Standard Clearance	.014-.075 (.36-1.91)
Output Shaft End Play	.012-.035 (.30-.89)
Planetary Pinion Gear Clearance	.008-.020 (.20-.51)
Torque Converter Depth	.669 (16.99)

TORQUE SPECIFICATIONS

TORQUE SPECIFICATIONS

Application	Ft. Lbs. (N.m)
Center Support-To-Case Bolt	19 (26)
Converter-To-Drive Plate Bolt	
Geo & Suzuki	48 (65)
Kia	20 (27)
Cooler Union Nut	26 (35)
Extension Housing-To-Case Bolt	26 (35)
Oil Pump-To-Case Bolt	15 (21)
Transmission Case-To-Converter Housing Bolt	
10-mm	25 (34)
12-mm	42 (57)
Transmission Mounting Bolt	37 (50)

Application	INCH Lbs. (N.m)
Control Shaft Lever Bolt	115 (13)
Lock Pawl Bracket Bolt	66 (7.5)
Oil Pan Bolt	40 (4.5)
Oil Pump Housing Bolt	80 (9)
Oil Strainer Bolt	49 (5.5)
Park/Neutral Position Switch	
Shift Shaft Set Nut	44 (5)
Shift Switch Lock Bolt	44 (5)
Throttle Cam Bolt	71 (8)
Upper Valve Body-To-Lower	
Valve Body Bolt	49 (5.5)
Valve Assembly-To-Case Bolt	89 (10)

Suzuki: Sidekick (1995)

NOTE: For Kia without OBD-II electronic controls, see KIA AW372LE ELECTRONIC CONTROLS article.

APPLICATION

APPLICATION

Vehicle	Transmission Model
1995 Sidekick	.... AW03-72LE

DESCRIPTION

Automatic transmission is electronically controlled. Transmission shifting and torque converter lock-up are controlled by Transmission Control Module (TCM).

The TCM receives information from various input devices and uses this information to control shift solenoids No. 1 and 2 on transmission valve body for transmission shifting, and Torque Converter Clutch (TCC) solenoid for torque converter lock-up.

An Overdrive (OD) switch is mounted on shift lever. When OD switch is depressed to ON position, transmission will shift into 4th gear when shift lever is in "D" position, and OD OFF light on instrument panel will go off. When OD switch is released to OFF position, transmission will shift into 3rd gear, and OD OFF light on instrument panel will illuminate. The OD OFF light is located on instrument panel.

OPERATION

TCM

The TCM receives information from various input devices and uses this information to control shift solenoids No. 1 and 2 on transmission valve body for transmission shifting, and TCC solenoid for torque converter lock-up.

The TCM contains a self-diagnostic system, which will store a trouble code if failures or problems are present in electronic control system. Trouble code can be retrieved to determine problem area. See SELF-DIAGNOSTIC SYSTEM. Note location of TCM. *See Fig. 1.*

TCM INPUT DEVICES

Brakelight Switch Signal – Brakelight switch delivers input signal to TCM, indicating vehicle braking. Brakelight switch is located on brake pedal support.

Cruise Control Electronic Control Unit (ECU) – Cruise control unit delivers an input signal to control overdrive operation in accordance with vehicle speed when cruise control is operating. When in overdrive with cruise control on, if vehicle speed drops 2 MPH less than the set speed, overdrive is released to prevent reduction in vehicle speed. Once vehicle speed is more than the set speed, the overdrive is resumed. If coolant temperature is low, transmission will not shift into overdrive. Cruise control unit is located next to TCM. *See Fig. 1.*

Engine Coolant Temperature (ECT) Sensor – ECT sensor delivers input signal to TCM, indicating engine coolant temperature. ECT sensor is located on front of engine. *See Fig. 2.*

Overdrive (OD) Switch – The OD switch provides an input signal to TCM to indicate when overdrive is selected by operator. When OD switch is depressed to ON position, transmission will shift into 4th gear when shift lever is in "D" position, and OD OFF light on instrument panel will go off. The OD OFF light is located on instrument panel. When OD switch is released to OFF position, transmission will shift into 3rd gear, and OD OFF light on instrument panel will illuminate. The OD switch is mounted on shift lever.

Park/Neutral Position (PNP) Switch Signal – PNP switch delivers an input signal to TCM indicating shift lever position. Switch is located on side of transmission.

Throttle Position (TP) Sensor – TP sensor delivers a variable throttle position input signal to TCM. TP sensor is located on side of throttle body.

Vehicle Speed Sensor (VSS) – Vehicle speed signal is delivered to TCM by No. 1 and No. 2 speed sensors.

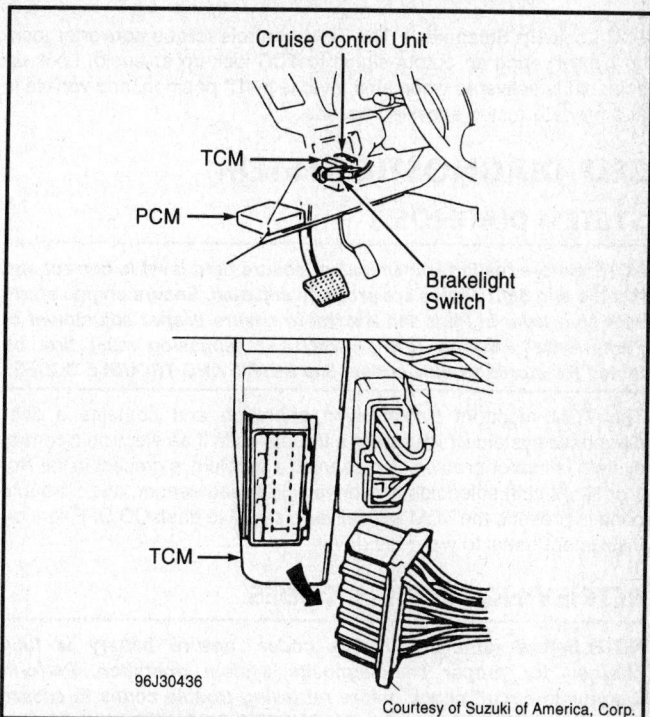

Fig. 1: Locating TCM Location

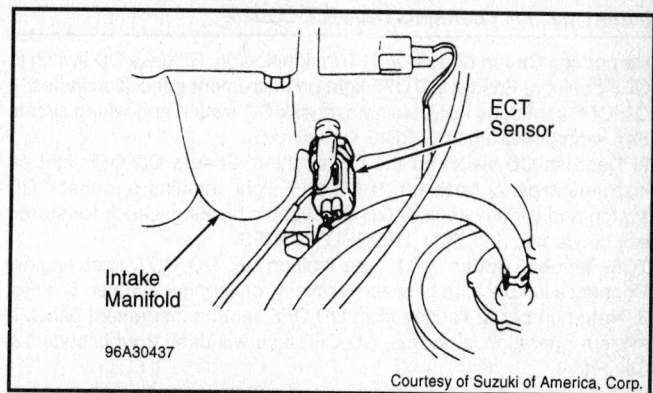

Fig. 2: Locating ECT Sensor

TCM OUTPUT DEVICES

No. 1 & No. 2 Shift Solenoids – The TCM controls transmission shifting by delivering an output signal to operate proper shift solenoid. Shift solenoids are located on transmission valve body. Shift solenoids are operated in accordance with shift lever range. If a shift solenoid malfunctions, TCM will select a gear. See FAIL SAFE GEAR POSITION table.

FAIL SAFE GEAR POSITION

Application	Solenoid No. 1 Failure	Solenoid No. 2 Failure	Solenoid No. 1 & 2 Failure
"D"			
1st Gear	3rd	1st	OD
2nd Gear	3rd	OD	OD
3rd Gear	3rd	OD	OD
OD Gear	OD	OD	OD
"2"			
1st Gear	3rd	1st	3rd
2nd Gear	3rd	3rd	3rd
"L"			
1st Gear	1st	1st	1st

3-218

AUTOMATIC TRANSMISSIONS
AW03-72LE Electronic Controls (Except OBD-II) (Cont.)

TCC Lock-Up Solenoid – The TCM controls torque converter lock-up by delivering an output signal to TCC lock-up solenoid. Lock-up solenoid is activated when shift lever is in "D" position, and vehicle is at a predetermined specified speed.

SELF-DIAGNOSTIC SYSTEM

SYSTEM DIAGNOSIS

NOTE: Before testing transmission, ensure fluid level is correct and throttle and shift cables are properly adjusted. Ensure engine starts with shift lever in Park and Neutral to ensure proper adjustment of Park/Neutral Position (PNP) switch. Transmission must first be tested for stored trouble codes. See RETRIEVING TROUBLE CODES.

The TCM monitors transmission operation and contains a self-diagnostic system which stores a trouble code if an electronic control system failure or problem is present. If a problem is present in the No. 1 or No. 2 shift solenoids and/or vehicle speed sensor, and a trouble code is present, the TCM will deliver a signal to flash OD OFF light on instrument panel to warn the driver.

RETRIEVING TROUBLE CODES

NOTE: Before retrieving trouble codes, ensure battery is fully charged for proper self-diagnostic system operation. Perform diagnostic circuit check before retrieving trouble codes to ensure operation of OD OFF light. See DIAGNOSTIC CIRCUIT CHECK. Trouble codes must be cleared from TCM memory once repairs have been performed. See CLEARING TROUBLE CODES.

Diagnostic Circuit Check – **1)** Turn ignition on. Release OD switch to OFF position. Ensure OD OFF light on instrument panel illuminates. If OD OFF light does not illuminate, check OD switch and wiring circuit. See wiring diagram in WIRING DIAGRAMS.
2) Depress OD switch to the ON position. Ensure OD OFF light on instrument panel goes off. If OD OFF light remains on, check OD switch and wiring circuit. If OD OFF light is blinking, check for stored trouble codes. See TCM TROUBLE CODES.
TCM Trouble Codes – **1)** Turn ignition on. DO NOT start engine. Connect a jumper wire between terminals on monitor coupler. *See Fig. 3.* Note number of flashes from OD OFF light on instrument panel. If system operation is normal, OD OFF light will flash trouble code 12. *See Fig. 4.*
2) If system is operating normally, and no trouble codes are present, turn ignition off and remove jumper wire. Perform manual shifting test to determine if problem is electrical or mechanical. See MANUAL SHIFTING TEST under TRANSMISSION SHIFT TESTING. Check system by symptom. See SYMPTOM TROUBLE SHOOTING.
3) If a trouble code is present, OD OFF light will flash a trouble code. The number of flashes will equal first digit of trouble code. After a one second pause, second digit will be displayed. *See Fig. 4.*
4) If more than one trouble code is present, next trouble code will be displayed after a 3 second pause. Smallest number trouble code will be displayed first. Trouble codes will be repeated. Once trouble code is obtained, determine probable cause. See TROUBLE CODE IDENTIFICATION table.

NOTE: Manufacturer does not provide diagnostic trouble code testing information. Only symptom trouble shooting and component testing procedures are given. For additional component information, see appropriate ENGINE PERFORMANCE article in 1995 MITCHELL® IMPORTED CARS, LIGHT TRUCKS & VANS SERVICE & REPAIR MANUAL.

TROUBLE CODE IDENTIFICATION

Trouble Code	[1] Probable Cause
12	System Operation Normal
21	No. 1 Shift Solenoid Open Circuit
22	No. 1 Shift Solenoid Short Circuit
23	No. 2 Shift Solenoid Open Circuit
24	No. 2 Shift Solenoid Short Circuit
25	TCC Solenoid Open Circuit
26	TCC Solenoid Short Circuit
31	Vehicle Speed Sensor Open Or Short Circuit
32	Throttle Position Sensor Short Circuit
33	Throttle Position Sensor Open Circuit
34	Defective Park/Neutral Position Switch
36	[2] No Signal-Both Vehicle Speed Sensors

[1] – Check listed component for probable cause. Also check wiring and connections of specified component.
[2] – No signal from both transmission and speedometer mounted vehicle speed sensors.

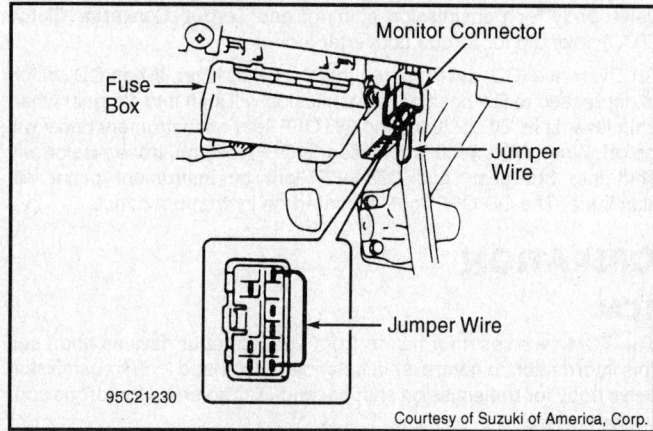

Fig. 3: Identifying Monitor Coupler Terminals

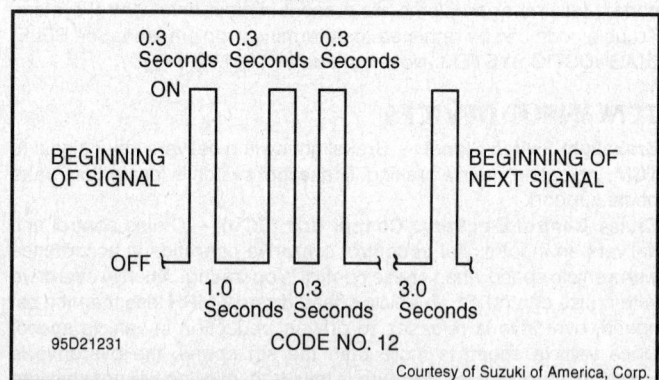

Fig. 4: Identifying Trouble Code Displays

CLEARING TROUBLE CODES

Once repairs have been performed, trouble codes must be cleared from TCM memory. To clear, disconnect negative battery cable for at least 10 seconds.

TRANSMISSION SHIFT TESTING

MANUAL SHIFTING TEST

NOTE: Perform manual shifting test if no trouble codes are present. Manual shifting test determines if problem is an electrical or mechanical related problem.

AUTOMATIC TRANSMISSIONS
AW03-72LE Electronic Controls (Except OBD-II) (Cont.)

3-219

1) Start and operate vehicle until normal operating temperature is achieved. Disconnect TCM harness connector. *See Fig. 1.* Road test vehicle and ensure transmission gear changes correspond with shift lever position. See GEAR APPLICATION table.

2) If an abnormality is present, problem is mechanically related. If all gears are correct, perform trouble shooting in accordance with symptom. See SYMPTOM TROUBLE SHOOTING. Turn ignition off.

3) Reconnect TCM harness connector. Clear trouble codes from TCM memory, as disconnecting electrical connector may set a trouble code. See CLEARING TROUBLE CODES.

GEAR APPLICATION

Shift Lever Position	Gear
"D"	Overdrive
"2"	3rd Gear
"L"	1st Gear
"R"	Reverse
"P"	Park

SYMPTOM TROUBLE SHOOTING

DOES NOT SHIFT

1) Ensure engine and transmission are at normal operating temperature. Retrieve trouble codes. See RETRIEVING TROUBLE CODES. If a trouble code is present, repair as needed. Clear trouble codes. See CLEARING TROUBLE CODES. If no trouble codes are present, go to next step.

2) Perform manual shifting test. See MANUAL SHIFTING TEST under TRANSMISSION SHIFT TESTING. Raise and support vehicle. Access TCM harness connector (leave connected). *See Fig. 1.* Go to next step.

3) Using a DVOM, measure voltage (backprobe) between chassis ground and TCM harness connector terminal S1, then terminal S2 while operating vehicle through all gears with shift selector in "D" position. *See Fig. 5.* Record readings and compare with table. See SHIFT SOLENOID VOLTAGE table. Go to next step.

SHIFT SOLENOID VOLTAGE

Application	1st Gear	2nd Gear	3rd Gear	OD Gear
No. 1 Shift Solenoid	10-14 Volts	10-14 Volts	0 Volt	0 Volt
No. 2 Shift Solenoid	0 Volt	10-14 Volts	10-14 Volts	0 Volt

4) If any reading is not as specified, go to next step. If all readings are as specified, inspect shift solenoids. See SHIFT SOLENOIDS under COMPONENT TESTING. If shift solenoids are okay, inspect and repair circuits between TCM and shift solenoids as needed. If circuits are okay, replace TCM and retest.

5) Repeat vehicle operation through all gears while monitoring voltage between chassis ground and TCM harness connector terminal "L", then terminal "2". Reading should be zero volts at each terminal. If readings are not as specified, replace Park/Neutral Position (PNP) switch and retest. If both readings are zero volts, replace TCM and retest.

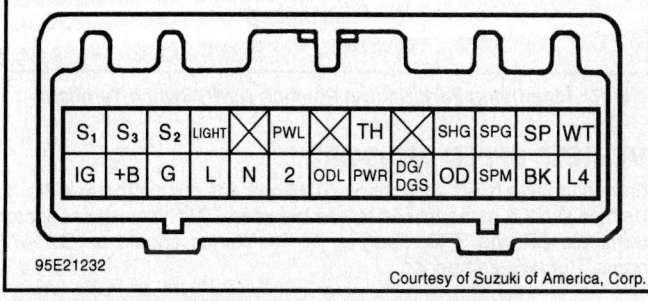

95E21232

Courtesy of Suzuki of America, Corp.

Fig. 5: Identifying TCM Harness Connector Terminals

INCORRECT SHIFT SPEEDS

1) Ensure engine and transmission are at normal operating temperature. Retrieve trouble codes. See RETRIEVING TROUBLE CODES. If a trouble code is present, repair as needed. Clear trouble codes. See CLEARING TROUBLE CODES. If no trouble codes are present, go to next step.

2) Access TCM harness connector (leave connected). *See Fig. 1.* Using a DVOM, measure voltage (backprobe) between chassis ground and TCM harness connector terminal TH. *See Fig. 5.* Go to next step.

3) Slowly depress accelerator pedal to Wide Open Throttle (WOT). Monitor voltage while depressing throttle pedal. Voltage should decrease as throttle is depressed. Voltage should be within the following range: battery voltage multiplied by .95 (idle position) to battery voltage multiplied by .39 (WOT). Go to next step.

4) If voltage is not within range in step 3), or changes erratically, inspect Throttle Position (TP) sensor. See appropriate ENGINE PERFORMANCE article in 1995 MITCHELL® IMPORTED CARS, LIGHT TRUCKS & VANS SERVICE & REPAIR MANUAL. If voltage is within range, turn ignition off and go to next step.

5) Disconnect TCM harness connector. Disconnect speedometer cable from transmission. Using a DVOM, measure resistance between chassis ground and TCM harness connector terminal SPM. *See Fig. 5.* Monitor DVOM while turning speedometer cable. Go to next step.

6) If reading pulses between zero ohms and infinity 4 times per revolution, go to next step. If reading is not as specified, inspect for a broken speedometer cable, faulty sensor in speedometer or faulty circuit between speedometer and TCM.

7) Ensure ignition is off. Reconnect TCM harness connector. Turn ignition on. Using a DVOM, measure voltage (backprobe) between chassis ground and TCM harness connector terminal PWR. *See Fig. 5.* If reading is 5 volts with shift selector in "N" position, and zero volts in "P" position, replace TCM and retest. If readings are not as specified, replace PNP switch and retest. If problem is still present, inspect and repair circuits between PNP switch and TCM.

NO UPSHIFT TO OVERDRIVE

1) Ensure engine and transmission are at normal operating temperature. Retrieve trouble codes. See RETRIEVING TROUBLE CODES. If a trouble code is present, repair as needed. Clear trouble codes. See CLEARING TROUBLE CODES. If no trouble codes are present, go to next step.

2) Perform manual shifting test. See MANUAL SHIFTING TEST under TRANSMISSION SHIFT TESTING. Reconnect TCM harness connector. Raise and support vehicle. Using a DVOM, measure voltage (backprobe) between chassis ground and TCM harness connector terminal S1, then terminal S2 while operating vehicle through all gears with shift selector in "D" position. *See Fig. 5.* Record readings and compare with table. See SHIFT SOLENOID VOLTAGE table. Go to next step.

SHIFT SOLENOID VOLTAGE

Application	1st Gear	2nd Gear	3rd Gear	OD Gear
No. 1 Shift Solenoid	10-14 Volts	10-14 Volts	0 Volt	0 Volt
No. 2 Shift Solenoid	0 Volt	10-14 Volts	10-14 Volts	0 Volt

3) If any reading is not within specification, go to next step. If all readings are within specification, inspect shift solenoids. See SHIFT SOLENOIDS under COMPONENT TESTING. If shift solenoids are okay, inspect and repair circuits between TCM and shift solenoids as needed. If circuits are okay, replace TCM and retest.

4) Repeat vehicle operation through all gears while monitoring voltage between chassis ground and TCM harness connector terminal "L", then terminal "2". If reading is zero volts for both circuits, go to next step. If reading is not as specified, replace Park/Neutral Position (PNP) switch and retest.

3-220

AUTOMATIC TRANSMISSIONS
AW03-72LE Electronic Controls (Except OBD-II) (Cont.)

5) Measure voltage (backprobe) between chassis ground and TCM harness connector terminal OD. See Fig. 5. If reading is 5 volts with OD switch in OFF position, and zero volts in ON position, go to next step. If reading is not as specified, inspect OD switch and applicable circuits. See wiring diagram in WIRING DIAGRAMS. Repair as needed.

6) Measure voltage (backprobe) between chassis ground and TCM harness connector terminal WT. See Fig. 5. If reading is zero volts with engine coolant temperature below 77°F (25°C), and battery voltage with engine coolant temperature above 86°F (30°C), go to step 8). If reading is not as specified, go to next step.

7) Inspect ECT sensor. See ENGINE COOLANT TEMPERATURE sensor under COMPONENT TESTING. If ECT tests okay, see appropriate ENGINE PERFORMANCE article in 1995 MITCHELL® IMPORTED CARS, LIGHT TRUCKS & VANS SERVICE & REPAIR MANUAL for further diagnostic information.

8) Measure voltage (backprobe) between chassis ground and TCM harness connector terminal L4. If reading is zero volts with transfer case in 4WD position, and battery voltage in 2WD position, replace TCM and retest. If reading is not as specified, replace 4WD switch (located on side of transfer case).

NO TCC LOCK-UP

1) Ensure engine and transmission are at normal operating temperature. Retrieve trouble codes. See RETRIEVING TROUBLE CODES. If a trouble code is present, repair as needed. Clear trouble codes. See CLEARING TROUBLE CODES. If no trouble codes are present, go to next step.

2) Raise and support vehicle. Using a DVOM, measure voltage (backprobe) between chassis ground and TCM harness connector terminal S3 while operating vehicle through all forward gears with shift selector in "D" position. See Fig. 5. Go to next step.

3) Ensure mode switch is in "N" (normal) position. Accelerate to 35 MPH. If battery voltage is present, inspect TCC solenoid. See SHIFT SOLENOIDS under COMPONENT TESTING. Replace as needed and retest. If battery voltage is not present, measure voltage (backprobe) between chassis ground and TCM harness connector terminal BK. See Fig. 5. Go to next step.

4) Depress and release brake pedal while monitoring voltage. If reading is zero volts with pedal released, and battery voltage with pedal depressed, go to next step. If reading is not as specified, inspect brake switch and circuit. Repair as needed.

5) Measure voltage (backprobe) between chassis ground and TCM harness connector terminal WT. See Fig. 5. If reading is zero volts with engine coolant temperature below 77°F (25°C), and battery voltage with engine coolant temperature above 86°F (30°C), go to step 7). If reading is not as specified, go to next step.

6) Inspect ECT sensor. See ENGINE COOLANT TEMPERATURE SENSOR under COMPONENT TESTING. If ECT is okay, see appropriate ENGINE PERFORMANCE article in 1995 MITCHELL® IMPORTED CARS, LIGHT TRUCKS & VANS SERVICE & REPAIR MANUAL for further diagnostic information.

7) Measure voltage (backprobe) between chassis ground and TCM harness connector terminal L4. If reading is zero volts with transfer case in 4WD position, and battery voltage in 2WD position, replace TCM and retest. If reading is not as specified, replace 4WD switch (located on side of transfer case).

COMPONENT TESTING

SOLENOIDS

1) Obtain access to TCM. See Fig. 1. Ensure ignition is off. Disconnect TCM harness connector. Turn ignition on. Using a fused jumper wire, connect one end to TCM harness connector terminal +B. With other end, probe terminals S1, S2 and S3, one at a time. See Fig. 5. Ensure a "clicking" sound can be heard when battery voltage is applied. Replace solenoid if no sound is heard.

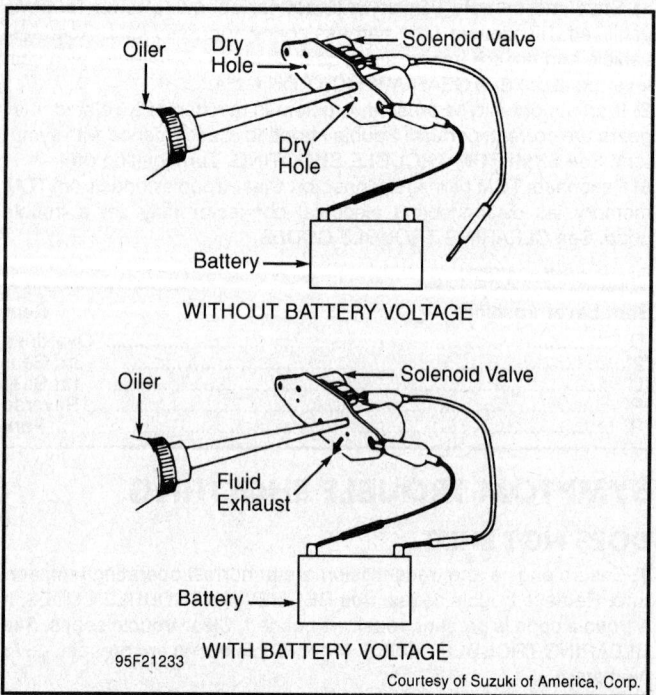

95F21233

Courtesy of Suzuki of America, Corp.

Fig. 6: Checking Solenoids

2) To check solenoid seals, apply battery voltage to solenoid. Apply ATF to solenoid with battery voltage connected. See Fig. 6. ATF should pass through solenoid. Remove battery voltage. Ensure ATF does not pass through solenoid. Replace solenoid if defective.

PARK/NEUTRAL POSITION (PNP) SWITCH

Disconnect PNP switch harness connector. Switch is located on side of transmission. Using a DVOM, check for continuity between specified terminals in accordance with shift lever position. See Fig. 7. Replace switch if defective.

PARK/NEUTRAL POSITION SWITCH CONTINUITY

Shift Lever Position	Continuity Between Terminals
"P"	5 & 6, 8 & 9
"R"	4 & 9
"N"	5 & 6, 7 & 9
"D"	3 & 9
"2"	2 & 9
"L"	1 & 9

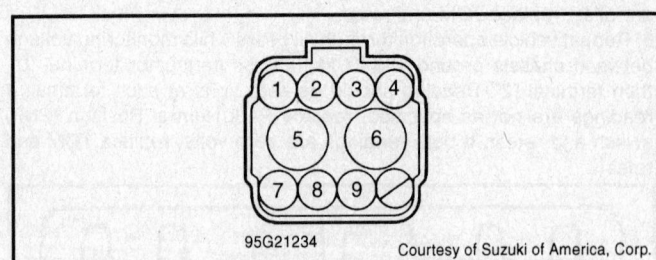

95G21234

Courtesy of Suzuki of America, Corp.

Fig. 7: Identifying Park/Neutral Position (PNP) Switch Terminals

VEHICLE SPEED SENSOR

Ensure ignition is off. Disconnect TCM harness connector. See Fig. 1. Using a DVOM, measure resistance between TCM harness connector terminals SP and SPG. See Fig. 5. Resistance should be 387-473 ohms. Replace as needed.

WIRING DIAGRAMS

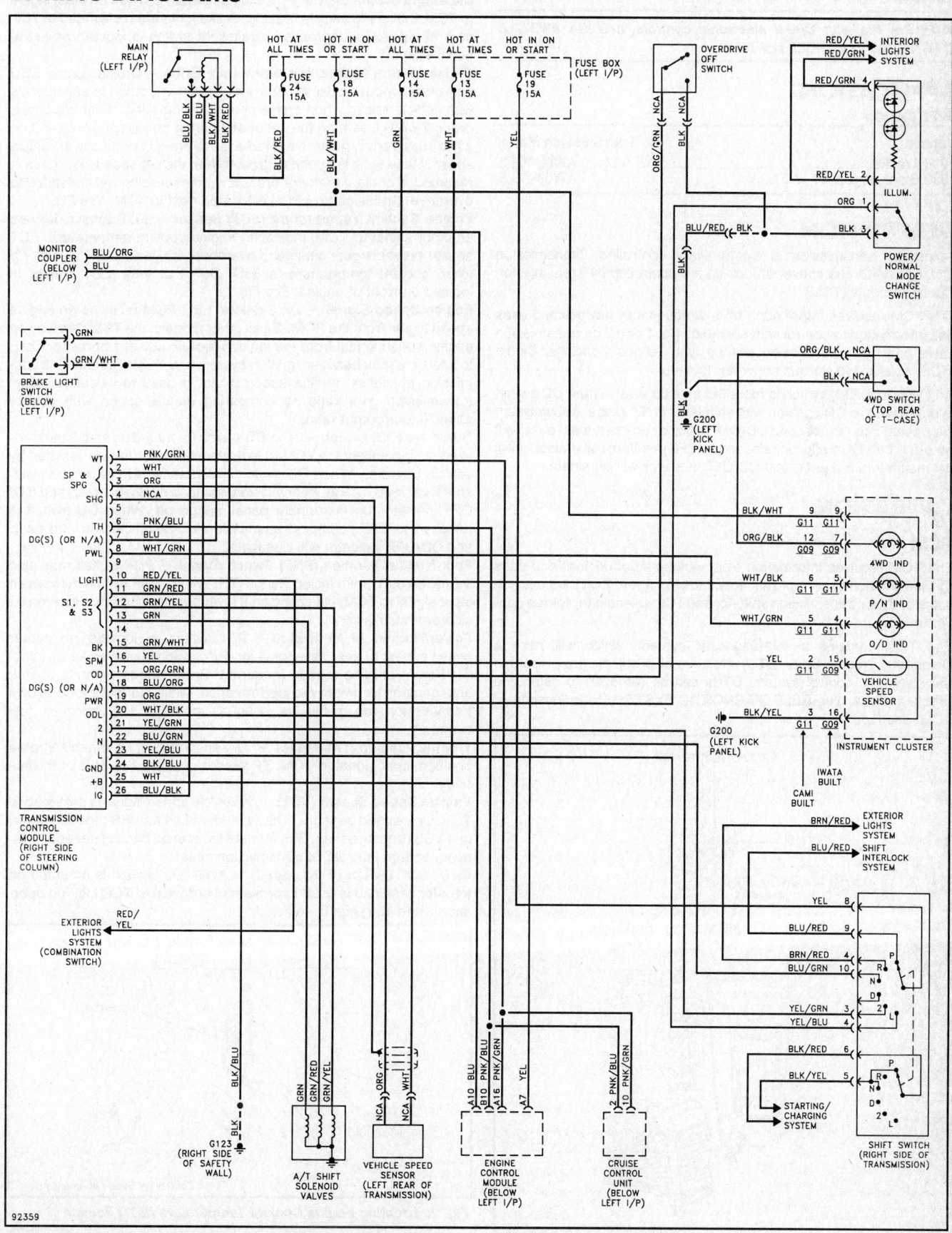

Fig. 8: Transmission Wiring Diagram (1995 Suzuki Sidekick)

AUTOMATIC TRANSMISSIONS
AW03-72LE Electronic Controls (With OBD-II)

Geo: Tracker (1996)
Suzuki: Sidekick, X-90 (1996)

NOTE: For Kia with OBD-II electronic controls, see KIA AW372LE ELECTRONIC CONTROLS article.

APPLICATION

APPLICATION

Vehicle	Transmission Model
1996 Tracker	AW03-72LE
1996 Sidekick & X-90	AW03-72LE

DESCRIPTION

Automatic transmission is electronically controlled. Transmission shifting and torque converter lock-up are controlled by Transmission Control Module (TCM).

The TCM receives information from various input devices and uses this information to control shift solenoids No. 1 and 2 on transmission valve body for transmission shifting, and Torque Converter Clutch (TCC) solenoid for torque converter lock-up.

An Overdrive (OD) switch is mounted on shift lever. When OD switch is depressed to ON position with shift lever in "D" range, transmission will upshift into 4th gear and OD/OFF indicator on instrument panel will go off. When OD switch is released to OFF position, transmission will downshift into 3rd gear, and OD/OFF indicator will illuminate.

OPERATION

TCM

The TCM receives information from various input devices and uses this information to control shift solenoids No. 1 and 2 on transmission valve body for transmission shifting, and TCC solenoid for torque converter lock-up.

The TCM contains a self-diagnostic system, which will store a Diagnostic Trouble Code (DTC) if failures or problems are present in the electronic control system. DTCs can be retrieved to determine problem areas. See SELF-DIAGNOSTIC SYSTEM. Note location of TCM. *See Fig. 1.*

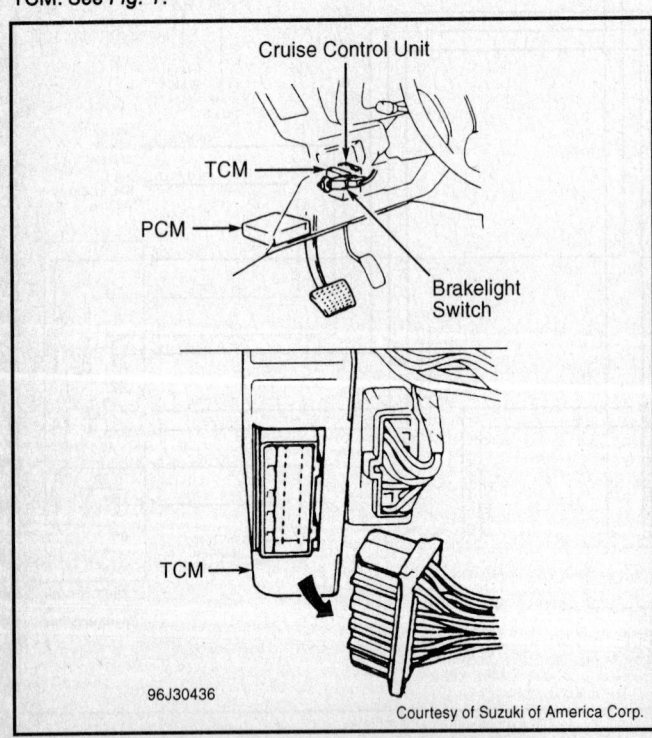

Fig. 1: Locating Transmission Control Module (TCM)

TCM INPUT DEVICES

Brakelight Switch Signal – Brakelight switch delivers an input signal to TCM, indicating vehicle braking. Brakelight switch disengages TCC as brake pedal is depressed. Brakelight switch is located on brake pedal support.

Cruise Control Electronic Control Unit (ECU) – Cruise control ECU delivers an input signal to control overdrive operation in accordance with vehicle speed when cruise control is operating. If vehicle speed drops 2 MPH less than the set speed during cruise control operation while in overdrive, overdrive is released to prevent reduction in vehicle speed. Once vehicle speed is greater than the set speed, overdrive is resumed. If coolant temperature is low, transmission will not shift into overdrive. Cruise control ECU is located next to TCM. *See Fig. 1.*

Engine Coolant Temperature (ECT) Sensor – ECT sensor delivers an input signal to TCM, indicating engine coolant temperature. ECT sensor prevents gear change to overdrive (4th gear) and TCC lock-up when coolant temperature is 86°F (30°C) or less. ECT sensor is located on front of engine. *See Fig. 2.*

Engine Speed Signal – On Sidekick 1.8L, TCM receives an engine speed signal from the PCM. On all other models, the TCM receives an engine speed signal from the ignition system noise suppressor filter, located in circuit between ignition system and TCM. To monitor transmission efficiency, engine speed signal is used to calculate actual transmission gear ratio by comparing engine speed with vehicle speed (input/output ratio).

Overdrive (OD) Switch – The OD switch (mounted on shift lever) provides an input signal to TCM to indicate when overdrive is selected by vehicle operator. When OD switch is depressed to ON position with shift lever in "D" range, transmission will upshift into 4th gear, and OD/OFF indicator on instrument panel will go off. When OD switch is released to OFF position, transmission will downshift into 3rd gear, and OD/OFF indicator will illuminate.

Park/Neutral Position (PNP) Switch Signal – PNP switch may also be known as Transmission Range (TR) switch. PNP switch delivers an input signal to TCM, indicating shift lever position. Switch is located on side of transmission.

Power/Normal (P/N) Switch – P/N switch is located on center console, next to gear selector lever. P/N switch allows driver to select 2 different shifting modes (patterns). Power mode extends upshift engagement for improved performance, while Normal mode allows transmission to upshift as soon as possible for improved fuel economy.

Throttle Position (TP) Sensor – TP sensor delivers a variable throttle position input signal to TCM. TP sensor is located on side of throttle body.

Vehicle Speed Sensor (VSS) – A vehicle speed signal is delivered to TCM by 2 speed sensors. They are identified as VSS (speedometer) and VSS (transmission). Sensors are located on back of speedometer head, and on left rear of transmission case.

4WD "LO" Switch (If Equipped) – 4WD "LO" switch is mounted on transfer case and is used to prevent overdrive and TCC lock-up operation when 4L range is selected.

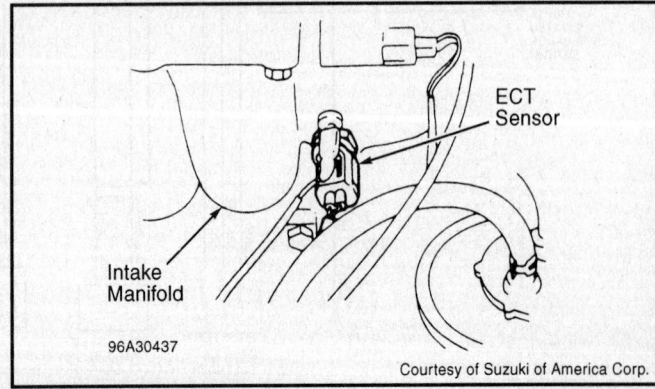

Fig. 2: Locating Engine Coolant Temperature (ECT) Sensor

AUTOMATIC TRANSMISSIONS
AW03-72LE Electronic Controls (With OBD-II) (Cont.)

3-223

TCM OUTPUT DEVICES

OD/OFF Indicator – OD/OFF indicator, located in instrument cluster, indicates OD is disabled when illuminated. Indicator also informs driver of a transmission related system problem, and can be used to display DTCs.

Power Indicator – Power indicator, located in instrument cluster, informs driver that power shifting mode has been selected.

Shift Solenoids No. 1 & 2 – The TCM controls transmission shifting by delivering an output signal to operate appropriate shift solenoid. Shift solenoids are located on transmission valve body. Shift solenoids are operated in accordance with shift lever range. If a shift solenoid malfunctions, TCM will select a gear. See FAIL SAFE GEAR POSITION table.

FAIL SAFE GEAR POSITION

Application	Solenoid No. 1 Failure	Solenoid No. 2 Failure	Solenoid No. 1 & 2 Failure
"D"			
1st Gear	3rd	1st	OD
2nd Gear	3rd	OD	OD
3rd Gear	3rd	OD	OD
OD Gear	OD	OD	OD
"2"			
1st Gear	3rd	1st	3rd
2nd Gear	3rd	3rd	3rd
"L"			
1st Gear	1st	1st	1st

TCC Lock-Up Solenoid – The TCM controls torque converter lock-up by delivering an output signal to TCC lock-up solenoid. Lock-up solenoid is activated when shift lever is in "D" position, and vehicle is at a predetermined specified speed. Lock-up will not occur until engine temperature is greater than 86°F (30°C).

SELF-DIAGNOSTIC SYSTEM

SYSTEM DIAGNOSIS

NOTE: The TCM On-Board Diagnostic (OBD) system check must be used as the starting point for any transmission electrical repairs. This will direct technician to the next logical step, save diagnostic time and prevent unnecessary replacement of functional components. See TCM ON-BOARD DIAGNOSTIC (OBD) SYSTEM CHECK.

The TCM continuously monitors transmission operation and contains a self-diagnostic system which stores a Diagnostic Trouble Code (DTC) if an electronic control system problem or component failure is present. Two kinds of DTCs are used in the self-diagnostic system for diagnosis. A 2-digit "Flash Code" DTC, and a 4-digit OBD-II DTC. Flash Code DTC is stored in the TCM and will illuminate OD/OFF indicator when set. OBD-II DTC is stored in the Powertrain Control Module (PCM) and illuminates the Malfunction Indicator Light (MIL) when set.

DTCs may be retrieved using 2 methods. If OD/OFF indicator or MIL indicates a system malfunction, retrieve DTCs using desired method. See RETRIEVING TROUBLE CODES.

RETRIEVING TROUBLE CODES

NOTE: Before retrieving trouble codes, ensure battery is fully charged for proper self-diagnostic system operation. Perform TCM On-Board Diagnostic (OBD) system check before retrieving trouble codes to ensure proper operation of OD/OFF indicator. See TCM ON-BOARD DIAGNOSTIC (OBD) SYSTEM CHECK. Trouble codes must be cleared from PCM and TCM memory once repairs have been performed. See CLEARING TROUBLE CODES.

NOTE: If a trouble code cannot be retrieved, and a transmission fault is present, perform manual shifting test to determine if fault is caused by an electrical or mechanical related problem. See MANUAL SHIFTING TEST under TRANSMISSION SHIFT TESTING.

Flash Code Method – **1)** Using a fused jumper wire, jumper 6-pin Data Link Connector (DLC) No. 2 (Black), terminal No. 1 (Blue/Green wire on Sidekick 1.8L; Blue/Orange wire on all others) and terminal No. 4 (Black wire) together. DLC is located in right front of engine compartment, next to washer fluid reservoir. *See Fig. 3.*

2) Turn ignition on. Observe OD/OFF indicator. Indicator will flash a number of times to indicate first digit of DTC, followed by a 1.5 second pause and an additional number of flashes to indicate second digit of DTC. If multiple DTCs are set, a 2.5 second pause will separate each DTC beginning with smallest number DTC first.

3) If no malfunctions are present, OD/OFF indicator will flash once, pause for 1.5 seconds, and flash 2 additional times. This indicates DTC 12 (system operation normal). If a DTC is present, identify DTC and diagnose accordingly. See FLASH CODE/DTC IDENTIFICATION table, then proceed to DIAGNOSTIC TESTING. After repairs are made, clear DTCs. See CLEARING TROUBLE CODES. Test drive vehicle and ensure OD/OFF indicator or MIL does not illuminate.

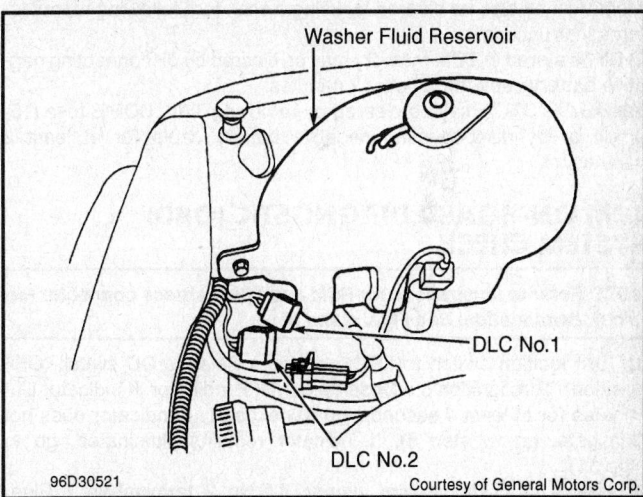

96D30521   Courtesy of General Motors Corp.

Fig. 3: Locating DLC No. 2 (Sidekick 1.6L, X-90 & Tracker Shown; Sidekick 1.8L Is Similar)

3-224

AUTOMATIC TRANSMISSIONS
AW03-72LE Electronic Controls (With OBD-II) (Cont.)

Scan Tool Method – 1) Using a Tech-1 or other OBD-II compatible scan tool, interface PCM by connecting to OBD-II 16-pin DLC, located under instrument panel to left of steering column. Retrieve DTCs following scan tool manufacturers instructions.

2) If a DTC is present, identify DTC and diagnose accordingly. See FLASH CODE/DTC IDENTIFICATION table, then proceed to DIAGNOSTIC TESTING. After repairs are made, clear DTCs. See CLEARING TROUBLE CODES. Test drive vehicle and ensure OD/OFF indicator or MIL does not illuminate.

FLASH CODE/DTC IDENTIFICATION

Flash Code/DTC	Condition
12/ [1]	System Operation Normal
[2] [3]/P1715	Park/Neutral Position Switch Circuit
21 & 22/P0753	No. 1 Shift Solenoid Circuit
23 & 24/P0758	No. 2 Shift Solenoid Circuit
25 & 26/P0743 Or P0773	TCC Solenoid Circuit
27/P0751	No. 1 Shift Solenoid Performance
28/P0756	No. 2 Shift Solenoid Performance
29/P0741 Or P0771	TCC Circuit Performance
31/P0720	VSS (Transmission) Circuit
32 & 33/P1700	TP Sensor Circuit
34/P0705	Transmission Range Switch Circuit
35/P1710	VSS (Speedometer) Back-Up Signal Circuit
37/P1875	4WD "LO" Switch Circuit
51/P1705	ECT Sensor Signal Input
52/P0725	Engine Speed Input Circuit

[1] – No DTC set.
[2] – No Flash Code set. Use scan tool method to retrieve trouble code.
[3] – DTC P1715 applies to Tracker only.

CLEARING TROUBLE CODES

Sidekick & X-90 – 1) DTCs stored in PCM memory may be cleared by disconnecting negative battery cable for at least 2 minutes. Memory may also be cleared by using a scan tool following manufactures instructions.

2) DTCs stored in TCM memory may be cleared by disconnecting negative battery cable for at least 2 minutes.

Tracker – DTCs may be cleared by removing TAIL DOME fuse (15-amp), or by disconnecting negative battery cable for at least 2 minutes.

TCM ON-BOARD DIAGNOSTIC (OBD) SYSTEM CHECK

NOTE: Refer to Illustrations for PCM and TCM harness connector terminal identification. See Figs. 4 and 5.

1) Turn ignition switch to LOCK position. Release OD switch (OFF position). Turn ignition on. Observe OD/OFF indicator. If indicator illuminates for at least 4 seconds, go to next step. If indicator does not illuminate, go to step **5)**. If indicator remains illuminated, go to step **11)**.

2) Using a fused jumper wire, jumper DLC No. 2, terminal No. 1 (Blue/Green wire on Sidekick 1.8L; Blue/Orange wire on all others) to ground. *See Fig. 3.* If indicator flashes DTC 12, electrical system is operating normally at this time. Check for mechanical related problems. See appropriate overhaul article for further diagnosis. If indicator flashes any DTC other than DTC 12, go to next step. If indicator does not flash a DTC, go to step **4)**.

3) Turn ignition switch to LOCK position. Retrieve DTCs using desired method. See RETRIEVING TROUBLE CODES. If any DTCs are set, identify DTC and diagnose accordingly. See FLASH CODE/DTC IDENTIFICATION table. If no DTCs are set, check for mechanical related problems. See appropriate overhaul article for further diagnosis.

4) Turn ignition switch to LOCK position. Disconnect TCM harness connector. Using a DVOM, measure resistance of (Blue/Green wire on Sidekick 1.8L; Blue/Orange wire on all others) between DLC No. 2, terminal No. 1 and TCM harness connector terminal No. 18. If resistance is less than 2 ohms, inspect TCM for poor harness connection. Repair as necessary. If connection is okay, replace TCM. If resistance is not as specified, repair open in appropriate wire between TCM and DLC No. 2. Repeat step **1)**.

5) Turn ignition switch to LOCK position. Using a test light connected to battery positive, probe TCM harness connector terminal No. 20 (White/Black wire). Turn ignition on. If test light illuminates, go to next step. If test light does not illuminate, go to step **8)**.

6) Turn ignition switch to LOCK position. Remove instrument cluster. See appropriate INSTRUMENT PANELS article in ACCESSORIES & EQUIPMENT in appropriate MITCHELL® manual. Inspect OD/OFF indicator bulb. If bulb is okay, go to next step. If bulb filament is open, replace bulb and repeat step **1)**.

7) Using a DVOM, measure resistance in White/Black wire between TCM harness connector terminal No. 20 and OD/OFF indicator bulb terminal at instrument cluster harness connector. If resistance is less than 2 ohms, repair open in instrument cluster printed circuit and/or open in power circuit to instrument cluster. If resistance is not as specified, repair open in White/Black wire between TCM and OD/OFF indicator bulb. Repeat step **1)**.

8) Using a test light connected to ground, probe TCM harness connector terminal No. 26 (Black/White wire on Sidekick 1.8L; Blue/Black wire on all others). If test light illuminates, go to next step. If test light does not illuminate, repair open in appropriate wire between TCM and main relay. Repeat Step **1)**.

9) Using a test light connected to ground, probe TCM harness connector terminal No. 25 (White wire). If test light illuminates, go to next step. If test light does not illuminate, repair open in White wire between TCM and TAIL DOME fuse (15-amp). Repeat Step **1)**.

10) Using a DVOM, measure resistance between ground and TCM harness connector terminal No. 24 (Black/Blue wire). If resistance is 2 ohms or less, inspect TCM for poor harness connection. Repair as necessary. If connection is okay, replace TCM. If resistance is not as specified, repair open in Black/Blue wire between TCM and ground. Repeat step **1)**.

11) Turn ignition switch to LOCK position. Disconnect TCM harness connector. Using a DVOM, measure resistance between ground and TCM harness connector terminal No. 20 (White/Black wire). If resistance is 2 ohms or less, repair White/Black wire for a short to ground between TCM and instrument cluster. If resistance is not as specified, go to next step.

12) Remove console and disconnect OD switch harness connector. Using a DVOM, measure resistance between OD switch terminals while depressing switch. If DVOM display changes from open circuit to less than 2 ohms, go to next step. If DVOM display is not as specified, replace OD switch and repeat step **1)**.

13) Using a DVOM, measure resistance between TCM harness connector terminal No. 17 (Orange/Green wire) and OD switch harness connector terminal No. 2 (Orange/Green wire). If resistance is 2 ohms or less, replace TCM. If resistance is not as specified, repair Orange/Green wire for a short to ground between TCM and OD switch. Repeat step **1)**.

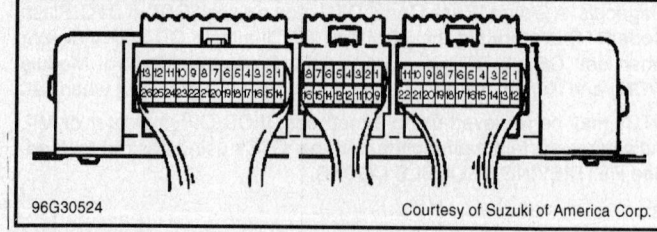

96G30524   Courtesy of Suzuki of America Corp.

Fig. 4: Identifying PCM Harness Connector Terminals

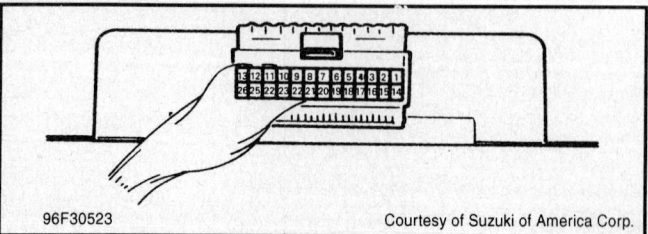

96F30523   Courtesy of Suzuki of America Corp.

Fig. 5: Identifying TCM Harness Connector Terminals

AUTOMATIC TRANSMISSIONS
AW03-72LE Electronic Controls (With OBD-II) (Cont.)

3-225

TRANSMISSION SHIFT TESTING
MANUAL SHIFTING TEST

NOTE: Perform manual shifting test if no trouble codes are present. Manual shifting test determines if fault is an electrical or mechanical related problem. Before proceeding, ensure vehicle is at normal operating temperature, ATF level is correct and throttle and shift cables are properly adjusted. Check if engine starts with shift lever in "P" and "N" positions to ensure proper adjustment of Park/Neutral Position (PNP) switch.

1) Start and operate vehicle until normal operating temperature is achieved. Disconnect TCM harness connector. See Fig. 1. Road test vehicle and ensure transmission gear changes correspond with shift lever position. See GEAR APPLICATION table.

2) If an abnormality is present, problem is mechanically related. If all gears applications are correct, perform trouble shooting in accordance with symptom. See SYMPTOM DIAGNOSIS in appropriate AUTOMATIC TRANSMISSIONS OVERHAUL article.

3) Turn ignition off. Reconnect TCM harness connector. Clear trouble codes from TCM memory, as disconnecting electrical connector may set a trouble code. See CLEARING TROUBLE CODES under SELF-DIAGNOSTIC SYSTEM.

GEAR APPLICATION

Shift Lever Position	Gear
"D"	Overdrive
"2"	3rd Gear
"L"	1st Gear
"R"	Reverse
"P"	Park

DIAGNOSTIC TESTING

NOTE: When trouble shooting transmission, first perform a functional check of the self-diagnostic system. See TCM ON-BOARD DIAGNOSTIC (OBD) SYSTEM CHECK under SELF-DIAGNOSTIC SYSTEM. If a DTC is retrieved, perform appropriate DTC test. If no DTCs are retrieved, and a transmission fault is present, perform manual shifting test to determine if fault is caused by an electrical or mechanical related problem. See MANUAL SHIFTING TEST under TRANSMISSION SHIFT TESTING.

NOTE: If "Flash Code" (2-digit code) method was used to retrieve DTCs, convert DTC into OBD-II 4-digit code for use in the following DTC tests. See FLASH CODE/DTC IDENTIFICATION table. See appropriate wiring diagram in WIRING DIAGRAMS to aid in component location, wire color and wire terminal identification.

DTC P0705: TRANSMISSION RANGE (TR) SENSOR CIRCUIT FAULT

NOTE: DTC P0705 will set if TR switch signal is not inputted for 25 seconds at 37 MPH or greater. DTC also sets when "D" range signal and an additional range signal is inputted simultaneously for 10 seconds.

1) Turn ignition switch to LOCK position. Disconnect TCM harness connector. Turn ignition on. Using a DVOM, measure voltage between ground and TCM harness connector terminal No. 9 (Green/Blue wire on Sidekick 1.8L; Green wire on all others) while moving gear selector through all gear ranges. If reading is 12 volts in "D" range, and less than one volt in any other range, go to next step. If reading is not as specified, go to step 7).

2) Using a DVOM, measure voltage between ground and TCM harness connector terminal No. 23 (Green/Blue wire) while moving gear selector through all gear ranges. If reading is 12 volts in "L" range, and less than one volt in any other range, go to next step. If reading is not as specified, go to step 11).

3) Using a DVOM, measure voltage between ground and TCM harness connector terminal No. 22 (Orange/Blue wire) while moving gear selector through all gear ranges. If reading is 12 volts in "N" range, and less than one volt in any other range, go to next step. If reading is not as specified, go to step 15).

4) Using a DVOM, measure voltage between ground and TCM harness connector terminal No. 21 (Green/Orange wire on Sidekick 1.8L; Green/Red wire on all others) while moving gear selector through all gear ranges. If reading is 12 volts in "2" range, and less than one volt in any other range, go to next step. If reading is not as specified, go to step 19).

5) Inspect TCM harness connector for poor terminal contact. Repair as necessary and retest. If contacts are okay, go to next step.

6) Turn ignition switch to LOCK position. Reconnect TCM harness connector. Clear DTCs. See CLEARING TROUBLE CODES under SELF-DIAGNOSTIC SYSTEM. Road test vehicle and recheck for DTCs. If DTC P0705 resets, replace TCM. If DTC P0705 does not reset, fault is not present at this time. Check for an intermittent problem. See DIAGNOSTIC AIDS.

7) Turn ignition switch to LOCK position. Disconnect TR switch harness connector. Turn ignition on. Using a DVOM, measure voltage between ground and TCM harness connector terminal No. 9 (Green/Blue wire on Sidekick 1.8L; Green wire on all others). If reading is one volt or less, go to next step. If reading is not as specified, repair appropriate wire for a short to power between TR switch and TCM.

8) Turn ignition off. Using a DVOM, measure resistance between ground and TCM harness connector terminal No. 9 (Green/Blue wire on Sidekick 1.8L; Green wire on all others). If resistance is less than 2 ohms, repair appropriate wire for a short to ground between TR switch and TCM. If resistance is not as specified, go to next step.

9) Using a DVOM, measure resistance between TCM harness connector terminal No. 9 (Green/Blue wire on Sidekick 1.8L; Green wire on all others) and TR switch harness connector terminal No. 9 (Yellow/Green wire on Sidekick 1.8L; Green wire on all others). If resistance is less than 2 ohms, go to next step. If resistance is not as specified, repair open in appropriate wire between TR switch and TCM.

10) Turn ignition on. Using a DVOM, measure voltage between ground and TR switch harness connector terminal No. 6 (Yellow wire). If reading is 11-14 volts, check TR switch for proper adjustment. See ADJUSTMENTS in appropriate AUTOMATIC TRANSMISSION SERVICING article. If adjustment is okay, replace TR switch. If reading is not as specified, repair open in Yellow wire between TR switch and TURN BACK fuse (15-amp).

11) Turn ignition switch to LOCK position. Disconnect TR switch harness connector. Turn ignition on. Using a DVOM, measure voltage between ground and TCM harness connector terminal No. 23 (Green/Blue wire). If reading is one volt or less, go to next step. If reading is not as specified, repair Green/Blue wire for a short to power between TR switch and TCM.

12) Turn ignition off. Using a DVOM, measure resistance between ground and TCM harness connector terminal No. 23 (Green/Blue wire). If resistance is less than 2 ohms, repair Green/Blue wire for a short to ground between TR switch and TCM. If resistance is not as specified, go to next step.

13) Using a DVOM, measure resistance between TCM harness connector terminal No. 23 (Green/Blue wire) and TR switch harness connector terminal No. 5 (Green/Blue wire on Sidekick 1.8L; Yellow/Blue wire on all others). If resistance is less than 2 ohms, go to next step. If resistance is not as specified, repair open in appropriate wire between TR switch and TCM.

14) Turn ignition on. Using a DVOM, measure voltage between ground and TR switch harness connector terminal No. 6 (Yellow wire). If reading is 11-14 volts, check TR switch for proper adjustment. See ADJUSTMENTS in appropriate AUTOMATIC TRANSMISSION SERVICING article. If adjustment is okay, replace TR switch. If reading is not as specified, repair open in Yellow wire between TR switch and TURN BACK fuse (15-amp).

3-226

AUTOMATIC TRANSMISSIONS
AW03-72LE Electronic Controls (With OBD-II) (Cont.)

15) Turn ignition switch to LOCK position. Disconnect TR switch harness connector. Turn ignition on. Using a DVOM, measure voltage between ground and TCM harness connector terminal No. 22 (Orange/Blue wire). If reading is one volt or less, go to next step. If reading is not as specified, repair Orange/Blue wire for a short to power between TR switch and TCM.

16) Turn ignition off. Using a DVOM, measure resistance between ground and TCM harness connector terminal No. 22 (Orange/Blue wire). If resistance is less than 2 ohms, repair Orange/Blue wire for a short to ground between TR switch and TCM. If resistance is not as specified, go to next step.

17) Using a DVOM, measure resistance between TCM harness connector terminal No. 22 (Orange/Blue wire) and TR switch harness connector terminal No. 10 (Orange/Blue wire on Sidekick 1.8L; Blue/Green wire on all others). If resistance is less than 2 ohms, go to next step. If resistance is not as specified, repair open in appropriate wire between TR switch and TCM.

18) Turn ignition on. Using a DVOM, measure voltage between ground and TR switch harness connector terminal No. 6 (Yellow wire). If reading is 11-14 volts, check TR switch for proper adjustment. See ADJUSTMENTS in appropriate AUTOMATIC TRANSMISSION SERVICING article. If adjustment is okay, replace TR switch. If reading is not as specified, repair open in Yellow wire between TR switch and TURN BACK fuse (15-amp).

19) Turn ignition switch to LOCK position. Disconnect TR switch harness connector. Turn ignition on. Using a DVOM, measure voltage between ground and TCM harness connector terminal No. 21 (Green/Orange wire on Sidekick 1.8L; Green/Red wire on all others). If reading is one volt or less, go to next step. If reading is not as specified, repair appropriate wire for a short to power between TR switch and TCM.

20) Turn ignition off. Using a DVOM, measure resistance between ground and TCM harness connector terminal No. 21 (Green/Orange wire on Sidekick 1.8L; Green/Red wire on all others). If resistance is less than 2 ohms, repair appropriate wire for a short to ground between TR switch and TCM. If resistance is not as specified, go to next step.

21) Using a DVOM, measure resistance between TCM harness connector terminal No. 21 (Green/Orange wire on Sidekick 1.8L; Green/Red wire on all others) and TR switch harness connector terminal No. 4 (Green/Orange wire on Sidekick 1.8L; Yellow/Green wire on all others). If resistance is less than 2 ohms, go to next step. If resistance is not as specified, repair open in appropriate wire between TR switch and TCM.

22) Turn ignition on. Using a DVOM, measure voltage between ground and TR switch harness connector terminal No. 6 (Yellow wire). If reading is 11-14 volts, check TR switch for proper adjustment. See ADJUSTMENTS in appropriate AUTOMATIC TRANSMISSION SERVICING article. If adjustment is okay, replace TR switch. If reading is not as specified, repair open in Yellow wire between TR switch and TURN BACK fuse (15-amp).

Diagnostic Aids – An intermittent condition may be caused by a poor connection, damaged wire insulation or a wire which is broken inside the insulation. Inspect TCM harness connector for damaged, corroded or backed-out terminal pins. Repair as necessary and retest system.

DTC P0720: VEHICLE SPEED SENSOR (VSS) CIRCUIT FAULT

NOTE: DTC P0720 will set when 4WD "LO" switch is open, and no VSS (transmission) signal is received while 2000 VSS (speedometer) signal pulses are received during 2 driving cycles.

1) Turn ignition switch to LOCK position. Disconnect TCM harness connector. Using a DVOM, measure resistance between TCM harness connector terminal No. 2 (White wire) and terminal No. 3 (Orange wire). If resistance is 387-473 ohms, go to step 6). If resistance is not as specified, go to next step.

2) Disconnect VSS (transmission). Using a DVOM, measure resistance between VSS terminals (sensor side). If resistance is 387-473 ohms, go to next step. If resistance is not as specified, replace VSS.

3) Using a DVOM, measure resistance between TCM harness connector terminal No. 3 (Orange wire) and VSS harness connector terminal No. 1 (Orange wire). If resistance is less than 2 ohms, go to next step. If resistance is not as specified, repair open in Orange wire between VSS and TCM.

4) Using a DVOM, measure resistance between TCM harness connector terminal No. 2 (White wire) and VSS harness connector terminal No. 2 (White wire). If resistance is less than 2 ohms, go to next step. If resistance is not as specified, repair open in White wire between VSS and TCM.

5) Reconnect all harness connectors. Clear DTCs. See CLEARING TROUBLE CODES under SELF-DIAGNOSTIC SYSTEM. Road test vehicle and recheck for DTCs. If DTC P0720 resets, replace TCM. If DTC P0720 does not reset, fault is not present at this time. Check for an intermittent problem. See DIAGNOSTIC AIDS.

Diagnostic Aids – An intermittent condition may be caused by a poor connection, damaged wire insulation or a wire which is broken inside the insulation. Inspect TCM harness connector for damaged, corroded or backed-out terminal pins. Repair as necessary and retest system.

DTC P0725: ENGINE SPEED INPUT CIRCUIT FAULT (EXCEPT SIDEKICK 1.8L)

NOTE: DTC P0725 will set if no engine speed signal is detected with ECT sensor signal being inputted (engine running) for 5 seconds, and occurring during 2 driving cycles.

Preliminary Check – Attempt to start engine. If engine starts, go to step 1). If engine does not start, diagnose ignition system. See appropriate BASIC DIAGNOSTIC PROCEDURES article in ENGINE PERFORMANCE in appropriate MITCHELL® manual.

1) Inspect noise suppressor filter. See NOISE SUPPRESSOR FILTER under COMPONENT TESTING. Replace if necessary. If noise suppressor filter is okay turn ignition switch to LOCK position. Disconnect TCM harness connector. Turn ignition on. Using a DVOM, measure voltage between ground and TCM harness connector terminal No. 4 (Brown wire). If reading is 11-14 volts, go to next step. If reading is not as specified, go to step 5)

2) Inspect TCM harness connector terminal No. 4 (Brown wire) for poor terminal contact. Repair as necessary and retest system. If connection is okay, go to next step.

3) Turn ignition switch to LOCK position. Reconnect TCM harness connector. Clear DTCs. See CLEARING TROUBLE CODES under SELF-DIAGNOSTIC SYSTEM. Start engine and run for 5 minutes. If DTC P0725 resets, go to next step. If DTC P0725 does not reset, fault is not present at this time. Check for an intermittent problem. See DIAGNOSTIC AIDS.

4) Replace noise suppressor filter with a known-good unit. Clear, then recheck for DTCs as noted in step 3). If DTC P0725 resets, replace TCM. If DTC P0725 does not reset, replace noise suppressor filter.

5) Disconnect noise suppressor filter harness connector. Using a DVOM, measure resistance between ground and TCM harness connector terminal No. 4 (Brown wire). If resistance is 2 ohms or less, repair Brown wire for a short to ground between TCM and noise suppressor filter. If resistance is not as specified, repair open or high resistance in Brown wire between TCM and noise suppressor filter.

Diagnostic Aids – An intermittent condition may be caused by a poor connection, damaged wire insulation or a wire which is broken inside the insulation. Inspect TCM harness connector for damaged, corroded or backed-out terminal pins. Repair as necessary and retest system.

DTC P0725: ENGINE SPEED INPUT CIRCUIT FAULT (SIDEKICK 1.8L)

NOTE: DTC P0725 will set if no engine speed signal is detected with ECT sensor signal being inputted (engine running) for 5 seconds, and occurring during 2 driving cycles.

Preliminary Check – Attempt to start engine. If engine starts, go to step 1). If engine does not start, diagnose ignition system. See appropriate BASIC DIAGNOSTIC PROCEDURES article in ENGINE PERFORMANCE in appropriate MITCHELL® manual.

1) Turn ignition switch to LOCK position. Inspect PCM and TCM harness connectors for poor connections. Repair as necessary and retest system. If connections are okay, go to next step.
2) Check Brown/White wire between 16-pin PCM harness connector terminal No. 10 and TCM harness connector terminal No. 4 for an open or short. Repair as necessary. If wire is okay, replace PCM and retest system.

DTC P0741 OR P0771: TORQUE CONVERTER CLUTCH (TCC) CIRCUIT PERFORMANCE

NOTE: DTC P0741 or P0771 will set while operating vehicle in 3rd or 4th gear in "D" range if TCC control of TCM does not agree with actual operation of TCC, even though TCC control solenoid valve is electrically in good condition. This DTC is commonly caused by a stuck TCC control solenoid valve and/or clogged valve body fluid passage.

1) Turn ignition on. Clear DTCs. See CLEARING TROUBLE CODES under SELF-DIAGNOSTIC SYSTEM. Start engine and allow it to reach normal operating temperature. Road test vehicle and check for correct upshift speeds and TCC operation. See ROAD TEST under TESTING in appropriate overhaul article. After road test, recheck for DTCs. If DTC P0741 or P0771 resets, go to next step. If DTC P0741 or P0771 does not reset, fault is not present at this time.
2) Inspect TCC solenoid valve operation. See SHIFT SOLENOIDS & TORQUE CONVERTER CLUTCH (TCC) SOLENOID under COMPONENT TESTING. Replace if necessary. If TCC solenoid tests okay, go to next step.
3) Inspect valve body condition. Check for leaks or obstructions in fluid passages. Overhaul if necessary. See VALVE BODY ASSEMBLY under COMPONENT DISASSEMBLY & REASSEMBLY in appropriate overhaul article. If valve body and fluid passages are okay, replace torque converter.

DTC P0743 OR P0773: TORQUE CONVERTER CLUTCH (TCC) CIRCUIT FAULT

NOTE: DTC P0743 or P0773 will set if voltage detected at TCM terminal No. 12 is 2 volts or less when TCC control solenoid valve is on, or 5.5 volts or greater when off.

1) Turn ignition switch to LOCK position. Disconnect TCM harness connector. Using a DVOM, measure resistance between ground and TCM harness connector terminal No. 12 (Green/Yellow wire). If resistance is 11-15 ohms at room temperature, go to step 4). If resistance is not as specified, go to next step.
2) Disconnect TCC control solenoid valve harness connector closest to transmission. Using a DVOM, measure resistance between ground and TCM harness connector terminal No. 12 (Green/Yellow wire). If resistance is less than 2 ohms, repair Green/Yellow wire for a short to ground between TCM and TCC control solenoid valve. If resistance is not as specified, go to next step.
3) Using a DVOM, measure resistance of Green/Yellow wire between TCM harness connector terminal No. 12 and harness connector which was disconnected in step 2). If resistance is less than 2 ohms, remove transmission oil pan and inspect internal wire harness for damage. Repair as necessary. If harness is okay, replace TCC control solenoid valve. If resistance is not as specified, repair open in Green/Yellow wire between TCM and TCC control solenoid valve.

4) Turn ignition on. Using a DVOM, measure voltage between ground and TCM harness connector terminal No. 12 (Green/Yellow wire). If reading is less than one volt, go to next step. If reading is not as specified, repair Green/Yellow wire for a short to power between TCM and TCC control solenoid valve.
5) Inspect all harness connectors for poor connections. Repair as necessary and retest system. If harness connections are okay, go to next step.
6) Reconnect TCM harness connector. Clear DTCs. See CLEARING TROUBLE CODES under SELF-DIAGNOSTIC SYSTEM. Road test vehicle and recheck for DTCs. If DTC P0743 or P0773 resets, replace TCM. If DTC P0743 or P0773 does not reset, fault is not present at this time. Check for an intermittent problem. See DIAGNOSTIC AIDS.

Diagnostic Aids – Check for poor connections at component and in-line harness connectors before replacing components. After repairs, recheck self-diagnostic system to ensure proper operation. See TCM ON-BOARD DIAGNOSTIC (OBD) SYSTEM CHECK under SELF-DIAGNOSTIC SYSTEM.

DTC P0751: NO. 1 SHIFT SOLENOID PERFORMANCE

NOTE: DTC P0751 will set while running in "D" range if gear change control from TCM to the transmission does not agree with actual gear position, even though No. 1 shift solenoid is electrically in good condition. This DTC is commonly caused by a stuck No. 1 shift solenoid, stuck 2-3 shift valve and/or clogged valve body fluid passage.

1) Turn ignition on. Clear DTCs. See CLEARING TROUBLE CODES under SELF-DIAGNOSTIC SYSTEM. Start engine and allow it to reach normal operating temperature. Road test vehicle and check for correct upshift speeds and TCC apply. See ROAD TEST under TESTING in appropriate overhaul article. After road test, recheck for DTCs. If DTC P0751 resets, go to next step. If DTC P0751 does not reset, fault is not present at this time.
2) Inspect No. 1 shift solenoid operation. See SHIFT SOLENOIDS & TORQUE CONVERTER CLUTCH (TCC) SOLENOID under COMPONENT TESTING. Replace if necessary. If No. 1 shift solenoid tests okay, go to next step.
3) Inspect valve body condition. Check for leaks or obstructions in fluid passages. Overhaul if necessary. See VALVE BODY ASSEMBLY under COMPONENT DISASSEMBLY & REASSEMBLY in appropriate overhaul article. If valve body and fluid passages are okay, repair faulty direct clutch.

DTC P0753: NO. 1 SHIFT SOLENOID CIRCUIT FAULT

NOTE: DTC P0753 will set when voltage detected at TCM terminal No. 13 is 2 volts or less when No. 1 shift solenoid is on, or 5.5 volts or greater when off.

1) Turn ignition switch to LOCK position. Disconnect TCM harness connector. Using a DVOM, measure resistance between ground and TCM harness connector terminal No. 13 (Green wire on Sidekick 1.8L; Green/Orange wire on all others). If resistance is 11-15 ohms at room temperature, go to step 4). If resistance is not as specified, go to next step.
2) Disconnect No. 1 shift solenoid harness connector closest to transmission. Using a DVOM, measure resistance between ground and TCM harness connector terminal No. 13 (Green wire on Sidekick 1.8L; Green/Orange wire on all others). If resistance is less than 2 ohms, repair appropriate wire for a short to ground between TCM and No. 1 shift solenoid. If resistance is not as specified, go to next step.
3) Using a DVOM, measure resistance in (Green wire on Sidekick 1.8L; Green/Orange wire on all others) between TCM harness connector terminal No. 13 and harness connector which was disconnected in step 2). If resistance is less than 2 ohms, remove transmission oil pan and inspect internal wire harness for damage. Repair as necessary. If harness is okay, replace No. 1 shift solenoid. If resistance is not as specified, repair open in appropriate wire between TCM and No. 1 shift solenoid.

AUTOMATIC TRANSMISSIONS
AW03-72LE Electronic Controls (With OBD-II) (Cont.)

3-228

4) Turn ignition on. Using a DVOM, measure voltage between ground and TCM harness connector terminal No. 13 (Green wire on Sidekick 1.8L; Green/Orange wire on all others). If reading is less than one volt, go to next step. If reading is not as specified, repair appropriate wire for a short to power between TCM and No. 1 shift solenoid.

5) Inspect all harness connectors for poor connections. Repair as necessary and retest system. If harness connections are okay, go to next step.

6) Reconnect TCM harness connector. Clear DTCs. See CLEARING TROUBLE CODES under SELF-DIAGNOSTIC SYSTEM. Road test vehicle and recheck for DTCs. If DTC P0753 resets, replace TCM. If DTC P0753 does not reset, fault is not present at this time. Check for an intermittent problem. See DIAGNOSTIC AIDS.

Diagnostic Aids – Check for poor connections at component and in-line harness connectors before replacing components. After repairs, recheck self-diagnostic system to ensure proper operation. See TCM ON-BOARD DIAGNOSTIC (OBD) SYSTEM CHECK under SELF-DIAGNOSTIC SYSTEM.

DTC P0756: NO. 2 SHIFT SOLENOID PERFORMANCE

NOTE: DTC P0756 will set while running in "D" range if gear change control from TCM to the transmission does not agree with actual gear position, even though No. 2 shift solenoid is electrically in good condition. This DTC is commonly caused by a stuck 1-2 or 3-4 shift valve, or clogged valve body fluid passage.

1) Turn ignition on. Clear DTCs. See CLEARING TROUBLE CODES under SELF-DIAGNOSTIC SYSTEM. Start engine and allow it to reach normal operating temperature. Road test vehicle and check for correct upshift speeds and TCC apply. See ROAD TEST under TESTING in appropriate overhaul article. After road test, recheck for DTCs. If DTC P0756 resets, go to next step. If DTC P0756 does not reset, fault is not present at this time.

2) Inspect No. 2 shift solenoid operation. See SHIFT SOLENOIDS & TORQUE CONVERTER CLUTCH (TCC) SOLENOID under COMPONENT TESTING. Replace if necessary. If No. 2 shift solenoid tests okay, go to next step.

3) Inspect valve body condition. Check for leaks or obstructions in fluid passages. Overhaul if necessary. See VALVE BODY ASSEMBLY under COMPONENT DISASSEMBLY & REASSEMBLY in appropriate overhaul article. If valve body and fluid passages are okay, repair faulty 2nd Brake.

DTC P0758: NO. 2 SHIFT SOLENOID CIRCUIT FAULT

NOTE: DTC P0758 will set when voltage detected at TCM terminal No. 11 is 2 volts or less when No. 2 shift solenoid is on, or 5.5 volts or greater when off.

1) Turn ignition switch to LOCK position. Disconnect TCM harness connector. Using a DVOM, measure resistance between ground and TCM harness connector terminal No. 11 (Green/Red wire). If resistance is 11-15 ohms at room temperature, go to step 4). If resistance is not as specified, go to next step.

2) Disconnect No. 2 shift solenoid harness connector closest to transmission. Using a DVOM, measure resistance between ground and TCM harness connector terminal No. 11 (Green/Red wire). If resistance is less than 2 ohms, repair Green/Red wire for a short to ground between TCM and No. 2 shift solenoid. If resistance is not as specified, go to next step.

3) Using a DVOM, measure resistance in Green/Red wire between TCM harness connector terminal No. 11 and harness connector which was disconnected in step 2). If resistance is less than 2 ohms, remove transmission oil pan and inspect internal wire harness for damage. Repair as necessary. If harness is okay, replace No. 2 shift solenoid. If resistance is not as specified, repair open in Green/Red wire between TCM and No. 2 shift solenoid.

4) Turn ignition on. Using a DVOM, measure voltage between ground and TCM harness connector terminal No. 11 (Green/Red wire). If reading is less than one volt, go to next step. If reading is not as specified, repair Green/Red wire for a short to power between TCM and No. 2 shift solenoid.

5) Inspect all harness connectors for poor connections. Repair as necessary and retest system. If harness connections are okay, go to next step.

6) Reconnect TCM harness connector. Clear DTCs. See CLEARING TROUBLE CODES under SELF-DIAGNOSTIC SYSTEM. Road test vehicle and recheck for DTCs. If DTC P0758 resets, replace TCM. If DTC P0758 does not reset, fault is not present at this time. Check for an intermittent problem. See DIAGNOSTIC AIDS.

Diagnostic Aids – Check for poor connections at component and in-line harness connectors before replacing components. After repairs, recheck self-diagnostic system to ensure proper operation. See TCM ON-BOARD DIAGNOSTIC (OBD) SYSTEM CHECK under SELF-DIAGNOSTIC SYSTEM.

DTC P1700: THROTTLE POSITION (TP) SENSOR CIRCUIT FAULT (EXCEPT SIDEKICK 1.8L)

NOTE: DTC P1700 will set if "ON" time of 64 Hz pulse signal from PCM to TCM is less than .4 milli seconds or greater than 12 milli seconds.

1) If DTCs P0122 or P0123 are currently set in PCM, diagnose these DTCs first. See appropriate SELF-DIAGNOSTICS article in ENGINE PERFORMANCE in appropriate MITCHELL® manual. If specified DTCs are not currently set, go to next step.

2) Turn ignition switch to LOCK position. Disconnect 26-pin PCM harness connector. Turn ignition on. Using a DVOM, measure voltage between ground and 26-pin PCM harness connector terminal No. 10 (Pink/Blue wire). If reading is 10-14 volts, go to next step. If reading is not as specified, go to step 5).

3) Inspect 26-pin PCM harness connector terminal No. 10 (Pink/Blue wire) for poor terminal contact. Repair as necessary and retest system. If connection is okay, go to next step.

4) Turn ignition switch to LOCK position. Reconnect PCM harness connector. Clear DTCs. See CLEARING TROUBLE CODES under SELF-DIAGNOSTIC SYSTEM. Road test vehicle and recheck for DTCs. If DTC P1700 resets, replace PCM. If DTC P1700 does not reset, fault is not present at this time. Check for an intermittent problem. See DIAGNOSTIC AIDS.

5) Turn ignition switch to LOCK position. Disconnect TCM harness connector. Using a DVOM, measure resistance between ground and 26-pin PCM harness connector terminal No. 10 (Pink/Blue wire). If resistance is less than 2 ohms, repair Pink/Blue wire for a short to ground between PCM and TCM. If resistance is not as specified, go to next step.

6) Using a DVOM, measure resistance between 26-pin PCM harness connector terminal No. 10 (Pink/Blue wire) and TCM harness connector terminal No. 6 (Pink/Blue wire). If resistance is less than 2 ohms, go to next step. If resistance is not as specified, repair open in Pink/Blue wire between PCM and TCM.

7) Reconnect TCM and PCM harness connectors. Clear DTCs. See CLEARING TROUBLE CODES under SELF-DIAGNOSTIC SYSTEM. Road test vehicle and recheck for DTCs. If DTC P1700 resets, replace TCM. If DTC P1700 does not reset, fault is not present at this time. Check for an intermittent problem. See DIAGNOSTIC AIDS.

Diagnostic Aids – An intermittent condition may be caused by a poor connection, damaged wire insulation or a wire which is broken inside the insulation. Inspect TCM harness connector for damaged, corroded or backed-out terminal pins. Repair as necessary and retest system.

AUTOMATIC TRANSMISSIONS
AW03-72LE Electronic Controls (With OBD-II) (Cont.)

3-229

DTC P1700: THROTTLE POSITION (TP) SENSOR CIRCUIT FAULT (SIDEKICK 1.8L)

NOTE: *DTC P1700 will set if "ON" time of 64 Hz pulse signal from PCM to TCM is less than .4 milli seconds or greater than 12 milli seconds.*

1) If DTCs P0122 or P0123 are currently set in PCM, diagnose these DTCs first. See appropriate SELF-DIAGNOSTICS article in ENGINE PERFORMANCE in appropriate MITCHELL® manual. If specified DTCs are not currently set, go to next step.
2) Turn ignition switch to LOCK position. Disconnect 22-pin PCM harness connector. Turn ignition on. Using a DVOM, measure voltage between ground and 22-pin PCM harness connector terminal No. 18 (Pink/Blue wire). If reading is 10-14 volts, go to next step. If reading is not as specified, go to step 5).
3) Inspect 22-pin PCM harness connector terminal No. 18 (Pink/Blue wire) for poor terminal contact. Repair as necessary and retest system. If connection is okay, go to next step.
4) Turn ignition switch to LOCK position. Reconnect PCM harness connector. Clear DTCs. See CLEARING TROUBLE CODES under SELF-DIAGNOSTIC SYSTEM. Road test vehicle and recheck for DTCs. If DTC P1700 resets, replace PCM. If DTC P1700 does not reset, fault is not present at this time. Check for an intermittent problem. See DIAGNOSTIC AIDS.
5) Turn ignition switch to LOCK position. Disconnect TCM harness connector. Using a DVOM, measure resistance between ground and 22-pin PCM harness connector terminal No. 18 (Pink/Blue wire). If resistance is less than 2 ohms, repair Pink/Blue wire for a short to ground between PCM and TCM. If resistance is not as specified, go to next step.
6) Using a DVOM, measure resistance between 22-pin PCM harness connector terminal No. 18 (Pink/Blue wire) and TCM harness connector terminal No. 6 (Pink/Blue wire). If resistance is less than 2 ohms, go to next step. If resistance is not as specified, repair open in Pink/Blue wire between PCM and TCM.
7) Reconnect TCM and PCM harness connectors. Clear DTCs. See CLEARING TROUBLE CODES under SELF-DIAGNOSTIC SYSTEM. Road test vehicle and recheck for DTCs. If DTC P1700 resets, replace TCM. If DTC P1700 does not reset, fault is not present at this time. Check for an intermittent problem. See DIAGNOSTIC AIDS.

Diagnostic Aids – An intermittent condition may be caused by a poor connection, damaged wire insulation or a wire which is broken inside the insulation. Inspect TCM harness connector for damaged, corroded or backed-out terminal pins. Repair as necessary and retest system.

DTC P1705: ENGINE COOLANT TEMPERATURE (ECT) SENSOR SIGNAL INPUT CIRCUIT FAULT

NOTE: *DTC P1705 will set when the following coolant temperature signals are detected by the TCM while engine is running:*
- *10 hz (100 milli seconds/cycle) signal at zero percent "ON" (10-14 volts) for 2.5 seconds.*
- *10 hz (100 milli seconds/cycle) signal at zero percent "ON" (about zero volt) after 15 minutes from engine start-up.*

1) If DTCs P0117 or P0118 are currently set in PCM, diagnose these DTCs first. See appropriate SELF-DIAGNOSTICS article in ENGINE PERFORMANCE in appropriate MITCHELL® manual. If specified DTCs are not currently set, go to next step.
2) Turn ignition switch to LOCK position. Disconnect 22-pin PCM harness connector. Disconnect main relay, located at center of instrument panel, behind blower speed selector switch. Turn ignition on. Using a DVOM, measure voltage between ground and 22-pin PCM harness connector terminal No. 16 (terminal No. 17 on Sidekick 1.8L) (Pink/Green wire). If reading is 10-14 volts, go to next step. If reading is not as specified, go to step 5).
3) Inspect 22-pin PCM harness connector terminal No. 16 (terminal No. 17 on Sidekick 1.8L) (Pink/Green wire) for poor terminal contact. Repair as necessary and retest system. If connection is okay, go to next step.

4) Turn ignition switch to LOCK position. Reconnect main relay and PCM harness connector. Clear DTCs. See CLEARING TROUBLE CODES under SELF-DIAGNOSTIC SYSTEM. Start engine and run for 15 minutes. Recheck for DTCs. If DTC P1705 resets, replace PCM. If DTC P1705 does not reset, fault is not present at this time. Check for an intermittent problem. See DIAGNOSTIC AIDS.
5) Turn ignition switch to LOCK position. Disconnect TCM harness connector. Using a DVOM, measure resistance between ground and 22-pin PCM harness connector terminal No. 16 (terminal No. 17 on Sidekick 1.8L) (Pink/Green wire). If resistance is less than 2 ohms, repair Pink/Green wire for a short to ground between PCM and TCM. If resistance is not as specified, go to next step.
6) Using a DVOM, measure resistance between 22-pin PCM harness connector terminal No. 16 (terminal No. 17 on Sidekick 1.8L) (Pink/Green wire) and TCM harness connector terminal No. 1 (Pink/Green wire). If resistance is less than 2 ohms, go to next step. If resistance is not as specified, repair open in Pink/Green wire between PCM and TCM.
7) Reconnect TCM and PCM harness connectors. Clear DTCs. See CLEARING TROUBLE CODES under SELF-DIAGNOSTIC SYSTEM. Start engine and run for 15 minutes. Recheck for DTCs. If DTC P1705 resets, replace TCM. If DTC P1705 does not reset, fault is not present at this time. Check for an intermittent problem. See DIAGNOSTIC AIDS.

Diagnostic Aids – An intermittent condition may be caused by a poor connection, damaged wire insulation or a wire which is broken inside the insulation. Inspect TCM harness connector for damaged, corroded or backed-out terminal pins. Repair as necessary and retest system.

DTC P1710: VEHICLE SPEED SENSOR (VSS) BACK-UP SIGNAL CIRCUIT FAULT (SIDEKICK)

NOTE: *DTC P1710 will set when 4WD "LO" switch is open, and no VSS (speedometer) signal is received while 10 VSS (transmission) signal pulses are received and fault occurred 500 times continuously during 2 drive cycles.*

1) If DTC P0500 is also set in PCM memory, diagnose this DTC first. See appropriate SELF-DIAGNOSTICS article in ENGINE PERFORMANCE in appropriate MITCHELL® manual. If specified DTC is not currently set, go to next step.
2) Turn ignition switch to LOCK position. Disconnect TCM harness connector. Raise and support vehicle. Place gear selector lever in "N" position. Lock left rear wheel. Go to next step.
3) Using a DVOM, check for continuity between ground and TCM harness connector terminal No. 16 (Yellow wire) while slowly turning right rear wheel. If reading toggles between continuity and infinity a few times for each wheel revolution, check for a poor connection at TCM. Repair as necessary. If connection is okay, replace TCM. If reading is not as specified, repair open in Yellow wire between TCM and VSS.

DTC P1710: VEHICLE SPEED SENSOR (VSS) BACK-UP SIGNAL CIRCUIT FAULT (TRACKER)

NOTE: *DTC P1710 will set when 4WD "LO" switch is open, and no VSS (speedometer) signal is received while 10 VSS (transmission) signal pulses are received and fault occurred 500 times continuously during 2 drive cycles.*

1) If DTC P0500 is also set in PCM memory, diagnose this DTC first. See appropriate SELF-DIAGNOSTICS article in ENGINE PERFORMANCE in appropriate MITCHELL® manual. If specified DTC is not currently set, go to next step.
2) Turn ignition switch to LOCK position. Disconnect TCM harness connector. Raise and support vehicle. Lock left rear wheel. Using a DVOM, measure resistance between ground and TCM harness connector terminal No. 16 (Yellow wire) while slowly rotating right rear wheel one full revolution. If resistance toggles between continuity and infinity a few times for each wheel revolution, reconnect TCM harness connector and go to step 5). If resistance is not as specified, go to next step.

3-230

AUTOMATIC TRANSMISSIONS
AW03-72LE Electronic Controls (With OBD-II) (Cont.)

3) Remove instrument cluster. See appropriate INSTRUMENT PANELS article in ACCESSORIES & EQUIPMENT in appropriate MITCHELL® manual. Rotate right rear wheel while observing speedometer cable end. If speedometer cable spins, go to next step. If speedometer cable does not spin, check for broken or disconnected speedometer cable.

4) Using a DVOM, measure resistance between VSS (speedometer) output terminals while rotating speedometer shaft. If resistance toggles between continuity and infinity 4 times for each revolution, go to next step. If resistance is not as specified, replace VSS (speedometer).

5) Using a DVOM, measure resistance between 13-pin instrument cluster harness connector terminal No. 4 (Yellow wire) and TCM harness connector terminal No. 16 (Yellow wire). If resistance is 2 ohms or less, go to next step. If resistance is not as specified, repair open in Yellow wire between instrument cluster and TCM.

6) Inspect TCM and instrument cluster harness connectors for poor terminal contact. Repair as necessary and retest system. If connections are okay, go to next step.

7) Turn ignition switch to LOCK position. Reinstall instrument cluster. Reconnect TCM harness connector. Clear DTCs. See CLEARING TROUBLE CODES under SELF-DIAGNOSTIC SYSTEM. Road test vehicle and recheck for DTCs. If DTC P1710 resets, replace TCM. If DTC P1710 does not reset, fault is not present at this time. Check for an intermittent problem. See DIAGNOSTIC AIDS.

Diagnostic Aids – An intermittent condition may be caused by a poor connection, damaged wire insulation or a wire which is broken inside the insulation. Inspect TCM harness connector for damaged, corroded or backed-out terminal pins. Repair as necessary and retest system.

DTC P1715: PARK/NEUTRAL POSITION (PNP) SWITCH CIRCUIT FAULT (TRACKER)

NOTE: DTC P1715 will set when the following occurs:
- *Engine speed changed from less than 300 RPM to greater than 500 RPM when vehicle speed was zero and TR switch is open ("R", "D", "2" or "L" positions).*
- *TR switch closed signal ("P" or "N" position) is detected for 10 seconds while engine is running at greater than 2000 RPM and vehicle under load.*

1) Place gear selector lever in "P" position. Depress brake pedal firmly. Turn ignition switch to START position. If engine cranks, go to next step. If engine does not crank, diagnose starting circuit. See TROUBLE SHOOTING article in GENERAL INFORMATION in appropriate MITCHELL® IMPORTED CARS, LIGHT TRUCKS & VANS SERVICE & REPAIR manual.

2) Turn ignition switch to LOCK position. Using a DVOM, measure voltage (backprobe) between ground and 22-pin PCM harness connector terminal No. 22 (Black/Red wire). Turn ignition on. If reading is one volt or less, leave DVOM connected and go to next step. If reading is not as specified, repair open or high resistance in Black/Red wire between PCM and circuit splice (S224).

3) With parking brake applied and brake pedal firmly depressed, shift gear selector lever through "R", "D", "2" and "L" positions while observing DVOM. If reading is 10-14 volts in each specified gear position, go to step **7)**. If reading is not as specified, leave DVOM connected and go to next step.

4) Turn ignition switch to LOCK position. Disconnect TR switch harness connector. Turn ignition on. Observe DVOM. If reading is 10-14 volts, leave DVOM connected and go to next step. If reading is not as specified, go to step **6)**.

5) Turn ignition switch to LOCK position. Raise and support vehicle. Place gear selector lever in "N" position. Loosen TR switch selector shaft nut and TR switch bolt. Pivot TR switch full clockwise. Slowly pivot TR switch counterclockwise until DVOM displays continuity. If continuity is obtained, tighten TR switch bolt to 15 ft. lbs. (20 N.m) and TR switch selector nut to 14 ft. lbs. (19 N.m). Reconnect all harness connectors and go to step **7)**. If continuity cannot be obtained, replace TR switch.

6) Turn ignition switch to LOCK position. Disconnect 22-pin PCM harness connector. Using a DVOM, check for continuity between ground and 22-pin PCM harness connector terminal No. 22 (Black/Red wire). If continuity is not present, go to next step. If continuity is present, repair Black/Red wire for a short to ground between PCM and TR switch.

7) Remove PCM and substitute with a known-good PCM. Perform DTC CONFIRMATION PROCEDURE. If DTC P1715 resets, inspect Black/Red wire and all other connections between PCM and TCM which may result in an open circuit or a short to ground. Repair as necessary and retest system. If DTC P1715 does not reset, replace PCM.

DTC Confirmation Procedure – **1)** Turn ignition switch to LOCK position. Start engine and allow it to reach normal operating temperature. Clear DTCs. See CLEARING TROUBLE CODES under SELF-DIAGNOSTIC SYSTEM.

2) Road test vehicle at 43 MPH with gear selector in "D" position for 10 seconds, then increase vehicle speed to 53 MPH for 10 seconds. Stop vehicle and check for DTCs.

DTC P1875: 4WD "LO" SWITCH CIRCUIT FAULT

NOTE: DTC P1875 will set while driving faster than 3 MPH with throttle angle greater than 5 percent for at least 20 seconds and the following conditions are present:
- *Vehicle speed sensed by VSS (speedometer) is greater than 6 MPH less than speed sensed by VSS (transmission) when 4WD "LO" switch is open.*
- *Vehicle speed sensed by VSS (speedometer) is more than 6 MPH greater than speed sensed by VSS (transmission) when 4WD "LO" switch is closed.*

1) Turn ignition switch to LOCK position. Disconnect TCM harness connector. Place transfer case gear selector in "2H" position. Using a DVOM, measure resistance between ground and TCM harness connector terminal No. 14 (Orange/White wire) while shifting transfer case gear selector from "2H" position to "4H" position, then to "N" position. If resistance is less than 2 ohms in specified positions, go to step **5)**. If resistance is not as specified, go to next step.

2) Place transfer case gear selector in "4L" position. Using a DVOM, measure resistance between ground and TCM harness connector terminal No. 14 (Orange/White wire). If resistance is less than 2 ohms, go to next step. If resistance is not as specified, go to step **6)**.

3) Inspect all harness connections for poor contact. Repair as necessary and retest system. If harness connections are okay, go to next step.

4) Reconnect TCM harness connector. Clear DTCs. See CLEARING TROUBLE CODES under SELF-DIAGNOSTIC SYSTEM. Road test vehicle at 19 MPH with gear selector lever in "D" position and transfer case gear selector in 2WD range. Stop vehicle, place gear selector lever in "P" position and transfer case gear selector in "4L" position. Road test vehicle at 19 MPH with gear selector lever in "D" position for about 30 seconds. If DTC P1875 resets, repeat step **1)**. If DTC resets for a second time, replace TCM. If DTC does not reset, fault is not present at this time. Check for an intermittent problem. See DIAGNOSTIC AIDS.

5) Disconnect 4WD "LO" switch harness connector. Using a DVOM, measure resistance between ground and TCM harness connector terminal No. 14 (Orange/White wire). If resistance is less than 2 ohms, repair Orange/White wire for a short to ground between TCM and 4WD "LO" switch. If resistance is not as specified, replace 4WD "LO" switch.

6) Disconnect 4WD "LO" switch harness connector. Using a DVOM, measure resistance between 4WD "LO" switch harness connector terminal No. 1 (Orange/White wire) and TCM harness connector terminal No. 14 (Orange/White wire). If resistance is less than 2 ohms, replace 4WD "LO" switch. If resistance is not as specified, repair open in Orange/White wire between TCM and 4WD "LO" switch.

Diagnostic Aids – An intermittent condition may be caused by a poor connection, damaged wire insulation or a wire which is broken inside the insulation. Inspect TCM harness connector for damaged, corroded or backed-out terminal pins. Repair as necessary and retest system.

COMPONENT TESTING

PARK/NEUTRAL POSITION (PNP) SWITCH

Disconnect PNP switch harness connector. Switch is located on side of transmission. Using a DVOM, check for continuity between specified terminals in accordance with shift lever position. See Fig. 6. Replace switch if defective.

PARK/NEUTRAL POSITION SWITCH CONTINUITY

Shift Lever Position	Continuity Between Terminals
"P"	2 & 3, 6 & 7
"R"	6 & 8
"N"	2 & 3, 6 & 10
"D"	6 & 9
"2"	4 & 6
"L"	5 & 6

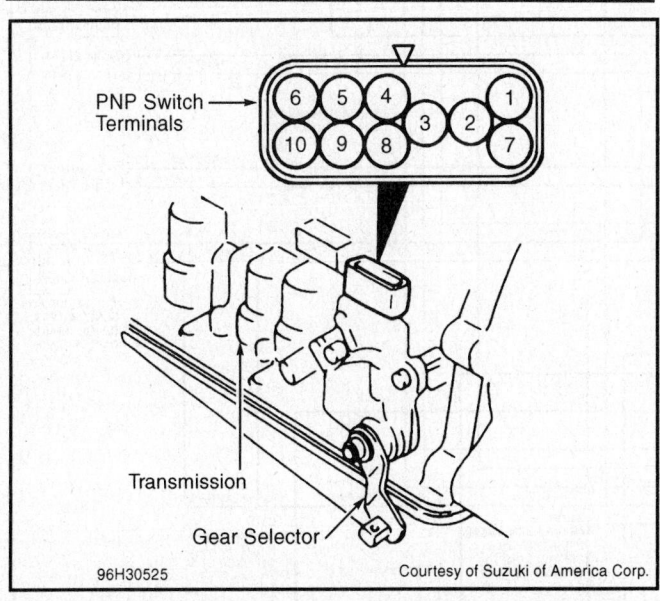

Fig. 6: Identifying Park/Neutral Position (PNP) Switch Terminals

SHIFT SOLENOIDS & TORQUE CONVERTER CLUTCH (TCC) SOLENOID

1) Obtain access to TCM. See Fig. 1. Ensure ignition is off. Disconnect TCM harness connector. Turn ignition on. Using a fused jumper wire, connect one end to TCM harness connector terminal No. 25 (White wire). With other end, probe terminals No. 11 (Green/Red wire), No. 12 (Green/Yellow wire) and No. 13 (Green wire on Sidekick 1.8L; Green/Orange wire on all others), one at a time. Ensure a "clicking" sound can be heard when battery voltage is applied. Replace appropriate solenoid if no sound is heard.

2) To check solenoid seals, apply battery voltage to solenoid. Apply ATF to solenoid with battery voltage connected. See Fig. 7. ATF should pass through solenoid. Remove battery voltage. Ensure ATF does not pass through solenoid. Replace appropriate solenoid if defective.

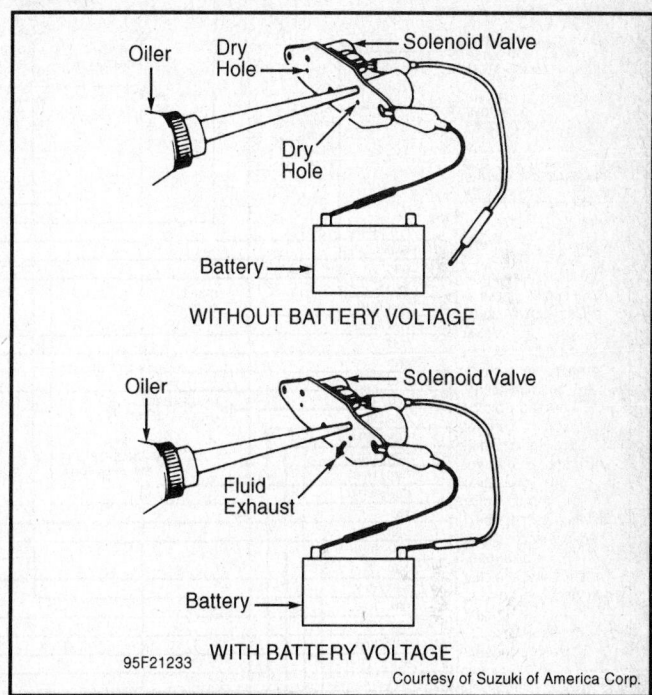

Fig. 7: Checking Solenoids

VEHICLE SPEED SENSOR (TRANSMISSION)

Ensure ignition is off. Disconnect TCM harness connector. See Fig. 1. Using a DVOM, measure resistance between TCM harness connector terminals No. 2 (White wire) and No. 3 (Orange wire). Resistance should be 387-473 ohms. Replace as needed.

3-232

AUTOMATIC TRANSMISSIONS
AW03-72LE Electronic Controls (With OBD-II) (Cont.)

WIRING DIAGRAMS

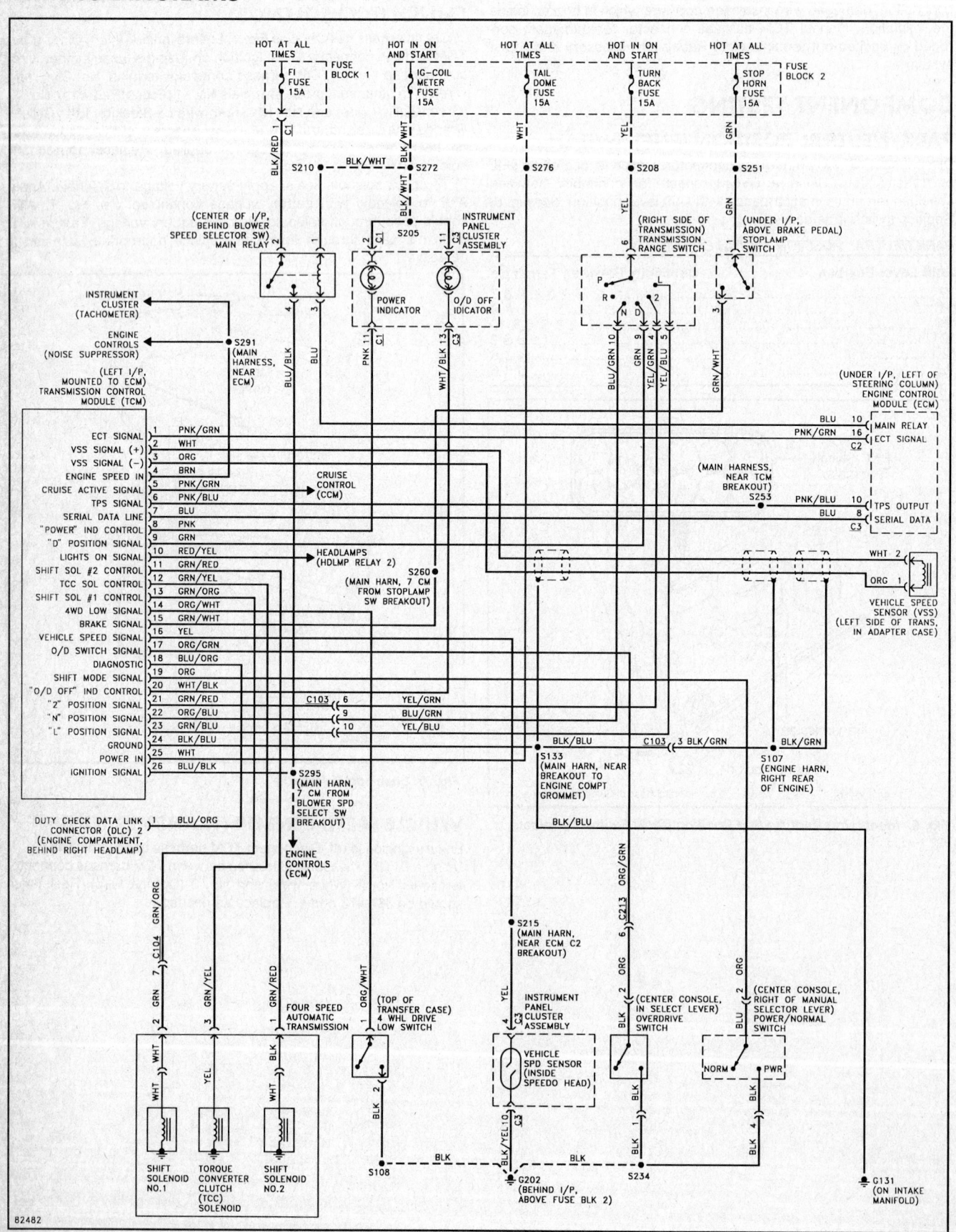

Fig. 8: Transmission Wiring Diagram (1996 Geo Tracker)

82482

AUTOMATIC TRANSMISSIONS
AW03-72LE Electronic Controls (With OBD-II) (Cont.)

3-233

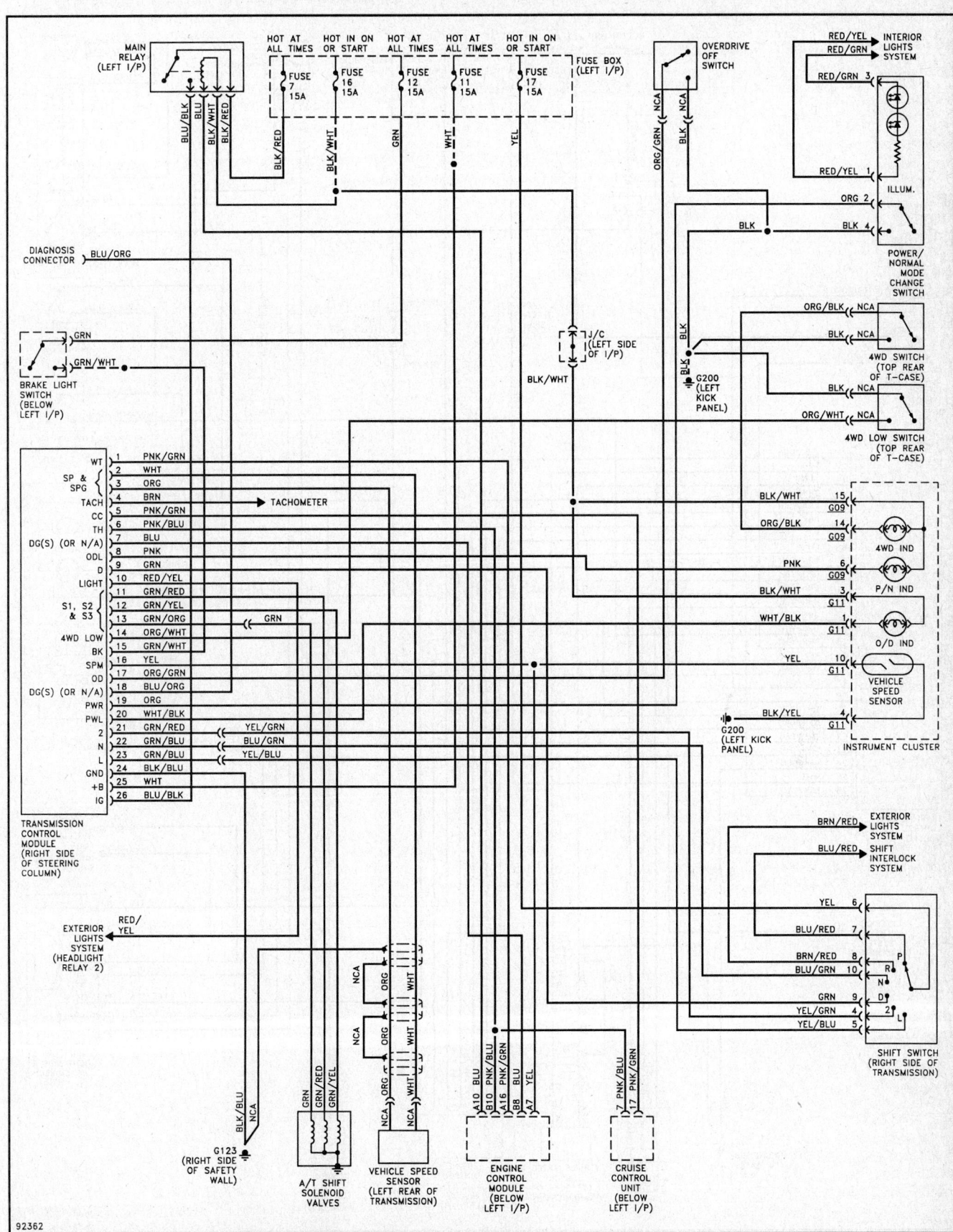

Fig. 9: Transmission Wiring Diagram (1996 Suzuki Sidekick & X-90 1.6L)

92362

AUTOMATIC TRANSMISSIONS
AW03-72LE Electronic Controls (With OBD-II) (Cont.)

3-234

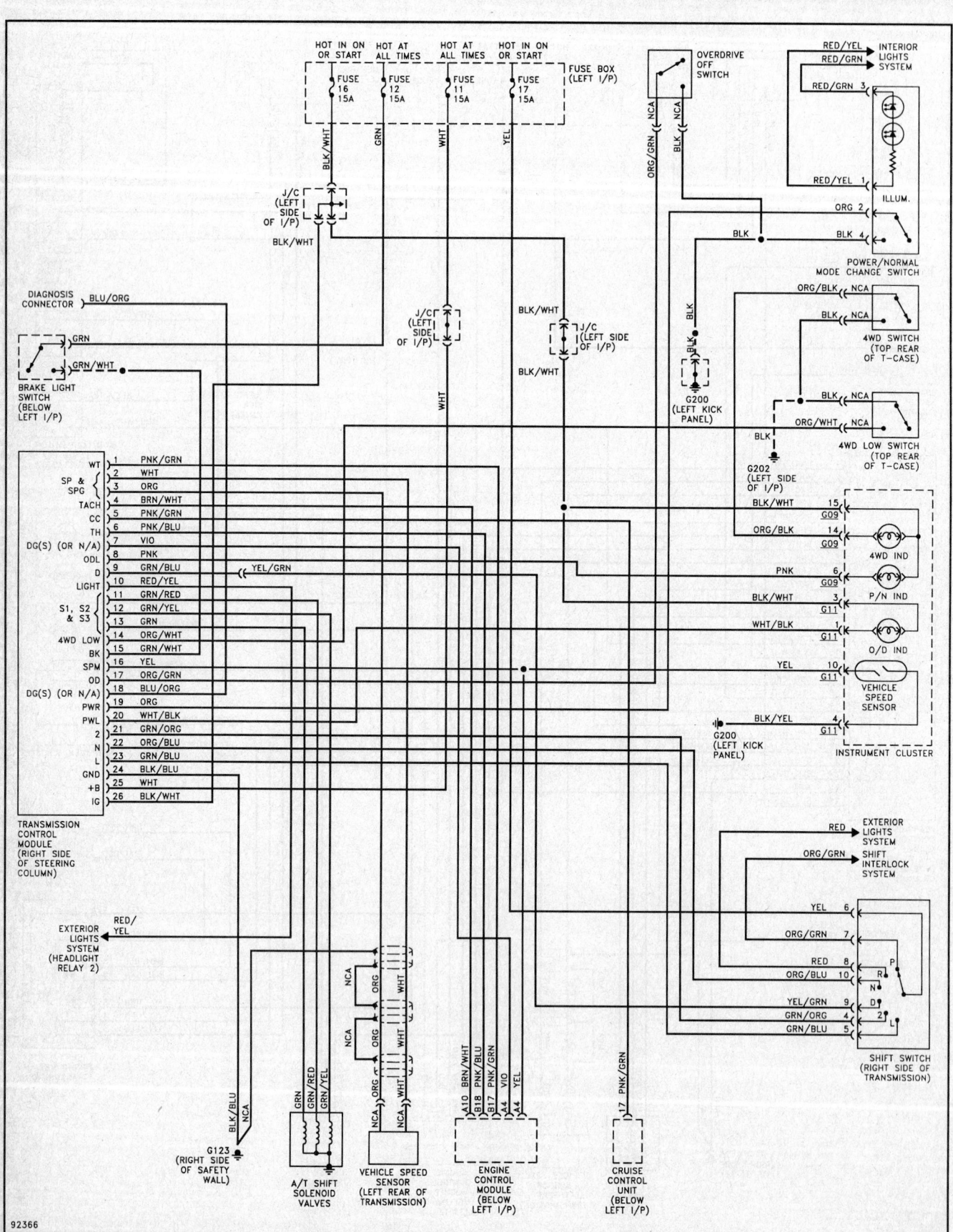

Fig. 10: Transmission Wiring Diagram (1996 Suzuki Sidekick 1.8L)

92366

A6, Cabriolet, 90

APPLICATION & LABOR TIMES

APPLICATION & LABOR TIMES

Vehicle Application	Labor Times [1] R & I	[2] Overhaul	Trans. Model
1995-96			
A6	5.6	9.4	01N (CLR)
Cabriolet & 90	5.6	9.4	097 (AZB)

[1] – Removal and installation of transmission from vehicle chassis.
[2] – On bench overhaul for transaxle and differential.
    DOES NOT include removal and installation.

IDENTIFICATION

Volkswagen Audi Group (VAG) transaxle type is cast into transaxle case above left output shaft flange. Transaxle code and build date are located on front top of transaxle case.

DESCRIPTION & OPERATION

Transaxle includes a 4-speed automatic transmission, a torque converter, a final drive and solenoid-operated valve body. See Fig. 1.

Under normal conditions, all shifts are controlled by a Transaxle Control Unit (TCU). See Fig. 9. Fourth gear is an overdrive gear.

NOTE: TCU may be referred to as Transmission Control Module (TCM).

Type 097 transaxle uses a standard torque converter. During 3rd gear (non-TCU controlled) and 4th gear operation, the 3rd-4th apply clutch is engaged. This locks the impeller shaft and small planetary drive shaft together, creating a direct coupling between the engine and transaxle.

Overdrive (4th gear) is engaged by the 3rd-4th apply clutch and 2nd-4th brake clutch.

During 3rd gear operation (TCU controlled), the transaxle engages 1st-3rd apply clutch and reverse clutch. This engages the turbine shaft to the large planetary drive shaft (through the 1st-3rd and reverse apply clutches), activating the torque converter.

Type 01N transaxle uses a lockup converter that is actuated in 2nd, 3rd and 4th. Overdrive (4th gear) is engaged by the 3rd-4th apply clutch and 2nd-4th brake clutch.

The transmission elements consist of a planetary gear set, one-way roller clutch, 3 apply clutches and 2 brake clutches. See Fig. 2. Power from the transmission is connected to the pinion through drive gears. A ring gear and differential assembly are connected to flanges which spin the drive axles.

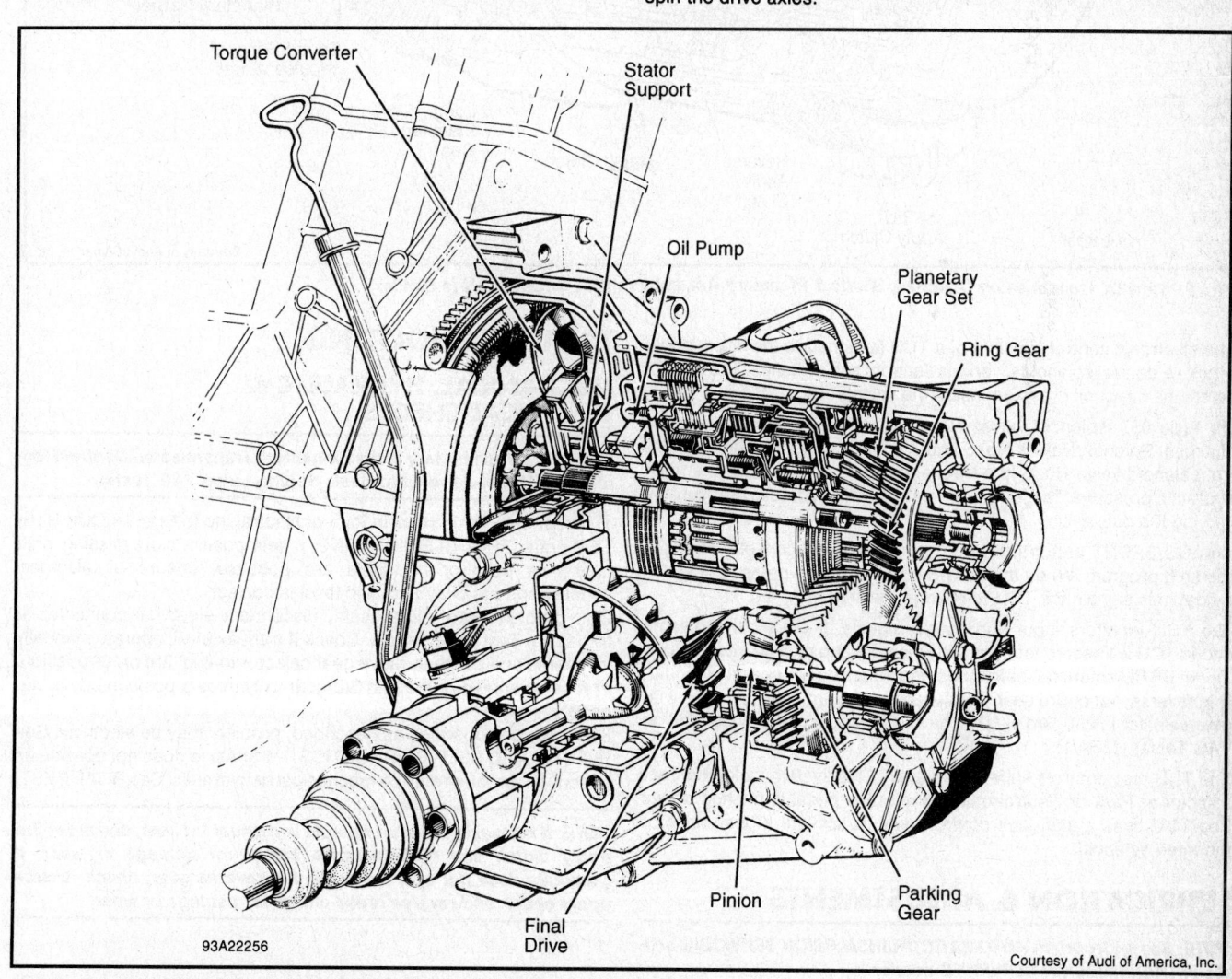

93A22256

Courtesy of Audi of America, Inc.

Fig. 1: Cut-Away View Of Transaxle Components (097 Shown, 01N Is Similar)

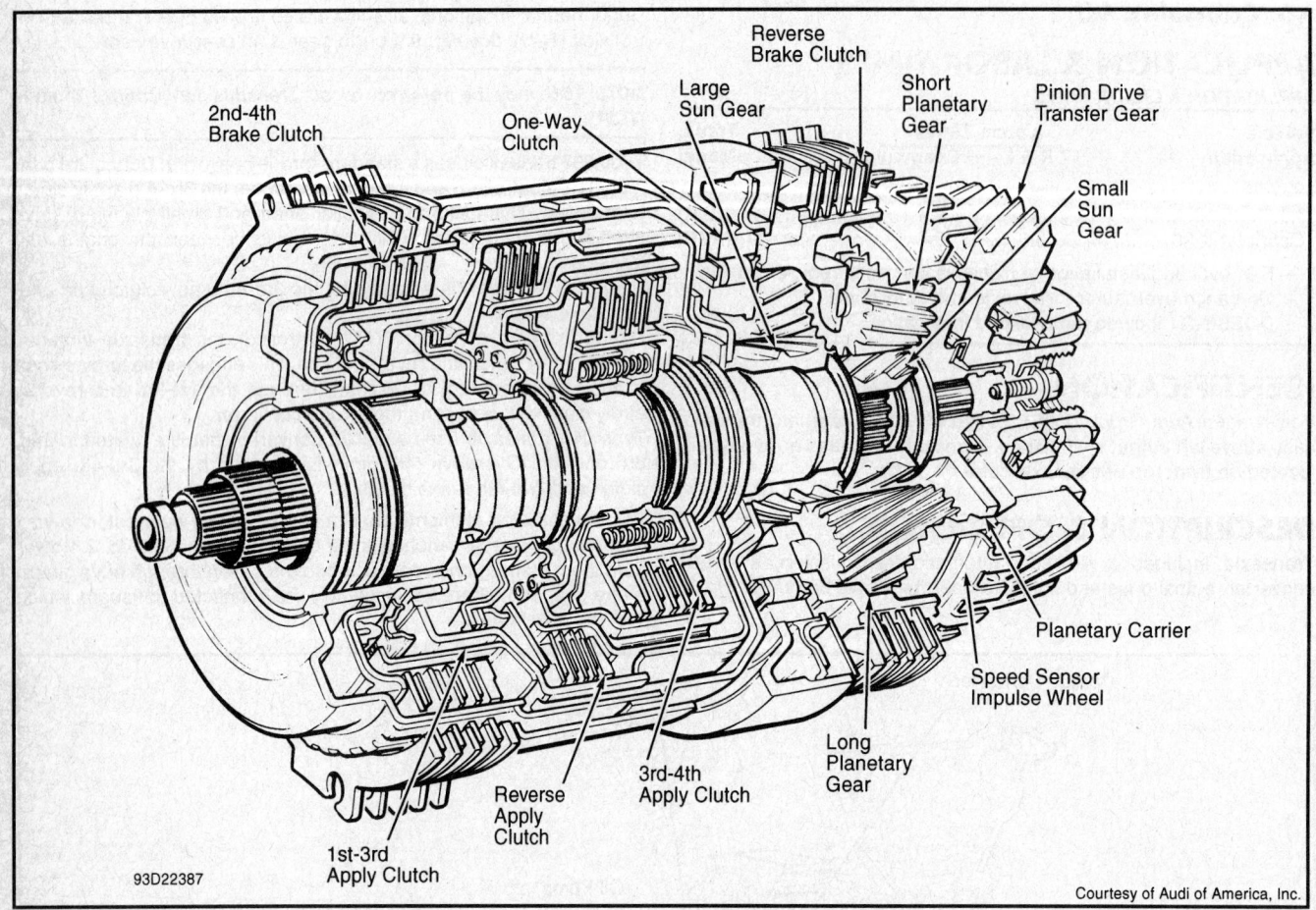

2nd-4th Brake Clutch

One-Way Clutch

Reverse Brake Clutch

Large Sun Gear

Short Planetary Gear

Pinion Drive Transfer Gear

Small Sun Gear

Planetary Carrier

Speed Sensor Impulse Wheel

Long Planetary Gear

3rd-4th Apply Clutch

Reverse Apply Clutch

1st-3rd Apply Clutch

93D22387

Courtesy of Audi of America, Inc.

Fig. 2: View Of Transmission Clutches, Shafts & Planetary Assemblies (097 Shown, 01N Is Similar)

The electronic control consists of a TCU (attached to the brake pedal bracket), control solenoids, various sensors and switches. The control solenoids direct oil pressure inside the valve body.

On Type 097, solenoid valves No. 1-4 control the apply and brake clutches. Solenoid valves No. 5 and 7 control shift smoothness. Control solenoid valve No. 6 is a frequency valve and controls the main hydraulic pressure. The TCU controls the main hydraulic pressure by varying the duty cycle.

An ECO/SPORT button (located on gear selector console) changes the shift program. When the ECO/SPORT button is pressed (SPORT mode), this signals the TCU to change the shift program.

The TCU monitors input and output signals. If electrical problems occur, TCU will record faults in TCU memory and may go into fail-safe mode. If TCU enters fail-safe mode, the transaxle will operate manually in reverse, 1st or 3rd gear. In fail-safe mode, 3rd gear operates with gear selector in 2nd, 3rd or "D". The TCU memory can only be read on VAG Tester (1551/1).

The TCU also controls shift-lock system. This system locks the gear selector in Park or Neutral unless the brake pedal is pushed down. The TCU uses a shift-lock control relay to activate a gear-selector mounted solenoid.

LUBRICATION & ADJUSTMENTS

NOTE: See appropriate AUTOMATIC TRANSMISSION SERVICING article in TRANSMISSION SERVICING section.

TROUBLE SHOOTING

MECHANICAL, HYDRAULIC & ELECTRICAL CHECKS

CAUTION: When battery is disconnected, Transmission Control Module (TCM) must be reset to Basic Setting using VAG Tester.

1) If gear selector is stuck in Park or Neutral, go to SHIFT-LOCK SYSTEM under TROUBLE SHOOTING. If gear positions are missing, shift quality is poor or no shifts are possible, ensure all electrical connections are okay and fluid level is correct.

2) If problems are still present, disconnect electrical connector at transaxle. Test drive vehicle. Check if transaxle will operate manually in reverse and 1st gear. Move gear selector to 2nd, 3rd or "D" position. Transaxle should operate in 3rd gear only in all 3 positions (2nd, 3rd or "D").

3) If transaxle operates as described, problem may be electrical. See ELECTRONIC SELF-DIAGNOSTICS. If transaxle does not operate as described, problem may be mechanical or hydraulic. See ROAD TEST.

NOTE: If transaxle does not operate in manual 1st gear, check 1st-3rd apply clutch and reverse brake clutch for damage or wear. If transaxle does not operate in manual reverse gear, check reverse apply clutch and reverse brake clutch for damage or wear.

ROAD TEST

WARNING: DO NOT exceed safe or legal speed limits during road test.

NOTE: Information from manufacturer available for Type 097 only.

1) Road test vehicle. Move ECO/SPORT switch to ECO. From a stop, perform full throttle upshifts with transaxle in "D". Note upshift speeds.
2) With vehicle at a speed above kickdown speed, press throttle pedal down and note kickdown shift speeds. Repeat road test with ECO/SPORT switch in SPORT position. Compare vehicle shift speeds to shift speed specifications. See SHIFT SPEED SPECIFICATIONS table.

SHIFT SPEED SPECIFICATIONS

Application [1]	Full Throttle (MPH)	Kickdown (MPH)
ECO Mode		
1-2	21-25	36-40
2-3	43-47	65-69
3-3 [1]	65-69	65-69
3-4	92-96	107-111
4-3	62-57	108-104
3-3 [2]	39-35	63-60
3-2	30-27	63-60
2-1	7-4	30-27
SPORT Mode		
1-2	36-40	36-40
2-3	65-69	65-69
3-3 [2]	88-92	88-92
3-4	107-111	107-111
4-3	87-83	108-104
3-3 [3]	42-38	63-60
3-2	41-37	63-60
2-1	6-12	30-27

[1] – Information from manufacturer available for Type 097 only.
[2] – Transaxle shifts from non-TCU controlled to TCU-controlled operation.
[3] – Transaxle shifts from TCU-controlled to non-TCU controlled operation.

3) If transaxle does not shift within specified MPH range, determine affected elements. See APPLY & BRAKE CLUTCH APPLICATION. See Fig. 3.

4) If all apply and brake clutch elements are affected, check oil pump, oil filter, cooler lines, solenoid valve No. 6, operation of ECO/SPORT switch, condition of torque converter and/or engine. Repair as necessary.
5) If one or more apply and brake clutch elements are affected, remove valve body. Locate appropriate fluid circuit in transaxle case and valve body. See Figs. 4-10. Check for leaks and blockage. Repair as necessary.
6) If hydraulic circuits are okay or problems with apply and brake clutch elements are mechanical, repair transaxle.

NOTE: If transaxle does not operate in manual 1st gear, check 1st-3rd apply clutch and reverse brake clutch for damage or wear. If transaxle does not operate in manual reverse gear, check reverse apply clutch and reverse brake clutch for damage or wear.

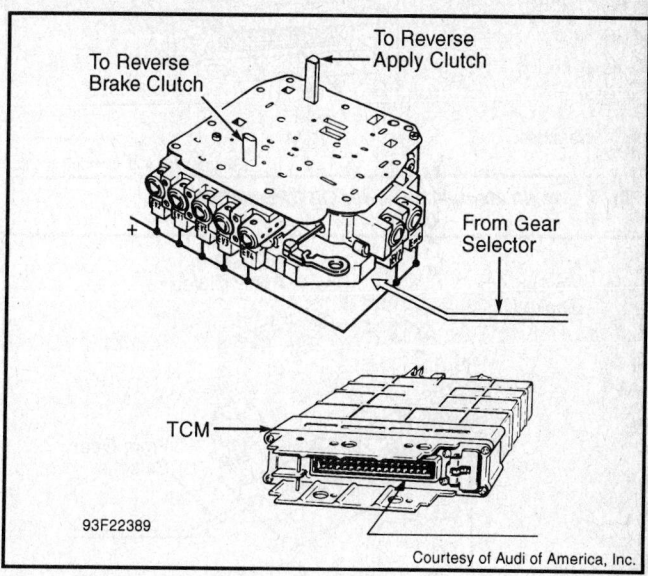

Fig. 4: Reverse Gear Oil Circuits (097)

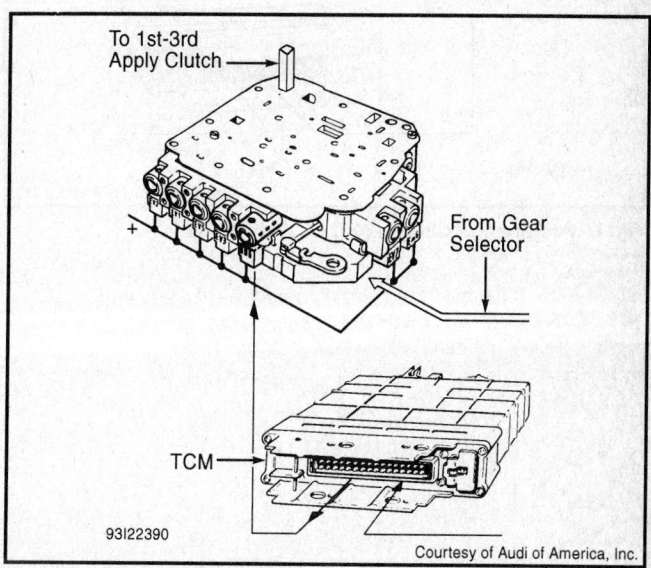

Fig. 5: 1st (In "D") Gear Oil Circuits (097)

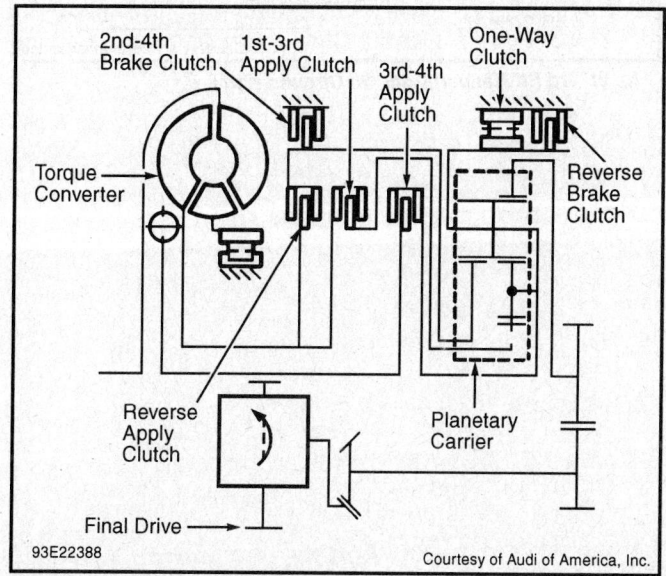

Fig. 3: Locating Transaxle Elements

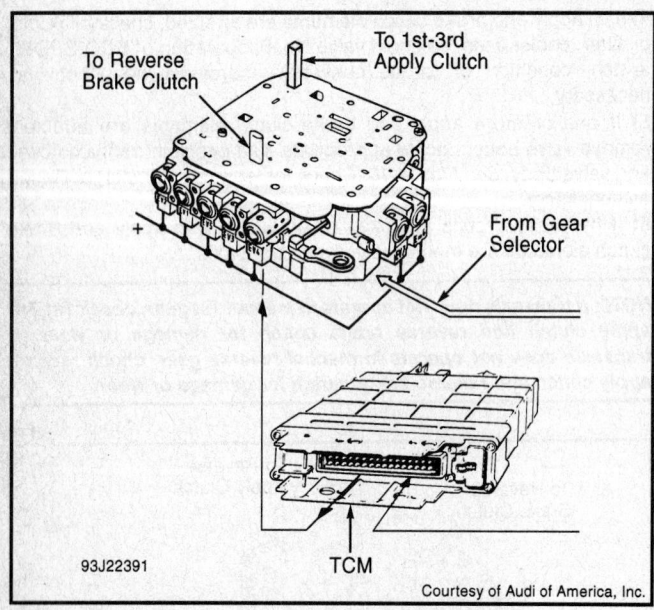

Fig. 6: *1st (In Manual 1st) Gear Oil Circuits (097)*

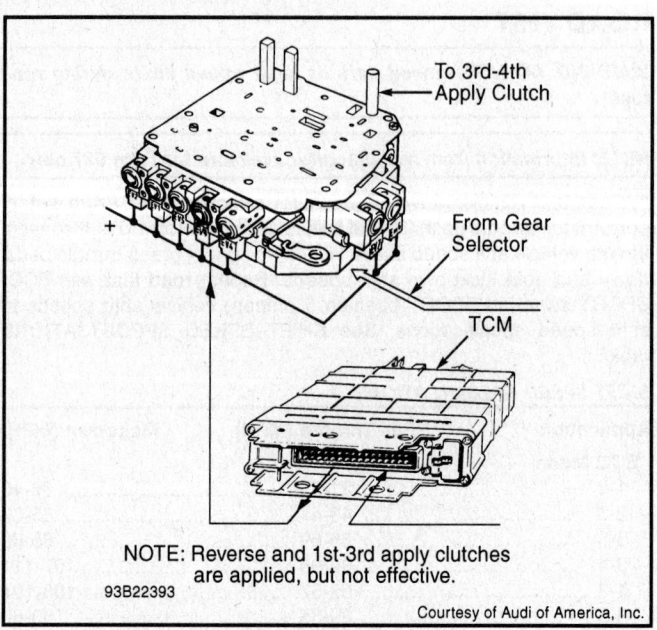

NOTE: Reverse and 1st-3rd apply clutches are applied, but not effective.

Fig. 8: *3rd (In "D") Gear Oil Circuits (097)*

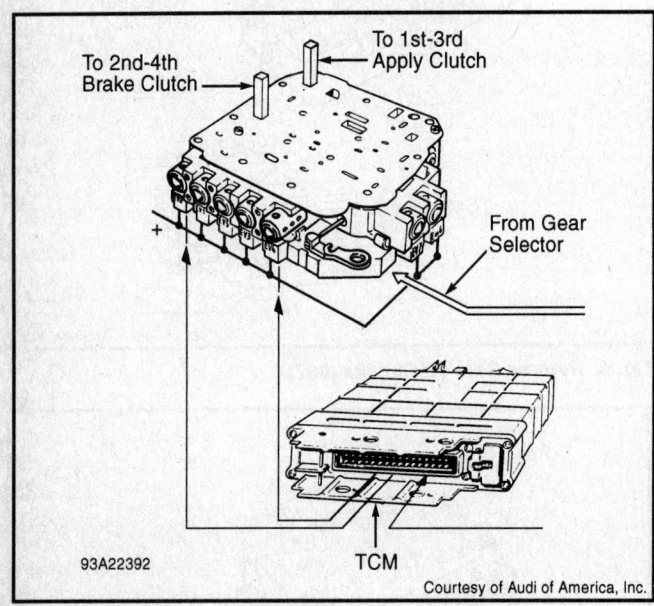

Fig. 7: *2nd Gear Oil Circuits (097)*

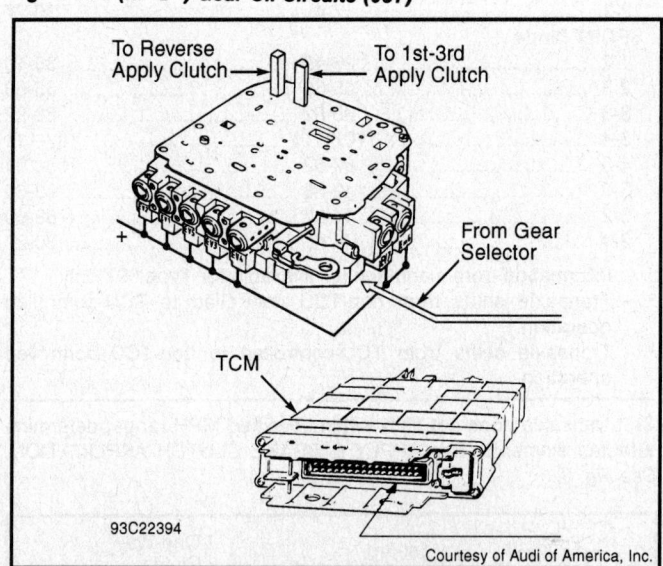

Fig. 9: *3rd (In Manual) Gear Oil Circuits (097)*

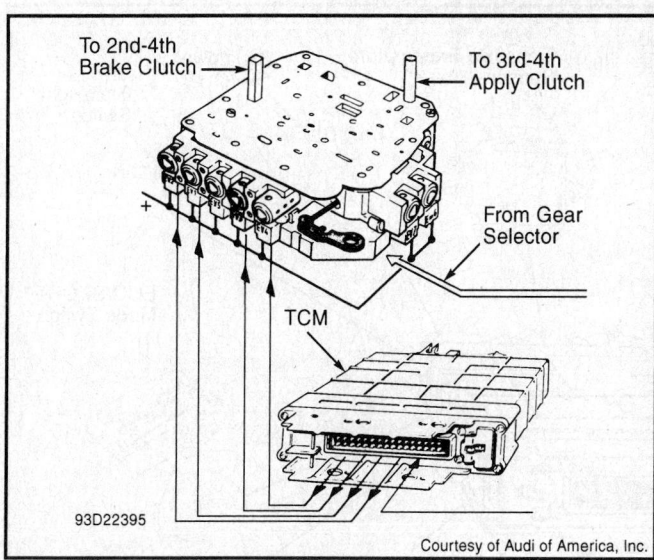

Fig. 10: *4th Gear Oil Circuits (097)*

APPLY & BRAKE CLUTCH APPLICATION

APPLY & BRAKE CLUTCH APPLICATION [1]

Gear Selector Position	Elements In Use
"D" (Drive)	
1st Gear	1st-3rd Apply & One-Way Clutch Holding
2nd Gear	1st-3rd Apply & 2nd-4th Brake
3rd Gear [2]	1st-3rd, 3rd-4th & Reverse Apply Clutches
4th Gear	3rd-4th Apply & 2nd-4th Brake
3rd (Drive)	
1st Gear	1st-3rd Apply & One-Way Clutch Holding
2nd Gear	1st-3rd Apply & 2nd-4th Brake
3rd Gear [2]	1st-3rd, 3rd-4th & Reverse Apply Clutches
3rd (Manual)	
3rd Gear [3]	1st-3rd Apply & Reverse Apply
2nd (Drive)	
1st Gear	1st-3rd Apply & One-Way Clutch Holding
2nd Gear	1st-3rd Apply & 2nd-4th Brake
1st (Manual)	
1st Gear	1st-3rd Apply & Reverse Brake
Reverse	Reverse Apply & Reverse Brake
Park & Neutral	All Apply & Brake Clutches Released Or Ineffective

[1] – Information not available for Type 01N
[2] – 1st-3rd and reverse apply clutches are engaged. However, main power path is the 3rd-4th apply clutch.
[3] – These elements are in use during TCU fail-safe mode.

SHIFT LOCK SYSTEM

OPERATION

1) A mechanical control cable prevents ignition key from being removed unless gear selector is in Park. With ignition key removed, gear selector locks in Park. See Fig. 11.

NOTE: If battery is disconnected or discharged, gear selector can be moved out of Park by turning ignition key to START position.

2) All models are equipped with an electronic shift lock system. TCU controls shift lock system. See Fig. 12. This system locks gear selector in Park or Neutral position unless brake pedal is pushed down. TCU uses shift lock control relay to release a solenoid mounted on gear selector assembly.

NOTE: Shift lock relay will not lock gear selector when vehicle speed is greater than 3 MPH.

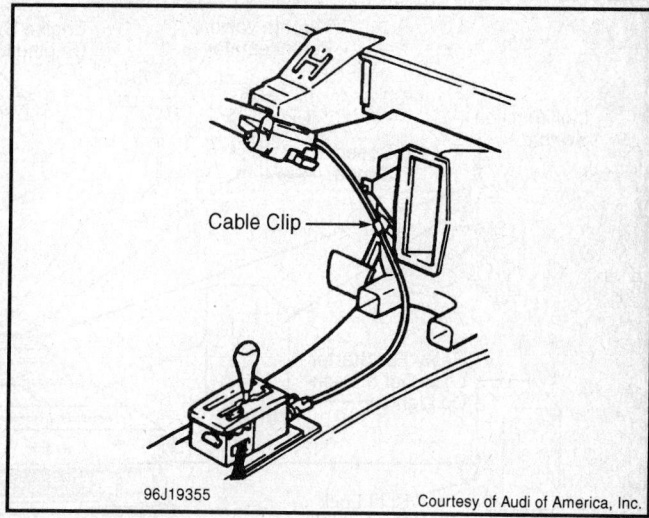

Fig. 11: *Identifying Shift-Lock Components*

FUNCTIONAL CHECK

1) With ignition key removed, ensure gear selector cannot be moved from Park. Insert key in ignition switch.

2) Turn ignition switch on. Ensure gear selector can only be moved with brake pedal pressed down. Move gear selector to Neutral position.

3) Without pressing brake pedal, ensure gear selector cannot move out of Neutral. Press brake pedal down. Ensure it is now possible to move gear selector.

4) If shift lock system does not operate as described, adjust gear selector, solenoid and control cable. If shift lock system does not operate after adjustments are made, check electrical system of shift lock system with Tester (VAG 1551/1).

5) See testing information under ELECTRONIC SELF-DIAGNOSTICS. *See Figs. 19-24.* If any problems are found, service harness or components. If no problems are found, TCU may be defective. If shift lock system still does not operate correctly, check for worn or damaged parts and replace as necessary. *See Fig. 13.*

NOTE: Perform the following adjustments in order given.

ADJUSTMENT

Control Cable – **1)** Remove cable housing mounting screws at gear selector console. Loosen lock screw.

2) Move gear selector to Drive position. Turn ignition on. Move control cable until a .060" (1.5 mm) feeler gauge fits between lock flap and lock pin. See Fig. 14.

3) Turn ignition off. Turn ignition on. Ensure gap is still .060" (1.5 mm). Turn ignition off and on several times and recheck gap. Install cable housing to gear selector console.

Gear Selector Solenoid – Move gear selector to Reverse. Remove screws, and raise top of gear selector housing. Ensure gap between gear selector and gear selector solenoid is .04" (1.0 mm). See Fig. 15. If necessary, loosen mounting screws and adjust. DO NOT install top of gear selector housing at this time.

Gear Selector – **1)** Move gear selector to Neutral. Energize solenoid and ensure lower part of gear selector is centered over solenoid.

2) Install top of gear selector housing. Position gear selector housing so gear selector is centered between Reverse and Drive. See Fig. 16. Tighten gear selector housing screws.

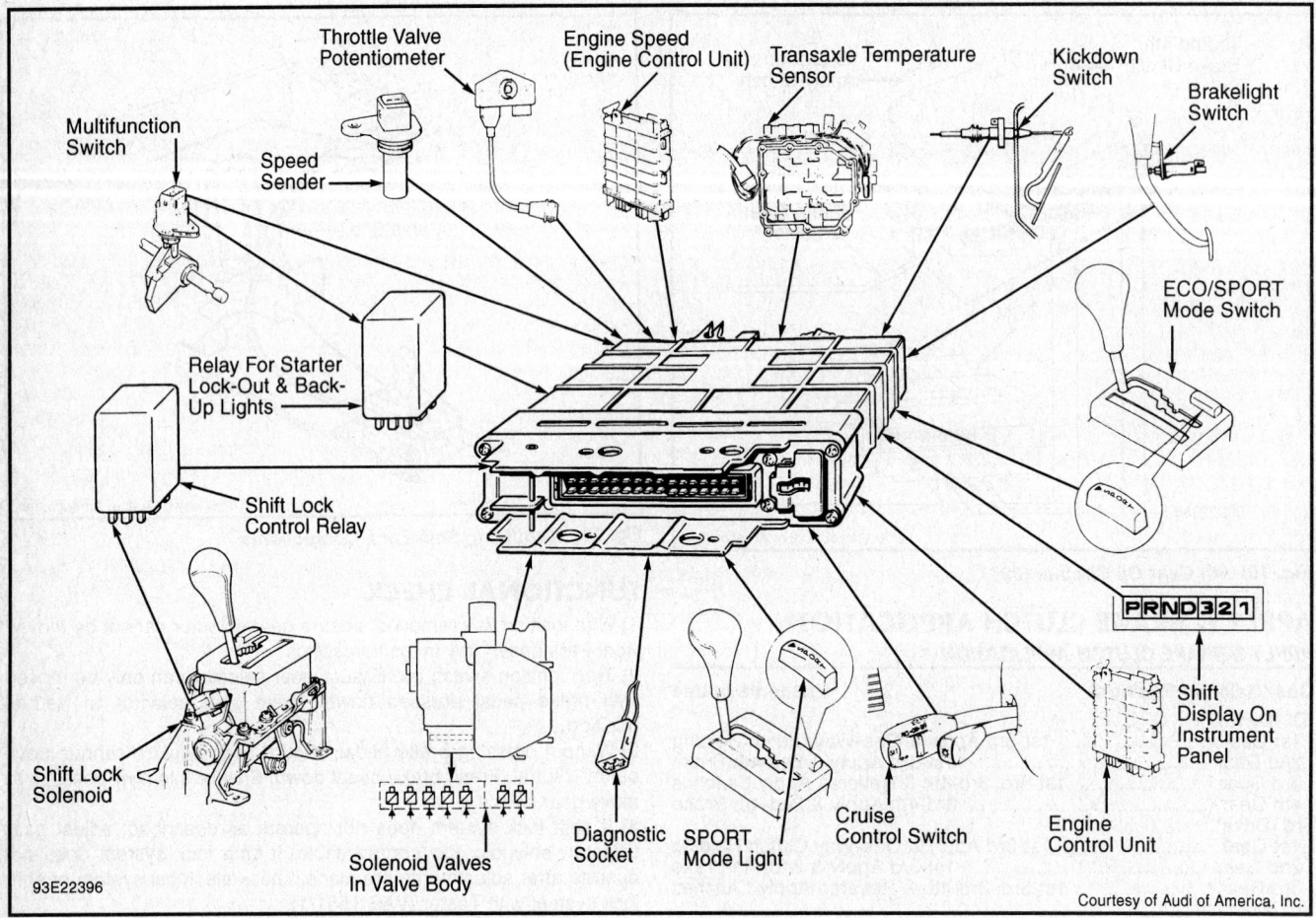

Fig. 12: Identifying TCU & Shift-Lock Electrical Components

REMOVAL & INSTALLATION

Control Cable – 1) Remove center console cover. Disconnect negative battery cable and wait 30 seconds. Disconnect voltage supply connector for air bag. Voltage supply connector is located at base of steering wheel on 90, or behind center console side trim on Cabriolet.

2) Using Torx wrench, remove air bag retaining screws from rear side of steering wheel. Remove air bag. Remove steering wheel. Remove dash panel.

3) Place gear selector in Neutral position. Remove cable housing mounting screws at gear selector console.

4) Remove cover from top of ignition switch. Remove spring clip holding cable housing to ignition assembly. Lift and tilt cable housing upward. Rotate control cable 1/4 turn until control cable unhooks from ignition switch. *See Fig. 17.*

NOTE: DO NOT kink control cable. If control cable is kinked, gear selector may not move.

5) Remove clip holding cable housing to A/C-heater housing. Remove cable housing from vehicle. To install cable housing, reverse removal procedure. Adjust control cable. See ADJUSTMENT (CONTROL CABLE) procedure under SHIFT-LOCK SYSTEM.

ELECTRONIC SELF-DIAGNOSTICS

1) Electronic control consists of TCU (attached to brake pedal bracket), control solenoids, and various sensors and switches. TCU monitors input and output signals. *See Fig. 12.*

2) If TCU detects problems in transaxle-related circuits or devices, TCU may record a trouble code in memory. To obtain trouble codes, use VAG Tester (1551/1). *See Fig. 18.* All trouble code and related testing information are contained in tester. See DIAGNOSTIC TROUBLE CODE (DTC) DEFINITIONS table.

DIAGNOSTIC TROUBLE CODE (DTC) DEFINITIONS

DTC	Definition
00000	No Communication
00258	Solenoid Valve No. 1
00260	Solenoid Valve No. 2
00262	Solenoid Valve No. 3
00263	[1] Transmission
00264	Solenoid Valve No. 4
00266	Solenoid Valve No. 5
00268	Solenoid Valve No. 6
00270	Solenoid Valve No. 7
00281	Vehicle Speed Sensor
00293	Transmission Range Switch
00296	[1] Kickdown Switch
00297	[2] Vehicle Speed Sensor
00299	[1] TR Program Switch
00300	Transmission Temperature sensor
00518	TPS Out Of Range
00526	[1] Brake Light Switch
00529	RPM Information Missing
00532	Supply Battery Voltage Low
00545	Engine/Transmission Electrical Connection
00596	[2] Shorted Solenoid Wiring
00638	Engine/Transmission Electrical Connection
00641	ATF Temperature Out Of Range
00652	TR Controller Incorrect Signal
00660	Kickdown Switch/TPS Incorrect Signal
01236	Shift Lock Solenoid
65535	Control Module Malfunctioning

[1] – Type 097
[2] – Type 01N

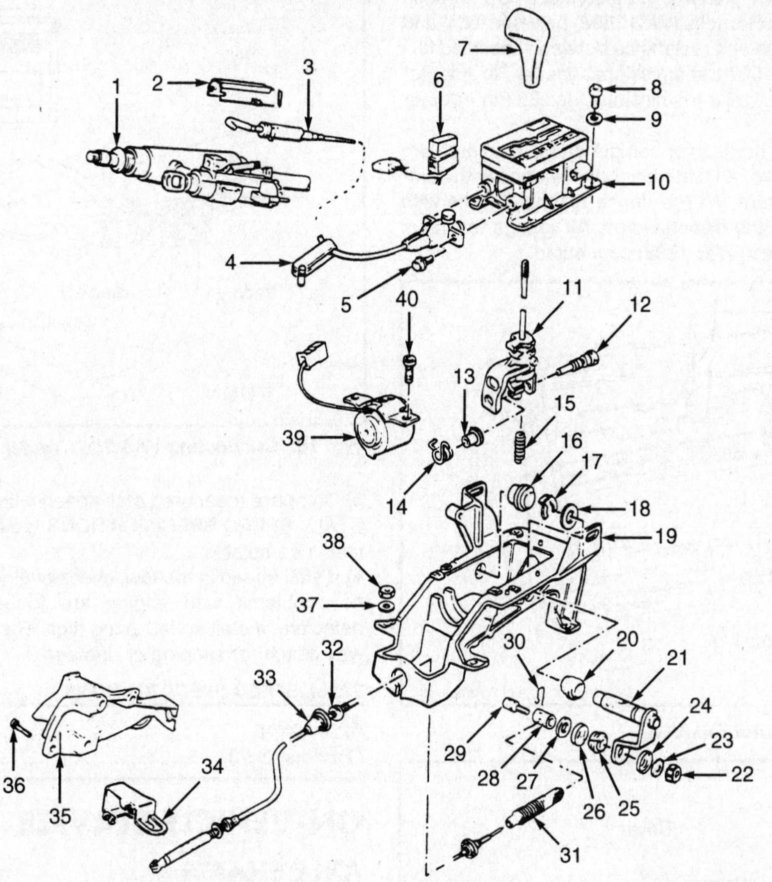

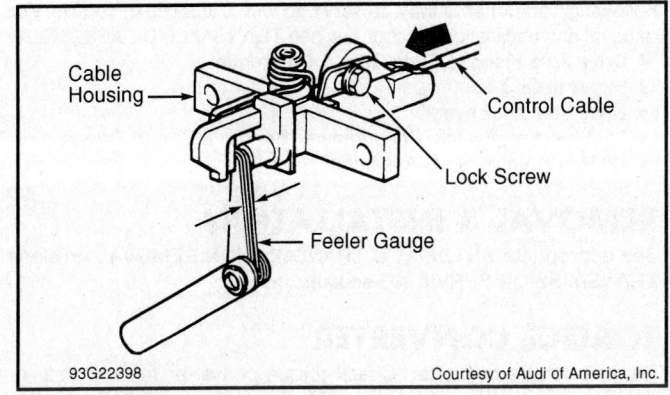

1. Ignition Switch	11. Gear Selector	21. Shift Lever	31. Bellows
2. Cover	12. Guide Pin	22. Nut	32. Shift Cable & Tube
3. Control Cable	13. Bushing	23. Washer	33. Grommet
4. Clip	14. Spring	24. Boot	34. Retaining Clip
5. Screw	15. Coil Spring	25. Bushing	35. Gear Box Support
6. ECO/SPORT Mode Switch	16. Bushing	26. Boot	36. Screw
7. Knob	17. Circlip	27. Washer	37. Washer
8. Screw	18. Washer	28. Clamping Sleeve	38. Nut
9. Washer	19. Gear Selector Console	29. Locking Pin	39. Gear Selector Lock Solenoid
10. Gear Selector Housing	20. Bushing	30. Spring Clip	40. Screw

93F22397

Courtesy of Audi of America, Inc.

Fig. 13: Exploded View Of Shift Lock & Gear Selector Console Assembly (097 Is Shown; 01N Is Similar)

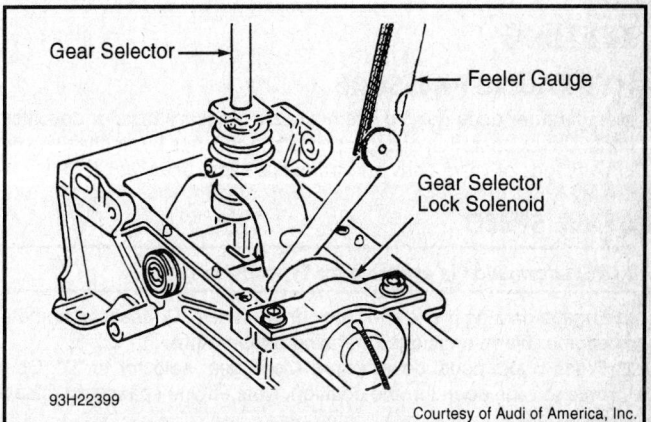

93G22398

Courtesy of Audi of America, Inc.

Fig. 14: Adjusting Control Cable

93H22399

Courtesy of Audi of America, Inc.

Fig. 15: Adjusting Gear Selector Solenoid

3) If tester is not available, turn ignition off. Disconnect TCU harness connector. Install Back-Probe Harness (VAG 1598) between TCU and TCU harness. Measure voltage and resistance between specified terminals of TCU connector. For 097 transmissions, use 38 Pin Adapter (1598/9). *See Figs. 19-21.* For 01N transmissions, use 68 Pin Adapter (1598/18). *See Figs. 22-24.*

4) If problem is found, service harness or component(s). If no problem is found, TCU may be defective. All testing should be done with components at ambient temperature. All resistance testing is done with Back-Probe Harness (VAG 1598) disconnected. All voltage testing is done with Back-Probe Harness (VAG 1598) connected.

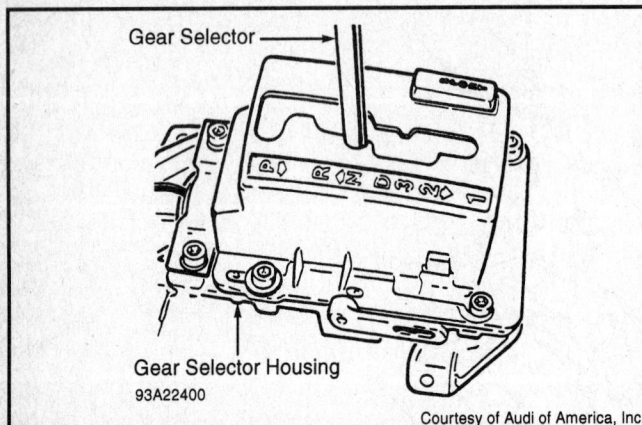

Fig. 16: *Adjusting Gear Selector Position*

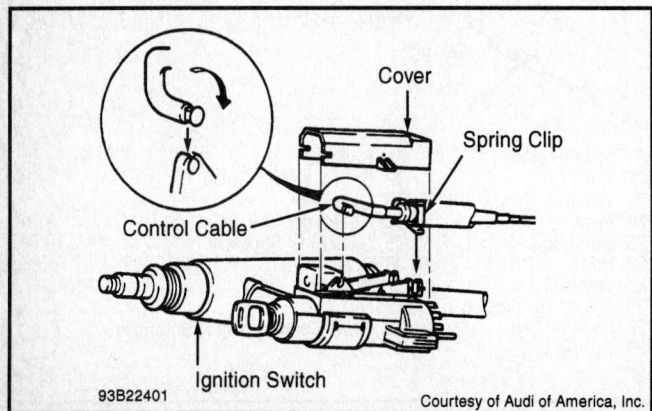

Fig. 17: *Removing Control Cable From Ignition Switch*

TESTING

HYDRAULIC PRESSURE

Manufacturer does not provide hydraulic pressure tests or specifications. Check operation of apply and brake clutches by air checking fluid passages of valve body and transaxle case. *See Figs. 4-10.*

STALL SPEED

NOTE: Information is available for Type 097 only.

1) Engage parking brake and block drive wheels. Connect tachometer to engine. Warm engine to operating temperature.

2) Press brake pedal down firmly. Move gear selector to "D". Open throttle to wide open throttle position. Note engine speed and release throttle pedal.

CAUTION: DO NOT operate engine at stall speed for more than 5 seconds. If you need to repeat stall speed test, wait 20 seconds.

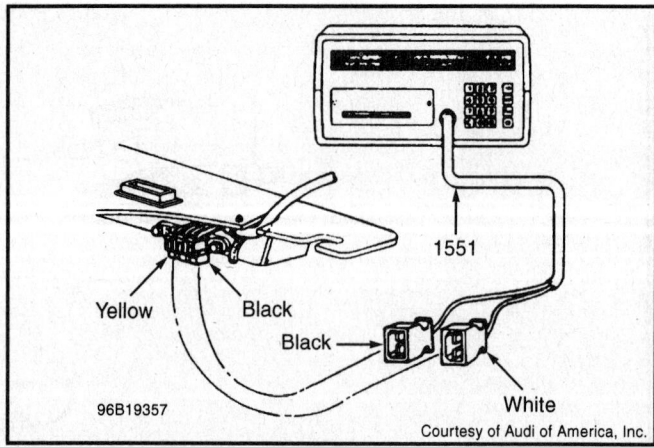

Fig. 18: *Connecting VAG 1551 Tester*

3) Compare measured stall speed with stall speed specification. See STALL SPEED SPECIFICATIONS table. If stall speed is within range, test is complete.

4) If stall speed is too low, check engine condition and adjustments. If no problems with engine are found, torque converter may be defective. If stall speed is too high, check 1st-3rd apply clutch or one-way clutch for slipping or damage.

STALL SPEED SPECIFICATIONS

Application	RPM
Cabriolet & 90	2650-2850

ON-VEHICLE SERVICE

AXLE SHAFTS

See appropriate AXLE SHAFTS article in AXLE SHAFTS & TRANSFER CASES section.

OIL COOLER FLUSHING

1) On Type 097, remove external oil filter. On both types, remove oil lines and allow fluid to drain. Using pressurized solvent, flush remaining fluid and debris from oil lines and cooler. Repeat flushing if necessary.

2) Use pressurized shop air to remove solvent from oil lines and oil cooler. Install a new external oil filter.

TRANSAXLE COMPONENTS

Following components may be serviced with transaxle in vehicle. For removal and installation procedures, see TRANSAXLE DISASSEMBLY.

- Drive Axle Flanges, Ring Gear & Differential
- External Oil Filter
- Gear Selector Lever
- Multifunction Switch, Speedometer Sender & Speed Sensor
- Oil Pan & Valve Body Assembly

REMOVAL & INSTALLATION

See appropriate AUTOMATIC TRANSMISSION REMOVAL article in TRANSMISSION SERVICING section.

TORQUE CONVERTER

Remove torque converter. Check torque converter for any wear or damage, and replace if necessary. If torque converter is being reused, fluid must be drained. Slightly tilt torque converter on bench and siphon old fluid from converter.

Test step	VAG 1598 terminals	Component to be tested	− Test conditions • Additional steps	Specified value or results	If test results NOT within specifications
			Switch multimeter to voltage measuring range 20 V		
1	19 + 1	Transmission Control Module (TCM) voltage supply	− Switch ignition ON	Approx. Battery Positive Voltage (B+)	− Check wire from terminal 1 to Ground (GND) − Check wire from terminal 19 for continuity with D/8 in relay panel
2	10 + 29	Throttle Position (TP) sensor	− Switch ignition ON • TP sensor disconnected	4.6 – 5 V	− Replace Transmission Control Module (TCM) − Return system to basic setting
	9 + 29		• Closed throttle position (CTP)	0.156 V min. 0.800 V max.	− Calibrate TP sensor; replace if necessary
			• Wide open throttle (WOT)	3.50 V min. 4.68 V max.	− Return system to basic setting
3	19 + 20	Shift lock solenoid	− Switch ignition ON • Selector lever in position P or N	Approx. Battery Positive Voltage (B+)	− Replace TCM − Return system to basic setting
			• Brakes applied	0 V	− Check signal from brake light switch Test step 4 − Replace TCM if necessary − Return system to basic setting
4	26 + 1	Signal from brake light switch	− Switch ignition ON • Brakes not applied	0 V	− Check brake light switch and wiring according to wiring diagram
			• Brakes applied	Approx. Battery Positive Voltage (B+)	

96D19359

Courtesy of Audi of America, Inc.

Fig. 19: Testing TCU Harness & Components Type 097 (1 Of 3)

TRANSAXLE DISASSEMBLY

TRANSMISSION UNIT

1) Remove torque converter. Using Support Plate (VW353 and VW309), mount transaxle on work bench. Remove oil pan and valve body assembly. Remove sealing plug from transaxle case. See Figs. 25 and 27.

2) Measure and record turbine shaft end play. See Fig. 26. Remove oil pump bolts. Using two M8 bolts, press oil pump from front of transaxle. See Fig. 29.

3) Remove turbine shaft complete with 2nd-4th brake clutch, support tube, 1st-3rd and reverse apply clutch assemblies. Remove impeller shaft and 3rd-4th apply clutch assembly. See Figs. 29 and 30.

4) Remove sealing plug from pinion drive transfer gear end of transaxle. Engage parking gear. Using a screwdriver, lock small sun gear drive shell to large sun gear drive shell. See Fig. 31. Remove bolt from end of small planetary drive shaft, and remove shaft.

5) Remove small sun gear drive shell, large sun gear drive shell, circlips and one-way clutch. Remove planetary carrier and bearing assembly. Remove reverse brake clutch assembly. See Figs. 28 and 33.

FINAL DRIVE & TRANSFER GEARS

1) Drain gear oil. Attach INCH-lb. torque wrench to a 1 5/8" (41 mm) socket wrench. See Fig. 82. Measure and record total roller bearing turning torque and backlash. These measurements are required if roller bearings, ring gear and pinion gear are reused.

2) Engage parking pawl. Using a 7/8" (22 mm) Allen wrench socket, remove fastener nut. See Fig. 34. Remove pinion drive transfer gear assembly from transaxle case. See Fig. 32.

3) Remove speedometer sender. On left axle flange, remove bolt and remove axle flange. On right axle flange, remove circlip. Using Puller (18-1) and Drift (3236), remove right axle flange. See Fig. 35.

4) Remove differential ring gear cover. Remove differential assembly from transaxle case. See Fig. 32.

5) Remove sealing plug from pinion cover. Using INCH-lb. torque wrench, measure turning force of pinion bearings. Record measurement for reassembly.

6) Ensure parking pawl is engaged. Remove nut from pinion. Remove pinion drive gear cover bolts. Install 2 bolts into threaded holes, and remove cover. See Fig. 36.

7) Using Puller (20-10) and Puller Arms (V 172), remove pinion drive gear. See Fig. 37. Remove parking gear from pinion. Remove pinion and bearing from transaxle.

Test step	VAG 1598 terminals	Component to be tested	– Test conditions • Additional steps	Specified value or results	If test results NOT within specifications
5	34 + 1	Multi-function transmission range (TR) switch Multi-function switch	– Switch ignition ON • Gear selector lever positions R, N, D, 3 and 2	4.5 – 5 V	– Check wire routing according to wiring diagram – Replace multi-function TR switch
			• Gear selector lever positions P and 1	0 – 0.8 V	
			• Gear selector lever position R	Approx. Battery Positive Voltage (B+)	
	15 + 1		• Gear selector lever positions P, R, 2 and 1	4.5 – 5 V	
			• Gear selector lever positions N, D, and 3	0 – 0.8 V	
	35 + 1		• Gear selector lever positions P, R, N and D	4.5 – 5 V	
			• Gear selector lever positions 3, 2, and 1	0 – 0.8 V	
	16 + 1		• Gear selector lever positions P, R, and N	Approx. Battery Positive Voltage (B+)	
			• Gear selector lever positions D, 3, 2, and 1	0 – 0.8 V	
Switch multimeter to resistance measuring range Ω					
6	22 + 18	Solenoid valve 1	– Switch ignition OFF	55 – 65 Ω	– Check harness routing according to wiring diagram
	22 + 1		• TCM removed	$\infty \, \Omega$ [1]	– Replace valve body
7	23 + 18	Solenoid valve 2	– Switch ignition OFF	55 – 65 Ω	– Check harness routing according to wiring diagram
	23 + 1		• TCM removed	$\infty \, \Omega$ [1]	– Replace valve body
8	3 + 18	Solenoid valve 3	– Switch ignition OFF	55 – 65 Ω	– Check harness routing according to wiring diagram
	3 + 1		• TCM disconnected	$\infty \, \Omega$ [1]	– Replace valve body
9	2 + 18	Solenoid valve 4	– Switch ignition OFF	55 – 65 Ω	– Check harness routing according to wiring diagram
	2 + 1		• TCM disconnected	$\infty \, \Omega$ [1]	– Replace valve body
10	24 + 18	Solenoid valve 5	– Switch ignition OFF	55 – 65 Ω	– Check harness routing according to wiring diagram
	24 + 1		• TCM disconnected	$\infty \, \Omega$ [1]	– Replace valve body

[1] Be sure multimeter is switched to greatest resistance measuring range.

96H19361

Courtesy of Audi of America, Inc.

Fig. 20: Testing TCU Harness & Components Type 097 (2 Of 3)

Test step	VAG 1598 terminals	Component to be tested	– Test conditions • Additional steps	Specified value or results	If test results NOT within specifications
11	25 + 18	Solenoid valve 6	– Switch ignition OFF	4.5 – 6.5 Ω	– Check harness routing according to wiring diagram
	25 + 1		• TCM disconnected	∞ Ω[1]	– Replace valve body
12	21 + 18	Solenoid valve 7	– Switch ignition OFF	55 – 65 Ω	– Check harness routing according to wiring diagram
	21 + 1		• TCM disconnected	∞ Ω[1]	– Replace valve body
13	19 + 20	Shift lock solenoid	– Switch ignition OFF • TCM disconnected	14 – 25 Ω	– Check harness routing according to wiring diagram – Replace magnet for shift lock
14	1 + 17	Kick down switch	– Switch ignition OFF • TCM disconnected • Accelerator pedal not depressed	∞ Ω[1]	– Check harness routing according to wiring diagram – Adjust or replace accelerator cable
			– Depress accelerator fully	less than 1.5 Ω	
15	32 + 33	Vehicle Speed Sensor (VSS)	– Switch ignition OFF – Set ohmmeter to 2 kΩ scale • TCM disconnected	800 Ω min. 900 Ω max.	– Check harness routing according to wiring diagram – Replace VSS
16	36 + 1	Transmission Range (TR) program switch	– Switch ignition OFF • TCM disconnected		– Check harness routing according to wiring diagram – Replace TR program switch
			• TR program switch not activated	∞ Ω[1]	
			• TR program switch activated	less than 1.5 Ω	
17	30 + 18	Transmission fluid (ATF) temperature sensor	– Switch ignition OFF – Set multimeter to 2 MΩ scale • TCM disconnected		– Check harness routing according to wiring diagram – Replace ATF temperature sensor
			• ATF temperature approx. 20°C (68°F)	0.247 MΩ	
			– Set multimeter to 200 kΩ scale		
			• ATF temperature approx. 60°C (140°F)	48.8 k Ω	
			• ATF temperature approx. 120°C (216°F)	7.4 k Ω	

[1] Be sure multimeter is switched to greatest resistance measuring range.

96J19363

Courtesy of Audi of America, Inc.

Fig. 21: Testing TCU Harness & Components Type 097 (3 Of 3)

Test Step	VAG 1598/18 sockets	Component tested	♦ Test conditions – Additional tasks	Specified value	Corrective Steps in Case of Deviation
			Switch to measuring range: voltage measurement 20V		
1	23 + 1	Voltage supply from Transmission Control Module (TCM)	♦ Ignition on	approx. Battery Positive Voltage (B+)	– Check wiring per wiring diagram – Check wiring from pin 1 to Ground – Check wiring from pin 23 to terminal 15 of central electrical system
2	29 + 1	Shift Lock Solenoid	♦ Ignition on	approx. Battery Positive Voltage (B+)	– Check wiring per wiring diagram – Replace Shift Lock Solenoid
3	15 + 1	Brake Light Switch	♦ Ignition on ♦ Brake pedal not depressed	≤1 V	– Check wiring per wiring diagram – Replace Brake Light Switch
			– Brake pedal depressed	approx. Battery Positive Voltage (B+)	
4	60 + 1	Cruise control voltage supply	♦ Ignition on	approx. Battery Positive Voltage (B+)	– Check wiring per wiring diagram – Check wiring from pin 1 to Ground – Check wiring from pin 60 to terminal 15 in central electrical system – Check fuse No. 11
5	63 + 1	Multi–Function Transmission Range Switch	♦ Ignition on – Selector lever R, N, D, 3 and 2	Infinite Ω [1]	– Check wiring per wiring diagram – Check connector on Multi–Function Transmission Range Switch for corrosion, if necessary replace – Replace Multi–Function Transmission Range Switch
			– Selector lever position P and 1	≤1.5 V	
	40 + 1		– Selector lever position P, R, 2 and 1	Infinite Ω [1]	
			– Selector lever position N, D and 3	≤1.5 V	
	62 + 1		– Selector lever position P, R, N and D	Infinite Ω [1]	
			– Selector lever position 3, 2 and 1	≤1.5 V	
	18 + 1		**Switch on measuring range: voltage measurement 20V**		
			– Selector lever position P, R and N	approx. Battery Positive Voltage (B+)	
			– Selector lever position D, 3, 2 and 1	≤1 V	

96B19365

Courtesy of Audi of America, Inc.

Fig. 22: Testing TCU Harness & Components Type 01N (1 Of 3)

Switch to measuring range: voltage measurement 200 Ω					
Test Step	VAG 1598/18 sockets	Component tested	♦ Test conditions – Additional tasks	Specified value	Corrective Steps in Case of Deviation
6	55 + 67	Solenoid Valve 1	♦ Ignition off	55 to 75 Ω	– Check wiring per wiring diagram
	55 + 1			Infinite Ω [1]	– Replace conductor strip or valve body
7	54 + 67	Solenoid Valve 2	♦ Ignition off	55 to 75 Ω	– Check wiring per wiring diagram
	54 + 1			Infinite Ω [1]	– Replace conductor strip or valve body
8	9 + 67	Solenoid Valve 3	♦ Ignition off	55 to 75 Ω	– Check wiring per wiring diagram
	9 + 1			Infinite Ω [1]	– Replace conductor strip or valve body
9	47 + 67	Solenoid Valve 4	♦ Ignition off	55 to 75 Ω	– Check wiring per wiring diagram
	47 + 1			Infinite Ω [1]	– Replace conductor strip or valve body
10	56 + 67	Solenoid Valve 5	♦ Ignition off	55 to 75 Ω	– Check wiring per wiring diagram
	56 + 1			Infinite Ω [1]	– Replace conductor strip or valve body
11	58 + 22	Solenoid Valve 6	♦ Ignition off	4 to 6 Ω	– Check wiring per wiring diagram
	58 + 1			Infinite Ω [1]	– Replace conductor strip or valve body
	22 + 1				
12	10 + 67	Solenoid Valve 7	♦ Ignition off	55 to 75 Ω	– Check wiring per wiring diagram
	10 + 1			Infinite Ω [1]	– Replace conductor strip or valve body
13	23 + 29	Shift Lock Solenoid	♦ Ignition off	10 to 20 Ω	– Check wiring per wiring diagram – Replace Shift Lock Solenoid
14	1 + 16	Kick Down Switch	♦ Ignition off ♦ Brake pedal not depressed	Infinite Ω [1]	– Check wiring per wiring diagram – Adjust or replace Accelerator Pedal cable
			– push Accelerator Pedal down until kick down	less than 1.5 Ω	

[1] Switch multimeter to highest Ω range

96D19367

Courtesy of Audi of America, Inc.

Fig. 23: Testing TCU Harness & Components Type 01N (2 Of 3)

Switch to measuring range: voltage measurement 20 K Ω					
Test Step	VAG 1598/18 sockets	Component tested	♦ Test conditions – Additional tasks	Specified value	Corrective Steps in Case of Deviation
15	20 + 65	Vehicle Speed Sensor (VSS)	♦ Ignition off		– Check wiring per wiring diagram
			min	0.75 K Ω	– Replace Vehicle Speed Sensor
			max	1.0 K Ω	
16	1 + 43	Sheathing for (VSS)	♦ Ignition off ♦ Ignition on	Infinite Ω [1]	– Check wiring per wiring diagram
17	20 + 65	Transmission Vehicle Speed Sensor	♦ Ignition off		– Check wiring per wiring diagram
			min	0.75 K Ω	– Transmission Vehicle Speed Sensor
			max	1.0 K Ω	
18	1 + 43	Sheathing for (VSS)	♦ Ignition off ♦ Ignition on	Infinite Ω [1]	– Check wiring per wiring diagram
19	6 + 67	Transmission Fluid-Temperature Sensor	♦ Ignition off		– Check wiring per wiring diagram
			♦ ATF temperature		– Replace conductor strip
			approx. 20°C	250 K Ω	
			– Switch multimeter to 200 K Ω		
			approx. 60°C	48.8 K Ω	
			approx. 120°C	7.4 K Ω	

[1] Switch multimeter to highest Ω range

96F19369

Courtesy of Audi of America, Inc.

Fig. 24: Testing TCU Harness & Components Type 01N (3 Of 3)

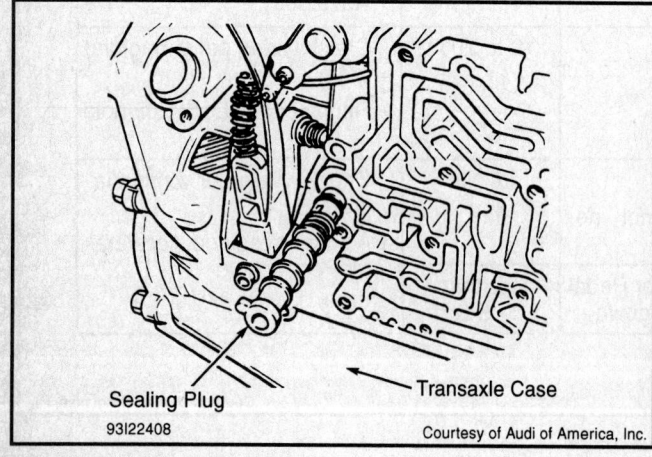

Sealing Plug

← Transaxle Case

93I22408

Courtesy of Audi of America, Inc.

Fig. 25: Locating Sealing Plug

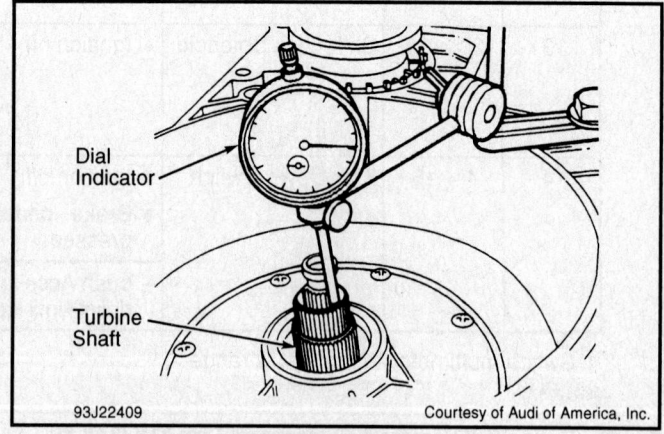

Dial Indicator

Turbine Shaft

93J22409

Courtesy of Audi of America, Inc.

Fig. 26: Checking Turbine Shaft End Play

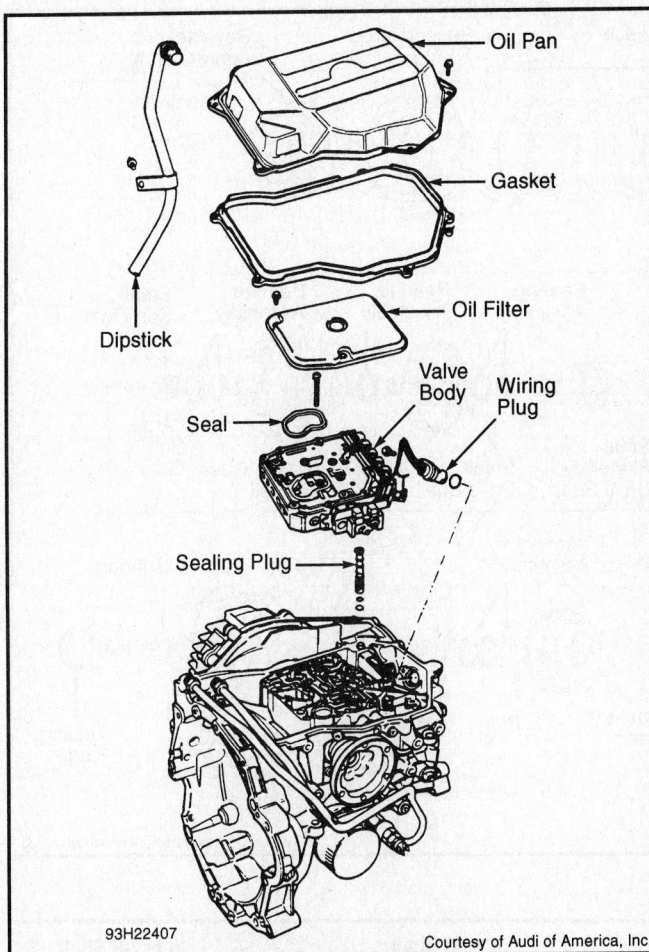

Fig. 27: Exploded View Of Oil Pan & Valve Body

COMPONENT DISASSEMBLY & REASSEMBLY

FINAL DRIVE

1) Disassemble differential. *See Fig. 38.* If necessary, apply heat to remove ring gear and bearings from differential housing. To reassemble differential, reverse disassembly.

2) Heat ring gear to 212°F (100°C). Install alignment pins to differential carrier, and install ring gear. *See Fig. 39.*

NOTE: If ring gear and/or bearings are replaced, check differential side bearing preload and ring gear position. See FINAL DRIVE & TRANSFER GEARS under TRANSAXLE REASSEMBLY.

3) Using Puller (VAG 1582) and Bearing Puller Adapter (VAG 1582-6), remove roller bearing from pinion. *See Fig. 40.* Using hydraulic press, Support (VW 402) and Adapter (VW 20-40), install roller bearing to pinion. *See Fig. 41.*

4) Check all bearing races in transaxle case. Using hydraulic press, replace bearing race(s). Replace each roller bearing and race as a set.

OIL PUMP & 2ND-4TH BRAKE CLUTCH PISTON

NOTE: Information is available for Type 097 only.

Disassemble oil pump and 2nd-4th brake clutch piston. Check for worn or damaged parts and replace as necessary. Replace all seals and reassemble. *See Fig. 42.*

NOTE: Specifications are not available.

ONE-WAY CLUTCH

NOTE: Information is available for Type 097 only.

1) Disassemble one-way clutch. Check for worn or damaged parts and replace as necessary. Compress each spring and install into cage. *See Fig. 43.*

2) Hold cage assembly with large lugs up. Install cage assembly into outer ring. *See Fig. 44.* Rotate cage clockwise until lugs touch stop. *See Fig. 45.* Install piston into outer ring. Piston should rotate freely in counter clockwise direction when installed. *See Fig. 46.*

PLANETARY CARRIER

Inspection & Adjustment – 1) Inspect planetary carrier, pinion gears, sun gears and related parts for wear or damage. Replace parts as necessary.

2) Assemble sun gear drive shells, planetary carrier, small sun gear, pinion drive transfer gear and all related bearings and washers onto small planetary drive shaft. *See Fig. 28.*

3) Install adjustment shim, washer and bolt to pinion drive transfer gear end of small planetary drive shaft. Using a screwdriver, lock small sun gear drive shell to large sun gear drive shell. *See Fig. 31.* Tighten bolt to 22 ft. lbs. (30 N.m).

4) Place assembly on Measuring Plate (VW 472/1). Place Dial Indicator Support (VW 382/7) on top of assembly. *See Fig. 47.* Measure end play of small sun gear drive shaft.

5) If end play is not .009-.014 (.23-.37 mm), replace adjustment shim. Adjustment shims range from .049 (1.26 mm) to .128" (3.25 mm) in .004" (.10 mm) increments.

APPLY CLUTCH PLATE APPLICATIONS

NOTE: Information is available for Type 097 only.

APPLY CLUTCH PLATE APPLICATIONS (097)

Application	Number Of Plates
Reverse Clutch	
Inner	5
Outer	5
1st-3rd Clutch	
Inner	5
Outer	4
3rd-4th Clutch	
Inner	5
Outer	4

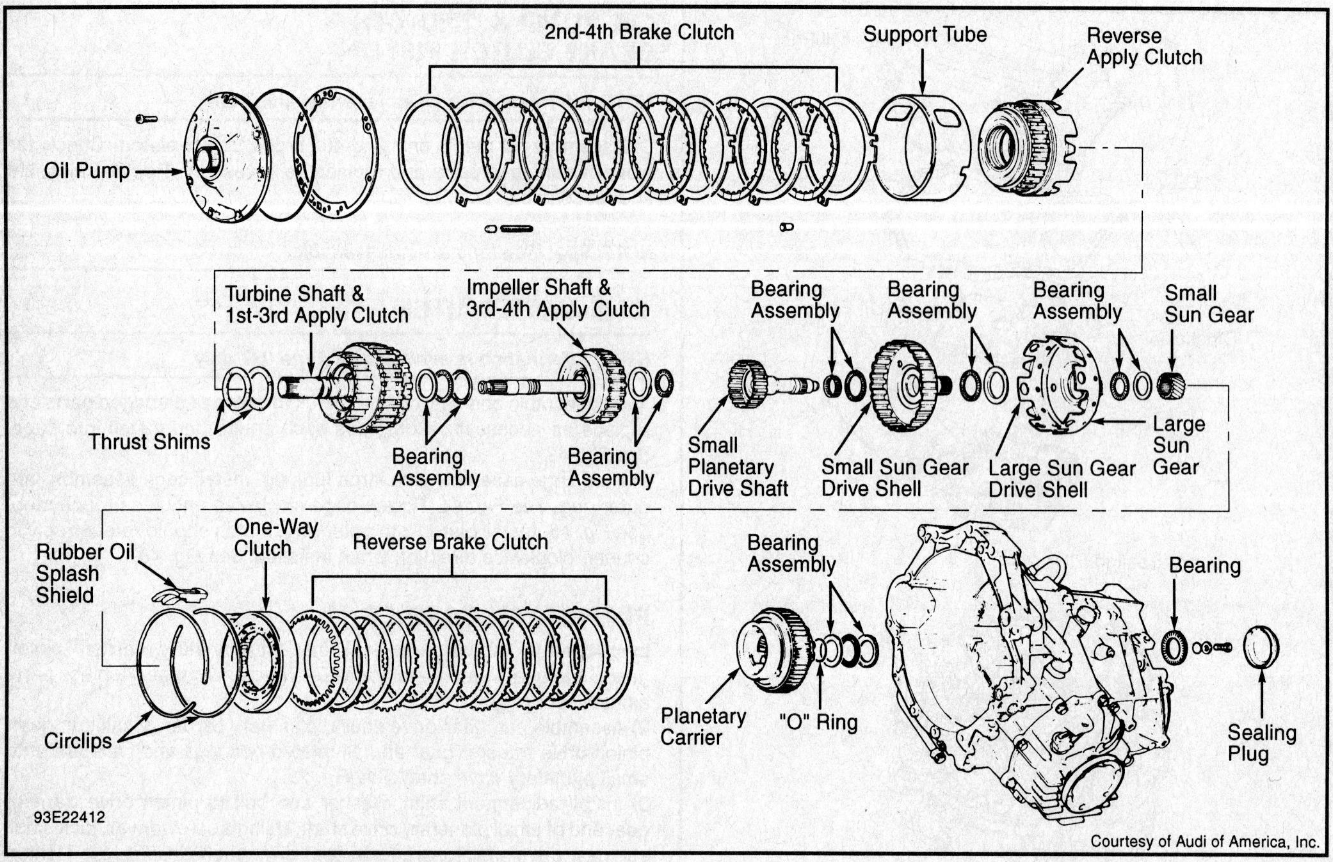

2nd-4th Brake Clutch   Support Tube   Reverse Apply Clutch

Oil Pump →

Turbine Shaft & 1st-3rd Apply Clutch   Impeller Shaft & 3rd-4th Apply Clutch   Bearing Assembly   Bearing Assembly   Bearing Assembly   Small Sun Gear

Thrust Shims   Bearing Assembly   Bearing Assembly   Small Planetary Drive Shaft   Small Sun Gear Drive Shell   Large Sun Gear Drive Shell   Large Sun Gear

Rubber Oil Splash Shield   One-Way Clutch   Reverse Brake Clutch   Bearing Assembly   Bearing

Circlips   Planetary Carrier   "O" Ring   Sealing Plug

93E22412

Courtesy of Audi of America, Inc.

Fig. 28: Exploded View Of Transmission Components

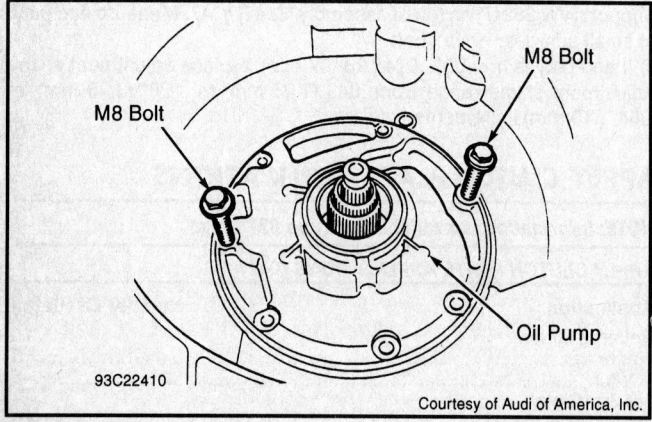

M8 Bolt   M8 Bolt

Oil Pump

93C22410

Courtesy of Audi of America, Inc.

Fig. 29: Removing Oil Pump

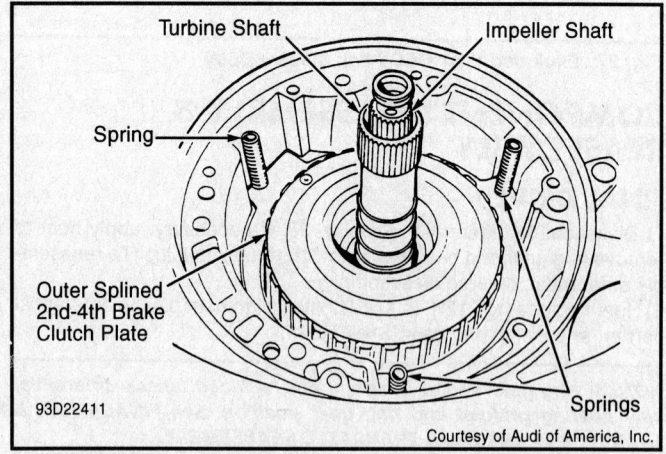

Turbine Shaft   Impeller Shaft

Spring

Outer Splined 2nd-4th Brake Clutch Plate   Springs

93D22411

Courtesy of Audi of America, Inc.

Fig. 30: Removing Turbine Shaft With 2nd-4th Brake Clutch & 1st-3rd Apply Clutch

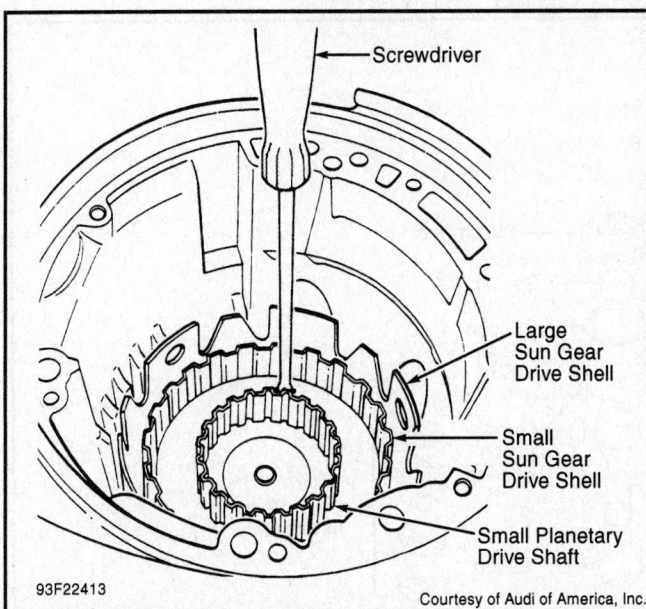

Fig. 31: Locking Small Sun Gear Drive Shell

93F22413

Courtesy of Audi of America, Inc.

REVERSE APPLY CLUTCH

NOTE: Soak all friction-faced clutch plates in ATF for at least 15 minutes before installation.

NOTE: Information is available for type 097 only.

1) Mark circlip for installation reference and remove. Disassemble clutch plates. *See Fig. 48.* Compress spring support, and remove circlip. Remove clutch piston.
2) Check for worn or damaged parts and replace as necessary. Ensure check ball in clutch housing is not damaged. Piston seal is part of piston. If damaged, replace reverse apply clutch piston. Reassemble reverse apply clutch. See APPLY CLUTCH PLATE APPLICATIONS table.

NOTE: Assembled clutch clearance specification is not available from manufacturer. Ensure thrust plate is installed with shouldered side facing circlip.

REVERSE & 2ND-4TH BRAKE CLUTCHES

Reverse and 2nd-4th brake clutches are disassembled and reassembled during transaxle disassembly and reassembly. See TRANSAXLE DISASSEMBLY and TRANSAXLE REASSEMBLY.

TRANSAXLE CASE

1) Remove multifunction switch, all seals, manual valve assembly, parking pawl and sensors. If necessary, remove parking pawl pin, detent spring screws and operating rod for manual valve from case. *See Figs. 49-55.* Inspect bushings and bearing races, and replace if necessary.
2) Install new "O" ring to gear change shaft. Install gear change shaft. Install parking pawl pin (if removed). Using a center punch, peen parking pawl pin. Install operating rod for manual valve, detent spring screws, multifunction switch and new seals. *See Figs. 50-55.*

NOTE: Install pinion oil seal with higher shoulder facing parking gear. Install pinion oil seal after all differential and transfer gear roller bearing preload adjustments and settings are complete. See FINAL DRIVE & TRANSFER GEARS under TRANSAXLE REASSEMBLY.

TRANSFER GEARS

Using Puller (VAG 1582) and Bearing Puller Adapter (VAG 1582-3), remove tapered bearing from pinion drive transfer gear. *See Fig. 53.* Using hydraulic press, Support (VW 402) and Adapter (VW 40-21), install bearing to pinion drive transfer gear. *See Fig 54.* Set pinion drive transfer and pinion drive gears aside.

VALVE BODY

NOTE: Disassembly and reassembly procedures are not available from manufacturer.

1ST-3RD APPLY CLUTCH

NOTE: Information from manufacturer available for Type 097 only.

1) Remove support ring. Mark circlip for installation reference, and remove circlip. Disassemble clutch plates. *See Fig. 57.* Remove diaphragm spring circlip. Compress spring support, and remove circlip. *See Fig. 56.* Remove spring plates and clutch piston.
2) Remove piston rings from piston. Piston seal is part of piston. If damaged, replace 1st-3rd apply clutch piston. Remove seal rings from turbine shaft. Check for worn or damaged parts and replace as necessary. Ensure check ball in clutch housing is not damaged.
3) Install new seal rings to clutch piston, and install piston in clutch housing. Install plate springs with curved sides facing piston. Install operating ring with curved side facing springs. Compress spring support and install circlip. *See Fig. 56.*
4) Install diaphragm spring with curved side facing piston. Install circlip. *See Fig. 58.* Install bottom thrust plate with smooth side facing clutch plate. Install one inner splined and one outer splined clutch plate into clutch housing. *See Fig. 57.*
5) Place inner plate carrier on bench. Install remaining clutch plates to inner plate carrier. See APPLY CLUTCH PLATE APPLICATIONS. Insert top thrust plate with smooth side facing clutch plate. Install support ring and snap in place. *See Fig. 59.*
6) Install inner plate carrier into clutch housing. Install circlip in clutch housing. *See Fig. 60.*

3RD-4TH APPLY CLUTCH

NOTE: Soak all friction-faced clutch plates in ATF for at least 15 minutes before installation.

NOTE: Information is available for Type 097 only.

1) Mark circlip for installation reference and remove. Disassemble clutch plates and round ring. *See Fig. 61.* Compress spring support ring, and remove circlip. Remove diaphragm spring circlip and diaphragm spring. Remove clutch piston.
2) Remove front impeller seal rings. DO NOT remove inner impeller seal rings unless damaged. Check for worn or damaged parts and replace as necessary.
3) Ensure check ball in clutch housing is not damaged. Piston seal is part of piston. If damaged, replace 3rd-4th apply clutch piston. Reassemble 3rd-4th apply clutch. See APPLY CLUTCH PLATE APPLICATIONS table.

NOTE: Assembled clutch clearance specification is not available from manufacturer. Ensure curved side of diaphragm spring faces piston. Ensure rounded side of round ring and rounded side of thrust plate face each other. Ensure top thrust plate is installed with shouldered side facing circlip.

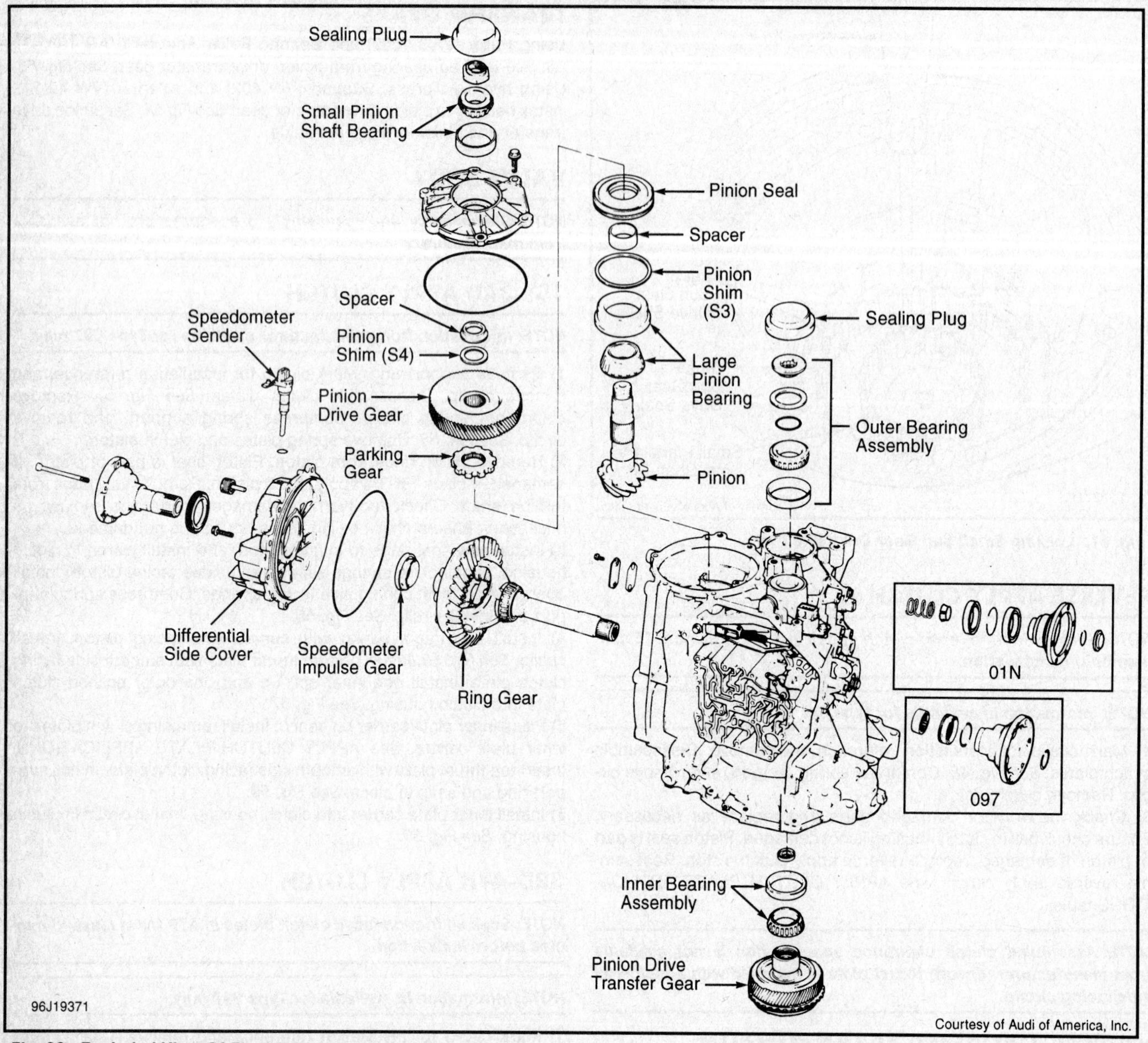

Sealing Plug

Small Pinion
Shaft Bearing

Pinion Seal

Spacer

Pinion
Shim
(S3)

Sealing Plug

Spacer

Speedometer
Sender

Pinion
Shim (S4)

Large
Pinion
Bearing

Outer Bearing
Assembly

Pinion
Drive Gear

Parking
Gear

Pinion

Differential
Side Cover

Speedometer
Impulse Gear

Ring Gear

01N

097

Inner Bearing
Assembly

Pinion Drive
Transfer Gear

96J19371

Courtesy of Audi of America, Inc.

Fig. 32: Exploded View Of Final Drive & Transfer Gear Assembly

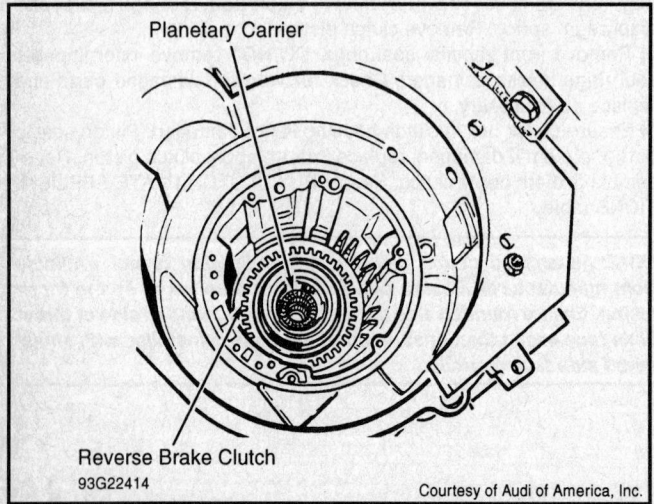

Planetary Carrier

Reverse Brake Clutch

93G22414

Courtesy of Audi of America, Inc.

Fig. 33: Removing Planetary Carrier & Reverse Brake Clutch

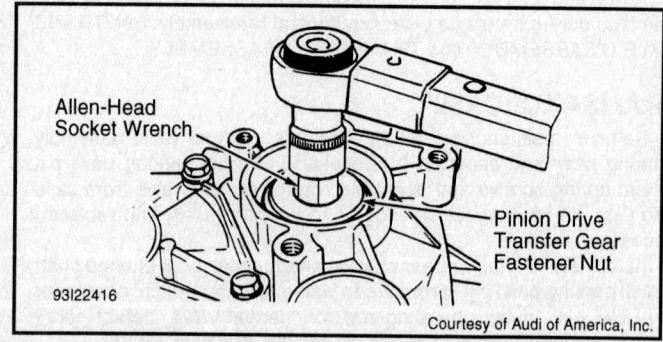

Allen-Head
Socket Wrench

Pinion Drive
Transfer Gear
Fastener Nut

93I22416

Courtesy of Audi of America, Inc.

Fig. 34: Removing Transfer Drive Gear Fastener Nut

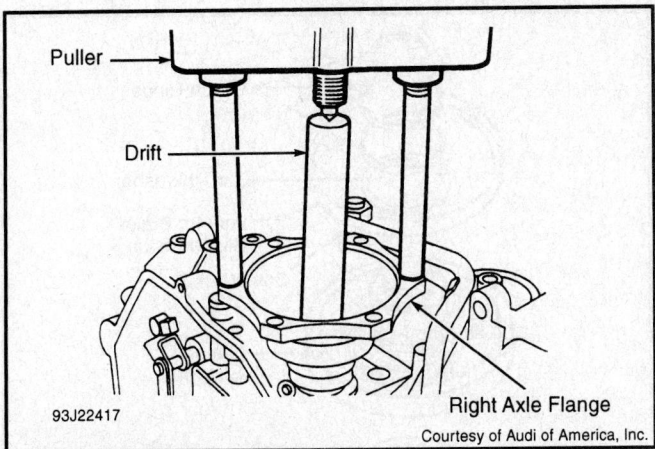

Fig. 35: Removing Right Axle Flange

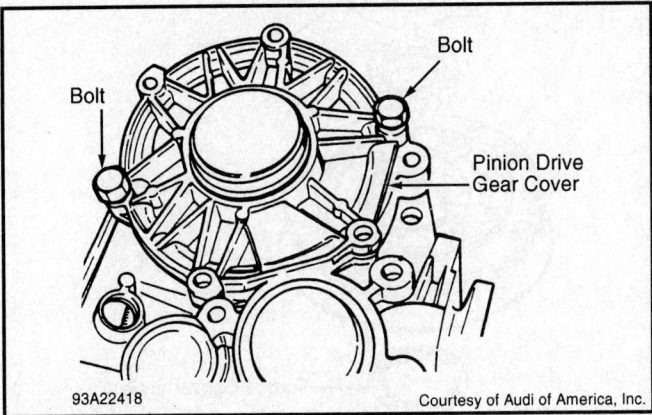

Fig. 36: Removing Pinion Drive Gear Cover

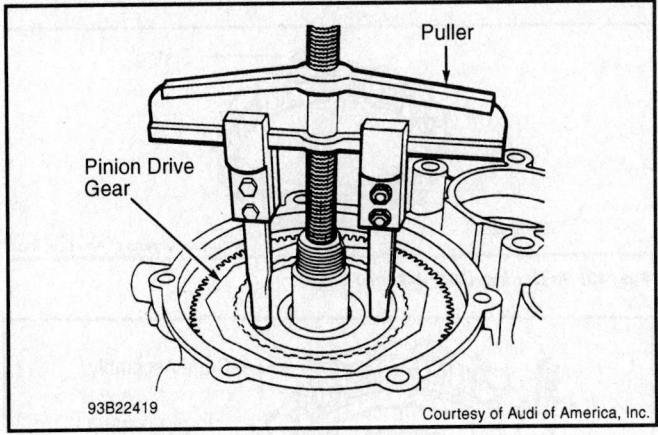

Fig. 37: Removing Pinion Drive Gear

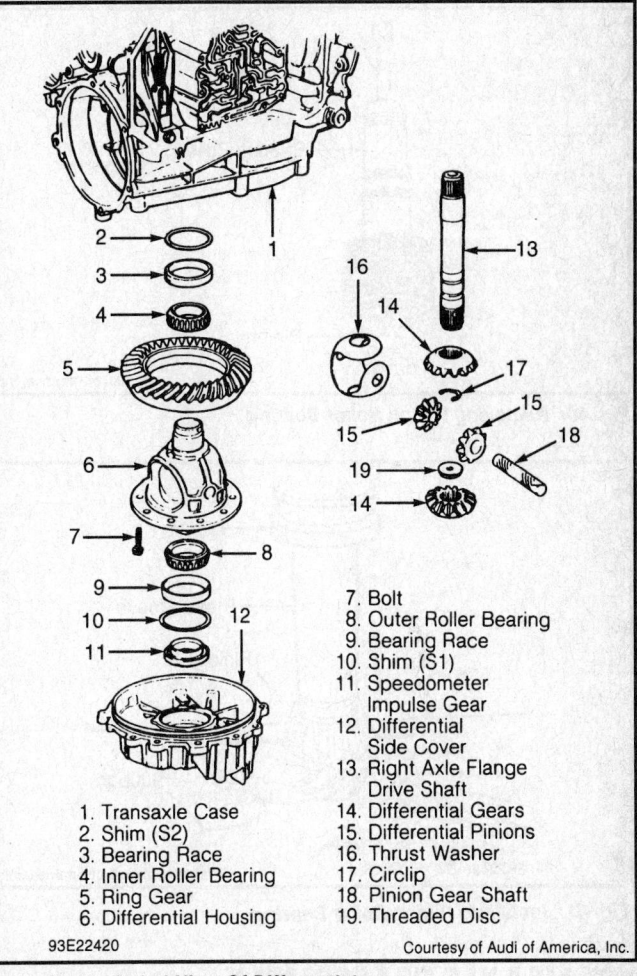

1. Transaxle Case
2. Shim (S2)
3. Bearing Race
4. Inner Roller Bearing
5. Ring Gear
6. Differential Housing

7. Bolt
8. Outer Roller Bearing
9. Bearing Race
10. Shim (S1)
11. Speedometer Impulse Gear
12. Differential Side Cover
13. Right Axle Flange Drive Shaft
14. Differential Gears
15. Differential Pinions
16. Thrust Washer
17. Circlip
18. Pinion Gear Shaft
19. Threaded Disc

Fig. 38: Exploded View Of Differential

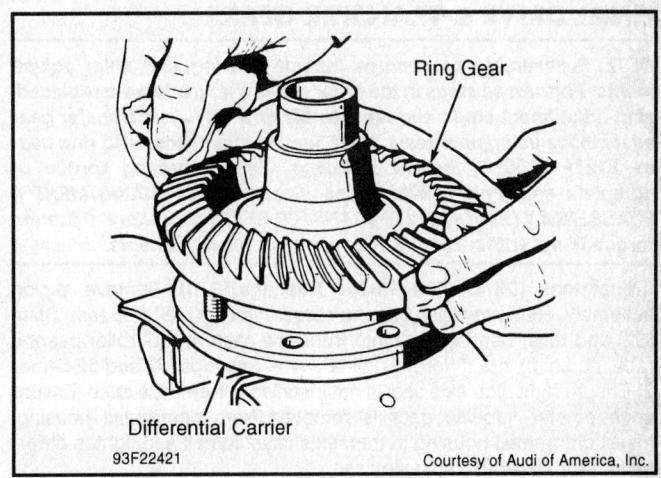

Fig. 39: Installing Ring Gear

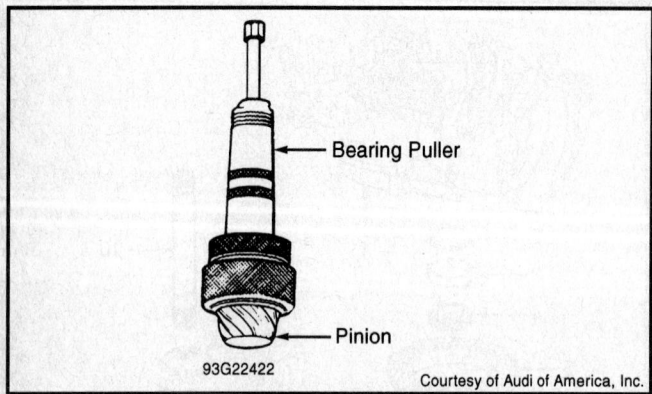

Fig. 40: Removing Pinion Roller Bearing

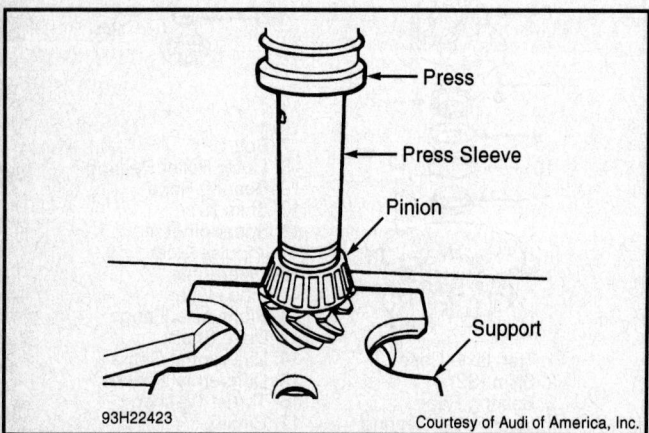

Fig. 41: Installing Pinion Roller Bearing

TRANSAXLE REASSEMBLY

FINAL DRIVE & TRANSFER GEARS

NOTE: Reassembly procedures include bearing and shim adjustments. Perform all steps in the order given. If no parts were replaced, skip adjustment steps and reassemble final drive and transfer gear assemblies using new seals. Heat bearing inner races and ring gear to 212°F (100°C) before installing. Ensure turning torque of complete assembly is within specifications. See ADJUSTMENT & REASSEMBLY (PINION DRIVE TRANSFER GEAR) procedure. If turning torque is not within specifications, check all adjustments.

Adjustment (Differential Roller Bearings) – 1) Remove pinion assembly. Remove roller bearing races. Install a .06" (1.5 mm) Shim (S2) and roller bearing race into transaxle case. Install roller bearing race (no shim) into differential side cover. *See Figs. 32 and 62-64.*
2) Ensure right side axle seal is not installed in transaxle case. Ensure speedometer impulse gear is removed from differential housing. Insert differential housing in transaxle case. Install and tighten differential side cover to transaxle case.
3) Position Adapter Plate (VW 385-17) and Dial Indicator Assembly (VW 387) on transaxle case. *See Fig. 65.* Move differential housing up and down (DO NOT rotate). Measure and record end play.

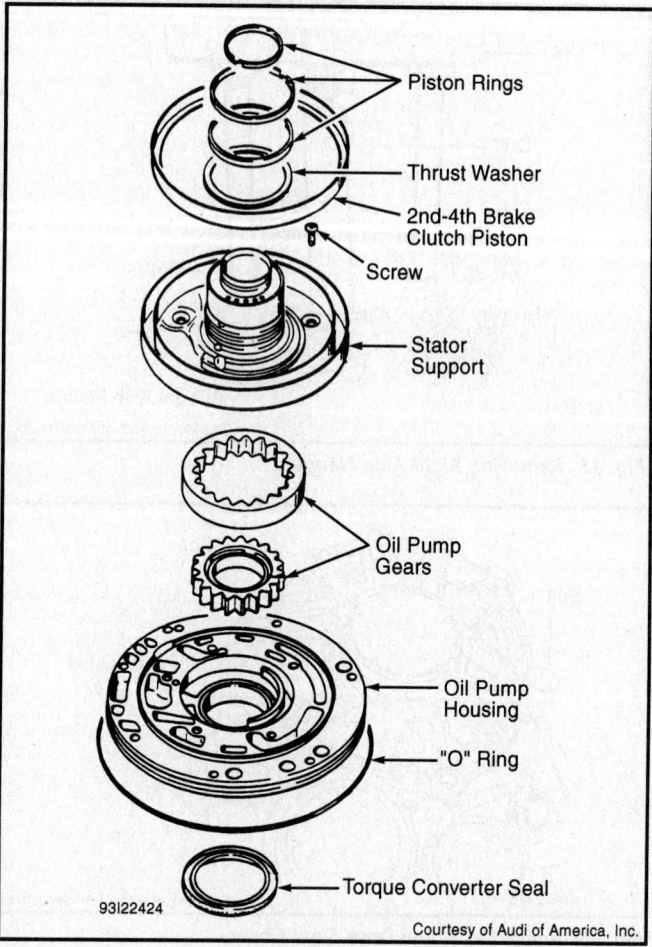

Fig. 42: Exploded View Of Oil Pump & 2nd-4th Brake Clutch Piston

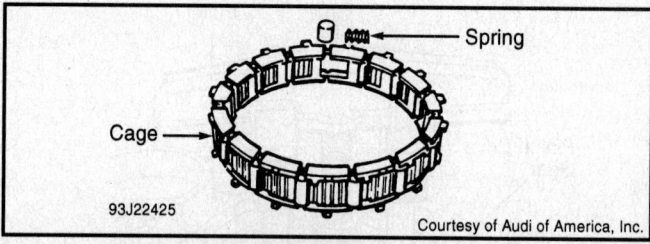

Fig. 43: Installing Springs Into Cage

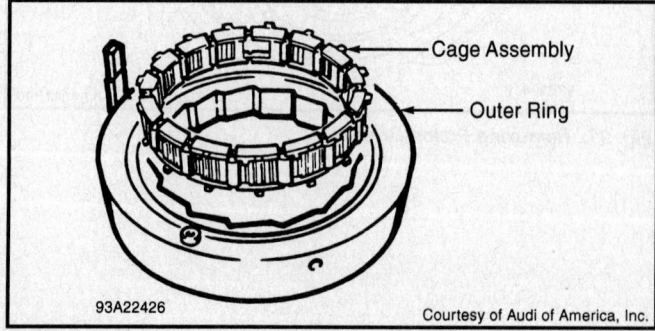

Fig. 44: Installing Cage Assembly Into Outer Ring

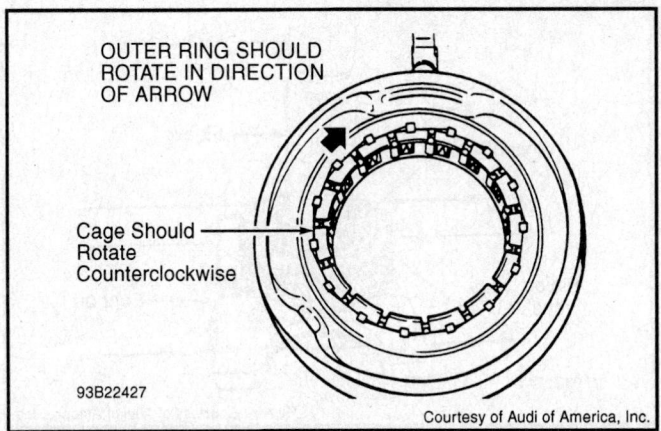

Fig. 45: Rotate Cage Clockwise Until Stop

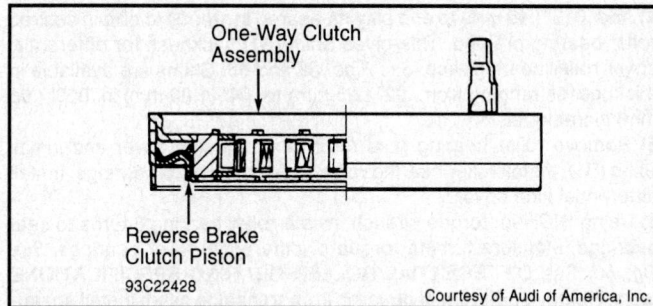

Fig. 46: Installing Piston Into One-Way Clutch

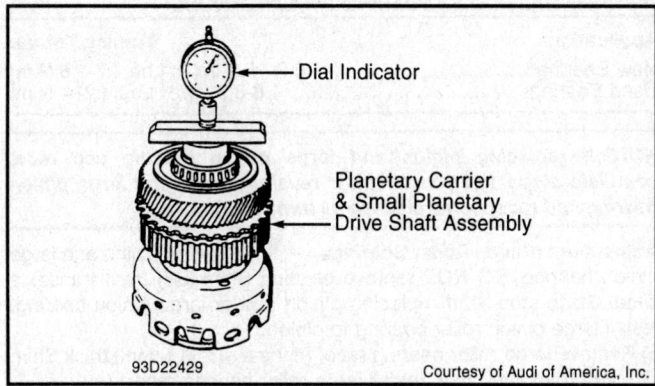

Fig. 47: Adjusting Planetary Carrier End Play

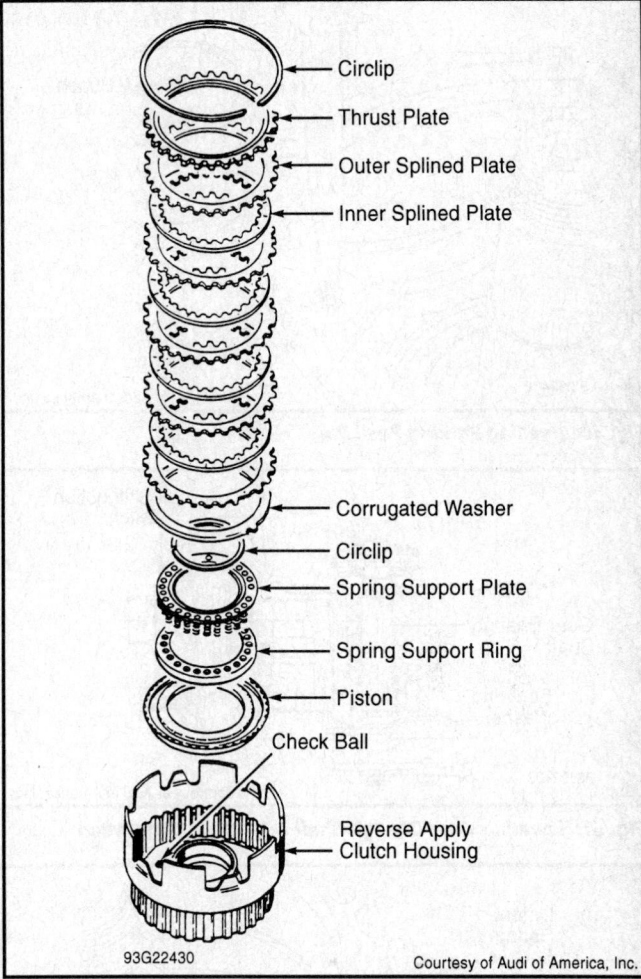

Fig. 48: Exploded View Of Reverse Apply Clutch

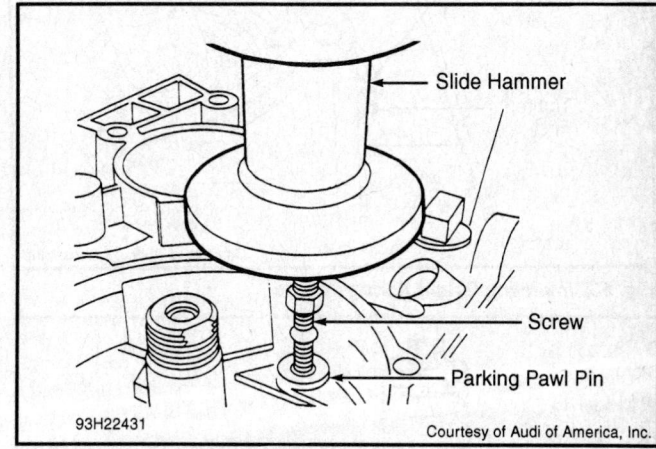

Fig. 49: Removing Parking Pawl Pin

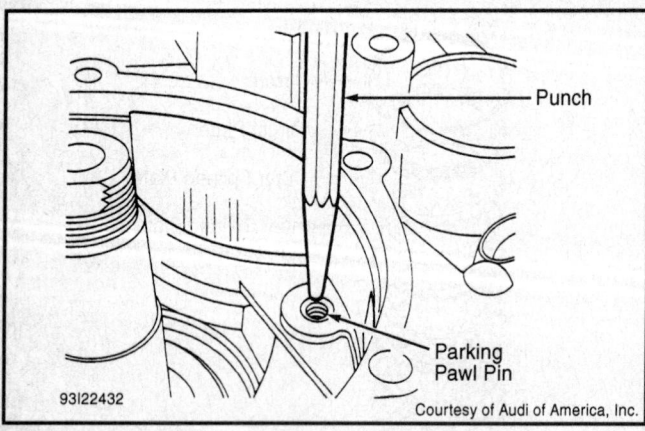

Fig. 50: Peening Parking Pawl Pin

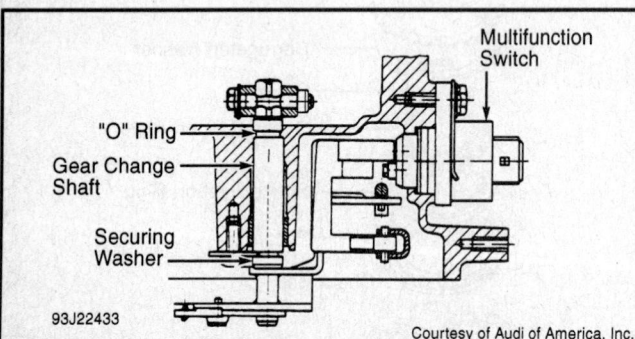

Fig. 51: Locating Gear Change Shaft & Multifunction Switch

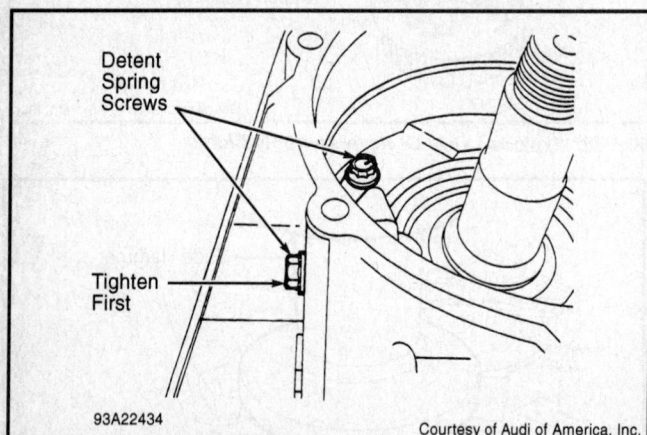

Fig. 52: Installing Detent Spring Screws

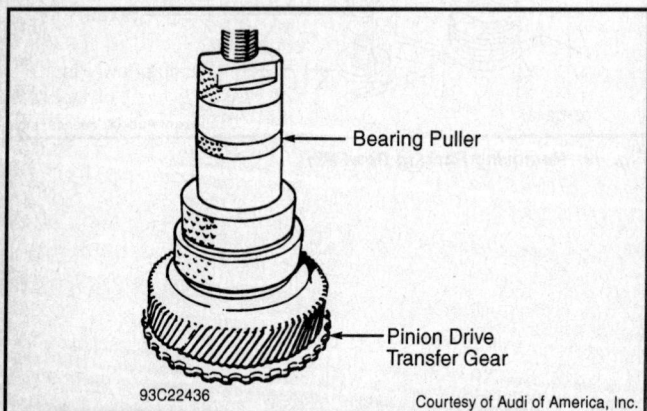

Fig. 53: Removing Pinion Drive Transfer Gear Roller Bearing

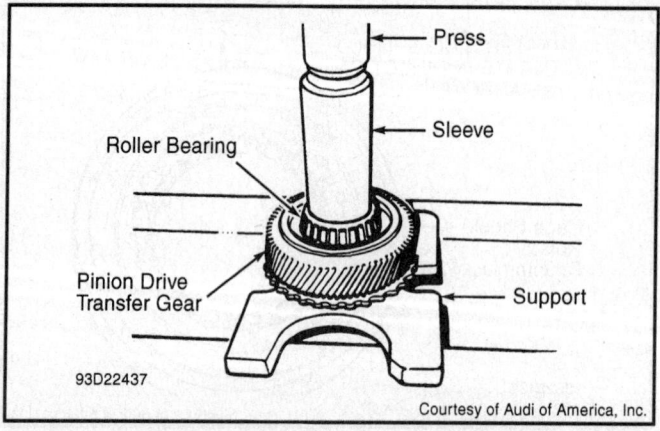

Fig. 54: Installing Pinion Drive Transfer Gear Roller Bearing

4) Add .016" (.40 mm) to end play measured in step **3)** to obtain desired roller bearing preload. This gives Shim (S1) thickness for differential cover roller bearing race. See Figs. 32 and 62. Shims are available in thicknesses ranging from .02" (.55 mm) to .04" (1.00 mm) in .002" (.05 mm) increments.

5) Remove roller bearing race for differential side cover and install Shim (S1). Install roller bearing race. Apply gear oil to bearings. Install differential side cover.

6) Using INCH-lb. torque wrench, rotate roller bearing 8 turns to seat bearings. Measure turning torque of differential roller bearings. See Fig. 66. See DIFFERENTIAL ROLLER BEARING SPECIFICATIONS table. Remove differential housing from transaxle case. Install speedometer impulse gear and set aside.

DIFFERENTIAL ROLLER BEARING SPECIFICATIONS

Application	Turning Torque
New Bearings	6.2-13.3 INCH Lbs. (.7-1.5 N.m)
Used Bearings	1.8-3.5 INCH Lbs. (.2-.4 N.m)

NOTE: If replacing pinion and large pinion bearing and race, complete steps 1) through 18). If reusing pinion and large pinion bearing and race, perform steps 1) through 9) only.

Adjustment (Pinion Roller Bearings) – **1)** If reusing pinion and large pinion bearing, DO NOT remove existing Shim (S3) from transaxle case. Go to step **3)**. If replacing pinion and/or large pinion bearing, install large pinion roller bearing to pinion.

2) Remove large roller bearing race. Place a .06" (1.5 mm) thick Shim (S3) into transaxle case. Install large roller bearing race.

3) Ensure parking lock lug is installed in transaxle case. Install small pinion roller bearing race in pinion cover. See Fig. 67. Install pinion and spacer into transaxle case. See Figs. 32 and 62.

4) Install parking gear (rounded side facing pinion drive gear), pinion drive gear and a .094" (2.40 mm) thick Shim (S4) on pinion. See Fig. 68.

5) Install shouldered spacer with wide side facing pinion drive gear. Install pinion cover. Install outer roller bearing. Install pinion nut. See Fig. 69. Tighten pinion cover bolts to 18 ft. lbs. (25 N.m).

6) Engage parking gear. Tighten pinion nut to 177 ft. lbs. (240 N.m). Position Adapter Plate (VW 385-17) and Dial Indicator Assembly (VW 387) on transaxle case. See Fig. 70. Move pinion up and down (DO NOT rotate). Measure and record end play.

7) Add .010" (.25 mm) to end play measured in step **6)**. This is Shim (S4) thickness required to preload pinion cover roller bearing. See Fig. 62. Shims are available in thickness ranging from .040-.094" (1.00-2.40 mm), in .001" (.025 mm) increments.

8) Remove pinion nut, pinion cover and shouldered spacer. Install Shim (S4). Install shouldered spacer. Apply gear oil to bearings. Install pinion cover and pinion nut. Tighten pinion nut to 250 ft. lbs. (339 N.m) to seat bearings. Loosen nut and retighten to 177 ft. lbs. (240 N.m).

9) Using INCH-lb. torque wrench, rotate roller bearing 8 turns to settle bearings. Measure turning torque of pinion roller bearings. See Fig. 71. See PINION ROLLER BEARING SPECIFICATIONS table.

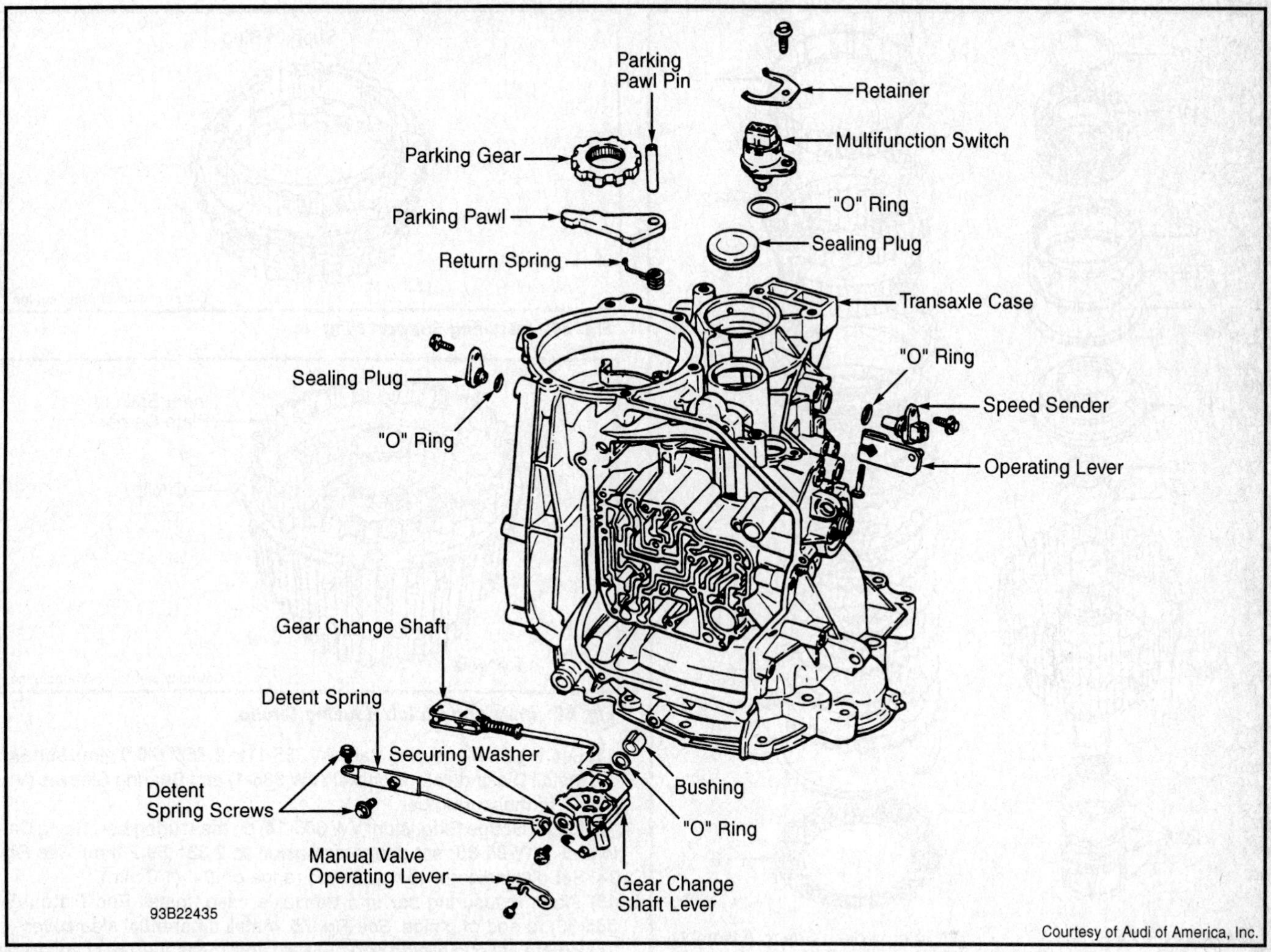

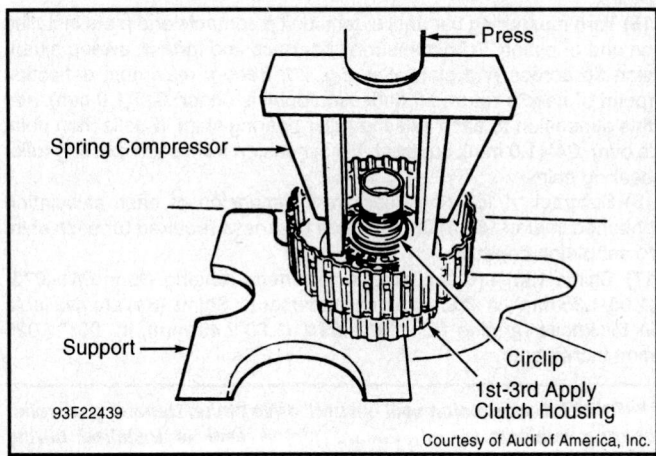

Parking Pawl Pin
Retainer
Multifunction Switch
Parking Gear
Parking Pawl
"O" Ring
Return Spring
Sealing Plug
Transaxle Case
Sealing Plug
"O" Ring
"O" Ring
Speed Sender
Operating Lever
Gear Change Shaft
Detent Spring
Securing Washer
Detent Spring Screws
Bushing
"O" Ring
Manual Valve Operating Lever
Gear Change Shaft Lever

93B22435

Courtesy of Audi of America, Inc.

Fig. 55: Exploded View Of Transaxle Case Components

Press
Spring Compressor
Support
Circlip
1st-3rd Apply Clutch Housing

93F22439

Courtesy of Audi of America, Inc.

Fig. 56: Removing & Installing Spring Circlip

10) If reusing large pinion roller bearing and Shim (S3), go to ADJUSTMENT (RING GEAR BACKLASH) procedure. Identify ring gear markings. *See Fig. 72.* Determine running clearance deviation "r" between pinion and ring gear. See RING GEAR MARKINGS table.

PINION ROLLER BEARING SPECIFICATIONS

Application	Turning Torque
New Bearings	11.9-23.4 INCH Lbs. (1.34-2.64 N.m)
Used Bearings	[1] Same As Before Disassembly

[1] – Recorded during disassembly. See FINAL DRIVE & TRANSFER GEARS under TRANSAXLE DISASSEMBLY.

RING GEAR MARKINGS

Marking [1]	Identifies
1141 – "1"	Ratio Of Ring & Pinion Gears – 41:11
312 – "2"	Ring & Pinion Match Set No.
"r" – "3"	Deviation No. In 1/100 mm
Ro (59.2)	Standard Length Of Factory Set Up
R	Axis Of Ring Gear & Face Of Pinion
Vo	Hypoid Offset

[1] – See Fig. 72 for marking examples.

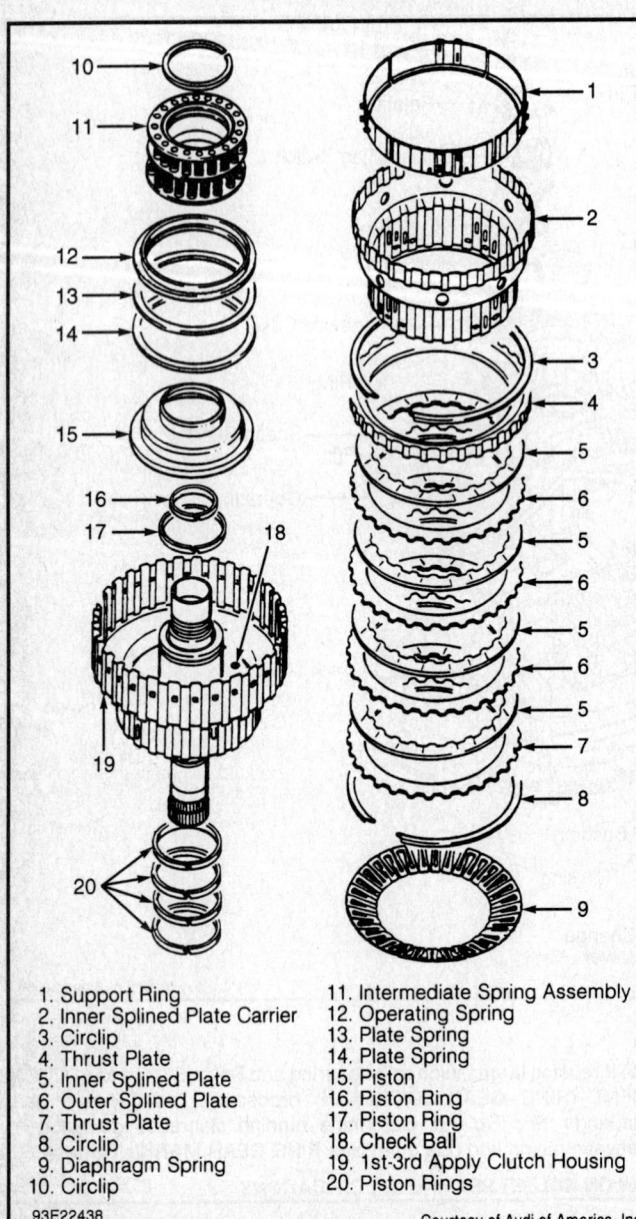

1. Support Ring
2. Inner Splined Plate Carrier
3. Circlip
4. Thrust Plate
5. Inner Splined Plate
6. Outer Splined Plate
7. Thrust Plate
8. Circlip
9. Diaphragm Spring
10. Circlip
11. Intermediate Spring Assembly
12. Operating Spring
13. Plate Spring
14. Plate Spring
15. Piston
16. Piston Ring
17. Piston Ring
18. Check Ball
19. 1st-3rd Apply Clutch Housing
20. Piston Rings

93E22438

Courtesy of Audi of America, Inc.

Fig. 57: Exploded View Of 1st-3rd Apply Clutch

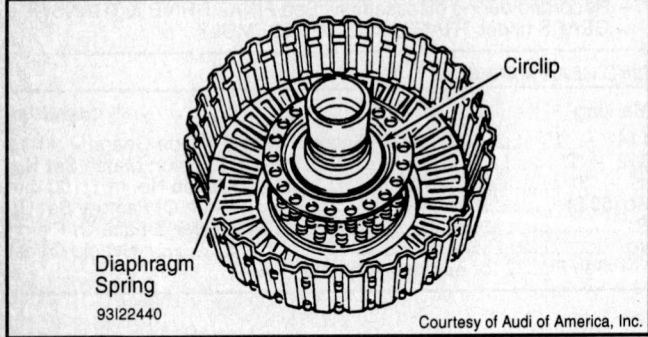

93I22440

Courtesy of Audi of America, Inc.

Fig. 58: Installing Diaphragm Spring & Circlip

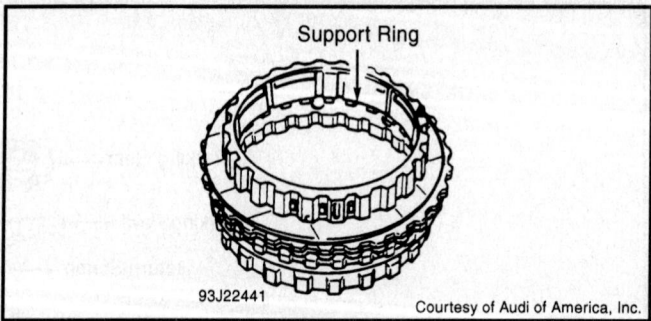

93J22441

Courtesy of Audi of America, Inc.

Fig. 59: Installing Support Ring

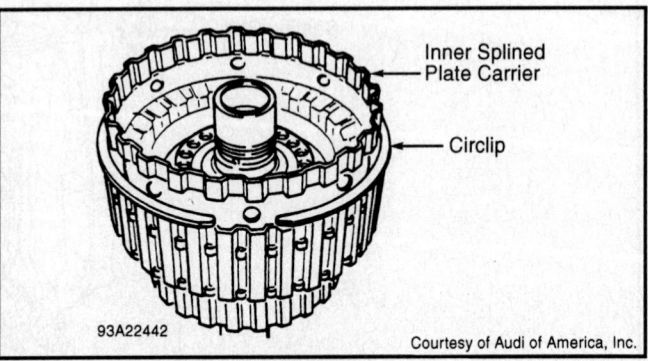

93A22442

Courtesy of Audi of America, Inc.

Fig. 60: Installing Clutch Housing Circlip

11) Set ring on Measuring Bar (VW 385-1) to 2.756" (70.0 mm). *See Fig. 73.* Install Dial Indicator Adapter (VW 385-1) and Bearing Sleeves (VW 385-2) to measuring bar.

12) Install Gauge Extension (VW 385-14) on measuring bar. Using Calibrator (VW-85-30) set gauge extension to 2.33" (59.2 mm). *See Fig. 74.* Set dial indicator to measuring range of .04" (1.0 mm).

13) Place measuring bar into transaxle case. Install End Plate (VW 385-33) to end of pinion. *See Fig. 75.* Install differential side cover.

14) Rotate second sliding ring outward until measuring bar can still be moved by hand. This centers measuring bar in differential bearing races.

15) Turn measuring bar until extension tip contacts end plate installed on end of pinion. Turn measuring bar back and forth to sweep extension tip across end plate. *See Fig. 76.* Record maximum deflection (point of needle return). If deflection point is under .04" (1.0 mm), add this dimension to each existing roller bearing shim. If deflection point is over .04" (1.0 mm), subtract this dimension from each existing roller bearing shim.

16) Subtract "r" (on ring gear) from dimension of each calculation obtained in step **15)**. This calculates thickness required for each shim to set pinion depth.

17) Shims (S3) are available in thickness ranging from .041-.073" (1.05-1.85 mm), in .002" (.05 mm) increments. Shims (S4) are available in thickness ranging from .040-.094" (1.00-2.40 mm), in .001" (.025 mm) increments.

WARNING: Leave pinion seal out until drive pinion transfer gear roller bearing preload is set. Ensure pinion seal is installed during reassembly. See FINAL DRIVE ASSEMBLY procedure.

18) Remove pinion, and install large pinion roller bearing Shim (S3). Install pinion. Repeat steps **8)** and **9)**. Record turning torque. This specification is required to set drive pinion transfer gear roller bearing preload.

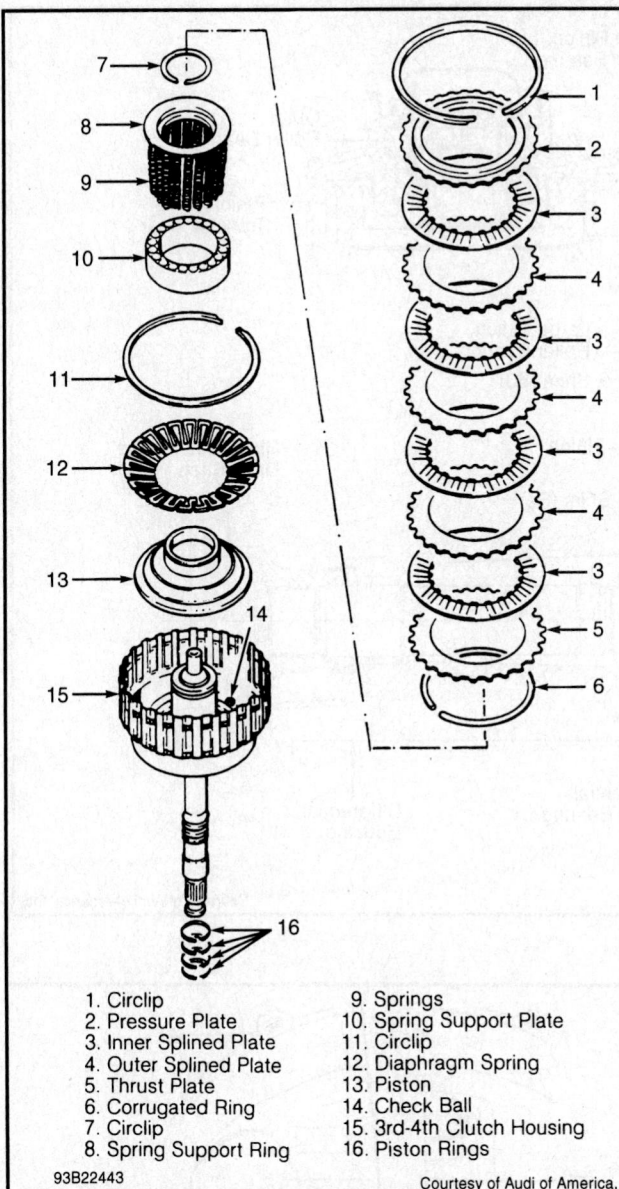

Fig. 61: Exploded View Of 3rd-4th Apply Clutch

1. Circlip
2. Pressure Plate
3. Inner Splined Plate
4. Outer Splined Plate
5. Thrust Plate
6. Corrugated Ring
7. Circlip
8. Spring Support Ring
9. Springs
10. Spring Support Plate
11. Circlip
12. Diaphragm Spring
13. Piston
14. Check Ball
15. 3rd-4th Clutch Housing
16. Piston Rings

93B22443

Courtesy of Audi of America, Inc.

Adjustment (Ring Gear Backlash) – **1)** Ensure pinion is installed to correct pinion depth and roller bearing preload. If not, see appropriate steps in ADJUSTMENT (PINION ROLLER BEARINGS) procedure.

2) Install differential housing and differential side cover. Rotate differential to seat bearings. Mount Dial Indicator Assembly (VW 387) to transaxle case. *See Fig. 77.*

3) Install Setting Adapters (VW 521-4 and 521-8) on differential. Set Measuring Lever (VW 388) to 2.756" (70.0 mm). Using Bearing Separator (Kukko 172), hold pinion from turning. *See Fig. 78.*

4) Hold ring gear against pinion. Set dial indicator to zero. Rotate ring gear, and record backlash. Check backlash at 3 more places on ring gear.

5) If backlash readings vary more than .002" (.06 mm), recheck ring gear installation or ring gear and pinion for damage. *See Figs. 38 and 62.* If backlash readings vary less than .002" (.06 mm), ring gear and pinion installation is okay.

6) Backlash should be .006-.010" (.15-.25 mm). If not, calculate shim thickness required to correct ring gear backlash. Shims are available in thickness ranging from .02-.04" (.55-1.00 mm), in .002" (.05 mm) increments.

7) Ensure roller bearing preload is maintained. Install shims and recheck ring gear backlash. *See Figs. 77 and 78.*

Adjustment & Reassembly (Pinion Drive Transfer Gear) – **1)** Ensure inner race for roller bearing is installed in transaxle case.

2) Install pinion drive transfer gear with roller bearing and axial needle bearing into transaxle case. *See Figs. 32 and 62.* Align lugs on outer roller bearing to fit between lugs on inner roller bearing. *See Fig. 79.*

3) Install outer roller bearing (without dished washer or shim) on pinion drive transfer gear. *See Figs. 32 and 62.* Engage parking gear. Using an Allen-head socket, tighten fastener nut to 74 ft. lbs. (100 N.m). *See Fig. 80.*

4) Remove fastener nut. Using a dial indicator, measure distance between pinion drive transfer gear and inner race of roller bearing. *See Fig. 81.* Add thickness of dished washer .58" (1.50 mm).

5) Add dished washer thickness to distance measured in step **3)**. Subtract .007" (.18 mm) to obtain shim thickness for desired roller bearing preload. Shims are available in thickness ranging from .063-.100" (1.60-2.55 mm), in .001" (.025 mm) increments.

6) Install selected shim. Install dished washer with cupped side facing away from fastener nut. Apply ATF to bearings. Install and tighten fastener nut to 185 ft. lbs. (250 N.m) to seat bearings.

7) Using INCH-lb. torque wrench, measure combined turning torque of pinion, differential and transfer gear roller bearings. *See Fig. 82.* See TRANSFER GEAR ROLLER BEARING SPECIFICATIONS table.

TRANSFER GEAR ROLLER BEARING SPECIFICATIONS

Application	Turning Torque
New Bearings	
Without Pinion &	
Differential Bearings	11.9-23.4 INCH Lbs. (1.34-2.64 N.m)
With Pinion &	
Differential Bearings	44.3 INCH Lbs. (5.0 N.m)
Used Bearings	[1] Same As Before Disassembly

[1] – Recorded during disassembly. See FINAL DRIVE & TRANSFER GEARS under TRANSAXLE DISASSEMBLY.

8) Remove fastener nut. If necessary, select a shim and recheck roller bearing preload. If roller bearing preload is okay, apply Locking Compound (AMV 100 01) to shaft side of roller bearing. *See Fig. 83.*

9) Align lugs with notches of opposite roller bearing. *See Fig. 79.* Install axial needle bearing with flat side facing drive shaft. Engage parking gear lug. Install fastener nut and tighten to 185 ft. lbs. (250 N.m).

Final Drive Assembly – **1)** Remove differential assembly. Remove pinion cover, parking gear, pinion drive gear and pinion assembly from transaxle case. Install pinion oil seal with higher shoulder facing parking gear. *See Fig. 32.*

2) Install Seal Protector (3187) over pinion oil seal. *See Fig. 84.* Install pinion, and remove seal protector. Install parking gear, pinion drive gear assembly and selected shims. *See Figs. 32 and 55.*

3) Install and tighten pinion nut to 177 ft. lbs. (240 N.m). Using a punch, flatten edge of nut against flat on pinion.

4) Install differential assembly. Install and tighten differential cover bolts to 18 ft. lbs. (25 N.m). Install "O" ring to right drive axle flange.

5) Install circlip to end of axle. Using Puller (VW 3244), install right drive axle flange to transaxle. *See Fig. 85.* Install left drive axle flange. Tighten attaching bolt to 18 ft. lbs. (25 N.m). Install speedometer sender.

TRANSMISSION

NOTE: Soak all friction-faced clutch plates in ATF for at least 15 minutes before installation. Apply assembly lubrication to all bushings, washers, shims and bearings before installation. See Fig. 28.

1) Install "O" ring and planetary carrier. Install small sun gear, axial needle bearing and washers. Install end plate shim. *See Fig. 85.*

2) Install reverse brake clutch plates. *See Fig. 87.* See BRAKE CLUTCH PLATE APPLICATIONS table. Using Assembly Ring (VW 3267), install one-way clutch and secure using circlip. *See Figs. 88 and 89.*

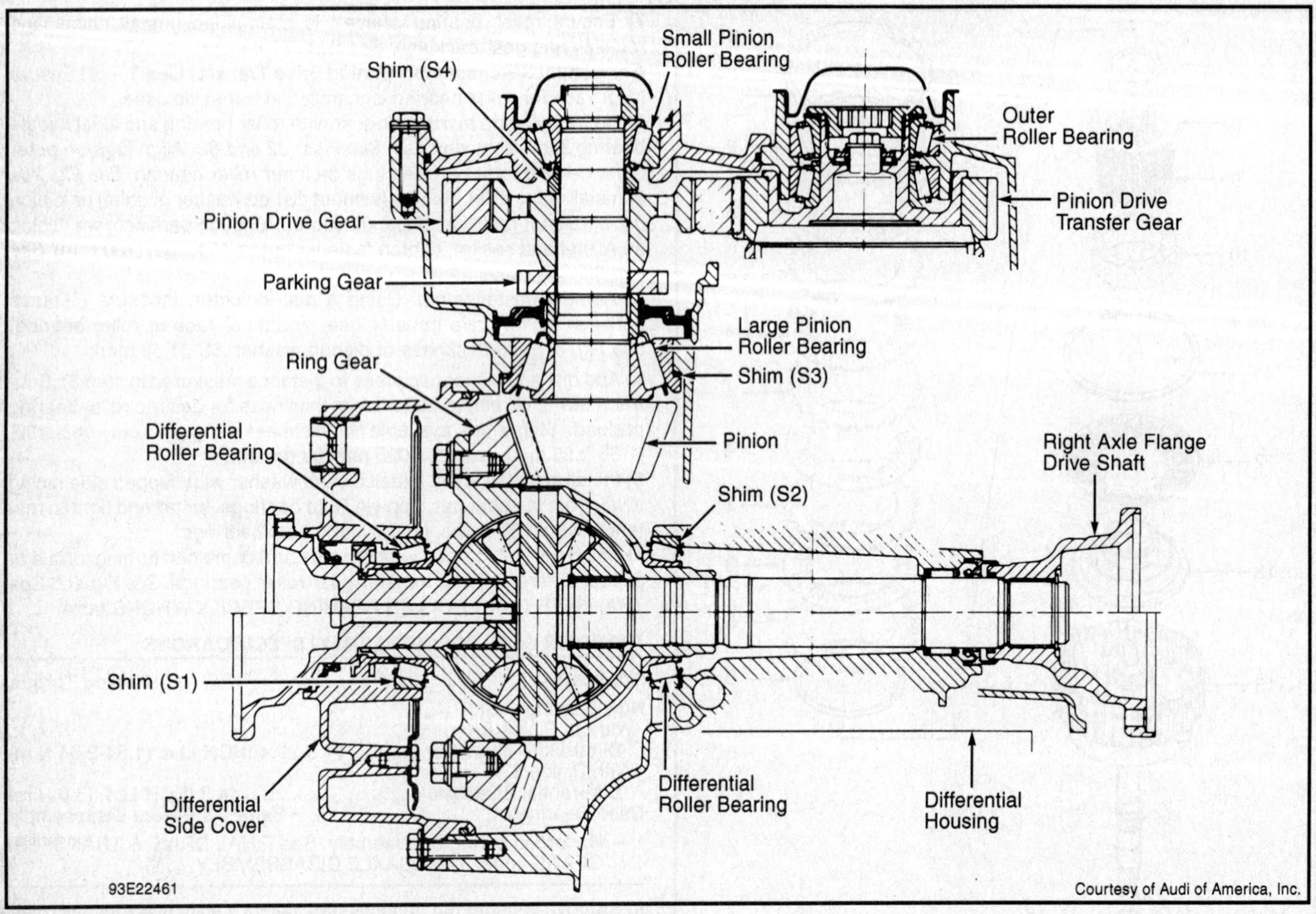

Shim (S4)

Small Pinion
Roller Bearing

Outer
Roller Bearing

Pinion Drive
Transfer Gear

Pinion Drive Gear

Parking Gear

Large Pinion
Roller Bearing

Shim (S3)

Ring Gear

Pinion

Differential
Roller Bearing

Right Axle Flange
Drive Shaft

Shim (S2)

Shim (S1)

Differential
Side Cover

Differential
Roller Bearing

Differential
Housing

93E22461

Courtesy of Audi of America, Inc.

Fig. 62: Locating Final Drive Roller Bearings, Races & Adjustment Shims

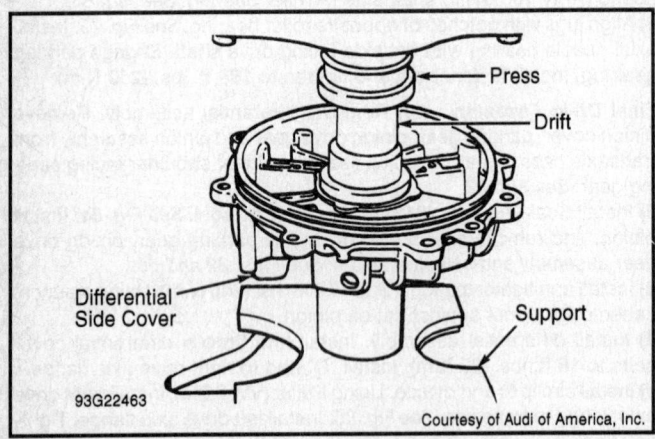

Press

Drift

Differential
Side Cover

Support

93G22463

Courtesy of Audi of America, Inc.

**Fig. 63: Installing Differential Housing Cover
Roller Bearing Race**

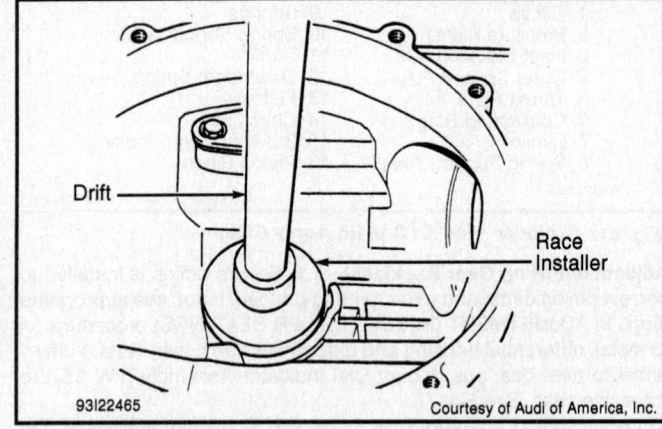

Drift

Race
Installer

93I22465

Courtesy of Audi of America, Inc.

Fig. 64: Installing Roller Bearing Race To Transaxle Case

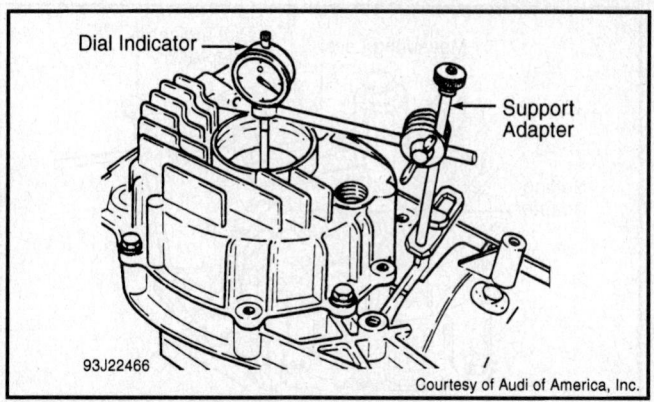

Fig. 65: Checking Roller Bearing End Play

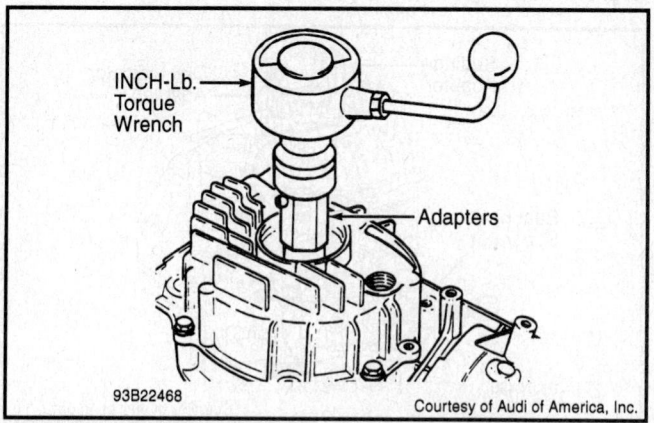

Fig. 66: Measuring Differential Roller Bearing Turning Torque

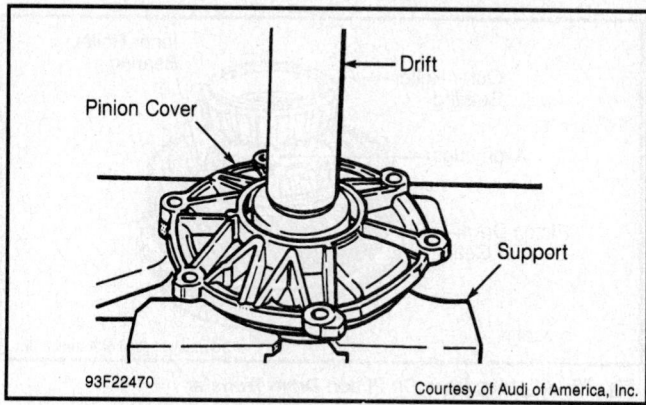

Fig. 67: Installing Small Pinion Bearing Roller Race

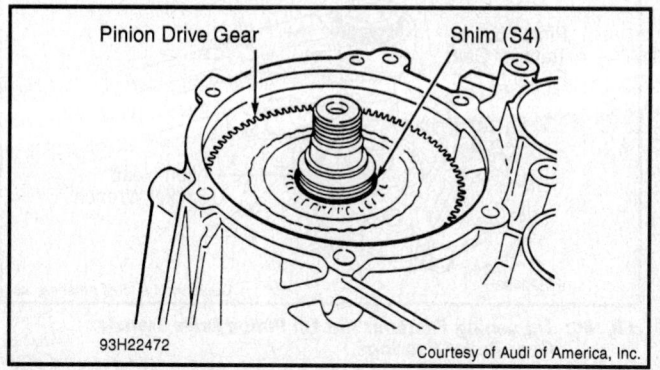

Fig. 68: Installing Shim (S4) On Pinion Drive Gear

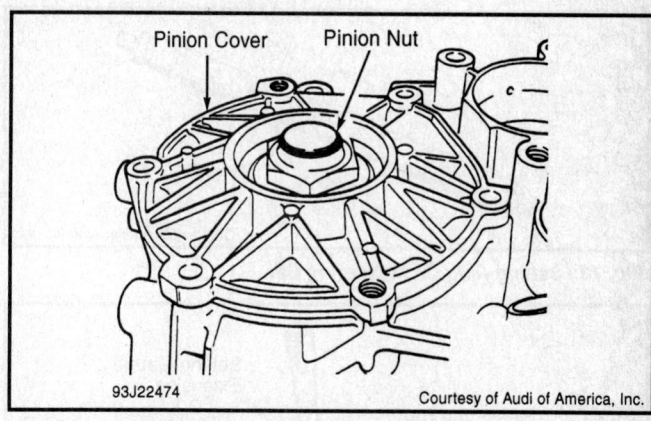

Fig. 69: Installing Pinion Cover & Pinion Nut

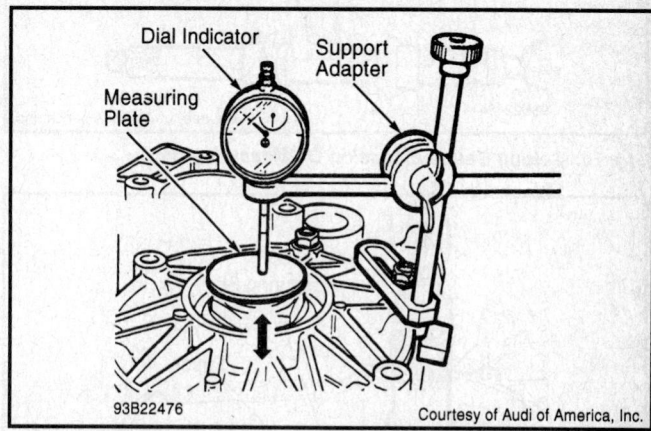

Fig. 70: Checking Pinion Roller Bearing End Play

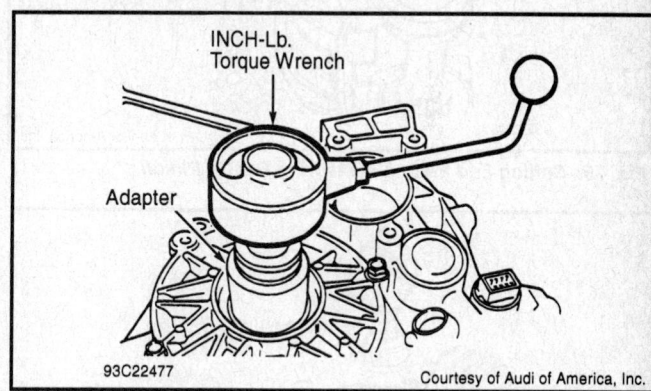

Fig. 71: Checking Pinion Roller Bearing Preload

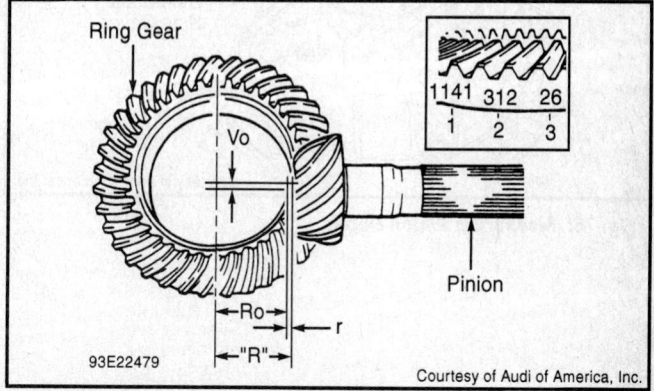

Fig. 72: Locating Ring Gear Markings

AUTOMATIC TRANSMISSIONS
Audi Type 01N & 097 (Cont.)

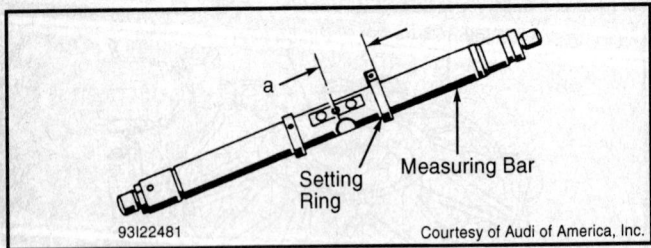

Fig. 73: Setting Ring On Measuring Bar

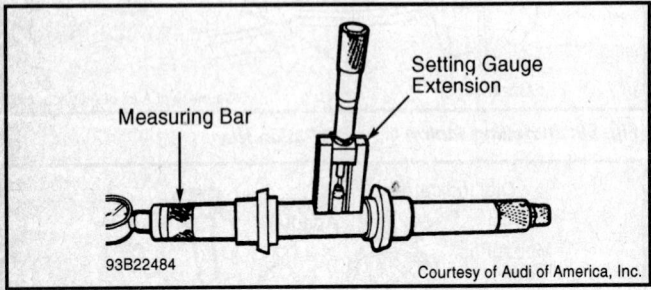

Fig. 74: Setting Gauge Extension On Measuring Bar

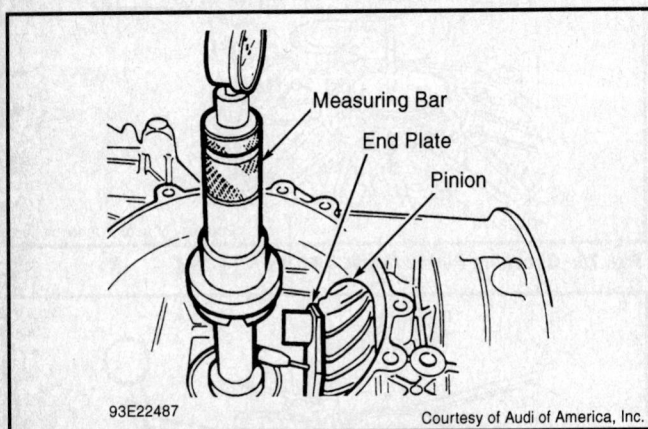

Fig. 75: Setting End Plate & Measuring Bar On Pinion

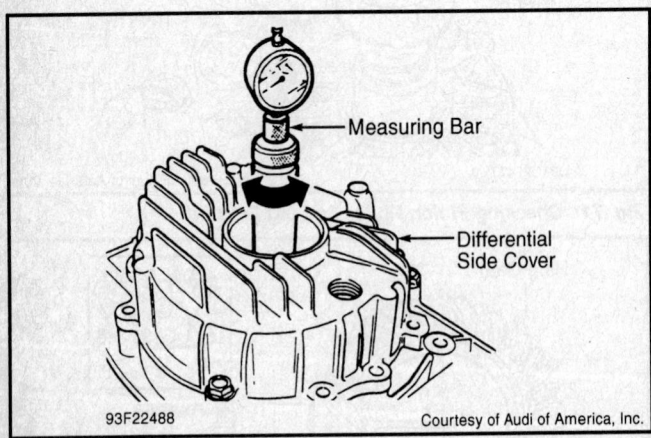

Fig. 76: Measuring Pinion Depth

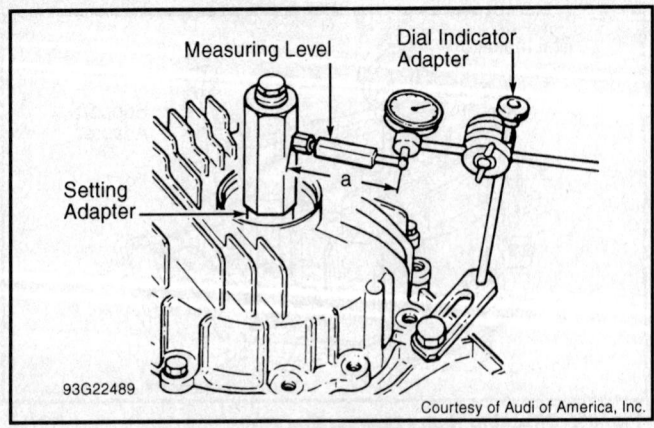

Fig. 77: Mounting Dial Indicator Adapter

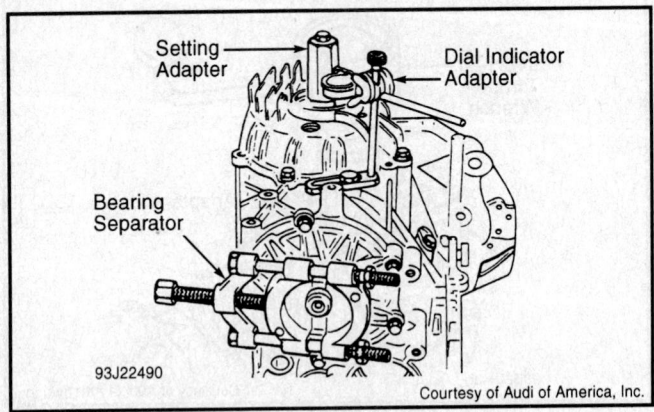

Fig. 78: Checking Ring Gear Backlash

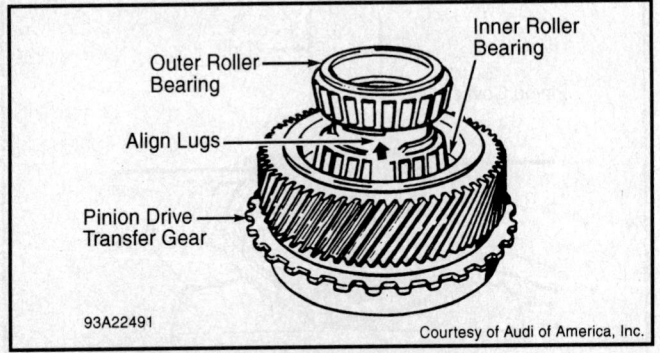

Fig. 79: Aligning Lugs On Pinion Drive Transfer Gear Roller Bearings

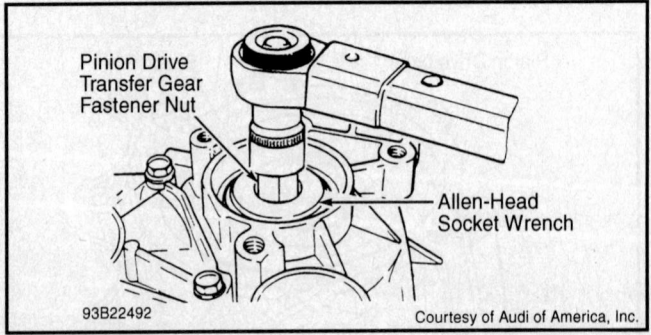

Fig. 80: Tightening Fastener Nut On Pinion Drive Transfer Gear Roller Bearings

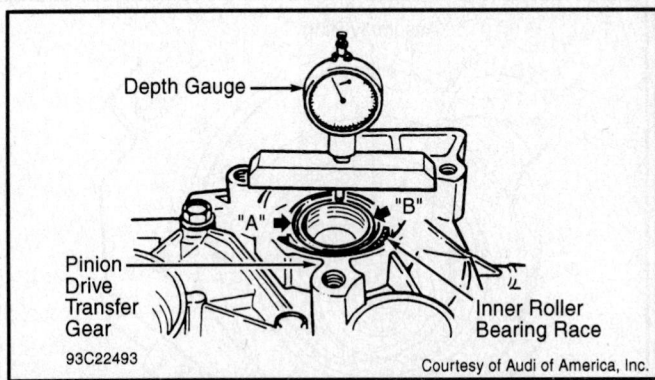

Fig. 81: Checking Distance Between Pinion Drive Transfer Gear & Inner Race Of Roller Bearings

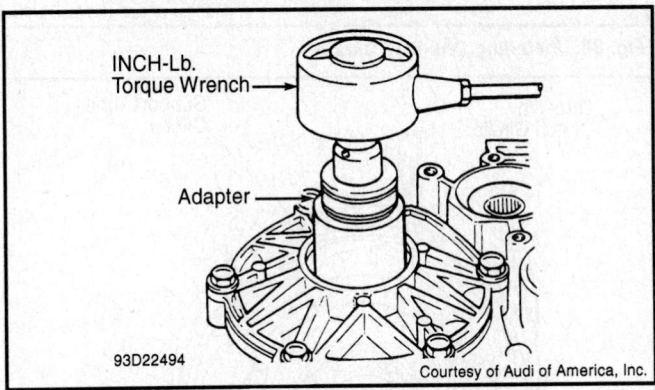

Fig. 82: Measuring Combined Turning Torque Of Pinion, Differential & Transfer Gear Roller Bearings

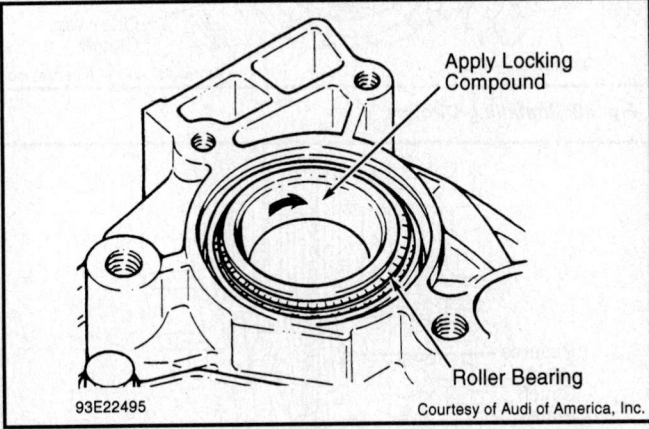

Fig. 83: Applying Locking Fluid To Shaft Side Of Roller Bearing

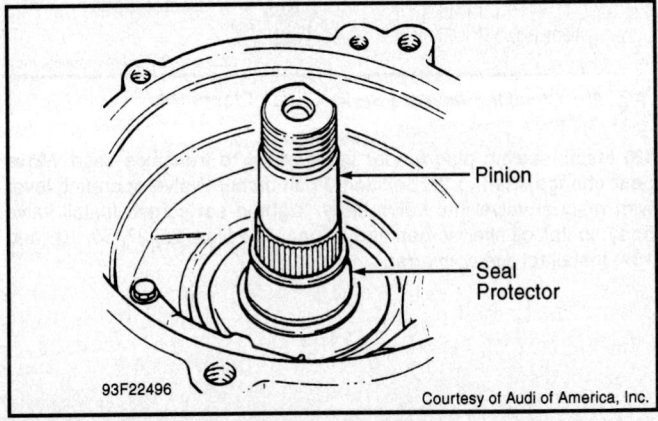

Fig. 84: Using Seal Protector To Install Pinion Drive Gear

3) Using a feeler gauge, check installed reverse brake clutch clearance. See Fig. 90. Clearance should be .047-.071" (1.2-1.8 mm). If clearance is not as specified, replace end plate shim. End plate shims are available in thicknesses ranging from .04" (1.0 mm) to .07" (1.9 mm) in .004" (.10 mm) increments. More than one shim can be used to obtain correct thickness.

BRAKE CLUTCH PLATE APPLICATIONS

Application [1]	Number Of Plates
Reverse Clutch	
Inner	5
Outer	5
2nd-4th Clutch	
Inner	6
Outer	7

[1] – Information is available for Type 097 only.

4) Install rubber oil splash shield and lower circlip for support tube. See Fig. 89. Install washers, bearing and large sun gear. Install large sun gear drive shell. See Fig. 91.
5) Install small sun gear drive shell. Install small planetary drive shaft. See Figs. 28, 92 and 93. Using a screwdriver, lock small sun gear drive shell to large sun gear drive shell. See Fig. 94. Install adjustment shim, washer and bolt on end of small planetary drive shaft. Tighten bolt to 22 ft. lbs. (30 N.m).
6) Ensure end play is .009-.014" (.23-.37 mm). If end play is not as specified, recheck assembly or adjustment. See PLANETARY CARRIER under COMPONENT DISASSEMBLY & REASSEMBLY.
7) Install bearing, washer, and impeller shaft and 3rd-4th apply clutch. See Fig. 95. Install bearing, washer and 1st-3rd apply clutch with turbine shaft assembly. See Fig. 96. Install thrust shims on 1st-3rd apply clutch housing. Install reverse apply clutch and support tube. See Fig. 97.

NOTE: Turbine shaft end play was measured before disassembly. If end play is okay, use original thrust shims. If end play is not okay, calculate difference and install required thrust shims.

8) For checking purposes, install oil pump gasket and oil pump. See Fig. 28. Position dial indicator and Support (VW 387) on transaxle case. See Fig. 98.
9) Position dial indicator on turbine shaft, and apply .040" (1.0 mm) preload. Move turbine shaft up and down. Turbine shaft end play should be .019-.047" (.50-1.20 mm).
10) If end play is okay, go to next step. If end play is not okay, install required thrust shims. Thrust shims are available in thicknesses ranging from .04" (1.0 mm) to .07" (1.8 mm) in .008" (.20 mm) increments. Recheck turbine shaft end play.
11) Remove oil pump and oil pump gasket. Install reverse apply clutch (if necessary) and support tube. Ensure groove on support tube engages wedge of one-way clutch. See Figs. 28 and 97.
12) Install .12" (3.0 mm) thick outer splined plate into transaxle case. See Fig. 99. Install 3 springs and cap springs. Install 2nd-4th brake clutch plates. See Fig. 100. See BRAKE CLUTCH PLATE APPLICATIONS table. Install 3 spring caps to springs.
13) DO NOT install top outer splined clutch plate. Determine clearance of 2nd-4th brake clutch. Press 2nd-4th brake clutch assembly down. Using a depth gauge, measure distance from top of oil pump flange to 2nd-4th brake clutch (inner splined). See Fig. 101.
14) Place a straightedge across top of piston. Place gasket on oil pump flange. Using depth gauge, measure distance from straightedge to oil pump flange gasket. See Fig. 102. Subtract thickness of straightedge.
15) Subtract distance measured in step **13)** from distance calculated in step **14)**. This gives 2nd-4th brake clutch-to-piston distance.
16) Subtract .14" (3.6 mm) from value calculated in step **15)**. This determines thickness of last outer splined 2nd-4th brake clutch plate. Outer splined 2nd-4th brake clutch plates are available in thickness ranging from .040-.108" (1.00-2.75 mm), in .010" (.25 mm) increments.

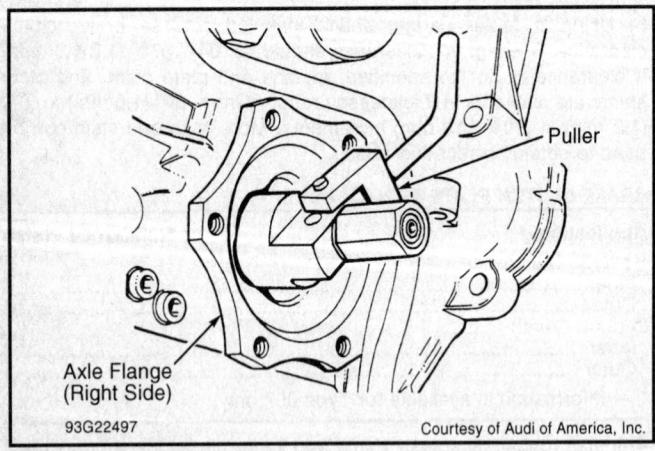

93G22497   Courtesy of Audi of America, Inc.

Fig. 85: Installing Right Drive Axle

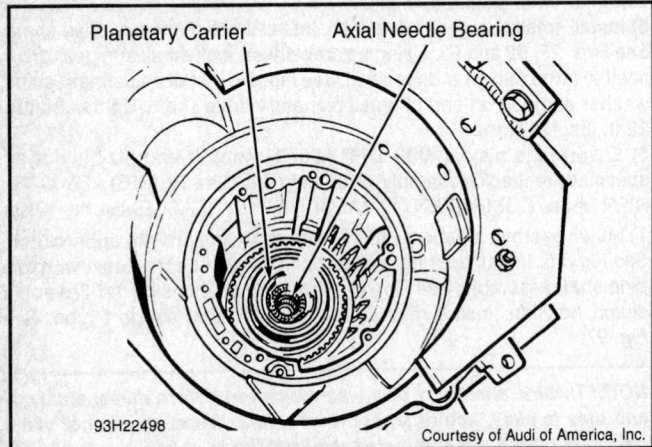

93H22498   Courtesy of Audi of America, Inc.

Fig. 86: Installing Planetary Carrier & Axial Needle Bearing

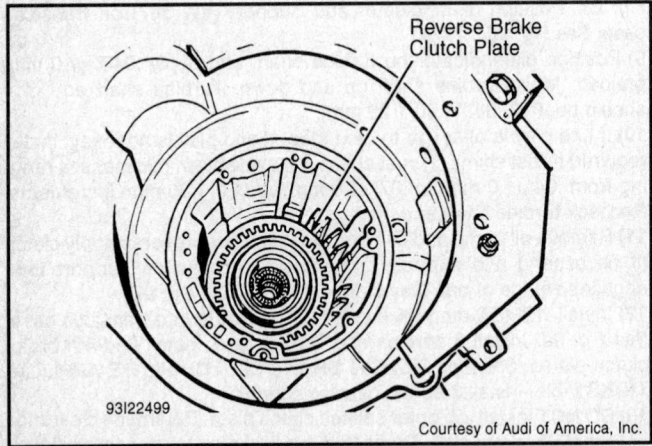

93I22499   Courtesy of Audi of America, Inc.

Fig. 87: Installing Reverse Brake Clutch Plates

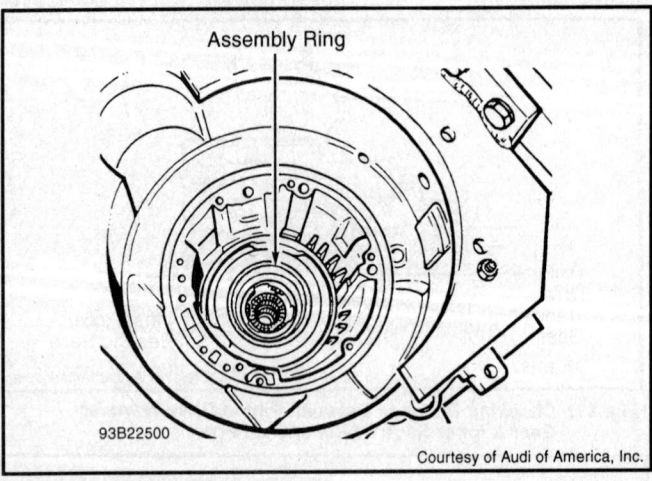

93B22500   Courtesy of Audi of America, Inc.

Fig. 88: Installing One-Way Clutch

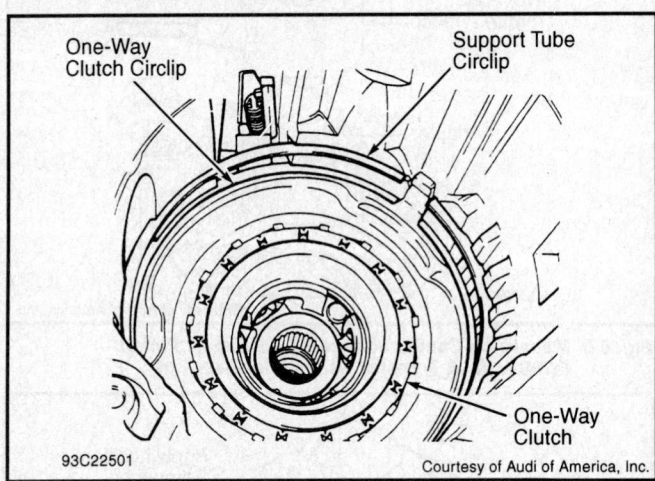

93C22501   Courtesy of Audi of America, Inc.

Fig. 89: Installing Circlips

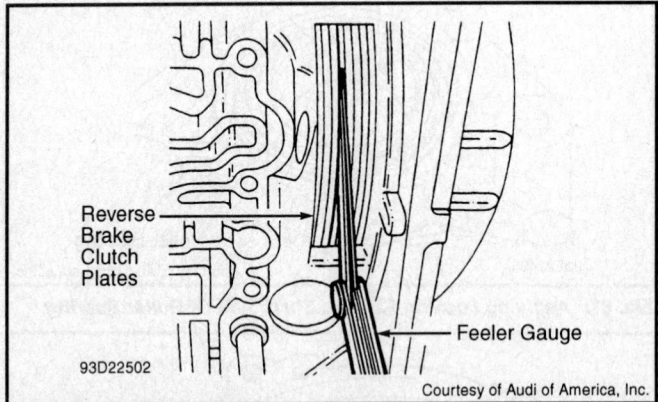

93D22502   Courtesy of Audi of America, Inc.

Fig. 90: Checking Reverse Brake Clutch Clearance

17) Install 3 spring caps and last outer 2nd-4th brake clutch plate. Install waved spring washer. Install oil pump gasket. Install "O" ring to oil pump, and install oil pump. Install pinion sealing plug to transaxle case.

NOTE: Factory uses .14" (3.6 mm) value to allow for waved spring washer being installed with 2nd-4th brake clutch plates.

18) Install sealing plug (under valve body) to transaxle case. Move gear change shaft to "P" position. Push manual valve operating lever with manual valve into valve body. Tighten set screw. Install valve body. Install oil filter screen and oil pan. See Figs. 25, 27, 55, 103 and 104. Install torque converter.

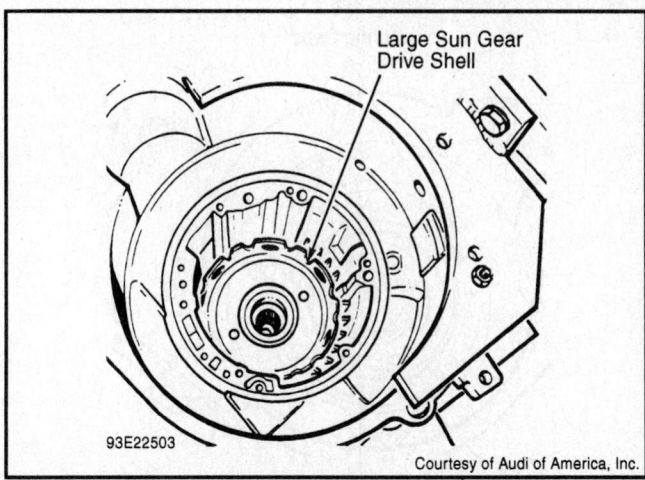

Fig. 91: Installing Large Sun Gear Drive Shell

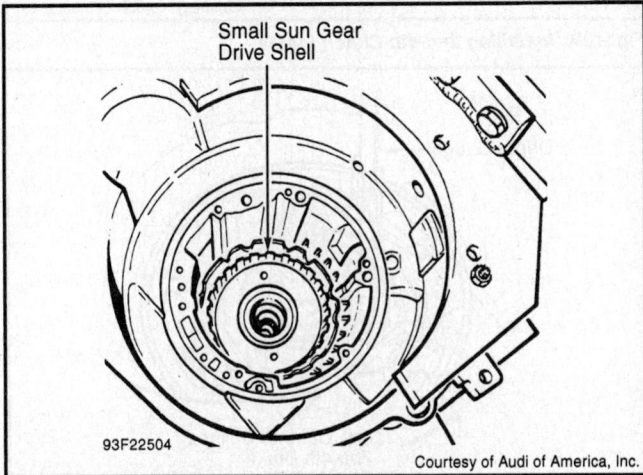

Fig. 92: Installing Small Sun Gear Drive Shell

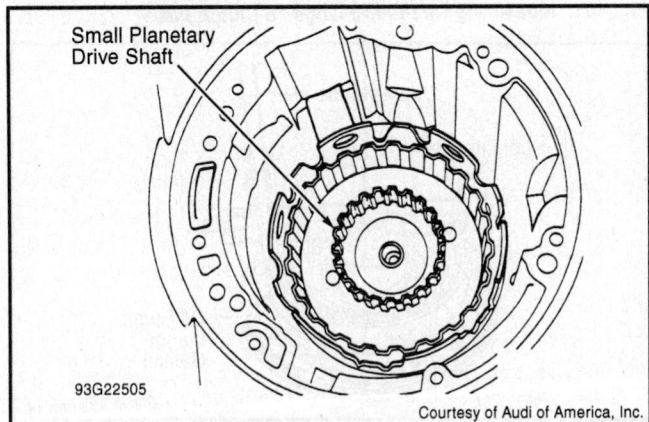

Fig. 93: Installing Small Planetary Drive Shaft

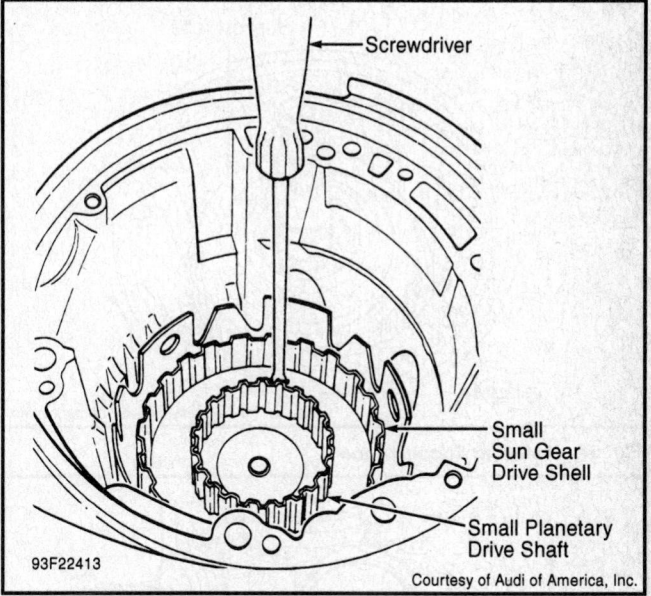

Fig. 94: Holding Small Sun Gear Drive Shell

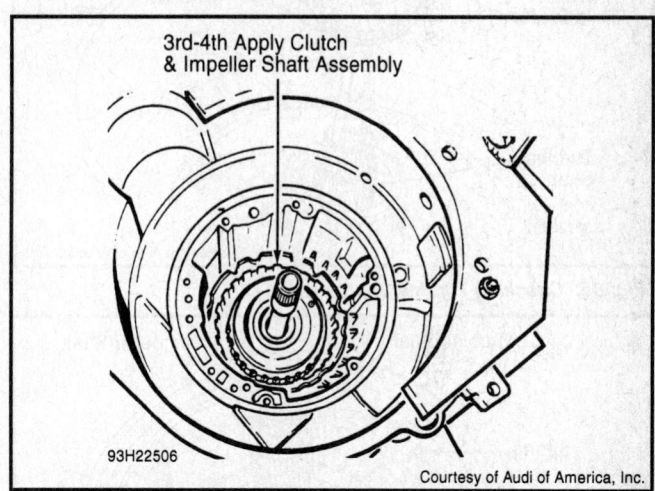

Fig. 95: Installing 3rd-4th Apply Clutch & Impeller Shaft

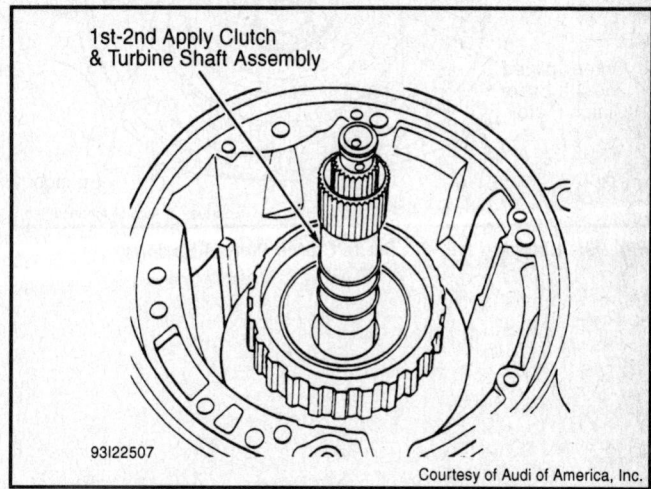

Fig. 96: Installing 1st-3rd Apply Clutch & Turbine Shaft

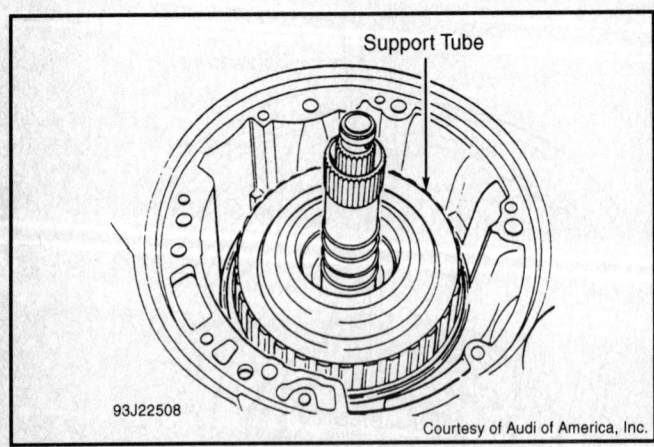

Fig. 97: Installing Support Tube

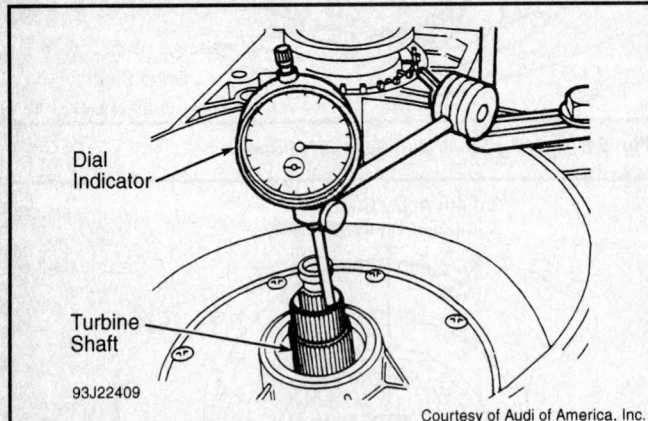

Fig. 98: Checking Turbine Shaft End Play

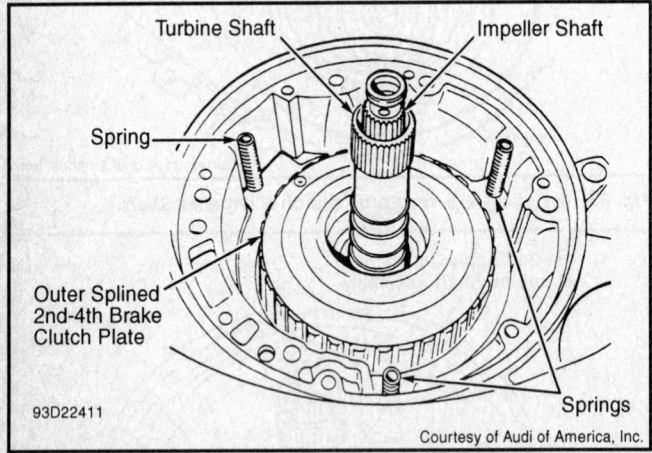

Fig. 99: Installing 2nd-4th Brake Clutch Plate & Springs

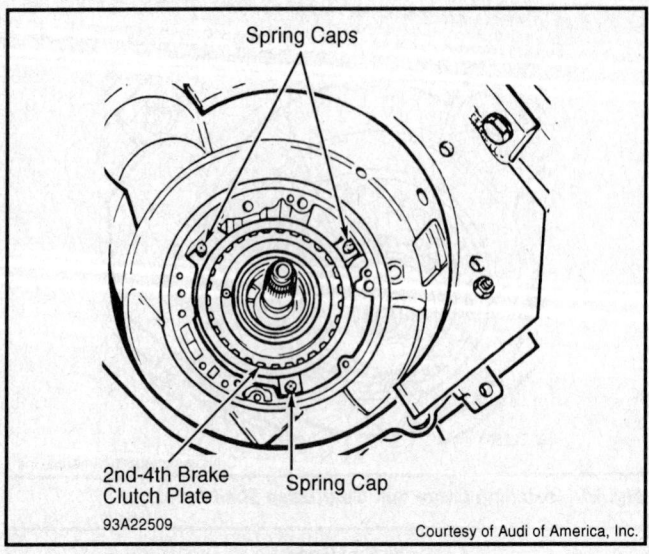

Fig. 100: Installing 2nd-4th Clutch Plates

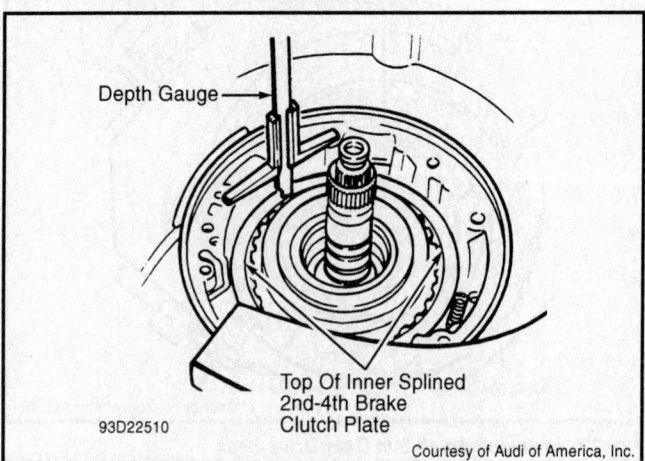

Fig. 101: Measuring Oil Pump Flange-To-Clutch Plate

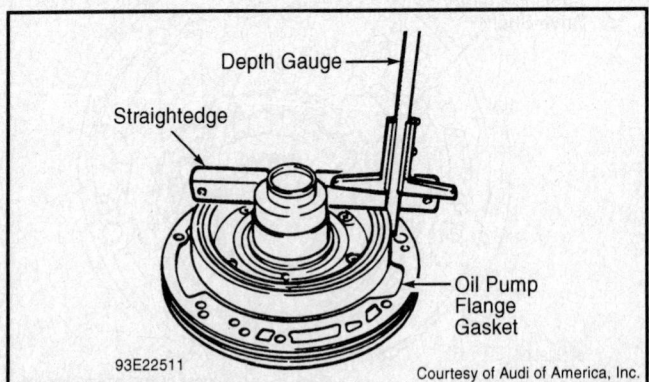

Fig. 102: Measuring Height Of Piston

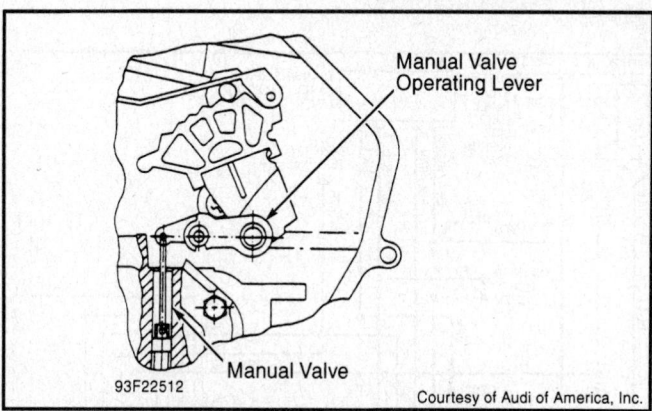

Fig. 103: Installing Manual Valve Operating Lever

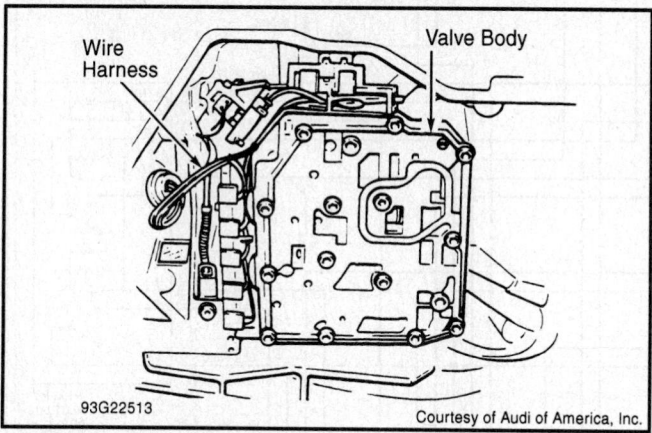

Fig. 104: Installing Valve Body

TORQUE SPECIFICATIONS

TORQUE SPECIFICATIONS

Application	Ft. Lbs. (N.m)
Differential Housing Cover Bolts	18 (25)
Drive Axle Attaching Bolt (Left Side Only)	18 (25)
Drive Axle Flange Bolts	59 (80)
Oil Cooler Banjo Bolts	22 (30)
Oil Cooler Union Fitting	44 (60)
Oil Filter (On Transaxle Case)	18 (25)
Pinion Cover Bolts	18 (25)
Pinion Drive Transfer Gear Nut	185 (250)
Pinion Nut	177 (240)
Ring Gear Bolts	66 (90)
Small Planetary Drive Shaft Bolt	22 (30)
Subframe-To-Transaxle Support Nut	
097	30 (40)
01N	82 (110)
Torque Converter Nuts	
097	44 (60)
01N	63 (85)
Transaxle-To-Engine Bolts	
097	
10-mm Diameter	44 (60)
12-mm Diameter	59 (80)
01N	
10-mm Diameter	33 (45)
12-mm Diameter	48 (65)
Transaxle-To-Transaxle Support Bolts	30 (40)

Application	INCH Lbs. (N.m)
Detent Spring Screws	89 (10)
Oil Filter (In Pan) Bolts	71 (8)
Oil Pan Bolts	84 (9.4)
Oil Pump-To-Transaxle Bolts	89 (10) Plus 90°
Valve Body Bolts	44 (5)

TRANSMISSION SPECIFICATIONS

TRANSMISSION SPECIFICATIONS

Application	In. (mm)
Clutch Clearance	
Apply Clutches	[1]
Brake Clutches	
2nd-4th	[2]
Reverse	.047-.071 (1.2-1.8)
Gear & Shaft End Play	
Planetary Carrier	.009-.014 (.23-.37)
Ring Gear Backlash	.006-.010 (.15-.25)
Turbine Shaft	.019-.047 (.50-1.20)

[1] – Assembled clutch clearance is not available.
[2] – See TRANSMISSION under TRANSAXLE REASSEMBLY.

TECHNICAL SERVICE BULLETINS

ERRATIC OR HARD SHIFTS

1991 80, 90 & 100 (VW TSB Group 37, No. 93-03, 5-30-93) – These models may have hard or erratic shifts. This may be caused by a loose or corroded connector at the multi-function switch. Check multi-function switch connector and repair as necessary. If no problems are found, check computer memory for any stored diagnostic codes and service system as required.

REVISED FINAL DRIVE FLUID

1993-94 Cabriolet, 90 & 100 (VW TSB Group 37, No. 93-02, 6-15-93) – The final drive fluid used in automatic transaxles has been changed. Use SAE 75W/90 Synthetic Final Drive Fluid (G 052 145 A2) only. Drain fluid. Fill final drive with 1.1 qts. (1.0L) of synthetic fluid. DO NOT mix fluids.

NO "D" RANGE, OTHER RANGES OKAY

1993-94 Cabriolet, 90 & 100 (VW TSB Group 38, No. 93-02, 5-30-93) – Some vehicles may not move in "D" range, but work okay in all other ranges. This may be caused by a misadjusted manual valve.

NOTE: Scan Tester (VAG 1551) will indicate Diagnostic Trouble Code (DTC) 00652 (gear monitoring).

To correct this, remove oil pan. Place gear selector in Park position. Loosen adjustment bolt. Push operating rod with manual valve into valve body as far as possible. Tighten adjustment bolt. Install oil pan and fill with fluid. Using scan tester, clear stored diagnostic codes. Return engine and transaxle to base settings. Road test vehicle. Check for any diagnostic trouble codes.

SHIFT LOCK SOLENOID, CLICKING

1993-1996 90, 1994-1996 Cabriolet (VW TSB Group 37, No. 96-01, 3-8-96) – Condition can be caused by one or more exterior lights inoperative. If a vehicle exhibits this condition, check for inoperative exterior lights and repair or replace as necessary.

AUTOMATIC TRANSMISSIONS
Audi Type 01N & 097 (Cont.)

WIRING DIAGRAMS

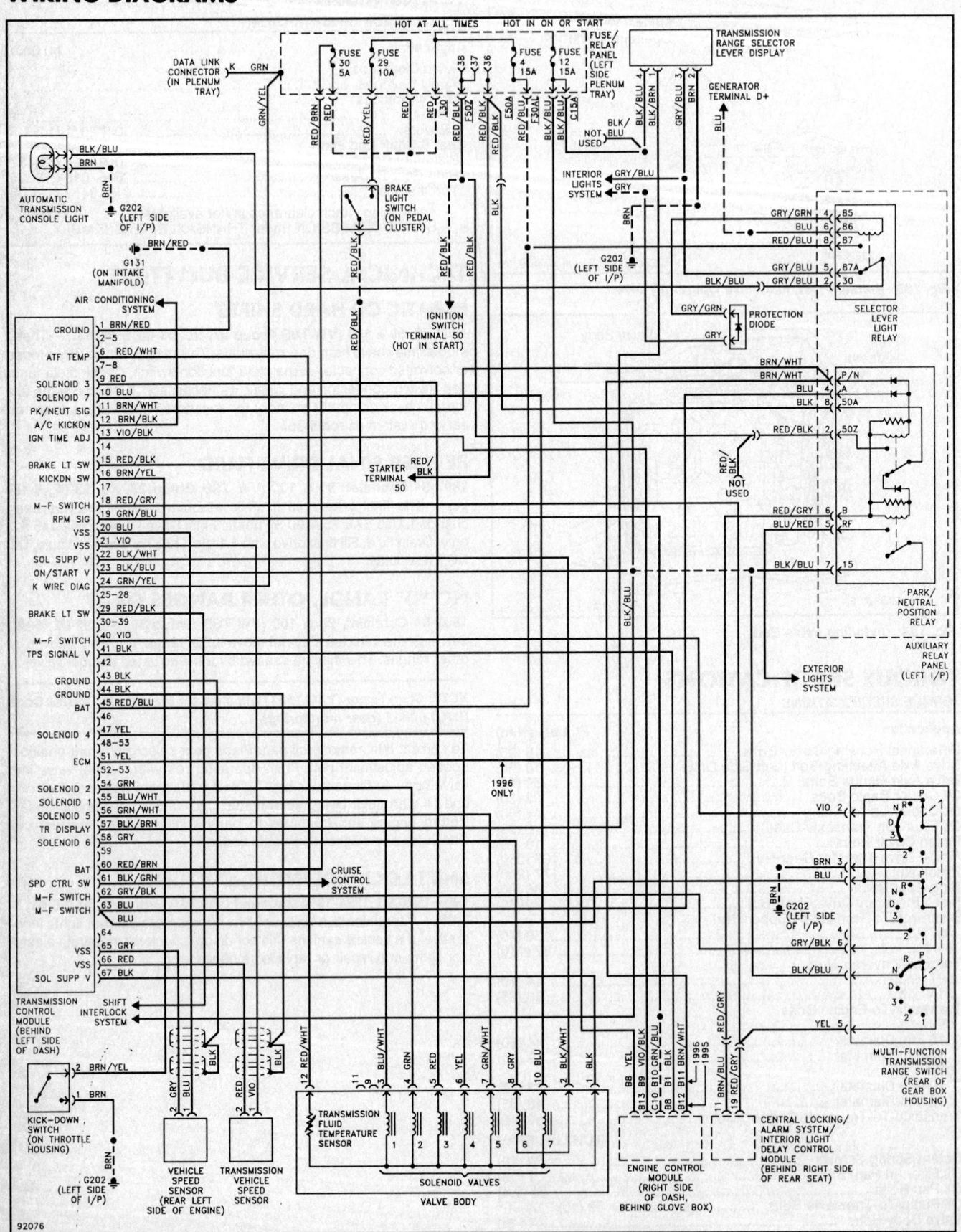

Fig. 105: *1995-96 Audi Cabriolet (Type 097) & 1995 Audi 90 (Type 097) Transaxle Wiring Diagram*

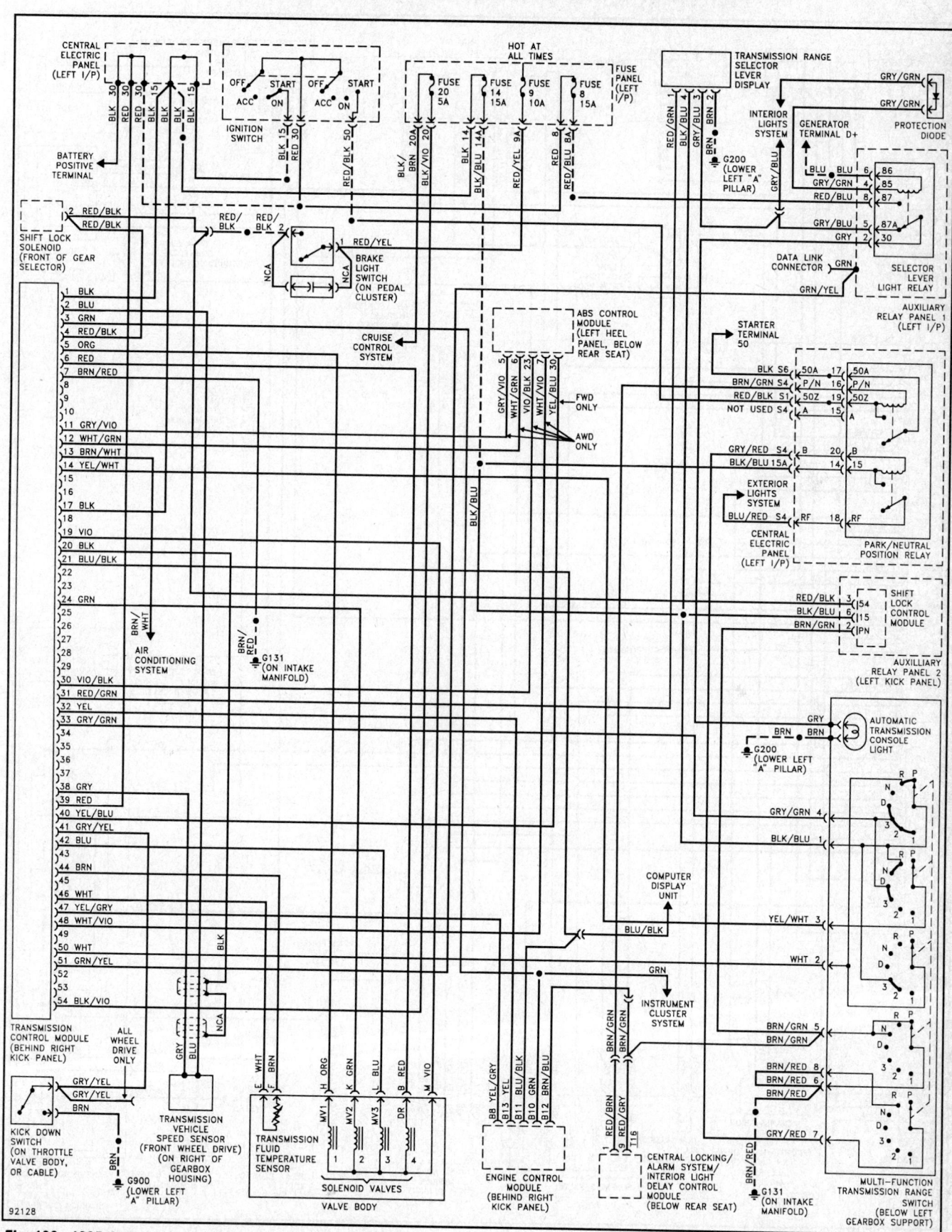

Fig. 106: *1995 Audi A6 (Type 01N) Transaxle Wiring Diagram*

92128

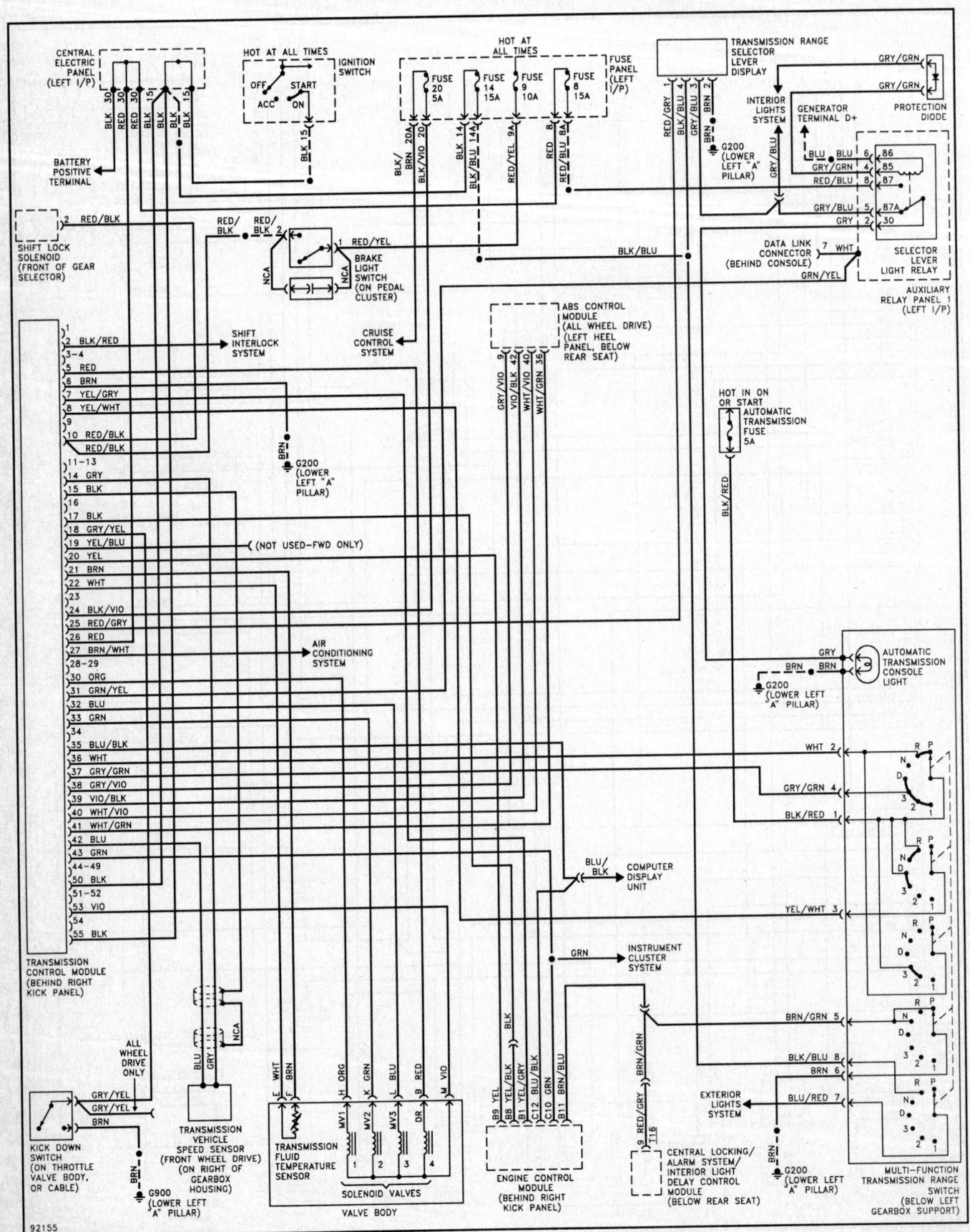

Fig. 107: *1996 Audi A6 (Type 01N) Transaxle Wiring Diagram*

92155

A4, A4 AWD

APPLICATION & LABOR TIMES

APPLICATION & LABOR TIMES

Vehicle Application	Labor Times		Trans. Type (Code)
	[1] R & I	[2] Overhaul	
1996			
A4	7.6	N/A	01V (DCS [3], DDT [4])
A4 AWD	10.0	N/A	01V (CJP)

[1] – Removal and installation of transmission from vehicle chassis.
[2] – On bench overhaul for transmission and differential. DOES NOT include removal and installation.
[3] – From 4/95, 2.72 differential gearing.
[4] – From 9/96, 3.09 differential gearing.

IDENTIFICATION

Volkswagen Audi Group (VAG) transaxle type is cast into transaxle case above left output shaft flange. Transaxle code and build date are located on front top of transaxle case. *See Fig. 1.*

DESCRIPTION & OPERATION

Transaxle includes a 5-speed automatic transmission, a torque converter with clutch, a final drive and solenoid-operated valve body. Under normal conditions, all shifts are controlled by a Transaxle Control Unit (TCU), 4th and 5th gears are overdrive gears.

NOTE: TCU may be referred to as Transmission Control Module (TCM).

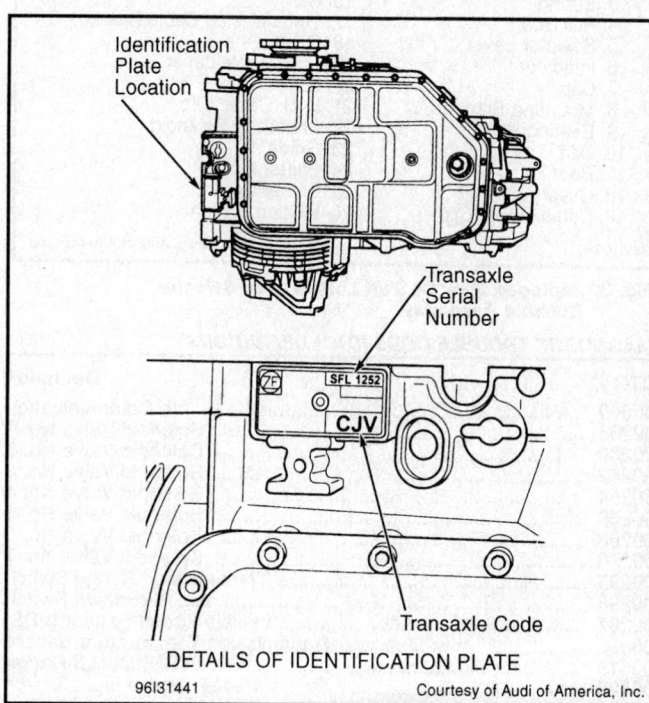

Identification Plate Location

Transaxle Serial Number

ZF   SFL 1252

CJV

Transaxle Code

DETAILS OF IDENTIFICATION PLATE

96l31441   Courtesy of Audi of America, Inc.

Fig. 1: Locating Transaxle Identification Plate

The electronic control consists of a TCU (attached to the brake pedal bracket), control solenoids, various sensors and switches. The control solenoids direct oil pressure inside the valve body.

The TCU monitors input and output signals. If electrical problems occur, TCU will record faults in TCU memory and may go into fail-safe mode. The TCU memory can only be read on VAG Tester (1551).

The TCU also controls shift-lock system. This system locks the gear selector in Park or Neutral unless the brake pedal is pushed down. The TCU uses a shift-lock control relay to release a gear-selector mounted solenoid.

LUBRICATION & ADJUSTMENTS

NOTE: See appropriate AUTOMATIC TRANSMISSION SERVICING article in TRANSMISSION SERVICING section.

TROUBLE SHOOTING

MECHANICAL & ELECTRICAL CHECKS

CAUTION: When battery is disconnected, Transmission Control Module (TCM) must be reset to Basic Setting using VAG Tester (1551).

If gear selector is stuck in Park or Neutral, go to SHIFT-LOCK SYSTEM under TROUBLE SHOOTING. If gear positions are missing, shift quality is poor or no shifts are possible, ensure all electrical connections are okay and fluid level is correct. Check for Diagnostic Trouble Codes (DTCs).

FAIL-SAFE FUNCTION

When one or more components or sensors fail, the TCU will substitute functions and continue to operate. If a critical component fails, and the TCU is active, transmission will shift into 4th gear with torque converter clutch disengaged and entire gear display will light. Reverse can be engaged and selector lock will not work. If a critical component fails, and the TCU is inactive, symptoms will be the same, but OBD codes cannot be accessed.

SHIFT LOCK SYSTEM

Operation – A mechanical control cable prevents ignition key from being removed unless gear selector is in Park. With ignition key removed, gear selector locks in Park. *See Fig. 2.*

NOTE: If battery is disconnected or discharged, gear selector can be moved out of Park by turning ignition key to START position.

All models are equipped with an electronic shift lock system. TCU controls shift lock system. This system locks gear selector in Park or Neutral position unless brake pedal is pushed down. TCU uses shift lock control relay to release a solenoid mounted on gear selector assembly.

NOTE: Shift lock relay will not lock gear selector when vehicle speed is greater than 3 MPH.

Functional Check – 1) With ignition key removed, ensure gear selector cannot be moved from Park. Insert key in ignition switch.
2) Turn ignition on. Ensure gear selector can only be moved with brake pedal pressed down. Move gear selector to Neutral position.
3) Without pressing brake pedal, ensure gear selector cannot move out of Neutral. Press brake pedal down. Ensure it is now possible to move gear selector.
4) If shift lock system does not operate as described, check electrical system of shift lock system with VAG Tester (1551). If Tester is not available, see testing information under ELECTRONIC SELF-DIAGNOSTICS. *See Figs. 7-11.*
5) If any problems are found, service harness or components. If shift lock system still does not operate correctly, check for worn or damaged parts and replace as necessary. *See Fig. 3.* If no problems are found, TCU may be defective.

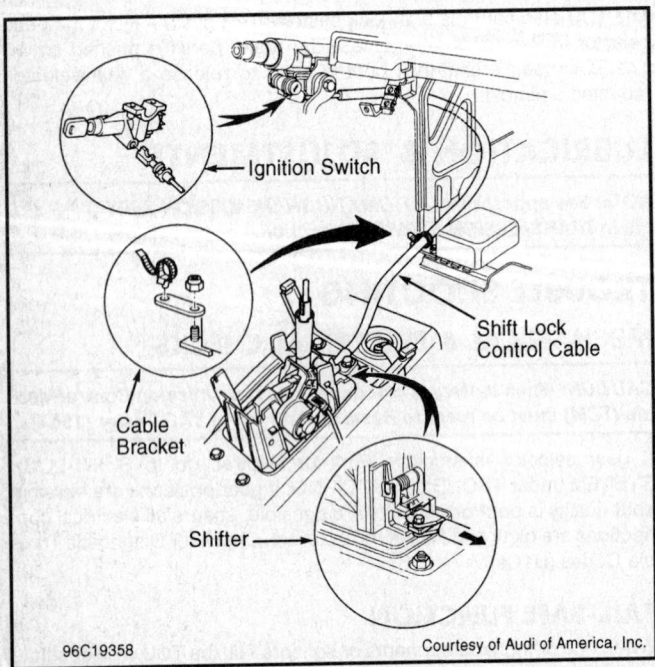

Fig. 2: Identifying Shift-Lock Components

NOTE: Perform the following adjustments in order given.

Adjustment (Control Cable) – **1)** Remove cable housing mounting screws at gear selector console. Loosen lock screw.

2) Move gear selector to Drive position. Turn ignition on. Move control cable until a .060" (1.5 mm) feeler gauge fits between lock flap and lock pin.

3) Turn ignition off. Turn ignition on. Ensure gap is still .060" (1.5 mm). Turn ignition off and on several times and recheck gap. Install cable housing to gear selector console.

Removal & Installation (Control Cable) – **1)** Remove center console cover. Disconnect negative battery cable and wait 30 seconds. Disconnect voltage supply connector for air bag.

2) Using Torx wrench, remove air bag retaining screws from rear side of steering wheel. Remove air bag. Remove steering wheel. Remove dash panel.

3) Place gear selector in Neutral position. Remove cable housing mounting screws at gear selector console.

4) Remove cover from top of ignition switch. Remove spring clip holding cable housing to ignition assembly. Lift and tilt cable housing upward. Rotate control cable 1/4 turn until control cable unhooks from ignition switch. *See Fig. 4.*

NOTE: DO NOT kink control cable. If control cable is kinked, gear selector may not move.

5) Remove clip holding cable housing to A/C-heater housing. Remove cable housing from vehicle. To install cable housing, reverse removal procedure. Adjust control cable. See ADJUSTMENT (CONTROL CABLE) procedure.

ELECTRONIC SELF-DIAGNOSTICS

1) Electronic control consists of TCU (attached to brake pedal bracket), control solenoids, and various sensors and switches. TCU monitors input and output signals.

2) If TCU detects problems in transaxle-related circuits or devices, TCU may record a trouble code in memory. To obtain trouble codes, use VAG Tester (1551). *See Fig. 5.* All trouble code and related testing information is contained in tester. See DIAGNOSTIC TROUBLE CODE DEFINITIONS table.

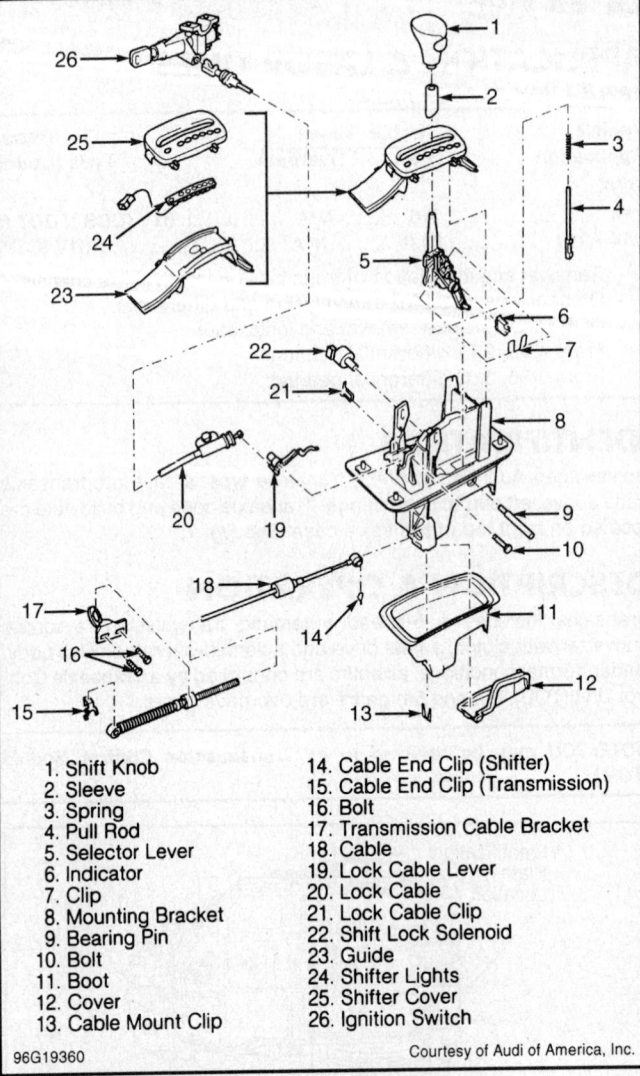

1. Shift Knob
2. Sleeve
3. Spring
4. Pull Rod
5. Selector Lever
6. Indicator
7. Clip
8. Mounting Bracket
9. Bearing Pin
10. Bolt
11. Boot
12. Cover
13. Cable Mount Clip
14. Cable End Clip (Shifter)
15. Cable End Clip (Transmission)
16. Bolt
17. Transmission Cable Bracket
18. Cable
19. Lock Cable Lever
20. Lock Cable
21. Lock Cable Clip
22. Shift Lock Solenoid
23. Guide
24. Shifter Lights
25. Shifter Cover
26. Ignition Switch

96G19360   Courtesy of Audi of America, Inc.

Fig. 3: Exploded View Of Shift Lock & Gear Selector Console Assembly

DIAGNOSTIC TROUBLE CODE (DTC) DEFINITIONS

DTC	Definition
00000	No Communication
00258	Solenoid Valve No. 1
00260	Solenoid Valve No. 2
00262	Solenoid Valve No. 3
00264	Solenoid Valve No. 4
00266	Solenoid Valve No. 5
00268	Solenoid Valve No. 6
00270	Solenoid Valve No. 7
00293	Transmission Range Switch
00296	Kickdown Switch
00297	Vehicle Speed Sensor (VSS)
00300	Transmission Temperature Sensor
00518	TPS Out Of Range
00526	Brake Light Switch
00529	RPM Information Missing
00532	Supply Battery Voltage Low
00543	RPM Information Maximum Exceeded
00545	Engine/Transmission Electrical Connection
00638	Engine/Transmission Electrical Connection
00652	TR Controller Incorrect Signal
00668	Supply Voltage Low
01044	Control Module Coded Wrong
01192	Torque Converter Clutch RPM Deviation
01236	Shift Lock Solenoid
17101	Transmission Input Speed Sensor
18192	High/Downshift Wire
18193	High/Downshift Wire
65535	Control Module Malfunctioning

3) If tester is not available, turn ignition off. Disconnect TCU harness connector. Install Back-Probe Harness (VAG 1598) and 88-Pin Adapter (1598/20) between TCU and TCU harness. Measure voltage and resistance between specified terminals of TCU connector. *See Figs. 6-10.*

4) If problem is found, service harness or component(s). If no problem is found, TCU may be defective. All testing should be done with components at ambient temperature. All resistance testing is done with Back-Probe Harness (VAG 1598) disconnected. All voltage testing is done with Back-Probe Harness (VAG 1598) connected.

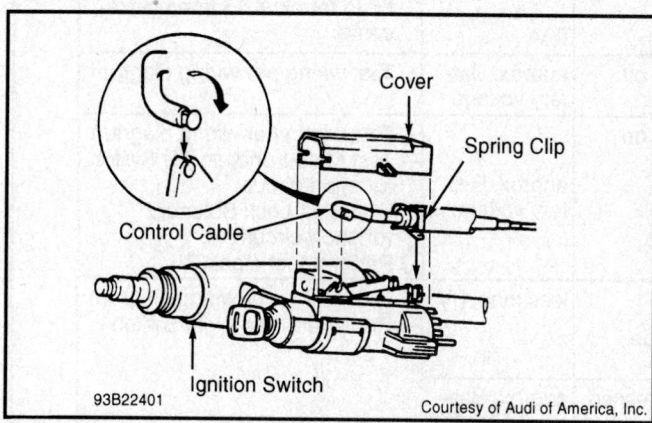

Fig. 4: Removing Control Cable From Ignition Switch

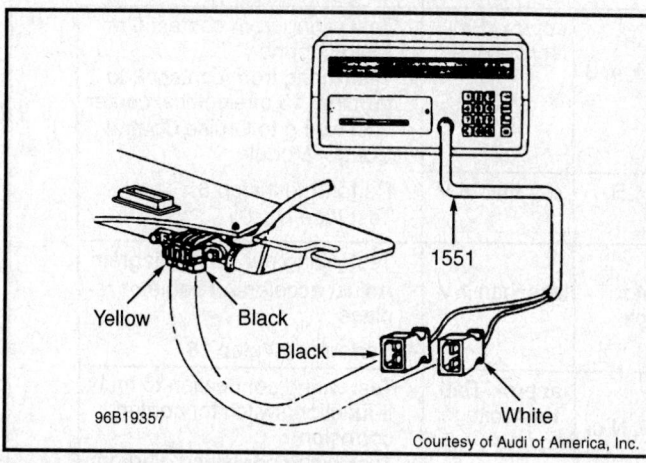

Fig. 5: Connecting Scan Tool (VAG 1551)

ON-VEHICLE SERVICE

DRIVE AXLE SHAFTS

See appropriate AXLE SHAFTS article in AXLE SHAFTS & TRANSFER CASES section.

OIL COOLER FLUSHING

1) Remove oil lines and allow fluid to drain. Using pressurized solvent, flush remaining fluid and debris from oil lines and cooler. Repeat flushing if necessary.

2) Use pressurized shop air to remove solvent from oil lines and oil cooler. Install a new external oil filter.

REMOVAL & INSTALLATION

See appropriate AUTOMATIC TRANSMISSION REMOVAL article in TRANSMISSION SERVICING section.

TORQUE CONVERTER

Remove torque converter. Check torque converter for any wear or damage, and replace if necessary. If torque converter is being reused, drain old fluid. Tilt converter on bench and siphon out all fluid.

COMPONENT DISASSEMBLY & REASSEMBLY

Information is not available.

TORQUE SPECIFICATIONS
TORQUE SPECIFICATIONS

Application	Ft. Lbs. (N.m)
Differential Housing Cover Bolts	17 (23)
Drive Axle Attaching Bolt (Left Side Only)	18 (25)
Drive Axle Flange Bolts	59 (80)
Oil Cooler Union Fitting	18 (25)
Torque Converter Nuts	63 (85)
Transaxle-To-Engine Bolts	
10-mm Diameter	33 (45)
12-mm Diameter	48 (65)
Transaxle-To-Transaxle Support Bolts	30 (40)

	INCH Lbs. (N.m)
Oil Filter (In Pan) Bolts	53 (6)
Oil Pan Bolts	10 (7)
Valve Body Bolts	70 (8)

			Switch on measuring range: Voltage measurement 20 V		
Test step	VAG 1598/22 Sockets	Test of	Test conditions - Additional operations	Specification	Corrective steps
1	54 + 28 55 + 34 55 + 6	Supply voltage of Transmission Control Module	Ignition switched on	approx. Battery voltage	- Test wiring per wiring diagram - Test wiring from contact 6, 34 or 28 to Ground - Test wiring from contact 54 or 55 to terminal 15 of electrical center
	54 + 55			0 V	
	26 + 6	Vehicle voltage terminal 30 of TCM	Ignition switched off	approx. Battery voltage	- Test wiring per wiring diagram
2	2 + 6	Shift Lock Solenoid	Ignition switched on	approx. Battery voltage	- Test wiring per wiring diagram - Test Multi-Function TR Switch for short circuit - Test Shift Lock Solenoid for short circuit - Perform test step 17
3	10 + 6 10 + 28	Brake Light Switch	Ignition on - Brake pedal not depressed	less than 1 V	- Test wiring per wiring diagram - Replace Brake Light Switch
			- Brake pedal depressed	approx. Battery voltage	
4	9 + 6 9 + 28	Supply voltage for Cruise Control, Control Module	Ignition on Selector lever in D, 4, 3	approx. Battery voltage	- Test wiring from contact 6 or 28 to Ground - Test wiring from contact 9 to terminal 15 of electrical center - Test wiring to Cruise Control, Control Module
			Selector lever in P, R, N, 2	less than 5 V	- Perform test step 6 - Test fuse No. 31
5	18 + 54	Kick Down Switch	Ignition on - Depress Accelerator Pedal as far as kick down	less than 1 V	- Test wiring per wiring diagram - Adjust accelerator cable or replace - Perform test step 18
6	36 + 34 36 + 6 36 + 28	Multi-Function TR Switch	Ignition on - Selector lever in P, N or D	approx. Battery voltage	- Test wiring connection to multi-function switch for contact corrosion - Test wiring per wiring diagram
			- Selector lever in R, 4, 3 and 2	less than 1 V	- Test fuse No. 31
	8 + 34 8 + 6 8 + 28		Ignition on - Selector lever in R, N and 4	approx. Battery voltage	- Test supply voltage - Perform test step 2
			- Selector lever in P, D, 3 and 2	less than 1 V	- Test wiring connection of control module to 8–pin connector
	37 + 34 37 + 6 37 + 28		- Selector lever in N, D, 4 and 2	approx. Battery voltage	- Replace Multi-Function Switch
			- Selector lever in P, R and 3	less than 1 V	- Perform test step 7
	9 + 34 9 + 6 9 + 28		- Selector lever in D, 4 and 3	approx. Battery voltage	- Perform test step 4, if necessary
			- Selector lever in P, R, N and 2	less than 1 V	

96B19373

Courtesy of Audi of America, Inc.

Fig. 6: Testing TCU Harness & Components Type 01V (1 Of 5)

Test step	VAG 1598/22 Sockets	Test of	Test conditions - Additional operations	Specifica-tion (Ω)	Corrective steps
7	36 + 8	Multi-Function TR Switch	Ignition off - Selector lever in N	less than 20	- Check wiring connection to multi-function switch for contact corrosion
			- Selector lever in P, R, D, 4, 3, 2	infinite [1]	
	37 + 9		Ignition off - Selector lever in D and 4	less than 20	- Test wiring connection from 88–pin control module to 8–pin connector
			- Fuse 31 removed [2] - Selector lever in P, R, N, 3, 2	infinite [1]	- Replace Multi-Function TR Switch
	37 + 36		Ignition off - Selector lever in N, D	less than 20	
			- Selector lever in P, R, 4, 3, 2	infinite [1]	
	1 + 7 [3]		- Selector lever in P, N	infinite [1]	
			- Selector lever in 2, 3, 4, D	less than 20	
8	6 + 34 28 + 34	Ground connections of Transmission Control Module	Ignition off	less than 1	- Test wiring per wiring diagram
	34 + Ground to Battery			less than 1	
9	52 + 53	Supply wiring of solenoid valves	Ignition off	less than 1	- Test wiring connection of control module to 16–pin connector - Perform test step 1 - Test wiring harness in transmission
10	52 + 30	Solenoid Valve 1	Ignition off Control module disconnected	25 to 35	- Test 16–pin wiring connection to transmission for contact corrosion
	30 + 34			infinite [1]	- Perform test step 9
11	52 + 33	Solenoid Valve 2	Ignition off Control module disconnected	25 to 35	- Test wiring connection from 88–pin control module to 16–pin connector
	33 + 34			infinite [1]	- Test wiring harness in transmission; replace if necessary
12	52 + 32	Solenoid Valve 3	Ignition off Control module disconnected	25 to 35	- Test relevant solenoid valves for short circuit; replace if necessary
	32 + 34			infinite [1]	Remove and install valve body
13	52 + 5	Solenoid Valve 4	Ignition off Control module disconnected	6 to 8	
	5 + 34			infinite [1]	Electrical malfunctions are recognized by On Board Diagnostic (OBD).

Switch on measuring range: Resistance measurement 200

[1] Set multimeter to maximum range
[2] Fuse for voltage supply of Multi-Function TR Switch
[3] Disconnect contacts on connector to Multi-Function TR Switch

96D19375

Courtesy of Audi of America, Inc.

Fig. 7: Testing TCU Harness & Components Type 01V (2 Of 5)

			Switch on measuring range: Resistance measurement 200		
Test step	VAG 1598/22 Sockets	Test of	Test conditions - Additional operations	Specification (Ω)	Corrective steps
14	52 + 1	Solenoid Valve 5	Ignition off Control module disconnected	6 to 8	- Test 16–pin wiring connection to transmission for contact corrosion
	1 + 34			infinite [1]	- Perform test step 9
15	52 + 29	Solenoid Valve 6	Ignition off Control module disconnected	6 to 8	- Test wiring connection from 88–pin control module to 16–pin connector
	29 + 34			infinite [1]	- Test wiring harness in transmission, replace if necessary
16	52 + 4	Solenoid Valve 7	Ignition off Control module disconnected	6 to 8	- Test relevant solenoid valves for short circuit; replace if necessary
	4 + 34			infinite [1]	Remove and install valve body
17	2 + 36	Shift Lock Solenoid	Ignition off - Selector lever in "P"	14 to 28	- Test wiring per wiring diagram - Replace shift lock solenoid; service selector mechanism - Perform test step 2
18	18 + 34	Kick-Down Switch	Ignition off Control module disconnected - Accelerator not depressed	infinite [1]	- Test wiring per wiring diagram - Adjust accelerator cable or replace
			- Depress Accelerator Pedal as far as kick-down	less than 1.5	

19	14 + 42	Transmission Vehicle Speed Sensor	Ignition off
			        min.
			        max.
				0.80 k
				1.20 k
					- Test wiring per wiring diagram

	14 + 34 14 + 54 42 + 54 42 + 34			infinite [1]	- Replace Transmission Vehicle Speed Sensor
	15 + 34 15 + 54	Screening of Circuit	Ignition off	infinite [1]	- Test wiring per wiring diagram

20	16 + 44	Transmission Input Speed Sensor	Ignition off
			Control module disconnected
			        min.
			        max.
				230
				300
					- Test wiring per wiring diagram

	44 + 34 44 + 54 16 + 54 16 + 34			infinite [1]	- Replace Transmission Input Speed Sensor
	23 + 34 23 + 54	Screening of Circuit	Ignition off	infinite [1]	- Test wiring per wiring diagram

[1] Set multimeter to maximum range

96F19377

Courtesy of Audi of America, Inc.

Fig. 8: Testing TCU Harness & Components Type 01V (3 Of 5)

Switch on measuring range: Resistance measurement 20 k					
Test step	VAG 1598/22 Sockets	Test of	Test conditions - Additional operations	Specification (Ω)	Corrective steps
21	21 + 22	Transmission Fluid Temperature Sensor	Ignition off Control module disconnected ATF temperature approx. 20 °C approx. 60 °C approx. 120 °C	 approx. 0.83 k[2] approx. 1.28 k[2] approx. 1.88 k[2]	- Test wiring connection from the 88-pin control module to the 16-pin connector - Test wiring harness in transmission; replace if necessary - Tramsmission fluid temp sensor is integrated in the wiring harness (in transmission)
	21 + 32 22 + 28		Ignition off	infinite [1]	
	21 + 54 22 + 54			infinite [1]	

[1] Set multimeter to maximum range
[2] Permissible tolerance: + 0.1 k

Switch on measuring range: Resistance measurement 2 M					
Test step	VAG 1598/22 Sockets	Test of	Test conditions - Additional operations	Specification (Ω)	Corrective steps
22	41 + 28 41 + 34 41 + 55	wiring connection to engine control module (throttle valve signal)	Ignition off Engine control module disconnected	infinite [1]	- Test wiring per wiring diagram
	41 + xx[2]			less than 1.5	
23	35 + 28 35 + 34	wiring connection to engine control module (consumption signal)	Ignition off Engine control module disconnected	greater than 40 k	- Test wiring per wiring diagram - Test board computer ⇒ Electrical System
	35 + xx[2]			less than1.5	
	35 + 34 35 + 28	Note: This step is a voltage check	Ignition on Engine control module disconnected	greater than 5 Volts	
24	40 + 28 40 + 34	wiring connection to engine control module (engine speed signal)	Ignition off Engine control module disconnected	15...80 k	- Test wiring per wiring diagram - Test board computer ⇒ Electrical System
	40 + xx[2]			less than 1.5	
25	20 + 28 20 + 34 20 + 55	wiring connection to engine control module (engine intervention)	Ignition off Engine control module disconnected	infinite [1]	- Test wiring per wiring diagram
	20 + xx[2]			less than 1.5	
26	51 + 28 51 + 34 51 + 55	wiring connection to engine control module (up/downshift signal)	Ignition off Control module disconnected	infinite	- Test wiring per wiring diagram
	51 + xx[2]			less than 1.5	

[1] Set multimeter to maximum range
[2] Check continuity of wire to ECU harness. See wiring diagram.

96H19379

Courtesy of Audi of America, Inc.

Fig. 9: Testing TCU Harness & Components Type 01V (4 Of 5)

AUTOMATIC TRANSMISSIONS
Audi Type 01V (Cont.)

Switch on measuring range: Resistance measurement 2 M					
Test step	VAG 1598/22 Sockets	Test of	Test conditions - Additional operations	Specification (Ω)	Corrective steps
27	1 + 7	Multi-function TR Switch	Ignition off - Selector lever in P, R, N, D, 4, 3, 2,	infinite 1)	- Check connector to multifunction switch for contact corrosion, water penetration or loose fit.
	2 + 3		Ignition off - Selector lever in N	≤ 20	
			Ignition off - Selector lever in P, R, D, 4, 3, 2	infinite 1)	
	4 + 5		Ignition off - Selector lever in D, 4	≤ 20	
			- Fuse 31 removed - Selector lever in P, R, N, 3, 2	infinite 1)	Replace Multi-function TR Switch
	2 + 4		Ignition off - Selector lever in N, D	≤ 20	
			- Selector lever in P, R, 4, 3, 2	infinite 1)	
27	1 + 2	Multi-function TR Switch	Ignition off - Selector lever in P, N, D	≤ 20	- Check connector to multifunction switch for contact corrosion, water penetration or loose fit.
			- Selector lever in R, 4, 3, 2	infinite1)	- Replace Multi-function TR Switch
	6 + 7	Signal of Multi-function TR Switch	Ignition off - Selector lever in R, D, 4, 3, 2	infinite1)	- Replace Multi-function TR Switch
	6 + 7		Ignition off - Selector lever in P, N	≤ 20	Check signal for ECM

1) Set multimeter to maximum range

96A19356

Courtesy of Audi of America, Inc.

Fig. 10: Testing TCU Harness & Components Type 01V (5 Of 5)

WIRING DIAGRAMS

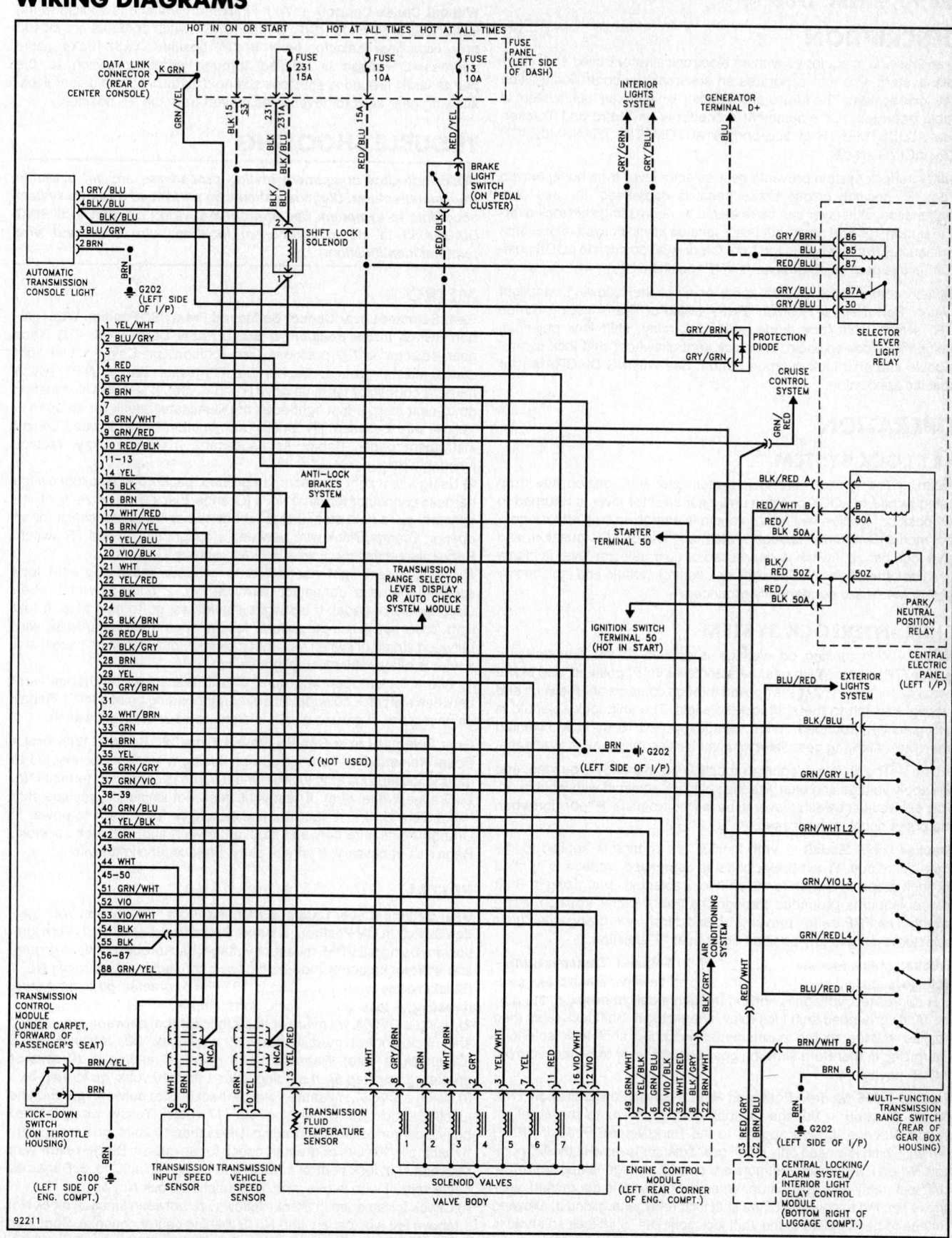

Fig. 11: *1996 A4 & A4 AWD Transaxle Wiring Diagram (Type 01V)*

AUTOMATIC TRANSMISSIONS
Geo Shift Interlock Systems

Metro, Prizm, Tracker

DESCRIPTION

Transmission is equipped with an electronically controlled shift interlock system. Prizm incorporates an electronically controlled ignition key lock system. The Metro and Tracker ignition key lock system is cable operated. For adjustment procedures on Metro and Tracker, see ADJUSTMENTS in appropriate AUTOMATIC TRANSMISSION SERVICING article.

Shift interlock system prevents gear selector lever from being moved from "P" position unless brake pedal is depressed. In case of a malfunction, shift lever can be released by depressing shift lock override button, located near shift lever. Ignition key lock system prevents ignition key from being moved from ON or ACC position to LOCK position unless gear selector lever is in "P" position.

System components include some or all of the following: stoplight switch, Park/Neutral Position (PNP) switch or Transmission Range (TR) switch, shift lock diode, shift lock relay, shift lock solenoid, ignition key lock solenoid, shift lock control switch, shift lock control module and shift lock override button. See WIRING DIAGRAMS for specific application.

OPERATION

KEY LOCK SYSTEM

Prizm – The ignition key lock system prevents ignition key from being turned to LOCK position until gear selector lever is returned to "P" position. Ignition key lock solenoid is energized by shift lock control module whenever ignition switch is in ON or ACC position, and shift lock control switch is depressed or gear selector lever is in any position other than "P". The shift lock control module and ignition key lock solenoid are permanently grounded.

SHIFT INTERLOCK SYSTEM

Metro – With ignition on, voltage is applied to the Transmission Range (TR) switch. With gear selector lever in "P" position, and brake pedal depressed, voltage is applied through contacts of TR switch and stoplight switch to the shift lock solenoid. The shift lock solenoid is permanently grounded. With voltage applied, shift lock solenoid energizes, allowing gear selector lever locking mechanism to release.

Prizm – The shift lock control module is permanently grounded, and will apply voltage and energize the shift lock solenoid with ignition on. This allows gear selector lever to be moved from the "P" position when the brake pedal is depressed.

Tracker (1995 Model) – With ignition on, voltage is applied to the shift lock diode. When brake pedal is depressed, voltage is applied through stoplight switch to the shift lock solenoid, energizing it. Shift lock solenoid is grounded through the Park/Neutral Position (PNP) switch. The PNP switch prevents solenoid from energizing when gear selector lever is in any position other than "P" position.

Tracker (1996 Models Equipped With 3-Speed Transmission) – Voltage is applied at all times to the stoplight switch. When brake pedal is depressed, voltage is applied through stoplight switch to the permanently grounded shift lock relay, energizing it. Shift lock relay then applies voltage to the permanently grounded shift lock solenoid, energizing it, therefore allowing gear selector lever to be moved from the "P" position.

Tracker (1996 Models Equipped With 4-Speed Transmission With Cruise Control) – Voltage is applied at all times to the stoplight switch. Voltage is also applied to the Park/Neutral Position (PNP) switch, which is closed only when gear selector lever is in the "P" position. When PNP switch contacts are closed, voltage is applied to the shift lock relay with ignition on. When brake pedal is depressed, voltage is applied to coil side of the shift lock relay, energizing it, allowing voltage to be supplied to the shift lock solenoid. Shift lock solenoid is permanently grounded, therefore it energizes and allows gear selector lever to be moved from "P" position.

Tracker (1996 Models Equipped With 4-Speed Transmission Without Cruise Control) – With ignition on, voltage is applied to the Park/Neutral Position (PNP) switch. PNP switch contacts are closed only with gear selector lever in "P" position. With brake pedal depressed, voltage is applied through stoplight switch to the permanently grounded shift lock solenoid. In turn, solenoid energizes, allowing gear selector lever to be moved from the "P" position.

TROUBLE SHOOTING

NOTE: Individual component testing procedures are not available from manufacturer. Diagnosis should be performed on entire system according to symptom. See appropriate wiring diagram in WIRING DIAGRAMS to aid in component location, wire color and wire terminal identification.

METRO

Gear Selector Lever Cannot Be Moved From "P" Position With Ignition Switch In ON Position, & Brake Pedal Depressed – 1) Place gear selector in "P" position. Turn ignition on. Using a test light connected to ground, backprobe Transaxle Range (TR) switch harness connector terminal No. 8 (Yellow wire). If test light illuminates, go to next step. If test light does not illuminate, check for an open in Yellow wire between TR switch and junction block, located behind instrument panel. Repair as necessary. If wire is okay, replace junction block.

2) Using a test light connected to ground, backprobe stoplight switch harness connector terminal No. 4 (Orange/Black wire). If test light illuminates, go to next step. If test light does not illuminate, check for an open in Orange/Black wire between stoplight switch and TR switch. Repair as necessary. If wire is okay, replace TR switch.

3) Using a test light connected to ground, backprobe shift lock solenoid harness connector terminal No. 2 (Orange/White wire). Depress brake pedal. If test light illuminates, go to next step. If test light does not illuminate, check for an open in Orange/White wire between stoplight switch and shift lock solenoid. Repair as necessary. If wire is okay, replace stoplight switch.

4) Check for an open in ground circuit (Black wire or Orange wire) between shift lock solenoid and circuit grounding point (G407). Repair as necessary. If ground circuit is okay, replace stoplight switch.

Gear Selector Lever Can Be Moved From "P" Position With Brake Pedal Released – Turn ignition on. Using a test light connected to ground, backprobe shift lock solenoid harness connector terminal No. 2 (Orange/White wire). If test light does not illuminate, replace shift lock solenoid. If test light illuminates, check for a short to power in Orange/White wire between stoplight switch and shift lock solenoid. Repair as necessary. If wire is okay, replace stoplight switch.

PRIZM

Gear Selector Lever Cannot Be Moved From "P" Position With Ignition Switch In ON Position, & Brake Pedal Depressed – 1) Turn ignition on. Using a DVOM, measure voltage (backprobe) between ground and shift lock control module harness connector C2, terminal No. 1 (Black/Yellow wire). If reading is 10 volts or greater, go to next step. If reading is less than 10 volts, go to step 3).

2) Using a DVOM, measure voltage (backprobe) between ground and shift lock control module harness connector C2, terminal No. 2 (Green/White wire). Depress brake pedal. If reading is 10 volts or greater, go to step 5). If reading is less than 10 volts, go to step 6).

3) Using a DVOM, measure voltage (backprobe) between ground and junction block No. 3, terminal No. 17 (Black/Yellow wire), located behind center console. If reading is less than 10 volts, go to next step. If reading is 10 volts or greater, check for an open in Black/Yellow wire between shift lock control module and junction block No. 3. Repair as necessary. If wire is okay, replace junction block No. 3.

4) Check for an open in Black/Yellow wire between junction block No. 1 (above left kick panel), and No. 3 (behind center console). Repair as necessary. If wire is okay, replace junction block No. 1.

5) Turn ignition switch to LOCK position. Disconnect shift lock control module harness connector C2. Using a test light connected to battery positive, probe shift lock control module harness connector C2, terminal No. 4 (White/Black wire). If test light illuminates, go to step 13). If test light does not illuminate, go to step 14).

6) Using a DVOM, measure voltage (backprobe) between ground and junction block No. 3 harness connector C3, terminal No. 2 (Green/White wire). Depress brake pedal. If reading is less than 10 volts, go to next step. If reading is 10 volts or greater, go to step 8).

7) Using a DVOM, measure voltage (backprobe) between ground and junction block No. 1 harness connector C5, terminal No. 18 (Green/White wire). Depress brake pedal. If reading is less than 10 volts, go to step 9). If reading is 10 volts or greater, go to step 10).

8) Check for an open in Green/White wire between junction block No. 3 and shift lock control module. Repair as necessary. If wire is okay, replace junction block No. 3.

9) Using a test light connected to ground, backprobe stoplight switch harness connector terminal No. 2 (Red/White wire). If test light illuminates, go to step 11). If test light does not illuminate, go to step 12).

10) Check for an open in Green/White wire between junction blocks No. 1 and 3. Repair as necessary. If wire is okay, replace junction block No. 1.

11) Check for an open in Green/White wire between stoplight switch and junction block No. 1. Repair as necessary. If wire is okay, adjust or replace stoplight switch.

12) Check for an open in Red/White wire between junction block No. 1 and stoplight switch. Repair as necessary. If wire is okay, replace junction block No. 1.

13) Disconnect shift lock control module harness connector C1. Ensure gear selector lever is in "P" position. Using a DVOM, measure resistance between shift lock control module harness connector C1 (harness side), terminals No. 1 (Green/Red wire) and No. 2 (Green wire). If resistance is 20 ohms or less, go to step 15). If resistance is greater than 20 ohms, replace shift lock control switch.

14) Using a test light connected to battery positive, backprobe junction block No. 3 harness connector C1, terminal No. 20 (White/Black wire). If test light does not illuminate, go to step 16). If test light illuminates, check for an open in White/Black wire between shift lock control module and junction block No. 3. Repair as necessary. If wire is okay, replace junction block No. 3.

15) Disconnect shift lock control module harness connector C3. Using a DVOM, measure resistance between shift lock control module harness connector C3 (harness side), terminals No. 1 (Blue wire) and No. 2 (Blue/Red wire). If resistance is 21-27 ohms, replace shift lock control module. If resistance is not as specified, replace shift lock solenoid.

16) Using a test light connected to battery positive, probe junction connector No. 3, terminal No. 14 (White/Black wire). Junction connectors (No. 1 and 3) are located between junction block No. 3 harness connector C1 and circuit grounding point (G200). If test light does not illuminate, go to next step. If test light illuminates, check for an open in White/Black wire between junction block No. 3 and junction connector No. 3. Repair as necessary. If wire is okay, replace junction connector No. 3.

17) Check for an open in White/Black wire between junction connector No. 3 and junction connector No. 1, or in White/Black wire between junction connector No. 1 and circuit grounding point (G200). Repair as necessary. If wire is okay, replace junction connector No. 1.

Gear Selector Lever Can Be Moved From "P" Position Without Depressing Brake Pedal – 1) Turn ignition on. Using a DVOM, measure voltage (backprobe) between ground and shift lock control module harness connector C2, terminal No. 2 (Green/White wire). If reading is 10 volts or greater, go to next step. If reading is less than 10 volts, go to step 3).

2) Disconnect stoplight switch harness connector. Using a DVOM, measure voltage between ground and stoplight switch harness connector terminal No. 1 (Green/White wire). If reading is 10 volts or greater, leave DVOM connected and go to step 4). If reading is less than 10 volts, adjust or replace stoplight switch.

3) Using a DVOM, measure voltage (backprobe) between ground and shift lock control module harness connector C3, terminal No. 2 (Blue/Red wire). If reading is 10 volts or greater, replace shift lock control module. If reading is less than 10 volts, replace shift lock solenoid.

4) Disconnect junction block No. 1, harness connector C6. Observe voltage reading on DVOM. If reading is less than 10 volts, go to next step. If reading is 10 volts or greater, check Green/White wire between stoplight switch and junction block No. 1 for a short to power. Repair as necessary. If wire is okay, replace junction block No. 1.

5) Check Green/White wire between junction blocks No. 1 and 3, or Green/White wire between junction block No. 3 and shift lock control module for a short to power. Repair as necessary. If wire is okay, replace junction block No. 3.

Ignition Key Cannot Be Removed From Ignition Switch With Gear Selector In "P" Position – 1) Turn ignition on. Using a DVOM, measure voltage (backprobe) between ground and shift lock control module harness connector C1, terminal No. 3 (Green/White wire). If reading is less than 10 volts, go to next step. If reading is 10 volts or greater, go to step 3).

2) Turn ignition switch to ACC position. Disconnect shift lock control module harness connector C1. Using a DVOM, measure voltage between ground and shift lock control module harness connector (module side) C1, terminal No. 3 (Green/White wire). Turn ignition on. If reading is 10 volts or greater, replace shift lock control switch. If reading is less than 10 volts, replace shift lock control module.

3) Turn ignition switch to ACC position. Disconnect ignition key lock solenoid harness connector. Turn ignition switch to LOCK position and attempt to remove ignition key from switch. If ignition key can be removed, go to next step. If ignition key cannot be removed, replace ignition key lock solenoid.

4) Check Blue/Black wire between shift lock control module and key lock solenoid for a short to power. Repair as necessary. If wire is okay, replace shift lock control module.

Ignition Key Can Be Removed From Ignition Switch With Gear Selector In Any Position – 1) Turn ignition on. Using a DVOM, measure voltage (backprobe) between ground and shift lock control module harness connector C2, terminal No. 5 (Gray wire). If reading is 10 volts or greater, go to next step. If reading is less than 10 volts, go to step 3).

2) Using a DVOM, measure voltage (backprobe) between ground and shift lock control module harness connector C1, terminal No. 3 (Green/White wire). If reading is 10 volts or greater, leave DVOM connected and go to step 4). If reading is less than 10 volts, replace shift lock control module.

3) Using a DVOM, measure voltage (backprobe) between ground and audio alarm module harness connector terminal No. 1 (Gray wire). If reading is 10 volts or greater, go to step 5). If reading is less than 10 volts, replace audio alarm module and retest system. Replace junction block No. 1 if system remains inoperative.

4) Observe voltage reading while depressing gear selector lever button. If reading is less than 2 volts, go to step 6). If reading is not as specified, go to step 7).

5) Check for an open in Gray wire between audio alarm module and junction block No. 3, or in Gray wire between junction block No. 3 and shift lock control module. Repair as necessary. If wire is okay, replace junction block No. 3.

6) Using a DVOM, measure voltage (backprobe) between ground and shift lock control module harness connector C2, terminal No. 6 (Blue/Black wire). If reading is 6-9 volts, go to step 8). If reading is not as specified, replace shift lock control module.

7) Turn ignition switch to LOCK position. Engage parking brake and move gear selector to "R" position. Disconnect shift lock control module harness connector C1. Measure resistance between shift lock control module harness connector (harness side) C1, terminals No. 2 (Green wire) and No. 3 (Green/White wire). If resistance is 2 ohms or greater, replace shift lock control solenoid. If resistance is less than 2 ohms, replace shift lock control module.

8) Using a test light connected to battery positive, backprobe ignition key lock solenoid harness connector terminal No. 1 (White/Black

wire). If test light illuminates, go to next step. If test light does not illuminate, check for an open in White/Black wire between ignition key lock solenoid and junction block No. 2, or White/Black wire between junction block No. 2 and circuit grounding point (G203). Repair as necessary. If wire is okay, replace junction block No. 2.

9) Turn ignition switch to LOCK position. Disconnect ignition key lock solenoid harness connector. Using a DVOM, measure resistance between key lock solenoid harness connector (solenoid side) terminals No. 1 and 2 (Blue wires). If resistance is 12-17 ohms, repair open in Blue/Black wire between shift lock control module and ignition key lock solenoid. If resistance is not as specified, replace ignition key lock solenoid.

TRACKER

System Diagnosis (1995 Models) – 1) Turn ignition on. Attempt to move gear selector lever from "P" position. If selector cannot be moved to another gear position, go to next step. If selector can be moved to another gear position, go to step **15)**.

2) Attempt to move gear selector lever from "P" position with brake pedal depressed. If selector can be moved to another gear position, system functions normally at this time. If selector cannot be moved to another gear position, go to next step.

3) Using a test light connected to ground, backprobe stoplight switch harness connector terminal No. 1 (Green wire). If test light illuminates, go to next step. If test light does not illuminate, repair open in Green wire between instrument panel fuse block and stoplight switch.

4) Using a test light connected to ground, backprobe stoplight switch harness connector terminal No. 3 (Green/White wire). Depress and hold brake pedal. If test light illuminates, go to next step. If test light does not illuminate, replace stoplight switch.

5) Using a test light connected to ground, backprobe shift lock relay harness connector terminal No. 1 (Green/White wire). Depress and hold brake pedal. If test light illuminates, go to next step. If test light does not illuminate, repair open in Green/White wire between stoplight switch and shift lock relay.

6) Using a test light connected to ground, backprobe shift lock diode harness connector terminal No. 1 (Yellow/Blue wire). If test light illuminates, go to next step. If test light does not illuminate, repair open in Yellow/Blue wire between instrument panel fuse block and shift lock diode.

7) Using a test light connected to ground, backprobe shift lock diode harness connector terminal No. 2 (Blue/Black wire). If test light illuminates, go to next step. If test light does not illuminate, replace shift lock diode.

8) Using a test light connected to ground, backprobe shift lock relay harness connector terminal No. 2 (Blue/Black wire). If test light illuminates, go to next step. If test light does not illuminate, repair open in Blue/Black wire between shift lock diode and shift lock relay.

9) Turn ignition off. Ensure gear selector is in "P" position. Disconnect shift lock relay. Using a DVOM, measure resistance between chassis ground and shift lock relay harness connector terminal No. 3 (Blue/Red wire). If resistance is .3 ohms or less, go to next step. If resistance is greater than .3 ohms, go to step **13)**.

10) Reconnect shift lock relay. Turn ignition on. Using a test light connected to ground, backprobe shift lock relay harness connector terminal No. 4 (Blue/Green wire). If test light illuminates, go to next step. If test light does not illuminate, replace shift lock relay.

11) Turn ignition off. Disconnect shift lock relay and shift lock solenoid harness connectors. Using a DVOM, measure resistance between shift lock relay harness connector terminal No. 4 (Blue/Green wire) and shift lock solenoid harness connector terminal No. 2 (Blue/Green wire). If resistance is .3 ohms or less, go to next step. If resistance is greater than .3 ohms, repair open in Blue/Green wire between shift lock relay and shift lock solenoid.

12) Using a DVOM, measure resistance between shift lock relay harness connector terminal No. 3 (Blue/Red wire) and shift lock solenoid harness connector terminal No. 2 (Blue/Red wire). If resistance is .3 ohms or less, replace shift lock solenoid. If resistance is greater than

.3 ohms, repair open in Red/Blue wire between shift lock solenoid and circuit splice (S259), located in main harness behind center of instrument panel.

13) Ensure gear selector lever is in "P" position. Disconnect Park/Neutral Position (PNP) switch harness connector C2. Using a DVOM, measure resistance between PNP switch harness connector terminals No. 2 (Blue/Red wire) and No. 4 (Black/Green wire). If resistance is .3 ohms or less, go to next step. If resistance is greater than .3 ohms, replace PNP switch.

14) Using a DVOM, measure resistance between chassis ground and PNP switch harness connector C2, terminal No. 4 (Black/Green wire). If resistance is .3 ohms or less, repair open in Blue/Red wire between PNP switch and circuit splice (S259), located in main harness behind center of instrument panel. If resistance is greater than .3 ohms, repair open in Black/Green wire between PNP switch and circuit grounding point (G125).

15) Disconnect shift lock solenoid. Using a test light connected to ground, probe shift lock solenoid harness connector terminal No. 1 (Blue/Green wire). If test light illuminates, go to next step. If test light does not illuminate, replace shift lock solenoid.

16) Disconnect shift lock relay. Using a test light connected to ground, probe shift lock relay harness connector terminal No. 4 (Blue/Green wire). If test light illuminates, repair Blue/Green wire for a short to power. If test light does not illuminate, go to next step.

17) Disconnect stoplight switch. Using a test light connected to ground, probe stoplight switch harness connector terminal No. 3 (Green/White wire). If test light illuminates, repair Green/White wire for a short to power. If test light does not illuminate, replace stoplight switch.

System Diagnosis (1996 Models Equipped With 3-Speed Automatic, Or 1996 Models Equipped With 4-Speed Automatic & Cruise Control) – 1) It is important to perform the following checks listed in the following Note before proceeding.

NOTE: Ensure STOP HORN fuse (15-amp), WIPER WASHER fuse (15-amp) and TURN BACK fuse (15-amp) are okay. Check for poor connections at circuit grounding points (G202). See appropriate wiring diagram in WIRING DIAGRAMS. Repair as necessary.

Turn ignition on. Attempt to move gear selector lever from "P" position. If selector cannot be moved to another gear position, go to next step. If selector can be moved to another gear position, go to step **14)**.

2) Attempt to move gear selector lever from "P" position with brake pedal depressed. If selector can be moved to another gear position, system functions normally at this time. If selector cannot be moved to another gear position, go to next step.

3) Using a test light connected to ground, backprobe stoplight switch harness connector terminal No. 1 (Green wire). If test light illuminates, go to next step. If test light does not illuminate, repair open in Green wire between instrument panel fuse block and stoplight switch.

4) Using a test light connected to ground, backprobe stoplight switch harness connector terminal No. 3 (Green/White wire). Depress and hold brake pedal. If test light illuminates, go to next step. If test light does not illuminate, check stoplight switch for proper adjustment. If adjustment is okay, replace stoplight switch.

5) Using a test light connected to ground, backprobe shift lock relay harness connector terminal No. 1 (Green/White wire). Depress and hold brake pedal. If test light illuminates, go to next step (3-speed), or step **11)** (4-speed). If test light does not illuminate, repair open in Green/White wire between stoplight switch and shift lock relay.

6) Using a test light connected to ground, backprobe shift lock relay harness connector terminal No. 2 (Yellow/Blue wire on 3-speed; Orange/Green wire on 4-speed). If test light illuminates, go to next step. If test light does not illuminate, repair open in appropriate wire between instrument panel fuse block and shift lock relay.

7) Turn ignition off. Disconnect shift lock relay. Using a DVOM, measure resistance between chassis ground and shift lock relay harness connector terminal No. 3 (Black wire). If resistance is .3 ohms or less, go to next step. If resistance is greater than .3 ohms, repair open Black wire between shift lock relay and chassis grounding point (G202).

8) Reconnect shift lock relay. Using a test light connected to ground, backprobe shift lock relay harness connector terminal No. 4 (Blue/Green wire). Depress and hold brake pedal. If test light illuminates, go to next step. If test light does not illuminate, replace shift lock relay.

9) Turn ignition off. Disconnect shift lock relay and shift lock solenoid harness connectors. Using a DVOM, measure resistance between shift lock relay harness connector terminal No. 4 (Blue/Green wire) and shift lock solenoid harness connector terminal No. 2 (Blue/Green wire). If resistance is .3 ohms or less, go to next step. If resistance is greater than .3 ohms, repair open in Blue/Green wire between shift lock relay and shift lock solenoid.

10) Using a DVOM, measure resistance between chassis ground and shift lock solenoid harness connector terminal No. 1 (Black wire). If resistance is .3 ohms or less, replace shift lock solenoid. If resistance is greater than .3 ohms, repair open in Black wire between shift lock solenoid and chassis grounding point (G202).

11) Ensure gear selector is in "P" position. Using a test light connected to ground, backprobe shift lock relay harness connector terminal No. 2 (Yellow/Blue wire on 3-speed; Orange/Green wire on 4-speed). If test light illuminates, go to step **7)**. If test light does not illuminate, go to next step.

12) Using a test light connected to ground, backprobe Transmission Range (TR) switch harness connector terminal No. 7 (Blue/Red wire). If test light illuminates, repair open in Blue/Red wire between TR switch and shift lock relay. If test light does not illuminate, go to next step.

13) Using a test light connected to ground, backprobe TR switch harness connector terminal No. 6 (Yellow wire). If test light illuminates, replace TR switch. If test light does not illuminate, repair open in Yellow wire between TR switch and instrument panel fuse block.

14) Disconnect shift lock solenoid. Using a test light connected to ground, probe shift lock solenoid harness connector terminal No. 2 (Blue/Green wire). If test light does not illuminate, replace shift lock solenoid. If test light illuminates, go to next step.

15) Disconnect shift lock relay. Using a test light connected to ground, probe shift lock relay harness connector terminal No. 4 (Blue/Green wire). If test light illuminates, repair Blue/Green wire between shift lock relay and shift lock solenoid for a short to power. If test light does not illuminate, go to next step.

16) Disconnect stoplight switch. Using a test light connected to ground, probe stoplight switch harness connector terminal No. 3 (Green/White wire). If test light illuminates, repair Green/White wire between stoplight switch and shift lock relay for a short to power. If test light does not illuminate, replace stoplight switch.

System Diagnosis (1996 Models Equipped With 4-Speed Automatic Without Cruise Control) – 1) Turn ignition on. Attempt to move gear selector lever from "P" position. If selector cannot be moved to another gear position, go to next step. If selector can be moved to another gear position, go to step **9)**.

2) Attempt to move gear selector lever from "P" position with brake pedal depressed. If selector can be moved to another gear position, system functions normally at this time. If selector cannot be moved to another gear position, go to next step.

3) Using a test light connected to ground, backprobe stoplight switch harness connector terminal No. 2 (Orange/Green wire). If test light illuminates, go to next step. If test light does not illuminate, go to step **7)**.

4) Using a test light connected to ground, backprobe stoplight switch harness connector terminal No. 4 (Blue/Green wire). Depress and hold brake pedal. If test light illuminates, go to next step. If test light does not illuminate, check stoplight switch for proper adjustment. If adjustment is okay, replace stoplight switch.

5) Disconnect shift lock solenoid. Using a test light connected to ground, probe shift lock solenoid harness connector terminal No. 2 (Blue/Green wire). Depress and hold brake pedal. If test light illuminates, go to next step. If test light does not illuminate, repair open in Blue/Green wire between shift lock solenoid and stoplight switch.

6) Turn ignition off. Using a DVOM, measure resistance between chassis ground and shift lock solenoid harness connector terminal No. 1 (Black wire). If resistance is .3 ohms or less, replace shift lock solenoid. If resistance is greater than .3 ohms, repair open in Black wire between shift lock solenoid and chassis grounding point (G202).

7) Ensure gear selector is in "P" position. Using a test light connected to ground, backprobe Transmission Range (TR) switch harness connector terminal No. 7 (Blue/Red wire). If test light does not illuminate, go to next step. If test light illuminates, repair open in Blue/Red wire or Orange/Green wire between TR switch and stoplight switch.

8) Using a test light connected to ground, backprobe TR switch harness connector terminal No. 6 (Yellow wire). If test light illuminates, replace TR switch. If test light does not illuminate, repair open in Yellow wire between TR switch and instrument panel fuse block.

9) Disconnect shift lock solenoid. Using a test light connected to ground, probe shift lock solenoid harness connector terminal No. 2 (Blue/Green wire). If test light does not illuminate, replace shift lock solenoid. If test light illuminates, check stoplight switch for proper adjustment. If adjustment is okay, repair Blue/Green wire between stoplight switch and shift lock solenoid for a short to power.

REMOVAL & INSTALLATION

IGNITION KEY LOCK SOLENOID

Removal & Installation (Prizm) – 1) Disconnect negative battery cable. Remove 2 cover plates from knee bolster. Remove hood release cable from hood latch release lever and bracket. Remove 4 bolts and knee bolster from instrument panel.

2) Disconnect harness connector from ABS Data Link Connector (DLC) (if equipped). Disconnect ignition key lock solenoid harness connector. Remove 2 screws and ignition key lock solenoid from ignition switch. To install, reverse removal procedure.

SHIFT LOCK CONTROL MODULE

Removal (Prizm) – 1) Disconnect negative battery cable. Move gear selector lever to "L" position. Remove center console trim bezel from center console. Disconnect rear defogger switch, hazard switch and cigar lighter harness connectors at rear of center console trim bezel.

2) Remove center trim bezel and center console tray. Remove radio from vehicle. Remove rear console. Return gear selector lever to "P" position. Remove selector trim bezel from center console. Remove right-side kick panel.

3) Remove glove box. Remove 2 cover plates from knee bolster. Remove hood release cable from hood latch release lever and bracket. Remove knee bolster from instrument panel. Disconnect harness connector from ABS Data Link Connector (DLC) (if equipped). Remove center console.

4) Remove illumination light from shift indicator. Remove 4 screws from shift indicator. Position shift indicator to allow access to shift lock control module. Disconnect harness connectors from shift lock solenoid/shift lock control switch assembly and shift lock control module. Remove shift lock control module from gear selector lever.

Installation (Prizm) – To install, reverse removal procedure. Before completion of installation, temporarily connect negative battery cable and ensure proper shift lock operation.

SHIFT LOCK RELAY

Removal & Installation (Tracker) – Disconnect negative battery cable. Pull shift lock relay from mounting bracket. Shift lock relay is located under left side of instrument panel, above brake pedal (1995 models), or on right side of engine compartment, between battery and fuse box (1996 models). Disconnect harness connector. To install, reverse removal procedure.

SHIFT LOCK SOLENOID

Removal & Installation (Metro) – 1) Disconnect negative battery cable. Remove gear selector knob. Remove console. Remove upper, slide and lower covers from gear selector lever. Disconnect shift lock solenoid harness connector.

2) Remove shift lock solenoid from gear selector lever housing. To install, reverse procedure. Adjust position of solenoid lock plate, if necessary. Ensure proper operation.

Removal & Installation (Tracker) – Disconnect negative battery cable. Remove console from floor. Disconnect shift lock solenoid harness connector under carpet. Remove shift lock solenoid from gear selector lever. To install, reverse removal procedure.

SHIFT LOCK SOLENOID & CONTROL SWITCH

Removal & Installation (Prizm) – 1) Disconnect negative battery cable. Move gear selector lever to "L" position. Remove center console trim bezel from center console. Disconnect rear defogger switch, hazard switch and cigar lighter harness connectors at rear of center console trim bezel.

2) Remove center trim bezel and center console tray. Remove radio from vehicle. Remove rear console. Return gear selector lever to "P" position. Remove selector trim bezel from center console. Remove right-side kick panel.

3) Remove glove box. Remove 2 cover plates from knee bolster. Remove hood release cable from hood latch release lever and bracket. Remove knee bolster from instrument panel. Disconnect harness connector from ABS Data Link Connector (DLC) (if equipped). Remove center console.

4) Remove illumination light from shift indicator. Remove 4 screws from shift indicator. Position shift indicator to allow access to shift lock solenoid/shift lock control switch assembly and disconnect harness connector. Remove 2 screws and solenoid/switch assembly from gear selector lever.

5) To install, reverse removal procedure. Before completion of installation, temporarily connect negative battery cable and ensure proper shift lock operation.

STOPLIGHT SWITCH

Removal & Installation (Metro) – 1) Disconnect negative battery cable. remove steering column joint cover. Disconnect stoplight switch harness connector. Remove stoplight switch from brake pedal bracket.

2) To install, reverse removal procedure. To adjust, pull brake pedal up toward steering wheel and hold. Adjust clearance between end of threaded portion of stoplight switch and brake pedal contact plate to .020-.039" (.5-1.0 mm). Tighten stoplight switch lock nut.

Removal & Installation (Prizm) – 1) Disconnect negative battery cable. Remove 2 cover plates from knee bolster. Remove hood release cable from hood latch release lever and bracket. Remove knee bolster from instrument panel. Disconnect harness connector from ABS Data Link Connector (DLC) (if equipped).

2) Remove left-side ventilation duct from left-side duct outlet. Disconnect stoplight switch harness connector. Loosen stoplight switch lock nut. Turn stoplight switch counterclockwise and remove from brake pedal bracket.

3) Install stoplight switch onto brake pedal bracket and turn clockwise until plunger makes contact with pedal lever. Adjust distance between end of stoplight switch plunger and end of threaded portion of stoplight switch to .020-.090" (.5-2.3 mm). Tighten lock nut. To complete installation, reverse removal procedure.

Removal & Installation (Tracker) – 1) Disconnect negative battery cable. Disconnect stoplight switch harness connector. Remove stoplight switch adjustment nut. Unscrew stoplight switch from brake pedal bracket.

2) To install, reverse removal procedure. To adjust, pull brake pedal up toward steering wheel and hold. Adjust clearance between end of threaded portion of stoplight switch and brake pedal return cushion to .060-.080" (1.5-2.0 mm). Tighten stoplight switch lock nut.

TRANSMISSION RANGE (TR) SWITCH

NOTE: TR switch may also be known as Park/Neutral Position (PNP) switch. See ON-VEHICLE SERVICE in appropriate AUTOMATIC TRANSMISSION OVERHAUL article.

WIRING DIAGRAMS

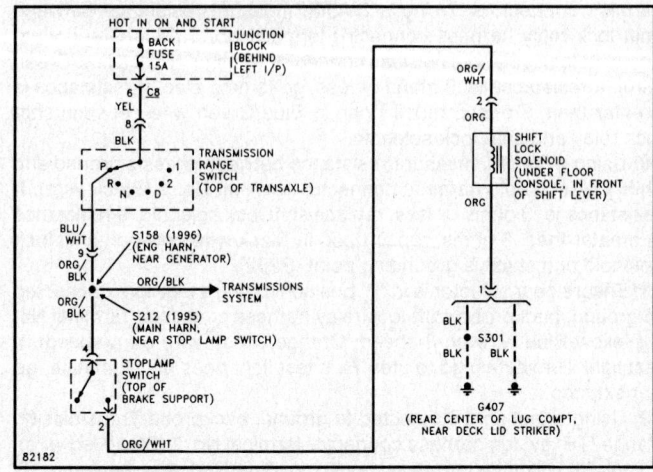

Fig. 1: *Shift Interlock System Wiring Diagram (1995-96 Metro)*

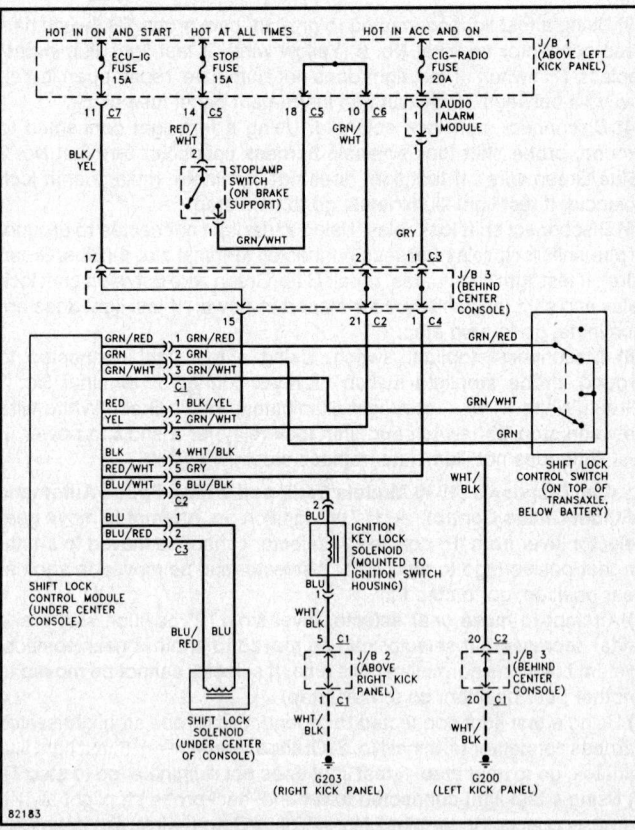

Fig. 2: *Shift Interlock System Wiring Diagram (1995-96 Prizm)*

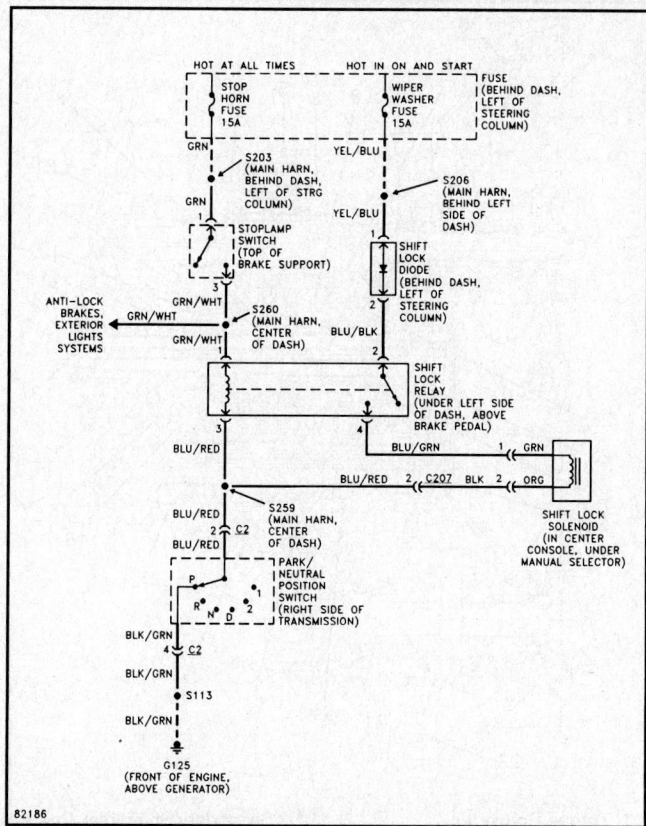

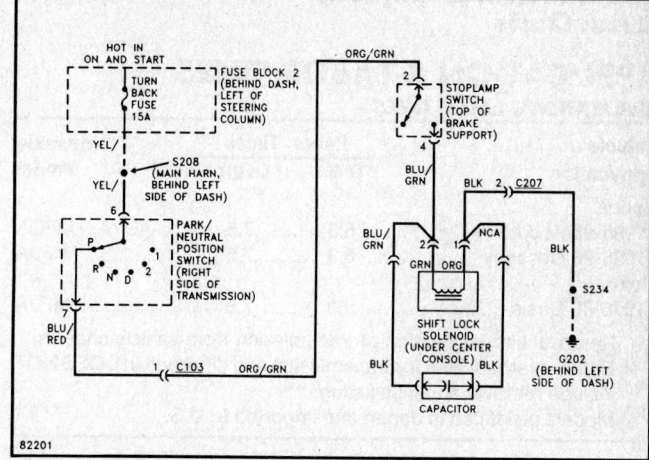

Fig. 5: Shift Interlock System Wiring Diagram (1996 Tracker – 4-Speed Without Cruise Control)

Fig. 3: Shift Interlock System Wiring Diagram (1995 Tracker)

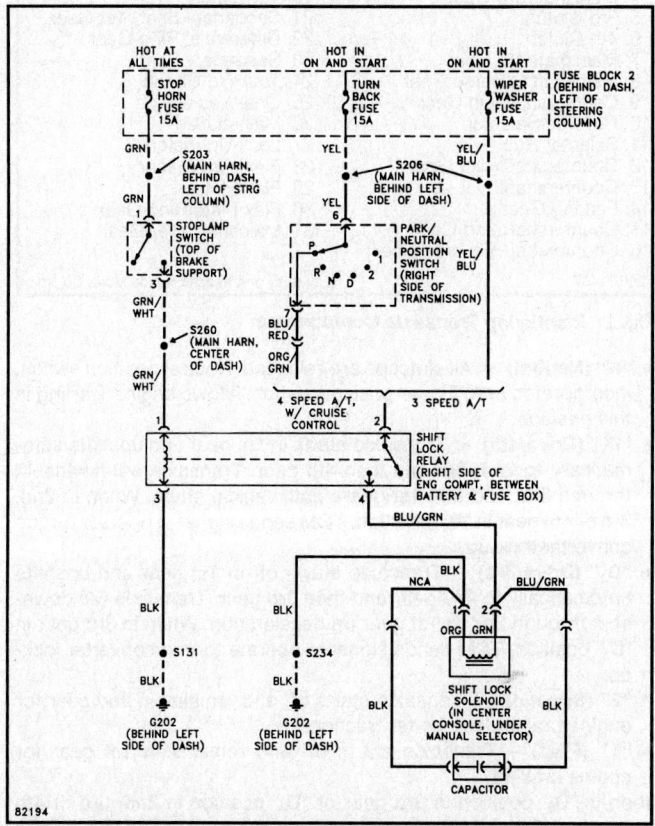

Fig. 4: Shift Interlock System Wiring Diagram (1996 Tracker – 3-Speed & 4-Speed With Cruise Control)

AUTOMATIC TRANSMISSIONS
Honda AOYA, MPJA & MPOA

Honda: Accord, Odyssey
Isuzu: Oasis

APPLICATION & LABOR TIMES

APPLICATION & LABOR TIMES

Vehicle Application	Labor Times		Transaxle Model
	[1] R & I	[2] Overhaul	
Honda			
1995-96 Accord (4-Cyl)	6.3	7.5	AOYA, [3] MPOA
1995-96 Odyssey	6.3	7.5	MPJA
Isuzu			
1995-96 Oasis	6.3	7.5	MPJA

[1] – Removal and installation of transmission from vehicle chassis.
[2] – Bench overhaul time for transmission and differential. DOES NOT include removal and installation.
[3] – Models produced in Japan and imported to U.S.

IDENTIFICATION

Transaxle model and serial number are stamped on the transaxle. *See Fig. 1.* Model and serial number may be required when ordering replacement components.

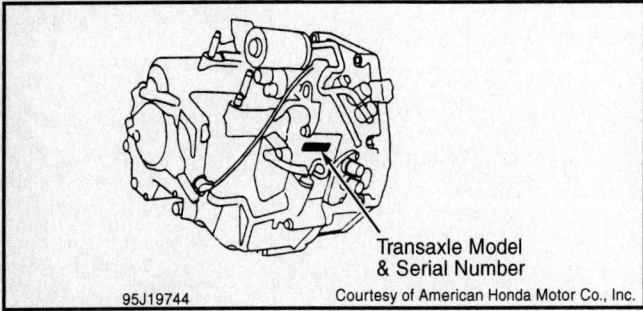

Transaxle Model & Serial Number

95J19744   Courtesy of American Honda Motor Co., Inc.

Fig. 1: Identifying Transaxle Model & Serial Number Location

DESCRIPTION

Automatic transaxle is electronically controlled and has 4 forward speeds and one reverse speed. Transaxle consists of clutches, mainshaft, countershaft, secondary shaft, shift control solenoid valves, lock-up control solenoid valves and lock-up torque converter. *See Fig. 2.*

Valve assembly consists of main valve body, secondary valve body, servo body, regulator valve body and throttle valve body. Transaxle shifting and torque converter lock-up are controlled by Transmission Control Module (TCM).

OPERATION

Shift lever has 7 positions. When shift lever is moved, manual valve on main valve body is moved by the shift cable. Shift lever also changes position of A/T gear position switch, mounted near shift lever. The A/T gear position switch delivers an input signal to the TCM to indicate shift lever position. The TCM uses input signal and operates shift control solenoid valves to control transaxle shifting.

When certain transaxle gear combinations are engaged by clutches, power is transmitted from mainshaft to countershaft by the secondary shaft to provide different gears. Shift lever positions operate as follows:

- **"P" (Park)** – Front wheels lock as parking pawl engages with parking gear on countershaft. All clutches are released. Neutral position switch, incorporated in A/T gear position switch, allows engine starting in this position.
- **"R" (Reverse)** – Reverse selector is engaged with countershaft reverse gear and 4th clutch is applied. Back-up light switch, incorporated in A/T gear position switch, allows back-up lights to operate.

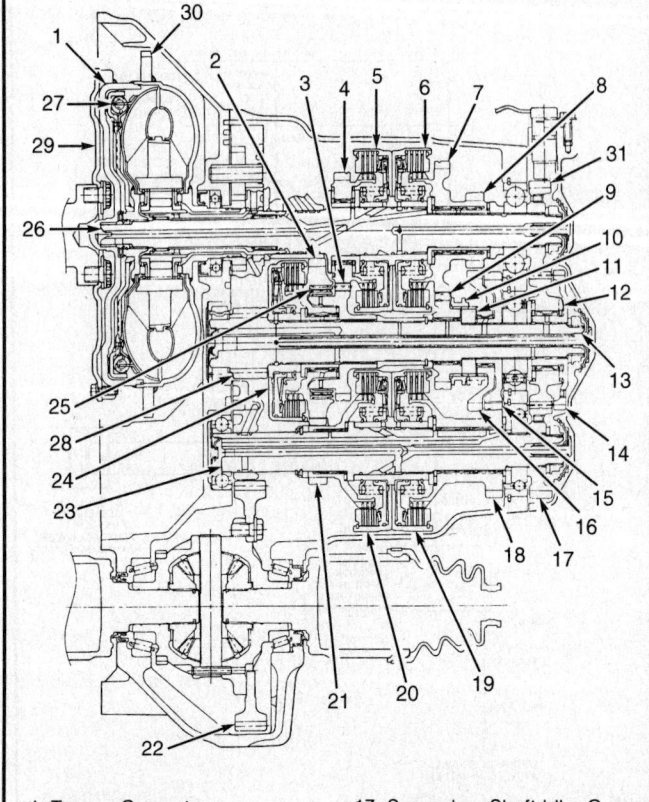

1. Torque Converter
2. Countershaft 1st Gear
3. Countershaft 3rd Gear
4. Mainshaft 3rd Gear
5. 3rd Clutch
6. 4th Clutch
7. Mainshaft 4th Gear
8. Mainshaft Reverse Gear
9. Countershaft 4th Gear
10. Reverse Selector
11. Selector Hub
12. Countershaft Idler Gear
13. Countershaft
14. Parking Gear
15. Countershaft 2nd Gear
16. Countershaft Reverse Gear
17. Secondary Shaft Idler Gear
18. Secondary Shaft 2nd Gear
19. 2nd Clutch
20. 1st Clutch
21. Secondary Shaft 1st Gear
22. Differential Ring Gear
23. Secondary Shaft
24. 1st-Hold Clutch
25. One-Way Clutch
26. Mainshaft
27. Lock-Up Piston
28. Final Drive Gear
29. Flex Plate
30. Flex Plate Ring Gear
31. Mainshaft Idler Gear

96G31407   Courtesy of American Honda Motor Co., Inc.

Fig. 2: Identifying Transaxle Components

- **"N" (Neutral)** – All clutches are released. Neutral position switch, incorporated in A/T gear position switch, allows engine starting in this position.
- **"D_4" (Drive/4th)** – Transaxle starts in 1st gear and upshifts automatically to 2nd, 3rd and then 4th gear. Transaxle will downshift through 3rd, 2nd and 1st gears until vehicle stops. When in 2nd, 3rd or 4th gear in "D_4" position, TCM sends signal to operate torque converter lock-up.
- **"D_3" (Drive/3rd)** – Transaxle starts off in 1st gear and upshifts automatically to 2nd gear and then 3rd gear. Transaxle will downshift through 2nd to 1st gear on deceleration. When in 3rd gear in "D_3" position, TCM sends signal to operate torque converter lock-up.
- **"2" (Second)** – Transaxle starts off and remains in 2nd gear for engine braking and better traction.
- **"1" (First)** – Transaxle starts off and remains in 1st gear for engine braking.

When in "D_3" position in 3rd gear or "D_4" position in 2nd, 3rd or 4th gear, torque converter lock-up exists and transaxle mainshaft rotates at the same speed as engine crankshaft. Under certain conditions, torque converter lock-up clutch is applied during deceleration when in

3rd and 4th gears. Torque converter lock-up is controlled by the TCM. The TCM receives various input signals and operates lock-up control solenoid valves. Operation of lock-up control solenoid valves controls the modulator pressure.

The TCM contains a logic control system which controls transaxle shifting while vehicle is ascending or descending on a slope or reducing vehicle speed. For more information on calculation of gradient program in TCM, see HONDA AOYA, MPJA & MPOA ELECTRONIC CONTROLS article.

The TCM contains self-diagnostic system which stores DTC if failure or problem exists in transaxle electronic control system. DTCs may be retrieved to determine transaxle problem area. For information on electronic transaxle components, see HONDA AOYA, MPJA & MPOA ELECTRONIC CONTROLS article.

Transaxle is equipped with shift and key interlock systems. Shift interlock system prevents shift lever from being moved from "P" position unless brake pedal is depressed and accelerator pedal is in idle position. In case of a malfunction, shift lever can be released by placing ignition key in release slot near shift lever. Key interlock system prevents ignition key from being removed from ignition switch unless shift lever is in "P" position. For additional information on interlock systems, see HONDA AOYA, MPJA & MPOA ELECTRONIC CONTROLS article.

The A/T gear position indicator on instrument panel contains lights to indicate which position A/T gear position switch on shift lever is in. For information and testing of A/T gear position indicator, see HONDA AOYA, MPJA & MPOA ELECTRONIC CONTROLS article.

LUBRICATION & ADJUSTMENTS

See appropriate AUTOMATIC TRANSMISSION SERVICING article in TRANSMISSION SERVICING section.

TROUBLE SHOOTING

Transaxle malfunctions may be caused by poor engine performance, improper adjustments, or failure of hydraulic, mechanical or electronic components. Always begin by checking fluid level, fluid condition and cable adjustments. Perform road test to determine if problem has been corrected. If problem still exists, several tests must be performed on transaxle. See TESTING.

SYMPTOM DIAGNOSIS

Use the following symptoms to identify components or signals that may be the cause of the fault:

Delayed Shift From "N" To "D₃" Or "D₄"
- 1st clutch defective.
- Foreign material in 1st orifice.

Delayed Shift From "N" To "R"
- Servo valve stuck.
- 1-2 shift valve stuck.
- 4th clutch defective.
- Servo control valve stuck.

Engine Runs But Vehicle Does Not Move In Any Gear
- Low fluid.
- ATF pump worn or binding.
- Regulator valve stuck or spring worn.
- Mainshaft worn or damaged.
- Shift cable broken or out of adjustment.
- Final drive gears worn or damaged.
- Flexplate defective.
- ATF strainer clogged.

Erratic Upshift, All Shifts
- PCM defective.

Erratic 1-2 Upshift
- Shift control solenoid valve "A" defective.
- PCM defective.

Erratic 2-3 Upshift
- Shift control solenoid valve "B" defective.
- PCM defective.

Erratic 3-4 Upshift
- Shift control solenoid valve "A" defective.
- PCM defective.

Excessive Idle Vibration
- ATF pump worn or binding.
- Engine output low.
- Flexplate defective.
- Lock-up shift valve stuck.
- Lock-up piston defective.

Flare On Start From "D₃", Stall RPM High In "D₄", "D₃", "2" & "1"
- Low fluid.
- ATF pump worn or binding.
- Regulator valve stuck or spring worn.
- Shift cable broken or out of adjustment.
- ATF strainer clogged.
- Converter check valve stuck.

Flare On Start From "D₃", Stall RPM High In "D₄", "D₃" & "1"
- Shift cable broken or out of adjustment.
- One way clutch worn or damaged.
- 1st clutch defective.

Flare On Start From "D₃", Stall RPM High In "2"
- Shift cable broken or out of adjustment.
- 2nd clutch defective.

Flare On Start From "D₃", Stall RPM Is Within Specification
- To much fluid.

Flare On Start From "D₃", Stall RPM Is Low
- Torque converter one-way clutch defective.
- Engine throttle cable out of adjustment.
- Engine output low.
- Lock-up shift valve stuck.
- Lock-up piston defective.

Flare On 2-3 Upshift
- Throttle valve "B" stuck.
- Throttle control cable out of adjustment.
- 3rd accumulator stuck.
- 2nd orifice control valve stuck.
- Foreign material in main orifice.
- Foreign material in 3rd orifice.
- 3rd clutch defective.
- Main orifice control valve stuck.

Flare On 3-4 Upshift
- Throttle valve "B" stuck.
- Throttle control cable out of adjustment.
- 4th accumulator stuck.
- Foreign material in main orifice.
- Orifice control valve stuck.
- Foreign material in 4th orifice.
- 4th clutch defective.
- Main orifice control valve stuck.

Harsh Shift When Manually Shifting To "1"
- 1st-hold accumulator defective.

Harsh 1-2 Upshift
- 2nd clutch defective.
- Throttle valve "B" stuck.
- Throttle control cable out of adjustment.
- 2nd accumulator stuck.
- Main orifice control valve stuck.

Harsh 2-3 Upshift
- Throttle valve "B" stuck.
- Throttle control cable out of adjustment.
- 3rd accumulator stuck.
- 2nd orifice control valve stuck.
- 3rd clutch defective.
- Main orifice control valve stuck.
- 3rd clutch defective.
- 2nd check ball stuck.
- Foreign material in separator plate orifice.

Harsh 3-4 Upshift
- Throttle valve "B" stuck.
- Throttle control cable out of adjustment.
- 4th accumulator stuck.

- Orifice control valve stuck.
- Foreign material in 3rd orifice.
- 4th clutch defective.
- 4th check ball stuck.
- Foreign material in separator plate orifice.
- Main orifice control valve stuck.

Harsh 2-1 Downshifts
- Throttle valve "B" stuck.
- Throttle control cable out of adjustment.
- 2nd accumulator stuck.
- Foreign material in 2nd orifice.
- Orifice control valve stuck.

Harsh 3-2 Downshifts
- Throttle valve "B" stuck.
- Throttle control cable out of adjustment.
- 3rd accumulator stuck.
- Orifice control valve stuck.
- 3rd check ball stuck.
- Main orifice control valve stuck.

Harsh 4-3 Downshifts
- Throttle valve "B" stuck.
- Throttle control cable out of adjustment.
- 4th accumulator stuck.
- 4th check ball stuck.
- 3rd kickdown valve stuck.
- Main orifice control valve stuck.

Lock-Up Clutch Does Not Disengage
- Throttle valve "B" stuck.
- Throttle control cable out of adjustment.
- Lock-up timing valve stuck.
- Lock-up shift valve stuck.
- Lock-up piston defective.
- Lock-up control valve stuck.
- Lock-up control solenoid valve "A" defective.
- Lock-up control solenoid valve "B" defective.
- PCM defective.

Lock-Up Clutch Not Smooth
- Throttle valve "B" stuck.
- Throttle control cable out of adjustment.
- Converter check valve stuck.
- Lock-up timing valve stuck.
- Lock-up shift valve stuck.
- Lock-up piston defective.
- Lock-up control valve stuck.
- Lock-up control solenoid valve "A" defective.
- Lock-up control solenoid valve "B" defective.
- PCM defective.

Lock-Up Clutch Does Not Engage
- Throttle valve "B" stuck.
- Throttle control cable out of adjustment.
- Converter check valve stuck.
- Lock-up timing valve stuck.
- Lock-up shift valve stuck.
- Lock-up piston defective.
- Lock-up control valve stuck.
- Lock-up control solenoid valve "A" defective.
- Lock-up control solenoid valve "B" defective.
- PCM defective.

No Engine Braking In "1"
- 1st-hold clutch defective.
- 1st-hold accumulator defective.

No Shift
- Modulator valve stuck.
- Shift control solenoid valve "A" defective.
- Shift control solenoid valve "B" defective.
- PCM defective.

No Shift, Stuck In 4th Gear
- Shift control solenoid valve "A" defective.
- Shift control solenoid valve "B" defective.
- PCM defective.

No 1-3 Shift From "D₃"
- 2-3 shift valve stuck.
- PCM defective.

No 1-4 Shift From "D₄"
- 2-3 shift valve stuck.
- 3-4 shift valve stuck.
- PCM defective.

Noise From Transaxle In All Gears
- ATF pump worn or binding.
- Case ball bearing worn or damaged.

Slips In All Gears
- ATF pump worn or binding.
- Pressure regulator stuck.
- ATF strainer plugged.

Slips In Reverse
- 4th clutch defective.
- 4th accumulator defective.
- Servo valve stuck.
- Feed pipe "O" ring broken.

Slips In 1st Gear
- 1st clutch defective.
- 1st accumulator defective.
- Feed pipe "O" ring broken.
- One-way clutch defective.

Slips In 2nd Gear
- 2nd clutch defective.
- 2-3 shift valve stuck.
- Clutch pressure control valve stuck.
- 2nd accumulator defective.
- Sealing rings/guide worn.

Slips In 3rd Gear
- 3rd clutch defective.
- 3-4 shift valve stuck.
- Clutch pressure control valve stuck.
- 3rd accumulator defective.
- Sealing rings/guide worn.

Slips In 4th Gear
- 4th clutch defective.
- Clutch pressure control valve stuck.
- 4th accumulator defective.
- Feed pipe "O" ring broken.

Shift Lever Operation Rough Or Binding
- Shift cable broken or out of adjustment.
- Shift cable problem.

Stall RPM High, All Clutch Pressures Okay
- Converter check valve stuck.

Vehicle Moves In All Gears Except "2"
- Shift cable broken or out of adjustment.
- 2nd gears worn or damaged.
- 2nd clutch defective.
- 2nd accumulator stuck.

Vehicle Moves In All Gears Except "R"
- Servo valve stuck.
- Shift cable broken or out of adjustment.
- Reverse gears worn or damaged.
- 4th clutch defective.

Vehicle Moves In "R" & "2" Only
- Shift cable broken or out of adjustment.
- One way clutch worn or damaged.
- 1st gears worn or damaged.
- 1st clutch defective.
- 1st accumulator defective.

Vehicle Moves In "N"
- 1st clutch defective.
- 2nd clutch defective.
- To much fluid.
- 3rd clutch defective.
- 4th clutch defective.
- Needle bearing worn or damaged.
- Thrust washer worn or damaged.
- Clutch clearance incorrect.

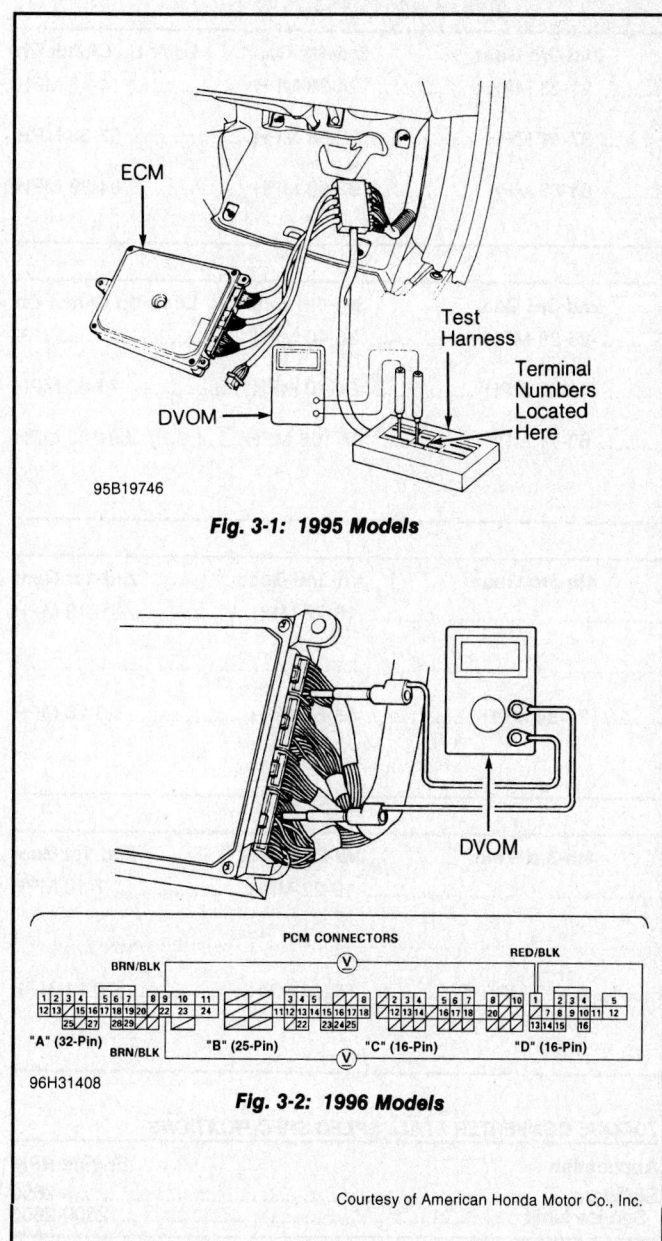

95B19746

Fig. 3-1: 1995 Models

DVOM

PCM CONNECTORS

BRN/BLK

RED/BLK

"A" (32-Pin)   BRN/BLK   "B" (25-Pin)   "C" (16-Pin)   "D" (16-Pin)

96H31408

Fig. 3-2: 1996 Models

Courtesy of American Honda Motor Co., Inc.

Fig. 3: Measuring TP Sensor Voltage

Vehicle Will Not Accelerate To Speeds Above 31 MPH
- Torque converter one-way clutch defective.

Vibration In All Gears
- Flexplate defective.

Will Not Shift Into "P" Position
- Shift cable broken or out of adjustment.
- Shift cable problem.

TESTING

ROAD TEST

NOTE: If shift lever cannot be moved from "P" position with brake pedal depressed and accelerator at idle position, check shift interlock system. See HONDA AOYA, MPJA & MPOA ELECTRONIC CONTROLS article.

1) Warm engine to normal operating temperature. Apply parking brake and block wheels. Start engine. Move shift lever to "D_4" position while depressing brake pedal. Depress accelerator pedal and release it suddenly. Engine should not stall.

2) Repeat step 1) with shift lever in "D_3" position. Ensure engine does not stall. Shut engine off. Manufacturer recommends monitoring of Throttle Position (TP) sensor voltage when performing road test to ensure proper throttle opening for verifying shift points and lock-up of torque converter.

NOTE: On 1996 models, the Engine Control Module (ECM) is referred to as Powertrain Control Module (PCM), components are the same, only the terminology has changed. Throughout this article ECM will be used.

3) Remove door sill molding on passenger's side. Pull carpet back for access to ECM, located on passenger's side, below carpet. See Fig. 3.

4) On 1995 models, remove ECM cover located above ECM. Ensure ignition is off. Install Test Harness (07LAJ-PT3010A) between ECM and ECM electrical connectors.

5) Install Digital Volt-Ohmmeter (DVOM) on test harness with positive lead at terminal D11 and negative lead at terminal D22 for monitoring of throttle position sensor voltage. Terminal numbers are on top of test harness. See Fig. 3. Ensure DVOM is set for measuring voltage.

6) On 1996 models, remove ECM cover located above ECM. Turn ECM over to gain access to connectors. Install Backprobe Test Set (07SAZ-001000A) or equivalent between ECM and DVOM leads. See Fig. 3.

7) Using DVOM, with positive lead at terminal D1 and negative lead at terminal A9 or A22. Ensure digital volt-ohmmeter is set for measuring voltage.

8) On all models, road test vehicle and check for abnormal noise and clutch slippage. Specified clutch is applied in designated gear. See CLUTCH APPLICATION table.

9) Ensure upshift and downshift points and lock-up of torque converter are correct in relation to throttle position sensor voltage or throttle opening and vehicle speed with shift lever in "D_4" position. See appropriate TRANSAXLE UPSHIFT SPECIFICATIONS and TRANSAXLE DOWNSHIFT SPECIFICATIONS tables.

10) With shift lever in "D_4" position, accelerate to about 35 MPH so transaxle is in 4th gear. Move shift lever to "2" position. Ensure engine braking occurs.

CAUTION: DO NOT shift from "D_4" to "2" at speeds over 63 MPH or transaxle may be damaged.

11) Place shift lever in "1" position. Accelerate from a stop at full throttle. Check for abnormal noise or clutch slippage. Upshifts and downshifts should not occur in this shift lever position.

12) Place shift lever in "2" position. Accelerate from a stop at full throttle. Check for abnormal noise or clutch slippage. Upshifts and downshifts should not occur in this shift lever position.

CLUTCH APPLICATION

Shift Lever Position	Elements In Use
"P" & "N"	No Clutches Are Applied
"R"	4th Clutch
"D_4"	
1st Gear	1st Clutch, One-Way Clutch
2nd Gear	[1] 2nd Clutch
3rd Gear	[1] 3rd Clutch
4th Gear	[1] 4th Clutch
"D_3"	
1st Gear	1st Clutch, One-Way Clutch
2nd Gear	[1] 2nd Clutch
3rd Gear	[1] 3rd Clutch
"2"	[1] 2nd Clutch
"1"	1st-Hold Clutch, 1st Clutch, One-Way Clutch

[1] – The 1st clutch engages but driving power is not transmitted, as one-way clutch slips.

TRANSAXLE UPSHIFT SPECIFICATIONS (AOYA – MPOA)

Application [1]	1st-2nd Gear	2nd-3rd Gear	3rd-4th Gear	Lock-Up Clutch On
Throttle Position Sensor Voltage .83 Volt	11-13 MPH	21-23 MPH	24-33 MPH	14-17 MPH
Throttle Position Sensor Voltage 2.18 Volts				
Accelerating From Stop	17-21 MPH	37-41 MPH	52-58 MPH	57-63 MPH
Full Throttle				
Accelerating From Stop	31-35 MPH	64-68 MPH	92-98 MPH	84-89 MPH

[1] – Shift lever in "D₄" position.

TRANSAXLE UPSHIFT SPECIFICATIONS (MPJA)

Application [1]	1st-2nd Gear	2nd-3rd Gear	3rd-4th Gear	Lock-Up Clutch On
Throttle Position Sensor Voltage .83 Volt	12-15 MPH	25-29 MPH	36-40 MPH	[2]
Throttle Position Sensor Voltage 2.18 Volts				
Accelerating From Stop	19-23 MPH	41-46 MPH	64-70 MPH	76-82 MPH
Full Throttle				
Accelerating From Stop	34-39 MPH	63-71 MPH	97-108 MPH	89-100 MPH

[1] – Shift lever in "D₄" position.
[2] – Specification is not available from manufacturer.

TRANSAXLE DOWNSHIFT SPECIFICATIONS (AOYA – MPOA)

Application [1]	Lock-Up Clutch Off	4th-3rd Gear	3rd-2nd Gear	2nd-1st Gear
Throttle Position Sensor Voltage .83 Volt	12-16 MPH	[2]	18-22 MPH	6-10 MPH
Throttle Position Sensor Voltage 2.18 Volts				
Vehicle Slowing By Grade Or Load	46-52 MPH	[2]	[2]	[2]
Full Throttle				
Vehicle Slowing By Grade Or Load	79-84 MPH	78-84 MPH	55-60 MPH	23-28 MPH

[1] – Shift lever in "D₄" position.
[2] – Specification is not available from manufacturer.

TRANSAXLE DOWNSHIFT SPECIFICATIONS (MPJA)

Application [1]	Lock-Up Clutch Off	4th-3rd Gear	3rd-2nd Gear	2nd-1st Gear
Throttle Position Sensor Voltage .83 Volt	12-16 MPH	[2]	19-22 MPH	7-10 MPH
Throttle Position Sensor Voltage 2.18 Volts				
Vehicle Slowing By Grade Or Load	49-55 MPH	[2]	[2]	[2]
Full Throttle				
Vehicle Slowing By Grade Or Load	85-96 MPH	83-93 MPH	57-64 MPH	26-31 MPH

[1] – Shift lever in "D₄" position.
[2] – Specification is not available from manufacturer.

13) Place shift lever in "R" position. Accelerate from a stop at full throttle. Check for abnormal noise or clutch slippage.

14) Park vehicle on a slope. Apply parking brake. Place shift lever in "P" position. Release parking brake. Ensure vehicle does not move. If vehicle moves, check for defective shift cable or parking components.

15) Ensure ignition is off. Remove test harness or backprobe set and reinstall electrical connectors, ECM cover, carpet and door sill molding.

TORQUE CONVERTER STALL SPEED TEST

CAUTION: DO NOT perform torque converter stall speed test for more than 10 seconds or transaxle may be damaged. DO NOT move shift lever while increasing engine speed.

1) Apply parking brake. Block front wheels. Connect tachometer and start engine. Ensure A/C is off. Warm engine to normal operating temperature. Place shift lever in "2" position.

2) Fully depress brake pedal. Fully depress accelerator for 6-8 seconds and note engine speed. This is the torque converter stall speed.

3) Allow transaxle to cool for 2 minutes. Repeat test procedure with shift lever in "D₄", "1" and "R" positions.

4) Ensure torque converter stall speed is within specification. Torque converter stall speed should be the same in "D₄", "2", "1" and "R" positions. See TORQUE CONVERTER STALL SPEED SPECIFICATIONS table. If torque converter stall speed is not within specification, see TORQUE CONVERTER STALL SPEED TROUBLE SHOOTING table for possible causes.

TORQUE CONVERTER STALL SPEED SPECIFICATIONS

Application	Engine RPM
Standard	2650
Service Limit	2500-2800

TORQUE CONVERTER STALL SPEED TROUBLE SHOOTING

Torque Converter Stall Speed Test Results	Probable Cause
Stall Speed RPM High In "D₄", "2", "1" & "R"	Low Fluid Level, Low Oil Pump Output, Clogged Fluid Strainer, Pressure Regulator Valve Stuck Closed, Slipping Clutch
Stall Speed RPM High In "R"	Slipping 4th Clutch
Stall Speed RPM High In "2" & "D₄"	Slipping 2nd Clutch
Stall Speed RPM High In "1"	Slipping 1st Clutch, Defective One-Way Clutch
Stall Speed RPM Low In "D₄", "2", "1" & "R"	Engine Output Low, Torque Converter One-Way Clutch Slipping

HYDRAULIC PRESSURE TEST

Pressure Test Preparation – Ensure transaxle fluid level is correct. Warm engine to normal operating temperature. Apply parking brake, and block rear wheels. Raise and support vehicle so front wheels can rotate.

HYDRAULIC PRESSURE TEST SPECIFICATIONS

Application	Shift Lever Position	Pressure psi (kPa)
Line Pressure		
Engine Speed At 2000 RPM	"P" Or "N"	113-130 (780-880)
Clutch Pressure		
1st Clutch		
Engine Speed At 2000 RPM	"1" Or "D₄"	113-130 (780-880)
1st-Hold Clutch		
Engine Speed At 2000 RPM	"1"	113-130 (780-880)
2nd Clutch		
Engine Speed At 2000 RPM	"2"	113-130 (780-880)
Throttle Control Lever Fully Closed [1]	"D₄"	64-71 (440-490)
Throttle Control Lever Open More Than 3/16 [2]	"D₄"	113-130 (780-880)
3rd Clutch		
Throttle Control Lever Fully Closed [1]	"D₄"	67-75 (460-520)
Throttle Control Lever Open More Than 3/16 [2]	"D₄"	113-130 (780-880)
4th Clutch		
Engine Speed At 2000 RPM	"R"	113-130 (780-880)
Throttle Control Lever Fully Closed [1]		
1995	"D₄"	68-75 (470-520)
1996	"D₄"	67-75 (460-520)
Throttle Control Lever Open More Than 3/16 [2]	"D₄"	113-130 (780-880)
Clutch Low Pressure		
Throttle Control Lever Fully Closed [1]		
2nd Or 3rd Clutch	"D₄"	64-71 (440-490)
4th Clutch		
1995	"D₄"	68-75 (470-520)
1996	"D₄"	67-75 (460-520)
Clutch High Pressure		
Throttle Control Lever Lifted Upward		
1/2 Distance Of Throttle Control Lever Travel		
2nd, 3rd Or 4th Clutch	"D₄"	113-130 (780-880)
Throttle "B" Pressure		
Throttle Control Lever Fully Closed [3]	"D₃" Or "D₄"	0 (0)
Throttle Control Lever Fully Open [3]	"D₃" Or "D₄"	113-130 (780-880)

[1] – Check pressure with engine speed at 2000 RPM. Fully closed position is with throttle control lever on transaxle in released position and not being pulled upward by T.V. cable.

[2] – Check pressure with engine speed at 2000 RPM. Open position is with transaxle T.V. lever being pulled upward 3/16 the distance of throttle control lever travel on 1996 models and 1/4 the distance of throttle control lever travel on 1995 models.

[3] – Check pressure with engine speed at 1000 RPM.

Line Pressure Test – 1) With engine off, remove pressure tap plug from line pressure tap on transaxle. *See Fig. 4.* Attach pressure gauge to line pressure tap using NEW washer. Tighten hose fitting to 13 ft. lbs. (18 N.m).

2) With shift lever in "P" position, start and operate engine at 2000 RPM. Note line pressure. Place shift lever in "N" position and note line pressure with engine at 2000 RPM.

3) Ensure line pressure is within specification. See appropriate HYDRAULIC PRESSURE TEST SPECIFICATIONS table. If line pressure is not within specification, see HYDRAULIC PRESSURE TEST TROUBLE SHOOTING table. Shut engine off.

4) Remove pressure gauge set. Using NEW seal washer, install and tighten pressure tap plug to specification. See TORQUE SPECIFICATIONS.

NOTE: Clutch pressure should be checked at each clutch pressure tap on transaxle. See Fig. 4.

Clutch Pressure Test – 1) With engine off, remove pressure tap plug from appropriate clutch pressure tap on transaxle. *See Fig. 4.* Attach pressure gauge to appropriate pressure tap using NEW washer. Tighten hose fitting to 13 ft. lbs. (18 N.m).

NOTE: Clutch pressure on some applications may vary with position of Throttle Valve (T.V.) lever on the transaxle. The T.V. cable must be disconnected for some tests. Ensure shift lever is in proper position when checking clutch pressures.

2) Raise and support vehicle allowing wheels to rotate freely. Start and operate engine at 2000 RPM. Note clutch pressure reading with shift lever in proper position. See appropriate HYDRAULIC PRESSURE TEST SPECIFICATIONS table.

3) Ensure clutch pressure is within specification. If clutch pressure is not within specification, see HYDRAULIC PRESSURE TEST TROUBLE SHOOTING table. Shut engine off.

4) Remove pressure gauge set. Using NEW seal washer, install and tighten pressure tap plug to specification. See TORQUE SPECIFICATIONS.

Low/High Pressure Test – 1) The low/high pressure is tested at 2nd, 3rd and 4th clutch pressure taps on transaxle. *See Fig. 4.* Disconnect Throttle Valve (T.V.) cable from transaxle T.V. lever.

NOTE: When disconnecting T.V. cable, unhook cable from transaxle T.V. lever. DO NOT loosen lock nuts used for cable adjustment.

2) With engine off, remove pressure tap plug from appropriate clutch pressure tap on transaxle. Attach pressure gauge to appropriate pressure tap using NEW washer. Tighten hose fitting to 13 ft. lbs. (18 N.m).

3) Start engine and allow to idle long enough to maintain normal operating temperature. Move shift lever to "D₄" position. Slowly increase engine speed until pressure is indicated on pressure gauge. Release throttle, allowing engine to idle, and note low pressure reading.

4) With engine idling, lift transaxle T.V. lever upward about half the distance of lever travel. Increase engine speed and note highest pressure reading.

5) Repeat procedure on remaining clutches. Ensure low/high pressure is within specification. See appropriate HYDRAULIC PRESSURE TEST SPECIFICATIONS table. If low/high pressure is not within specification, see HYDRAULIC PRESSURE TEST TROUBLE SHOOTING table.

6) Shut engine off. Remove pressure gauge set. Using NEW seal washer, install and tighten pressure tap plug to specification. See TORQUE SPECIFICATIONS. Reconnect T.V. cable.

Throttle Valve "B" Pressure Test – 1) Disconnect Throttle Valve (T.V.) cable from transaxle T.V. lever. With engine off, remove pressure tap plug from throttle valve "B" pressure tap. See Fig. 4.

NOTE: When disconnecting T.V. cable, unhook cable from transaxle T.V. lever. DO NOT loosen lock nuts used for cable adjustment.

2) Attach pressure gauge to throttle valve "B" pressure tap using NEW washer. Tighten hose fitting to 13 ft. lbs. (18 N.m).

3) Start engine and operate at 1000 RPM with shift lever in "D₄" position. No pressure should exist with transaxle T.V. lever closed (released position). Lift transaxle T.V. lever to fully open position. Note throttle valve "B" pressure reading.

4) Ensure throttle valve "B" pressure is within specification. See appropriate HYDRAULIC PRESSURE TEST SPECIFICATIONS table. If pressure is not within specification, see HYDRAULIC PRESSURE TEST TROUBLE SHOOTING table. Shut engine off.

5) Remove pressure gauge. Using NEW seal washer, install and tighten pressure tap plug to specification. See TORQUE SPECIFICATIONS. Reconnect T.V. cable.

HYDRAULIC PRESSURE TEST TROUBLE SHOOTING

Application	Probable Cause
Line Pressure	
Low Or No Pressure	Defective Torque Converter, Defective Torque Converter Check Valve, Defective Oil Pump Pressure Regulator, Defective Oil Pump
Clutch Pressure	
Low Or No 1st Clutch Pressure	Defective 1st Clutch
Low Or No 1st-Hold Clutch Pressure	Defective 1st-Hold Clutch
Low Or No 2nd Clutch Pressure	Defective 2nd Clutch
Low Or No 3rd Clutch Pressure	Defective 3rd Clutch
Low Or No 4th Clutch Pressure	Defective 4th Clutch, Defective Servo Valve On 4th Clutch
Low/High Pressure	
Low Or No 2nd Clutch Pressure	Defective 2nd Clutch
Low Or No 3rd Clutch Pressure	Defective 3rd Clutch
Low Or No 4th Clutch Pressure	Defective 4th Clutch
Throttle Valve "B" Pressure	
Low Or No Pressure	Defective Throttle Valve "B"

ON-VEHICLE SERVICE

AXLE SHAFTS

See AXLE SHAFTS article in AXLE SHAFTS & TRANSFER CASES.

OIL COOLER FLUSHING

NOTE: Oil cooler flushing should be preformed before reinstalling transaxle.

1) Attach Oil Cooler Flusher (J38405-A) to oil cooler lines. See Fig. 5. Fill oil cooler flusher tank 2/3 full with Flushing Fluid (J35944-20). DO NOT use any other flushing fluid.

2) Ensure water and air valves on oil cooler flusher are off. Apply 80-120 psi (550-829 kPa) air pressure to oil cooler flusher. Turn oil cooler flusher water valve on so water will flow through oil cooler for 10 seconds. Replace oil cooler if water will not flow through oil cooler. Shut water valve off.

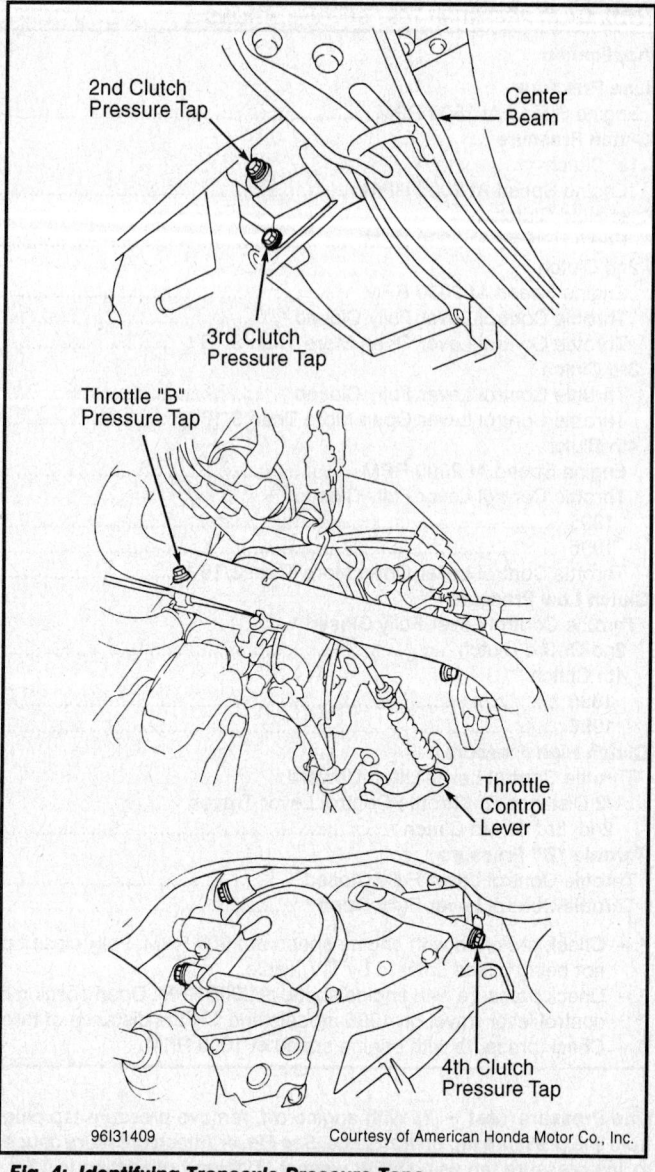

Fig. 4: Identifying Transaxle Pressure Taps

96I31409   Courtesy of American Honda Motor Co., Inc.

3) Depress and hold mixing trigger on oil cooler flusher downward. Turn water valve on and flush oil cooler for 2 minutes. Turn air valve on for 5 seconds every 15-20 seconds to create a surging action.

4) Turn water valve off. Release mixing trigger. Disconnect oil cooler flusher and reverse hoses so oil cooler can be flushed in the opposite direction.

5) Repeat steps 2) and 3). Turn water valve off. Release mixing trigger. Turn water valve on. Rinse oil cooler for at least one minute. Once oil cooler is flushed in both directions, turn water off. Turn air valve on for 2 minutes or until no moisture is visible from drain hose.

CAUTION: Ensure no moisture exists in oil cooler, as it can damage transaxle.

6) Turn air off. Disconnect oil cooler flusher. Reconnect inlet line on oil cooler. Once transaxle is installed, attach drain hose on return line and place in oil container. Ensure transaxle is in "P" position. Fill transaxle with ATF.

7) Start engine and operate for approximately 30 seconds or until one quart (.9L) of ATF is discharged from return line. Shut engine off. Remove drain hose. Reinstall return line. Fill transaxle to proper level.

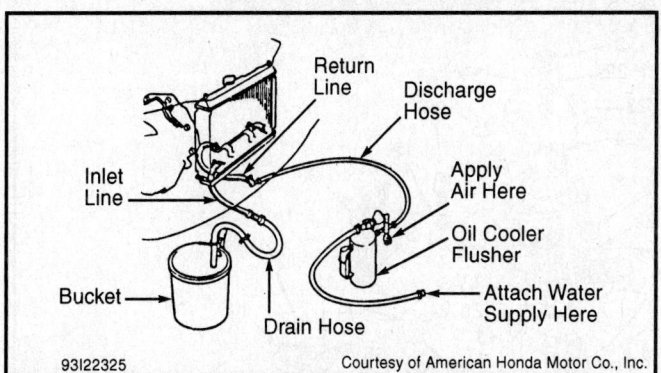

Fig. 5: Installing Oil Cooler Flusher

REMOVAL & INSTALLATION

ELECTRICAL COMPONENTS

See HONDA AOYA, MPJA & MPOA ELECTRONIC CONTROLS article.

TRANSAXLE

See appropriate AUTOMATIC TRANSMISSION REMOVAL article in TRANSMISSION SERVICING.

TORQUE CONVERTER

Torque converter consists of pump, turbine and stator assembled as a unit. Torque converter cannot be serviced and must be replaced if defective.

NOTE: For torque converter stall speed test, see TORQUE CONVERTER STALL SPEED TEST under TESTING.

TRANSAXLE DISASSEMBLY

VALVE BODIES & INTERNAL COMPONENTS

1) Remove bolts, right side cover and gasket. *See Fig. 6.* Install Mainshaft Holder (07GAB-PF50100 or 07GAB-PF50101) on mainshaft to secure mainshaft from rotating. *See Fig. 7.*

CAUTION: DO NOT use Impact wrench to remove lock nuts from countershaft, mainshaft and secondary shaft.

2) Engage parking pawl with parking gear. Using hammer and chisel, cut lock tabs on countershaft, mainshaft and secondary shaft lock nuts. Remove lock nuts and spring washers. *See Fig. 6.*

NOTE: Mainshaft lock nut has left-hand thread.

3) Remove mainshaft holder once all lock nuts are removed. Using puller, remove parking gear from countershaft. Using puller, remove idler gears from mainshaft and secondary shaft.
4) Remove countershaft idler gear, needle bearing, thrust needle bearing and thrust washer from countershaft. Remove parking pawl, parking pawl spring, parking pawl shaft and parking pawl stop.
5) Remove throttle control lever and spring from throttle control shaft. Remove ATF cooler pipe-to-hanger bolt. Remove transaxle housing bolts.
6) Remove bolts from reverse idler gear shaft holder. Screw bolt into center of shaft on reverse idler gear shaft holder. *See Fig. 8.* Pull reverse idler gear shaft holder with shaft and needle bearing from transaxle housing.

NOTE: Transaxle housing will not separate from torque converter housing if reverse idler gear shaft holder is not removed and reverse idler gear repositioned.

7) Move reverse idler gear outward to disengage from countershaft reverse gear. *See Fig. 9.* Align spring pin with groove in transaxle housing by rotating control shaft. Using Puller (07HAC-PK4010A), remove transaxle housing. *See Fig. 10.*
8) Remove reverse idler gear from transaxle housing. Remove countershaft 2nd gear, countershaft reverse gear, thrust washer, thrust needle bearing and secondary shaft 2nd gear together from countershaft and secondary shaft. *See Fig. 11.*
9) Remove bolt, bolt lock, shift fork, reverse selector hub and reverse selector. Remove needle bearings, thrust needle bearing and splined washer from secondary shaft.
10) Remove secondary shaft, mainshaft and countershaft assemblies. Remove differential assembly from torque converter housing. Remove bolt and servo detent base. *See Fig. 12.* Remove bolts and fluid strainer.

CAUTION: To prevent bolt damage, ensure accumulator cover is held downward when removing bolts. Use care when removing bolts and accumulator cover, as accumulator cover is under spring tension.

11) Remove oil feedpipes from servo body and main valve body. Remove bolts and accumulator cover. *See Fig. 12.* Remove bolts, servo body and servo separator plate.
12) Remove secondary valve body and secondary separator plate. Use care not to lose check balls in secondary valve body. Remove bolts, throttle valve body and throttle separator plate.
13) Remove bolt and regulator valve body. Remove stop shaft, "O" ring and stator shaft. Disconnect detent spring from detent arm. Remove control shaft from torque converter housing. Remove detent arm shaft and detent arm from main valve body.
14) Remove bolts and main valve body. Use care not to lose check balls in main valve body. Remove bolts and 1st-2nd accumulator body.
15) Remove oil pump driven gear shaft, oil pump driven gear and oil pump drive gear. Remove main separator plate and dowel pins. Remove lock-up control solenoid valve assembly and shift control solenoid valve assembly (if necessary).

COMPONENT DISASSEMBLY & REASSEMBLY

MAIN VALVE BODY

CAUTION: When disassembling main valve body, place main valve body components in order, and mark spring locations for reassembly reference. DO NOT use force to remove components. DO NOT use magnet to remove check balls, as check balls may become magnetized. Note direction of valve cap installation before removing from main valve body.

Disassembly – Disassemble main valve body. *See Fig. 13.* Use care when removing valve caps or spring seats, as they are under spring pressure.
Cleaning & Inspection – 1) Clean components with solvent and dry with compressed air. Replace main valve body if any parts are worn or damaged.
2) Ensure all valves slide freely in their bores. If valves do not slide freely, polish burrs or rough areas using No. 600 sandpaper soaked for 30 minutes in ATF. Thoroughly clean main valve body and components if polishing was needed.
3) Ensure spring free length is within specification. See SPRING SPECIFICATIONS table. Replace springs if not within specification.

NOTE: Oil pump clearance must be checked in main valve body. See OIL PUMP under COMPONENT DISASSEMBLY & REASSEMBLY.

Reassembly – Coat all components and bores with ATF. To reassemble, reverse disassembly procedure. Install NEW filter. Ensure all components are installed in correct location. *See Fig. 13.*

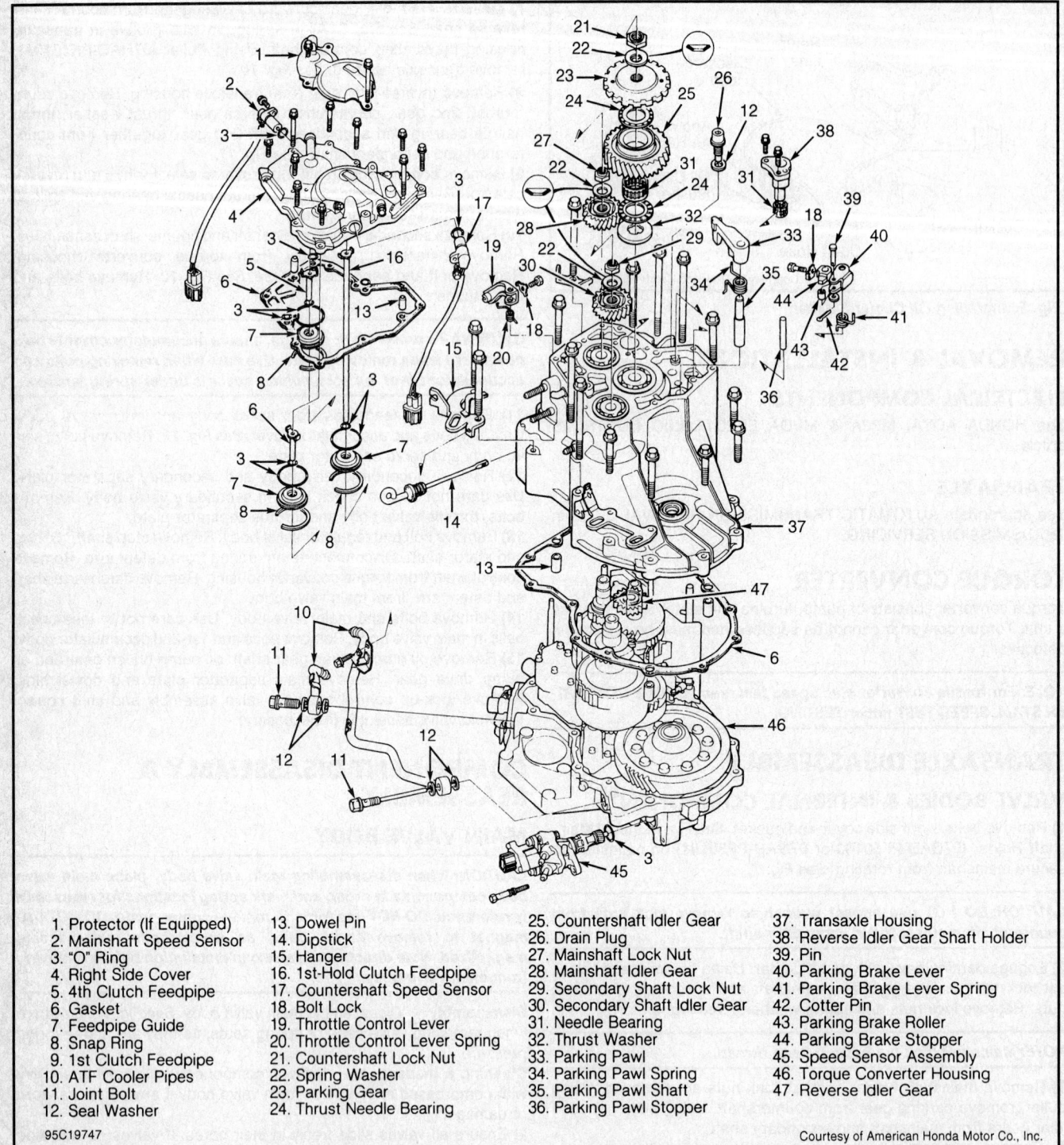

1. Protector (If Equipped)	13. Dowel Pin	25. Countershaft Idler Gear	37. Transaxle Housing
2. Mainshaft Speed Sensor	14. Dipstick	26. Drain Plug	38. Reverse Idler Gear Shaft Holder
3. "O" Ring	15. Hanger	27. Mainshaft Lock Nut	39. Pin
4. Right Side Cover	16. 1st-Hold Clutch Feedpipe	28. Mainshaft Idler Gear	40. Parking Brake Lever
5. 4th Clutch Feedpipe	17. Countershaft Speed Sensor	29. Secondary Shaft Lock Nut	41. Parking Brake Lever Spring
6. Gasket	18. Bolt Lock	30. Secondary Shaft Idler Gear	42. Cotter Pin
7. Feedpipe Guide	19. Throttle Control Lever	31. Needle Bearing	43. Parking Brake Roller
8. Snap Ring	20. Throttle Control Lever Spring	32. Thrust Washer	44. Parking Brake Stopper
9. 1st Clutch Feedpipe	21. Countershaft Lock Nut	33. Parking Pawl	45. Speed Sensor Assembly
10. ATF Cooler Pipes	22. Spring Washer	34. Parking Pawl Spring	46. Torque Converter Housing
11. Joint Bolt	23. Parking Gear	35. Parking Pawl Shaft	47. Reverse Idler Gear
12. Seal Washer	24. Thrust Needle Bearing	36. Parking Pawl Stopper	

95C19747

Courtesy of American Honda Motor Co., Inc.

Fig. 6: Exploded View Of Right Side Cover & Components

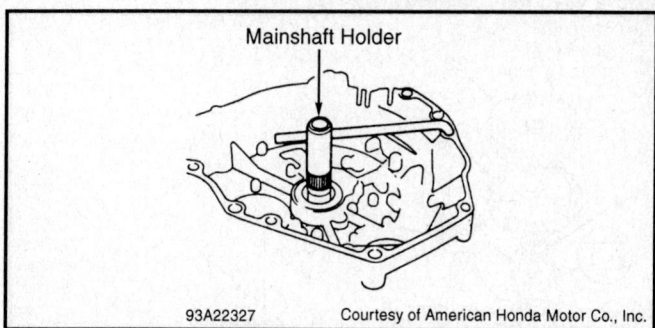

Fig. 7: Installing Mainshaft Holder

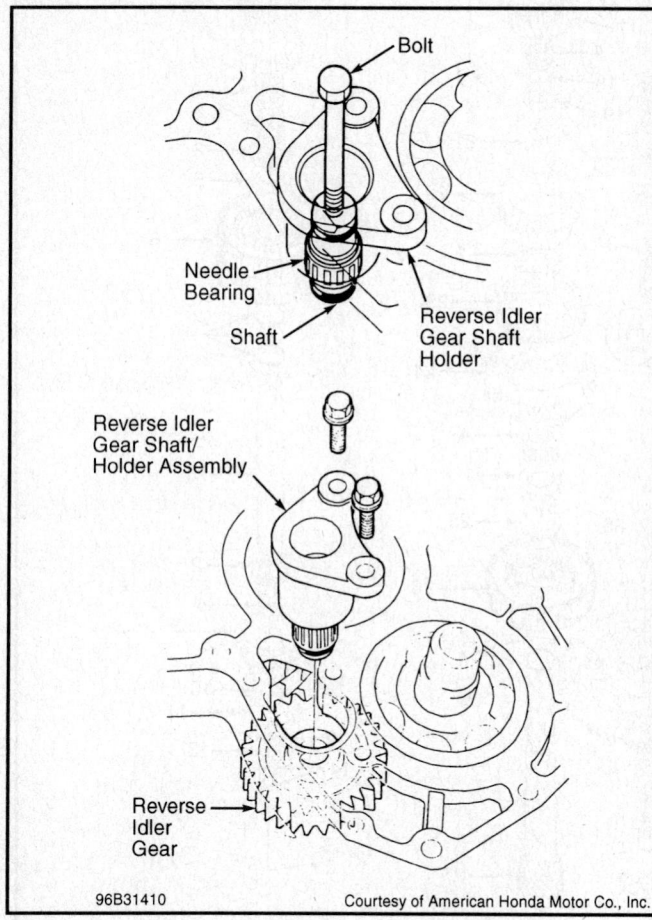

Fig. 8: Removing Idler Gear Shaft Holder & Components

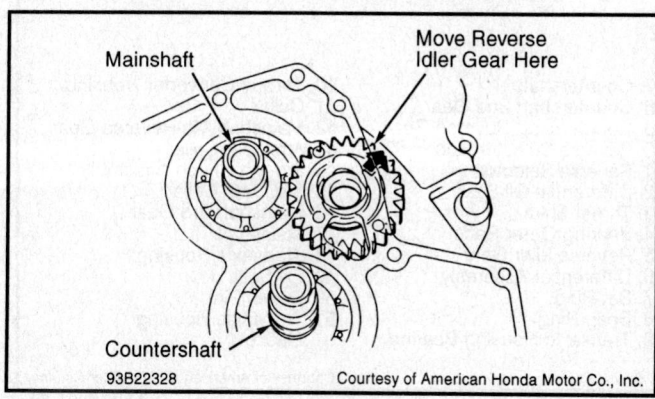

Fig. 9: Positioning Reverse Idler Gear

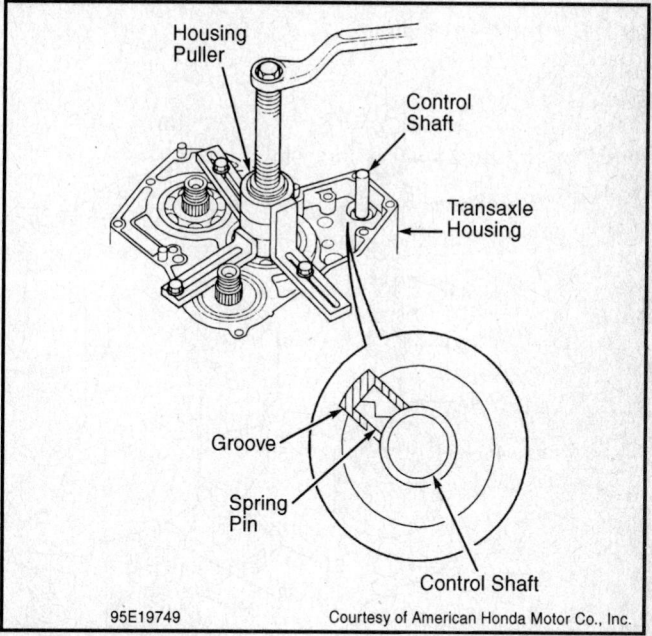

Fig. 10: Aligning Spring Pin & Removing Transaxle Housing

SPRING SPECIFICATIONS

Application	Free Length In. (mm)
Main Valve Body	
Clutch Pressure Control Valve Spring	1.299 (33.00)
Cooler Relief Valve Spring	1.843 (46.81)
Lock-Up Control Valve Spring	¹
Lock-Up Shift Valve Spring	2.902 (73.70)
Main Orifice Control Valve Spring	1.933 (49.10)
Modulator Valve Spring	1.299 (33.00)
1-2 Shift Valve Spring	1.591 (40.40)
2-3 Shift Valve Spring	2.244 (57.00)
Regulator Valve Body	
Lock-Up Timing Valve Spring	2.012 (51.10)
Regulator Valve Spring "A"	
AOYA – MPOA	3.457 (87.80)
MPJA	3.488 (88.60)
Regulator Valve Spring "B"	1.732 (44.00)
Stator Reaction Spring	1.193 (30.30)
Torque Converter Check Valve Spring	1.504 (38.20)
Secondary Valve Body	
Servo Control Valve Spring	2.071 (52.60)
Orifice Control Valve Spring	2.067 (52.50)
2nd Orifice Control Valve Spring	2.614 (66.40)
3rd Kickdown Valve Spring	1.902 (48.30)
3-4 Shift Valve Spring	2.244 (57.00)
4th Exhaust Valve Spring	1.921 (48.80)
Servo Body	
1st-Hold Accumulator Spring	2.547 (64.70)
3rd Accumulator Spring	3.921 (99.60)
4th Accumulator Spring	3.547 (90.10)
Throttle Valve Body	
Relief Valve Spring	1.539 (39.10)
Throttle Valve "B" Spring	²
Throttle Valve "B" Adjusting Spring	1.181 (30.00)
1st-2nd Accumulator Body	
1st Accumulator Spring "A"	4.315 (109.60)
1st Accumulator Spring "B"	2.776 (70.50)
2nd Accumulator Spring	3.583 (91.00)

¹ – Spring free length may be 1.496" (38.00 mm), 1.516" (38.50 mm) or 1.535" (39.00 mm)

² – Spring free length may be 1.634" (41.50 mm) or 1.638" (41.60 mm).

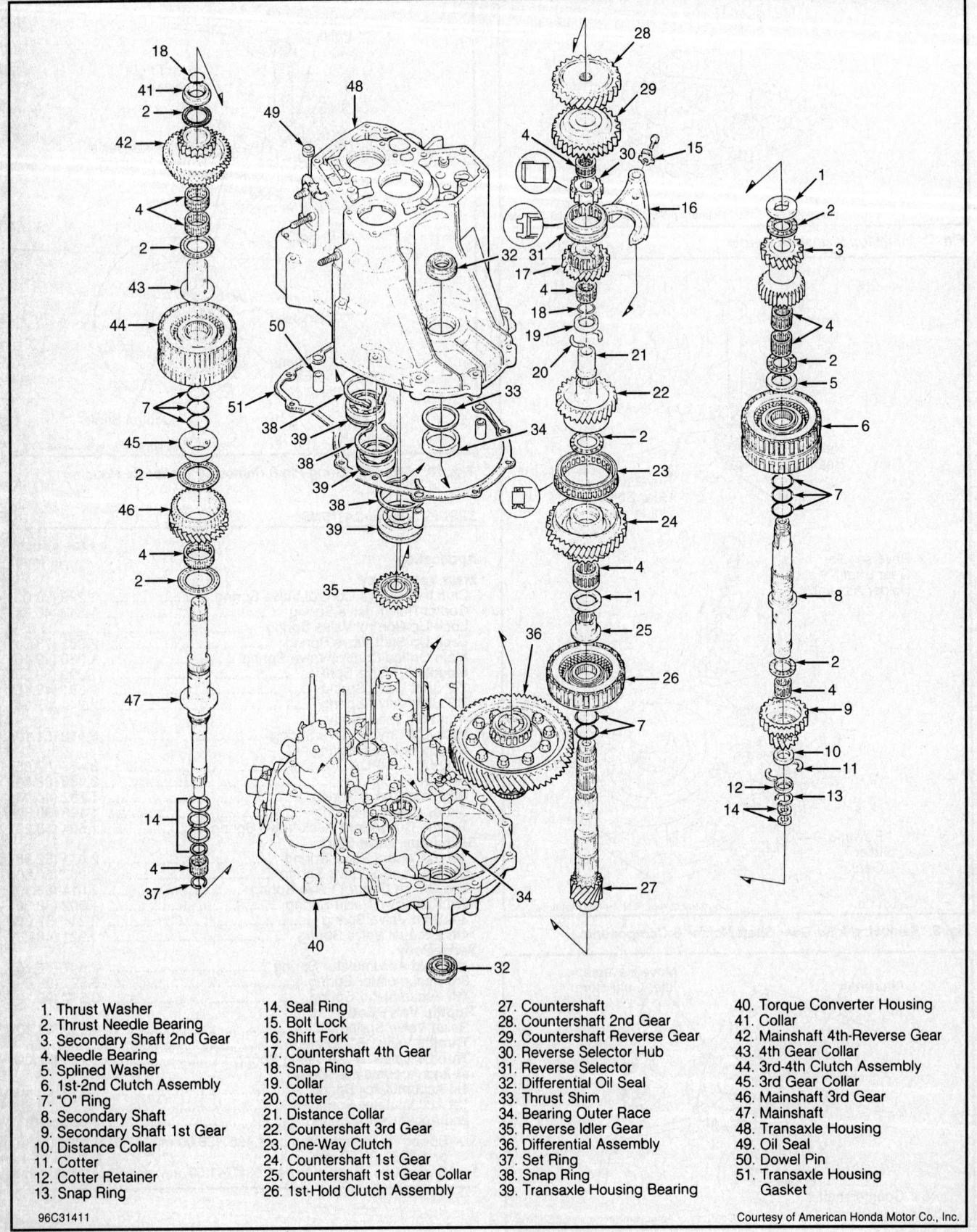

1. Thrust Washer
2. Thrust Needle Bearing
3. Secondary Shaft 2nd Gear
4. Needle Bearing
5. Splined Washer
6. 1st-2nd Clutch Assembly
7. "O" Ring
8. Secondary Shaft
9. Secondary Shaft 1st Gear
10. Distance Collar
11. Cotter
12. Cotter Retainer
13. Snap Ring
14. Seal Ring
15. Bolt Lock
16. Shift Fork
17. Countershaft 4th Gear
18. Snap Ring
19. Collar
20. Cotter
21. Distance Collar
22. Countershaft 3rd Gear
23. One-Way Clutch
24. Countershaft 1st Gear
25. Countershaft 1st Gear Collar
26. 1st-Hold Clutch Assembly
27. Countershaft
28. Countershaft 2nd Gear
29. Countershaft Reverse Gear
30. Reverse Selector Hub
31. Reverse Selector
32. Differential Oil Seal
33. Thrust Shim
34. Bearing Outer Race
35. Reverse Idler Gear
36. Differential Assembly
37. Set Ring
38. Snap Ring
39. Transaxle Housing Bearing
40. Torque Converter Housing
41. Collar
42. Mainshaft 4th-Reverse Gear
43. 4th Gear Collar
44. 3rd-4th Clutch Assembly
45. 3rd Gear Collar
46. Mainshaft 3rd Gear
47. Mainshaft
48. Transaxle Housing
49. Oil Seal
50. Dowel Pin
51. Transaxle Housing
   Gasket

96C31411

Courtesy of American Honda Motor Co., Inc.

Fig. 11: Exploded View Of Transaxle Housing & Components

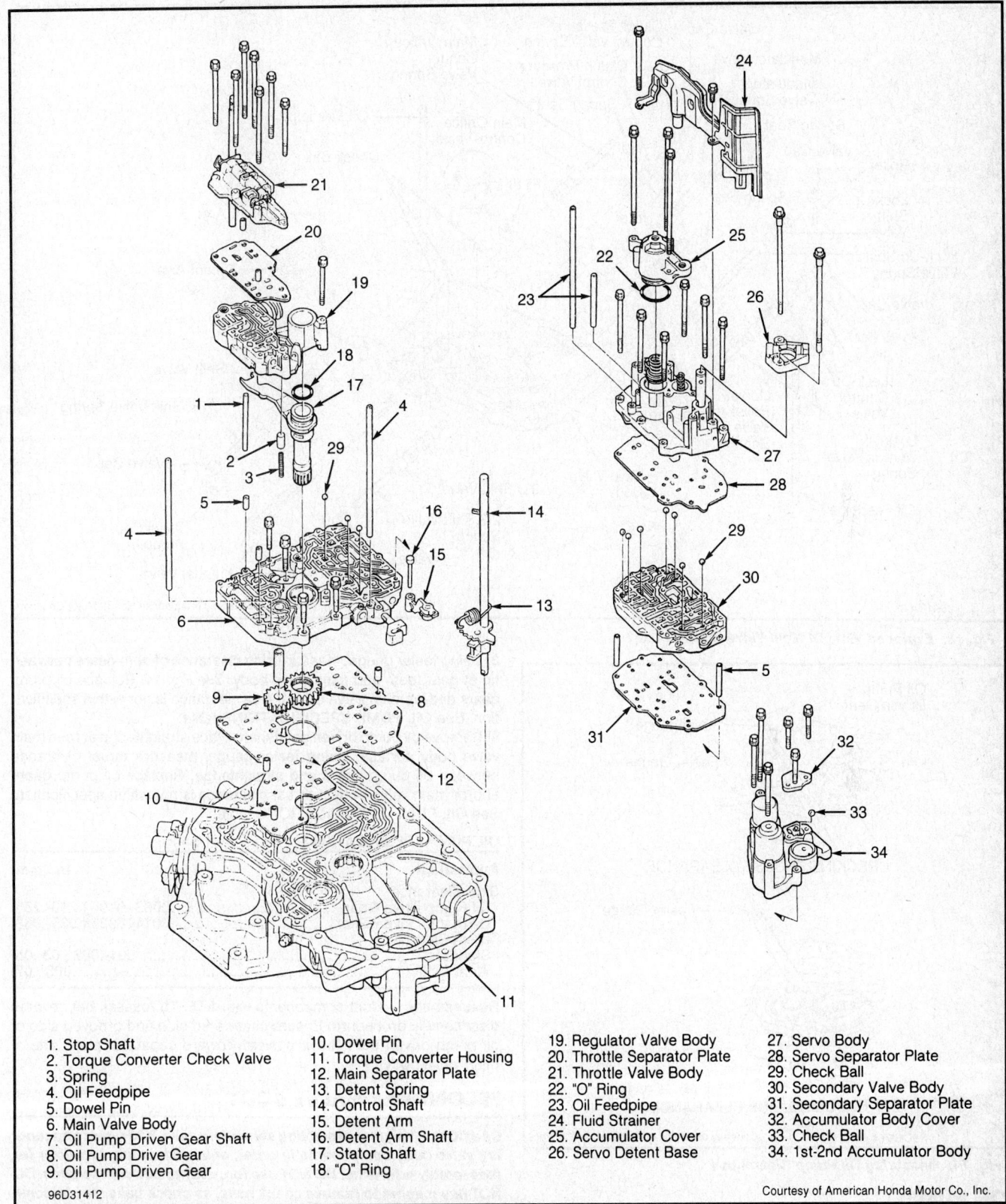

1. Stop Shaft
2. Torque Converter Check Valve
3. Spring
4. Oil Feedpipe
5. Dowel Pin
6. Main Valve Body
7. Oil Pump Driven Gear Shaft
8. Oil Pump Drive Gear
9. Oil Pump Driven Gear
10. Dowel Pin
11. Torque Converter Housing
12. Main Separator Plate
13. Detent Spring
14. Control Shaft
15. Detent Arm
16. Detent Arm Shaft
17. Stator Shaft
18. "O" Ring
19. Regulator Valve Body
20. Throttle Separator Plate
21. Throttle Valve Body
22. "O" Ring
23. Oil Feedpipe
24. Fluid Strainer
25. Accumulator Cover
26. Servo Detent Base
27. Servo Body
28. Servo Separator Plate
29. Check Ball
30. Secondary Valve Body
31. Secondary Separator Plate
32. Accumulator Body Cover
33. Check Ball
34. 1st-2nd Accumulator Body

96D31412

Courtesy of American Honda Motor Co., Inc.

Fig. 12: Exploded View Of Torque Converter Housing & Components

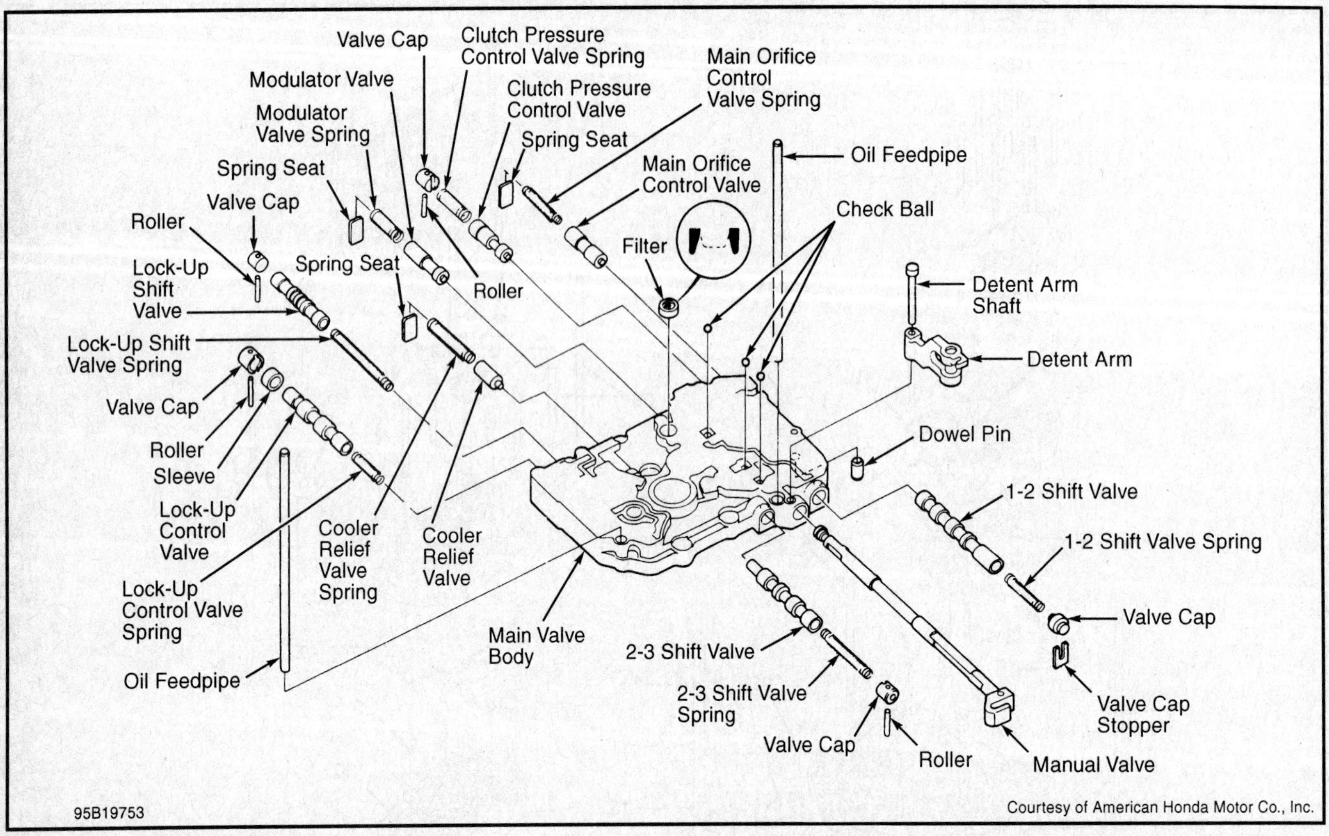

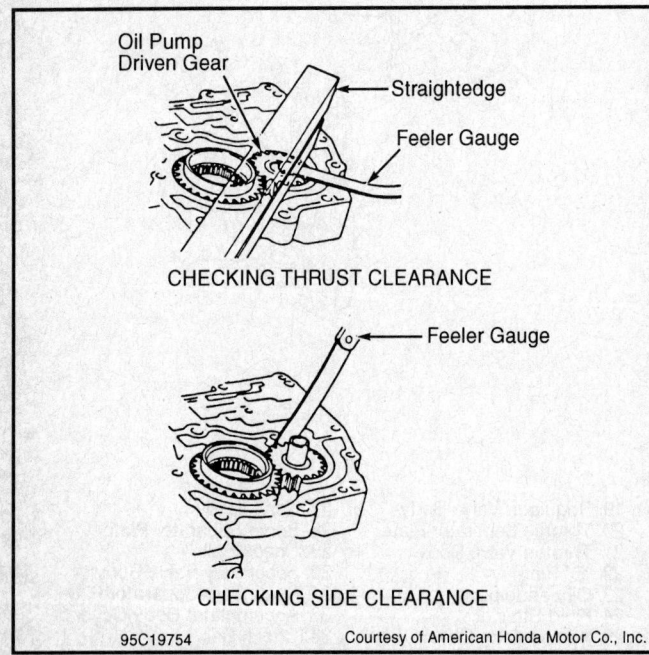

Courtesy of American Honda Motor Co., Inc.

95B19753

Fig. 13: Exploded View Of Main Valve Body

Fig. 14: Measuring Oil Pump Clearances

95C19754   Courtesy of American Honda Motor Co., Inc.

OIL PUMP

Disassembly – Note direction of oil pump gear installation in main valve body. Remove oil pump driven gear shaft and oil pump gears from main valve body (if not previously removed).

Cleaning & Inspection – 1) Clean components with solvent and dry with compressed air. Inspect components and replace if damaged.

2) Install oil pump gears and oil pump driven gear shaft in main valve body. Ensure chamfered and grooved side of oil pump driven gear is facing upward (toward separator plate side of main valve body).

3) Using feeler gauge, measure side clearance of both gears between tip of gear teeth and main valve body. See Fig. 14. Replace oil pump gears and/or main valve body if side clearance is not within specification. See OIL PUMP SPECIFICATIONS table.

4) Remove oil pump driven gear shaft. Place straightedge across main valve body surface. Using feeler gauge, measure thrust clearance between oil pump gears and straightedge. Replace oil pump gears and/or main valve body if thrust clearance is not within specification. See OIL PUMP SPECIFICATIONS table.

OIL PUMP SPECIFICATIONS

Application	In. (mm)
Side Clearance	
Oil Pump Drive Gear	.0083-.0104 (.210-.265)
Oil Pump Driven Gear	.0014-.0025 (.035-.063)
Thrust Clearance	
Standard	.001-.002 (.03-.05)
Wear Limit	.003 (.07)

Reassembly – Coat components with ATF. To reassemble, reverse disassembly procedure. Ensure chamfered side and grooved side of oil pump driven gear faces upward (toward separator plate side of main valve body).

SECONDARY VALVE BODY

CAUTION: When disassembling secondary valve body, place secondary valve body components in order, and mark spring locations for reassembly reference. DO NOT use force to remove components. DO NOT use magnet to remove check balls, as check balls may become magnetized. Note direction of valve cap installation before removing from secondary valve body.

Disassembly – Disassemble secondary valve body. See Fig. 15. Use care when removing valve caps or spring seats, as they are under spring pressure.

Cleaning & Inspection – 1) Clean components with solvent and dry with compressed air. Replace secondary valve body if any parts are worn or damaged.

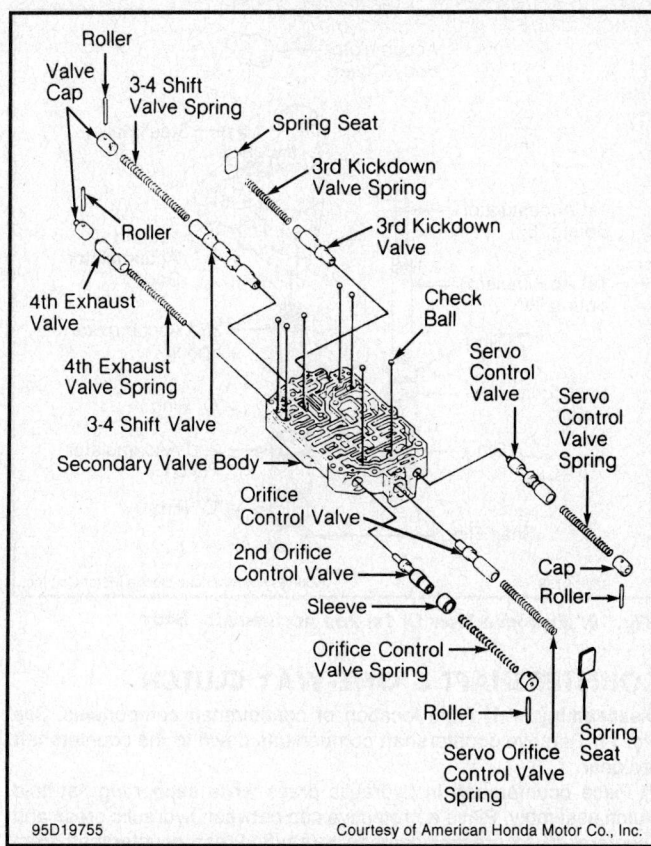

95D19755   Courtesy of American Honda Motor Co., Inc.

Fig. 15: Exploded View Of Secondary Valve Body

2) Ensure all valves slide freely in their bores. If valves do not slide freely, polish burrs or rough areas using No. 600 sandpaper soaked for 30 minutes in ATF. Thoroughly clean secondary valve body and components if polishing was needed.

3) Ensure spring free length is within specification. See SPRING SPECIFICATIONS table. Replace springs if not within specification.

Reassembly – Coat all components and bores with Dexron-II ATF. To reassemble, reverse disassembly procedure. Ensure all components are installed in correct location. See Fig. 15.

REGULATOR VALVE BODY

CAUTION: Regulator spring cap is under spring pressure. Ensure regulator spring cap is held downward when removing stopper bolt.

Disassembly – Hold regulator spring cap downward. Remove stopper bolt. Slowly remove regulator spring cap and components from regulator valve body. See Fig. 16.

Cleaning & Inspection – **1)** Clean components with solvent and dry with compressed air. Replace regulator valve body if any parts are worn or damaged.

2) Ensure all valves slide freely in their bores. If valves do not slide freely, polish burrs or rough areas using No. 600 sandpaper soaked for 30 minutes in ATF. Thoroughly clean regulator valve body and components if polishing was needed.

3) Ensure spring free length is within specification. See SPRING SPECIFICATIONS table. Replace springs if not within specification.

Reassembly – Coat all components and bores with Dexron-II ATF. To reassemble, reverse disassembly procedure. Install NEW filter. Ensure all components are installed in correct location. See Fig. 16. Tighten stopper bolt to specification. See TORQUE SPECIFICATIONS.

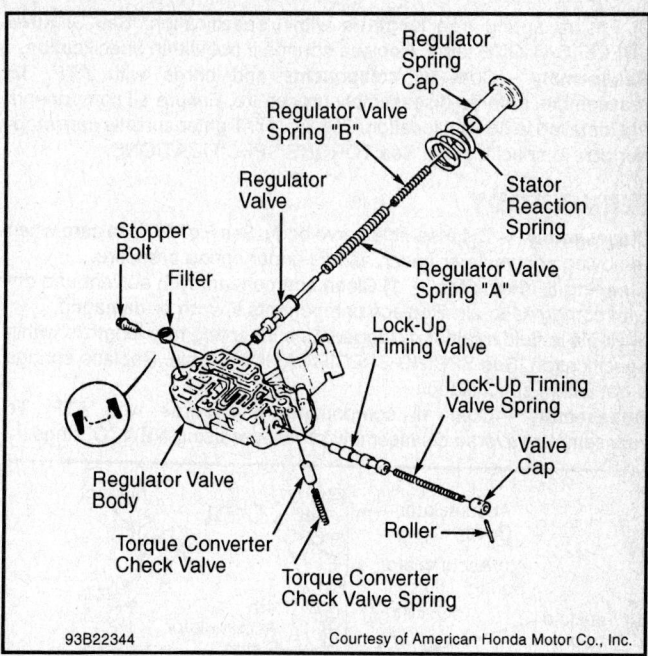

93B22344   Courtesy of American Honda Motor Co., Inc.

Fig. 16: Exploded View Of Regulator Valve Body

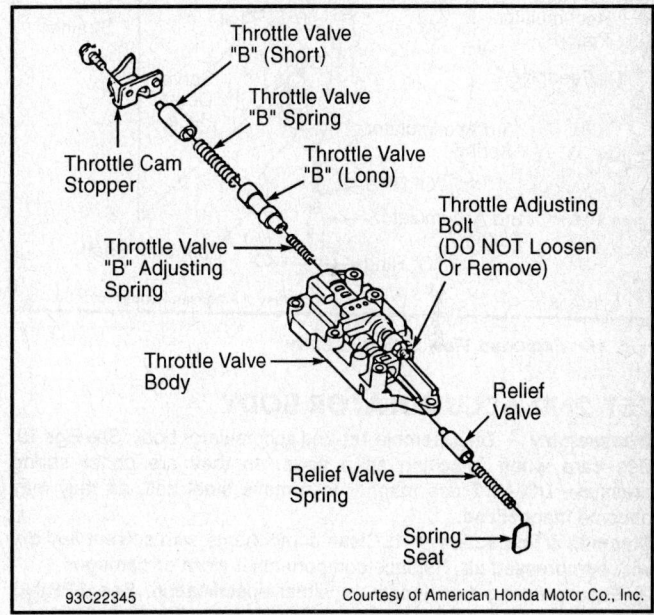

93C22345   Courtesy of American Honda Motor Co., Inc.

Fig. 17: Exploded View Of Throttle Valve Body

THROTTLE VALVE BODY

NOTE: DO NOT loosen or remove throttle adjusting bolt.

Disassembly – Disassemble throttle valve body. See Fig. 17. Use care when removing throttle cam stopper and spring seat, as they are under spring pressure.

Cleaning & Inspection – **1)** Clean components with solvent and dry with compressed air. Replace throttle valve body if any parts are worn or damaged.

2) Ensure all valves slide freely in the bore. If valves do not slide freely, polish burrs or rough areas using No. 600 sandpaper soaked for 30 minutes in ATF. Thoroughly clean throttle valve body and components if polishing was needed.

3) Ensure spring free length is within specification. See SPRING SPECIFICATIONS table. Replace springs if not within specification.

Reassembly – Coat all components and bores with ATF. To reassemble, reverse disassembly procedure. Ensure all components are installed in correct location. *See Fig. 17.* Tighten throttle cam stopper bolt to specification. See TORQUE SPECIFICATIONS.

SERVO BODY

Disassembly – Disassemble servo body. *See Fig. 18.* Use care when removing accumulator cover, as it is under spring pressure.

Cleaning & Inspection – **1)** Clean components with solvent and dry with compressed air. Replace components if worn or damaged.

2) Replace fluid strainer if clogged. Ensure spring free length is within specification. See SPRING SPECIFICATIONS table. Replace springs if not within specification.

Reassembly – Coat all components and bores with ATF. To reassemble, reverse disassembly procedure using NEW "O" rings.

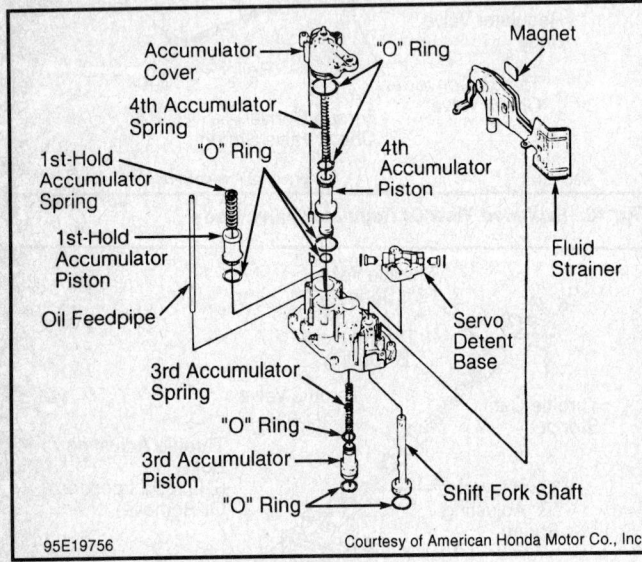

95E19756   Courtesy of American Honda Motor Co., Inc.

Fig. 18: Exploded View Of Servo Body

1ST-2ND ACCUMULATOR BODY

Disassembly – Disassemble 1st-2nd accumulator body. *See Figs 19.* Use care when removing snap rings, as they are under spring pressure. DO NOT use magnet to remove steel ball, as they may become magnetized.

Cleaning & Inspection – **1)** Clean components with solvent and dry with compressed air. Replace components if worn or damaged.

2) Ensure spring free length is within specification. See SPRING SPECIFICATIONS table. Replace springs if not within specification.

Reassembly – Coat all components and bores with ATF. To reassemble, reverse disassembly procedure using NEW "O" rings.

MAINSHAFT

Disassembly – Note location of mainshaft components. *See Fig. 11.* Remove mainshaft components.

Cleaning & Inspection – Clean components with solvent and dry with compressed air. Inspect splines for excessive wear. Check bearing surfaces for scoring or wear. Inspect all needle bearings for galling and rough movement.

Reassembly – Lubricate all components with Dexron-II ATF. Reassemble mainshaft. Ensure thrust needle bearings are installed with unrolled edge of bearing retainer facing washer. Before installing NEW "O" rings on mainshaft, wrap splines on mainshaft with tape to prevent damage to "O" rings.

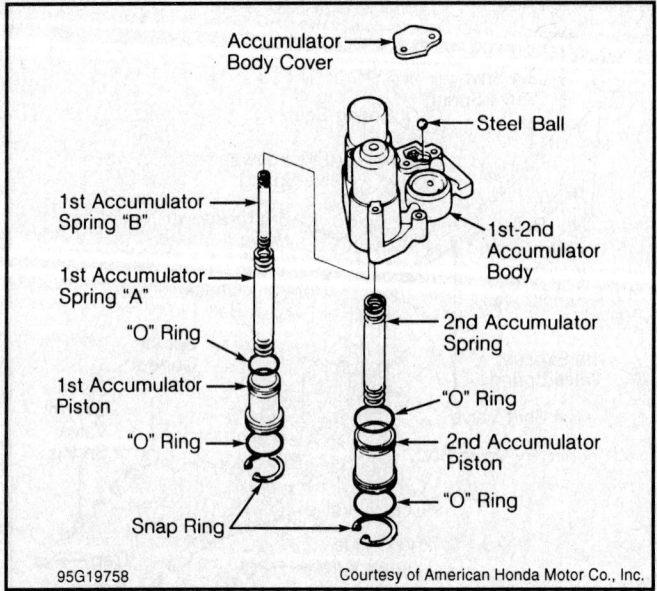

95G19758   Courtesy of American Honda Motor Co., Inc.

Fig. 19: Exploded View Of 1st-2nd Accumulator Body

COUNTERSHAFT & ONE-WAY CLUTCH

Disassembly – **1)** Note location of countershaft components. *See Fig. 11.* Remove countershaft components down to the countershaft 3rd gear.

2) Place countershaft in hydraulic press while supporting 1st-hold clutch assembly. Place a protective cap between hydraulic press and countershaft to prevent damage to shaft. Press countershaft from countershaft 3rd gear and 1st-hold clutch assembly.

3) Separate countershaft 3rd gear with countershaft 1st gear from 1st-hold clutch assembly. Remove needle bearing, thrust washer and countershaft 1st gear collar from 1st-hold clutch assembly.

4) To separate countershaft 3rd gear from countershaft 1st gear, hold countershaft 1st gear and rotate countershaft 3rd gear counterclockwise. Remove countershaft 3rd gear.

5) Note direction of one-way clutch installation in countershaft 1st gear. Gently pry one-way clutch from countershaft 1st gear.

Cleaning & Inspection – **1)** Clean components with solvent and dry with compressed air. Inspect splines for excessive wear. Check bearing surfaces for scoring or wear.

2) Inspect all needle bearings for galling and rough movement. Inspect one-way clutch for damage.

Reassembly – **1)** Lubricate all components with ATF. Install countershaft 1st gear collar, thrust washer and needle bearing on 1st-hold clutch assembly.

2) Install one-way clutch in countershaft 1st gear with large flange area toward countershaft 1st gear. *See Fig. 20.* Install thrust needle bearing on countershaft 1st gear. Install countershaft 3rd gear on countershaft 1st gear. Hold countershaft 1st gear. Ensure countershaft 3rd gear rotates counterclockwise.

3) Install countershaft 1st gear with countershaft 3rd gear on 1st-hold clutch assembly. Using press, press countershaft into countershaft 3rd gear and 1st-hold clutch assembly. Ensure all splines are aligned when installing countershaft. Ensure final drive gear on countershaft contacts 1st-hold clutch assembly.

4) Reassemble countershaft components. Ensure thrust needle bearings are installed with unrolled edge of bearing retainer facing washer. Before installing NEW "O" rings on countershaft, wrap splines on countershaft with tape to prevent damage to "O" rings.

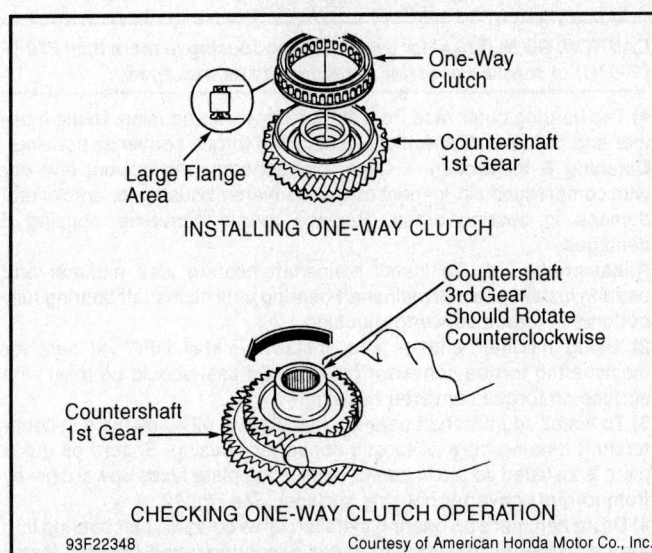

Fig. 20: Installing & Checking One-Way Clutch Operation

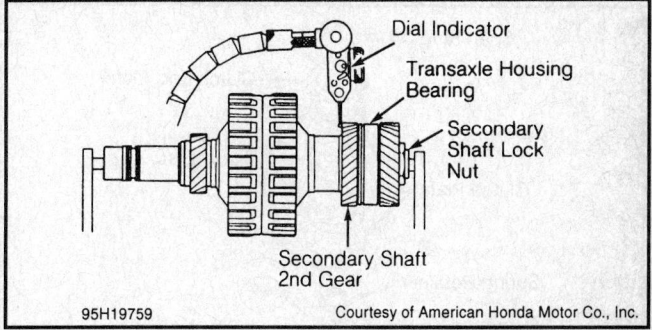

Fig. 21: Checking Secondary Shaft 2nd Gear Clearance

SECONDARY SHAFT

Disassembly – Note location of secondary shaft components. *See Fig. 11.* Remove secondary shaft components.

Cleaning & Inspection – Clean components with solvent and dry with compressed air. Inspect splines for excessive wear. Check bearing surfaces for scoring or wear. Inspect all needle bearings for galling and rough movement.

Reassembly – **1)** Lubricate all components with ATF. Reassemble secondary shaft without "O" rings. Ensure thrust needle bearings are installed with unrolled edge of bearing retainer facing washer.

2) Remove transaxle housing bearing for secondary shaft from transaxle housing. Install transaxle housing bearing for secondary shaft on secondary shaft. Using press, press secondary shaft idler gear on secondary shaft. Install spring washer and used secondary shaft lock nut on secondary shaft. *See Fig. 21.*

3) Tighten secondary shaft lock nut to 22 ft. lbs. (30 N.m). Attach dial indicator on secondary shaft with stem against secondary shaft 2nd gear. Push secondary shaft 2nd gear inward (toward 1st-2nd clutch assembly) and zero dial indicator.

4) Pull secondary shaft 2nd gear outward and note secondary shaft 2nd gear clearance. Check secondary shaft 2nd gear clearance at 3 places on secondary shaft. Average the 3 readings to obtain secondary shaft 2nd gear clearance.

5) Install different thickness splined washer on secondary shaft if secondary shaft 2nd gear clearance is not .003-.006" (.07-.15 mm). Different thickness splined washers are available. See SPLINED WASHER SPECIFICATIONS table. Install different thickness splined washer (if necessary) and recheck clearance.

SPLINED WASHER SPECIFICATIONS

Washer Number	Part Number	Thickness In. (mm)
1	90406-PX4-700	.159 (4.05)
2	90407-PX4-700	.161 (4.10)
3	90408-PX4-700	.163 (4.15)
4	90409-PX4-700	.165 (4.20)
5	90410-PX4-700	.167 (4.25)
6	90411-PX4-700	.169 (4.30)
7	90412-PX4-700	.171 (4.35)
8	90413-PX4-700	.173 (4.40)
9	90414-PX4-700	.175 (4.45)

6) Remove secondary shaft lock nut, spring washer, secondary shaft idler gear and transaxle housing bearing. Lubricate all components with ATF.

7) Reassemble secondary shaft. Ensure thrust needle bearings are installed with unrolled edge of bearing retainer facing washer. Before installing NEW "O" rings on secondary shaft, wrap splines on secondary shaft with tape to prevent damage to "O" rings.

CLUTCH ASSEMBLIES

NOTE: *The 1st-2nd and 3rd-4th clutch assemblies are equipped with 2 different styles of clutch pistons, if replacement is necessary, ensure proper type clutch is used. See Figs. 22-23. Ensure spring compressor is making full contact with spring retainer or damage will occur.*

Disassembly – **1)** Remove snap ring, clutch end plate, clutch discs and clutch plates. *See Figs. 22-23.*

2) Note direction of disc spring installation. Remove disc spring. On all clutches, using spring compressor, compress return spring. Remove snap ring. Release and remove spring compressor. Remove spring retainer and return spring.

3) Wrap shop towel around clutch drum. Apply light air pressure to oil passage on clutch drum to remove clutch piston. Remove "O" rings.

Cleaning & Inspection – Clean metal components with solvent and dry with compressed air. Ensure check valve on rear of clutch piston is thoroughly cleaned and securely fastened on clutch piston. Inspect components for damage and replace if necessary. Ensure no rough edges exist on "O" ring sealing areas.

Reassembly – **1)** Lubricate all components with ATF. Install NEW "O" rings. Install clutch piston in clutch drum. Slightly rotate clutch piston back and forth during installation to prevent damaging "O" rings.

CAUTION: *DO NOT apply excessive force on clutch piston or "O" rings will be damaged.*

2) Install return spring. On 1st-hold clutch, ensure return spring is installed in correct direction. *See Fig. 22.* On all clutches, install spring retainer in clutch drum. Place snap ring on spring retainer. Using spring compressor, compress return spring. Install snap ring. Release and remove spring compressor.

3) Install disc spring. Ensure disc spring is installed in proper direction. *See Figs. 22-23.*

CAUTION: *Ensure clutch discs are soaked in ATF for at least 30 minutes before installing.*

4) Alternately install clutch plates and clutch discs starting with clutch plate. Install clutch end plate with flat side toward clutch disc. *See Fig. 24.* Install snap ring.

5) Using dial indicator, measure clutch clearance between clutch end plate and top clutch disc. *See Fig. 25.* Zero dial indicator with clutch end plate lowered, and then lift clutch end plate upward against snap ring. Distance measured is clutch clearance.

6) Measure clutch clearance at 3 different locations. Ensure clutch clearance is within specification. See CLUTCH CLEARANCE SPECIFICATIONS table.

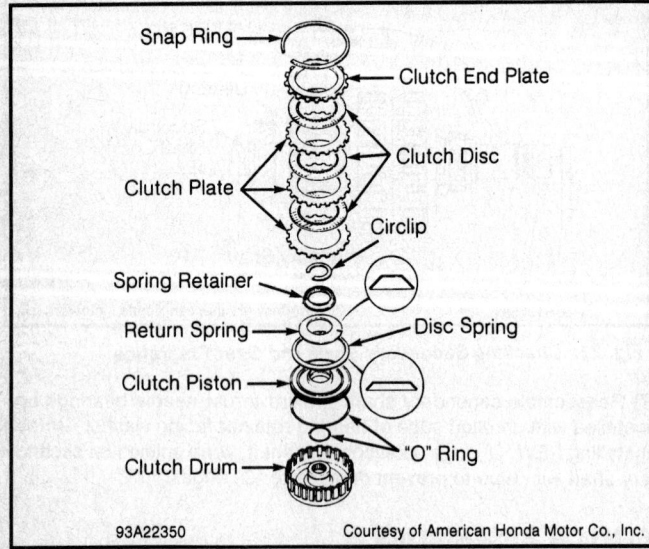

93A22350   Courtesy of American Honda Motor Co., Inc.

Fig. 22: Exploded View Of 1st-Hold Clutch

7) If clutch clearance is not within specification, install different thickness clutch end plate. See CLUTCH END PLATE SPECIFICATIONS table.

NOTE: If thickest clutch end plate is installed and clutch clearance still exceeds specification, replace clutch discs and clutch plates.

CLUTCH CLEARANCE SPECIFICATIONS

Application	In. (mm)
1st & 2nd Clutches	.026-.033 (.65-.85)
1st-Hold Clutch	.031-.039 (.80-1.00)
3rd & 4th Clutches	.016-.024 (.40-.60)

CLUTCH END PLATE SPECIFICATIONS

Plate Number	Part [1] Number	Thickness In. (mm)
1	22551-PX4-003	.083 (2.10)
2	22552-PX4-003	.087 (2.20)
3	22553-PX4-003	.091 (2.30)
4	22554-PX4-003	.094 (2.40)
5	22555-PX4-003	.098 (2.50)
6	22556-PX4-003	.102 (2.60)
7	22557-PX4-003	.106 (2.70)
8	22558-PX4-003	.110 (2.80)
9	22559-PX4-003	.114 (2.90)

[1] – On 1st-hold clutch the center portion of part number may be POX instead of PX4.

TORQUE CONVERTER HOUSING

Disassembly – 1) If removing countershaft bearing from torque converter housing, use slide hammer to remove countershaft bearing. Remove oil guide plate from bore in torque converter housing. *See Fig. 12.*

CAUTION: DO NOT heat torque converter housing to more than 212°F (100°C) or torque converter housing may be damaged.

2) If removing secondary shaft bearing from torque converter housing, use heat gun to heat torque converter housing around secondary shaft bearing to 212°F (100°C). Tap secondary shaft bearing from torque converter housing. Remove oil guide plate from bore in torque converter housing. *See Fig. 12.*

3) Remove mainshaft bearing and oil seal using hammer and bearing driver. If removing bearing outer race for differential assembly from torque converter housing, use heat gun to heat torque converter housing around bearing outer race to 212°F (100°C).

CAUTION: DO NOT heat torque converter housing to more than 212°F (100°C) or torque converter housing may be damaged.

4) Tap bearing outer race from torque converter housing. Using hammer and drift, tap differential oil seal from torque converter housing.
Cleaning & Inspection – Clean components with solvent and dry with compressed air. Inspect torque converter housing for cracks and damage in bearing areas. Replace torque converter housing if damaged.
Reassembly – 1) To install mainshaft bearing, use hammer and bearing installer. Install mainshaft bearing until mainshaft bearing fully bottoms in torque converter housing.
2) Using hammer and oil seal installer, install NEW oil seal for mainshaft in torque converter housing. Oil seal should be even with surface on torque converter housing.
3) To install countershaft bearing, install NEW oil guide plate in countershaft bearing bore of torque converter housing. Ensure oil guide plate is installed so tab in center of oil guide plate faces upward (away from torque converter housing surface). *See Fig. 12.*
4) Using hammer and bearing installer, drive countershaft bearing into torque converter housing. To install secondary shaft bearing, install NEW oil guide plate in secondary shaft bearing bore of torque converter housing.
5) Ensure oil guide plate is installed so tab in center of oil guide plate faces upward (away from torque converter housing surface). Ensure oil guide is installed to a depth of 0-.001" (0-.03 mm), zero being flush and .001" is past flush.
6) Using hammer and bearing installer, drive secondary shaft bearing into torque converter housing.
7) To install bearing outer race for differential assembly, use hammer and bearing race installer. Install bearing outer race until race is even with surface on torque converter housing.

CAUTION: DO NOT install thrust shim in torque converter housing below differential bearing outer race. Thrust shim must be installed in transaxle housing.

8) To install differential oil seal, using hammer and oil seal installer, install NEW oil seal in torque converter housing until oil seal is fully seated.

TRANSAXLE HOUSING

NOTE: DO NOT remove snap rings for bearing replacement unless necessary for cleaning snap ring groove. Expand snap ring enough to push bearing out.

Disassembly – 1) Expand snap ring. Press transaxle housing bearings (for mainshaft, countershaft and secondary shaft) from transaxle housing. Using hammer and drift, tap differential oil seal from transaxle housing.

CAUTION: DO NOT heat transaxle housing to more than 212°F (100°C) or transaxle housing may be damaged.

2) If removing bearing outer race for differential assembly, use heat gun to heat transaxle housing around bearing outer race to 212°F (100°C).
3) Tap bearing outer race from transaxle housing. Remove thrust shim, located below differential bearing outer race from transaxle housing.
Cleaning & Inspection – Clean components with solvent and dry with compressed air. Inspect transaxle housing for cracks and damage in bearing areas. Replace transaxle housing if damaged.

NOTE: Ensure original thickness thrust shim is installed. If any components have been changed, differential assembly bearing preload must be checked. See DIFFERENTIAL ASSEMBLY BEARING PRELOAD under TRANSAXLE REASSEMBLY.

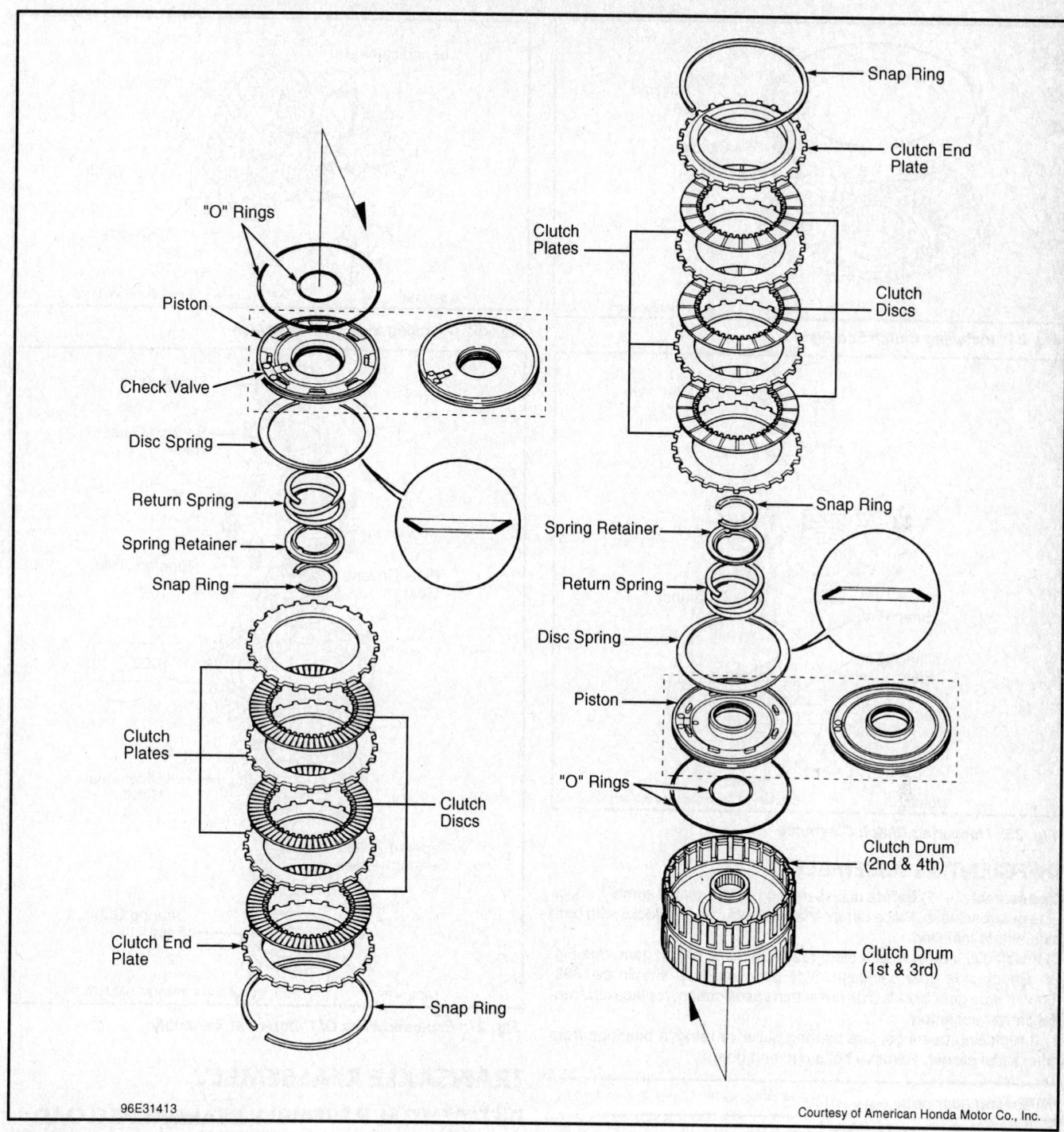

Labels (left column): "O" Rings, Piston, Check Valve, Disc Spring, Return Spring, Spring Retainer, Snap Ring, Clutch Plates, Clutch Discs, Clutch End Plate, Snap Ring

Labels (right column): Snap Ring, Clutch End Plate, Clutch Plates, Clutch Discs, Snap Ring, Spring Retainer, Return Spring, Disc Spring, Piston, "O" Rings, Clutch Drum (2nd & 4th), Clutch Drum (1st & 3rd)

96E31413

Courtesy of American Honda Motor Co., Inc.

Fig. 23: Exploded View Of Clutches

Reassembly – 1) Install thrust shim in transaxle housing. Using hammer and bearing race installer, install bearing outer race until race is fully seated in transaxle housing.

2) To install transaxle housing bearing for mainshaft, countershaft and secondary shaft, expand snap ring and install bearing part way into transaxle housing. Release snap ring.

3) Press bearing into transaxle housing until snap ring engages with groove on bearing. Ensure snap ring end gap is 0-.276" (0-7 mm). If snap ring end gap is not within specification, reseat or replace snap ring.

CAUTION: Ensure transaxle housing bearings are installed with groove of bearing facing inside of transaxle housing so snap ring engages in bearing when bearing is fully installed.

4) To install differential oil seal, use hammer and oil seal installer, install NEW oil seal into transaxle housing until oil seal is fully seated.

RIGHT SIDE COVER

Disassembly – Remove snap rings retaining clutch feedpipes in right side cover. Remove feedpipe guides, 4th clutch feedpipe, 1st-hold clutch feedpipe, 1st clutch feedpipe and "O" rings from right side cover. *See Fig. 6.*

Cleaning & Inspection – Clean components with solvent and dry with compressed air. Inspect components for cracks or damage. Replace components if necessary.

Reassembly – To reassemble, reverse disassembly procedure using NEW "O" rings. Ensure lugs on clutch feedpipes align with grooves in right side cover.

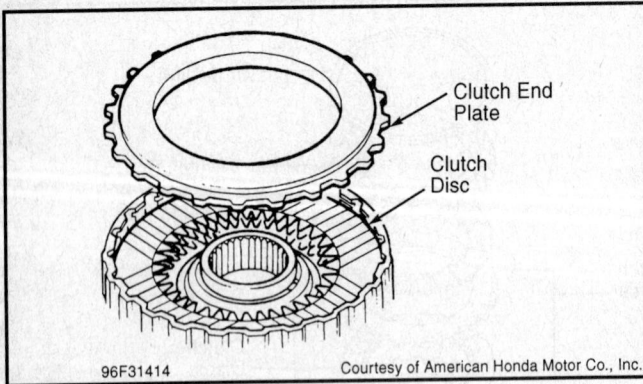

Fig. 24: Installing Clutch End Plate

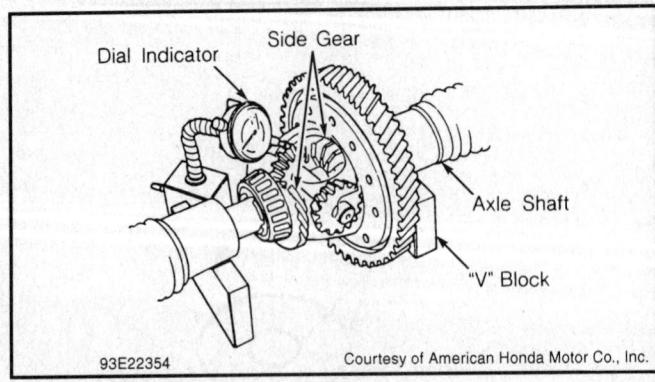

Fig. 26: Checking Side Gear Backlash

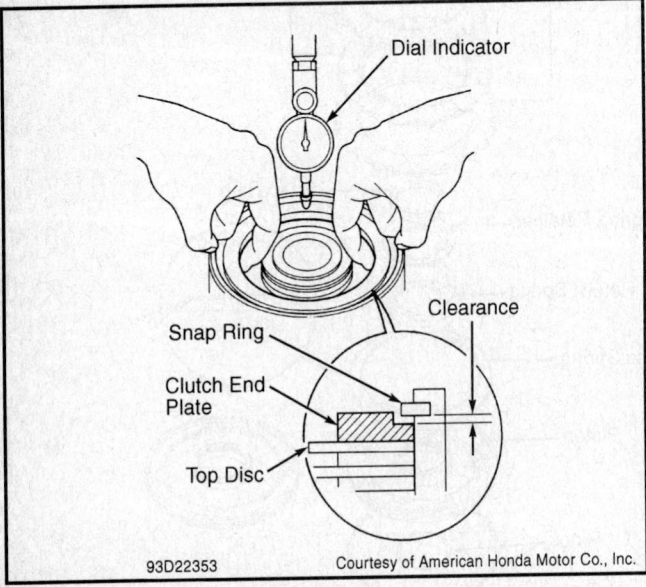

Fig. 25: Measuring Clutch Clearance

DIFFERENTIAL ASSEMBLY

Disassembly – 1) Before disassembling differential assembly, check side gear backlash. Place differential assembly on "V" blocks with both axle shafts installed.

2) Install dial indicator with stem resting against pinion gear. *See Fig. 26.* Check side gear backlash. Side gear backlash should be .002-.006". If side gear backlash is not within specification, replace differential carrier assembly.

3) If replacing bearings, use bearing puller to remove bearings from differential carrier. Remove bolts and ring gear.

NOTE: Ring gear bolts have left-hand threads.

Cleaning & Inspection – Clean components with solvent and dry with compressed air. Inspect components for wear and damage. Inspect differential bearings for rough rotation. Replace components if necessary.

CAUTION: Ring gear must be installed with chamfered edge on inside of ring gear toward differential carrier.

Reassembly – 1) Install ring gear on differential carrier. Ensure chamfered edge on inside of ring gear is toward differential carrier.

2) Install and tighten ring gear bolts in crisscross pattern to specification. See TORQUE SPECIFICATIONS. *See Fig. 27.* Press NEW bearings on differential carrier (if removed). Bearing preload must be reset if bearings are replaced.

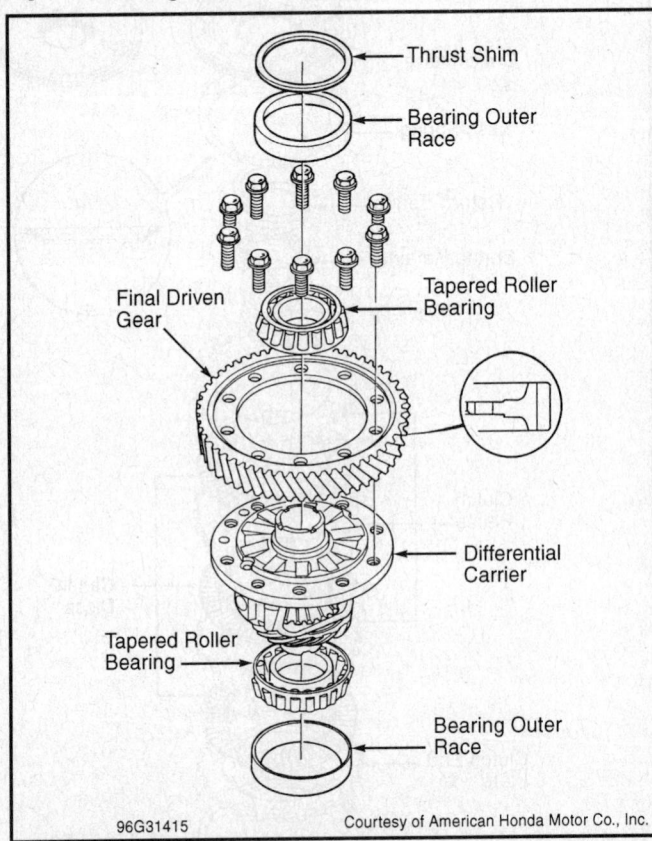

Fig. 27: Exploded View Of Differential Assembly

TRANSAXLE REASSEMBLY

DIFFERENTIAL ASSEMBLY BEARING PRELOAD

NOTE: If transaxle housing, torque converter housing, differential carrier, bearings, thrust shim or differential bearing outer races are replaced, differential assembly bearing preload must be checked.

CAUTION: DO NOT heat transaxle housing to more than 212°F (100°C) or transaxle housing may be damaged.

1) Using heat gun, heat transaxle housing around bearing outer race for differential assembly to 212°F (100°C). Tap bearing outer race from transaxle housing. Remove thrust shim, located below differential bearing outer race, from transaxle housing.

2) Allow transaxle housing to cool to room temperature. Select thrust shim "I" with a thickness of .102" (2.60 mm). See THRUST SHIM SPECIFICATIONS table. Do not reuse original shim.

CAUTION: DO NOT use more than 2 thrust shims when adjusting differential assembly bearing preload.

THRUST SHIM SPECIFICATIONS

Thrust Shim I.D. Letter	Part Number	Thickness In. (mm)
A	41441-PK4-000	.087 (2.20)
B	41442-PK4-000	.089 (2.25)
C	41443-PK4-000	.091 (2.30)
D	41444-PK4-000	.093 (2.35)
E	41445-PK4-000	.094 (2.40)
F	41446-PK4-000	.096 (2.45)
G	41447-PK4-000	.098 (2.50)
H	41448-PK4-000	.100 (2.55)
I [1]	41449-PK4-000	.102 (2.60)
J	41450-PK4-000	.104 (2.65)
K	41451-PK4-000	.106 (2.70)
L	41452-PK4-000	.108 (2.75)
M	41453-PK4-000	.110 (2.80)
N	41454-PK4-000	.112 (2.85)
O	41455-PK4-000	.114 (2.90)
P	41456-PK4-000	.116 (2.95)
O	41457-PK4-000	.118 (3.00)
R	41458-PK4-000	.120 (3.05)

[1] – This is the standard thrust shim.

3) Install thrust shim in transaxle housing. Using hammer and bearing race installer, install bearing outer race until race is fully seated in transaxle housing.

4) Install gasket on torque converter housing. Do not apply sealer at this time. Install differential assembly in torque converter housing. Install transaxle housing on torque converter housing without mainshaft, countershaft and secondary shaft installed.

CAUTION: Ensure gasket is installed when checking differential assembly bearing preload.

5) Install and tighten transaxle housing bolts to 40 ft. lbs. (54 N.m) in sequence. See Fig. 28. Rotate differential assembly several revolutions to seat bearings.

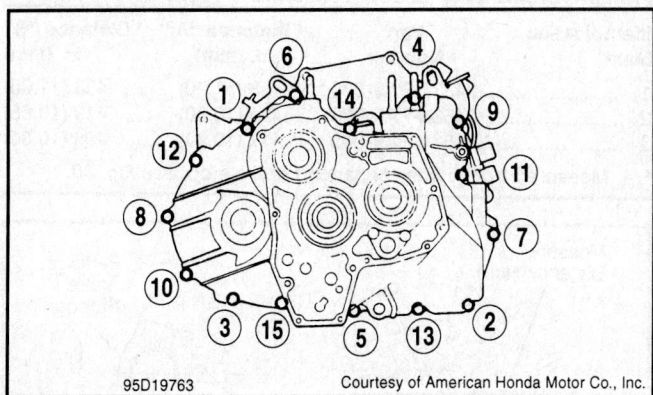

95D19763   Courtesy of American Honda Motor Co., Inc.

Fig. 28: Transaxle Housing Bolt Tightening Sequence

6) Install Preload Adapter (07HAJ-PK40201) into differential assembly. See Fig. 29. Install INCH-lb. torque wrench on preload adapter. Measure differential assembly bearing preload by checking starting torque required to rotate differential assembly in both directions at room temperature.

7) Ensure differential assembly bearing preload is within specification. See DIFFERENTIAL ASSEMBLY BEARING PRELOAD SPECIFICATIONS table.

DIFFERENTIAL ASSEMBLY BEARING PRELOAD SPECIFICATIONS

Application	[1] INCH Lbs. (N.m)
New Bearings	24-35 (2.8-4.0)
Used Bearings	22-32 (2.5-3.7)

[1] – This is the starting torque required to rotate differential assembly.

8) If differential assembly bearing preload is not within specification, select proper thickness thrust shim to obtain correct reading. See THRUST SHIM SPECIFICATIONS table.

9) Changing thrust shim by one size will increase or decrease differential assembly bearing preload about 2.60-3.50 INCH lbs. (.3-.4 N.m). Increase thrust shim thickness to increase differential assembly bearing preload. Decrease thrust shim thickness to decrease differential assembly bearing preload.

CAUTION: DO NOT use more than 2 thrust shims when adjusting differential assembly bearing preload.

10) If adjusting differential assembly bearing preload, remove transaxle housing from torque converter housing. Remove differential bearing outer race from transaxle housing. Install correct thrust shim. Using hammer and bearing race installer, install bearing outer race in transaxle housing.

11) Recheck differential assembly bearing preload. Once correct differential assembly bearing preload is obtained, remove transaxle housing, gasket and differential assembly from torque converter housing.

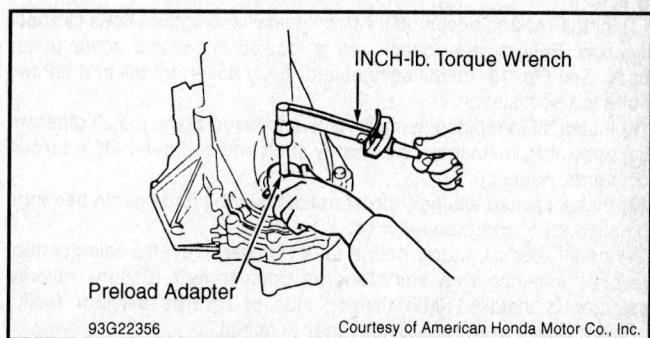

93G22356   Courtesy of American Honda Motor Co., Inc.

Fig. 29: Checking Differential Bearing Preload

VALVE BODIES & INTERNAL COMPONENTS

NOTE: If transaxle housing, torque converter housing, differential carrier, bearings, thrust shim or bearing outer races for differential assembly are replaced, differential assembly bearing preload must be checked. See DIFFERENTIAL ASSEMBLY BEARING PRELOAD under TRANSAXLE REASSEMBLY.

NOTE: Coat all components with ATF before reassembly.

1) Install main separator plate and 3 dowel pins on torque converter housing. Install oil pump drive gear, oil pump driven gear and oil pump driven gear shaft.

CAUTION: Ensure oil pump driven gear is installed with grooved and chamfered side facing downward, toward main separator plate. Ensure oil pump tolerances are within specification. See OIL PUMP under COMPONENT DISASSEMBLY & REASSEMBLY.

2) Install main valve body. Loosely install all main valve body bolts. Once all bolts are installed, tighten main valve body bolts to specification. See TORQUE SPECIFICATIONS.

CAUTION: *Ensure oil pump gears rotate smoothly and oil pump driven gear shaft moves freely once main valve body is installed. If components do not operate correctly, loosen main valve body bolts and realign oil pump gears and oil pump driven gear shaft. Failure to align oil pump driven gear shaft may result in seized oil pump gears or shaft.*

3) Ensure filter and check balls are installed in main valve body. *See Fig. 13.* Install stator shaft, NEW "O" ring and stop shaft. Install dowel pins, spring and torque converter check valve in main valve body.

4) Install regulator valve body and retaining bolt on main valve body. Ensure filter is installed on regulator valve body. *See Fig. 12.* Install dowel pins and throttle separator plate on regulator valve body.

5) Install secondary separator plate and dowel pins on main valve body. Install control shaft on torque converter housing. Ensure control shaft engages with manual valve on main valve body.

6) Install detent arm and detent arm shaft on main valve body. Install detent spring and hook on detent arm and control shaft.

7) Install secondary valve body on secondary separator plate. Ensure check balls are installed in secondary valve body. *See Fig. 15.*

8) Install servo separator plate and servo body on secondary valve body. Install and tighten servo body bolts to specification.

9) Install oil feedpipe and 4th accumulator cover on servo body. Install and tighten 4th accumulator cover bolts to specification.

10) Install fluid strainer. Install and tighten fluid strainer bolts to specification. Install servo detent base. Install and tighten bolts to specification.

11) Install 1st-2nd accumulator body. Install and tighten bolts to specification. Ensure steel check ball is located in 1st-2nd accumulator body. *See Fig. 19.* Install accumulator body cover. Install and tighten bolts to specification.

12) Install oil feedpipes in main valve and servo body. Install differential assembly, mainshaft, secondary shaft and countershaft in torque converter housing.

13) Install splined washer, thrust needle bearing and needle bearings on secondary shaft. *See Fig. 11.*

14) Install needle bearing, countershaft 4th gear, reverse selector hub, reverse selector with shift fork on countershaft. Ensure reverse selector is installed with flanged side of reverse selector facing upward (away from torque converter housing).

15) Install needle bearing on reverse selector hub. Rotate shift fork shaft on servo body so large chamfered hole aligns with hole in shift fork. Install shift fork bolt and NEW lock washer. Tighten bolt to specification. Bend over tabs on bolt lock.

16) Install secondary shaft 2nd gear, thrust needle bearing and thrust washer on secondary shaft. Install countershaft reverse gear and countershaft 2nd gear on countershaft.

17) Install reverse idler gear in transaxle case. Install NEW gasket and dowel pins on torque converter housing. Align spring pin with groove in transaxle housing by rotating control shaft. *See Fig. 10.*

18) Install transaxle housing with transmission hanger, throttle control cable bracket and harness bracket on torque converter housing. Install and tighten bolts to specification in sequence using several steps. *See Fig. 28.* Engage reverse idler gear with countershaft reverse gear.

19) Install NEW "O" rings on shaft for reverse idler gear shaft holder. *See Fig. 8.* Coat shaft, needle bearing and NEW "O" rings with grease.

20) Install shaft in reverse idler gear shaft holder. Ensure flat area on shaft engages with flat area on reverse idler gear shaft holder. Install reverse idler gear shaft holder with needle bearing on transaxle housing. Install and tighten bolts to specification.

21) Install parking brake lever spring and parking brake lever on control shaft. *See Fig. 6.* Install bolt and NEW bolt lock on parking brake lever. DO NOT tighten bolt at this time.

22) Install Mainshaft Holder (07GAB-PF50100 or 07GAB-PF50101) on mainshaft to secure mainshaft from rotating. *See Fig. 7.* Install mainshaft idler gear on mainshaft. Install old mainshaft lock nut on mainshaft. Mainshaft has left-hand threads.

23) Tighten mainshaft lock nut to 166 ft. lbs. (230 N.m) to seat mainshaft idler gear on mainshaft. DO NOT use hammer to install mainshaft idler gear on mainshaft or impact wrench to tighten lock nut.

24) Install secondary shaft idler gear on secondary shaft. Install thrust washer, thrust needle bearing, needle bearing, countershaft idler gear and parking gear on countershaft. *See Fig. 6.*

25) Install old secondary shaft lock nut on secondary shaft. Tighten secondary shaft lock nut to 166 ft. lbs. (230 N.m) while holding countershaft idler gear to seat secondary shaft idler gear on secondary shaft. DO NOT use hammer to install secondary shaft idler gear on secondary shaft or impact wrench to tighten lock nut.

26) Place 24-mm socket at center of parking gear. Install a 10 x 1.25-mm bolt in end of countershaft. Install parking pawl shaft, parking pawl stopper, parking pawl spring and parking pawl. Engage parking pawl with parking gear.

27) Tighten bolt to pull parking gear onto countershaft. DO NOT use hammer to install parking gear on countershaft. Remove bolt and socket.

28) Install old countershaft lock nut on countershaft. Tighten countershaft lock nut to 166 ft. lbs. (230 N.m) to seat parking gear on countershaft. DO NOT use impact wrench to tighten lock nut.

29) Remove lock nuts from mainshaft, countershaft and secondary shaft. Install NEW spring washers and NEW lock nuts on mainshaft, countershaft and secondary shaft. Ensure spring washers are installed so large area of spring washer is against lock nut. *See Fig. 6.*

30) Tighten lock nuts to specification. See TORQUE SPECIFICATIONS. DO NOT use impact wrench to tighten lock nuts. Stake lock nuts against shaft. Remove mainshaft holder.

CAUTION: *Ensure all lock nuts are securely staked against the shaft.*

31) Place parking brake lever in "P" position. Ensure parking pawl fully engages with parking gear. If parking pawl does not fully engage, measure parking brake stop distance between parking pawl shaft and pin on parking brake stop. *See Fig. 30.*

32) Parking brake stop distance should be 2.54-2.58" (64.5-65.6 mm). If parking brake stop distance is not within specification, install different size parking brake stop.

33) Parking brake stop is available in different sizes. See PARKING BRAKE STOP SPECIFICATIONS table.

PARKING BRAKE STOP SPECIFICATIONS

Identification Mark	Part Number	[1] Distance "A" In. (mm)	[1] Distance "B" In. (mm)
1	24537-PA9-003	.433 (11.00)	.433 (11.00)
2	24538-PA9-003	.425 (10.80)	.419 (10.65)
3	24539-PA9-003	.417 (10.60)	.406 (10.30)

[1] – Measured from center of parking brake stop. *See Fig. 30.*

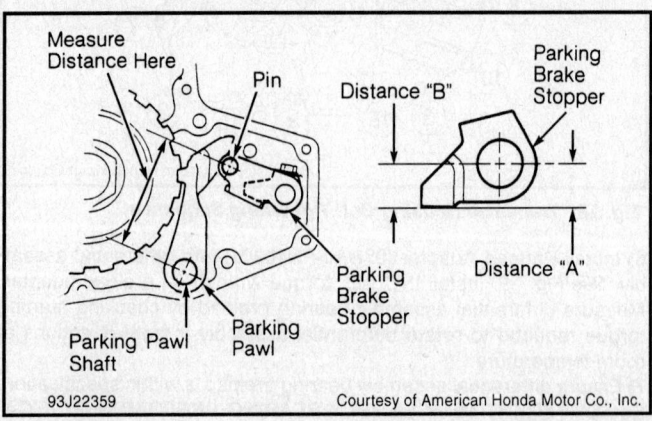

93J22359   Courtesy of American Honda Motor Co., Inc.

Fig. 30: Measuring Parking Brake Sop Distance & Parking Brake Stop

34) Tighten parking brake lever bolt to specification. Bend over tabs on bolt lock. Using NEW gasket, install right side cover. Install and tighten bolts to specification.

35) To install remaining components, reverse removal procedure. Use NEW seal washers when installing joint bolts for ATF cooler pipes. Tighten all fasteners to specification.

CAUTION: If transaxle failure existed, flush oil cooler. See OIL COOLER FLUSHING under ON-VEHICLE SERVICE.

TRANSAXLE SPECIFICATIONS
TRANSAXLE SPECIFICATIONS

Application	Specification
Clutch Clearance	
1st & 2nd Clutches	.026-.033" (.65-.85 mm)
1st-Hold Clutch	.031-.039" (.80-1.00 mm)
3rd & 4th Clutches	.016-.024" (.40-.60 mm)
Differential Bearing Preload [1]	
New Bearings	24-35 INCH lbs. (2.8-4.0 N.m)
Used Bearings	22-32 INCH lbs. (2.5-3.7 N.m)
Oil Pump Clearances	
Side Clearance	
Oil Pump Drive Gear	.0083-.0104" (.210-.265 mm)
Oil Pump Driven Gear	.0014-.0025" (.035-.063 mm)
Thrust Clearance	
Standard	.001-.002" (.03-.05 mm)
Wear Limit	.003" (.07 mm)
Secondary Shaft 2nd Gear Clearance	.003-.006" (.07-.15 mm)
Side Gear Backlash	.002-.006" (.05-.15 mm)
Parking Brake Stop Distance	2.54-2.58" (64.5-65.6 mm)

[1] – This is the starting torque required to rotate differential assembly.

TORQUE SPECIFICATIONS
TORQUE SPECIFICATIONS

Application	Ft. Lbs. (N.m)
Countershaft Lock Nut	123 (167)
Joint Bolt	21 (29)
Mainshaft Lock Nut	123 (167)
Main Valve Body Bolt	
6-mm Bolt	[1]
8-mm Bolt	13 (18)
Pressure Tap Plug	13 (18)
Ring Gear Bolt	74 (100)
Secondary Shaft Lock Nut	123 (167)
Speed Sensor Assembly Bolt	13 (18)
Transaxle Housing Bolt [2]	40 (54)

	INCH Lbs. (N.m)
Accumulator Body Cover Bolt	106 (12.0)
Accumulator Cover Bolt	106 (12.0)
Fluid Strainer Bolt	106 (12.0)
Lock-Up Control Solenoid Valve Assembly Bolt	106 (12.0)
Parking Brake Lever Bolt	124 (14.0)
Regulator Valve Body Bolt	106 (12.0)
Reverse Idler Gear Shaft Holder Bolt	106 (12.0)
Right Side Cover Bolt	106 (12.0)
Servo Detent Base Bolt	106 (12.0)
Servo Body Bolt	106 (12.0)
Shift Control Solenoid Valve Assembly Bolt	106 (12.0)
Shift Fork Bolt	124 (14.0)
Stop Bolt	106 (12.0)
Throttle Cam Stop Bolt	71 (8.0)
Throttle Valve Body Bolt	106 (12.0)
1st-2nd Accumulator Body Bolt	106 (12.0)

[1] – Tighten bolt to 106 INCH lbs. (12.0 N.m).
[2] – Tighten bolts to specification in sequence. *See Fig. 28.*

WIRING DIAGRAMS

See HONDA AOYA, MPJA & MPOA ELECTRONIC CONTROLS article.

AUTOMATIC TRANSMISSIONS
Honda AOYA, MPJA & MPOA Electronic Controls

Honda: Accord, Odyssey
Isuzu: Oasis

APPLICATION

APPLICATION

Vehicle	Transaxle Model
Honda	
Accord (4-Cyl.)	AOYA, [1] MPOA
Odyssey	MPJA
Isuzu	
Oasis	MPJA

[1] – Models manufactured in Japan for U.S. sales.

CAUTION: Vehicle is equipped with a Supplemental Restraint System (SRS). When servicing vehicle, use care to avoid accidental air bag deployment. All SRS electrical connections and wiring harness are covered with Yellow insulation. SRS-related components are located in steering column, center console, instrument panel and lower panel on instrument panel. DO NOT use electrical test equipment on these circuits. It may be necessary to deactivate SRS before servicing components. See AIR BAG SERVICING article in APPLICATIONS & IDENTIFICATION section.

DESCRIPTION

NOTE: On 1995 models, transaxle electronic components are controlled by Transmission Control Module (TCM). On 1996 models, transaxle electronic components are controlled by Powertrain Control Module (PCM). These modules perform same function. On 1995 models, there are separate modules for engine and transmission controls (ECM and TCM). On 1996 models, engine and transmission components are controlled by the PCM.

Automatic transaxle is electronically controlled. Transaxle shifting and torque converter lock-up are controlled by PCM/TCM. The PCM/TCM receives information from various input devices and uses this information to control shift and lock-up control solenoid valves.

The PCM/TCM contains a grade logic control system which controls transaxle shifting while vehicle is ascending or descending on a slope or reducing vehicle speed.

The transaxle is equipped with shift and key interlock systems. Shift interlock system prevents shift lever from being moved from Park unless brake pedal is depressed and accelerator is in idle position. In case of a malfunction, shift lever can be released by placing ignition key in key release slot near shift lever. Key interlock system prevents ignition key from being removed from ignition lock assembly unless shift lever is in Park.

The A/T gear position indicator on instrument panel contains lights to indicate which position A/T gear position switch on shift lever is in.

OPERATION

A/T GEAR POSITION INDICATOR

With ignition in RUN or START position, voltage is supplied to A/T gear position indicator, located on instrument panel. *See Fig. 1.* When shift lever is moved to designated gear position, A/T gear position switch completes the ground circuit for A/T gear position indicator on instrument panel. The light on A/T gear position indicator will be illuminated to indicate shift lever gear position. The PCM/TCM controls operation of the "D₄" light on A/T gear position indicator on instrument panel. The A/T gear position switch is located on driver's side of shift lever. *See Fig. 5.*

When headlights are turned on, voltage is supplied on Red/Black wire terminal on A/T gear position indicator. This changes light illumination from fixed illumination to being controlled by the dash light dimmer input on the Red wire.

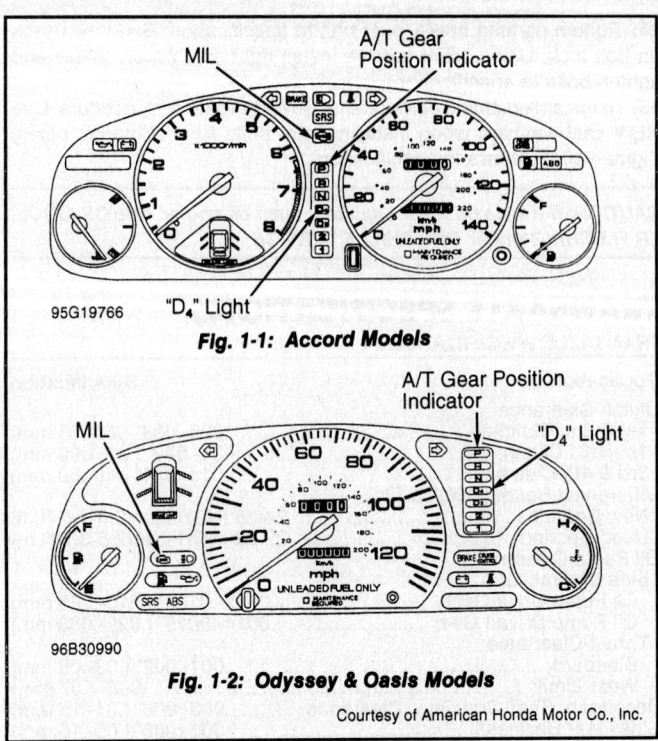

Fig. 1-1: Accord Models

Fig. 1-2: Odyssey & Oasis Models

Courtesy of American Honda Motor Co., Inc.

Fig. 1: Identifying A/T Gear Position Indicator, "D₄" Light & MIL

GRADE LOGIC CONTROL SYSTEM

The grade logic control system is available on all models. The PCM/TCM compares actual driving conditions with driving conditions memorized in the PCM/TCM, based on input signals from vehicle speed sensor, throttle position sensor, engine coolant temperature sensor, brakelight switch and A/T gear position switch. The PCM/TCM uses these input signals to control shifting while vehicle is ascending or descending a slope or during deceleration.

When PCM/TCM determines vehicle is ascending a slope with shift lever in "D₄" position, the PCM/TCM extends engagement of 3rd gear to prevent transaxle from frequently shifting between 3rd and 4th gears to provide smooth vehicle operation. Shift points between 3rd and 4th gear are stored in PCM/TCM which allows the most suitable gear selection depending on changing conditions.

When PCM/TCM determines vehicle is descending a slope with shift lever in "D₄" position, the PCM/TCM changes upshift speed from 3rd to 4th gear with throttle fully closed so speed becomes faster than the set speed for driving on a flat surface to widen the 3rd gear driving area. This, in conjunction with engine braking from torque converter lock-up operation on deceleration, provides smooth vehicle operation. When vehicle is decelerating on a gradual hill with transaxle in 4th gear or when applying brakes on a steep hill, the transaxle will downshift to 3rd gear. When vehicle accelerates, transaxle will shift into 4th gear.

When vehicle enters a corner and needs to decelerate first and then accelerate, the PCM/TCM reduces the number of times transaxle shifts to obtain smooth vehicle operation. When vehicle is decelerating from speeds greater than 27 MPH, PCM/TCM shifts transaxle from 4th gear to 3rd gear earlier than normal to prepare for upcoming acceleration and provide smooth vehicle operation.

SHIFT & KEY INTERLOCK SYSTEMS

Shift Interlock System – Shift interlock system prevents shift lever from being moved from Park unless brake pedal is depressed and accelerator is in idle position. In case of a malfunction, shift lever can be released by placing ignition key in release slot near shift lever. Voltage is provided to shift lock solenoid when ignition is on.

When brake pedal is depressed, battery voltage is applied to the PCM/TCM from brakelight switch. With accelerator pedal in idle position, a low voltage is applied to the PCM/TCM from the throttle position sensor. The TCM then supplies voltage to shift lock circuit in the interlock control unit. When A/T gear position switch is in Park position, interlock control unit then operates shift lock solenoid by controlling the ground circuit. When shift lock solenoid is energized, shift lever is released and can be moved.

Shift lock solenoid is located on passenger's side of shift lever. *See Fig. 2.* The A/T gear position switch is located on driver's side of shift lever. *See Fig. 5.* Interlock control unit is located behind instrument panel and contains a Gray 8-pin electrical connector. *See Fig. 3.*

Key Interlock System – Key interlock system prevents ignition key from being removed from ignition lock assembly on steering column unless shift lever is in Park. Voltage is provided to key interlock switch from No. 30 fuse (20-amp) on Accord models or No. 30 fuse (15-amp) on Odyssey and Oasis models in engine compartment fuse/relay box. Engine compartment fuse/relay box is located on passenger's side rear corner of engine compartment, near firewall.

When ignition key is in ignition lock assembly, key interlock switch closes, providing voltage to key interlock solenoid and interlock control unit.

If shift lever is not in Park, interlock control unit energizes key interlock solenoid by completing ground circuit. When key interlock solenoid is energized, ignition key cannot be removed from ignition lock assembly. Key interlock switch and solenoid are located on ignition lock assembly. *See Fig. 2.* Interlock control unit is located behind instrument panel and contains a Gray 8-pin electrical connector. *See Fig. 3.*

POWERTRAIN/TRANSMISSION CONTROL MODULE (PCM/TCM)

The PCM/TCM receives information from various input devices and uses information to control lock-up and shift control solenoid valves. *See Fig. 4.* The PCM/TCM contains a self-diagnostic system which will store flash code and Diagnostic Trouble Code (DTC) if failure or problem exists in the transaxle electronic control system. Flash code/DTC can be retrieved to determine transaxle problem area.

For information on self-diagnostic system, see SELF-DIAGNOSTIC SYSTEM. The PCM/TCM is located below carpet, under passenger's side of instrument panel. *See Fig. 5.*

PCM/TCM INPUT DEVICES

Air Conditioning Signal – The A/C clutch relay provides input signal to PCM/TCM to indicate A/C operation. The A/C clutch relay is located at driver's side front corner of engine compartment. *See Fig. 5.*

Brake Switch – Brakelight switch delivers input signal to PCM/TCM to indicate vehicle braking. Brakelight switch is located on brake pedal support. *See Fig. 5.*

Engine Coolant Temperature (ECT) Sensor – Engine Coolant Temperature (ECT) sensor delivers input signal to PCM/TCM to indicate engine coolant temperature. Engine coolant temperature sensor is located on cylinder head, below the distributor. *See Fig. 5.*

Engine Speed Signal – An engine speed or RPM signal is delivered to PCM/TCM from ignition control module in the distributor.

Engine Control Module (ECM) – On 1995 models, an upshift and downshift comparative input signal and shift acknowledgment input signal are sent between ECM and TCM. A 5-volt reference signal also exists between ECM and the TCM. The ECM is located below carpet, under passenger's side of instrument panel. *See Fig. 5.*

Service Check Connector – Service check connector is used when retrieving flash codes for transaxle electronic control system diagnosis. When jumper wire is installed between service check connector electrical terminals, an input is delivered to PCM/TCM to display flash codes on "D₄" light on A/T gear position indicator on instrument panel. Service check connector is a 2-pin Blue connector, located at lower passenger's corner of glove box, near kick panel. *See Fig. 6.*

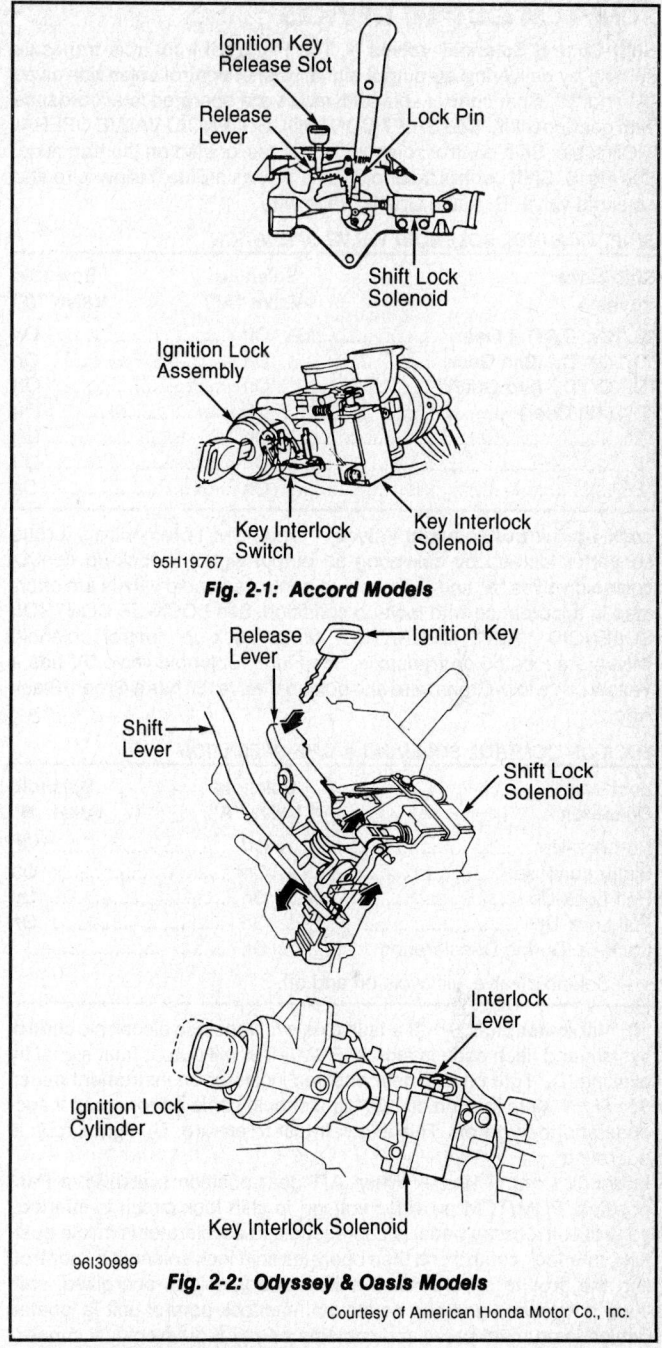

95H19767

Fig. 2-1: Accord Models

96I30989

Fig. 2-2: Odyssey & Oasis Models

Courtesy of American Honda Motor Co., Inc.

Fig. 2: Identifying Shift Lock Solenoid, Key Interlock Switch & Key Interlock Solenoid

Mainshaft & Countershaft Speed Sensor – Mainshaft speed sensor delivers an input signal to PCM/TCM to indicate the speed of the mainshaft in the transaxle. Countershaft speed sensor delivers an input signal to PCM/TCM to indicate the speed of the countershaft in the transaxle. Countershaft and mainshaft speed sensors are located on transaxle. *See Fig. 5.*

Throttle Position (TP) Sensor – TP sensor delivers an input signal to PCM/TCM to indicate throttle position. TP sensor is mounted on throttle body. *See Fig. 5.*

Vehicle Speed Sensor (VSS) – Sensor (VSS) delivers an input signal to PCM/TCM to indicate the vehicle speed. Vehicle speed sensor is located on rear of transaxle. *See Fig. 5.*

PCM/TCM OUTPUT DEVICES

Shift Control Solenoid Valves – The PCM/TCM controls transaxle shifting by delivering an output signal to shift control solenoid valves "A" and "B". Shift control solenoid valves are operated in accordance with gear position. See SHIFT CONTROL SOLENOID VALVE OPERATION table. Shift control solenoid valves are located on the transaxle. *See Fig. 5.* Shift control solenoid valve "A" has a Blue/Yellow wire and solenoid valve "B" has a Green/White wire.

SHIFT CONTROL SOLENOID VALVE OPERATION

Shift Lever Position	Solenoid Valve "A"	Solenoid Valve "B"
"D₃" Or "D₄" (1st Gear)	Off	On
"D₃" Or "D₄" (2nd Gear)	On	On
"D₃" Or "D₄" (3rd Gear)	On	Off
"D₄" (4th Gear)	Off	Off
"R"	On	Off
"1"	On	Off
"2"	On	On

Lock-Up Control Solenoid Valves – The PCM/TCM controls torque converter lock-up by delivering an output signal to lock-up control solenoid valves "A" and "B". Lock-up control solenoid valves are operated in accordance with lock-up condition. See LOCK-UP CONTROL SOLENOID VALVE OPERATION table. Lock-up control solenoid valves are located on transaxle. *See Fig. 5.* Solenoid valve "A" has a Yellow or Yellow/Green wire and solenoid valve "B" has a Green/Black wire.

LOCK-UP CONTROL SOLENOID VALVE OPERATION

Lock-Up Condition	Solenoid Valve "A"	Solenoid Valve "B"
No Lock-Up	Off	Off
Slight Lock-Up	On	Off
Half Lock-Up	On	On
Full Lock-Up	On	On
Lock-Up During Deceleration	On	¹

¹ – Solenoid valve will cycle on and off.

"D₄" Indicator Light – If a fault exists in transaxle electronic control system and flash code is stored, PCM/TCM will output fault signal by blinking "D₄" light on A/T gear position indicator on instrument panel. *See Fig. 1.* With ignition on, "D₄" light should come on for about 2 seconds and then go off. This is a self-test to ensure "D₄" light circuit is operating.

Interlock Control Unit – When A/T gear position switch is in Park position, PCM/TCM provides voltage to shift lock circuit in interlock control unit if brake pedal is depressed and accelerator is in idle position. Interlock control unit then operates shift lock solenoid by controlling the ground circuit. When shift lock solenoid is energized, shift lever is released and can be moved. Interlock control unit is located behind instrument panel and contains a Gray 8-pin electrical connector. *See Fig. 3.*

Self-Diagnosis Signal – If an abnormality exists in transaxle electronic control system and flash code or DTC is stored in PCM/TCM memory, PCM/TCM will deliver an output signal to turn on and blink "D₄" light on A/T gear position indicator on instrument panel. *See Fig. 1.* On 1996 models, DTC can be retrieved using scan tool connected to Data Link Connector (DLC). DLC is located behind ash tray on Accord models and on right side of front console on Odyssey and Oasis models. On all models, flash code can be retrieved to identify problem area by installing jumper wire between service check connector electrical terminals. Flash codes with be displayed by blinking "D₄" light on A/T gear position indicator on instrument panel.

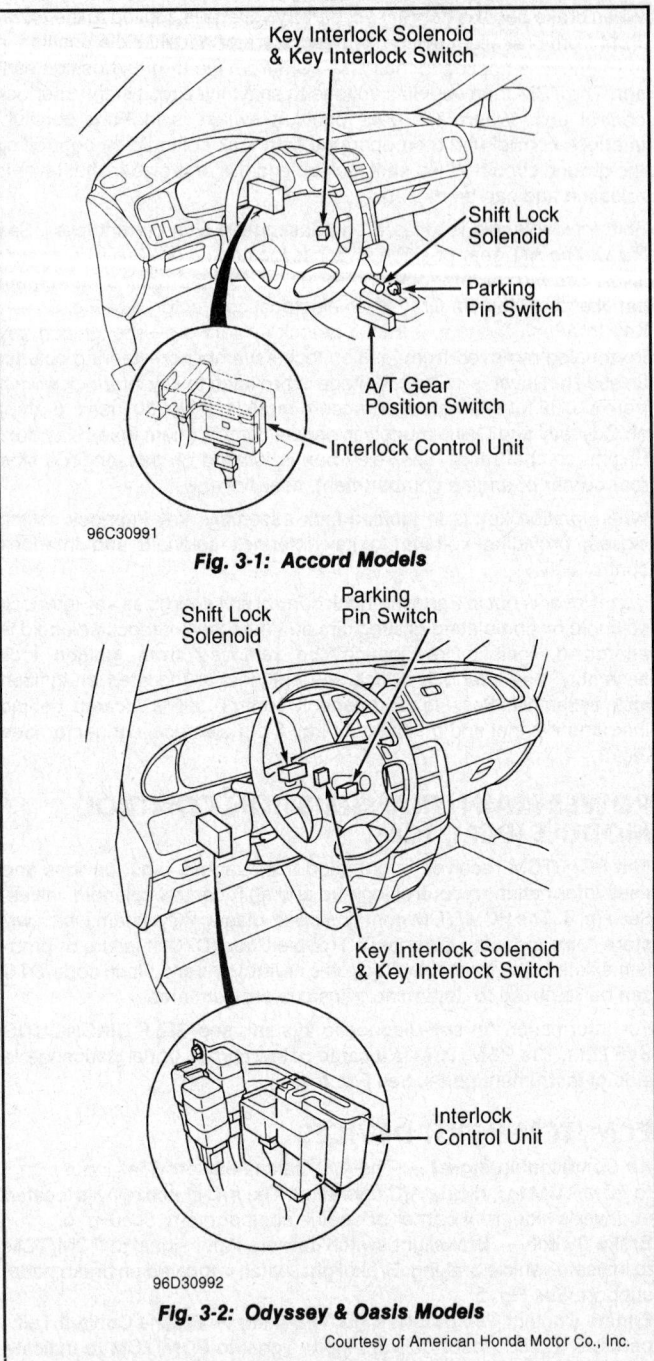

96C30991

Fig. 3-1: Accord Models

96D30992

Fig. 3-2: Odyssey & Oasis Models

Courtesy of American Honda Motor Co., Inc.

Fig. 3: Identifying Interlock Control Unit

SELF-DIAGNOSTIC SYSTEM

SYSTEM DIAGNOSIS

The PCM/TCM monitors transaxle operation. The PCM/TCM contains a self-diagnostic system which stores fault code if failure or problem exists. Fault code may also be referred to as Diagnostic Trouble Code (DTC). If fault code is stored, PCM/TCM will blink "D₄" light on A/T gear position indicator on instrument panel. Fault code can be retrieved for diagnosing transaxle electronic control system. See RETRIEVING FAULT CODES.

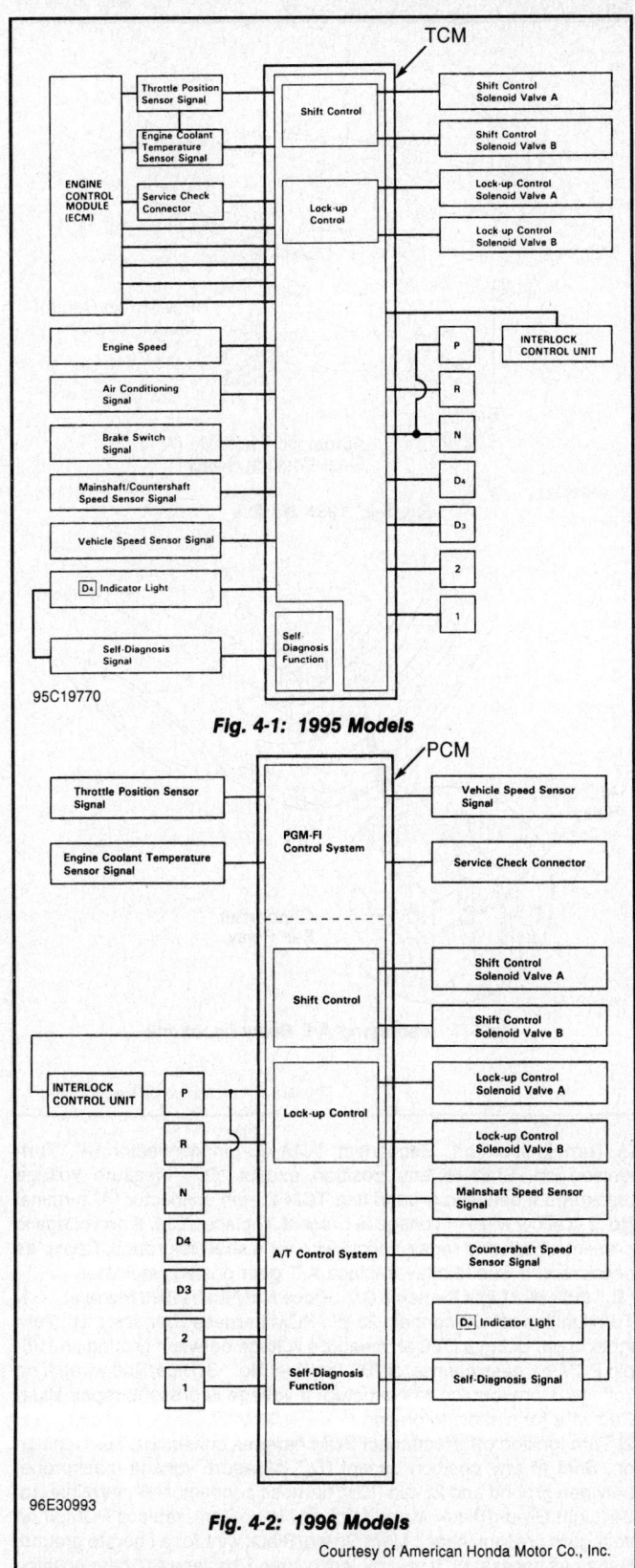

95C19770

Fig. 4-1: 1995 Models

96E30993

Fig. 4-2: 1996 Models

Courtesy of American Honda Motor Co., Inc.

Fig. 4: Identifying Input & Output Devices

RETRIEVING FAULT CODES

NOTE: When diagnosing transaxle, ensure "D₄" light on A/T gear position indicator on instrument panel is not turned on by problem in PGM-FI system. The PGM-FI system controls the fuel injection system. To repair PGM-FI system, see appropriate SELF-DIAGNOSTICS article in ENGINE PERFORMANCE in appropriate MITCHELL® manual.

NOTE: Before any diagnostic procedure, obtain radio anti-theft code from customer. Note radio preset stations, as radio stations and clock setting will be cleared and must be reset. Radio anti-theft code must be re-entered for radio operation.

Retrieving DTCs Using Scan Tool (1996) – 1) If fault code exists, "D₄" light on A/T gear position on instrument panel will blink when ignition is turned on. To retrieve DTC using scan tool, turn ignition off.
2) Connect scan tool to 16-pin Data Link Connector (DLC) located behind ash tray on Accord models and on right side of front console on Odyssey and Oasis models. Turn ignition on. Scan tool will indicate DTCs. Follow scan tool manufacturers instructions.
3) Once DTC is obtained, turn ignition off. Determine probable cause and symptom. See DTC/FLASH CODE IDENTIFICATION (1996) table. If any other codes except those listed are displayed, see appropriate SELF-DIAGNOSTICS article in ENGINE PERFORMANCE in appropriate MITCHELL® manual. For trouble shooting of fault codes, see DIAGNOSTIC TESTS (1996). If "D₄" light does not flash or stays on, see appropriate "D₄" INDICATOR LIGHT CIRCUIT CHECK.

NOTE: Flash Codes can be retrieved on all years/models but are the only codes available on 1995 models.

Retrieving Flash Codes Using "D₄" Light – 1) If flash code exists, "D₄" light on A/T gear position on instrument panel will blink when ignition is turned on. To retrieve flash code, turn ignition off.
2) Install jumper wire between service check connector terminals. Service check connector is a Gray 2-pin connector located on the PCM/TCM cover, below passenger's side of instrument panel. *See Fig. 6.* This will place PCM/TCM in self-diagnostic mode.

CAUTION: DO NOT use the 3-pin connector located next to service check connector.

3) Turn ignition on. Flash codes with be displayed by blinking "D₄" light on A/T gear position indicator on instrument panel.

NOTE: If Malfunction Indicator Light (MIL) on instrument panel also starts blinking, PGM-FI system must be checked. See appropriate SELF-DIAGNOSTICS article in ENGINE PERFORMANCE in appropriate MITCHELL® manual.

4) Note number of blinks from "D₄" light. A short blink indicates a single digit Flash Code. A long blink equals 10 short blinks. For example, if "D₄" light blinks once, this is a Flash Code No. 1. If "D₄" light blinks one long blink and then 4 short blinks, this is a Flash Code No. 14. *See Fig. 7.*
5) Once Flash Code is obtained, turn ignition off. Remove jumper wire from service check connector. Determine probable cause and symptom. See appropriate CODE IDENTIFICATION table. If any other Flash Codes except those listed are displayed, PCM/TCM is defective. For trouble shooting of Flash Codes, see appropriate DIAGNOSTIC TESTS.
6) If customer describes symptoms listed in either CODE IDENTIFICATION table for Flash Code No. 3, 6, or 11 and "D₄" indicator light is off, it may be necessary to test drive vehicle to recreate the symptom and then check for Flash Code with ignition still on. If "D₄" light does not flash or stays on, see appropriate "D₄" INDICATOR LIGHT CIRCUIT CHECK.

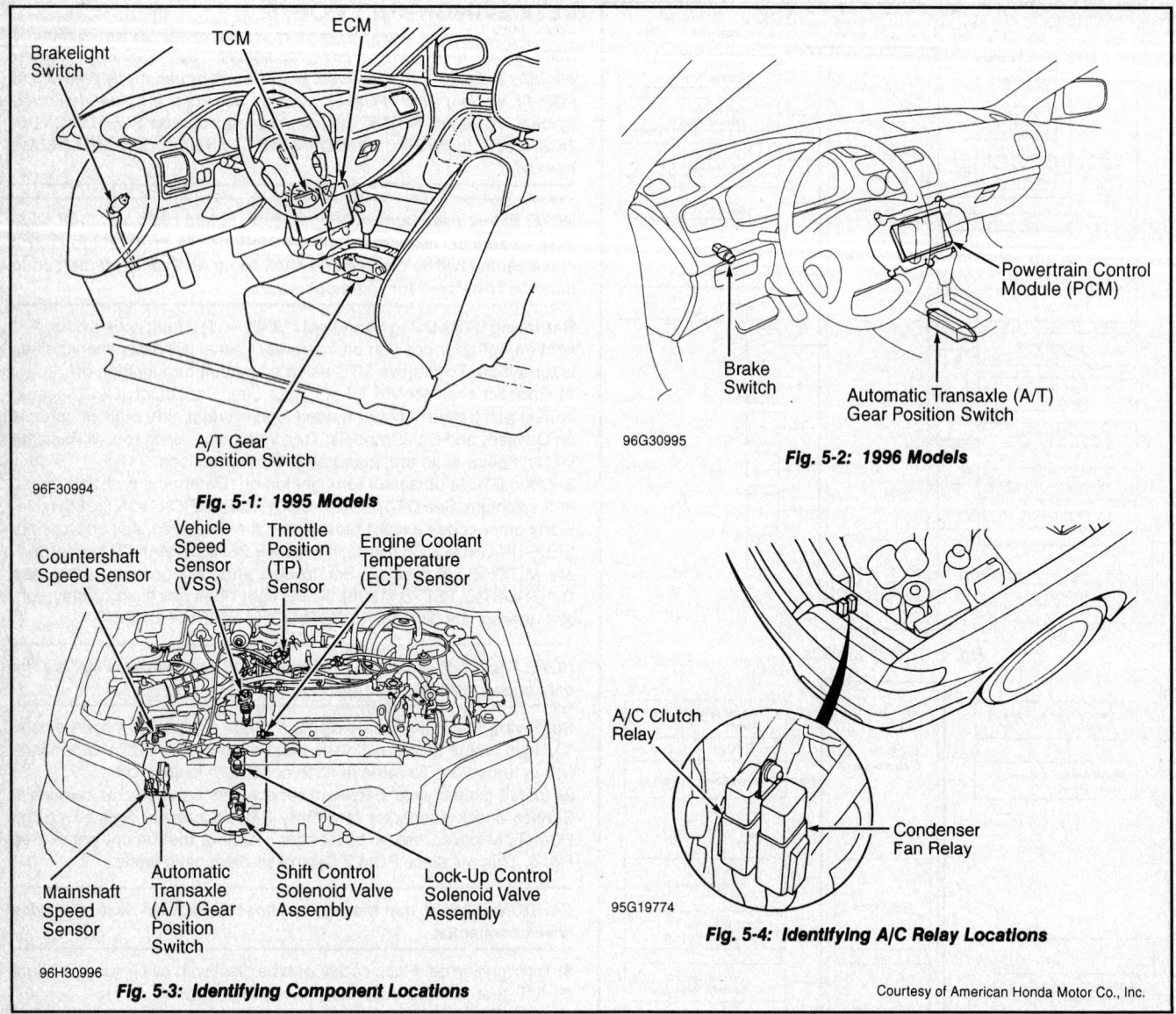

Fig. 5-1: 1995 Models
96F30994

Fig. 5-2: 1996 Models
96G30995

Fig. 5-3: Identifying Component Locations
96H30996

Fig. 5-4: Identifying A/C Relay Locations
95G19774

Courtesy of American Honda Motor Co., Inc.

Fig. 5: Identifying PCM/TCM Input & Output Device Locations

"D₄" INDICATOR LIGHT CIRCUIT CHECK

"D₄" Indicator Light Remains On & Does Not Flash (1995 Accord) – 1) Turn ignition off. Disconnect TCM 26-pin connector. Connect Test Harness (07LAJ-PT3010A) to 26-pin electrical connector. *See Fig. 8.* DO NOT connect test harness to TCM. Turn ignition on. Using a DVOM, measure voltage between ground and test harness terminal A8. If no voltage is present, go to next step. If voltage is present, check and repair Blue/Red wire for a short to power between TCM and gauge assembly.

2) Connect test harness to TCM. Shift to any position except "D₄". Measure voltage between ground and test harness connector terminal A17. If voltage is present, replace TCM. If no voltage is present, check and repair Light Green/Black wire for a short to ground. Repair as necessary. If wire is okay, replace A/T gear position indicator.

"D₄" Indicator Light Remains On & Does Not Flash (1995 Odyssey) – 1) Turn ignition off. Disconnect TCM 26-pin connector "A". Turn ignition on. Using a DVOM, measure voltage between ground and TCM 26-pin connector "A" terminal No. 17 (Blue/Red wire). If no voltage is present, go to next step. If voltage is present, check and repair Blue/Red wire for a short to power between TCM and gauge assembly.

2) Turn ignition off. Reconnect TCM 26-pin connector "A". Turn ignition on. Shift to any position except "D₄". Measure voltage (backprobe) between ground and TCM 26-pin connector "A" terminal No. 9 (Yellow wire). If voltage is present, replace TCM. If no voltage is present, check and repair Yellow wire for a short to ground. Repair as necessary. If wire is okay, replace A/T gear position indicator.

"D₄" Indicator Light Remains On & Does Not Flash (1996 Models) – 1) Turn ignition off. Disconnect 25-pin PCM harness connector "B". Turn ignition on. Using a DVOM, measure voltage between ground and 25-pin PCM harness connector "B", terminal No. 13 (Blue/Red wire). If no voltage is present, go to next step. If voltage is present, repair Blue/Red wire for a short to power.

2) Turn ignition off. Reconnect PCM harness connector. Turn ignition on. Shift to any position except "D₄". Measure voltage (backprobe) between ground and 25-pin PCM harness connector "B", terminal No. 24 (Light Green/Black wire). If voltage is present, replace PCM. If no voltage is present, check Light Green/Black wire for a short to ground. Repair as necessary. If no problem is found, replace A/T gear position indicator.

"D₄" Indicator Light Does Not Come On (1995 Accord) – 1) Turn ignition on. Ensure SCS service connector is not connected to service check connector. Shift to "D₄" position. If "D₄" indicator light does not come on, go to next step. If "D₄" indicator light comes on, check for loose TCM connectors and replace TCM with known good part as necessary and retest.

2) Turn ignition off. Disconnect TCM 26-pin connector. Connect Test Harness (07LAJ-PT3010A) to 26-pin electrical connector. See Fig. 8. DO NOT connect test harness to TCM. Using a DVOM, check for continuity between ground and test harness connector terminals A25 and A26. If continuity is present, go to next step. If continuity is not present, check and repair open or poor connection in appropriate Brown/Black wires.

3) Turn ignition on. Measure voltage between test harness terminals A23 or A24 and A25 or A26. If battery voltage is present, go to next step. If battery voltage is not present, check and repair open or short in Black/Yellow wire between A23 and/or A24 terminals and fuse No. 15 (7.5-amp) in fuse/relay box on driver's side of instrument panel, near steering column.

4) Turn ignition off. Connect test harness to TCM. Turn ignition on. Using a DVOM, measure voltage between test harness connector terminal A8 and terminals A25 or A26. Voltage should be present for 2 seconds. If DVOM indicates voltage as specified, check for an open or short in Blue/Red wire between TCM and gauge assembly. Repair as necessary. If no voltage was indicated, go to next step.

5) Turn ignition off. Disconnect test harness connector from TCM. Check for continuity between test harness connector terminal A8 and gauge assembly 16-pin connector terminal No. C3 (Blue/Red wire). If continuity is present, go to next step. If continuity is not present, check and repair Blue/Red wire between test harness connector and gauge assembly.

6) Check for loose TCM connectors or faulty A/T gear position switch. Repair as necessary. If no problem is found, replace TCM with a known good part and retest.

"D₄" Indicator Light Does Not Come On (1995 Odyssey) – 1) Turn ignition on. Ensure SCS service connector is not connected to service check connector. Shift to "D₄" position. If "D₄" indicator light does not come on, go to next step. If "D₄" indicator light comes on, check for loose TCM connectors and replace TCM with known good part as necessary and retest.

2) Turn ignition off. Disconnect TCM 26-pin connector "A". Using a DVOM, check for continuity between ground and TCM 26-pin connector "A" terminals No. 13 and No. 26 (Brown/Black wires). If continuity is present, go to next step. If continuity is not present, check and repair open or poor connection in appropriate Brown/Black wire.

3) Turn ignition on. Measure voltage at TCM 26-pin connector "A", between terminals No. 12 (Black/Yellow wire) and No. 13 (Brown/Black wire), then between terminals No. 25 (Black/Yellow wire) and No. 26 (Brown/Black wire). If battery voltage is present, go to next step. If battery voltage is not present, check and repair open or short in appropriate wire between TCM and fuse/relay box on driver's side of instrument panel, near steering column.

4) Turn ignition off. Reconnect TCM 26-pin connector "A". Using a DVOM, measure voltage (backprobe) between TCM 26-pin connector "A" terminal No. 17 (Blue/Red wire) and terminals No. 13 or No. 26 (Brown/Black wires). Turn ignition on. Voltage should be present for 2 seconds. If DVOM indicates voltage as specified, go to next step. If no voltage was indicated, go to step 6).

5) Turn ignition off. Disconnect TCM 26-pin connector "A". Check for continuity between TCM 26-pin connector "A" terminal No. 17 (Blue/Red wire) and gauge assembly 16-pin connector "C" terminal C14 (Blue/Red wire). If continuity is present, go to next step. If continuity is not present, check and repair Blue/Red wire between TCM 26-pin connector "A" and gauge assembly.

7) Check for loose TCM connectors or faulty A/T gear position switch. Repair as necessary. If no problem is found, replace TCM with a known good part and retest.

"D₄" Indicator Light Does Not Come On (1996 Models) – 1) Turn ignition on. Ensure service connector shorting tool is not connected to service check connector. Shift to "D₄" position. If "D₄" indicator light does not illuminate, go to next step. If "D₄" indicator light illuminates, check for loose TCM harness connections. Replace TCM with a known-good unit if necessary and retest.

2) Turn ignition off. Disconnect 32-pin PCM harness connector "A". Using a DVOM, check for continuity between ground and 32-pin PCM harness connector "A", terminals No. 9 and 22 (Brown/Black wires). If continuity is present, go to next step. If continuity is not present, repair open or poor connection in appropriate Brown/Black wire.

3) Turn ignition on. Measure voltage at 32-pin PCM harness connector "A", between terminals No. 9 (Yellow/Black wire) and No. 11 (Brown/Black wire), then between terminals No. 24 (Yellow/Black wire) and No. 22 (Brown/Black wire). If battery voltage is present, go to next step. If battery voltage is not present, repair open or short in appropriate Yellow/Black wire between TCM and engine compartment fuse/relay box.

4) Turn ignition off. Reconnect PCM harness connector. Connect a DVOM (backprobe) between 25-pin PCM harness connector "B", terminal No. 13 (Blue/Red wire) and 32-pin PCM harness connector "A", terminals No. 9 or 22 (Brown/Black wires). Turn ignition on. Voltage should be present for 2 seconds. If DVOM indicates voltage as specified, go to next step. If no voltage was indicated, go to step 6).

5) Check for an open or short in Blue/Red wire between PCM and gauge assembly. Repair as necessary. If no problem is found, repair faulty "D₄" indicator bulb or gauge assembly printed circuit board.

6) Turn ignition off. Disconnect 25-pin PCM harness connector "B". Check Blue/Red wire for continuity between 25-pin PCM harness connector "B", terminal No. 13 and Gauge assembly 16-pin harness connector terminal C3. If continuity is present, go to next step. If continuity is not present, repair open in Red/Blue wire.

7) Check for loose TCM harness connectors or faulty A/T gear position switch. Repair as necessary. If no problem is found, replace TCM with a known-good unit and retest.

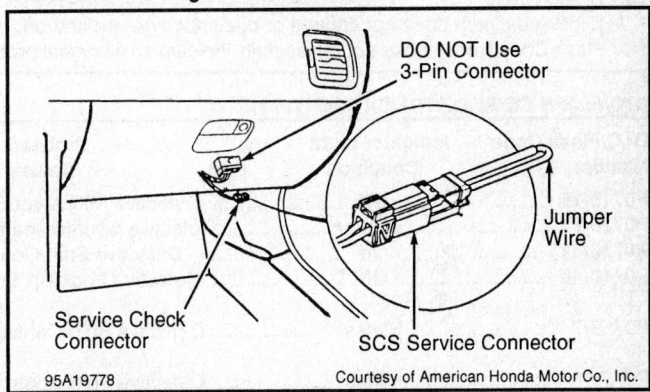

Fig. 6: Identifying Service Check Connector

95A19778   Courtesy of American Honda Motor Co., Inc.

CLEARING CODES

NOTE: PCM/TCM memory can NOT be cleared using scan tool, the following procedure must be used. Before clearing fault codes, obtain radio anti-theft code from customer. Note radio preset stations, as radio stations and clock setting will be cleared and must be reset. Radio anti-theft code must be reset for radio operation.

1) Once repairs have been performed, fault codes must be cleared. Ensure ignition is off. Remove No. 39 BACK-UP/RADIO fuse (7.5-amp) in engine compartment fuse/relay box for 10 seconds. Engine compartment fuse/relay box is located on passenger's side rear corner of engine compartment, near firewall. This clears PCM/TCM and ECM memories.

2) Reinstall fuse. To re-enter radio anti-theft code, turn ignition and radio on. When the word "CODE" is displayed on radio, re-enter radio anti-theft code by using the radio station preset buttons. Reset clock and radio stations.

FLASH CODE IDENTIFICATION (1995)

Flash Code [1] Number	Indicator Light [2] Condition	Probable [3] Cause	[4] [5] Symptom
1	Blinks	Defective Lock-Up Control Solenoid "A"	Lock-Up Clutch Does Not Engage Or Remains Engaged, Unstable Idle Speed
2	Blinks	Defective Lock-Up Control Solenoid "B"	Lock-Up Clutch Does Not Engage
3	Blinks Or Remains Off	Defective Throttle Position Sensor	Lock-Up Clutch Does Not Engage
4	Blinks	Defective Vehicle Speed Sensor	Lock-Up Clutch Does Not Engage
5	Blinks	Defective A/T Gear Position Switch	Lock-Up Clutch Does Not Engage, Fails To Shift Other Than 2nd-4th Gears
6	Off	Defective A/T Gear Position Switch	Lock-Up Clutch Does Not Engage, Lock-Up Clutch Engages & Disengages Fails To Shift Other Than 2nd-4th Gears
7	Blinks	Defective Shift Control Solenoid "A"	Fails To Upshift, Remains In 4th Gear
8	Blinks	Defective Shift Control Solenoid "B"	Remains In 1st Or 4th Gear
9	Blinks	Defective Countershaft Speed Sensor	Lock-Up Clutch Does Not Engage
10	Blinks	Defective Engine Coolant Temp. Sensor	Lock-Up Clutch Does Not Engage
11	Off	Defective Ignition Coil (Ignitor)	Lock-Up Clutch Does Not Engage
13	Blinks	Defective Baro Sensor Or Circuit	Not Specific
14	Off	Shorted Or Open FAS Wire Between TCM Terminal & ECM, Faulty ECM	Transaxle Jerks Hard When Shifting
15 [6]	Off	Defective Mainshaft Speed Sensor	Transaxle Jerks Hard When Shifting

[1] – Number of blinks from "D₄" indicator light on A/T gear position indicator on instrument panel with jumper wire installed in service check connector.

[2] – Operation of "D₄" indicator light without jumper wire installed in service check connector.

[3] – Check listed component for probable cause. Also check wiring and connections of specified component.

[4] – If transaxle fails to shift from Park with brake pedal depressed, check brakelight signal. See BRAKELIGHT SIGNAL under TROUBLE SHOOTING.

[5] – If lock-up clutch does not engage or does not cycle on and off, check A/C signal. See A/C SIGNAL under TROUBLE SHOOTING.

[6] – Flash Code No. 15 does not necessarily indicate an electrical problem, as flash code may also be caused by an internal transaxle problem.

DTC/FLASH CODE IDENTIFICATION (1996)

DTC/Flash Code [1] Number	Indicator Light [2] Condition	Probable [3] Cause	[4] Symptom
P0715/15	Off	Defective Mainshaft Speed Sensor	Transaxle Jerks Hard When Shifting
P0720/9	Blinks	Defective Countershaft Speed Sensor	Lock-Up Clutch Does Not Engage
P0730/41	Off	Defective Shift Control System	Fails To Shift, Stuck In 1st Or 4th Gears
P0740/40	Off	Defective Lock-Up Control System	Lock-Up Clutch Does Not Engage Or Remains Engaged, Unstable Engine Idle
P0753/7	Blinks	Defective Shift Control Solenoid "A"	Remains In 4th Gear, Fails To Shift Other Than 1st-4th, 2nd-4th Or 2nd-3rd Gears
P0758/8	Blinks	Defective Shift Control Solenoid "B"	Remains In 1st Or 4th Gear
P1705/5	Blinks	Defective A/T Gear Position Switch	Lock-Up Clutch Does Not Engage, Fails To Shift Other Than 2nd-4th Gears
P1706/6	Off	Defective A/T Gear Position Switch	Lock-Up Clutch Does Not Engage, Lock-Up Clutch Engages & Disengages, Fails To Shift Other Than 2nd-4th Gears
P1753/1	Blinks	Defective Lock-Up Control Solenoid "A"	Lock-Up Clutch Does Not Engage Or Remains Engaged, Unstable Engine Idle
P1758/2	Blinks	Defective Lock-Up Control Solenoid "B"	Lock-Up Clutch Does Not Engage

[1] – This is the number of blinks from "D₄" light on A/T gear position indicator on instrument panel with jumper wire installed in service check connector. Flash Codes can be retrieved on all years/models but are the only codes available on 1995 models.

[2] – This is operation of "D₄" light on A/T gear position indicator on instrument panel.

[3] – Specified component for probable cause. Also check wiring and connections for the specified component.

[4] – If transaxle fails to shift from Park with brake pedal depressed, check brakelight signal. See BRAKELIGHT SIGNAL under TROUBLE SHOOTING.

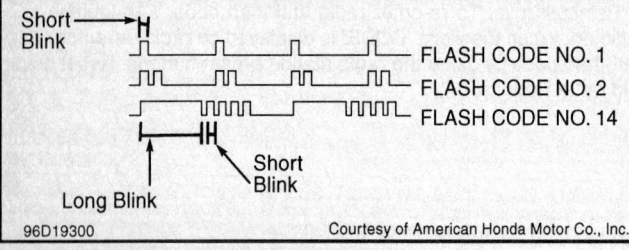

Short Blink
FLASH CODE NO. 1
FLASH CODE NO. 2
FLASH CODE NO. 14
Long Blink — Short Blink
96D19300   Courtesy of American Honda Motor Co., Inc.

Fig. 7: Identifying Fault Code Displays

TROUBLE SHOOTING

A/C SIGNAL (1995 ACCORD & ODYSSEY)

NOTE: If no A/C signal exists, torque converter lock-up clutch may not engage or cycle on and off.

1) Start engine. Turn blower switch and A/C switch to the ON position. Check if A/C compressor clutch engages.

2) If A/C compressor clutch does not engage, check A/C compressor clutch and wiring. If A/C compressor clutch engages, turn engine off. Disconnect 26-pin connector from TCM, located underneath carpet, under passenger's side of instrument panel. *See Fig. 5.*

3) Connect voltmeter between Red/Blue wire at terminal A24 (Accord) or A22 (Odyssey) and Brown/Black wire at terminal A13 or A26 (Accord) or terminal A25 or A26 (Odyssey) of 26-pin connector. Start engine. Note voltage with the A/C compressor off.

4) If battery voltage does not exist, proceed to step **5)**. If battery voltage exists, A/C signal is okay. Check for loose TCM electrical connections. If electrical connections are okay, substitute TCM with a known good unit and recheck operation.

5) If battery voltage does not exist, check for open circuit in Red/Blue wire between terminal A24 (Accord) or A22 (Odyssey) and A/C clutch relay. A/C clutch relay is located at driver's side front corner of engine compartment. *See Fig. 5.*

BRAKELIGHT SIGNAL (1995 ACCORD & ODYSSEY)

NOTE: If no brakelight signal exists, transaxle may fail to shift from Park with brake pedal depressed.

1) Ensure brakelights come on when brake pedal is depressed. If brakelights do not come on, ensure No. 30 fuse (20-amp) in engine compartment fuse box is okay. Engine compartment fuse/relay box is located on passenger's side rear corner of engine compartment, near firewall. If fuse is okay, check and repair brakelight signal circuit.

2) If brakelights operate, ensure ignition is off. Remove passenger's side door sill molding. Pull carpet back for access to TCM, located below carpet, under passenger's side of instrument panel. *See Fig. 5.*

3) On Accord, remove cover located above ECM and TCM. Remove TCM and turn TCM over. Disconnect 26-pin and 22-pin electrical connectors from TCM. Connect Test Harness (07LAJ-PT3010A) to 26-pin and 22-pin electrical connectors. *See Fig. 8.* DO NOT connect test harness to TCM. Using Digital Volt-Ohmmeter (DVOM), measure voltage between terminals D2 and A25 or A26 on test harness with brake pedal depressed. Terminal numbers are located on test harness.

4) On Odyssey, disconnect 26-pin and 22-pin electrical connectors from TCM. Using Digital Volt-Ohmmeter (DVOM), measure voltage between TCM 22-pin connector "B" terminal No. 12 (Green/White wire) and TCM 26-pin connector "A" terminals No. 13 or No. 26 (Brown/Black wires). *See Fig. 32.*

5) If battery voltage exists, brakelight signal to TCM is okay. Check for loose TCM electrical connections. If electrical connections are okay, substitute TCM with a known good unit and recheck operation.

6) If battery voltage does not exist, check for open circuit in the Green/White wire between terminal D2 and brakelight switch. Brakelight switch is located on brake pedal support. *See Fig. 5.*

7) Ensure ignition is off. Remove test harness. Reinstall electrical connectors on TCM. Reinstall remaining components.

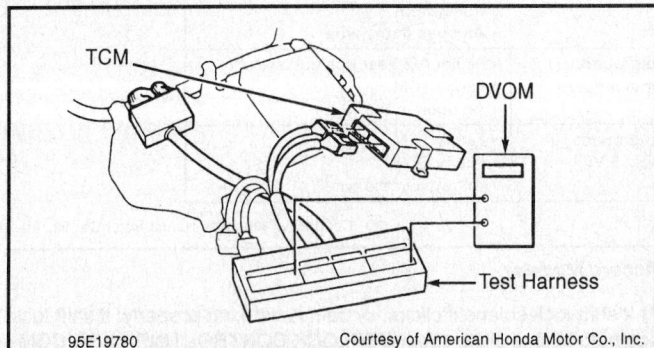

Fig. 8: Installing Test Harness

BRAKELIGHT SIGNAL (1996)

NOTE: If no brakelight signal exists, transaxle may fail to shift from Park with brake pedal depressed.

1) Ensure brakelights come on when brake pedal is depressed. If brakelights do not come on, ensure No. 30 fuse (20-amp) for Accord models or No. 30 fuse (15-amp) for Odyssey and Oasis models in engine compartment fuse box is okay. Engine compartment fuse/relay box is located on passenger's side rear corner of engine compartment, near firewall. If fuse is okay, check and repair brakelight signal circuit.

2) If brakelights operate, ensure ignition is off. Remove passenger's side door sill molding. Pull carpet back for access to PCM, located below carpet, under passenger's side of instrument panel. *See Fig. 5.*

3) Disconnect 32-pin and 16-pin electrical connectors from PCM. Using Digital Volt-Ohmmeter (DVOM), measure voltage between terminals D5 (Green/White wire) and A9 or A22 (Brown/Black wires). *See Figs. 33 and 34.*

4) If battery voltage exists, brakelight signal to TCM is okay. Check for loose PCM electrical connections. If electrical connections are okay, substitute PCM with a known good unit and recheck operation.

5) If battery voltage does not exist, check for open circuit in the Green/White wire between terminal D5 and brakelight switch. Brakelight switch is located on brake pedal support. *See Fig. 5.*

SYSTEM TESTING

A/T GEAR POSITION INDICATOR

NOTE: If necessary, refer to wiring schematic when checking component wiring. See Figs. 13 and 14.

1) Remove instrument panel gauge assembly from instrument panel. On Accord models, disconnect all electrical connectors from rear of instrument panel gauge assembly. *See Fig. 9.* The 22-pin connector and 16-pin connectors are used for testing A/T gear position indicator.

2) On Odyssey and Oasis models, disconnect all electrical connectors from rear of instrument panel gauge assembly. The 2 outer 16-pin connectors are used for testing A/T gear position indicator. *See Fig. 10.*

3) On all models, check for voltage and continuity at electrical connectors as specified. *See Figs. 9 and 10.*

4) If necessary to check ground connections, G401, G402 or G404, see GROUND CONNECTION LOCATIONS table. *See Figs. 11 and 12.*

GROUND CONNECTION LOCATIONS

Ground Connection	Location
G401	
Odyssey & Oasis Models	Left Pillar Underdash
G402	
Accord Models	Behind Passenger's Side Kick Panel
Odyssey & Oasis Models	Right Pillar Underdash
G404	
Accord Models	Driver's Side Of Instrument Panel, Near Console
Odyssey & Oasis Models	Right Pillar Underdash

5) If necessary, check No. 1 fuse (10-amp), fuse is located in fuse/relay box, near driver's side kick panel. If necessary, check No. 32 fuse (15-amp), fuse is located in engine compartment fuse/relay box. Engine compartment fuse/relay box is located on passenger's side rear corner of engine compartment, near firewall.

6) If necessary to access PCM/TCM, the PCM/TCM is located underneath carpet, under passenger's side of instrument panel. *See Fig. 5.*

7) On 1995 models, if necessary to access ECM, the ECM is located underneath carpet, under passenger's side of instrument panel.

8) If necessary to access A/T gear position switch, switch is located on driver's side of shift lever.

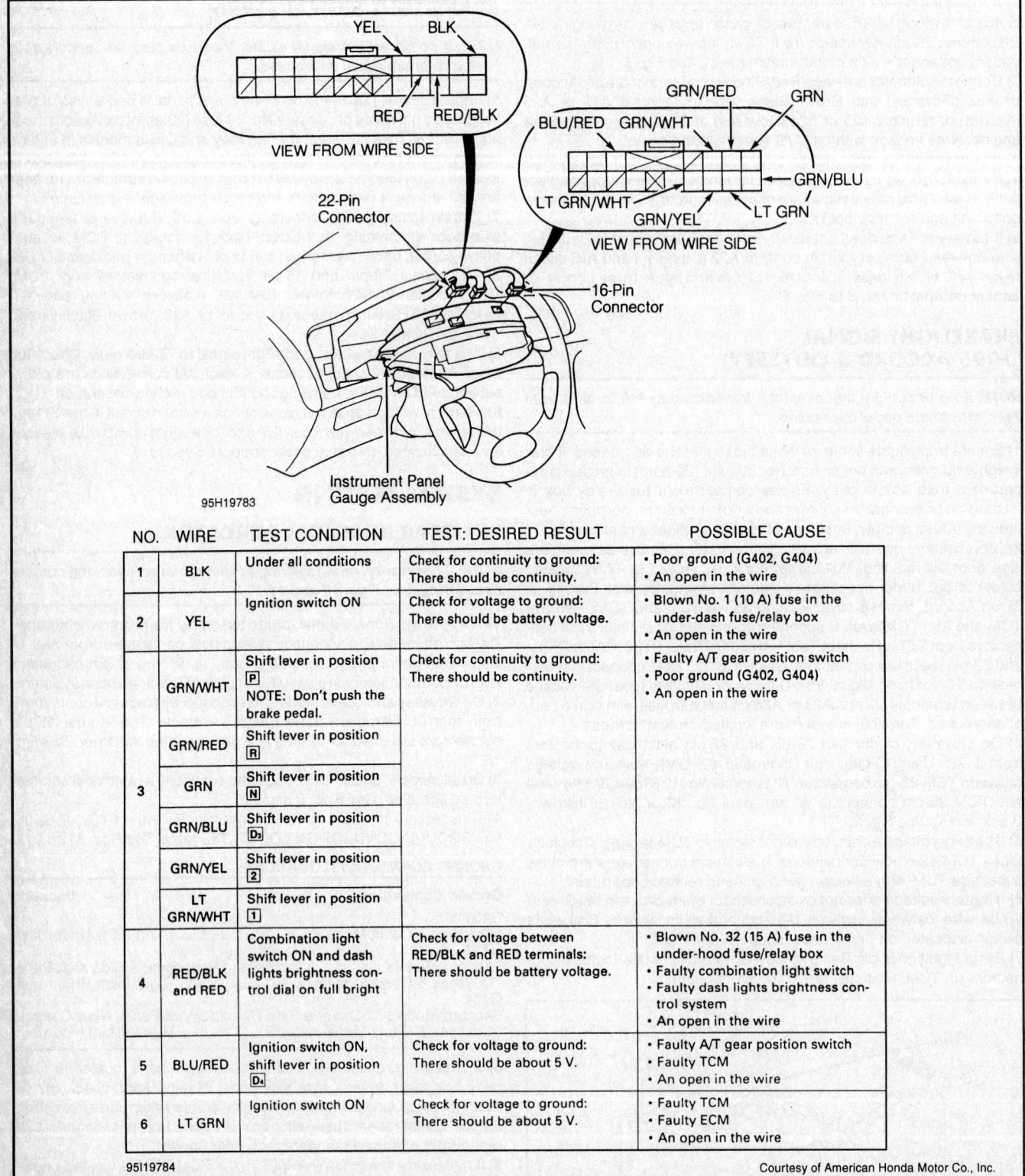

NO.	WIRE	TEST CONDITION	TEST: DESIRED RESULT	POSSIBLE CAUSE
1	BLK	Under all conditions	Check for continuity to ground: There should be continuity.	• Poor ground (G402, G404) • An open in the wire
2	YEL	Ignition switch ON	Check for voltage to ground: There should be battery voltage.	• Blown No. 1 (10 A) fuse in the under-dash fuse/relay box • An open in the wire
3	GRN/WHT	Shift lever in position P NOTE: Don't push the brake pedal.	Check for continuity to ground: There should be continuity.	• Faulty A/T gear position switch • Poor ground (G402, G404) • An open in the wire
	GRN/RED	Shift lever in position R		
	GRN	Shift lever in position N		
	GRN/BLU	Shift lever in position D₃		
	GRN/YEL	Shift lever in position 2		
	LT GRN/WHT	Shift lever in position 1		
4	RED/BLK and RED	Combination light switch ON and dash lights brightness control dial on full bright	Check for voltage between RED/BLK and RED terminals: There should be battery voltage.	• Blown No. 32 (15 A) fuse in the under-hood fuse/relay box • Faulty combination light switch • Faulty dash lights brightness control system • An open in the wire
5	BLU/RED	Ignition switch ON, shift lever in position D₄	Check for voltage to ground: There should be about 5 V.	• Faulty A/T gear position switch • Faulty TCM • An open in the wire
6	LT GRN	Ignition switch ON	Check for voltage to ground: There should be about 5 V.	• Faulty TCM • Faulty ECM • An open in the wire

95I19784   Courtesy of American Honda Motor Co., Inc.

Fig. 9: Identifying Connectors & Testing A/T Gear Position Indicator (Accord Models)

SHIFT & KEY INTERLOCK SYSTEMS

NOTE: If necessary, refer to wiring schematic when checking component wiring. See Figs. 15 and 16.

1) To check system operation, ensure shift lever is in Park. Turn ignition on. Depress brake pedal with accelerator pedal in idle position.

2) If shift lock solenoid clicks, system is working properly. If shift lock solenoid fails to click, see INTERLOCK CONTROL UNIT under COMPONENT TESTING. If shift lever cannot be moved from Park, check for proper installation procedure of shift lock solenoid. See SHIFT LOCK SOLENOID under REMOVAL & INSTALLATION. If shift lock solenoid installation is okay, test A/T gear position switch, see A/T GEAR POSITION SWITCH.

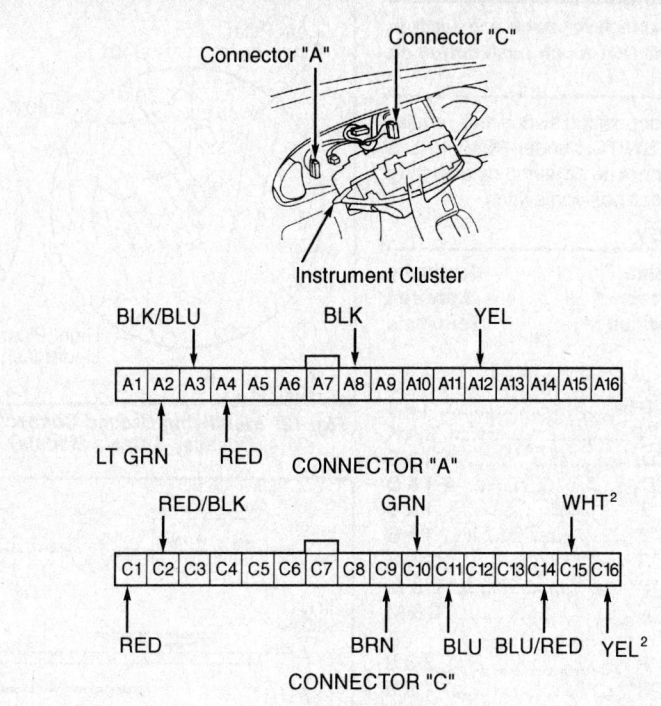

BLK/BLU   BLK   YEL

| A1 | A2 | A3 | A4 | A5 | A6 | A7 | A8 | A9 | A10 | A11 | A12 | A13 | A14 | A15 | A16 |

LT GRN   RED   **CONNECTOR "A"**

RED/BLK   GRN   WHT[2]

| C1 | C2 | C3 | C4 | C5 | C6 | C7 | C8 | C9 | C10 | C11 | C12 | C13 | C14 | C15 | C16 |

RED   BRN   BLU   BLU/RED   YEL[2]

CONNECTOR "C"

Cavity	Wire	Test condition	Test: Desired result	Possible cause if result is not obtained
A2	LT GRN	Ignition switch ON (II)	Check for voltage to ground: There should be about 5 V.	• PCM • An open in the wire
A8	BLK	Under all conditions	Check for continuity to ground: There should be continuity.	• Poor ground (G401, G402, G404) • An open in the wire
A12	YEL[1]	Ignition switch ON (II)	Check for voltage to ground: There should be battery voltage.	• Blown No. 1 (10 A) fuse in the under-dash fuse/relay box • An open in the wire
C1	RED	Under all conditions	Check for continuity to ground: There should be continuity.	• Poor ground (G401, G402, G404) • An open in the wire
C2	RED/BLK	Ignition switch ON (II) Combination light switch ON	Check for voltage to ground: There should be battery voltage.	• Blown No. 32 (15 A) fuse in the under-hood fuse/relay box • Combination light switch • An open in the wire
C14	BLU/RED	Ignition switch ON (II) Shift lever in position D₄	Check for voltage to ground: There should be about 5 V.	• PCM • A/T gear position switch • An open in the wire
A3	BLK/BLU	Shift lever in position P	Check for continuity to ground: There should be continuity.	• A/T gear position switch • Poor ground (G401, G402, G404) • An open in the wire
C15	WHT[2]	Shift lever in position R		
A4	RED	Shift lever in position N		
C16	YEL[2]	Shift lever in position D₄		
C10	GRN	Shift lever in position D₃		
C11	BLU	Shift lever in position 2		
C9	BRN	Shift lever in position 1		

96I30997   Courtesy of American Honda Motor Co., Inc.

Fig. 10: Identifying Connectors & Testing A/T Gear Position Indicator (Odyssey & Oasis Models)

COMPONENT TESTING

A/T GEAR POSITION SWITCH

NOTE: The A/T gear position switch contains back-up light switch and neutral position switch. These switches can be checked when checking A/T gear position switch.

1) The A/T gear position switch is located on driver's side of shift lever. *See Fig. 5.* Remove center console.

2) On Accord, disconnect 2-pin and 12-pin electrical connectors at A/T gear position switch and note terminal identification. On Odyssey and Oasis, disconnect 10-pin electrical connectors at A/T gear position switch and note terminal identification. *See Fig. 17.* Using ohmmeter, check continuity between specified terminals in relation to shift lever position. See A/T GEAR POSITION SWITCH CONTINUITY table.

NOTE: *Check continuity while moving shift lever back and forth in free play area of each gear position. DO NOT touch push button on shift lever when checking continuity.*

3) If continuity is not as specified, A/T gear position switch may require adjustment. See A/T GEAR POSITION SWITCH under REMOVAL & INSTALLATION. If correct continuity cannot be obtained by adjusting A/T gear position switch, replace A/T gear position switch.

A/T GEAR POSITION SWITCH CONTINUITY

Application	Shift Lever Position	Continuity Between Terminals
Accord		
A/T Gear Position Switch	"P"	F & I
	"R"	I & J
	"N"	I & K
	"D₄"	A, I & E
	"D₃"	A, I & D
	"2"	A, I & C
	"1"	I & B
Back-Up Light Switch	"R"	G & H
Neutral Position Switch	"P"	L & M
	"N"	L & M
Odyssey & Oasis		
A/T Gear Position Switch	"P"	1, 3 & 8
	"R"	1 & 9
	"N"	1, 3 & 10
	"D₄"	1, 2 & 4
	"D₃"	1, 2 & 5
	"2"	1, 2 & 6
	"1"	1 & 7

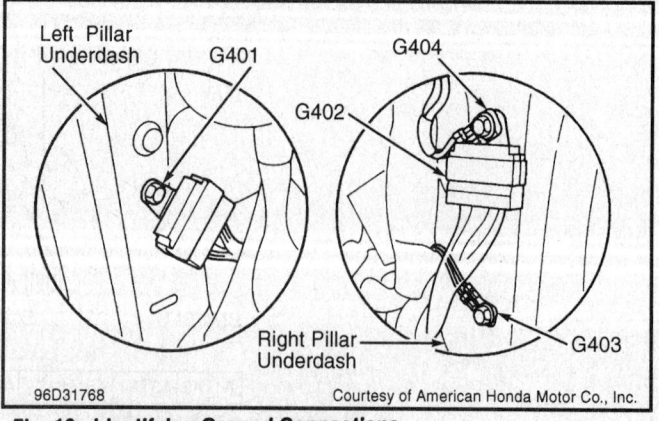

Fig. 12: Identifying Ground Connections (Odyssey & Oasis Models)

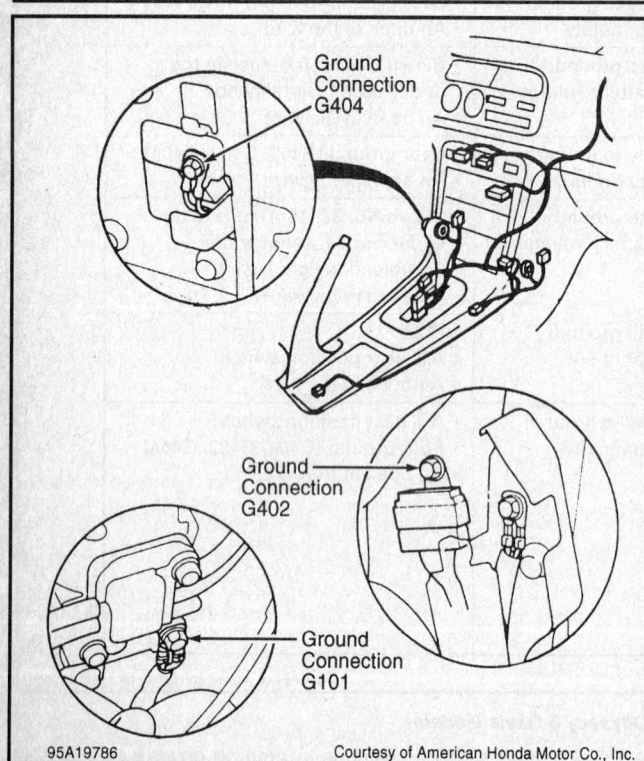

Fig. 11: Identifying Ground Connections (Accord Models)

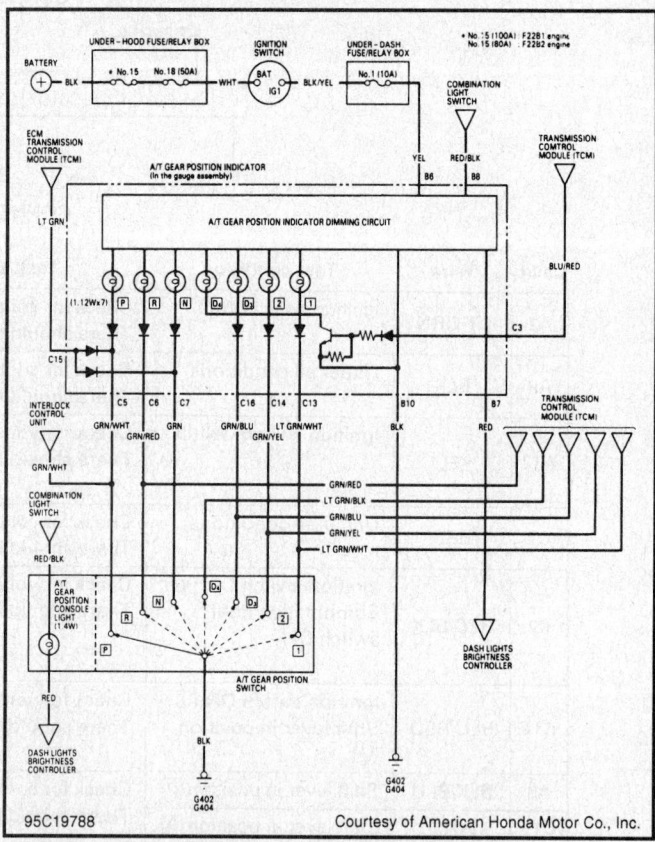

Fig. 13: A/T Gear Position Indicator Wiring Schematic (Accord Models)

BRAKELIGHT SWITCH

1) Disconnect electrical connector from brakelight switch and note terminal identification. *See Fig. 18.*

2) Using ohmmeter, check for continuity between terminals "A" and "D" with brake pedal released. Continuity should exist.

3) Using ohmmeter, check continuity between terminals "B" and "C" with brake pedal depressed. Continuity should exist.

4) If continuity is not as specified, ensure brake pedal is properly adjusted so brakelight switch can obtain proper travel for switch operation. If proper brakelight switch travel exists, replace brakelight switch.

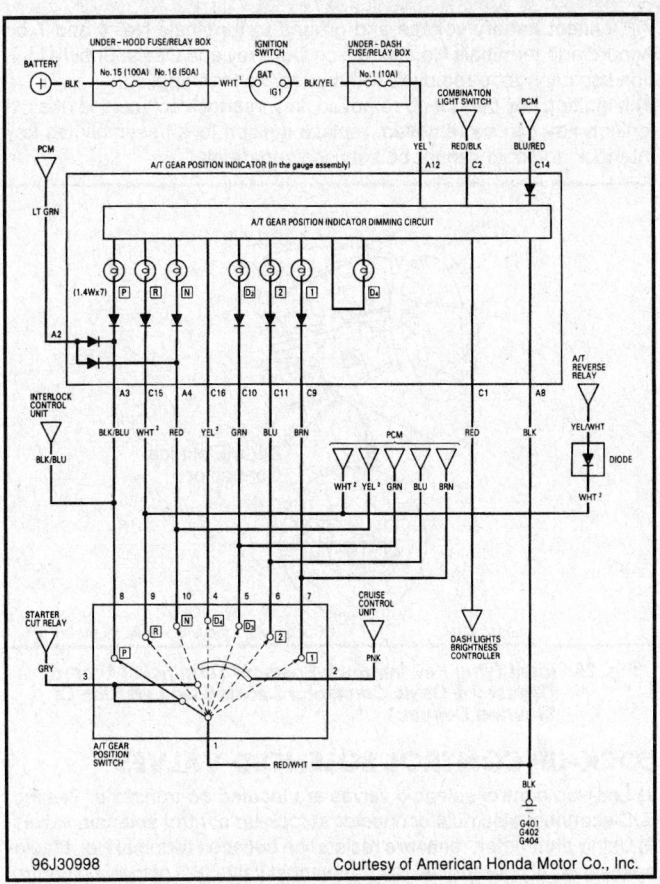

Fig. 14: A/T Gear Position Indicator Wiring Schematic (Odyssey & Oasis Models)

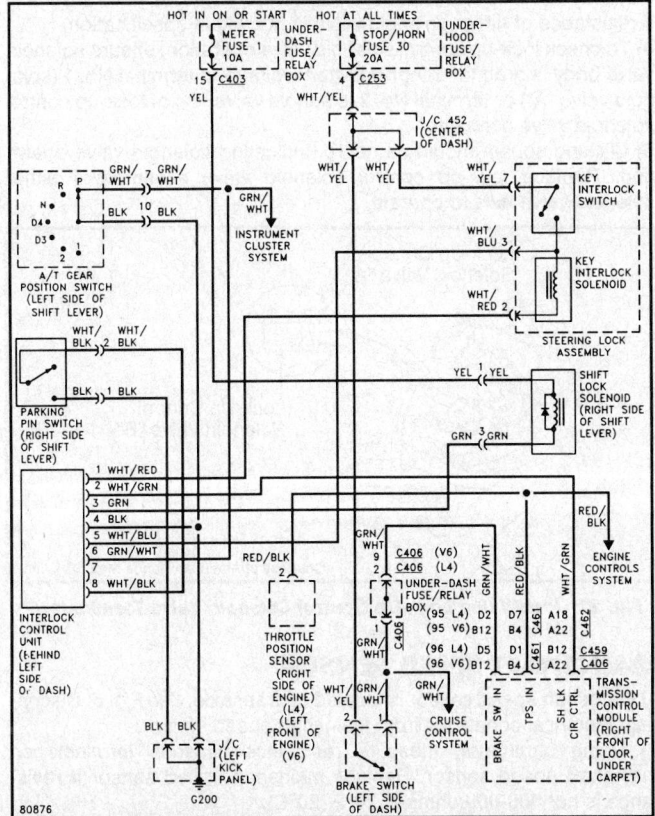

Fig. 15: Shift & Key Interlock System Wiring Schematic (Accord Models)

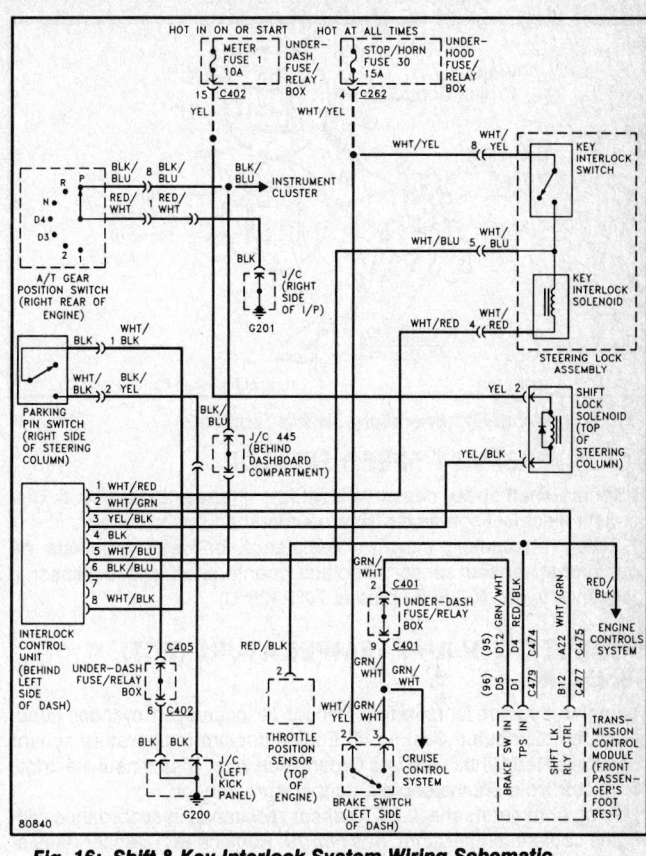

Fig. 16: Shift & Key Interlock System Wiring Schematic (Odyssey & Oasis Models)

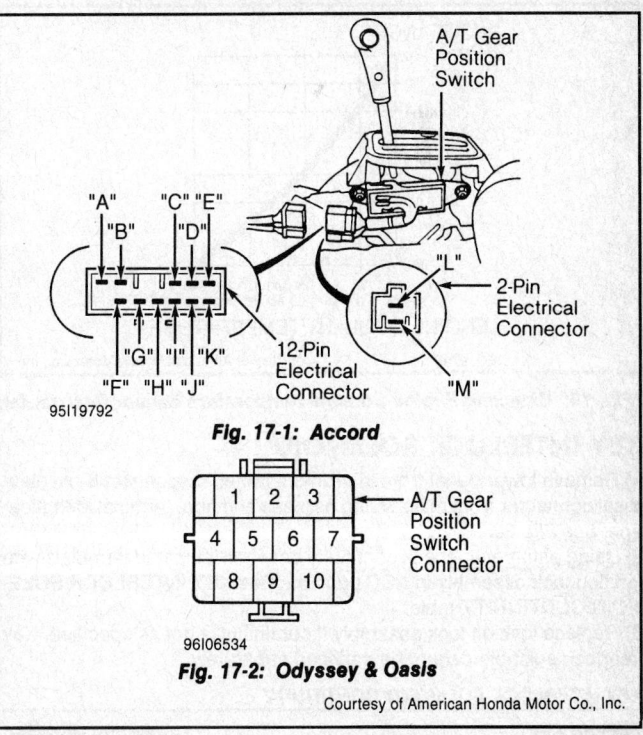

Fig. 17-1: Accord

Fig. 17-2: Odyssey & Oasis

Courtesy of American Honda Motor Co., Inc.

Fig. 17: Identifying A/T Gear Position Switch Terminals

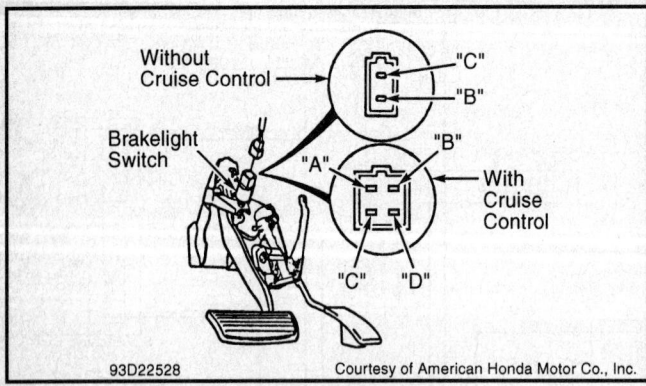

Fig. 18: Identifying Brakelight Switch Terminals

COUNTERSHAFT SPEED SENSOR

1) Countershaft speed sensor is located on transaxle. See Fig. 5. Disconnect electrical connector from countershaft speed sensor.

2) Using ohmmeter, measure resistance between terminals on countershaft speed sensor. Replace countershaft speed sensor if resistance is not 400-600 ohms at 70°F (20°C).

ENGINE COOLANT TEMPERATURE (ECT) SENSOR

1) Engine coolant temperature sensor is located on cylinder head, below the distributor. See Fig. 5. Engine coolant temperature sensor contains a Red/White wire and Green/Blue wire. Disconnect electrical connector from engine coolant temperature sensor.

2) Using ohmmeter, check ECT sensor resistance in accordance with engine coolant temperature. See Fig. 19. Replace ECT sensor if resistance is not within specification.

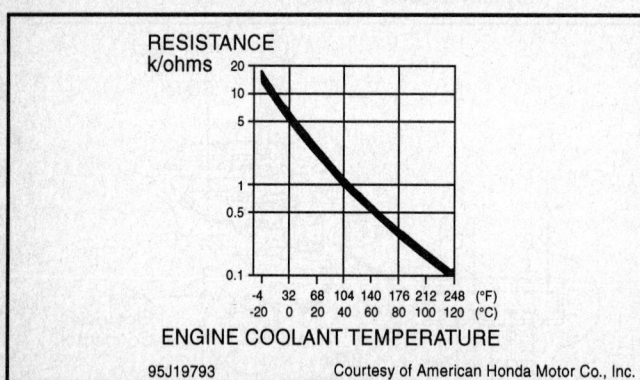

Fig. 19: Checking Engine Coolant Temperature Sensor Resistance

KEY INTERLOCK SOLENOID

1) Remove lower panel from instrument panel. Disconnect 8-pin electrical connector from main wiring harness and note terminal identification. See Fig. 20.

2) Using ohmmeter, check continuity between indicated terminals with ignition lock assembly in ACC position. See KEY INTERLOCK SOLENOID CONTINUITY table.

3) Replace ignition lock assembly if continuity is not as specified. Key interlock solenoid cannot be serviced separately.

KEY INTERLOCK SOLENOID CONTINUITY

Ignition Key Position	Continuity Between Terminals
Key Installed	
Accord	4, 6 & 7
Odyssey & Oasis	4, 5 & 8
Key Removed	
Accord	6 & 7
Odyssey & Oasis	4 & 5

4) Connect battery voltage and ground to terminals No. 4 and 7 on Accord and terminals No. 4 and 8 on Odyssey and Oasis. Ensure ignition key cannot be removed with battery voltage applied.

5) If ignition key cannot be removed, key interlock solenoid is okay. If ignition key can be removed, replace ignition lock assembly, as key interlock solenoid cannot be serviced separately.

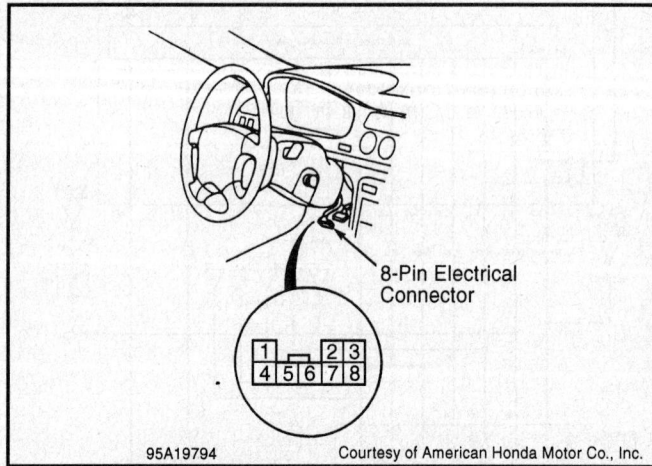

Fig. 20: Identifying Key Interlock Solenoid Terminals (Accord; Odyssey & Oasis Connector Located On Left Side Of Steering Column)

LOCK-UP CONTROL SOLENOID VALVES

1) Lock-up control solenoid valves are located on transaxle. See Fig. 5. Disconnect electrical connector at lock-up control solenoid valves.

2) Using ohmmeter, measure resistance between terminal No. 1 (solenoid valve "A") or terminal No. 2 (solenoid valve "B") of lock-up control solenoid valve connector and body ground. See Fig. 21.

3) Resistance should be 12-24 ohms on Accord and 14-25 ohms on Odyssey and Oasis. Replace lock-up control solenoid valve assembly if resistance of either solenoid valve is not within specification.

4) To check lock-up control solenoid valve operation, ensure solenoid valve body is grounded. Apply battery voltage to terminal No. 1 (solenoid valve "A") or terminal No. 2 (solenoid valve "B") of lock-up control solenoid valve connector.

5) Clicking sound should be heard, indicating solenoid valve operation. Replace lock-up control solenoid valve assembly if either solenoid valve fails to operate.

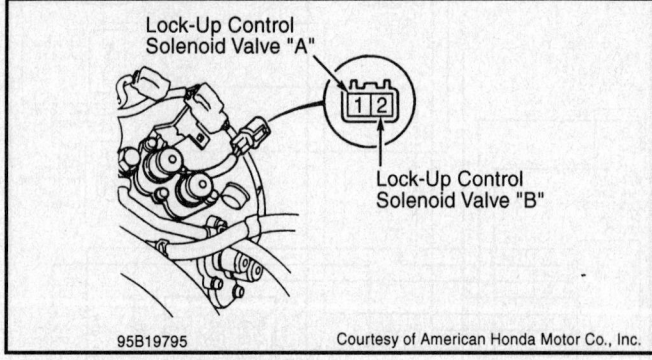

Fig. 21: Identifying Lock-Up Control Solenoid Valve Terminals

MAINSHAFT SPEED SENSOR

1) Mainshaft speed sensor is located on transaxle. See Fig. 5. Disconnect electrical connector from mainshaft speed sensor.

2) Using ohmmeter, measure resistance between terminals on mainshaft speed sensor. Replace mainshaft speed sensor if resistance is not 400-600 ohms at 70°F (20°C).

SHIFT CONTROL SOLENOID VALVES

1) Shift control solenoid valves are located on the transaxle. *See Fig. 5.* Disconnect electrical connector at shift control solenoid valves.

2) Using ohmmeter, measure resistance between terminal No. 1 (solenoid valve "A") or terminal No. 3 (solenoid valve "B") of shift control solenoid valve connector and body ground. *See Fig. 22.*

3) Resistance should be 12-24 ohms on Accord and 14-25 ohms on Odyssey and Oasis. Replace shift control solenoid valve assembly if resistance of either solenoid valve is not within specification.

4) To check shift control solenoid valve operation, ensure solenoid valve body is grounded. Apply battery voltage to terminal No. 1 (solenoid valve "A") or terminal No. 3 (solenoid valve "B") of shift control solenoid valve connector.

5) Clicking sound should be heard, indicating solenoid valve operation. Replace shift control solenoid valve assembly if either solenoid valve fails to operate.

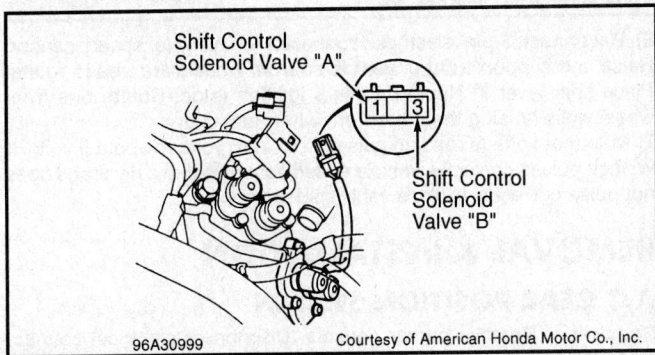

Fig. 22: Identifying Shift Control Solenoid Valve Terminals

SHIFT LOCK SOLENOID

1) Remove center console. Disconnect 3-pin electrical connector from main wiring harness and note terminal identification. *See Fig. 23.*

CAUTION: Battery voltage must be applied to correct shift lock solenoid terminals, or diode inside shift lock solenoid will be damaged.

2) Momentarily connect battery positive terminal to terminal "A" and battery negative terminal to terminal "B" on Accord and connect battery positive terminal to terminal No. 1 and battery negative terminal to terminal No. 2 on Odyssey and Oasis. Ensure shift lock solenoid operates with battery voltage applied. Replace shift lock solenoid if it does not operate.

THROTTLE POSITION (TP) SENSOR

TP sensor should input a .5-volt reference signal to PCM/TCM at closed throttle and approximately 4.5-volt signal at full throttle. Voltage should change smoothly as throttle valve is opened and closed. If voltage is not correct, check throttle position sensor wiring circuit. See WIRING DIAGRAMS. Individual component testing not available from manufacturer.

NOTE: On 1995 models, if problem in throttle position sensor exists, throttle position sensor may set Fault Code No. 3 in TCM. See RETRIEVING FAULT CODES under SELF-DIAGNOSTIC SYSTEM

VEHICLE SPEED SENSOR (VSS)

Accord – 1) Vehicle speed sensor is located on rear of transaxle, near distributor. *See Fig. 5.* Ensure No. 1 fuse (10-amp) in fuse/relay box near driver's side kick panel is okay. Replace fuse if necessary. If fuse is okay, disconnect 3-pin electrical connector at vehicle speed sensor.

2) Turn ignition on. Using voltmeter, measure voltage between Yellow wire and Black wire of 3-pin electrical connector. If battery voltage exists, proceed to step **5)**. If battery voltage does not exist, proceed to step **3)**.

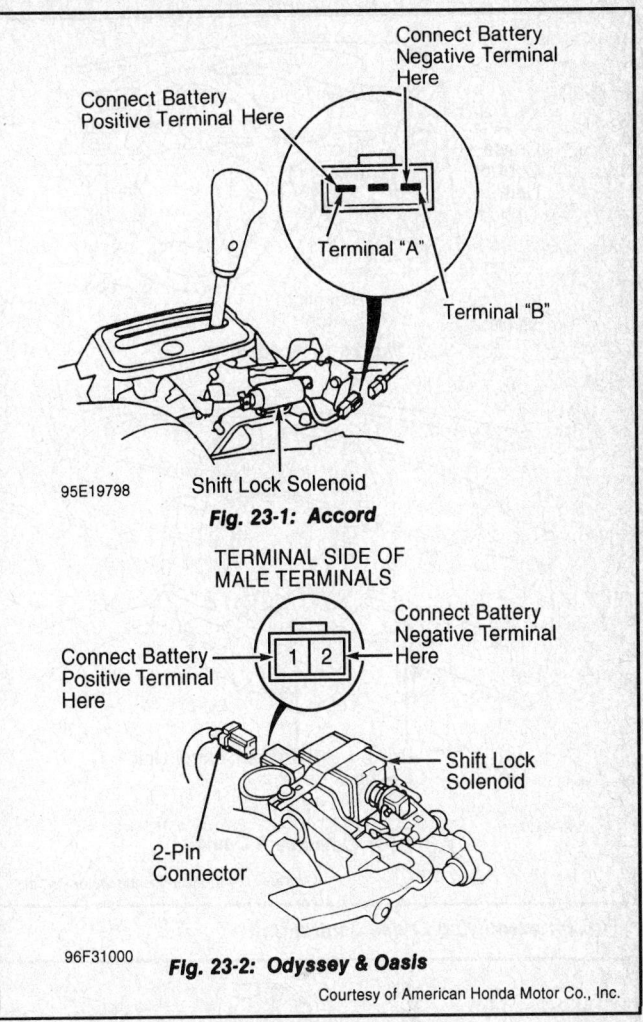

Fig. 23-1: Accord

Fig. 23-2: Odyssey & Oasis

Courtesy of American Honda Motor Co., Inc.

Fig. 23: Identifying Shift Lock Solenoid Connector & Terminals

3) Using ohmmeter, check for continuity between Black wire of 3-pin electrical connector and body ground. If continuity exists, repair open circuit in Yellow wire between 3-pin electrical connector and No. 1 fuse (10-amp) in fuse/relay box near driver's side kick panel.

4) If continuity does not exist, check for open circuit in Black wire between 3-pin electrical connector and ground connection G101. See WIRING DIAGRAMS. Ground connection G101 is located on bolt at end of intake manifold, near brake master cylinder. *See Fig. 12.*

5) Using voltmeter, measure voltage between Orange and Black wires of 3-pin electrical connector. If about 5 volts exist, proceed to step **6)**. If about 5 volts does not exist, repair open circuit or short circuit to ground in Orange wire. The Orange wire goes to instrument panel gauge assembly, TCM, ECM and cruise control unit on 1995 models and to instrument panel gauge assembly, PCM and cruise control unit on 1996 models.

NOTE: Cruise control unit is located on driver's side of instrument panel and contains a 14-pin electrical connector. See Fig. 24.

6) Connect Test Harness (07LAJ-PT30200A) between vehicle speed sensor and wiring harness. *See Fig. 25.* Raise and support front of vehicle so front wheels are free to rotate.

7) Connect Green clip on test harness to positive (+) lead on voltmeter. Connect Red clip on test harness to negative (–) lead on voltmeter.

8) Place shift lever in Neutral. Ensure ignition is on. Rotate one front wheel while holding the other front wheel stationary.

9) Note that voltage reading pulses from zero volts to about 5 volts. If voltage pulses correctly, vehicle speed sensor is okay. If voltage does not pulse correctly, replace vehicle speed sensor.

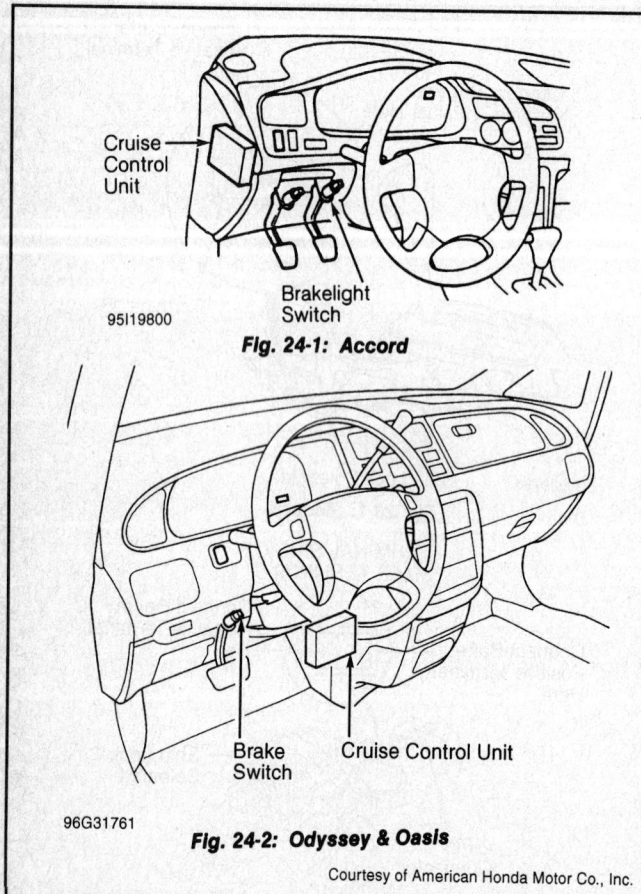

Fig. 24-1: Accord

95I19800

Fig. 24-2: Odyssey & Oasis

96G31761

Courtesy of American Honda Motor Co., Inc.

Fig. 24: Identifying Cruise Control Unit

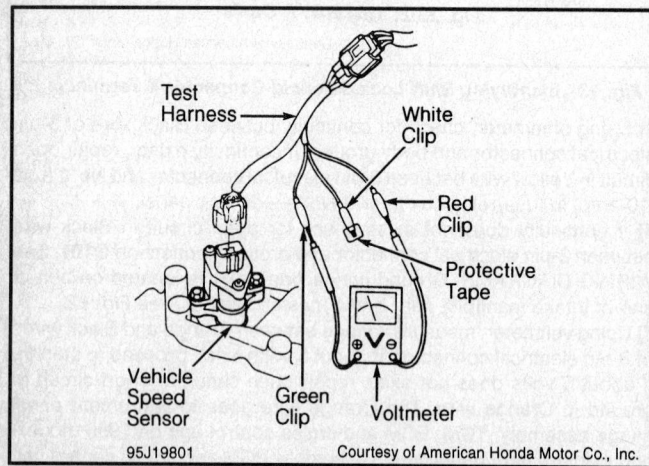

Fig. 25: Installing Test Harness For Testing VSS

95J19801 Courtesy of American Honda Motor Co., Inc.

Odyssey & Oasis – 1) Vehicle speed sensor is located on rear of transaxle, below engine thermostat housing. See Fig. 5. Ensure No. 1 fuse (10-amp) in fuse/relay box near driver's side kick panel is okay. Replace fuse if necessary. If fuse is okay, disconnect 3-pin electrical connector at vehicle speed sensor.
2) Connect Test Harness (07LAJ-PT30200A) to VSS engine harness only. Connect Red test harness clip to positive lead of DVOM. Check continuity between Red test harness clip and ground.
3) If continuity does not exist, check for open circuit in Black wire between VSS and ground connection G101. See WIRING DIAGRAMS. Ground connection G101 is located at back of engine near master cylinder. If continuity exists, connect test harness to VSS and go to next step.

4) Connect White test harness clip to positive lead of DVOM. Connect Red test harness clip to negative lead of DVOM. Turn ignition on. Using voltmeter, check for battery voltage. If battery voltage exists, proceed to next step. If battery voltage does not exist, repair open Yellow wire between VSS 3-pin electrical connector and No. 1 fuse (10-amp) in fuse/relay box near driver's side kick panel.
5) Connect Green test harness clip to positive lead of DVOM. Connect Red test harness clip to negative lead of DVOM. If about 5 volts or more exist, proceed to next step. If about 5 volts does not exist, repair open in Orange wire. The Orange wire goes to instrument panel gauge assembly, TCM, ECM and cruise control unit on 1995 models and to instrument panel gauge assembly, PCM and cruise control unit on 1996 models.

NOTE: *Cruise control unit is located behind driver's side of instrument panel, just above brakelight switch and contains a 14-pin electrical connector. See Fig. 24.*

6) Reconnect 3-pin electrical connector on vehicle speed sensor. Raise and support front of vehicle so front wheels are free to rotate. Place shift lever in Neutral. Ensure ignition is on. Rotate one front wheel while holding the other front wheel stationary.
7) Note that voltage reading pulses from zero volts to about 5 volts. If voltage pulses correctly, vehicle speed sensor is okay. If voltage does not pulse correctly, replace vehicle speed sensor.

REMOVAL & INSTALLATION
A/T GEAR POSITION SWITCH
Removal – Remove center console. Disconnect electrical connectors from A/T gear position switch. Remove nuts and A/T gear position switch.
Installation – 1) Ensure parking brake is applied. Place switch slider on A/T gear position switch in neutral position. See Fig. 26. Place shift lever in Neutral.
2) Install A/T gear position switch and nuts. DO NOT tighten nuts at this time. The A/T gear position switch must be adjusted.
3) On Accord, to adjust A/T gear position switch, place shift lever in "P" position. Ensure retaining nuts are loose. Note electrical connector terminal identification. See Fig. 17.
4) Connect ohmmeter between terminals "F" and "I". Move A/T gear position switch toward rear of console until continuity exists between terminals "F" and "I". Free play at lock pin should be about .079" (2.0 mm). See Fig. 26.
5) Tighten nuts. On all models, check A/T gear position switch for correct continuity in all gears and schronization with indicator lights. See A/T GEAR POSITION SWITCH under COMPONENT TESTING. If proper adjustment cannot be obtained, check for damaged shift lever detent or bracket. Install electrical connector and cover on center console.

BRAKELIGHT SWITCH
Removal & Installation (Accord) – 1) Disconnect electrical connector from brakelight switch located on brake pedal support. Remove lock nut.
2) Unscrew brakelight switch. To install, screw brakelight switch inward until brakelight plunger is fully depressed.
3) Back off brakelight switch 1/4 turn. Install and tighten lock nut. Install electrical connector. Ensure brakelights and cruise control operate properly.
Removal & Installation (Odyssey & Oasis) – 1) Disconnect electrical connector from brakelight switch located on brake pedal support. Remove lock nut.
2) Unscrew brakelight switch. To install, screw brakelight switch inward until brakelight plunger is fully depressed.
3) Back off brakelight switch until clearance between threaded end on brakelight switch and pad on pedal is .012-.039" (.30-1.00 mm). Install and tighten lock nut. Install electrical connector. Ensure brakelights and cruise control operate properly.

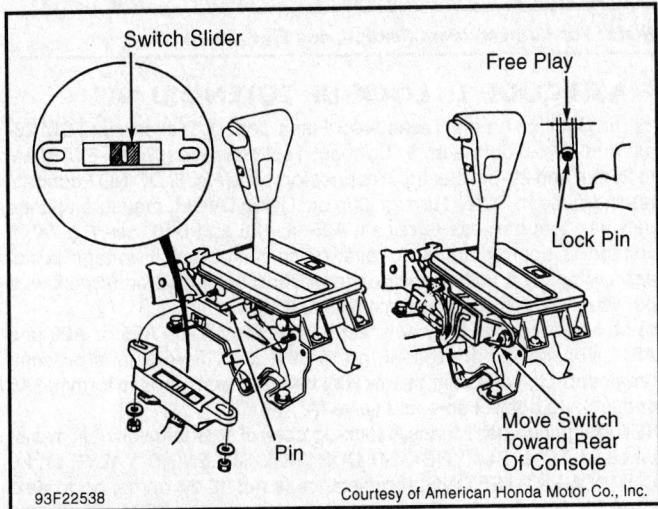

Fig. 26: Installing A/T Gear Position Switch

COUNTERSHAFT SPEED SENSOR

Removal & Installation – Countershaft speed sensor is located on transaxle. *See Fig. 5*. Remove bolt, countershaft speed sensor and "O" ring. To install, reverse removal procedure using NEW "O" ring. Tighten bolt to specification. See TORQUE SPECIFICATIONS.

ENGINE COOLANT TEMPERATURE (ECT) SENSOR

Removal – Engine coolant temperature sensor is located on cylinder head, below the distributor. *See Fig. 5*. Engine coolant temperature sensor contains a Red/White wire and Green/Blue wire on. Drain cooling system. Remove engine coolant temperature sensor.

Installation – 1) Install and tighten engine coolant temperature sensor. When refilling cooling system, open air bleeder screw on thermostat housing.

2) Fill cooling system until coolant flows from air bleeder screw. Tighten air bleeder screw to specification. See TORQUE SPECIFICATIONS. Finish filling cooling system.

KEY INTERLOCK SOLENOID

Removal & Installation – Key interlock solenoid cannot be serviced separately. Entire ignition lock assembly must be replaced.

LOCK-UP CONTROL SOLENOID VALVES

Removal & Installation – 1) Lock-up control solenoid valves are located on transaxle. *See Fig. 5*. Disconnect electrical connector at lock-up control solenoid valves.

2) Remove bolts, lock-up control solenoid valve assembly and gasket. To install, reverse removal procedure using NEW gasket. Tighten bolts to specification. See TORQUE SPECIFICATIONS.

MAINSHAFT SPEED SENSOR

Removal & Installation – Mainshaft speed sensor is located on transaxle. *See Fig. 5*. Remove bolt, mainshaft speed sensor and "O" ring. To install, reverse removal procedure using NEW "O" ring. Tighten bolt to specification. See TORQUE SPECIFICATIONS.

SHIFT CONTROL SOLENOID VALVES

Removal & Installation – 1) Shift control solenoid valves are located on transaxle. *See Fig. 5*. Disconnect electrical connector at shift control solenoid valves.

2) Remove bolts, shift control solenoid valve assembly and gasket. To install, reverse removal procedure using NEW gasket. Tighten bolts to specification. See TORQUE SPECIFICATIONS.

SHIFT LOCK SOLENOID

Removal (Accord) – Remove center console. Disconnect electrical connector at shift lock solenoid. Remove clip or pin from shift lock solenoid. Remove nuts and shift lock solenoid.

Installation – 1) Install shift lock solenoid with NEW nuts snugly installed. Install clip or pin and electrical connector.

2) Turn ignition on with solenoid energized. Ensure clearance between top of shift lock lever and lock pin groove is .145-.185" (3.7-4.7 mm). *See Fig. 27*.

3) If clearance is not as specified, loosen nuts and reposition shift lock solenoid until correct clearance is obtained. Once correct clearance is obtained, tighten nuts to specification. See TORQUE SPECIFICATIONS.

4) Turn ignition off with solenoid de-energized. Ensure lock pin is blocked by shift lock lever. *See Fig. 27*. Check solenoid operation several times.

Removal (Odyssey & Oasis) – Remove steering column covers. Disconnect electrical connector at shift lock solenoid. Remove shift lock extension. Remove detent spring washer and shift lock solenoid.

Installation – Reverse removal procedure. Ensure shift lock stop does not protrude with ignition off. *See Fig. 28*. Measure shift lock stop protrusion with ignition on. Ensure shift lock stop protrudes more than .300" (7.50 mm).

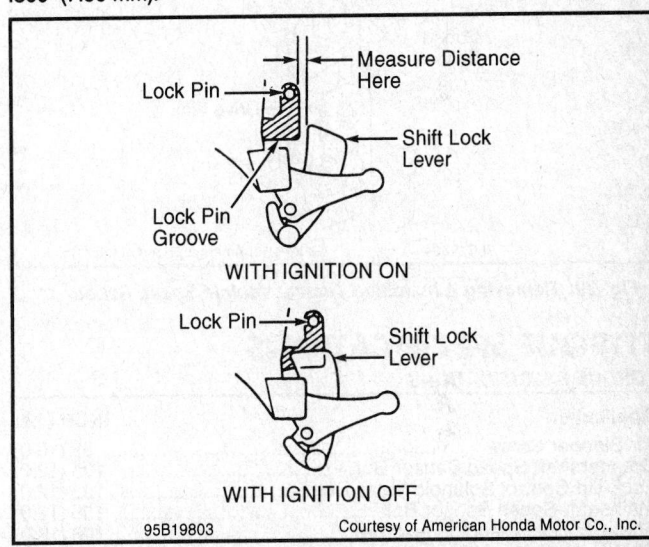

Fig. 27: Checking Shift Lock Solenoid Operation (Accord)

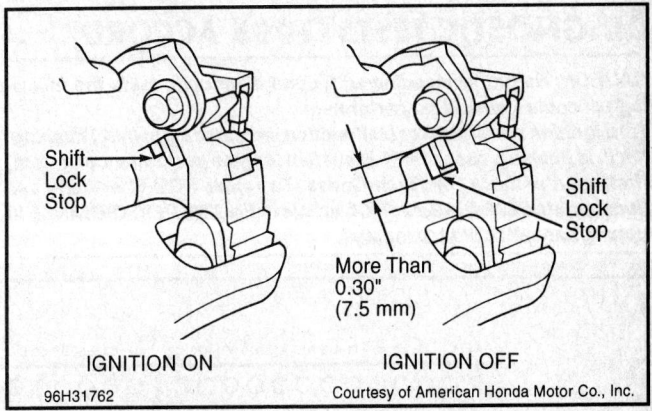

Fig. 28: Checking Shift Lock Solenoid Operation (Odyssey & Oasis)

PCM/TCM

Removal & Installation – The PCM/TCM is located below carpet, under passenger's side of instrument panel. *See Fig. 5.* Replacement information not available.

THROTTLE POSITION (TP) SENSOR

Removal & Installation – Throttle position sensor is mounted on throttle body. Replacement information is not available.

VEHICLE SPEED SENSOR (VSS)

Removal & Installation – **1)** Vehicle speed sensor is located on rear of transaxle, near distributor. *See Fig. 5.*
2) Disconnect electrical connector at vehicle speed sensor. Remove bolts and vehicle speed sensor. Use care not to lose drive link located between vehicle speed sensor and housing. *See Fig. 29.* To install, reverse removal procedure.

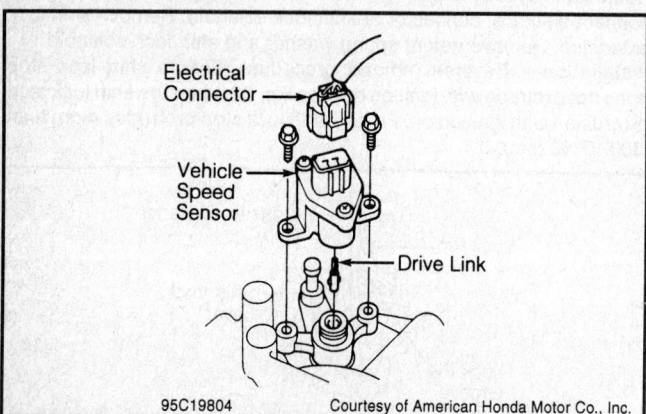

95C19804   Courtesy of American Honda Motor Co., Inc.

Fig. 29: Removing & Installing Typical Vehicle Speed Sensor

TORQUE SPECIFICATIONS

TORQUE SPECIFICATIONS

Application	INCH Lbs.
Air Bleeder Screw	89 (10.0)
Countershaft Speed Sensor Bolt	106 (12.0)
Lock-Up Control Solenoid Valve Bolt	106 (12.0)
Mainshaft Speed Sensor Bolt	106 (12.0)
Shift Control Solenoid Valve Bolt	106 (12.0)
Shift Lock Solenoid Nut	89 (10.0)

DIAGNOSTIC TESTS (1995 ACCORD)

CAUTION: Before proceeding with code diagnostic tests the following procedure should be performed:
Turn ignition on. Check for Malfunction Indicator Light (MIL) flashing. If MIL is flashing, repair PGM-FI system (engine performance system) first, then recheck for Flash Codes. To repair PGM-FI system, see appropriate SELF-DIAGNOSTICS article in ENGINE PERFORMANCE in appropriate MITCHELL® manual.

NOTE: For terminal identification, see Figs. 30 and 31.

FLASH CODE 1: LOCK-UP SOLENOID "A"

1) Turn ignition on and recheck for Flash Code 1. Disconnect TCM 26-pin and 22-pin connectors. Connect Test Harness (07LAJ-PT3010A) to 26-pin and 22-pin electrical connectors. *See Fig. 8.* DO NOT connect test harness to TCM. Turn ignition on. Using DVOM, measure voltage between test harness terminals A25 or A26 and D18. *See Fig. 30.* If voltage is approximately 5 volts, go to next step. If voltage is not approximately 5 volts, repair open or short in Light Green/Black wire between test harness terminal D18 and ECM.
2) Measure voltage between test harness terminals A25 or A26 and A6. If voltage is not present, go to next step. If voltage is present, repair short to voltage in Yellow wire between test harness terminal A6 and lock-up control solenoid valve "A".
3) Turn ignition off. Measure lock-up control solenoid valve "A" resistance at TCM. See LOCK-UP CONTROL SOLENOID VALVE under COMPONENT TESTING. If resistance is not 12-24 ohms, go to next step. If resistance is 12-24 ohms, check for loose TCM connectors and replace TCM with known good part, as necessary.
4) Disconnect lock-up control solenoid valve connector. Check for continuity between test harness terminals A25 or A26 and A6. If continuity does not exist, go to next step. If continuity exists, repair short to ground in Yellow wire between test harness terminal A6 and lock-up control solenoid valve "A".
5) Measure resistance between lock-up control solenoid valve connector (solenoid side) Yellow wire and ground. If resistance is not 12-24 ohms, replace lock-up control solenoid valve assembly. If resistance is 12-24 ohms, check and repair open Yellow wire between lock-up control solenoid valve connector and lock-up control solenoid valve.

FLASH CODE 2: LOCK-UP SOLENOID "B"

1) Turn ignition on and recheck for Flash Code 2. Disconnect TCM 26-pin and 22-pin connectors. Connect Test Harness (07LAJ-PT3010A) to 26-pin and 22-pin electrical connectors. *See Fig. 8.* DO NOT connect test harness to TCM. Using DVOM, measure voltage between test harness terminals A25 or A26 and D18. *See Fig. 30.* If voltage is approximately 5 volts, go to next step. If voltage is not approximately 5 volts, repair open or short in Light Green/Black wire between test harness terminal D18 and ECM.
2) Measure voltage between test harness terminals A25 or A26 and A4. If voltage is not present, go to next step. If voltage is present, repair short to voltage in Green/Black wire between test harness terminal A4 and lock-up control solenoid valve "B".
3) Turn ignition off. Measure lock-up control solenoid valve "B" resistance at TCM. See LOCK-UP CONTROL SOLENOID VALVE under COMPONENT TESTING. If resistance is not 12-24 ohms, go to next step. If resistance is 12-24 ohms, check for loose TCM connectors and replace TCM with known good part, as necessary.
4) Disconnect lock-up control solenoid valve connector. Check for continuity between test harness terminals A25 or A26 and A4. If continuity does not exist, go to next step. If continuity exists, repair short to ground in Green/Black wire between test harness terminal A4 and lock-up control solenoid valve "B".

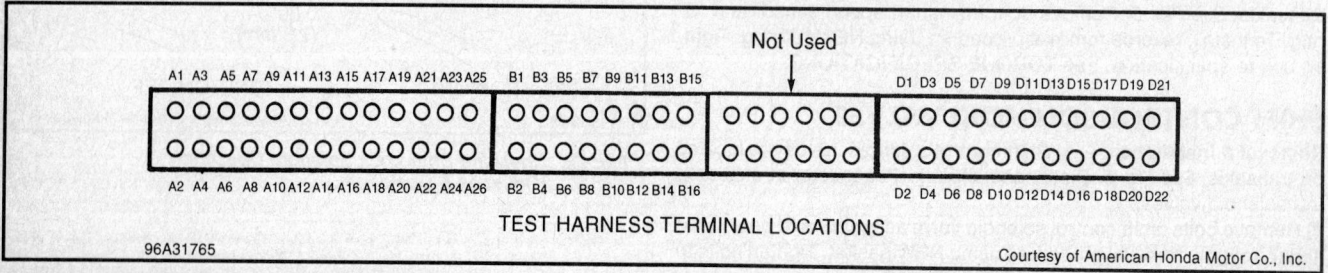

Not Used

TEST HARNESS TERMINAL LOCATIONS

96A31765   Courtesy of American Honda Motor Co., Inc.

Fig. 30: Identifying Test Harness Terminals

5) Measure resistance between lock-up control solenoid valve connector (solenoid side) Green/Black wire and ground. If resistance is not 12-24 ohms, replace lock-up control solenoid valve assembly. If resistance is 12-24 ohms, check and repair open Green/Black wire between lock-up control solenoid valve connector and lock-up control solenoid valve.

FLASH CODE 3: TP SENSOR

1) Turn ignition on and recheck for Flash Code 3. Disconnect TCM 26-pin and 22-pin connectors. Connect Test Harness (07LAJ-PT3010A) to 26-pin and 22-pin electrical connectors. See Fig. 8. DO NOT connect test harness to TCM.

2) Using DVOM, measure voltage between test harness terminals A25 or A26 and D18. See Fig. 30. If voltage is approximately 5 volts, go to next step. If voltage is not approximately 5 volts, repair open or short in Light Green/Black wire between test harness terminal D18 and ECM.

3) Turn ignition off. Connect Test Harness to TCM. Turn ignition on. Measure voltage between test harness terminals A25 or A26 and D7. If voltage is .4-.6 volts, check for loose TCM connectors and replace TCM with known good part, as necessary. If voltage is not .4-.6 volts, repair open or short in Red/Black wire between TCM test harness and TP sensor.

FLASH CODE 4: VEHICLE SPEED SENSOR (VSS)

1) Ensure speedometer operates correctly. If speedometer operates properly, go to next step. If speedometer does not operate properly, see VEHICLE SPEED SENSOR (VSS) under COMPONENT TESTING.

2) Raise and support vehicle. Block one front wheel. Place gear selector in neutral. Turn ignition off. Disconnect TCM 22-pin and TCM 26-pin connectors. Connect Test Harness (07LAJ-PT3010A) to 26-pin and 22-pin electrical connectors. See Fig. 8. DO NOT connect test harness to TCM.

3) Turn ignition on. While rotating unblocked front wheel, measure voltage between test harness terminals A25 or A26 and D9. See Fig. 30.

4) If voltage alternates from zero to 5 volts, check for loose TCM connectors and replace TCM with known good part, as necessary. If voltage does not alternate from zero to 5 volts, check and repair short or open in Orange wire between test harness terminal D9 and VSS. If wire is okay, see VEHICLE SPEED SENSOR (VSS) under COMPONENT TESTING.

FLASH CODE 5: A/T GEAR POSITION SWITCH

NOTE: FLASH CODE 5 is set when TCM receives 2 gear position signals at same time.

1) Turn ignition on. If any A/T gear position indicator light stays on when gear selector is moved from that gear, go to next step. If all A/T gear position indicator lights go off when gear selector is moved from that gear, system is okay at this time.

2) Turn ignition off. Disconnect TCM 26-pin and 22-pin connectors. Connect Test Harness (07LAJ-PT3010A) between TCM and electrical connectors. See Fig. 8. Turn ignition on. Shift to all gear positions except reverse. Using DVOM, measure voltage between test harness terminals A25 or A26 and A21. See Fig. 30. If battery voltage is present, go to next step. If battery voltage is not present, check and repair short in Green/Red wire between test harness connector and A/T gear position indicator or A/T gear position switch. If Green/Red wire is okay, check for loose TCM connectors and replace TCM with known good part, as necessary.

3) Shift to all gear positions except "N" and "P". Measure voltage between test harness terminals A25 or A26 and A19. If battery voltage is present, go to next step. If battery voltage is not present, check and repair short in Light Green wire between test harness connector and A/T gear position indicator or repair short in Green/White or Green wire between A/T gear position indicator and A/T gear position switch. If wires are okay, check for loose TCM connectors and replace TCM with known good part, as necessary.

4) Shift to all gear positions except "D₄". Measure voltage between test harness terminals A25 or A26 and A17. If battery voltage is present, go to next step. If battery voltage is not present, check and repair short in Light Green/Black wire between test harness connector and A/T gear position switch. If Light Green/Black wire is okay, check for loose TCM connectors and replace TCM with known good part, as necessary.

5) Shift to all gear positions except "D₃". Measure voltage between test harness terminals A25 or A26 and A15. If battery voltage is present, go to next step. If battery voltage is not present, check and repair short in Green/Blue wire between test harness connector and A/T gear position indicator or A/T gear position switch. If Green/Blue wire is okay, check for loose TCM connectors and replace TCM with known good part, as necessary.

6) Shift to all gear positions except "2". Measure voltage between test harness terminals A25 or A26 and A13. If battery voltage is present, go to next step. If battery voltage is not present, check and repair short in Green/Yellow wire between test harness connector and A/T gear position indicator or A/T gear position switch. If Green/Yellow wire is okay, check for loose TCM connectors and replace TCM with known good part, as necessary.

7) Shift to all gear positions except "1". Measure voltage between test harness terminals A25 or A26 and A11. If battery voltage is present, check for loose TCM connectors and replace TCM with known good part, as necessary. If battery voltage is not present, check and repair short in Light Green/White wire between test harness connector and A/T gear position indicator or A/T gear position switch. If Light Green/White wire is okay, check for loose TCM connectors and replace TCM with known good part, as necessary.

FLASH CODE 6: A/T GEAR POSITION SWITCH

1) Turn ignition off. Disconnect TCM 26-pin and 22-pin connectors. Connect Test Harness (07LAJ-PT3010A) between TCM and electrical connectors. See Fig. 8. Turn ignition on. Shift to reverse position. Using DVOM, measure voltage between test harness terminals A25 or A26 and A21. See Fig. 30. If battery voltage is present, go to next step. If battery voltage is not present, check and repair open in Green/Red wire between test harness connector and A/T gear position switch.

2) Shift to "N" and "P" position. Measure voltage between test harness terminals A25 or A26 and A19. If battery voltage is present, go to next step. If battery voltage is not present, check and repair open in Light Green wire between test harness connector and A/T gear position indicator.

3) Shift to "D₄" position. Measure voltage between test harness terminals A25 or A26 and A17. If battery voltage is present, go to next step. If battery voltage is not present, check and repair open in Light Green/Black wire between test harness connector and A/T gear position switch.

4) Shift to "D₃" position. Measure voltage between test harness terminals A25 or A26 and A15. If battery voltage is present, go to next step. If battery voltage is not present, check and repair open in Green/Blue wire between test harness connector and A/T gear position switch.

5) Shift to "2" position. Measure voltage between test harness terminals A25 or A26 and A13. If battery voltage is present, go to next step. If battery voltage is not present, check and repair open in Green/Yellow wire between test harness connector and A/T gear position switch.

6) Shift to "1" position. Measure voltage between test harness terminals A25 or A26 and A11. If battery voltage is present, check for loose TCM connectors and replace TCM with known good part, as necessary. If battery voltage is not present, check and repair open in Light Green/White wire between test harness connector and A/T gear position switch.

FLASH CODE 7: SHIFT SOLENOID "A"

1) Turn ignition on and recheck for Flash Code 7. Disconnect TCM 26-pin and TCM 22-pin connectors. Connect Test Harness (07LAJ-PT3010A) to 26-pin and 22-pin electrical connectors. See Fig. 8. DO NOT connect test harness to TCM. Turn ignition on. Using DVOM,

measure voltage between test harness terminals A25 or A26 and D18. *See Fig. 30.* If voltage is approximately 5 volts, go to next step. If voltage is not approximately 5 volts, repair open or short in Light Green/Black wire between test harness terminal D18 and ECM.

2) Measure voltage between test harness terminals A25 or A26 and A5. If voltage is not present, go to next step. If voltage is present, repair short to voltage in Blue/Yellow wire between test harness terminal A6 and shift control solenoid valve "A".

3) Turn ignition off. Measure shift control solenoid valve "A" resistance at TCM. See SHIFT CONTROL SOLENOID VALVE under COMPONENT TESTING. If resistance is not 12-24 ohms, go to next step. If resistance is 12-24 ohms, check for loose TCM connectors and replace TCM with known good part, as necessary.

4) Disconnect shift control solenoid valve connector. Check for continuity between test harness terminals A25 or A26 and A5. If continuity does not exist, go to next step. If continuity exists, repair short to ground in Blue/Yellow wire between test harness terminal A5 and shift control solenoid valve "A".

5) Measure resistance between shift control solenoid valve connector (solenoid side) Blue/Yellow wire and ground. If resistance is not 12-24 ohms, replace shift control solenoid valve assembly. If resistance is 12-24 ohms, check and repair open Blue/Yellow wire between shift control solenoid valve connector and shift control solenoid valve.

FLASH CODE 8: SHIFT SOLENOID "B"

1) Turn ignition on and recheck for Flash Code 8. Disconnect TCM 26-pin and 22-pin connectors. Connect Test Harness (07LAJ-PT3010A) to 26-pin and 22-pin electrical connectors. *See Fig. 8.* DO NOT connect test harness to TCM. Using DVOM, measure voltage between test harness terminals A25 or A26 and D18. *See Fig. 30.* If voltage is approximately 5 volts, go to next step. If voltage is not approximately 5 volts, repair open or short in Light Green/Black wire between test harness terminal D18 and ECM.

2) Measure voltage between test harness terminals A25 or A26 and A3. If voltage is not present, go to next step. If voltage is present, repair short to voltage in Green/White wire between test harness terminal A3 and shift control solenoid valve "B".

3) Turn ignition off. Measure shift control solenoid valve "B" resistance at TCM. See SHIFT CONTROL SOLENOID VALVE under COMPONENT TESTING. If resistance is not 12-24 ohms, go to next step. If resistance is 12-24 ohms, check for loose TCM connectors and replace TCM with known good part, as necessary.

4) Disconnect shift control solenoid valve connector. Check for continuity between test harness terminals A25 or A26 and A3. If continuity does not exist, go to next step. If continuity exists, repair short to ground in Green/White wire between test harness terminal A3 and shift control solenoid valve "B".

5) Measure resistance between shift control solenoid valve connector (solenoid side) Green/White wire and ground. If resistance is not 12-24 ohms, replace shift control solenoid valve assembly. If resistance is 12-24 ohms, check and repair open Green/White wire between shift control solenoid valve connector and shift control solenoid valve.

FLASH CODE 9: COUNTERSHAFT SPEED SENSOR

1) Ensure countershaft speed sensor is installed properly. See COUNTERSHAFT SPEED SENSOR under REMOVAL & INSTALLATION. Disconnect countershaft speed sensor connector and measure resistance between sensor connector terminals. See COUNTERSHAFT SPEED SENSOR under COMPONENT TESTING.

2) If resistance is not 400-600 ohms, replace countershaft speed sensor. If resistance is 400-600 ohms, disconnect TCM 22-pin connector. Connect Test Harness (07LAJ-PT3010A) to 22-pin electrical connector. *See Fig. 8.* DO NOT connect test harness to TCM. Check continuity between ground and test harness terminals D15 and D17. *See Fig. 30.*

3) If continuity exists, repair short to ground in Blue/Green or Blue/Yellow wires between test harness connector and countershaft speed sensor. If continuity does not exist, reconnect countershaft speed sensor connector. Measure resistance between test harness terminals D15 and D17.

4) If resistance is 400-600 ohms, check for loose TCM connectors and replace TCM with known good part, as necessary. If resistance is not 400-600 ohms, repair open Blue/Green or Blue/Yellow wires between test harness connector and countershaft speed sensor connector.

FLASH CODE 10: ECT SENSOR

1) Turn ignition on and recheck for Flash Code 10. Disconnect TCM 26-pin and 22-pin connectors. Connect Test Harness (07LAJ-PT3010A) to 26-pin and 22-pin electrical connectors. *See Fig. 8.* DO NOT connect test harness to TCM.

2) Using DVOM, measure voltage between test harness terminals A25 or A26 and D18. *See Fig. 30.* If voltage is approximately 5 volts, go to next step. If voltage is not approximately 5 volts, repair open or short in Light Green/Black wire between test harness terminal D18 and ECM.

3) Turn ignition off. Connect test harness connectors to TCM. Turn ignition on. Start engine and warm to normal operating temperature. Measure voltage between test harness terminals A25 or A26 and D5. *See Fig. 30.* If voltage is not less than one volt, repair open Red/White wire between TCM and ECT sensor. If voltage is less than one volt, check for loose TCM connectors and replace TCM with known good part, as necessary.

FLASH CODE 11: IGNITION COIL

1) Disconnect TCM 26-pin connector. Turn ignition on. Using DVOM, measure voltage between TCM 26-pin connector terminals A9 (Blue wire) and A25 or A26 (Brown/Black wires). *See Fig. 31.*

2) If battery voltage is present, check for loose TCM connectors and replace TCM with known good part, as necessary. If battery voltage is not present, repair open or short in Blue wire between ignition coil and TCM 26-pin connector.

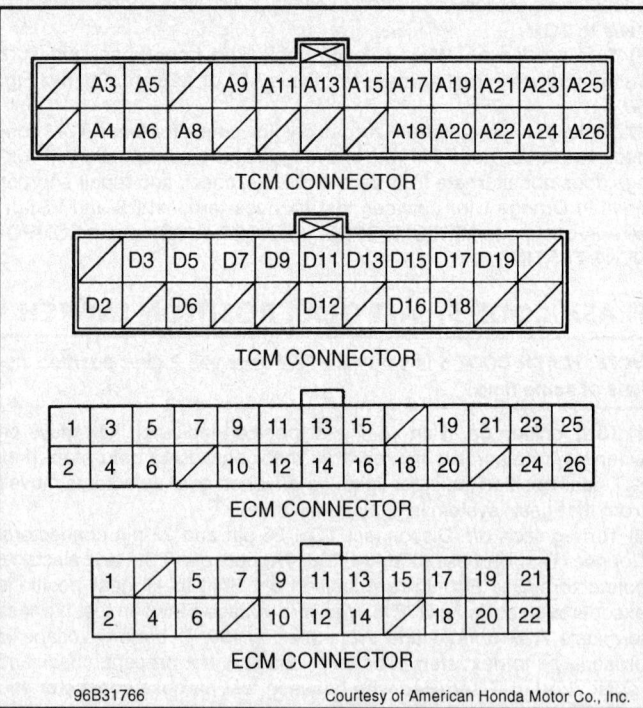

96B31766   Courtesy of American Honda Motor Co., Inc.

Fig. 31: Identifying TCM & ECM Connector Terminals

FLASH CODE 13: BARO SIGNAL

NOTE: *Baro sensor is built into ECM.*

1) Check for Flash Code 13. If code is present, go to next step. If Code 13 is not present, clear codes. See CLEARING CODES. If MIL light is still on and indicates Code 13, replace ECM with known good part, as necessary. If MIL light is not on or does not indicate Code 13, go to next step.

2) Turn ignition off. Disconnect TCM 22-pin 26-pin connectors. Connect Test Harness (07LAJ-PT3010A) to 26-pin and 22-pin electrical connectors. *See Fig. 8.* DO NOT connect test harness to TCM. Turn ignition on. Measure voltage between test harness terminals A25 or A26 and D18. *See Fig. 30.* If voltage is approximately 5 volts, go to next step. If voltage is not approximately 5 volts, repair open or short in Light Green/Black wire between test harness terminal D18 and ECM.

3) Turn ignition off. Disconnect TCM and ECM 22-pin connectors. Check for continuity of Blue/White wire between ECM 22-pin connector terminal D5 and TCM 22-pin connector terminal D3. *See Fig. 31.* If continuity exists, go to next step. If continuity does not exist, repair open Blue/White wire between ECM and TCM.

4) Check for continuity between ECM 22-pin connector terminal D5 (Blue/White wire) and ground or TCM 22-pin connector terminal D3 (Blue/White wire) and ground. If continuity does not exist, check for loose TCM connectors and replace TCM with known good part, as necessary. If continuity exists, repair short to ground in Blue/White wire.

FLASH CODE 14: FAS SIGNAL

1) Turn ignition on and recheck for Flash Code 14. Start engine and warm to normal operating temperature. Shift to park. Connect Test Harness (07LAJ-PT3010A) between TCM and electrical connectors. *See Fig. 8.* Turn ignition on and wait 2 seconds. Using DVOM, measure voltage between test harness terminals A25 or A26 and D16. *See Fig. 30..* If voltage is not approximately 5 volts, go to next step. If voltage is approximately 5 volts, check for loose TCM connectors and replace TCM with known good part, as necessary.

2) Turn ignition off. Disconnect test harness from TCM. Turn ignition on. Measure voltage between test harness terminals A25 or A26 and D16. *See Fig. 31.* If voltage is approximately 5 volts, check for loose TCM connectors and replace TCM with known good part, as necessary. If voltage is not approximately 5 volts, go to next step.

3) Turn ignition off. Disconnect ECM 26-pin connector. Check for continuity of between test harness terminals A25 or A26 and D16. If continuity exists, repair short in Brown/White wire between TCM and ECM. If continuity does not exist, go to next step.

4) Disconnect 26-pin and 22-pin connectors from test harness. Check for continuity between ECM 26-pin connector terminal A18 and TCM 22-pin connector terminal D16. If continuity exists, check for loose TCM connectors and replace TCM with known good part, as necessary. If continuity does not exist, repair open in Brown/White wire between TCM and ECM.

FLASH CODE 15: MAINSHAFT SPEED SENSOR

NOTE: FLASH CODE 15 doesn't always mean an electrical problem in mainshaft speed sensor or circuit, this DTC can also be caused by a mechanical problem in transaxle.

1) Ensure mainshaft and countershaft speed sensors are installed properly. See COUNTERSHAFT or MAINSHAFT SPEED SENSOR under REMOVAL & INSTALLATION. Disconnect mainshaft speed sensor connector and measure resistance between sensor connector terminals. See MAINSHAFT SPEED SENSOR under COMPONENT TESTING.

2) If resistance is not 400-600 ohms, replace mainshaft speed sensor. If resistance is 400-600 ohms, disconnect TCM 22-pin connector. Connect Test Harness (07LAJ-PT3010A) to 22-pin electrical connector. *See Fig. 8.* DO NOT connect test harness to TCM. Check continuity between test harness terminals D12 and D19 and ground. *See Fig. 30.*

3) If continuity exists, repair short to ground in Orange/Blue or White/Blue wires between test harness terminals and mainshaft speed sensor. If continuity does not exist, reconnect mainshaft speed sensor connector. Measure resistance between test harness terminals D12 and D19.

4) If resistance is not 400-600 ohms, go to next step. If resistance is 400-600 ohms, perform FLASH CODE 9 diagnostic, check for loose TCM connectors and replace TCM with known good part, as necessary.

5) Disconnect mainshaft speed sensor connector. Check continuity of Orange/Blue wire between test harness terminal D19 and mainshaft speed sensor connector. If continuity exists, go to next step. If continuity does not exist, repair open Orange/Blue wire between test harness connector and mainshaft speed sensor connector.

6) Check continuity of White/Blue wire between test harness terminal D12 and mainshaft speed sensor connector. If continuity exists, check for loose TCM connectors and replace TCM with known good part, as necessary. If continuity does not exist, repair open White/Blue wire between test harness connector and mainshaft speed sensor connector.

DIAGNOSTIC TESTS (1995 ODYSSEY)

NOTE: For terminal identification, see Fig. 32.

FLASH CODE 1: LOCK-UP CONTROL SOLENOID VALVE "A"

1) Disconnect TCM 26-pin connector "A" and TCM 22-pin connector "B". Turn ignition on. Using DVOM, measure voltage between TCM 22-pin connector "B" terminal No. 20 (Light Green/Black wire) and TCM 26-pin connector "A" terminals No. 13 or No. 26 (Brown/Black wires). *See Fig. 32.* If voltage is approximately 5 volts, go to next step. If voltage is not approximately 5 volts, repair open or short in Light Green/Black wire between TCM 22-pin connector "B" and ECM.

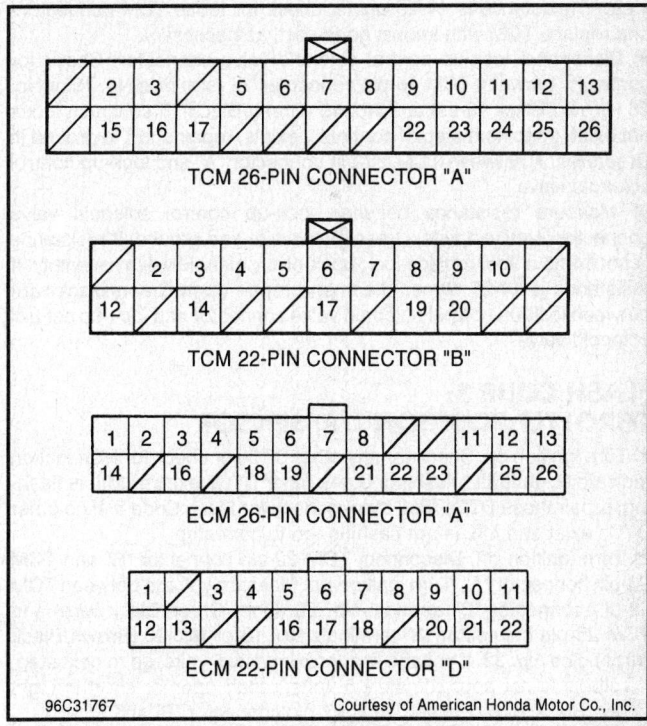

TCM 26-PIN CONNECTOR "A"

TCM 22-PIN CONNECTOR "B"

ECM 26-PIN CONNECTOR "A"

ECM 22-PIN CONNECTOR "D"

96C31767 Courtesy of American Honda Motor Co., Inc.

Fig. 32: Identifying TCM & ECM Connector Terminals

2) Measure voltage between TCM 26-pin connector "A" terminals No. 13 or No. 26 (Brown/Black wires) and No. 16 (Yellow wire). If voltage is not present, go to next step. If voltage is present, repair short to voltage in Yellow wire.

3) Turn ignition off. Measure lock-up control solenoid valve "A" resistance at TCM. See LOCK-UP CONTROL SOLENOID VALVE under COMPONENT TESTING. If resistance is not 14-25 ohms, go to next step. If resistance is 14-25 ohms, check for loose TCM connectors and replace TCM with known good part, as necessary.

4) Disconnect lock-up control solenoid valve connector. Check for continuity between TCM 26-pin connector "A" terminals No. 13 or No. 26 (Brown/Black wires) and No. 16 (Yellow wire). If continuity does not exist, go to next step. If continuity exists, repair short to ground in Yellow wire between TCM 26-pin connector "A" and lock-up control solenoid valve.

5) Measure resistance between lock-up control solenoid valve connector (solenoid side) Yellow wire and ground. If resistance is not 14-25 ohms, replace lock-up control solenoid valve assembly. If resistance is 14-25 ohms, check and repair open Yellow wire between lock-up control solenoid valve connector and lock-up control solenoid valve.

FLASH CODE 2:
LOCK-UP CONTROL SOLENOID VALVE "B"

1) Disconnect TCM 26-pin connector "A" and TCM 22-pin connector "B". Turn ignition on. Using DVOM, measure voltage between TCM 22-pin connector "B" terminal No. 20 (Light Green/Black wire) and TCM 26-pin connector "A" terminals No. 13 or No. 26 (Brown/Black wires). See Fig. 32. If voltage is approximately 5 volts, go to next step. If voltage is not approximately 5 volts, repair open or short in Light Green/Black wire between TCM 22-pin connector for "B" and ECM.

2) Measure voltage between TCM 26-pin connector "A" terminals No. 13 or No. 26 (Brown/Black wires) and No. 15 (Green/Black wire). If voltage is not present, go to next step. If voltage is present, repair short to voltage in Green/Black wire.

3) Turn ignition off. Measure lock-up control solenoid valve "B" resistance at TCM. See LOCK-UP CONTROL SOLENOID VALVE under COMPONENT TESTING. If resistance is not 14-25 ohms, go to next step. If resistance is 14-25 ohms, check for loose TCM connectors and replace TCM with known good part, as necessary.

4) Disconnect lock-up control solenoid valve connector. Check for continuity between TCM 26-pin connector "A" terminals No. 13 or No. 26 (Brown/Black wires) and No. 15 (Green/Black). If continuity does not exist, go to next step. If continuity exists, repair short to ground in Green/Black between TCM 26-pin connector "A" and lock-up control solenoid valve.

5) Measure resistance between lock-up control solenoid valve connector (solenoid side) Green/Black wire and ground. If resistance is not 14-25 ohms, replace lock-up control solenoid valve assembly. If resistance is 14-25 ohms, check and repair open Green/Black wire between lock-up control solenoid valve connector and lock-up control solenoid valve.

FLASH CODE 3:
THROTTLE POSITION (TP) SENSOR

1) Turn ignition on. Check for any other DTCs or check for Malfunction Indicator Light (MIL) flashing. If any other DTCs exist or MIL is flashing, repair those DTCs first, then recheck for Flash Code 3. If no other DTCs exist and MIL is not flashing, go to next step.

2) Turn ignition off. Disconnect TCM 22-pin connector "B" and TCM 26-pin connector "A". Turn ignition on. Measure voltage between TCM 22-pin connector "B" terminal No. 20 (Light Green/Black wire) and TCM 26-pin connector "A" terminals No. 13 or No. 26 (Brown/Black wires). See Fig. 32. If voltage is approximately 5 volts, go to next step. If voltage is not approximately 5 volts, repair open or short in Light Green/Black wire between TCM 22-pin connector "B" and ECM.

3) Measure voltage between TCM 22-pin connector "B" terminal No. 4 (Red/Black wire) and TCM 26-pin connector "A" terminals No. 13 or No. 26 (Brown/Black wires). If voltage is .4-.6 volts, check for loose TCM connectors and replace TCM with known good part, as necessary. If voltage is not .4-.6 volts, repair open or short in Red/Black wire between TCM and TP sensor.

FLASH CODE 4: VEHICLE SPEED SENSOR (VSS)

1) Ensure speedometer operates correctly. If speedometer operates properly, go to next step. If speedometer does not operate properly, see VEHICLE SPEED SENSOR (VSS) under COMPONENT TESTING.

2) Raise and support vehicle. Block one front wheel. Place gear selector in "N" position. Turn ignition off. Disconnect TCM 22-pin connector "B" and TCM 26-pin connector "A". Turn ignition on. While rotating unblocked front wheel, measure voltage between TCM 22-pin connector "B" terminal No. 5 (Orange wire) and TCM 26-pin connector "A" terminals No. 13 or No. 26 (Brown/Black wires). See Fig. 32.

3) If voltage alternates from zero to 5 volts, check for loose TCM connectors and replace TCM with known good part, as necessary. If voltage does not alternate from zero to 5 volts, check and repair short or open in Orange wire between TCM and VSS. If wire is okay, see VEHICLE SPEED SENSOR (VSS) under COMPONENT TESTING.

FLASH CODE 5:
A/T GEAR POSITION SWITCH (SHORT)

NOTE: FLASH CODE 5 is set when TCM receives 2 gear position signals at same time.

1) Turn ignition on. If any A/T gear position indicator light stays on when gear selector is moved from that gear, go to next step. If all A/T gear position indicator lights go off when gear selector is moved from that gear, system is okay at this time.

2) Shift to all gear positions except reverse. Using DVOM, measure voltage between TCM 26-pin connector "A" terminals No. 13 or No. 26 (Brown/Black wires) and No. 11 (White wire). See Fig. 32. If battery voltage is present, go to next step. If battery voltage is not present, check and repair short in White wire between TCM 26-pin connector "A" and A/T gear position indicator or A/T gear position switch. If White wire is okay, check for loose TCM connectors and replace TCM with known good part, as necessary.

3) Shift to all gear positions except "N" and "P". Measure voltage between TCM 26-pin connector "A" terminals No. 13 or No. 26 (Brown/Black wires) and No. 10 (Light Green wire). If battery voltage is present, go to next step. If battery voltage is not present, check and repair short in Light Green wire between TCM 26-pin connector "A" and A/T gear position indicator or A/T gear position switch. If White wire is okay, check for loose TCM connectors and replace TCM with known good part, as necessary.

4) Shift to all gear positions except "D4". Measure voltage between TCM 26-pin connector "A" terminals No. 13 or No. 26 (Brown/Black wires) and No. 9 (Yellow wire). If battery voltage is present, go to next step. If battery voltage is not present, check and repair short in Yellow wire between TCM 26-pin connector "A" and A/T gear position switch. If Yellow wire is okay, check for loose TCM connectors and replace TCM with known good part, as necessary.

5) Shift to all gear positions except "D3". Measure voltage between TCM 26-pin connector "A" terminals No. 13 or No. 26 (Brown/Black wires) and No. 8 (Green wire). If battery voltage is present, go to next step. If battery voltage is not present, check and repair short in Green wire between TCM 26-pin connector "A" and A/T gear position indicator or A/T gear position switch. If Green wire is okay, check for loose TCM connectors and replace TCM with known good part, as necessary.

6) Shift to all gear positions except "2". Measure voltage between TCM 26-pin connector "A" terminals No. 13 or No. 26 (Brown/Black wires) and No. 7 (Blue wire). If battery voltage is present, go to next step. If battery voltage is not present, check and repair short in Blue wire between TCM 26-pin connector "A" and A/T gear position indicator or A/T gear position switch. If Blue wire is okay, check for loose TCM connectors and replace TCM with known good part, as necessary.

7) Shift to all gear positions except "1". Measure voltage between TCM 26-pin connector "A" terminals No. 13 or No. 26 (Brown/Black wires) and No. 6 (Brown wire). If battery voltage is present, check for loose TCM connectors and replace TCM with known good part, as necessary. If battery voltage is not present, check and repair short in Brown wire between TCM 26-pin connector "A" and A/T gear position indicator or A/T gear position switch. If Brown wire is okay, check for loose TCM connectors and replace TCM with known good part, as necessary.

FLASH CODE 6:
A/T GEAR POSITION SWITCH (OPEN)

1) Turn ignition on. If any A/T gear position indicator light stays on when gear selector is moved from that gear, go to next step. If all A/T gear position indicator lights go off when gear selector is moved from that gear, system is okay at this time.

2) Shift to reverse. Using DVOM, measure voltage between TCM 26-pin connector "A" terminals No. 13 or No. 26 (Brown/Black wires) and No. 11 (White wire). See Fig. 32. If voltage is present, go to next step. If voltage is not present, check and repair open in White wire between TCM 26-pin connector "A" and A/T gear position switch.

3) Shift to "N" or "P". Measure voltage between TCM 26-pin connector "A" terminals No. 13 or No. 26 (Brown/Black wires) and No. 10 (Light Green wire). If voltage is present, go to next step. If voltage is not present, check and repair open in Light Green wire between TCM 26-pin connector "A" and A/T gear position indicator.

4) Shift to "D₄" position. Measure voltage between TCM 26-pin connector "A" terminals No. 13 or No. 26 (Brown/Black wires) and No. 9 (Yellow wire). If voltage is present, go to next step. If voltage is not present, check and repair open in Yellow wire between TCM 26-pin connector "A" and A/T gear position switch.

5) Shift to "D₃" position. Measure voltage between TCM 26-pin connector "A" terminals No. 13 or No. 26 (Brown/Black wires) and No. 8 (Green wire). If voltage is present, go to next step. If voltage is not present, check and repair open in Green wire between TCM 26-pin connector "A" and A/T gear position switch.

6) Shift to "2" position. Measure voltage between TCM 26-pin connector "A" terminals No. 13 or No. 26 (Brown/Black wires) and No. 7 (Blue wire). If voltage is present, go to next step. If voltage is not present, check and repair open in Blue wire between TCM 26-pin connector "A" and A/T gear position switch.

7) Shift to "1" position. Measure voltage between TCM 26-pin connector "A" terminals No. 13 or No. 26 (Brown/Black wires) and No. 6 (Brown wire). If voltage is present, check for loose TCM connectors and replace TCM with known good part, as necessary. If voltage is not present, check and repair open in Brown wire between TCM 26-pin connector "A" and A/T gear position switch.

FLASH CODE 7:
SHIFT CONTROL SOLENOID VALVE "A"

1) Disconnect TCM 26-pin connector "A" and TCM 22-pin connector "B". Turn ignition on. Using DVOM, measure voltage between TCM 22-pin connector "B" terminal No. 20 (Light Green/Black wire) and TCM 26-pin connector "A" terminals No. 13 or No. 26 (Brown/Black wires). See Fig. 32. If voltage is approximately 5 volts, go to next step. If voltage is not approximately 5 volts, repair open or short in Light Green/Black wire between TCM 22-pin connector "B" and ECM.

2) Measure voltage between TCM 26-pin connector "A" terminals No. 13 or No. 26 (Brown/Black wires) and No. 3 (Blue/Yellow wire). If voltage is not present, go to next step. If voltage is present, repair short to voltage in Blue/Yellow wire.

3) Turn ignition off. Measure shift control solenoid valve "A" resistance at TCM. See SHIFT CONTROL SOLENOID VALVE under COMPONENT TESTING. If resistance is not 14-25 ohms, go to next step. If resistance is 14-25 ohms, check for loose TCM connectors and replace TCM with known good part, as necessary.

4) Disconnect shift control solenoid valve connector. Check for continuity between TCM 26-pin connector "A" terminals No. 13 or No. 26 (Brown/Black wires) and No. 3 (Blue/Yellow wire). If continuity does not exist, go to next step. If continuity exists, repair short to ground in Blue/Yellow wire between TCM 26-pin connector "A" and shift control solenoid valve.

5) Measure resistance between shift control solenoid valve connector (solenoid side) Blue/Yellow wire and ground. If resistance is not 14-25 ohms, replace shift control solenoid valve assembly. If resistance is 14-25 ohms, check and repair open Blue/Yellow wire between shift control solenoid valve connector and shift control solenoid valve.

FLASH CODE 8:
SHIFT CONTROL SOLENOID VALVE "B"

1) Disconnect TCM 26-pin connector "A" and TCM 22-pin connector "B". Turn ignition on. Using DVOM, measure voltage between TCM 22-pin connector "B" terminal No. 20 (Light Green/Black wire) and TCM 26-pin connector "A" terminals No. 13 or No. 26 (Brown/Black wires). See Fig. 32. If voltage is approximately 5 volts, go to next step. If voltage is not approximately 5 volts, repair open Light Green/Black wire between TCM 22-pin connector "B" and ECM.

2) Measure voltage between TCM 26-pin connector "A" terminals No. 13 or No. 26 (Brown/Black wires) and No. 2 (Green/White wire). If voltage is not present, go to next step. If voltage is present, repair short to voltage in Green/White wire.

3) Turn ignition off. Measure shift control solenoid valve "B" resistance at TCM. See SHIFT CONTROL SOLENOID VALVE under COMPONENT TESTING. If resistance is not 14-25 ohms, go to next step. If resistance is 14-25 ohms, check for loose TCM connectors and replace TCM with known good part, as necessary.

4) Disconnect shift control solenoid valve connector. Check for continuity between TCM 26-pin connector "A" terminals No. 13 or No. 26 (Brown/Black wires) and No. 2 (Green/White wire). If continuity does not exist, go to next step. If continuity exists, repair short to ground in Green/White wire between TCM 26-pin connector "A" and shift control solenoid valve.

5) Measure resistance between shift control solenoid valve connector (solenoid side) Green/White wire and ground. If resistance is not 14-25 ohms, replace shift control solenoid valve assembly. If resistance is 14-25 ohms, check and repair open Green/White wire between shift control solenoid valve connector and shift control solenoid valve.

FLASH CODE 9:
COUNTERSHAFT SPEED SENSOR

1) Ensure countershaft speed sensor is installed properly. See COUNTERSHAFT SPEED SENSOR under REMOVAL & INSTALLATION. Disconnect countershaft speed sensor connector and measure resistance between sensor connector terminals. See COUNTERSHAFT SPEED SENSOR under COMPONENT TESTING.

2) If resistance is not 400-600 ohms, replace countershaft speed sensor. If resistance is 400-600 ohms, disconnect TCM 22-pin connector "B". Check continuity between ground and TCM 22-pin connector "B" terminals No. 8 (Blue/Yellow wire) and No. 9 (Blue/Green wire). See Fig. 32.

3) If continuity exists, repair short to ground in Blue/Yellow or Blue/Green wires between TCM and countershaft speed sensor. If continuity does not exist, reconnect countershaft speed sensor connector. Measure resistance between TCM 22-pin connector "B" terminals No. 8 (Blue/Yellow wire) and No. 9 (Blue/Green wire).

4) If resistance is not 400-600 ohms, check for loose TCM connectors or repair open Green or Blue wires between TCM 22-pin connector and countershaft speed sensor connector. If resistance is 400-600 ohms, check for loose TCM connectors and replace TCM with known good part, as necessary.

FLASH CODE 10:
ENGINE COOLANT TEMP. (ECT) SENSOR

1) Turn ignition on. Check for any other DTCs or check for Malfunction Indicator Light (MIL) flashing. If any other DTCs exists or MIL is flashing, repair those DTCs first, then recheck for Flash Code 10. If no other DTCs exist and MIL is not flashing, go to next step.

2) Turn ignition off. Disconnect TCM 22-pin connector "B" and TCM 26-pin connector "A". Turn ignition on. Measure voltage between TCM 22-pin connector "B" terminal No. 20 (Light Green/Black wire) and TCM 26-pin connector "A" terminals No. 13 or No. 26 (Brown/Black wires). See Fig. 32. If voltage is approximately 5 volts, go to next step. If voltage is not approximately 5 volts, repair open or short in Light Green/Black wire between TCM 22-pin connector "B" and ECM.

3) Measure voltage between TCM 22-pin connector "B" terminal No. 3 (Red/White wire) and TCM 26-pin connector "A" terminals No. 13 or No. 26 (Brown/Black wires). If voltage is less than one volt, check for loose TCM connectors and replace TCM with known good part, as necessary. If voltage is equal to or greater than one volt, repair open Red/White wire between TCM and ECT sensor.

FLASH CODE 11: IGNITION COIL

1) Disconnect TCM 26-pin connector "A". Start engine. Using DVOM, measure voltage between TCM 26-pin connector "A" terminals No. 5 (Blue wire) and No. 13 or No. 26 (Brown/Black wires). *See Fig. 32.*
2) If battery voltage is present, check for loose TCM connectors and replace TCM with known good part, as necessary. If battery voltage is not present, repair open or short in Blue wire between ignition coil and TCM 26-pin connector "A".

FLASH CODE 13: BAROMETRIC PRESSURE (BARO) SENSOR

NOTE: Baro sensor is built into ECM.

1) Turn ignition off. Disconnect TCM 22-pin connector "B" and TCM 26-pin connector "A". Turn ignition on. Measure voltage between TCM 22-pin connector "B" terminal No. 20 (Light Green/Black wire) and TCM 26-pin connector "A" terminals No. 13 or No. 26 (Brown/Black wires). *See Fig. 32.* If voltage is approximately 5 volts, go to next step. If voltage is not approximately 5 volts, repair open or short in Light Green/Black wire between TCM 22-pin connector "B" and ECM.
2) Turn ignition off. Disconnect ECM 22-pin connector "D". ECM is located under passenger side of dash. *See Fig. 5.* Check continuity of Blue/White wire between ECM 22-pin connector "D" terminal No. 3 and TCM 22-pin connector "B" terminal No. 2. *See Fig. 32.* If continuity exists, go to next step. If continuity does not exist, repair open Blue/White wire between ECM and TCM.
3) Check for continuity between ECM 22-pin connector "D" terminal No. 3 (Blue/White wire) and ground or TCM 22-pin connector "B" terminal No. 2 (Blue/White wire) and ground. If continuity does not exist, check for loose TCM connectors and replace TCM with known good part, as necessary. If continuity exists, repair short to ground in Blue/White wire.

FLASH CODE 14: FAS SIGNAL

1) Start engine and warm to normal operating temperature. Shift to Park position. Cycle key off and on and wait for 2 seconds. Using DVOM, measure voltage between TCM 22-pin connector "B" terminal No. 19 (Brown/White wire) TCM 26-pin connector "A" terminals No. 13 and No. 26 (Brown/Black wires). *See Fig. 32..* If voltage is approximately 5 volts, go to next step. If voltage is not approximately 5 volts, check for loose TCM connectors and replace TCM with known good part, as necessary.
2) Turn ignition off. Disconnect TCM 22-pin connector "B". Turn ignition on. Measure voltage between ECM 26-pin connector "A" terminal No. 22 (Brown/White wire) and terminal No. 26 (Brown/Black wire). *See Fig. 32.* If voltage is not approximately 5 volts, go to step **4)**. If voltage is approximately 5 volts, go to next step.
3) Turn ignition off. Check for continuity of Brown/White wire between ECM 26-pin connector "A" terminal No. 22 and TCM 22-pin connector "B" terminal No. 19. If continuity does not exist, repair open Brown/White wire between TCM and ECM. If continuity exists, check for loose TCM connectors and replace TCM with known good part, as necessary.
4) Turn ignition off. Disconnect ECM 26-pin connector "A". Check for continuity of Brown/White wires between ECM 26-pin connector "A" terminal No. 22 and ground or TCM 22-pin connector "B" terminal No. 19 and ground. If continuity does not exist, check for loose TCM connectors and replace TCM with known good part, as necessary. If continuity exists, repair short in Brown/White wire between TCM and ECM.

FLASH CODE 15: MAINSHAFT SPEED SENSOR

NOTE: FLASH CODE 15 doesn't always mean an electrical problem in mainshaft speed sensor or circuit, this DTC can also be caused by a mechanical problem in transaxle.

1) Ensure mainshaft and countershaft speed sensors are installed properly. See COUNTERSHAFT or MAINSHAFT SPEED SENSOR under REMOVAL & INSTALLATION. Disconnect mainshaft speed sensor connector and measure resistance between sensor connector terminals. See MAINSHAFT SPEED SENSOR under COMPONENT TESTING.
2) If resistance is not 400-600 ohms, replace mainshaft speed sensor. If resistance is 400-600 ohms, disconnect TCM 22-pin connector "B". Check continuity between ground and TCM 22-pin connector "B" terminals No. 10 (Orange/Blue wire) and No. 17 (White/Blue wire). *See Fig. 32.*
3) If continuity exists, repair short to ground in Orange/Blue and White/Blue wires between TCM and mainshaft speed sensor. If continuity does not exist, reconnect mainshaft speed sensor connector. Measure resistance between TCM 22-pin connector "B" terminals No. 10 (Orange/Blue wire) and No. 17 (White/Blue wire).
4) If resistance is not 400-600 ohms, go to next step. If resistance is 400-600 ohms, perform Flash Code 9 diagnostics, and check for loose TCM connectors and replace TCM with known good part, as necessary.
5) Disconnect mainshaft speed sensor connector. Check continuity of Orange/Blue wire between TCM 22-pin connector "B" terminal No. 10 and mainshaft speed sensor connector. If continuity exists, go to next step. If continuity does not exist, repair open Orange/Blue wire between TCM 22-pin connector and mainshaft speed sensor connector.
6) Check continuity of White/Blue wire between TCM 22-pin connector "B" terminal No. 17 and mainshaft speed sensor connector. If continuity exists, check for loose TCM connectors and replace TCM with known good part, as necessary. If continuity does not exist, repair open White/Blue wire between TCM 22-pin connector and mainshaft speed sensor connector.

DIAGNOSTIC TESTS (1996)

NOTE: Terminal identification, circuit description and terminal voltage is included in PIN VOLTAGE CHARTS. See Figs. 33 and 34.

DTC P0715 (FLASH CODE 15): MAINSHAFT SPEED SENSOR

NOTE: DTC P0715 (FLASH CODE 15) doesn't always mean an electrical problem in mainshaft speed sensor or circuit, this DTC can also be caused by a mechanical problem in transaxle.

1) Ensure mainshaft and countershaft speed sensors are installed properly. See COUNTERSHAFT or MAINSHAFT SPEED SENSOR under REMOVAL & INSTALLATION. Disconnect mainshaft speed sensor connector and measure resistance between sensor connector terminals. See MAINSHAFT SPEED SENSOR under COMPONENT TESTING.
2) If resistance is not 400-600 ohms, replace mainshaft speed sensor. If resistance is 400-600 ohms, disconnect PCM 25-pin connector "B". Check continuity between ground and PCM 25-pin connector "B" terminals No. 15 (Orange/Blue wire) and No. 14 (White/Blue wire). *See Figs. 33 and 34.*
3) If continuity exists, repair short to ground in Orange/Blue and White/Blue wires between PCM and mainshaft speed sensor. If continuity does not exist, reconnect mainshaft speed sensor connector. Measure resistance between PCM 25-pin connector "B" terminals No. 15 (Orange/Blue wire) and No. 14 (White/Blue wire).

4) If resistance is not 400-600 ohms, go to next step. If resistance is 400-600 ohms, perform DTC P0720 (FLASH CODE 9) diagnostic, check for loose PCM connectors and replace PCM with known good part, as necessary.

5) Disconnect mainshaft speed sensor connector. Check continuity of Red wire between PCM 25-pin connector "B" terminal No. 15 (Orange/Blue wire) and mainshaft speed sensor connector. If continuity exists, go to next step. If continuity does not exist, repair open Orange/Blue wire between PCM 25-pin connector and mainshaft speed sensor connector.

6) Check continuity of White wire between PCM 25-pin connector "B" terminal No. 14 (White/Blue wire) and mainshaft speed sensor connector. If continuity exists, check for loose PCM connectors and replace PCM with known good part, as necessary. If continuity does not exist, repair open White/Blue wire between PCM 25-pin connector and mainshaft speed sensor connector.

DTC P0720 (FLASH CODE 9): COUNTERSHAFT SPEED SENSOR

1) Ensure countershaft speed sensor is installed properly. See COUNTERSHAFT SPEED SENSOR under REMOVAL & INSTALLATION. Disconnect countershaft speed sensor connector and measure resistance between sensor connector terminals. See COUNTERSHAFT SPEED SENSOR under COMPONENT TESTING.

2) If resistance is not 400-600 ohms, replace countershaft speed sensor. If resistance is 400-600 ohms, disconnect PCM 25-pin connector "B". Check continuity between ground and PCM 25-pin connector "B" terminals No. 23 (Blue/Green wire) and No. 22 (Blue/Yellow wire). See Figs. 33 and 34.

3) If continuity exists, repair short to ground in Blue/Green or Blue/Yellow wires between PCM and countershaft speed sensor. If continuity does not exist, reconnect countershaft speed sensor connector. Measure resistance between PCM 25-pin connector "B" terminals No. 23 (Blue/Green wire) and No. 22 (Blue/Yellow wire).

4) If resistance is not 400-600 ohms, check for loose PCM connectors and replace PCM with known good part, as necessary. If resistance is 400-600 ohms, repair open Blue/Green or Blue/Yellow wires between PCM 25-pin connector and countershaft speed sensor connector.

DTC P0730 (FLASH CODE 41): SHIFT CONTROL SYSTEM

1) Do not perform this DTC test until all other DTCs have been repaired. Road test vehicle at over 12 MPH for more than 30 seconds in 2nd, 3rd and 4th gear. Using scan tool, check for any other DTCs. If any other DTCs exist, repair those DTCs first, then recheck for DTC P0730. If no other DTCs exist, go to next step.

2) Test clutch pressure. See HYDRAULIC PRESSURE TEST under TESTING in HONDA AOYA, MPJA & MPOA overhaul article. If clutch pressure is within specification, go to next step. If clutch pressure is not within specification, repair hydraulic system as necessary. See HYDRAULIC PRESSURE TROUBLE SHOOTING table under HYDRAULIC PRESSURE TEST in HONDA AOYA, MPJA & MPOA overhaul article.

3) Replace shift control solenoid valve assembly. See SHIFT CONTROL SOLENOID VALVES under REMOVAL & INSTALLATION. Turn ignition off and clear codes. See CLEARING CODES. Road test vehicle at over 12 MPH for more than 30 seconds in 2nd, 3rd and 4th gear. Recheck DTCs. If P0730 returns, repair internal components as necessary. If P0730 does not return, system is okay.

DTC P0740 (FLASH CODE 40): LOCK-UP CONTROL SYSTEM

1) Do not perform this DTC test until all other DTCs have been repaired. Using scan tool, check for any other DTCs. If any other DTCs exist, repair those DTCs first, then recheck for DTC P0740. If no other DTCs exist, go to next step.

2) Test line pressure. See HYDRAULIC PRESSURE TEST under TESTING in AUTOMATIC TRANSMISSIONS HONDA AOYA, MPJA & MPOA overhaul article. If line pressure is within specification, go to next step. If line pressure is not within specification, repair hydraulic system as necessary. See HYDRAULIC PRESSURE TROUBLE SHOOTING table under HYDRAULIC PRESSURE TEST in HONDA AOYA, MPJA & MPOA overhaul article.

3) Test clutch pressure. If clutch pressure is within specification, go to next step. If clutch pressure is not within specification, repair hydraulic system as necessary. See HYDRAULIC PRESSURE TROUBLE SHOOTING table under HYDRAULIC PRESSURE TEST in HONDA AOYA, MPJA & MPOA overhaul article.

4) Replace lock-up control solenoid valve assembly. See LOCK-UP CONTROL SOLENOID VALVES under REMOVAL & INSTALLATION. Turn ignition off and clear codes. See CLEARING CODES. Road test vehicle at over 50 MPH for more than one minute. Recheck DTCs. If P0740 returns, go to next step. If P0740 does not return, system is okay.

5) Replace torque converter. Turn ignition off and clear codes. See CLEARING CODES. Road test vehicle at over 50 MPH for more than one minute. Recheck DTCs. If P0740 returns, replace transaxle. If P0740 does not return, system is okay.

DTC P0753 (FLASH CODE 7): SHIFT CONTROL SOLENOID VALVE "A"

1) Disconnect PCM 32-pin connector "A" and PCM 25-pin connector "B". Turn ignition on. Using DVOM, measure voltage between PCM 25-pin connector "B" terminal No. 3 (Blue/Yellow wire) and PCM 32-pin connector "A" terminals No. 9 (Black/Red wire) or No. 22 (Brown/Black wire). See Figs. 33 and 34. If voltage is present, repair short to power in Blue/Yellow wire between PCM 25-pin connector "B" and shift solenoid "A". If voltage is not present, go to next step.

2) Turn ignition off. Measure shift control solenoid valve "A" resistance at PCM. See SHIFT CONTROL SOLENOID VALVE under COMPONENT TESTING. If resistance is not 14-25 ohms, go to next step. If resistance is 14-25 ohms, check for loose PCM connectors and replace PCM with known good part, as necessary.

3) Disconnect shift control solenoid valve connector. Check for continuity between PCM 32-pin connector "A" terminal No. 9 (Black/Red wire) or No. 22 (Brown/Black wire) and PCM 25-pin connector "B" terminal No. 3 (Blue/Yellow wire). If continuity does not exist, go to next step. If continuity exists, repair short to ground in Blue/Yellow wire between PCM 32-pin connector "A" and shift solenoid valve "A".

4) Measure resistance between shift control solenoid valve connector (solenoid side) Blue/Yellow wire and ground. If resistance is not 14-25 ohms, replace shift control solenoid valve assembly. If resistance is 14-25 ohms, check and repair open Blue/Yellow wire between shift control solenoid valve connector and shift solenoid valve "A".

DTC P0758 (FLASH CODE 8): SHIFT CONTROL SOLENOID VALVE "B"

1) Disconnect PCM 32-pin connector "A" and PCM 25-pin connector "B". Turn ignition on. Using DVOM, measure voltage between PCM 25-pin connector "B" terminal No. 11 (Green/White wire) and PCM 32-pin connector "A" terminal No. 9 (Black/Red wire) or No. 22 (Brown/Black wire). See Figs. 33 and 34. If voltage is approximately 5 volts, repair short to power in Green/White wire between PCM 25-pin connector "B" and shift solenoid "A". If voltage is not approximately 5 volts, go to next step.

2) Turn ignition off. Measure shift control solenoid valve "A" resistance at PCM. See SHIFT CONTROL SOLENOID VALVE under COMPONENT TESTING. If resistance is not 14-25 ohms, go to next step. If resistance is 14-25 ohms, check for loose PCM connectors and replace PCM with known good part, as necessary.

3) Disconnect shift control solenoid valve connector. Check for continuity between PCM 32-pin connector "A" terminal No. 9 (Black/Red wire) or No. 22 (Brown/Black wire) and PCM 25-pin connector "B" terminal No. 11 (Green/White wire). If continuity does not exist, go to next step. If continuity exists, repair short to ground in Green/White wire between PCM 32-pin connector "A" and shift solenoid valve "A".

4) Measure resistance between shift control solenoid valve connector (solenoid side) Green/White wire and ground. If resistance is not 14-25 ohms, replace shift control solenoid valve assembly. If resistance is 14-25 ohms, check and repair open Green/White wire between shift control solenoid valve connector and shift solenoid valve "A".

DTC P1705 (FLASH CODE 5): A/T GEAR POSITION SWITCH (SHORT)

NOTE: DTC P1705 is set when PCM receives 2 gear position signals at same time.

1) Turn ignition on. If any A/T gear position indicator light stays on when gear selector is moved from that gear, go to next step. If all A/T gear position indicator lights go off when gear selector is moved from that gear, system is okay at this time.

2) Shift to all gear positions except reverse. Using DVOM, measure voltage between PCM 32-pin connector "A" terminal No. 9 (Black/Red wire) or No. 22 (Brown/Black wire) and PCM 25-pin connector "B" terminal No. 16 (Green/Red wire). *See Figs. 33 and 34.* If battery voltage is present, go to next step. If battery voltage is not present, check and repair short in Green/Red wire between PCM 25-pin connector "B" and A/T gear position indicator or A/T gear position switch. If Green/Red wire is okay, check for loose PCM connectors and replace PCM with known good part, as necessary.

3) Shift to all gear positions except "N" and "P". Measure voltage between PCM 32-pin connector "A" terminal No. 9 (Black/Red wire) or No. 22 (Brown/Black wire) and PCM 25-pin connector "B" terminal No. 25 (Light Green wire). If about 5 volts is present, go to next step. If about 5 volts is not present, check and repair short in Light Green wire between PCM 25-pin connector "B" and A/T gear position indicator or A/T gear position switch. If Light Green wire is okay, check for loose PCM connectors and replace PCM with known good part, as necessary.

4) Shift to all gear positions except "D₄". Measure voltage between PCM 32-pin connector "A" terminal No. 9 (Black/Red wire) or No. 22 (Brown/Black wire) and PCM 25-pin connector "B" terminal No. 24 (Light Green/Black wire). If about 5 volts is present, go to next step. If about 5 volts is not present, check and repair short in Light Green/Black wire between PCM 25-pin connector "B" and A/T gear position switch. If Light Green/Black wire is okay, check for loose PCM connectors and replace PCM with known good part, as necessary.

5) Shift to all gear positions except "D₃". Measure voltage between PCM 32-pin connector "A" terminal No. 9 (Black/Red wire) or No. 22 (Brown/Black wire) and PCM 25-pin connector "B" terminal No. 8 (Light Green/Blue wire). If battery voltage is present, go to next step. If battery voltage is not present, check and repair short in Green/Blue wire between PCM 25-pin connector "B" and A/T gear position indicator or A/T gear position switch. If Green/Blue wire is okay, check for loose PCM connectors and replace PCM with known good part, as necessary.

6) Shift to all gear positions except "2". Measure voltage between PCM 32-pin connector "A" terminal No. 9 (Black/Red wire) or No. 22 (Brown/Black wire) and PCM 25-pin connector "B" terminal No. 17 (Green/Yellow wire). If battery voltage is present, go to next step. If battery voltage is not present, check and repair short in Green/Yellow wire between PCM 25-pin connector "B" and A/T gear position indicator or A/T gear position switch. If Green/Yellow wire is okay, check for loose PCM connectors and replace PCM with known good part, as necessary.

7) Shift to all gear positions except "1". Measure voltage between PCM 32-pin connector "A" terminal No. 9 (Black/Red wire) or No. 22 (Brown/Black wire) and PCM 25-pin connector "B" terminal No. 18 (Light Green/White wire). If battery voltage is present, check for loose PCM connectors and replace PCM with known good part, as necessary. If battery voltage is not present, check and repair short in Light Green/White wire between PCM 25-pin connector "B" and A/T gear position indicator or A/T gear position switch. If Light Green/White wire is okay, check for loose PCM connectors and replace PCM with known good part, as necessary.

DTC P1706 (FLASH CODE 6): A/T GEAR POSITION SWITCH (OPEN)

1) Turn ignition on. If any A/T gear position indicator light stays on when gear selector is moved from that gear, go to next step. If all A/T gear position indicator lights go off when gear selector is moved from that gear, system is okay at this time.

2) Shift to reverse. Using DVOM, measure voltage between PCM 32-pin connector "A" terminal No. 9 (Black/Red wire) or No. 22 (Brown/Black wire) and PCM 25-pin connector "B" terminal No. 16 (Green/Red wire). *See Figs. 33 and 34.* If voltage is not present, go to next step. If voltage is present, check and repair open in Green/Red wire between PCM 25-pin connector "B" and A/T gear position switch.

3) Shift to "N" or "P". Measure voltage between PCM 32-pin connector "A" terminal No. 9 (Black/Red wire) or No. 22 (Brown/Black wire) and PCM 25-pin connector "B" terminal No. 25 (Light Green wire). If voltage is not present, go to next step. If voltage is present, check and repair open in Light Green wire between PCM 25-pin connector "B" and A/T gear position switch.

4) Shift to "D₄" position. Measure voltage between PCM 32-pin connector "A" terminal No. 9 (Black/Red wire) or No. 22 (Brown/Black wire) and PCM 25-pin connector "B" terminal No. 24 (Light Green/Black wire). If voltage is not present, go to next step. If voltage is present, check and repair open in Light Green/Black wire between PCM 25-pin connector "B" and A/T gear position switch.

5) Shift to "D₃" position. Measure voltage between PCM 32-pin connector "A" terminal No. 9 (Black/Red wire) or No. 22 (Brown/Black wire) and PCM 25-pin connector "B" terminal No. 8 (Green/Blue wire). If voltage is not present, go to next step. If voltage is present, check and repair open in Green/Blue wire between PCM 25-pin connector "B" and A/T gear position switch.

6) Shift to "2" position. Measure voltage between PCM 32-pin connector "A" terminal No. 9 (Black/Red wire) or No. 22 (Brown/Black wire) and PCM 25-pin connector "B" terminal No. 17 (Green/Yellow wire). If voltage is not present, go to next step. If voltage is present, check and repair open in Green/Yellow wire between PCM 25-pin connector "B" and A/T gear position switch.

7) Shift to "1" position. Measure voltage between PCM 32-pin connector "A" terminal No. 9 (Black/Red wire) or No. 22 (Brown/Black wire) and PCM 25-pin connector "B" terminal No. 18 (Light Green/White wire). If voltage is not present, check for loose PCM connectors and replace PCM with known good part, as necessary. If voltage is present, check and repair open in Light Green/White wire between PCM 25-pin connector "B" and A/T gear position switch.

DTC P1753 (FLASH CODE 1): LOCK-UP CONTROL SOLENOID VALVE "A"

1) Disconnect PCM 32-pin connector "A" and PCM 25-pin connector "B". Turn ignition on. Using DVOM, measure voltage between PCM 25-pin connector "B" terminal No. 5 (Yellow wire) and PCM 32-pin connector "A" terminal No. 9 (Black/Red wire) or No. 22 (Brown/Black wire). *See Figs. 33 and 34.* If voltage is present, go to next step. If voltage is not present, repair open or short in Yellow wire between PCM 25-pin connector "B" and lock-up control solenoid valve.

2) Turn ignition off. Measure lock-up control solenoid valve "A" resistance at PCM. See LOCK-UP CONTROL SOLENOID VALVE under COMPONENT TESTING. If resistance is not 14-25 ohms, go to next step. If resistance is 14-25 ohms, check for loose PCM connectors and replace PCM with known good part, as necessary.

3) Disconnect lock-up control solenoid valve connector. Check for continuity between PCM 32-pin connector "A" terminal No. 9 (Black/Red wire) or No. 22 (Brown/Black wire) and PCM 25-pin connector "B" terminal No. 5 (Yellow wire). If continuity does not exist, go to next step. If continuity exists, repair short to ground in Yellow wire between PCM 25-pin connector "B" and lock-up control solenoid valve.

4) Measure resistance between lock-up control solenoid valve connector (solenoid side) Yellow wire and ground. If resistance is not 14-25 ohms, replace lock-up control solenoid valve assembly. If resistance is 14-25 ohms, check and repair open Yellow wire between lock-up control solenoid valve connector and lock-up control solenoid valve.

DTC P1758 (FLASH CODE 2): LOCK-UP CONTROL SOLENOID VALVE "B"

1) Disconnect PCM 32-pin connector "A" and PCM 25-pin connector "B". Turn ignition on. Using DVOM, measure voltage between PCM 25-pin connector "B" terminal No. 4 (Green/Black wire) and PCM 32-pin connector "A" terminal No. 9 (Black/Red wire) or No. 22 (Brown/Black wire). *See Figs. 33 and 34.* If voltage is present, go to next step. If voltage is not present, repair open or short in Green/Black wire between PCM 25-pin connector "B" and lock-up control solenoid valve "B".

2) Turn ignition off. Measure lock-up control solenoid valve "B" resistance at PCM. See LOCK-UP CONTROL SOLENOID VALVE under COMPONENT TESTING. If resistance is not 14-25 ohms, go to next step. If resistance is 14-25 ohms, check for loose PCM connectors and replace PCM with known good part, as necessary.

3) Disconnect lock-up control solenoid valve connector. Check for continuity between PCM 32-pin connector "A" terminal No. 9 (Black/Red wire) or No. 22 (Brown/Black wire) and PCM 25-pin connector "B" terminal No. 4 (Green/Black wire). If continuity does not exist, go to next step. If continuity exists, repair short to ground in Green/Black between PCM 25-pin connector "B" and lock-up control solenoid valve "B".

PIN VOLTAGE CHARTS

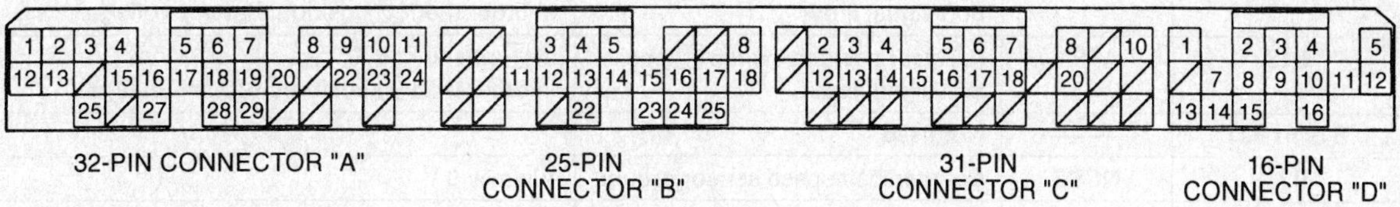

PCM TERMINAL LOCATIONS

PCM CONNECTOR "A" (32-PIN)

Terminal Number	Signal	Description	Measuring Conditions/Terminal Voltage
A1 to A8		See appropriate SELF-DIAGNOSTICS article in ENGINE PERFORMANCE in appropriate MITCHELL® manual.	
A9	LG1	Ground	
A10	PG1	Ground	
A11	IGP1	Power supply system	With ignition switch ON (II): Battery voltage With ignition switch OFF: 0 V
A12 to A21		See appropriate SELF-DIAGNOSTICS article in ENGINE PERFORMANCE in appropriate MITCHELL® manual.	
A22	LG2	Ground	
A23	PG2	Ground	
A24	IGP2	Power supply system	With ignition switch ON (II): Battery voltage With ignition switch OFF: 0 V
A25 to A32		See appropriate SELF-DIAGNOSTICS article in ENGINE PERFORMANCE in appropriate MITCHELL® manual.	

PCM CONNECTOR "B" (25-PIN)

Terminal Number	Signal	Description	Measuring Conditions/Terminal Voltage
B1 to B2	———	Not used	
B3	SHA	Shift control solenoid valve A control	In D_4 2nd gear and 3rd gear: Battery voltage In D_4 1st gear and 4th gear: 0 V
B4	LCB	Lock-up control solenoid valve B control	During half and full lock-up and during deceleration: Battery voltage During no lock-up: 0 V
B5	LCA	Lock-up control solenoid valve A control	When lock-up is ON: Battery voltage With no lock-up: 0 V
B6 to B7	———	Not used	
B8	ATP D3	A/T gear position switch D_3 position signal input	In D_3 position: 0 V in other than D_3 position: Battery voltage
B9 to B10	———	Not used	
B11	SHB	Shift control solenoid valve B control	in D_4 1st gear and 2nd gear: Battery voltage In D_4 3rd gear and 4th gear: 0 V
B12	ILU	Interlock control	When ignition switch is ON (II), brake pedal depressed and accelerator pedal released: 12 V
B13	D_4 IND	D4 Indicator light control	When ignition switch is first turned ON (II): Battery voltage for two seconds

96I31763   Courtesy of American Honda Motor Co., Inc.

Fig. 33: Pin Voltage Chart & Terminal Identification (1996 1 Of 2)

4) Measure resistance between lock-up control solenoid valve connector (solenoid side) Green/Black wire and ground. If resistance is not 14-25 ohms, replace lock-up control solenoid valve assembly. If resistance is 14-25 ohms, check and repair open Green/Black wire between lock-up control solenoid valve connector and lock-up control solenoid valve.

PCM CONNECTOR "B" (25-PIN CONT.)

Terminal Number	Signal	Description	Measuring Conditions/Terminal Voltage
B14	NMSG	Mainshaft speed sensor ground	Always: 0 V
B15	NM	Mainshaft speed sensor signal input	Depending on vehicle speed: Pulsing signal When vehicle is stopped: 0 V
B16	ATP R	A/T gear position switch ℝ position signal input	In ℝ position: 0 V in other than ℝ position: Battery voltage
B17	ATP 2	A/T gear position switch ② position signal input	In ② position: 0 V in other than ② position: Battery voltage
B18	ATP 1	A/T gear position switch ① position signal input	In ① position: 0 V in other than ① position: Battery voltage
B19 to B21	——	Not used	
B22	NCSG	Countershaft speed sensor ground	Always: 0 V
B23	NC	Countershaft speed sensor signal input	Depending on vehicle speed: Pulsing signal When vehicle is stopped: 0 V
B24	ATP D4	A/T gear position switch D4 position signal input	In D4 position: 0 V in other than D4 position: Battery voltage
B25	ATP PN	A/T gear position switch ℙ and ℕ position signals input	In ℙ and ℕ positions: 0V in other than ℙ and ℕ positions: Battery voltage

PCM CONNECTOR "C" (31-PIN)

Terminal Number	Signal	Description	Measuring Conditions/Terminal Voltage
C1 to C6	See appropriate SELF-DIAGNOSTICS article in ENGINE PERFORMANCE in appropriate MITCHELL® manual.		
C7	SCS	Service check signal	With ignition switch ON (II) and service check connector is open: 5 V With ignition switch ON (II) and service check connector connected with special tool: 0 V
C8 to C9	See appropriate SELF-DIAGNOSTICS article in ENGINE PERFORMANCE in appropriate MITCHELL® manual.		
C10	VBU	Back-up power system	Always battery voltage
C11 to C31	See appropriate SELF-DIAGNOSTICS article in ENGINE PERFORMANCE in appropriate MITCHELL® manual.		

PCM CONNECTOR "D" (16-PIN)

Terminal Number	Signal	Description	Measuring Conditions/Terminal Voltage
D1 to D4	See appropriate SELF-DIAGNOSTICS article in ENGINE PERFORMANCE in appropriate MITCHELL® manual.		
D5	STOP SW	Brake switch signal input	With ignition switch ON (II) and brake pedal depressed: Battery voltage With ignition switch ON (II) and brake pedal released: 0 V
D6 to D16	See appropriate SELF-DIAGNOSTICS article in ENGINE PERFORMANCE in appropriate MITCHELL® manual.		

96J31764

Courtesy of American Honda Motor Co., Inc.

Fig. 34: Pin Voltage Chart (1996 2 Of 2)

WIRING DIAGRAMS

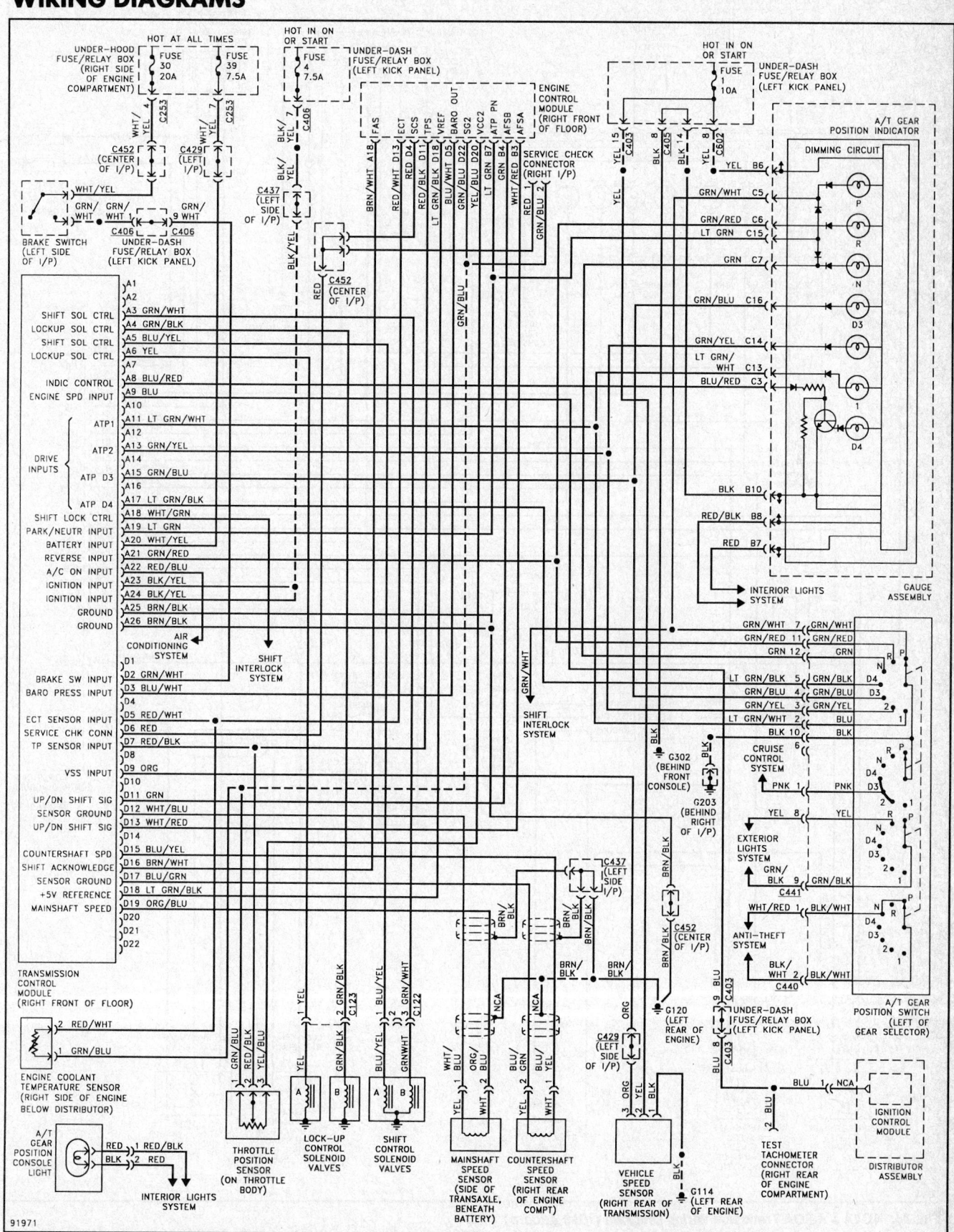

Fig. 35: AOYA & MPOA Transaxle Wiring Diagram (1995 Accord)

91971

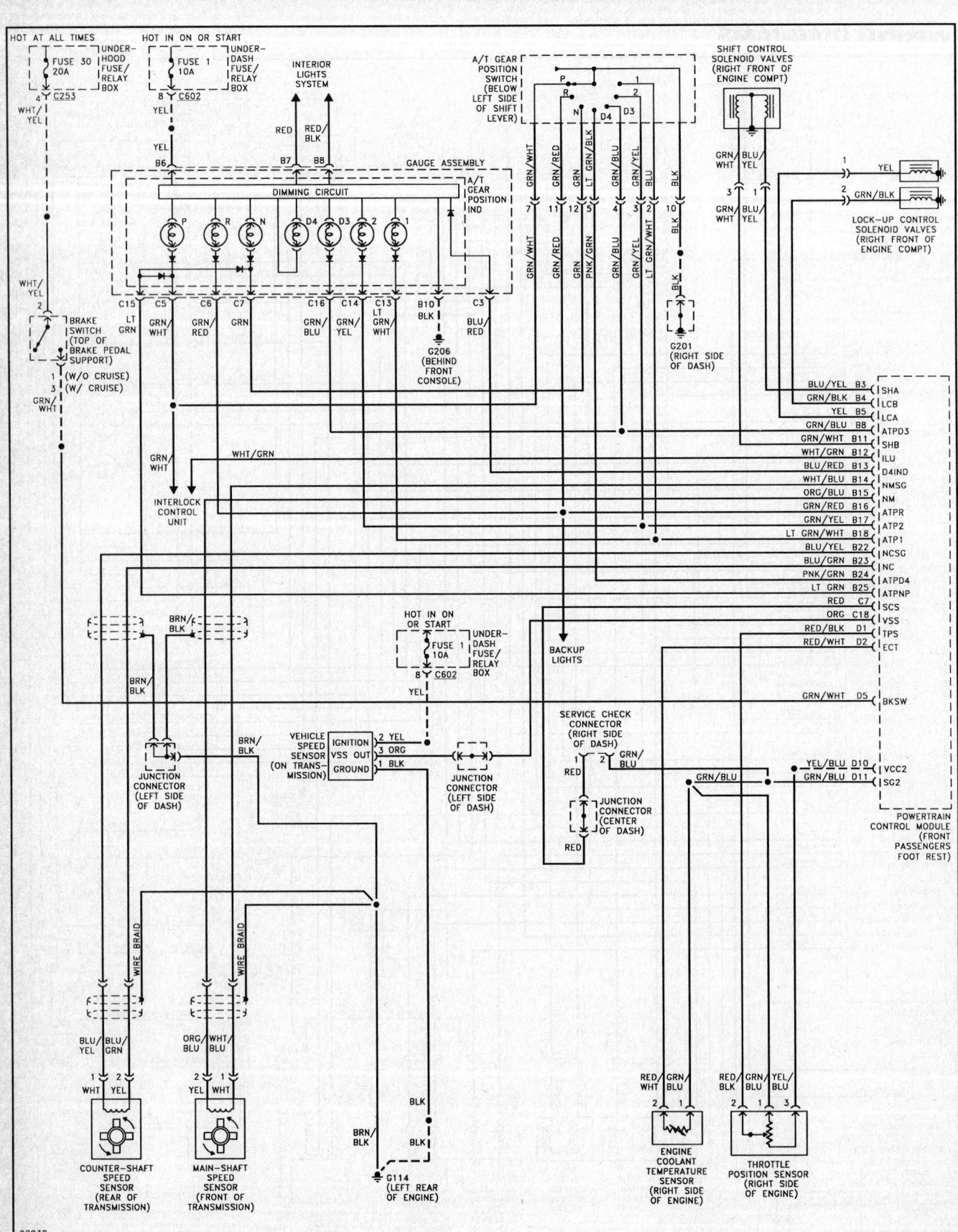

Fig. 36: AOYA & MPOA Transaxle Wiring Diagram (1996 Accord)

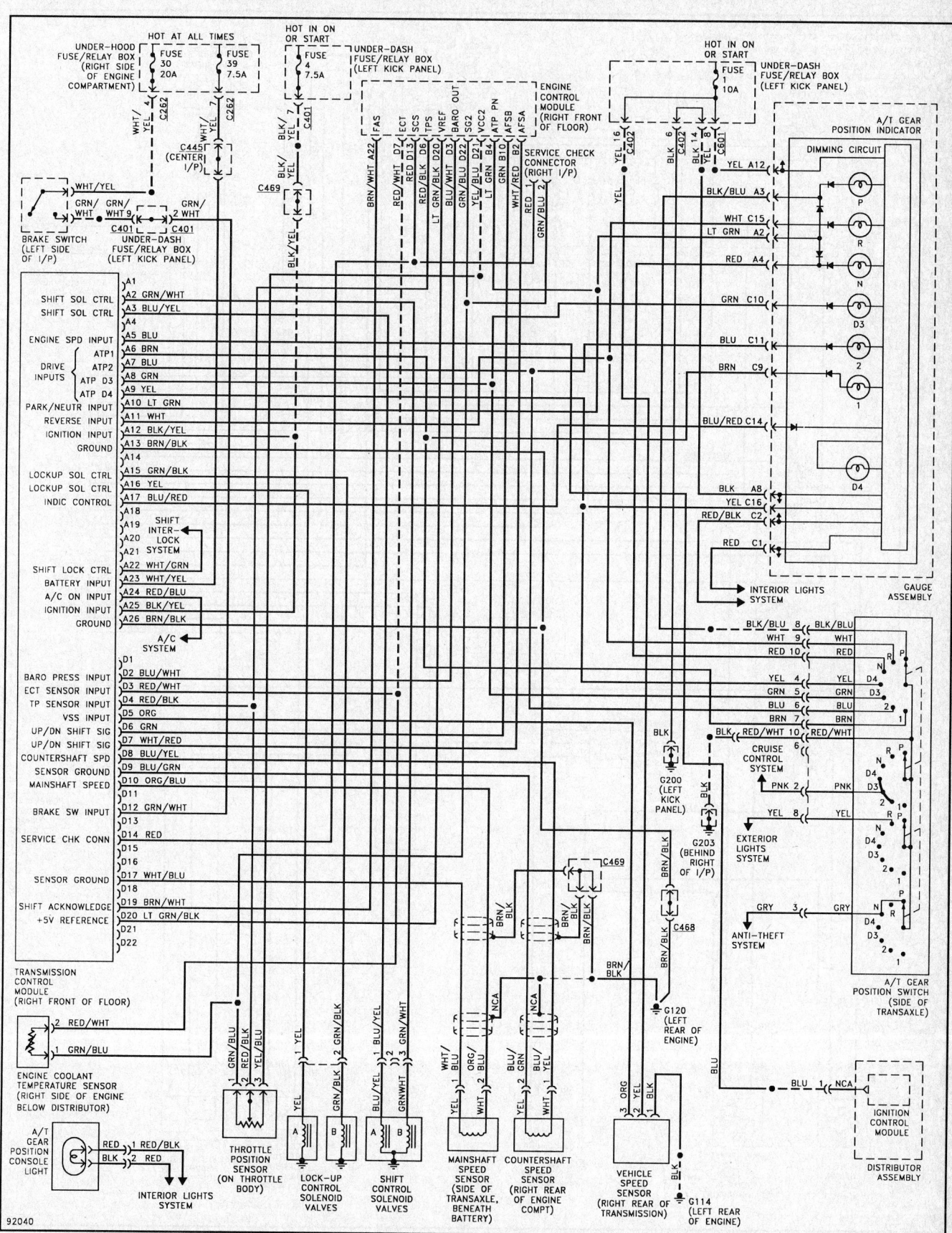

Fig. 37: *MPJA Transaxle Wiring Diagram (1995 Odyssey & Oasis)*

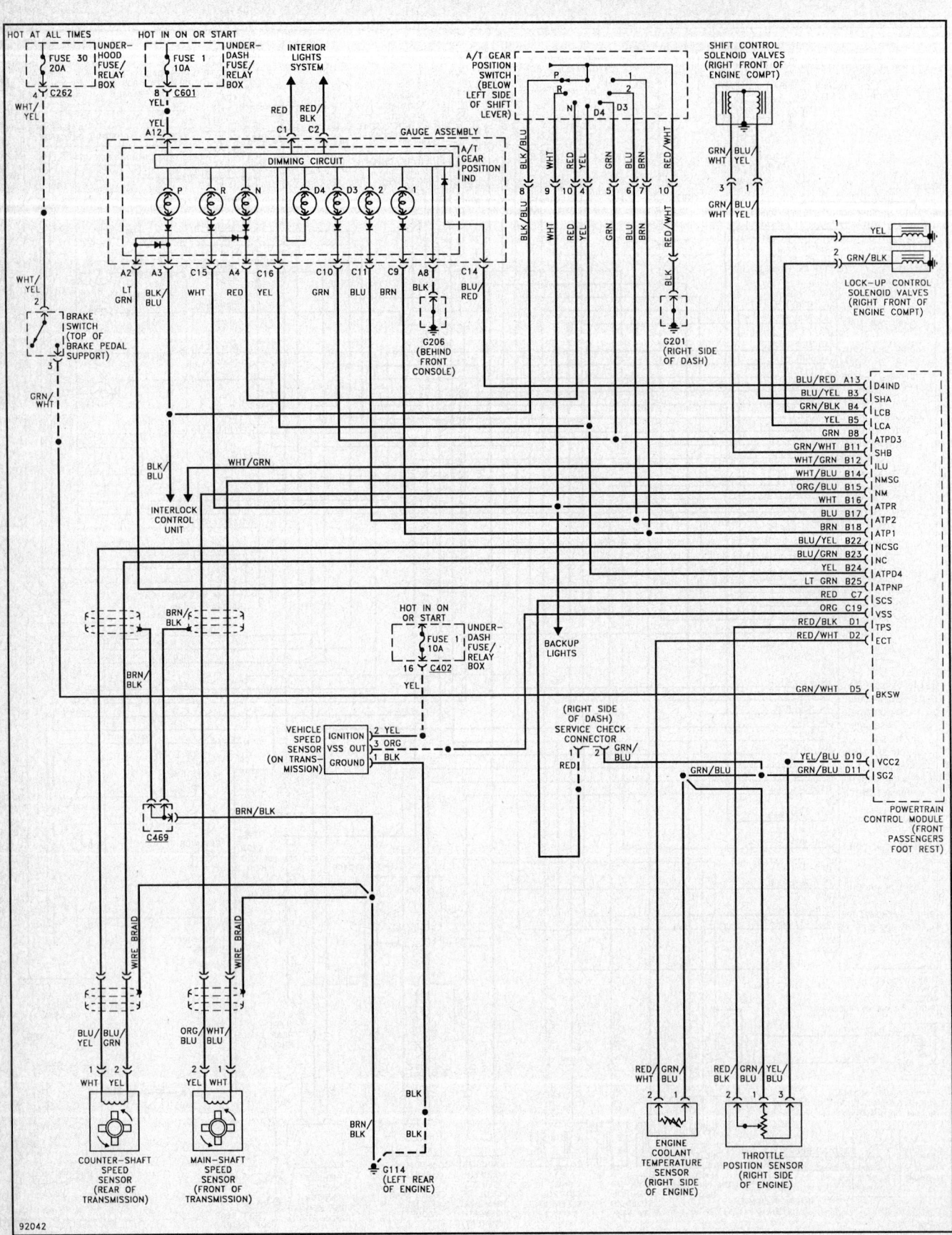

Fig. 38: MPJA Transaxle Wiring Diagram (1996 Odyssey & Oasis)

Civic (1996)

APPLICATION & LABOR TIMES

APPLICATION & LABOR TIMES

Vehicle Application	Labor Times		Trans. Model
	¹ R & I	² Overhaul	
Civic (1996)	4.1	6.2	A4RA

¹ – Removal and installation of transaxle from vehicle chassis.
² – Bench overhaul time for transaxle and differential. DOES NOT include removal and installation.

IDENTIFICATION

Transaxle model and serial number are stamped on the transaxle. *See Fig. 1.* Model and serial number may be required when ordering replacement components.

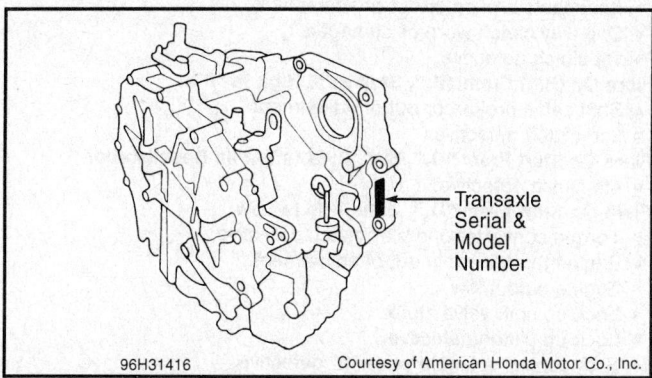

96H31416   Courtesy of American Honda Motor Co., Inc.

Transaxle Serial & Model Number

Fig. 1: Locating Transaxle Model & Serial Number

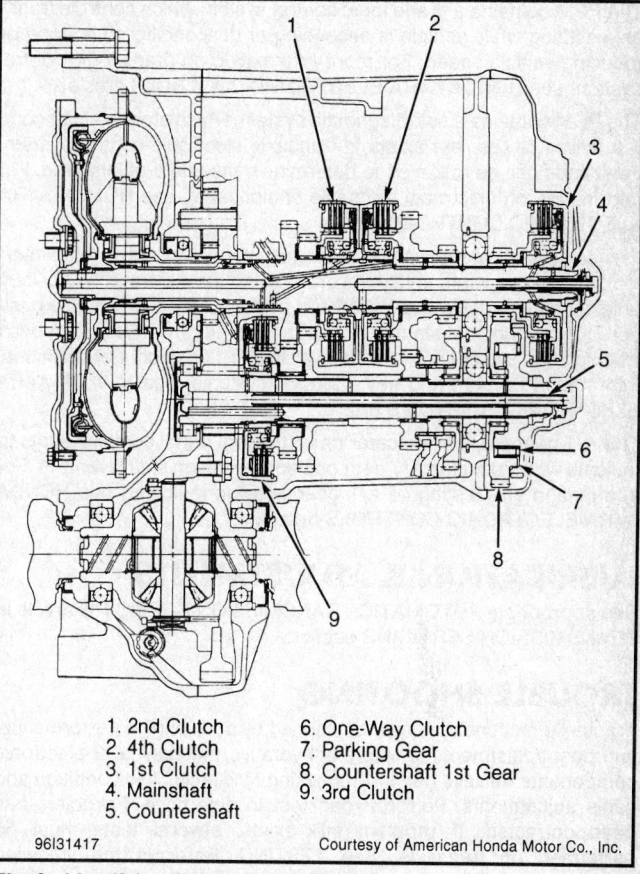

1. 2nd Clutch
2. 4th Clutch
3. 1st Clutch
4. Mainshaft
5. Countershaft
6. One-Way Clutch
7. Parking Gear
8. Countershaft 1st Gear
9. 3rd Clutch

96I31417   Courtesy of American Honda Motor Co., Inc.

Fig. 2: Identifying Transaxle Components

DESCRIPTION

Automatic transaxle is electronically controlled with 4 forward speeds and one reverse speed. Transaxle consists of clutches, mainshaft, countershaft, shift control solenoid valves, lock-up control solenoid valves, linear solenoid and a 3 element lock-up torque converter. *See Fig. 2.*

Valve bodies include; main valve body, secondary valve body, regulator valve body, servo body and lock-up valve body. Main valve body assembly consists of manual valve, 1-2 shift valve, 2nd orifice control valve, Clutch Pressure Back-up (CPB) valve, modulator valve, servo control valve, relief valve and ATF pump gears. Secondary valve body consists of 2-3 and 3-4 shift valves, 3-4 orifice control valve, 4th exhaust valve and Clutch Pressure Control (CPC) valve. Regulator valve body consists of pressure regulator valve, torque converter check valve, cooler relief valve and lock-up control valve. Servo body consists of servo valve and incorporates accumulators. Lock-up valve body consists of lock-up shift valve and lock-up timing valve.

The linear solenoid and shift control solenoid valve A/B are bolted to transaxle housing. Lock-up control solenoid valve A/B is bolted to torque converter housing.

Transaxle shifting and torque converter lock-up are controlled by the Powertrain Control Module (PCM) which receives input signals from various sensors. The PCM determines appropriate shift point and activates appropriate shift control solenoid valve, lock-up control solenoid valves or linear solenoid.

OPERATION

Shift lever has 6 positions. When shift lever is moved, the spool type manual valve on main valve body is moved by the shift cable. Shift lever also changes position of the A/T gear position switch, mounted on the transaxle. The A/T gear position switch delivers an input signal

to PCM indicating shift lever position. The PCM uses this input signal for controlling shift control solenoid valves. The PCM determines appropriate shift point and activates proper shift control solenoid valve for transaxle shifting.

When transaxle gear combinations are engaged by clutches, power is transmitted from mainshaft to countershaft to provide different gears. Shift lever positions operate as follows:

- **"P" (Park)** – Front wheels lock as parking pawl engages with parking gear on countershaft. All clutches are released. Neutral position switch, incorporated in A/T gear position switch, allows engine starting in this position.
- **"R" (Reverse)** – Reverse selector is engaged with countershaft reverse gear and 4th clutch is applied. Back-up light switch, incorporated in A/T gear position switch, operates back-up lights.
- **"N" (Neutral)** – All clutches are released. Neutral position switch, incorporated in A/T gear position switch allows engine starting in this position.
- **"D₄" (Drive)** – Transaxle starts in 1st gear and upshifts automatically to 2nd, 3rd and then 4th gear. Transaxle will downshift through 3rd, 2nd and 1st gears until vehicle stops. When in 3rd or 4th gear in this range, PCM sends signal to operate torque converter lock-up.
- **"D₃" (Drive)** – Transaxle starts in 1st gear and upshifts automatically to 2nd gear and then 3rd gear. Transaxle will downshift through all gears on deceleration. When in 3rd gear in this range, PCM sends signal to operate torque converter lock-up.
- **"2" (Second)** – Transaxle starts off and remains in 2nd gear for engine braking and better traction.

When in "D₃" position in 3rd gear or "D₄" position in 3rd or 4th gear, torque converter lock-up exists and transaxle mainshaft rotates at the same speed as engine crankshaft. Torque converter lock-up is controlled by the PCM. The PCM receives various input signals and operates lock-up control solenoid valves.

The PCM contains a grade logic control system which controls transaxle shifting while vehicle is ascending or descending on a slope or reducing vehicle speed. For more information on grade logic control system, see HONDA A4RA ELECTRONIC CONTROLS article.

The PCM contains a self-diagnostic system, which stores a fault code if a failure or problem exists in transaxle electronic control system. Fault code can be retrieved to determine transaxle problem area. For information on electronic transaxle components, see HONDA A4RA ELECTRONIC CONTROLS article.

Transaxle is equipped with shift and key interlock systems. Shift interlock system prevents shift lever from being moved from "P" position unless brake pedal is depressed and accelerator pedal is in idle position. Key interlock system prevents ignition key from being removed from ignition switch unless shift lever is in "P" position. For additional information on shift and key interlock systems, see HONDA A4RA ELECTRONIC CONTROLS article.

The A/T gear position indicator on instrument panel contains lights to indicate which position A/T gear position switch on shift lever is in. For information and testing of A/T gear position indicator, see HONDA A4RA ELECTRONIC CONTROLS article.

LUBRICATION & ADJUSTMENTS

See appropriate AUTOMATIC TRANSMISSION SERVICING article in TRANSMISSION SERVICING section.

TROUBLE SHOOTING

Transaxle malfunctions may be caused by poor engine performance, improper adjustments or failure of hydraulic, mechanical or electronic components. Always begin by checking fluid level, fluid condition and cable adjustments. Perform road test to determine if problem has been corrected. If problem still exists, several tests must be performed on transaxle. See TESTING. Refer to the following symptoms and check the specified components:

Delayed Shift From "N" To "D_3" Or "D_4"
- 1st clutch defective.
- Foreign material in 1st orifice.

Delayed Shift From "N" To "R"
- Servo valve stuck.
- 1-2 shift valve stuck.
- 4th clutch defective.
- Servo control valve stuck.

Engine Runs But Vehicle Does Not Move In Any Gear
- Low fluid.
- ATF pump worn or binding.
- Regulator valve stuck.
- Mainshaft worn or damaged.
- Shift cable broken or out of adjustment.
- Final drive gears worn or damaged.
- Flexplate defective.
- ATF strainer clogged.

Erratic Upshift, All Shifts
- Engine throttle cable out of adjustment.
- PCM defective.
- Countershaft speed sensor defective.

Erratic 1-2 Upshift
- 1-2 shift valve stuck.
- Shift control solenoid valve "A" defective.
- PCM defective.

Erratic 2-3 Upshift
- 2-3 shift valve stuck.
- Shift control solenoid valve "B" defective.
- PCM defective.

Erratic 3-4 Upshift
- 3-4 shift valve stuck.
- Shift control solenoid valve "A" defective.
- PCM defective.

Excessive Idle Vibration
- Low fluid.
- ATF pump worn or binding.
- Linear solenoid assembly defective.
- Engine output low.
- Flexplate defective.
- Lock-up shift valve stuck.
- Lock-up piston defective.
- Shift control solenoid valve "A" defective.
- PCM defective.

Flare On Start From "D_3", Stall RPM High In "D_4", "D_3" & "2"
- Low fluid.
- ATF pump worn or binding.
- Regulator valve stuck.
- Shift cable broken or out of adjustment.
- ATF strainer clogged.
- Converter check valve stuck.

Flare On Start From "D_3", Stall RPM High In "D_4", "D_3" & "2"
- Shift cable broken or out of adjustment.
- One way clutch worn or damaged.
- 1st clutch defective.

Flare On Start From "D_3", Stall RPM High In "2"
- Shift cable broken or out of adjustment.
- 2nd clutch defective.

Flare On Start From "D_3", Stall RPM Is Within Specification
- 4th clutch defective.

Flare On Start From "D_3", Stall RPM Is Low
- Torque converter one-way clutch defective.
- Engine throttle cable out of adjustment.
- Engine output low.
- Lock-up shift valve stuck.
- Lock-up piston defective.
- Shift control solenoid valve "A" defective.
- PCM defective.

Flare On 2-3 Upshift
- 3rd clutch defective.
- Linear solenoid assembly defective.
- CPC valve stuck.
- 2nd accumulator stuck.
- 2nd orifice control valve stuck.
- Lock-up control solenoid valve "B" defective.
- PCM defective.

Flare On 3-4 Upshift
- 4th clutch defective.
- Linear solenoid assembly defective.
- CPC valve stuck.
- 3rd accumulator stuck.
- Lock-up control solenoid valve "B" defective.
- PCM defective.

Harsh 1-2 Upshift
- 2nd clutch defective.
- Linear solenoid assembly defective.
- CPC valve stuck.
- Foreign material in main orifice.

Harsh 2-3 Upshift
- 3rd clutch defective.
- Linear solenoid assembly defective.
- CPC valve stuck.
- 2nd accumulator stuck.
- 2nd orifice control valve stuck.
- Foreign material in main orifice.
- Lock-up control solenoid valve "A" defective.
- Lock-up control solenoid valve "B" defective.
- PCM defective.
- Mainshaft speed sensor defective.
- Countershaft speed sensor defective.

Harsh 3-4 Upshift
- 4th clutch defective.
- Linear solenoid assembly defective.
- CPC valve stuck.
- 3rd accumulator stuck.
- 3-4 orifice control valve stuck.
- Foreign material in main orifice.
- Lock-up control solenoid valve "A" defective.
- Lock-up control solenoid valve "B" defective.
- PCM defective.
- Mainshaft speed sensor defective.
- Countershaft speed sensor defective.

Harsh 2-1 Downshifts
- Linear solenoid assembly defective.
- CPC valve stuck.
- 2nd accumulator stuck.
- CPB valve stuck.
- PCM defective.
- Foreign material in 2nd exhaust orifice.
- Mainshaft speed sensor defective.
- Countershaft speed sensor defective.

Harsh 3-2 Downshifts
- 2nd clutch defective.
- Linear solenoid assembly defective.
- CPC valve stuck.
- 3rd accumulator defective.
- CPB valve stuck.
- PCM defective.
- Foreign material in 3rd exhaust orifice.
- Mainshaft speed sensor defective.
- Countershaft speed sensor defective.

Harsh 4-3 Downshifts
- 3rd clutch defective.
- Linear solenoid assembly defective.
- CPC valve stuck.
- 4th accumulator defective.
- CPB valve stuck.
- PCM defective.
- Foreign material in 4th exhaust orifice.
- Mainshaft speed sensor defective.
- Countershaft speed sensor defective.

Lock-Up Clutch Does Not Disengage
- Linear solenoid assembly defective.
- Lock-up timing valve stuck.
- Lock-up shift valve stuck.
- Lock-up control valve stuck.
- Lock-up piston defective.
- Lock-up control solenoid valve "A" defective.
- Lock-up control solenoid valve "B" defective.
- Countershaft speed sensor defective.

Lock-Up Clutch Not Smooth
- Linear solenoid assembly defective.
- Converter check valve stuck.
- Lock-up timing valve stuck.
- Lock-up shift valve stuck.
- Lock-up control valve stuck.
- Lock-up piston defective.
- Lock-up control solenoid valve "A" defective.
- Lock-up control solenoid valve "B" defective.
- Countershaft speed sensor defective.

Lock-Up Clutch Does Not Engage
- Linear solenoid assembly defective.
- Converter check valve stuck.
- Lock-up timing valve stuck.
- Lock-up shift valve stuck.
- Lock-up control valve stuck.
- Lock-up piston defective.
- Lock-up control solenoid valve "A" defective.
- Lock-up control solenoid valve "B" defective.
- Countershaft speed sensor defective.

No Shift
- Linear solenoid assembly defective.
- CPC valve stuck.
- Modulator valve stuck.
- Shift control solenoid valve "A" defective.
- Shift control solenoid valve "B" defective.
- PCM defective.

No Shift, Stuck In 4th Gear
- Shift control solenoid valve "A" defective.
- Shift control solenoid valve "B" defective.
- PCM defective.

No 1-3 Shift From "D₃"
- 2-3 shift valve stuck.
- Shift control solenoid valve "B" defective.
- PCM defective.

No 1-4 Shift From "D₄"
- 2-3 shift valve stuck.
- 3-4 shift valve stuck.
- Shift control solenoid valve "A" defective.
- PCM defective.

Noise From Transaxle In All Gears
- ATF pump worn or binding.
- Case ball bearing worn or damaged.

Shift Lever Operation Not Smooth
- Shift cable broken or out of adjustment.
- Shift cable problem.

Stall RPM High, All Clutch Pressures Okay
- Converter check valve stuck.

Vehicle Moves In All Gears Except "2"
- Shift cable broken or out of adjustment.
- 2nd clutch defective.
- 2nd gears worn or damaged.
- 2nd accumulator defective.

Vehicle Moves In All Gears Except "R"
- Servo valve stuck.
- Shift cable broken or out of adjustment.
- 4th clutch defective.
- Reverse gears worn or damaged.

Vehicle Moves In "R" & "2" Only
- Shift cable broken or out of adjustment.
- One way clutch worn or damaged.
- 1st gears worn or damaged.
- 1st clutch defective.
- Foreign material in 1st orifice.
- 1st accumulator defective.

Vehicle Moves In "N"
- 1st clutch defective.
- 2nd clutch defective.
- 3rd clutch defective.
- 4th clutch defective.
- To much fluid.
- Foreign material in main orifice.
- Needle bearing worn or damaged.
- Thrust washer worn or damaged.
- Clutch clearance incorrect.

Vehicle Will Not Accelerate To A Speed Greater Than 31 MPH
- Torque converter one-way clutch defective.

Vibration In All Gears
- Flexplate defective.

Will Not Shift Into "P" Position
- Shift cable broken or out of adjustment.
- Shift cable problem.

TESTING

ROAD TEST

NOTE: If shift lever cannot be moved from "P" position with brake pedal depressed and accelerator pedal at idle position, check shift interlock system. See HONDA A4RA ELECTRONIC CONTROLS article.

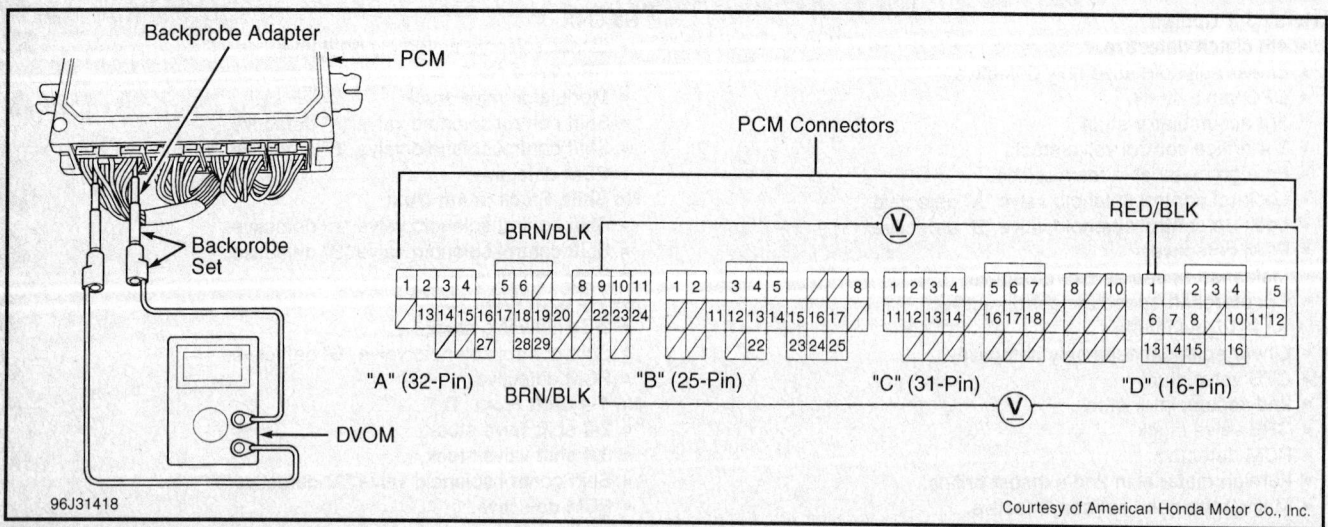

Fig. 3: Installing Backprobe Test Set

CAUTION: Vehicle is equipped with an air bag system (Supplemental Restraint System (SRS). All wires have Yellow insulation and are located underdash or in instrument panel area. To avoid injury from accidental deployment, read and carefully follow all SERVICE PRECAUTIONS and DISABLING & ACTIVATING AIR BAG SYSTEM procedures in APPLICATIONS & IDENTIFICATIONS.

1) Warm engine to normal operating temperature. Apply parking brake and block wheels. Start engine. Move shift lever to "D_4" position while depressing brake pedal. Depress accelerator pedal and release it suddenly. Engine should not stall.

2) Repeat step 1) in "D_3" position. Ensure engine does not stall. Manufacturer recommends monitoring of throttle position sensor voltage when performing road test to ensure proper throttle opening for verifying shift points.

3) Ensure ignition is off. Remove passenger side kick panel. Remove PCM bracket and remove PCM from bracket. Install Backprobe Test Set (07SAZ-001000A) or equivalent between PCM and Digital Volt-Ohmmeter (DVOM) leads. See Fig. 3.

4) Using DVOM, with positive lead at terminal D1 and negative lead at terminal A9 or A22. See Fig. 3. Ensure digital volt-ohmmeter is set for measuring voltage.

5) Road test vehicle and check for abnormal noise and clutch slippage. Specified clutch is applied in designated gears. See CLUTCH APPLICATION table.

6) Note that shift points and lock-up clutch operation are within specification in accordance with throttle position sensor voltage. See TRANSAXLE UPSHIFT SPECIFICATIONS and TRANSAXLE DOWNSHIFT SPECIFICATIONS tables.

7) With shift lever in "D_4" position, accelerate to about 35 MPH so transaxle is in 4th gear. Move shift lever to "2" position. Ensure engine braking occurs.

CAUTION: DO NOT shift from "D_4" to "2" at speeds greater than 62 MPH or transaxle may be damaged.

8) Place shift lever in "2" position. Accelerate from a stop at full throttle. Check for abnormal noise or clutch slippage. Upshifts and downshifts should not occur in this range.

9) Place shift lever in "R" position. Accelerate from a stop at full throttle. Check for abnormal noise or clutch slippage.

10) Park vehicle on a slope. Apply parking brake and place shift lever in "P" position. Release parking brake. Ensure vehicle does not move. If vehicle moves, check for defective shift cable or parking components.

11) Ensure ignition is off. Reinstall electrical connectors, PCM bracket and PCM.

CLUTCH APPLICATION

Shift Lever Position	Elements In Use
"P" & "N"	No Clutches Are Applied
"R"	4th Clutch
"D_4"	
1st Gear	1st Clutch
2nd Gear	[1] 1st clutch, 2nd Clutch
3rd Gear	[1] 1st clutch, 3rd Clutch
4th Gear	[1] 1st clutch, 4th Clutch
"D_3"	
1st Gear	1st Clutch
2nd Gear	[1] 1st clutch, 2nd Clutch
3rd Gear	[1] 1st clutch, 3rd Clutch
"2"	[1] 1st clutch, 2nd Clutch

[1] – The 1st clutch engages, but driving power is not transmitted, as one-way clutch slips.

TRANSAXLE UPSHIFT SPECIFICATIONS (EXCEPT VTEC)

"D_4" Position & Condition	1st-2nd Gear	2nd-3rd Gear	3rd-4th Gear	Lock-Up Clutch On
TPS Voltage .75 Volt	9-12 MPH	20-23 MPH	28-33 MPH	22-25 MPH
TPS Voltage 2.25 Volts	22-26 MPH	41-47 MPH	59-65 MPH	61-67 MPH
TPS Voltage 4.5 Volts (Full Throttle)	33-39 MPH	64-73 MPH	102-113 MPH	99-110 MPH

TRANSAXLE DOWNSHIFT SPECIFICATIONS (EXCEPT VTEC)

"D_4" Position & Condition	Lock-Up Clutch Off	4th-3rd Gear	3rd-2nd Gear	2nd-1st Gear
TPS Voltage .75 Volt	19-22 MPH	[1]	[1]	[2] 7-10 MPH
TPS Voltage 4.5 Volts (Full Throttle)	96-107 MPH	86-97 MPH	54-61 MPH	25-31 MPH

[1] – Specification not available from manufacturer.
[2] – Downshift from 3rd to 1st gear.

TRANSAXLE UPSHIFT SPECIFICATIONS (VTEC)

"D₄" Position & Condition	1st-2nd Gear	2nd-3rd Gear	3rd-4th Gear	Lock-Up Clutch On
TPS Voltage .75 Volt	9-12 MPH	20-23 MPH	28-33 MPH	22-25 MPH
TPS Voltage 2.25 Volts	22-26 MPH	41-47 MPH	59-65 MPH	61-67 MPH
TPS Voltage 4.5 Volts (Full Throttle)	32-38 MPH	62-71 MPH	97-108 MPH	96-107 MPH

TRANSAXLE DOWNSHIFT SPECIFICATIONS (VTEC)

"D₄" Position & Condition	Lock-Up Clutch Off	4th-3rd Gear	3rd-2nd Gear	2nd-1st Gear
TPS Voltage .75 Volt	19-22 MPH	¹	¹	² 7-10 MPH
TPS Voltage 4.5 Volts (Full Throttle)	92-103 MPH	86-97 MPH	54-61 MPH	25-31 MPH

¹ – Specification not available from manufacturer.
² – Downshift from 3rd to 1st gear.

TORQUE CONVERTER STALL SPEED TEST

CAUTION: DO NOT perform torque converter stall speed test for more than 10 seconds or transaxle may be damaged. DO NOT move shift lever while increasing engine speed.

1) Apply parking brake and block all wheels. Connect tachometer. Start engine. Ensure A/C is off. Warm engine to normal operating temperature. Place shift lever in "2" position.
2) Fully depress brake pedal. Fully depress accelerator for 6-8 seconds and note engine speed. This is the torque converter stall speed.
3) Allow transaxle to cool for 2 minutes at idle in "N" or "P". Repeat test procedure in "D₄", "2" and "R" positions.
4) Torque converter stall speed should be the same in "D₄", "2" and "R" positions. Torque converter stall speed should be 2550-2850 RPM. If torque converter stall speed is not within specification, see TORQUE CONVERTER STALL SPEED TROUBLE SHOOTING table for possible causes.

TORQUE CONVERTER STALL SPEED TROUBLE SHOOTING

Torque Converter Stall Speed Test Results	Probable Cause
Stall Speed RPM High In "D₄", "2" & "R"	Low Fluid Level, Low Oil Pump Output, Clogged Fluid Strainer, Pressure Regulator Valve Stuck Closed, Slipping Clutch
Stall Speed RPM High In "R"	Slipping 4th Clutch
Stall Speed RPM High In "2"	Slipping 2nd Clutch Defective One-Way Clutch
Stall Speed RPM Low In "D₄", "2" & "R"	Engine Output Low, Torque Converter One-Way Clutch Slipping

HYDRAULIC PRESSURE TEST

Test Preparation – Ensure transaxle fluid level is correct. Warm engine to normal operating temperature. Apply parking brake and block rear wheels. Raise and support vehicle so front wheels can rotate. Attach tachometer.
Pressure Testing – 1) With engine off, remove pressure tap plug from appropriate pressure tap on transaxle. *See Fig. 4.* Attach pressure gauge to appropriate pressure tap using NEW washer. Tighten hose fitting to 13 ft. lbs. (18 N.m).
2) Start and operate engine at 2000 RPM for all pressure readings. Measure line pressure, 1st clutch, 2nd clutch, 3rd clutch and 4th clutch in order. With shift lever in appropriate position, measure each line pressure.
3) Line pressure should be within specification. See HYDRAULIC PRESSURE TEST SPECIFICATIONS table. If line pressure is not within specification, see HYDRAULIC PRESSURE TEST TROUBLE SHOOTING table.
4) For 2nd, 3rd or 4th clutch measurement, disconnect linear solenoid connector. *See Fig. 5* Apply battery voltage to linear solenoid connector terminals. With shift lever in appropriate position, measure each

line pressure at 2000 RPM. Line pressure should be within specification. See HYDRAULIC PRESSURE TEST SPECIFICATIONS table. If line pressure is not within specification, see HYDRAULIC PRESSURE TEST TROUBLE SHOOTING table. Shut engine off.
5) Remove pressure gauge set. Using NEW seal washer, install and tighten pressure tap plug to specification. See TORQUE SPECIFICATIONS.

HYDRAULIC PRESSURE TEST TROUBLE SHOOTING

Application	Probable Cause
Line Pressure	
Low Or No Line Pressure	Defective Torque Converter, Defective Torque Converter Check Valve, Defective Oil Pump Pressure Regulator, Defective Oil Pump
Clutch Pressure	
Low Or No 1st Clutch Pressure	Defective 1st Clutch
Low Or No 2nd Clutch Pressure	Defective 2nd Clutch
Low Or No 3rd Clutch Pressure	Defective 3rd Clutch
Low Or No 4th Clutch Pressure	Defective 4th Clutch, Defective Servo Valve

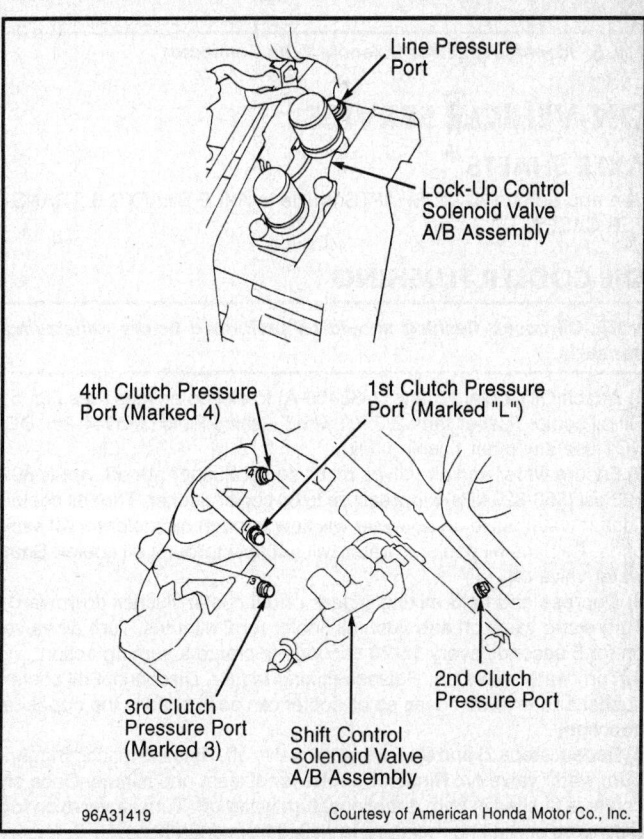

96A31419   Courtesy of American Honda Motor Co., Inc.

Fig. 4: Identifying Transaxle Pressure Taps

HYDRAULIC PRESSURE TEST SPECIFICATIONS

Application	Shift Lever Position	psi. (kPa)
Line Pressure	"P" Or "N"	120-128 (830-880)
Clutch Pressure		
With Linear Solenoid Disconnected		
1st Clutch	"D₄"	110-128 (780-880)
2nd Clutch	"D₄"	110-128 (780-880)
3rd Clutch	"D₄"	110-128 (780-880)
4th Clutch	"D₄"	110-128 (780-880)
	"R"	110-128 (780-880)
With Voltage Applied To Linear Solenoid		
1st Clutch	"D₄"	0-21 (0-150)
2nd Clutch	"D₄"	0-21 (0-150)
3rd Clutch	"D₄"	0-21 (0-150)
4th Clutch	"D₄"	0-21 (0-150)
	"R"	0-21 (0-150)

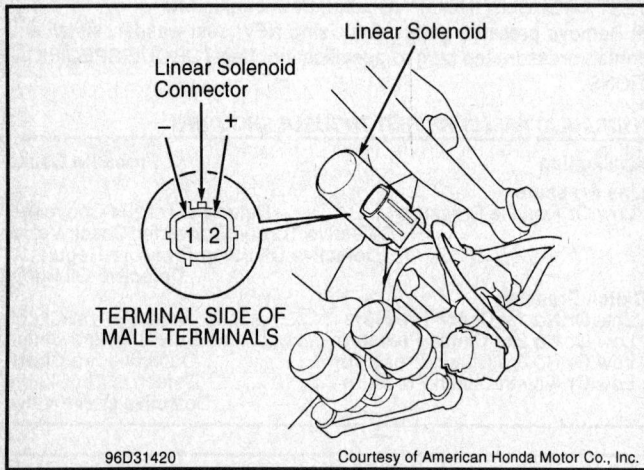

96D31420   Courtesy of American Honda Motor Co., Inc.

Fig. 5: Identifying Linear Solenoid 2-Pin Connector

ON-VEHICLE SERVICE

AXLE SHAFTS

See appropriate AXLE SHAFTS article in AXLE SHAFTS & TRANSFER CASES.

OIL COOLER FLUSHING

NOTE: Oil cooler flushing should be preformed before reinstalling transaxle.

1) Attach Oil Cooler Flusher (J38405-A) to oil cooler lines. *See Fig. 6.* Fill oil cooler flusher tank 2/3 full with Flushing Fluid (J35944-20). DO NOT use any other flushing fluid.
2) Ensure water and air valves on oil cooler flusher are off. Apply 80-120 psi (550-829 kPa) air pressure to oil cooler flusher. Turn oil cooler flusher water valve on so water will flow through oil cooler for 10 seconds. Replace oil cooler if water will not flow through oil cooler. Shut water valve off.
3) Depress and hold mixing trigger on oil cooler flusher downward. Turn water valve on and flush oil cooler for 2 minutes. Turn air valve on for 5 seconds every 15-20 seconds to create a surging action.
4) Turn water valve off. Release mixing trigger. Disconnect oil cooler flusher and reverse hoses so oil cooler can be flushed in the opposite direction.
5) Repeat steps **2)** and **3)**. Turn water valve off. Release mixing trigger. Turn water valve on. Rinse oil cooler for at least one minute. Once oil cooler is flushed in both directions, turn water off. Turn air valve on for 2 minutes or until no moisture is visible from drain hose.

CAUTION: Ensure no moisture exists in oil cooler, as it can damage transaxle.

6) Turn air off. Disconnect oil cooler flusher. Reconnect inlet line on oil cooler. Once transaxle is installed, attach drain hose on return line and place in oil container. Ensure transaxle is in "P" position. Fill transaxle with ATF.
7) Start engine and operate for approximately 30 seconds or until one quart (.9L) of ATF is discharged from return line. Shut engine off. Remove drain hose. Reinstall return line. Fill transaxle to proper level.

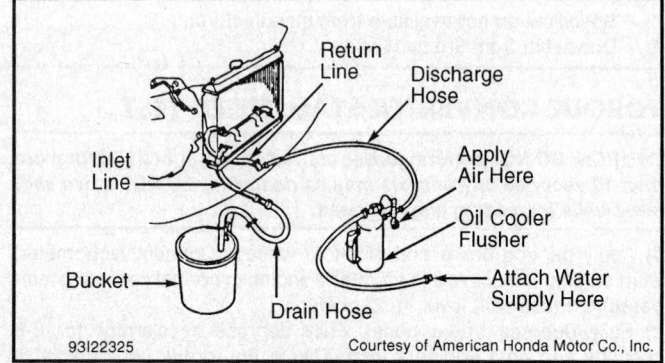

93122325   Courtesy of American Honda Motor Co., Inc.

Fig. 6: Installing Oil Cooler Flusher

REMOVAL & INSTALLATION

ELECTRICAL COMPONENTS

See HONDA A4RA ELECTRONIC CONTROLS article.

TRANSAXLE

See appropriate AUTOMATIC TRANSMISSION REMOVAL article in TRANSMISSION SERVICING.

TORQUE CONVERTER

Torque converter consists of pump, turbine and stator assembled as a unit. Torque converter cannot be serviced and must be replaced if defective.

NOTE: For torque converter stall speed test, see TORQUE CONVERTER STALL SPEED TEST under TESTING.

TRANSAXLE DISASSEMBLY

VALVE BODIES & INTERNAL COMPONENTS

1) Remove bolts, right side cover and gasket. *See Fig. 7.* Install Mainshaft Holder (07GAB-PF50101) on mainshaft to secure mainshaft from rotating. *See Fig. 8.*

CAUTION: DO NOT use impact wrench to remove lock nuts from countershaft, mainshaft and secondary shaft.

2) Engage parking pawl with parking gear. Using hammer and chisel, cut lock tabs on countershaft and mainshaft lock nuts. Remove lock nuts and spring washers. *See Fig. 7.*

NOTE: Mainshaft and countershaft lock nut has left-hand thread.

3) Remove mainshaft holder once lock nuts are removed. Remove 1st clutch, mainshaft 1st gear assembly and mainshaft 1st gear collar from mainshaft. Remove parking pawl, parking pawl spring and parking pawl shaft. Remove parking brake lever from control shaft.
4) Using puller, remove parking gear, one-way clutch and countershaft 1st gear from countershaft. Using puller, remove idler gears from mainshaft and secondary shaft.

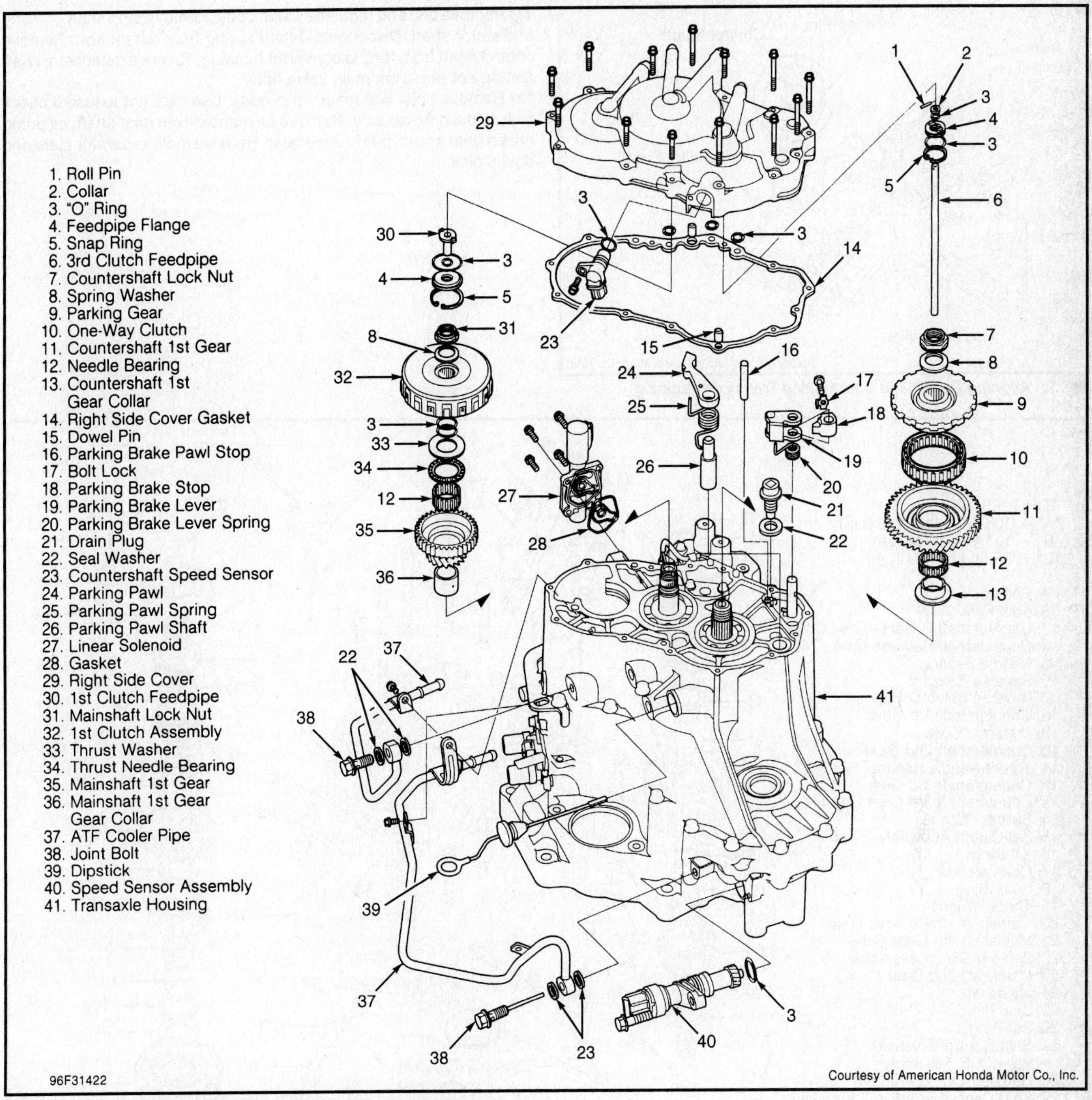

1. Roll Pin
2. Collar
3. "O" Ring
4. Feedpipe Flange
5. Snap Ring
6. 3rd Clutch Feedpipe
7. Countershaft Lock Nut
8. Spring Washer
9. Parking Gear
10. One-Way Clutch
11. Countershaft 1st Gear
12. Needle Bearing
13. Countershaft 1st Gear Collar
14. Right Side Cover Gasket
15. Dowel Pin
16. Parking Brake Pawl Stop
17. Bolt Lock
18. Parking Brake Stop
19. Parking Brake Lever
20. Parking Brake Lever Spring
21. Drain Plug
22. Seal Washer
23. Countershaft Speed Sensor
24. Parking Pawl
25. Parking Pawl Spring
26. Parking Pawl Shaft
27. Linear Solenoid
28. Gasket
29. Right Side Cover
30. 1st Clutch Feedpipe
31. Mainshaft Lock Nut
32. 1st Clutch Assembly
33. Thrust Washer
34. Thrust Needle Bearing
35. Mainshaft 1st Gear
36. Mainshaft 1st Gear Gear Collar
37. ATF Cooler Pipe
38. Joint Bolt
39. Dipstick
40. Speed Sensor Assembly
41. Transaxle Housing

96F31422

Courtesy of American Honda Motor Co., Inc.

Fig. 7: Exploded View Of Right Side Cover & Components

5) Remove needle bearing and countershaft 1st gear collar from countershaft. Remove ATF cooler lines and dipstick.

6) Remove mainshaft speed sensor. Remove transaxle housing bolts and hanger. Align spring pin with groove in transaxle housing by rotating control shaft. Using Puller (07HAC-PK4010A), remove transaxle housing. See Fig. 9.

7) Remove countershaft reverse gear, collar and needle bearing. See Fig. 10. Remove bolt, lock washer, shift fork and reverse selector.

8) Remove mainshaft and countershaft assemblies at same time. Remove differential assembly from torque converter housing.

9) Remove oil feedpipes from servo body, secondary valve body and main valve body. Remove bolts and fluid strainer. Remove bolt and servo detent base. See Fig. 11. Remove bolts, servo body and servo separator plate.

10) Remove secondary valve body, stop shaft and secondary separator plate. Remove bolts, lock-up valve body and separator plate.

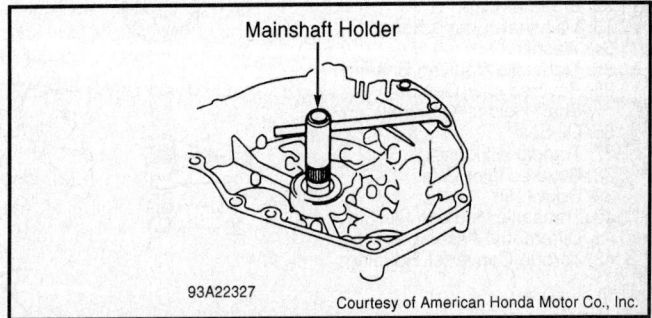

Mainshaft Holder

93A22327

Courtesy of American Honda Motor Co., Inc.

Fig. 8: Installing Mainshaft Holder

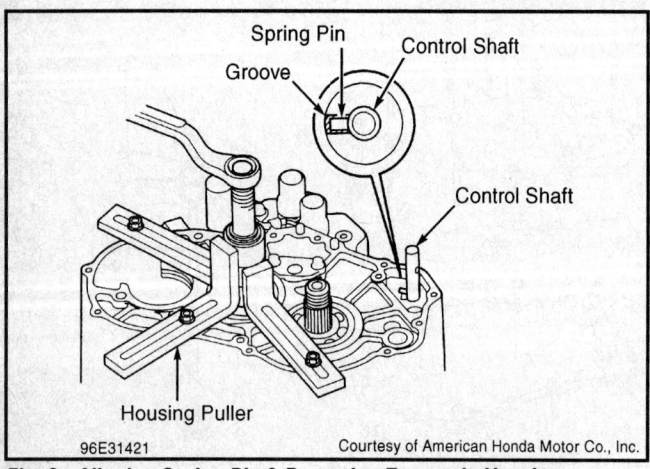

Spring Pin
Control Shaft
Groove
Control Shaft
Housing Puller
96E31421
Courtesy of American Honda Motor Co., Inc.

Fig. 9: Aligning Spring Pin & Removing Transaxle Housing

11) Remove bolt and regulator valve body. Remove stop shaft, "O" ring and stator shaft. Disconnect detent spring from detent arm. Remove control shaft from torque converter housing. Remove detent arm shaft and detent arm from main valve body.

12) Remove bolts and main valve body. Use care not to lose 8 check balls in main valve body. Remove oil pump driven gear shaft, oil pump driven gear and oil pump drive gear. Remove main separator plate and dowel pins.

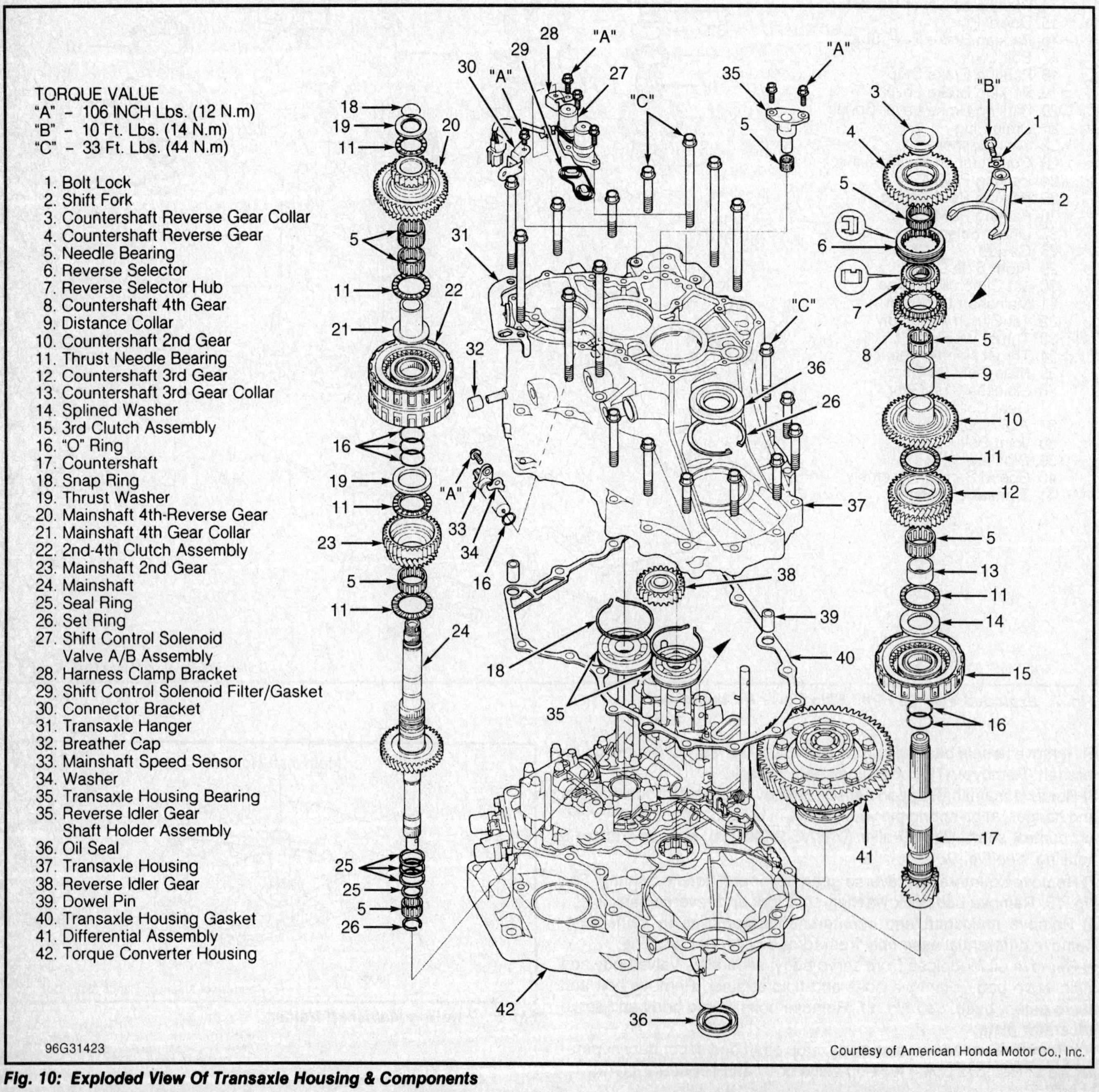

TORQUE VALUE
"A" – 106 INCH Lbs. (12 N.m)
"B" – 10 Ft. Lbs. (14 N.m)
"C" – 33 Ft. Lbs. (44 N.m)

1. Bolt Lock
2. Shift Fork
3. Countershaft Reverse Gear Collar
4. Countershaft Reverse Gear
5. Needle Bearing
6. Reverse Selector
7. Reverse Selector Hub
8. Countershaft 4th Gear
9. Distance Collar
10. Countershaft 2nd Gear
11. Thrust Needle Bearing
12. Countershaft 3rd Gear
13. Countershaft 3rd Gear Collar
14. Splined Washer
15. 3rd Clutch Assembly
16. "O" Ring
17. Countershaft
18. Snap Ring
19. Thrust Washer
20. Mainshaft 4th-Reverse Gear
21. Mainshaft 4th Gear Collar
22. 2nd-4th Clutch Assembly
23. Mainshaft 2nd Gear
24. Mainshaft
25. Seal Ring
26. Set Ring
27. Shift Control Solenoid Valve A/B Assembly
28. Harness Clamp Bracket
29. Shift Control Solenoid Filter/Gasket
30. Connector Bracket
31. Transaxle Hanger
32. Breather Cap
33. Mainshaft Speed Sensor
34. Washer
35. Transaxle Housing Bearing
35. Reverse Idler Gear Shaft Holder Assembly
36. Oil Seal
37. Transaxle Housing
38. Reverse Idler Gear
39. Dowel Pin
40. Transaxle Housing Gasket
41. Differential Assembly
42. Torque Converter Housing

96G31423
Courtesy of American Honda Motor Co., Inc.

Fig. 10: Exploded View Of Transaxle Housing & Components

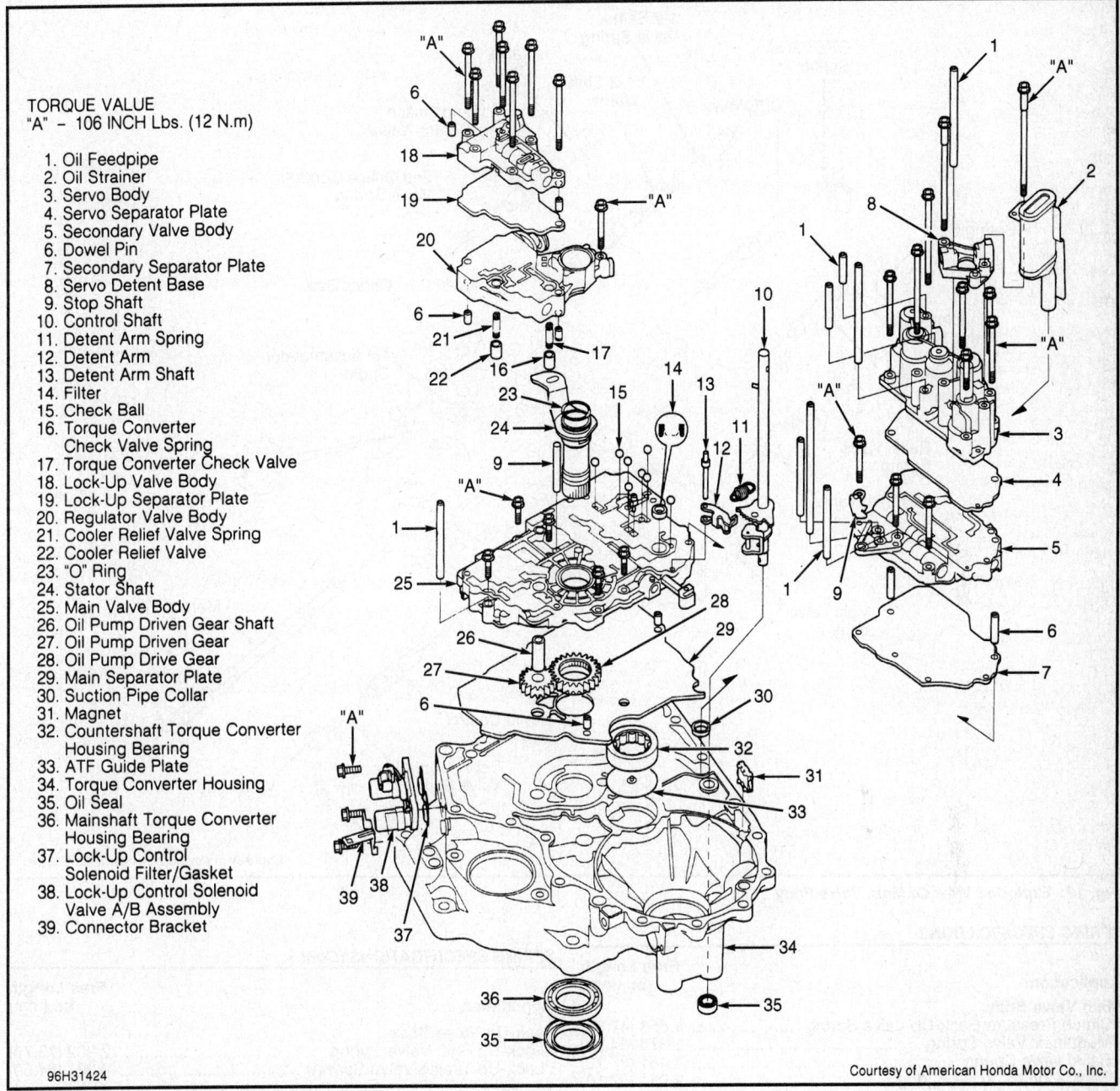

TORQUE VALUE
"A" – 106 INCH Lbs. (12 N.m)

1. Oil Feedpipe
2. Oil Strainer
3. Servo Body
4. Servo Separator Plate
5. Secondary Valve Body
6. Dowel Pin
7. Secondary Separator Plate
8. Servo Detent Base
9. Stop Shaft
10. Control Shaft
11. Detent Arm Spring
12. Detent Arm
13. Detent Arm Shaft
14. Filter
15. Check Ball
16. Torque Converter
   Check Valve Spring
17. Torque Converter Check Valve
18. Lock-Up Valve Body
19. Lock-Up Separator Plate
20. Regulator Valve Body
21. Cooler Relief Valve Spring
22. Cooler Relief Valve
23. "O" Ring
24. Stator Shaft
25. Main Valve Body
26. Oil Pump Driven Gear Shaft
27. Oil Pump Driven Gear
28. Oil Pump Drive Gear
29. Main Separator Plate
30. Suction Pipe Collar
31. Magnet
32. Countershaft Torque Converter
   Housing Bearing
33. ATF Guide Plate
34. Torque Converter Housing
35. Oil Seal
36. Mainshaft Torque Converter
   Housing Bearing
37. Lock-Up Control
   Solenoid Filter/Gasket
38. Lock-Up Control Solenoid
   Valve A/B Assembly
39. Connector Bracket

96H31424

Courtesy of American Honda Motor Co., Inc.

Fig. 11: Exploded View Of Torque Converter Housing & Components

COMPONENT DISASSEMBLY & REASSEMBLY

MAIN VALVE BODY

CAUTION: When disassembling main valve body, place main valve body components in order, and mark spring locations for reassembly reference. DO NOT use force to remove components. DO NOT use magnet to remove check balls, as check balls may become magnetized. Note direction of valve cap installation before removing from main valve body.

Disassembly – Disassemble main valve body. *See Fig. 12.* Use care when removing valve caps or spring seats, as they are under spring pressure.

Cleaning & Inspection – 1) Clean components with solvent and dry with compressed air. Replace main valve body if any parts are worn or damaged.

2) Ensure all valves slide freely in their bores. If valves do not slide freely, polish burrs or rough areas using No. 600 sandpaper soaked for 30 minutes in ATF. Thoroughly clean main valve body and components if polishing was needed.

3) Ensure spring free length is within specification. See SPRING SPECIFICATIONS table. Replace springs if not within specification.

NOTE: Oil pump clearance must be checked in main valve body. See OIL PUMP.

Reassembly – Coat all components and bores with ATF. To reassemble, reverse disassembly procedure. Install NEW filter. Ensure all components are installed in correct location. *See Fig. 12.*

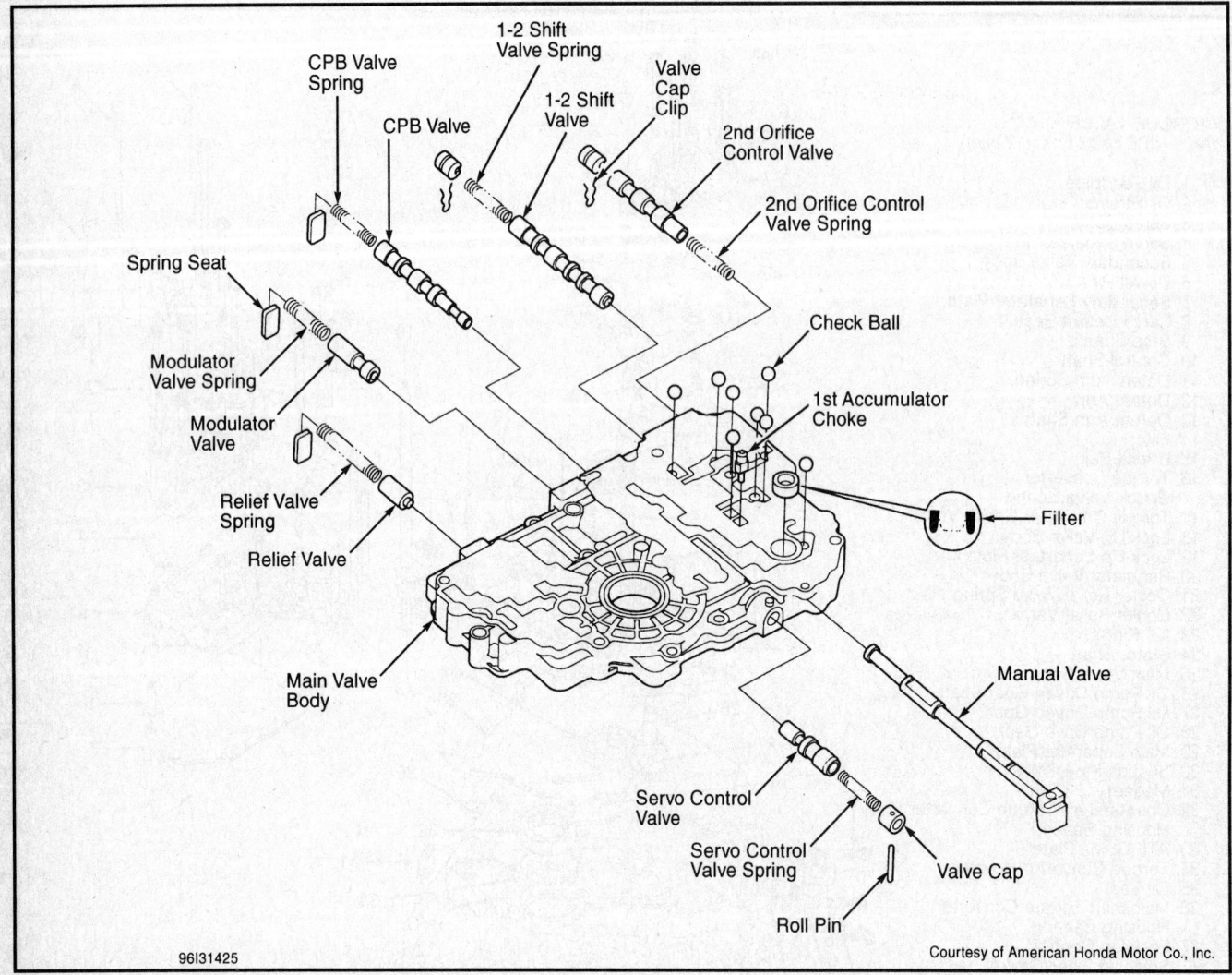

96I31425

Courtesy of American Honda Motor Co., Inc.

Fig. 12: Exploded View Of Main Valve Body

SPRING SPECIFICATIONS

Application	Free Length In. (mm)
Main Valve Body	
Clutch Pressure Back-Up Valve Spring	1.858 (47.20)
Modulator Valve Spring	1.370 (34.80)
Relief valve Spring	1.461 (37.10)
Servo Control Valve Spring	2.051 (52.10)
1-2 Shift Valve Spring	1.626 (41.30)
2nd Orifice Control Valve Spring	1.370 (34.80)
Regulator Valve Body	
Cooler Relief Valve Spring	1.331 (33.80)
Lock-Up Timing Valve Spring	1.496 (38.00)
Regulator Valve Spring "A"	3.457 (87.80)
Regulator Valve Spring "B"	1.732 (44.00)
Stator Reaction Spring	1.193 (30.30)
Torque Converter Check Valve Spring	1.331 (33.80)
Secondary Valve Body	
2-3 Shift Valve Spring	2.244 (57.00)
3-4 Orifice Control Valve Spring	1.476 (37.50)
3-4 Shift Valve Spring	2.244 (57.00)
4th Exhaust Valve Spring	1.433 (46.40)
Servo Body	
1st Accumulator Spring	3.508 (89.10)
2nd Accumulator Spring "A"	1.535 (39.00)
2nd Accumulator Spring "B"	.815 (20.70)
2nd Accumulator Spring "C"	2.677 (68.00)
3rd Accumulator Spring "A"	3.516 (89.30)
3rd Accumulator Spring "B"	2.583 (65.60)
4th Accumulator Spring "A"	3.425 (87.00)
4th Accumulator Spring "B"	2.031 (51.60)

SPRING SPECIFICATIONS (Cont.)

Application	Free Length In. (mm)
Lock-Up Valve Body	
Lock-Up Shift Valve Spring	2.902 (73.70)
Lock-Up Timing Valve Spring	3.327 (84.50)

OIL PUMP

Disassembly – Note direction of oil pump gear installation in main valve body. Remove oil pump driven gear shaft and oil pump gears from main valve body (if not previously removed).

Cleaning & Inspection – **1)** Clean components with solvent and dry with compressed air. Inspect components and replace if damaged.

2) Install oil pump gears and oil pump driven gear shaft in main valve body. Ensure chamfered and grooved side of oil pump driven gear is facing upward (toward separator plate side of main valve body).

3) Using feeler gauge, measure side clearance of both gears between tip of gear teeth and main valve body. See Fig. 13. Replace oil pump gears and/or main valve body if side clearance is not within specification. See OIL PUMP SPECIFICATIONS table.

4) Remove oil pump driven gear shaft. Place straightedge across main valve body surface. Using feeler gauge, measure thrust clearance between oil pump gears and straightedge. Replace oil pump gears and/or main valve body if thrust clearance is not within specification. See OIL PUMP SPECIFICATIONS table.

OIL PUMP SPECIFICATIONS

Application	In. (mm)
Side Clearance	
Oil Pump Drive Gear	.0041-.0052 (.105-.133)
Oil Pump Driven Gear	.0014-.0025 (.035-.065)
Thrust Clearance	
Standard	.001-.002 (.03-.05)
Wear Limit	.003 (.07)

Reassembly – Coat components with ATF. To reassemble, reverse disassembly procedure. Ensure chamfered and grooved side of oil pump driven gear is facing upward (toward separator plate side of main valve body).

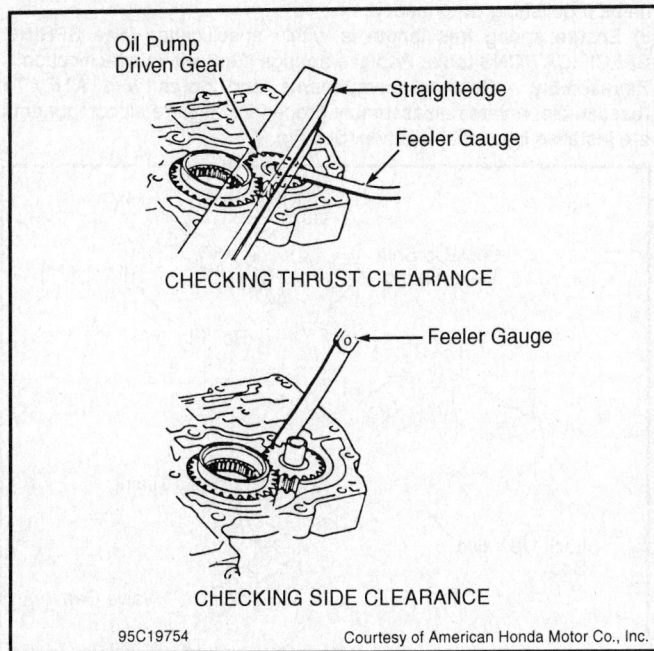

CHECKING THRUST CLEARANCE

CHECKING SIDE CLEARANCE

95C19754   Courtesy of American Honda Motor Co., Inc.

Fig. 13: Measuring Oil Pump Clearances

SECONDARY VALVE BODY

CAUTION: Clutch Pressure Control (CPC) valve is installed in secondary valve body, behind lock bolt. See Fig. 14. DO NOT remove lock bolt. If CPC valve becomes frozen, replace secondary valve body assembly.

Disassembly – When disassembling secondary valve body, place secondary valve body components in order, and mark spring locations for reassembly reference. DO NOT use force to remove components. DO NOT use magnet to remove check balls, as check balls may become magnetized. Note direction of valve cap installation before removing from secondary valve body. See Fig. 14. Use care when removing valve caps, sleeves or spring seats, as they are under spring pressure.

Cleaning & Inspection – 1) Clean components with solvent and dry with compressed air. Replace secondary valve body if any parts are worn or damaged.

2) Ensure all valves slide freely in their bores. If valves do not slide freely, polish burrs or rough areas using No. 600 sandpaper soaked for 30 minutes in ATF. Sandpaper can be rolled into a tube shape for deburring valve bores. Thoroughly clean secondary valve body and components if polishing was needed.

3) Ensure spring free length is within specification. See SPRING SPECIFICATIONS table. Replace springs if not within specification.

Reassembly – Coat all components and bores with Dexron-II ATF. To reassemble, reverse disassembly procedure. Ensure all components are installed in correct location. See Fig. 14.

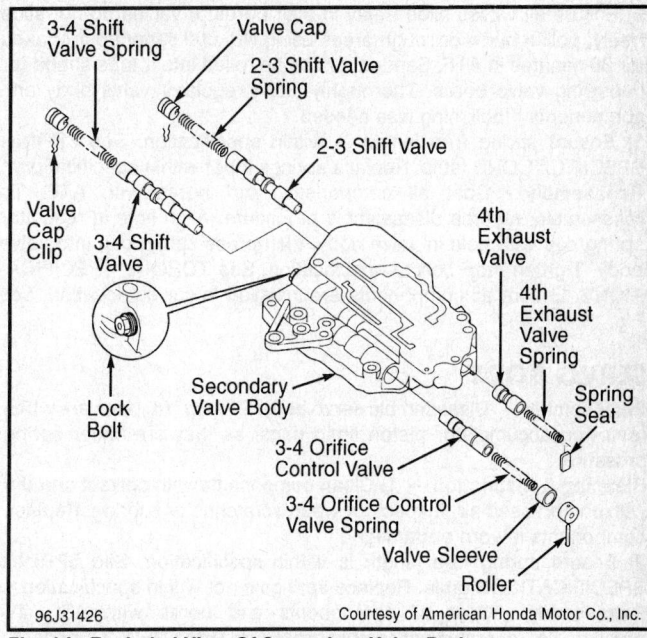

96J31426   Courtesy of American Honda Motor Co., Inc.

Fig. 14: Exploded View Of Secondary Valve Body

REGULATOR VALVE BODY

CAUTION: Regulator spring cap is under spring pressure. Ensure regulator spring cap is held downward when removing stop bolt.

Disassembly – Hold regulator spring cap downward. Remove stop bolt. Slowly remove regulator spring cap and components from regulator valve body. See Fig. 15.

Cleaning & Inspection – 1) Clean components with solvent and dry with compressed air. Replace regulator valve body if any parts are worn or damaged.

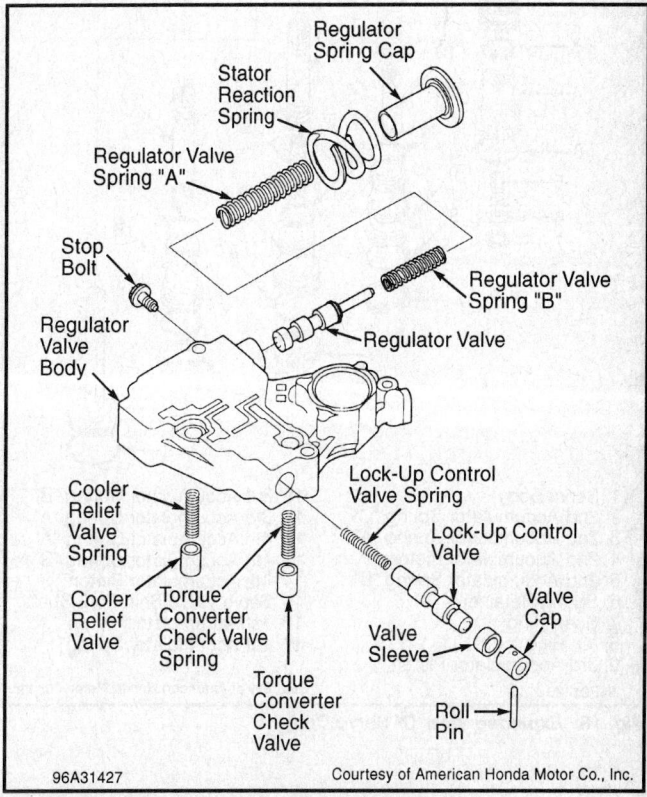

96A31427   Courtesy of American Honda Motor Co., Inc.

Fig. 15: Exploded View Of Regulator Valve Body

2) Ensure all valves slide freely in their bores. If valves do not slide freely, polish burrs or rough areas using No. 600 sandpaper soaked for 30 minutes in ATF. Sandpaper can be rolled into a tube shape for deburring valve bores. Thoroughly clean regulator valve body and components if polishing was needed.

3) Ensure spring free length is within specification. See SPRING SPECIFICATIONS table. Replace springs if not within specification.

Reassembly – Coat all components and bores with ATF. To reassemble, reverse disassembly procedure. Align hole in regulator spring cap with hole in valve body, then press spring cap into valve body. Tighten stop bolt to specification. See TORQUE SPECIFICATIONS. Ensure all components are installed in correct location. See Fig. 15.

SERVO BODY

Disassembly – Disassemble servo body. See Fig. 16. Use care when removing accumulator piston snap rings, as they are under spring pressure.

Cleaning & Inspection – **1)** Clean components with solvent and dry with compressed air. Inspect for wear, scratches or scoring. Replace components if worn or damaged.

2) Ensure spring free length is within specification. See SPRING SPECIFICATIONS table. Replace springs if not within specification.

Reassembly – Coat all components and bores with ATF. To reassemble, reverse disassembly procedure using NEW "O" rings.

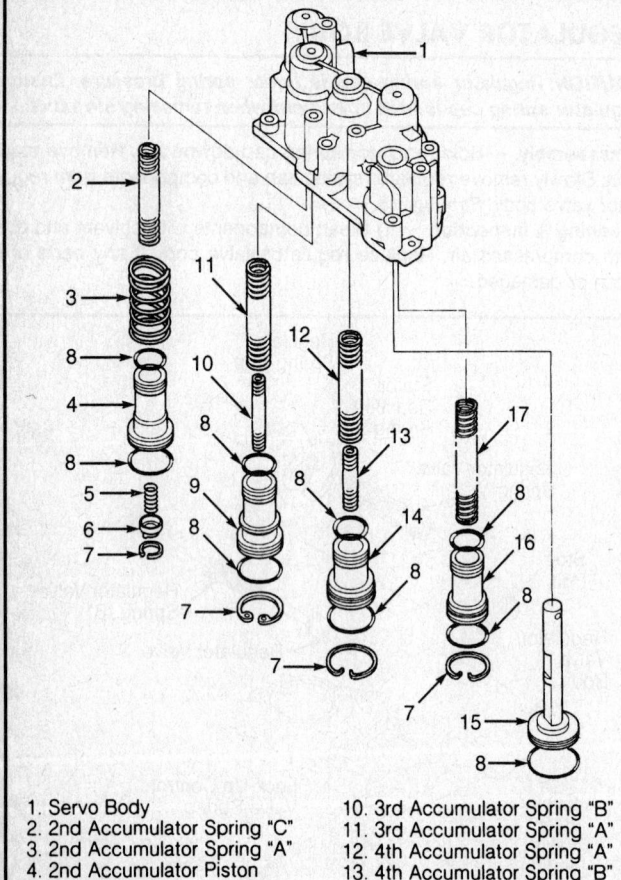

1. Servo Body
2. 2nd Accumulator Spring "C"
3. 2nd Accumulator Spring "A"
4. 2nd Accumulator Piston
5. 2nd Accumulator Spring "B"
6. Spring Retainer
7. Snap Ring
8. "O" Ring
9. 3rd Accumulator Piston
10. 3rd Accumulator Spring "B"
11. 3rd Accumulator Spring "A"
12. 4th Accumulator Spring "A"
13. 4th Accumulator Spring "B"
14. 4th Accumulator Piston
15. Servo Valve Shift Fork Shaft
16. 1st Accumulator Piston
17. 1st Accumulator Spring

96B31428   Courtesy of American Honda Motor Co., Inc.

Fig. 16: Exploded View Of Servo Body

LOCK-UP VALVE BODY

Disassembly – Disassemble lock-up valve body. See Fig. 17. Place lock-up valve body components in order, and mark spring locations for reassembly reference. DO NOT use force to remove components. Note direction of valve cap installation before removing from secondary valve body.

Cleaning & Inspection – **1)** Clean components with solvent and dry with compressed air. Replace lock-up valve body if any parts are worn or damaged.

2) Ensure all valves slide freely in the bore. If valves do not slide freely, polish burrs or rough areas using No. 600 sandpaper soaked for 30 minutes in ATF. Sandpaper can be rolled into a tube shape for deburring valve bores. Thoroughly clean lock-up valve body and components if polishing was needed.

3) Ensure spring free length is within specification. See SPRING SPECIFICATIONS table. Replace springs if not within specification.

Reassembly – Coat all components and bores with ATF. To reassemble, reverse disassembly procedure. Ensure all components are installed in correct location. See Fig. 17.

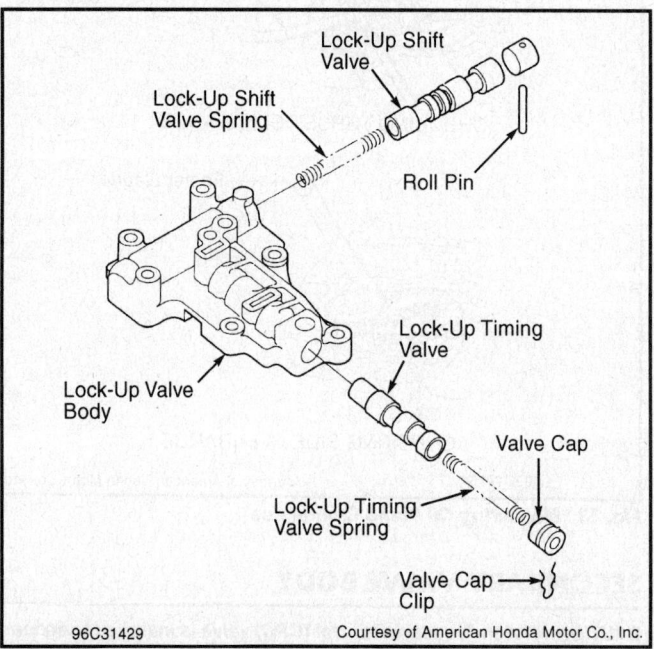

96C31429   Courtesy of American Honda Motor Co., Inc.

Fig. 17: Exploded View Of Lock-Up Valve Body

MAINSHAFT

NOTE: Mainshaft lock nut has left hand threads.

Disassembly – Note location of mainshaft components. See Fig. 10. Remove mainshaft components.

Cleaning & Inspection – Clean components with solvent and dry with compressed air. Inspect splines for excessive wear. Check bearing surfaces for scoring, scratches or wear. Inspect all needle bearings for galling and rough movement.

Adjustments – **1)** Lubricate all components with ATF. Reassemble mainshaft components in illustration without "O" rings. See Fig. 18. Ensure thrust needle bearings are installed with unrolled edge of bearing retainer facing washer.

2) Remove transaxle housing bearing for mainshaft from transaxle housing. Install transaxle housing bearing for mainshaft on mainshaft. Tighten mainshaft lock nut to 22 ft. lbs. (30 N.m).

3) Push 2nd gear in towards 2nd clutch. Using a feeler gauge, measure clearance thrust between 2nd and 3rd gear. See Fig. 19. Check mainshaft clearance at 3 places. Average the 3 readings to obtain mainshaft clearance.

4) Ensure mainshaft clearance is .002-.005" (.05-.13 mm). If clearance is not as specified, replace selective thrust washer with appropriate washer. See SELECTIVE THRUST WASHER SPECIFICATIONS table. After replacing selective thrust washer, recheck clearance.

SELECTIVE THRUST WASHER SPECIFICATIONS

Washer Number	Part Number	Thickness In. (mm)
1	90441-P4P-010	.157 (4.00)
2	90442-P4P-010	.159 (4.05)
3	90443-P4P-010	.161 (4.10)
4	90444-P4P-010	.163 (4.15)
5	90445-P4P-010	.165 (4.20)
6	90446-P4P-010	.167 (4.25)
7	90447-P4P-010	.169 (4.30)
8	90448-P4P-010	.171 (4.35)
9	90449-P4P-010	.173 (4.40)
10	90450-P4P-000	.175 (4.45)

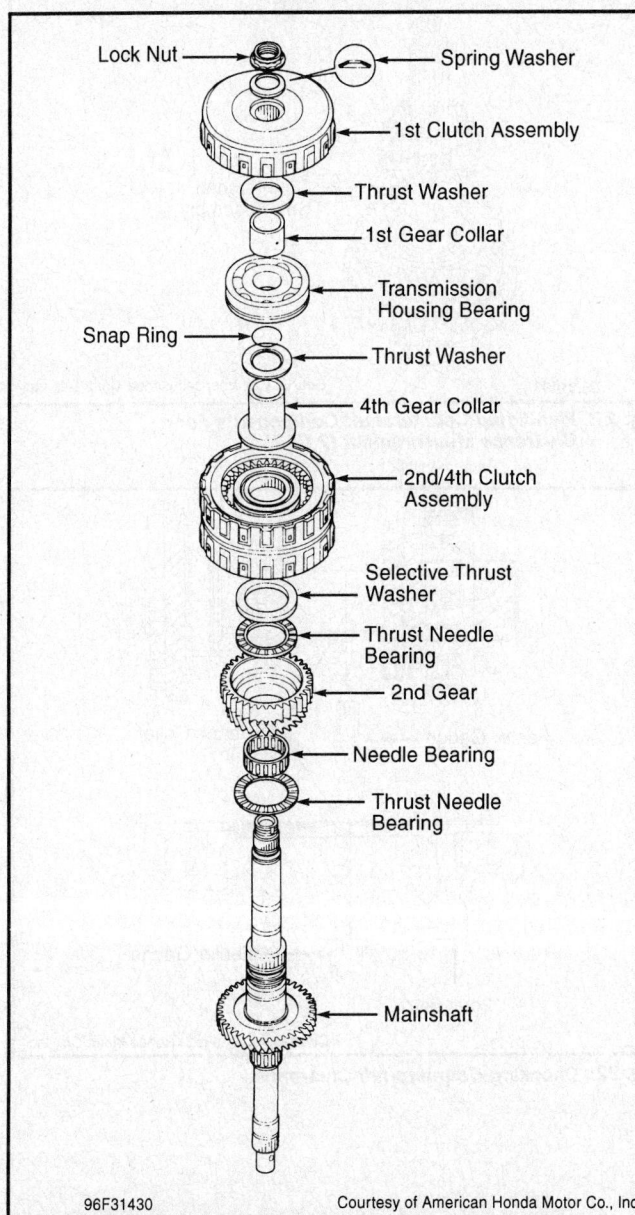

Lock Nut — Spring Washer
1st Clutch Assembly
Thrust Washer
1st Gear Collar
Transmission Housing Bearing
Snap Ring
Thrust Washer
4th Gear Collar
2nd/4th Clutch Assembly
Selective Thrust Washer
Thrust Needle Bearing
2nd Gear
Needle Bearing
Thrust Needle Bearing
Mainshaft

96F31430   Courtesy of American Honda Motor Co., Inc.

Fig. 18: Identifying Mainshaft Components For Clearance Measurement

Reassembly – Lubricate all components with ATF. Reassemble mainshaft. See Fig. 10. Ensure thrust needle bearings are installed with unrolled edge of bearing retainer facing washer. Before installing NEW "O" rings on mainshaft, wrap splines on mainshaft with tape to prevent damage to "O" rings.

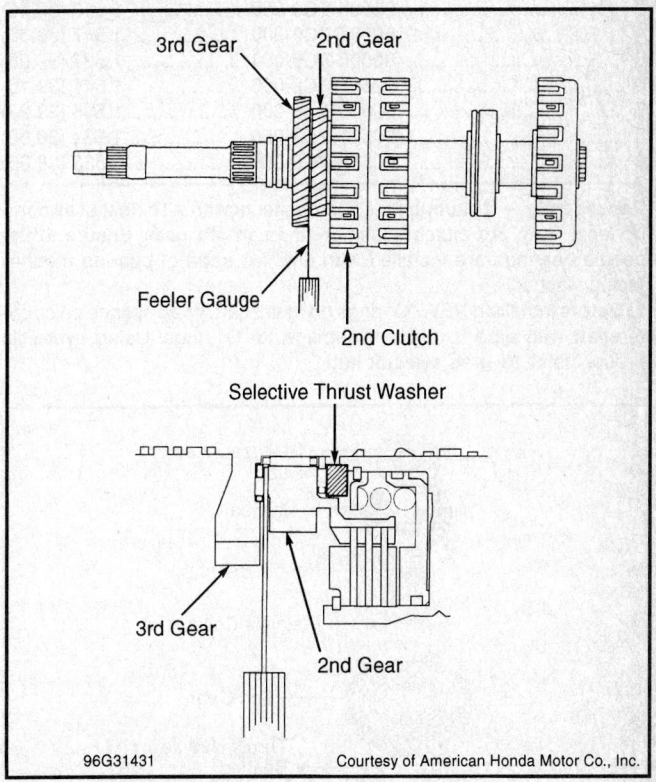

3rd Gear   2nd Gear
Feeler Gauge
2nd Clutch
Selective Thrust Washer
3rd Gear
2nd Gear

96G31431   Courtesy of American Honda Motor Co., Inc.

Fig. 19: Checking Mainshaft Clearance

COUNTERSHAFT

NOTE: Countershaft lock nut has left hand threads.

Disassembly – 1) Note location of countershaft components. See Fig. 10. Remove countershaft components down to reverse selector hub.

2) Place countershaft in hydraulic press while supporting 4th gear. Press countershaft from countershaft 4th gear. Disassemble remainder of countershaft assembly.

Cleaning & Inspection – Clean components with solvent and dry with compressed air. Inspect splines for excessive wear. Check bearing surfaces for scoring, scratches or wear. Inspect all needle bearings for galling and rough movement.

Adjustments – 1) Lubricate all components with ATF. Reassemble countershaft components in illustration without "O" rings. See Fig. 20. Ensure thrust needle bearings are installed with unrolled edge of bearing retainer facing washer. Using hydraulic press, install reverse selector hub.

2) Remove transaxle housing bearing for countershaft from transaxle housing. Install transaxle housing bearing for countershaft on countershaft with remaining components. See Fig. 21. Tighten countershaft lock nut to 22 ft. lbs. (30 N.m).

3) Using a feeler gauge, measure clearance between 2nd gear and distance collar. See Fig. 22. Check countershaft clearance at 3 places. Average the 3 readings to obtain countershaft clearance.

4) Ensure countershaft clearance is .002-.005" (.05-.13 mm). If clearance is not as specified, replace distance collar with appropriate collar. See DISTANCE COLLAR SPECIFICATIONS table. After replacing distance collar, recheck clearance.

DISTANCE COLLAR SPECIFICATIONS

Collar Number	Part Number	Thickness In. (mm)
1	90503-PC9-000	1.535 (39.00)
2	90504-PC9-000	1.539 (39.10)
3	90505-PC9-000	1.543 (39.20)
4	90507-PC9-000	1.547 (39.30)
5	90508-PC9-000	1.537 (39.05)
6	90509-PC9-000	1.541 (39.15)
7	90510-PC9-000	1.545 (39.25)
8	90511-PC9-000	1.531 (38.90)
9	90512-PC9-000	1.533 (38.95)

Reassembly – **1)** Lubricate all components with ATF. Install all components from 3rd clutch assembly through 4th gear. Ensure thrust needle bearings are installed with unrolled edge of bearing retainer facing washer.

2) Before installing NEW "O" rings on mainshaft, wrap splines on countershaft with tape to prevent damage to "O" rings. Using hydraulic press, install reverse selector hub.

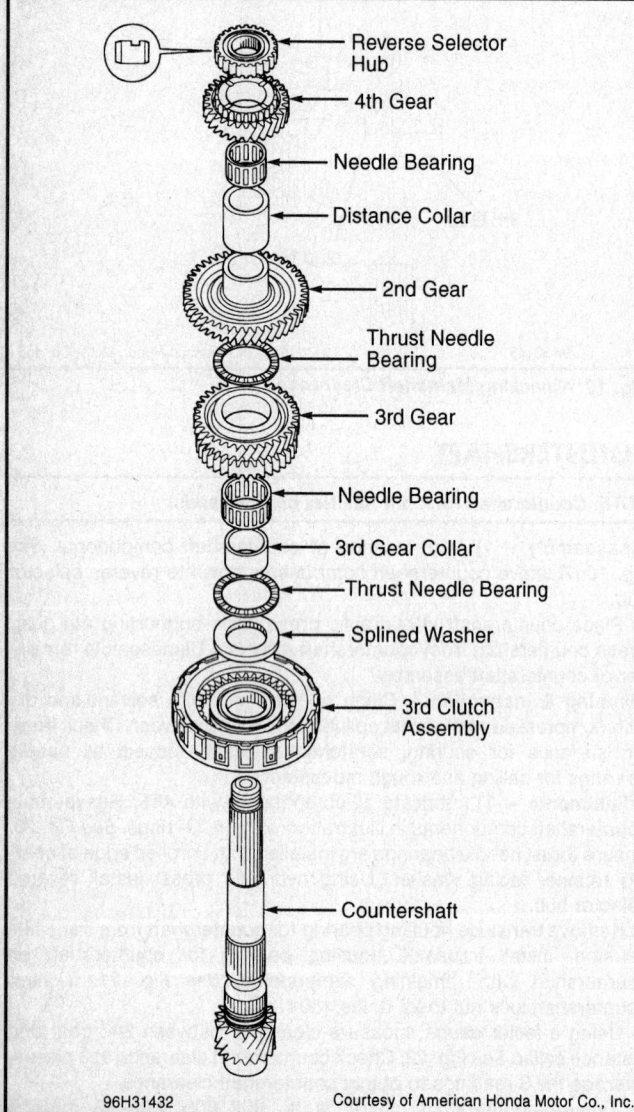

96H31432

Courtesy of American Honda Motor Co., Inc.

Fig. 20: Identifying Countershaft Components For Clearance Measurement (1 Of 2)

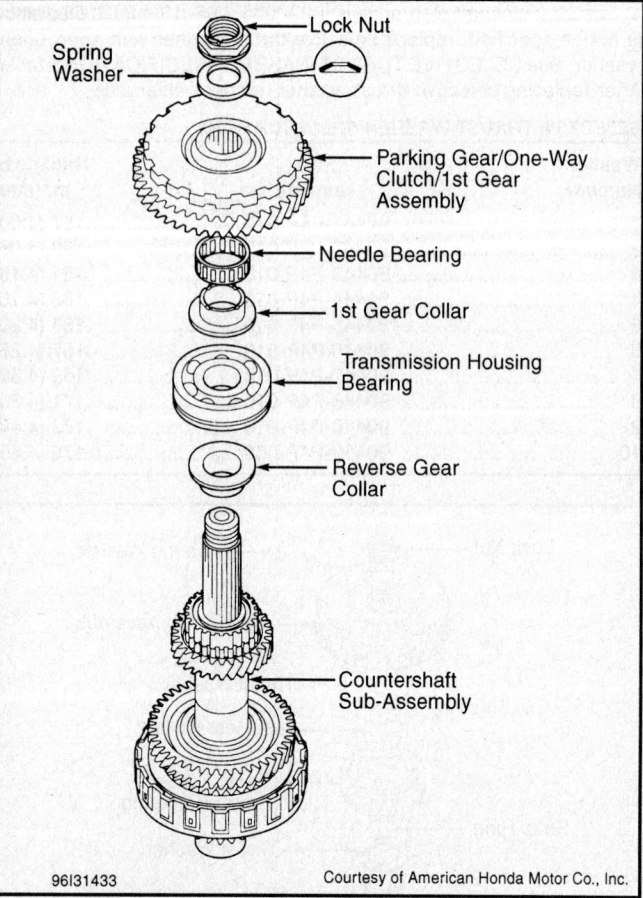

96I31433

Courtesy of American Honda Motor Co., Inc.

Fig. 21: Identifying Countershaft Components For Clearance Measurement (2 Of 2)

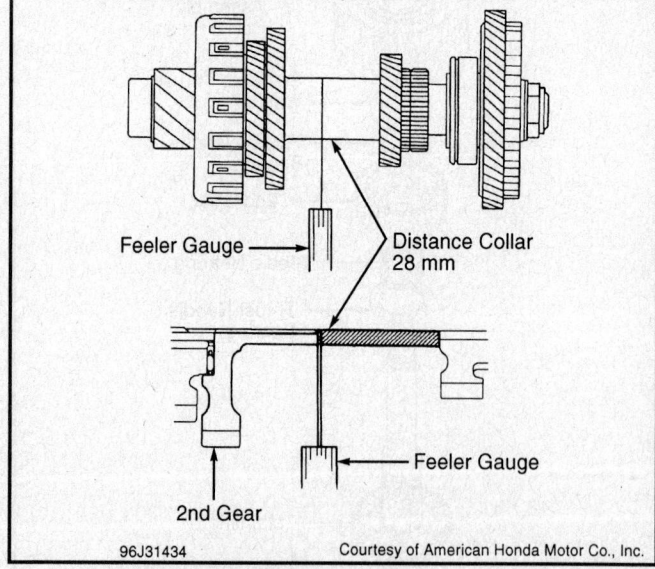

96J31434

Courtesy of American Honda Motor Co., Inc.

Fig. 22: Checking Countershaft Clearance

ONE-WAY CLUTCH

Disassembly – Separate countershaft 1st gear from parking gear by rotating parking gear counterclockwise while holding countershaft 1st gear. *See Fig. 23.* Remove one-way clutch by prying up with end of screwdriver.

Inspection – Check parking gear and 1st gear for wear and scoring. Check one-way clutch for damage and movement in wrong direction. One-way clutch should only turn in direction shown. *See Fig. 23.*

Reassembly – Reverse disassembly procedure for reassembly. Ensure one-way clutch is installed correctly. *See Fig. 24.* Check one-way clutch rotation. One-way clutch is defective if parking gear will rotate clockwise. *See Fig. 23.*

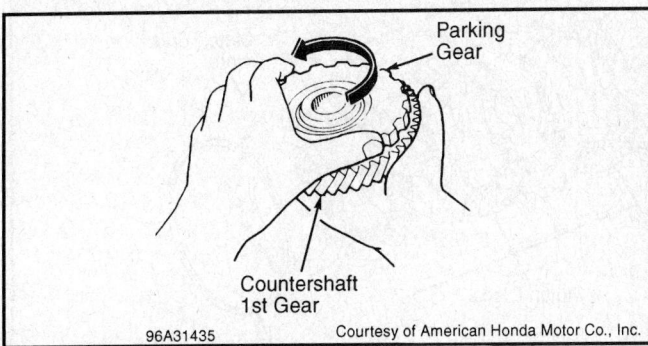

96A31435   Courtesy of American Honda Motor Co., Inc.

Fig. 23: Removing & Checking One-Way Clutch Operation

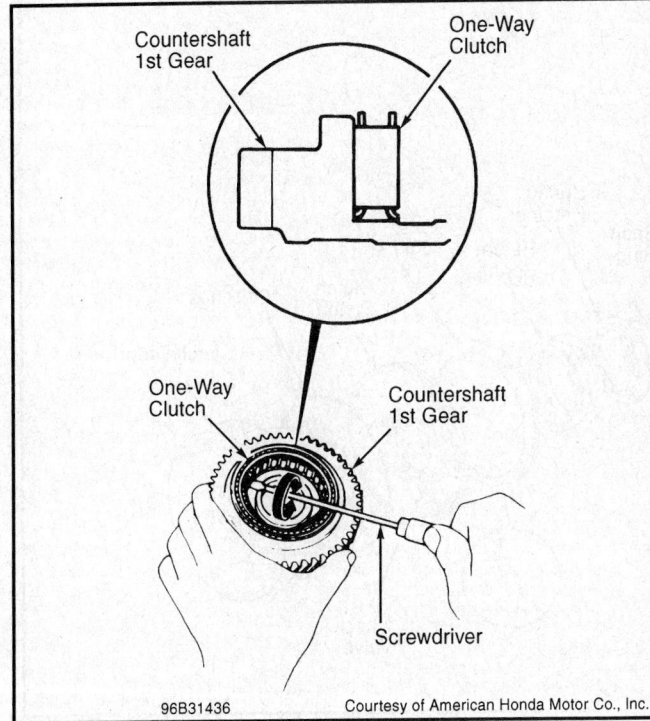

96B31436   Courtesy of American Honda Motor Co., Inc.

Fig. 24: Installing One-Way Clutch

CLUTCH ASSEMBLIES

NOTE: Ensure spring compressor is making full contact with spring retainer or damage will occur.

Disassembly – 1) Remove snap ring, clutch end plate, clutch discs and clutch plates. *See Figs. 25-26.*

2) Note direction of disc spring installation. On all clutches except 2nd clutch, remove disc spring. The 2nd clutch is not equipped with a disc spring. Using spring compressor, compress return spring. Remove snap ring. Release and remove spring compressor. Remove spring retainer and return spring.

3) Wrap shop towel around clutch drum. Apply light air pressure to oil passage on clutch drum to remove clutch piston. Remove "O" rings.

Cleaning & Inspection – Clean metal components with solvent and dry with compressed air. Ensure check valve on rear of clutch piston is thoroughly cleaned and securely fastened on clutch piston. Inspect components for damage and replace if necessary. Ensure no rough edges exist on "O" ring sealing areas.

Reassembly – 1) Lubricate all components with ATF. Install NEW "O" rings. Install clutch piston in clutch drum. Slightly rotate clutch piston during installation to prevent damaging "O" rings.

CAUTION: DO NOT apply excessive force on clutch piston or "O" rings will be damaged.

2) Install return spring. Install spring retainer in clutch drum. Place snap ring on spring retainer. Using spring compressor, compress return spring. Install snap ring. Release and remove spring compressor.

3) Install disc spring (except 2nd clutch). Ensure disc spring is installed in proper direction. *See Figs. 25-26.*

CAUTION: Ensure clutch discs are soaked in ATF for at least 30 minutes before installing.

4) Alternately install clutch plates and clutch discs starting with clutch plate. Install clutch end plate with flat side toward clutch disc. Install snap ring.

5) Using dial indicator, measure clutch clearance between clutch end plate and top clutch disc. *See Fig. 27.* Zero dial indicator with clutch end plate lowered, and then lift clutch end plate upward against snap ring. Distance measured is clutch clearance.

6) Measure clutch clearance at 3 different locations. Ensure clutch clearance is within specification. See CLUTCH CLEARANCE SPECIFICATIONS table.

7) If clutch clearance is not within specification, install different thickness clutch end plate. See CLUTCH END PLATE SPECIFICATIONS table.

NOTE: If thickest clutch end plate is installed and clutch clearance still exceeds specification, replace clutch discs and clutch plates.

CLUTCH CLEARANCE SPECIFICATIONS

Application	In. (mm)
1st & 2nd Clutches	.026-.033 (.65-.85)
3rd & 4th Clutches	.016-.024 (.40-.60)

CLUTCH END PLATE SPECIFICATIONS

Plate Number	Part Number	Thickness In. (mm)
1	22551-P4R-003	.083 (2.10)
2	22552-P4R-003	.087 (2.20)
3	22553-P4R-003	.091 (2.30)
4	22554-P4R-003	.094 (2.40)
5	22555-P4R-003	.098 (2.50)
6	22556-P4R-003	.102 (2.60)
7	22557-P4R-003	.106 (2.70)
8	22558-P4R-003	.110 (2.80)
9	22559-P4R-003	.114 (2.90)

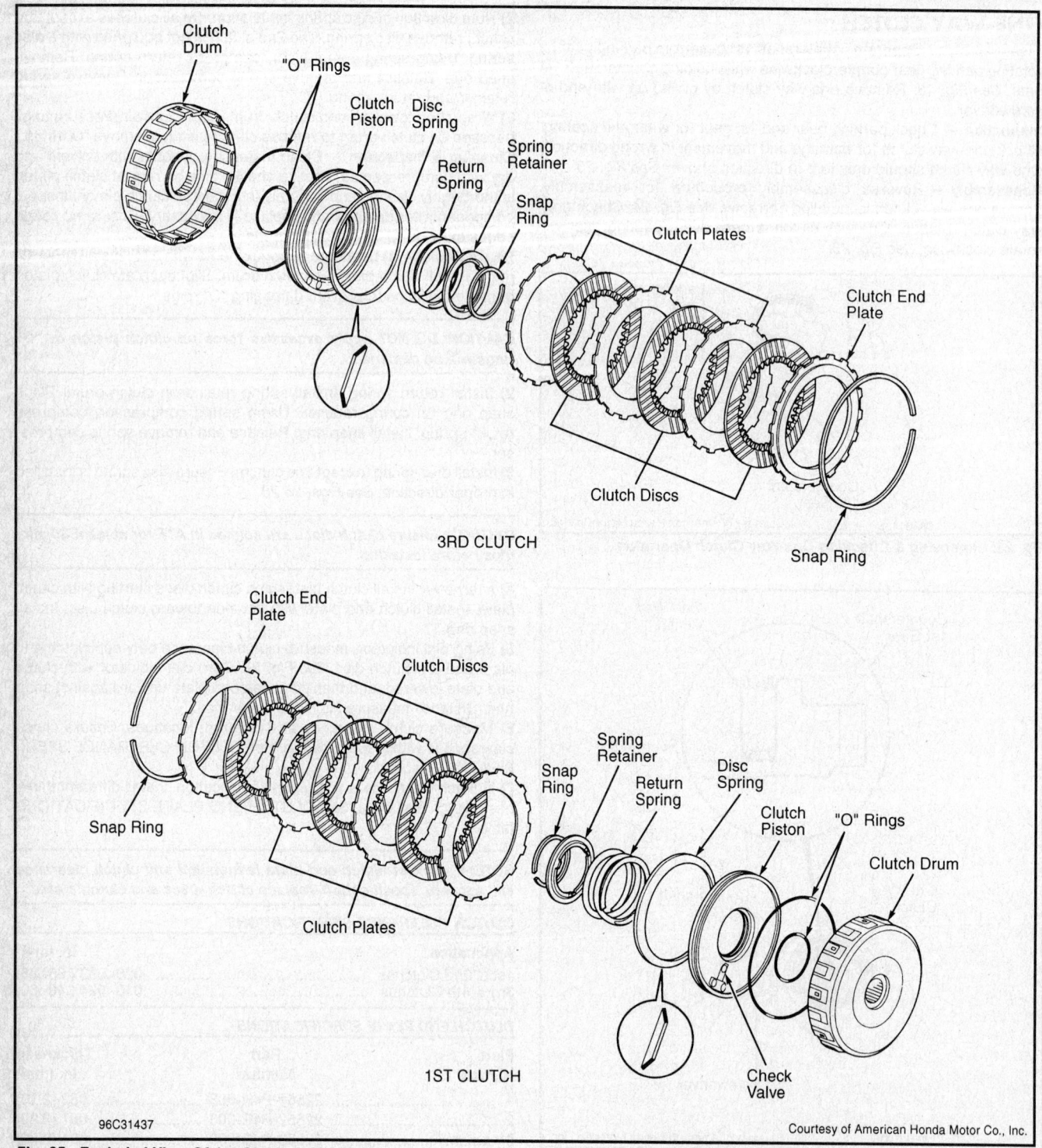

3RD CLUTCH

1ST CLUTCH

96C31437

Courtesy of American Honda Motor Co., Inc.

Fig. 25: Exploded View Of 1st Clutch & 3rd Clutch

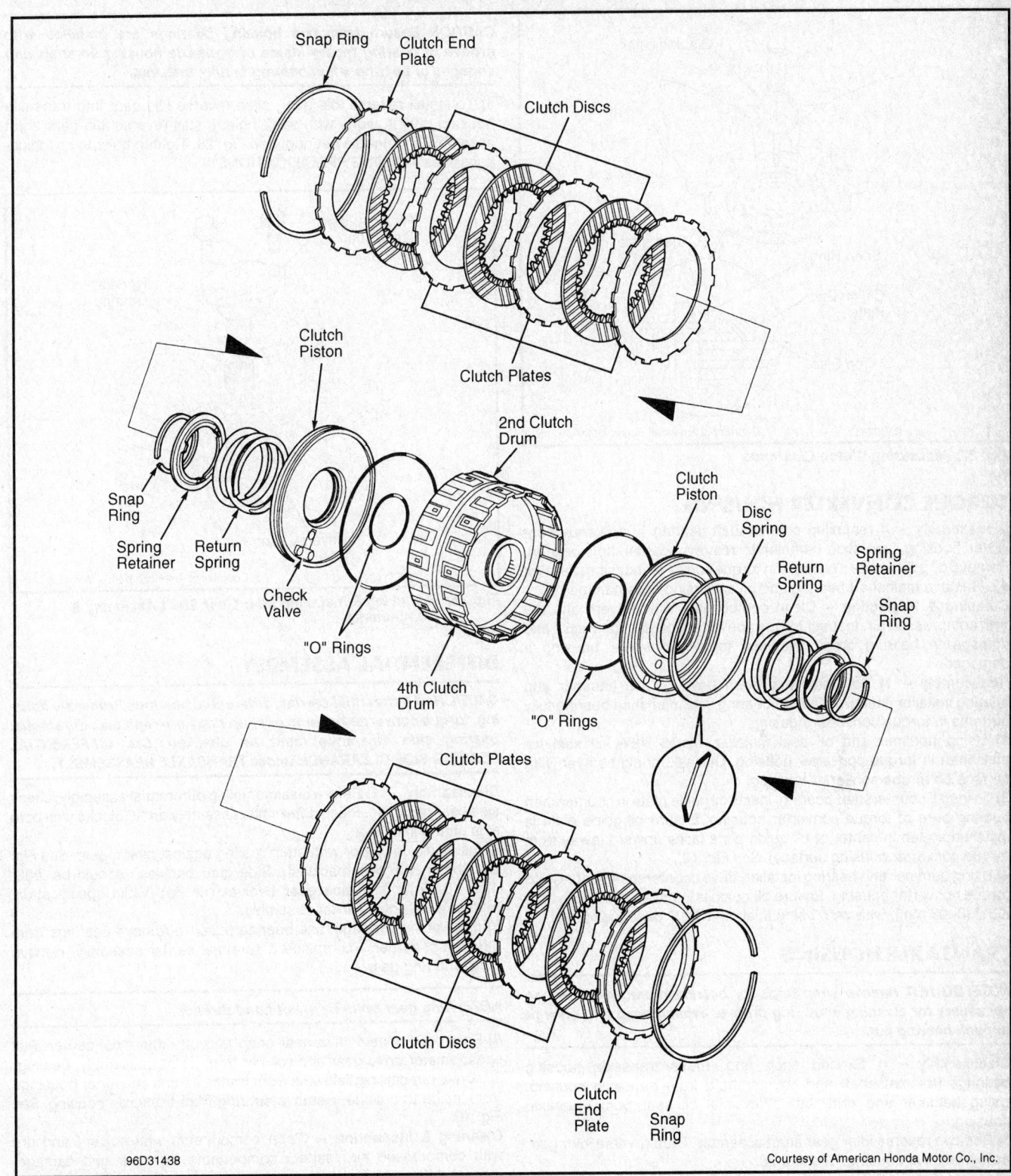

96D31438

Courtesy of American Honda Motor Co., Inc.

Fig. 26: Exploded View Of 2nd-4th Clutches

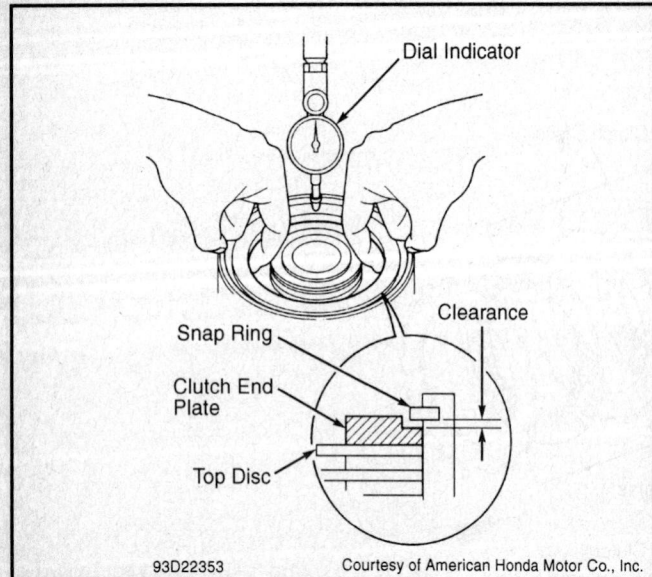

Fig. 27: Measuring Clutch Clearance

TORQUE CONVERTER HOUSING

Disassembly – If removing countershaft bearing from torque converter housing, use slide hammer to remove countershaft bearing. Remove oil guide plate from bore in torque converter housing. *See Fig. 12.* Remove mainshaft bearing and oil seal using slide hammer.

Cleaning & Inspection – Clean components with solvent and dry with compressed air. Inspect torque converter housing for cracks and damage in bearing areas. Replace torque converter housing if damaged.

Reassembly – **1)** To install mainshaft bearing, use hammer and bearing installer. Install mainshaft bearing until mainshaft bearing fully bottoms in torque converter housing.

2) Using hammer and oil seal installer, install NEW oil seal for mainshaft in torque converter housing. Oil seal should be even with surface on torque converter housing.

3) To install countershaft bearing, install oil guide plate in countershaft bearing bore of torque converter housing. Ensure oil guide plate is installed so tab in center of oil guide plate faces upward (away from torque converter housing surface). *See Fig. 12.*

4) Using hammer and bearing installer, drive countershaft bearing into torque converter housing. Ensure oil guide is installed to a depth of 0-.001" (0-.03 mm), with zero being flush and .001" past flush (inset).

TRANSAXLE HOUSING

NOTE: DO NOT remove snap rings for bearing replacement unless necessary for cleaning snap ring groove. Expand snap ring enough to push bearing out.

Disassembly – **1)** Expand snap ring. Press transaxle housing bearings (for mainshaft and countershaft) from transaxle housing. Using hammer and drift, tap differential oil seal from transaxle housing.

2) Remove reverse idler gear shaft assembly. Slide reverse idler gear from transaxle housing. *See Fig. 28.*

Cleaning & Inspection – Clean components with solvent and dry with compressed air. Inspect transaxle housing for cracks and damage in bearing areas. Replace transaxle housing if damaged.

Reassembly – **1)** To install transaxle housing bearing for mainshaft and countershaft, expand snap ring and install bearing part of the way into transaxle housing. Release snap ring.

2) Press bearing into transaxle housing until snap ring engages with groove on bearing. Ensure snap ring end gap is 0-.276" (0-7 mm). If snap ring end gap is not within specification, reseat or replace snap ring.

CAUTION: Ensure transaxle housing bearings are installed with groove of bearing facing inside of transaxle housing so snap ring engages in bearing when bearing is fully installed.

3) To install reverse idle gear, slide reverse idle gear into transaxle housing until it aligns with shaft hole. Install reverse idle gear shaft assembly and needle bearing. *See Fig. 28.* Tighten bolts to specifications. See TORQUE SPECIFICATIONS.

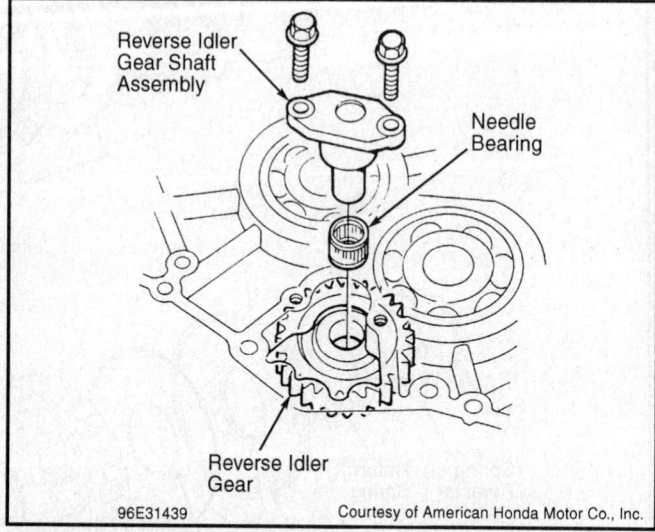

Fig. 28: Removing & Installing Idler Gear Shaft Assembly & Components

DIFFERENTIAL ASSEMBLY

CAUTION: If differential carrier, differential bearings, transaxle housing, torque converter housing or snap rings are replaced, differential bearing side clearance must be checked. See DIFFERENTIAL BEARING SIDE CLEARANCE under TRANSAXLE REASSEMBLY.

Disassembly – **1)** Before disassembling differential assembly, check side gear backlash. Place differential assembly on "V" blocks with both axle shafts installed.

2) Install dial indicator with stem resting against pinion gear. *See Fig. 29.* Check side gear backlash. Side gear backlash should be .002-.006" (5-15 mm). If side gear backlash is not within specification, replace differential carrier assembly.

3) If replacing bearings, use bearing puller to remove bearings from differential carrier. To replace differential carrier assembly, remove bolts and ring gear.

NOTE: Ring gear bolts have left-hand threads.

4) Pry speedometer drive gear snap ring off differential carrier. Pull speedometer drive gear and roll pin from carrier assembly. *See Fig. 30.* Drive out differential seals from transaxle and converter housings from inside to outside. Remove set ring from transaxle housing. *See Fig. 10.*

Cleaning & Inspection – Clean components with solvent and dry with compressed air. Inspect components for wear and damage. Inspect differential bearings for rough rotation. Replace components if necessary.

CAUTION: Ring gear must be installed with chamfered edge on inside of ring gear toward differential carrier.

Reassembly – **1)** Install speedometer drive gear roll pin. Install speedometer drive gear with chamfered side facing carrier. Align cutout in speedometer drive gear with roll pin.

2) Align speedometer drive gear snap ring hooked end with pinion shaft. *See Fig. 31.* Install snap ring in differential groove.

3) Install ring gear on differential carrier. Ensure chamfered edge on inside of ring gear is toward differential carrier. Install and tighten ring gear bolts in crisscross pattern to specification. See TORQUE SPECIFICATIONS. *See Fig. 27.*

4) Press NEW bearings on differential carrier (if removed). Install .098" (2.50 mm) set ring in transaxle housing.

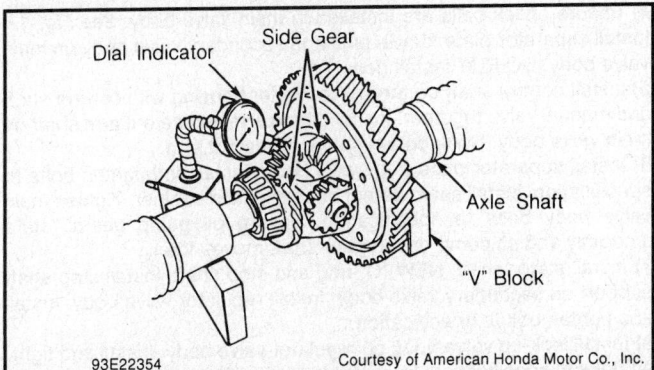

Fig. 29: Checking Side Gear Backlash

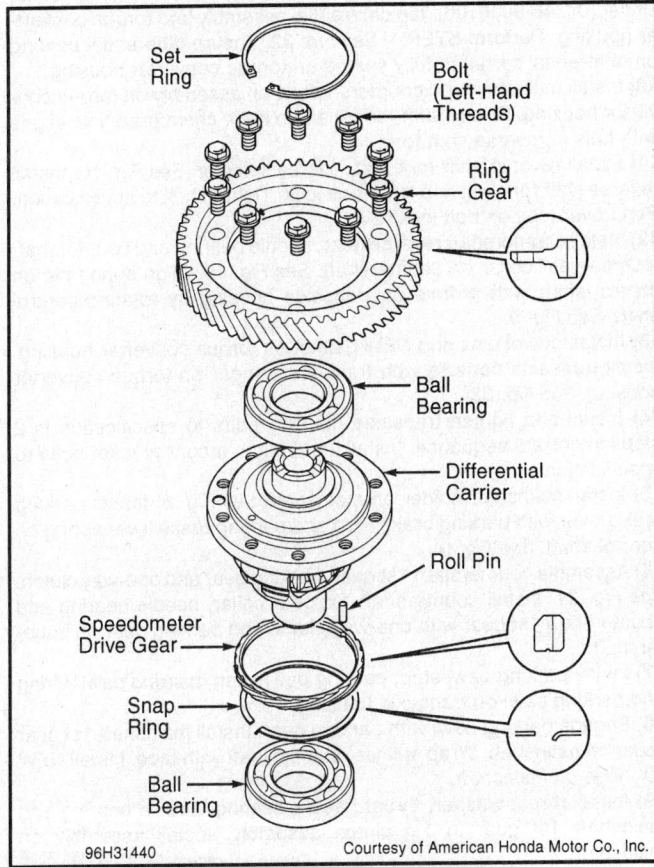

Fig. 30: Exploded View Of Differential Assembly

TRANSAXLE REASSEMBLY

DIFFERENTIAL BEARING SIDE CLEARANCE

CAUTION: If differential carrier, differential bearings, transaxle housing, torque converter housing or snap rings are replaced, differential bearing side clearance must be checked.

1) Install .098" (2.50 mm) thick set ring in transaxle housing. This is the snap ring that differential bearing seats against. Ensure set ring is fully seated.

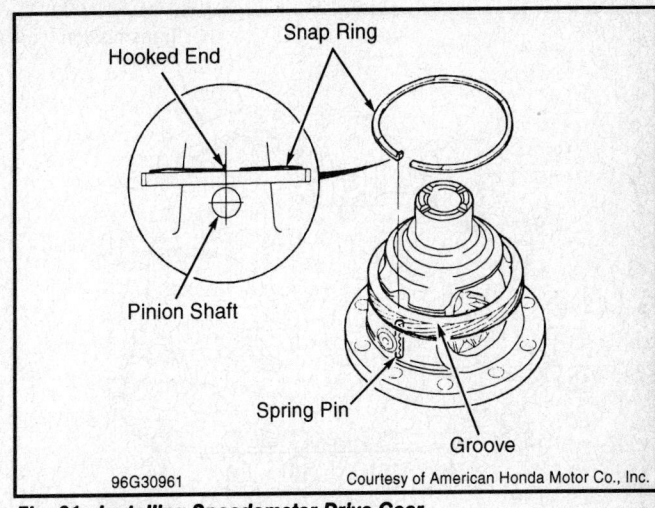

Fig. 31: Installing Speedometer Drive Gear

2) Tap differential assembly into torque converter housing using Driver (07746-0030100). Perform STEP 1. *See Fig. 32.* Ensure differential bearing on differential carrier is fully seated on torque converter housing.

3) Install gasket and transaxle housing on torque converter housing. Install and tighten transaxle housing bolts to 33 ft. lbs. (45 N.m) in 2 steps using proper sequence. *See Fig. 33.*

4) Using driver, tap on transaxle housing side of differential assembly to fully seat differential bearings. Perform STEP 2. *See Fig. 32.* Ensure differential bearings are fully seated in both housings.

5) Using feeler gauge, measure differential bearing side clearance between snap ring and bearing on transaxle housing. *See Fig. 34.* Replace set ring if differential bearing side clearance exceeds .006" (.15 mm). Different thickness set rings are available. See SET RING SPECIFICATIONS table. Recheck differential bearing side clearance. Remove transaxle housing and differential assembly.

SET RING SPECIFICATIONS

Part Number	Thickness In. (mm)
90414-689-000	.098 (2.50)
90415-689-000	.102 (2.60)
90416-689-000	.106 (2.70)
90417-689-000	.110 (2.80)
90418-689-000	.114 (2.90)
90419-PH8-000	.118 (3.00)

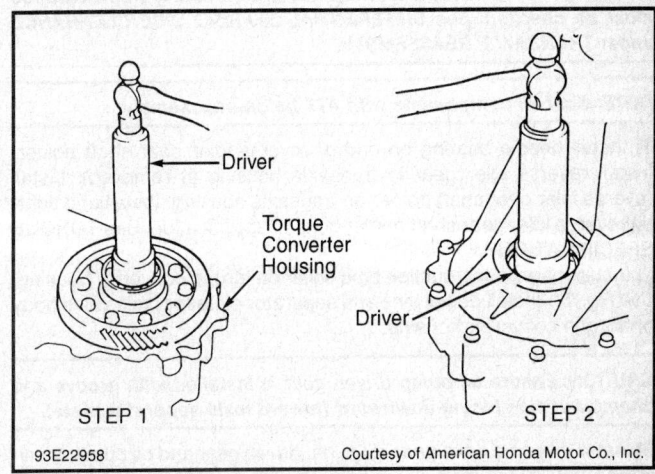

Fig. 32: Installing Differential Assembly

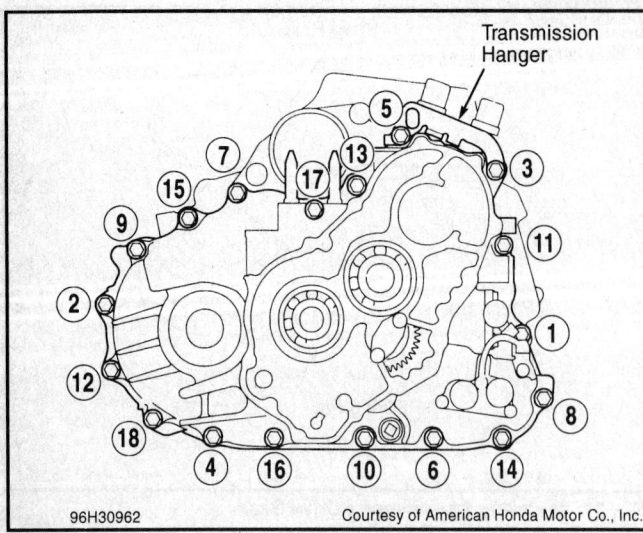

96H30962   Courtesy of American Honda Motor Co., Inc.

Fig. 33: Transaxle Housing Bolt Tightening Sequence

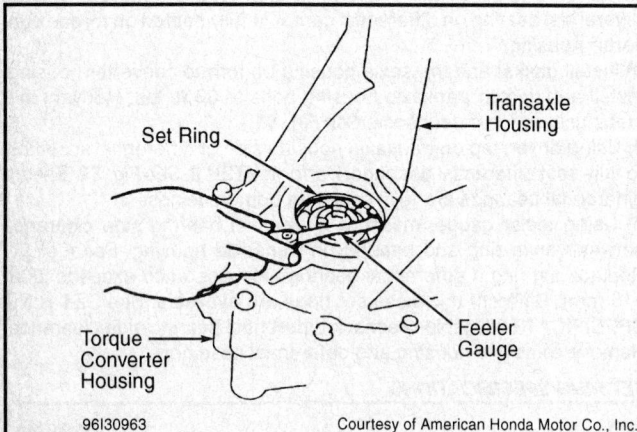

96I30963   Courtesy of American Honda Motor Co., Inc.

Fig. 34: Checking Differential Bearing Side Clearance

VALVE BODIES & INTERNAL COMPONENTS

NOTE: If transaxle housing, torque converter housing, differential carrier, bearings, thrust shim or bearing outer races for differential assembly are replaced, differential assembly bearing side clearance must be checked. See DIFFERENTIAL BEARING SIDE CLEARANCE under TRANSAXLE REASSEMBLY.

NOTE: Coat all components with ATF before reassembly.

1) Install needle bearing on end of reverse idler gear shaft holder. Install reverse idler gear in transaxle housing (if removed). Install reverse idler gear shaft holder on transaxle housing. Install and tighten reverse idler gear shaft holder bolts to specification. See TORQUE SPECIFICATIONS.
2) Install magnet and suction pipe collar on torque converter housing. *See Fig. 11.* Install dowel pins and separator plate for main valve body on torque converter housing.

CAUTION: Ensure oil pump driven gear is installed with groove and chamfered side facing downward (toward main separator plate).

3) Install oil pump drive gear, oil pump driven gear and oil pump driven gear shaft. Install main valve body. Install and loosely tighten main valve body bolts.

CAUTION: Ensure oil pump gears rotate smoothly and oil pump driven gear shaft moves freely once main valve body is installed. If components do not operate correctly, loosen bolts, and realign oil pump gears and oil pump driven gear shaft. Failure to align oil pump driven gear shaft may result in seized oil pump gears or shaft.

4) Ensure check balls are installed in main valve body. *See Fig. 12.* Install separator plate, dowel pins and secondary valve body on main valve body. DO NOT install bolts.
5) Install control shaft on torque converter housing with control shaft and manual valve together. Install detent arm and detent arm shaft on main valve body. Hook detent spring on detent arm.
6) Install separator plate and servo body. Install and tighten bolts to specification. Install servo detent base and fluid strainer. Tighten main valve body bolts to specification. Ensure oil pump gears rotate smoothly and oil pump driven gear shaft moves freely.
7) Install stator shaft, NEW "O" ring and stop shaft. Install stop shaft support on secondary valve body. Install regulator valve body. Install and tighten bolt to specification.
8) Install lock-up valve body on regulator valve body. Install and tighten bolts to specification. Install oil feedpipes in main valve body, secondary valve body and servo body. *See Fig. 11.*
9) Install differential assembly in torque converter housing. Using Driver (07746-0030100), tap differential assembly into torque converter housing. Perform STEP 1. *See Fig. 32.* Ensure differential bearing on differential carrier is fully seated on torque converter housing.
10) Install mainshaft and countershaft as an assembly on torque converter housing. Rotate shift fork shaft so large chamfered hole aligns with hole in reverse shift fork.
11) Install reverse shift fork and reverse selector. *See Fig. 10.* Install reverse shift fork bolt and NEW bolt lock. Tighten bolt to specification. Bend over tabs on bolt lock.
12) Install countershaft reverse gear, needle bearing and countershaft reverse gear collar on countershaft. *See Fig. 10.* Align spring pin on control shaft with groove on transaxle housing by rotating control shaft. *See Fig. 9.*
13) Install dowel pins and NEW gasket on torque converter housing. Install transaxle housing with transaxle hanger on torque converter housing. *See Fig. 33.*
14) Install and tighten transaxle housing bolts to specification in 2 steps in correct sequence. Install and tighten mount bracket bolts to specification.
15) Install mainshaft holder on mainshaft. *See Fig. 8.* Install parking brake lever with parking brake stop and parking brake lever spring on control shaft. *See Fig. 9.*
16) Assemble countershaft 1st gear, parking gear and one-way clutch. *See Fig. 24.* Install countershaft 1st gear collar, needle bearing and countershaft 1st gear with one-way clutch and parking gear on countershaft.
17) Install parking pawl stop, parking pawl shaft, parking pawl spring and parking pawl on transaxle housing.
18) Engage parking pawl with parking gear. Install mainshaft 1st gear collar on mainshaft. Wrap splines on mainshaft with tape. Install NEW "O" rings on mainshaft.
19) Install thrust washer, thrust needle bearing, needle bearing and mainshaft 1st gear in 1st clutch assembly. Install assembly on mainshaft.

NOTE: Countershaft and mainshaft lock nuts have left hand threads. Ensure spring washers are installed in correct direction. See Figs. 18 and 21.

20) Install NEW spring washers and lock nuts on countershaft and mainshaft. Tighten lock nuts to specifications. See TORQUE SPECIFICATIONS. Stake thread area of lock nut against threads on mainshaft and countershaft.
21) Place parking brake lever in "P" position. Ensure parking pawl engages parking gear. Measure parking brake stop distance between parking pawl shaft and pin on parking brake lever. *See Fig. 35.*

22) Parking brake stop distance should be 2.87-2.91" (72.9-73.9 mm). If parking brake stop distance is not within specification install different size parking brake stop, and recheck parking brake stop distance. Parking brake stop is available in 3 different sizes. See PARKING BRAKE STOP SPECIFICATIONS table.

PARKING BRAKE STOP SPECIFICATIONS

Identification Mark	Part Number	[1] Distance "L_1" In. (mm)	[1] Distance "L_2" In. (mm)
1	24537-PA9-003	.433 (11.00)	.433 (11.00)
2	24538-PA9-003	.425 (10.80)	.419 (10.65)
3	24539-PA9-003	.417 (10.60)	.406 (10.30)

[1] – Measured from center of parking brake stop. See Fig. 35.

23) Once correct parking brake stop distance is obtained, tighten parking brake stop bolt to specification. Bend over tabs on bolt lock. Using NEW gasket and install right side cover. Install and tighten bolts to specification.

24) To install remaining components, reverse removal procedure. Use NEW seal washers when installing joint bolts for cooler pipes. Use NEW "O" ring when installing mainshaft or countershaft speed sensors. Tighten all fasteners to specification.

CAUTION: If transaxle failed internally, flush oil cooler. See OIL COOLER FLUSHING under ON-VEHICLE SERVICE.

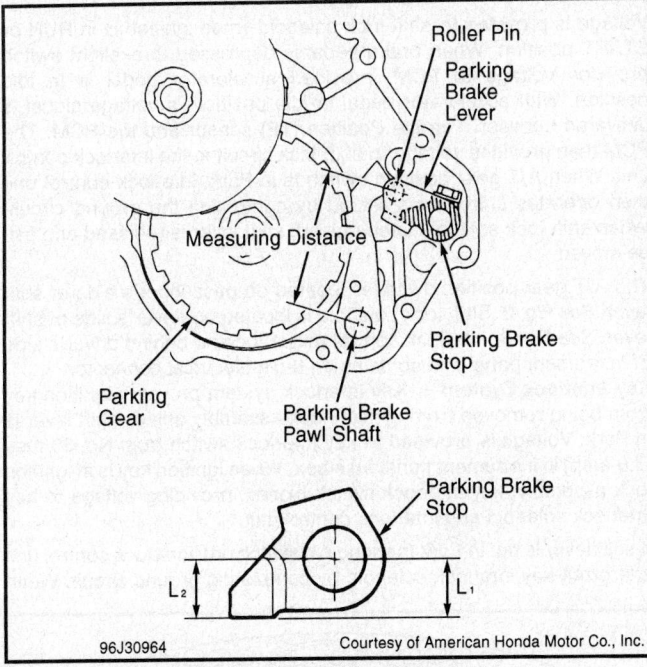

Fig. 35: Measuring Parking Brake Stop Distance

96J30964 — Courtesy of American Honda Motor Co., Inc.

TORQUE SPECIFICATIONS
TORQUE SPECIFICATIONS

Application	Ft. Lbs. (N.m)
Countershaft Lock Nut	76 (103)
Drain Plug	36 (49)
Joint Bolt	21 (29)
Mainshaft Lock Nut	58 (78)
Mount Bracket Bolt	47 (64)
Parking Brake Stop Bolt	10 (14)
Pressure Tap Plug	13 (18)
Reverse Shift Fork Bolt	10 (14)
Ring Gear Bolt	74 (100)
Transaxle Housing Bolt [1]	33 (45)
Vehicle Speed Sensor Bolt	16 (22)

Application	INCH Lbs. (N.m)
Countershaft Speed Sensor Bolt	106 (12.0)
Lock-Up Valve Body Bolt	106 (12.0)
Mainshaft Speed Sensor Bolt	106 (12.0)
Main Valve Body Bolt	106 (12.0)
Needle Bearing Stop Bolt	106 (12.0)
Regulator Valve Body Bolt	106 (12.0)
Reverse Idler Gear Shaft Holder Bolt	106 (12.0)
Right Side Cover Bolt	106 (12.0)
Secondary Valve Body Bolt	106 (12.0)
Servo Body Bolt	106 (12.0)
Servo Detent Base Bolt	106 (12.0)
Stop Bolt	106 (12.0)
Throttle Cam Stop Bolt	106 (12.0)
Throttle Control Lever Bolt	69 (7.8)

[1] – Tighten bolts to specification in sequence. See Fig. 33.

TRANSAXLE SPECIFICATIONS
TRANSAXLE SPECIFICATIONS

Application	Specification
Clutch Clearance	
1st & 2nd Clutches	.026-.033" (.65-.85 mm)
3rd & 4th Clutches	.016-.024" (.40-.60 mm)
Differential Bearing Side Clearance	[1] .006" (.15 mm)
Countershaft 2nd Gear Clearance	.002-.005" (.05-.13 mm)
Mainshaft End Play	.004-.007" (.11-.18 mm)
Oil Pump Clearances	
Side Clearance	
Oil Pump Drive Gear	.0083-.0104" (.210-.265 mm)
Oil Pump Driven Gear	.0028-.0049" (.070-.125 mm)
Thrust Clearance	
Standard	.0010-.0020" (.030-.050 mm)
Wear Limit	.0028" (.070 mm)
Parking Brake Stop Distance	2.87-2.91" (72.9-73.9 mm)

[1] – This is the maximum clearance. Replace set ring with different thickness set ring if clearance exceeds specification.

WIRING DIAGRAMS

For appropriate wiring diagram, see HONDA A4RA ELECTRONIC CONTROLS article.

Civic

APPLICATION

APPLICATION

Vehicle	Transaxle Model
1996 Civic	A4RA

CAUTION: Vehicle is equipped with a Supplemental Restraint System (SRS). When servicing vehicle, use care to avoid accidental air bag deployment. All SRS electrical connections and wiring harness are covered with Yellow Insulation. SRS-related components are located in steering column, center console, instrument panel and lower panel on instrument panel. DO NOT use electrical test equipment on these circuits. It may be necessary to deactivate SRS before servicing components. See AIR BAG SERVICING article in APPLICATIONS & IDENTIFICATIONS.

NOTE: Obtain radio anti-theft code from customer before disconnecting negative battery cable. Radio anti-theft code must be re-entered into radio once negative battery cable is reconnected. To re-enter radio anti-theft code, turn ignition and radio on. When the word CODE is displayed on radio, re-enter radio anti-theft code by using the radio station preset buttons.

DESCRIPTION

Automatic transaxle is electronically controlled. Transaxle shifting and torque converter lock-up are controlled by Powertrain Control Module (PCM). PCM is located below instrument panel behind passenger-side kick panel. PCM receives information from various input devices and uses this information to control shift and lock-up control solenoid valves.

The PCM contains a grade logic control system which controls transaxle shifting while vehicle is ascending or descending a slope or reducing vehicle speed. Transaxle is equipped with shift and key interlock systems. Shift interlock system prevents shift lever from being moved from Park unless brake pedal is depressed and accelerator pedal is in idle position. In case of a malfunction, shift lever can be released by placing ignition key in key release slot near shift lever. Key interlock system prevents ignition key from being removed from ignition lock assembly unless shift lever is in Park.

The A/T gear position indicator on instrument panel contains lights to indicate which position A/T gear position switch on shift lever is in.

OPERATION

A/T GEAR POSITION INDICATOR

With ignition in RUN or START position, voltage is supplied to A/T gear position indicator, located on instrument panel. *See Fig. 1.* When shift lever is moved to designated gear position, A/T gear position switch completes the ground circuit for A/T gear position indicator on instrument panel. The light on A/T gear position indicator is illuminated to indicate the shift lever gear position. The A/T gear position switch is located on passenger's side of shift lever. *See Fig. 2.*

When headlights are turned on, voltage is supplied to Red/Black wire through fuse No. 30 (7.5-amp) at A/T gear position indicator. This changes brightness control from fixed setting to control by the dash light dimmer input on the Red wire.

GRADE LOGIC CONTROL SYSTEM

The PCM compares actual driving conditions with driving conditions memorized in the PCM, based on input signals from Vehicle Speed Sensor (VSS), Throttle Position (TP) sensor, Engine Coolant Temperature (ECT) sensor, Barometric Pressure (Baro) sensor, brakelight switch signal and A/T gear position switch. The PCM uses these input signals to control shifting while vehicle is ascending or descending a slope, or during deceleration.

When PCM determines vehicle is ascending a slope with shift lever in "D₄" position, PCM extends engagement of 3rd gear to prevent transaxle from frequently shifting between 3rd and 4th gears. Shift points between 3rd and 4th gear are stored in PCM which allows the most suitable gear selection depending on conditions.

When PCM determines vehicle is descending a slope with shift lever in "D₄" position, PCM changes upshift speed from 3rd to 4th gear when throttle is fully closed. This widens the 3rd gear operating range from that programmed for level surface operation and, in conjunction with engine braking from torque converter lock-up, provides smooth vehicle operation. When vehicle is decelerating on a gradual hill in 4th gear, or when applying brakes on a steep hill, the transaxle will downshift to 3rd gear. When vehicle accelerates, transaxle will upshift into 4th gear.

When vehicle decelerates from speeds greater than 30 MPH, PCM shifts transaxle from 4th gear to 2nd gear earlier than normal to reduce the number of times the transaxle shifts. This allows smoother acceleration and vehicle operation.

SHIFT & KEY INTERLOCK SYSTEMS

Shift Interlock System – Shift interlock system prevents shift lever from being moved from Park unless brake pedal is depressed and accelerator pedal is in idle position. Shift lever cannot be moved from Park if brake and accelerator pedal are depressed at the same time. In case of a malfunction, shift lever can be released by placing ignition key in key release slot near shift lever.

Voltage is provided to shift lock solenoid when ignition is in RUN or START position. When brake pedal is depressed, brakelight switch provides voltage to PCM, provided accelerator pedal is in idle position. With accelerator pedal in idle position, a voltage signal is delivered between Throttle Position (TP) sensor and the PCM. The PCM then provides voltage to shift lock circuit in the interlock control unit. When A/T gear position switch is in Park, interlock control unit then operates shift lock solenoid by controlling the ground circuit. When shift lock solenoid is energized, shift lever is released and can be moved.

The A/T gear position switch is located on passenger's side of shift lever. *See Fig. 2.* Shift lock solenoid is located on driver's side of shift lever. *See Fig. 3.* Interlock control unit is located behind driver's side of instrument panel and contains an 8-pin electrical connector.

Key Interlock System – Key interlock system prevents ignition key from being removed from ignition lock assembly unless shift lever is in Park. Voltage is provided to key interlock switch from No. 33 fuse (7.5-amp) in instrument panel fuse box. When ignition key is in ignition lock assembly, key interlock switch closes, providing voltage to key interlock solenoid and interlock control unit.

If shift lever is not in Park (parking pin switch on), interlock control unit energizes key interlock solenoid by completing ground circuit. When

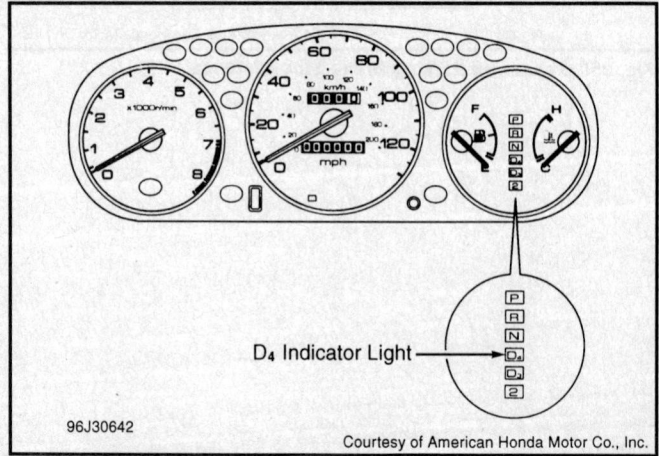

D₄ Indicator Light

96J30642

Courtesy of American Honda Motor Co., Inc.

Fig. 1: Identifying A/T Gear Position Indicator

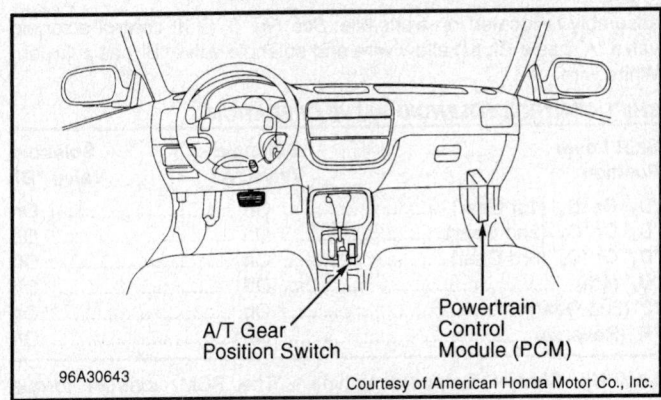

Fig. 2: Locating A/T Gear Position Switch & PCM

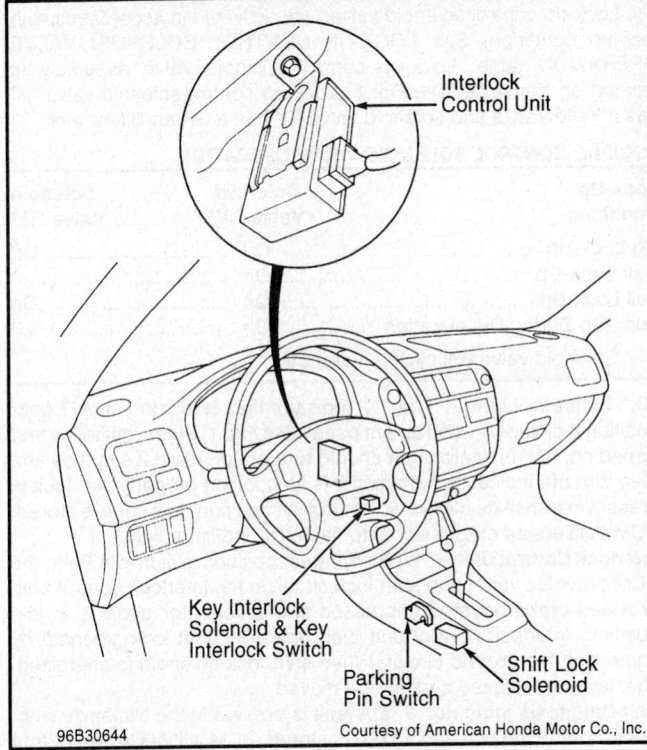

Fig. 3: Locating Shift & Key Interlock System Components

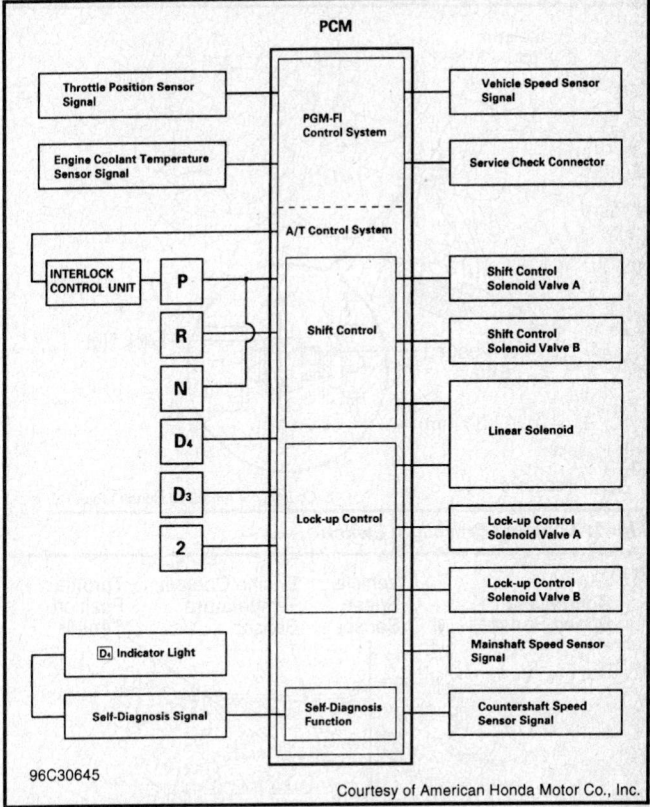

Fig. 4: Identifying PCM Input & Output Devices

PCM INPUT DEVICES

Barometric Pressure Signal – The PCM contains a built-in barometric pressure sensor to determine atmospheric pressure. The PCM is located below instrument panel, behind passenger-side kick panel. *See Fig. 2.*

Brake Switch Signal – Brakelight switch delivers an input signal to PCM, indicating vehicle braking. Brakelight switch is also used in determining grade logic control. Brakelight switch is located on brake pedal support. *See Fig. 5.*

Engine Coolant Temperature (ECT) Signal – ECT sensor delivers an input signal to PCM, indicating engine coolant temperature. The ECT sensor is located on cylinder head, below distributor and contains a Red/White wire and Green/Black wire in the electrical connector. *See Fig. 6.*

Mainshaft & Countershaft Speed Signal – Mainshaft speed signal is delivered to PCM. Mainshaft speed sensor is located on right side of transaxle. *See Fig. 6.* Countershaft speed signal is delivered to PCM. Countershaft speed sensor is located on left side of transaxle.

Service Check Connector – Service check connector is used when retrieving flash codes for transaxle electronic control system diagnosis. When jumper wire is installed between electrical terminals of service check connector, an input is delivered to PCM to display flash codes on "D₄" indicator light. Service check connector is a 2-pin Blue colored electrical connector located at passenger's corner of instrument panel. *See Fig. 7.*

Shift Position Signal – Shift position signal is delivered to PCM by the A/T gear position switch, located on passenger's side of shift lever. *See Fig. 2.*

Throttle Position (TP) Sensor Signal – Throttle Position (TP) sensor delivers an input signal to PCM to indicate throttle position. The TP sensor is mounted on throttle body. *See Fig. 6.*

Vehicle Speed Sensor (VSS) Signal – VSS delivers an input signal to PCM to indicate vehicle speed. The VSS is located on top of transaxle. *See Fig. 6.*

key interlock solenoid is energized, ignition key cannot be removed from ignition lock assembly. Key interlock switch and key interlock solenoid are located on ignition lock assembly. *See Fig. 3.* Parking pin switch is located on driver's side of shift lever. Interlock control unit is located behind driver's side of instrument panel and contains an 8-pin electrical connector.

POWERTRAIN CONTROL MODULE (PCM)

The PCM receives information from various input devices and uses this information to control shift and lock-up control solenoid valves. *See Fig. 4.* The PCM contains a self-diagnostic system which will store a fault code if a failure is present in transaxle electronic control system. Fault code may also be referred to as Diagnostic Trouble Code (DTC) or flash code. DTC or flash code may be retrieved to determine transaxle problem area. See SELF-DIAGNOSTIC SYSTEM. The PCM is located behind passenger-side kick panel. *See Fig. 2.*

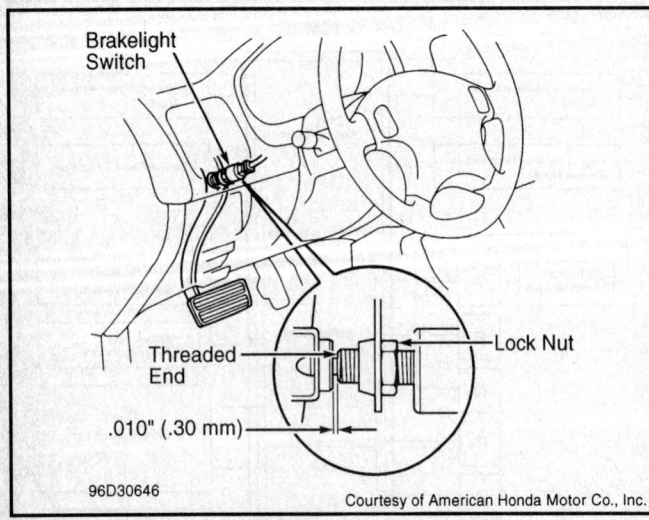

Fig. 5: Locating Brakelight Switch

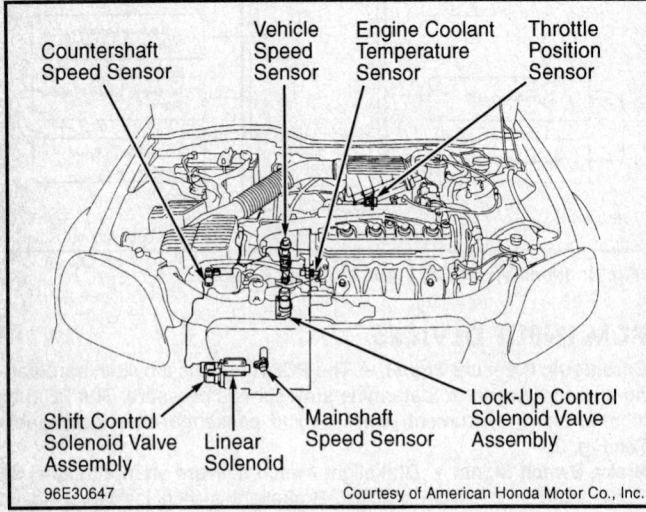

Fig. 6: Locating Input & Output Devices

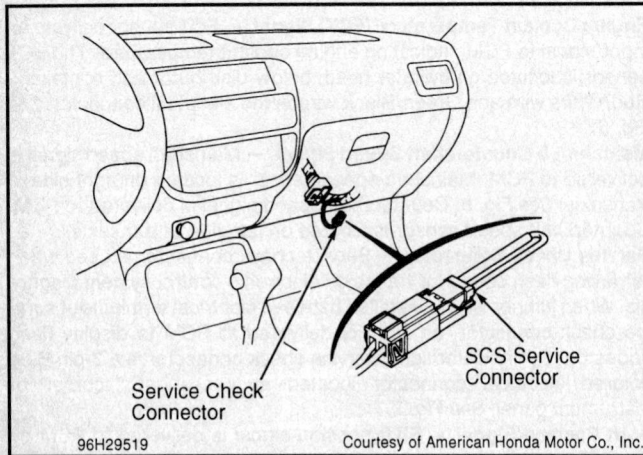

Fig. 7: Locating Service Check Connector

PCM OUTPUT DEVICES

Shift Control Solenoid Valves – The PCM controls transaxle shifting by delivering an output signal to shift control solenoid valves "A" and "B" on shift control solenoid valve assembly. Solenoid valves are operated in accordance with gear position. See SHIFT CONTROL SOLENOID VALVE OPERATION table. Shift control solenoid valve

assembly is located on transaxle. *See Fig. 6.* Shift control solenoid valve "A" has a Blue/Yellow wire and solenoid valve "B" has a Green/White wire.

SHIFT CONTROL SOLENOID VALVE OPERATION

Shift Lever Position	Solenoid Valve "A"	Solenoid Valve "B"
"D$_3$" Or "D$_4$" (1st Gear)	Off	On
"D$_3$" Or "D$_4$" (2nd Gear)	On	On
"D$_3$" Or "D$_4$" (3rd Gear)	On	Off
"D$_4$" (4th)	Off	Off
"2" (2nd Gear)	On	On
"R" (Reverse)	On	Off

Lock-Up Control Solenoid Valves – The PCM controls torque converter lock-up by delivering an output signal to lock-up control solenoid valves "A" and "B" on lock-up control solenoid valve assembly. Lock-up control solenoid valves are activated in accordance with lock-up condition. See LOCK-UP CONTROL SOLENOID VALVE OPERATION table. Lock-up control solenoid valve assembly is located on transaxle. *See Fig. 6.* Lock-up control solenoid valve "A" has a Yellow wire and solenoid valve "B" has a Green/Black wire.

LOCK-UP CONTROL SOLENOID VALVE OPERATION

Lock-Up Condition	Solenoid Valve "A"	Solenoid Valve "B"
No Lock-Up	Off	Off
Half Lock-Up	On	[1]
Full Lock-Up	On	On
Lock-Up During Deceleration	On	[1]

[1] – Solenoid valve will cycle on and off.

"D$_4$" Indicator Light – The "D$_4$" indicator light is located on A/T gear position indicator on instrument panel. *See Fig. 1.* When ignition is first turned on, "D$_4$" indicator light should turn on for about 2 seconds and then turn off, indicating light circuit is functioning properly. If a fault is present in transaxle electronic control system and fault code is stored, PCM delivers an output signal to flash "D$_4$" indicator light.

Interlock Control Unit – When A/T gear position switch is in Park, the PCM provides voltage to shift lock circuit in the interlock control unit, provided brake pedal is depressed and accelerator pedal is in idle position. Interlock control unit then operates shift lock solenoid by controlling the ground circuit. When shift lock solenoid is energized, shift lever is released and can be moved.

Self-Diagnosis Indicator – If a fault is present in the transaxle electronic control system and a DTC is stored, PCM will deliver an output signal (flash code) to turn on and flash "D$_4$" light. The "D$_4$" light is located on the A/T gear position indicator on instrument panel. *See Fig. 1.* Flash code can be retrieved to identify problem area by installing a jumper wire between service check connector terminals. DTC (4-digit) "P" code can be retrieved to identify problem area using a scan tool connected to Data Link Connector (DLC). Flash codes will be displayed by flashing "D$_4$" light.

SELF-DIAGNOSTIC SYSTEM

SYSTEM DIAGNOSIS

PCM monitors transaxle operation. The PCM contains a self-diagnostic system which stores a Diagnostic Trouble Code (DTC) if a transaxle electronic control system failure is present. If a DTC is stored, PCM will turn on and flash "D$_4$" light on A/T gear position indicator on instrument panel. *See Fig. 1.* If a transaxle electronic control system failure is suspected, and "D$_4$" light on A/T gear position indicator does not flash or remains on, see appropriate test under "D$_4$" INDICATOR LIGHT CIRCUIT CHECK. DTCs can be retrieved using a scan tool connected to Data Link Connector (DLC) located under instrument panel, on driver's side. Flash code may also be retrieved for diagnosing transaxle electronic control system.

"D₄" INDICATOR LIGHT CIRCUIT CHECK

"D₄" Indicator Light Does Not Come On – **1)** Turn ignition on. Ensure service connector shorting tool is not connected to service check connector. Shift to "D₄" position. If "D₄" indicator light does not illuminate, go to next step. If "D₄" indicator light illuminates, check for loose PCM harness connections. Replace PCM with a known-good unit if necessary and retest.

2) Turn ignition off. Disconnect 32-pin PCM harness connector "A". Using a DVOM, check for continuity between ground and 32-pin PCM harness connector "A", terminals No. 9 and 22 (Brown/Black wires). If continuity is present, go to next step. If continuity is not present, repair open or poor connection in appropriate Brown/Black wire.

3) Turn ignition on. Measure voltage at 32-pin PCM harness connector "A", between terminals No. 9 (Brown/Black wire) and No. 11 (Yellow/Black wire), then between terminals No. 22 (Brown/Black wire) and No. 24 (Yellow/Black wire). If battery voltage is present, go to next step. If battery voltage is not present, repair open or short in appropriate wire between PCM and PGM-FI main relay and/or engine compartment fuse/relay box.

4) Turn ignition off. Reconnect PCM harness connector. Connect a DVOM (backprobe) between 25-pin PCM harness connector "B", terminal No. 13 (Blue/Red wire) and 32-pin PCM harness connector "A", terminals No. 9 or 22 (Brown/Black wires). Turn ignition on. Voltage should be present for 2 seconds. If DVOM indicates voltage as specified, go to next step. If no voltage was indicated, go to step **6)**.

5) Check for an open in Blue/Red wire between PCM and gauge assembly. Repair as necessary. If no problem is found, repair faulty "D₄" indicator bulb or gauge assembly printed circuit board.

6) Check for loose PCM harness connectors or faulty A/T gear position switch. Repair as necessary. If no problem is found, replace PCM with a known-good unit and retest.

"D₄" Indicator Light Remains On Constantly (Not Flashing) – **1)** Turn ignition off. Disconnect 25-pin PCM harness connector "B". Turn ignition on. Using a DVOM, measure voltage between ground and 25-pin PCM harness connector "B", terminal No. 13 (Blue/Red wire). If no voltage is present, go to next step. If voltage is present, repair Blue/Red wire for a short to power.

2) Turn ignition off. Reconnect PCM harness connector. Turn ignition on. Shift to any position except "D₄". Measure voltage (backprobe) between ground and 25-pin PCM harness connector "B", terminal No. 24 (Yellow wire). If voltage is present, replace PCM. If no voltage is present, check Yellow wire for a short to ground. Repair as necessary. If no problem is found, replace A/T gear position indicator.

RETRIEVING FAULT CODES

NOTE: During diagnostics, ensure "D₄" indicator light on A/T gear position indicator on instrument panel is not turned on by a fault in the PGM-FI system. The PGM-FI system controls the fuel injection system. To repair PGM-FI system, see appropriate SELF-DIAGNOSTICS article in ENGINE PERFORMANCE in appropriate MITCHELL® manual. After PGM-FI system has been repaired, clear fault codes. See CLEARING FAULT CODES. After fault codes have been cleared, road test vehicle for several minutes at over 30 MPH and recheck fault codes.

NOTE: Before any diagnostic procedure, obtain radio anti-theft code from customer. Note radio preset stations, as radio stations and clock setting will be cleared and must be reset. Radio anti-theft code must be re-entered for radio operation.

Retrieving DTCs Using Scan Tool – **1)** If a DTC is present, "D₄" light on instrument panel will flash when ignition is turned on. To retrieve DTC using scan tool, turn ignition off.

2) Connect scan tool to 16-pin Data Link Connector (DLC) located under instrument panel, on driver's side. Turn ignition on. Scan tool will indicate DTCs. Follow scan tool manufactures instructions.

3) Once DTC is obtained, turn ignition off. Determine probable cause and symptom. See DTC/FLASH CODE IDENTIFICATION table. If any

other DTCs except those listed are displayed, see appropriate SELF-DIAGNOSTICS article in ENGINE PERFORMANCE in appropriate MITCHELL® manual. For trouble shooting of DTCs, see DIAGNOSTIC TESTS. If "D₄" light does not flash or remains on, see appropriate test under "D₄" INDICATOR LIGHT CIRCUIT CHECK.

Retrieving Flash Codes Using "D₄" Light – **1)** If a flash code is present, "D₄" light on instrument panel will flash when ignition is turned on. To retrieve flash code, turn ignition off.

2) Install a jumper wire between service check connector electrical terminals. Service check connector is a Blue 2-pin electrical connector, located under passenger's side of instrument panel. See Fig. 7.

3) Turn ignition on. Flash codes will be displayed by short and long flashes of "D₄" light on instrument panel. If the Malfunction Indicator Light (MIL) also flashes, see appropriate SELF-DIAGNOSTICS article in ENGINE PERFORMANCE in appropriate MITCHELL® manual. Repair MIL codes first.

4) A short flash indicates a single digit flash code. A long flash equals 10 short flashes. For example, if "D₄" light flashes once, this is a Flash Code No. 1. If "D₄" light flashes one long, then 5 short flashes, this is a Flash Code No. 15. See Fig. 8.

5) Once flash code is obtained, turn ignition off. Remove jumper wire from service check connector. Determine probable cause and symptom. See DTC/FLASH CODE IDENTIFICATION table. If any other flash codes except those listed are displayed, PCM is defective. For trouble shooting of flash codes, see DIAGNOSTIC TESTS.

NOTE: If customer describes symptoms for DTC P1706 (Flash Code No. 6), it is necessary to test drive vehicle to recreate the symptom, then check for trouble code with ignition still on.

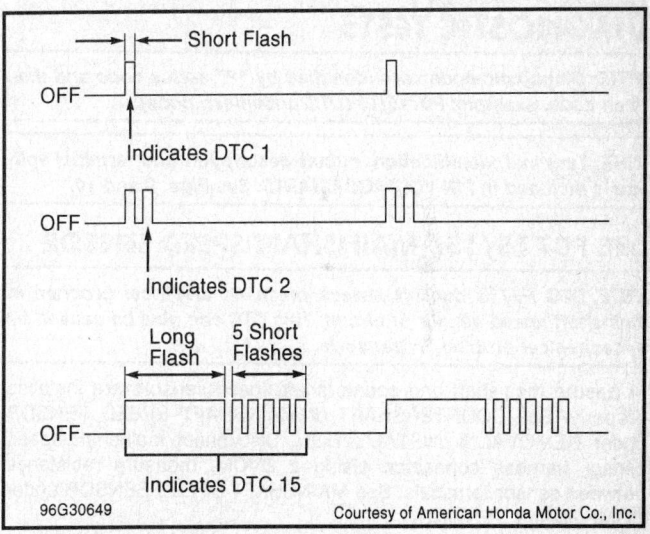

Fig. 8: Identifying Flash Code Displays

CLEARING FAULT CODES

NOTE: PCM memory can NOT be cleared using scan tool. The following procedure must be used. Before clearing fault codes, obtain radio anti-theft code from customer. Note radio preset stations, as radio stations and clock setting will be cleared and must be reset. Radio anti-theft code must be reset for radio operation.

1) Once repairs have been performed, fault codes must be cleared from PCM memory. Ensure ignition is off. Remove BACK-UP fuse (7.5 amp) from engine compartment fuse/relay box for at least 10 seconds. This will clear PCM memory.

2) Reinstall fuse. To re-enter radio anti-theft code, turn radio on. When the word CODE is displayed on radio, re-enter radio anti-theft code by using the radio station preset buttons. Reset clock and radio stations.

DTC/FLASH CODE IDENTIFICATION

DTC/Flash Code [1] Number	Indicator Light [2] Condition	Probable [3] Cause	[4] Symptom
P0715/15	Off	Defective Mainshaft Speed Sensor	Transaxle Jerks Hard When Shifting
P0720/9	Flashes	Defective Countershaft Speed Sensor	Lock-Up Clutch Does Not Engage
P0730/41	Off	Defective Shift Control System	Fails To Shift, Stuck In 1st Or 4th Gears
P0740/40	Off	Defective Lock-Up Control System	Lock-Up Clutch Does Not Engage Or Remains Engaged, Unstable Engine Idle
P0753/7	Flashes	Defective Shift Control Solenoid "A"	Remains In 4th Gear, Fails To Shift Other Than 1st-4th, 2nd-4th Or 2nd-3rd Gears
P0758/8	Flashes	Defective Shift Control Solenoid "B"	Remains In 1st Or 4th Gear
P1705/5	Flashes	Defective A/T Gear Position Switch	Lock-Up Clutch Does Not Engage, Fails To Shift Other Than 2nd-4th Gears
P1706/6	Off	Defective A/T Gear Position Switch	Lock-Up Clutch Does Not Engage, Lock-Up Clutch Engages & Disengages, Fails To Shift Other Than 2nd-4th Gears
P1753/1	Flashes	Defective Lock-Up Control Solenoid "A"	Lock-Up Clutch Does Not Engage Or Remains Engaged, Unstable Engine Idle
P1758/2	Flashes	Defective Lock-Up Control Solenoid "B"	Lock-Up Clutch Does Not Engage
P1768/16	Flashes	Defective Linear Control Solenoid "B"	Lock-Up Clutch Does Not Engage, Transaxle Jerks Hard When Shifting

[1] – Number of flashes from "D4" light on instrument panel with jumper wire installed in service check connector.
[2] – Operation of "D4" light on instrument panel.
[3] – Specified component for probable cause. Also check wiring and connections related to specified component.
[4] – If transaxle fails to shift from Park with brake pedal depressed and accelerator pedal in idle position, check brakelight signal. See BRAKE-LIGHT SIGNAL under TROUBLE SHOOTING.

DIAGNOSTIC TESTS

NOTE: Diagnostic codes are identified by "P" series code and then flash code, example: P0715/15 (DTC code/flash code).

NOTE: Terminal identification, circuit description and terminal voltage is included in PIN VOLTAGE CHARTS. See Figs. 9 and 10.

DTC P0715/15: MAINSHAFT SPEED SENSOR

NOTE: DTC P0715 doesn't always mean an electrical problem in mainshaft speed sensor or circuit. This DTC can also be caused by a mechanical problem in transaxle.

1) Ensure mainshaft and countershaft speed sensors are installed properly. See COUNTERSHAFT or MAINSHAFT SPEED SENSOR under REMOVAL & INSTALLATION. Disconnect mainshaft speed sensor harness connector. Using a DVOM, measure resistance between sensor terminals. See MAINSHAFT SPEED SENSOR under COMPONENT TESTING.
2) If resistance is not 400-600 ohms, replace mainshaft speed sensor. If resistance is 400-600 ohms, disconnect 25-pin PCM harness connector "B". Check for continuity between ground and 25-pin PCM harness connector "B", terminals No. 15 (Red wire) and No. 14 (White wire). *See Figs. 9 and 10.*
3) If continuity is present, repair short to ground in Red or White wire between PCM and mainshaft speed sensor. If continuity is not present, reconnect mainshaft speed sensor harness connector. Measure resistance between 25-pin PCM harness connector "B", terminals No. 15 (Red wire) and No. 14 (White wire).
4) If resistance is not 400-600 ohms, go to next step. If resistance is 400-600 ohms, go to DTC P0720 (FLASH CODE 9). Check for loose PCM harness connectors. Replace PCM with a known-good unit if necessary.
5) Disconnect mainshaft speed sensor harness connector. Check Red wire for continuity between 25-pin PCM harness connector "B", terminal No. 15 and mainshaft speed sensor harness connector. If continuity is present, go to next step. If continuity is not present, repair open in Red wire between 25-pin PCM harness connector and mainshaft speed sensor harness connector.

6) Check White wire for continuity between 25-pin PCM harness connector "B", terminal No. 14 and mainshaft speed sensor harness connector. If continuity is present, check for loose PCM harness connectors. Replace PCM with a known-good unit if necessary. If continuity is not present, repair open in White wire between 25-pin PCM harness connector and mainshaft speed sensor harness connector.

DTC P0720/9: COUNTERSHAFT SPEED SENSOR

1) Ensure countershaft speed sensor is installed properly. See COUNTERSHAFT SPEED SENSOR under REMOVAL & INSTALLATION. Disconnect countershaft speed sensor harness connector. Using a DVOM, measure resistance between sensor terminals. See COUNTERSHAFT SPEED SENSOR under COMPONENT TESTING.
2) If resistance is not 400-600 ohms, replace countershaft speed sensor. If resistance is 400-600 ohms, disconnect 25-pin PCM harness connector "B". Check continuity between ground and 25-pin PCM harness connector "B", terminals No. 22 (Green wire) and No. 23 (Blue wire). *See Figs. 9 and 10.*
3) If continuity is present, repair short to ground in Green or Blue wire between PCM and countershaft speed sensor. If continuity is not present, reconnect countershaft speed sensor harness connector. Measure resistance between 25-pin PCM harness connector "B", terminals No. 22 (Green wire) and No. 23 (Blue wire).
4) If resistance is 400-600 ohms, check for loose PCM harness connectors. Replace PCM with a known-good unit if necessary. If resistance is not 400-600 ohms, repair loose connection or open in Green or Blue wire between 25-pin PCM harness connector and countershaft speed sensor harness connector.

DTC P0730/41: SHIFT CONTROL SYSTEM

NOTE: Do NOT perform this test procedure until all other DTCs have been repaired first.

1) Road test vehicle at over 12 MPH for more than 30 seconds in 2nd, 3rd and 4th gear. Using scan tool, check for any other DTCs. If any other DTCs are present, repair those DTCs first, then recheck for DTC P0730. If no other DTCs are present, go to next step.
2) Test clutch pressure. See HYDRAULIC PRESSURE TEST under TESTING in appropriate overhaul article. If clutch pressure is within specification, go to next step. If clutch pressure is not within specifica-

tion, repair hydraulic system as necessary. See HYDRAULIC PRESSURE TEST TROUBLE SHOOTING table under HYDRAULIC PRESSURE TEST in appropriate overhaul article.

3) Replace shift control solenoid valve assembly. See SHIFT CONTROL SOLENOID VALVES under REMOVAL & INSTALLATION. Turn ignition off and clear codes. See CLEARING FAULT CODES. Road test vehicle at over 12 MPH for more than 30 seconds in 2nd, 3rd and 4th gear. Recheck DTCs. If P0730 returns, go to next step. If P0730 does not return, system is okay.

4) Replace linear shift control solenoid valve assembly. See SHIFT CONTROL SOLENOID VALVES under REMOVAL & INSTALLATION. Turn ignition off and clear codes. See CLEARING FAULT CODES. Road test vehicle at over 12 MPH for more than 30 seconds in 2nd, 3rd and 4th gear. Recheck DTCs. If P0730 returns, repair internal components as necessary. If P0730 does not return, system is okay.

DTC P0740/40: LOCK-UP CONTROL SYSTEM

NOTE: Do NOT perform this test procedure until all other DTCs have been repaired first.

1) Using scan tool, check for any other DTCs. If any other DTCs are present, repair those DTCs first, then recheck for DTC P0740. If no other DTCs are present, go to next step.

2) Test line pressure. See HYDRAULIC PRESSURE TEST under TESTING in appropriate overhaul article. If line pressure is within specification, go to next step. If line pressure is not within specification, repair hydraulic system as necessary. See HYDRAULIC PRESSURE TEST TROUBLE SHOOTING table under HYDRAULIC PRESSURE TEST in appropriate overhaul article.

3) Test clutch pressure. If clutch pressure is within specification, go to next step. If clutch pressure is not within specification, repair hydraulic system as necessary. See HYDRAULIC PRESSURE TEST TROUBLE SHOOTING table under HYDRAULIC PRESSURE TEST in appropriate overhaul article.

4) Replace lock-up control solenoid valve assembly. See LOCK-UP CONTROL SOLENOID VALVES under REMOVAL & INSTALLATION. Turn ignition off and clear codes. See CLEARING FAULT CODES. Road test vehicle at over 50 MPH for more than one minute. Recheck DTCs. If P0740 returns, go to next step. If P0740 does not return, system is okay.

5) Replace linear shift control solenoid valve assembly. See SHIFT CONTROL SOLENOID VALVES under REMOVAL & INSTALLATION. Turn ignition off and clear codes. See CLEARING FAULT CODES. Road test vehicle at over 50 MPH for more than one minute. Recheck DTCs. If P0740 returns, go to next step. If P0740 does not return, system is okay.

6) Replace torque converter. Turn ignition off and clear codes. See CLEARING FAULT CODES. Road test vehicle at over 50 MPH for more than one minute. Recheck DTCs. If P0740 returns, replace transaxle. If P0740 does not return, system is okay.

DTC P0753/7:
SHIFT CONTROL SOLENOID VALVE "A"

1) Disconnect 32-pin PCM harness connector "A" and 25-pin PCM harness connector "B". Turn ignition on. Using DVOM, measure voltage between 25-pin PCM harness connector "B", terminal No. 3 (Blue/Yellow wire) and 32-pin PCM harness connector "A", terminals No. 9 or No. 22 (Brown/Black wires). *See Figs. 9 and 10.* If voltage is not present, go to next step. If voltage is present, repair short to power in Blue/Yellow wire between 25-pin PCM harness connector "B" and shift control solenoid valve "A".

2) Turn ignition off. Measure resistance of shift control solenoid valve "A" between 25-pin PCM harness connector "B", terminal No. 3 (Blue/Yellow wire) and 32-pin PCM harness connector "A", terminals No. 9 or No. 22 (Brown/Black wires). *See Figs. 9 and 10.* If resistance is not 14-25 ohms, go to next step. If resistance is 14-25 ohms, check for loose PCM harness connectors. Replace PCM with a known-good unit if necessary.

3) Disconnect shift control solenoid valve harness connector. Check for continuity between 25-pin PCM harness connector "B", terminal No. 3 (Blue/Yellow wire) and 32-pin PCM harness connector "A", terminals No. 9 or No. 22 (Brown/Black wires). *See Figs. 9 and 10.* If continuity is not present, go to next step. If continuity is present, repair short to ground in Blue/Yellow wire between 25-pin PCM harness connector "B" and shift control solenoid valve "A".

4) Measure resistance between shift control solenoid valve harness connector (solenoid side) Blue/Yellow wire and ground. If resistance is not 14-25 ohms, replace shift control solenoid valve. If resistance is 14-25 ohms, repair open in Blue/Yellow wire between shift control solenoid valve "A" and 25-pin PCM harness connector "B".

DTC P0758/8:
SHIFT CONTROL SOLENOID VALVE "B"

1) Disconnect 32-pin PCM harness connector "A" and 25-pin PCM harness connector "B". Turn ignition on. Using a DVOM, measure voltage between 25-pin PCM harness connector "B", terminal No. 11 (Green/White wire) and 32-pin PCM harness connector "A", terminals No. 9 or No. 22 (Brown/Black wires). *See Figs. 9 and 10.* If voltage is not present, go to next step. If voltage is present, repair short to power in Green/White wire between 25-pin PCM harness connector "B" and shift control solenoid valve "B".

2) Turn ignition off. Measure resistance of shift control solenoid valve "A" between 25-pin PCM harness connector "B", terminal No. 11 (Green/White wire) and 32-pin PCM harness connector "A", terminals No. 9 or No. 22 (Brown/Black wires). *See Figs. 9 and 10.* If resistance is not 14-25 ohms, go to next step. If resistance is 14-25 ohms, check for loose PCM harness connectors. Replace PCM with a known-good unit if necessary.

3) Disconnect shift control solenoid valve harness connector. Check for continuity between 25-pin PCM harness connector "B", terminal No. 11 (Green/White wire) and 32-pin PCM harness connector "A", terminals No. 9 or No. 22 (Brown/Black wires). *See Figs. 9 and 10.* If continuity is not present, go to next step. If continuity is present, repair short to ground in Green/White wire between 25-pin PCM harness connector "B" and shift control solenoid valve "B".

4) Measure resistance between shift control solenoid valve harness connector (solenoid side) Green/White wire and ground. If resistance is not 14-25 ohms, replace shift control solenoid valve. If resistance is 14-25 ohms, repair open in Green/White wire between shift control solenoid valve "B" and 25-pin PCM harness connector "B".

DTC P1705/5:
A/T GEAR POSITION SWITCH (SHORT)

NOTE: DTC P1705 is set when PCM receives 2 gear position signals at the same time.

1) Turn ignition on. If any A/T gear position indicator lights stay on when gear selector is moved from that gear, go to next step. If all A/T gear position·indicator lights turn off when gear selector is moved from that gear, system is okay at this time.

2) Shift through all gear positions except Reverse. Using a DVOM, measure voltage between 25-pin PCM harness connector "B", terminal No. 16 (White wire) and 32-pin PCM harness connector "A", terminals No. 9 or No. 22 (Brown/Black wires). *See Figs. 9 and 10.* If battery voltage is present, go to next step. If battery voltage is not present, check and repair short in White wire between 25-pin PCM harness connector "B" and A/T gear position indicator or A/T gear position switch. If White wire is okay, check for loose PCM harness connectors. Replace PCM with a known-good unit if necessary.

3) Shift through all gear positions except Neutral and Park. Measure voltage between 25-pin PCM harness connector "B", terminal No. 25 (Light Green wire) and 32-pin PCM harness connector "A", terminals No. 9 or No. 22 (Brown/Black wires). If battery voltage is present, go to next step. If battery voltage is not present, check and repair short in Light Green wire between 25-pin PCM harness connector "B" and A/T gear position indicator or A/T gear position switch. If Light Green wire is okay, check for loose PCM harness connectors. Replace PCM with a known-good unit if necessary.

4) Shift through all gear positions except "D⁴". Measure voltage between 25-pin PCM harness connector "B", terminal No. 24 (Yellow wire) and 32-pin PCM harness connector "A", terminals No. 9 or No. 22 (Brown/Black wires). If battery voltage is present, go to next step. If battery voltage is not present, check and repair short in Yellow wire between 25-pin PCM harness connector "B" and A/T gear position switch. If Yellow wire is okay, check for loose PCM harness connectors. Replace PCM with a known-good unit if necessary.

5) Shift through all gear positions except "D³". Measure voltage between 25-pin PCM harness connector "B" terminal No. 8 (Green wire) and 32-pin PCM harness connector "A", terminals No. 9 or No. 22 (Brown/Black wires). If battery voltage is present, go to next step. If battery voltage is not present, check and repair short in Green wire between 25-pin PCM harness connector "B" and A/T gear position indicator or A/T gear position switch. If Green wire is okay, check for loose PCM harness connectors. Replace PCM with a known-good unit if necessary.

6) Shift through all gear positions except "2". Measure voltage between 25-pin PCM harness connector "B", terminal No. 17 (Blue wire) and 32-pin PCM harness connector "A", terminals No. 9 or No. 22 (Brown/Black wires). If battery voltage is present, check for loose PCM connectors. Replace PCM with a known-good unit if necessary. If battery voltage is not present, check and repair short in Blue wire between 25-pin PCM harness connector "B" and A/T gear position indicator or A/T gear position switch. If Blue wire is okay, check for loose PCM harness connectors. Replace PCM with a known-good unit if necessary.

DTC P1706/6:
A/T GEAR POSITION SWITCH (OPEN)

1) Turn ignition on. If any A/T gear position indicator lights stay on when gear selector is moved from that gear, go to next step. If all A/T gear position indicator lights turn off when gear selector is moved from that gear, system is okay at this time.

2) Shift to Reverse. Using a DVOM, measure voltage between 25-pin PCM harness connector "B", terminal No. 16 (White wire) and 32-pin PCM harness connector "A", terminals No. 9 or No. 22 (Brown/Black wires). *See Figs. 9 and 10.* If voltage is not present, go to next step. If voltage is present, check and repair open in White wire between 25-pin PCM harness connector "B" and A/T gear position switch.

3) Shift to Neutral or Park. Measure voltage between 25-pin PCM harness connector "B", terminal No. 25 (Light Green wire) and 32-pin PCM

harness connector "A", terminal No. 9 or No. 22 (Brown/Black wires). If voltage is not present, go to next step. If voltage is present, check and repair open in Light Green wire between 25-pin PCM harness connector "B" and A/T gear position indicator.

4) Shift to "D₄" position. Measure voltage between 25-pin PCM harness connector "B", terminal No. 24 (Yellow wire) and 32-pin PCM harness connector "A", terminals No. 9 or No. 22 (Brown/Black wires). If voltage is not present, go to next step. If voltage is present, check and repair open in Yellow wire between 25-pin PCM harness connector "B" and A/T gear position switch.

5) Shift to "D₃" position. Measure voltage between 25-pin PCM harness connector "B", terminal No. 8 (Green wire) and 32-pin PCM harness connector "A", terminals No. 9 or No. 22 (Brown/Black wires). If voltage is not present, go to next step. If voltage is present, check and repair open in Green wire between 25-pin PCM harness connector "B" and A/T gear position switch.

6) Shift to "2" position. Measure voltage between 25-pin PCM harness connector "B", terminal No. 17 (Blue wire) and 32-pin PCM harness connector "A", terminals No. 9 or No. 22 (Brown/Black wires). If voltage is not present, check for loose PCM harness connectors. Replace PCM with a known-good unit if necessary. If voltage is present, check and repair open in Blue wire between 25-pin PCM harness connector "B" and A/T gear position switch.

DTC P1753/1:
LOCK-UP CONTROL SOLENOID VALVE "A"

1) Disconnect 32-pin PCM harness connector "A" and 25-pin PCM harness connector "B". Turn ignition on. Using a DVOM, measure voltage between 25-pin PCM harness connector "B", terminal No. 5 (Yellow wire) and 32-pin PCM harness connector "A", terminals No. 9 or No. 22 (Brown/Black wires). *See Figs. 9 and 10.* If voltage is not present, go to next step. If voltage is present, repair short to power in Yellow wire between 25-pin PCM harness connector "B" and lock-up control solenoid valve "A".

2) Turn ignition off. Measure resistance between 25-pin PCM harness connector "B", terminal No. 5 (Yellow wire) and 32-pin PCM harness connector "A", terminals No. 9 or No. 22 (Brown/Black wires). If resistance is not 14-25 ohms, go to next step. If resistance is 14-25 ohms, check for loose PCM harness connectors. Replace PCM with a known-good unit if necessary.

3) Disconnect lock-up control solenoid valve harness connector. Check for continuity between 25-pin PCM harness connector "B", terminal No. 5 (Yellow wire) and 32-pin PCM harness connector "A", terminals No. 9 or No. 22 (Brown/Black wires). If continuity is not present, go to next step. If continuity is present, repair short to ground in Yellow wire between 25-pin PCM harness connector "B" and lock-up control solenoid valve "A".

4) Measure resistance between ground and Yellow wire at lock-up control solenoid valve harness connector (solenoid side). If resistance is not 14-25 ohms, replace lock-up control solenoid valve assembly. If resistance is 14-25 ohms, check and repair open in Yellow wire between lock-up control solenoid valve harness connector and lock-up control solenoid valve "A".

DTC P1758/2:
LOCK-UP CONTROL SOLENOID VALVE "B"

1) Disconnect 32-pin PCM harness connector "A" and 25-pin PCM harness connector "B". Turn ignition on. Using a DVOM, measure voltage between 25-pin PCM harness connector "B", terminal No. 4 (Green/Black wire) and 32-pin PCM harness connector "A", terminals No. 9 or No. 22 (Brown/Black wires). *See Figs. 9 and 10.* If voltage is not present, go to next step. If voltage is present, repair short to power in Green/Black wire between 25-pin PCM harness connector "B" and lock-up control solenoid valve "B".

2) Turn ignition off. Measure resistance between 25-pin PCM harness connector "B", terminal No. 4 (Green/Black wire) and 32-pin PCM harness connector "A", terminals No. 9 or No. 22 (Brown/Black wires). If resistance is not 14-25 ohms, go to next step. If resistance is 14-25 ohms, check for loose PCM harness connectors. Replace PCM with a known-good unit if necessary.

3) Disconnect lock-up control solenoid valve harness connector. Check for continuity between 25-pin PCM harness connector "B", terminal No. 4 (Green/Black wire) and 32-pin PCM harness connector "A", terminals No. 9 or No. 22 (Brown/Black wires). If continuity is not present, go to next step. If continuity is present, repair short to ground in Green/Black wire between 25-pin PCM harness connector "B" and lock-up control solenoid valve "B".

4) Measure resistance between ground and Green/Black wire at lock-up control solenoid valve harness connector (solenoid side). If resistance is not 14-25 ohms, replace lock-up control solenoid valve assembly. If resistance is 14-25 ohms, check and repair open in Green/Black wire between lock-up control solenoid valve harness connector and lock-up control solenoid valve "B".

DTC P1768/16: LINEAR SOLENOID

1) Disconnect linear solenoid harness connector. Using a DVOM, measure resistance of linear solenoid. If resistance is 4-9 ohms, go to next step. If resistance is not 4-9 ohms, replace linear solenoid.

2) Disconnect 25-pin PCM harness connector "B". Check for continuity between ground and 25-pin PCM harness connector "B", terminals No. 1 (White wire), then No. 2 (Red wire). See Figs. 9 and 10. If continuity is not present, go to next step. If continuity is present, repair short between White and Red wires.

3) Reconnect linear solenoid harness connector. Measure resistance between 25-pin PCM harness connector "B", terminals No. 1 (White wire) and No. 2 (Red wire). If resistance is 4-9 ohms, check for loose PCM harness connectors. Replace PCM with a known-good unit if necessary. If resistance is not 4-9 ohms, repair open or poor connection in White wire or Red wire between 25-pin PCM harness connector "B" and linear solenoid.

TROUBLE SHOOTING

BRAKELIGHT SIGNAL

NOTE: If no brakelight signal is present, transaxle may fail to shift from Park with brake pedal depressed and accelerator pedal in idle position.

1) Ensure brakelights come on when brake pedal is depressed. If brakelights come on, go to next step. If brakelights do not come on, check fuse No. 52 (15-amp) in engine compartment fuse/relay box. If fuse is okay, repair brakelight signal circuit.

2) Ensure ignition is off. Disconnect 32-pin PCM harness connector "A", and 16-pin PCM harness connector "D". Using a DVOM, measure voltage between 16-pin PCM harness connector "D", terminal No. 5 (Green/White wire) and 32-pin PCM harness connector "A", terminals No. 9 or No. 22 (Brown/Black wires) with brake pedal depressed. See Figs. 9 and 10. If battery voltage is present, go to next step. If battery voltage is not present, repair open in Green/White wire.

3) Brakelight signal is okay at this time. Check for loose PCM harness connectors. Replace PCM with a known-good unit if necessary and retest.

SYSTEM TESTING

A/T GEAR POSITION INDICATOR

NOTE: For system testing, refer to wiring schematic when checking component wiring. See Fig. 13. To check individual components, see COMPONENT TESTING.

1) Remove instrument panel gauge assembly from instrument panel. Disconnect 14-pin harness connector from rear of instrument panel gauge assembly. See Fig. 11.

2) Using a DVOM, check for voltage and continuity at harness connector terminals as specified. See Fig. 12. If necessary, check ground connections G401 or G402. Ground connection G401 is located behind driver's side of instrument panel, above kick panel. Ground connection G402 is located behind passenger's side of instrument panel, above kick panel.

3) If all voltage and continuity checks are okay, but indicator is still faulty, replace printed circuit board.

SHIFT & KEY INTERLOCK SYSTEMS

NOTE: For system testing, refer to appropriate wiring diagram when checking component wiring. See WIRING DIAGRAMS. To check individual components, see COMPONENT TESTING.

1) To check system operation, ensure shift lever is in Park. Turn ignition on. Depress brake pedal with accelerator pedal in idle position.

2) If shift lock solenoid clicks, system is working properly. If shift lock solenoid fails to click, see INTERLOCK CONTROL UNIT under COMPONENT TESTING. If shift lever cannot be moved from Park, check for proper installation of shift lock solenoid. If shift lock solenoid installation is okay, test A/T gear position switch, see A/T GEAR POSITION SWITCH under COMPONENT TESTING.

COMPONENT TESTING

A/T GEAR POSITION SWITCH

NOTE: A/T gear position switch also contains back-up light switch and neutral position switch. Back-up light switch and neutral position switch can also be checked when checking A/T gear position switch.

1) Remove center console. Disconnect 14-pin harness connector from A/T gear position switch. Note harness connector terminal identification. See Fig. 14.

2) Using a DVOM, check continuity between specified terminal(s) with shift lever in indicated positions. See A/T GEAR POSITION SWITCH CONTINUITY table.

NOTE: Check continuity while moving shift lever back and forth in free play area of each gear position. DO NOT touch push button on shift lever when checking continuity.

3) If continuity is not as specified, A/T gear position switch may require adjustment. See A/T GEAR POSITION SWITCH under REMOVAL & INSTALLATION. If correct continuity cannot be obtained by adjusting A/T gear position switch, replace switch assembly.

A/T GEAR POSITION SWITCH CONTINUITY

Application	Shift Lever Position	Continuity Between Terminals No.
With Cruise Control		
A/T Gear Position Switch	"P"	1 & 12
	"R"	1 & 13
	"N"	1 & 14
	"D₄"	1, 7 & 9
	"D₃"	1, 6 & 9
	"2"	1, 5 & 9
Back-Up Light Switch	"R"	3 & 4
Neutral Position Switch	"P"	10 & 11
	"N"	10 & 11
Without Cruise Control		
A/T Gear Position Switch	"P"	1 & 12
	"R"	1 & 13
	"N"	1 & 14
	"D₄"	1 & 7
	"D₃"	1 & 6
	"2"	1 & 5
Back-Up Light Switch	"R"	3 & 4
Neutral Position Switch	"P"	10 & 11
	"N"	10 & 11

AUTOMATIC TRANSMISSIONS
Honda A4RA Electronic Controls (Cont.)

PIN VOLTAGE CHARTS

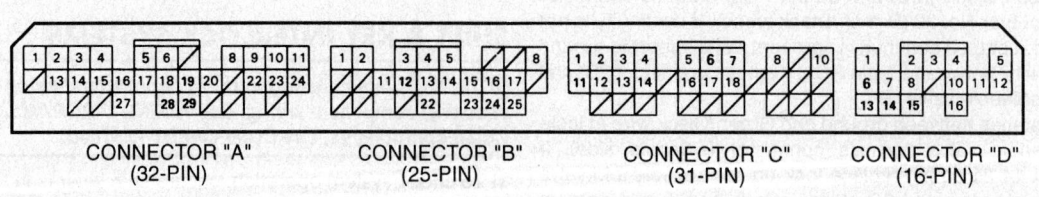

CONNECTOR "A" (32-PIN)   CONNECTOR "B" (25-PIN)   CONNECTOR "C" (31-PIN)   CONNECTOR "D" (16-PIN)

Terminal Number	Signal	Description	Measuring Conditions/Terminal Voltage
A1 to A8		Engine Control	
A9	LG1	Ground	
A10	PG1	Ground	
A11	IGP1	Power supply system	With ignition switch ON (II): Battery voltage With ignition switch OFF: 0 V
A12 to A21		Engine Control	
A22	LG2	Ground	
A23	PG2	Ground	
A24	IGP2	Power supply system	With ignition switch ON (II): Battery voltage With ignition switch OFF: 0 V
A25 to A32		Engine Control	
B1	LS–	Linear solenoid power supply negative electrode	Ignition switch ON (II): Pulsing signal
B2	LS+	Linear solenoid power supply positive electrode	Ignition switch ON (II): Pulsing signal
B3	SHA	Shift control solenoid valve A control	In 2nd gear and 3rd gear in D_3, D_4 position, and in 2 position: Battery voltage In 1st gear and 4th gear in D_3, D_4 position: 0 V
B4	LCB	Lock-up control solenoid valve B control	When full lock-up: Battery voltage When half lock-up: Pulsing signal
B5	LCA	Lock-up control solenoid valve A control	When lock-up is ON: Battery voltage With no lock-up: 0 V
B6 to B7	—	Not used	
B8	ATP D3	A/T gear position switch D_3 position signal input	In D_3 position: 0 V In other than D_3 position: Battery voltage
B9 to B10	—	Not used	

96A30650

Courtesy of American Honda Motor Co., Inc.

Fig. 9: Pin Voltage Chart & Terminal Identification (1 Of 2)

Terminal Number	Signal	Description	Measuring Conditions/Terminal Voltage
B11	SHB	Shift control solenoid valve B control	In 1st gear and 2nd gear in D3, D4 position, and in 2 position: Battery voltage In 3rd gear and 4th gear in D3, D4 position: 0 V
B12	SLU	Interlock control	When ignition switch is ON (II), brake pedal depressed and accelerator pedal released: 0 V
B13	D4 IND	D4 Indicator light control	When ignition switch is first turned ON (II): Battery voltage for two seconds In D4 position: Battery voltage
B14	NMSG	Mainshaft speed sensor ground	Always: 0 V
B15	NM	Mainshaft speed sensor signal input	Depending on engine speed: Pulsing signal When engine is stopped: 0 V
B16	ATP R	A/T gear position switch R position signal input	In R position: 0 V In other than R position: Battery voltage
B17	ATP 2	A/T gear position switch 2 position signal input	In 2 position: 0 V In other than 2 position: Battery voltage
B18 to B21	—	Not used	
B22	NCSG	Countershaft speed sensor ground	Always: 0 V
B23	NC	Countershaft speed sensor signal input	Depending on vehicle speed: Pulsing signal When vehicle is stopped: 0 V
B24	ATP D4	A/T gear position switch D4 position signal input	In D4 position: 0 V In other than D4 position: 5 V
B25	ATP PN	A/T gear position switch P and N position signals input	In P and N positions: 0 V In other than P and N positions: Battery voltage
C1 to C6		Engine Control	
C7	SCS	Service check signal	With ignition switch ON (II) and service check connector open: 5 V With ignition switch ON (II) and service check connector connected with special tool: 0 V
C8 to C9		Engine Control	
C10	VBU	Back-up power system	Always battery voltage
C11 to C31		Engine Control	
D1 to D4		Engine Control	
D5	STOP SW	Brake switch signal input	With ignition switch ON (II) and brake pedal depressed: Battery voltage With ignition switch ON (II) and brake pedal released: 0 V
D6 to D16		Engine Control	

96B30651

Courtesy of American Honda Motor Co., Inc.

Fig. 10: Pin Voltage Chart & Terminal Identification (2 Of 2)

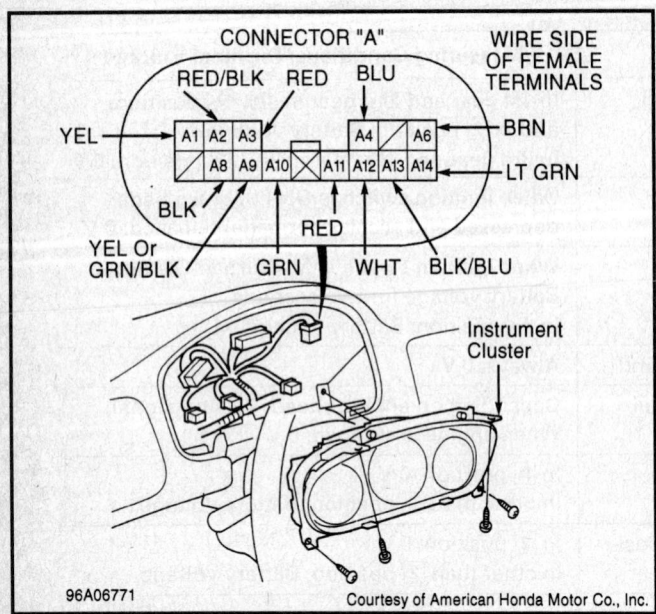

Fig. 11: Identifying Instrument Panel Gauge Assembly Harness Connector Terminals

Cavity	Wire	Test Condition	Test: Desired Result	Possible Cause If Result Is Not Obtained
A1	YEL	Ignition switch ON (II)	Check for voltage to ground: There should be battery voltage.	• Blown No. 25 (7.5 A) fuse in the under-dash fuse/relay box • An open in the wire
A2	RED/BLK	Combination light switch ON and dash lights brightness control dial on full bright	Check for voltage between RED/BLK and RED terminals: There should be battery voltage.	• Blown No. 30 (7.5 A) fuse in the under-dash fuse/relay box • Faulty combination light switch • Faulty dash lights brightness controller • An open in the wire
A3	RED			
A4	BLU	Shift lever in ② or Ⓛ	Check for continuity to ground: There should be continuity. NOTE: There should be no continuity in any other position.	• Faulty A/T gear position switch • An open in the wire
A10	GRN	Shift lever in D₃ or Ⓢ		
A11	RED	Shift lever in Ⓝ		
A12	WHT	Shift lever in Ⓡ		
A13	BLK/BLU	Shift lever in Ⓟ NOTE: Don't push the brake pedal.		
A9	YEL	Ignition switch ON (II) and shift lever in any position except D₄	Check for voltage to ground: There should be battery voltage for two seconds after the ignition switch is turned ON (II), and then less than 1 V.	• Faulty PCM • An open in the wire
A8	BLK	Under all conditions	Check for continuity to ground: There should be continuity.	• Poor ground (G401, G402) • An open in the wire
A14	LT GRN	Ignition switch ON (II)	Check for voltage to ground: • There should be battery voltage • There should be about 5 V	• Faulty PCM • An open in the wire

96I31599

Courtesy of American Honda Motor Co., Inc.

Fig. 12: Testing A/T Gear Position Indicator

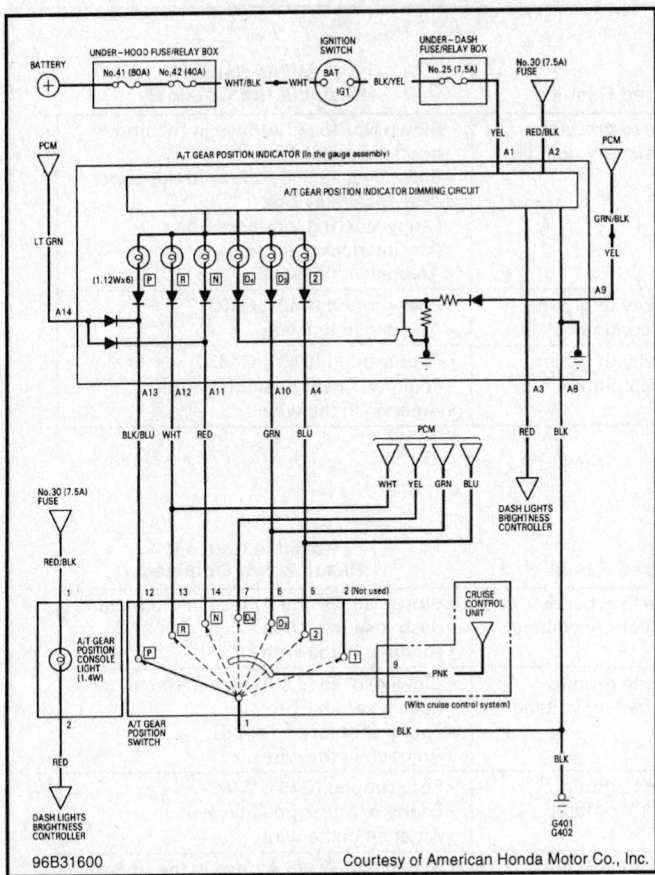

Fig. 13: A/T Gear Position Indicator System Wiring Schematic

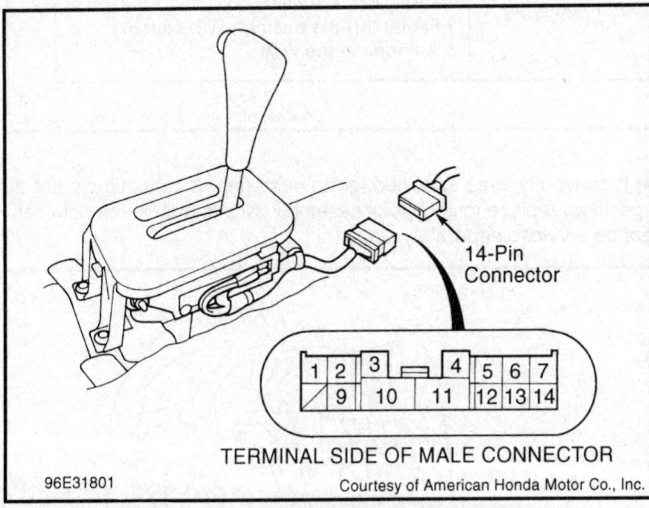

Fig. 14: Identifying A/T Gear Position Switch Harness Connector Terminals

BRAKELIGHT SWITCH

1) Disconnect harness connector from brakelight switch located on brake pedal support. *See Fig. 5.*

2) On models with cruise control, using a DVOM, check for continuity between terminals No. 1 (Light Green wire) and No. 2 (Gray wire) with brake pedal released. Continuity should be present.

3) On all models, using a DVOM, check for continuity between terminals No. 3 (Green/White wire) and No. 4 (White/Green wire) with brake pedal depressed. Continuity should be present.

4) If continuity is not as specified, ensure brake pedal is properly adjusted so brakelight switch has proper travel for switch operation. If brakelight switch travel is okay, replace brakelight switch.

COUNTERSHAFT SPEED SENSOR

Disconnect harness connector from countershaft speed sensor located on top of transaxle. *See Fig. 6.* Using a DVOM, measure resistance between sensor terminals. Replace countershaft speed sensor if resistance is not 400-600 ohms.

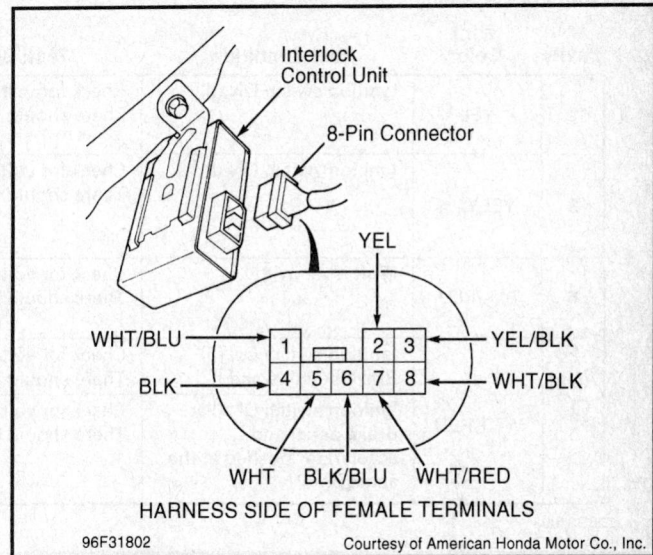

Fig. 15: Identifying Interlock Control Unit Harness Connector Terminals

Key Interlock System:

Cavity	Wire Color	Test Condition	Test: Desired Result	Possible Cause If Result Is Not Obtained
1	WHT/BLU	Ignition switch turned to ACC (I) and key pushed in	Check for voltage to ground: There should be battery voltage.	• Blown No. 48 (30 A) fuse in the under-hood fuse/relay box • Blown No. 33 (7.5 A) fuse in the under-dash fuse/relay box • Faulty steering lock assembly (key interlock solenoid) • An open in the wire
5	WHT			
4	BLK	Under all conditions	Check for continuity to ground: There should be continuity.	• Poor ground (G401, G402) • An open in the wire
6	BLK/BLU	Shift lever in [P]	Check for continuity to ground: There should be continuity.	• Poor ground (G401, G402) • Faulty A/T gear position switch • An open in the wire

Reconnect the 8P connector to the interlock control unit.

Shift Lock System:

Cavity	Wire Color	Test Condition	Test: Desired Result	Possible Cause If Result Is Not Obtained
2	YEL	Ignition switch ON (II)	Check for voltage to ground: There should be battery voltage.	• Blown No. 25 (7.5 A) fuse in the under-dash fuse/relay box • An open in the wire
3	YEL/BLK	Ignition switch ON (II)	Check for voltage to ground: There should be battery voltage.	• Blown No. 25 (7.5 A) fuse in the under-dash fuse/relay box • Faulty shift lock solenoid • An open in the wire
6	BLK/BLU	Shift lever in [P]	Check for voltage to ground: There should be 1 V or less.	• Poor ground (G401, G402) • Faulty A/T gear position switch • An open in the wire
7	WHT/RED	Ignition switch ON (II) Brake pedal pushed	Check for voltage to ground: There should be 1 V or less.	• Blown No. 52 (15 A) fuse in the under-hood fuse/relay box • Faulty PCM • Faulty brake switch • Faulty throttle position (TP) sensor • An open in the wire
		Ignition switch ON (II) Brake pedal and accelerator pushed at the same time	Check for voltage to ground: There should be battery voltage.	

96G31803

Courtesy of American Honda Motor Co., Inc.

Fig. 16: Testing Interlock Control Unit

INTERLOCK CONTROL UNIT

1) Remove lower panel from instrument panel. Disconnect 8-pin harness connector from interlock control unit. Interlock control unit is located behind center of instrument panel. *See Fig. 3.* Inspect terminals for poor connection, corrosion or bending. Repair as necessary.

2) Using a DVOM, check for continuity or voltage between specified terminals or body ground. *See Figs. 15 and 16.* If necessary, check ground connections G401 or G402. Ground connection G401 is located behind driver's side of instrument panel, above kick panel. Ground connection G402 is located behind passenger's side of instrument panel, above kick panel.

3) If necessary, check fuse No. 48 (30-amp) in engine compartment fuse/relay box, and fuse No. 33 (7.5-amp) in instrument panel fuse/relay box.

KEY INTERLOCK SOLENOID

1) Remove lower cover and knee bolster from driver's side of instrument panel for access to key interlock solenoid 7-pin harness connector. *See Fig. 17.*

2) Disconnect key interlock solenoid 7-pin harness connector from main wiring harness. Note harness connector terminal identification.

3) Using a DVOM, check continuity between designated terminals with ignition lock assembly in ACC position. See KEY INTERLOCK SOLENOID CONTINUITY SPECIFICATIONS table.

4) If continuity is as specified, go to next step. If continuity is not as specified, replace ignition lock assembly. Key interlock solenoid cannot be serviced separately.

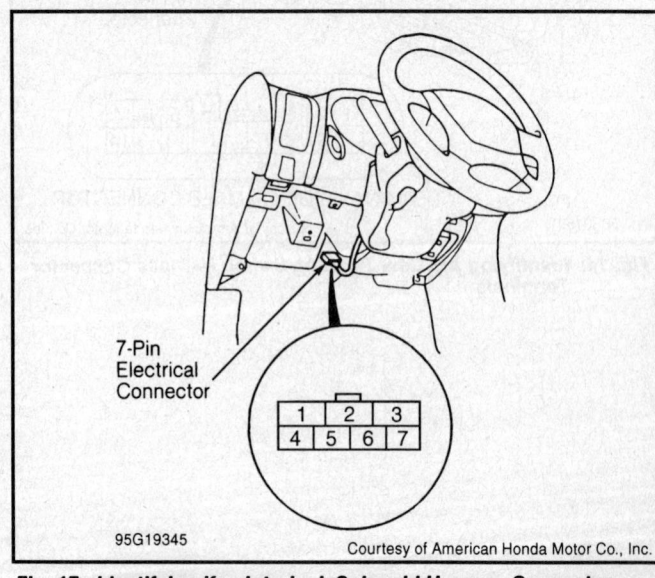

7-Pin Electrical Connector

95G19345

Courtesy of American Honda Motor Co., Inc.

Fig. 17: Identifying Key Interlock Solenoid Harness Connector & Terminals

5) Connect battery voltage and ground to terminals No. 5 and No. 7. Ensure ignition key cannot be removed with battery voltage applied.

6) If ignition key cannot be removed, key interlock solenoid is okay. If ignition key can be removed, replace ignition lock assembly. Key interlock solenoid cannot be serviced separately.

KEY INTERLOCK SOLENOID CONTINUITY SPECIFICATIONS

Ignition Key Position	Continuity Between Terminals No.
Key Pushed In	5, 6 & 7
Key Released	5 & 6

LINEAR SOLENOID

1) Linear solenoid is located on side of transaxle. See Fig. 6. Disconnect harness connector at linear solenoid.

2) Using a DVOM, check resistance between solenoid terminals. Resistance should be 4-9 ohms. Replace linear solenoid assembly if resistance is not as specified.

3) Check linear solenoid operation. Apply battery voltage to terminal No. 2, and ground terminal No. 1. See Fig. 18. A clicking sound should be heard, indicating solenoid operation. Replace linear solenoid assembly if solenoid fails to operate.

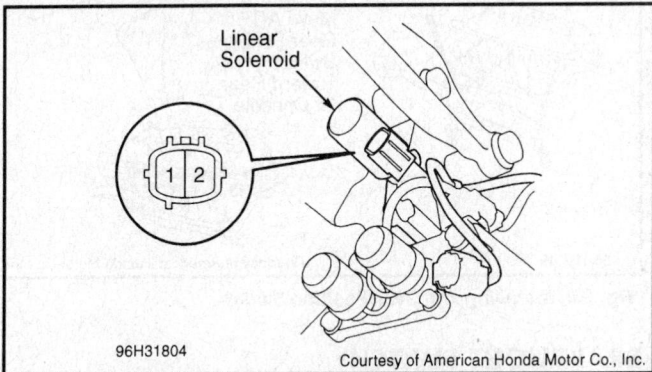

96H31804   Courtesy of American Honda Motor Co., Inc.

Fig. 18: Identifying Linear Solenoid Connector Terminals

LOCK-UP CONTROL SOLENOID VALVES

1) Lock-up control solenoid valve assembly is located on transaxle. See Fig. 6. Disconnect harness connector at lock-up control solenoid valve assembly.

2) Using a DVOM, check resistance between terminal No. 1 (solenoid valve "B"), or terminal No. 2 (solenoid valve "A") and body ground. See Fig. 19.

3) Resistance should be 14-25 ohms. Replace lock-up control solenoid valve assembly if resistance of either solenoid valve is not within specification.

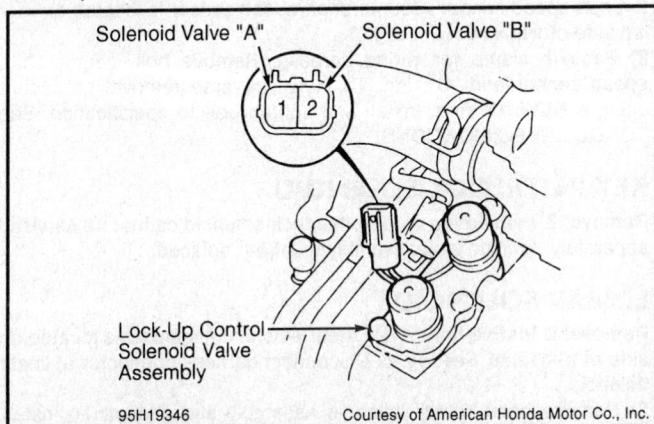

95H19346   Courtesy of American Honda Motor Co., Inc.

Fig. 19: Identifying Lock-Up Control Solenoid Valve Harness Connector Terminals

4) Check lock-up control solenoid valve operation. Ensure solenoid valve body is grounded. Apply battery voltage to terminal No. 1 (solenoid valve "B") or terminal No. 2 (solenoid valve "A").

5) A clicking sound should be heard, indicating solenoid valve operation. Replace lock-up control solenoid valve assembly if either solenoid valve fails to operate.

MAINSHAFT SPEED SENSOR

Disconnect harness connector from mainshaft speed sensor located on top of transaxle. See Fig. 6. Using a DVOM, measure resistance between sensor terminals. Replace mainshaft speed sensor if resistance is not 400-600 ohms.

PARKING PIN SWITCH

1) Remove center console. Disconnect parking pin switch 4-pin harness connector. Parking pin switch is located on left side of shifter assembly.

2) Using a DVOM, check for continuity between parking pin switch terminals. See Fig. 20. Continuity should be present between terminals No. 3 and 4 when shift lever is in any position other than "P", or when shift lever is in "P" position with button depressed.

3) Continuity should not be present between terminals No. 3 and 4 with shift lever in "P" position and button released.

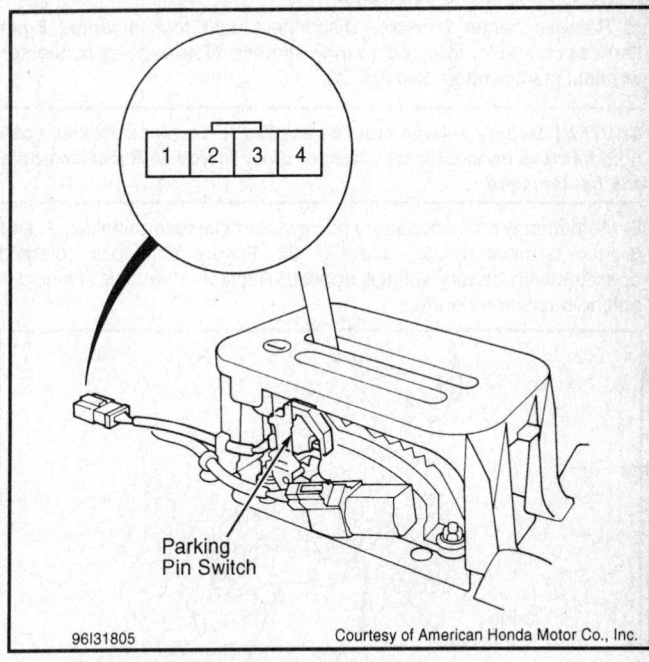

96I31805   Courtesy of American Honda Motor Co., Inc.

Fig. 20: Identifying Parking Pin Switch Harness Connector Terminals

SHIFT CONTROL SOLENOID VALVES

1) Shift control solenoid valves are located on transaxle. See Fig. 6. Disconnect harness connector at shift control solenoid valves.

2) Using a DVOM, measure resistance between terminal No. 1 (solenoid valve "A"), or terminal No. 2 (solenoid valve "B") and ground. See Fig. 21.

3) Resistance should be 14-25 ohms. Replace shift control solenoid valve assembly if resistance of either solenoid valve is not within specification.

4) Check shift control solenoid valve operation. Ensure solenoid valve body is grounded. Apply battery voltage to terminal No. 1 (solenoid valve "A") or terminal No. 2 (solenoid valve "B").

5) A clicking sound should be heard, indicating solenoid valve operation. Replace shift control solenoid valve assembly if either solenoid valve fails to operate.

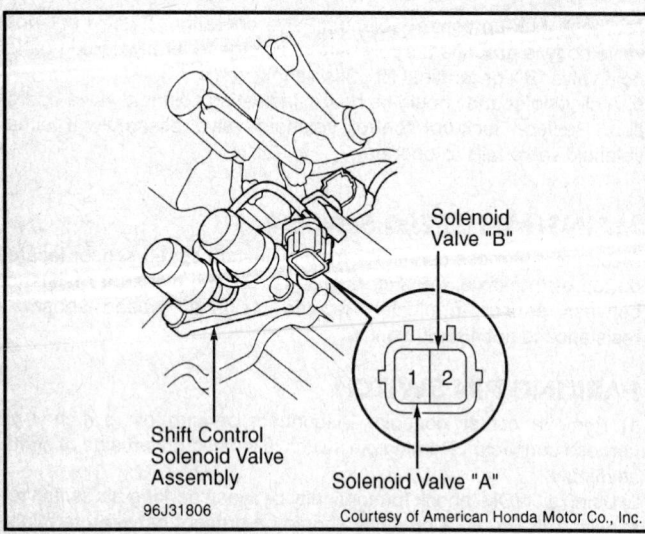

Fig. 21: *Identifying Shift Control Solenoid Valve Harness Connector Terminals*

SHIFT LOCK SOLENOID

1) Remove center console. Disconnect shift lock solenoid 2-pin harness connector from main wiring harness. Note harness connector terminal identification. *See Fig. 22.*

CAUTION: Battery voltage must be applied to correct shift lock solenoid harness connector terminals or diode inside shift lock solenoid will be damaged.

2) Momentarily connect battery positive terminal to terminal No. 1, and ground terminal No. 2'. *See Fig. 22.* Ensure shift lock solenoid operates with battery voltage applied. Replace shift lock solenoid if solenoid fails to operate.

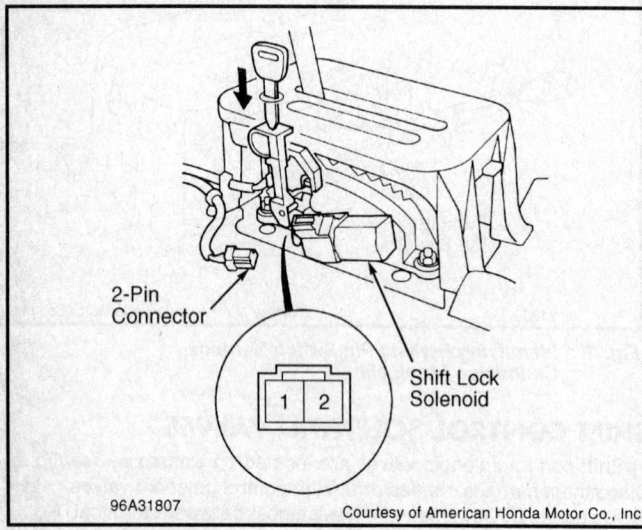

Fig. 22: *Identifying Shift Lock Solenoid Harness Connector Terminals*

REMOVAL & INSTALLATION

A/T GEAR POSITION SWITCH

Removal – Remove center console. Disconnect 14-pin harness connector from A/T gear position switch. Remove retaining nuts and A/T gear position switch.
Installation – **1)** Ensure parking brake is applied. Place switch slider on A/T gear position switch in Neutral. *See Fig. 23.* Place shift lever in Neutral.

2) Install A/T gear position switch and retaining nuts. DO NOT tighten nuts at this time. The A/T gear position switch must be adjusted.
3) To adjust A/T gear position switch, place shift lever in Park. Ensure retaining nuts are loose. Note 14-pin harness connector terminal identification. *See Fig. 14.*
4) Connect a DVOM between terminals No. 1 and 7. Move A/T gear position switch toward rear of console until continuity is present between terminals No. 1 and 7. Free play at lock pin should be .079" (2.0 mm). *See Fig. 23.*
5) Tighten retaining nuts. Check A/T gear position switch for correct continuity in all gears. See A/T GEAR POSITION SWITCH under COMPONENT TESTING. If proper adjustment cannot be obtained, check for damaged shift lever detent or bracket. Reconnect harness connector and install center console.

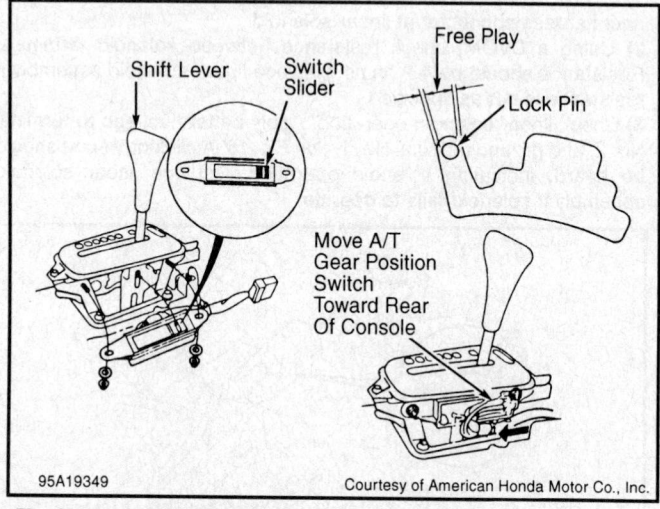

Fig. 23: *Installing A/T Gear Position Switch*

BRAKELIGHT SWITCH

Removal & Installation – **1)** Disconnect harness connector from brakelight switch. Remove lock nut from brakelight switch. Unscrew brakelight switch and remove. To install, screw brakelight switch inward until brakelight plunger is fully depressed.
2) Back off brakelight switch 1/4 turn. Ensure .010" (.30 mm) clearance is present between threaded end of brakelight switch and pad area on brake pedal *See Fig. 5.* Install and tighten lock nut. Reconnect harness electrical connector. Ensure brakelights and cruise control operate properly.

COUNTERSHAFT SPEED SENSOR

Removal & Installation – **1)** Disconnect harness connector at countershaft speed sensor. Countershaft speed sensor is located on rear left side of transaxle. *See Fig. 6.*
2) Remove clamp for wiring harness. Remove bolt, countershaft speed sensor and "O" ring. To install, reverse removal procedure using a NEW "O" ring. Install and tighten bolt to specification. See TORQUE SPECIFICATIONS.

KEY INTERLOCK SOLENOID

Removal & Installation – Key interlock solenoid cannot be serviced separately. Ignition lock assembly must be replaced.

LINEAR SOLENOID

Removal & Installation – **1)** Linear solenoid assembly is located on side of transaxle. *See Fig. 6.* Disconnect harness connector at linear solenoid.
2) Remove bolts, linear solenoid assembly and gasket. To install, reverse removal procedure using a NEW gasket. Tighten bolts to specification. See TORQUE SPECIFICATIONS.

LOCK-UP CONTROL SOLENOID VALVES

Removal & Installation – 1) Lock-up control solenoid valve assembly is located on transaxle. *See Fig. 6.* Disconnect harness connector at lock-up control solenoid valves.

2) Remove bolts, lock-up control solenoid valve assembly and gasket. To install, reverse removal procedure using a NEW gasket. Tighten bolts to specification. See TORQUE SPECIFICATIONS.

MAINSHAFT SPEED SENSOR

Removal & Installation – 1) Disconnect harness connector at mainshaft speed sensor. Mainshaft speed sensor is located on side of transaxle. *See Fig. 6.*

2) Remove clamp for wiring harness. Remove bolt, mainshaft speed sensor and "O" ring. To install, reverse removal procedure using a NEW "O" ring. Install and tighten bolt to specification. See TORQUE SPECIFICATIONS.

SHIFT CONTROL SOLENOID VALVES

Removal & Installation – 1) Shift control solenoid valve assembly is located on transaxle. *See Fig. 6.* Disconnect harness connector at shift control solenoid valves.

2) Remove bolts, shift control solenoid valve assembly and gasket. To install, reverse removal procedure using a NEW gasket. Tighten bolts to specification. See TORQUE SPECIFICATIONS.

TORQUE SPECIFICATIONS

TORQUE SPECIFICATIONS

Application	INCH Lbs. (N.m)
A/T Gear Position Switch Nut	84 (9.5)
Countershaft Speed Sensor Bolt	106 (12.0)
Linear Solenoid Assembly Bolt	106 (12.0)
Lock-Up Control Solencid Valve Assembly Bolt	106 (12.0)
Mainshaft Speed Sensor Bolt	106 (12.0)
Shift Control Solenoid Valve Assembly Bolt	106 (12.0)

WIRING DIAGRAMS

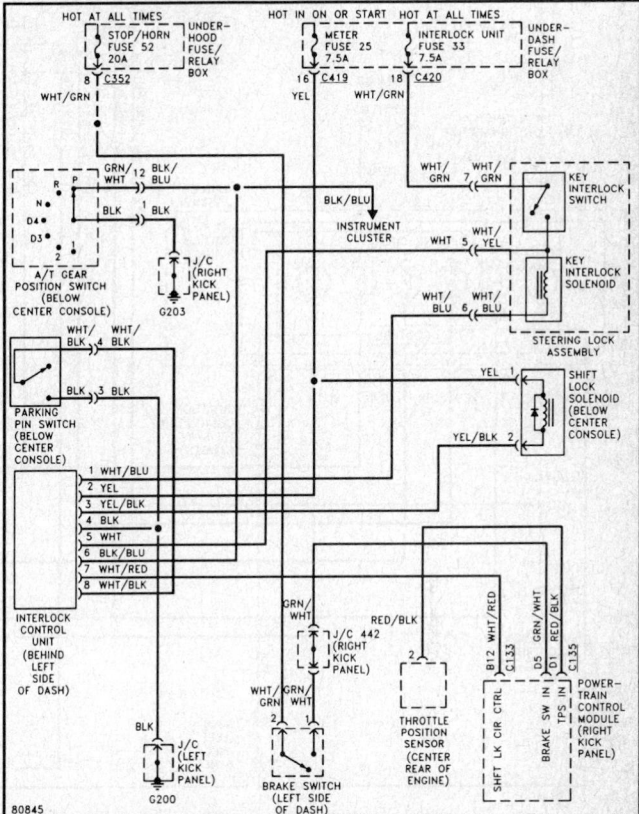

Fig. 24: Shift Interlock System Wiring Diagram (1996 Civic)

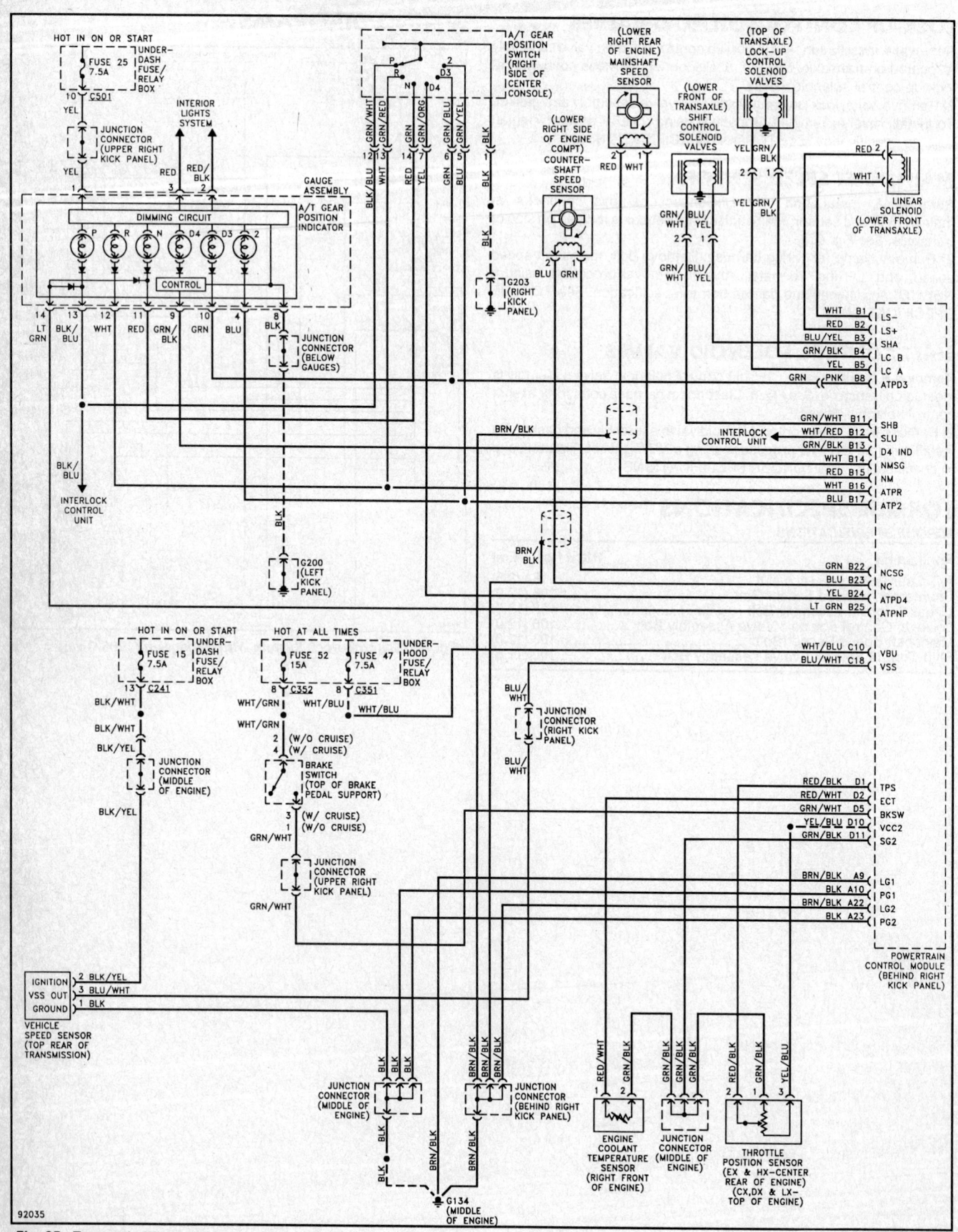

Fig. 25: Transaxle Wiring Diagram (1996 Civic)

92035

Civic (1995), Civic Del Sol

APPLICATION & LABOR TIMES

APPLICATION & LABOR TIMES

Vehicle Application	Labor Times		Trans. Model
	¹ R & I	² Overhaul	
1995 Civic	4.1	6.2	A24A
1995 Civic Del Sol	4.1	6.2	S24A
1996 Civic Del Sol	4.1	6.2	S24A

¹ – Removal and installation of transmission from vehicle chassis.

² – Bench overhaul time for transmission and differential. DOES NOT include removal and installation.

IDENTIFICATION

Transaxle model and serial number are stamped on the transaxle. *See Fig. 1.* Model and serial number may be required when ordering replacement components.

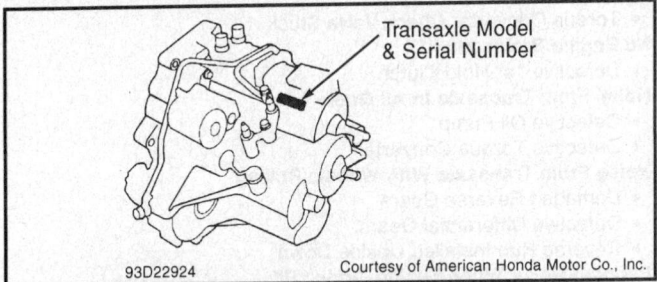

Transaxle Model & Serial Number

93D22924   Courtesy of American Honda Motor Co., Inc.

Fig. 1: Identifying Transaxle Model & Serial Number Location

DESCRIPTION

Transaxle has 4 forward speeds and one reverse. Transaxle consists of hydraulically actuated clutches, mainshaft, countershaft, sub-shaft, lock-up control solenoid valves and lock-up torque converter. *See Fig. 2.* Valve assembly consists of main valve body, secondary valve body, servo body, modulator valve body, lock-up valve body, regulator valve body and governor body. Torque converter lock-up is controlled by the lock-up control solenoid valves. The lock-up control solenoid valves are controlled by the Engine Control Module (ECM).

OPERATION

Shift lever has 7 positions. When shift lever is moved, manual valve on main valve body is moved by the shift cable. When certain transaxle gear combinations are engaged by clutches, power is transmitted from the mainshaft to the countershaft through the sub-shaft shaft to provide different gears. Shift lever positions operate as follows:

- **"P" (Park)** – Front wheels locked as parking pawl engages with parking gear on countershaft. All clutches are released. Neutral position switch, incorporated in A/T gear position switch, allows engine starting in this position.
- **"R" (Reverse)** – Reverse selector engages with countershaft reverse gear and 4th clutch is applied. Back-up light switch, incorporated in A/T gear position switch, allows back-up lights to be operated.
- **"N" (Neutral)** – All clutches are released. Neutral position switch, incorporated in A/T gear position switch, allows engine starting in this position.
- **"D₄" (Drive/4th)** – Transaxle starts in 1st gear and upshifts automatically to 2nd, 3rd and 4th gears. Transaxle will downshift through 3rd, 2nd and 1st gears until vehicle stops. When in 2nd, 3rd or 4th gear in this range, torque converter lock-up will operate through signal delivered by ECM.
- **"D₃" (Drive/3rd)** – Transaxle starts off in 1st gear and upshifts automatically to 2nd gear and 3rd gear. On deceleration, transaxle will downshift through 2nd gear to 1st gear. When in 3rd gear in this range, torque converter lock-up will operate through signal delivered from ECM.

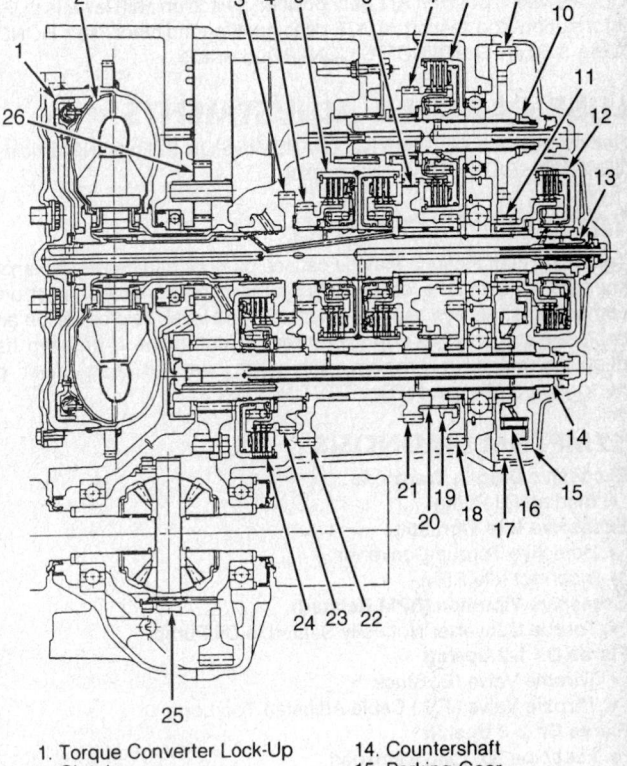

1. Torque Converter Lock-Up Clutch	14. Countershaft
2. Torque Converter	15. Parking Gear
3. Mainshaft 3rd Gear	16. One-Way Clutch
4. Mainshaft 2nd Gear	17. Countershaft 1st Gear
5. 2nd-4th Clutch	18. Countershaft Reverse Gear
6. Mainshaft 4th-Reverse Gear	19. Reverse Selector
7. Sub-Shaft 4th Gear	20. Reverse Selector Hub
8. 1st-Hold Clutch	21. Countershaft 4th Gear
9. Sub-Shaft 1st Gear	22. Countershaft 2nd Gear
10. Sub-Shaft	23. Countershaft 3rd Gear
11. Mainshaft 1st Gear	24. 3rd Clutch
12. 1st Clutch	25. Differential Assembly
13. Mainshaft	26. Oil Pump

93E22925   Courtesy of American Honda Motor Co., Inc.

Fig. 2: Identifying Transaxle Components

- **"2" (Second)** – Transaxle starts off and remains in 2nd gear for engine braking and better traction.
- **"1" (First)** – Transaxle starts off and remains in 1st gear for engine braking.

When in "D₄", 2nd, 3rd and 4th gears, or "D₃" 3rd gear, torque converter lock-up exists and transaxle mainshaft rotates at the same speed as engine crankshaft. Under certain conditions, torque converter lock-up clutch is applied during deceleration when in 2nd, 3rd and 4th gears. Torque converter lock-up is controlled by the ECM. The ECM receives various input signals and operates lock-up control solenoid valves. Operation of lock-up control solenoid valves controls the modulator pressure.

The ECM contains a self-diagnostic system, which will store fault code if failure or problem exists in lock-up control solenoid valve or wiring circuit. Fault code can be retrieved to determine transaxle problem area. For information on lock-up control solenoid valve controls, see HONDA A24A & S24A ELECTRONIC CONTROLS article.

Transaxle is equipped with shift and key interlock systems. Shift interlock system prevents shift lever from being moved from "P" position unless brake pedal is depressed and accelerator is in idle position. In case of a malfunction, shift lever can be released by placing ignition key in release slot near shift lever. Key interlock system prevents ignition key from being removed from ignition switch unless shift lever is in "P" position. For additional information on interlock systems, see HONDA A24A & S24A ELECTRONIC CONTROLS article.

AUTOMATIC TRANSMISSIONS
Honda A24A & S24A (Cont.)

The A/T gear position indicator on instrument panel contains lights to indicate which position A/T gear position switch on shift lever is in. For information and testing of A/T gear position indicator, see HONDA A24A & S24A ELECTRONIC CONTROLS article.

LUBRICATION & ADJUSTMENTS

See appropriate AUTOMATIC TRANSMISSION SERVICING article in TRANSMISSION SERVICING section.

TROUBLE SHOOTING

Transaxle malfunctions may be caused by poor engine performance, improper adjustments, or failure of hydraulic, mechanical or electronic components. Always begin by checking fluid level, fluid condition and cable adjustments. Perform road test to determine if problem has been corrected. If problem still exists, several tests must be performed on transaxle. See TESTING.

SYMPTOM DIAGNOSIS

Excessive Drag In Transaxle
- Binding Oil Pump

Excessive Idle Vibration
- Defective Torque Converter
- Incorrect Idle RPM

Excessive Vibration (RPM Related)
- Torque Converter Not Fully Seated In Oil Pump

Flares On 1-2 Upshift
- Throttle Valve "B" Stuck
- Throttle Valve (T.V.) Cable Adjusted Too Long

Flares On 2-3 Upshift
- Feedpipe "O" Ring Damaged
- Throttle Valve "B" Stuck
- Throttle Valve (T.V.) Cable Adjusted Too Long
- 2-3 Orifice Control Valve Stuck

Flares On 3-4 Upshift
- Feedpipe "O" Ring Damaged
- Throttle Valve "B" Stuck
- Throttle Valve (T.V.) Cable Adjusted Too Long
- 2/3-4 Orifice Control Valve Stuck

Gear Whine That Changes With RPM & Shifts
- Defective 1st Clutch
- Defective 3rd Gears

Gear Whine That Changes With Speed
- Defective Differential Gears
- Shift Fork Bent

Harsh Downshift At Closed Throttle
- Throttle Valve "B" Stuck

Harsh Kickdown Shifts
- Clutch Pressure Control Valve Stuck
- Throttle Valve (T.V.) Cable Adjusted Too Short
- 4-3 Kickdown Valve Stuck
- 4th Exhaust Valve Stuck

Harsh Shift When Manually Shifting To "1"
- Defective 1st-Hold Accumulator

Harsh Upshifts & Downshifts
- Clutch Pressure Control Valve Stuck
- Improper Type ATF
- Incorrect Clutch Clearance
- Throttle Valve "B" Stuck
- Throttle Valve (T.V.) Cable Adjusted Too Short
- 2-3 Orifice Control Valve Stuck
- 4-3 Kickdown Valve Stuck

Harsh 1-2 Upshift
- Defective 2nd Clutch
- Throttle Valve (T.V.) Cable Adjusted Too Short

Harsh 2-1 Kickdown Shift
- Defective One-Way Clutch

Harsh 2-3 Upshift
- Clutch Pressure Control Valve Stuck
- Defective 3rd Clutch
- Throttle Valve (T.V.) Cable Adjusted Too Short
- 2-3 Orifice Control Valve Stuck

Harsh 3-4 Upshift
- Clutch Pressure Control Valve Stuck
- Defective 4th Clutch
- Throttle Valve (T.V.) Cable Adjusted Too Short
- 2/3-4 Orifice Control Valve Stuck

Lock-Up Clutch Does Not Lock-Up Smoothly
- Defective Torque Converter
- Lock-Up Control Valve Stuck
- Lock-Up Shift Valve Stuck

Lock-Up Clutch Does Not Operate Properly
- Improperly Adjusted Throttle Valve (T.V.) Cable
- Lock-Up Control Valve Stuck
- Lock-Up Shift Valve Stuck
- Lock-Up Timing Valve Stuck
- Throttle Valve "B" Stuck
- Torque Converter Check Valve Stuck

No Engine Braking In "1"
- Defective 1st-Hold Clutch

Noise From Transaxle In All Gears
- Defective Oil Pump
- Defective Torque Converter

Noise From Transaxle With Wheels Rolling
- Damaged Reverse Gears
- Defective Differential Gears
- Reverse Hub Installed Upside Down

Popping Noise When Taking Off In "R"
- Damaged Reverse Gears
- Shift Fork Bent
- Worn Reverse Selector

Ratcheting Noise When Shifting To "R"
- Damaged Reverse Gears
- Defective Oil Pump
- Regulator Valve Stuck
- Shift Fork Bent
- Worn Reverse Selector

Ratcheting Noise When Shifting From "R" To "P" Or "N"
- Damaged Reverse Gears
- Damaged 4th Gears
- Shift Fork Bent
- Worn Reverse Selector

Shifts Erratically
- Improperly Installed Valves Or Springs
- Modulator Valve Stuck
- Throttle Valve (T.V.) Cable Adjusted Too Short

Slips In All Gears
- Defective Oil Pump
- Fluid Strainer Clogged
- Regulator Valve Stuck

Slips In 1st Gear
- Defective One-Way Clutch
- Defective 1st Clutch Or 1st Accumulator
- Feedpipe "O" Ring Damaged

Slips In Reverse
- Defective 4th Clutch Or 4th Accumulator
- Servo Valve Stuck

Slips In 2nd Gear
- Clutch Pressure Control Valve Stuck
- Defective Seal Rings Or Guide
- Defective 2nd Clutch Or 2nd Accumulator
- 2-3 Shift Valve Stuck

Slips In 3rd Gear
- Clutch Pressure Control Valve Stuck
- Defective 3rd Clutch Or 3rd Accumulator
- Feedpipe "O" Ring Damaged
- 3-4 Shift Valve Stuck

Slips In 4th Gear
- Clutch Pressure Control Valve Stuck
- Defective 4th Clutch Or 4th Accumulator

Upshifts Late
- Modulator Valve Stuck

Vehicle Locks In "R"
- Parking Brake Lever Installed Upside Down
- Shift Fork Retaining Bolt Not Installed

Vehicle Moves In All Gears Except "R"
- Defective Or Improperly Adjusted Shift Cable
- Defective Or Worn Reverse Gears
- Defective 4th Clutch
- Servo Control Valve Stuck
- Servo Valve Stuck
- Shift Fork Bent
- Worn Reverse Selector

Vehicle Moves In All Gears Except "2"
- Defective Seal Rings Or Guide
- Defective 2nd Clutch Or 2nd Accumulator

Vehicle Moves In "N"
- Defective Or Improperly Adjusted Shift Cable
- Defective 1st, 2nd, 3rd Or 4th Clutch
- Incorrect Gear Or Clutch Clearance

Vehicle Moves In "R" & "2" Only
- Defective One-Way Clutch
- Defective 1st Clutch Or 1st Accumulator
- Feedpipe "O" Ring Damaged

Vehicle Will Not Move
- Defective Oil Pump
- Defective Or Improperly Adjusted Shift Cable
- Fluid Strainer Clogged
- Regulator Valve Stuck

Vehicle Will Not Move In "D_3" Or "D_4"
- One-Way Clutch Installed Upside Down

Will Not Downshift To 1st Gear
- Defective 1st-Hold Clutch
- 1-2 Shift Valve Stuck

Will Not Shift Into 4th Gear When In "D_4"
- Defective Or Improperly Adjusted Shift Cable
- 3-4 Shift Valve Stuck
- 4th Accumulator Stuck
- 4th Exhaust Valve Stuck

Will Not Upshift (Stays In 1st Gear)
- Clutch Pressure Control Valve Stuck
- Modulator Valve Stuck
- 1-2 Shift Valve Stuck

TESTING

ROAD TEST

NOTE: If shift lever cannot be moved from "P" position with brake pedal depressed and accelerator at idle position, check shift interlock system. See HONDA A24A & S24A ELECTRONIC CONTROLS article.

1) Warm engine to normal operating temperature. Apply parking brake and block wheels. Start engine. Move shift lever to "D_4" position while depressing brake pedal. Depress accelerator pedal and release it suddenly. Engine should not stall.

2) Repeat step 1) with shift lever in "D_3" position. Ensure engine does not stall. Manufacturer recommends monitoring of Throttle Position (TP) sensor voltage when performing road test to ensure proper throttle opening for verifying shift points and lock-up of torque converter.

3) Remove door sill molding and lower dash panel on passenger's side and remove small cover on passenger's side kick panel. Pull carpet back for access to the Powertrain Control Module (PCM), located on passenger's side, below carpet. See Fig. 3.

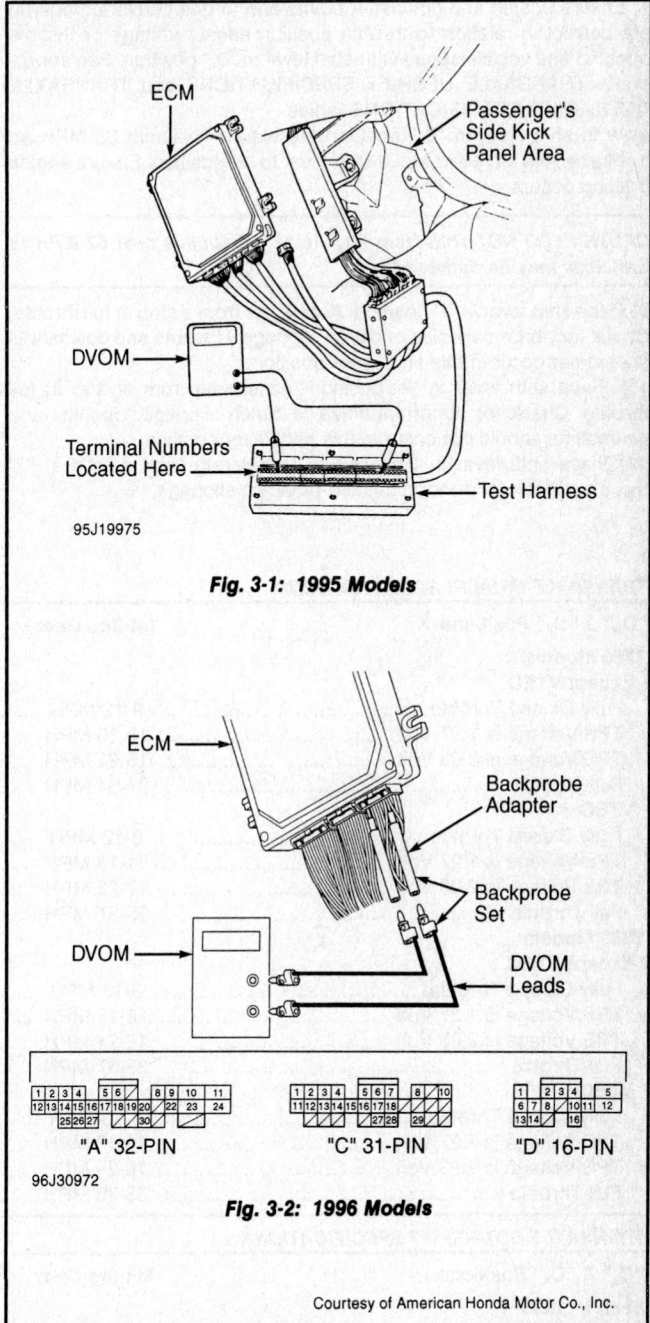

Fig. 3-1: *1995 Models*

Fig. 3-2: *1996 Models*

Courtesy of American Honda Motor Co., Inc.

Fig. 3: *Measuring TP Sensor Voltage*

4) Remove PCM cover located above PCM. Ensure ignition is off. On 1995 models, install Test Harness (07LAJ-PT3010A) between PCM and PCM electrical connectors. Install Digital Volt-Ohmmeter (DVOM) on test harness with positive lead at terminal D11 and negative lead at terminal D22 to monitor throttle position sensor voltage. Terminal numbers are on top of test harness. *See Fig. 3.*

5) On 1996 models, install Backprobe Test Set (07SAZ-001000A) or equivalent between PCM and DVOM leads. *See Fig. 3.* Using DVOM, with positive lead at terminal D1 and negative lead at terminal D11. *See Fig. 3.* Ensure Digital Volt-Ohmmeter (DVOM) is set for measuring voltage.

6) On all models, road test vehicle and check for abnormal noise and clutch slippage. See CLUTCH APPLICATION table for clutch engagement.

7) Ensure upshift and downshift points and torque converter lock-up are correct in relation to throttle position sensor voltage or throttle opening and vehicle speed with shift lever in "D₄" position. See appropriate TRANSAXLE UPSHIFT SPECIFICATIONS and TRANSAXLE DOWNSHIFT SPECIFICATIONS tables.

8) With shift lever in "D₄" position, accelerate to about 35 MPH so transaxle is in 4th gear. Move shift lever to "2" position. Ensure engine braking occurs.

CAUTION: DO NOT shift from "D₄" to "2" at speeds over 62 MPH or transaxle may be damaged.

---

9) Place shift lever in "1" position. Accelerate from a stop at full throttle. Check for abnormal noise or clutch slippage. Upshifts and downshifts should not occur in this shift lever position.

10) Place shift lever in "2" position. Accelerate from a stop at full throttle. Check for abnormal noise or clutch slippage. Upshifts and downshifts should not occur in this shift lever position.

11) Place shift lever in "R" position. Accelerate from a stop at full throttle. Check for abnormal noise or clutch slippage.

12) Park vehicle on a slope. Apply parking brake. Place shift lever in "P" position. Release parking brake. Ensure vehicle does not move. If vehicle moves, check for defective shift cable or parking components.

13) Ensure ignition is off. Remove test harness and reinstall electrical connectors, PCM cover, carpet and door sill molding.

CLUTCH APPLICATION

Shift Lever Position	Elements In Use
"P" & "N"	No Clutches Are Applied
"R"	4th Clutch
"D₄"	
1st Gear	1st Clutch
2nd Gear	¹ 2nd Clutch
3rd Gear	¹ 3rd Clutch
4th Gear	¹ 4th Clutch
"D₃"	
1st Gear	1st Clutch
2nd Gear	¹ 2nd Clutch
3rd Gear	¹ 3rd Clutch
"2"	¹ 2nd Clutch
"1"	1st-Hold Clutch & 1st Clutch

¹ – The 1st clutch engages, but driving power is not transmitted, as one-way clutch slips.

TRANSAXLE UPSHIFT SPECIFICATIONS

"D₃" & "D₄" Positions	1st-2nd Gear	2nd-3rd Gear	3rd-4th Gear
1995 Models			
Except VTEC			
Fully Closed Throttle	9-12 MPH	23-25 MPH	31-33 MPH
TPS Voltage is 1.27 Volt	13-16 MPH	31-33 MPH	41-45 MPH
TPS Voltage is 2.03 Volt	16-21 MPH	38-45 MPH	51-59 MPH
Full Throttle	31-34 MPH	57-61 MPH	89-95 MPH
VTEC			
Fully Closed Throttle	9-12 MPH	23-25 MPH	31-33 MPH
TPS Voltage is 1.27 Volt	14-16 MPH	32-35 MPH	42-46 MPH
TPS Voltage is 2.03 Volt	17-22 MPH	41-48 MPH	53-61 MPH
Full Throttle	35-37 MPH	65-69 MPH	94-101 MPH
1996 Models			
Except VTEC			
Fully Closed Throttle	9-13 MPH	23-27 MPH	31-35 MPH
TPS Voltage is 1.27 Volt	13-17 MPH	31-35 MPH	41-47 MPH
TPS Voltage is 2.03 Volt	16-24 MPH	38-50 MPH	52-63 MPH
Full Throttle	33-37 MPH	59-67 MPH	92-103 MPH
VTEC			
Fully Closed Throttle	9-13 MPH	23-27 MPH	31-35 MPH
TPS Voltage is 1.27 Volt	13-17 MPH	31-35 MPH	41-47 MPH
TPS Voltage is 2.03 Volt	16-24 MPH	38-50 MPH	51-63 MPH
Full Throttle	33-38 MPH	61-68 MPH	94-104 MPH

TRANSAXLE DOWNSHIFT SPECIFICATIONS

"D₃" & "D₄" Positions	4th-3rd Gear	3rd-2nd Gear	2nd-1st Gear
1995 Models			
Except VTEC			
Fully Closed Throttle	¹	18-20 MPH	6-8 MPH
Fully Open Throttle	75-81 MPH	51-56 MPH	25-28 MPH
VTEC			
Fully Closed Throttle	¹	18-20 MPH	6-8 MPH
Fully Open Throttle	81-87 MPH	58-62 MPH	24-26 MPH
1996 Models			
Except VTEC			
Fully Closed Throttle	¹	18-22 MPH	6-9 MPH
Fully Open Throttle	79-89 MPH	54-62 MPH	24-28 MPH
VTEC			
Fully Closed Throttle	¹	18-22 MPH	5-9 MPH
Fully Open Throttle	81-91 MPH	55-63 MPH	25-29 MPH

¹ – Specification is not available from manufacturer.

HYDRAULIC PRESSURE TEST SPECIFICATIONS (Cont.)

Application	Shift Lever Position	Pressure psi (kPa)
Clutch Pressure (Cont.)		
1996 Models		
Engine Speed At 2000 RPM	"R"	114-128 (800-900)
Transaxle T.V. Lever Fully Closed [1]	"D₄"	50-57 (350-400)
Transaxle T.V. Lever Open More Than 1/8 [2]	"D₄"	114-128 (800-900)
Clutch Low Pressure		
Transaxle T.V. Lever Fully Closed [1]		
2nd, 3rd Or 4th Clutch	"D₄"	50-57 (350-400)
Clutch High Pressure		
1995 Models		
Except VTEC		
Transaxle T.V. Lever Lifted Upward		
1/8 Distance Of T.V. Lever Travel		
2nd, 3rd Or 4th Clutch	"D₄"	107-121 (750-850)
VTEC		
Transaxle T.V. Lever Lifted Upward		
1/8 Distance Of T.V. Lever Travel		
2nd, 3rd Or 4th Clutch	"D₄"	114-128 (800-900)
1996 Models		
Transaxle T.V. Lever Lifted Upward		
1/8 Distance Of T.V. Lever Travel		
2nd, 3rd Or 4th Clutch	"D₄"	114-128 (800-900)
Throttle Valve Pressure		
Throttle Valve "A"		
1995 Models		
Transaxle T.V. Lever Fully Open [3]	"D₃" Or "D₄"	68-71 (480-500)
1996 Models		
Except VTEC		
Transaxle T.V. Lever Fully Open [3]	"D₃" Or "D₄"	73-75 (510-530)
VTEC		
Transaxle T.V. Lever Fully Open [3]	"D₃" Or "D₄"	75-78 (530-550)
Throttle Valve "B"		
1995 Models		
Except VTEC		
Transaxle T.V. Lever Fully Open [3]	"D₃" Or "D₄"	107-121 (750-850)
VTEC		
Transaxle T.V. Lever Fully Open [3]	"D₃" Or "D₄"	114-128 (800-900)
1996 Models		
Transaxle T.V. Lever Fully Open [3]	"D₃" Or "D₄"	114-128 (800-900)
Governor Pressure [4]		
1995 Models	"D₃" Or "D₄"	25-27 (179-192)
1996 Models		
Except VTEC	"D₃" Or "D₄"	25-27 (179-192)
VTEC	"D₃" Or "D₄"	25-28 (179-194)

[1] – Check pressure with engine speed at 2000 RPM. T.V. cable must be disconnected. Fully closed position is with transaxle T.V. lever in released position and not being pulled upward by T.V. cable.

[2] – Check pressure with engine speed at 2000 RPM. T.V. cable must be disconnected. Open position is with transaxle T.V. lever being pulled upward 1/8 the distance of lever travel.

[3] – Check pressure with engine speed at 1000 RPM. Open position is with transaxle T.V. lever being pulled fully upward.

[4] – Check governor pressure with vehicle speed at 38 MPH.

3) Start engine and allow to idle. Move shift lever to "D₄" position. Slowly increase engine speed until pressure is indicated on pressure gauge. Release throttle, allowing engine to idle and note clutch low pressure reading.

4) With engine idling, lift transaxle T.V. lever upward approximately half the distance of lever travel. Increase engine speed and note highest pressure reading. This is the clutch high pressure.

5) Repeat procedure on remaining clutches. Ensure clutch low/high pressure is within specification. See appropriate HYDRAULIC PRESSURE TEST SPECIFICATIONS table. If clutch low/high pressure is not within specification, see HYDRAULIC PRESSURE TROUBLE SHOOTING table. Shut engine off.

6) Remove pressure gauge set. Using NEW seal washer, install and tighten pressure tap plug to specification. See TORQUE SPECIFICATIONS. Reconnect T.V. cable.

NOTE: Throttle valve pressure must be checked at throttle valve "A" and "B" pressure taps on transaxle.

Throttle Valve Pressure Test – 1) Disconnect Throttle Valve (T.V.) cable from transaxle T.V. lever. With engine off, remove pressure tap plug from throttle valve "A" or "B" pressure tap. *See Fig. 4.*

NOTE: When disconnecting T.V. cable, unhook cable from transaxle T.V. lever. DO NOT loosen lock nuts used for cable adjustment.

2) Attach pressure gauge to appropriate throttle valve pressure tap using NEW seal washer. Tighten hose fitting to 13 ft. lbs. (18 N.m).

3) Start engine and operate at 1000 RPM with shift lever in "D₃" or "D₄" position. Approximately 0-.7 psi (0-5 kPa) should exist with transaxle T.V. lever closed (released position).

4) Lift transaxle T.V. lever on transaxle to fully open position. Note throttle valve pressure reading.

5) Ensure throttle valve pressure is within specification. See appropriate HYDRAULIC PRESSURE TEST SPECIFICATIONS table. If pressure is not within specification, see HYDRAULIC PRESSURE TROUBLE SHOOTING table. Shut engine off.

6) Remove pressure gauge set. Using NEW seal washer, install and tighten pressure tap plug to specification. See TORQUE SPECIFICATIONS. Reconnect T.V. cable.

HYDRAULIC PRESSURE TROUBLE SHOOTING

Application	Probable Cause
Line Pressure	
Low Or No Pressure	Defective Torque Converter, Defective Torque Converter Check Valve, Defective Oil Pump Pressure Regulator, Defective Oil Pump
Clutch Pressure	
Low Or No 1st Clutch Pressure	Defective 1st Clutch
Low Or No 1st-Hold Clutch Pressure	Defective 1st-Hold Clutch
Low Or No 2nd Clutch Pressure	Defective 2nd Clutch
Low Or No 3rd Clutch Pressure	Defective 3rd Clutch
Low Or No 4th Clutch Pressure	Defective 4th Clutch, Defective Servo Valve On 4th Clutch
Clutch Low/High Pressure	
Low Or No 2nd Clutch Pressure	Defective 2nd Clutch
Low Or No 3rd Clutch Pressure	Defective 3rd Clutch
Low Or No 4th Clutch Pressure	Defective 4th Clutch
Throttle Valve Pressure	
High, Low Or No Throttle Valve "A" Pressure	Defective Throttle Valve "A", Defective Modulator Valve
High, Low Or No Throttle Valve "B" Pressure	Defective Throttle Valve "B"
Governor Pressure	
Low Or No Pressure	Defective Governor Valve

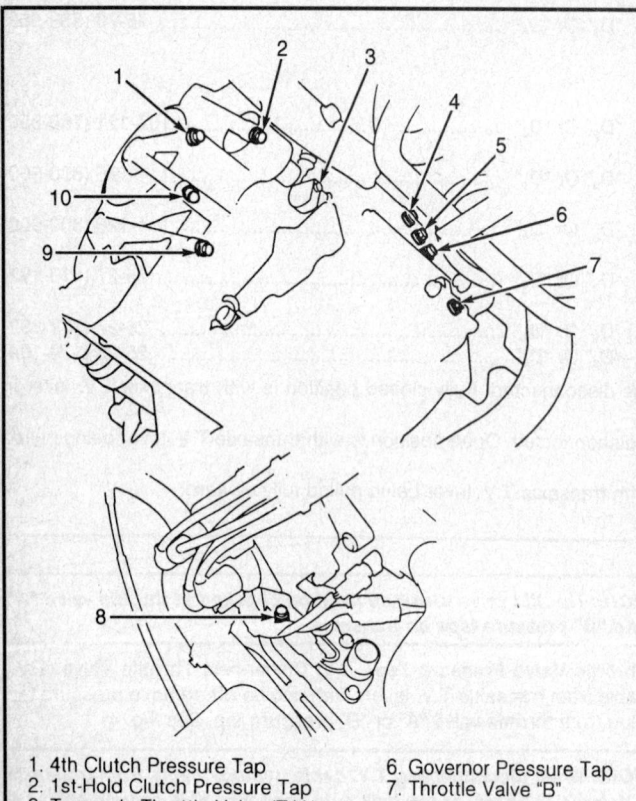

1. 4th Clutch Pressure Tap
2. 1st-Hold Clutch Pressure Tap
3. Transaxle Throttle Valve (T.V.) Lever
4. Throttle Valve "A" Pressure Tap
5. 2nd Clutch Pressure Tap
6. Governor Pressure Tap
7. Throttle Valve "B" Pressure Tap
8. Line Pressure Tap
9. 3rd Clutch Pressure Tap
10. 1st Clutch Pressure Tap

93F22926   Courtesy of American Honda Motor Co., Inc.

Fig. 4: Identifying Transaxle Pressure Taps

Governor Pressure Test – **1)** With engine off, remove pressure plug from governor pressure tap on transaxle. *See Fig. 4.* Attach pressure gauge to pressure tap using NEW seal washer. Tighten hose fitting to 13 ft. lbs. (18 N.m).

2) Start engine. Place shift lever in "D₃" or "D₄" position. Accelerate to 38 MPH and note governor pressure.

3) Ensure governor pressure is within specification. See appropriate HYDRAULIC PRESSURE TEST SPECIFICATIONS table. If governor pressure is not within specification, see HYDRAULIC PRESSURE TROUBLE SHOOTING table. Shut engine off.

4) Remove pressure gauge set. Using NEW seal washer, install and tighten pressure tap plug to specification. See TORQUE SPECIFICATIONS.

ON-VEHICLE SERVICE

AXLE SHAFTS

See appropriate AXLE SHAFTS article in AXLE SHAFTS & TRANSFER CASES section.

OIL COOLER FLUSHING

1) Attach Oil Cooler Flusher (J38405-A) to oil cooler lines. *See Fig. 5.* Fill oil cooler flusher tank 2/3 full with Flushing Fluid (J35944-20). DO NOT use any other flushing fluid.

2) Ensure water and air valves on oil cooler flusher are off. Apply 80-120 psi (550-829 kPa) air pressure to oil cooler flusher. Turn oil cooler flusher water valve on so water will flow through oil cooler for 10 seconds. Replace oil cooler if water will not flow through oil cooler. Shut water valve off.

3) Depress and hold mixing trigger on oil cooler flusher downward. Turn water valve on and flush oil cooler for 2 minutes. Turn air valve on for 5 seconds every 15-20 seconds to create a surging action. Turn water valve off. Release mixing trigger.

4) Disconnect oil cooler flusher and reverse hoses so oil cooler can be flushed in opposite direction. Repeat steps **2)** and **3)**.

5) Turn water valve on. Rinse oil cooler for at least one minute. Once oil cooler is flushed in both directions, turn water off. Turn air valve on for 2 minutes or until no moisture is visible from drain hose.

CAUTION: Ensure no moisture exists in oil cooler, as moisture can damage transaxle.

---

6) Turn air off. Disconnect oil cooler flusher. Reconnect inlet line on oil cooler. Once transaxle is installed, attach drain hose on return line and place in oil container. Ensure transaxle is in "P" position. Fill transaxle with ATF.

7) Start engine and operate for approximately 30 seconds or until one quart (.9L) of ATF is discharged from return line. Shut engine off. Remove drain hose. Reinstall return line. Fill transaxle to proper level.

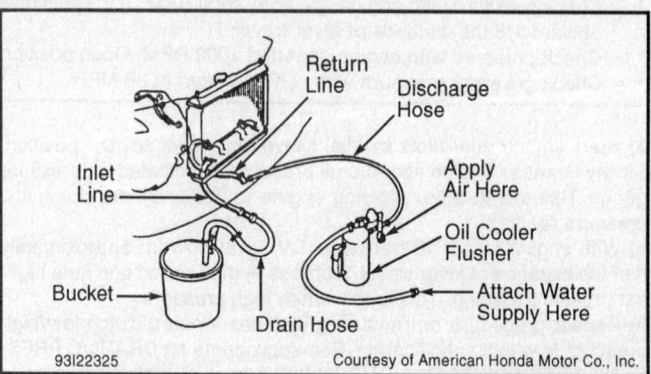

93122325   Courtesy of American Honda Motor Co., Inc.

Fig. 5: Installing Oil Cooler Flusher

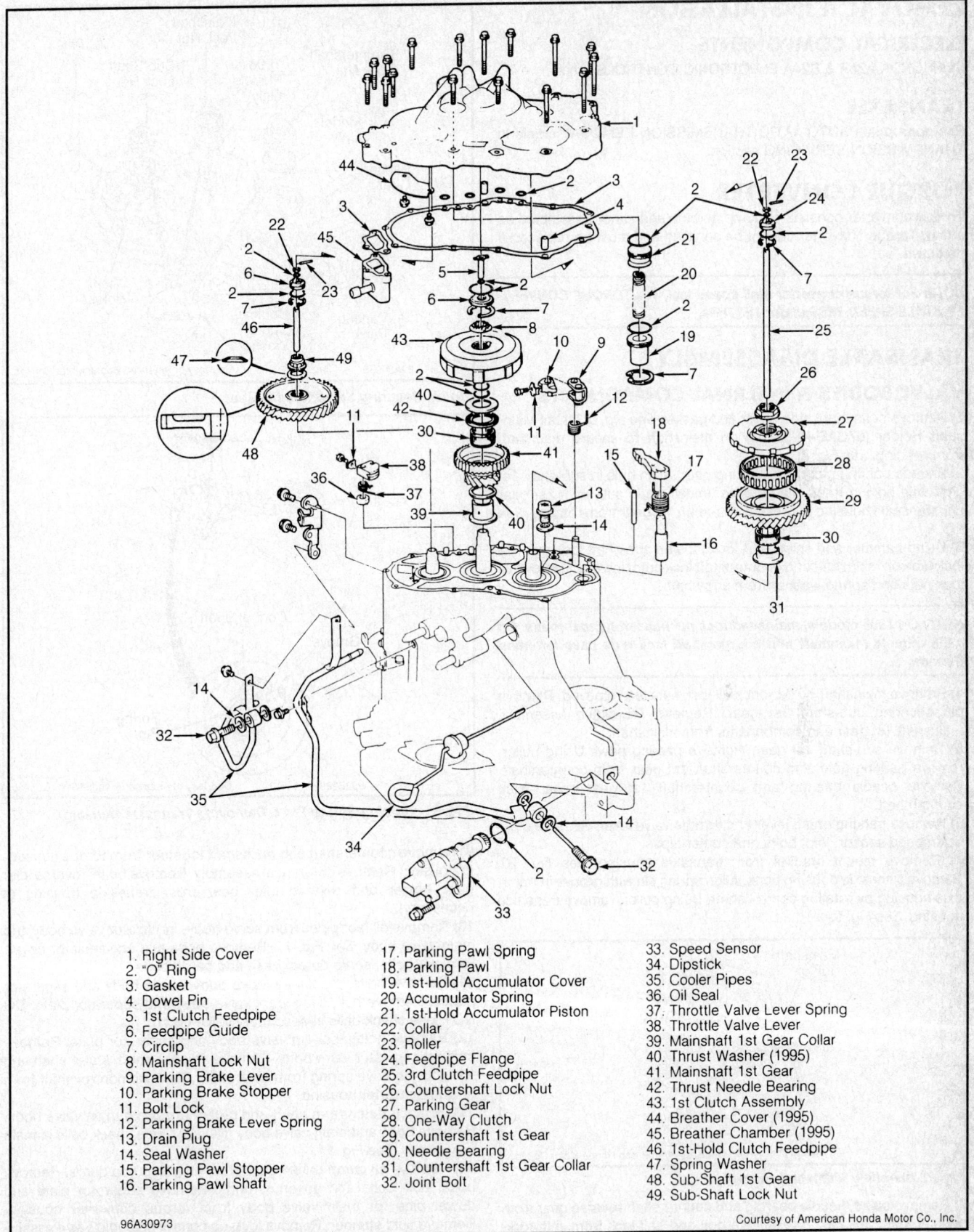

1. Right Side Cover
2. "O" Ring
3. Gasket
4. Dowel Pin
5. 1st Clutch Feedpipe
6. Feedpipe Guide
7. Circlip
8. Mainshaft Lock Nut
9. Parking Brake Lever
10. Parking Brake Stopper
11. Bolt Lock
12. Parking Brake Lever Spring
13. Drain Plug
14. Seal Washer
15. Parking Pawl Stopper
16. Parking Pawl Shaft

17. Parking Pawl Spring
18. Parking Pawl
19. 1st-Hold Accumulator Cover
20. Accumulator Spring
21. 1st-Hold Accumulator Piston
22. Collar
23. Roller
24. Feedpipe Flange
25. 3rd Clutch Feedpipe
26. Countershaft Lock Nut
27. Parking Gear
28. One-Way Clutch
29. Countershaft 1st Gear
30. Needle Bearing
31. Countershaft 1st Gear Collar
32. Joint Bolt

33. Speed Sensor
34. Dipstick
35. Cooler Pipes
36. Oil Seal
37. Throttle Valve Lever Spring
38. Throttle Valve Lever
39. Mainshaft 1st Gear Collar
40. Thrust Washer (1995)
41. Mainshaft 1st Gear
42. Thrust Needle Bearing
43. 1st Clutch Assembly
44. Breather Cover (1995)
45. Breather Chamber (1995)
46. 1st-Hold Clutch Feedpipe
47. Spring Washer
48. Sub-Shaft 1st Gear
49. Sub-Shaft Lock Nut

96A30973

Courtesy of American Honda Motor Co., Inc.

Fig. 6: Exploded View Of Right Side Cover & Components

AUTOMATIC TRANSMISSIONS
Honda A24A & S24A (Cont.)

REMOVAL & INSTALLATION

ELECTRICAL COMPONENTS

See HONDA A24A & S24A ELECTRONIC CONTROLS article.

TRANSAXLE

See appropriate AUTOMATIC TRANSMISSION REMOVAL article in TRANSMISSION SERVICING section.

TORQUE CONVERTER

Torque converter consists of pump, turbine and stator assembled as a unit. Torque converter cannot be serviced and must be replaced if defective.

NOTE: *For torque converter stall speed test, see TORQUE CONVERTER STALL SPEED TEST under TESTING.*

TRANSAXLE DISASSEMBLY

VALVE BODIES & INTERNAL COMPONENTS

1) Remove bolts, right side cover and gasket. *See Fig. 6.* Install Mainshaft Holder (07GAB-PF50101) on mainshaft to secure mainshaft from rotating. *See Fig. 7.*

2) Engage parking pawl with parking gear. Align hole in sub-shaft 1st gear with hole in transaxle housing. Install pin in sub-shaft 1st gear and transaxle housing to prevent sub-shaft 1st gear from rotating. *See Fig. 8.*

3) Using hammer and chisel, cut lock tabs on sub-shaft lock nut. Pry lock tabs on mainshaft and countershaft lock nuts upward. Remove all lock nuts and spring washer from sub-shaft.

NOTE: *On 1995 models, mainshaft lock nut has left-hand threads. On 1996 models mainshaft and countershaft lock nuts have left-hand threads.*

---

4) Remove mainshaft holder once all lock nuts are removed. Remove pin securing sub-shaft 1st gear. Remove 1st clutch assembly, mainshaft 1st gear and components from mainshaft.

5) Remove sub-shaft 1st gear. Remove parking pawl. Using puller, remove parking gear and countershaft 1st gear from countershaft. Remove needle bearing and countershaft 1st gear collar from countershaft.

6) Remove parking brake lever and throttle valve lever. Remove dipstick, speed sensor, joint bolts and cooler pipes.

7) Remove mount bracket from transaxle housing. *See Fig. 10.* Remove transaxle housing bolts. Align spring pin with groove in transaxle housing by rotating control shaft. Using puller, remove transaxle housing. *See Fig. 9.*

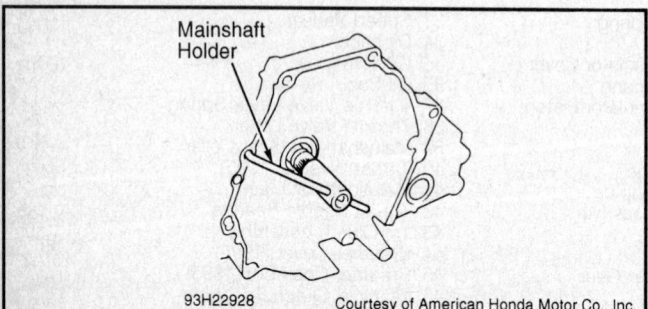

Fig. 7: *Installing Mainshaft Holder*

8) Remove collar, needle bearing and countershaft reverse gear from countershaft. *See Fig. 10.* Remove bolt and bolt lock from shift fork. Remove shift fork and reverse selector from countershaft.

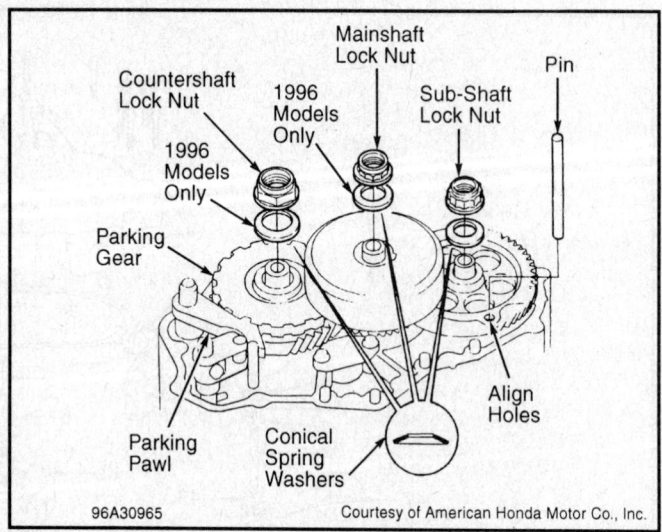

Fig. 8: *Securing Sub-Shaft 1st Gear*

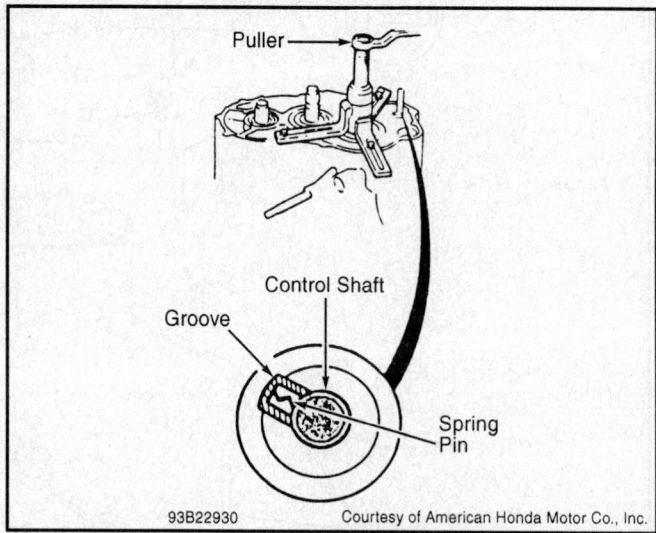

Fig. 9: *Aligning Spring Pin & Removing Transaxle Housing*

9) Remove countershaft and mainshaft together from torque converter housing. Remove differential assembly. Remove bolts, reverse idler gear holder and reverse idler gear from transaxle housing (if necessary).

10) Remove oil feedpipes from servo body, modulator valve body and main valve body. *See Fig. 11.* Remove bolts and accumulator cover. Remove bolts, servo detent base and baffle plate.

11) Remove bolts, modulator valve body, servo body and separator plates. Remove bolt, secondary valve body and separator plate. DO NOT lose check balls in secondary valve body.

12) Remove bolts, lock-up valve body and separator plate. Remove bolt and regulator valve body. Remove stopper shaft, stator shaft and "O" ring. Remove spring from detent arm. Remove control shaft from torque converter housing.

13) Remove detent arm shaft and detent arm from main valve body. Remove bolts and main valve body. DO NOT lose check balls in main valve body. *See Fig. 11.*

14) Remove oil pump driven gear shaft and oil pump gears. Remove bolts, bolt locks and governor body. Remove separator plate and dowel pins for main valve body from torque converter housing. Remove fluid strainer. Remove lock-up control solenoid valve assembly (if necessary).

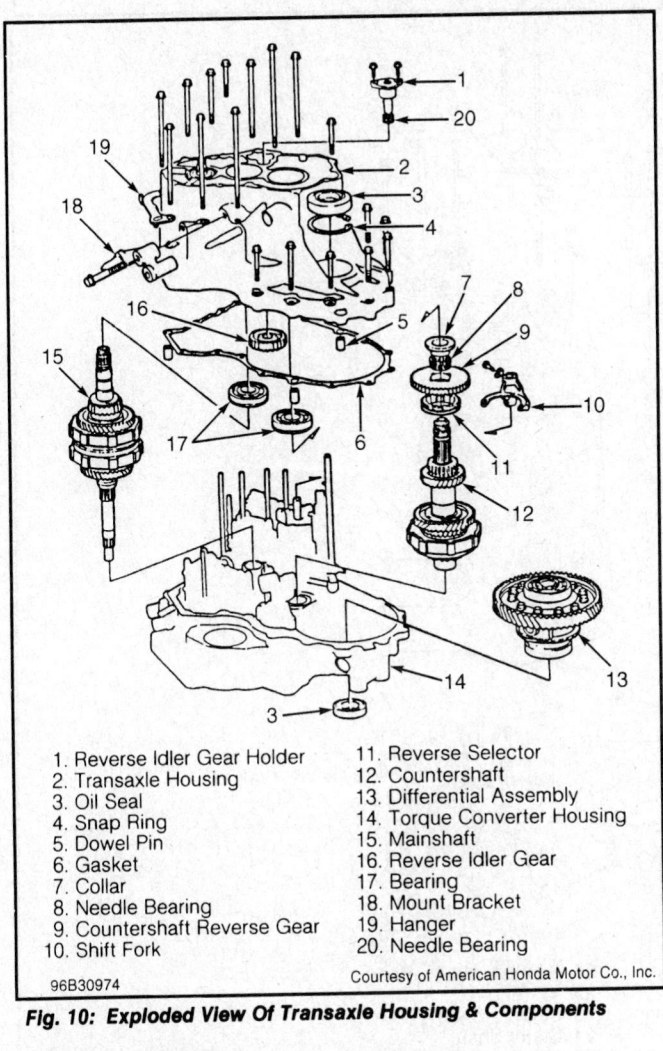

1. Reverse Idler Gear Holder
2. Transaxle Housing
3. Oil Seal
4. Snap Ring
5. Dowel Pin
6. Gasket
7. Collar
8. Needle Bearing
9. Countershaft Reverse Gear
10. Shift Fork
11. Reverse Selector
12. Countershaft
13. Differential Assembly
14. Torque Converter Housing
15. Mainshaft
16. Reverse Idler Gear
17. Bearing
18. Mount Bracket
19. Hanger
20. Needle Bearing

96B30974   Courtesy of American Honda Motor Co., Inc.

Fig. 10: Exploded View Of Transaxle Housing & Components

COMPONENT DISASSEMBLY & REASSEMBLY

VALVE BODY CLEANING & INSPECTION

NOTE: The following procedure should be used when servicing valves and valve bodies after disassembly.

1) Clean components with solvent and dry with compressed air. Replace valve body as an assembly if any parts are worn or damaged.
2) Ensure all valves slide freely in their bores. If valves do not slide freely, polish burrs or rough areas using No. 600 sandpaper soaked in ATF for at least 30 minutes. Sandpaper can be rolled into a tube shape for deburring valve bores. Thoroughly clean main valve body and components if polishing was needed.
3) Ensure spring free length is within specification. See appropriate SPRING SPECIFICATIONS table. Replace springs if not within specification.

MAIN VALVE BODY

CAUTION: When disassembling main valve body, place components in order and mark spring locations for reassembly reference. DO NOT use force to remove components. DO NOT use magnet to remove check balls, as check balls may become magnetized. Note direction of valve cap installation before removing from main valve body.

Disassembly – Disassemble main valve body. See Fig. 12. Use care when removing valve covers, valve cap or spring seats, as they are under spring pressure.

NOTE: Oil pump clearance must be checked in main valve body. See OIL PUMP under COMPONENT DISASSEMBLY & REASSEMBLY.

Reassembly – Coat all components and bores with ATF. To reassemble, reverse disassembly procedure. Ensure all components are installed in correct location. See Fig. 12. Tighten valve cover bolts to specification. See TORQUE SPECIFICATIONS.

SPRING SPECIFICATIONS

Application	Free Length In. (mm)
Main Valve Body	
Relief Valve Spring	1.461 (37.10)
1-2 Shift Valve Ball Spring	.421 (10.70)
1-2 Shift Valve Spring	2.079 (52.80)
2-3 Shift Valve Ball Spring	.524 (13.30)
2-3 Shift Valve Spring	2.571 (65.30)
3-2 Timing Valve Spring	1.795 (45.60)
3-4 Shift Valve Ball Spring	.445 (11.30)
3-4 Shift Valve Spring	1.280 (32.50)
4th Exhaust Valve Spring	1.705 (43.30)
Regulator Valve Body	
Cooler Check Valve Spring	1.331 (33.80)
Lock-Up Control Valve Spring	1.512 (38.40)
Regulator Valve Spring "A"	
1995 Models	
Except VTEC	3.362 (85.40)
VTEC	3.457 (87.80)
1996 Models	3.457 (87.80)
Regulator Valve Spring "B"	1.732 (44.00)
Stator Reaction Spring	1.193 (30.30)
Torque Converter Check Valve Spring	1.331 (33.80)
Secondary Valve Body	
Clutch Pressure Control Valve Spring	.980 (24.90)
Governor Cut Valve Spring	1.752 (44.50)
Reverse Control Valve Spring	1.575 (40.00)
Servo Control Valve Spring	1.343 (34.10)
2nd-On Orifice Control Valve Spring	.949 (24.10)
2-1 Timing Valve Spring	1.299 (33.00)
2-3 Orifice Control Valve Spring	1.307 (33.20)
4-3 Kickdown Valve Spring	1.177 (29.90)
Servo Body	
Throttle Valve "A" Adjusting Spring	1.063 (27.00)
Throttle Valve "A" Spring	[1]
Throttle Valve "B" Adjusting Spring	1.181 (30.00)
Throttle Valve "B" Spring	[2]
1st Accumulator Spring "A"	4.012 (101.90)
1st Accumulator Spring "B"	1.929 (49.00)
2nd Accumulator Spring	3.031 (77.00)
2/3-4 Orifice Control Valve Spring	2.043 (51.90)
3rd Accumulator Spring	3.614 (91.80)
4th Accumulator Spring	3.547 (90.10)
Modulator Valve Body	
Modulator Valve Spring	
1995 Models	[3]
1996 Models	[4]
Lock-Up Valve Body	
Lock-Up Shift Valve Spring	2.902 (73.70)
Lock-Up Timing Valve Spring	2.421 (61.50)
Governor Body	
Governor Spring "A"	1.295 (32.90)
Governor Spring "B"	[5]

[1] – Spring free length may be .870" (22.10 mm), .874" (22.20 mm) or .878" (22.30 mm).
[2] – Spring free length may be 1.634" (41.50 mm) or 1.638" (41.60 mm).
[3] – Spring free length may be 1.071" (27.20 mm) or 1.035" (26.30 mm).
[4] – Spring free length may be 1.071" (27.20 mm) or 1.087" (27.60 mm).
[5] – Spring free length may be 1.094" (27.80 mm) or 1.146" (29.10 mm).

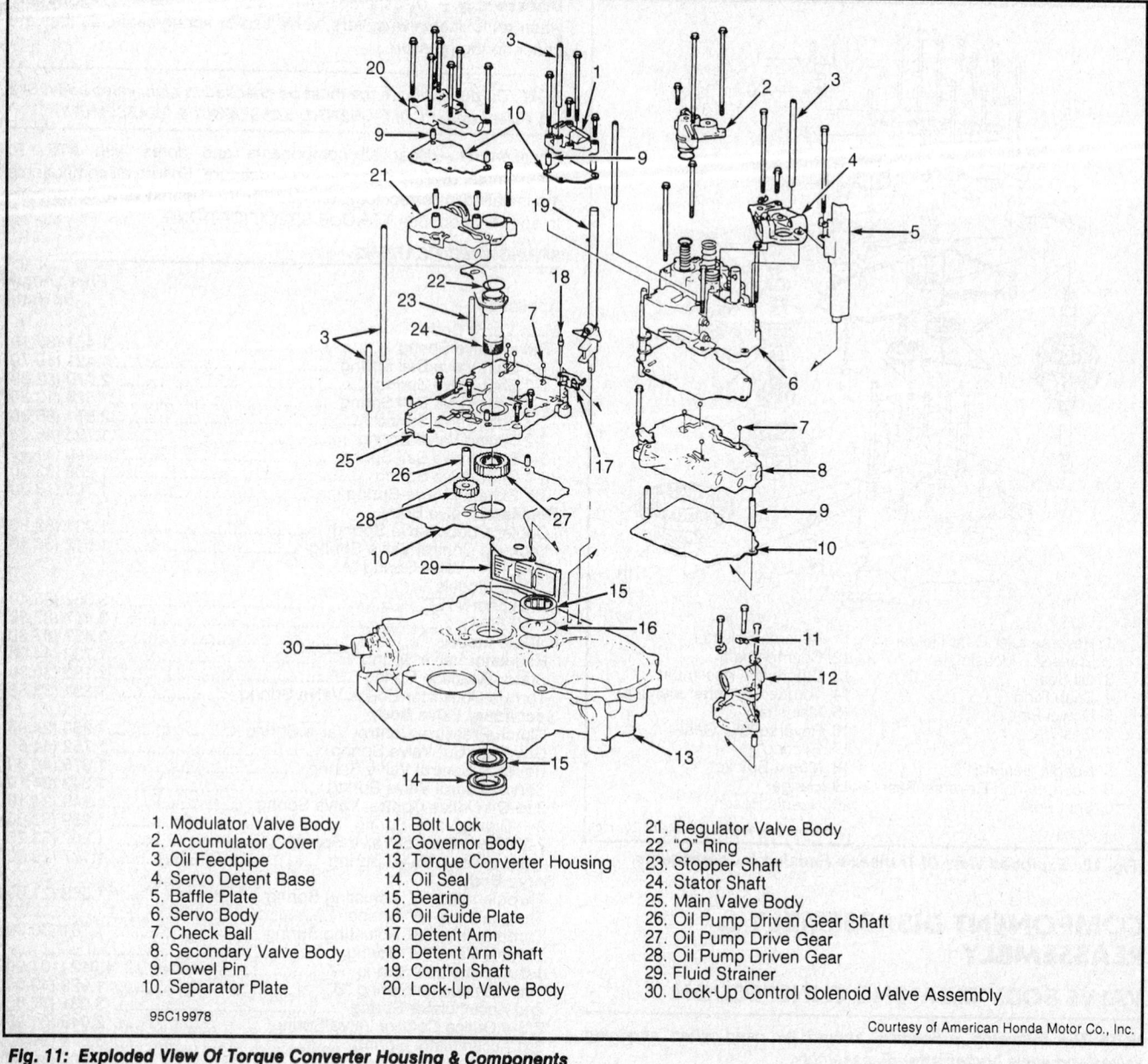

1. Modulator Valve Body
2. Accumulator Cover
3. Oil Feedpipe
4. Servo Detent Base
5. Baffle Plate
6. Servo Body
7. Check Ball
8. Secondary Valve Body
9. Dowel Pin
10. Separator Plate
11. Bolt Lock
12. Governor Body
13. Torque Converter Housing
14. Oil Seal
15. Bearing
16. Oil Guide Plate
17. Detent Arm
18. Detent Arm Shaft
19. Control Shaft
20. Lock-Up Valve Body
21. Regulator Valve Body
22. "O" Ring
23. Stopper Shaft
24. Stator Shaft
25. Main Valve Body
26. Oil Pump Driven Gear Shaft
27. Oil Pump Drive Gear
28. Oil Pump Driven Gear
29. Fluid Strainer
30. Lock-Up Control Solenoid Valve Assembly

95C19978

Courtesy of American Honda Motor Co., Inc.

Fig. 11: Exploded View Of Torque Converter Housing & Components

OIL PUMP

Disassembly – Note direction of oil pump gear installation in main valve body. Remove oil pump driven gear shaft and oil pump gears from main valve body (if not previously removed).

Cleaning & Inspection – **1)** Clean components with solvent and dry with compressed air. Inspect components and replace if damaged.

2) Install oil pump gears and oil pump driven gear shaft in main valve body. Ensure chamfered and grooved side of oil pump driven gear is facing upward (toward separator plate side of main valve body).

3) Using feeler gauge, measure side clearance of both gears between tip of gear teeth and main valve body. See Fig. 13. Replace oil pump gears and/or main valve body if side clearance is not within specification. See OIL PUMP SPECIFICATIONS table.

4) Remove oil pump driven gear shaft. Place straightedge across main valve body surface. Using feeler gauge, measure thrust clearance between oil pump gears and straightedge. Replace oil pump gears and/or main valve body if thrust clearance is not within specification. See OIL PUMP SPECIFICATIONS table.

OIL PUMP SPECIFICATIONS

Application	In. (mm)
Side Clearance	
Oil Pump Drive Gear	.0083-.0104 (.210-.265)
Oil Pump Driven Gear	
1995	.0028-.0049 (.070-.125)
1996	.0014-.0025 (.035-.065)
Thrust Clearance	
Standard	.0016-.0024 (.034-.056)
Wear Limit	.0028 (.070)

Reassembly – Coat components with ATF. To reassemble, reverse disassembly procedure. Ensure chamfered and grooved side of oil pump driven gear is facing upward (toward separator plate side of main valve body).

TORQUE CONVERTER LOCK-UP SPECIFICATIONS

Application & Shift Lever Position	Lock-Up Clutch On	Lock-Up Clutch Off
1995 Models		
Except VTEC		
"D₃" Position		
Fully Closed Throttle	60-64 MPH	57-61 MPH
TPS Voltage Is 2.03 Volt	66-70 MPH	57-61 MPH
Full Throttle	82-86 MPH	78-82 MPH
"D₄" Position		
Fully Closed Throttle	15-17 MPH	14-16 MPH
TPS Voltage Is 2.03 Volt	66-70 MPH	54-58 MPH
Full Throttle	88-91 MPH	85-88 MPH
VTEC		
"D₃" Position		
Fully Closed Throttle	60-64 MPH	57-61 MPH
TPS Voltage Is 2.03 Volt	66-70 MPH	57-61 MPH
Full Throttle	82-86 MPH	79-83 MPH
"D₄" Position		
Fully Closed Throttle	15-17 MPH	14-16 MPH
TPS Voltage Is 2.03 Volt	66-70 MPH	54-58 MPH
Full Throttle	94-98 MPH	90-94 MPH
1996 Models		
Except VTEC		
"D₃" Position		
Fully Closed Throttle	61-65 MPH	58-62 MPH
TPS Voltage Is 2.03 Volt	66-70 MPH	58-62 MPH
Full Throttle	85-89 MPH	85-89 MPH
"D₄" Position		
Fully Closed Throttle	16-18 MPH	14-16 MPH
TPS Voltage Is 2.03 Volt	66-70 MPH	53-57 MPH
Full Throttle	91-95 MPH	85-89 MPH
VTEC		
"D₃" Position		
Fully Closed Throttle	61-65 MPH	58-62 MPH
TPS Voltage Is 2.03 Volt	66-70 MPH	58-62 MPH
Full Throttle	85-89 MPH	85-89 MPH
"D₄" Position		
Fully Closed Throttle	16-17 MPH	14-16 MPH
TPS Voltage Is 2.03 Volt	66-70 MPH	53-57 MPH
Full Throttle	93-97 MPH	86-90 MPH

TORQUE CONVERTER STALL SPEED TEST

CAUTION: DO NOT perform torque converter stall speed test for more than 10 seconds, or transaxle may be damaged. DO NOT move shift lever while increasing engine speed.

1) Apply parking brake. Block all wheels. Connect tachometer and start engine. Ensure A/C is off. Warm engine to normal operating temperature. Place shift lever in "2" position.
2) Fully depress brake pedal. Fully depress accelerator for 6-8 seconds and note engine speed. This is torque converter stall speed.
3) Allow transaxle to cool for 2 minutes. Repeat test procedure with shift lever in "D₄", "1" and "R" positions.
4) Torque converter stall speed should be the same in "D₄", "2", "1" and "R" and within specification. See TORQUE CONVERTER STALL SPEED SPECIFICATIONS table. If torque converter stall speed is not within specification, see TORQUE CONVERTER STALL SPEED TROUBLE SHOOTING table for possible problem areas.

TORQUE CONVERTER STALL SPEED SPECIFICATIONS

Application	Engine RPM
1995 Models	
Standard	2600
Service Limit	2400-2800
1996 Models	
Standard	2700
Service Limit	2500-2900

TORQUE CONVERTER STALL SPEED TROUBLE SHOOTING

Torque Converter Stall Speed Test Results	Probable Cause
Stall Speed RPM High In "D₄", "2", "1" & "R"	Low Fluid Level, Low Oil Pump Output, Clogged Fluid Strainer, Pressure Regulator Valve Stuck Closed, Slipping Clutch
Stall Speed RPM High In "R"	Slipping 4th Clutch
Stall Speed RPM High In "D₄"	Slipping 1st Clutch, Defective One-Way Clutch
Stall Speed RPM High In "2"	Slipping 2nd Clutch
Stall Speed RPM High In "1"	Slipping 1st-Hold Or 1st Clutch, Defective One-Way Clutch
Stall Speed RPM Low In "D₄", "2", "1" & "R"	Engine Output Low, Torque Converter One-Way Clutch Slipping

HYDRAULIC PRESSURE TEST

Pressure Test Preparation – Ensure transaxle fluid level is correct. Warm engine to normal operating temperature. Apply parking brake. Block rear wheels. Raise and support vehicle so front wheels can rotate.
Line Pressure Test – **1)** With engine off, remove pressure tap plug from line pressure tap on transaxle. *See Fig. 4.* Attach pressure gauge to line pressure tap using NEW seal washer. Tighten hose fitting to 13 ft. lbs. (18 N.m).
2) With shift lever in "P", start and operate engine at 2000 RPM. Note line pressure. Place shift lever in "N" and note line pressure.
3) Ensure line pressure is within specification. See appropriate HYDRAULIC PRESSURE TEST SPECIFICATIONS table. If line pressure is not within specification, see HYDRAULIC PRESSURE TROUBLE SHOOTING table. Shut engine off.
4) Remove pressure gauge set. Using NEW seal washer, install and tighten pressure tap plug to specification. See TORQUE SPECIFICATIONS.

NOTE: Check clutch pressure at each clutch pressure tap on transaxle. See Fig. 4.

Clutch Pressure Test – **1)** With engine off, remove pressure tap plug from appropriate clutch pressure tap on transaxle. *See Fig. 4.* Attach pressure gauge to appropriate pressure tap using NEW seal washer. Tighten hose fitting to 13 ft. lbs. (18 N.m).

NOTE: Clutch pressure on some applications may vary with position of Throttle Valve (T.V.) lever on transaxle. The T.V. cable must be disconnected for some tests. Ensure shift lever is in proper position when checking clutch pressures.

2) Start and operate engine at 2000 RPM. Note clutch pressure with shift lever in appropriate position. See appropriate HYDRAULIC PRESSURE TEST SPECIFICATIONS table.
3) Ensure clutch pressure is within specification. If clutch pressure is not within specification, see HYDRAULIC PRESSURE TROUBLE SHOOTING table. Shut engine off.
4) Remove pressure gauge set. Using NEW seal washer, install and tighten pressure tap plug to specification. See TORQUE SPECIFICATIONS.
Clutch Low/High Pressure Test – **1)** Clutch low/high pressure is tested at 2nd, 3rd and 4th clutch pressure taps on transaxle. *See Fig. 4.* Disconnect Throttle Valve (T.V.) cable from transaxle T.V. lever.

NOTE: When disconnecting T.V. cable, unhook cable from transaxle T.V. lever. DO NOT loosen lock nuts used for cable adjustment.

2) With engine off, remove pressure tap plug from appropriate clutch pressure tap on transaxle. Attach pressure gauge to appropriate pressure tap using NEW seal washer. Tighten hose fitting to 13 ft. lbs. (18 N.m).

HYDRAULIC PRESSURE TEST SPECIFICATIONS

Application	Shift Lever Position	Pressure psi (kPa)
Line Pressure		
1995 Models		
Except VTEC		
Engine Speed At 2000 RPM	"P" Or "N"	107-121 (750-850)
VTEC		
Engine Speed At 2000 RPM	"P" Or "N"	114-128 (800-900)
1996 Models		
Engine Speed At 2000 RPM	"P" Or "N"	114-128 (800-900)
Clutch Pressure		
1st Clutch		
1995 Models		
Except VTEC		
Engine Speed At 2000 RPM	"1" Or "D₄"	107-121 (750-850)
VTEC		
Engine Speed At 2000 RPM	"1" Or "D₄"	114-128 (800-900)
1996 Models		
Engine Speed At 2000 RPM	"1" Or "D₄"	114-128 (800-900)
1st-Hold Clutch		
1995 Models		
Except VTEC		
Engine Speed At 2000 RPM	"1"	107-121 (750-850)
VTEC		
Engine Speed At 2000 RPM	"1"	114-128 (800-900)
1996 Models		
Engine Speed At 2000 RPM	"1"	114-128 (800-900)
2nd Clutch		
1995 Models		
Except VTEC		
Engine Speed At 2000 RPM	"2"	107-121 (750-850)
Transaxle T.V. Lever Fully Closed [1]	"D₄"	50-57 (350-400)
Transaxle T.V. Lever Open More Than 1/8 [2]	"D₄"	107-121 (750-850)
VTEC		
Engine Speed At 2000 RPM	"2"	114-128 (800-900)
Transaxle T.V. Lever Fully Closed [1]	"D₄"	50-57 (350-400)
Transaxle T.V. Lever Open More Than 1/8 [2]	"D₄"	114-128 (800-900)
1996 Models		
Engine Speed At 2000 RPM	"2"	114-128 (800-900)
Transaxle T.V. Lever Fully Closed [1]	"D₄"	50-57 (350-400)
Transaxle T.V. Lever Open More Than 1/8 [2]	"D₄"	114-128 (800-900)
3rd Clutch		
1995 Models		
Except VTEC		
Transaxle T.V. Lever Fully Closed [1]	"D₄"	50-57 (350-400)
Transaxle T.V. Lever Open More Than 1/8 [2]	"D₄"	107-121 (750-850)
VTEC		
Transaxle T.V. Lever Fully Closed [1]	"D₄"	50-57 (350-400)
Transaxle T.V. Lever Open More Than 1/8 [2]	"D₄"	114-128 (800-900)
1996 Models		
Transaxle T.V. Lever Fully Closed [1]	"D₄"	50-57 (350-400)
Transaxle T.V. Lever Open More Than 1/8 [2]	"D₄"	114-128 (800-900)
4th Clutch		
1995 Models		
Except VTEC		
Engine Speed At 2000 RPM	"R"	107-121 (750-850)
Transaxle T.V. Lever Fully Closed [1]	"D₄"	50-57 (350-400)
Transaxle T.V. Lever Open More Than 1/8 [2]	"D₄"	107-121 (750-850)
VTEC		
Engine Speed At 2000 RPM	"R"	114-128 (800-900)
Transaxle T.V. Lever Fully Closed [1]	"D₄"	50-57 (350-400)
Transaxle T.V. Lever Open More Than 1/8 [2]	"D₄"	114-128 (800-900)

[1] – Check pressure with engine speed at 2000 RPM. T.V. cable must be disconnected. Fully closed position is with transaxle T.V. lever in released position and not being pulled upward by T.V. cable.

[2] – Check pressure with engine speed at 2000 RPM. T.V. cable must be disconnected. Open position is with transaxle T.V. lever being pulled upward 1/8 the distance of lever travel.

[3] – Check pressure with engine speed at 1000 RPM. Open position is with transaxle T.V. lever being pulled fully upward.

[4] – Check governor pressure with vehicle speed at 38 MPH.

Elantra, Sonata

APPLICATION

APPLICATION

Vehicle	Transaxle Model
1995 Elantra	KM175
1995-96 Sonata 2.0L	KM175

DESCRIPTION

Automatic transaxle is electronically controlled. Transaxle shifting is controlled by Transmission Control Module (TCM). Damper clutch lock-up (torque converter lock-up) is controlled by TCM.

The TCM receives information from input devices and transmits electrical signal to appropriate Shift Control Solenoid Valves (SCSV) and Pressure Control Solenoid Valve (PCSV), mounted on valve body assembly for controlling transaxle shifting. TCM controls damper clutch (torque converter lock-up) by operating Damper Clutch Control Solenoid Valve (DCCSV), located on valve body assembly.

An overdrive switch is mounted on shift lever. When overdrive switch is depressed to the ON position, transaxle will automatically upshift to overdrive and overdrive off indicator light on instrument panel will not be illuminated.

When overdrive switch is released to the OFF position, transaxle will not upshift to overdrive and overdrive off indicator light on instrument panel will be illuminated.

A range switch is located on console, near shift lever. On Sonata models, range switch contains a PWR (power) mode and NORM (normal) mode. When range switch is depressed to PWR (power) mode, an input signal is delivered to TCM, and TCM changes shift points to provide maximum performance. When range switch is released to the NORM (normal) mode, an input signal is delivered to TCM, and TCM changes shift points to provide maximum fuel economy. When engine coolant temperature is less than 68°F (20°C), transaxle will remain in NORM (normal) mode even if range switch is in PWR (power) mode. When range switch is in NORM (normal) mode and vehicle speed exceeds 60 MPH, transaxle will not downshift when accelerator pedal is depressed. Range switch must be in PWR (power) mode for transaxle to downshift.

On Elantra models, range switch contains a ECON (economy) mode and NORM (normal) mode. When range switch is depressed to the NORM (normal) mode, an input signal is delivered to TCM, and TCM changes shift points to provide maximum performance. When range switch is released to the ECON (economy) mode, an input signal is delivered to TCM, and TCM changes shift points to provide maximum fuel economy. When engine coolant temperature is less than 68°F (20°C), transaxle will remain in ECON (economy) mode even if range switch is in NORM (normal) mode. When range switch is in ECON (economy) mode and vehicle speed exceeds 60 MPH, transaxle will not downshift when accelerator pedal is depressed. Range switch must be in NORM (normal) mode for transaxle to downshift.

On all models, the TCM contains self-diagnostic system, which stores fault code if failure or problem exists in transaxle electronic control system. Fault codes may be retrieved to determine transaxle problem area. Fault code may be referred to as Diagnostic Trouble Code (DTC). For information on self-diagnostic system, see SELF-DIAGNOSIS under SELF-DIAGNOSTIC SYSTEM.

Electronic control system contains a fail-safe system in the event that an electronic component should malfunction. The fail-safe system will provide transaxle operation until the malfunction is repaired. If failures exists in certain electronic components for a repeated number of times, transaxle may remain in 2nd or 3rd gear. This is referred to as fail-safe mode. Park, Neutral and Reverse gears will operate in fail-safe mode, but only one forward gear will operate.

Transaxle is equipped with shift and key interlock systems. Shift interlock system prevents shift lever from being moved from Park position unless brake pedal is depressed, ignition is on and release button on side of shift lever is depressed. Key interlock system prevents ignition key from being turned to LOCK position unless shift lever is in Park position. For additional information, see SHIFT & KEY INTERLOCK SYSTEMS under OPERATION.

OPERATION

SHIFT & KEY INTERLOCK SYSTEMS

Shift interlock system prevents shift lever from being moved from Park position unless brake pedal is depressed, ignition is on and release button on side of shift lever is depressed. In case of a malfunction, shift lever can be released by depressing release button.

On Elantra models, release button is located on front corner of console, near driver's side of shift lever. On Sonata models, release button is located on front corner of console, near driver's side of shift lever.

The A/T and key lock control unit controls operation of A/T shift lock solenoid for shift lever operation. The key interlock system prevents ignition key from being turned to LOCK position unless shift lever is in Park position. The A/T and key lock control unit controls operation of key lock solenoid.

The shift and key interlock systems consists of A/T and key lock control unit, A/T shift lock solenoid, park position/key lock switch, key lock solenoid and brakelight switch.

The A/T and key lock control unit is located below center of instrument panel at center console, or near passenger's side kick panel, depending on vehicle application. See Fig. 1. The A/T shift lock solenoid and park position/key lock switch are located on shift lever. See Fig. 2. Brakelight switch is mounted near brake pedal. Key lock solenoid is located on ignition lock assembly on steering column.

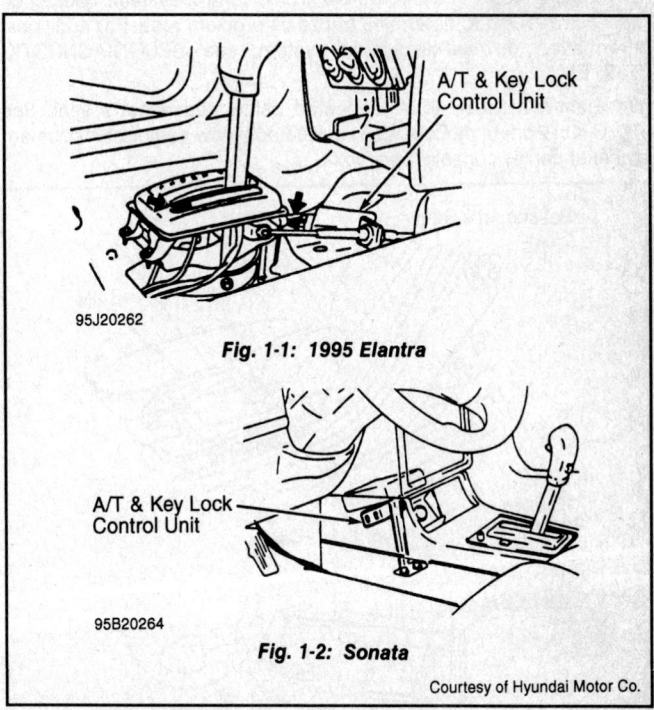

95J20262

Fig. 1-1: 1995 Elantra

95B20264

Fig. 1-2: Sonata

Courtesy of Hyundai Motor Co.

Fig. 1: Identifying A/T & Key Lock Control Unit

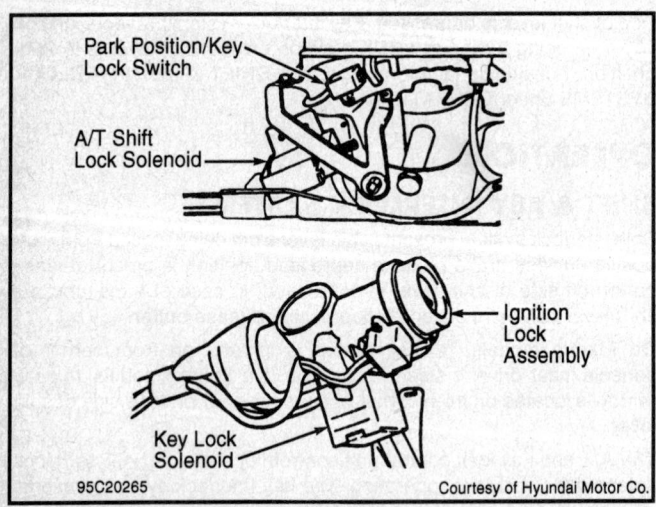

95C20265   Courtesy of Hyundai Motor Co.

Fig. 2: Identifying A/T Shift Lock Solenoid, Key Lock Solenoid &
Park Position/Key Lock Switch

TRANSMISSION CONTROL MODULE (TCM)

The TCM receives information from input devices and transmits electrical signal to appropriate Shift Control Solenoid Valves (SCSV) and Pressure Control Solenoid Valve (PCSV) to control transaxle shifting. Shift control and pressure control solenoid valves are located on valve body assembly. TCM controls damper clutch (torque converter lockup) by operating Damper Clutch Control Solenoid Valve (DCCSV), located on valve body assembly.

TCM contains self-diagnostic system, which stores fault code if failure or problem exists in transaxle electronic control system. Fault code may be retrieved to determine transaxle problem area. For additional information on self-diagnostic system, see SELF-DIAGNOSTIC SYSTEM.

On Elantra models, TCM is located below passenger's seat. *See Fig. 3.* On Sonata models, TCM is located below center of instrument panel at center console. *See Fig. 4.*

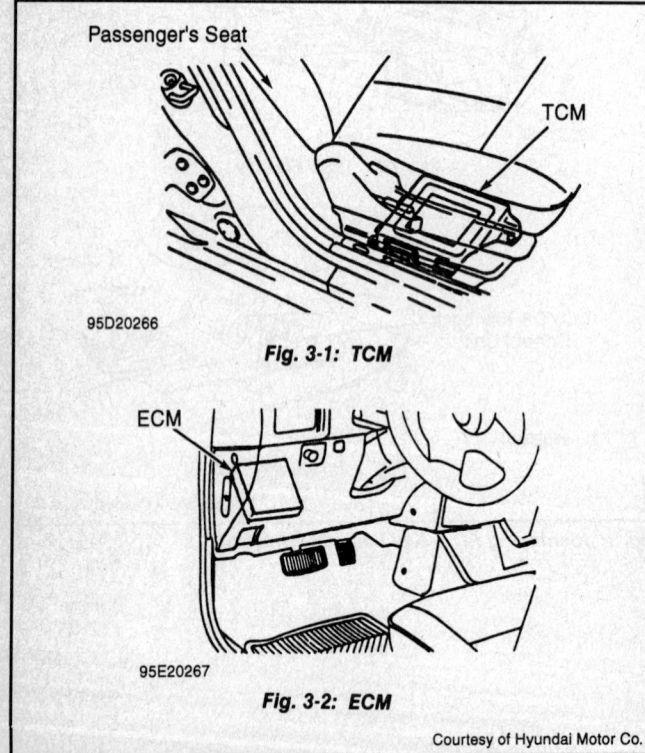

95D20266

Fig. 3-1: TCM

95E20267

Fig. 3-2: ECM

Courtesy of Hyundai Motor Co.

Fig. 3: Identifying TCM & Engine Control Module (ECM)
(Elantra)

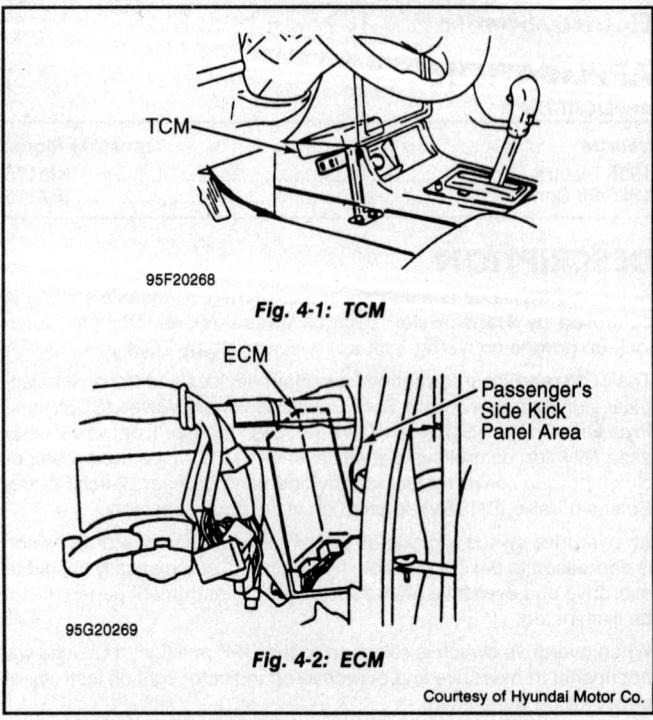

95F20268

Fig. 4-1: TCM

95G20269

Fig. 4-2: ECM

Courtesy of Hyundai Motor Co.

Fig. 4: Identifying TCM & Engine Control Module (ECM)
(Sonata)

TCM INPUT DEVICES

A/C Operation Signal – An A/C operation signal is delivered from the A/C clutch relay to the TCM to indicate A/C operation. The A/C clutch relay is located in engine compartment fuse/relay box.

Idle Switch (1995 Elantra & 1995 Sonata) – Idle switch is a contact-type switch, which opens when throttle is depressed and closes when throttle is released. Idle switch delivers input signal to TCM to indicate position of throttle valve. Idle switch is located on throttle body. *See Fig. 5.* Idle switch may also be referred to as idle position switch.

Kickdown Servo Switch – Kickdown servo switch delivers input signal to TCM to indicate kickdown servo position. Kickdown servo switch may also be referred to as kickdown switch. Kickdown servo switch is located on kickdown servo on transaxle. *See Fig. 5.*

Oil Temperature Sensor – Oil temperature sensor delivers input signal to TCM to indicate transaxle oil temperature. Oil temperature sensor is located on bottom of valve body assembly. *See Fig. 5.*

Overdrive Switch – Overdrive switch is mounted on shift lever. When overdrive switch is depressed to the ON position, transaxle will automatically upshift to overdrive and overdrive off indicator light on instrument panel will not be illuminated. When overdrive switch is released to the OFF position, transaxle will not upshift to overdrive and overdrive off indicator light on instrument panel will be illuminated.

Pulse Generators "A" & "B" – Pulse generators "A" and "B" deliver input signals to TCM to indicate the speed of transaxle internal components. Pulse generators "A" and "B" are mounted on the transaxle. *See Fig. 5.*

Range Switch – Range switch is located on console, near shift lever. On Sonata models, range switch contains a PWR (power) mode and NORM (normal) mode. When range switch is depressed to PWR (power) mode, an input signal is delivered to TCM, and TCM changes shift points to provide maximum performance. When range switch is released to the NORM (normal) mode, an input signal is delivered to TCM, and TCM changes shift points to provide maximum fuel economy. When engine coolant temperature is less than 68°F (20°C), transaxle will remain in NORM (normal) mode even if range switch is in PWR (power) mode. When range switch is in NORM (normal) mode and vehicle speed exceeds 60 MPH, transaxle will not downshift when accelerator pedal is depressed. Range switch must be in PWR (power) mode for transaxle to downshift.

On Elantra models, range switch contains a ECON (economy) mode and NORM (normal) mode. When range switch is depressed to the NORM (normal) mode, an input signal is delivered to TCM, and TCM changes shift points to provide maximum performance. When range switch is released to the ECON (economy) mode, an input signal is delivered to TCM, and TCM changes shift points to provide maximum fuel economy. When engine coolant temperature is less than 68°F (20°C), transaxle will remain in ECON (economy) mode even if range switch is in NORM (normal) mode. When range switch is in ECON (economy) mode and vehicle speed exceeds 60 MPH, transaxle will not downshift when accelerator pedal is depressed. Range switch must be in NORM (normal) mode for transaxle to downshift.

Throttle Position Sensor (TPS) – Throttle position sensor delivers an input signal to TCM to indicate throttle position. Throttle position sensor is mounted on side of throttle body.

Transaxle Range Switch – When shift lever is moved, shift cable moves the manual control lever which operates the transaxle range switch. Transaxle range switch delivers an input signal to TCM to indicate shift lever position. The TCM uses input signal and operates shift control solenoid valves to control transaxle shifting. Transaxle range switch is mounted below manual control lever on transaxle. See Fig. 5. Transaxle range switch may also be referred to as inhibitor switch.

Vehicle Speed Sensor (VSS) – Vehicle speed sensor delivers an input signal to TCM to indicate vehicle speed. Vehicle speed sensor is located on rear of speedometer on instrument panel gauge assembly. See Fig. 5. Vehicle speed sensor may also be referred to as vehicle speed reed switch.

TCM OUTPUT DEVICES

Damper Clutch Control Solenoid Valve – The TCM controls damper clutch (torque converter lock-up) operation by delivering an output signal to Damper Clutch Control Solenoid Valve (DCCSV). Damper clutch control solenoid valve is operated in accordance with gear position. See DAMPER CLUTCH CONTROL SOLENOID VALVE OPERATION table. The damper clutch control solenoid valve is located on valve body assembly. See Fig. 6.

DAMPER CLUTCH CONTROL SOLENOID VALVE OPERATION

Gear Position	Solenoid Operation
Park & Neutral	Off
Reverse	Off
1st Gear	Off
2nd Gear	On
3rd Gear	On
4th Gear	On
During Lock-Up	Off

Pressure Control Solenoid Valve (PCSV) – The TCM controls transaxle shifting by delivering an output signal to pressure control solenoid valve. Pressure control solenoid valve may also be referred to as oil pressure control solenoid valve. Pressure control solenoid valve is operated in accordance with gear position. See PRESSURE CONTROL SOLENOID VALVE OPERATION table. Pressure control solenoid valve is mounted on valve body assembly. See Fig. 6.

PRESSURE CONTROL SOLENOID VALVE OPERATION

Gear Position	Solenoid Operation
Park & Neutral	Off
Reverse	Off
1st Gear	On
2nd Gear	Off
3rd Gear	Off
4th Gear	Off
During Lock-Up	On

Shift Control Solenoid Valve (SCSV) – The TCM controls transaxle shifting by delivering an output signal to shift control solenoid valves "A" and "B". Shift control solenoid valves are operated in accordance with gear position. See SHIFT CONTROL SOLENOID VALVE OPERATION table. Shift control solenoid valves are located on valve body assembly. See Fig. 6. Shift control solenoid valve "A" has a Blue/Black wire and shift control solenoid valve "B" has a Red wire.

SHIFT CONTROL SOLENOID VALVE OPERATION

Gear Position	SCSV "A"	SCSV "B"
Park & Neutral	Off	Off
Reverse	Off	Off
1st Gear	On	On
2nd Gear	Off	On
3rd Gear	Off	Off
4th Gear	On	Off
During Lock-Up	On	On

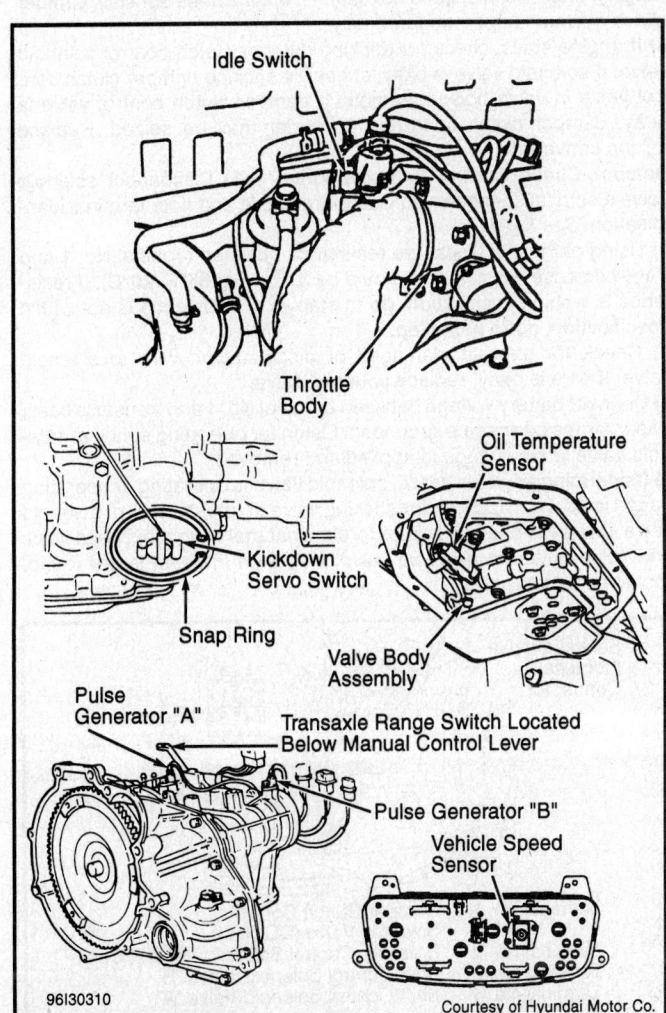

Idle Switch

Throttle Body

Oil Temperature Sensor

Kickdown Servo Switch

Snap Ring

Valve Body Assembly

Pulse Generator "A"

Transaxle Range Switch Located Below Manual Control Lever

Pulse Generator "B"

Vehicle Speed Sensor

96I30310

Courtesy of Hyundai Motor Co.

Fig. 5: Locating TCM Input Devices

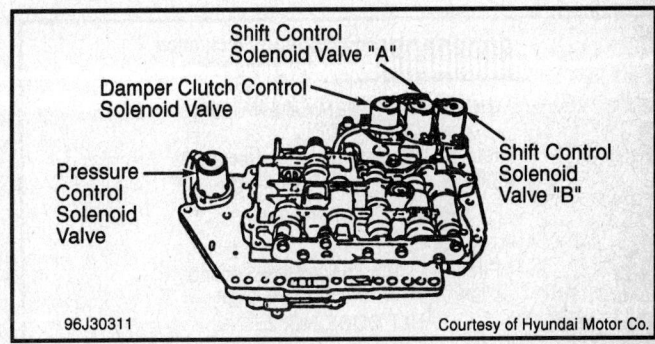

Shift Control Solenoid Valve "A"

Damper Clutch Control Solenoid Valve

Pressure Control Solenoid Valve

Shift Control Solenoid Valve "B"

96J30311

Courtesy of Hyundai Motor Co.

Fig. 6: Identifying Control Solenoid Valves

SELF-DIAGNOSTIC SYSTEM

SYSTEM DIAGNOSIS

The TCM contains self-diagnostic system, which stores fault code in TCM memory if failure or problem exists in transaxle electronic control system. Fault code can be retrieved for diagnosing transaxle electronic control system. See RETRIEVING FAULT CODES.

RETRIEVING FAULT CODES

NOTE: Fault codes may be retrieved using scan tester or voltmeter.

1) On 1995 Elantra and 1995 Sonata, locate data link connector near fuse box at driver's side kick panel. On 1996 Sonata, locate data link connector on lower right side of driver's lower instrument panel.

2) If using scan tester, connect scan tester to data link connector and cigarette lighter. If using voltmeter, connect voltmeter between ground terminal and diagnostic output terminal on data link connector. *See Fig. 7.*

3) Turn ignition on. If using scan tester, note fault code displays on scan tester using scan tester manufacturer's instructions.

4) If using voltmeter, note fluctuations of voltmeter needle. If system is operating normal and no fault codes are displayed, voltmeter will display several consecutive short fluctuations. *See Fig. 8.*

5) If fault codes exists, fault codes will be displayed by short and long fluctuations of voltmeter. The first fluctuation indicates first digit of fault code. Following fluctuations indicate the second digit of fault code. *See Fig. 8.*

6) Record fault codes in the order they are displayed. If transaxle is not in fail-safe mode and does not remain in 2nd or 3rd gear, a maximum of 10 fault codes may be stored in the TCM memory. The same fault code may be stored as many as 3 times.

7) If number of stored fault codes exceeds the maximum of 10 fault codes, previously stored fault codes will be erased beginning with the oldest fault code.

8) If transaxle is in fail-safe mode and remains in 2nd or 3rd gear, a special fail-safe fault code will be stored in the TCM memory. Only 3 fail-safe mode fault codes may be stored in the TCM memory at one time.

9) When transaxle is in fail-safe mode and remains in 2nd or 3rd gear, fail safe-mode fault codes will be cancelled when ignition is turned off. Transaxle will no longer remain in 2nd or 3rd gear, but fail-safe mode fault code will be stored in the TCM memory.

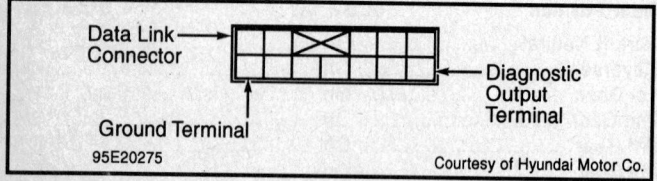

Data Link Connector → Diagnostic Output Terminal

Ground Terminal

95E20275 — Courtesy of Hyundai Motor Co.

Fig. 7: Identifying Data Link Connector Terminals

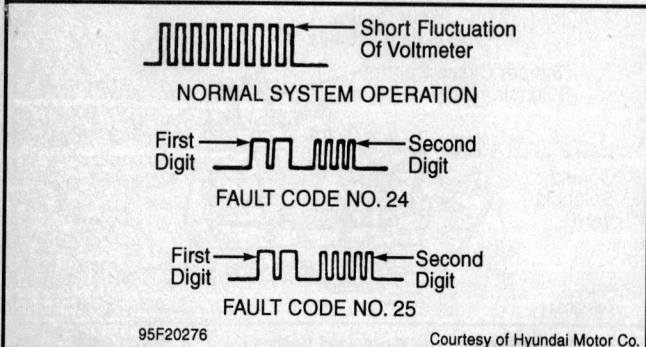

Short Fluctuation Of Voltmeter

NORMAL SYSTEM OPERATION

First Digit — Second Digit

FAULT CODE NO. 24

First Digit — Second Digit

FAULT CODE NO. 25

95F20276 — Courtesy of Hyundai Motor Co.

Fig. 8: Identifying Fault Code Displays

10) To identify fault code and items to be checked or adjusted, see FAULT CODE IDENTIFICATION table. To check electrical system components, see ELECTRONIC SYSTEM & COMPONENT TESTING under ELECTRONIC TROUBLE SHOOTING.

11) Once all repairs are performed, ensure fault codes are cleared from the TCM memory. See CLEARING FAULT CODES under SELF-DIAGNOSTIC SYSTEM

CLEARING FAULT CODES

WARNING: When battery is disconnected, vehicle computer and memory systems may lose memory data. Driveability problems may exist until computer systems have completed a relearn cycle. See COMPUTER RELEARN PROCEDURES in APPLICATIONS & IDENTIFICATION section before disconnecting battery.

Once all repairs are performed, fault codes must be cleared from TCM memory. To clear fault codes, disconnect negative battery cable for a few seconds.

ELECTRONIC TROUBLE SHOOTING

ELECTRONIC SYSTEM & COMPONENT TESTING

Damper Clutch System – 1) Install tachometer. Apply parking brake. Start engine and allow to idle. Ensure engine idle is correctly adjusted. If engine idle is not correct, adjust as necessary.

2) With engine idling, apply brake pedal. Place shift lever in "R" or "D" range. If engine stalls, go to next step. If engine does not stall, damper clutch system is operating normally.

3) If engine stalls, check for sticking damper clutch control solenoid valve. If solenoid valve is okay, check for sticking damper clutch control valve in valve body assembly. If damper clutch control valve is okay, damper clutch in torque converter may be seized. Replace torque converter.

Damper Clutch Control Solenoid Valve – 1) Disconnect solenoid valve electrical connector on side of transaxle and note terminal identification. *See Fig. 9.*

2) Using ohmmeter, measure resistance between terminal No. 1 and transaxle case. Resistance should be 3 ohms at 68°F (20°C). If resistance is within specification, go to step 4). If resistance is not within specification, go to next step.

3) Check for shorted, damaged or disconnected wire to solenoid valve. If wire is okay, replace solenoid valve.

4) Connect battery voltage between terminal No. 1 and transaxle case. Ensure transaxle case is grounded. Listen for operating sound at solenoid valve when voltage is applied and removed.

5) If operating sound is heard, solenoid valve is operating. If operating sound is not heard, check for sticking valve at release side of solenoid valve. If valve is okay, check for foreign material caught between valve and valve guide on solenoid valve. If foreign material is not found, replace solenoid valve.

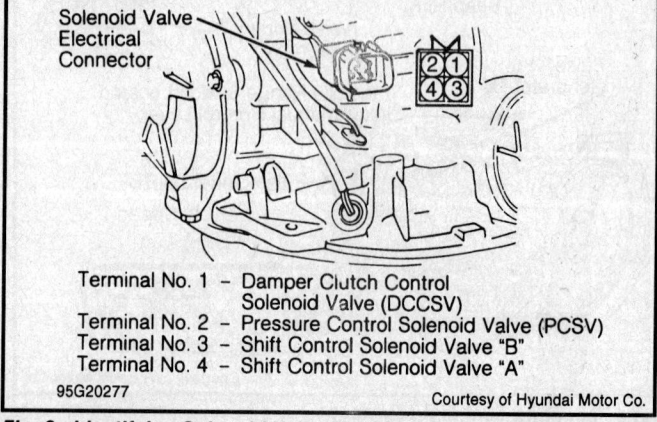

Solenoid Valve Electrical Connector

Terminal No. 1 – Damper Clutch Control Solenoid Valve (DCCSV)
Terminal No. 2 – Pressure Control Solenoid Valve (PCSV)
Terminal No. 3 – Shift Control Solenoid Valve "B"
Terminal No. 4 – Shift Control Solenoid Valve "A"

95G20277 — Courtesy of Hyundai Motor Co.

Fig. 9: Identifying Solenoid Valve Electrical Connector & Connector Terminals

FAULT CODE IDENTIFICATION

Fault Code Number	Probable Cause	Fail-Safe Mode	[1] Items To Check Or Replace
11	High TPS Output	No	Check TPS Operation, Adjustment & Wiring Circuit, Check Idle Switch, Check For Fault Code No. 24
12	Low TPS Output	No	Check TPS Operation, Adjustment & Wiring Circuit, Check Idle Switch, Check For Fault Code No. 24
13	Defective TPS	No	Check TPS Operation, Adjustment & Wiring Circuit
14	Improperly Adjusted TPS	No	Check TPS Adjustment
15	Open Oil Temperature Sensor Circuit (Low Temperature Side)	No	Check Oil Temperature Sensor & Wiring Circuit
16	Shorted Oil Temperature Sensor Circuit (High Temperature Side)	No	Check Oil Temperature Sensor & Wiring Circuit
17	Oil Temperature Sensor Open Circuit (High Temperature Side) Or Shorted Circuit (Low Temperature Side)	No	Check Oil Temperature Sensor & Wiring Circuit
21	Open Kickdown Servo Switch Circuit	No	Check Kickdown Servo Switch & Wiring Circuit
22	Shorted Kickdown Servo Switch Circuit	No	Check Kickdown Servo Switch & Wiring Circuit
23	Ignition Pulse Signal Circuit	No	Check For Open Circuit To Pin No. 9 (White Wire) On 14-Pin Connector At TCM
24	Idle Switch Circuit	No	Check Idle Switch & Wiring Circuit
31	Open Pulse Generator "A" Circuit	No	Check Pulse Generator "A" & Wiring Circuit, Check Vehicle Speed Sensor
32	Open Pulse Generator "B" Circuit	No	Check Pulse Generator "B" & Wiring Circuit, Check Vehicle Speed Sensor
41	Open Shift Control Solenoid Valve "A" Circuit	No	Check Shift Control Solenoid Valve "A" & Wiring Circuit
42	Shorted Shift Control Solenoid Valve "A" Circuit	No	Check Shift Control Solenoid Valve "A" & Wiring Circuit
43	Open Shift Control Solenoid Valve "B" Circuit	No	Check Shift Control Solenoid Valve "B" & Wiring Circuit
44	Shorted Shift Control Solenoid Valve "B" Circuit	No	Check Shift Control Solenoid Valve "B" & Wiring Circuit
45	Open Pressure Control Solenoid Valve Circuit	No	Check Pressure Control Solenoid Valve & Wiring Circuit
46	Shorted Pressure Control Solenoid Valve Circuit	No	Check Pressure Control Solenoid Valve & Wiring Circuit
47	Open Damper Clutch Control Solenoid Valve Circuit	No	Check Damper Clutch Control Solenoid Valve & Wiring Circuit
48	Shorted Damper Clutch Control Solenoid Valve Circuit	No	Check Damper Clutch Control Solenoid Valve & Wiring Circuit
49	Defective Damper Clutch Control System	No	Check Damper Clutch Hydraulic Circuit, Check Damper Clutch Control Solenoid Valve, Defective TCM
51	Incorrect 1st Gear Shift [2]	No	Check Pulse Generators "A", "B" & Wiring Circuits, Rear Clutch Or Low-Reverse Brake Slipping
52	Incorrect 2nd Gear Shift [2]	No	Check Pulse Generator "A" & Wiring Circuit, Rear Clutch Or Kickdown Brake Slipping
53	Incorrect 3rd Gear Shift [2]	No	Check Pulse Generators "A", "B" & Wiring Circuits, Front, End Or Rear Clutch Slipping
54	Incorrect 4th Gear Shift [2]	No	Check Pulse Generator "A" & Wiring Circuit, End Clutch Or Kickdown Brake Slipping
81	Open Pulse Generator "A" Circuit	Yes	Check Pulse Generator "A" & Wiring Circuit, Check Vehicle Speed Sensor
82	Open Pulse Generator "B" Circuit	Yes	Check Pulse Generator "B" & Wiring Circuit, Check Vehicle Speed Sensor
83	Open Or Shorted Shift Control Solenoid Valve "A" Circuit	Yes	Check Shift Control Solenoid Valve "A" & Wiring Circuit
84	Open Or Shorted Shift Control Solenoid Valve "B" Circuit	Yes	Check Shift Control Solenoid Valve "B" & Wiring Circuit
85	Open Or Shorted Pressure Control Solenoid Valve	Yes	Check Pressure Control Solenoid Valve & Wiring Circuit
86	Transaxle Shifting Non-Synchronous	Yes	[3]

[1] – To check items listed, see ELECTRONIC SYSTEM & COMPONENT TESTING under ELECTRONIC TROUBLE SHOOTING. For adjustment of components, see ADJUSTMENTS.

[2] – Shift speed does not correspond to engine speed.

[3] – See Fault Codes No. 51, 52, 53 Or 54 for items to be checked in relation to improper gear operation.

Idle Switch (1995 Elantra & 1995 Sonata) – 1) Disconnect wiring harness electrical connector at idle switch, located on throttle body. *See Fig. 5.*

2) To check idle switch power supply, turn ignition on. Using voltmeter, measure voltage between idle switch connector terminal and ground. Voltage should be greater than 4 volts. If voltage is not as specified, check wiring circuit to idle switch. See WIRING DIAGRAMS.

3) To check idle switch operation, connect ohmmeter between idle switch connector terminal and ground. With accelerator pedal depressed, no continuity should exist. With accelerator pedal released (idle position), continuity should exist. If continuity is not as specified, check for improperly adjusted throttle or cruise control cables. If cable adjustment is okay, replace idle switch.

Kickdown Servo Switch – 1) Disconnect electrical connector for kickdown servo switch. Kickdown servo switch is located on kickdown servo on transaxle. *See Fig. 5.*

2) Using ohmmeter, check continuity between kickdown servo switch connector terminal and ground. If continuity exists, go to next step. If continuity does not exist, check for poor connection, damaged or disconnected wire to kickdown servo switch. If connections and wire are okay, replace kickdown servo switch.

3) Apply brakes. Start engine and allow to idle. Place shift lever in "L" position. Using ohmmeter, check continuity between kickdown servo switch connector terminal and ground.

4) If continuity does not exist, kickdown servo switch is okay. Replace kickdown servo switch if continuity exists.

Overdrive Switch – 1) Disconnect electrical connector for overdrive switch and note switch terminal identification. *See Fig. 10 or 11.* Overdrive switch is mounted on shift lever.

2) Depress overdrive switch to the ON position. Using ohmmeter, ensure continuity exists between specified terminals. See OVERDRIVE SWITCH CONTINUITY SPECIFICATIONS table.

3) Release overdrive switch to the OFF position. Using ohmmeter, ensure continuity exists between specified terminals. See OVERDRIVE SWITCH CONTINUITY SPECIFICATIONS table. Replace overdrive switch if continuity is not as specified.

OVERDRIVE SWITCH CONTINUITY SPECIFICATIONS

Application & Switch Position	Continuity Between Terminals
1995 Elantra	
ON Position	1 & 2
OFF Position	1 & 3
Sonata	
ON Position	2 & 5
OFF Position	1 & 2

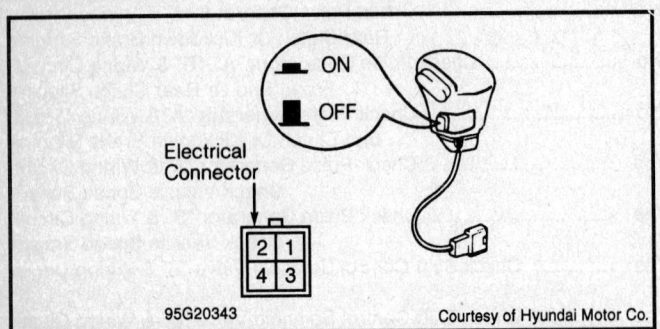

Fig. 10: Identifying Overdrive Switch Terminals (Elantra)

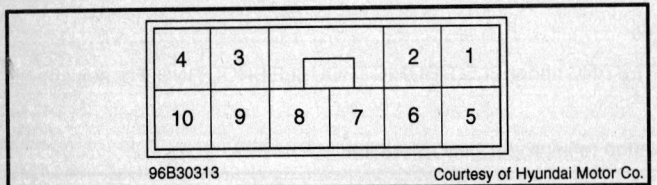

Fig. 11: Identifying Overdrive Switch Terminals (Sonata)

Oil Temperature Sensor (1995 Elantra & 1995 Sonata) – 1) Disconnect oil temperature sensor electrical connector. Note electrical connector terminals. *See Fig. 12.*

2) Using ohmmeter, check resistance between terminals No. 1 and No. 2, or No. 2 and No. 3 while varying temperature from low to high temperature.

3) If resistance reading changes smoothly as temperature is varied from low to high, oil temperature sensor is okay. If resistance reading does not change smoothly, or continuity does not exist, check wiring harness to oil temperature sensor. If wiring harness is okay, replace oil temperature sensor.

Oil Temperature Sensor (1996 Sonata) – 1) Disconnect oil temperature sensor electrical connector. Using ohmmeter, check resistance between connector terminals while varying temperature from low to high temperature.

2) If resistance reading changes smoothly as temperature is varied from low to high, oil temperature sensor is okay. If resistance reading does not change smoothly, or continuity does not exist, check wiring harness to oil temperature sensor. If wiring harness is okay, replace oil temperature sensor.

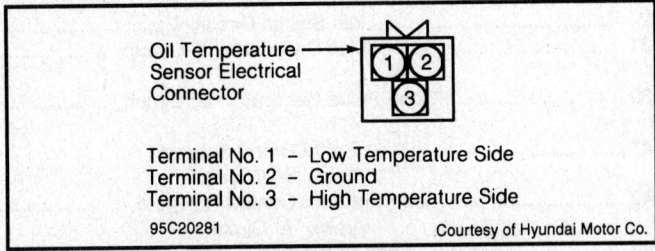

Fig. 12: Identifying Oil Temperature Sensor Electrical Connector Terminals (1995 Elantra & 1995 Sonata)

Pressure Control Solenoid Valve (PCSV) – 1) Disconnect solenoid valve electrical connector on side of transaxle and note terminal identification. *See Fig. 9.*

2) Using ohmmeter, measure resistance between terminal No. 2 and transaxle case. Resistance should be 2.6-3.2 ohms at 68°F (20°C). If resistance is within specification, go to step **4)**. If resistance is not within specification, go to next step.

3) Check for shorted, damaged or disconnected wire to solenoid valve. If wire is okay, replace solenoid valve.

4) Connect battery voltage to terminal No. 2 and transaxle case. Ensure transaxle case is grounded. Listen for operating sound at solenoid valve when voltage is applied and removed.

5) If operating sound is heard, solenoid valve is operating. If operating sound is not heard, check for foreign material caught between valve and valve guide on solenoid valve. If foreign material is not found, replace solenoid valve.

Pulse Generator "A" Or "B" – 1) To check pulse generator resistance, disconnect pulse generator electrical connector. Note terminal identification. *See Fig. 13.*

2) Using ohmmeter, measure resistance between terminals No. 1 and No. 2 for pulse generator "A", or terminals No. 3 and No. 4 for pulse generator "B". *See Fig. 13.* Resistance should be 215-275 ohms at 68°F (20°C).

3) If resistance is within specification, pulse generator is okay. If resistance is not within specification, check for shorted, damaged or disconnected wire to pulse generator. If wire is okay, replace pulse generator.

4) To check pulse generator with oscilloscope, raise and support vehicle so front wheels are free to rotate. Ensure pulse generator electrical connector is connected.

5) Start engine. Place shift lever in "L" position. Increase engine speed to 1000 RPM. Using oscilloscope, check voltage wave pattern between terminals No. 1 and No. 2 for pulse generator "A", or terminals No. 3 and No. 4 for pulse generator "B".

6) Voltage should be at least 1000 millivolts for pulse generator "A" and 500 millivolts for pulse generator "B". *See Fig. 14.*

7) If very low voltage is obtained, check for faulty installation of pulse generator. If pulse generator installation is okay, replace appropriate pulse generator. If noise exists in oscilloscope wave pattern, check for improper grounding of pulse generator circuit wire. If wire is okay, replace appropriate pulse generator.

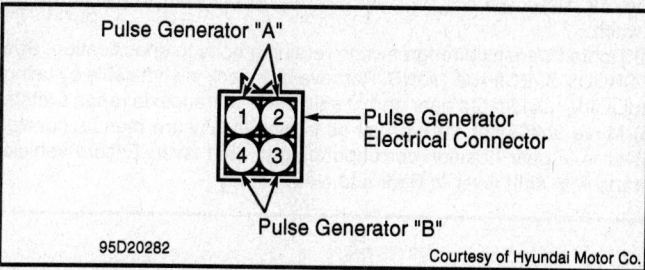

Fig. 13: Identifying Pulse Generator Electrical Connector Terminals

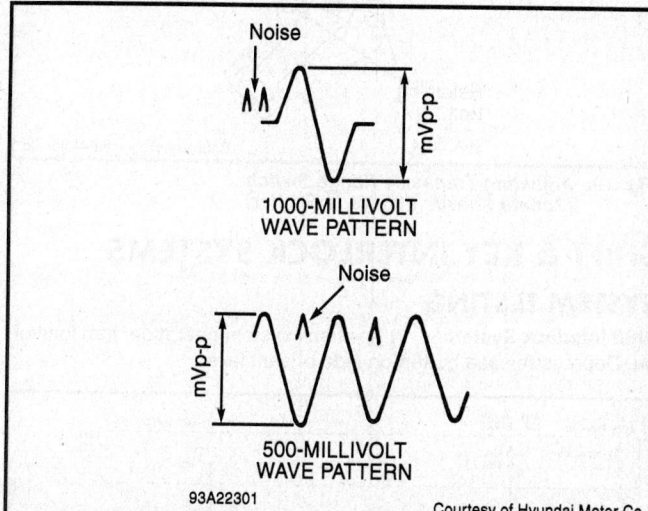

Fig. 14: Identifying Pulse Generator Oscilloscope Wave Patterns

Range Switch – 1) Disconnect electrical connector for range switch and note switch terminal identification. See Fig. 15 or 16. Range switch is located on console, near shift lever.
2) Using ohmmeter, ensure continuity exists between specified terminals in relation to switch position. See RANGE SWITCH CONTINUITY SPECIFICATIONS. Replace range switch if continuity is not as specified.

RANGE SWITCH CONTINUITY SPECIFICATIONS

Application & Switch Position	Continuity Between Terminals
1995 Elantra	
ECON	1 & 4
NORM	1 & 2
Sonata	
NORM	1 & 3, 2 & 4
PWR	1 & 3, 2 & 5

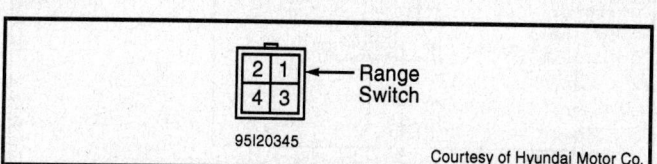

Fig. 15: Identifying Range Switch Terminals (1995 Elantra)

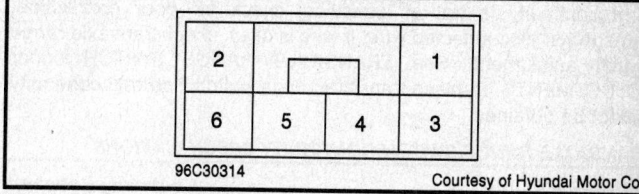

Fig. 16: Identifying Range Switch Terminals (Sonata)

Shift Control Solenoid Valve (SCSV) "A" Or "B" – 1) Disconnect solenoid valve electrical connector on side of transaxle and note terminal identification. See Fig. 9.
2) Using ohmmeter, measure resistance between terminal No. 3 (solenoid valve "B") or terminal No. 4 (solenoid valve "A") and transaxle case. Resistance should be 21-24 ohms at 68°F (20°C). If resistance is within specification, go to step **4)**. If resistance is not within specification, go to next step.
3) Check for shorted, damaged or disconnected wire to solenoid valve. If wire is okay, replace solenoid valve.
4) Connect battery voltage between terminal No. 3 (solenoid valve "B") or terminal No. 4 (solenoid valve "A") and ground. Listen for operating sound at solenoid valve when voltage is applied and removed.
5) If operating sound is heard, solenoid valve is operating. If operating sound is not heard, check for foreign material caught in solenoid valve. If foreign material is not found, replace solenoid valve.

Throttle Position Sensor – 1) Note TPS connector terminal identification. See Fig. 17. Using ohmmeter, measure resistance between terminals No. 1 and No. 4 on TPS. Resistance should be 3500-6500 ohms at 68°F (20°C). If resistance is not as specified, check wire harness. If wire harness is okay, replace TPS.
2) Start engine and warm to normal operating temperature. Using ohmmeter, measure resistance between terminals No. 1 and No. 3 with engine idling. Resistance should be 400 ohms at 68°F (20°C). If resistance is not as specified, adjust TPS. See THROTTLE POSITION SENSOR (TPS) under ADJUSTMENTS.
3) Check resistance between terminals No. 1 and No. 3 as throttle is operated from idle to wide open position. If TPS is operating correctly, resistance should change smoothly. If resistance does not change smoothly, replace TPS.

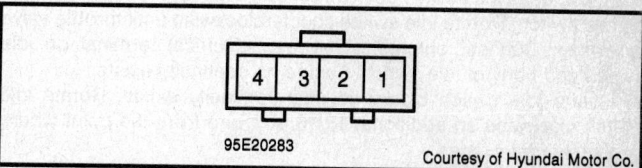

Fig. 17: Identifying Throttle Position Sensor (TPS) Terminals

Transaxle Control Module (TCM) – 1) Ensure ignition is off. Disconnect electrical connectors from TCM. On Elantra models, TCM is located below passenger's seat. See Fig. 3. On Sonata models, TCM is located below center of instrument panel at center console. See Fig. 4.
2) Connect known good TCM to electrical connectors and road test vehicle. If malfunction does not occur, replace original TCM. If problem occurs, original TCM is okay. Check sensors and wire harness.

NOTE: For additional wiring and circuit information, see WIRING DIAGRAMS.

Transaxle Range Switch – 1) Transaxle range switch is mounted on transaxle. See Fig. 5. Transaxle range switch may also be referred to as inhibitor switch. Note transaxle range switch connector terminals. See Fig. 18.
2) Apply parking brake. Using ohmmeter, ensure continuity exists between specified terminals in relation to shift lever position. See TRANSAXLE RANGE SWITCH CONTINUITY SPECIFICATIONS table.

) If continuity is not as specified, check for poor connection, damaged or disconnected wire. If wire is okay, check transaxle range switch adjustment. See TRANSAXLE RANGE SWITCH under ADJUSTMENTS. Replace transaxle range switch if correct continuity cannot be obtained.

TRANSAXLE RANGE SWITCH CONTINUITY SPECIFICATIONS

Shift Lever Position	Continuity Between Terminals
"P"	3 & 4, 10 & 11
"R"	3 & 12, 8 & 9
"N"	3 & 5, 10 & 11
"D"	1 & 3
"2"	3 & 6
"L"	2 & 3

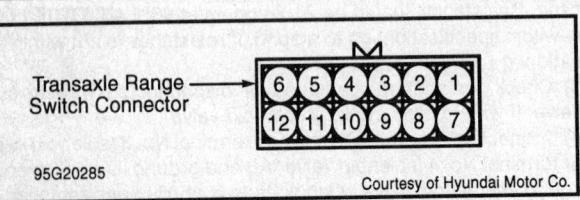

Transaxle Range Switch Connector →

95G20285

Courtesy of Hyundai Motor Co.

Fig. 18: Identifying Transaxle Range Switch Connector Terminals

Vehicle Speed Sensor – On 1995 Elantra, Vehicle Speed Sensor (VSS) is located on rear of speedometer on instrument panel gauge assembly. See Fig. 5. On Sonata, Vehicle Speed Sensor (VSS) is located on transaxle. On all models, vehicle speed sensor should change from continuity to no continuity 4 times with each revolution of speedometer cable shaft. Replace vehicle speed sensor if operation is not as specified.

ADJUSTMENTS

IDLE SWITCH

1995 Elantra & 1995 Sonata – 1) Idle switch is preset at the factory and adjustment should not be required unless idle switch is replaced. Loosen tension on accelerator cable.

2) Disconnect electrical connector from idle switch, located on throttle body, opposite the throttle position sensor. See Fig. 5. Loosen lock nut on idle switch. Rotate idle switch counterclockwise until throttle valve is closed. Connect ohmmeter between electrical terminal on idle switch and body of idle switch. Ensure no continuity exists.

3) Rotate idle switch clockwise until continuity exists. Rotate idle switch clockwise an additional 15/16 of a turn from the point where continuity first existed.

4) Remove ohmmeter. Hold idle switch from rotating and tighten lock nut. Install electrical connector on idle switch. Adjust accelerator cable. Start engine. Ensure idle speed is within specification. Check and adjust TPS. See THROTTLE POSITION SENSOR (TPS) under ADJUSTMENTS.

1996 Sonata – Idle switch is incorporated in Throttle Position Switch (TPS), mounted on throttle body. See THROTTLE POSITION SWITCH (TPS) for adjustment.

THROTTLE POSITION SENSOR (TPS)

1) Connect voltmeter between TPS terminals No. 1 and No. 3. See Fig. 17. Turn ignition on.

2) If voltage is .48-.52 volts, TPS setting is okay. If voltage is not as specified, go to next step.

3) Loosen TPS bolts enough to allow rotation of TPS. Turn TPS clockwise to increase output voltage. When specified voltage is obtained, tighten bolts and retest. See TORQUE SPECIFICATIONS. If specified voltage cannot be obtained, replace TPS and readjust.

TRANSAXLE RANGE SWITCH

1) Transaxle range switch is mounted below manual control lever on transaxle. See Fig. 5. Apply parking brake. Place shift lever in Neutral position.

2) Disconnect shift cable from manual control lever. Place manual control lever on transaxle in Neutral position.

3) Loosen transaxle range switch retaining bolts. Rotate transaxle range switch body until the .47" (12.0 mm) wide end of manual control lever aligns with wide flange area on transaxle range switch. See Fig. 19. Use care not to allow "O" ring to fall from transaxle range switch.

4) Tighten transaxle range switch retaining bolts to specification. See TORQUE SPECIFICATIONS. Remove any slack in shift cable by using adjusting nut located near end of shift cable at transaxle range switch.

5) Move shift lever through all gear ranges. Ensure manual control lever is in gear position corresponding to shift lever. Ensure vehicle starts with shift lever in Park and Neutral only.

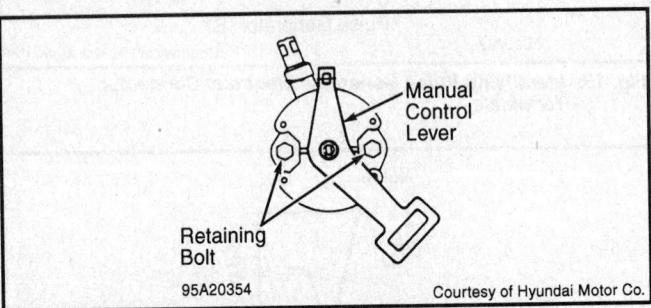

Manual Control Lever

Retaining Bolt

95A20354

Courtesy of Hyundai Motor Co.

Fig. 19: Adjusting Transaxle Range Switch (Sonata Shown; Elantra Is Similar)

SHIFT & KEY INTERLOCK SYSTEMS

SYSTEM TESTING

Shift Interlock System – 1) To check system operation, turn ignition on. Depress release button on side of shift lever.

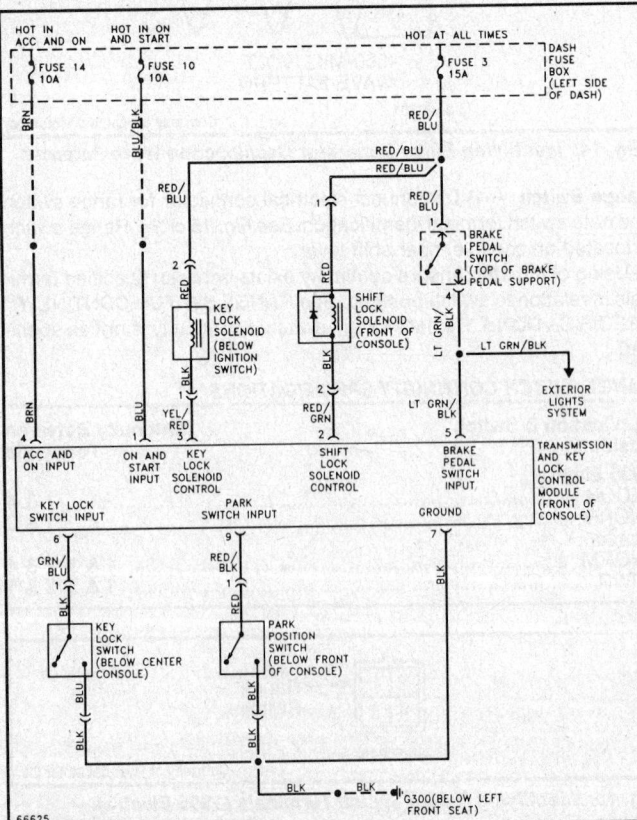

66625

Fig. 20: Shift & Key Interlock System Wiring Schematic (Elantra)

2) With brake pedal released, shift lever should not move from Park. Depress brake pedal. Shift lever should now move from Park.

3) If shift interlock system operation is not as specified, it may be necessary to check brakelight switch and A/T shift lock solenoid. See BRAKELIGHT SWITCH and A/T SHIFT LOCK SOLENOID under SHIFT & KEY INTERLOCK SYSTEM COMPONENT TESTING.

Key Interlock System – **1)** With shift lever in any gear position except Park, ensure ignition key cannot be turned to LOCK position. Place shift lever in Park. Ensure ignition key can now be turned to LOCK position.

2) If key interlock system operation is not as specified, it may be necessary to check key lock solenoid. See KEY LOCK SOLENOID under SHIFT & KEY INTERLOCK SYSTEM COMPONENT TESTING.

COMPONENT TESTING

A/T & Key Lock Control Unit – The A/T and key lock control unit is located below center of instrument panel at center console, or near passenger's side kick panel, depending on vehicle application. *See Fig. 1.* To test A/T and Key Lock Control Unit input circuit, see A/T & KEY LOCK CONTROL UNIT CIRCUIT table. *See Fig. 22.* No other testing information is available from the manufacturer.

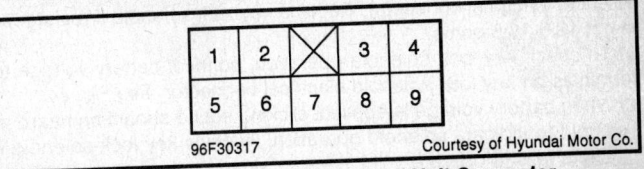

Fig. 22: Identifying A/T & Key Lock Control Unit Connector Terminals

A/T Shift Lock Solenoid – **1)** Disconnect electrical connector at A/T shift lock solenoid, located on shift lever. *See Fig. 1.*

2) Using ohmmeter measure resistance between terminals on A/T shift lock solenoid electrical connector. Replace A/T shift lock solenoid if resistance is not 12-16 ohms.

3) To check A/T shift lock solenoid operation, connect battery voltage to terminals on A/T shift lock solenoid electrical connector. *See Fig. 23.*

4) When battery voltage is applied, clicking sound should be heard at solenoid to indicate solenoid operation. Replace A/T shift lock solenoid if solenoid fails to operate.

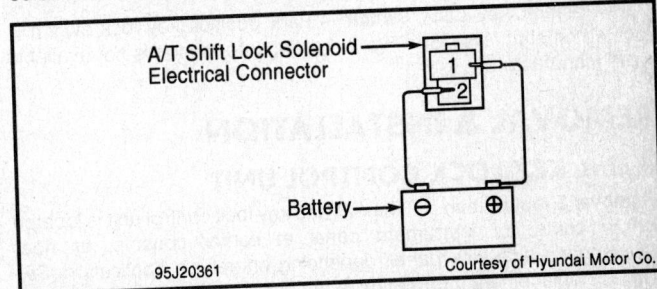

Fig. 23: Testing A/T Shift Lock Solenoid Operation

Brakelight Switch – **1)** Disconnect brakelight switch electrical connector. Brakelight switch is mounted near brake pedal.

2) Using ohmmeter, check for continuity between electrical terminals on brakelight switch with brake pedal depressed. Continuity should exist.

3) Using ohmmeter, check for continuity between electrical terminals on brakelight switch with brake pedal released. Continuity should not exist.

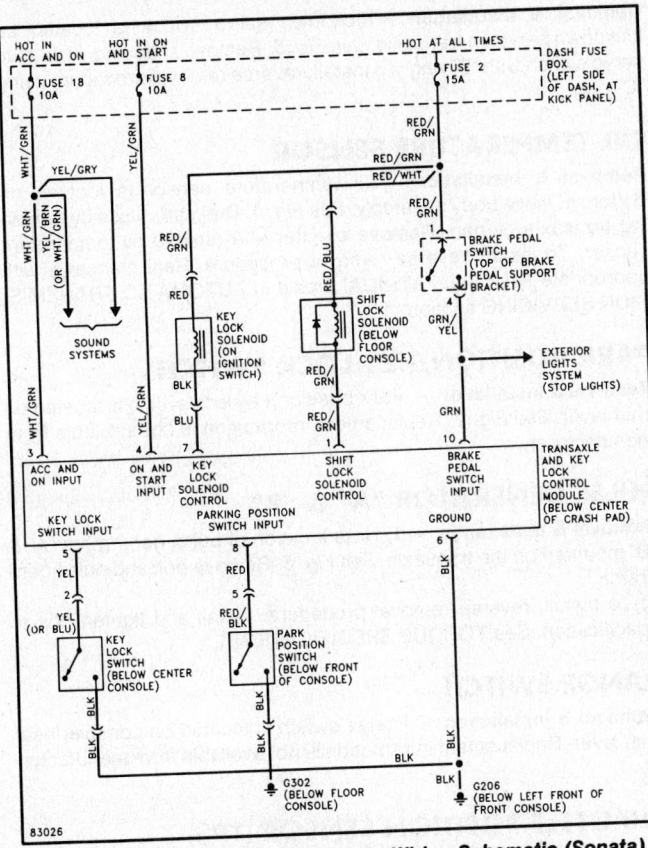

Fig. 21: Shift & Key Interlock System Wiring Schematic (Sonata)

A/T & KEY LOCK CONTROL UNIT CIRCUIT

Elantra Terminal No.	Sonata Terminal No.	Circuit	Test Condition	[1] Measured Output
1	4	Ignition Source	Ignition On	Battery Voltage
			Ignition Off	No Voltage
2	1	Shift Lock Solenoid	At All Times	Battery Voltage
3	7	Key Lock Solenoid	At All Times	Battery Voltage
		ACC Source	Ignition Switch In ACC Position	Battery Voltage
4	3		Ignition Off	No Voltage
5	2	Brake Light Switch	Brake Pedal Depressed	Battery Voltage
			Brake Pedal Not Depressed	No Voltage
7	6	Ground	At All Times	Continuity
9	8	Parking Position Switch	Shift Lever In "P" Position	Continuity
			Shift Lever In Any Other Position	No Continuity

[1] – Measured output is measured between specified terminal and ground.

4) If operation is not as specified, ensure brake pedal is properly adjusted so brakelight switch can obtain proper travel for switch operation. If proper brakelight switch travel exists, replace brakelight switch.

Key Lock Solenoid – **1)** Disconnect electrical connector at key lock solenoid. Key lock solenoid is located in ignition lock assembly on steering column.

2) Using ohmmeter measure resistance between terminals on key lock solenoid electrical connector. Replace key lock solenoid if resistance is not 12.5-16.5 ohms.

3) To check key lock solenoid operation, connect battery voltage to terminals on key lock solenoid electrical connector. See Fig. 24.

4) When battery voltage is applied, clicking sound should be heard at solenoid to indicate solenoid operation. Replace key lock solenoid if solenoid fails to operate.

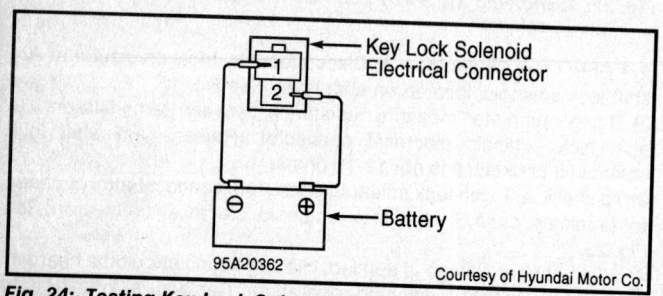

Fig. 24: Testing Key Lock Solenoid Operation

Park Position/Key Lock Switch – Park position/key lock switch is located on shift lever. See Fig. 2. Testing information is not available from manufacturer.

REMOVAL & INSTALLATION

A/T & KEY LOCK CONTROL UNIT

Removal & Installation – The A/T and key lock control unit is located below center of instrument panel at center console, or near passenger's side kick panel, depending on vehicle application. See Fig. 1. Replacement information is not available from manufacturer.

A/T SHIFT LOCK SOLENOID

Removal & Installation – The A/T shift lock solenoid is located on shift lever. See Fig. 2. Replacement information is not available from manufacturer.

BRAKELIGHT SWITCH

Removal & Installation – **1)** Disconnect electrical connector at brakelight switch, mounted near brake pedal. Remove lock nut. Unscrew brakelight switch.

2) To install, screw brakelight switch inward until clearance between threaded end on brakelight switch and brake pedal is .020-.039" (.50-1.00 mm). Install and tighten lock nut. Install electrical connector. Ensure brakelights operate properly.

DAMPER CLUTCH, PRESSURE CONTROL & SHIFT CONTROL SOLENOID VALVES

Removal – **1)** Valve body assembly must be removed for servicing of control solenoid valves. Remove valve body assembly. See VALVE BODY ASSEMBLY under REMOVAL & INSTALLATION in HYUNDAI KM175 AUTOMATIC TRANSMISSIONS article.

2) Note location of appropriate control solenoid valve on valve body assembly. See Fig. 6. Remove bolts and appropriate control solenoid valve.

Installation – To install, reverse removal procedure. Ensure proper procedure is used when installing valve body assembly. Fill transaxle with Mopar Plus-Type 7176 ATF.

IDLE SWITCH

Removal & Installation (1995 Elantra & 1995 Sonata) – Idle switch is screwed into the throttle body on opposite side of throttle position sensor. Replacement information is not available from manufacturer. Idle switch must be adjusted if removed from throttle body. See IDLE SWITCH under ADJUSTMENTS.

KEY LOCK SOLENOID

Removal & Installation – Key lock solenoid is located in ignition lock assembly on steering column. Replacement information is not available from manufacturer.

KICKDOWN SERVO SWITCH

Removal & Installation – Kickdown servo switch is located on kickdown servo on transaxle. See Fig. 5. Remove snap ring, kickdown servo switch with "D" ring. To install, reverse removal procedure using "D" ring.

OIL TEMPERATURE SENSOR

Removal & Installation – Oil temperature sensor is located on bottom of valve body assembly. See Fig. 5. Drain transaxle by removing transaxle oil pan. Remove oil filter and remove oil temperature sensor. To install, reverse removal procedure. Refill transaxle with appropriate fluid. See HYUNDAI article in AUTOMATIC TRANSMISSION SERVICING section.

PARK POSITION/KEY LOCK SWITCH

Removal & Installation – Park position/key lock switch is located on shift lever. See Fig. 2. Replacement information is not available from manufacturer.

PULSE GENERATOR "A" & "B"

Removal & Installation – **1)** Note location of pulse generators "A" & "B" mounted on the transaxle. See Fig. 5. Remove bolt and pulse generator.

2) To install, reverse removal procedure. Install and tighten bolt to specification. See TORQUE SPECIFICATIONS.

RANGE SWITCH

Removal & Installation – Range switch is located on console, near shift lever. Replacement information is not available from manufacturer.

THROTTLE POSITION SENSOR (TPS)

Removal & Installation – **1)** Disconnect electrical connector at throttle position sensor, mounted on side of throttle body. Remove bolts and throttle position sensor.

2) To install, reverse removal procedure. Install and tighten throttle position sensor bolts to specification. See TORQUE SPECIFICATIONS. Adjust throttle position sensor. See THROTTLE POSITION SENSOR (TPS) under ADJUSTMENTS.

TRANSAXLE CONTROL MODULE (TCM)

Removal & Installation – On Elantra models, TCM is located below passenger's seat. See Fig. 3. On Sonata models, TCM is located below center of instrument panel at center console. See Fig. 4. On all models, replacement information is not available from manufacturer.

TRANSAXLE RANGE SWITCH

Removal & Installation – **1)** Transaxle range switch is mounted below manual control lever on transaxle. See Fig. 5. Disconnect shift cable and electrical connector at transaxle range switch.

2) Remove lock nut and manual control lever. Remove transaxle range switch retaining bolts and transaxle range switch.

3) To install, reverse removal procedure. DO NOT tighten transaxle range switch retaining bolts until switch is adjusted. Tighten manual control lever lock nut to specification. See TORQUE SPECIFICATIONS.

4) Adjust transaxle range switch. See TRANSAXLE RANGE SWITCH under ADJUSTMENTS.

VEHICLE SPEED SENSOR (VSS)

Removal & Installation – On Elantra, vehicle speed sensor is located on rear of speedometer on instrument panel gauge assembly. *See Fig. 5.* On Sonata, vehicle speed sensor is located on transaxle. Replacement information is not available from manufacturer.

TORQUE SPECIFICATIONS

TORQUE SPECIFICATIONS

Application	Ft. Lbs. (N.m)
Manual Control Lever Lock Nut	12-15 (16-20)
	INCH Lbs. (N.m)
Pulse Generator Bolt	89-106 (10.0-12.0)
Throttle Position Sensor Retaining Bolt	13-22 (1.5-2.2)
Transaxle Range Switch Retaining Bolt	89-106 (10.0-12.0)

AUTOMATIC TRANSMISSIONS
Hyundai KM175 Electronic Controls (Cont.)

WIRING DIAGRAMS

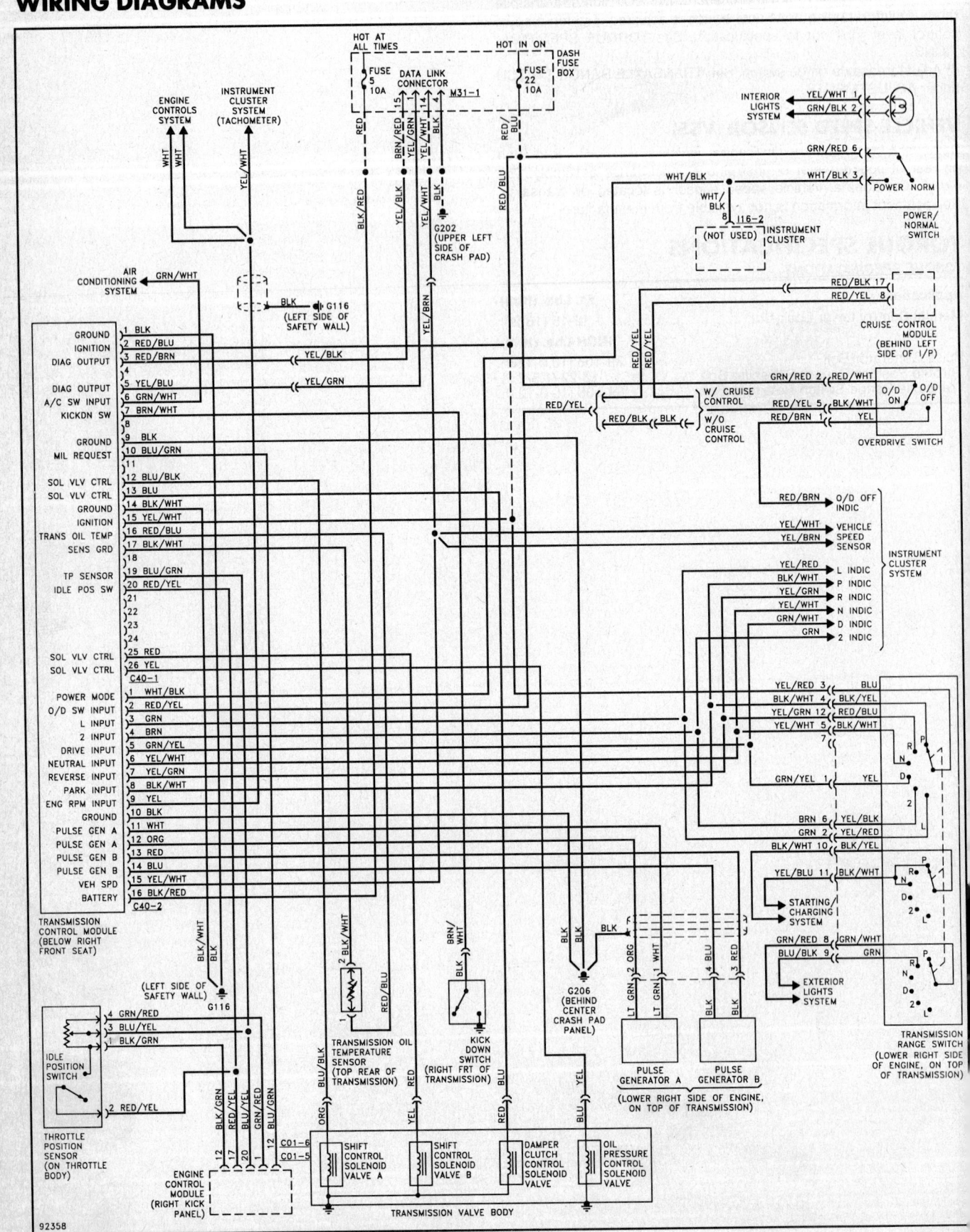

Fig. 25: Transaxle Wiring Diagram (1995 Elantra)

92358

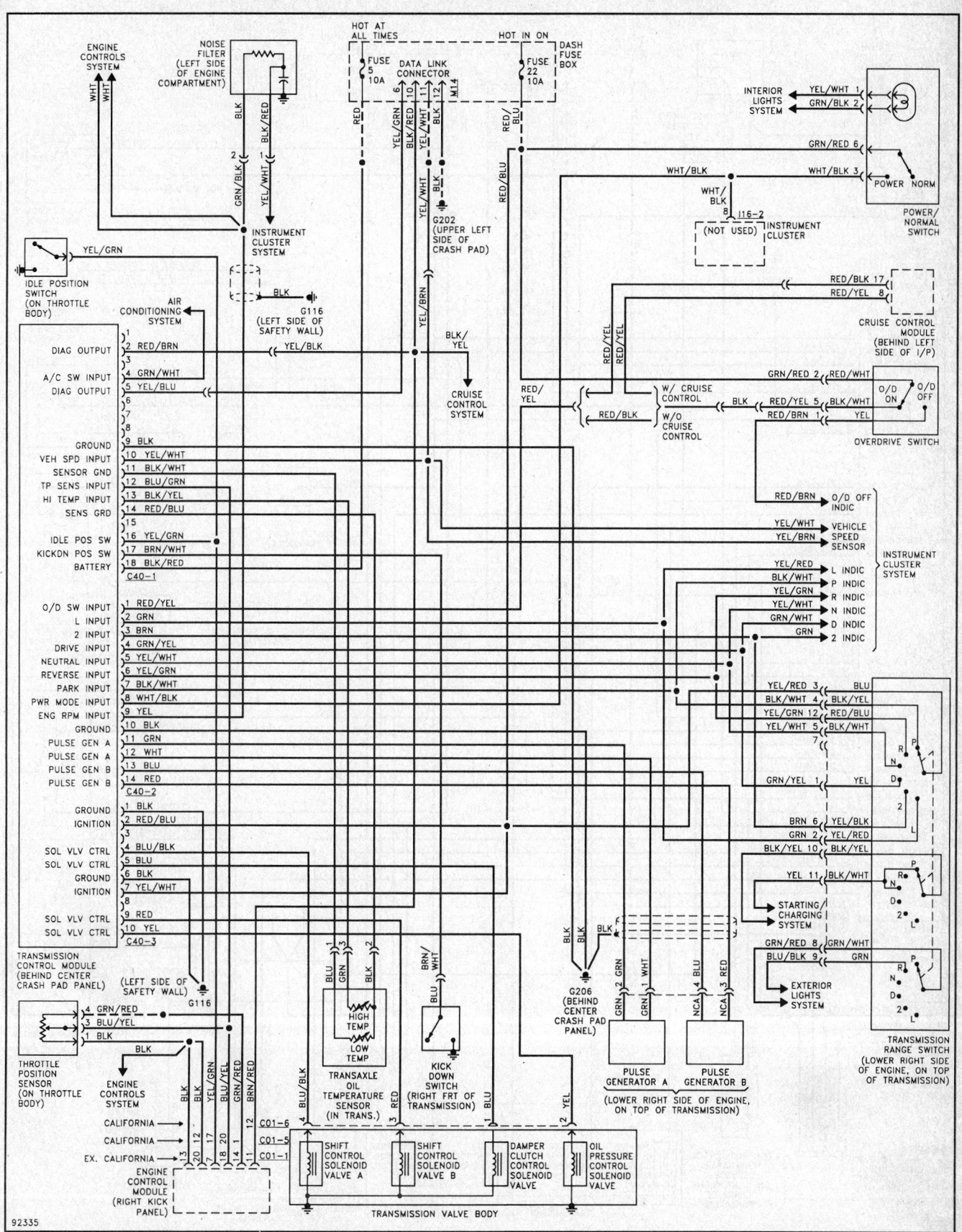

Fig. 26: Transaxle Wiring Diagram (1995 Sonata 2.0L)

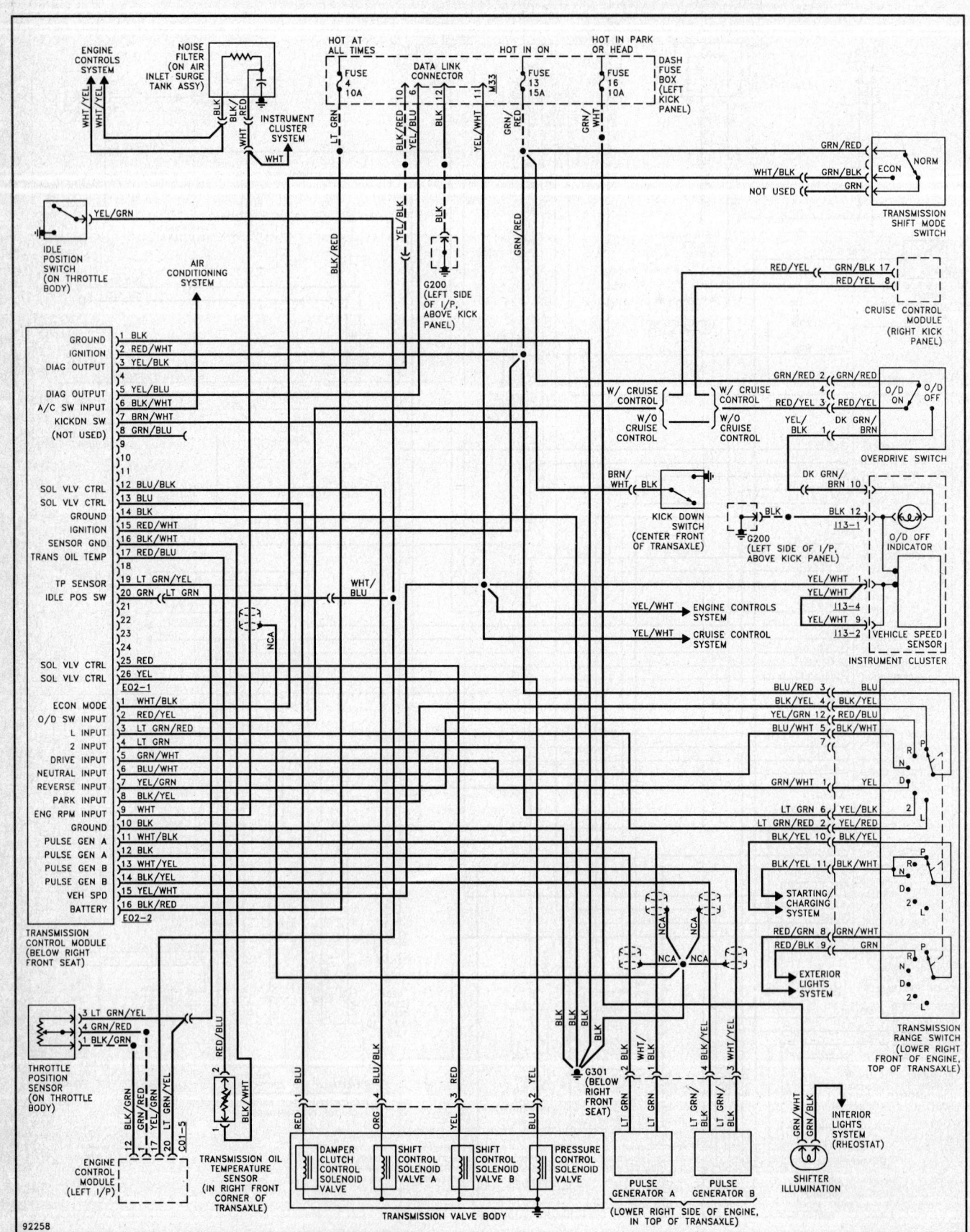

Fig. 27: Transaxle Wiring Diagram (1996 Sonata 2.0L)

XJS, XJ6

IDENTIFICATION

AUTOMATIC TRANSMISSION APPLICATIONS

Model	Transmission
1995	
XJS (4.0L)	ZF 4HP 24-E
XJ6	ZF 4HP 24-E
1996	
XJS & XJ6	ZF 4HP 24-E

DESCRIPTION

Automatic transmission is electronically controlled. Transmission shifting and torque converter lock-up are controlled by Transmission Control Module (TCM). The TCM receives information from various input devices and uses this information to control shift solenoids and pressure regulator solenoid. This information is used in conjunction with transmission speed sensor signal, and inputs from engine management system to calculate optimum shift points and control parameters for shift pressure and ignition retard to enhance shift quality.

If a major fault occurs, TCM removes all electrical power to transmission and the transmission reverts to a mechanical default (limp-home) condition. This condition allows only mechanical selection of reverse and one forward gear, either 3rd or 4th, depending on conditions at time of default. The transmission warning indicator light on instrument cluster will illuminate to inform driver of a problem. In some instances, indicator light may be turned off by turning ignition off and restarting engine. Transmission should still be diagnosed.

Transmission is capable of 2 different shift modes, Normal (N) mode and Sport (S) mode. For additional information, see SHIFT MODES under OPERATION. Transmission is equipped with shift interlock system. Shift lock system prevents gearshift lever movement from Park position unless brake pedal is depressed and ignition is on (position II). System also prevents ignition switch from being placed in LOCK position unless gearshift lever is in Park position.

OPERATION

SHIFT MODES

NOTE: Transmission is capable of 2 different shift modes, Normal (N) mode and Sport (S) mode. Shift mode may be selected by using rocker switch mounted on center console, near gearshift lever. Shift modes are used to change transmission shift points for various vehicle operating conditions.

Normal Mode – Normal mode is selected by depressing "N" on rocker switch mounted on center console, near gearshift lever. Normal mode provides standard transmission shift points.

Sport Mode – Sport mode is obtained by depressing "S" on rocker switch mounted on center console, near gearshift lever. Sport mode slightly increases engine speed at which transmission shift points occur for maximum performance. When Sport mode is selected with ignition on, SPORT indicator light on instrument cluster will illuminate.

TRANSMISSION CONTROL MODULE (TCM)

The TCM receives information from various input devices and uses this information to control the following output devices: shift solenoids, pressure regulator solenoid and lockup solenoid.

The TCM contains a self-diagnostic system which stores a Diagnostic Trouble Code (DTC) if a failure or problem is present in the transmission electronic control system. If a failure occurs in a monitored circuit, automatic transmission failure indicator light will illuminate to inform driver of a problem. Indicator light is located at top left of instrument panel.

DTCs may be retrieved to determine transmission problem area. For information on retrieving DTCs, see SELF-DIAGNOSTIC SYSTEM. For TCM locations, see WIRING DIAGRAMS.

SELF-DIAGNOSTIC SYSTEM

SYSTEM CHECK

1) Turn ignition on. Automatic transmission failure indicator light should illuminate for 2-4 seconds, then go off, indicating light circuit is operating properly. Indicator light is located at top left of instrument cluster.

2) Indicator light may flash briefly during engine start-up, but should stay off during engine operation. If indicator light stays on, TCM has detected a system fault. See RETRIEVING CODES.

RETRIEVING CODES

Turn ignition off. Connect Jaguar Portable Diagnostic Unit (PDU) scan tool or generic scan tool to 16-pin Data Link Connector (DLC). *See Fig. 1.* Turn ignition on. If using PDU scan tool, follow PDU screen prompts. If using generic scan tool, follow scan tool manufacturer's operating instructions. Check for and note any DTCs. See DIAGNOSTIC TROUBLE CODE IDENTIFICATION table for probable cause.

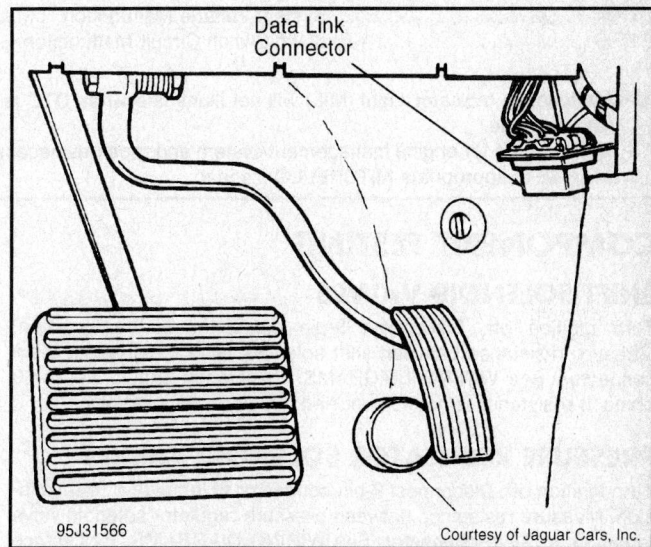

95J31566 Courtesy of Jaguar Cars, Inc.

Fig. 1: Locating 16-Pin Data Link Connector (DLC)

CLEARING CODES

NOTE: Some models have an anti-theft code built into the radio circuit. Clearing codes by disconnecting negative battery cable cancels clock and radio settings; make note of settings before clearing codes. After codes are cleared, the radio will not function until code is entered.

To clear codes or to reset Powertrain Control Module (PCM), use PDU scan tool or generic scan tool following manufacturer's instructions. Codes can also be cleared by turning ignition off and disconnecting negative battery terminal for 30 seconds. Disconnect scan tool from DLC, or reconnect negative battery terminal.

DIAGNOSTIC TROUBLE CODE (DTC) IDENTIFICATION

Code	Description	Probable Cause
P0603	Control Module Memory Fault	TCM
P0605	Internal Control Module ROM Test Fault	TCM
P0702	Electronic Transmission Control System Fault Error	TCM Internal Relay
P0705	Transmission Rotary Switch Malfunction	Open In Rotary Switch Circuit Or Rotary Switch
P0706	Transmission Rotary Switch Circuit Range/Performance	Open In Rotary Switch Circuit Or Rotary Switch
P0712 [1]	Transmission Fluid Temperature Sensor (TFT) Low Input	Faulty TFT Sensor Or Wiring Harness
P0713 [1]	Transmission Fluid Temperature Sensor High Input	Faulty TFT Sensor Or Wiring Harness
P0721	Output Speed Sensor Circuit Range/Performance	Faulty Speed Sensor Or Wiring Harness
P0722	No Output Speed Sensor Circuit Signal	Faulty Speed Sensor Or Wiring Harness
P0726	Engine Speed Input Circuit Range/Performance	[2] Wiring Harness Or Faulty Signal From ECM
P0727	No Engine Speed Input Signal	[2] Wiring Harness Or Faulty Signal From ECM
P0743	Electronic Torque Converter Clutch System Fault	Faulty Solenoid Valve Or Wiring Harness
P0748	Electronic Pressure Control Solenoid Fault	Faulty Pressure Control Solenoid Valve Or Wiring Harness
P0753	Shift Solenoid "A" Fault	Faulty Shift Solenoid Valve Or Wiring Harness
P0758	Shift Solenoid "B" Fault	Faulty Shift Solenoid Valve Or Wiring Harness
P1608	Transmission Control Module (TCM) Fault	TCM
P1780 [1]	Torque Reduction Signal Malfunction	[2] Wiring Harness Or Faulty Signal From ECM
P1781 [1]	Torque Signal Malfunction	[2] Wiring Harness Or Faulty Signal From ECM
P1782 [1]	Traction Control Input Signal Fault	Short To Ground In TRAC Active Circuit
P1785 [1]	Transmission Indicator Light Malfunction	Wiring Harness, Indicator Bulb Or Instrument Cluster
P1790	Throttle Position Signal System Range/Performance	[2] Wiring Harness Or Faulty Signal From ECM
P1791	Throttle Position Signal Fault	Ignition System, Fuel System Or Engine Mechanical
P1792	Sport Mode Indicator	Wiring Harness, Indicator Bulb Or Instrument Cluster
P1794	System Voltage Malfunction	Blown Fuses, Wiring Harness Or TCM
P1796	Kickdown Switch Circuit Malfunction	Wiring Harness, Switch Out Of Adjustment Or Faulty Switch

[1] – Malfunction Indicator Light (MIL) will not illuminate when DTC is set. Jaguar Portable Diagnostic Unit (PDU) scan tool must be used to retrieve code.

[2] – Check DTCs for engine management system and repair as necessary. See appropriate SELF-DIAGNOSTICS article in ENGINE PERFORMANCE in appropriate MITCHELL® manual.

COMPONENT TESTING

SHIFT SOLENOID VALVES

Turn ignition off. Disconnect 9-pin connector at transmission. Measure resistance between shift solenoid valve terminals at 9-pin connector. See WIRING DIAGRAMS. Resistance should be 28-60 ohms. If resistance is not as specified, replace solenoid valve.

PRESSURE REGULATOR SOLENOID VALVE

Turn ignition off. Disconnect 9-pin connector at left side of transmission. Measure resistance between pressure regulator solenoid valve terminals at 9-pin connector. See WIRING DIAGRAMS. Resistance should be 5-7 ohms. If resistance is not as specified, replace solenoid valve.

AUTOMATIC TRANSMISSIONS
Jaguar ZF 4HP 24-E Electronic Controls (Cont.)

3-787

WIRING DIAGRAMS

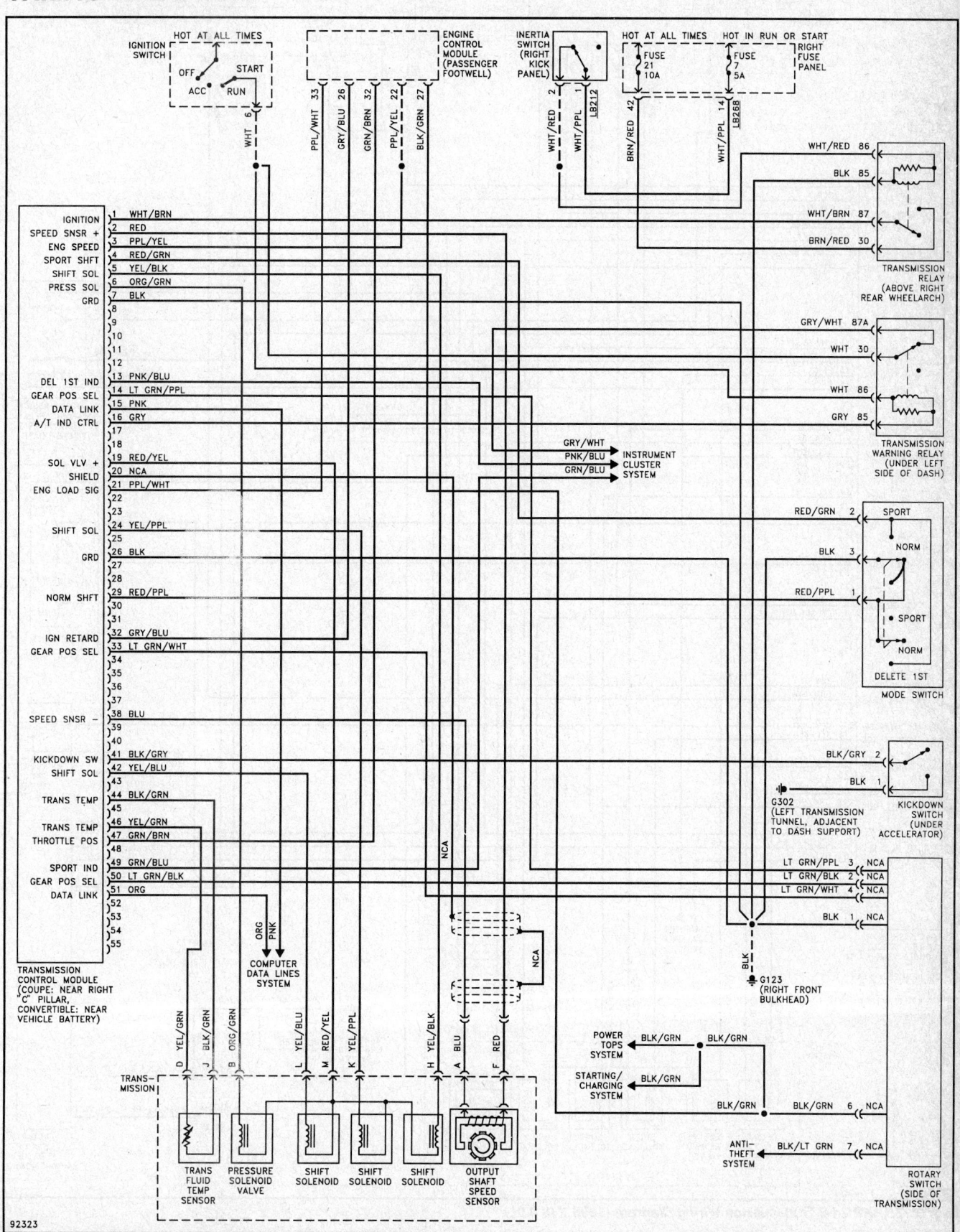

Fig. 2: *ZF 4HP 24-E Transmission Wiring Diagram (1995 XJS 4.0L)*

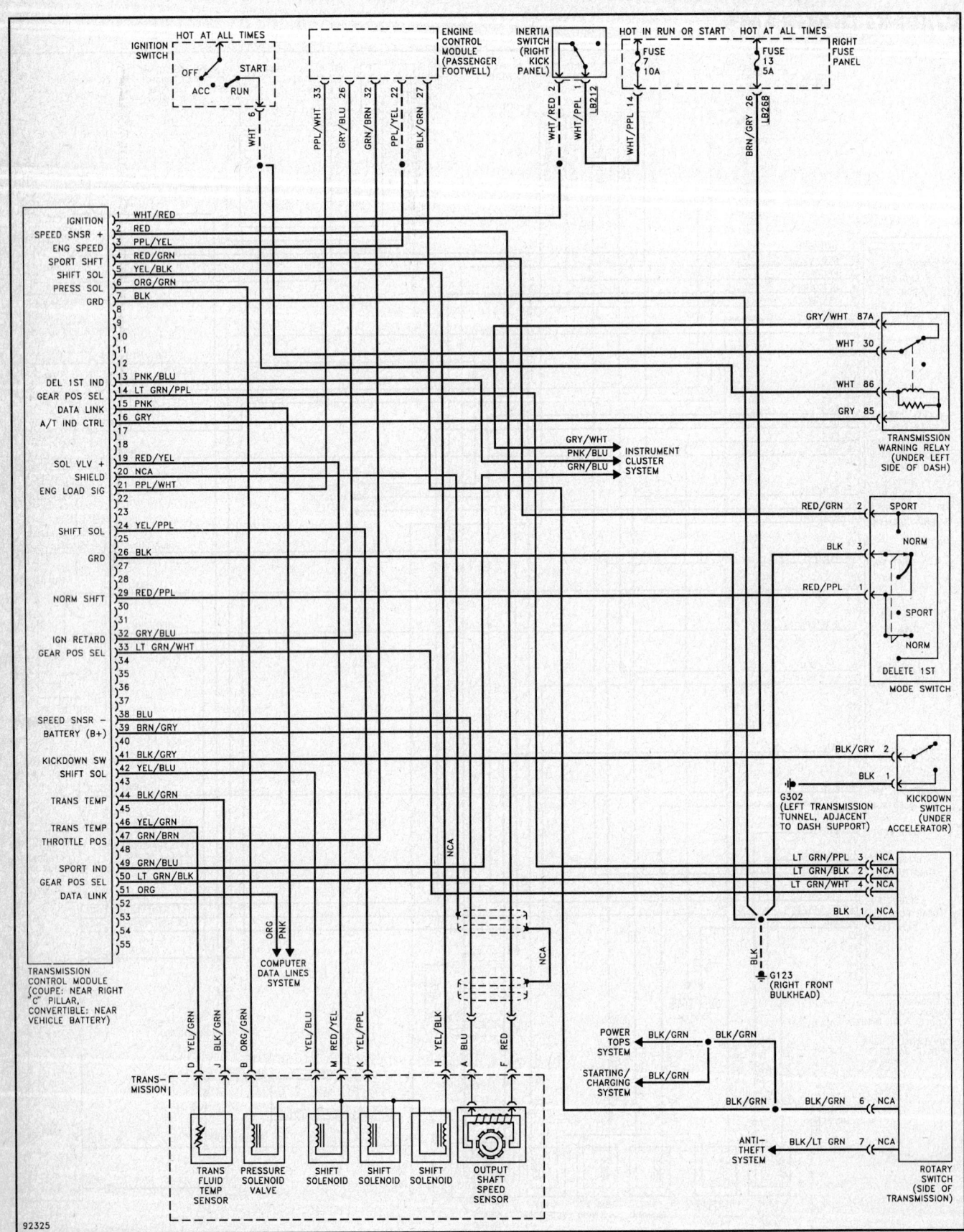

Fig. 3: ZF 4HP 24-E Transmission Wiring Diagram (1996 XJS 4.0L)

AUTOMATIC TRANSMISSIONS
Jaguar ZF 4HP 24-E Electronic Controls (Cont.)

3-789

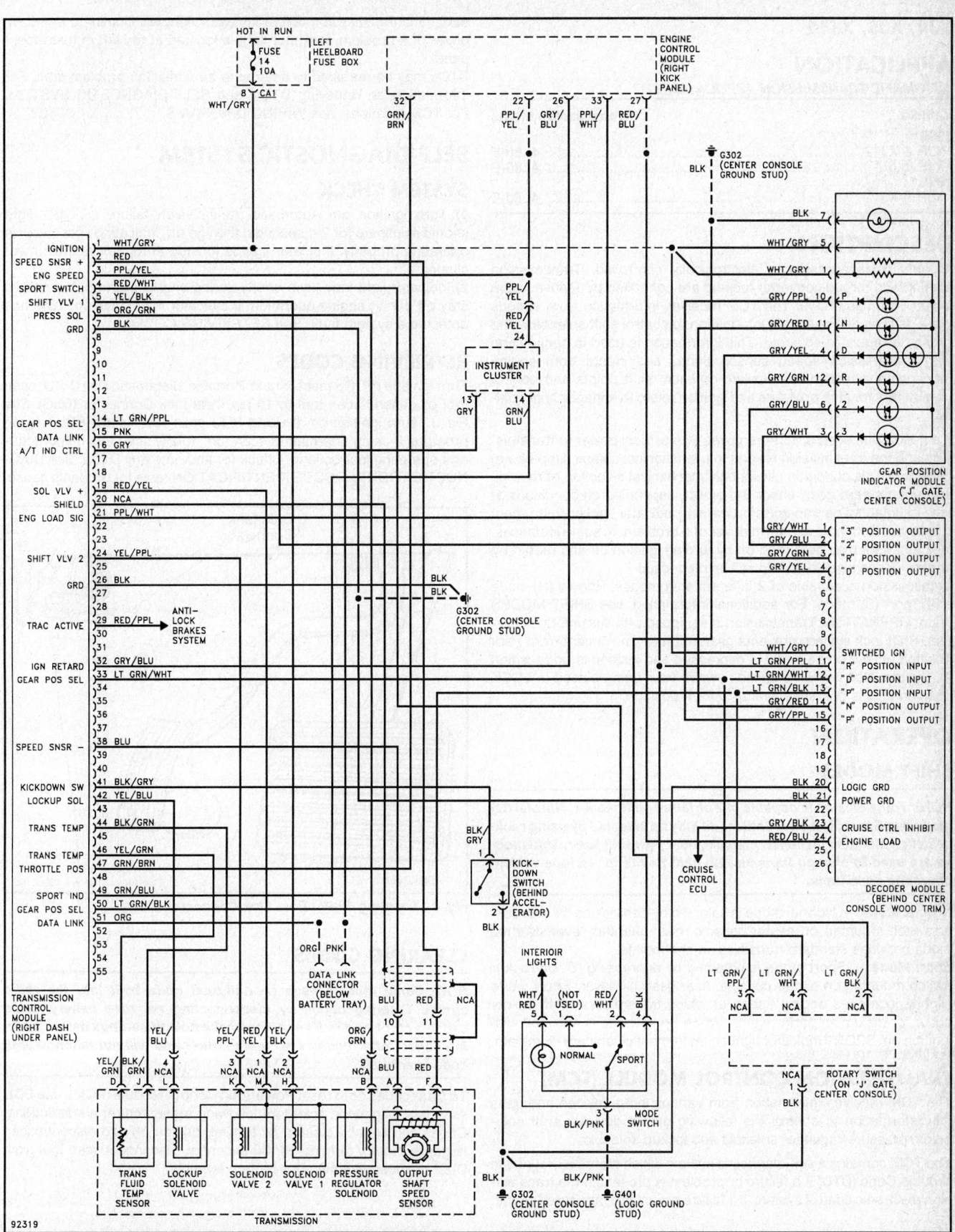

Fig. 4: ZF 4HP 24-E Transmission Wiring Diagram (1995-96 XJ6)

AUTOMATIC TRANSMISSIONS
Jaguar 4L80-E Electronic Controls

XJR, XJS, XJ12

APPLICATION

AUTOMATIC TRANSMISSION APPLICATIONS

Vehicle	Transmission Model
1995	
XJR & XJ12	4L80-E
XJS (6.0L)	4L80-E
1996	
XJR & XJ12	4L80-E

DESCRIPTION

Automatic transmission is electronically controlled. Transmission shifting and torque converter lock-up are controlled by Transmission Control Module (TCM). The TCM receives information from various input devices and uses this information to control shift solenoids and pressure regulator solenoid. This information is used in conjunction with transmission speed sensor signal, and inputs from engine management system to calculate optimum shift points and control parameters for shift pressure and ignition retard to enhance shift quality.

If a major fault occurs, TCM removes all electrical power to transmission and the transmission reverts to a mechanical default (limp-home) condition. This condition allows only mechanical selection of reverse and one forward gear, either 3rd or 4th, depending on conditions at time of default. The transmission warning indicator light on instrument cluster will illuminate to inform driver of a problem. In some instances, indicator light may be turned off by turning ignition off and restarting engine. Transmission should still be diagnosed.

Transmission is capable of 2 different shift modes, Normal (N) mode and Sport (S) mode. For additional information, see SHIFT MODES under OPERATION. Transmission is equipped with shift interlock system. Shift lock system prevents gearshift lever movement from Park position unless brake pedal is depressed and ignition is on (position II). System also prevents ignition switch from being placed in LOCK position unless gearshift lever is in Park position.

OPERATION

SHIFT MODES

NOTE: Transmission is capable of 2 different shift modes, Normal (N) mode and Sport (S) mode. Shift mode may be selected by using rocker switch mounted on center console, near gearshift lever. Shift modes are used to change transmission shift points for various vehicle operating conditions.

Normal Mode – Normal mode is selected by depressing "N" on rocker switch mounted on center console, near gearshift lever. Normal mode provides standard transmission shift points.

Sport Mode – Sport mode is obtained by depressing "S" on rocker switch mounted on center console, near gearshift lever. Sport mode slightly increases engine speed at which transmission shift points occur for maximum performance. When Sport mode is selected with ignition on, SPORT indicator light on instrument cluster will illuminate.

TRANSMISSION CONTROL MODULE (TCM)

The TCM receives information from various input devices and uses this information to control the following output devices: shift solenoids, pressure regulator solenoid and lockup solenoid.

The TCM contains a self-diagnostic system which stores a Diagnostic Trouble Code (DTC) if a failure or problem is present in the transmission electronic control system. If a failure occurs in a monitored circuit,

automatic transmission failure indicator light will illuminate to inform driver of a problem. Indicator light is located at top left of instrument panel.

DTCs may be retrieved to determine transmission problem area. For information on retrieving DTCs, see SELF-DIAGNOSTIC SYSTEM. For TCM locations, see WIRING DIAGRAMS.

SELF-DIAGNOSTIC SYSTEM

SYSTEM CHECK

1) Turn ignition on. Automatic transmission failure indicator light should illuminate for 2-4 seconds, then go off, indicating light circuit is operating properly. Indicator light is located at top left of instrument cluster.

2) Indicator light may flash briefly during engine start-up, but should stay off during engine operation. If indicator light stays on, TCM has detected a system fault. See RETRIEVING CODES.

RETRIEVING CODES

Turn ignition off. Connect Jaguar Portable Diagnostic Unit (PDU) scan tool or generic scan tool to 16-pin Data Link Connector (DLC). *See Fig. 1.* Turn ignition on. If using PDU scan tool, follow PDU screen prompts. If using aftermarket scan tool, follow scan tool manufacturer's operating instructions. Check for and note any DTCs. See DIAGNOSTIC TROUBLE CODE IDENTIFICATION table for probable cause.

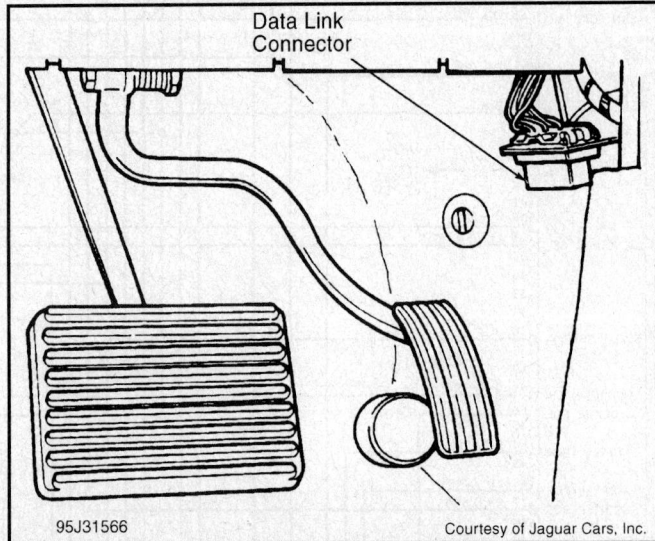

Fig. 1: Locating 16-Pin Data Link Connector (DLC)

95J31566   Courtesy of Jaguar Cars, Inc.

CLEARING CODES

NOTE: Some models have an anti-theft code built into the radio circuit. Clearing codes by disconnecting negative battery cable cancels clock and radio settings; make note of settings before clearing codes. After codes are cleared, the radio will not function until code is entered.

To clear codes or to reset Powertrain Control Module (PCM), use PDU scan tool or generic scan tool following manufacturer's instructions. Codes can also be cleared by turning ignition off and disconnecting negative battery terminal for 30 seconds. Disconnect scan tool from DLC, or reconnect negative battery terminal.

DIAGNOSTIC TROUBLE CODE (DTC) IDENTIFICATION

Code	Description	Probable Cause
P0603	Control Module Memory Fault	TCM
P0703 [1]	Brake Switch Circuit Fault	Faulty Brake Switch Or Wiring Harness
P0706	Transmission Range Sensor Fault	Wiring Harness Or Faulty Pressure Switch Manifold
P0712	Transmission Fluid Temperature Sensor (TFT) Low Input	Faulty TFT Sensor Or Wiring Harness
P0713	Transmission Fluid Temperature Sensor High Input	Faulty TFT Sensor Or Wiring Harness
P0715	Input Speed Sensor Malfunction	Faulty Input Speed Sensor Or Wiring Harness
P0716	Input Speed Sensor Circuit Range/Performance	Faulty Input Speed Sensor Or Wiring Harness
P0720	Output Speed Sensor Malfunction	Faulty Output Speed Sensor Or Wiring Harness
P0721	Output Speed Sensor Circuit Range/Performance	Faulty Output Speed Sensor Or Wiring Harness
P0726	Engine Speed Input Circuit Range/Performance	[2] Wiring Harness Or Faulty Signal From ECM
P0727	No Engine Speed Input Signal	[2] Wiring Harness Or Faulty Signal From ECM
P0730	Incorrect Gear Ratio	Wiring Harness, Faulty Speed Sensor, Pressure Switch Manifold, Low Fluid Level Or Mechanical Failure
P0741	Torque Converter Clutch Always Off	Wiring Harness, Faulty Torque Converter Clutch Solenoid Or Mechanical Failure
P0742	Torque Converter Clutch Always On	Wiring Harness, Faulty Torque Converter Clutch Solenoid Or Mechanical Failure
P0743	Torque Converter Clutch System Fault	Wiring Harness, Faulty Torque Converter Clutch Solenoid Or Mechanical Failure
P0748 [1]	Electronic Pressure Control Solenoid Fault	[3] Wiring Harness Or Faulty Force Motor
P0751	Shift Solenoid "A" Performance Fault	Faulty Shift Solenoid Valve, Wiring Harness Or Blown Fuse
P0753	Shift Solenoid "A" Electrical Fault	Faulty Shift Solenoid Valve, Wiring Harness Or Blown Fuse
P0756	Shift Solenoid "B" Performance Fault	Faulty Shift Solenoid Valve, Wiring Harness Or Blown Fuse
P0758	Shift Solenoid "B" Electrical Fault	Faulty Shift Solenoid Valve, Wiring Harness Or Blown Fuse
P0780 [1]	Shift Malfunction	Mechanical Wear/Failure
P1739	Transmission Slipping	Wiring Harness, Blown Fuse, Faulty Torque Converter Clutch Or Mechanical Wear
P1780	Torque Reduction Signal Malfunction	[2] Wiring Harness Or Faulty Signal From ECM
P1781	Engine Torque Signal Malfunction	[2] Wiring Harness Or Faulty Signal From ECM
P1782 [1]	Traction Control Input Signal Fault	Short To Ground In TRAC Active Circuit
P1783 [1]	High Transmission Temperature Condition	[4]
P1791	Throttle Position Signal Fault	[2] Wiring Harness Or Faulty Signal From ECM
P1794	System Voltage Malfunction	Blown Fuses, Wiring Harness Or TCM
P1796 [1]	Kickdown Switch Circuit Malfunction	Wiring Harness, Switch Out Of Adjustment Or Faulty Switch

[1] – Malfunction Indicator Light (MIL) will not illuminate when DTC is set. Jaguar Portable Diagnostic Unit (PDU) scan tool must be used to retrieve code.

[2] – Check DTCs for engine management system and repair as necessary. See appropriate SELF-DIAGNOSTICS article in ENGINE PERFORMANCE in appropriate MITCHELL® manual.

[3] – Force motor is mounted in transmission housing and acts as a transmission torque fluid pressure regulator.

[4] – No information available from manufacturer.

COMPONENT TESTING

SHIFT SOLENOID VALVES

Disconnect 14-pin connector at left side of transmission. Measure resistance between shift solenoid valve terminals at 14-pin connector. See WIRING DIAGRAMS. Resistance should be about 40 ohms. If resistance is not as specified, replace solenoid valve.

VARIABLE FORCE MOTOR

Disconnect 14-pin connector at left side of transmission. Measure resistance between variable force motor terminals at 14-pin connector. See WIRING DIAGRAMS. Resistance should be about 4-5 ohms. If resistance is not as specified, replace variable force motor.

INPUT & OUTPUT SPEED SENSORS

Turn ignition off. Disconnect 14-pin connector at left side of transmission. Measure resistance between input or output speed sensor terminals at 14-pin connector. See WIRING DIAGRAMS. Resistance should be 1000-1500 ohms. If resistance is not as specified, replace sensor.

WIRING DIAGRAMS

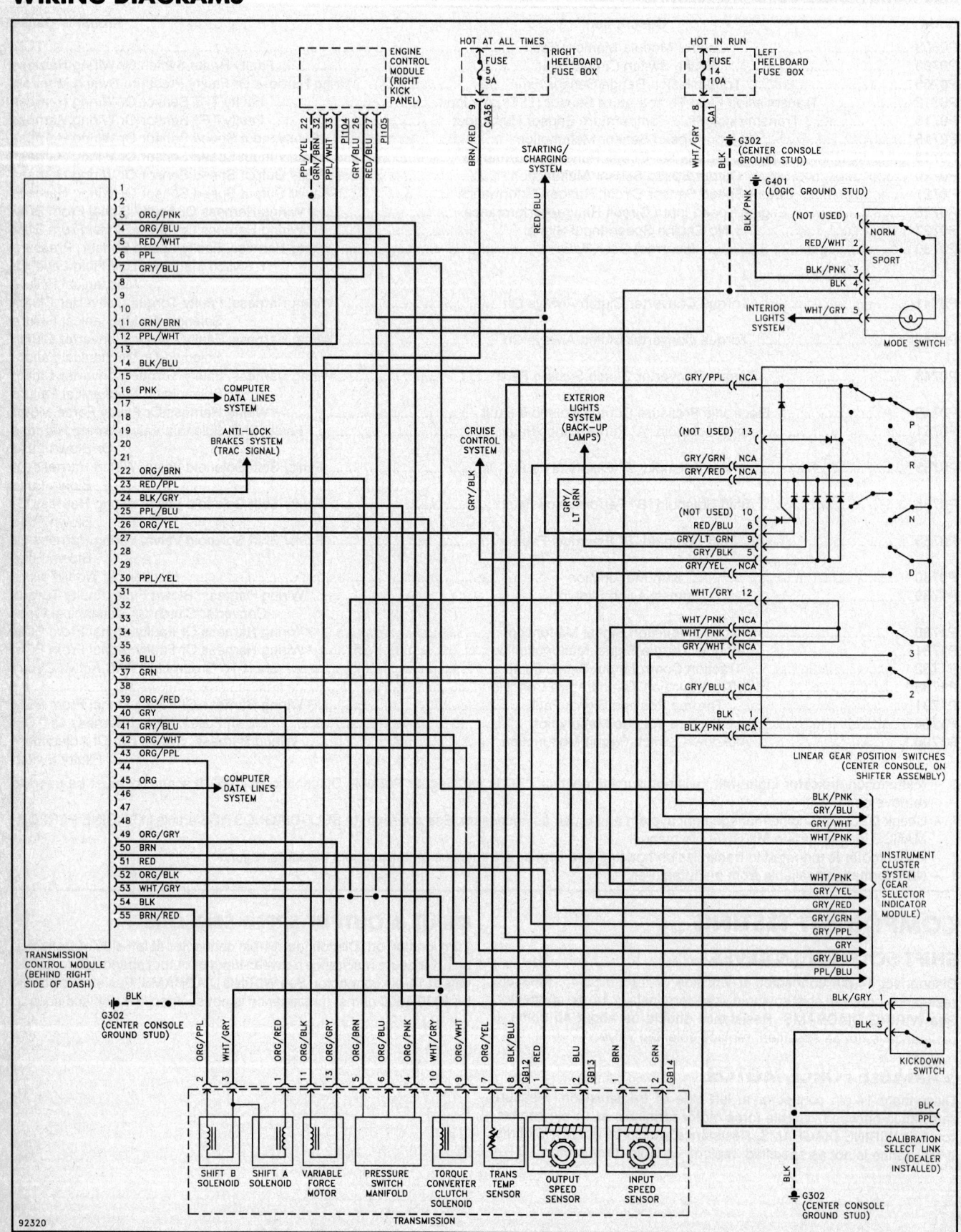

Fig. 2: 4L80-E Transmission Wiring Diagram (1995-96 XJR)

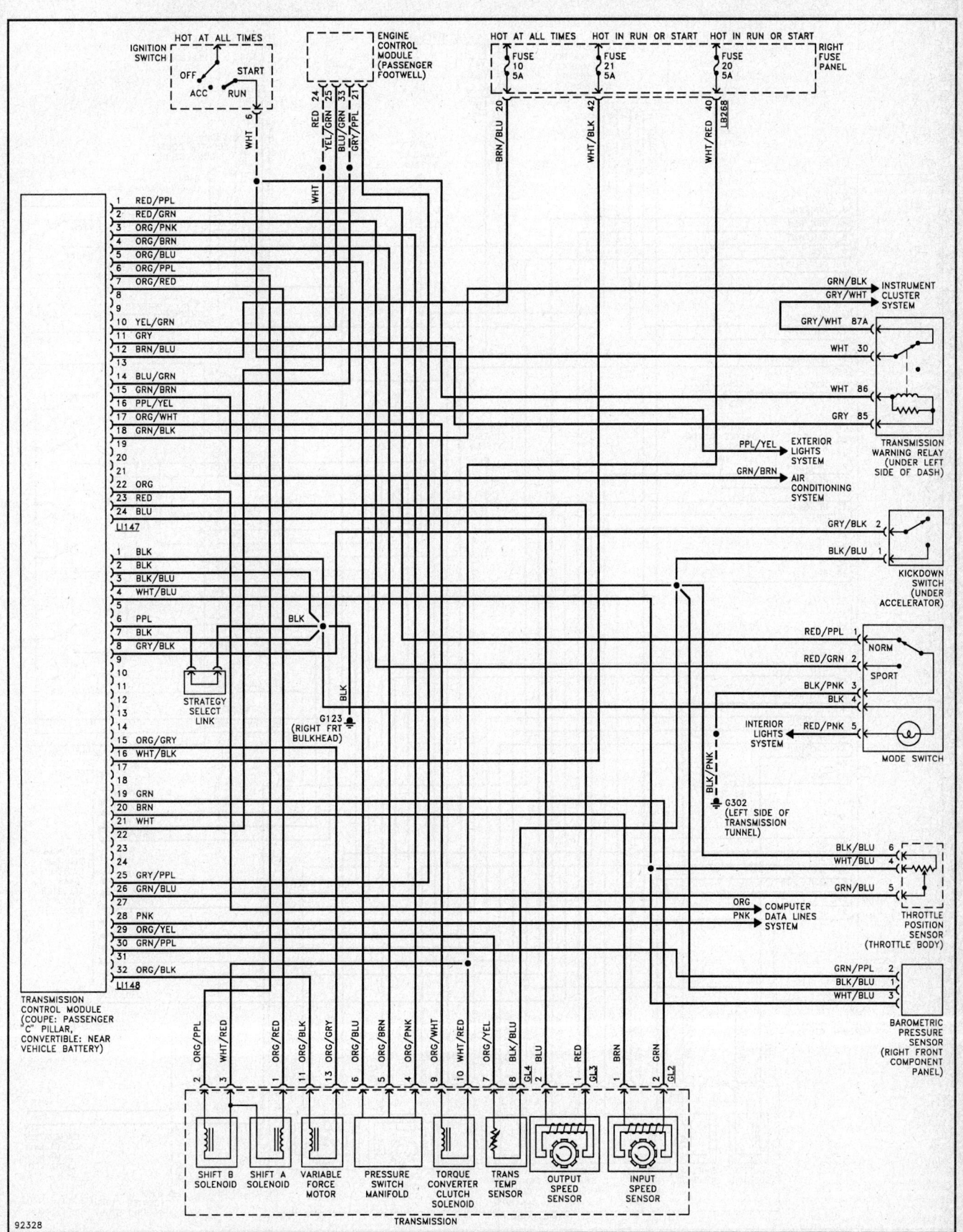

Fig. 3: 4L80-E Transmission Wiring Diagram (1995 XJS 6.0L)

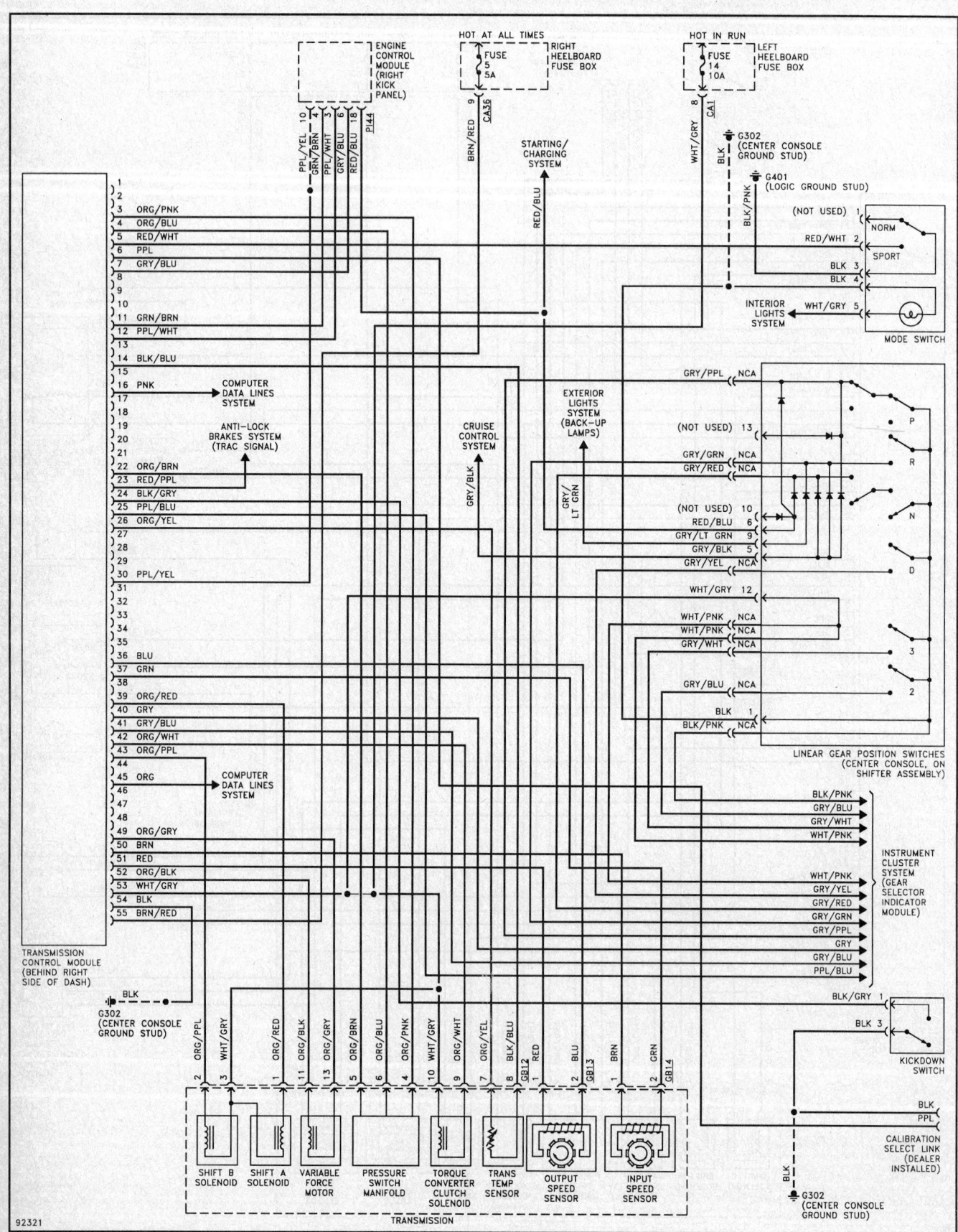

Fig. 4: 4L80-E Transmission Wiring Diagram (1995-96 XJ12)

Sportage
APPLICATION

Vehicle	Transmission Model
1995-96 Kia Sportage	AW372LE

CAUTION: Vehicle is equipped with Supplemental Restraint System (SRS). When servicing vehicle, use care to avoid accidental air bag deployment. SRS-related components are located in steering column, center console and instrument panel. DO NOT use electrical test equipment on these circuits. If necessary, deactivate SRS before servicing components. See AIR BAG SERVICING article in APPLICATIONS & IDENTIFICATIONS section.

DESCRIPTION

Automatic transmission is a 4-speed electronically controlled transmission. Two solenoids that control shift changes are located in valve body. Solenoids are controlled by a Transmission Control Module (TCM). TCM receives information from various input devices and uses this information to control shift solenoids for transmission shifting and lock-up solenoid for torque converter lock-up.

A HOLD switch is mounted on the shift lever. HOLD function may be activated in "D", "2" or "L" gears by pressing HOLD button. In "L" and "2" positions vehicle is held in these gears and no upshift or downshift takes place. This function is used for driving up steep inclines or for engine braking assistance when descending steep grades. If activated in "D" position a 1-2 and 2-3 upshift is permitted when starting from a stop but after the 2-3 upshift the vehicle is locked in "D" until it comes to a complete stop. The 1-2 and 2-3 upshift pattern is changed to a "short shift" specification. This function is used for starting off or driving on slippery surfaces. Pushing HOLD button again deactivates system.

A mode select switch is located near shift lever on center console. Mode select switch has a POWER (PWR) and a ECONOMY (ECO) operating position. When mode select switch is depressed (PWR position), transmission upshift and downshifts will occur at a higher vehicle speed than with switch released. An indicator light on instrument panel indicates mode select switch is in PWR position.

OPERATION
TCM

TCM receives information from various input devices and uses this information to control solenoids on transmission valve body for transmission shifting and torque converter lock-up.

TCM contains a self-diagnostic system, which will store trouble code(s) if failure or problem exists in electronic control system. Trouble code can be retrieved to determine problem area. See SELF-DIAGNOSTIC SYSTEM. TCM is located under left side of instrument panel, left of steering column near relay block.

TCM INPUT DEVICES

Brakelight Switch – Brakelight switch delivers input signal to TCM, indicating vehicle braking. Brakelight switch is located on pedal support.

Coolant Temperature Sensor (CTS) – Coolant temperature sensor delivers input signal to TCM, indicating engine coolant temperature. Coolant temperature sensor is mounted to thermostat housing, facing alternator.

HOLD Switch – HOLD switch delivers input to TCM to indicate gears preferred by operator. Switch is located on shift lever handle.

Mode Select (POWER/ECONOMY) Switch – Mode select switch delivers an input signal to TCM to indicate transmission shift points selected by the operator. Switch is located on center console beside shifter.

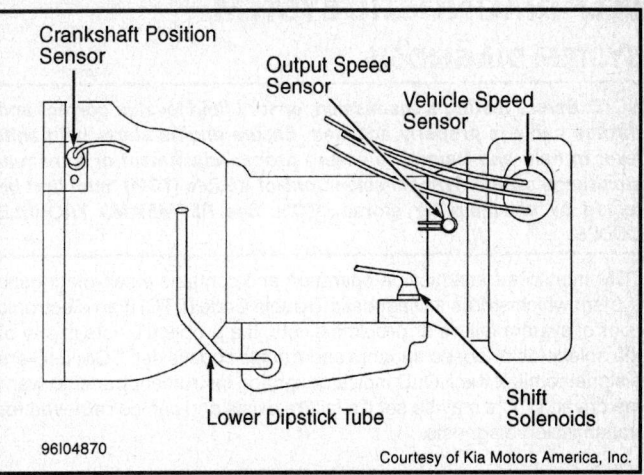

Fig. 1: *Locating Various Transmission Sensors*

Output Shaft Speed Sensor – Transmission speed is input to TCM by output shaft speed sensor. Sensor is located on side of transmission. *See Fig. 1.*

Throttle Position (TP) Sensor – TP sensor delivers an input signal to TCM indicating throttle position. TP sensor is located on side of throttle body.

Transmission Range Switch – Transmission range switch delivers an input signal to TCM indicating shift lever position. Switch is located on side of transmission.

Vehicle Speed Sensor – Vehicle speed signal is delivered to TCM by vehicle speed sensor. Speed sensor is driven by output shaft of transfer case and indicates actual vehicle speed. *See Fig. 1.*

TCM OUTPUT DEVICES

Shift Solenoids "A" & "B" – The TCM controls transmission shifting by delivering an output signal to operate proper solenoid. See SOLENOID OPERATION table. Solenoids are located on transmission valve body.

SOLENOID OPERATION

Shift Lever Position	Solenoid "A"	Solenoid "B"
"D" (Drive)		
1st Gear	On	Off
2nd Gear	On	On
3rd Gear	Off	On
4th Gear	Off	Off
"2" (Second)		
1st Gear	On	Off
2nd Gear	On	On
"L" (Low)		
1st Gear	On	Off
"R" (Reverse)	On	Off
"N" Or "P"		
(Neutral Or Park)	On	Off

TCC Control Solenoid – The TCM controls torque converter lock-up by delivering an output signal to TCC solenoid. Lock-up solenoid is activated when shift lever is in "D", engine is normal operating temperature and vehicle is at specified speed. TCC solenoid is located on transmission valve body.

HOLD Indicator Light – Receives signal from TCM to indicate switch position.

POWER/ECONOMY Mode Indicator Light – Receives signal from TCM to indicate mode switch position.

SELF-DIAGNOSTIC SYSTEM

SYSTEM DIAGNOSIS

NOTE: Before testing transmission, ensure fluid level is correct and throttle cable is properly adjusted. Ensure engine starts with shift lever in Park and Neutral to ensure proper adjustment of transmission range switch. Transmission Control Module (TCM) must first be tested by checking for stored DTC's. See RETRIEVING TROUBLE CODES.

TCM monitors transmission operation and contains a self-diagnostic system which stores a Diagnostic Trouble Code (DTC) if an electronic control system failure or problem exists. If a problem exists in any of the solenoids or speed sensors and trouble code is set, TCM delivers a signal to blink the HOLD indicator light on instrument panel to warn the driver. DTC's may be set if a failure exists and can be retrieved for transmission diagnosis.

RETRIEVING TROUBLE CODES

NOTE: Before retrieving DTC's, ensure proper battery voltage exists for proper self-diagnosis system operation.

Using HOLD Indicator Light (1995 Models) – 1) Raise hood and access Data Link Connector (DLC) on right side of engine compartment, mounted on air filter housing near mass air flow sensor.

2) Connect jumper wire between terminals No. 12 and 18 on DLC connector. *See Fig. 2.* Turn ignition switch to ON position. If DTC exists, HOLD indicator light will flash every 4 seconds. Long (1.2 second duration) flash indicates first digit and short (.4 second duration) flash indicates second digit.

3) If more than one DTC exists, next code will be displayed after pause of 4 seconds. Lowest number code will be displayed first. Trouble codes will be repeated. Once DTC(s) is obtained, determine probable cause and symptom. See DIAGNOSTIC TROUBLE CODE IDENTIFICATION table. For trouble shooting of codes, see DIAGNOSTIC TESTING. Turn ignition off. and remove jumper wire.

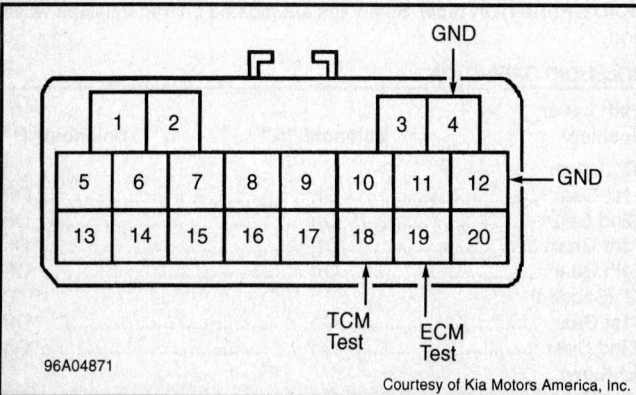

Fig. 2: Identifying DLC Connector Terminals (1995 Models)

Using Scan Tool (1996 Models) – Ensure ignition is in OFF position. Connect scan tool to Data Link Connector (DLC) located under left side of instrument panel, near center console. *See Fig. 3.* Turn ignition switch to ON position. Check for stored DTC's. See DIAGNOSTIC TROUBLE CODE IDENTIFICATION table. For trouble shooting of codes, see DIAGNOSTIC TESTING. Turn ignition off. and remove jumper wire.

NOTE: Once repairs have been performed, DTC's must be cleared from TCM memory and vehicle test driven. See CLEARING TROUBLE CODES. Accelerate vehicle to 31 MPH for 1 minute. Fully depress accelerator pedal to force downshift. Release accelerator pedal and slow vehicle to stop. Perform retrieval procedure to ensure DTC's have been cleared and no new DTC's exist.

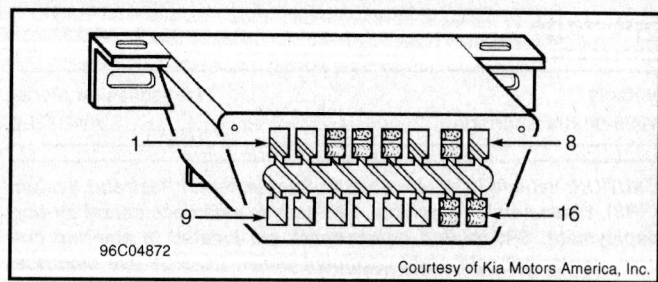

Fig. 3: Identifying DLC Connector Terminals (1996 Models)

DIAGNOSTIC TROUBLE CODE IDENTIFICATION

DTC No.	¹ Probable Cause
1995 Models	
6	Vehicle Speed Sensor
12	Throttle Position Sensor
55	Input Shaft Speed Sensor
60	Shift Solenoid "A"
61	Shift Solenoid "B"
63	TCC Solenoid
1996 Models	
P0501	Vehicle Speed Sensor
P1121	Throttle Position Sensor
P0722	Output Shaft Speed Sensor
P0753	Shift Solenoid "A"
P0758	Shift Solenoid "B"
P0743	TCC Solenoid

¹ – Check listed component for probable cause. Also check wiring and connection of specified component.

CLEARING TROUBLE CODES

To clear DTC's stored in TCM, disconnect negative battery cable for at least 10 seconds.

COMPONENT LOCATION

COMPONENT LOCATION

Description	Location
Coolant Temperature Sensor	Mounted to thermostat housing, facing alternator.
Electronic Control Module	Behind lower right side of instrument panel, near right kick panel.
Output Speed Sensor	See Fig. 1
Solenoids "A" & "B"	Mounted to Valve Body
TCC Solenoid	Mounted to Valve Body
Transmission Control Unit	Behind left side of instrument panel, next to relay block.
Vehicle Speed Sensor	See Figs. 1 And 4

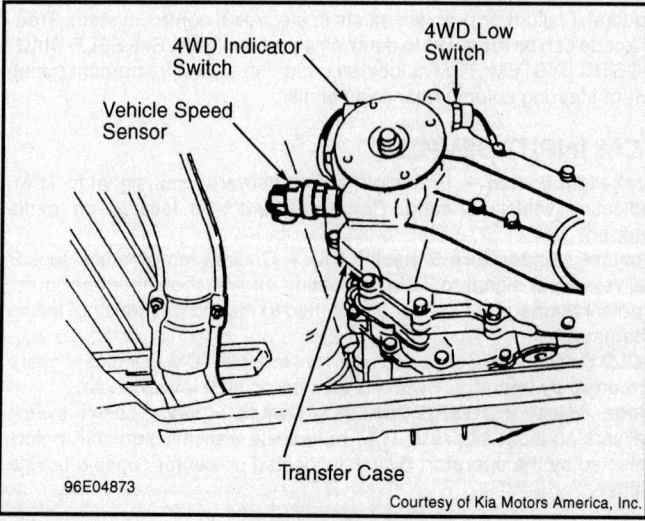

Fig. 4: Locating Transfer Case Mounted Sensors & Switches

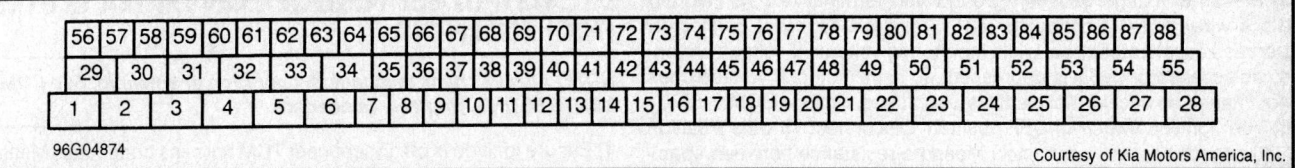

Fig. 5: Identifying Electronic Control Module Harness Connector Terminals

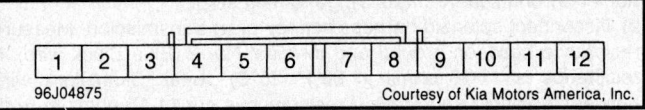

Fig. 6: Identifying Instrument Cluster C250 Harness Connector

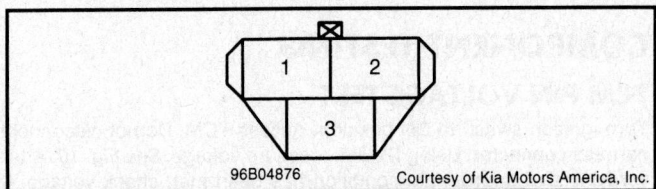

Fig. 7: Identifying Transmission Solenoid Connector

HARNESS CONNECTOR IDENTIFICATION

HARNESS CONNECTOR IDENTIFICATION

Component	See Fig.
Electronic Control Module	5
Instrument Cluster (C250 Connector)	6
Transmission Shift Solenoids	7
Transmission Control Unit	9
Throttle Position Sensor	8

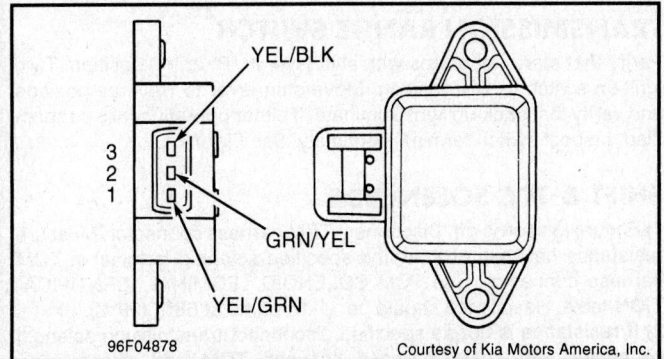

Fig. 8: Identifying Throttle Position Sensor Harness Connector

DIAGNOSTIC TESTS

NOTE: For connector terminal identification, see CONNECTOR IDEN-TIFICATION. For circuit identification, see appropriate wiring diagram in WIRING DIAGRAMS.

DTC 6/P0501: VEHICLE SPEED SENSOR

1) Disconnect TCM harness connector. Raise and support rear wheels. Start and run engine. Place transmission in Drive and allow rear wheels to turn. Measure voltage between ground and terminal No. 5 (Blue/Green wire) on TCM harness connector. If 0-5 volt pulse is present, replace TCM. If 0-5 volt pulse is not present, go to next step.

2) Remove instrument cluster. Access instrument cluster harness connector (White 12-pin) C250. With rear wheels rotating, measure voltage between ground and terminal No. 3 (Blue/Green wire) on instrument cluster harness connector. If 0-5 volt pulse is present, repair Blue/Green wire between TCM and instrument cluster. If 0-5 volt pulse is not present, go to next step.

3) Measure voltage between ground and terminal No. 2 (Blue/Black wire) on instrument cluster connector C250. If 0-5 volt pulse is present, replace speedometer. If 0-5 volt pulse is not present, go DTC 55/P0722 test.

DTC 12/P1121: THROTTLE POSITION SENSOR

1) Turn ignition on. Using voltmeter, backprobe TCM harness connector. Do not disconnect connector. Measure voltage between ground and terminal No. 6 (Light Green wire). Depress accelerator pedal while monitoring voltage. Go to next step.

2) If voltage changes as accelerator pedal is depressed, replace TCM. If voltage does not change as accelerator pedal is depressed, go to next step.

3) Measure voltage between ground and terminal No. 38 (Light Green wire) on ECM connector C211. Do not disconnect connector. Depress accelerator pedal while monitoring voltage. If voltage changes as accelerator pedal is depressed, repair Light Green wire between TCM and ECM. If voltage does not change as accelerator pedal is depressed, go to next step.

4) Measure voltage between ground and terminal No. 12 (Yellow/Green wire) on ECM harness connector. If 5 volts is present, go to next step. If 5 volts is not present, replace ECM.

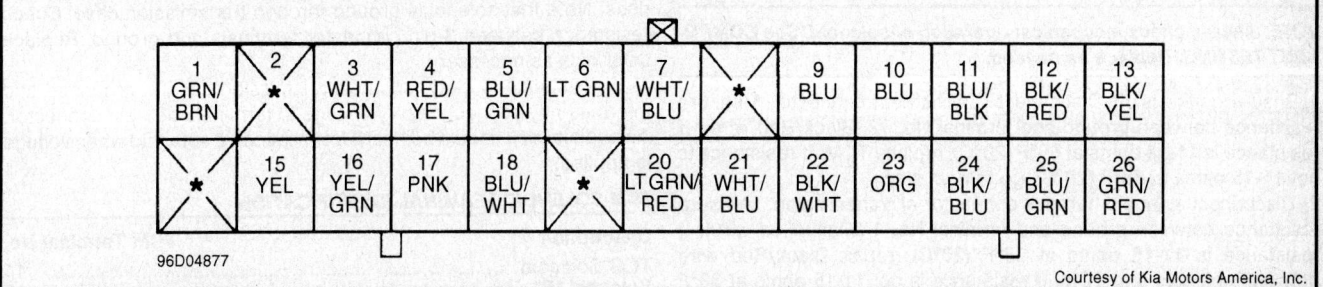

Fig. 9: Identifying Transmission Control Unit Harness Connector

5) Measure voltage between ground and terminal No. 73 (Yellow/Black wire) on ECM connector C211. Do not disconnect connector. Depress accelerator pedal while monitoring voltage. If voltage changes as accelerator pedal is depressed, go to next step. If voltage does not change as accelerator pedal is depressed, replace ECM.

6) Turn ignition switch to OFF position. Disconnect Throttle Position (TP) sensor harness connector. Measure resistance between specified terminals. See TP SENSOR RESISTANCE table. If resistance measurements are within specification, repair circuit(s) between TP sensor and ECM. If resistance is not within specification, replace TP sensor.

TP SENSOR RESISTANCE

Between Terminals	Ohms
Throttle Fully Open	
1 & 2	2000
1 & 3	2500
2 & 3	1000
Throttle Fully Closed	
1 & 2	2000
1 & 3	1500
2 & 3	2000

DTC 55/P0722: OUTPUT SPEED SENSOR

1) Raise and support rear wheels. Start and run engine. Place transmission in "D" and allow rear wheels to turn. Using voltmeter, backprobe TCM harness connector. Do not disconnect connector. Measure voltage between terminals No. 4 (Red/Yellow wire) and No. 10 (Blue wire). If voltage varies between 2-3 volts, replace TCM. If voltage does not vary between 2-3 volts, go to next step.

2) Stop wheels from turning and place transmission in "P". Turn off engine. Disconnect output shaft speed sensor. Measure resistance between sensor component connector terminals. If resistance is 387-473 ohms at 68°F (20°C), check for open or short circuit(s) between output speed sensor and TCM. Repair as needed. If resistance is not 387-473 ohms at 68°F (20°C), replace output speed sensor.

DTC 60/P0753: SHIFT SOLENOID "A"

NOTE: Always check mechanical operation of solenoid. See COMPONENT TESTING. Replace as needed.

1) Ensure ignition is off. Disconnect TCM harness connector. Measure resistance between ground and terminal No. 13 (Black/Yellow wire). If resistance is 11-15 ohms at 68°F (20°C), replace TCM. If resistance is not 11-15 ohms at 68°F (20°C), go to next step.

2) Disconnect solenoid harness connector at transmission. Measure resistance between ground and terminal No. 3 (Black/Yellow wire). If resistance is 11-15 ohms at 68°F (20°C), repair Black/Yellow wire between solenoid and TCM. If resistance is not 11-15 ohms at 68°F (20°C), replace solenoid "A".

DTC 61/P0758: SHIFT SOLENOID "B"

NOTE: Always check mechanical operation of solenoid. See COMPONENT TESTING. Replace as needed.

1) Ensure ignition is off. Disconnect TCM harness connector. Measure resistance between ground and terminal No. 12 (Black/Red wire). If resistance is 11-15 ohms at 68°F (20°C), replace TCM. If resistance is not 11-15 ohms at 68°F (20°C), go to next step.

2) Disconnect solenoid harness connector at transmission. Measure resistance between ground and terminal No. 1 (Black/Red wire). If resistance is 11-15 ohms at 68°F (20°C), repair Black/Red wire between solenoid and TCM. If resistance is not 11-15 ohms at 68°F (20°C), replace solenoid "B".

DTC 63/P0743: TORQUE CONVERTER CLUTCH (TCC) SOLENOID

NOTE: Always check mechanical operation of solenoid. See COMPONENT TESTING. Replace as needed.

1) Ensure ignition is off. Disconnect TCM harness connector. Measure resistance between ground and terminal No. 11 (Blue/Black wire). If resistance is 11-15 ohms at 68°F (20°C), replace TCM. If resistance is not 11-15 ohms at 68°F (20°C), go to next step.

2) Disconnect solenoid harness connector at transmission. Measure resistance between ground and terminal No. 2 (Blue/Black wire). If resistance is 11-15 ohms at 68°F (20°C), repair Blue/Black wire between solenoid and TCM. If resistance is not 11-15 ohms at 68°F (20°C), replace TCC solenoid.

COMPONENT TESTING

TCM PIN VOLTAGE TEST

Turn ignition switch to ON position. Access TCM. Do not disconnect harness connector. Using DVOM, measure voltage. See Fig. 10. After verifying that appropriate condition has been met, check voltage. If voltage is not within specification, replace TCM.

BRAKE PEDAL SWITCH

Disconnect brake pedal switch harness connector. Connect ohmmeter leads to specified switch terminals. See Fig. 11. Monitor ohmmeter while operating switch. If continuity does not change, replace switch.

POWER/ECONOMY SWITCH

Disconnect power/economy switch harness connector. Connect ohmmeter leads to specified switch terminals. See Fig. 12. Monitor ohmmeter while operating switch. If continuity does not change, replace switch.

TRANSMISSION RANGE SWITCH

Verify that starter operates with shift lever in "P" or "N" position. Turn ignition switch to ON position. Move shift lever to Reverse position and verify that back-up light illuminate. If either operation fails as specified, inspect switch terminal continuity. See Fig. 13.

SHIFT & TCC SOLENOIDS

1) Ensure ignition is off. Disconnect TCM harness connector. Measure resistance between ground and specified solenoid terminal at TCM harness connector. See TCM SOLENOID TERMINAL IDENTIFICATION table. Resistance should be 11-15 ohms at 68°F (20°C).

2) If resistance is not as specified disconnect transmission solenoid connector and check harness between TCM and transmission connector for short or open. See appropriate wiring diagram in WIRING DIAGRAMS. If harness is okay, go to next step.

3) Disconnect 3-pin transmission solenoid connector from vehicle harness. Note that solenoids ground through transmission case. Check resistance between 3-pin connector terminals and ground. Replace solenoids as necessary.

4) If resistance is okay, ensure transmission case is grounded and intermittently connect battery voltage to terminals of 3-pin connector. An audible click should be heard from specified solenoid when voltage is applied.

TCM SOLENOID TERMINAL IDENTIFICATION

Description	TCM Terminal No.
TCC Solenoid	11
Solenoid "B"	12
Solenoid "A"	13

TERM	DESCRIPTION	CONNECT	CONDITION	VOLTAGE
1	HOLD Switch	1 and Ground	Hold Switch ON	0V
1	HOLD Switch	1 and Ground	Hold Switch OFF	B+
2	not used	–	–	–
3	Eng Coolant Temp Snsr	3 and Ground	Engine cold	B+
4	Input/Turbine Speed Snsr	4 and Ground	Wheels stopped	0V or 5V
4	Input/Turbine Speed Snsr	4 and Ground	Wheels turning	0V – 5V pulse
5	Vehicle Speed Sensor	5 and Ground	Wheels stopped	0V or 5V
5	Vehicle Speed Sensor	5 and Ground	Wheels turning	0V – 5V pulse
6	Throttle Position Sensor	6 and Ground	Engine running	0V – B+ pulse
7	Power/Economy Switch	7 and Ground	Power/Economy Switch OFF	0V
7	Power/Economy Switch	7 and Ground	Power/Economy Switch ON	B+
8	not used	–	–	–
9	N range	9 and Ground	Key ON, Trans in N range	B+
9	N range	9 and Ground	Key ON, Trans not in N range	0V
10	Input/Turbine Speed Snsr	10 and Ground	Wheels stopped	0V or 5V
10	Input/Turbine Speed Snsr	10 and Ground	Wheels turning	0V – 5V pulse
11	Torq Conv Clutch Sol	11 and Ground	Key OFF	0V
11	Torq Conv Clutch Sol	11 and Ground	Key ON	B+
12	Shift Solenoid B	12 and Ground	Key OFF	0V
12	Shift Solenoid B	12 and Ground	Key ON	0V
13	Shift Solenoid A	13 and Ground	Key OFF	0V
13	Shift Solenoid A	13 and Ground	Key ON	B+
14	not used	–	–	–
15	4WD Low Switch	15 and Ground	4WD Low Switch OFF	0V
15	4WD Low Switch	15 and Ground	4WD Low Switch ON	B+
16	Data Link Connector	16 and Ground	–	0V
17	Data Link Connector	17 and Ground	–	0V
18	HOLD Indicator	18 and Ground	Hold Switch ON	0V
18	HOLD Indicator	18 and Ground	Hold Switch OFF	B+
19	not used	–	–	–
20	Power Indicator	20 and Ground	Power/Economy Switch OFF	B+
20	Power Indicator	20 and Ground	Power/Economy Switch ON	0V
21	L range	21 and Ground	Key ON, Trans in L range	B+
21	L range	21 and Ground	Key ON, Trans not in L range	0V
22	2 range	22 and Ground	Key ON, Trans in 2 range	B+
22	2 range	22 and Ground	Key ON, Trans not in 2 range	0V
23	Brake Pedal Switch	23 and Ground	Brake Pedal depressed	B+
23	Brake Pedal Switch	23 and Ground	Brake Pedal released	0V
24	Ground	24 and Ground	–	0V
25	Battery	25 and Ground	–	B+
26	Ignition	26 and Ground	Key ON	B+
26	Ignition	26 and Ground	Key OFF	0V

96G04869

Courtesy of Kia Motors America, Inc.

Fig. 10: TCM Pin Voltage Table

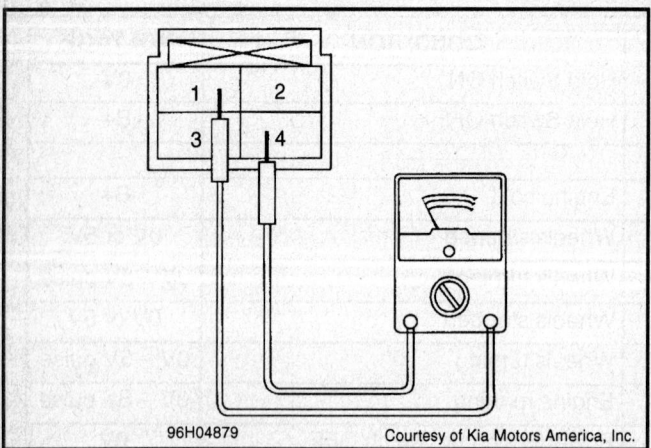

Fig. 11: **Testing Brake Pedal Switch**

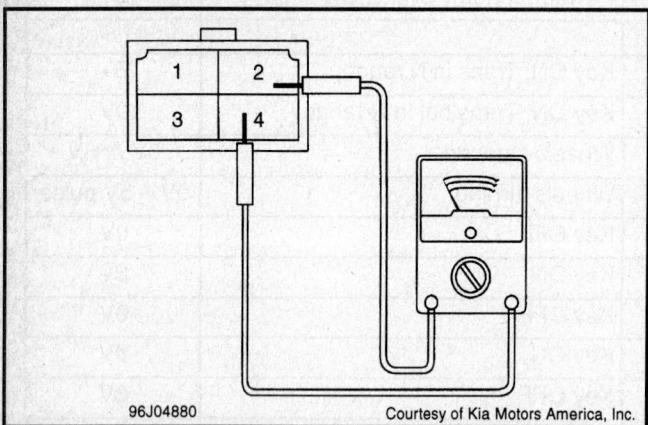

Fig. 12: **Testing Power/Economy Switch**

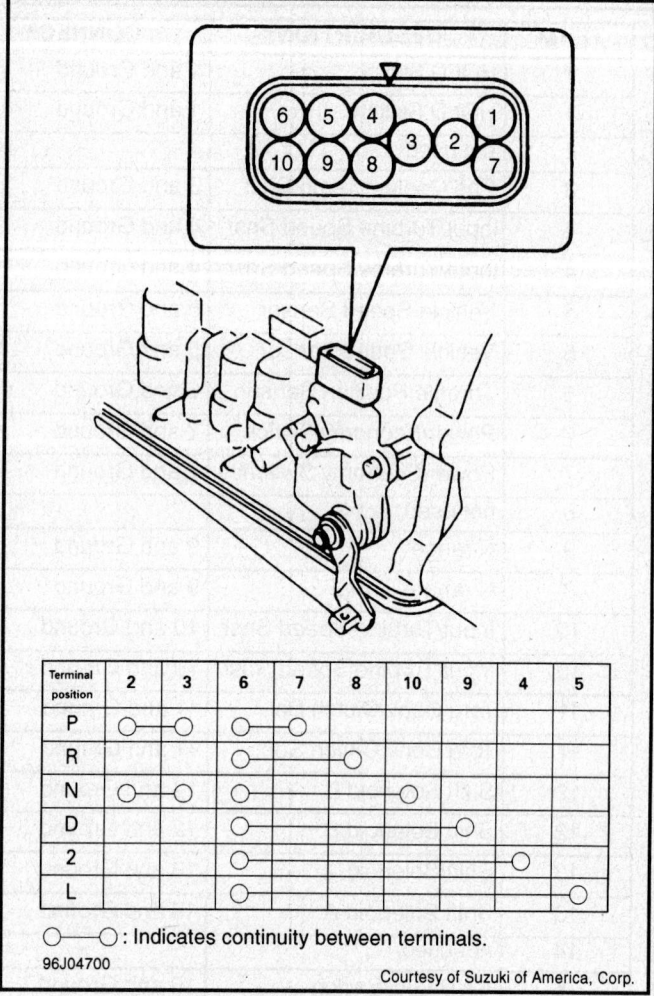

Terminal position	2	3	6	7	8	10	9	4	5
P	○	○	○	○					
R			○		○				
N	○	○	○			○			
D			○				○		
2			○					○	
L			○						○

○——○ : Indicates continuity between terminals.

Fig. 13: **Testing Transmission Range Switch**

WIRING DIAGRAMS

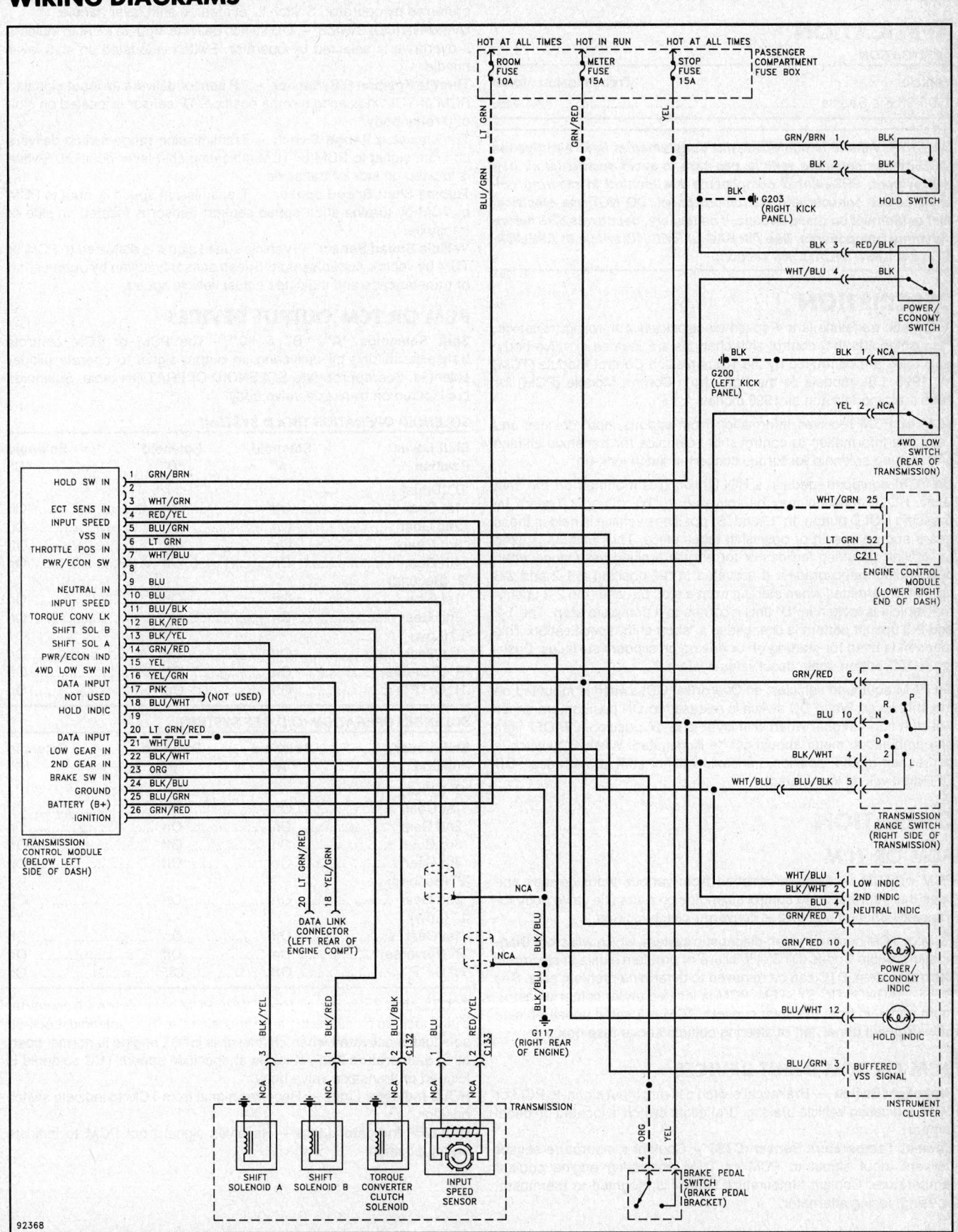

Fig. 14: Transmission Wiring Diagram (1995-96 Sportage)

AUTOMATIC TRANSMISSIONS
Kia FA4A-EL Electronic Controls

Sephia

APPLICATION

APPLICATION

Vehicle	Transmission Model
1995-96 Kia Sephia	FA4A-EL

CAUTION: Vehicle is equipped with Supplemental Restraint System (SRS). When servicing vehicle, use care to avoid accidental air bag deployment. SRS-related components are located in steering column, center console and instrument panel. DO NOT use electrical test equipment on these circuits. If necessary, deactivate SRS before servicing components. See AIR BAG SERVICING article in APPLICATIONS & IDENTIFICATIONS section.

DESCRIPTION

Automatic transaxle is a 4-speed electronically controlled transaxle. Four solenoids that control shift changes are located in valve body. Solenoids are controlled by the Transmission Control Module (TCM) for 1995 1.6L models or the Powertrain Control Module (PCM) for 1995 1.8L models and all 1996 models.

TCM or PCM receives information from various input devices and uses this information to control shift solenoids for transaxle shifting and lock-up solenoid for torque converter clutch lock-up.

On TCM equipped models, a HOLD switch is mounted on the shift lever. HOLD function may be activated in "D", "S" or "L" gears by pressing HOLD button. In "L" and "S" positions vehicle is held in these gears and no upshift or downshift takes place. This function is used for driving up steep inclines or for engine braking assistance when descending steep grades. If activated in "D" position a 1-2 and 2-3 upshift is permitted when starting from a stop but after the 2-3 upshift the vehicle is locked in "D" until it comes to a complete stop. The 1-2 and 2-3 upshift pattern is changed to a "short shift" specification. This function is used for starting off or driving on slippery surfaces. Pushing HOLD button again deactivates system.

On PCM equipped vehicles, an Overdrive (OD) switch is mounted on the shift lever. When OD switch is released to ON position, transaxle will shift into 4th gear when shift lever is in "D" position. OD OFF light on combination meter should not be illuminated. When OD switch is depressed to OFF position, transaxle will not shift into 4th gear. OD OFF light will be illuminated.

OPERATION

PCM OR TCM

PCM or TCM receives information from various input devices and uses this information to control solenoids on transaxle valve body for transaxle shifting and torque converter clutch lock-up.

PCM or TCM contains a self-diagnostic system, which will store Diagnostic Trouble Codes (DTC's) if failure or problem exists in electronic control system. DTC can be retrieved to determine problem area. See SELF-DIAGNOSTIC SYSTEM. PCM is located under center of instrument panel, in front of center console. TCM is located under left side of instrument panel, left of steering column above fuse box.

PCM OR TCM INPUT DEVICES

Brakelight Switch – Brakelight switch delivers input signal to PCM or TCM, indicating vehicle braking. Brakelight switch is located on pedal support.
Coolant Temperature Sensor (CTS) – Coolant temperature sensor delivers input signal to PCM or TCM, indicating engine coolant temperature. Coolant temperature sensor is mounted to thermostat housing, facing alternator.

HOLD Switch – HOLD switch delivers input to TCM to indicate gears preferred by operator. Switch is located on shift lever handle.
Overdrive (OD) Switch – OD switch delivers input to PCM to indicate if overdrive is selected by operator. Switch is located on shift lever handle.
Throttle Position (TP) Sensor – TP sensor delivers an input signal to PCM or TCM indicating throttle position. TP sensor is located on side of throttle body.
Transmission Range Switch – Transmission range switch delivers an input signal to PCM or TCM indicating shift lever position. Switch is located on side of transaxle.
Turbine Shaft Speed Sensor – Transmission speed is input to PCM or TCM by turbine shaft speed sensor. Sensor is located on side of transaxle.
Vehicle Speed Sensor – Vehicle speed signal is delivered to PCM or TCM by vehicle speed sensor. Speed sensor is driven by output shaft of transfer case and indicates actual vehicle speed.

PCM OR TCM OUTPUT DEVICES

Shift Solenoids "A", "B" & "C" – The PCM or TCM controls transaxle shifting by delivering an output signal to operate proper solenoid. See appropriate SOLENOID OPERATION table. Solenoids are located on transaxle valve body.

SOLENOID OPERATION (HOLD SYSTEM)

Shift Lever Position	Solenoid "A"	Solenoid "B"	Solenoid "C"
"D" (Drive)			
1st Gear	Off	On	On
2nd Gear	On	On	On
3rd Gear	On	Off	Off
4th Gear	On	Off	On
"2" (Second)			
1st Gear	Off	On	On
2nd Gear	On	On	On
"L" (Low)			
1st Gear	Off	On	On
"R" (Reverse)	On	Off	Off
"N" Or "P"	Off	OfF	On

SOLENOID OPERATION (O/D OFF SYSTEM)

Shift Lever Position	Solenoid "A"	Solenoid "B"	Solenoid "C"
"D" (Drive)			
1st Gear	Off	On	On
2nd Gear	On	On	On
3rd Gear	On	Off	Off
4th Gear	On	Off	On
"2" (Second)			
2nd Gear	On	On	Off
"L" (Low)			
1st Gear	Off	On	Off
"R" (Reverse)	On	Off	Off
"N" Or "P"	Off	OfF	On

TCC Control Solenoid – The TCM or PCM controls torque converter clutch lock-up by delivering an output signal to TCC solenoid. Lock-up solenoid is activated when shift lever is in "D", engine is normal operating temperature and vehicle is at specified speed. TCC solenoid is located on transaxle valve body.
HOLD Indicator Light – Receives signal from TCM to indicate switch position.
O/D OFF Indicator Light – Receives signal from PCM to indicate switch position.

SELF-DIAGNOSTIC SYSTEM

SYSTEM DIAGNOSIS

NOTE: Before testing transaxle, ensure fluid level is correct and throttle cable is properly adjusted. Ensure engine starts with shift lever in Park and Neutral to ensure proper adjustment of transaxle range switch. Powertrain Control Module (PCM) or Transmission Control Module (TCM) must first be tested by checking for stored codes. See RETRIEVING TROUBLE CODES.

PCM or TCM (depending on model) monitors transaxle operation and contains a self-diagnostic system which stores a DTC if an electronic control system failure or problem exists. If a problem exists in any of the solenoids or speed sensors and DTC is set, PCM or TCM delivers a signal to blink the HOLD or O/D OFF (as equipped) indicator light on instrument panel to warn the driver. DTC's may be set if a failure exists and can be retrieved for transaxle diagnosis.

RETRIEVING TROUBLE CODES

NOTE: Before retrieving DTC's, ensure proper battery voltage exists for proper self-diagnosis system operation.

Using HOLD Indicator Light (1995 Models Except 1.8L Models) – 1) Raise hood and access Data Link Connector (DLC) on left center of bulkhead in engine compartment. *See Fig. 1.*

2) Connect jumper wire between terminals No. 12 and 18 on DLC connector. *See Fig. 2.* Turn ignition switch to ON position. If DTC exists, HOLD indicator light will flash every 4 seconds. Long (1.2 second duration) flash indicates first digit and short (.4 second duration) flash indicates second digit.

3) If more than one DTC exists, next code will be displayed after pause of 4 seconds. Lowest number code will be displayed first. DTC's will be repeated. Once DTC(s) is obtained, determine probable cause and symptom. See DIAGNOSTIC TROUBLE CODE IDENTIFICATION table. For trouble shooting of codes, see DIAGNOSTIC TESTING. Turn ignition off and remove jumper wire.

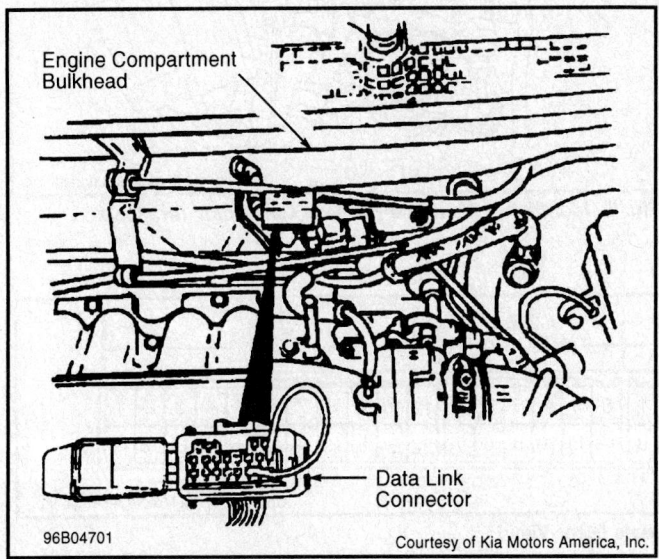

96B04701   Courtesy of Kia Motors America, Inc.

Fig. 1: Locating DLC Connector (1995 1.6L Models)

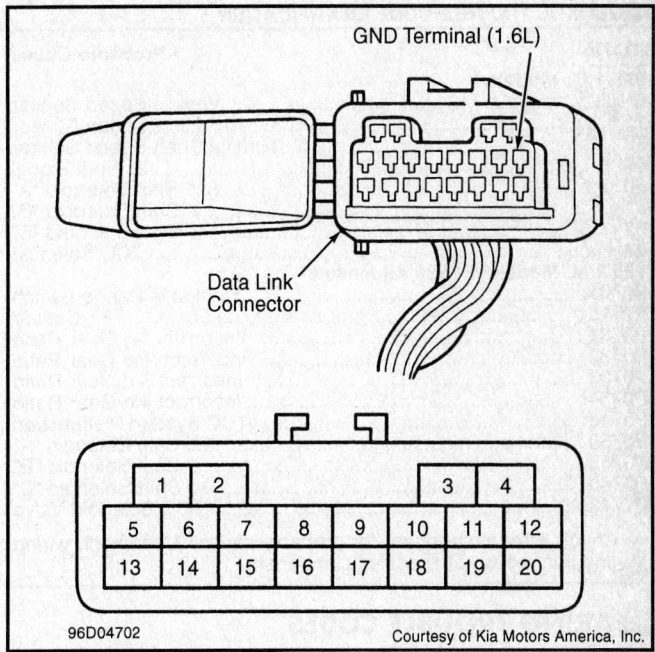

96D04702   Courtesy of Kia Motors America, Inc.

Fig. 2: Identifying DLC Connector Terminals (1995 1.6L Models)

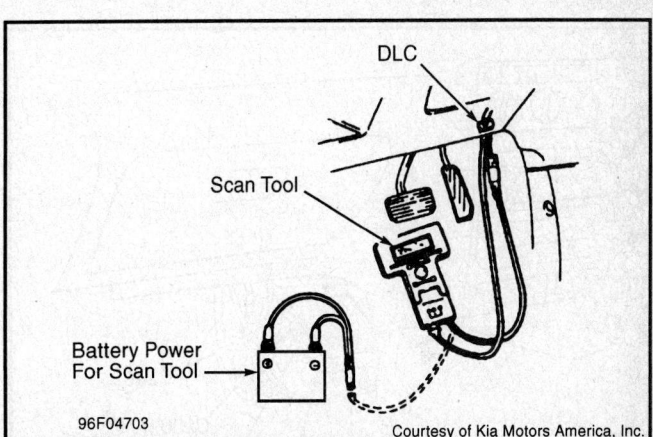

96F04703   Courtesy of Kia Motors America, Inc.

Fig. 3: Identifying DLC Connector Location (1995 1.8L & 1996 Models)

Using Scan Tool (1995 1.8L Models & 1996 Models) – Ensure ignition is in OFF position. Connect scan tool to Data Link Connector (DLC) located under left side of instrument panel, near center console. *See Fig. 3.* Turn ignition switch to ON position. Check for stored DTC's. See DIAGNOSTIC TROUBLE CODE IDENTIFICATION table. For trouble shooting of codes, see DIAGNOSTIC TESTING. Turn ignition off and remove jumper wire.

NOTE: Once repairs have been performed, DTC's must be cleared from PCM or TCM memory and vehicle test driven. See CLEARING TROUBLE CODES. Accelerate vehicle to 31 MPH for 1 minute. Fully depress accelerator pedal to force downshift. Release accelerator pedal and slow vehicle to stop. Perform retrieval procedure to ensure DTC's have been cleared and no new DTC's exist.

DIAGNOSTIC TROUBLE CODE IDENTIFICATION

DTC No.	¹ Probable Cause
1995 1.6L Models	
6	Vehicle Speed Sensor
12	Throttle Position Sensor
55	Turbine Shaft Speed Sensor
57	Shift Signal
60	Shift Solenoid "A"
61	Shift Solenoid "B"
62	Shift Solenoid "C"
63	TCC Solenoid
1995 1.8L Models & 1996 All Models	
P0705	Transaxle Range Switch
P0715	TFT Sensor
P0731	Incorrect 1st Gear Ratio
P0732	Incorrect 2nd Gear Ratio
P0733	Incorrect 3rd Gear Ratio
P0734	Incorrect 4th Gear Ratio
P0740	TCC System Malfunction
P0750	Shift Solenoid "A"
P0755	Shift Solenoid "B"
P0760	Shift Solenoid "C"
P1743	TCC Solenoid Valve

¹ – Check listed component for probable cause. Also check wiring and connection of specified component.

CLEARING TROUBLE CODES

To clear DTC's stored in PCM or TCM, disconnect negative battery cable for at least 10 seconds.

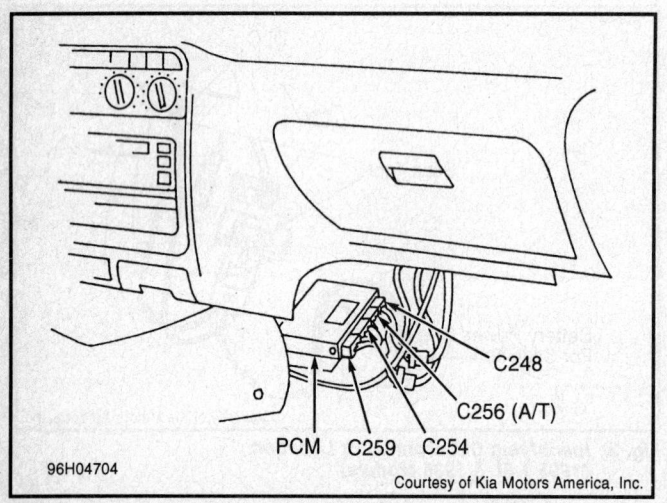

96H04704
Courtesy of Kia Motors America, Inc.

Fig. 4: Locating Powertrain Control Module & Connectors

COMPONENT LOCATION
COMPONENT LOCATION

Description	Location
Coolant Temperature Sensor	Mounted on end of cylinder head, left side.
Engine Control Module	Located under center of instrument panel.
Powertrain Control Module	See Fig. 4.
Solenoids "A", "B" & "C"	Mounted to Valve Body
TCC Solenoid	Mounted to Valve Body
Transmission Control Unit	Behind left side of instrument panel, next to relay block.
Turbine Shaft Speed Sensor	Mounted to top of transaxle, near mount bracket.
Vehicle Speed Sensor	Mounted on transaxle, near differential.

HARNESS CONNECTOR IDENTIFICATION
HARNESS CONNECTOR IDENTIFICATION

Component	See Fig.
Powertrain Control Module	5
Transaxle	6
Transaxle Control Module	7
Vehicle Speed Sensor	8 & 9

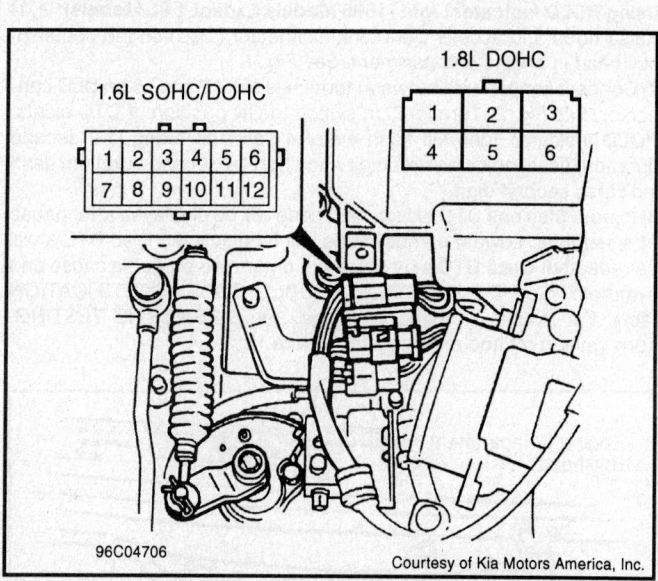

96C04706
Courtesy of Kia Motors America, Inc.

Fig. 6: Identifying Transaxle Harness Connector Terminals

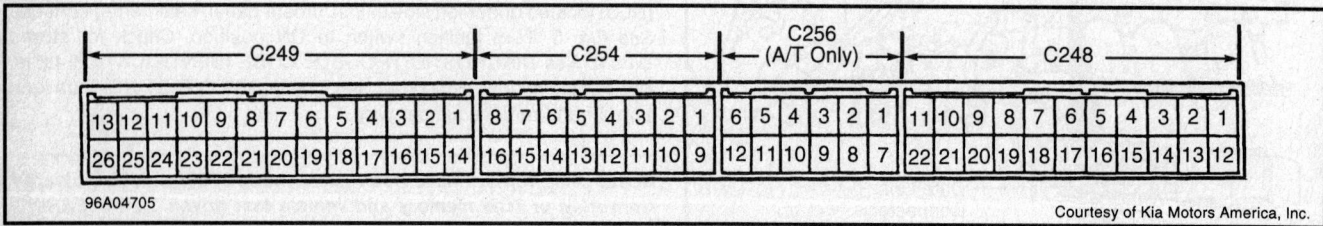

96A04705
Courtesy of Kia Motors America, Inc.

Fig. 5: Identifying Powertrain Control Module Harness Connector Terminals (Rear View)

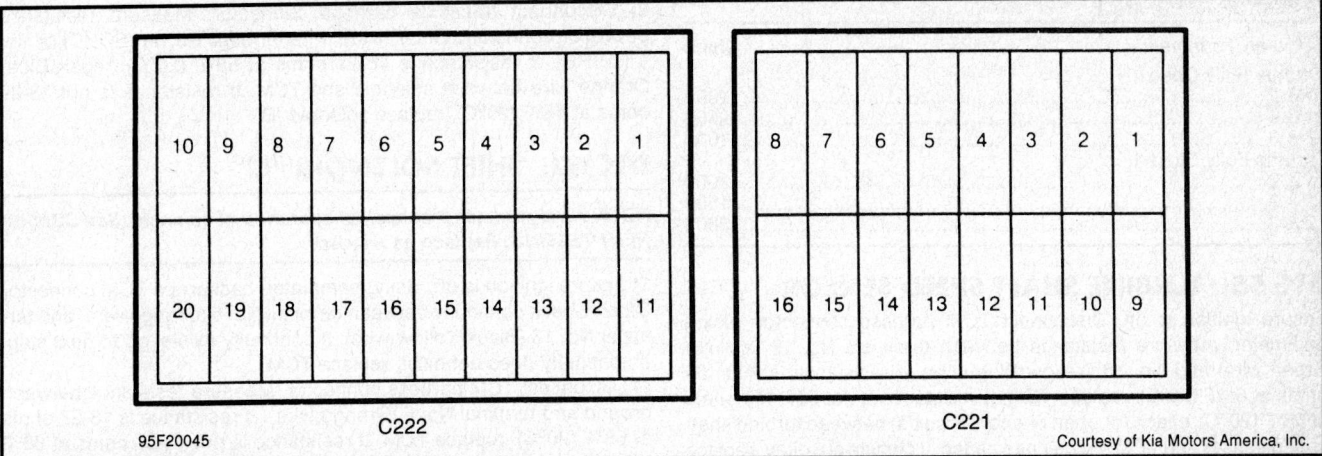

Fig. 7: *Identifying Transaxle Control Module Harness Connector Terminals*

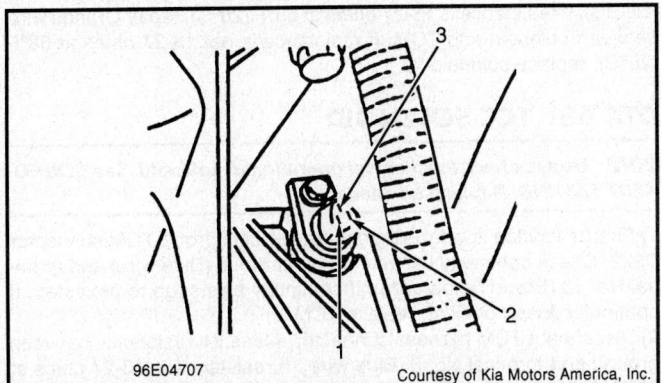

Fig. 8: *Identifying Vehicle Speed Sensor Terminals*

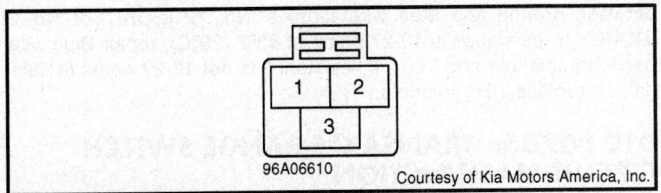

Fig. 9: *Identifying Vehicle Speed Sensor Harness Connector Terminals*

DIAGNOSTIC TESTS

NOTE: For connector terminal identification, see HARNESS CONNECTOR IDENTIFICATION table. For circuit identification, see appropriate wiring diagram in WIRING DIAGRAMS.

DTC 6: VEHICLE SPEED SENSOR

1) Disconnect TCM harness connector. Raise and support front wheels. Start and run engine. Place transaxle in Drive and allow front wheels to turn. Measure voltage between ground and terminal No. 16 (Green/Red wire) on TCM harness connector C221. If 1-10 volt pulse is present, replace TCM. If 1-10 volt pulse is not present, go to next step.
2) Remove instrument cluster. Access instrument cluster harness connector (White 20-pin) C229. With rear wheels rotating, measure voltage between ground and terminal No. 13 (Green/Red wire) on instrument cluster harness connector. If 1-10 volt pulse is present, repair Green/Red wire between TCM and instrument cluster. If 1-10 volt pulse is not present, go to next step.

3) Measure voltage between ground and terminal No. 6 (Pink wire) on instrument cluster connector C229. If 1-10 volt pulse is present, replace speedometer. If 1-10 volt pulse is not present, go to next step.
4) Stop wheels from turning. Place shift lever in Park and turn off engine. Turn ignition to ON position. Disconnect vehicle speed sensor harness connector. Measure voltage between ground and terminal No. 3 (Black/Yellow wire) on speed sensor harness connector. If battery voltage is present, go to next step. If battery voltage is not present, repair Black/Yellow wire between sensor and METER (15-amp) fuse.
5) Turn ignition off. Check continuity between ground and terminal No. 2 (Black wire) on vehicle speed sensor harness connector. If continuity exists, replace vehicle speed sensor. If continuity does not exist, repair open Black wire.

DTC 12: THROTTLE POSITION SENSOR

1) Turn ignition on. Using voltmeter, backprobe TCM harness connector. Do not disconnect connector. Measure voltage between ground and terminal No. 20 (Light Green/Orange wire) TCM connector C222. Depress accelerator pedal while monitoring voltage. Go to next step.
2) If voltage changes as accelerator pedal is depressed, replace TCM. If voltage does not change as accelerator pedal is depressed, go to next step.
3) Measure voltage between ground and terminal No. 1 (Light Green/Red wire) on TCM connector C222. If 5 volts is present, go to next step. If 5 volts is not present, replace TCM.
4) Turn ignition switch to OFF position. Disconnect Throttle Position (TP) sensor harness connector. Measure resistance between specified component terminals. See TP SENSOR RESISTANCE table. *See Fig. 10.* If resistance measurements are within specification, repair circuit(s) between TP sensor and TCM. If resistance is not within specification, replace TP sensor.

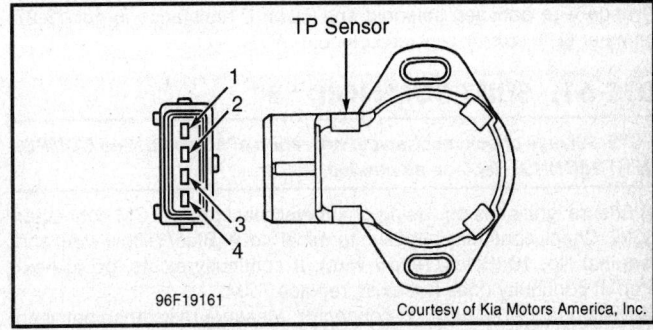

Fig. 10: *Identifying Throttle Position Sensor Terminals*

TP SENSOR RESISTANCE

Between Terminals	Ohms
Throttle Fully Open	
1 & 2	2000
1 & 3	2500
2 & 3	1000
Throttle Fully Closed	
1 & 2	2000
1 & 3	1500
2 & 3	2000

DTC 55: TURBINE SHAFT SPEED SENSOR

Ensure ignition is off. Disconnect TCM harness connector. Using ohmmeter, measure resistance between terminals No. 15 (Yellow/Green wire) and No. 16 (Yellow/Blue wire). If resistance is 200-400 ohms at 68°F (20°C), replace TCM. If resistance is not 387-473 ohms at 68°F (20°C), check for open or short circuit(s) between turbine shaft speed sensor and TCM. Repair as needed. If circuits are okay, replace turbine shaft speed sensor.

DTC 57: SHIFT SIGNAL

1) Ensure ignition is off. Using ohmmeter, backprobe TCM connector C222. Check continuity between terminal No. 3 (Blue/Orange wire) and terminal No. 18 (Black/Yellow wire). If continuity exists, go to next step. If continuity does not exist, replace TCM.
2) Ensure ignition is off. Disconnect TCM harness connector. Disconnect Electronic Control Module (ECM) harness connectors. On SOHC models, check continuity of White/Yellow wire between terminal No. 21 on ECM harness connector C248 (22-pin connector) and terminal No. 7 on TCM harness connector C222. Repair as needed. If continuity exists, go to step 4).
3) On DOHC models, check continuity of Green wire between terminal No. 8 on ECM harness connector C248 (22-pin connector) and terminal No. 7 on TCM harness connector C222. Repair as needed. If continuity exists, go to next step.
4) Possible cause of code 57 is malfunctioning ECM. Substitute ECM with known good unit and retest. Replace as needed.

DTC 60: SHIFT SOLENOID "A"

NOTE: Always check mechanical operation of solenoid. See COMPONENT TESTING. Replace as needed.

1) Ensure ignition is off. Using ohmmeter, backprobe TCM connector C222. Check continuity between terminal No. 3 (Blue/Orange wire) and terminal No. 18 (Black/Yellow wire). If continuity exists, go to next step. If continuity does not exist, replace TCM.
2) Disconnect TCM harness connector. Measure resistance between ground and terminal No. 3 (Blue/Orange wire). If resistance is 13-27 ohms at 68°F (20°C), replace TCM. If resistance is not 13-27 ohms at 68°F (20°C), go to next step.
3) Disconnect transaxle harness connector. Measure resistance between ground and Blue/Orange wire terminal No. 5 (SOHC) or No. 1 (DOHC). If resistance is 13-27 ohms at 68°F (20°C), repair Blue/Orange wire between solenoid and TCM. If resistance is not 13-27 ohms at 68°F (20°C), replace solenoid "A".

DTC 61: SHIFT SOLENOID "B"

NOTE: Always check mechanical operation of solenoid. See COMPONENT TESTING. Replace as needed.

1) Ensure ignition is off. Using ohmmeter, backprobe TCM connector C222. Check continuity between terminal No. 4 (Blue/Yellow wire) and terminal No. 18 (Black/Yellow wire). If continuity exists, go to next step. If continuity does not exist, replace TCM.
2) Disconnect TCM harness connector. Measure resistance between ground and terminal No. 4 (Blue/Yellow wire). If resistance is 13-27 ohms at 68°F (20°C), replace TCM. If resistance is not 13-27 ohms at 68°F (20°C), go to next step.

3) Disconnect transaxle harness connector. Measure resistance between ground and Blue/Yellow wire terminal No. 11 (SOHC) or No. 4 (DOHC). If resistance is 13-27 ohms at 68°F (20°C), repair Blue/Orange wire between solenoid and TCM. If resistance is not 13-27 ohms at 68°F (20°C), replace solenoid "B".

DTC 62: SHIFT SOLENOID "C"

NOTE: Always check mechanical operation of solenoid. See COMPONENT TESTING. Replace as needed.

1) Ensure ignition is off. Using ohmmeter, backprobe TCM connector C222. Check continuity between terminal No. 5 (Orange wire) and terminal No. 18 (Black/Yellow wire). If continuity exists, go to next step. If continuity does not exist, replace TCM.
2) Disconnect TCM harness connector. Measure resistance between ground and terminal No. 5 (Orange wire). If resistance is 13-27 ohms at 68°F (20°C), replace TCM. If resistance is not 13-27 ohms at 68°F (20°C), go to next step.
3) Disconnect transaxle harness connector. Measure resistance between ground and Orange wire terminal No. 6 (SOHC) or No. 5 (DOHC). If resistance is 13-27 ohms at 68°F (20°C), repair Orange wire between solenoid and TCM. If resistance is not 13-27 ohms at 68°F (20°C), replace solenoid "C".

DTC 63: TCC SOLENOID

NOTE: Always check mechanical operation of solenoid. See COMPONENT TESTING. Replace as needed.

1) Ensure ignition is off. Using ohmmeter, backprobe TCM connector C222. Check continuity between terminal No. 6 (Blue wire) and terminal No. 18 (Black/Yellow wire). If continuity exists, go to next step. If continuity does not exist, replace TCM.
2) Disconnect TCM harness connector. Measure resistance between ground and terminal No. 6 (Blue wire). If resistance is 13-27 ohms at 68°F (20°C), replace TCM. If resistance is not 13-27 ohms at 68°F (20°C), go to next step.
3) Disconnect transaxle harness connector. Measure resistance between ground and Blue wire terminal No. 12 (SOHC) or No. 3 (DOHC). If resistance is 13-27 ohms at 68°F (20°C), repair Blue wire between solenoid and TCM. If resistance is not 13-27 ohms at 68°F (20°C), replace TCC solenoid.

DTC P0705: TRANSAXLE RANGE SWITCH CIRCUIT MALFUNCTION

Condition – Engine speed is greater than 531 RPM and vehicle speed is more than 55 MPH. No signal is received from range switch. Vehicle speed is more than 12 MPH with "D" range and "N" position switches on. Possible causes for either condition are:
- Transaxle range switch malfunction.
- Damaged wiring or connectors between transaxle range switch and PCM.
- PCM failure.

Diagnostic Procedure – 1) Ensure all appropriate connections are clean and tight. Repair as needed. Turn ignition on. Using voltmeter, backprobe PCM connector C248. Measure voltage between ground and specified terminal. See DTC P0705 TEST table. If all voltages are within specification, go to step 6). If any voltage is not within specification, go to next step.
2) Check continuity of circuits between transaxle range switch and PCM. See appropriate wiring diagram in WIRING DIAGRAMS. Repair as needed. If all circuits are okay, go to next step.
3) Disconnect negative battery cable. Disconnect transaxle range switch harness connector. Inspect continuity of transaxle range switch internal circuits. See TRANSAXLE RANGE SWITCH (PCM EQUIPPED MODELS) in COMPONENT TESTING. Replace as needed. If switch is okay, go to next step.

DTC P0705 TEST

PCM Terminal No.	Measured Voltage	Range Switch Position
17	0	"P" Or "N"
17	12-14	"R", "D", "2" Or "1"
9	12-14	"D"
9	0	All Except "D"
4	12-14	"2"
4	0	All Except "2"
10	12-14	"1"
10	0	All Except "1"

4) Leave negative battery cable disconnected. Disconnect PCM harness connector C248. Disconnect ignition switch harness connector C213. Connector C213 is located at base of steering column. Connector is Black with Black/White wire input circuit and Black/Blue wire output circuit.

5) Check continuity between terminal No. 17 (Black/Blue wire) on PCM harness connector C248 and output circuit of ignition switch harness connector C213. Repair as needed. If continuity exists, go to next step.

6) Reconnect negative battery cable. Road test vehicle. Retrieve DTC's. If code P0705 is still present, replace PCM. If code is no longer present, problem may be caused by poor connection. Repair as needed.

DTC P0710: TRANSAXLE FLUID TEMPERATURE (TFT) SENSOR CIRCUIT MALFUNCTION

Condition – Vehicle speed is more than 12 MPH and voltage input to PCM is less than .097 volts or greater than 4.941 volts. Possible causes for condition are:

- Transaxle fluid temperature sensor malfunction.
- Damaged wiring or connectors between transaxle fluid temperature sensor and PCM.

Diagnostic Procedure – **1)** Ensure all appropriate connections are clean and tight. Repair as needed. Turn ignition on. Access PCM connectors. Using voltmeter, backprobe harness connectors. Do not disconnect connectors. Go to next step.

2) Measure voltage between ground and terminal No. 3 (White/Black wire) on PCM connector C254. Voltage should be about 4.0 volts at 68°F (20°C) or 1.5 volts at 256°F (130°C). If voltage is within specifications, go to step **6)**. If voltage is not within specifications, go to next step.

3) Turn ignition off. Disconnect PCM harness connector C254. Measure resistance between terminals No. 3 (White/Black wire) and No. 8 (Black/Yellow wire). See TFT SENSOR SPECIFICATIONS. If resistance is within specification, go to step **6)**. If resistance is not within specification, go to next step.

4) Disconnect transaxle 6-pin harness connector. Measure resistance between terminals No. 2 (Black/Brown wire) and No. 6 (Violet/White wire). See TFT SENSOR SPECIFICATIONS. If resistance is within specification, go to step **6)**. If resistance is not within specification, replace TFT sensor.

5) Check continuity of circuit between TFT sensor and PCM. See appropriate wiring diagram in WIRING DIAGRAMS. Repair as needed. If circuit is okay, go to next step.

TFT SENSOR SPECIFICATIONS

K/Ohms	Ambient Temperature
124.8-142.0	-20°F (-4°C)
52.0-57.4	0°F (32°C)
23.4-25.0	20°F (68°C)
11.1-12.1	40°F (104°C)
5.6-6.3	60°F (140°C)
3.0-3.4	80°F (176°C)
1.7-2.0	100°F (212°C)
1.1-1.2	120°F (248°C)
.86-.92	130°F (266°C)

6) Reconnect all harness connectors. Road test vehicle. Retrieve DTC's. If code P0710 is still present, replace PCM. If code is no longer present, problem may be caused by poor connection. Repair as needed.

DTC P0715: TURBINE SHAFT SPEED SENSOR

Condition – Turbine shaft speed sensor signal is not input to PCM when vehicle is above 25 MPH and shift lever is in "D", "2" or "1" position. Possible causes for condition are:

- Turbine shaft speed sensor malfunction.
- Damaged wiring or connectors between turbine shaft speed sensor and PCM.

Diagnostic Procedure – **1)** Ensure all appropriate connections are clean and tight. Repair as needed. Turn ignition on. Access PCM connectors. Using voltmeter, backprobe harness connectors. Do not disconnect connectors. Go to next step.

2) Measure voltage between terminals No. 6 (Yellow/Green wire) and No. 12 (Yellow/Blue wire) on PCM harness connector C256. Voltage should be .1-1.1 volts with engine running in Park or Neutral. If voltage is within specification, go to step **6)**. If voltage is not within specification, go to next step.

3) Turn ignition off. Disconnect negative battery cable. Disconnect PCM harness connector C256. Measure resistance between terminals No. 6 (Yellow/Green wire) and No. 12 (Yellow/Blue wire). If resistance is 200-400 ohms, go to step **6)**. If resistance is not 200-400 ohms, go to next step.

4) Disconnect turbine shaft speed sensor. Measure resistance between component terminals. If resistance is 200-400 ohms, go to step **6)**. If resistance is not 200-400 ohms, replace turbine shaft speed sensor.

5) Check continuity of circuits between turbine shaft speed sensor and PCM. See appropriate wiring diagram in WIRING DIAGRAMS. Repair as needed. If circuits are okay, go to next step.

6) Reconnect all harness connectors. Road test vehicle. Retrieve DTC's. If code P0715 is still present, replace PCM. If code is no longer present, problem may be caused by poor connection. Repair as needed.

DTC P0731: INCORRECT 1ST GEAR RATIO

Condition – Shift solenoids "A", "B", "C", vehicle speed sensor, turbine shaft speed sensor and TFT sensor function normally and vehicle speed is 12-32 MPH in 1st gear. Turbine shaft speed sensor and vehicle speed sensor signals indicate that gear ratio is above set value. Possible causes are:

- Low ATF level.
- Low line pressure.
- Control valve stuck.
- Solenoid valve malfunction.
- PCM malfunction.
- Forward clutch, 3-4 brake band, one-way clutch No. 1 slippage.

Diagnostic Procedure – **1)** Inspect ATF level and condition. Correct as needed. If fluid level and condition is okay, check line pressure. See TESTING in FA4A-EL & GF4A-EL overhaul article. Follow repair recommendations if line pressure is not within specifications. If line pressure is okay, go to next step.

2) Perform stall speed test. See TESTING in FA4A-EL & GF4A-EL overhaul article. Follow repair recommendations if stall speed is not within specifications. If stall speed is okay, go to next step.

3) Perform time lag test. See TESTING in FA4A-EL & GF4A-EL overhaul article. Follow repair recommendations if time lag is not within specifications. If time lag is okay, go to next step.

4) Perform road test. See TESTING in FA4A-EL & GF4A-EL overhaul article. Follow repair recommendations if transaxle shift speeds or shift feel is not as specified. If vehicle shifts at correct speeds and shift feel is acceptable, go to next step.

5) Clear DTC's. See CLEARING CODES. Retrieve DTC's. If code P0731 is still present, replace PCM. If code is no longer present, problem may be caused by intermittent clutch slippage. Further investigation may be required.

DTC P0732: INCORRECT 2ND GEAR RATIO

Condition – Shift solenoids "A", "B", "C", vehicle speed sensor, turbine shaft speed sensor and TFT sensor function normally and vehicle speed is 17-60 MPH in 2nd gear with 3/8ths throttle opening. Turbine shaft speed sensor and vehicle speed sensor signals indicate that gear ratio is above set value. Possible causes are:

- Low ATF level.
- Low line pressure.
- Control valve stuck.
- Solenoid valve malfunction.
- PCM malfunction.
- Forward clutch, 2-4 brake band, one-way clutch No. 1 slippage.

Diagnostic Procedure – **1)** Inspect ATF level and condition. Correct as needed. If fluid level and condition is okay, check line pressure. See TESTING in FA4A-EL & GF4A-EL overhaul article. Follow repair recommendations if line pressure is not within specifications. If line pressure is okay, go to next step.
2) Perform stall speed test. See TESTING in FA4A-EL & GF4A-EL overhaul article. Follow repair recommendations if stall speed is not within specifications. If stall speed is okay, go to next step.
3) Perform time lag test. See TESTING in FA4A-EL & GF4A-EL overhaul article. Follow repair recommendations if time lag is not within specifications. If time lag is okay, go to next step.
4) Perform road test. See TESTING in FA4A-EL & GF4A-EL overhaul article. Follow repair recommendations if transaxle shift speeds or shift feel is not as specified. If vehicle shifts at correct speeds and shift feel is acceptable, go to next step.
5) Clear DTC's. See CLEARING CODES. Retrieve DTC's. If code P0732 is still present, replace PCM. If code is no longer present, problem may be caused by intermittent clutch slippage. Further investigation may be required.

DTC P0733: INCORRECT 3RD GEAR RATIO

Condition – Shift solenoids "A", "B", "C", vehicle speed sensor, turbine shaft speed sensor and TFT sensor function normally and vehicle speed is 19-32 MPH in 3rd gear. Turbine shaft speed sensor and vehicle speed sensor signals indicate that gear ratio is above set value. Possible causes are:

- Low ATF level.
- Low line pressure.
- Control valve stuck.
- Solenoid valve malfunction.
- PCM malfunction.
- Forward clutch, 3-4 brake band, one-way clutch No. 1 slippage.

Diagnostic Procedure – **1)** Inspect ATF level and condition. Correct as needed. If fluid level and condition is okay, check line pressure. See TESTING in FA4A-EL & GF4A-EL overhaul article. Follow repair recommendations if line pressure is not within specifications. If line pressure is okay, go to next step.
2) Perform stall speed test. See TESTING in FA4A-EL & GF4A-EL overhaul article. Follow repair recommendations if stall speed is not within specifications. If stall speed is okay, go to next step.
3) Perform time lag test. See TESTING in FA4A-EL & GF4A-EL overhaul article. Follow repair recommendations if time lag is not within specifications. If time lag is okay, go to next step.
4) Perform road test. See TESTING in FA4A-EL & GF4A-EL overhaul article. Follow repair recommendations if transaxle shift speeds or shift feel is not as specified. If vehicle shifts at correct speeds and shift feel is acceptable, go to next step.
5) Clear DTC's. See CLEARING CODES. Retrieve DTC's. If code P0733 is still present, replace PCM. If code is no longer present, problem may be caused by intermittent clutch slippage. Further investigation may be required.

DTC P0734: INCORRECT 4TH GEAR RATIO

Condition – Shift solenoids "A", "B", "C", vehicle speed sensor, turbine shaft speed sensor and TFT sensor function normally and vehicle speed is 44-65 MPH in 4th gear. Turbine shaft speed sensor and vehicle speed sensor signals indicate that gear ratio is above set value. Possible causes are:

- Low ATF level.
- Low line pressure.
- Control valve stuck.
- Solenoid valve malfunction.
- PCM malfunction.
- 2-4 brake band and 3-4 clutch slippage.

Diagnostic Procedure – **1)** Inspect ATF level and condition. Correct as needed. If fluid level and condition is okay, check line pressure. See TESTING in FA4A-EL & GF4A-EL overhaul article. Follow repair recommendations if line pressure is not within specifications. If line pressure is okay, go to next step.
2) Perform stall speed test. See TESTING in FA4A-EL & GF4A-EL overhaul article. Follow repair recommendations if stall speed is not within specifications. If stall speed is okay, go to next step.
3) Perform time lag test. See TESTING in FA4A-EL & GF4A-EL overhaul article. Follow repair recommendations if time lag is not within specifications. If time lag is okay, go to next step.
4) Perform road test. See TESTING in FA4A-EL & GF4A-EL overhaul article. Follow repair recommendations if transaxle shift speeds or shift feel is not as specified. If vehicle shifts at correct speeds and shift feel is acceptable, go to next step.
5) Clear DTC's. See CLEARING CODES. Retrieve DTC's. If code P0734 is still present, replace PCM. If code is no longer present, problem may be caused by intermittent clutch slippage. Further investigation may be required.

DTC P0740: TORQUE CONVERTER CLUTCH MALFUNCTION

Condition – Shift solenoids "A", "B", "C", vehicle speed sensor, turbine shaft speed sensor and TFT sensor function normally and vehicle speed is 44-65 MPH. Difference in number of engine revolutions and reverse and forward drum revolutions is more than 100 with transaxle in 4th gear and TCC engaged. Possible causes are:

- Low ATF level.
- Low line pressure.
- Torque converter slippage.
- Control valve stuck.
- TCC solenoid valve malfunction.
- PCM malfunction.

Diagnostic Procedure – **1)** Inspect ATF level and condition. Correct as needed. If fluid level and condition is okay, check line pressure. See TESTING in FA4A-EL & GF4A-EL overhaul article. Follow repair recommendations if line pressure is not within specifications. If line pressure is okay, go to next step.
2) Inspect TCC control valve in valve body. See FA4A-EL & GF4A-EL overhaul article. Follow repair recommendations if valve operation is faulty. If valve is okay, go to next step.
3) Clear DTC's. See CLEARING CODES. Retrieve DTC's. If code P0740 is still present, replace PCM. If code is no longer present, problem may be caused by intermittent TCC slippage. Further investigation may be required.

DTC P0750: SHIFT SOLENOID "A" MALFUNCTION

Possible Causes
- Short or open circuit between PCM and solenoid.
- PCM malfunction.
- Shift solenoid malfunction.

Diagnostic Procedure – **1)** Ensure all appropriate connections are clean and tight. Repair as needed. Turn ignition on. Access PCM connectors. Using voltmeter, backprobe harness connectors. Do not disconnect connectors. Go to next step.
2) Measure voltage between ground and terminal No. 1 (Blue/Orange wire) on PCM connector C256. Battery voltage should be present with solenoid on and zero voltage with solenoid off. If voltage is within specifications, go to step **6)**. If voltage is not within specifications, go to next step.

3) Turn ignition off. Disconnect PCM harness connector C256. Measure resistance between ground and terminal No. 1 (Blue/Orange wire). If resistance is 13-27 ohms, go to step **6)**. If resistance is not 13-27 ohms, go to next step.

4) Disconnect transaxle 6-pin harness connector. Measure resistance between terminals No. 1 (Pink/Blue wire) and No. 6 (Violet/White wire). If resistance is 13-27 ohms, go to step **6)**. If resistance is not 13-27 ohms, go to next step.

5) Check continuity of circuit between shift solenoid "A" and PCM. See appropriate wiring diagram in WIRING DIAGRAMS. Repair as needed. If circuit is okay, go to next step.

6) Reconnect all harness connectors. Road test vehicle. Retrieve DTC's. If code P0750 is still present, replace PCM. If code is no longer present, problem may be caused by poor connection. Repair as needed.

DTC P0755: SHIFT SOLENOID "B" MALFUNCTION

Possible Causes
- Short or open circuit between PCM and solenoid.
- PCM malfunction.
- Shift solenoid malfunction.

Diagnostic Procedure – 1) Ensure all appropriate connections are clean and tight. Repair as needed. Turn ignition on. Access PCM connectors. Using voltmeter, backprobe harness connectors. Do not disconnect connectors. Go to next step.

2) Measure voltage between ground and terminal No. 7 (Blue/Yellow wire) on PCM connector C256. Battery voltage should be present with solenoid on and zero voltage with solenoid off. If voltage is within specifications, go to step **6)**. If voltage is not within specifications, go to next step.

3) Turn ignition off. Disconnect PCM harness connector C256. Measure resistance between ground and terminal No. 1 (Blue/Yellow wire). If resistance is 13-27 ohms, go to step **6)**. If resistance is not 13-27 ohms, go to next step.

4) Disconnect transaxle 6-pin harness connector. Measure resistance between terminals No. 4 (Gray/Blue wire) and No. 6 (Violet/White wire). If resistance is 13-27 ohms, go to step **6)**. If resistance is not 13-27 ohms, go to next step.

5) Check continuity of circuit between shift solenoid "B" and PCM. See appropriate wiring diagram in WIRING DIAGRAMS. Repair as needed. If circuit is okay, go to next step.

6) Reconnect all harness connectors. Road test vehicle. Retrieve DTC's. If code P0755 is still present, replace PCM. If code is no longer present, problem may be caused by poor connection. Repair as needed.

DTC P0760: SHIFT SOLENOID "C" MALFUNCTION

Possible Causes
- Short or open circuit between PCM and solenoid.
- PCM malfunction.
- Shift solenoid malfunction.

Diagnostic Procedure – 1) Ensure all appropriate connections are clean and tight. Repair as needed. Turn ignition on. Access PCM connectors. Using voltmeter, backprobe harness connectors. Do not disconnect connectors. Go to next step.

2) Measure voltage between ground and terminal No. 2 (Orange wire) on PCM connector C256. Battery voltage should be present with sole-noid on and zero voltage with solenoid off. If voltage is within specifications, go to step **6)**. If voltage is not within specifications, go to next step.

3) Turn ignition off. Disconnect PCM harness connector C256. Measure resistance between ground and terminal No. 2 (Orange wire). If resistance is 13-27 ohms, go to step **6)**. If resistance is not 13-27 ohms, go to next step.

4) Disconnect transaxle 6-pin harness connector. Measure resistance between terminals No. 5 (Orange wire) and No. 6 (Violet/White wire). If resistance is 13-27 ohms, go to step **6)**. If resistance is not 13-27 ohms, go to next step.

5) Check continuity of circuit between shift solenoid "C" and PCM. See appropriate wiring diagram in WIRING DIAGRAMS. Repair as needed. If circuit is okay, go to next step.

6) Reconnect all harness connectors. Road test vehicle. Retrieve DTC's. If code P0760 is still present, replace PCM. If code is no longer present, problem may be caused by poor connection. Repair as needed.

DTC P1743: TORQUE CONVERTER CLUTCH SOLENOID MALFUNCTION

Possible Causes
- Short or open circuit between PCM and solenoid.
- PCM malfunction.
- TCC shift solenoid malfunction.

Diagnostic Procedure – 1) Ensure all appropriate connections are clean and tight. Repair as needed. Turn ignition on. Access PCM connectors. Using voltmeter, backprobe harness connectors. Do not disconnect connectors. Go to next step.

2) Measure voltage between ground and terminal No. 8 (Blue wire) on PCM connector C256. Battery voltage should be present with solenoid on and zero voltage with solenoid off. If voltage is within specifications, go to step **6)**. If voltage is not within specifications, go to next step.

3) Turn ignition off. Disconnect PCM harness connector C256. Measure resistance between ground and terminal No. 8 (Blue wire). If resistance is 13-27 ohms, go to step **6)**. If resistance is not 13-27 ohms, go to next step.

4) Disconnect transaxle 6-pin harness connector. Measure resistance between terminals No. 3 (Brown wire) and No. 6 (Violet/White wire). If resistance is 13-27 ohms, go to step **6)**. If resistance is not 13-27 ohms, go to next step.

5) Check continuity of circuit between shift solenoid "A" and PCM. See appropriate wiring diagram in WIRING DIAGRAMS. Repair as needed. If circuit is okay, go to next step.

6) Reconnect all harness connectors. Road test vehicle. Retrieve DTC's. If code P1743 is still present, replace PCM. If code is no longer present, problem may be caused by poor connection. Repair as needed.

COMPONENT TESTING

PCM & TCM TERMINAL VOLTAGE TESTS

Turn ignition switch to ON position. Access PCM or TCM. Do not disconnect harness connector. Using DVOM, measure voltage. *See Figs. 11-15.* After verifying that appropriate condition has been met, check voltage. If voltage is not within specification, replace PCM or TCM (as applicable).

Terminal	Connection to	Voltmeter + terminal	Voltmeter – terminal	Voltage	Condition
C221/1	—	—	—	—	—
C221/2 (Output)	Data link connector (DLC) (TCM FAIL)	C221/2	Ground	Approximately 12V	Normal
				Below 1.5V or Approximately 12V (fluctuating)	If malfunction present (HOLD indicator flashing)
				Code signal	TCM terminal grounded
C221/3 (Input)	Data link connector (TCM TEST)	C221/3		Approximately 12V	Normal
				Below 1.5V	TCM terminal grounded
C221/4 (Input)	Transaxle fluid temperature sensor	C221/4		Approximately 4.95V-1.12V (ATF temperature) -20°F (-30°C) 302°F (150°C)	While warming up ATF Note: Approximately 4.6V: ATF temperature 68°F (20°C) Approximately 1.5V: ATF temperature 266°F (130°C)
C221/5	—	—	—	—	—
C221/6	—	—	—	—	—
C221/7	Closed throttle powition switch	—	—	—	Closed throttle position switch
C221/8 (Input)	Closed throttle position switch	C221/8	Ground	Approximately 12V	Closed throttle position switch OFF (Throttle valve open)
				Below 1.5V	Closed throttle position switch ON (Throttle valve fully closed)
C221/9 (Output)	HOLD indicator	C221/9		Below 1.5V	HOLD mode
				Approximately 12V	Normal mode
C221/10	—	—	—	—	—
C221/11 (Input)	Brake pedal position switch	C221/11		Approximately 12V	Brake pedal depressed
				Below 1.5V	Brake pedal released
C221/12 (Input)	HOLD switch	1H	Ground	Below 1.5V	Switch depressed
				Approximately 12V	Switch released
C221/13 (Ground)	Battery ground	1J	Ground	Below 1.5V	—
C221/14	—	—	—	—	—

96G04708

Courtesy of Kia Motors America, Inc.

Fig. 11: TCM Pin Voltage Table (1.6L SOHC, 1 Of 2)

Terminal	Connection to	Voltmeter		Voltage	Condition
		+ terminal	− terminal		
C221/15 (Input)	Engine control module (Engine coolant temperature signal)	C221/15	Ground	Approximately 12V	Above 162°F (72°C)
				Below 1.5V	Below 153°F (67°C)
C221/16 (Input)	Vehicle speed sensor	C221/16		Approximately 3V-4V	While driving
				Approximately 3V-4V or below 1.5V	Vehicle stopped
C222/1 (Input)	Throttle position (TP) sensor	C222/1		Approximately 5V	Ignition switch ON
				Below 1.5V	Ignition switch OFF
C222/2	—	—	—	—	—
C222/3 (Output)	Shift solenoid A	C222/3	Ground	Approximately 12V or Below 1.5V	—
C222/4 (Output)	Shift solenoid B	C222/4		Approximately 12V or Below 1.5V	—
C222/5 (Output)	Shift solenoid C	C222/5		Approximately 12V or Below 1.5V	—
C222/6 (Output)	Torque converter clutch solenoid	C222/6	Ground	Approximately 12V	Lock−up
				Below 1.5V	Other
C222/7 (Output)	Engine control module (Shift Signal)	C222/7		Approximately 12V	Downshift with throttle valve opening 2/8 or more
				Below 1.5V	Others
C222/8 (Memory power)	Battery	C222/8		Approximately 12V	Constant
C222/9 (Battery power)	Battery	C222/9		Approximately 12V	Ignition ON
				Below 1.5V	Ignition OFF
C222/10 (Battery power)	Battery	C222/10		Approximately 12V	Ignition ON
				Below 1.5V	Ignition OFF
C222/11 (Input)	Transaxle range switch (P and N ranges)	C222/11	Ground	Below 1.5V	P and N ranges
				Approximately 12V	Other ranges
C222/12 (Input)	Transaxle range switch (D range)	C222/12		Approximately 12V	D range
				Below 1.5V	Other ranges
C222/13 (Input)	Transaxle range switch (S range)	C222/13		Approximately 12V	S range
				Below 1.5V	Other ranges
C222/14 (Input)	Transaxle range switch (L range)	C222/14	Ground	Approximately 12V	L range
				Below 1.5V	Other ranges
C222/15 (Input)	Input/turbine speed sensor*	C222/15		Above 1V (AC)	Engine running (N range)
				Approx. 0V (AC)	Engine stopped
C222/16 (Ground)	Input/turbine speed sensor	C222/16		Below 1.5V	—
C222/17	—	—	—	—	—
C222/18 (Ground)	Battery ground	C222/18	Ground	Below 1.5V	Constant
C222/19	—	—	—	—	—
C222/20 (Input)	Throttle Position (TP) sensor	C222/20	Ground	Approximately .4-4.4V	Throttle valve fully closed to fully open

* Checked in AC voltage range

96I04709

Courtesy of Kia Motors America, Inc.

Fig. 12: TCM Pin Voltage Table (1.6L SOHC, 2 Of 2)

AUTOMATIC TRANSMISSIONS
Kia FA4A-EL Electronic Controls (Cont.)

Terminal	Connection to	Voltmeter + terminal	Voltmeter − terminal	Voltage	Condition
C222/1	—	—		—	—
C221/2 (Output)	Data link connector (DLC) (TCM FAIL)	C221/2		Approximately 12V	Normal
				Below 1.5V or Approximately 12V (fluctuating)	If malfunction present (HOLD indicator flashing)
				Code signal	TCM terminal grounded
C221/3 (Input)	Data link connector (TCM TEST)	C221/3	Ground	Approximately 12V	Normal
				Below 1.5V	TCM terminal grounded
C221/4 (Input)	Transaxle fluid temperature sensor	C221/4		Approximately 4.95V-1.12V (ATF temperature) -20°F (-30°C) 302°F (150°C)	While warming-up ATF Note: Approximately 4.6: ATF temperature 68°F (20°C) Approximately 1.5V: ATF temperature 266°F (130°C)
C221/5	—	—	—	—	—
C221/6	—	—	—	—	—
C221/7	—	—	—	—	—
C221/8 (Input)	Closed throttle position switch	C221/8		Approximately 12V	Closed throttle position switch OFF (Throttle valve open)
				Below 1.5V	Closed throttle position switch ON (Throttle valve fully closed)
C221/9 (Output)	HOLD indicator	C221/9	Ground	Below 1.5V	HOLD mode
				Approximately 12V	Normal mode
C221/10	Engine control module Transaxle range switch signal	C2221/10		Below 1.0V	P or N ranges
				Approximately 12V	Other ranges
C221/11 (Input)	Brake pedal position switch	C221/11		Approximately 12V	Brake pedal depressed
				Below 1.5V	Brake pedal released
C221/12 (Input)	HOLD switch	1H		Below 1.5V	HOLD switch depressed
				Approximately 12V	HOLD switch released
C221/13 (Ground)	Battery ground	1J	Ground	Below 1.5V	—
C221/14	—	—	—	—	—

96A04710

Courtesy of Kia Motors America, Inc.

Fig. 13: TCM Pin Voltage Table (1.6L DOHC, 1 Of 2)

Terminal	Connection to	Voltmeter		Voltage	Condition
		+ terminal	− terminal		
C221/15 (Input)	Engine control module (Engine coolant temperature signal)	C221/15	Ground	Approximately 12V	Above 162°F (72°C)
				Below 1.5V	Below 153°F (67°C)
C221/16 (Input)	Vehicle speed sensor	C221/16		Approximately 3V-4V	While driving
				Approximately 3V-4V or below 1.5V	Vehicle stopped
C222/1 (Input)	Throttle position (TP) sensor	C222/1		Approximately 5V	Ignition switch ON
				Below 1.5V	Ignition switch OFF
C222/2	—	—	—	—	—
C222/3 (Output)	Shift solenoid A	C222/3	Ground	Approximately 12V or Below 1.5V	—
C222/4 (Output)	Shift solenoid B	C222/4		Approximately 12V or Below 1.5V	—
C222/5 (Output)	Shift solenoid C	C222/5		Approximately 12V or Below 1.5V	—
C222/6 (Output)	Torque converter clutch solenoid	C222/6		Approximately 12V	Lock−up
				Below 1.5V	Other
C222/7 (Output)	Engine control module (Shift Signal)	C222/7	Ground	Approximately 12V	Downshift with throttle valve opening 2/8 or more
				Below 1.5V	Others
C222/8 (Memory power)	Battery	C222/8		Approximately 12V	Constant
C222/9 (Battery power)	Battery	C222/9		Approximately 12V	Ignition ON
				Below 1.5V	Ignition OFF
C222/10 (Battery power)	Battery	C222/10		Approximately 12V	Ignition ON
				Below 1.5V	Ignition OFF
C222/11 (Input)	Transaxle range switch (P and N ranges)	C222/11	Ground	Below 1.5V	P and N ranges
				Approximately 12V	Other ranges
C222/12 (Input)	Transaxle range switch (D range)	C222/12		Approximately 12V	D range
				Below 1.5V	Other ranges
C222/13 (Input)	Transaxle range switch (S range)	C222/13	Ground	Approximately 12V	S range
				Below 1.5V	Other ranges
C222/14 (Input)	Transaxle range switch (L range)	C222/14		Approximately 12V	L range
				Below 1.5V	Other ranges
C222/15 (Input)	Input/turbine speed sensor*	C222/15		Above 1V (AC)	Engine running (N range)
				Approx. 0V (AC)	Engine stopped
C222/16 (Ground)	Input/turbine speed sensor	C222/16		Below 1.5V	—
C222/17	—	—	—	—	—
C222/18 (Ground)	Battery ground		Ground	Below 1.5V	Constant
C222/19	—	—	—	—	—
C222/20 (Input)	Throttle Position (TP) sensor		Ground	Approximately .4-4.4V	Throttle valve fully closed to fully open

* Checked in AC voltage range

96C04711

Courtesy of Kia Motors America, Inc.

Fig. 14: TCM Pin Voltage Table (1.6L DOHC, 2 Of 2)

AUTOMATIC TRANSMISSIONS
Kia FA4A-EL Electronic Controls (Cont.)

Terminal	Signal	Connected to	Test Condition		Voltage	Possible Malfunction
C256-1	Shift solenoid A control	Shift solenoid A	During shifting		B+	Shift solenoid A
			Others		Below 1.0	
C256-2	Shift solenoid C control	Shift solenoid C	During shifting		B+	Shift solenoid C
			Others		Below 1.0	
C256-3	O/D OFF indicator light control	O/D OFF indicator light	Ignition switch ON	O/D OFF mode	Below 2.0	Instrument cluster O/D OFF indicator
				Others	B+	
C256-4	2 range	Transaxle range switch (2 range)	Idle	2 range	B+	Transaxle range switch
				Others	Below 1.0	
C256-5	O/D switch	O/D switch	Ignition switch ON	O/D OFF switch pressed	Below 1.0	Transaxle range switch
				O/D OFF switch released	B+	
C256-6	Input/ turbine speed sensor	Input/turbine speed sensor (turbine)	Ignition switch ON		Approx 1.0	Input/turbine speed sensor
			Idle			
C256-7	Shift solenoid B control	Shift solenoid B	During shifting		B+	Shift solenoid B
			Others		Below 1.0	
C256-8	Torque converter clutch solenoid control	Torque converter clutch solenoid	During shifting		B+	Torque converter clutch solenoid valve
			Others		Below 1.0	
C256-9	D range	Transaxle range switch (D range)	Idle	D range	B+	Transaxle range switch
				Others	Below 1.0	
C256-10	1 range	Transaxle range switch (1 range)	Idle	1 range	B+	Transaxle range switch
				Other	Below 1.0	
C256-11	-	-	-		-	-
C256-12	Input/ turbine speed sensor ground	Input/turbine speed sensor (ground)	Constant		Below 1.0	PCM C236-12 terminal continuity harness

96E04712

Courtesy of Kia Motors America, Inc.

Fig. 15: PCM Pin Voltage Table (1.8L DOHC)

O/D OFF SWITCH

1) Remove center console to access switch connector. Turn ignition switch on. Using voltmeter, backprobe harness connector. *See Fig. 16.* With O/D OFF switch in released position, measure voltage on terminals No. 3 and 6.

2) Battery voltage should be present on terminal No. 3 and zero voltage on terminal No. 6. Depress switch. Zero voltage should be present on both terminals. If voltage is as specified, switch is functioning correctly. If voltage is not as specified, go to next step.

3) Turn ignition off. Disconnect O/D OFF switch harness connector. *See Fig. 16.* Check continuity between terminals No. 3 and 6 on switch harness connector. Continuity should exist with switch depressed. If continuity is as specified, switch is okay. Inspect circuits to ground and PCM. Repair as needed. If continuity is not as specified, replace switch.

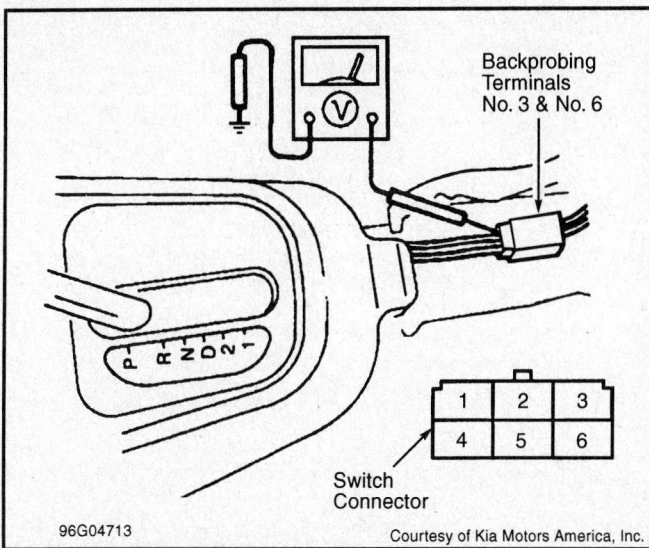

96G04713   Courtesy of Kia Motors America, Inc.

Fig. 16: Identifying O/D OFF Switch Terminals

SHIFT & TCC SOLENOIDS

1) Ensure ignition is off. Disconnect PCM or TCM harness connector. Measure resistance between ground and specified solenoid terminal at PCM or TCM harness connector. See appropriate SOLENOID TERMINAL IDENTIFICATION table. Resistance should be 13-27 ohms at 68°F (20°C).

2) If resistance is not as specified disconnect transmission solenoid connector and check harness between PCM or TCM and transmission connector for short or open. See appropriate wiring diagram in WIRING DIAGRAMS. If harness is okay, go to next step.

3) Disconnect transmission solenoid connector from vehicle harness. Note that solenoids ground through transmission case. Check resistance between connector terminals and ground. Replace solenoids as necessary.

PCM SOLENOID TERMINAL IDENTIFICATION

Description	PCM Terminal No.
Connector C256	
Solenoid "A"	1
Solenoid "B"	7
Solenoid "C"	2
TCC Solenoid	8

TCM SOLENOID TERMINAL IDENTIFICATION

Description	PCM Terminal No.
Connector C112	
Solenoid "A"	5
Solenoid "B"	11
Solenoid "C"	6
TCC Solenoid	12

4) If resistance is okay, ensure transmission case is grounded and intermittently connect battery voltage to terminals of connector. An audible click should be heard from specified solenoid when voltage is applied.

TRANSAXLE FLUID TEMPERATURE (TFT) SENSOR

See DTC P0710 under DIAGNOSTIC TESTS.

TRANSMISSION RANGE SWITCH

Verify that starter operates with shift lever in Park or Neutral position. Turn ignition switch to ON position. Move shift lever to "R" position and verify that back-up lights illuminate. If either operation fails as specified, inspect switch terminal continuity. *See Fig. 17 or 18.*

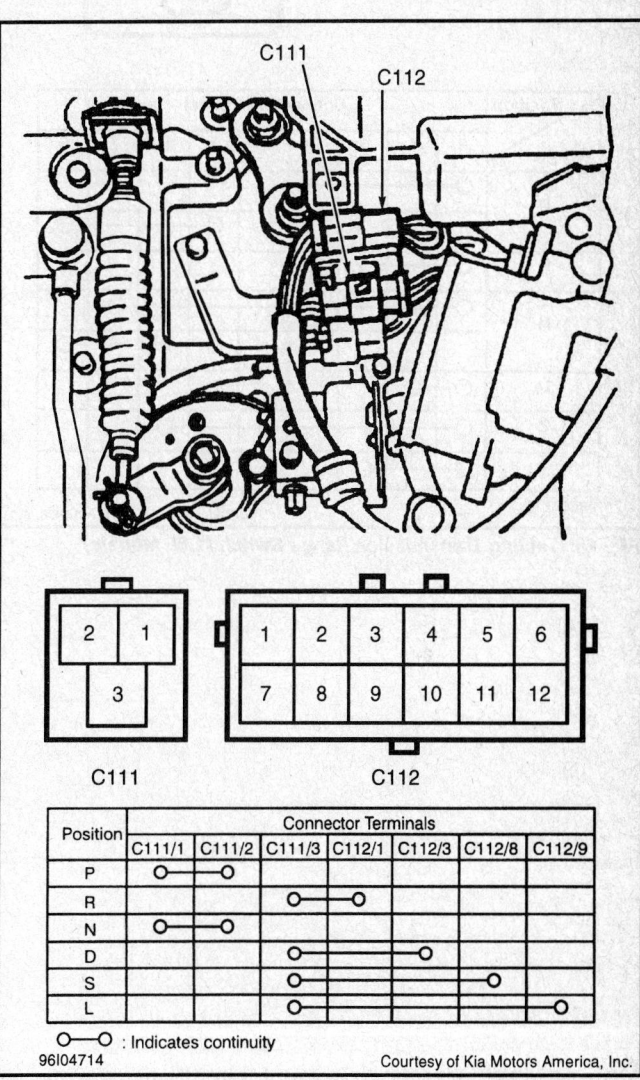

Position	Connector Terminals						
	C111/1	C111/2	C111/3	C112/1	C112/3	C112/8	C112/9
P	O——O						
R				O——O			
N	O——O						
D			O—		—O		
S			O—			—O	
L			O—				—O

O——O : Indicates continuity

96I04714   Courtesy of Kia Motors America, Inc.

Fig. 17: Testing Transmission Range Switch (1.6L Models)

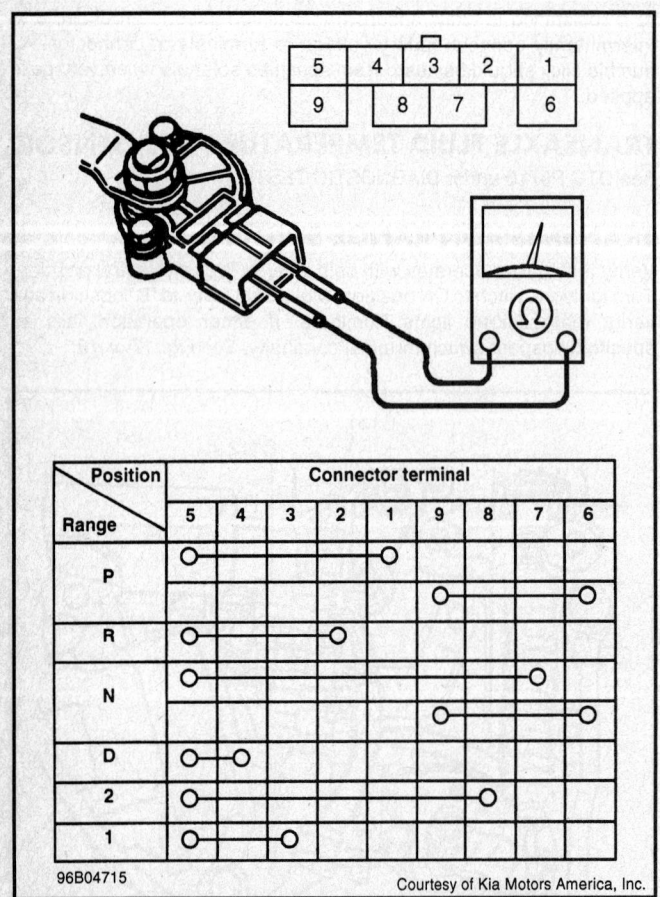

Position	Connector terminal								
Range	5	4	3	2	1	9	8	7	6
P	○				○				
						○			○
R	○			○					
N	○							○	
						○			○
D	○	○							
2	○						○		
1	○		○						

96B04715   Courtesy of Kia Motors America, Inc.

Fig. 18: Testing Transmission Range Switch (1.8L Models)

TURBINE SHAFT SPEED SENSOR

See DTC NO. P0715 under DIAGNOSTIC TESTING.

VEHICLE SPEED SENSOR

Raise and support front of vehicle. Turn ignition on. Using voltmeter, backprobe between terminal No. 1 on sensor connector and ground. *See Fig. 8.* Rotate front wheels. If voltage pulses between 1 and 10 volts, inspect circuits between ground and PCM or TCM. See approprite wiring diagram in WIRING DIAGRAMS. Repair as needed. If circuits are okay, replace vehicle speed sensor.

WIRING DIAGRAMS

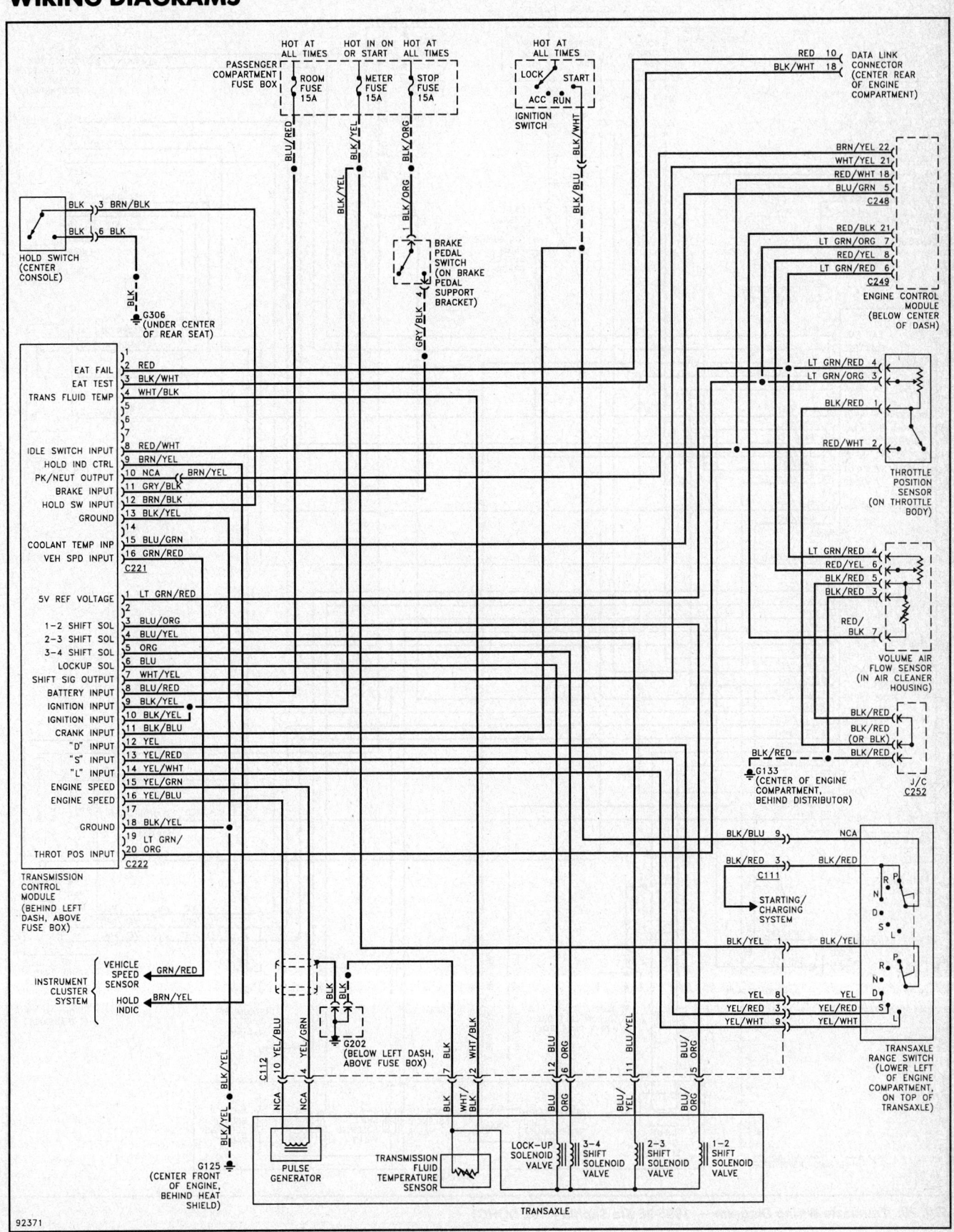

Fig. 19: Transaxle Wiring Diagram – 1995-96 Kia Sephia (1.6L SOHC)

92371

AUTOMATIC TRANSMISSIONS
Kia FA4A-EL Electronic Controls (Cont.)

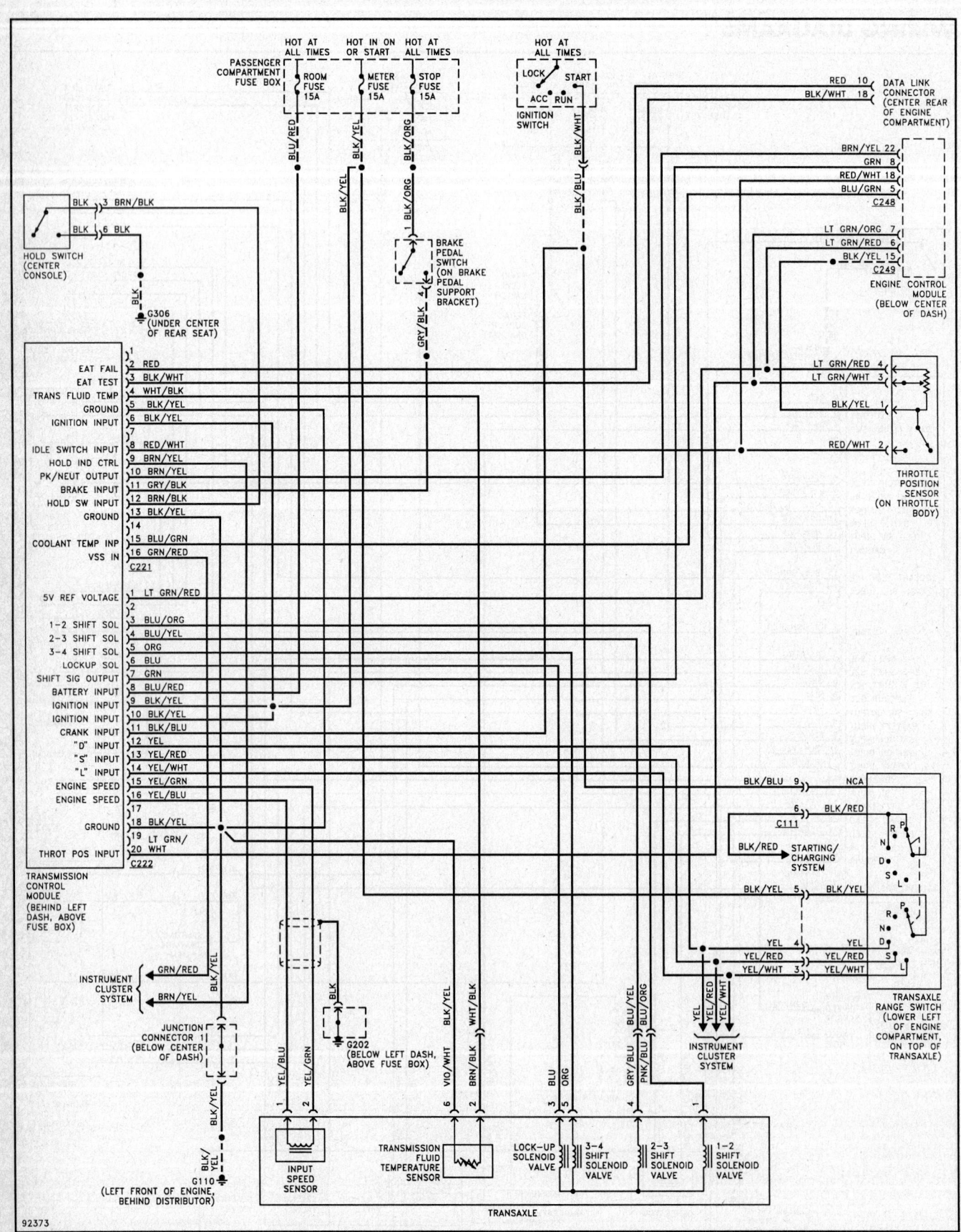

***Fig. 20:** Transaxle Wiring Diagram – 1995-96 Kia Sephia (1.6L DOHC)*

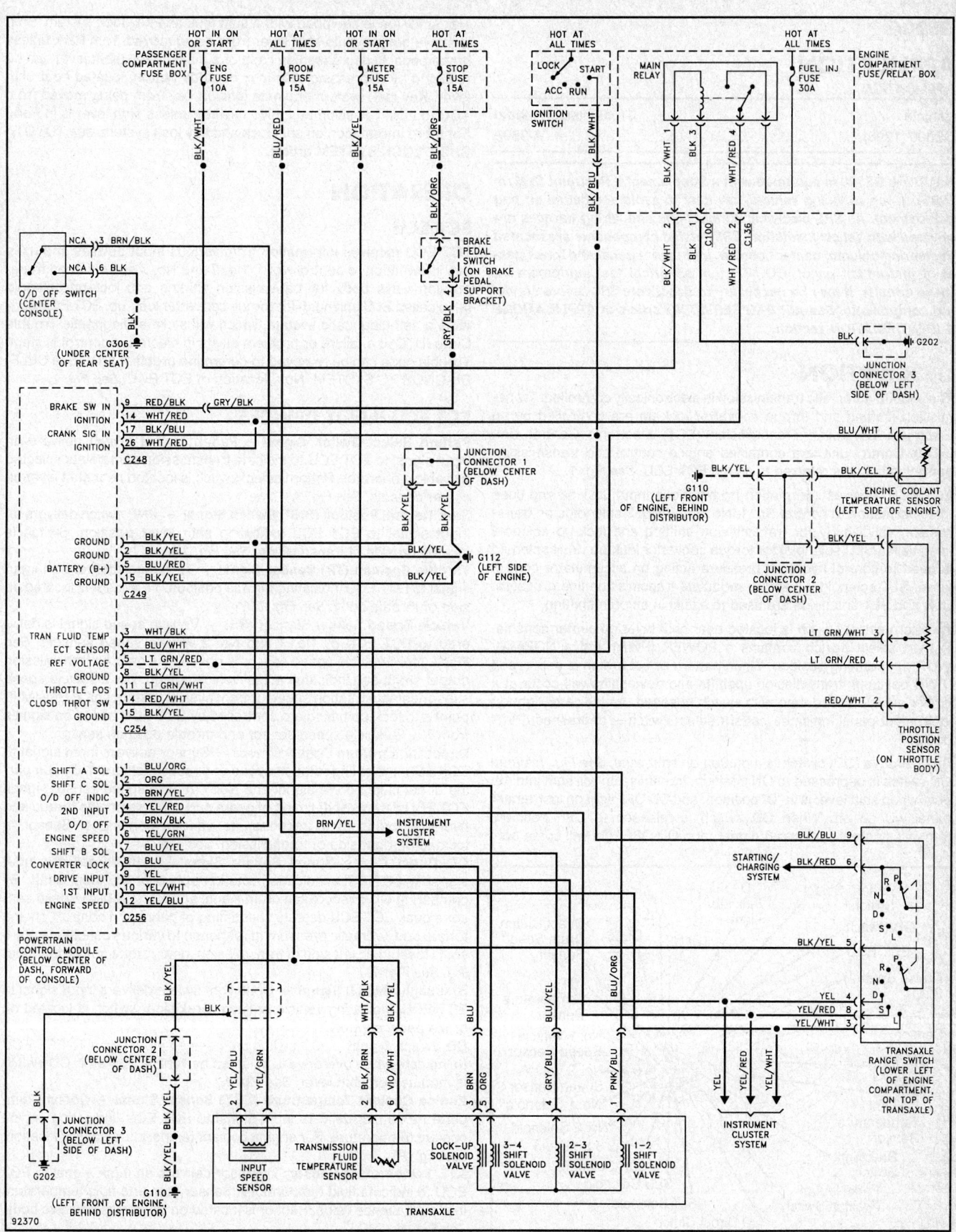

Fig. 21: Transaxle Wiring Diagram – 1995-96 Kia Sephia (1.8L DOHC)

92370

AUTOMATIC TRANSMISSIONS
Lexus A-350E Electronic Controls

GS300

APPLICATION

APPLICATION

Vehicle	Transmission Model
GS300 (1996)	A-350E

CAUTION: GS300 is equipped with a Supplemental Restraint System (SRS). When servicing vehicle, use care to avoid accidental air bag deployment. All SRS electrical connections and wiring harness are covered with Yellow insulation. SRS-related components are located in steering column, center console, instrument panel and lower panel of instrument panel. DO NOT use electrical test equipment on these circuits. It may be necessary to deactivate SRS before servicing components. See AIR BAG SERVICING article in APPLICATIONS & IDENTIFICATION section.

DESCRIPTION

The A-350E automatic transmission is electronically controlled. Transmission shifting and torque converter lock-up are controlled by an Electronic Controlled Transmission (ECT) Electronic Control Unit (ECU). Control unit is a combined engine control and transmission control unit and is referred to as the ECT ECU. *See Fig. 1.*

ECT ECU receives information from various input devices and uses this information to control No. 1, No. 2 and No. 3 solenoids on transmission valve body for transmission shifting and lock-up solenoid (also called SLU solenoid) for torque converter lock-up. SLN solenoid is used to control hydraulic pressure acting on accumulator control valve. SLT solenoid is used to modulate transmission line pressure. SLN and SLT solenoids are used to assist in smooth shifting.

A pattern select switch is located near shift lever on center console. Pattern select switch contains a POWER (PWR) and a NORMAL (NORM) operating position. When pattern select switch is depressed (PWR position), transmission upshifts and downshifts will occur at a higher vehicle speed than with switch released. An indicator light on instrument panel indicates pattern select switch is depressed (PWR position).

An Overdrive (OD) switch is mounted on shift lever. *See Fig. 1.* When OD switch is depressed to ON position, transmission will shift into 4th gear when shift lever is in "D" position, and OD OFF light on instrument panel will go off. When OD switch is released to OFF position, transmission will shift into 3rd gear, and OD OFF light will come on.

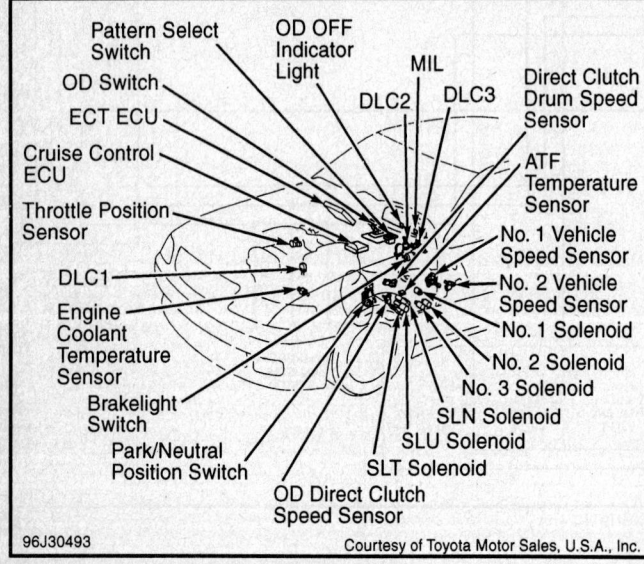

Pattern Select Switch
OD Switch
ECT ECU
Cruise Control ECU
Throttle Position Sensor
DLC1
Engine Coolant Temperature Sensor
Brakelight Switch
Park/Neutral Position Switch

OD OFF Indicator Light
MIL
DLC2   DLC3

Direct Clutch Drum Speed Sensor
ATF Temperature Sensor
No. 1 Vehicle Speed Sensor
No. 2 Vehicle Speed Sensor
No. 1 Solenoid
No. 2 Solenoid
No. 3 Solenoid
SLN Solenoid
SLU Solenoid
SLT Solenoid
OD Direct Clutch Speed Sensor

96J30493   Courtesy of Toyota Motor Sales, U.S.A., Inc.

Fig. 1: Identifying Input & Output Devices

Transmission is equipped with a shift lock and key lock system. Shift lock system prevents shift lever from being moved from Park unless brake pedal is depressed. In case of a malfunction, shift lever can be released by depressing shift lock override button, located near shift lever. Key lock system prevents ignition key from being moved from ACC to LOCK position on ignition switch unless shift lever is in Park. For more information on shift lock and key lock system, see TOYOTA SHIFT LOCK SYSTEM article.

OPERATION

ECT ECU

ECT ECU receives information from various input devices and uses this information to control No. 1, No. 2 and No. 3 solenoids on transmission valve body for transmission shifting and lock-up solenoid (also called SLU solenoid) for torque converter lock-up. ECT ECU contains a self-diagnostic system, which will store a Diagnostic Trouble Code (DTC) if a failure or problem exists in electronic control system. Trouble code can be retrieved to determine problem area. See SELF-DIAGNOSTIC SYSTEM. Note location of ECT ECU. *See Fig. 1.*

ECT ECU INPUT DEVICES

Pattern Select Switch Signal – Pattern select switch delivers an input signal to ECT ECU to indicate transmission shift points selected by vehicle operator. Pattern select switch is located near shift lever on center console. *See Fig. 1.*

Park/Neutral Position (PNP) Switch Signal – PNP switch delivers an input signal to ECT ECU indicating shift lever position. Switch is located on side of transmission. *See Fig. 1.*

Throttle Position (TP) Sensor Signal – TP sensor delivers an input signal to ECT ECU indicating throttle position. TP sensor is located on side of throttle body. *See Fig. 1.*

Vehicle Speed Sensor Signal (VSS) – Vehicle speed signal is delivered to ECT ECU by No. 1 and No. 2 vehicle speed sensors. *See Fig. 1.* No. 1 vehicle speed sensor is driven by a gear on transmission output shaft, and indicates actual vehicle speed. No. 2 vehicle speed sensor detects rotation speed of transmission output shaft. Gear shift point and lock-up timing are controlled by ECT ECU based on signals from No. 2 vehicle speed sensor and throttle position sensor.

Direct Clutch Drum Speed Sensor – Sensor delivers input signal to ECT ECU, indicating rotation speed of direct clutch drum. By comparing direct clutch drum signal and No. 1 vehicle speed sensor signal, ECT ECU detects shift timing of gears and controls engine torque and hydraulic pressure in response to various conditions. Sensor is located on right side of transmission. *See Fig. 1.*

OD Direct Clutch Speed Sensor Signal – Sensor delivers input signal to ECT ECU, indicating rotation speed of OD input shaft. By comparing OD direct clutch drum signal and No. 2 vehicle speed sensor signal, ECT ECU detects shift timing of gears and controls engine torque and hydraulic pressure in response to various conditions. Sensor is located on left side of transmission, near torque converter housing. *See Fig. 1.*

Brakelight Switch Signal – Brakelight switch delivers input signal to ECT ECU, indicating vehicle braking. Brakelight switch is located on brake pedal support.

OD Switch Signal – OD switch provides an input signal to ECT ECU to indicate when overdrive is selected by vehicle operator. OD switch is mounted on shift lever. *See Fig. 1.*

Engine Coolant Temperature (ECT) Sensor Signal – Coolant temperature sensor delivers input signal to ECT ECU, indicating engine coolant temperature. For engine coolant temperature sensor location, *see Fig. 17.*

ATF Temperature Sensor – Sensor delivers an input signal to ECT ECU to indicate fluid temperature. Sensor converts fluid temperature into a resistance value. Sensor is located on transmission valve body. *See Fig. 1.*

Cruise Control Electronic Control Unit (ECU) – Cruise control ECU delivers an input signal to control overdrive operation in accordance with vehicle speed when cruise control is operating. *See Fig. 1*

Lexus A-350E Electronic Controls (Cont.)

ECT ECU OUTPUT DEVICES

No. 1, No. 2 & No. 3 Solenoids – ECT ECU controls transmission shifting by delivering an output signal to operate proper solenoid. Solenoids are located on transmission valve body. See Fig. 1. Solenoids are operated in accordance with shift lever position. If a solenoid malfunctions, fail-safe gear may be selected. See Fig. 2.

NOTE: In some gears, ECT ECU provides a fail-safe system which will place transmission in designated gear depending on solenoid failure.

Lock-Up Solenoid – ECT ECU controls torque converter lock-up by delivering an output signal to lock-up solenoid. Lock-up solenoid (also called SLU solenoid) is activated when shift lever is in "D" position and vehicle is at specified speed. Lock-up solenoid is located on transmission valve body. See Fig. 1.

SLT Solenoid – Throttle pressure applied to primary regulator valve, which modulates line pressure, causes SLT solenoid to precisely and minutely modulate and generate line pressure according to accelerator pedal effort, if engine power output is detected. This reduces fluctuation of line pressure and provides smooth shifting. When ECT ECU receives throttle valve opening angle signal, duty cycle ratio signal is sent to SLT solenoid, activating solenoid. SLT solenoid is located on transmission valve body. See Fig. 1.

SLN Solenoid – SLN solenoid controls hydraulic pressure acting on accumulator control valve when transmission shifts and assists in smooth shifting. ECT ECU determines optimum control pressure according to signals from TP sensor, vehicle speed sensor and direct clutch drum speed sensor, and volume of current flow to SLN solenoid. Amount of current flow to SLN solenoid is controlled by duty cycle ratio of ECT ECU output signal, causing a momentary change in hydraulic pressure acting on clutches during gear shifting. When duty cycle ratio is high, pressure is low. SLN solenoid is located on transmission valve body. See Fig. 1.

SELF-DIAGNOSTIC SYSTEM

SYSTEM DIAGNOSIS

NOTE: Before testing transmission, ensure fluid level is correct and throttle and shift cables are properly adjusted. Ensure engine starts with shift lever in "P" (Park) and "N" (Neutral) to ensure proper adjustment of park/neutral position switch. Transmission must first be tested by checking for stored trouble codes. See RETRIEVING TROUBLE CODES.

ECT ECU monitors engine and transmission operation and contains a self-diagnostic system which stores diagnostic trouble code(s). A Malfunction Indicator Light (MIL), located on instrument panel, will illuminate if a system or component fails and sets a DTC.

Position	NORMAL				SHIFT SOLENOID No.1 MALFUNCTIONING				SHIFT SOLENOID No.2 MALFUNCTIONING				SHIFT SOLENOID No.3 MALFUNCTIONING			
	Solenoid valve			Gear	Solenoid valve			Gear	Solenoid valve			Gear	Solenoid valve			Gear
	No.1	No.2	No.3		No.1	No.2	No.3		No.1	No.2	No.3		No.1	No.2	No.3	
D	OFF	ON	ON	1st	×	ON	ON	1st	ON↑OFF	×	ON	4th	OFF	ON	×	2nd
	OFF	ON	OFF	2nd	×	ON	OFF	2nd	ON↑OFF	×	ON↑OFF	4th	OFF	ON	×	2nd
	ON	ON	ON	3rd	×	OFF↑ON	ON	4th	ON	×	ON	4th	ON	ON	×	3.5th
	ON	OFF	ON	4th	×	OFF	ON	4th	ON	×	ON	4th	OFF↑ON	OFF	×	O/D
	OFF	OFF	OFF	O/D	×	OFF	OFF	O/D	OFF	×	OFF	O/D	OFF	OFF	×	O/D
S	OFF	ON	ON	1st	×	ON	ON	1st	ON↑OFF	×	ON	4th	OFF	ON	×	2nd
	ON	ON	ON	3rd	×	OFF↑ON	ON	4th	ON	×	ON	4th	ON	ON	×	3.5th
	ON	OFF	ON	4th	×	OFF	ON	4th	ON	×	ON	4th	OFF↑ON	OFF	×	O/D
L	OFF	ON	ON	1st	×	ON	ON	1st	OFF	×	ON	1st	OFF	ON	×	2nd
	ON	ON	ON	3rd	×	ON	OFF↑ON	2nd	ON	×	ON	3rd	ON	ON	×	3.5th

Position	SHIFT SOLENOID No.1, No.2 MALFUNCTIONING				SHIFT SOLENOID No.1, No.3 MALFUNCTIONING				SHIFT SOLENOID No.2, No.3 MALFUNCTIONING				SHIFT SOLENOID No.1, No.2, No.3 MALFUNCTIONING			
	Solenoid valve			Gear	Solenoid valve			Gear	Solenoid valve			Gear	Solenoid valve			Gear
	No.1	No.2	No.3		No.1	No.2	No.3		No.1	No.2	No.3		No.1	No.2	No.3	
D	×	×	ON	4th	×	ON	×	2nd	OFF	×	×	O/D	×	×	×	O/D
	×	×	ON↑OFF	4th	×	ON	×	2nd	OFF	×	×	O/D	×	×	×	O/D
	×	×	ON	4th	×	OFF↑ON	×	O/D	OFF↑ON	×	×	O/D	×	×	×	O/D
	×	×	ON	4th	×	OFF	×	O/D	OFF↑ON	×	×	O/D	×	×	×	O/D
	×	×	OFF	O/D	×	OFF	×	O/D	OFF	×	×	O/D	×	×	×	O/D
S	×	×	ON	4th	×	ON	×	2nd	OFF	×	×	O/D	×	×	×	O/D
	×	×	ON	4th	×	OFF↑ON	×	O/D	OFF↑ON	×	×	O/D	×	×	×	O/D
	×	×	ON	4th	×	OFF	×	O/D	OFF↑ON	×	×	O/D	×	×	×	O/D
L	×	×	ON	1st	×	ON	×	2nd	OFF	×	×	2nd	×	×	×	2nd
	×	×	ON↑OFF	2nd	×	ON	×	2nd	ON	×	×	3.5th	×	×	×	2nd

×: Malfunctions ↑: Fail safe function 3.5th is the gear ratio between the 3rd and 4th

96A30494

Courtesy of Toyota Motor Sales, U.S.A., Inc.

Fig. 2: Checking No. 1, No. 2 & No. 3 Solenoid Operation

MIL illuminates with ignition switch in ON position, engine off (KOEO). Once engine is started, MIL should go out. If MIL remains illuminated, ECT ECU has detected a malfunction or abnormality in system. If MIL does not illuminate, inspect circuit and light. See WIRING DIAGRAM.

If malfunction does not reoccur in 3 trips, MIL goes off, but Diagnostic Trouble Code (DTC) remains recorded in ECT ECU memory. Trouble codes may only be retrieved using an appropriate scan tool or Lexus scan tool connected to 16-pin Data Link Connector (DLC3), located at lower left corner of instrument panel. See Figs. 3 and 4. Scan tool also provides freeze-frame data and can be used to clear trouble codes.

ECT ECU records engine operating condition (fuel system, calculated load, coolant temperature, fuel trim (mixture), engine speed, vehicle speed, etc.) with 1st malfunction ONLY. Information is ONLY for 1st recorded failure, even if more than one code has been recorded. Freeze-frame data is only updated when all trouble codes have been cleared, or a misfire or fuel-trim malfunction has occurred.

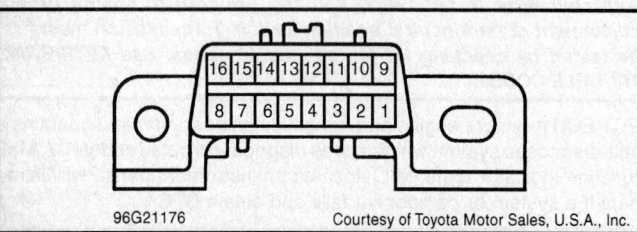

Fig. 3: Identifying Data Link Connector (DLC3) Terminals

RETRIEVING TROUBLE CODES

NOTE: Before retrieving trouble codes, ensure sufficient battery voltage exists for proper self-diagnosis system operation. Ensure proper operation of MIL light.

NOTE: MIL will illuminate for all trouble codes.

NOTE: For additional engine performance or other system related trouble codes present that are not listed in DIAGNOSTIC TROUBLE CODE (DTC) IDENTIFICATION table, see appropriate MITCHELL® ENGINE PERFORMANCE publication for IMPORTED CARS, LIGHT TRUCKS & VANS.

ECT ECU Codes – 1) Connect scan tool to Data Link Connector (DLC3). DLC3 is located at lower left corner of instrument panel. See Fig. 4.
2) Turn ignition on. Turn on scan tool. Retrieve any trouble codes stored in memory following scan tool instructions. See DIAGNOSTIC TROUBLE CODE (DTC) IDENTIFICATION table.
3) Trouble codes recorded may not have illuminated MIL. When certain malfunctions or trouble codes initially occur, they will be temporarily stored in ECT ECU memory, but MIL will not illuminate.
4) Second time malfunction or trouble code is detected, MIL will illuminate, provided ignition is turned off and then back on after malfunction

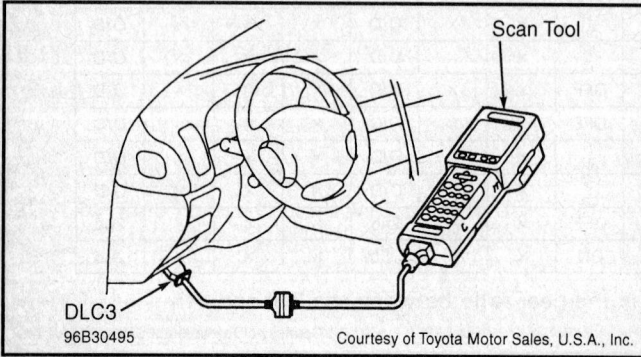

Scan Tool

DLC3
96B30495   Courtesy of Toyota Motor Sales, U.S.A., Inc.

Fig. 4: Connecting Scan Tool To Data Link Connector (DLC3)

or trouble code was first detected. This process is referred to as 2 trip detection logic and only applies to specific trouble codes.
5) Record freeze-frame data. If using Lexus scan tool, ensure tool is in NORMAL mode. CHECK MODE will erase all codes.

DIAGNOSTIC TROUBLE CODE (DTC) IDENTIFICATION

DTC	[1] Probable Cause
P0500	No. 1 Vehicle Speed Sensor
P0710	ATF Temperature Sensor
P0715	OD Direct Clutch Speed Sensor
P0750	No. 1 Solenoid
P0753	No. 1 Solenoid Circuit
P0755	No. 2 Solenoid
P0758	No. 2 Solenoid Circuit
P0760	No. 3 Solenoid
P0763	No. 3 Solenoid Circuit
P0770	[2] Lock-Up Solenoid
P0773	Lock-Up Solenoid Circuit
P1700	No. 2 Vehicle Speed Sensor Circuit
P1705	Direct Clutch Drum Speed Sensor Circuit
P1760	SLT Solenoid Circuit
P1765	SLN Solenoid Circuit
P1780	Park/Neutral Position Switch

[1] – Check listed component for probable cause. Check wiring and connections of specified component.
[2] – Also called SLU solenoid.

CLEARING TROUBLE CODES

Once repairs have been performed, trouble codes must be cleared from ECT ECU memory. DTCs may be cleared by following methods:
- Scan tool (follow manufacturers instructions).
- Remove EFI fuse (15-amp) from engine compartment relay box on left fender panel, for 10 seconds or more to clear memory in ECT ECU.
- Disconnect negative battery cable (memory for electronic components will be also be canceled).

DIAGNOSTIC TESTS

When trouble shooting transmission, first check for stored trouble codes and repair as necessary. If no trouble codes exist, perform manual shift test to determine if problem area is in electrical circuits or a mechanical transmission problem. See MANUAL SHIFT TEST.

NOTE: Manufacturer recommends using Check Harness (09990-0100) connected to ECT ECU when performing circuit tests at ECT ECU harness connector. Harness connects between ECT ECU terminals and ECT ECU harness connector. See Fig. 7. Check harness test terminals are same as ECT ECU harness connector terminals. ECT ECU is located under passenger side floor mat. See Fig. 1.

DTC P0500:
NO. 1 VEHICLE SPEED SENSOR (VSS) FAULT

Circuit Description – No. 1 Vehicle Speed Sensor (VSS), driven by transmission output shaft, outputs a pulse signal to combination meter. Combination meter converts signal to a more precise waveform for ECT ECU. DTC is set when ECT ECU does not detect any signal while vehicle is in motion. Possible causes are:
- Open or short in vehicle speed sensor circuit.
- No. 1 VSS failure.
- Combination meter malfunction.
- ECT ECU malfunction.

Diagnosis & Repair Procedure – 1) Test drive vehicle and determine if speedometer is functioning properly. If speedometer is okay, go to next step. If speedometer is not functioning, go to step **4)**.
2) Raise and support vehicle. Shift transmission into Neutral. Access ECT ECU harness connector and install check harness. See Fig. 7. Disconnect Blue power steering ECU connector and cruise control ECU connector. See Fig. 1. Power steering ECU connector is located behind instrument panel, above steering column.

3) Turn ignition on. Using DVOM, measure voltage between ECT ECU terminal SP1 and ground while rotating rear wheel. *See Fig. 9.* If voltage is not 4.5-5.5 volts, check and repair open circuit between combination meter and ECT ECU. See WIRING DIAGRAM. If voltage is as specified, replace ECT ECU and retest.

4) Check odometer operation. If odometer does not operate, go to step **6).** If odometer works, check trip meter operation. If trip meter operates while driving, replace speedometer. If trip meter does not operate, remove combination meter. Disconnect combination meter Orange 23-pin connector. Connect jumper wires from harness connector terminals B1, B13, B15 and B23 to combination meter terminals B1, B13, B15 and B23. *See Fig. 5.*

5) Turn ignition on. Using DVOM, measure voltage between terminals B13 and B15 at combination meter. Rotate rear wheel. If voltage is zero to 11 volts or more for each revolution of drive shaft, replace speedometer. If voltage is not as specified, replace combination meter circuit plate.

6) Disconnect combination meter Orange 23-pin connector. *See Fig. 5.* Inspect connector on wire harness side. Turn ignition on. Using DVOM, measure voltage between terminals B13 and B15 at combination meter. Rotate rear wheel. If voltage is not zero to 11 volts or more for each revolution of drive shaft, go to next step. If voltage is as specified, replace combination meter circuit plate.

7) Inspect No. 1 speed sensor operation. See NO. 1 VEHICLE SPEED SENSOR (VSS) under COMPONENT TESTS. Replace as necessary. If speed sensor is okay, inspect wiring circuit between combination meter harness connector terminals B13, B15 and speed sensor. Repair as necessary.

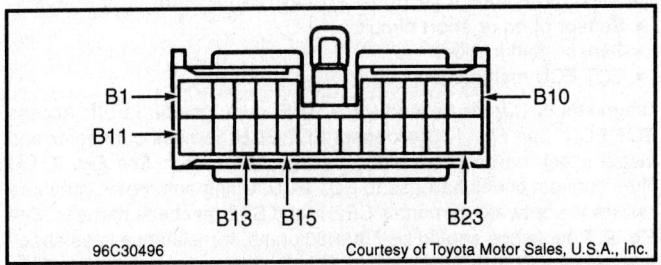

Fig. 5: Identifying Combination Meter 23-Pin Connector Terminals

DTC P0710: ATF TEMPERATURE SENSOR

Circuit Description – ATF temperature sensor converts fluid temperature into a resistance value which in input to ECT ECU. DTC is set when temperature sensor resistance is less than 79 ohms, or after engine has been operating for 15 minutes or more, temperature sensor resistance is more than 156 k/ohms. Either condition must be set for .5 second or more. Possible causes are:
- Open or short in ATF temperature sensor circuit.
- ATF temperature sensor malfunction.
- ECT ECU malfunction.

Diagnosis & Repair Procedure – 1) Raise and support vehicle. Remove transmission oil pan. Disconnect ATF temperature sensor connector (Orange wires). Remove sensor from valve body. Connect ohmmeter leads between sensor terminals.

2) Submerge sensor in container of water. Heat water while measuring sensor resistance. At 50°F (10°C), sensor resistance should be 6.45 k/ohms. At 230°F (110°C), sensor resistance should be 250 ohms. If resistance is not as specified, replace sensor. If resistance is as specified, inspect and repair wiring harness circuits between sensor and ECT ECU. If circuits are okay, replace ECT ECU.

DTC P0715: OD DIRECT CLUTCH SPEED SENSOR

Circuit Description – OD direct clutch speed sensor, located at left front side of transmission near torque converter housing, detects OD input shaft RPM from rotation of OD direct clutch drum. By comparing OD direct clutch speed signal and No. 2 vehicle speed sensor signal, ECT ECU detects shift timing of gears and controls engine torque and

hydraulic pressure in response to various conditions. This assists in smooth shifting. DTC is set when gear change cannot be performed, gear position is 1st , 3rd or 4th, output shaft RPM is 1000 RPM or more, input shaft RPM is 300 RPM or less, speed sensor operation is normal, and No. 1, No. 2 and No. 3 solenoid operation is normal. All conditions must be set for 5 seconds or more. Possible causes are:
- Open or short in OD direct clutch speed sensor circuit.
- OD direct clutch speed sensor malfunction.
- ECT ECU malfunction.

Diagnosis & Repair Procedure – 1) Ensure ignition is off. Access ECT ECU. *See Fig. 1.* Disconnect ECT ECU harness connector and install check harness to ECT ECU harness connector. *See Fig. 7.* DO NOT connect check harness to ECT ECU. Using ohmmeter, measure resistance between terminal NCO+ and terminal NCO- at check harness. *See Fig. 9.* Resistance should be 560-680 ohms. If resistance is within specification, replace ECT ECU. If resistance is not within specification, go to next step.

2) Remove OD direct clutch speed sensor from transmission. Measure resistance between sensor terminals. Resistance should be 560-680 ohms. If resistance is not as specified, replace sensor. If resistance is as specified, check and repair circuits between sensor and ECT ECU.

3) Check voltage between sensor terminals when a magnet is put close to tip of speed sensor. *See Fig. 6.* If a low intermittent voltage is generated, sensor is okay. If no voltage is generated, replace speed sensor.

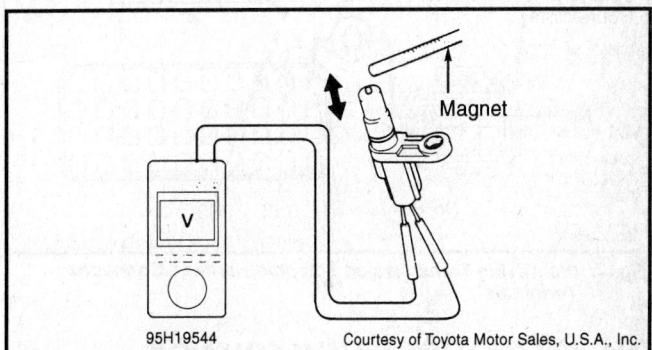

Fig. 6: Testing Speed Sensors

DTC P0750, P0755 & P0760: NO. 1, NO. 2 & NO. 3 SOLENOID FAULT

Circuit Description – ECT ECU uses signal from No. 1 vehicle speed sensor to determine actual gear position. ECT ECU compares actual gear with shift schedule in memory to detect mechanical trouble of solenoids and/or valve body. DTC is set if during normal driving gear required by ECT ECU does not match actual gear after 2 trips have been completed. Possible causes are:
- No. 1, No. 2 and/or No. 3 solenoid is stuck open or closed.
- Valve body is clogged or valve(s) is stuck.

Diagnosis & Repair Procedure – Remove and inspect operation of solenoids. See appropriate solenoid test under COMPONENT TESTS. If solenoids are okay, inspect valve body. See TOYOTA A-340 SERIES & A-350 SERIES overhaul article.

DTC P0753, P0758 & P0763: NO. 1, NO. 2 & NO. 3 SOLENOID CIRCUIT

Circuit Description – Shifting is performed in combination with ON and OFF position of shift solenoids controlled by ECT ECU. If an open or short circuit occurs in any shift solenoid, ECT ECU reverts to fail-safe mode. *See Fig. 2.* ECT ECU turns SLU solenoid off at same time. DTCs are output when a open or short circuit occurs. Possible causes are:
- No. 1, No. 2 and/or No. 3 solenoid circuit.
- No. 1, No. 2 and/or No. 3 solenoid malfunction.
- ECT ECU malfunction.

Diagnosis & Repair Procedure – 1) Ensure ignition is off. Access ECT ECU. *See Fig. 1.* Disconnect ECT ECU harness connector and install check harness on wiring harness connector. DO NOT connect check harness to ECT ECU. Using ohmmeter, measure resistance between terminal S1, S2 and/or S3 at check harness and ground. *See Fig. 7.* If resistance is 11-15 ohms, replace ECT ECU and retest. If resistance is not within specification, go to next step.

2) Disconnect solenoid harness connectors (next to PNP switch) at transmission. Check continuity between terminals No. 2, 4 and 8 of transmission harness connectors and corresponding terminal of check harness. *See Figs. 7 and 9.*

3) If continuity exists for all circuits, go to next step. If continuity does not exist for any circuit, inspect and repair circuit(s) as needed.

4) Measure resistance between transmission connector terminals No. 2, 4 and 8, and ground. *See Fig. 7.* If resistance is 11-15 ohms, replace solenoid. If resistance is not as specified, replace transmission sub-harness as needed.

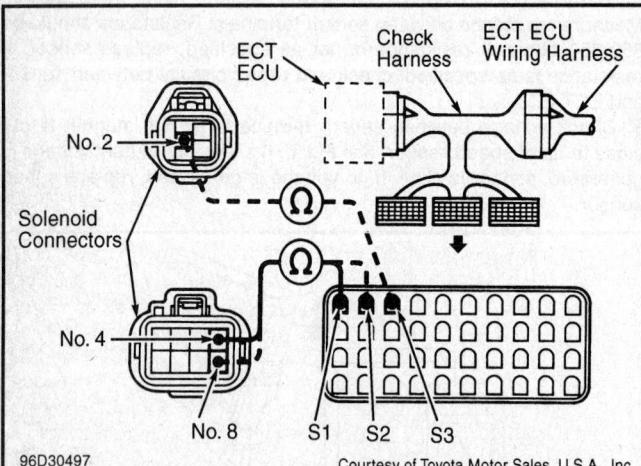

Fig. 7: Identifying Transmission Solenoid Harness Connector Terminals

DTC P0770: LOCK-UP/SLU SOLENOID

Circuit Description – ECT ECU uses signals from throttle position sensor and airflow meter to monitor engagement of Torque Converter Clutch (TCC). ECT ECU compares engagement condition of TCC with lock-up schedule in memory to detect mechanical trouble of SLU solenoid, valve body and torque converter. DTC is set when TCC lock-up does not occur during appropriate speed, or lock-up does not release at appropriate speed. Possible causes are:
- Lock-up solenoid is stuck open or closed.
- Valve body clogged or valve stuck.
- TCC malfunction.

Diagnosis & Repair Procedure – Raise and support vehicle. Remove transmission oil pan. Disconnect solenoid connector (Brown and Yellow wires). Using ohmmeter, measure resistance between solenoid connector terminals. If resistance is not 3.4-3.8 ohms, inspect and repair transmission sub-harness as needed. If sub-harness is okay, replace ECT ECU. If resistance is 3.4-3.8 ohms, remove solenoid and check operation. See appropriate solenoid test under COMPONENT TESTS. If solenoid is okay, inspect valve body. See TOYOTA A-340 SERIES & A-350 SERIES overhaul article.

DTC P0773: LOCK-UP/SLU SOLENOID CIRCUIT

Circuit Description – Lock-up solenoid is turned on and off by signals from ECT ECU. Amount of current flow to solenoid is controlled by duty cycle ratio of ECT ECU output signal. The higher the duty cycle ratio, the higher the lock-up hydraulic pressure becomes during lock-up operation. DTC is output when ECT ECU outputs a duty

signal to lock-up solenoid in 90 percent or higher duty cycle ratio. Current to solenoid is 350-550 milliamps or less. Possible causes are:
- Lock-up solenoid open or short circuit.
- Lock-up solenoid malfunction.
- ECT ECU malfunction.

Diagnosis & Repair Procedure – Raise and support vehicle. Remove transmission oil pan. Disconnect solenoid connector (Brown and Yellow wires). Using ohmmeter, measure resistance between solenoid connector terminals. If resistance is not 3.4-3.8 ohms, inspect and repair transmission sub-harness as needed. If sub-harness is okay, replace ECT ECU. If resistance is 3.4-3.8 ohms, remove and inspect operation of solenoid. See appropriate solenoid test under COMPONENT TESTS. If solenoid is okay, inspect valve body. See TOYOTA A-340 SERIES & A-350 SERIES overhaul article.

DTC P1700: NO. 2 VEHICLE SPEED SENSOR (VSS) CIRCUIT

Circuit Description – No. 2 vehicle speed sensor detects transmission output shaft RPM and sends signals to ECT ECU. An AC voltage is generated in No. 2 vehicle speed sensor coil as rotor mounted on output shaft rotates. This voltage is sent to ECT ECU. Gear shift point and lock-up timing are controlled by ECT ECU based on signals from No. 2 vehicle speed sensor and throttle position sensor. If No. 2 vehicle speed sensor malfunctions, ECT ECU uses input signals from No. 1 vehicle speed sensor as a back-up signal. DTC is output when no signal is detected from No. 2 vehicle speed sensor while No. 1 vehicle speed sensor sends 4 pulses to ECT ECU. Vehicle speed is more than 5.6 MPH for at least 4 seconds. Possible causes are:
- Sensor open or short circuit.
- Sensor malfunction.
- ECT ECU malfunction.

Diagnosis & Repair Procedure – 1) Ensure ignition is off. Access ECT ECU. *See Fig. 1.* Disconnect ECT ECU harness connector and install check harness on wiring harness connector. *See Fig. 7.* DO NOT connect check harness to ECT ECU. Using ohmmeter, measure resistance between terminals SP2+ and SP2- at check harness. *See Fig. 9.* Resistance should be 560-680 ohms. If resistance is as specified, replace ECT ECU and retest. If resistance is not within specification, go to next step.

2) Remove No. 2 vehicle speed sensor from transmission. Measure resistance between sensor terminals. Resistance should be 560-680 ohms. If resistance is not as specified, replace sensor. If resistance is as specified, check and repair circuits between sensor and ECT ECU.

3) Check voltage between sensor terminals when a magnet is put close to tip of speed sensor. *See Fig. 6.* If a low intermittent voltage is generated, sensor is okay. If no voltage is generated, replace speed sensor.

DTC P1705: DIRECT CLUTCH DRUM SPEED SENSOR CIRCUIT (NC2 REVOLUTION SENSOR CIRCUIT)

Circuit Description – Direct clutch drum speed sensor detects rotation speed of direct clutch drum. By comparing direct clutch drum speed signal and vehicle speed sensor signal, ECT ECU monitors shifts and appropriately controls engine torque and hydraulic pressure in response to various conditions. Gear shift performance is smooth. DTC is output when gear change is not being performed, gear position is 1st, 2nd, 4th or OD, output shaft RPM is 1000 RPM or more, input shaft RPM is 300 RPM or less, and shift solenoids and No. 1 and No. 2 vehicle speed sensors are operation normal. Possible causes are:
- Sensor open or short circuit.
- Sensor malfunction.
- ECT ECU malfunction.

Diagnosis & Repair Procedure – 1) Ensure ignition is off. Access ECT ECU. *See Fig. 1.* Disconnect ECT ECU harness connector and install check harness on wiring harness connector. *See Fig. 7.* DO NOT connect check harness to ECT ECU. Using ohmmeter, measure resistance between terminals NC2+ and NC2- at check harness. *See*

Fig. 9. Resistance should be 560-680 ohms. If resistance is as specified, replace ECT ECU and retest. If resistance is not within specification, go to next step.

2) Remove direct clutch drum speed sensor from transmission. Measure resistance between sensor terminals. Resistance should be 560-680 ohms. If resistance is not as specified, replace sensor. If resistance is as specified, check and repair circuits between sensor and ECT ECU.

3) Check voltage between sensor terminals when a magnet is put close to tip of speed sensor. *See Fig. 6.* If a low intermittent voltage is generated, sensor is okay. If no voltage is generated, replace speed sensor.

DTC P1760: SLT SOLENOID CIRCUIT (LINE PRESSURE CONTROL)

Circuit Description – Throttle pressure is applied to primary regulator valve, which modulates line pressure, causes SLT solenoid to precisely modulate line pressure according to accelerator pedal effort, or engine power output detected. This reduces fluctuation of line pressure and provides smooth shifting. Upon receiving throttle valve opening angle signal, ECT ECU controls line pressure by sending predetermined duty cycle ratio to SLT solenoid, activating solenoid, modulating line pressure and generating throttle pressure. DTC is output when voltage at SLT- terminal at ECT ECU is zero or 12 volts for one second or more, indicating a solenoid duty cycle is not present. Possible causes are:

- SLT solenoid open or short circuit.
- SLT solenoid malfunction.
- ECT ECU malfunction.

Diagnosis & Repair Procedure – Raise and support vehicle. Remove transmission oil pan. Disconnect solenoid connector (Orange and Green wires). Using ohmmeter, measure resistance between solenoid connector terminals. If resistance is not 3.7-4.1 ohms, inspect and repair transmission sub-harness as needed. If sub-harness is okay, replace ECT ECU. If resistance is 3.7-4.1 ohms, remove and inspect operation of solenoid. See appropriate solenoid test under COMPONENT TESTS. If solenoid is okay, inspect valve body. See TOYOTA A-340 SERIES & A-350 SERIES overhaul article.

DTC P1765: SLN SOLENOID CIRCUIT (ACCUMULATOR BACK PRESSURE MODULATION)

Circuit Description – SLN solenoid controls hydraulic pressure acting on accumulator control valve. ECT ECU determines optimum operating pressure according to signals from throttle position sensor, vehicle speed sensor and direct clutch speed sensor. DTC is output when ECT ECU output signal to SLN solenoid is 90 percent or higher duty cycle ratio. Current flow to SLN solenoid is 230-430 milliamps or less. Possible causes are:

- SLN solenoid open or short circuit.
- SLN solenoid malfunction.
- ECT ECU malfunction.

Diagnosis & Repair Procedure – Ensure ignition is off. Raise and support vehicle. Remove transmission oil pan. Disconnect SLN solenoid connector (Red and Blue wires). Using an ohmmeter, measure resistance between solenoid connector terminals. Ensure resistance is 5.1-5.5 ohms. If resistance is not as specified, inspect and repair circuit(s) between SLN solenoid and ECT ECU. See WIRING DIAGRAM. Also conduct performance check of solenoid. See SLN, SLT & SLU SOLENOID under COMPONENT TESTS. Replace as needed. If solenoid is okay, replace ECT ECU and retest.

DTC P1780: PARK/NEUTRAL POSITION (PNP) SWITCH

Circuit Description – PNP switch verifies shift lever position and sends signals to ECT ECU. If no signal is received from PNP switch, ECT ECU defaults to drive ("D") position. DTC is output when ECT ECU detects 2 or more circuits are on. Vehicle speed has to be above 44 MPH for 30 seconds or more with engine speed at 2000-2500 RPM. Possible causes are:

- Short in PNP switch circuit.
- PNP switch malfunction.
- ECT ECU malfunction.

Diagnosis & Repair Procedure – **1)** Turn ignition off. Access ECT ECU. Disconnect ECT ECU harness connector. Install check harness between ECT ECU and wiring harness. *See Fig. 7.* Turn ignition on. Using DVOM, measure voltage at terminals NSW, "R", "2" and "L" of check harness between terminal and body ground with gear selector in each shift position. *See Fig. 9.*

2) Ensure 9-14 volts is present at NSW terminal at ECT ECU harness connector in all shift positions. Ensure 7.5-14 volts is present at terminals "R", "2" and "L" at ECT ECU harness connector with gear selector in "R", "2" and "L" position. If voltage is not as specified, check park/neutral position switch. See PARK/NEUTRAL POSITION (PNP) SWITCH under COMPONENT TESTS. If switch is okay, check and repair circuit(s) between PNP switch and ECT ECU. See WIRING DIAGRAM.

MANUAL SHIFT TEST

NOTE: Perform manual shift test if no trouble codes exist. Manual shift test determines if problem area is in electrical circuits or a mechanical transmission problem.

1) With ignition off, disconnect electrical connectors for solenoids from transmission. Road test vehicle and ensure transmission gear changes correspond with shift lever position. See GEAR APPLICATION table.

2) If abnormality exists, a mechanical transmission problem exists. Turn ignition off. Reconnect electrical connector. Clear trouble codes from ECT ECU memory, as disconnecting electrical connector may set a trouble code. See CLEARING TROUBLE CODES under SELF-DIAGNOSTIC SYSTEM.

GEAR APPLICATION

Shift Lever Position	Gear
"D"	Overdrive
"2"	3rd
"L"	1st
"R"	Reverse
"P"	Park

CIRCUIT TESTS

BRAKELIGHT SIGNAL

1) Inspect operation of brakelights. Repair as needed. If switch is suspect, see BRAKELIGHT SWITCH under COMPONENT TESTS. If circuit is suspect, diagnose and repair as necessary. See WIRING DIAGRAM.

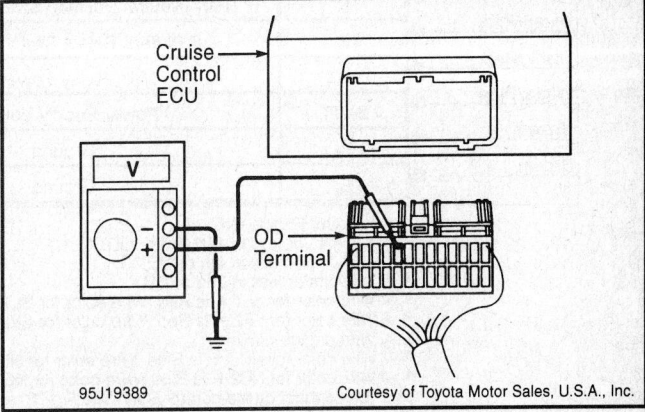

95J19389   Courtesy of Toyota Motor Sales, U.S.A., Inc.

Fig. 8: Identifying Cruise Control ECU Terminals

2) Connect scan tool to DLC3. *See Fig. 4*. Turn ignition on. Read STP signal while depressing and releasing brake pedal. Ensure signal cycles when pressing brake pedal. If signal cycles, replace ECT ECU. If signal does not cycle, inspect and repair circuit between brakelight switch and ECT ECU. If circuit is okay, replace ECT ECU.

OVERDRIVE CANCEL SIGNAL

1) Access ECT ECU. *See Fig. 1*. Connect check harness to ECT ECU. Turn ignition on. Measure voltage between terminal OD1 of check harness connector and ground. *See Fig. 9*. If voltage is 4-6 volts, substitute known good ECT ECU and retest. If voltage is not 4-6 volts, go to next step.

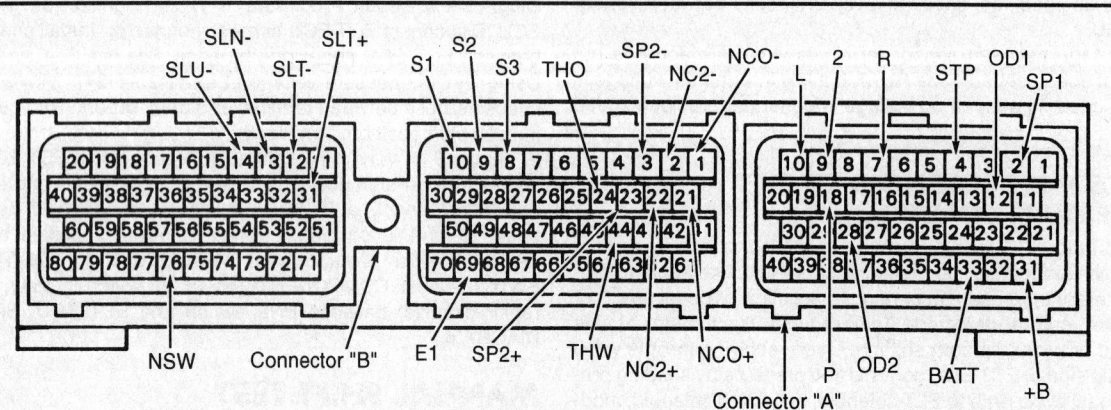

	Terminal ID.	Function/Description	Voltage Value (DC Volts Unless Otherwise Specified)
Blue/Yellow	S1	No. 1 Solenoid	9-14 Volts With KOEO [1] [2]
Green/Yellow	S2	No. 2 Solenoid	9-14 Volts With KOEO [1] [3]
Black	S3	No. 3 Solenoid	9-14 Volts With KOEO [1] [4]
Blue	SLU-	Lock-Up Solenoid	3 Volts Or Less With KOEO [1]
Green/White	SLN-	SLN Solenoid	3 Volts Or Less With KOEO [1]
[5]	SLT+, SLT-	SLT Solenoid	3 Volts Or Less With KOEO [1]
[6]	SP2+, SP2-	No. 2 Vehicle Speed Sensor	1.5 Volts Or Less, Or 4-6 Volts [7]
[8]	NCO+, NCO-	OD Direct Clutch Speed Sensor	1.5 Volts Or Less, Or 4-6 Volts [7]
[9]	NC2+, NC2-	Direct Clutch Drum Speed Sensor	1.5 Volts Or Less, Or 4-6 Volts [7]
Green/White	STP	Brakelight Switch Signal	7.5-14 Volts With Pedal Depressed
Pink	THW	Engine Coolant Temperature Sensor Signal	1.5 Volts Or Less @ 176°F (80°C)
Violet/White	SP1	No. 1 Vehicle Speed Sensor Signal	1.5 Volts Or Less, Or 4-6 Volts [1] [10]
Yellow	THO	ATF Temperature Sensor	1.5 Volts Or Less @ 230°F (110°C)
Violet	OD1	OD Output To Cruise Control ECU	9-14 Volts With KOEO [1]
Black/Red	OD2	Overdrive Switch Signal	9-14 Volts With Switch On
Black	NSW	Ignition Switch Signal	9-14 Volts In "P" Or "N", KOEO [1]
Green/Orange	2 (S)	Park/Neutral Position Switch "2" Signal	7.5-14 Volts In "2", KOEO [1]
Green/Black	L	Park/Neutral Position Switch "L" Signal	7.5-14 Volts In "L", KOEO [1]
Red/Black	R	Park/Neutral Position Switch "R" Signal	7.5-14 Volts With KOEO [1]
Blue/White	P	Pattern Select Switch Signal	7.5-14 Volts In PWR Position
Black/Red	+B	EFI Main Relay Power Supply	9-14 Volts With KOEO [1]
White/Blue	BATT	Power Supply Voltage	9-14 Volts (Constant)
Brown	E₁	Ground	Not Applicable
Brown	E₂	Ground	Not Applicable

[1] – Key On, Engine Off.
[2] – 1.5 volts or less in 1st, 2nd or OD.
[3] – 1.5 volts or less in 4th or OD.
[4] – 1.5 volts or less in 2nd or OD.
[5] – Wire color for SLT+ is Red. Wire color for SLT- is Blue.
[6] – Wire color for SP2+ is Red. Wire color for SP2- is Green.
[7] – With engine running.
[8] – Wire color for NCO+ is Blue. Wire color for NCO- is Yellow.
[9] – Wire color for NC2+ is Blue. Wire color for NC2- is Yellow.
[10] – Disconnect cruise control ECU. *See Fig. 1*.

96E30498

Courtesy of Toyota Motor Sales, U.S.A., Inc.

Fig. 9: ECT ECU Pin Voltage Table (Component Connector View)

2) Turn ignition off. Disconnect cruise control ECU harness connector, located behind instrument panel, near passenger's side kick panel. Turn ignition on. Measure voltage between terminal OD and ground. *See Fig. 8.* If 4-6 volts is present, replace cruise control ECU and retest. If 4-6 volts is not present, inspect and repair circuit between cruise control ECU and ECT ECU.

ECT ECU VOLTAGES

Access ECT ECU. *See Fig. 1.* Turn ignition on. Connect check harness to ECT ECU. Using voltmeter, measure voltage at check harness connector. Check voltage between selected terminal and E_1 terminal. Voltage should be as specified. *See Fig. 9.*

COMPONENT TESTS

NO. 1 VEHICLE SPEED SENSOR (VSS)

1) Disconnect electrical connector from No. 1 VSS, located on top of transmission. *See Fig. 1.* Connect positive battery lead to terminal No. 1 and negative lead to terminal No. 2. Connect positive lead of voltmeter to terminal No. 3 and negative lead to terminal No. 2. *See Fig. 10.*

2) Raise and support one vehicle rear wheel. Rotate wheel and monitor voltmeter. Ensure voltage changes from zero to 11 volts. Voltage should change 4 times per each revolution of speedometer cable shaft. Replace speed sensor if voltage does not change as specified.

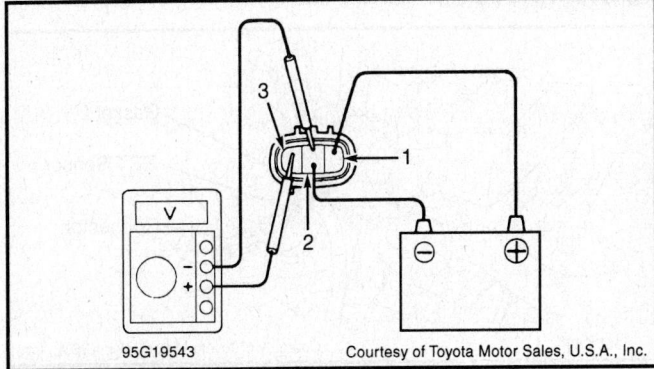

Fig. 10: Checking No. 1 Vehicle Speed Sensor

NO. 1 & NO. 2 SOLENOIDS

1) To check solenoid seals, remove suspect solenoid. Connect battery voltage to solenoid. Apply 71 psi (5 kg/cm²) to solenoid with battery voltage connected. *See Fig. 11.*

2) With battery voltage applied, air should pass through solenoid. Disconnect voltage to solenoid. Ensure air does not pass through solenoid. Replace solenoid if defective.

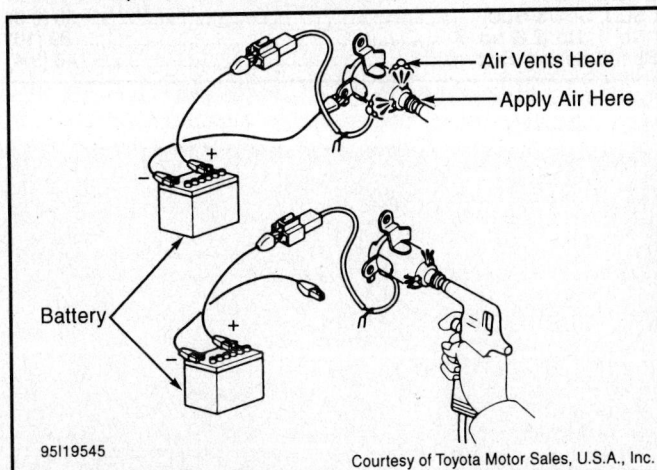

Fig. 11: Checking Solenoids

NO. 3 SOLENOID

1) To check solenoid seals, remove suspect solenoid. Connect battery voltage to solenoid. Apply 71 psi (5 kg/cm²) to solenoid with battery voltage connected. *See Fig. 11.*

2) With battery voltage applied, air should not pass through solenoid. Disconnect voltage to solenoid. Ensure air does pass through solenoid. Replace solenoid if defective.

SLN, SLT & SLU SOLENOID

Raise and support vehicle. Remove transmission oil pan. Remove appropriate solenoid. To check solenoid operation, connect positive battery voltage to solenoid terminal No. 1. Ensure a 8-10 watt bulb is placed in-line of positive lead. *See Fig. 12.* Connect negative lead to terminal No. 2 and monitor valve's movement. Replace as needed.

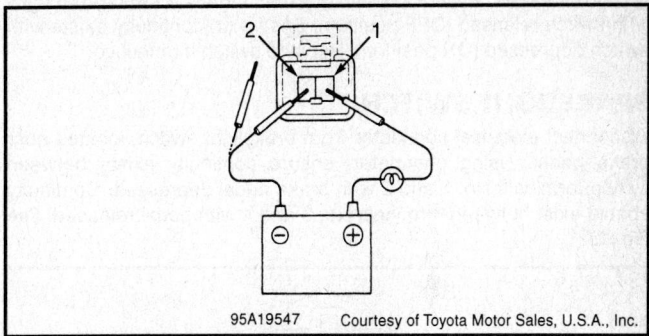

Fig. 12: Testing SLN, SLT & SLU Solenoid

PARK/NEUTRAL POSITION (PNP) SWITCH

Disconnect harness connector at park/neutral position switch. Switch is located on side of transmission. Using ohmmeter, check for continuity between specified terminals in accordance with shift lever position. *See Fig. 13.* Replace PNP switch if defective.

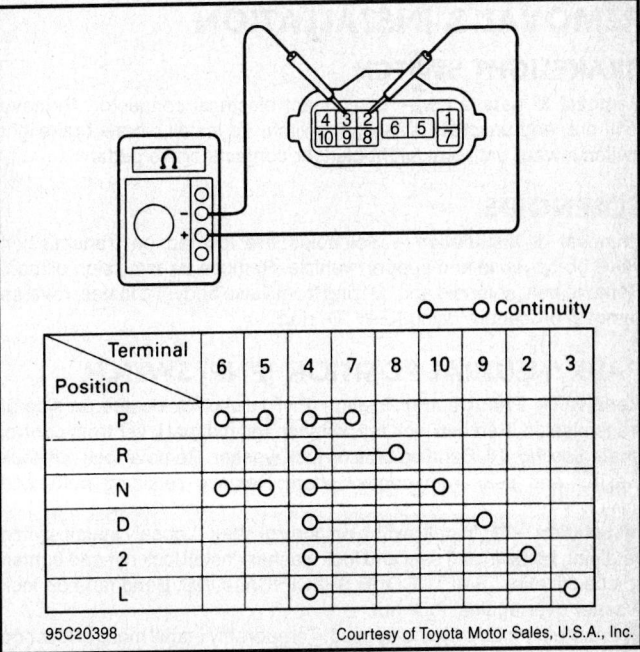

O——O Continuity

Terminal Position	6	5	4	7	8	10	9	2	3
P	O——O		O——O						
R			O——————O						
N	O——O		O——————————O					
D			O——————————————O				
2			O——————————————————O		
L			O——————————————————————O

Fig. 13: Testing Park/Neutral Position (PNP) Switch

PATTERN SELECT SWITCH

Disconnect electrical connector from pattern select switch. Using ohmmeter, ensure continuity exists between terminals No. 1 and 2 with switch in PWR position. *See Fig. 14.* No continuity should exist in NORM position. Replace switch as necessary.

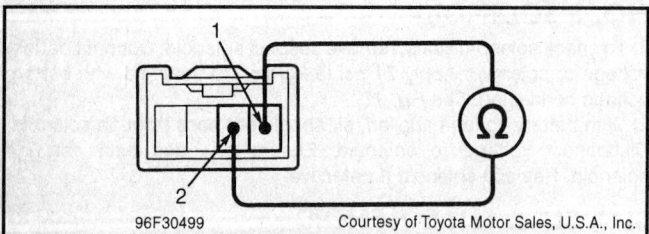

Fig. 14: Identifying Pattern Select Switch Terminals

OVERDRIVE (OD) SWITCH

Disconnect electrical connector from OD switch, located on shift lever. Using ohmmeter, ensure continuity exists between switch terminals with switch released (OFF position). Ensure no continuity exists with switch depressed (ON position). Replace switch if defective.

BRAKELIGHT SWITCH

Disconnect electrical connector from brakelight switch, located near brake pedal. Using ohmmeter, ensure continuity exists between switch terminals No. 1 and 2 with brake pedal depressed. Continuity should exist between terminals No. 3 and 4 with pedal released. See Fig. 15.

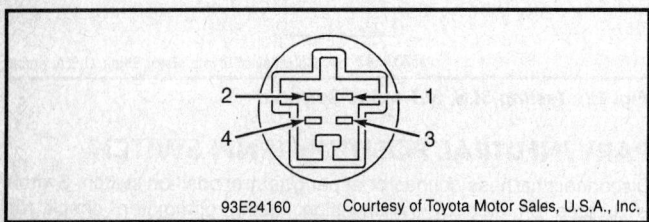

Fig. 15: Identifying Brakelight Switch Terminals

REMOVAL & INSTALLATION

BRAKELIGHT SWITCH

Removal & Installation – Disconnect electrical connector. Remove lock nut, and unscrew brakelight switch. To install, screw brakelight switch inward until brakelight plunger contacts brake pedal.

SOLENOIDS

Removal & Installation – Solenoids are located on transmission valve body. Raise and support vehicle. Remove transmission oil pan. Remove bolt, solenoid and "O" ring from valve body. To install, reverse removal procedure using NEW "O" ring.

PARK/NEUTRAL POSITION (PNP) SWITCH

Removal – Park/Neutral Position (PNP) switch is located on side of transmission. Remove lock nut, washer and manual lever from control shaft. See Fig. 16. Bend up tabs on lock washer. Remove lock nut, lock washer and seal from control shaft. Remove retaining bolts and switch.
Installation – **1)** Install switch on control shaft. Loosely install switch retaining bolts. Install seal and lock washer. Install lock nut and tighten to specification. See TORQUE SPECIFICATIONS. Bend tabs on lock washer over against lock nut.
2) Ensure parking brake is applied. Temporarily install manual lever on control shaft. Place shift lever in Neutral. Remove manual lever. Rotate park/neutral position switch and align neutral basic line on PNP switch with groove. See Fig. 16.
3) Hold PNP switch in this position. Tighten retaining bolts to specification. To install remaining components, reverse removal procedure.

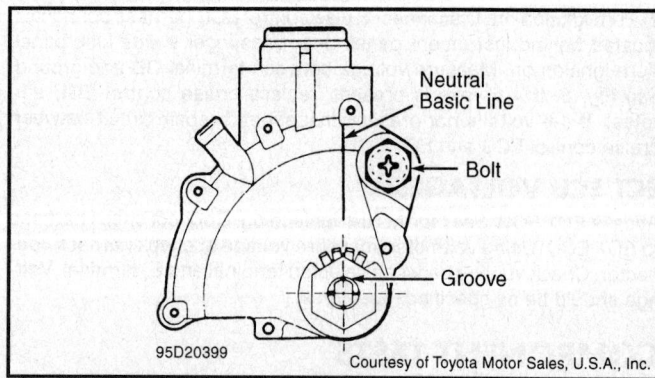

Fig. 16: Removing & Installing PNP Switch

OVERDRIVE (OD) SWITCH

Overdrive (OD) switch is mounted on shift lever. See Fig. 1. Replacement information not available from manufacturer.

ENGINE COOLANT TEMPERATURE SENSOR

Removal & Installation – Drain cooling system. Disconnect engine coolant temperature sensor connector. See Fig. 17. Remove coolant temperature sensor. To install, reverse removal procedure. Refill cooling system and check for leaks.

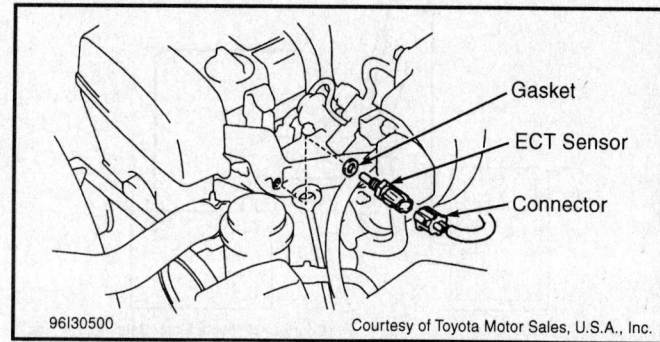

Fig. 17: Identifying ECT Sensor Location

TORQUE SPECIFICATIONS
TORQUE SPECIFICATIONS

Application	INCH Lbs. (N.m)
PNP Switch	
Bolt	15 (13)
Nut	35 (3.9)
Solenoid Bolt	
SLN, SLT & SLU	56 (6.3)
No. 1, No. 2 & No. 3	89 (10)
Speed Sensor Bolt	48 (5.4)

WIRING DIAGRAMS

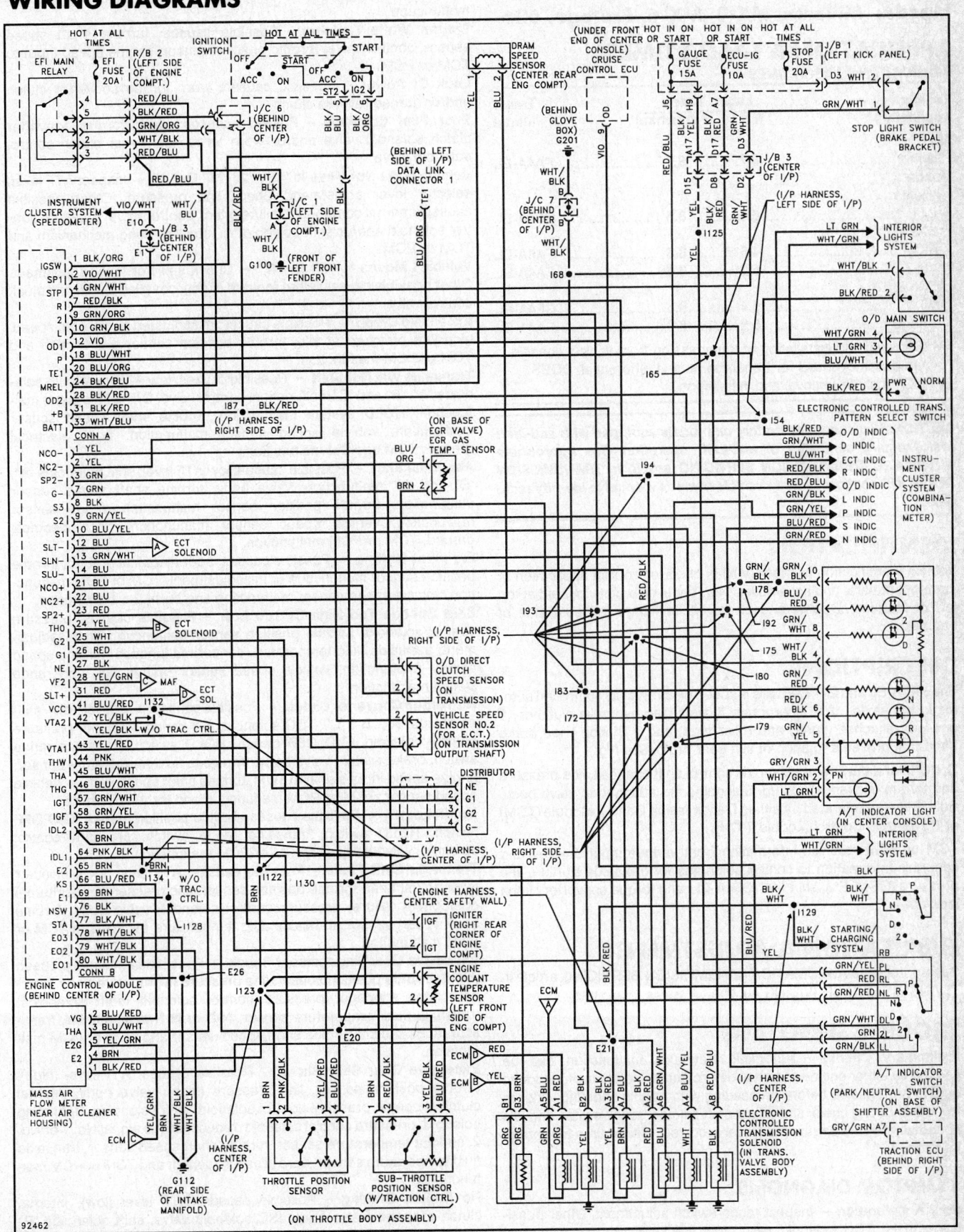

Fig. 18: Transmission Wiring Diagram (1996 Lexus GS300)

92462

AUTOMATIC TRANSMISSIONS
Mazda FA4A-EL & GF4A-EL

Kia: Sephia
Mazda: Millenia, MX-3, MX-6, Protege, 626

APPLICATION & LABOR TIMES

APPLICATION & LABOR TIMES

Vehicle Application	Labor Times		Trans. Model
	[1] R & I	[2] Overhaul	
Kia			
Sephia	4.7	8.6	FA4A-EL
Mazda			
Millenia			
2.5L	6.5	8.6	GF4A-EL
MX-3			
4-Cyl	4.5	8.6	FA4A-EL
V6	5.2	8.6	FA4A-EL
MX-6 & 626			
V6	6.4	8.6	GF4A-EL
Protege	5.2	8.6	FA4A-EL

[1] – Removal and installation of transmission from vehicle chassis.

[2] – On bench overhaul for transmission and differential. DOES NOT include removal and installation.

CAUTION: Disconnecting battery on models equipped with anti-theft radio require canceling of anti-theft operation. See appropriate AUTOMATIC TRANSMISSION SERVICING article in TRANSMISSION SERVICING section. Refer to vehicle owner's manual to identify radio type.

IDENTIFICATION

Vehicle Identification Number (VIN) is used for correct application of component parts and assemblies. Number is on a plate located at top left of instrument panel and on transaxle flange (exhaust side of engine).

DESCRIPTION

The FA4A-EL and GF4A-EL are 4-speed electronically controlled automatic transaxles that incorporate 5 multi-disc hydraulic clutches, 2 one-way clutches (sprag and roller type) and a friction lined brake band that prevents rotation of sun gear drum. *See Fig. 1.*

ON/OFF and duty cycle solenoids control shift changes, line pressure and torque converter lock-up. Solenoids are attached to valve body. Solenoids are operated by either Transmission Control Module (TCM) or Powertrain Control Module (PCM).

TCM or PCM receives information from various input devices and uses this information to control solenoids for transaxle shifting, line pressure (GF4A-EL), shift feel (GF4A-EL) and torque converter clutch lock-up.

LUBRICATION & ADJUSTMENTS

See appropriate AUTOMATIC TRANSMISSION SERVICING article in TRANSMISSION SERVICING section.

TROUBLE SHOOTING

Preliminary Checks – Automatic transaxle malfunction can be caused by either engine or transaxle problems. Isolate malfunction to engine or transaxle before proceeding with trouble shooting. Prior to trouble shooting check and adjust shift linkage, range switch and idle speed as needed. Ensure fluid level is correct. Check tires for correct inflation.

SYMPTOM DIAGNOSIS

Poor Acceleration – Inspect range switch adjustment. Other possible causes: TCC solenoid valve, low line pressure, worn internal clutches, sticking pressure regulator, pressure modifier valve and or solenoid reducing valve, low engine power output and TCM or PCM malfunction.

Surges While Cruising – Possible causes: turbine shaft speed sensor, control valve, throttle position sensor, engine speed input to TCM or PCM.

Lack Of Power – Possible causes: worn torque converter clutch and/or burned reverse clutch.

Poor Fuel Economy – Possible causes: worn torque converter clutch solenoid valve and/or worn torque converter clutch control solenoid valve.

Vehicle Does Not Move In "D", "2", "1" Or "R" – Inspect ATF level, selector lever adjustment. Check line pressure. Other possible causes: internal component failure, stuck control valve, pressure control solenoid and/or shift solenoid "A", stuck parking mechanism and TCM or PCM.

Vehicles Moves In "P" Or "N" – Check selector lever adjustment. Other possible causes: worn forward clutch, coasting clutch and stuck control valve.

Excessive Creep – Possible causes: misadjusted engine idle speed, high line pressure at idle, throttle position sensor malfunction and TCM or PCM malfunction.

Transaxle Will Not Shift – Possible causes: low ATF level, shift solenoids "A", "B" and "C" malfunction, control valve, O/D OFF system malfunction, HOLD system malfunction, turbine shaft speed sensor malfunction, vehicle speed sensor malfunction, poor electrical ground, TCM or PCM malfunction.

Abnormal Shift – Possible causes: low ATF level, shift solenoids "A", "B" and "C" malfunction, valve body, turbine shaft speed sensor malfunction, throttle position sensor malfunction, range sensor malfunction, vehicle speed sensor malfunction, poor electrical ground, TCM or PCM malfunction.

Frequent Shifting – Possible causes: poor electrical ground, throttle position sensor malfunction or misadjustment, TCM or PCM malfunction, vehicle speed sensor malfunction and burnt 2-4 brake band.

Shift Speeds Too High Or Too Low – Possible causes: pressure control solenoid, throttle position sensor malfunction or misadjustment, transaxle fluid temperature sensor malfunction, turbine speed sensor malfunction, vehicle speed sensor malfunction and range switch malfunction.

No Torque Converter Clutch – Possible causes: ATF level (low), shift solenoids "A", "B", "C", TCC solenoid, 3-2 timing solenoid, pressure control solenoid, O/D OFF switch, HOLD switch, transaxle range switch, brake switch, valve body, transaxle fluid temperature sensor, engine speed input signal to TCM, turbine shaft speed sensor, vehicle speed sensor, TCM or PCM malfunction and torque converter.

No Kickdown – Possible causes: throttle position sensor, O/D OFF switch, HOLD switch, transaxle range switch, pressure control solenoid, valve body and TCM or PCM malfunction.

Transaxle Shift Flare – Possible causes: ATF level (low), selector lever adjustment, throttle position sensor, line pressure(low), internal component failure, pressure control solenoid, valve body, turbine shaft speed sensor, transaxle fluid temperature sensor and TCM or PCM malfunction.

Excessive Gear Engagement Shock – Possible causes: idle speed (high), throttle position sensor, line pressure (high), valve body, internal clutch slippage, pressure control solenoid, shift solenoids, transaxle fluid temperature sensor, N-D or N-R accumulator, transaxle range switch, turbine shaft speed sensor and TCM or PCM malfunction.

Excessive Gear Shift Shock – Possible causes: ATF level (high), throttle position sensor, line pressure (high), valve body, internal clutch slippage, pressure control solenoid, shift solenoids, 3-2 timing solenoid, pressure control solenoid, reduce torque signal No. 1 or No. 2, coolant temperature sensor, turbine shaft speed sensor, transaxle fluid temperature sensor, baro pressure sensor and TCM or PCM malfunction.

No Engine Braking – Possible causes: ATF level (low), internal clutch slippage, valve body, ISC solenoid valve, shift solenoids "B" and/or "C" and TCM or PCM malfunction.

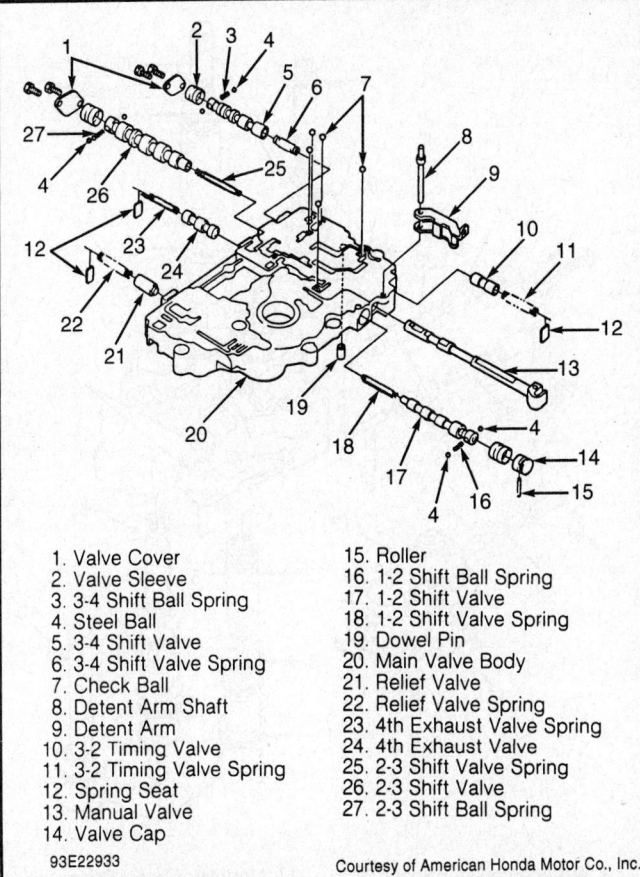

1. Valve Cover
2. Valve Sleeve
3. 3-4 Shift Ball Spring
4. Steel Ball
5. 3-4 Shift Valve
6. 3-4 Shift Valve Spring
7. Check Ball
8. Detent Arm Shaft
9. Detent Arm
10. 3-2 Timing Valve
11. 3-2 Timing Valve Spring
12. Spring Seat
13. Manual Valve
14. Valve Cap
15. Roller
16. 1-2 Shift Ball Spring
17. 1-2 Shift Valve
18. 1-2 Shift Valve Spring
19. Dowel Pin
20. Main Valve Body
21. Relief Valve
22. Relief Valve Spring
23. 4th Exhaust Valve Spring
24. 4th Exhaust Valve
25. 2-3 Shift Valve Spring
26. 2-3 Shift Valve
27. 2-3 Shift Ball Spring

93E22933   Courtesy of American Honda Motor Co., Inc.

Fig. 12: Exploded View Of Main Valve Body

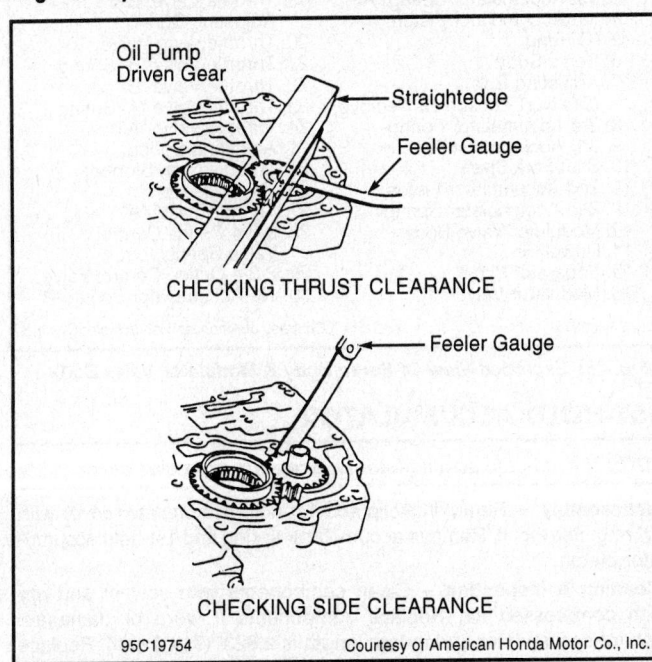

CHECKING THRUST CLEARANCE

CHECKING SIDE CLEARANCE

95C19754   Courtesy of American Honda Motor Co., Inc.

Fig. 13: Measuring Oil Pump Clearances

REGULATOR VALVE BODY

CAUTION: Regulator spring cap is under spring pressure. Ensure regulator spring cap is held downward when removing stopper bolt.

Disassembly – Hold regulator spring cap downward. Remove stopper bolt. Slowly remove regulator spring cap and components from regulator valve body. *See Fig. 14.*

Reassembly – Coat all components and bores with ATF. To reassemble, reverse disassembly procedure. Ensure all components are installed in correct location. *See Fig. 14.* Tighten stopper bolt to specification. See TORQUE SPECIFICATIONS.

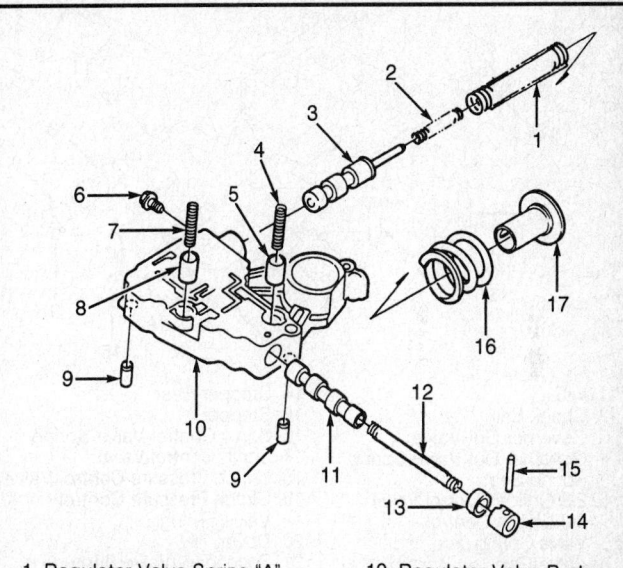

1. Regulator Valve Spring "A"
2. Regulator Valve Spring "B"
3. Regulator Valve
4. Torque Converter Check Valve Spring
5. Torque Converter Check Valve
6. Stopper Bolt
7. Cooler Check Valve Spring
8. Cooler Check Valve
9. Dowel Pin
10. Regulator Valve Body
11. Lock-Up Control Valve
12. Lock-Up Control Valve Spring
13. Sleeve
14. Valve Cap
15. Roller
16. Stator Reaction Spring
17. Regulator Spring Cap

93F22934   Courtesy of American Honda Motor Co., Inc.

Fig. 14: Exploded View Of Regulator Valve Body

SECONDARY VALVE BODY

CAUTION: When disassembling secondary valve body, place components in order and mark spring locations for reassembly reference. DO NOT use force to remove components. DO NOT use magnet to remove check balls, as check balls may become magnetized. Note direction of valve cap installation before removing from secondary valve body.

Disassembly – Disassemble secondary valve body. *See Fig. 15.* Use care when removing valve caps or spring seats, as they are under spring pressure.

Reassembly – Coat all components and bores with ATF. To reassemble, reverse disassembly procedure. Install NEW filter. Ensure all components are installed in correct location. *See Fig. 15.*

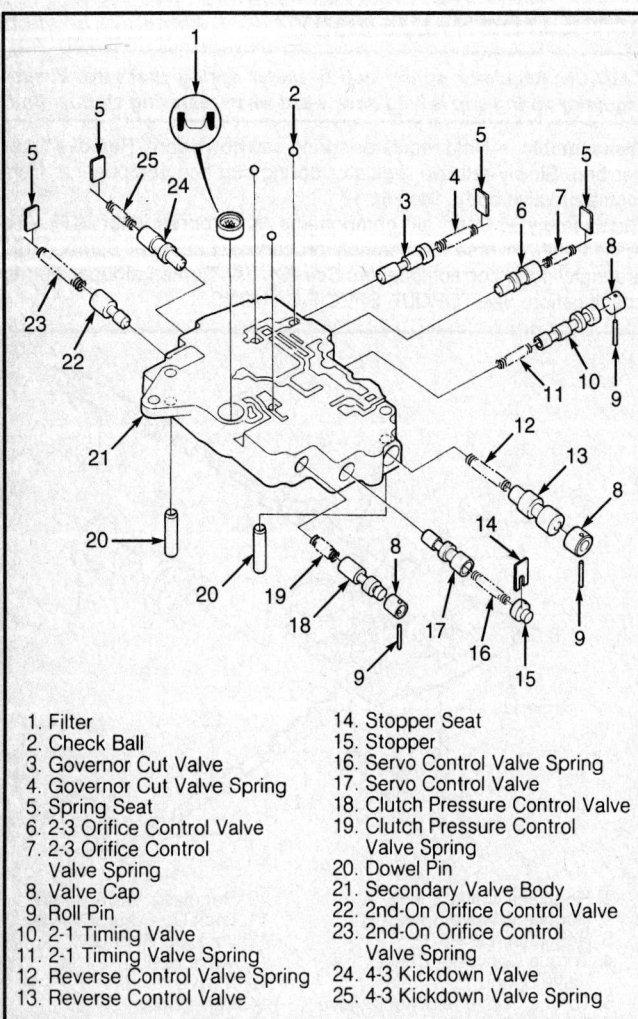

1. Filter
2. Check Ball
3. Governor Cut Valve
4. Governor Cut Valve Spring
5. Spring Seat
6. 2-3 Orifice Control Valve
7. 2-3 Orifice Control Valve Spring
8. Valve Cap
9. Roll Pin
10. 2-1 Timing Valve
11. 2-1 Timing Valve Spring
12. Reverse Control Valve Spring
13. Reverse Control Valve
14. Stopper Seat
15. Stopper
16. Servo Control Valve Spring
17. Servo Control Valve
18. Clutch Pressure Control Valve
19. Clutch Pressure Control Valve Spring
20. Dowel Pin
21. Secondary Valve Body
22. 2nd-On Orifice Control Valve
23. 2nd-On Orifice Control Valve Spring
24. 4-3 Kickdown Valve
25. 4-3 Kickdown Valve Spring

96B30966   Courtesy of American Honda Motor Co., Inc.

Fig. 15: Exploded View Of Secondary Valve Body

SERVO BODY & MODULATOR VALVE BODY

Disassembly – Disassemble servo body and modulator valve body. *See Fig. 16*. Use care when removing spring seats, as they are under spring pressure.

Reassembly – Coat all components and bores with ATF. To reassemble, reverse disassembly procedure using NEW "O" rings. Tighten throttle cam stopper bolt to specification. See TORQUE SPECIFICATIONS.

LOCK-UP VALVE BODY

Disassembly – Note direction of valve cap installation before removing from lock-up valve body. Disassemble lock-up valve body. *See Fig. 17*. Use care when removing valve caps, as they are under spring pressure.

Reassembly – Coat all components and bores with ATF. To reassemble, reverse disassembly procedure. *See Fig. 17*.

GOVERNOR BODY

Disassembly – To disassemble, refer to illustration for exploded view of governor body. *See Fig. 18*.

Cleaning & Inspection – **1)** Clean components with solvent and dry with compressed air. Replace components if worn or damaged. Ensure components slide smoothly in governor housing.

2) Ensure spring free length is within specification. See SPRING SPECIFICATIONS table. Replace springs if not within specification.

Reassembly – Coat all components and bores with ATF. To reassemble, reverse disassembly procedure using NEW bolt locks and NEW filters. *See Fig. 18*. Tighten governor housing-to-governor shaft bolts to specification. See TORQUE SPECIFICATIONS.

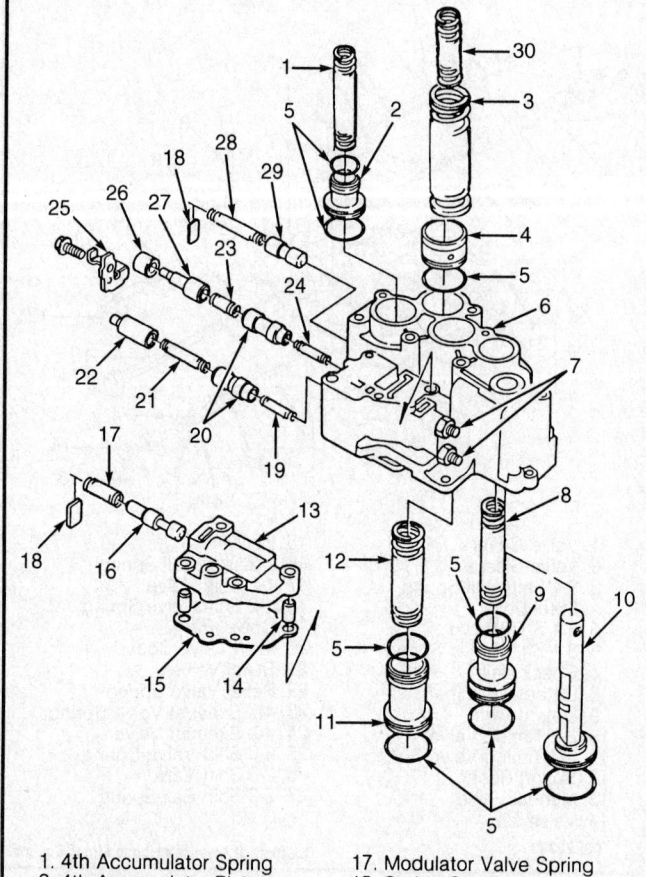

1. 4th Accumulator Spring
2. 4th Accumulator Piston
3. 1st Accumulator Spring "A"
4. 1st Accumulator Piston
5. "O" Ring
6. Servo Body
7. Adjusting Bolt (DO NOT Loosen Or Remove)
8. 3rd Accumulator Spring
9. 3rd Accumulator Piston
10. Shift Fork Shaft
11. 2nd Accumulator Piston
12. 2nd Accumulator Spring
13. Modulator Valve Body
14. Dowel Pin
15. Separator Plate
16. Modulator Valve
17. Modulator Valve Spring
18. Spring Seat
19. Throttle Valve "B" Adjusting Spring
20. Throttle Long Valve
21. Throttle Valve "B" Spring
22. Throttle Valve "B"
23. Throttle Valve "A" Spring
24. Throttle Valve "A" Adjusting Spring
25. Throttle Cam Stopper
26. Valve Sleeve
27. Throttle Valve "A"
28. 2/3-4 Orifice Control Valve Spring
29. 2/3-4 Orifice Control Valve
30. 1st Accumulator Spring "B"

96C30975   Courtesy of American Honda Motor Co., Inc.

Fig. 16: Exploded View Of Servo Body & Modulator Valve Body

1ST-HOLD ACCUMULATOR

NOTE: *The 1st-hold accumulator is located in right side cover.*

Disassembly – Remove circlip and 1st-hold accumulator cover with "O" ring. *See Fig. 6*. Remove accumulator spring and 1st-hold accumulator piston.

Cleaning & Inspection – Clean components with solvent and dry with compressed air. Replace components if worn or damaged. Ensure accumulator spring free length is 2.823" (71.70 mm). Replace spring if not as specified.

Reassembly – Coat all components and bores with ATF. To reassemble, reverse disassembly procedure using NEW "O" rings.

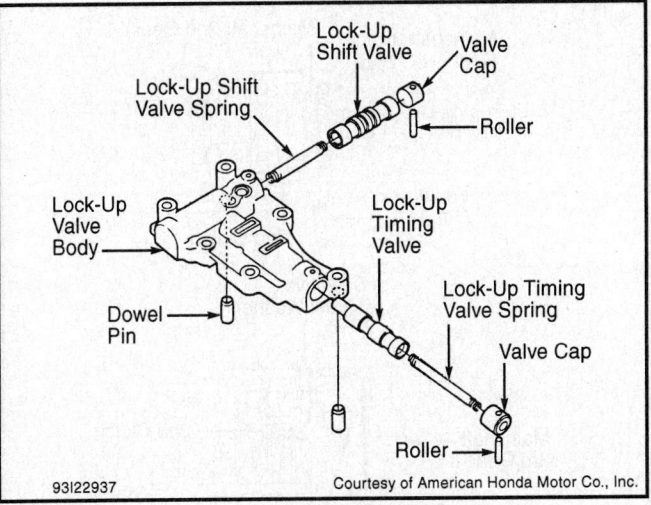

Fig. 17: Exploded View Of Lock-Up Valve Body

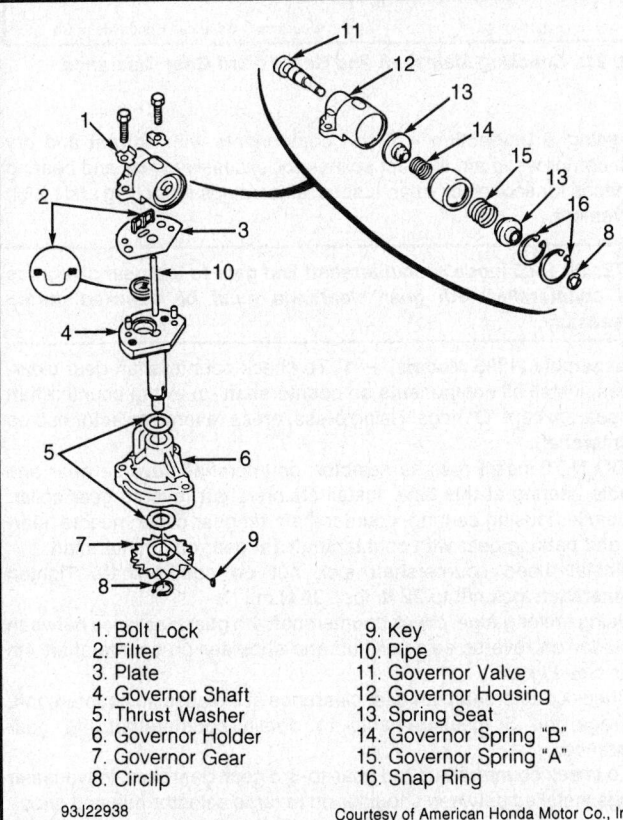

1. Bolt Lock	9. Key
2. Filter	10. Pipe
3. Plate	11. Governor Valve
4. Governor Shaft	12. Governor Housing
5. Thrust Washer	13. Spring Seat
6. Governor Holder	14. Governor Spring "B"
7. Governor Gear	15. Governor Spring "A"
8. Circlip	16. Snap Ring

93J22938   Courtesy of American Honda Motor Co., Inc.

Fig. 18: Exploded View Of Governor Body

MAINSHAFT

NOTE: Mainshaft lock nut has left hand threads. On 1996 models, mainshaft has beveled spring washer below lock nut.

Disassembly – Note location of mainshaft components. See Fig. 19. Remove mainshaft components.
Cleaning & Inspection – Clean components with solvent and dry with compressed air. Inspect splines for excessive wear and bearing surfaces for scoring or wear. Inspect all bearings for galling and rough movement.

NOTE: Mainshaft 2nd gear-to-3rd gear clearance must be checked during reassembly.

Reassembly – 1) To check mainshaft 2nd gear-to-3rd gear clearance, install proper components, except "O" rings, on mainshaft. See Fig. 20.
2) Install beveled spring washer, if equipped. Install used mainshaft lock nut on mainshaft. Tighten mainshaft lock nut to 22 ft. lbs. (30 N.m). Hold mainshaft 2nd gear against 2nd clutch.
3) Using feeler gauge, measure clearance between mainshaft 2nd gear and mainshaft 3rd gear. Check mainshaft clearance at 3 places on mainshaft. Average the 3 measurements to obtain mainshaft 2nd gear-to-3rd gear clearance. See Fig. 21.
4) Replace selective thrust washer, located between mainshaft 2nd gear and 2nd clutch if mainshaft 2nd gear-to-3rd gear clearance is not .002-.005" (.05-.13 mm). Different thickness thrust washers are available. See appropriate THRUST WASHER SPECIFICATIONS table. Replace thrust washer if necessary and recheck mainshaft 2nd gear-to-3rd gear clearance.
5) Once correct thickness thrust washer is obtained, lubricate all components with ATF. Reassemble mainshaft using NEW "O" rings.
6) Ensure thrust needle bearings are installed with unrolled edge of bearing retainer facing washer. Before installing NEW "O" rings on mainshaft, wrap splines on mainshaft with tape to prevent damage to "O" rings.

THRUST WASHER SPECIFICATIONS (1995)

Washer Number	Part Number	Thickness In. (mm)
1	90441-PC9-010	.138 (3.50)
2	90442-PC9-010	.140 (3.55)
3	90443-PC9-010	.142 (3.60)
4	90444-PC9-010	.144 (3.65)
5	90445-PC9-010	.146 (3.70)
6	90446-PC9-010	.148 (3.75)
7	90447-PC9-010	.150 (3.80)
8	90448-PC9-010	.152 (3.85)
9	90449-PC9-010	.154 (3.90)

THRUST WASHER SPECIFICATIONS (1996)

Washer Number	Part Number	Thickness In. (mm)
1	90441-P4P-000	.157 (4.00)
2	90442-P4P-000	.159 (4.05)
3	90443-P4P-000	.161 (4.10)
4	90444-P4P-000	.163 (4.15)
5	90445-P4P-000	.165 (4.20)
6	90446-P4P-000	.167 (4.25)
7	90447-P4P-000	.169 (4.30)
8	90448-P4P-000	.171 (4.35)
9	90449-P4P-000	.173 (4.40)
10	90450-P4P-000	.175 (4.45)

COUNTERSHAFT

NOTE: On 1996 models, countershaft lock nut has left hand threads and beveled spring washer below lock nut. On 1995 models, separating countershaft 2nd gear and countershaft 3rd gear are cotters and a needle thrust bearing, 1996 models do not have the cotters.

Disassembly – 1) Note location of countershaft components. See Fig. 22. Remove countershaft components down to the reverse selector hub.
2) Place countershaft in hydraulic press while supporting countershaft 4th gear. Place a protective cap between hydraulic press and countershaft to prevent damage to countershaft.
3) Press countershaft from reverse selector hub. Remove remaining components from countershaft.

AUTOMATIC TRANSMISSIONS
Honda A24A & S24A (Cont.)

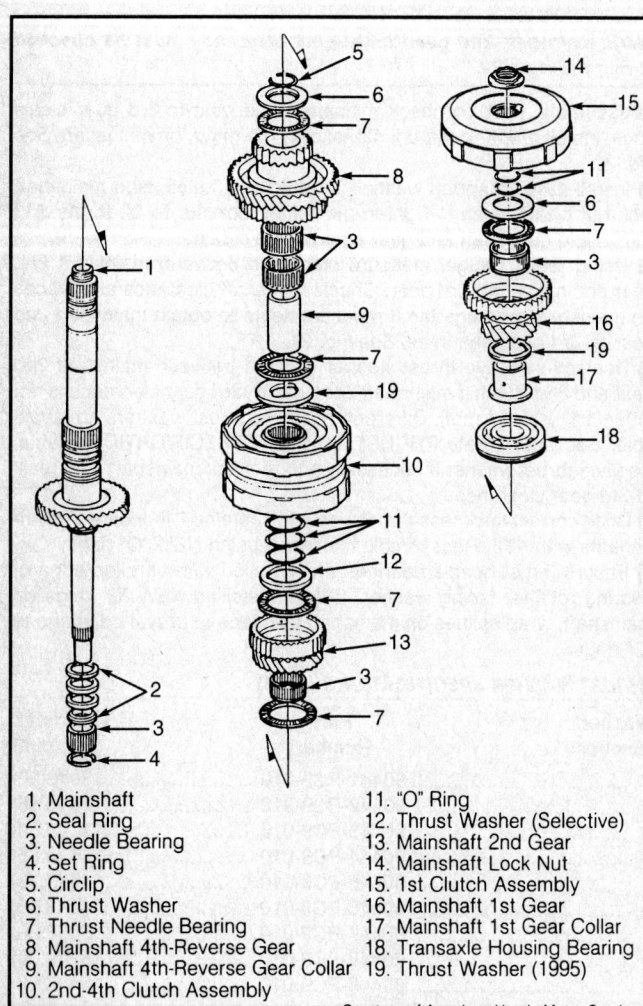

1. Mainshaft
2. Seal Ring
3. Needle Bearing
4. Set Ring
5. Circlip
6. Thrust Washer
7. Thrust Needle Bearing
8. Mainshaft 4th-Reverse Gear
9. Mainshaft 4th-Reverse Gear Collar
10. 2nd-4th Clutch Assembly
11. "O" Ring
12. Thrust Washer (Selective)
13. Mainshaft 2nd Gear
14. Mainshaft Lock Nut
15. 1st Clutch Assembly
16. Mainshaft 1st Gear
17. Mainshaft 1st Gear Collar
18. Transaxle Housing Bearing
19. Thrust Washer (1995)

96C30967   Courtesy of American Honda Motor Co., Inc.

Fig. 19: Exploded View Of Mainshaft & Components

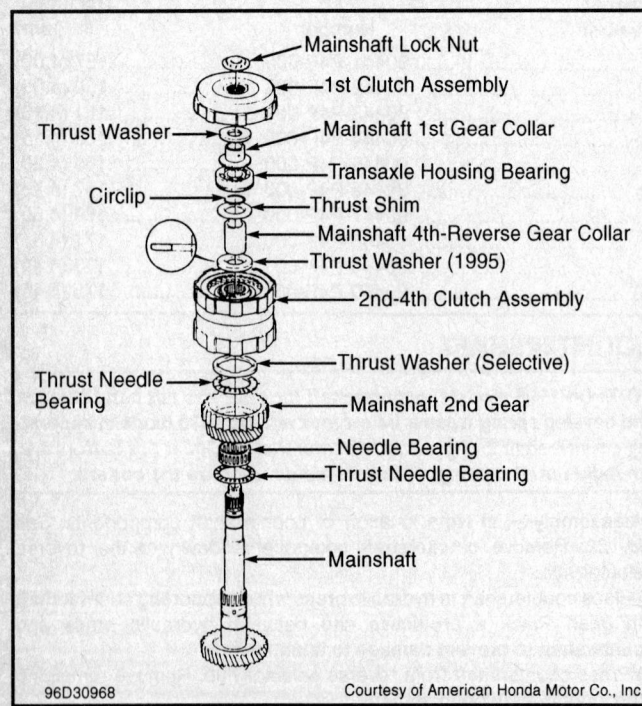

96D30968   Courtesy of American Honda Motor Co., Inc.

Fig. 20: Assembling Mainshaft For Checking Mainshaft 2nd Gear-To-3rd Gear Clearance

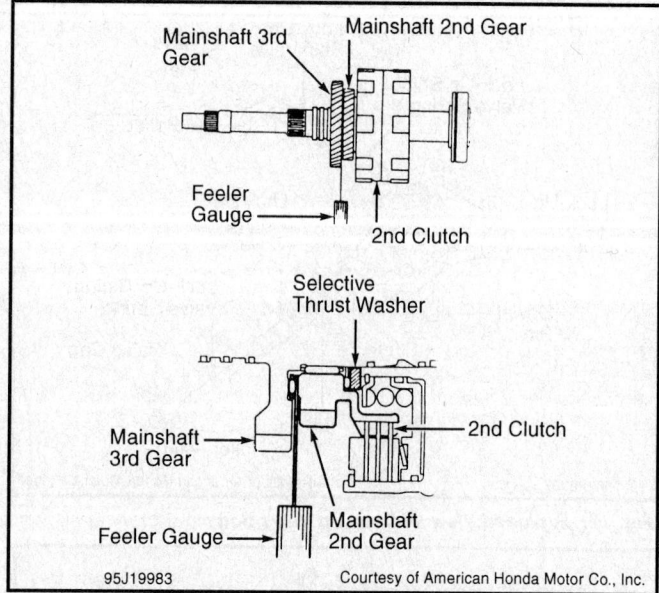

95J19983   Courtesy of American Honda Motor Co., Inc.

Fig. 21: Checking Mainshaft 2nd Gear-To-3rd Gear Clearance

Cleaning & Inspection – Clean components with solvent and dry with compressed air. Inspect splines for excessive wear and bearing surfaces for scoring or wear. Inspect all bearings for galling and rough movement.

NOTE: On 1995 models, countershaft 2nd gear-to-3rd gear clearance and countershaft 4th gear clearance must be checked during reassembly.

Reassembly (1995 Models) – **1)** To check countershaft gear clearances, install all components on countershaft up to the countershaft 4th gear, except "O" rings. Using press, press reverse selector hub on countershaft.
2) DO NOT install reverse selector, countershaft reverse gear and needle bearing at this time. Install countershaft reverse gear collar, transaxle housing bearing, countershaft 1st gear collar, needle bearing and parking gear with countershaft 1st gear on countershaft.
3) Install used countershaft lock nut on countershaft. Tighten countershaft lock nut to 22 ft. lbs. (30 N.m).
4) Using feeler gauge, check countershaft 4th gear clearance between shoulder on reverse selector hub and shoulder on countershaft 4th gear. See Fig. 23.
5) Check countershaft 4th gear clearance at 3 places on countershaft. Average the 3 measurements to obtain countershaft 4th gear clearance.
6) To check countershaft 2nd gear-to-3rd gear clearance, leave feeler gauge installed between shoulder on reverse selector hub and shoulder on countershaft 4th gear. Slide countershaft 3rd gear fully outward (away from countershaft 2nd gear). Using a second feeler gauge, measure clearance between countershaft 2nd gear and countershaft 3rd gear. See Fig. 23.
7) Slide countershaft 3rd gear fully inward (toward countershaft 2nd gear). Using feeler gauge, measure clearance between countershaft 2nd gear and countershaft 3rd gear. Calculate difference between 2 measurements to determine countershaft 2nd gear-to-3rd gear clearance.
8) Check countershaft 2nd gear-to-3rd gear clearance at 3 places on countershaft. Average the 3 measurements to obtain countershaft 2nd gear-to-3rd gear clearance. Remove feeler gauges.

9) Replace distance collar if countershaft 4th gear clearance is not .002-.005" (.05-.13 mm). Different length distance collars are available. See DISTANCE COLLAR SPECIFICATIONS table. Install different distance collar if necessary and recheck countershaft 4th gear clearance.

10) Replace splined washer if countershaft 2nd gear-to-3rd gear clearance is not .002-.005" (.05-.13 mm). Different thickness splined washers are available. See SPLINED WASHER SPECIFICATIONS table. Install different thickness splined washer if necessary and recheck countershaft 2nd-3rd gear clearance.

11) Once correct gear clearances are obtained, lubricate all components with ATF. Reassemble countershaft using NEW "O" rings.

12) Ensure thrust needle bearings are installed with unrolled edge of bearing retainer facing washer. Before installing NEW "O" rings on countershaft, wrap splines on countershaft with tape to prevent damage to "O" rings.

DISTANCE COLLAR SPECIFICATIONS

Collar Number	Part Number	Thickness In. (mm)
1	90503-PC9-000	1.535 (39.00)
2	90504-PC9-000	1.539 (39.10)
3	90505-PC9-000	1.543 (39.20)
4	90507-PC9-000	1.547 (39.30)
5	90508-PC9-000	1.537 (39.05)
6	90509-PC9-000	1.541 (39.15)
7	90510-PC9-000	1.545 (39.25)
8	90511-PC9-000	1.531 (38.90)
9	90512-PC9-000	1.533 (38.95)

SPLINED WASHER SPECIFICATIONS

Washer Number	Part Number	Thickness In. (mm)
1	90411-PF4-000	.118 (3.00)
2	90412-PF4-000	.120 (3.05)
3	90413-PF4-000	.122 (3.10)
4	90414-PF4-000	.124 (3.15)
5	90415-PF4-000	.126 (3.20)
6	90416-PF4-000	.128 (3.25)
7	90417-PF4-000	.130 (3.30)
8	90418-PF4-000	.132 (3.35)
9	90419-PF4-000	.134 (3.40)
10	90411-P24-J00	.136 (3.45)
11	90412-P24-J00	.138 (3.50)
12	90413-P24-J00	.140 (3.55)
13	90414-P24-J00	.142 (3.60)

NOTE: On 1996 models, countershaft 4th gear clearance must be checked during reassembly.

Reassembly (1996 Models) – 1) To check countershaft gear clearances, install all components on countershaft up to the countershaft 4th gear, except "O" rings. Using press, press reverse selector hub on countershaft.

2) DO NOT install reverse selector, countershaft reverse gear and needle bearing at this time. Install countershaft reverse gear collar, transaxle housing bearing, countershaft 1st gear collar, needle bearing and parking gear with countershaft 1st gear on countershaft.

3) Install beveled spring washer and used countershaft lock nut on countershaft. Tighten countershaft lock nut to 22 ft. lbs. (30 N.m).

4) Using feeler gauge, check countershaft 4th gear clearance between shoulder on reverse selector hub and shoulder on countershaft 4th gear. See Fig. 23.

5) Check countershaft 4th gear clearance at 3 places on countershaft. Average the 3 measurements to obtain countershaft 4th gear clearance.

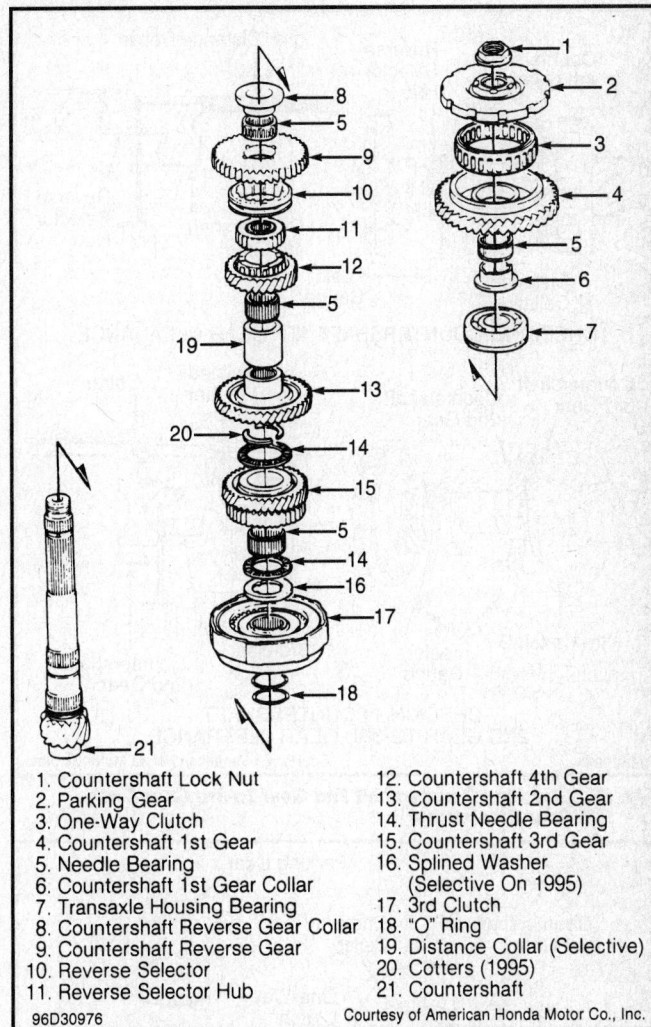

1. Countershaft Lock Nut
2. Parking Gear
3. One-Way Clutch
4. Countershaft 1st Gear
5. Needle Bearing
6. Countershaft 1st Gear Collar
7. Transaxle Housing Bearing
8. Countershaft Reverse Gear Collar
9. Countershaft Reverse Gear
10. Reverse Selector
11. Reverse Selector Hub
12. Countershaft 4th Gear
13. Countershaft 2nd Gear
14. Thrust Needle Bearing
15. Countershaft 3rd Gear
16. Splined Washer (Selective On 1995)
17. 3rd Clutch
18. "O" Ring
19. Distance Collar (Selective)
20. Cotters (1995)
21. Countershaft

96D30976

Courtesy of American Honda Motor Co., Inc.

Fig. 22: Exploded View Of Countershaft & Components

6) Replace distance collar if countershaft 4th gear clearance is not .004-.007" (.10-.18 mm). Different length distance collars are available. See DISTANCE COLLAR SPECIFICATIONS table. Install different distance collar if necessary and recheck countershaft 4th gear clearance.

7) Once correct gear clearances are obtained, lubricate all components with ATF. Reassemble countershaft using NEW "O" rings.

8) Ensure thrust needle bearings are installed with unrolled edge of bearing retainer facing washer. Before installing NEW "O" rings on countershaft, wrap splines on countershaft with tape to prevent damage to "O" rings.

PARKING GEAR & ONE-WAY CLUTCH

Disassembly –1) To separate parking gear from countershaft 1st gear, hold countershaft 1st gear and rotate parking gear counterclockwise. Remove parking gear.

2) Note direction of one-way clutch installation in countershaft 1st gear. Using screwdriver, gently pry one-way clutch from countershaft 1st gear.

Cleaning & Inspection – Clean components with solvent and dry with compressed air. Inspect components for damage.

Reassembly –1) Lubricate all components with ATF. Install one-way clutch with large flange area toward countershaft 1st gear. See Fig. 24.

2) Install parking gear. To check one-way clutch operation, hold countershaft 1st gear. Ensure parking gear rotates counterclockwise.

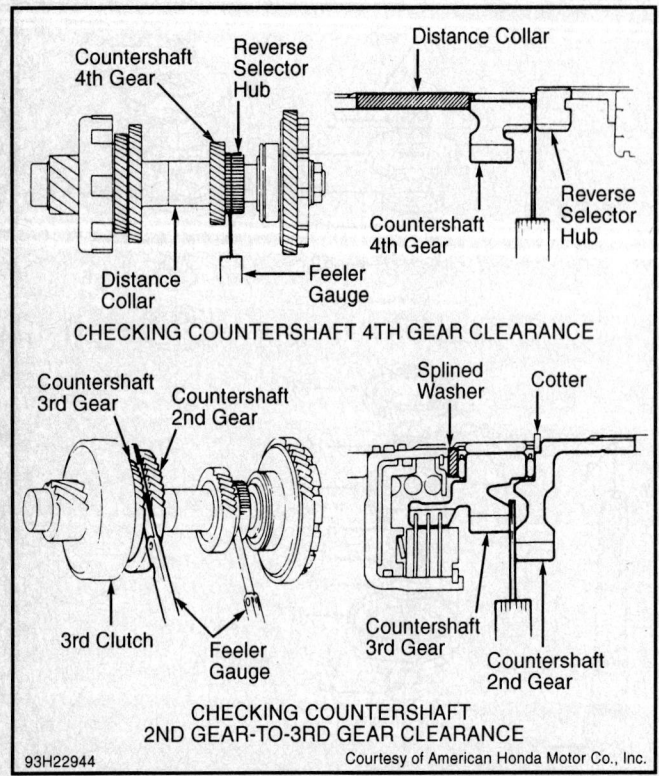

CHECKING COUNTERSHAFT 4TH GEAR CLEARANCE

CHECKING COUNTERSHAFT
2ND GEAR-TO-3RD GEAR CLEARANCE

93H22944   Courtesy of American Honda Motor Co., Inc.

Fig. 23: Checking Countershaft 2nd Gear-To-3rd Gear & 4th Gear Clearances

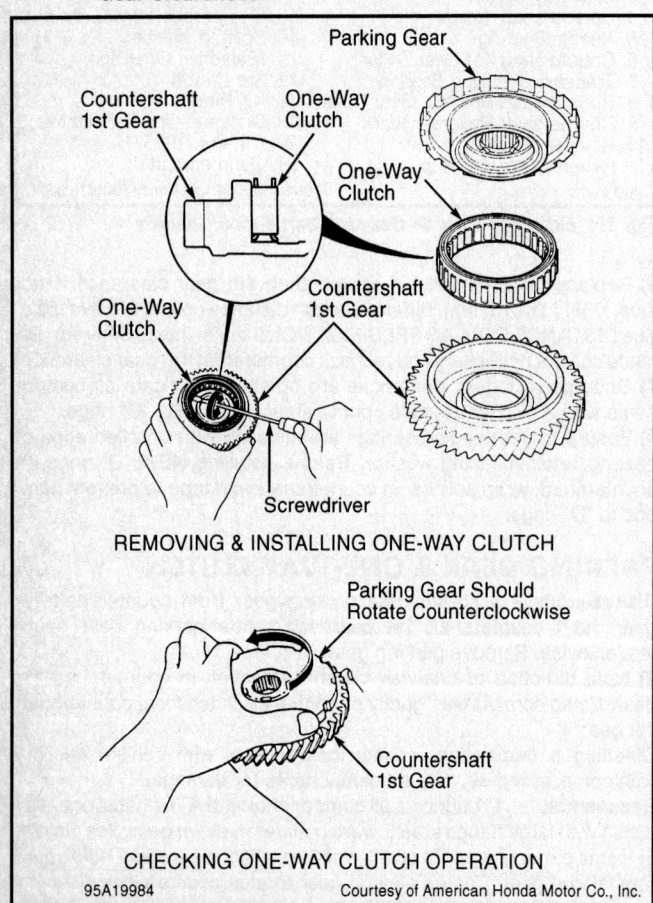

REMOVING & INSTALLING ONE-WAY CLUTCH

CHECKING ONE-WAY CLUTCH OPERATION

95A19984   Courtesy of American Honda Motor Co., Inc.

Fig. 24: Installing & Checking One-Way Clutch Operation

SUB-SHAFT & COMPONENTS

Disassembly – 1) Tap on sub-shaft to remove oil guide cap from transaxle housing. See Fig. 25.

2) On all models, remove sub-shaft, 1st-hold clutch, sub-shaft 4th gear and components from transaxle housing.

3) If removing transaxle housing bearing, expand snap ring. Using press, press transaxle housing bearing from transaxle housing. Remove snap ring (if necessary).

4) If removing needle bearing from transaxle housing, remove needle bearing stopper bolt and needle bearing stopper. Using hammer and drift, tap needle bearing from transaxle housing.

Cleaning & Inspection – 1) Clean components with solvent and dry with compressed air. Inspect splines for excessive wear and bearing surfaces for scoring or wear.

2) Inspect all needle bearings for galling and rough movement. Inspect sub-shaft 4th gear for damage.

Reassembly – 1) Lubricate all components with ATF. If installing NEW needle bearing in transaxle housing, using press, press needle bearing into transaxle housing.

CAUTION: Ensure transaxle housing bearing is installed with groove facing toward outside of transaxle housing so snap ring will engage with bearing.

---

2) If installing transaxle housing bearing in transaxle housing, install snap ring (if removed). Expand snap ring. Using press, press transaxle housing bearing part way into transaxle housing.

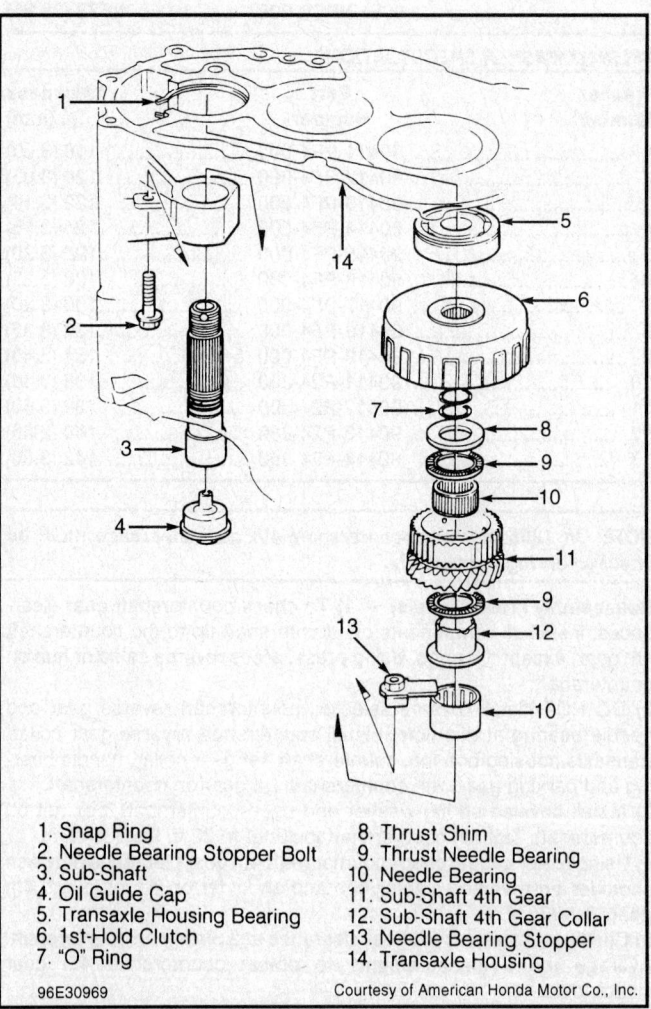

1. Snap Ring
2. Needle Bearing Stopper Bolt
3. Sub-Shaft
4. Oil Guide Cap
5. Transaxle Housing Bearing
6. 1st-Hold Clutch
7. "O" Ring
8. Thrust Shim
9. Thrust Needle Bearing
10. Needle Bearing
11. Sub-Shaft 4th Gear
12. Sub-Shaft 4th Gear Collar
13. Needle Bearing Stopper
14. Transaxle Housing

96E30969   Courtesy of American Honda Motor Co., Inc.

Fig. 25: Exploded View Of Typical Sub-Shaft & Components

3) Release snap ring. Continue pressing transaxle housing bearing into transaxle housing until snap ring engages in bearing. Ensure snap ring is fully seated. Snap ring end gap clearance should be 0-.280" (0-7 mm). If snap ring end gap is too large, reseat or replace snap ring.

4) Reassemble sub-shaft. Ensure thrust needle bearings are installed with unrolled edge of bearing retainer facing washer.

5) Use NEW "O" rings on sub-shaft. Before installing "O" rings on sub-shaft, wrap splines on sub-shaft with tape to prevent damage to "O" rings. Install sub-shaft and components in transaxle housing.

6) Install and tighten needle bearing stopper bolt to specification. See TORQUE SPECIFICATIONS. Tap NEW oil guide cap into transaxle housing. Ensure oil guide cap is fully seated in transaxle housing.

CLUTCH ASSEMBLIES

NOTE: The 2nd/4th and 1st-Hold clutch assemblies are equipped with 2 different styles of clutch pistons, if replacement is necessary, ensure same design as original type clutch is used. See Fig. 26. Ensure spring compressor is making full contact with spring retainer or damage will occur.

Disassembly – 1) Remove snap ring, clutch end plate, clutch discs and clutch plates. *See Fig. 26.*

2) Note direction of disc spring installation on all clutches. Remove disc springs.

3) Using spring compress, compress return spring. Remove snap ring. Release and remove spring compressor. Remove spring retainer and return spring.

4) Wrap shop towel around clutch drum. Apply light air pressure to oil passage on clutch drum to remove clutch piston. Remove "O" rings.

Cleaning & Inspection – 1) Clean metal components with solvent and dry with compressed air. Ensure check valve on rear of clutch piston (if equipped) is thoroughly cleaned and securely fastened on clutch piston.

2) Inspect components for damage. Replace if necessary. Ensure no rough edges exist on "O" ring sealing areas.

Reassembly – 1) Lubricate all components with ATF. Install NEW "O" rings. Install clutch piston in clutch drum. Slightly rotate clutch piston during installation to prevent damaging "O" rings.

CAUTION: DO NOT apply excessive force on clutch piston or "O" rings will be damaged.

2) Install return spring and spring retainer in clutch drum. Place snap ring on spring retainer. Using spring compressor, compress return spring. Install snap ring. Remove spring compressor.

3) Install disc spring on all clutches. Ensure disc spring is installed in proper direction. *See Fig. 26.*

CAUTION: Soak clutch discs in ATF for at least 30 minutes before installing.

4) Alternately install clutch plates and clutch discs starting with clutch plate. Install clutch end plate with flat side toward clutch disc. Install snap ring.

5) Using dial indicator, measure clutch clearance between clutch end plate and top clutch disc. *See Fig. 27.* Zero dial indicator with clutch end plate lowered, and then lift clutch end plate upward against snap ring. Distance measured is clutch clearance.

6) Measure clutch clearance at 3 different locations. Clutch clearance should be within specification. See CLUTCH CLEARANCE SPECIFICATIONS table.

7) If clutch clearance is not within specification, install different thickness clutch end plate. See CLUTCH END PLATE SPECIFICATIONS table.

NOTE: If thickest clutch end plate is installed and clutch clearance still exceeds specification, replace clutch discs and clutch plates.

CLUTCH CLEARANCE SPECIFICATIONS

Application	Clutch Clearance In. (mm)
1st & 2nd Clutches	.026-.033 (.65-.85)
1st-Hold Clutch	.020-.031 (.50-.80)
3rd & 4th Clutches	.016-.024 (.40-.60)

CLUTCH END PLATE SPECIFICATIONS

Plate Number	Part Number	Thickness In. (mm)
1st-Hold Clutch		
1	22551-PS5-003	.083 (2.10)
2	22552-PS5-003	.087 (2.20)
3	22553-PS5-003	.091 (2.30)
4	22554-PS5-003	.094 (2.40)
5	22555-PS5-003	.098 (2.50)
6	22556-PS5-003	.102 (2.60)
7	22557-PS5-003	.106 (2.70)
1st, 2nd, 3rd & 4th Clutches		
1	22551-PC9-000	.094 (2.40)
2	22552-PC9-000	.098 (2.50)
3	22553-PC9-000	.102 (2.60)
4	22554-PC9-000	.106 (2.70)
5	22555-PC9-000	.110 (2.80)
6	22556-PC9-000	.114 (2.90)
7	22557-PC9-000	.118 (3.00)
8	22558-PC9-000	.122 (3.10)
9	22559-PC9-000	.126 (3.20)
10	22560-PC9-000	.130 (3.30)
11	22561-PC9-000	.083 (2.10)
12	22562-PC9-000	.087 (2.20)
13	22563-PC9-000	.091 (2.30)

TORQUE CONVERTER HOUSING

Disassembly – 1) Remove countershaft bearing from torque converter housing using slide hammer (if necessary). Remove oil guide plate from torque converter housing. *See Fig. 11.*

2) Using hammer and bearing remover/installer, remove mainshaft bearing and oil seal from torque converter housing. Using hammer and drift, tap differential oil seal from torque converter housing.

Cleaning & Inspection – Clean components with solvent and dry with compressed air. Inspect torque converter housing for cracks and damage in bearing areas. Replace torque converter housing if damaged.

Reassembly – 1) Coat all components with ATF. To install mainshaft bearing, use hammer and bearing remover/installer, install bearing in until bearing bottoms in torque converter housing.

2) Using hammer and oil seal installer, install NEW mainshaft oil seal in torque converter housing. Oil seal should be flush with torque converter housing surface.

3) To install countershaft bearing, install oil guide plate in countershaft bearing bore of torque converter housing. Ensure oil guide plate is installed so tab in center faces upward (away from torque converter housing surface). *See Fig. 11.* Ensure oil guide is installed to a depth of 0-.001" (0-.03 mm), zero being flush and .001" is past flush (inset). Using hammer and bearing installer, install countershaft bearing into torque converter housing.

CAUTION: If any differential components, transaxle housing, torque converter housing, snap rings or differential bearings are replaced, differential bearing side clearance must be checked. See DIFFERENTIAL BEARING SIDE CLEARANCE under TRANSAXLE REASSEMBLY.

4) Once correct differential bearing side clearance is obtained, using hammer and oil seal installer, install NEW differential oil seal in torque converter housing. Ensure oil seal is fully seated in torque converter housing.

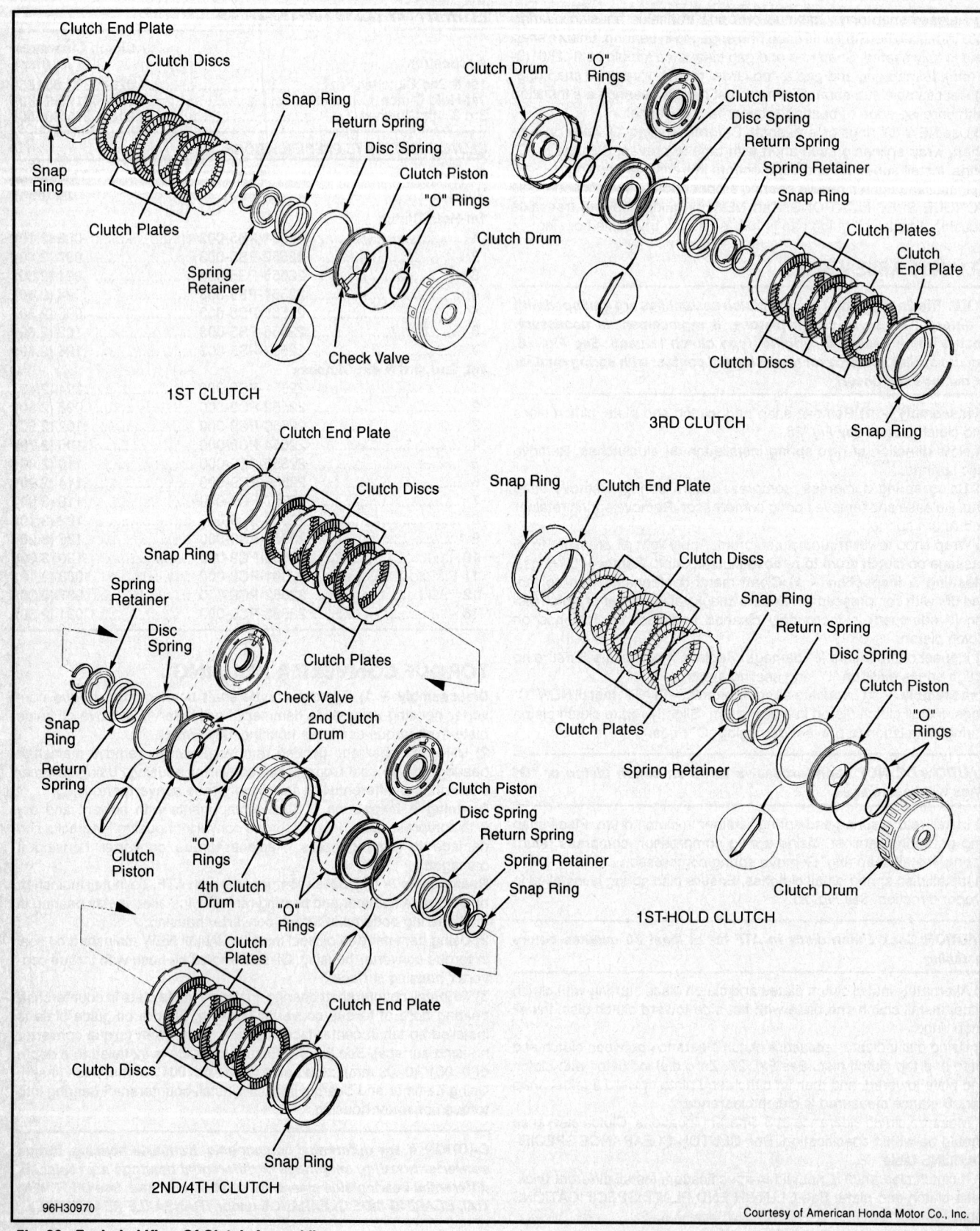

1ST CLUTCH

Clutch End Plate
Clutch Discs
Snap Ring
Return Spring
Disc Spring
Clutch Piston
"O" Rings
Clutch Drum
Snap Ring
Clutch Plates
Spring Retainer
Check Valve

3RD CLUTCH

Clutch Drum
"O" Rings
Clutch Piston
Disc Spring
Return Spring
Spring Retainer
Snap Ring
Clutch Plates
Clutch End Plate
Clutch Discs
Snap Ring

2ND/4TH CLUTCH

Clutch End Plate
Clutch Discs
Snap Ring
Spring Retainer
Disc Spring
Snap Ring
Return Spring
Clutch Piston
"O" Rings
4th Clutch Drum
"O" Rings
Clutch Plates
Clutch Discs
Snap Ring
Check Valve
2nd Clutch Drum
Clutch Plates
Clutch Piston
Disc Spring
Return Spring
Spring Retainer
Snap Ring

1ST-HOLD CLUTCH

Snap Ring
Clutch End Plate
Clutch Discs
Snap Ring
Return Spring
Disc Spring
Clutch Piston
"O" Rings
Clutch Plates
Spring Retainer
Clutch Drum

96H30970

Courtesy of American Honda Motor Co., Inc.

Fig. 26: Exploded View Of Clutch Assemblies

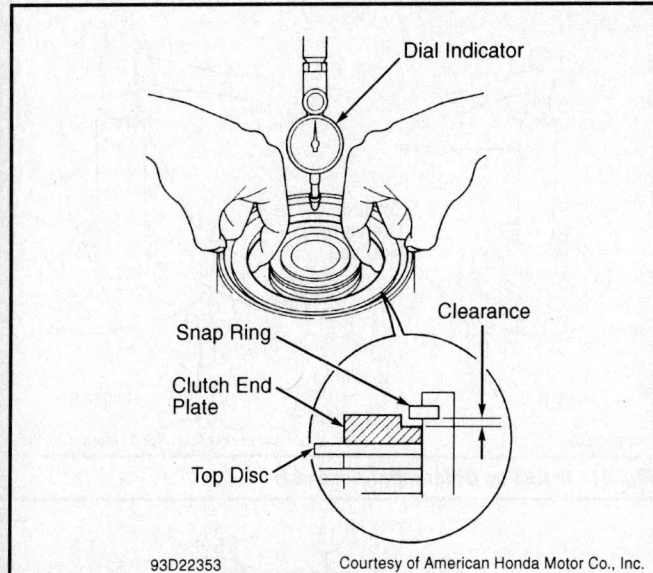

93D22353   Courtesy of American Honda Motor Co., Inc.

Fig. 27: Measuring Clutch Clearance

TRANSAXLE HOUSING

Disassembly – 1) Expand snap ring, and press mainshaft, countershaft and sub-shaft bearings from transaxle housing. Using hammer and drift, tap differential oil seal from transaxle housing.

2) DO NOT remove snap ring from transaxle housing unless necessary to clean groove in transaxle housing. Using hammer and drift, tap differential oil seal from transaxle housing.

Cleaning & Inspection – Clean components with solvent and dry with compressed air. Inspect transaxle housing for cracks and damage in bearing areas. Replace transaxle housing if damaged.

Reassembly – 1) Coat all components with ATF. To install mainshaft, countershaft and sub-shaft bearings, expand snap ring and install bearing part way into transaxle housing.

CAUTION: Ensure bearings are installed with groove of bearing facing inside of transaxle housing so snap ring engages in bearing when bearing is fully installed. Ensure snap ring fully engages in bearing. Snap ring end gap clearance should be 0-.280" (0-7 mm). If snap ring end gap is too large, reseat or replace snap ring.

2) Release snap ring. Press bearing into transaxle housing until snap ring engages with groove on bearing.

CAUTION: If differential carrier, differential bearings, transaxle housing, torque converter housing or snap rings are replaced, differential bearing side clearance must be checked. See DIFFERENTIAL BEARING SIDE CLEARANCE under TRANSAXLE REASSEMBLY.

3) Once correct differential bearing side clearance is obtained, using hammer and oil seal installer, install NEW differential oil seal in transaxle housing. Ensure oil seal is fully seated in transaxle housing.

DIFFERENTIAL ASSEMBLY

Disassembly – 1) Before disassembling differential assembly, check pinion gear backlash. Place differential assembly on "V" blocks with both axle shafts installed.

2) Install dial indicator with stem resting against pinion gear. *See Fig. 28.* Check pinion gear backlash. Pinion gear backlash should be .003-.006" (.08-.15 mm). Replace differential assembly if pinion gear backlash is not within specification.

3) If replacing differential bearings, use bearing puller to remove differential bearings from differential carrier. Remove bolts and ring gear.

NOTE: Ring gear bolts have left-hand threads.

4) If removing speedometer drive gear, remove snap ring, speedometer drive gear and dowel pin. *See Fig. 29.*

Cleaning & Inspection – Clean components with solvent and dry with compressed air. Inspect components for wear and damage. Replace components as necessary.

Reassembly – 1) Install dowel pin for speedometer drive gear in differential carrier. Install speedometer drive gear on differential carrier.

CAUTION: Ensure chamfered side on inside of speedometer drive gear is toward differential carrier. See Fig. 29. Ensure cutout area on speedometer drive gear aligns with dowel pin.

2) Install snap ring so hooked end is facing upward and snap ring end gap is properly positioned in relation to pinion shaft in differential carrier. *See Fig. 30.* Ensure snap ring seats in groove on differential carrier.

CAUTION: Ensure ring gear is installed on differential carrier with chamfered side on inside of ring gear toward differential carrier.

3) Install ring gear on differential carrier with chamfered side on inside of ring gear toward differential carrier. *See Fig. 29.*

4) Install and tighten ring gear bolts to specification. See TORQUE SPECIFICATIONS. Using driver, install NEW differential bearings on differential carrier (if removed).

CAUTION: If differential carrier, differential bearings, transaxle housing, torque converter housing or snap rings are replaced, differential bearing side clearance must be checked. See DIFFERENTIAL BEARING SIDE CLEARANCE under TRANSAXLE REASSEMBLY.

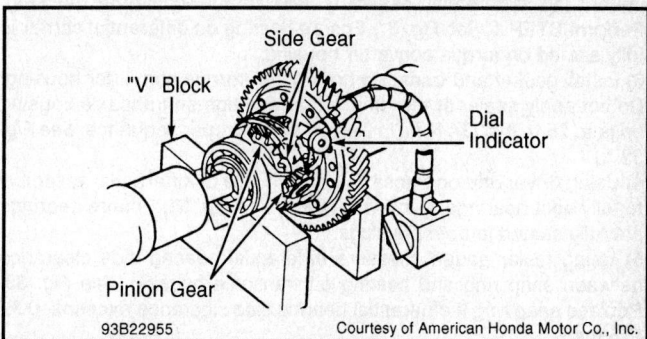

93B22955   Courtesy of American Honda Motor Co., Inc.

Fig. 28: Checking Pinion Gear Backlash

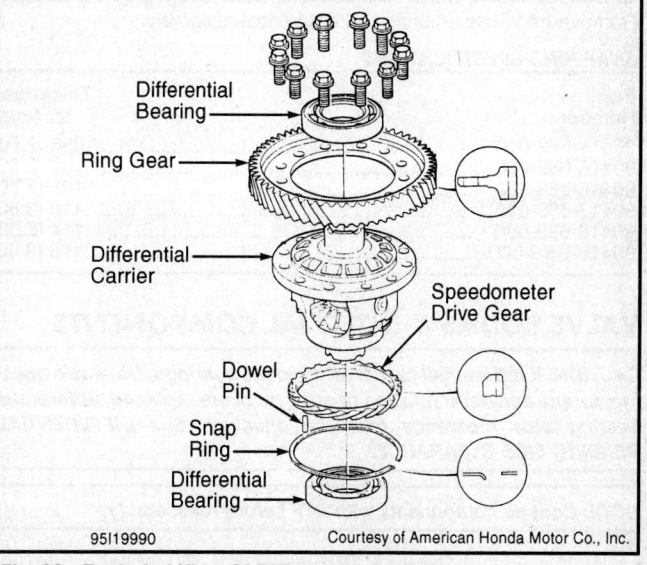

95I19990   Courtesy of American Honda Motor Co., Inc.

Fig. 29: Exploded View Of Differential Assembly

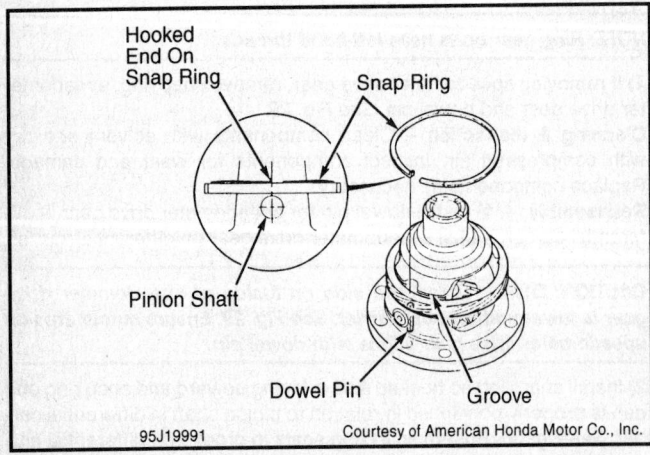

Fig. 30: *Installing Speedometer Drive Gear Retaining Snap Ring*

TRANSAXLE REASSEMBLY

DIFFERENTIAL BEARING SIDE CLEARANCE

CAUTION: If differential carrier, differential bearings, transaxle housing, torque converter housing or snap rings are replaced, differential bearing side clearance must be checked.

1) Ensure differential oil seal is not installed in transaxle housing. Install .098" (2.50 mm) thick snap ring in transaxle housing. This is the snap ring that differential bearing seats against. Ensure snap ring is fully seated.

2) Install differential assembly on torque converter housing. Using driver, tap differential assembly into torque converter housing. Perform STEP 1. *See Fig. 31.* Ensure bearing on differential carrier is fully seated on torque converter housing.

3) Install gasket and transaxle housing on torque converter housing. Do not apply sealer at this time. Install and tighten transaxle housing bolts to 25 ft. lbs. (34 N.m) in 2 steps using proper sequence. *See Fig. 32.*

4) Using driver, tap on transaxle housing side of differential assembly to fully seat bearings. Perform STEP 2. *See Fig. 31.* Ensure bearings are fully seated in both housings.

5) Using feeler gauge, measure differential bearing side clearance between snap ring and bearing on transaxle housing. *See Fig. 33.* Replace snap ring if differential bearing side clearance exceeds .006" (.15 mm).

6) Different thickness snap rings are available. See SNAP RING SPECIFICATIONS table. Recheck differential bearing side clearance. Remove transaxle housing and differential assembly.

SNAP RING SPECIFICATIONS

Part Number	Thickness In. (mm)
90414-689-000	.098 (2.50)
90415-689-000	.102 (2.60)
90416-689-000	.106 (2.70)
90417-689-000	.110 (2.80)
90418-689-000	.114 (2.90)
90419-PH8-000	.118 (3.00)

VALVE BODIES & INTERNAL COMPONENTS

CAUTION: If differential carrier, differential bearings, transaxle housing, torque converter housing or snap rings are replaced, differential bearing side clearance must be checked. See DIFFERENTIAL BEARING SIDE CLEARANCE.

NOTE: Coat all components with ATF before reassembly.

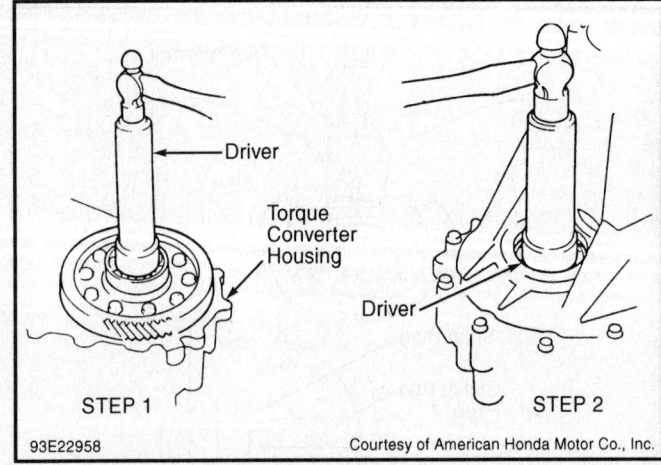

Fig. 31: *Installing Differential Assembly*

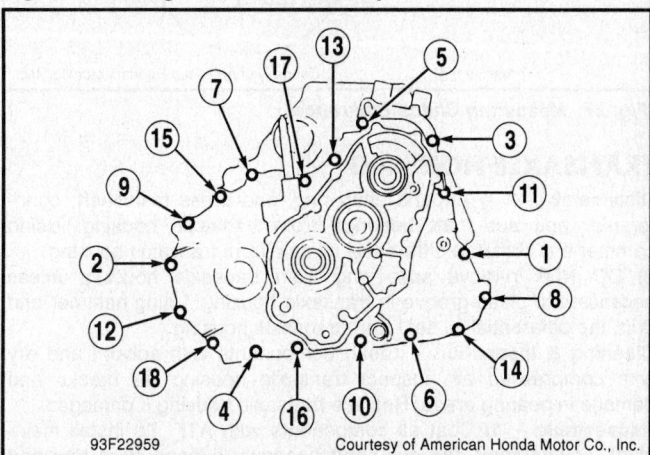

Fig. 32: *Transaxle Housing Bolt Tightening Sequence*

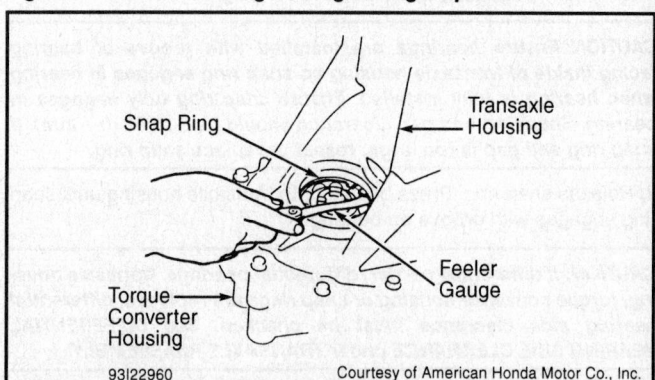

Fig. 33: *Checking Differential Bearing Side Clearance*

1) Install needle bearing on end of reverse idler gear holder. Install reverse idler gear in transaxle housing. Install reverse idler gear holder on transaxle housing. Install and tighten reverse idler gear holder bolts to specification. See TORQUE SPECIFICATIONS.

2) Install fluid strainer on torque converter housing. Install dowel pins and separator plate for main valve body on torque converter housing.

CAUTION: Ensure oil pump driven gear is installed with groove and chamfered side facing downward (toward main separator plate).

3) Install oil pump drive gear, oil pump driven gear and oil pump driven gear shaft. Install main valve body. Install and slightly tighten main valve body bolts.

CAUTION: *Ensure oil pump gears rotate smoothly and oil pump driven gear shaft moves freely once main valve body is installed. If components do not operate correctly, loosen main valve body bolts, and realign oil pump gears and oil pump driven gear shaft. Failure to align oil pump driven gear shaft may result in seized oil pump gears or shaft.*

4) Ensure check balls are installed in main valve body. See Fig. 12. Install separator plate, dowel pins, secondary valve body and retaining bolt.

5) Install control shaft on torque converter housing. Ensure control shaft engages with manual valve on main valve body.

6) Install detent arm and detent arm shaft on main valve body. Hook detent spring on detent arm and control shaft.

7) Ensure check balls and filter are installed on secondary valve body. See Fig. 15. Install separator plate and servo body. Install and tighten secondary valve body and servo body bolts to specification.

8) Install dowel pins, separator plate and modulator valve body. Install and tighten bolts to specification. Install accumulator cover. Install and tighten bolts to specification.

9) Install baffle plate and servo detent base. Install bolts and NEW bolt locks on servo detent base. Tighten bolts to specification. Bend over tabs on bolt locks.

10) Install dowel pin and governor body. Install bolts and NEW bolt locks on governor body. Tighten bolts to specification. Bend over tabs on bolt locks.

11) Tighten main valve body bolts to specification. Ensure oil pump gears rotate smoothly and oil pump driven gear shaft moves freely once main valve body is installed. If components do not operate correctly, loosen main valve body bolts, and realign oil pump gears and oil pump driven gear shaft. Failure to align oil pump driven gear shaft may result in seized oil pump gears or shaft.

12) Install stator shaft, NEW "O" ring and stopper shaft. Install regulator valve body with one retaining bolt.

13) Install dowel pins, separator plate and lock-up valve body. Install and tighten regulator valve body and lock-up valve body bolts to specification. Install all oil feedpipes. See Fig. 11.

14) Install sub-shaft assembly. See SUB-SHAFT & COMPONENTS under COMPONENT DISASSEMBLY & REASSEMBLY. Install differential assembly in torque converter housing. Using driver, tap differential assembly into torque converter housing. Perform STEP 1. See Fig. 31. Ensure bearing on differential carrier is fully seated on torque converter housing.

15) Install mainshaft and countershaft as an assembly on torque converter housing. Rotate shift fork shaft on servo body so large chamfered hole aligns with hole in reverse shift fork.

16) Install shift fork and reverse selector. See Fig. 10. Install shift fork bolt and NEW bolt lock. Tighten bolt to specification. Bend over tabs on bolt lock.

17) Install countershaft reverse gear, needle bearing and collar on countershaft. Align spring pin on control shaft with groove on transaxle housing by rotating control shaft. See Fig. 9. Install dowel pins and NEW gasket on torque converter housing.

18) Install transaxle housing on torque converter housing. Install and tighten transaxle housing bolts to specification in 2 steps using proper sequence. See Fig. 32.

19) Install mount bracket on transaxle housing. Install and tighten mount bracket bolts to specification.

20) Install mainshaft holder on mainshaft to secure mainshaft from rotating. See Fig. 7. Install parking brake lever and parking brake lever spring on control shaft. See Fig. 6.

21) Install countershaft 1st gear collar, needle bearing and countershaft 1st gear with one-way clutch and parking gear on countershaft.

22) Install parking brake stopper, bolt and NEW bolt lock. DO NOT tighten bolt at this time. Install parking pawl stopper, parking pawl shaft, parking pawl spring and parking pawl.

NOTE: *On 1996 models, countershaft lock nut has left hand threads. DO NOT use impact wrench to tighten lock nut.*

23) Engage parking pawl with parking gear. Install old beveled spring washer (1996) and old countershaft lock nut on countershaft. Tighten countershaft lock nut to 77 ft. lbs. (105 N.m) to seat parking gear and countershaft 1st gear on countershaft. Remove old countershaft lock nut from countershaft.

24) Install sub-shaft 1st gear on sub-shaft. Install mainshaft 1st gear collar on mainshaft. Apply tape to mainshaft splines to prevent damage to "O" rings. Install NEW "O" rings on mainshaft.

25) Install needle bearing, thrust needle bearing, thrust washer and mainshaft 1st gear in 1st clutch assembly and install on mainshaft. See Fig. 6.

26) Ensure sub-shaft 1st gear is installed in proper direction. Align hole in sub-shaft 1st gear with hole in transaxle housing.

27) Install pin in sub-shaft 1st gear and transaxle housing to prevent sub-shaft 1st gear from rotating while tightening lock nut. See Fig. 8. Install NEW beveled spring washer on sub-shaft, countershaft (1996) and mainshaft (1996).

CAUTION: *Ensure beveled spring washers are installed with largest area away from lock nut. See Fig. 6.*

NOTE: *Mainshaft has left-hand threads. Countershaft in 1996 has left hand-threads. DO NOT use impact wrench to tighten lock nuts.*

28) Install NEW lock nuts on countershaft, mainshaft and sub-shaft. Tighten lock nuts to specification. Remove pin from sub-shaft 1st gear. Remove mainshaft holder.

29) Stake flange area of mainshaft lock nut against 1st clutch assembly. Stake flange area of countershaft lock nut against parking gear. Stake thread area of sub-shaft lock nut against threads of sub-shaft.

CAUTION: *Ensure all lock nuts are securely staked.*

30) Place parking brake lever in "P" position. Ensure parking pawl fully engages parking gear.

31) If parking pawl does not fully engage, measure parking brake stopper distance between parking pawl shaft and pin on parking brake lever. See Fig. 34.

32) Parking brake stopper distance should be 3.100-3.140" (78.75-79.75 mm). If parking brake stopper distance is not within specification, install different size parking brake stopper, and recheck parking brake stopper distance.

33) Parking brake stopper is available in different sizes. See PARKING BRAKE STOPPER SPECIFICATIONS table.

PARKING BRAKE STOPPER SPECIFICATIONS

I.D. Mark	Part Number	[1] Distance "A" In. (mm)	[1] Distance "B" In. (mm)
1	24537-PA9-003	.433 (11.00)	.433 (11.00)
2	24538-PA9-003	.425 (10.80)	.419 (10.65)
3	24539-PA9-003	.417 (10.60)	.406 (10.30)

[1] – Measured from center of parking brake stopper. See Fig. 34.

34) Tighten parking brake stopper bolt to specification. Bend over tabs on bolt lock. Using NEW gasket, install right side cover. Install and tighten bolts to specification.

35) To install remaining components, reverse removal procedure. Ensure NEW seal washers are used when installing joint bolts for cooler pipes. Tighten all fasteners to specification.

CAUTION: *If transaxle failure existed, flush oil cooler. See OIL COOLER FLUSHING under ON-VEHICLE SERVICE.*

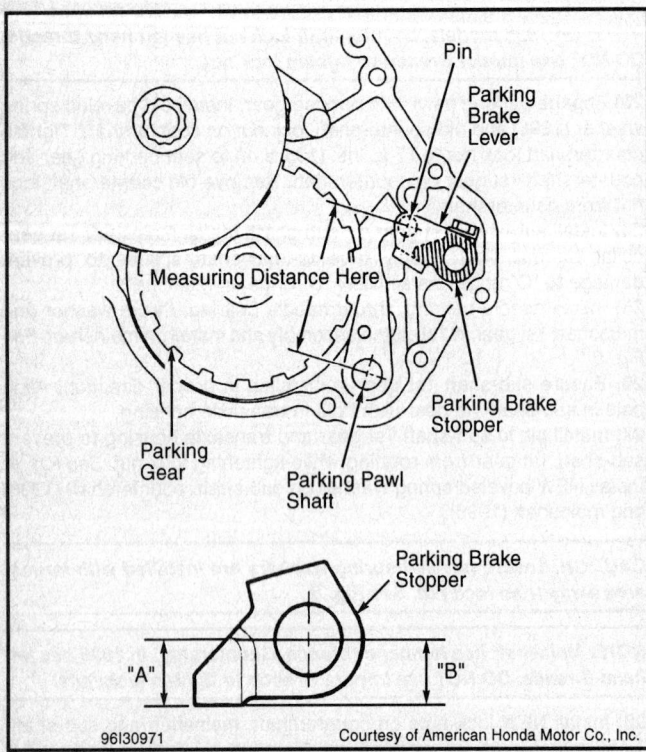

Fig. 34: Measuring Parking Brake Stopper Distance & Parking
Brake Stopper

TRANSAXLE SPECIFICATIONS

TRANSAXLE SPECIFICATIONS

Application	Specification
Clutch Clearance	
1st & 2nd Clutches	.026-.033" (.65-.85 mm)
1st-Hold Clutch	.020-.031" (.50-.80 mm)
3rd & 4th Clutches	.016-.024" (.40-.60 mm)
Differential Bearing Side Clearance	[1] .006" (.15 mm)
Differential Pinion Gear Backlash	.003-.006" (.08-.15 mm)
Gear Clearances	
Countershaft	
1995	
2nd Gear-To-3rd Gear Clearance	.002-.005" (.05-.13 mm)
4th Gear Clearance	.002-.005" (.05-.13 mm)
1996	
4th Gear Clearance	.004-.007" (.10-.18 mm)
Mainshaft	
2nd Gear-To-3rd Gear Clearance	.002-.005" (.05-.13 mm)
Oil Pump Clearances	
Side Clearance	
Oil Pump Drive Gear	.0083-.0104" (.210-.265 mm)
Oil Pump Driven Gear	
1995	.0028-.0049" (.070-.125 mm)
1996	.0014-.0025" (.035-.065 mm)
Thrust Clearance	
Standard	.0016-.0024" (.034-.056 mm)
Wear Limit	.0028" (.070 mm)
Parking Brake Stopper Distance	3.100-3.140" (78.75-79.75 mm)

[1] – This is the maximum clearance. Replace snap ring with different
thickness snap ring if clearance exceeds specification.

TORQUE SPECIFICATIONS

TORQUE SPECIFICATIONS

Application	Ft. Lbs. (N.m)
Cooler Pipes	21 (29)
Countershaft Lock Nut	77 (105)
Drain Plug	36 (49)
Joint Bolt	21 (29)
Mainshaft Lock Nut	58 (80)
Mount Bracket Bolt	36 (49)
Pressure Tap Plug	13 (18)
Ring Gear Bolt	76 (103)
Speed Sensor Bolt	16 (22)
Sub-Shaft Lock Nut	70 (95)
Transaxle Housing Bolt [1]	33 (45)

Application	INCH Lbs. (N.m)
Accumulator Cover Bolt	106 (12.0)
Breather Cover Bolt	97 (11.0)
Governor Body Bolt	106 (12.0)
Governor Housing-To-Governor Shaft Bolt	106 (12.0)
Lock-Up Control Solenoid Valve Assembly Bolt	106 (12.0)
Lock-Up Valve Body Bolt	106 (12.0)
Main Valve Body Bolt	106 (12.0)
Modulator Valve Body Bolt	106 (12.0)
Needle Bearing Stopper Bolt	106 (12.0)
Parking Brake Stopper Bolt	124 (14.0)
Regulator Valve Body Bolt	106 (12.0)
Reverse Idler Gear Holder Bolt	106 (12.0)
Right Side Cover Bolt	108 (12.0)
Secondary Valve Body Bolt	106 (12.0)
Servo Body Bolt	106 (12.0)
Servo Detent Base Bolt	106 (12.0)
Shift Fork Bolt	124 (14.0)
Stopper Bolt	106 (12.0)
Throttle Cam Stopper Bolt	106 (12.0)
Valve Cover Bolt	71 (8.0)

[1] – Tighten bolts to specification in sequence. *See Fig. 32.*

Civic, Civic Del Sol

APPLICATION

APPLICATION

Vehicle	Transaxle Model
1995 Civic	A24A
1995-96 Civic Del Sol	S24A

CAUTION: Vehicle is equipped with a Supplemental Restraint System (SRS). When servicing vehicle, use care to avoid accidental air bag deployment. All SRS electrical connections and wiring harness are covered with Yellow insulation. SRS-related components are located in steering column, center console, instrument panel and lower panel on instrument panel. DO NOT use electrical test equipment on these circuits. It may be necessary to deactivate SRS before servicing components. See AIR BAG SERVICING article in APPLICATIONS & IDENTIFICATION section.

NOTE: If negative battery cable is to be disconnected, obtain radio anti-theft code from customer before disconnecting negative battery cable. Radio anti-theft code must be re-entered into radio once negative battery cable is reconnected. To re-enter radio anti-theft code, turn ignition and radio on. When the word "CODE" is displayed on radio, re-enter radio anti-theft code by using the radio station preset buttons.

DESCRIPTION

Automatic transaxle torque converter lock-up is controlled by the Engine Control Module (ECM). This is the ECM used for controlling the electronic fuel injection system and torque converter lock-up. The ECM receives information from various input devices and uses information for controlling torque converter lock-up by operating the lock-up control solenoid valves.

Transaxle is equipped with shift and key interlock systems. Shift interlock system prevents shift lever from being moved from Park unless brake pedal is depressed and accelerator is in idle position. In case of a malfunction, shift lever can be released by placing ignition key in ignition key release slot near shift lever. Key interlock system prevents ignition key from being removed from ignition lock assembly on steering column unless shift lever is in Park.

The A/T gear position indicator on instrument panel contains lights to indicate which position A/T gear position switch on shift lever is in.

OPERATION

A/T GEAR POSITION INDICATOR

With ignition in RUN or START position, voltage is supplied to A/T gear position indicator, located on instrument panel. See Fig. 1. When shift lever is moved to designated gear position, A/T gear position switch completes the ground circuit for A/T gear position indicator on instrument panel. The light on A/T gear position indicator will be illuminated to indicate shift lever gear position. The A/T gear position switch is mounted on passenger's side of shift lever. See Fig. 2.

When headlights are turned on, voltage is supplied on Red/Black wire terminal on A/T gear position indicator. This changes light illumination from fixed illumination to being controlled by the dash light dimmer input on the Red wire.

SHIFT & KEY INTERLOCK SYSTEMS

Shift Interlock System – Shift interlock system prevents shift lever from being moved from Park unless brake pedal is depressed and accelerator is in idle position. In case of a malfunction, shift lever can be released by placing ignition key in release slot near shift lever. Voltage is provided to shift lock solenoid when ignition is on.

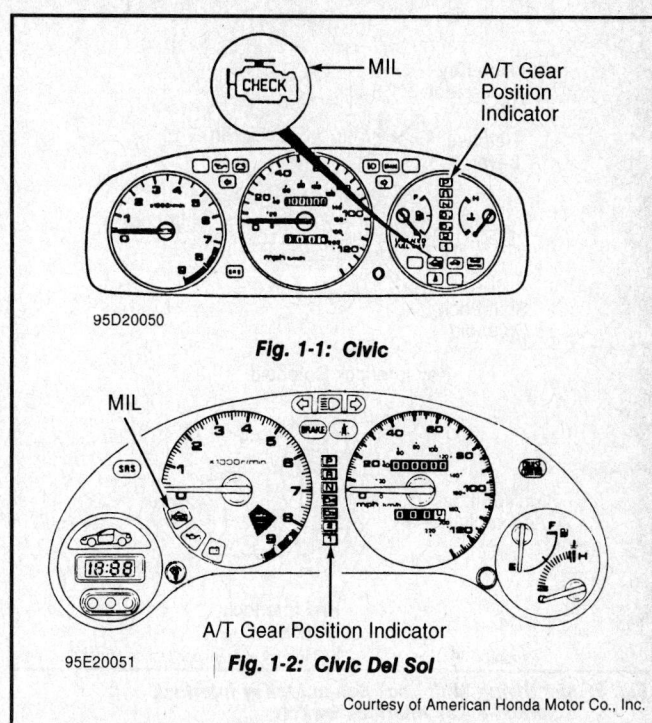

95D20050

Fig. 1-1: Civic

95E20051 | **Fig. 1-2: Civic Del Sol**

A/T Gear Position Indicator

Courtesy of American Honda Motor Co., Inc.

Fig. 1: Identifying A/T Gear Position Indicator & MIL Light

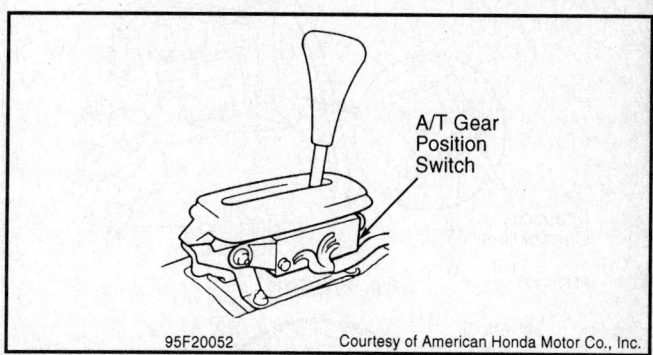

A/T Gear Position Switch

95F20052   Courtesy of American Honda Motor Co., Inc.

Fig. 2: Identifying A/T Gear Position Switch

When brake pedal is depressed, battery voltage is supplied to the Engine Control Module (ECM) on the Green/White wire from brakelight switch. With accelerator pedal is in idle position, a low-voltage signal is sent from throttle position sensor to the ECM. When the A/T gear position switch is in Park, ECM provides voltage to shift lock circuit in the interlock control unit, provided brake pedal is depressed and accelerator is in idle position. Interlock control unit then operates shift lock solenoid by controlling the ground circuit. When shift lock solenoid is energized, shift lever is released and can be moved.

The A/T gear position switch is mounted on passenger's side of shift lever. See Fig. 1. Shift lock solenoid is located on driver's side of shift lever. See Fig. 3. The ECM is located behind carpet, near passenger's side kick panel. See Fig. 6. Interlock control unit is located below driver's side of instrument panel on Civic and to right of instrument cluster on Civic Del Sol. Interlock control unit contains a Gray colored 8-pin electrical connector. See Fig. 4.

Key Interlock System – Key interlock system prevents ignition key from being removed from ignition lock assembly unless shift lever is in Park position. Voltage is provided to key interlock switch from fuse No. 42 (20-amp on Civic and 15-amp on Civic Del Sol) in engine compartment fuse/relay box. Engine compartment fuse/relay box is located on passenger's side rear corner of engine compartment, near battery.

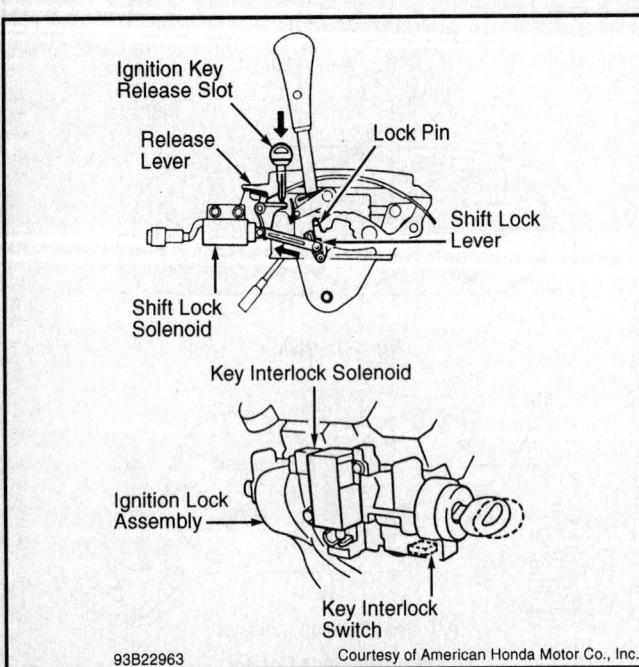

Fig. 3: Identifying Shift Lock Solenoid, Key Interlock Solenoid & Key Interlock Switch

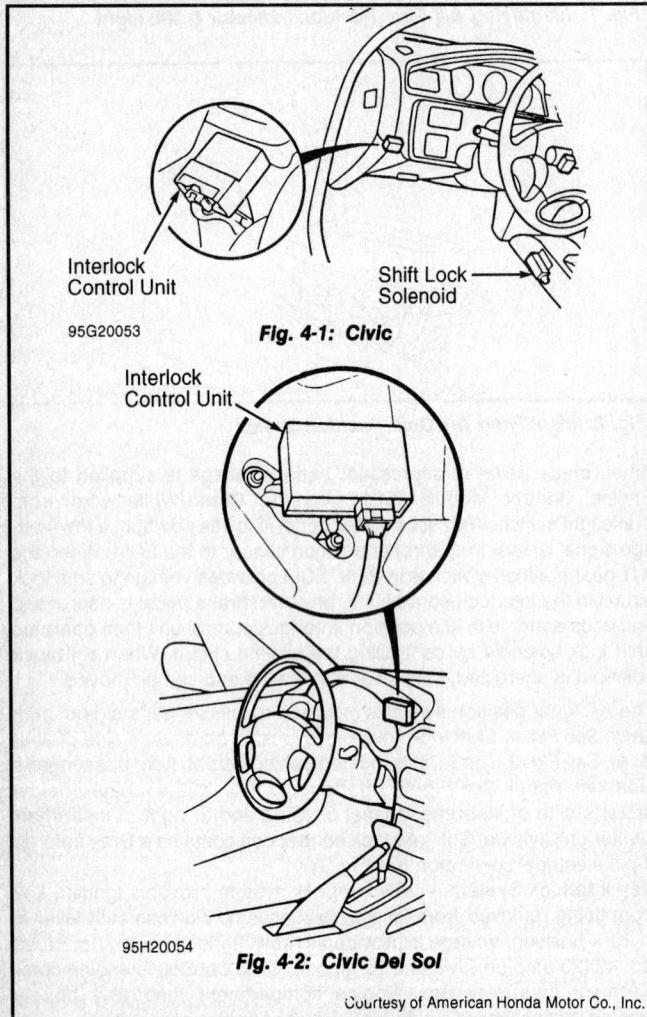

Fig. 4-1: Civic

Fig. 4-2: Civic Del Sol

Fig. 4: Identifying Interlock Control Unit

When ignition key is installed in ignition lock assembly, key interlock switch closes, providing voltage to key interlock solenoid and interlock control unit.

If shift lever is not in Park, interlock control unit activates key interlock solenoid by completing ground circuit, preventing ignition key from being removed from ignition lock assembly. Key interlock switch and solenoid are located on ignition lock assembly. *See Fig. 3.* Interlock control unit is located below driver's side of instrument panel and contains a Gray 8-pin electrical connector. *See Fig. 4.*

ENGINE CONTROL MODULE (ECM) & LOCK-UP CONTROL SOLENOID VALVES

The ECM controls electronic fuel injection system and torque converter lock-up. The ECM receives information from various input devices and uses information to control torque converter lock-up by operating lock-up control solenoid valves "A" and "B". Solenoid valves are operated in accordance with lock-up condition. See LOCK-UP CONTROL SOLENOID VALVE OPERATION table.

Lock-up control solenoid valves are located on transaxle, below distributor. *See Fig. 5.* Lock-up control solenoid valve "A" has a Yellow wire and solenoid valve "B" has a Green/Black wire.

The ECM contains a self-diagnostic system which will store code if failure or problem exists in lock-up control solenoid valves or wiring circuit. Fault code may also be referred to as Diagnostic Trouble Code (DTC). Flash code can be displayed and DTC can be retrieved using scan tool to determine whether problem exists in lock-up control solenoid valves, wiring circuit or gear position switch circuit (1996). For information on self-diagnostic system, see SELF-DIAGNOSTIC SYSTEM. The ECM is located behind carpet, near passenger's side kick panel. *See Fig. 6.*

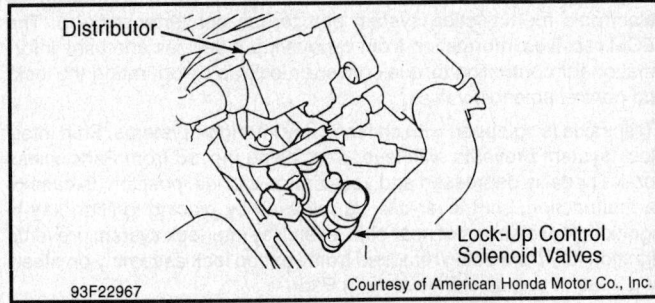

Fig. 5: Identifying Lock-Up Control Solenoid Valves

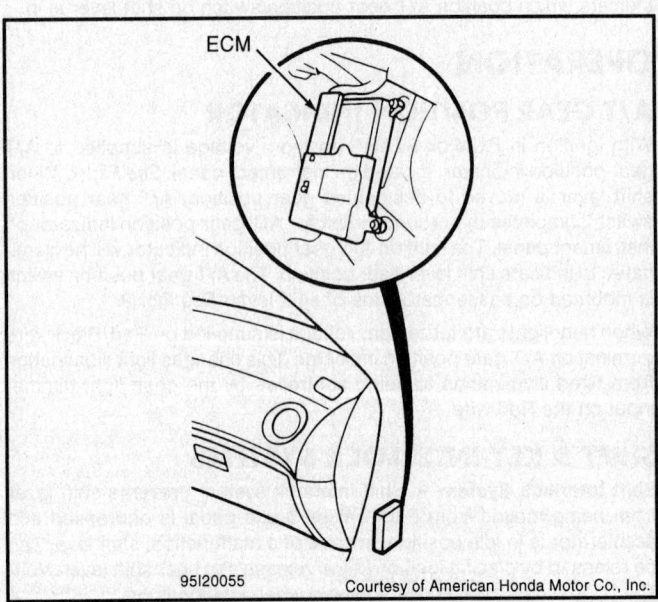

Fig. 6: Identifying Engine Control Module (ECM)

LOCK-UP CONTROL SOLENOID VALVE OPERATION

Lock-Up Condition	Solenoid Valve "A"	Solenoid Valve "B"
No Lock-Up	Off	Off
Slight Lock-Up	On	1
Half Lock-Up	On	On
Full Lock-Up	On	On
Lock-Up During Deceleration	On	1

1 – Solenoid valve will cycle on and off.

SELF-DIAGNOSTIC SYSTEM

SYSTEM DIAGNOSIS

The Engine Control Module (ECM) contains a self-diagnostic system, which will store Diagnostic Trouble Code (DTC) if failure or problem exists in lock-up control solenoid valves, wiring circuit or gear position switch circuit (1996). If DTC code is stored, ECM will turn on Malfunction Indicator Light (MIL) on instrument panel displaying flash code and store DTC in memory. *See Fig. 1.* Flash Codes can be retrieved on all years/models but are the only codes available on 1995 models. On 1996 models, DTC can be retrieved from ECM memory using scan tool at Data Link Connector (DLC) located on right side of center console behind inspection cover.

NOTE: The MIL will also be turned on if problem exists in electronic fuel injection system.

RETRIEVING DTCS & FLASH CODES

NOTE: DTC/Flash Codes must be retrieved if MIL on instrument panel remains on. See Fig. 1. If torque converter lock-up does not operate and MIL is not on, perform diagnostic circuit check to ensure proper operation of MIL. See DIAGNOSTIC CIRCUIT CHECK procedure.

NOTE: Before any diagnostic procedure, obtain radio anti-theft code from customer. Note radio preset stations, as radio stations and clock setting will be cleared and must be reset. Radio anti-theft code must be re-entered for radio operation.

Diagnostic Circuit Check – Turn ignition on. Ensure Malfunction Indicator Light (MIL) on the instrument panel comes on for about 2 seconds and then goes off. *See Fig. 1.* If MIL does not come on or remains on after 2 seconds, light circuit must be checked. See see appropriate SELF-DIAGNOSTICS article in ENGINE PERFORMANCE in appropriate MITCHELL® manual. If MIL comes on for about 2 seconds and then goes off, go to RETRIEVING DTCS USING SCAN TOOL or RETRIEVING FLASH CODES USING MIL LIGHT.

Retrieving DTCs Using Scan Tool – **1)** If DTC exists, MIL light on instrument panel will blink when ignition is turned on. To retrieve DTC using scan tool, turn ignition off.

2) Connect scan tool to 16-pin Data Link Connector (DLC) located on right side of center console behind inspection cover. Turn ignition on. Scan tool will indicate DTCs. Follow scan tool manufacturers instructions.

3) Once DTC is obtained, turn ignition off. Determine probable cause and symptom and see TROUBLE SHOOTING. If any other codes except those listed are displayed, see appropriate SELF-DIAGNOSTICS article in ENGINE PERFORMANCE in appropriate MITCHELL® manual.

Retrieving Flash Codes Using MIL Light – **1)** To retrieve flash codes, ensure ignition is off. Install jumper wire between terminals of service check connector, located behind passenger-side kick panel, near glove box. *See Fig. 7.*

CAUTION: Service check connector is a 2-pin Blue colored connector. DO NOT use 3-pin connector located near service check connector.

2) Turn ignition on. Note number of blinks from MIL on instrument panel. A short blink indicates number one and a long blink indicates number 10.

3) For example, a Flash Code No. 3 is indicated by MIL blinking 3 times. *See Fig. 8.* Flash Code No. 13 is indicated by one long blink and then 3 short blinks. If more than one flash code exists, flash codes will be displayed one after another.

4) If failure or problem exists in lock-up control solenoid valves or wiring circuit, Flash Code No. 19 will be displayed. See TROUBLE SHOOTING. If any other flash code besides Flash Code No. 19 exists, electronic fuel injection system must be checked. See appropriate SELF-DIAGNOSTICS article in ENGINE PERFORMANCE in appropriate MITCHELL® manual.

5) Once flash codes are retrieved, turn ignition off. Remove jumper wire from service check connector. Clear flash codes from ECM memory. See CLEARING CODES under SELF-DIAGNOSTIC SYSTEM.

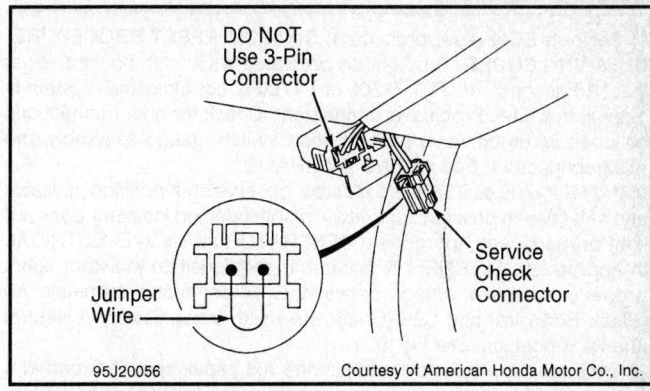

Fig. 7: Identifying Service Check Connector

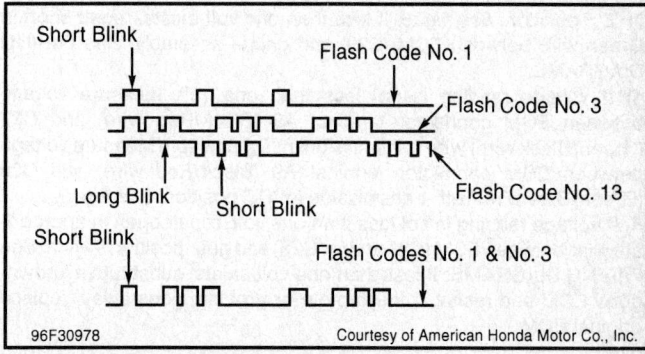

Fig. 8: Identifying Flash Code Displays

CLEARING CODES

NOTE: Before clearing codes, note radio preset stations, as radio stations and clock setting will be cleared and must be reset. Before clearing codes, obtain radio anti-theft code from customer. Radio anti-theft code must be re-entered for radio operation.

1) Once repairs have been performed, codes must be cleared from ECM memory. Use scan tool and follow manufacturers instructions. If scan tool is not being used, remove No. 32 BACK-UP fuse (7.5-amp) in engine compartment fuse box for 10 seconds. Engine compartment fuse/relay box is located on passenger's side rear corner of engine compartment, near battery.

2) Reinstall fuse. To re-enter radio anti-theft code, turn ignition and radio on. When the word "CODE" is displayed on radio, re-enter radio anti-theft code by using the radio station preset buttons. Reset clock and radio stations.

TROUBLE SHOOTING

NOTE: If transaxle fails to shift from Park, check brakelight signal and shift interlock system. See BRAKELIGHT SIGNAL under TROUBLE SHOOTING and SHIFT & KEY INTERLOCK SYSTEMS under SYSTEM TESTING. If ignition key can be removed from ignition lock assembly with shift lever in any position other than Park, check key interlock system. See SHIFT & KEY INTERLOCK SYSTEMS under SYSTEM TESTING.

DTC P1705 & P1706:
A/T GEAR POSITION SWITCH

NOTE: 1996 Civic Del Sol only. DTC 1705 indicates a problem in A/T gear position switch circuit. DTC 1706 indicates no signal in A/T gear position switch circuit.

1) Perform ECM reset procedure. See ECM RESET PROCEDURE/CLEARING CODES. Turn ignition on. Select each shift position for at least 15 seconds. If DTC P1705 or P1706 is not indicated, system is okay at this time. Problem is intermittent. Check for poor connections or loose wires between gear position switch, gauge assembly and ECM connectors. See WIRING DIAGRAMS.
2) If DTC P1705 or P1706 is indicated, observe shift position indicator and select each position separately. If shift position indicator does not light properly, see appropriate GENERATOR article in ELECTRICAL in appropriate MITCHELL® manual. If shift position indicator lights properly, measure voltage between ECM connector terminals A9 (Black/Red wire) and C29 (Green wire) with transmission in Neutral and Park position. See Fig. 9.
3) If voltage reading is not less than one volt, repair open in Green wire between ECM (C29) and gauge assembly. See WIRING DIAGRAMS. If less than one volt exists, measure voltage between ECM connector terminals A9 (Black/Red wire) and C29 (Green wire) with transmission in "D₄" position. See Fig. 9. If less than one volt exists, repair short in Green wire between ECM (C29) and gauge assembly. See WIRING DIAGRAMS.
4) If voltage reading is not less than one volt, measure voltage between ECM connector terminal A9 (Black/Red wire) and C27 (Green/Black wire) with transmission in "D₄" position. Measure voltage between ECM connector terminal A9 (Black/Red wire) and C28 (Green/Blue wire) with transmission in "D₃" position. See Fig. 9.
5) If voltage reading is not less than one volt, repair open in appropriate wire between ECM (C27 and/or C28) and gear position switch. See WIRING DIAGRAMS. If less than one volt exists, substitute a known-good ECM and recheck. If symptom or problem goes away, replace original ECM.

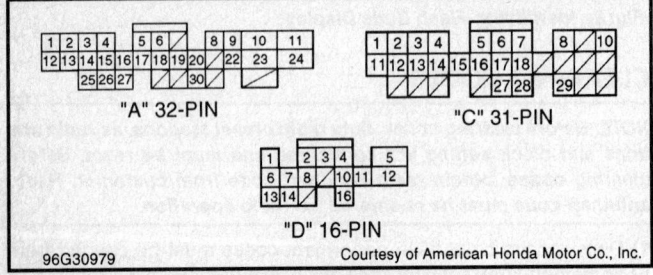

Fig. 9: Identifying ECM Connector Terminals

"A" 32-PIN   "C" 31-PIN   "D" 16-PIN

96G30979   Courtesy of American Honda Motor Co., Inc.

DTC P1753 & P1758 (FLASH CODE 19):
A/T LOCK-UP CONTROL SOLENOID VALVE

NOTE: DTCs 1753 and P1758 (Flash Code 19) indicate a problem in A/T lock-up control solenoid valve.

1) Perform ECM reset procedure. See CLEARING CODES. Test-drive vehicle several miles, ensure transmission upshifts and downshifts several times. If DTCs P1753 and/or P1758 (Flash Code 19) are not indicated, system is okay at this time. Problem is intermittent. Check for poor connections or loose wires between lock-up control solenoid A/B and ECM connectors. Lock-up control solenoid valves are located on transaxle, below distributor. See Fig. 5. See WIRING DIAGRAMS. On 1995 models, check connectors C426 and C303. See Fig. 10.
2) On all models, if DTC P1753 or P1758 (Flash Code 19) is indicated, turn ignition off. On 1995 models, go to step 7). On 1996 models, go to next step.

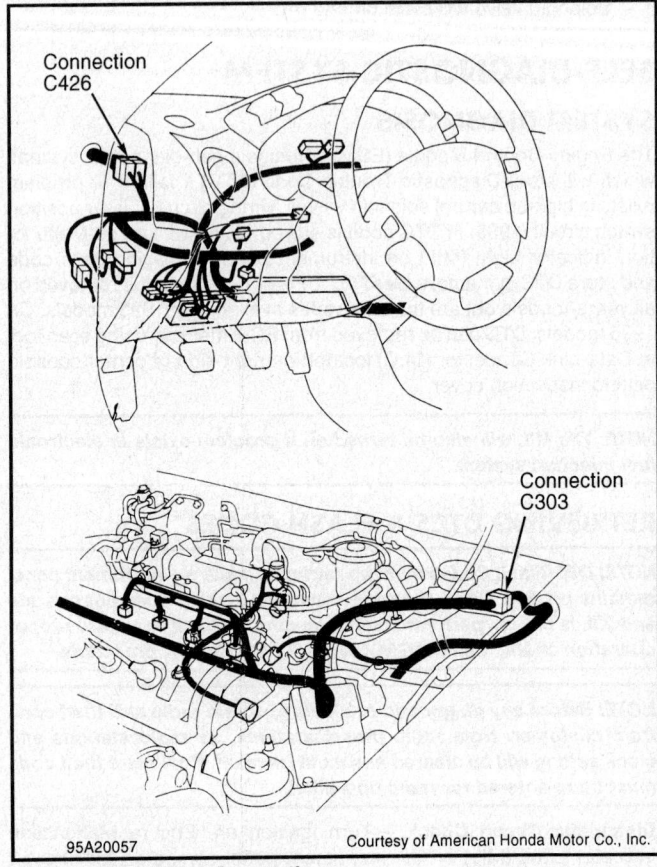

Connection C426

Connection C303

95A20057   Courtesy of American Honda Motor Co., Inc.

Fig. 10: Identifying Connections

3) Disconnect ECM connector "A". See Fig. 9. Disconnect lock-up control solenoid connector. Lock-up control solenoid 2-pin connector is located at lower front of transmission and contains Green/Black and Yellow wires. Check for continuity between ground and ECM connector terminals A25 (Green/Black wire) and A26 (Yellow wire) individually.
4) If continuity exists, repair short to ground in appropriate wire between ECM connector and lock-up control solenoid connector. See WIRING DIAGRAMS. If continuity does not exist, reconnect lock-up control solenoid connector. Check resistance between ECM connector terminal A9 (Black/Red wire) and terminals A25 (Green/Black wire) and A26 (Yellow wire) individually.
5) If resistance is 10-22 ohms, substitute a known-good ECM and recheck. If symptom or problem goes away, replace original ECM. If resistance is not 10-22 ohms, check for continuity in Green/Black wire between ECM connector terminal A25 and lock-up control solenoid connector. Check for continuity in Yellow wire between ECM connector terminal A26 and lock-up control solenoid connector.
6) If continuity exists, replace lock-up control solenoid valve. If continuity does not exist, repair open in appropriate wire between ECM and lock-up control solenoid connector. See WIRING DIAGRAMS.
7) Remove bolts and ECM cover. Disconnect wiring harness from ECM. Connect Test Harness (07LAJ-PT3010A) to wiring harness only. DO NOT connect test harness to ECM. See Fig. 11.

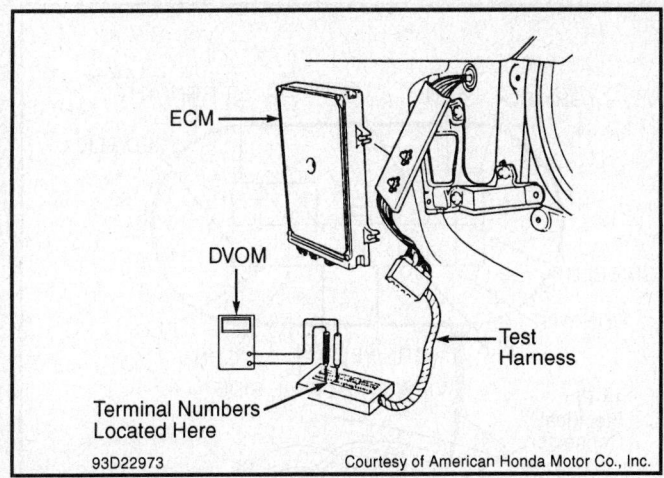

ECM

DVOM

Test Harness

Terminal Numbers Located Here

93D22973

Courtesy of American Honda Motor Co., Inc.

Fig. 11: Installing Test Harness

8) Disconnect electrical connector from lock-up control solenoid valves located on transaxle, below distributor. See Fig. 5.

9) Using Digital Volt-Ohmmeter (DVOM), check continuity between body ground and test harness terminals A19 and A17. Terminal A19 is for lock-up control solenoid valve "A" and terminal A17 is for control solenoid valve "B". Terminal numbers are stamped on top of test harness. See Fig. 11.

10) If continuity does not exist, proceed to step 11). If continuity exists at terminal A19, repair short circuit in Yellow wire (solenoid valve "A") between ECM and lock-up control solenoid valve electrical connector. If continuity exists at terminal A17, repair short circuit in Green/Black wire (solenoid valve "B") between ECM and lock-up control solenoid valve electrical connector.

11) Reconnect electrical connector at lock-up control solenoid valves. Using DVOM, check resistance between test harness terminal A26 and terminals A19 and A17. If resistance is not 14-25 ohms, proceed to step 12). If resistance is 14-25 ohms, substitute a known good ECM and recheck system operation. If system operates okay, replace original ECM.

12) Using DVOM, check continuity on Yellow wire (solenoid valve "A") or Green/Black wire (solenoid valve "B") between ECM and lock-up control solenoid valve electrical connector.

13) If continuity exists on Yellow wire or Green/Black wire, replace lock-up control solenoid valve assembly. See LOCK-UP CONTROL SOLENOID VALVES under REMOVAL & INSTALLATION.

14) If continuity does not exist on Yellow wire or Green/Black wire, repair open circuit in Yellow wire or Green/Black wire between ECM and lock-up control solenoid valve electrical connector.

15) Once all repairs are completed, remove test harness. Reconnect wiring harness at ECM. Reinstall ECM cover, carpet and sill molding. Clear codes from ECM memory. See CLEARING CODES under SELF-DIAGNOSTIC SYSTEM.

BRAKELIGHT SIGNAL

NOTE: If no brakelight signal exists, transaxle may fail to shift from Park with brake pedal depressed.

1) Ensure brakelights come on when brake pedal is depressed. If brakelights do not come on, ensure STOP/HORN fuse in engine compartment fuse/relay box is okay.

2) Engine compartment fuse/relay box is located on passenger's side rear corner of engine compartment, near battery. If fuse is okay, repair brakelight signal circuit and check brakelight switch. See BRAKELIGHT SWITCH under COMPONENT TESTING.

3) If brakelights come on, ensure ignition is off. Remove sill molding from passenger's side door opening. Pull carpet back to access ECM. The ECM is located behind carpet, near passenger's side kick panel. See Fig. 6. Remove bolts and ECM cover.

4) On 1995 models, disconnect wiring harness from ECM. Connect Test Harness (07LAJ-PT3010A) to wiring harness only. DO NOT connect test harness to ECM. See Fig. 11.

5) Depress brake pedal. Using Digital Volt-Ohmmeter (DVOM), check voltage between test harness terminals A26 and D2 on test harness. Terminal numbers are stamped on top of test harness. See Fig. 11.

6) On 1996 models, using DVOM, measure voltage between ECM terminals A9 and D5. See Fig. 9. On all models, if battery voltage exists, brakelight signal to ECM is okay. Check for loose ECM electrical connections. If electrical connections are okay, substitute ECM with a known good unit and recheck operation.

7) If battery voltage does not exist, repair open circuit in Green/White wire between brakelight switch and ECM. Brakelight switch is located above brake pedal.

8) Remove test harness. Reconnect wiring harness at ECM. Reinstall ECM cover, carpet and sill molding.

SYSTEM TESTING

A/T GEAR POSITION INDICATOR

NOTE: If necessary, refer to wiring schematic when checking component wiring. See Fig. 14.

1) Remove instrument panel gauge assembly from instrument panel. Disconnect 14-pin electrical connector from rear of instrument panel gauge assembly. See Fig. 12.

2) Check for voltage and continuity at electrical connectors as specified. See Fig. 12. If necessary to check ground connections G201 or G401, ground connection G201 is located at passenger's side front corner of engine compartment, on inner fender panel. Ground connection G401 is located behind driver's side of instrument panel, above kick panel. See Fig. 13.

3) If necessary to check fuse No. 15 (10-amp), fuse is located in fuse box on driver's side of instrument panel, near steering column. If necessary to access ECM, the ECM is located behind carpet, near passenger's side kick panel. See Fig. 6.

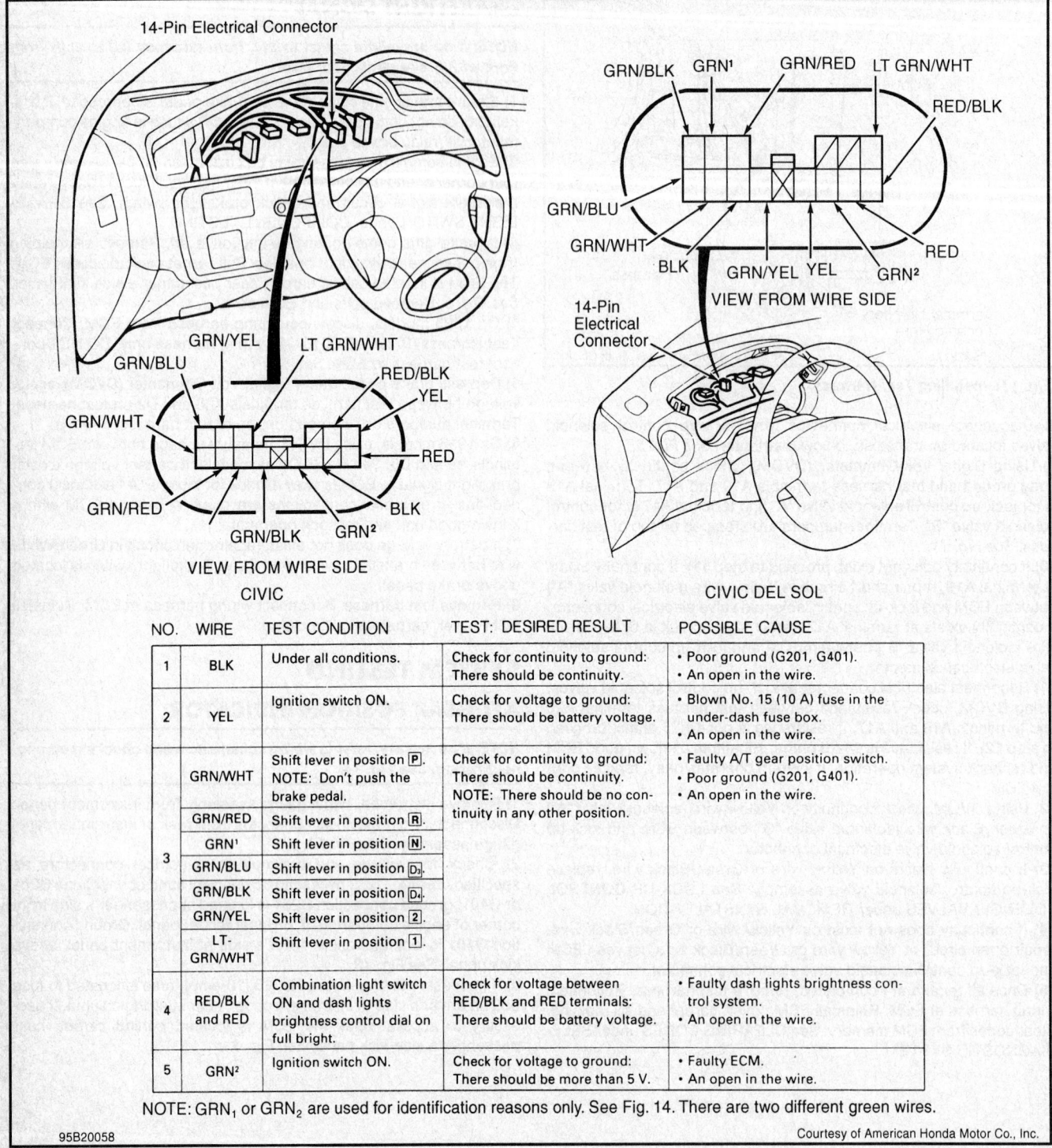

NO.	WIRE	TEST CONDITION	TEST: DESIRED RESULT	POSSIBLE CAUSE
1	BLK	Under all conditions.	Check for continuity to ground: There should be continuity.	• Poor ground (G201, G401). • An open in the wire.
2	YEL	Ignition switch ON.	Check for voltage to ground: There should be battery voltage.	• Blown No. 15 (10 A) fuse in the under-dash fuse box. • An open in the wire.
3	GRN/WHT	Shift lever in position [P]. NOTE: Don't push the brake pedal.	Check for continuity to ground: There should be continuity. NOTE: There should be no continuity in any other position.	• Faulty A/T gear position switch. • Poor ground (G201, G401). • An open in the wire.
	GRN/RED	Shift lever in position [R].		
	GRN^1	Shift lever in position [N].		
	GRN/BLU	Shift lever in position [D₃].		
	GRN/BLK	Shift lever in position [D₄].		
	GRN/YEL	Shift lever in position [2].		
	LT-GRN/WHT	Shift lever in position [1].		
4	RED/BLK and RED	Combination light switch ON and dash lights brightness control dial on full bright.	Check for voltage between RED/BLK and RED terminals: There should be battery voltage.	• Faulty dash lights brightness control system. • An open in the wire.
5	GRN^2	Ignition switch ON.	Check for voltage to ground: There should be more than 5 V.	• Faulty ECM. • An open in the wire.

NOTE: GRN$_1$ or GRN$_2$ are used for identification reasons only. See Fig. 14. There are two different green wires.

95B20058   Courtesy of American Honda Motor Co., Inc.

Fig. 12: Identifying 14-Pin Electrical Connector & Testing A/T Gear Position Indicator

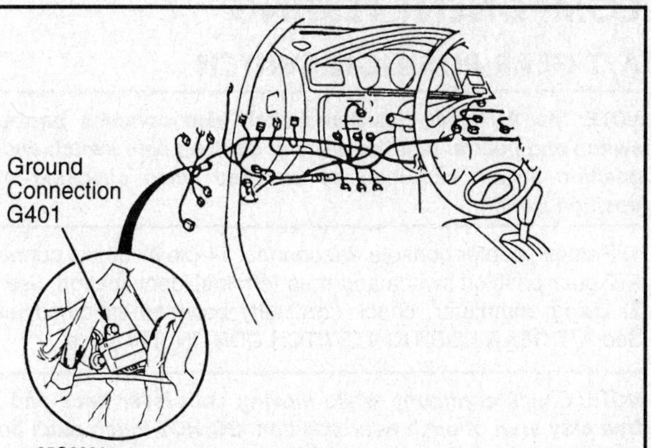

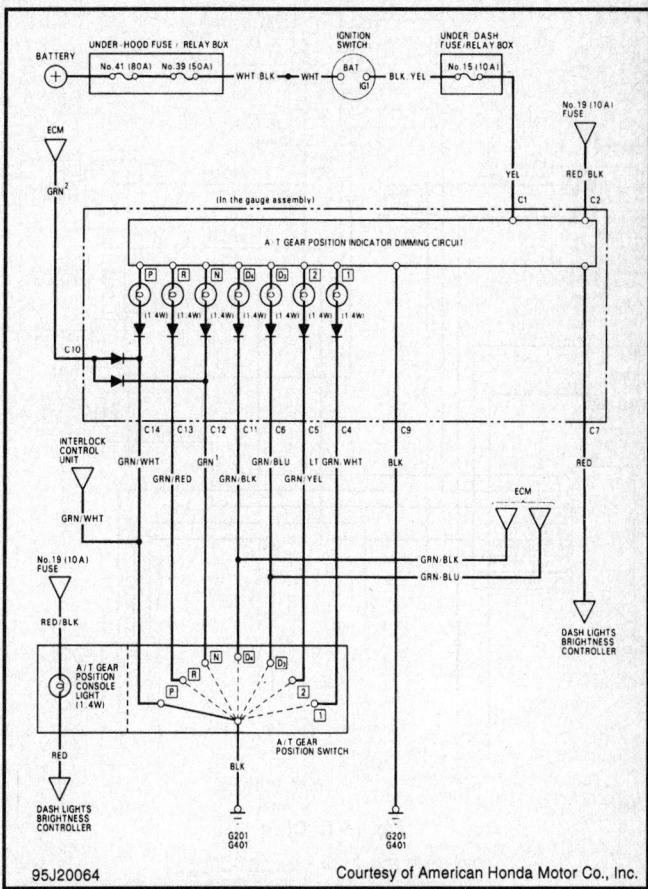

Fig. 13-1: Civic

95G20061

Ground Connection G401

Ground Connection G401

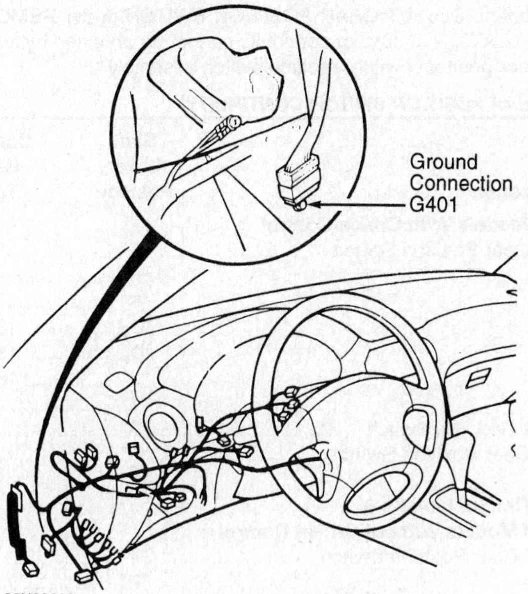

95H20062

Fig. 13-2: Civic Del Sol

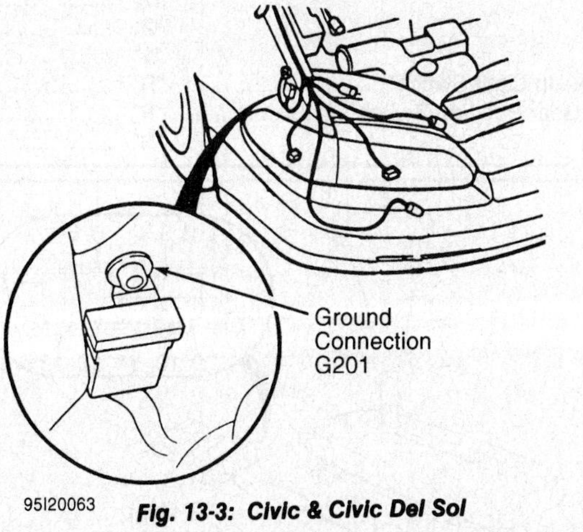

Ground Connection G201

95I20063

Fig. 13-3: Civic & Civic Del Sol

Courtesy of American Honda Motor Co., Inc.

Fig. 13: Identifying Ground Connections

95J20064   Courtesy of American Honda Motor Co., Inc.

Fig. 14: A/T Gear Position Indicator Wiring Schematic

SHIFT & KEY INTERLOCK SYSTEMS

NOTE: For system testing, refer to wiring schematic when checking component wiring. See Fig. 15. To check individual components, see COMPONENT TESTING.

1) To check system operation, ensure shift lever is in Park. Turn ignition on. Depress brake pedal with accelerator pedal in idle position.
2) If shift lock solenoid clicks, system is working properly. If shift lock solenoid fails to click, see INTERLOCK CONTROL UNIT under COMPONENT TESTING. If shift lever cannot be moved from Park, check for proper installation procedure of shift lock solenoid. See SHIFT LOCK SOLENOID under REMOVAL & INSTALLATION. If shift lock solenoid installation is okay, test A/T gear position switch, see A/T GEAR POSITION SWITCH.

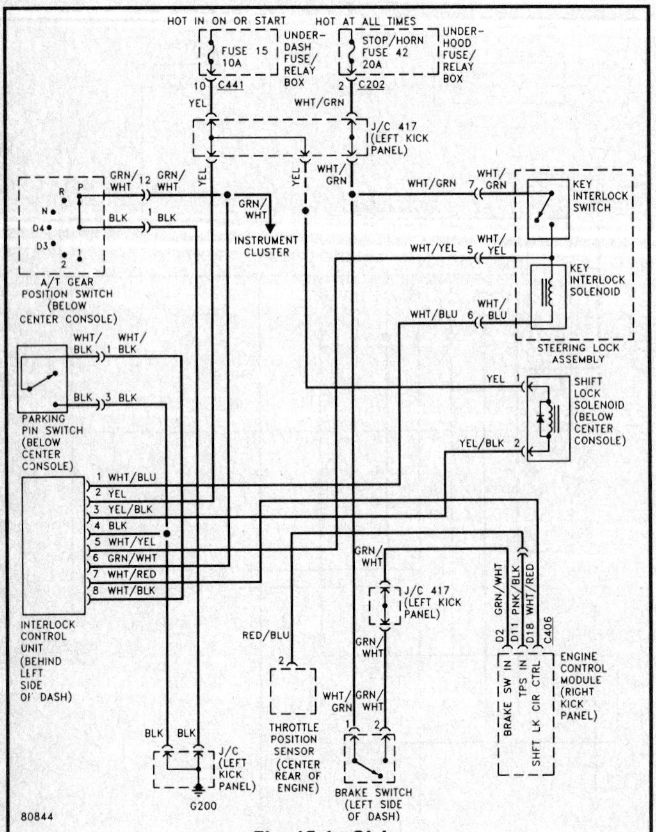

Fig. 15-1: Civic

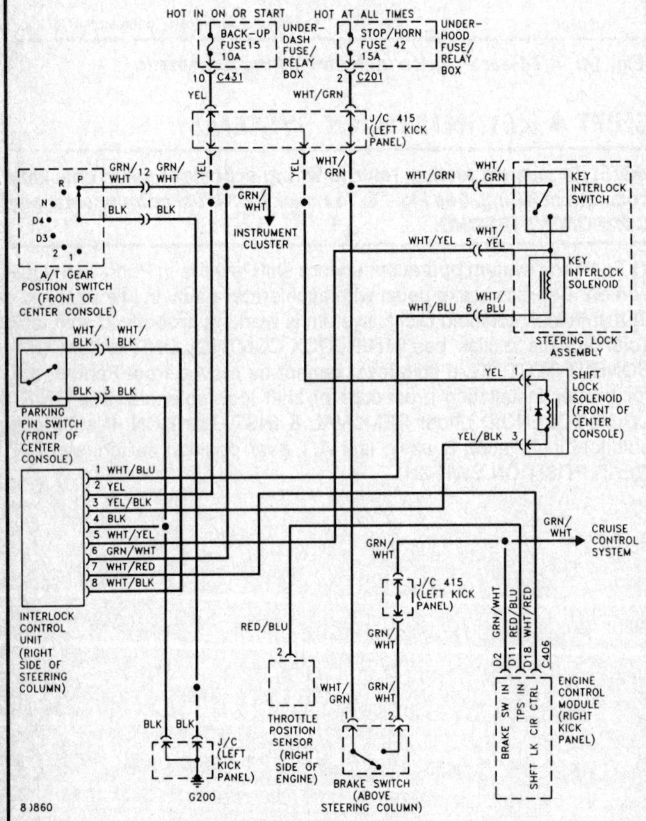

Fig. 15-2: Civic Del Sol

Fig. 15: Shift & Key Interlock System Wiring Schematic

COMPONENT TESTING

A/T GEAR POSITION SWITCH

NOTE: The A/T gear position switch also contains back-up light switch and neutral position switch. Back-up light switch and neutral position switch can also be checked when checking A/T gear position switch.

1) Remove center console. Disconnect 14-pin electrical connector for A/T gear position switch and note terminal identification. *See Fig. 16.*
2) Using ohmmeter, check continuity between indicated terminals. See A/T GEAR POSITION SWITCH CONTINUITY table.

NOTE: Check continuity while moving shift lever back and forth in free play area of each gear position. DO NOT touch push button on shift lever when checking continuity.

3) If continuity is not as specified, A/T gear position switch may require adjustment. See A/T GEAR POSITION SWITCH under REMOVAL & INSTALLATION. If correct continuity cannot be obtained by adjusting A/T gear position switch, replace switch assembly.

A/T GEAR POSITION SWITCH CONTINUITY

Application	Shift Lever Position	Continuity Between Terminal
Civic Models With Cruise Control		
A/T Gear Position Switch	"P"	7 & 10
	"R"	7 & 9
	"N"	7 & 8
	"D_4"	13, 7 & 1
	"D_3"	13, 7 & 2
	"2"	13, 7 & 3
	"1"	7 & 6
Back-Up Light Switch	"R"	4 & 5
A/T Gear Position Switch	"P"	11 & 12
	"N"	11 & 12
Civic Del Sol Models &		
Civic Models Without Cruise Control		
A/T Gear Position Switch	"P"	7 & 10
	"R"	7 & 9
	"N"	7 & 8
	"D_4"	7 & 1
	"D_3"	7 & 2
	"2"	7 & 3
	"1"	7 & 6
Back-Up Light Switch	"R"	4 & 5
A/T Gear Position Switch	"P"	11 & 12
	"N"	11 & 12

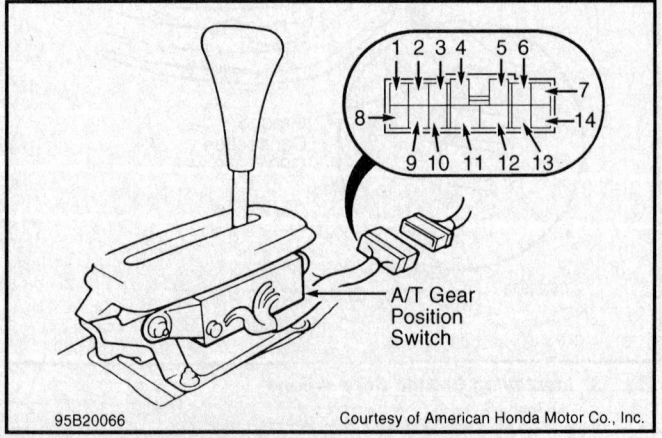

Fig. 16: Identifying A/T Gear Position Switch Terminals

Courtesy of American Honda Motor Co., Inc.

BRAKELIGHT SWITCH

1) Disconnect electrical connector from brakelight switch, located near brake pedal. Note brake switch terminal identification. *See Fig. 18.*

2) On models with cruise control, using ohmmeter, check continuity between terminals "A" and "D" with brake pedal released. Continuity should exist.

3) On all models, using ohmmeter, check continuity between terminals "B" and "C" with brake pedal depressed. Continuity should exist.

4) If continuity is not as specified, ensure brake pedal is properly adjusted so switch has proper travel for switch operation. If proper brakelight switch travel exists, replace brakelight switch.

INTERLOCK CONTROL UNIT

NOTE: It may be necessary to consult wiring schematic when checking any interlock system component wiring. See Fig. 15.

1) Remove lower panel from instrument panel. Disconnect 8-pin connector from interlock control unit. Interlock control unit is located under left side of instrument panel on Civic and to right of instrument cluster on Civic Del Sol. *See Fig. 4.* Inspect terminals for corrosion or bending, repair as necessary.

2) Using DVOM, check for continuity or voltage between specified terminals or body ground. *See Fig. 17.* If necessary to check ground connections G201 or G401, ground connection G201 is located in right front corner of engine compartment. Ground connection G401 is located behind driver's side of instrument panel. *See Fig. 13.*

3) If necessary to check No. 15 fuse (10-amp), fuse is located in the fuse/relay box behind driver's side kick panel. Fuse No. 42 (15 or 20-amp), is located in the fuse/relay box in engine compartment.

KEY INTERLOCK SOLENOID

1) Remove lower cover and knee bolster from driver's side of instrument panel for access to key interlock solenoid 7-pin electrical connector. *See Fig. 19.*

2) Disconnect key interlock solenoid 7-pin electrical connector from main wiring harness. Note electrical connector terminal identification.

3) Using ohmmeter, check continuity between indicated terminals with ignition lock assembly in ACC position. See KEY INTERLOCK SOLENOID CONTINUITY table.

4) If continuity is as specified, proceed to next step. Replace ignition lock assembly if continuity is not as specified. Key interlock solenoid cannot be serviced separately.

Shift Lock System:

No.	Wire	Test condition	Test: Desired result	Possible cause if result is not obtained
1	YEL	Ignition switch ON (II)	Check for voltage to ground: There should be battery voltage.	• Blown No. 15 (10 A) fuse in the under-dash fuse/relay box • An open in the wire
2	WHT/RED	Ignition switch ON (II), brake pedal depressed	Check for voltage to ground: There should be 1 V or less.	• Faulty ECM • An open in the wire • Faulty brake switch • Faulty throttle position (TP) sensor (see section 11)
		Ignition switch ON (II), brake pedal and accelerator depressed at the same time	Check for voltage to ground: There should be about 3 V.	
3	GRN/WHT	Shift lever in position P	Check for continuity to ground: There should be continuity.	• Faulty A/T gear position switch • Poor ground (G201, G401) • An open in the wire
4	YEL/BLK	Ignition switch ON (II)	Check for voltage to ground: There should be battery voltage.	• Blown No. 15 (10 A) fuse in the under-dash fuse/relay box • Faulty shift lock solenoid • An open in the wire

Key Interlock System:

No.	Wire	Test condition	Test: Desired result	Possible cause if result is not obtained
1	BLK	Under all conditions	Check for continuity to ground: There should be continuity.	• Poor ground (G201, G401) • An open in the wire
2	GRN/WHT	Shift lever in position P	Check for continuity to ground: There should be continuity.	• Faulty A/T gear position switch • Poor ground (G201, G401) • An open in the wire
3	WHT/YEL	Ignition switch turned to ACC and key pushed in	Check for voltage to ground: There should be battery voltage.	• Blown No. 42 (15 A) on Civic and (20A) on Civic Del Sol fuse in the under-hood fuse/relay box • Faulty steering lock assembly (key interlock solenoid) • An open in the wire
	WHT/BLU			
4	WHT/BLK	Shift lever in position P and push button pushed	Check for continuity to ground: There should be continuity.	• Faulty parking pin switch • Poor ground (G201, G401) • An open in the wire
		Shift lever in position P and push button released	Check for continuity to ground: There should be no continuity.	• Faulty parking pin switch • Short to ground • An open in the wire

96E30977

Courtesy of American Honda Motor Co., Inc.

Fig. 17: Testing Interlock Control Unit

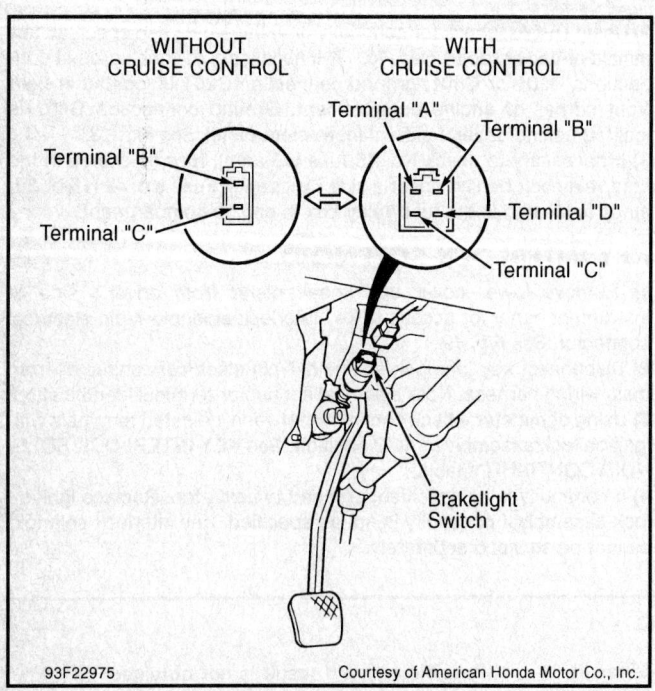

Fig. 18: *Identifying Brakelight Switch Terminals*

5) Connect battery voltage and ground to terminals "A" and "B". Ensure ignition key cannot be removed with battery voltage applied.

6) If ignition key cannot be removed, key interlock solenoid is okay. If ignition key can be removed, replace ignition lock assembly. Key interlock solenoid cannot be serviced separately.

KEY INTERLOCK SOLENOID CONTINUITY

Ignition Key Position	Continuity Between Terminals
Key Installed	A, B & C
Key Removed	B & C

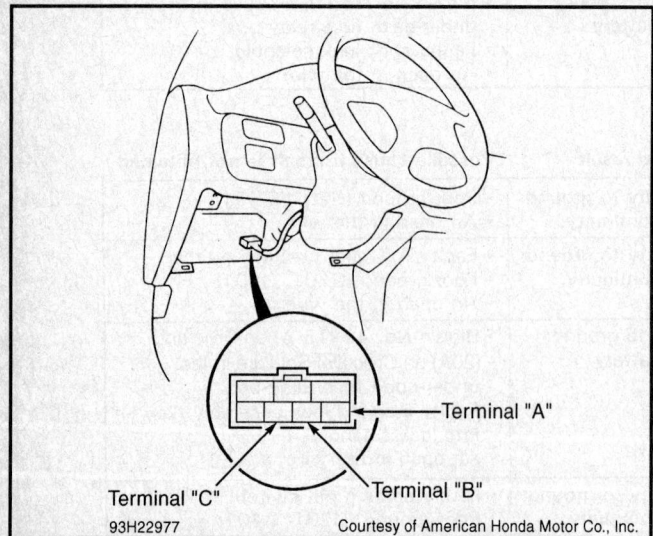

Fig. 19: *Identifying Key Interlock Solenoid Electrical Connector & Terminals*

LOCK-UP CONTROL SOLENOID VALVES

1) Lock-up control solenoid valves are located on transaxle, below distributor. *See Fig. 5.* Disconnect electrical connector at lock-up control solenoid valves.

2) Using ohmmeter, check resistance between terminal No. 1 (solenoid valve "A") or terminal No. 2 (solenoid valve "B") and body ground. *See Fig. 20.*

3) Resistance should be 14-25 ohms on Civic models or 14-16 ohms on Civic Del Sol models. On all models, replace lock-up control solenoid valve assembly if resistance of either solenoid valve is not within specification.

4) To check lock-up control solenoid valve operation, ensure solenoid valve body is grounded. Apply battery voltage to terminal No. 1 (solenoid valve "A") or terminal No. 2 (solenoid valve "B"). Clicking sound should be heard, indicating solenoid valve operation. Replace lock-up control solenoid valve assembly if either solenoid valve fails to operate.

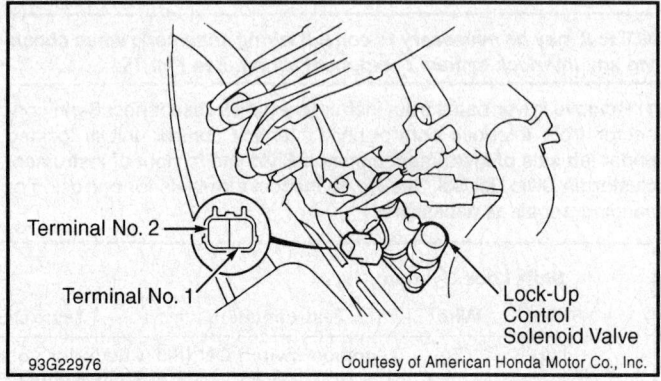

Fig. 20: *Identifying Lock-Up Control Solenoid Valve Terminals*

PARKING PIN SWITCH

1) Remove center console. Disconnect parking pin switch 2-pin connector. Parking pin switch is located on left side of shifter assembly.

2) Using an ohmmeter, check continuity between parking pin switch terminals. Continuity should exist when shift lever is pushed to right. Continuity should not exist with shift lever in stationary position. If continuity is not as described, replace parking pin switch.

SHIFT LOCK SOLENOID

1) Remove center console. Disconnect shift lock solenoid 2-pin electrical connector from main wiring harness. Note electrical connector terminal identification. *See Fig. 21.*

CAUTION: Battery voltage must be applied to correct shift lock solenoid electrical connector terminals or diode inside shift lock solenoid will be damaged.

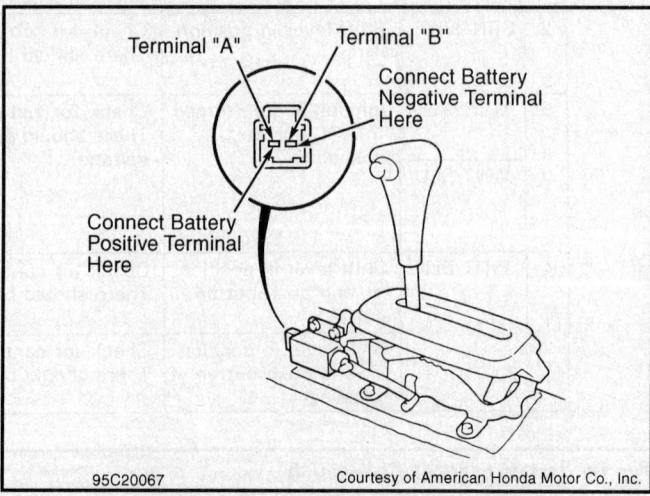

Fig. 21: *Identifying Shift Lock Solenoid Electrical Connector Terminals*

2) Momentarily connect battery positive terminal to terminal "A" and battery negative terminal to terminal "B". *See Fig. 21.* Ensure shift lock solenoid operates with battery voltage applied. Replace shift lock solenoid if solenoid fails to operate.

THROTTLE POSITION (TP) SENSOR

Throttle position sensor should input a .5-volt reference signal to ECM at closed throttle. At full throttle, signal should be approximately 4.5 volts. Voltage should change smoothly as throttle valve is opened and closed. If voltage is not as specified, check throttle position sensor wiring circuit. See WIRING DIAGRAMS. Individual component testing not available from manufacturer.

NOTE: If problem in throttle position sensor exists, throttle position sensor may set DTC P0122 or P0123/Flash Code No. 7 in ECM. See appropriate SELF-DIAGNOSTICS article in ENGINE PERFORMANCE in appropriate MITCHELL® manual.

REMOVAL & INSTALLATION

A/T GEAR POSITION SWITCH

Removal – Remove center console. Disconnect electrical connector from A/T gear position switch. Remove nuts and A/T gear position switch.

Installation – 1) Ensure parking brake is applied. Place switch slider on A/T gear position switch in neutral position. *See Fig. 22.* Place shift lever in Neutral.

2) Install A/T gear position switch and nuts. DO NOT tighten nuts at this time. The A/T gear position switch must be adjusted.

3) To adjust A/T gear position switch, place shift lever in Park. Ensure retaining nuts are loose. Note electrical connector terminal identification. *See Fig. 16.*

4) Connect ohmmeter between terminals No. 7 and 10. Move A/T gear position switch toward rear of console until continuity exists between terminals No. 7 and 10. Free play at lock pin should be about .079" (2.0 mm). *See Fig. 22.*

5) Tighten nuts. Check A/T gear position switch for correct continuity in all gears. See A/T GEAR POSITION SWITCH under COMPONENT TESTING. If proper adjustment cannot be obtained, check for damaged shift lever detent or bracket. Install electrical connector and center console.

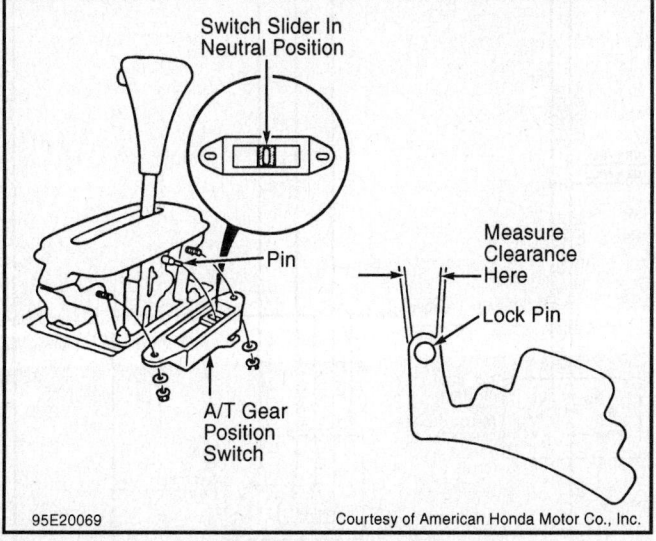

Fig. 22: Removing & Installing A/T Gear Position Switch

BRAKELIGHT SWITCH

Removal & Installation – 1) Disconnect electrical connector from brakelight switch. Remove lock nut from brakelight switch. Unscrew

brakelight switch. To install, screw brakelight switch inward until brakelight switch plunger is fully depressed.

2) Back off brakelight switch 1/4 turn. Ensure .010" (.30 mm) clearance exists between threaded end of brakelight switch and pad area on brake pedal. Install and tighten lock nut. Install electrical connector. Ensure brakelights and cruise control operate properly.

KEY INTERLOCK SOLENOID

Removal & Installation – Key interlock solenoid cannot be serviced separately, as entire ignition lock assembly must be replaced.

LOCK-UP CONTROL SOLENOID VALVES

Removal & Installation – 1) Lock-up control solenoid valves are located on transaxle, below distributor. *See Fig. 5.* Disconnect electrical connector at lock-up control solenoid valves.

2) Remove bolts, lock-up control solenoid valve assembly and gasket. To install, reverse removal procedure using NEW filter/gasket. Tighten bolts to specification. See TORQUE SPECIFICATIONS.

SHIFT LOCK SOLENOID

Removal – Remove center console. Disconnect electrical connector at shift lock solenoid. Remove collar and pin from shift lock solenoid. Remove nuts and shift lock solenoid.

Installation – 1) Install shift lock solenoid with NEW nuts snugly installed. Install pin, collar and electrical connector.

2) Turn ignition on. With shift lock solenoid energized, ensure clearance between top of shift lock lever and lock pin groove is .078-.118" (2.0-3.0 mm). *See Fig. 23.*

3) If clearance is not as specified, loosen nuts and reposition shift lock solenoid until correct clearance is obtained. Once correct clearance is obtained, tighten nuts to specification. See TORQUE SPECIFICATIONS.

4) Turn ignition off. With solenoid de-energized, ensure lock pin is blocked by shift lock lever. *See Fig. 23.* Check solenoid operation several times to ensure correct operation.

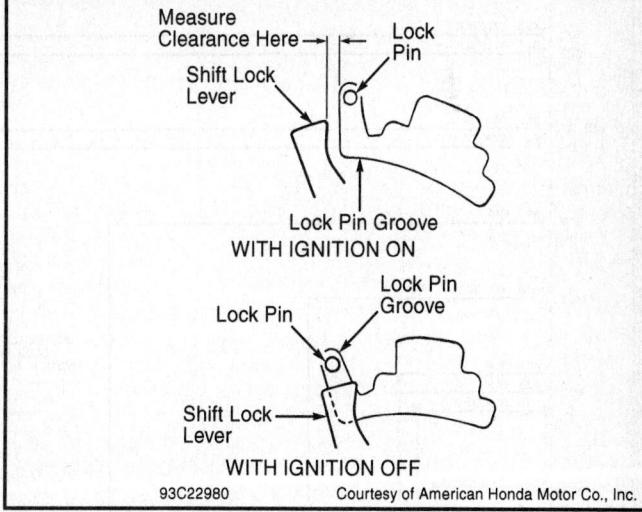

Fig. 23: Checking Shift Lock Solenoid Operation

THROTTLE POSITION (TP) SENSOR

Removal & Installation – Throttle position sensor is mounted on side of throttle body. Replacement information is not available from manufacturer.

TORQUE SPECIFICATIONS

TORQUE SPECIFICATIONS

Application	INCH Lbs. (N.m)
Lock-Up Control Solenoid Valve Bolt	106 (12.0)
Shift Lock Solenoid Nut	89 (10.0)

WIRING DIAGRAMS

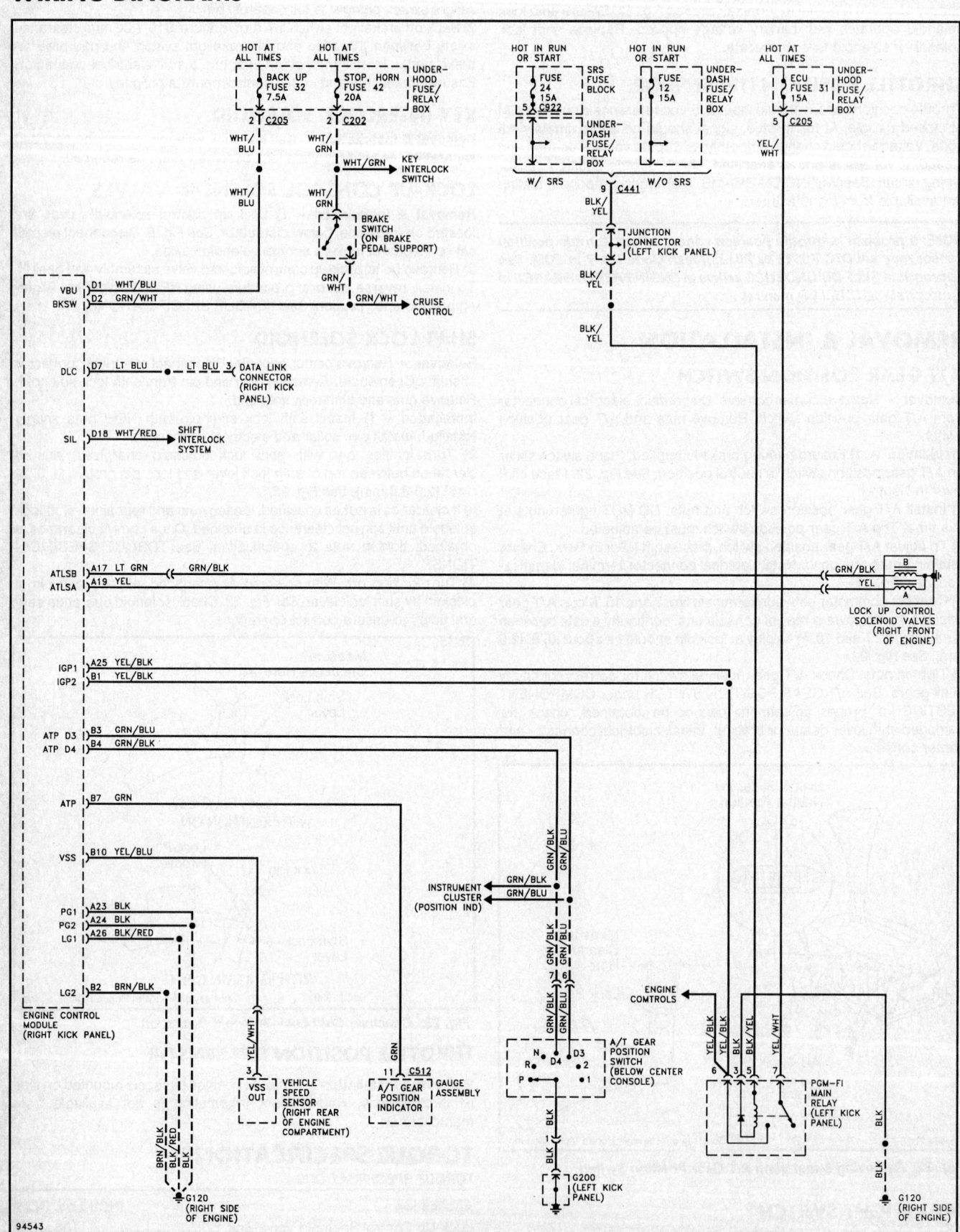

Fig. 24: Transaxle Wiring Diagram (1995 Civic)

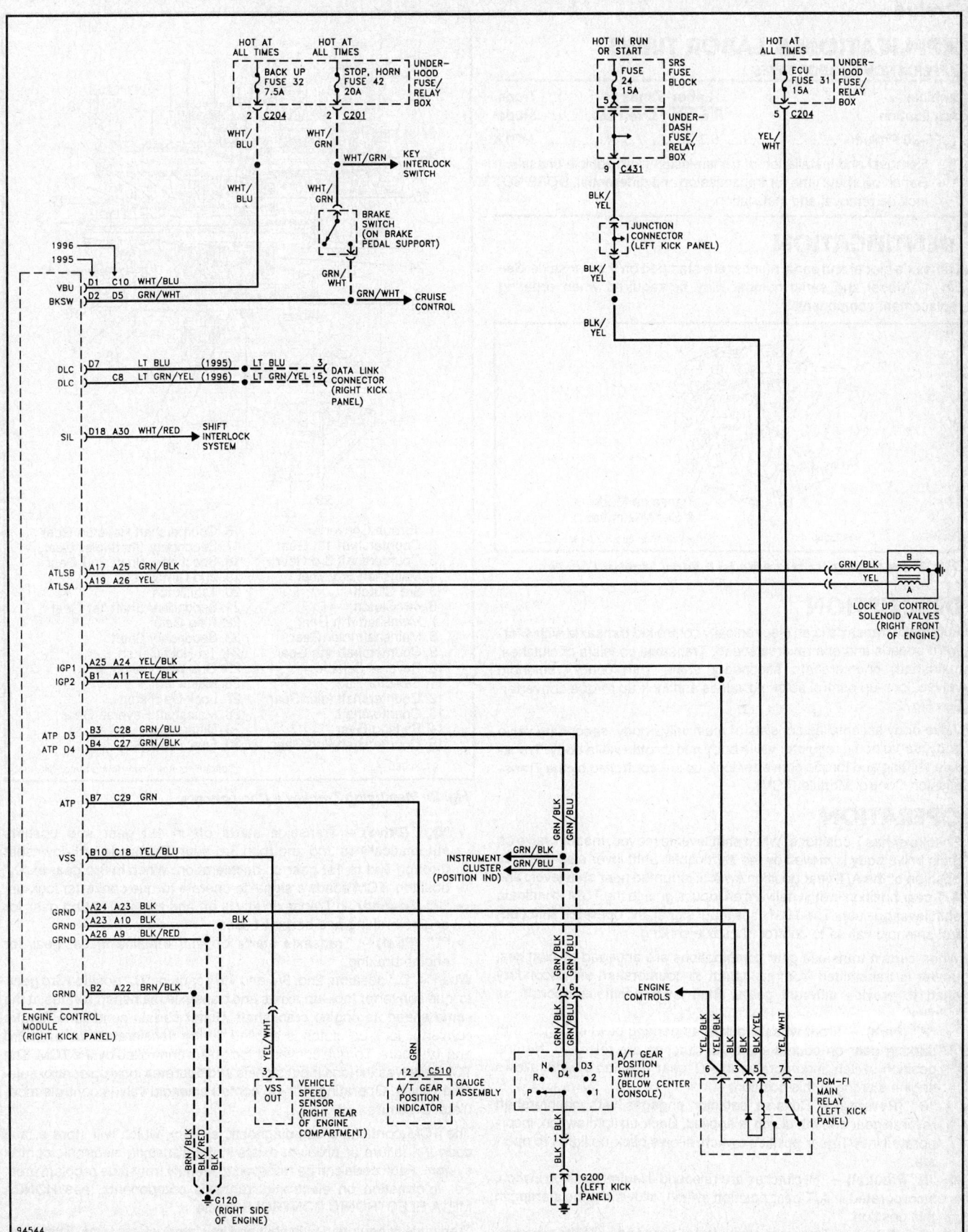

Fig. 25: Transaxle Wiring Diagram (1995-96 Civic Del Sol)

AUTOMATIC TRANSMISSIONS
Honda MP1A

Prelude

APPLICATION & LABOR TIMES

APPLICATION & LABOR TIMES

Vehicle Application	Labor Times		Trans. Model
	[1] R & I	[2] Overhaul	
1995-96 Prelude	6.3	7.5	MP1A

[1] – Removal and installation of transmission from vehicle chassis.
[2] – Bench overhaul time for transmission and differential. DOES NOT include removal and installation.

IDENTIFICATION

Transaxle model and serial number are stamped on the transaxle. *See Fig. 1.* Model and serial number may be required when ordering replacement components.

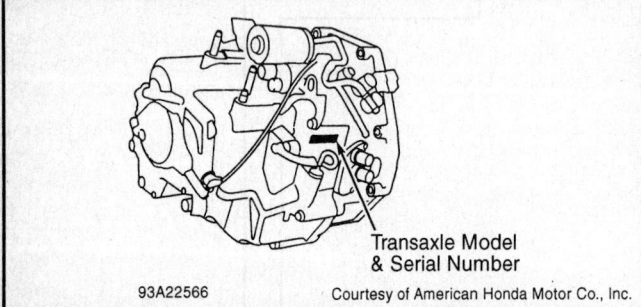

Transaxle Model
& Serial Number

93A22566   Courtesy of American Honda Motor Co., Inc.

Fig. 1: Identifying Transaxle Model & Serial Number Location

DESCRIPTION

Automatic transaxle is an electronically controlled transaxle with 4 forward speeds and one reverse speed. Transaxle consists of clutches, mainshaft, countershaft, secondary shaft, shift control solenoid valves, lock-up control solenoid valves and lock-up torque converter. *See Fig. 2.*

Valve body assemblies consists of main valve body, secondary valve body, servo body, regulator valve body and throttle valve body. Transaxle shifting and torque converter lock-up are controlled by the Transmission Control Module (TCM).

OPERATION

Shift lever has 7 positions. When shift lever is moved, manual valve on main valve body is moved by the shift cable. Shift lever also changes position of the A/T gear position switch, mounted near shift lever. The A/T gear position switch delivers an input signal to the TCM to indicate shift lever position. The TCM uses input signal and operates shift control solenoid valves to control transaxle shifting.

When certain transaxle gear combinations are engaged by clutches, power is transmitted from mainshaft to countershaft via secondary shaft to provide different gears. Shift lever positions operate as follows:

- **"P" (Park)** – Front wheels locked as parking pawl engages with parking gear on countershaft. All clutches are released. Neutral position switch, incorporated in A/T gear position switch, allows engine starting in this position.
- **"R" (Reverse)** – Reverse selector engages with countershaft reverse gear and 4th clutch is applied. Back-up light switch, incorporated in A/T gear position switch, allows back-up lights to operate.
- **"N" (Neutral)** – All clutches are released. Neutral position switch, incorporated in A/T gear position switch, allows engine starting in this position.
- **"D₄" (Drive)** – Transaxle starts in 1st gear and upshifts automatically to 2nd, 3rd then 4th gears. Transaxle will downshift through 3rd, 2nd and 1st gears until vehicle stops. When in 2nd, 3rd or 4th gear in "D₄" position, TCM sends a signal to operate torque converter lock-up.

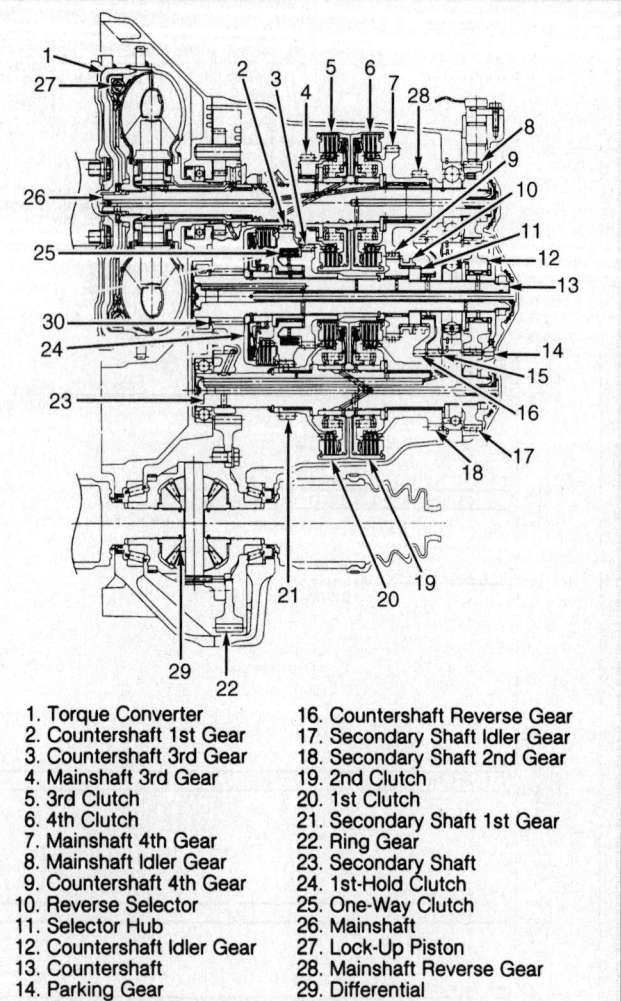

1. Torque Converter	16. Countershaft Reverse Gear
2. Countershaft 1st Gear	17. Secondary Shaft Idler Gear
3. Countershaft 3rd Gear	18. Secondary Shaft 2nd Gear
4. Mainshaft 3rd Gear	19. 2nd Clutch
5. 3rd Clutch	20. 1st Clutch
6. 4th Clutch	21. Secondary Shaft 1st Gear
7. Mainshaft 4th Gear	22. Ring Gear
8. Mainshaft Idler Gear	23. Secondary Shaft
9. Countershaft 4th Gear	24. 1st-Hold Clutch
10. Reverse Selector	25. One-Way Clutch
11. Selector Hub	26. Mainshaft
12. Countershaft Idler Gear	27. Lock-Up Piston
13. Countershaft	28. Mainshaft Reverse Gear
14. Parking Gear	29. Differential
15. Countershaft 2nd Gear	30. Final Drive Gear

96J30980   Courtesy of American Honda Motor Co., Inc.

Fig. 2: Identifying Transaxle Components

- **"D₃" (Drive)** – Transaxle starts off in 1st gear and upshifts automatically to 2nd and then 3rd gear. Transaxle will downshift through 2nd to 1st gear on deceleration. When in 3rd gear in "D₃" position, TCM sends a signal to operate torque converter lock-up.
- **"2" (Second)** – Transaxle starts off and remains in 2nd gear for engine braking and better traction.
- **"1" (First)** – Transaxle starts off and remains in 1st gear for engine braking.

When in "D₄" position, 2nd, 3rd and 4th gears, or "D₃" position 3rd gear, torque converter lock-up exists and transaxle mainshaft rotates at the same speed as engine crankshaft. Under certain conditions, torque converter lock-up clutch is applied during deceleration when in 3rd and 4th gears. Torque converter lock-up is controlled by the TCM. The TCM receives various input signals and operates lock-up control solenoid valves. Operating lock-up control solenoid valves controls modulator pressure.

The TCM contains a self-diagnostic system, which will store a fault code if a failure or problem exists in the transaxle electronic control system. Fault code can be retrieved to identify transaxle problem area. For information on electronic transaxle components, see HONDA MP1A ELECTRONIC CONTROLS article.

Transaxle is equipped with shift and key interlock systems. Shift interlock system prevents shift lever from being moved from "P" position unless brake pedal is depressed and accelerator is in idle position. In case of a malfunction, shift lever can be released by placing ignition key in release slot near shift lever. Key interlock system prevents ignition key from being removed from ignition switch unless shift lever is in "P" position. For additional information on shift and key interlock systems, see HONDA MP1A ELECTRONIC CONTROLS article.

The A/T gear position indicator on instrument panel contains lights to indicate which position A/T gear position switch on shift lever is in. For information and testing of A/T gear position indicator, see HONDA MP1A ELECTRONIC CONTROLS article.

LUBRICATION & ADJUSTMENTS

See appropriate AUTOMATIC TRANSMISSION SERVICING article in TRANSMISSION SERVICING section.

SYMPTOM TROUBLE SHOOTING

Transaxle malfunctions may be caused by poor engine performance, improper adjustments or failure of hydraulic, mechanical or electronic components. Always begin by checking fluid level, fluid condition and cable adjustments. Perform road test to determine if problem has been corrected. If problem still exists, perform several tests on transaxle. See TESTING.

Excessive Drag
- Binding Oil Pump

Excessive Idle Vibration
- Defective Torque Converter
- Incorrect Idle RPM

Excessive Vibration (RPM Related)
- Torque Converter Not Fully Seated In Oil Pump

Flares On 1-2 Upshift
- Clutch Pressure Control Valve Stuck
- Throttle Valve "B" Stuck
- Throttle Valve (T.V.) Cable Adjusted Too Long

Flares On 2-3 Upshift
- Clutch Pressure Control Valve Stuck
- Defective Seal Rings Or Guide
- Throttle Valve "B" Stuck
- Throttle Valve (T.V.) Cable Adjusted Too Long
- 2nd Orifice Control Valve Stuck

Flares On 3-4 Upshift
- Clutch Pressure Control Valve Stuck
- Defective Seal Rings Or Guide
- Orifice Control Valve Stuck
- Throttle Valve "B" Stuck
- Throttle Valve (T.V.) Cable Adjusted Too Long

Gear Whine That Changes With RPM & Shifts
- Damaged Mainshaft Or Countershaft
- Damaged Secondary Shaft Idler Gears
- Defective 1st Clutch
- Defective 3rd Gears

Gear Whine That Changes With Speed
- Defective Differential Gears
- Shift Fork Bent

Harsh Downshift At Closed Throttle
- Clutch Pressure Control Valve Stuck
- Throttle Valve "B" Stuck
- Throttle Valve (T.V.) Cable Adjusted Too Short

Harsh Kickdown Shifts
- Clutch Pressure Control Valve Stuck
- Throttle Valve "B" Stuck
- Throttle Valve (T.V.) Cable Adjusted Too Short
- 3rd Kickdown Valve Stuck
- 3-2 Kickdown Valve Stuck
- 4th Exhaust Valve Stuck

Harsh Shift When Manually Shifting To "1"
- Defective 1st-Hold Accumulator

Harsh Upshifts & Downshifts
- Clutch Pressure Control Valve Stuck
- Improper ATF Type
- Incorrect Clutch Clearance
- Orifice Control Valve Stuck

- Throttle Valve "B" Stuck
- Throttle Valve (T.V.) Cable Adjusted Too Short
- 2nd Orifice Control Valve Stuck
- 3rd Kickdown Valve Stuck
- 3-2 Kickdown Valve Stuck

Harsh 1-2 Upshift
- Clutch Pressure Control Valve Stuck
- Defective 2nd Clutch
- Throttle Valve "B" Stuck
- Throttle Valve (T.V.) Cable Adjusted Too Short

Harsh 2-1 Kickdown Shift
- Defective One-Way Clutch

Harsh 2-3 Upshift
- Clutch Pressure Control Valve Stuck
- Defective 3rd Clutch
- Throttle Valve "B" Stuck
- Throttle Valve (T.V.) Cable Adjusted Too Short
- 2nd Orifice Control Valve Stuck

Harsh 3-4 Upshift
- Clutch Pressure Control Valve Stuck
- Defective 4th Clutch
- Orifice Control Valve Stuck
- Throttle Valve "B" Stuck
- Throttle Valve (T.V.) Cable Adjusted Too Short

Lock-Up Clutch Does Not Lock-Up Smoothly
- Defective Torque Converter
- Lock-Up Control Valve Stuck
- Lock-Up Shift Valve Stuck

Lock-Up Clutch Does Not Operate Properly
- Improperly Adjusted Throttle Valve (T.V.) Cable
- Lock-Up Control Valve Stuck
- Lock-Up Shift Valve Stuck
- Lock-Up Timing Valve Stuck
- Throttle Valve "B" Stuck
- Torque Converter Check Valve Stuck

No Engine Braking In "1"
- Defective 1st-Hold Clutch

Noise From Transaxle In All Gears
- Defective Oil Pump
- Defective Torque Converter

Noise From Transaxle When Wheels Rolling
- Damaged Reverse Gears
- Defective Differential Gears
- Reverse Selector Hub Installed Upside Down

Popping Noise When Taking Off In "R"
- Damaged Reverse Gears
- Shift Fork Bent
- Worn Reverse Selector

Ratcheting Noise When Shifting To "R"
- Damaged Reverse Gears
- Defective Oil Pump
- Pressure Regulator Stuck
- Shift Fork Bent
- Worn Reverse Selector

Ratcheting Noise When Shifting From "R" To "P" Or "N"
- Damaged Reverse Gears
- Damaged 4th Gears
- Shift Fork Bent
- Worn Reverse Selector

Shifts Erratically
- Improperly Installed Valves Or Springs
- Modulator Valve Stuck
- Throttle Valve (T.V.) Cable Adjusted Too Short
- 3-2 Kickdown Valve Stuck

Slips In All Gears
- Defective Oil Pump
- Fluid Strainer Clogged
- Pressure Regulator Stuck

Slips In Reverse
- Defective 4th Clutch Or 4th Accumulator
- Feedpipe "O" Ring Damaged
- Servo Valve Stuck

Slips In 1st Gear
- Defective One-Way Clutch
- Defective 1st Clutch Or 1st Accumulator
- Feedpipe "O" Ring Damaged

Slips In 2nd Gear
- Clutch Pressure Control Valve Stuck
- Defective Seal Rings Or Guide
- Defective 2nd Clutch Or 2nd Accumulator
- 2-3 Shift Valve Stuck

Slips In 3rd Gear
- Clutch Pressure Control Valve Stuck
- Defective Seal Rings Or Guide
- Defective 3rd Clutch Or 3rd Accumulator
- 3-4 Shift Valve Stuck

Slips In 4th Gear
- Clutch Pressure Control Valve Stuck
- Defective 4th Clutch Or 4th Accumulator
- Feedpipe "O" Ring Damaged

Upshifts Late
- Modulator Valve Stuck

Vehicle Locks In "R"
- Parking Brake Lever Installed Upside Down
- Shift Fork Retaining Bolt Not Installed

Vehicle Moves In All Gears Except "R"
- Defective Or Improperly Adjusted Shift Cable
- Defective Or Worn Reverse Gears
- Defective 4th Clutch
- Servo Control Valve Stuck
- Servo Valve Stuck
- Shift Fork Bent
- Worn Reverse Selector

Vehicle Moves In All Gears Except "2"
- Defective Seal Rings Or Guide
- Defective 2nd Clutch Or 2nd Accumulator

Vehicle Moves In "N"
- Defective Or Improperly Adjusted Shift Cable
- Defective 1st, 2nd, 3rd Or 4th Clutch
- Incorrect Gear Or Clutch Clearance

Vehicle Moves In "R" & "2" Only
- Defective One-Way Clutch
- Defective 1st Clutch Or 1st Accumulator
- Feedpipe "O" Ring Damaged

Vehicle Will Not Move
- Defective Oil Pump
- Defective Or Improperly Adjusted Shift Cable
- Fluid Strainer Clogged
- Pressure Regulator Stuck

Vehicle Will Not Move In "D₃" Or "D₄"
- One-Way Clutch Installed Upside Down

Will Not Downshift To 1st Gear
- Defective 1st-Hold Clutch
- 1-2 Shift Valve Stuck

Will Not Shift Into 4th Gear When In "D₄"
- Defective Or Improperly Adjusted Shift Cable
- Defective 4th Accumulator
- 3-4 Shift Valve Stuck
- 4th Exhaust Valve Stuck

Will Not Upshift (Stays In Low Gear)
- Clutch Pressure Control Valve Stuck
- Modulator Valve Stuck
- 1-2 Shift Valve Stuck

TESTING
ROAD TEST

NOTE: If shift lever cannot be moved from "P" position with brake pedal depressed and accelerator at idle position, check shift interlock system. See HONDA MP1A ELECTRONIC CONTROLS article.

1) Warm engine to normal operating temperature. Apply parking brake and block wheels. Start engine. Move shift lever to "D₄" position while depressing brake pedal. Depress accelerator pedal and release it suddenly. Engine should not stall.

2) Repeat step 1) with shift lever in "D₃" position. Ensure engine does not stall. Shut engine off. Manufacturer recommends monitoring of Throttle Position (TP) sensor voltage when performing road test to ensure proper throttle opening for verifying shift points and lock-up of torque converter.

3) Remove door sill molding on passenger's side and remove small cover on passenger's side kick panel. Pull carpet back for access to Engine Control Module (ECM), located on passenger's side, below carpet. See Fig. 3.

4) Remove ECM cover located above ECM. Ensure ignition is off. On 1995 models, install Test Harness (07LAJ-PT3010A) between ECM and ECM electrical connectors. See Fig. 3. Install Digital Volt-Ohmmeter (DVOM) on test harness with positive lead at terminal D11 and negative lead at terminal D22 for monitoring of throttle position sensor voltage. Terminal numbers are on top of test harness. See Fig. 3.

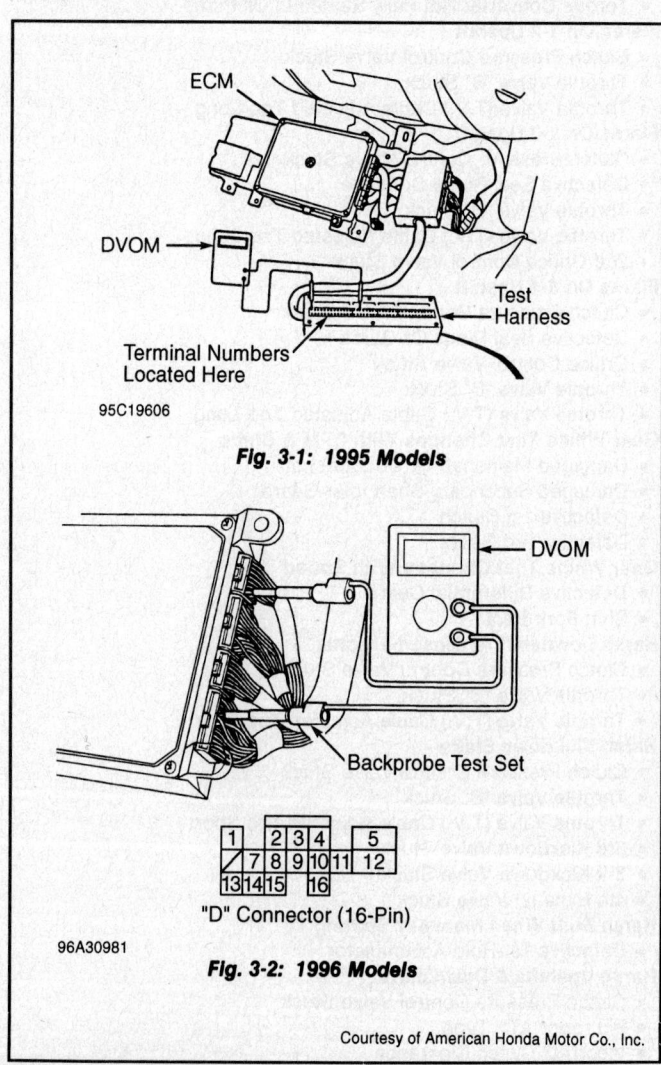

95C19606

Fig. 3-1: 1995 Models

"D" Connector (16-Pin)

96A30981

Fig. 3-2: 1996 Models

Courtesy of American Honda Motor Co., Inc.

Fig. 3: Measuring TP Sensor Voltage

TRANSAXLE UPSHIFT SPECIFICATIONS

Application [1]	1st-2nd Gear	2nd-3rd Gear	3rd-4th Gear	Lock-Up Clutch On
2.2L SOHC				
Throttle Position Sensor Voltage .83 Volt				
Coasting Downhill From Stop	13-15 MPH	26-28 MPH	36-40 MPH	14-17 MPH
Throttle Position Sensor Voltage 2.18 Volts				
Accelerating From Stop	17-21 MPH	37-41 MPH	57-63 MPH	61-67 MPH
Full Throttle				
Accelerating From Stop	29-34 MPH	60-65 MPH	88-94 MPH	81-86 MPH
2.3L DOHC				
Throttle Position Sensor Voltage .83 Volt				
Coasting Downhill From Stop	13-15 MPH	26-28 MPH	36-40 MPH	14-17 MPH
Throttle Position Sensor Voltage 2.18 Volts				
Accelerating From Stop	18-22 MPH	36-40 MPH	54-60 MPH	58-64 MPH
Full Throttle				
Accelerating From Stop	29-34 MPH	57-62 MPH	83-88 MPH	80-85 MPH

[1] – Shift lever in "D₄" position.

TRANSAXLE DOWNSHIFT SPECIFICATIONS

Application [1]	Lock-Up Clutch Off	4th-3rd Gear	3rd-2nd Gear	2nd-1st Gear
2.2L SOHC				
Throttle Position Sensor Voltage .83 Volt				
Coasting Or Braking To A Stop	13-16 MPH	[2]	18-22 MPH	6-10 MPH
Throttle Position Sensor Voltage 2.18 Volts				
Vehicle Slowing By Grade Or Load	53-59 MPH	[2]	[2]	[2]
Full Throttle				
Vehicle Slowing By Grade Or Load	77-82 MPH	76-82 MPH	52-57 MPH	21-26 MPH
2.3L DOHC				
Throttle Position Sensor Voltage .83 Volt				
Coasting Or Braking To A Stop	13-16 MPH	[2]	18-22 MPH	6-10 MPH
Throttle Position Sensor Voltage 2.18 Volts				
Vehicle Slowing By Grade Or Load	48-54 MPH	[2]	[2]	[2]
Full Throttle				
Vehicle Slowing By Grade Or Load	73-80 MPH	73-79 MPH	51-56 MPH	24-29 MPH

[1] – Shift lever in "D₄" position.
[2] – Specification is not available from manufacturer.

5) On 1996 models, install Backprobe Test Set (07SAZ-001000A) or equivalent between PCM and DVOM leads. *See Fig. 3.* Using DVOM, with positive lead at terminal D1 and negative lead at terminal D11. *See Fig. 3.* Ensure DVOM is set for measuring voltage.

6) On all models, road test vehicle and check for abnormal noise and clutch slippage. Specified clutch is applied in designated gear. See CLUTCH APPLICATION table.

7) Ensure upshift and downshift points and lock-up of torque converter are correct in relation to throttle position sensor voltage or throttle opening and vehicle speed with shift lever in "D₄" position. See TRANSAXLE UPSHIFT SPECIFICATIONS and TRANSAXLE DOWNSHIFT SPECIFICATIONS tables.

8) With shift lever in "D₄" position, accelerate to about 35 MPH so transaxle is in 4th gear. Move shift lever to "2" position. Ensure engine braking occurs.

CAUTION: DO NOT shift from "D₄" to "2" at speeds over 63 MPH or transaxle may be damaged.

9) Place shift lever in "1" position. Accelerate from a stop at full throttle. Check for abnormal noise or clutch slippage. Upshifts and downshifts should not occur in this shift lever position.

10) Place shift lever in "2" position. Accelerate from a stop at full throttle. Check for abnormal noise or clutch slippage. Upshifts and downshifts should not occur in this shift lever position.

11) Place shift lever in "R" position. Accelerate from a stop at full throttle. Check for abnormal noise or clutch slippage.

12) Park vehicle on a slope. Apply parking brake. Place shift lever in "P" position. Release parking brake. Ensure vehicle does not move. If vehicle moves, check for defective shift cable or parking components.

13) Ensure ignition is off. Remove test harness and reinstall electrical connectors, ECM cover, carpet and door sill molding.

CLUTCH APPLICATION

Shift Lever Position	Elements In Use
"P" & "N"	No Clutches Are Applied
"R"	4th Clutch
"D₄"	
1st Gear	1st Clutch, One-Way Clutch
2nd Gear	[1] 2nd Clutch
3rd Gear	[1] 3rd Clutch
4th Gear	[1] 4th Clutch
"D₃"	
1st Gear	1st Clutch, One-Way Clutch
2nd Gear	[1] 2nd Clutch
3rd Gear	[1] 3rd Clutch
"2"	[1] 2nd Clutch
"1"	1st-Hold Clutch, 1st Clutch, One-Way Clutch

[1] – The 1st clutch engages but driving power is not transmitted, as one-way clutch slips.

TORQUE CONVERTER STALL SPEED TEST

CAUTION: DO NOT perform torque converter stall speed test for more than 10 seconds or transaxle may be damaged. DO NOT move shift lever while increasing engine speed.

1) Apply parking brake. Block front wheels. Connect tachometer and start engine. Ensure A/C is off. Warm engine to normal operating temperature. Place shift lever in "2" position.

2) Fully depress brake pedal. Fully depress accelerator for 6-8 seconds and note engine speed. This is the torque converter stall speed.

3) Allow transaxle to cool for 2 minutes. Repeat test procedure with shift lever in "D₄", "1" and "R" positions.

4) Ensure torque converter stall speed is within specification. Torque converter stall speed should be the same in "D₄", "2", "1" and "R" positions. See TORQUE CONVERTER STALL SPEED SPECIFICATIONS table. If torque converter stall speed is not within specification, see TORQUE CONVERTER STALL SPEED TROUBLE SHOOTING table for possible causes.

TORQUE CONVERTER STALL SPEED SPECIFICATIONS

Application	Engine RPM
2.2L SOHC	
Standard	2500
Service Limit	2350-2650
2.3L DOHC	
Standard	2750
Service Limit	2600-2900

TORQUE CONVERTER STALL SPEED TROUBLE SHOOTING

Torque Converter Stall Speed Test Results	Probable Cause
Stall Speed RPM High In "D₄", "2", "1" & "R"	Low Fluid Level, Low Oil Pump Output, Clogged Fluid Strainer, Pressure Regulator Valve Stuck Closed, Slipping Clutch
Stall Speed RPM High In "R"	Slipping 4th Clutch
Stall Speed RPM High In "D₄"	Slipping Clutch
Stall Speed RPM High In "2"	Slipping 2nd Clutch
Stall Speed RPM High In "1"	Slipping 1st-Hold Or 1st Clutch, Defective One-Way Clutch
Stall Speed RPM Low In "D₄", "2", "1" & "R"	Engine Output Low, Torque Converter One-Way Clutch Slipping

HYDRAULIC PRESSURE TEST

Pressure Test Preparation – Ensure transaxle fluid level is correct. Warm engine to normal operating temperature. Apply parking brake. Block rear wheels. Raise and support vehicle so front wheels can rotate.

Line Pressure Test – 1) With engine off, remove pressure tap plug from line pressure tap on transaxle. *See Fig. 4.* Attach pressure gauge to line pressure tap using NEW aluminum washer. Tighten hose fitting to 13 ft. lbs. (18 N.m).

2) With shift lever in "P" position, start and operate engine at 2000 RPM. Note line pressure. Place shift lever in "N" position and note line pressure with engine at 2000 RPM.

3) Line pressure should be within specification. See appropriate HYDRAULIC PRESSURE TEST SPECIFICATIONS table. If line pressure is not within specification, see HYDRAULIC PRESSURE TEST TROUBLE SHOOTING table. Shut engine off.

4) Remove pressure gauge set. Using NEW aluminum seal washer, install and tighten pressure tap plug to specification. See TORQUE SPECIFICATIONS.

NOTE: Check clutch pressure at each clutch pressure tap on transaxle. See Fig. 4.

Clutch Pressure Test – 1) With engine off, remove pressure tap plug from appropriate clutch pressure tap on transaxle. *See Fig. 4.* Attach pressure gauge to appropriate pressure tap using NEW aluminum washer. Tighten hose fitting to 13 ft. lbs. (18 N.m).

NOTE: Clutch pressure on some applications may vary with position of Throttle Valve (T.V.) lever on transaxle. The T.V. cable must be disconnected for some tests. Ensure shift lever is in proper position when checking clutch pressures.

2) Start and operate engine at 2000 RPM. Note clutch pressure reading with shift lever in appropriate position. See appropriate HYDRAULIC PRESSURE TEST SPECIFICATIONS table.

3) Ensure clutch pressure is within specification. If clutch pressure is not within specification, see HYDRAULIC PRESSURE TEST TROUBLE SHOOTING table. Shut engine off.

4) Remove pressure gauge set. Using NEW aluminum seal washer, install and tighten pressure tap plug to specification. See TORQUE SPECIFICATIONS.

Low/High Pressure Test – 1) The low/high pressure is tested at 2nd, 3rd and 4th clutch pressure taps on transaxle. *See Fig. 4.* Disconnect Throttle Valve (T.V.) cable from transaxle T.V. lever.

NOTE: When disconnecting T.V. cable, unhook cable from transaxle T.V. lever. DO NOT loosen lock nuts used for cable adjustment.

2) With engine off, remove pressure tap plug from appropriate clutch pressure tap on transaxle. Attach pressure gauge to appropriate pressure tap using NEW aluminum washer. Tighten hose fitting to 13 ft. lbs. (18 N.m).

3) Start engine and allow to idle. Move shift lever to "D₄" position. Slowly increase engine speed until pressure is indicated on pressure gauge. Release throttle, allowing engine to idle and note low pressure reading.

4) With engine idling, lift transaxle T.V. lever upward approximately half the distance of lever travel. Increase engine speed and note highest pressure reading.

5) Repeat procedure for remaining clutches. Ensure low/high pressure is within specification. See appropriate HYDRAULIC PRESSURE TEST SPECIFICATIONS table. If low/high pressure is not within specification, see HYDRAULIC PRESSURE TEST TROUBLE SHOOTING table.

6) Shut engine off. Remove pressure gauge set. Using NEW aluminum seal washer, install and tighten pressure tap plug to specification. See TORQUE SPECIFICATIONS. Reconnect T.V. cable.

Throttle Valve "B" Pressure Test – 1) Disconnect T.V. cable from transaxle T.V. lever. With engine off, remove pressure tap plug from throttle valve "B" pressure tap. *See Fig. 4.*

NOTE: When disconnecting T.V. cable, unhook cable from transaxle T.V. lever. DO NOT loosen lock nuts used for cable adjustment.

2) Attach pressure gauge to throttle valve "B" pressure tap using NEW aluminum washer. Tighten hose fitting to 13 ft. lbs. (18 N.m).

3) Start engine and operate at 1000 RPM with shift lever in "D₄" position. No pressure should exist with transaxle T.V. lever released (closed position).

4) Lift transaxle T.V. lever fully upward (open position). Note throttle valve "B" pressure reading.

5) Ensure throttle valve "B" pressure is within specification. See appropriate HYDRAULIC PRESSURE TEST SPECIFICATIONS table. If pressure is not within specification, see HYDRAULIC PRESSURE TEST TROUBLE SHOOTING table. Shut engine off.

6) Remove pressure gauge set. Using NEW aluminum seal washer, install and tighten pressure tap plug to specification. See TORQUE SPECIFICATIONS. Reconnect T.V. cable.

HYDRAULIC PRESSURE TEST TROUBLE SHOOTING

Application	Probable Cause
Line Pressure	
Low Or No Line Pressure	Defective Torque Converter, Defective Torque Converter Check Valve, Defective Pressure Regulator, Defective Oil Pump
Clutch Pressure	
Low Or No 1st Clutch Pressure	Defective 1st Clutch
Low Or No 1st-Hold Clutch Pressure	Defective 1st-Hold Clutch
Low Or No 2nd Clutch Pressure	Defective 2nd Clutch
Low Or No 3rd Clutch Pressure	Defective 3rd Clutch
Low Or No 4th Clutch Pressure	Defective 4th Clutch, Defective Servo Valve On 4th Clutch
Low/High Pressure	
Low Or No 2nd Clutch Pressure	Defective 2nd Clutch
Low Or No 3rd Clutch Pressure	Defective 3rd Clutch
Low Or No 4th Clutch Pressure	Defective 4th Clutch
Throttle Valve "B" Pressure	
Low Or No Pressure	Defective Throttle Valve "B"

HYDRAULIC PRESSURE TEST SPECIFICATIONS (2.2L SOHC)

Application	Shift Lever Position	Pressure psi. (kPa)
Line Pressure		
With Engine At 2000 RPM	"P" Or "N"	107-121 (750-850)
Clutch Pressure		
1st Clutch		
With Engine At 2000 RPM	"1" Or "D$_4$"	107-121 (750-850)
1st-Hold Clutch		
With Engine At 2000 RPM	"1"	107-121 (750-850)
2nd Clutch		
With Engine At 2000 RPM	"2"	107-121 (750-850)
With Transaxle T.V. Lever Fully Closed [1]	"D$_4$"	64-71 (450-500)
With Transaxle T.V. Lever Open More Than 3/16 [2]	"D$_4$"	107-121 (750-850)
3rd Clutch		
With Transaxle T.V. Lever Fully Closed [1]	"D$_4$"	64-71 (450-500)
With Transaxle T.V. Lever Open More Than 3/16 [2]	"D$_4$"	107-121 (750-850)
4th Clutch		
With Engine At 2000 RPM	"R"	107-121 (750-850)
With Transaxle T.V. Lever Fully Closed [1]	"D$_4$"	68-75 (480-530)
With Transaxle T.V. Lever Open More Than 3/16 [2]	"D$_4$"	107-121 (750-850)
Low Pressure		
With Transaxle T.V. Lever Fully Closed [1]		
2nd Or 3rd Clutch	"D$_4$"	64-71 (450-500)
4th Clutch	"D$_4$"	68-75 (480-530)
High Pressure		
With Transaxle T.V. Lever Lifted Upward		
1/2 Distance Of T.V. Lever Travel		
2nd, 3rd Or 4th Clutch	"D$_4$"	107-121 (750-850)
Throttle Valve "B" Pressure		
With Transaxle T.V. Lever Fully Open [3]	"D$_4$"	107-121 (750-850)

[1] – Pressure is checked with engine at 2000 RPM. The T.V. cable must be disconnected. Fully closed position is with transaxle T.V. lever in released position and not being pulled upward by the T.V. cable.

[2] – Pressure is checked with engine at 2000 RPM. The T.V. cable must be disconnected. Open position is with transaxle T.V. lever being pulled upward 3/16 of lever travel distance.

[3] – Pressure is checked with engine at 1000 RPM. Open position is with transaxle T.V. lever being pulled fully upward.

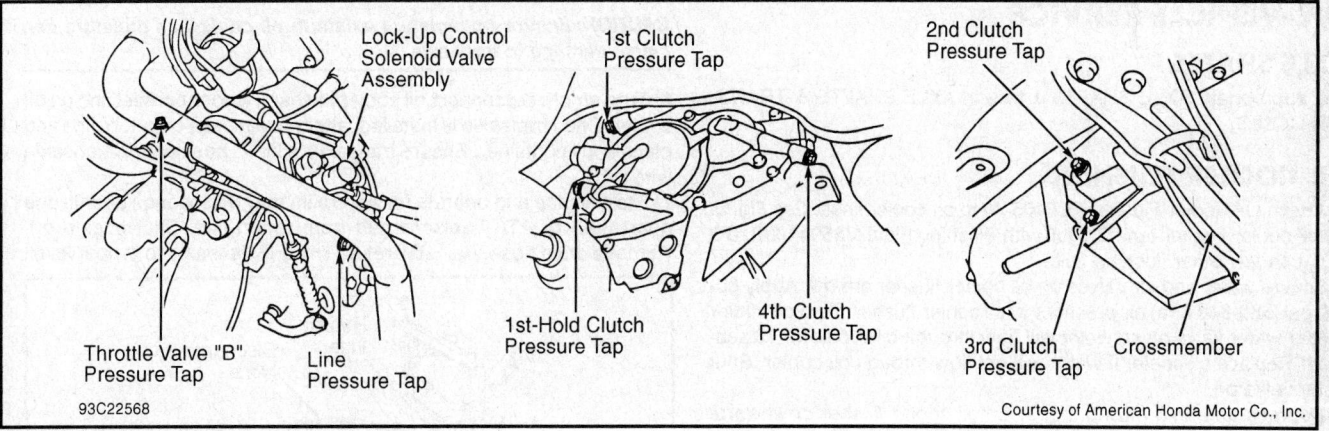

93C22568

Courtesy of American Honda Motor Co., Inc.

Fig. 4: Identifying Transaxle Pressure Taps

HYDRAULIC PRESSURE TEST SPECIFICATIONS (2.3L DOHC)

Application	Shift Lever Position	Pressure psi. (kPa)
Line Pressure		
With Engine At 2000 RPM	"P" Or "N"	114-128 (800-900)
Clutch Pressure		
1st Clutch		
With Engine At 2000 RPM	"1" Or "D₄"	114-128 (800-900)
1st-Hold Clutch		
With Engine At 2000 RPM	"1"	114-128 (800-900)
2nd Clutch		
With Engine At 2000 RPM	"2"	114-128 (800-900)
With Transaxle T.V. Lever Fully Closed [1]	"D₄"	64-71 (450-500)
With Transaxle T.V. Lever Open More Than 3/16 [2]	"D₄"	114-128 (800-900)
3rd Clutch		
With Transaxle T.V. Lever Fully Closed [1]	"D₄"	64-71 (450-500)
With Transaxle T.V. Lever Open More Than 3/16 [2]	"D₄"	114-128 (800-900)
4th Clutch		
With Engine At 2000 RPM	"R"	114-128 (800-900)
With Transaxle T.V. Lever Fully Closed [1]	"D₄"	68-75 (480-530)
With Transaxle T.V. Lever Open More Than 3/16 [2]	"D₄"	114-128 (800-900)
Low Pressure		
With Transaxle T.V. Lever Fully Closed [1]		
2nd Or 3rd Clutch	"D₄"	64-71 (450-500)
4th Clutch	"D₄"	68-75 (480-530)
High Pressure		
With Transaxle T.V. Lever Lifted Upward		
1/2 Distance Of T.V. Lever Travel		
2nd, 3rd Or 4th Clutch	"D₄"	114-128 (800-900)
Throttle Valve "B" Pressure		
With Transaxle T.V. Lever Fully Open [3]	"D₄"	114-128 (800-900)

[1] – Clutch pressure is checked with engine at 2000 RPM. The T.V. cable must be disconnected. Fully closed position is with transaxle T.V. lever in released position and not being pulled upward by the T.V. cable.

[2] – Clutch pressure is checked with engine at 2000 RPM. The T.V. cable must be disconnected. Open position is with transaxle T.V. lever being pulled upward 3/16 of lever travel distance.

[3] – Pressure is checked with engine at 1000 RPM. Open position is with transaxle T.V. lever being pulled fully upward.

ON-VEHICLE SERVICE

AXLE SHAFTS

See appropriate AXLE SHAFTS article in AXLE SHAFTS & TRANSFER CASES.

OIL COOLER FLUSHING

1) Attach Oil Cooler Flusher (J38405-A) to oil cooler lines. *See Fig. 5.* Fill oil cooler flusher tank 2/3 full with Flushing Fluid (J35944-20). DO NOT use any other flushing fluid.

2) Ensure water and air valves on oil cooler flusher are off. Apply 80-120 psi (560-840 kPa) air pressure to oil cooler flusher. Turn oil cooler flusher water valve on so water will flow through oil cooler for 10 seconds. Replace oil cooler if water will not flow through oil cooler. Shut water valve off.

3) Depress and hold mixing trigger on oil cooler flusher downward. Turn water valve on and flush oil cooler for 2 minutes. Turn air valve on for 5 seconds every 15-20 seconds to create a surging action.

4) Turn water valve off. Release mixing trigger. Disconnect oil cooler flusher and reverse hoses so oil cooler can be flushed in the opposite direction.

5) Repeat steps 2) and 3). Turn water valve off and release mixing trigger. Turn water valve on and rinse oil cooler for at least one minute. Once oil cooler is flushed in both directions, turn water off. Turn air valve on for 2 minutes or until no moisture is visible from drain hose.

CAUTION: Ensure no moisture exists in oil cooler, as moisture can cause damage to transaxle.

6) Turn air off. Disconnect oil cooler flusher. Reconnect inlet line on oil cooler. Once transaxle is installed, attach drain hose on return line and place in oil container. Ensure transaxle is in "P" position. Fill transaxle with ATF.

7) Start engine and operate for approximately 30 seconds or until one quart (.9L) of ATF is discharged from return line. Shut engine off. Remove drain hose. Reinstall return line. Fill transaxle to proper level.

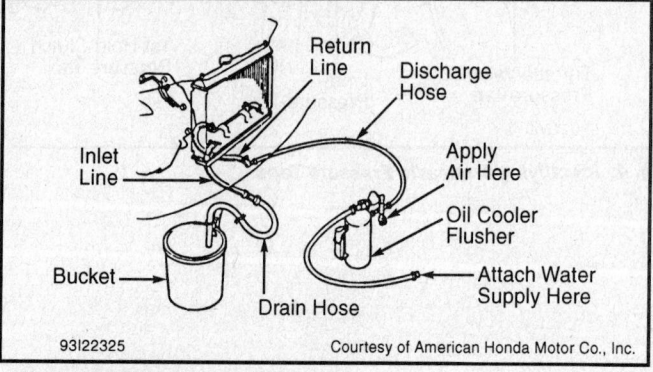

93122325   Courtesy of American Honda Motor Co., Inc.

Fig. 5: Installing Oil Cooler Flusher

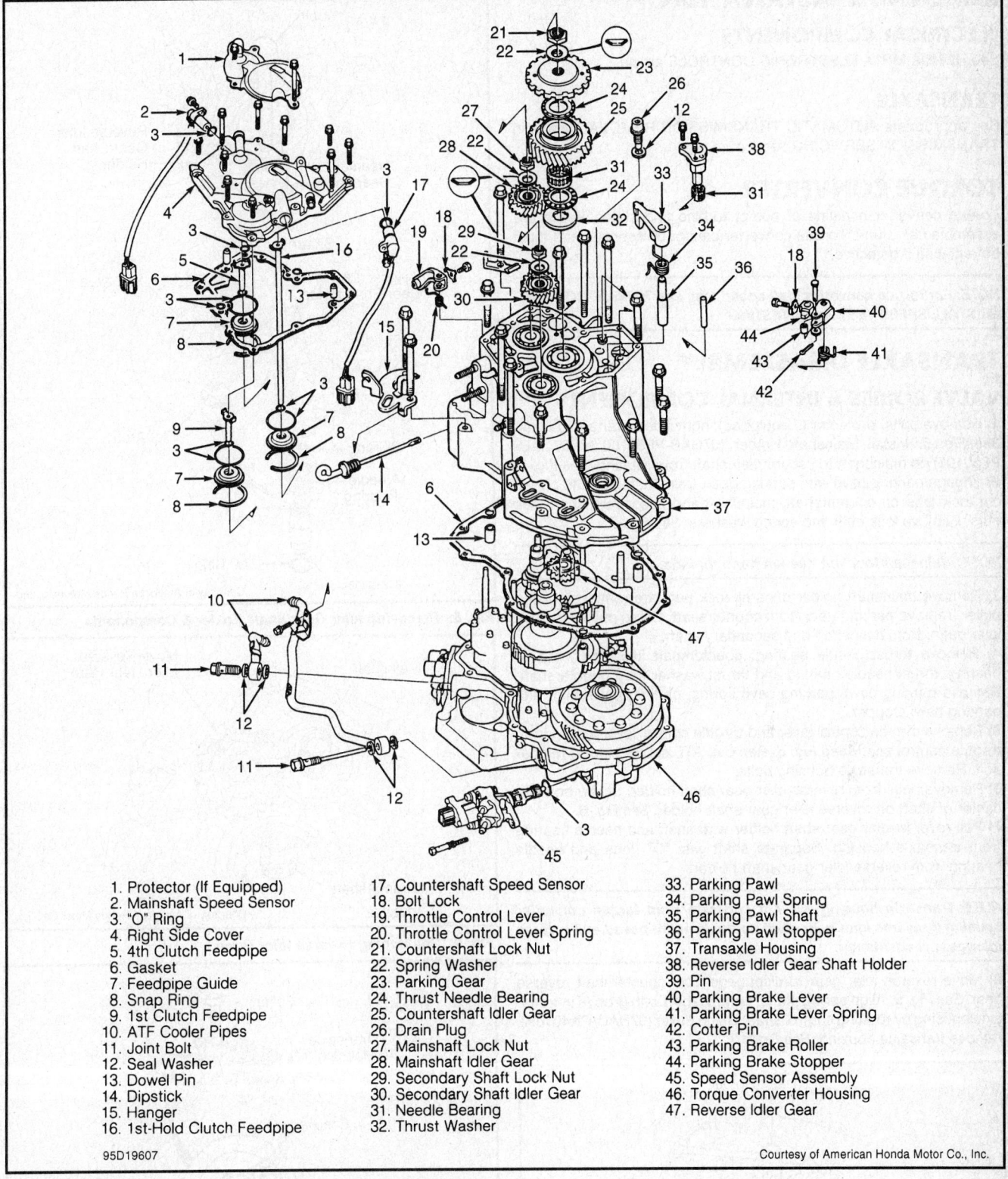

1. Protector (If Equipped)
2. Mainshaft Speed Sensor
3. "O" Ring
4. Right Side Cover
5. 4th Clutch Feedpipe
6. Gasket
7. Feedpipe Guide
8. Snap Ring
9. 1st Clutch Feedpipe
10. ATF Cooler Pipes
11. Joint Bolt
12. Seal Washer
13. Dowel Pin
14. Dipstick
15. Hanger
16. 1st-Hold Clutch Feedpipe
17. Countershaft Speed Sensor
18. Bolt Lock
19. Throttle Control Lever
20. Throttle Control Lever Spring
21. Countershaft Lock Nut
22. Spring Washer
23. Parking Gear
24. Thrust Needle Bearing
25. Countershaft Idler Gear
26. Drain Plug
27. Mainshaft Lock Nut
28. Mainshaft Idler Gear
29. Secondary Shaft Lock Nut
30. Secondary Shaft Idler Gear
31. Needle Bearing
32. Thrust Washer
33. Parking Pawl
34. Parking Pawl Spring
35. Parking Pawl Shaft
36. Parking Pawl Stopper
37. Transaxle Housing
38. Reverse Idler Gear Shaft Holder
39. Pin
40. Parking Brake Lever
41. Parking Brake Lever Spring
42. Cotter Pin
43. Parking Brake Roller
44. Parking Brake Stopper
45. Speed Sensor Assembly
46. Torque Converter Housing
47. Reverse Idler Gear

95D19607

Courtesy of American Honda Motor Co., Inc.

Fig. 6: Exploded View Of Typical Right Side Cover & Components

REMOVAL & INSTALLATION

ELECTRICAL COMPONENTS

See HONDA MP1A ELECTRONIC CONTROLS article.

TRANSAXLE

See appropriate AUTOMATIC TRANSMISSION REMOVAL article in TRANSMISSION SERVICING section.

TORQUE CONVERTER

Torque converter consists of pump, turbine and stator, which are assembled as a unit. Torque converter cannot be serviced and must be replaced if defective.

NOTE: For torque converter stall speed test, see TORQUE CONVERTER STALL SPEED TEST under TESTING.

TRANSAXLE DISASSEMBLY

VALVE BODIES & INTERNAL COMPONENTS

1) Remove bolts, protector (if equipped), right side cover and gasket. *See Fig. 6.* Install Mainshaft Holder (07GAB-PF50100 or 07GAB-PF50101) on mainshaft to secure mainshaft from rotating. *See Fig. 7.*
2) Engage parking pawl with parking gear. Using hammer and chisel, cut lock tabs on countershaft, mainshaft and secondary shaft lock nuts. Remove lock nuts and spring washers. *See Fig. 6.*

NOTE: Mainshaft lock nut has left-hand threads.

3) Remove mainshaft holder once all lock nuts are removed. Using puller, remove parking gear from countershaft. Using puller, remove idler gears from mainshaft and secondary shaft.
4) Remove thrust needle bearing, countershaft idler gear, needle bearing, thrust needle bearing and thrust washer from countershaft. Remove parking pawl, parking pawl spring, parking pawl shaft and parking pawl stopper.
5) Remove throttle control lever and throttle control lever spring from throttle control shaft. *See Fig. 6.* Remove ATF cooler pipe-to-hanger bolt. Remove transaxle housing bolts.
6) Remove bolts from reverse idler gear shaft holder. Screw bolt into center of shaft on reverse idler gear shaft holder. *See Fig. 8.*
7) Pull reverse idler gear shaft holder with shaft and needle bearing from transaxle housing. Separate shaft with "O" rings and needle bearing from reverse idler gear shaft holder.

NOTE: Transaxle housing will not separate from torque converter housing if reverse idler gear shaft holder is not removed and reverse idler gear repositioned.

8) Move reverse idler gear to disengage from countershaft reverse gear. *See Fig. 9.* Align spring pin on control shaft with groove in transaxle housing by rotating control shaft. Using Puller (07HAC-PK4010A), remove transaxle housing. *See Fig. 10.*

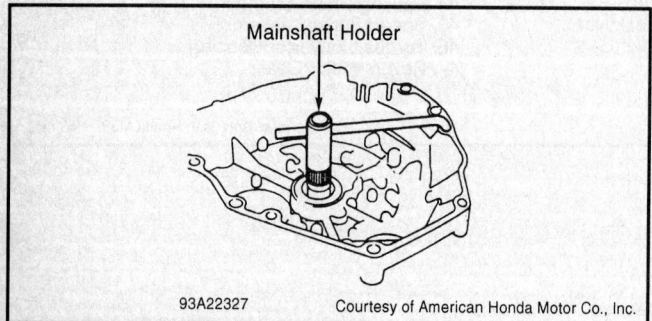

93A22327   Courtesy of American Honda Motor Co., Inc.

Fig. 7: Installing Mainshaft Holder

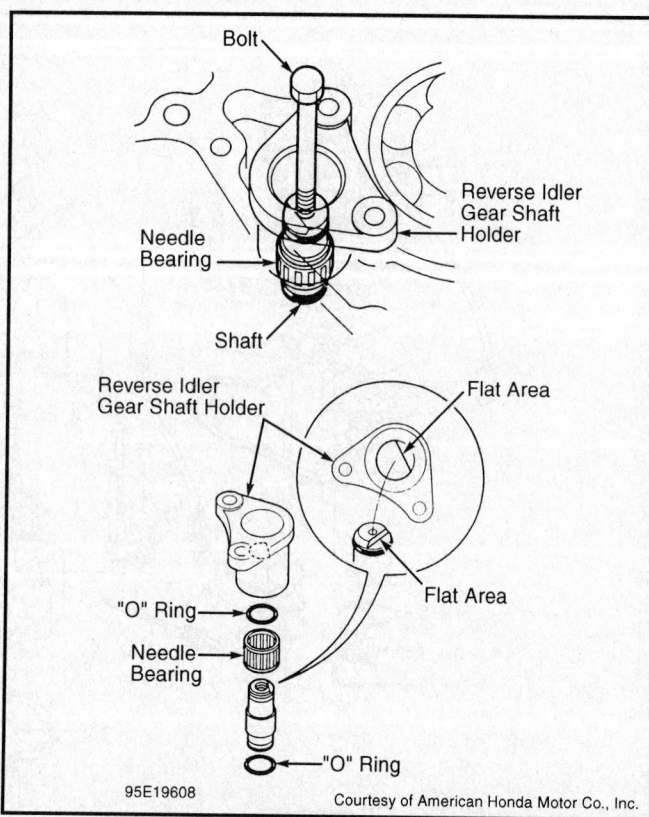

95E19608   Courtesy of American Honda Motor Co., Inc.

Fig. 8: Removing Idler Gear Shaft Holder & Components

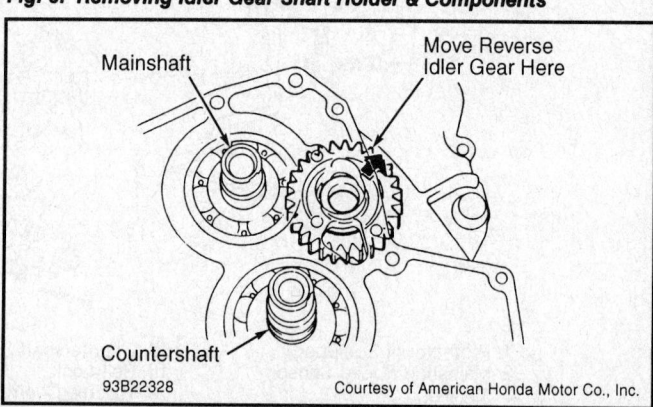

93B22328   Courtesy of American Honda Motor Co., Inc.

Fig. 9: Positioning Reverse Idler Gear

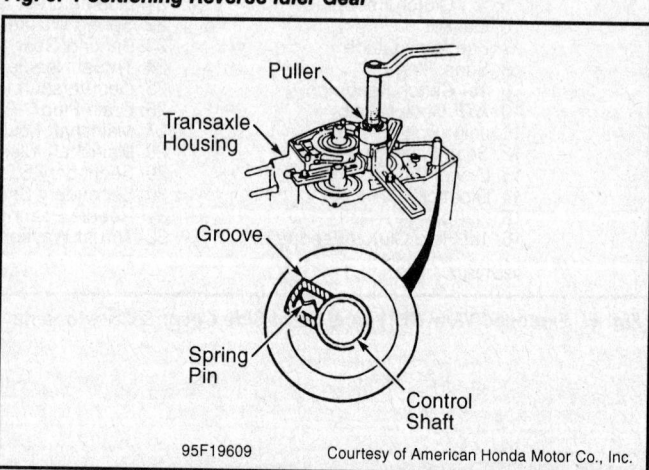

95F19609   Courtesy of American Honda Motor Co., Inc.

Fig. 10: Aligning Spring Pin & Removing Transaxle Housing

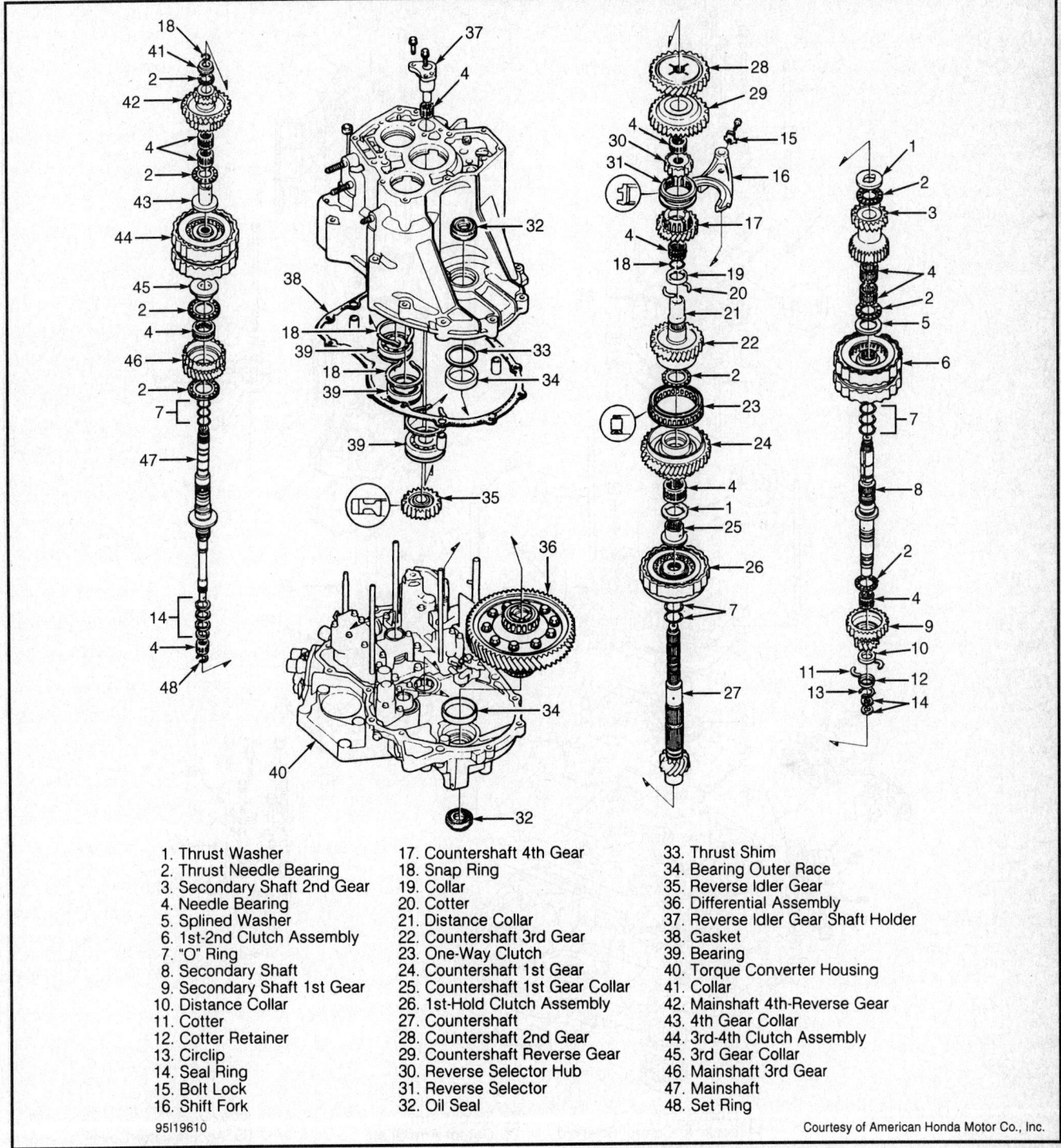

Fig. 11: Exploded View Of Transaxle Housing & Components

1. Thrust Washer
2. Thrust Needle Bearing
3. Secondary Shaft 2nd Gear
4. Needle Bearing
5. Splined Washer
6. 1st-2nd Clutch Assembly
7. "O" Ring
8. Secondary Shaft
9. Secondary Shaft 1st Gear
10. Distance Collar
11. Cotter
12. Cotter Retainer
13. Circlip
14. Seal Ring
15. Bolt Lock
16. Shift Fork

17. Countershaft 4th Gear
18. Snap Ring
19. Collar
20. Cotter
21. Distance Collar
22. Countershaft 3rd Gear
23. One-Way Clutch
24. Countershaft 1st Gear
25. Countershaft 1st Gear Collar
26. 1st-Hold Clutch Assembly
27. Countershaft
28. Countershaft 2nd Gear
29. Countershaft Reverse Gear
30. Reverse Selector Hub
31. Reverse Selector
32. Oil Seal

33. Thrust Shim
34. Bearing Outer Race
35. Reverse Idler Gear
36. Differential Assembly
37. Reverse Idler Gear Shaft Holder
38. Gasket
39. Bearing
40. Torque Converter Housing
41. Collar
42. Mainshaft 4th-Reverse Gear
43. 4th Gear Collar
44. 3rd-4th Clutch Assembly
45. 3rd Gear Collar
46. Mainshaft 3rd Gear
47. Mainshaft
48. Set Ring

95I19610

Courtesy of American Honda Motor Co., Inc.

9) Remove reverse idler gear from transaxle housing. Remove countershaft 2nd gear, countershaft reverse gear, thrust washer, thrust needle bearing and secondary shaft 2nd gear together from countershaft and secondary shaft. *See Fig. 11.*

10) Remove bolt, bolt lock, shift fork, reverse selector hub and reverse selector from countershaft. Remove needle bearings, thrust needle bearing and splined washer from secondary shaft.

11) Remove secondary shaft, mainshaft and countershaft assemblies from torque converter housing. Remove differential assembly from torque converter housing. Remove cable control lever from end of control shaft. Remove bolts, bolt locks (if equipped) and servo detent base. *See Fig. 12.* Remove bolts and fluid strainer.

CAUTION: Accumulator cover is under spring tension. Hold accumulator cover downward when removing bolts in a crisscross pattern to prevent bolt damage.

12) Using care, remove bolts, accumulator cover and "O" ring. Remove oil feedpipes from servo body and main valve body. Remove bolts, servo body and servo separator plate.

13) Remove secondary valve body and secondary separator plate. Use care not to lose check balls in secondary valve body. Remove bolts, throttle valve body and throttle valve separator plate.

14) Remove "E" clip and throttle control shaft from throttle valve body. Remove bolt and regulator valve body. Remove stopper shaft, stator shaft and "O" ring .

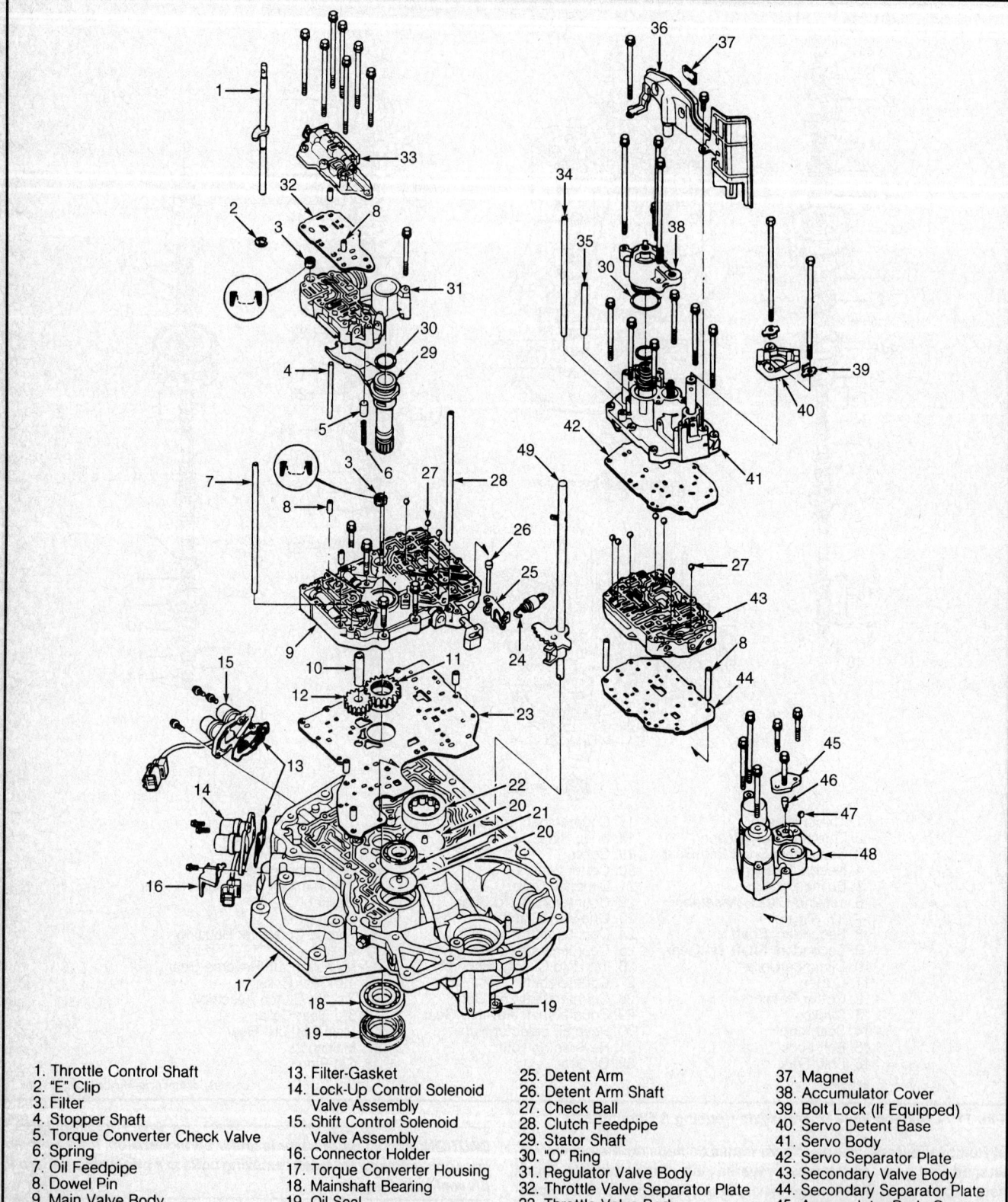

1. Throttle Control Shaft
2. "E" Clip
3. Filter
4. Stopper Shaft
5. Torque Converter Check Valve
6. Spring
7. Oil Feedpipe
8. Dowel Pin
9. Main Valve Body
10. Oil Pump Driven Gear Shaft
11. Oil Pump Drive Gear
12. Oil Pump Driven Gear

13. Filter-Gasket
14. Lock-Up Control Solenoid Valve Assembly
15. Shift Control Solenoid Valve Assembly
16. Connector Holder
17. Torque Converter Housing
18. Mainshaft Bearing
19. Oil Seal
20. Oil Guide Plate
21. Secondary Shaft Bearing
22. Countershaft Bearing
23. Main Separator Plate
24. Detent Spring

25. Detent Arm
26. Detent Arm Shaft
27. Check Ball
28. Clutch Feedpipe
29. Stator Shaft
30. "O" Ring
31. Regulator Valve Body
32. Throttle Valve Separator Plate
33. Throttle Valve Body
34. Oil Feedpipe
35. Oil Feedpipe
36. Fluid Strainer

37. Magnet
38. Accumulator Cover
39. Bolt Lock (If Equipped)
40. Servo Detent Base
41. Servo Body
42. Servo Separator Plate
43. Secondary Valve Body
44. Secondary Separator Plate
45. Accumulator Body Cover
46. 1st Accumulator Choke
47. Steel Ball
48. 1st-2nd Accumulator Body
49. Control Shaft

95J19611

Courtesy of American Honda Motor Co., Inc.

Fig. 12: Exploded View Of Torque Converter Housing & Components

15) Disconnect detent spring from detent arm. Remove control shaft from torque converter housing. Remove detent arm shaft, detent arm and detent spring. *See Fig. 12.*

16) Remove bolts and main valve body. Use care not to lose check balls in main valve body. Remove bolts and 1st-2nd accumulator body.

17) Remove oil pump driven gear shaft, oil pump driven and drive gears, main separator plate and dowel pins. Remove lock-up control solenoid valve assembly and shift control solenoid valve assembly (if necessary).

COMPONENT DISASSEMBLY & REASSEMBLY

MAIN VALVE BODY

CAUTION: When disassembling main valve body, place main valve body components in order and mark spring locations for reassembly reference. DO NOT use force to remove components. DO NOT use magnet to remove check balls, as check balls may become magnetized. Note direction of valve cap installation before removing from main valve body.

Disassembly – Disassemble main valve body. *See Fig. 13.* Use care when removing valve caps or spring seats, as they are under spring pressure.

Cleaning & Inspection – 1) Clean components with solvent and dry with compressed air. Replace main valve body as an assembly if any parts are worn or damaged.

2) Ensure all valves slide freely in bores. If valves do not slide freely, polish burrs or rough areas using No. 600 sandpaper soaked in ATF for at least 30 minutes. Thoroughly clean main valve body and components if polishing was needed.

3) Ensure spring free length is within specification. See SPRING SPECIFICATIONS table. Replace springs if not within specification.

NOTE: Oil pump clearance must be checked in main valve body. See OIL PUMP under COMPONENT DISASSEMBLY & REASSEMBLY.

Reassembly – Coat all components and bores with ATF. To reassemble, reverse disassembly procedure. Install NEW filter. Ensure all components are installed in correct location. *See Fig. 13.*

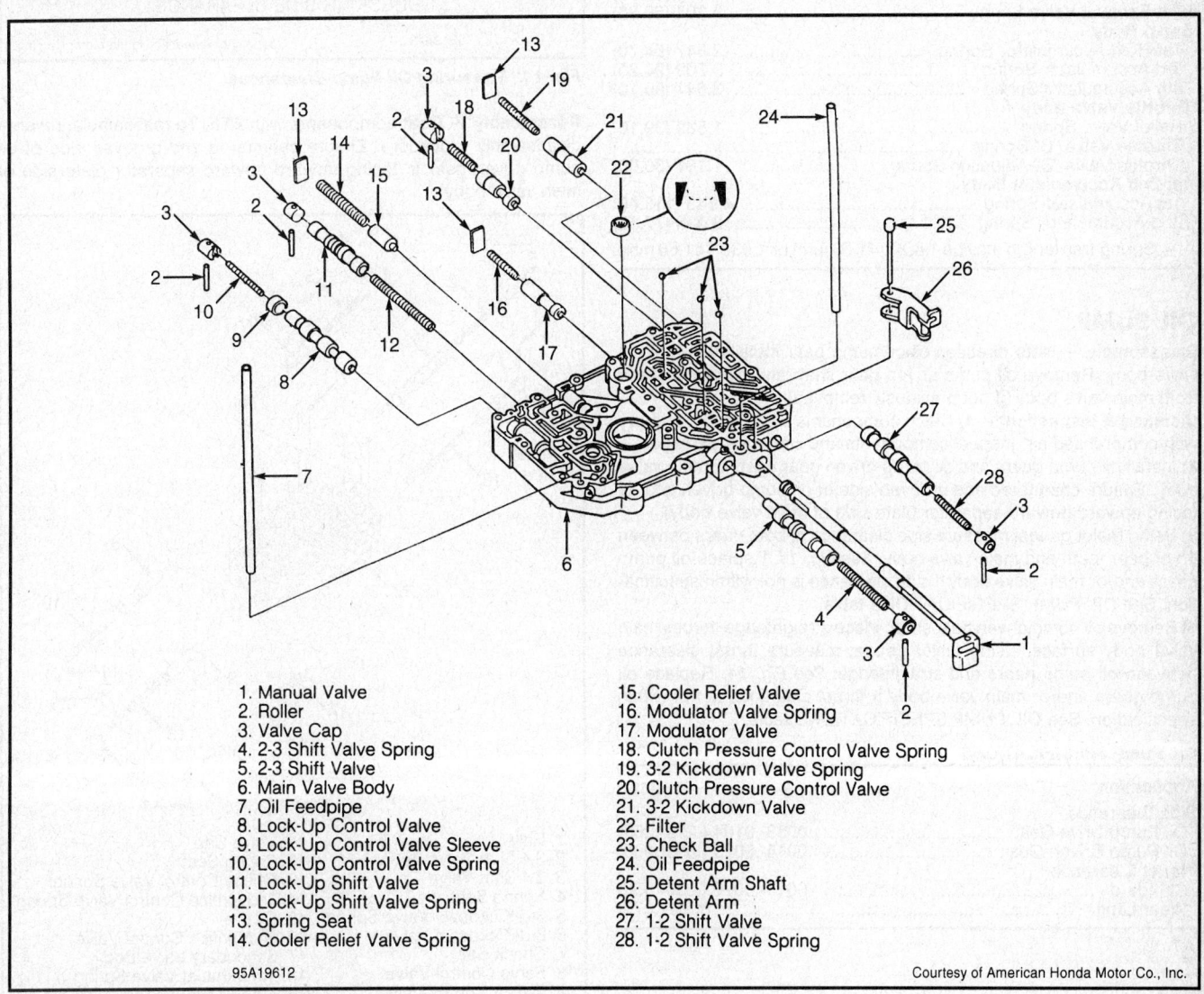

1. Manual Valve
2. Roller
3. Valve Cap
4. 2-3 Shift Valve Spring
5. 2-3 Shift Valve
6. Main Valve Body
7. Oil Feedpipe
8. Lock-Up Control Valve
9. Lock-Up Control Valve Sleeve
10. Lock-Up Control Valve Spring
11. Lock-Up Shift Valve
12. Lock-Up Shift Valve Spring
13. Spring Seat
14. Cooler Relief Valve Spring
15. Cooler Relief Valve
16. Modulator Valve Spring
17. Modulator Valve
18. Clutch Pressure Control Valve Spring
19. 3-2 Kickdown Valve Spring
20. Clutch Pressure Control Valve
21. 3-2 Kickdown Valve
22. Filter
23. Check Ball
24. Oil Feedpipe
25. Detent Arm Shaft
26. Detent Arm
27. 1-2 Shift Valve
28. 1-2 Shift Valve Spring

95A19612

Courtesy of American Honda Motor Co., Inc.

Fig. 13: Exploded View Of Main Valve Body

SPRING SPECIFICATIONS

Application	Free Length In. (mm)
Main Valve Body	
Clutch Pressure Control Valve Spring	1.299 (33.00)
Cooler Relief Valve Spring	1.843 (46.81)
Lock-Up Control Valve Spring	1.496 (38.00)
Lock-Up Shift Valve Spring	2.902 (73.70)
Modulator Valve Spring	1.299 (33.00)
1-2 Shift Valve Spring	1.626 (41.30)
2-3 Shift Valve Spring	2.244 (57.00)
3-2 Kickdown Valve Spring	1.846 (46.90)
Regulator Valve Body	
Lock-Up Timing Valve Spring	2.012 (51.10)
Regulator Valve Spring "A"	
2.2L SOHC	3.362 (85.40)
2.3L DOHC	3.457 (87.80)
Regulator Valve Spring "B"	1.732 (44.00)
Stator Reaction Spring	1.193 (30.30)
Torque Converter Check Valve Spring	1.504 (38.20)
Secondary Valve Body	
Orifice Control Valve Spring	2.067 (52.50)
Servo Control Valve Spring	2.071 (52.60)
2nd Orifice Control Valve Spring	2.295 (58.30)
3rd Kickdown Valve Spring	1.902 (48.30)
3-4 Shift Valve Spring	2.244 (57.00)
4th Exhaust Valve Spring	2.394 (60.80)
Servo Body	
1st-Hold Accumulator Spring	2.547 (64.70)
3rd Accumulator Spring	3.709 (94.20)
4th Accumulator Spring	3.547 (90.10)
Throttle Valve Body	
Relief Valve Spring	1.539 (39.10)
Throttle Valve "B" Spring	[1]
Throttle Valve "B" Adjusting Spring	1.181 (30.00)
1st-2nd Accumulator Body	
1st Accumulator Spring	4.543 (115.40)
2nd Accumulator Spring	3.035 (77.10)

[1] – Spring free length may be 1.634" (41.50 mm) or 1.638" (41.60 mm).

OIL PUMP

Disassembly – Note direction of oil pump gear installation in main valve body. Remove oil pump driven gear shaft and oil pump gears from main valve body (if not previously removed).

Cleaning & Inspection – 1) Clean components with solvent and dry with compressed air. Inspect components and replace if damaged.

2) Install oil pump gears and oil pump driven gear shaft in main valve body. Ensure chamfered and grooved side of oil pump driven gear is facing upward (toward separator plate side of main valve body).

3) Using feeler gauge, measure side clearance of both gears between tip of gear teeth and main valve body. *See Fig. 14.* Replace oil pump gears and/or main valve body if side clearance is not within specification. See OIL PUMP SPECIFICATIONS table.

4) Remove oil pump driven gear shaft. Place straightedge across main valve body surface. Using feeler gauge, measure thrust clearance between oil pump gears and straightedge. *See Fig. 14.* Replace oil pump gears and/or main valve body if thrust clearance is not within specification. See OIL PUMP SPECIFICATIONS table.

OIL PUMP SPECIFICATIONS

Application	In. (mm)
Side Clearance	
Oil Pump Drive Gear	.0083-.0104 (.210-.265)
Oil Pump Driven Gear	.0014-.0025 (.035-.063)
Thrust Clearance	
Standard	.0010-.0020 (.030-.050)
Wear Limit	.0028 (.070)

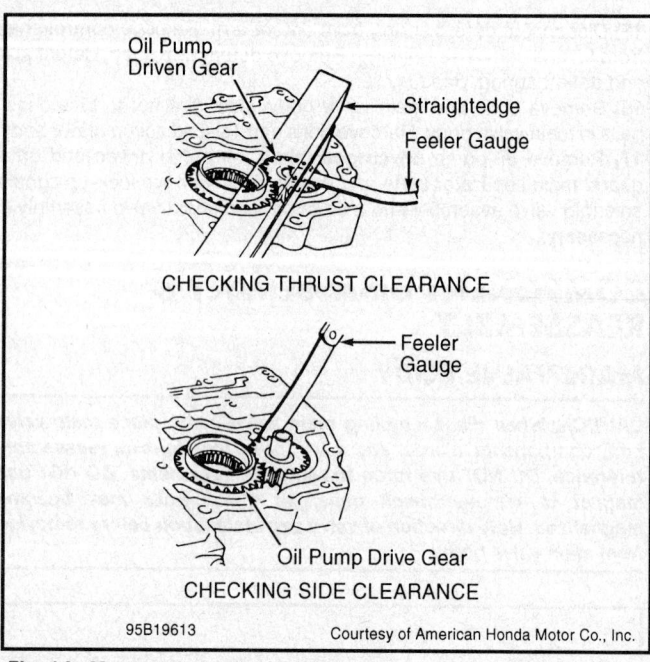

CHECKING THRUST CLEARANCE

CHECKING SIDE CLEARANCE

95B19613   Courtesy of American Honda Motor Co., Inc.

Fig. 14: Measuring Oil Pump Clearances

Reassembly – Coat components with ATF. To reassemble, reverse disassembly procedure. Ensure chamfered and grooved side of oil pump driven gear is facing upward (toward separator plate side of main valve body).

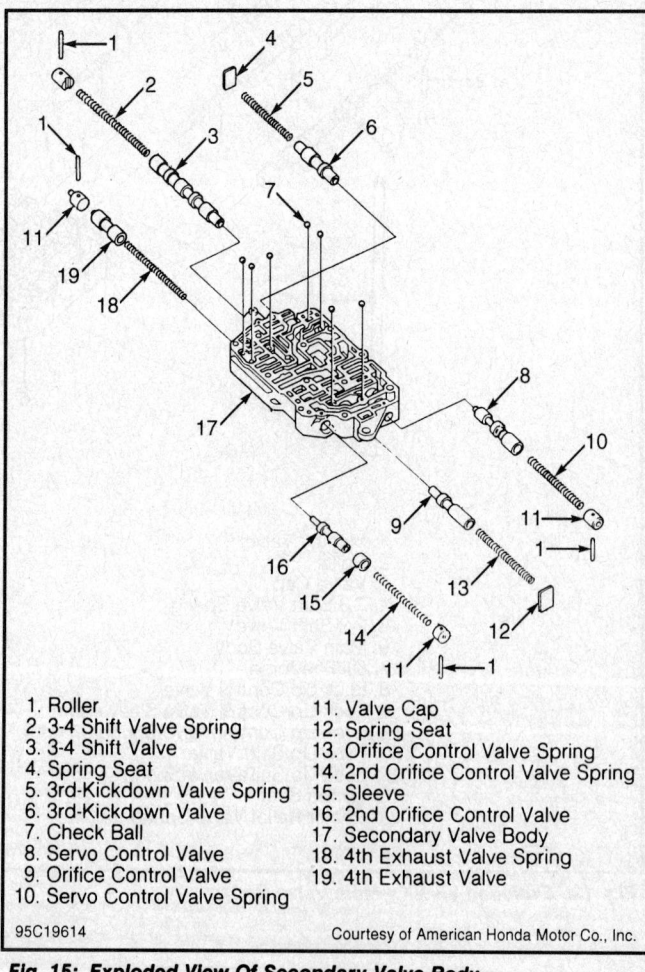

1. Roller
2. 3-4 Shift Valve Spring
3. 3-4 Shift Valve
4. Spring Seat
5. 3rd-Kickdown Valve Spring
6. 3rd-Kickdown Valve
7. Check Ball
8. Servo Control Valve
9. Orifice Control Valve
10. Servo Control Valve Spring
11. Valve Cap
12. Spring Seat
13. Orifice Control Valve Spring
14. 2nd Orifice Control Valve Spring
15. Sleeve
16. 2nd Orifice Control Valve
17. Secondary Valve Body
18. 4th Exhaust Valve Spring
19. 4th Exhaust Valve

95C19614   Courtesy of American Honda Motor Co., Inc.

Fig. 15: Exploded View Of Secondary Valve Body

SECONDARY VALVE BODY

CAUTION: When disassembling secondary valve body, place secondary valve body components in order and mark spring locations for reassembly reference. DO NOT use force to remove components. DO NOT use magnet to remove check balls, as check balls may become magnetized. Note direction of valve cap installation before removing from secondary valve body.

Disassembly – Disassemble secondary valve body. *See Fig. 15.* Use care when removing valve caps or spring seats, as they are under spring pressure.

Cleaning & Inspection – 1) Clean components with solvent and dry with compressed air. Replace secondary valve body as an assembly if any parts are worn or damaged.

2) Ensure all valves slide freely in bore. If valves do not slide freely, polish burrs or rough areas using No. 600 sandpaper soaked in ATF for at least 30 minutes. Thoroughly clean secondary valve body and components if polishing was needed.

3) Ensure spring free length is within specification. See SPRING SPECIFICATIONS table. Replace springs if not within specification.

Reassembly – Coat all components and bores with ATF. To reassemble, reverse disassembly procedure. Ensure all components are installed in correct location. *See Fig. 15.*

REGULATOR VALVE BODY

CAUTION: Regulator spring cap is under spring pressure. Ensure regulator spring cap is held downward when removing stopper bolt.

Disassembly – Hold regulator spring cap downward. Remove stopper bolt. Slowly remove regulator spring cap and components from regulator valve body. *See Fig. 16.*

Cleaning & Inspection – 1) Clean components with solvent and dry with compressed air. Replace regulator valve body as an assembly if any parts are worn or damaged.

2) Ensure all valves slide freely in bore. If valves do not slide freely, polish burrs or rough areas using No. 600 sandpaper soaked in ATF for at least 30 minutes. Thoroughly clean regulator valve body and components if polishing was needed.

3) Ensure spring free length is within specification. See SPRING SPECIFICATIONS table. Replace springs if not within specification.

Reassembly – Coat all components and bores with ATF. To reassemble, reverse disassembly procedure. Install NEW filter. Ensure all components are installed in correct location. *See Fig. 16.* Tighten stopper bolt to specification. See TORQUE SPECIFICATIONS.

THROTTLE VALVE BODY

NOTE: DO NOT loosen or remove throttle adjusting bolt.

Disassembly – Disassemble throttle valve body. *See Fig. 17.* Use care when removing throttle cam stopper and spring seat, as they are under spring pressure.

Cleaning & Inspection – 1) Clean components with solvent and dry with compressed air. Replace throttle valve body as an assembly if any parts are worn or damaged.

2) Ensure all valves slide freely in bore. If valves do not slide freely, polish burrs or rough areas using No. 600 sandpaper soaked in ATF for at least 30 minutes. Thoroughly clean throttle valve body and components if polishing was needed.

3) Ensure spring free length is within specification. See SPRING SPECIFICATIONS table. Replace springs if not within specification.

Reassembly – Coat all components and bores with ATF. To reassemble, reverse disassembly procedure. Ensure all components are installed in correct location. *See Fig. 17.* Tighten throttle cam stopper bolt to specification. See TORQUE SPECIFICATIONS.

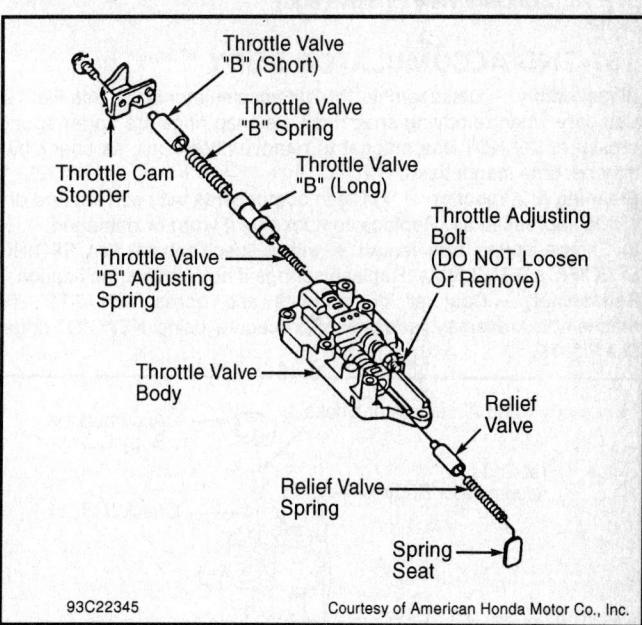

93C22345   Courtesy of American Honda Motor Co., Inc.

Fig. 17: Exploded View Of Throttle Valve Body

SERVO BODY

Disassembly – Disassemble servo body. *See Fig. 18.* Use care when removing accumulator cover, as it is under spring pressure.

Cleaning & Inspection – 1) Clean components with solvent and dry with compressed air. Replace components if worn or damaged.

2) Replace fluid strainer if clogged. Ensure spring free length is within specification. See SPRING SPECIFICATIONS table. Replace springs if not within specification.

Reassembly – Coat all components and bores with ATF. To reassemble, reverse disassembly procedure using NEW "O" rings. *See Fig. 18.*

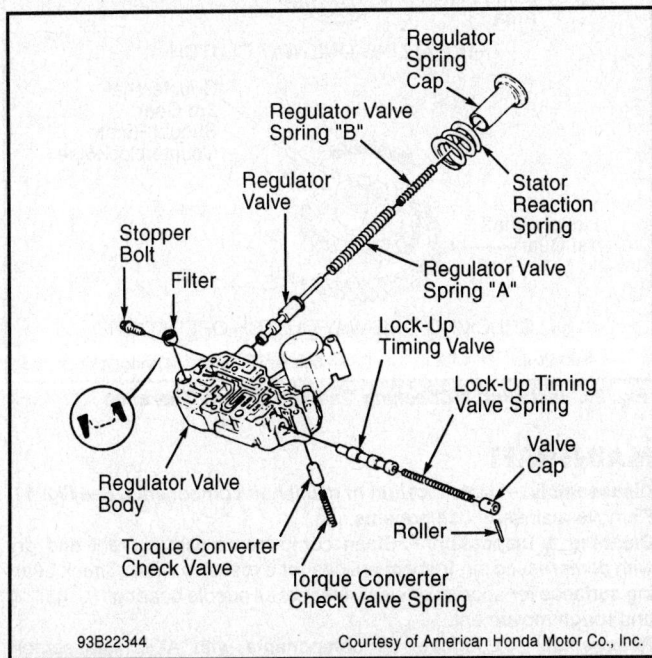

93B22344   Courtesy of American Honda Motor Co., Inc.

Fig. 16: Exploded View Of Regulator Valve Body

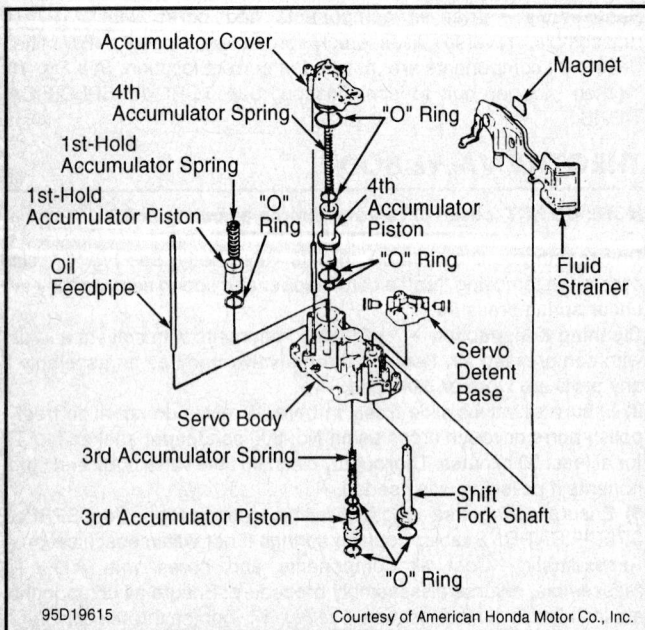

Fig. 18: Exploded View Of Servo Body

1ST-2ND ACCUMULATOR BODY

Disassembly – Disassemble 1st-2nd accumulator body. See Fig. 19. Use care when removing snap rings, as snap rings are under spring pressure. DO NOT use magnet to remove check ball, as check ball may become magnetized.

Cleaning & Inspection – **1)** Clean components with solvent and dry with compressed air. Replace components if worn or damaged.
2) Ensure spring free length is within specification. See SPRING SPECIFICATIONS table. Replace springs if not within specification.

Reassembly – Coat all components and bores with ATF. To reassemble, reverse disassembly procedure using NEW "O" rings. See Fig. 19.

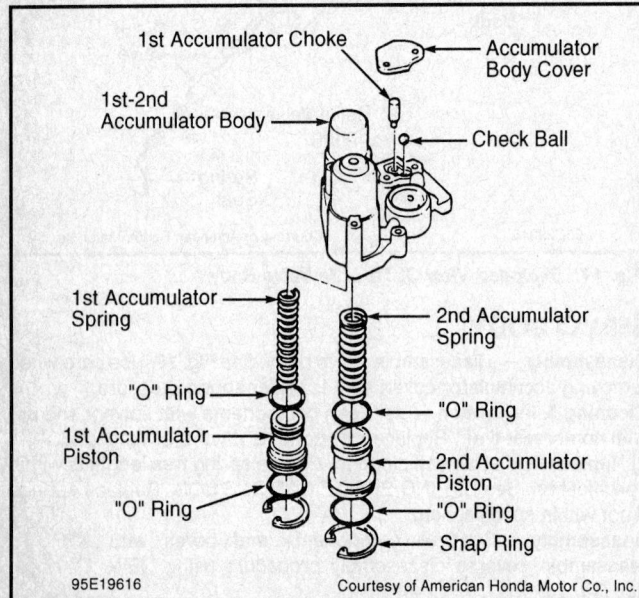

Fig. 19: Exploded View Of 1st-2nd Accumulator Body

COUNTERSHAFT & ONE-WAY CLUTCH

Disassembly – **1)** Note location of countershaft components. See Fig. 11. Remove countershaft components down to the countershaft 3rd gear.

2) Place countershaft in hydraulic press while supporting 1st-hold clutch assembly. Place a protective cap between hydraulic press and countershaft to prevent damage to shaft. Press countershaft from countershaft 3rd gear and 1st-hold clutch assembly.
3) Separate countershaft 3rd gear with countershaft 1st gear from 1st-hold clutch assembly. Remove needle bearing, thrust washer and countershaft 1st gear collar from 1st-hold clutch assembly.
4) To separate countershaft 3rd gear from countershaft 1st gear, hold countershaft 1st gear and rotate countershaft 3rd gear counterclockwise. Remove countershaft 3rd gear and thrust needle bearing from countershaft 1st gear.
5) Note direction of one-way clutch installation in countershaft 1st gear. Gently pry one-way clutch from countershaft 1st gear.

Cleaning & Inspection – **1)** Clean components with solvent and dry with compressed air. Inspect splines for excessive wear. Check bearing surfaces for scoring or wear.
2) Inspect all needle bearings for galling and rough movement. Inspect one-way clutch for damage.

Reassembly – **1)** Lubricate all components with ATF. Install countershaft 1st gear collar, thrust washer and needle bearing on 1st-hold clutch assembly.
2) Install one-way clutch in countershaft 1st gear with large flange area toward countershaft 1st gear. See Fig. 20. Install thrust needle bearing on countershaft 1st gear. Install countershaft 3rd gear on countershaft 1st gear. Hold countershaft 1st gear. Ensure countershaft 3rd gear rotates counterclockwise.
3) Install countershaft 1st gear with countershaft 3rd gear on 1st-hold clutch assembly. Using press, press countershaft into countershaft 3rd gear and 1st-hold clutch assembly. Ensure all splines are aligned when installing countershaft. Ensure final drive gear on countershaft contacts 1st-hold clutch assembly.
4) Reassemble countershaft components. Ensure thrust needle bearings are installed with unrolled edge of bearing retainer facing washer. Before installing NEW "O" rings on countershaft, wrap splines on countershaft with tape to prevent damage to "O" rings.

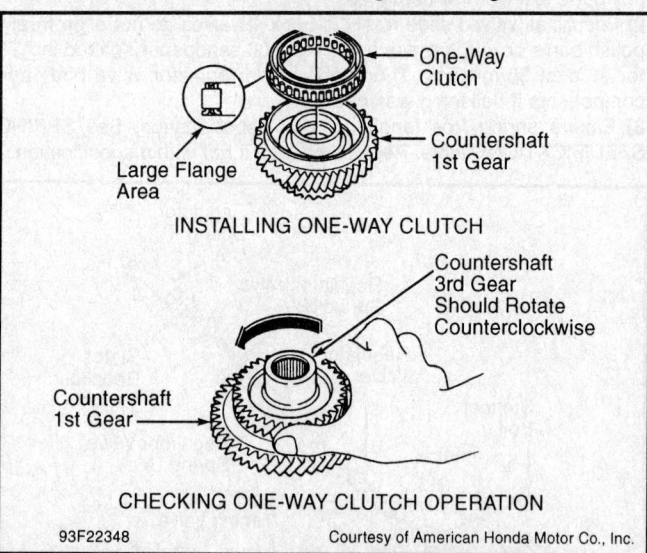

Fig. 20: Installing & Checking One-Way Clutch Operation

MAINSHAFT

Disassembly – Note location of mainshaft components. See Fig. 11. Remove mainshaft components.

Cleaning & Inspection – Clean components with solvent and dry with compressed air. Inspect splines for excessive wear. Check bearing surfaces for scoring or wear. Inspect all needle bearings for galling and rough movement.

Reassembly – Lubricate all components with ATF. Reassemble mainshaft. See Fig. 11. Ensure thrust needle bearings are installed with unrolled edge of bearing retainer facing washer. Before installing NEW "O" rings on mainshaft, wrap splines on mainshaft with tape to prevent damage to "O" rings.

SECONDARY SHAFT

Disassembly – Note location of secondary shaft components. *See Fig. 11.* Remove secondary shaft components.

Cleaning & Inspection – Clean components with solvent and dry with compressed air. Inspect splines for excessive wear. Check bearing surfaces for scoring or wear. Inspect all needle bearings for galling and rough movement.

Reassembly – 1) Lubricate all components with ATF. Reassemble secondary shaft without "O" rings. Ensure thrust needle bearings are installed with unrolled edge of bearing retainer facing washer.

2) Remove secondary shaft bearing from transaxle housing. Install secondary shaft bearing, secondary shaft idler gear, spring washer and used lock nut on secondary shaft.

3) Tighten lock nut to 22 ft. lbs. (30 N.m). Attach dial indicator on secondary shaft with stem against secondary shaft 2nd gear. *See Fig. 21.* Push secondary shaft 2nd gear inward (toward 1st-2nd clutch) and zero dial indicator.

4) Pull secondary shaft 2nd gear outward and note axial clearance. This is the secondary shaft 2nd gear clearance. Check secondary shaft 2nd gear clearance at 3 places on secondary shaft 2nd gear. Average the 3 measurements to obtain secondary shaft 2nd gear clearance.

5) Replace splined washer located next to 1st-2nd clutch assembly if secondary shaft 2nd gear clearance is not .002-.005" (.04-.12 mm). Different thickness splined washers are available. See SPLINED WASHER SPECIFICATIONS table. Install different thickness splined washer (if necessary) and recheck clearance.

SPLINED WASHER SPECIFICATIONS

Washer Number	Part Number	Thickness In. (mm)
1	90406-PX4-700	.159 (4.05)
2	90407-PX4-700	.161 (4.10)
3	90408-PX4-700	.163 (4.15)
4	90409-PX4-700	.165 (4.20)
5	90410-PX4-700	.167 (4.25)
6	90411-PX4-700	.169 (4.30)
7	90412-PX4-700	.171 (4.35)
8	90413-PX4-700	.173 (4.40)
9	90414-PX4-700	.175 (4.45)

6) Remove lock nut, spring washer, secondary shaft idler gear and secondary shaft bearing. Lubricate all components with ATF.

7) Reassemble secondary shaft. Ensure thrust needle bearings are installed with unrolled edge of bearing retainer facing washer. Before installing NEW "O" rings on secondary shaft, wrap splines on secondary shaft with tape to prevent damage to "O" rings.

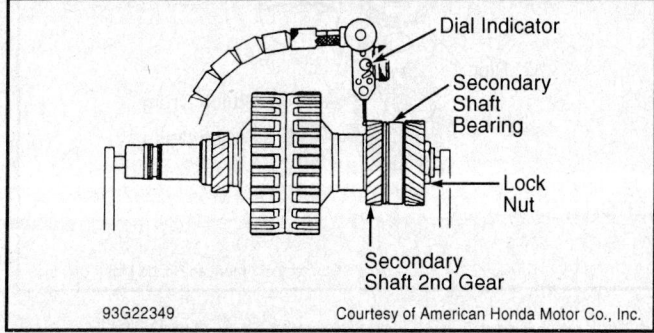

93G22349   Courtesy of American Honda Motor Co., Inc.

Fig. 21: Checking Secondary Shaft 2nd Gear Clearance

CLUTCH ASSEMBLIES

Disassembly – 1) Remove snap ring, clutch end plate, clutch discs and clutch plates. *See Figs. 22 and 23.*

2) On some 1st, 3rd and 4th clutches, disc spring may not be staked on clutch piston. Note direction of disc spring installation. Remove disc spring if disc spring is not staked on clutch piston.

3) Using spring compress, compress return spring. Remove circlip. Release and remove spring compressor. Remove spring retainer and return spring.

4) Wrap shop towel around clutch drum. Apply light air pressure to oil passage on clutch drum to remove clutch piston. Remove "O" rings.

Cleaning & Inspection – 1) Clean metal components with solvent and dry with compressed air. Ensure check valve on rear of clutch piston is thoroughly cleaned and securely fastened on clutch piston.

2) Inspect components for damage. Replace if necessary. Ensure no rough edges exist on "O" ring sealing areas.

3) On some 1st, 3rd and 4th clutches, disc spring may be staked on clutch piston. If disc spring is staked on clutch piston, ensure disc spring is securely staked to clutch piston.

Reassembly – 1) Lubricate all components with ATF. Install NEW "O" rings. Install clutch piston in clutch drum. Slightly rotate clutch piston back and forth during installation to prevent damaging "O" rings.

CAUTION: DO NOT apply excessive force on clutch piston or "O" rings will be damaged.

---

2) Install return spring and spring retainer in clutch drum. Place circlip on spring retainer. Using spring compressor, compress return spring. Install circlip. Remove spring compressor.

3) On 1st, 3rd and 4th clutches, install disc spring if disc spring is not staked on clutch piston. Install disc spring on 1st-hold clutch. Ensure disc spring is installed in proper direction. *See Figs. 22 and 23.*

CAUTION: Soak clutch discs in ATF for at least 30 minutes before installing.

---

4) Alternately install clutch plates and clutch discs starting with clutch plate. Install clutch end plate with flat side toward clutch disc. Install snap ring.

NOTE: The 2nd clutch on 2.3L DOHC uses 4 clutch discs and 4 clutch plates, while 2nd clutch on 2.2L SOHC only uses 3 clutch discs and 3 clutch plates.

---

5) Using dial indicator, measure clutch clearance between clutch end plate and top clutch disc. *See Fig. 24.* Zero dial indicator with clutch end plate lowered, and then lift clutch end plate upward against snap ring. Distance measured is clutch clearance.

6) Measure clutch clearance at 3 different locations. Clutch clearance should be within specification. See CLUTCH CLEARANCE SPECIFICATIONS table.

7) If clutch clearance is not within specification, install different thickness clutch end plate. See CLUTCH END PLATE SPECIFICATIONS table.

NOTE: If thickest clutch end plate is installed and clutch clearance still exceeds specification, replace clutch discs and clutch plates.

CLUTCH CLEARANCE SPECIFICATIONS

Application	In. (mm)
1st & 2nd Clutches	.026-.033 (.65-.85)
1st-Hold Clutch	.031-.039 (.80-1.00)
3rd & 4th Clutches	.016-.024 (.40-.60)

CLUTCH END PLATE SPECIFICATIONS

Plate Number	Part Number	Thickness In. (mm)
1	22551-PX4-003	.083 (2.10)
2	22552-PX4-003	.087 (2.20)
3	22553-PX4-003	.091 (2.30)
4	22554-PX4-003	.094 (2.40)
5	22555-PX4-003	.098 (2.50)
6	22556-PX4-003	.102 (2.60)
7	22557-PX4-003	.106 (2.70)
8	22558-PX4-003	.110 (2.80)
9	22559-PX4-003	.114 (2.90)

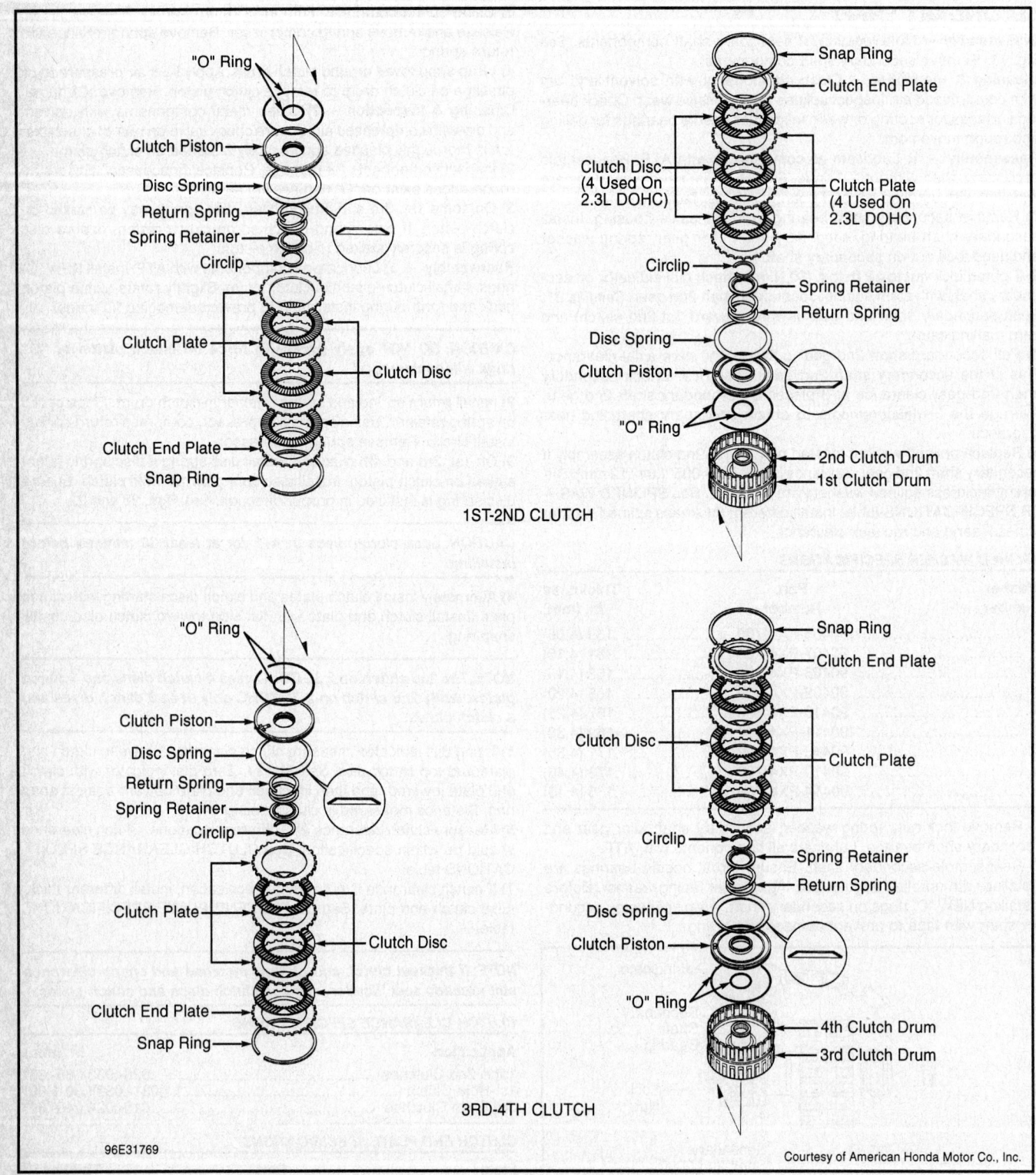

1ST-2ND CLUTCH

3RD-4TH CLUTCH

96E31769

Courtesy of American Honda Motor Co., Inc.

Fig. 22: Exploded View Of 1st-2nd & 3rd-4th Clutches

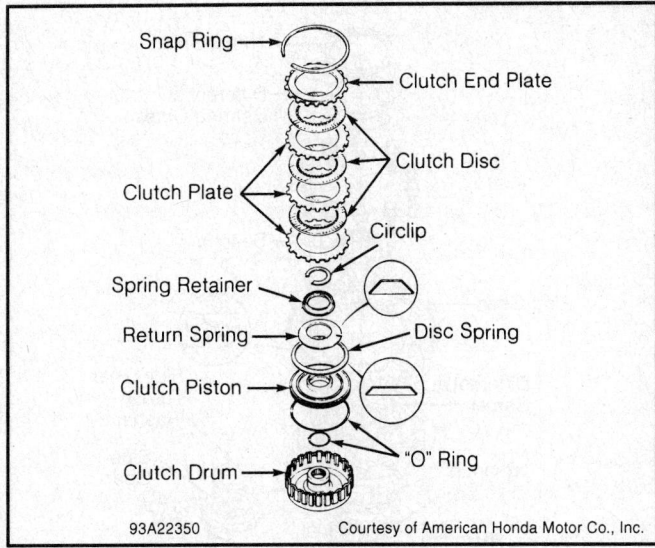

93A22350   Courtesy of American Honda Motor Co., Inc.

Fig. 23: Exploded View Of 1st-Hold Clutch

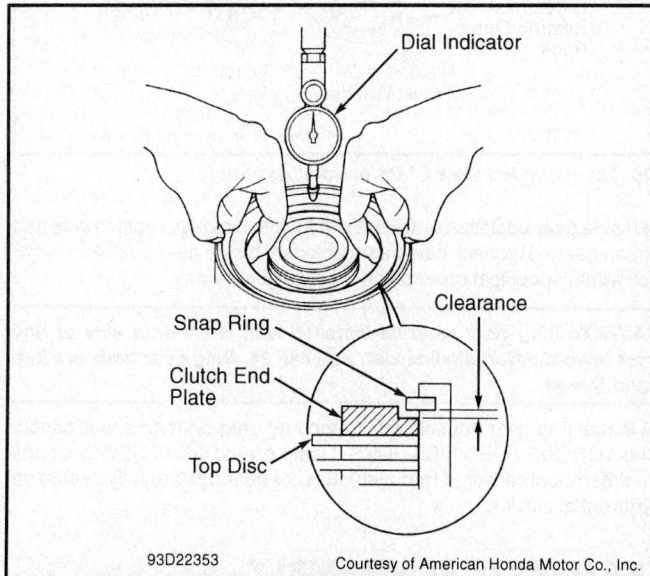

93D22353   Courtesy of American Honda Motor Co., Inc.

Fig. 24: Measuring Clutch Clearance

TORQUE CONVERTER HOUSING

Disassembly – 1) Remove countershaft bearing from torque converter housing using slide hammer (if necessary). Remove oil guide plate from torque converter housing. *See Fig. 12.*

CAUTION: DO NOT heat torque converter housing to more than 212°F (100°C) or torque converter housing may be damaged.

---

2) If removing secondary shaft bearing, use heat gun to heat torque converter housing around secondary shaft bearing to 212°F (100°C). Tap secondary shaft bearing from torque converter housing.
3) Remove oil guide plate from torque converter housing. *See Fig. 12.* Using hammer and bearing remover/installer, remove mainshaft bearing and oil seal from torque converter housing.
4) If removing differential bearing outer race from torque converter housing, use heat gun to heat torque converter housing around differential bearing outer race to 212°F (100°C).
5) Tap bearing race from torque converter housing. Using hammer and drift, tap differential oil seal from torque converter housing.
Cleaning & Inspection – Clean components with solvent and dry with compressed air. Inspect torque converter housing for cracks and damage in bearing areas. Replace torque converter housing if damaged.

Reassembly – 1) To install mainshaft bearing, use hammer and bearing remover/installer, install bearing until bearing bottoms in torque converter housing.
2) Using hammer and oil seal installer, install NEW mainshaft oil seal in torque converter housing. Oil seal should be flush with torque converter housing surface.
3) To install countershaft bearing, install NEW oil guide plate in countershaft bearing bore of torque converter housing. Ensure oil guide plate is installed so tab in center of oil guide plate faces upward (away from torque converter housing surface). *See Fig. 12.*
4) Using hammer and bearing installer, install countershaft bearing into torque converter housing. To install secondary shaft bearing, install NEW oil guide plate in secondary shaft bearing bore of torque converter housing.
5) Ensure oil guide plate is installed so tab in center of oil guide plate is facing upward (away from torque converter housing surface). Ensure oil guide is installed to a depth of 0-.001" (0-.03 mm), zero being flush and .001" is past flush. *See Fig. 12.* Using hammer and bearing installer, install secondary shaft bearing into torque converter housing.
6) To install differential bearing outer race, use hammer and bearing race installer, install differential bearing outer race in torque converter housing until race is even with torque converter housing surface.

CAUTION: DO NOT install thrust shim in torque converter housing below differential bearing outer race. Thrust shim must be installed in transaxle housing.

---

7) To install differential oil seal, use hammer and oil seal installer, install NEW oil seal into torque converter housing until oil seal is fully seated.

TRANSAXLE HOUSING

Disassembly – 1) Expand snap ring, and press mainshaft, countershaft and secondary shaft bearings from transaxle housing. Using hammer and drift, tap differential oil seal from transaxle housing.

CAUTION: DO NOT heat transaxle housing to more than 212°F (100°C) or housing may be damaged.

---

2) If removing differential bearing outer race, use heat gun to heat transaxle housing around differential bearing outer race to 212°F (100°C).
3) Tap differential bearing outer race from transaxle housing. Remove thrust shim, located below differential bearing outer race from transaxle housing.
Cleaning & Inspection – Clean components with solvent and dry with compressed air. Inspect transaxle housing for cracks and damage in bearing areas. Replace transaxle housing if damaged.

NOTE: Ensure original thickness thrust shim is installed. If any components have been changed, differential assembly bearing preload must be checked. See DIFFERENTIAL ASSEMBLY BEARING PRELOAD under TRANSAXLE REASSEMBLY.

Reassembly – 1) Install thrust shim. Using hammer and bearing race installer, install differential bearing outer race in transaxle housing.
2) To install mainshaft, countershaft and secondary shaft bearings, expand snap ring and install bearing part way into transaxle housing. Release snap ring.
3) Press bearing into transaxle housing until snap ring engages with groove on bearing. Ensure snap ring end gap is 0-.276" (0-7 mm). If snap ring end gap is not within specification, reseat or replace snap ring.

CAUTION: Ensure bearings are installed with groove of bearing facing inside of transaxle housing so snap ring engages in bearing when bearing is fully installed. Ensure snap ring fully engages in bearing.

---

4) To install differential oil seal, use hammer and oil seal installer, install NEW oil seal into transaxle housing until oil seal is fully seated.

RIGHT SIDE COVER

Disassembly – Remove snap rings retaining clutch feedpipes in right side cover. Remove feedpipe guides, clutch feedpipes and "O" rings from right side cover. See Fig. 6.

Cleaning & Inspection – Clean components with solvent and dry with compressed air. Inspect components for cracks or damage. Replace components as necessary.

Reassembly – To reassemble, reverse disassembly procedure using NEW "O" rings.

DIFFERENTIAL ASSEMBLY

Disassembly – 1) Before disassembling differential assembly, check side gear backlash. Place differential assembly on "V" blocks with both axle shafts installed.

2) Install dial indicator with stem resting against pinion gear. See Fig. 25. Check side gear backlash. Side gear backlash should be .002-.006" (.05-.15 mm).

3) If side gear backlash is not within specification, different thickness pinion gear thrust washer should be installed during reassembly. See PINION GEAR THRUST WASHER SPECIFICATIONS table.

4) If replacing bearings, use bearing puller to remove bearings from differential carrier. Remove bolts and ring gear.

NOTE: Ring gear bolts have left-hand threads.

---

5) Drive pin from differential carrier. See Fig. 26. Remove pinion shaft, pinion gears, side gears and thrust washers.

PINION GEAR THRUST WASHER SPECIFICATIONS

Part Number	Thickness In. (mm)
41351-PG1-000	.028 (.70)
41352-PG1-000	.029 (.75)
41353-PG1-000	.031 (.80)
41354-PG1-000	.032 (.85)
41355-PG1-000	.035 (.90)
41356-PG1-000	.036 (.95)
41357-PG1-000	.039 (1.00)
41358-PG1-000	.041 (1.05)

Cleaning & Inspection – Clean components with solvent and dry with compressed air. Inspect components for wear and damage. Replace components as necessary.

Reassembly – 1) Coat both sides of pinion gears and side gears with grease. Install side gears and side gear thrust washers in differential carrier.

2) Install pinion gears and pinion gear thrust washers in differential carrier so they are exactly opposite each other. Rotate pinion gears until they align with pinion shaft hole in differential carrier. Install pinion shaft and pin.

3) Recheck side gear backlash. If side gear backlash is not within specification, select different thickness pinion gear thrust washers. Ensure both pinion gear thrust washers are the same thickness.

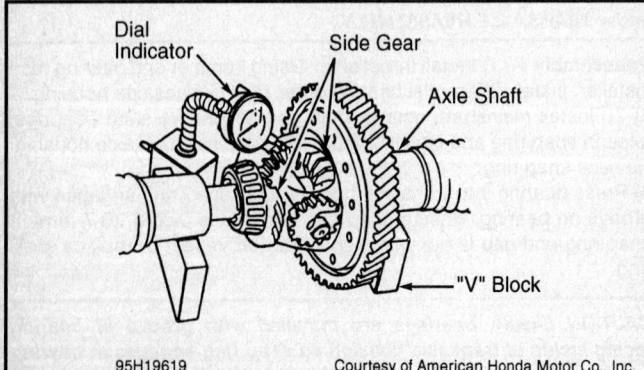

95H19619   Courtesy of American Honda Motor Co., Inc.

Fig. 25: Checking Side Gear Backlash

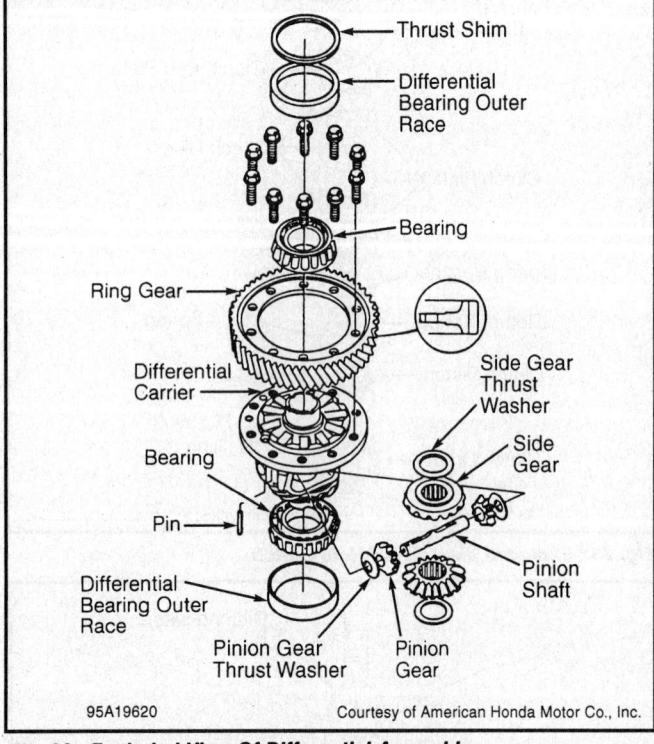

95A19620   Courtesy of American Honda Motor Co., Inc.

Fig. 26: Exploded View Of Differential Assembly

4) If side gear backlash is still not within specification, replace side and pinion gears. Recheck side gear backlash. If side gear backlash is still not within specification, replace differential carrier.

CAUTION: Ring gear must be installed with chamfered side of ring gear toward differential carrier. See Fig. 26. Ring gear bolts are left-hand thread.

---

5) Install ring gear. Install and tighten ring gear bolts to specification. See TORQUE SPECIFICATIONS. Using press, install NEW bearings on differential carrier (if removed). Ensure bearings are fully seated on differential carrier.

TRANSAXLE REASSEMBLY

DIFFERENTIAL ASSEMBLY BEARING PRELOAD

NOTE: If transaxle housing, torque converter housing, differential carrier, bearings, thrust shim or differential bearing outer races are replaced, differential assembly bearing preload must be checked.

CAUTION: DO NOT heat transaxle housing to more than 212°F (100°C), or housing may be damaged.

---

1) Using heat gun, heat transaxle housing around differential bearing outer race and thrust shim to 212°F (100°C). Tap differential bearing outer race from transaxle housing. Remove thrust shim, located below differential bearing outer race, from transaxle housing.

2) Allow transaxle housing to cool to room temperature. Select thrust shim so total thickness of thrust shim is .102" (2.60 mm). See THRUST SHIM SPECIFICATIONS table.

CAUTION: DO NOT use more than 2 thrust shims when adjusting differential assembly bearing preload.

THRUST SHIM SPECIFICATIONS

Thrust Shim I.D. Letter	Part Number	Thickness In. (mm)
A	41441-PK4-000	.087 (2.20)
B	41442-PK4-000	.089 (2.25)
C	41443-PK4-000	.091 (2.30)
D	41444-PK4-000	.093 (2.35)
E	41445-PK4-000	.094 (2.40)
F	41446-PK4-000	.096 (2.45)
G	41447-PK4-000	.098 (2.50)
H	41448-PK4-000	.100 (2.55)
I [1]	41449-PK4-000	.102 (2.60)
J	41450-PK4-000	.104 (2.65)
K	41451-PK4-000	.106 (2.70)
L	41452-PK4-000	.108 (2.75)
M	41453-PK4-000	.110 (2.80)
N	41454-PK4-000	.112 (2.85)
O	41455-PK4-000	.114 (2.90)
P	41456-PK4-000	.116 (2.95)
O	41457-PK4-000	.118 (3.00)
R	41458-PK4-000	.120 (3.05)

[1] – This is the standard thrust shim.

3) Install thrust shim in transaxle housing. Using hammer and bearing race installer, install differential bearing outer race in transaxle housing. Ensure differential bearing outer race is fully seated in transaxle housing.

4) Install gasket on torque converter housing. Do not apply sealer at this time. Install differential assembly in torque converter housing. Install transaxle housing on torque converter housing without mainshaft, countershaft and secondary shaft installed.

CAUTION: Ensure gasket is installed when checking differential assembly bearing preload.

5) Install and tighten transaxle housing-to-torque converter housing bolts to 40 ft. lbs. (54 N.m) in sequence. *See Fig. 27.* Rotate differential assembly several revolutions to seat bearings.

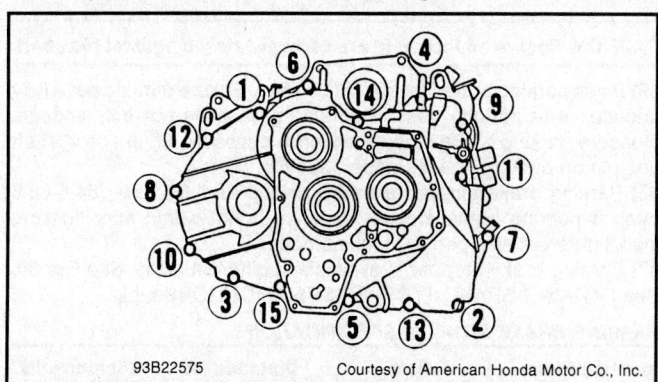

93B22575   Courtesy of American Honda Motor Co., Inc.

Fig. 27: Transaxle Housing Bolt Tightening Sequence

6) Install Preload Adapter (07HAJ-PK40201) into differential assembly. *See Fig. 28.* Install INCH-lb. torque wrench on preload adapter. Measure differential assembly bearing preload by checking starting torque required to rotate differential assembly in both directions at room temperature.

7) Differential assembly bearing preload should be within specification. See DIFFERENTIAL ASSEMBLY BEARING PRELOAD SPECIFICATIONS table.

DIFFERENTIAL ASSEMBLY BEARING PRELOAD SPECIFICATIONS [1]

Application	INCH Lbs. (N.m)
New Bearings	24-35 (2.8-4.0)
Used Bearings	22-32 (2.5-3.7)

[1] – This is the starting torque required to rotate differential assembly.

8) If differential assembly bearing preload is not within specification, select proper thickness thrust shim to obtain correct reading. See THRUST SHIM SPECIFICATIONS table.

9) Changing thrust shim to the next size will increase or decrease bearing preload about 2.60-3.50 INCH lbs. (.3-.4 N.m). Increase thrust shim thickness to increase differential assembly bearing preload. Decrease thrust shim thickness to decrease bearing preload.

CAUTION: DO NOT use more than 2 thrust shims when adjusting differential assembly bearing preload.

10) If adjusting differential assembly bearing preload, remove transaxle housing from torque converter housing. Remove differential bearing outer race from transaxle housing. Install correct thrust shim. Using hammer and bearing race installer, install differential bearing outer race in transaxle housing.

11) Reinstall transaxle housing and recheck differential assembly bearing preload. Once correct differential assembly bearing preload is obtained, remove transaxle housing, gasket and differential assembly from torque converter housing.

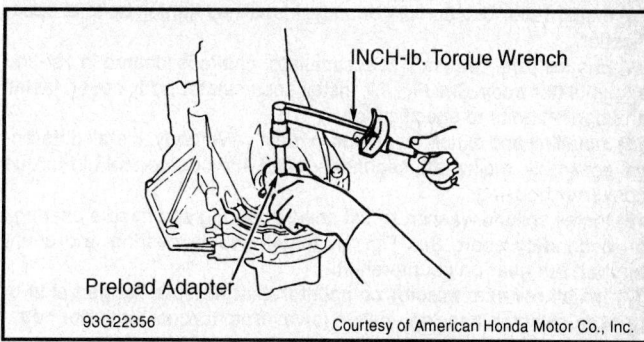

INCH-lb. Torque Wrench

Preload Adapter

93G22356   Courtesy of American Honda Motor Co., Inc.

Fig. 28: Checking Differential Bearing Preload

VALVE BODIES & INTERNAL COMPONENTS

NOTE: If transaxle housing, torque converter housing, differential carrier, bearings, thrust shim or differential bearing outer races are replaced, differential assembly bearing preload must be checked. See DIFFERENTIAL ASSEMBLY BEARING PRELOAD under TRANSAXLE REASSEMBLY.

NOTE: Coat all components with ATF before reassembly.

1) Install main separator plate and 3 dowel pins on torque converter housing. Install oil pump drive gear, oil pump driven gear and oil pump driven gear shaft.

CAUTION: Ensure oil pump driven gear is installed with groove and chamfered side facing downward (toward main separator plate).

2) Install main valve body. Loosely install all main valve body bolts. Once all bolts are installed, tighten main valve body bolts to specification. See TORQUE SPECIFICATIONS.

CAUTION: Ensure oil pump gears rotate smoothly and oil pump driven gear shaft moves freely once main valve body is installed. If components do not operate correctly, loosen main valve body bolts and realign oil pump gears and oil pump driven gear shaft. Failure to align oil pump driven gear shaft may result in seized oil pump gears or shaft.

3) Ensure filter and check balls are installed in main valve body. *See Fig. 13.* Install stator shaft, NEW "O" ring and stopper shaft. Install dowel pins in main valve body. Install spring and torque converter check valve in regulator valve body.

4) Install regulator valve body and bolt on main valve body. Ensure filter is installed on regulator valve body. *See Fig. 12.* Install dowel pins and throttle valve separator plate on regulator vale body.

5) Install throttle control shaft on throttle valve body using NEW "E" clip. Install throttle valve body. Install and tighten throttle valve body and regulator valve body bolts to specification.

6) Install secondary separator plate and dowel pins on main valve body. See Fig. 12. Install control shaft on torque converter housing. Ensure control shaft engages with manual valve on main valve body.

7) Install detent arm and detent arm shaft on main valve body. See Fig. 12. Install detent spring and hook on detent arm and control shaft.

8) Install cable control lever on end of control shaft. Install secondary valve body on secondary separator plate. Ensure check balls are installed in secondary valve body. See Fig. 15.

9) Install servo separator plate and servo body on secondary valve body. Install and tighten servo body bolts to specification.

10) Install oil feedpipes and accumulator cover on servo body. Install and tighten accumulator cover bolts to specification.

11) Install fluid strainer. Install and tighten fluid strainer bolts to specification.

12) Install servo detent base. Install NEW bolt locks (if equipped) on servo detent base bolts. Install and tighten bolts to specification. Bend over tabs on bolt locks.

13) Install 1st-2nd accumulator body. Install and tighten bolts to specification.

14) Ensure steel ball and 1st accumulator choke is located in 1st-2nd accumulator body. See Fig. 19. Install accumulator body cover. Install and tighten bolts to specification.

15) Install oil and clutch feedpipes in main valve body. Install differential assembly, mainshaft, secondary shaft and countershaft in torque converter housing.

16) Install splined washer, thrust needle bearing and needle bearings on secondary shaft. See Fig. 11. Install needle bearing and countershaft 4th gear on countershaft.

17) Install reverse selector on countershaft. Ensure flanged side of reverse selector is facing upward (away from torque converter housing). Install shift fork and reverse selector hub.

18) Rotate shift fork shaft on servo body so large chamfered hole aligns with hole in shift fork. Install shift fork bolt and NEW bolt lock. Tighten bolt to specification. Bend over tabs on bolt lock.

19) Install secondary shaft 2nd gear, thrust needle bearing and thrust washer on secondary shaft. Install needle bearing, countershaft reverse gear and countershaft 2nd gear on countershaft.

20) Install reverse idler gear in transaxle case with largest chamfered area facing upward (away from transaxle housing). See Fig. 29.

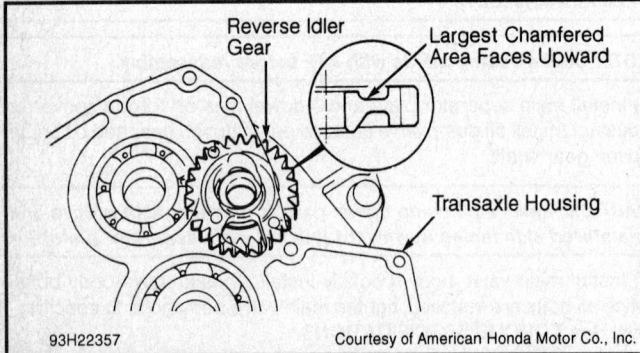

Reverse Idler Gear

Largest Chamfered Area Faces Upward

Transaxle Housing

93H22357   Courtesy of American Honda Motor Co., Inc.

Fig. 29: Installing Reverse Idler Gear

21) Install dowel pins and NEW gasket on torque converter housing. Align spring pin with groove in transaxle housing by rotating control shaft. See Fig. 10.

22) Install transaxle housing on torque converter housing. Install and tighten bolts to specification in sequence using several steps. See Fig. 27. Engage reverse idler gear with countershaft reverse gear.

23) Install NEW "O" rings on shaft for reverse idler shaft holder. See Fig. 8. Coat shaft, needle bearing and NEW "O" rings with grease.

24) Install shaft in reverse idler gear shaft holder. Ensure flat area on shaft engages with flat area on reverse idler gear shaft holder. See Fig. 8.

25) Install reverse idler gear shaft holder with needle bearing on transaxle housing. Install and tighten bolts to specification.

26) Install parking brake lever spring and parking brake lever on control shaft. See Fig. 6. Install bolt and NEW bolt lock on parking brake lever. DO NOT tighten bolt at this time.

NOTE: Mainshaft lock nut has left hand threads.

---

27) Install Mainshaft Holder (07GAB-PF50100 or 07GAB-PF50101) on mainshaft to secure mainshaft from rotating. See Fig. 7. Install mainshaft idler gear on mainshaft. Install old mainshaft lock nut on mainshaft. Mainshaft has left-hand threads.

28) Tighten mainshaft lock nut to 166 ft. lbs. (230 N.m) to seat mainshaft idler gear on mainshaft. DO NOT use hammer to install mainshaft idler gear on mainshaft or impact wrench to tighten lock nut.

29) Install secondary shaft idler gear on secondary shaft. Install thrust washer, thrust needle bearing, needle bearing, countershaft idler gear and parking gear on countershaft. See Fig. 6.

30) Install old secondary shaft lock nut on secondary shaft. Tighten secondary shaft lock nut to 166 ft. lbs. (230 N.m) while holding countershaft idler gear to seat secondary shaft idler gear on secondary shaft. DO NOT use hammer to install secondary shaft idler gear on secondary shaft or impact wrench to tighten lock nut.

31) Place 24-mm socket at center of parking gear. Install a 10 x 1.25-mm bolt in end of countershaft. Install parking pawl shaft, parking pawl stopper, parking pawl spring and parking pawl. See Fig. 6. Engage parking pawl with parking gear.

32) Tighten bolt to pull parking gear onto the countershaft. DO NOT use hammer to install parking gear on countershaft. Remove bolt and socket. Install old countershaft lock nut on countershaft. Tighten countershaft lock nut to 166 ft. lbs. (230 N.m) to seat parking gear on countershaft. DO NOT use impact wrench to tighten lock nut.

33) Remove lock nuts from mainshaft, countershaft and secondary shaft. Install NEW spring washers and NEW lock nuts on mainshaft, countershaft and secondary shaft. Ensure spring washers are installed so large area of spring washer is against lock nut. See Fig. 6.

34) Tighten lock nuts to specification. DO NOT use impact wrench to tighten lock nuts. Stake lock nuts against shaft. Remove mainshaft holder.

CAUTION: Ensure all lock nuts are securely staked against the shaft.

---

35) Place parking brake lever in "P" position. Ensure parking pawl fully engages with parking gear. If parking pawl does not fully engage, measure parking brake stopper distance between parking pawl shaft and pin on parking brake stopper. See Fig. 30.

36) Parking brake stopper distance should be 2.54-2.58" (64.5-65.6 mm). If parking brake stopper distance is not within specification, install different size parking brake stopper.

37) Parking brake stopper is available in different sizes. See Fig. 30. See PARKING BRAKE STOPPER SPECIFICATIONS table.

PARKING BRAKE STOPPER SPECIFICATIONS

Identification Mark	Part Number	[1] Distance "A" In. (mm)	[1] Distance "B" In. (mm)
1	24537-PA9-003	.433 (11.00)	.433 (11.00)
2	24538-PA9-003	.425 (10.80)	.419 (10.65)
3	24539-PA9-003	.417 (10.60)	.406 (10.30)

[1] – Measured from center of parking brake stopper. See Fig. 30.

38) Tighten parking brake lever bolt to specification. Bend over tabs on bolt lock. Using NEW gasket, install right side cover. Install and tighten bolts to specification.

39) To install remaining components, reverse removal procedure. Use NEW seal washers when installing joint bolts for ATF cooler pipes. Tighten all fasteners to specification.

CAUTION: If transaxle failure existed, flush oil cooler. See OIL COOLER FLUSHING under ON-VEHICLE SERVICE.

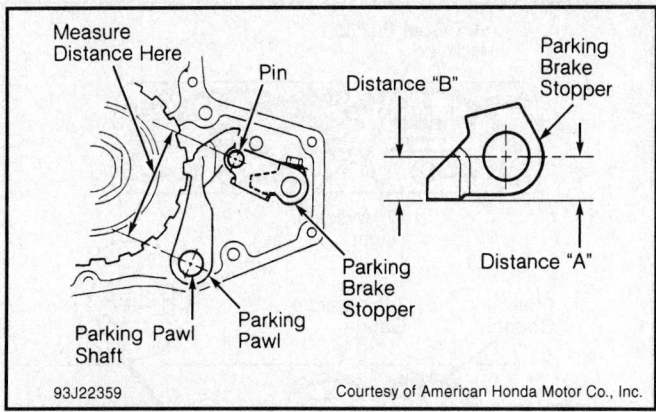

Courtesy of American Honda Motor Co., Inc.

93J22359

Fig. 30: Measuring Parking Brake Stopper Distance & Parking Brake Stopper

TORQUE SPECIFICATIONS
TORQUE SPECIFICATIONS

Application	Ft. Lbs. (N.m)
Countershaft Lock Nut	123 (167)
Joint Bolt	21 (29)
Main Valve Body Bolt	
6-mm Bolt	1
8-mm Bolt	13 (18)
Mainshaft Lock Nut	123 (167)
Pressure Tap Plug	13 (18)
Ring Gear Bolt	76 (103)
Secondary Shaft Lock Nut	123 (167)
Speed Sensor Assembly Bolt	13 (18)
Transaxle Housing Bolt [2]	40 (54)

	INCH Lbs. (N.m)
Accumulator Body Cover Bolt	106 (12.0)
Accumulator Cover Bolt	106 (12.0)
Countershaft Speed Sensor Bolt	106 (12.0)
Fluid Strainer Bolt	106 (12.0)
Lock-Up Control Solenoid Valve Assembly Bolt	106 (12.0)
Mainshaft Speed Sensor Bolt	106 (12.0)
Parking Brake Lever Bolt	124 (14.0)
Regulator Valve Body Bolt	106 (12.0)
Reverse Idler Gear Shaft Holder Bolt	106 (12.0)
Right Side Cover Bolt	106 (12.0)
Servo Body Bolt	106 (12.0)
Servo Detent Base Bolt	106 (12.0)
Shift Control Solenoid Valve Assembly Bolt	106 (12.0)
Shift Fork Bolt	124 (14.0)
Stopper Bolt	106 (12.0)
Throttle Cam Stopper Bolt	71 (8.0)
Throttle Valve Body Bolt	106 (12.0)
1st-2nd Accumulator Body Bolt	106 (12.0)

[1] – Tighten bolt to 106 INCH lbs. (12.0 N.m).
[2] – Tighten bolts to specification in sequence. *See Fig. 27.*

TRANSAXLE SPECIFICATIONS
TRANSAXLE SPECIFICATIONS

Application	Specification
Clutch Clearance	
1st & 2nd Clutches	.026-.033" (.65-.85 mm)
1st-Hold Clutch	.031-.039" (.80-1.00 mm)
3rd & 4th Clutches	.016-.024" (.40-.60 mm)
Differential Bearing Preload [1]	
New Bearings	24-35 INCH lbs. (2.8-4.0 N.m)
Used Bearings	22-32 INCH lbs. (2.5-3.7 N.m)
Oil Pump Clearances	
Side Clearance	
Oil Pump Drive Gear	.0083-.0104" (.210-.265 mm)
Oil Pump Driven Gear	.0014-.0025" (.035-.063 mm)
Thrust Clearance	
Standard	.0010-.0020" (.030-.050 mm)
Wear Limit	.0028" (.070 mm)
Secondary Shaft 2nd	
Gear Clearance	.003-.006" (.07-.15 mm)
Side Gear Backlash	.002-.006" (.05-.15 mm)
Parking Brake Stopper Distance	2.54-2.58" (64.5-65.6 mm)

[1] – This is the starting torque required to rotate differential assembly.

WIRING DIAGRAMS

For appropriate wiring diagram, see HONDA MP1A ELECTRONIC CONTROLS article in AUTOMATIC TRANSMISSIONS.

AUTOMATIC TRANSMISSIONS
Honda MP1A Electronic Controls

Prelude

APPLICATION

APPLICATION

Vehicle	Transaxle Model
1995-96 Prelude	MP1A

CAUTION: Vehicle is equipped with a Supplemental Restraint System (SRS). When servicing vehicle, use care to prevent accidental air bag deployment. All SRS electrical connections and wiring harness are covered with Yellow insulation. SRS-related components are located in steering column, center console, instrument panel and lower panel on instrument panel. DO NOT use electrical test equipment on these circuits. It may be necessary to deactivate SRS before servicing components. See AIR BAG SERVICING article in APPLICATIONS & IDENTIFICATION section.

NOTE: If negative battery cable is to be disconnected, obtain radio anti-theft code from customer before disconnecting negative battery cable. Radio anti-theft code must be re-entered into radio once negative battery cable is reconnected. To re-enter radio anti-theft code, turn ignition and radio on. When the word "CODE" is displayed on radio, re-enter radio anti-theft code by using the radio station preset buttons.

DESCRIPTION

NOTE: On 1995 models, transaxle electronic components are controlled by Transmission Control Module (TCM). On 1996 models, transaxle electronic components are controlled by Powertrain Control Module (PCM). These modules perform same function. On 1995 models, there are separate modules for engine and transmission controls (ECM and TCM). On 1996 models, engine and transmission components are controlled by the PCM.

Automatic transaxle is electronically controlled. Transaxle shifting and torque converter lock-up are controlled by PCM/TCM. The PCM/TCM receives information from various input devices and uses information to control lock-up and shift control solenoid valves.

Transaxle is equipped with shift and key interlock systems. Shift interlock system prevents shift lever from being moved from Park unless brake pedal is depressed and accelerator is in idle position. In case of a malfunction, shift lever can be released by placing ignition key in release slot near shift lever. Key interlock system prevents ignition key from being removed from ignition lock assembly unless shift lever is in Park.

The A/T gear position indicator on instrument panel contains lights to indicate which position A/T gear position switch on shift lever is in.

OPERATION

A/T GEAR POSITION INDICATOR

With ignition in RUN or START position, voltage is supplied to A/T gear position indicator, located on instrument panel. *See Fig. 1.* When shift lever is moved to designated gear position, A/T gear position switch completes the ground circuit for A/T gear position indicator on instrument panel. The light on A/T gear position indicator will be illuminated to indicate shift lever gear position. The PCM/TCM controls operation of the "D₄" indicator light on A/T gear position indicator on instrument panel. The A/T gear position switch is mounted on driver's side of shift lever. *See Fig. 4.*

When headlights are turned on, voltage is supplied on Red/Black wire terminal on A/T gear position indicator. This changes light illumination from fixed illumination to being controlled by the dash light dimmer input on the Red wire.

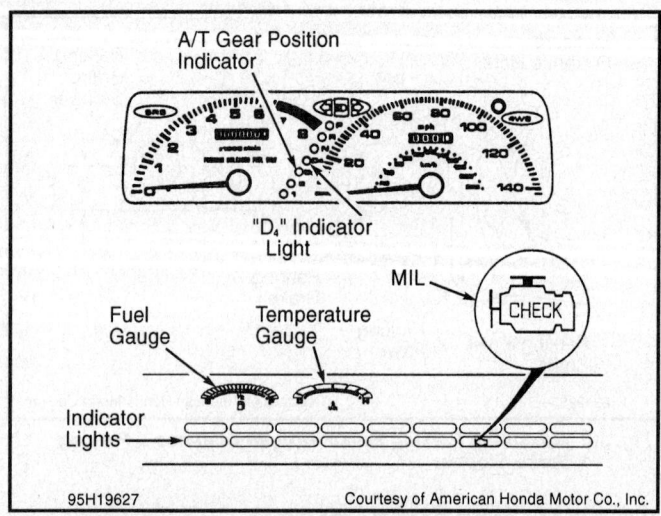

Courtesy of American Honda Motor Co., Inc.

Fig. 1: Identifying A/T Gear Position Indicator, "D₄" Light & MIL Light

SHIFT & KEY INTERLOCK SYSTEMS

Shift Interlock System – Shift interlock system prevents shift lever from being moved from Park unless brake pedal is depressed and accelerator is in idle position. In case of a malfunction, shift lever can be released by placing ignition key in release slot near shift lever. Voltage is provided to shift lock solenoid when ignition is on.

When brake pedal is depressed, battery voltage is applied to the PCM/TCM from brakelight switch. With accelerator pedal in idle position, a low voltage is applied to the PCM/TCM from the throttle position sensor. The PCM/TCM then supplies voltage to shift lock circuit in the interlock control unit. When A/T gear position switch is in Park position, interlock control unit then operates shift lock solenoid by controlling the ground circuit. When shift lock solenoid is energized, shift lever is released and can be moved.

Shift lock solenoid is mounted on driver's side of shift lever. *See Fig. 2.* The A/T gear position switch is located on side of shift lever. *See Fig. 4.* Interlock control unit is located above driver's side kick panel and contains a Gray 8-pin electrical connector. *See Fig. 4.*

Key Interlock System – Key interlock system prevents ignition key from being removed from ignition lock assembly unless shift lever is in Park. Voltage is provided to key interlock switch from No. 46 fuse

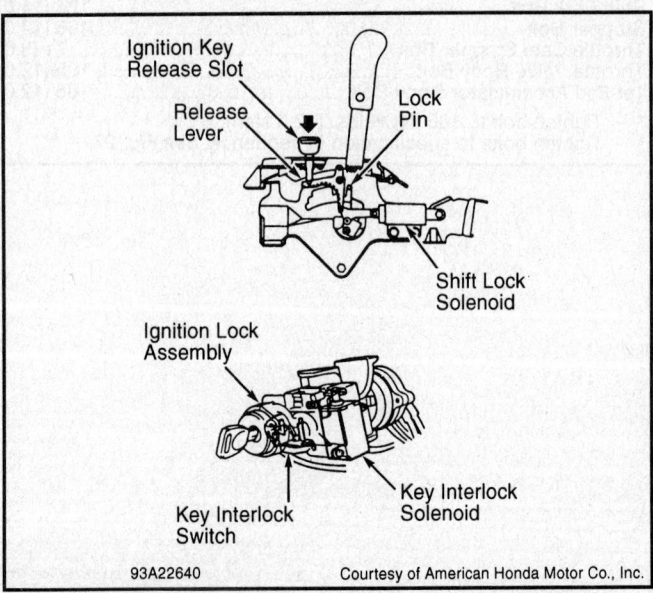

Courtesy of American Honda Motor Co., Inc.

Fig. 2: Identifying Shift & Key Interlock System Components

(15-amp) in engine compartment fuse box. Engine compartment fuse box is located on passenger's side rear corner of engine compartment, near firewall. When ignition key is installed in ignition lock assembly, key interlock switch closes, providing voltage to key interlock solenoid and interlock control unit.

If shift lever is not in Park, interlock control unit activates key interlock solenoid by completing the ground circuit, preventing ignition key from being removed from ignition lock assembly. Key interlock switch and solenoid are located on ignition lock assembly. See Fig. 2. Interlock control unit is located above driver's side kick panel and contains a Gray 8-pin electrical connector. See Fig. 4.

TRANSMISSION CONTROL MODULE (PCM/TCM)

The PCM/TCM receives information from various input devices and uses information to control lock-up and shift control solenoid valves. See Fig. 3. The PCM/TCM contains a self-diagnostic system, which will store fault code if failure or problem exists in the transaxle electronic control system. Fault code can be retrieved to determine transaxle problem area. Fault code may also be referred to as Diagnostic Trouble Code (DTC).

For information on self-diagnostic system, see SELF-DIAGNOSTIC SYSTEM. The PCM/TCM is located behind passenger's side kick panel. See Fig. 4.

PCM/TCM INPUT DEVICES

Air Conditioning Signal – The A/C clutch relay provides input signal to PCM/TCM to indicate A/C operation. The A/C clutch relay is located at driver's side front corner of engine compartment. See Fig. 4.

Brake Switch Signal – Brakelight switch provides input signal to PCM/TCM to indicate vehicle braking. Brakelight switch is located on brake pedal support. See Fig. 4.

Engine Coolant Temperature Sensor Signal – Engine Coolant Temperature (ECT) sensor delivers input signal to PCM/TCM to indicate engine coolant temperature. Engine coolant temperature sensor is located on cylinder head, below the distributor and contains a Green/White wire and a Yellow/Blue wire in the electrical connector. See Fig. 3.

Engine Speed Signal – An engine speed or RPM signal is delivered to PCM/TCM from ignition control module in the distributor.

Engine Control Module (ECM) – An upshift and downshift comparative input signal and shift acknowledgment input signal are sent between ECM and PCM/TCM. A 5-volt reference signal also exists between ECM and the PCM/TCM. The ECM is located on passenger's side floor panel, below the carpet. See Fig. 4.

Service Check Connector – Service check connector is used when retrieving codes for transaxle electronic control system diagnosis. When jumper wire is installed between service check connector electrical terminals, an input is delivered to PCM/TCM to display flash codes on "D$_4$" indicator light on A/T gear position indicator on instrument panel. Service check connector is a 2-pin Blue or Gray connector, located below center of instrument panel, near center console. See Fig. 5.

Mainshaft & Countershaft Speed Sensor Signal – Mainshaft speed sensor delivers an input signal to PCM/TCM to indicate the speed of the mainshaft in the transaxle. Countershaft speed sensor delivers an input signal to PCM/TCM to indicate the speed of the countershaft in the transaxle. Countershaft and mainshaft speed sensors are located on transaxle. See Fig. 4.

Throttle Position Sensor Signal – Throttle position sensor delivers an input signal to PCM/TCM to indicate throttle position. Throttle position sensor is mounted on throttle body. See Fig. 4.

Vehicle Speed Sensor Signal – Vehicle Speed Sensor (VSS) delivers an input signal to PCM/TCM to indicate the vehicle speed. Vehicle speed sensor is located on transaxle, below thermostat housing. See Fig. 4.

PCM/TCM OUTPUT DEVICES

Shift Control Solenoid Valves – The PCM/TCM controls transaxle shifting by delivering an output signal to shift control solenoid valves "A" and "B". Shift control solenoid valves are operated in accordance with gear position. See SHIFT CONTROL SOLENOID VALVE OPERATION table. Shift control solenoid valves are located on the transaxle. See Fig. 4. Shift control solenoid valve "A" has a Blue/Yellow wire and solenoid valve "B" has a Green/White wire.

SHIFT CONTROL SOLENOID VALVE OPERATION

Shift Lever Position	Solenoid Valve "A"	Solenoid Valve "B"
"D$_3$" Or "D$_4$" (1st Gear)	Off	On
"D$_3$" Or "D$_4$" (2nd Gear)	On	On
"D$_3$" Or "D$_4$" (3rd Gear)	On	Off
"D$_4$" (4th Gear)	Off	Off
"R"	On	Off
"1"	On	Off
"2"	On	On

Lock-Up Control Solenoid Valves – The PCM/TCM controls torque converter lock-up by delivering an output signal to lock-up control solenoid valves "A" and "B". Lock-up control solenoid valves are operated in accordance with lock-up condition. See LOCK-UP CONTROL SOLENOID VALVE OPERATION table. Lock-up control solenoid valves are located on the transaxle. See Fig. 4. Lock-up control solenoid valve "A" has a Yellow wire and solenoid valve "B" has a Green/Black wire.

LOCK-UP CONTROL SOLENOID VALVE OPERATION

Lock-Up Condition	Solenoid Valve "A"	Solenoid Valve "B"
No Lock-Up	Off	Off
Slight Lock-Up	On	[1]
Half Lock-Up	On	On
Full Lock-Up	On	On
Lock-Up During Deceleration	On	[1]

[1] – Solenoid valve will cycle on and off.

95I19628   Courtesy of American Honda Motor Co., Inc.

Fig. 3: Identifying Input & Output Devices

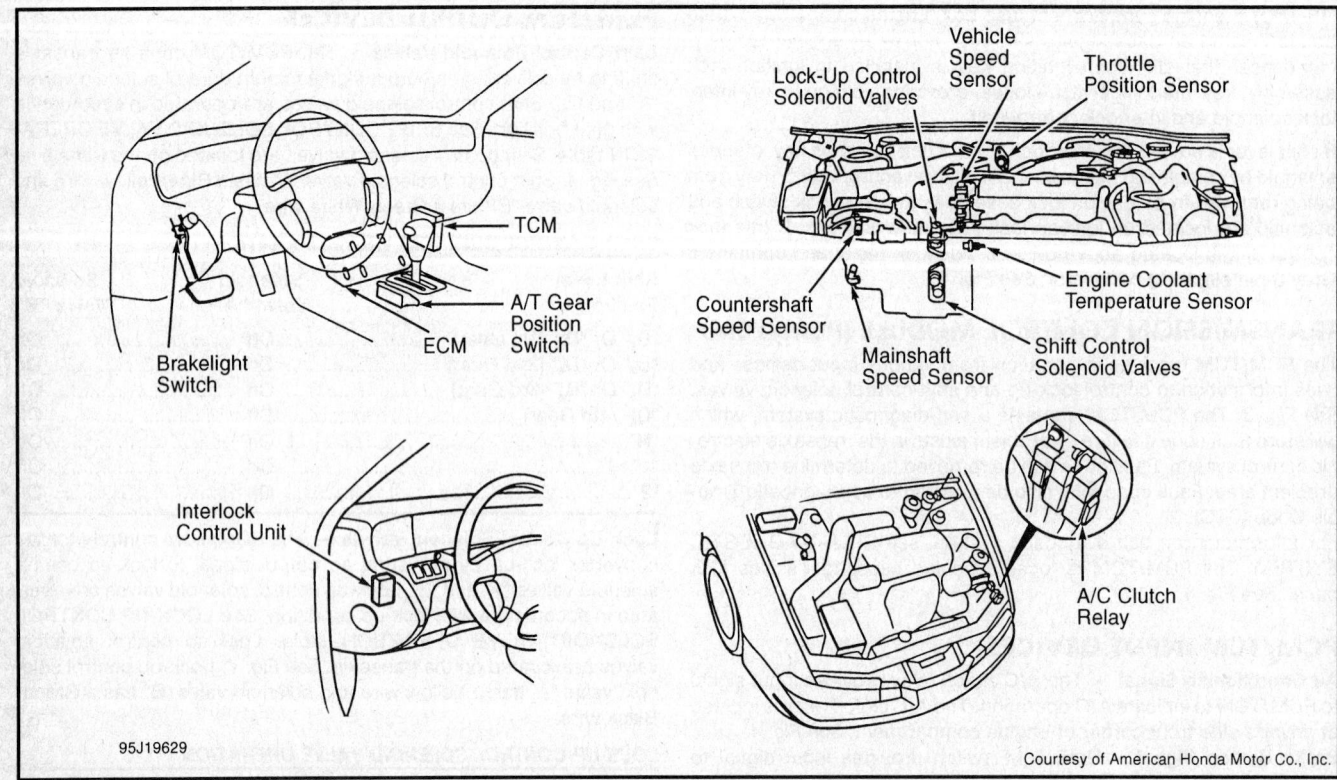

95J19629

Courtesy of American Honda Motor Co., Inc.

Fig. 4: Identifying PCM/TCM Input & Output Device Locations

"D₄" Indicator Light – If a fault exists in transaxle electronic control system and fault code is stored, PCM/TCM will output flash signal by blinking "D₄" indicator light on A/T gear position indicator on instrument panel. See Fig. 1.

Interlock Control Unit – When A/T gear position switch is in Park position, PCM/TCM provides voltage to shift lock circuit in interlock control unit if brake pedal is depressed and accelerator is in idle position. Interlock control unit then operates shift lock solenoid by controlling the ground circuit. When shift lock solenoid is energized, shift lever is released and can be moved. Interlock control unit is located above driver's side kick panel and contains a Gray 8-pin electrical connector. See Fig. 4.

Self-Diagnostic Indicator – If an abnormality exists in transaxle electronic control system and fault code is stored in PCM/TCM memory, PCM/TCM will deliver an output signal to turn on and blink "D₄" indicator light on A/T gear position indicator on instrument panel. See Fig. 1. Flash code can be retrieved to identify problem area by installing jumper wire between service check connector electrical terminals. Flash codes with be displayed by blinking "D₄" indicator light on A/T gear position indicator on instrument panel.

SELF-DIAGNOSTIC SYSTEM

SYSTEM DIAGNOSIS

The PCM/TCM monitors transaxle operation. PCM/TCM contains a self-diagnostic system, which stores a DTC if a transaxle electronic control system failure or problem exists. If DTC is stored, PCM/TCM will blink "D₄" indicator light on A/T gear position indicator on instrument panel. If a transaxle electronic control system failure or problem is suspected and "D₄" light on A/T gear position indicator does not flash, perform diagnostic circuit check to ensure proper operation of "D₄" light. On 1995 models, see DIAGNOSTIC CHARTS. On 1996 models, see appropriate "D₄" test under DIAGNOSTIC TESTING (1996). Flash Codes can be retrieved on all years/models but are the only codes available on 1995 models. On 1996 models, DTC can be retrieved using scan tool at Data Link Connector (DLC) located under drink holder in center console. See RETRIEVING CODES.

RETRIEVING CODES

NOTE: When diagnosing transaxle, ensure "D₄" indicator light on A/T gear position indicator on instrument panel is not turned on by problem in PGM-FI system. The PGM-FI system controls the fuel injection system. To repair PGM-FI system, see appropriate SELF-DIAGNOSTICS article in ENGINE PERFORMANCE in appropriate MITCHELL® manual.

NOTE: Before any diagnostic procedure, obtain radio anti-theft code from customer. Note radio preset stations, as radio stations and clock setting will be cleared and must be reset. Radio anti-theft code must be re-entered for radio operation.

Retrieving DTCs Using Scan Tool (1996) – **1)** If fault code exists, "D₄" light on A/T gear position on instrument panel will blink when ignition is turned on. To retrieve DTC using scan tool, turn ignition off.
2) Connect scan tool to 16-pin Data Link Connector (DLC) located under drink holder in center console. Turn ignition on. Scan tool will indicate DTCs. Follow scan tool manufacturers instructions.
3) Once DTC is obtained, turn ignition off. Determine probable cause and symptom. See DTC/FLASH CODE IDENTIFICATION (1996) table. If any other codes except those listed are displayed, see appropriate SELF-DIAGNOSTICS article in ENGINE PERFORMANCE in appropriate MITCHELL® manual. For trouble shooting of fault codes, see DIAGNOSTIC TESTING (1996) under DIAGNOSTIC TESTING. If "D₄" light does not flash or stays on, see appropriate "D₄" test under DIAGNOSTIC TESTING (1996).

NOTE: Flash Codes can be retrieved on all years/models but are the only codes available on 1995 models.

Retrieving Flash Codes Using "D₄" Light – **1)** If flash code exists, "D₄" light on A/T gear position on instrument panel will blink when ignition is turned on. To retrieve flash code, turn ignition off.
2) Install jumper wire between service check connector terminals. Service check connector is a Gray 2-pin connector located on the PCM cover, below passenger's side Cont. of instrument panel. See Fig. 5. This will place PCM/TCM in self-diagnostic mode.

FLASH CODE IDENTIFICATION (1995)

Fault Code [1] Number	Indicator Light [2] Condition	Probable [3] Cause	[4] [5] Symptom
1	Blinks	Defective Lock-Up Control Solenoid "A"	Lock-Up Clutch Does Not Engage Or Remains Engaged, Unstable Idle Speed
2	Blinks	Defective Lock-Up Control Solenoid "B"	Lock-Up Clutch Does Not Engage
3	Blinks Or Remains Off	Defective Throttle Position Sensor	Lock-Up Clutch Does Not Engage
4	Blinks	Defective Vehicle Speed Sensor	Lock-Up Clutch Does Not Engage
5	Blinks	Defective A/T Gear Position Switch	Lock-Up Clutch Does Not Engage, Fails To Shift Other Than 2nd-4th Gears
6	Off	Defective A/T Gear Position Switch	Lock-Up Clutch Does Not Engage, Lock-Up Clutch Engages & Disengages Fails To Shift Other Than 2nd-4th Gears
7	Blinks	Defective Shift Control Solenoid "A"	Fails To Upshift, Remains In 4th Gear
8	Blinks	Defective Shift Control Solenoid "B"	Remains In 1st Or 4th Gear
9	Blinks	Defective Countershaft Speed Sensor	Lock-Up Clutch Does Not Engage
10	Blinks	Defective Engine Coolant Temp. Sensor	Lock-Up Clutch Does Not Engage
11	Off	Defective Ignition Coil (Ignitor)	Lock-Up Clutch Does Not Engage
14	Off	Shorted Or Open Wire Between PCM/TCM Terminal D16 & ECM, Faulty ECM	Transaxle Jerks Hard When Shifting
15 [6]	Off	Defective Mainshaft Speed Sensor	Transaxle Jerks Hard When Shifting

[1] – Number of blinks from "D₄" indicator light on A/T gear position indicator on instrument panel with jumper wire installed in service check connector.

[2] – Operation of "D₄" indicator light without jumper wire installed in service check connector.

[3] – Check listed component for probable cause. Also check wiring and connections of specified component.

[4] – If transaxle fails to shift from Park with brake pedal depressed, check brakelight signal. See BRAKELIGHT SIGNAL under TROUBLE SHOOTING.

[5] – If lock-up clutch does not engage or does not cycle on and off, check A/C signal. See A/C SIGNAL under TROUBLE SHOOTING.

[6] – Flash Code No. 15 does not necessarily indicate an electrical problem, as flash code may also be caused by an internal transaxle problem.

DTC/FLASH CODE IDENTIFICATION (1996)

DTC/Flash Code [1] Number	Indicator Light [2] Condition	Probable [3] Cause	[4] Symptom
P0715/15	Off	Defective Mainshaft Speed Sensor	Transaxle Jerks Hard When Shifting
P0720/9	Blinks	Defective Countershaft Speed Sensor	Lock-Up Clutch Does Not Engage
P0730/41	Off	Defective Shift Control System	Fails To Shift, Stuck In 1st Or 4th Gears
P0740/40	Off	Defective Lock-Up Control System	Lock-Up Clutch Does Not Engage Or Remains Engaged, Unstable Engine Idle
P0753/7	Blinks	Defective Shift Control Solenoid "A"	Remains In 4th Gear, Fails To Shift Other Than 1st-4th, 2nd-4th Or 2nd-3rd Gears
P0758/8	Blinks	Defective Shift Control Solenoid "B"	Remains In 1st Or 4th Gear
P1705/5	Blinks	Defective A/T Gear Position Switch	Lock-Up Clutch Does Not Engage, Fails To Shift Other Than 2nd-4th Gears
P1706/6	Off	Defective A/T Gear Position Switch	Lock-Up Clutch Does Not Engage, Lock-Up Clutch Engages & Disengages, Fails To Shift Other Than 2nd-4th Gears
P1753/1	Blinks	Defective Lock-Up Control Solenoid "A"	Lock-Up Clutch Does Not Engage Or Remains Engaged, Unstable Engine Idle
P1758/2	Blinks	Defective Lock-Up Control Solenoid "B"	Lock-Up Clutch Does Not Engage Or Remains Engaged, Unstable Engine Idle

[1] – This is the number of blinks from "D₄" light on A/T gear position indicator on instrument panel with jumper wire installed in service check connector. Flash Codes can be retrieved on all years/models but are the only codes available on 1995 models.

[2] – This is operation of "D₄" light on A/T gear position indicator on instrument panel.

[3] – Specified component for probable cause. Also check wiring and connections for the specified component.

[4] – If transaxle fails to shift from Park with brake pedal depressed, check brakelight signal. See BRAKELIGHT SIGNAL under TROUBLE SHOOTING.

CAUTION: DO NOT use the 3-pin connector located next to service check connector.

3) Turn ignition on. Flash codes with be displayed by blinking "D₄" light on A/T gear position indicator on instrument panel.

NOTE: If Malfunction Indicator Light (MIL) on instrument panel also starts blinking, PGM-FI system must be checked. See appropriate SELF-DIAGNOSTICS article in ENGINE PERFORMANCE in appropriate MITCHELL® manual.

4) Note number of blinks from "D₄" light. A short blink indicates a single digit Flash Code. A long blink equals 10 short blinks. For example, if "D₄" light blinks once, this is a Flash Code No. 1. If "D₄" light blinks one long blink and then 4 short blinks, this is a Flash Code No. 14. See Fig. 6.

5) Once Flash Code is obtained, turn ignition off. Remove jumper wire from service check connector. Determine probable cause and symptom. See appropriate CODE IDENTIFICATION table. If any other Flash Codes except those listed are displayed, PCM/TCM is defective. For trouble shooting of Flash Codes, see DIAGNOSTIC TESTING.

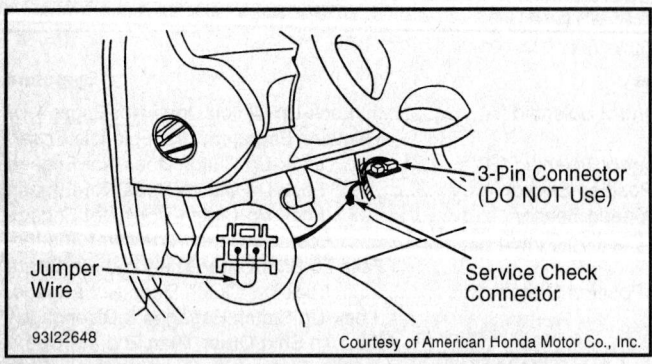

Fig. 5: Installing Jumper Wire In Service Check Connector

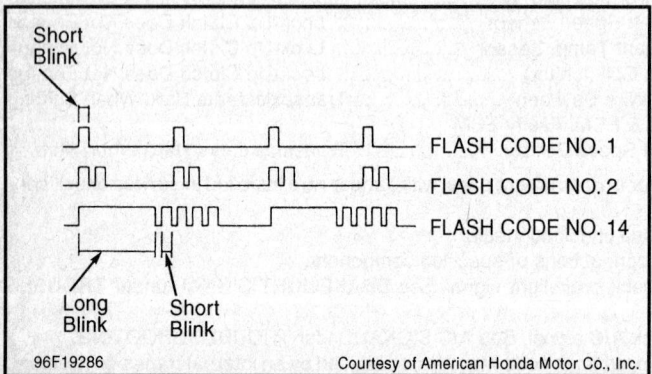

Fig. 6: Identifying Flash Code Displays

6) If customer describes symptoms listed in either CODE IDENTIFICATION table for Flash Code No. 3, 6, or 11 and "D₄" indicator light is off, it may be necessary to test drive vehicle to recreate the symptom and then check for Flash Code with ignition still on.

CLEARING CODES

NOTE: Before clearing codes, obtain radio anti-theft code from customer. Note radio preset stations, as radio stations and clock setting will be cleared and must be reset. Radio anti-theft code must be re-entered for radio operation.

1) Once repairs have been performed, codes must be cleared from PCM/TCM memory. Ensure ignition is off. Remove No. 43 clock-radio fuse (10-amp) in engine compartment fuse box for 10 seconds. Engine compartment fuse box is located on passenger's side rear corner of engine compartment, near firewall.

NOTE: PCM (1996) memory can NOT be cleared using scan tool, clock-radio fuse must be removed.

2) This will clear PCM/TCM and ECM memories. Reinstall fuse. To re-enter radio anti-theft code, turn ignition and radio on. When the word "CODE" is displayed on radio, re-enter radio anti-theft code by using the radio station preset buttons. Reset clock and radio stations.

TROUBLE SHOOTING

A/C SIGNAL (1995)

NOTE: If A/C signal exists, torque converter lock-up clutch may not engage or cycle on and off.

1) Start engine. Turn blower switch and A/C switch to the ON position. Check if A/C compressor clutch engages.

2) If A/C compressor clutch does not engage, check A/C compressor clutch and wiring. If A/C compressor clutch engages, turn engine off. Ensure ignition is off. Remove passenger's side door sill molding and passenger's side kick panel. Pull carpet back for access to PCM/TCM, located behind passenger's side kick panel. *See Fig. 4.*

3) Disconnect 26-pin connector from PCM/TCM, located behind passenger's side kick panel. *See Fig. 4.* Connect voltmeter between terminal A22 (Red/Blue wire) and terminal A25 (Black/Red wire) or terminal A26 (Brown/Black wire) of 26-pin connector. Start engine. Note voltage with A/C compressor off.

4) If battery voltage does not exist, go to step 5). If battery voltage exists, A/C signal is okay. Check for loose PCM/TCM electrical connections. If electrical connections are okay, substitute PCM/TCM with a known good unit and recheck operation.

5) If battery voltage does not exist, check for open circuit in Red/Blue wire between terminal A22 and A/C clutch relay. A/C clutch relay is located at driver's side front corner of engine compartment. *See Fig. 4.*

6) Reinstall electrical connector on PCM/TCM. Reinstall passenger's side kick panel and passenger's side door sill molding.

BRAKELIGHT SIGNAL (1995)

NOTE: If no brakelight signal exists, transaxle may fail to shift from Park with brake pedal depressed and accelerator pedal in idle position.

1) Ensure brakelights come on when brake pedal is depressed. If brakelights come on, go to next step. If brakelights do not come on, check No. 41 fuse (15-amp) in engine compartment fuse box. Engine compartment fuse box is located on passenger's side rear corner of engine compartment, near firewall. If fuse is okay, repair brakelight signal circuit.

2) Ensure ignition is off. Remove passenger's side door sill molding and passenger's side kick panel. Pull carpet back for access to TCM, located behind passenger's side kick panel. *See Fig. 4.* Disconnect 26-pin and 22-pin electrical connectors from PCM/TCM.

3) Connect Test Harness (07LAJ-PT3010A) to 26-pin and 22-pin electrical connectors. *See Fig. 7.* DO NOT connect test harness to PCM/TCM.

4) Using Digital Volt-Ohmmeter (DVOM), measure voltage between terminals D2 and A25 or A26 on test harness with brake pedal depressed. Terminal numbers are located on test harness. *See Fig. 7.*

5) If battery voltage exists, brakelight signal to PCM/TCM is okay. Check for loose PCM/TCM electrical connections. If electrical connections are okay, substitute PCM/TCM with a known good unit and recheck operation.

6) If battery voltage does not exist, check for open circuit in Green/White wire between terminal D2 and brakelight switch. Brakelight switch is located on brake pedal support. *See Fig. 4.*

7) Ensure ignition is off. Remove test harness. Reinstall electrical connectors on PCM/TCM. Reinstall passenger's side kick panel and passenger's side door sill molding.

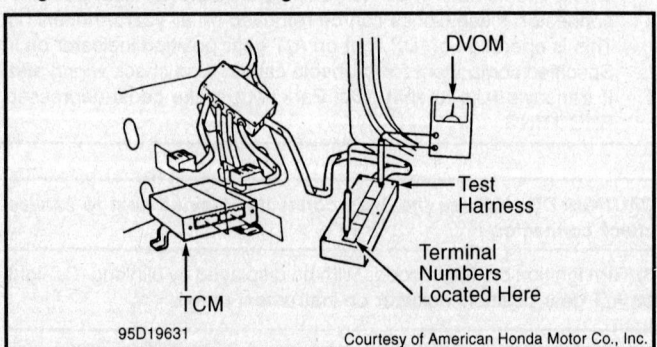

Fig. 7: Installing Test Harness

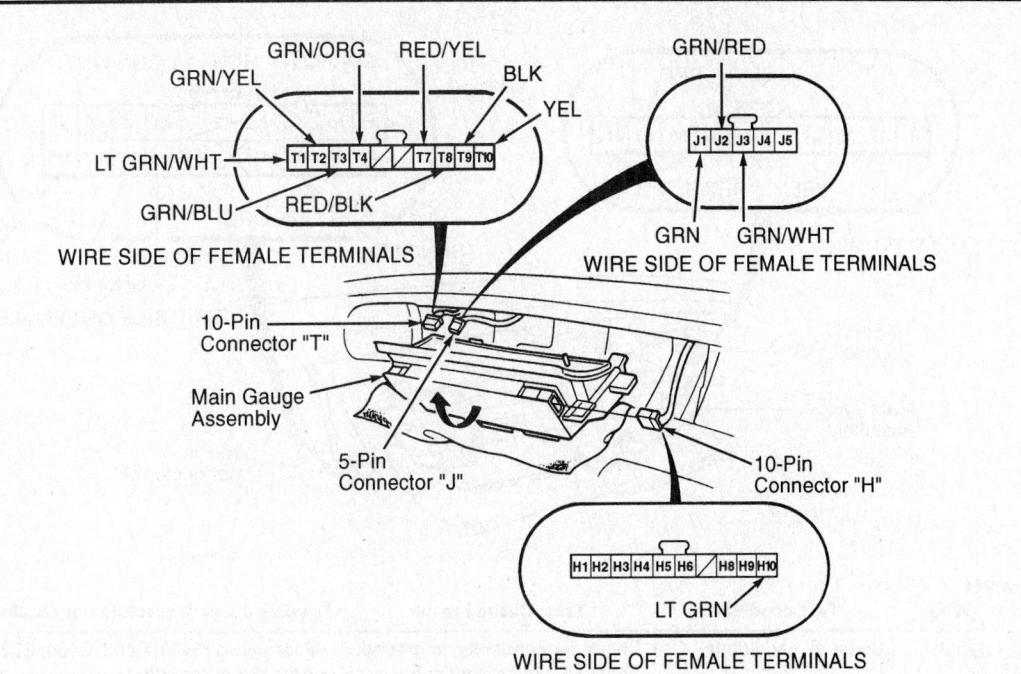

WIRE SIDE OF FEMALE TERMINALS

10-Pin Connector "T"

Main Gauge Assembly

5-Pin Connector "J"

10-Pin Connector "H"

WIRE SIDE OF FEMALE TERMINALS

Terminal No.	Wire	Test condition	Test: Desired result	Possible cause if result is not obtained
T9	BLK	Under all conditions	Check for continuity to ground: There should be continuity.	• Poor ground (G401, G402, G404, G521) • An open in the wire
T10	YEL	Ignition switch ON	Check for voltage to ground: There should be battery voltage.	• Blown No. 1 (10 A) fuse (In the under-dash fuse/relay box) • An open in the wire
J3	GRN/WHT	Shift lever in P NOTE: Don't push the brake pedal.	Check for continuity to ground: There should be continuity. NOTE: There should be no continuity in any other position.	• Faulty A/T gear position switch • Poor ground (G401, G402, G404, G521) • An open in the wire
J2	GRN/RED	Shift lever in R		
J1	GRN	Shift lever in N		
T3	GRN/BLU	Shift lever in D3		
T2	GRN/YEL	Shift lever in 2		
T1	LT GRN/ WHT	Shift lever in 1		
T7 · T8	RED/YEL and RED/BLK	Combination light switch ON, and dash lights brightness control dial on full bright	Check for voltage between T8 and T7 terminals: There should be battery voltage.	• Faulty dash lights brightness control system • An open in the wire
T4	GRN/ORN	Ignition switch ON, and shift lever in any position except D4	Check for voltage to ground: There should be battery voltage for two seconds after the ignition switch is turned ON, and less than 1 volt two seconds later.	• Faulty transmission control module (TCM) • An open in the wire
H10	LT GRN	Ignition switch ON	Check for voltage to ground: There should be more than 11 volts.	• Faulty ECM or TCM • An open in the wire

96C30983

Courtesy of American Honda Motor Co., Inc.

Fig. 8: Identifying Connectors & Testing A/T Gear Position Indicator

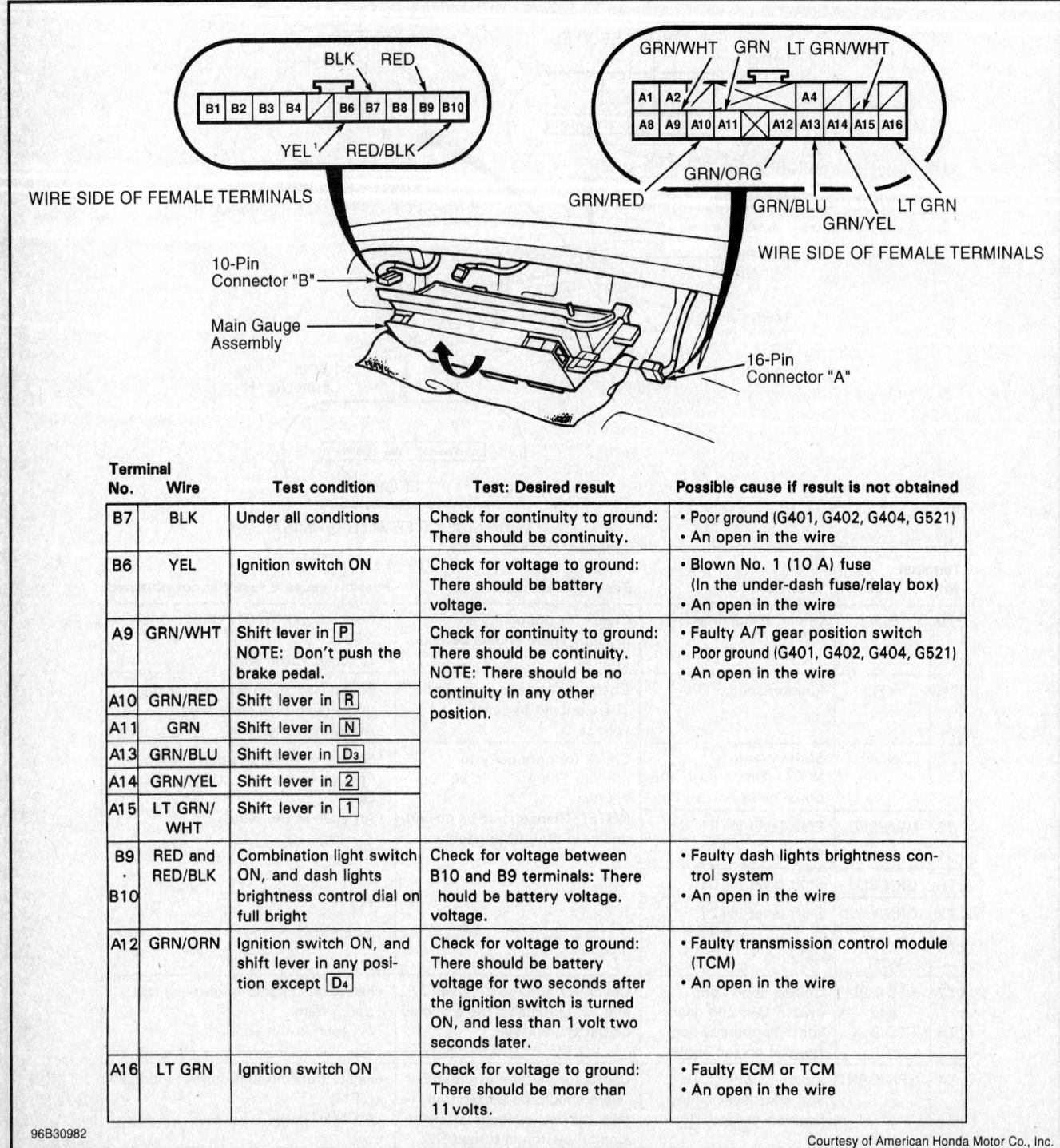

Terminal No.	Wire	Test condition	Test: Desired result	Possible cause if result is not obtained
B7	BLK	Under all conditions	Check for continuity to ground: There should be continuity.	• Poor ground (G401, G402, G404, G521) • An open in the wire
B6	YEL	Ignition switch ON	Check for voltage to ground: There should be battery voltage.	• Blown No. 1 (10 A) fuse (In the under-dash fuse/relay box) • An open in the wire
A9	GRN/WHT	Shift lever in P NOTE: Don't push the brake pedal.	Check for continuity to ground: There should be continuity. NOTE: There should be no continuity in any other position.	• Faulty A/T gear position switch • Poor ground (G401, G402, G404, G521) • An open in the wire
A10	GRN/RED	Shift lever in R		
A11	GRN	Shift lever in N		
A13	GRN/BLU	Shift lever in D₃		
A14	GRN/YEL	Shift lever in 2		
A15	LT GRN/WHT	Shift lever in 1		
B9 • B10	RED and RED/BLK	Combination light switch ON, and dash lights brightness control dial on full bright	Check for voltage between B10 and B9 terminals: There hould be battery voltage. voltage.	• Faulty dash lights brightness control system • An open in the wire
A12	GRN/ORN	Ignition switch ON, and shift lever in any position except D₄	Check for voltage to ground: There should be battery voltage for two seconds after the ignition switch is turned ON, and less than 1 volt two seconds later.	• Faulty transmission control module (TCM) • An open in the wire
A16	LT GRN	Ignition switch ON	Check for voltage to ground: There should be more than 11 volts.	• Faulty ECM or TCM • An open in the wire

96B30982   Courtesy of American Honda Motor Co., Inc.

Fig. 9: Identifying Connectors & Testing A/T Gear Position Indicator

BRAKELIGHT SIGNAL (1996)

NOTE: If no brakelight signal exists, transaxle may fail to shift from Park with brake pedal depressed and accelerator pedal in idle position.

1) Ensure brakelights come on when brake pedal is depressed. If brakelights come on, go to next step. If brakelights do not come on, check No. 41 fuse (15-amp) in engine compartment fuse box, located at passenger's side rear corner of engine compartment. If fuse is okay, repair brakelight signal circuit.

2) Ensure ignition is off. Disconnect the 32-pin connector "A" and 16-pin connector "B" electrical connectors from PCM, located behind driver's side kick panel. See Fig. 7.

3) Using Digital Volt-Ohmmeter (DVOM), measure voltage between terminals D5 and A9 or A22 with brake pedal depressed. If battery voltage exists, brakelight signal to PCM is okay. Check for loose PCM electrical connections. If electrical connections are okay, substitute PCM with a known good unit and recheck operation.

4) If battery voltage does not exist, check for open circuit in the Green/White wire between terminal D5 and brakelight switch. Brakelight switch is located on brake pedal support. See Fig. 4.

SYSTEM TESTING

A/T GEAR POSITION INDICATOR

NOTE: If necessary, refer to wiring schematic when checking component wiring. See Fig. 11.

1) Remove instrument panel gauge assembly from instrument panel. On models with luminescent gauges, disconnect connector "J" (5-pin), connector "H" (16-pin) and connector "T" (10-pin) from rear of instrument panel gauge assembly. *See Fig. 8.*

2) On models without luminescent gauges, disconnect connector "A" (16-pin) and connector "B" (10-pin) from rear of instrument panel gauge assembly. *See Fig. 9.*

3) On all models, check for voltage and continuity at electrical connectors as specified. *See Figs. 8 and 9.*

4) If necessary to check ground connections, G401, G402, G404 or G521, see GROUND CONNECTION LOCATIONS table. *See Fig. 10.*

GROUND CONNECTION LOCATIONS

Ground Connection	Location
G401	Behind Passenger's Kick Panel, Above PCM/TCM
G402	Driver's Side Of Center Console, Near Shift Lever
G404	Passenger's Side Of Center Console, Near Shift Lever
G521	Below Driver's Seat, Near Seat Mount Rail

5) If necessary to check No. 13 fuse (10-amp), fuse is located in the fuse/relay box behind driver's side kick panel. *See Fig. 4.* If necessary to access PCM/TCM, PCM/TCM is located behind passenger's side kick panel.

6) If necessary to access A/T gear position switch, A/T gear position switch is mounted on driver's side of shift lever. *See Fig. 4.*

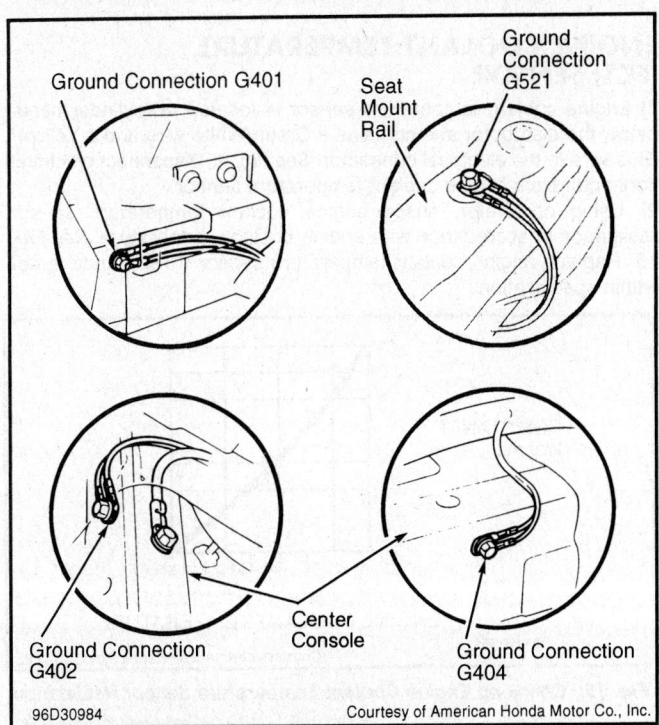

Fig. 10: Identifying Ground Connections

SHIFT & KEY INTERLOCK SYSTEMS

NOTE: For system testing, refer to wiring schematic when checking component wiring. See Fig. 12. To check individual components, see COMPONENT TESTING.

1) To check system operation, ensure shift lever is in Park. Turn ignition on. Depress brake pedal with accelerator pedal in idle position.

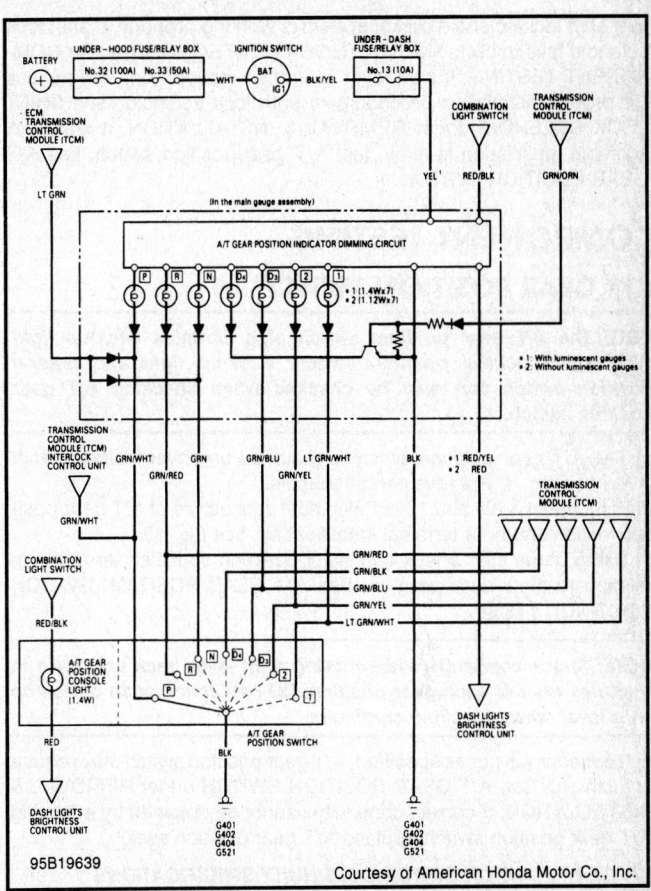

Fig. 11: A/T Gear Position Indicator Wiring Schematic

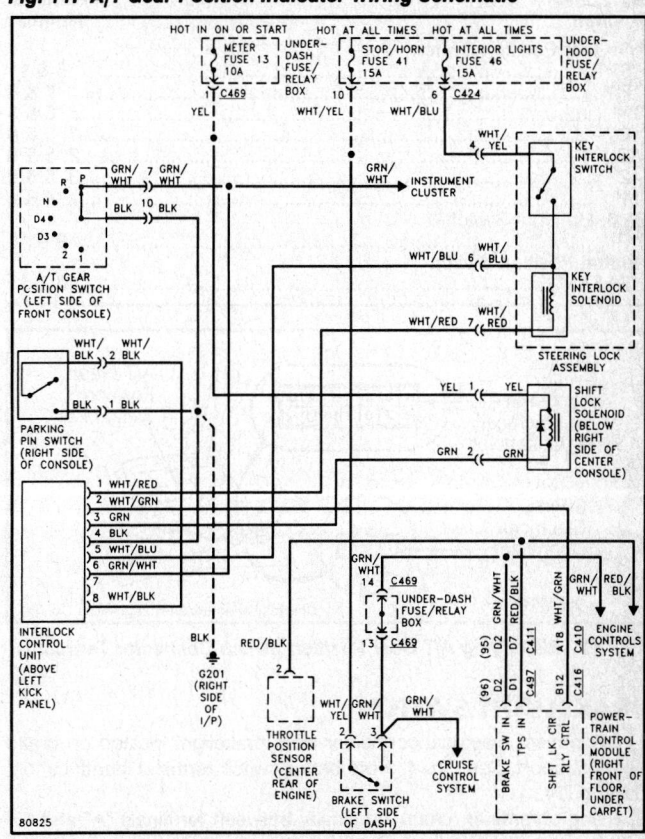

Fig. 12: Shift & Key Interlock System Wiring Schematic

2) If shift lock solenoid clicks, system is working properly. If shift lock solenoid fails to click, see INTERLOCK CONTROL UNIT under COMPONENT TESTING. If shift lever cannot be moved from Park, check for proper installation procedure of shift lock solenoid. See SHIFT LOCK SOLENOID under REMOVAL & INSTALLATION. If shift lock solenoid installation is okay, test A/T gear position switch, see A/T GEAR POSITION SWITCH.

COMPONENT TESTING

A/T GEAR POSITION SWITCH

NOTE: The A/T gear position switch also contains back-up light switch and neutral position switch. Back-up light and neutral position switch can also be checked when checking A/T gear position switch.

1) The A/T gear position switch is mounted on driver's side of shift lever. *See Fig. 4.* Remove center console.
2) Disconnect 3-pin and 12-pin electrical connectors at A/T gear position switch and note terminal identification. *See Fig. 13.*
3) Using ohmmeter, check continuity between specified terminals in relation to shift lever position. See A/T GEAR POSITION SWITCH CONTINUITY table.

NOTE: Check continuity while moving shift lever back and forth in free play area of each gear position. DO NOT touch push button on shift lever when checking continuity.

4) If continuity is not as specified, A/T gear position switch may require adjustment. See A/T GEAR POSITION SWITCH under REMOVAL & INSTALLATION. If correct continuity cannot be obtained by adjusting A/T gear position switch, replace A/T gear position switch.

A/T GEAR POSITION SWITCH CONTINUITY SPECIFICATIONS

Shift Lever Position	Terminal Number
A/T Gear Position Switch	
"P"	8 & 11
"R"	7 & 8
"N"	6 & 8
"D$_4$"	1, 5 & 8
"D$_3$"	2, 5 & 8
"2"	3, 5 & 8
"1"	4 & 8
Back-Up Light Switch	
"R"	9 & 10
Neutral Position Switch	
"P" & "N"	13 & 15

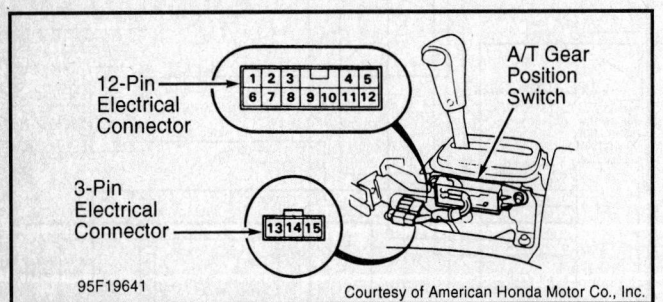

Fig. 13: Identifying A/T Gear Position Switch Connector Terminals

BRAKELIGHT SWITCH

1) Disconnect electrical connector from brakelight located on brake pedal support. *See Fig. 4.* Note brake switch terminal identification. *See Fig. 14.*
2) Using ohmmeter, check continuity between terminals "A" and "D" with brake pedal released. Continuity should exist.
3) Check continuity between terminals "B" and "C" with brake pedal depressed. Continuity should exist.

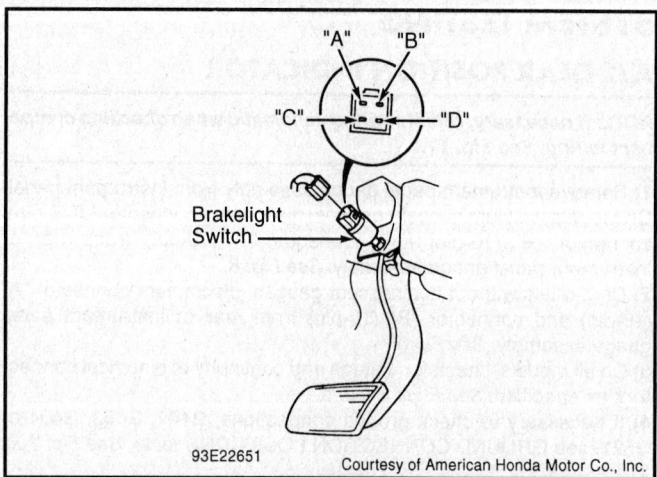

Fig. 14: Identifying Brakelight Switch Terminals

4) If continuity is not as specified, ensure brake pedal is properly adjusted so brakelight switch has proper travel for switch operation. If proper brakelight switch travel exists, replace brakelight switch.

COUNTERSHAFT SPEED SENSOR

1) Countershaft speed sensor is located on transaxle. *See Fig. 4.* Disconnect electrical connector from countershaft speed sensor.
2) Using ohmmeter, measure resistance between terminals on countershaft speed sensor. Replace countershaft speed sensor if resistance is not 400-600 ohms at 70°F (20°C).

ENGINE COOLANT TEMPERATURE (ECT) SENSOR

1) Engine coolant temperature sensor is located on cylinder head, below the distributor and contains a Green/White wire and a Yellow/Blue wire in the electrical connector. *See Fig. 4.* Disconnect electrical connector from engine coolant temperature sensor.
2) Using ohmmeter, check engine coolant temperature sensor resistance in accordance with engine coolant temperature. *See Fig. 15.* Replace engine coolant temperature sensor if resistance is not within specification.

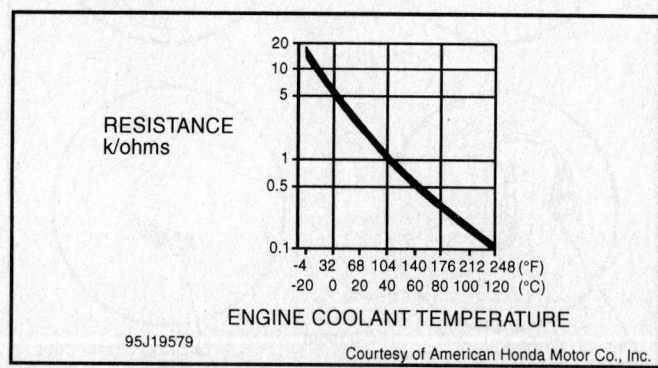

Fig. 15: Checking Engine Coolant Temperature Sensor Resistance

INTERLOCK CONTROL UNIT

1) Remove lower panel from instrument panel. Disconnect 8-pin connector from interlock control unit. Interlock control unit is located under left side of instrument panel. *See Fig. 4.* Inspect terminals for poor connection, corrosion or bending, repair as necessary.
2) Using DVOM, check for continuity or voltage between specified terminals or body ground. *See Fig. 16.* If necessary to check ground connections G401, G402, G404 or G521, see GROUND CONNECTIONS LOCATIONS table under SYSTEM TESTING. *See Fig. 10.*

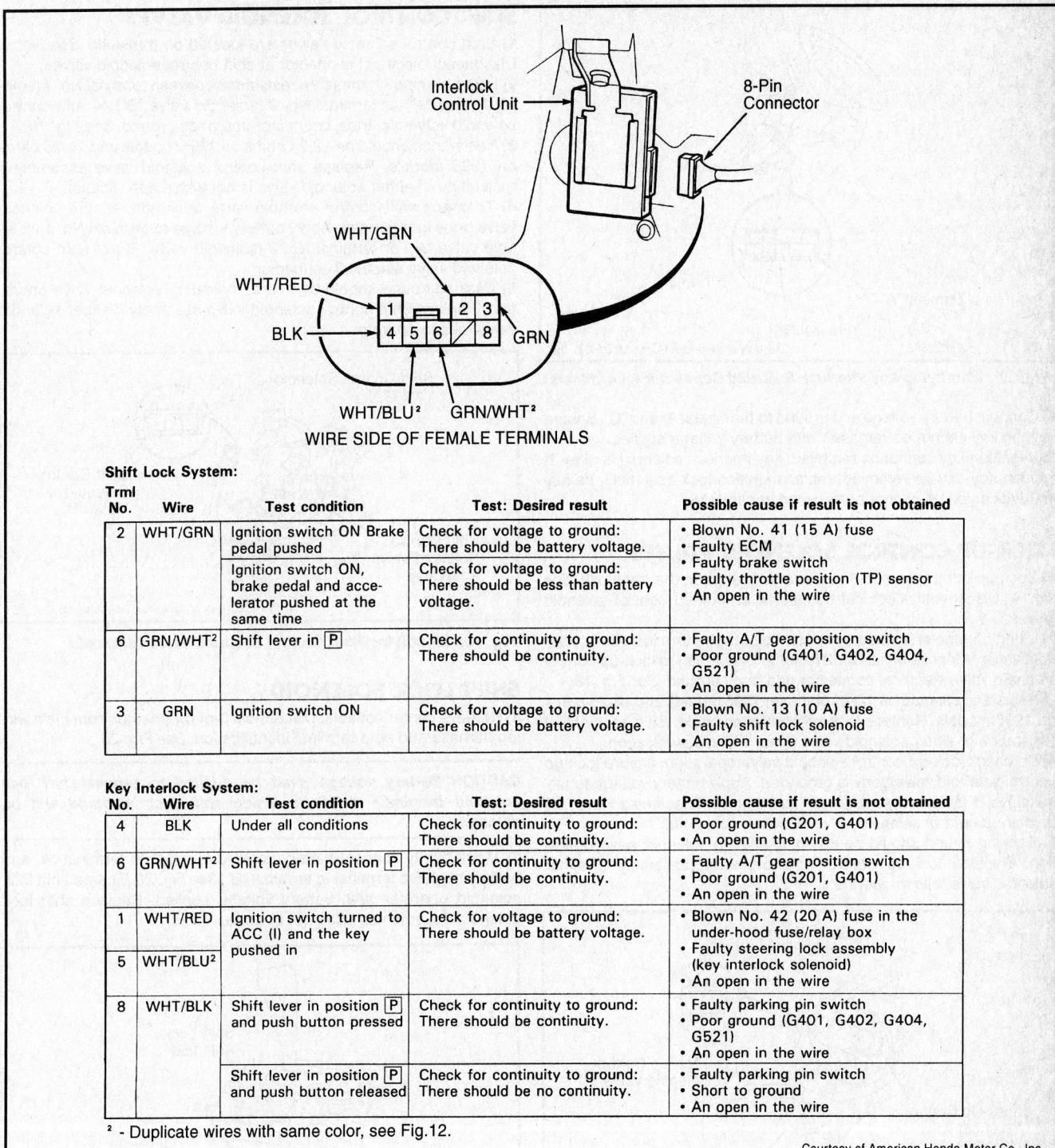

Courtesy of American Honda Motor Co., Inc.

96F30986

Fig. 16: Testing Interlock Control Unit

3) If necessary to check No. 41 fuse (15-amp) in engine compartment fuse box, located at passenger's side rear corner of engine compartment. If necessary to check No. 13 fuse (10-amp), fuse is located in fuse box on driver's side of instrument panel, near steering column. If necessary to access PCM/TCM, the PCM/TCM is located behind glove box. *See Fig. 4.*

KEY INTERLOCK SOLENOID

1) Remove lower panel from steering column. Disconnect 8-pin electrical connector from main wiring harness and note terminal identification. *See Fig. 17.*

2) Using ohmmeter, check continuity between designated terminals with ignition lock assembly in ACC position. See KEY INTERLOCK SOLENOID CONTINUITY SPECIFICATIONS table.

3) Replace ignition lock assembly if continuity is not as specified, as key interlock solenoid cannot be serviced separately.

KEY INTERLOCK SOLENOID CONTINUITY SPECIFICATIONS

Ignition Key Position	Continuity Between Terminals
Key Installed	"A", "B" & "C"
Key Removed	"B" & "C"

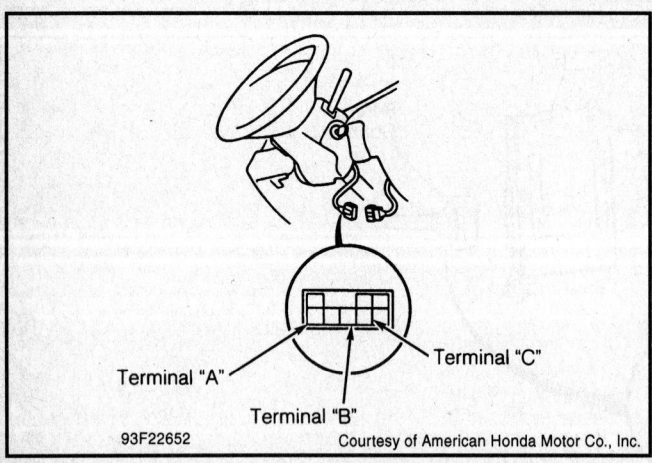

Terminal "A"

Terminal "B"

Terminal "C"

93F22652   Courtesy of American Honda Motor Co., Inc.

Fig. 17: Identifying Key Interlock Solenoid Connector & Terminals

4) Connect battery voltage and ground to terminals "A" and "C'. Ensure ignition key cannot be removed with battery voltage applied.
5) If ignition key cannot be removed, key interlock solenoid is okay. If ignition key can be removed, replace ignition lock assembly, as key interlock solenoid cannot be serviced separately.

LOCK-UP CONTROL SOLENOID VALVES

1) Lock-up control solenoid valves are located on the transaxle. See Fig. 4. Disconnect electrical connector at lock-up control solenoid valves.
2) Using ohmmeter, measure resistance between terminal No. 1 (solenoid valve "A") or terminal No. 2 (solenoid valve "B") of lock-up control solenoid valve electrical connector and body ground. See Fig. 18.
3) Resistance should be 12-24 ohms on 1995 models and 14-25 ohms on 1996 models. Replace lock-up control solenoid valve assembly if resistance of either solenoid valve is not within specification.
4) To check lock-up control solenoid valve operation, ensure lock-up control solenoid valve body is grounded. Apply battery voltage to terminal No. 1 (solenoid valve "A") or terminal No. 2 (solenoid valve "B") of lock-up control solenoid valve electrical connector.
5) Clicking sound should be heard, indicating solenoid valve operation. Replace lock-up control solenoid valve assembly if either solenoid valve fails to operate.

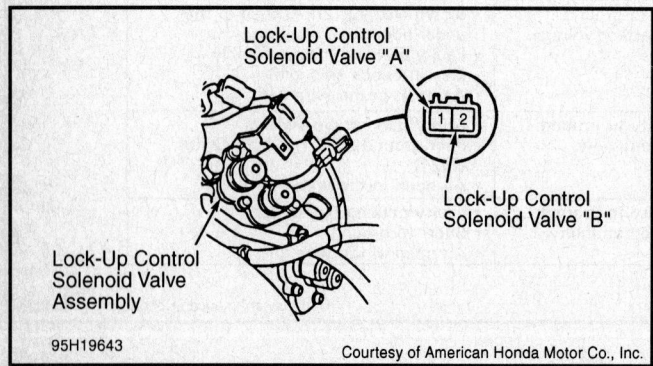

Lock-Up Control Solenoid Valve "A"

Lock-Up Control Solenoid Valve "B"

Lock-Up Control Solenoid Valve Assembly

95H19643   Courtesy of American Honda Motor Co., Inc.

Fig. 18: Identifying Lock-Up Control Solenoid Valve Terminals

MAINSHAFT SPEED SENSOR

1) Mainshaft speed sensor is located on transaxle. See Fig. 4. Disconnect electrical connector from mainshaft speed sensor.
2) Using ohmmeter, measure resistance between terminals on mainshaft speed sensor. Replace mainshaft speed sensor if resistance is not 400-600 ohms at 70°F (20°C).

SHIFT CONTROL SOLENOID VALVES

1) Shift control solenoid valves are located on transaxle. See Fig. 4. Disconnect electrical connector at shift control solenoid valves.
2) Using ohmmeter, measure resistance between terminal No. 1 (solenoid valve "A") or terminal No. 2 (solenoid valve "B") of shift control solenoid valve electrical connector and body ground. See Fig. 19.
3) Resistance should be 12-24 ohms on 1995 models and 14-25 ohms on 1996 models. Replace shift control solenoid valve assembly if resistance of either solenoid valve is not within specification.
4) To check shift control solenoid valve operation, ensure solenoid valve body is grounded. Apply battery voltage to terminal No. 1 (solenoid valve "A") or terminal No. 2 (solenoid valve "B") of shift control solenoid valve electrical connector.
5) Clicking sound should be heard, indicating solenoid valve operation. Replace shift control solenoid valve assembly if either valve fails to operate.

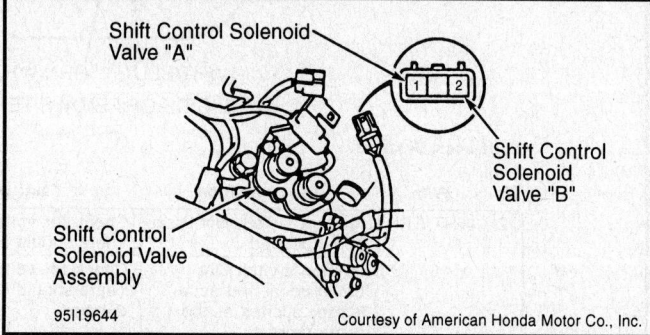

Shift Control Solenoid Valve "A"

Shift Control Solenoid Valve "B"

Shift Control Solenoid Valve Assembly

95l19644   Courtesy of American Honda Motor Co., Inc.

Fig. 19: Identifying Shift Control Solenoid Valve Terminals

SHIFT LOCK SOLENOID

1) Remove center console. Disconnect 3-pin connector from main wiring harness and note terminal identification. See Fig. 20.

CAUTION: Battery voltage must be applied to proper shift lock solenoid terminals or diode inside shift lock solenoid will be damaged.

2) Momentarily connect battery positive terminal to terminal "A" and battery negative terminal to terminal "B". See Fig. 20. Ensure shift lock solenoid operates with battery voltage applied. Replace shift lock solenoid if it solenoid does not operate.

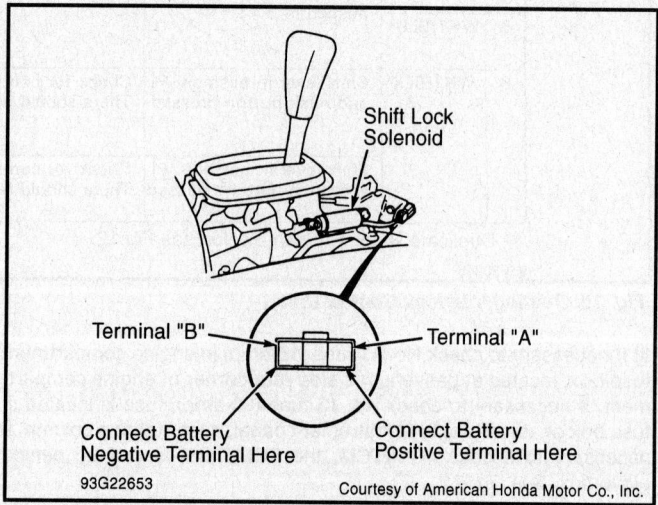

Shift Lock Solenoid

Terminal "B"

Terminal "A"

Connect Battery Negative Terminal Here

Connect Battery Positive Terminal Here

93G22653   Courtesy of American Honda Motor Co., Inc.

Fig. 20: Identifying Shift Lock Solenoid Connector & Terminals

THROTTLE POSITION (TP) SENSOR

TP sensor should input a .5-volt reference signal to TCM at closed throttle and approximately 4.5-volt signal at full throttle. Voltage should change smoothly as throttle valve is opened and closed. If voltage is not correct, check throttle position sensor wiring circuit. See WIRING DIAGRAMS. Individual component testing not available from manufacturer.

NOTE: On 1995 models, if problem in throttle position sensor exists, throttle position sensor may set Flash Code No. 3 in TCM. See RETRIEVING CODES under SELF-DIAGNOSTIC SYSTEM

VEHICLE SPEED SENSOR (VSS)

1) Vehicle speed sensor is located on transaxle, below thermostat housing. *See Fig. 4.* Ensure No. 23 fuse (15-amp) for vehicles equipped without luminescent gauges and No. 13 fuse (10-amp) for vehicles equipped with luminescent gauges in fuse/relay box behind driver's side kick panel is okay. Replace fuse if necessary. If fuse is okay, disconnect 3-pin electrical connector at vehicle speed sensor.

2) Turn ignition on. Using voltmeter, measure voltage between the Black/Yellow wire and Black wire of 3-pin electrical connector. If battery voltage exists, proceed to step 5). If battery voltage does not exist, proceed to step 3).

3) Using ohmmeter, check for continuity between Black wire of 3-pin electrical connector and body ground. If continuity exists, repair open circuit in Black/Yellow wire between 3-pin electrical connector and appropriate fuse in fuse/relay box behind driver's side kick panel.

4) If continuity does not exist, check for open circuit in Black wire between 3-pin electrical connector and ground connection G101. See WIRING DIAGRAMS. Ground connection G101 is located on bolt at thermostat housing.

5) Using voltmeter, measure voltage between Orange and Black wires of 3-pin electrical connector. If about 5 volts exist, proceed to next step. If about 5 volts does not exist, repair open circuit or short circuit to ground in Orange wire. The Orange wire goes to instrument panel gauge assembly, PCM/TCM and cruise control unit.

NOTE: Cruise control unit is located behind driver's side of instrument panel, near steering column. See Fig. 21.

6) Reconnect 3-pin electrical connector on vehicle speed sensor. Raise and support front of vehicle so front wheels are free to rotate. Using voltmeter, backprobe Orange wire on 3-pin electrical connector and connect it to body ground.

7) Place shift lever in Neutral. Ensure ignition is on. Rotate one front wheel while holding the other front wheel stationary.

8) Note that voltage reading pulses from zero volts to about 5 volts. If voltage pulses correctly, vehicle speed sensor is okay. If voltage does not pulse correctly, replace vehicle speed sensor.

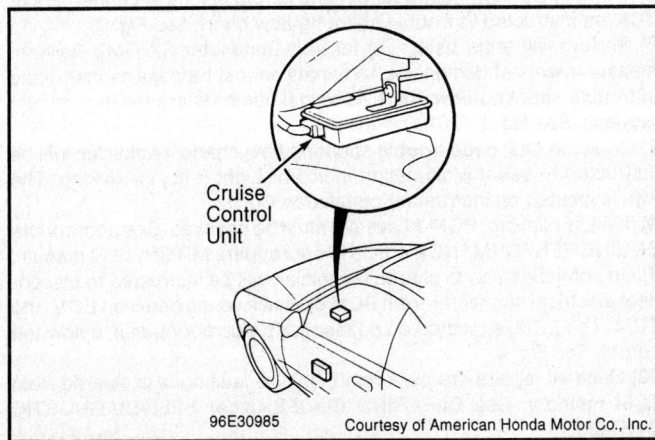

Cruise Control Unit

96E30985   Courtesy of American Honda Motor Co., Inc.

Fig. 21: Identifying Cruise Control Unit

REMOVAL & INSTALLATION

A/T GEAR POSITION SWITCH

Removal – Remove center console. Disconnect electrical connectors from A/T gear position switch. Remove nuts and A/T gear position switch.

Installation – 1) Ensure parking brake is applied. Place switch slider on A/T gear position switch in neutral position. *See Fig. 22.* Place shift lever in Neutral.

2) Install A/T gear position switch and nuts. DO NOT tighten nuts at this time, as A/T gear position switch must be adjusted.

3) To adjust A/T gear position switch, place shift lever in Park. Ensure retaining nuts are loose. Note electrical connector terminal identification. *See Fig. 14.*

4) Connect ohmmeter between terminals No. 8 and 11. Move A/T gear position switch toward rear of console until continuity exists between terminals No. 8 and 11. Free play at lock pin should be .079" (2.0 mm) maximum. *See Fig. 22.*

5) Tighten nuts. Check A/T gear position switch for correct continuity in all gears. See A/T GEAR POSITION SWITCH under COMPONENT TESTING. If proper adjustment cannot be obtained, check for damaged shift lever detent or bracket. Install electrical connector and center console.

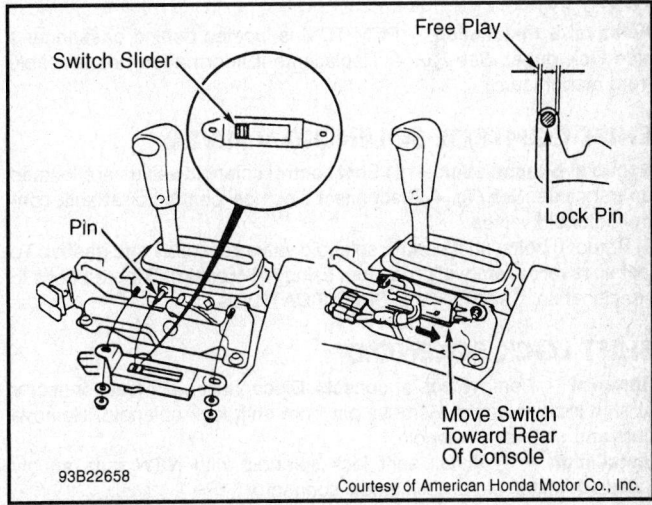

Switch Slider

Free Play

Pin

Lock Pin

Move Switch Toward Rear Of Console

93B22658   Courtesy of American Honda Motor Co., Inc.

Fig. 22: Installing A/T Gear Position Switch

BRAKELIGHT SWITCH

Removal & Installation – 1) Disconnect electrical connector. Remove lock nut and unscrew brakelight switch. To install, screw brakelight switch inward until brakelight plunger is fully depressed.

2) Back off brakelight switch 1/4 turn. Install and tighten lock nut. Install electrical connector. Ensure brakelights and cruise control operate properly.

COUNTERSHAFT SPEED SENSOR

Removal & Installation – Countershaft speed sensor is located on transaxle. *See Fig. 4.* Remove bolt, countershaft speed sensor and "O" ring. To install, reverse removal procedure using NEW "O" ring. Tighten bolt to specification. See TORQUE SPECIFICATIONS.

ENGINE COOLANT TEMPERATURE (ECT) SENSOR

Removal – Engine coolant temperature sensor is located on cylinder head, below the distributor and contains a Green/White wire and a Yellow/Blue wire in the electrical connector. *See Fig. 3.* Drain cooling system. Remove engine coolant temperature sensor.

Installation – 1) Install and tighten engine coolant temperature sensor. When refilling cooling system, open air bleed bolt on thermostat housing.

2) Fill cooling system until coolant flows from air bleed bolt. Tighten air bleed bolt to specification. See TORQUE SPECIFICATIONS. Finish filling cooling system.

KEY INTERLOCK SOLENOID

Removal & Installation – Key interlock solenoid cannot be serviced separately. Entire ignition lock assembly must be replaced.

LOCK-UP CONTROL SOLENOID VALVES

Removal & Installation – 1) Lock-up control solenoid valves are located on the transaxle. See Fig. 4. Disconnect electrical connector at lock-up control solenoid valves.
2) Remove bolts, lock-up control solenoid valve assembly and gasket. To install, reverse removal procedure using NEW gasket. Tighten bolts to specification. See TORQUE SPECIFICATIONS.

MAINSHAFT SPEED SENSOR

Removal & Installation – Mainshaft speed sensor is located on transaxle. See Fig. 4. Remove bolt, mainshaft speed sensor and "O" ring. To install, reverse removal procedure using NEW "O" ring. Tighten bolt to specification. See TORQUE SPECIFICATIONS.

PCM/TCM

Removal & Installation – PCM/TCM is located behind passenger's side kick panel. See Fig. 4. Replacement information not available from manufacturer.

SHIFT CONTROL SOLENOID VALVES

Removal & Installation – 1) Shift control solenoid valves are located on transaxle. See Fig. 4. Disconnect electrical connector at shift control solenoid valves.
2) Remove bolts, shift control solenoid valve assembly and gasket. To install, reverse removal procedure using NEW gasket. Tighten bolts to specification. See TORQUE SPECIFICATIONS.

SHIFT LOCK SOLENOID

Removal – Remove center console. Disconnect electrical connector at shift lock solenoid. Remove pin from shift lock solenoid. Remove nuts and shift lock solenoid.
Installation – 1) Install shift lock solenoid with NEW nuts snugly installed. Install pin and electrical connector.
2) Turn ignition on (solenoid energized), ensure clearance between top of shift lock lever and lock pin groove is .094-.134" (2.4-3.4 mm). See Fig. 23.

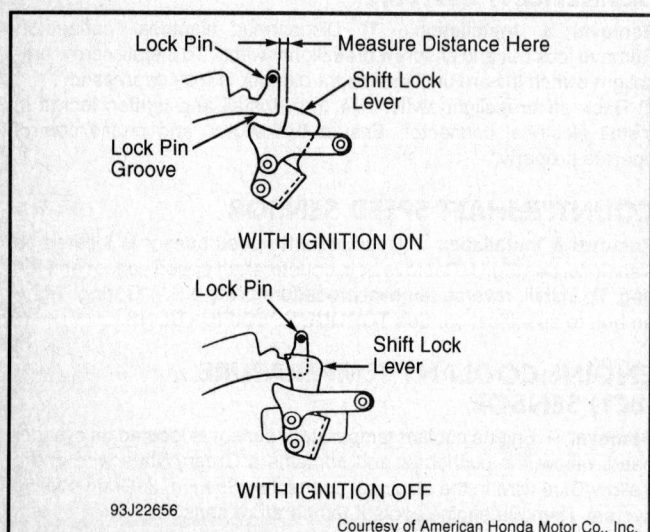

WITH IGNITION ON

WITH IGNITION OFF

93J22656
Courtesy of American Honda Motor Co., Inc.

Fig. 23: Checking Shift Lock Solenoid Operation

3) If clearance is not as specified, loosen nuts and reposition shift lock solenoid until correct clearance is obtained. Once correct clearance is obtained, tighten nuts to specification. See TORQUE SPECIFICATIONS.
4) Turn ignition off (solenoid de-energized). Ensure lock pin is blocked by shift lock lever. See Fig. 23. Check solenoid operation several times.

THROTTLE POSITION SENSOR

Removal & Installation – Throttle position sensor is mounted on throttle body. Replacement information is not available from manufacturer.

VEHICLE SPEED SENSOR (VSS)

NOTE: When servicing vehicle speed sensor, DO NOT lose vehicle speed sensor drive shaft located between vehicle speed sensor and power steering speed sensor.

Removal & Installation – Vehicle speed sensor is located on transaxle, below thermostat housing. See Fig. 4. Disconnect electrical connector at vehicle speed sensor. Remove bolts and vehicle speed sensor. To install, reverse removal procedure.

TORQUE SPECIFICATIONS

TORQUE SPECIFICATIONS

Application	INCH Lbs.
Air Bleed Bolt	89 (10.0)
Countershaft Speed Sensor Bolt	106 (12.0)
Lock-Up Control Solenoid Valve Bolt	106 (12.0)
Mainshaft Speed Sensor Bolt	106 (12.0)
Shift Control Solenoid Valve Bolt	106 (12.0)
Shift Lock Solenoid Nut	89 (10.0)

DIAGNOSTIC TESTING

FLOW CHART USAGE (1995)

1) Use appropriate trouble shooting flow chart corresponding to fault code. Ensure ignition is off before disconnecting electrical connectors from TCM. The TCM is located behind passenger's side kick panel. *See Fig. 4.*
2) The TCM has a 26-pin and 22-pin electrical connectors. These are referenced as connectors 26P and 22P in trouble shooting flow charts.
3) Test Harness (07LAJ-PT3010A) may be required for use with trouble shooting flow chart. To install test harness, ensure ignition is off.
4) Remove passenger's side door sill molding and passenger's side kick panel. Pull carpet back for access to TCM, located behind driver's side kick panel. *See Fig. 4.* Disconnect 26-pin and 22-pin electrical connectors from TCM.
5) Connect test harness to 26-pin and 22-pin electrical connectors or TCM as instructed in trouble shooting flow chart. *See Fig. 7.*
6) Perform all tests using Digital Volt-Ohmmeter (DVOM). Perform measurements at designated terminals on test harness as instructed in trouble shooting flow chart. Terminal numbers are located on test harness. *See Fig. 7.*
7) On some fault code trouble shooting flow charts, technician will be instructed to see if Malfunction Indicator Light (MIL) is blinking. The MIL is located on instrument panel. *See Fig. 1.*
8) If MIL is blinking, PGM-FI system must be checked. See appropriate ENGINE PERFORMANCE article in appropriate MITCHELL® manual.
9) On some flash code charts, technician will be instructed to disconnect electrical connector from ECM or check wiring between ECM and TCM. The ECM is located on passenger's side floor panel, below the carpet. *See Fig. 4.*
10) Once all repairs are performed, ensure fault code is cleared from TCM memory. See CLEARING CODES under SELF-DIAGNOSTIC SYSTEM.

NOTE: The following charts and illustrations are courtesy of American Honda Motor Co., Inc.

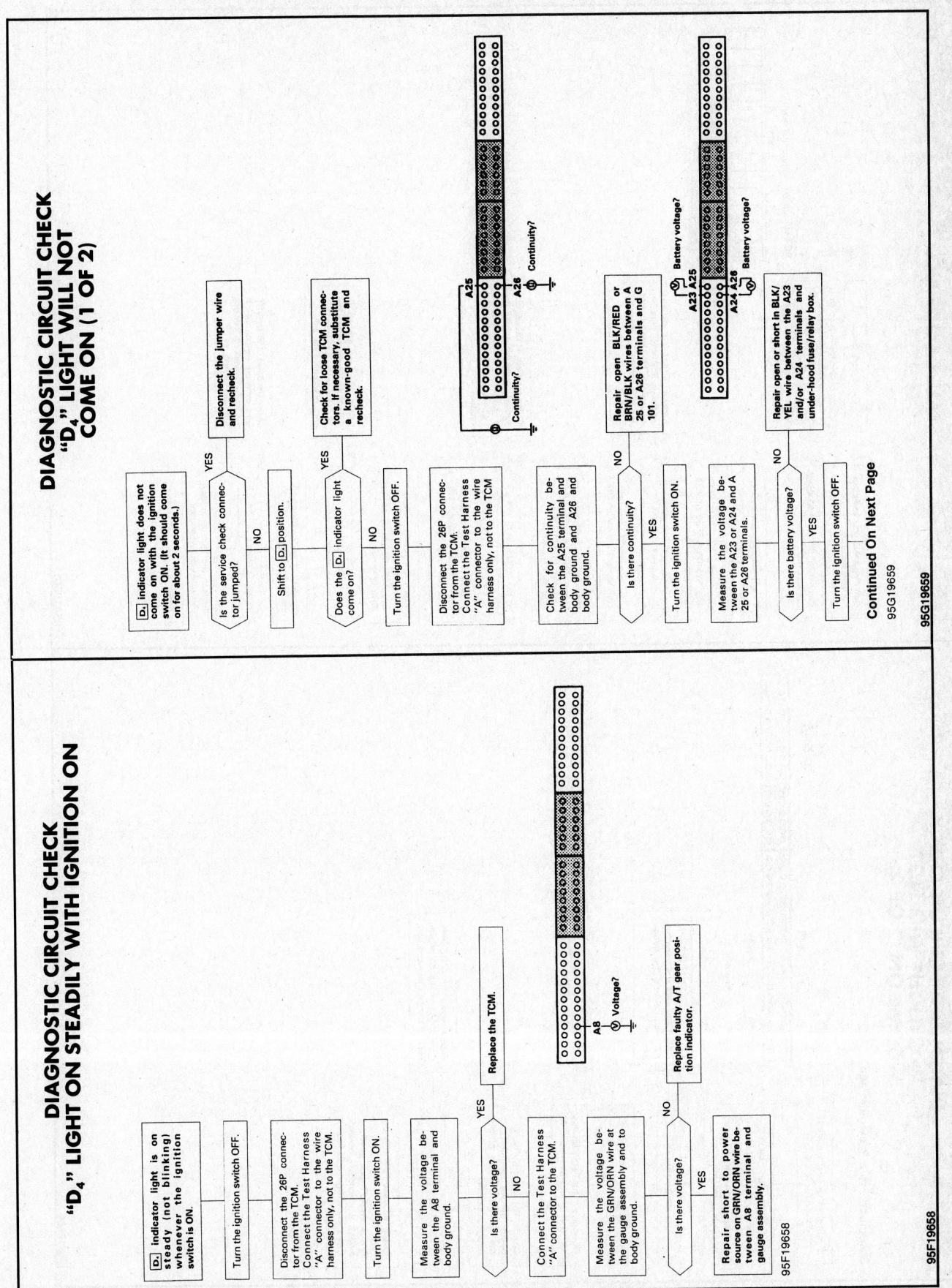

DIAGNOSTIC CIRCUIT CHECK "D4" LIGHT WILL NOT COME ON (1 OF 2)

D4 indicator light does not come on with the ignition switch ON. (It should come on for about 2 seconds.)

Is the service check connector jumped?

YES → Disconnect the jumper wire and recheck.

NO → Shift to D4 position.

Does the D4 indicator light come on?

YES → Check for loose TCM connectors. If necessary, substitute a known-good TCM and recheck.

NO → Turn the ignition switch OFF.

Disconnect the 26P connector from the TCM. Connect the Test Harness "A" connector to the wire harness only, not to the TCM.

Check for continuity between the A25 terminal and body ground and A26 and body ground.

A25 Continuity?

A26 Continuity?

Is there continuity?

NO → Repair open BLK/RED or BRN/BLK wires between A 25 or A26 terminals and G 101.

YES → Turn the ignition switch ON.

Measure the voltage between the A23 or A24 and A 25 or A26 terminals.

A23 A25 Battery voltage?

A24 A26 Battery voltage?

Is there battery voltage?

NO → Repair open or short in BLK/ YEL wire between the A23 and/or A24 terminals and under-hood fuse/relay box.

YES → Turn the ignition switch OFF.

Continued On Next Page

95G19659

95G19659

DIAGNOSTIC CIRCUIT CHECK "D4" LIGHT ON STEADILY WITH IGNITION ON

D4 indicator light is on steady (not blinking) whenever the ignition switch is ON.

Turn the ignition switch OFF.

Disconnect the 26P connector from the TCM. Connect the Test Harness "A" connector to the wire harness only, not to the TCM.

Turn the ignition switch ON.

Measure the voltage between the A8 terminal and body ground.

A8 Voltage?

Is there voltage?

YES → Replace the TCM.

NO → Connect the Test Harness "A" connector to the TCM.

Measure the voltage between the GRN/ORN wire at the gauge assembly and to body ground.

Is there voltage?

NO → Replace faulty A/T gear position indicator.

YES → Repair short to power source on GRN/ORN wire between A8 terminal and gauge assembly.

95F19658

95F19658

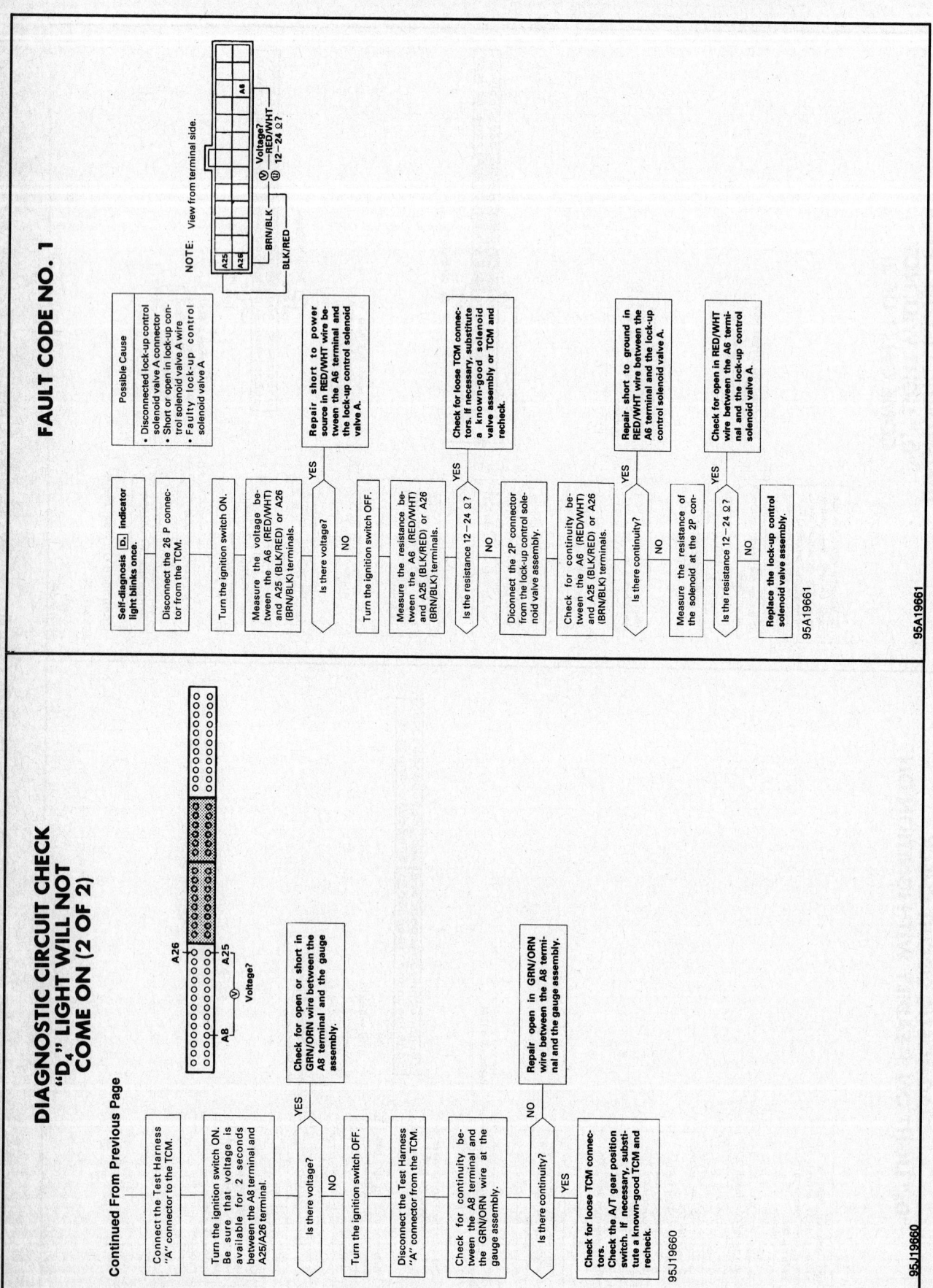

FAULT CODE NO. 1

NOTE: View from terminal side.

A25
A26
BRN/BLK
BLK/RED
A8
RED/WHT
Voltage?
12 — 24 Ω?

Possible Cause
• Disconnected lock-up control solenoid valve A connector • Short or open in lock-up control solenoid valve A wire • Faulty lock-up control solenoid valve A

Self-diagnosis D₄ indicator light blinks once.

Disconnect the 26 P connector from the TCM.

Turn the ignition switch ON.

Measure the voltage between the A6 (RED/WHT) and A25 (BLK/RED) or A26 (BRN/BLK) terminals.

Is there voltage? — YES → Repair short to power source in RED/WHT wire between the A6 terminal and the lock-up control solenoid valve A.

NO

Turn the ignition switch OFF.

Measure the resistance between the A6 (RED/WHT) and A25 (BLK/RED) or A26 (BRN/BLK) terminals.

Is the resistance 12—24 Ω? — YES → Check for loose TCM connectors. If necessary, substitute a known-good solenoid valve assembly or TCM and recheck.

NO

Disconnect the 2P connector from the lock-up control solenoid valve assembly.

Check for continuity between the A6 (RED/WHT) and A25 (BLK/RED) or A26 (BRN/BLK) terminals.

Is there continuity? — YES → Repair short to ground in RED/WHT wire between the A6 terminal and the lock-up control solenoid valve A.

NO

Measure the resistance of the solenoid at the 2P connector.

Is the resistance 12—24 Ω? — YES → Check for open in RED/WHT wire between the A6 terminal and the lock-up control solenoid valve A.

NO

Replace the lock-up control solenoid valve assembly.

95A19661

95J19661

DIAGNOSTIC CIRCUIT CHECK
"D₄" LIGHT WILL NOT COME ON (2 OF 2)

Continued From Previous Page

A26
A8   A25
Voltage?

Connect the Test Harness "A" connector to the TCM.

Turn the ignition switch ON. Be sure that voltage is available for 2 seconds between the A8 terminal and A25/A26 terminal.

Is there voltage? — YES → Check for open or short in GRN/ORN wire between the A8 terminal and the gauge assembly.

NO

Turn the ignition switch OFF.

Disconnect the Test Harness "A" connector from the TCM.

Check for continuity between the A8 terminal and the GRN/ORN wire at the gauge assembly.

Is there continuity? — NO → Repair open in GRN/ORN wire between the A8 terminal and the gauge assembly.

YES

Check for loose TCM connectors.
Check the A/T gear position switch. If necessary, substitute a known-good TCM and recheck.

95J19660

95J19660

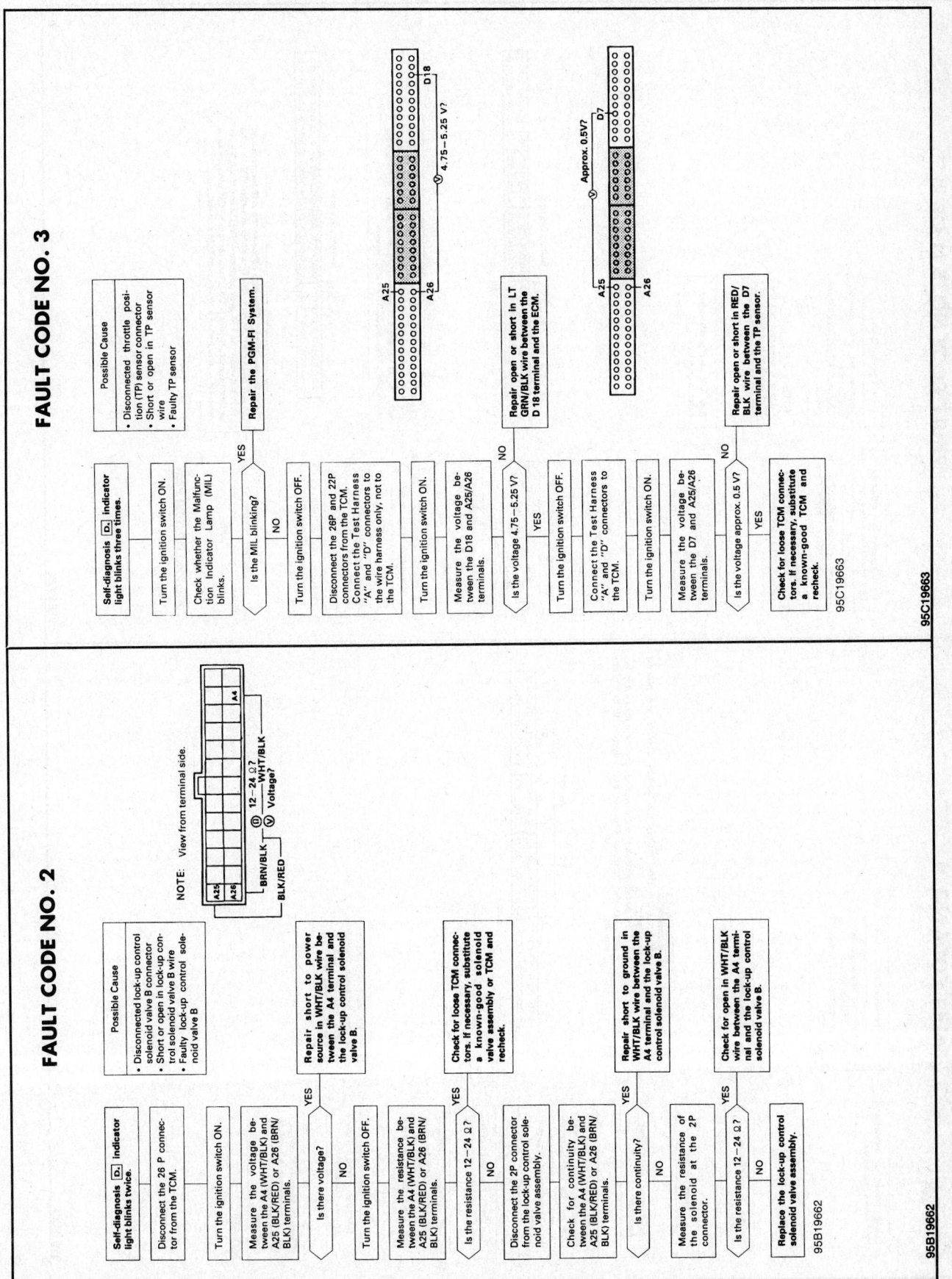

FAULT CODE NO. 2

Possible Cause
- Disconnected lock-up control solenoid valve B connector
- Short or open in lock-up control solenoid valve B wire
- Faulty lock-up control solenoid valve B

Self-diagnosis [D₄] indicator light blinks twice.

Disconnect the 26 P connector from the TCM.

Turn the ignition switch ON.

Measure the voltage between the A4 (WHT/BLK) and A25 (BLK/RED) or A26 (BRN/BLK) terminals.

Is there voltage? — YES → Repair short to power source in WHT/BLK wire between the A4 terminal and the lock-up control solenoid valve B.

NO ↓

Turn the ignition switch OFF.

Measure the resistance between the A4 (WHT/BLK) and A25 (BLK/RED) or A26 (BRN/BLK) terminals.

Is the resistance 12–24 Ω? — YES → Check for loose TCM connectors. If necessary, substitute a known-good solenoid valve assembly or TCM and recheck.

NO ↓

Disconnect the 2P connector from the lock-up control solenoid valve assembly.

Check for continuity between the A4 (WHT/BLK) and A25 (BLK/RED) or A26 (BRN/BLK) terminals.

Is there continuity? — YES → Repair short to ground in WHT/BLK wire between the A4 terminal and the lock-up control solenoid valve B.

NO ↓

Measure the resistance of the solenoid at the 2P connector.

Is the resistance 12–24 Ω? — YES → Check for open in WHT/BLK wire between the A4 terminal and the lock-up control solenoid valve B.

NO ↓

Replace the lock-up control solenoid valve assembly.

NOTE: View from terminal side.
Ⓡ 12–24 Ω? Ⓥ Voltage?
BRN/BLK WHT/BLK BLK/RED
A25 A26 A4

95B19662

FAULT CODE NO. 3

Possible Cause
- Disconnected throttle position (TP) sensor connector
- Short or open in TP sensor wire
- Faulty TP sensor

Self-diagnosis [D₄] indicator light blinks three times.

Turn the ignition switch ON.

Check whether the Malfunction Indicator Lamp (MIL) blinks.

Is the MIL blinking? — YES → Repair the PGM-FI System.

NO ↓

Turn the ignition switch OFF.

Disconnect the 26P and 22P connectors from the TCM. Connect the Test Harness "A" and "D" connectors to the wire harness only, not to the TCM.

Turn the ignition switch ON.

Measure the voltage between the D18 and A25/A26 terminals.

Is the voltage 4.75–5.25 V? — NO → Repair open or short in LT GRN/BLK wire between the D18 terminal and the ECM.

YES ↓

Turn the ignition switch OFF.

Connect the Test Harness "A" and "D" connectors to the TCM.

Turn the ignition switch ON.

Measure the voltage between the D7 and A25/A26 terminals.

Is the voltage approx. 0.5 V? — NO → Repair open or short in RED/BLK wire between the D7 terminal and the TP sensor.

YES ↓

Check for loose TCM connectors. If necessary, substitute a known-good TCM and recheck.

D18 4.75–5.25 V?
A25 A26

Approx. 0.5 V? D7
A25 A26

95C19663

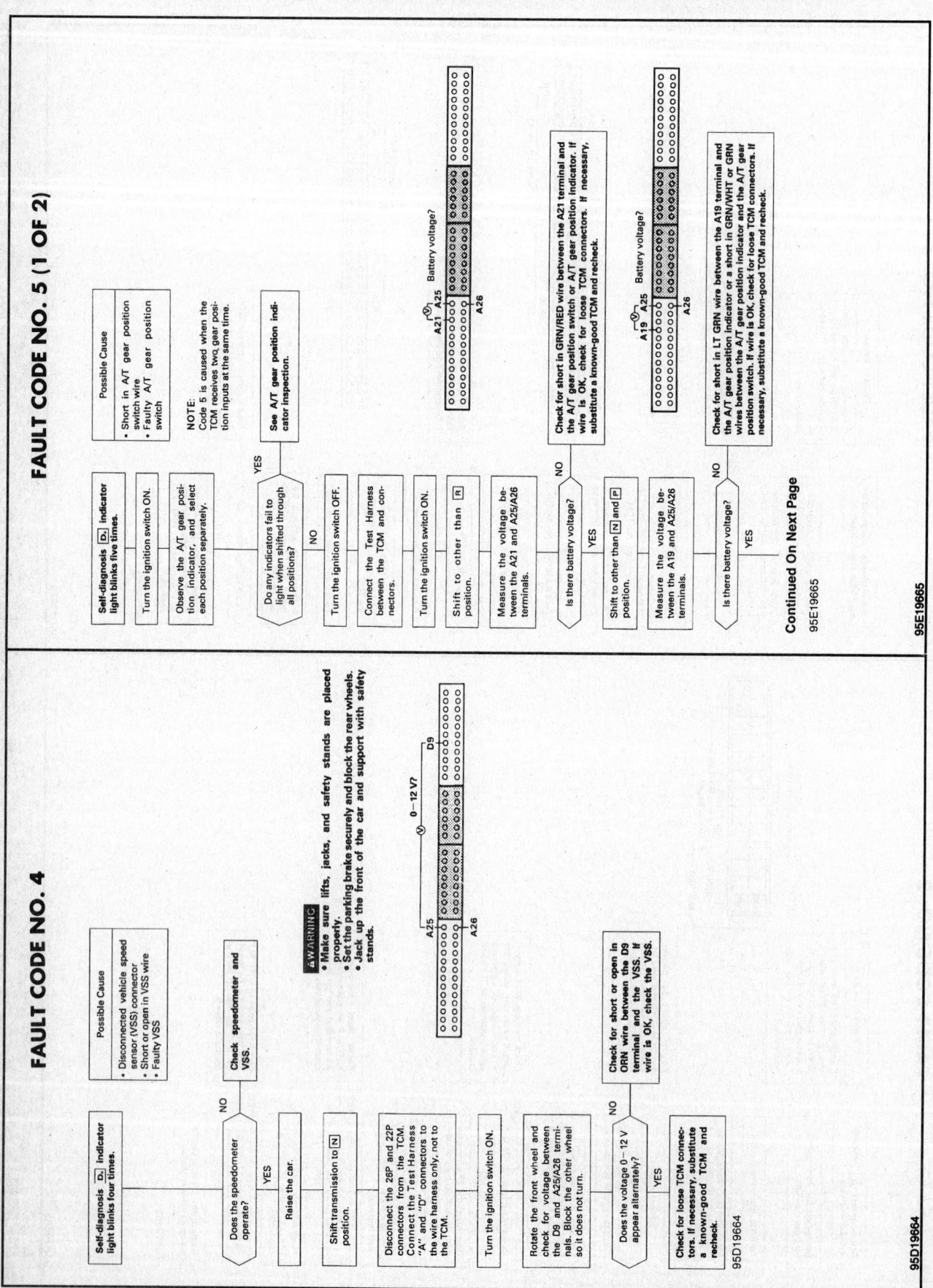

FAULT CODE NO. 4

Self-diagnosis [D₄] **indicator light blinks four times.**

Possible Cause
- Disconnected vehicle speed sensor (VSS) connector
- Short or open in VSS wire
- Faulty VSS

Check speedometer and VSS.

Does the speedometer operate? — NO

YES

Raise the car.

Shift transmission to [N] position.

Disconnect the 26P and 22P connectors from the TCM. Connect the Test Harness "A" and "D" connectors to the wire harness only, not to the TCM.

Turn the ignition switch ON.

⚠WARNING
- **Make sure lifts, jacks, and safety stands are placed properly.**
- **Set the parking brake securely and block the rear wheels.**
- **Jack up the front of the car and support with safety stands.**

Rotate the front wheel and check for voltage between the D9 and A25/A26 terminals. Block the other wheel so it does not turn.

Does the voltage 0-12 V appear alternately? — NO

Check for short or open in ORN wire between the D9 terminal and the VSS. If wire is OK, check the VSS.

YES

Check for loose TCM connectors. If necessary, substitute a known-good TCM and recheck.

95D19664

FAULT CODE NO. 5 (1 OF 2)

Possible Cause
- Short in A/T gear position switch wire
- Faulty A/T gear position switch

NOTE:
Code 5 is caused when the TCM receives two gear position inputs at the same time.

Self-diagnosis [D₅] **indicator light blinks five times.**

Turn the ignition switch ON.

Observe the A/T gear position indicator, and select each position separately.

See A/T gear position indicator inspection.

YES

Do any indicators fail to light when shifted through all positions?

NO

Turn the ignition switch OFF.

Connect the Test Harness between the TCM and connectors.

Turn the ignition switch ON.

Shift to other than [R] position.

Measure the voltage between the A21 and A25/A26 terminals.

Is there battery voltage? — NO

Check for short in GRN/RED wire between the A21 terminal and the A/T gear position switch or A/T gear position indicator. If wire is OK, check for loose TCM connectors. If necessary, substitute a known-good TCM and recheck.

YES

Shift to other than [N] and [P] position.

Measure the voltage between the A19 and A25/A26 terminals.

Is there battery voltage? — NO

Check for short in LT GRN wire between the A19 terminal and the A/T gear position indicator or a short in GRN/WHT or GRN wires between the A/T gear position indicator and the A/T gear position switch. If wire is OK, check for loose TCM connectors. If necessary, substitute a known-good TCM and recheck.

YES

Continued On Next Page

95E19665

95E19665

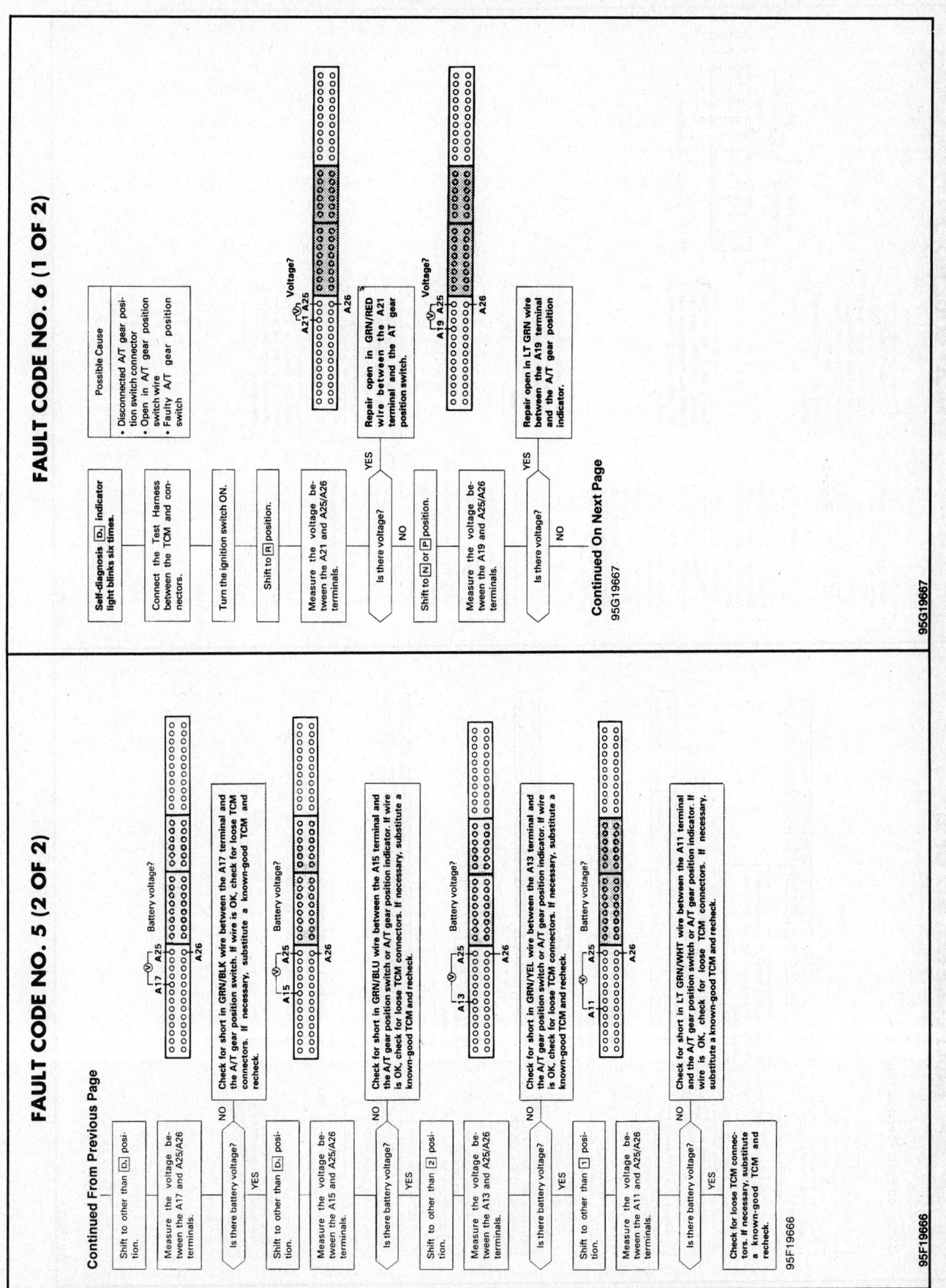

FAULT CODE NO. 6 (1 OF 2)

Possible Cause
- Disconnected A/T gear position switch connector
- Open in A/T gear position switch wire
- Faulty A/T gear position switch

Self-diagnosis D₄ indicator light blinks six times.

Connect the Test Harness between the TCM and connectors.

Turn the ignition switch ON.

Shift to R position.

Measure the voltage between the A21 and A25/A26 terminals.

Is there voltage?
YES — Repair open in GRN/RED wire between the A21 terminal and the AT gear position switch.
NO

Shift to N or P position.

Measure the voltage between the A19 and A25/A26 terminals.

Is there voltage?
YES — Repair open in LT GRN wire between the A19 terminal and the A/T gear position indicator.
NO

Continued On Next Page
95G19667

95G19667

FAULT CODE NO. 5 (2 OF 2)

Continued From Previous Page

Shift to other than D₄ position.

Measure the voltage between the A17 and A25/A26 terminals.

Is there battery voltage?
NO — Check for short in GRN/BLK wire between the A17 terminal and the A/T gear position switch. If wire is OK, check for loose TCM connectors. If necessary, substitute a known-good TCM and recheck.
YES

Shift to other than D₃ position.

Measure the voltage between the A15 and A25/A26 terminals.

Is there battery voltage?
NO — Check for short in GRN/BLU wire between the A15 terminal and the A/T gear position switch or A/T gear position indicator. If wire is OK, check for loose TCM connectors. If necessary, substitute a known-good TCM and recheck.
YES

Shift to other than 2 position.

Measure the voltage between the A13 and A25/A26 terminals.

Is there battery voltage?
NO — Check for short in GRN/YEL wire between the A13 terminal and the A/T gear position switch or A/T gear position indicator. If wire is OK, check for loose TCM connectors. If necessary, substitute a known-good TCM and recheck.
YES

Shift to other than 1 position.

Measure the voltage between the A11 and A25/A26 terminals.

Is there battery voltage?
NO — Check for short in LT GRN/WHT wire between the A11 terminal and the A/T gear position switch or A/T gear position indicator. If wire is OK, check for loose TCM connectors. If necessary, substitute a known-good TCM and recheck.
YES

Check for loose TCM connectors. If necessary, substitute a known-good TCM and recheck.

95F19666

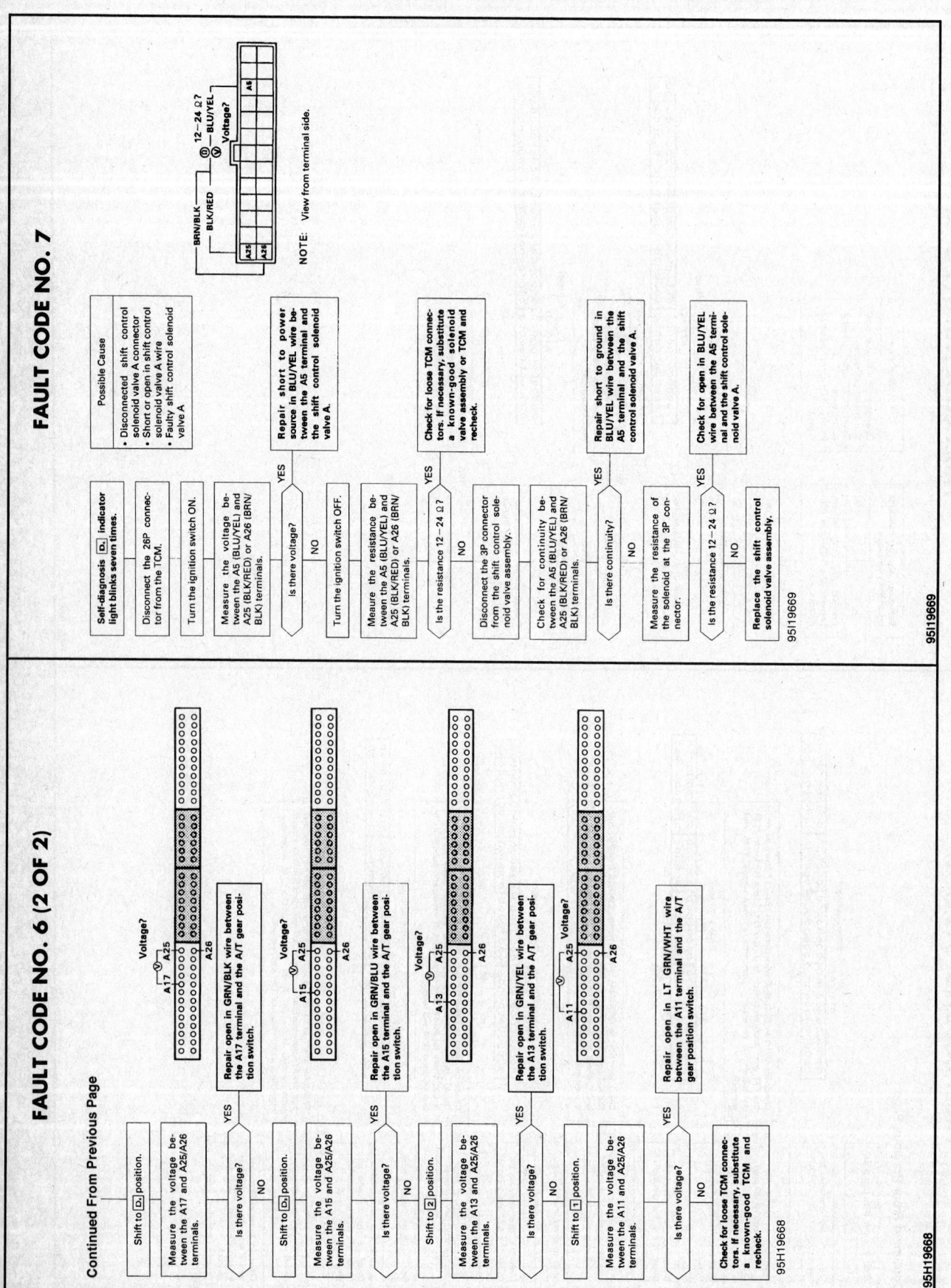

FAULT CODE NO. 7

BRN/BLK
BLK/RED
⑤ 12–24 Ω?
BLU/YEL
Ⓥ Voltage?
A5
A25
A26

NOTE: View from terminal side.

Possible Cause
- Disconnected shift control solenoid valve A connector
- Short or open in shift control solenoid valve A wire
- Faulty shift control solenoid valve A

Self-diagnosis ☐D₄☐ indicator light blinks seven times.

Disconnect the 26P connector from the TCM.

Turn the ignition switch ON.

Measure the voltage between the A5 (BLU/YEL) and A25 (BLK/RED) or A26 (BRN/BLK) terminals.

Is there voltage? — YES — Repair short to power source in BLU/YEL wire between the A5 terminal and the shift control solenoid valve A.

NO

Turn the ignition switch OFF.

Meaure the resistance between the A5 (BLU/YEL) and A25 (BLK/RED) or A26 (BRN/BLK) terminals.

Is the resistance 12–24 Ω? — YES — Check for loose TCM connectors. If necessary, substitute a known-good solenoid valve assembly or TCM and recheck.

NO

Disconnect the 3P connector from the shift control solenoid valve assembly.

Check for continuity between the A5 (BLU/YEL) and A25 (BLK/RED) or A26 (BRN/BLK) terminals.

Is there continuity? — YES — Repair short to ground in BLU/YEL wire between the A5 terminal and the shift control solenoid valve A.

NO

Measure the resistance of the solenoid at the 3P connector.

Is the resistance 12–24 Ω? — YES — Check for open in BLU/YEL wire between the A5 terminal and the shift control solenoid valve A.

NO

Replace the shift control solenoid valve assembly.

95H9669

95H9669

FAULT CODE NO. 6 (2 OF 2)

Continued From Previous Page

Shift to ☐D₄☐ position.

Measure the voltage between the A17 and A25/A26 terminals.

Ⓥ Voltage?
A17 A25
A26

Is there voltage? — YES — Repair open in GRN/BLK wire between the A17 terminal and the A/T gear position switch.

NO

Shift to ☐D₃☐ position.

Measure the voltage between the A15 and A25/A26 terminals.

Ⓥ Voltage?
A15 A25
A26

Is there voltage? — YES — Repair open in GRN/BLU wire between the A15 terminal and the A/T gear position switch.

NO

Shift to ☐2☐ position.

Measure the voltage between the A13 and A25/A26 terminals.

Ⓥ Voltage?
A13 A25
A26

Is there voltage? — YES — Repair open in GRN/YEL wire between the A13 terminal and the A/T gear position switch.

NO

Shift to ☐1☐ position.

Measure the voltage between the A11 and A25/A26 terminals.

Ⓥ Voltage?
A11 A25
A26

Is there voltage? — YES — Repair open in LT GRN/WHT wire between the A11 terminal and the A/T gear position switch.

NO

Check for loose TCM connectors. If necessary, substitute a known-good TCM and recheck.

95H19668

95H19668

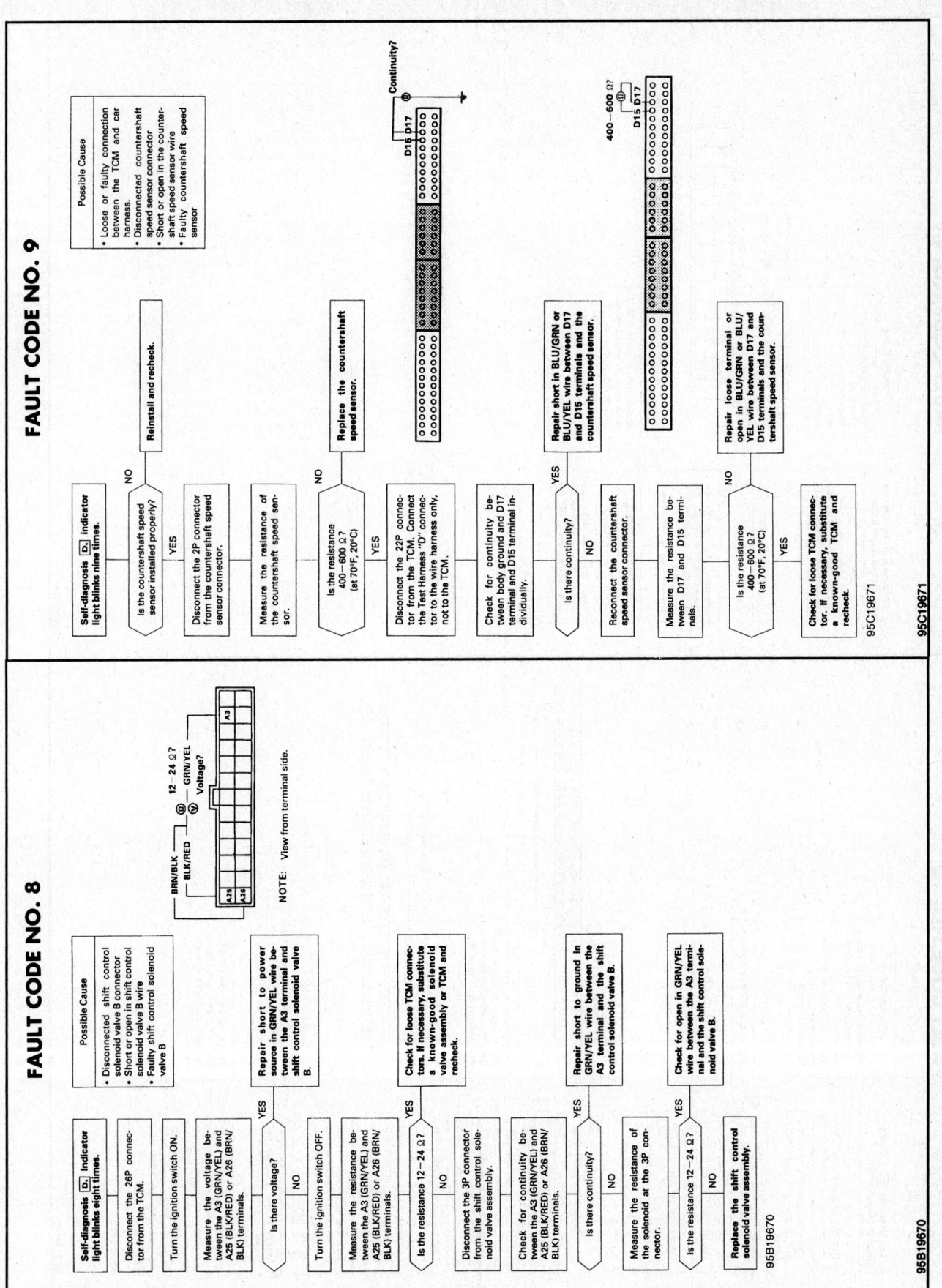

FAULT CODE NO. 8

Self-diagnosis [D₄] indicator light blinks eight times.

Possible Cause
- Disconnected shift control solenoid valve B connector
- Short or open in shift control solenoid valve B wire
- Faulty shift control solenoid valve B

Disconnect the 26P connector from the TCM.

Turn the ignition switch ON.

Measure the voltage between the A3 (GRN/YEL) and A25 (BLK/RED) or A26 (BRN/BLK) terminals.

Is there voltage? — YES → Repair short to power source in GRN/YEL wire between the A3 terminal and shift control solenoid valve B.

NO

Turn the ignition switch OFF.

Measure the resistance between the A3 (GRN/YEL) and A25 (BLK/RED) or A26 (BRN/BLK) terminals.

Is the resistance 12—24 Ω? — YES → Check for loose TCM connectors. If necessary, substitute a known-good solenoid valve assembly or TCM and recheck.

NO

Disconnect the 3P connector from the shift control solenoid valve assembly.

Check for continuity between the A3 (GRN/YEL) and A25 (BLK/RED) or A26 (BRN/BLK) terminals.

Is there continuity? — YES → Repair short to ground in GRN/YEL wire between the A3 terminal and the shift control solenoid valve B.

NO

Measure the resistance of the solenoid at the 3P connector.

Is the resistance 12—24 Ω? — YES → Check for open in GRN/YEL wire between the A3 terminal and the shift control solenoid valve B.

NO

Replace the shift control solenoid valve assembly.

95B19670

BRN/BLK
BLK/RED
Ⓡ 12—24 Ω?
Ⓥ GRN/YEL Voltage?
A3
A25
A26

NOTE: View from terminal side.

FAULT CODE NO. 9

Self-diagnosis [D₄] indicator light blinks nine times.

Possible Cause
- Loose or faulty connection between the TCM and car harness.
- Disconnected countershaft speed sensor connector
- Short or open in the countershaft speed sensor wire
- Faulty countershaft speed sensor

Is the countershaft speed sensor installed properly? — NO → Reinstall and recheck.

YES

Disconnect the 2P connector from the countershaft speed sensor connector.

Measure the resistance of the countershaft speed sensor.

Is the resistance 400—600 Ω? (at 70°F, 20°C) — NO → Replace the countershaft speed sensor.

YES

Disconnect the 22P connector from the TCM. Connect the Test Harness "D" connector to the wire harness only, not to the TCM.

Check for continuity between body ground and D17 terminal and D15 terminal individually.

Is there continuity? — YES → Repair short in BLU/GRN or BLU/GRN or BLU/YEL wire between D17 and D15 terminals and the countershaft speed sensor.

NO

Reconnect the countershaft speed sensor connector.

Measure the resistance between D17 and D15 terminals.

Is the resistance 400—600 Ω? (at 70°F, 20°C) — NO → Repair loose terminal or open in BLU/GRN or BLU/YEL wire between D17 and D15 terminals and the countershaft speed sensor.

YES

Check for loose TCM connector. If necessary, substitute a known-good TCM and recheck.

D15 D17 Continuity?

400—600 Ω? D15 D17

95C19671

95C19671

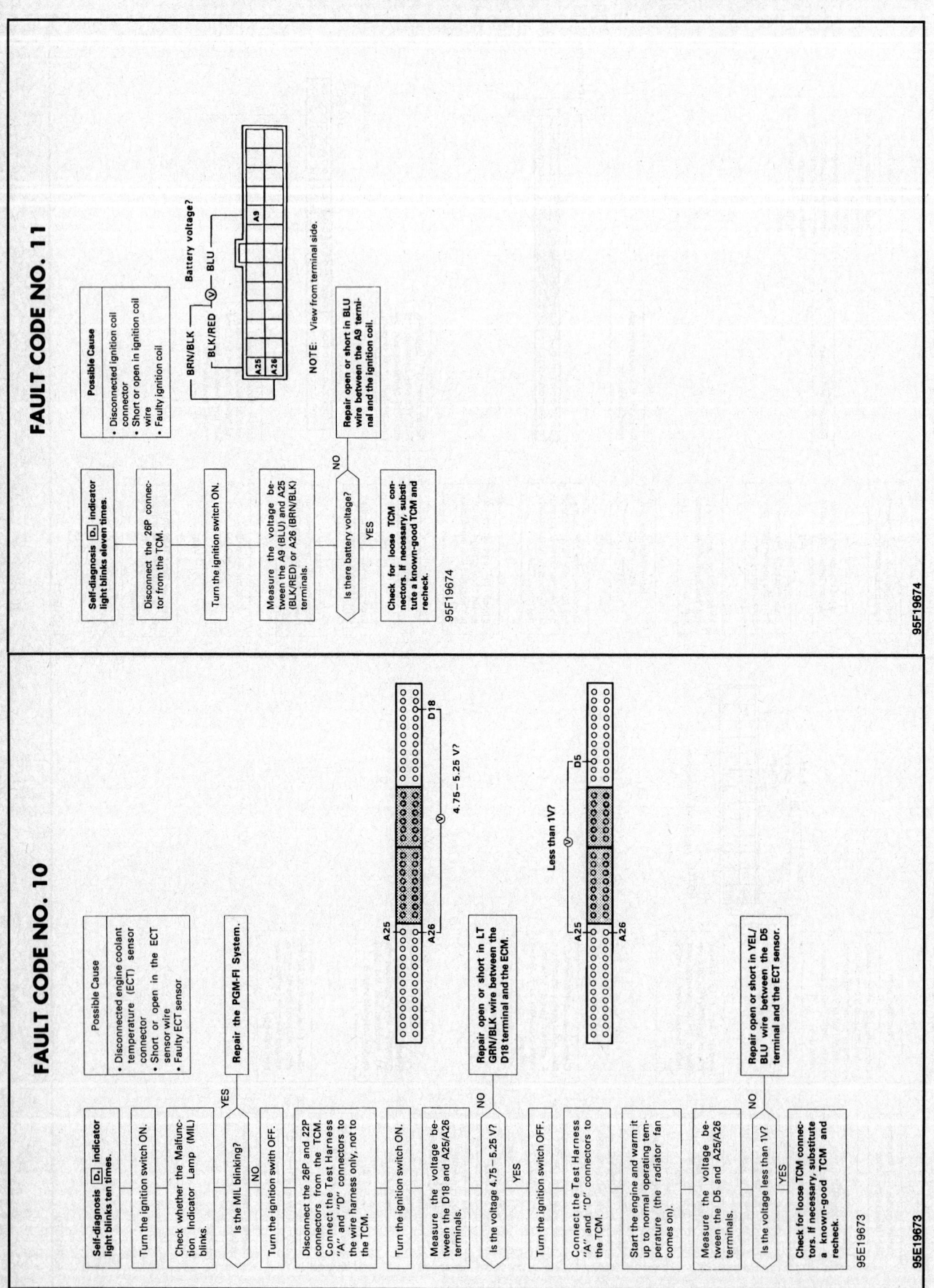

FAULT CODE NO. 11

Self-diagnosis D₄ indicator light blinks eleven times.

Possible Cause
- Disconnected ignition coil connector
- Short or open in ignition coil wire
- Faulty ignition coil

Disconnect the 26P connector from the TCM.

Turn the ignition switch ON.

Measure the voltage between the A9 (BLU) and A25 (BLK/RED) or A26 (BRN/BLK) terminals.

Is there battery voltage? — NO → Repair open or short in BLU wire between the A9 terminal and the ignition coil.

YES

Check for loose TCM connectors. If necessary, substitute a known-good TCM and recheck.

Battery voltage?

BRN/BLK
BLK/RED — V — BLU
A25 A26 A9

NOTE: View from terminal side.

95F19674

95F19674

FAULT CODE NO. 10

Self-diagnosis D₄ indicator light blinks ten times.

Possible Cause
- Disconnected engine coolant temperature (ECT) sensor connector
- Short or open in the ECT sensor wire
- Faulty ECT sensor

Check whether the Malfunction Indicator Lamp (MIL) blinks.

Is the MIL blinking? — YES → Repair the PGM-FI System.

NO

Turn the ignition switch OFF.

Disconnect the 26P and 22P connectors from the TCM. Connect the Test Harness "A" and "D" connectors to the wire harness only, not to the TCM.

Turn the ignition switch ON.

Measure the voltage between the D18 and A25/A26 terminals.

Is the voltage 4.75 — 5.25 V? — NO → Repair open or short in LT GRN/BLK wire between the D18 terminal and the ECM.

YES

Turn the ignition switch OFF.

Connect the Test Harness "A" and "D" connectors to the TCM.

Start the engine and warm it up to normal operating temperature (the radiator fan comes on).

Measure the voltage between the D5 and A25/A26 terminals.

Is the voltage less than 1V? — NO → Repair open or short in YEL/BLU wire between the D5 terminal and the ECT sensor.

YES

Check for loose TCM connectors. If necessary, substitute a known-good TCM and recheck.

A25
A26
D18
4.75 — 5.25 V?

Less than 1V?
A25
A26
D5

95E19673

95E19673

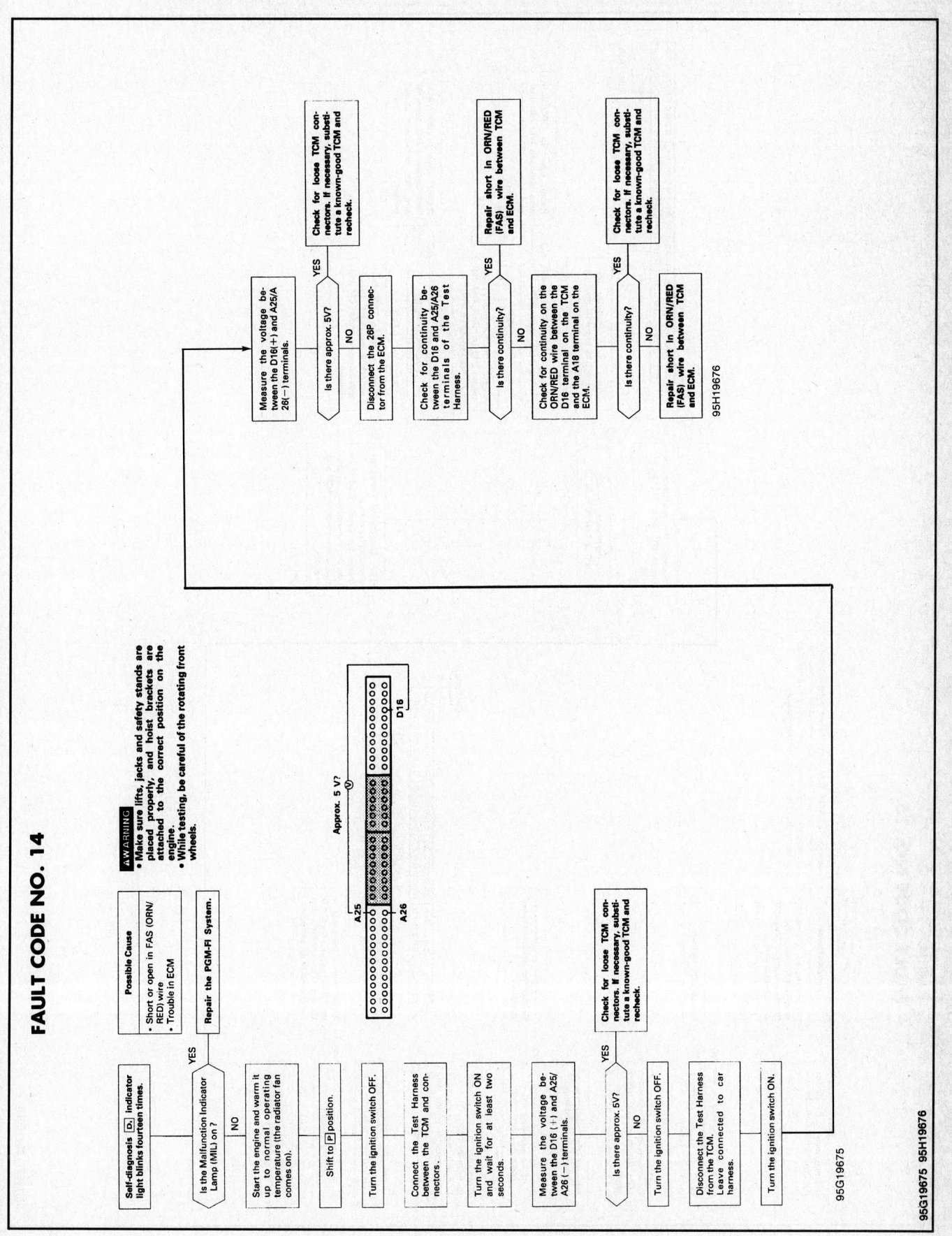

FAULT CODE NO. 14

Self-diagnosis [D₄] indicator light blinks fourteen times.

Possible Cause
- Short or open in FAS (ORN/RED) wire
- Trouble in ECM

⚠ WARNING
- Make sure lifts, jacks and safety stands are placed properly, and hoist brackets are attached to the correct position on the engine.
- While testing, be careful of the rotating front wheels.

Is the Malfunction Indicator Lamp (MIL) on ?
→ YES → Repair the PGM-FI System.
↓ NO

Start the engine and warm it up to normal operating temperature (the radiator fan comes on).

Shift to [P] position.

Turn the ignition switch OFF.

Connect the Test Harness between the TCM and connectors.

Turn the ignition switch ON and wait for at least two seconds.

Measure the voltage between the D16 (+) and A25/A26 (−) terminals.

Is there approx. 5V?
→ YES → Check for loose TCM connectors. If necessary, substitute a known-good TCM and recheck.
↓ NO

Turn the ignition switch OFF.

Disconnect the Test Harness from the TCM. Leave connected to car harness.

Turn the ignition switch ON.

Approx. 5 V?

A25
A26
D16

Measure the voltage between the D16(+) and A25/A26(−) terminals.

Is there approx. 5V?
→ YES → Check for loose TCM connectors. If necessary, substitute a known-good TCM and recheck.
↓ NO

Disconnect the 26P connector from the ECM.

Check for continuity between the D16 and A25/A26 terminals of the Test Harness.

Is there continuity?
→ YES → Repair short in ORN/RED (FAS) wire between TCM and ECM.
↓ NO

Check for continuity on the ORN/RED wire between the TCM D16 terminal on the TCM and the A18 terminal on the ECM.

Is there continuity?
→ YES → Check for loose TCM connectors. If necessary, substitute a known-good TCM and recheck.
↓ NO

Repair short in ORN/RED (FAS) wire between TCM and ECM.

95H19676

95G19675

95G19675 95H19676

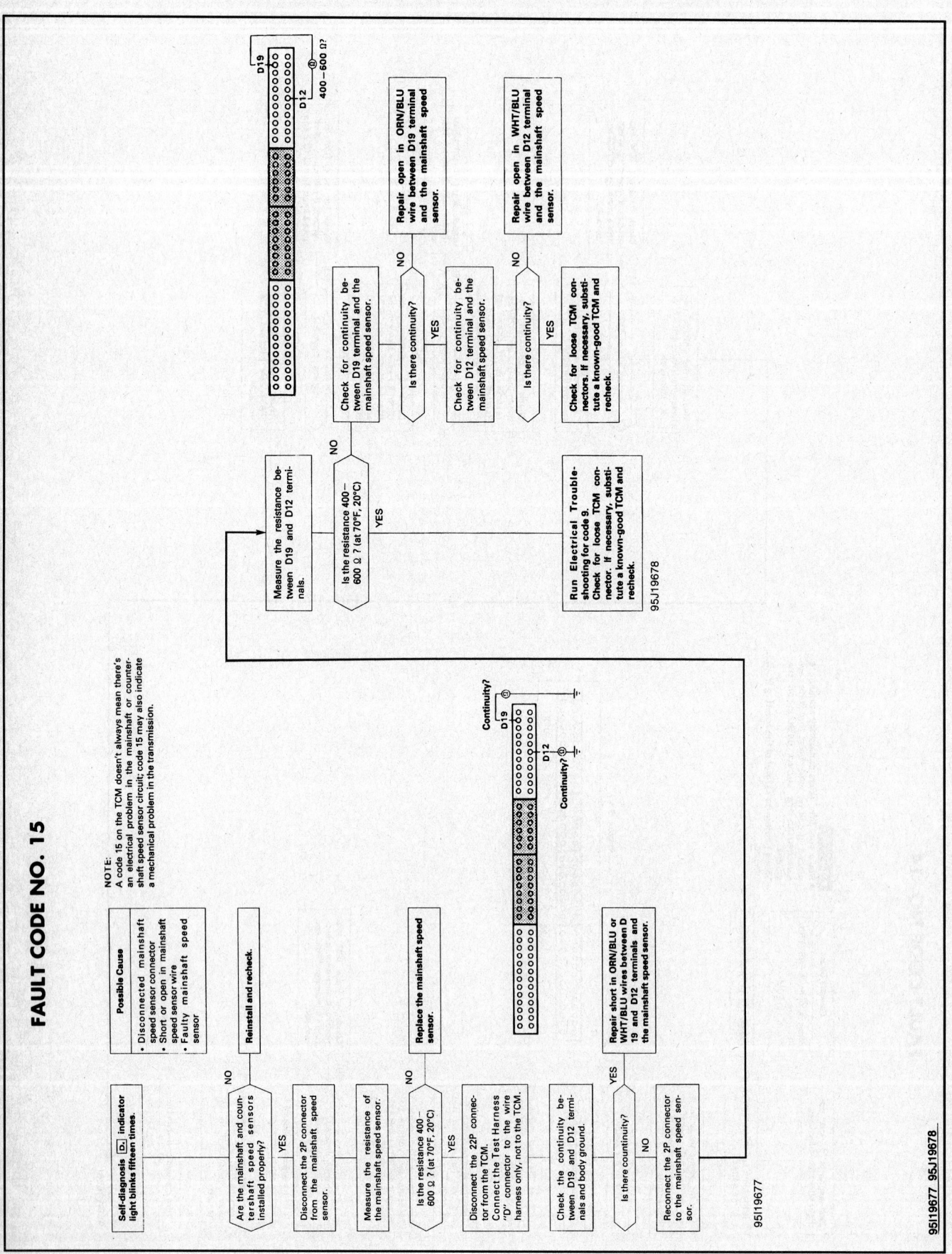

FAULT CODE NO. 15

NOTE:
A code 15 on the TCM doesn't always mean there's an electrical problem in the mainshaft or countershaft speed sensor circuit; code 15 may also indicate a mechanical problem in the transmission.

Possible Cause
- Disconnected mainshaft speed sensor connector
- Short or open in mainshaft speed sensor wire
- Faulty mainshaft speed sensor

Self-diagnosis ⓓ indicator light blinks fifteen times.

Are the mainshaft and countershaft speed sensors installed properly?

Reinstall and recheck.

Disconnect the 2P connector from the mainshaft speed sensor.

Measure the resistance of the mainshaft speed sensor.

Is the resistance 400—600 Ω? (at 70°F, 20°C)

Replace the mainshaft speed sensor.

Disconnect the 22P connector from the TCM. Connect the Test Harness "D" connector to the wire harness only, not to the TCM.

Check the continuity between D19 and D12 terminals and body ground.

Is there countinuity?

Repair short in ORN/BLU or WHT/BLU wires between D 19 and D12 terminals and the mainshaft speed sensor.

Reconnect the 2P connector to the mainshaft speed sensor.

Measure the resistance between D19 and D12 terminals.

Is the resistance 400—600 Ω? (at 70°F, 20°C)

Run Electrical Troubleshooting for code 9. Check for loose TCM connector. If necessary, substitute a known-good TCM and recheck.

Check for continuity between D19 terminal and the mainshaft speed sensor.

Is there continuity?

Repair open in ORN/BLU wire between the D19 terminal and the mainshaft speed sensor.

Check for continuity between D12 terminal and the mainshaft speed sensor.

Is there continuity?

Repair open in WHT/BLU wire between the D12 terminal and the mainshaft speed sensor.

Check for loose TCM connectors. If necessary, substitute a known-good TCM and recheck.

400—600 Ω?

95J19678

95J19677

95J19677 95J19678

DIAGNOSTIC TESTING (1996)

NOTE: Terminal identification, circuit description and terminal voltage is included in PIN VOLTAGE CHARTS. See Figs. 24 and 25.

DTC P0715 (FLASH CODE 15): MAINSHAFT SPEED SENSOR

NOTE: DTC P0715 (FLASH CODE 15) doesn't always mean an electrical problem in mainshaft speed sensor or circuit, this DTC can also be caused by a mechanical problem in transaxle.

1) Ensure mainshaft and countershaft speed sensors are installed properly. See COUNTERSHAFT or MAINSHAFT SPEED SENSOR under REMOVAL & INSTALLATION. Disconnect mainshaft speed sensor connector and measure resistance between sensor connector terminals. See MAINSHAFT SPEED SENSOR under COMPONENT TESTING.
2) If resistance is not 400-600 ohms, replace mainshaft speed sensor. If resistance is 400-600 ohms, disconnect PCM 25-pin connector "B". Check continuity between ground and PCM 25-pin connector "B" terminals No. 15 (Orange/Blue wire) and No. 14 (White/Blue wire). *See Figs. 24 and 25.*
3) If continuity exists, repair short to ground in Orange/Blue and White/Blue wires between PCM and mainshaft speed sensor. If continuity does not exist, reconnect mainshaft speed sensor connector. Measure resistance between PCM 25-pin connector "B" terminals No. 15 (Orange/Blue wire) and No. 14 (White/Blue wire).
4) If resistance is not 400-600 ohms, go to next step. If resistance is 400-600 ohms, perform DTC P0720 (FLASH CODE 9) diagnostic, check for loose PCM connectors and replace PCM with known good part, as necessary.
5) Disconnect mainshaft speed sensor connector. Check continuity of Red wire between PCM 25-pin connector "B" terminal No. 15 (Orange/Blue wire) and mainshaft speed sensor connector. If continuity exists, go to next step. If continuity does not exist, repair open Orange/Blue wire between PCM 25-pin connector and mainshaft speed sensor connector.
6) Check continuity of White wire between PCM 25-pin connector "B" terminal No. 14 (White/Blue wire) and mainshaft speed sensor connector. If continuity exists, check for loose PCM connectors and replace PCM with known good part, as necessary. If continuity does not exist, repair open White/Blue wire between PCM 25-pin connector and mainshaft speed sensor connector.

DTC P0720 (FLASH CODE 9): COUNTERSHAFT SPEED SENSOR

1) Ensure countershaft speed sensor is installed properly. See COUNTERSHAFT SPEED SENSOR under REMOVAL & INSTALLATION. Disconnect countershaft speed sensor connector and measure resistance between sensor connector terminals. See COUNTERSHAFT SPEED SENSOR under COMPONENT TESTING.
2) If resistance is not 400-600 ohms, replace countershaft speed sensor. If resistance is 400-600 ohms, disconnect PCM 25-pin connector "B". Check continuity between ground and PCM 25-pin connector "B" terminals No. 23 (Blue/Green wire) and No. 22 (Blue/Yellow wire). *See Figs. 24 and 25.*
3) If continuity exists, repair short to ground in Blue/Green or Blue/Yellow wires between PCM and countershaft speed sensor. If continuity does not exist, reconnect countershaft speed sensor connector. Measure resistance between PCM 25-pin connector "B" terminals No. 23 (Blue/Green wire) and No. 22 (Blue/Yellow wire).
4) If resistance is not 400-600 ohms, check for loose PCM connectors and replace PCM with known good part, as necessary. If resistance is 400-600 ohms, repair open Blue/Green or Blue/Yellow wires between PCM 25-pin connector and countershaft speed sensor connector.

DTC P0730 (FLASH CODE 41): SHIFT CONTROL SYSTEM

NOTE: Do NOT perform this DTC test until all other DTCs have been repaired first.

1) Road test vehicle at over 12 MPH for more than 30 seconds in 2nd, 3rd and 4th gear. Using scan tool, check for any other DTCs. If any other DTCs exist, repair those DTCs first, then recheck for DTC P0730 (FLASH CODE 41). If no other DTCs exist, go to next step.
2) Test clutch pressure. See HYDRAULIC PRESSURE TEST under TESTING in HONDA MP1A overhaul article. If clutch pressure is within specification, go to next step. If clutch pressure is not within specification, repair hydraulic system as necessary. See HYDRAULIC PRESSURE TROUBLE SHOOTING table under HYDRAULIC PRESSURE TEST in HONDA MP1A overhaul article.
3) Replace shift control solenoid valve assembly. See SHIFT CONTROL SOLENOID VALVES under REMOVAL & INSTALLATION. Turn ignition off and clear codes. See CLEARING CODES. Road test vehicle at over 12 MPH for more than 30 seconds in 2nd, 3rd and 4th gear. Recheck DTCs. If P0730 (FLASH CODE 41) returns, repair internal components as necessary. If P0730 (FLASH CODE 41) does not return, system is okay.

DTC P0740 (FLASH CODE 40): LOCK-UP CONTROL SYSTEM

NOTE: Do NOT perform this DTC test until all other DTCs have been repaired first.

1) Using scan tool, check for any other DTCs. If any other DTCs exist, repair those DTCs first, then recheck for DTC P0740 (FLASH CODE 40). If no other DTCs exist, go to next step.
2) Test line pressure. See HYDRAULIC PRESSURE TEST under TESTING in HONDA MP1A overhaul article. If clutch pressure is within specification, go to next step. If line pressure is not within specification, repair hydraulic system as necessary. See HYDRAULIC PRESSURE TROUBLE SHOOTING table under HYDRAULIC PRESSURE TEST in HONDA MP1A overhaul article.
3) Test clutch pressure. If clutch pressure is within specification, go to next step. If clutch pressure is not within specification, repair hydraulic system as necessary. See HYDRAULIC PRESSURE TROUBLE SHOOTING table under HYDRAULIC PRESSURE TEST in HONDA MP1A overhaul article.
4) Replace lock-up control solenoid valve assembly. See LOCK-UP CONTROL SOLENOID VALVES under REMOVAL & INSTALLATION. Turn ignition off and clear codes. See CLEARING CODES. Road test vehicle at over 50 MPH for more than one minute. Recheck DTCs. If P0740 (FLASH CODE 40) returns, go to next step. If P0740 (FLASH CODE 40) does not return, system is okay.
5) Replace torque converter. Turn ignition off and clear codes. See CLEARING CODES. Road test vehicle at over 50 MPH for more than one minute. Recheck DTCs. If P0740 (FLASH CODE 40) returns, replace transaxle. If P0740 (FLASH CODE 40) does not return, system is okay.

DTC P0753 (FLASH CODE 7): SHIFT CONTROL SOLENOID VALVE "A"

1) Disconnect PCM 32-pin connector "A" and PCM 25-pin connector "B". Turn ignition on. Using DVOM, measure voltage between PCM 25-pin connector "B" terminal No. 3 (Blue/Yellow wire) and PCM 32-pin connector "A" terminals No. 9 (Black/Red wire) or No. 22 (Brown/Black wire). *See Figs. 24 and 25.* If voltage is present, repair short to power in Blue/Yellow wire between PCM 25-pin connector "B" and shift solenoid "A". If voltage is not present, go to next step.

2) Turn ignition off. Measure shift control solenoid valve "A" resistance at PCM. See SHIFT CONTROL SOLENOID VALVE under COMPONENT TESTING. If resistance is not 14-25 ohms, go to next step. If resistance is 14-25 ohms, check for loose PCM connectors and replace PCM with known good part, as necessary.

3) Disconnect shift control solenoid valve connector. Check for continuity between PCM 32-pin connector "A" terminal No. 9 (Black/Red wire) or No. 22 (Brown/Black wire) and PCM 25-pin connector "B" terminal No. 3 (Blue/Yellow wire). If continuity does not exist, go to next step. If continuity exists, repair short to ground in Blue/Yellow wire between PCM 32-pin connector "A" and shift solenoid valve "A".

4) Measure resistance between shift control solenoid valve connector (solenoid side) Blue/Yellow wire and ground. If resistance is not 14-25 ohms, replace shift control solenoid valve assembly. If resistance is 14-25 ohms, check and repair open Blue/Yellow wire between shift control solenoid valve connector and shift solenoid valve "A".

DTC P0758 (FLASH CODE 8): SHIFT CONTROL SOLENOID VALVE "B"

1) Disconnect PCM 32-pin connector "A" and PCM 25-pin connector "B". Turn ignition on. Using DVOM, measure voltage between PCM 25-pin connector "B" terminal No. 11 (Green/Yellow wire) and PCM 32-pin connector "A" terminal No. 9 (Black/Red wire) or No. 22 (Brown/Black wire). *See Figs. 24 and 25.* If voltage is approximately 5 volts, repair short to power in Green/Yellow wire between PCM 25-pin connector "B" and shift solenoid "A". If voltage is not approximately 5 volts, go to next step.

2) Turn ignition off. Measure shift control solenoid valve "A" resistance at PCM. See SHIFT CONTROL SOLENOID VALVE under COMPONENT TESTING. If resistance is not 14-25 ohms, go to next step. If resistance is 14-25 ohms, check for loose PCM connectors and replace PCM with known good part, as necessary.

3) Disconnect shift control solenoid valve connector. Check for continuity between PCM 32-pin connector "A" terminal No. 9 (Black/Red wire) or No. 22 (Brown/Black wire) and PCM 25-pin connector "B" terminal No. 11 (Green/Yellow wire). If continuity does not exist, go to next step. If continuity exists, repair short to ground in Green/Yellow wire between PCM 32-pin connector "A" and shift solenoid valve "A".

4) Measure resistance between shift control solenoid valve connector (solenoid side) Green/Yellow wire and ground. If resistance is not 14-25 ohms, replace shift control solenoid valve assembly. If resistance is 14-25 ohms, check and repair open Green/Yellow wire between shift control solenoid valve connector and shift solenoid valve "A".

DTC P1705 (FLASH CODE 5): A/T GEAR POSITION SWITCH (SHORT)

NOTE: DTC P1705 is set when PCM receives 2 gear position signals at same time.

1) Turn ignition on. If any A/T gear position indicator light stays on when gear selector is moved from that gear, go to next step. If all A/T gear position indicator lights go off when gear selector is moved from that gear, system is okay at this time. Fault that set code is intermittent.

2) Shift to all gear positions except Reverse. Using DVOM, measure voltage between PCM 32-pin connector "A" terminal No. 9 (Black/Red wire) or No. 22 (Brown/Black wire) and PCM 25-pin connector "B" terminal No. 16 (Green/Red wire). *See Figs. 24 and 25.* If battery voltage is present, go to next step. If battery voltage is not present, check and repair short in Green/Red wire between PCM 25-pin connector "B" and A/T gear position indicator or A/T gear position switch. If Green/Red wire is okay, check for loose PCM connectors and replace PCM with known good part, as necessary.

3) Shift to all gear positions except Neutral and Park. Measure voltage between PCM 32-pin connector "A" terminal No. 9 (Black/Red wire) or No. 22 (Brown/Black wire) and PCM 25-pin connector "B" terminal No. 25 (Light Green wire). If about 5 volts is present, go to next step. If about 5 volts is not present, check and repair short in Light Green wire

between PCM 25-pin connector "B" and A/T gear position indicator or A/T gear position switch. If Light Green wire is okay, check for loose PCM connectors and replace PCM with known good part, as necessary.

4) Shift to all gear positions except "D₄". Measure voltage between PCM 32-pin connector "A" terminal No. 9 (Black/Red wire) or No. 22 (Brown/Black wire) and PCM 25-pin connector "B" terminal No. 24 (Green/Black wire). If about 5 volts is present, go to next step. If about 5 volts is not present, check and repair short in Green/Black wire between PCM 25-pin connector "B" and A/T gear position switch. If Green/Black wire is okay, check for loose PCM connectors and replace PCM with known good part, as necessary.

5) Shift to all gear positions except "D₃". Measure voltage between PCM 32-pin connector "A" terminal No. 9 (Black/Red wire) or No. 22 (Brown/Black wire) and PCM 25-pin connector "B" terminal No. 8 (Green/Blue wire). If battery voltage is present, go to next step. If battery voltage is not present, check and repair short in Green/Blue wire between PCM 25-pin connector "B" and A/T gear position indicator or A/T gear position switch. If Green/Blue wire is okay, check for loose PCM connectors and replace PCM with known good part, as necessary.

6) Shift to all gear positions except "2". Measure voltage between PCM 32-pin connector "A" terminal No. 9 (Black/Red wire) or No. 22 (Brown/Black wire) and PCM 25-pin connector "B" terminal No. 17 (Green/Yellow wire). If battery voltage is present, go to next step. If battery voltage is not present, check and repair short in Green/Yellow wire between PCM 25-pin connector "B" and A/T gear position indicator or A/T gear position switch. If Green/Yellow wire is okay, check for loose PCM connectors and replace PCM with known good part, as necessary.

7) Shift to all gear positions except "1". Measure voltage between PCM 32-pin connector "A" terminal No. 9 (Black/Red wire) or No. 22 (Brown/Black wire) and PCM 25-pin connector "B" terminal No. 18 (Light Green/White wire). If battery voltage is present, check for loose PCM connectors and replace PCM with known good part, as necessary. If battery voltage is not present, check and repair short in Light Green/White wire between PCM 25-pin connector "B" and A/T gear position indicator or A/T gear position switch. If Light Green/White wire is okay, check for loose PCM connectors and replace PCM with known good part, as necessary.

DTC P1706 (FLASH CODE 6): A/T GEAR POSITION SWITCH (OPEN)

1) Turn ignition on. If any A/T gear position indicator light stays on when gear selector is moved from that gear, go to next step. If all A/T gear position indicator lights go off when gear selector is moved from that gear, system is okay at this time.

2) Shift to reverse. Using DVOM, measure voltage between PCM 32-pin connector "A" terminal No. 9 (Black/Red wire) or No. 22 (Brown/Black wire) and PCM 25-pin connector "B" terminal No. 16 (Green/Red wire). *See Figs. 24 and 25.* If voltage is not present, go to next step. If voltage is present, check and repair open in Green/Red wire between PCM 25-pin connector "B" and A/T gear position switch.

3) Shift to Neutral or Park. Measure voltage between PCM 32-pin connector "A" terminal No. 9 (Black/Red wire) or No. 22 (Brown/Black wire) and PCM 25-pin connector "B" terminal No. 25 (Light Green wire). If voltage is not present, go to next step. If voltage is present, check and repair open in Light Green wire between PCM 25-pin connector "B" and A/T gear position switch.

4) Shift to "D₄" position. Measure voltage between PCM 32-pin connector "A" terminal No. 9 (Black/Red wire) or No. 22 (Brown/Black wire) and PCM 25-pin connector "B" terminal No. 24 (Green/Black wire). If voltage is not present, go to next step. If voltage is present, check and repair open in Green/Black wire between PCM 25-pin connector "B" and A/T gear position switch.

5) Shift to "D₃" position. Measure voltage between PCM 32-pin connector "A" terminal No. 9 (Black/Red wire) or No. 22 (Brown/Black wire) and PCM 25-pin connector "B" terminal No. 8 (Green/Blue wire). If voltage is not present, go to next step. If voltage is present, check and repair open in Green/Blue wire between PCM 25-pin connector "B" and A/T gear position switch.

PIN VOLTAGE CHARTS

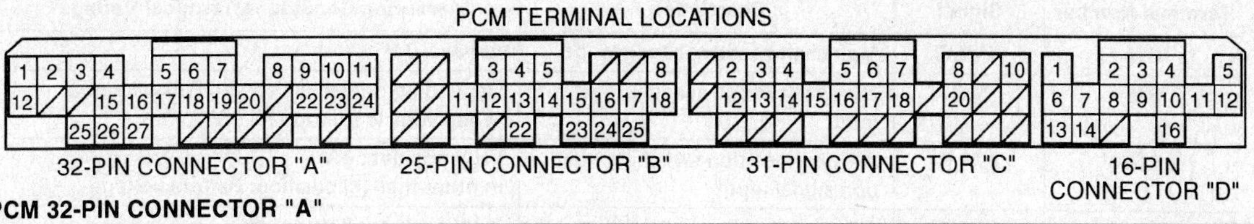

PCM TERMINAL LOCATIONS

32-PIN CONNECTOR "A" 25-PIN CONNECTOR "B" 31-PIN CONNECTOR "C" 16-PIN CONNECTOR "D"

PCM 32-PIN CONNECTOR "A"

Terminal Number	Signal	Description	Measuring Conditions/Terminal Voltage
A1 to A8	See appropriate SELF-DIAGNOSTICS article in ENGINE PERFORMANCE in appropriate MITCHELL® manual.		
A9	LG1	Ground	
A10	PG1	Ground	
A11	IGP1	Power supply system	With ignition switch ON (II): Battery voltage With ignition switch OFF: 0 V
A12 to A21	See appropriate SELF-DIAGNOSTICS article in ENGINE PERFORMANCE in appropriate MITCHELL® manuel.		
A22	LG2	Ground	
A23	PG2	Ground	
A24	IGP2	Power supply system	With ignition switch ON (II): Battery voltage With ignition switch OFF: 0 V
A25 to A32	See appropriate SELF-DIAGNOSTICS article in ENGINE PERFORMANCE in appropriate MITCHELL® manual.		

PCM 25-PIN CONNECTOR "B"

Terminal Number	Signal	Description	Measuring Conditions/Terminal Voltage
B1 to B2	————	Not used	
B3	SHA	Shift control solenoid valve A control	In [1], [2] position, in 2nd and 3rd gear in [D3], [D4] position: Battery voltage In 1st gear in [D3], [D4] position, in 4th gear in [D4] position: 0 V
B4	LCB	Lock-up control solenoid valve B control	During half and full lock-up and during deceleration: Battery voltage During no lock-up: 0 V
B5	LCA	Lock-up control solenoid valve A control	When lock-up is ON: Battery voltage With no lock-up: 0 V
B6 to B7	————	Not used	
B8	ATP D3	A/T gear position switch [D3] position signal input	In [D3] position: 0 V in other than [D3] position: Battery voltage
B9 to B10	————	Not used	
B11	SHB	Shift control solenoid valve B control	In [2] position, in 1st and 2nd gear in [D3], [D4] position: Battery voltage In [1] position, in 3rd gear in [D3], [D4] position, in 4th gear in [D4] position: 0 V
B12	ILU	Interlock control	When ignition switch is ON (II), brake pedal depressed and accelerator pedal released: Battery voltage
B13	D4 IND	D4 Indicator light control	When ignition switch is first turned ON (II): Battery voltage for two seconds In [D4] position: Battery voltage

96G30987

Courtesy of American Honda Motor Co., Inc.

Fig. 24: Pin Voltage Chart & Terminal Identification (1 Of 2)

6) Shift to "2" position. Measure voltage between PCM 32-pin connector "A" terminal No. 9 (Black/Red wire) or No. 22 (Brown/Black wire) and PCM 25-pin connector "B" terminal No. 17 (Green/Yellow wire). If voltage is not present, go to next step. If voltage is present, check and repair open in Green/Yellow wire between PCM 25-pin connector "B" and A/T gear position switch.

7) Shift to "1" position. Measure voltage between PCM 32-pin connector "A" terminal No. 9 (Black/Red wire) or No. 22 (Brown/Black wire) and PCM 25-pin connector "B" terminal No. 18 (Light Green/White wire). If voltage is not present, check for loose PCM connectors and replace PCM with known good part, as necessary. If voltage is present, check and repair open in Light Green/White wire between PCM 25-pin connector "B" and A/T gear position switch.

PCM 25-PIN CONNECTOR "B" (Cont.)

Terminal Number	Signal	Description	Measuring Conditions/Terminal Voltage
B14	NMSG	Mainshaft speed sensor ground	Always: 0 V
B15	NM	Mainshaft speed sensor signal input	Depending on vehicle speed: Pulsing signal When vehicle is stopped: 0 V
B16	ATP R	A/T gear position switch Ⓡ position signal input	In Ⓡ position: 0 V in other than Ⓡ position: Battery voltage
B17	ATP 2	A/T gear position switch ② position signal input	In ② position: 0 V in other than ② position: Battery voltage
B18	ATP 1	A/T gear position switch ① position signal input	In ① position: 0 V in other than ① position: Battery voltage
B19 to B21	——	Not used	
B22	NCSG	Countershaft speed sensor ground	Always: 0 V
B23	NC	Countershaft speed sensor signal input	Depending on vehicle speed: Pulsing signal When vehicle is stopped: 0 V
B24	ATP D4	A/T gear position switch D₄ position signal input	In D₄ position: 0 V in other than D₄ position: 5 V
B25	ATP PN	A/T gear position switch Ⓟ and Ⓝ position signals input	In Ⓟ and Ⓝ positions: 0V in other than Ⓟ and Ⓝ positions: 5 V

PCM 31-PIN CONNECTOR "C"

Terminal Number	Signal	Description	Measuring Conditions/Terminal Voltage
C1 to C6	See appropriate SELF-DIAGNOSTICS article in ENGINE PERFORMANCE in appropriate MITCHELL® manual.		
C7	SCS	Service check signal	With ignition switch ON (II) and service check connector open: 5 V With ignition switch ON (II) and service check connector connected with special tool: 0 V
C8 to C9	See appropriate SELF-DIAGNOSTICS article in ENGINE PERFORMANCE in appropriate MITCHELL® manual.		
C10	VBU	Back-up power system	Always battery voltage
C11 to C31	See appropriate SELF-DIAGNOSTICS article in ENGINE PERFORMANCE in appropriate MITCHELL® manual.		

PCM 16-PIN CONNECTOR "D"

Terminal Number	Signal	Description	Measuring Conditions/Terminal Voltage
D1 to D4	See appropriate SELF-DIAGNOSTICS article in ENGINE PERFORMANCE in appropriate MITCHELL® manual.		
D5	STOP SW	Brake switch signal input	With ignition switch ON (II) and brake pedal depressed: Battery voltage With ignition switch ON (II) and brake pedal released: 0 V
D6 to D16	See appropriate SELF-DIAGNOSTICS article in ENGINE PERFORMANCE in appropriate MITCHELL® manual.		

96H30988

Courtesy of American Honda Motor Co., Inc.

Fig. 25: Pin Voltage Chart (2 Of 2)

DTC P1753 (FLASH CODE 1): LOCK-UP CONTROL SOLENOID VALVE "A"

1) Disconnect PCM 32-pin connector "A" and PCM 25-pin connector "B". Turn ignition on. Using DVOM, measure voltage between PCM 25-pin connector "B" terminal No. 5 (Red/White wire) and PCM 32-pin connector "A" terminal No. 9 (Black/Red wire) or No. 22 (Brown/Black wire). *See Figs. 24 and 25.* If voltage is present, go to next step. If voltage is not present, repair open or short in Red/White wire between PCM 25-pin connector "B" and lock-up control solenoid valve.

2) Turn ignition off. Measure lock-up control solenoid valve "A" resistance at PCM. See LOCK-UP CONTROL SOLENOID VALVE under COMPONENT TESTING. If resistance is not 14-25 ohms, go to next step. If resistance is 14-25 ohms, check for loose PCM connectors and replace PCM with known good part, as necessary.

3) Disconnect lock-up control solenoid valve connector. Check for continuity between PCM 32-pin connector "A" terminal No. 9 (Black/Red wire) or No. 22 (Brown/Black wire) and PCM 25-pin connector "B" terminal No. 5 (Red/White wire). If continuity does not exist, go to next step. If continuity exists, repair short to ground in Red/White wire between PCM 25-pin connector "B" and lock-up control solenoid valve.

4) Measure resistance between lock-up control solenoid valve connector (solenoid side) Yellow wire and ground. If resistance is not 14-25 ohms, replace lock-up control solenoid valve assembly. If resistance is 14-25 ohms, check and repair open Yellow wire between lock-up control solenoid valve connector and lock-up control solenoid valve.

DTC P1758 (FLASH CODE 2): LOCK-UP CONTROL SOLENOID VALVE "B"

1) Disconnect PCM 32-pin connector "A" and PCM 25-pin connector "B". Turn ignition on. Using DVOM, measure voltage between PCM 25-pin connector "B" terminal No. 4 (White/Black wire) and PCM 32-pin connector "A" terminal No. 9 (Black/Red wire) or No. 22 (Brown/Black wire). See Figs. 24 and 25. If voltage is present, go to next step. If voltage is not present, repair open or short in White/Black wire between PCM 25-pin connector "B" and lock-up control solenoid valve "B".

2) Turn ignition off. Measure lock-up control solenoid valve "B" resistance at PCM. See LOCK-UP CONTROL SOLENOID VALVE under COMPONENT TESTING. If resistance is not 14-25 ohms, go to next step. If resistance is 14-25 ohms, check for loose PCM connectors and replace PCM with known good part, as necessary.

3) Disconnect lock-up control solenoid valve connector. Check for continuity between PCM 32-pin connector "A" terminal No. 9 (Black/Red wire) or No. 22 (Brown/Black wire) and PCM 25-pin connector "B" terminal No. 4 (White/Black wire). If continuity does not exist, go to next step. If continuity exists, repair short to ground in White/Black between PCM 25-pin connector "B" and lock-up control solenoid valve "B".

4) Measure resistance between lock-up control solenoid valve connector (solenoid side) Green/Black wire and ground. If resistance is not 14-25 ohms, replace lock-up control solenoid valve assembly. If resistance is 14-25 ohms, check and repair open Green/Black wire between lock-up control solenoid valve connector and lock-up control solenoid valve.

"D₄" INDICATOR LIGHT ON CONSTANTLY

1) Turn ignition off. Disconnect 25-pin PCM harness connector "B". Turn ignition on. Using a DVOM, measure voltage between ground and 25-pin PCM harness connector "B", terminal No. 13 (Green/Black wire). If no voltage is present, go to next step. If voltage is present, repair Green/Black wire for a short to power.

2) Turn ignition off. Reconnect PCM harness connector. Turn ignition on. Shift to any position except "D₄". Measure voltage (backprobe) between ground and 25-pin PCM harness connector "B", terminal No. 24 (Green/Black wire). If voltage is present, replace PCM. If no voltage is present, check Green/Black wire for a short to ground. Repair as necessary. If no problem is found, replace A/T gear position indicator.

"D₄" INDICATOR LIGHT DOES NOT COME ON

1) Turn ignition on. Ensure service connector shorting tool or jumper wire is not connected to service check connector. Shift to "D₄" position. If "D₄" indicator light does not illuminate, go to next step. If "D₄" indicator light illuminates, check for loose PCM harness connections. Replace PCM with a known-good unit if necessary and retest.

2) Turn ignition off. Disconnect 32-pin PCM harness connector "A". Using a DVOM, check for continuity between ground and 32-pin PCM harness connector "A", terminal No. 9 (Black/Red wire) and terminal No. 22 (Brown/Black wire). If continuity is present, go to next step. If continuity is not present, repair open or poor connection in Black/Red or Brown/Black wire.

3) Turn ignition on. Measure voltage at 32-pin PCM harness connector "A", between terminals No. 9 (Black/Red wire) and No. 11 (Yellow/Black wire), then between terminals No. 24 (Yellow/Black wire) and No. 22 (Brown/Black wire). If battery voltage is present, go to next step. If battery voltage is not present, repair open or short in appropriate Yellow/Black wire between PCM and engine compartment fuse/relay box.

4) Turn ignition off. Reconnect PCM harness connector. Connect a DVOM (backprobe) between 25-pin PCM harness connector "B", terminal No. 13 (Green/Black wire) and 32-pin PCM harness connector "A", terminal No. 9 (Black/Red wire) or terminal No. 22 (Brown/Black wires). Turn ignition on. Voltage should be present for 2 seconds. If DVOM indicates voltage as specified, go to next step. If no voltage was indicated, go to step 6).

5) Check for an open in Green/Black wire between PCM and gauge assembly. Repair as necessary. If no problem is found, repair faulty "D₄" indicator bulb or gauge assembly printed circuit board.

6) Turn ignition off. Disconnect 25-pin PCM harness connector "B". Check Green/Black wire for continuity between 25-pin PCM harness connector "B", terminal No. 13 and gauge assembly 16-pin harness connector terminal C3. If continuity is present, go to next step. If continuity is not present, repair open in Green/Black wire.

7) Check for loose PCM harness connectors or faulty A/T gear position switch. Repair as necessary. If no problem is found, replace PCM with a known-good unit and retest.

WIRING DIAGRAMS

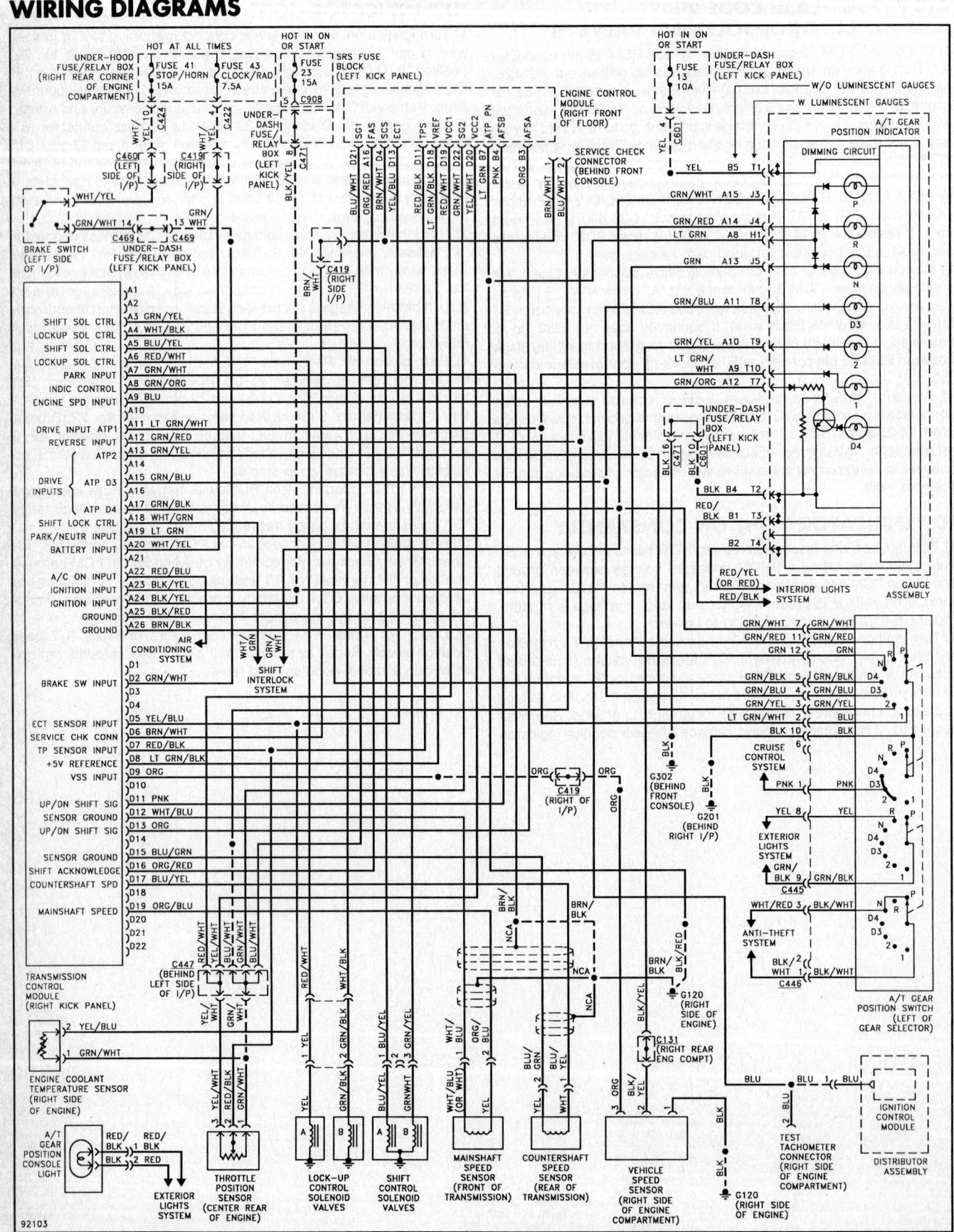

Fig. 26: Transaxle Wiring Diagram (1995 Prelude)

92103

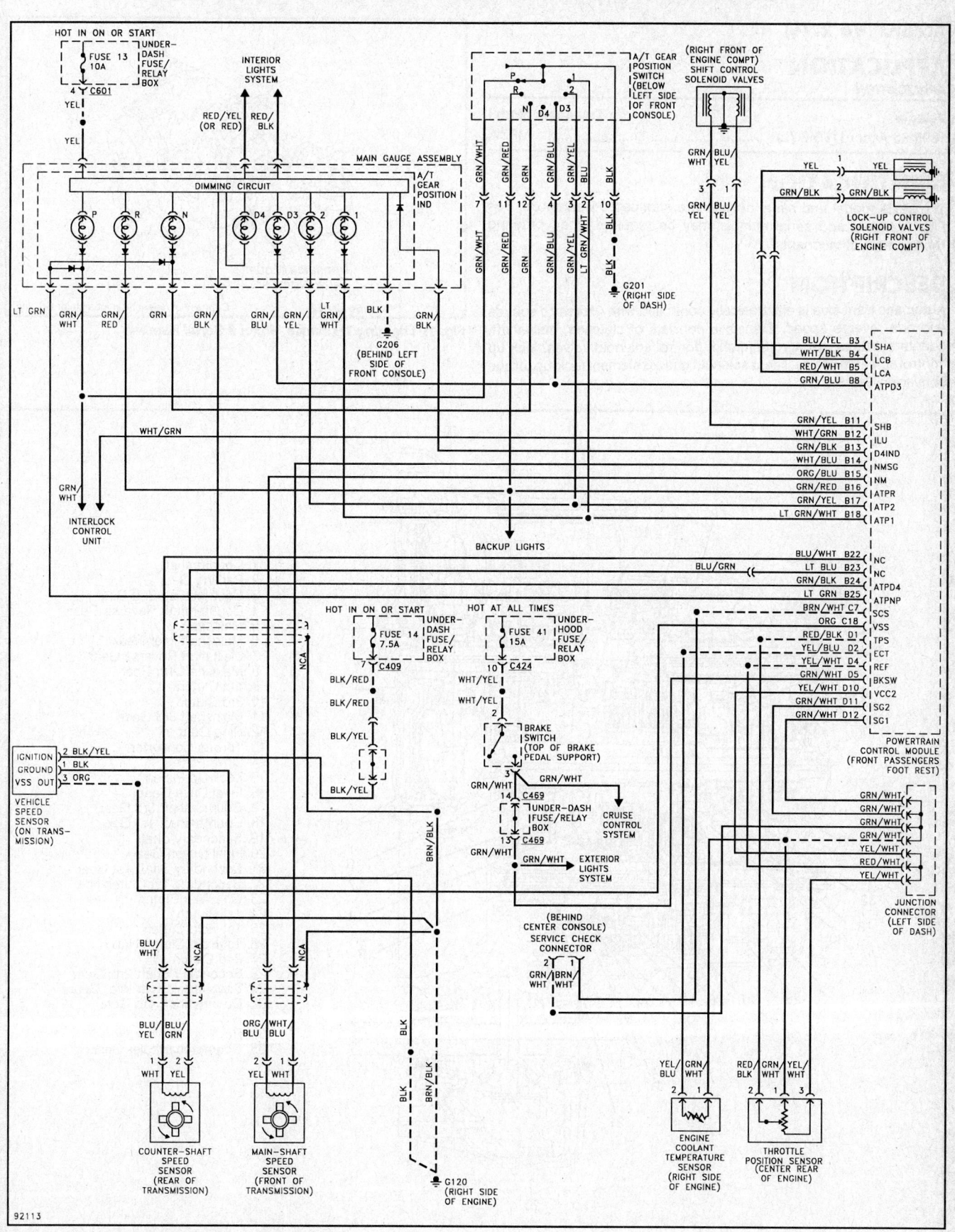

Fig. 27: Transaxle Wiring Diagram (1996 Prelude)

Accord (V6 2.7L)

APPLICATION

APPLICATION

Vehicle	Transaxle Model
1995-96 Accord (V6 2.7L)	MPZA

IDENTIFICATION

Transaxle model and serial number are stamped on transaxle. *See Fig. 1.* Model and serial number may be required when ordering replacement components.

DESCRIPTION

Automatic transaxle is electronically controlled with 4 forward speeds and one reverse speed. Transaxle consists of clutches, mainshaft, countershaft, secondary shaft, shift control solenoid valves, lock-up control solenoid valves, linear solenoid and a 3 element lock-up torque converter. *See Fig. 2.*

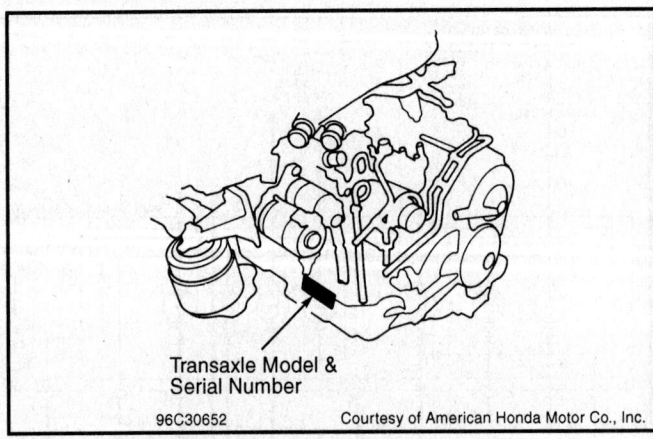

Transaxle Model &
Serial Number

96C30652   Courtesy of American Honda Motor Co., Inc.

Fig. 1: Locating Transaxle Model & Serial Number

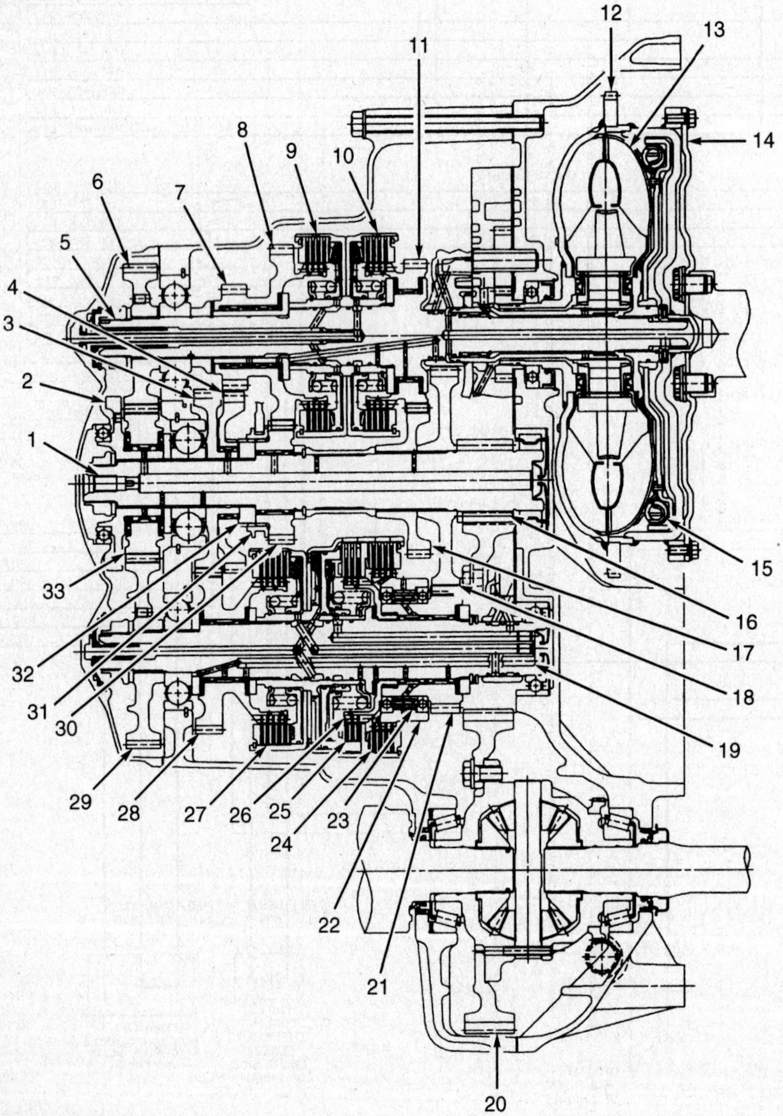

1. Countershaft
2. Parking Gear
3. Countershaft 2nd Gear
4. Countershaft Reverse Gear
5. Mainshaft
6. Mainshaft Idler Gear
7. Mainshaft Reverse Gear
8. Mainshaft 4th Gear
9. 4th Clutch
10. 3rd Clutch
11. Mainshaft 3rd Gear
12. Ring Gear
13. Torque Converter
14. Drive Plate
15. Lock-Up Piston
16. Final Drive Gear
17. Countershaft 3rd Gear
18. Countershaft 1st Gear
19. Secondary Shaft
20. Final Driven Gear
21. Secondary Shaft 1st Gear
22. Secondary 1st Clutch Hub
23. One-Way Clutch
24. 1st Clutch
25. 1st-Hold Clutch
26. 1st-Hold Clutch Hub
27. 2nd Clutch
28. Secondary Shaft 2nd Gear
29. Secondary Shaft Idler Gear
30. Countershaft 4th Gear
31. Reverse Selector
32. Reverse Selector Hub
33. Countershaft Idler Gear

96D30653   Courtesy of American Honda Motor Co., Inc.

Fig. 2: Cut-Away View Of Transaxle Components

Valve bodies include; main valve body, secondary valve body, regulator valve body, servo body, lock-up valve body and accumulator valve body. Main valve body assembly consists of manual valve, 1-2 shift valve, 2nd orifice control valve, 2-3 shift valve, 3rd kickdown valve, modulator valve, cooler relief valve, lock-up shift valve and main body valve. Secondary valve body consists of 2nd kickdown valve, 3-4 shift valve, main orifice control valve, servo control valve, servo orifice control valve and 4th exhaust valve. Regulator valve body consists of regulator valve, torque converter check valve and lock-up control valve. Servo body consists of servo valve and incorporates accumulators. Lock-up valve body consists of lock-up timing valve and relief valve. Accumulator valve body consists of 1st and 2nd accumulator pistons.

The linear solenoid/throttle valve body assembly is attached to outside of transaxle housing. Shift control solenoid valves "A" and "B", and lock-up control solenoid valves "A" and "B" are bolted to outside of torque converter housing.

Transaxle shifting and torque converter lock-up are controlled by the Transmission Control Module (TCM), which receives input signals from various sensors. The TCM determines appropriate shift point and activates appropriate shift control solenoid valve, lock-up control solenoid valves or linear solenoid.

OPERATION

Shift lever has 7 positions. When shift lever is moved, manual valve on main valve body is moved by the shift cable. When certain transaxle gear combinations are engaged by clutches, power is transmitted from mainshaft to the countershaft and through the secondary shaft to provide different gears. Shift lever positions operate as follows:

- **"P" (Park)** – Front wheels are locked as parking pawl engages with parking gear on countershaft. All clutches are released. Neutral position switch, incorporated in A/T gear position switch, allows engine starting in this position.
- **"R" (Reverse)** – Reverse selector engages with countershaft reverse gear and 4th gear clutch is applied. Backup light switch, incorporated in A/T gear position switch, allows back-up lights to operate.
- **"N" (Neutral)** – All clutches are released. Neutral position switch, incorporated in A/T gear position switch, allows engine starting in this position.
- **"D₄" (Drive/4th)** – Transaxle starts in 1st gear and upshifts automatically to 2nd, 3rd and 4th gears. Transaxle will downshift through 3rd, 2nd and 1st gears until vehicle stops. When in 2nd, 3rd or 4th gear in "D₄" position, TCM sends signal to operate torque converter lock-up.
- **"D₃" (Drive/3rd)** – Transaxle starts off in 1st gear and upshifts automatically to 2nd gear and 3rd gear. On deceleration, transaxle will downshift through 2nd gear to 1st gear. When in 3rd gear in "D₃" position, TCM sends signal to operate torque converter lock-up.
- **"2" (Second)** – Transaxle starts off and remains in 2nd gear for engine braking and better traction.
- **"1" (First)** – Transaxle starts off and remains in 1st gear for engine braking.

When in "D₃" position in 3rd gear, or "D₄" position in 2nd, 3rd or 4th gear, torque converter lock-up is present and transaxle mainshaft rotates at the same speed as engine crankshaft. Under certain conditions, torque converter lock-up clutch is applied during deceleration when in 3rd and 4th gears. Torque converter lock-up is controlled by TCM. The TCM receives various input signals and operates lock-up control solenoid valves. Operation of lock-up control solenoid valves controls modulator pressure.

The TCM contains a grade logic control system which controls transaxle shifting while vehicle is ascending or descending on a slope or when reducing vehicle speed. For more information on grade logic control system, see HONDA MPZA ELECTRONIC CONTROLS article.

The TCM contains a self-diagnostic system, which will store a Diagnostic Trouble Code (DTC) if a failure is present in the transaxle electronic control system. The DTC can be retrieved to determine transaxle problem area. For information on electronic transaxle components, see HONDA MPZA ELECTRONIC CONTROLS article.

Transaxle is equipped with shift and key interlock systems. Shift interlock system prevents shift lever from being moved from "P" position unless brake pedal is depressed and accelerator pedal is in idle position. In case of a malfunction, shift lever can be released by placing ignition key in release slot near shift lever. Key interlock system prevents ignition key from being removed from ignition switch unless shift lever is in "P" position. For additional information on interlock systems, see HONDA MPZA ELECTRONIC CONTROLS article.

The A/T gear position indicator on instrument panel contains lights to indicate which position A/T gear position switch on shift lever is in. For information and testing of A/T gear position indicator, see HONDA MPZA ELECTRONIC CONTROLS article.

LUBRICATION & ADJUSTMENTS

See appropriate AUTOMATIC TRANSMISSION SERVICING article in TRANSMISSION SERVICING section.

TROUBLE SHOOTING

Transaxle malfunctions may be caused by poor engine performance, improper adjustments or failure of hydraulic, mechanical or electronic components. Always begin by checking fluid level, fluid condition and cable adjustments. Perform road test to determine if problem has been corrected. If problem is still present, several tests must be performed on transaxle. See TESTING.

Engine Runs, But Vehicle Does Not Move In Any Gear Position
- Low ATF
- Mainshaft Worn/Damaged
- Countershaft Worn/Damaged
- Secondary Shaft Worn/Damaged
- Final Gears Worn/Damaged
- Oil Pump Worn Or Binding
- Regulator Valve Stuck Or Spring Worn
- Oil Filter Clogged
- Shift Cable Broken/Out Of Adjustment
- Drive Plate Defective Or Transaxle Misassembly

Vehicle Moves In "R" & "2", But Not In "D₃", "D₄" Or "1" Position
- 1st Gears Worn/Damaged
- 1st Clutch Defective
- One-Way Clutch Worn/Damaged
- 1st Accumulator Defective
- Shift Cable Broken/Out Of Adjustment

Vehicle Moves In "D₃", "D₄", "1" & "R", But Not In "2" Position
- 2nd Gears Worn/Damaged
- 2nd Clutch Defective
- One-Way Clutch Worn/Damaged
- 2nd Accumulator Defective
- Shift Cable Broken/Out Of Adjustment

Vehicle Moves In "D₃", "D₄", "2" & "1", But Not In "R" Position
- 4th Clutch Defective
- Reverse Gears Worn/Damaged
- Reverse Idler Gear Worn/Damaged
- Servo Valve Stuck
- Shift Cable Broken/Out Of Adjustment

Vehicle Moves In "N" Position
- ATF Over Filled
- 1st Clutch Defective
- 2nd Clutch Defective
- 3rd Clutch Defective
- 4th Clutch Defective
- Needle Bearing Worn/Damaged
- Thrust Washer Worn/Damaged
- Clutch Clearance Incorrect

Excessive Idle Vibration
- Binding Oil Pump
- Lock-Up Shift Valve Stuck
- Engine Output Low
- Lock-Up Piston Defective
- Drive Plate Defective Or Transaxle Misassembly

Excessive Vibration (All Engine Speeds)
- Drive Plate Defective Or Transaxle Misassembly

Poor Acceleration & Flares On Starting Off In "R" Position With The Following Stall Conditions:

Stall RPM High In "D₄", "D₃", "2" & "1" Position
- Low ATF
- Oil Pump Worn Or Binding
- Regulator Valve Stuck Or Spring Worn
- Torque Converter Check Valve Stuck
- Oil Filter Clogged
- Shift Cable Broken/Out Of Adjustment
- Torque Converter One-Way Clutch Worn/Damaged

Stall RPM High In "1" Position
- 1st Clutch Defective
- One-Way Clutch Worn/Damaged
- Shift Cable Broken/Out Of Adjustment

Stall RPM High In "2" Position
- 2nd Clutch Defective
- Shift Cable Broken/Out Of Adjustment

Stall RPM Within Specification
- ATF Over Filled

Stall RPM Low
- Lock-Up Shift Valve Stuck
- Engine Output Low
- Engine Throttle Cable Out Of Adjustment
- Lock-Up Piston Defective

Does Not Shift
- Lock-Up Shift Valve Stuck
- Shift Control Solenoid Valve "A" Defective
- Shift Control Solenoid Valve "B" Defective
- TCM Defective

Fails To Shift In "D₃" Position; From 1st To 3rd Gear
- 2-3 Shift Valve Stuck
- TCM Defective

Fails To Shift In "D₄" Position; From 1st To 4th Gear
- 2-3 Shift Valve Stuck
- 3-4 Shift Valve Stuck
- TCM Defective

Erratic 1-2 Upshift, 2-3 Upshift & 3-4 Upshift
- TCM Defective

Erratic 1-2 Upshift
- Shift Control Solenoid Valve "A" Defective
- TCM Defective

Erratic 2-3 Upshift
- Shift Control Solenoid Valve "B" Defective
- TCM Defective

Erratic 3-4 Upshift
- Shift Control Solenoid Valve "A" Defective
- TCM Defective

Harsh Upshift (1-2)
- 2nd Clutch Defective
- 2nd Accumulator Defective
- Main Orifice Control Valve Stuck
- Linear Solenoid Defective

Harsh Upshift (2-3)
- 3rd Clutch Defective
- 3rd Accumulator Defective
- 2nd Orifice Control Valve Stuck
- Main Orifice Control Valve Stuck
- Linear Solenoid Defective

Harsh Upshift (3-4)
- 4th Clutch Defective
- 4th Accumulator Defective
- Servo Orifice Control Valve Stuck
- Main Orifice Control Valve Stuck
- Linear Solenoid Defective

Harsh Downshift (2-1)
- 2nd Accumulator Defective
- 2nd Check Ball Stuck
- Main Orifice Control Valve Stuck
- Linear Solenoid Defective

Harsh Downshift (3-2)
- 3rd Accumulator Defective
- 3rd Check Ball Stuck
- 2nd Kickdown Valve Stuck
- Main Orifice Control Valve Stuck
- 4th Exhaust Valve Stuck
- Linear Solenoid Defective

Harsh Downshift (4-3)
- 4th Accumulator Defective
- 4th Check Ball Stuck
- 3rd Kickdown Valve Stuck
- Main Orifice Control Valve Stuck
- 4th Exhaust Valve Stuck
- Linear Solenoid Defective

Flares On 2-3 Upshift
- 3rd Clutch Defective
- 3rd Accumulator Defective
- Foreign Material In Main Orifice
- Foreign Material In 3rd Orifice
- 2nd Orifice Control Valve Stuck
- Linear Solenoid Defective

Flares On 3-4 Upshift
- 4th Clutch Defective
- 4th Accumulator Defective
- Foreign Material In Main Orifice
- Foreign Material In 4th Orifice
- Servo Orifice Control Valve Stuck
- Linear Solenoid Defective

Excessive Shock On 2-3 Upshift
- 3rd Clutch Defective
- 3rd Accumulator Defective
- 2nd Check Ball Stuck
- 2nd Orifice Control Valve Stuck
- Foreign Material In Separator Plate Orifice
- Linear Solenoid Defective

Excessive Shock On 3-4 Upshift
- 4th Clutch Defective
- 4th Accumulator Defective
- 3rd Check Ball Stuck
- Servo Orifice Control Valve Stuck
- Foreign Material In Separator Plate Orifice
- Linear Solenoid Defective

Late Shift From "N" Position To "D₄" Or "D₃" Position
- 1st Clutch Defective
- Foreign Material In 1st Orifice

Late Shift From "N" Position To "R" Position
- 4th Clutch Defective
- Servo Valve Stuck
- 1-2 Shift Valve Stuck
- Servo Control Valve Stuck

Noise From Transaxle In All Gears
- Torque Converter Housing Or Transaxle Housing Ball Bearing Worn/Damaged
- Oil Pump Worn Or Binding

Vehicle Does Not Accelerate Greater Than 31 MPH
- Torque Converter One-Way Clutch Defective

Shift Lever Does Not Operate Smoothly
- Shift Cable Broken/Out Of Adjustment
- Joint In Shift Cable & Transmission Or Body Worn

Fails To Shift; Stuck In 4th Gear
- Shift Control Solenoid Valve "A" Defective
- Shift Control Solenoid Valve "B" Defective
- TCM Defective

Transaxle Will Not Shift Into "P" Position
- Shift Cable Broken/Out Of Adjustment
- Joint In Shift Cable & Transmission Or Body Worn

Stall RPM High; All Clutch Pressures Within Specification
- 1st Clutch Defective
- 2nd Clutch Defective
- One-Way Clutch Worn/Damaged
- Torque Converter Check Valve Stuck

Lock-Up Clutch Does Not Disengage
- Lock-Up Shift Valve Stuck
- Lock-Up Control Valve Stuck
- Lock-Up Timing Valve Stuck
- Lock-Up Control Solenoid Valve "A" Defective
- Lock-Up Control Solenoid Valve "B" Defective
- Linear Solenoid Defective
- TCM Defective
- Lock-Up Piston Defective

Lock-Up Clutch Does Not Operate Smoothly
- Torque Converter Check Valve Stuck
- Lock-Up Shift Valve Stuck
- Lock-Up Control Valve Stuck
- Lock-Up Timing Valve Stuck
- Lock-Up Control Solenoid Valve "A" Defective
- Lock-Up Control Solenoid Valve "B" Defective
- Linear Solenoid Defective
- TCM Defective
- Lock-Up Piston Defective

Lock-Up Clutch Does Not Engage
- Torque Converter Check Valve Stuck
- Lock-Up Shift Valve Stuck
- Lock-Up Control Valve Stuck
- Lock-Up Timing Valve Stuck
- Lock-Up Control Solenoid Valve "A" Defective
- Lock-Up Control Solenoid Valve "B" Defective
- Linear Solenoid Defective
- TCM Defective
- Lock-Up Piston Defective

Excessive Shock When Shifting Into "1" Position
- 1st-Hold Clutch Defective
- 1st-Hold Accumulator Defective
- Foreign Material In Separator Plate Orifice

No Engine Braking In "1" Position
- 1st-Hold Clutch Defective
- 1st-Hold Accumulator Defective
- Foreign Material In 1st-Hold Orifice

TESTING

CAUTION: Vehicle is equipped with a Supplemental Restraint System (SRS). All wires have Yellow insulation and are located underdash or in instrument panel area. To avoid injury from accidental deployment, read and carefully follow all SERVICE PRECAUTIONS and DISABLING & ACTIVATING AIR BAG SYSTEM procedures in APPLICATIONS & IDENTIFICATIONS.

ROAD TEST

NOTE: If shift lever cannot be moved from "P" position with brake pedal depressed and accelerator at idle position, check shift interlock system. See HONDA MPZA ELECTRONIC CONTROLS article.

1) Warm engine to normal operating temperature. Apply parking brake and block wheels. Start engine. Move shift lever to "D₄" position while depressing brake pedal. Depress accelerator pedal and release it suddenly. Engine should not stall.

2) Repeat step 1) with shift lever in "D₃" position. Ensure engine does not stall. Manufacturer recommends monitoring of Throttle Position (TP) sensor voltage when performing road test. This ensures proper throttle opening for verifying shift points and lock-up of torque converter.

3) Remove right-side door sill molding. Pull carpet back to expose TCM. Remove ECM cover mounting nuts and turn TCM over. Ensure ignition is off. Using a DVOM, measure voltage (backprobe) between 22-pin TCM harness connector "B", terminal No. 4 (Red/Black wire) and 26-pin TCM harness connector "A", terminals No. 13 or 26 (Brown/Black wires). *See Fig. 3.*

4) Install scan tool. Road test vehicle on a flat road in "D₄" position. Monitor TP sensor voltage and ensure shift points occur at specified speeds. *See Fig. 4.* Also check for abnormal transaxle noise and clutch slippage. See CLUTCH APPLICATION table.

CLUTCH APPLICATION

Shift Lever Position	Elements In Use
"P" Or "N"	No Clutches Are Applied
"R"	4th Clutch
"D₄"	
1st Gear	1st Clutch & ¹ One-Way Clutch
2nd Gear	² 1st Clutch & 2nd Clutch
3rd Gear	² 1st Clutch & 3rd Clutch
4th Gear	² 1st Clutch & 4th Clutch
"D₃"	
1st Gear	1st Clutch & ¹ One-Way Clutch
2nd Gear	² 1st Clutch & 2nd Clutch
3rd Gear	² 1st Clutch & 3rd Clutch
"2"	² 1st Clutch & 2nd Clutch
"1"	1st-Hold Clutch, 1st Clutch & ¹ One-Way Clutch

¹ – One-way clutch engages on acceleration and slips on deceleration. No engine braking occurs.
² – The 1st clutch engages, but driving power is not transmitted, as one-way clutch slips.

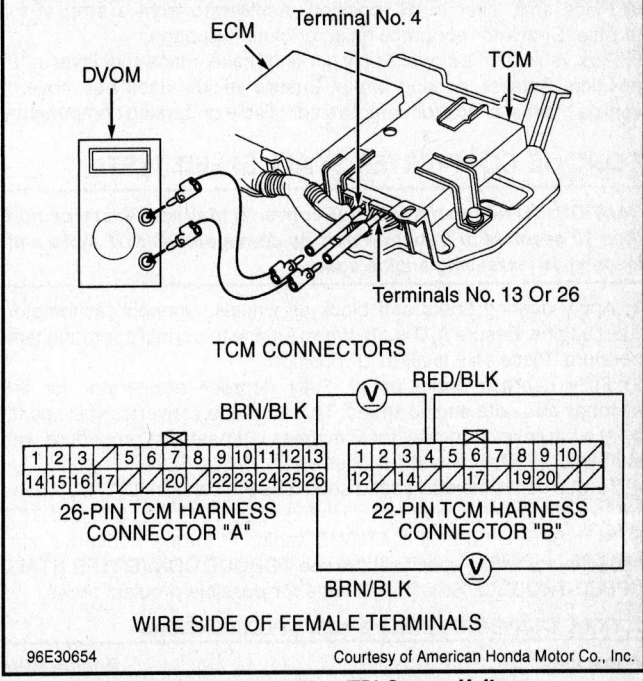

TCM CONNECTORS

WIRE SIDE OF FEMALE TERMINALS

96E30654   Courtesy of American Honda Motor Co., Inc.

Fig. 3: Measuring Throttle Position (TP) Sensor Voltage

5) With shift lever in "D₄" position, accelerate to about 35 MPH so transaxle is in 4th gear. Move shift lever to "2" position. Ensure engine braking occurs.

6) Place shift lever in "1" position. Accelerate from a stop at full throttle. Check for abnormal noise or clutch slippage. Upshifts and downshifts should not occur in this shift lever position.

● Upshift			1st → 2nd	2nd → 3rd	3rd → 4th	Lock-Up Clutch ON
Throttle position sensor voltage: 0.67 V		MPH	8 – 9	18 – 20	26 – 30	14 – 16
Coasting down-hill from a stop		KM/H	13 – 15	29 – 32	42 – 48	22 – 26
Throttle position sensor voltage: 2.26 V		MPH	19 – 21	35 – 39	52 – 55	60 – 65
Acceleration from a stop		KM/H	30 – 34	56 – 62	83 – 89	97 – 105
Full throttle		MPH	31 – 35	57 – 61	85 – 89	89 – 94
Acceleration from a stop		KM/H	50 – 56	92 – 98	137 – 143	143 – 151

● Downshift			Lock-Up Clutch OFF	4th → 3rd	3rd → 2nd	2nd → 1st
Throttle position sensor voltage: 0.67 V		MPH	13 – 16	18 – 21	———	6 – 8 (3rd → 1st)
Coasting or braking to a stop		KM/H	21 – 25	29 – 33	———	9 – 13 (3rd → 1st)
Throttle position sensor voltage: 2.26 V		MPH	51 – 56	———	———	———
When car is slowed by increased grade, wind, etc.		KM/H	82 – 90	———	———	———
Full throttle		MPH	83 – 88	79 – 83	52 – 55	25 – 29
When car is slowed by increased grade, wind, etc.		KM/H	134 – 142	127 – 133	83 – 89	41 – 47

96F30655   Courtesy of American Honda Motor Co., Inc.

Fig. 4: Checking Upshift & Downshift Speeds

7) Place shift lever in "2" position. Accelerate from a stop at full throttle. Check for abnormal noise or clutch slippage. Upshifts and downshifts should not occur in this shift lever position.

8) Place shift lever in "R" position. Accelerate from a stop at full throttle. Check for abnormal noise or clutch slippage.

9) Park vehicle on a slope. Apply parking brake. Place shift lever in "P" position. Release parking brake. Ensure vehicle does not move. If vehicle moves, check for defective shift cable or parking components.

TORQUE CONVERTER STALL SPEED TEST

CAUTION: DO NOT perform torque converter stall speed test for more than 10 seconds or transaxle may be damaged. DO NOT move shift lever while increasing engine speed.

1) Apply parking brake and block all wheels. Connect tachometer. Start engine. Ensure A/C is off. Warm engine to normal operating temperature. Place shift lever in "2" position.

2) Fully depress brake pedal. Fully depress accelerator for 6-8 seconds and note engine speed. This is torque converter stall speed.

3) Allow transaxle to cool for 2 minutes. Repeat test procedure with shift lever in "D₄", "1" and "R" positions.

4) Torque converter stall speed should be the same in "D₄", "2", "1" and "R" positions and within specification. See TORQUE CONVERTER STALL SPEED SPECIFICATIONS table. If torque converter stall speed is not within specification, see TORQUE CONVERTER STALL SPEED TROUBLE SHOOTING table for possible problem areas.

TORQUE CONVERTER STALL SPEED SPECIFICATIONS

Application	Engine RPM
Standard	2450
Service Limit	2300-2600

TORQUE CONVERTER STALL SPEED TROUBLE SHOOTING

Torque Converter Stall Speed Test Results	Probable Cause
Stall Speed RPM High In "D₄", "2", "1" & "R"	Low Fluid Level, Low Oil Pump Output, Clogged Oil Filter, Pressure Regulator Valve Stuck Closed, Slipping Clutch
Stall Speed RPM High In "R"	Slipping 4th Clutch
Stall Speed RPM High In "2" & "D₄"	Slipping 2nd Clutch
Stall Speed RPM High In "1"	Slipping 1st Clutch, Slipping One-Way Clutch
Stall Speed RPM Low In "D₄", "2", "1" & "R"	Engine Output Low, Torque Converter One-Way Clutch Slipping

HYDRAULIC PRESSURE TEST

Pressure Test Preparation – Ensure transaxle fluid level is correct. Warm engine to normal operating temperature. Apply parking brake and block rear wheels. Raise and support vehicle so front wheels can rotate.

Pressure Test (Line, Clutch & Throttle Pressure) – 1) With engine off, remove appropriate pressure tap plugs to be tested. See Fig. 5. Attach Pressure Gauge Set (07406-0020400) and Low Pressure Gauge (07406-0070300) to appropriate pressure taps. Tighten hose fittings to 13 ft. lbs. (18 N.m).

NOTE: Apply battery voltage to linear solenoid terminal "B", and ground terminal "A" when checking pressures with throttle fully closed. See Fig. 6.

2) Disconnect linear solenoid harness connector. See Fig. 6. With shift lever in "P" or "N" position, start and operate engine at 2000 RPM. Note pressure at specified shift lever and throttle positions. See Fig. 5.

3) If pressure is not within specification, check for probable cause and repair as necessary. See Fig. 5. Turn engine off.

4) Using a NEW seal washer, install and tighten pressure tap plugs to 13 ft. lbs. (18 N.m).

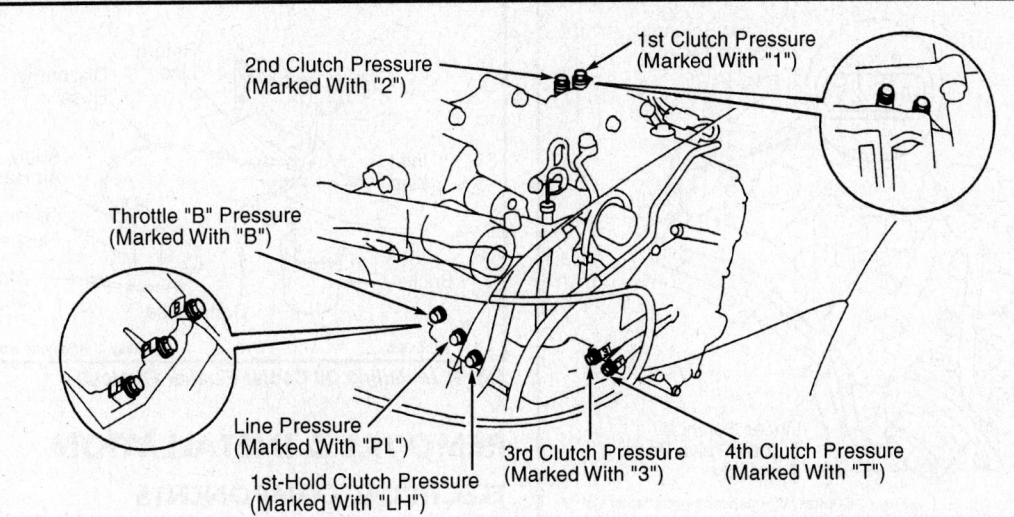

2nd Clutch Pressure (Marked With "2")
1st Clutch Pressure (Marked With "1")
Throttle "B" Pressure (Marked With "B")
Line Pressure (Marked With "PL")
1st-Hold Clutch Pressure (Marked With "LH")
3rd Clutch Pressure (Marked With "3")
4th Clutch Pressure (Marked With "T")

PRESSURE	SHIFT LEVER POSITION	SYMPTOM	PROBABLE CAUSE	FLUID PRESSURE	
				Standard	Service Limit
Line	N or P	No (or low) line pressure	Torque converter, ATF pump, pressure regulator, torque converter check valve	490 kPa (5.0 kgf/cm², 71 psi) Fully-closed throttle	440 kPa (4.5 kgf/cm², 64 psi) Fully-closed throttle
1st Clutch	1 or D4	No or low 1st clutch pressure	1st Clutch	840 kPa (8.5 kgf/cm², 120 psi) Fully-opened throttle	780 kPa (8.0 kgf/cm², 110 psi) Fully-opened throttle
1st-hold Clutch	1	No or low 1st-hold clutch pressure	1st-hold Clutch		
2nd Clutch	2	No or low 2nd clutch pressure	2nd Clutch		
2nd Clutch	D4	No or low 2nd clutch pressure			
3rd Clutch		No or low 3rd clutch pressure	3rd Clutch		
4th Clutch		No or low 4th clutch pressure	4th Clutch		
	R		Servo Valve or 4th Clutch		
Throttle "B"	D4	Pressure too high	Linear Solenoid/ Throttle Valve Body Assembly	0 kPa (0 kgf/cm², 0 psi) Fully-closed throttle	_____
		No or low throttle B pressure		590 kPa (6.0 kgf/cm², 85 psi) Fully-opened throttle	540 kPa (5.5 kgf/cm², 78 psi) Fully-opened throttle

96G30656

Courtesy of American Honda Motor Co., Inc.

Fig. 5: Testing Line, Clutch & Throttle Pressures

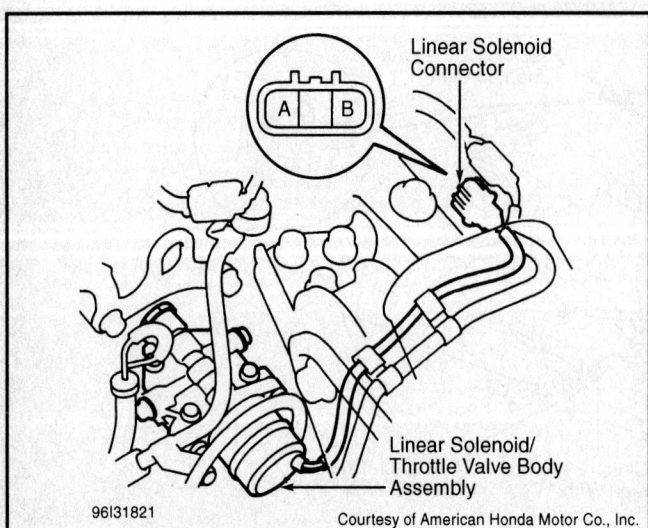

Fig. 6: Locating & Identifying Linear Solenoid Harness Connector Terminals

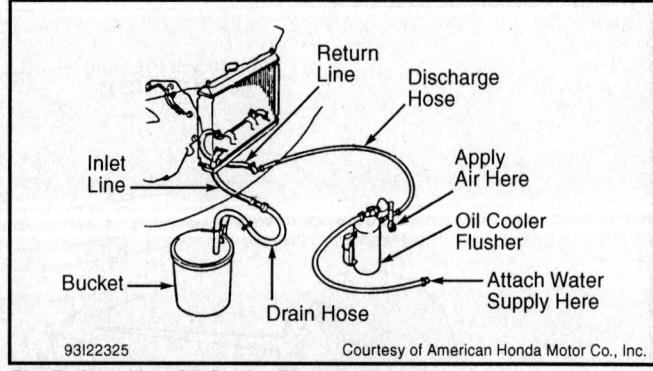

Fig. 7: Installing Oil Cooler Flusher (Typical)

ON-VEHICLE SERVICE

AXLE SHAFTS

See appropriate article in AXLE SHAFTS & TRANSFER CASES section.

OIL COOLER FLUSHING

1) Attach Oil Cooler Flusher (J38405-A) to oil cooler lines. *See Fig. 7.* Fill oil cooler flusher tank 2/3 full with Flushing Fluid (J35944-20). DO NOT use any other flushing fluid.
2) Ensure water and air valves on oil cooler flusher are off. Apply 80-120 psi (550-829 kPa) air pressure to oil cooler flusher. Turn oil cooler flusher water valve on so water will flow through oil cooler for 10 seconds. Shut water valve off. Replace oil cooler if water will not flow through oil cooler.
3) Depress and hold mixing trigger on oil cooler flusher downward. Turn water valve on and flush oil cooler for 2 minutes. Turn air valve on for 5 seconds every 15-20 seconds to create a surging action.
4) Turn water valve off. Release mixing trigger. Disconnect oil cooler flusher and reverse hoses so oil cooler can be flushed in the opposite direction.
5) Repeat steps **2)** and **3)**. Turn water valve off. Release mixing trigger. Turn water valve on and rinse oil cooler for at least one minute. Once oil cooler is flushed in both directions, turn water off. Turn air valve on for 2 minutes or until no moisture is visible from drain hose.

CAUTION: Ensure no moisture is present in oil cooler, as it can damage transaxle.

6) Turn air off. Disconnect oil cooler flusher. Reconnect inlet line on oil cooler. Once transaxle is installed, attach drain hose on return line and place in oil container. Ensure transaxle is in "P" position. Fill transaxle with Honda ATF.
7) Start engine and operate for approximately 30 seconds or until one quart (.9L) of ATF is discharged from return line. Shut engine off. Remove drain hose. Reinstall return line. Fill transaxle to proper level.

REMOVAL & INSTALLATION

ELECTRICAL COMPONENTS

See HONDA MPZA ELECTRONIC CONTROLS article.

TRANSAXLE

See appropriate AUTOMATIC TRANSMISSION REMOVAL article in TRANSMISSION SERVICING section.

TORQUE CONVERTER

Torque converter consists of pump, turbine and stator assembled as a unit. Torque converter cannot be serviced and must be replaced if defective.

NOTE: For torque converter stall speed test, see TORQUE CONVERTER STALL SPEED TEST under TESTING.

TRANSAXLE DISASSEMBLY

LEFT-SIDE COVER

NOTE: Refer to illustration during disassembly. See Fig. 8.

1) Remove mainshaft speed sensor harness connector from bracket. Remove 16 left-side cover bolts and remove cover. Install Mainshaft Holder (07GAB-PF50100 or 07GAB-PF5101) on mainshaft. *See Fig. 9.*

NOTE: Countershaft and secondary shaft lock nuts have LEFT-HAND threads. Save removed lock nuts for use in installation of press fit idler gears and parking gear.

2) Engage parking brake pawl with parking gear. Using a chisel, remove lock tabs from each shaft lock nut. Remove lock nuts and conical washers from each shaft.
3) Remove mainshaft holder. Using a puller, remove parking gear. *See Fig. 10.* Remove thrust needle bearing, countershaft idler gear, needle bearing, thrust needle bearing and splined washer from countershaft.
4) Using a puller, remove idler gears from mainshaft and secondary shaft. Remove parking brake pawl, spring, shaft and stop shaft from transaxle housing. Remove bolt securing parking brake stop.
5) Remove lock washer, parking brake stop, lever and spring from control shaft. Remove connectors from connector bracket on ATF cooler lines. Remove joint bolts and ATF cooler lines.

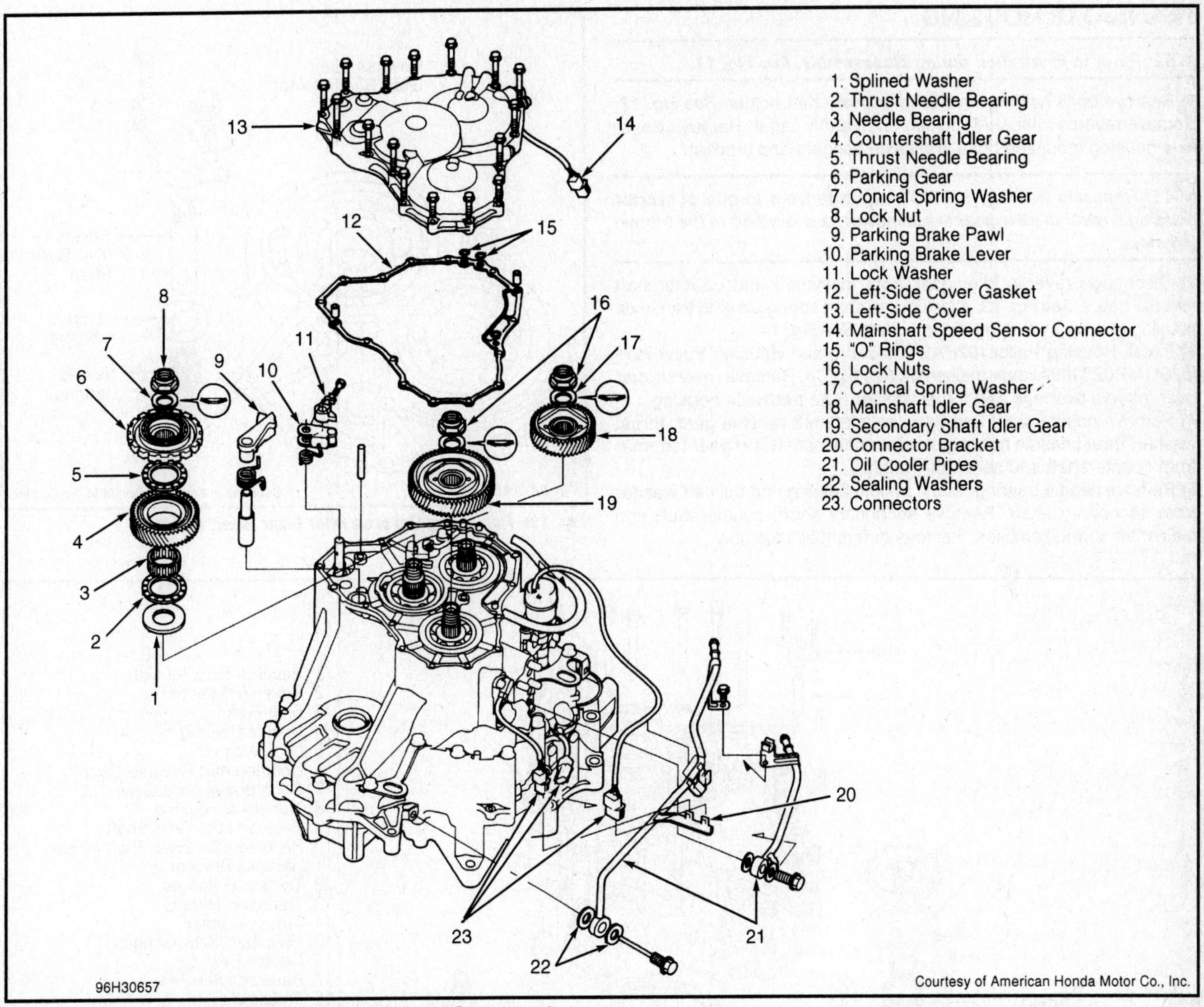

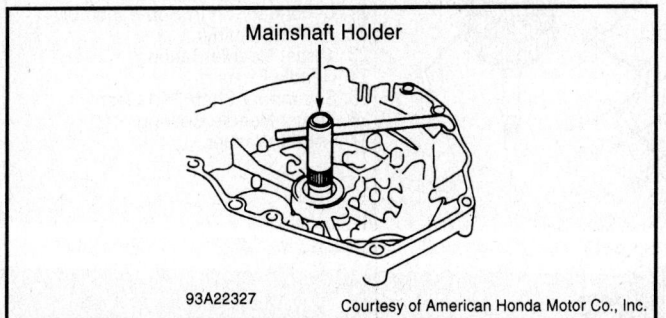

1. Splined Washer
2. Thrust Needle Bearing
3. Needle Bearing
4. Countershaft Idler Gear
5. Thrust Needle Bearing
6. Parking Gear
7. Conical Spring Washer
8. Lock Nut
9. Parking Brake Pawl
10. Parking Brake Lever
11. Lock Washer
12. Left-Side Cover Gasket
13. Left-Side Cover
14. Mainshaft Speed Sensor Connector
15. "O" Rings
16. Lock Nuts
17. Conical Spring Washer
18. Mainshaft Idler Gear
19. Secondary Shaft Idler Gear
20. Connector Bracket
21. Oil Cooler Pipes
22. Sealing Washers
23. Connectors

96H30657

Courtesy of American Honda Motor Co., Inc.

Fig. 8: Exploded View Of Left-Side Cover & Related Components

Mainshaft Holder

93A22327

Courtesy of American Honda Motor Co., Inc.

Fig. 9: Installing Mainshaft Holder

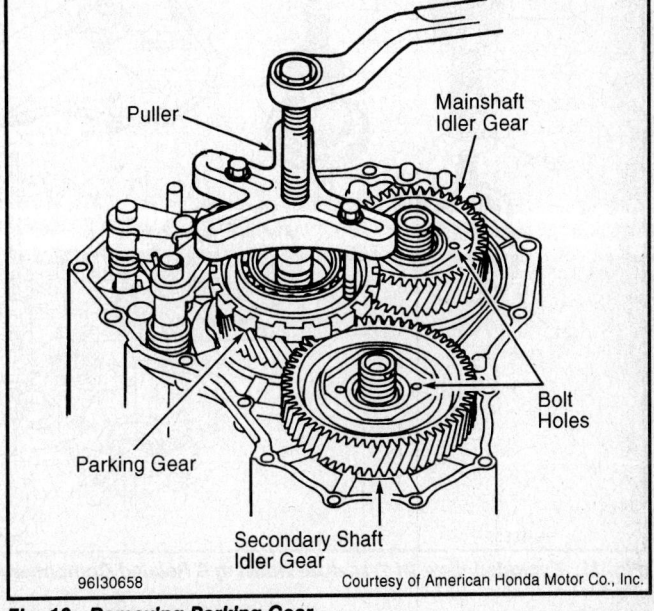

Puller

Mainshaft Idler Gear

Bolt Holes

Parking Gear

Secondary Shaft Idler Gear

96I30658

Courtesy of American Honda Motor Co., Inc.

Fig. 10: Removing Parking Gear

TRANSAXLE HOUSING

NOTE: Refer to illustration during disassembly. See Fig. 11.

1) Remove bolts holding reverse idler gear shaft holder. *See Fig. 12.* Remove reverse idler shaft holder, shaft and washer. Remove transaxle housing mounting bolts, transaxle hangers and bracket.

NOTE: Transaxle housing will NOT separate from torque converter housing if reverse idler gear is not moved as described in the following step.

2) Disengage reverse idler gear from mainshaft and countershaft reverse gears. *See Fig. 13.* Align control shaft spring pin with transaxle housing groove by turning control shaft. *See Fig. 14.*
3) Install Housing Puller (07HAC-PK4010A) and Housing Puller Arm (07SCA-P0Z0100A) over mainshaft. *See Fig. 14.* Remove reverse idler gear, needle bearings and thrust washer from transaxle housing.
4) Remove countershaft 2nd gear, countershaft reverse gear, thrust washer, thrust needle bearing and secondary shaft 2nd gear together from countershaft and secondary shaft.
5) Remove needle bearing, thrust needle bearing and splined washer from secondary shaft. Remove secondary shaft, countershaft and mainshaft sub-assemblies. Remove differential assembly.

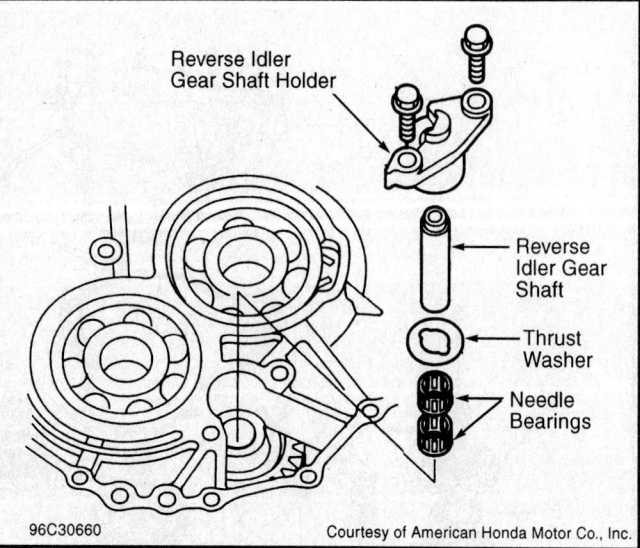

96C30660   Courtesy of American Honda Motor Co., Inc.

Fig. 12: Removing Reverse Idler Gear Shaft Holder

1. Reverse Selector Hub
2. Reverse Selector
3. Shift Fork
4. Needle Bearing
5. Lock Washer
6. Countershaft Reverse Gear
7. Countershaft 2nd Gear
8. Transaxle Housing
9. Reverse Idler Gear Shaft
10. Reverse Idler Gear Shaft Holder
11. Harness Bracket
12. Transaxle Hanger
13. Transaxle Hanger
14. Thrust Washer
15. Mainshaft Sub-Assembly
16. Needle Bearings
17. Reverse Idler Gear
18. Thrust Washer
19. Differential Assembly
20. Countershaft Sub-Assembly
21. Secondary Shaft Sub-Assembly
22. Splined Washer
23. Thrust Needle Bearing
24. Needle Bearing
25. Secondary Shaft 2nd Gear
26. Thrust Needle Bearing
27. Thrust Washer

96J30659   Courtesy of American Honda Motor Co., Inc.

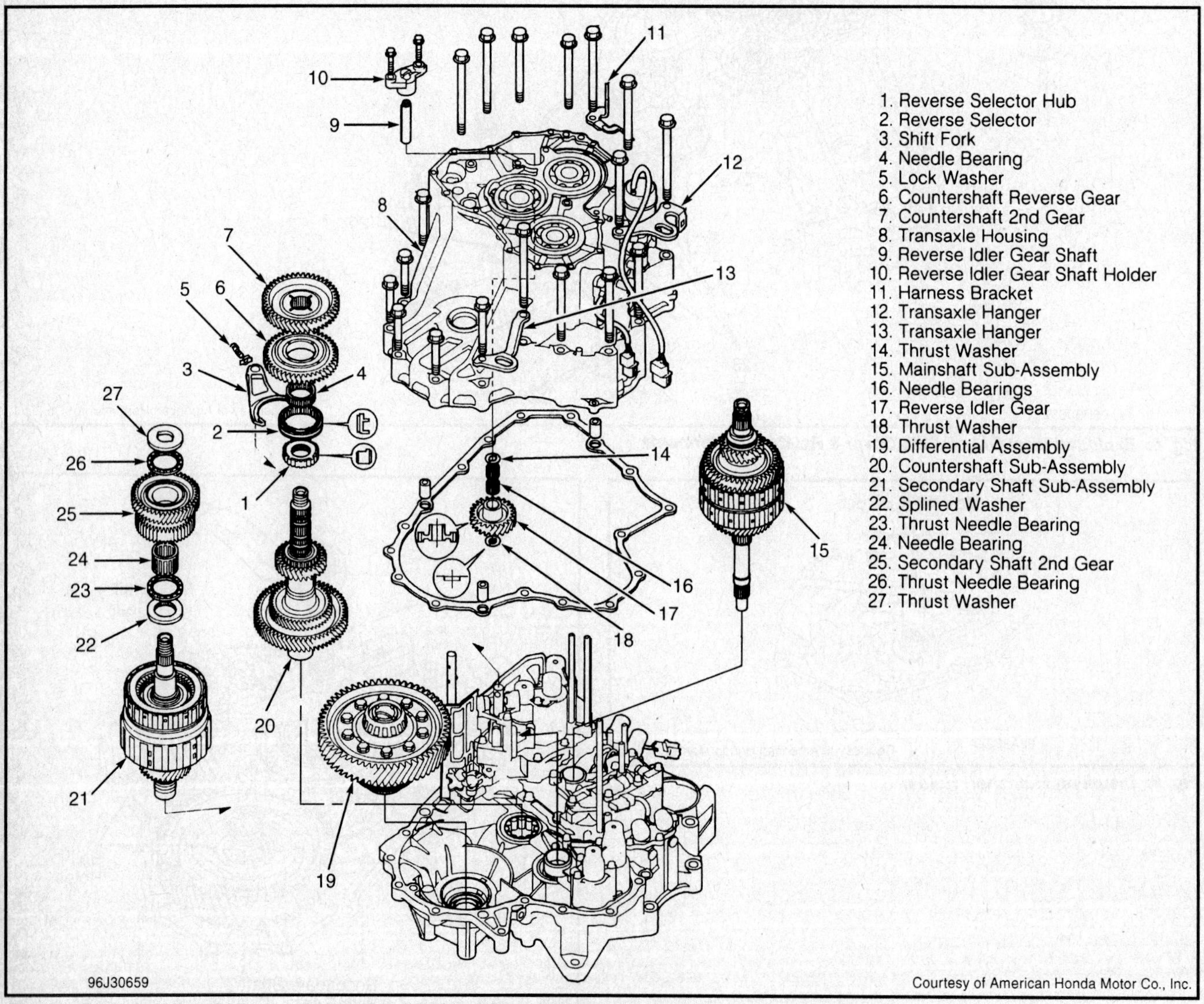

Fig. 11: Exploded View Of Transaxle Housing & Related Components

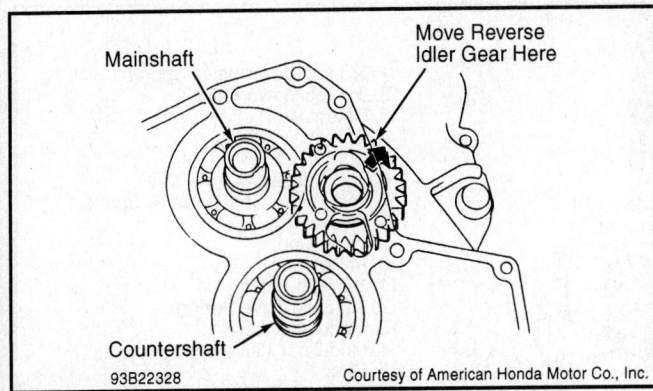

Fig. 13: Disengaging Reverse Idler Gear

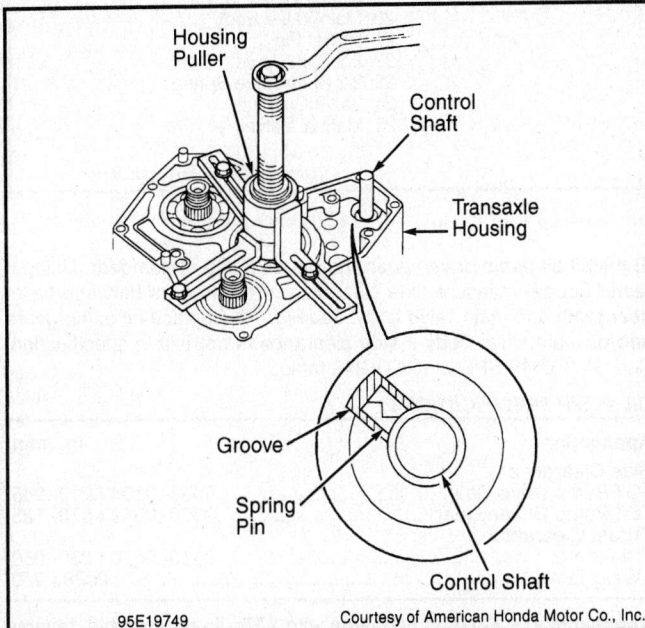

Fig. 14: Control Shaft Alignment & Housing Removal

TORQUE CONVERTER HOUSING/VALVE BODY

1) Remove 2 ATF feed pipes from lock-up valve body, 2 pipes from servo body, one pipe from main valve body and one pipe from accumulator body. Remove 2 bolts and servo detent base.

CAUTION: 4th accumulator is spring loaded. Press down on accumulator cover during bolt removal to prevent stripping servo body threads. DO NOT let check balls fall from secondary valve body during removal.

---

2) Remove oil filter and 4th accumulator cover. Remove servo body and separator plate. Remove secondary valve body, separator plate and dowel pins. Remove lock-up valve body, separator plate and dowel pins.
3) Remove regulator valve body with torque converter check valve and spring. Remove stator shaft and stop shaft. Remove detent spring from detent arm. Separate control shaft from manual valve. Remove control shaft from torque converter housing.

CAUTION: DO NOT let check balls fall from main valve body during removal.

---

4) Remove detent arm and detent arm shaft from main valve body. Remove main valve body. Remove accumulator body. Remove oil pump driven gear shaft and oil pump gears. Remove main separator plate and 3 dowel pins.

MAIN VALVE BODY

CAUTION: When disassembling main valve body, place main valve body components in order and mark spring locations for reassembly reference. DO NOT use force to remove components. DO NOT use magnet to remove check balls, as check balls may become magnetized. Note direction of valve cap installation before removing from main valve body.

Disassembly – Disassemble main valve body. *See Fig. 15.* Use care when removing valve caps or spring seat, as they are under spring pressure.
Cleaning & Inspection – **1)** Clean components with solvent and dry with compressed air. Replace main valve body if any parts are worn or damaged.
2) Ensure all valves slide freely in their bores. If valves do not slide freely, polish burrs or rough areas using No. 600 sandpaper soaked in ATF for at least 30 minutes. Thoroughly clean main valve body and components if polishing was needed.
3) Ensure spring free length is within specification. See SPRING SPECIFICATIONS table. Replace springs if not within specification.

NOTE: Oil pump clearance must be checked in main valve body. See OIL PUMP under COMPONENT DISASSEMBLY & REASSEMBLY.

Reassembly – Coat all components and bores with ATF. To reassemble, reverse disassembly procedure. Ensure all components are installed in correct location. *See Fig. 15.*

SPRING SPECIFICATIONS

Application	Free Length In. (mm)
Accumulator Valve Body	
2nd Accumulator Spring "B"	2.028 (51.50)
2nd Accumulator Spring "A"	3.953 (100.40)
2nd Accumulator Spring "C"	.610 (15.50)
Lubrication Check Valve Spring	1.720 (43.70)
1st Accumulator Spring "B"	2.834 (72.00)
1st Accumulator Spring "A"	4.028 (102.30)
Lock-Up Valve Body	
Relief Valve Spring	1.587 (40.30)
Lock-Up Timing Valve Spring	2.126 (54.00)
Main Valve Body	
2-3 Shift Valve Spring	1.693 (43.00)
3rd Kick-Down Valve Spring	1.831 (46.50)
2nd Orifice Control Valve Spring	1.657 (42.10)
1-2 Shift Valve Spring	1.626 (41.30)
Modulator Valve Spring	1.299 (33.00)
	Or 1.276 (32.40)
Cooler Relief Valve Spring	1.843 (46.80)
Lock-Up Shift Valve Spring	2.480 (63.00)
Regulator Valve Body	
Stator Reaction Spring	1.311 (30.30)
Regulator Valve Spring "A"	2.819 (71.60)
Regulator Valve Spring "B"	1.732 (44.00)
Lock-Up Control Valve Spring	1.469 (37.30)
Torque Converter Check Valve Spring	1.398 (35.50)
Secondary Valve Body	
2nd Kickdown Valve Spring	1.780 (45.20)
3-4 Shift Valve Spring	2.244 (57.00)
Main Orifice Control Valve Spring	1.555 (39.50)
Servo Control Valve Spring	1.280 (32.50)
Servo Orifice Control Valve Spring	1.906 (48.40)
4th Exhaust Valve Spring	1.280 (32.50)
Servo Body	
3rd Accumulator Spring "B"	1.969 (50.00)
3rd Accumulator Spring "A"	4.118 (104.60)
4th Accumulator Spring	4.087 (103.80)
1st-Hold Accumulator Spring "B"	3.012 (76.50)
1st-Hold Accumulator Spring "A"	3.843 (97.60)

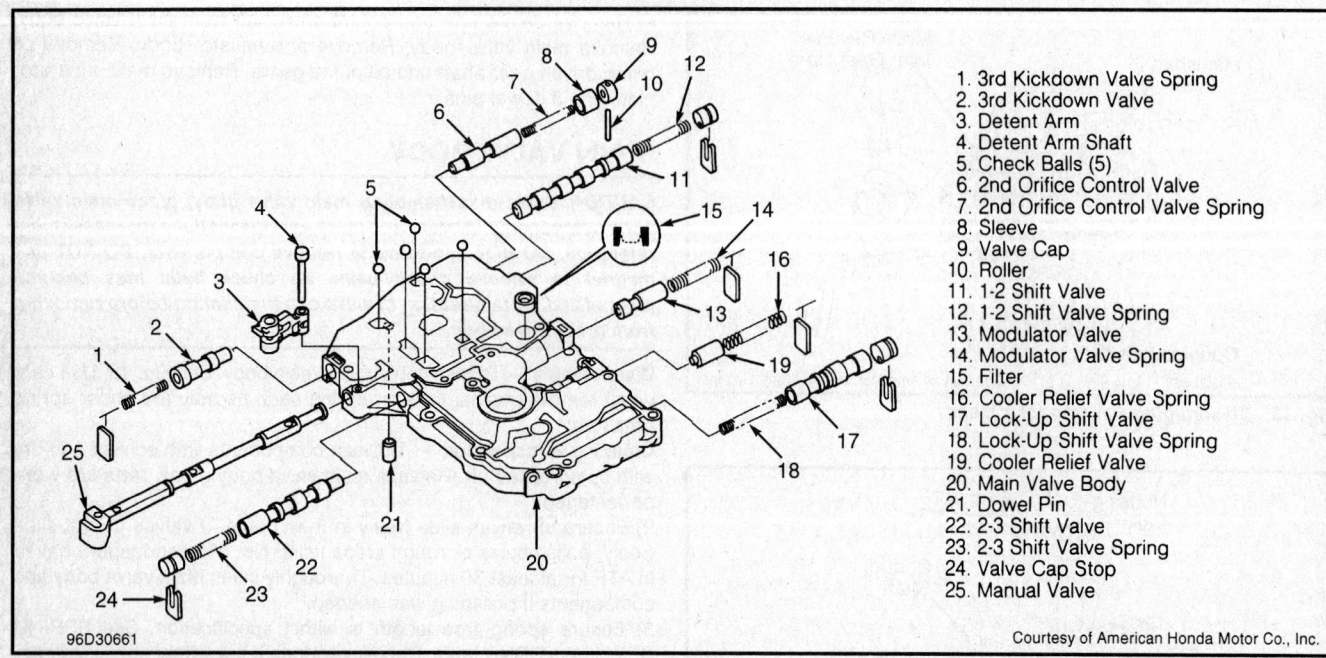

1. 3rd Kickdown Valve Spring
2. 3rd Kickdown Valve
3. Detent Arm
4. Detent Arm Shaft
5. Check Balls (5)
6. 2nd Orifice Control Valve
7. 2nd Orifice Control Valve Spring
8. Sleeve
9. Valve Cap
10. Roller
11. 1-2 Shift Valve
12. 1-2 Shift Valve Spring
13. Modulator Valve
14. Modulator Valve Spring
15. Filter
16. Cooler Relief Valve Spring
17. Lock-Up Shift Valve
18. Lock-Up Shift Valve Spring
19. Cooler Relief Valve
20. Main Valve Body
21. Dowel Pin
22. 2-3 Shift Valve
23. 2-3 Shift Valve Spring
24. Valve Cap Stop
25. Manual Valve

96D30661   Courtesy of American Honda Motor Co., Inc.

Fig. 15: Exploded View Of Main Valve Body

OIL PUMP

Disassembly – Note direction of oil pump gear installation in main valve body. Remove oil pump driven gear shaft and oil pump gears from main valve body (if not previously removed).

Cleaning & Inspection – 1) Clean components with solvent and dry with compressed air. Inspect components and replace if damaged.

2) Install oil pump gears in main valve body. Ensure chamfered and grooved side of oil pump driven gear is facing upward (toward separator plate side of main valve body).

3) Place straightedge across main valve body surface. Using a feeler gauge, measure thrust clearance between oil pump driven gear and straightedge. See Fig. 16. Replace oil pump gears and/or main valve body if thrust clearance is not within specification. See OIL PUMP SPECIFICATIONS table.

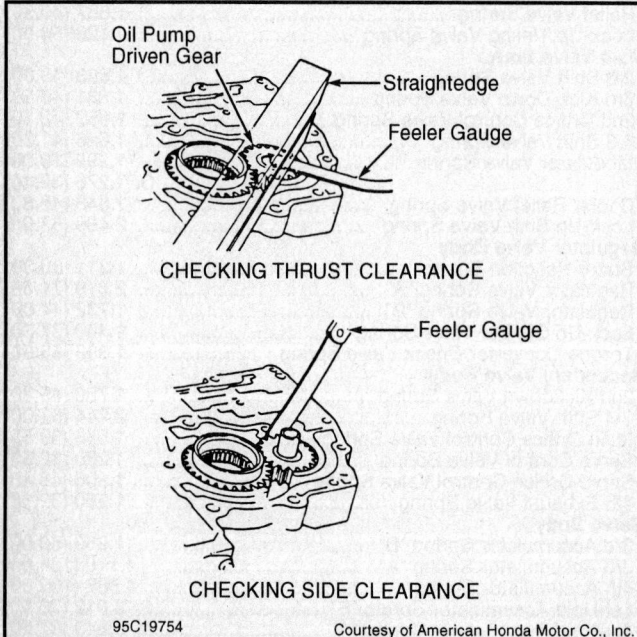

CHECKING THRUST CLEARANCE

CHECKING SIDE CLEARANCE

95C19754   Courtesy of American Honda Motor Co., Inc.

Fig. 16: Checking Oil Pump Clearances

4) Install oil pump driven gear shaft in oil pump driven gear. Using a feeler gauge, measure side clearance of both gears between tip of gear teeth and main valve body. See Fig. 16. Replace oil pump gears and/or main valve body if side clearance is not within specification. See OIL PUMP SPECIFICATIONS table.

OIL PUMP SPECIFICATIONS

Application	In. (mm)
Side Clearance	
Oil Pump Drive Gear	.0083-.0104 (.210-.265)
Oil Pump Driven Gear	.0028-.0049 (.070-.125)
Thrust Clearance	
Standard	.0010-.0020 (.030-.050)
Wear Limit	.0028 (.070)

Reassembly – Coat components with ATF. To reassemble, reverse disassembly procedure. Ensure chamfered and grooved side of oil pump driven gear faces upward (toward separator plate side of main valve body).

REGULATOR VALVE BODY

CAUTION: Regulator spring cap is under spring pressure. Ensure regulator spring cap is held down when removing stopper bolt. Use care when removing valve cap, as valve cap is under spring pressure.

Disassembly – Note direction of valve cap installation before removing from regulator valve body. Hold regulator spring cap down, and remove stopper bolt. Slowly remove regulator spring cap and components from regulator valve body. See Fig. 17.

Cleaning & Inspection – 1) Clean components with solvent and dry with compressed air. Replace regulator valve body assembly if any parts are worn or damaged.

2) Ensure all valves slide freely in their bores. If valves do not slide freely, polish burrs or rough areas using No. 600 sandpaper soaked in ATF for at least 30 minutes. Thoroughly clean regulator valve body and components if polishing was needed.

3) Ensure spring free length is within specification. See SPRING SPECIFICATIONS table. Replace springs if not within specification.

Reassembly – Coat all components and bores with ATF. To reassemble, reverse disassembly procedure. Ensure all components are installed in correct location. See Fig. 17. Tighten stopper bolt to specification. See TORQUE SPECIFICATIONS.

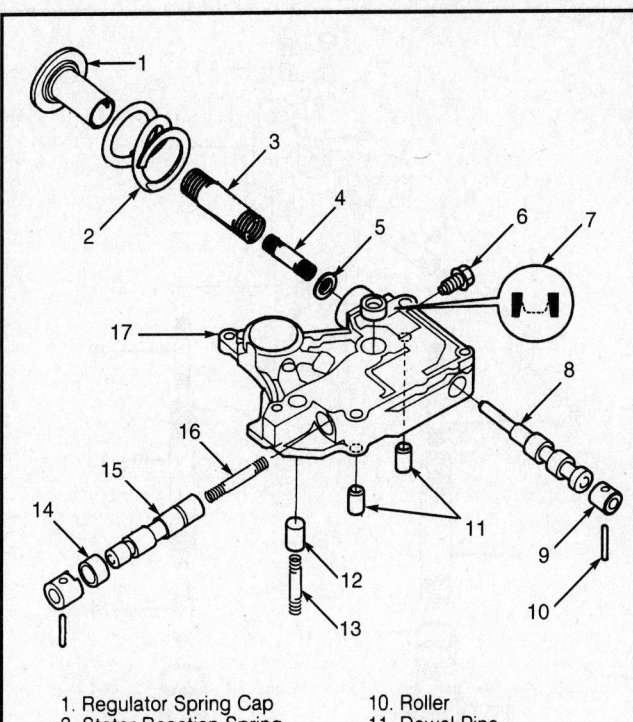

1. Regulator Spring Cap
2. Stator Reaction Spring
3. Regulator Valve Spring "A"
4. Regulator Valve Spring "B"
5. Regulator Spring Seat
6. Stop Bolt
7. Filter
8. Regulator Valve
9. Valve Cap
10. Roller
11. Dowel Pins
12. Torque Converter Check Valve
13. Torque Converter Check Valve Spring
14. Sleeve
15. Lock-Up Control Valve
16. Lock-Up Control Valve Spring
17. Regulator Valve Body

96E30662

Courtesy of American Honda Motor Co.,

Fig. 17: Exploded View Of Regulator Valve Body

LOCK-UP VALVE BODY

Disassembly – Note direction of valve cap installation before removing from lock-up valve body. Disassemble lock-up valve body. *See Fig. 18.* Use care when removing valve caps, as they are under spring pressure.

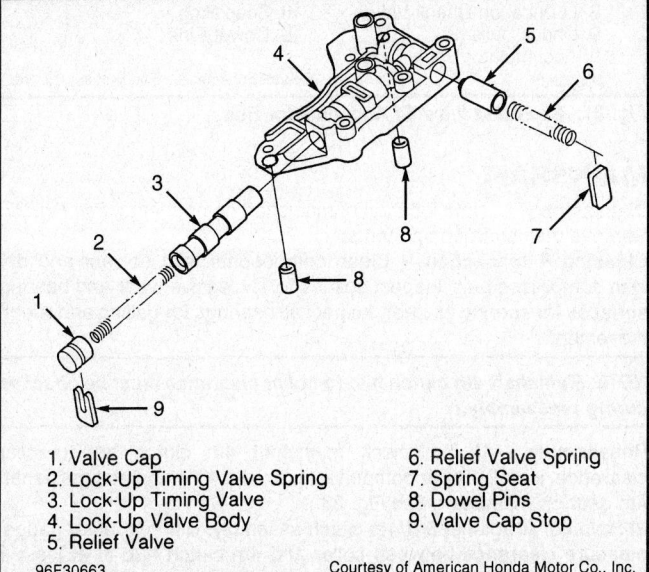

1. Valve Cap
2. Lock-Up Timing Valve Spring
3. Lock-Up Timing Valve
4. Lock-Up Valve Body
5. Relief Valve
6. Relief Valve Spring
7. Spring Seat
8. Dowel Pins
9. Valve Cap Stop

96F30663

Courtesy of American Honda Motor Co., Inc.

Fig. 18: Exploded View Of Lock-Up Valve Body

Cleaning & Inspection – 1) Clean components with solvent and dry with compressed air. Replace lock-up valve body assembly if any parts are worn or damaged.
2) Ensure all valves slide freely in their bores. If valves do not slide freely, polish burrs or rough areas using No. 600 sandpaper soaked for 30 minutes in ATF. Thoroughly clean lock-up valve body and components if polishing was needed.
3) Ensure spring free length is within specification. See SPRING SPECIFICATIONS table. Replace springs if not within specification.
Reassembly – Coat all components and bores with ATF. To reassemble, reverse disassembly procedure. *See Fig. 18.*

SECONDARY VALVE BODY

CAUTION: When disassembling secondary valve body, place secondary valve body components in order and mark spring locations for reassembly reference. DO NOT use force to remove components. DO NOT use magnet to remove check balls, as check balls may become magnetized. Note direction of valve cap installation before removing from secondary valve body.

Disassembly – Disassemble secondary valve body. *See Fig. 19.* Use care when removing valve caps or spring seats, as they are under spring pressure.
Cleaning & Inspection – 1) Clean components with solvent and dry with compressed air. Replace secondary valve body assembly if any parts are worn or damaged.
2) Ensure all valves slide freely in their bores. If valves do not slide freely, polish burrs or rough areas using No. 600 sandpaper soaked for 30 minutes in ATF. Thoroughly clean secondary valve body and components if polishing was needed.
3) Ensure spring free length is within specification. See SPRING SPECIFICATIONS table. Replace springs if not within specification.
Reassembly – Coat all components and bores with ATF. To reassemble, reverse disassembly procedure. Ensure all components are installed in correct location. *See Fig. 19.*

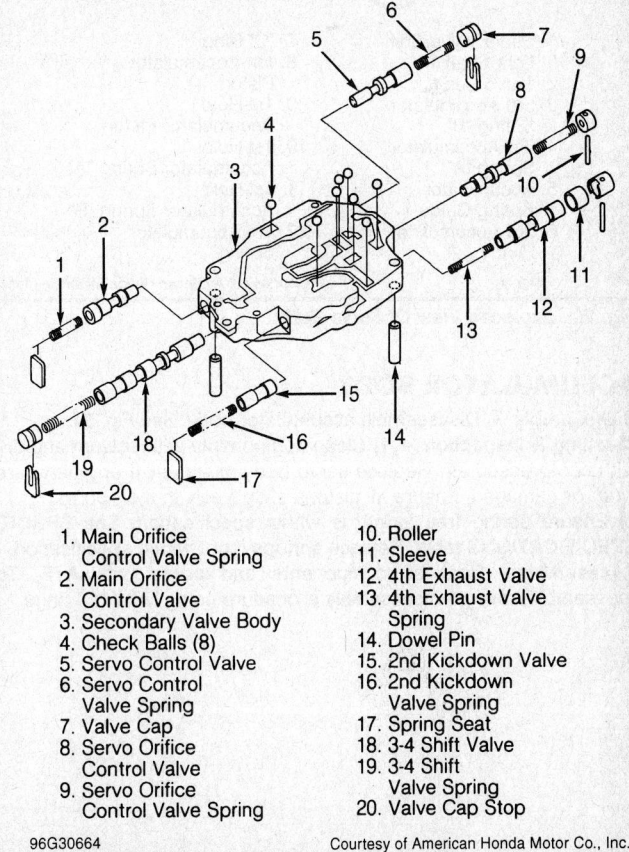

1. Main Orifice Control Valve Spring
2. Main Orifice Control Valve
3. Secondary Valve Body
4. Check Balls (8)
5. Servo Control Valve
6. Servo Control Valve Spring
7. Valve Cap
8. Servo Orifice Control Valve
9. Servo Orifice Control Valve Spring
10. Roller
11. Sleeve
12. 4th Exhaust Valve
13. 4th Exhaust Valve Spring
14. Dowel Pin
15. 2nd Kickdown Valve
16. 2nd Kickdown Valve Spring
17. Spring Seat
18. 3-4 Shift Valve
19. 3-4 Shift Valve Spring
20. Valve Cap Stop

96G30664

Courtesy of American Honda Motor Co., Inc.

Fig. 19: Exploded View Of Secondary Valve Body

SERVO BODY

Disassembly – Disassemble servo body. *See Fig. 20.*

Cleaning & Inspection – 1) Clean components with solvent and dry with compressed air. Replace servo body assembly if any parts are worn or damaged. Ensure all pistons slide freely in their bores.
2) Ensure spring free length is within specification. See SPRING SPECIFICATIONS table. Replace springs if not within specification.

Reassembly – Coat all components and bores with ATF. To reassemble, reverse disassembly procedure using NEW "O" rings.

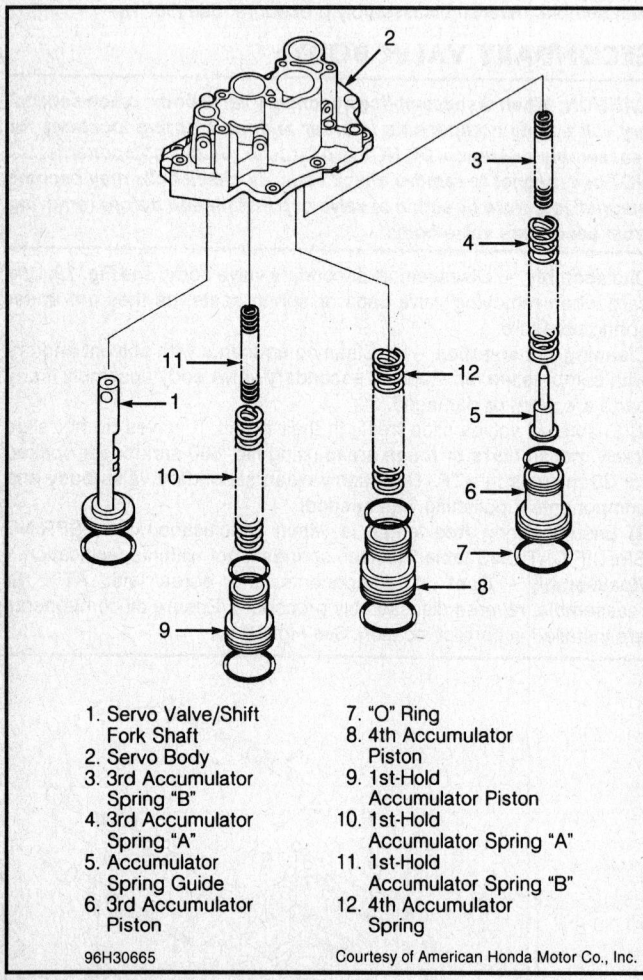

1. Servo Valve/Shift Fork Shaft	7. "O" Ring
2. Servo Body	8. 4th Accumulator Piston
3. 3rd Accumulator Spring "B"	9. 1st-Hold Accumulator Piston
4. 3rd Accumulator Spring "A"	10. 1st-Hold Accumulator Spring "A"
5. Accumulator Spring Guide	11. 1st-Hold Accumulator Spring "B"
6. 3rd Accumulator Piston	12. 4th Accumulator Spring

96H30665   Courtesy of American Honda Motor Co., Inc.

Fig. 20: Exploded View Of Servo Body

ACCUMULATOR BODY

Disassembly – Disassemble accumulator body. *See Fig. 21.*

Cleaning & Inspection – 1) Clean components with solvent and dry with compressed air. Replace servo body assembly if any parts are worn or damaged. Ensure all pistons slide freely in their bores.
2) Ensure spring free length is within specification. See SPRING SPECIFICATIONS table. Replace springs if not within specification.

Reassembly – Coat all components and bores with ATF. To reassemble, reverse disassembly procedure using NEW "O" rings.

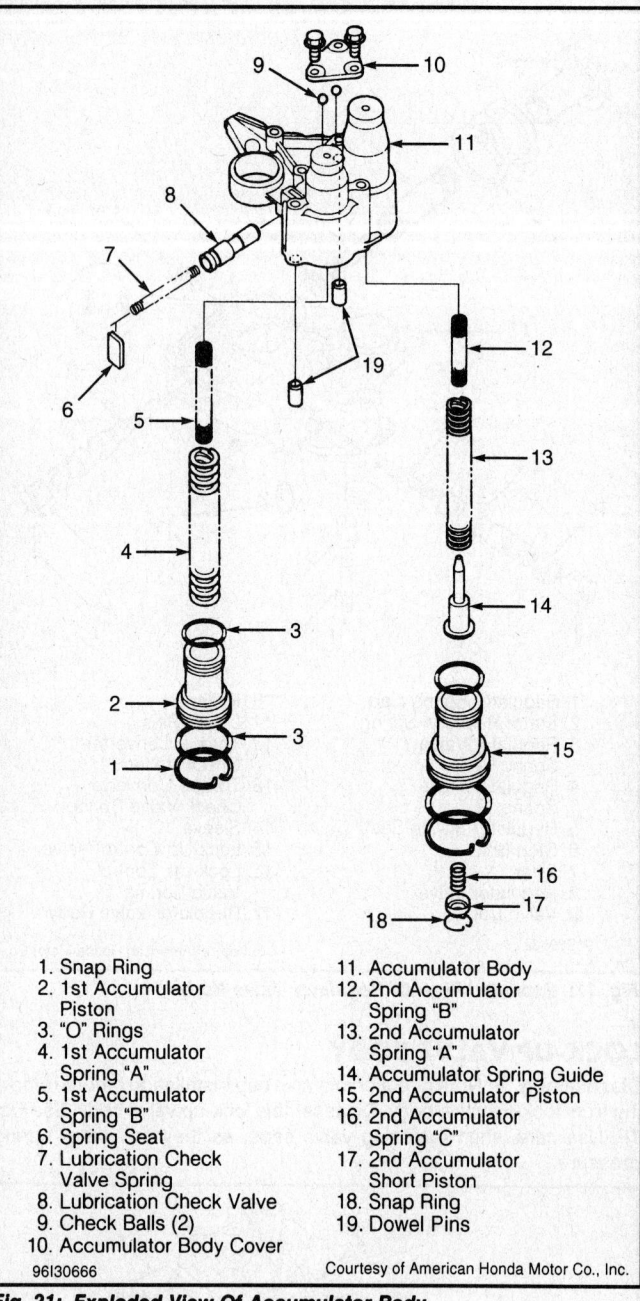

1. Snap Ring	11. Accumulator Body
2. 1st Accumulator Piston	12. 2nd Accumulator Spring "B"
3. "O" Rings	13. 2nd Accumulator Spring "A"
4. 1st Accumulator Spring "A"	14. Accumulator Spring Guide
5. 1st Accumulator Spring "B"	15. 2nd Accumulator Piston
6. Spring Seat	16. 2nd Accumulator Spring "C"
7. Lubrication Check Valve Spring	17. 2nd Accumulator Short Piston
8. Lubrication Check Valve	18. Snap Ring
9. Check Balls (2)	19. Dowel Pins
10. Accumulator Body Cover	

96I30666   Courtesy of American Honda Motor Co., Inc.

Fig. 21: Exploded View Of Accumulator Body

MAINSHAFT

Disassembly – Note location of mainshaft components. *See Fig. 22.* Remove mainshaft components.

Cleaning & Inspection – Clean components with solvent and dry with compressed air. Inspect splines for excessive wear and bearing surfaces for scoring or wear. Inspect all bearings for galling and rough movement.

NOTE: Mainshaft 4th clutch hub-to-collar clearance must be checked during reassembly.

Reassembly – 1) To check mainshaft 4th clutch hub-to-collar clearance, install proper components, except "O" rings and mainshaft 4th gear on mainshaft. *See Fig. 23.*
2) Hold collar against 3rd/4th clutch assembly. Using a feeler gauge, measure clearance between collar and 4th clutch hub in at least 3 places. *See Fig. 24.* Use average measurement as actual clearance. Specified clearance is .001-.004" (.03-.11 mm).

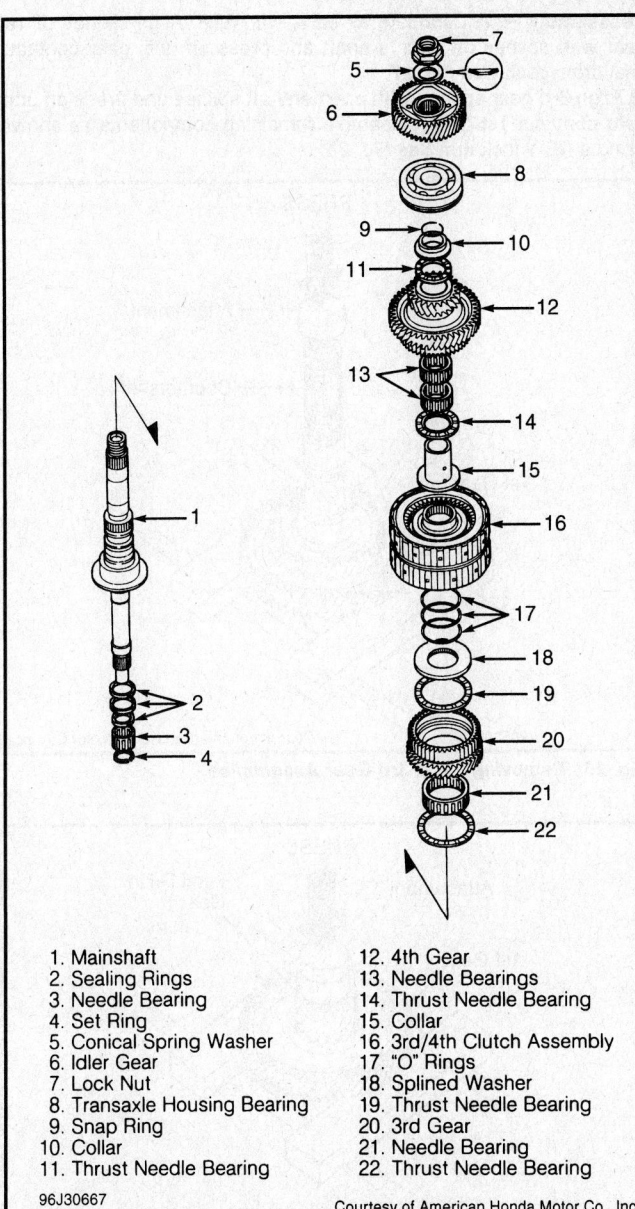

1. Mainshaft
2. Sealing Rings
3. Needle Bearing
4. Set Ring
5. Conical Spring Washer
6. Idler Gear
7. Lock Nut
8. Transaxle Housing Bearing
9. Snap Ring
10. Collar
11. Thrust Needle Bearing
12. 4th Gear
13. Needle Bearings
14. Thrust Needle Bearing
15. Collar
16. 3rd/4th Clutch Assembly
17. "O" Rings
18. Splined Washer
19. Thrust Needle Bearing
20. 3rd Gear
21. Needle Bearing
22. Thrust Needle Bearing

96J30667　　　　　　　　Courtesy of American Honda Motor Co., Inc.

Fig. 22: Exploded View Of Mainshaft Assembly

3) If clearance is not as specified, remove splined washer and measure thickness. Different thickness splined washers are available. Select and install a new splined washer to obtain proper clearance. See MAINSHAFT SPLINED WASHER THICKNESS table.

4) Once correct thickness splined washer is obtained, lubricate all components with ATF. Reassemble mainshaft using a NEW lock nut. Before installing NEW "O" rings on mainshaft, wrap splines with tape.

MAINSHAFT SPLINED WASHER THICKNESS

Washer Number	Part Number	Thickness In. (mm)
1	90414-P0Z-000	.191 (4.85)
2	90415-P0Z-000	.193 (4.90)
3	90416-P0Z-000	.195 (4.95)
4	90417-P0Z-000	.197 (5.00)
5	90418-P0Z-000	.199 (5.05)
6	90419-P0Z-000	.201 (5.10)

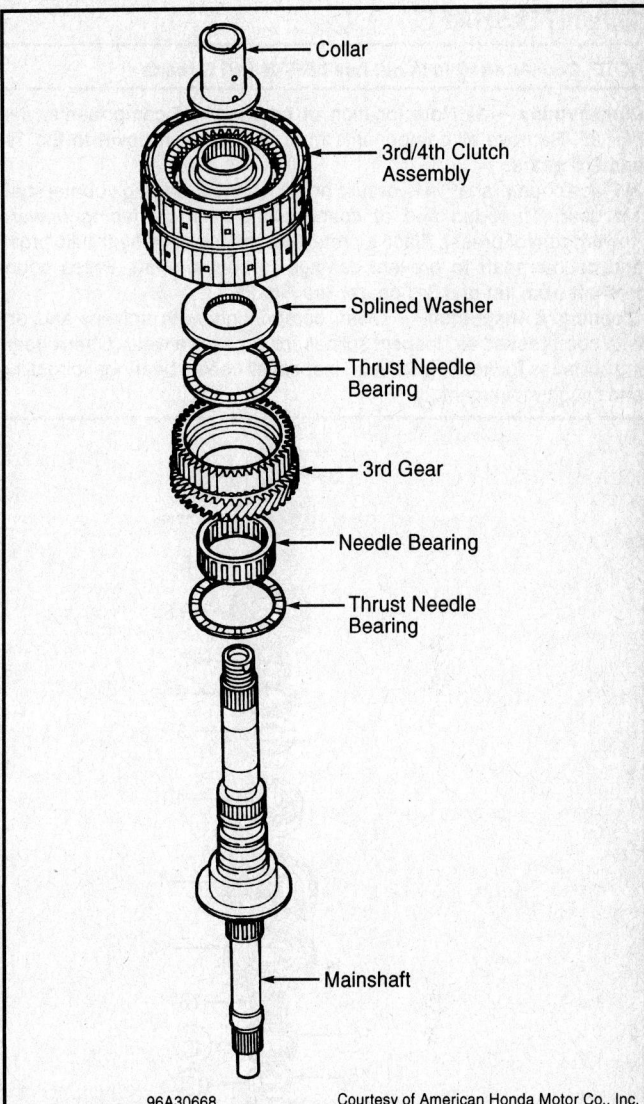

96A30668　　　　　　　　Courtesy of American Honda Motor Co., Inc.

Fig. 23: Installed Components For Clearance Check

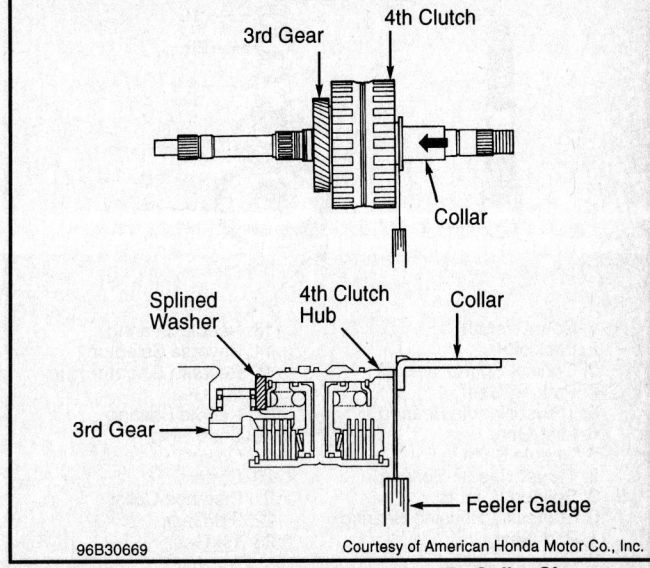

96B30669　　　　　　　　Courtesy of American Honda Motor Co., Inc.

Fig. 24: Measuring Mainshaft 4th Clutch Hub-To-Collar Clearance

COUNTERSHAFT

NOTE: Countershaft lock nut has LEFT-HAND threads.

Disassembly – 1) Note location of countershaft components. *See Fig. 25.* Remove all components from countershaft down to the 1st and 3rd gears.

2) Place countershaft in hydraulic press while supporting countershaft 1st gear. Threaded end of countershaft must be facing upward (toward ram of press). Place a protective cap between hydraulic press and countershaft to prevent damage to countershaft. Press countershaft from 1st and 3rd gears. *See Fig. 26.*

Cleaning & Inspection – Clean components with solvent and dry with compressed air. Inspect splines for excessive wear. Check bearing surfaces for scoring or wear. Inspect all needle bearings for galling and rough movement.

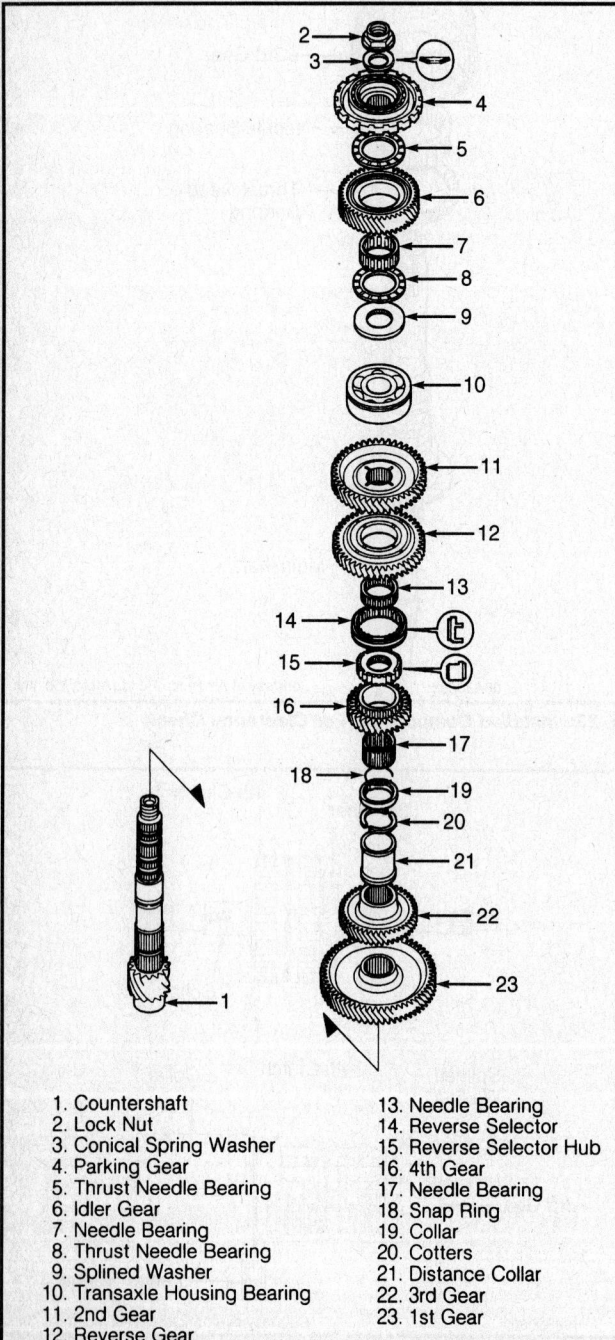

1. Countershaft
2. Lock Nut
3. Conical Spring Washer
4. Parking Gear
5. Thrust Needle Bearing
6. Idler Gear
7. Needle Bearing
8. Thrust Needle Bearing
9. Splined Washer
10. Transaxle Housing Bearing
11. 2nd Gear
12. Reverse Gear
13. Needle Bearing
14. Reverse Selector
15. Reverse Selector Hub
16. 4th Gear
17. Needle Bearing
18. Snap Ring
19. Collar
20. Cotters
21. Distance Collar
22. 3rd Gear
23. 1st Gear

96E30670   Courtesy of American Honda Motor Co., Inc.

Fig. 25: Exploded View Of Countershaft Components

Reassembly – 1) Lubricate all parts with ATF. Align splines of 1st gear with splines on countershaft and press on until gear contacts final drive gear. *See Fig. 27.*

2) Align 3rd gear splines with countershaft splines and press on until gear contacts 1st gear. Assemble remaining components as shown using a NEW lock nut. *See Fig. 25.*

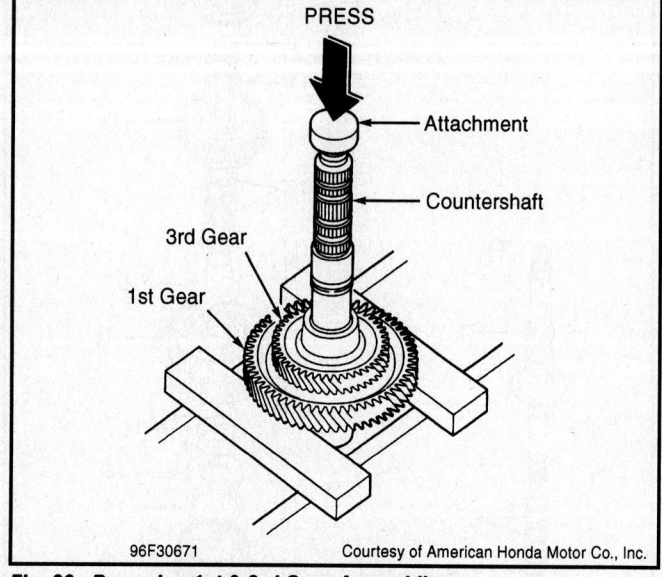

96F30671   Courtesy of American Honda Motor Co., Inc.

Fig. 26: Removing 1st & 3rd Gear Assemblies

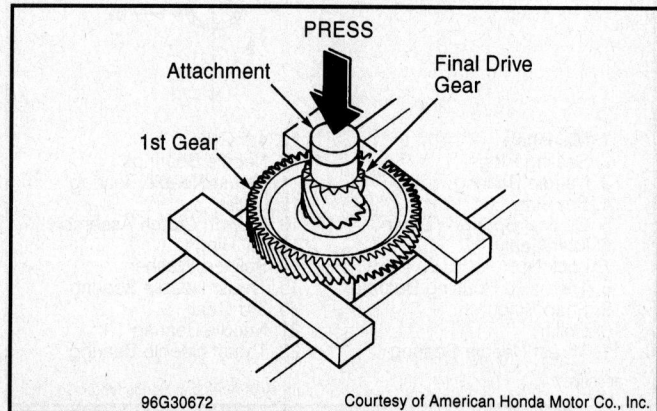

96G30672   Courtesy of American Honda Motor Co., Inc.

Fig. 27: Installing 1st Gear

SECONDARY SHAFT

NOTE: Secondary shaft lock nut has LEFT-HAND threads.

Disassembly – Note location of secondary shaft components. *See Fig. 28.* Remove secondary shaft components.

Cleaning & Inspection – Clean components with solvent and dry with compressed air. Inspect splines for excessive wear. Check bearing surfaces for scoring or wear. Inspect all needle bearings for galling and rough movement.

Reassembly (2nd Gear) – 1) Lubricate all components with ATF. Reassemble specified secondary shaft components without "O" rings. *See Fig. 29.* Position dial indicator against 2nd gear. Hold thrust washer against clutch assembly. Measure 2nd gear axial clearance in at least 3 places while moving 2nd gear. *See Fig. 30.* Use average measurement as actual clearance. Specified clearance is .003-.006" (.07-.15 mm).

2) If clearance is not as specified, remove splined washer under 2nd gear and measure thickness. Different thickness splined washers are available. Select and install a new splined washer to obtain proper clearance. See 2ND GEAR SPLINED WASHER THICKNESS table.

3) Once correct thickness splined washer is obtained, lubricate all components with ATF. Reassemble using a NEW lock nut. Before installing NEW "O" rings on secondary shaft, wrap splines with tape.

2ND GEAR SPLINED WASHER THICKNESS

Washer Number	Part Number	Thickness In. (mm)
1	90406-P0Z-000	.193 (4.90)
2	90407-P0Z-000	.195 (4.95)
3	90408-P0Z-000	.197 (5.00)
4	90409-P0Z-000	.199 (5.05)
5	90410-P0Z-000	.201 (5.10)
6	90411-P0Z-000	.203 (5.15)
7	90412-P0Z-000	.205 (5.20)

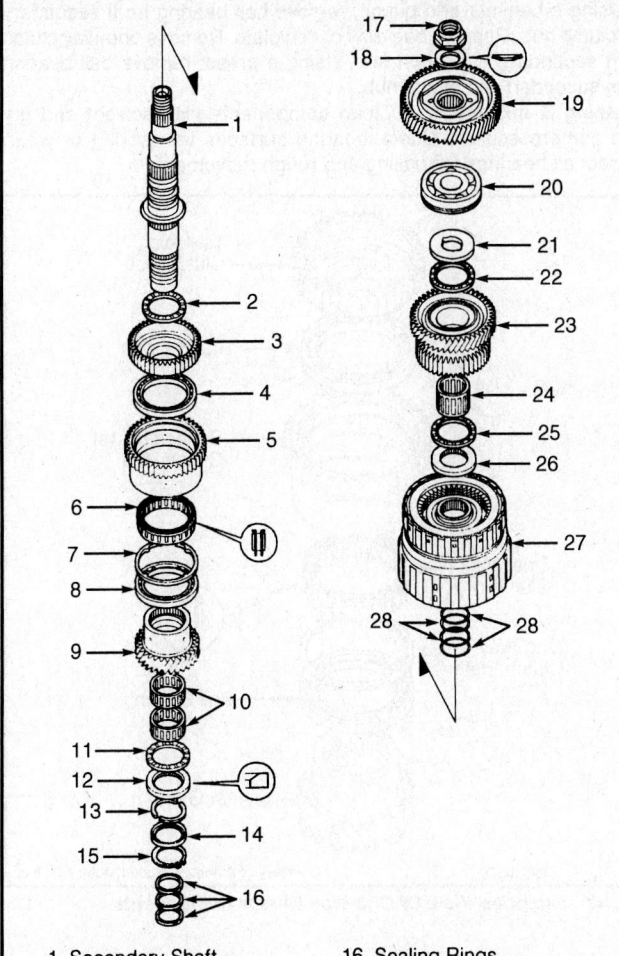

1. Secondary Shaft
2. Thrust Needle Bearing
3. 1st-Hold Clutch Hub
4. Ball Bearing
5. Secondary 1st Clutch Hub
6. One-Way Clutch
7. One-Way Clutch Plate
8. Ball Bearing
9. 1st Gear
10. Needle Bearings
11. Thrust Needle Bearing
12. Splined Washer
13. Cotters
14. Cotter Retainer
15. Snap Ring
16. Sealing Rings
17. Lock Nut
18. Conical Spring Washer
19. Idler Gear
20. Transaxle Housing Bearing
21. Thrust Washer
22. Thrust Needle Bearing
23. 2nd Gear
24. Needle Bearing
25. Thrust Needle Bearing
26. Splined Washer
27. 1st/1st-Hold/2nd Clutch Assembly
28. "O" Rings

96H30673   Courtesy of American Honda Motor Co., Inc.

Fig. 28: Exploded View Of Secondary Shaft Components

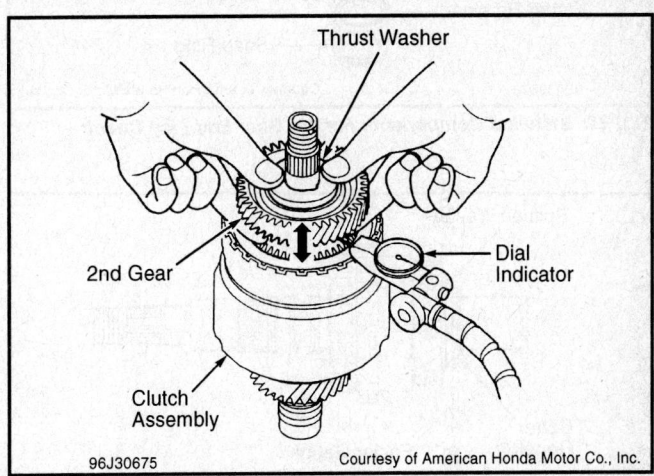

- Thrust Washer
- Thrust Needle Bearing
- 2nd Gear
- Needle Bearing
- Thrust Needle Bearing
- Splined Washer
- 1st/1st-Hold/2nd Clutch Assembly
- Secondary Shaft

96I30674   Courtesy of American Honda Motor Co., Inc.

Fig. 29: Installed Components For 2nd Gear End Play Check

Thrust Washer

2nd Gear

Dial Indicator

Clutch Assembly

96J30675   Courtesy of American Honda Motor Co., Inc.

Fig. 30: Measuring 2nd Gear End Play

Reassembly (1st Gear) – 1) Lubricate all components with ATF. Reassemble specified secondary shaft components. *See Fig. 31.* Using a feeler gauge, measure clearance between splined washer and cotter retainer in at least 3 places. *See Fig. 32.* Use average measurement as actual clearance. Specified clearance is .003-.006" (.07-.15 mm).

2) If clearance is not as specified, remove splined washer and measure thickness. Different thickness splined washers are available. Select and install a new splined washer to obtain proper clearance. See 1ST GEAR SPLINED WASHER THICKNESS table.

3) Once correct thickness splined washer is obtained, lubricate all components with ATF and reassemble. Before installing NEW "O" rings on secondary shaft, wrap splines with tape.

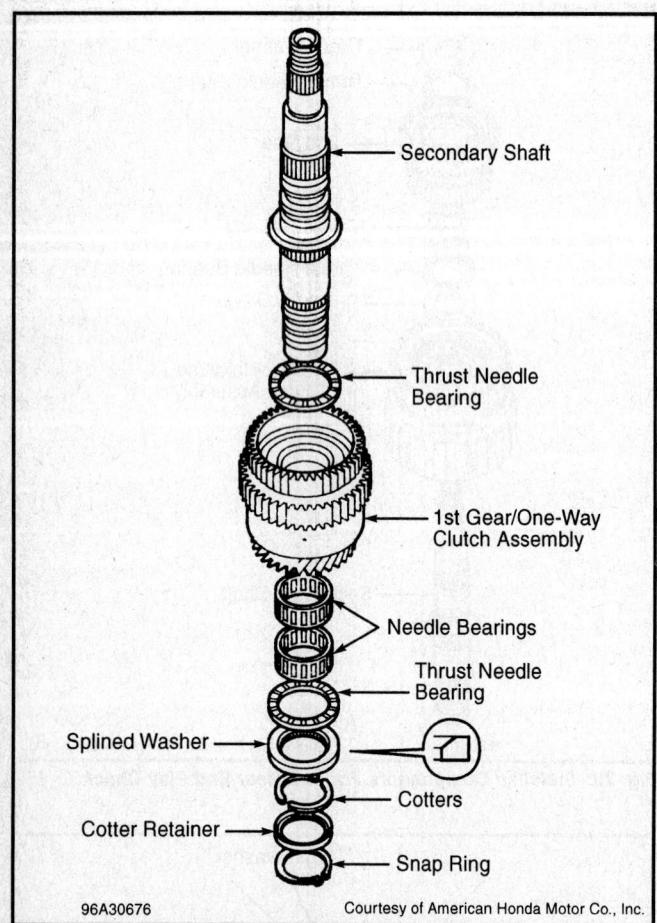

Fig. 31: Installed Components For 1st Gear End Play Check

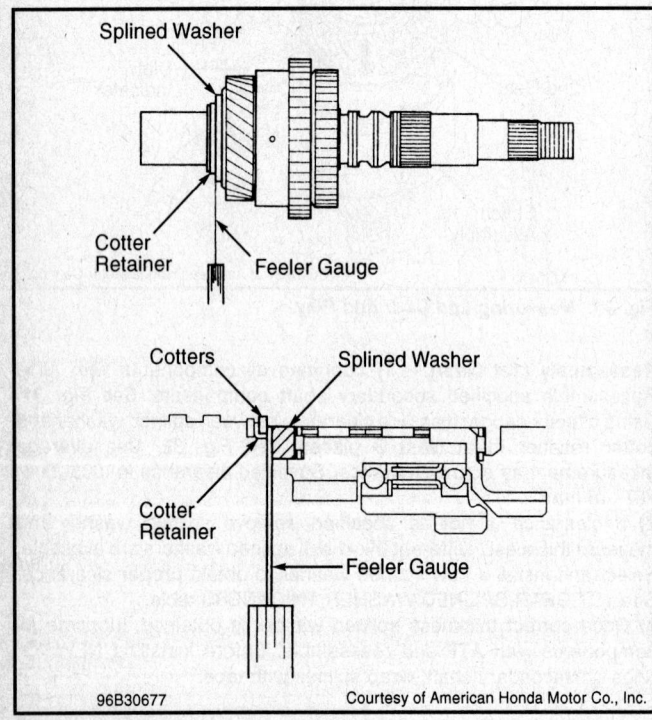

Fig. 32: Measuring 1st Gear End Play

1ST GEAR SPLINED WASHER THICKNESS

Washer Number	Part Number	Thickness In. (mm)
1	90502-P0Z-000	.270 (6.85)
2	90503-P0Z-000	.272 (6.90)
3	90504-P0Z-000	.274 (6.95)
4	90505-P0Z-000	.276 (7.00)
5	90506-P0Z-000	.278 (7.05)
6	90507-P0Z-000	.280 (7.10)

SECONDARY SHAFT ONE-WAY CLUTCH

Disassembly – 1) Note location of one-way clutch components. *See Fig. 33.* Using a press, remove 1st-hold clutch hub from secondary 1st clutch hub. Separate secondary 1st clutch hub from 1st gear by turning secondary 1st clutch hub clockwise.

2) Using a hammer and punch, remove ball bearing from secondary 1st clutch hub. Remove one-way clutch plate. Remove one-way clutch from secondary 1st clutch hub. Using a press, remove ball bearing from secondary 1st clutch hub.

Cleaning & Inspection – Clean components with solvent and dry with compressed air. Check bearing surfaces for scoring or wear. Inspect all bearings for galling and rough movement.

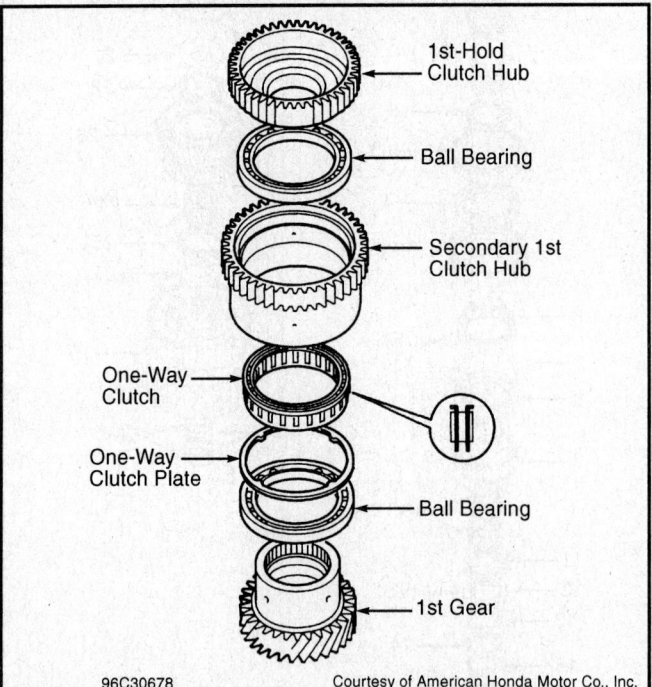

Fig. 33: Exploded View Of One-Way Clutch Components

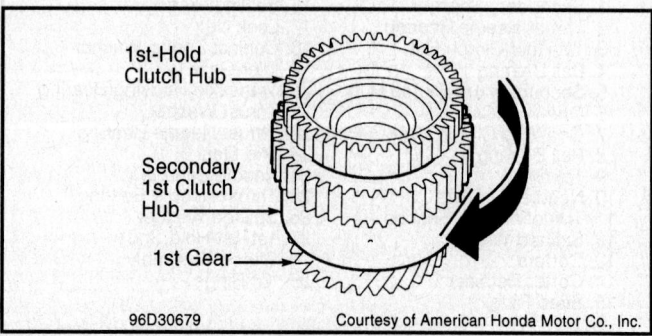

Fig. 34: One-Way Clutch Rotation

Reassembly – 1) Lubricate all components with ATF. Using a press, install ball bearing in gear side of secondary 1st clutch hub. Install one-way clutch in secondary 1st clutch hub in direction shown. *See Fig. 33.* Install one-way clutch plate in secondary 1st clutch hub.

2) Using a press, install ball bearing in secondary 1st clutch hub. Assemble secondary 1st clutch hub and 1st gear by holding 1st gear and turning secondary 1st clutch hub clockwise.

3) Using a press, install 1st-hold clutch hub in 1st gear. Ensure one-way clutch rotates in proper direction. *See Fig. 34.*

CLUTCH ASSEMBLIES

Disassembly – 1) Remove snap ring, clutch end plate, clutch discs and clutch plates. *See Figs. 35 and 36.*

2) Remove disc spring (except 1st-hold clutch). Install appropriate clutch spring compressor. Compress return spring and remove circlip.

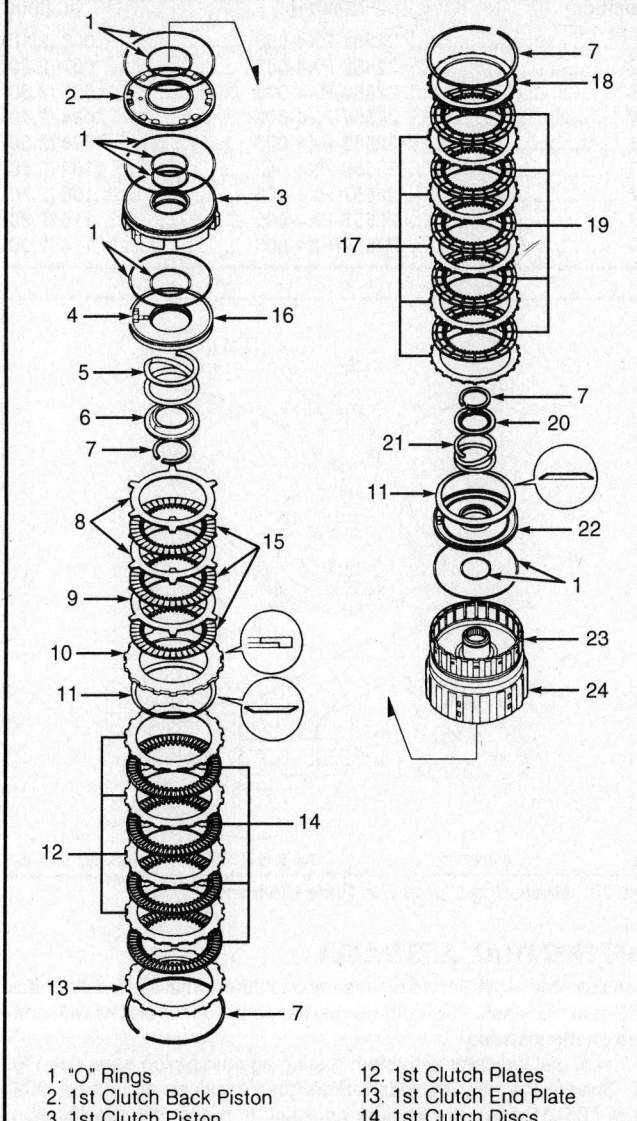

1. "O" Rings	12. 1st Clutch Plates
2. 1st Clutch Back Piston	13. 1st Clutch End Plate
3. 1st Clutch Piston	14. 1st Clutch Discs
4. Check Ball	15. 1st-Hold Clutch Discs
5. Return Spring	16. 1st-Hold Clutch Piston
6. Spring Retainer	17. Clutch Plates
7. Snap Ring	18. Clutch End Plate
8. 1st-Hold Clutch Plates	19. Clutch Discs
9. 1st-Hold Clutch End Plate	20. Spring Retainer
10. 1st-Hold Clutch Plate "B"	21. Return Spring
11. Disc Spring	22. 2nd Clutch Piston
	23. 2nd Clutch Drum
	24. 1st/1st-Hold Clutch Drum

96G30680   Courtesy of American Honda Motor Co., Inc.

Fig. 35: Exploded View Of 1st/1st-Hold/2nd Clutch Assemblies

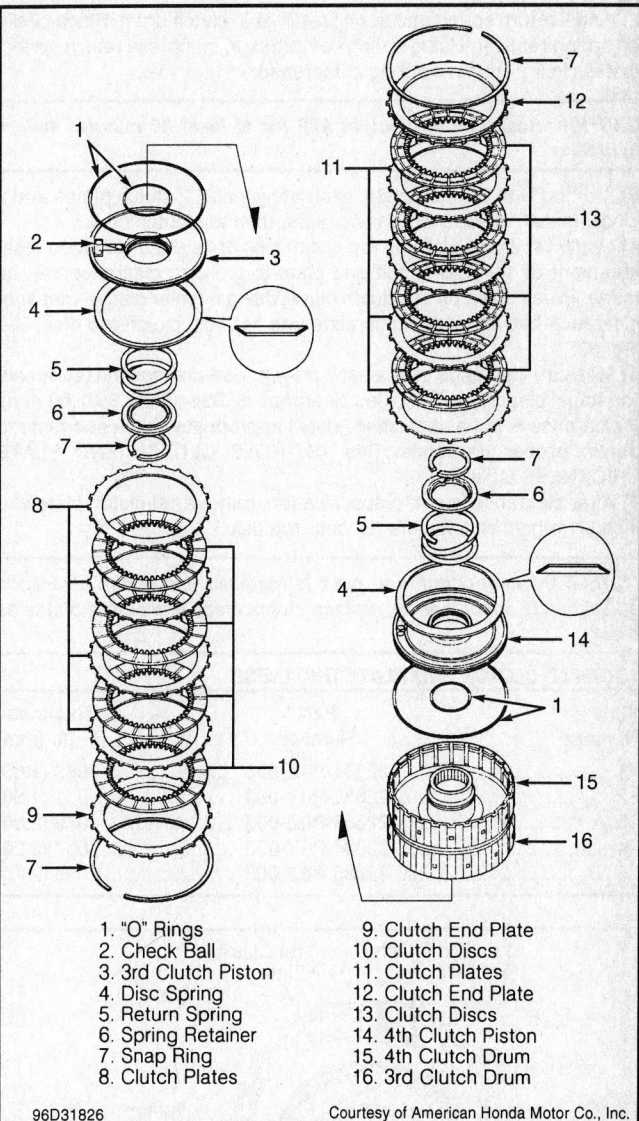

1. "O" Rings	9. Clutch End Plate
2. Check Ball	10. Clutch Discs
3. 3rd Clutch Piston	11. Clutch Plates
4. Disc Spring	12. Clutch End Plate
5. Return Spring	13. Clutch Discs
6. Spring Retainer	14. 4th Clutch Piston
7. Snap Ring	15. 4th Clutch Drum
8. Clutch Plates	16. 3rd Clutch Drum

96D31826   Courtesy of American Honda Motor Co., Inc.

Fig. 36: Exploded View Of 3rd/4th Clutch Assemblies

Release and remove spring compressor. Remove spring retainer and return spring.

3) Wrap shop towel around clutch drum. Apply light air pressure to oil passage on clutch drum to remove clutch piston. Remove "O" rings.

4) Install secondary shaft with old "O" rings in 1st/1st-hold/2nd clutch drum. Remove 1st clutch piston by applying air pressure to secondary shaft fluid passage.

5) Remove 1st/1st-hold/2nd clutch drum from secondary shaft. Remove 1st-hold clutch piston by applying air pressure to 1st clutch piston fluid passage. Remove 1st clutch back piston by applying air pressure to outside of 1st clutch drum.

Cleaning & Inspection – 1) Clean metal components with solvent and dry with compressed air. Ensure check valve on rear of clutch piston is thoroughly cleaned and securely fastened on clutch piston.

2) Inspect components for damage. Replace if necessary. Ensure no rough edges are present on "O" ring sealing areas.

Reassembly (1st-Hold Clutch) – 1) Lubricate all components with ATF. Install NEW "O" rings. Install clutch piston in clutch drum. Slightly rotate clutch piston back and forth during installation to prevent damaging "O" rings.

CAUTION: DO NOT apply excessive force on clutch piston or "O" rings will be damaged.

2) Install return spring and spring retainer in clutch drum. Place circlip on spring retainer. Using spring compressor, compress return spring. Install circlip. Remove spring compressor.

CAUTION: Soak clutch discs in ATF for at least 30 minutes before installing.

3) Starting with a clutch plate, alternately install 2 clutch plates and 2 discs. Install 1st-hold clutch end plate, then top clutch disc.

4) Install 1st clutch plate on top clutch disc of 1st-hold clutch so measurement of 1st-hold clutch end plate-to-top disc clearance can be made. Press down on 1st clutch plate. Using a feeler gauge, measure clearance between 1st clutch plate and 1st-hold clutch top disc. See Fig. 37.

5) Measure clearance in at least 3 places. Use average measurement for actual clearance. Specified clearance is .024-.039" (.60-1.00 mm). If clearance is not as specified, install appropriate clutch end plate to obtain proper clearance. See 1ST-HOLD CLUTCH END PLATE THICKNESS table.

6) After clearance is set to specification, remove 1st clutch plate and install 1st-hold clutch plate "B" onto top disc.

NOTE: If thickest clutch end plate is installed and clutch clearance still exceeds specification, replace clutch discs and clutch plates as a set.

1ST-HOLD CLUTCH END PLATE THICKNESS

Plate Number	Part Number	Thickness In. (mm)
1	22681-P0Z-003	.063 (1.60)
2	22682-P0Z-003	.071 (1.80)
N/A	22683-P0Z-003	.079 (2.00)
4	22684-P0Z-003	.087 (2.20)
5	22685-P0Z-003	.095 (2.40)

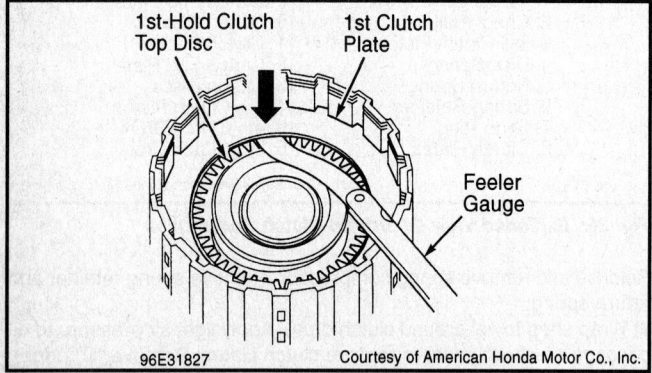

Fig. 37: Measuring 1st Clutch Plate-To-1st-Hold Clutch Top Disc Clearance

Reassembly (1st, 2nd & 3rd/4th Clutches) – 1) Install disc spring into clutch drum. Starting with a clutch plate, alternately install clutch plates and discs. Install clutch end plate with flat side toward disc. Install snap ring.

2) Using a dial indicator, measure clearance between clutch end plate and top disc. Zero dial indicator with clutch end plate lowered, and lift up to snap ring for measurement. See Fig. 38.

3) Take measurements in at least 3 places. Use average measurement for actual clearance. Ensure clearance is within specification. See TRANSAXLE SPECIFICATIONS table.

4) If clearance is not as specified, install appropriate clutch end plate to obtain proper clearance. See appropriate CLUTCH END PLATE THICKNESS table.

NOTE: If thickest clutch end plate is installed and clutch clearance still exceeds specification, replace clutch discs and clutch plates as a set.

1ST CLUTCH END PLATE THICKNESS

Plate Number	Part Number	Thickness In. (mm)
1	22551-P0Z-003	.083 (2.10)
2	22552-P0Z-003	.087 (2.20)
3	22553-P0Z-003	.091 (2.30)
4	22554-P0Z-003	.094 (2.40)
5	22555-P0Z-003	.098 (2.50)
6	22556-P0Z-003	.102 (2.60)
7	22557-P0Z-003	.106 (2.70)
8	22558-P0Z-003	.110 (2.80)
9	22559-P0Z-003	.114 (2.90)

2ND, 3RD & 4TH CLUTCH END PLATE THICKNESS

Plate Number	Part Number	Thickness In. (mm)
1	22551-PX4-003	.083 (2.10)
2	22552-PX4-003	.087 (2.20)
3	22553-PX4-003	.091 (2.30)
4	22554-PX4-003	.094 (2.40)
5	22555-PX4-003	.098 (2.50)
6	22556-PX4-003	.102 (2.60)
7	22557-PX4-003	.106 (2.70)
8	22558-PX4-003	.110 (2.80)
9	22559-PX4-003	.114 (2.90)

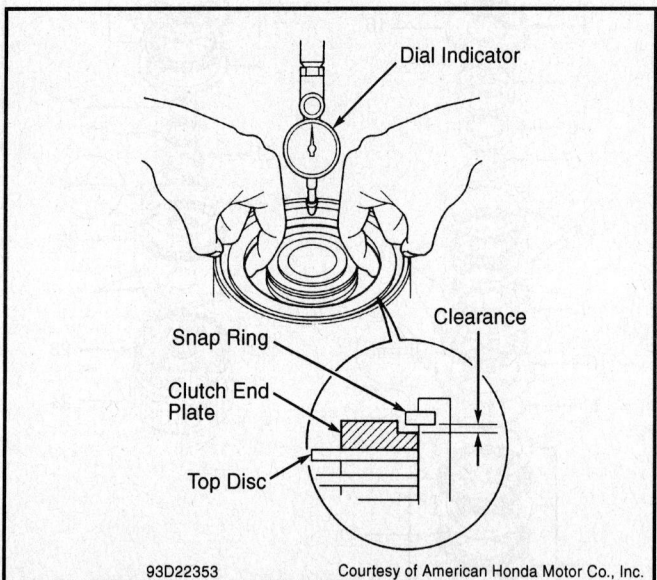

Fig. 38: Measuring Clutch End Plate Clearance

DIFFERENTIAL ASSEMBLY

Disassembly – 1) Before disassembling differential assembly, check side gear backlash. Place differential assembly on "V" blocks with both axle shafts installed.

2) Install dial indicator with stem resting against pinion gear. See Fig. 39. Check side gear backlash. Side gear backlash should be .002-.006" (.05-.15 mm). If side gear backlash is not within specification, replace differential carrier.

CAUTION: Ring gear must be installed with chamfered side of ring gear toward differential carrier. See Fig. 40. Ring gear bolts are LEFT-HAND thread.

3) If replacing bearings, use bearing puller to remove bearings from differential carrier. Remove bolts and ring gear.

Cleaning & Inspection – Clean components with solvent and dry with compressed air. Inspect components for wear and damage. Replace components as necessary.

Reassembly – If installing NEW bearings, bearing preload must be checked and adjusted. See DIFFERENTIAL ASSEMBLY BEARING PRELOAD under TRANSAXLE REASSEMBLY. Install ring gear and tighten ring gear bolts to 75 ft. lbs. (102 N.m).

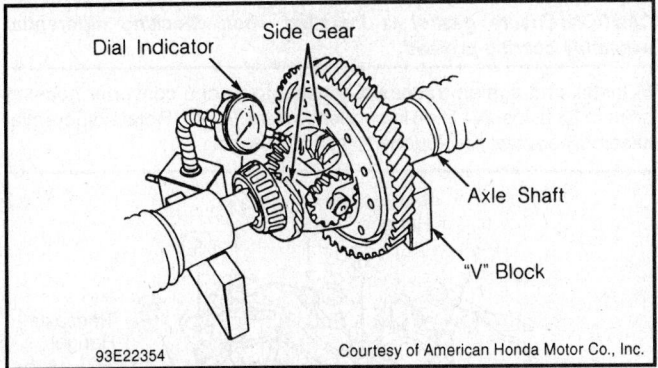

93E22354   Courtesy of American Honda Motor Co., Inc.

Fig. 39: Checking Side Gear Backlash

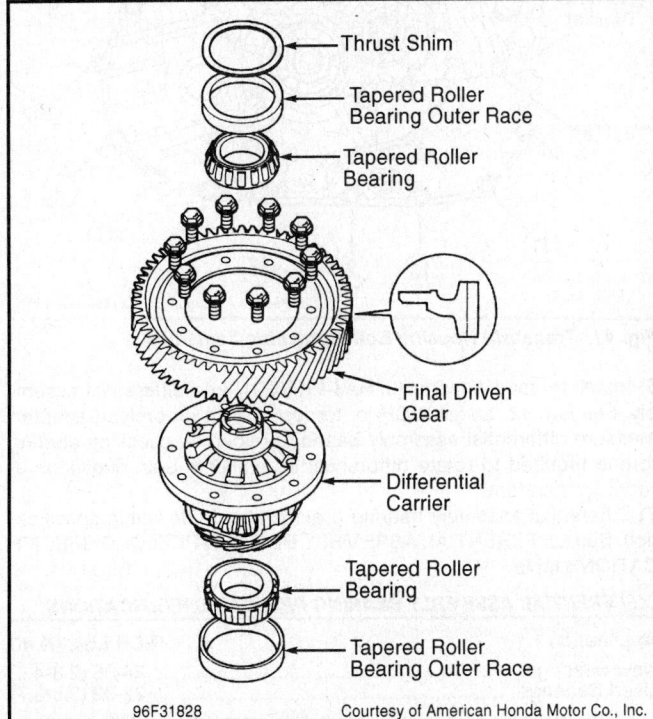

96F31828   Courtesy of American Honda Motor Co., Inc.

Fig. 40: Exploded View Of Differential Assembly

TORQUE CONVERTER HOUSING

Disassembly – **1)** Remove countershaft bearing from torque converter housing using a slide hammer (if necessary). Remove oil guide plate from torque converter housing.

CAUTION: DO NOT heat torque converter housing to more than 212°F (100°C) or torque converter housing may be damaged.

---

2) Remove secondary shaft bearing from torque converter housing using a slide hammer (if necessary). Remove oil guide plate from torque converter housing.
3) Remove snap ring from mainshaft bearing. Remove oil seal and mainshaft bearing from torque converter housing using a slide hammer (if necessary).
4) If removing differential bearing outer race from torque converter housing, use heat gun to heat torque converter housing around differential bearing outer race to 212°F (100°C).

5) Tap bearing race from torque converter housing. Using a hammer and drift, tap differential oil seal from torque converter housing.
Cleaning & Inspection – Clean components with solvent and dry with compressed air. Inspect torque converter housing for cracks and damage in bearing areas. Replace torque converter housing if damaged.
Reassembly – **1)** To install mainshaft bearing, use a hammer and bearing remover/installer to install bearing until bearing bottoms in torque converter housing.
2) Using a hammer and oil seal installer, install NEW mainshaft oil seal in torque converter housing. Oil seal should be flush with torque converter housing surface.
3) To install countershaft bearing, install oil guide plate in countershaft bearing bore of torque converter housing. Ensure oil guide plate is installed so tab in center of oil guide plate faces upward (away from torque converter housing surface).
4) Using a hammer and bearing installer, install countershaft bearing into torque converter housing. To install secondary shaft bearing, install oil guide plate in secondary shaft bearing bore of torque converter housing.
5) Ensure oil guide plate is installed so tab in center of oil guide plate is facing upward (away from torque converter housing surface). Ensure oil guide is installed to a depth of 0-.001" (0-.03 mm), zero being flush and .001" is past flush. Using a hammer and bearing installer, install secondary shaft bearing into torque converter housing.

CAUTION: DO NOT install thrust shim in torque converter housing below differential bearing outer race. Thrust shim must be installed in transaxle housing. Outer bearing race in torque converter housing is not a press fit.

---

6) Install differential bearing outer race. To install differential oil seal, use a hammer and oil seal installer. Install NEW oil seal into torque converter housing until oil seal is fully seated.

TRANSAXLE HOUSING

Disassembly – **1)** Expand snap ring and press mainshaft, countershaft and secondary shaft bearings from transaxle housing. Using a hammer and drift, tap differential oil seal from transaxle housing.

CAUTION: DO NOT heat transaxle housing to more than 212°F (100°C) or housing may be damaged.

---

2) If removing differential bearing outer race, use heat gun to heat transaxle housing around differential bearing outer race to 212°F (100°C).
3) Tap differential bearing outer race from transaxle housing. Remove thrust shim, located below differential bearing outer race from transaxle housing.
Cleaning & Inspection – Clean components with solvent and dry with compressed air. Inspect transaxle housing for cracks and damage in bearing areas. Replace transaxle housing if damaged.

NOTE: Ensure original thickness thrust shim is installed. If any components have been changed, differential assembly bearing preload must be checked. See DIFFERENTIAL ASSEMBLY BEARING PRELOAD under TRANSAXLE REASSEMBLY.

Reassembly – **1)** Install thrust shim. Using a hammer and bearing race installer, install differential bearing outer race in transaxle housing.
2) To install mainshaft, countershaft and secondary shaft bearings, expand snap ring and install bearing part way into transaxle housing. Release snap ring.
3) Press bearing into transaxle housing until snap ring engages with groove on bearing. Ensure snap ring end gap is 0-.276" (0-7.0 mm). If snap ring end gap is not within specification, reseat or replace snap ring.

CAUTION: Ensure bearings are installed with groove of bearing facing inside of transaxle housing so snap ring engages in bearing when bearing is fully installed. Ensure snap ring fully engages in bearing.

4) To install differential oil seal, use a hammer and oil seal installer. Install NEW oil seal into transaxle housing until oil seal is fully seated.

LEFT-SIDE COVER

Disassembly – Remove snap rings retaining clutch feedpipes in left-side cover. Remove feedpipe guides, clutch feedpipes and "O" rings from left-side cover.
Cleaning & Inspection – Clean components with solvent and dry with compressed air. Inspect components for cracks or damage. Replace components as necessary.
Reassembly – To reassemble, reverse disassembly procedure using NEW "O" rings.

TRANSAXLE REASSEMBLY

DIFFERENTIAL ASSEMBLY BEARING PRELOAD

NOTE: If transaxle housing, torque converter housing, differential carrier, bearings, thrust shim or differential bearing outer races are replaced, differential assembly bearing preload must be checked.

CAUTION: DO NOT heat transaxle housing to more than 212°F (100°C), or housing may be damaged.

1) Using heat gun, heat transaxle housing around differential bearing outer race and thrust shim to 212°F (100°C). Tap differential bearing outer race from transaxle housing. Remove thrust shim, located below differential bearing outer race, from transaxle housing.
2) Allow transaxle housing to cool to room temperature. Select thrust shim so total thickness of thrust shim is .085" (2.15 mm). See THRUST SHIM SPECIFICATIONS table.

CAUTION: DO NOT use more than 2 thrust shims when adjusting differential assembly bearing preload.

THRUST SHIM SPECIFICATIONS

Thrust Shim I.D. Letter	Part Number	Thickness In. (mm)
A	41381-PG4-000	.035 (.90)
B	41382-PG4-000	.037 (.95)
C	41383-PG4-000	.039 (1.00)
D [1]	41384-PG4-000	.041 (1.05)
E [1]	41385-PG4-000	.043 (1.10)
F	41386-PG4-000	.045 (1.15)
G	41387-PG4-000	.047 (1.20)
H	41388-PG4-000	.049 (1.25)
I	41389-PG4-000	.051 (1.30)
J	41390-PG4-000	.053 (1.35)
K [2]	41391-PG4-000	.085 (2.15)
L	41392-PG4-000	.087 (2.20)
M	41393-PG4-000	.089 (2.25)
N	41394-PG4-000	.091 (2.30)
O	41395-PG4-000	.093 (2.35)
P	41396-PG4-000	.094 (2.40)
Q	41397-PG4-000	.096 (2.45)

[1] – This is the standard thrust shim combination when adjusting preload with 2 shims.
[2] – This is the standard thrust shim when adjusting preload with one shim.

3) Install thrust shim in transaxle housing. Using a hammer and bearing race installer, install differential bearing outer race in transaxle housing. Ensure differential bearing outer race is fully seated in transaxle housing.

4) Install gasket on torque converter housing. Do not apply sealer at this time. Install differential assembly in torque converter housing. Install transaxle housing on torque converter housing without mainshaft, countershaft and secondary shaft installed.

CAUTION: Ensure gasket is installed when checking differential assembly bearing preload.

5) Install and tighten transaxle housing-to-torque converter housing bolts to 33 ft. lbs. (44 N.m) in sequence. See Fig. 41. Rotate differential assembly several revolutions to seat bearings.

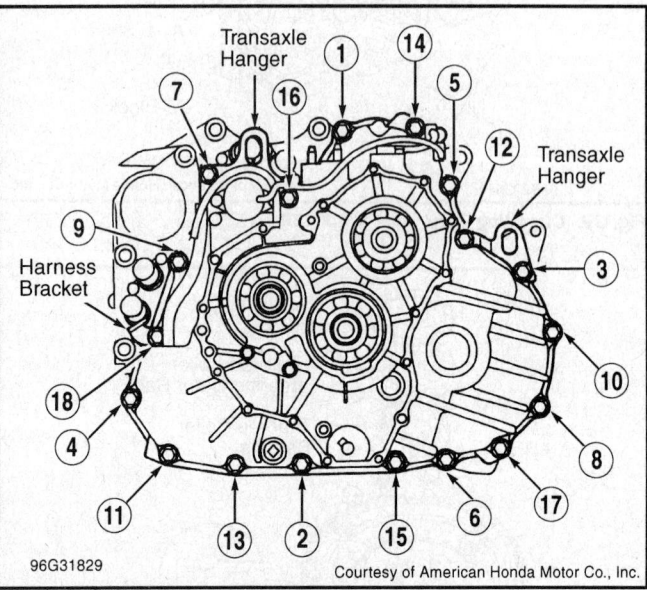

96G31829   Courtesy of American Honda Motor Co., Inc.

Fig. 41: Transaxle Housing Bolt Tightening Sequence

6) Install Preload Adapter (07HAJ-PK40201) into differential assembly. *See Fig. 42.* Install INCH-lb. torque wrench on preload adapter. Measure differential assembly bearing preload by checking starting torque required to rotate differential assembly in both directions at room temperature.
7) Differential assembly bearing preload should be within specification. See DIFFERENTIAL ASSEMBLY BEARING PRELOAD SPECIFICATIONS table.

DIFFERENTIAL ASSEMBLY BEARING PRELOAD SPECIFICATIONS [1]

Application	INCH Lbs. (N.m)
New Bearings	24-35 (2.8-4.0)
Used Bearings	22-32 (2.5-3.7)

[1] – This is the starting torque required to rotate differential assembly.

8) If differential assembly bearing preload is not within specification, select proper thickness thrust shim to obtain correct reading. See THRUST SHIM SPECIFICATIONS table.
9) Changing thrust shim to the next size will increase or decrease bearing preload about 2.60-3.50 INCH lbs. (.3-.4 N.m). Increase thrust shim thickness to increase differential assembly bearing preload. Decrease thrust shim thickness to decrease bearing preload.

CAUTION: DO NOT use more than 2 thrust shims when adjusting differential assembly bearing preload.

10) If adjusting differential assembly bearing preload, remove transaxle housing from torque converter housing. Remove differential bearing outer race from transaxle housing. Install correct thrust shim. Using a hammer and bearing race installer, install differential bearing outer race in transaxle housing.
11) Reinstall transaxle housing and recheck differential assembly bearing preload. Once correct differential assembly bearing preload is obtained, remove transaxle housing, gasket and differential assembly from torque converter housing.

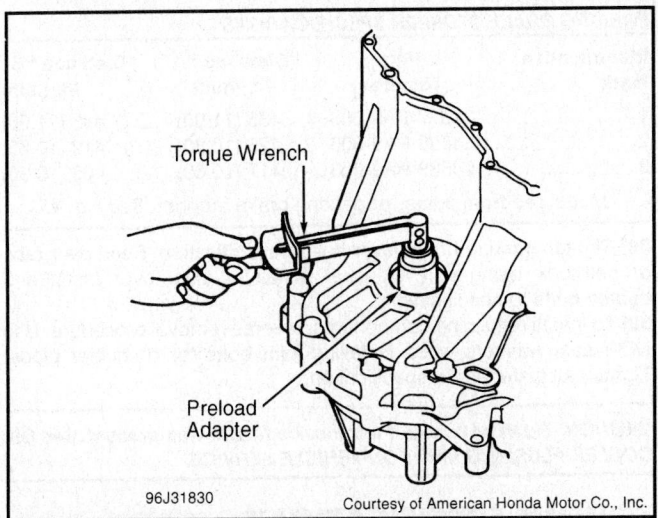

96J31830 Courtesy of American Honda Motor Co., Inc.

Fig. 42: Checking Differential Bearing Preload

VALVE BODIES & INTERNAL COMPONENTS

NOTE: If transaxle housing, torque converter housing, differential carrier, bearings, thrust shim or differential bearing outer races are replaced, differential assembly bearing preload must be checked. See DIFFERENTIAL ASSEMBLY BEARING PRELOAD under TRANSAXLE REASSEMBLY.

NOTE: Coat all components with ATF before reassembly.

1) Install main separator plate and 3 dowel pins on torque converter housing. Install oil pump drive gear, oil pump driven gear and oil pump driven gear shaft.

CAUTION: Ensure oil pump driven gear is installed with groove and chamfered side facing downward (toward main separator plate).

2) Install main valve body. Loosely install all main valve body bolts. Once all bolts are installed, tighten main valve body bolts to specification. See TORQUE SPECIFICATIONS.

CAUTION: Ensure oil pump gears rotate smoothly and oil pump driven gear shaft moves freely once main valve body is installed. If components do not operate correctly, loosen main valve body bolts and realign oil pump gears and oil pump driven gear shaft. Failure to align oil pump driven gear shaft may result in seized oil pump gears or shaft.

3) Ensure check balls are installed in main valve body. See Fig. 15. Install stator shaft, NEW "O" ring and stop shaft. Install dowel pins in main valve body. Install spring and torque converter check valve in main valve body.

4) Install regulator valve body and bolt on main valve body. Install dowel pins and separator plate on regulator vale body. Install lock-up valve body.

5) Install control shaft in transmission housing with manual valve together. Install detent arm and arm shaft in main valve body. Hook detent spring to detent arm.

6) Install secondary valve body. Ensure check balls are installed in secondary valve body. See Fig. 19. Install servo separator plate and servo body. Install 4th accumulator cover, oil filter, servo detent base and accumulator body. Tighten bolts to specification.

7) Install one oil feed pipe in main valve body, 2 oil feed pipes in servo body, 2 oil feed pipes in lock-up valve body and one oil feed pipe in accumulator body.

8) Install differential assembly, countershaft sub-assembly, mainshaft sub-assembly and secondary shaft sub-assembly in torque converter housing. Install splined washer, thrust needle bearing and needle bearing on secondary shaft.

9) Install needle bearings, reverse selector hub and reverse selector with shift fork on countershaft in direction shown. See Fig. 43.

10) Rotate shift fork shaft on servo body so large chamfered hole aligns with hole in shift fork. Install shift fork bolt and NEW bolt lock. Tighten bolt to specification. Bend over tabs on bolt lock.

11) Install secondary shaft 2nd gear, thrust needle bearing and thrust washer on secondary shaft. Install needle bearing, countershaft reverse gear and countershaft 2nd gear on countershaft.

12) Install reverse idler gear in transaxle case with largest chamfered area facing upward (away from transaxle housing).

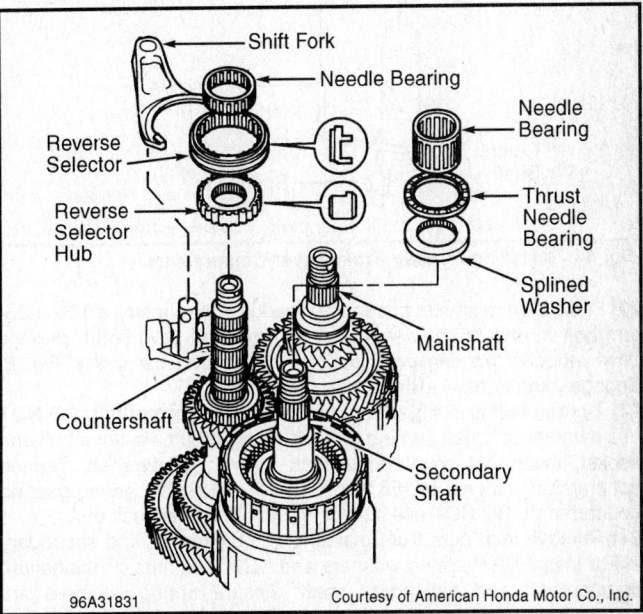

96A31831 Courtesy of American Honda Motor Co., Inc.

Fig. 43: Installing Shift Fork & Reverse Selector

13) Install dowel pins and NEW gasket on torque converter housing. Align spring pin with groove in transaxle housing by rotating control shaft. See Fig. 14.

14) Install transaxle housing on torque converter housing. Install and tighten bolts to specification in sequence using several steps. See Fig. 41. Engage reverse idler gear with countershaft reverse gear.

15) Coat reverse idler gear shaft and needle bearings with grease. Install shaft in reverse idler gear shaft holder.

16) Install reverse idler gear shaft holder with needle bearings in transaxle housing. Install and tighten bolts to specification.

17) Install parking brake lever spring and parking brake lever on control shaft. See Fig. 44. Install bolt and NEW lock washer on parking brake lever. DO NOT tighten bolt at this time.

NOTE: Mainshaft lock nut has LEFT-HAND threads.

18) Install Mainshaft Holder (07GAB-PF50100 or 07GAB-PF50101) on mainshaft to secure mainshaft from rotating. See Fig. 9. Install mainshaft idler gear on mainshaft. Install old mainshaft lock nut on mainshaft. Mainshaft has LEFT-HAND threads.

19) Tighten mainshaft lock nut to 166 ft. lbs. (225 N.m) to seat mainshaft idler gear on mainshaft. DO NOT use hammer to install mainshaft idler gear on mainshaft or impact wrench to tighten lock nut.

20) Install secondary shaft idler gear on secondary shaft. Install splined washer, thrust needle bearing, needle bearing, countershaft idler gear, thrust needle bearing and parking gear on countershaft. See Fig. 8.

21) Install old secondary shaft lock nut on secondary shaft. Tighten secondary shaft lock nut to 166 ft. lbs. (225 N.m) while holding countershaft idler gear to seat secondary shaft idler gear on secondary shaft. DO NOT use hammer to install secondary shaft idler gear on secondary shaft or impact wrench to tighten lock nut.

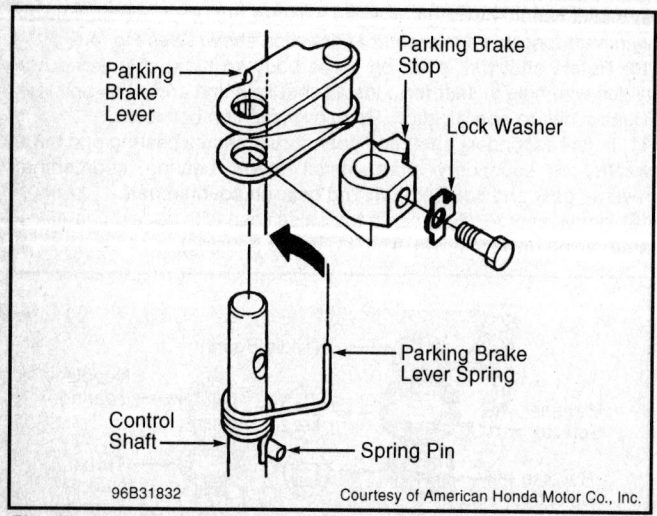

96B31832 — Courtesy of American Honda Motor Co., Inc.

Fig. 44: Installing Parking Brake Lever Components

22) Place 24-mm socket at center of parking gear. Install a 10 x 1.25-mm bolt in end of countershaft. Install parking pawl shaft, parking pawl stopper, parking pawl spring and parking pawl. See Fig. 8. Engage parking pawl with parking gear.

23) Tighten bolt to pull parking gear onto the countershaft. DO NOT use hammer to install parking gear on countershaft. Remove bolt and socket. Install old countershaft lock nut on countershaft. Tighten countershaft lock nut to 166 ft. lbs. (225 N.m) to seat parking gear on countershaft. DO NOT use impact wrench to tighten lock nut.

24) Remove lock nuts from mainshaft, countershaft and secondary shaft. Install NEW spring washers and NEW lock nuts on mainshaft, countershaft and secondary shaft. Ensure spring washers are installed so large area of spring washer is against lock nut.

25) Tighten lock nuts to specification. DO NOT use impact wrench to tighten lock nuts. Stake lock nuts against shaft. Remove mainshaft holder.

CAUTION: Ensure all lock nuts are securely staked against the shaft.

26) Place parking brake lever in "P" position. Ensure parking pawl fully engages with parking gear. If parking pawl does not fully engage, measure parking brake stopper distance between parking pawl shaft and pin on parking brake stopper. See Fig. 45.

27) Parking brake stopper distance should be 2.88-2.92" (73.2-74.2 mm). If parking brake stopper distance is not within specification, install different size parking brake stopper.

28) Parking brake stopper is available in different sizes. See PARKING BRAKE STOPPER SPECIFICATIONS table.

PARKING BRAKE STOPPER SPECIFICATIONS

Identification Mark	Part Number	[1] Distance "A" In. (mm)	[1] Distance "B" In. (mm)
1	24537-PA9-003	.433 (11.00)	.433 (11.00)
2	24538-PA9-003	.425 (10.80)	.419 (10.65)
3	24539-PA9-003	.417 (10.60)	.406 (10.30)

[1] – Measured from center of parking brake stopper. See Fig. 45.

29) Tighten parking brake lever bolt to specification. Bend over tabs on bolt lock. Using a NEW gasket, install left-side cover. Install and tighten bolts to specification.

30) To install remaining components, reverse removal procedure. Use NEW seal washers when installing joint bolts for oil cooler pipes. Tighten all fasteners to specification.

CAUTION: Flush oil cooler if a transaxle failure was present. See OIL COOLER FLUSHING under ON-VEHICLE SERVICE.

TORQUE SPECIFICATIONS
TORQUE SPECIFICATIONS

Application	Ft. Lbs. (N.m)
Countershaft Lock Nut	123 (167)
Joint Bolt	21 (29)
Main Valve Body Bolt	
6-mm Bolt	[1]
8-mm Bolt	13 (18)
Mainshaft Lock Nut	123 (167)
Pressure Tap Plug	13 (18)
Reverse Idler Gear Shaft Holder Bolt	20 (27)
Ring Gear Bolt	75 (102)
Secondary Shaft Lock Nut	123 (167)
Transaxle Housing Bolt [2]	33 (44)

Application	INCH Lbs. (N.m)
Accumulator Body Bolt	106 (12.0)
Countershaft Speed Sensor Bolt	106 (12.0)
Left-Side Cover Bolt	106 (12.0)
Lock-Up Control Solenoid Valve Assembly Bolt	106 (12.0)
Linear Solenoid/Throttle Valve Body Bolt	106 (12.0)
Mainshaft Speed Sensor Bolt	106 (12.0)
Oil Filter Bolt	106 (12.0)
Parking Brake Lever Bolt	120 (14.0)
Regulator Valve Body Bolt	106 (12.0)
Servo Body Bolt	106 (12.0)
Servo Detent Base Bolt	106 (12.0)
Shift Control Solenoid Valve Assembly Bolt	106 (12.0)
Shift Fork Bolt	120 (14.0)
4th Accumulator Cover Bolt	106 (12.0)

[1] – Tighten bolt to 106 INCH lbs. (12.0 N.m).
[2] – Tighten bolts to specification in sequence. See Fig. 41.

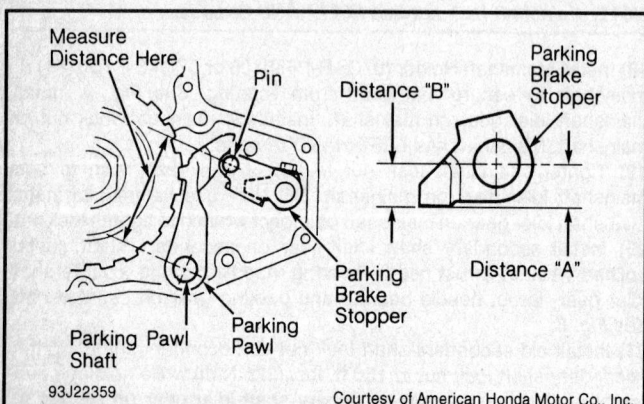

93J22359 — Courtesy of American Honda Motor Co., Inc.

Fig. 45: Measuring Parking Brake Stopper Distance & Parking Brake Stopper

TRANSAXLE SPECIFICATIONS

TRANSAXLE SPECIFICATIONS

Application	Specification
Clutch Clearance	
1st Clutch	.030-.037" (.75-.95 mm)
2nd Clutch	.028-.035" (.70-.90 mm)
1st-Hold Clutch	.024-.039" (.60-1.00 mm)
3rd Clutch	.026-.033" (.65-.85 mm)
4th Clutch	.022-.030" (.55-.75 mm)
Differential Bearing Preload [1]	
New Bearings	24-35 INCH lbs. (2.8-4.0 N.m)
Used Bearings	22-32 INCH lbs. (2.5-3.7 N.m)
Oil Pump Clearances	
Side Clearance	
Oil Pump Drive Gear	.0083-.0104" (.210-.265 mm)
Oil Pump Driven Gear	.003-.005" (.070-.125 mm)
Thrust Clearance	
Standard	.0010-.0020" (.030-.050 mm)
Wear Limit	.0028" (.070 mm)
Secondary Shaft 1st	
Gear Clearance	.003-.006" (.07-.15 mm)
Secondary Shaft 2nd	
Gear Clearance	.003-.006" (.07-.15 mm)
Differential Side Gear Backlash	.002-.006" (.05-.15 mm)
Parking Brake Stopper Distance	2.88-2.92" (73.2-74.2 mm)
4th Clutch Hub-To-Mainshaft End Play	.001-.004" (.03-.11 mm)

[1] – This is the starting torque required to rotate differential assembly.

WIRING DIAGRAMS

For appropriate wiring diagram, see HONDA MPZA ELECTRONIC CONTROLS article.

AUTOMATIC TRANSMISSIONS
Honda MPZA Electronic Controls

Accord (V6 2.7L)

APPLICATION

APPLICATION

Vehicle	Transaxle Model
1995-96 Accord (V6 2.7L)	MPZA

CAUTION: Vehicle is equipped with a Supplemental Restraint System (SRS). When servicing vehicle, use care to avoid accidental air bag deployment. All SRS electrical connections and wiring harnesses are covered with Yellow Insulation. SRS-related components are located in steering column, center console, instrument panel and lower panel on instrument panel. DO NOT use electrical test equipment on these circuits. It may be necessary to deactivate SRS before servicing components. See AIR BAG SERVICING article in APPLICATIONS & IDENTIFICATIONS.

NOTE: Obtain radio anti-theft code from vehicle owner before disconnecting negative battery cable. Radio anti-theft code must be re-entered into radio once negative battery cable is reconnected. To re-enter radio anti-theft code, turn ignition and radio on. When CODE is displayed on radio, re-enter radio anti-theft code by using radio station preset buttons.

DESCRIPTION

Automatic transaxle is electronically controlled. Transaxle shifting and torque converter lock-up are controlled by Transmission Control Module (TCM). TCM is located below instrument panel under front lower panel on passenger's side. TCM receives information from various input devices and uses this information to control shift, linear and lock-up control solenoid valves.

The TCM contains a grade logic control system which controls transaxle shifting while vehicle is ascending or descending a slope, or reducing vehicle speed. Transaxle is equipped with shift and key interlock systems. Shift interlock system prevents shift lever from being moved from Park unless brake pedal is depressed and accelerator pedal is in idle position. In case of a malfunction, shift lever can be released by placing ignition key in key release slot near shift lever. Key interlock system prevents ignition key from being removed from ignition lock assembly unless shift lever is in Park.

The A/T gear position indicator on instrument panel contains lights to indicate which position A/T gear position switch on shift lever is in.

OPERATION

A/T GEAR POSITION INDICATOR

With ignition in RUN or START position, voltage is supplied to A/T gear position indicator, located on instrument panel. *See Fig. 1*. When shift lever is moved to designated gear position, A/T gear position switch completes the ground circuit for A/T gear position indicator. The light on A/T gear position indicator will illuminate to indicate shift lever gear position. The A/T gear position switch is located on driver's side of shift lever. *See Fig. 2*.

When headlights are turned on, voltage is applied to A/T gear position indicator dimming circuit through Red/Black wire from combination light switch. Brightness of dash lights is controlled through Red wire from brightness controller.

GRADE LOGIC CONTROL SYSTEM

The TCM compares actual driving conditions with driving conditions memorized in the TCM, based on input signals from Vehicle Speed Sensor (VSS), Throttle Position (TP) sensor, Engine Coolant Temperature (ECT) sensor, Barometric Pressure (BARO) sensor, brakelight switch signal and A/T gear position switch. The TCM uses these input signals to control shifting while vehicle is ascending or descending a slope, or during deceleration.

When the TCM determines vehicle is ascending a slope with shift lever in "D₄" position, TCM extends engagement of 3rd gear to prevent transaxle from frequently shifting between 3rd and 4th gears. Shift points between 3rd and 4th gear are stored in TCM, which allows the most suitable gear selection depending on conditions.

When the TCM determines vehicle is descending a slope with shift lever in "D₄" position, TCM changes upshift speed from 3rd to 4th gear when throttle is fully closed. This widens the 3rd gear operating range from that programmed for level surface operation and, in conjunction with engine braking from torque converter lock-up, provides smooth vehicle operation. When vehicle is decelerating on a gradual hill in 4th gear, or when applying brakes on a steep hill, the transaxle will downshift to 3rd gear. When vehicle accelerates, transaxle will upshift into 4th gear.

When vehicle decelerates from speeds greater than 30 MPH, TCM shifts transaxle from 4th gear to 2nd gear earlier than normal to reduce the number of times transaxle shifts. This allows smoother acceleration and vehicle operation.

SHIFT & KEY INTERLOCK SYSTEMS

Shift Interlock System – Shift interlock system prevents shift lever from being moved from Park unless brake pedal is depressed and accelerator pedal is in idle position. Shift lever cannot be moved from Park if brake and accelerator pedal are depressed at the same time. In case of a malfunction, shift lever can be released by placing ignition key in key release slot near shift lever.

Voltage is provided to shift lock solenoid when ignition is in RUN or START position. When brake pedal is depressed, brakelight switch provides voltage to TCM, provided accelerator pedal is in idle position. With accelerator pedal in idle position, a voltage signal is delivered between Throttle Position (TP) sensor and the TCM. The TCM then provides voltage to shift lock circuit in the interlock control unit. When A/T gear position switch is in Park, interlock control unit operates shift lock solenoid by controlling the ground circuit. When shift lock solenoid is energized, shift lever is released and can be moved.

The A/T gear position switch and shift lock solenoid are located on driver's side of shift lever. *See Fig. 2*. Interlock control unit is located behind driver's side of instrument panel and contains an 8-pin harness connector. *See Fig. 2*.

Key Interlock System – Key interlock system prevents ignition key from being removed from ignition lock assembly unless shift lever is in Park. Voltage is provided to key interlock switch from fuse No. 30 (20-amp) in engine compartment fuse/relay box. When ignition key is in ignition lock assembly, key interlock switch closes, providing voltage to key interlock solenoid and interlock control unit.

If shift lever is not in Park (parking pin switch on), interlock control unit energizes key interlock solenoid by completing the ground circuit. When key interlock solenoid is energized, ignition key cannot be removed from ignition lock assembly. Key interlock switch and key interlock solenoid are located on ignition lock assembly. *See Fig. 2*. Parking pin switch is located on left side of shift lever. Interlock control unit is located behind driver's side of instrument panel and contains an 8-pin harness connector. *See Fig. 2*.

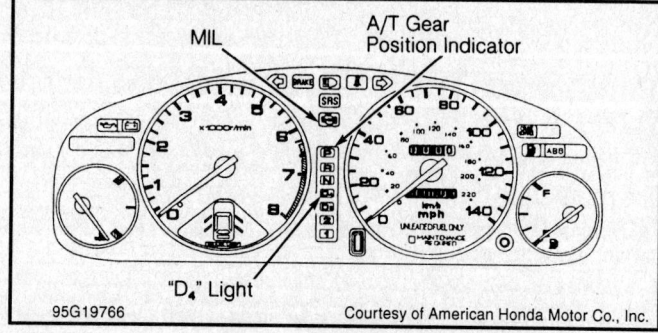

95G19766   Courtesy of American Honda Motor Co., Inc.

Fig. 1: Locating A/T Gear Position Indicator & MIL Light

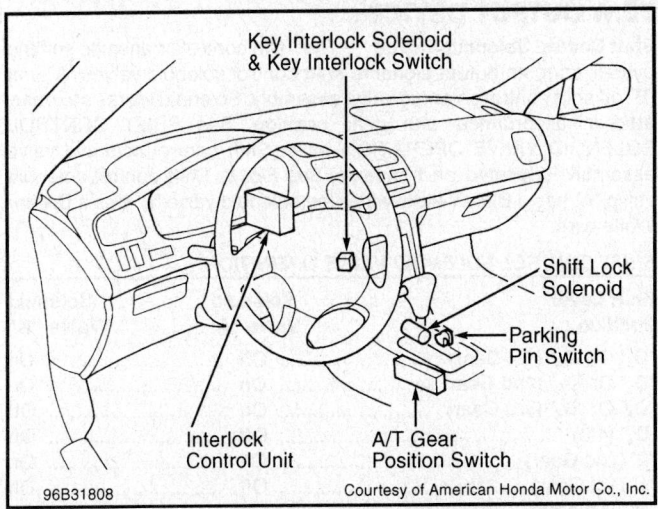

Fig. 2: Locating Shift & Key Interlock System Components

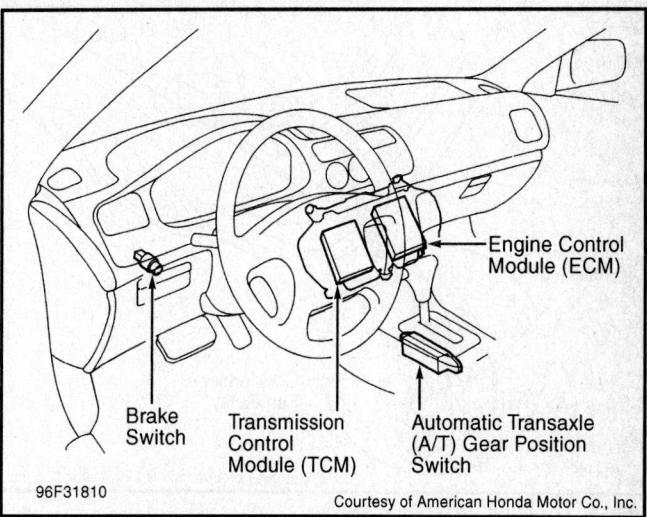

Fig. 4: Locating ECM, TCM, A/T Gear Position Switch & Brakelight Switch

TRANSMISSION CONTROL MODULE (TCM)

The TCM receives information from various input devices and uses this information to control shift, linear and lock-up control solenoid valves. See Fig. 3. The TCM contains a self-diagnostic system which stores a fault code if a failure is present in transaxle electronic control system. Fault code may also be referred to as Diagnostic Trouble Code (DTC) or flash code. DTC or flash code may be retrieved to determine transaxle problem area. See SELF-DIAGNOSTIC SYSTEM. The TCM is located behind center of instrument panel. See Fig. 4.

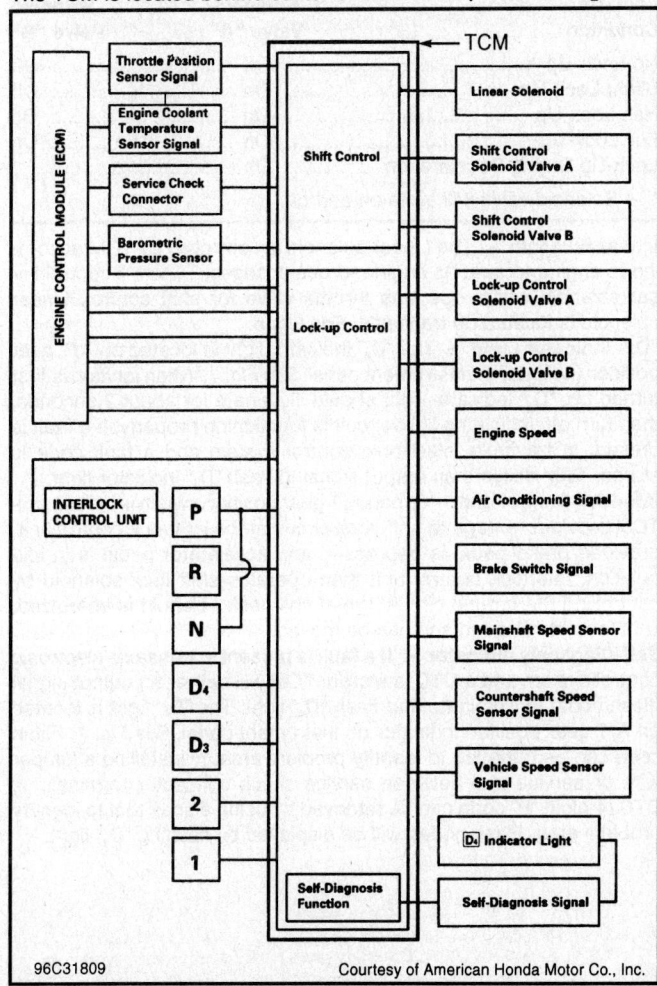

Fig. 3: Identifying TCM Input & Output Devices

TCM INPUT DEVICES

Air Conditioning Signal – The A/C clutch relay delivers an input signal to TCM, indicating A/C operation. The A/C clutch relay is located at front left corner of engine compartment, near radiator. See Fig. 5.

Barometric Pressure Signal – Barometric pressure signal is delivered between Engine Control Module (ECM) and the TCM. The ECM contains a built-in barometric pressure sensor to determine atmospheric pressure. The ECM is located behind center of instrument panel. See Fig. 4.

Brake Switch Signal – Brakelight switch delivers an input signal to TCM, indicating vehicle braking. Brakelight switch is also used in determining grade logic control. Brakelight switch is located on brake pedal support. See Fig. 4.

Engine Coolant Temperature (ECT) Signal – ECT sensor delivers an input signal to TCM, indicating engine coolant temperature. The ECT sensor is located on cylinder head, below distributor and contains a Red/White wire and Green/Blue wire in the electrical connector. See Fig. 6.

Engine Speed – Engine speed signal (RPM) is delivered to TCM from ignition control module in distributor assembly.

Engine Control Module (ECM) – Upshift, downshift and shift acknowledgment signals are delivered between the ECM and TCM. A 5-volt reference signal is present between ECM and TCM. The ECM is located behind center of instrument panel. See Fig. 4.

Mainshaft & Countershaft Speed Signal – Mainshaft speed signal is delivered to TCM. Mainshaft speed sensor is located on side of transaxle. See Fig. 6. Countershaft speed signal is delivered to TCM. Countershaft speed sensor is located on top of transaxle. See Fig. 6.

Service Check Connector – Service check connector is used when retrieving flash codes for transaxle electronic control system diagnosis. When a jumper wire is installed between electrical terminals of service check connector, an input signal is delivered to TCM to display flash codes on "D₄" indicator light. Service check connector is a 2-pin Blue colored harness connector located at passenger's corner of instrument panel. See Fig. 7.

Shift Position Signal – Shift position signal is delivered to TCM by the A/T gear position switch, located on driver's side of shift lever. See Fig. 2 or 4.

Throttle Position (TP) Sensor Signal – Throttle Position (TP) sensor delivers an input signal to TCM to indicate throttle position. The TP sensor is mounted on throttle body. See Fig. 6.

Vehicle Speed Sensor Signal – Vehicle Speed Sensor (VSS) delivers an input signal to TCM to indicate vehicle speed. The VSS is located on top of transaxle. See Fig. 6.

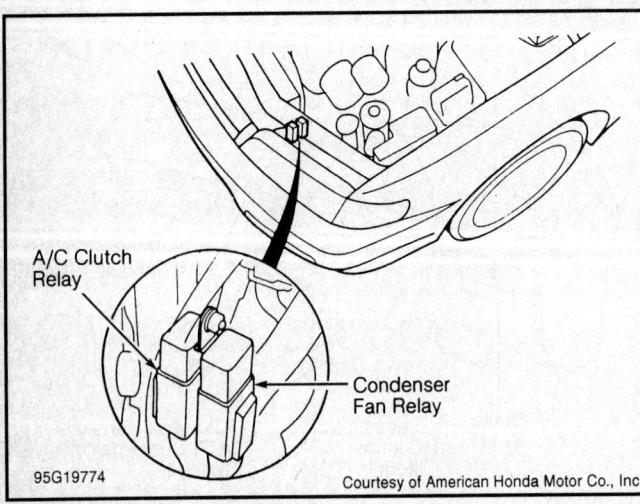

Fig. 5: Locating A/C Clutch Relay

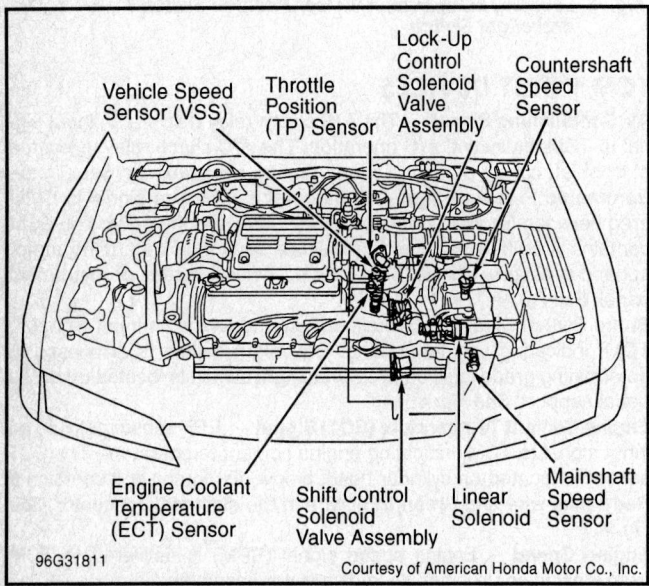

Fig. 6: Locating Input & Output Devices

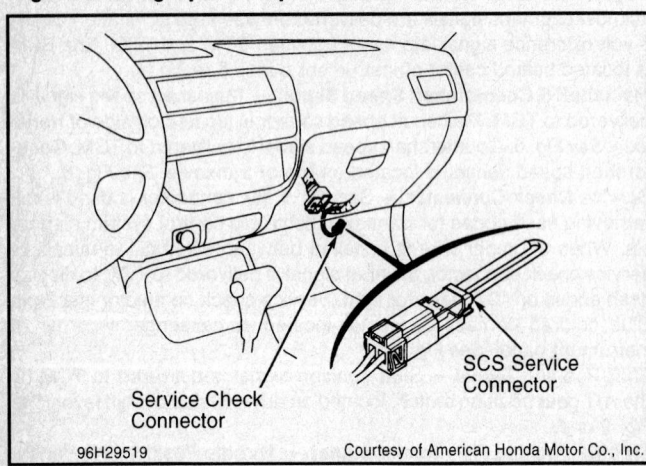

Fig. 7: Locating Service Check Connector

TCM OUTPUT DEVICES

Shift Control Solenoid Valves – The TCM controls transaxle shifting by delivering an output signal to shift control solenoid valves "A" and "B" on shift control solenoid valve assembly. Solenoid valves are operated in accordance with gear position. See SHIFT CONTROL SOLENOID VALVE OPERATION table. Shift control solenoid valve assembly is located on transaxle. *See Fig. 6.* Shift control solenoid valve "A" has a Blue/Yellow wire, and solenoid valve "B" has a Green/White wire.

SHIFT CONTROL SOLENOID VALVE OPERATION

Shift Lever Position	Solenoid Valve "A"	Solenoid Valve "B"
"D₃" Or "D₄" (1st Gear)	Off	On
"D₃" Or "D₄" (2nd Gear)	On	On
"D₃" Or "D₄" (3rd Gear)	On	Off
"D₄" (4th)	Off	Off
"2" (2nd Gear)	On	On
"1" (1st Gear)	Off	On
"R" (Reverse)	On	Off

Lock-Up Control Solenoid Valves – The TCM controls torque converter lock-up by delivering an output signal to lock-up control solenoid valves "A" and "B" on lock-up control solenoid valve assembly. Lock-up control solenoid valves are activated in accordance with lock-up condition. See LOCK-UP CONTROL SOLENOID VALVE OPERATION table. Lock-up control solenoid valve assembly is located on transaxle. *See Fig. 6.* Lock-up control solenoid valve "A" has a Yellow wire, and solenoid valve "B" has a Green/Black wire.

LOCK-UP CONTROL SOLENOID VALVE OPERATION

Lock-Up Condition	Solenoid Valve "A"	Solenoid Valve "B"
No Lock-Up	Off	Off
Slight Lock-Up	On	Off
Half Lock-Up	On	On
Full Lock-Up	On	On
Lock-Up During Deceleration	On	[1]

[1] – Solenoid valve will cycle on and off.

Linear Solenoid – The Linear solenoid is controlled by TCM according to engine torque. As engine torque changes, TCM will control linear solenoid which operates throttle valve for shift control. Linear solenoid is located on transaxle. *See Fig. 6.*

"D₄" Indicator Light – The "D₄" indicator light is located on A/T gear position indicator on instrument panel. *See Fig. 1.* When ignition is first turned on, "D₄" indicator light should illuminate for about 2 seconds, then turn off, indicating light circuit is functioning properly. If a fault is present in transaxle electronic control system and a fault code is stored, TCM delivers an output signal to flash "D₄" indicator light.

Interlock Control Unit – When A/T gear position switch is in Park, the TCM provides voltage to shift lock circuit at the interlock control unit, provided brake pedal is depressed and accelerator pedal is in idle position. Interlock control unit then operates shift lock solenoid by controlling the ground circuit. When shift lock solenoid is energized, shift lever is released and can be moved.

Self-Diagnosis Indicator – If a fault is present in transaxle electronic control system and a DTC is stored, TCM will deliver an output signal (flash code) to illuminate and flash "D₄" light. The "D₄" light is located on A/T gear position indicator on instrument panel. *See Fig. 1.* Flash code can be retrieved to identify problem area by installing a jumper wire or service tool between service check connector terminals. A DTC (4-digit) "P" code can be retrieved by using a scan tool to identify problem area. Flash codes will be displayed by flashing "D₄" light.

SELF-DIAGNOSTIC SYSTEM

SYSTEM DIAGNOSIS

TCM monitors transaxle operation. TCM contains a self-diagnostic system which stores a DTC if a transaxle electronic control system failure is present. If a DTC is stored, TCM will illuminate and flash "D₄" light on A/T gear position indicator on instrument panel. *See Fig. 1.* If a transaxle electronic control system failure is suspected, and "D₄" light on A/T gear position indicator does not flash, perform appropriate test under "D₄" INDICATOR LIGHT CIRCUIT CHECK. DTCs can be retrieved using a scan tool connected to Data Link Connector (DLC) located behind ashtray. Flash code may also be retrieved for diagnosing transaxle electronic control system.

"D₄" INDICATOR LIGHT CIRCUIT CHECK

"D₄" Indicator Light Does Not Come On – **1)** Turn ignition on. Ensure service connector shorting tool is not connected to service check connector. Shift to "D₄" position. If "D₄" indicator light does not illuminate, go to next step. If "D₄" indicator light illuminates, check for loose TCM harness connections. Replace TCM with a known-good unit if necessary and retest.

2) Turn ignition off. Disconnect 26-pin TCM harness connector "A". Using a DVOM, check for continuity between ground and 26-pin TCM harness connector "A", terminals No. 13 and 26 (Brown/Black wires). If continuity is present, go to next step. If continuity is not present, repair open or poor connection in appropriate Brown/Black wire.

3) Turn ignition on. Measure voltage at 26-pin TCM harness connector "A", between terminals No. 12 (Black/Yellow wire) and No. 13 (Brown/Black wire), then between terminals No. 25 (Black/Yellow wire) and No. 26 (Brown/Black wire). If battery voltage is present, go to next step. If battery voltage is not present, repair open or short in appropriate Black/Yellow wire between TCM and engine compartment fuse/relay box.

4) Turn ignition off. Reconnect TCM harness connector. Connect a DVOM (backprobe) between 26-pin TCM harness connector "A", terminal No. 17 (Blue/Red wire) and terminals No. 13 or 26 (Brown/Black wires). Turn ignition on. Voltage should be present for 2 seconds. If DVOM indicates voltage as specified, go to next step. If no voltage was indicated, go to step **6)**.

5) Check for an open or short in Blue/Red wire between TCM and gauge assembly. Repair as necessary. If no problem is found, repair faulty "D₄" indicator bulb or gauge assembly printed circuit board.

6) Turn ignition off. Disconnect 26-pin TCM harness connector "A". Check Blue/Red wire for continuity between 26-pin TCM harness connector "A", terminal No. 17 and gauge assembly harness connector terminal C3. If continuity is present, go to next step. If continuity is not present, repair open in Red/Blue wire.

7) Check for loose TCM harness connectors or faulty A/T gear position switch. Repair as necessary. If no problem is found, replace TCM with a known-good unit and retest.

"D₄" Indicator Light Remains On Constantly (Not Flashing) – **1)** Turn ignition off. Disconnect 26-pin TCM harness connector "A". Turn ignition on. Using a DVOM, measure voltage between ground and 26-pin TCM harness connector "A", terminal No. 17 (Blue/Red wire). If no voltage is present, go to next step. If voltage is present, repair Blue/Red wire for a short to power.

2) Turn ignition off. Reconnect TCM harness connector. Turn ignition on. Shift to any position except "D₄". Measure voltage (backprobe) between ground and 26-pin TCM harness connector "A", terminal No. 9 (Light Green/Black wire). If voltage is present, replace TCM. If no voltage is present, check Light Green/Black wire for a short to ground. Repair as necessary. If no problem is found, replace A/T gear position indicator.

RETRIEVING FAULT CODES

NOTE: *During diagnostics, ensure "D₄" indicator light on A/T gear position indicator is not turned on by a fault in the PGM-FI system. The PGM-FI system controls the fuel injection system. To repair PGM-FI system, see appropriate SELF-DIAGNOSTICS article in ENGINE PERFORMANCE in appropriate MITCHELL® manual. After PGM-FI system as been repaired, clear fault codes. See CLEARING FAULT CODES. After fault codes have been cleared, road test vehicle for several minutes at over 30 MPH and recheck fault codes.*

NOTE: *Before any diagnostic procedure, obtain radio anti-theft code from customer. Note radio preset stations, as radio stations and clock setting will be cleared and must be reset. Radio anti-theft code must be re-entered for radio operation.*

Retrieving DTCs Using Scan Tool – **1)** If a DTC is present, "D₄" light on A/T gear position indicator will flash when ignition is turned on. To retrieve DTC using scan tool, turn ignition off.

2) Connect scan tool to 16-pin Data Link Connector (DLC) located behind ashtray. Turn ignition on. Scan tool will indicate DTCs. Follow scan tool manufactures instructions.

3) Once DTC is obtained, turn ignition off. Determine probable cause and symptom. See DTC/FLASH CODE IDENTIFICATION table. If any other DTCs except those listed are displayed, see appropriate SELF-DIAGNOSTICS article in ENGINE PERFORMANCE in appropriate MITCHELL® manual. For trouble shooting of DTCs, see DIAGNOSTIC TESTS. If "D₄" light does not flash or remains on, see appropriate test under "D₄" INDICATOR LIGHT CIRCUIT CHECK.

Retrieving Flash Codes Using "D₄" Light – **1)** If a flash code is present, "D₄" light on A/T gear position indicator will flash when ignition is turned on. To retrieve flash code, turn ignition off.

2) Install a jumper wire or service tool between service check connector electrical terminals. Service check connector is a Blue 2-pin electrical connector located under passenger's side of instrument panel. *See Fig. 7.*

3) Turn ignition on. Flash codes will be displayed by short and long flashes of "D₄" light on A/T gear position indicator. If the Malfunction Indicator Light (MIL) is also flashing, see appropriate SELF-DIAGNOSTICS article in ENGINE PERFORMANCE in appropriate MITCHELL® manual. Repair MIL light codes first.

4) A short flash indicates a single digit flash code. A long flash equals 10 short flashes. For example, if "D₄" light flashes once, this is a Flash Code No. 1. If "D₄" light flashes one long, then 5 short flashes, this is a Flash Code No. 15. *See Fig. 8.*

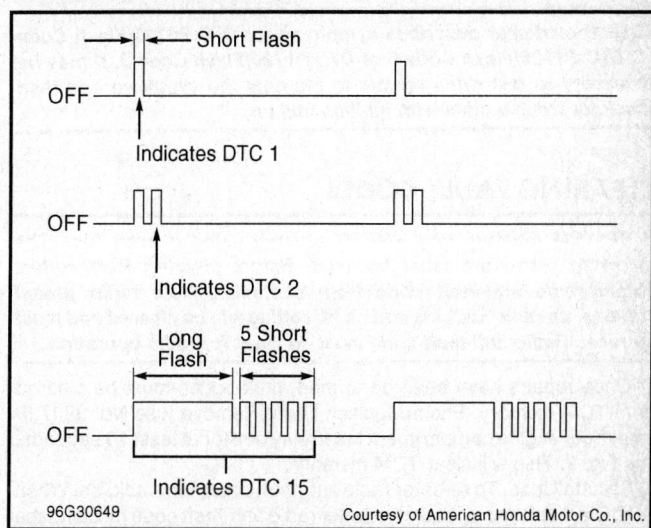

Fig. 8: Identifying Flash Code Displays

DTC/FLASH CODE IDENTIFICATION

DTC/Flash Code [1] Number	Indicator Light [2] Condition	Probable [3] Cause	[4] [5] Symptom
P0715/15	Off	Defective Mainshaft Speed Sensor	Transaxle Jerks Hard When Shifting
P0720/9	Flashes	Defective Countershaft Speed Sensor	Lock-Up Clutch Does Not Engage
P0725/11	Off	Defective Ignition Coil	Lock-Up Clutch Does Not Engage
P0730	Off	Defective Shift Control System	Fails To Shift, Stuck In 1st Or 4th Gears
P0740	Off	Defective Lock-Up Control System	Lock-Up Clutch Does Not Engage Or Remains Engaged, Unstable Engine Idle
P0753/7	Flashes	Defective Shift Control Solenoid "A"	Remains In 4th Gear, Fails To Shift Other Than 1st-4th, 2nd-4th Or 2nd-3rd Gears
P0758/8	Flashes	Defective Shift Control Solenoid "B"	Remains In 1st Or 4th Gear
P1705/5	Flashes	Defective A/T Gear Position Switch	Lock-Up Clutch Does Not Engage, Fails To Shift Other Than 2nd-4th Gears
P1706/6	Off	Defective A/T Gear Position Switch	Lock-Up Clutch Does Not Engage, Lock-Up Clutch Engages & Disengages, Fails To Shift Other Than 2nd-4th Gears
P1753/1	Flashes	Defective Lock-Up Control Solenoid "A"	Lock-Up Clutch Does Not Engage Or Remains Engaged, Unstable Engine Idle
P1758/2	Flashes	Defective Lock-Up Control Solenoid "B"	Lock-Up Clutch Does Not Engage
P1768/16	Flashes	Defective Linear Control Solenoid "B"	Lock-Up Clutch Does Not Engage, Transaxle Jerks Hard When Shifting
P1786/14	Flashes	Shorted Or Open FAS Wire Between TCM Terminal B19 & ECM, Defective ECM	Transaxle Jerks Hard When Shifting
P1790/3	Flashes Or Remains Off	Defective Throttle Position Sensor	Lock-Up Clutch Does Not Engage
P1791/4	Flashes	Defective Vehicle Speed Sensor	Lock-Up Clutch Does Not Engage
P1792/10	Flashes	Defective Engine Coolant Temp. Sensor	Lock-Up Clutch Does Not Engage
P1794/13	Flashes	Defective Baro Sensor	No Specific Symptoms

[1] – Number of blinks from "D4" light on A/T gear position indicator with jumper wire or service tool installed in service check connector.

[2] – Operation of "D4" light on A/T gear position indicator.

[3] – Specified component for probable cause. Also check wiring and connections for the specified component.

[4] – If transaxle fails to shift from Park with brake pedal depressed and accelerator pedal in idle position, check brakelight signal. See BRAKE-LIGHT SIGNAL under TROUBLE SHOOTING.

[5] – If lock-up clutch does not engage or does not cycle on and off, check A/C signal. See A/C SIGNAL under TROUBLE SHOOTING.

5) Once flash code is obtained, turn ignition off. Remove jumper wire or service tool from service check connector. Determine probable cause and symptom. See DTC/FLASH CODE IDENTIFICATION table. If any other flash codes except those listed are displayed, TCM is defective. For trouble shooting of flash codes, see DIAGNOSTIC TESTS.

NOTE: If customer describes symptoms for DTC P0725/Flash Code 11, DTC P1706/Flash Code 6 or DTC P1790/Flash Code 3, it may be necessary to test drive vehicle to recreate the symptom and then check for trouble code with ignition still on.

CLEARING FAULT CODES

NOTE: TCM memory can NOT be cleared using a scan tool. The following procedure must be used. Before clearing fault codes, obtain radio anti-theft code from customer. Note radio preset stations, as radio stations and clock setting will be cleared and must be reset. Radio anti-theft code must be reset for radio operation.

1) Once repairs have been performed, fault codes must be cleared from TCM memory. Ensure ignition is off. Remove fuse No. 39 (7.5-amp) from engine compartment fuse/relay box for at least 10 seconds. *See Fig. 9.* This will clear TCM memory.
2) Reinstall fuse. To re-enter radio anti-theft code, turn radio on. When CODE is displayed on radio, re-enter radio anti-theft code by using the radio station preset buttons. Reset clock and radio stations.

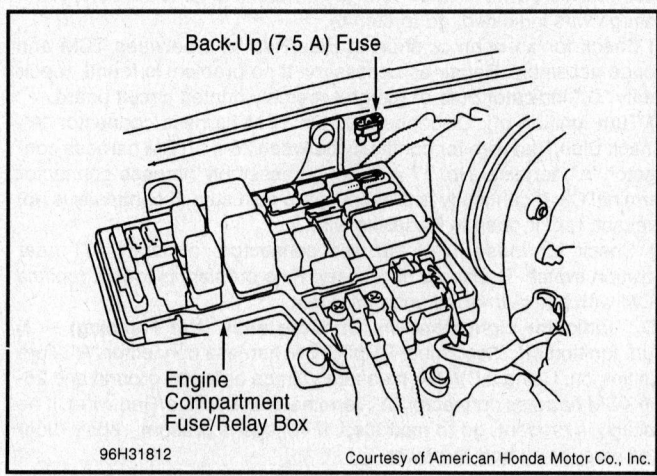

Back-Up (7.5 A) Fuse

Engine Compartment Fuse/Relay Box

96H31812 — Courtesy of American Honda Motor Co., Inc.

Fig. 9: Locating Fuse No. 39 (7.5-Amp)

DIAGNOSTIC TESTS

NOTE: Diagnostic codes are identified by "P" series code and then flash code, example: P0715/15 (DTC code/flash code).

NOTE: During diagnostic testing, refer to illustrations for harness connector and wire terminal identification. See Figs. 10-12.

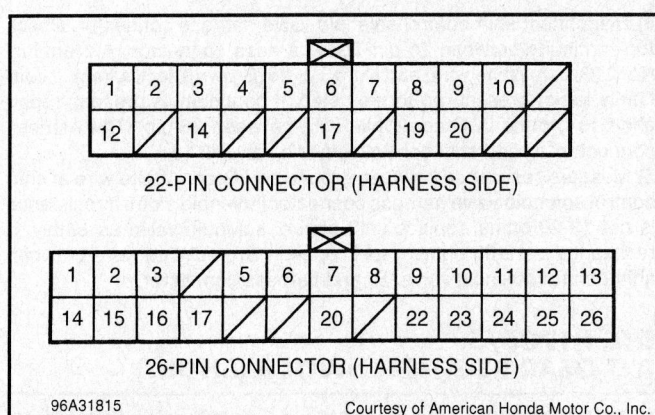

22-PIN CONNECTOR (HARNESS SIDE)

26-PIN CONNECTOR (HARNESS SIDE)

96A31815   Courtesy of American Honda Motor Co., Inc.

Fig. 10: Identifying TCM Harness Connectors & Terminals

DTC P0715/15: MAINSHAFT SPEED SENSOR

NOTE: DTC P0715 does NOT confirm an electrical problem in mainshaft speed sensor or circuit. This DTC can also be caused by a mechanical problem in transaxle.

1) Ensure mainshaft and countershaft speed sensors are installed properly. See COUNTERSHAFT or MAINSHAFT SPEED SENSOR under REMOVAL & INSTALLATION. Disconnect mainshaft speed sensor harness connector. Using a DVOM, measure resistance between sensor terminals. See MAINSHAFT SPEED SENSOR under COMPONENT TESTING.
2) If resistance is not 400-600 ohms, replace mainshaft speed sensor. If resistance is 400-600 ohms, disconnect 22-pin TCM harness connector "B". Check for continuity between ground and 22-pin TCM harness connector "B", terminals No. 10 (Orange/Blue wire) and No. 17 (White/Blue wire). *See Fig. 10.*
3) If continuity is present, repair short to ground in Orange/Blue wire or White/Blue wire between TCM and mainshaft speed sensor. If continuity is not present, reconnect mainshaft speed sensor harness connector. Measure resistance between 22-pin PCM harness connector "B", terminals No. 10 (Orange/Blue wire) and No. 17 (White/Blue wire).
4) If resistance is not 400-600 ohms, go to next step. If resistance is 400-600 ohms, go to DTC P0720 (FLASH CODE 9). Check for loose TCM harness connectors. Replace TCM with a known-good unit if necessary.
5) Disconnect mainshaft speed sensor harness connector. Check Orange/Blue wire for continuity between 22-pin TCM harness connector "B", terminal No. 10 and mainshaft speed sensor harness connector. If continuity is present, go to next step. If continuity is not present, repair open in Orange/Blue wire between 22-pin TCM harness connector and mainshaft speed sensor harness connector.
6) Check White/Blue wire for continuity between 22-pin TCM harness connector "B", terminal No. 17 and mainshaft speed sensor harness connector. If continuity is present, check for loose TCM harness connectors. Replace TCM with a known-good unit if necessary. If continuity is not present, repair open in White/Blue wire between 22-pin TCM harness connector and mainshaft speed sensor harness connector.

DTC P0720/9: COUNTERSHAFT SPEED SENSOR

1) Ensure countershaft speed sensor is installed properly. See COUNTERSHAFT SPEED SENSOR under REMOVAL & INSTALLATION. Disconnect countershaft speed sensor harness connector. Using a DVOM, measure resistance between sensor terminals. See COUNTERSHAFT SPEED SENSOR under COMPONENT TESTING.
2) If resistance is not 400-600 ohms, replace countershaft speed sensor. If resistance is 400-600 ohms, disconnect 22-pin TCM harness connector "B". Check for continuity between ground and 22-pin TCM harness connector "B", terminals No. 8 (Blue/Yellow wire) and No. 9 (Blue/Green wire). *See Fig. 10.*

3) If continuity is present, repair short to ground in Blue/Yellow wire or Blue/Green wire between TCM and countershaft speed sensor. If continuity is not present, reconnect countershaft speed sensor harness connector. Measure resistance between 22-pin TCM harness connector "B", terminals No. 8 (Blue/Yellow wire) and No. 9 (Blue/Green wire).
4) If resistance is 400-600 ohms, check for loose TCM harness connectors. Replace TCM with a known-good unit if necessary. If resistance is not 400-600 ohms, repair loose connection or open in Blue/Yellow wire or Blue/Green wire between 22-pin TCM harness connector and countershaft speed sensor harness connector.

DTC P0725/11: IGNITION COIL

1) Disconnect 26-pin TCM harness connector "A". Turn ignition on. Using a DVOM, measure voltage between 26-pin TCM harness connector "A", terminal No. 5 (Blue wire) and terminals No. 13 or 26 (Brown/Black wires). *See Fig. 10.*
2) If battery voltage is present, check for loose TCM harness connectors. Replace TCM with a known-good unit if necessary. If battery voltage is not present, repair open or short in Blue wire between ignition coil and 26-pin TCM harness connector "A".

DTC P0730: SHIFT CONTROL SYSTEM

NOTE: DO NOT perform this DTC test until all other DTCs have been repaired first.

1) Road test vehicle at over 12 MPH for more than 30 seconds in 2nd, 3rd and 4th gear. Using scan tool, check for any other DTCs. If any other DTCs are present, repair those DTCs first, then recheck for DTC P0730. If no other DTCs are present, go to next step.
2) Test clutch pressure. See HYDRAULIC PRESSURE TEST under TESTING in appropriate overhaul article. If clutch pressure is within specification, go to next step. If clutch pressure is not within specification, repair hydraulic system as necessary. See HYDRAULIC PRESSURE TROUBLE SHOOTING table under HYDRAULIC PRESSURE TEST in appropriate overhaul article.
3) Replace shift control solenoid valve assembly. See SHIFT CONTROL SOLENOID VALVES under REMOVAL & INSTALLATION. Turn ignition off and clear codes. See CLEARING FAULT CODES under SELF-DIAGNOSTIC SYSTEM. Road test vehicle at over 12 MPH for more than 30 seconds in 2nd, 3rd and 4th gear. Recheck DTCs. If P0730 returns, go to next step. If P0730 does not return, system is okay.
4) Replace linear solenoid assembly. See LINEAR SOLENOID under REMOVAL & INSTALLATION. Turn ignition off and clear codes. See CLEARING FAULT CODES under SELF-DIAGNOSTIC SYSTEM. Road test vehicle at over 12 MPH for more than 30 seconds in 2nd, 3rd and 4th gear. Recheck DTCs. If P0730 returns, replace transaxle. If P0730 does not return, system is okay.

DTC P0740: LOCK-UP CONTROL SYSTEM

NOTE: DO NOT perform this DTC test until all other DTCs have been repaired first.

1) Using scan tool, check for any other DTCs. If any other DTCs are present, repair those DTCs first, then recheck for DTC P0740. If no other DTCs are present, go to next step.
2) Test line pressure. See HYDRAULIC PRESSURE TEST under TESTING in appropriate overhaul article. If line pressure is within specification, go to next step. If line pressure is not within specification, repair hydraulic system as necessary. See HYDRAULIC PRESSURE TROUBLE SHOOTING table under HYDRAULIC PRESSURE TEST in appropriate overhaul article.
3) Test clutch pressure. If clutch pressure is within specification, go to next step. If clutch pressure is not within specification, repair hydraulic system as necessary. See HYDRAULIC PRESSURE TROUBLE SHOOTING table under HYDRAULIC PRESSURE TEST in appropriate overhaul article.

4) Replace lock-up control solenoid valve assembly. See LOCK-UP CONTROL SOLENOID VALVES under REMOVAL & INSTALLATION. Turn ignition off and clear codes. See CLEARING FAULT CODES under SELF-DIAGNOSTIC SYSTEM. Road test vehicle at over 50 MPH for more than one minute. Recheck DTCs. If P0740 returns, go to next step. If P0740 does not return, system is okay.

5) Replace linear solenoid assembly. See LINEAR SOLENOID under REMOVAL & INSTALLATION. Turn ignition off and clear codes. See CLEARING FAULT CODES under SELF-DIAGNOSTIC SYSTEM. Road test vehicle at over 50 MPH for more than one minute. Recheck DTCs. If P0740 returns, go to next step. If P0740 does not return, system is okay.

6) Replace torque converter. Turn ignition off and clear codes. See CLEARING FAULT CODES under SELF-DIAGNOSTIC SYSTEM. Road test vehicle at over 50 MPH for more than one minute. Recheck DTCs. If P0740 returns, replace transaxle. If P0740 does not return, system is okay.

DTC P0753/7:
SHIFT CONTROL SOLENOID VALVE "A"

1) Disconnect 26-pin TCM harness connector "A" and 22-pin TCM harness connector "B". Turn ignition on. Using a DVOM, measure voltage between 22-pin TCM harness connector "B", terminal No. 20 (Light Green/Black wire) and 26-pin TCM harness connector "A", terminals No. 13 or 26 (Brown/Black wires). See Fig. 10. If voltage is about 5 volts, go to next step. If voltage is not as specified, repair open or short in Light Green/Black wire between 22-pin TCM harness connector "B" and ECM.

2) Measure voltage between 26-pin TCM harness connector "A", terminal No. 3 (Blue/Yellow wire) and terminals No. 13 or 26 (Brown/Black wires). If voltage is not present, go to next step. If voltage is present, repair Blue/Yellow wire for a short to power.

3) Turn ignition off. Measure resistance between 26-pin TCM harness connector "A", terminal No. 3 (Blue/Yellow wire) and terminals No. 13 or 26 (Brown/Black wires). If resistance is not 12-20 ohms, go to next step. If resistance is 12-20 ohms, check for loose TCM harness connectors. Replace TCM with a known-good unit if necessary.

4) Disconnect shift control solenoid valve harness connector. Check for continuity between 26-pin TCM harness connector "A", terminal No. 3 (Blue/Yellow wire) and terminals No. 13 or 26 (Brown/Black wires). If continuity is not present, go to next step. If continuity is present, repair Blue/Yellow wire for a short to ground between 26-pin TCM harness connector "A" and shift control solenoid valve "A".

5) Measure resistance between ground and Blue/Yellow wire at shift control solenoid valve harness connector (solenoid side). If resistance is not 12-20 ohms, replace shift control solenoid valve assembly. If resistance is 12-20 ohms, repair open in Blue/Yellow wire between shift control solenoid valve "A" and harness connector.

DTC P0758/8:
SHIFT CONTROL SOLENOID VALVE "B"

1) Disconnect 26-pin TCM harness connector "A" and 22-pin TCM harness connector "B". Turn ignition on. Using a DVOM, measure voltage between 22-pin TCM harness connector "B", terminal No. 20 (Light Green/Black wire) and 26-pin TCM harness connector "A", terminals No. 13 or 26 (Brown/Black wires). See Fig. 10. If voltage is about 5 volts, go to next step. If voltage is not as specified, repair open or short in Light Green/Black wire between 22-pin TCM harness connector "B" and ECM.

2) Measure voltage between 26-pin TCM harness connector "A", terminal No. 2 (Green/White wire) and terminals No. 13 or 26 (Brown/Black wires). If voltage is not present, go to next step. If voltage is present, repair short to power in Green/White wire.

3) Turn ignition off. Measure resistance between 26-pin TCM harness connector "A", terminal No. 2 (Green/White wire) and terminals No. 13 or 26 (Brown/Black wires). If resistance is not 12-20 ohms, go to next step. If resistance is 12-20 ohms, check for loose TCM harness connectors. Replace TCM with a known-good unit if necessary.

4) Disconnect shift control solenoid valve harness connector. Check for continuity between 26-pin TCM harness connector "A", terminal No. 2 (Green/White wire) and No. 13 or 26 (Brown/Black wires). If continuity is not present, go to next step. If continuity is present, repair short to ground in Green/White wire between 26-pin TCM harness connector "A" and shift control solenoid valve "B".

5) Measure resistance between ground and Green/White wire at shift control solenoid valve harness connector (solenoid side). If resistance is not 12-20 ohms, replace shift control solenoid valve assembly. If resistance is 12-20 ohms, repair open in Green/White wire between shift control solenoid valve "B" and harness connector.

DTC P1705/5:
A/T GEAR POSITION SWITCH (SHORT)

NOTE: DTC P1705 is set when TCM receives 2 gear position signals at the same time.

1) Turn ignition on. If any A/T gear position indicator lights remain illuminated when gear selector is moved from that gear, go to next step. If all A/T gear position indicator lights turn off when gear selector is moved from that gear, system is okay at this time.

2) Shift through all gear positions except Reverse. Using a DVOM, measure voltage between 26-pin TCM harness connector "A", terminal No. 11 (Green/Red wire) and terminals No. 13 or 26 (Brown/Black wires). See Fig. 10. If battery voltage is present, go to next step. If battery voltage is not present, check for a short in Green/Red wire between 26-pin TCM harness connector "A" and A/T gear position indicator, or A/T gear position switch. Repair as necessary. If Green/Red wire is okay, check for loose TCM harness connectors. Replace TCM with a known-good unit if necessary.

3) Shift through all gear positions except Neutral and Park. Measure voltage between 26-pin TCM harness connector "A", terminal No. 10 (Light Green wire) and terminals No. 13 or 26 (Brown/Black wires). If battery voltage is present, go to next step. If battery voltage is not present, check for a short in Light Green wire between 26-pin TCM harness connector "A" and A/T gear position indicator, or A/T gear position switch. Repair as necessary. If Light Green wire is okay, check for loose TCM harness connectors. Replace TCM with a known-good unit if necessary.

4) Shift through all gear positions except "D₄". Measure voltage between 26-pin TCM harness connector "A", terminal No. 9 (Light Green/Black wire) and terminals No. 13 or 26 (Brown/Black wires). If battery voltage is present, go to next step. If battery voltage is not present, check for a short in Light Green/Black wire between 26-pin TCM harness connector "A" and A/T gear position switch. Repair as necessary. If Light Green/Black wire is okay, check for loose TCM harness connectors. Replace TCM with a known-good unit if necessary.

5) Shift through all gear positions except "D³". Measure voltage between 26-pin TCM harness connector "A", terminal No. 8 (Green/Blue wire) and terminals No. 13 or 26 (Brown/Black wires). If battery voltage is present, go to next step. If battery voltage is not present, check for a short in Green/Blue wire between 26-pin TCM harness connector "A" and A/T gear position indicator, or A/T gear position switch. Repair as necessary. If Green/Blue wire is okay, check for loose TCM harness connectors. Replace TCM with a known-good unit if necessary.

6) Shift through all gear positions except "2". Measure voltage between 26-pin TCM harness connector "A", terminal No. 7 (Green/Yellow wire) and terminals No. 13 or 26 (Brown/Black wires). If battery voltage is present, go to next step. If battery voltage is not present, check for a short in Green/Yellow wire between 26-pin TCM harness connector "A" and A/T gear position indicator, or A/T gear position switch. Repair as necessary. If Green/Yellow wire is okay, check for loose TCM harness connectors. Replace TCM with a known-good unit if necessary.

7) Shift through all gear positions except "1". Measure voltage between 26-pin TCM harness connector "A", terminal No. 6 (Light Green/White wire) and terminals No. 13 or 26 (Brown/Black wires). If battery voltage is present, check for loose TCM harness connectors. Replace TCM with a known-good unit if necessary. If battery voltage is not present, check for a short in Light Green/White wire between 26-pin TCM harness connector "A" and A/T gear position indicator, or A/T gear position switch. Repair as necessary. If Light Green/White wire is okay, check for loose TCM harness connectors. Replace TCM with a known-good unit if necessary.

DTC P1706/6:
A/T GEAR POSITION SWITCH (OPEN)

1) Turn ignition on. If any A/T gear position indicator lights remain on when gear selector is moved from that gear, go to next step. If all A/T gear position indicator lights turn off when gear selector is moved from that gear, system is okay at this time.

2) Shift to Reverse. Using a DVOM, measure voltage between 26-pin TCM harness connector "A", terminal No. 11 (Green/Red wire) and terminals No. 13 or 26 (Brown/Black wires). See Fig. 10. If voltage is not present, go to next step. If voltage is present, repair open in Green/Red wire between 26-pin TCM harness connector "A" and A/T gear position switch.

3) Shift to Neutral or Park. Measure voltage between 26-pin TCM harness connector "A", terminal No. 10 (Light Green wire) and terminals No. 13 or 26 (Brown/Black wires). If voltage is not present, go to next step. If voltage is present, repair open in Light Green wire between 26-pin TCM harness connector "A" and A/T gear position indicator.

4) Shift to "D$_4$" position. Measure voltage between 26-pin TCM harness connector "A", terminal No. 9 (Light Green/Black wire) and terminals No. 13 or 26 (Brown/Black wires). If voltage is not present, go to next step. If voltage is present, repair open in Light Green/Black wire between 26-pin TCM harness connector "A" and A/T gear position switch.

5) Shift to "D$_3$" position. Measure voltage between 26-pin TCM harness connector "A", terminal No. 8 (Green/Blue wire) and terminals No. 13 or 26 (Brown/Black wires). If voltage is not present, go to next step. If voltage is present, repair open in Green/Blue wire between 26-pin TCM harness connector "A" and A/T gear position switch.

6) Shift to "2" position. Measure voltage between 26-pin TCM harness connector "A", terminal No. 7 (Green/Yellow wire) and terminals No. 13 or 26 (Brown/Black wires). If voltage is not present, go to next step. If voltage is present, repair open in Green/Yellow wire between 26-pin TCM harness connector "A" and A/T gear position switch.

7) Shift to "1" position. Measure voltage between 26-pin TCM harness connector "A", terminal No. 6 (Light Green/White wire) and terminals No. 13 or 26 (Brown/Black wires). If voltage is not present, check for loose TCM harness connectors. Replace TCM with a known-good unit if necessary. If voltage is present, repair open in Light Green/White wire between 26-pin TCM harness connector "A" and A/T gear position switch.

DTC P1753/1:
LOCK-UP CONTROL SOLENOID VALVE "A"

1) Disconnect 26-pin TCM harness connector "A" and 22-pin TCM harness connector "B". Turn ignition on. Using a DVOM, measure voltage between 22-pin TCM harness connector "B", terminal No. 20 (Light Green/Black wire) and 26-pin TCM harness connector "A", terminals No. 13 or 26 (Brown/Black wires). See Fig. 10. If voltage is about 5 volts, go to next step. If voltage is not as specified, repair open or short in Light Green/Black wire between 22-pin TCM harness connector "B" and ECM.

2) Measure voltage between 26-pin TCM harness connector "A", terminal No. 16 (Yellow wire) and terminals No. 13 or 26 (Brown/Black wires). If voltage is not present, go to next step. If voltage is present, repair short to power in Yellow wire.

3) Turn ignition off. Measure resistance between 26-pin TCM harness connector "A", terminal No. 16 (Yellow wire) and terminals No. 13 or 26 (Brown/Black wires). If resistance is not 12-20 ohms, go to next step.

If resistance is 12-20 ohms, check for loose TCM harness connectors. Replace TCM with a known-good unit if necessary.

4) Disconnect lock-up control solenoid valve harness connector. Check for continuity between 26-pin TCM harness connector "A", terminal No. 16 (Yellow wire) and terminals No. 13 or 26 (Brown/Black wires). If continuity is not present, go to next step. If continuity is present, repair short to ground in Yellow wire between 26-pin TCM harness connector "A" and lock-up control solenoid valve "A".

5) Measure resistance of Yellow wire between ground and lock-up control solenoid valve harness connector (solenoid side). If resistance is not 12-20 ohms, replace lock-up control solenoid valve assembly. If resistance is 12-20 ohms, repair open in Yellow wire between lock-up control solenoid valve "A" and harness connector.

DTC P1758/2:
LOCK-UP CONTROL SOLENOID VALVE "B"

1) Disconnect 26-pin TCM harness connector "A" and 22-pin TCM harness connector "B". Turn ignition on. Using a DVOM, measure voltage between 22-pin TCM harness connector "B", terminal No. 20 (Light Green/Black wire) and 26-pin TCM harness connector "A", terminals No. 13 or 26 (Brown/Black wires). See Fig. 10. If voltage is about 5 volts, go to next step. If voltage is not as specified, repair open or short in Light Green/Black wire between 22-pin TCM harness connector "B" and ECM.

2) Measure voltage between 26-pin TCM harness connector "A", terminal No. 15 (Green/Black wire) and terminals No. 13 or 26 (Brown/Black wires). If voltage is not present, go to next step. If voltage is present, repair short to power in Green/Black wire.

3) Turn ignition off. Measure resistance between 26-pin TCM harness connector "A", terminal No. 15 (Green/Black wire) and terminals No. 13 or 26 (Brown/Black wires). If resistance is not 12-20 ohms, go to next step. If resistance is 12-20 ohms, check for loose TCM harness connectors. Replace TCM with a known-good unit if necessary.

4) Disconnect lock-up control solenoid valve harness connector. Check for continuity between 26-pin TCM harness connector "A", terminal No. 15 (Green/Black wire) and terminals No. 13 or 26 (Brown/Black wires). If continuity is not present, go to next step. If continuity is present, repair short to ground in Green/Black wire between 26-pin TCM harness connector "A" and lock-up control solenoid valve "B".

5) Measure resistance of Green/Black wire between ground and lock-up control solenoid valve harness connector (solenoid side). If resistance is not 12-20 ohms, replace lock-up control solenoid valve assembly. If resistance is 12-20 ohms, repair open in Green/Black wire between lock-up control solenoid valve harness connector "B" and harness connector.

DTC P1768/16: LINEAR SOLENOID

1) Disconnect linear solenoid harness connector. Using a DVOM, measure resistance of linear solenoid. If resistance is about 5 ohms, go to next step. If resistance is not as specified, replace linear solenoid assembly.

2) Disconnect 22-pin TCM harness connector "B" and 26-pin TCM harness connector "A". Check for continuity between ground and 22-pin TCM harness connector "B", terminal No. 1 (Red wire), then between ground and 26-pin TCM harness connector "A", terminal No. 1 (White wire). See Fig. 10. If continuity is not present, go to next step. If continuity is present, repair short between Red wire and White wire.

3) Reconnect linear solenoid harness connector. Measure resistance between 22-pin TCM harness connector "B", terminal No. 1 (Red wire) and 26-pin TCM harness connector "A", terminal No. 1 (White wire). If resistance is about 5 ohms, check for loose TCM harness connectors. Replace TCM with a known-good unit if necessary. If resistance is not as specified, repair open or poor connection in Red wire or White wire between linear solenoid and 22-pin TCM harness connector "B", or 26-pin TCM harness connector "A".

DTC P1786/14: FAS SIGNAL

1) Start engine and allow it to reach normal operating temperature. Shift to Park. Cycle key off and on and wait for 2 seconds. Using a

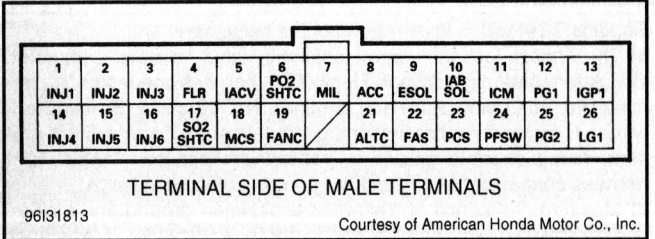

1	2	3	4	5	6	7	8	9	10	11	12	13
INJ1	INJ2	INJ3	FLR	IACV	PO2 SHTC	MIL	ACC	ESOL	IAB SOL	ICM	PG1	IGP1
14	15	16	17	18	19		21	22	23	24	25	26
INJ4	INJ5	INJ6	SO2 SHTC	MCS	FANC		ALTC	FAS	PCS	PFSW	PG2	LG1

TERMINAL SIDE OF MALE TERMINALS

96I31813

Courtesy of American Honda Motor Co., Inc.

Fig. 11: Identifying 26-Pin ECM Harness Connector "A" Terminals

DVOM, measure voltage between 22-pin TCM harness connector "B", terminal No. 19 (Brown/White wire) and 26-pin TCM harness connector "A", terminals No. 13 or 26 (Brown/Black wires). *See Fig. 10*. If voltage is about 5 volts, check for loose TCM harness connectors. Replace TCM with a known-good unit if necessary. If voltage is not as specified, go to net step.

2) Turn ignition off. Disconnect 22-pin TCM harness connector "B". Turn ignition on. Measure voltage between 26-pin ECM harness connector "A", terminals No. 22 (Brown/White wire) and No. 26 (Brown/Black wire). *See Fig. 11*. If voltage is about 5 volts, go to next step. If voltage is not as specified, go to step **4)**.

3) Turn ignition off. Check Brown/White wire for continuity between 26-pin ECM harness connector "A", terminal No. 22 and 22-pin TCM harness connector "B", terminal No. 19. If continuity is not present, repair open in Brown/White wire between ECM and TCM. If continuity is present, check for loose TCM harness connectors. Replace TCM with a known-good unit if necessary.

4) Turn ignition off. Disconnect 26-pin ECM harness connector "A". Check for continuity between ground and 26-pin ECM harness connector "A", terminal No. 22 (Brown/White wire), or between ground and 22-pin TCM harness connector "B", terminal No. 19 (Brown/White wire). If continuity is not present, check for loose TCM harness connectors. Replace TCM with a known-good unit if necessary. If continuity is present, repair short in Yellow wire between ECM and TCM.

DTC P1790/3:
THROTTLE POSITION (TP) SENSOR

1) Turn ignition on. Using scan tool, check for any other DTCs. Check for flashing Malfunction Indicator Light (MIL). If any other DTCs are present or MIL is flashing, repair those DTCs first, then recheck for DTC P1790. If no other DTCs are present, and MIL is not flashing, go to next step.

2) Turn ignition off. Disconnect 22-pin TCM harness connector "B" and 26-pin TCM harness connector "A". Turn ignition on. Measure voltage between 22-pin TCM harness connector "B", terminal No. 20 (Light Green/Black wire) and 26-pin TCM harness connector "A", terminals No. 13 or 26 (Brown/Black wires). *See Fig. 10*. If voltage is about 5 volts, go to next step. If voltage is not as specified, repair open or short in Light Green/Black wire between 22-pin TCM harness connector "B" and ECM.

3) Measure voltage between 22-pin TCM harness connector "B", terminal No. 4 (Red/Black wire) and 26-pin TCM harness connector "A", terminals No. 13 or 26 (Brown/Black wires). If voltage is .4-.6 volt, check for loose TCM harness connectors. Replace TCM with a known-good unit if necessary. If voltage is not as specified, repair open or short in Red/Black wire between TCM and TP sensor.

DTC P1791/4: VEHICLE SPEED SENSOR (VSS)

1) Ensure speedometer operates properly. If speedometer operates properly, go to next step. If speedometer does not operate properly, see VEHICLE SPEED SENSOR (VSS) under COMPONENT TESTING.

2) Raise and support vehicle. Block one front wheel. Place gear selector in Neutral. Turn ignition off. Disconnect 22-pin TCM harness connector "B" and 26-pin TCM harness connector "A". Turn ignition on. While rotating unblocked front wheel and using a DVOM, measure voltage between 22-pin TCM harness connector "B", terminal No. 5 (Orange wire) and 26-pin TCM harness connector "A", terminals No. 13 or 26 (Brown/Black wires). *See Fig. 10*.

3) If voltage alternates from zero to about 5 volts, check for loose TCM harness connectors. Replace TCM with a known-good unit if necessary. If voltage does not alternate as specified, check for an open or short in Orange wire between TCM and VSS. If wire is okay, see VEHICLE SPEED SENSOR (VSS) under COMPONENT TESTING.

DTC P1792/10:
ENGINE COOLANT TEMPERATURE (ECT) SENSOR

1) Turn ignition on. Using scan tool, check for any other DTCs. Check for flashing Malfunction Indicator Light (MIL). If any other DTCs are present or MIL is flashing, repair those DTCs first, then recheck for DTC P1792. If no other DTCs are present and MIL is not flashing, go to next step.

2) Turn ignition off. Disconnect 22-pin TCM harness connector "B" and 26-pin TCM harness connector "A". Turn ignition on. Measure voltage between 22-pin TCM harness connector "B", terminal No. 20 (Light Green/Black wire) and 26-pin TCM harness connector "A", terminals No. 13 or 26 (Brown/Black wires). *See Fig. 10*. If voltage is about 5 volts, go to next step. If voltage is not as specified, repair open or short in Light Green/Black wire between 22-pin TCM harness connector "B" and ECM.

3) Turn ignition off. Reconnect TCM harness connectors. Start engine and allow it to reach normal operating temperature. Measure voltage (backprobe) between 22-pin TCM harness connector "B", terminal No. 3 (Red/White wire) and 26-pin TCM harness connector "A", terminals No. 13 or 26 (Brown/Black wires). If voltage is less than one volt, check for loose TCM harness connectors. Replace TCM with a known-good unit if necessary. If voltage is equal to or greater than one volt, repair open or short in Red/White wire between TCM and ECT sensor.

DTC P1794/13:
BAROMETRIC PRESSURE (BARO) SENSOR

NOTE: Baro sensor is built into ECM.

1) Turn ignition off. Disconnect 22-pin TCM harness connector "B" and 26-pin TCM harness connector "A". Turn ignition on. Using a DVOM, measure voltage between 22-pin TCM harness connector "B", terminal No. 20 (Light Green/Black wire) and 26-pin TCM harness connector "A", terminals No. 13 or 26 (Brown/Black wires). *See Fig. 10*. If voltage is about 5 volts, go to next step. If voltage is not as specified, repair open or short in Light Green/Black wire between 22-pin TCM harness connector "B" and ECM.

2) Turn ignition off. Disconnect 22-pin ECM harness connector "D". Check Blue/White wire for continuity between 22-pin ECM harness connector "D", terminal No. 3 and 22-pin TCM harness connector "B" terminal No. 2. *See Fig. 12*. If continuity is present, go to next step. If continuity is not present, repair open in Blue/White wire between ECM and TCM.

3) Check for continuity between ground and 22-pin ECM harness connector "D", terminal No. 3 (Blue/White wire), or between ground and 22-pin TCM harness connector "B", terminal No. 2 (Blue/White wire). If continuity is not present, check for loose TCM harness connectors. Replace TCM with a known-good unit if necessary. If continuity is present, repair short to ground in Blue/White wire.

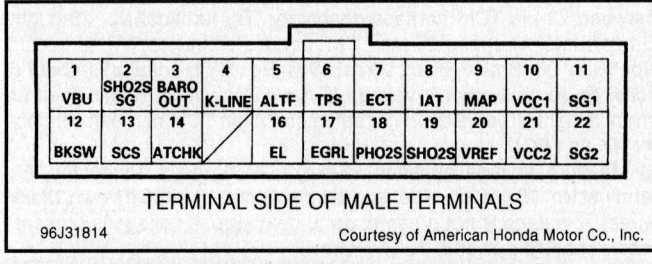

1	2	3	4	5	6	7	8	9	10	11
VBU	SHO2S SG	BARO OUT	K-LINE	ALTF	TPS	ECT	IAT	MAP	VCC1	SG1
12	13	14		16	17	18	19	20	21	22
BKSW	SCS	ATCHK		EL	EGRL	PHO2S	SHO2S	VREF	VCC2	SG2

TERMINAL SIDE OF MALE TERMINALS

96J31814

Courtesy of American Honda Motor Co., Inc.

Fig. 12: Identifying ECM Harness Connector "D" Terminals

TROUBLE SHOOTING

A/C SIGNAL

NOTE: If no A/C signal is present, torque converter lock-up clutch may not engage or cycle on and off.

1) Start engine. Turn blower switch and A/C switch to the ON position. Check if A/C compressor clutch engages.

2) If A/C compressor clutch does not engage, check A/C system. See appropriate AUTOMATIC or MANUAL A/C-HEATER SYSTEMS article in appropriate MITCHELL® AIR CONDITIONING & HEATING SERVICE & REPAIR manual. If A/C compressor clutch engages, turn engine off. Disconnect 26-pin TCM harness connector "A".

3) Start engine. Using a DVOM, measure voltage between 26-pin TCM harness connector "A", terminal No. 24 (Red/Blue wire) and terminals No. 13 or 26 (Brown/Black wire). Note voltage with A/C compressor off.

4) If battery voltage is not present, go to next step. If battery voltage is present, A/C signal is okay. Check for loose TCM harness connections. If harness connections are okay, substitute TCM with a known-good unit and recheck.

5) Repair open Red/Blue wire between 26-pin TCM harness connector "A", terminal No. 24 and A/C compressor clutch relay. The A/C compressor clutch relay is located at left front corner of engine compartment, near radiator. *See Fig. 5.*

BRAKELIGHT SIGNAL

NOTE: If no brakelight is present, transaxle may fail to shift from Park with brake pedal depressed and accelerator pedal in idle position.

1) Ensure brakelights come on when brake pedal is depressed. If brakelights come on, go to next step. If brakelights do not come on, check fuse No. 30 (20-amp) in engine compartment fuse/relay box. If fuse is okay, repair brakelight signal circuit.

2) Ensure ignition is off. Disconnect 26-pin TCM harness connector "A" and 22-pin TCM harness connector "B". Using a DVOM, measure voltage between 22-pin TCM harness connector "B", terminal No. 12 (Green/White wire) and 26-pin TCM harness connector "A", terminals No. 13 or 26 (Brown/Black wires) with brake pedal depressed. If battery voltage is present, brakelight signal to TCM is okay. Check for loose TCM harness connections. If harness connections are okay, substitute TCM with a known-good unit and recheck.

3) If battery voltage is not present, repair open in Green/White wire between 22-pin TCM harness connector "B", terminal No. 12 and brakelight switch. Brakelight switch is located on brake pedal support. *See Fig. 4.*

SYSTEM TESTING

A/T GEAR POSITION INDICATOR

NOTE: If necessary, refer to wiring schematic when checking component wiring. See Fig. 13.

1) Remove instrument panel gauge assembly from instrument panel. Disconnect harness connectors from rear of instrument panel gauge assembly. *See Fig. 14.*

2) Using a DVOM, check for voltage and continuity at specified harness connectors and terminals. *See Fig. 15.* If necessary, check ground connections G402 or G404. Ground connection G402 is located at passenger's side front corner, behind instrument panel. Ground connection G404 is located behind driver's side of center console. *See Fig. 16.*

3) If necessary, check fuse No. 1 (10-amp) located in instrument panel fuse/relay box, or fuse No. 32 (15-amp) located in engine compartment fuse/relay box.

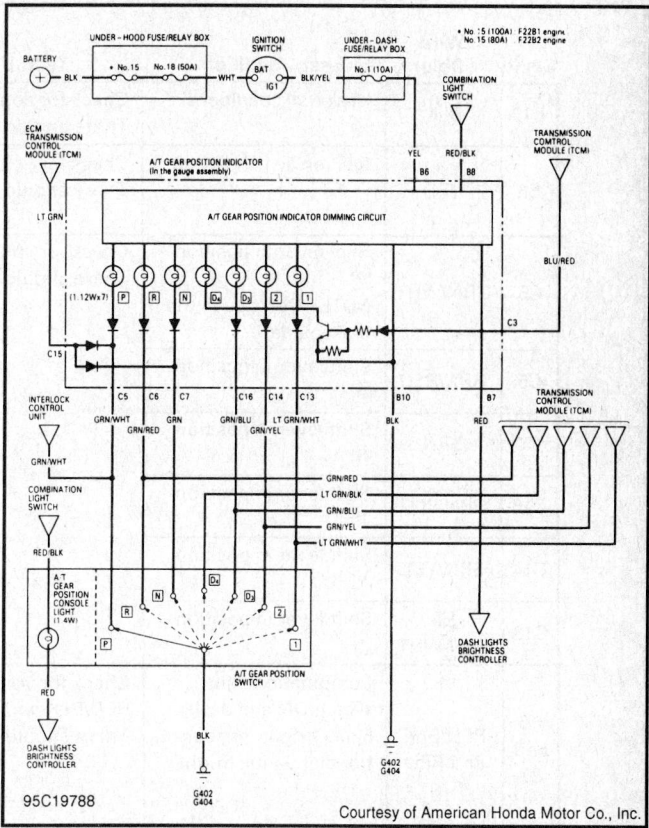

Fig. 13: A/T Gear Position Indicator Wiring Schematic

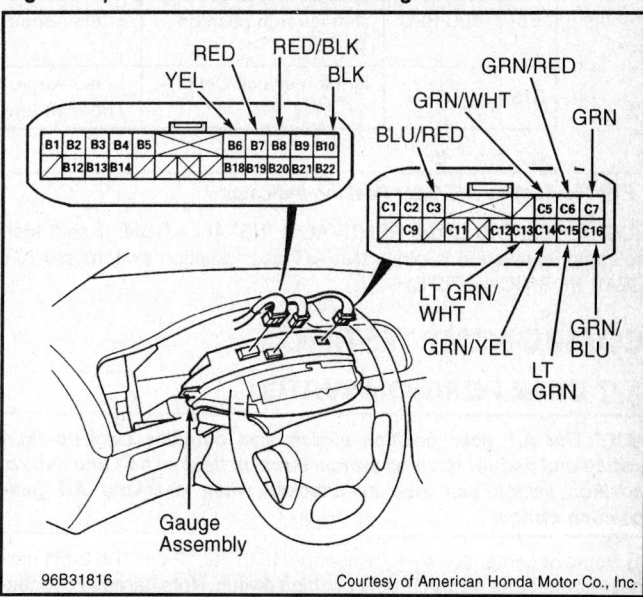

Fig. 14: Identifying Instrument Panel Gauge Assembly Harness Connectors

SHIFT & KEY INTERLOCK SYSTEMS

NOTE: For system testing, refer to appropriate wiring diagram. See WIRING DIAGRAMS. To check individual components, see COMPONENT TESTING.

1) To check system operation, ensure shift lever is in Park. Turn ignition on. Depress brake pedal with accelerator pedal in idle position.

2) If shift lock solenoid clicks, system is working properly. If shift lock solenoid fails to click, see INTERLOCK CONTROL UNIT under COMPONENT TESTING. If shift lever cannot be moved from Park, check for proper installation procedure of shift lock solenoid. See SHIFT

Cavity	Wire Color	Test Condition	Test: Desired Result	Possible Cause If Result Is Not Obtained
B10	BLK	Under all conditions	Check for continuity to ground: There should be continuity.	• Poor ground (G402, G404) • An open in the wire
B6	YEL	Ignition switch ON (II)	Check for voltage to ground: There should be battery voltage.	• Blown No. 1 (10 A) fuse in the under-dash fuse/relay box • An open in the wire
C5	GRN/WHT	Shift lever in position P NOTE: Don't push the brake pedal.	Check for continuity to ground: There should be continuity.	• Faulty A/T gear position switch • Poor ground (G402, G404) • An open in the wire
C6	GRN/RED	Shift lever in position R		
C7	GRN	Shift lever in position N		
C16	GRN/BLU	Shift lever in position D₃		
C14	GRN/YEL	Shift lever in position 2		
C13	LT GRN/WHT	Shift lever in position 1		
B8 and B7	RED/BLK and RED	Combination light switch ON and dash lights brightness control dial on full bright	Check for voltage between RED/BLK and RED terminals: There should be battery voltage.	• Blown No. 32 (15 A) fuse in the under-hood fuse/relay box • Faulty combination light switch • Faulty dash lights brightness control system • An open in the wire
C3	BLU/RED	Ignition switch ON (II), shift lever in position D₄	Check for voltage to ground: There should be about 5 V.	• Faulty A/T gear position switch • Faulty PCM • An open in the wire
C15	LT GRN	Ignition switch ON (II)	Check for voltage to ground: There should be about 5 V.	• Faulty PCM • An open in the wire

96C31817   Courtesy of American Honda Motor Co., Inc.

Fig. 15: Testing A/T Gear Position Indicator

LOCK SOLENOID under REMOVAL & INSTALLATION. If shift lock solenoid installation is okay, test A/T gear position switch, see A/T GEAR POSITION SWITCH.

COMPONENT TESTING

A/T GEAR POSITION SWITCH

NOTE: The A/T gear position switch also contains back-up light switch and neutral position switch. Back-up light switch and neutral position switch can also be checked when checking A/T gear position switch.

1) Remove center console. Disconnect both the 12-pin and 2-pin harness connectors from A/T gear position switch. Note harness connector terminal identification. *See Fig. 17.*

2) Using a DVOM, check for continuity between specified terminal(s) with shift lever in indicated positions. See A/T GEAR POSITION SWITCH CONTINUITY table.

NOTE: Check for continuity while moving shift lever back and forth in free play area of each gear position. DO NOT touch push button on shift lever when checking continuity.

3) If continuity is not as specified, A/T gear position switch may require adjustment. See A/T GEAR POSITION SWITCH under REMOVAL & INSTALLATION. If correct continuity cannot be obtained by adjusting A/T gear position switch, replace switch assembly.

A/T GEAR POSITION SWITCH CONTINUITY

Application	Shift Lever Position	Continuity Between Terminals
With Cruise Control		
A/T Gear Position Switch	"P"	F & I
	"R"	I & J
	"N"	I & K
	"D₄"	A, E & I
	"D₃"	A, D & I
	"2"	A, C & I
	"1"	B & I
Back-Up Light Switch	"R"	G & H
Neutral Position Switch	"P"	L & M
	"N"	L & M
Without Cruise Control		
A/T Gear Position Switch	"P"	F & I
	"R"	I & J
	"N"	I & K
	"D₄"	E & I
	"D₃"	D & I
	"2"	C & I
	"1"	B & I
Back-Up Light Switch	"R"	G & H
Neutral Position Switch	"P"	L & M
	"N"	L & M

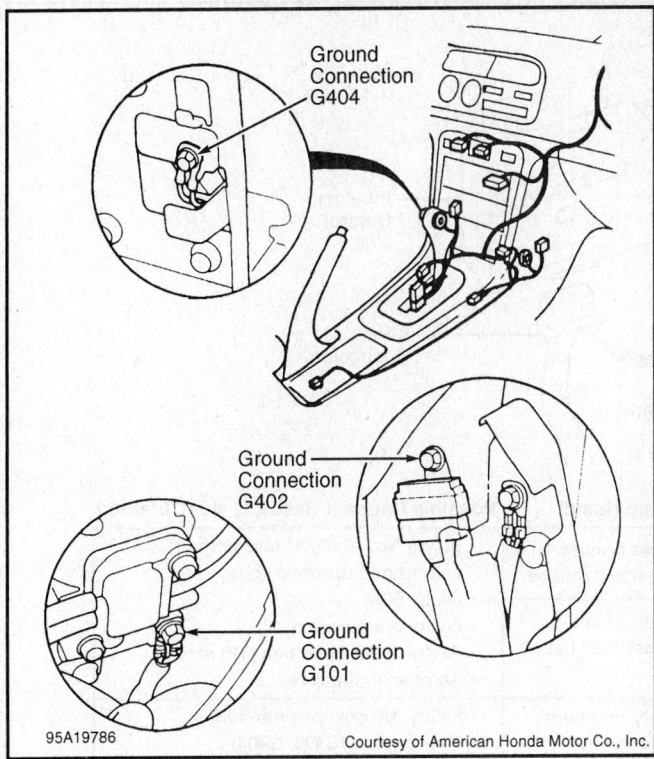

Fig. 16: Locating Ground Connections

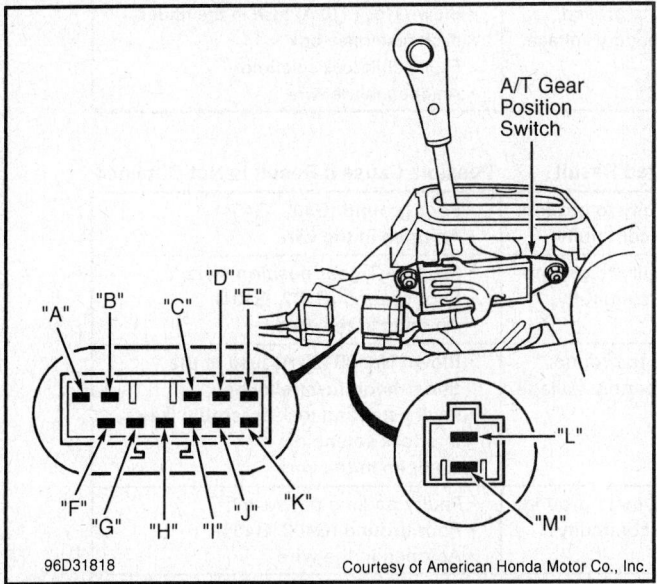

Fig. 17: Identifying A/T Gear Position Switch Harness Connector Terminals

BRAKELIGHT SWITCH

1) Disconnect harness connector from brakelight switch, located on brake pedal support. *See Fig. 4.* Note brakelight switch terminal identification. *See Fig. 18.*

2) On models with cruise control, using a DVOM, check for continuity between terminals "B" and "C" with brake pedal depressed. Continuity should be present. Continuity should not be present with brake pedal released.

3) On models without cruise control, using a DVOM, check for continuity between terminals "A" and "B" with brake pedal depressed. Continuity should be present. Continuity should not be present with brake pedal released.

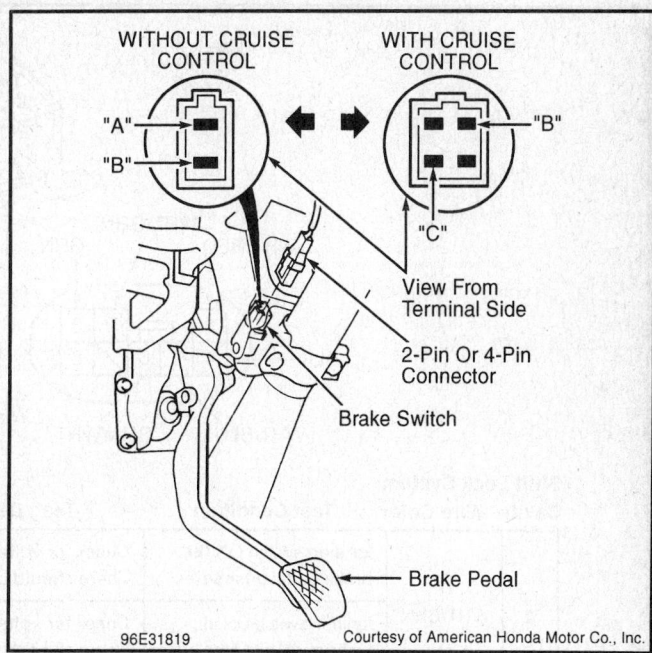

Fig. 18: Identifying Brakelight Switch Terminals

4) If continuity is not as specified, ensure brake pedal is properly adjusted so brakelight switch has proper travel for switch operation. If brakelight switch travel is okay, replace brakelight switch.

COUNTERSHAFT SPEED SENSOR

Disconnect harness connector from countershaft speed sensor located on top of transaxle. *See Fig. 6.* Using a DVOM, measure resistance between sensor terminals. Replace countershaft speed sensor if resistance is not 400-600 ohms.

ENGINE COOLANT TEMPERATURE (ECT) SENSOR

1) Sensor is located on cylinder head, below distributor and contains a Red/White wire and Green/Blue wire in the harness connector. *See Fig. 6.*

2) Disconnect harness connector from sensor. Using a DVOM, measure sensor resistance in accordance with coolant temperature. *See Fig. 19.* Replace ECT sensor if resistance is not as specified.

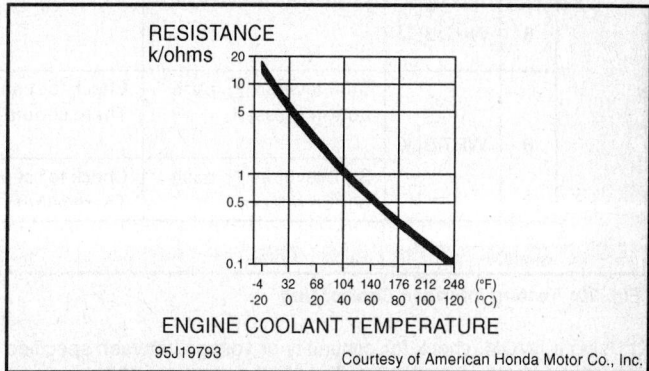

Fig. 19: Measuring ECT Sensor Resistance

INTERLOCK CONTROL UNIT

1) Disconnect 8-pin harness connector from interlock control unit. Interlock control unit is located behind center of instrument panel. *See Fig. 2.* Inspect terminals for poor connection, corrosion or bending. Repair as necessary.

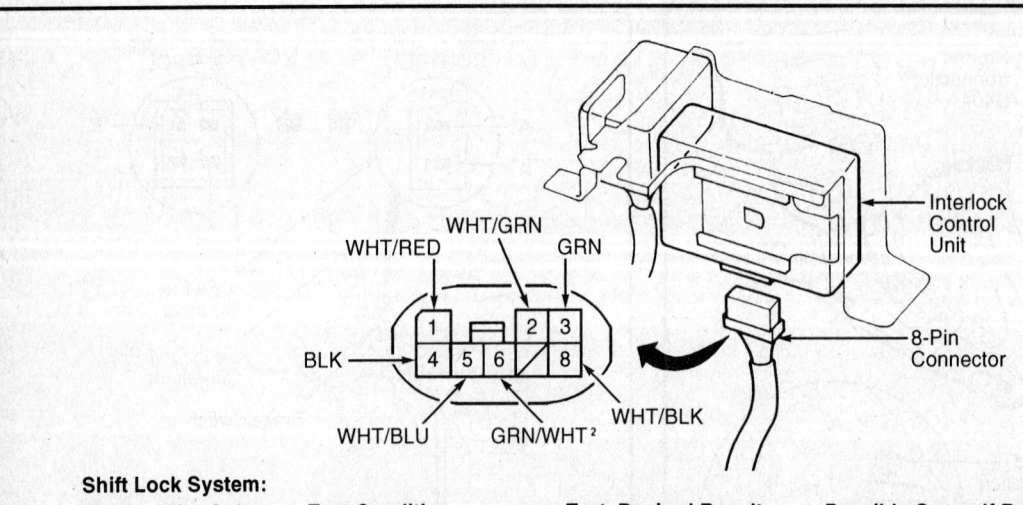

Shift Lock System:

Cavity	Wire Color	Test Condition	Test: Desired Result	Possible Cause If Result Is Not Obtained
2	WHT/GRN	Ignition switch ON (II), brake pedal pushed	Check for voltage to ground: There should be battery voltage.	• Blown No. 30 (20 A) fuse in the under-hood fuse/relay box • Faulty PCM • Faulty brake switch • Faulty throttle position (TP) sensor • An open in the wire
		Ignition switch ON (II), brake pedal and accelerator pushed at the same time	Check for voltage to ground: There should be less than battery voltage.	
6	GRN/WHT²	Shift lever in P	Check for continuity to ground: There should be continuity.	• Faulty A/T gear position switch • Poor ground (G402, G404) • An open in the wire
3	GRN	Ignition switch ON (II)	Check for voltage to ground: There should be battery voltage.	• Blown No. 1 (10 A) fuse in the under-dash fuse/relay box • Faulty shift lock solenoid • An open in the wire

Key Interlock System:

Cavity	Wire Color	Test Condition	Test: Desired Result	Possible Cause If Result Is Not Obtained
4	BLK	Under all conditions	Check for continuity to ground: There should be continuity.	• Poor ground (G402, G404) • An open in the wire
6	GRN/WHT²	Shift lever in P	Check for continuity to ground: There should be continuity.	• Faulty A/T gear position switch • Poor ground (G402, G404) • An open in the wire
1	WHT/RED	Ignition switch turned to ACC (I), the key pushed all the way in	Check for voltage to ground: There should be battery voltage.	• Blown No. 30 (20 A) fuse in the under-hood fuse/relay box • Faulty steering lock assembly (key interlock solenoid) • An open in the wire
5	WHT/BLU			
8	WHT/BLK	Shift lever in P, push button pressed	Check for continuity to ground: There should be continuity.	• Faulty parking pin switch • Poor ground (G402, G404) • An open in the wire
		Shift lever in P, push button released	Check for continuity to ground: There should be no continuity.	• Faulty parking pin switch • Short to ground

96H31820

Courtesy of American Honda Motor Co., Inc.

Fig. 20: Testing Interlock Control Unit

2) Using a DVOM, check for continuity or voltage between specified terminals or body ground. *See Fig. 20.* If necessary, check ground connections G402 or G404. Ground connection G402 is located at passenger's side front corner, behind instrument panel. Ground connection G404 is located behind driver's side of center console. *See Fig. 16.*

3) If necessary, check fuse No. 30 (20-amp) in engine compartment fuse box, or fuse No. 1 fuse (10-amp) in instrument panel fuse/relay box.

KEY INTERLOCK SOLENOID

1) Remove lower cover and knee bolster from driver's side of instrument panel for access to key interlock solenoid 8-pin harness connector. *See Fig. 21.*

2) Disconnect key interlock solenoid 8-pin harness connector from main wiring harness. Note harness connector terminal identification.

3) Using a DVOM, check for continuity between designated terminals with ignition lock assembly in ACC position. See KEY INTERLOCK SOLENOID CONTINUITY SPECIFICATIONS table.

4) If continuity is as specified, go to next step. If continuity is not as specified, replace ignition lock assembly. Key interlock solenoid cannot be serviced separately.

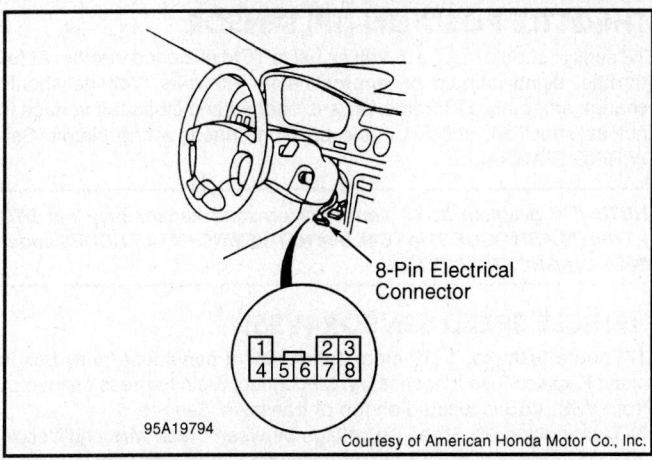

Fig. 21: Identifying Key Interlock Solenoid Harness Connector & Terminals

5) Connect battery voltage and ground to terminals No. 4 and 7. Ensure ignition key cannot be removed with battery voltage applied.

6) If ignition key cannot be removed, key interlock solenoid is okay. If ignition key can be removed, replace ignition lock assembly. Key interlock solenoid cannot be serviced separately.

KEY INTERLOCK SOLENOID CONTINUITY SPECIFICATIONS

Ignition Key Position	Continuity Between Terminals
Key Pushed In	4, 6 & 7
Key Released	6 & 7

LINEAR SOLENOID

1) Linear solenoid is located on transaxle. See Fig. 6. Disconnect harness connector at linear solenoid.

2) Using a DVOM, measure resistance between solenoid terminals. Resistance should be 4.6-5.2 ohms. Replace linear solenoid assembly if resistance is not as specified.

3) Check linear solenoid operation. Apply battery voltage to terminal "A" and ground terminal "B". See Fig. 22. A clicking sound should be heard, indicating solenoid operation. Replace linear solenoid assembly if solenoid fails to operate.

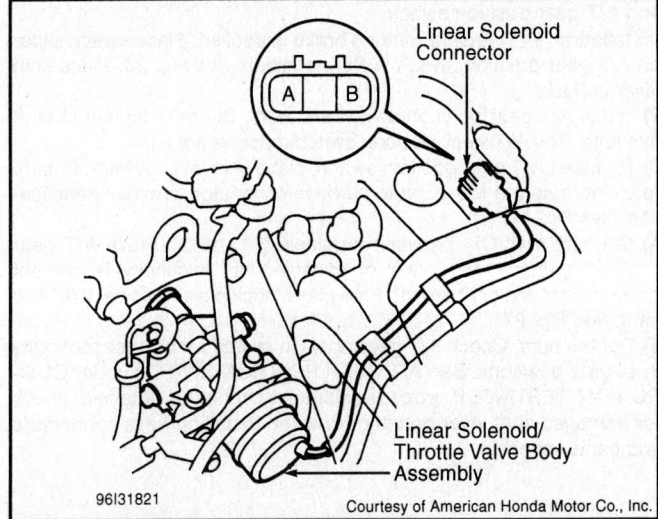

Fig. 22: Identifying Linear Solenoid Harness Connector Terminals

LOCK-UP CONTROL SOLENOID VALVES

1) Lock-up control solenoid valves are located on transaxle. Disconnect harness connector at lock-up control solenoid valves. See Fig. 6.

2) Using a DVOM, measure resistance between ground and terminal No. 1 (solenoid valve "B"), then between ground and terminal No. 3 (solenoid valve "A"). See Fig. 23.

3) Resistance should be 12-20 ohms. Replace lock-up control solenoid valve assembly if resistance of either solenoid valve is not within specification.

4) Check lock-up control solenoid valve operation. Ensure solenoid valve body is grounded. Apply battery voltage to terminal No. 1 (solenoid valve "B") or terminal No. 3 (solenoid valve "A").

5) A clicking sound should be heard, indicating solenoid valve operation. Replace lock-up control solenoid valve assembly if either solenoid valve fails to operate.

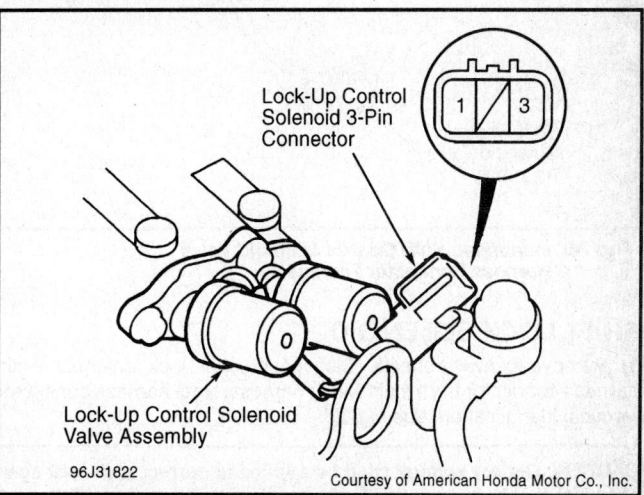

Fig. 23: Identifying Lock-Up Control Solenoid Valve Harness Connector Terminals

MAINSHAFT SPEED SENSOR

Disconnect harness connector from mainshaft speed sensor located on side of transaxle. See Fig. 6. Using a DVOM, measure resistance between sensor terminals. Replace mainshaft speed sensor if resistance is not 400-600 ohms.

PARKING PIN SWITCH

1) Remove center console. Disconnect parking pin switch 2-pin harness connector. Parking pin switch is located on left side of shifter assembly.

2) Using a DVOM, check for continuity between parking pin switch terminals. Continuity should be present when shift lever button is depressed. Continuity should not be present with shift lever button released. If continuity is not as described, replace parking pin switch.

SHIFT CONTROL SOLENOID VALVES

1) Shift control solenoid valves are located on transaxle. See Fig. 6. Disconnect harness connector at shift control solenoid valves.

2) Using a DVOM, measure resistance between ground and terminal No. 1 (solenoid valve "A"), then between ground and terminal No. 3 (solenoid valve "B"). See Fig. 24.

3) Resistance should be 12-20 ohms. Replace shift control solenoid valve assembly if resistance of either solenoid valve is not within specification.

4) Check shift control solenoid valve operation. Ensure solenoid valve body is grounded. Apply battery voltage to terminal No. 1 (solenoid valve "A") or terminal No. 3 (solenoid valve "B").

5) A clicking sound should be heard, indicating solenoid valve operation. Replace shift control solenoid valve assembly if either solenoid valve fails to operate.

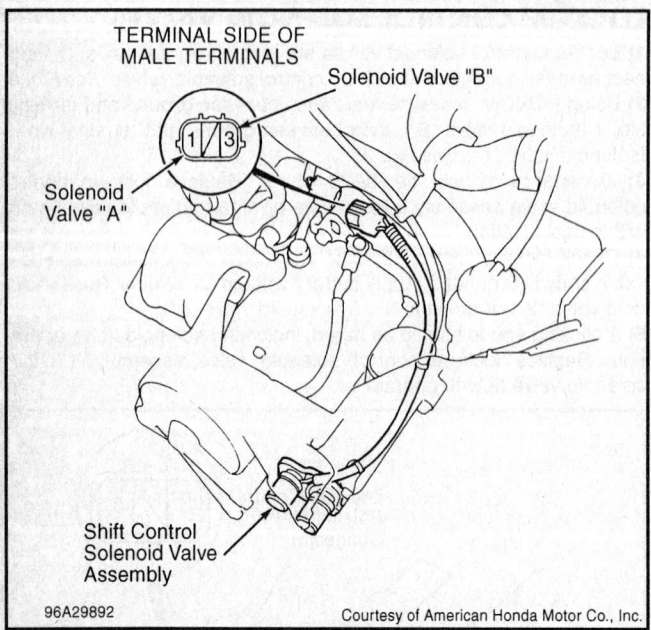

Fig. 24: Identifying Shift Control Solenoid Valve Harness Connector Terminals

SHIFT LOCK SOLENOID

1) Remove center console. Disconnect shift lock solenoid 3-pin harness connector from main wiring harness. Note harness connector terminal identification. *See Fig. 25.*

CAUTION: Battery voltage must be applied to correct shift lock solenoid electrical connector terminals or diode inside shift lock solenoid will be damaged.

---

2) Momentarily connect battery positive terminal to terminal "A", and battery negative terminal to terminal "B". *See Fig. 25.* Ensure shift lock solenoid operates with battery voltage applied. Replace shift lock solenoid if solenoid fails to operate.

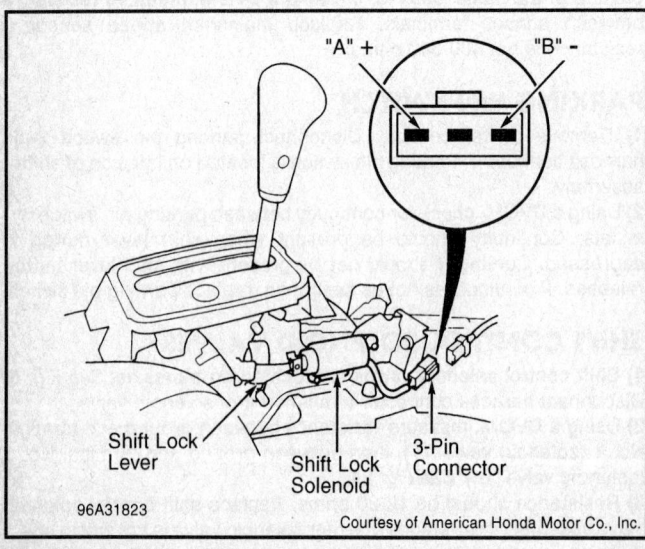

Fig. 25: Identifying Shift Lock Solenoid Harness Connector Terminals

THROTTLE POSITION (TP) SENSOR

TP sensor should input a .5-volt signal to TCM at closed throttle. At full throttle, signal should be approximately 4.5 volts. Voltage should change smoothly as throttle valve is opened and closed. If voltage is not as specified, check throttle position sensor wiring circuit. See WIRING DIAGRAMS.

NOTE: If a problem in TP sensor is present, sensor may set DTC P1790 (FLASH CODE 3) in TCM. See RETRIEVING FAULT CODES under SELF-DIAGNOSTIC SYSTEM.

VEHICLE SPEED SENSOR (VSS)

1) Ensure fuse No. 1 (10-amp) in instrument panel fuse/relay box is okay. Replace fuse if necessary. Disconnect 3-pin harness connector from VSS. VSS is located on top of transaxle. *See Fig. 6.*

2) Turn ignition on. Measure voltage between Black wire and Yellow wire on harness side of 3-pin harness connector. If battery voltage is present, go to step **4)**. If battery voltage is not present, check for continuity between Black wire of 3-pin harness connector and ground.

3) If continuity is present, repair open in Yellow wire between 3-pin harness connector and fuse No. 1 (10-amp) in instrument panel fuse/relay box. If continuity is not present, repair open in Black wire to VSS and ground. Ground is located on left rear of engine.

4) Measure voltage between Orange wire and Black wire of 3-pin harness connector. Voltage should be about 5 volts. If voltage is as specified, go to next step. If voltage is not as specified, check for an open or short to ground in Orange wire.

5) Reinstall 3-pin harness connector on VSS. Raise and support vehicle so front wheels can rotate. Connect a DVOM (backprobe) between ground and Orange wire on 3-pin harness connector.

6) Turn ignition on. Place shift lever in Neutral. Slowly rotate one front wheel while holding remaining front wheel from rotating and note voltage reading.

7) Ensure voltage pulses from zero volts to about 5 volts. If voltage pulses as specified, VSS is okay. If voltage does not pulse as specified, replace VSS. See VEHICLE SPEED SENSOR under REMOVAL & INSTALLATION.

REMOVAL & INSTALLATION
A/T GEAR POSITION SWITCH

Removal – Remove center console. Disconnect both the 12-pin and 2-pin harness connectors from A/T gear position switch. Remove nuts and A/T gear position switch.

Installation – 1) Ensure parking brake is applied. Place switch slider on A/T gear position switch in Park position. *See Fig. 26.* Place shift lever in Park.

2) Install A/T gear position switch and nuts. DO NOT tighten nuts at this time. The A/T gear position switch must be adjusted.

3) To adjust A/T gear position switch, place shift lever in Park. Ensure retaining nuts are loose. Note harness connector terminal identification. *See Fig. 17.*

4) Connect a DVOM between terminals "F" and "I". Move A/T gear position switch toward rear of console until continuity is present between terminals "F" and "I". Free play at lock pin should be .079" (2.0 mm). *See Fig. 27.*

5) Tighten nuts. Check A/T gear position switch for correct continuity in all gear positions. See A/T GEAR POSITION SWITCH under COMPONENT TESTING. If proper adjustment cannot be obtained, check for damaged shift lever detent or bracket. Install harness connectors and center console.

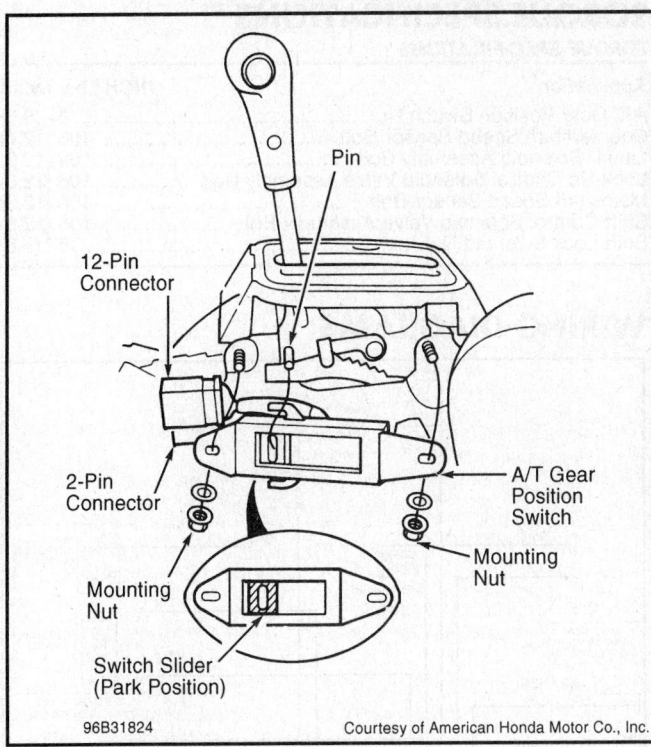

Fig. 26: Installing A/T Gear Position Switch

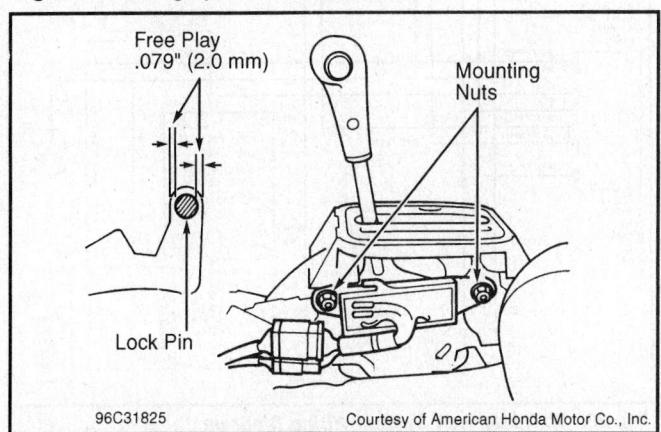

Fig. 27: Adjusting Shift Lever Free Play

BRAKELIGHT SWITCH

Removal & Installation – 1) Disconnect harness connector from brakelight switch. Remove lock nut from brakelight switch. Unscrew brakelight switch and remove. To install, screw brakelight switch inward until brakelight plunger is fully depressed.

2) Back off brakelight switch 1/4 turn. Ensure .010" (.30 mm) clearance is present between threaded end of brakelight switch and pad area on brake pedal. See Fig. 28. Install and tighten lock nut. Install harness connector. Ensure brakelights and cruise control operate properly.

COUNTERSHAFT SPEED SENSOR

Removal & Installation – 1) Disconnect harness connector at countershaft speed sensor. Countershaft speed sensor is located on top of transaxle. See Fig. 6.

2) Remove clamp for the wiring harness. Remove bolt, countershaft speed sensor and "O" ring. To install, reverse removal procedure using a NEW "O" ring. Install and tighten bolt to specification. See TORQUE SPECIFICATIONS.

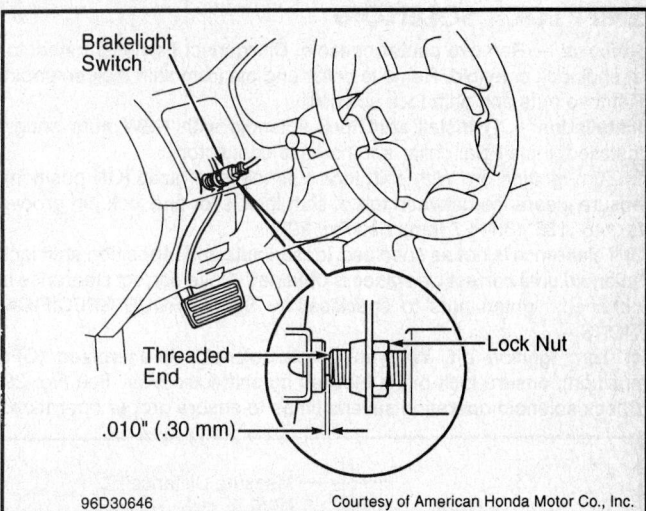

Fig. 28: Adjusting Brakelight Switch

ENGINE COOLANT TEMPERATURE (ECT) SENSOR

Removal & Installation – 1) The ECT sensor is located on cylinder head, below distributor and contains a Red/White wire and Green/Blue wire in the harness connector. See Fig. 6. Drain cooling system. Remove engine coolant temperature sensor.

2) To install, reverse removal procedure. Fill cooling system to top of radiator neck. Warm engine until cooling fan turns on and off twice. Finish filling cooling system.

KEY INTERLOCK SOLENOID

Removal & Installation – Key interlock solenoid cannot be serviced separately, as entire ignition lock assembly must be replaced.

LINEAR SOLENOID

Removal & Installation – 1) Linear solenoid assembly is located on transaxle. See Fig. 6. Disconnect harness connector at linear solenoid.

2) Remove bolts, linear solenoid assembly and gasket. To install, reverse removal procedure using a NEW gasket. Tighten bolts to specification. See TORQUE SPECIFICATIONS.

LOCK-UP CONTROL SOLENOID VALVES

Removal & Installation – 1) Lock-up control solenoid valve assembly is located on transaxle. See Fig. 6. Disconnect harness connector at lock-up control solenoid valves.

2) Remove bolts, lock-up control solenoid valve assembly and gasket. To install, reverse removal procedure using a NEW gasket. Tighten bolts to specification. See TORQUE SPECIFICATIONS.

MAINSHAFT SPEED SENSOR

Removal & Installation – 1) Disconnect harness connector at mainshaft speed sensor. Mainshaft speed sensor is located on side of transaxle. See Fig. 6.

2) Remove clamp for the wiring harness. Remove bolt, mainshaft speed sensor and "O" ring. To install, reverse removal procedure using a NEW "O" ring. Install and tighten bolt to specification. See TORQUE SPECIFICATIONS.

SHIFT CONTROL SOLENOID VALVES

Removal & Installation – 1) Shift control solenoid valve assembly is located on transaxle. See Fig. 6. Disconnect harness connector at shift control solenoid valves.

2) Remove bolts, shift control solenoid valve assembly and gasket. To install, reverse removal procedure using a NEW gasket. Tighten bolts to specification. See TORQUE SPECIFICATIONS.

SHIFT LOCK SOLENOID

Removal – Remove center console. Disconnect harness connector at shift lock solenoid. Remove collar and pin from shift lock solenoid. Remove nuts and shift lock solenoid.

Installation – 1) Install shift lock solenoid with NEW nuts snugly installed. Install pin, collar and harness connector.

2) Turn ignition on. With shift lock solenoid energized (ON position), ensure clearance between top of shift lock lever and lock pin groove is .145-.185" (3.7-4.7 mm). See Fig. 29.

3) If clearance is not as specified, loosen nuts and reposition shift lock solenoid until correct clearance is obtained. Once correct clearance is obtained, tighten nuts to specification. See TORQUE SPECIFICATIONS.

4) Turn ignition off. With shift lock solenoid de-energized (OFF position), ensure lock pin is blocked by shift lock lever. See Fig. 29. Check solenoid operation several times to ensure proper operation.

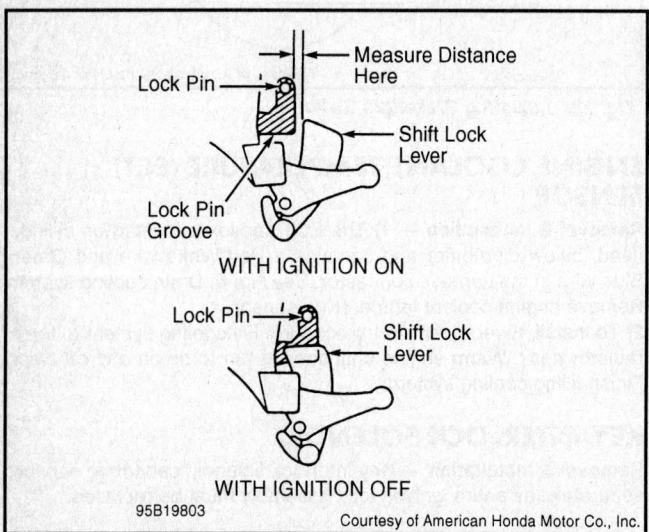

Fig. 29: Checking Shift Lock Solenoid Adjustment & Operation

THROTTLE POSITION (TP) SENSOR

Removal & Installation – TP sensor is mounted on side of throttle body. Replacement information is not available.

VEHICLE SPEED SENSOR (VSS)

Removal & Installation – 1) Disconnect harness connector from VSS, located on top of transaxle. See Fig. 6.

2) Remove bolts and VSS. To install, reverse removal procedure. Install and tighten bolt to 13 ft. lbs (17 N.m).

TORQUE SPECIFICATIONS
TORQUE SPECIFICATIONS

Application	INCH Lbs. (N.m)
A/T Gear Position Switch Nut	84 (9.5)
Countershaft Speed Sensor Bolt	106 (12.0)
Linear Solenoid Assembly Bolt	106 (12.0)
Lock-Up Control Solenoid Valve Assembly Bolt	106 (12.0)
Mainshaft Speed Sensor Bolt	106 (12.0)
Shift Control Solenoid Valve Assembly Bolt	106 (12.0)
Shift Lock Solenoid Nut	87 (9.8)

WIRING DIAGRAMS

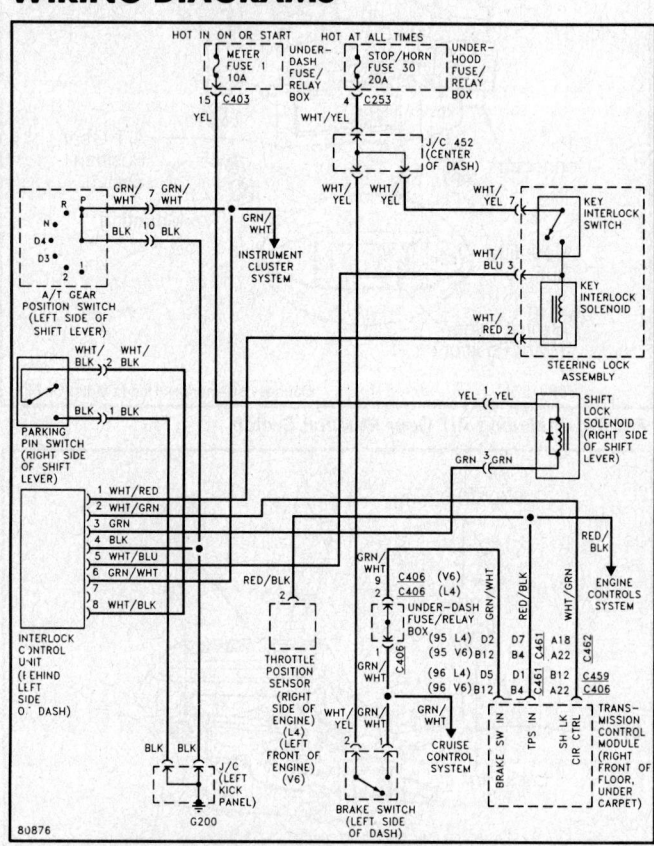

Fig. 30: Shift Interlock System Wiring Diagram (1995-96 Accord – V6 2.7L)

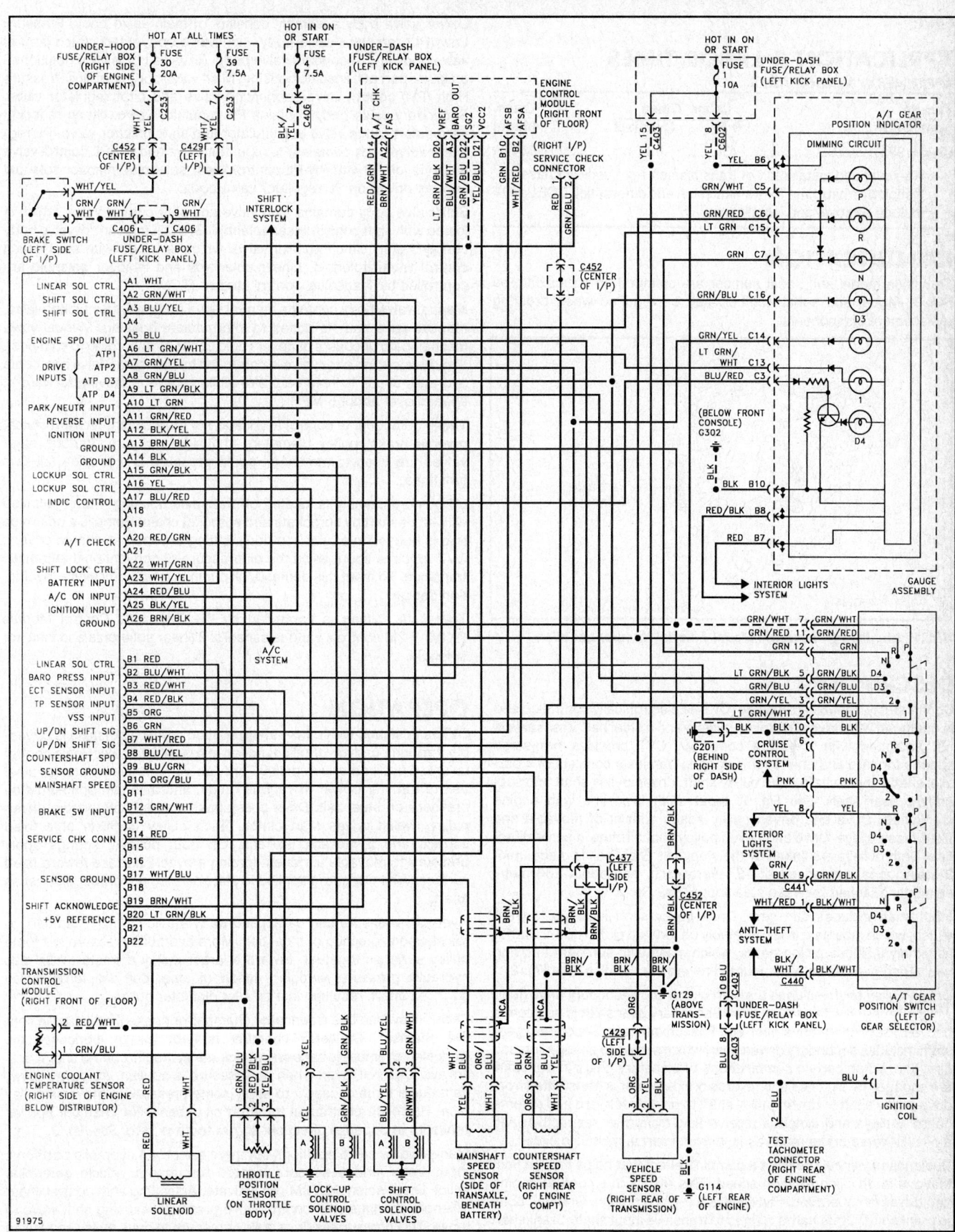

Fig. 31: Transaxle Wiring Diagram (1995-96 Accord – V6 2.7L)

91975

AUTOMATIC TRANSMISSIONS
Honda M4VA CVT

Civic

APPLICATION & LABOR TIMES

APPLICATION & LABOR TIMES

Vehicle Application	Labor Times		Trans. Model
	[1] R & I	[2] Overhaul	
Civic (1996)	4.1	6.2	M4VA

[1] – Removal and installation of transmission from vehicle chassis.
[2] – Bench overhaul time for transmission and differential. DOES NOT include removal and installation.

IDENTIFICATION

Transaxle model and serial number are stamped on transaxle. *See Fig. 1.* Model and serial number may be required when ordering replacement components.

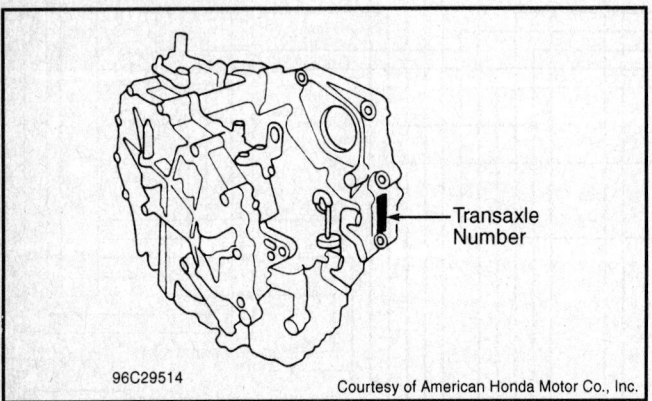

96C29514

Courtesy of American Honda Motor Co., Inc.

Fig. 1: Identifying Transaxle Model & Serial Number Location

DESCRIPTION

Continuously Variable Transaxle (CVT) is electronically controlled and is equipped with drive and driven pulleys and a steel belt. Transaxle is not equipped with a torque converter. CVT provides non-stage speeds forward and one reverse speed. Transaxle consists of 4 parallel shafts: input shaft, drive pulley shaft, driven pulley shaft and secondary gear shaft. *See Fig. 2.* Input shaft is in line with engine crankshaft. Drive and driven pulley shafts consist of movable and fixed face pulleys. Drive and driven pulley shafts rotate in same direction. Both pulleys are linked by the steel belt. Steel belt is made up of 2 steel loops, comprised of 12 layers each, and about 280 metal elements attached between steel loops. *See Fig. 3.*

Input shaft includes sun gear. Drive pulley shaft includes forward clutch, which mounts carrier assembly on forward clutch drum. Carrier assembly includes pinion gears, which mesh with sun gear and ring gear. Ring gear has a hub-mounted reverse brake disc. *See Fig. 2.*

Driven pulley shaft includes the start clutch and secondary drive gear, which is integral with parking gear. Secondary gear shaft is positioned between secondary drive gear and final driven gear. Secondary gear shaft includes secondary driven gear, which serves to change rotation direction. When certain combinations of planetary gears in transaxle are engaged by clutches and reverse brake, power is transmitted from drive pulley shaft to driven pulley shaft to provide forward and reverse gears. Pulleys and clutches receive fluid from their respective feed pipes. Reverse brake receives fluid from internal hydraulic circuit.

Dual mass flywheel provides a damping effect that helps reduce fluctuations in driveline rotation speed. This results in smoother engine and drivetrain operation. Flywheel is a 2-piece design. One half bolts to crankshaft. Other half is splined to transaxle input shaft. Crankshaft half drives input shaft half using torsion springs, viscous damping chambers that contain grease and a friction surface. Torsion springs allow controlled movement between the 2 surfaces. Grease chambers and friction surface act as dampers.

Lower valve body assembly consists of main valve body, Pressure Low (PL) regulator valve body, shift valve body, start clutch control valve body and secondary valve body. All valve bodies are positioned on lower part of transaxle housing. Main valve body contains Pressure High (PH) control valve, lubrication valve and pitot regulator valve. Secondary valve body contains PH regulator valve, clutch reducing valve, start clutch valve accumulator and shift inhibitor valve. PL regulator valve body contains PL regulator valve and PH-PL control valve which is joined with PH-PL control linear solenoid. Inhibitor solenoid valve is bolted on PL regulator valve body.

Shift valve body contains shift valve and shift control valve, which is joined with shift control linear solenoid. Start clutch control valve body contains start clutch control valve, which is joined with start clutch control linear solenoid. Linear solenoids and inhibitor solenoid are controlled by Transaxle Control Module (TCM).

Manual valve body contains manual valve and reverse inhibitor valve. Manual valve body is bolted to intermediate housing. Manual valve mechanically uncovers or covers fluid passage according to shift position. Reverse inhibitor valve is controlled by pressure. Valve intercepts hydraulic circuit to reverse brake while vehicle is moving forward at speeds over about 6 MPH.

These components control application of start clutch, forward clutch, reverse brake, pulley diameters and side pressure. Various other valves are used to modify oil pump pressure and provide fail-safe functions.

Oil pump assembly is located on transaxle housing. Pump is linked with input shaft by sprockets and sprocket chain. Pump is a gear type that is housed in a cast iron body, sitting between aluminum covers. CVT requires about twice the oil pressure of conventional automatic transaxle. To meet this demand, oil pump is a high efficiency, low friction design.

Transaxle shifting is controlled by the Transaxle Control Module (TCM). TCM controls various sensors, 3 linear solenoids and inhibitor solenoid.

OPERATION

CVT is designed with a fail-safe operation mode. Transaxle is driveable through purely hydraulic function in the event of electronic control failure. Drive and driven pulleys provide variable diameters for steel belt to transfer power at various ratios, and maintain optimum side pressure on steel belt. Drive pulley pushes steel belt, driving driven pulley, which drives start clutch. Each pulley consists of a fixed surface and a movable surface. On both pulleys, springs apply pressure to movable surfaces, forcing movable surface toward fixed surface. When torque is applied to steel belt, it tries to wedge surfaces apart.

Hydraulic pressure can be applied to hydraulic control chambers to resist wedging action of steel belt. More hydraulic pressure will force pulley surfaces together, toward a larger pulley diameter. With less hydraulic pressure, wedging action of steel belt will force pulley surfaces apart, resulting in a smaller diameter pulley.

Each pulley also has a cancellor chamber opposite the hydraulic control chamber. Cancellor chamber is kept full of lubrication oil. Cancellor chamber is necessary because hydraulic control chamber is always full of oil, even when no pressure is applied. As pulley spins, centrifugal force causes it to apply some pressure to movable pulley face. However, centrifugal force on oil in cancellor chamber applies pressure in opposite direction, so net force is zero. *See Fig. 3.*

Manual valve has 6 positions but there are only 4 hydraulic positions. Input from various sensors located throughout vehicle determine which linear solenoid TCM will activate. Activating shift control linear solenoid changes shift control valve pressure, causing shift valve to move. This pressurizes drive pulley pressure to drive pulley and driven pulley, which changes their effective pulley ratio. Activating start clutch control linear solenoid moves start clutch control valve. Start clutch control valve uncovers port to allow start clutch pressure to start clutch, which engages start clutch. Start clutch slips to allow

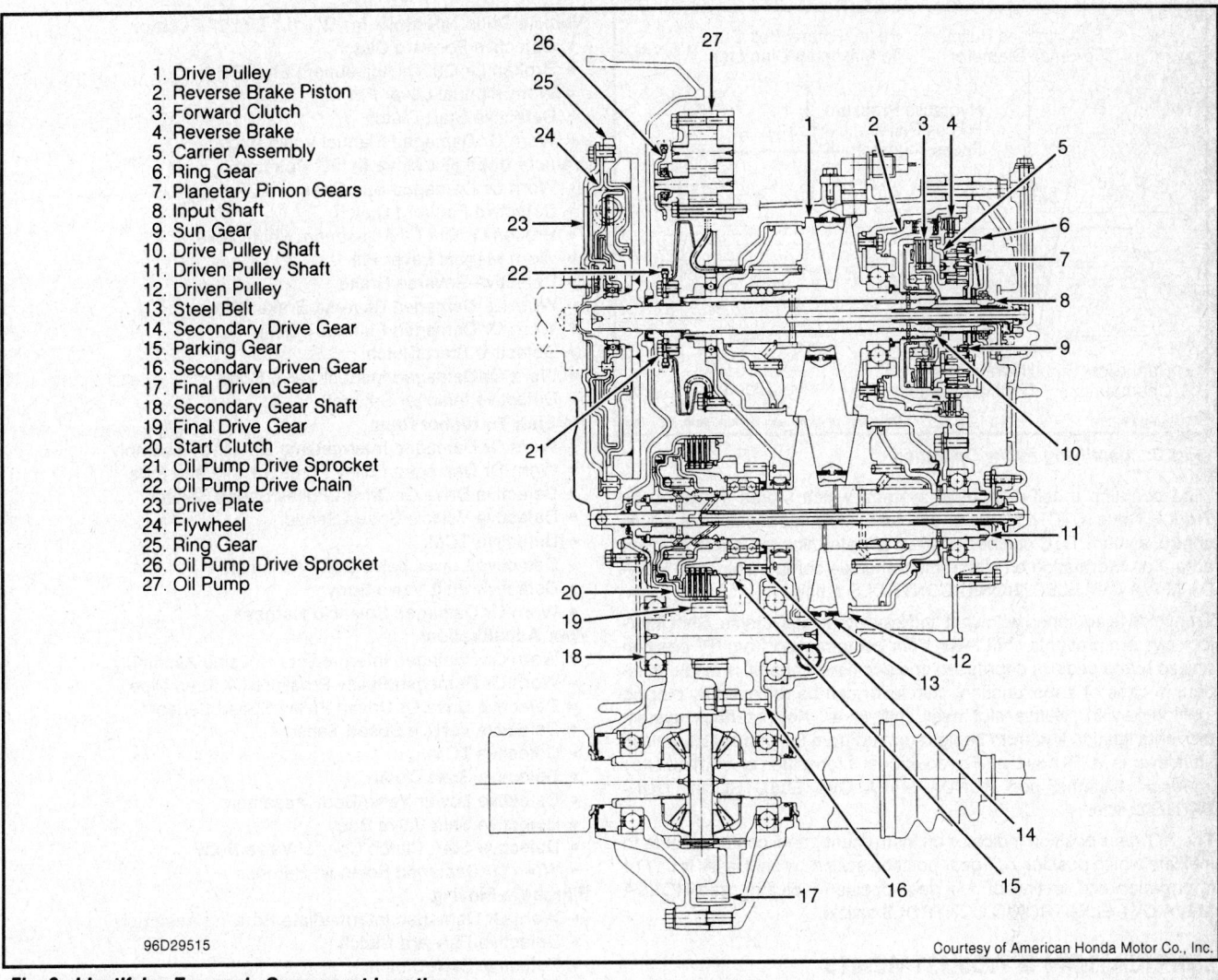

1. Drive Pulley
2. Reverse Brake Piston
3. Forward Clutch
4. Reverse Brake
5. Carrier Assembly
6. Ring Gear
7. Planetary Pinion Gears
8. Input Shaft
9. Sun Gear
10. Drive Pulley Shaft
11. Driven Pulley Shaft
12. Driven Pulley
13. Steel Belt
14. Secondary Drive Gear
15. Parking Gear
16. Secondary Driven Gear
17. Final Driven Gear
18. Secondary Gear Shaft
19. Final Drive Gear
20. Start Clutch
21. Oil Pump Drive Sprocket
22. Oil Pump Drive Chain
23. Drive Plate
24. Flywheel
25. Ring Gear
26. Oil Pump Drive Sprocket
27. Oil Pump

96D29515

Courtesy of American Honda Motor Co., Inc.

Fig. 2: Identifying Transaxle Component Locations

engine to idle in gear when vehicle is stopped, controls slippage when starting from a stop and locks up during normal driving for maximum power transfer efficiency and fuel economy.

Reverse inhibitor solenoid is an on/off type solenoid which operates reverse inhibitor valve to prevent reverse engagement until vehicle speed is less than 6 MPH. Start clutch control solenoid controls pressure applied to start clutch. Low pressure is applied at a stop, increased pressure is applied during acceleration, or full pressure is applied during normal driving conditions. PH/PL control solenoid is used to control amount of side pressure applied to steel belt by pulleys. Under high load situations, solenoid allows high side pressure to be applied to prevent belt slippage. Under lower load situations, it reduces amount of side pressure to reduce friction and improve fuel economy. Shift control solenoid operates shift valve to determine amount of PH or PL pressure to be applied to drive and driven pulley's hydraulic control chambers. This determines exact drive ratio.

When shift lever is moved, manual valve on main valve body is moved by shift cable. Shift lever also changes position of A/T gear position switch, mounted on the shift lever. The A/T gear position switch delivers an input signal to TCM to indicate shift lever position. TCM uses this input signal to control solenoids. TCM determines appropriate shift point and activates proper solenoid for transaxle shifting.

When transaxle gear combinations are engaged by clutches and brake, power is transmitted to provide appropriate gears. Shift lever positions operate as follows:

- **"P" (Park)** – Front wheels lock as parking pawl engages with parking gear on driven pulley shaft. All clutches are released. Neutral safety switch, incorporated in A/T gear position switch, allows engine starting in this position. All hydraulic pressure is blocked at manual valve.
- **"R" (Reverse)** – Reverse brake is engaged. Back-up light switch, incorporated in A/T gear position switch, allows back-up lights to operate. Hydraulic pressure is directed to reverse brake.
- **"N" (Neutral)** – All clutches are released. Neutral safety switch, incorporated in A/T gear position switch, allows engine starting in this position. All hydraulic pressure is blocked at manual valve.
- **"D" (Drive)** – Transaxle automatically adjusts gear ratio to keep engine at most efficient speed for current driving conditions. Hydraulic pressure is directed to forward clutch.
- **"S" (Second)** – Transaxle shifts into a lower gear for better acceleration and increased engine braking. Used for rapid acceleration at highway speeds. Hydraulic pressure is directed to forward clutch.
- **"L" (Low)** – Transaxle shifts into lowest gear for increased power on hills and for engine braking. Hydraulic pressure is directed to forward clutch.

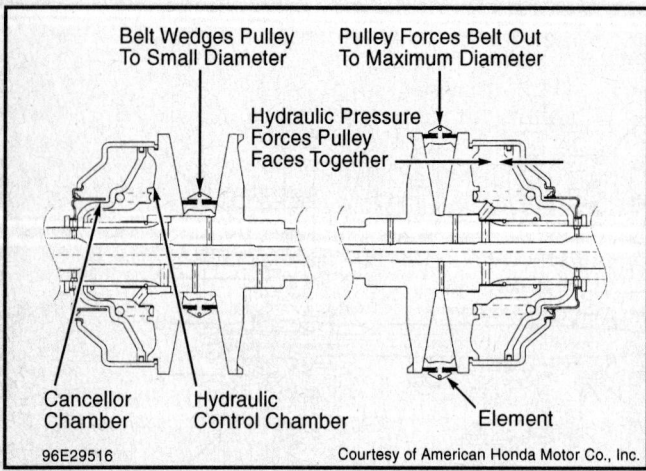

Belt Wedges Pulley To Small Diameter

Pulley Forces Belt Out To Maximum Diameter

Hydraulic Pressure Forces Pulley Faces Together

Cancellor Chamber

Hydraulic Control Chamber

Element

96E29516

Courtesy of American Honda Motor Co., Inc.

Fig. 3: Identifying Pulley Operation

TCM contains a self-diagnostic system, which stores a Diagnostic Trouble Code (DTC) if failure or problem exists in transaxle electronic control system. DTC can be retrieved to determine transaxle problem area. For information on electronic transaxle components, see HONDA M4VA CVT ELECTRONIC CONTROLS article.

Transaxle is equipped with shift and key interlock systems. Shift interlock system prevents shift lever from being moved from "P" position unless brake pedal is depressed and accelerator pedal is in idle position. In case of a malfunction, shift lever can be released by placing ignition key in release slot near shift lever. Key interlock system prevents ignition key from being removed from ignition switch unless shift lever is in "P" position. For additional information on shift and key interlock systems, see HONDA M4VA CVT ELECTRONIC CONTROLS article.

The A/T gear position indicator on instrument panel contains lights to indicate which position A/T gear position switch on shift lever is in. For information and testing of A/T gear position indicator, see HONDA M4VA CVT ELECTRONIC CONTROLS article.

LUBRICATION & ADJUSTMENTS

See appropriate AUTOMATIC TRANSMISSION SERVICING article in TRANSMISSION SERVICING section.

TROUBLE SHOOTING

Transaxle malfunctions may be caused by poor engine performance, improper adjustments or failure of hydraulic, mechanical or electronic components. Always begin by checking fluid level, fluid condition and cable adjustments. Perform road test to determine if problem has been corrected. If problem still exists, several tests must be performed on transaxle. See TESTING.

SYMPTOM DIAGNOSIS

Engine Runs But Vehicle Does Not Move In Any Gear Position
- Low Fluid Level
- Worn Oil Pump
- Worn Or Damaged Oil Pump Chain Or Sprocket
- Worn Or Damaged Input Shaft
- Worn Or Damaged Sun Gear
- Worn Or Damaged Final Driven Gear
- Worn Or Damaged Secondary Drive Or Driven Gear
- Worn Or Damaged Flywheel Or Drive Plate
- Worn Or Damaged Intermediate Housing Assembly
- Defective Forward Clutch
- Defective Start Clutch
- Plugged Oil Filter Or Strainer
- Defective Lower Valve Body Assembly
- Defective PL Regulator Valve Body Assembly
- Defective Start Clutch Control Valve Body
- Worn Or Damaged Manual Valve Body

Vehicle Does Not Move In "D", "L" Or "S" Position
- Defective Forward Clutch
- Broken Or Out Of Adjustment Shift Cable
- Worn Manual Lever Pin
- Defective Start Clutch
- Worn Or Damaged Manual Valve Body

Vehicle Does Not Move In "R" Position
- Worn Or Damaged Sun Gear
- Defective Forward Clutch
- Broken Or Out Of Adjustment Shift Cable
- Worn Manual Lever Pin
- Defective Reverse Brake
- Worn Or Damaged Reverse Brake Piston
- Worn Or Damaged Planetary Gear
- Defective Start Clutch
- Worn Or Damaged Manual Valve Body
- Defective Inhibitor Solenoid

No Shift To Higher Ratio
- Worn Or Damaged Intermediate Housing Assembly
- Worn Or Damaged Pulley Pressure Oil Feed Pipe
- Defective Drive Or Driven Pulley Speed Sensor
- Defective Vehicle Speed Sensor
- Defective TCM
- Defective Lower Valve Body Assembly
- Defective Shift Valve Body
- Worn Or Damaged Solenoid Harness

Poor Acceleration
- Worn Or Damaged Intermediate Housing Assembly
- Worn Or Damaged Pulley Pressure Oil Feed Pipe
- Defective Drive Or Driven Pulley Speed Sensor
- Defective Vehicle Speed Sensor
- Defective TCM
- Defective Start Clutch
- Defective Lower Valve Body Assembly
- Defective Shift Valve Body
- Defective Start Clutch Control Valve Body
- Worn Or Damaged Solenoid Harness

Flares On Moving
- Worn Or Damaged Intermediate Housing Assembly
- Defective Forward Clutch
- Defective Start Clutch
- Worn Or Damaged Start Clutch Pressure Oil Feed Pipe
- Defective Lower Valve Body Assembly
- Defective PL Regulator Valve Body Assembly
- Defective Start Clutch Control Valve Body
- Worn Or Damaged Solenoid Harness

Excessive Shock When Depressing & Releasing Accelerator Pedal
- Worn Or Damaged Intermediate Housing Assembly
- Defective Forward Clutch
- Defective Start Clutch
- Worn Or Damaged Start Clutch Pressure Oil Feed Pipe
- Defective Lower Valve Body Assembly
- Defective PL Regulator Valve Body Assembly
- Defective Start Clutch Control Valve Body

No Engine Braking
- Worn Or Damaged Intermediate Housing Assembly
- Defective Start Clutch
- Worn Or Damaged Start Clutch Pressure Oil Feed Pipe
- Defective Lower Valve Body Assembly
- Defective PL Regulator Valve Body Assembly
- Defective Start Clutch Control Valve Body

Vehicle Does Not Accelerate In "R" Position
- Worn Or Damaged Intermediate Housing Assembly
- Defective Reverse Brake
- Worn Or Damaged Reverse Brake Piston
- Worn Or Damaged Planetary Gear
- Defective Start Clutch
- Defective Lower Valve Body Assembly
- Defective PL Regulator Valve Body Assembly
- Defective Start Clutch Control Valve Body

Vehicle Moves In "N" Position (Shift Cable Adjustment Is Okay)
- Defective Forward Clutch
- Incorrect Clutch/Reverse Brake Clearance
- Worn Or Damaged Reverse Brake Return Spring/Retainer

Late Shift From "N" To "D" Or "D" To "N" Position
- Defective Forward Clutch
- Broken Or Out Of Adjustment Shift Cable
- Worn Manual Lever Pin
- Worn Or Damaged Manual Valve Body
- Incorrect Clutch/Reverse Brake Clearance

Late Shift From "N" To "R" Or "R" To "N" Position
- Broken Or Out Of Adjustment Shift Cable
- Worn Manual Lever Pin
- Defective Reverse Brake
- Worn Or Damaged Reverse Brake Piston
- Worn Or Damaged Manual Valve Body
- Incorrect Clutch/Reverse Brake Clearance

Engine Stops When Shifted From "N" To "D" Position
- Worn Or Damaged Intermediate Housing Assembly
- Defective Forward Clutch
- Defective Start Clutch
- Defective Lower Valve Body Assembly
- Defective Shift Valve Body
- Defective Start Clutch Control Valve Body

Engine Stops When Shifted From "N" To "R" Position
- Worn Or Damaged Intermediate Housing Assembly
- Worn Or Damaged Reverse Brake Piston
- Worn Or Damaged Planetary Gear
- Defective Start Clutch
- Worn Or Damaged Carrier Thrust Needle Bearing
- Worn Or Damaged Carrier Thrust Washer
- Defective Lower Valve Body Assembly
- Defective Shift Valve Body
- Defective Start Clutch Control Valve Body

Noise From Transaxle In "R" Position

NOTE: Some gear noise in "R" position is normal due to planetary gear action.

- Worn Or Damaged Sun Gear
- Defective Reverse Brake
- Worn Or Damaged Reverse Brake Piston
- Worn Or Damaged Planetary Gear
- Worn Or Damaged Carrier Thrust Needle Bearing
- Worn Or Damaged Carrier Thrust Washer

Excessive Idle Vibration
- Worn Oil Pump
- Worn Or Damaged Oil Pump Chain Or Sprocket
- Worn Or Damaged Drive Plate Or Flywheel
- Low Engine Output
- Defective Flywheel

Noise From Transaxle In "N" Or "P" Position
- Worn Or Damaged Oil Pump
- Worn Or Damaged Oil Pump Chain Or Sprocket
- Worn Or Damaged Planetary Gear
- Worn Or Damaged Input Shaft Needle Bearing
- Worn Or Damaged Carrier Thrust Needle Bearing
- Defective Flywheel Assembly

Hunting Engine Speed
- Defective TCM
- Defective Lower Valve Body Assembly
- Defective Shift Valve Body
- Defective Start Clutch Control Valve Body

Vibration In All Positions
- Worn Or Damaged Drive Plate Or Flywheel
- Defective Flywheel

Shift Lever Does Not Operate Smoothly
- Out Of Adjustment Or Broken Shift Cable
- Worn Or Damaged Control Lever
- Worn Or Damaged Manual Valve Body

Transaxle Will Not Shift Out Of Or Into "P" Position
- Out Of Adjustment Or Broken Shift Cable
- Worn Or Damaged Control Lever
- Worn Or Damaged Parking Pawl Or Shaft
- Worn Or Damaged Detent Lever
- Worn Or Damaged Parking Rod Assembly
- Worn Or Damaged Parking Gear
- Worn Or Damaged Parking Pawl Spring

Vehicle Does Not Accelerate To More Than A Certain Speed
- Worn Or Damaged Intermediate Housing Assembly
- Defective Start Clutch
- Defective Forward Clutch
- Defective Drive Or Driven Pulley Speed Sensor
- Defective Vehicle Speed Sensor
- Defective TCM
- Defective Lower Valve Body Assembly
- Defective Shift Valve Body

Excessive Shock On Start Off
- Defective Start Clutch Control Valve Body

Flares When Accelerating At Low Speed
- Defective Start Clutch
- Worn Or Damaged Start Clutch Pressure Oil Feed Pipe
- Defective Start Clutch Control Valve Body

Excessive Vibration In "D", "L", "S' & "R" Positions
- Defective Start Clutch
- Worn Or Damaged Start Clutch Pressure Oil Feed Pipe
- Defective Start Clutch Control Valve Body

Low Engine Speed In "D", "L", "S' & "R" Positions
- Defective Start Clutch
- Worn Or Damaged Start Clutch Pressure Oil Feed Pipe
- Defective Start Clutch Control Valve Body

Stall Speed High
- Defective Start Clutch
- Defective Forward Clutch
- Defective Start Clutch Control Valve Body

Stall Speed Low
- Worn Or Damaged Intermediate Housing Assembly
- Defective Start Clutch
- Low Engine Output
- Defective Shift Valve Body
- Defective Start Clutch Control Valve Body

Shudder On Starting Off
- Defective Start Clutch
- Fluid Deteriorated

TESTING

ROAD TEST

NOTE: If shift lever cannot be moved from "P" position with brake pedal depressed and accelerator pedal at idle position, check shift interlock system. See HONDA M4VA CVT ELECTRONIC CONTROLS article.

---

1) Warm engine to normal operating temperature. Apply parking brake and block wheels. Start engine. Move shift lever to "D" position while depressing brake pedal. Depress accelerator pedal and release it suddenly. Engine should not stall. Park vehicle on slope and apply parking brake. Ensure shift lever is in "P" position. Release parking brake. Ensure vehicle does not move forward.

2) Manufacturer recommends monitoring of Throttle Position (TP) sensor voltage when performing road test to ensure proper throttle opening for verifying vehicle speed and engine RPM. TP sensor voltage may be monitored using appropriate scan tool. If scan tool is not available, go to next step.

3) Remove driver's side kick panel. Unbolt TCM. Ensure ignition is off. Connect Backprobe Test Set (07SAZ-001000A) or equivalent between TCM harness connectors and Digital Volt-Ohmmeter (DVOM). Connect backprobe adapters with positive lead at terminal B4 and negative lead at terminals A4 or A17 to monitor throttle position sensor voltage. See Fig. 4.

4) Test drive vehicle on flat highway in specified gear position and at specified throttle angle opening and vehicle speed. Ensure engine RPM is as specified at specified MPH. See ENGINE RPM-TO-VEHICLE SPEED SPECIFICATIONS table.

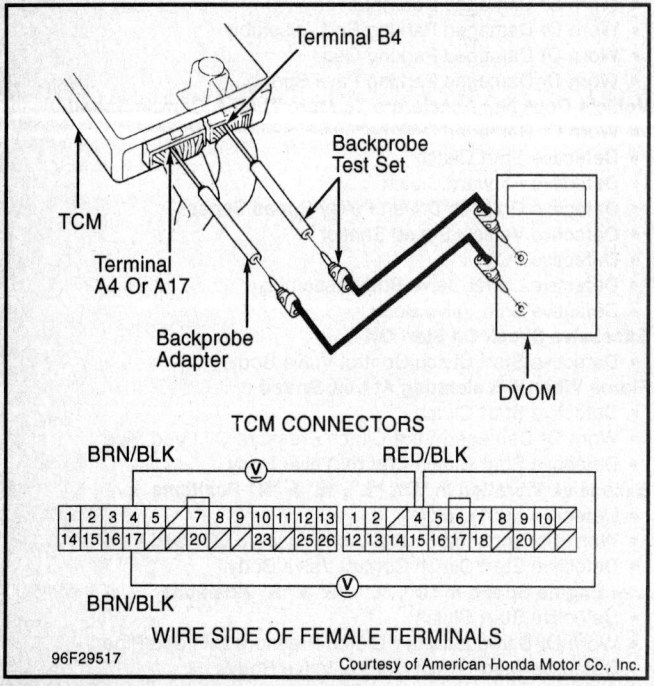

Terminal B4

Backprobe Test Set

TCM

Terminal A4 Or A17

Backprobe Adapter

DVOM

TCM CONNECTORS

BRN/BLK   RED/BLK

| 1 | 2 | 3 | 4 | 5 | | 7 | 8 | 9 | 10 | 11 | 12 | 13 | 1 | 2 | | 4 | 5 | 6 | 7 | 8 | 9 | 10 |
|14|15|16|17| |20| | |23| |25|26| |12|13|14|15|16|17|18| |20| |

BRN/BLK

WIRE SIDE OF FEMALE TERMINALS

96F29517   Courtesy of American Honda Motor Co., Inc.

Fig. 4: Measuring TP Sensor Voltage

STALL SPEED TEST

CAUTION: DO NOT perform stall speed test for more than 10 seconds or transaxle may be damaged. DO NOT move shift lever while increasing engine speed. Ensure pressure gauge is removed prior to stall speed testing.

1) Apply parking brake and block all wheels. Connect tachometer and start engine. Ensure A/C is off. Warm engine to normal operating temperature. Place shift lever in "D" position.
2) Fully depress brake pedal. Fully depress accelerator for 6-8 seconds and note engine speed.
3) Allow transaxle to cool for 2 minutes. Repeat test procedure in "S", "L" and "R" positions.
4) Stall speed should be 2800-3100 RPM in "S", "L" and "R" positions. Stall speed should be 2350-2650 RPM in "D" position. If stall speed is not within specification, see STALL SPEED TROUBLE SHOOTING table for possible causes.

STALL SPEED TROUBLE SHOOTING

Stall Speed Gear Positions	Probable Cause
Stall Speed RPM High In "D", "S", "L" & "R"	Low Fluid Level, Low Oil Pump Output, Clogged Fluid Strainer, PH Regulator Valve Stuck Closed, Slipping Forward Clutch Defective Start Clutch
Stall Speed RPM High In "R"	Slipping Reverse Brake Defective Start Clutch
Stall Speed RPM Low In "D", "S", "L" & "R"	Engine Output Low, Faulty Start Clutch Stuck Shift Valve

HYDRAULIC PRESSURE TEST

CAUTION: When measuring drive and driven pulley pressure when "D" indicator light indicates a problem, an oil pressure gauge that measures 711 psi (4902 kPa) or more must be used.

NOTE: Drive pulley pressure may be above 498 psi (3434 kPa) when there is a transaxle problem that causes TCM to go into fail-safe mode.

1) Ensure transaxle fluid level is correct. Warm engine to normal operating temperature. Apply parking brake. Block rear wheels. Raise and support vehicle so front wheels can rotate.

ENGINE RPM-TO-VEHICLE SPEED SPECIFICATIONS

TP Sensor Voltage (Throttle Angle)	Shift Lever Position	25 MPH	37 MPH	62 MPH
0.75 Volt (Quarter Throttle)	Drive	1250-1650 RPM	N/A	N/A
2.25 Volts (Half Throttle)	Drive	2500-3100 RPM	2650-3250 RPM	2700-3300 RPM
4.50 Volts (Full Throttle)	Drive	3950-4550 RPM	4650-5250 RPM	5200-5800 RPM
0.75 Volt (Quarter Throttle)	Second	1800-2200 RPM	2200-2800 RPM	3550-4150 RPM
2.25 Volts (Half Throttle)	Second	2950-3550 RPM	3250-3850 RPM	4050-4650 RPM
4.50 Volts (Full Throttle)	Second	4100-4700 RPM	5100-5700 RPM	5900-6500 RPM
0.75 Volt (Quarter Throttle)	Low	3100-3700 RPM	3650-4250 RPM	4450-5050 RPM
2.25 Volts (Half Throttle)	Low	3500-4100 RPM	4050-4650 RPM	4800-5400 RPM
4.50 Volts (Full Throttle)	Low	4100-4700 RPM	5100-5700 RPM	5900-6500 RPM

HYDRAULIC PRESSURE TEST SPECIFICATIONS

Application	Shift Lever Position	psi. (kPa)
Forward Clutch With Engine At 1500 RPM	"D"	200-253 (1379-1744)
Reverse Brake With Engine At 1500 RPM	"R"	200-253 (1379-1744)
Drive Pulley With Engine At 1500 RPM	"N"	30-100 (207-690)
Driven Pulley With Engine At 1500 RPM	"N"	210-330 (1448-2275)
Lubrication With Engine At 3000 RPM	"N"	30 (207)

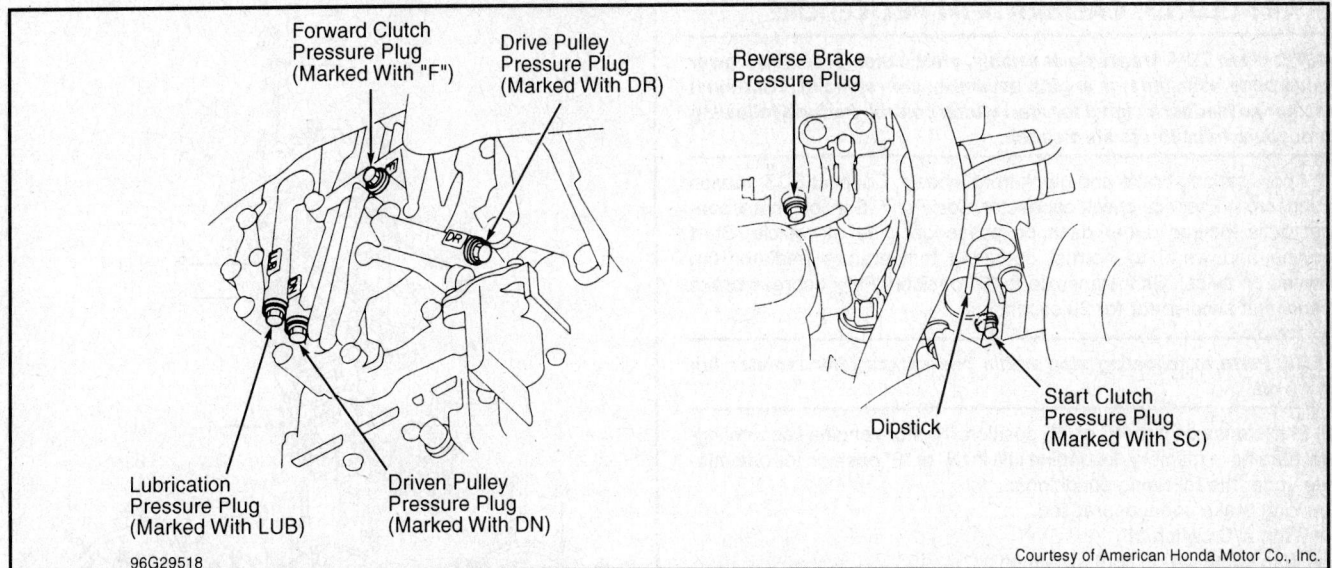

Fig. 5: Identifying Transaxle Pressure Plug Locations

2) With engine off, remove pressure plug from appropriate pressure port on transaxle. Connect appropriate pressure gauge to appropriate pressure port. See Fig. 5. Tighten fitting to 13 ft. lbs. (18 N.m).

3) With shift lever in "D" position, start and operate engine at 1500 RPM. With pressure gauge connected to "F" pressure port, note hydraulic pressure reading for forward clutch.

4) Shift transaxle into "R" position. With pressure gauge connected to reverse brake pressure port, note hydraulic pressure reading for reverse brake.

5) Shift transaxle into "N" position. With pressure gauge connected to "DR" or "DN" pressure port, note hydraulic pressure reading for drive pulley and driven pulley.

6) With transaxle still in "N" position, measure lubrication pressure at 3000 RPM with pressure gauge connected to LUB pressure port.

7) All hydraulic pressures should be within specification. See HYDRAULIC PRESSURE TEST SPECIFICATIONS table. If hydraulic pressures are not within specification, see HYDRAULIC PRESSURE TEST TROUBLE SHOOTING table. Install pressure plug into pressure port using NEW sealing washer. Tighten plug to 13 ft. lbs. (18 N.m).

HYDRAULIC PRESSURE TEST TROUBLE SHOOTING

Pressure Symptom	Probable Cause
Low Or No Forward Clutch	Forward Clutch,
Low Or No Reverse Brake	Reverse Brake
Low Or No Drive Pulley	Oil Pump, Shift Valve PH Or PL Regulator Valve
Drive Pulley Pressure Too High	PH Or PL Regulator Valve, Shift Valve, Shift Control Solenoid
Low Or No Driven Pulley	Oil Pump, PH Regulator Valve, Shift Valve, Shift Control Solenoid
Driven Pulley Pressure Too High	PH Regulator Valve
Low Or No Lubrication	Oil Pump, Lubrication Valve

ON-VEHICLE SERVICE

AXLE SHAFTS

See appropriate article in AXLE SHAFTS & TRANSFER CASES section.

LOWER VALVE BODY ASSEMBLY

Lower valve body assembly consists of main valve body, Pressure Low (PL) regulator valve body, shift valve body, start clutch control valve body and secondary valve body. See LOWER VALVE BODY ASSEMBLY under REMOVAL & INSTALLATION.

OIL COOLER FLUSHING

1) Attach Oil Cooler Flusher (J38405-A) to oil cooler lines. See Fig. 6. Fill oil cooler flusher tank 2/3 full with Flushing Fluid (J35944-20). DO NOT use any other flushing fluid.

2) Ensure water and air valves on oil cooler flusher are off. Apply 80-120 psi (550-829 kPa) air pressure to oil cooler flusher. Turn oil cooler flusher water valve on so water flows through oil cooler for 10 seconds. Replace oil cooler if water will not flow through oil cooler. Shut water valve off.

3) Depress and hold mixing trigger on oil cooler flusher downward. Turn water valve on and flush oil cooler for 2 minutes. Turn air valve on for 5 seconds every 15-20 seconds to create a surging action.

4) Turn water valve off. Release mixing trigger. Disconnect oil cooler flusher and reverse hoses so oil cooler can be flushed in opposite direction.

5) Repeat steps **2)** and **3)**. Turn water valve off. Release mixing trigger. Turn water valve on and rinse oil cooler for at least one minute. Once oil cooler is flushed in both directions, turn water off. Turn air valve on until no moisture is visible from drain hose.

***

CAUTION: Ensure no moisture exists in oil cooler, as it can damage transaxle.

***

6) Turn air off. Disconnect oil cooler flusher. Reconnect inlet line on oil cooler. Once transaxle is installed, attach drain hose on return line and place in oil container. Ensure transaxle is in "P" position. Fill transaxle with ATF.

7) Start engine and operate for about 30 seconds or until one quart (.9L) of ATF is discharged from return line. Shut engine off. Remove drain hose. Reinstall return line. Fill transaxle to proper level.

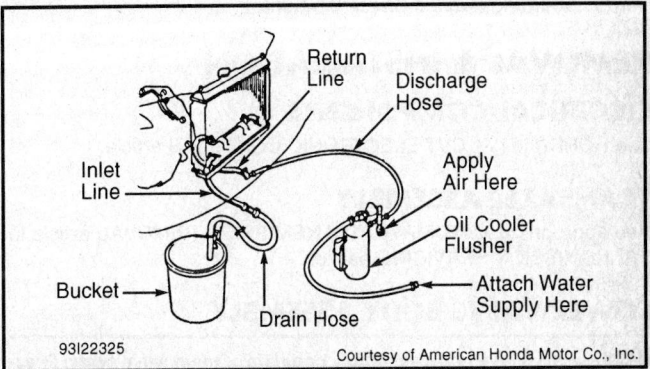

Fig. 6: Installing Oil Cooler Flusher

START CLUTCH CALIBRATION PROCEDURE

NOTE: When TCM, transaxle assembly, start clutch assembly, lower valve body assembly or engine assembly are replaced, TCM must memorize feedback signal for start clutch control. Perform following procedure to calibrate start clutch.

1) Apply parking brake and block front wheels. Connect SCS service connector to service check connector. *See Fig. 7.* Service check connector is located under dash on passenger side of vehicle. Start engine and warm to normal operating temperature (radiator fan comes on twice). Shift transaxle to "D" position. Fully depress brake pedal and accelerator for 20 seconds.

NOTE: Perform following step within one minute after radiator fan goes off.

2) Shift transaxle into "N" or "P" position. To store engine vacuum signal reading in memory, let engine idle in "N" or "P" position for one minute under the following conditions:
- With brake pedal depressed.
- With A/C switch off.
- With combination light switch off.
- With heater fan switch off.
- Turn off all other electrical systems.

3) Shift transaxle into "D" position and let engine idle for 2 minutes to store feedback signal in memory under same conditions as in step **2)**. Connect scan tool to vehicle. Using scan tool, ensure TCM has completed start clutch calibration. Disconnect SCS service connector from service check connector.

NOTE: TCM will not store feedback signal when fluid temperature is less than 104°F (40°C) even if engine coolant temperature reaches normal operating temperature. Repeat these procedures until start clutch calibration is completed.

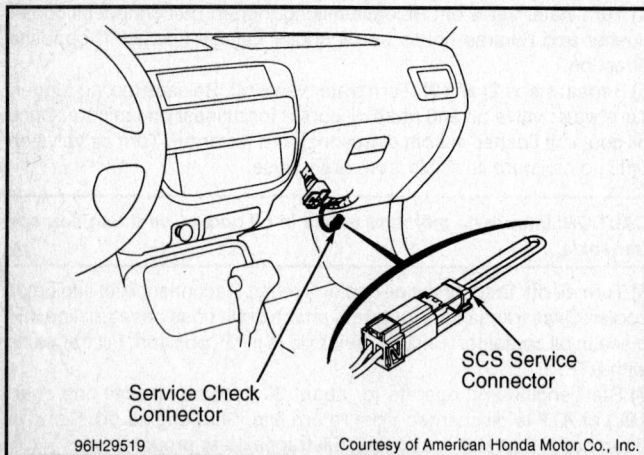

96H29519   Courtesy of American Honda Motor Co., Inc.

Fig. 7: *Locating Service Check Connector*

REMOVAL & INSTALLATION

ELECTRICAL COMPONENTS

See HONDA M4VA CVT ELECTRONIC CONTROLS article.

TRANSAXLE ASSEMBLY

See appropriate AUTOMATIC TRANSMISSION REMOVAL article in TRANSMISSION SERVICING section.

LOWER VALVE BODY ASSEMBLY

NOTE: Lower valve body assembly consists of main valve body, Pressure Low (PL) regulator valve body, shift valve body, start clutch control valve body and secondary valve body.

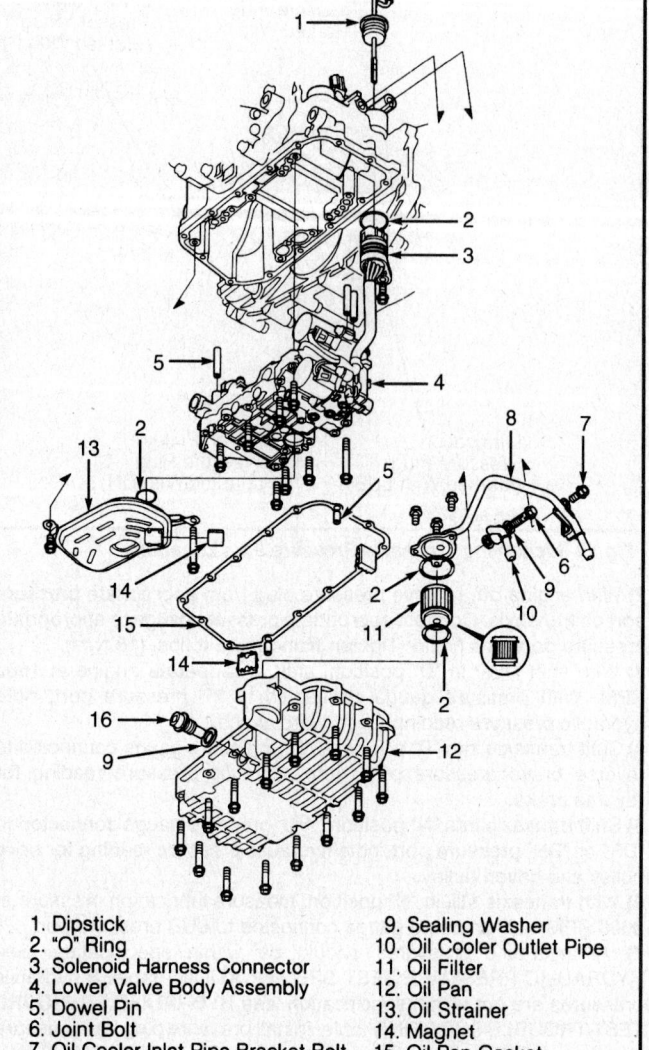

1. Dipstick
2. "O" Ring
3. Solenoid Harness Connector
4. Lower Valve Body Assembly
5. Dowel Pin
6. Joint Bolt
7. Oil Cooler Inlet Pipe Bracket Bolt
8. Oil Cooler Inlet Pipe Assembly
9. Sealing Washer
10. Oil Cooler Outlet Pipe
11. Oil Filter
12. Oil Pan
13. Oil Strainer
14. Magnet
15. Oil Pan Gasket
16. Drain Plug

96A29520   Courtesy of American Honda Motor Co., Inc.

Fig. 8: *Identifying Lower Valve Body Assembly & Components*

Removal – 1) Raise and support vehicle. Drain fluid by removing drain plug and sealing washer from rear of transaxle. *See Fig. 8.* Disconnect 8-pin connector from solenoid harness connector.
2) Remove oil cooler hoses at oil cooler pipes. Turn ends of oil cooler hoses up and plug to prevent oil loss. Remove right front mount/bracket. Remove oil cooler outlet pipe, bracket bolt and 14 oil pan bolts. Remove oil strainer. Remove bolt securing solenoid harness connector. Remove 8 bolts and lower valve body assembly. *See Fig. 8.*

NOTE: If necessary to disassemble lower valve body assembly, see LOWER VALVE BODY ASSEMBLY under COMPONENT DISASSEMBLY & REASSEMBLY.

Installation – To install, reverse removal procedure using NEW "O" rings, gasket and sealing washers. Tighten all bolts to specification. See TORQUE SPECIFICATIONS. Tighten drain plug to specification. Perform START CLUTCH CALIBRATION PROCEDURE under ON-VEHICLE SERVICE.

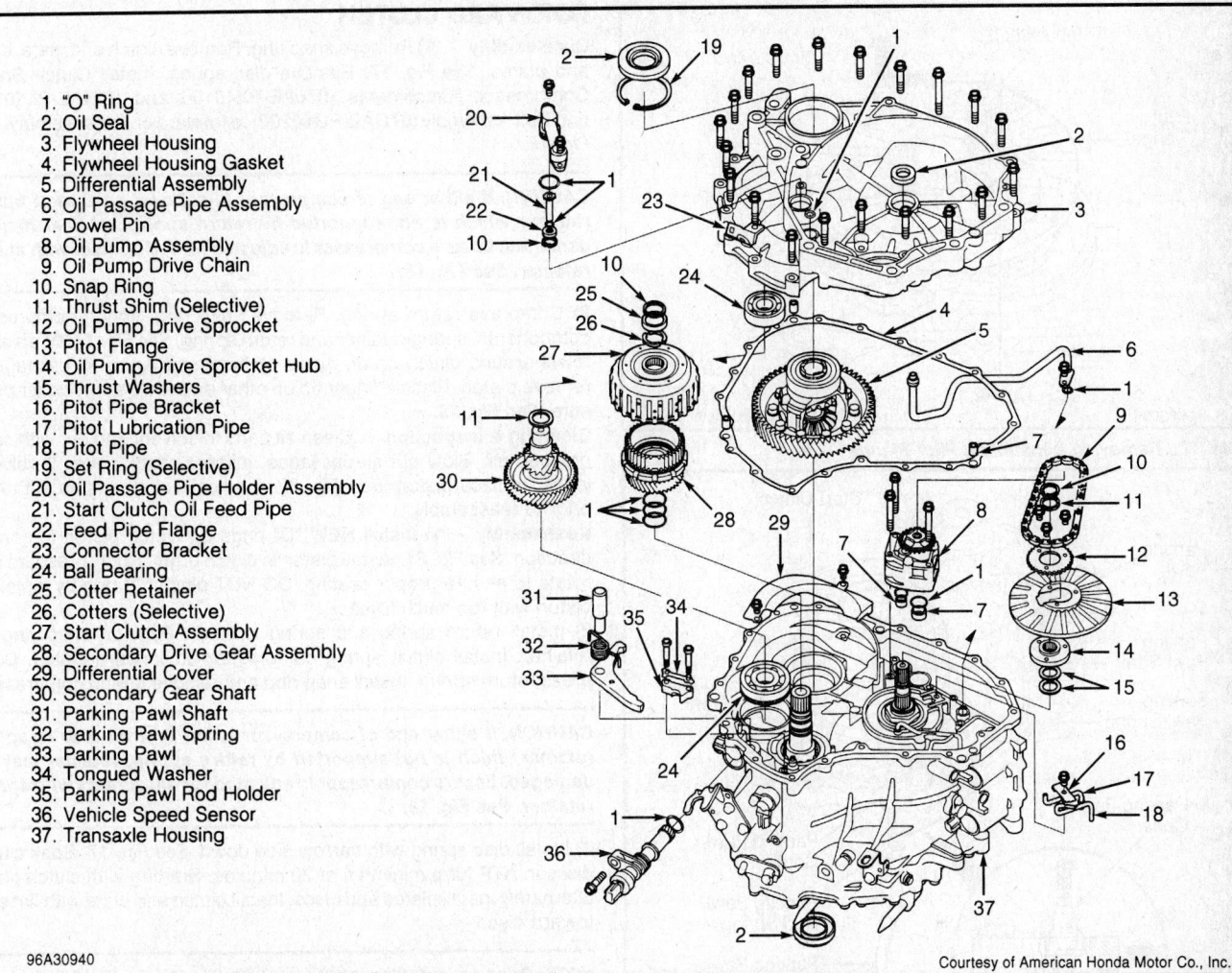

1. "O" Ring
2. Oil Seal
3. Flywheel Housing
4. Flywheel Housing Gasket
5. Differential Assembly
6. Oil Passage Pipe Assembly
7. Dowel Pin
8. Oil Pump Assembly
9. Oil Pump Drive Chain
10. Snap Ring
11. Thrust Shim (Selective)
12. Oil Pump Drive Sprocket
13. Pitot Flange
14. Oil Pump Drive Sprocket Hub
15. Thrust Washers
16. Pitot Pipe Bracket
17. Pitot Lubrication Pipe
18. Pitot Pipe
19. Set Ring (Selective)
20. Oil Passage Pipe Holder Assembly
21. Start Clutch Oil Feed Pipe
22. Feed Pipe Flange
23. Connector Bracket
24. Ball Bearing
25. Cotter Retainer
26. Cotters (Selective)
27. Start Clutch Assembly
28. Secondary Drive Gear Assembly
29. Differential Cover
30. Secondary Gear Shaft
31. Parking Pawl Shaft
32. Parking Pawl Spring
33. Parking Pawl
34. Tongued Washer
35. Parking Pawl Rod Holder
36. Vehicle Speed Sensor
37. Transaxle Housing

96A30940

Courtesy of American Honda Motor Co., Inc.

Fig. 9: Exploded View Of Flywheel & Transaxle Housing Components

TRANSAXLE DISASSEMBLY

1) Remove oil passage pipe holder assembly. Remove 20 bolts and flywheel housing. Remove oil pump drive sprocket, then remove oil pump drive chain. See Fig. 9. Move pitot flange toward it's cutout, then remove pitot flange. See Fig. 10.

2) Remove snap ring securing oil pump drive sprocket hub. Remove thrust shim, oil pump drive sprocket hub and thrust washers. Remove differential assembly and secondary gear shaft. Remove parking pawl shaft, parking pawl spring and parking pawl. See Fig. 11. Remove snap ring securing start clutch. Remove cotter retainer and cotters. See Fig. 9.

3) Set Start Clutch Remover (07TAE-P4V0120) on start clutch. Attach pawl of remover to parking gear. See Fig. 12. Remove start clutch and secondary drive gear assembly.

CAUTION: DO NOT place pawl of remover on start clutch guide. If pawl of remover contacts start clutch guide, start clutch guide may be damaged.

4) Remove 14 right side cover bolts and remove cover. Remove manual valve body pipes. Remove snap ring securing ring gear. Remove thrust shim and ring gear. Remove snap ring securing reverse brake discs and plates. Remove reverse brake end plate, discs, plates and spring. See Fig. 13.

5) Remove carrier assembly with thrust washers and thrust needle bearing from forward clutch. Remove sun gear with thrust washer and thrust needle bearing. Remove input shaft by pulling upward. Remove snap ring securing forward clutch. Remove snap ring securing forward clutch end plate. Remove end plate.

6) Reinstall carrier assembly on forward clutch. Secure carrier with forward clutch end plate snap ring. Remove forward clutch and carrier assembly together. Install Reverse Brake Spring Compressor (07TAE-P4V0110) on reverse brake. Compress reverse brake return spring and remove snap ring. See Fig. 14.

CAUTION: If spring retainer tab is on reverse brake piston, spring retainer may be damaged. Ensure spring retainer tab is not on piston. See Fig. 15.

7) Remove spring compressor and remove spring retainer/return spring assembly. Remove reverse brake pressure plug. See Fig. 5. Apply compressed air to pressure port and remove reverse brake piston.

8) Remove snap ring retainer from driven pulley shaft. Remove 5 bolts and remove manual valve body. Remove roller and push control shaft assembly toward outside of transaxle housing. Remove 4 bolts and intermediate housing. See Fig. 13.

COMPONENT DISASSEMBLY & REASSEMBLY

MANUAL VALVE BODY

Disassembly & Reassembly – Remove spring seat, spring and reverse inhibitor valve. Remove manual valve from valve body. Clean all parts in solvent and dry with compressed air. Blow out all passages. Inspect valve body for wear, scratches and scoring. See Fig. 16. To reassemble, reverse disassembly procedures.

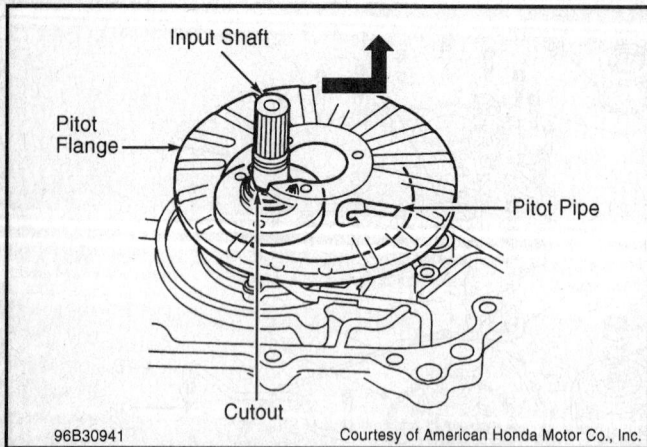

Fig. 10: Removing & Installing Pitot Flange

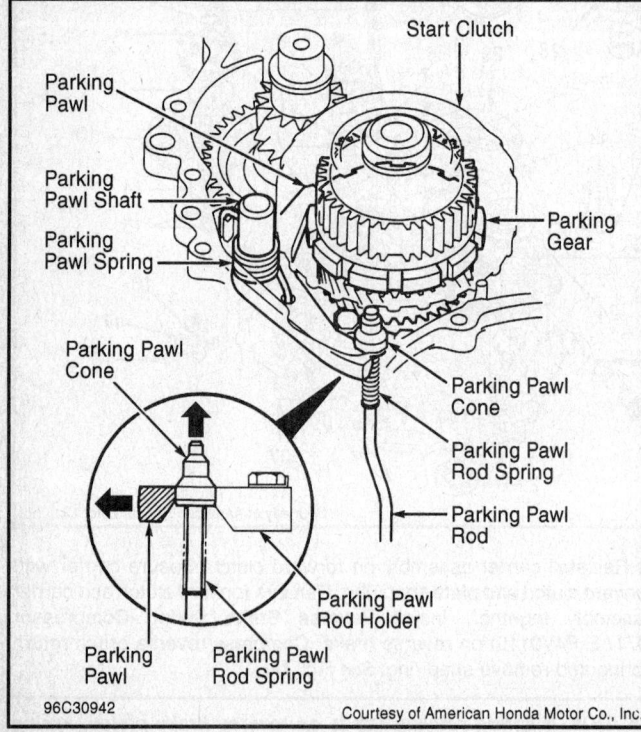

Fig. 11: Identifying Parking Pawl Components

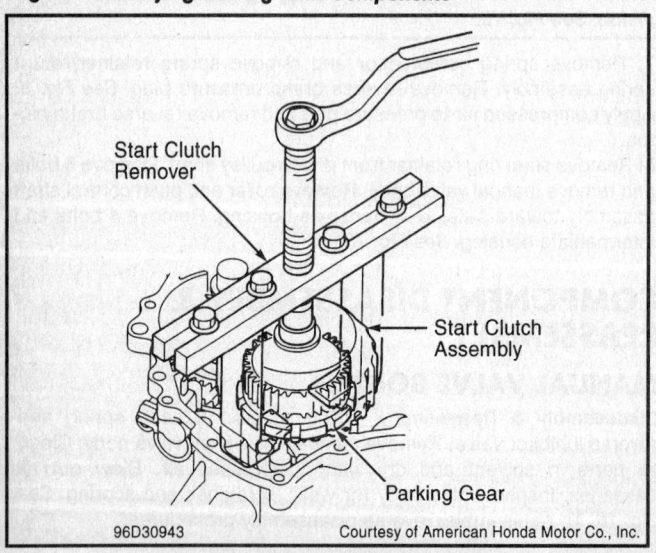

Fig. 12: Removing Start Clutch & Secondary Drive Gear Assembly

FORWARD CLUTCH

Disassembly – 1) Remove snap ring. Remove clutch end plate, discs and plates. See Fig. 17. Remove disc spring. Install Clutch Spring Compressor Attachments (07LAE-PX40100 and 07HAE-PL50100) and Bolt Assembly (07GAE-PG40200) to forward clutch assembly. See Fig. 18.

CAUTION: If either end of compressor is set over an area of spring retainer which is not supported by return spring, retainer may be damaged. Ensure compressor is adjusted for full contact with spring retainer. See Fig. 18.

2) Compress return spring. Remove snap ring, spring compressor components, spring retainer and return spring. See Fig. 17. Wrap shop towel around clutch drum. Apply compressed air to oil passage to remove piston. Place a finger tip on other end while applying air pressure. See Fig. 19.

Cleaning & Inspection – Clean all parts in solvent and dry with compressed air. Blow out all passages. Inspect check valve. If valve is loose, replace piston. See Fig. 20. Lubricate components with ATF prior to reassembly.

Reassembly – 1) Install NEW "O" rings on clutch piston in correct direction. See Fig. 21. Install piston in clutch drum. Apply pressure and rotate to ensure proper seating. DO NOT pinch "O" ring by installing piston with too much force.

2) Install return spring and spring retainer. Position snap ring on retainer. Install clutch spring compressor on forward clutch. Compress return spring. Install snap ring and remove spring compressor.

CAUTION: If either end of compressor is set over an area of spring retainer which is not supported by return spring, retainer may be damaged. Ensure compressor is adjusted for full contact with spring retainer. See Fig. 18.

3) Install disc spring with narrow side down. See Fig. 17. Soak clutch discs in ATF for a minimum of 30 minutes. Starting with clutch plate, alternately install plates and discs. Install clutch end plate with flat side toward disc.

NOTE: Prior to installing plates and discs, ensure inside of clutch drum is free of dirt or other foreign matter.

4) Install snap ring. Ensure snap ring end gap is .31" (7.9 mm). Using a dial indicator, measure clearance between clutch end plate and top disc. Zero dial indicator with clutch end plate lowered and lift plate up to snap ring. See Fig. 22.

5) Distance clutch end plate moves is clearance between clutch end plate and top disc. Measure clearance in at least 3 places and use average as actual measurement. Clearance should be .016-.024" (.40-.60 mm).

6) If clearance is not within specification, select a NEW clutch end plate, then recheck. End plates are available in thicknesses between .138" (3.50 mm) and .185" (4.70 mm), in increments of .004" (.10 mm). See Fig. 23. After replacing clutch end plate, ensure clearance is within specification.

NOTE: If thickest clutch end plate is installed, but clearance is still over specification, replace clutch discs and plates.

DIFFERENTIAL ASSEMBLY

Disassembly – 1) Prior to disassembly, place differential assembly on "V"-blocks and install both axles. Using dial indicator, measure pinion gear backlash. See Fig. 24. Backlash should be .002-.006" (.05-.15 mm). If backlash is not as specified, replace differential carrier.

2) Remove final driven gear from differential carrier. Final driven gear bolts have left-hand threads. Using appropriate bearing puller, remove differential carrier bearings (if necessary). See Fig. 25.

Cleaning & Inspection – Check bearings for wear and rough rotation. Inspect final driven gear teeth for damage. Replace components as necessary.

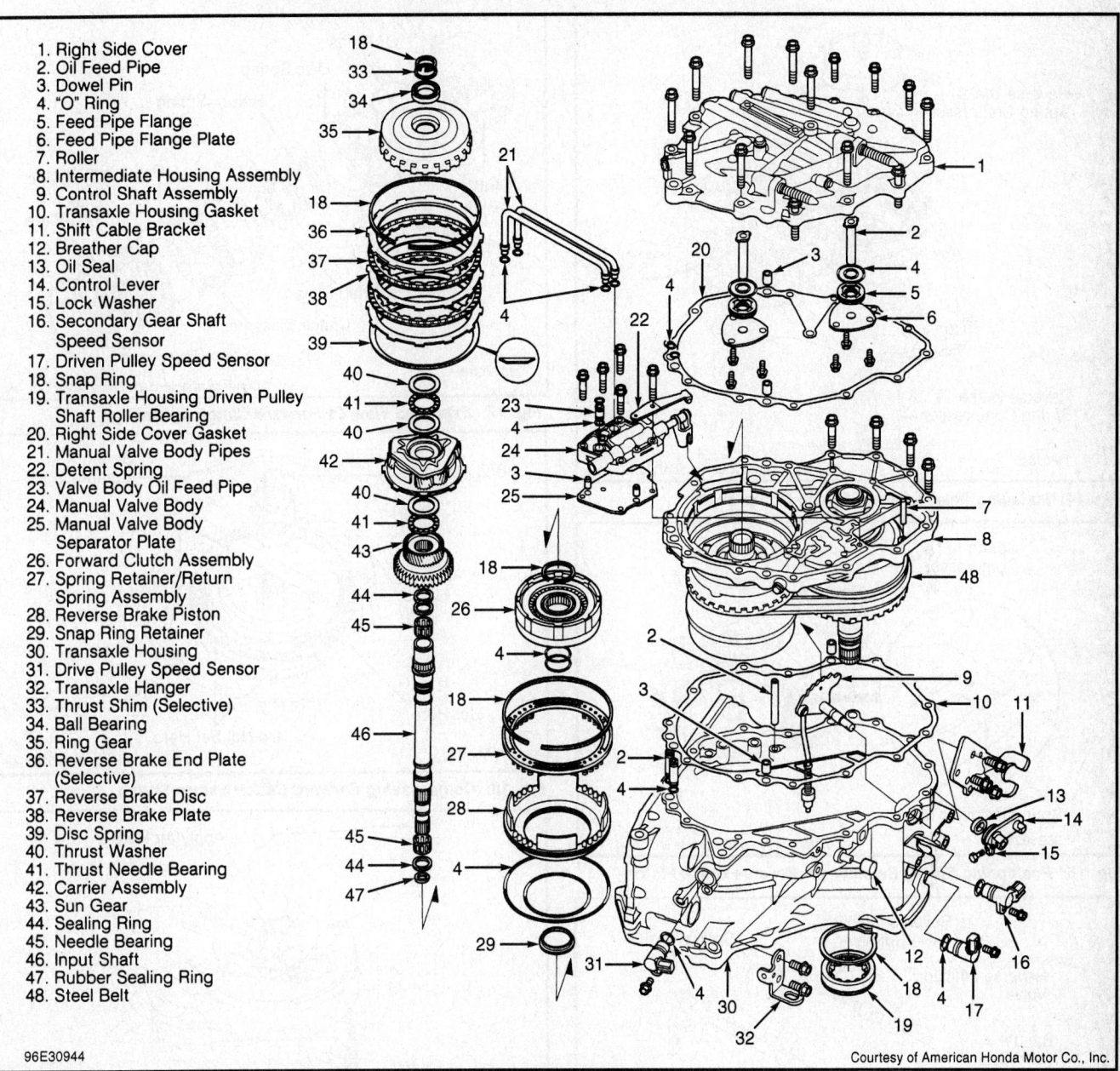

1. Right Side Cover
2. Oil Feed Pipe
3. Dowel Pin
4. "O" Ring
5. Feed Pipe Flange
6. Feed Pipe Flange Plate
7. Roller
8. Intermediate Housing Assembly
9. Control Shaft Assembly
10. Transaxle Housing Gasket
11. Shift Cable Bracket
12. Breather Cap
13. Oil Seal
14. Control Lever
15. Lock Washer
16. Secondary Gear Shaft Speed Sensor
17. Driven Pulley Speed Sensor
18. Snap Ring
19. Transaxle Housing Driven Pulley Shaft Roller Bearing
20. Right Side Cover Gasket
21. Manual Valve Body Pipes
22. Detent Spring
23. Valve Body Oil Feed Pipe
24. Manual Valve Body
25. Manual Valve Body Separator Plate
26. Forward Clutch Assembly
27. Spring Retainer/Return Spring Assembly
28. Reverse Brake Piston
29. Snap Ring Retainer
30. Transaxle Housing
31. Drive Pulley Speed Sensor
32. Transaxle Hanger
33. Thrust Shim (Selective)
34. Ball Bearing
35. Ring Gear
36. Reverse Brake End Plate (Selective)
37. Reverse Brake Disc
38. Reverse Brake Plate
39. Disc Spring
40. Thrust Washer
41. Thrust Needle Bearing
42. Carrier Assembly
43. Sun Gear
44. Sealing Ring
45. Needle Bearing
46. Input Shaft
47. Rubber Sealing Ring
48. Steel Belt

96E30944

Courtesy of American Honda Motor Co., Inc.

Fig. 13: Exploded View Of Right Side Cover & Intermediate Housing Components

Reassembly – To reassemble, reverse disassembly procedure. Install NEW bearings using appropriate driver and press. Install final driven gear on differential carrier with chamfered side of gear on inner bore, facing differential carrier. Tighten bolts to 74 ft. lbs. (101 N.m).

TRANSAXLE & FLYWHEEL HOUSING OIL SEALS

Disassembly & Reassembly – **1)** Remove oil seal from transaxle housing and flywheel housing using pin punch and hammer. Install a 3.15" (80 mm) set ring into flywheel housing. DO NOT install oil seal. Using appropriate driver, install differential assembly into transaxle housing.

2) Install flywheel housing and tighten bolts to 21 ft. lbs. (29 N.m). Using feeler gauge, measure clearance between 3.15" (80 mm) set ring and outer race of bearing in flywheel housing. See Fig. 26. Clearance should be .006" (.15 mm). If clearance is more than specified, select and install NEW set ring, then go to next step. Set ring is available in thicknesses between .098" (2.50 mm) and 1.18" (3.00 mm). If set ring-to-bearing outer race clearance is less than specification, set ring does not need replacement.

3) Remove flywheel housing. Install correct thickness set ring. Install oil seal in transaxle housing and flywheel housing using appropriate driver, pilot, adapter and hammer. Ensure oil seal in flywheel housing is installed to correct depth. See Fig. 27.

DRIVEN PULLEY SHAFT BEARING

Disassembly & Reassembly – **1)** Expand snap ring with snap ring pliers, then push bearing out using driver, adapter and press. See Fig. 28. DO NOT remove snap ring unless it is necessary to clean groove in housing. Lubricate parts with ATF. Expand snap ring with pliers. Insert NEW bearing part-way into housing using driver and adapter. Install bearing with groove facing outside housing.

2) Release pliers, then push bearing down into housing until ring snaps in place around bearing. After installing bearing, ensure snap ring is seated in bearing and housing grooves. See Fig. 29. Ensure snap ring operates properly and snap ring end gap is 0-.35" (0-9 mm).

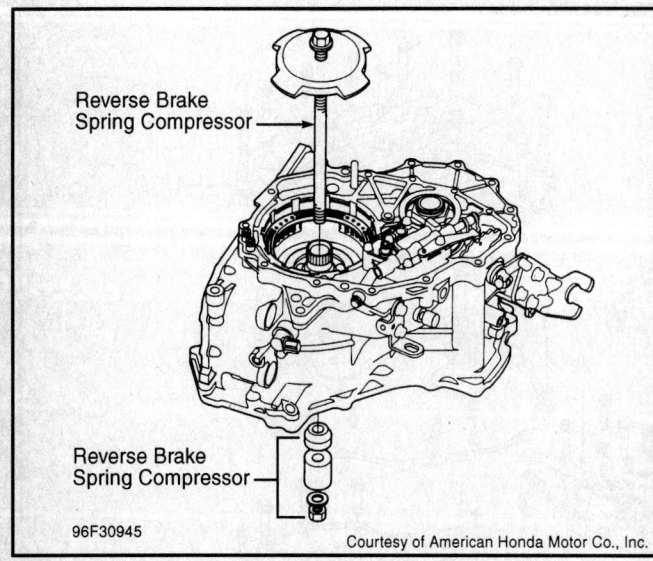

Fig. 14: Installing Reverse Brake Spring Compressor

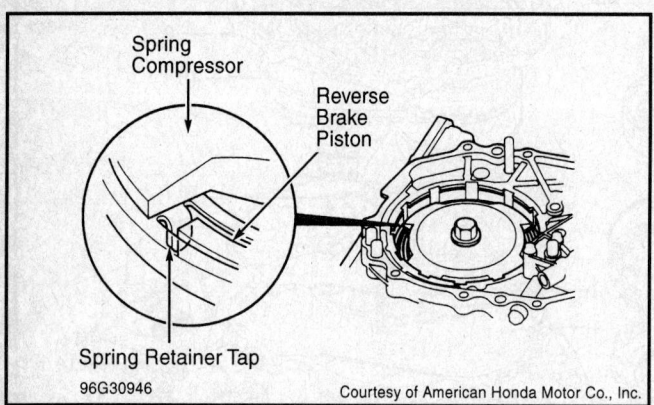

Fig. 15: Positioning Spring Retainer On Reverse Brake Piston

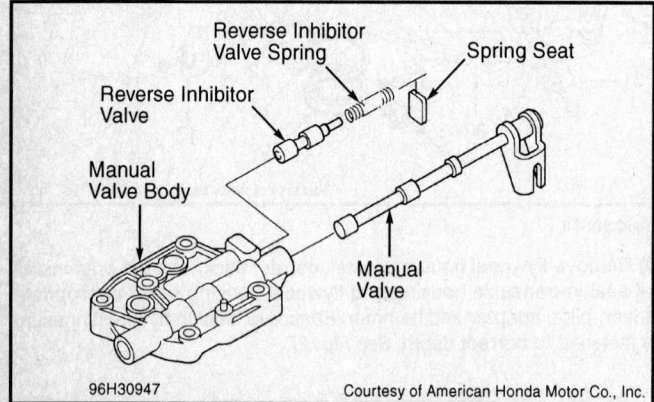

Fig. 16: Identifying Manual Valve Body Components

SECONDARY GEAR SHAFT BEARING

Disassembly & Reassembly – Using slide hammer and bearing puller, remove secondary gear shaft bearing from transaxle housing and flywheel housing. Using adapter, driver and press, install NEW secondary gear shaft bearing until it bottoms in transaxle housing or flywheel housing.

RING GEAR BEARING

Disassembly & Reassembly – Remove ring gear bearing using pin punch and hammer. Using adapter, driver and press, install NEW ring gear bearing until it bottoms in ring gear.

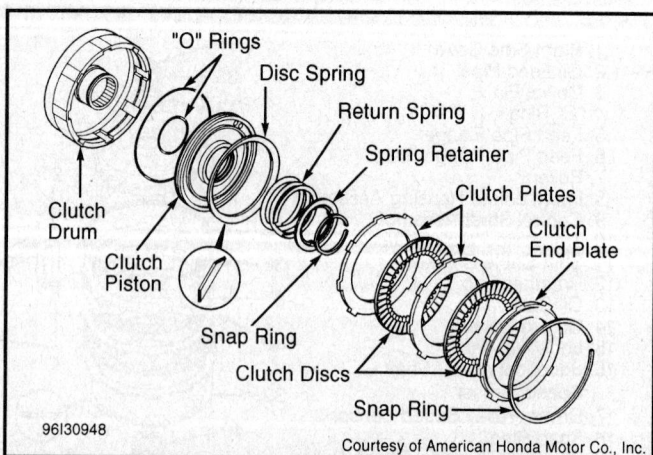

Fig. 17: Exploded View Of Forward Clutch Assembly

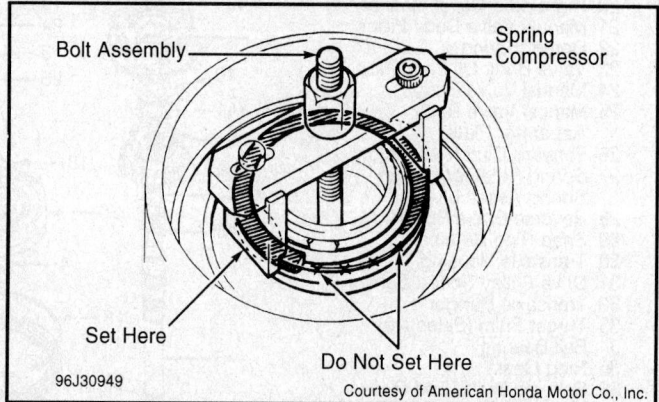

Fig. 18: Compressing Forward Clutch Return Spring

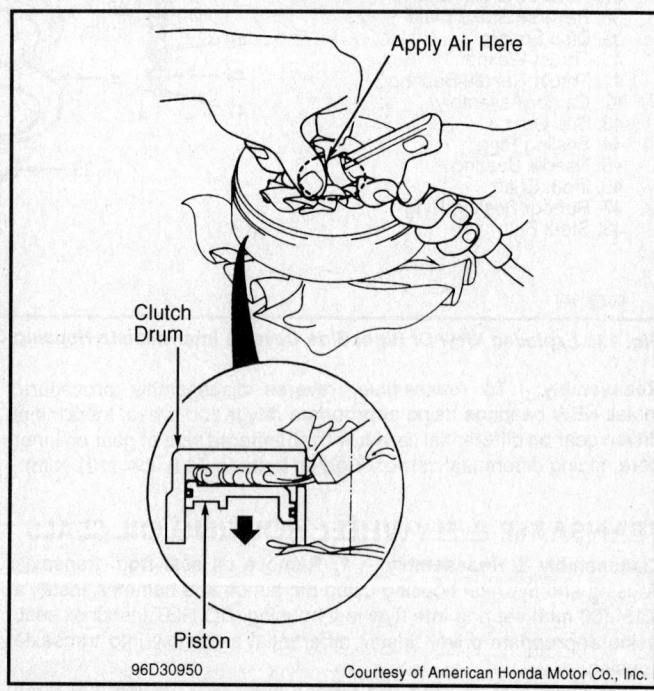

Fig. 19: Removing Forward Clutch Piston

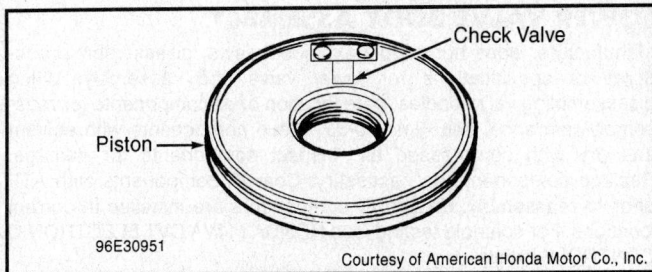

Fig. 20: Checking Forward Clutch Piston Check Valve

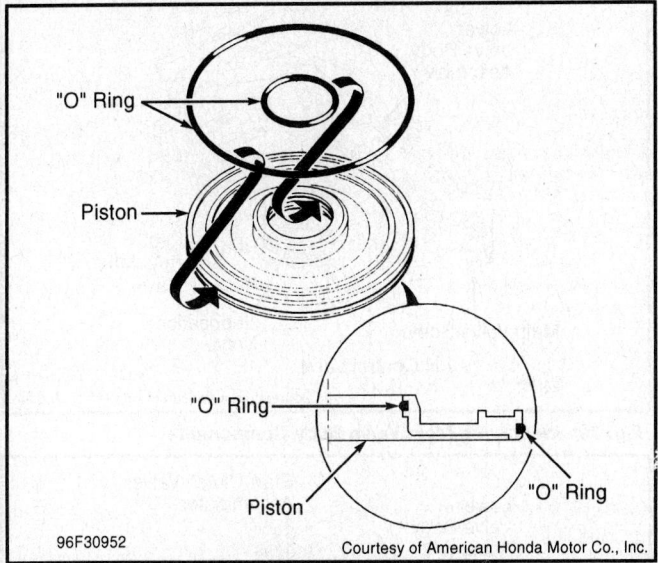

Fig. 21: Installing Forward Clutch Piston "O" Rings

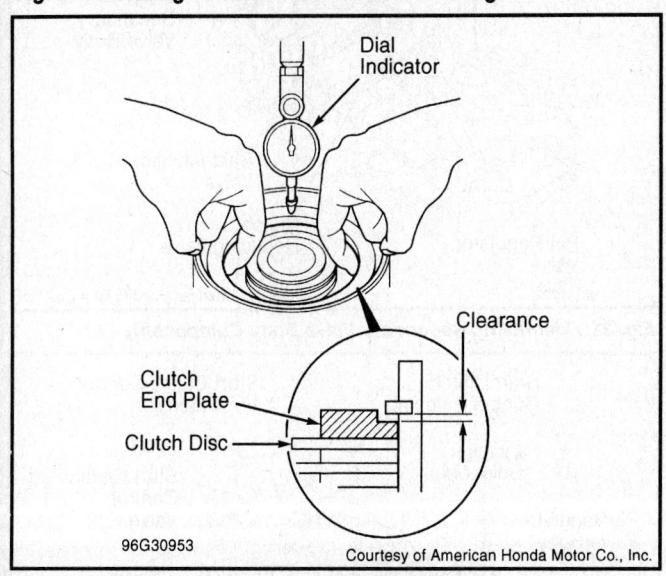

Fig. 22: Measuring Forward Clutch Clearance

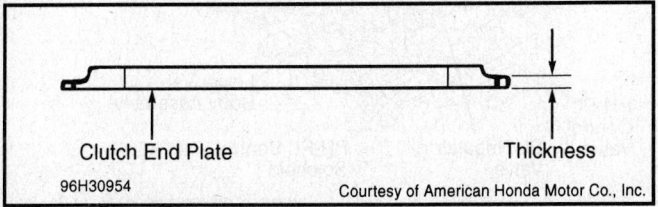

Fig. 23: Measuring Forward Clutch End Plate Thickness

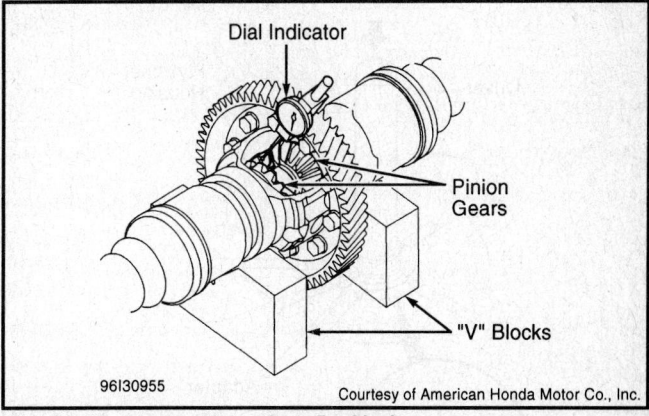

Fig. 24: Measuring Pinion Gear Backlash

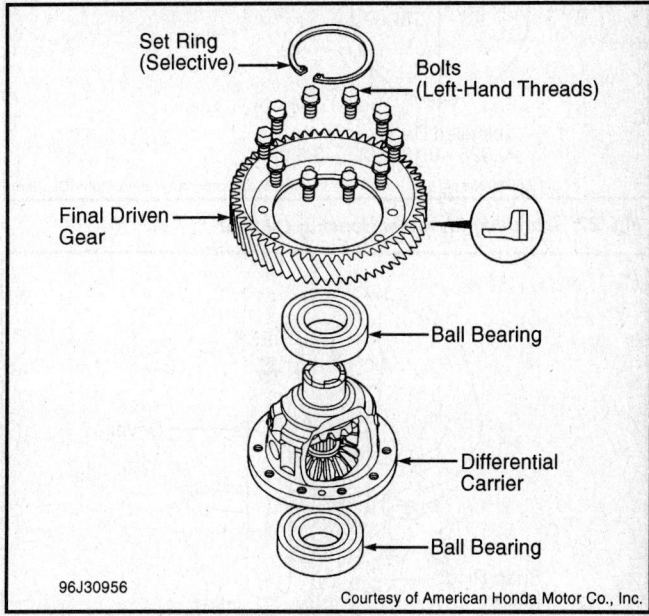

Fig. 25: Identifying Differential Assembly Components

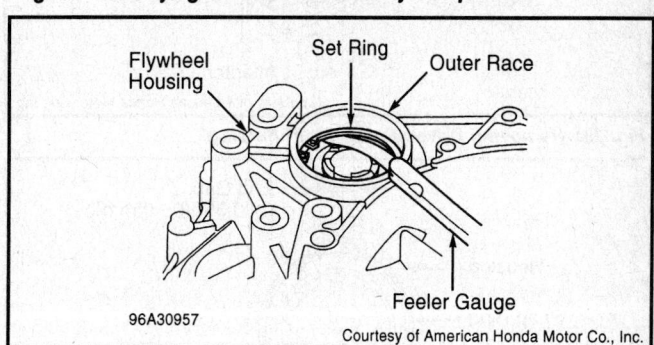

Fig. 26: Measuring Set Ring Clearance

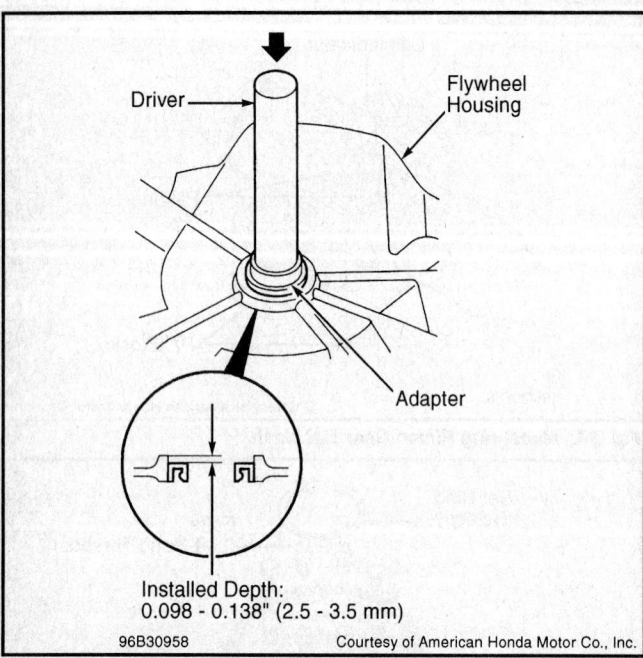

Fig. 27: Installing Flywheel Housing Oil Seal

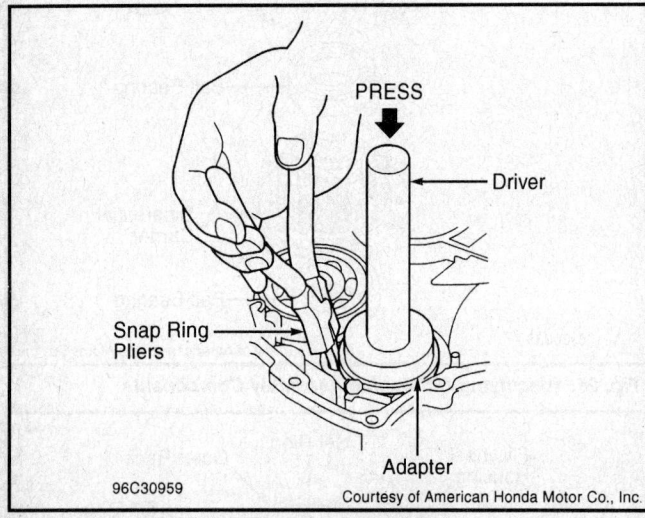

Fig. 28: Removing Driven Pulley Shaft Bearing

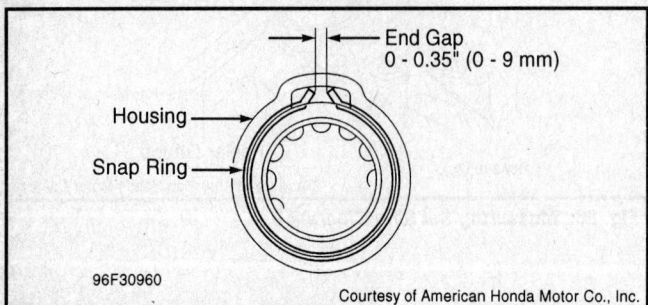

Fig. 29: Measuring Snap Ring End Gap

CONTROL SHAFT ASSEMBLY

Disassembly & Reassembly – Remove bolt and lock washer. Remove control lever from control shaft. Remove control shaft assembly. *See Fig. 13.* To reassemble, reverse disassembly procedures.

LOWER VALVE BODY ASSEMBLY

Manufacturer does not supply exploded views, disassembly procedures or specifications for lower valve body assembly. When disassembling valve bodies, note location of all components for reassembly reference. *See Figs. 30-33.* Clean components with solvent and dry with compressed air. Inspect components for damage. Replace components as necessary. Coat all components with ATF prior to reassembly. Ensure all components are installed in correct locations. For solenoid testing, see HONDA M4VA CVT ELECTRONIC CONTROLS article.

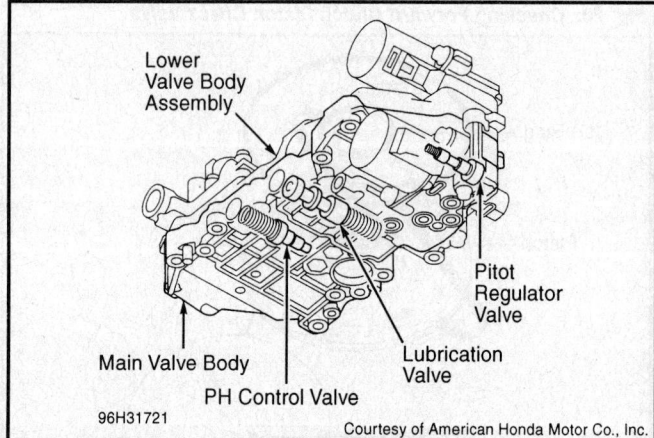

Fig. 30: Identifying Main Valve Body Components

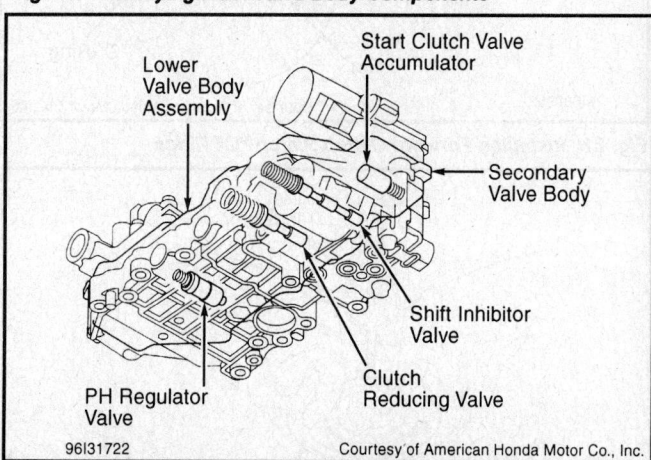

Fig. 31: Identifying Secondary Valve Body Components

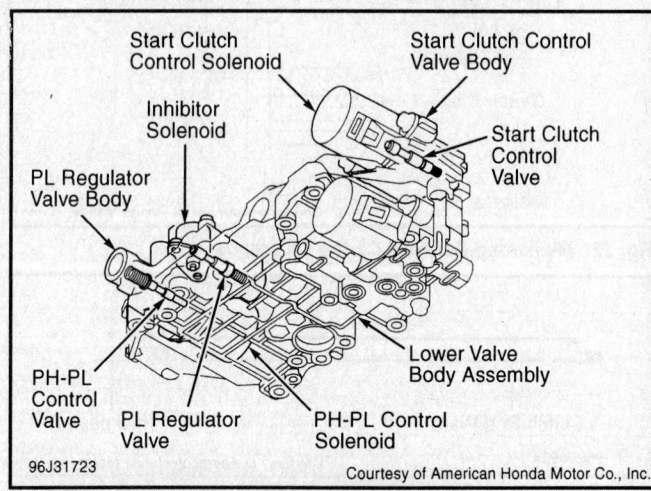

Fig. 32: Identifying PL Regulator & Start Clutch Control Valve Body Components

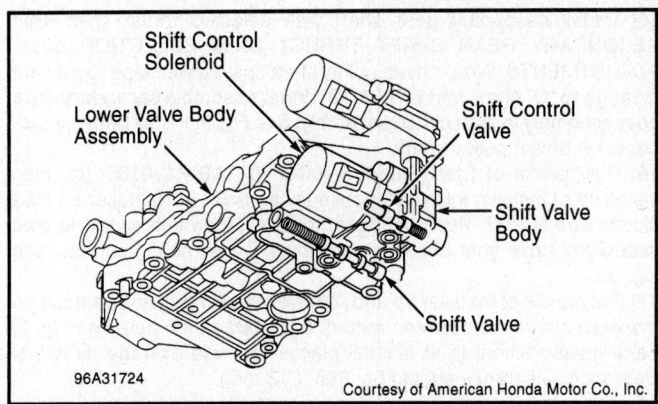

96A31724

Courtesy of American Honda Motor Co., Inc.

Fig. 33: Identifying Shift Valve Body Components

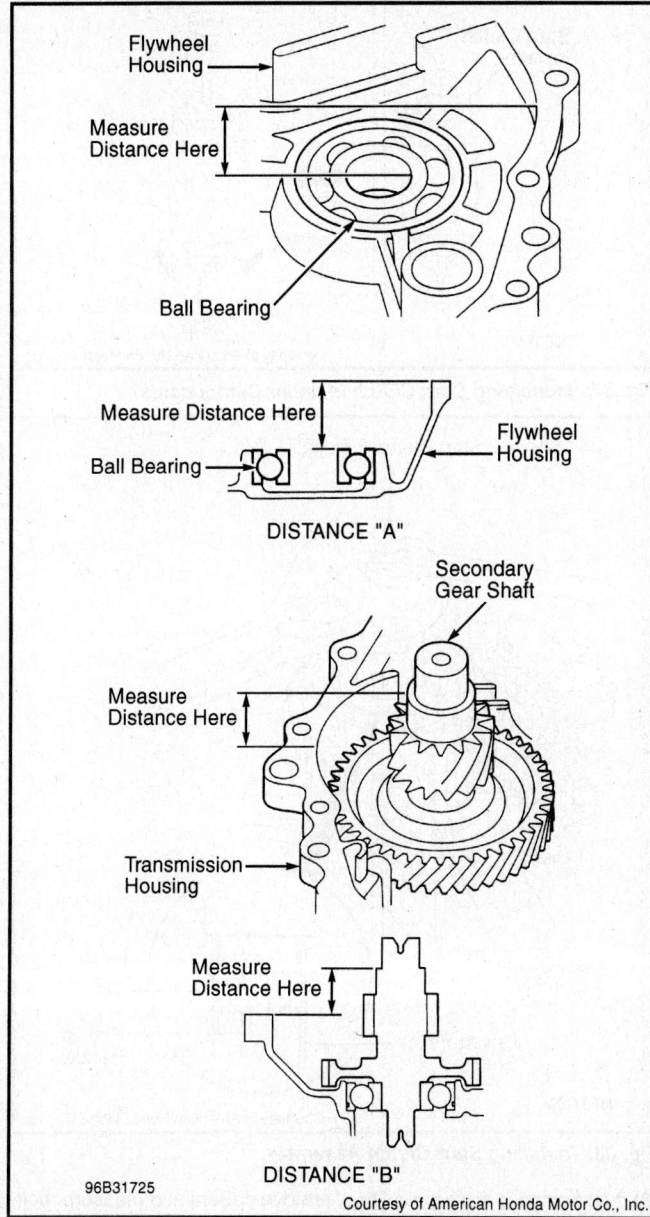

96B31725

Courtesy of American Honda Motor Co., Inc.

Fig. 34: Calculating Secondary Gear Shaft Thrust Shim Thickness

ADJUSTMENTS

SECONDARY GEAR SHAFT THRUST SHIM SELECTION

NOTE: Perform this procedure prior to transaxle reassembly.

1) Measure distance "A" between flywheel housing surface and ball bearing. *See Fig. 34.* Install secondary gear shaft in transaxle housing. Measure distance "B" between transaxle housing surface and thrust shim washer mounting surface of secondary gear shaft. *See Fig. 34.*
2) Calculate thrust shim thickness using following formula: Measurement "A" minus measurement "B" plus flywheel housing gasket thickness of .020" (.50 mm). Shim is available in thicknesses between .110" (2.80 mm) and .150" (3.80 mm) in increments of .004" (.10 mm).

TRANSAXLE REASSEMBLY

NOTE: When TCM, transaxle assembly, start clutch assembly, lower valve body assembly or engine assembly are replaced, TCM must memorize feedback signal for start clutch control. Perform START CLUTCH CALIBRATION PROCEDURE under ON-VEHICLE SERVICE to calibrate start clutch after installing transaxle.

1) Install long oil feed pipe in transaxle housing. Install 2 oil feed pipes with NEW "O" rings in transaxle housing. Install 2 dowel pins and NEW transaxle housing gasket on transaxle housing. *See Fig. 13.* Push control shaft assembly toward outside of transaxle housing, then install intermediate housing assembly.
2) Install manual valve body separator plate and 2 dowel pins on intermediate housing. Install manual valve body with detent spring. Pull control shaft assembly back, then install roller on intermediate housing. Install reverse brake piston in intermediate housing.
3) Install spring retainer/return spring assembly on reverse brake piston. Install return springs on spring guides of reverse brake piston. Install reverse brake spring compressor on reverse brake return spring. *See Fig. 14.*

CAUTION: If spring retainer tab is on reverse brake piston, spring retainer may be damaged. Ensure spring retainer tab is not on piston. See Fig. 15.

4) Compress return springs, then install snap ring in intermediate housing above spring retainer. Ensure snap ring end gap is a minimum of .59" (15 mm). Soak reverse brake discs in ATF for a minimum of 30 minutes. Install disc spring on reverse brake piston.
5) Starting with a reverse brake plate, alternately install reverse brake plate and discs. Install reverse brake end plate and snap ring. Using a dial indicator, measure clearance between reverse brake end plate and top disc. *See Fig. 35.*
6) Zero dial indicator with reverse brake end plate lowered. Lift end plate up toward snap ring. Take measurement in at least 3 places and use average as actual clearance. Clearance should be .018-.030" (.46-.76 mm).
7) If clearance is not as specified, remove reverse brake end plate and measure plate thickness. Select and install NEW reverse brake end plate, then recheck clearance. End plate is available in thicknesses between .142" (3.61 mm) and .200" (5.08 mm) in increments of .008" (.20 mm).

NOTE: If thickest reverse brake end plate is installed, but clearance is still over specification, replace reverse brake discs and plates.

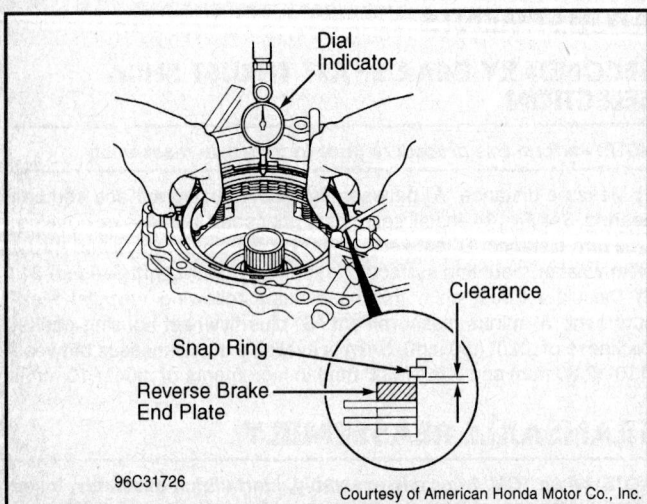

Fig. 35: Measuring Reverse Brake End Plate Clearance

8) After replacing reverse brake end plate, ensure clearance is within specification. Remove snap ring, reverse brake end plate, discs, plates and disc spring. Install snap ring retainer on drive pulley shaft.

9) Wrap drive pulley shaft splines with tape to prevent damage to "O" rings. Install NEW "O" rings. Install forward clutch assembly on drive pulley shaft. Install snap ring. Ensure outside diameter of snap ring is 1.63" (41.4 mm) maximum. Install input shaft in drive pulley shaft.

10) Install sun gear in forward clutch. See Fig. 13. Install thrust needle bearing and thrust washer on sun gear. Install carrier assembly on forward clutch. Install thrust washer, thrust needle bearing and thrust washer on carrier assembly. Install ring gear and thrust shim. Install snap ring.

11) Ensure outside diameter of snap ring is 1.21" (30.7 mm) maximum. Using feeler gauge, measure clearance between thrust shim and snap ring. Take measurement in at least 3 places and use average as actual clearance. Clearance should be .0004-.0043" (.010-.110 mm). See Fig. 36.

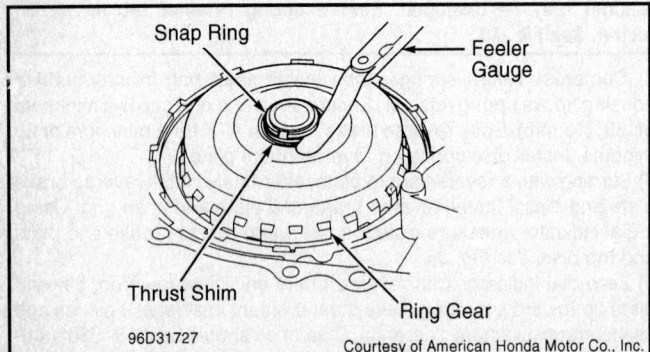

Fig. 36: Measuring Ring Gear Thrust Shim-To-Snap Ring Clearance

12) If clearance is not as specified, remove thrust shim and measure shim thickness. Select and install NEW thrust shim, then recheck clearance. Thrust shim is available in thicknesses between .041" (1.05 mm) and .072" (1.82 mm) in increments of .003" (.07 mm). After replacing thrust shim, ensure clearance is within specification and snap ring outside diameter is correct.

13) Install disc spring with narrow end down. See Fig. 13. Starting with a reverse brake plate, alternately install reverse brake plates and discs. Install selected reverse brake plate, then install snap ring. Ensure outside diameter of snap ring is .71" (18 mm) maximum.

14) Install manual valve body pipes with NEW "O" rings on manual valve body and intermediate housing. Install 2 dowel pins and NEW right side cover gasket on intermediate housing. See Fig. 13. Install NEW "O" rings on oil feed pipes. Install right side cover. Install parking pawl, spring and shaft on transaxle housing. Move control lever to any gear position except "P" position.

15) Install secondary gear shaft with selected thrust shim. See SECONDARY GEAR SHAFT THRUST SHIM SELECTION under ADJUSTMENTS. Wrap driven pulley shaft splines with tape to prevent damage to "O" rings. Install NEW "O" rings. Assemble secondary drive gear assembly in start clutch assembly. See Fig. 9. Install both components on driven pulley shaft.

16) Pull handle of Start Clutch Installer (07TAE-P4V0130) up, then install tip of installer into driven pulley shaft hole. Set installer on start clutch. See Fig. 37. Push handle of installer, then tighten nut to seat secondary drive gear assembly on driven pulley shaft securely. See Fig. 38.

17) Pull handle of installer up and remove installer. Install cotters, then measure clearance between cotters and start clutch hub. See Fig. 9. Take measurement in at least 3 places and use average as actual clearance. Clearance should be .005" (.13 mm).

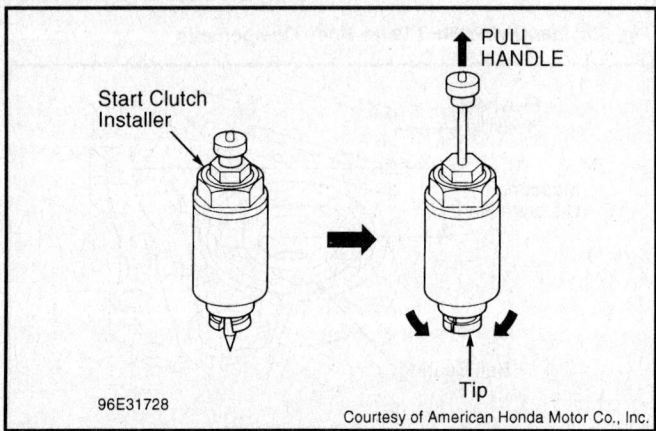

Fig. 37: Identifying Start Clutch Installer Components

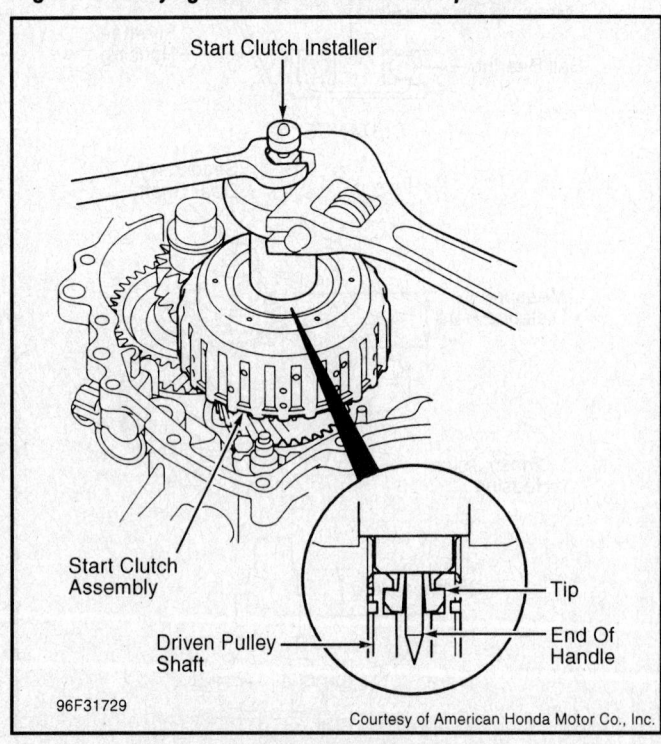

Fig. 38: Installing Start Clutch Assembly

18) If clearance is not as specified, remove cotters and measure their thickness. Select and install NEW cotters, then recheck clearance. Cotters are available in thicknesses between .114" (2.90 mm) and .126" (3.20 mm) in increments of .004" (.10 mm). After replacing cotters, ensure clearance is within specification.

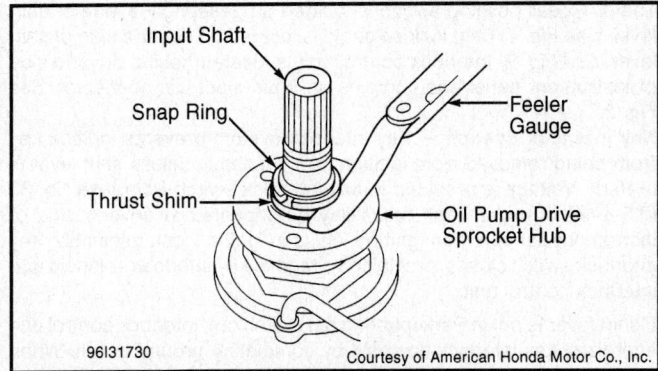

96I31730

Courtesy of American Honda Motor Co., Inc.

Fig. 39: Measuring Oil Pump Drive Sprocket Hub Thrust Shim-To-Snap Ring Clearance

19) Install cotter retainer and snap ring. Ensure outside diameter of snap ring is 1.33" (33.9 mm) maximum. Install thrust washers, oil pump drive sprocket hub and thrust shim on input shaft. See Fig. 9. Install snap ring. Ensure outside diameter of snap ring is 1.04" (26.3 mm) maximum.

20) Measure clearance between thrust shim and snap ring. See Fig. 39. Take measurement in at least 3 places and use average as actual clearance. Clearance should be .015-.026" (.37-.65 mm). If clearance is not as specified, remove thrust shim and measure shim thickness.

21) Select and install NEW thrust shim, then recheck clearance. Thrust shims are available in thicknesses between .026" (.65 mm) and .095" (2.40 mm) in increments of .004" (.10 mm). After replacing thrust shims, ensure clearance is within specification and snap ring outside diameter is correct.

22) Install pitot flange using cutout to clear pitot pipes. See Fig. 10. Install oil pump drive sprocket. Install oil pump drive chain on oil pump drive and driven sprockets. Install and tighten sprocket bolts to specification. See TORQUE SPECIFICATIONS. Install differential assembly. Install oil passage pipe assembly using NEW "O" rings. See Fig. 9.

23) Install 3 dowel pins and NEW flywheel housing gasket on transaxle housing. Install flywheel housing and connector bracket (20 bolts). Install oil passage pipe holder assembly. See Fig. 9.

24) Install solenoid harness connector with NEW "O" ring. Install lower valve body assembly with 3 dowel pins (8 bolts). Install oil strainer with NEW "O" ring. Assemble oil pan, oil filter and oil cooler inlet pipe. See Fig. 8. Install oil pan with 2 dowel pins and NEW oil pan gasket. Install oil cooler inlet pipe bracket bolt. Install oil cooler outlet pipe with joint bolt and NEW sealing washers. See Fig. 8.

TRANSAXLE SPECIFICATIONS

TRANSAXLE SPECIFICATIONS

Application	Specification In. (mm)
Clearance	
Cotters-To-Start Clutch Hub	.005 (.13)
Forward Clutch	.016-.024 (.40-.60)
Flywheel Housing Set Ring-To-Outer Race	.006 (.15)
Oil Pump Drive Sprocket Hub	.015-.026 (.37-.65)
Reverse Brake	.018-.030 (.46-.76)
Ring Gear Thrust Shim-to-Snap Ring	.0004-.0043 (.010-.110)
Differential Pinion Gear Backlash	.002-.006 (.05-.15)
Snap Ring Diameter	
Cotter Retainer (Minimum)	1.33 (33.9)
Forward Clutch (Maximum)	1.63 (41.4)
Reverse Brake (Minimum)	.71 (18)
Ring Gear (Maximum)	1.21 (30.7)
Oil Pump Drive Sprocket Hub (Maximum)	1.04 (26.3)
Snap Ring End Gap	
Driven Pulley Shaft Bearing	0-0.35 (0-9)
Reverse Brake (Minimum)	.59 (15)

TORQUE SPECIFICATIONS

TORQUE SPECIFICATIONS

Application	Ft. Lbs. (N.m)
Control Lever Bolt	10 (14)
Flywheel Housing Bolt	21 (29)
Intermediate Housing Bolt	21 (29)
Joint Bolt	21 (29)
Oil Cooler Inlet Pipe Bracket Bolt	19 (26)
Oil Cooler Outlet Pipe Bolt	21 (29)
Oil Pan Drain Plug	36 (49)
Oil Pump Assembly Bolt	19 (26)
Pressure Plug	13 (18)
Ring Gear Bolt	74 (101)
Right Side Cover Bolt	
6-mm Bolt	[1]
8-mm Bolt	27 (37)
Shift Cable Bracket Bolt	19 (26)
Vehicle Speed Sensor Bolt	16 (22)

Application	INCH Lbs. (N.m)
All Other Speed Sensor Bolts	106 (12.0)
Lower Valve Body Assembly Bolt	106 (12.0)
Lower Valve Body Assembly-To-Transaxle Housing Bolt	106 (12.0)
Manual Valve Bolt	106 (12.0)
Oil Filter Bolt	106 (12.0)
Oil Pan Bolt	106 (12.0)
Oil Passage Pipe Holder Assembly Bolt	106 (12.0)
Oil Passage Pipe Assembly Bolt	106 (12.0)
Oil Pump Drive Sprocket Bolt	106 (12.0)
Oil Strainer Bolt	106 (12.0)
Solenoid Harness Bolt	106 (12.0)

[1] – Tighten bolt to 106 INCH lbs. (12.0 N.m).

WIRING DIAGRAMS

For wiring diagram, see HONDA M4VA CVT ELECTRONIC CONTROLS article.

AUTOMATIC TRANSMISSIONS
Honda M4VA CVT Electronic Controls

Civic

APPLICATION

APPLICATION

Vehicle	Transaxle Model
1996 Civic	M4VA

CAUTION: Vehicle is equipped with a Supplemental Restraint System (SRS). When servicing vehicle, use care to avoid accidental air bag deployment. All SRS electrical connections and wiring harness are covered with Yellow insulation. SRS-related components are located in steering column, center console, instrument panel and lower panel on instrument panel. DO NOT use electrical test equipment on these circuits. It may be necessary to deactivate SRS before servicing components. See AIR BAG SERVICING article in APPLICATIONS & IDENTIFICATIONS.

DESCRIPTION

Continuously Variable Transaxle is electronically controlled. Transaxle shifting is controlled by Transmission Control Module (TCM). TCM is located below instrument panel behind left kick panel. TCM receives information from various input devices and uses this information to operate 4 solenoids and "D" indicator light to control shift (pulley ratio) control, belt side pressure control, start clutch control, reverse inhibitor control and for self-diagnosis.

Transaxle is equipped with shift and key interlock systems. Shift interlock system prevents shift lever from being moved from Park unless brake pedal is depressed and accelerator pedal is in idle position. In case of a malfunction, shift lever can be released by placing ignition key in key release slot near shift lever. Key interlock system prevents ignition key from being removed from ignition lock assembly unless shift lever is in Park.

The A/T gear position indicator on instrument panel contains lights to indicate which position A/T gear position switch, on shift lever, is in.

OPERATION

A/T GEAR POSITION INDICATOR

With ignition in RUN or START position, voltage is supplied to A/T gear position indicator, located on instrument panel. *See Fig. 1.* When shift lever is moved to designated gear position, A/T gear position switch completes the ground circuit for A/T gear position indicator on instrument panel. The light on A/T gear position indicator will be illuminated to indicate the shift lever gear position. The A/T gear position switch is located on passenger's side of shift lever.

When headlights are turned on, voltage is supplied to Red/Black wire through fuse No. 30 (7.5-amp) at A/T gear position indicator. This changes brightness control from fixed setting to control by the dash light dimmer input on the Red wire.

SHIFT & KEY INTERLOCK SYSTEMS

Shift Interlock System – Shift interlock system prevents shift lever from being moved from Park unless brake pedal is depressed and accelerator pedal is in idle position. Shift lever cannot be moved from Park if brake and accelerator pedal are depressed at the same time. In case of a malfunction, shift lever can be released by placing ignition key in key release slot near shift lever.

Voltage is provided to shift lock solenoid when ignition is in RUN or START position. When brake pedal is depressed, brakelight switch provides voltage to TCM, provided accelerator pedal is in idle position. With accelerator pedal in idle position, a voltage signal is delivered between Throttle Position (TP) sensor and TCM. TCM then provides voltage to shift lock circuit in interlock control unit. When A/T gear position switch is in Park, interlock control unit operates shift lock solenoid by controlling the ground circuit. When shift lock solenoid is energized, shift lever is released and can be moved.

The A/T gear position switch is located on passenger's side of shift lever. *See Fig. 4.* Shift lock solenoid is located on driver's side of shift lever. *See Fig. 2.* Interlock control unit is located behind driver's side of instrument panel and contains an 8-pin electrical connector. *See Fig. 2.*

Key Interlock System – Key interlock system prevents ignition key from being removed from ignition lock assembly unless shift lever is in Park. Voltage is provided to key interlock switch from fuse No. 33 (7.5-amp) in under dash fuse/relay box, located at driver's side of instrument panel. When ignition key is in ignition lock assembly, key interlock switch closes, providing voltage to key interlock solenoid and interlock control unit.

If shift lever is not in Park (parking pin switch on), interlock control unit energizes key interlock solenoid by completing ground circuit. When key interlock solenoid is energized, ignition key cannot be removed from ignition lock assembly. Key interlock switch and key interlock solenoid are located on ignition lock assembly. *See Fig. 2.* Parking pin switch is located on driver's side of shift lever. Interlock control unit is located behind driver's side of instrument panel and contains an 8-pin electrical connector. *See Fig. 2.*

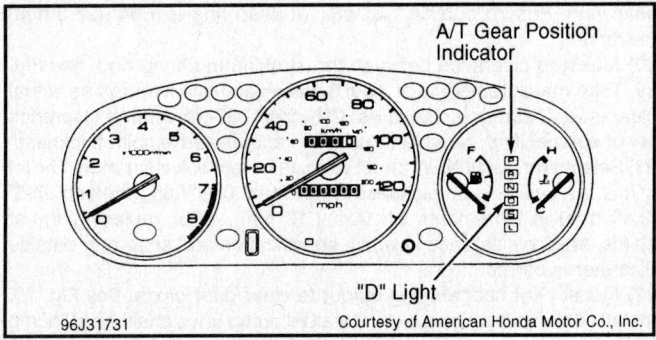

96J31731   Courtesy of American Honda Motor Co., Inc.

Fig. 1: Identifying A/T Gear Position Indicator Light

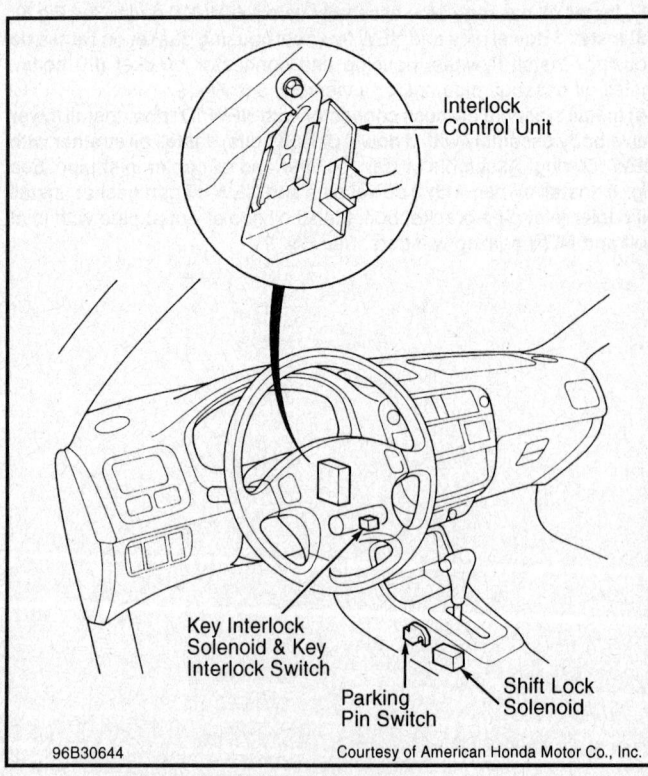

96B30644   Courtesy of American Honda Motor Co., Inc.

Fig. 2: Locating Shift & Key Interlock System Components

TRANSMISSION CONTROL MODULE

Transmission Control Module (TCM) receives information from various input devices and uses this information to control various solenoids. *See Fig. 3.* TCM contains self-diagnostic system which stores fault code if failure or problem exists in transaxle electronic control system. Fault code may also be referred to as Diagnostic Trouble Code (DTC) or flash code. DTC or flash code may be retrieved to determine transaxle problem area. See SELF-DIAGNOSTIC SYSTEM. TCM is located behind driver's side kick panel. *See Fig. 4.*

TCM determines desired pulley ratio by looking at road speed and throttle opening, and choosing a target engine RPM. TCM calculates correct pulley ratio to achieve target engine RPM. For example, at wide open throttle, target RPM will be relatively high for good acceleration. At highway cruising speed with low throttle opening, target RPM will be relatively low for low engine noise and good fuel economy.

TCM also considers shift lever position in determining target RPM. CVT will operate through it's entire range of ratios in each shift lever position. However, for any given road speed and throttle opening, target RPM will be different.

TCM uses a different target RPM for each shift position. For example, at medium road speed of 50 MPH, one half throttle opening in "L" position, target RPM will be about 3000 RPM. At same road speed and throttle opening in "S" position, target RPM will be about 2500 RPM. For same conditions in "D" position, target RPM will be less than 2000 RPM.

When throttle is closed and vehicle is at a stop or at very low speed in a forward gear, TCM operates start clutch control solenoid to apply a small amount of pressure to start clutch. This provides a "creep" function on transaxle, and allows driver to operate vehicle with brake pedal only at very low speeds, or to start out from a stop on a hill without vehicle rolling backward. In "D" position, TCM monitors brakelight switch and reduces creep force when brake is applied. This helps reduce engine vibration and improves fuel economy.

For any given pulley ratio, TCM knows what the relative speeds of both pulleys should be. By comparing inputs from 2 pulley speed sensors, TCM can determine if there is any slippage in steel belt and pulleys. TCM knows ratio between start clutch and secondary gear shaft. By comparing input from driven pulley speed sensor to secondary gear shaft speed sensor input, TCM can determine if there is improper slippage in start clutch.

TCM stores a MAP sensor value in memory as a guide for controlling start clutch pressure during "creep" function. If battery is disconnected, TCM is unplugged, Engine Control Module (ECM) is unplugged, or back-up fuse (7.5-amp) is removed, perform START CLUTCH CALIBRATION PROCEDURE to ensure TCM memorizes a new MAP sensor feedback signal.

TCM INPUT DEVICES

Manifold Absolute Pressure (MAP) Signal – Absolute pressure signal is delivered between Engine Control Module (ECM) and TCM. TCM uses this information along with other inputs to determine correct side pressure. MAP sensor is located near throttle position sensor. *See Fig. 4.*

Brakelight Switch Signal – Brakelight switch delivers input signal to TCM, indicating vehicle braking. Brakelight switch is located on brake pedal support. *See Fig. 4.*

Engine Control Module (ECM) – An upshift and downshift signal and a shift acknowledgment signal is delivered between ECM and TCM. A 5-volt reference signal exists between ECM and TCM. ECM is located behind passenger's side kick panel, below instrument panel. *See Fig. 4.*

Drive Pulley & Driven Pulley Speed Sensor Signal – Drive pulley speed signal is delivered to TCM. Drive pulley speed sensor is located on side of transaxle near dipstick. *See Fig. 4.* Driven pulley speed signal is delivered to TCM. Driven pulley speed sensor is located on top of transaxle.

Secondary Gear Shaft Speed Sensor Signal – Speed signal is delivered to TCM. Secondary gear shaft speed sensor is located on side of transaxle near vehicle speed sensor. *See Fig. 4.*

Service Check Connector – Service check connector is used when retrieving flash codes for transaxle electronic control system diagnosis. When jumper wire is installed between electrical terminals of service check connector, an input is delivered to TCM to display flash codes on "D" indicator light. Service check connector is a Blue 2-pin electrical connector located at passenger's corner of instrument panel. *See Fig. 5.*

Shift Position Signal – Shift position signal is delivered to TCM by the A/T gear position switch, located on passenger's side of shift lever. *See Fig. 4.*

Throttle Position (TP) Sensor Signal – Throttle Position (TP) sensor delivers input signal to TCM to indicate throttle position. TP sensor is mounted on throttle body. *See Fig. 4.*

Vehicle Speed Sensor (VSS) Signal – Vehicle speed sensor delivers input signal to TCM to indicate vehicle speed. VSS is located on top of transaxle. *See Fig. 4.*

TCM OUTPUT DEVICES

Shift Control Solenoid – TCM delivers an output signal to shift control solenoid to adjust pulley positions and achieve desired pulley ratio. TCM then monitors engine RPM, pulley speed sensors, secondary gear shaft speed sensor and vehicle speed sensor to ensure desired ratio has been achieved. Shift control solenoid is located on transaxle lower valve body assembly.

Reverse Inhibitor Solenoid – TCM monitors vehicle speed sensor and if driver selects reverse when vehicle speed is more than 6 MPH, TCM opens reverse inhibitor solenoid. This action bleeds pressure from reverse inhibitor valve, preventing reverse engagement. Reverse inhibitor solenoid is located on transaxle lower valve body assembly.

Start Clutch Control Solenoid – TCM receives input from vehicle speed sensor, gear position switch, throttle position sensor, MAP sensor and brakelight switch to determine correct amount of pressure to apply to start clutch. TCM operates start clutch control solenoid to apply appropriate amount of pressure. Start clutch control solenoid is located on transaxle lower valve body assembly.

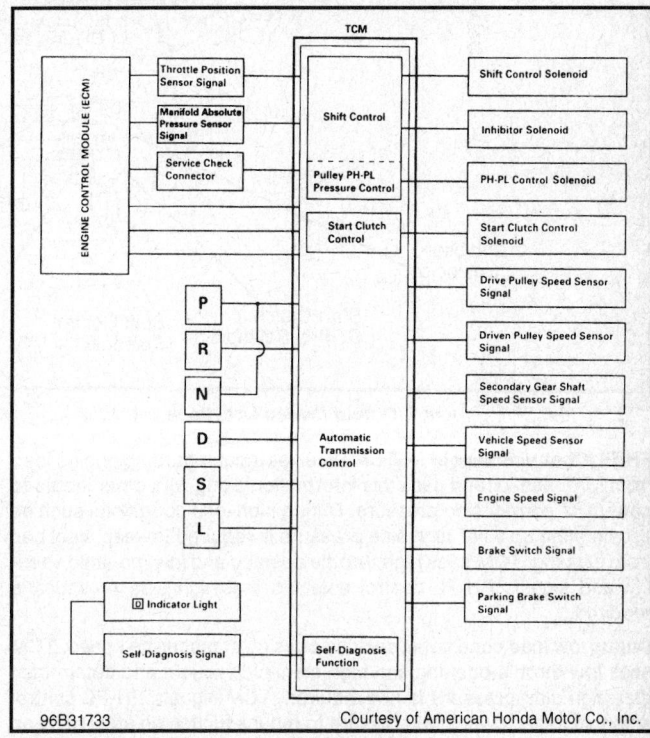

Fig. 3: Identifying Input & Output Devices

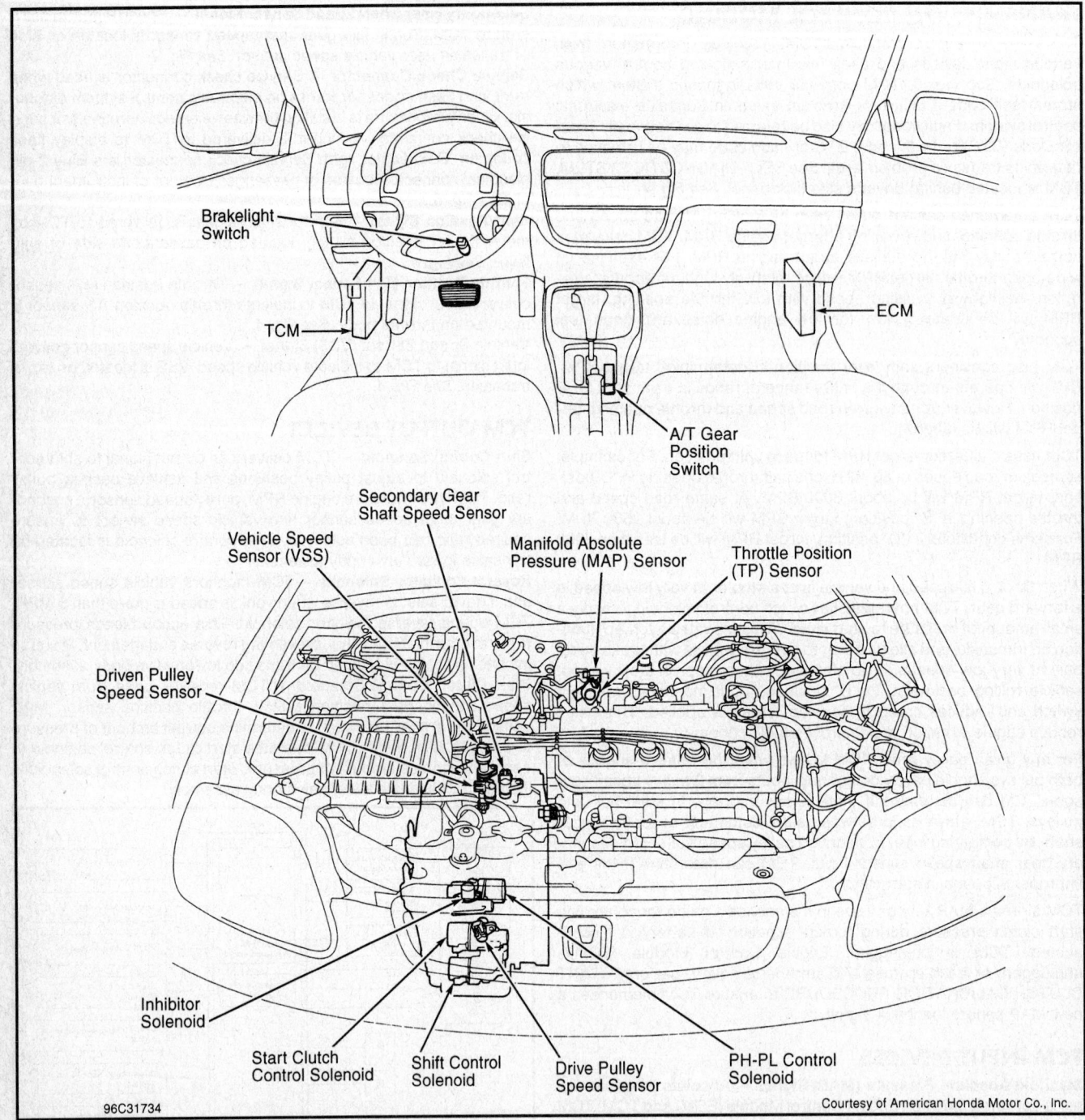

96C31734

Courtesy of American Honda Motor Co., Inc.

Fig. 4: Identifying Input & Output Device Locations

PH-PL Control Solenoid – TCM receives input regarding engine load from MAP sensor and uses this information along with other inputs to determine correct side pressure. During high load conditions such as accelerating up a hill, high side pressure is required to keep steel belt from slipping. TCM sees high throttle opening and low manifold vacuum and signals PH-PL control solenoid that high side pressure is required.

During low load conditions, such as cruising at moderate speed, TCM sees low throttle opening and high manifold vacuum and determines that high side pressure is not required. TCM signals PH-PL control solenoid to set lower side pressure to reduce friction on steel belt and improve fuel economy.

START CLUTCH CALIBRATION PROCEDURE

NOTE: When TCM, transaxle assembly, start clutch assembly, lower valve body assembly or engine assembly are replaced, TCM must memorize feedback signal for start clutch control. Perform following procedure to calibrate start clutch.

1) Apply parking brake and block front wheels. Connect SCS service connector to service check connector. *See Fig. 5.* Service check connector is located under dash on passenger side of vehicle. Start engine and warm to normal operating temperature (radiator fan comes on twice). Shift transaxle to "D" position. Fully depress brake pedal and accelerator for 20 seconds.

NOTE: Perform following step within one minute after radiator fan goes off.

2) Shift transaxle into "N" or "P" position. To store engine vacuum signal reading in memory, let engine idle in "N" or "P" position for one minute under the following conditions:

- With brake pedal depressed.
- With A/C switch off.
- With combination light switch off.
- With heater fan switch off.
- Turn off all other electrical systems.

3) Shift transaxle into "D" position and let engine idle for 2 minutes to store feedback signal in memory under same conditions as in step **2)**. Connect scan tool to vehicle. Using scan tool, ensure TCM has completed start clutch calibration. Disconnect SCS service connector from service check connector.

NOTE: TCM will not store feedback signal when fluid temperature is less than 104°F (40°C) even if engine coolant temperature reaches normal operating temperature. Repeat these procedures until start clutch calibration is completed.

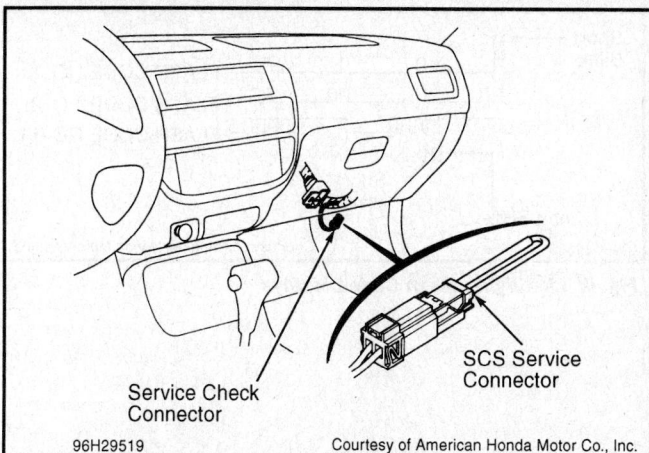

Fig. 5: Locating Service Check Connector

SELF-DIAGNOSTIC SYSTEM

SYSTEM DIAGNOSIS

TCM monitors transaxle operation. TCM contains a self-diagnostic system which stores a Diagnostic Trouble Code (DTC) if a transaxle electronic control system failure or problem exists. If DTC is stored,

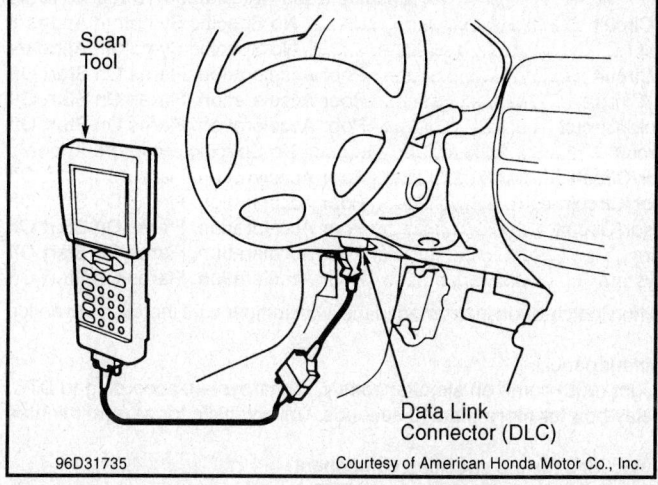

Fig. 6: Locating 16-Pin Data Link Connector (DLC)

TCM will turn on and blink "D" light on A/T gear position indicator on instrument panel. *See Fig. 1.* If a transaxle electronic control system failure or problem is suspected and "D" light on A/T gear position indicator does not flash, perform indicator light circuit check to ensure proper operation of "D" light. See "D" INDICATOR LIGHT CIRCUIT CHECK. DTC can be retrieved using scan tool at 16-pin Data Link Connector (DLC) located near left kick panel. *See Fig. 6.* Flash code may also be retrieved for diagnosing transaxle electronic control system.

"D" INDICATOR LIGHT CIRCUIT CHECK

"D" Indicator Light Does Not Come On – 1) Turn ignition on. Ensure SCS service connector is not connected to service check connector. Shift to "D" position. If "D" indicator light does not come on, go to next step. If "D" indicator light comes on, check for loose TCM connectors and replace TCM with known good part as necessary and retest.

2) Turn ignition off. Disconnect TCM 26-pin connector "A". Using a DVOM, check for continuity between ground and TCM 26-pin connector "A" terminals No. 13 and No. 26 (Black wires). If continuity is present, go to next step. If continuity is not present, check and repair open or poor connection in appropriate Black wire.

3) Turn ignition on. Measure voltage at TCM 26-pin connector "A", between terminals No. 12 (Black/White wire) and No. 13 (Black wire), then between terminals No. 25 (Black/White wire) and No. 26 (Black wire). If battery voltage is present, go to next step. If battery voltage is not present, check and repair open or short in appropriate wire between TCM and fuse No. 15 (7.5-amp) in fuse/relay box on driver's side of instrument panel, near steering column.

4) Turn ignition off. Reconnect TCM 26-pin connector "A". Using a DVOM, measure voltage (backprobe) between TCM 26-pin connector "A" terminal No. 20 (Green/Black wire) and terminals No. 13 or No. 26 (Black wires). Turn ignition on. Voltage should be present for 2 seconds. If DVOM indicates voltage as specified, go to next step. If no voltage was indicated, go to step **6)**.

5) Check for an open in Green/Black wire between TCM and gauge assembly. Repair as necessary. If wire is okay, repair faulty "D" indicator bulb or gauge assembly printed circuit board.

6) Turn ignition off. Disconnect TCM 26-pin connector "A". Check for continuity between TCM 26-pin connector "A" terminal No. 20 (Green/Black wire) and gauge assembly 14-pin connector terminal No. 9 (Green/Black wire). If continuity is present, go to next step. If continuity is not present, check and repair Green/Black wire between TCM 26-pin connector "A" and gauge assembly.

7) Check for loose TCM connectors or faulty A/T gear position switch. Repair as necessary. If no problem is found, replace TCM with a known good part and retest.

"D" Indicator Light Remains On Constantly (Not Flashing) – 1) Turn ignition off. Disconnect TCM 26-pin connector "A". Turn ignition on. Using a DVOM, measure voltage between ground and TCM 26-pin connector "A" terminal No. 20 (Green/Black wire). If no voltage is present, go to next step. If voltage is present, check and repair Green/Black wire for a short to power between TCM and gauge assembly.

2) Turn ignition off. Reconnect TCM 26-pin connector "A". Turn ignition on. Shift to any position except "D". Measure voltage (backprobe) between ground and TCM 26-pin connector "A" terminal No. 9 (Yellow wire). If voltage is present, replace TCM. If no voltage is present, check and repair Yellow wire for a short to ground. Repair as necessary. If wire is okay, replace A/T gear position indicator.

RETRIEVING CODES

NOTE: During diagnostics, ensure "D" indicator light on A/T gear position indicator on instrument panel is not turned on by a DTC in PGM-FI system. PGM-FI system controls fuel injection system. To repair PGM-FI system, see appropriate SELF-DIAGNOSTICS article in ENGINE PERFORMANCE in appropriate MITCHELL® manual. After PGM-FI system as been repaired, disconnect 7.5-amp back-up fuse located in underhood fuse/relay box for more than 10 seconds to reset TCM memory. See Fig. 7. Drive vehicle for several minutes at a speed over 30 MPH, then recheck.

NOTE: *Disconnecting 7.5-amp back-up fuse also cancels radio preset stations and clock setting. Note radio preset stations and clock setting prior to removing fuse.*

Retrieving DTC's Using Scan Tool – 1) If DTC exists, "D" light on A/T gear position on instrument panel will blink when ignition is turned on. To retrieve DTC using scan tool, turn ignition off.

2) Connect scan tool to 16-pin Data Link Connector (DLC) located near left kick panel. *See Fig. 6.* Turn ignition on. Scan tool will indicate DTC's. Follow scan tool manufacturer's instructions.

3) Once DTC is obtained, turn ignition off. Determine probable cause and symptom. See DTC/FLASH CODE IDENTIFICATION table. If any other DTC's except those listed are displayed, see appropriate SELF-DIAGNOSTICS article in ENGINE PERFORMANCE in appropriate MITCHELL® manual. For trouble shooting of DTC's, see DIAGNOSTIC TESTS. If "D" light does not flash or stays on, see "D" INDICATOR LIGHT CIRCUIT CHECK.

Retrieving Flash Codes Using "D" Light – 1) If flash code exists, "D" light on A/T gear position indicator on instrument panel will blink when ignition is turned on. To retrieve flash code, turn ignition off.

2) Install SCS service connector between service check connector electrical terminals. Service check connector is a Blue 2-pin electrical connector, located under passenger's side of instrument panel. *See Fig. 5.*

3) Turn ignition on. Flash codes will be displayed by short and long blinks of "D" light on A/T gear position indicator on instrument panel. If Malfunction Indicator Light (MIL) is also flashing, see appropriate SELF-DIAGNOSTICS article in ENGINE PERFORMANCE in appropriate MITCHELL® manual. Repair MIL codes first.

4) A short blink indicates a single digit flash code. A long blink equals 10 short blinks. For example, if "D" light blinks once, this is a Flash Code No. 1. If "D" light blinks one long blink and then 4 short blinks, this is a Flash Code No. 14. *See Fig. 8.*

5) Once flash code is obtained, turn ignition off. Remove SCS service connector from service check connector. Determine probable cause and symptom. See DTC/FLASH CODE IDENTIFICATION table. If any other flash codes except those listed are displayed, TCM is defective. For trouble shooting of flash codes, see DIAGNOSTIC TESTS.

NOTE: *If customer describes symptoms for DTC P01706/Flash Code No. 6, it may be necessary to test drive vehicle to recreate the symptom and then check for code with ignition still on.*

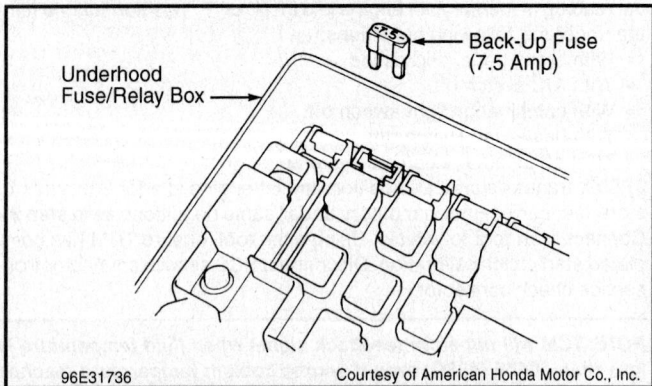

Fig. 7: Identifying Back-Up Fuse (7.5-Amp) Location

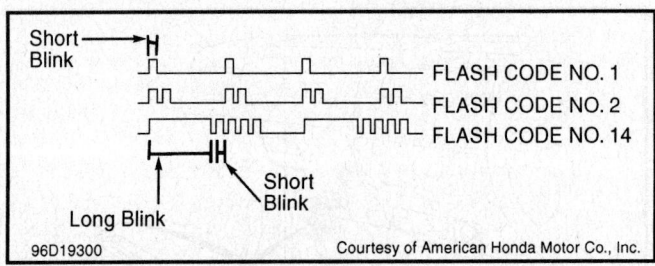

Fig. 8: Identifying Flash Code Displays

DTC/FLASH CODE IDENTIFICATION

DTC/ [1] Number	Indicator Light [2][3] Condition	Probable [4] Cause	Symptom
P0725/11	Blinks	Defective Ignition Coil/Circuit	Poor Acceleration, Flares On Start Off
P1655/37	Blinks	Defective ECM, TCM Or Circuit	Poor Creeping Power, Brake Pedal Released
P1705/5	Blinks	Defective A/T Gear Position Switch/Circuit	Transaxle Shifts Using "D" Position In Any Positions
P1706/6 [5]	Off	Defective A/T Gear Position Switch/Circuit	Transaxle Shifts Using "D" Position In Any Positions
P1790/3	Blinks	Defective TP Sensor/Circuit	Engine RPM Does Not Increase, Transaxle Does Not Kick Down, Or Transaxle Does Not Change To Higher Ratio
P1791/4	Blinks	Defective Vehicle Speed Sensor/Circuit	No Specific Symptom Appears
P1793/12	Blinks	Defective MAP Sensor/Circuit	No Specific Symptom Appears
P1870/30	Blinks	Defective Shift Control Solenoid/Circuit	Poor Acceleration, Flares On Start Off
P1873/31	Blinks	Defective PH-PL Control Solenoid/Circuit	Poor Acceleration, Flares On Start Off
P1879/32	Blinks	Defective Start Clutch Control Solenoid/Circuit	Poor Acceleration, Flares On Start Off
P1882/33	Blinks	Defective Inhibitor Solenoid/Circuit	No Specific Symptom Appears
P1885/34	Blinks	Defective Drive Pulley Speed Sensor/Circuit	Poor Acceleration, Flares On Start Off
P1886/35	Blinks	Defective Driven Pulley Speed Sensor/Circuit	Poor Acceleration, Flares On Start Off
P1888/36	Blinks	Defective Secondary Gear Shaft Sensor/Circuit	Poor Acceleration, Flares On Start Off
P1890/42	Blinks	Defective Shift Control System	Poor Acceleration, Flares On Start Off
P1891/43	Blinks	Defective Start Clutch Control System	Poor Acceleration, Flares On Start Off

[1] – This is the number of blinks (flash code) from "D" light on A/T gear position indicator on instrument panel with jumper wire installed in service check connector.

[2] – This is operation of "D" light on A/T gear position indicator on instrument panel.

[3] – If "D" light on A/T gear position indicator and Malfunction Indicator Light (MIL) come on simultaneously, repair system according to DTC, then reset memory by removing BACK-UP fuse in underhood fuse/relay box for more than 10 seconds. Drive vehicle for several minutes at speed more than 30 MPH, then recheck DTC.

[4] – Specified component for probable cause. Also check wiring and tronnections for the specified component.

[5] – If customer describes this symptom, recreate symptom by test driving vehicle to verify, then check DTC.

CLEARING CODES

NOTE: TCM memory can also be cleared using scan tool. If scan tool is not available, the following procedure must be used. Note radio preset stations, as radio stations and clock setting will be cleared and must be reset.

Once repairs have been performed, codes must be cleared from TCM memory. Ensure ignition is off. Remove back-up fuse (7.5-amp) from underhood fuse/relay box in engine compartment, located near battery, for at least 10 seconds. *See Fig. 7.* This will clear TCM and ECM memories. Reset clock and radio stations.

DIAGNOSTIC TESTS

NOTE: Terminal identification, circuit description and terminal voltage is included in PIN VOLTAGE CHARTS. See Figs. 10 and 11.

DTC P0725 (FLASH CODE 11): IGNITION COIL

1) Disconnect TCM 26-pin connector "A". Start engine. Using DVOM, measure voltage between TCM 26-pin connector "A" terminals No. 5 (Blue wire) and No. 13 or No. 26 (Black wires). *See Fig. 10.*
2) If battery voltage is present, check for loose TCM connectors and replace TCM with known good part as necessary. If battery voltage is not present, check and repair open or short in Blue wire between ignition coil and TCM 26-pin connector "A".

DTC P1655 (FLASH CODE 37): TCM CIRCUITS TMA & TMP SIGNALS

1) Turn ignition off. Disconnect TCM 22-pin connector "B" and ECM 31-pin connector "C". *See Fig. 9.* Using DVOM, check continuity between TCM 22-pin connector "B" terminal No. 7 (Gray wire) and ECM 31-pin connector "C" terminal No. 9 (Gray wire). *See Fig. 9.* If continuity exists, go to next step. If continuity does not exist, check and repair open in Gray wire between TCM and ECM.
2) Check continuity between TCM 22-pin connector "B" terminal No. 7 (Gray wire) and ground, and between ECM 31-pin connector "C" terminal No. 9 (Gray wire) and ground. *See Fig. 9.* If continuity does not exist, go to next step. If continuity exists, check and repair short to ground in Gray wire.
3) Reconnect TCM 22-pin connector "B" and ECM 31-pin connector "C". Turn ignition on. Using DVOM, measure voltage between ECM 31-pin connector "C" terminal No. 9 (Gray wire) and ground. If about 10 volts is not present, go to next step. If about 10 volts is present, check for loose ECM connectors and replace ECM with known good part as necessary.
4) Turn ignition off. Disconnect TCM 22-pin connector "B" and ECM 31-pin connector "C". *See Fig. 9.* Using DVOM, check continuity

between TCM 22-pin connector "B" terminal No. 6 (Pink wire) and ECM 31-pin connector "C" terminal No. 30 (Pink wire). *See Fig. 9.* If continuity exists, go to next step. If continuity does not exist, check and repair open in Pink wire between TCM and ECM.
5) Check continuity between TCM 22-pin connector "B" terminal No. 6 (Pink wire) and ground, and between ECM 31-pin connector "C" terminal No. 30 (Pink wire) and ground. *See Fig. 9.* If continuity does not exist, go to next step. If continuity exists, check and repair short to ground in Pink wire.
6) Reconnect TCM 22-pin connector "B" and ECM 31-pin connector "C". Turn ignition on. Using DVOM, measure voltage between TCM 22-pin connector "B" terminal No. 6 (Pink wire) and ground. If about 5 volts is not present, replace TCM. If about 5 volts is present, check for loose TCM connectors and replace TCM with known good part as necessary.

DTC P1705 (FLASH CODE 5): A/T GEAR POSITION SWITCH (SHORT)

NOTE: DTC P1705/5 is set when TCM receives 2 gear position signals at same time.

1) Turn ignition on. If any A/T gear position indicator light stays on when gear selector is moved from that gear, go to next step. If all A/T gear position indicator lights go off when gear selector is moved from that gear, system is okay at this time.
2) Shift to all gear positions except "R" position. Using DVOM, measure voltage between TCM 26-pin connector "A" terminals No. 13 or No. 26 (Black wires) and No. 11 (White wire). *See Fig. 10.* If about 10 volts is present, go to next step. If about 10 volts is not present, check and repair short in White wire between TCM 26-pin connector "A" and A/T gear position indicator or A/T gear position switch. If White wire is okay, check for loose TCM connectors and replace TCM with known good part as necessary.
3) Shift to all gear positions except "N" and "P" positions. Measure voltage between TCM 26-pin connector "A" terminals No. 13 or No. 26 (Black wires) and No. 10 (Light Green wire). If about 10 volts is present, go to next step. If about 10 volts is not present, check and repair short in Light Green wire between TCM 26-pin connector "A" and A/T gear position indicator or A/T gear position switch. If Light Green wire is okay, check for loose TCM connectors and replace TCM with known good part as necessary.
4) Shift to all gear positions except "D" position. Measure voltage between TCM 26-pin connector "A" terminals No. 13 or No. 26 (Black wires) and No. 9 (Yellow wire). If about 10 volts is present, go to next step. If about 10 volts is not present, check and repair short in Yellow wire between TCM 26-pin connector "A" and A/T gear position switch. If Yellow wire is okay, check for loose TCM connectors and replace TCM with known good part as necessary.
5) Shift to all gear positions except "S" position. Measure voltage between TCM 26-pin connector "A" terminals No. 13 or No. 26 (Black wires) and No. 8 (Green wire). If about 10 volts is present, go to next step. If about 10 volts is not present, check and repair short in Green wire between TCM 26-pin connector "A" and A/T gear position indicator or A/T gear position switch. If Green wire is okay, check for loose TCM connectors and replace TCM with known good part as necessary.
6) Shift to all gear positions except "L" position. Measure voltage between TCM 26-pin connector "A" terminals No. 13 or No. 26 (Black wires) and No. 7 (Blue wire). If about 10 volts is present, check for loose TCM connectors and replace TCM with known good part as necessary. If about 10 volts is not present, check and repair short in Blue wire between TCM 26-pin connector "A" and A/T gear position indicator or A/T gear position switch. If Blue wire is okay, check for loose TCM connectors and replace TCM with known good part as necessary.

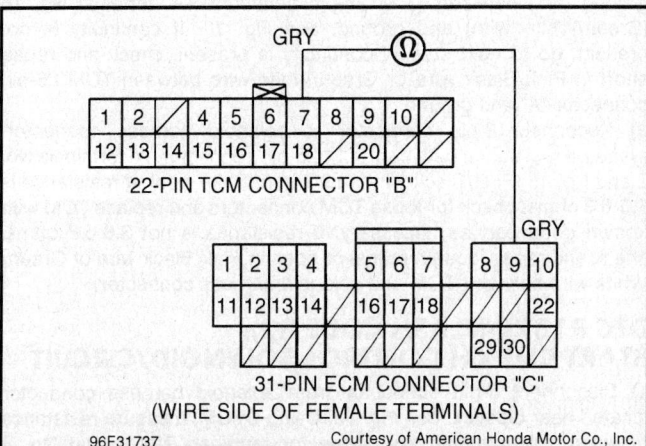

Fig. 9: Identifying 31-Pin ECM Connector "C" & TCM 22-Pin Connector "B" Terminal Locations

DTC P1706 (FLASH CODE 6): A/T GEAR POSITION SWITCH (OPEN)

1) Turn ignition on. If any A/T gear position indicator light stays on when gear selector is moved from that gear, go to next step. If all

A/T gear position indicator lights go off when gear selector is moved from that gear, system is okay at this time.

2) Shift to "R" position. Using DVOM, measure voltage between TCM 26-pin connector "A" terminals No. 13 or No. 26 (Black wires) and No. 11 (White wire). *See Fig. 10.* If voltage is not present, go to next step. If voltage is present, check and repair open in White wire between TCM 26-pin connector "A" and A/T gear position switch.

3) Shift to "N" or "P" position. Measure voltage between TCM 26-pin connector "A" terminals No. 13 or No. 26 (Black wires) and No. 10 (Light Green wire). If voltage is not present, go to next step. If voltage is present, check and repair open in Light Green wire between TCM 26-pin connector "A" and A/T gear position indicator.

4) Shift to "D" position. Measure voltage between TCM 26-pin connector "A" terminals No. 13 or No. 26 (Black wires) and No. 9 (Yellow wire). If voltage is present, go to next step. If voltage is present, check and repair open in Yellow wire between TCM 26-pin connector "A" and A/T gear position switch.

5) Shift to "S" position. Measure voltage between TCM 26-pin connector "A" terminals No. 13 or No. 26 (Black wires) and No. 8 (Green wire). If voltage is not present, go to next step. If voltage is present, check and repair open in Green wire between TCM 26-pin connector "A" and A/T gear position switch.

6) Shift to "L" position. Measure voltage between TCM 26-pin connector "A" terminals No. 13 or No. 26 (Black wires) and No. 7 (Blue wire). If voltage is not present, check for loose TCM connectors and replace TCM with known good part as necessary. If voltage is present, check and repair open in Blue wire between TCM 26-pin connector "A" and A/T gear position switch.

DTC P1790 (FLASH CODE 3): THROTTLE POSITION (TP) SENSOR

1) Turn ignition on. Using scan tool, check for any other DTC's or check for Malfunction Indicator Light (MIL) flashing. If any other DTC's exist or MIL is flashing, repair those DTC's first, then recheck for DTC P1790. If no other DTCs exist and MIL is not flashing, go to next step.

2) Turn ignition off. Disconnect TCM 22-pin connector "B" and TCM 26-pin connector "A". Turn ignition on. Using DVOM, measure voltage between TCM 22-pin connector "B" terminal No. 20 (White/Red wire) and TCM 26-pin connector "A" terminals No. 13 or No. 26 (Black wires). *See Figs. 10 and 11.* If about 5 volts is present, go to next step. If about 5 volts is not present, check and repair open or short in White/Red wire between TCM 22-pin connector "B" and ECM.

3) Measure voltage between TCM 22-pin connector "B" terminal No. 4 (Red/Black wire) and TCM 26-pin connector "A" terminals No. 13 or No. 26 (Black wires). If voltage is .4-.6 volts, check for loose TCM connectors and replace TCM with known good part as necessary. If voltage is not .4-.6 volts, check and repair open or short in Red/Black wire between TCM and TP sensor.

DTC P1791 (FLASH CODE 4): VEHICLE SPEED SENSOR (VSS)

1) Ensure speedometer operates correctly. If speedometer operates properly, go to next step. If speedometer does not operate properly, see VEHICLE SPEED SENSOR (VSS) under COMPONENT TESTING.

2) Raise and support vehicle. Block one front wheel. Place shift lever in "N" position. Turn ignition off. Disconnect TCM 22-pin connector "B" and TCM 26-pin connector "A". Turn ignition on. While rotating unblocked front wheel, measure voltage between TCM 22-pin connector "B" terminal No. 5 (Blue/White wire) and TCM 26-pin connector "A" terminals No. 13 or No. 26 (Black wires). *See Figs. 10 and 11.*

3) If voltage alternates from zero to 5 volts, check for loose TCM connectors and replace TCM with known good part as necessary. If voltage does not alternate from zero to 5 volts, check and repair short or open in Blue/White wire between TCM and VSS. If wire is okay, see VEHICLE SPEED SENSOR (VSS) under COMPONENT TESTING.

DTC P1793 (FLASH CODE 12): MANIFOLD ABSOLUTE PRESSURE (MAP) SENSOR

1) Turn ignition on. Using scan tool, check for any other DTC's or check for Malfunction Indicator Light (MIL) flashing. If any other DTC's

exist or MIL is flashing, repair those DTC's first, then recheck for DTC P1793. If no other DTC's exist and MIL is not flashing, go to next step.

2) Turn ignition off. Disconnect TCM 22-pin connector "B" and TCM 26-pin connector "A". Turn ignition on. Using DVOM, measure voltage between TCM 22-pin connector "B" terminal No. 20 (White/Red wire) and TCM 26-pin connector "A" terminals No. 13 or No. 26 (Black wires). *See Figs. 10 and 11.* If about 5 volts is present, go to next step. If about 5 volts is not present, check and repair open or short in White/Red wire between TCM 22-pin connector "B" and ECM.

3) Measure voltage between TCM 22-pin connector "B" terminal No. 2 (Red/Green wire) and TCM 26-pin connector "A" terminals No. 13 or No. 26 (Black wires). If about 3 volts is present, check for loose TCM connectors and replace TCM with known good part as necessary. If about 3 volts is not present, check and repair open or short in Red/Green wire between TCM and MAP sensor.

DTC P1870 (FLASH CODE 30): SHIFT CONTROL SOLENOID/CIRCUIT

1) Disconnect 8-pin connector from solenoid harness connector located near dipstick. *See Fig. 12.* Using DVOM, measure resistance between solenoid harness connector terminals No. 3 and No. 7 (Blue/White wire and Green/Yellow wire). If resistance is 3.8-6.8 ohms, go to next step. If resistance is not 3.8-6.8 ohms, replace lower valve body assembly. See HONDA M4VA CVT overhaul article.

2) Disconnect TCM 26-pin connector "A". Check continuity between TCM 26-pin connector "A" terminal No. 3 (Green/Yellow wire) and ground, and between TCM 26-pin connector "A" terminal No. 16 (Blue/Yellow wire) and ground. *See Fig. 10.* If continuity is not present, go to next step. If continuity is present, check and repair short in Green/Yellow wire or Blue/Yellow wire between TCM 26-pin connector "A" and ground.

3) Reconnect 8-pin connector to solenoid harness connector. Measure resistance between TCM 26-pin connector "A" terminals No. 3 and No. 16 (Green/Yellow wire and Blue/Yellow wire). If resistance is 3.8-6.8 ohms, check for loose TCM connectors and replace TCM with known good part as necessary. If resistance is not 3.8-6.8 ohms, check and repair loose terminal or open in Green/Yellow wire or Blue/Yellow wire between TCM and solenoid harness connector.

DTC P1873 (FLASH CODE 31): PH-PL CONTROL SOLENOID/CIRCUIT

1) Disconnect 8-pin connector from solenoid harness connector located near dipstick. *See Fig. 12.* Using DVOM, measure resistance between solenoid harness connector terminals No. 2 and No. 6 (Green/White wire and Pink/Black wire). If resistance is 3.8-6.8 ohms, go to next step. If resistance is not 3.8-6.8 ohms, replace lower valve body assembly. See HONDA M4VA CVT overhaul article.

2) Disconnect TCM 26-pin connector "A". Check continuity between TCM 26-pin connector "A" terminal No. 2 (Pink/Black wire) and ground, and between TCM 26-pin connector "A" terminal No. 15 (Green/White wire) and ground. *See Fig. 10.* If continuity is not present, go to next step. If continuity is present, check and repair short in Pink/Black wire or Green/White wire between TCM 26-pin connector "A" and ground.

3) Reconnect 8-pin connector to solenoid harness connector. Measure resistance between TCM 26-pin connector "A" terminals No. 2 and No. 15 (Pink/Black wire and Green/White wire). If resistance is 3.8-6.8 ohms, check for loose TCM connectors and replace TCM with known good part as necessary. If resistance is not 3.8-6.8 ohms, check and repair loose terminal or open in Pink/Black wire or Green/White wire between TCM and solenoid harness connector.

DTC P1879 (FLASH CODE 32): START CLUTCH CONTROL SOLENOID/CIRCUIT

1) Disconnect 8-pin connector from solenoid harness connector located near dipstick. *See Fig. 12.* Using DVOM, measure resistance between solenoid harness connector terminals No. 4 and No. 8 (Yellow wire and Pink/Blue wire). If resistance is 3.8-6.8 ohms, go to next step. If resistance is not 3.8-6.8 ohms, replace lower valve body assembly. See HONDA M4VA CVT overhaul article.

2) Disconnect TCM 26-pin connector "A". Check continuity between TCM 26-pin connector "A" terminal No. 1 (Pink/Blue wire) and ground, and between TCM 26-pin connector "A" terminal No. 14 (Yellow wire) and ground. See Fig. 10. If continuity is not present, go to next step. If continuity is present, check and repair short in Pink/Blue wire or Yellow wire between TCM 26-pin connector "A" and ground.

3) Reconnect 8-pin connector to solenoid harness connector. Measure resistance between TCM 26-pin connector "A" terminals No. 1 and No. 14 (Pink/Blue wire and Yellow wire). If resistance is 3.8-6.8 ohms, check for loose TCM connectors and replace TCM with known good part as necessary. If resistance is not 3.8-6.8 ohms, check and repair loose terminal or open in Pink/Blue wire or Yellow wire between TCM and solenoid harness connector.

DTC P1882 (FLASH CODE 33): INHIBITOR SOLENOID/CIRCUIT

1) Disconnect 8-pin connector from solenoid harness connector located near dipstick. See Fig. 12. Using DVOM, measure resistance between solenoid harness connector terminal No. 5 (Green/Black wire) and ground. If resistance is 11.7-21.0 ohms, go to next step. If resistance is not 11.7-21.0 ohms, replace lower valve body assembly. See HONDA M4VA CVT overhaul article.

2) Disconnect TCM 22-pin connector "B". Check continuity between TCM 22-pin connector "B" terminal No. 1 (Green/Black wire) and ground. See Fig. 11. If continuity is not present, go to next step. If continuity is present, check and repair short in Green/Black wire between TCM 22-pin connector "B" and ground.

3) Reconnect 8-pin connector to solenoid harness connector. Measure resistance between TCM 22-pin connector "B" terminal No. 1 (Green/Black wire) and ground. If resistance is 11.7-21.0 ohms, check for loose TCM connectors and replace TCM with known good part as necessary. If resistance is not 11.7-21.0 ohms, check and repair loose terminal or open in Green/Black wire between TCM and solenoid harness connector.

DTC P1885 (FLASH CODE 34): DRIVE PULLEY SPEED SENSOR/CIRCUIT

1) Ensure drive pulley speed sensor is installed correctly. Adjust as necessary. Disconnect 2-pin connector from drive pulley speed sensor, located near dipstick. See Fig. 12. Using DVOM, measure resistance between drive pulley speed sensor connector terminals. If resistance is 350-600 ohms, go to next step. If resistance is not 350-600 ohms, replace drive pulley speed sensor.

2) Disconnect TCM 22-pin connector "B". Check continuity between TCM 22-pin connector "B" terminal No. 10 (Red/Blue wire) and ground, and between TCM 22-pin connector "B" terminal No. 17 (Green wire) and ground. See Fig. 11. If continuity is not present, go to next step. If continuity is present, check and repair short in Red/Blue wire or Green wire between TCM 22-pin connector "B" and drive pulley speed sensor.

3) Reconnect drive pulley speed sensor connector. Measure resistance between TCM 22-pin connector "B" terminals No. 10 and No. 17 (Red/Blue wire and Green wire). If resistance is 350-600 ohms, check for loose TCM connectors and replace TCM with known good part as necessary. If resistance is not 350-600 ohms, check and repair loose terminal or open in Red/Blue wire or Green wire between TCM and drive pulley speed sensor.

DTC P1886 (FLASH CODE 35): DRIVEN PULLEY SPEED SENSOR/CIRCUIT

1) Ensure driven pulley speed sensor is installed correctly. Adjust as necessary. Disconnect 2-pin connector from driven pulley speed sensor, located on top of transaxle, near shift cable. See Fig. 4. Using DVOM, measure resistance between driven pulley speed sensor connector terminals. If resistance is 350-600 ohms, go to next step. If resistance is not 350-600 ohms, replace driven pulley speed sensor.

2) Disconnect TCM 22-pin connector "B". Check continuity between TCM 22-pin connector "B" terminal No. 8 (Red/Blue wire) and ground, and between TCM 22-pin connector "B" terminal No. 9 (White wire) and ground. See Fig. 11. If continuity is not present, go to next step.

If continuity is present, check and repair short in Red/Blue wire or White wire between TCM 22-pin connector "B" and driven pulley speed sensor.

3) Reconnect driven pulley speed sensor connector. Measure resistance between TCM 22-pin connector "B" terminals No. 8 and No. 9 (Red/Blue wire and White wire). If resistance is 350-600 ohms, check for loose TCM connectors and replace TCM with known good part as necessary. If resistance is not 350-600 ohms, check and repair loose terminal or open in Red/Blue wire or White wire between TCM and driven pulley speed sensor.

DTC P1888 (FLASH CODE 36): SECONDARY GEAR SHAFT SPEED SENSOR/CIRCUIT

1) Ensure secondary gear shaft speed sensor is installed correctly. Adjust as necessary. Disconnect 2-pin connector from secondary gear shaft speed sensor, located on top of transaxle, near shift cable. See Fig. 4. Using DVOM, measure resistance between secondary gear shaft speed sensor connector terminals. If resistance is 350-600 ohms, go to next step. If resistance is not 350-600 ohms, replace secondary gear shaft speed sensor.

2) Disconnect TCM 22-pin connector "B". Check continuity between TCM 22-pin connector "B" terminal No. 15 (White/Red wire) and ground, and between TCM 22-pin connector "B" terminal No. 16 (Orange/Blue wire) and ground. See Fig. 11. If continuity is not present, go to next step. If continuity is present, check and repair short in White/Red wire or Orange/Blue wire between TCM 22-pin connector "B" and secondary gear shaft speed sensor.

3) Reconnect secondary gear shaft speed sensor connector. Measure resistance between TCM 22-pin connector "B" terminals No. 15 and No. 16 (White/Red wire and Orange/Blue wire). If resistance is 350-600 ohms, check for loose TCM connectors and replace TCM with known good part as necessary. If resistance is not 350-600 ohms, check and repair loose terminal or open in White/Red wire or Orange/Blue wire between TCM and secondary gear shaft speed sensor.

DTC P1890 (FLASH CODE 42): SHIFT CONTROL SYSTEM

1) Check for any other DTC's indicated by "D" light. If any other DTC's exist, repair those DTC's first, then recheck for DTC P1890. If no other DTC's exist, go to next step.

2) Perform STALL SPEED TEST procedure under TESTING in HONDA M4VA CVT overhaul article. If stall speed is more than 3500 RPM, replace transaxle. If stall speed is less than 2000 RPM, replace lower valve body assembly. If stall speed is more than 2000 RPM, perform ROAD TEST procedure under TESTING in HONDA M4VA CVT overhaul article. If engine RPM is as specified in ROAD TEST, replace lower valve body assembly. If engine RPM is not as specified in ROAD TEST, replace transaxle.

DTC P1891 (FLASH CODE 43): START CLUTCH CONTROL SYSTEM

1) Check for any other DTC's indicated by "D" light. If any other DTC's exist, repair those DTC's first, then recheck for DTC P1891. If no other DTC's exist, go to next step.

2) Turn ignition off. Disconnect 8-pin connector from solenoid harness connector, located near dipstick. See Fig. 12. Start engine and shift transaxle into "D" position. If vehicle does not move ("creep"), replace start clutch assembly. If vehicle moves, turn ignition off.

3) Reconnect 8-pin connector to solenoid harness connector. Start engine and shift transaxle into "D" position. If vehicle does not move ("creep"), replace lower valve body assembly. If vehicle moves, and "creeping" speed is about 3 MPH, perform STALL SPEED TEST procedure under TESTING in HONDA M4VA CVT overhaul article.

4) If stall speed is more than 3500 RPM, replace start clutch assembly. If stall speed is less than 3500 RPM, ensure engine is at normal operating temperature (radiator fan comes on). Start engine and shift transaxle into "D" position. If vehicle does not move ("creep"), replace start clutch assembly. If vehicle moves, system is working correctly.

PIN VOLTAGE CHARTS

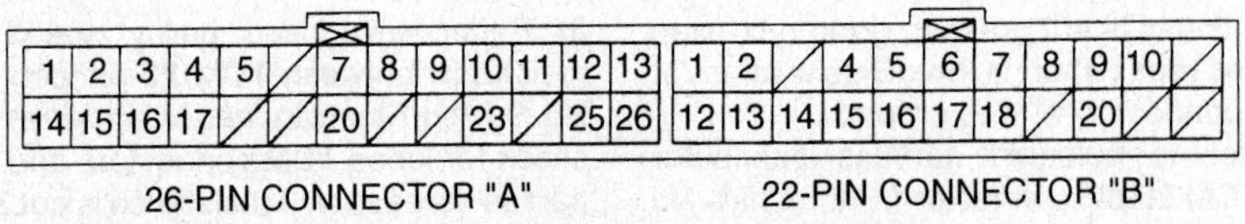

```
┌─┬─┬─┬─┬─┬─┬─┬─┬─┬──┬──┬──┬──┐   ┌─┬─┬─┬─┬─┬─┬─┬─┬─┬──┐
│1│2│3│4│5│╱│7│8│9│10│11│12│13│   │1│2│╱│4│5│6│7│8│9│10│
├─┼─┼─┼─┼─┼─┼─┼─┼─┼──┼──┼──┼──┤   ├─┼─┼─┼─┼─┼─┼─┼─┼─┼──┤
│14│15│16│17│╱│╱│20│╱│23│╱│25│26│  │12│13│14│15│16│17│18│╱│20│╱│
└──┴──┴──┴──┴─┴─┴──┴─┴──┴─┴──┴──┘  └──┴──┴──┴──┴──┴──┴──┴─┴──┴─┘
         26-PIN CONNECTOR "A"              22-PIN CONNECTOR "B"
                      TCM TERMINAL LOCATIONS
```

Terminal Number	Signal	Description	Measuring Conditions/Terminal Voltage
A1	SC LS–	Start clutch control solenoid power supply negative electrode	Engine idling, P position: Approx. 0.4 V
A2	HLC LS–	PH-PL control solenoid power supply negative electrode	Engine idling, P position: Approx. 0.7 V
A3	SH LS–	Shift control solenoid power supply negative electrode	Engine idling, P position: Approx. 0.8 V
A4	LG1	Ground	
A5	NE	Engine speed signal input	With engine running: Pulsing signal
A6	——	Not used	
A7	ATP L	A/T gear position switch L position signal input	In L position: 0 V / In other than L position: Approx. 10 V
A8	ATP S	A/T gear position switch S position signal input	In S position: 0 V / In other than S position: Approx. 10 V
A9	ATP D	A/T gear position switch D position signal input	In D position: 0 V / In other than D position: Approx. 10 V
A10	ATP PN	A/T gear position switch N and P position signals input	In N or P position: 0 V / In other than N or P position: Approx. 5 V
A11	ATP R	A/T gear position switch R position signal input	In R position: 0 V / In other than R position: Approx. 10 V
A12	IG1	Power supply system	With ignition switch ON (II): Battery voltage / With ignition switch OFF: 0 V
A13	PG1	Ground	
A14	SC LS+	Start clutch control solenoid power supply positive electrode	Engine idling, P position: Approx. 2.5 V
A15	HLC LS+	PH-PL control solenoid power supply positive electrode	Engine idling, P position: Approx. 5.0 V
A16	SH LS+	Shift control solenoid power supply positive electrode	Engine idling, P position: Approx. 6.0 V
A17	LG1	Ground	
A18	——	Not used	
A19	——	Not used	
A20	D IND	D indicator light control	When D indicator light comes on: Approx. 10 V / When D indicator light OFF: 0 V
A21	——	Not used	
A22	——	Not used	
A23	VBU	Back-up power system	Always battery voltage
A24	——	Not used	
A25	IG1	Power supply system	With ignition switch ON (II): Battery voltage / With ignition switch OFF: 0 V
A26	PG1	Ground	

96G31738

Courtesy of American Honda Motor Co., Inc.

Fig. 10: Pin Voltage Chart & Terminal Identification (1 Of 2)

Terminal Number	Signal	Description	Measuring Conditions/Terminal Voltage
B1	SOL INH	Inhibitor solenoid control	With inhibitor solenoid ON: Battery voltage With inhibitor solenoid OFF: 0 V
B2	MAP (PB)	Manifold Absolute Pressure (MAP) sensor signal input	With ignition switch ON (II): Approx. 2.5 V With engine idling: Approx. 1.0 V (depending on engine speed)
B3		Not used	
B4	TPS	Throttle Position (TP) sensor signal input	With ignition switch ON (II) and throttle fully open: 4.14 – 4.82 V With ignition switch ON (II) and throttle fully closed: 0.44 – 0.56 V
B5	VSS	Vehicle Speed Sensor (VSS) signal input	With ignition switch ON (II) and rotating front wheels: 0 – 5 V cycle
B6	TMB	Data communication with ECM: Transmission control data output	With ignition switch ON (II): Pulsing signal
B7	TMA	Data communication with ECM: PGM-FI control data input	With ignition switch ON (II): Pulsing signal
B8	NDN SG	Driven pulley speed sensor ground	
B9	NDN	Driven pulley speed sensor signal input	In other than N and P position: Pulsing signal
B10	NDR	Drive pulley speed sensor signal input	In other than N and P position: Pulsing signal
B11	——	Not used	
B12	STOP SW	Brake switch signal input	With brake pedal depressed: Battery voltage With brake pedal released: 0 V
B13	DIAG-H (TXD/RXD)	Data communication: Diagnostic trouble code output	With ignition switch ON (II): Approx. 5 V
B14	SCS	Service check signal	With ignition switch ON (II) and service check connector open: Approx. 5 V With ignition switch ON (II) and service check connector connected with special tool: 0 V
B15	VEL	Secondary gear shaft speed sensor signal input	Depending on vehicle speed: Pulsing signal When vehicle is stopped: 0 V
B16	VEL SG	Secondary gear shaft speed sensor ground	
B17	NDR SG	Drive pulley speed sensor ground	
B18	HBRK SW	Parking brake switch signal input	With parking brake lever pulled: 0 V With parking brake lever released: Battery voltage
B19	——	Not used	
B20	VREF	+5 V reference	With ignition switch ON (II): Approx. 5 V
B21	——	Not used	
B22	——	Not used	

96H31739

Courtesy of American Honda Motor Co., Inc.

Fig. 11: Pin Voltage Chart (2 Of 2)

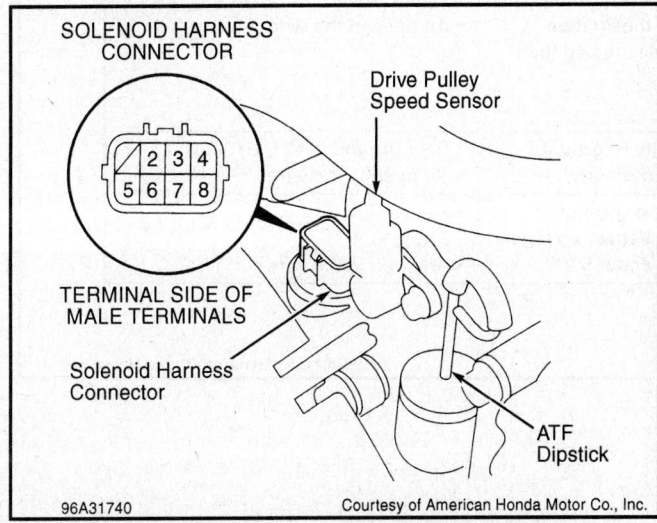

96A31740

Courtesy of American Honda Motor Co., Inc.

Fig. 12: Identifying Solenoid Harness Connector Terminals & Drive Pulley Speed Sensor Location

SYSTEM TESTING
A/T GEAR POSITION INDICATOR

NOTE: If necessary, refer to wiring schematic when checking component wiring. See Fig. 14.

1) Remove instrument panel gauge assembly from instrument panel. Disconnect 14-pin electrical connector "A" from rear of instrument panel gauge assembly. *See Fig. 13.*

2) Check for voltage and continuity at electrical connector as specified. *See Fig. 13.* If necessary, check ground connections G401 or G402. G401 ground connection is located at driver's side kick panel, above Gray 14-pin connector. G402 ground connection is located at upper passenger's side kick panel, below White 20-pin junction connector, near PGM-FI main relay.

NOTE: Ground connections are made through main wiring harness.

3) If necessary, check fuse No. 25 (7.5-amp). Fuse is located in fuse box on driver's side of instrument panel, near steering column. If necessary, access TCM. TCM is located behind driver's side kick panel. *See Fig. 4.* If necessary to access ECM, ECM is located behind passenger's side kick panel, below instrument panel. *See Fig. 4.*

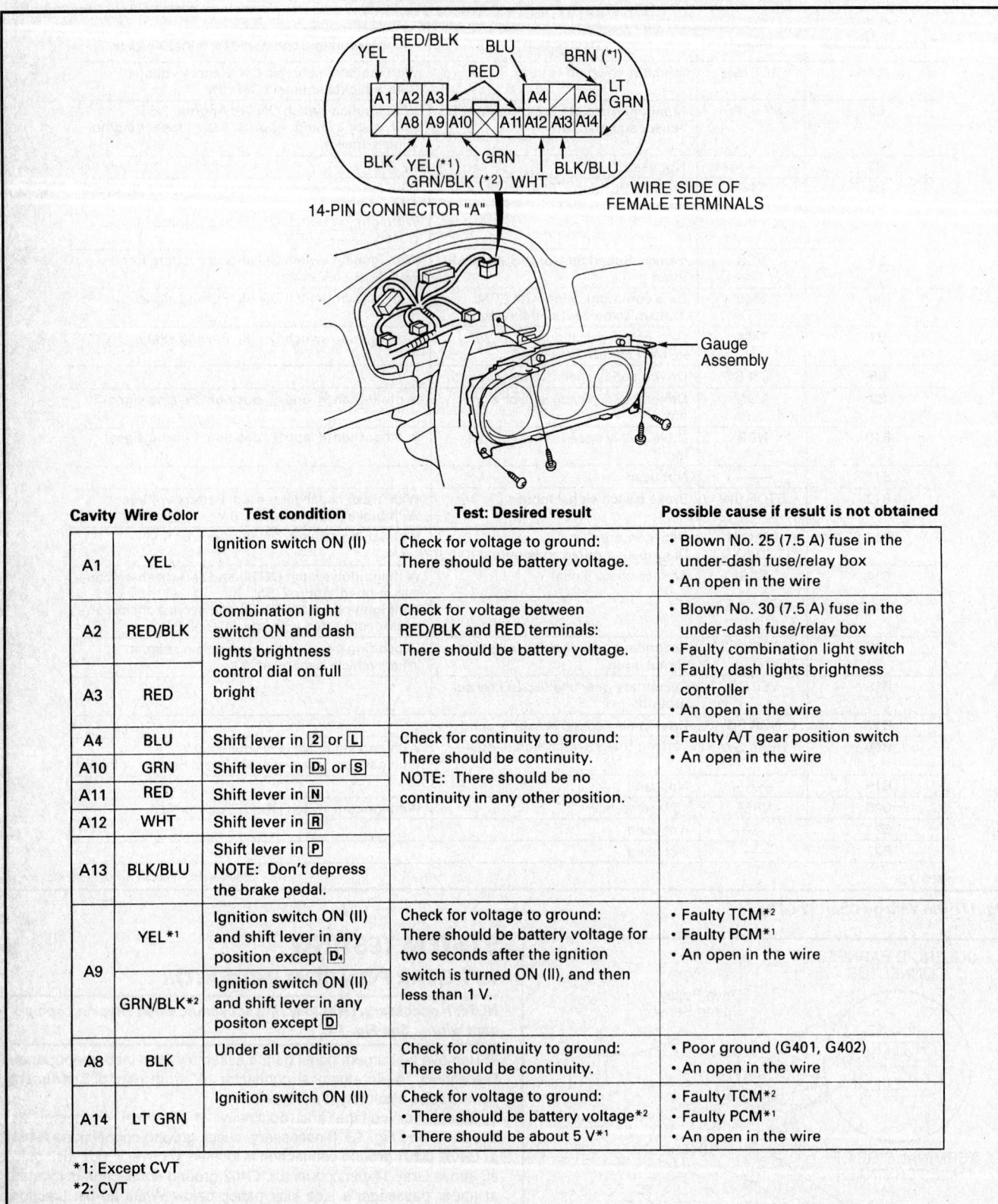

Cavity	Wire Color	Test condition	Test: Desired result	Possible cause if result is not obtained
A1	YEL	Ignition switch ON (II)	Check for voltage to ground: There should be battery voltage.	• Blown No. 25 (7.5 A) fuse in the under-dash fuse/relay box • An open in the wire
A2	RED/BLK	Combination light switch ON and dash lights brightness control dial on full bright	Check for voltage between RED/BLK and RED terminals: There should be battery voltage.	• Blown No. 30 (7.5 A) fuse in the under-dash fuse/relay box • Faulty combination light switch • Faulty dash lights brightness controller • An open in the wire
A3	RED			
A4	BLU	Shift lever in ② or Ⓛ	Check for continuity to ground: There should be continuity. NOTE: There should be no continuity in any other position.	• Faulty A/T gear position switch • An open in the wire
A10	GRN	Shift lever in D₃ or Ⓢ		
A11	RED	Shift lever in Ⓝ		
A12	WHT	Shift lever in Ⓡ		
A13	BLK/BLU	Shift lever in Ⓟ NOTE: Don't depress the brake pedal.		
A9	YEL*1	Ignition switch ON (II) and shift lever in any position except D₄	Check for voltage to ground: There should be battery voltage for two seconds after the ignition switch is turned ON (II), and then less than 1 V.	• Faulty TCM*² • Faulty PCM*¹ • An open in the wire
	GRN/BLK*²	Ignition switch ON (II) and shift lever in any positon except Ⓓ		
A8	BLK	Under all conditions	Check for continuity to ground: There should be continuity.	• Poor ground (G401, G402) • An open in the wire
A14	LT GRN	Ignition switch ON (II)	Check for voltage to ground: • There should be battery voltage*² • There should be about 5 V*¹	• Faulty TCM*² • Faulty PCM*¹ • An open in the wire

*1: Except CVT
*2: CVT

96B31741

Courtesy of American Honda Motor Co., Inc.

Fig. 13: Testing A/T Gear Position Indicator

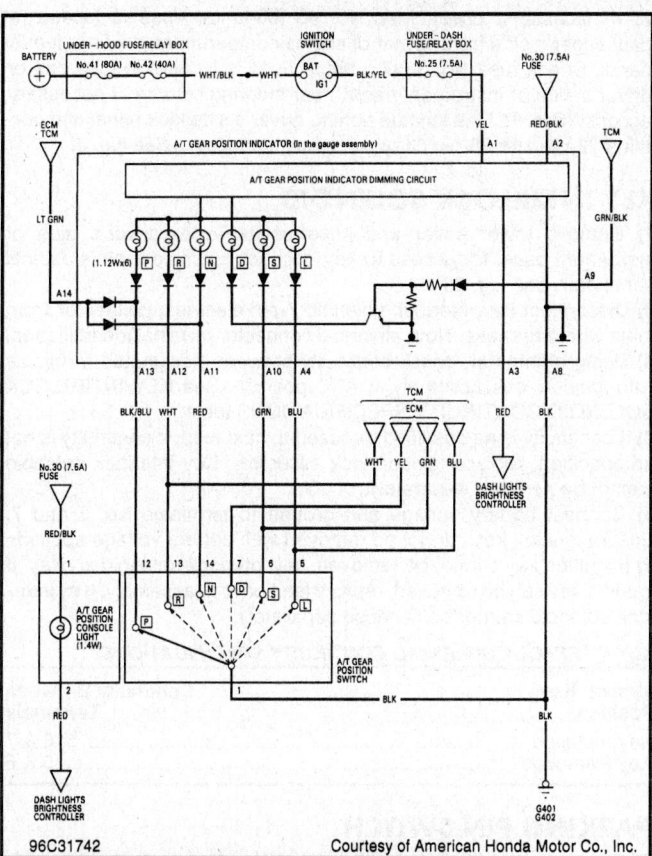

Fig. 14: A/T Gear Position Indicator Wiring Schematic

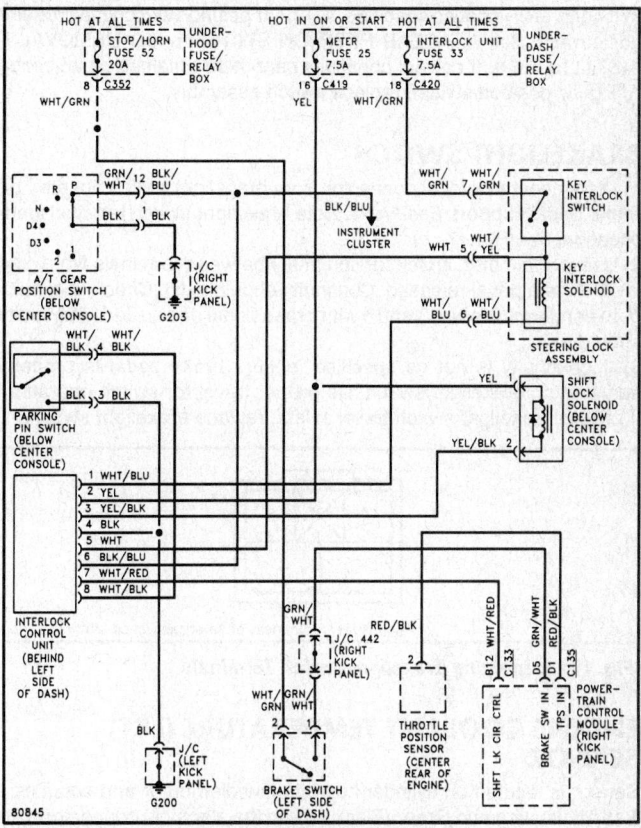

Fig. 15: Shift Interlock System Wiring Schematic

SHIFT & KEY INTERLOCK SYSTEMS

NOTE: For system testing, refer to wiring schematic when checking component wiring. See Fig. 15. To check individual components, see COMPONENT TESTING.

1) To check system operation, ensure shift lever is in Park. Turn ignition on. Depress brake pedal with accelerator pedal in idle position. If shift lock solenoid clicks, system is working properly. If shift lock solenoid fails to click, see INTERLOCK CONTROL UNIT under COMPONENT TESTING.

2) If shift lever cannot be moved from Park, check for proper installation procedure of shift lock solenoid. See SHIFT LOCK SOLENOID under REMOVAL & INSTALLATION. If shift lock solenoid installation is okay, test A/T gear position switch, see A/T GEAR POSITION SWITCH.

COMPONENT TESTING

A/T GEAR POSITION SWITCH

NOTE: The A/T gear position switch also contains back-up light switch and neutral position switch. Back-up light switch and neutral position switch can also be checked when checking A/T gear position switch.

1) Remove center console. Disconnect 14-pin electrical connector from A/T gear position switch. Note electrical connector terminal identification. *See Fig. 16.*

2) Using ohmmeter, check continuity between specified terminal(s) with shift lever in indicated positions. See A/T GEAR POSITION SWITCH CONTINUITY table.

NOTE: Check continuity while moving shift lever back and forth in free play area of each gear position. DO NOT touch push button on shift lever when checking continuity.

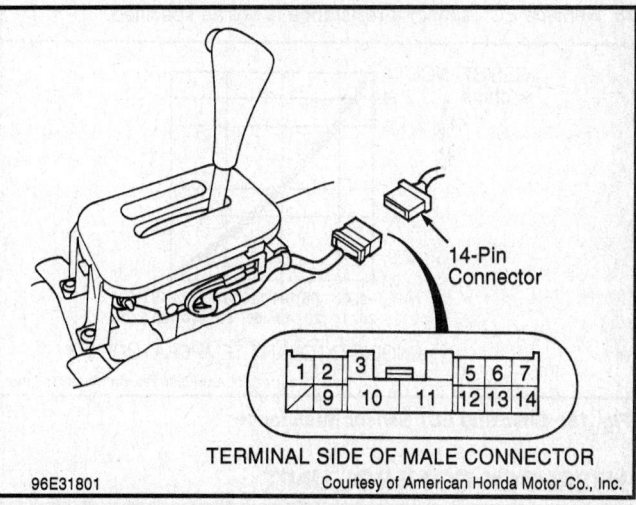

Fig. 16: Identifying A/T Gear Position Switch Harness Connector Terminals

A/T GEAR POSITION SWITCH CONTINUITY

Application	Shift Lever Position	Continuity Between Terminals No.
A/T Gear Position Switch	"P"	1 & 12
	"R"	1 & 13
	"N"	1 & 14
	D	1 & 7
	"S"	1 & 6
	"L"	1 & 5
Back-Up Light Switch	"R"	3 & 4
Neutral Position Switch	"P"	10 & 11
	"N"	10 & 11

3) If continuity is not as specified, A/T gear position switch may require adjustment. See A/T GEAR POSITION SWITCH under REMOVAL & INSTALLATION. If correct continuity cannot be obtained by adjusting A/T gear position switch, replace switch assembly.

BRAKELIGHT SWITCH

1) Disconnect electrical connector from brakelight switch, located on brake pedal support. See Fig. 4. Note brakelight switch terminal identification. See Fig. 17.

2) Using ohmmeter, check for continuity between terminals No. 1 and 2 with brake pedal released. Continuity should exist. Check continuity between terminals No. 3 and 4 with brake pedal depressed. Continuity should exist.

3) If continuity is not as specified, ensure brake pedal is properly adjusted so brakelight switch has proper travel for switch operation. If proper brakelight switch travel exists, replace brakelight switch.

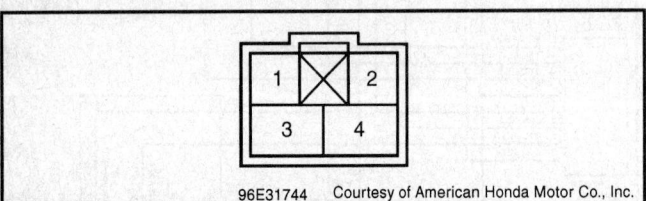

96E31744   Courtesy of American Honda Motor Co., Inc.

Fig. 17: Identifying Brakelight Switch Terminals

ENGINE COOLANT TEMPERATURE (ECT) SENSOR

Sensor is located on cylinder head, below distributor and contains a Red/White wire and Green/Black wire in the electrical connector. Disconnect electrical connector from sensor. Using ohmmeter, check sensor resistance in accordance with coolant temperature. See Fig. 18. Replace ECT sensor if resistance is not as specified.

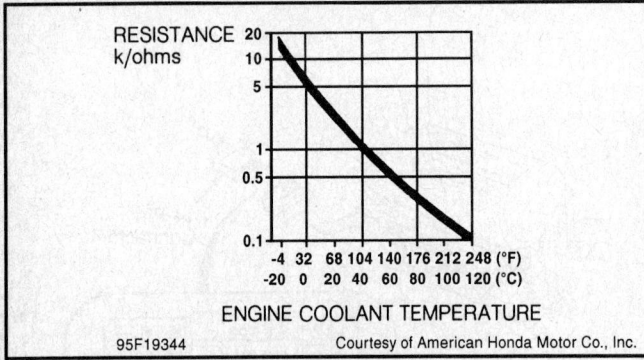

95F19344   Courtesy of American Honda Motor Co., Inc.

Fig. 18: Checking ECT Sensor Resistance

INTERLOCK CONTROL UNIT

NOTE: When testing shift lock system, reconnect 8-pin connector to interlock control unit. See Fig. 19.

1) Remove lower panel from instrument panel. Disconnect 8-pin connector from interlock control unit. Interlock control unit is located under left side of instrument panel. See Fig. 2. Inspect terminals for poor connection, corrosion or bending, repair as necessary.

2) Using DVOM, check for continuity or voltage between specified terminals or body ground. See Fig. 19. If necessary, check ground connections G401 or G402. G401 ground connection is located at driver's side kick panel, above Gray 14-pin connector. G402 ground connection is located at upper passenger's side kick panel, below White 20-pin junction connector, near PGM-FI main relay.

NOTE: Ground connections are made through main wiring harness.

3) If necessary, check fuse No. 48 (30-amp). Fuse is located at passenger's side front corner of engine compartment, on inner fender panel. Check fuse No. 33 (7.5 amp). Fuse is located in fuse box on driver's side of instrument panel, near steering column. If necessary, access TCM. TCM is located behind driver's side kick panel and contains 22-pin and 26-pin Gray electrical connectors. See Fig. 4.

KEY INTERLOCK SOLENOID

1) Remove lower cover and knee bolster from driver's side of instrument panel for access to key interlock solenoid 7-pin electrical connector. See Fig. 20.

2) Disconnect key interlock solenoid 7-pin electrical connector from main wiring harness. Note electrical connector terminal identification.

3) Using ohmmeter, check continuity between designated terminals with ignition lock assembly in ACC position. See KEY INTERLOCK SOLENOID CONTINUITY SPECIFICATIONS table.

4) If continuity is as specified, proceed to next step. If continuity is not as specified, replace ignition lock assembly. Key interlock solenoid cannot be serviced separately.

5) Connect battery voltage and ground to terminals No. 5 and 7. Ensure ignition key cannot be removed with battery voltage applied.

6) If ignition key cannot be removed, key interlock solenoid is okay. If ignition key can be removed, replace ignition lock assembly. Key interlock solenoid cannot be serviced separately.

KEY INTERLOCK SOLENOID CONTINUITY SPECIFICATIONS

Ignition Key Position	Continuity Between Terminals
Key Installed	5, 6 & 7
Key Removed	5 & 6

PARKING PIN SWITCH

1) Remove center console. Disconnect parking pin switch 4-pin connector. Parking pin switch is located on left side of shift lever assembly. See Fig. 21.

2) Using an ohmmeter, check continuity between parking pin switch terminals No. 3 and 4. Continuity should exist when shift lever button is depressed in "P" position, or if shift lever is in any position except "P". Continuity should not exist with shift lever in "P" position and button is released. If continuity is not as described, replace parking pin switch.

CONTROL & INHIBITOR SOLENOIDS

1) Control solenoids and inhibitor solenoid are located on transaxle. See Fig. 4. Disconnect 8-pin solenoid harness connector, located near dipstick. See Fig. 12.

2) Using ohmmeter, check resistance between appropriate terminals of solenoid harness connector. See SOLENOID TERMINAL IDENTIFICATION table. Resistance for PH-PL control solenoid, shift control solenoid and start clutch control solenoid should be 3.8-6.8 ohms. Resistance for inhibitor solenoid should be 11.7-20.0 ohms. Replace lower valve body assembly if resistance for any solenoid is not within specification.

3) If readings for solenoids are as specified, check solenoid operation. Connect jumper wire to positive battery terminal and lowest terminal number used for each solenoid when testing resistance in previous step. Connect jumper wire to negative battery terminal and highest terminal number used for each solenoid when testing resistance in previous step. Clicking sound should be heard, indicating solenoid operation. Replace lower valve body assembly if any solenoid does not operate.

SOLENOID TERMINAL IDENTIFICATION

Solenoid Application	Terminal No. (+ & −)
Inhibitor	5 & Ground
PH-PL Control	2 & 6
Shift Control	3 & 7
Start Clutch Control	4 & 8

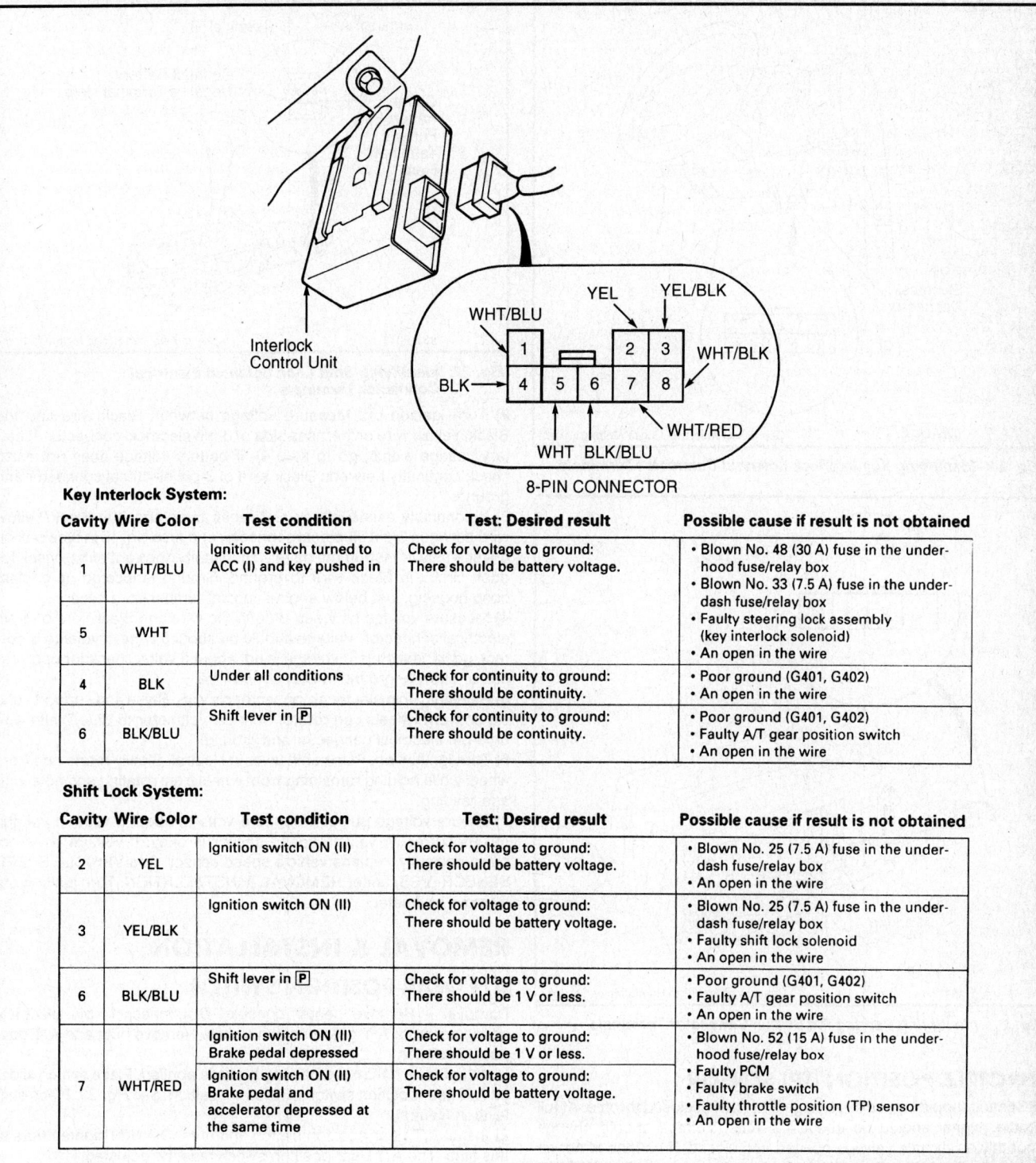

Fig. 19: Testing Interlock Control Unit

Key Interlock System:

Cavity	Wire Color	Test condition	Test: Desired result	Possible cause if result is not obtained
1	WHT/BLU	Ignition switch turned to ACC (I) and key pushed in	Check for voltage to ground: There should be battery voltage.	• Blown No. 48 (30 A) fuse in the under-hood fuse/relay box • Blown No. 33 (7.5 A) fuse in the under-dash fuse/relay box • Faulty steering lock assembly (key interlock solenoid) • An open in the wire
5	WHT			
4	BLK	Under all conditions	Check for continuity to ground: There should be continuity.	• Poor ground (G401, G402) • An open in the wire
6	BLK/BLU	Shift lever in P	Check for continuity to ground: There should be continuity.	• Poor ground (G401, G402) • Faulty A/T gear position switch • An open in the wire

Shift Lock System:

Cavity	Wire Color	Test condition	Test: Desired result	Possible cause if result is not obtained
2	YEL	Ignition switch ON (II)	Check for voltage to ground: There should be battery voltage.	• Blown No. 25 (7.5 A) fuse in the under-dash fuse/relay box • An open in the wire
3	YEL/BLK	Ignition switch ON (II)	Check for voltage to ground: There should be battery voltage.	• Blown No. 25 (7.5 A) fuse in the under-dash fuse/relay box • Faulty shift lock solenoid • An open in the wire
6	BLK/BLU	Shift lever in P	Check for voltage to ground: There should be 1 V or less.	• Poor ground (G401, G402) • Faulty A/T gear position switch • An open in the wire
7	WHT/RED	Ignition switch ON (II) Brake pedal depressed	Check for voltage to ground: There should be 1 V or less.	• Blown No. 52 (15 A) fuse in the under-hood fuse/relay box • Faulty PCM • Faulty brake switch • Faulty throttle position (TP) sensor • An open in the wire
		Ignition switch ON (II) Brake pedal and accelerator depressed at the same time	Check for voltage to ground: There should be battery voltage.	

96F31745

Courtesy of American Honda Motor Co., Inc.

SHIFT LOCK SOLENOID

1) Remove center console. Disconnect shift lock solenoid 2-pin electrical connector from main wiring harness. Note electrical connector terminal identification. *See Fig. 22.*

CAUTION: Battery voltage must be applied to correct shift lock solenoid electrical connector terminals or diode inside shift lock solenoid will be damaged.

2) Momentarily connect battery positive terminal to terminal "A" and battery negative terminal to terminal "B". *See Fig. 22.* Ensure shift lock solenoid operates with battery voltage applied. Replace shift lock solenoid if solenoid fails to operate.

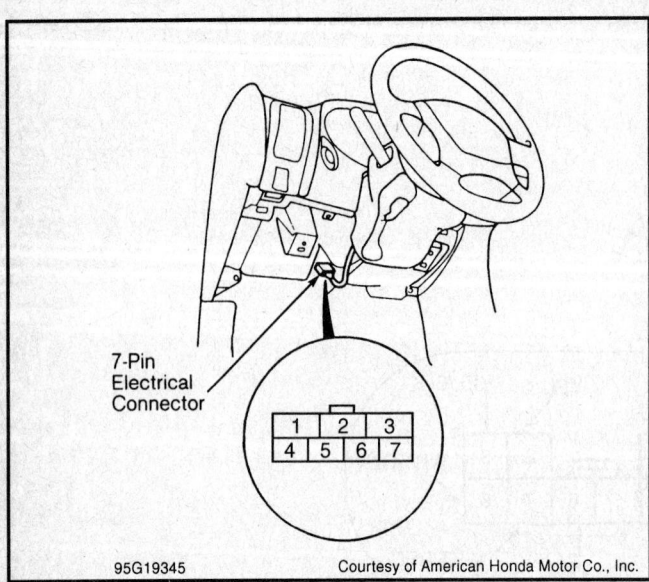

95G19345   Courtesy of American Honda Motor Co., Inc.

Fig. 20: Identifying Key Interlock Solenoid Connector Terminals

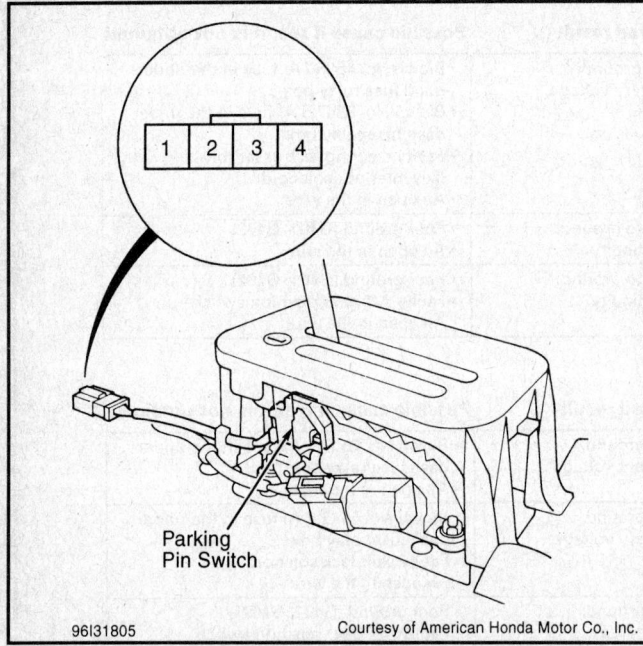

96I31805   Courtesy of American Honda Motor Co., Inc.

Fig. 21: Identifying Parking Pin Switch Connector Terminals

THROTTLE POSITION (TP) SENSOR

TP sensor should input a .5-volt signal to TCM at closed throttle. At full throttle, signal should be about 4.5 volts. Voltage should change smoothly as throttle valve is opened and closed. If voltage is not as specified, check throttle position sensor wiring circuit. See WIRING DIAGRAMS.

NOTE: If problem in TP sensor exists, sensor may set DTC P1790/3 in TCM. See RETRIEVING CODES under SELF-DIAGNOSTIC SYSTEM.

VEHICLE SPEED SENSOR (VSS)

1) Ensure fuse No. 15 fuse (7.5-amp) in fuse box on driver's side of instrument panel, near steering column is okay. Replace fuse if necessary. Disconnect 3-pin electrical connector from Vehicle Speed Sensor (VSS). VSS is located on top of transaxle. See Fig. 4.

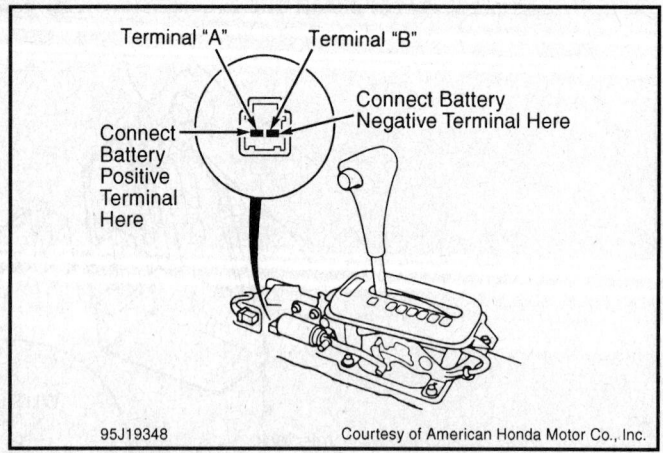

95J19348   Courtesy of American Honda Motor Co., Inc.

Fig. 22: Identifying Shift Lock Solenoid Electrical Connector Terminals

2) Turn ignition on. Measure voltage between Black wire and the Black/Yellow wire on harness side of 3-pin electrical connector. If battery voltage exists, go to step 4). If battery voltage does not exist, check continuity between Black wire of 3-pin electrical connector and ground.

3) If continuity exists, check and repair open circuit in Black/Yellow wire between 3-pin electrical connector and fuse No. 15 in fuse box on driver's side of instrument panel. If continuity does not exist, check for open circuit in Black wire to ground. Ground is located on coolant hose housing, just below engine coolant temperature sensor.

4) Measure voltage between Blue/White wire and Black wire of 3-pin electrical connector. Voltage should be about 5 volts. If voltage is correct, go to next step. If voltage is not about 5 volts, check for open circuit or short to ground in Blue/White wire.

5) Reinstall 3-pin electrical connector on VSS. Raise and support vehicle so front wheels can rotate. Connect voltmeter to Blue/White wire on 3-pin electrical connector and ground.

6) Turn ignition on. Place shift lever in Neutral. Slowly rotate one front wheel while holding remaining front wheel from rotating and note voltage reading.

7) Ensure voltage pulses from zero volts to about 5 volts. If voltage pulses correctly, vehicle speed sensor is okay. If voltage does not pulse correctly, replace vehicle speed sensor. See VEHICLE SPEED SENSOR (VSS) under REMOVAL & INSTALLATION. Turn ignition off. Remove voltmeter.

REMOVAL & INSTALLATION

A/T GEAR POSITION SWITCH

Removal – Remove center console. Disconnect 14-pin electrical connector from A/T gear position switch. Remove nuts and A/T gear position switch.

Installation – 1) Ensure parking brake is applied. Place switch slider on A/T gear position switch in Neutral position. See Fig. 23. Place shift lever in Neutral.

2) Install A/T gear position switch and nuts. DO NOT tighten nuts at this time. The A/T gear position switch must be adjusted.

3) To adjust A/T gear position switch, place shift lever in Park. Ensure retaining nuts are loose. Note 14-pin electrical connector terminal identification. See Fig. 16.

4) Connect ohmmeter between terminals No. 1 and No. 7. Move A/T gear position switch toward rear of console until continuity exists between terminals No. 1 and No. 7. Free play at lock pin should be .079" (2.0 mm). See Fig. 23.

5) Tighten nuts. Check A/T gear position switch for correct continuity in all gears. See A/T GEAR POSITION SWITCH under COMPONENT TESTING. If proper adjustment cannot be obtained, check for damaged shift lever detent or bracket. Install electrical connector and center console.

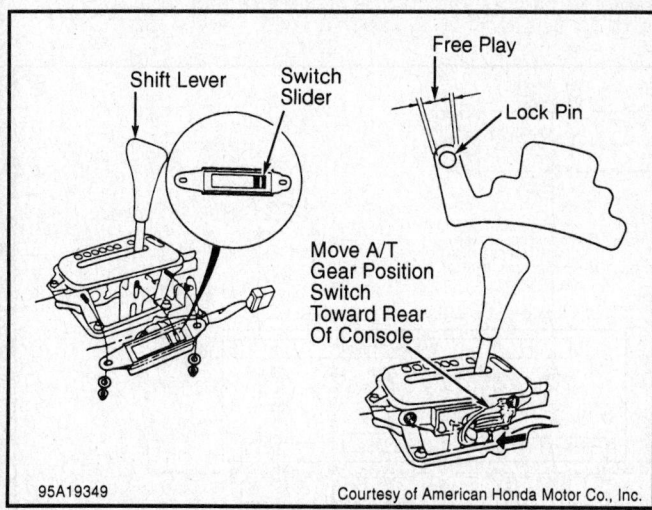

95A19349   Courtesy of American Honda Motor Co., Inc.

Fig. 23: Installing A/T Gear Position Switch

BRAKELIGHT SWITCH

Removal & Installation – 1) Disconnect electrical connector from brakelight switch. Remove lock nut from brakelight switch. Unscrew brakelight switch and remove. To install, screw brakelight switch inward until brakelight plunger is fully depressed.

2) Back off brakelight switch 1/4 turn. Ensure .012" (.30 mm) clearance exists between threaded end of brakelight switch and pad area on brake pedal. Install and tighten lock nut. Install electrical connector. Ensure brakelights operate properly.

DRIVE, DRIVEN & SECONDARY GEAR SHAFT SPEED SENSORS

Removal & Installation – 1) Disconnect electrical connector at appropriate speed sensor. Drive pulley speed sensor is located near dipstick. *See Fig. 12.* Driven pulley and secondary gear shaft speed sensors are located on top of transaxle. *See Fig. 4.*

2) Remove appropriate speed sensor and "O" ring. To install, reverse removal procedure using NEW "O" ring. Install and tighten bolt to specification. See TORQUE SPECIFICATIONS.

ENGINE COOLANT TEMPERATURE (ECT) SENSOR

Removal & Installation – ECT sensor is located on cylinder head, below distributor and contains a Red/White wire and Green/Black wire in electrical connector. Drain cooling system. Remove engine coolant temperature sensor. Install and tighten engine coolant temperature sensor. Fill cooling system to top of radiator neck. Warm engine until cooling fan turns on and off twice. Finish filling cooling system.

KEY INTERLOCK SOLENOID

Removal & Installation – Key interlock solenoid cannot be serviced separately, as entire ignition lock assembly must be replaced.

CONTROL & INHIBITOR SOLENOIDS

Manufacturer recommends replacement of lower control valve assembly if any solenoid is defective. See LOWER VALVE BODY ASSEMBLY under REMOVAL & INSTALLATION in HONDA M4VA CVT overhaul article.

THROTTLE POSITION (TP) SENSOR

Removal & Installation – TP sensor is mounted on side of throttle body. Replacement information is not available.

VEHICLE SPEED SENSOR (VSS)

Removal & Installation – Disconnect electrical connector from vehicle speed sensor, located on top of transaxle. *See Fig. 4.* Remove bolts and vehicle speed sensor. To install, reverse removal procedure. Install and tighten bolts to specification.

TORQUE SPECIFICATIONS
TORQUE SPECIFICATIONS

Application	INCH Lbs. (N.m)
A/T Gear Position Switch Nut	87 (9.8)
Drive Pulley Speed Sensor Bolt	106 (12.0)
Driven Pulley Speed Sensor Bolt	106 (12.0)
Secondary Gear Shaft Speed Sensor Bolt	106 (12.0)
Shift Control Solenoid Valve Assembly Bolt	106 (12.0)
Shift Lock Solenoid Screw	27 (3.0)
Vehicle Speed Sensor Bolt	87 (9.8)

AUTOMATIC TRANSMISSIONS
Honda M4VA CVT Electronic Controls (Cont.)

WIRING DIAGRAMS

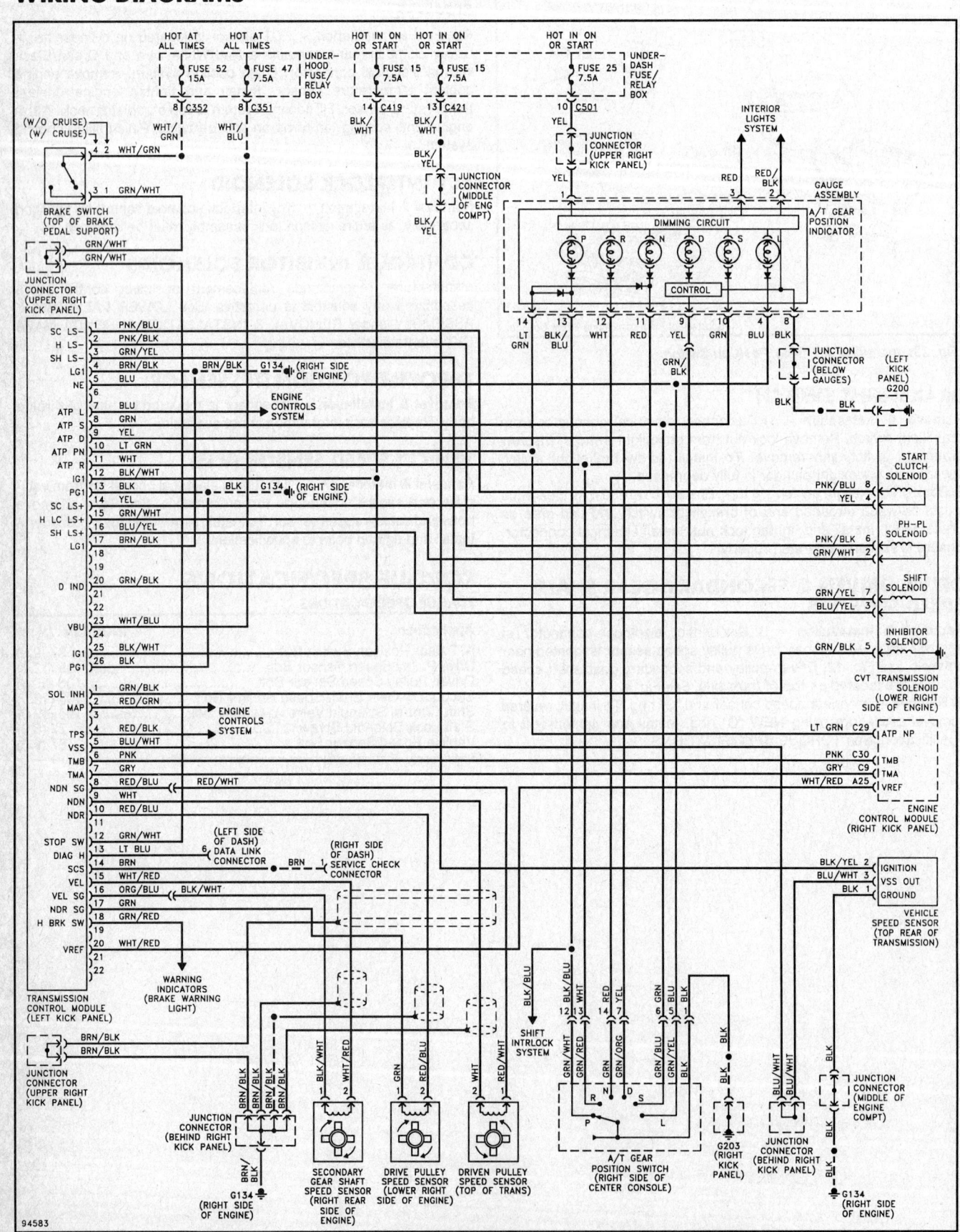

Fig. 24: Transaxle Wiring Diagram (1996 Civic With CVT Transaxle)

AUTOMATIC TRANSMISSIONS
Hydra-Matic 3L30

Geo: Tracker
Suzuki: Sidekick

APPLICATION & LABOR TIMES

APPLICATION & LABOR TIMES

Vehicle Application	Labor Times [1] R & I	[2] Overhaul	Trans. Model
Geo			
1995-96 Tracker			
2WD	4.8	7.1	3L30
4WD	5.8	7.1	3L30
Suzuki			
1995-96 Sidekick			
2WD	4.8	7.1	3L30
4WD	5.8	7.1	3L30

[1] – Removal and installation of transmission from vehicle chassis.
[2] – Bench overhaul time for transmission. DOES NOT include removal and installation.

IDENTIFICATION

Transmission is identified by identification plate attached to transmission case, located on left side, above oil pan. Vehicle Identification Number (VIN) may also be used in identifying transmission. VIN locations are at top left of instrument panel and driver's-side door post. VIN is used to ensure correct application of component parts and assemblies.

DESCRIPTION & OPERATION

Automatic transmission provides 3 forward speeds and reverse. Main internal components are; oil pump, Torque Converter w/Clutch (TCC), reverse clutch, 2nd clutch, 3rd clutch, one-way clutch (sprag type), compound planetary gear set, low brake, governor and valve body. *See Fig. 1.*

Gear shifting is controlled by valve body. Components that regulate shifting schedules are; governor, modulator and kick-down valve. TCC is operated by an electric solenoid. TCC solenoid operation depends on signals provided by the Engine Coolant Temperature (ECT) sensor, brake switch, Throttle Position (TP) sensor, Vehicle Speed Sensor (VSS) and gear position.

LUBRICATION & ADJUSTMENTS

See appropriate AUTOMATIC TRANSMISSION SERVICING article in TRANSMISSION SERVICING section.

TROUBLE SHOOTING

NOTE: Poor engine performance can have a negative effect on transmission performance.

Preliminary Checks – Ensure fluid level is correct. Inspect and adjust shift linkage and park/neutral position switch (if necessary). Check idle speed RPM and adjust as necessary. Road test vehicle to ensure proper engine performance.

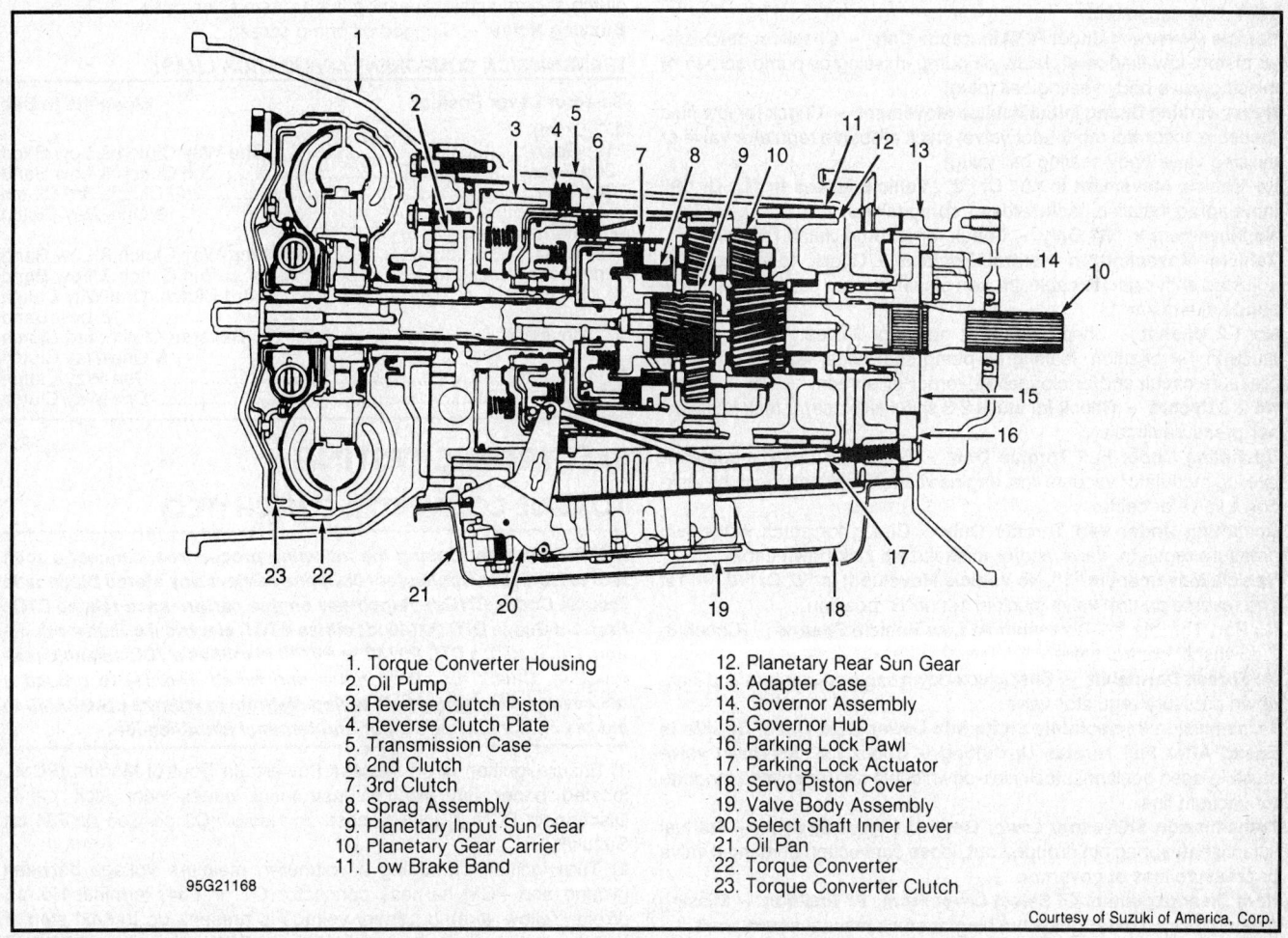

1. Torque Converter Housing
2. Oil Pump
3. Reverse Clutch Piston
4. Reverse Clutch Plate
5. Transmission Case
6. 2nd Clutch
7. 3rd Clutch
8. Sprag Assembly
9. Planetary Input Sun Gear
10. Planetary Gear Carrier
11. Low Brake Band
12. Planetary Rear Sun Gear
13. Adapter Case
14. Governor Assembly
15. Governor Hub
16. Parking Lock Pawl
17. Parking Lock Actuator
18. Servo Piston Cover
19. Valve Body Assembly
20. Select Shaft Inner Lever
21. Oil Pan
22. Torque Converter
23. Torque Converter Clutch

95G21168

Courtesy of Suzuki of America, Corp.

Fig. 1: Cross-Sectional View Of 3L30 Transmission

SYMPTOM DIAGNOSIS

Low Fluid Level – Check for fluid leak out of filler tube, external fluid leak(s) and faulty vacuum modulator.

Fluid Leak From Filler Tube – Check for high fluid level, engine coolant in transmission fluid, pinched breather hose and leak in oil pump suction circuit.

Low Fluid Pressure – Check for low fluid level, clogged oil pump screen, leak in oil pump suction circuit, leak in oil pressure circuit, pressure regulator valve malfunction and/or missing valve body sealing ball (plug).

High Fluid Pressure – Check for leaking modulator vacuum line, malfunctioning modulator, leaking engine vacuum system or faulty pressure regulator valve.

Excessive Smoke From Exhaust – Inspect vacuum modulator.

No Torque Converter Clutch Application – Check for 12-volt power supply to transmission, good ground in transmission, faulty harness connections, defective pressure switch, sticking converter clutch control valve, cut or leaking TCC solenoid valve "O" ring, damaged or mispositioned oil pump wear plate, incorrectly tightened converter housing-to-oil pump bolts and/or cut turbine shaft "O" ring.

No Torque Converter Clutch Release Or Shudder – Check for sticking TCC control valve, restricted TCC apply passage, low fluid level, low fluid pressure, poor engine performance and/or cut turbine shaft "O" ring.

No Vehicle Movement In Any Range – Check fluid level, clogged oil pump screen, disconnected manual valve link or manual select shaft inner lever, broken input shaft, pressure regulator valve stuck in open position or faulty oil pump.

No Vehicle Movement In Any Gear Position – Check for parking pawl disengagement.

Vehicle Movement Under RPM Increase Only – Check for stuck servo piston, low fluid level, faulty oil pump, missing oil pump screen or missing valve body sealing ball (plug).

Heavy Jerking During Initial Vehicle Movement – Check for low fluid pressure, incorrect modulator valve, stuck pressure regulator valve or missing valve body sealing ball (plug).

No Vehicle Movement In "D" Or "2", Vehicle Moves In "L" Or "R" – Input sprag installed backwards or sprag failure.

No Movement In "R" Only – Check for reverse clutch failure.

Vehicle Movement In Neutral Position – Check for improperly adjusted shift selector cable, broken planetary gear carrier and/or low band adjustment.

No 1-2 Upshift – Check for stuck governor valves, 1-2 shift valve stuck in 1st position, leaking oil pump seal rings, leak in governor pressure circuit and/or clogged governor oil screen.

No 2-3 Upshift – Check for stuck 2-3 shift valve and/or leak in governor pressure circuit.

Upshifting Under Full Throttle Only – Check for faulty modulator, leaking modulator vacuum line, engine vacuum leak and/or stuck kickdown valve or cable.

Upshifting Under Part Throttle Only – Check for stuck kick-down pressure regulator valve and/or misadjusted kick-down cable.

Vehicle Movement In "1", No Vehicle Movement In "2" Or "R" – 1st and reverse control valve stuck in 1st or "R" position.

No Part Throttle 3-2 Downshift At Low Vehicle Speeds – Check 3-2 downshift control valve.

No Forced Downshift – Check kick-down cable adjustment and kick-down pressure regulator valve.

Transmission Immediately Shifts Into Lower Gear Once Throttle Is Eased After Full Throttle Upshifting – Check for kick-down valve stuck in open position, stuck kick-down cable and/or spliced modulator vacuum line.

Transmission Shifts Into Lower Gear At Higher Speeds – Manual select shaft spring pin dropped out, loose connection at manual valve or pressure loss at governor.

Hard Disengagement Of Select Lever From "P" Position – Missing parking lock actuator guide bushing or stuck manual select shaft.

Engine Flare, 1-2 Shift – Check for low fluid pressure, missing valve body sealing ball (plug), leaking 2nd clutch piston seals, 2nd clutch piston check ball stuck open, broken or cracked 2nd clutch piston, 2nd clutch piston plates worn or leaking oil pump hub sealing rings.

Engine Flare, 2-3 Shift – Check for low fluid pressure, low band adjustment, missing valve body sealing ball (plug), leaking 3rd clutch piston seals, 3rd clutch piston check ball stuck open, broken or cracked 3rd clutch piston and/or worn input shaft bushing.

Harsh 1-2 Shift – Check for high fluid pressure, stuck 1-2 accumulator valve and/or broken 2nd clutch spring cushion.

Harsh 2-3 Shift – Check for high fluid pressure or incorrect low band adjustment.

Harsh 3-2 Manual Downshift – Check for stuck open high speed downshift valve and low band adjustment.

Harsh 3-2 Coasting Downshift – Check for stuck open low speed downshift timing valve.

High Speed Downshift Flare – Check for low fluid pressure or low band adjustment

Low Speed Forced Downshift Flare – Check for low fluid pressure, low band adjustment, closed high speed downshift timing valve and/or one-way clutch does not lock on 3-1 downshifting.

No Engine Braking In Low – Check select cable adjustment and/or stuck manual low control valve.

No Engine Braking In "2" Range – Check select cable adjustment.

Transmission Does Not Hold In Park – Improperly adjusted select cable, broken parking lock actuator spring or damaged parking pawl and governor hub.

Excessive Noise In All Ranges – Check backlash between sun gear and planetary gears, loose planetary carrier lock plate, defective thrust bearing, worn bushings or loose converter housing bolt contacting torque converter.

Screeching Noise When Starting – Torque converter failure.

Short Vibrating, Hissing Noise Shortly Before 1-2 Upshift – Reverse clutch spring cushion wearing into transmission case.

Buzzing Noise – Clogged oil pump screen.

TRANSMISSION COMPONENT APPLICATION CHART

Selector Lever Position	Elements In Use
"D" (Drive)	
1st Gear	One-Way Clutch & Low Band
2nd Gear	2nd Clutch & Low Band
3rd Gear	2nd Clutch, 3rd Clutch & One-Way Clutch
"2" (Intermediate)	
1st Gear	One-Way Clutch & Low Band
2nd Gear	2nd Clutch & Low Band
"L" (1st Gear)	3rd Clutch, One-Way Clutch & Low Band
"R" (Reverse)	Reverse Clutch, 3rd Clutch & One-Way Clutch
"N" (Neutral)	One-Way Clutch
"P" (Park)	One-Way Clutch

ELECTRONIC TESTING

TORQUE CONVERTER CLUTCH (TCC)

NOTE: Before performing the following procedures, connect a scan tool to Data Link Connector (DLC) and retrieve any stored Diagnostic Trouble Codes (DTCs). Repair any engine performance-related DTCs first. On Geo, a DTC P0740 identifies a TCC electrical circuit malfunction. On Suzuki, a DTC P0740 or P0770 identifies a TCC solenoid malfunction. Check for blown fuses and repair short(s) to ground if necessary. See appropriate wiring diagram in WIRING DIAGRAMS to aid in component, wire color and terminal identification.

1) Ensure ignition is off. Access Powertrain Control Module (PCM), located under left side of instrument panel, near kick panel. Disconnect PCM 22-pin harness connector (C2 on Geo or E34 on Suzuki).
2) Turn ignition on. Using a voltmeter, measure voltage between ground and PCM harness connector C2 or E34, terminal No. 16 (White/Yellow wire). If battery voltage is present, go to next step. If battery voltage is not present, check TCC relay. See TORQUE CONVERTER CLUTCH (TCC) RELAY. Replace if necessary. If relay is okay, go to step 4).

3) Start engine and allow it to reach normal operating temperature. Raise and support vehicle to allow rear wheels to spin freely. Shift selector lever to "D" position and accelerate. If voltage reading decreases to 0-1 volt at about 47 MPH, check TCC relay. See TORQUE CONVERTER CLUTCH (TCC) RELAY. Replace if necessary. If relay is okay, go to step **6)**. If voltage reading is not as specified, go to step **5)**.

4) Check for poor TCC relay harness connection. Check White/Yellow wire between TCC relay and PCM for an open or short to ground. Check Blue/Black wire between TCC relay and main relay for an open or short to ground. Repair as necessary. If no problems are found, substitute a known-good PCM and retest system.

5) Check for poor harness connections at PCM. Repair as necessary. If no problems are found, substitute a known-good PCM and retest system.

6) Turn ignition off. Disconnect TCC relay. Turn ignition on. Using a voltmeter, measure voltage between ground and TCC relay harness connector terminal No. 2 (Black/White wire). If reading is battery voltage, go to next step. If reading is not as specified, repair open in Black/White wire.

7) Check TCC solenoid. See TORQUE CONVERTER CLUTCH (TCC) SOLENOID. Replace if necessary. If solenoid is okay, go to next step.

8) Check White wire between TCC relay and TCC solenoid for an open or poor connection. Repair as necessary. If no problem is found, check for low fluid pressure, misadjusted kick-down cable or other internal transmission problems.

TORQUE CONVERTER CLUTCH (TCC) RELAY

1) Turn ignition off. Remove TCC relay. Using an ohmmeter, measure resistance between relay terminals No. 1 and 3. *See Fig. 2.* Resistance should be 90-110 ohms. Continuity should not be present between terminals No. 2 and 4.

2) Apply battery voltage to terminal No. 1, and ground terminal No. 3. Continuity should now be present between terminals No. 2 and 4. Replace relay if it does not test as specified.

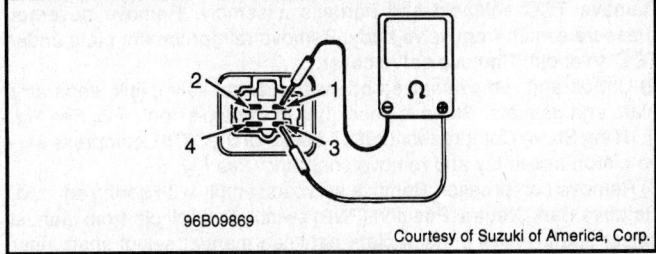

96B09869

Courtesy of Suzuki of America, Corp.

Fig. 2: Identifying TCC Relay Terminals

TORQUE CONVERTER CLUTCH (TCC) SOLENOID

1) Remove TCC solenoid from transmission. Using Orifice Plug (09922-85811), plug one oil passage on TCC solenoid. Using an oiler, add ATF to remaining oil passage. *See Fig. 3.* Oil should exhaust from solenoid.

2) Using fused jumper wires, apply battery voltage and ground to TCC solenoid terminals. Solenoid should click and not allow any oil to exhaust. Replace TCC solenoid if it does not test as specified.

TESTING

TIME LAG TEST

1) Engine and transmission must be at normal operating temperature. Start engine and ensure idle RPM is within specification with A/C off. Apply service and parking brakes. Using stop watch, measure time until engagement shock is felt when selector lever is shifted from "N" to "D" position.

2) Allow one minute intervals between tests. Perform time measurements 2 more times and calculate average value. Time should be less than 1.2 seconds. Repeat test procedure to test time lag when

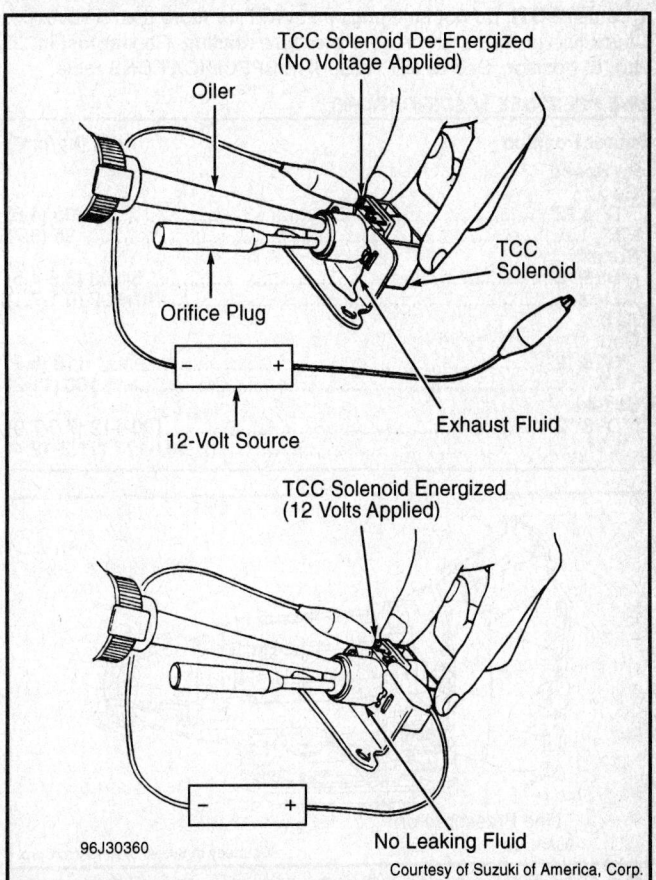

96J30360

Courtesy of Suzuki of America, Corp.

Fig. 3: Testing TCC Solenoid

selector lever is shifted from "N" to "R" position. Time lag should be less than 1.5 seconds. If results are not within specification, inspect internal components.

ROAD TEST

1) Ensure vehicle is at operating temperature. Shift transmission into drive. Accelerate vehicle and ensure vehicle upshifts from 1st to 2nd, then to 3rd gear. TCC should apply while in 3rd gear.

2) Depress accelerator pedal to 1/2 position. TCC should release, then transmission should downshift to 2nd gear. Accelerate to cruising speed until TCC is applied. Using left foot, very lightly apply brake pedal. TCC should disengage.

3) Release accelerator pedal. As vehicle is slowing down, manually shift into 2nd gear, then into low position. Ensure transmission shifts into lower gears and engine braking occurs. Stop vehicle and shift into reverse. Lightly accelerate vehicle to confirm reverse operation. Stop vehicle on slight incline. Shift vehicle into park. Ensure vehicle does not move.

HYDRAULIC PRESSURE TESTS

Line Pressure Test – 1) Ensure transmission fluid is at normal operating temperature. Raise and support vehicle. Place a wood block between distributor housing and firewall to prevent damage to distributor cap when lowering transmission.

2) Support transmission with jack. Unbolt cross member and lower transmission to gain access to pressure port. Connect appropriate pressure gauge to line pressure test port on transmission. *See Fig. 4.*

3) Apply service brake and shift transmission to "D" position. Release brake and allow wheels to accelerate to approximately 28 MPH. Allow engine to idle (approximately 1500 RPM). Check line pressure and record pressure reading. Repeat test in "2" and "L" position.

4) Apply brakes. Shift transmission to "D" position. Disconnect modulator vacuum line. Depress accelerator pedal to Wide Open

Throttle (WOT). Do not hold engine at WOT for more than 5 seconds. Check line pressure and record pressure reading. Repeat test in "2" and "L" position. See LINE PRESSURE SPECIFICATIONS table.

LINE PRESSURE SPECIFICATIONS

Shifter Position	psi (kg/cm²)
Idle Speed	
Geo	
"D" & "2"	65 (4.6)
"L"	95 (6.7)
Suzuki	
"D" & "2"	54-63 (3.8-4.5)
"L"	87-102 (6.1-7.1)
WOT	
Geo	
"D" & "2"	118 (8.3)
"L"	160 (11.2)
Suzuki	
"D" & "2"	100-112 (7.0-7.9)
"L"	161-177 (11.3-12.4)

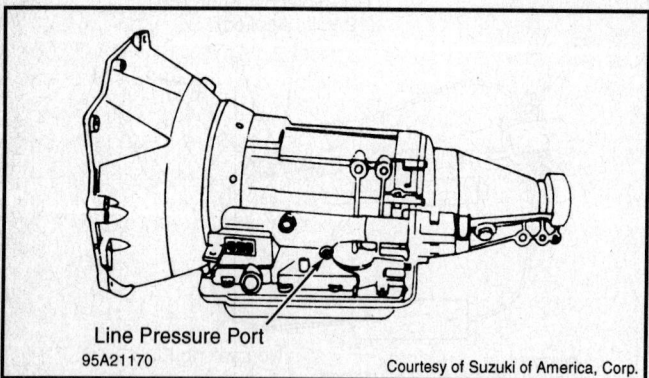

Line Pressure Port
95A21170   Courtesy of Suzuki of America, Corp.

Fig. 4: Identifying Pressure Test Port

VACUUM MODULATOR

NOTE: A faulty vacuum modulator can cause:
- Harsh upshift and downshifts.
- Delayed upshifts.
- Soft upshifts and downshifts.
- Slips in "L", "D" and "R".
- Transmission overheating.
- Burnt transmission fluid.

1) Remove modulator. Hold modulator so vacuum fitting points downward. Replace modulator if full of transmission fluid.
2) Connect vacuum pump. Apply 20 In. Hg of vacuum. Ensure modulator operates and holds vacuum. Replace if necessary.

ON-VEHICLE SERVICE

EXTENSION HOUSING & GOVERNOR ASSEMBLY

Removal – 1) Raise and support vehicle. Place reference marks on drive shaft and companion flange. Remove drive shaft, speedometer cable and speedometer driven gear. Support transmission with jack. Remove transmission-to-cross-member bolts and rear mount from extension housing.
2) Remove extension housing bolts and remove extension housing. Note bolt length and location. On 4WD vehicles, remove transfer case and adaptor. See appropriate article in AXLE SHAFTS & TRANSFER CASES section.
3) Remove snap ring, speedometer drive gear and remaining snap ring from output shaft. Remove governor assembly (if applicable).

Installation To install, reverse removal procedure. Ensure output shaft bolt hole is aligned with governor assembly. Install extension housing and new gasket. Clean all bolt threads.

SHIFT LINKAGE

For shift linkage adjustment, see ADJUSTMENTS in appropriate AUTOMATIC TRANSMISSION SERVICING article.

KICKDOWN CABLE/THROTTLE CABLE

For kickdown or throttle cable adjustment, see ADJUSTMENTS in appropriate AUTOMATIC TRANSMISSION SERVICING article.

REMOVAL & INSTALLATION

For transmission removal and installation procedure, see REMOVAL & INSTALLATION in appropriate AUTOMATIC TRANSMISSION REMOVAL article.

TORQUE CONVERTER

NOTE: Torque converter is a sealed unit and must be serviced as a complete assembly. Perform the following tests to check torque converter condition. Torque converter and transmission cooler must be thoroughly cleaned and flushed if transmission fluid is contaminated.

STATOR (ONE-WAY CLUTCH) TEST

Insert finger into splined inner race of roller clutch and try to turn race in both directions. Clutch should lock when rotated counterclockwise, and turn freely when rotated clockwise. Replace torque converter if clutch fails test.

TRANSMISSION DISASSEMBLY

1) Remove oil pan and filter. Remove manual detent roller assembly. Remove TCC solenoid and harness assembly. Remove governor pressure switch from valve body. Remove reinforcement plate under TCC solenoid. Remove servo cover.
2) Unbolt and remove valve body with manual valve, link, separator plate and gaskets. Remove check ball in transmission case. See Fig. 5. Using Servo Compressor (09927-66020 or J-23075), compress servo piston assembly and remove snap ring. See Fig. 6.
3) Remove compressor. Remove servo assembly with spring and rod. Remove Park/Neutral Position (PNP) switch. Pull roll pin from manual select shaft. Place a metal plate between manual select shaft inner lever and case. Loosen nut on end of shaft and remove. Remove lever and select shaft.
4) Remove extension housing or transfer case. Remove modulator and modulator plunger. Remove roll pin from kickdown valve sleeve. Remove remaining kickdown valve components. See Fig. 7. Remove speedometer gear retaining snap ring, gear and snap ring.
5) Remove governor hub. Remove governor from hub. Remove small filter screen from hub. See Fig. 8. Remove "O" ring from input shaft. Remove bolts securing converter housing to transmission case.
6) Remove housing, oil pump and reverse clutch piston as complete assembly. Remove 2nd and 3rd clutch assemblies. See Fig. 8. Remove remaining reverse clutch plate and pressure plate.
7) Remove planetary gear. Remove thrust bearing from top of sun gear if bearing did not stay with planetary gear. Remove rear sun gear assembly. Remove low brake band and any remaining thrust bearing and washer.
8) Remove manual select shaft inner lever and parking lock actuator assembly. Separate 2nd clutch from 3rd clutch. Remove electrical harness connector.

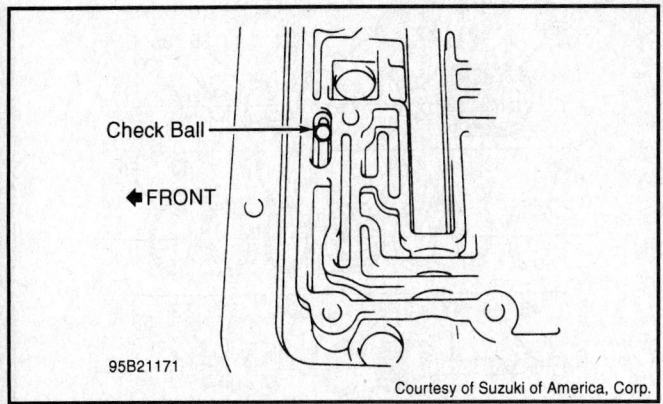

Fig. 5: Locating Transmission Case Check Ball

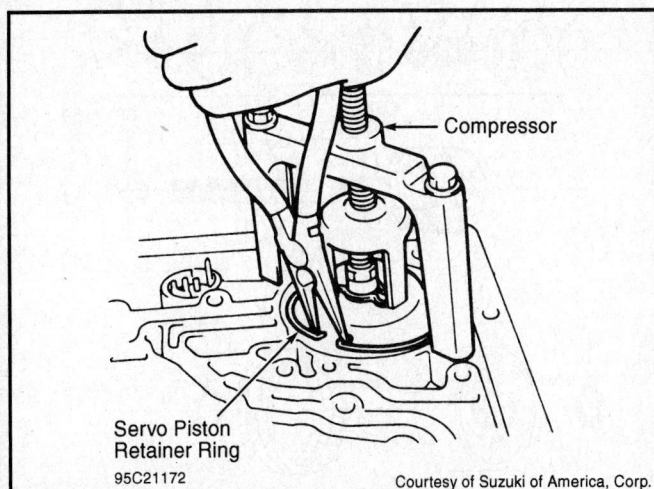

Fig. 6: Compressing Servo Piston Assembly

COMPONENT DISASSEMBLY & REASSEMBLY

GOVERNOR BODY

Disassembly & Reassembly – Depress secondary valve spring and remove secondary valve spring retainer. *See Fig. 9.* Remove components from governor body. Inspect valves for scoring, nicks or burrs. Polish with crocus cloth. To assemble, reverse disassembly procedures. Ensure valves move freely.

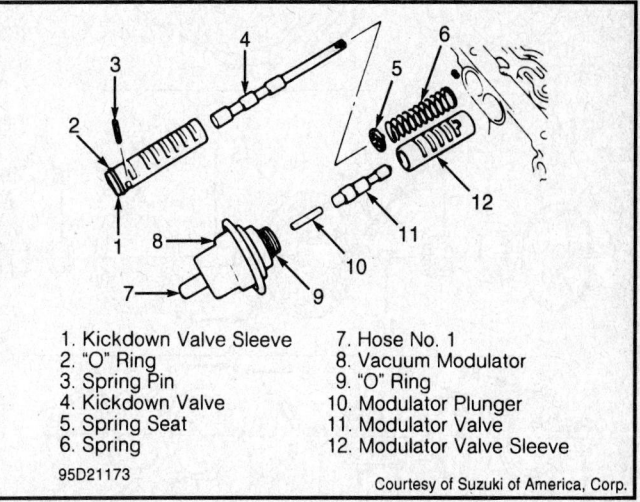

1. Kickdown Valve Sleeve
2. "O" Ring
3. Spring Pin
4. Kickdown Valve
5. Spring Seat
6. Spring
7. Hose No. 1
8. Vacuum Modulator
9. "O" Ring
10. Modulator Plunger
11. Modulator Valve
12. Modulator Valve Sleeve

Fig. 7: Exploded View Of Modulator & Kick-Down Assemblies

SERVO PISTON ASSEMBLY

Disassembly & Reassembly – Loosen adjusting stud nut and remove. Compress piston and remove clip. *See Fig. 11.* Clean all parts and inspect for wear or damage. To reassemble, reverse disassembly procedure.

VALVE BODY SPRING SPECIFICATIONS (GEO)

Description	Diameter In. (mm)	Free Length In. (mm)	Color
1-2 Shift Control Valve	[1]	[1]	[1]
1-2 Shift Valve	.750 (19.1)	2.438 (61.9)	[1]
2-3 Shift Control Valve	.687 (17.4)	1.750 (44.5)	[1]
3-2 Control Valve	.438 (11.1)	1.750 (44.5)	[1]
Detent Pressure Regulator	.500 (12.7)	1.625 (41.3)	[1]
High Speed Downshift Valve	.438 (11.1)	1.313 (33.4)	[1]
Low Speed Downshift Valve	.438 (11.1)	1.375 (34.9)	[1]
Low Reverse Control Valve	.438 (11.1)	1.313 (33.4)	[1]
1-2 Accumulator Valve	.500 (12.7)	1.063 (27.0)	[1]

[1] – Information not available from manufacturer.

VALVE BODY SPRING SPECIFICATIONS (SUZUKI)

Description	Diameter In. (mm)	Free Length In. (mm)	Color
1-2 Shift Control Valve	.31 (8)	.53 (13.5)	Black
1-2 Shift Valve	.72 (18.3)	2.46 (62.5)	Lt. Blue
2-3 Shift Control Valve	.72 (18.3)	2.13 (54)	Brown/Yellow
3-2 Control Valve	.41 (10.3)	1.61 (41)	Silver
Detent Pressure Regulator	.47 (12)	1.57 (40)	Yellow/Green
High Speed Downshift Valve	.48 (12.2)	1.31 (33.2)	Blue/Pink
Low Speed Downshift Valve	.4 (10.3)	1.30 (33)	Blue/Green
Low Reverse Control Valve	.4 (10.3)	1.34 (34)	Light Green
1-2 Accumulator Valve	.52 (13.3)	.67 (17)	Green/Yellow

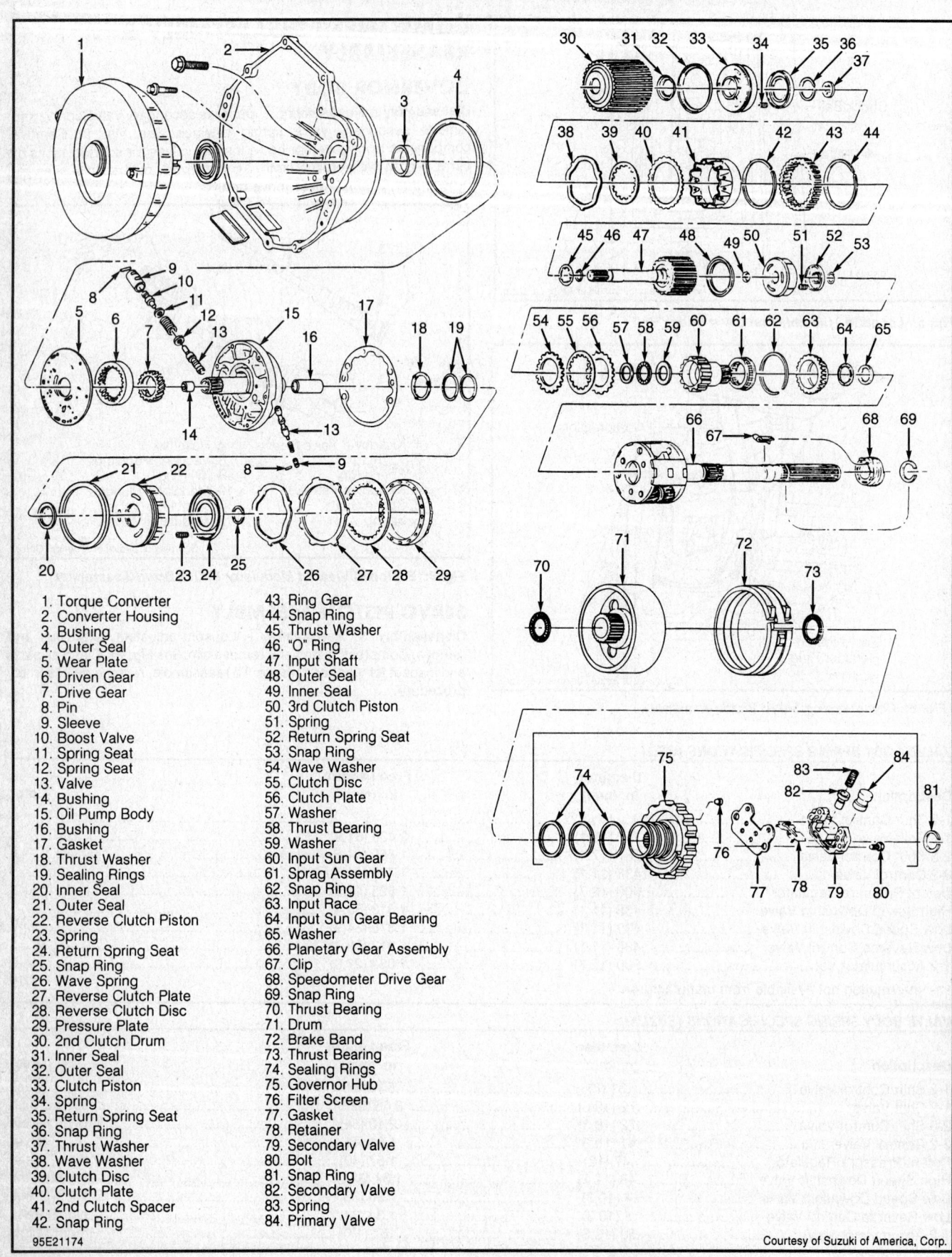

1. Torque Converter
2. Converter Housing
3. Bushing
4. Outer Seal
5. Wear Plate
6. Driven Gear
7. Drive Gear
8. Pin
9. Sleeve
10. Boost Valve
11. Spring Seat
12. Spring Seat
13. Valve
14. Bushing
15. Oil Pump Body
16. Bushing
17. Gasket
18. Thrust Washer
19. Sealing Rings
20. Inner Seal
21. Outer Seal
22. Reverse Clutch Piston
23. Spring
24. Return Spring Seat
25. Snap Ring
26. Wave Spring
27. Reverse Clutch Plate
28. Reverse Clutch Disc
29. Pressure Plate
30. 2nd Clutch Drum
31. Inner Seal
32. Outer Seal
33. Clutch Piston
34. Spring
35. Return Spring Seat
36. Snap Ring
37. Thrust Washer
38. Wave Washer
39. Clutch Disc
40. Clutch Plate
41. 2nd Clutch Spacer
42. Snap Ring

43. Ring Gear
44. Snap Ring
45. Thrust Washer
46. "O" Ring
47. Input Shaft
48. Outer Seal
49. Inner Seal
50. 3rd Clutch Piston
51. Spring
52. Return Spring Seat
53. Snap Ring
54. Wave Washer
55. Clutch Disc
56. Clutch Plate
57. Washer
58. Thrust Bearing
59. Washer
60. Input Sun Gear
61. Sprag Assembly
62. Snap Ring
63. Input Race
64. Input Sun Gear Bearing
65. Washer
66. Planetary Gear Assembly
67. Clip
68. Speedometer Drive Gear
69. Snap Ring
70. Thrust Bearing
71. Drum
72. Brake Band
73. Thrust Bearing
74. Sealing Rings
75. Governor Hub
76. Filter Screen
77. Gasket
78. Retainer
79. Secondary Valve
80. Bolt
81. Snap Ring
82. Secondary Valve
83. Spring
84. Primary Valve

95E21174

Courtesy of Suzuki of America, Corp.

Fig. 8: Exploded View Of Transmission Assembly

VALVE BODY ASSEMBLY

NOTE: All valve body components must be installed in original location. Lay all components in sequence during removal for reassembly reference.

Disassembly – Remove manual valve. Individually remove each valve retaining pins. Remove all components. *See Fig. 10.*

Inspection – Clean all parts in solvent. Dry with compressed air. Ensure all valve body passages are clear. Inspect valves for scoring or roughness. Ensure valves slide freely in bores. Inspect valve springs for damage, squareness and collapsed coils. Measure spring free length and outer diameter. Replace spring if not within specification. See appropriate VALVE BODY SPRING SPECIFICATIONS table.

Reassembly – Install valves, springs, plugs and retaining pins in proper order and location. Use a liberal amount of transmission fluid. Ensure valves move freely and snap back when moved.

CONVERTER HOUSING, OIL PUMP & REVERSE CLUTCH ASSEMBLY

Disassembly – **1)** Remove selective thrust washer from oil pump shaft (if necessary). Remove bolts and separate converter housing from oil pump. Remove pump wear plate. Mark pump gears with reference marks and remove gears.

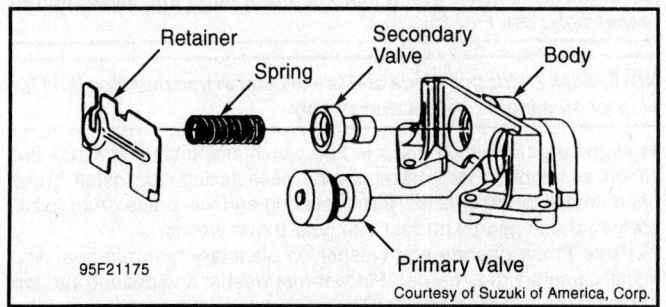

95F21175
Courtesy of Suzuki of America, Corp.

Fig. 9: Exploded View Of Governor Assembly

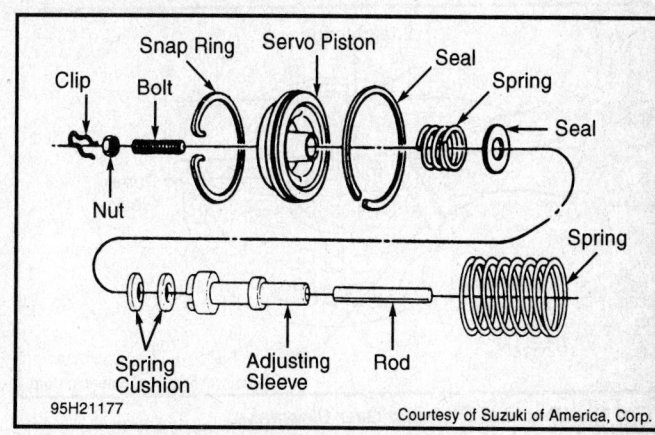

95H21177
Courtesy of Suzuki of America, Corp.

Fig. 11: Exploded View Of Servo Piston Assembly

2) Using appropriate compressor, compress reverse clutch spring seat. Remove snap ring. Remove reverse clutch piston. *See Fig. 8.* If necessary, remove valve assemblies from oil pump by removing retaining pins.

Inspection – Clean all components in solvent. Inspect valves and valve bores for scoring, burrs and nicks. Polish valves with crocus cloth (as needed). Using straightedge and feeler gauge, inspect pump to gear clearance. *See Fig. 12.* Clearance should be .0005-.0032" (.02-.08 mm).

Reassembly – **1)** Place wear plate on pump and align bolt holes. Install NEW oil seal in converter housing. Place converter housing on oil pump. Loosely install bolts. Install oil pump Aligning Sleeve (09927-66010 or J-23082-01) through converter housing into pump. Tighten bolts to specification. See TORQUE SPECIFICATIONS.

2) Install reverse clutch piston onto rear face of pump. Place springs onto piston. Install spring seat. Compress spring seat and install snap ring.

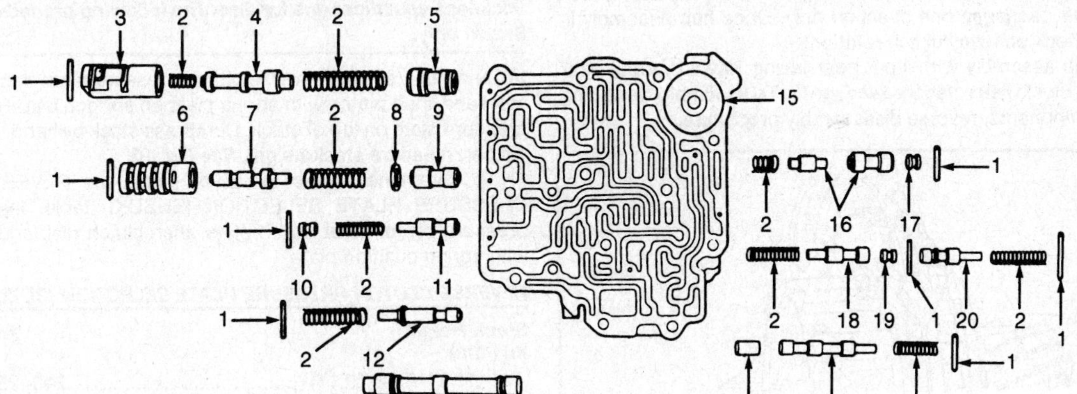

1. Pin
2. Spring
3. Sleeve
4. 1-2 Shift Control Valve
5. 1-2 Shift Valve
6. Sleeve
7. 2-3 Shift Control Valve
8. Spring Seat
9. 2-3 Shift Valve
10. Plug
11. 3-2 Control Valve
12. Detent Pressure Regulator Valve
13. Link
14. Manual Valve
15. 1-2 Accumulator Piston Assembly
16. 1-2 Accumulator Valve
17. Plug
18. Low Speed Downshift Timing Valve
19. Intermediate Valve
20. High Speed Downshift Timing Valve
21. Reverse Control Valve
22. Manual Low Control Valve

95G21176
Courtesy of Suzuki of America, Corp.

Fig. 10: Exploded View Of Valve Body Assembly

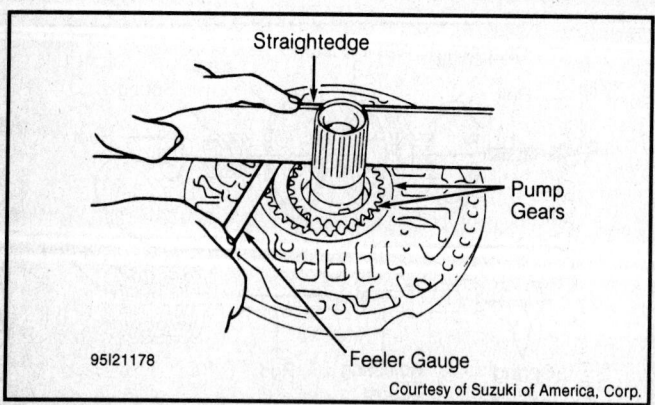

Fig. 12: Checking Oil Pump Gear Clearance

2ND CLUTCH ASSEMBLY

Disassembly – 1) Remove snap ring from 2nd clutch drum. Remove ring gear, snap ring and spacer. *See Fig. 8.* Remove clutch plates and discs. Remove bronze thrust washer.
2) Using appropriate spring compressor, compress spring seat and remove snap ring. Remove spring seat, return springs and piston.
Inspection & Reassembly – Apply compressed air to piston check ball. Ensure air passes in one direction only. To assemble 2nd clutch assembly, reverse disassembly procedure.

3RD CLUTCH ASSEMBLY

Disassembly – 1) Mount 3rd clutch assembly in soft-jawed vise. Compress retaining ring using several thin blade screwdrivers. Insert screwdrivers in slots in drum and push up on inside clutch plate to force snap ring from groove.
2) Remove 3rd clutch hub, clutch plates, thrust bearing and washer. *See Figs. 8 and 13.* Disassemble 3rd clutch hub. Note direction of sprag assembly.
3) Using appropriate spring compressor, compress return spring seat and remove snap ring. Remove spring seat, return springs and piston.
Inspection & Reassembly – 1) Apply compressed air to piston check ball. Ensure air passes in one direction only. Once hub assembly is assembled, check one-way clutch rotation.
2) Holding hub assembly with input gear facing forward, input gear should lock in clockwise rotation. *See Fig. 13.* To assemble remaining 3rd clutch components, reverse disassembly procedure.

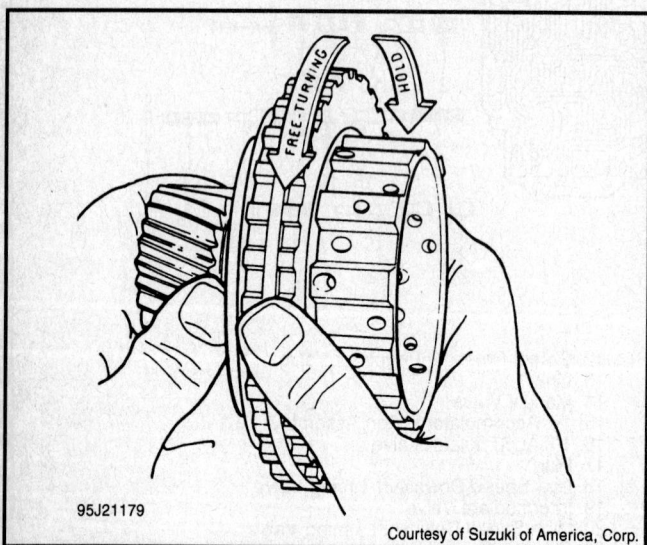

Fig. 13: Checking 3rd Clutch Hub Rotation

PLANETARY GEAR CARRIER

Inspection – Visually check carrier for distortion and damage. Using feeler gauge, check planetary pinion gear clearance. *See Fig. 14.* Clearance should be .005-.035" (.13-.85 mm). Replace as needed.

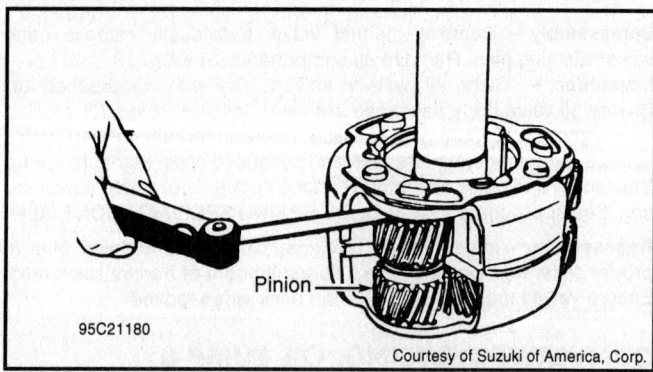

Fig. 14: Checking Planetary Gear Pinion Gear Clearance

TRANSMISSION REASSEMBLY

NOTE: Ensure correct thrust bearing and washer placement during reassembly. See Fig. 15.

NOTE: Soak all friction discs and brake band in transmission fluid for at least 15 minutes before reassembly.

1) Align tangs of clutch discs in 2nd clutch assembly and install 3rd clutch assembly. Place transmission case facing up. Install brake band. Install thrust washer, thrust bearing and low brake drum (planetary rear sun gear) with rear sun gear thrust washer.
2) Place thrust bearing and washer on planetary rear sun gear and install planetary gear carrier. Place thrust washer and bearing into top of planetary carrier. Insert 2nd/3rd clutch assemblies into case.

NOTE: Manufacturer does not provide reverse clutch pressure plate thickness specifications for Geo. The following procedure applies to Suzuki only.

3) Determine correct reverse clutch pressure plate thickness. Stack steel and lined plates with spring plate on surface plate. Place current pressure plate on top of stack. Compress stack by hand. Using vernier caliper, measure stack height. *See Fig. 16.*
4) To determine correct pressure plate, see REVERSE CLUTCH PRESSURE PLATE SELECTION (SUZUKI) table. Install selected pressure place, steel clutch plate, then clutch disc and repeat. End with spring cushion plate.

REVERSE CLUTCH PRESSURE PLATE SELECTION (SUZUKI)

Stack Height In. (mm)	Pressure Plate In. (mm)
.741-.750 (18.82-19.11)	.248-.252 (6.30-6.40)
.730-.741 (18.53-18.81)	.259-.263 (6.59-6.69)
.718-.729 (18.24-18.52)	.271-.275 (6.88-6.98)
.707-.718 (17.95-18.23)	.282-.286 (7.17-7.27)

5) Determine correct input shaft thrust washer. Place Depth Measuring Tool (09923-46010 or J-23085) on flange of case. *See Fig. 17.* Loosen thumb screw and allow plunger to contact thrust face of 2nd clutch housing. Tighten thumb screw.
6) Remove measuring tool. Using feeler gauge, measure length of plunger protrusion. Select appropriate thrust washer to obtain .014-.031" (.36-.79 mm) end play and install. See SELECTIVE THRUST WASHER SELECTION table.

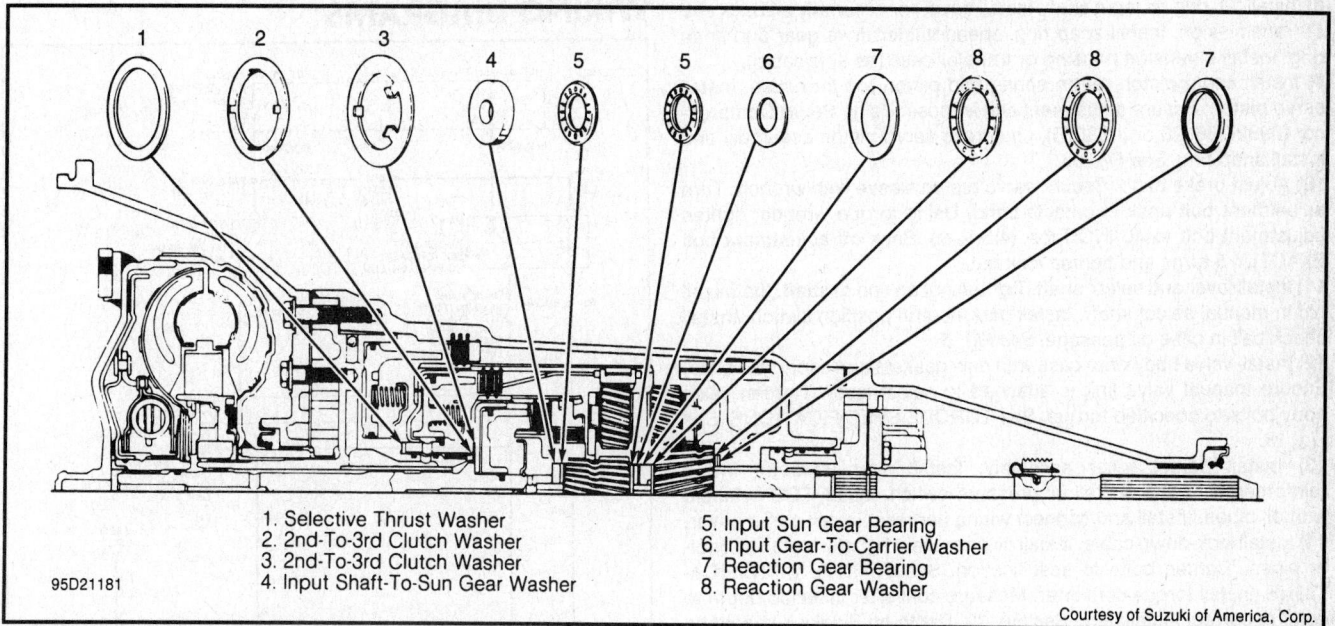

1. Selective Thrust Washer
2. 2nd-To-3rd Clutch Washer
3. 2nd-To-3rd Clutch Washer
4. Input Shaft-To-Sun Gear Washer
5. Input Sun Gear Bearing
6. Input Gear-To-Carrier Washer
7. Reaction Gear Bearing
8. Reaction Gear Washer

95D21181

Courtesy of Suzuki of America, Corp.

Fig. 15: Identifying Transmission Thrust Bearings & Washers

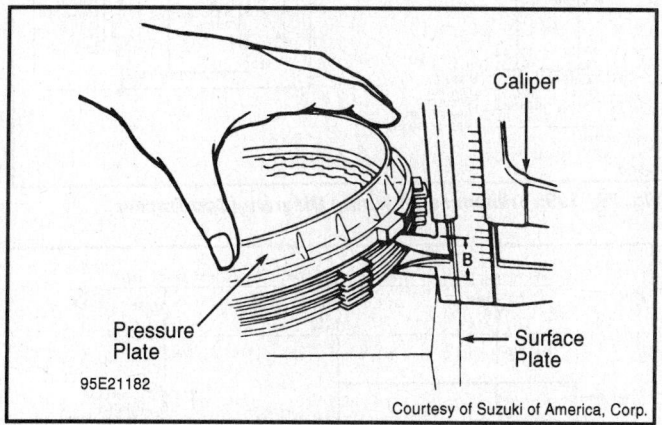

95E21182

Courtesy of Suzuki of America, Corp.

Fig. 16: Measuring Reverse Clutch Stack Height (Suzuki)

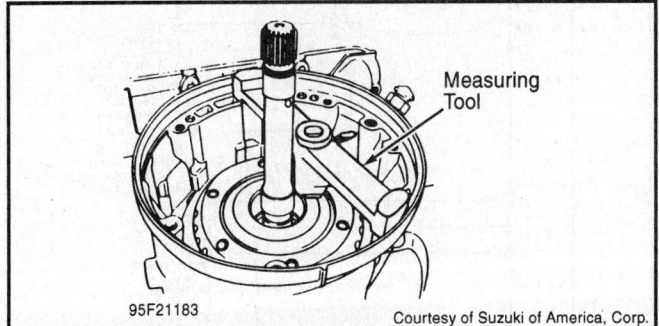

95F21183

Courtesy of Suzuki of America, Corp.

Fig. 17: Measuring 2nd Clutch Drum Depth

SELECTIVE THRUST WASHER SELECTION

I.D No.	Color	Thickness
2	Yellow	.060-.074 (1.52-1.88)
3	Red	.068-.079 (1.73-2.01)
4	Black	.075-.084 (1.91-2.13)
5	Natural	.083-.089 (2.11-2.26)
6	Green	.090-.094 (2.29-2.39)
7	Blue	.095-.102 (2.41-2.59)

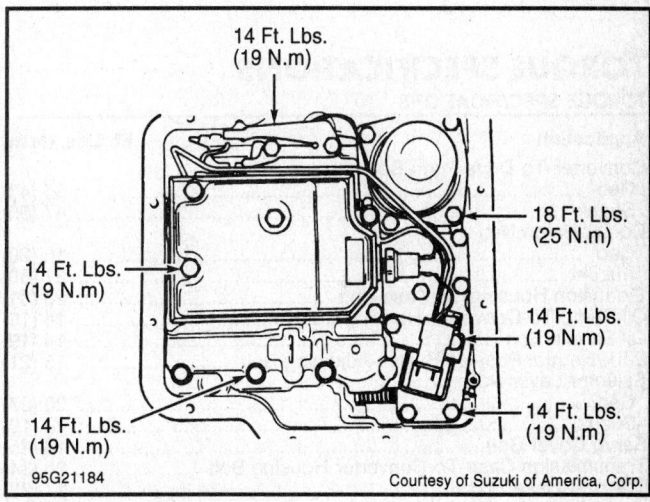

95G21184

Courtesy of Suzuki of America, Corp.

Fig. 18: Installing Valve Body

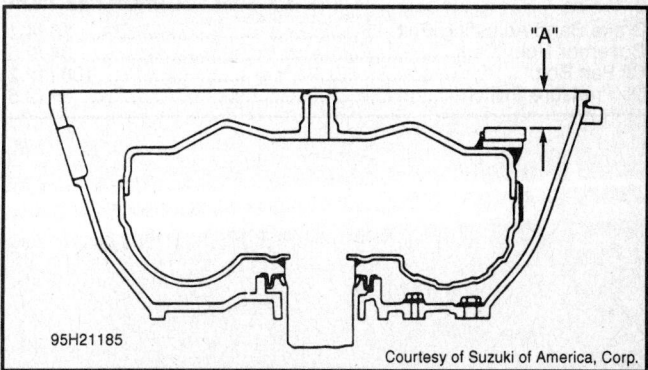

95H21185

Courtesy of Suzuki of America, Corp.

Fig. 19: Measuring Torque Converter Installation

7) Install reverse clutch, oil pump and converter housing assembly. Install bolts and tighten to specification. See TORQUE SPECIFICATIONS. Inspect input shaft end play. Ensure end play is .014-.031" (.36-.79 mm). If end play is not within specification, select alternate thrust washer and remeasure.

8) Install "O" ring on input shaft. Install governor assembly on back end of transmission. Install snap ring, speedometer drive gear and snap ring. Install extension housing or transfer case (as applicable).

9) Install servo piston return spring and piston rod into case. Install servo piston. Ensure adjustment bolt is loose. Using Servo Compressor (09927-66020 or J-23075), compress servo piston assembly and install snap ring. *See Fig. 6.*

10) Adjust brake band. Secure servo piston sleeve with wrench. Turn adjustment bolt until it contacts band. Using torque wrench, tighten adjustment bolt to 40 INCH lbs. (4.5 N.m). Back off adjustment bolt EXACTLY 5 turns and tighten lock nut.

11) Install lever and select shaft. Tighten nut on end of shaft. Install roll pin in manual select shaft. Install park/neutral position switch. Install check ball in case oil passage. *See Fig. 5.*

12) Install valve body onto case with new gaskets and separator plate. Ensure manual valve link is attached to select lever. Tighten valve body bolts to specified torque. See TORQUE SPECIFICATIONS. *See Fig. 18.*

13) Install detent roller assembly. Install filter (screen). Install reinforcement plate. Install oil pressure switch. Install TCC solenoid with oil pipes. Install and connect wiring harness. Install servo cover.

14) Install kick-down cable. Install oil pan with magnets. Install oil cooler pipes. Tighten bolts to specification. See TORQUE SPECIFICATIONS. Install torque converter. Measure converter installed depth to confirm correct installation. *See Fig. 19.* Depth on Sidekick should be 1.21-1.33" (30.67-33.83 mm). Depth on Tracker should be .83-.91" (21.2-23.2 mm).

TORQUE SPECIFICATIONS

TORQUE SPECIFICATIONS

Application	Ft. Lbs. (N.m)
Converter-To-Drive Plate Bolt	
Geo	35 (48)
Suzuki	47 (65)
Cooler Union Nut	
Geo	15 (20)
Suzuki	21 (30)
Extension Housing-To-Case Bolt	23 (31)
Oil Pump-To-Converter Housing Bolt	14 (19)
Oil Screen Bolt	14 (19)
Park/Neutral Position Switch Adjusting Bolt	15 (21)
Selector Lever Nut	
Geo	20 (27)
Suzuki	14 (19)
Servo Cover Bolt	18 (25)
Transmission Case-To-Converter Housing Bolt	25 (34)
Transfer Case Bolt	17 (23)
Valve Assembly-To-Case Bolt	14 (19)
	INCH Lbs. (N.m)
Brake Band Adjusting Bolt	36 (4.1)
Governor Bolt	84 (9.5)
Oil Pan Bolt	108 (12.2)
Oil Pressure Switch	84 (9.5)

WIRING DIAGRAMS

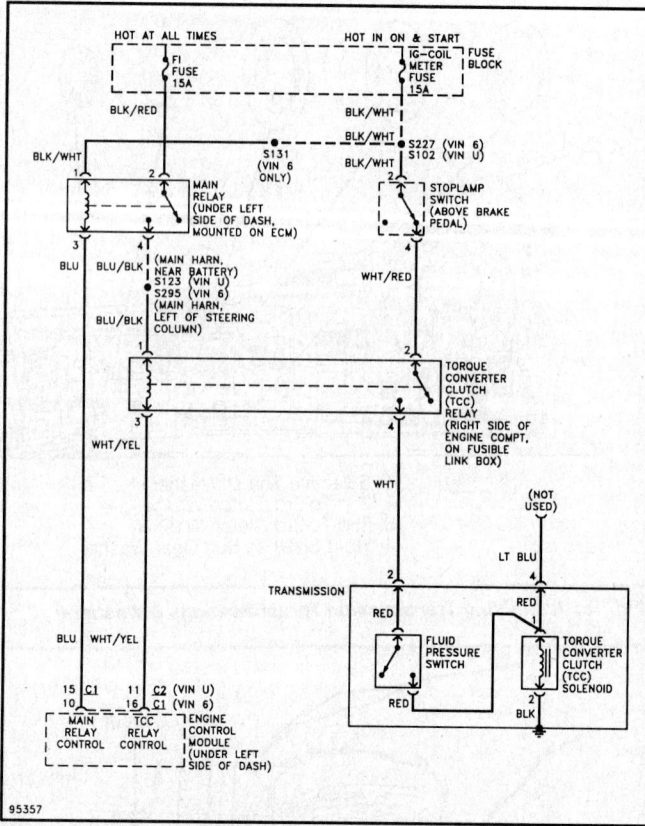

Fig. 20: 1995 Transmission Wiring Diagram (Geo Tracker)

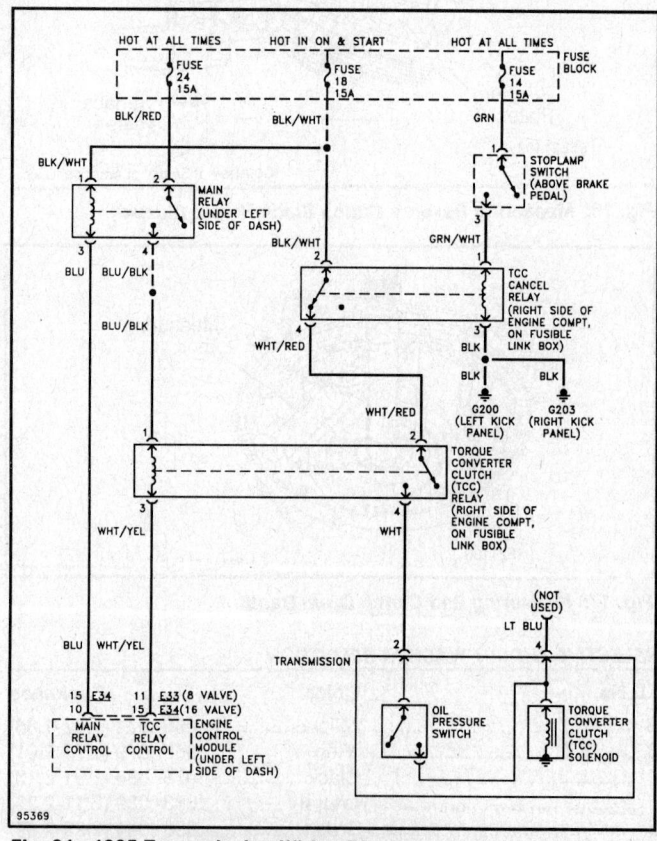

Fig. 21: 1995 Transmission Wiring Diagram (Suzuki Sidekick 1.6L – With Cruise Control)

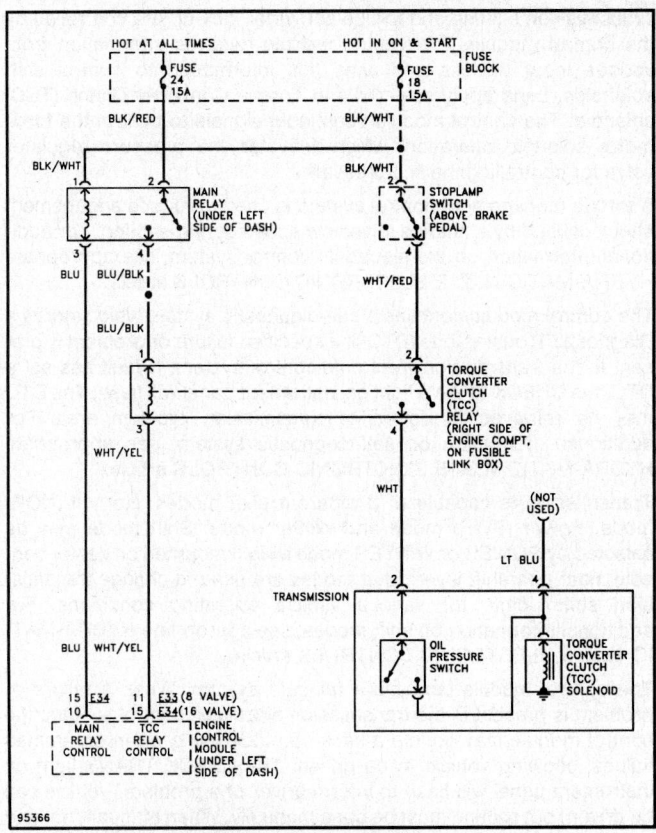

**Fig. 22: 1995 Transmission Wiring Diagram
(Suzuki Sidekick 1.6L – Without Cruise Control)**

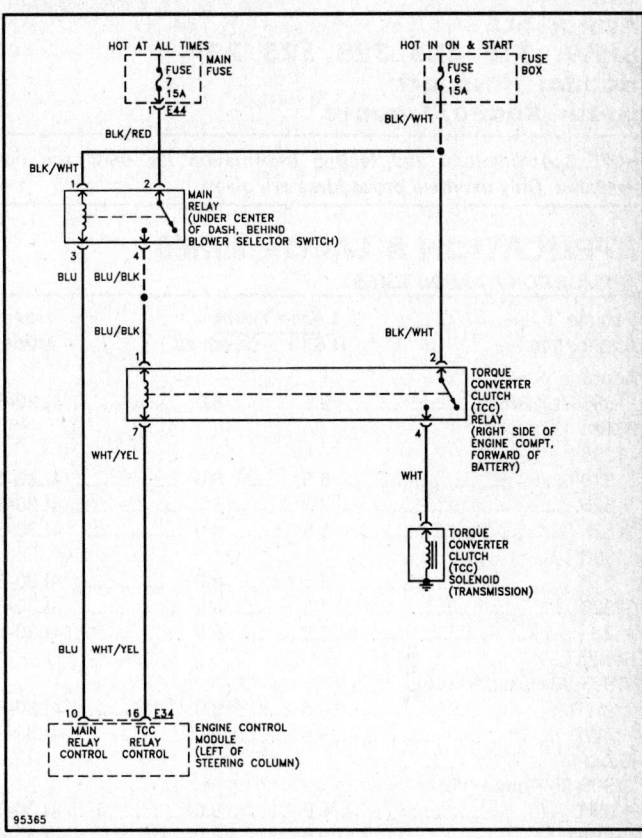

Fig. 24: 1996 Transmission Wiring Diagram (Suzuki Sidekick 1.6L)

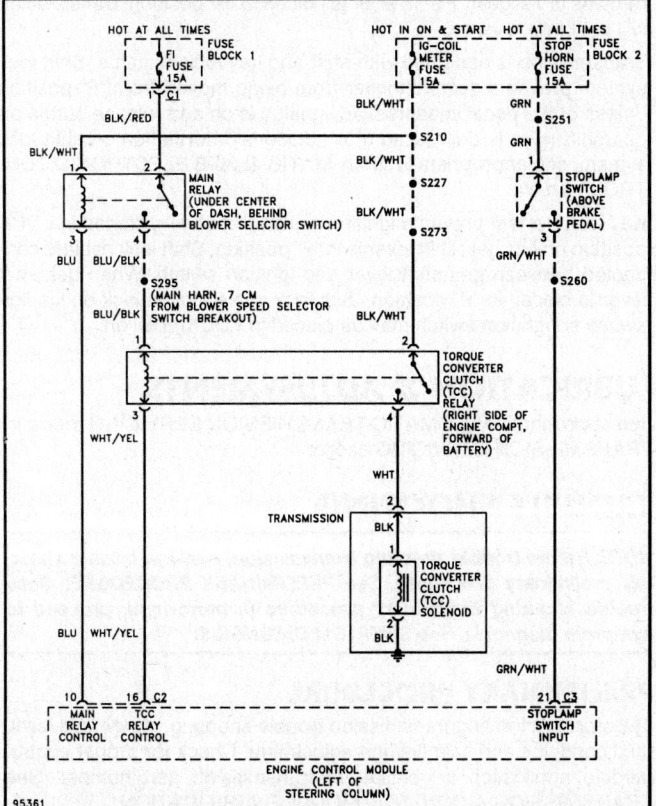

Fig. 23: 1996 Transmission Wiring Diagram (Geo Tracker)

AUTOMATIC TRANSMISSIONS
Hydra-Matic 4L30-E

Acura: SLX
BMW: 318, 325, 328, 525, Z3
Honda: Passport
Isuzu: Rodeo, Trooper

NOTE: Specifications and testing information for BMW are not available. Only overhaul procedures are given.

APPLICATION & LABOR TIMES

APPLICATION & LABOR TIMES

Vehicle Application	Labor Times R & I [1]	Overhaul [2]	Trans. Model
Acura			
1996 SLX (V6)	9.6	8.0	4L30-E
BMW			
1995			
318	5.5	8.0	4L30-E
325	7.3	8.0	4L30-E
525	5.5	8.0	4L30-E
1996			
318	5.5	8.0	4L30-E
328	7.3	8.0	4L30-E
Z3	5.2	8.0	4L30-E
Honda			
1995-96 Passport (V6)			
2WD	8.6	8.0	4L30-E
4WD	9.6	8.0	4L30-E
Isuzu			
1995-96 Rodeo (V6)			
2WD	8.6	8.0	4L30-E
4WD	9.6	8.0	4L30-E
1995-96 Trooper (V6)	9.6	8.0	4L30-E

[1] – Removal and installation of transmission from vehicle chassis.
[2] – Bench overhaul time for transmission. DOES NOT include removal and installation.

IDENTIFICATION

Identification plate is located on side of transmission case. *See Fig. 1.* Identification plate information may be required when ordering replacement components.

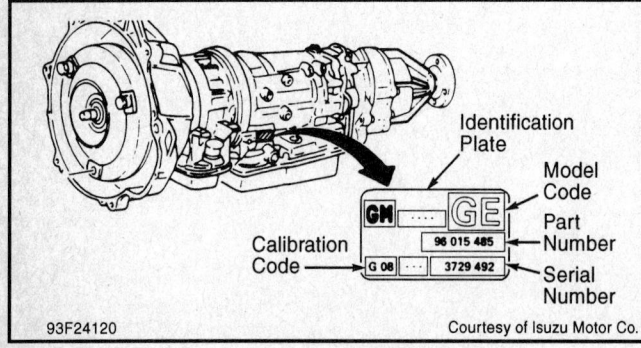

Fig. 1: Locating Transmission Identification Plate

93F24120   Courtesy of Isuzu Motor Co.

DESCRIPTION & OPERATION

NOTE: The transmission electronic control system is controlled by Transmission Control Module (TCM) on 1995 models, and Powertrain Control Module (PCM) on 1996 models. In this article, both units will be referred to as "control module".

Automatic transmission is electronically controlled, providing 4 forward speeds and one reverse speed. Transmission consists of a torque converter, clutches, planetary gears and brake band. *See Fig. 2.* On 4WD models, transfer case is bolted to rear of transmission.

Transmission shifting and torque converter lock-up are controlled by the control module. The control module receives information from various input devices and uses this information to control shift solenoids, band apply solenoid and Torque Converter Clutch (TCC) solenoid. The control module uses input signals to control the force motor solenoid operation, which activates the pressure regulator valve for controlling the line pressure.

A torque management control system is used to reduce engagement shock caused by a change in vehicle speed during shifting. For additional information on the electronic control system, see appropriate HYDRA-MATIC 4L30-E ELECTRONIC CONTROLS article.

The control module contains a self-diagnostic system which stores a Diagnostic Trouble Code (DTC) if a specified failure or problem is present in the transmission electronic control system. If fault has set a DTC, the CHECK TRANS light on instrument panel will flash. The DTC may be retrieved to determine transmission problem area. For additional information on self-diagnostic system, see appropriate HYDRA-MATIC 4L30-E ELECTRONIC CONTROLS article.

Transmission is capable of 3 different shift modes, Normal (NOR) mode, Power (PWR) mode and Winter mode. Shift mode may be selected by POWER or WINTER mode switch mounted on center console, near gearshift lever. Shift modes are used to change transmission shift points for various vehicle operating conditions. For additional information on shift modes, see appropriate HYDRA-MATIC 4L30-E ELECTRONIC CONTROLS article.

The control module contains a fail-safe system. When a failure or problem is present in the transmission electronic control system, the control module may go into a back-up mode using pre-programmed values, allowing vehicle to be driven. The CHECK TRANS light on instrument panel will flash to inform driver of a problem. Vehicle can be driven, but shifting must be done manually. When manually shifting transmission, if shift lever is placed in "D" or "3" position, transmission remains in 4th gear. If shift lever is placed in "2" position, transmission remain in 3rd gear. If shift lever is placed in "L" position, transmission remains in 1st gear. If shift lever is placed in "R" position, transmission will shift into reverse.

Transmission is equipped with shift and key lock systems. Shift lock system prevents gearshift lever from being moved from "P" position unless brake pedal is depressed, ignition is on and release button on gearshift lever is depressed. For additional information on shift lock system, see appropriate HYDRA-MATIC 4L30-E ELECTRONIC CONTROLS article.

Key lock system prevents ignition switch from being placed in LOCK position unless gearshift lever is in "P" position. Shift lock cable is connected between gearshift lever and ignition switch. When gearshift lever is placed in "P" position, shift lock cable moves lock on ignition switch so ignition switch may be placed in LOCK position.

LUBRICATION & ADJUSTMENTS

See appropriate AUTOMATIC TRANSMISSION SERVICING article in TRANSMISSION SERVICING section.

TROUBLE SHOOTING

NOTE: Before trouble shooting transmission, perform trouble shooting preliminary procedure. See PRELIMINARY PROCEDURE. Once trouble shooting preliminary procedure is performed, proceed to symptom diagnosis. See SYMPTOM DIAGNOSIS.

PRELIMINARY PROCEDURE

1) Before performing transmission trouble shooting, check fluid level, fluid condition and shift linkage adjustment. Check for proper control module application in relation to transmission part number. See TRANSMISSION & CONTROL MODULE VERIFICATION.
2) Check for stored DTCs. See RETRIEVING DIAGNOSTIC TROUBLE CODES under SELF-DIAGNOSTIC SYSTEM in appropriate HYDRA-MATIC 4L30-E ELECTRONIC CONTROLS article.

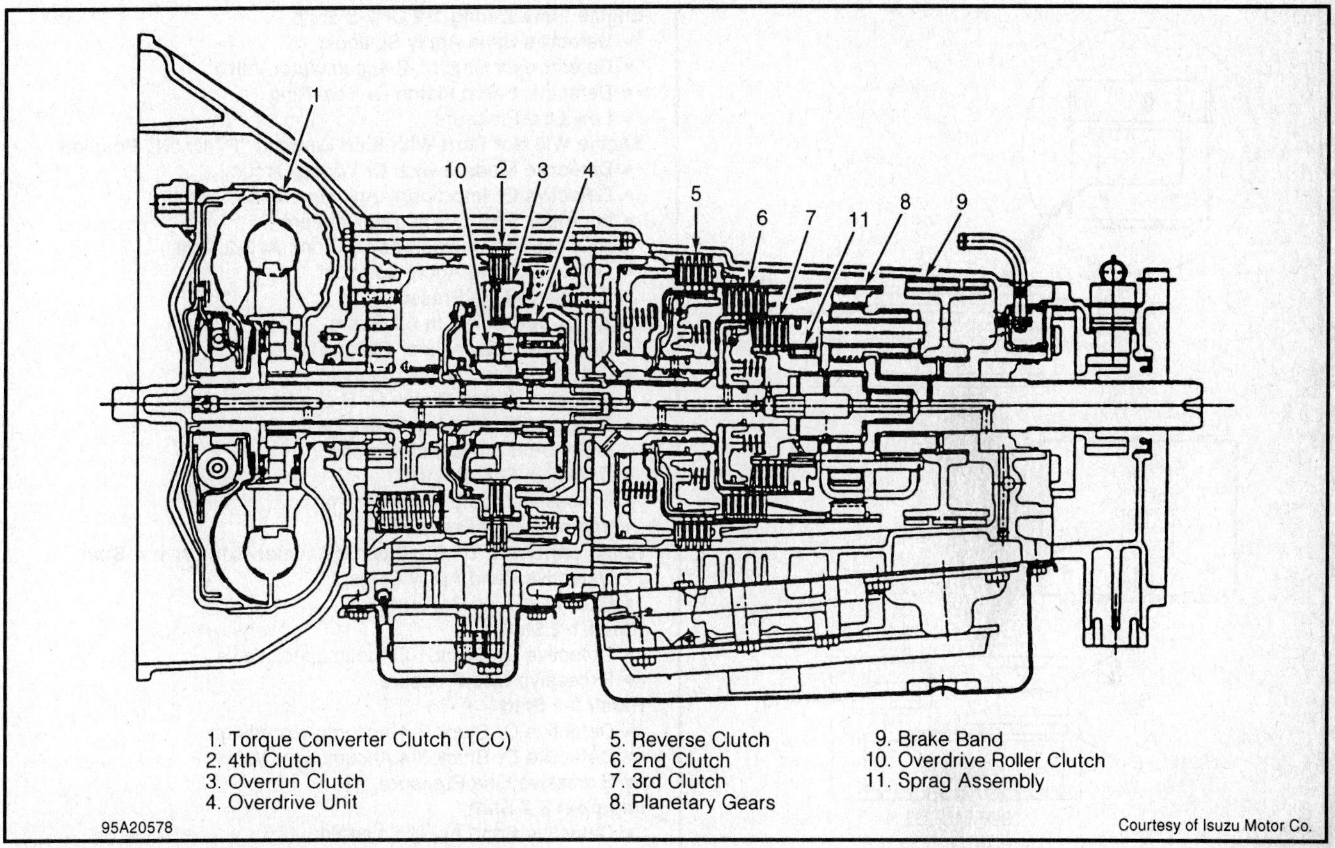

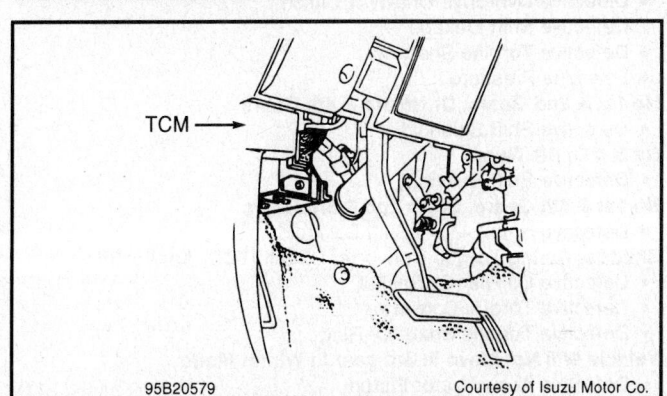

1. Torque Converter Clutch (TCC)
2. 4th Clutch
3. Overrun Clutch
4. Overdrive Unit

5. Reverse Clutch
6. 2nd Clutch
7. 3rd Clutch
8. Planetary Gears

9. Brake Band
10. Overdrive Roller Clutch
11. Sprag Assembly

95A20578   Courtesy of Isuzu Motor Co.

Fig. 2: Identifying Transmission Component Locations

3) Perform road test, torque converter stall speed test and hydraulic pressure test to identify problem. See ROAD TEST, TORQUE CONVERTER STALL SPEED TEST and HYDRAULIC PRESSURE TEST under TRANSMISSION TESTING.

TRANSMISSION & CONTROL MODULE VERIFICATION

NOTE: Transmission and control module verification should be performed to ensure proper control module is used in accordance with transmission application.

1) Note transmission part number stamped on identification plate on side of transmission case. *See Fig. 1.*

2) Note location of control module (mounted below driver's side of instrument panel on 1995 models, or behind center of instrument panel on 1996 models) and Isuzu part number stamped on unit. *See Figs. 3, 4 and 5.*

3) Using transmission part number and control module part number, ensure proper control module is installed. See TRANSMISSION & CONTROL MODULE APPLICATION table. Replace control module if incorrect unit is installed.

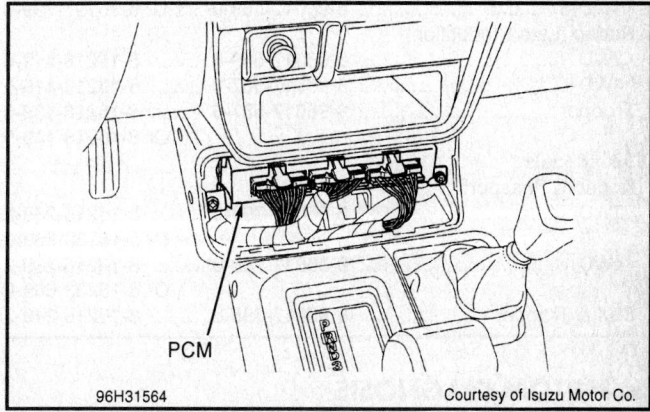

TCM

95B20579   Courtesy of Isuzu Motor Co.

Fig. 3: Locating Control Module (1995 Models)

PCM

96H31564   Courtesy of Isuzu Motor Co.

Fig. 4: Locating Control Module (1996 Models)

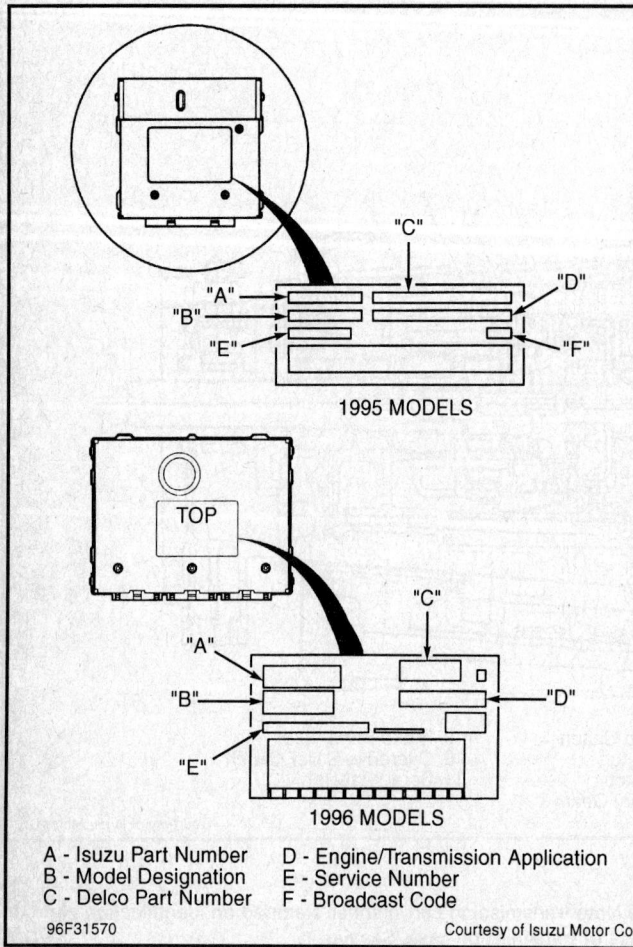

1995 MODELS

TOP

1996 MODELS

A - Isuzu Part Number
B - Model Designation
C - Delco Part Number
D - Engine/Transmission Application
E - Service Number
F - Broadcast Code

96F31570

Courtesy of Isuzu Motor Co.

Fig. 5: Locating Control Module Part Number

TRANSMISSION & CONTROL MODULE APPLICATION

Vehicle Application	Transmission Part No.	Control Module Isuzu Part No.
1995 Models		
Rodeo (Early Production)		
2WD	8-96017-175-0	8-16197-799-0
4WD	8-96017-169-0	8-16197-799-0
Rodeo (Late Production)		
2WD	8-96017-589-0	8-16218-419-0
4WD	8-96017-587-0	8-16218-419-0
Trooper	8-96017-587-0	8-16218-439-0 Or 8-16218-449-0
1996 Models		
Rodeo & Passport		
2WD	8-96017-799-0	8-16215-239-2 Or 8-16233-869-0
4WD	8-96017-798-0	8-16215-239-2 Or 8-16233-869-0
SLX & Trooper	8-96017-798-0	8-16215-249-3

SYMPTOM DIAGNOSIS

Delayed Gear Engagement In "D" & "R" Positions
- Defective Teflon Seal Rings On Turbine Shaft
- Low Line Pressure

Delayed Gear Engagement In "R" Position Only
- Defective Main Valve Body-To-Transmission Case Gasket
- Low Line Pressure
- Missing Check Balls In Valve Body
- Restricted Orifice At Transfer Plate And Valve Body

Engine Flare During 1-2 Or 2-3 Shift
- Defective Band Apply Solenoid
- Defective Or Stuck 1-2 Accumulator Valve
- Defective Servo Piston Or Seal Ring
- Low Line Pressure

Engine Will Not Start With Shift Lever In "P" Or "N" Position
- Defective Mode Switch Or Wiring Circuit
- Defective Or Improperly Adjusted Mode Switch
- Improper Shift Linkage Adjustment

Harsh Coasting Downshifts Or Clunk At 3-2 Shift
- Defective Band Apply Solenoid
- Excessive Line Pressure

Harsh Or Soft Shifts In All Gears
- Defective Accumulator Piston Or Servo
- Defective Band Apply Solenoid
- Defective Clutch Plates Or Brake Band
- Defective Or Missing Check Ball In 2nd And 3rd Clutch Pistons
- Defective Seal Rings
- Excessive Clutch Piston Travel
- Improper Line Pressure

Harsh Shift Into "D" Position Or Accelerating From A Stop
- Defective Band Apply Solenoid
- Excessive Line Pressure

Harsh 1-2 Shift
- Defective Or Stuck 1-2 Accumulator Valve
- Excessive Line Pressure

Harsh 3-4 Shift
- Defective Or Stuck 3-4 Accumulator Piston
- Defective Or Stuck 3-4 Accumulator Valve
- Excessive Line Pressure

Improper 3-2 Shift
- Defective Band Apply Solenoid
- Low Line Pressure

Intermittent 4-2 Downshift At Steady Speed
- Defective Mode Switch Or Wiring
- Defective Transmission Speed Sensor Or Wiring

No Engine Braking
- Damaged Piston Seal Ring On Overrun Clutch Piston
- Defective Or Stuck Overrun Lock-Out Valve On Center Support
- Defective Teflon Seal Rings On Turbine Shaft
- Defective Turbine Shaft
- Defective 3-4 Accumulator Piston
- Excessive Overrun Clutch Piston Travel
- Low Line Pressure

No Forward Or Reverse Gears
- Defective Overdrive One-Way Clutch
- Defective Shift Linkage
- Defective Turbine Shaft
- Low Line Pressure

No 1st & 2nd Gears, Or No 3rd & 4th Gears
- Defective Shift Solenoid

No 3rd Or 4th Gears
- Defective Shift Solenoid

No 1st & 4th Gears, Or No 2nd & 3rd Gears
- Defective Shift 1-2/3-4 Shift Solenoid

Shudder During Torque Converter Clutch (TCC) Application
- Defective Oil Filer Or Gasket
- Defective Torque Converter
- Defective Turbine Shaft "O" Ring

Vehicle Will Not Move In 3rd gear In Winter Mode
- Defective Accumulator Piston
- Defective Or Missing Check Ball In 2nd Clutch Piston
- Defective 2nd Clutch Seals
- Excessive 2nd Clutch Piston Travel
- Internal Hydraulic Pressure Leakage

Whine Or Buzzing Noise From Transmission
- Defective Oil Filter Gasket
- Low Fluid Level
- Restricted Oil Filter

ELECTRICAL SYSTEM & COMPONENT TESTING

For electrical system and component testing, see appropriate HYDRA-MATIC 4L30-E ELECTRONIC CONTROLS article.

TRANSMISSION TESTING

NOTE: *Before beginning any testing, check fluid level, fluid condition and shift linkage adjustment. Check for any stored diagnostic trouble codes. See RETRIEVING DIAGNOSTIC TROUBLE CODES under SELF-DIAGNOSTIC SYSTEM in appropriate HYDRA-MATIC 4L30-E ELECTRONIC CONTROLS article.*

ROAD TEST

NOTE: *If road test is performed with engine coolant temperature less than 158°F (70°C), shift speeds will be delayed during light throttle application and occur at a slightly higher speed. When TECH 1 scan tool is connected to data link connector, maximum line pressure will be obtained, resulting in harsh shifts.*

NOTE: *Engine coolant temperature must be greater than 158°F (70°C) for TCC operation. The TCC operates in 2nd gear kickdown when engine coolant temperature is greater than 158°F (70°C). TCC operates in 2nd, 3rd and 4th gear when transmission fluid temperature is greater than 284°F (140°C).*

1) If a stored diagnostic trouble code is present, clear diagnostic trouble codes from control module memory. See CLEARING DIAGNOSTIC TROUBLE CODES under SELF-DIAGNOSTICS SYSTEM in appropriate HYDRA-MATIC 4L30-E ELECTRONIC CONTROLS article.

2) Start and warm engine to normal operating temperature. Road test vehicle and check for abnormal noise, clutch slippage and shift firmness. Specified clutch and brake are applied in designated gear. See CLUTCH & BAND APPLICATION table.

3) Ensure upshift and downshift speeds are correct in relation to throttle opening and position of POWER or WINTER mode switches mounted on center console, near gearshift lever. See appropriate UPSHIFT SPECIFICATIONS and DOWNSHIFT SPECIFICATIONS tables.

4) Ensure Torque Converter Clutch (TCC) operation is correct to gear application in relation to throttle opening with shift lever in "D" position. See appropriate TCC SPECIFICATIONS table.

5) During road test, if CHECK TRANS light on instrument panel starts flashing, a diagnostic trouble code is stored in control module memory. Check stored diagnostic trouble code and repair as necessary.

6) During road test, if a problem is present, but CHECK TRANS light on instrument panel did not flash, turn engine off. Disconnect control module harness connectors. See Fig. 3 or 4.

7) Repeat road test, while manually shifting the transmission. With shift lever in "L" position, transmission should remain in 1st gear. With shift lever in "2" position, transmission should remain in 3rd gear. With shift lever in "3" or "D" position, transmission should remain in 4th gear. Shut engine off. Reconnect control module harness connectors.

8) If problem is still present, see SYMPTOM DIAGNOSIS under TROUBLE SHOOTING. If problem is not present with harness connectors disconnected at control module, check wiring connections and control module ground circuits.

CLUTCH & BAND APPLICATION

Shift Lever Position	Elements In Use
"P"	Overrun Clutch
"R"	Overdrive Roller Clutch, Overrun Clutch, Reverse Clutch & Sprag Assembly
"N"	Overrun Clutch
"D"	
1st Gear	Overdrive Roller Clutch, Overrun Clutch, Sprag Assembly & Brake Band
2nd Gear	Overdrive Roller Clutch, Overrun Clutch, 2nd Clutch & Brake Band
3rd Gear	Overdrive Roller Clutch, Overrun Clutch, 3rd Clutch & 2nd Clutch
4th Gear	2nd Clutch, 3rd Clutch & 4th Clutch
"3"	
1st Gear	Overdrive Roller Clutch, Overrun Clutch, Sprag Assembly & Brake Band
2nd Gear	Overdrive Roller Clutch, Overrun Clutch, 2nd Clutch & Brake Band
3rd Gear	Overdrive Roller Clutch, Overrun Clutch, 3rd Clutch & 2nd Clutch
"2"	
1st Gear	Overdrive Roller Clutch, Overrun Clutch, 3rd Clutch, Sprag Assembly & Brake Band
2nd Gear	Overdrive Roller Clutch, Overrun Clutch, 2nd Clutch & Brake Band
"L"	
1st Gear	Overdrive Roller Clutch, Overrun Clutch, 3rd Clutch, Sprag Assembly & Brake Band

TCC SPECIFICATIONS (1995 PASSPORT & RODEO) [1]

Shift Mode	Gear Range	MPH
TCC ON		
Normal	2nd	47-50
	3rd	34-38
	4th	40-45
Power	2nd	47-50
	3rd	50-53
	4th	50-53
TCC OFF		
Normal	2nd	43-47
	3rd	29-33
	4th	37-41
Power	2nd	43-47
	3rd	44-48
	4th	47-50

[1] – Specification is taken with throttle opening at 9 percent, and gearshift lever in "D" position.

TCC SPECIFICATIONS (1995 TROOPER) [1]

Shift Mode	Gear Range	MPH
TCC ON		
Normal	2nd	45-48
	3rd	33-37
	4th	39-43
Power	2nd	45-49
	3rd	48-52
	4th	48-52
TCC OFF		
Normal	2nd	42-45
	3rd	28-32
	4th	36-40
Power	2nd	42-45
	3rd	42-46
	4th	45-48

[1] – Specification is taken with throttle opening at 9 percent, and gearshift lever in "D" position.

TCC SPECIFICATIONS (1996 PASSPORT & RODEO) ¹

Shift Mode	Gear Range	MPH
TCC ON		
Normal	2nd	49-53
	3rd	36-40
	4th	43-47
Power	2nd	49-53
	3rd	52-56
	4th	52-56
TCC OFF		
Normal	2nd	46-50
	3rd	30-34
	4th	40-44
Power	2nd	46-50
	3rd	47-51
	4th	50-54

¹ – Specification is taken with throttle opening at 9 percent, and gearshift lever in "D" position.

TCC SPECIFICATIONS (1996 SLX & TROOPER) ¹

Shift Mode	Gear Range	MPH
TCC ON		
Normal	2nd	45-48
	3rd	33-37
	4th	48-52
Power	2nd	45-48
	3rd	48-52
	4th	48-52
TCC OFF		
Normal	2nd	42-45
	3rd	28-32
	4th	45-49
Power	2nd	42-45
	3rd	42-46
	4th	45-48

¹ – Specification is taken with throttle opening at 9 percent, and gearshift lever in "D" position.

UPSHIFT SPECIFICATIONS (1995-96 PASSPORT & RODEO)

Shift Lever Position	1st-2nd MPH	2nd-3rd MPH	3rd-4th MPH
Normal Mode			
"D"			
Full Throttle	32-35	64-68	96-99
Half Throttle	21-24	37-41	62-66
"3"			
Full Throttle	32-35	64-68	
Half Throttle	21-24	37-41	
"2"			
Full Throttle	32-35		
Half Throttle	21-24		
Power Mode			
"D"			
Full Throttle	32-35	64-68	109-113
Half Throttle	24-28	48-52	80-84
"3"			
Full Throttle	32-35	64-68	
Half Throttle	24-28	48-52	
"2"			
Full Throttle	32-35		
Half Throttle	24-28		

UPSHIFT SPECIFICATIONS (1995 TROOPER)

Shift Lever Position	1st-2nd MPH	2nd-3rd MPH	3rd-4th MPH
Normal Mode			
"D"			
Full Throttle	30-34	62-66	92-96
Half Throttle	20-24	36-40	60-64
"3"			
Full Throttle	30-34	62-66	
Half Throttle	20-24	36-40	
"2"			
Full Throttle	30-34		
Half Throttle	20-24		
Power Mode			
"D"			
Full Throttle	30-34	62-66	105-109
Half Throttle	23-27	46-50	77-81
"3"			
Full Throttle	30-34	62-66	
Half Throttle	23-27	46-50	
"2"			
Full Throttle	30-34		
Half Throttle	23-27		

UPSHIFT SPECIFICATIONS (1996 SLX & TROOPER)

Shift Lever Position	1st-2nd MPH	2nd-3rd MPH	3rd-4th MPH
Normal Mode			
"D"			
Full Throttle	24-28	50-54	81-85
Half Throttle	18-22	36-40	70-74
"3"			
Full Throttle	30-34	62-66	
Half Throttle	20-24	36-40	
"2"			
Full Throttle	30-34		
Half Throttle	20-24		
Power Mode			
"D"			
Full Throttle	27-31	52-56	82-86
Half Throttle	23-27	45-49	78-82
"3"			
Full Throttle	30-34	62-66	
Half Throttle	23-27	46-50	
"2"			
Full Throttle	30-34		
Half Throttle	23-27		

DOWNSHIFT SPECIFICATIONS (1995-96 PASSPORT & RODEO)

Shift Lever Position	4th-3rd MPH	3rd-2nd MPH	2nd-1st MPH
Normal Mode			
"D"			
Full Throttle	90-94	56-60	25-29
Half Throttle	43-47	22-26	10-14
Closed Throttle	17-21	10-14	8-12
"3"			
Full Throttle		56-60	25-29
Half Throttle		22-26	10-14
Closed Throttle		10-14	8-12
"2"			
Full Throttle		61-65	26-30
Half Throttle		61-65	10-14
Closed Throttle		53-57	8-12
Power Mode			
"D"			
Full Throttle	103-107	58-62	26-30
Half Throttle	63-67	34-38	14-17
Closed Throttle	30-33	16-19	8-12
"3"			
Full Throttle		58-62	26-30
Half Throttle		34-38	14-17
Closed Throttle		16-19	8-12
"2"			
Full Throttle		61-65	26-30
Half Throttle		61-65	14-17
Closed Throttle		53-57	8-12

DOWNSHIFT SPECIFICATIONS (1995 TROOPER)

Shift Lever Position	4th-3rd MPH	3rd-2nd MPH	2nd-1st MPH
Normal Mode			
"D"			
Full Throttle	87-91	54-58	24-28
Half Throttle	42-46	21-25	9-13
Closed Throttle	17-20	9-13	8-12
"3"			
Full Throttle		54-58	24-28
Half Throttle		21-25	9-13
Closed Throttle		9-13	8-12
"2"			
Full Throttle		59-63	25-29
Half Throttle		59-63	9-13
Closed Throttle		51-55	8-12
Power Mode			
"D"			
Full Throttle	100-104	56-60	25-29
Half Throttle	61-65	33-37	13-17
Closed Throttle	29-32	15-19	8-12
"3"			
Full Throttle		56-60	25-29
Half Throttle		33-37	13-17
Closed Throttle		15-19	8-12
"2"			
Full Throttle		59-63	25-29
Half Throttle		59-63	13-17
Closed Throttle		51-55	8-12

DOWNSHIFT SPECIFICATIONS (1996 SLX & TROOPER)

Shift Lever Position	4th-3rd MPH	3rd-2nd MPH	2nd-1st MPH
Normal Mode			
"D"			
Full Throttle	69-73	44-48	9-13
Half Throttle	40-44	20-24	14-18
Closed Throttle	17-21	12-16	8-12
"3"			
Full Throttle		54-58	24-28
Half Throttle		21-25	9-13
Closed Throttle		9-13	8-12
"2"			
Full Throttle		59-63	25-29
Half Throttle		59-63	9-13
Closed Throttle		51-55	8-12
Power Mode			
"D"			
Full Throttle	74-78	46-50	19-23
Half Throttle	58-62	31-35	13-17
Closed Throttle	28-32	14-18	8-12
"3"			
Full Throttle		56-60	25-29
Half Throttle		33-37	13-17
Closed Throttle		15-19	8-12
"2"			
Full Throttle		59-63	25-29
Half Throttle		59-63	13-17
Closed Throttle		51-55	8-12

TORQUE CONVERTER STALL SPEED TEST

CAUTION: DO NOT perform torque converter stall speed test for more than 5 seconds or transmission may be damaged. Transmission must be cooled between tests by placing gearshift lever in "N" position and operating engine at 1200 RPM for at least one minute.

1) Apply parking brake. Block all wheels. Connect tachometer and start engine. Warm engine to normal operating temperature. Ensure transmission fluid level is correct.
2) Fully depress brake pedal. Place gearshift lever in "D" position. Fully depress accelerator for no more than 5 seconds and note highest engine speed. This is the torque converter stall speed.
3) Place gearshift lever in "N" position. Operate engine at 1200 RPM for at least one minute to cool transmission. Repeat test procedure with gearshift lever in "3", "2", "L" and "R" positions.
4) Ensure torque converter stall speed is within specification. See TORQUE CONVERTER STALL SPEED SPECIFICATIONS table. If torque converter stall speed is not within specification, an internal torque converter or transmission failure is present.

TORQUE CONVERTER STALL SPEED SPECIFICATIONS

Application	Engine RPM
Passport & Rodeo	2000-2300
1995 Trooper	
DOHC	2050-2350
SOHC	2000-2300
1996 SLX & Trooper	
SOHC	2000-2300

HYDRAULIC PRESSURE TEST

Pressure Test Preparation – Warm engine to normal operating temperature. Ensure transmission fluid level is correct. Apply parking brake. Block all wheels.

NOTE: If TECH 1 scan tool is connected to data link connector, or if transmission is in back-up mode, maximum line pressure will be obtained.

Line Pressure Test – 1) With engine off, remove pressure tap plug from line pressure tap, located near torque converter housing on driver's side of transmission case, just above adapter case oil pan. *See Fig. 6.*

2) Install oil pressure gauge on line pressure tap. Start engine and allow it to idle.

3) Line pressure is checked in each transmission shift mode with engine idling and at torque converter stall speed with gearshift lever in specified position. Shift mode may be selected by POWER or WINTER mode switch mounted on center console, near gearshift lever. When neither power or winter mode are selected, transmission will remain in normal mode.

4) With engine idling, place gearshift lever in specified position and note line pressure. See LINE PRESSURE SPECIFICATIONS table. Line pressure should be within specification. See LINE PRESSURE SPECIFICATIONS table.

5) To check line pressure at torque converter stall speed, fully depress brake pedal. Place gearshift lever in "D" position and in proper shift mode. Fully depress accelerator no more than 5 seconds and note line pressure reading.

CAUTION: *DO NOT perform line pressure test for more than 5 seconds at torque converter stall speed or transmission may be damaged. Transmission must be cooled between pressure tests by placing gearshift lever in "N" position and operating engine at 1200 RPM for at least one minute.*

---

6) Place gearshift lever in "N" position. Operate engine at 1200 RPM for at least one minute to cool transmission. Repeat line pressure test procedure at torque converter stall speed with gearshift lever in "3", "2", "L" and "R" positions in proper shift mode.

7) Line pressure should be within specification. See appropriate LINE PRESSURE SPECIFICATIONS table. If line pressure is not within specification, see LINE PRESSURE TROUBLE SHOOTING table. Turn engine off.

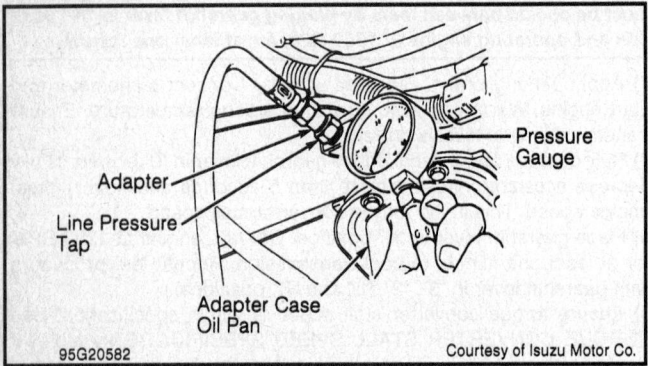

95G20582   Courtesy of Isuzu Motor Co.

Fig. 6: Checking Line Pressure

LINE PRESSURE SPECIFICATIONS (1995-96 BMW)

Engine RPM	Shift Lever Position	Line Pressure psi (kPa)
1500	"P" Or "N"	152 (1048)

LINE PRESSURE SPECIFICATIONS (1995 PASSPORT & RODEO)

Shift Mode	Shift Lever Position	Line Pressure psi (kPa)
Engine Idling		
Normal & Power	"D", "3", "2" & "L"	48 (330)
Winter	"D"	46-52 (316-358)
Normal, Power & Winter	"R"	65-74 (450-508)
At Stall Speed		
Normal & Power	"D", "3", "2" & "L"	150-161 (1031-1111)
Winter	"D"	150-161 (1031-1111)
Normal, Power & Winter	"R"	210-227 (1449-1562)

8) Remove pressure gauge and adapter. Apply Loctite 242 on threads of pressure tap plug. Install and tighten pressure tap plug to specification. See TORQUE SPECIFICATIONS.

LINE PRESSURE SPECIFICATIONS (1995 1/2-96 PASSPORT & RODEO)

Shift Mode	Shift Lever Position	Line Pressure psi (kPa)
Engine Idling		
Normal & Power	"D", "3", "2" & "L"	55 (380)
Winter	"D"	46-52 (316-358)
Normal, Power & Winter	"R"	68-76 (470-520)
At Stall Speed		
Normal & Power	"D", "3", "2" & "L"	150-161 (1031-1111)
Winter	"D"	150-161 (1031-1111)
Normal, Power & Winter	"R"	210-227 (1449-1562)

LINE PRESSURE SPECIFICATIONS (1995-96 SLX & TROOPER)

Shift Mode	Shift Lever Position	Line Pressure psi (kPa)
Engine Idling		
Normal & Power	"D", "3", "2" & "L"	55 (380)
Winter	"D"	46-52 (316-358)
Normal, Power & Winter	"R"	68-76 (470-520)
At Stall Speed		
Normal & Power	"D", "3", "2" & "L"	150-161 (1031-1111)
Winter	"D"	150-161 (1031-1111)
Normal, Power & Winter	"R"	210-227 (1449-1562)

LINE PRESSURE TEST TROUBLE SHOOTING

Application	Probable Cause
High Line Pressure [1]	Defective Throttle Position (TP) Sensor, Force Motor Solenoid Plunger Stuck, Defective Force Motor Solenoid Or Wiring Circuit, Stuck Feed Limit Valve In Adapter Case Valve Body Loose Torque Converter Housing Bolts, Stuck Pressure Regulator Valve Or Boost Valve In Oil Pump, Missing Check Balls In Valve Bodies, Defective Seals Or Gaskets
Low Line Pressure	Low Fluid Level, Defective Throttle Position (TP) Sensor, Restricted Or Damaged Oil Filter, Force Motor Solenoid Plunger Stuck, Stuck Feed Limit Valve In Adapter Case Valve Body, Loose Torque Converter Housing Bolts, Stuck Pressure Regulator Valve Or Boost Valve In Oil Pump, Restricted Pressure Regulator Valve Oil Passages, Defective Oil Pump, Missing Check Balls In Valve Bodies, Defective Seals Or Gaskets

[1] – When TECH 1 scan tool is connected to data link connector, or if transmission is in back-up mode, maximum line pressure will be obtained.

ON-VEHICLE SERVICE
ELECTRICAL COMPONENTS

For servicing of electrical components, see appropriate HYDRA-MATIC 4L30-E ELECTRONIC CONTROLS article.

BRAKE BAND ADJUSTMENT

1) Drain fluid. Remove bolts, main case oil pan and gasket. *See Fig. 8.* Remove bolts, servo cover and gasket. Loosen lock nut on servo adjusting screw.

2) Using an INCH-lb. torque wrench, tighten servo adjusting screw to 40 INCH lbs. (4.5 N.m). Back off servo adjusting screw 5 revolutions. Hold sleeve on servo piston. Tighten lock nut to 14 ft. lbs. (19 N.m). Ensure servo adjusting screw does not rotate while tightening lock nut.

3) Using a NEW gasket, install servo cover. Install and tighten bolts to specification. See TORQUE SPECIFICATIONS. Using a NEW gasket, install main case oil pan. Install and tighten bolts to specification. Fill transmission with Dexron-III ATF.

SHIFT LOCK CABLE ADJUSTMENT

Key lock system prevents ignition switch from being placed in LOCK position unless gearshift lever is in "P" position. Shift lock cable is connected between gearshift lever and ignition switch. When gearshift lever is placed in "P" position, check that ignition switch may be placed in LOCK position. If ignition switch cannot be placed in LOCK position, perform the following shift lock cable adjustment.

1) Place ignition switch in LOCK position. Ensure gearshift lever is in "P" position. Remove console components for access to shift lock cable at gearshift lever.
2) Adjust cable screw cap on gearshift lever side of shift lock cable to provide slack in shift lock cable so a gap of .059-.098" (1.50-2.5 mm) exists between rod on steering lock side and the stopper. See Fig. 7.
3) Tighten lock nut "A" against bracket while pulling cable screw cap toward instrument panel side (front) of center console. See Fig. 7. This prevents slack in the inner cable.
4) Loosen lock nut "A" 2 turn to provide slack in the inner cable. Hold lock nut "A" and tighten lock nut "B" to 35 INCH lbs. (4 N.m). To recheck system operation, ensure gearshift lever cannot be moved from "P" position with ignition switch in LOCK position.
5) Ensure ignition switch can be turned to LOCK position only when gearshift lever is in "P" position. If operation is not as specified, readjust shift lock cable.

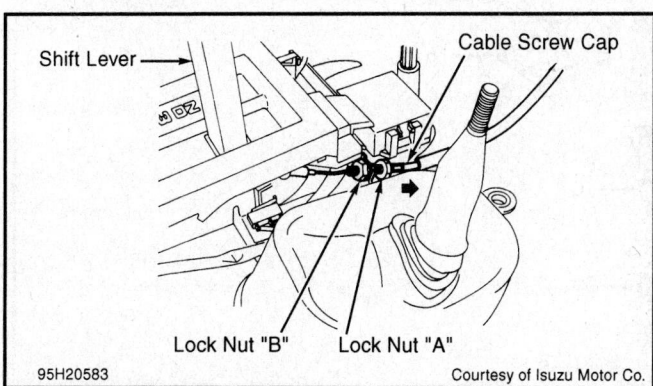

Fig. 7: Adjusting Shift Lock Cable

REMOVAL & INSTALLATION

ELECTRICAL COMPONENTS

For servicing of electrical components, see appropriate HYDRA-MATIC 4L30-E ELECTRONIC CONTROLS article.

TRANSFER CASE

See appropriate TRANSFER CASE article in AXLE SHAFTS & TRANSFER CASES section.

TRANSMISSION

See appropriate AUTOMATIC TRANSMISSION REMOVAL article in TRANSMISSION SERVICING section.

TORQUE CONVERTER

Torque converter cannot be serviced and must be replaced if defective.

NOTE: For torque converter stall speed test, see TORQUE CONVERTER STALL SPEED TEST under TRANSMISSION TESTING.

TRANSMISSION DISASSEMBLY

VALVE BODIES & INTERNAL COMPONENTS

Disassembly – 1) Remove torque converter. Remove "O" ring from end of turbine shaft. On 4WD models, remove transfer case from rear of transmission.
2) On all models, remove screws, cover and mode switch and wiring harness. See Fig. 8. Remove bolts, adapter case oil pan and gasket.
3) Disconnect electrical connectors at solenoids on adapter case valve body. Note location of adapter case valve body bolts for reassembly reference. Remove bolts, adapter case valve body, transfer plate and transfer plate gaskets.
4) Remove wiring harness for solenoids on adapter case valve body. Remove bolts, main case oil pan, magnet and gasket. Remove bolts and oil filter.
5) Remove bolts and manual detent. Disconnect wiring harness at solenoids on main valve body and the case 4-pin connector. Remove 4-pin connector.
6) Remove bolts, servo cover and gasket. Position transmission case with main valve body facing upward. Note location of main valve body bolts for reassembly reference. Note position of manual valve link, as long end fits into manual valve and short end fits into range selector.
7) Remove bolts, main valve body with manual valve link, transfer plate gaskets and transfer plate. Note location of 2 check balls in transmission case. See Fig. 9. Remove check balls from transmission case.
8) Using spring compressor, compress servo piston and return spring. Remove servo piston retaining snap ring. Slowly release spring compressor. Remove servo piston, apply rod and return spring. See Fig. 8.
9) Remove bolt and speed sensor with "O" ring from extension housing. On 2WD models, remove drive shaft companion flange nut, drive shaft companion flange and "O" ring from rear of transmission. On all models, remove bolts, extension housing and gasket from transmission case.
10) Remove retaining ring, speed sensor drive gear and parking lock gear with seal ring from output shaft. Position transmission case in vertical position with torque converter housing facing upward.
11) If removing oil pump assembly from torque converter housing, loosen but DO NOT remove the 5 inner bolts on torque converter housing. These are the oil pump assembly-to-torque converter housing bolts.
12) On all applications, remove torque converter housing-to-adapter case bolts. These are the 7 outer bolts. Remove torque converter housing, outer seal ring, oil pump, gasket and selective thrust washer.
13) Remove 4th clutch retainer from turbine shaft. See Fig. 10. Pull upward on turbine shaft and lift overrun clutch assembly and 4th clutch plates and clutch discs from transmission case. Remove thrust bearing, overdrive internal gear and thrust washer.
14) Remove adapter case and center support assembly with 4th clutch piston. See Fig. 11. Remove seal ring, selective thrust washer and "O" rings from transmission case.
15) Using spring compressor, compress 4th clutch retainer and spring assembly. Remove snap ring from adapter case. Remove spring compressor, snap ring and 4th clutch retainer and spring assembly.
16) To remove 4th clutch piston from adapter case, hold adapter case and pull 4th clutch piston from adapter case. Remove converter housing-to-main case bolts.
17) While holding intermediate shaft, twist and pull out 2nd and 3rd clutch assemblies with reverse clutch plates and clutch discs from transmission case while holding onto output shaft. See Fig. 11. Separate 2nd and 3rd clutch assemblies. Remove thrust washer, reverse clutch plates and pressure plate.
18) Remove bearing, washer, planetary carrier and thrust bearing assembly from transmission case. See Fig. 11. Remove reaction sun gear, needle bearing, brake drum, brake band and thrust bearing assembly.
19) For reassembly reference, measure height of spring pin in relation to transmission case. Spring pin retains selector shaft in transmission case. See Fig. 12.

AUTOMATIC TRANSMISSIONS
Hydra-Matic 4L30-E (Cont.)

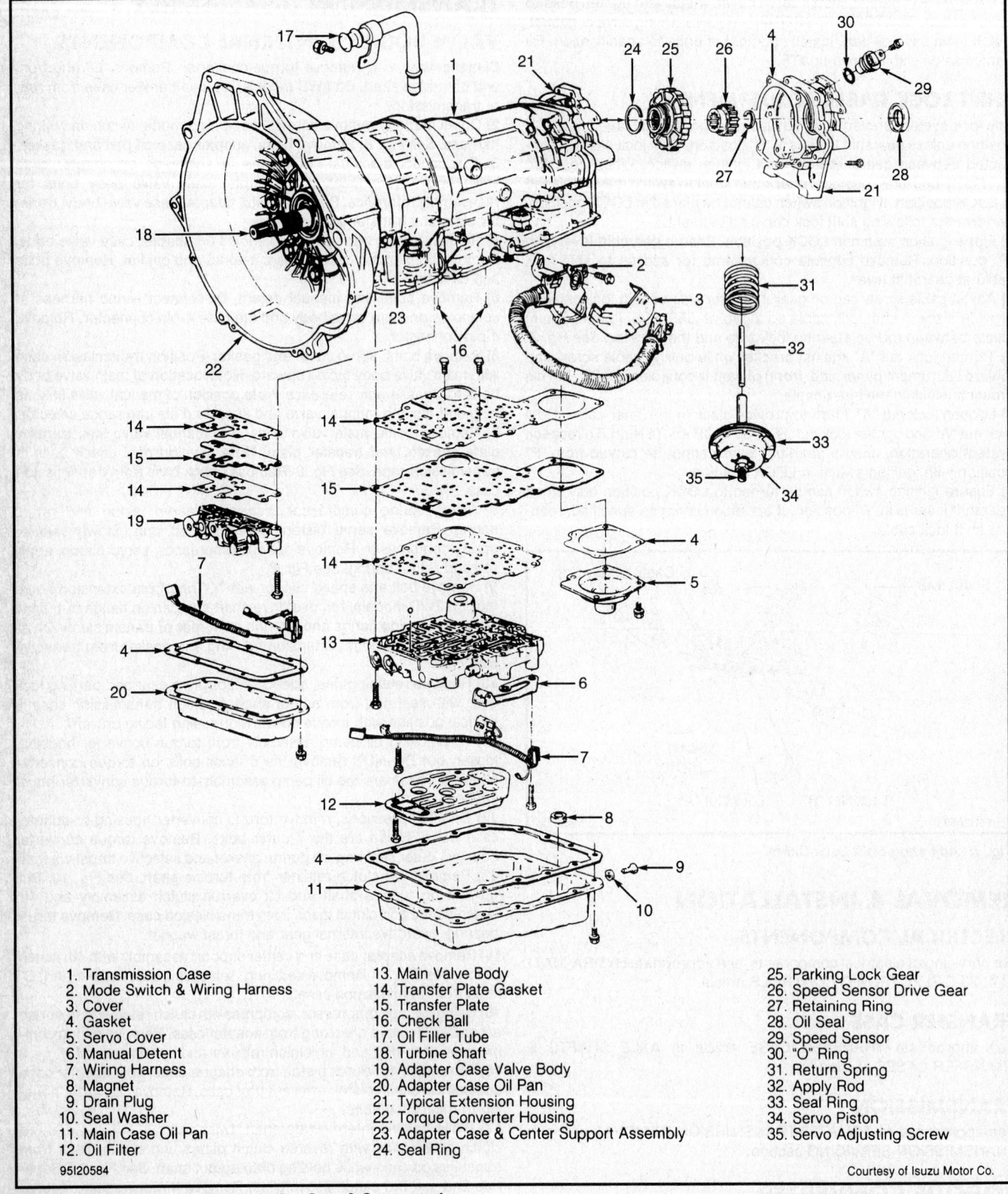

1. Transmission Case	13. Main Valve Body	25. Parking Lock Gear
2. Mode Switch & Wiring Harness	14. Transfer Plate Gasket	26. Speed Sensor Drive Gear
3. Cover	15. Transfer Plate	27. Retaining Ring
4. Gasket	16. Check Ball	28. Oil Seal
5. Servo Cover	17. Oil Filler Tube	29. Speed Sensor
6. Manual Detent	18. Turbine Shaft	30. "O" Ring
7. Wiring Harness	19. Adapter Case Valve Body	31. Return Spring
8. Magnet	20. Adapter Case Oil Pan	32. Apply Rod
9. Drain Plug	21. Typical Extension Housing	33. Seal Ring
10. Seal Washer	22. Torque Converter Housing	34. Servo Piston
11. Main Case Oil Pan	23. Adapter Case & Center Support Assembly	35. Servo Adjusting Screw
12. Oil Filter	24. Seal Ring	

95120584

Courtesy of Isuzu Motor Co.

Fig. 8: Exploded View Of Transmission Case & Components

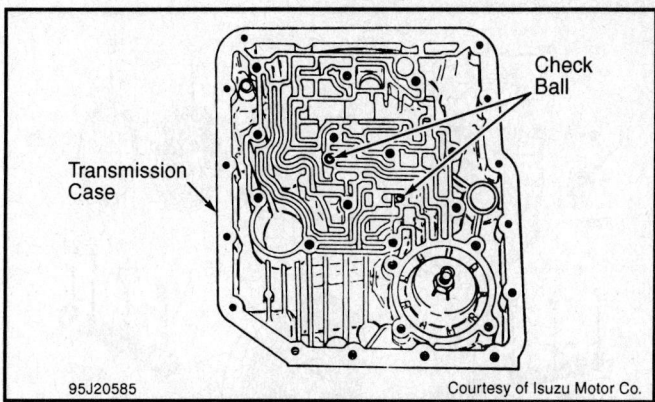

Fig. 9: Identifying Check Ball Locations In Transmission Case

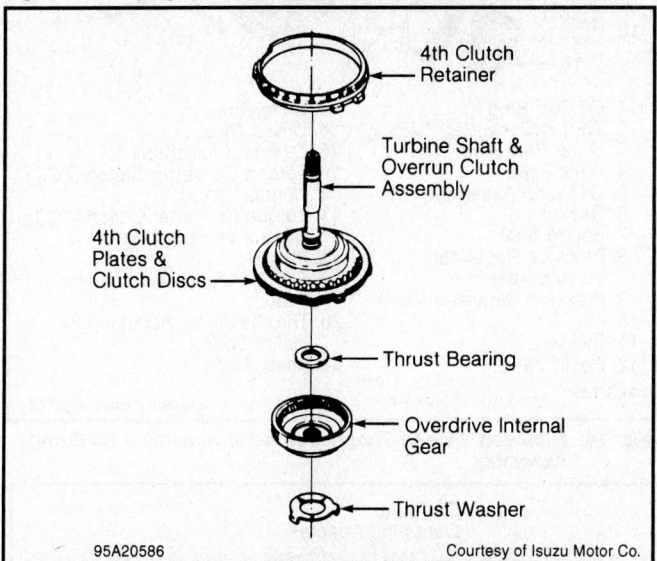

Fig. 10: *Removing & Installing 4th Clutch Retainer, Turbine Shaft, Overrun Clutch Housing, 4th Clutch Plates, Overdrive Internal Gear, Thrust Bearing & Thrust Washer*

20) Insert wire into center of spring pin to prevent spring pin from collapsing during removal. Protect machined surface of transmission case. Remove spring pin.

21) Remove selector shaft nut from end of selector shaft. Remove parking lock and range selector lever with actuator rod from selector shaft. Remove selector shaft.

COMPONENT DISASSEMBLY & REASSEMBLY

PLANETARY CARRIER

Cleaning & Inspection – 1) Clean components with solvent and dry with compressed air. Inspect all gears and shafts for chipped gears, excessive wear and damage. Replace components as necessary.

2) Using feeler gauge, measure planetary carrier pinion end clearance. See Fig. 13. Planetary carrier pinion end clearance should be .005-.035" (.13-.89 mm). Replace planetary carrier if pinion end clearance is not within specification.

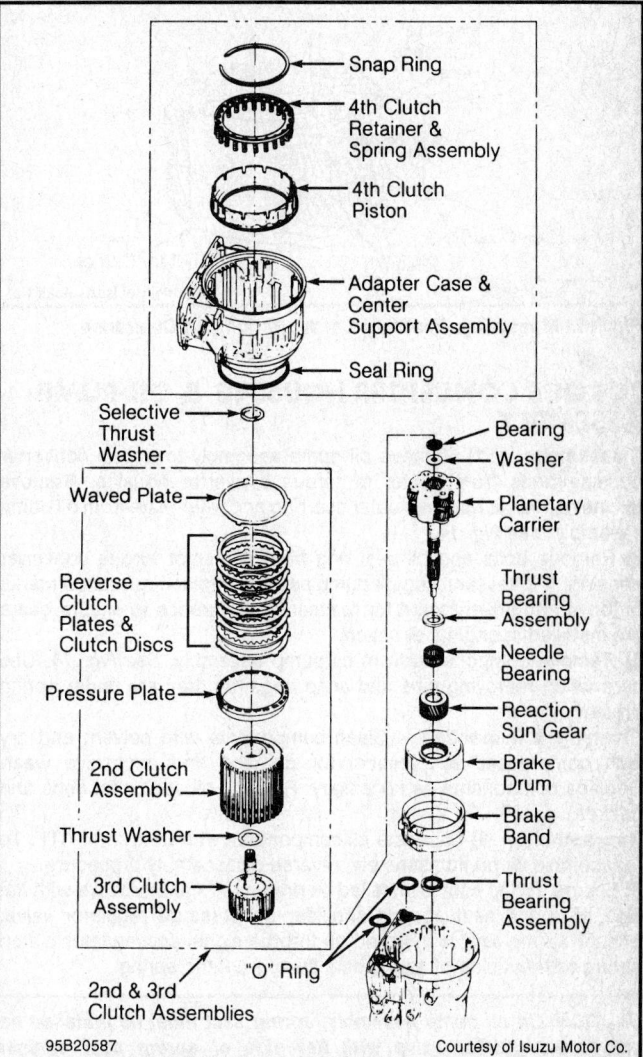

Fig. 11: *Removing & Installing Adapter Case, 2nd & 3rd Clutch Assemblies, Planetary Carrier & Components*

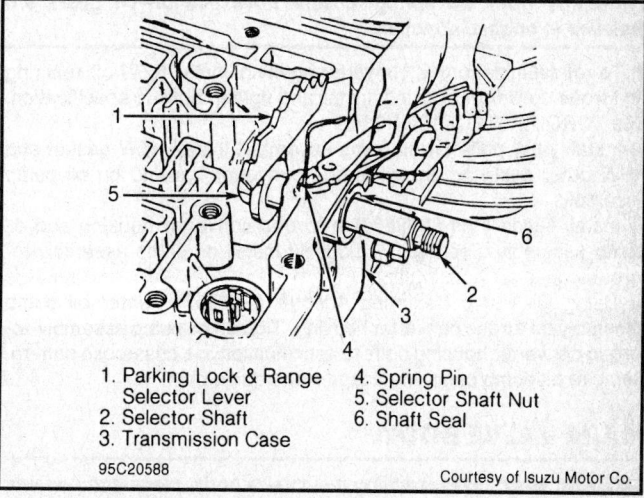

1. Parking Lock & Range Selector Lever
2. Selector Shaft
3. Transmission Case
4. Spring Pin
5. Selector Shaft Nut
6. Shaft Seal

Fig. 12: *Identifying Spring Pin, Selector Shaft, Parking Lock & Range Selector Lever*

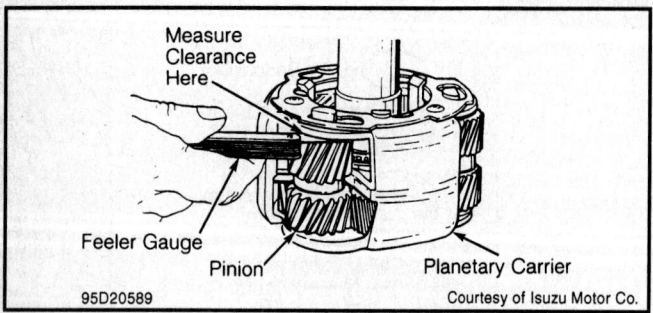

Fig. 13: Measuring Planetary Carrier Pinion End Clearance

TORQUE CONVERTER HOUSING & OIL PUMP ASSEMBLY

Disassembly – 1) Remove oil pump assembly-to-torque converter housing bolts from center of torque converter housing. Remove torque converter housing, outer seal ring and wear plate from oil pump assembly. *See Fig. 14.*

2) Remove bolts and oil seal ring from center of torque converter housing. If disassembling oil pump assembly, place reference marks on drive and driven gears for reassembly reference to ensure gears are installed in original direction.

3) Remove components from oil pump assembly. *See Fig. 14.* Use care when removing pins and snap rings, as they are under spring pressure.

Cleaning & Inspection – Clean components with solvent and dry with compressed air. Inspect for damage and excessive wear. Replace components as necessary. Replace oil seal, seal rings and gasket.

Reassembly – 1) Lubricate all components with Dexron-III ATF. To reassemble oil pump assembly, reverse disassembly procedure.

2) Ensure spring seat is installed on pressure regulator valve with flat side of spring seat against shoulder on pressure regulator valve. Ensure spring seat is installed on throttle signal accumulator piston spring with flat side of spring seat away from the spring.

CAUTION: On oil pump assembly, spring seat must be installed on pressure regulator valve with flat side of spring seat against shoulder on pressure regulator valve. Spring seat must be installed on throttle signal accumulator piston spring with flat side of spring seat away from the spring. Ensure drive and driven gears are installed in original direction.

3) To reassemble torque converter housing, install NEW oil seal ring on torque converter housing. Install and tighten bolts to specification. See TORQUE SPECIFICATIONS.

4) Install wear plate on oil pump assembly. Install NEW gasket and NEW outer seal ring. Install torque converter housing on oil pump assembly.

5) Install Guide Pins (J-38588) in torque converter housing and oil pump assembly. *See Fig. 15.* Loosely install oil pump assembly-to-torque converter housing bolts.

6) Using Oil Pump Centering Adapter (J-38557), center oil pump assembly on torque converter housing. Tighten oil pump assembly-to-torque converter housing bolts to specification in a crisscross pattern. Remove oil pump centering adapter and guide pins.

MAIN VALVE BODY

CAUTION: When disassembling main valve body, place components in order and mark spring locations for reassembly reference. DO NOT use force to remove components from main valve body. Remove solenoids by pulling on metal tip. DO NOT pull on electrical connector housing on solenoid.

Disassembly – 1) Remove transfer plate-to-main valve body bolts. Remove transfer plate gaskets and transfer plate from main valve body. Note location of check ball in main valve body. *See Fig. 16.*

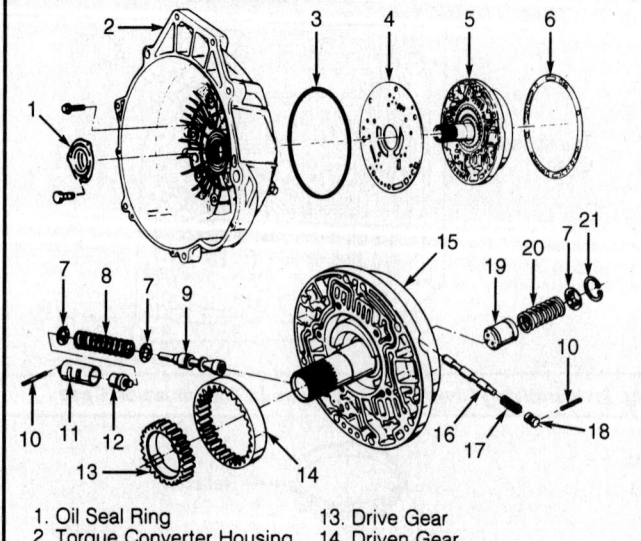

1. Oil Seal Ring
2. Torque Converter Housing
3. Outer Seal Ring
4. Wear Plate
5. Oil Pump Assembly
6. Gasket
7. Spring Seat
8. Pressure Regulator Valve Spring
9. Pressure Regulator Valve
10. Pin
11. Sleeve
12. Boost Valve
13. Drive Gear
14. Driven Gear
15. Oil Pump Assembly
16. Torque Converter Clutch (TCC) Control Valve
17. Torque Converter Clutch (TCC) Control Valve Spring
18. Plug
19. Throttle Signal Accumulator Piston
20. Throttle Signal Accumulator Piston Spring
21. Snap Ring

Fig. 14: Exploded View Of Torque Converter Housing & Oil Pump Assembly

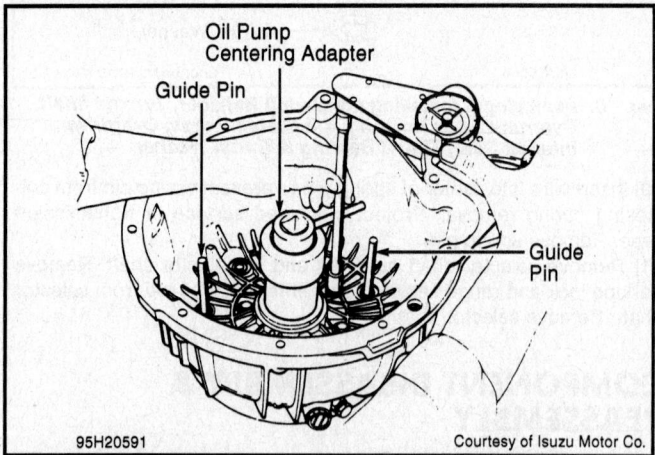

Fig. 15: Installing Torque Converter Housing On Oil Pump Assembly

2) Remove components from main valve body. Use care when removing pins and plugs, as components are under spring tension.

Cleaning & Inspection – Clean components with solvent and dry with compressed air. Inspect components for damage or signs of wear. Replace components as required. Ensure valves slide freely in bores on main valve body.

Reassembly – 1) Lubricate all components with Dexron-III ATF. To reassemble, reverse disassembly procedure using NEW transfer plate gaskets. Ensure components are installed in correct location. *See Fig. 16.*

2) Use guide pins in main valve body when installing transfer plate gaskets and transfer plate on main valve body. Install and tighten transfer plate-to-main valve body bolts to specification. See TORQUE SPECIFICATIONS.

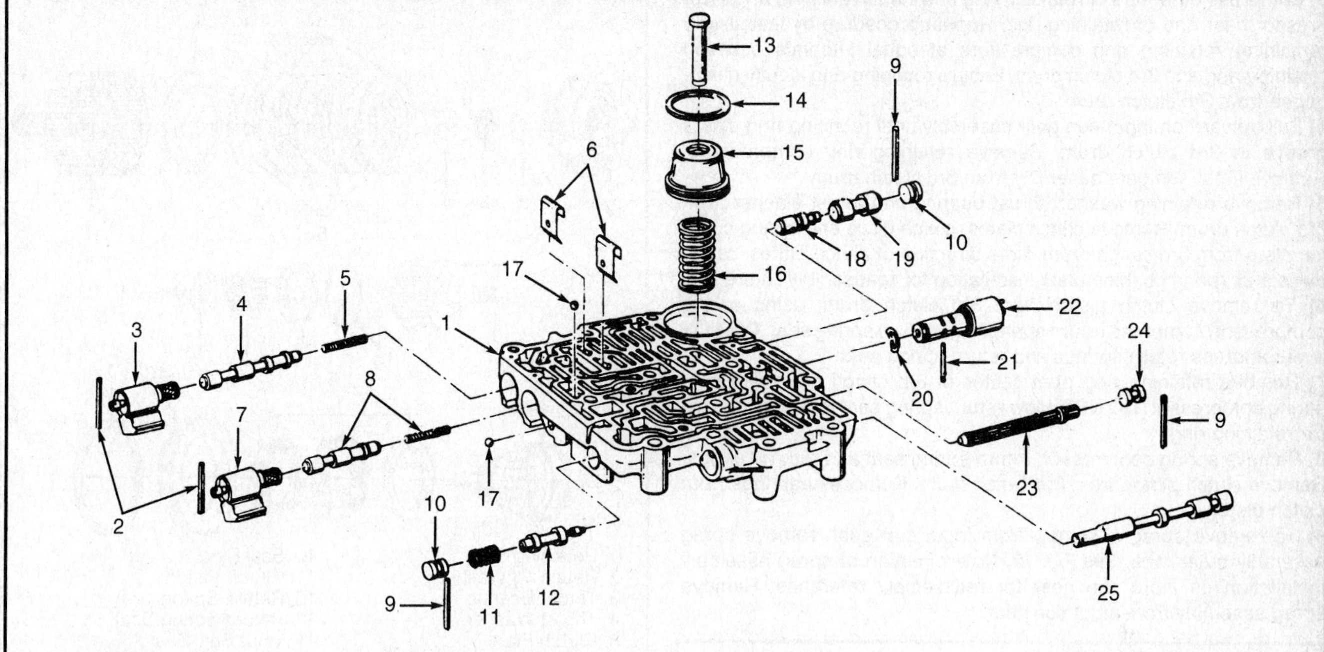

1. Main Valve Body	8. 2-3 Shift Valve & Spring
2. Spring Pin	9. Spring Pin
3. 1-2/3-4 Shift Solenoid	10. Plug
4. 1-2/3-4 Shift Valve	11. Low Pressure Control Valve Spring
5. 1-2/3-4 Shift Valve Spring	12. Low Pressure Control Valve
6. Retainer	13. Pin
7. 2-3 Shift Solenoid	

14. Seal	20. Waved Washer
15. Accumulator Piston	21. Pin
16. Spring	22. Band Control Solenoid
17. Check Ball	23. Screen Assembly
18. 1-2 Accumulator Control Valve	24. Plug
19. 1-2 Accumulator Valve	25. Manual Valve

95I20592

Courtesy of Isuzu Motor Co.

Fig. 16: Exploded View Of Main Valve Body

ADAPTER CASE VALVE BODY

CAUTION: When disassembling adapter case valve body, place components in order, and mark spring locations for reassembly reference. DO NOT use force to remove components from adapter case valve body.

Disassembly – 1) Remove components from adapter case valve body. See Fig. 17.

2) Use care when removing spring pins and plugs, as components are under spring tension. When removing plug for screen assembly, screw a 5-mm bolt in center of plug to aid in plug removal.

Cleaning & Inspection – Clean components with solvent and dry with compressed air. Inspect components for damage or signs of wear. Replace components as required. Ensure valves slide freely in bores on adapter case valve body.

Reassembly – 1) Lubricate all components with Dexron-III ATF. To reassemble, reverse disassembly procedure using NEW "O" rings.

2) Ensure force motor solenoid is positioned with electrical connections on solenoid facing toward mounting surface on adapter case valve body. Tighten force motor solenoid and torque converter clutch solenoid retaining bolts to specification. See TORQUE SPECIFICATIONS.

3RD CLUTCH & SPRAG ASSEMBLY

Disassembly – 1) Place 3rd clutch drum and intermediate shaft upright, using overdrive internal gear as a support. See Fig. 18.

2) Locate end of retaining ring at opening on side of 3rd clutch drum. Using screwdriver, compress one end of retaining ring and install one Retaining Ring Compressor (J-38450) near end of retaining ring to hold retaining ring clear of groove in 3rd clutch drum. See Fig. 18.

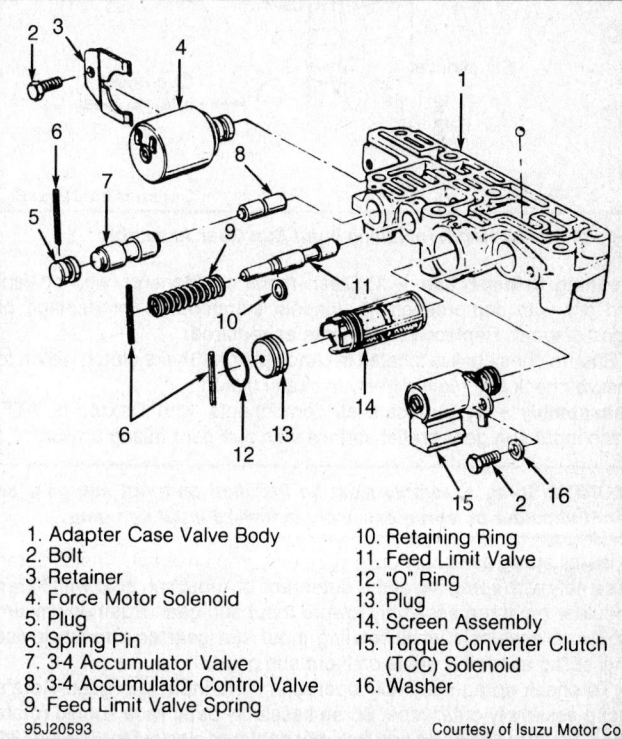

1. Adapter Case Valve Body	10. Retaining Ring
2. Bolt	11. Feed Limit Valve
3. Retainer	12. "O" Ring
4. Force Motor Solenoid	13. Plug
5. Plug	14. Screen Assembly
6. Spring Pin	15. Torque Converter Clutch
7. 3-4 Accumulator Valve	(TCC) Solenoid
8. 3-4 Accumulator Control Valve	16. Washer
9. Feed Limit Valve Spring	

95J20593

Courtesy of Isuzu Motor Co.

Fig. 17: Exploded View Of Adapter Case Valve Body

3) Compress other end of retaining ring and install retaining ring compressor near end of retaining ring. Repeat procedure by installing 3 remaining retaining ring compressors at equal intervals between retaining ring and 3rd clutch drum. Ensure retaining ring is fully disengaged from 3rd clutch drum.

4) Pull upward on input sun gear assembly until retaining ring clears groove in 3rd clutch drum. Remove retaining ring compressors. Remove input sun gear assembly from 3rd clutch drum.

5) Remove retaining washer, thrust bearing and thrust washer from 3rd clutch drum. Remove clutch plates, clutch discs and spring cushion plate from 3rd clutch drum. Note direction of clutch plates, clutch discs and spring cushion plate installation for reassembly reference.

6) To remove clutch piston from 3rd clutch drum, using spring compressor, compress return springs and return spring seat. DO NOT overcompress return springs and return spring seat.

7) Remove retaining ring from center of 3rd clutch drum. Release spring compressor. DO NOT allow return spring seat to bind in groove for retaining ring.

8) Remove spring compressor, return spring seat and return springs. Remove clutch piston from 3rd clutch drum. Remove seal rings from clutch piston.

9) To remove sprag assembly from input sun gear, remove sprag assembly outer race. *See Fig. 19.* Note direction of sprag assembly installation on input sun gear for reassembly reference. Remove sprag assembly from input sun gear.

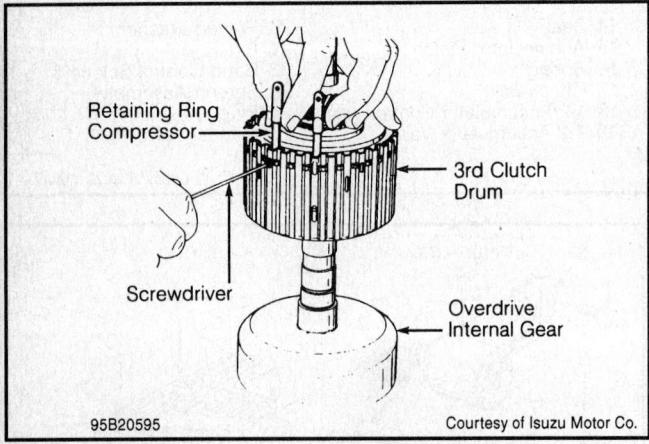

Fig. 18: Removing & Installing Input Sun Gear Assembly

Cleaning & Inspection – 1) Clean metal components with solvent and dry with compressed air. Inspect components for damage or signs of wear. Replace components as required.

2) Ensure check ball is located in clutch piston. Shake clutch piston to ensure check ball moves freely in clutch piston.

Reassembly – 1) Lubricate all components with Dexron-III ATF. Place input sun gear on flat surface with sun gear facing upward.

CAUTION: Sprag assembly must be installed on input sun gear so flared shoulder on sprag assembly is toward input sun gear.

---

2) Install sprag assembly outer race on sprag assembly. Install sprag assembly with sprag assembly outer race on input sun gear with flared shoulder on sprag assembly toward input sun gear. Push downward on sprag assembly while rotating input sun gear counterclockwise until sprag assembly seats on input sun gear.

3) To check sprag assembly operation, hold input sun gear. Rotate sprag assembly outer race. Sprag assembly outer race should rotate freely counterclockwise and lock when rotated clockwise. *See Fig. 20.* If sprag assembly operation is not as specified, sprag assembly is incorrectly installed on input sun gear.

CAUTION: Ensure sprag assembly outer race rotates freely counterclockwise and locks when rotated clockwise. See Fig. 20.

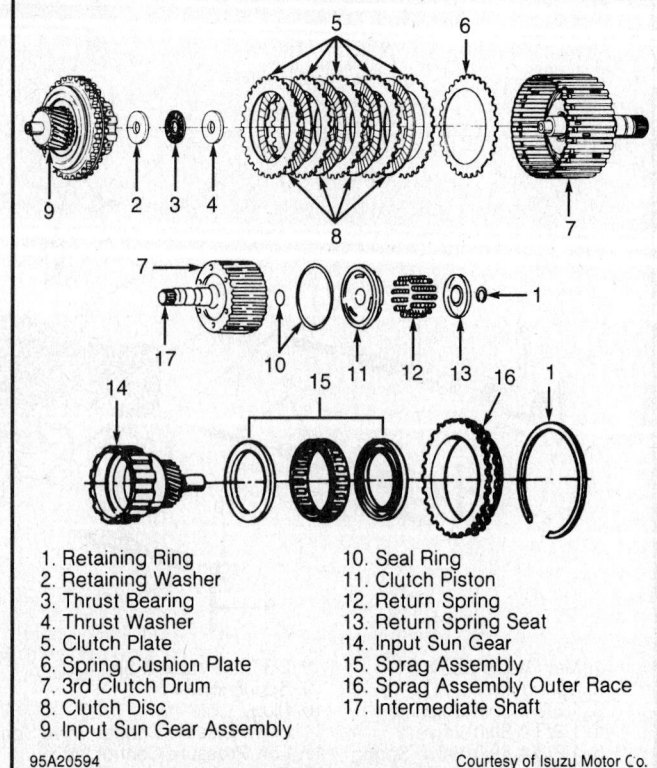

1. Retaining Ring
2. Retaining Washer
3. Thrust Bearing
4. Thrust Washer
5. Clutch Plate
6. Spring Cushion Plate
7. 3rd Clutch Drum
8. Clutch Disc
9. Input Sun Gear Assembly
10. Seal Ring
11. Clutch Piston
12. Return Spring
13. Return Spring Seat
14. Input Sun Gear
15. Sprag Assembly
16. Sprag Assembly Outer Race
17. Intermediate Shaft

Fig. 19: Exploded View Of 3rd Clutch & Sprag Assembly

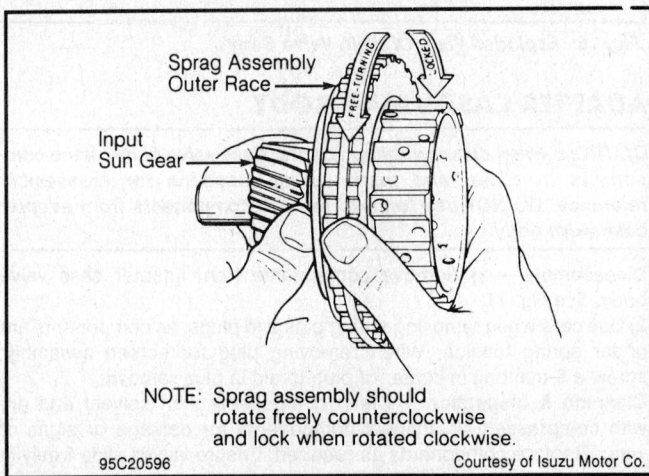

NOTE: Sprag assembly should rotate freely counterclockwise and lock when rotated clockwise.

Fig. 20: Checking Sprag Assembly Operation

4) Install NEW seal rings on clutch piston so lip on seal ring faces toward shaft end of 3rd clutch drum (toward front of transmission). Lubricate seal rings with Dexron-III ATF.

5) Install clutch piston in 3rd clutch drum. Use care not to damage seal rings. Install return springs and return spring seat.

6) Using spring compressor, compress return springs and return spring seat. Use care to not allow return spring seat to bind in groove for retaining ring or overcompress return springs and return spring seat.

7) Install retaining ring at center of 3rd clutch drum. Remove spring compressor. Place 3rd clutch drum and intermediate shaft upright, using overdrive internal gear as a support.

CAUTION: Spring cushion plate must be installed in 3rd clutch drum so beveled side of spring cushion plate is toward 3rd clutch drum. See Fig. 19.

8) Install spring cushion plate in 3rd clutch drum with beveled side of spring cushion plate toward 3rd clutch drum. *See Fig. 19.*

9) Install clutch plates and clutch discs in 3rd clutch drum, starting with clutch plate and alternating with clutch disc.

10) Install thrust washer, thrust bearing and retaining washer on 3rd clutch drum. Install input sun gear assembly on 3rd clutch assembly.

11) Ensure splines on sprag assembly fully engages with tangs on clutch discs. Rotate input sun gear assembly back and forth to ensure sprag assembly outer race engages with 3rd clutch drum.

12) Install retaining ring compressors at each side of retaining ring. Using screwdriver, compress retaining ring while pushing downward on sprag assembly outer race until retaining ring aligns with groove on 3rd clutch drum.

13) Remove retaining ring compressors. Ensure retaining ring fully engages in groove in 3rd clutch drum.

2ND CLUTCH

Disassembly – 1) Remove retaining ring, ring gear, retaining ring and spacer from 2nd clutch drum. *See Fig. 21.*

2) Remove clutch plates, clutch discs and waved plate from 2nd clutch drum. Note direction of clutch plates, clutch discs and waved plate installation for reassembly reference.

3) To remove clutch piston from 2nd clutch drum, using spring compressor, compress return springs and return spring seat. Remove retaining ring from center of 2nd clutch drum.

4) Release spring compressor. DO NOT allow return spring seat to bind in groove for retaining ring. Remove spring compressor, return spring seat and return springs.

5) Remove clutch piston from 2nd clutch drum. Remove seal rings from clutch piston.

Cleaning & Inspection – 1) Clean metal components with solvent and dry with compressed air. Inspect components for damage or signs of wear. Replace components as required.

2) Ensure check ball is located in clutch piston. Shake clutch piston to ensure check ball moves freely in clutch piston.

Reassembly – 1) Lubricate all components with Dexron-III ATF. Install NEW seal rings on clutch piston so lip on seal ring faces toward inside of 2nd clutch drum (toward front of transmission).

2) Install clutch piston in 2nd clutch drum. Use care not to damage seal rings. Install return springs and return spring seat.

3) Using spring compressor, compress return springs and return spring seat. Use care to not allow return spring seat to bind in groove for retaining ring.

4) Install retaining ring at center of 2nd clutch drum. Remove spring compressor. Install waved plate in 2nd clutch drum. Ensure waved plate is installed in original direction.

5) Install clutch plates and clutch discs in 2nd clutch drum, starting with clutch plate and alternating with clutch disc. *See Fig. 21.*

6) Install spacer with proper end of spacer facing clutch plate. *See Fig. 21.* Install retaining ring, ring gear and remaining retaining ring.

3-4 ACCUMULATOR

Disassembly – 1) The 3-4 accumulator is located in adapter case. *See Fig. 22.* Using spring compressor, depress cover. Remove snap ring from adapter case. Remove spring compressor.

2) Using slide hammer screwed into the center of cover, pull cover from adapter case. Remove spring and 3-4 accumulator piston. Remove all seal rings.

Cleaning & Inspection – Clean metal components with solvent and dry with compressed air. Inspect components for damage or signs of wear. Replace components as required.

Reassembly – To reassemble, reverse disassembly procedure using NEW seal rings. Lubricate seal rings with Dexron-III ATF.

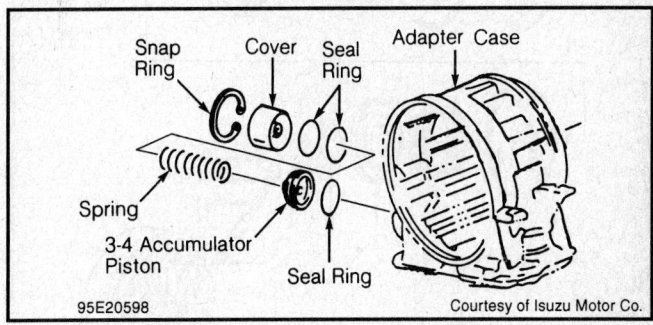

95E20598   Courtesy of Isuzu Motor Co.

Fig. 22: Exploded View Of 3-4 Accumulator Piston

REVERSE CLUTCH PISTON & CENTER SUPPORT

Disassembly – 1) Using Spring Compressor (J-23327), compress return springs and return spring seat on center support. *See Fig. 23.* DO NOT over compress return springs and return spring seat or damage to return spring seat may result.

2) Remove retaining ring. Remove spring compressor, return spring seat and return springs. Remove rear clutch piston. *See Fig. 24.*

3) Remove bolts, center support, gasket, transfer plate and gasket from adapter case. *See Fig. 24.* Remove restrictor from adapter case. *See Fig. 25.*

4) Remove retainer plate from side of center support. *See Fig. 24.* Remove plug, overrun lock-out valve spring and overrun lock-out valve from center support.

Cleaning & Inspection – Clean components with solvent and dry with compressed air. Inspect components for damage or signs of wear. Replace components as required.

Reassembly – 1) Lubricate all metal components with Dexron-III ATF. Install overrun lock-out valve in center support so small long diameter is toward the overrun lock-out valve spring area in center support. *See Fig. 24.* Install overrun lock-out valve spring.

CAUTION: Ensure overrun lock-out valve is installed in center support with small long diameter toward overrun lock-out valve spring area in center support. See Fig. 24.

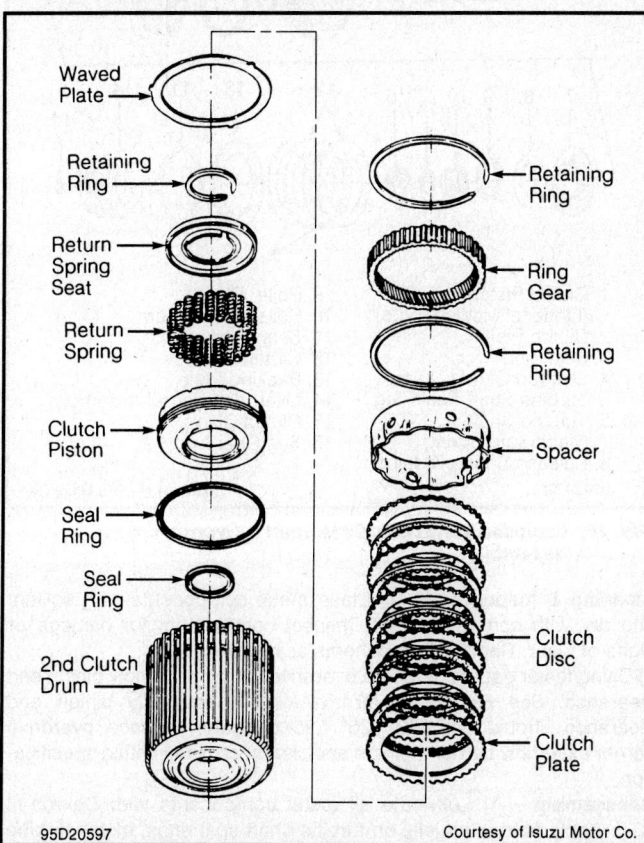

95D20597   Courtesy of Isuzu Motor Co.

Fig. 21: Exploded View Of 2nd Clutch

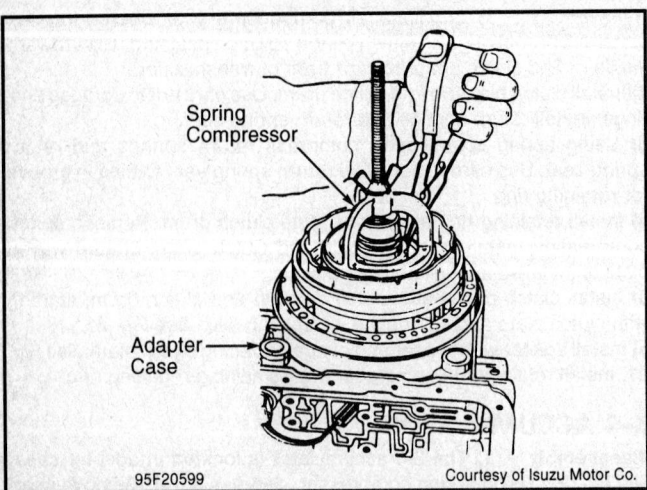

Fig. 23: Compressing Return Springs On Rear Clutch

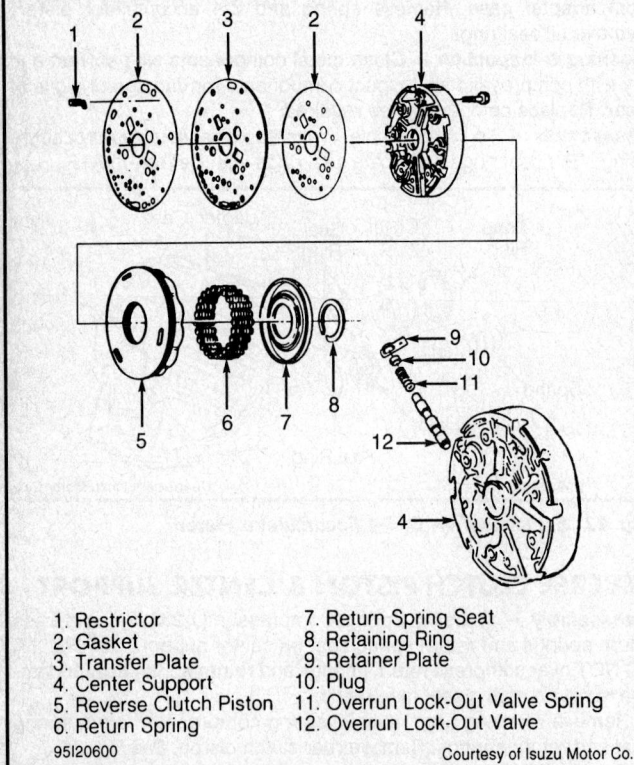

1. Restrictor
2. Gasket
3. Transfer Plate
4. Center Support
5. Reverse Clutch Piston
6. Return Spring
7. Return Spring Seat
8. Retaining Ring
9. Retainer Plate
10. Plug
11. Overrun Lock-Out Valve Spring
12. Overrun Lock-Out Valve

95I20600   Courtesy of Isuzu Motor Co.

Fig. 24: Exploded View Of Reverse Clutch Piston & Center Support

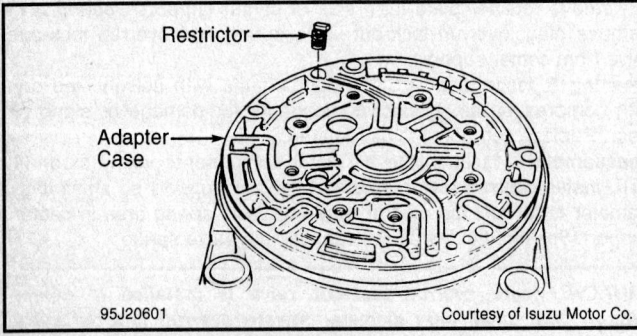

Fig. 25: Removing & Installing Restrictor In Adapter Case

2) Install plug and retainer plate on center support. Install restrictor in rear of adapter case. See Fig. 25.

3) Using NEW gaskets, install transfer plate and center support on adapter case. Install and tighten center support bolts to specification. See TORQUE SPECIFICATIONS.

4) Install reverse clutch piston on center support. Install return springs and return spring seat. Using spring compressor, compress return springs and return spring seat. Install retaining ring. Remove spring compressor.

TURBINE SHAFT & OVERRUN CLUTCH ASSEMBLY

Disassembly – 1) Position overrun clutch assembly upright, using overdrive internal gear as a support. Remove snap ring and overdrive carrier assembly. See Fig. 26.

2) Remove sun gear and turbine shaft. Remove snap ring, backing plate, clutch discs and clutch plates. Note direction of clutch discs and clutch plate installation for reassembly reference.

3) Using spring compressor, compress release spring retainer and diaphragm spring. Remove snap ring from center of overrun clutch drum. Remove spring compressor.

4) Remove roller clutch cam, roller clutch, release spring retainer and diaphragm spring. Remove clutch piston from overrun clutch drum. Remove seal rings from clutch piston if seal rings are not molded onto clutch piston. Remove turbine shaft seal rings from turbine shaft.

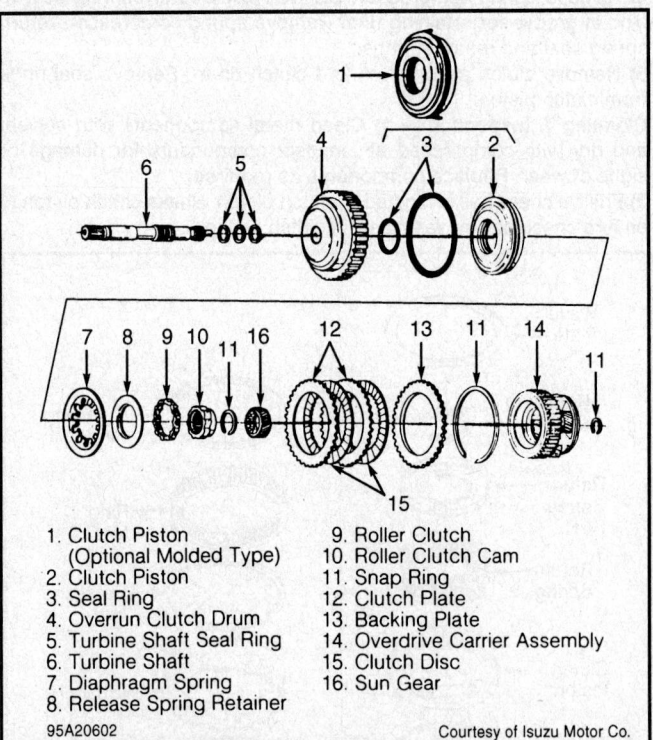

1. Clutch Piston (Optional Molded Type)
2. Clutch Piston
3. Seal Ring
4. Overrun Clutch Drum
5. Turbine Shaft Seal Ring
6. Turbine Shaft
7. Diaphragm Spring
8. Release Spring Retainer
9. Roller Clutch
10. Roller Clutch Cam
11. Snap Ring
12. Clutch Plate
13. Backing Plate
14. Overdrive Carrier Assembly
15. Clutch Disc
16. Sun Gear

95A20602   Courtesy of Isuzu Motor Co.

Fig. 26: Exploded View Of Turbine Shaft & Overrun Clutch Assembly

Cleaning & Inspection – 1) Clean metal components with solvent and dry with compressed air. Inspect components for damage or signs of wear. Replace components as required.

2) Using feeler gauge, measure overdrive carrier assembly pinion end clearance. See Fig. 27. Overdrive carrier assembly pinion end clearance should be .009-.025" (.25-.64 mm). Replace overdrive carrier assembly carrier if pinion end clearance is not within specification.

Reassembly – 1) Lubricate all metal components with Dexron-III ATF. Apply petroleum jelly on turbine shaft seal rings. Install turbine shaft seal rings on turbine shaft.

2) Install NEW seal rings on clutch piston if seal rings are not molded onto clutch piston. Install clutch piston in overrun clutch drum. Use care not to damage seal rings.

CAUTION: Diaphragm spring must be installed in proper direction in overrun clutch drum. See Fig. 24.

3) Install diaphragm spring in overrun clutch drum. Ensure diaphragm spring is installed in proper direction on overrun clutch drum. *See Fig. 26.*

4) Install release spring retainer, roller clutch and roller clutch cam in overrun clutch drum. Using spring compressor, compress release spring retainer and diaphragm spring. Install snap ring at center of overrun clutch drum. Remove spring compressor.

5) Install clutch plates and clutch discs in overrun clutch drum, starting with clutch plate and alternating with clutch disc. *See Fig. 26.*

CAUTION: Sun gear must be installed with countersunk area on sun gear facing toward overrun clutch drum.

6) Install backing plate and snap ring. Install turbine shaft on overrun clutch drum. Install sun gear with countersunk area on sun gear facing toward overrun clutch drum.

7) Install overdrive carrier assembly. Rotate overdrive carrier assembly counterclockwise during installation until roller clutch fully engages overdrive carrier assembly. Rotate overdrive carrier assembly and listen for looseness in the rollers on roller clutch. Install snap ring on end of turbine shaft.

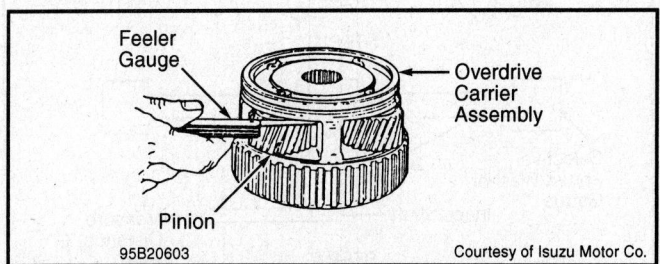

Fig. 27: Measuring Overdrive Carrier Assembly Pinion End Clearance

TRANSMISSION REASSEMBLY

VALVE BODIES & INTERNAL COMPONENTS

NOTE: Lubricate all components with Dexron-III ATF before reassembly. Coat all thrust bearings assemblies with petroleum jelly before installing.

1) Install NEW shaft seal for selector shaft in transmission case. Install selector shaft. Install spring pin in transmission case. *See Fig. 12.* DO NOT install spring flush with surface on transmission case.

2) Install parking lock and range selector lever with actuator rod on selector shaft. Install and tighten selector shaft nut to specification. See TORQUE SPECIFICATIONS.

3) Install brake band in transmission case. Ensure servo pin area aligns with servo hole. Install thrust bearing assembly in rear of transmission case.

4) Install brake drum, reaction sun gear and needle bearing. *See Fig. 11.* Install thrust bearing assembly on output shaft on planetary carrier.

5) Pinions on planetary carrier must be properly aligned. Each pinion is marked with 2 dots to indicate master tooth space and a single dot to indicate the master tooth. Planetary carrier is marked with double lines which should align with the 2 dots on 2 opposite pinions. Single lines on planetary carrier should align with single dot on the other 2 pinions. *See Fig. 28.*

6) Properly align all pinion on planetary carrier. Install 2nd and 3rd clutch assemblies on planetary carrier. If pinions are properly aligned, 2nd and 3rd clutch assembly should fit easily on planetary carrier.

7) Rotate 3rd clutch and ensure pinions with 2 dots are at tooth No. 1 and 46 on ring gear in 2nd clutch assembly. *See Fig. 28.* Pinions with one dot should be between tooth No. 23 and 24 on ring gear in 2nd clutch assembly. If not as specified, realign as necessary.

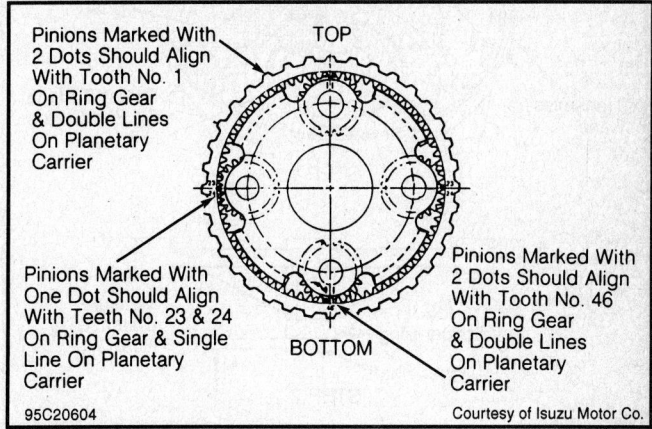

Fig. 28: Aligning Pinions On Planetary Carrier

8) Once correct pinion alignment is obtained, install planetary carrier in transmission case. Install washer and bearing on planetary carrier. *See Fig. 11.*

9) Install thrust washer on 2nd clutch. Ensure tangs on thrust washer engage with slots on second clutch. Align tangs on clutch plates in 2nd clutch. Install 3rd clutch assembly in 2nd clutch drum.

10) Install assembled 2nd and 3rd clutch assemblies in transmission case. Ensure planetary carrier is properly aligned. Rotate output shaft and clutch assemblies to ensure proper engagement.

11) Install pressure plate in transmission case. Ensure pressure plate is installed in proper direction with lip side facing upward. *See Fig. 11.* Tang side on pressure plate must be toward main valve body surface on transmission case.

12) Install reverse clutch plates and clutch discs, starting with clutch plate and alternating with clutch disc. Install waved plate with center tang facing valve body surface on transmission case.

13) The 2nd clutch end play must now be checked. Install Selective Thrust Washer Gauge (J-23085-A) on transmission case, against intermediate shaft. Move inner shaft on selective thrust washer gauge downward against thrust surface on 2nd clutch hub. Perform STEP 1. *See Fig. 29.* Tighten thumb screw on selective thrust washer gauge.

14) Remove selective thrust washer gauge from transmission case. Install spacer ring on inner shaft of selective thrust washer gauge. Measure distance "G" from end of inner shaft to surface on spacer ring. Perform STEP 2. *See Fig. 29.*

15) Using dimension "G", determine color code of selective thrust washer that fits on the center support. See SELECTIVE THRUST WASHER SPECIFICATIONS table. This should provide a final 2nd clutch end play of .014-.031" (.36-.79 mm).

SELECTIVE THRUST WASHER SPECIFICATIONS

Dimension "G" In. (mm)	Color Code
.060-.064 (1.53-1.63)	Yellow
.068-.072 (1.72-1.82)	Red
.075-.079 (1.91-2.01)	Black
.083-.087 (2.10-2.20)	Natural
.090-.094 (2.29-2.39)	Green
.098-.102 (2.48-2.58)	Blue

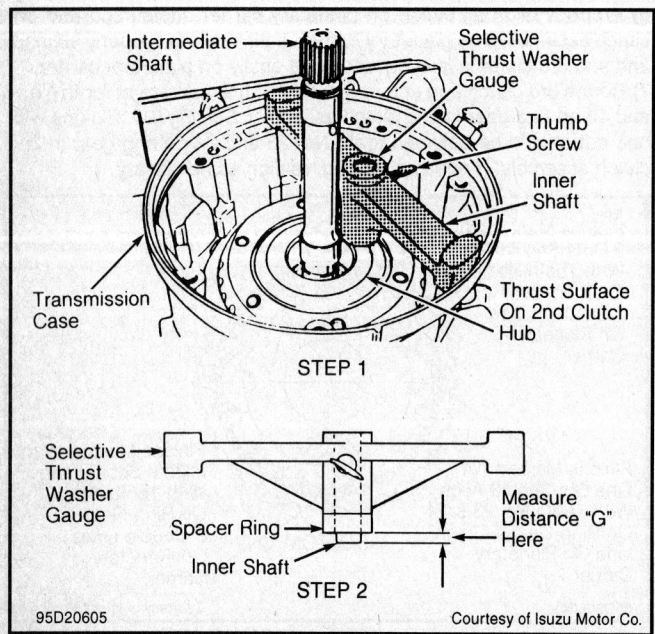

Fig. 29: *Measuring 2nd Clutch End Play*

Dimension "G" In. (mm)	Color Code
.060-.064 (1.53-1.63)	Yellow
.068-.072 (1.72-1.82)	Red
.075-.079 (1.91-2.01)	Black
.083-.087 (2.10-2.20)	Natural
.090-.094 (2.29-2.39)	Green
.098-.102 (2.48-2.58)	Blue

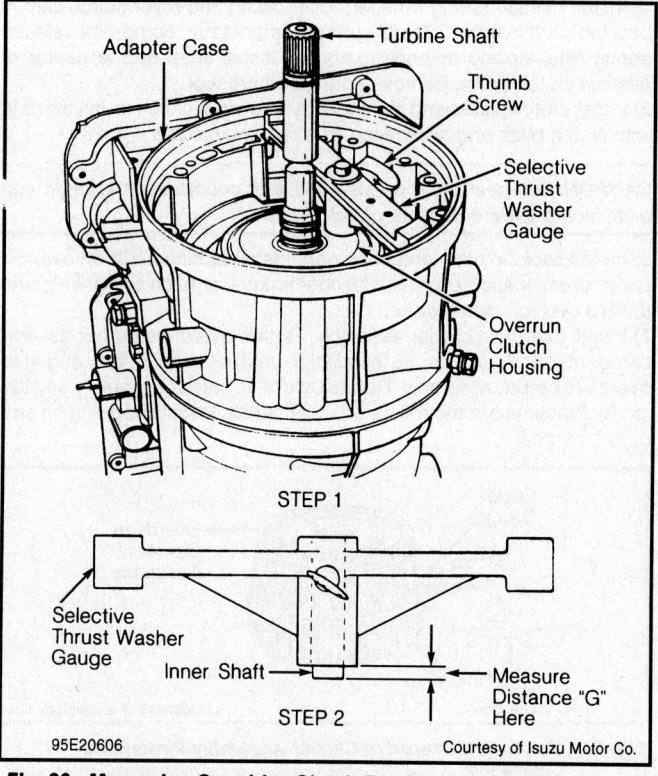

Fig. 30: *Measuring Overdrive Clutch End Play*

16) Install NEW seal rings on 4th clutch piston. Lubricate seal rings with Dexron-III ATF. Install 4th clutch piston in adapter case. Use care not to damage seal rings.

17) Install 4th clutch retainer and spring assembly on 4th clutch piston. *See Fig. 11.* Using spring compressor, compress 4th clutch spring retainer and spring assembly. Install snap ring in adapter case. Remove spring compressor.

18) Apply petroleum jelly on selective thrust washer. Install selective thrust washer on center support. Install NEW "O" rings on front of transmission case and NEW seal ring on adapter case. *See Fig. 11.*

19) Install guide pins in front of transmission case for aligning adapter case. Install adapter case and center support assembly on transmission case.

20) Install thrust washer on adapter case. Ensure tangs on thrust washer engage with slots in adapter case. Apply petroleum jelly on thrust bearing and install at center of overdrive internal gear with Black side of thrust bearing facing upward. *See Fig. 10.*

21) Install overdrive internal gear with thrust bearing on turbine shaft and overrun clutch assembly. Install turbine shaft and overrun clutch assembly with overdrive internal gear in adapter case.

22) Install 4th clutch plates and clutch discs in following order: clutch plate, clutch disc, clutch plate, clutch plate, clutch disc and clutch plate. Clutch plates must be installed with short tang facing toward adapter case valve body surface.

23) Install 4th clutch retainer with notch area toward adapter case valve body surface. Overdrive clutch end play must now be checked.

24) Install Selective Thrust Washer Gauge (J-23085-A) on adapter case, against turbine shaft. Move inner shaft on selective thrust washer gauge downward against thrust surface on overrun clutch housing. Perform STEP 1. *See Fig. 30.* Tighten thumb screw on selective thrust washer gauge.

25) Remove selective thrust washer gauge from adapter case. Measure distance "G" from end of inner shaft to surface on selective thrust washer gauge. Perform STEP 2. *See Fig. 30*

26) Using dimension "G", determine color code of selective thrust washer that fits on rear of oil pump assembly. See SELECTIVE THRUST WASHER SPECIFICATIONS table. This should provide a final overdrive clutch end play of .004-.031" (.10-.80 mm).

27) Install NEW outer seal ring on torque converter housing and NEW gasket on oil pump assembly. *See Fig. 14.* Apply petroleum jelly on selective thrust and install on rear of oil pump assembly. Ensure selective thrust washer is fully seated on oil pump assembly.

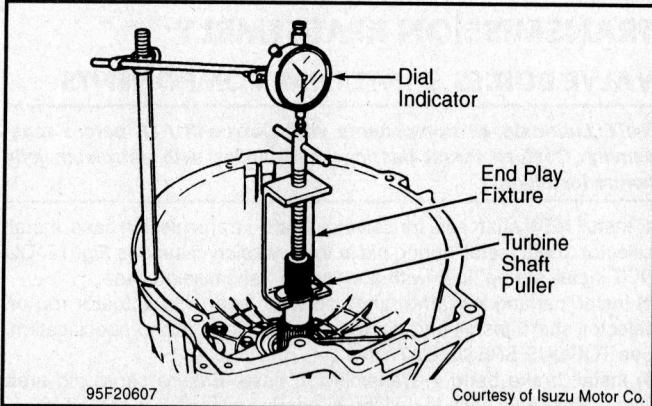

Fig. 31: *Measuring Turbine Shaft End Play*

28) Install torque converter housing with oil pump assembly on adapter case. Install and tighten torque converter housing-to-adapter case bolts to specification. Ensure oil pump gears rotate freely.

29) Install dial indicator, Turbine Shaft Puller (J-25022) and End Play Fixture (J-24773-1) onto turbine shaft. *See Fig. 31.* Pull turbine shaft upward until slight resistance is felt. Zero dial indicator.

30) Continue to pull turbine shaft upward and note turbine shaft end play. Turbine shaft end play should be .004-.031" (.10-.80 mm). Remove dial indicator, turbine shaft puller and end play fixture.

31) If turbine shaft end play is not within specification, different thickness selective thrust washer must be installed on rear of oil pump assembly. Repeat steps **24)** through **26)** for selective thrust washer selection procedure.

32) On 2WD models, install NEW bearing in extension housing if replacement is required. On all models, install NEW oil seal in extension housing. Install NEW seal ring on parking lock gear if seal ring is damaged. See Fig. 8.

33) Install parking lock gear, speed sensor drive gear and retaining ring on output shaft. See Fig. 8. Using NEW gasket, install extension housing. Ensure parking pawl shaft and actuator rod are aligned with extension housing. Install and tighten extension housing bolts to specification.

34) On 2WD models, install drive shaft companion flange and NEW "O" ring on output shaft. Install and tighten drive shaft companion flange nut to specification.

35) On all models, using a NEW "O" ring, install speed sensor. Install and tighten bolt to specification. Position transmission with output shaft facing upward. Install dial indicator on extension housing with stem of dial indicator against output shaft. Zero dial indicator.

36) Manually push output shaft upward and note output shaft end play. Output shaft end play should be .014-.031" (.36-.80 mm). If output shaft end play is not within specification, different thickness selective thrust washer must be installed on center support. Repeat steps **13)** through **15)** for selective thrust washer selection procedure.

37) Ensure brake band is correctly positioned, rotate output shaft if necessary. Install NEW seal ring on servo piston if necessary. Install apply rod in transmission case with rounded end of rod toward the brake band.

38) Install return spring and servo piston. Use care not to damage seal ring on servo piston. Using spring compressor, compress servo piston and return spring. Install servo piston retaining snap ring. Remove spring compressor.

39) To adjust brake band, loosen lock nut on servo adjusting screw. See Fig. 8. Using an INCH-lb. torque wrench, tighten servo adjusting screw to 40 INCH lbs. (4.5 N.m).

40) Back off servo adjusting screw 5 revolutions. Hold sleeve on servo piston. Tighten lock nut to 14 ft. lbs. (19 N.m). Ensure servo adjusting screw does not rotate while tightening lock nut.

41) Install 2 check balls in transmission case. See Fig. 9. Install case 4-pin connector and wiring harness. Install guide pins for main valve body in transmission case.

42) Install assembled main valve body and manual valve link assembly. Manual valve link must be extended, as long end fits into manual valve and short end fits into range selector. Remove guide pins. Install and tighten main valve body bolts to specification. Install electrical connectors at solenoids on main valve body.

43) Using a NEW gasket, install servo cover. Install and tighten bolts to specification. Install manual detent on main valve body. See Fig. 8. Install and tighten bolts to specification.

44) Install a NEW oil filter. Install and tighten bolts to specification. Using NEW gasket, install main case oil pan. Install and tighten bolts to specification.

45) Install 5-pin electrical connector in adapter case. Using NEW transfer plate gaskets, install adapter case valve body and transfer plate. Install and tighten bolts to specification. Install electrical connectors at solenoids on adapter case valve body.

46) Using a NEW gasket, install adapter case oil pan. Install and tighten bolts to specification. Using a NEW seal ring, install oil filler tube. Install and tighten bolt to specification.

47) Install and adjust mode switch. For mode switch adjustment, see appropriate HYDRA-MATIC 4L30-E ELECTRONIC CONTROLS article. Install NEW "O" ring on end of turbine shaft. Install torque converter.

TORQUE SPECIFICATIONS
TORQUE SPECIFICATIONS

Application	Ft. Lbs. (N.m)
Adapter Case Valve Body Bolt	15 (20)
Center Support Bolt	18 (24)
Drive Shaft Companion Flange Nut	76 (103)
Extension Housing Bolt	24 (33)
Main Valve Body Bolt	15 (20)
Manual Detent Bolt	15 (20)
Oil Filter Bolt	15 (20)
Oil Pan Drain Plug	28 (38)
Oil Pan Overfill Plug	28 (38)
Oil Pump Assembly-To-Torque Converter Housing Bolt	15 (20)
Selector Shaft Nut	16 (22)
Servo Cover Bolt	18 (24)
Torque Converter Housing-To-Adapter Case Bolt	29 (39)

Application	INCH Lbs. (N.m)
Adapter Case Oil Pan Bolt	97 (11)
Force Motor Solenoid Bolt	89 (10)
Main Case Oil Pan Bolt	97 (11)
Mode Switch Bolt	115 (13)
Oil Seal Ring Bolt	27 (3)
Pressure Tap Plug	106 (12)
Speed Sensor Bolt	80 (9)
Torque Converter Clutch Solenoid Bolt	89 (10)
Transfer Plate-To-Main Valve Body Bolt	115 (13)

TRANSMISSION SPECIFICATIONS
TRANSMISSION SPECIFICATIONS

Application	Specification In. (mm)
Output Shaft End Play	.014-.031 (.36-.80)
Overdrive Carrier Assembly Pinion End Clearance	.009-.025 (.25-.64)
Overdrive Clutch End Play [1]	.004-.031 (.10-.80)
Planetary Carrier Pinion End Clearance	.005-.035 (.13-.89)
Turbine Shaft End Play	.004-.031 (.10-.80)
2nd Clutch End Play [1]	.014-.031 (.36-.79)

[1] – For measuring procedure, see TRANSMISSION REASSEMBLY.

TECHNICAL SERVICE BULLETINS

DELAYED GEAR ENGAGEMENT

Isuzu TSB SB96-05-L002 (July 1996) – Some 1991-96 Rodeo and 1990-96 Trooper vehicles equipped with 4L30-E automatic transmission may experience a noticeable delay from the time that gear selection is made to the time that gear engagement occurs. This usually occurs after vehicle has been parked for an extended period of time (e.g., overnight) and only on the initial gear engagement when shifting into Drive or Reverse. This delay may be caused by torque converter drain-down.

This condition does not affect transmission operation once torque converter refills, and is not harmful to transmission. However, if it is necessary to eliminate this condition, replace scarf cut seal ring located on the first grove of turbine shaft with a solid seal ring, using Turbine Shaft Seal Kit (8-96041-327-0). See REPAIR PROCEDURE.

Repair Procedure – 1) Remove scarf cut seal ring located in first groove of turbine shaft (closest to torque converter). See Fig. 32. Lubricate turbine shaft groove and NEW seal ring with petroleum jelly. Place NEW seal ring over turbine shaft and position onto first groove. Go to next step.

NOTE: Solid seal ring is made of a silicone based material. This material will stretch during installation, causing an increase in seal ring diameter. To ensure proper seal ring functioning, seal ring must be resized. To resize seal ring, use sizing tool supplied with Turbine Shaft Seal Kit (8-96041-327-0).

WIRING DIAGRAMS

For wiring diagrams, see appropriate HYDRA-MATIC 4L30-E ELECTRONIC CONTROLS article.

TECHNICAL SERVICE BULLETINS

DELAYED GEAR ENGAGEMENT

Isuzu TSB SB96-05-L002 (July 1996) – Some 1991-96 Rodeo and 1990-96 Trooper vehicles equipped with 4L30-E automatic transmission may experience a noticeable delay from the time that gear selection is made to the time that gear engagement occurs. This usually occurs after vehicle has been parked for an extended period of time (e.g., overnight) and only on the initial gear engagement when shifting into Drive or Reverse. This delay may be caused by torque converter drain-down.

This condition does not affect transmission operation once torque converter refills, and is not harmful to transmission. However, if it is necessary to eliminate this condition, replace scarf cut seal ring located on the first grove of turbine shaft with a solid seal ring, using Turbine Shaft Seal Kit (8-96041-327-0). See REPAIR PROCEDURE.

Repair Procedure – 1) Remove scarf cut seal ring located in first groove of turbine shaft (closest to torque converter). *See Fig. 32.* Lubricate turbine shaft groove and NEW seal ring with petroleum jelly. Place NEW seal ring over turbine shaft and position onto first groove. Go to next step.

NOTE: Solid seal ring is made of a silicone based material. This material will stretch during installation, causing an increase in seal ring diameter. To ensure proper seal ring functioning, seal ring must be resized. To resize seal ring, use sizing tool supplied with Turbine Shaft Seal Kit (8-96041-327-0).

---

2) Place sizing tool over turbine shaft and push downward until tool contacts overrun clutch. *See Fig. 33.* Wait 5 minutes, then remove and discard sizing tool. Reassemble transmission.

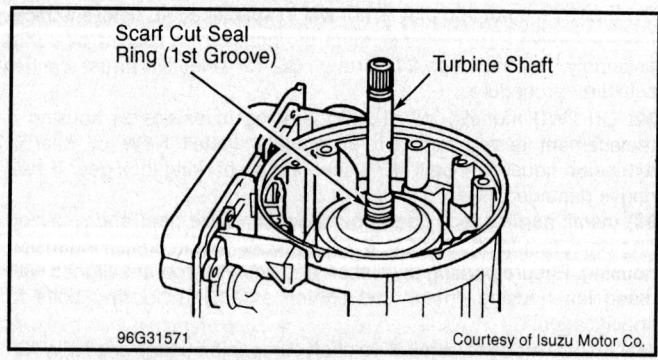

Fig. 32: Locating Scarf Cut Seal Ring

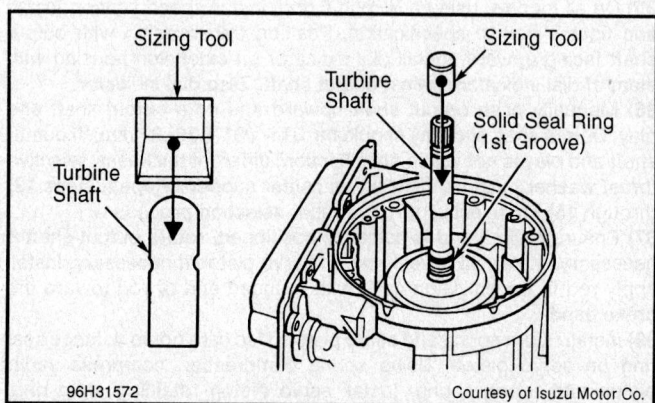

Fig. 33: Installing Sizing Tool

1995 Hydra-Matic 4L30-E Electronic Controls

1995 Honda: Passport
1995 Isuzu: Rodeo, Trooper

APPLICATION

APPLICATION

Vehicle	Transmission Model
Honda	
1995 Passport [1]	4L30-E
Isuzu	
1995 Rodeo (3.2L V6) [1]	4L30-E
1995 Trooper	4L30-E

[1] – Early and late production.

DESCRIPTION

Automatic transmission is electronically controlled. Transmission shifting and torque converter lock-up are controlled by Transmission Control Module (TCM). The TCM receives information from various input devices and uses this information to control shift solenoids, band apply solenoid and Torque Converter Clutch (TCC) solenoid. The TCM uses input signals to control the force motor solenoid operation, which operates the pressure regulator valve to control line pressure.

A torque management control system is used. The torque management control system uses TCM to deliver a spark advance signal to Engine Control Module (ECM) during transmission shifting. This controls engine torque and reduces engagement shock caused by a change in vehicle speed.

The TCM contains a fail-safe system. When a failure or problem is present in the transmission electronic control system, the TCM may go into a back-up mode using pre-programmed values, allowing vehicle to be driven. The CHECK TRANS light on instrument panel will flash to inform driver of a problem. Vehicle can be driven, but shifting must be done manually. For additional information, see TRANSMISSION CONTROL MODULE (TCM) under OPERATION.

Transmission is capable of 3 different shift modes, Normal (NOR) mode, Power (PWR) mode and Winter mode. For additional information, see SHIFT MODES under OPERATION.

Transmission is equipped with shift and key lock systems. Shift lock system prevents gearshift lever movement from "P" position unless brake pedal is depressed, ignition is on and release button on gearshift lever is depressed. Key lock system prevents ignition switch from being placed in LOCK position unless gearshift lever is in "P" position. For additional information on shift and key lock systems, see SHIFT & KEY LOCK SYSTEMS under OPERATION.

OPERATION

SHIFT & KEY LOCK SYSTEMS

Shift Lock System – Shift lock system prevents gearshift lever movement from "P" position unless brake pedal is depressed, ignition is on and release button on gearshift lever is depressed. Shift lock system uses a safety lock controller and shift lock solenoid for controlling gearshift lever operation. When brake pedal is depressed, brake switch delivers an input signal to safety lock controller to indicate that brakes are applied, allowing gearshift lever movement from "P" position. Safety lock controller and shift lock solenoid are located near gearshift lever. See Fig. 1. For testing of shift lock system, see SHIFT LOCK SYSTEM under SYSTEM TESTING.

Key Lock System – Shift lock cable is connected between gearshift lever and ignition switch. When gearshift lever is placed in "P" position, shift lock cable moves lock on ignition switch so ignition switch may be placed in LOCK position. For testing of key lock system, see KEY LOCK SYSTEM under SYSTEM TESTING.

SHIFT MODES

NOTE: Transmission is capable of 3 different shift modes, Normal (NOR) mode, Power (PWR) mode and Winter mode. Shift mode may be selected by using POWER or WINTER mode switch mounted on center console, near gearshift lever. Shift modes are used to change transmission shift points for various vehicle operating conditions.

Normal Mode – Normal mode is obtained when neither Power mode or Winter mode are selected. Normal mode provides standard transmission shift points.

Power Mode – Power mode is obtained by using POWER mode switch on center console, near gearshift lever. Power mode slightly increases engine speed at which transmission shift points occur for maximum performance. Power mode may be selected in any forward gear position. When Power mode is selected with ignition on, POWER DRIVE indicator light on instrument panel will illuminate. On early production 1995 Passport and Rodeo models, POWER DRIVE indicator light is located at center of instrument panel, just above the air vents. On late production 1995 Passport and Rodeo models and 1995 Trooper models, POWER DRIVE indicator light is located in instrument cluster.

Winter Mode – Winter mode is obtained by using WINTER mode switch on center console, near gearshift lever. Winter mode is activated when all of the following conditions are present.
- Accelerator opening is approximately 8 percent or less.
- Kickdown switch is off.
- Gearshift lever is in "D" position.
- Transmission fluid temperature is 120°F (248°C) or less.
- Vehicle speed is 7 MPH or less.
- WINTER mode switch is on.

When in Winter mode, transmission starts off in 3rd gear to aid in vehicle traction on ice and snow. When Winter mode is selected with ignition on, WINTER DRIVE indicator light will illuminate. On early production 1995 Passport and Rodeo models, WINTER DRIVE indicator light is located at center of instrument panel, just above the air vents. On late production 1995 Passport and Rodeo models and 1995 Trooper models, WINTER DRIVE indicator light is located in instrument cluster.

On all models, Winter mode is canceled when any of the following conditions are present.
- Ignition is turned off.
- Gearshift lever is placed in "3", "2" or "L" position.
- Transmission fluid temperature is 140°F (284°C) or greater.
- Vehicle speed exceeds 22 MPH.
- WINTER mode switch is turned off.

Winter mode should only by used on slippery road conditions. Operation of Winter mode during normal driving conditions will result in decreased performance and sluggish acceleration.

TRANSMISSION CONTROL MODULE (TCM)

The TCM receives information from various input devices and uses this information to control the following output devices: shift solenoids, band apply solenoid, Torque Converter Clutch (TCC) solenoid and force motor solenoid.

The TCM contains a self-diagnostic system which stores a Diagnostic Trouble Code (DTC) if a failure or problem is present in the transmis-

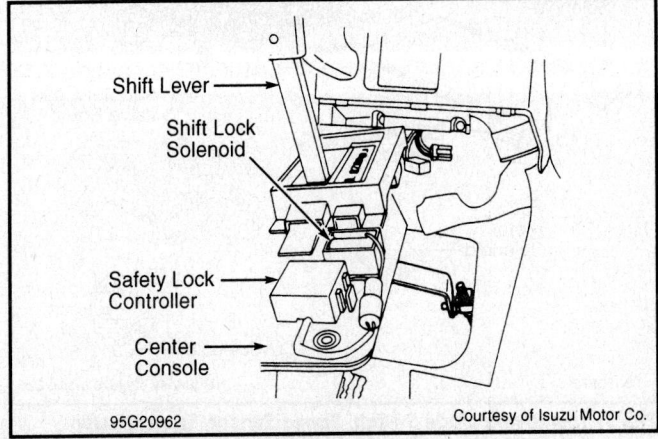

Shift Lever

Shift Lock Solenoid

Safety Lock Controller

Center Console

95G20962   Courtesy of Isuzu Motor Co.

Fig. 1: Identifying Safety Lock Controller

3-572

AUTOMATIC TRANSMISSIONS
1995 Hydra-Matic 4L30-E Electronic Controls (Cont.)

sion electronic control system. If a certain failure or problem is present, CHECK TRANS light will flash to inform driver of a problem. See DTC IDENTIFICATION table. On early production 1995 Passport and Rodeo models, CHECK TRANS light is located at center of instrument panel, just above the air vents. On late production 1995 Passport and Rodeo models, CHECK TRANS light is located in instrument cluster. On 1995 Trooper models, CHECK TRANS light is located on left side of instrument panel, below air vent.

DTCs may be retrieved to determine transmission problem area. For information on retrieving DTCs, see SELF-DIAGNOSTIC SYSTEM. The TCM contains a fail-safe system. When a certain failure or problem is present in the transmission electronic control system, the TCM may go into back-up mode using pre-programmed values, allowing vehicle to be driven. The CHECK TRANS light may flash to inform driver of a problem. See DTC IDENTIFICATION table.

Vehicle can be driven in back-up mode, but shifting must be done manually. When manually shifting transmission, if gearshift lever is placed in "D" or "3" position, transmission remains in 4th gear. If gearshift lever is placed in "2" position, transmission remains in 3rd gear. If gearshift lever is placed in "L" position, transmission remains in 1st gear. If gearshift lever is placed in "R" position, transmission will shift into reverse. Back-up mode may be cleared by turning ignition off, then back on again.

For additional information on the self-diagnostic system, see SELF-DIAGNOSTIC SYSTEM. The TCM is located above driver-side kick panel. See Fig. 2.

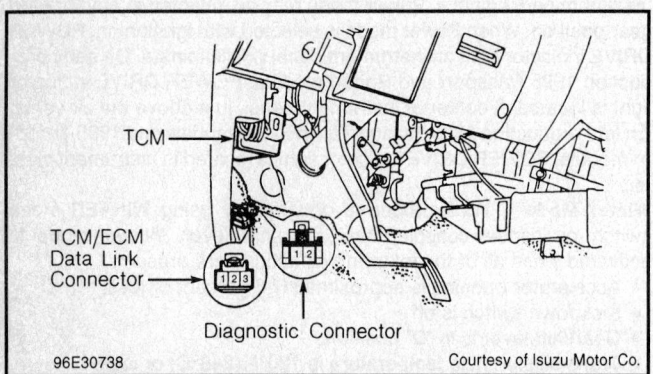

Fig. 2: Identifying TCM, Diagnostic Connector & TCM/ECM Data Link Connector (Passport & Rodeo Shown; Trooper Is Similar)

TCM INPUT DEVICES

A/C Signal – The A/C compressor relay delivers an input signal to TCM to indicate A/C operation. The A/C compressor relay is located in fuse/relay box at passenger's side front corner of engine compartment.

Barometric Sensor (High Altitude Vehicles Only) – Barometric sensor delivers an input signal to TCM to indicate altitude. The TCM uses input signal to control transmission hydraulic pressures to provide smooth shifts at high altitude. Barometric sensor is located at driver's side front corner of engine compartment, behind headlight.

Brakelight Switch – Brakelight switch delivers an input signal to TCM to indicate vehicle braking. Brakelight switch is located near brake pedal. Brakelight switch may be referred to as brake switch.

Cruise Control Signal – Transmission will downshift when an overdrive OFF signal is received from cruise control unit. Cruise control unit is located behind passenger's side kick panel. Cruise control unit may also be referred to as cruise control module.

Diagnostic Connector – Diagnostic connector will deliver an input signal to display a Diagnostic Trouble Code (DTC) using CHECK TRANS light on instrument panel. Diagnostic connector may be referred to as Data Link Connector (DLC). See Fig. 2.

Engine Coolant Temperature (ECT) Sensor – ECT sensor delivers an input signal to Engine Control Module (ECM) to indicate engine coolant temperature. The TCM receives engine coolant temperature

input signal from the ECM. ECT sensor is located on coolant pipe at rear of cylinder head.

Engine Speed Or RPM Signal – An engine speed or RPM signal is delivered to TCM from ignition control module, located below ignition coils.

Kickdown Switch – Kickdown switch delivers an input signal to TCM to indicate if accelerator pedal is fully depressed. Kickdown switch is located on accelerator pedal.

Mode Switch – Mode switch delivers an input signal to TCM to indicate shift lever position. Mode switch is located on side of transmission. See Fig. 3.

POWER Mode Switch – POWER mode switch delivers an input signal to TCM to indicate when POWER mode switch is positioned in the Power mode. POWER mode switch is located on center console, near gearshift lever.

Speed Sensor – Speed sensor delivers an input signal to TCM to indicate transmission output shaft speed. Speed sensor is located on extension housing on rear of transmission. See Fig. 3. Speed sensor may be referred to as magnetic sensor.

Throttle Position Sensor (TPS) – The TPS delivers an input signal to TCM to indicate throttle position. The TPS sensor is mounted on side of throttle body.

Transmission Oil Temperature Sensor – Transmission oil temperature sensor delivers an input signal to TCM to indicate transmission oil

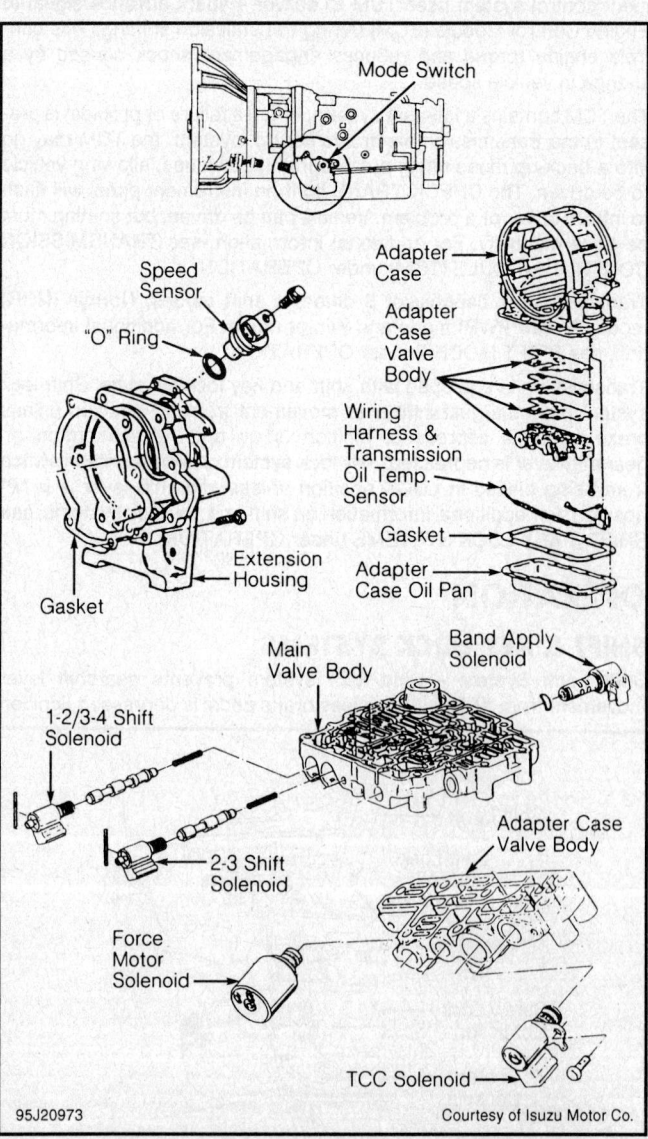

Fig. 3: Identifying Mode Switch, Speed Sensor, Transmission Oil Temperature Sensor, Shift Solenoids & TCC Solenoid

AUTOMATIC TRANSMISSIONS
1995 Hydra-Matic 4L30-E Electronic Controls (Cont.)

3-575

SYSTEM TESTING

SHIFT LOCK SYSTEM

NOTE: Shift lock system prevents shift lever movement from "P" position unless brake pedal is depressed, ignition is on and release button on gearshift lever is depressed.

1) Shift lock system uses a safety lock controller, shift lock solenoid and brakelight or stoplight switch for controlling shift lock system. Safety lock controller and shift lock solenoid are located near gearshift lever. *See Fig. 1.*

2) For system testing, see shift lock system wiring diagram. See WIRING DIAGRAMS. No other testing information is available.

KEY LOCK SYSTEM

NOTE: Shift lock cable is connected between gearshift lever and ignition switch. When gearshift lever is placed in "P" position, shift lock cable moves lock on ignition switch so ignition switch may be placed in LOCK position.

1) To check system operation, ensure gearshift lever cannot be moved from "P" position with ignition switch in LOCK position.

2) Ensure ignition switch can be turned to LOCK position only when gearshift lever is in "P" position. If operation is not as specified, adjust shift lock cable. See SHIFT LOCK CABLE ADJUSTMENT under ON-VEHICLE SERVICE in appropriate overhaul article.

TECH 1 SCAN TOOL OPERATING MODES

NOTE: TECH 1 scan tool may be operated in different modes for transmission diagnosis.

OPERATING MODE DESCRIPTION & USAGE

FO: Data List Mode – 1) This mode continuously monitors data parameters. The FO: Data List mode may be selected from select mode on TECH 1 scan tool. When using this mode, current values of various sensors and system operating signals are displayed under specified conditions.

2) Comparing displayed data in relation to the correct value and condition from FO: Data List Quick Check, the technician may determine which test or DTC trouble shooting flow chart to use for system diagnosis. *See Fig. 5 and 6.*

3) If all values are correct, perform F5: Actuator Test. See F5: ACTUATOR TEST MODE. If value is not as specified, perform diagnosis for specified test or DTC. For trouble shooting of specified test or DTC, see appropriate TROUBLE SHOOTING FLOW CHARTS.

TECH 1 DISPLAY	CONDITONS	CORRECT VALUE	FOR DIAGNOSIS SEE
BATTERY VOLTAGE	Ignition ON	9 V $\leq$ voltage $\leq$ 15.5 V (V)	DTC 25 or 26
FORCE MOTOR CUR.	Engine at idle speed	approx. 0.9 A	DTC 35
CALCULAT. PRESS.	Parking brake on Selector lever position "D"	approx. 4.0 bar	
SOLENOID 1-2/3-4	Vehicle traveling at a speed of: approx. 50 km/h (32 mph) with selector lever in position "2" or approx. 70 km/h (44 mph) with selector lever in position "3"	ACTIVE	DTC 31 or 41
SOLENOID 2-3	Vehicle traveling at a speed of: approx. 10 km/h (6 mph) with selector lever in position "L" or approx. 30 km/h (18 mph) with selector lever in position "2"	ACTIVE	DTC 32 or 42
BAND APPLY SOL.	Engine at idle speed Selector lever position "L"	approx. 99% DC	DTC 34 or 44
TCC SOLENOID	Vehicle traveling at a speed of approx. 80 km/h (50 mph) Selector lever position "D"	ON	DTC 33 or 43
TCC SLIP RPM	Constant engine speed Selector lever position "D" TCC on	0 ± 10 RPM	DTC 33 or 43
BRAKE SWITCH	Ignition ON Brake pedal pressed	ACTIVE	DTC 55 or 56
AT INPUT SPEED	Engine speed $\leq$ 200 rpm Output speed > 1024 rpm Selector lever position "D", "3", "2", "L"	Engine speed: (RPM)	DTC 13 or 62
AT OUTPUT SPEED	Output speed $\leq$ 0 rpm Engine speed > 3000 rpm Selector lever position "D", "3", "2", "L"	Output speed: (RPM)	DTC 11 or 13
BAROMETER SENSOR	Engine at idle speed	0.9 ~ 1.0 bar approx. 0.02 V	–
SELECTOR POS.	Ignition ON Shift through all selector lever positions	Dependent on selector lever position P, R, N, D, 3, 2, L	DTC 53 or 54
C/C O/D LOCKOUT	When O/D OFF signal detected while cruise control system is in use	ACTIVE	–
ACTUAL GEAR	Vehicle traveling at a speed of approx. 100 km/h (62 mph) Selector lever position "D"	- 4 -	DTC 61

Courtesy of Isuzu Motor Co.

96F30739

Fig. 5: FO: Data List Quick Check (1 Of 2)

3-576

AUTOMATIC TRANSMISSIONS
1995 Hydra-Matic 4L30-E Electronic Controls (Cont.)

TECH 1 DISPLAY	CONDITONS	CORRECT VALUE	FOR DIAGNOSIS SEE
SELECTOR PIN A	Ignition ON Selector lever position: "P", "R", "3" or "2"	ACTIVE	DTC 53 or 54
SELECTOR PIN B	Ignition ON Selector lever position: "R", "N", "D" or "3"	ACTIVE	DTC 53 or 54
SELECTOR PIN C	Ignition ON Selector lever position: "D", "3", "2" or "L"	ACTIVE	DTC 53 or 54
SELECTOR PIN P	Ignition ON Selector lever position: "P", "N", "3" or "L"	ACTIVE	DTC 53 or 54
TPS SIGNAL	Ignition ON Throttle body in idle speed position Throttle body in full load position	0.1 V to 0.96 V (0%) 4.9 V or less (99%)	DTC 21 or 22
KICK DOWN SWITCH	Ignition ON Depress accelerator pedal to stop	ACTIVE	DTC 52
A/C REQUEST	Engine running. Air conditioning ON. Compressor engaged.	ACTIVE	CHECK WIRE FROM TCM CONNECTOR A-64 TERMINAL D8 FOR OPEN CIRCUIT.
TRANSM. OIL TEMP.	Engine running	70 - 120°C/158 - 248°F approx. 1.00 ~ 3.10 V	DTC 15 or 16
COOLANT TEMP SW.	Ignition ON: Engine warm	COLD (≤ 63°C) WARM (> 70°C)	DTC 51
WINTER SW. (-D-)	Ignition ON Selector lever position "D" Press "WINTER" switch	ACTIVE	TRANSMIS-SION OPERATING MODE TEST
WINTER LAMP	Engine running Selector lever position "D" Press "WINTER" switch	ON	
POWER SWITCH	Ignition ON Press "POWER" switch	ACTIVE	TRANSMIS-SION OPERATING MODE TEST
POWER LAMP	Engine running Press "POWER" switch	ON	

96I30740   Courtesy of Isuzu Motor Co.

Fig. 6: FO: Data List Quick Check (2 Of 2)

F2: Diagnostic Trouble Code (DTC) Mode – The F2: Diagnostic Trouble Code (DTC) mode may be selected from select mode on TECH 1 scan tool. When using this mode, DTC may be retrieved from TCM for system diagnosis.

F3: Snapshot Mode – 1) The F3: Snapshot mode may be selected from select mode on TECH 1 scan tool. When using this mode, data is stored by TECH 1 scan tool. Stored data may be displayed to aid in diagnosing intermittent problems for system diagnosis. Intermittent problems may be caused by damaged wiring, loose or dirty connections or improperly routed wiring.

2) When using this mode, the technician may specify a trigger condition and the TCM stores data before and after the trigger condition.

F4: Clear Codes – The F4: Clear Codes mode may be selected from select mode on TECH 1 scan tool. This mode is used to clear DTCs from TCM memory.

F5: Actuator Test Mode – 1) The F5: Actuator Test mode may be selected from select mode on TECH 1 scan tool. This mode is used to check correct operation of electronic system actuators.

2) When using F5: Actuator Test mode, ensure parking brake is applied, wheels are blocked, gearshift lever is in "N" position and ignition is on with engine off. By comparing displayed data in relation to the correct result from F5: Actuator Test Quick Check, the technician may determine which test or DTC trouble shooting flow chart to use for system diagnosis. *See Fig. 7.*

3) If correct result is not obtained, perform diagnosis for specified test or DTC. For trouble shooting of specified test or DTC, see appropriate TROUBLE SHOOTING FLOW CHARTS.

AUTOMATIC TRANSMISSIONS
1995 Hydra-Matic 4L30-E Electronic Controls (Cont.)

3-577

Before performing actuator test, ensure shift lever is in "N" position, ignition is on with engine off.

TECH 1 DISPLAY	NOTES	CORRECT RESULT	FOR DIAGNOSIS SEE
SOLEN. 1-2/3-4	Press arrow up (ON) Press arrow down (OFF)	"Click" heard from transmission	DTC 31 or 41
SOLENOID 2-3	Press arrow up (ON) Press arrow down (OFF)	"Click" heard from transmission	DTC 32 or 42
SHIFT SOLENOID	Press arrow up (ON) Press arrow down (OFF)	"Click" heard from transmission	DTC 82
TCC SOLENOID	Not used	–	–
TCC HIGH (D)	Press arrow up (ON) Press arrow down (OFF)	"Click" heard from transmission	DTC 33 or 43 / DTC 64 or 65
ATF LAMP	Press arrow up (ON) Press arrow down (OFF)	A/T OIL TEMP lamp ON	A/T OIL TEMPERATURE INDICATOR TEST
POWER LAMP	Press arrow up (ON) Press arrow down (OFF)	POWER lamp ON	TRANSMISSION OPERATING MODE TEST
WINTER LAMP	Press arrow up (ON) Press arrow down (OFF)	WINTER lamp ON	
CHK. TRN. LAMP	Press arrow up (ON) Press arrow down (OFF)	CHECK TRANS lamp ON	CHECK TRANS CHECK
ABS OFF LAMP	Not used	–	–

- If CHECK TRANS light operation is not as specified, proceed to appropriate CHECK LIGHT TEST trouble shooting chart. See TROUBLE SHOOTING FLOW CHARTS.

95J20981

Courtesy of Isuzu Motor Co.

Fig. 7: F5: Actuator Test Mode Check

COMPONENT TESTING

A/C COMPRESSOR RELAY

Passport & Rodeo – 1) Remove A/C compressor relay from fuse/relay box at passenger's side front corner of engine compartment. Note A/C compressor terminal identification. See Fig. 8.
2) Using a DVOM, ensure continuity is present between terminals No. 1 and 2. Continuity should not exist between terminals No. 1 and 3.
3) Connect battery voltage to terminals No. 4 and 5. Ensure continuity is now present between terminals No. 1 and 3, and continuity is not present between terminals No. 1 and 2. Disconnect battery. Replace A/C compressor relay if defective.
Trooper – 1) Remove A/C compressor relay from fuse/relay box at passenger's side front corner of engine compartment. Note A/C compressor terminal identification. See Fig. 8.
2) Using a DVOM, ensure continuity is not present between terminals No. 2 and 4. Connect battery voltage to terminals No. 1 and 3. Ensure continuity is now present between terminals No. 2 and 4. Disconnect battery. Replace A/C compressor relay if defective.

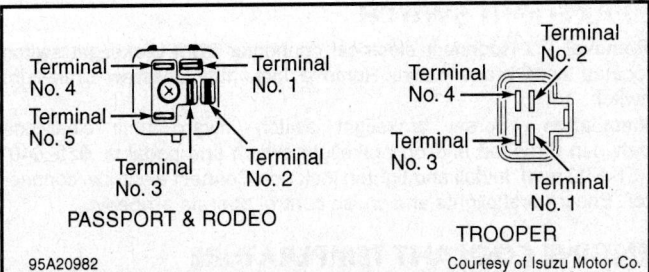

95A20982

Courtesy of Isuzu Motor Co.

Fig. 8: Identifying A/C Compressor Relay Terminals

BAROMETRIC SENSOR

Barometric sensor is located at driver's side front corner of engine compartment, behind headlight. Component testing information is not available from manufacturer.

BAND APPLY SOLENOID

Band apply solenoid is located on main valve body. See Fig. 3. Component testing information is not available from manufacturer.

BRAKELIGHT SWITCH

Without Cruise Control – 1) Disconnect electrical connector from brakelight switch. Brakelight switch is located near brake pedal.
2) Using a DVOM, ensure continuity is not present between terminals on brakelight switch with brake pedal released. Ensure continuity is present between terminals on brakelight switch with brake pedal depressed.
3) If continuity is not as specified, ensure brake pedal is properly adjusted so brakelight switch can obtain proper travel for switch operation. If brakelight switch travel is okay, replace brakelight switch.
With Cruise Control – 1) Disconnect electrical connector from brakelight switch and note terminal identification. See Fig. 9. Brakelight switch is located near brake pedal.
2) Using a DVOM, ensure continuity is present between specified terminals in relation to brake pedal position. See BRAKELIGHT SWITCH CONTINUITY SPECIFICATIONS table.
3) If continuity is not as specified, ensure brake pedal is properly adjusted so brakelight switch can obtain proper travel for switch operation. If brakelight switch travel is okay, replace brakelight switch.

BRAKELIGHT SWITCH CONTINUITY SPECIFICATIONS

Condition	Continuity Between Terminals No.
Brake Pedal Released	2 & 3
Brake Pedal Depressed	1 & 4

3-578

AUTOMATIC TRANSMISSIONS
1995 Hydra-Matic 4L30-E Electronic Controls (Cont.)

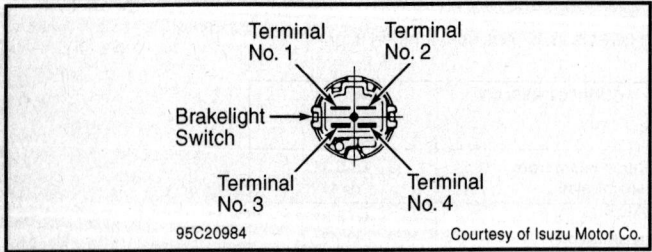

Fig. 9: Identifying Brakelight Switch Terminals

ENGINE COOLANT TEMPERATURE (ECT) SENSOR

ECT sensor is located on coolant pipe at rear of cylinder head. ECT sensor contains a Gray wire and Gray/Black wire in harness connector. Component testing information is not available from manufacturer.

FORCE MOTOR SOLENOID

Force motor solenoid is located on adapter case valve body. *See Fig. 3.* Component testing information is not available from manufacturer.

KICKDOWN SWITCH

Kickdown switch is located on accelerator pedal. Component testing information is not available from manufacturer.

MODE SWITCH

1) Mode switch is located on side of transmission. *See Fig. 3.* Remove necessary covers for access to mode switch electrical connector. Disconnect mode switch electrical connector and note terminal identification. *See Fig. 10.*
2) Using a DVOM, check continuity between specified terminals in relation to shift lever position. See MODE SWITCH CONTINUITY table. If continuity is not as specified, mode switch may require adjustment. See MODE SWITCH under REMOVAL & INSTALLATION. Replace mode switch if specified continuity cannot be obtained by adjusting.

MODE SWITCH CONTINUITY

Shift Lever Position	Continuity Between Terminals
"P"	3, 5 & 8
"R"	5, 7 & 8
"N"	3, 5 & 7
"D"	5, 6 & 7
"3"	3, 5, 6, 7 & 8
"2"	5, 6 & 8
"L"	3, 5 & 6

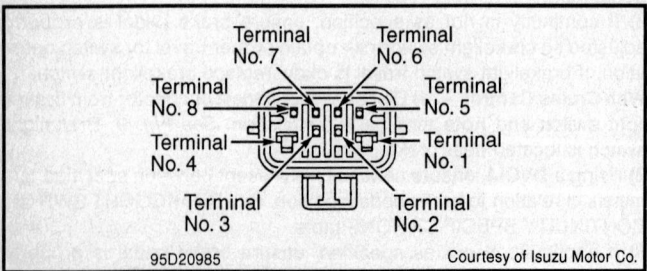

Fig. 10: Identifying Mode Switch Terminals

POWER MODE SWITCH

POWER mode switch is located on center console, near gearshift lever. Component testing information is not available from manufacturer.

SHIFT SOLENOID

The 1-2/3-4 and 2-3 shift solenoids are located on main valve body. *See Fig. 3.* Component testing information is not available from manufacturer.

SPEED SENSOR

Speed sensor is located on extension housing on rear of transmission. *See Fig. 3.* Speed sensor may be referred to as magnetic sensor. Component testing information is not available from manufacturer.

THROTTLE POSITION SENSOR (TPS)

The TPS sensor is mounted on side of throttle body. Component testing information is not available from manufacturer.

TORQUE CONVERTER CLUTCH (TCC) SOLENOID

Torque Converter Clutch (TCC) solenoid is located on adapter case valve body. *See Fig. 3* Component testing information is not available from manufacturer.

TRANSMISSION OIL TEMPERATURE SENSOR

Transmission oil temperature sensor is located on wiring harness in adapter case oil pan. *See Fig. 3.* Component testing information is not available from manufacturer.

WINTER MODE SWITCH

WINTER mode switch is mounted on center console, near gearshift lever. Component testing information is not available from manufacturer.

REMOVAL & INSTALLATION

A/C COMPRESSOR RELAY

Removal & Installation – Remove A/C compressor relay from fuse/relay box at passenger's side front corner of engine compartment. To install, reverse removal procedure.

BAND APPLY SOLENOID

Removal – **1)** Band apply solenoid is located on main valve body. *See Fig. 3.* Disconnect negative battery cable. Remove exhaust pipe (if necessary) to access main case oil pan. Remove bolts, main case oil pan, magnet and gasket. Remove bolts and oil filter. Disconnect electrical connectors at band apply solenoid.
2) Remove spring pin used to retain band apply solenoid in main valve body. Remove band apply solenoid and gasket from main valve body by pulling on metal tip. DO NOT pull on electrical connector housing on band apply solenoid.
Installation – To install, reverse removal procedure using NEW gaskets and oil filter. Ensure spring pin is fully seated in main valve body. Install and tighten oil filter and main case oil pan bolts to specification. See TORQUE SPECIFICATIONS. Fill transmission with Dexron-III ATF.

BRAKELIGHT SWITCH

Removal – Disconnect electrical connector from brakelight switch located near brake pedal. Remove lock nut. Unscrew brakelight switch.
Installation – Screw brakelight switch inward until clearance between threaded end on brakelight switch and pedal is .020-.040" (.51-1.02 mm). Install and tighten lock nut. Connect electrical connector. Ensure brakelights and cruise control operate properly.

ENGINE COOLANT TEMPERATURE (ECT) SENSOR

Removal – **1)** ECT sensor is located on coolant pipe at rear of cylinder head, and contains a Gray wire and a Gray/Black wire in electrical connector.

AUTOMATIC TRANSMISSIONS
1995 Hydra-Matic 4L30-E Electronic Controls (Cont.)

3-579

2) Disconnect negative battery cable. Drain cooling system. It may be necessary to remove fuel inlet manifold for access to ECT sensor. Remove ECT sensor.

Installation – Apply thread sealant to threads of ECT sensor. Install and tighten ECT sensor to specification. See TORQUE SPECIFICATIONS. Fill cooling system.

FORCE MOTOR SOLENOID

Removal – **1)** Force motor solenoid is located on adapter case valve body. *See Fig. 3.* Disconnect negative battery cable.

2) Remove exhaust pipe (if necessary) for access to adapter case oil pan. Remove bolts, adapter case oil pan and gasket. Disconnect electrical connectors at force motor solenoid. Remove bolt and force motor solenoid.

Installation – **1)** Install force motor solenoid on adapter case valve body. Ensure force motor solenoid is installed with electrical connector terminals facing upward, toward transmission.

2) Install and tighten force motor solenoid bolt to specification. See TORQUE SPECIFICATIONS. Using a NEW gasket, install adapter case oil pan. Install and tighten bolts to specification. To install remaining components, reverse removal procedure. Fill transmission with Dexron-III ATF.

KICKDOWN SWITCH

Removal & Installation – Kickdown switch is located on accelerator pedal. Replacement information not available from manufacturer.

MODE SWITCH

Removal – **1)** Disconnect negative battery cable. Apply parking brake. Place gearshift lever in "N" position. Remove mode switch cover for access to mode switch located on side of transmission. *See Fig. 3.* Remove shift lever nut and disconnect shift lever from mode switch.

2) Remove bolts and heat protector from torque converter housing for access to wiring and mode switch. Remove air cleaner assembly. Disconnect mode switch harness connector. Remove clips for mode switch wiring. Remove mode switch retaining bolts and mode switch.

Installation – **1)** Install mode switch with retaining bolts. DO NOT tighten mode switch retaining bolts at this time. Mode switch must be adjusted. To adjust mode switch, rotate mode switch until slot in housing on mode switch aligns with selector shaft bushing. Insert a 3/32" punch into slot. *See Fig. 11.*

2) Tighten mode switch retaining bolts to specification. See TORQUE SPECIFICATIONS. Install shift lever on mode switch and tighten shift lever nut to specification. Install mode switch cover on mode switch. Install heat protector. Install and tighten bolts to specification. Install air cleaner assembly.

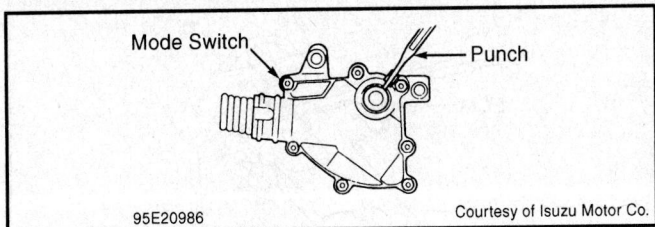

95E20986   Courtesy of Isuzu Motor Co.

Fig. 11: Adjusting Mode Switch

POWER MODE SWITCH

Removal & Installation – POWER mode switch is located on center console, near gearshift lever. Replacement information is not available from manufacturer.

SHIFT SOLENOID

Removal – **1)** The 1-2/3-4 and 2-3 shift solenoids are located on main valve body. *See Fig. 3.* Disconnect negative battery cable. Remove exhaust pipe (if necessary) to access main case oil pan. Remove bolts, main case oil pan, magnet and gasket. Remove bolts and oil filter. Disconnect electrical connectors at appropriate shift solenoid.

2) Remove spring pin used to retain shift solenoid in main valve body. Remove shift solenoid and gasket from main valve body by pulling on metal tip. DO NOT pull on electrical connector housing on shift solenoid.

Installation – To install, reverse removal procedure using NEW gaskets and oil filter. Ensure spring pin is fully seated in main valve body. Install and tighten oil filter and main case oil pan bolts to specification. See TORQUE SPECIFICATIONS. Fill transmission with Dexron-III ATF.

SPEED SENSOR

Removal – **1)** Disconnect electrical connector at speed sensor located on extension housing on rear of transmission. *See Fig. 3.* Remove speed sensor bolt, speed sensor and "O" ring.

2) To install, reverse removal procedure using a NEW "O" ring. Install and tighten speed sensor bolt to specification. See TORQUE SPECIFICATIONS.

TCM

CAUTION: When replacing TCM, it is critical that correct TCM is paired with transmission. Note transmission and TCM identification numbers and consult dealer for latest application. Failure to pair proper components can result in poor transmission performance. When handling TCM, DO NOT touch terminal pins on TCM, as static electricity may damage TCM.

Removal & Installation – Ensure ignition is off. Disconnect harness connectors at TCM, located below driver's side of instrument panel, near kick panel. *See Fig. 2.* Remove TCM. To install, reverse removal procedure.

TCM MEM-CAL

CAUTION: The following procedure must be performed to ensure static electricity does not damage TCM MEM-CAL. Before removing TCM MEM-CAL from package, ground package to a good vehicle ground. DO NOT touch terminal pins on TCM MEM-CAL. Always touch a good vehicle ground before touching TCM MEM-CAL.

Removal – **1)** Ensure ignition is off. Disconnect negative battery cable. Disconnect harness connectors at TCM, located below driver's side of instrument panel, near kick panel. *See Fig. 2.*

2) Remove access cover on TCM to expose TCM MEM-CAL. *See Fig. 12.* Using 2 fingers, pinch both retaining clips on each end of TCM MEM-CAL together. Remove TCM MEM-CAL from TCM.

CAUTION: When installing TCM MEM-CAL in TCM, small notch on TCM MEM-CAL must align with small notch on TCM MEM-CAL socket in TCM. See Fig. 12. TCM MEM-CAL must be installed into TCM MEM-CAL socket until a "click" sound is heard to ensure TCM MEM-CAL is fully seated.

Installation – **1)** Ensure TCM MEM-CAL contains correct replacement part number and install in TCM. Ensure small notch on TCM MEM-CAL aligns with small notch in TCM socket. *See Fig. 12.*

2) Press TCM MEM-CAL into socket until a "click" sound is heard to ensure TCM MEM-CAL is fully seated. Install access cover on TCM. Reinstall TCM and harness connectors. To complete installation, reverse removal procedure.

3-580

AUTOMATIC TRANSMISSIONS
1995 Hydra-Matic 4L30-E Electronic Controls (Cont.)

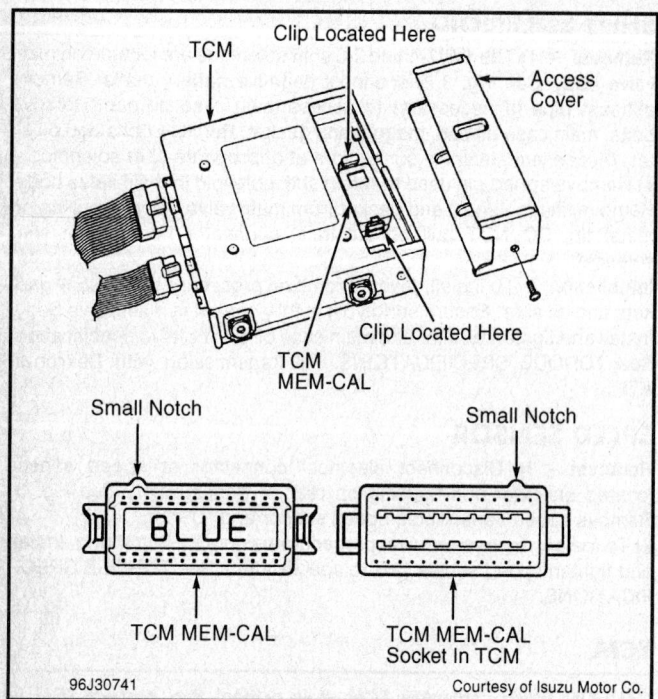

Fig. 12: Removing & Installing TCM MEM-CAL

THROTTLE POSITION SENSOR (TPS)

Removal & Installation – 1) Disconnect harness connector at TPS sensor mounted on side of throttle body. Remove TPS bolts and TPS. **2)** To install, ensure throttle is closed. Install TPS on throttle body and throttle shaft. Align TPS with bolt holes. Install and tighten TPS bolts to specification. See TORQUE SPECIFICATIONS. Install harness connector.

TORQUE CONVERTER CLUTCH (TCC) SOLENOID

Removal – 1) The TCC solenoid is located on adapter case valve body. *See Fig. 3.* Disconnect negative battery cable.
2) Remove exhaust pipe (if necessary) to access adapter case oil pan. Remove bolts, adapter case oil pan and gasket. Disconnect electrical connector at TCC solenoid. Remove bolt, TCC solenoid and "O" ring.
Installation – 1) Using a NEW "O" ring, install TCC solenoid on adapter case valve body. Install and tighten TCC solenoid bolt to specification. See TORQUE SPECIFICATIONS.
2) Using a NEW gasket, install adapter case oil pan. Install and tighten bolts to specification. To install remaining components, reverse removal procedure. Fill transmission with Dexron-III ATF.

TRANSMISSION OIL TEMPERATURE SENSOR

Removal & Installation – Transmission oil temperature sensor is located on wiring harness in adapter case oil pan. *See Fig. 3.* Replacement information not available from manufacturer.

WINTER MODE SWITCH

Removal & Installation – Winter mode switch is located on center console, near gearshift lever. Replacement information not available from manufacturer.

TORQUE SPECIFICATIONS
TORQUE SPECIFICATIONS

Application	Ft. Lbs. (N.m)
Engine Coolant Temperature Sensor	22 (30)
Oil Filter Bolt	15 (20)
Shift Lever Nut	17 (23)

TORQUE SPECIFICATIONS (Cont.)

Application	INCH Lbs. (N.m)
Adapter Case Oil Pan Bolt	96 (10.8)
Force Motor Solenoid Bolt	87 (9.8)
Heat Protector Bolt	52 (5.9)
Main Case Oil Pan Bolt	96 (10.8)
Mode Switch Retaining Bolt	113 (12.8)
Speed Sensor Bolt	78 (8.8)
TCC Solenoid Bolt	87 (9.8)
TPS Bolt	18 (2.0)

TROUBLE SHOOTING FLOW CHARTS

FLOW CHART USAGE

1) Use trouble shooting flow chart in accordance with problem area or corresponding to DTC. When using trouble shooting flow charts, technician may be instructed to disconnect specified harness connector and check circuit at specified terminal on harness connector. For harness connector and terminal identification, *See Figs. 14-18.*
2) When using some trouble shooting flow charts, technician may be instructed to go to TCM MEM-CAL REPLACEMENT. For this procedure, see TCM MEM-CAL under REMOVAL & INSTALLATION.
3) When using some trouble shooting flow charts, technician may be instructed to go to INTERMITTENT CONDITIONS. For this procedure, see INTERMITTENT CONDITIONS under TROUBLE SHOOTING.
4) When using some trouble shooting flow charts, technician may be instructed to check ECM for stored trouble codes. See appropriate SELF-DIAGNOSTICS article in ENGINE PERFORMANCE in appropriate MITCHELL® manual for proper procedure.
5) When using trouble shooting flow charts, technician may be instructed to use TECH 1 scan tool to check specified data. Technician may be instructed to access TCM or ECM.

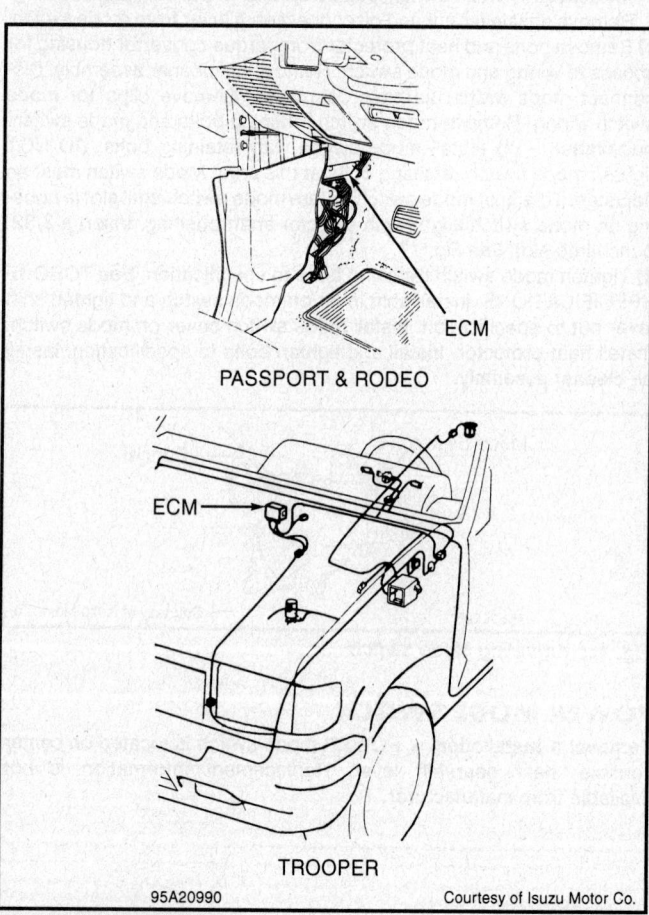

Fig. 13: Locating ECM

AUTOMATIC TRANSMISSIONS
1995 Hydra-Matic 4L30-E Electronic Controls (Cont.)

3-581

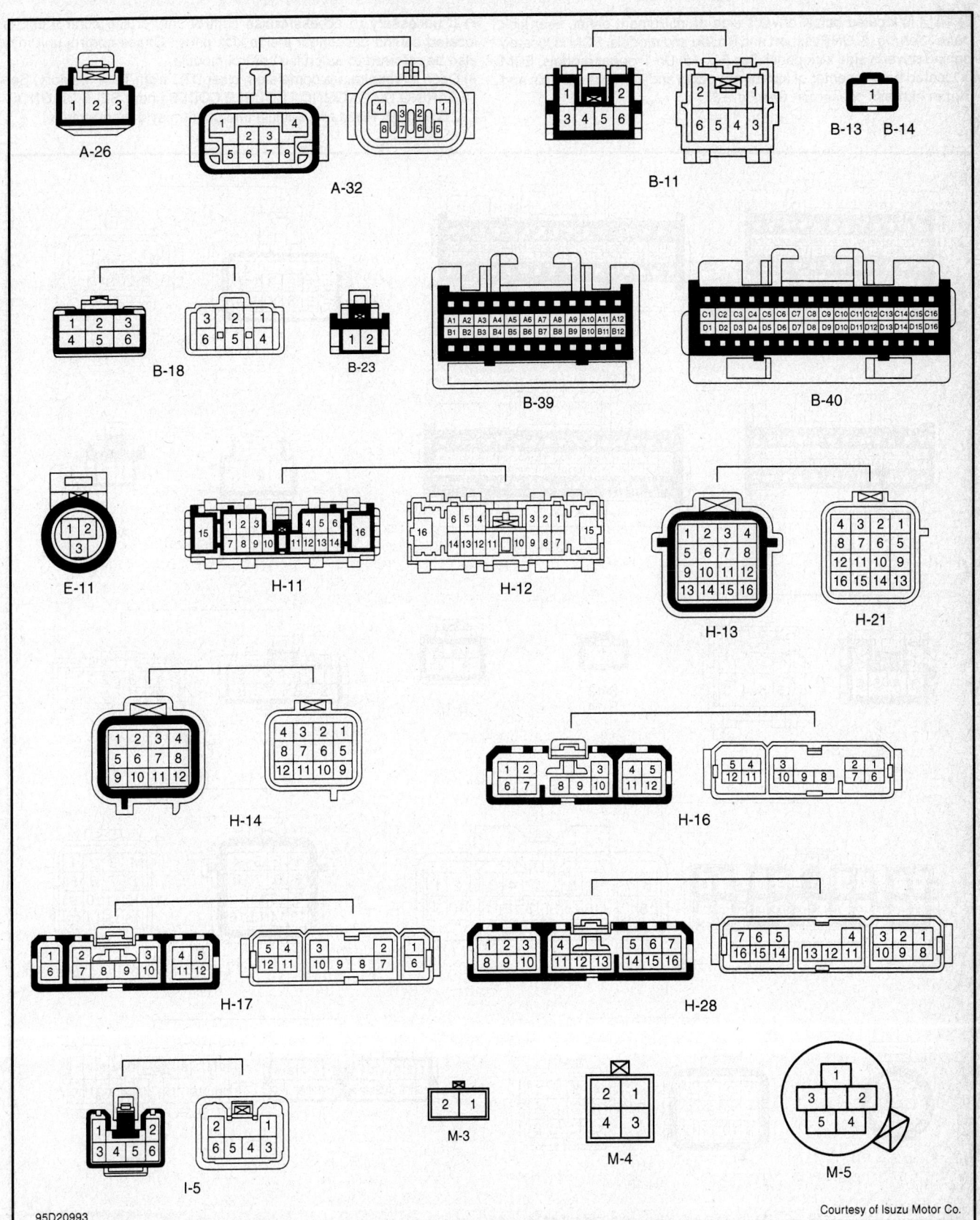

Fig. 14: Identifying Harness Connectors & Terminals (Early Production 1995 Passport & Rodeo)

95D20993

Courtesy of Isuzu Motor Co.

3-582

AUTOMATIC TRANSMISSIONS
1995 Hydra-Matic 4L30-E Electronic Controls (Cont.)

6) TCM is located below driver's side of instrument panel, near kick panel. *See Fig. 2.* On Passport and Rodeo and models, ECM is located behind driver's side kick panel. *See Fig. 13.* On Trooper models, ECM is located behind center of instrument panel and contains a 24-pin and 32-pin harness connector. *See Fig. 13.*

7) If necessary to access cruise control unit, cruise control unit is located behind passenger's side kick panel. Cruise control unit may also be referred to as cruise control module.

8) Once all repairs are completed, clear DTC from TCM memory. See CLEARING DIAGNOSTIC TROUBLE CODES under SELF-DIAGNOSTIC SYSTEM. Road test vehicle and confirm system operation.

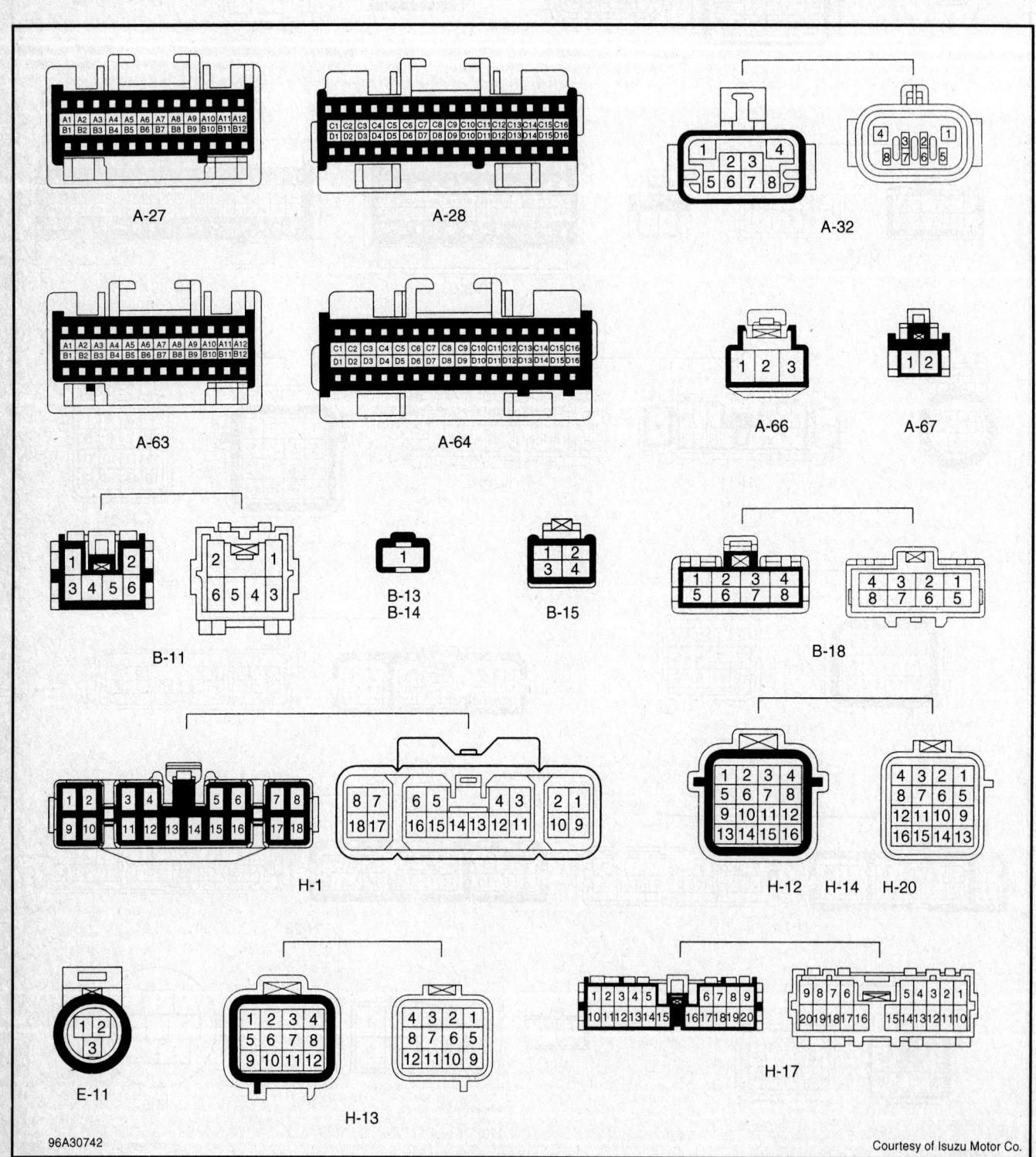

Fig. 15: Identifying Harness Connectors & Terminals (Late Production 1995 Passport & Rodeo – Part 1 Of 2)

AUTOMATIC TRANSMISSIONS
1995 Hydra-Matic 4L30-E Electronic Controls (Cont.)

3-583

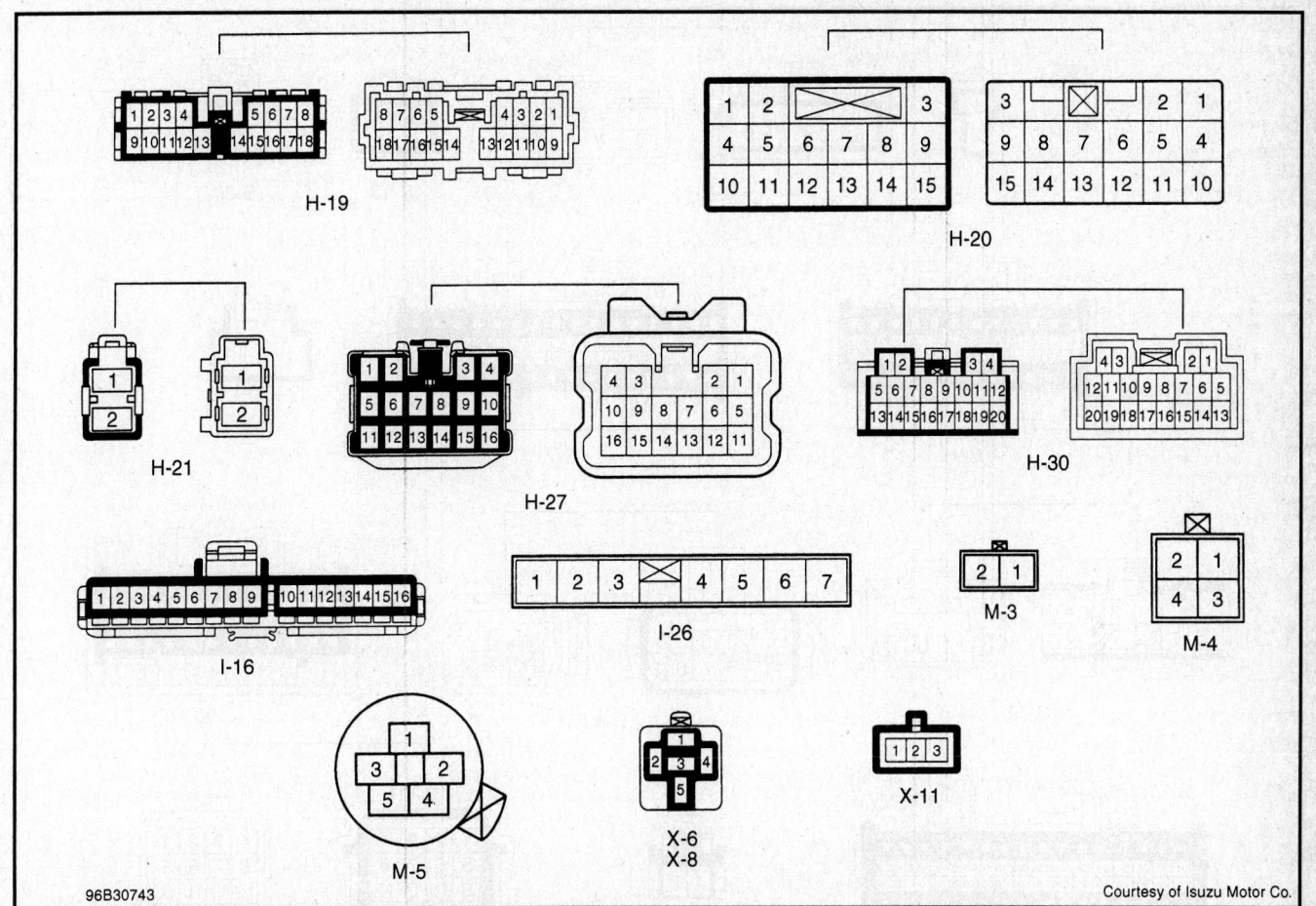

96B30743

Courtesy of Isuzu Motor Co.

Fig. 16: Identifying Harness Connectors & Terminals (Late Production 1995 Passport & Rodeo – Part 2 Of 2)

3-584

AUTOMATIC TRANSMISSIONS
1995 Hydra-Matic 4L30-E Electronic Controls (Cont.)

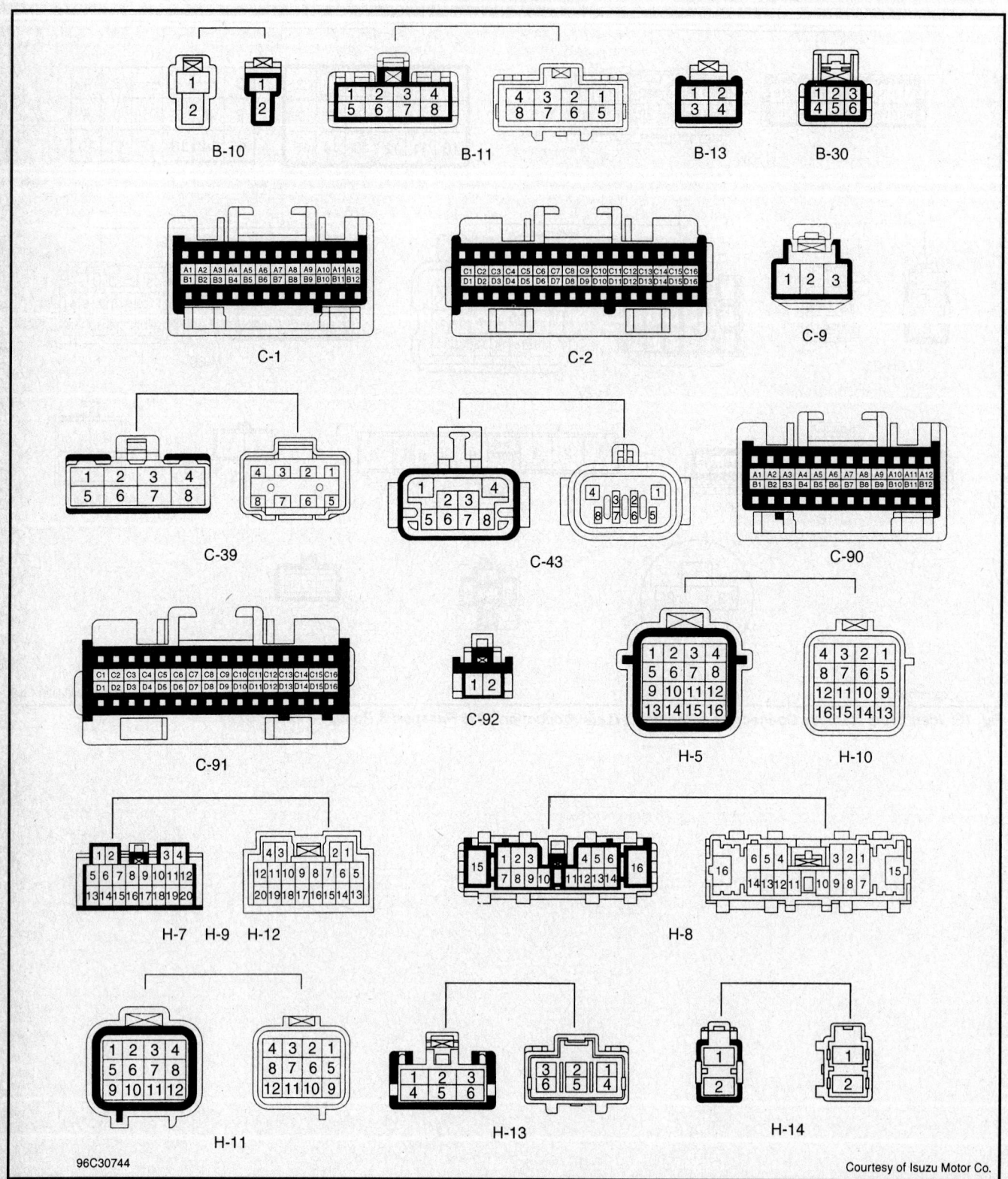

Fig. 17: Identifying Harness Connectors & Terminals (1995 Trooper – Part 1 Of 2)

96C30744

Courtesy of Isuzu Motor Co.

AUTOMATIC TRANSMISSIONS
1995 Hydra-Matic 4L30-E Electronic Controls (Cont.)

3-585

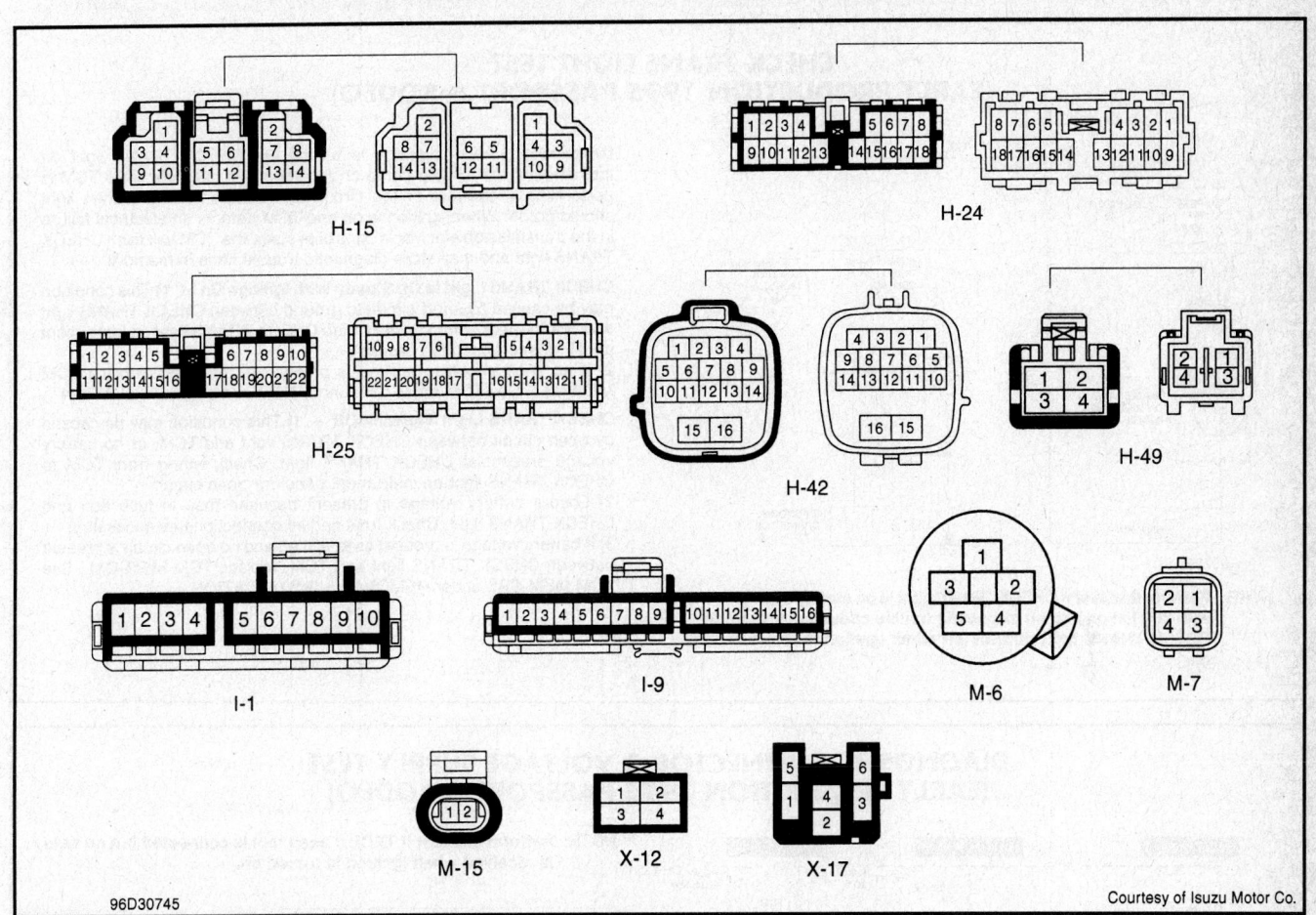

96D30745

Courtesy of Isuzu Motor Co.

Fig. 18: Identifying Harness Connectors & Terminals (1995 Trooper – Part 2 Of 2)

3-586

AUTOMATIC TRANSMISSIONS
1995 Hydra-Matic 4L30-E Electronic Controls (Cont.)

CHECK TRANS LIGHT TEST
(EARLY PRODUCTION 1995 PASSPORT & RODEO)

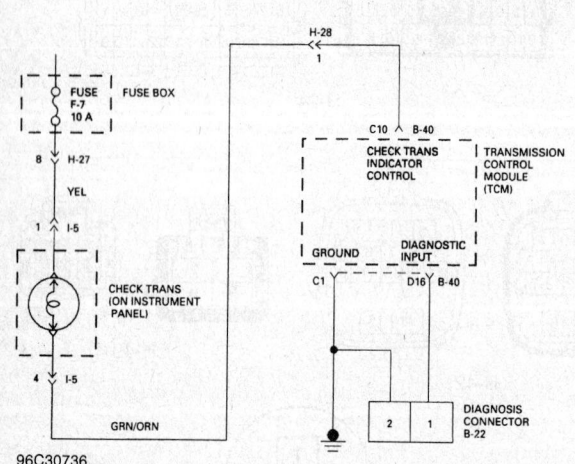

96C30736

NOTE: Perform this test if CHECK TRANS light is on steady at all times with ignition on and no diagnostic trouble codes are stored, or CHECK TRANS light remains off when ignition is first turned on.

Description – When ignition is turned on, CHECK TRANS light on instrument panel should come on for about 2-4 seconds while TCM is performing a self-test of the circuit and components and then light should go off. When ignition is on and TCM detects an electrical failure in the transmission electronic control system, the TCM will flash CHECK TRANS light and may store diagnostic trouble code in memory.

CHECK TRANS Light Is On Steady With Ignition On – 1) This condition may be caused by short circuit to ground between CHECK TRANS light and TCM. Check wiring from TCM to CHECK TRANS light on instrument panel for short circuit to ground.

2) If no short circuit to ground is present in the wiring, replace TCM MEM-CAL. See TCM MEM-CAL under REMOVAL & INSTALLATION.

CHECK TRANS Light Remains Off – 1) This condition may be caused by open circuit between CHECK TRANS light and TCM, or no battery voltage present at CHECK TRANS light. Check wiring from TCM to CHECK TRANS light on instrument panel for open circuit.

2) Ensure battery voltage is present between fuse in fuse box and CHECK TRANS light. Check fuse and all connections as necessary.

3) If battery voltage is present as specified and no open circuit is present between CHECK TRANS light and TCM, replace TCM MEM-CAL. See TCM MEM-CAL under REMOVAL & INSTALLATION.

DIAGNOSTIC CONNECTOR & VOLTAGE SUPPLY TEST
(EARLY PRODUCTION 1995 PASSPORT & RODEO)

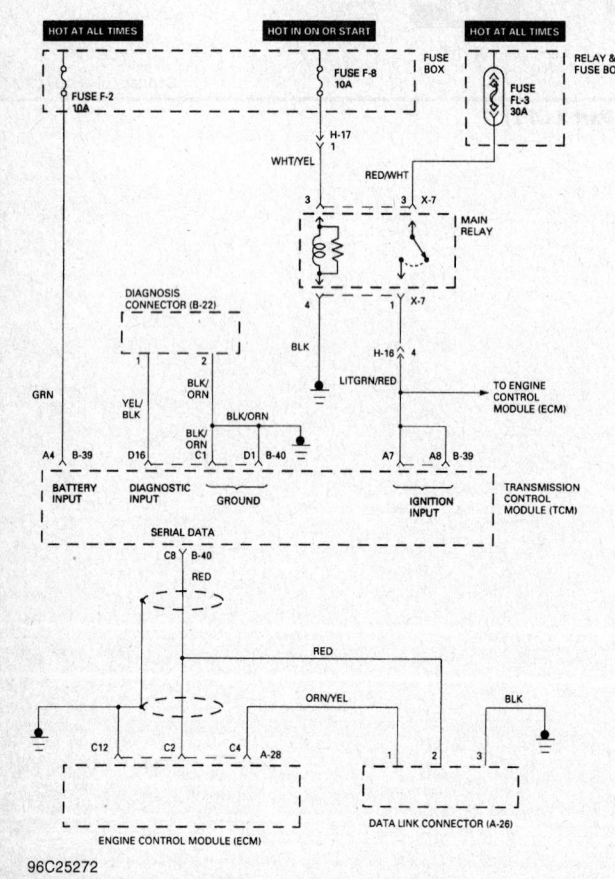

96C25272

NOTE: Perform this test if TECH 1 scan tool is connected but no data is received when ignition is turned on.

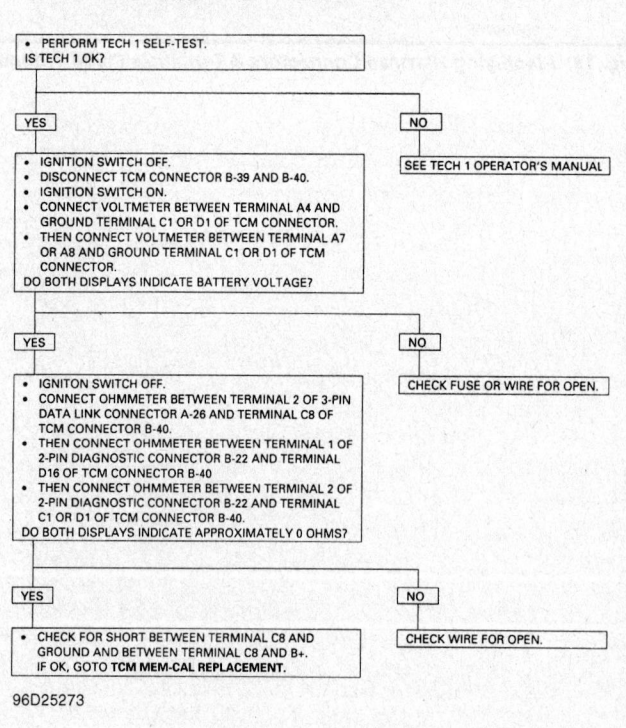

96D25273

AUTOMATIC TRANSMISSIONS
1995 Hydra-Matic 4L30-E Electronic Controls (Cont.)

3-587

TRANSMISSION OPERATING MODE TEST
(EARLY PRODUCTION 1995 PASSPORT & RODEO)

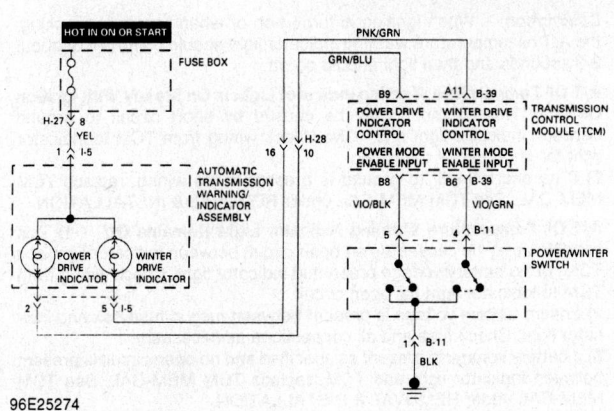

96E25274

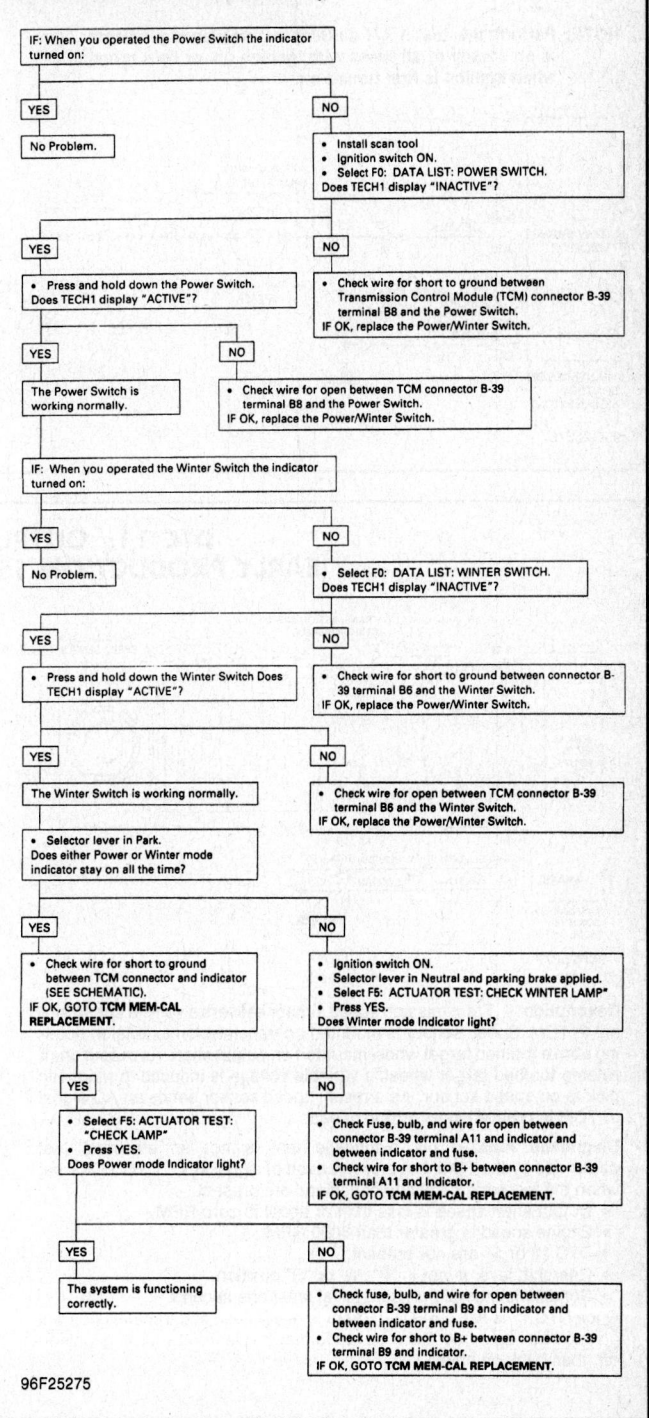

96F25275

Description – The TCM controls transmission shifting and operation using 3 different shift modes, Normal mode, Power mode and Winter mode. Driver selects shift mode by using power or winter mode switch mounted on center console, near gearshift lever. Power mode slightly increases engine speed at which transmission shift points occur for maximum performance.

In Winter mode, transmission starts off in 3rd gear to aid in vehicle traction on ice and snow. When Winter mode is selected, the TCM overrides the Power or Normal mode. Winter mode will be activated when all of the following conditions are present.

- Accelerator opening is at approximately 7 percent or less.
- Kickdown switch is off.
- Gearshift lever is in "D" position.
- Transmission fluid temperature is 140°F (248°C) or less.
- Vehicle speed is less than 7 MPH.
- WINTER mode switch is on.

Winter mode will be canceled when any of the following conditions are present.

- Ignition is turned off.
- Kickdown switch is on for more than 3 seconds.
- Gearshift lever is placed in "3", "2" or "L" position.
- Transmission fluid temperature is 140°F (284°C) or greater.
- Vehicle speed exceeds 20 MPH.
- WINTER mode switch is turned off.

When Winter or Power mode are canceled, transmission operates in Normal mode. Normal mode provides standard transmission shift points.

3-588

AUTOMATIC TRANSMISSIONS
1995 Hydra-Matic 4L30-E Electronic Controls (Cont.)

A/T OIL TEMP. INDICATOR TEST
(EARLY PRODUCTION 1995 PASSPORT & RODEO)

NOTE: Perform this test if A/T oil temperature warning indicator light is on steady at all times with ignition on, or light remains off when ignition is first turned on.

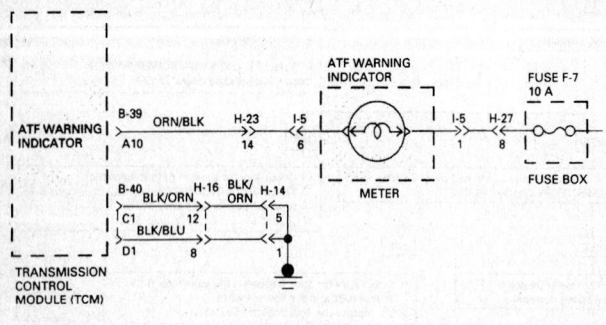

96G25276

Description – When ignition is turned on or when engine is cranking, the A/T temperature warning indicator light should come on for about 2-3 seconds and then light should go off.

A/T Oil Temperature Warning Indicator Light Is On Steady With Ignition On – **1)** This condition may be caused by short circuit to ground between indicator light and TCM. Check wiring from TCM to indicator light for short circuit to ground.
2) If no short circuit to ground is present in the wiring, replace TCM MEM-CAL. See TCM MEM-CAL under REMOVAL & INSTALLATION.

A/T Oil Temperature Warning Indicator Light Remains Off – **1)** This condition may be caused by an open circuit between indicator light and TCM, or no battery voltage present at indicator light. Check wiring from TCM to indicator light for open circuit.
2) Ensure battery voltage is present between fuse in fuse box and indicator light. Check fuse and all connections as necessary.
3) If battery voltage is present as specified and no open circuit is present between indicator light and TCM, replace TCM MEM-CAL. See TCM MEM-CAL under REMOVAL & INSTALLATION.

DTC 11: OUTPUT SPEED FAILURE
(EARLY PRODUCTION 1995 PASSPORT & RODEO)

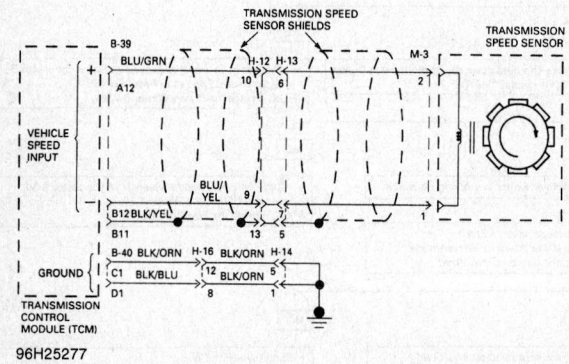

96H25277

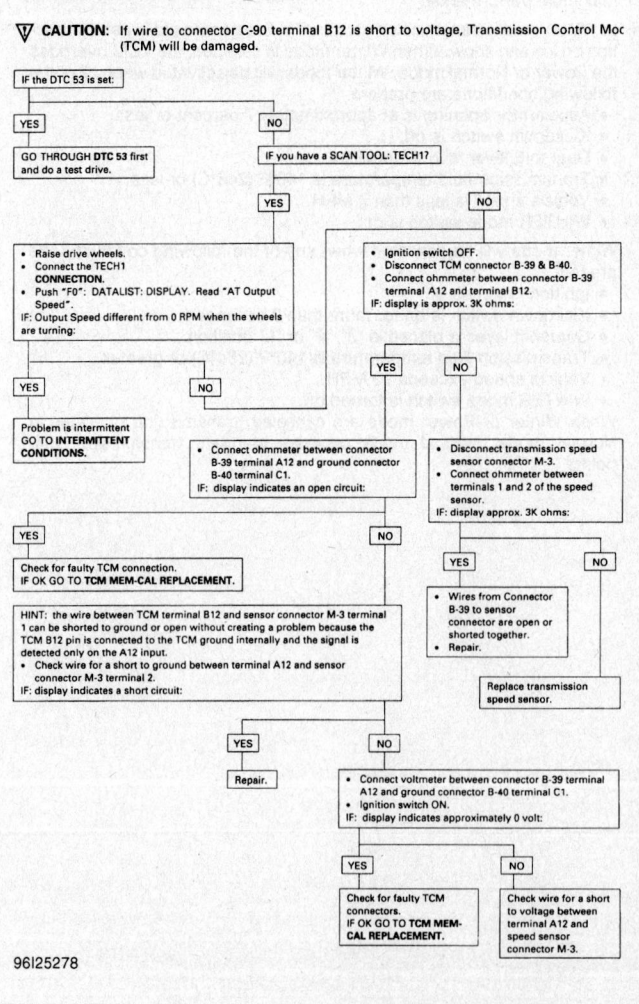

96I25278

Description – Transmission speed sensor delivers a vehicle speed signal to TCM. Speed sensor is mounted on transmission extension housing above toothed target wheel mounted on output shaft. As output shaft rotates toothed target wheel, a variable voltage is induced in magnetic pickup on speed sensor. As a result, speed sensor sends an AC signal to TCM in proportion to vehicle speed.

Diagnostic Aids – This diagnostic test is not an electrical test performed by the TCM, but a comparison of signal input. DTC 11 will set when the following detection conditions are present.
- Output shaft speed is less than or equal to zero RPM.
- Engine speed is greater than 3000 RPM.
- DTC 13 or 54 are not present.
- Gearshift lever is not in "P", "N" or "R" position.
- Conditions must be present for at least one second.
Once DTC 11 is set, CHECK TRANS light will flash and transmission will go into back-up mode. Back-up mode may be cleared by turning ignition off, then back on again.

AUTOMATIC TRANSMISSIONS
1995 Hydra-Matic 4L30-E Electronic Controls (Cont.)

3-589

DTC 13: ENGINE SPEED FAILURE
(EARLY PRODUCTION 1995 PASSPORT & RODEO)

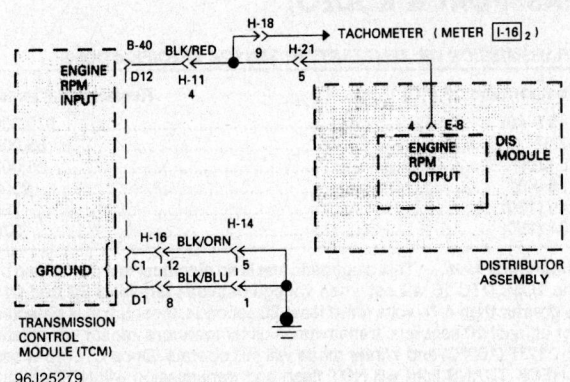

96J25279

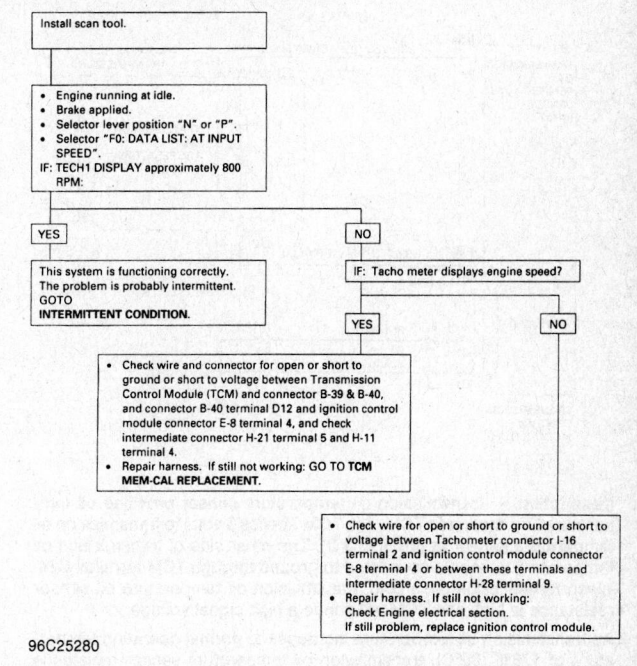

96C25280

Description – Ignition control module sends a engine speed or RPM signal to TCM. Engine Control Module (ECM) also receives signal from ignition control module. In Neutral at idle, engine speed should be approximately 800 RPM.

Diagnostic Aids – This diagnostic test is not an electrical test performed by the TCM, but a comparison of signal input. DTC 13 will set when the following detection conditions are present.
- Output speed is greater than 1024 RPM.
- Engine speed is equal to or less than 200 RPM.
- Acceleration is greater than one MPH.
- DTC 11, 54 or 62 are not present.
- Gearshift lever is not in "P" or "N" position.
- Conditions must be present for at least .5 second.

Once DTC 13 is set, CHECK TRANS light will flash and transmission will go into back-up mode. Back-up mode may be cleared by turning ignition off, then back on again.

3-590

AUTOMATIC TRANSMISSIONS
1995 Hydra-Matic 4L30-E Electronic Controls (Cont.)

DTC 15: TRANSMISSION OIL TEMP. SENSOR CIRCUIT
(SHORT CIRCUIT TO B+ OR OPEN CIRCUIT)
(EARLY PRODUCTION 1995 PASSPORT & RODEO)

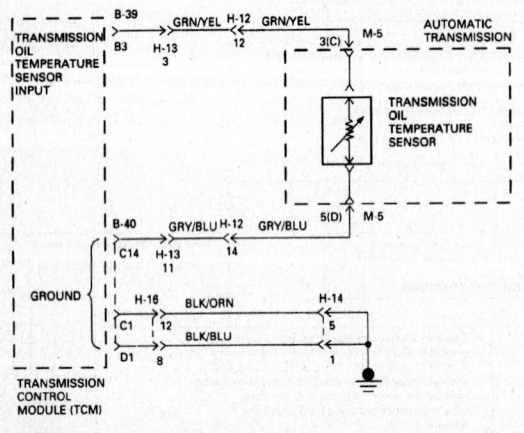

96H30681

Description – Transmission oil temperature sensor provides oil temperature information to TCM. The TCM applies 5 volts to transmission oil temperature sensor at terminal 3(C). The other side of transmission oil temperature sensor is connected to ground through TCM terminal C14. When transmission oil is cold, transmission oil temperature oil sensor resistance is high and TCM will sense a high signal voltage.

As transmission oil temperature increases to normal operating temperature of 176°F (80°C), transmission oil temperature sensor resistance becomes less and voltage decreases to approximately 3.5 volts. When DTC 15 is set, the transmission will use a warm value for operation, but TECH 1 scan tool will display the actual oil temperature. Transmission oil temperature resistance will change in relation to temperature. See TRANSMISSION OIL TEMPERATURE SENSOR SPECIFICATIONS table.

TRANSMISSION OIL TEMPERATURE SENSOR SPECIFICATIONS

Temperature °F (°C)	Resistance (Ohms)
–40 (–40)	672,000
32 (0)	65,000
68 (20)	25,000
176 (80)	2500
248 (120)	780
304 (150)	370

Diagnostic Aids – This diagnostic test is an electrical test performed by the TCM. DTC 15 will set when voltage between terminals B3 and C14 is greater than 4.74 volts for at least 20 seconds. If condition is detected for at least 20 seconds, transmission oil temperature sensor will default to 212°F (100°C) and Winter mode will still operate. Once DTC 15 is set, CHECK TRANS light will NOT flash and transmission will NOT go into back-up mode. System will return to normal operation when voltage between terminals B3 and C14 is equal to or less than 4.74 volts.

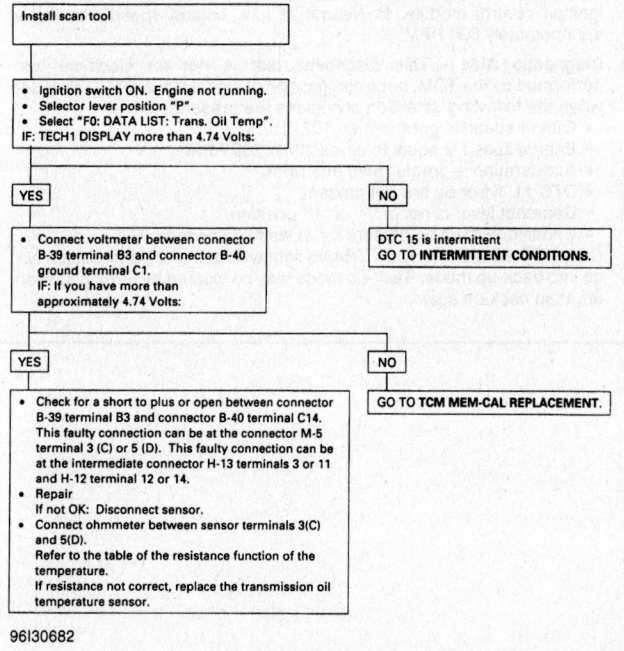

96I30682

AUTOMATIC TRANSMISSIONS
1995 Hydra-Matic 4L30-E Electronic Controls (Cont.)

3-591

DTC 16: TRANSMISSION OIL TEMP. SENSOR CIRCUIT
(SHORT CIRCUIT TO GROUND)
(EARLY PRODUCTION 1995 PASSPORT & RODEO)

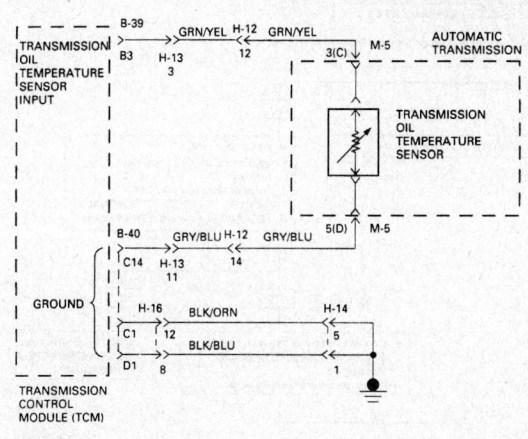

96H30681

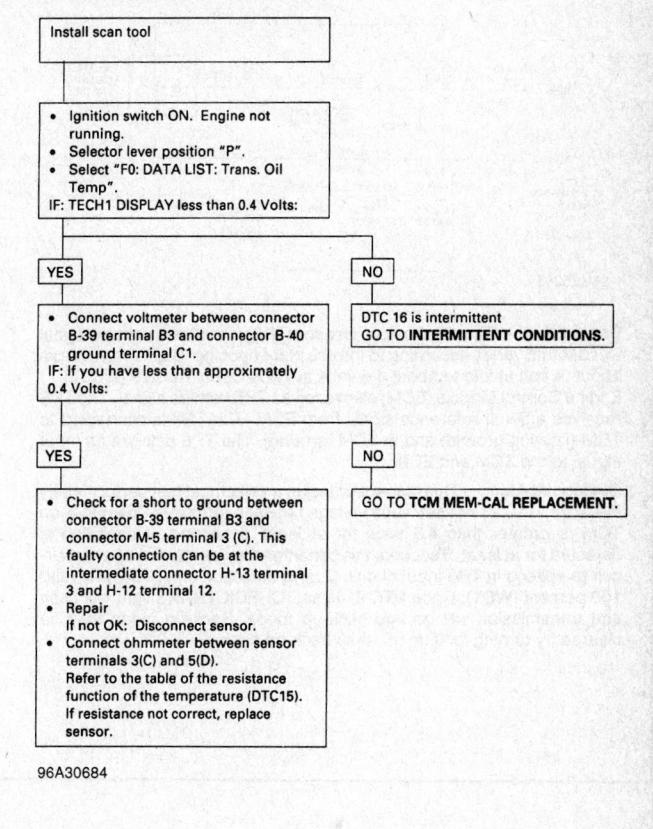

96A30684

Description – Transmission oil temperature sensor provides oil temperature information to TCM. The TCM applies 5 volts to transmission oil temperature sensor at terminal 3(C). The other side of transmission oil temperature sensor is connected to ground through TCM terminal C14.

When transmission oil is cold, transmission oil temperature oil sensor resistance is high and TCM will sense a high signal voltage. As transmission oil temperature increases to normal operating temperature of 176°F (80°C), transmission oil temperature sensor resistance becomes less and voltage decreases to approximately 3.5 volts. When DTC 16 is set, the transmission will use a warm value for operation, but TECH 1 scan tool will display the actual oil temperature.

Diagnostic Aids – This diagnostic test is an electrical test performed by the TCM. DTC 16 will set when voltage between terminals B3 and C14 is less than .4 volt for at least 20 seconds. If condition is detected for at least 20 seconds, transmission oil temperature sensor will default to 212°F (100°C) and Winter mode will still operate. Once DTC 16 is set, CHECK TRANS light will NOT flash and transmission will NOT go into back-up mode. System will return to normal operation when voltage between terminals B3 and C14 is equal to or greater than .4 volt.

3-592

AUTOMATIC TRANSMISSIONS
1995 Hydra-Matic 4L30-E Electronic Controls (Cont.)

DTC 21: THROTTLE POSITION SENSOR CIRCUIT (SHORT CIRCUIT TO B+)
(EARLY PRODUCTION 1995 PASSPORT & RODEO)

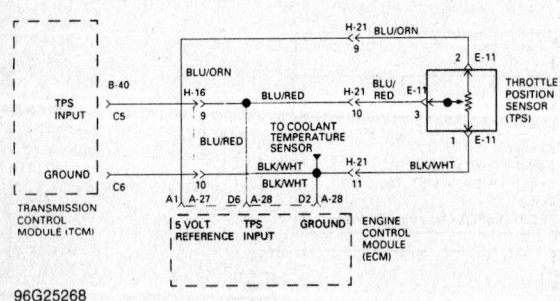

96G25268

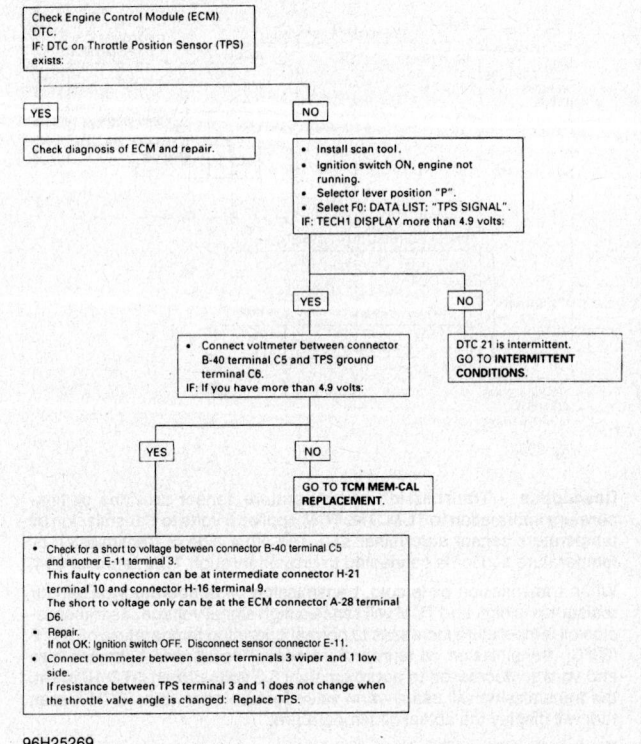

96H25269

Description – Throttle Position Sensor (TPS) provides a voltage signal to TCM that varies according to throttle plate opening. Signal varies from about .4 volt at idle to about 4.6 volts at Wide Open Throttle (WOT). Engine Control Module (ECM) also receives TPS voltage signal. The TPS receives a 5-volt reference signal from ECM. The TPS is connected to TCM (floating ground) and at ECM (ground). The TPS delivers an input signal to the TCM and ECM.

Diagnostic Aids – This diagnostic test is an electrical test performed by the TCM. DTC 21 will set when voltage between terminals C5 and C6 on TCM is greater than 4.9 volts for at least .5 second. If condition is detected for at least .5 second, this condition may be caused by short circuit to voltage in TPS input circuit. During detection time, TCM will read 100 percent (WOT). Once DTC 21 is set, CHECK TRANS light will flash and transmission will go into back-up mode. Back-up mode may be cleared by turning ignition off, then back on again.

AUTOMATIC TRANSMISSIONS
1995 Hydra-Matic 4L30-E Electronic Controls (Cont.)

3-593

DTC 22: THROTTLE POSITION SENSOR CIRCUIT
(SHORT CIRCUIT TO GROUND OR OPEN CIRCUIT)
(EARLY PRODUCTION 1995 PASSPORT & RODEO)

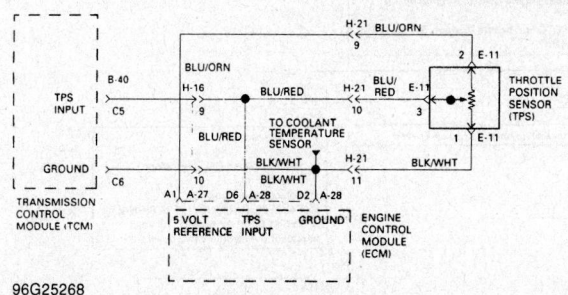

96G25268

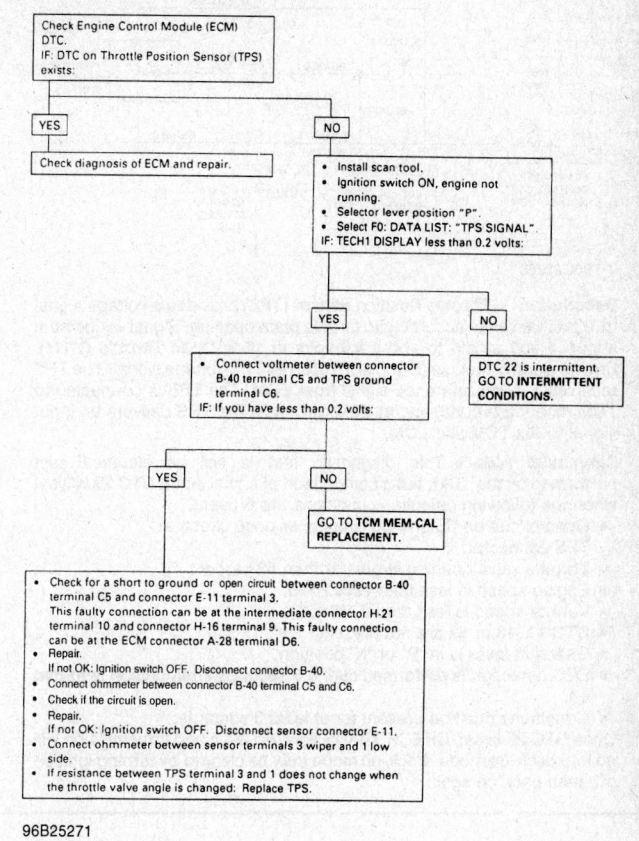

Description – Throttle Position Sensor (TPS) provides a voltage signal to TCM that varies according to throttle plate opening. Signal varies from about .4 volt at idle to about 4.6 volts at Wide Open Throttle (WOT). Engine Control Module (ECM) also receives TPS voltage signal. The TPS receives a 5-volt reference signal from ECM at terminal. The TPS is connected to TCM (floating ground) and at ECM (ground). The TPS delivers an input signal to the TCM and ECM.

Diagnostic Aids – This diagnostic test is an electrical test performed by the TCM. DTC 22 will set when the following detection conditions are present.
- Short circuit on TPS input signal to TCM ground or open circuit on TPS circuit.
- Voltage between terminals C5 and C6 on TCM is less than .2 volts for at least .5 second.

If condition is detected for at least .5 second, during detection time, TCM will read zero percent (idle position). Once DTC 22 is set, CHECK TRANS light will flash and transmission will go into back-up mode. Back-up mode may be cleared by turning ignition off, then back on again.

96B25271

3-594

AUTOMATIC TRANSMISSIONS
1995 Hydra-Matic 4L30-E Electronic Controls (Cont.)

DTC 23: THROTTLE POSITION SENSOR CIRCUIT (CONNECTOR OPEN CIRCUIT)
(EARLY PRODUCTION 1995 PASSPORT & RODEO)

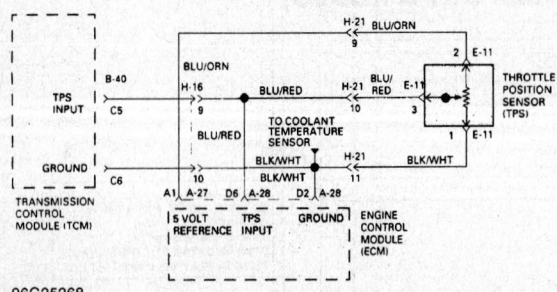

96G25268

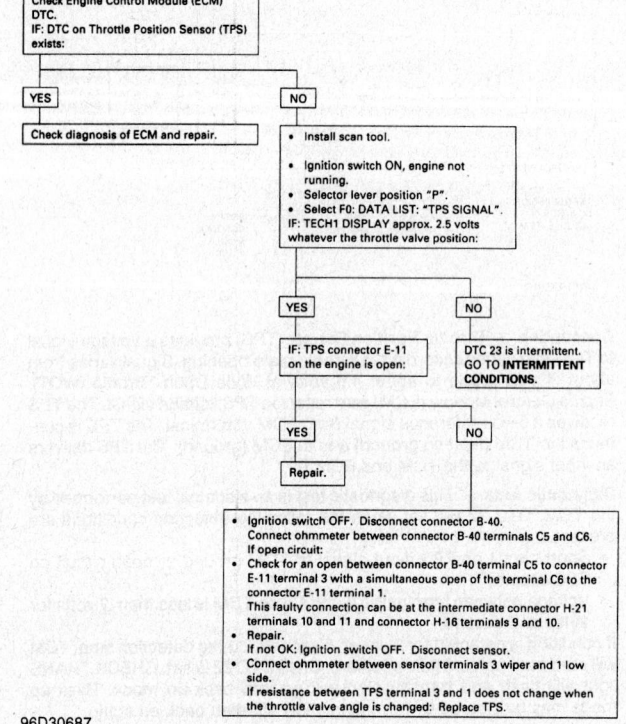

96D30687

Description – Throttle Position Sensor (TPS) provides a voltage signal to TCM that varies according to throttle plate opening. Signal varies from about .4 volt at idle to about 4.6 volts at Wide Open Throttle (WOT). Engine Control Module (ECM) also receives TPS voltage signal. The TPS receives a 5-volt reference signal from ECM. The TPS is connected to TCM (floating ground) and at ECM (ground). The TPS delivers an input signal to the TCM and ECM.

Diagnostic Aids – This diagnostic test is not an electrical test performed by the TCM, but a comparison of signal input. DTC 23 will set when the following detection conditions are present.

- Open circuit on C5 and C6 circuits, or open circuit at TPS connector.
- Throttle valve opening is greater than 42 percent.
- Engine speed is less than 2200 RPM.
- Vehicle speed is less than 2 MPH.
- DTC 11, 13 or 62 are not present.
- Gearshift lever is in "P" or "N" position.
- DTC detection is performed during 6 seconds after ignition is turned on.
- Conditions must be present for at least 3 seconds.

Once DTC 23 is set, CHECK TRANS light will flash and transmission will go into back-up mode. Back-up mode may be cleared by turning ignition off, then back on again.

AUTOMATIC TRANSMISSIONS
1995 Hydra-Matic 4L30-E Electronic Controls (Cont.)

3-595

DTC 25: SUPPLY VOLTAGE TOO LOW
(EARLY PRODUCTION 1995 PASSPORT & RODEO)

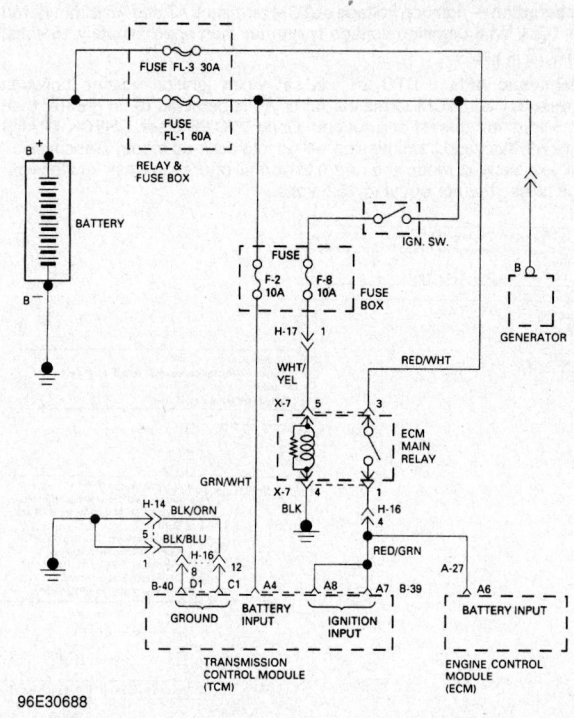

96E30688

SUPPLY VOLTAGE SPECIFICATIONS

Transmission Oil Temperature °F (°C)	Minimum Voltage
Code Set Condition	
–40 (–40)	8.7
194 (90)	9.0
304 (150)	9.2
Back-Up Mode Recovery	
–40 (–40)	9.2
194 (90)	9.5
304 (150)	9.6

Once DTC 25 is set, CHECK TRANS light will flash and transmission will go into back-up mode. Transmission will exit back-up mode and return to normal operation when ignition voltage increases to minimum specified voltage for indicated temperature range. See BACK-UP MODE RECOVERY in SUPPLY VOLTAGE SPECIFICATIONS table.

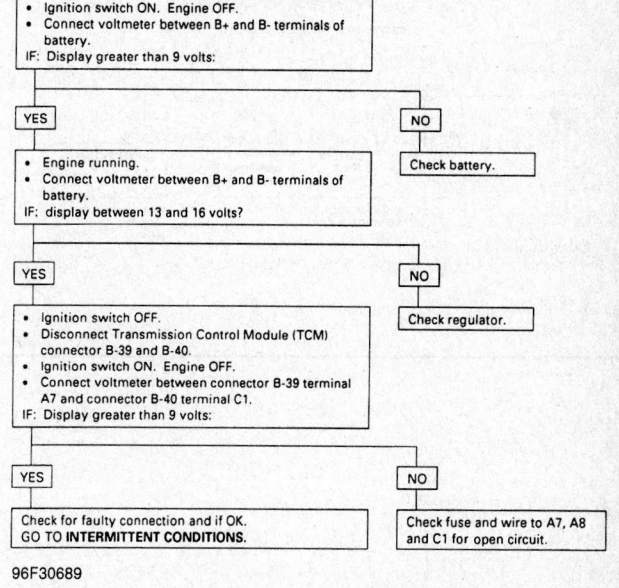

96F30689

Description – Ignition voltage at TCM terminals A7 and A8 is monitored by TCM. When ignition voltage is less than approximately 9 volts, DTC 25 is set. Minimum voltage requirement will vary with transmission oil temperature.

Diagnostic Aids – This diagnostic test is an electrical test performed by the TCM. DTC 25 will set when ignition voltage between ground C1 and TCM terminals A7 and A8 is detected to be less than minimum required for at least one second. See CODE SET CONDITION in SUPPLY VOLTAGE SPECIFICATIONS table.

3-596

AUTOMATIC TRANSMISSIONS
1995 Hydra-Matic 4L30-E Electronic Controls (Cont.)

DTC 26: SUPPLY VOLTAGE TOO HIGH
(EARLY PRODUCTION 1995 PASSPORT & RODEO)

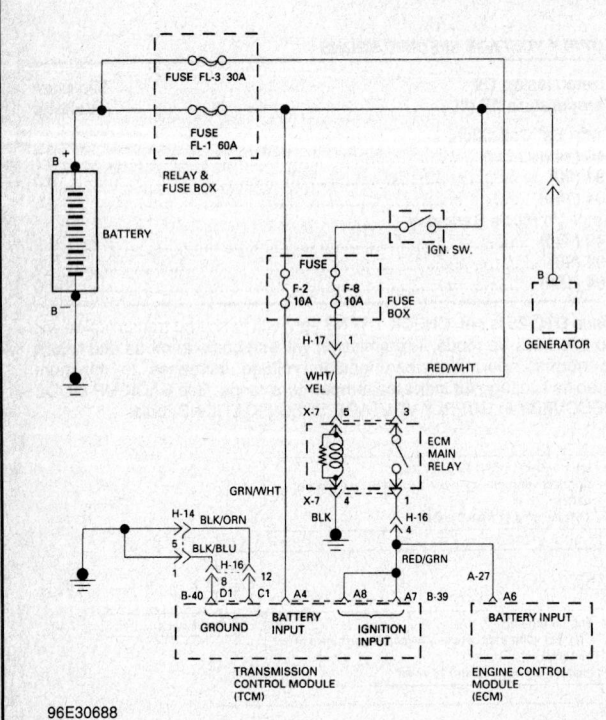

Description – Ignition voltage at TCM terminals A7 and A8 is monitored by TCM. When ignition voltage is greater than approximately 16 volts, DTC 26 is set.

Diagnostic Aids – DTC 26 will set when ignition voltage between ground C1 and TCM terminals A7 or A8 is detected to be greater than 15.5 volts for at least one second. Once DTC 26 is set, CHECK TRANS light will flash and transmission will go into back-up mode. Transmission will exit back-up mode and return to normal operation when ignition voltage is less than or equal to 15.5 volts.

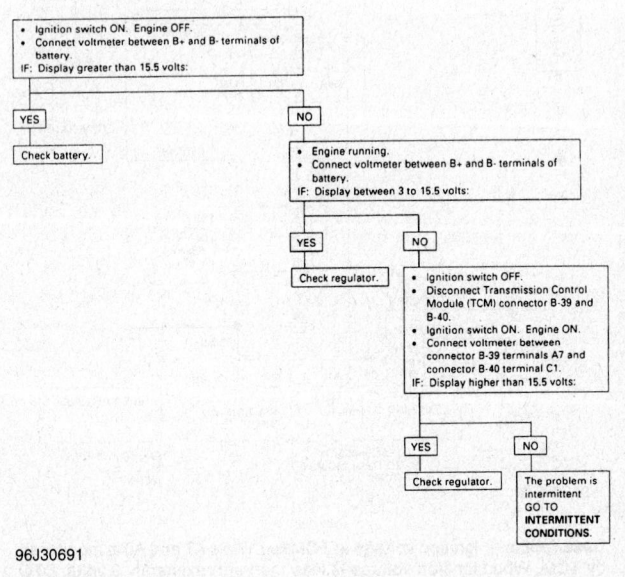

96E30688

96J30691

AUTOMATIC TRANSMISSIONS
1995 Hydra-Matic 4L30-E Electronic Controls (Cont.)

3-597

DTC 31: 1-2/3-4 SHIFT SOLENOID CIRCUIT
(SHORT CIRCUIT TO GROUND OR OPEN CIRCUIT)
(EARLY PRODUCTION 1995 PASSPORT & RODEO)

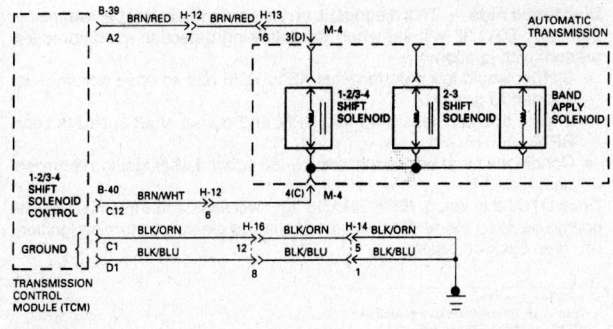

96A30692

Description – The 1-2/3-4 shift solenoid is a normally closed solenoid located on main valve body. In 2nd or 3rd gear, the TCM energizes shift solenoid to open fluid inlet port. When port is open, fluid pressure then actuates shift valve. Shift solenoid is activated by applying voltage to one side (high side) of shift solenoid and grounding the other side (low side) of shift solenoid.

High Side Driver (HSD) is a circuit of the TCM that acts as a switch between shift solenoid and supply voltage. High side of shift solenoid is permanently supplied voltage, except in back-up mode or when ignition is off. The TCM continually monitors shift solenoid connection to the Low Side Driver (LSD) for either high or low voltage. The LSD is a circuit of the TCM used as a switch between shift solenoid and ground. When shift solenoid is turned on, the TCM completes ground circuit for shift solenoid.

When ignition is turned on before engine is cranked, the TCM activates shift solenoids and band apply solenoid to check operating circuits of each solenoid for short or open circuit. To do so, the gear is set to 4th gear, 3rd gear, 1st gear, 1st gear with band applied and 4th gear with no HSD. Each one of the 5 tests requires .15 second. If engine is cranked before end of all tests, remaining tests are not performed.

Diagnostic Aids – This diagnostic test is an electrical test performed by the TCM. DTC 31 will set when the following detection conditions are present with ignition on.
- Shift solenoid low side terminal A2 to TCM has an open circuit or is shorted to ground.
- Engine speed is less than 480 RPM and output shaft speed is zero RPM.
- Conditions must be present for .15-1.03 seconds after ignition is turned on.

Once DTC 31 is set, CHECK TRANS light will flash and transmission will go into back-up mode. Back-up mode may be cleared by turning ignition off, then back on again.

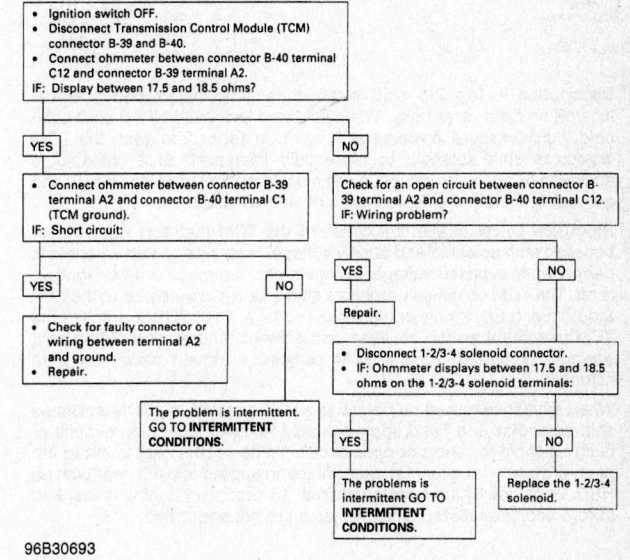

96B30693

DTC 32: 2-3 SHIFT SOLENOID CIRCUIT
(SHORT CIRCUIT TO GROUND OR OPEN CIRCUIT)
(EARLY PRODUCTION 1995 PASSPORT & RODEO)

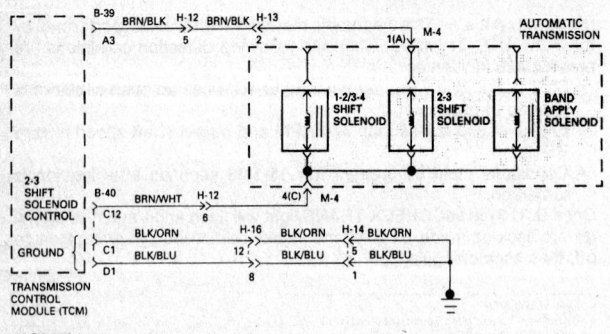

96C30694

Description – The 2-3 shift solenoid is a normally open solenoid located on main valve body. When fluid port is opened by 2-3 shift solenoid, fluid pressure actuates shift valve. In 1st or 2nd gear, the TCM energizes shift solenoid to close fluid inlet port. Shift solenoid is activated by applying voltage to one side (high side) of shift solenoid and grounding the other side (low side) of shift solenoid.

High Side Driver (HSD) is a circuit of the TCM that acts as a switch between shift solenoid and supply voltage. High side of shift solenoid is permanently supplied voltage, except in back-up mode or when ignition is off. The TCM continually monitors shift solenoid connection to the Low Side Driver (LSD) for either high or low voltage. The LSD is a circuit of the TCM used as a switch between shift solenoid and ground. When shift solenoid is turned on, the TCM completes ground circuit for shift solenoid.

When ignition is turned on before engine is cranked, the TCM activates shift solenoids and band apply solenoid to check operating circuits of each solenoid for short or open circuit. To do so, the gear is set to 4th gear, 3rd gear, 1st gear, 1st gear with band applied and 4th gear with no HSD. Each one of the 5 tests requires .15 second. If engine is cranked before end of all tests, remaining tests are not performed.

Diagnostic Aids – This diagnostic test is an electrical test performed by the TCM. DTC 32 will set when the following detection conditions are present with ignition on.

- Shift solenoid low side terminal A3 to TCM has an open circuit, or is shorted to ground.
- Engine speed is less than 480 RPM and output shaft speed is zero RPM.
- Conditions must be present for .15-.88 second after ignition is turned on.

Once DTC 32 is set, CHECK TRANS light will flash and transmission will go into back-up mode. Back-up mode may be cleared by turning ignition off, then back on again.

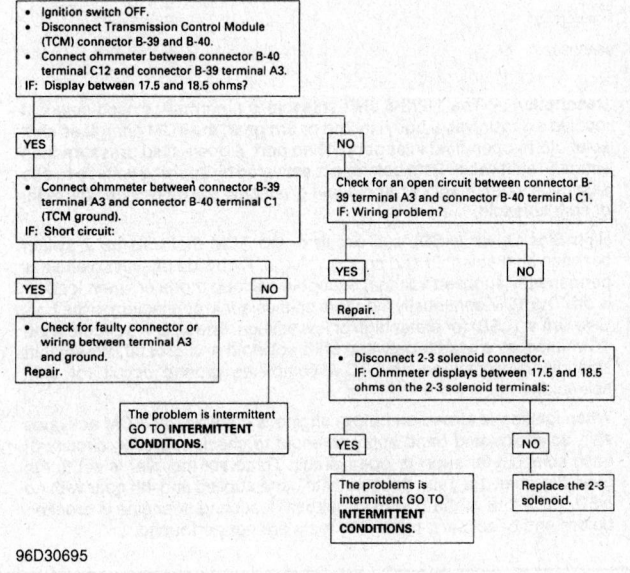

96D30695

AUTOMATIC TRANSMISSIONS
1995 Hydra-Matic 4L30-E Electronic Controls (Cont.)

3-599

DTC 33: TCC SOLENOID CIRCUIT (SHORT CIRCUIT TO B+ OR OPEN CIRCUIT)
(EARLY PRODUCTION 1995 PASSPORT & RODEO)

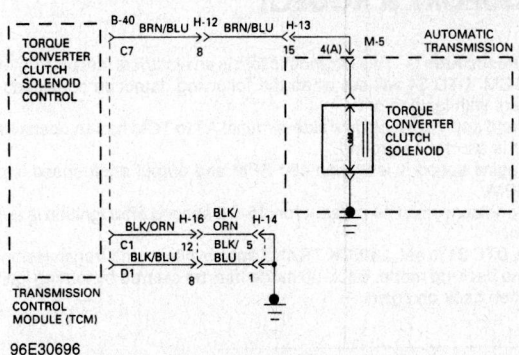

96E30696

Description – Torque Converter Clutch (TCC) solenoid is located on adapter case valve body. TCM energizes TCC solenoid to open fluid port. When fluid port is open, line pressure actuates converter clutch control valve which exhausts the fluid and torque converter clutch engages. TCM allows torque converter clutch to engage only when:

- Transmission is at normal operating temperature.
- Brake pedal is in released position.
- Transmission is in 2nd, 3rd or 4th gear.
- Engine is at normal operating temperature.
- Shift pattern requests TCC apply.
- Shift is finished.
- DTC 43, 55, 64 or 65 are not present.

TCC solenoid is activated by applying voltage to one side (high side) of TCC solenoid and grounding the other side (low side) of TCC solenoid. High Side Driver (HSD) is a circuit of the TCM that acts as a switch between TCC solenoid and supply voltage. High side of TCC solenoid is used to turn TCC solenoid on or off, as low side of TCC solenoid is permanently connected to ground. When transmission is in back-up mode or ignition is turned off, TCC solenoid is turned off.

The TCM continually monitors TCC solenoid connection to HSD for either high or low voltage. The only test performed is when engine is cranked and TCC solenoid is turned on. If this circuit is shorted to battery voltage, TCC solenoid is constantly on and shifts may be firm.

In 1st gear, TCC is hydraulically off whatever position TCC solenoid is in. Vehicle may be driven with TCC solenoid shorted to battery voltage. Engine may stall when driver is braking, if vehicle is stopped with transmission in 2nd gear with TCC applied. The 3-2 shifts will be very firm.

Diagnostic Aids – This diagnostic test is an electrical test performed by the TCM. DTC 33 will set when TCC solenoid high side to TCM terminal C7 contains open circuit or is shorted to battery voltage and condition is present for .13 second. If DTC 33 is set, the TCC will be shut off and CHECK TRANS light will flash. Transmission will NOT go into back-up mode. Transmission will return to normal operation by turning ignition off, then back on again.

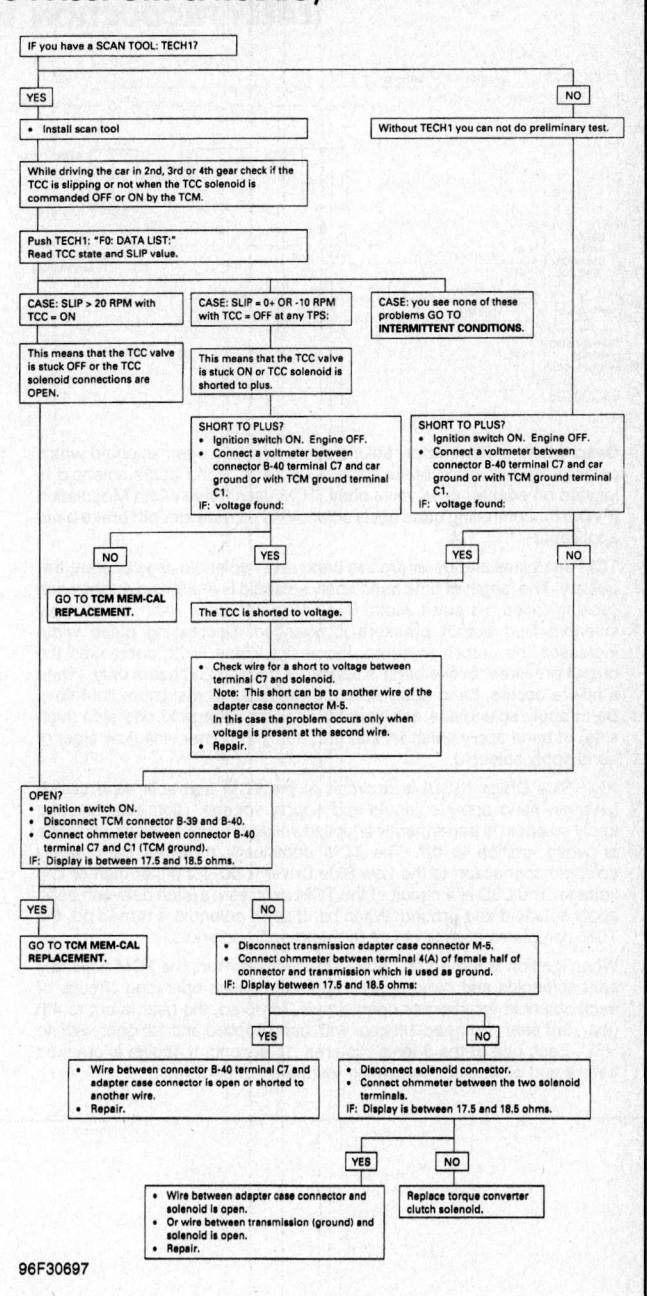

96F30697

3-600

AUTOMATIC TRANSMISSIONS
1995 Hydra-Matic 4L30-E Electronic Controls (Cont.)

DTC 34: BAND APPLY SOLENOID CIRCUIT
(SHORT CIRCUIT TO GROUND OR OPEN CIRCUIT)
(EARLY PRODUCTION 1995 PASSPORT & RODEO)

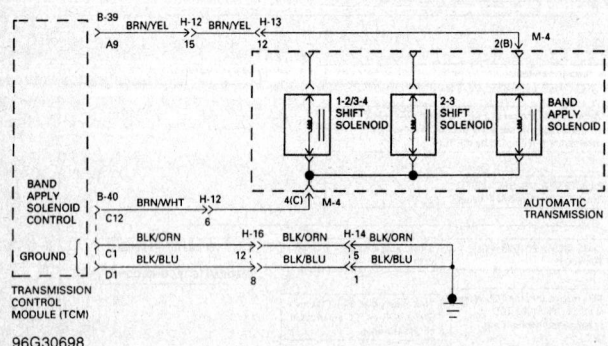

96G30698

Description – Band apply solenoid is a normally open solenoid which controls fluid flow for brake band application. Band apply solenoid is located on adapter case valve body. TCM uses Pulse Width Modulation (PWM) for controlling band apply solenoid to provide smooth brake band application.

TCM energizes and de-energizes band apply solenoid at a constant frequency. The length of time band apply solenoid is energized during each cycle is called the pulse width. By varying the pulse width, band apply solenoid fluid output pressure is changed. Decreasing pulse width increases the output pressure. Increasing pulse width decreases the output pressure. Brake band is applied in 1st and 2nd gears only. When a failure occurs, band apply solenoid regulates at maximum fluid flow. Band apply solenoid is activated by applying voltage to one side (high side) of band apply solenoid and grounding the other side (low side) of band apply solenoid.

High Side Driver (HSD) is a circuit of the TCM that acts as a switch between band apply solenoid and supply voltage. High side of band apply solenoid is permanently supplied voltage, except in back-up mode or when ignition is off. The TCM continually monitors band apply solenoid connection to the Low Side Driver (LSD) for either high or low voltage. The LSD is a circuit of the TCM used as a switch between band apply solenoid and ground. When band apply solenoid is turned on, the TCM completes ground circuit for band apply solenoid.

When ignition is turned on before engine is cranked, the TCM activates shift solenoids and band apply solenoid to check operating circuits of each solenoid for short or open circuit. To do so, the gear is set to 4th gear, 3rd gear, 1st gear, 1st gear with band applied and 4th gear with no HSD. Each one of the 5 tests requires .15 second. If engine is cranked before end of all tests, remaining tests are not performed.

Diagnostic Aids – This diagnostic test is an electrical test performed by the TCM. DTC 34 will set when the following detection conditions are present with ignition on.

- Band apply solenoid low side terminal A9 to TCM has an open circuit, or is shorted to ground.
- Engine speed is less than 480 RPM and output shaft speed is zero RPM.
- Conditions must be present for .15-.75 second after ignition is turned on.

Once DTC 34 is set, CHECK TRANS light will flash and transmission will go into back-up mode. Back-up mode may be cleared by turning ignition off, then back on again.

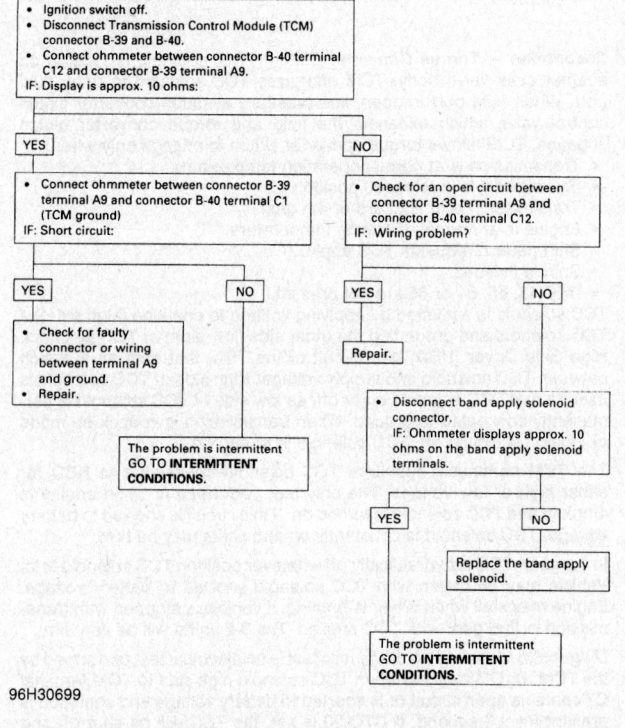

96H30699

AUTOMATIC TRANSMISSIONS
1995 Hydra-Matic 4L30-E Electronic Controls (Cont.)

3-601

DTC 35: FORCE MOTOR SOLENOID CIRCUIT
(SHORT CIRCUIT TO B+ OR GROUND)
(EARLY PRODUCTION 1995 PASSPORT & RODEO)

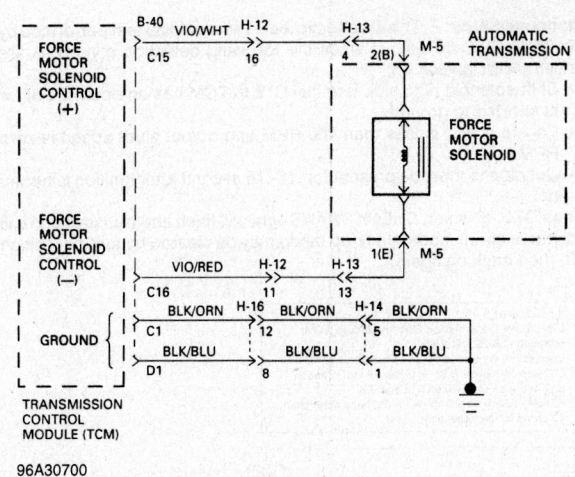

96A30700

Description – Force motor solenoid is a variable position solenoid used to regulate line pressure. Force motor solenoid is located on adapter case valve body. The TCM uses Throttle Position Sensor (TPS) information and vehicle speed to determine appropriate line pressure for a given load. TCM regulates line pressure by applying a varying applied amperage of .1-1.1 amps to force motor solenoid. TCM then monitors return amperage on the return line.

Line pressure may vary from less than 50 psi (3.5 kg/cm²) to more than 200 psi (14.1 kg/cm²). Line pressure is proportional to current applied on force motor solenoid. High current produces low line pressure and low current produces high line pressure.

Diagnostic Aids – This diagnostic test is an electrical test performed by the TCM. DTC 35 sets when return line amperage is greater than .2 amp from the commanded amperage. Once DTC 35 is set, CHECK TRANS light will flash and transmission will go into back-up mode. Back-up mode may be cleared by turning ignition off, then back on again.

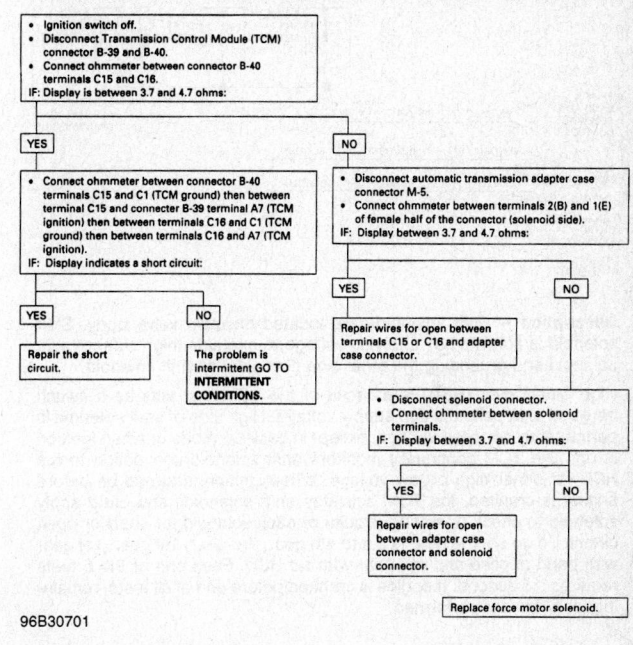

96B30701

3-602

AUTOMATIC TRANSMISSIONS
1995 Hydra-Matic 4L30-E Electronic Controls (Cont.)

DTC 36: SHIFT SOLENOID CIRCUIT
(SHORT CIRCUIT TO GROUND OR OPEN CIRCUIT)
(EARLY PRODUCTION 1995 PASSPORT & RODEO)

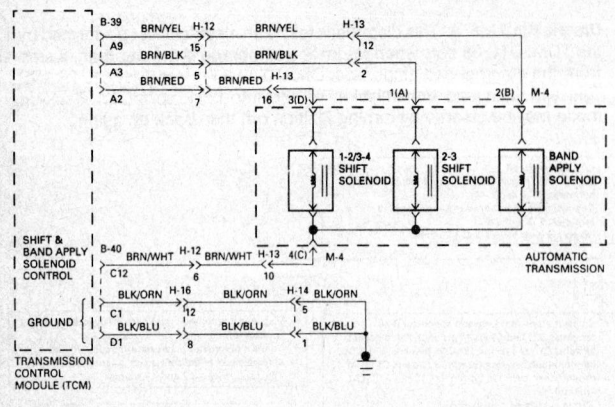

96C30702

Description – Shift solenoids are located on main valve body. Shift solenoid is activated by applying voltage to one side (high side) of shift solenoid and grounding the other side (low side) of shift solenoid.

High Side Driver (HSD) is a circuit of the TCM that acts as a switch between shift solenoid and supply voltage. High side of shift solenoid is permanently supplied voltage, except in back-up mode or when ignition is off. The TCM continually monitors shift solenoid connection to the HSD for either high or low voltage. When ignition is turned on before engine is cranked, the TCM activates shift solenoids and band apply solenoid to check operating circuits of each solenoid for short or open circuit. To do so, the gear is set to 4th gear, 3rd gear, 1st gear, 1st gear with band applied and 4th gear with no HSD. Each one of the 5 tests requires .15 second. If engine is cranked before end of all tests, remaining tests are not performed.

Diagnostic Aids – This diagnostic test is an electrical test performed by the TCM. DTC 36 will set when the following detection conditions are present with ignition on.
- Shift solenoid high side terminal C12 to TCM has an open circuit, or is shorted to ground.
- Engine speed is less than 480 RPM and output shaft speed is zero RPM.
- Conditions must be present for .15-.75 second after ignition is turned on.

Once DTC 36 is set, CHECK TRANS light will flash and transmission will go into back-up mode. Back-up mode may be cleared by turning ignition off, then back on again.

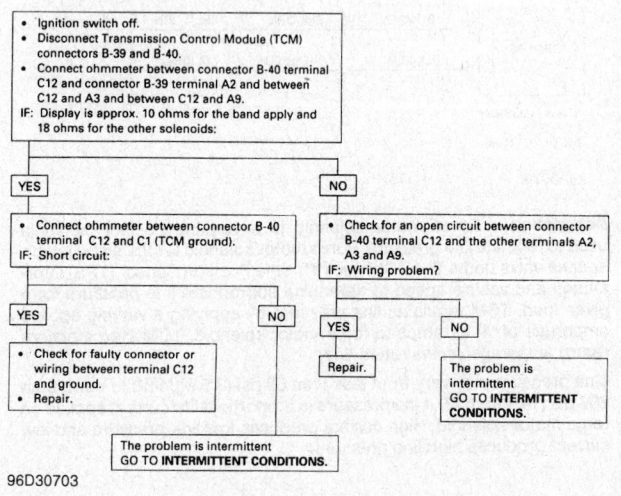

96D30703

DTC 37: TORQUE MANAGEMENT SERIAL LINE FAULTY
(EARLY PRODUCTION 1995 PASSPORT & RODEO)

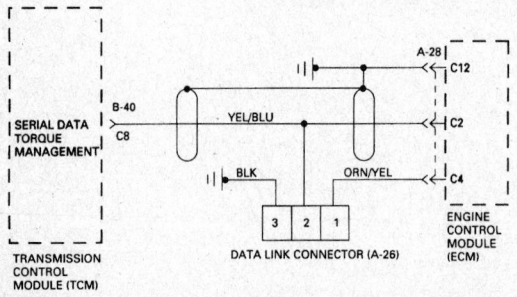

96E30704

Description – Torque management uses TCM to deliver a spark advance signal to Engine Control Module (ECM) during transmission shifting. This controls engine torque and reduces engagement shock caused by changing of vehicle speed. Each time transmission shifts with torque management active, TCM delivers a signal to the ECM.

Diagnostic Aids – This diagnostic test is not an electrical test performed by the TCM, but a comparison of signal input. DTC 37 will set when a torque management failure is present, or ECM does not acknowledge signal from TCM when transmission shifts with torque management active. Once DTC 37 is set, CHECK TRANS light will flash and transmission will go into back-up mode. Back-up mode may be cleared by turning ignition off, then back on again.

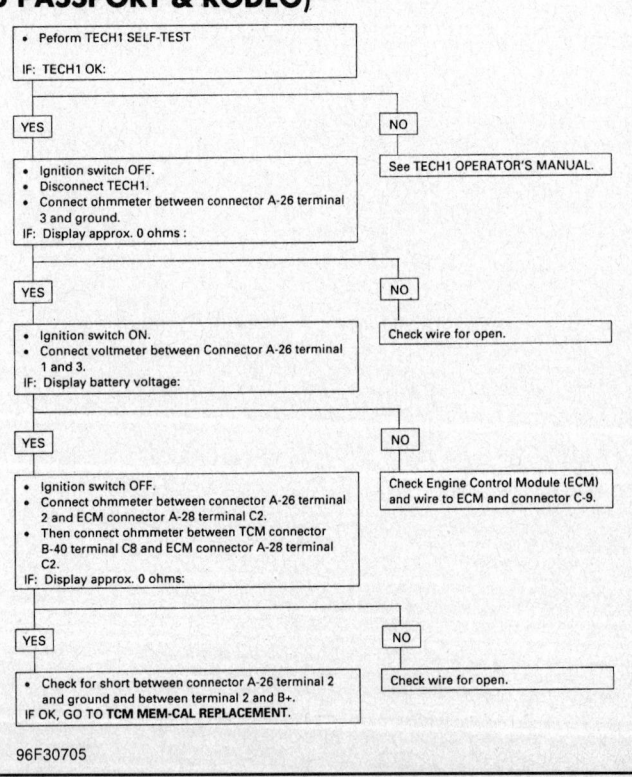

96F30705

AUTOMATIC TRANSMISSIONS
1995 Hydra-Matic 4L30-E Electronic Controls (Cont.)

3-603

DTC 41: 1-2/3-4 SHIFT SOLENOID CIRCUIT (SHORT CIRCUIT TO B+) (EARLY PRODUCTION 1995 PASSPORT & RODEO)

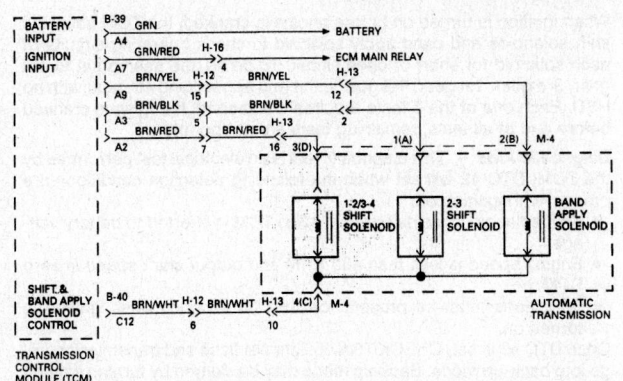

96G30706

Description – The 1-2/3-4 shift solenoid is a normally closed solenoid located on main valve body. In 2nd or 3rd gear, the TCM energizes shift solenoid to open fluid inlet port. When port is open, fluid pressure then actuates shift valve. Shift solenoid is activated by applying voltage to one side (high side) of shift solenoid and grounding other side (low side) of shift solenoid.

High Side Driver (HSD) is a circuit of the TCM that acts as a switch between shift solenoid and supply voltage. High side of shift solenoid is permanently supplied voltage, except in back-up mode or when ignition is off. The TCM continually monitors shift solenoid connection to the Low Side Driver (LSD) for either high or low voltage. The LSD is a circuit of the TCM used as a switch between shift solenoid and ground. When shift solenoid is turned on, the TCM completes the ground circuit for shift solenoid.

When ignition is turned on before engine is cranked, the TCM activates shift solenoids and band apply solenoid to check operating circuits of each solenoid for short or open circuit. To do so, the gear is set to 4th gear, 3rd gear, 1st gear, 1st gear with band applied and 4th gear with no HSD. Each one of the 5 tests requires .15 second. If engine is cranked before end of all tests, remaining tests are not performed.

Diagnostic Aids – This diagnostic test is an electrical test performed by the TCM. DTC 41 will set when the following detection conditions are present with ignition on.

- Shift solenoid low side terminal A2 to TCM is shorted to battery voltage.
- Engine speed is less than 480 RPM and output shaft speed is zero RPM.
- Conditions must be present for .15-.88 second after ignition is turned on.

Once DTC 41 is set, CHECK TRANS light will flash and transmission will go into back-up mode. Back-up mode may be cleared by turning ignition off, then back on again.

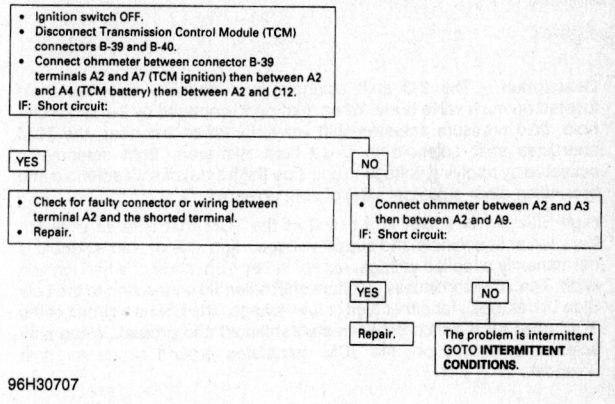

96H30707

3-604

AUTOMATIC TRANSMISSIONS
1995 Hydra-Matic 4L30-E Electronic Controls (Cont.)

DTC 42: 2-3 SHIFT SOLENOID CIRCUIT (SHORT CIRCUIT TO B+)
(EARLY PRODUCTION 1995 PASSPORT & RODEO)

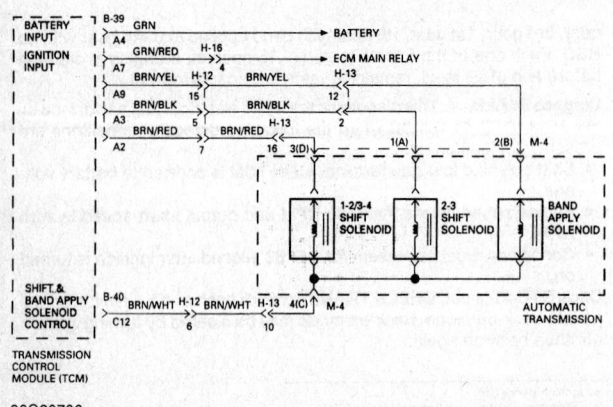

96G30706

Description – The 2-3 shift solenoid is a normally open solenoid located on main valve body. When fluid port is opened by 2-3 shift solenoid, fluid pressure actuates shift valve. In 1st or 2nd gear, the TCM energizes shift solenoid to close fluid inlet port. Shift solenoid is activated by applying voltage to one side (high side) of shift solenoid and grounding other side (low side) of shift solenoid.

High Side Driver (HSD) is a circuit of the TCM that acts as a switch between shift solenoid and supply voltage. High side of shift solenoid is permanently supplied voltage, except in back-up mode or when ignition is off. The TCM continually monitors shift solenoid connection to the Low Side Driver (LSD) for either high or low voltage. The LSD is a circuit of the TCM used as a switch between shift solenoid and ground. When shift solenoid is turned on, the TCM completes ground circuit for shift solenoid.

When ignition is turned on before engine is cranked, the TCM activates shift solenoids and band apply solenoid to check operating circuits of each solenoid for short or open circuit. To do so, the gear is set to 4th gear, 3rd gear, 1st gear, 1st gear with band applied and 4th gear with no HSD. Each one of the 5 tests requires .15 second. If engine is cranked before end of all tests, remaining tests are not performed.

Diagnostic Aids – This diagnostic test is an electrical test performed by the TCM. DTC 42 will set when the following detection conditions are present with ignition on.

- Shift solenoid low side terminal A3 to TCM is shorted to battery voltage.
- Engine speed is less than 480 RPM and output shaft speed is zero RPM.
- Conditions must be present for .15-1.03 seconds after ignition is turned on.

Once DTC 42 is set, CHECK TRANS light will flash and transmission will go into back-up mode. Back-up mode may be cleared by turning ignition off, then back on again.

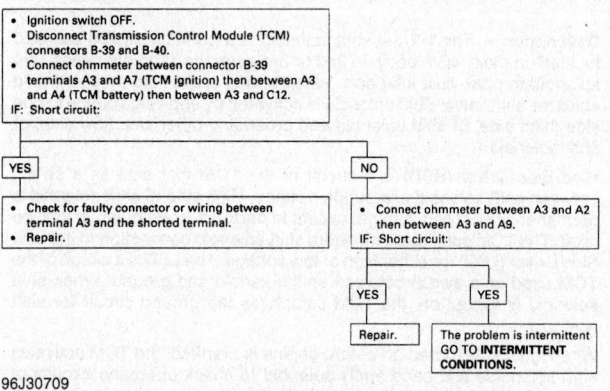

96J30709

DTC 43: TCC SOLENOID CIRCUIT (SHORT CIRCUIT TO GROUND)
(EARLY PRODUCTION 1995 PASSPORT & RODEO)

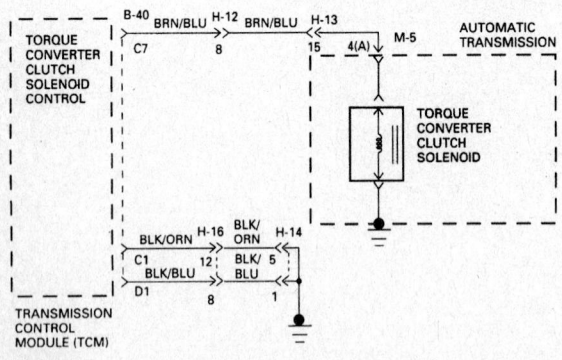

96C30710

Description – Torque Converter Clutch (TCC) solenoid is located on adapter case valve body. TCM energizes TCC solenoid to open fluid port. When fluid port is open, line pressure actuates converter clutch control valve which exhausts the fluid and torque converter clutch engages. TCM allows torque converter clutch to engage only when:

- Transmission is at normal operating temperature.
- Brake pedal is in released position.
- Transmission is in 2nd, 3rd or 4th gear.
- Engine is at normal operating temperature.
- Shift pattern requests TCC apply.
- Shift is finished.
- DTC 33, DTC 55, DTC 64 Or DTC 65 are not present.

TCC solenoid is activated by applying voltage to one side (high side) of TCC solenoid and grounding other side (low side) of TCC solenoid. High Side Driver (HSD) is a circuit of the TCM that acts as a switch between TCC solenoid and supply voltage. High side of TCC solenoid is used to turn TCC solenoid on or off, as low side of TCC solenoid is permanently connected to ground. When transmission is in back-up mode or ignition is turned off, TCC solenoid is turned off.

The TCM continually monitors TCC solenoid connection to HSD for either high or low voltage. The only test performed is when engine is cranked and TCC solenoid is turned on.

Diagnostic Aids – This diagnostic test is an electrical test performed by the TCM. DTC 43 will set when TCC solenoid high side to TCM terminal C7 is shorted to ground and condition is present for .07 second after ignition is turned on. If DTC 43 is set, the TCC will be shut off. The CHECK TRANS light will NOT flash and transmission will NOT go into back-up mode. Transmission will return to normal operation by turning ignition off, then back on again.

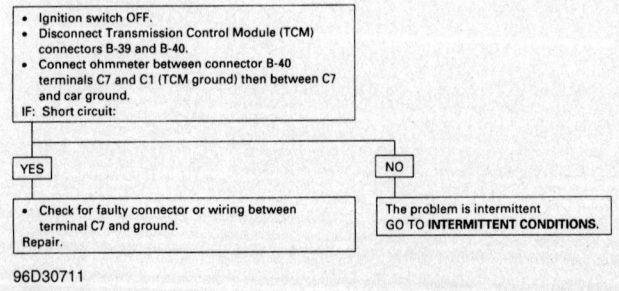

96D30711

DTC 44: BAND APPLY SOLENOID CIRCUIT (SHORT CIRCUIT TO B+)
(EARLY PRODUCTION 1995 PASSPORT & RODEO)

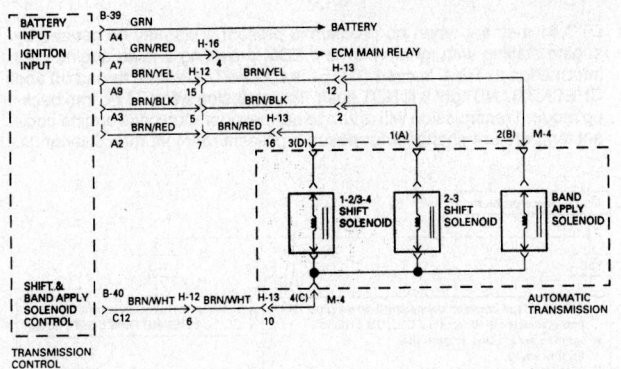

96G30706

Description – Band apply solenoid is a normally open solenoid which controls fluid flow for brake band application. Band apply solenoid is located on adapter case valve body. TCM uses Pulse Width Modulation (PWM) for controlling band apply solenoid to provide smooth brake band application.

TCM energizes and de-energizes band apply solenoid at a constant frequency. The length of time band apply solenoid is energized during each cycle is called the pulse width. By varying the pulse width, band apply solenoid fluid output pressure is changed. Decreasing pulse width increases the output pressure. Increasing pulse width decreases the output pressure. Brake band is applied in 1st and 2nd gears only. When a failure occurs, band apply solenoid regulates at maximum fluid flow. Band apply solenoid is activated by applying voltage to one side (high side) of band apply solenoid and grounding the other side (low side) of band apply solenoid.

High Side Driver (HSD) is a circuit of the TCM that acts as a switch between band apply solenoid and supply voltage. High side of band apply solenoid is permanently supplied voltage, except in back-up mode or when ignition is off. The TCM continually monitors band apply solenoid connection to the Low Side Driver (LSD) for either high or low

voltage. The LSD is a circuit of the TCM used as a switch between band apply solenoid and ground. When band apply solenoid is turned on, the TCM completes ground circuit for band apply solenoid.

When ignition is turned on before engine is cranked, the TCM activates shift solenoids and band apply solenoid to check operating circuits of each solenoid for short or open circuit. To do so, the gear is set to 4th gear, 3rd gear, 1st gear, 1st gear with band applied and 4th gear with no HSD. Each one of the 5 tests requires .15 second. If engine is cranked before end of all tests, remaining tests are not performed.

Diagnostic Aids – This diagnostic test is an electrical test performed by the TCM. DTC 44 will set when the following detection conditions are present with ignition on.
- Band apply solenoid low side terminal A9 is shorted to battery voltage.
- Engine speed is less than 480 RPM and output shaft speed is zero RPM.
- Conditions must be present for .15-1.18 seconds after ignition is turned on.

Once DTC 44 is set, CHECK TRANS light will flash and transmission will go into back-up mode. Back-up mode may be cleared by turning ignition off, then back on again.

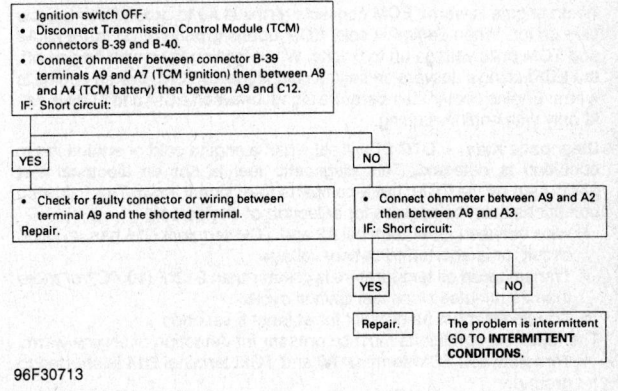

96F30713

DTC 46: SHIFT SOLENOID CIRCUIT (SHORT CIRCUIT TO B+)
(EARLY PRODUCTION 1995 PASSPORT & RODEO)

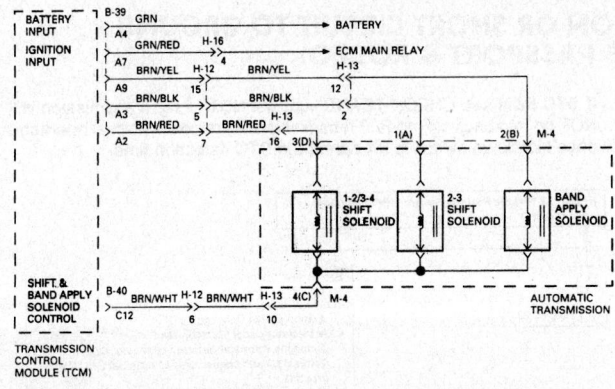

96G30706

Description – Shift solenoids are located on main valve body. Shift solenoids are activated by applying voltage to one side (high side) of shift solenoid and grounding the other side (low side) of shift solenoid. High Side Driver (HSD) is a circuit of TCM that acts as a switch between shift solenoid and supply voltage. High side of shift solenoid is permanently supplied voltage, except in back-up mode or when ignition is off. The TCM continually monitors shift solenoid connection to HSD for either high or low voltage.

When ignition is turned on before engine is cranked, the TCM activates shift solenoids and band apply solenoid to check operating circuits of each solenoid for short or open circuit. To do so, the gear is set to 4th

gear, 3rd gear, 1st gear, 1st gear with band applied and 4th gear with no HSD. Each one of the 5 tests requires .15 second. If engine is cranked before end of all tests, remaining tests are not performed.

Diagnostic Aids – This diagnostic test is an electrical test performed by the TCM. DTC 46 will set when the following detection conditions are present with ignition on.
- Shift solenoid high side terminal C12 to TCM is shorted to battery voltage.
- Engine speed is less than 480 RPM and output shaft speed is zero RPM.
- Conditions must be present for .15-1.34 seconds after ignition is turned on.

Once DTC 46 is set, CHECK TRANS light will flash and transmission will go into back-up mode. Back-up mode may be cleared by turning ignition off, then back on again.

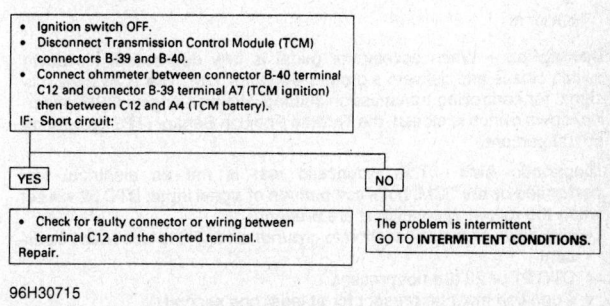

96H30715

3-606

AUTOMATIC TRANSMISSIONS
1995 Hydra-Matic 4L30-E Electronic Controls (Cont.)

DTC 51: ENGINE COOLANT TEMP. SENSOR CIRCUIT
(SHORT CIRCUIT TO B+, GROUND OR OPEN CIRCUIT)
(EARLY PRODUCTION 1995 PASSPORT & RODEO)

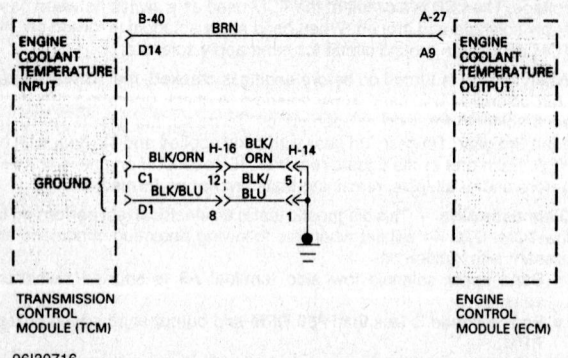

96I30716

Description – Engine Coolant Temperature (ECT) sensor delivers an engine coolant temperature signal to Engine Control Module (ECM). The ECM delivers a engine warm signal to TCM when ECM determines engine coolant temperature is greater than 158°F (70°C).

When engine is warm, ECM connects terminal A9 to ground using a low side driver. When engine is cold, ECM opens ground at on terminal A9 and TCM pulls voltage up to 5 volts. When ignition is on with engine off, the ECM always delivers an engine cold signal to TCM, even if engine is warm. Engine coolant temperature signal between ECM and TCM is valid only with engine running.

Diagnostic Aids – DTC 51 will set when a engine cold or engine warm condition is detected. This diagnostic test is not an electrical test performed by the TCM, but a comparison of signal input. The following conditions must be present for detection of engine cold.
- Wire between ECM terminal A9 and TCM terminal D14 has an open circuit, or is shorted to battery voltage.
- Transmission oil temperature is greater than 212°F (100°C), or more than 20 minutes since last ignition cycle.
- Conditions must be present for at least 6 seconds.

The following conditions must be present for detection of engine warm.
- Wire between ECM terminal A9 and TCM terminal D14 is shorted to ground.
- Transmission oil temperature is less than 32°F (0°C).
- Voltage on transmission oil temperature sensor must be less than 4.74 volts.
- Conditions must be present for at least 6 seconds.

DTC 51 may set when no problem is present. This may be caused by engine stalling with ignition on and ECM providing a false engine cold information to TCM. In case DTC 51 is set, the TCC will be turned off and CHECK TRANS light will NOT flash. Transmission will NOT go into back-up mode. Transmission will return to normal operation once engine coolant temperature change information is present for more than 6 seconds.

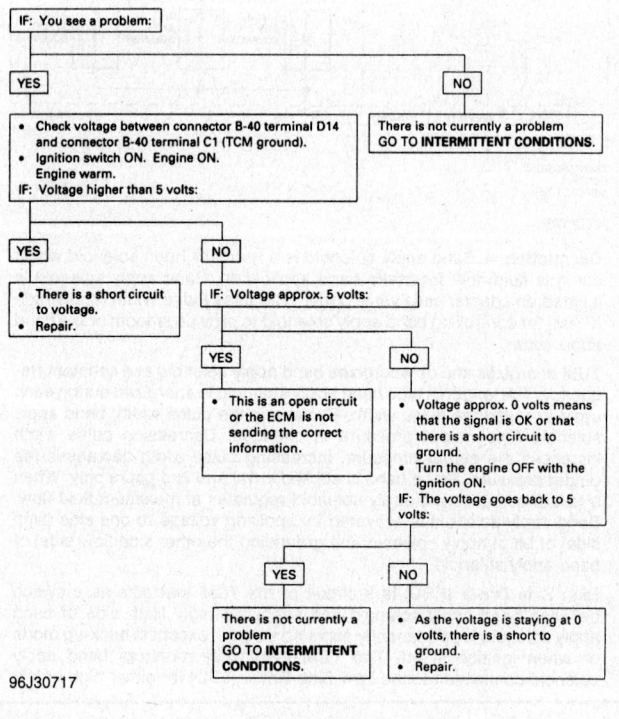

96J30717

DTC 52: KICKDOWN SWITCH ALWAYS ON OR SHORT CIRCUIT TO GROUND
(EARLY PRODUCTION 1995 PASSPORT & RODEO)

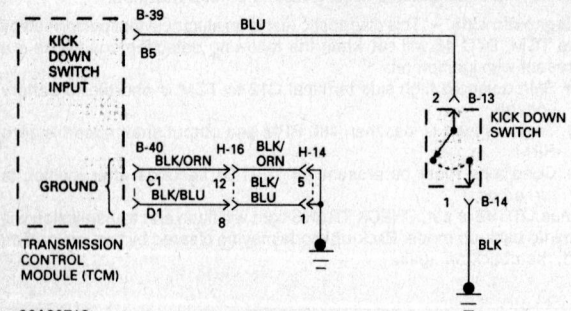

96A30718

Description – When accelerator pedal is fully depressed, kickdown switch closes and delivers a ground signal to TCM. The TCM uses this signal for controlling transmission shifting with high engine RPM. When kickdown switch is closed, the Throttle Position Sensor (TPS) is already at 100 percent.

Diagnostic Aids – This diagnostic test is not an electrical test performed by the TCM, but a comparison of signal input. DTC 52 will set when the following conditions are present.
- Kickdown switch is on (short to ground), and TPS is less than 70 percent.
- DTC 21 or 22 are not present.
- Condition must be present for at least one second.

If DTC 52 is set, CHECK TRANS light will NOT flash. Transmission will NOT go into back-up mode. Transmission will return to normal operation once kickdown switch is off during the DTC detection time.

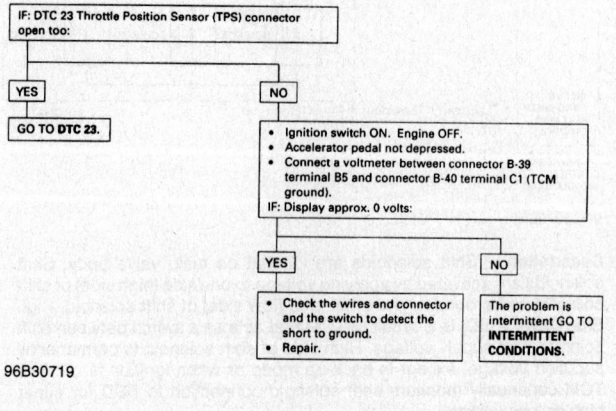

96B30719

AUTOMATIC TRANSMISSIONS
1995 Hydra-Matic 4L30-E Electronic Controls (Cont.)

3-607

DTC 53: MODE SWITCH IN "P", "N" OR "R" BAD POSITION
(EARLY PRODUCTION 1995 PASSPORT & RODEO)

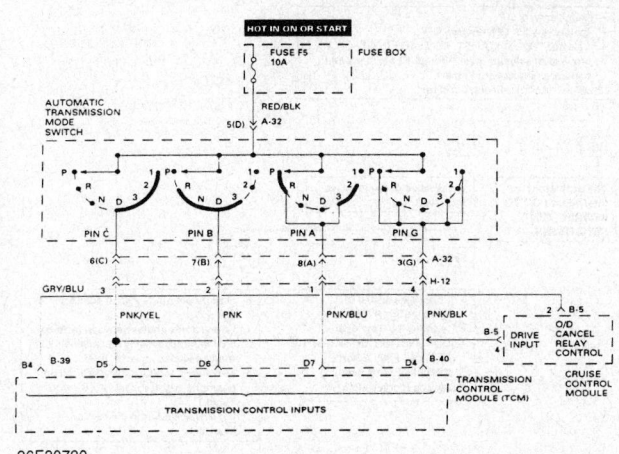

96E30720

Description – Mode switch delivers input signal to TCM to indicate gearshift lever position. Mode switch is located on side of transmission. Mode switch also provides information for engine cranking and control of back-up lights. Fuse F5 provides voltage to mode switch. If fuse F5 is open, mode switch will not operate and DTC 54 will be set. Ensure shift linkage is properly adjusted, as DTC 53 may be caused by improperly adjusted shift linkage.

Diagnostic Aids – This diagnostic test is not an electrical test performed by the TCM, but a comparison of signal input.
The following conditions must be present for detection of "P" or "N" bad position.
- A/T input speed is less than 3000 RPM.
- Throttle position sensor (TPS) is greater than 20 percent.
- Mode switch in "P" or "N" position.
- DTC 13, 21 or 22 are not present.
- Conditions must be present for at least 4 seconds.

After detection time, the default position is assumed for pressure calculation and shift pattern is always "D".
If DTC 53 is set due to previous conditions for "P" or "N" bad position, the CHECK TRANS light will NOT flash. Transmission will NOT go into back-up mode. To return to normal operation, maintain engine speed at greater than 3000 RPM with TPS higher than 20 percent when mode switch is not in "P" or "N" position. The following conditions must be present for detection of "R" bad position.
- A/T output speed is greater than 3200 RPM.
- Mode switch in "R" position.
- DTC 11 or 62 are not present.
- Conditions must be present for at least one second.

After detection time, the default position is assumed for pressure calculation and shift pattern is always "D".
If DTC 53 is set due to previous conditions for "R" bad position, the CHECK TRANS light will NOT flash. Transmission will NOT go into back-up mode. To return to normal operation, maintain output speed at greater than 3200 RPM when mode switch is not in "R" position.

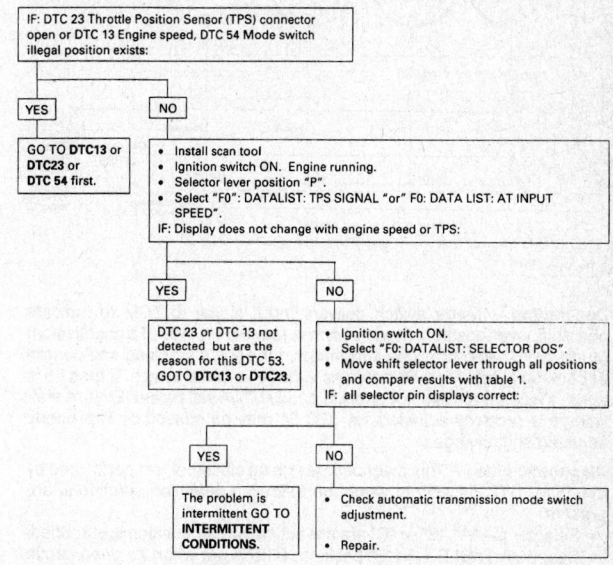

Table 1

	SHIFT SELECTOR POSITION						
TECH1 DISPLAY	P	R	N	D	3	2	L
SELECTOR PIN A	X	X			X	X	
SELECTOR PIN B		X	X	X	X		
SELECTOR PIN C				X	X	X	X
SELECTOR PIN P	X		X		X		X

Note: "X" indicates TECH1 displays "ACTIVE".

96F30721

3-608

AUTOMATIC TRANSMISSIONS
1995 Hydra-Matic 4L30-E Electronic Controls (Cont.)

DTC 54: MODE SWITCH ILLEGAL POSITION
(EARLY PRODUCTION 1995 PASSPORT & RODEO)

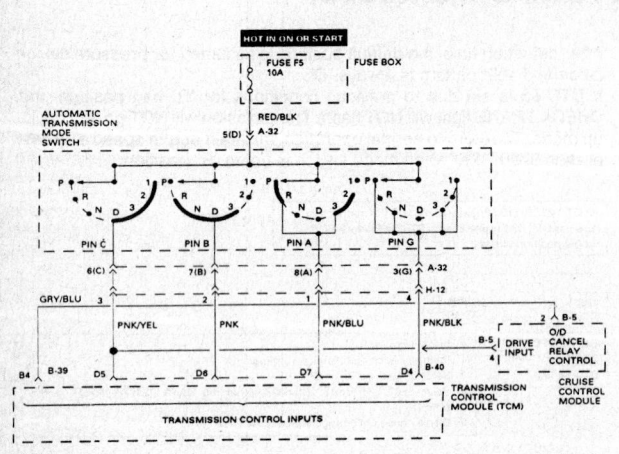

96E30720

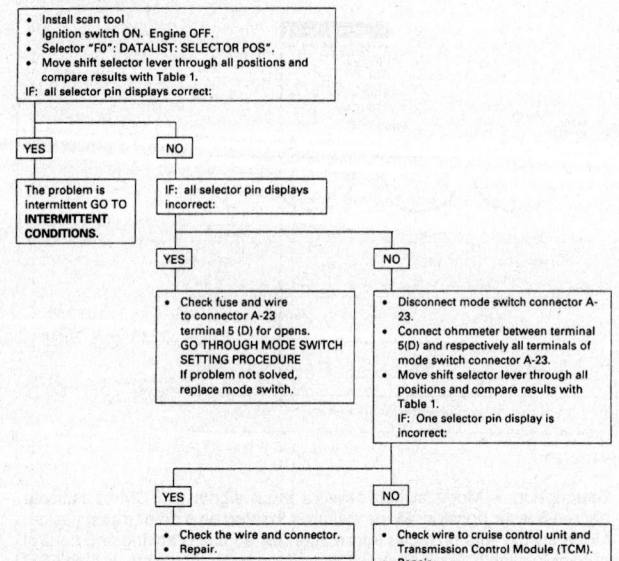

- Install scan tool
- Ignition switch ON. Engine OFF.
- Selector "F0": DATALIST: SELECTOR POS".
- Move shift selector lever through all positions and compare results with Table 1.
- IF: all selector pin displays correct:

YES → The problem is intermittent GO TO **INTERMITTENT CONDITIONS**.

NO → IF: all selector pin displays incorrect:

YES →
- Check fuse and wire to connector A-23 terminal 5 (D) for opens. GO THROUGH MODE SWITCH SETTING PROCEDURE If problem not solved, replace mode switch.

NO →
- Disconnect mode switch connector A-23.
- Connect ohmmeter between terminal 5(D) and respectively all terminals of mode switch connector A-23.
- Move shift selector lever through all positions and compare results with Table 1. IF: One selector pin display is incorrect:

YES →
- Check the wire and connector.
- Repair.

NO →
- Check wire to cruise control unit and Transmission Control Module (TCM).
- Repair.

Table 1

	SHIFT SELECTOR POSITION						
TECH1 DISPLAY	P	R	N	D	3	2	L
SELECTOR PIN A	X	X			X	X	
SELECTOR PIN B		X	X	X			
SELECTOR PIN C				X	X	X	X
SELECTOR PIN P	X		X		X		X

Note: "X" indicates TECH1 displays "ACTIVE 12V".

96H30723

Description – Mode switch delivers input signal to TCM to indicate gearshift lever position. Mode switch is located on side of transmission. Mode switch also provides information for engine cranking and control of back-up lights. Fuse F5 provides voltage to mode switch. If fuse F5 is open, mode switch will not operate and DTC 54 will be set. Ensure shift linkage is properly adjusted, as DTC 54 may be caused by improperly adjusted shift linkage.

Diagnostic Aids – This diagnostic test is an electrical test performed by the TCM. DTC 54 will set when the following detection conditions are present.
- Selector pin "A", "B" or "C" are not active and no position is identified.
- Based on TABLE 1, in "P" position, DTC is set when an open circuit or short to ground is present at pin "A".
- Conditions must be present for at least 5 seconds.
Once DTC 54 is set, CHECK TRANS light will flash and transmission will go into back-up mode. Back-up mode may be cleared by turning ignition off, then back on again.

DTC 55: BRAKE SWITCH CIRCUIT
(SHORT CIRCUIT TO GROUND OR OPEN CIRCUIT)
(EARLY PRODUCTION 1995 PASSPORT & RODEO)

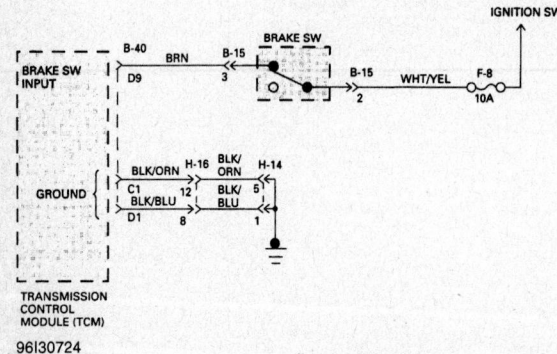

96I30724

Description – Brake switch delivers input signal to TCM to indicate vehicle braking. TCM uses input signal from brake switch for controlling Torque Converter Clutch (TCC). Brake switch may be referred to as brakelight switch.

Diagnostic Aids – This diagnostic test is not an electrical test performed by the TCM, but a comparison of signal input. DTC 55 will set when the following detection conditions are present.
- Brakes noted as being applied during acceleration from less than 6 MPH to more than 37 MPH within 6 seconds.
- After this acceleration, vehicle speed was greater than 37 MPH during at least 6 seconds.
- DTC 11 or 62 are not present.
- Conditions must be present for at least 5 times during ignition cycle.
If DTC 55 is set, CHECK TRANS light will NOT flash. Transmission will NOT go into back-up mode. To return to normal operation, brake must be released.

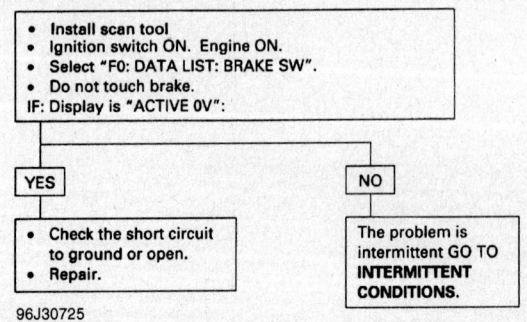

- Install scan tool
- Ignition switch ON. Engine ON.
- Select "F0: DATA LIST: BRAKE SW".
- Do not touch brake.
- IF: Display is "ACTIVE 0V":

YES →
- Check the short circuit to ground or open.
- Repair.

NO → The problem is intermittent GO TO **INTERMITTENT CONDITIONS**.

96J30725

AUTOMATIC TRANSMISSIONS
1995 Hydra-Matic 4L30-E Electronic Controls (Cont.)

3-609

DTC 56: BRAKE SWITCH CIRCUIT (SHORT CIRCUIT TO B+)
(EARLY PRODUCTION 1995 PASSPORT & RODEO)

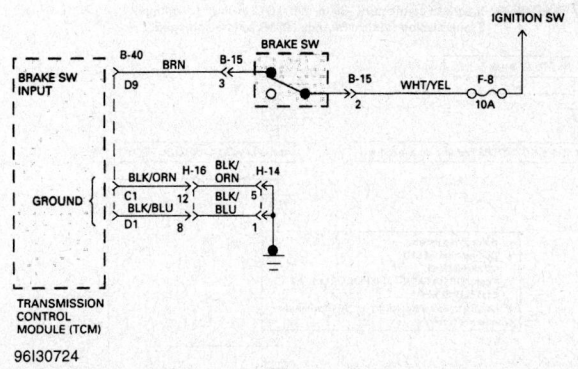

96130724

Description – Brake switch delivers input signal to TCM to indicate vehicle braking. TCM uses input signal from brake switch for controlling Torque Converter Clutch (TCC). Brake switch may be referred to as brakelight switch.

Diagnostic Aids – This diagnostic test is not an electrical test performed by the TCM, but a comparison of signal input. DTC 56 will set when the following detection conditions are present.

- Brakes noted as being released during deceleration from more than 37 MPH to less than 6 MPH within 6 seconds.
- Before deceleration, vehicle speed was greater than 37 MPH during at least 6 seconds.
- DTC 11 or 62 are not present.
- Conditions must be present for at least 5 times during ignition cycle.

If DTC 56 is set, CHECK TRANS light will NOT flash. Transmission will NOT go into back-up mode. To return to normal operation, brake must be released.

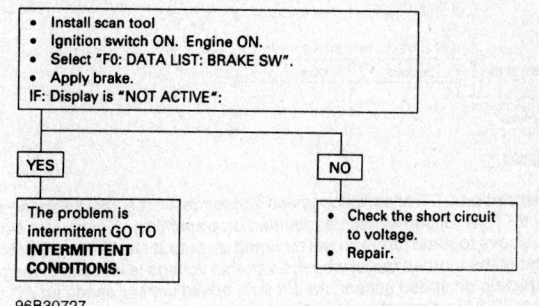

96B30727

DTC 61: GEAR ERROR
(EARLY PRODUCTION 1995 PASSPORT & RODEO)

Description – The TCM calculates slippage of Torque Converter Clutch (TCC) and transmission based upon engine speed, output speed and gear ratio. TCC should slip a specified amount at high engine speeds. Transmission should not slip more than a specified value when there is no shift.

Diagnostic Aids – This diagnostic test is not an electrical test performed by the TCM, but a comparison of signal input. DTC 56 will be set when the following detection conditions are present.

- Engine speed is greater than 3500 RPM.
- Slippage must be more than specified amount in specified gear: 1st gear =595 RPM, 2nd gear =556 RPM, 3rd gear =536 RPM, 4th gear =473 RPM.
- DTC 11, 13 or 62 are not present.
- Last change of shift solenoid was more than 3 seconds.
- Conditions must be present for at least 3 seconds.

Once DTC 61 is set, CHECK TRANS light will flash and transmission will go into back-up mode. Back-up mode may be cleared by turning ignition off, then back on again.

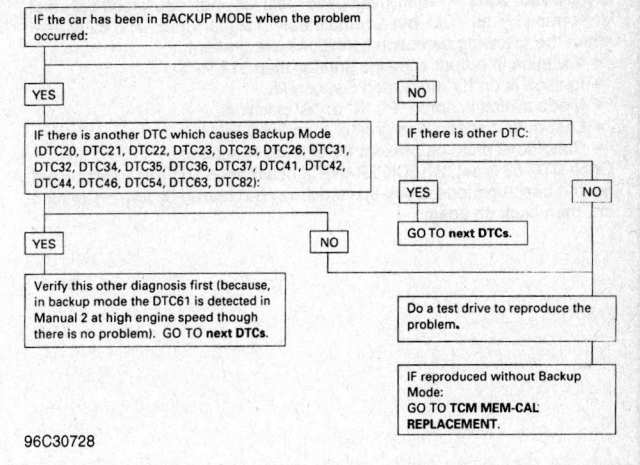

96C30728

3-610

AUTOMATIC TRANSMISSIONS
1995 Hydra-Matic 4L30-E Electronic Controls (Cont.)

DTC 62: DOWNSHIFT PROTECTION
(EARLY PRODUCTION 1995 PASSPORT & RODEO)

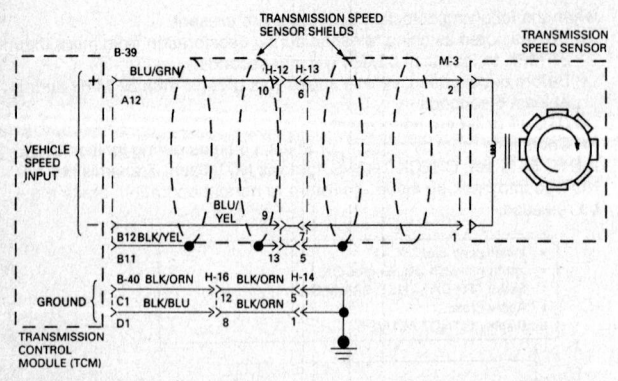

96H25277

Description – Transmission speed sensor delivers a vehicle speed signal to TCM. Speed sensor is mounted on transmission extension housing above toothed target wheel mounted on output shaft. As output shaft rotates the toothed target wheel, a variable voltage is induced in magnetic pickup on speed sensor. As a result, speed sensor sends an AC signal to TCM in proportion to vehicle speed.

Output speed information from transmission speed sensor is used to determine transmission shifting. If output speed information changes suddenly due to an open circuit or electrical interference, transmission will downshift. To avoid this, TCM constantly monitors variations of output speed. If variation in output speed is too great when output speed is greater than 2900 RPM, DTC 62 is set.

Diagnostic Aids – This diagnostic test is not an electrical test performed by the TCM, but a comparison of signal input. DTC 62 will set when the following detection conditions are present.
- Variation in output speed is greater than 512 RPM.
- Ignition is on for more than 5 seconds.
- Mode switch is not in "P", "N" or "R" position.
- Last output speed was greater than 2900 RPM.
- Conditions must be present for at least .1 second.

Once DTC 62 is set, CHECK TRANS light will flash and transmission will go into back-up mode. Back-up mode may be cleared by turning ignition off, then back on again.

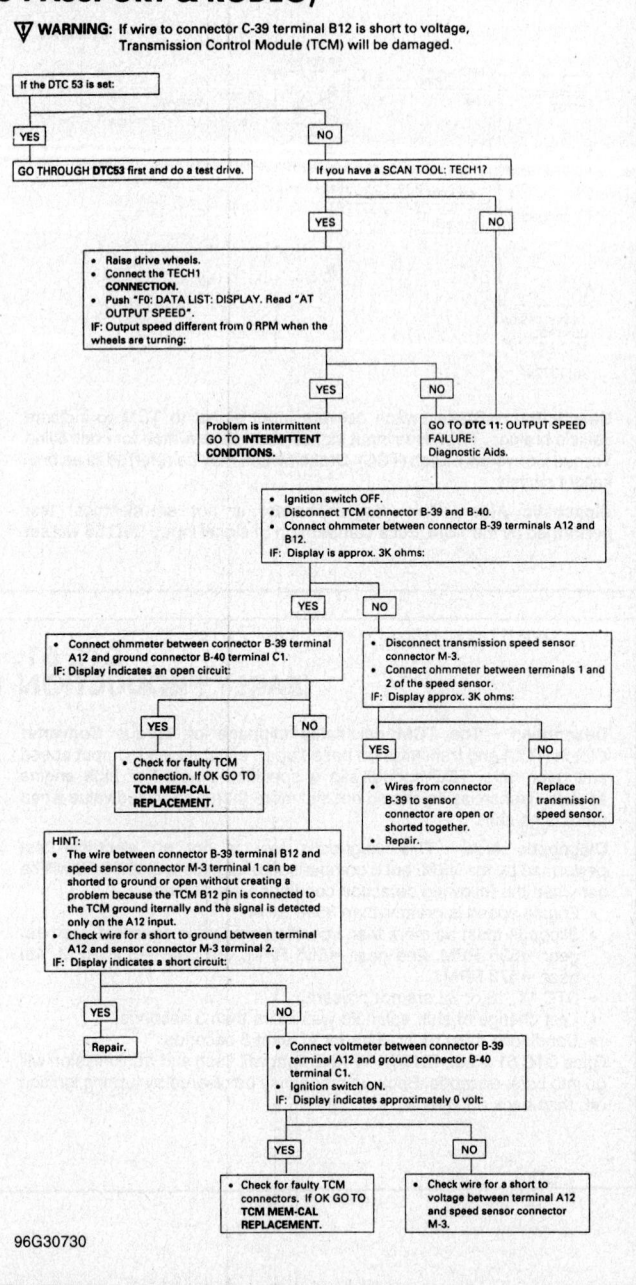

96G30730

DTC 63: EPROM CSUM FAILURE
(EARLY PRODUCTION 1995 PASSPORT & RODEO)

Description – The Erasable Programmable Read Only Memory (EPROM) is an electronic circuit that contains commands for controlling the TCM. The EPROM content is checked automatically approximately each second by the TCM. This procedure is called the Check Sum (CSUM) calculation. If CSUM is false, this means one command is altered. This may be due to a circuit failure or a bad contact between EPROM and TCM, resulting in DTC 63 being set. If all EPROM connections are bad, TCM will not operate. The CSUM cannot be calculated and detected. Nothing will operate, not even the CHECK TRANS light.

Diagnostic Aids – This diagnostic test is not an electrical test performed by the TCM, but a comparison of signal input. DTC 63 will set when the following detection conditions are present.
- Bad EPROM CSUM.
- Condition must be present for at least one second.

Once DTC 63 is set, CHECK TRANS light will flash and transmission will go into back-up mode. Back-up mode may be cleared by turning ignition off, then back on again. To solve the problem, check EPROM MEM-CAL connector. If condition is still present, replace TCM MEM-CAL. See TCM MEM-CAL under REMOVAL & INSTALLATION.

AUTOMATIC TRANSMISSIONS
1995 Hydra-Matic 4L30-E Electronic Controls (Cont.)

3-611

DTC 64: TCC VALVE STUCK ON
(EARLY PRODUCTION 1995 PASSPORT & RODEO)

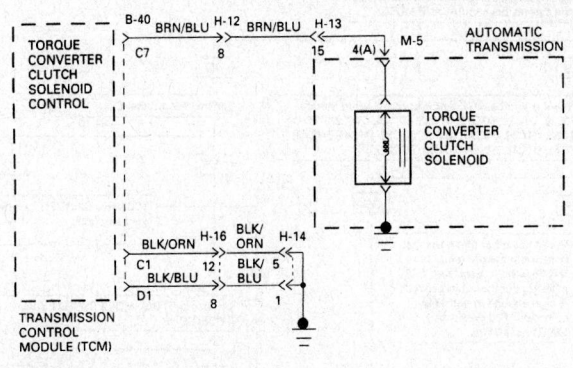

96E30696

Description – Torque Converter Clutch (TCC) solenoid is located on adapter case valve body. TCM energizes TCC solenoid to open fluid port. When fluid port is open, line pressure actuates converter clutch control valve which exhausts the fluid and torque converter clutch engages. TCM allows torque converter clutch to engage only when:

- Transmission is at normal operating temperature.
- Brake pedal is in released position.
- Transmission is in 2nd, 3rd or 4th gear.
- Engine is at normal operating temperature.

TCC solenoid is activated by applying voltage to one side (high side) of TCC solenoid with other side of TCC solenoid grounded.

Diagnostic Aids – This diagnostic test is not an electrical test performed by the TCM, but a comparison of signal input. DTC 64 will set when the following conditions are present.

- TCC should be off based upon shift pattern or conditions that turn TCC off and slippage is less than –20 RPM.
- TCC slippage is less than 20 RPM.
- Throttle position sensor (TPS) is greater than 25 percent.
- DTC 11, 13, 21 or 62 are not present.
- Gearshift lever is not in "P" or "N" position.
- Current gear is not 1st gear.
- Conditions must be present for at least 4 seconds.

If DTC 64 is set, CHECK TRANS light will NOT flash. Transmission will NOT go into back-up mode. To return to normal operation, cycle ignition switch.

If DTC 64 is set, the TCC will be turned off. If TCC remains on constantly due to short circuit, the hydraulic circuit will not apply TCC in 1st gear so engine does not stall. However, if driver brakes sharply in 2nd gear, engine may stall.

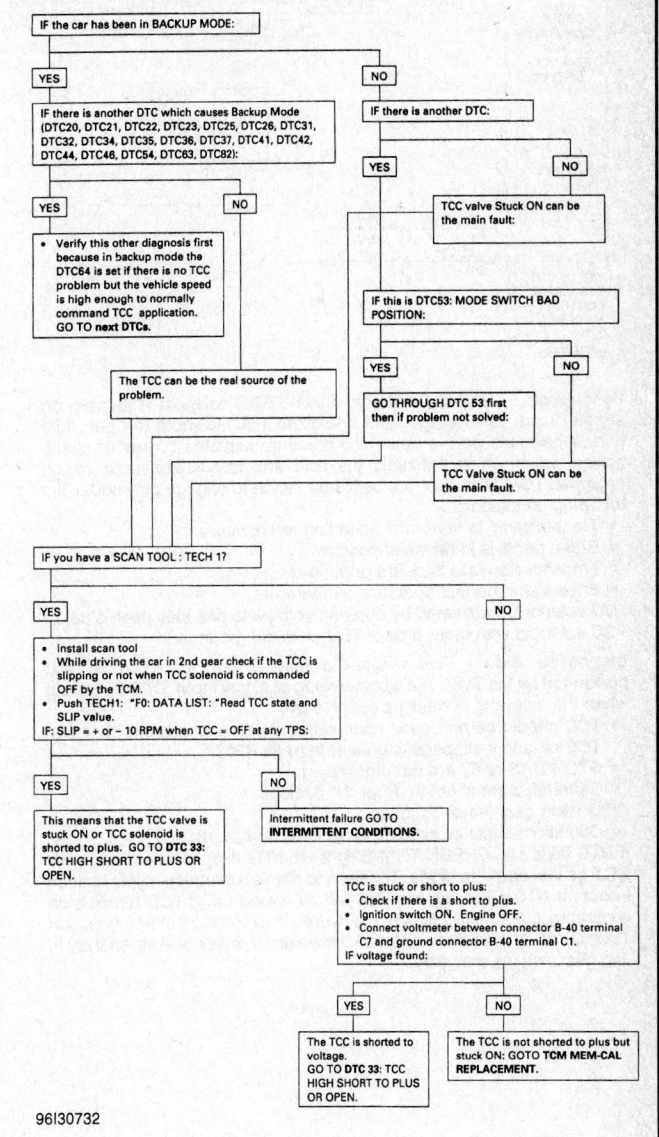

96I30732

3-612

AUTOMATIC TRANSMISSIONS
1995 Hydra-Matic 4L30-E Electronic Controls (Cont.)

DTC 65: TCC VALVE STUCK OFF
(EARLY PRODUCTION 1995 PASSPORT & RODEO)

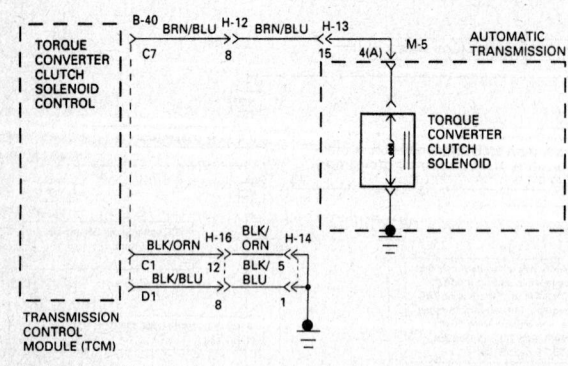

96E30696

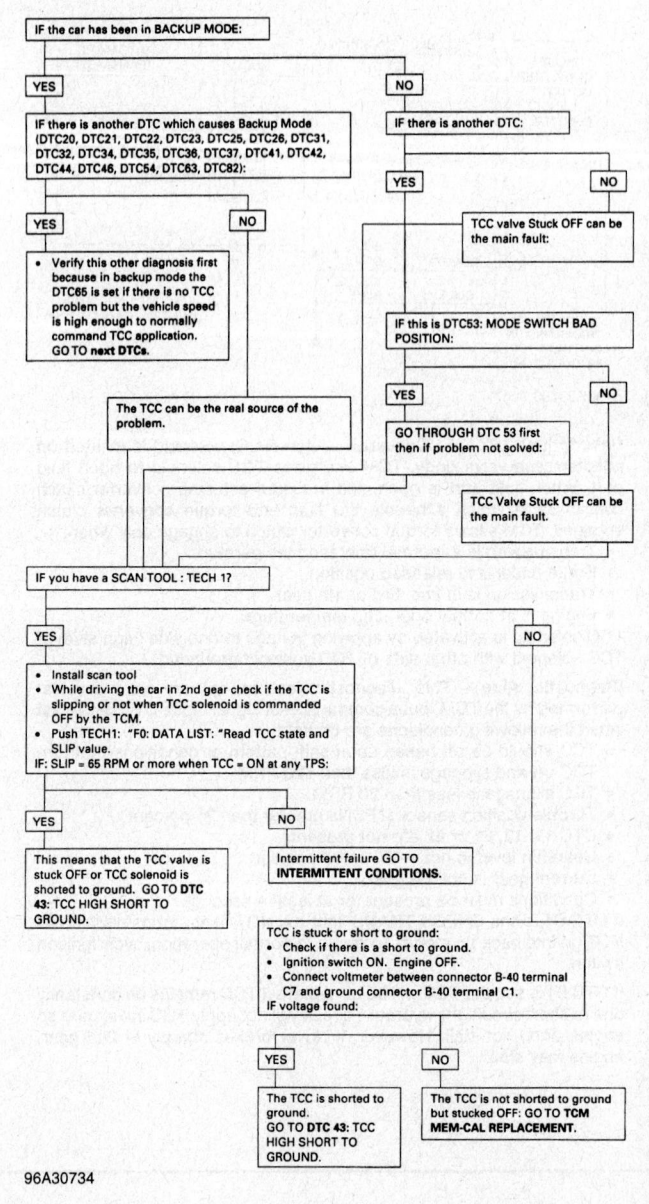

Description – Torque Converter Clutch (TCC) solenoid is located on adapter case valve body. TCM energizes TCC solenoid to open fluid port. When fluid port is open, line pressure actuates converter clutch control valve which exhausts the fluid and torque converter clutch engages. TCM allows torque converter clutch to engage only under the following conditions:
- Transmission is at normal operating temperature.
- Brake pedal is in released position.
- Transmission is in 2nd, 3rd or 4th gear.
- Engine is at normal operating temperature.

TCC solenoid is activated by applying voltage to one side (high side) of TCC solenoid with other side of TCC solenoid grounded.

Diagnostic Aids – This diagnostic test is not an electrical test performed by the TCM, but a comparison of signal input. DTC 65 will set when the following conditions are present.
- TCC should be on based upon shift pattern or conditions that turn TCC on and if slippage is greater than 65 RPM.
- DTC 11, 13 or 62 are not present.
- Gearshift lever is not in "P" or "N" position.
- Current gear is not 1st gear.
- Conditions must be present for at least 3 seconds.

If DTC 65 is set, CHECK TRANS light will NOT flash. Transmission will NOT go into back-up mode. To return to normal operation, cycle ignition switch. If DTC 65 is set, the TCC will be turned off. If TCC remains on constantly due to short circuit, the hydraulic circuit will not apply TCC in 1st gear so engine does not stall. However, if driver brakes sharply in 2nd gear, engine may stall.

96A30734

AUTOMATIC TRANSMISSIONS
1995 Hydra-Matic 4L30-E Electronic Controls (Cont.)

3-613

DTC 82: SHIFT OR BAND APPLY SOLENOIDS FAULTY DURING DRIVING
(EARLY PRODUCTION 1995 PASSPORT & RODEO)

Description – Shift solenoids are located on main valve body. Band apply solenoid is located on adapter case valve body. The TCM energizes solenoid to open or close fluid inlet port depending on solenoid application. Solenoid is activated by applying voltage to one side (high side) of solenoid and grounding the other side (low side) of solenoid.

High Side Driver (HSD) is a circuit of the TCM that acts as a switch between solenoid and supply voltage. High side of solenoid is permanently supplied voltage, except in back-up mode or when ignition is off. The Low Side Driver (LSD) is a circuit of TCM that used as a switch between solenoid and ground. When solenoid is turned on, the TCM completes ground circuit for the solenoid.

Diagnostic Aids – DTC 82 is set when a short circuit or open circuit is present in the wiring to solenoid when engine is cranked, and then car is driven. DTC 82 can only be set when TCM is activating the solenoid with the problem circuit. To know where problem area is located, cycle ignition switch to use TCM self-check of solenoids when engine is not cranked, but ignition is on. DTC 82 will set when the following detection conditions are present.

- HSD or LSD is improperly on.
- Condition must be present for at least .15 second.

Once DTC 82 is set, CHECK TRANS light will flash and transmission will go into back-up mode. Back-up mode may be cleared by turning ignition off, then back on again.

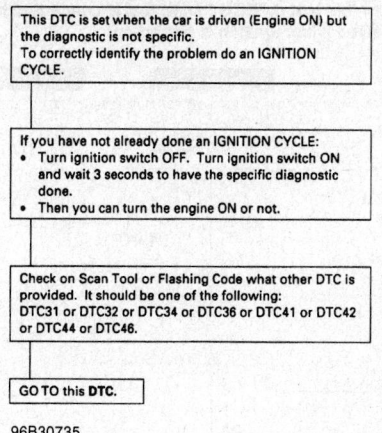

This DTC is set when the car is driven (Engine ON) but the diagnostic is not specific.
To correctly identify the problem do an IGNITION CYCLE.

If you have not already done an IGNITION CYCLE:
- Turn ignition switch OFF. Turn ignition switch ON and wait 3 seconds to have the specific diagnostic done.
- Then you can turn the engine ON or not.

Check on Scan Tool or Flashing Code what other DTC is provided. It should be one of the following:
DTC31 or DTC32 or DTC34 or DTC36 or DTC41 or DTC42 or DTC44 or DTC46.

GO TO this **DTC.**

96B30735

CHECK TRANS LIGHT TEST
(LATE PRODUCTION 1995 PASSPORT & RODEO)

NOTE: Perform this test if CHECK TRANS light is on steady at all times with ignition on and no diagnostic trouble codes stored, or CHECK TRANS LIGHT remains off when ignition is first turned on.

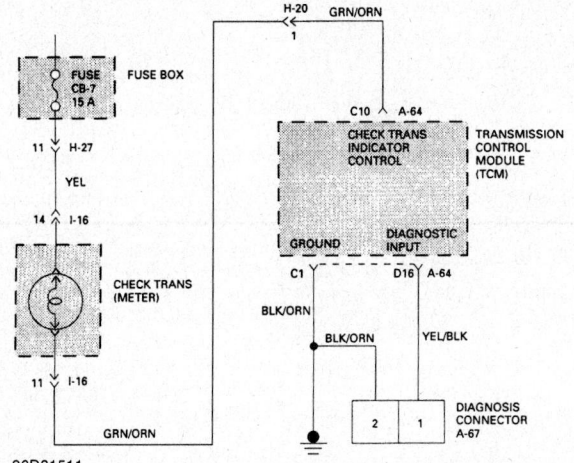

96D31511

Description – When ignition is turned on, CHECK TRANS light on instrument panel should come on for about 2-4 seconds while TCM is performing a self-test of the circuit and components, then light should go off. When ignition is on and TCM detects an electrical failure in the transmission electronic control system, the TCM will flash CHECK TRANS light and may store a diagnostic trouble code in memory.

CHECK TRANS Light Is On Steady With Ignition On – **1)** This condition may be caused by short circuit to ground between CHECK TRANS light and TCM. Check wiring from TCM to CHECK TRANS light on instrument panel for a short circuit to ground.
2) If no short circuit to ground is present in the wiring, replace TCM MEM-CAL. See TCM MEM-CAL under REMOVAL & INSTALLATION.

CHECK TRANS Light Remains Off – **1)** This condition may be caused by an open circuit between CHECK TRANS light and TCM, or no battery voltage present at CHECK TRANS light. Check wiring from TCM to CHECK TRANS light on instrument panel for an open circuit.
2) Ensure battery voltage is present between fuse in fuse box and CHECK TRANS light. Check fuse and all connections as necessary.
3) If battery voltage is present, and no open circuit is present between CHECK TRANS light and TCM, replace TCM MEM-CAL. See TCM MEM-CAL under REMOVAL & INSTALLATION.

3-614

AUTOMATIC TRANSMISSIONS
1995 Hydra-Matic 4L30-E Electronic Controls (Cont.)

DIAGNOSTIC CONNECTOR & VOLTAGE SUPPLY TEST
(LATE PRODUCTION 1995 PASSPORT & RODEO)

NOTE: Perform this test if TECH 1 scan tool is connected but no data is received when ignition is turned on.

TECH 1 REFERS TO CHART 1 WHEN THE EQUIPMENT IS CORRECTLY CONNECTED, BUT NO DATA (WITH IGNITION ON) IS RECEIVED FROM TECH 1.

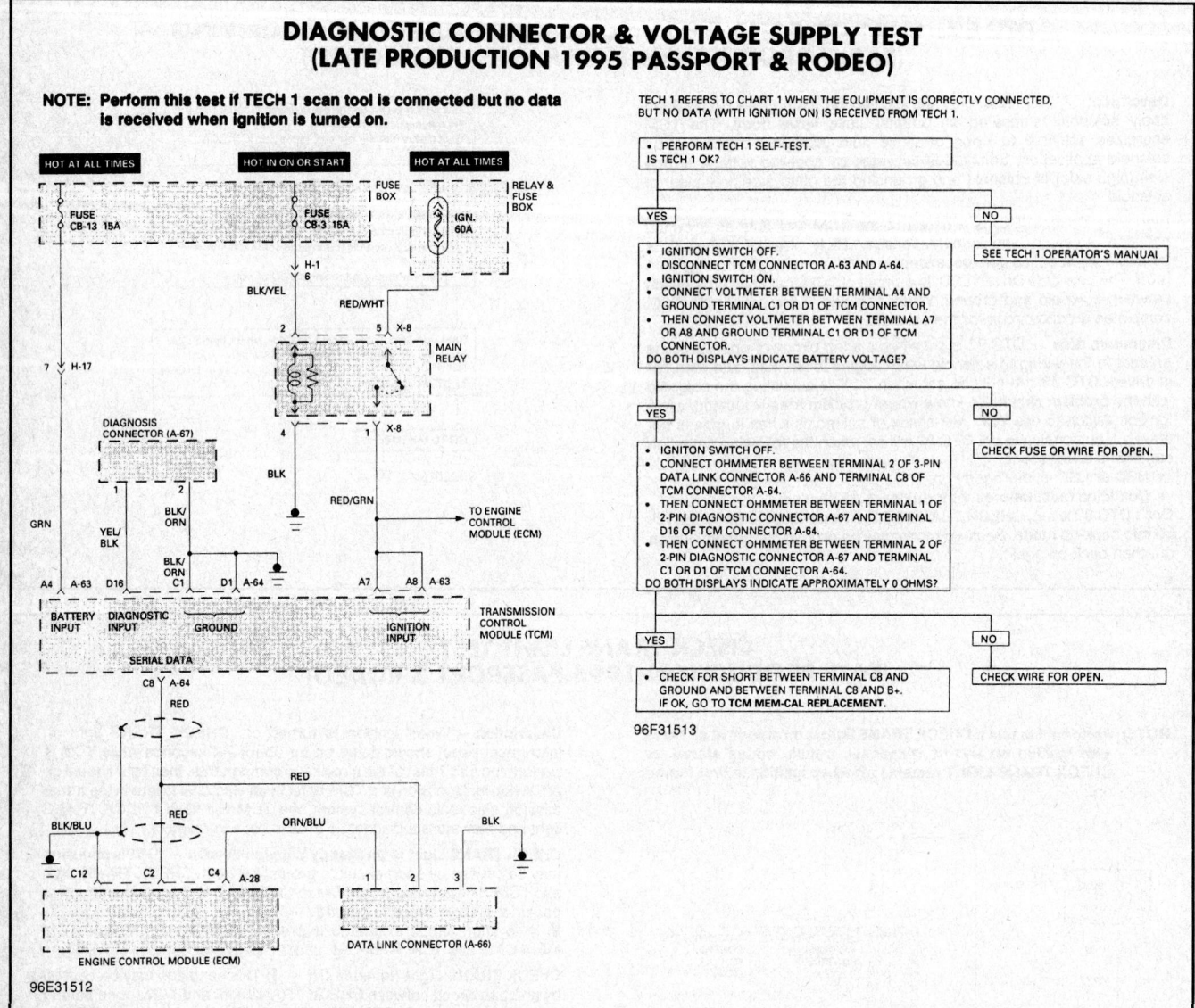

96E31512

96F31513

AUTOMATIC TRANSMISSIONS
1995 Hydra-Matic 4L30-E Electronic Controls (Cont.)

3-615

TRANSMISSION OPERATING MODE TEST
(LATE PRODUCTION 1995 PASSPORT & RODEO)

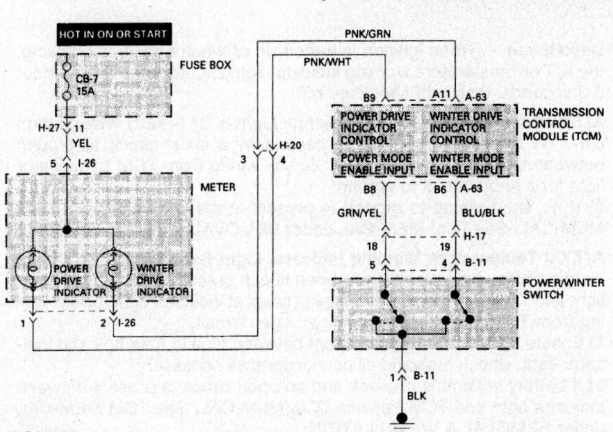

96G31514

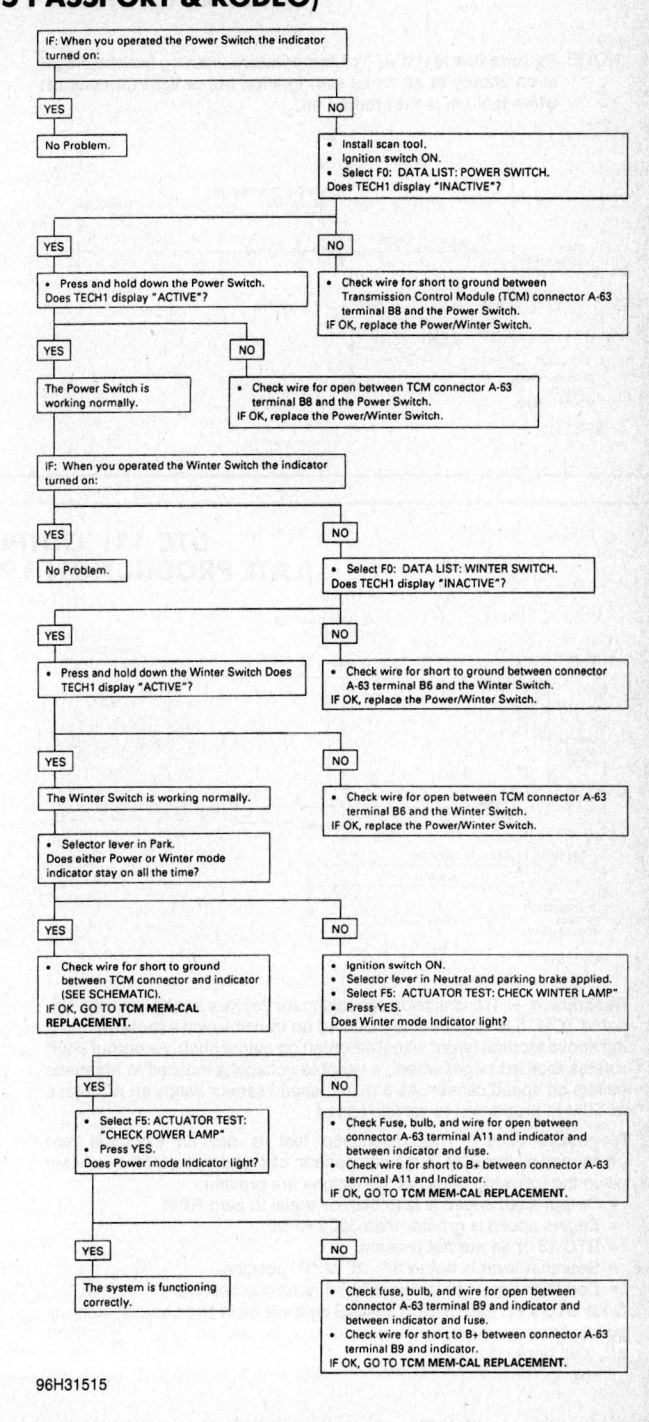

96H31515

Description – The TCM controls transmission shifting and operation using 3 different shift modes: Normal mode, Power mode and Winter mode. Driver selects shift mode by using POWER or WINTER mode switch mounted on center console, near gearshift lever. Power mode slightly increases engine speed at which transmission shift points occur for maximum performance.

In Winter mode, transmission starts off in 3rd gear to aid in vehicle traction on ice and snow. When Winter mode is selected, the TCM overrides the Power or Normal mode. Winter mode will be activated when all of the following conditions are present.

- Accelerator opening is at 7 percent or less.
- Kickdown switch is off.
- Gearshift lever is in "D" position.
- Transmission fluid temperature is 140°F (248°C) or less.
- Vehicle speed is less than 7 MPH.
- WINTER mode switch is on.

Winter mode will be canceled when any of the following conditions are present.

- Ignition is turned off.
- Kickdown switch is on for more than 3 seconds.
- Gearshift lever is placed in "3", "2" or "L" position.
- Transmission fluid temperature is 140°F (284°C) or greater.
- Vehicle speed exceeds 20 MPH.
- WINTER mode switch is turned off.

When Winter or Power mode are canceled, transmission operates in Normal mode. Normal mode provides standard transmission shift points.

3-616

AUTOMATIC TRANSMISSIONS
1995 Hydra-Matic 4L30-E Electronic Controls (Cont.)

A/T OIL TEMP. INDICATOR TEST
(LATE PRODUCTION 1995 PASSPORT & RODEO)

NOTE: Perform this test if A/T oil temperature warning indicator light is on steady at all times with ignition on, or light remains off when ignition is first turned on.

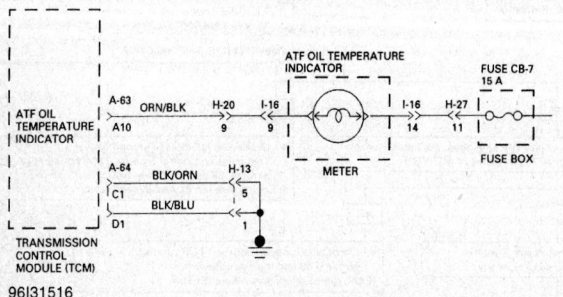

96I31516

Description – When ignition is turned on or when engine is cranking, the A/T oil temperature warning indicator light should come on for about 2-3 seconds, then light should go off.

A/T Oil Temperature Warning Indicator Light Is On Steady With Ignition On – 1) This condition may be caused by a short circuit to ground between indicator light and TCM. Check wiring from TCM to indicator light for a short circuit to ground.
2) If no short circuit to ground is present in the wiring, replace TCM MEM-CAL. See TCM MEM-CAL under REMOVAL & INSTALLATION.

A/T Oil Temperature Warning Indicator Light Remains Off – 1) This condition may be caused by an open circuit present between indicator light and TCM, or no battery voltage present at indicator light. Check wiring from TCM to indicator light for an open circuit.
2) Ensure battery voltage is present between fuse in fuse box and indicator light. Check fuse and all connections as necessary.
3) If battery voltage is present, and no open circuit is present between indicator light and TCM, replace TCM MEM-CAL. See TCM MEM-CAL under REMOVAL & INSTALLATION.

DTC 11: OUTPUT SPEED FAILURE
(LATE PRODUCTION 1995 PASSPORT & RODEO)

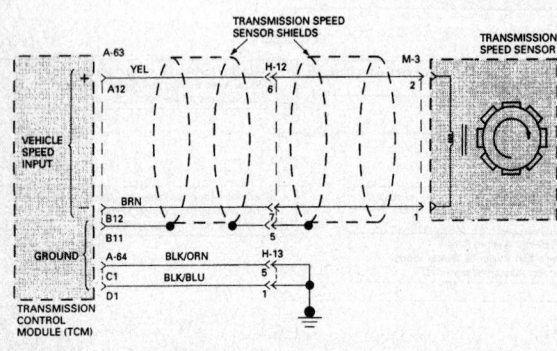

96J31517

Description – Transmission speed sensor delivers a vehicle speed signal to TCM. Speed sensor is mounted on transmission extension housing above toothed target wheel mounted on output shaft. As output shaft rotates toothed target wheel, a variable voltage is induced in magnetic pickup on speed sensor. As a result, speed sensor sends an AC signal to TCM in proportion to vehicle speed.

Diagnostic Aids – This diagnostic test is not an electrical test performed by the TCM, but a comparison of signal input. DTC 11 will set when the following detection conditions are present.
- Output shaft speed is less than or equal to zero RPM.
- Engine speed is greater than 3000 RPM.
- DTC 13 or 54 are not present.
- Gearshift lever is not in "P", "N" or "R" position.
- Conditions must be present for at least one second.

Once DTC 11 is set, CHECK TRANS light will flash and transmission will go into back-up mode. Back-up mode may be cleared by turning ignition off, then back on again.

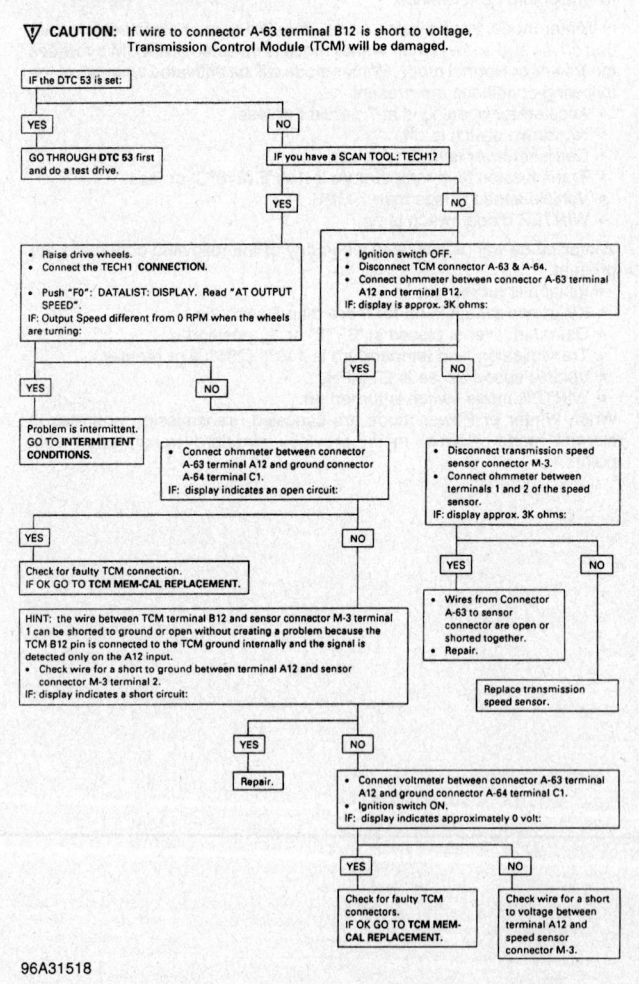

96A31518

DTC 13: ENGINE SPEED FAILURE
(LATE PRODUCTION 1995 PASSPORT & RODEO)

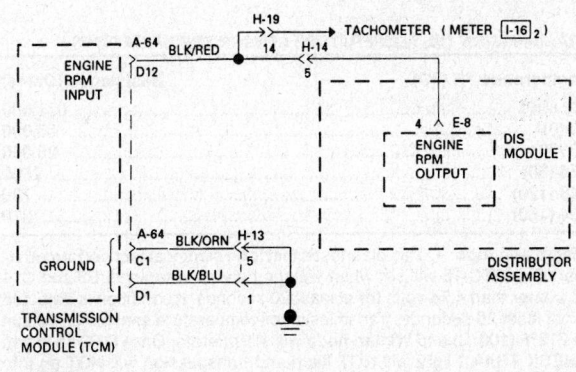

96B31519

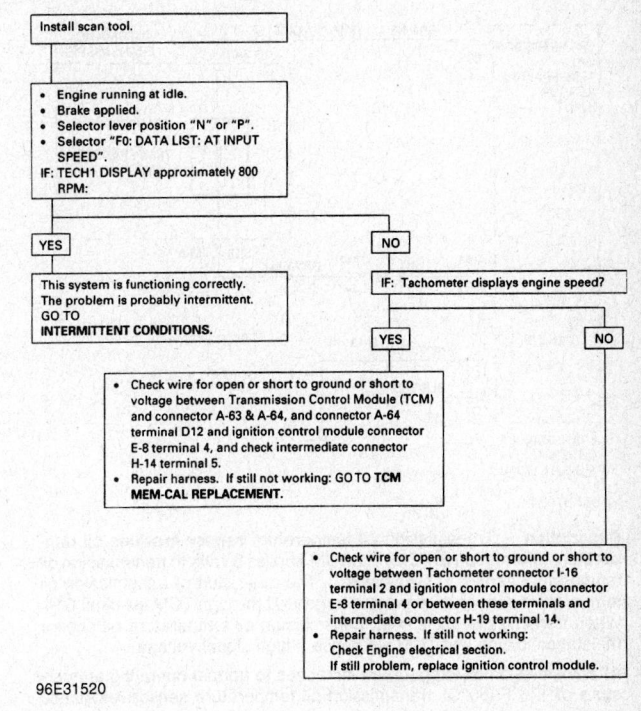

96E31520

Description – Ignition control module sends an engine speed or RPM signal to TCM. Engine Control Module (ECM) also receives a signal from ignition control module. In Neutral at idle, engine speed should be approximately 800 RPM.

Diagnostic Aids – This diagnostic test is not an electrical test performed by the TCM, but a comparison of signal input. DTC 13 will set when the following detection conditions are present.

- Output speed is greater than 1024 RPM.
- Engine speed is equal to or less than 200 RPM.
- Acceleration is greater than one MPH.
- DTC 11, 54 or 62 are not present.
- Gearshift lever is not in "P" or "N" position.
- Conditions must be present for at least .5 second.

Once DTC 13 is set, CHECK TRANS light will flash and transmission will go into back-up mode. Back-up mode may be cleared by turning ignition off, then back on again.

3-618

AUTOMATIC TRANSMISSIONS
1995 Hydra-Matic 4L30-E Electronic Controls (Cont.)

DTC 15: TRANSMISSION OIL TEMP. SENSOR CIRCUIT
(SHORT CIRCUIT TO B+ OR OPEN CIRCUIT)
(LATE PRODUCTION 1995 PASSPORT & RODEO)

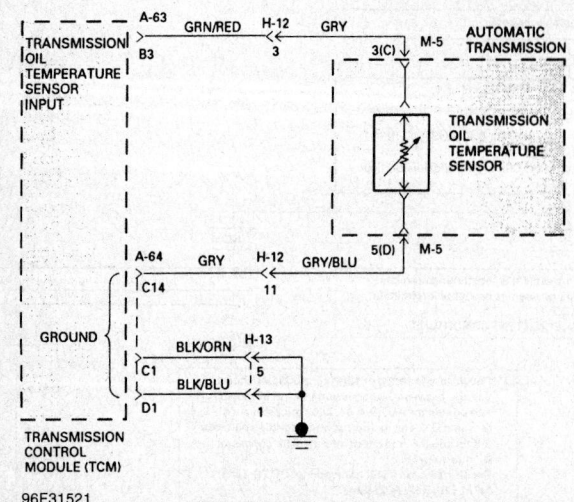

96F31521

Description – Transmission oil temperature sensor provides oil temperature information to TCM. The TCM applies 5 volts to transmission oil temperature sensor at terminal 3(C). The other side of transmission oil temperature sensor is connected to ground through TCM terminal C14. When transmission oil is cold, transmission oil temperature oil sensor resistance is high and TCM will sense a high signal voltage.

As transmission oil temperature increases to normal operating temperature of 176°F (80°C), transmission oil temperature sensor resistance becomes less and voltage decreases to approximately 3.5 volts. When DTC 15 is set, the transmission will use a warm value for operation, but TECH 1 scan tool will display the actual oil temperature. Transmission oil temperature resistance will change in relation to temperature. See TRANSMISSION OIL TEMPERATURE SENSOR SPECIFICATIONS table.

TRANSMISSION OIL TEMPERATURE SENSOR SPECIFICATIONS

Temperature °F (°C)	Resistance (Ohms)
-40 (-40)	672,000
32 (0)	65,000
68 (20)	25,000
176 (80)	2500
248 (120)	780
304 (150)	370

Diagnostic Aids – This diagnostic test is an electrical test performed by the TCM. DTC 15 will set when voltage between terminals B3 and C14 is greater than 4.74 volts for at least 20 seconds. If condition is detected for at least 20 seconds, transmission oil temperature sensor will default to 212°F (100°C) and Winter mode will still operate. Once DTC 15 is set, CHECK TRANS light will NOT flash and transmission will NOT go into back-up mode. System will return to normal operation when voltage between terminals B3 and C14 is equal to or less than 4.74 volts.

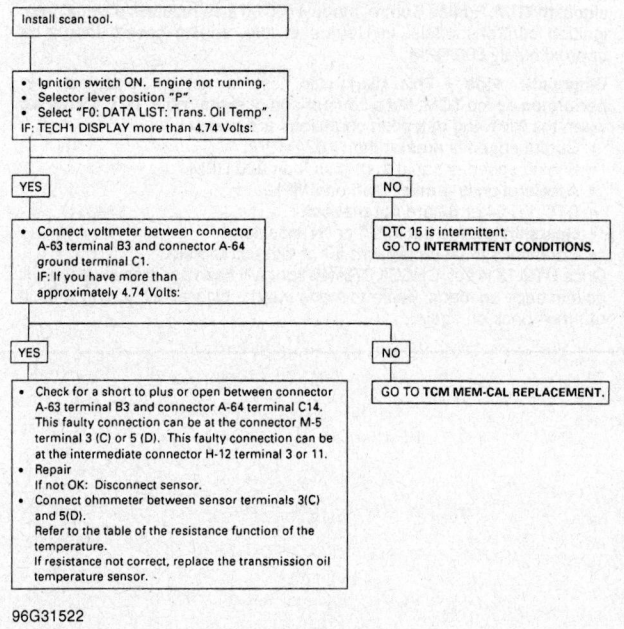

96G31522

AUTOMATIC TRANSMISSIONS
1995 Hydra-Matic 4L30-E Electronic Controls (Cont.)

3-619

DTC 16: TRANSMISSION OIL TEMP. SENSOR CIRCUIT
(SHORT CIRCUIT TO GROUND)
(LATE PRODUCTION 1995 PASSPORT & RODEO)

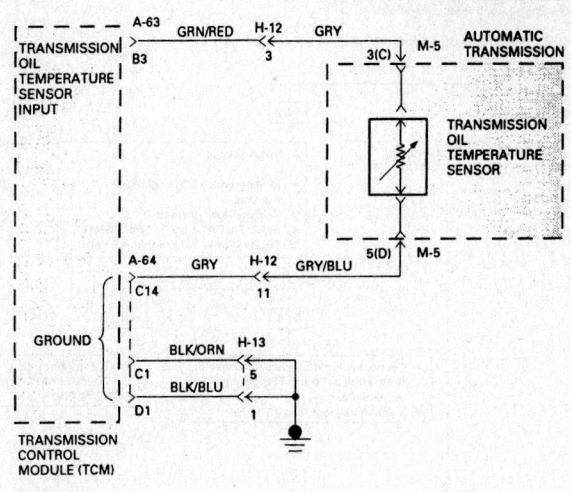

96F31521

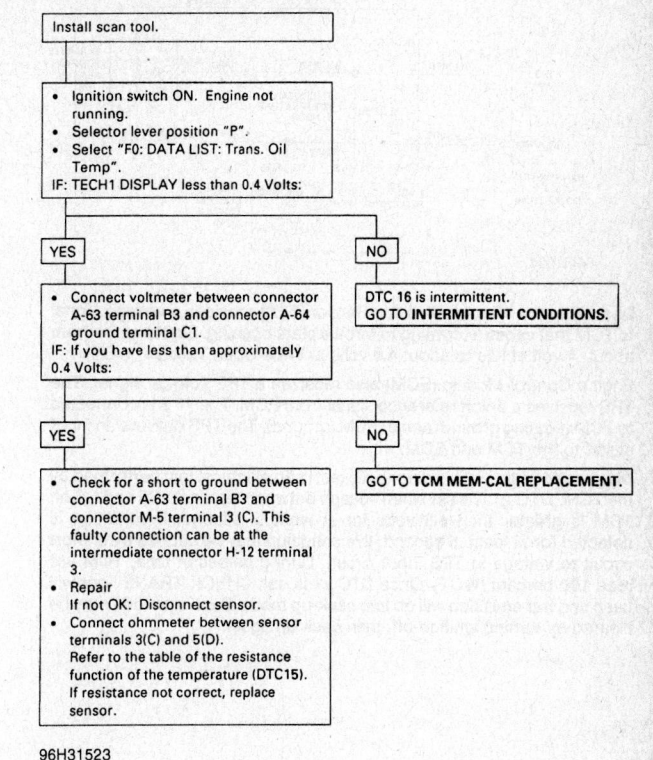

96H31523

Description – Transmission oil temperature sensor provides oil temperature information to TCM. The TCM applies 5 volts to transmission oil temperature sensor at terminal 3(C). The other side of transmission oil temperature sensor is connected to ground through TCM terminal C14.

When transmission oil is cold, transmission oil temperature sensor resistance is high and TCM will sense a high signal voltage. As transmission oil temperature increases to normal operating temperature of 176°F (80°C), transmission oil temperature sensor resistance becomes less and voltage decreases to approximately 3.5 volts. When DTC 16 is set, the transmission will use a warm value for operation, but TECH 1 scan tool will display the actual oil temperature.

Diagnostic Aids – This diagnostic test is an electrical test performed by the TCM. DTC 16 will set when voltage between terminals B3 and C14 is less than .4 volt for at least 20 seconds. If condition is detected for at least 20 seconds, transmission oil temperature sensor will default to 212°F (100°C) and Winter mode will still operate. Once DTC 16 is set, CHECK TRANS light will NOT flash and transmission will NOT go into back-up mode. System will return to normal operation when voltage between terminals B3 and C14 is equal to or greater than .4 volt.

3-620

AUTOMATIC TRANSMISSIONS
1995 Hydra-Matic 4L30-E Electronic Controls (Cont.)

DTC 21: THROTTLE POSITION SENSOR CIRCUIT (SHORT CIRCUIT TO B+)
(LATE PRODUCTION 1995 PASSPORT & RODEO)

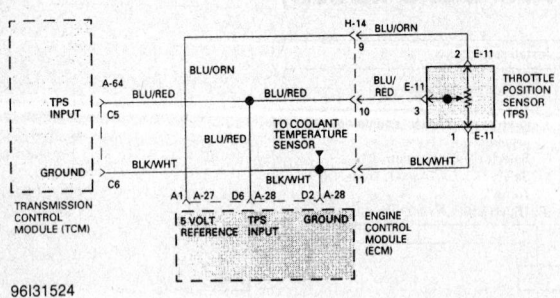

96I31524

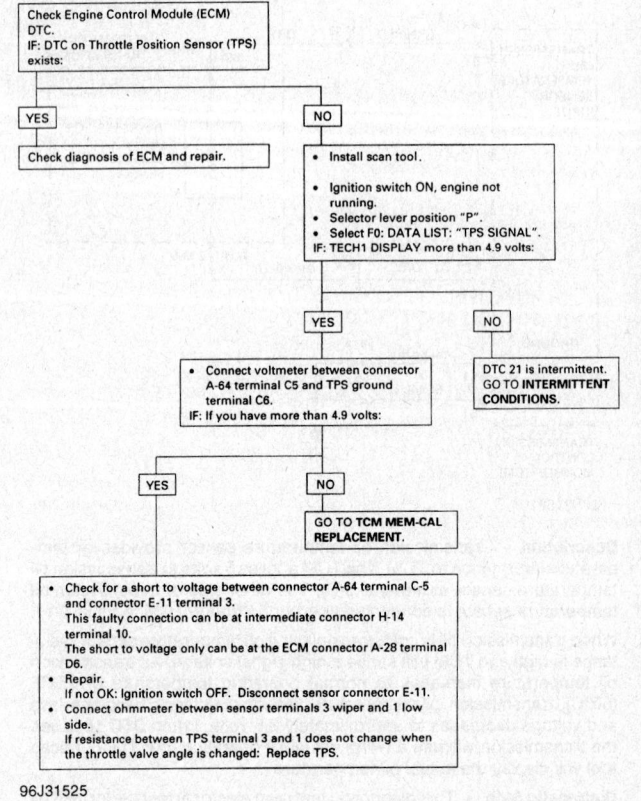

96J31525

Description – Throttle Position Sensor (TPS) provides a voltage signal to TCM that varies according to throttle plate opening. Signal varies from about .4 volt at idle to about 4.6 volts at Wide Open Throttle (WOT).

Engine Control Module (ECM) also receives a TPS voltage signal. The TPS receives a 5-volt reference signal from ECM. The TPS is connected to TCM (floating ground) and at ECM (ground). The TPS delivers an input signal to the TCM and ECM.

Diagnostic Aids – This diagnostic test is an electrical test performed by the TCM. DTC 21 will set when voltage between terminals C5 and C6 on TCM is greater than 4.9 volts for at least .5 second. If condition is detected for at least .5 second, this condition may be caused by a short circuit to voltage in TPS input circuit. During detection time, TCM will read 100 percent (WOT). Once DTC 21 is set, CHECK TRANS light will flash and transmission will go into back-up mode. Back-up mode may be cleared by turning ignition off, then back on again.

AUTOMATIC TRANSMISSIONS
1995 Hydra-Matic 4L30-E Electronic Controls (Cont.)

3-621

DTC 22: THROTTLE POSITION SENSOR CIRCUIT
(SHORT CIRCUIT TO GROUND OR OPEN CIRCUIT)
(LATE PRODUCTION 1995 PASSPORT & RODEO)

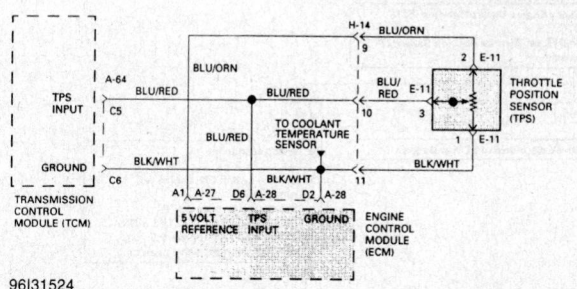

96I31524

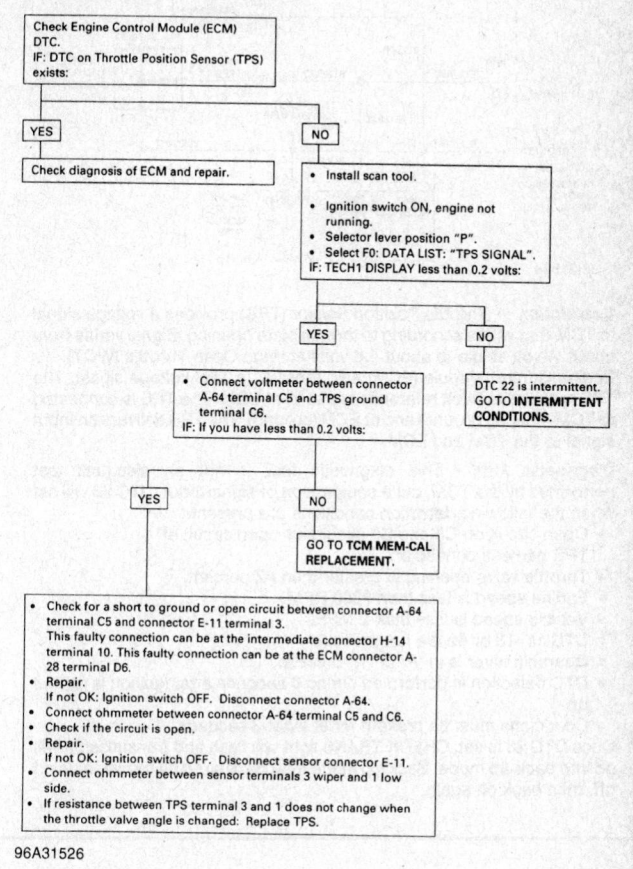

96A31526

Description – Throttle Position Sensor (TPS) provides a voltage signal to TCM that varies according to throttle plate opening. Signal varies from about .4 volt at idle to about 4.6 volts at Wide Open Throttle (WOT).

Engine Control Module (ECM) also receives a TPS voltage signal. The TPS receives a 5-volt reference signal from ECM at terminal. The TPS is connected to TCM (floating ground) and at ECM (ground). The TPS delivers an input signal to the TCM and ECM.

Diagnostic Aids – This diagnostic test is an electrical test performed by the TCM. DTC 22 will set when the following detection conditions are present.

- Short circuit on TPS input signal to TCM ground, or open circuit on TPS circuit.
- Voltage between terminals C5 and C6 on TCM is less than .2 volts for at least .5 second.

If condition is detected for at least .5 second during detection time, TCM will read zero percent (idle position). Once DTC 22 is set, CHECK TRANS light will flash and transmission will go into back-up mode. Back-up mode may be cleared by turning ignition off, then back on again.

3-622

AUTOMATIC TRANSMISSIONS
1995 Hydra-Matic 4L30-E Electronic Controls (Cont.)

DTC 23: THROTTLE POSITION SENSOR CIRCUIT (CONNECTOR OPEN CIRCUIT)
(LATE PRODUCTION 1995 PASSPORT & RODEO)

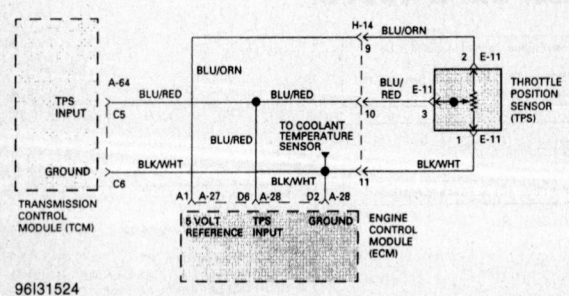

96I31524

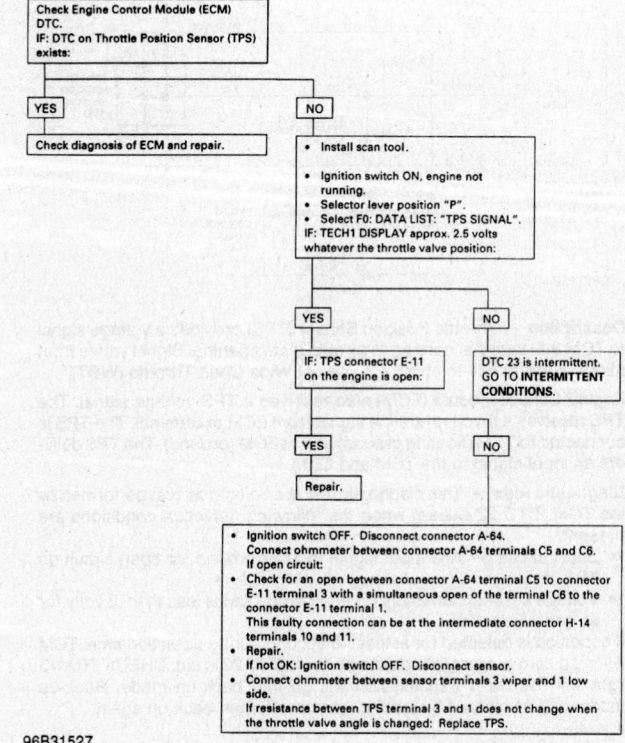

Description – Throttle Position Sensor (TPS) provides a voltage signal to TCM that varies according to throttle plate opening. Signal varies from about .4 volt at idle to about 4.6 volts at Wide Open Throttle (WOT). Engine Control Module (ECM) also receives a TPS voltage signal. The TPS receives a 5-volt reference signal from ECM. The TPS is connected to TCM (floating ground) and at ECM (ground). The TPS delivers an input signal to the TCM and ECM.

Diagnostic Aids – This diagnostic test is not an electrical test performed by the TCM, but a comparison of signal input. DTC 23 will set when the following detection conditions are present.

- Open circuit on C5 and C6 circuits or open circuit at TPS harness connector.
- Throttle valve opening is greater than 42 percent.
- Engine speed is less than 2200 RPM.
- Vehicle speed is less than 2 MPH.
- DTC 11, 13 or 62 are not present.
- Gearshift lever is in "P" or "N" position.
- DTC detection is performed during 6 seconds after ignition is turned on.
- Conditions must be present for at least 3 seconds.

Once DTC 23 is set, CHECK TRANS light will flash and transmission will go into back-up mode. Back-up mode may be cleared by turning ignition off, then back on again.

96B31527

AUTOMATIC TRANSMISSIONS
1995 Hydra-Matic 4L30-E Electronic Controls (Cont.)

3-623

DTC 25: SUPPLY VOLTAGE TOO LOW
(LATE PRODUCTION 1995 PASSPORT & RODEO)

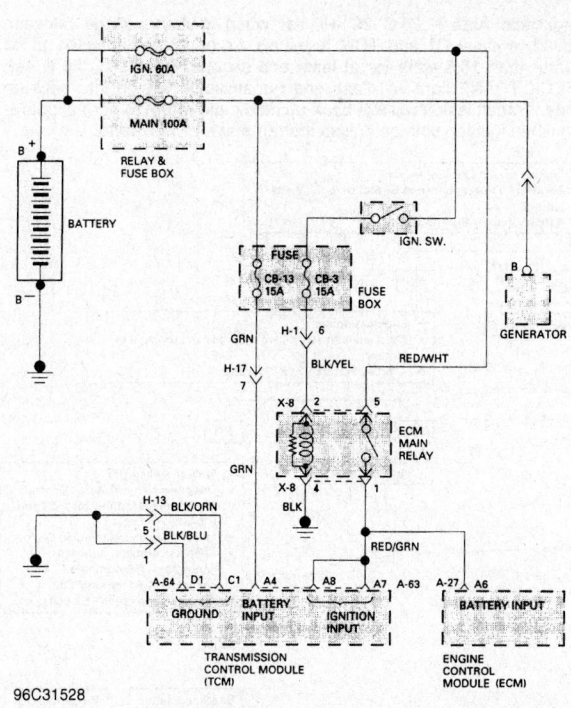

96C31528

Description – Ignition voltage at TCM terminals A7 and A8 are monitored by TCM. When ignition voltage is less than 9 volts, DTC 25 is set. Minimum voltage requirement will vary with transmission oil temperature.

Diagnostic Aids – This diagnostic test is an electrical test performed by the TCM. DTC 25 will set when ignition voltage between ground terminal C1 and TCM terminals A7 and A8 are detected to be less than minimum required for at least one second. See CODE SET CONDITION in SUPPLY VOLTAGE SPECIFICATIONS table.

SUPPLY VOLTAGE SPECIFICATIONS

Transmission Oil Temperature °F (°C)	Minimum Voltage
Code Set Condition	
-40 (-40)	8.7
194 (90)	9.0
304 (150)	9.2
Back-Up Mode Recovery	
-40 (-40)	9.2
194 (90)	9.5
304 (150)	9.6

Once DTC 25 is set, CHECK TRANS light will flash and transmission will go into back-up mode. Transmission will exit back-up mode and return to normal operation when ignition voltage increases to minimum specified voltage for indicated temperature range. See BACK-UP MODE RECOVERY in SUPPLY VOLTAGE SPECIFICATIONS table.

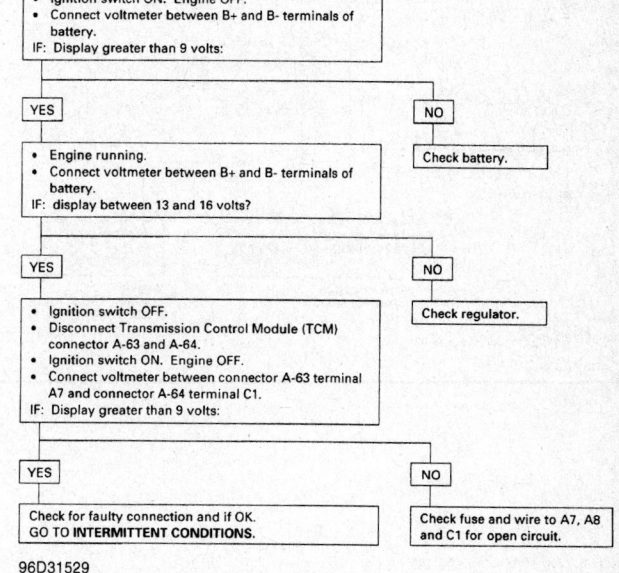

96D31529

3-624

AUTOMATIC TRANSMISSIONS
1995 Hydra-Matic 4L30-E Electronic Controls (Cont.)

DTC 26: SUPPLY VOLTAGE TOO HIGH
(LATE PRODUCTION 1995 PASSPORT & RODEO)

Description – Ignition voltage at TCM terminals A7 and A8 are monitored by TCM. When ignition voltage is greater than 15.5 volts, DTC 26 is set.

Diagnostic Aids – DTC 26 will set when ignition voltage between ground terminal C1 and TCM terminals A7 or A8 are detected to be greater than 15.5 volts for at least one second. Once DTC 26 is set, CHECK TRANS light will flash and transmission will go into back-up mode. Transmission will exit back-up mode and return to normal operation when ignition voltage is less than or equal to 15.5 volts.

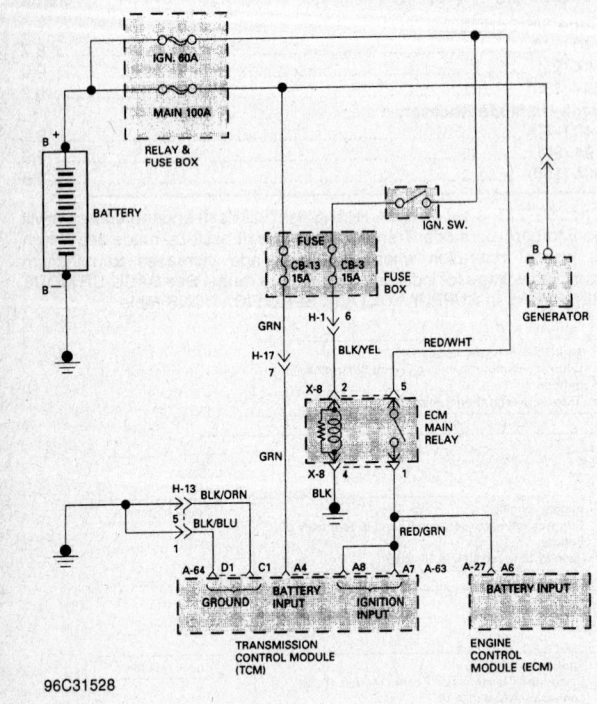

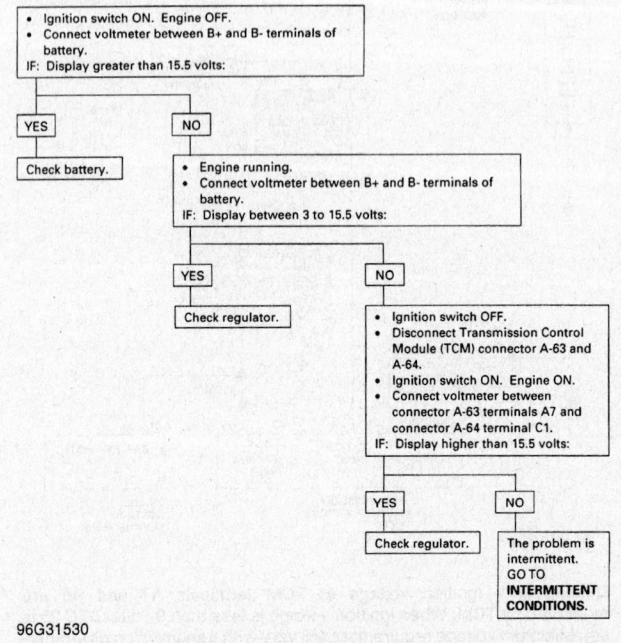

- Ignition switch ON. Engine OFF.
- Connect voltmeter between B+ and B- terminals of battery.
IF: Display greater than 15.5 volts:

YES → Check battery.

NO →
- Engine running.
- Connect voltmeter between B+ and B- terminals of battery.
IF: Display between 3 to 15.5 volts:

YES → Check regulator.

NO →
- Ignition switch OFF.
- Disconnect Transmission Control Module (TCM) connector A-63 and A-64.
- Ignition switch ON. Engine ON.
- Connect voltmeter between connector A-63 terminals A7 and connector A-64 terminal C1.
IF: Display higher than 15.5 volts:

YES → Check regulator.

NO → The problem is intermittent. GO TO **INTERMITTENT CONDITIONS.**

96C31528

96G31530

AUTOMATIC TRANSMISSIONS
1995 Hydra-Matic 4L30-E Electronic Controls (Cont.)

3-625

DTC 31: 1-2/3-4 SHIFT SOLENOID CIRCUIT
(SHORT CIRCUIT TO GROUND OR OPEN CIRCUIT)
(LATE PRODUCTION 1995 PASSPORT & RODEO)

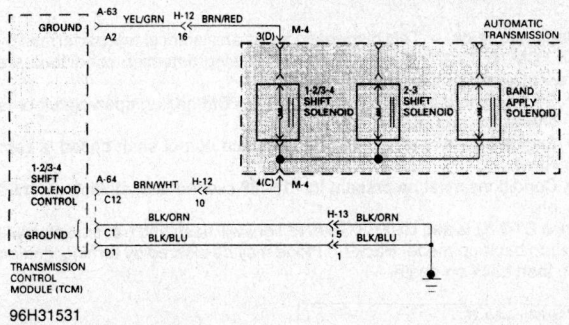

96H31531

Description – The 1-2/3-4 shift solenoid is a normally closed solenoid located on main valve body. In 2nd or 3rd gear, the TCM energizes shift solenoid to open fluid inlet port. When port is open, fluid pressure actuates shift valve. Shift solenoid is activated by applying voltage to one side (high side) of shift solenoid and grounding the other side (low side) of shift solenoid.

High Side Driver (HSD) is a circuit of the TCM which acts as a switch between shift solenoid and supply voltage. High side of shift solenoid is permanently supplied voltage, except in back-up mode or when ignition is off. The TCM continually monitors shift solenoid connection to the Low Side Driver (LSD) for either high or low voltage. The LSD is a circuit of the TCM used as a switch between shift solenoid and ground. When shift solenoid is turned on, the TCM completes a ground circuit for shift solenoid.

When ignition is turned on before engine is cranked, the TCM activates shift solenoids and band apply solenoid to check operating circuits of each solenoid for a short or an open circuit. To do so, the gear is set to 4th gear, 3rd gear, 1st gear, 1st gear with band applied and 4th gear with no HSD. Each one of the 5 tests requires .15 second. If engine is cranked before end of all tests, remaining tests are not performed.

Diagnostic Aids – This diagnostic test is an electrical test performed by the TCM. DTC 31 will set when the following detection conditions are present when ignition is on.

- Shift solenoid low side A2 to TCM has an open circuit or is shorted to ground.
- Engine speed is less than 480 RPM and output shaft speed is zero RPM.
- Conditions must be present for .15-1.03 seconds after ignition is turned on.

Once DTC 31 is set, CHECK TRANS light will flash and transmission will go into back-up mode. Back-up mode may be cleared by turning ignition off, then back on again.

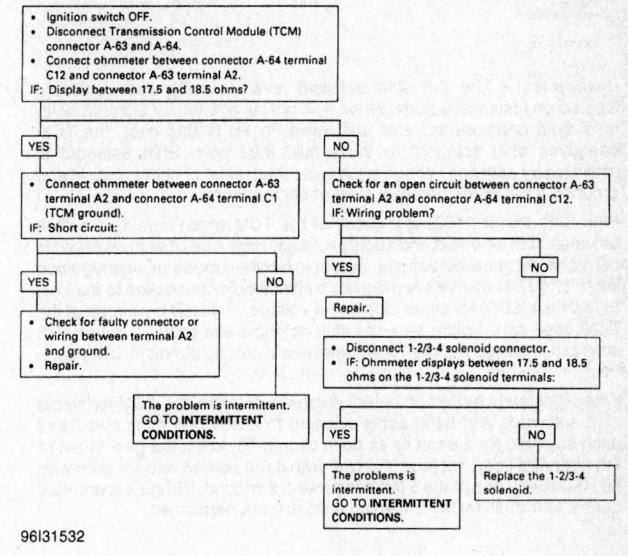

96I31532

3-626

AUTOMATIC TRANSMISSIONS
1995 Hydra-Matic 4L30-E Electronic Controls (Cont.)

DTC 32: 2-3 SHIFT SOLENOID CIRCUIT
(SHORT CIRCUIT TO GROUND OR OPEN CIRCUIT)
(LATE PRODUCTION 1995 PASSPORT & RODEO)

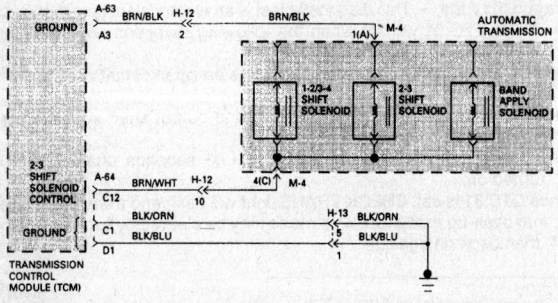

96J31533

Description – The 2-3 shift solenoid is a normally open solenoid located on main valve body. When fluid port is opened by 2-3 shift solenoid, fluid pressure actuates shift valve. In 1st or 2nd gear, the TCM energizes shift solenoid to close fluid inlet port. Shift solenoid is activated by applying voltage to one side (high side) of shift solenoid and grounding the other side (low side) of shift solenoid.

High Side Driver (HSD) is a circuit of the TCM which acts as a switch between shift solenoid and supply voltage. High side of shift solenoid is permanently supplied voltage, except in back-up mode or when ignition is off. The TCM continually monitors shift solenoid connection to the Low Side Driver (LSD) for either high or low voltage. The LSD is a circuit of the TCM used as a switch between shift solenoid and ground. When shift solenoid is turned on, the TCM completes a ground circuit for shift solenoid.

When ignition is turned on before engine is cranked, the TCM activates shift solenoids and band apply solenoid to check operating circuits of each solenoid for a short or an open circuit. To do so, the gear is set to 4th gear, 3rd gear, 1st gear, 1st gear with band applied and 4th gear with no HSD. Each one of the 5 tests requires .15 second. If engine is cranked before end of all tests, remaining tests are not performed.

Diagnostic Aids – This diagnostic test is an electrical test performed by the TCM. DTC 32 will set when the following detection conditions are present when ignition is on.

- Shift solenoid low side terminal A3 to TCM has an open circuit or is shorted to ground.
- Engine speed is less than 480 RPM and output shaft speed is zero RPM.
- Conditions must be present for .15-.88 second after ignition s turned on.

Once DTC 32 is set, CHECK TRANS light will flash and transmission will go into back-up mode. Back-up mode may be cleared by turning ignition off, then back on again.

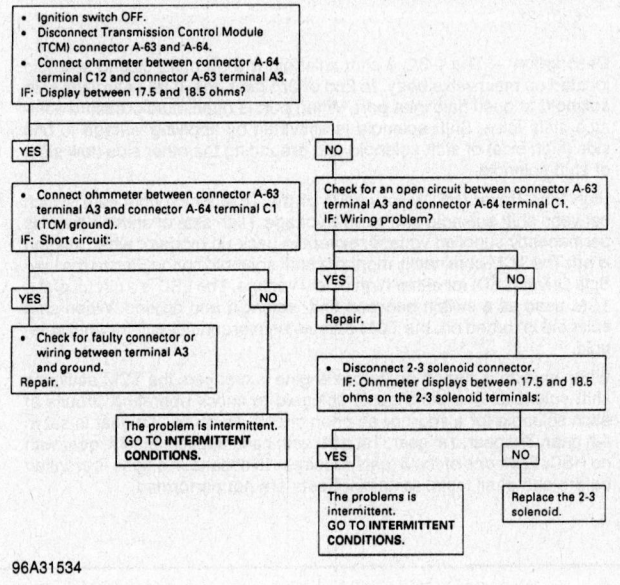

96A31534

AUTOMATIC TRANSMISSIONS
1995 Hydra-Matic 4L30-E Electronic Controls (Cont.)

3-627

DTC 33: TCC SOLENOID CIRCUIT (SHORT CIRCUIT TO B+ OR OPEN CIRCUIT)
(LATE PRODUCTION 1995 PASSPORT & RODEO)

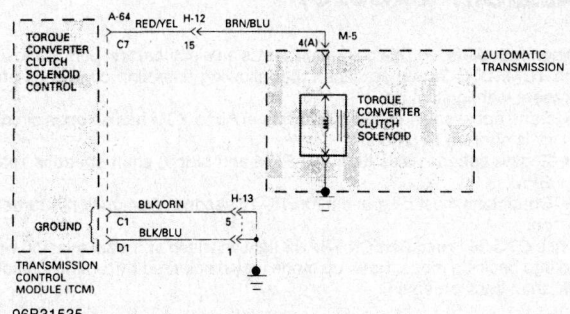

96B31535

Description – Torque Converter Clutch (TCC) solenoid is located on adapter case valve body. TCM energizes TCC solenoid to open fluid port. When fluid port is open, line pressure actuates converter clutch control valve which exhausts the fluid, allowing torque converter clutch to engage. TCM allows torque converter clutch to engage only when:

- Transmission is at normal operating temperature.
- Brake pedal is in released position.
- Transmission is in 2nd, 3rd or 4th gear.
- Engine is at normal operating temperature.
- Shift pattern requests TCC apply.
- Shift is finished.
- DTC 43, 55, 64 or 65 are not present.

TCC solenoid is activated by applying voltage to one side (high side) of TCC solenoid and grounding the other side (low side) of TCC solenoid. High Side Driver (HSD) is a circuit of the TCM which acts as a switch between TCC solenoid and supply voltage. High side of TCC solenoid is used to turn TCC solenoid on or off, as low side of TCC solenoid is permanently connected to ground. When transmission is in back-up mode or ignition is turned off, TCC solenoid is turned off.

The TCM continually monitors TCC solenoid connection to HSD for either high or low voltage. The only test performed is when engine is cranked and TCC solenoid is turned on. If this circuit is shorted to battery voltage, TCC solenoid is constantly on and shifts may be firm.

In 1st gear, TCC is hydraulically off, whatever position TCC solenoid is in. Vehicle may be driven with TCC solenoid shorted to battery voltage. Engine may stall when driver is braking, or if vehicle is stopped with transmission in 2nd gear with TCC applied. The 3-2 shifts will be very firm.

Diagnostic Aids – This diagnostic test is an electrical test performed by the TCM. DTC 33 will set when TCC solenoid high side to TCM terminal C7 contains an open circuit or is shorted to battery voltage and condition is present for .13 second. If DTC 33 is set, the TCC will be shut off and CHECK TRANS light will flash. Transmission will NOT go into back-up mode. Transmission will return to normal operation by turning ignition off, then back on again.

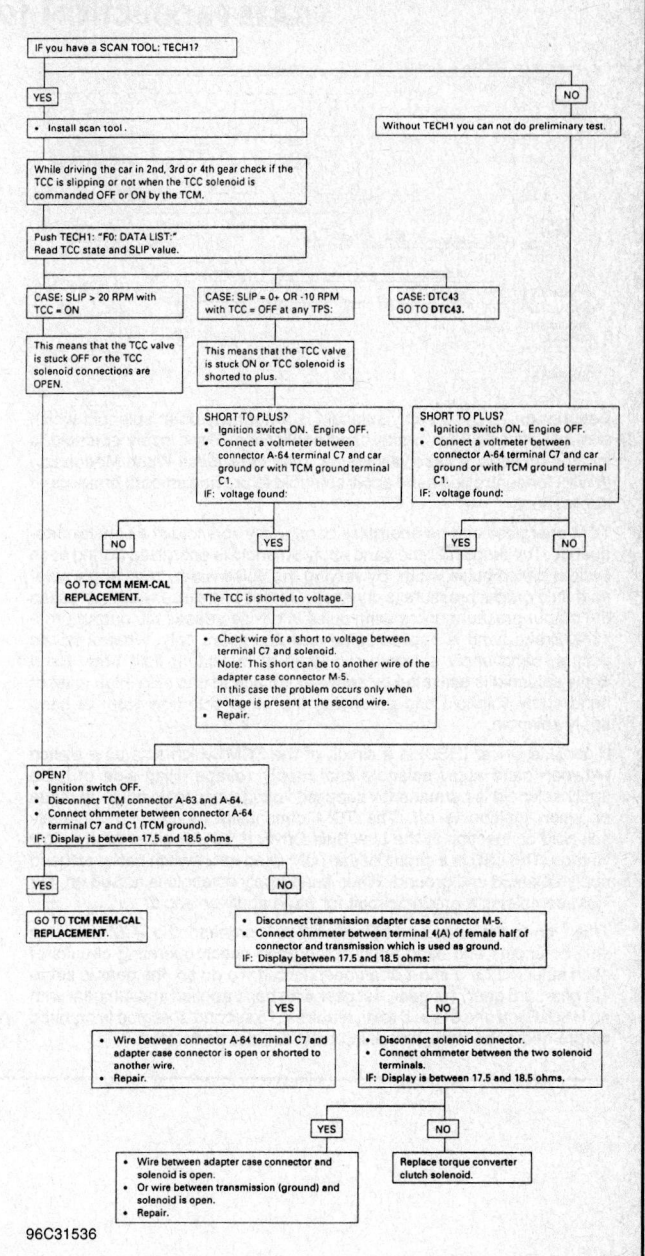

96C31536

3-628

AUTOMATIC TRANSMISSIONS
1995 Hydra-Matic 4L30-E Electronic Controls (Cont.)

**DTC 34: BAND APPLY SOLENOID CIRCUIT
(SHORT CIRCUIT TO GROUND OR OPEN CIRCUIT)
(LATE PRODUCTION 1995 PASSPORT & RODEO)**

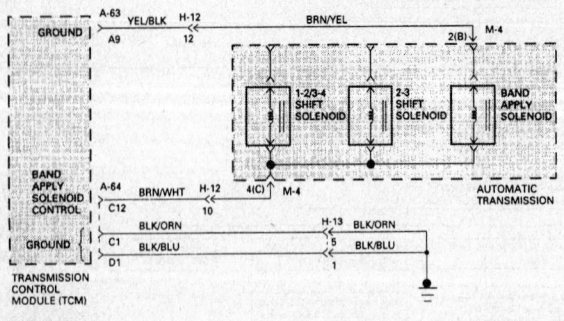

96D31537

Description – Band apply solenoid is a normally open solenoid which controls fluid flow for brake band application. Band apply solenoid is located on adapter case valve body. TCM uses Pulse Width Modulation (PWM) for controlling band apply solenoid to provide smooth brake band application.

TCM energizes and de-energizes band apply solenoid at a constant frequency. The length of time band apply solenoid is energized during each cycle is called pulse width. By varying the pulse width, band apply solenoid fluid output pressure is changed. Decreasing pulse width increases the output pressure. Increasing pulse width decreases the output pressure. Brake band is applied in 1st and 2nd gears only. When a failure occurs, band apply solenoid regulates at maximum fluid flow. Band apply solenoid is activated by applying voltage to one side (high side) of band apply solenoid and grounding the other side (low side) of band apply solenoid.

High Side Driver (HSD) is a circuit of the TCM which acts as a switch between band apply solenoid and supply voltage. High side of band apply solenoid is permanently supplied voltage, except in back-up mode or when ignition is off. The TCM continually monitors band apply solenoid connection to the Low Side Driver (LSD) for either high or low voltage. The LSD is a circuit of the TCM used as a switch between band apply solenoid and ground. When band apply solenoid is turned on, the TCM completes a ground circuit for band apply solenoid.

When ignition is turned on before engine is cranked, the TCM activates shift solenoids and band apply solenoid to check operating circuits of each solenoid for a short or an open circuit. To do so, the gear is set to 4th gear, 3rd gear, 1st gear, 1st gear with band applied and 4th gear with no HSD. Each one of the 5 tests requires .15 second. If engine is cranked before end of all tests, remaining tests are not performed.

Diagnostic Aids – This diagnostic test is an electrical test performed by the TCM. DTC 34 will set when the following detection conditions are present with ignition on.

- Band apply solenoid low side terminal A9 to TCM has an open circuit or is shorted to ground.
- Engine speed is less than 480 RPM and output shaft speed is zero RPM.
- Conditions must be present for .15-.75 second after ignition is turned on.

Once DTC 34 is set, CHECK TRANS light will flash and transmission will go into back-up mode. Back-up mode may be cleared by turning ignition off, then back on again.

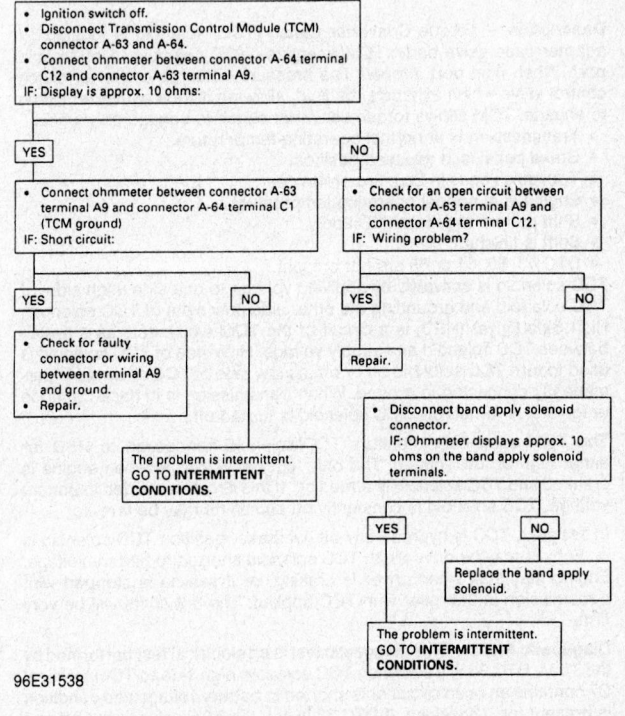

96E31538

AUTOMATIC TRANSMISSIONS
1995 Hydra-Matic 4L30-E Electronic Controls (Cont.)

3-629

DTC 35: FORCE MOTOR SOLENOID CIRCUIT
(SHORT CIRCUIT TO B+ OR GROUND)
(LATE PRODUCTION 1995 PASSPORT & RODEO)

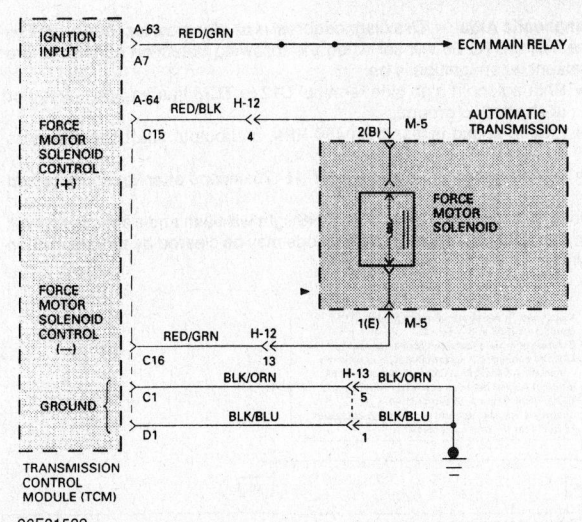

96F31539

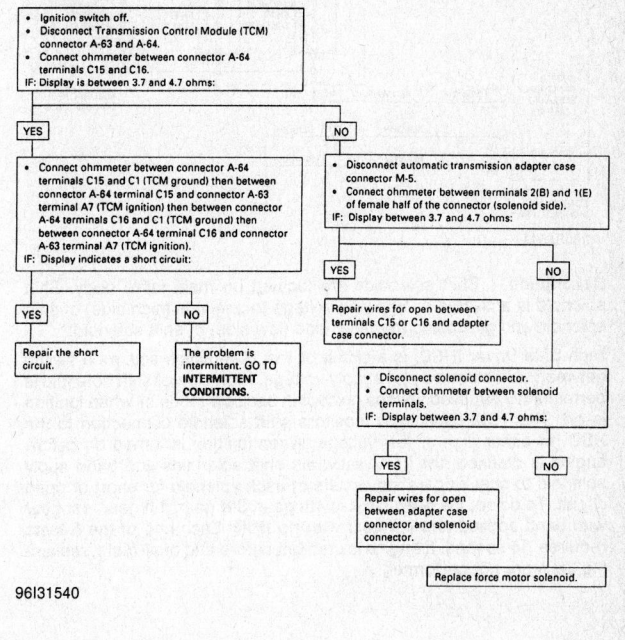

96I31540

Diagnostic Aids – This diagnostic test is an electrical test performed by the TCM. DTC 35 sets when return line amperage is greater than .2 amp from the commanded amperage. Once DTC 35 is set, CHECK TRANS light will flash and transmission will go into back-up mode. Back-up mode may be cleared by turning ignition off, then back on again.

Description – Force motor solenoid is a variable position solenoid used to regulate line pressure. Force motor solenoid is located on adapter case valve body. The TCM uses Throttle Position Sensor (TPS) information and vehicle speed to determine appropriate line pressure for a given load. TCM regulates line pressure by applying a varying applied amperage of .1-1.1 amps to force motor solenoid. TCM then monitors return amperage on the return line.

Line pressure may vary from less than 50 psi (3.5 kg/cm²) to more than 200 psi (14.1 kg/cm²). Line pressure is proportional to current applied on force motor solenoid. High current produces low line pressure and low current produces high line pressure.

3-630

AUTOMATIC TRANSMISSIONS
1995 Hydra-Matic 4L30-E Electronic Controls (Cont.)

DTC 36: SHIFT SOLENOID CIRCUIT
(SHORT CIRCUIT TO GROUND OR OPEN CIRCUIT)
(LATE PRODUCTION 1995 PASSPORT & RODEO)

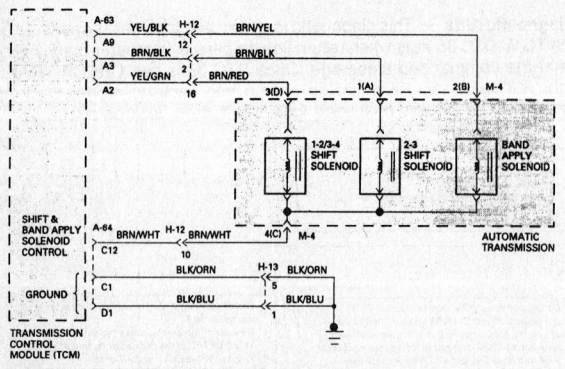

96J31541

Description – Shift solenoids are located on main valve body. Shift solenoid is activated by applying voltage to one side (high side) of shift solenoid and grounding the other side (low side) of shift solenoid.

High Side Driver (HSD) is a circuit of the TCM which acts as a switch between shift solenoid and supply voltage. High side of shift solenoid is permanently supplied voltage, except in back-up mode or when ignition is off. The TCM continually monitors shift solenoid connection to the HSD for either high or low voltage. When ignition is turned on before engine is cranked, the TCM activates shift solenoids and band apply solenoid to check operating circuits of each solenoid for short or open circuit. To do so, the gear is set to 4th gear, 3rd gear, 1st gear, 1st gear with band applied and 4th gear with no HSD. Each one of the 5 tests requires .15 second. If engine is cranked before end of all tests, remaining tests are not performed.

Diagnostic Aids – This diagnostic test is an electrical test performed by the TCM. DTC 36 will set when the following detection conditions are present when ignition is on.
- Shift solenoid high side terminal C12 to TCM has an open circuit or is shorted to ground.
- Engine speed is less than 480 RPM and output shaft speed is zero RPM.
- Conditions must be present for .15-.75 second after ignition is turned on.

Once DTC 36 is set, CHECK TRANS light will flash and transmission will go into back-up mode. Back-up mode may be cleared by turning ignition off, then back on again.

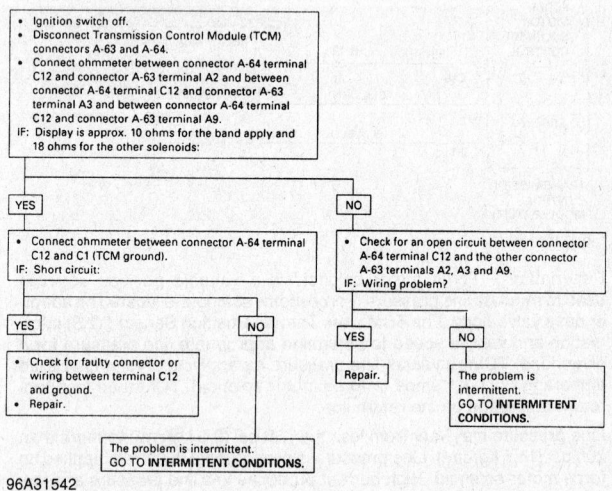

96A31542

DTC 37: TORQUE MANAGEMENT SERIAL LINE FAULTY
(LATE PRODUCTION 1995 PASSPORT & RODEO)

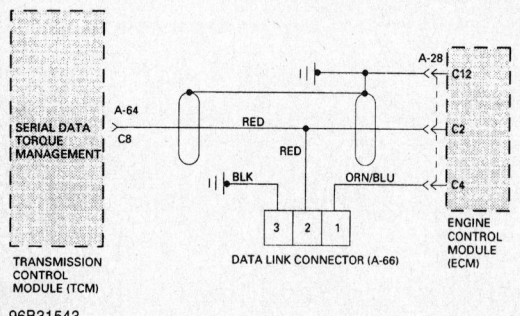

96B31543

Description – Torque management uses TCM to deliver a spark advance signal to Engine Control Module (ECM) during transmission shifting. This controls engine torque and reduces engagement shock caused by a change in vehicle speed. Each time transmission shifts with torque management active, TCM delivers a signal to the ECM.

Diagnostic Aids – This diagnostic test is not an electrical test performed by the TCM, but a comparison of signal input. DTC 37 will set when a torque management failure is present, or ECM does not acknowledge signal from TCM when transmission shifts with torque management active. Once DTC 37 is set, CHECK TRANS light will flash and transmission will go into back-up mode. Back-up mode may be cleared by turning ignition off, then back on again.

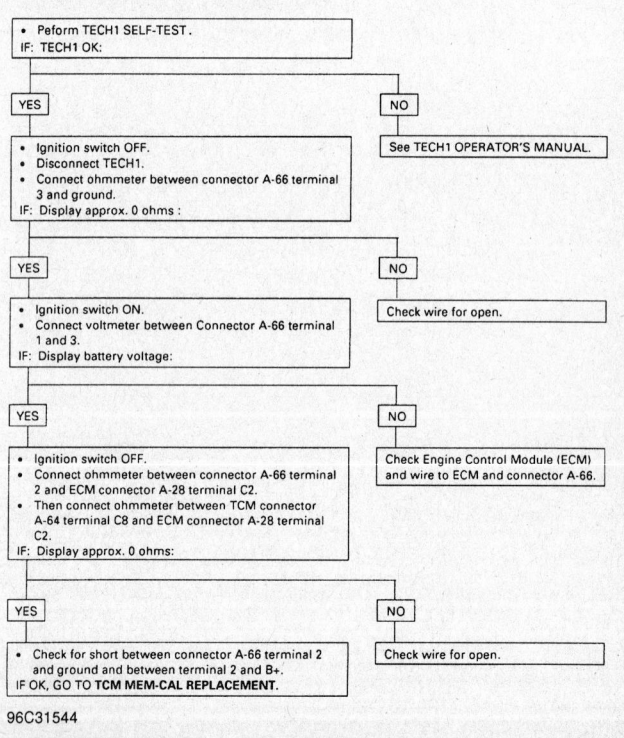

96C31544

AUTOMATIC TRANSMISSIONS
1995 Hydra-Matic 4L30-E Electronic Controls (Cont.)

3-631

DTC 41: 1-2/3-4 SHIFT SOLENOID CIRCUIT (SHORT CIRCUIT TO B+)
(LATE PRODUCTION 1995 PASSPORT & RODEO)

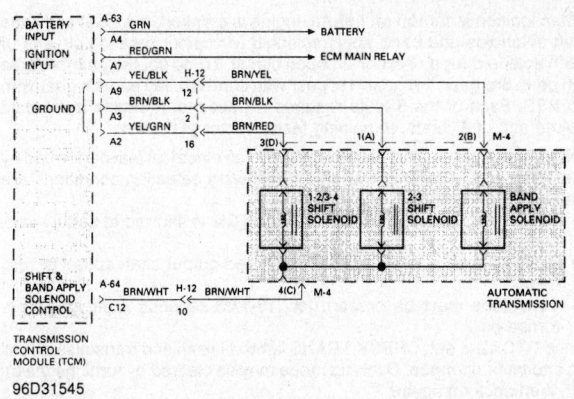

96D31545

Diagnostic Aids – This diagnostic test is an electrical test performed by the TCM. DTC 41 will set when the following detection conditions are present when ignition is on.

- Shift solenoid low side terminal A2 to TCM is shorted to battery voltage.
- Engine speed is less than 480 RPM and output shaft speed is zero RPM.
- Conditions must be present for .15-.88 second after ignition is turned on.

Once DTC 41 is set, CHECK TRANS light will flash and transmission will go into back-up mode. Back-up mode may be cleared by turning ignition off, then back on again.

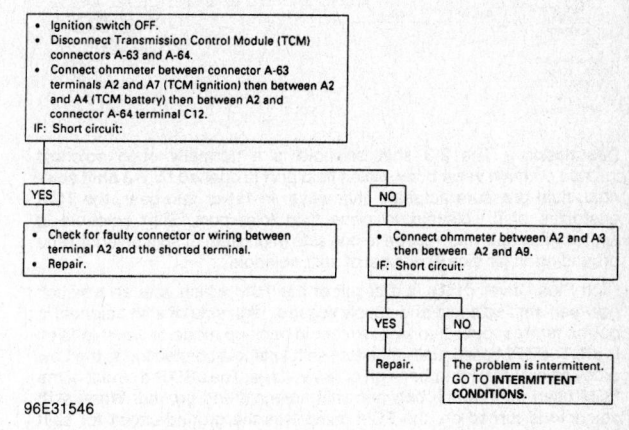

96E31546

Description – The 1-2/3-4 shift solenoid is a normally closed solenoid located on main valve body. In 2nd or 3rd gear, the TCM energizes shift solenoid to open fluid inlet port. When port is open, fluid pressure actuates shift valve. Shift solenoid is activated by applying voltage to one side (high side) of shift solenoid and grounding other side (low side) of shift solenoid.

High Side Driver (HSD) is a circuit of the TCM which acts as a switch between shift solenoid and supply voltage. High side of shift solenoid is permanently supplied voltage, except in back-up mode or when ignition is off. The TCM continually monitors shift solenoid connection to the Low Side Driver (LSD) for either high or low voltage. The LSD is a circuit of the TCM used as a switch between shift solenoid and ground. When shift solenoid is turned on, the TCM completes the ground circuit for shift solenoid.

When ignition is turned on before engine is cranked, the TCM activates shift solenoids and band apply solenoid to check operating circuits of each solenoid for a short or an open circuit. To do so, the gear is set to 4th gear, 3rd gear, 1st gear, 1st gear with band applied and 4th gear with no HSD. Each of the 5 tests requires .15 second. If engine is cranked before end of all tests, remaining tests are not performed.

3-632

AUTOMATIC TRANSMISSIONS
1995 Hydra-Matic 4L30-E Electronic Controls (Cont.)

DTC 42: 2-3 SHIFT SOLENOID CIRCUIT (SHORT CIRCUIT TO B+)
(LATE PRODUCTION 1995 PASSPORT & RODEO)

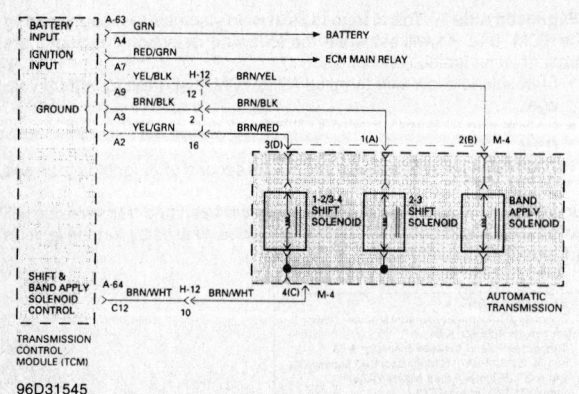

96D31545

Description – The 2-3 shift solenoid is a normally open solenoid located on main valve body. When fluid port is opened by 2-3 shift solenoid, fluid pressure actuates shift valve. In 1st or 2nd gear, the TCM energizes shift solenoid to close fluid inlet port. Shift solenoid is activated by applying voltage to one side (high side) of shift solenoid and grounding other side (low side) of shift solenoid.

High Side Driver (HSD) is a circuit of the TCM which acts as a switch between shift solenoid and supply voltage. High side of shift solenoid is permanently supplied voltage, except in back-up mode or when ignition is off. The TCM continually monitors shift solenoid connection to the Low Side Driver (LSD) for either high or low voltage. The LSD is a circuit of the TCM used as a switch between shift solenoid and ground. When shift solenoid is turned on, the TCM completes the ground circuit for shift solenoid.

When ignition is turned on before engine is cranked, the TCM activates shift solenoids and band apply solenoid to check operating circuits of each solenoid for a short or an open circuit. To do so, the gear is set to 4th gear, 3rd gear, 1st gear, 1st gear with band applied and 4th gear with no HSD. Each of the 5 tests requires .15 second. If engine is cranked before end of all tests, remaining tests are not performed.

Diagnostic Aids – This diagnostic test is an electrical test performed by the TCM. DTC 42 will set when the following detection conditions are present when ignition is on.

- Shift solenoid low side terminal A3 to TCM is shorted to battery voltage.
- Engine speed is less than 480 RPM and output shaft speed is zero RPM.
- Conditions must be present for .15-1.03 seconds After ignition is turned on.

Once DTC 42 is set, CHECK TRANS light will flash and transmission will go into back-up mode. Back-up mode may be cleared by turning ignition off, then back on again.

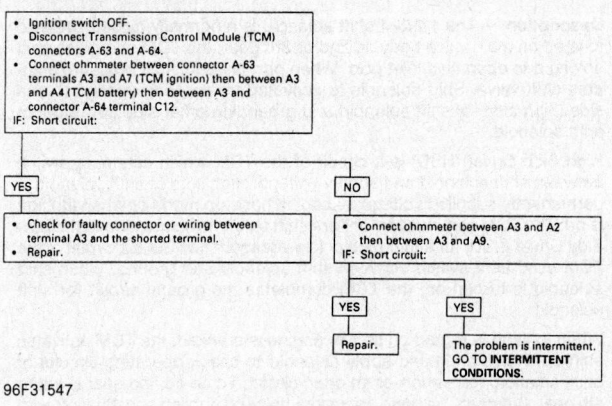

96F31547

AUTOMATIC TRANSMISSIONS
1995 Hydra-Matic 4L30-E Electronic Controls (Cont.)

3-633

DTC 43: TCC SOLENOID CIRCUIT (SHORT CIRCUIT TO GROUND)
(LATE PRODUCTION 1995 PASSPORT & RODEO)

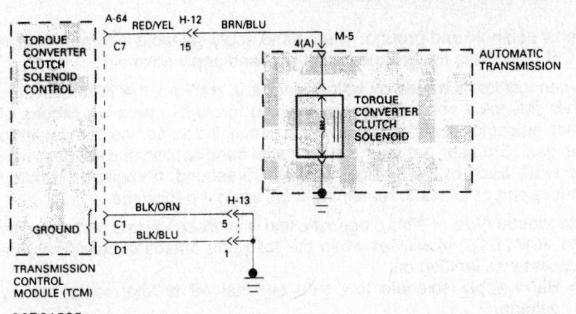

96B31535

Description – Torque Converter Clutch (TCC) solenoid is located on adapter case valve body. TCM energizes TCC solenoid to open fluid port. When fluid port is open, line pressure actuates converter clutch control valve which exhausts the fluid, allowing torque converter clutch to engage. TCM allows torque converter clutch to engage only when:
- Transmission is at normal operating temperature.
- Brake pedal is in released position.
- Transmission is in 2nd, 3rd or 4th gear.
- Engine is at normal operating temperature.
- Shift pattern requests TCC apply.
- Shift is finished.
- DTC 33, 55, 64 or 65 are not present.

TCC solenoid is activated by applying voltage to one side (high side) of TCC solenoid and grounding other side (low side) of TCC solenoid. High Side Driver (HSD) is a circuit of the TCM which acts as a switch between TCC solenoid and supply voltage. High side of TCC solenoid is used to turn TCC solenoid on or off, as low side of TCC solenoid is permanently connected to ground. When transmission is in back-up mode or ignition is turned off, TCC solenoid is turned off.

The TCM continually monitors TCC solenoid connection to HSD for either high or low voltage. The only test performed is when engine is cranked and TCC solenoid is turned on.

Diagnostic Aids – This diagnostic test is an electrical test performed by the TCM. DTC 43 will set when TCC solenoid high side to TCM terminal C7 is shorted to ground and condition is present for .07 second after ignition is turned on. If DTC 43 is set, the TCC will be shut off. The CHECK TRANS light will NOT flash and transmission will NOT go into back-up mode. Transmission will return to normal operation by turning ignition off, then back on again.

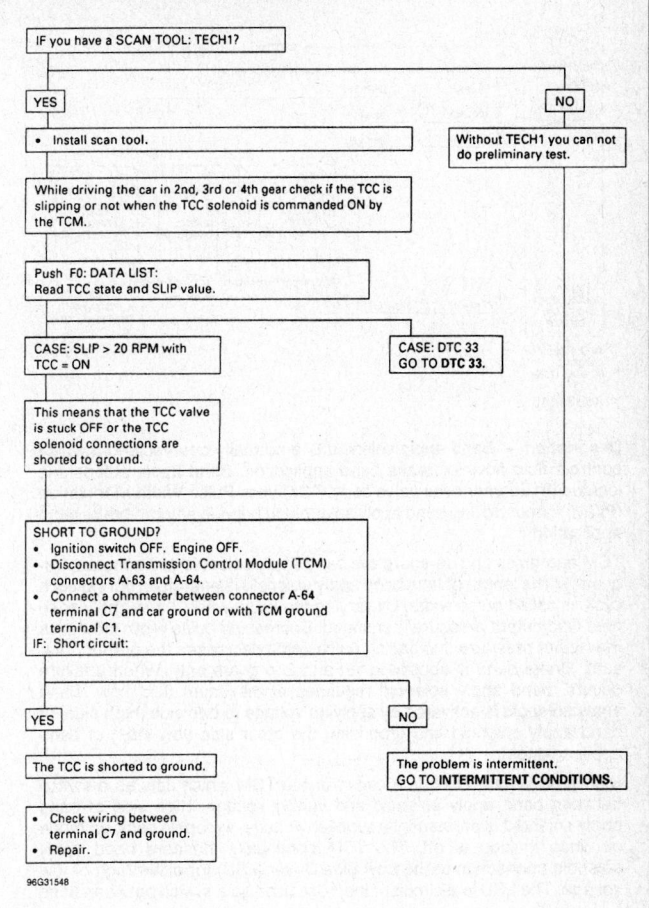

96G31548

3-634

AUTOMATIC TRANSMISSIONS
1995 Hydra-Matic 4L30-E Electronic Controls (Cont.)

DTC 44: BAND APPLY SOLENOID CIRCUIT (SHORT CIRCUIT TO B+)
(LATE PRODUCTION 1995 PASSPORT & RODEO)

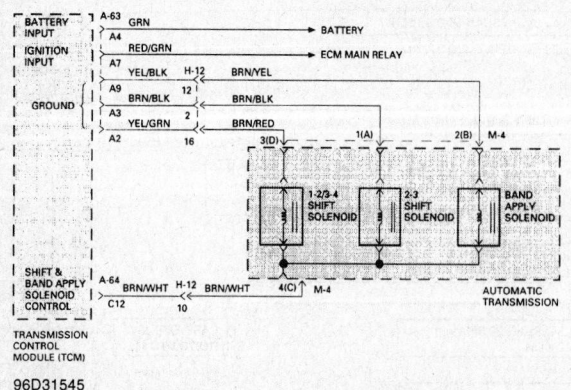

96D31545

Description – Band apply solenoid is a normally open solenoid which controls fluid flow for brake band application. Band apply solenoid is located on adapter case valve body. TCM uses Pulse Width Modulation (PWM) for controlling band apply solenoid to provide smooth brake band application.

TCM energizes and de-energizes band apply solenoid at a constant frequency. The length of time band apply solenoid is energized during each cycle is called pulse width. By varying the pulse width, band apply solenoid fluid output pressure is changed. Decreasing pulse width increases the output pressure. Increasing pulse width decreases the output pressure. Brake band is applied in 1st and 2nd gears only. When a failure occurs, band apply solenoid regulates at maximum fluid flow. Band apply solenoid is activated by applying voltage to one side (high side) of band apply solenoid and grounding the other side (low side) of band apply solenoid.

High Side Driver (HSD) is a circuit of the TCM which acts as a switch between band apply solenoid and supply voltage. High side of band apply solenoid is permanently supplied voltage, except in back-up mode or when ignition is off. The TCM continually monitors band apply solenoid connection to the Low Side Driver (LSD) for either high or low voltage. The LSD is a circuit of the TCM used as a switch between band

apply solenoid and ground. When band apply solenoid is turned on, the TCM completes the ground circuit for band apply solenoid.

When ignition is turned on before engine is cranked, the TCM activates shift solenoids and band apply solenoid to check operating circuits of each solenoid for a short or an open circuit. To do so, the gear is set to 4th gear, 3rd gear, 1st gear, 1st gear with band applied and 4th gear with no HSD. Each of the 5 tests requires .15 second. If engine is cranked before end of all tests, remaining tests are not performed.

Diagnostic Aids – This diagnostic test is an electrical test performed by the TCM. DTC 44 will set when the following detection conditions are present with ignition on.

- Band apply solenoid low side terminal A9 is shorted to battery voltage.
- Engine speed is less than 480 RPM and output shaft speed is zero RPM.
- Conditions must be present for .15-1.18 seconds after ignition is turned on.

Once DTC 44 is set, CHECK TRANS light will flash and transmission will go into back-up mode. Back-up mode may be cleared by turning ignition off, then back on again.

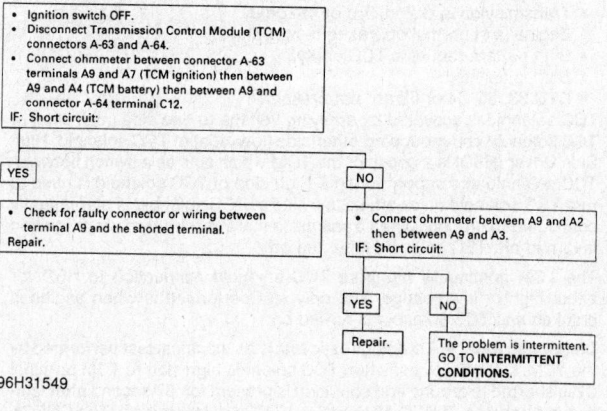

96H31549

AUTOMATIC TRANSMISSIONS
1995 Hydra-Matic 4L30-E Electronic Controls (Cont.)

3-635

DTC 46: SHIFT SOLENOID CIRCUIT (SHORT CIRCUIT TO B+)
(LATE PRODUCTION 1995 PASSPORT & RODEO)

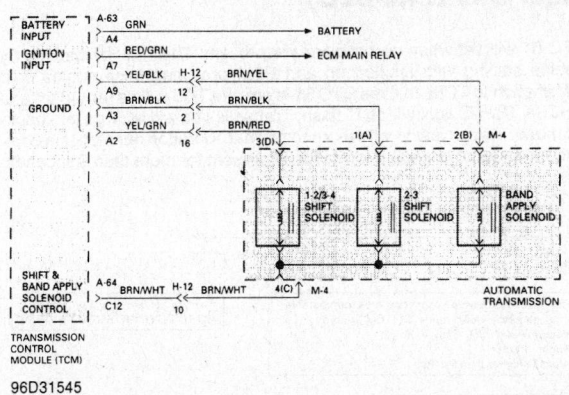

96D31545

Description – Shift solenoids are located on main valve body. Shift solenoids are activated by applying voltage to one side (high side) of shift solenoid and grounding the other side (low side) of shift solenoid.

High Side Driver (HSD) is a circuit of TCM which acts as a switch between shift solenoid and supply voltage. High side of shift solenoid is permanently supplied voltage, except in back-up mode or when ignition is off. The TCM continually monitors shift solenoid connection to HSD for either high or low voltage.

When ignition is turned on before engine is cranked, the TCM activates shift solenoids and band apply solenoid to check operating circuits of each solenoid for a short or an open circuit. To do so, the gear is set to 4th gear, 3rd gear, 1st gear, 1st gear with band applied and 4th gear with no HSD. Each of the 5 tests requires .15 second. If engine is cranked before end of all tests, remaining tests are not performed.

Diagnostic Aids – This diagnostic test is an electrical test performed by the TCM. DTC 46 will set when the following detection conditions are present when ignition is on.

- Shift solenoid high side terminal C12 to TCM is shorted to battery voltage.
- Engine speed is less than 480 RPM and output shaft speed is zero RPM.
- Conditions must be present for .15-1.34 seconds after ignition is turned on.

Once DTC 46 is set, CHECK TRANS light will flash and transmission will go into back-up mode. Back-up mode may be cleared by turning ignition off, then back on again.

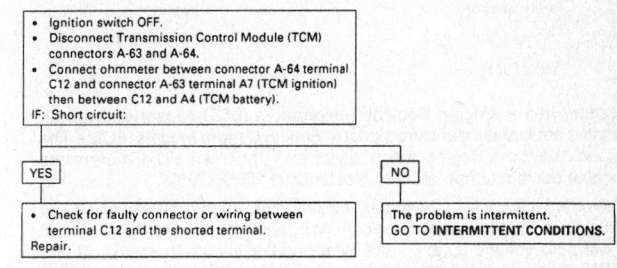

96B31550

3-636

AUTOMATIC TRANSMISSIONS
1995 Hydra-Matic 4L30-E Electronic Controls (Cont.)

DTC 51: ENGINE COOLANT TEMP. SENSOR CIRCUIT
(SHORT CIRCUIT TO B+, GROUND OR OPEN CIRCUIT)
(LATE PRODUCTION 1995 PASSPORT & RODEO)

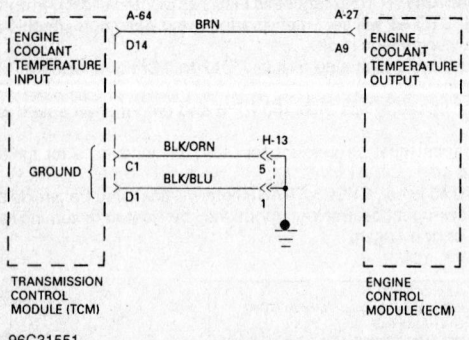

96C31551

Description – Engine Coolant Temperature (ECT) sensor delivers an engine coolant temperature signal to Engine Control Module (ECM). The ECM delivers a engine warm signal to TCM when ECM determines engine coolant temperature is greater than 158°F (70°C).

When engine is warm, ECM connects terminal A9 to ground using a low side driver. When engine is cold, ECM opens ground at terminal A9 and TCM pulls voltage up to 5 volts. When ignition is on with engine off, the ECM always delivers an engine cold signal to TCM, even if engine is warm. Engine coolant temperature signal between ECM and TCM is valid only with engine running.

Diagnostic Aids – DTC 51 will set when an engine cold or engine warm condition is detected. This diagnostic test is not an electrical test performed by the TCM, but a comparison of signal input. The following conditions must be present for detection of engine cold.
- Wire between ECM terminal A9 and TCM terminal D14 has an open circuit or is shorted to battery voltage.
- Transmission oil temperature is greater than 302°F (150°C) or more than 20 minutes since last ignition cycle.
- Conditions must be present for at least 6 seconds.

The following conditions must be present for detection of engine warm.
- Wire between ECM terminal A9 and TCM terminal D14 is shorted to ground.
- Transmission oil temperature is less than 32°F (0°C).
- Voltage on transmission oil temperature sensor circuit must be less than 4.74 volts.
- Conditions must be present for at least 6 seconds.

DTC 51 will set when no problem are present. This may be caused by engine stalling with ignition on and ECM providing false engine cold information to TCM. In case DTC 51 is set, the TCC will be turned off and CHECK TRANS light will NOT flash. Transmission will NOT go into back-up mode. Transmission will return to normal operation once engine coolant temperature change information is present for more than 6 seconds.

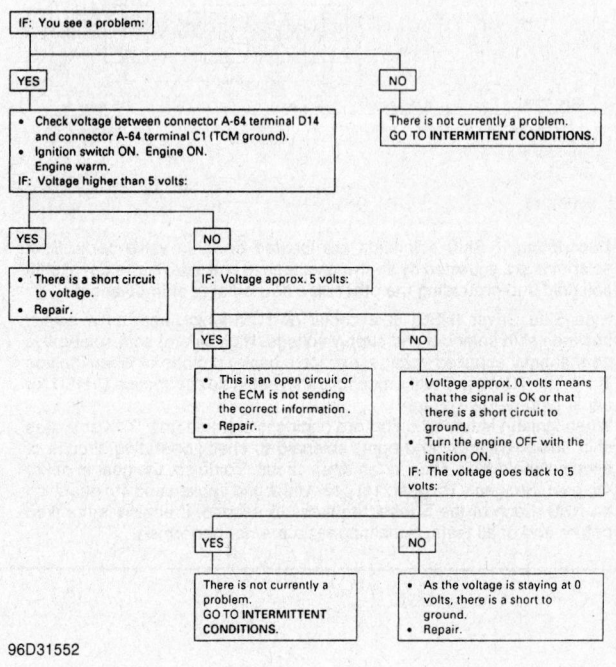

96D31552

AUTOMATIC TRANSMISSIONS
1995 Hydra-Matic 4L30-E Electronic Controls (Cont.)

3-637

DTC 52: KICKDOWN SWITCH ALWAYS ON OR SHORT CIRCUIT TO GROUND
(LATE PRODUCTION 1995 PASSPORT & RODEO)

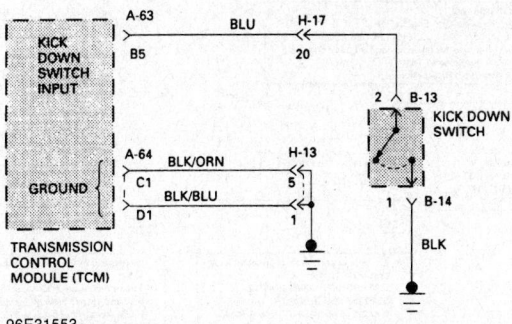

96E31553

Description – When accelerator pedal is fully depressed, kickdown switch closes and delivers a ground signal to TCM. The TCM uses this signal for controlling transmission shifting with high engine RPM. When kickdown switch is closed, the Throttle Position Sensor (TPS) is already at 100 percent.

Diagnostic Aids – This diagnostic test is not an electrical test performed by the TCM, but a comparison of signal input. DTC 52 will set when the following conditions are present.
- Kickdown switch is on (short to ground) and TPS is less than 70 percent.
- DTC 21 or 22 are not present.
- Condition must be present for at least one second.

If DTC 52 is set, CHECK TRANS light will NOT flash. Transmission will NOT go into back-up mode. Transmission will return to normal operation once kickdown switch is off during the DTC detection time.

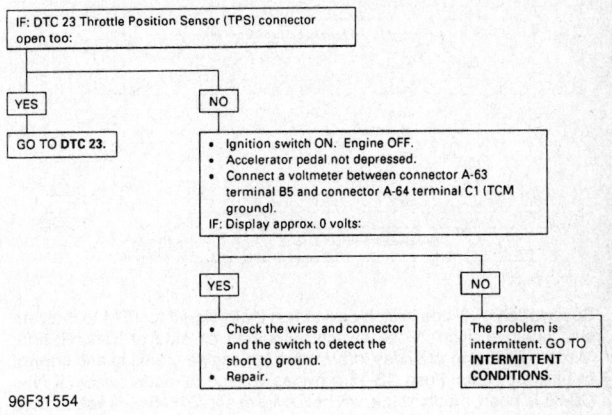

96F31554

DTC 53: MODE SWITCH IN "P", "N" OR "R" BAD POSITION
(LATE PRODUCTION 1995 PASSPORT & RODEO)

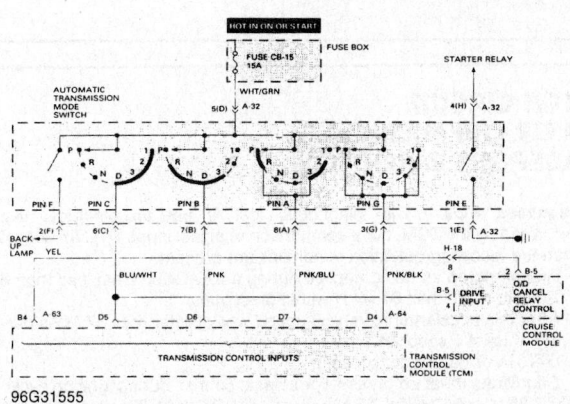

96G31555

Description – Mode switch delivers input signal to TCM to indicate gearshift lever position. Mode switch is located on side of transmission. Mode switch also provides information for engine cranking and control of back-up lights. Fuse CB-15 provides voltage to mode switch. If fuse CB-15 is open, mode switch will not operate and DTC 54 will be set. Ensure shift linkage is properly adjusted, as DTC 53 may be caused by improperly adjusted shift linkage.

Diagnostic Aids – This diagnostic test is not an electrical test performed by the TCM, but a comparison of signal input. The following conditions must be present for detection of "P" or "N" bad position.
- A/T input speed is less than 3000 RPM.
- Throttle position sensor (TPS) is greater than 20 percent.
- Mode switch in "P" or "N position.
- DTC 13, 21 or 22 are not present.
- Conditions must be present for at least 4 seconds.

After detection time, the default position is assumed for pressure calculation and shift pattern is always "D".
If DTC 53 is set due to previous conditions for "P" or "N" bad position, the CHECK TRANS light will NOT flash. Transmission will NOT go into back-up mode. To return to normal operation, maintain engine speed at greater than 3000 RPM with TPS higher than 20 percent when mode switch is not in "P" or "N" position.

The following conditions must be present for detection of "R" bad position.
- A/T output speed is greater than 3200 RPM.
- Mode switch in "R" position.
- DTC 11 or 62 are not present.
- Conditions must be present for at least one second.

After detection time, the default position is assumed for pressure calculation and shift pattern is always "D".
If DTC 53 is set due to previous conditions for "R" bad position, the CHECK TRANS light will NOT flash. Transmission will NOT go into back-up mode. To return to normal operation, maintain output speed at greater than 3200 RPM when mode switch is not in "R" position.

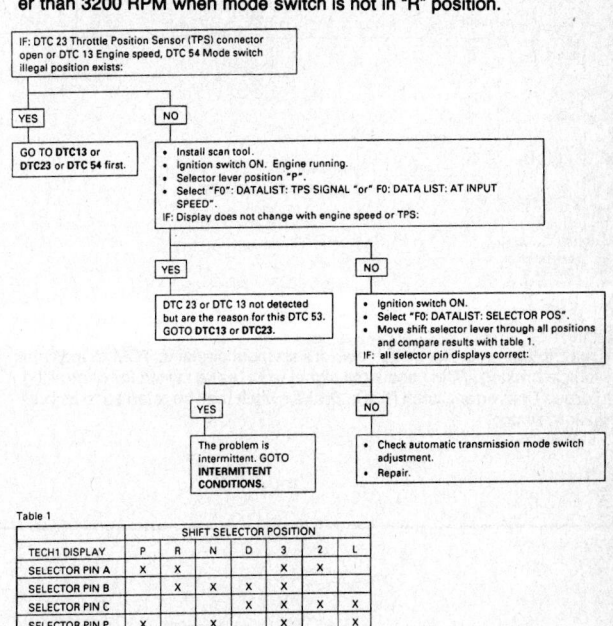

Table 1

	SHIFT SELECTOR POSITION					
TECH1 DISPLAY	P	R	N	D	3	2	L
SELECTOR PIN A	X	X			X	X	
SELECTOR PIN B		X	X	X	X		
SELECTOR PIN C				X	X	X	X
SELECTOR PIN P	X		X		X		X

Note: "X" indicates TECH1 displays "ACTIVE".

96H31556

3-638

AUTOMATIC TRANSMISSIONS
1995 Hydra-Matic 4L30-E Electronic Controls (Cont.)

DTC 54: MODE SWITCH ILLEGAL POSITION
(LATE PRODUCTION 1995 PASSPORT & RODEO)

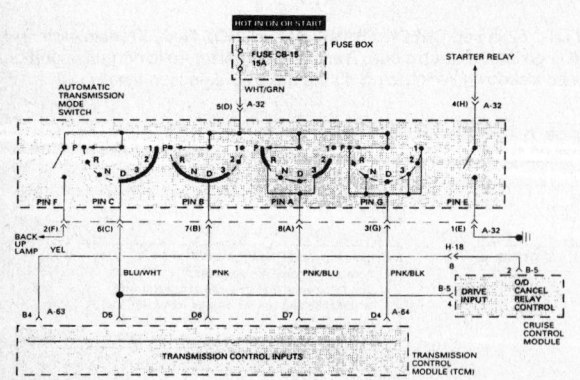

96G31555

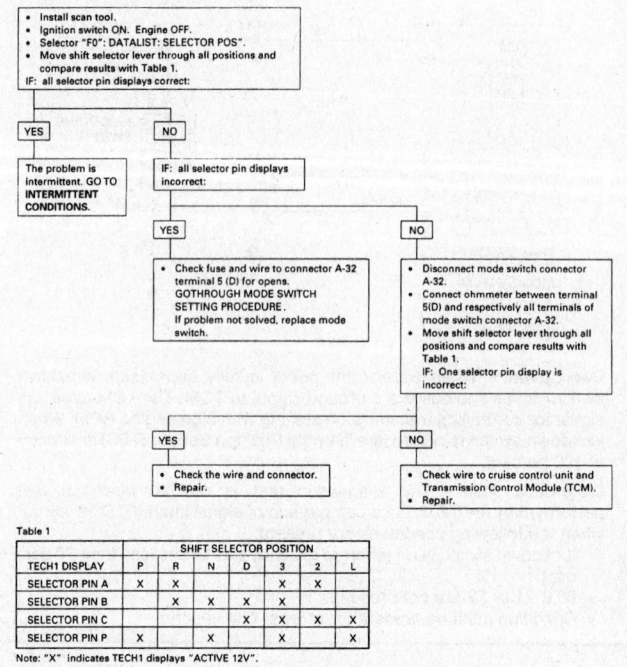

Description – Mode switch delivers an input signal to TCM to indicate shift lever position. Mode switch is located on side of transmission. Mode switch also provides information for engine cranking and control of back-up lights. Fuse CB-15 provides voltage to mode switch. If fuse CB-15 is open, mode switch will not operate and DTC 54 will set. Ensure shift linkage is properly adjusted, as DTC 54 may be caused by improperly adjusted shift linkage.

Diagnostic Aids – This diagnostic test is an electrical test performed by the TCM. DTC 54 will set when the following detection conditions are present.

- Selector pin "A", "B" or "C" are not active and no position is identified.
- Based on TABLE 1, in "P" position, DTC is set when an open circuit or a short to ground is present at pin "A".
- Conditions must be present for at least 5 seconds.

Once DTC 54 is set, CHECK TRANS light will flash and transmission will go into back-up mode. Back-up mode may be cleared by turning ignition off, then back on again.

Table 1

TECH1 DISPLAY	SHIFT SELECTOR POSITION						
	P	R	N	D	3	2	L
SELECTOR PIN A	X	X			X	X	
SELECTOR PIN B		X	X	X	X		
SELECTOR PIN C				X	X	X	X
SELECTOR PIN P	X		X		X		X

Note: "X" indicates TECH1 displays "ACTIVE 12V".

96I31557

DTC 55: BRAKE SWITCH CIRCUIT
(SHORT CIRCUIT TO GROUND OR OPEN CIRCUIT)
(LATE PRODUCTION 1995 PASSPORT & RODEO)

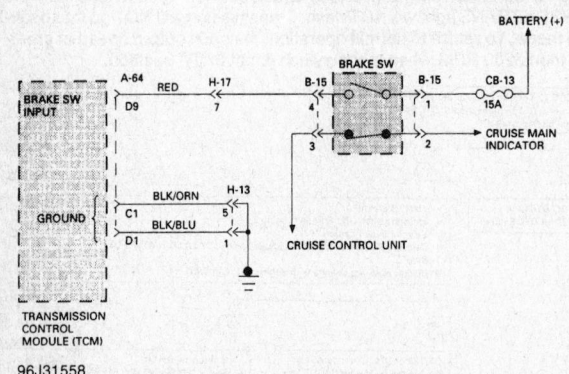

96J31558

Description – Brake switch delivers an input signal to TCM to indicate vehicle braking. TCM uses input signal from brake switch for controlling Torque Converter Clutch (TCC). Brake switch may be referred to as brakelight switch.

Diagnostic Aids – This diagnostic test is not an electrical test performed by the TCM, but a comparison of signal input. DTC 55 will be set when the following detection conditions are present.

- Brakes noted as being applied during acceleration from less than 6 MPH to more than 37 MPH within 6 seconds.
- After this acceleration, vehicle speed was greater than 37 MPH during at least 6 seconds.
- DTC 11 or 62 are not present.
- Conditions must be present for at least 5 times during ignition cycle.

If DTC 55 is set, CHECK TRANS light will NOT flash. Transmission will NOT go into back-up mode. To return to normal operation, brake must be released.

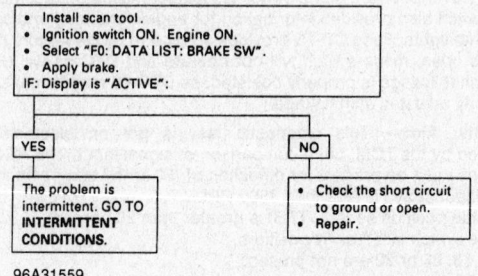

96A31559

AUTOMATIC TRANSMISSIONS
1995 Hydra-Matic 4L30-E Electronic Controls (Cont.)

3-639

DTC 56: BRAKE SWITCH CIRCUIT (SHORT CIRCUIT TO B+)
(LATE PRODUCTION 1995 PASSPORT & RODEO)

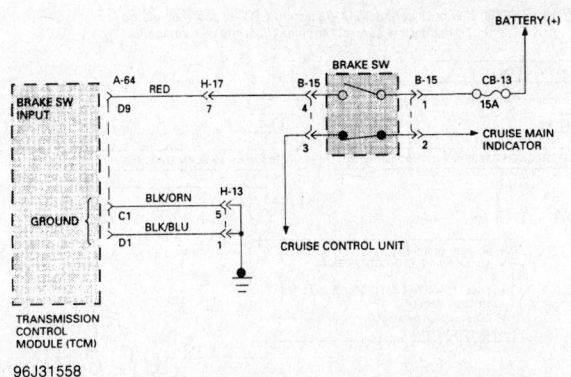

96J31558

Description – Brake switch delivers an input signal to TCM to indicate vehicle braking. TCM uses input signal from brake switch for controlling Torque Converter Clutch (TCC). Brake switch may be referred to as brakelight switch.

Diagnostic Aids – This diagnostic test is not an electrical test performed by the TCM, but a comparison of signal input. DTC 56 will set when the following detection conditions are present.

- Brakes noted as being released during deceleration from more than 37 MPH to less than 6 MPH within 6 seconds.
- Before deceleration, vehicle speed was greater than 37 MPH during at least 6 seconds.
- DTC 11 or 62 are not present.
- Conditions must be present for at least 5 times during ignition cycle.

If DTC 56 is set, CHECK TRANS light will NOT flash. Transmission will NOT go into back-up mode. To return to normal operation, brake must be released.

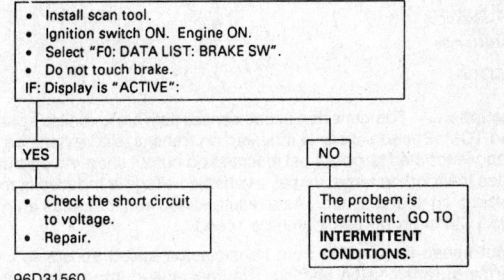

96D31560

DTC 61: GEAR ERROR
(LATE PRODUCTION 1995 PASSPORT & RODEO)

Description – The TCM calculates slippage of Torque Converter Clutch (TCC) and transmission based upon engine speed, output speed and gear ratio. TCC should slip a specified amount at high engine speeds. Transmission should not slip more than a specified value when there is no shift.

Diagnostic Aids – This diagnostic test is not an electrical test performed by the TCM, but a comparison of signal input. DTC 56 will set when the following detection conditions are present.

- Engine speed is greater than 3500 RPM.
- Slippage must be more than specified amount in specified gear: 1st gear =595 RPM, 2nd gear =556 RPM, 3rd gear =536 RPM, 4th gear =473 RPM.
- DTC 11, 13 or 62 are not present.
- Last change of shift solenoid took longer than 3 seconds.
- Conditions must be present for at least 3 seconds.

Once DTC 61 is set, CHECK TRANS light will flash and transmission will go into back-up mode. Back-up mode may be cleared by turning ignition off, then back on again.

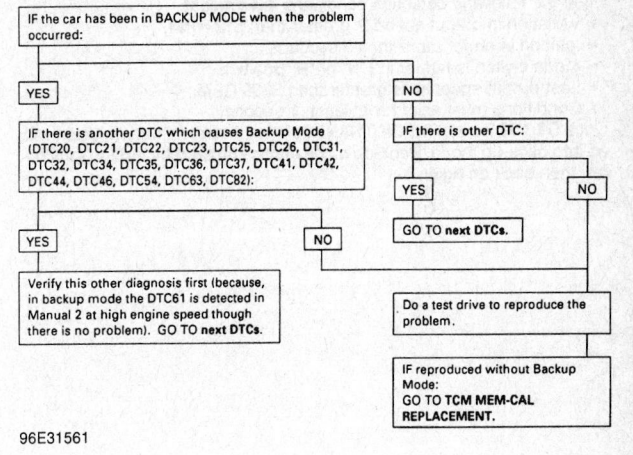

96E31561

3-640

AUTOMATIC TRANSMISSIONS
1995 Hydra-Matic 4L30-E Electronic Controls (Cont.)

DTC 62: DOWNSHIFT PROTECTION
(LATE PRODUCTION 1995 PASSPORT & RODEO)

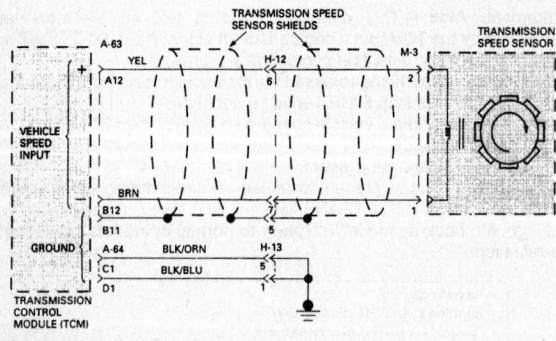

96J31517

Description – Transmission speed sensor delivers a vehicle speed signal to TCM. Speed sensor is mounted on transmission extension housing above toothed target wheel mounted on output shaft. As output shaft rotates the toothed target wheel, a variable voltage is induced in magnetic pickup on speed sensor. As a result, speed sensor sends an AC signal to TCM in proportion to vehicle speed.

Output speed information from transmission speed sensor is used to determine transmission shifting. If output speed information changes suddenly due to an open circuit or electrical interference, transmission will downshift. To avoid this, TCM constantly monitors variations of output speed. If variation in output speed is too great when output speed is greater than 2900 RPM, DTC 62 is set.

Diagnostic Aids – This diagnostic test is not an electrical test performed by the TCM, but a comparison of signal input. DTC 62 will set when the following detection conditions are present.
- Variation in output speed is greater than 512 RPM.
- Ignition is on for more than 5 seconds.
- Mode switch is not in "P", "N" or "R" position.
- Last output speed was greater than 2900 RPM.
- Conditions must exist for at least .1 second.

Once DTC 62 is set, CHECK TRANS light will flash and transmission will go into back-up mode. Back-up mode may be cleared by turning ignition off, then back on again.

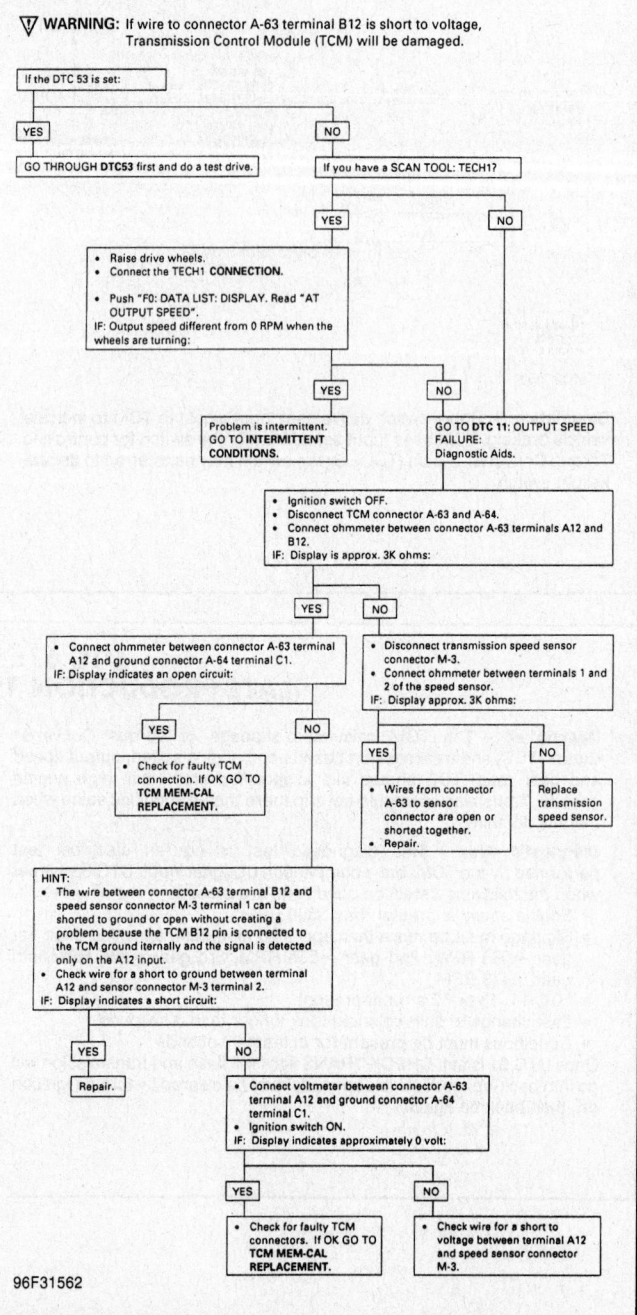

96F31562

DTC 63: EPROM CSUM FAILURE
(LATE PRODUCTION 1995 PASSPORT & RODEO)

Description – The Erasable Programmable Read Only Memory (EPROM) is an electronic circuit that contains commands for controlling the TCM. The EPROM content is checked automatically approximately each second by the TCM. This procedure is called the Check Sum (CSUM) calculation. If CSUM is false, this means one command is altered. This may be due to a circuit failure or a bad contact between EPROM and TCM, resulting in DTC 63 being set. If all EPROM connections are bad, TCM will not operate. The CSUM cannot be calculated and detected. Nothing will operate, including CHECK TRANS light.

Diagnostic Aids – This diagnostic test is not an electrical test performed by the TCM, but a comparison of signal input. DTC 63 will set when the following detection conditions are present.
- Bad EPROM CSUM.
- Condition must be present for at least one second.

Once DTC 63 is set, CHECK TRANS light will flash and transmission will go into back-up mode. Back-up mode may be cleared by turning ignition off, then back on again. To solve the problem, check EPROM MEM-CAL connector. If condition is still present, replace TCM MEM-CAL. See TCM MEM-CAL under REMOVAL & INSTALLATION.

AUTOMATIC TRANSMISSIONS
1995 Hydra-Matic 4L30-E Electronic Controls (Cont.)

3-641

DTC 82: SHIFT OR BAND APPLY SOLENOIDS FAULTY DURING DRIVING
(LATE PRODUCTION 1995 PASSPORT & RODEO)

Description – Shift solenoids are located on main valve body. Band apply solenoid is located on adapter case valve body. The TCM energizes solenoid to open or close fluid inlet port depending on solenoid application. Solenoid is activated by applying voltage to one side (high side) of solenoid and grounding the other side (low side) of solenoid.

High Side Driver (HSD) is a circuit of the TCM which acts as a switch between solenoid and supply voltage. High side of solenoid is permanently supplied voltage, except in back-up mode or when ignition is off. The Low Side Driver (LSD) is a circuit of TCM that is used as a switch between solenoid and ground. When solenoid is turned on, the TCM completes the ground circuit for the solenoid.

Diagnostic Aids – DTC 82 is set when a short circuit or open circuit is present in the wiring to solenoid when engine is cranked, and then car is driven. DTC 82 can only be set when TCM is activating the solenoid with the problem circuit. To locate problem area, cycle ignition switch to use TCM self-check of solenoids when engine is not cranked, but ignition is on. DTC 82 will set when the following detection conditions are present.
- HSD or LSD is improperly on.
- Condition must be present for at least .15 second.

Once DTC 82 is set, CHECK TRANS light will flash and transmission will go into back-up mode. Back-up mode may be cleared by turning ignition off, then back on again.

> This DTC is set when the car is driven (Engine ON) but the diagnostic is not specific.
> To correctly identify the problem do an IGNITION CYCLE.

> If you have not already done an IGNITION CYCLE:
> - Turn ignition switch OFF. Turn ignition switch ON and wait 3 seconds to have the specific diagnostic done.
> - Then you can turn the engine ON or not.

> Check on Scan Tool or Flashing Code what other DTC is provided. It should be one of the following: DTC31 or DTC32 or DTC34 or DTC36 or DTC41 or DTC42 or DTC44 or DTC46.

> GO TO this **DTC**.

96G31563

CHECK TRANS LIGHT TEST (1995 TROOPER)

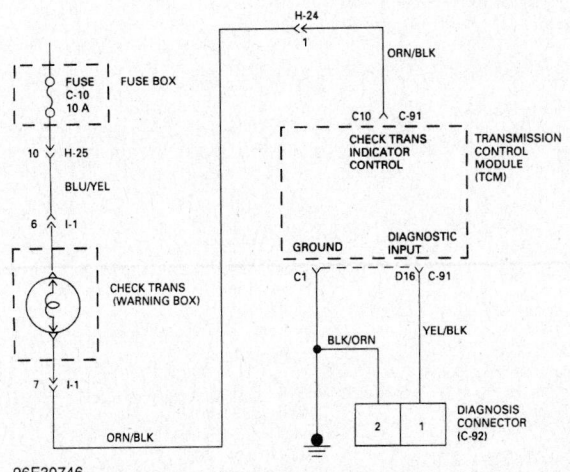

96E30746

Description – When ignition is turned on, CHECK TRANS light on instrument panel should illuminate for about 2-4 seconds while TCM is performing a self-test of the circuit and components, then light should go off. When ignition is on and TCM detects an electrical failure in the transmission electronic control system, TCM will flash CHECK TRANS light and may store a diagnostic trouble code in memory.

CHECK TRANS Light Is On Steady With Ignition On – 1) This condition may be caused by a short circuit to ground between CHECK TRANS light and TCM. Check wiring from TCM to CHECK TRANS light on instrument panel for short circuit to ground.
2) If no short circuit to ground is present in wiring, replace TCM MEM-CAL. See TCM MEM-CAL under REMOVAL & INSTALLATION.

CHECK TRANS Light Remains Off – 1) This condition may be caused by an open circuit between CHECK TRANS light and TCM, or no battery voltage is present at CHECK TRANS light. Check wiring from TCM to CHECK TRANS light on instrument panel for an open circuit.
2) Ensure battery voltage is present between fuse in fuse box and CHECK TRANS light. Check fuse and all connections as necessary.
3) If battery voltage is present, and no open circuit is present between CHECK TRANS light and TCM, replace TCM MEM-CAL. See TCM MEM-CAL under REMOVAL & INSTALLATION.

NOTE: Perform this test if CHECK TRANS light is on steady at all times with ignition on and no diagnostic trouble codes stored, or CHECK TRANS LIGHT remains off when ignition is first turned on.

3-642

AUTOMATIC TRANSMISSIONS
1995 Hydra-Matic 4L30-E Electronic Controls (Cont.)

DIAGNOSTIC CONNECTOR & VOLTAGE SUPPLY TEST (1995 TROOPER)

NOTE: Perform this test if TECH 1 scan tool is connected but no data is received when ignition is turned on.

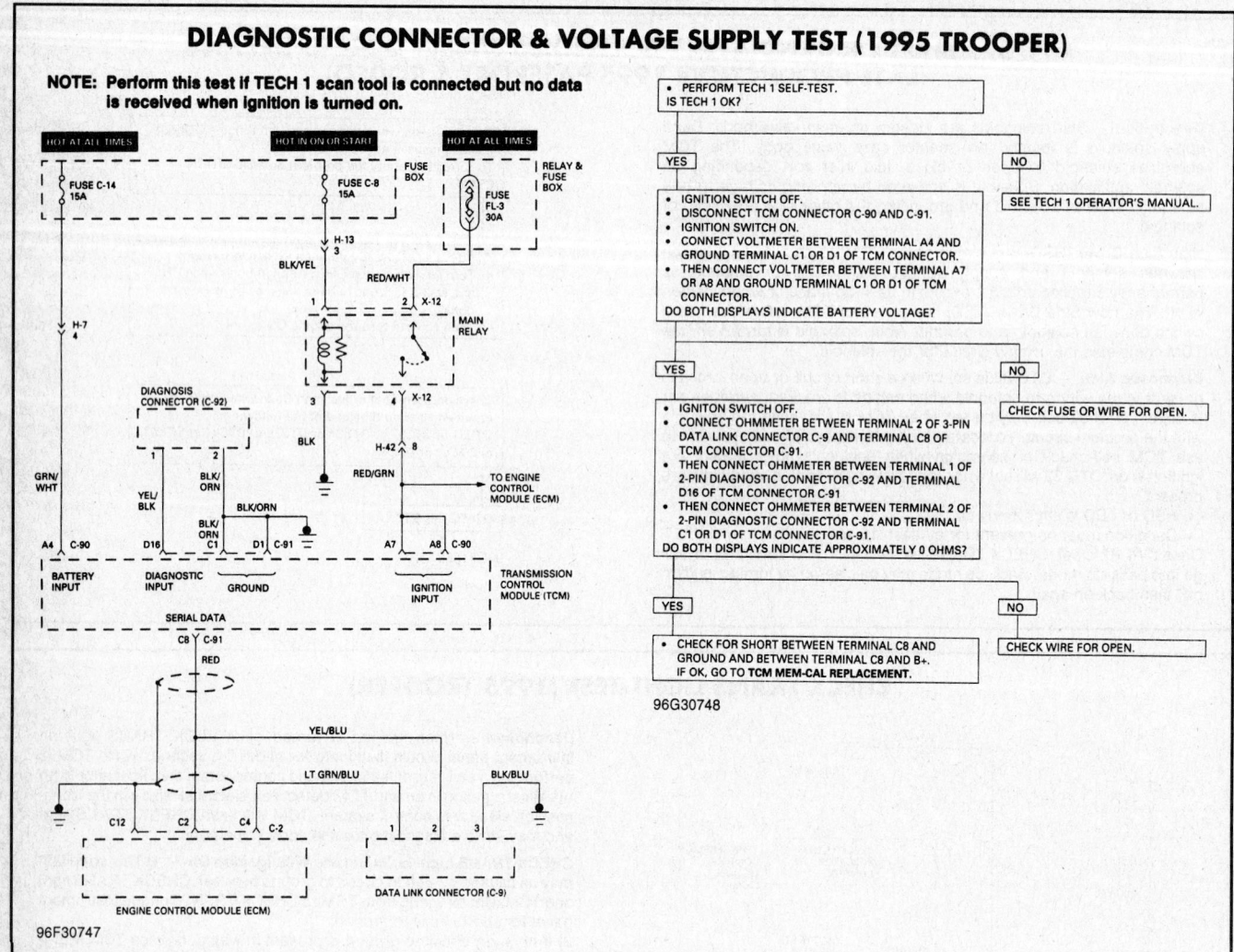

96F30747

96G30748

AUTOMATIC TRANSMISSIONS
1995 Hydra-Matic 4L30-E Electronic Controls (Cont.)

3-643

TRANSMISSION OPERATING MODE TEST (1995 TROOPER)

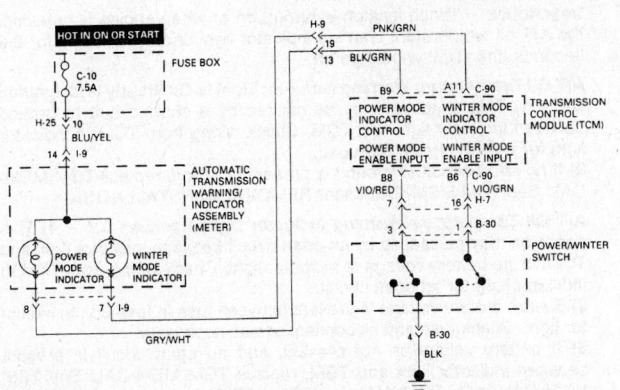

96H30749

Description – The TCM controls transmission shifting and operation using 3 different shift modes: Normal mode, Power mode and Winter mode. Driver selects shift mode by using POWER or WINTER mode switch mounted on center console, near gearshift lever. Power mode slightly increases engine speed at which transmission shift points occur for maximum performance.

In Winter mode, transmission starts off in 3rd gear to aid in vehicle traction on ice and snow. When Winter mode is selected, the TCM overrides the Power or Normal mode. Winter mode is activated when all of the following conditions are present.

- Accelerator opening is at approximately 7 percent or less.
- Kickdown switch is off.
- Gearshift lever is in "D" position.
- Transmission fluid temperature is 140°F (248°C) or less.
- Vehicle speed is less than 7 MPH.
- WINTER mode switch is on.

Winter mode is canceled when any of the following conditions are present.

- Ignition is turned off.
- Kickdown switch is on for more than 3 seconds.
- Gearshift lever is placed in "3", "2" or "L" position.
- Transmission fluid temperature is 140°F (284°C) or greater.
- Vehicle speed exceeds 20 MPH.
- WINTER mode switch is turned off.

When Winter or Power mode are canceled, transmission operates in Normal mode. Normal mode provides standard transmission shift points.

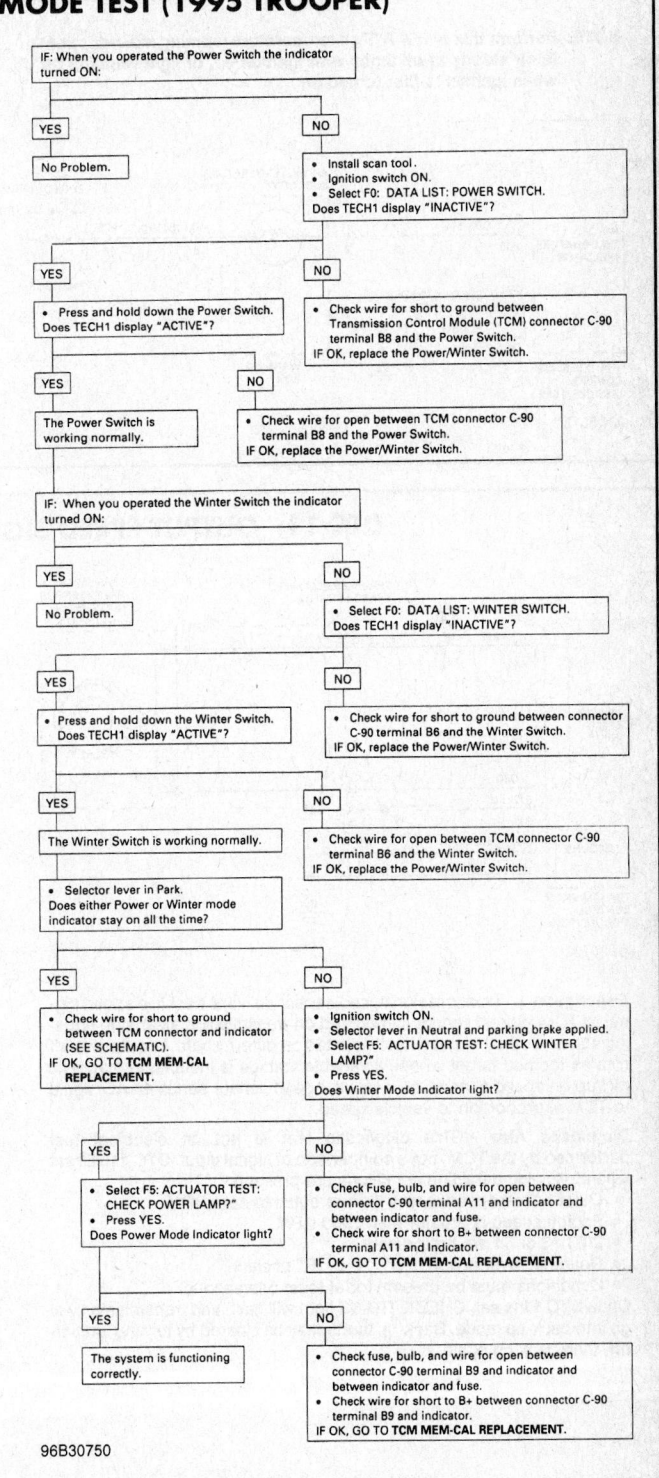

96B30750

3-644

AUTOMATIC TRANSMISSIONS
1995 Hydra-Matic 4L30-E Electronic Controls (Cont.)

A/T OIL TEMP. INDICATOR TEST (1995 TROOPER)

NOTE: Perform this test if A/T oil temperature warning indicator light is on steady at all times with ignition on, or light remains off when ignition is first turned on.

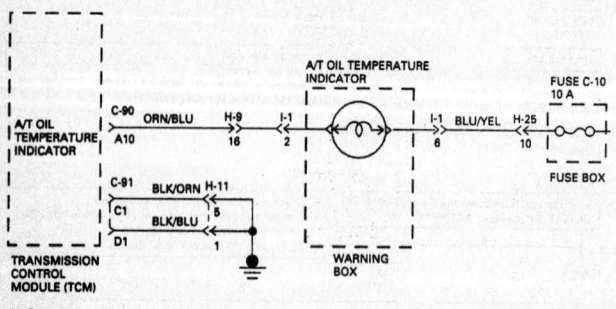

96C30751

Description – When ignition is turned on or when engine is cranking, the A/T oil temperature warning indicator light should come on for 2-3 seconds, then light should go off.

A/T Oil Temperature Warning Indicator Light Is On Steady With Ignition On – 1) This condition may be caused by a short circuit to ground between indicator light and TCM. Check wiring from TCM to indicator light for a short circuit to ground.

2) If no short circuit to ground is present in wiring, replace TCM MEMCAL. See TCM MEM-CAL under REMOVAL & INSTALLATION.

A/T Oil Temperature Warning Indicator Light Remains Off – 1) This condition may be caused by an open circuit between indicator light and TCM, or no battery voltage to indicator light. Check wiring from TCM to indicator light for an open circuit.

2) Ensure battery voltage is present between fuse in fuse box to indicator light. Check fuse and all connections as necessary.

3) If battery voltage is not present, and no open circuit is present between indicator light and TCM, replace TCM MEM-CAL. See TCM MEM-CAL under REMOVAL & INSTALLATION.

DTC 11: OUTPUT SPEED SIGNAL FAULT (1995 TROOPER)

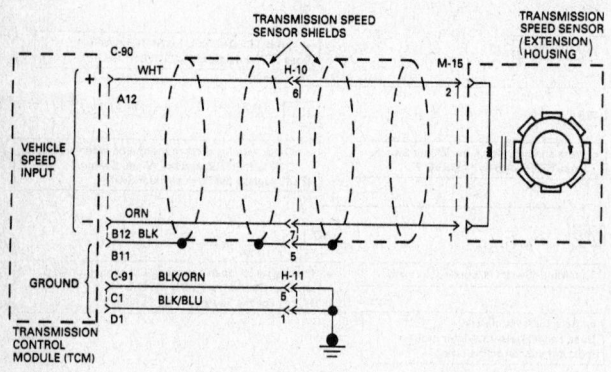

96D30752

Description – Transmission speed sensor delivers a vehicle speed signal to TCM. Speed sensor is mounted on transmission extension housing above toothed target wheel mounted on output shaft. As output shaft rotates toothed target wheel, a variable voltage is induced in magnetic pickup on speed sensor. As a result, speed sensor sends an AC signal to TCM in proportion to vehicle speed.

Diagnostic Aids – This diagnostic test is not an electrical test performed by the TCM, but a comparison of signal input. DTC 11 will set when following detection conditions are present.

- Output shaft speed is less than or equal to zero RPM.
- Engine speed is greater than 3000 RPM.
- DTC 13 or 54 are not present.
- Gearshift lever is not in "P", "N" or "R" position.
- Conditions must be present for at least one second.

Once DTC 11 is set, CHECK TRANS light will flash and transmission will go into back-up mode. Back-up mode may be cleared by turning ignition off, then back on again.

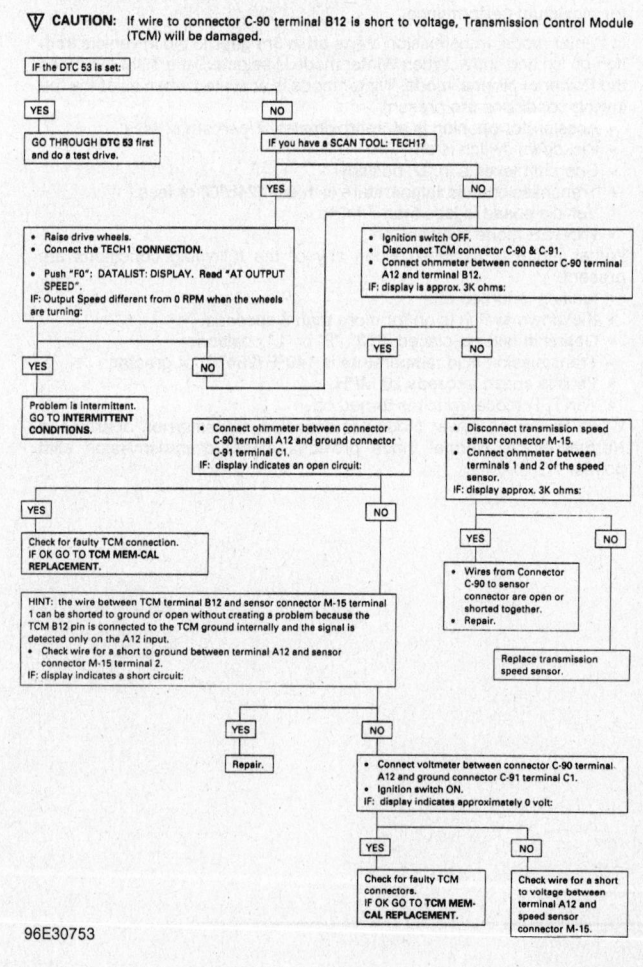

96E30753

AUTOMATIC TRANSMISSIONS
1995 Hydra-Matic 4L30-E Electronic Controls (Cont.)

3-645

DTC 13: ENGINE SPEED FAILURE (1995 TROOPER)

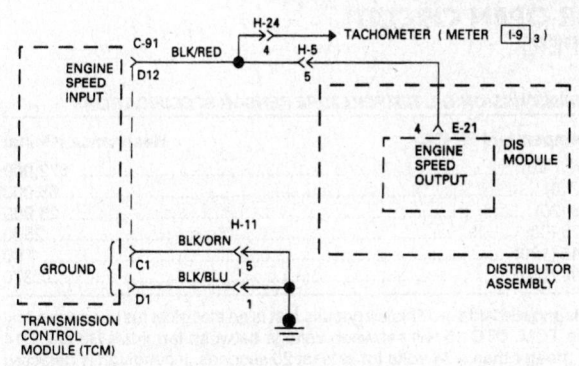

96F30754

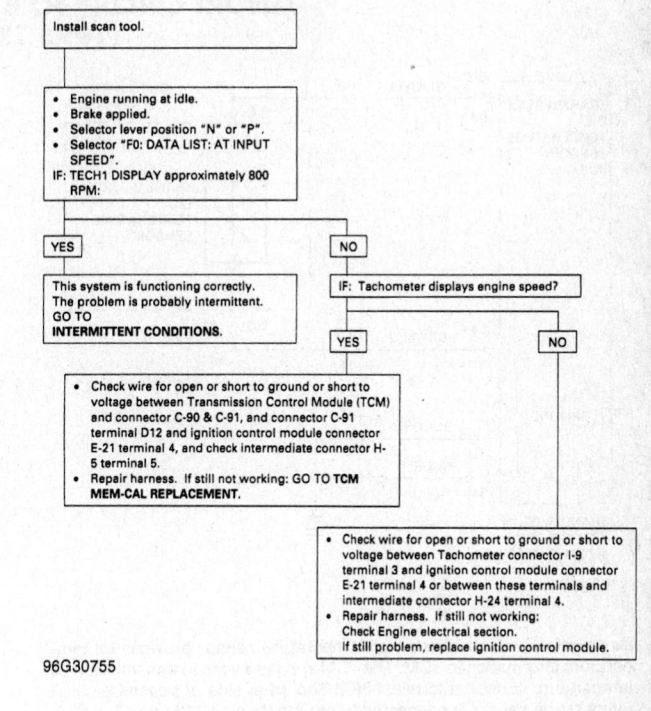

96G30755

Description – Ignition control module sends an engine speed or RPM signal to TCM. Engine Control Module (ECM) also receives a signal from ignition control module. In Neutral at idle, engine speed should be approximately 800 RPM.

Diagnostic Aids – This diagnostic test is not an electrical test performed by the TCM, but a comparison of signal input. DTC 13 will set when the following detection conditions are present.
- Output speed is greater than 1024 RPM.
- Engine speed is equal to or less than 200 RPM.
- Acceleration is greater than one MPH.
- DTC 11, 54 or 62 are not present.
- Gearshift lever is not in "P" or "N" position.
- Conditions must be present for at least .5 second.

Once DTC 13 is set, CHECK TRANS light will flash and transmission will go into back-up mode. Back-up mode may be cleared by turning ignition off, then back on again.

3-646

AUTOMATIC TRANSMISSIONS
1995 Hydra-Matic 4L30-E Electronic Controls (Cont.)

DTC 15: TRANSMISSION OIL TEMP. SENSOR CIRCUIT
(SHORT CIRCUIT TO B+ OR OPEN CIRCUIT)
(1995 TROOPER)

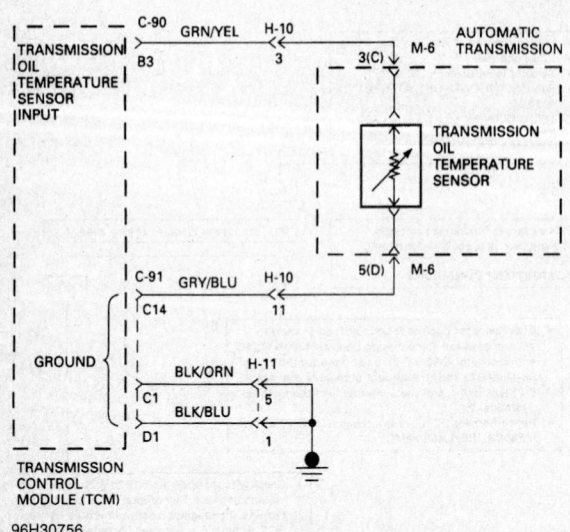

96H30756

Description – Transmission oil temperature sensor provides oil temperature information to TCM. The TCM applies 5 volts to transmission oil temperature sensor at terminal 3(C). The other side of transmission oil temperature sensor is connected to ground through TCM terminal C14. When transmission oil is cold, transmission oil temperature oil sensor resistance is high and TCM will sense a high signal voltage.

As transmission oil temperature increases to normal operating temperature of 176°F (80°C), transmission oil temperature sensor resistance becomes less and voltage decreases to approximately 3.5 volts. When DTC 15 is set, the transmission will use a warm value for operation, but TECH 1 scan tool will display the actual oil temperature. Transmission oil temperature resistance will change in relation to temperature. See TRANSMISSION OIL TEMPERATURE SENSOR SPECIFICATIONS table.

TRANSMISSION OIL TEMPERATURE SENSOR SPECIFICATIONS

Temperature °F (°C)	Resistance (Ohms)
-40 (-40)	672,000
32 (0)	65,000
68 (20)	25,000
176 (80)	2500
248 (120)	780
304 (150)	370

Diagnostic Aids – This diagnostic test is an electrical test performed by the TCM. DTC 15 will set when voltage between terminals B3 and C14 is greater than 4.74 volts for at least 20 seconds. If condition is detected for at least 20 seconds, transmission oil temperature sensor will default to 212°F (100°C) and Winter mode will still operate. Once DTC 15 is set, CHECK TRANS light will NOT flash and transmission will NOT go into back-up mode. System will return to normal operation when voltage between terminals B3 and C14 is equal to or less than 4.74 volts.

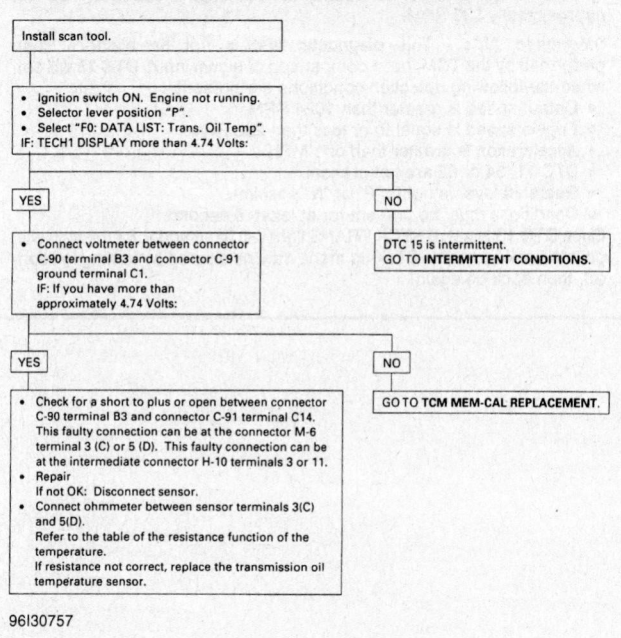

96I30757

AUTOMATIC TRANSMISSIONS
1995 Hydra-Matic 4L30-E Electronic Controls (Cont.)

3-647

DTC 16: TRANSMISSION OIL TEMP. SENSOR CIRCUIT
(SHORT CIRCUIT TO GROUND)
(1995 TROOPER)

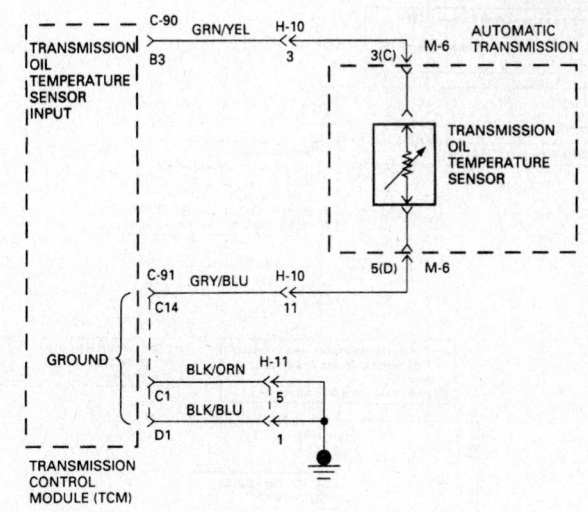

96H30756

Description – Transmission oil temperature sensor provides oil temperature information to TCM. The TCM applies 5 volts to transmission oil temperature sensor at terminal 3(C). The other side of transmission oil temperature sensor is connected to ground through TCM terminal C14.

When transmission oil is cold, transmission oil temperature sensor resistance is high and TCM will sense a high signal voltage. As transmission oil temperature increases to normal operating temperature of 176°F (80°C), transmission oil temperature sensor resistance becomes less and voltage decreases to approximately 3.5 volts. When DTC 16 is set, the transmission will use a warm value for operation, but TECH 1 scan tool will display the actual oil temperature.

Diagnostic Aids – This diagnostic test is an electrical test performed by the TCM. DTC 16 will set when voltage between terminals B3 and C14 is less than .4 volt for at least 20 seconds. If condition is detected for at least 20 seconds, transmission oil temperature sensor will default to 212°F (100°C) and Winter mode will still operate. Once DTC 16 is set, CHECK TRANS light will NOT flash and transmission will NOT go into back-up mode. System will return to normal operation when voltage between terminals B3 and C14 is equal to or greater than .4 volt.

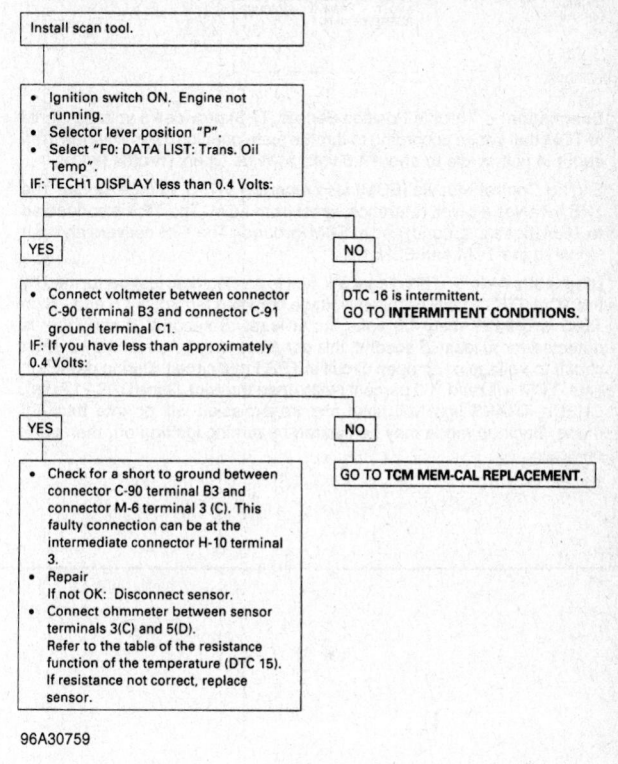

96A30759

3-648

AUTOMATIC TRANSMISSIONS
1995 Hydra-Matic 4L30-E Electronic Controls (Cont.)

DTC 21: THROTTLE POSITION SENSOR CIRCUIT (SHORT CIRCUIT TO B+)
(1995 TROOPER)

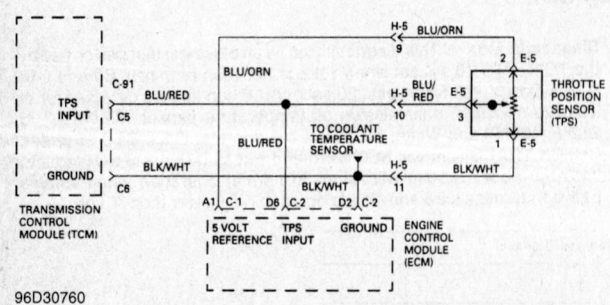

96D30760

Description – Throttle Position Sensor (TPS) provides a voltage signal to TCM that varies according to throttle plate opening. Signal varies from about .4 volt at idle to about 4.6 volts at Wide Open Throttle (WOT).

Engine Control Module (ECM) also receives a TPS voltage signal. The TPS receives a 5-volt reference signal from ECM. The TPS is connected to TCM (floating ground) and at ECM (ground). The TPS delivers an input signal to the TCM and ECM.

Diagnostic Aids – This diagnostic test is an electrical test performed by the TCM. DTC 21 will set when voltage between terminals C5 and C6 on TCM is greater than 4.9 volts for at least .5 second. If condition is detected for at least .5 second, this condition may be caused by a short circuit to voltage or an open circuit in TPS input circuit. During detection time, TCM will read 100 percent (wide open throttle). Once DTC 21 is set, CHECK TRANS light will flash and transmission will go into back-up mode. Back-up mode may be cleared by turning ignition off, then back on again.

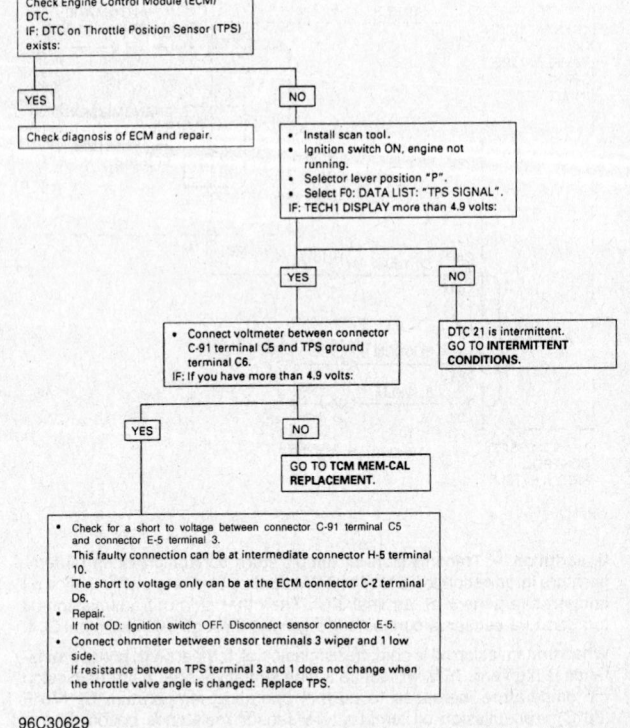

96C30629

AUTOMATIC TRANSMISSIONS
1995 Hydra-Matic 4L30-E Electronic Controls (Cont.)

3-649

DTC 22: THROTTLE POSITION SENSOR CIRCUIT
(SHORT CIRCUIT TO GROUND OR OPEN CIRCUIT)
(1995 TROOPER)

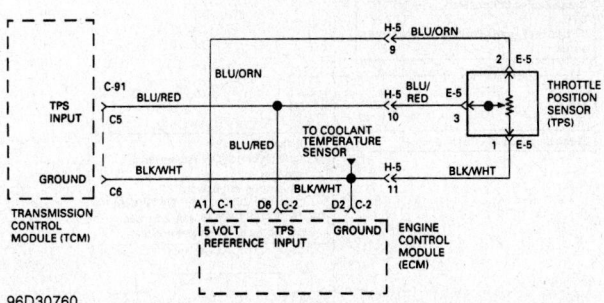

96D30760

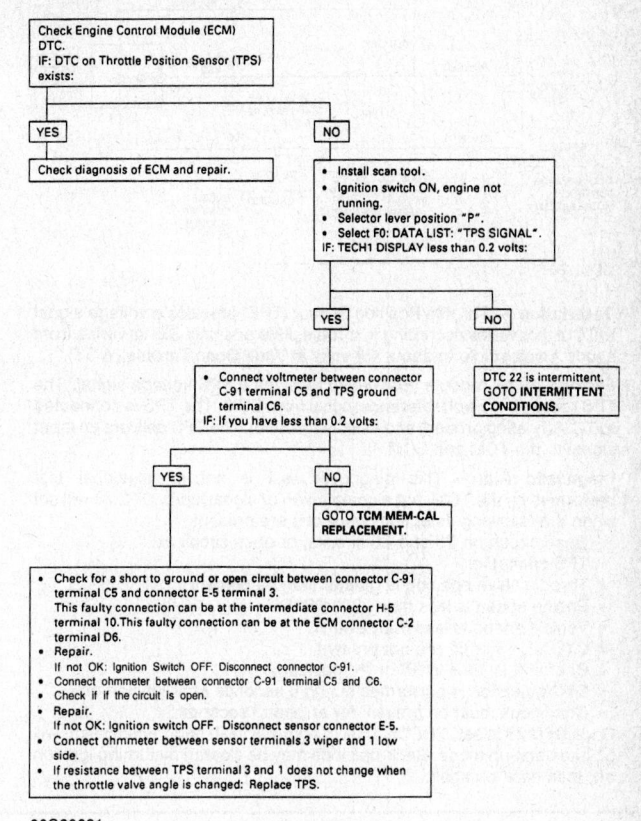

96G30631

Description – Throttle Position Sensor (TPS) provides a voltage signal to TCM that varies according to throttle plate opening. Signal varies from about .4 volt at idle to about 4.6 volts at Wide Open Throttle (WOT). Engine Control Module (ECM) also receives a TPS voltage signal. The TPS receives a 5-volt reference signal from ECM. The TPS is connected to TCM (floating ground) and at ECM (ground). The TPS delivers an input signal to the TCM and ECM.

Diagnostic Aids – This diagnostic test is an electrical test performed by the TCM. DTC 22 will set when the following detection conditions are present.
- Short circuit on TPS input signal to TCM ground, or open circuit on TPS circuit.
- Voltage between terminals C5 and C6 on TCM is less than .2 volt for at least .5 second.

If condition is detected for at least .5 second, during detection time, TCM will read zero percent (idle position). Once DTC 22 is set, CHECK TRANS light will flash and transmission will go into back-up mode. Back-up mode may be cleared by turning ignition off, then back on again.

3-650

AUTOMATIC TRANSMISSIONS
1995 Hydra-Matic 4L30-E Electronic Controls (Cont.)

DTC 23: THROTTLE POSITION SENSOR CIRCUIT (CONNECTOR OPEN CIRCUIT)
(1995 TROOPER)

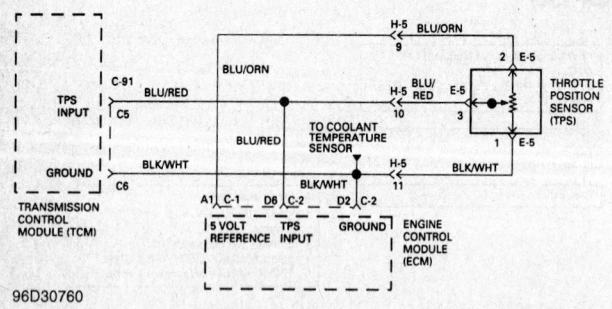

96D30760

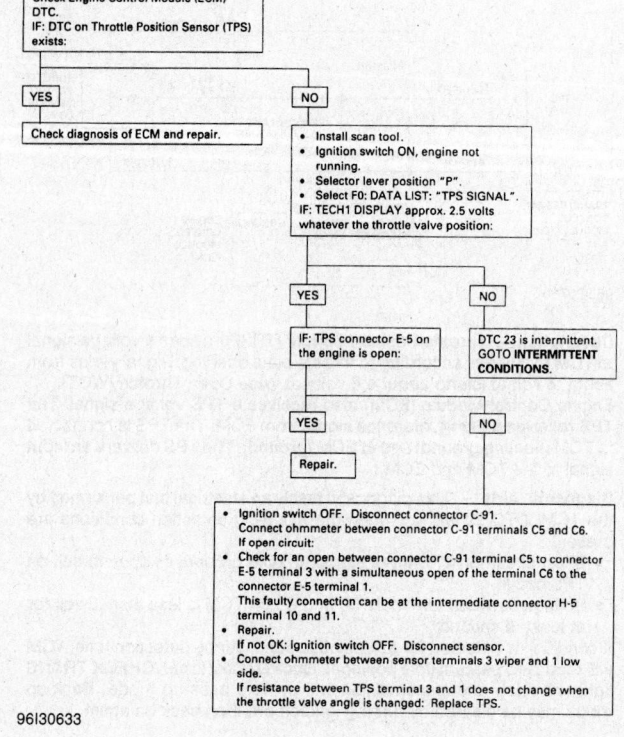

96I30633

Description – Throttle Position Sensor (TPS) provides a voltage signal to TCM that varies according to throttle plate opening. Signal varies from about .4 volt at idle to about 4.6 volts at Wide Open Throttle (WOT).

Engine Control Module (ECM) also receives a TPS voltage signal. The TPS receives a 5-volt reference signal from ECM. The TPS is connected to TCM (floating ground) and at ECM (ground). The TPS delivers an input signal to the TCM and ECM.

Diagnostic Aids – This diagnostic test is not an electrical test performed by the TCM, but a comparison of signal input. DTC 23 will set when the following detection conditions are present.
- Open circuit on C5 and C6 circuits, or open circuit at TPS connector.
- Throttle valve opening is greater than 42 percent.
- Engine speed is less than 2200 RPM.
- Vehicle speed is less than 2 MPH.
- DTC 11, 13 or 62 are not present.
- Gearshift lever is in "P" or "N" position.
- DTC detection is performed during 6 seconds after ignition on.
- Conditions must be present for at least 3 seconds.

Once DTC 23 is set, CHECK TRANS light will flash and transmission will go into back-up mode. Back-up mode may be cleared by turning ignition off, then back on again.

AUTOMATIC TRANSMISSIONS
1995 Hydra-Matic 4L30-E Electronic Controls (Cont.)

3-651

DTC 25: SUPPLY VOLTAGE TOO LOW (1995 TROOPER)

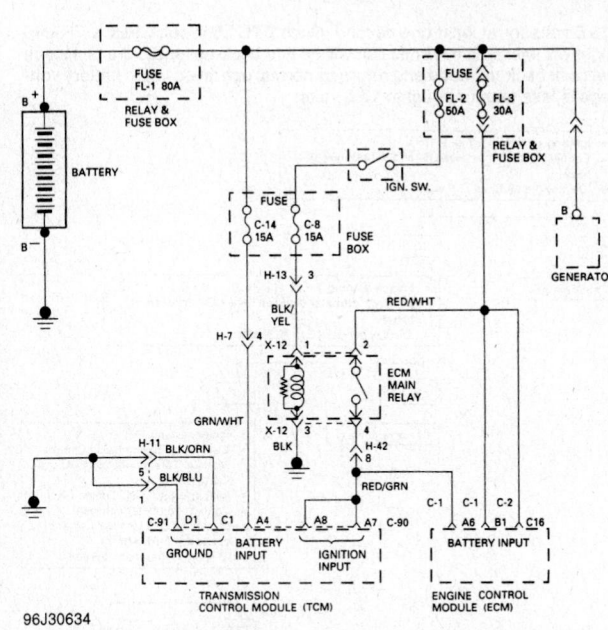

96J30634

Description – Ignition voltage at TCM terminals A7 and A8 are monitored by TCM. When ignition voltage is less than 9 volts, DTC 25 is set. Minimum voltage requirement will vary with transmission oil temperature.

Diagnostic Aids – This diagnostic test is an electrical test performed by the TCM. DTC 25 will set when ignition voltage between ground terminal C1 and TCM terminals A7 and A8 are detected to be less than minimum required for at least one second. See CODE SET CONDITION in SUPPLY VOLTAGE SPECIFICATIONS table.

SUPPLY VOLTAGE SPECIFICATIONS

Transmission Oil Temperature °F (°C)	Minimum Volts
Code Set Condition	
−40 (−40)	8.7
194 (90)	9.0
304 (150)	9.2
Back-Up Mode Recovery	
−40 (−40)	9.2
194 (90)	9.5
304 (150)	9.6

Once DTC 25 is set, CHECK TRANS light will flash and transmission will go into back-up mode. Transmission will exit back-up mode and return to normal operation when ignition voltage increases to minimum specified voltage for indicated temperature range. See BACK-UP MODE RECOVERY in SUPPLY VOLTAGE SPECIFICATIONS table.

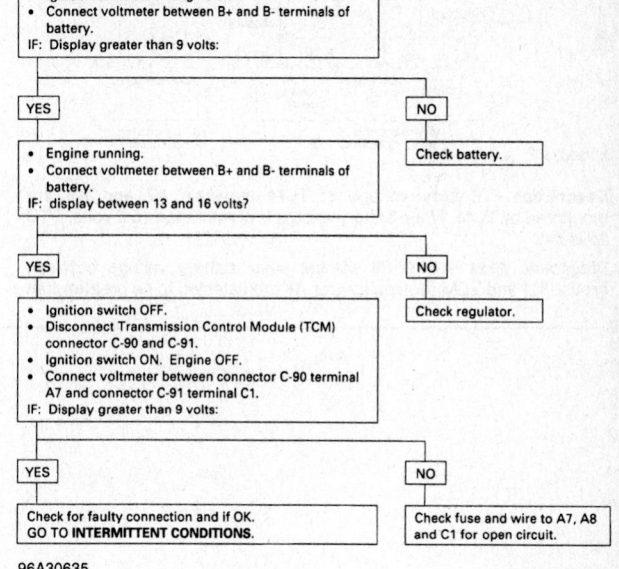

96A30635

3-652

AUTOMATIC TRANSMISSIONS
1995 Hydra-Matic 4L30-E Electronic Controls (Cont.)

DTC 26: SUPPLY VOLTAGE TOO HIGH (1995 TROOPER)

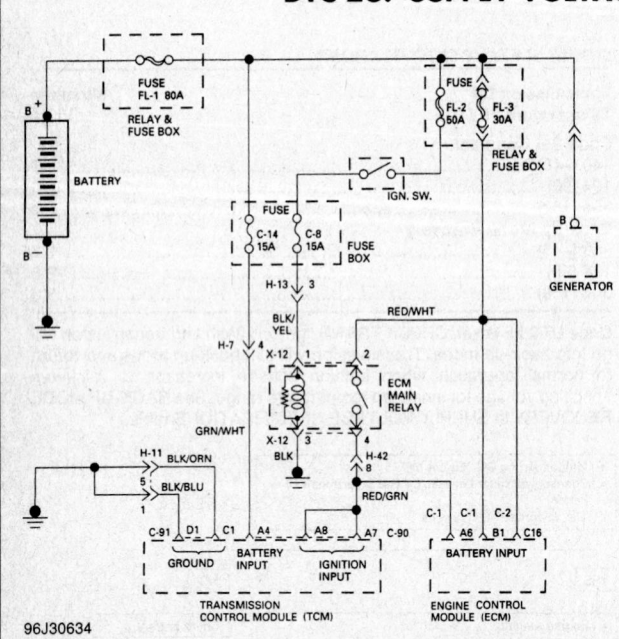

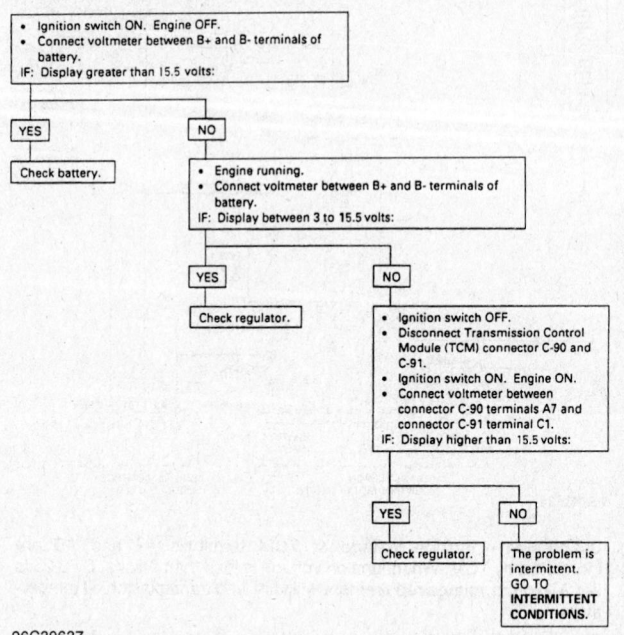

15.5 volts for at least one second. Once DTC 26 is set, CHECK TRANS light will flash and transmission will go into back-up mode. Transmission will exit back-up mode and return to normal operation when battery voltage is less than or equal to 15.5 volts.

- Ignition switch ON. Engine OFF.
- Connect voltmeter between B+ and B- terminals of battery.
- IF: Display greater than 15.5 volts:

YES → Check battery.

NO →
- Engine running.
- Connect voltmeter between B+ and B- terminals of battery.
- IF: Display between 3 to 15.5 volts:

YES → Check regulator.

NO →
- Ignition switch OFF.
- Disconnect Transmission Control Module (TCM) connector C-90 and C-91.
- Ignition switch ON. Engine ON.
- Connect voltmeter between connector C-90 terminals A7 and connector C-91 terminal C1.
- IF: Display higher than 15.5 volts:

YES → Check regulator.

NO → The problem is intermittent. GO TO **INTERMITTENT CONDITIONS.**

96C30637

96J30634

Description – Battery voltage at TCM terminals A7 and A8 are monitored by TCM. When battery voltage is greater than 15.5 volts, DTC 26 is set.

Diagnostic Aids – DTC 26 will set when battery voltage between ground C1 and TCM terminals A7 or A8 are detected to be greater than

AUTOMATIC TRANSMISSIONS
1995 Hydra-Matic 4L30-E Electronic Controls (Cont.)

3-653

DTC 31: 1-2/3-4 SHIFT SOLENOID CIRCUIT
(SHORT CIRCUIT TO GROUND OR OPEN CIRCUIT)
(1995 TROOPER)

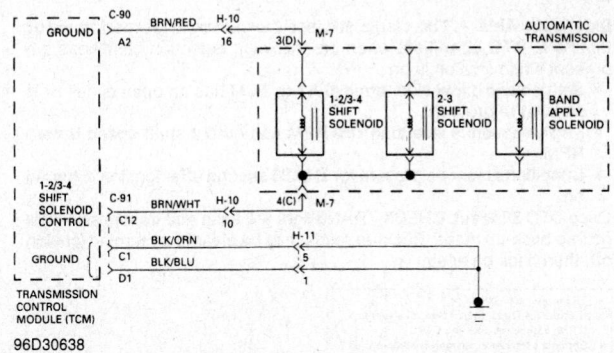

96D30638

Description – The 1-2/3-4 shift solenoid is a normally closed solenoid located on main valve body. In 2nd or 3rd gear, the TCM energizes shift solenoid to open fluid inlet port. When port is open, fluid pressure actuates shift valve. Shift solenoid is activated by applying voltage to one side (high side) of shift solenoid, and grounding the other side (low side) of shift solenoid.

High Side Driver (HSD) is a circuit of the TCM which acts as a switch between shift solenoid and supply voltage. High side of shift solenoid is permanently supplied voltage, except in back-up mode or when ignition is off. The TCM continually monitors shift solenoid connection to the Low Side Driver (LSD) for either high or low voltage. The LSD is a circuit of the TCM used as a switch between shift solenoid and ground. When shift solenoid is turned on, the TCM completes ground circuit for shift solenoid.

When ignition is turned on before engine is cranked, the TCM activates shift solenoids and band apply solenoid to check operating circuits of each solenoid for a short or open circuit. To do so, the gear is set to 4th gear, 3rd gear, 1st gear, 1st gear with band applied and 4th gear with no HSD. Each one of the 5 tests requires .15 second. If engine is cranked before end of all tests, remaining tests are not performed.

Diagnostic Aids – This diagnostic test is an electrical test performed by the TCM. DTC 31 will set when following detection conditions are present when ignition is on.
- Shift solenoid low side terminal A2 to TCM has an open circuit or is shorted to ground.
- Engine speed is less than 480 RPM and output shaft speed is zero RPM.
- Conditions must be present for .15-1.03 seconds after ignition is turned on.

Once DTC 31 is set, CHECK TRANS light will flash and transmission will go into back-up mode. Back-up mode may be cleared by turning ignition off, then back on again.

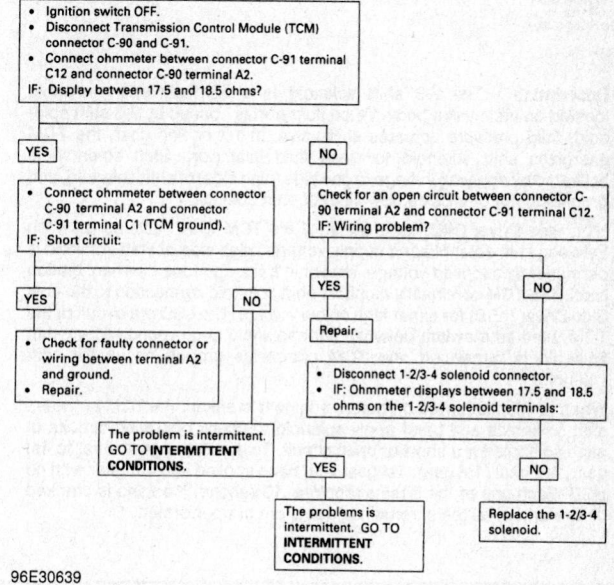

96E30639

3-654

AUTOMATIC TRANSMISSIONS
1995 Hydra-Matic 4L30-E Electronic Controls (Cont.)

DTC 32: 2-3 SHIFT SOLENOID CIRCUIT
(SHORT CIRCUIT TO GROUND OR OPEN CIRCUIT)
(1995 TROOPER)

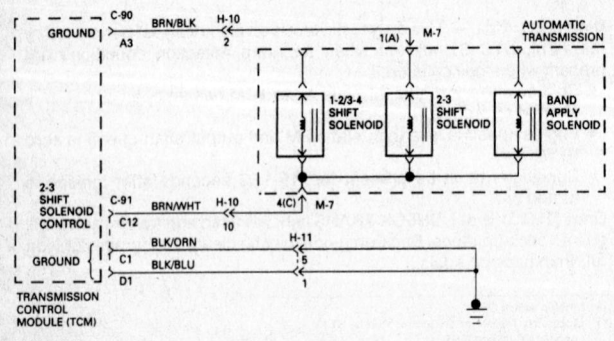

96H30640

Description – The 2-3 shift solenoid is a normally open solenoid located on main valve body. When fluid port is opened by 2-3 shift solenoid, fluid pressure actuates shift valve. In 1st or 2nd gear, the TCM energizes shift solenoid to close fluid inlet port. Shift solenoid is activated by applying voltage to one side (high side) of shift solenoid, and grounding the other side (low side) of shift solenoid.

High Side Driver (HSD) is a circuit of the TCM which acts as a switch between shift solenoid and supply voltage. High side of shift solenoid is permanently supplied voltage, except in back-up mode or when ignition is off. The TCM continually monitors shift solenoid connection to the Low Side Driver (LSD) for either high or low voltage. The LSD is a circuit of the TCM used as a switch between shift solenoid and ground. When shift solenoid is turned on, the TCM completes ground circuit for shift solenoid.

When ignition is turned on before engine is cranked, the TCM activates shift solenoids and band apply solenoid to check operating circuits of each solenoid for a short or open circuit. To do so, the gear is set to 4th gear, 3rd gear, 1st gear, 1st gear with band applied and 4th gear with no HSD. Each one of the 5 tests requires .15 second. If engine is cranked before end of all tests, remaining tests are not performed.

Diagnostic Aids – This diagnostic test is an electrical test performed by the TCM. DTC 32 will set when the following detection conditions are present when ignition is on.
- Shift solenoid low side terminal A3 to TCM has an open circuit or is shorted to ground.
- Engine speed is less than 480 RPM and output shaft speed is zero RPM.
- Conditions must be present for .15-.88 second after ignition is turned on.

Once DTC 32 is set, CHECK TRANS light will flash and transmission will go into back-up mode. Back-up mode may be cleared by turning ignition off, then back on again.

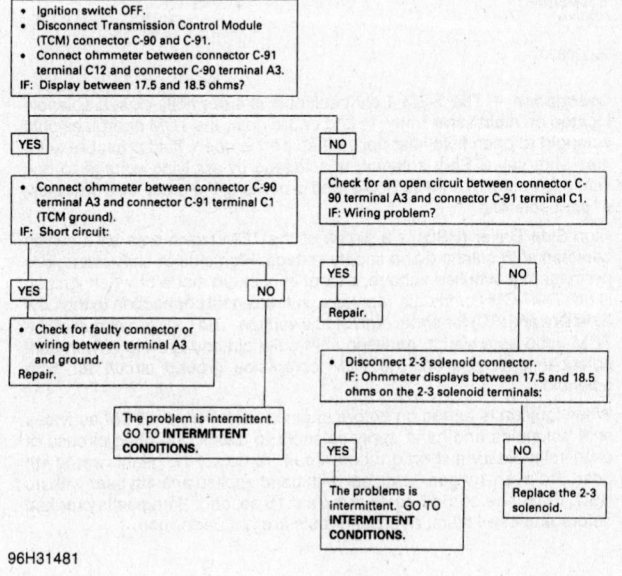

96H31481

AUTOMATIC TRANSMISSIONS
1995 Hydra-Matic 4L30-E Electronic Controls (Cont.)

3-655

DTC 33: TCC SOLENOID CIRCUIT (SHORT CIRCUIT TO B+ OR OPEN CIRCUIT) (1995 TROOPER)

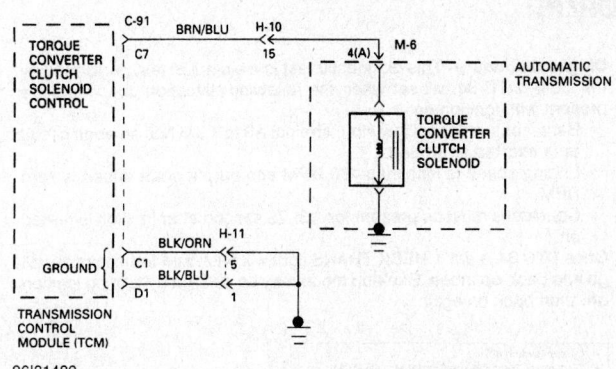

96I31482

Description – Torque Converter Clutch (TCC) solenoid is located on adapter case valve body. TCM energizes TCC solenoid to open fluid port. When fluid port is open, line pressure actuates converter clutch control valve which exhausts the fluid, allowing torque converter clutch to engage. TCM allows torque converter clutch to engage only when:

- Transmission is at normal operating temperature.
- Brake pedal is in released position.
- Transmission is in 2nd, 3rd or 4th gear.
- Engine is at normal operating temperature.
- Shift pattern requests TCC apply.
- Shift is finished.
- DTC 43, 55, 64 or 65 are not present.

TCC solenoid is activated by applying voltage to one side (high side) of TCC solenoid, and grounding the other side (low side) of TCC solenoid.

High Side Driver (HSD) is a circuit of the TCM which acts as a switch between TCC solenoid and supply voltage. High side of TCC solenoid is used to turn TCC solenoid on or off, as low side of TCC solenoid is permanently connected to ground. When transmission is in back-up mode or ignition is turned off, TCC solenoid is turned off.

The TCM continually monitors TCC solenoid connection to HSD for either high or low voltage. The only test performed is when engine is cranked and TCC solenoid is turned on. If this circuit is shorted to battery voltage, TCC solenoid is constantly on, and shifts may be firm.

In 1st gear, TCC is hydraulically OFF, whatever position TCC solenoid is in. Vehicle may be driven with TCC solenoid shorted to battery voltage. Engine may stall when driver is braking, or if vehicle is stopped with transmission in 2nd gear with TCC applied. The 3-2 shifts will be very firm.

Diagnostic Aids – This diagnostic test is an electrical test performed by the TCM. DTC 33 will set when TCC solenoid high side to TCM terminal C7 contains an open circuit or is shorted to battery voltage, and condition is present for .13 second. If DTC 33 is set, the TCC will be shut off and CHECK TRANS light will flash. Transmission will NOT go into back-up mode.
Transmission will return to normal operation by turning ignition off, then back on again.

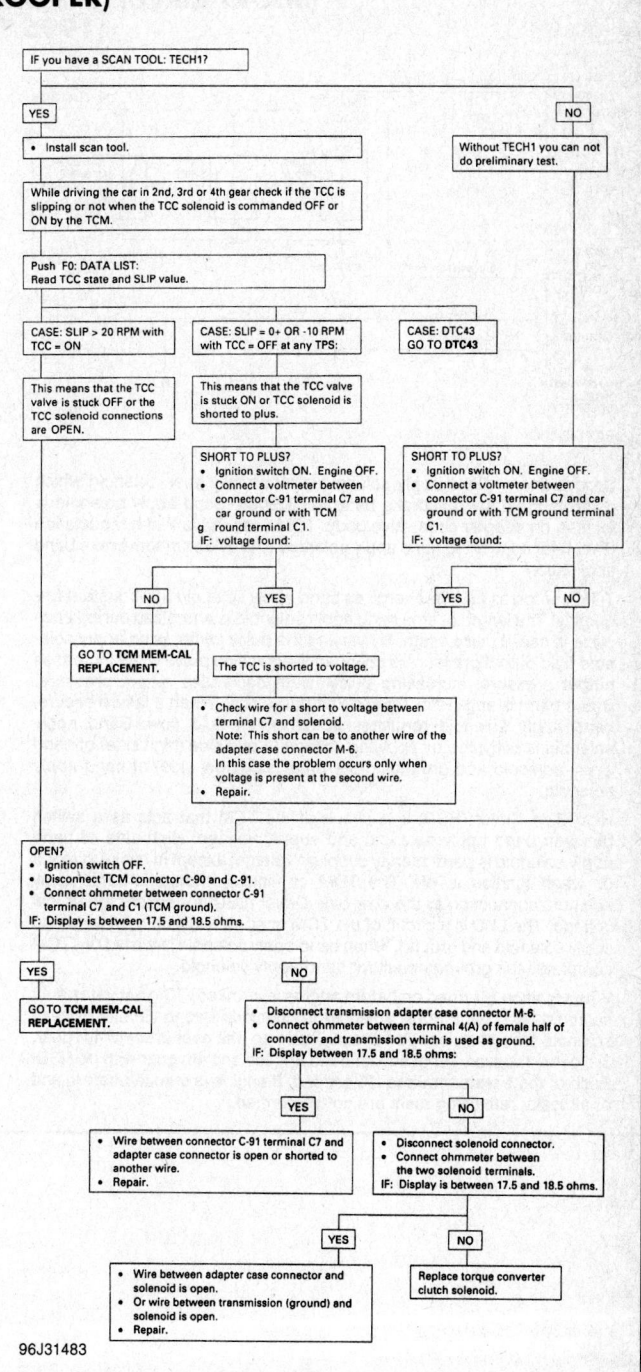

96J31483

3-656

AUTOMATIC TRANSMISSIONS
1995 Hydra-Matic 4L30-E Electronic Controls (Cont.)

DTC 34: BAND APPLY SOLENOID CIRCUIT
(SHORT CIRCUIT TO GROUND OR OPEN CIRCUIT)
(1995 TROOPER)

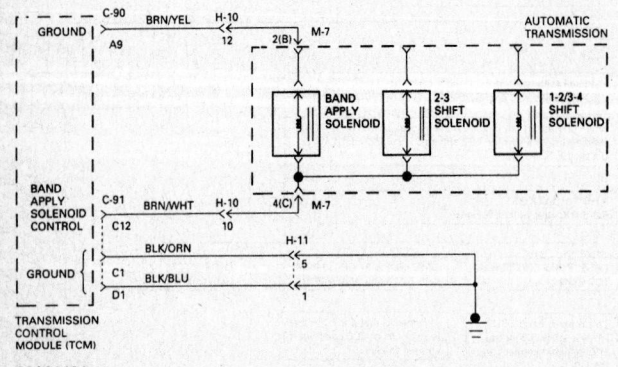

96A31484

Description – Band apply solenoid is a normally open solenoid which controls fluid flow for brake band application. Band apply solenoid is located on adapter case valve body. TCM uses Pulse Width Modulation (PWM) for controlling band apply solenoid to provide smooth brake band application.

TCM energizes and de-energizes band apply solenoid at a constant frequency. The length of time band apply solenoid is energized during each cycle is called pulse width. By varying the pulse width, band apply solenoid fluid output pressure is changed. Decreasing pulse width increases output pressure. Increasing pulse width decreases output pressure. Brake band is applied in 1st and 2nd gears only. When a failure occurs, band apply solenoid regulates at maximum fluid flow. Band apply solenoid is activated by applying voltage to one side (high side) of band apply solenoid and grounding the other side (low side) of band apply solenoid.

High Side Driver (HSD) is a circuit of the TCM that acts as a switch between band apply solenoid and supply voltage. High side of band apply solenoid is permanently supplied voltage, except in back-up mode or when ignition is off. The TCM continually monitors band apply solenoid connection to the Low Side Driver (LSD) for either high or low voltage. The LSD is a circuit of the TCM used as a switch between band apply solenoid and ground. When band apply solenoid is turned on, TCM completes the ground circuit for band apply solenoid.

When ignition is turned on before engine is cranked, TCM activates shift solenoids and band apply solenoid to check operating circuits of each solenoid for a short or open circuit. To do so, the gear is set to 4th gear, 3rd gear, 1st gear, 1st gear with band applied and 4th gear with no HSD. Each of the 5 tests requires .15 second. If engine is cranked before end of all tests, remaining tests are not performed.

Diagnostic Aids – This diagnostic test is a electrical test performed by the TCM. DTC 34 will set when the following detection conditions are present with ignition on.

- Band apply solenoid low side terminal A9 to TCM has an open circuit or is shorted to ground.
- Engine speed is less than 480 RPM and output shaft speed is zero RPM.
- Conditions must be present for .15-.75 second after ignition is turned on.

Once DTC 34 is set, CHECK TRANS light will flash and transmission will go into back-up mode. Back-up mode may be cleared by turning ignition off, then back on again.

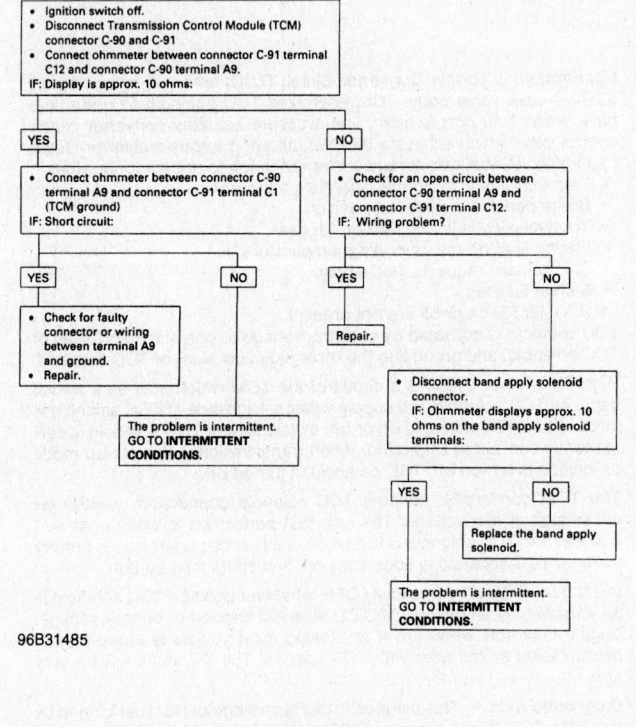

96B31485

AUTOMATIC TRANSMISSIONS
1995 Hydra-Matic 4L30-E Electronic Controls (Cont.)

3-657

DTC 35: FORCE MOTOR SOLENOID CIRCUIT
(SHORT CIRCUIT TO B+ OR GROUND)
(1995 TROOPER)

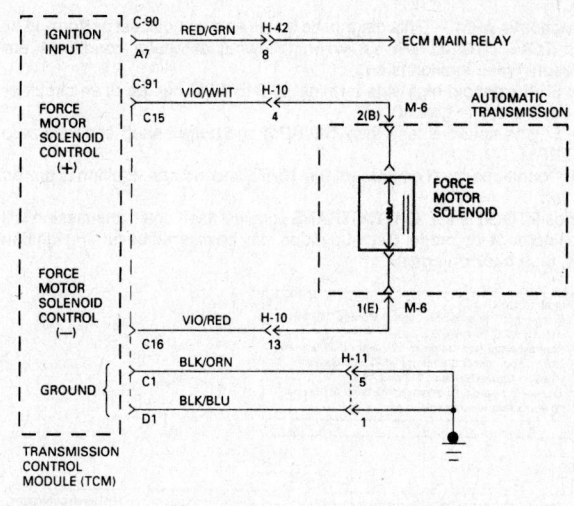

96C31486

Description – Force motor solenoid is a variable position solenoid used to regulate line pressure. Force motor solenoid is located on adapter case valve body. The TCM uses Throttle Position Sensor (TPS) information and vehicle speed to determine appropriate line pressure for a given load. TCM regulates line pressure by applying a varying applied amperage of .1-1.1 amps to force motor solenoid. TCM then monitors return amperage on the return line.

Line pressure may vary from less than 50 psi (3.5 kg/cm²) to greater than 200 psi (14.1 kg/cm²). Line pressure is proportional to current applied on force motor solenoid. High current produces low line pressure and low current produces high line pressure.

Diagnostic Aids – This diagnostic test is an electrical test performed by the TCM. DTC 35 sets when return line amperage is greater than .2 amp from the commanded amperage. Once DTC 35 is set, CHECK TRANS light will flash and transmission will go into back-up mode. Back-up mode may be cleared by turning ignition off, then back on again.

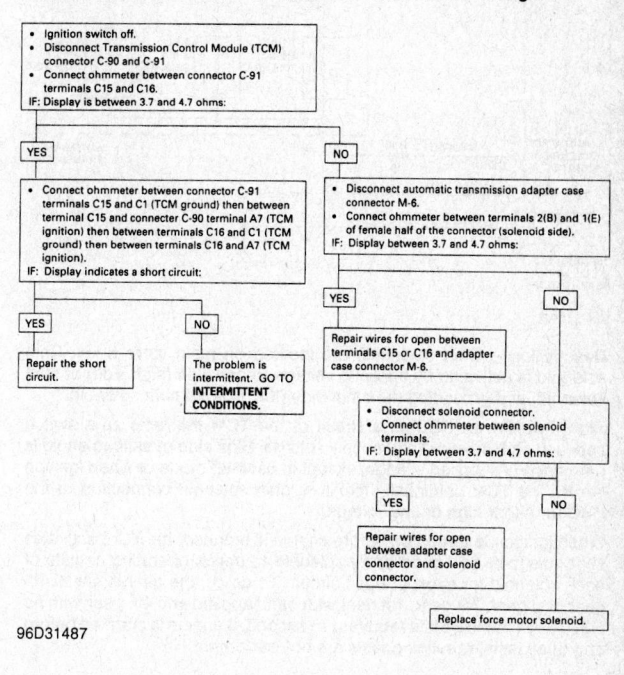

96D31487

3-658

AUTOMATIC TRANSMISSIONS
1995 Hydra-Matic 4L30-E Electronic Controls (Cont.)

DTC 36: SHIFT SOLENOID CIRCUIT
(SHORT CIRCUIT TO GROUND OR OPEN CIRCUIT)
(1995 TROOPER)

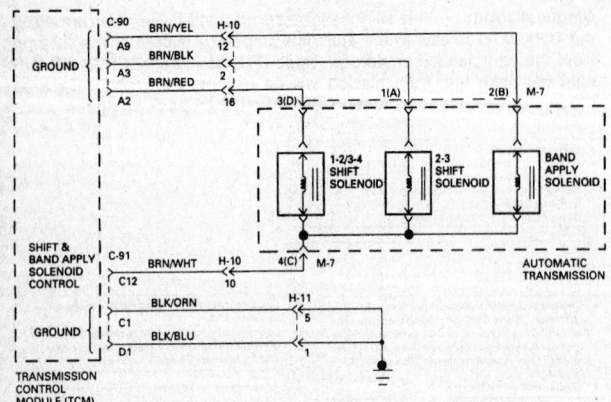

96E31488

Description – Shift solenoids are located on main valve body. Shift solenoid is activated by applying voltage to one side (high side) of shift solenoid, and grounding the other side (low side) of shift solenoid.

High Side Driver (HSD) is a circuit of the TCM that acts as a switch between shift solenoid and supply voltage. High side of shift solenoid is permanently supplied with voltage, except in back-up mode or when ignition is off. The TCM continually monitors shift solenoid connection to the HSD for either high or low voltage.

When ignition is turned on before engine is cranked, the TCM activates shift solenoids and band apply solenoid to check operating circuits of each solenoid for short or open circuit. To do so, the gear is set to 4th gear, 3rd gear, 1st gear, 1st gear with band applied and 4th gear with no HSD. Each of the 5 tests requires .15 second. If engine is cranked before end of all tests, remaining tests are not performed.

Diagnostic Aids – This diagnostic test is an electrical test performed by the TCM. DTC 36 will set when following detection conditions are present when ignition is on.
- Shift solenoid high side terminal C12 to TCM has an open circuit or is shorted to ground.
- Engine speed is less than 480 RPM and output shaft speed is zero RPM.
- Conditions must be present for .15-.75 second after ignition is turned on.

Once DTC 36 is set, CHECK TRANS light will flash and transmission will go into back-up mode. Back-up mode may be cleared by turning ignition off, then back on again.

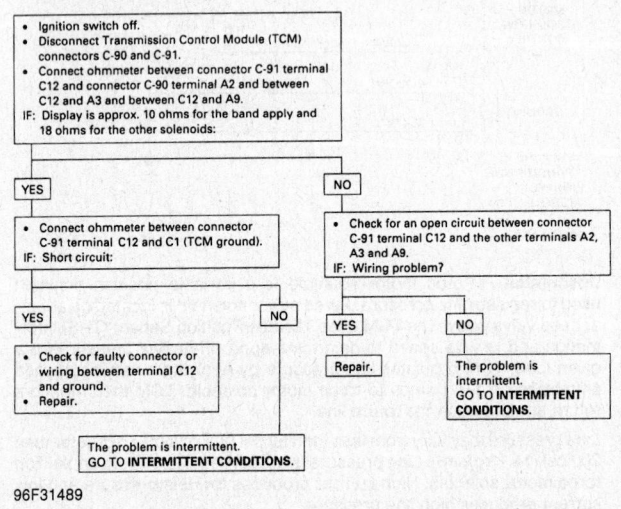

96F31489

DTC 37: TORQUE MANAGEMENT SERIAL LINE FAULTY (1995 TROOPER)

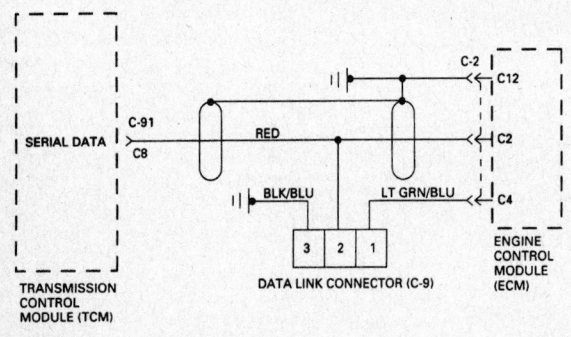

96I31490

Description – Torque management uses TCM to deliver a spark advance signal to Engine Control Module (ECM) during transmission shifting. This controls engine torque and reduces engagement shock caused by a change in vehicle speed. Each time transmission shifts with torque management active, TCM delivers a signal to ECM.

Diagnostic Aids – This diagnostic test is not an electrical test performed by the TCM, but a comparison of signal input. DTC 37 will set when a torque management failure is present, or ECM does not acknowledge a signal from TCM when transmission shifts with torque management active. Once DTC 37 is set, CHECK TRANS light will flash and transmission will go into back-up mode. Back-up mode may be cleared by turning ignition off, then back on again.

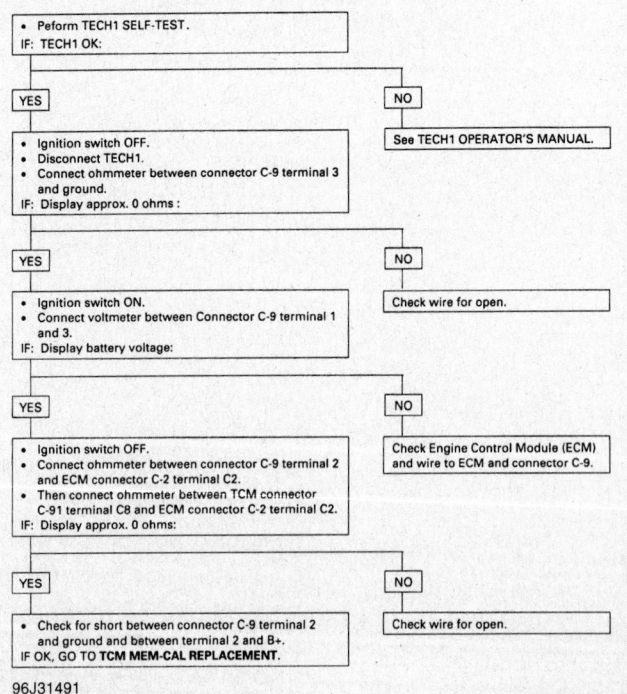

96J31491

AUTOMATIC TRANSMISSIONS
1995 Hydra-Matic 4L30-E Electronic Controls (Cont.)

3-659

DTC 41: 1-2/3-4 SHIFT SOLENOID CIRCUIT (SHORT CIRCUIT TO B+)
(1995 TROOPER)

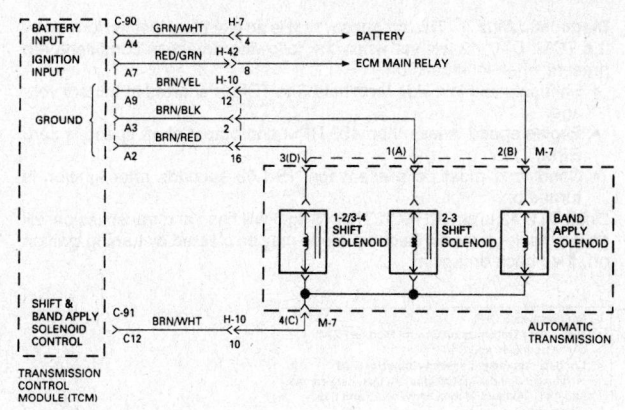

96A31492

Description – The 1-2/3-4 shift solenoid is a normally closed solenoid located on main valve body. In 2nd or 3rd gear, TCM energizes shift solenoid to open fluid inlet port. When port is open, fluid pressure actuates shift valve. Shift solenoid is activated by applying voltage to one side (high side) of shift solenoid, and grounding other side (low side) of shift solenoid.

High Side Driver (HSD) is a circuit of the TCM which acts as a switch between shift solenoid and supply voltage. High side of shift solenoid is permanently supplied voltage, except in back-up mode or when ignition is off. TCM continually monitors shift solenoid connection to Low Side Driver (LSD) for either high or low voltage. The LSD is a circuit of the TCM used as a switch between shift solenoid and ground. When shift solenoid is turned on, TCM completes the ground circuit for shift solenoid.

When ignition is turned on before engine is cranked, TCM activates shift solenoids and band apply solenoid to check operating circuits of each solenoid for a short or open circuit. To do so, the gear is set to 4th gear,

3rd gear, 1st gear, 1st gear with band applied and 4th gear with no HSD. Each of the 5 tests requires .15 second. If engine is cranked before end of all tests, remaining tests are not performed.

Diagnostic Aids – This diagnostic test is an electrical test performed by the TCM. DTC 41 will set when the following detection conditions are present when ignition is on.

- Shift solenoid low side terminal A2 to TCM is shorted to battery voltage.
- Engine speed is less than 480 RPM and output shaft speed is zero RPM.
- Conditions must be present for .15-.88 second after ignition is turned on.

Once DTC 41 is set, CHECK TRANS light will flash and transmission will go into back-up mode. Back-up mode may be cleared by turning ignition off, then back on again.

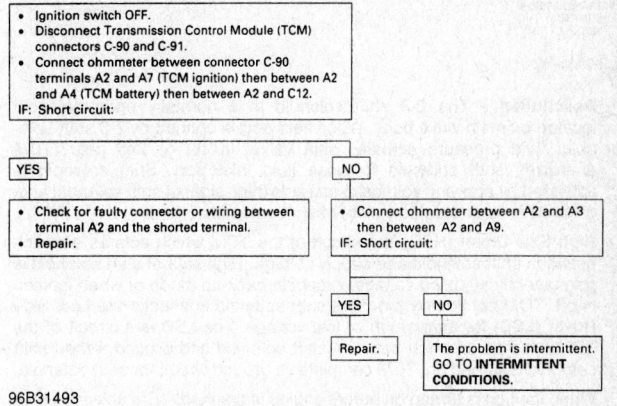

96B31493

3-660

AUTOMATIC TRANSMISSIONS
1995 Hydra-Matic 4L30-E Electronic Controls (Cont.)

DTC 42: 2-3 SHIFT SOLENOID CIRCUIT (SHORT CIRCUIT TO B+)
(1995 TROOPER)

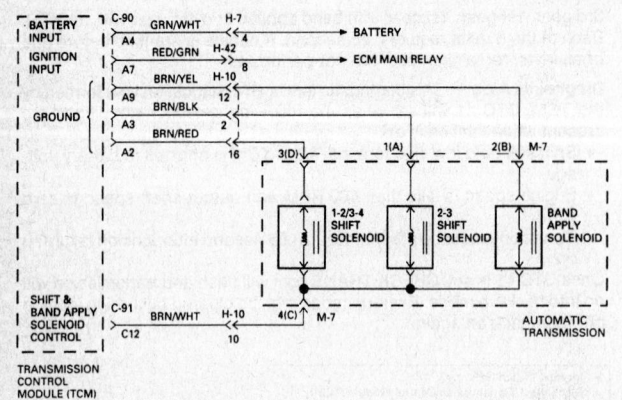

96A31492

Description – The 2-3 shift solenoid is a normally open solenoid located on main valve body. When fluid port is opened by 2-3 shift solenoid, fluid pressure actuates shift valve. In 1st or 2nd gear, TCM energizes shift solenoid to close fluid inlet port. Shift solenoid is activated by applying voltage to one side (high side) of shift solenoid and, grounding other side (low side) of shift solenoid.

High Side Driver (HSD) is a circuit of the TCM which acts as a switch between shift solenoid and supply voltage. High side of shift solenoid is permanently supplied voltage, except in back-up mode or when ignition is off. TCM continually monitors shift solenoid connection to Low Side Driver (LSD) for either high or low voltage. The LSD is a circuit of the TCM used as a switch between shift solenoid and ground. When shift solenoid is turned on, TCM completes a ground circuit for shift solenoid.

When ignition is turned on before engine is cranked, TCM activates shift solenoids and band apply solenoid to check operating circuits of each solenoid for a short or open circuit. To do so, the gear is set to 4th gear, 3rd gear, 1st gear, 1st gear with band applied and 4th gear with no HSD. Each of the 5 tests requires .15 second. If engine is cranked before end of all tests, remaining tests are not performed.

Diagnostic Aids – This diagnostic test is an electrical test performed by the TCM. DTC 42 will set when the following detection conditions are present when ignition is on.

- Shift solenoid low side terminal A3 to TCM is shorted to battery voltage.
- Engine speed is less than 480 RPM and output shaft speed is zero RPM.
- Conditions must be present for .15-1.03 seconds after ignition is turned on.

Once DTC 42 is set, CHECK TRANS light will flash and transmission will go into back-up mode. Back-up mode may be cleared by turning ignition off, then back on again.

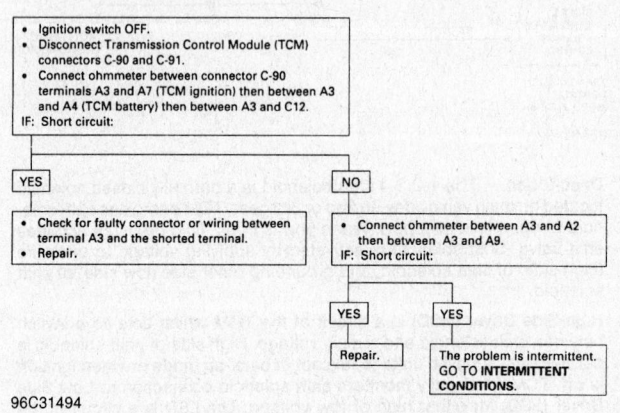

96C31494

AUTOMATIC TRANSMISSIONS
1995 Hydra-Matic 4L30-E Electronic Controls (Cont.)

3-661

DTC 43: TCC SOLENOID CIRCUIT (SHORT CIRCUIT TO GROUND)
(1995 TROOPER)

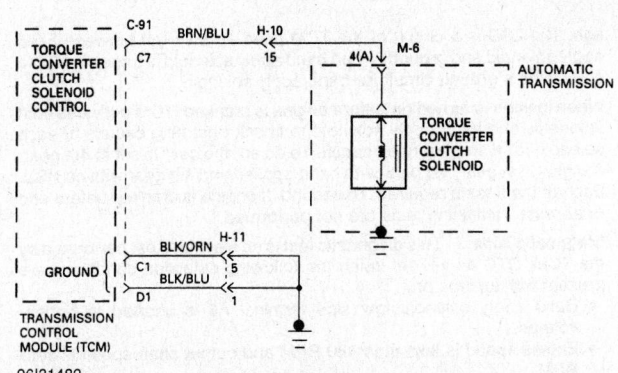

96I31482

Description – Torque Converter Clutch (TCC) solenoid is located on adapter case valve body. TCM energizes TCC solenoid to open fluid port. When fluid port is open, line pressure actuates converter clutch control valve which exhausts the fluid, engaging torque converter clutch. TCM allows torque converter clutch to engage only when:
- Transmission is at normal operating temperature.
- Brake pedal is in released position.
- Transmission is in 2nd, 3rd or 4th gear.
- Engine is at normal operating temperature.
- Shift pattern requests TCC apply.
- Shift is finished.
- DTC 33, 55, 64 or 65 are not present.

TCC solenoid is activated by applying voltage to one side (high side) of TCC solenoid, and grounding other side (low side) of TCC solenoid.

High Side Driver (HSD) is a circuit of the TCM which acts as a switch between TCC solenoid and supply voltage. High side of TCC solenoid is used to turn TCC solenoid on or off, as low side of TCC solenoid is permanently connected to ground. When transmission is in back-up mode or ignition is turned off, TCC solenoid is turned off.

The TCM continually monitors TCC solenoid connection to HSD for either high or low voltage. The only test performed is when engine is cranked and TCC solenoid is turned on.

Diagnostic Aids – This diagnostic test is an electrical test performed by the TCM. DTC 43 will set when TCC solenoid high side to TCM terminal C7 is shorted to ground and condition is present for .07 second after ignition is turned on. If DTC 43 is set, TCC will be shut off. CHECK TRANS light will NOT flash, and transmission will NOT go into back-up mode. Transmission will return to normal operation by turning ignition off, then back on again.

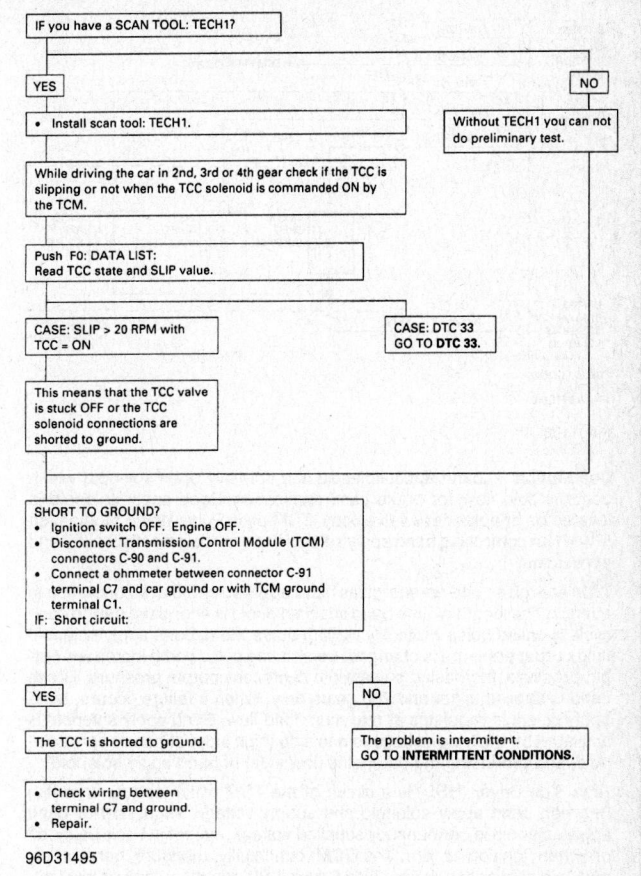

96D31495

3-662

AUTOMATIC TRANSMISSIONS
1995 Hydra-Matic 4L30-E Electronic Controls (Cont.)

DTC 44: BAND APPLY SOLENOID CIRCUIT (SHORT CIRCUIT TO B+)
(1995 TROOPER)

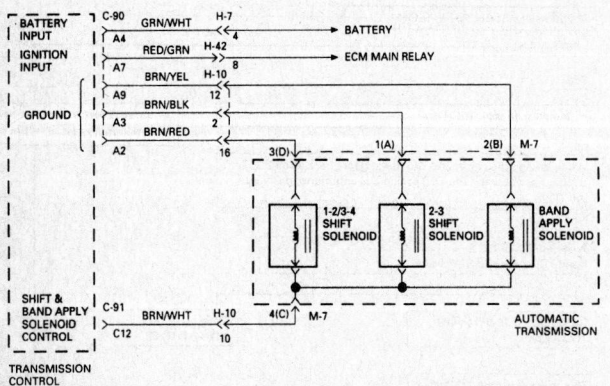

96A31492

Description – Band apply solenoid is a normally open solenoid which controls fluid flow for brake band application. Band apply solenoid is located on adapter case valve body. TCM uses Pulse Width Modulation (PWM) for controlling band apply solenoid to provide smooth brake band application.

TCM energizes and de-energizes band apply solenoid at a constant frequency. The length of time band apply solenoid is energized during each cycle is called pulse width. By varying pulse width, band apply solenoid fluid output pressure is changed. Decreasing pulse width increases output pressure. Increasing pulse width decreases output pressure. Brake band is applied in 1st and 2nd gears only. When a failure occurs, band apply solenoid regulates at maximum fluid flow. Band apply solenoid is activated by applying voltage to one side (high side) of band apply solenoid, and grounding the other side (low side) of band apply solenoid.

High Side Driver (HSD) is a circuit of the TCM which acts as a switch between band apply solenoid and supply voltage. High side of band apply solenoid is permanently supplied voltage, except in back-up mode or when ignition is off. The TCM continually monitors band apply solenoid connection to Low Side Driver (LSD) for either high or low voltage. The LSD is a circuit of the TCM used as a switch between band apply solenoid and ground. When band apply solenoid is turned on, TCM completes a ground circuit for band apply solenoid.

When ignition is turned on before engine is cranked, TCM activates shift solenoids and band apply solenoid to check operating circuits of each solenoid for a short or open circuit. To do so, the gear is set to 4th gear, 3rd gear, 1st gear, 1st gear with band applied and 4th gear with no HSD. Each of the 5 tests requires .15 second. If engine is cranked before end of all tests, remaining tests are not performed.

Diagnostic Aids – This diagnostic test is an electrical test performed by the TCM. DTC 44 will set when the following detection conditions are present with ignition on.
- Band apply solenoid low side terminal A9 is shorted to battery voltage.
- Engine speed is less than 480 RPM and output shaft speed is zero RPM.
- Conditions must be present for .15-1.18 seconds after ignition is turned on.

Once DTC 44 is set, CHECK TRANS light will flash and transmission will go into back-up mode. Back-up mode may be cleared by turning ignition off, then back on again.

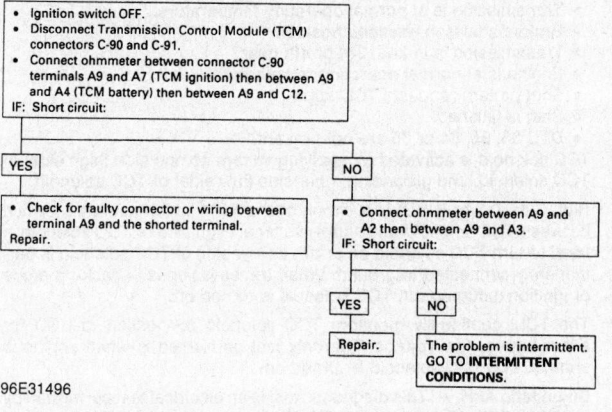

96E31496

AUTOMATIC TRANSMISSIONS
1995 Hydra-Matic 4L30-E Electronic Controls (Cont.)

3-663

DTC 46: SHIFT SOLENOID CIRCUIT (SHORT CIRCUIT TO B+)
(1995 TROOPER)

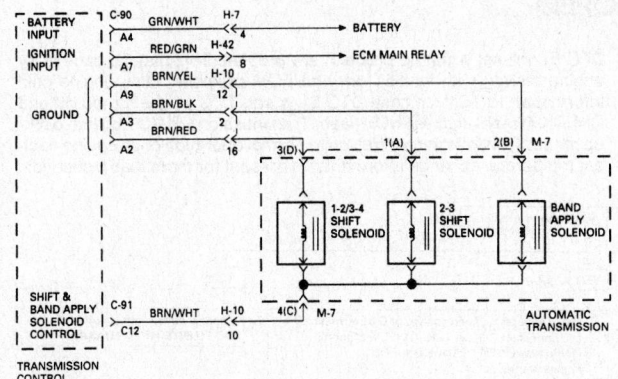

96A31492

Description – Shift solenoids are located on main valve body. Shift solenoids are activated by applying voltage to one side (high side) of shift solenoid, and grounding the other side (low side) of shift solenoid.

High Side Driver (HSD) is a circuit of TCM which acts as a switch between shift solenoid and supply voltage. High side of shift solenoid is permanently supplied voltage, except in back-up mode or when ignition is off. TCM continually monitors shift solenoid connection to HSD for either high or low voltage.

When ignition is turned on before engine is cranked, TCM activates shift solenoids and band apply solenoid to check operating circuits of each solenoid for a short or open circuit. To do so, the gear is set to 4th gear, 3rd gear, 1st gear, 1st gear with band applied and 4th gear with no HSD. Each of the 5 tests requires .15 second. If engine is cranked before end of all tests, remaining tests are not performed.

Diagnostic Aids – This diagnostic test is an electrical test performed by the TCM. DTC 46 will set when the following detection conditions are present when ignition is on.

- Shift solenoid high side terminal C12 to TCM is shorted to battery voltage.
- Engine speed is less than 480 RPM and output shaft speed is zero RPM.
- Conditions must be present for .15-1.34 seconds after ignition is turned on.

Once DTC 46 is set, CHECK TRANS light will flash and transmission will go into back-up mode. Back-up mode may be cleared by turning ignition off, then back on again.

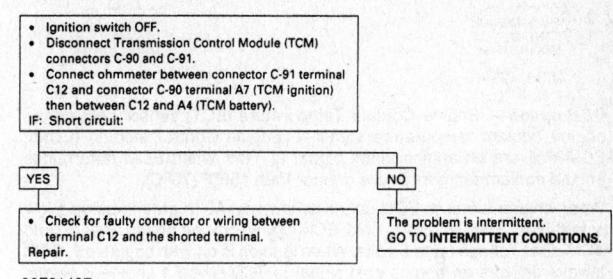

96F31497

3-664

AUTOMATIC TRANSMISSIONS
1995 Hydra-Matic 4L30-E Electronic Controls (Cont.)

DTC 51: ENGINE COOLANT TEMP. SENSOR CIRCUIT
(SHORT CIRCUIT TO B+, GROUND OR OPEN CIRCUIT)
(1995 TROOPER)

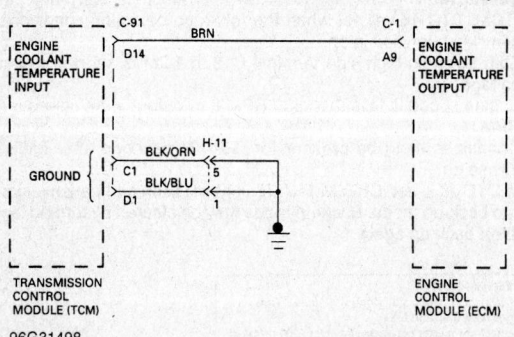

96G31498

Description – Engine Coolant Temperature (ECT) sensor delivers an engine coolant temperature signal to Engine Control Module (ECM). ECM delivers an engine warm signal to TCM when ECM determines engine coolant temperature is greater than 158°F (70°C).

When engine is warm, ECM connects terminal A9 to ground using a low side driver. When engine is cold, ECM opens ground on terminal A9 and TCM pulls voltage up to 5 volts. When ignition is on with engine off, ECM always delivers an engine cold signal to TCM, even if engine is warm. Engine coolant temperature signal between ECM and TCM is valid only with engine running.

Diagnostic Aids – DTC 51 will set when an engine cold or engine warm condition is detected. This diagnostic test is not an electrical test performed by the TCM, but a comparison of signal input.
The following conditions must be present for detection of engine cold.
- Wire between ECM terminal A9 and TCM terminal D14 is open or shorted to battery voltage.
- Transmission oil temperature is greater than 212°F (100°C), or more than 20 minutes since last ignition cycle.
- Conditions must be present for at least 6 seconds.
The following conditions must be present for detection of engine warm.
- Wire between ECM terminal A9 and TCM terminal D14 is shorted to ground.
- Transmission oil temperature is less than 32°F (0°C).
- Voltage on transmission oil temperature sensor circuit must be less than 4.74 volts.
- Conditions must be present for at least 6 seconds.

DTC 51 will set when no problem are present. This may be caused by engine stalling with ignition on, and ECM providing false engine cold information to TCM. In case DTC 51 is set, TCC will be turned off and CHECK TRANS light will NOT flash. Transmission will NOT go into back-up mode. Transmission will return to normal operation once engine coolant temperature change information is present for more than 6 seconds.

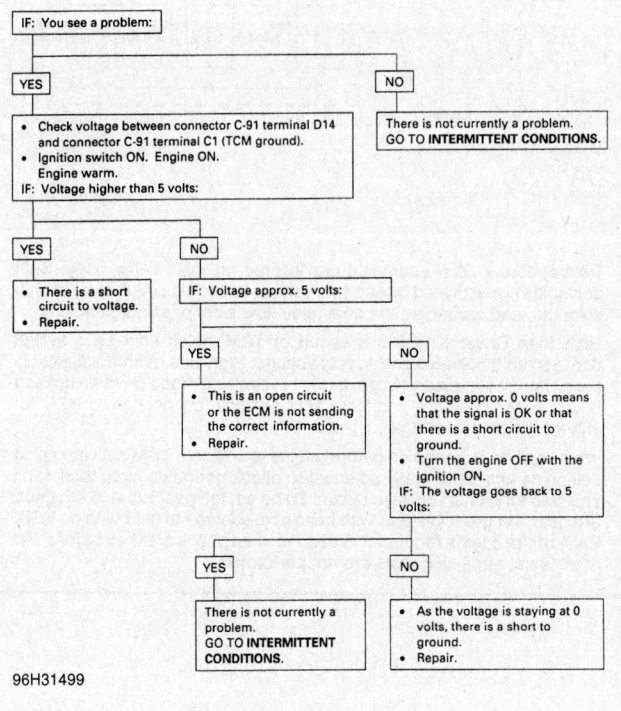

96H31499

AUTOMATIC TRANSMISSIONS
1995 Hydra-Matic 4L30-E Electronic Controls (Cont.)

3-665

DTC 52: KICKDOWN SWITCH ALWAYS ON OR SHORT CIRCUIT TO GROUND
(1995 TROOPER)

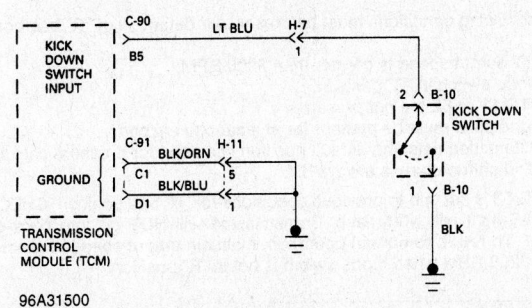

96A31500

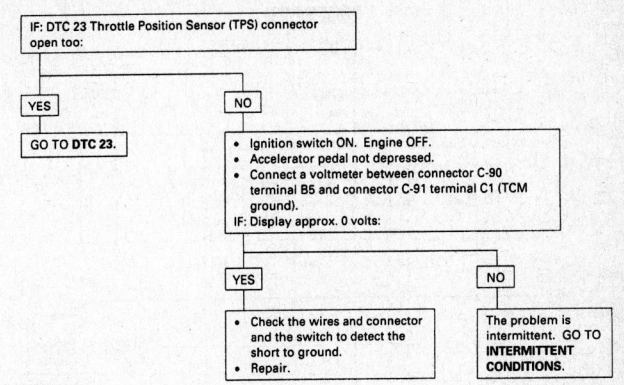

96B31501

Description – When accelerator pedal is fully depressed, kickdown switch closes and delivers a ground signal to TCM. TCM uses this signal for controlling transmission shifting with high engine RPM. When kickdown switch is closed, Throttle Position Sensor (TPS) is already at 100 percent.

Diagnostic Aids – This diagnostic test is not an electrical test performed by the TCM, but a comparison of signal input. DTC 52 will set when the following conditions are present.

- Kickdown switch is on (short to ground) and TPS is less than 70 percent.
- DTC 21 or 22 are not present.
- Condition must be present for at least one second.

If DTC 52 is set, CHECK TRANS light will NOT flash. Transmission will NOT go into back-up mode. Transmission will return to normal operation once kickdown switch is off during DTC detection time.

3-666

AUTOMATIC TRANSMISSIONS
1995 Hydra-Matic 4L30-E Electronic Controls (Cont.)

DTC 53: MODE SWITCH IN "P", "N" OR "R" BAD POSITION
(1995 TROOPER)

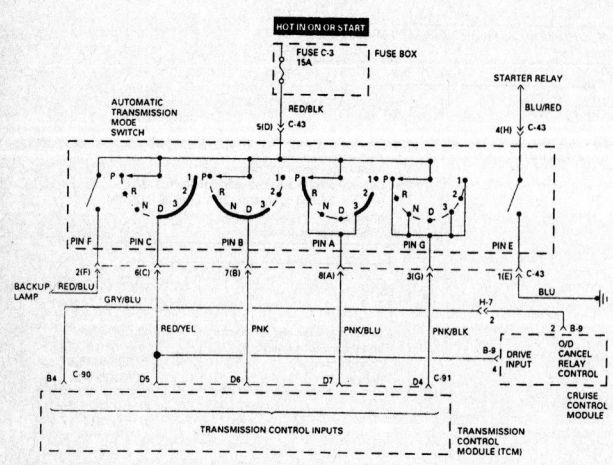

96C31502

Description – Mode switch delivers an input signal to TCM to indicate gearshift lever position. Mode switch is located on side of transmission. Mode switch also provides information for engine cranking and control of back-up lights. Fuse C-3 provides voltage to mode switch. If fuse C-3 is open, mode switch will not operate, and DTC 54 will be set. Ensure shift linkage is properly adjusted, as DTC 53 may be caused by improperly adjusted shift linkage.

Diagnostic Aids – This diagnostic test is not an electrical test performed by the TCM, but a comparison of signal input.
The following conditions must be present for detection of "P" or "N" bad position.
- A/T input speed is less than 3000 RPM.
- Throttle position sensor (TPS) is greater than 20 percent.
- Mode switch in "P" or "N" position.
- DTC 13, 21 or 22 are not present.
- Conditions must be present for at least 4 seconds.
After detection time, default position assumed for pressure calculation and shift pattern is always "D".

If DTC 53 is set due to previous conditions for "P" or "N" bad position, CHECK TRANS light will NOT flash. Transmission will NOT go into back-up mode. To return to normal operation, maintain engine speed at greater than 3200 RPM with TPS higher than 20 percent when mode switch is not in "P" or "N" position.

The following conditions must be present for detection of "R" bad position.
- A/T output speed is greater than 3200 RPM.
- Mode switch in "R" position.
- DTC 11 or 62 are not present.
- Conditions must be present for at least one second.
After detection time, the default position assumed for pressure calculation and shift pattern is always "D".

If DTC 53 is set due to previous conditions for "R" bad position, CHECK TRANS light will NOT flash. Transmission will NOT go into back-up mode. To return to normal operation, maintain output speed at greater than 3200 RPM when mode switch is not in "R" position.

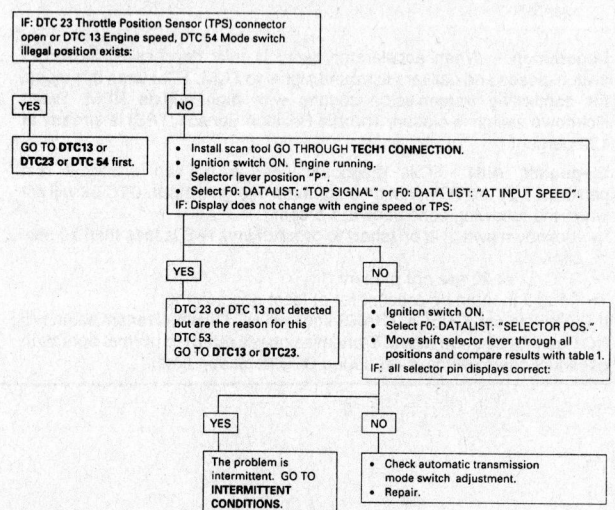

Table 1

	SHIFT SELECTOR POSITION						
TECH1 DISPLAY	P	R	N	D	3	2	L
SELECTOR PIN A	X	X				X	X
SELECTOR PIN B		X	X	X	X		
SELECTOR PIN C				X	X	X	X
SELECTOR PIN P	X		X		X		X

Note: "X" indicates TECH1 displays "ACTIVE".

96D31503

AUTOMATIC TRANSMISSIONS
1995 Hydra-Matic 4L30-E Electronic Controls (Cont.)

3-667

DTC 54: MODE SWITCH ILLEGAL POSITION
(1995 TROOPER)

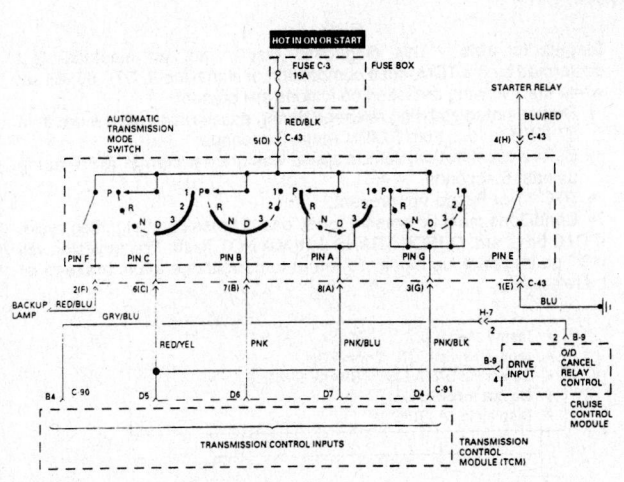

96C31502

- Install scan tool.
- Ignition switch ON. Engine OFF.
- Selector F0: DATALIST: "SELECTOR POS".
- Move shift selector lever through all positions and compare results with Table 1.
IF: all selector pin displays correct:

YES → The problem is intermittent. GO TO **INTERMITTENT CONDITIONS.**

NO → IF: all selector pin displays incorrect:

YES → Check fuse and wire to connector C-43 terminal 5 (D) for opens. GO THROUGH MODE SWITCH SETTING PROCEDURE (PAGE: 7A-157). If problem not solved, replace mode switch.

NO → Disconnect mode switch connector C-43.
- Connect ohmmeter between terminal 5(D) and respectively all terminals of mode switch connector C-43.
- Move shift selector lever through all positions and compare results with Table 1.
IF: One selector pin display is incorrect:

YES → Check the wire and connector. Repair.

NO → Check wire to cruise control unit and Transmission Control Module (TCM). Repair.

Table 1

	SHIFT SELECTOR POSITION						
TECH1 DISPLAY	P	R	N	D	3	2	L
SELECTOR PIN A	X	X			X	X	
SELECTOR PIN B		X	X	X	X		
SELECTOR PIN C				X	X	X	X
SELECTOR PIN P	X		X		X		X

Note: "X" indicates TECH1 displays "ACTIVE".

96E31504

Description – Mode switch delivers input signal to TCM to indicate shift lever position. Mode switch is located on side of transmission. Mode switch also provides information for engine cranking and control of back-up lights. Fuse C-3 provides voltage to mode switch. If fuse C-3 is open, mode switch will not operate and DTC 54 will be set. Ensure shift linkage is properly adjusted, as DTC 54 may be caused by improperly adjusted shift linkage.

Diagnostic Aids – This diagnostic test is an electrical test performed by the TCM. DTC 54 will set when the following detection conditions are present.
- Selector pin "A", "B" Or "C" are not active and no position is identified.
- Based on TABLE 1, in "P" position, DTC is set when an open circuit or short to ground is present at pin "A".
- Conditions must be present for at least 5 seconds.
Once DTC 54 is set, CHECK TRANS light will flash and transmission will go into back-up mode. Back-up mode may be cleared by turning ignition off, then back on again.

DTC 55: BRAKE SWITCH CIRCUIT
(SHORT CIRCUIT TO GROUND OR OPEN CIRCUIT)
(1995 TROOPER)

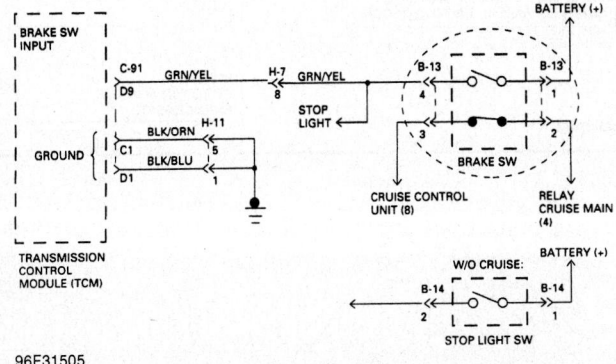

96F31505

Description – Brake switch delivers an input signal to TCM to indicate vehicle braking. TCM uses input signal from brake switch for controlling Torque Converter Clutch (TCC). Brake switch may be referred to as brakelight switch or stoplight switch.

Diagnostic Aids – This diagnostic test is not an electrical test performed by the TCM, but a comparison of signal input. DTC 55 will set when the following detection conditions are present.
- Brakes noted as being applied during acceleration from less than 6 MPH to more than 37 MPH within 6 seconds.
- After this acceleration, vehicle speed was greater than 37 MPH during at least 6 seconds.
- DTC 11 or 62 are not present.
- Conditions must be present for at least 5 times during ignition cycle.
If DTC 55 is set, CHECK TRANS light will NOT flash. Transmission will NOT go into back-up mode. To return to normal operation, brake must be released.

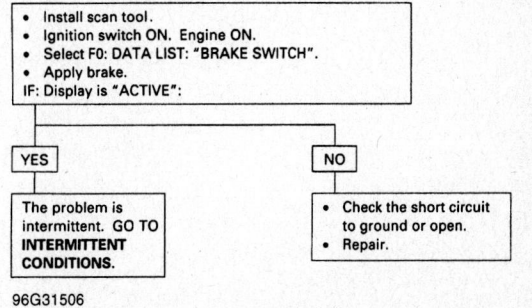

- Install scan tool.
- Ignition switch ON. Engine ON.
- Select F0: DATA LIST: "BRAKE SWITCH".
- Apply brake.
IF: Display is "ACTIVE":

YES → The problem is intermittent. GO TO **INTERMITTENT CONDITIONS.**

NO → Check the short circuit to ground or open. Repair.

96G31506

3-668

AUTOMATIC TRANSMISSIONS
1995 Hydra-Matic 4L30-E Electronic Controls (Cont.)

DTC 56: BRAKE SWITCH CIRCUIT (SHORT CIRCUIT TO B+)
(1995 TROOPER)

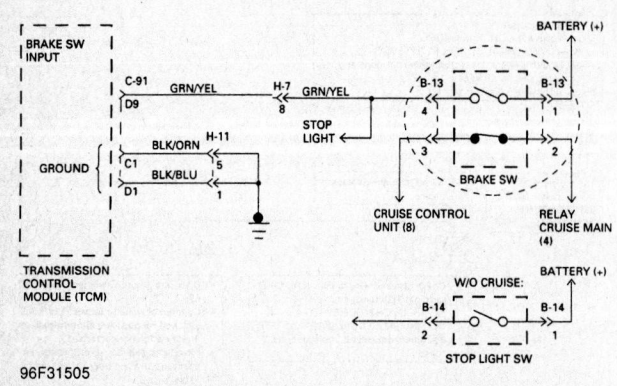

96F31505

Description – Brake switch delivers an input signal to TCM to indicate vehicle braking. TCM uses input signal from brake switch for controlling Torque Converter Clutch (TCC). Brake switch may be referred to as brakelight switch or stoplight switch.

Diagnostic Aids – This diagnostic test is not an electrical test performed by the TCM, but a comparison of signal input. DTC 56 will set when the following detection conditions are present.

- Brakes noted as being released during deceleration from more than 37 MPH to less than 6 MPH within 6 seconds.
- Before deceleration, vehicle speed was greater than 37 MPH during at least 6 seconds.
- DTC 11 or 62 are not present.
- Conditions must be present for at least 5 times during ignition cycle.

If DTC 56 is set, CHECK TRANS light will NOT flash. Transmission will NOT go into back-up mode. To return to normal operation, brake must be released.

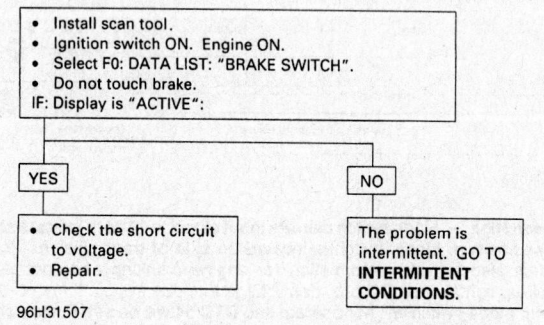

96H31507

DTC 61: GEAR ERROR (1995 TROOPER)

Description – The TCM calculates slippage of Torque Converter Clutch (TCC) and transmission based upon engine speed, output speed and gear ratio. TCC should slip a specified amount at high engine speeds. Transmission should not slip more than a specified value when there is no shift.

Diagnostic Aids – This diagnostic test is not an electrical test performed by the TCM, but a comparison of signal input. DTC 56 will set when the following detection conditions are present.

- Engine speed is greater than 3500 RPM.
- Slippage must be greater than specified amount in specified gear: 1st gear =595 RPM, 2nd gear =556 RPM, 3rd gear =536 RPM, 4th gear =528 RPM.
- DTC 11, 13 or 62 are not present.
- Last change of shift solenoid took longer than 3 seconds.
- Conditions must be present for at least 3 seconds.

Once DTC 61 is set, CHECK TRANS light will flash and transmission will go into back-up mode. Back-up mode may be cleared by turning ignition off, then back on again.

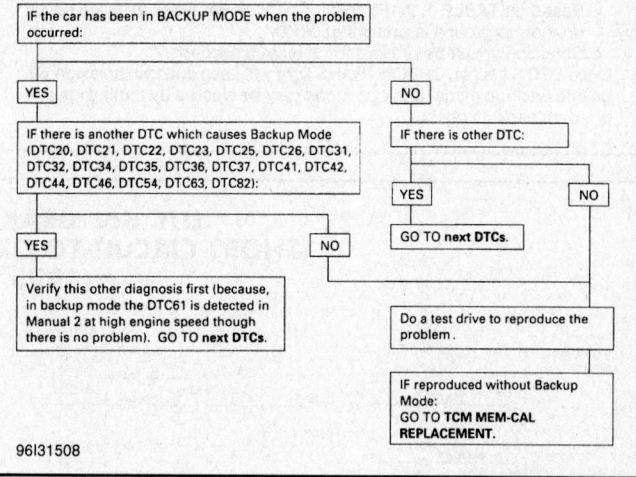

96I31508

AUTOMATIC TRANSMISSIONS
1995 Hydra-Matic 4L30-E Electronic Controls (Cont.)

3-669

DTC 62: DOWNSHIFT PROTECTION (1995 TROOPER)

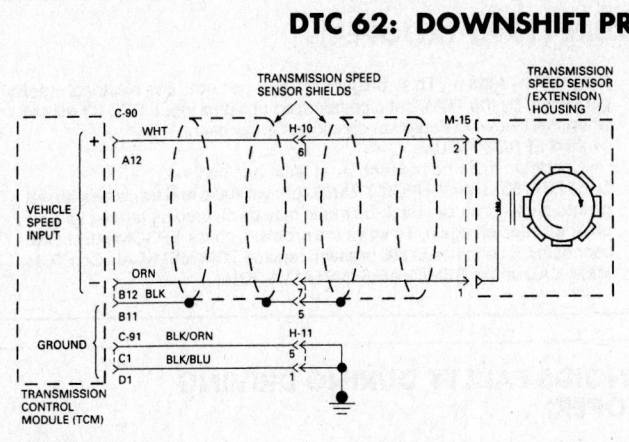

96D30752

Description – Transmission speed sensor delivers a vehicle signal to TCM. Speed sensor is mounted on transmission extension housing above toothed target wheel mounted on output shaft. As output shaft rotates the toothed target wheel, a variable voltage is induced in magnetic pickup on speed sensor. As a result, speed sensor sends an AC signal to TCM in proportion to vehicle speed.

Output speed information from transmission speed sensor is used to determine transmission shifting. If output speed information changes suddenly due to an open circuit or electrical interference, transmission will downshift. To avoid this, TCM constantly monitors variations of output speed. If variation in output speed is too great when output speed is greater than 2900 RPM, DTC 62 is set.

Diagnostic Aids – This diagnostic test is not an electrical test performed by the TCM, but a comparison of signal input. DTC 62 will set when the following detection conditions are present.
- Variation in output speed is greater than 512 RPM.
- Ignition is on for more than 5 seconds.
- Mode switch is not in "P", "N" or "R" position.
- Last output speed was greater than 2900 RPM.
- Conditions must be present for at least .1 second.

Once DTC 62 is set, CHECK TRANS light will flash and transmission will go into back-up mode. Back-up mode may be cleared by turning ignition off, then back on again.

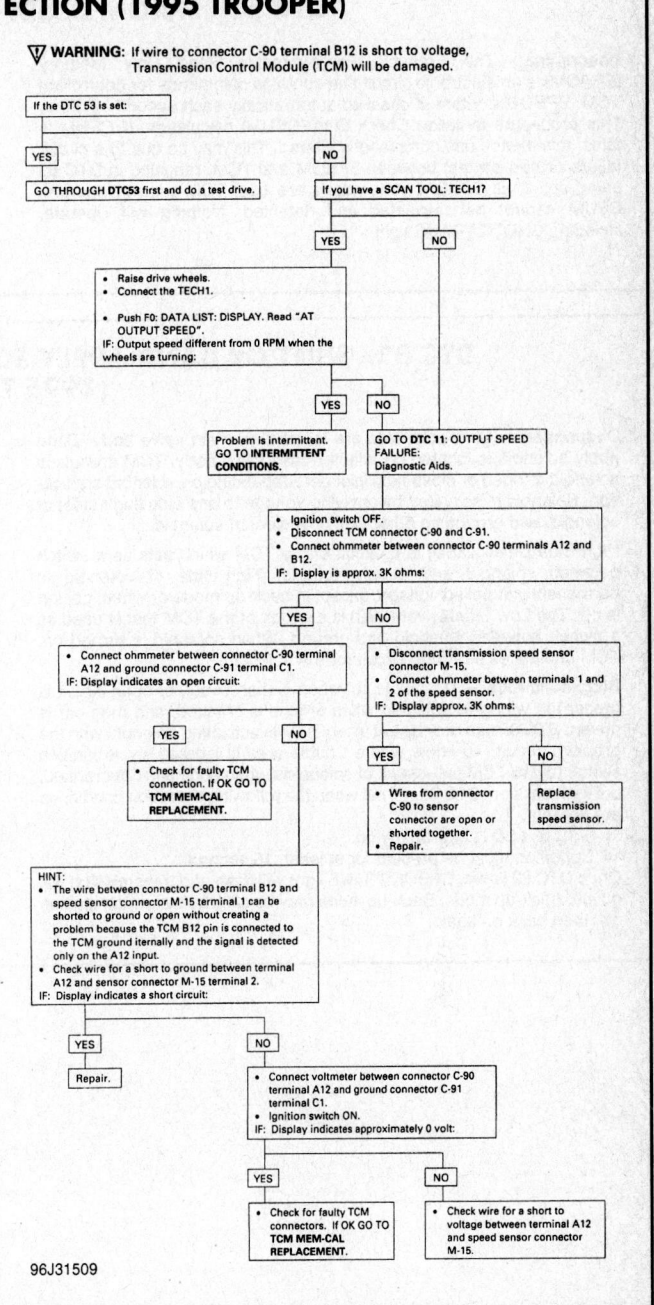

96J31509

3-670

AUTOMATIC TRANSMISSIONS
1995 Hydra-Matic 4L30-E Electronic Controls (Cont.)

DTC 63: EPROM CSUM FAILURE (1995 TROOPER)

Description – The Erasable Programmable Read Only Memory (EPROM) is an electronic circuit that contains commands for controlling TCM. EPROM content is checked automatically each second by TCM. This procedure is called Check Sum (CSUM) calculation. If CSUM is false, this means one command is altered. This may be due to a circuit failure or bad contact between EPROM and TCM, resulting in DTC 63 being set. If all EPROM connections are bad, TCM will not operate. CSUM cannot be calculated and detected. Nothing will operate, including CHECK TRANS light.

Diagnostic Aids – This diagnostic test is not an electrical test performed by the TCM, but a comparison of signal input. DTC 63 will set when the following detection conditions are present.
- Bad EPROM CSUM.
- Condition must be present for at least one second.

Once DTC 63 is set, CHECK TRANS light will flash and transmission will go into back-up mode. Back-up mode may be cleared by turning ignition off, then back on again. To solve the problem, check EPROM MEM-CAL connector. If condition is still present, replace TCM MEM-CAL. See TCM MEM-CAL under REMOVAL & INSTALLATION.

DTC 82: SHIFT OR BAND APPLY SOLENOIDS FAULTY DURING DRIVING (1995 TROOPER)

Description – Shift solenoids are located on main valve body. Band apply solenoid is located on adapter case valve body. TCM energizes solenoid to open or close fluid inlet port depending on solenoid application. Solenoid is activated by applying voltage to one side (high side) of solenoid, and grounding other side (low side) of solenoid.

High Side Driver (HSD) is a circuit of the TCM which acts as a switch between solenoid and supply voltage. High side of solenoid is permanently supplied voltage, except in back-up mode or when ignition is off. The Low Side Driver (LSD) is a circuit of the TCM that is used as a switch between solenoid and ground. When solenoid is turned on, TCM completes a ground circuit for the solenoid.

Diagnostic Aids – DTC 82 is set when a short circuit or open circuit is present in wiring to solenoid when engine is cranked, and then car is driven. DTC 82 can only be set when TCM is activating solenoid with the problem circuit. To know where trouble area is located, cycle ignition switch to use TCM self-check of solenoids when engine is not cranked, but ignition is on. DTC 82 will set when the following detection conditions are present.
- HSD or LSD is improperly on.
- Condition must be present for at least .15 second.

Once DTC 82 is set, CHECK TRANS light will flash and transmission will go into back-up mode. Back-up mode may be cleared by turning ignition off, then back on again.

> This DTC is set when the car is driven (Engine ON) but the diagnostic is not specific.
> To correctly identify the problem, do an IGNITION CYCLE.

> If you have not already done an IGNITION CYCLE:
> - Turn ignition switch OFF. Turn ignition switch ON and wait 3 seconds to have the specific diagnostic done.
> - Then you can turn the engine ON or not.

> Check on Scan Tool or Flashing Code what other DTC is provided. It should be one of the following:
> DTC31 or DTC32 or DTC34 or DTC36 or DTC41 or DTC42 or DTC44 or DTC46.

> GO TO this **DTC**.

96C31510

AUTOMATIC TRANSMISSIONS
1995 Hydra-Matic 4L30-E Electronic Controls (Cont.)

3-671

WIRING DIAGRAMS

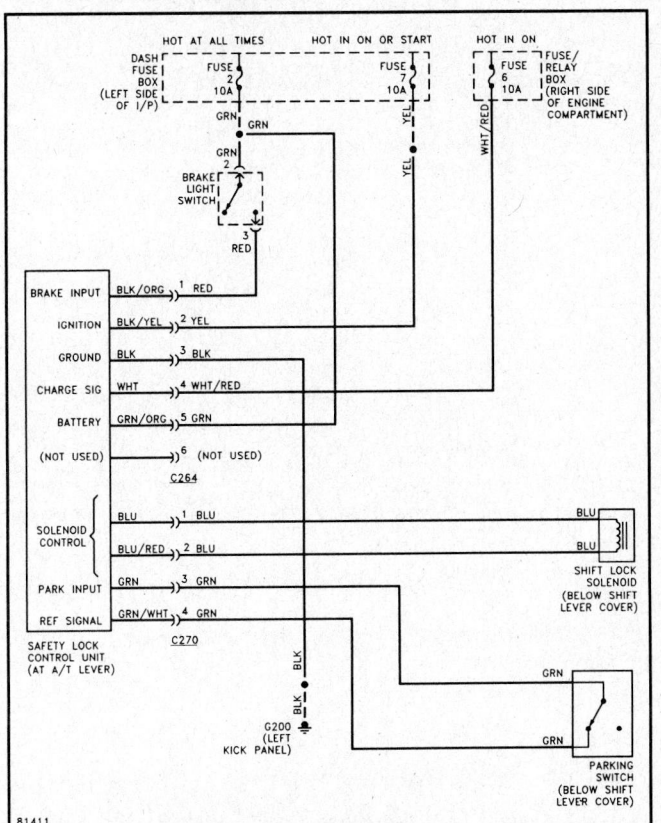

Fig. 19: Shift Lock System Wiring Diagram (1995 Passport – Early Production)

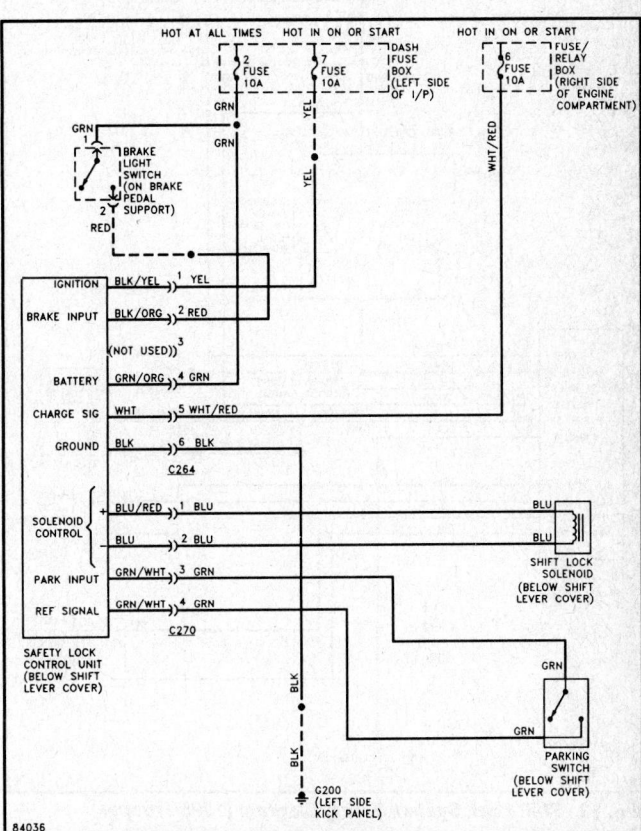

Fig. 21: Shift Lock System Wiring Diagram (1995 Rodeo – Early Production)

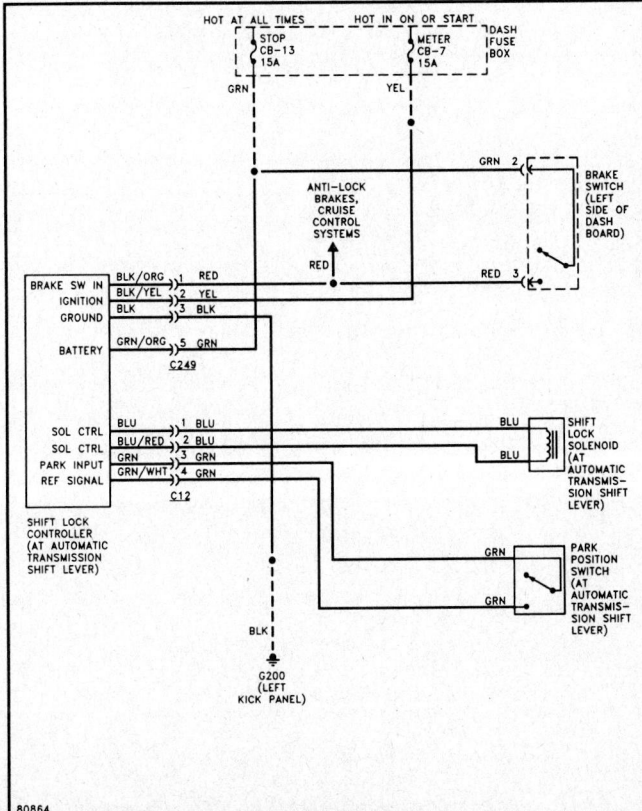

Fig. 20: Shift Lock System Wiring Diagram (1995 Passport – Late Production)

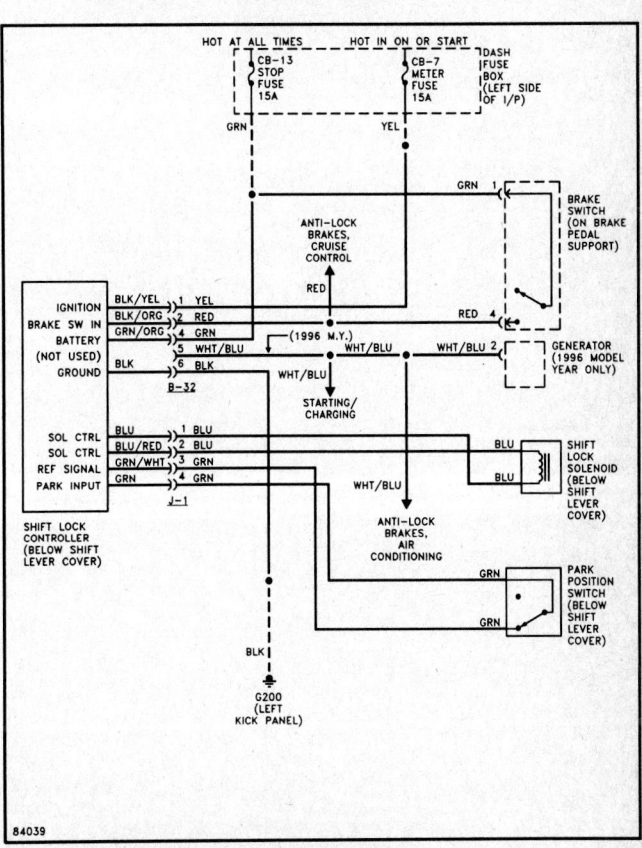

Fig. 22: Shift Lock System Wiring Diagram (1995 Rodeo – Late Production)

3-672

AUTOMATIC TRANSMISSIONS
1995 Hydra-Matic 4L30-E Electronic Controls (Cont.)

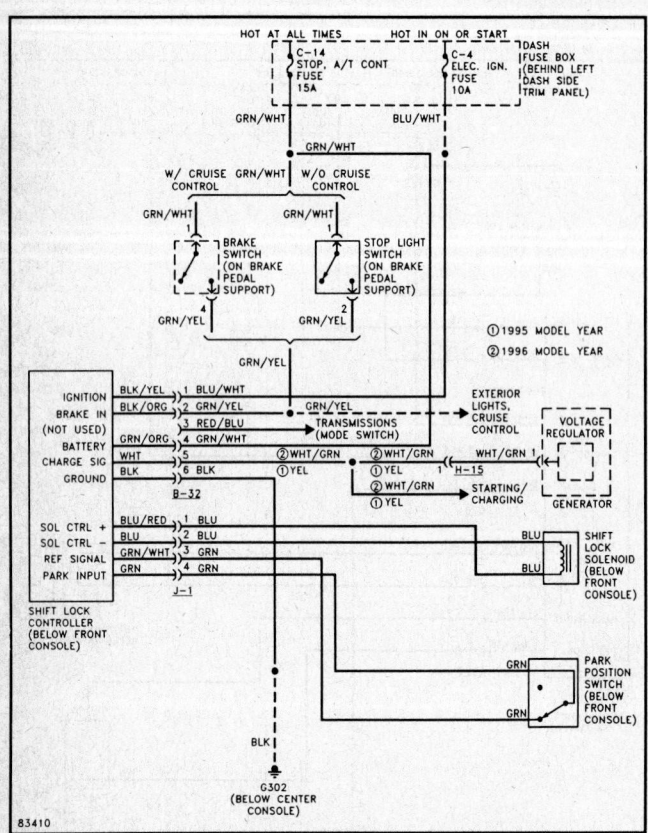

Fig. 23: Shift Lock System Wiring Diagram (1995 Trooper)

AUTOMATIC TRANSMISSIONS
1995 Hydra-Matic 4L30-E Electronic Controls (Cont.)

3-673

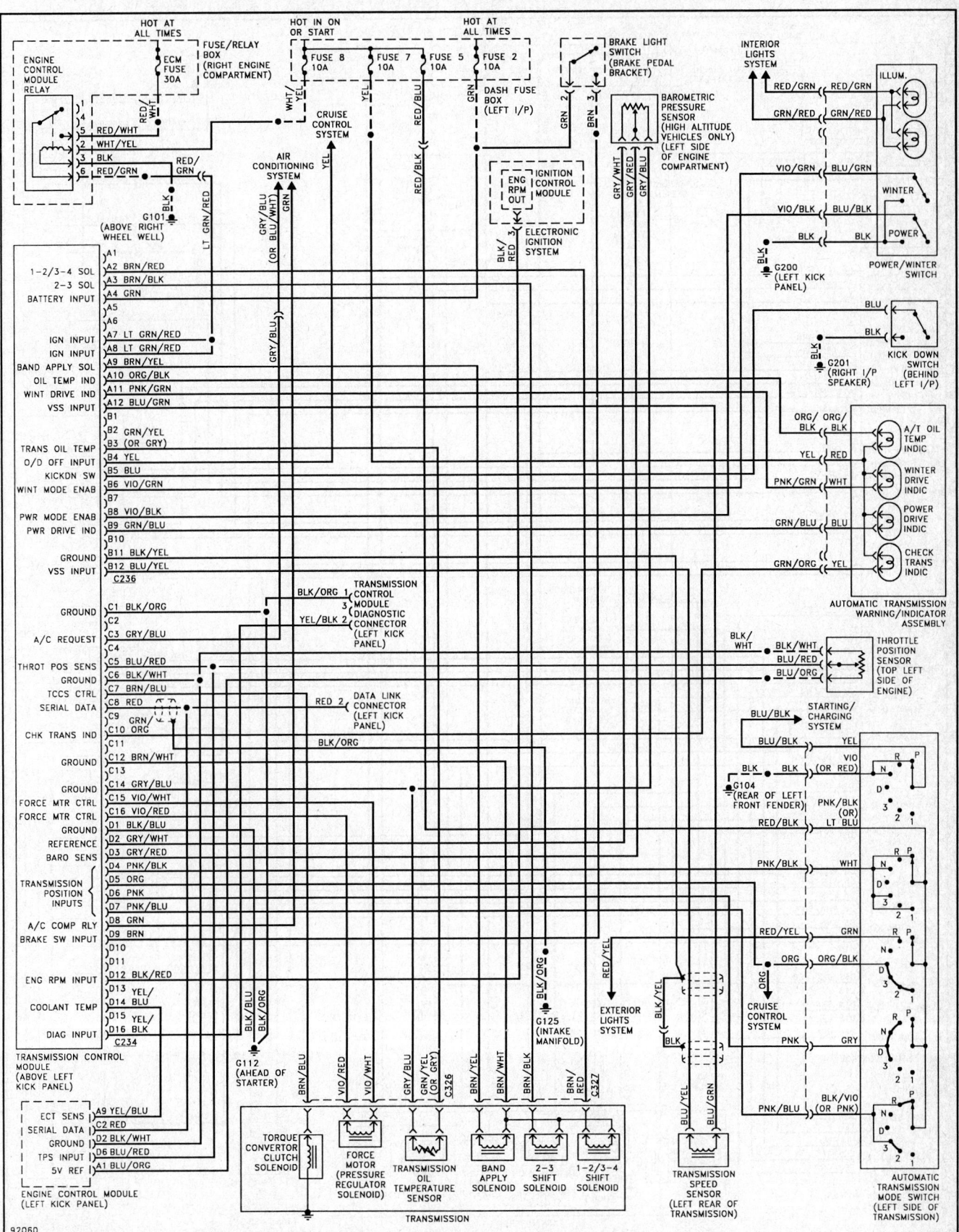

Fig. 24: 4L30-E Transmission Wiring Diagram (1995 Passport & Rodeo – Early Production)

3-674

AUTOMATIC TRANSMISSIONS
1995 Hydra-Matic 4L30-E Electronic Controls (Cont.)

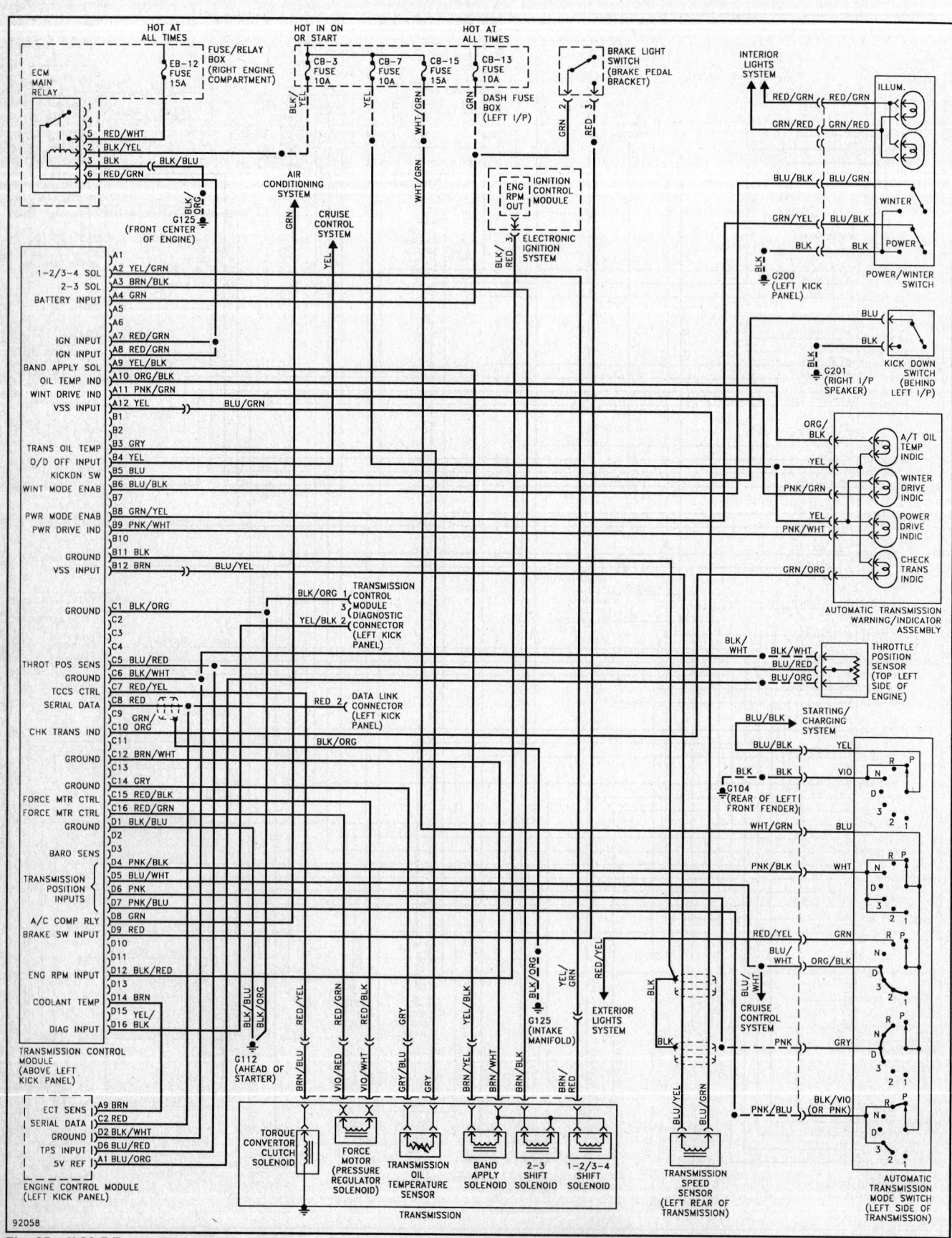

Fig. 25: 4L30-E Transmission Wiring Diagram (1995 Passport & Rodeo - Late Production)

3-675

AUTOMATIC TRANSMISSIONS
1995 Hydra-Matic 4L30-E Electronic Controls (Cont.)

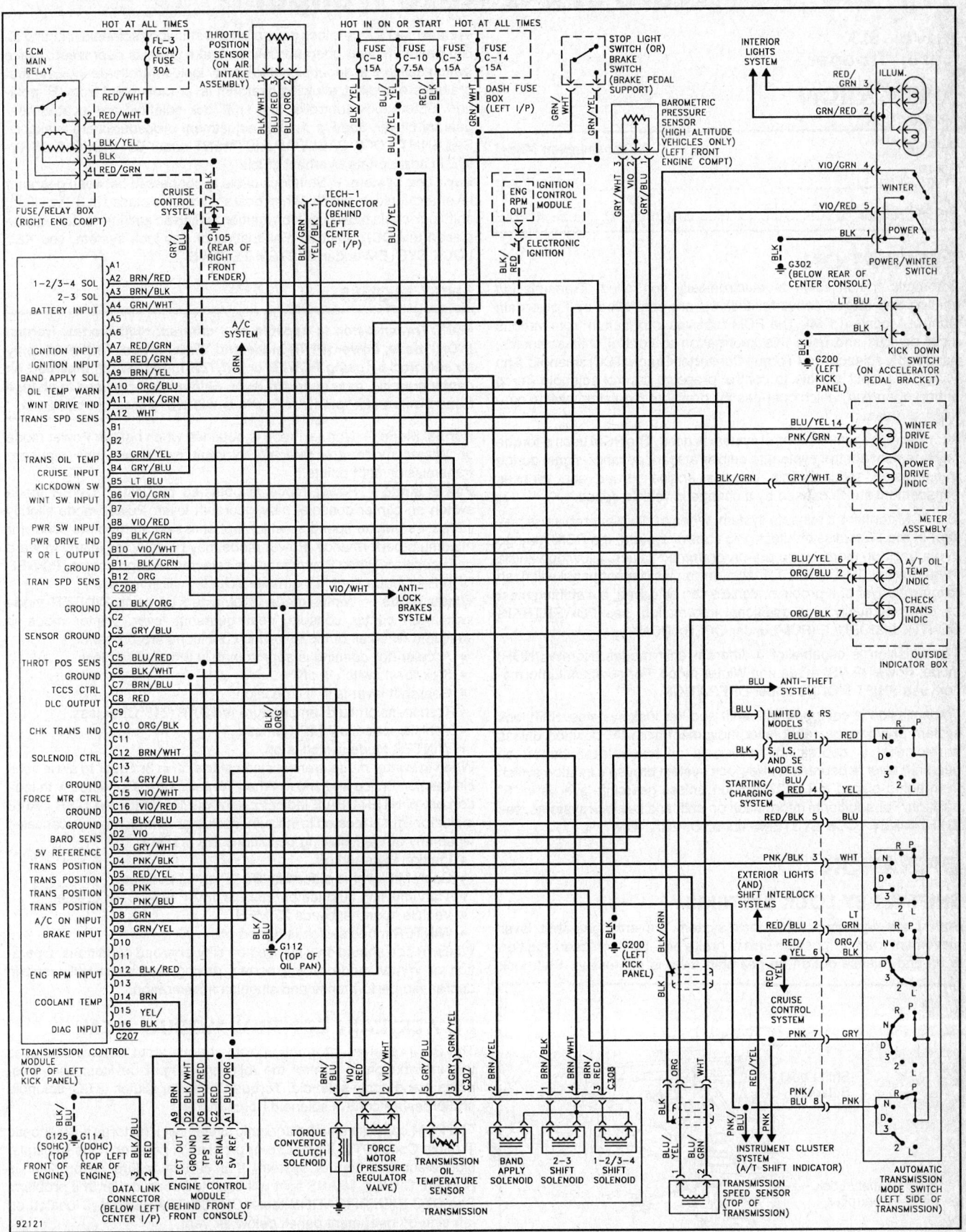

Fig. 26: 4L30-E Transmission Wiring Diagram (1995 Trooper)

AUTOMATIC TRANSMISSIONS
1996 Hydra-Matic 4L30-E Electronic Controls
Acura SLX & Izuzu Trooper

Acura: SLX
Isuzu: Trooper

APPLICATION

APPLICATION

Vehicle	Transmission Model
Acura	
1996 SLX	4L30-E
Isuzu	
1996 Trooper	4L30-E

DESCRIPTION

Automatic transmission is electronically controlled. Transmission shifting and torque converter lock-up are controlled by Powertrain Control Module (PCM). The PCM receives information from various input devices and uses this information to control shift solenoids, band apply solenoid and Torque Converter Clutch (TCC) solenoid. The PCM uses input signals to control pressure control solenoid (force motor) operation, which operates the pressure regulator valve to control line pressure.

A torque management control system is used. The PCM uses a torque management control system to deliver a spark advance signal during transmission shifting. This controls engine torque and reduces engagement shock caused by a change in vehicle speed.

The PCM contains a fail-safe system. When a failure or problem is present in the transmission electronic control system, the PCM may go into a back-up mode using pre-programmed values, allowing vehicle to be driven. The CHECK TRANS light on instrument panel will flash to inform driver of a problem. Vehicle can be driven, but shifting must be done manually. For additional information, see POWERTRAIN CONTROL MODULE (PCM) under OPERATION.

Transmission is capable of 3 different shift modes, Normal (NOR) mode, Power (PWR) mode and Winter mode. For additional information, see SHIFT MODES under OPERATION.

Transmission is equipped with shift and key lock systems. Shift lock system prevents gearshift lever movement from "P" position unless brake pedal is depressed, ignition is on and release button on gearshift lever is depressed. Key lock system prevents ignition switch from being placed in LOCK position unless gearshift lever is in "P" position. For additional information on shift and key lock systems, see SHIFT & KEY LOCK SYSTEMS under OPERATION.

OPERATION

SHIFT & KEY LOCK SYSTEMS

Shift Lock System – Shift lock system prevents gearshift lever movement from "P" position unless brake pedal is depressed, ignition is on and release button on gearshift lever is depressed. Shift lock

system uses a safety lock controller and shift lock solenoid for controlling gearshift lever operation. When brake pedal is depressed, brake switch delivers an input signal to safety lock controller to indicate that brakes are applied, allowing gearshift lever movement from "P" position. Safety lock controller and shift lock solenoid are located near gearshift lever. *See Fig. 1.* Only adjustment procedures are available. See SHIFT LOCK CABLE ADJUSTMENT under ON-VEHICLE SERVICE in appropriate overhaul article.

Key Lock System – Shift lock cable is connected between gearshift lever and ignition switch. When gearshift lever is placed in "P" position, shift lock cable moves lock on ignition switch so ignition switch may be placed in LOCK position. For testing of key lock system, see KEY LOCK SYSTEM under SYSTEM TESTING.

SHIFT MODES

NOTE: Transmission is capable of 3 different shift modes, Normal (NOR) mode, Power (PWR) mode and Winter mode. Shift mode may be selected by using POWER or WINTER mode switch mounted on center console, near gearshift lever. Shift modes are used to change transmission shift points for various vehicle operating conditions.

Normal Mode – Normal mode is obtained when neither Power mode or Winter mode are selected. Normal mode provides standard transmission shift points.

Power Mode – Power mode is obtained by using POWER mode switch on center console, near gearshift lever. Power mode slightly increases engine speed at which transmission shift points occur for maximum performance. Power mode may be selected in any forward gear position. When Power mode is selected with ignition on, POWER DRIVE indicator light in instrument cluster will illuminate.

Winter Mode – Winter mode is obtained by using WINTER mode switch on center console, near gearshift lever. Winter mode is activated when all of the following conditions are present.

- Accelerator opening is approximately 8 percent or less.
- Kickdown switch is off.
- Gearshift lever is in "D" position.
- Transmission fluid temperature is 120°F (248°C) or less.
- Vehicle speed is 7 MPH or less.
- WINTER mode switch is on.

When in Winter mode, transmission starts off in 3rd gear to aid in vehicle traction on ice and snow. When Winter mode is selected with ignition on, WINTER DRIVE indicator light will illuminate. WINTER DRIVE indicator light is located in instrument cluster. Winter mode is canceled when any of the following conditions are present.

- Ignition is turned off.
- Gearshift lever is placed in "3", "2" or "L" position.
- Transmission fluid temperature is 140°F (284°C) or greater.
- Vehicle speed exceeds 22 MPH.
- WINTER mode switch is turned off.

Winter mode should only by used on slippery road conditions. Operation of Winter mode during normal driving conditions will result in decreased performance and sluggish acceleration.

POWERTRAIN CONTROL MODULE (PCM)

The PCM receives information from various input devices and uses this information to control the following output devices: shift solenoids, band apply solenoid, Torque Converter Clutch (TCC) solenoid and pressure control solenoid (force motor).

The PCM contains a self-diagnostic system which stores a Diagnostic Trouble Code (DTC) if a failure or problem is present in the transmission electronic control system. If a certain failure or problem is present, CHECK TRANS light will flash to inform driver of a problem. See DTC IDENTIFICATION table. CHECK TRANS light is located on left side of instrument panel, below air vent.

DTCs may be retrieved to determine transmission problem area. For information on retrieving DTCs, see SELF-DIAGNOSTIC SYSTEM. The PCM contains a fail-safe system. When a certain failure or problem is present in the transmission electronic control system, the PCM

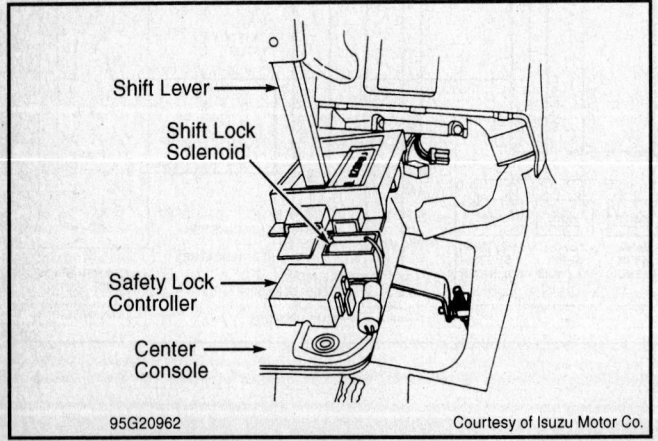

95G20962   Courtesy of Isuzu Motor Co.

Fig. 1: Identifying Safety Lock Controller

AUTOMATIC TRANSMISSIONS
1996 Hydra-Matic 4L30-E Electronic Controls
Acura SLX & Isuzu Trooper (Cont.)

3-677

may go into back-up mode using pre-programmed values, allowing vehicle to be driven. The CHECK TRANS light may flash to inform driver of a problem. See DTC IDENTIFICATION table.

Vehicle can be driven in back-up mode, but shifting must be done manually. When manually shifting transmission, if gearshift lever is placed in "D" or "3" position, transmission remains in 4th gear. If gearshift lever is placed in "2" position, transmission remains in 3rd gear. If gearshift lever is placed in "L" position, transmission remains in 1st gear. If gearshift lever is placed in "R" position, transmission will shift into reverse. Back-up mode may be cleared by turning ignition off, then back on again.

For additional information on the self-diagnostic system, see SELF-DIAGNOSTIC SYSTEM. The PCM is located below center of instrument panel. *See Fig. 2.*

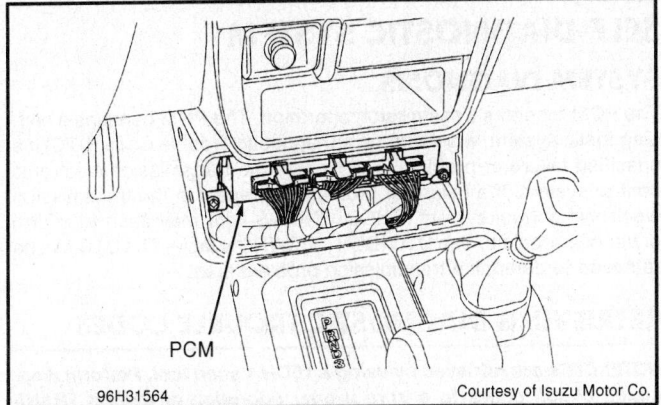

Fig. 2: Locating PCM

PCM INPUT DEVICES

A/C Signal – The A/C compressor relay delivers an input signal to PCM to indicate A/C operation. The A/C compressor relay is located in fuse/relay box at passenger's side front corner of engine compartment.

Brakelight Switch – Brakelight switch delivers an input signal to PCM to indicate vehicle braking. Brakelight switch is located near brake pedal. Brakelight switch may be referred to as brake switch.

Cruise Control Signal – Transmission will downshift when an overdrive OFF signal is received from cruise control unit. Cruise control unit is located behind passenger's side kick panel. Cruise control unit may also be referred to as cruise control module.

Diagnostic Connector – Diagnostic connector will deliver an input signal to display a Diagnostic Trouble Code (DTC) using CHECK TRANS light on instrument panel. Diagnostic connector may be referred to as Data Link Connector (DLC). *See Fig. 3.*

Engine Coolant Temperature (ECT) Sensor – ECT sensor delivers an input signal to PCM to indicate engine coolant temperature. ECT sensor is located on coolant pipe at rear of cylinder head.

Engine Speed Or RPM Signal – An engine speed or RPM signal is delivered to PCM from ignition control module, located below ignition coils.

Kickdown Switch – Kickdown switch delivers an input signal to PCM to indicate if accelerator pedal is fully depressed. Kickdown switch is located on accelerator pedal.

Mode Switch – Mode switch delivers an input signal to PCM to indicate shift lever position. Mode switch is located on side of transmission. *See Fig. 4.*

POWER Mode Switch – POWER mode switch delivers an input signal to PCM to indicate when POWER mode switch is positioned in the Power mode. POWER mode switch is located on center console, near gearshift lever.

Speed Sensor – Speed sensor delivers an input signal to PCM to indicate transmission output shaft speed. Speed sensor is located on extension housing on rear of transmission. *See Fig. 4.* Speed sensor may be referred to as magnetic sensor.

Throttle Position (TP) Sensor – The TP sensor delivers an input signal to PCM to indicate throttle position. The TP sensor is mounted on side of throttle body.

Transmission Oil Temperature Sensor – Transmission oil temperature sensor delivers an input signal to PCM to indicate transmission oil temperature. The PCM uses this input signal for controlling the Winter shift mode. The PCM also uses input signal for controlling the torque converter clutch and A/T oil temperature warning light. Transmission oil temperature sensor is located on wiring harness in adapter case oil pan. *See Fig. 4.*

WINTER Mode Switch – WINTER mode switch delivers an input signal to PCM to indicate when the WINTER mode switch is positioned in Winter mode. WINTER mode switch is located on center console, near gearshift lever.

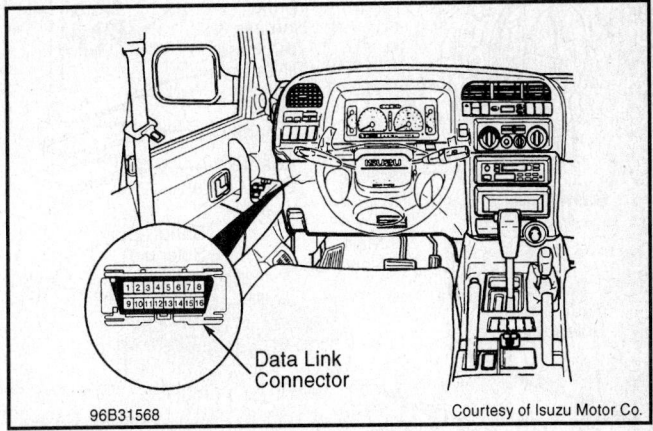

Fig. 3: Locating Data Link Connector (DLC)

PCM OUTPUT DEVICES

A/T Oil Temperature Warning Light – The PCM delivers an output signal to illuminate A/T oil temperature warning light if transmission oil temperature is greater than 284°F (140°C). Transmission oil temperature light will turn off when transmission oil temperature is less than 266°F (130°C). A/T temperature light is located in instrument cluster.

Anti-Lock Brake System (ABS) Signal – The TCM delivers an output signal to ABS controller when gearshift lever is in "R" or "L" position. The ABS controller uses this input signal for controlling ABS operation.

Band Apply Solenoid – The PCM delivers an output signal to operate band apply solenoid. Band apply solenoid (located on main valve body) regulates oil flow when a 3-2 downshift exists to prevent engine overspeed and shock control. *See Fig. 4.*

CHECK TRANS Light – The PCM delivers an output signal to flash CHECK TRANS light on instrument panel if a specified failure or problem is present in transmission electronic control system.

Diagnostic Connector – The PCM outputs various operating data to the diagnostic connector. Operating data may be obtained by connecting a scan tool to diagnostic connector. Diagnostic connector may be referred to as Data Link Connector (DLC).

POWER DRIVE Indicator Light – The PCM delivers an output signal to illuminate POWER DRIVE indicator light when POWER mode switch is placed in Power mode with ignition on. POWER DRIVE light is located in instrument cluster.

Pressure Control Solenoid (Force Motor) – The PCM delivers an output signal to operate pressure control solenoid, which operates pressure regulator valve to control line pressure. Pressure control solenoid is located on adapter case valve body. *See Fig. 4.*

Shift Solenoids – The PCM controls transmission shifting by delivering an output signal to 1-2/3-4 and 2-3 shift solenoids. Shift solenoids are operated in accordance with gear position. See SHIFT SOLENOID OPERATION table. Shift solenoids are located on main valve body. *See Fig. 4.*

3-678

AUTOMATIC TRANSMISSIONS
1996 Hydra-Matic 4L30-E Electronic Controls
Acura SLX & Isuzu Trooper (Cont.)

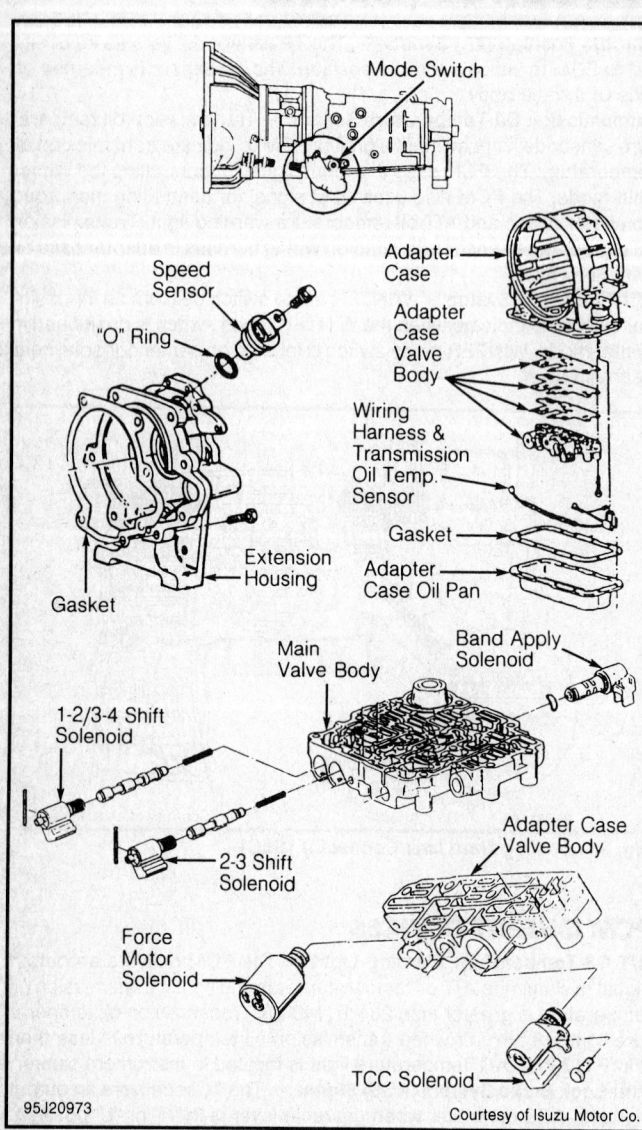

Fig. 4: Identifying Mode Switch, Speed Sensor, Transmission Oil Temperature Sensor, Shift Solenoids & TCC Solenoid

95J20973   Courtesy of Isuzu Motor Co.

Fig. 4: Identifying Mode Switch, Speed Sensor, Transmission Oil Temperature Sensor, Shift Solenoids & TCC Solenoid

SHIFT SOLENOID OPERATION

Gearshift Lever Position	1-2/3-4 Solenoid	2-3 Solenoid
"P" Or "N"	Off	On
"R"	Off	On
"D"		
1st Gear	Off	On
2nd Gear	On	On
3rd Gear	On	Off
4th Gear	Off	Off
"3"		
1st Gear	Off	On
2nd Gear	On	On
3rd Gear	On	Off
"2"		
1st Gear	Off	On
2nd Gear	On	On
"L"		
1st Gear	Off	On

Torque Converter Clutch (TCC) Solenoid – The PCM controls torque converter lock-up by delivering an output signal to TCC solenoid, located on adapter case valve body. *See Fig. 4.* Torque converter lock-up occurs only when all of the following conditions are present.

- Engine and transmission are at normal operating temperature.
- Brake pedal is released.
- Transmission is in 2nd, 3rd or 4th gear.

Torque Management Control Signal – The PCM delivers a spark advance output signal during transmission shifting. This reduces engagement shock caused by a change in vehicle speed.

WINTER DRIVE Indicator Light – The PCM delivers an output signal to illuminate WINTER DRIVE indicator light when WINTER mode switch is placed in Winter mode with ignition on. WINTER DRIVE indicator light is located in instrument cluster.

SELF-DIAGNOSTIC SYSTEM

SYSTEM DIAGNOSIS

The PCM monitors transmission operation. The PCM contains a self-diagnostic system, which stores a Diagnostic Trouble Code (DTC) if a specified failure or problem is present in the transmission electronic control system. If a failure or problem is present in the transmission electronic control system, CHECK TRANS light may flash to inform driver of a problem. See DTC IDENTIFICATION table. The DTC can be retrieved to determine transmission problem area.

RETRIEVING DIAGNOSTIC TROUBLE CODES

NOTE: DTCs are retrieved by using a TECH 1 scan tool. Perform diagnostic circuit check to ensure proper operation of CHECK TRANS light before attempting to retrieve DTCs. When using TECH 1 scan tool, different modes may be used. Follow scan tool manufacturer's instructions.

Diagnostic Circuit Check – **1)** Turn ignition on. CHECK TRANS light should illuminate for 2-3 seconds, then go off, indicating light circuit is operating properly.

2) If CHECK TRANS light functions as specified, DTCs can be retrieved. See PCM DIAGNOSTIC TROUBLE CODES. If CHECK TRANS light is flashing with ignition on, proceed to PCM DIAGNOSTIC TROUBLE CODES.

3) If CHECK TRANS light does not illuminate as specified, or remains off, proceed to CHECK TRANS LIGHT TEST under TROUBLE SHOOTING.

PCM Diagnostic Trouble Codes – **1)** Ensure ignition is off. Connect Adapter Cable (3000081) and scan tool to DLC. Connect scan tool to battery voltage (if required). Go to next step.

2) Turn ignition on. Using scan tool, note DTC displays on scan tool following scan tool manufacturer's instructions. Go to next step.

3) Once DTC is obtained, determine probable cause and symptom. See DTC IDENTIFICATION table. For trouble shooting of DTCs, see appropriate DTC test under DIAGNOSTIC TESTS. Turn ignition off. Remove scan tool.

AUTOMATIC TRANSMISSIONS
1996 Hydra-Matic 4L30-E Electronic Controls
Acura SLX & Isuzu Trooper (Cont.)

3-679

DTC IDENTIFICATION

DTC	Description
P0218	Transmission Fluid Over-Temperature
P0560	System Voltage Malfunction
P0705	Transmission Range Switch (Mode Switch) Illegal Position
P0706	Transmission Range Switch (Mode Switch) Performance
P0712	Transmission Fluid Temperature (TFT) Sensor Circuit (Low Input)
P0713	Transmission Fluid Temperature (TFT) Sensor Circuit (High Input)
P0719	TCC Brake Switch Circuit High (Stuck On)
P0722	Transmission Output Speed Sensor (OSS) (Low Input)
P0723	Transmission Output Speed Sensor (OSS) (Intermittent)
P0724	TCC Brake Switch Circuit Low (Stuck Off)
P0730	Transmission Incorrect Gear Ratio
P0742	TCC Circuit Stuck On
P0748	Pressure Control Solenoid (Force Motor) (Circuit Electrical)
P0751	Shift Solenoid "A" Performance (Without Input Speed)
P0753	Shift Solenoid "A" Electrical
P0756	Shift Solenoid "B" Performance (Without Input Speed)
P0758	Shift Solenoid "B" Electrical
P1790	ROM Transmission Side Bad Check Sum
P1792	EEPROM Transmission Side Bad Check Sum
P1835	Kickdown Switch Always On
P1850	Brake Band Apply Solenoid Malfunction
P1860	TCC PWM Solenoid Electrical
P1870	Transmission Component Slipping

CLEARING DIAGNOSTIC TROUBLE CODES

1) Using TECH 1 scan tool, use F4: Clear Code mode from main menu to clear DTC from PCM memory using scan tool manufacturer's instructions.

2) If DTC cannot be cleared from PCM memory, or if TECH 1 scan tool is not available, remove STOP-A/T CONT fuse (15-amp) from instrument panel fuse box for at least 10 seconds.

TROUBLE SHOOTING

CHECK TRANS LIGHT TEST

NOTE: *Perform this test if CHECK TRANS light is on steady at all times with ignition on and no diagnostic trouble codes are stored, or CHECK TRANS light remains off when ignition is first turned on.*

Description – When ignition is turned on, CHECK TRANS light on instrument panel should come on for about 2-3 seconds while PCM is performing a self-test of the circuit and components, then light should turn off. When ignition is on and PCM detects an electrical failure in the transmission electronic control system, the PCM will flash CHECK TRANS light and may store a diagnostic trouble code in memory.

CHECK TRANS Light Is On Steady With Ignition On – **1)** This condition may be caused by a short circuit to ground between CHECK TRANS light and PCM. Check wiring between PCM and CHECK TRANS light on instrument panel for a short circuit to ground.

2) If no short circuit to ground is present in the wiring, replace PCM. See PCM under REMOVAL & INSTALLATION.

CHECK TRANS Light Remains Off – **1)** This condition may be caused by an open circuit or short to power between CHECK TRANS light and PCM. Check wiring between PCM and CHECK TRANS light on instrument panel for an open circuit or short to power.

2) Ensure battery voltage is present between fuse in fuse box and CHECK TRANS light. Check fuse and all connections as necessary.

3) If battery voltage is present as specified and no open or short circuit is present between CHECK TRANS light and PCM, replace PCM. See PCM under REMOVAL & INSTALLATION.

INTERMITTENT CONDITIONS

If TECH 1 scan tool displays DTC as intermittent, or if after a test drive a DTC does not reappear though the detection conditions for the DTC, problem is most likely a faulty electrical connection or loose wiring. Intermittent problems are rarely present in electronic components such as the PCM, but rather in electrical connections or ground circuits. When an intermittent condition is present, perform the following procedure.

1) Check for loose connections at electrical terminal connectors. Check for improperly seated electrical connectors or damaged electrical terminals.

2) Check for loose or corroded ground connections. Check for pinched or damaged wiring. Check for improperly routed wiring which may cause electro-magnetic interference from spark plug wires, distributor wires, ignition coil and alternator.

3) Use F3: Snapshot mode to isolate the cause of an intermittent condition following scan tool manufacturer's instructions. Set Snapshot mode to trigger on suspected DTC, or if you notice the reported symptom during test drive, manually trigger Snapshot mode.

4) After Snapshot mode is triggered, command scan tool to play back flow of data recorded from each of the various sensors. Signs of an intermittent condition in a sensor circuit may cause a sudden jump in data values out of normal range.

SYSTEM TESTING

KEY LOCK SYSTEM

NOTE: *Shift lock cable is connected between gearshift lever and ignition switch. When gearshift lever is placed in "P" position, shift lock cable moves lock on ignition switch so ignition switch may be placed in LOCK position.*

1) To check system operation, ensure gearshift lever cannot be moved from "P" position with ignition switch in LOCK position.

2) Ensure ignition switch can be turned to LOCK position only when gearshift lever is in "P" position. If operation is not as specified, adjust shift lock cable. See SHIFT LOCK CABLE ADJUSTMENT under ON-VEHICLE SERVICE in appropriate overhaul article.

DIAGNOSTIC TESTS

NOTE: *Perform ON-BOARD DIAGNOSTIC (OBD) SYSTEM CHECK before proceeding with diagnostic tests. See appropriate BASIC DIAGNOSTIC PROCEDURES article in ENGINE PERFORMANCE in appropriate MITCHELL® manual.*

NOTE: *See appropriate wiring diagram under WIRING DIAGRAMS to aid in component location, wire color and terminal identification.*

DTC P0218:
TRANSMISSION FLUID OVER-TEMPERATURE

Conditions For Setting DTC:
- DTCs P0712 and P0713 are not present.
- Transmission fluid temperature is greater than 284°F (140°C).
- Conditions must be present for 21 seconds.

Diagnosis – **1)** Ensure engine is mechanically in good condition, and not cause of a transmission overheating problem. Ensure transmission fluid is at proper level. See CHECKING FLUID LEVEL under LUBRICATION in appropriate AUTOMATIC TRANSMISSION SERVICING article. Repair as necessary. Go to next step.

2) Install scan tool. Turn ignition on. Using scan tool, record DTC FAILURE RECORDS. Observe Transmission Fluid Temperature (TFT) sensor voltage reading on scan tool. If TFT sensor reading is less than .33 volt, go to next step. If reading is not as specified, see DIAGNOSTIC AIDS.

3-680

AUTOMATIC TRANSMISSIONS
1996 Hydra-Matic 4L30-E Electronic Controls
Acura SLX & Isuzu Trooper (Cont.)

3) Turn ignition off. Disconnect transmission harness connector H-10 (16-pin Blue connector). Turn ignition on. If TFT sensor signal voltage reading is greater than 4.92 volts, check for faulty wiring harness. If reading is not as specified, go to next step.

4) Check Green/Red wire between PCM and TFT sensor for a short to ground. Repair as necessary and go to step 6). If no problem is found, go to next step.

5) Inspect PCM for poor harness connections. Repair as necessary. If no problem is found, replace PCM and go to next step.

6) Using scan tool, select DTC, then CLEAR INFO function. Ensure transmission fluid temperature is less than 266°F (130°C) for at least 10 seconds. Review DTC INFO. If last test failed, or DTC P0218 is present, repeat step 1). If last test passed and no DTCs are present, testing is complete.

Diagnostic Aids – Inspect for poor harness connections and improper wire harness routing. An intermittent condition may be caused by a wire which is broken inside its insulation, or shorted to an additional circuit or chassis ground. Check harness connectors for damaged, corroded or backed-out terminal pins. Repair as necessary. Check for possible torque converter stator problem. Verify vehicle owners driving habits, trailer towing, etc.

DTC P0560: SYSTEM VOLTAGE MALFUNCTION

Conditions For Setting DTC (System Voltage Low):
- Engine speed is greater than 1000 RPM.
- System voltage is less than 10 volts at a maximum transmission temperature of 302°F (150°C).
- System voltage is less than 7.3 volts at a minimum transmission temperature of –40°F (–40°C).
  - Conditions must be present for 4 seconds.

Conditions For Setting DTC (System Voltage High):
- System voltage is greater than 16 volts for 2 seconds.

Diagnosis – 1) Install scan tool. Turn ignition on. Using scan tool, record DTC FAILURE RECORDS. Using a DVOM, measure voltage between battery terminals. Note reading for future reference. If reading is greater than 10.5 volts, go to next step. If reading is not as specified, charge or replace battery.

2) Start engine and allow it to reach normal operating temperature. Observe generator/check engine light. If light is illuminated, inspect and repair faulty charging system. If light is not illuminated, go to next step.

3) Increase engine speed to 1000-1500 RPM. Observe scan tool system voltage. If reading is within 13-15 volts, go to next step. If reading is not as specified, inspect and repair faulty charging system.

4) Turn ignition off. Disconnect PCM harness connectors C-1 (Red) and C-3 (Blue). Turn ignition on. Using a DVOM, measure voltage between ground and PCM harness connector C-1, terminal A4 (Red/White wire), then between ground and PCM harness connector C-3, terminal E16 (Red/Blue wire). Compare voltage readings with that of reading noted in step 1). If difference in voltage reading is greater than .5 volt, go to next step. If difference in voltage is not as specified, go to step 6).

5) Repair Red/White wire between PCM and battery for high resistance. Go to step 10).

6) Using a DVOM, measure voltage between ground and PCM harness connector C-3, terminal E16 (Red/Blue wire), then between ground and PCM harness connector C-3, terminal F16 (Red/Blue wire). Compare voltage readings with that of reading noted in step 1). If difference in voltage reading is greater than .5 volt, go to next step. If difference in voltage is not as specified, go to step 8).

7) Repair Red/Blue wire between PCM and PCM relay for high resistance. Go to step 10).

8) Check PCM harness connector C-1, terminal A4 (Red/White wire); harness connector C-3, terminal E16 (Red/Blue wire); and harness connector C-3, terminal F16 (Red/Blue wire) for damaged, corroded, or backed-out terminal pins. Repair as necessary and go to step 10). If no problem is found, go to next step.

9) Replace PCM. Go to next step.

10) Using scan tool, select DTC, then CLEAR INFO function. Start engine and allow it to reach normal operating temperature. PCM must see a system voltage of 10-16 volts. Review DTC INFO. If last test failed, or DTC P0560 is present, repeat step 1). If last test passed and no DTCs are present, testing is complete.

Diagnostic Aids – Inspect for poor harness connections and improper wire harness routing. An intermittent condition may be caused by a wire which is broken inside its insulation, or shorted to an additional circuit or chassis ground. Check harness connectors for damaged, corroded or backed-out terminal pins. Repair as necessary. Check for proper belt tension. Charging battery or jump starting may set DTC P0560.

DTC P0705: TRANSMISSION RANGE SWITCH (MODE SWITCH) ILLEGAL POSITION

Conditions For Setting DTC:
- Illegal range position detected for 5 seconds.

Diagnosis – 1) Ensure transmission linkage between gearshift lever and manual valve is adjusted properly. Check diagnostic circuit. See RETRIEVING DIAGNOSTIC TROUBLE CODES under SELF-DIAGNOSTIC SYSTEM. Go to next step.

2) Install scan tool. Turn ignition on. Using scan tool, record DTC FREEZE FRAME and FAILURE RECORDS. Observe scan tool while moving gearshift lever through all gear ranges. If scan tool display coincides with actual gear range selected, go to DIAGNOSTIC AIDS. If operation is not as specified, go to next step.

3) Turn ignition off. Disconnect mode switch harness connector C-43 (8-pin Black connector). Turn ignition on. Using a DVOM, measure voltage between ground and mode switch harness connector C-43, terminals No. 3 (Pink/Black wire), No. 6 (Blue/Black wire), No. 7 (Pink wire), then No. 8 (Pink/Blue wire). If battery voltage is present at all circuits, go to step 5). If battery voltage is not present at all circuits, go to next step.

4) Check for an open or short to ground in any circuit which did not indicate battery voltage. Repair as necessary and go to step 8). If no problem is found, go to step 6).

5) Ensure circuits checked in step 3) are not shorted together. To check, apply ground to each circuit while monitoring range switch display on scan tool. If more than one gear range is displayed at one time, go to step 7). If no problem is found, refer to RANGE SWITCH LOGIC TABLE. See Fig. 5.

6) Check PCM for poor harness connections. Repair a necessary. If no problem is found, replace PCM. Go to step 8).

7) Repair appropriate wire as necessary. Go to next step.

8) Using scan tool, select DTC, then CLEAR INFO function. Road test vehicle. Review DTC INFO. If last test failed, or DTC P0705 is present, repeat step 1). If last test passed and no DTCs are present, testing is complete.

Diagnostic Aids – Inspect for poor harness connections and improper wire harness routing. An intermittent condition may be caused by a wire which is broken inside its insulation, or shorted to an additional circuit or chassis ground. Check harness connectors for damaged, corroded or backed-out terminal pins. Repair as necessary. Refer to RANGE SWITCH LOGIC TABLE for additional information. See Fig. 5.

AUTOMATIC TRANSMISSIONS
1996 Hydra-Matic 4L30-E Electronic Controls
Acura SLX & Isuzu Trooper (Cont.)

3-681

Range Position	Range Switch Pin No.			
	8	7	6	3
Park	ON	OFF	OFF	ON
Reverse	ON	ON	OFF	OFF
Neutral	OFF	ON	OFF	ON
D4	OFF	ON	ON	OFF
D3	ON	ON	ON	ON
"2"	ON	OFF	ON	OFF
"L"	OFF	OFF	ON	ON
Illegal	OFF	OFF	OFF	OFF
Illegal	OFF	OFF	OFF	ON

96J31566

Courtesy of Isuzu Motor Co.

Fig. 5: Range Switch Logic Table

DTC P0706: TRANSMISSION RANGE SWITCH (MODE SWITCH) PERFORMANCE

Conditions For Setting DTC ("R" Bad Position):
- Engine is running.
- DTCs P0722 and P0723 are not present.
- Output speed greater than 3200 RPM.
- Range switch indicates "R".
- Conditions must be met for 4 seconds.

Conditions For Setting DTC ("P" Or "N" Bad Position):
- Engine is running.
- No TP sensor DTCs.
- Engine speed is less than 3000 RPM.
- TP sensor angle is greater than 20 percent.
- Range switch indicates "P" or "N".
- Conditions must be met for 4 seconds.

Diagnosis – 1) Ensure transmission linkage between gearshift lever and manual valve is adjusted properly. Check diagnostic circuit. See RETRIEVING DIAGNOSTIC TROUBLE CODES under SELF-DIAGNOSTIC SYSTEM. Go to next step.
2) Install scan tool. Turn ignition on. Using scan tool, record DTC FREEZE FRAME and FAILURE RECORDS. Observe scan tool while moving gearshift lever through all gear ranges. If scan tool display coincides with actual gear range selected, go to DIAGNOSTIC AIDS. If operation is not as specified, go to next step.
3) Turn ignition off. Disconnect mode switch harness connector C-43 (8-pin Black connector). Turn ignition on. Using a DVOM, measure voltage between ground and mode switch harness connector C-43, terminals No. 3 (Pink/Black wire), No. 6 (Blue/Black wire), No. 7 (Pink wire), then No. 8 (Pink/Blue wire). If battery voltage is present at all circuits, go to step **5)**. If battery voltage is not present at all circuits, go to next step.
4) Check for an open or short to ground in any circuit which did not indicate battery voltage. Repair as necessary and go to step **8)**. If no problem is found, go to step **6)**.
5) Ensure circuits checked in step **3)** are not shorted together. To check, apply ground to each circuit while monitoring range switch display on scan tool. If more than one gear range is displayed at one time, go to step **7)**. If no problem is found, refer to RANGE SWITCH LOGIC TABLE. See Fig. 5.
6) Check PCM for poor harness connections. Repair a necessary. If no problem is found, replace PCM. Go to step **8)**.
7) Repair appropriate wire as necessary. Go to next step.
8) Using scan tool, select DTC, then CLEAR INFO function. Road test vehicle. Review DTC INFO. If last test failed, or DTC P0705 is present, repeat step **1)**. If last test passed and no DTCs are present, testing is complete.

Diagnostic Aids – Inspect for poor harness connections and improper wire harness routing. An intermittent condition may be caused by a wire which is broken inside its insulation, or shorted to an additional circuit or chassis ground. Check harness connectors for damaged, corroded or backed-out terminal pins. Repair as necessary. Refer to RANGE SWITCH LOGIC TABLE for additional information. See Fig. 5.

DTC P0712: TRANS. FLUID TEMP. (TFT) SENSOR CIRCUIT LOW INPUT

Conditions For Setting DTC:
- DTC P0560 is not present.
- Ignition is on.
- TFT sensor indicates a voltage less than .4 volt.
- Conditions must be present for 20 seconds.

Diagnosis – 1) Perform transmission fluid checking procedure. See CHECKING FLUID LEVEL under LUBRICATION in appropriate AUTOMATIC TRANSMISSION SERVICING article. Fill if necessary and go to next step.
2) Install scan tool. Turn ignition on. Using scan tool, record DTC FREEZE FRAME and FAILURE RECORDS. If scan tool displays TFT sensor voltage less than .4 volt, go to next step. If reading is not as specified, go to DIAGNOSTIC AIDS.
3) Turn ignition off. Disconnect transmission harness connector H-10 (16-pin Blue connector). Turn ignition on. If TFT sensor voltage rises to 4.92 volts, go to next step. If reading is not as specified, go to step **9)**.
4) Turn ignition off. Using a DVOM, measure resistance between TFT sensor harness connector terminals (Green wire and Green/Red wire). Compare resistance readings with table. See TFT SENSOR RESISTANCE table. If resistance is within specification, go to DIAGNOSTIC AIDS. If resistance is not within specification, go to next step.

TFT SENSOR RESISTANCE

Temperature °F (°C)	Resistance (Ohms)
−40 (−40)	672,000
32 (0)	65,000
68 (20)	25,000
176 (80)	2,500
248 (120)	780
302 (150)	370

5) Disconnect transmission harness connector M-6 (5-pin Black connector). Using a DVOM, measure resistance between TFT sensor terminals (Green wire and Green/Red wire). Compare resistance readings with table. See TFT SENSOR RESISTANCE table. If

3-682

AUTOMATIC TRANSMISSIONS
1996 Hydra-Matic 4L30-E Electronic Controls
Acura SLX & Isuzu Trooper (Cont.)

resistance is within specification, go to DIAGNOSTIC AIDS. If resistance is not within specification, go to next step.

6) Remove transmission oil pan. Inspect internal wiring harness for a short to ground. If a short to ground is found, go to step 8). If no problem is found, go to next step.

7) Disconnect internal wiring harness at TFT sensor. Using a DVOM, measure resistance of TFT sensor. Compare resistance readings with table. See TFT SENSOR RESISTANCE table. If resistance is within specification, go to DIAGNOSTIC AIDS. If resistance is not within specification, go to next step.

8) Replace TFT sensor. Go to step 12).

9) Check Green/Red wire between TFT sensor and PCM for a short to ground. Repair as necessary and go to step 12). If no problem is found, go to next step.

10) Check PCM for poor harness connections. Repair as necessary and go to step 12). If no problem is found, go to next step.

11) Replace PCM. Go to next step.

12) Using scan tool, select DTC, then CLEAR INFO function. Ensure TFT sensor indicates a voltage greater than .33 volt for 2 seconds. Review DTC INFO. If last test failed, or DTC P0712 is present, repeat step 1). If last test passed and no DTCs are present, testing is complete.

Diagnostic Aids – Inspect for poor harness connections and improper wire harness routing. An intermittent condition may be caused by a wire which is broken inside its insulation, or shorted to an additional circuit or chassis ground. Check harness connectors for damaged, corroded or backed-out terminal pins. Repair as necessary. A scan tool which displays a TFT sensor temperature value at 212°F (100°C), may indicate a short to ground in Green/Red wire between TFT sensor and PCM.

DTC P0713: TRANS. FLUID TEMP. (TFT) SENSOR CIRCUIT HIGH INPUT

Conditions For Setting DTC:
- DTC P0560 is not present.
- Ignition is on.
- TFT sensor indicates a voltage greater than 4.86 volts.
- Conditions must be present for 20 seconds.

Diagnosis – 1) Perform transmission fluid checking procedure. See CHECKING FLUID LEVEL under LUBRICATION in appropriate AUTOMATIC TRANSMISSION SERVICING article. Fill if necessary and go to next step.

2) Install scan tool. Turn ignition on. Using scan tool, record DTC FREEZE FRAME and FAILURE RECORDS. If scan tool displays TFT sensor voltage greater than 4.86 volts, go to next step. If reading is not as specified, go to DIAGNOSTIC AIDS.

3) Turn ignition off. Disconnect transmission harness connector H-10 (16-pin Blue connector). Using a fused jumper wire, jumper Green wire and Green/Red wire together (engine harness side). Turn ignition on. If TFT sensor voltage drops to less than .4 volt, go to next step. If voltage does not drop as specified, go to step 9).

4) Turn ignition off. Using a DVOM, measure resistance between TFT sensor harness connector terminals (Green wire and Green/Red wire). Compare resistance readings with table. See TFT SENSOR RESISTANCE table. If resistance is within specification, go to DIAGNOSTIC AIDS. If resistance is not within specification, go to next step.

TFT SENSOR RESISTANCE

Temperature °F (°C)	Resistance (Ohms)
−40 (−40)	672,000
32 (0)	65,000
68 (20)	25,000
176 (80)	2,500
248 (120)	780
302 (150)	370

5) Disconnect transmission harness connector M-6 (5-pin Black connector). Using a DVOM, measure resistance between TFT sensor terminals (Green wire and Green/Red wire). Compare resistance readings with table. See TFT SENSOR RESISTANCE table. If resistance is within specification, go to DIAGNOSTIC AIDS. If resistance is not within specification, go to next step.

6) Remove transmission oil pan. Inspect internal wiring harness for an open. Repair as necessary and go to step 13). If no problem is found, go to next step.

7) Disconnect internal wiring harness at TFT sensor. Using a DVOM, measure resistance of TFT sensor. Compare resistance readings with table. See TFT SENSOR RESISTANCE table. If resistance is within specification, go to DIAGNOSTIC AIDS. If resistance is not within specification, go to next step.

8) Replace TFT sensor. Go to step 13).

9) Check Green/Red wire between TFT sensor and PCM for a short to power. Repair as necessary and go to step 13). If no problem is found, go to next step.

10) Check Green wire between TFT sensor and PCM for an open. Repair as necessary and go to step 13). If no problem is found, go to next step.

11) Check PCM for poor harness connections. Repair as necessary and go to step 13). If no problem is found, go to next step.

12) Replace PCM. Go to next step.

13) Using scan tool, select DTC, then CLEAR INFO function. Ensure TFT sensor indicates a voltage less than 4.92 volts for 2 seconds. Review DTC INFO. If last test failed, or DTC P0713 is present, repeat step 1). If last test passed and no DTCs are present, testing is complete.

Diagnostic Aids – Inspect for poor harness connections and improper wire harness routing. An intermittent condition may be caused by a wire which is broken inside its insulation, or shorted to an additional circuit or chassis ground. Check harness connectors for damaged, corroded or backed-out terminal pins. Repair as necessary. After transmission is operating, TFT sensor temperature value on scan tool should rise steadily to about 212°F (100°C), then stabilize.

DTC P0719: TCC BRAKE SWITCH CIRCUIT HIGH (STUCK ON)

Conditions For Setting DTC:
- DTCs P0722 and P0723 are not present.
- PCM detects a closed brake switch/circuit (12 volts) for 2 seconds, and the following events occur 7 consecutive times: vehicle speed is less than 5 MPH, then between 5 MPH and 20 MPH for 4 seconds; then vehicle speed is greater than 20 MPH for 4 seconds.

Diagnosis – 1) Install scan tool. Turn ignition on. If an ABS DTC is set, check appropriate fuse. Using scan tool, record DTC FREEZE FRAME and FAILURE RECORDS. Apply, then release brake pedal. If scan tool displays TCC brake switch as CLOSED with brake pedal applied, then OPEN when released, go to DIAGNOSTIC AIDS. If scan tool display is not as specified, go to next step.

2) Using a test light connected to ground, backprobe ignition feed circuit (Green/White wire) at brake switch. If test light illuminates, go to next step. If test light does not illuminate, go to step 4).

3) Using a test light connected to ground, backprobe Green/Yellow wire at brake switch. If test light does not illuminate, go to step 7). If test light illuminates, leave test light connected and go to step 5).

4) Check fuse C-14 (15-amp) in instrument panel fuse box. If fuse is blown, check for a short to ground. Repair as necessary. If fuse is okay, repair open in ignition feed circuit (Green/White wire) between brake switch and instrument panel fuse box. Go to step 13).

5) Disconnect brake switch harness connector. If test light remains illuminated, go to step 8). If test light is not illuminated, go to next step.

6) Using a DVOM, check for continuity between brake switch terminals. If continuity is present, go to step 9). If continuity is not present, go to step 10).

AUTOMATIC TRANSMISSIONS
1996 Hydra-Matic 4L30-E Electronic Controls
Acura SLX & Isuzu Trooper (Cont.)

3-683

7) Disconnect brake switch harness connector. Ensure ignition is on. Using a test light connected to ground, probe Green/Yellow wire terminal (harness side). If test light illuminates, leave test light connected and go to next step. If test light does not illuminate, go to step 10).

8) Turn ignition off. Disconnect PCM harness connector C-3 (Blue). Turn ignition on. If test light illuminates, check Green/Yellow wire between brake switch and PCM for a short to power. Repair as necessary and go to step 13). If no problem is found, go to step 10).

9) Replace brake switch. Go to step 13).

10) Turn ignition off. Reconnect PCM harness connector C-3 (Blue) if disconnected. Turn ignition on. Observe scan tool. If display shows TCC brake switch as OPEN, with brake pedal applied, then CLOSED with brake pedal released, go to DIAGNOSTIC AIDS. If scan tool display is not as specified, go to next step.

11) Check PCM for poor harness connections. Repair as necessary and go to step 13). If no problem is found, go to next step.

12) Replace PCM. Go to next step.

13) Using scan tool, select DTC, then CLEAR INFO function. Ensure PCM brake switch signal indicates zero volts for at least one second with brake pedal applied. Review DTC INFO. If last test failed, or DTC P0719 is present, repeat step 1). If last test passed and no DTCs are present, testing is complete.

Diagnostic Aids – Inspect for poor harness connections and improper wire harness routing. An intermittent condition may be caused by a wire which is broken inside its insulation, or shorted to an additional circuit or chassis ground. Check harness connectors for damaged, corroded or backed-out terminal pins. Repair as necessary. Check brake switch for proper mounting and adjustment.

DTC P0722: TRANSMISSION OUTPUT SPEED SENSOR (OSS) LOW INPUT

Conditions For Setting DTC:
- DTCs P0107, P0108, P0106, P1106, P1107, P0122 and P0123 are not present.
- Not in Park or Neutral.
- TP sensor angle is greater than 10 percent.
- Engine vacuum is between zero and 10.2 in. Hg.
- Engine speed is between 3000 RPM and 5000 RPM.
- Transmission speed is less than zero RPM.
- All conditions must be present for 5 seconds.

Diagnosis – 1) Install scan tool. Turn ignition on. Using scan tool, record DTC FREEZE FRAME and FAILURE RECORDS. Raise and support vehicle. Start engine. Place gearshift lever in any drive range. Observe TRANS OUTPUT SPEED parameter on scan tool. If scan tool indicates that transmission output speed increases as wheel speed increases, go to DIAGNOSTIC AIDS. If transmission output speed does not change as specified, go to next step.

2) Check speedometer operation. If operation is okay, go to next step. If operation is not okay, go to step 4).

3) Check for proper speedometer calibration. If calibration is okay, go to step 16). If calibration is not okay, go to next step.

4) Turn ignition off. Disconnect PCM harness connector C-3 (Blue). Using a DVOM, measure resistance between PCM harness connector C-3, terminal E1 (Red wire), and terminal E2 (White wire). If resistance is 3000 ohms, go to next step. If resistance is not as specified, go to step 6).

5) Using a DVOM, select AC volts. Turn driveshaft by rotating a rear wheel by hand. If reading is greater than .5 volt, go to step 7). If reading is not as specified, go to step 8).

6) Inspect Red wire and White wire between OSS and PCM for an open or poor connection. Repair as necessary and go to step 17). If no problem is found, go to step 8).

7) Reconnect PCM harness connector. Disconnect OSS harness connector. Turn ignition on. Using a DVOM, measure voltage between OSS Harness connector terminals. If reading is 4.0-5.1 volts, go to step 16). If reading is not a specified, go to step 10).

8) Remove OSS. Check output shaft speed sensor rotor for damage or misalignment. Repair as necessary and go to step 17). If no problem is found, go to next step.

9) Replace OSS. Go to step 17).

10) If reading in step 7) was less than 4.0 volts, go to step 12). If reading was not less than 4.0 volts in step 7), go to next step.

11) If reading in step 7) was greater than 5.1 volts, go to step 15).

12) Using a DVOM, measure voltage between ground and Red wire at OSS harness connector. If reading is 4.0-5.1 volts, go to next step. If reading is not as specified, go to step 14).

13) Repair open in White wire between OSS and PCM. Go to step 17).

14) Check Red wire between OSS and PCM for an open or short to ground. Repair as necessary and go to step 17). If no problem is found, go to step 16).

15) Repair short to power in Red wire between OSS and PCM. Go to step 17).

16) Replace PCM. Go to next step.

17) Using scan tool, select DTC, then CLEAR INFO function. Operate vehicle so scan tool indicates a transmission output speed greater than 101 RPM for 3 seconds. Review DTC INFO. If last test failed, or DTC P0722 is present, repeat step 1). If last test passed and no DTCs are present, testing is complete.

Diagnostic Aids – DTC P0722 will set when no output speed is detected at start-off. Inspect for poor harness connections and improper wire harness routing. An intermittent condition may be caused by a wire which is broken inside its insulation, or shorted to an additional circuit or chassis ground. Check harness connectors for damaged, corroded or backed-out terminal pins. Repair as necessary.

DTC P0723: TRANSMISSION OUTPUT SPEED SENSOR (OSS) INTERMITTENT

Conditions For Setting DTC (In Park Or Neutral):
- Transmission output speed change is greater than 7000 RPM.
- Condition is present for 6 seconds.
- Engine running time is greater than 2 seconds.

Conditions For Setting DTC (Not In Park Or Neutral):
- Transmission output speed change is greater than 512 RPM.
- Condition is present for .1 second.
- Engine running time is greater than 2 seconds.

Diagnosis – 1) Install scan tool. Turn ignition on. Using scan tool, record DTC FREEZE FRAME and FAILURE RECORDS. Raise and support vehicle. Start engine. Place gearshift lever in any drive range. Observe TRANS OUTPUT SPEED parameter on scan tool. If scan tool indicates that transmission output speed increases as wheel speed increases, go to DIAGNOSTIC AIDS. If transmission output speed does not change as specified, go to next step.

2) Check speedometer operation. If operation is okay, go to next step. If operation is not okay, go to step 4).

3) Check for proper speedometer calibration. If calibration is okay, go to step 16). If calibration is not okay, go to next step.

4) Turn ignition off. Disconnect PCM harness connector C-3 (Blue). Using a DVOM, measure resistance between PCM harness connector terminal E1 (Red wire), and terminal E2 (White wire). If resistance is 3000 ohms, go to next step. If resistance is not as specified, go to step 6).

5) Using a DVOM, select AC volts. Turn driveshaft by rotating a rear wheel by hand. If reading is greater than .5 volt, go to step 7). If reading is not as specified, go to step 8).

6) Inspect Red wire and White wire between OSS and PCM for an open or poor connection. Repair as necessary and go to step 17). If no problem is found, go to step 8).

7) Reconnect PCM harness connector. Disconnect OSS harness connector. Turn ignition on. Using a DVOM, measure voltage between OSS harness connector terminals. If reading is 4.0-5.1 volts, go to step 16). If reading is not a specified, go to step 10).

8) Remove OSS. Check output shaft speed sensor rotor for damage or misalignment. Repair as necessary and go to step 17). If no problem is found, go to next step.

3-684

AUTOMATIC TRANSMISSIONS
1996 Hydra-Matic 4L30-E Electronic Controls
Acura SLX & Isuzu Trooper (Cont.)

9) Replace OSS. Go to step **17**).

10) If reading in step **7**) was less than 4.0 volts, go to step **12**). If reading was not less than 4.0 volts in step **7**), go to next step.

11) If reading in step **7**) was greater than 5.1 volts, go to step **15**).

12) Using a DVOM, measure voltage between ground and Red wire at OSS harness connector. If reading is 4.0-5.1 volts, go to next step. If reading is not as specified, go to step **14**).

13) Repair open in White wire between OSS and PCM. Go to step **17**).

14) Check Red wire between OSS and PCM for an open or short to ground. Repair as necessary and go to step **17**). If no problem is found, go to step **16**).

15) Repair short to power in Red wire between OSS and PCM. Go to step **17**).

16) Replace PCM. Go to next step.

17) Using scan tool, select DTC, then CLEAR INFO function. Operate vehicle so scan tool indicates a transmission output speed greater than 101 RPM for 3 seconds. Review DTC INFO. If last test failed, or DTC P0723 is present, repeat step **1**). If last test passed and no DTCs are present, testing is complete.

Diagnostic Aids – DTC P0723 will set when output speed has been detected, then lost. Inspect for poor harness connections and improper wire harness routing. An intermittent condition may be caused by a wire which is broken inside its insulation, or shorted to an additional circuit or chassis ground. Check harness connectors for damaged, corroded or backed-out terminal pins. Repair as necessary.

DTC P0724:
TCC BRAKE SWITCH CIRCUIT LOW (STUCK OFF)
Conditions For Setting DTC:
- DTCs P0722 or P0723 are not present.
- PCM detects an open brake switch/circuit (zero volts) during decelerations, and the following events occur 7 consecutive times: vehicle speed is greater than 20 MPH for 4 seconds, then between 5 MPH and 20 MPH for 4 seconds; then vehicle speed is less than 5 MPH.

Diagnosis – **1)** Install scan tool. Turn ignition on. Using scan tool, record DTC FAILURE RECORDS. Apply, then release brake pedal. If scan tool displays TCC brake switch as CLOSED with brake pedal applied, then OPEN when released, go to DIAGNOSTIC AIDS. If scan tool display is not as specified, go to next step.

2) Using a test light connected to ground, backprobe ignition feed circuit (Green/White wire) at brake switch. If test light illuminates, go to next step. If test light does not illuminate, go to step **4**).

3) Using a test light connected to ground, backprobe Green/Yellow wire at brake switch. Apply brake pedal. If test light illuminates, go to step **6**). If test light does not illuminate, go to next step.

4) Check fuse C-14 (15-amp) in instrument panel fuse box. If fuse is blown, check for a short to ground. Repair as necessary. If fuse is okay, repair open in ignition feed circuit (Green/White wire) between brake switch and instrument panel fuse box. Go to step **10**).

5) Disconnect brake switch electrical connector. Using a DVOM, measure resistance between terminals No. 1 and 4 of brake switch. Apply brake pedal. If resistance is zero ohms, go to next step. If resistance is not as specified, go to step **7**).

6) Check Green/Yellow wire between PCM and brake switch for an open. Repair as necessary and go to step **10**). If no problem is found, go to step **8**).

7) Replace brake switch. Go to step **10**).

8) Check for poor PCM harness connections. Repair as necessary and go to step **10**). If no problem is found, go to next step.

9) Replace PCM. Go to next step.

10) Using scan tool, select DTC, then CLEAR INFO function. Ensure PCM brake switch signal indicates 12 volts for at least one second with brake pedal released. Review DTC INFO. If last test failed, or DTC P0724 is present, repeat step **1**). If last test passed and no DTCs are present, testing is complete.

Diagnostic Aids – Inspect for poor harness connections and improper wire harness routing. An intermittent condition may be caused by a wire which is broken inside its insulation, or shorted to an additional circuit or chassis ground. Check harness connectors for damaged, corroded or backed-out terminal pins. Repair as necessary. Check brake switch for proper mounting and adjustment.

DTC P0730:
TRANSMISSION INCORRECT GEAR RATIO
Conditions For Setting DTC:
- DTCs P0722 and P0723 are not present.
- Not in Park, Neutral or Reverse.
- Engine speed is greater than 3500 RPM.
- Three seconds since up-shift.
- Three seconds since down-shift.
- Three seconds since garage shift ("N" to "D").
- One of the following occurs: slip is greater than 595 RPM in 1st gear, greater than 556 RPM in 2nd gear, greater than 536 RPM in 3rd gear or greater than 528 RPM in 4th gear.
- Conditions must be present for 5.5 seconds.

Diagnosis – **1)** Inspect cooling system for leaks. Repair as necessary and go to step **6**). If no problem is found, go to next step.

2) Perform transmission fluid checking procedure. See CHECKING FLUID LEVEL under LUBRICATION in appropriate AUTOMATIC TRANSMISSION SERVICING article. Fill if necessary and go to next step.

3) Install scan tool. Turn ignition on. Using scan tool, record DTC FAILURE RECORDS. Test drive vehicle in 1st, 2nd, 3rd and "D" with engine speed greater than 3500 RPM for 5.5 seconds. Using scan tool in SNAPSHOT mode, record each gear ratio. Compare recorded value with GEAR RATIO SPECIFICATION table. If gear ratios match, go to DIAGNOSTIC AIDS. If gear ratios do not match, go to next step.

GEAR RATIO SPECIFICATION

Gear Range	Ratio
1st	2.73-2.99
2nd	1.54-1.71
3rd	0.93-1.05
4th	0.66-0.78

4) Perform hydraulic pressure test. See TRANSMISSION TESTING in appropriate overhaul article. Repair as necessary and go to step **6**). If no problem is found, go to next step.

5) Check for possible clutch slippage. See TROUBLE SHOOTING in appropriate overhaul article. Repair as necessary and go to next step.

6) Using scan tool, select DTC, then CLEAR INFO function. Select SPECIFIC DTC, then enter DTC P1871. Test drive vehicle in D4 with engine speed greater than 3500 RPM to obtain any of the following gear ratios for 7 seconds:
- 1st 1:2.73-1:2.99
- 2nd 1:1.54-1:1.71
- 3rd 1:0.93-1:1.05
- 4th 1:0.66-1:0.78

If last test failed, or DTC P0730 is present, repeat step **1**). If last test passed and no DTCs are present, testing is complete.

Diagnostic Aids – Check for intermittent output speed sensor circuit problems. Check for possible incorrect calibration (PCM part number, tire size or rear axle ratio).

DTC P0742: TORQUE CONVERTER CLUTCH (TCC) CIRCUIT STUCK ON
Conditions For Setting DTC:
- DTCs P0122, P0123, P0722, P0723 and P1860 are not present.
- TP angel is greater than 20 percent.
- Engine speed is greater than 500 RPM and less than 3000 RPM.
- Engine vacuum is between zero and 10.2 in. Hg.
- Commanded gear is not 1st.
- Gear range is D4.

AUTOMATIC TRANSMISSIONS
1996 Hydra-Matic 4L30-E Electronic Controls
Acura SLX & Isuzu Trooper (Cont.)

3-685

- TCC is commanded OFF.
- TCC slip speed is between –30 and 30 RPM for 4 seconds.
- Vehicle speed is greater than 15 MPH, and less than 75 MPH.
- Speed ratio is greater than .9 and less than 1.8.

Diagnosis – 1) Install scan tool. Turn ignition on. Using scan tool, record DTC FREEZE FRAME and FAILURE RECORDS. Verify TP sensor operation. If TP sensor value is .6-5.0 volts, go to next step. If TP sensor value is not as specified, go to DIAGNOSTIC AIDS.
2) Test drive vehicle in D4 range in 4th gear under steady acceleration, with TP sensor angle greater than 20 percent. Using scan tool, observe TCC SLIP SPEED parameter. If display indicates –30 to 30 RPM while TCC solenoid state is OFF, go to next step. If display is not as specified, go to DIAGNOSTIC AIDS.
3) TCC solenoid is mechanically stuck on. Check for the following:
- Clogged TCC solenoid exhaust orifice.
- TCC apply valve stuck in apply position.
- Misaligned or damaged valve body gaskets.
- Restricted release passage.

Repair as necessary and go to next step.
4) Using scan tool, select DTC, then CLEAR INFO function. Ensure TCC slip is between 200 and 2500 RPM for 4 seconds. Review DTC INFO. If last test failed, or DTC P0742 is present, repeat step **1)**. If last test passed and no DTCs are present, testing is complete.

Diagnostic Aids – If TCC is mechanically stuck on with parking brake applied and any gear range selected, TCC fluid will mechanically apply TCC, possibly causing engine to stall.

DTC P0748: PRESSURE CONTROL SOLENOID (FORCE MOTOR) CIRCUIT ELECTRICAL

Conditions For Setting DTC:
- DTC P0560 is not present.
- PCM detects that pressure control solenoid has reached its electrical high or low limit.

Diagnosis – 1) Install scan tool. Turn ignition on. Using scan tool, record DTC FAILURE RECORDS. Start engine. Ensure gearshift lever is in "P" position. Using scan tool, apply .1 amp through 1.0 amp while observing PC REF. CURRENT and PC ACT. CURRENT. If PC ACT. CURRENT is always within .16 amp, go to DIAGNOSTIC AIDS. If PC ACT. CURRENT is not as specified, go to next step.
2) Turn ignition off. Disconnect transmission harness connector M-6 (5-pin Black connector). Using a DVOM, measure resistance between terminals of pressure control solenoid (Violet/Red wire and Violet/White wire). If resistance is 3-7 ohms, go to step **6)**. If resistance is not as specified, go to next step.
3) Remove transmission oil pan. Disconnect internal wiring harness. Using a DVOM, measure resistance of pressure control solenoid. If resistance is 3-7 ohms, go to step **5)**. If resistance is not as specified, go to next step.
4) Replace pressure control solenoid. Go to step **8)**.
5) Repair open in internal wiring harness. Go to step **8)**.
6) Inspect pressure control solenoid circuit for an open, short or poor connection. Repair as necessary and go to step **8)**. If no problem is found, go to next step.
7) Replace PCM. Go to next step.
8) Using scan tool, select DTC, then CLEAR INFO function. Ensure pressure control solenoid duty cycle is not at its electrical high or low limit. Review DTC INFO. If last test failed, or DTC P0748 is present, repeat step **1)**. If last test passed and no DTCs are present, testing is complete.

Diagnostic Aids – Inspect for poor harness connections and improper wire harness routing. An intermittent condition may be caused by a wire which is broken inside its insulation, or shorted to an additional circuit or chassis ground. Check harness connectors for damaged, corroded or backed-out terminal pins. Repair as necessary.

DTC P0751: SHIFT SOLENOID "A" PERFORMANCE (WITHOUT INPUT SPEED)

NOTE: Shift solenoid "A" may also be known as 1-2/3-4 shift solenoid. Shift solenoid "B" may also be known as 2-3 shift solenoid.

Conditions For Setting DTC:
- DTCs P0122, P0123, P0722, P0723, P0742, P1860, P0753 and P0758 are not present.
- Gear range is D4.
- Vehicle speed is greater than 6.25 MPH.
- Transmission fluid temperature is 68-266°F (20-130°C).

All conditions above must be met, and the combination of conditions No. 1, 2, 3 and 4, or 1, 2, 3 and 5 occur 2 consecutive times.
Condition No. 1:
- Commanded 1-2 shift.
- TP angle is between 10 and 60 percent.
- TP angle is constant within plus or minus 5 percent.
- Vehicle speed is between 11 and 31 MPH.
- Within 2.2 seconds, engine speed in 2nd gear must be 100 RPM greater than last speed in 1st gear.

Condition No. 2:
- Commanded 2-3 shift.
- TP angle is between 15 and 60 percent.
- TP angle is constant within plus or minus 5 percent.
- Vehicle speed is between 20 and 45 MPH.
- Within 2.2 seconds, engine speed in 3rd gear must be 64 RPM less than last speed in 2nd gear.

Condition No. 3:
- Commanded 3-4 shift.
- TP angle is between 23 and 60 percent.
- TP angle is constant within plus or minus 5 percent.
- Vehicle speed is between 31 and 87 MPH.
- Within 2.2 seconds, engine speed in 4th gear must not be greater than last speed in 3rd gear.

Condition No. 4:
- Commanded 4th gear.
- TCC is ON.
- TP angle is between 15 and 60 percent.
- Speed ratio is between .85 and 1.2 (speed ratio = engine speed divided by output speed).
- TCC slip speed is between 100 and 2000 RPM for 3 seconds.

Condition No. 5:
- Commanded 4th gear.
- TCC is ON.
- TP angle is between 15 and 60 percent.
- Speed ratio is between .5 and .85.
- TCC slip speed is between –50 and 500 RPM for 3 seconds.

Diagnosis – 1) Install scan tool. Turn ignition on. Using scan tool, record DTC FREEZE FRAME and FAILURE RECORDS. Start engine. Apply brake pedal. Observe scan tool while moving gearshift lever through all gear ranges. If scan tool display coincides with actual gear range selected, go to next step. If operation is not as specified, go to RANGE SWITCH LOGIC TABLE. See Fig. 5.
2) Raise and support vehicle. With engine running, place gearshift lever in D4. Using scan tool, command 1st, 2nd, 3rd and 4th gears while accelerating vehicle. If 2-3 or 1-4 shift patterns are detected only, go to next step. If all shift patterns are detected, go to DIAGNOSTIC AIDS.
3) Check shift solenoid/hydraulic circuit for the following:
- Internal malfunction in one or both shift solenoids.
- Contamination in one or both shift solenoids.
- Damaged seals on one or both shift solenoids.

Repair as necessary and go to next step. If no problem is found, go to DIAGNOSTIC AIDS.
4) Using scan tool, select DTC, then CLEAR INFO function. Road test vehicle. Review DTC INFO. If last test failed, or DTC P0751 is present, repeat step **1)**. If last test passed and no DTCs are present, testing is complete.

3-686

AUTOMATIC TRANSMISSIONS
1996 Hydra-Matic 4L30-E Electronic Controls
Acura SLX & Isuzu Trooper (Cont.)

Diagnostic Aids – Verify transmission shift speeds are correct. See TRANSMISSION TESTING in appropriate overhaul article. Other transmission internal failures may cause more than one shift to occur. A shift solenoid "A" performance problem may set a shift solenoid "B" DTC P0756 or a transmission component slipping DTC P1870.

DTC P0753: SHIFT SOLENOID "A" ELECTRICAL

NOTE: Shift solenoid "A" may also be known as 1-2/3-4 shift solenoid. Shift solenoid "B" may also be known as 2-3 shift solenoid.

Conditions For Setting DTC:
- Ignition on.
- DTC P0560 is not present.
- PCM commands solenoid on and voltage remains high (battery voltage).
- PCM commands solenoid off and voltage remains low (zero voltage).
- Conditions must be present for .275 second.

Diagnosis – **1)** Install scan tool. Turn ignition on. Using scan tool, record DTC FREEZE FRAME and FAILURE RECORDS. If DTCs P0753, P0758 and P1860 are set, go to next step. If specified, DTCs are not set, go to DIAGNOSTIC AIDS.

2) Ensure ignition is on. Using a DVOM, measure voltage (backprobe) between ground and PCM harness connector C-3 (Blue), terminal E14 (Brown/White wire). If reading is 10-12 volts, go to next step. If reading is not as specified, go to step **4)**.

3) Turn ignition off. Disconnect PCM harness connector C-3. Turn ignition on. Using a DVOM, measure voltage between ground and PCM harness connector C-3, terminal F14 (Brown/Red wire). If reading is 10-12 volts, go to step **10)**. If reading is not as specified, go to next step.

4) Turn ignition off. Using a DVOM, measure resistance between PCM harness connector C-3, terminal E14 (Brown/White wire) and terminal F14 (Brown/Red wire). If resistance is 18-20 ohms, go to next step. If resistance is not as specified, go to step **6)**.

5) Disconnect PCM harness connectors C-1 (Red) and C-2 (White). Using a DVOM, check for continuity between ground and PCM harness connector C-3, terminal F14 (Brown/Red wire). If continuity is present, go to step **11)**. If no continuity is present, go to step **7)**.

6) Disconnect transmission harness connector H-10 (16-pin Blue connector). Using a DVOM, measure resistance between terminals No. 5 (Brown/Red wire) and No. 6 (Brown/White wire). If resistance is 18-20 ohms, go to step **13)**. If resistance is not as specified, go to step **8)**.

7) Using a DVOM, measure continuity between ground and PCM harness connector C-3 (Blue), terminal E14 (Brown/White wire). If continuity is present, go to step **12)**. If continuity is not present, go to step **9)**.

8) Disconnect transmission harness connector M-7 (4-pin Black connector). Using a DVOM, measure resistance between harness connector M-7, terminals No. 3 (Brown/Red wire) and No. 4 (Brown/White wire). If resistance is 18-20 ohms, go to step **14)**. If resistance is not as specified, go to step **15)**.

9) Check all PCM harness connections. If a problem is found, go to step **17)**. If no problem is found, go to step **16)**.

10) Repair Brown/Red wire between PCM harness connector C-3 (Blue) and shift solenoid "A" for a short to power. Go to step **18)**.

11) Repair Brown/Red wire between PCM harness connector C-3 (Blue) and shift solenoid "A" for a short to ground. Go to step **18)**.

12) Repair Brown/White wire between PCM harness connector C-3 (Blue) and shift solenoid "A" for a short to ground. Go to step **18)**.

13) Repair wiring harness between transmission harness connector H-10 (16-pin Blue connector) and PCM harness connector C-3 (Blue) for an open or poor connection. Go to step **18)**.

14) Repair open or poor connection in wiring harness between transmission harness connector H-10 (16-pin Blue connector) and transmission harness connector M-7 (4-pin Black connector). Go to step **18)**.

15) Replace shift solenoid "A". Go to step **18)**.

16) Replace PCM. Go to step **18)**.

17) Repair PCM harness connections. Go to next step.

18) Using scan tool, select DTC, then CLEAR INFO function. Operate vehicle and ensure that when shift solenoid "A" is commanded on, voltage drops to zero, then increases to battery voltage when commanded off. Review DTC INFO. If last test failed, or DTC P0753 is present, repeat step **1)**. If last test passed and no DTCs are present, testing is complete.

Diagnostic Aids – Inspect for poor harness connections and improper wire harness routing. An intermittent condition may be caused by a wire which is broken inside its insulation, or shorted to an additional circuit or chassis ground. Check harness connectors for damaged, corroded or backed-out terminal pins. Repair as necessary. An open ignition feed circuit can cause multiple DTCs to set. A shift solenoid "B" DTC P0756 may also set with a shift solenoid "A" failure.

DTC P0756: SHIFT SOLENOID "B" PERFORMANCE (WITHOUT INPUT SPEED)

NOTE: Shift solenoid "A" may also be known as 1-2/3-4 shift solenoid. Shift solenoid "B" may also be known as 2-3 shift solenoid.

Conditions For Setting DTC:
- DTCs P0106, P1106, P0107, P1107, P0108, P0122, P0123, P0722, P0723, P0742, P1860, P0753 and P0758 are not present.
- Vehicle speed is greater than 6.25 MPH.
- Gear range is D4.
- Engine vacuum is between zero and 10.2 in. Hg.
- Engine speed is less than 6000 RPM.
- Transmission temperature is 68-266°F (20-130°C).
- TCC is off.

All conditions above must be met, and either one of the following fail conditions occurs:
- Solenoid is stuck ON, and conditions No. 3 and 4 are present 2 consecutive times.
- Solenoid is stuck OFF, and conditions No. 1 and 3 are present 2 consecutive times.

Condition No. 1:
- TP angle is greater than 45 percent.
- 1st gear is commanded for 3 seconds.
- Speed ratio is between .5 and 2.65 (speed ratio = engine speed divided by output speed).
- Transmission output speed is between 320 and 2000 RPM.
- TCC slip speed is between –200 and –4000 RPM for 1.8 seconds.

Condition No. 2:
- Not used.

Condition No. 3:
- Commanded 2-3 shift.
- TP angle is between 10 and 60 percent.
- TP angle is within plus or minus 5 percent.
- 3rd gear is commanded for 2 seconds.
- 3rd gear speed ratio is higher than the last 2nd gear speed ratio minus .3 (scan tool value is numerically greater in 3rd gear).
- 3rd gear TCC slip speed is greater than or equal to last 2nd gear TCC slip speed plus 520 RPM for 2.1 seconds.
- Discontinue test if time since last commanded 2-3 shift is 6 seconds.

Condition No. 4:
- TP angle is greater than 10 percent.
- 4th gear is commanded for one second.
- Speed ratio is between 2.0 and 4.0.
- Transmission output speed is between zero and 8192 RPM.
- TCC slip speed is between 2000 and 5000 RPM form 3 seconds.

Diagnosis – **1)** Install scan tool. Turn ignition on. Using scan tool, record DTC FREEZE FRAME and FAILURE RECORDS. Start engine. Apply brake pedal. Observe scan tool while moving gearshift lever

AUTOMATIC TRANSMISSIONS
1996 Hydra-Matic 4L30-E Electronic Controls
Acura SLX & Isuzu Trooper (Cont.)

3-687

through all gear ranges. If scan tool display coincides with actual gear range selected, go to next step. If operation is not as specified, go to RANGE SWITCH LOGIC TABLE. *See Fig. 5.*

2) Raise and support vehicle. With engine running, place gearshift lever in D4. Using scan tool, command 1st, 2nd, 3rd and 4th gears while accelerating vehicle. If 1st gear was commanded and not achieved, or 4th gear was commanded and a gear range other than 4th occurred, go to next step. If all shift patterns are detected, go to DIAGNOSTIC AIDS.

3) Check shift solenoid/hydraulic circuit for the following:
- Internal malfunction in one or both shift solenoids.
- Contamination in one or both shift solenoids.
- Damaged seals on one or both shift solenoids.

Repair as necessary and go to next step. If no problem is found, go to DIAGNOSTIC AIDS.

4) Using scan tool, select DTC, then CLEAR INFO function. Road test vehicle. Review DTC INFO. If last test failed, or DTC P0756 is present, repeat step 1). If last test passed and no DTCs are present, testing is complete.

Diagnostic Aids – A shift solenoid "A" electrical failure can also set a shift solenoid "B" performance DTC P0756. A shift solenoid "B" electrical failure can also set a shift solenoid "B" performance DTC P0756.

DTC P0758: SHIFT SOLENOID "B" ELECTRICAL

NOTE: Shift solenoid "A" may also be known as 1-2/3-4 shift solenoid. Shift solenoid "B" may also be known as 2-3 shift solenoid.

Conditions For Setting DTC:
- Ignition on.
- DTC P0560 is not set.
- PCM commands solenoid on and voltage remains high (battery voltage).
- PCM commands solenoid off and voltage remains low (zero voltage).
- Conditions must be present for .275 second.

Diagnosis – 1) Install scan tool. Turn ignition on. Using scan tool, record DTC FREEZE FRAME and FAILURE RECORDS. If DTCs P0753, P0758 and P1860 are set, go to step 3). If specified, DTCs are not set, go to next step.

2) With engine running, apply brake pedal and place gearshift lever in "D" position. Press WINTER switch to select Winter mode. If scan tool displays DTC P0758 at 3rd gear, go to step 7). If display is not as specified, go to DIAGNOSTIC AIDS.

3) Turn ignition off. Disconnect PCM harness connectors C-2 (White) and C-3 (Blue). Turn ignition on. Using a DVOM, measure voltage between PCM harness connector C-2, terminal C2 (Brown/Black wire) and terminal C8 (Black/Pink wire). If reading is 10-12 volts, go to step 14). If reading is not as specified, go to next step.

4) Turn ignition off. Using a DVOM, measure resistance between PCM harness connector C-2, terminal C2 (Brown/Black wire) and PCM harness connector C-3, terminal E-14 (Brown/White wire). If resistance is 18-20 ohms, go to step 15). If resistance is not as specified, go to next step.

5) Disconnect transmission harness connector H-10 (16-pin Blue connector). Using a DVOM, measure resistance between transmission harness connector H-10, terminals No. 2 (Brown/Yellow wire) and No. 6 (Brown/White wire). If resistance is 18-20 ohms, go to step 16). If resistance is not as specified, go to next step.

6) Disconnect transmission harness connector M-7 (4-pin Black connector). Using a DVOM, measure resistance between transmission harness connector M-7, terminals No. 1 (Brown/Black wire) and No. 4 (Brown/White wire). If resistance is 18-20 ohms, go to step 17). If resistance is not as specified, go to step 18).

7) Turn ignition off. Disconnect PCM harness connectors C-2 (White) and C-3 (Blue). Using a DVOM, measure resistance between PCM harness connector C-2, terminal C2 (Brown/Black wire) and PCM harness connector C-3, terminal E14 (Brown/white wire). If resistance is between 18-20 ohms, go to next step. If resistance is not as specified, go to step 9).

8) Using a DVOM, check for continuity between PCM harness connector C-2, terminal C2 (Brown/Black wire) and ground. If continuity is present, go to step 19). If no continuity is present, go to step 10).

9) Disconnect transmission harness connector H-10 (16-pin Blue connector). Using a DVOM, measure resistance between transmission harness connector H-10, terminals No. 2 (Brown/Black wire) and No. 6 (Brown/White wire). If resistance is 18-20 ohms, go to step 20). If resistance is not as specified, go to step 11).

10) Using a DVOM, check for continuity between ground and PCM harness connector C-3, terminal E14 (Brown/White wire). If continuity is present, go to step 21). If no continuity is present, go to step 12).

11) Disconnect transmission harness connector M-7 (4-pin Black connector). Using a DVOM, measure resistance between harness connector M-7, terminals No. 1 (Brown/Black wire) and No. 4 (Brown/White wire). If resistance is 18-20 ohms, go to step 22). If resistance is not as specified, go to step 23).

12) Check all connections at PCM and transmission harness connector H-10. repair as necessary and go to step 25). If no problem is found, go to next step.

13) Reconnect PCM harness connectors C-2 and C-3. Start engine and repeat step 2). If scan tool displays DTC P0758 at 3rd gear, go to step 24). If display is not as specified, go to DIAGNOSTIC AIDS.

14) Repair Brown/Black wire between PCM harness connector C-2 and transmission harness connector M-7 for a short to power. Go to step 25).

15) PCM harness connector C-2, internal terminal C2 (Brown/Black wire) is shorted to power. Replace PCM. Go to step 25).

16) Repair wire harness between PCM and transmission harness connector H-10 for a short circuit. Go to step 25).

17) Repair wire harness between transmission harness connector H-10 and transmission harness connectors M-6 or M-7 for a short circuit. Go to step 25).

18) Shift solenoid "B" or its internal wiring harness is faulty. Repair as necessary. Go to step 25).

19) Repair Brown/Black wire between PCM harness connector C-2 and transmission harness connector M-7 for a short to ground. Go to step 25).

20) Brown/Black wire between PCM harness connector C-2 and transmission harness connector H-10 is open, or Brown/White wire between PCM harness connector C-3 and transmission harness connector H-10 is open. Repair as necessary. Go to step 25).

21) Repair Brown/White wire between PCM harness connector C-3 and transmission harness connector M-7 for a short to ground. Go to step 25).

22) Brown/Black wire between transmission harness connector H-10 and transmission harness connector M-7 is open, or Brown/White wire between transmission harness connector H-10 and transmission harness connector M-7 is open. Repair as necessary. Go to step 25).

23) Shift solenoid "B" or its internal wiring harness is faulty. Repair as necessary. Go to step 25).

24) Replace PCM. Go to next step.

25) Using scan tool, select DTC, then CLEAR INFO function. Operate vehicle and ensure that when shift solenoid "B" is commanded on, voltage drops to zero, then increases to battery voltage when commanded off. Review DTC INFO. If last test failed, or DTC P0758 is present, repeat step 1). If last test passed and no DTCs are present, testing is complete.

Diagnostic Aids – Inspect for poor harness connections and improper wire harness routing. An intermittent condition may be caused by a wire which is broken inside its insulation, or shorted to an additional circuit or chassis ground. Check harness connectors for damaged, corroded or backed-out terminal pins. Repair as necessary.

DTC P1790:
ROM TRANSMISSION SIDE BAD CHECK SUM
DTC P1792:
EEPROM TRANSMISSION SIDE BAD CHECK SUM

Conditions For Setting DTC:
- Check Sum (CSUM) error detected for one second.

3-688

AUTOMATIC TRANSMISSIONS
1996 Hydra-Matic 4L30-E Electronic Controls
Acura SLX & Isuzu Trooper (Cont.)

Diagnosis – 1) Install scan tool. Turn ignition on. Using scan tool, record DTC FAILURE RECORDS. If DTC P1790 is set, go to step **4**). If DTC P1790 is not set, go to next step.

2) If DTC P1792 is set, go to next step.

3) Remove PCM. Using Service Programming System (T-6), reprogram transmission EEPROM. Go to step **5**).

4) Replace PCM. Go to next step.

5) Using scan tool, select DTC, then CLEAR INFO function. Road test vehicle. Review DTC INFO. If last test failed, or DTCs P1790 or P1792 are present, repeat step **1**). If last test passed and no DTCs are present, testing is complete.

DTC P1835: KICKDOWN SWITCH ALWAYS ON
Conditions For Setting DTC:
- DTCs P0122 and P0123 are not present.
- TP angle is less than 70 percent.
- Kickdown switch is on.
- Conditions must be present for one second.

Diagnosis – 1) Install scan tool. Turn ignition on. Using scan tool, record DTC FAILURE RECORDS. If scan tool displays KICKDOWN SWITCH LOW (closed), go to next step. If display is not as specified, go to step **3**).

2) Turn ignition off. Disconnect PCM harness connector C-3 (Blue). Using a DVOM, check for continuity between ground and PCM harness connector C-3, terminal F11 (Light Blue wire). If continuity is present, go to step **4**). If no continuity is present, go to step **7**).

3) If scan tool displays kickdown switch ON when TP angle is less than 70 percent, go to step **5**). If display is not as specified, go to DIAGNOSTIC AIDS.

4) Disconnect kickdown switch electrical connector. Using a DVOM, check for continuity between kickdown switch terminals. If continuity is present, go to step **6**). If no continuity is present, go to step **8**).

5) Adjust kickdown switch. Scan tool should display kickdown switch ON when TP angle is greater than 95 percent. Go to step **9**).

6) Replace kickdown switch. Go to step **9**).

7) Replace PCM. Go to step **9**).

8) Repair Light Blue wire between PCM and kickdown switch for a short to ground. Go to next step.

9) Using scan tool, select DTC, then CLEAR INFO function. Ensure torque converter stator temperature switch circuit does not indicate a hot mode when transmission fluid temperature is less than 140°F (60°C) for at least 5 seconds. Review DTC INFO. If last test failed, or DTC P1835 is present, repeat step **1**). If last test passed and no DTCs are present, testing is complete.

Diagnostic Aids – Check wire harness for a short to ground between PCM and kickdown switch. Check for misadjusted or faulty kickdown switch.

DTC P1850:
BRAKE BAND APPLY SOLENOID MALFUNCTION
Conditions For Setting DTC:
- DTC P0560 is not present.
- Ignition on.
- PCM commands solenoid on, and voltage remains high (battery voltage).
- PCM commands solenoid off, and voltage remains low (zero voltage).
- Conditions met in 1.3 seconds.

Diagnosis – 1) Install scan tool. Turn ignition on. Using scan tool, record DTC FREEZE FRAME and FAILURE RECORDS. If DTCs P0753 and P0758 are set, go to next step. If specified DTCs are not present, go to step **3**).

2) Using a DVOM, measure voltage (backprobe) between PCM harness connector C-2 (White), terminal C8 (Black/Pink wire) and PCM harness connector C-3 (Blue), terminal E14 (Brown/White wire). If reading is 10-12 volts, go to step **4**). If reading is not as specified, go to step **5**).

3) Turn ignition off. Disconnect PCM harness connectors C-1 (Red) and C-3 (Blue). Using a DVOM, measure resistance between PCM harness connector C-1, terminal A16 (Brown/Yellow wire) and PCM harness connector C-3, terminal E14 (Brown/White wire). If resistance is 10-12 ohms, go to step **11**). If resistance is not as specified, go to step **12**).

4) Using a DVOM, measure voltage (backprobe) between PCM harness connector C-1, terminal A16 (Brown/Yellow wire) and PCM harness connector C-2, terminal C8 (Black/Red wire). If reading is 10-12 volts, go to step **25**). If reading is not as specified, go to step **3**).

5) Turn ignition off. Disconnect PCM harness connectors C-1 (Red) and C-3 (Blue). Using a DVOM, check for continuity between ground and PCM harness connector C-3, terminal E14 (Brown/White wire). If continuity is present, go to next step. If no continuity is present, go to step **8**).

6) Disconnect transmission harness connector H-10 (16-pin Blue connector). Using a DVOM, check for continuity between ground and transmission harness connector H-10, terminal No. 12 (Brown/Yellow wire). If continuity is present, go to next step. If no continuity is present, go to step **16**).

7) Disconnect transmission harness connector M-7 (4-pin Black connector). Using a DVOM, check for continuity between ground and transmission harness connector M-7, terminal No. 2 (Brown/Yellow wire). If continuity is present, go to step **17**). If no continuity is present, go to step **18**).

8) Disconnect PCM harness connector C-1 (Red). Using a DVOM, measure resistance between PCM harness connector C-1, terminal A16 (Brown/Yellow wire) and PCM harness connector C-3, terminal E14 (Brown/White wire). If resistance is 10-12 ohms, go to step **25**). If resistance is not as specified, go to next step.

9) Disconnect transmission harness connector H-10 (16-pin Blue connector). Using a DVOM, measure resistance between transmission harness connector H-10, terminals No. 6 (Brown/White wire) and No. 12 (Brown/Yellow wire). If resistance is 10-12 ohms, go to step **16**). If resistance is not as specified, go to next step.

10) Disconnect transmission harness connector M-7 (4-pin Black connector). Using a DVOM, measure resistance between transmission harness connector M-7, terminals No. 2 (Brown/Yellow wire) and No. 4 (Brown/White wire). If resistance is 10-12 ohms, go to step **19**). If resistance is not as specified, go to step **20**).

11) Using a DVOM, check for continuity between ground and PCM harness connector C-1, terminal A-16 (Brown/Yellow wire). If continuity is present, go to step **13**). If continuity is not present, go to step **25**).

12) Disconnect transmission harness connector H-10 (16-pin Blue connector). Using a DVOM, measure resistance between transmission harness connector H-10, terminals No. 6 (Brown/White wire) and No. 12 (Brown/Yellow wire). If resistance is 10-12 ohms, go to step **23**). If resistance is not as specified, go to step **14**).

13) Disconnect transmission harness connector H-10 (16-pin Blue connector). Using a DVOM, check for continuity between ground and transmission harness connector H-10, terminal No. 12 (Brown/Yellow wire). If continuity is present, go to step **15**). If no continuity is present, go to step **21**).

14) Disconnect transmission harness connector M-7 (4-pin Black connector). Using a DVOM, measure resistance between transmission harness connector M-7, terminals No. 2 (Brown/Yellow wire) and No. 4 (Brown/White wire). If resistance is 10-12 ohms, go to step **24**). If resistance is not as specified, go to step **20**).

15) Disconnect transmission harness connector M-7 (4-pin Black connector). Using a DVOM, check for continuity between ground and transmission harness connector M-7, terminal No. 2 (Brown/Yellow wire). If continuity is present, go to step **17**). If no continuity is present, go to step **22**).

16) Repair open in Brown/White wire between PCM harness connector C-3 and transmission harness connector H-10. Go to step **26**).

17) Brake band apply solenoid is faulty, or its internal wiring harness is shorted to ground. Repair as necessary. Go to step **26**).

AUTOMATIC TRANSMISSIONS
1996 Hydra-Matic 4L30-E Electronic Controls
Acura SLX & Isuzu Trooper (Cont.)

3-689

18) Repair short to ground in Brown/White wire between transmission harness connector M-7 and transmission harness connector H-10. Go to step 26).

19) Repair open in Brown/White wire between transmission harness connector M-7 and transmission harness connector H-10. Go to step 26).

20) Brake band apply solenoid is faulty, or its internal wiring harness is open. Repair as necessary. Go to step 26).

21) Repair short to ground in Brown/Yellow wire between PCM harness connector C-1 and transmission harness connector H-10. Go to step 26).

22) Repair short to ground in Brown/Yellow wire between transmission harness connector M-7 and transmission harness connector H-10. Go to step 26).

23) Repair open in Brown/Yellow wire between PCM harness connector C-1 and transmission harness connector H-10. Go to step 26).

24) Repair open in Brown/Yellow wire between transmission harness connector M-7 and transmission harness connector H-10. Go to step 26).

25) Check PCM harness connections. Repair as necessary. If connections are okay, replace PCM. Go to next step.

26) Using scan tool, select DTC, then CLEAR INFO function. Ensure that when 3-2 control solenoid is commanded on, voltage drops to zero, and when commanded off, voltage increases to battery voltage. Review DTC INFO. If last test failed, or DTC P1850 is present, repeat step 1). If last test passed and no DTCs are present, testing is complete.

Diagnostic Aids – Inspect for poor harness connections and improper wire harness routing. An intermittent condition may be caused by a wire which is broken inside its insulation, or shorted to an additional circuit or chassis ground. Check harness connectors for damaged, corroded or backed-out terminal pins. Repair as necessary.

DTC P1860: TCC PWM SOLENOID ELECTRICAL

Conditions For Setting DTC:
- DTCs P0560, P0751, P0753, P0756 and P0758 are not present.
- Ignition on.
- PCM commands solenoid on, and voltage remains low (zero voltage).
- PCM commands solenoid off, and voltage remains high (battery voltage).
- Conditions present for .15 second.

Diagnosis – 1) Install scan tool. Turn ignition on. Using scan tool, record DTC FREEZE FRAME and FAILURE RECORDS. If DTC P1860 is present, go to next step. If DTC P1860 is not present, go to step 3).

2) Using a DVOM, measure voltage (backprobe) between PCM harness connector C-2 (White), terminal D2 (Brown/Blue wire) and terminal C8 (Black/Pink wire). If reading is zero volts, go to step 4). If reading is not as specified, go to step 5).

3) Apply brake pedal and place gearshift lever in "D" position. Road test vehicle and increase vehicle speed until TCC shows ON in 4th gear. If scan tool displays DTC P1860 with TCC on, go to step 9). If DTC P1860 is not displayed, go to DIAGNOSTIC AIDS.

4) Turn ignition off. Disconnect PCM harness connector C-2 (White). Using a DVOM, measure resistance between PCM harness connector C-2, terminal D2 (Brown/Blue wire) and terminal C8 (Black/Pink wire). If resistance is 18-20 ohms, go to step 6). If resistance is not as specified, go to step 7).

5) Check Brown/Blue wire for a short to power between PCM harness connector C-2 and transmission harness connector M-6 (5-pin Black connector). Repair as necessary and go to step 18). If no problem is found, go to step 19).

6) Possible intermittent condition. Check wiring harness and terminals between PCM harness connector C-2 and transmission harness connector M-6. Repair as necessary and go to step 18). If no problem is found, go to step 19).

7) Disconnect transmission harness connector H-10 (16-pin Blue connector). Using a DVOM, measure resistance between ground and transmission harness connector H-10, terminal No. 11 (Brown/Blue wire). If resistance is 18-20 ohms, go to step 15). If resistance is not as specified, go to next step.

8) Disconnect transmission harness connector M-6 (5-pin Black connector. Using a DVOM, measure resistance between ground and transmission harness connector M-6, terminal No. 4 (Brown/Blue wire). If resistance is 18-20 ohms, go to step 16). If resistance is not as specified, go to step 17).

9) Turn ignition off. Disconnect PCM harness connector C-2 (White). Using a DVOM, measure resistance between PCM harness connector C-2, terminal D2 (Brown/Blue wire) and terminal C8 (Black/Pink wire). If resistance is 18-20 ohms, go to step 18). If resistance is not as specified, go to next step.

10) Disconnect transmission harness connector H-10 (16-pin Blue connector). Using a DVOM, measure resistance between ground and transmission harness connector H-10, terminal No. 11 (Brown/Blue wire). If resistance is 18-20 ohms, go to step 12). If resistance is not as specified, go to next step.

11) Disconnect transmission harness connector M-6 (5-pin Black connector. Using a DVOM, measure resistance between ground and transmission harness connector M-6, terminal No. 4 (Brown/Blue wire). If resistance is 18-20 ohms, go to step 13). If resistance is not as specified, go to step 14).

12) Repair Brown/Blue wire for a short to ground between PCM harness connector C-2 and transmission harness connector H-10. Go to step 20).

13) Repair wiring harness for a short to ground between transmission harness connector H-10 and transmission harness connector M-6. Go to step 20).

14) TCC PWM solenoid is faulty, or its internal wiring harness is shorted to ground. Repair as necessary. Go to step 20).

15) Repair open in Brown/Blue wire between PCM harness connector C-2 and transmission harness connector H-10. Go to step 20).

16) Repair open in Brown/Blue wire between transmission harness connector H-10 and transmission harness connector M-6. Go to step 20).

17) TCC PWM solenoid is faulty, or its internal wiring harness is open. Repair as necessary. Go to step 20).

18) Check PCM harness connections. Repair as necessary. If connections are okay, replace PCM. Go to step 20).

19) Check Brown/Blue wire connections at PCM harness connector C-2 and transmission harness connectors H-10 and M-6. Repair as necessary and go to next step.

20) Using scan tool, select DTC, then CLEAR INFO function. Ensure that when TCC PWM solenoid is commanded on, voltage increases to battery voltage, and when commanded off, voltage decreases to zero volts. Review DTC INFO. If last test failed, or DTC P1860 is present, repeat step 1). If last test passed and no DTCs are present, testing is complete.

Diagnostic Aids – Inspect for poor harness connections and improper wire harness routing. An intermittent condition may be caused by a wire which is broke inside its insulation, or shorted to an additional circuit or chassis ground. Check harness connectors for damaged, corroded or backed-out terminal pins. Repair as necessary.

DTC P1870:
TRANSMISSION COMPONENT SLIPPING

Conditions For Setting DTC:
The following conditions must be met for 3 TCC cycles with excessive TCC slip conditions.
- DTCs P0106, P1106, P0107, P1107, P0108, P0122, P0123, P0722, P0723, P0751, P0753, P0756, P0758 and P1860 are not present.
- No TCC solenoid DTC P0742.
- Engine speed is between 800 and 3360 RPM.
- Engine vacuum is between zero and 10.2 in. Hg.
- Gear range is D4.

3-690

AUTOMATIC TRANSMISSIONS
1996 Hydra-Matic 4L30-E Electronic Controls
Acura SLX & Isuzu Trooper (Cont.)

- TP angle is between 12 and 70 percent.
- TFT is between 68-286°F (20-141°C).
- TCC is on for 3 seconds.
- TCC slip speed is between 300 and 800 RPM for 10 seconds.
- Vehicle speed is between 24 and 69 MPH.
- Speed ratio is between .5 and .95.

Diagnosis – 1) Install scan tool. Turn ignition on. Using scan tool, record DTC FREEZE FRAME and FAILURE RECORDS. Apply brake pedal. Observe scan tool while moving gearshift lever through all gear ranges. If scan tool display matches each gear range selected, go to next step. If operation is not as specified, go to RANGE SWITCH LOGIC TABLE. *See Fig. 5.*

2) Road test vehicle in 4th gear with TCC engaged. Observe scan tool. If TCC SLIP SPEED is greater than 130 RPM for 8 seconds at any time with TCC engaged, see TROUBLE SHOOTING in appropriate overhaul article. If TCC SLIP SPEED never exceeds 130 RPM for 8 seconds, go to DIAGNOSTIC AIDS.

Diagnostic Aids – A malfunctioning range switch, faulty shift solenoids, faulty TCC solenoid or faulty TCC PWM solenoid may set DTC P1870. An internal transmission failure or incorrect engine speed may also set DTC P1870.

COMPONENT TESTING

NOTE: Some component testing information is not available from manufacturer. To aid in diagnosis of a certain component, refer to appropriate DTC test related to that component under DIAGNOSTIC TESTS.

A/C COMPRESSOR RELAY

1) Remove A/C compressor relay from fuse/relay box at passenger's side front corner of engine compartment. Note A/C compressor terminal identification. *See Fig. 6.*

2) Using a DVOM, ensure continuity is present between terminals No. 1 and 3. Continuity should not be present between terminals No. 2 and 4.

3) Apply battery voltage to terminals No. 1 and 3. Ensure continuity is now present between terminals No. 2 and 4. Replace A/C compressor relay if defective.

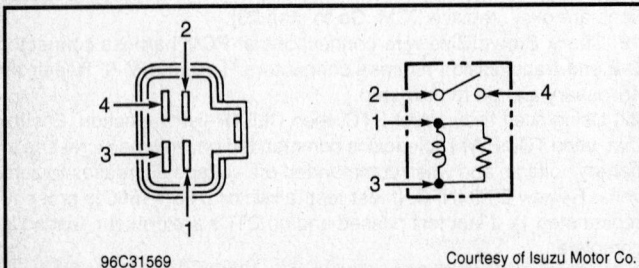

Fig. 6: Identifying A/C Compressor Relay Terminals

BAND APPLY SOLENOID

Band apply solenoid is located on main valve body. *See Fig. 4.* Component testing information is not available from manufacturer.

BRAKELIGHT SWITCH

Without Cruise Control – 1) Disconnect electrical connector from brakelight switch. Brakelight switch is located near brake pedal.

2) Using a DVOM, ensure continuity is present between terminals on brakelight switch only when brake pedal is depressed.

3) If continuity is not as specified, ensure brake pedal is properly adjusted so brakelight switch can obtain proper travel for switch operation. If brakelight switch travel is okay, replace brakelight switch.

With Cruise Control – 1) Disconnect electrical connector from brakelight switch and note terminal identification. *See Fig. 7.* Brakelight switch is located near brake pedal.

2) Using a DVOM, ensure continuity is present between specified terminals in relation to brake pedal position. See BRAKELIGHT SWITCH CONTINUITY SPECIFICATIONS table.

3) If continuity is not as specified, ensure brake pedal is properly adjusted so brakelight switch can obtain proper travel for switch operation. If brakelight switch travel is okay, replace brakelight switch.

BRAKELIGHT SWITCH CONTINUITY SPECIFICATIONS

Condition	Continuity Between Terminals No.
Brake Pedal Released	1 & 4
Brake Pedal Depressed	2 & 3

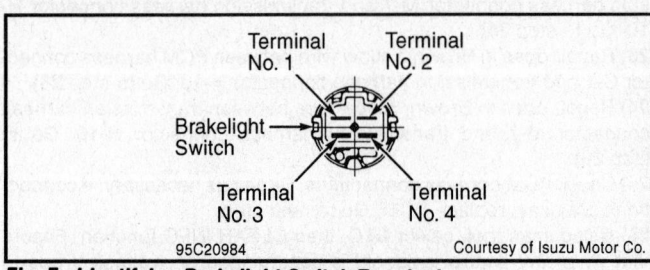

Fig. 7: Identifying Brakelight Switch Terminals

ENGINE COOLANT TEMPERATURE (ECT) SENSOR

ECT sensor is located on coolant pipe at rear of cylinder head. ECT sensor contains a Blue/Red wire and Blue/Yellow wire in harness connector. See appropriate SYSTEM & COMPONENT TESTING article in ENGINE PERFORMANCE in appropriate MITCHELL® manual.

KICKDOWN SWITCH

Kickdown switch is located on accelerator pedal. Component testing information is not available from manufacturer.

MODE SWITCH

1) Mode switch is located on side of transmission. *See Fig. 4.* Remove necessary covers for access to mode switch electrical connector. Disconnect mode switch electrical connector and note terminal identification. *See Fig. 8.*

2) Using a DVOM, check for continuity between specified terminals in relation to shift lever position. See MODE SWITCH CONTINUITY table. If continuity is not as specified, mode switch may require adjustment. See MODE SWITCH under REMOVAL & INSTALLATION. Replace mode switch if specified continuity cannot be obtained by adjusting.

MODE SWITCH CONTINUITY

Shift Lever Position	Continuity Between Terminals No.
"P"	3, 5 & 8
"R"	5, 7 & 8
"N"	3, 5 & 7
"D"	5, 6 & 7
"3"	3, 5, 6, 7 & 8
"2"	5, 6 & 8
"L"	3, 5 & 6

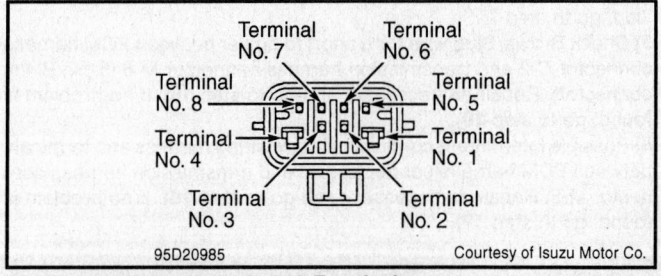

Fig. 8: Identifying Mode Switch Terminals

AUTOMATIC TRANSMISSIONS
1996 Hydra-Matic 4L30-E Electronic Controls
Acura SLX & Isuzu Trooper (Cont.)

3-691

POWER MODE SWITCH

POWER mode switch is located on center console, near gearshift lever. Component testing information is not available from manufacturer.

PRESSURE CONTROL SOLENOID (FORCE MOTOR)

Force motor solenoid is located on adapter case valve body. *See Fig. 4.* Component testing information is not available from manufacturer.

SHIFT SOLENOID

NOTE: Shift solenoid "A" may also be known as 1-2/3-4 shift solenoid. Shift solenoid "B" may also be known as 2-3 shift solenoid.

Shift solenoids "A" and "B" are located on main valve body. *See Fig. 4.* Component testing information is not available from manufacturer.

SPEED SENSOR

Speed sensor is located on extension housing on rear of transmission. *See Fig. 4.* Speed sensor may be referred to as magnetic sensor. See appropriate SYSTEM & COMPONENT TESTING article in ENGINE PERFORMANCE in appropriate MITCHELL® manual.

THROTTLE POSITION (TP) SENSOR

The TP sensor is mounted on side of throttle body. See appropriate SYSTEM & COMPONENT TESTING article in ENGINE PERFORMANCE in appropriate MITCHELL® manual.

TORQUE CONVERTER CLUTCH (TCC) SOLENOID

Torque Converter Clutch (TCC) solenoid is located on adapter case valve body. *See Fig. 4.* Component testing information is not available from manufacturer.

TRANSMISSION FLUID TEMPERATURE (TFT) SENSOR

Disconnect TFT sensor electrical connector. Using a DVOM, measure resistance between sensor terminals. Replace sensor if resistance is not within specification. See TFT SENSOR RESISTANCE table. TFT sensor is located in adapter case oil pan. *See Fig. 4.*

TFT SENSOR RESISTANCE

Temperature °F (°C)	Resistance (Ohms)
–40 (–40)	672,000
32 (0)	65,000
68 (20)	25,000
176 (80)	2,500
248 (120)	780
302 (150)	370

WINTER MODE SWITCH

WINTER mode switch is mounted on center console, near gearshift lever. Component testing information is not available from manufacturer.

REMOVAL & INSTALLATION

A/C COMPRESSOR RELAY

Removal & Installation – Remove A/C compressor relay from fuse/relay box at passenger's side front corner of engine compartment. To install, reverse removal procedure.

BAND APPLY SOLENOID

Removal – **1)** Band apply solenoid is located on main valve body. *See Fig. 4.* Disconnect negative battery cable. Remove exhaust pipe (if necessary) to access main case oil pan. Remove bolts, main case oil pan, magnet and gasket. Remove bolts and oil filter. Disconnect electrical connectors at band apply solenoid.

2) Remove spring pin used to retain band apply solenoid in main valve body. Remove band apply solenoid and gasket from main valve body by pulling on metal tip. DO NOT pull on electrical connector housing on band apply solenoid.

Installation – To install, reverse removal procedure using NEW gaskets and oil filter. Ensure spring pin is fully seated in main valve body. Install and tighten oil filter and main case oil pan bolts to specification. See TORQUE SPECIFICATIONS. Fill transmission with Dexron-III ATF.

BRAKELIGHT SWITCH

Removal & Installation – **1)** Disconnect electrical connector from brakelight switch located near brake pedal. Remove lock nut. Unscrew brakelight switch.

2) To install, screw brakelight switch inward until clearance between threaded end on brakelight switch and pedal is .020-.040" (.51-1.02 mm). Install and tighten lock nut. Connect electrical connector. Ensure brakelights and cruise control operate properly.

ENGINE COOLANT TEMPERATURE (ECT) SENSOR

Removal – **1)** ECT sensor is located on coolant pipe at rear of cylinder head, and contains a Blue/Red wire and a Blue/Yellow wire in electrical connector.

2) Disconnect negative battery cable. Drain cooling system. It may be necessary to remove fuel inlet manifold for access to ECT sensor. Remove ECT sensor.

Installation – Apply thread sealant to threads of ECT sensor. Install and tighten ECT sensor to specification. See TORQUE SPECIFICATIONS. Fill cooling system.

KICKDOWN SWITCH

Removal & Installation – Kickdown switch is located on accelerator pedal. Replacement information is not available from manufacturer.

MODE SWITCH

Removal – **1)** Disconnect negative battery cable. Apply parking brake. Place gearshift lever in "N" position. Remove mode switch cover for access to mode switch. *See Fig. 4.* Remove shift lever nut and disconnect shift lever from mode switch.

2) Remove bolts and heat protector from torque converter housing for access to wiring and mode switch. Remove air cleaner assembly. Disconnect mode switch harness connector. Remove clips for mode switch wiring. Remove mode switch retaining bolts and mode switch.

Installation – **1)** Install mode switch with retaining bolts. DO NOT tighten mode switch retaining bolts at this time. Mode switch must be adjusted. To adjust mode switch, rotate mode switch until slot in housing on mode switch aligns with selector shaft bushing. Insert a 3/32" punch into slot. *See Fig. 9.*

2) Tighten mode switch retaining bolts to specification. See TORQUE SPECIFICATIONS. Install shift lever on mode switch and tighten shift lever nut to specification. Install mode switch cover on mode switch. Install heat protector. Install and tighten bolts to specification. Install air cleaner assembly.

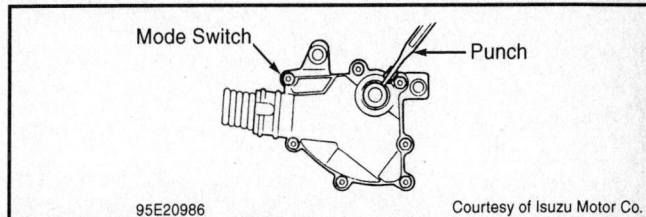

95E20986 Courtesy of Isuzu Motor Co.

Fig. 9: Adjusting Mode Switch

3-692

AUTOMATIC TRANSMISSIONS
1996 Hydra-Matic 4L30-E Electronic Controls
Acura SLX & Isuzu Trooper (Cont.)

PCM

Removal & Installation – Ensure ignition is off. Disconnect negative battery cable. Remove front console. Disconnect PCM harness connectors. Remove PCM and brackets. To install, reverse removal procedure.

POWER MODE SWITCH

Removal & Installation – POWER mode switch is located on center console, near gearshift lever. Replacement information is not available from manufacturer.

PRESSURE CONTROL SOLENOID (FORCE MOTOR)

Removal – **1)** Pressure control solenoid is located on adapter case valve body. *See Fig. 4.* Disconnect negative battery cable.

2) Remove exhaust pipe (if necessary) for access to adapter case oil pan. Remove bolts, adapter case oil pan and gasket. Disconnect electrical connectors at pressure control solenoid. Remove bolt and pressure control solenoid.

Installation – **1)** Install pressure control solenoid on adapter case valve body. Ensure pressure control solenoid is installed with electrical connector terminals facing upward, toward transmission.

2) Install and tighten pressure control solenoid bolt to specification. See TORQUE SPECIFICATIONS. Using a NEW gasket, install adapter case oil pan. Install and tighten bolts to specification. To install remaining components, reverse removal procedure. Fill transmission with Dexron-III ATF.

SHIFT SOLENOID

NOTE: Shift solenoid "A" may also be known as 1-2/3-4 shift solenoid. Shift solenoid "B" may also be known as 2-3 shift solenoid.

Removal – **1)** Shift solenoids "A" and "B" are located on main valve body. *See Fig. 4.* Disconnect negative battery cable. Remove exhaust pipe (if necessary) to access main case oil pan. Remove bolts, main case oil pan, magnet and gasket. Remove bolts and oil filter. Disconnect electrical connectors at appropriate shift solenoid.

2) Remove spring pin used to retain shift solenoid in main valve body. Remove shift solenoid and gasket from main valve body by pulling on metal tip. DO NOT pull on electrical connector housing on shift solenoid.

Installation – To install, reverse removal procedure using NEW gaskets and oil filter. Ensure spring pin is fully seated in main valve body. Install and tighten oil filter and main case oil pan bolts to specification. See TORQUE SPECIFICATIONS. Fill transmission with Dexron-III ATF.

SPEED SENSOR

Removal & Installation – **1)** Disconnect electrical connector at speed sensor located on rear of transmission. *See Fig. 4.* Remove speed sensor bolt, speed sensor and "O" ring.

2) To install, reverse removal procedure using a NEW "O" ring. Install and tighten speed sensor bolt to specification. See TORQUE SPECIFICATIONS.

THROTTLE POSITION (TP) SENSOR

Removal & Installation – **1)** Disconnect harness connector at TP sensor mounted on side of throttle body. Remove TP sensor bolts and TP sensor.

2) To install, ensure throttle is closed. Install TP sensor on throttle body and throttle shaft. Align TP sensor with bolt holes. Install and tighten TP sensor bolts to specification. See TORQUE SPECIFICATIONS. Install harness connector.

TORQUE CONVERTER CLUTCH (TCC) SOLENOID

Removal – **1)** The TCC solenoid is located on adapter case valve body. *See Fig. 4.* Disconnect negative battery cable.

2) Remove exhaust pipe (if necessary) to access adapter case oil pan. Remove bolts, adapter case oil pan and gasket. Disconnect electrical connector at TCC solenoid. Remove bolt, TCC solenoid and "O" ring.

Installation – **1)** Using a NEW "O" ring, install TCC solenoid on adapter case valve body. Install and tighten TCC solenoid bolt to specification. See TORQUE SPECIFICATIONS.

2) Using a NEW gasket, install adapter case oil pan. Install and tighten bolts to specification. To install remaining components, reverse removal procedure. Fill transmission with Dexron-III ATF.

TRANSMISSION FLUID TEMPERATURE (TFT) SENSOR

Removal & Installation – Transmission oil temperature sensor is located on wiring harness in adapter case oil pan. *See Fig. 4.* Replacement information is not available from manufacturer.

WINTER MODE SWITCH

Removal & Installation – WINTER mode switch is located on center console, near gearshift lever. Replacement information is not available from manufacturer.

TORQUE SPECIFICATIONS
TORQUE SPECIFICATIONS

Application	Ft. Lbs. (N.m)
ECT Sensor	22 (30)
Oil Filter Bolt	15 (20)
Shift Lever Nut	17 (23)
	INCH Lbs. (N.m)
Adapter Case Oil Pan Bolt	96 (10.8)
Heat Protector Bolt	52 (5.9)
Main Case Oil Pan Bolt	96 (10.8)
Mode Switch Retaining Bolt	113 (12.8)
Pressure Control Solenoid Bolt	87 (9.8)
Speed Sensor Bolt	78 (8.8)
TCC Solenoid Bolt	87 (9.8)
TP Sensor Bolt	18 (2.0)

AUTOMATIC TRANSMISSIONS
1996 Hydra-Matic 4L30-E Electronic Controls
Acura SLX & Isuzu Trooper (Cont.)

3-693

WIRING DIAGRAMS

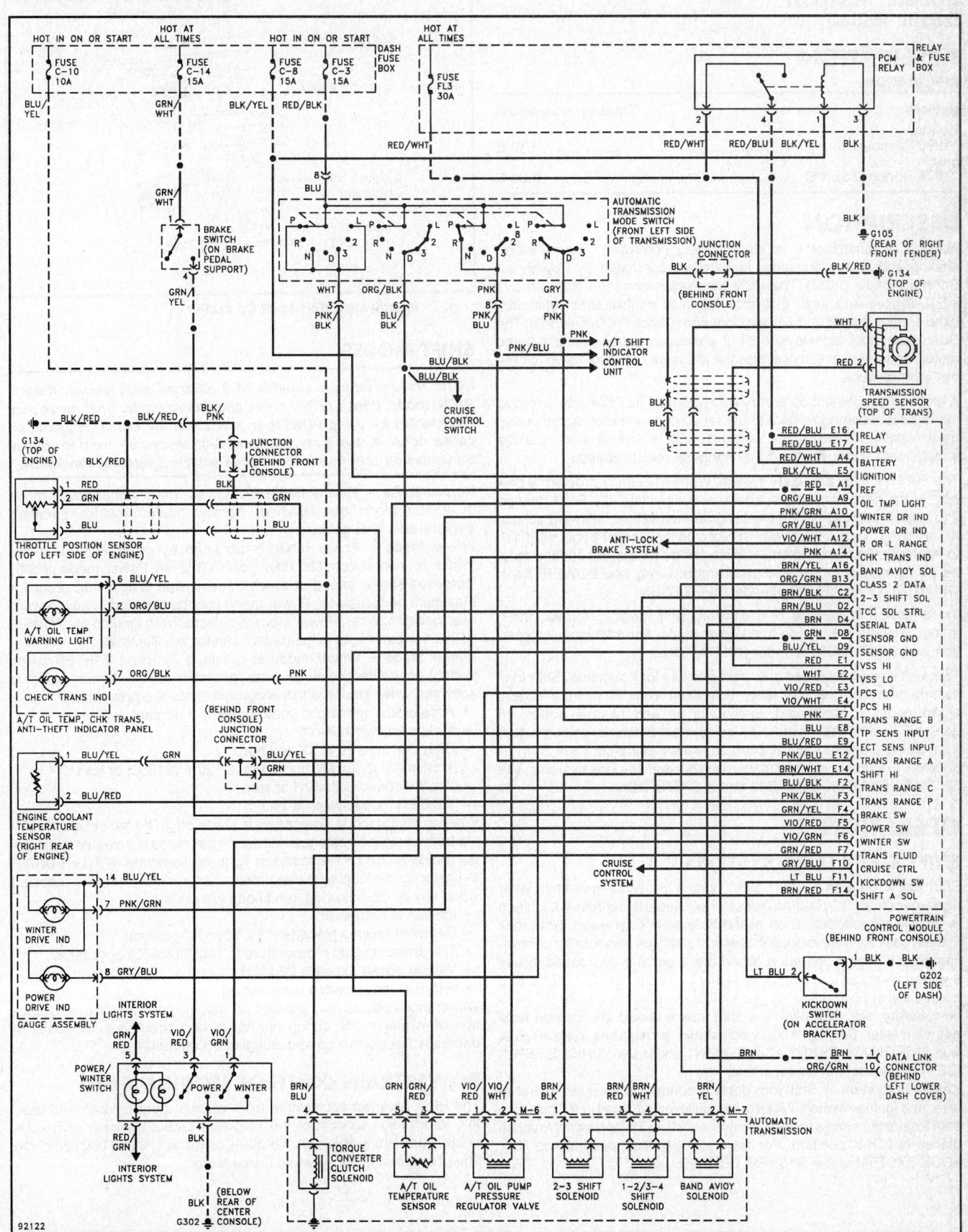

Fig. 10: 4L30-E Transmission Wiring Diagram (1996 SLX & Trooper)

Honda: Passport
Isuzu: Rodeo

APPLICATION

APPLICATION

Vehicle	Transmission Model
Honda	
1996 Passport	4L30-E
Isuzu	
1996 Rodeo (3.2L V6)	4L30-E

DESCRIPTION

Automatic transmission is electronically controlled. Transmission shifting and torque converter lock-up are controlled by Powertrain Control Module (PCM). The PCM receives information from various input devices and uses this information to control shift solenoids, band apply solenoid and Torque Converter Clutch (TCC) solenoid. The PCM uses input signals to control pressure control solenoid (force motor) operation, which operates the pressure regulator valve to control line pressure.

A torque management control system is used. The PCM uses a torque management control system to deliver a spark advance signal during transmission shifting. This controls engine torque and reduces engagement shock caused by a change in vehicle speed.

The PCM contains a fail-safe system. When a failure or problem is present in the transmission electronic control system, the PCM may go into a back-up mode using pre-programmed values, allowing vehicle to be driven. The CHECK TRANS light on instrument panel will flash to inform driver of a problem. Vehicle can be driven, but shifting must be done manually. For additional information, see POWERTRAIN CONTROL MODULE (PCM) under OPERATION.

Transmission is capable of 3 different shift modes, Normal (NOR) mode, Power (PWR) mode and Winter mode. For additional information, see SHIFT MODES under OPERATION.

Transmission is equipped with shift and key lock systems. Shift lock system prevents gearshift lever movement from "P" position unless brake pedal is depressed, ignition is on and release button on gearshift lever is depressed. Key lock system prevents ignition switch from being placed in LOCK position unless gearshift lever is in "P" position. For additional information on shift and key lock systems, see SHIFT & KEY LOCK SYSTEMS under OPERATION.

OPERATION

SHIFT & KEY LOCK SYSTEMS

Shift Lock System – Shift lock system prevents gearshift lever movement from "P" position unless brake pedal is depressed, ignition is on and release button on gearshift lever is depressed. Shift lock system uses a safety lock controller and shift lock solenoid for controlling gearshift lever operation. When brake pedal is depressed, brake switch delivers an input signal to safety lock controller to indicate that brakes are applied, allowing gearshift lever movement from "P" position. Safety lock controller and shift lock solenoid are located near gearshift lever. See Fig. 1. Only adjustment procedures are available. See SHIFT LOCK CABLE ADJUSTMENT under ON-VEHICLE SERVICE in appropriate overhaul article.

Key Lock System – Shift lock cable is connected between gearshift lever and ignition switch. When gearshift lever is placed in "P" position, shift lock cable moves lock on ignition switch so ignition switch may be placed in LOCK position. For testing of key lock system, see KEY LOCK SYSTEM under SYSTEM TESTING.

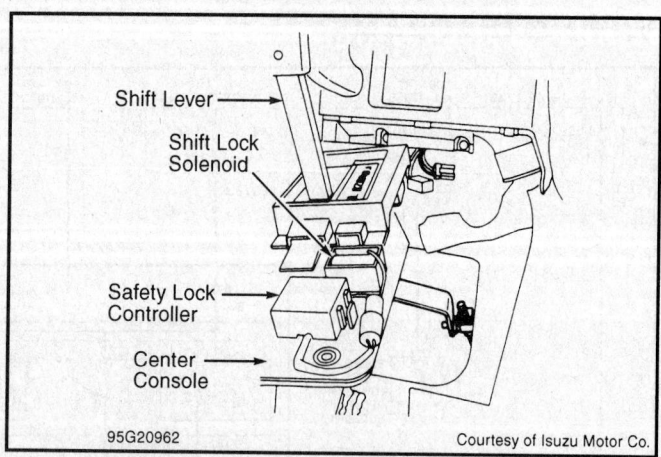

95G20962 Courtesy of Isuzu Motor Co.

Fig. 1: Identifying Safety Lock Controller

SHIFT MODES

NOTE: Transmission is capable of 3 different shift modes, Normal (NOR) mode, Power (PWR) mode and Winter mode. Shift mode may be selected by using POWER or WINTER mode switch mounted on center console, near gearshift lever. Shift modes are used to change transmission shift points for various vehicle operating conditions.

Normal Mode – Normal mode is obtained when neither Power mode or Winter mode are selected. Normal mode provides standard transmission shift points.

Power Mode – Power mode is obtained by using POWER mode switch on center console, near gearshift lever. Power mode slightly increases engine speed at which transmission shift points occur for maximum performance. Power mode may be selected in any forward gear position. When Power mode is selected with ignition on, POWER DRIVE indicator light in instrument cluster will illuminate.

Winter Mode – Winter mode is obtained by using WINTER mode switch on center console, near gearshift lever. Winter mode is activated when all of the following conditions are present.

- Accelerator opening is approximately 8 percent or less.
- Kickdown switch is off.
- Gearshift lever is in "D" position.
- Transmission fluid temperature is 120°F (248°C) or less.
- Vehicle speed is 7 MPH or less.
- WINTER mode switch is on.

When in Winter mode, transmission starts off in 3rd gear to aid in vehicle traction on ice and snow. When Winter mode is selected with ignition on, WINTER DRIVE indicator light will illuminate. WINTER DRIVE indicator light is located in instrument cluster. Winter mode is canceled when any of the following conditions are present.

- Ignition is turned off.
- Gearshift lever is placed in "3", "2" or "L" position.
- Transmission fluid temperature is 140°F (284°C) or greater.
- Vehicle speed exceeds 22 MPH.
- WINTER mode switch is turned off.

Winter mode should only by used on slippery road conditions. Operation of Winter mode during normal driving conditions will result in decreased performance and sluggish acceleration.

POWERTRAIN CONTROL MODULE (PCM)

The PCM receives information from various input devices and uses this information to control the following output devices: shift solenoids, band apply solenoid, Torque Converter Clutch (TCC) solenoid and pressure control solenoid (force motor).

AUTOMATIC TRANSMISSIONS
1996 Hydra-Matic 4L30-E Electronic Controls
Honda Passport & Isuzu Rodeo (Cont.)

3-695

The PCM contains a self-diagnostic system which stores a Diagnostic Trouble Code (DTC) if a failure or problem is present in the transmission electronic control system. If a certain failure or problem is present, CHECK TRANS light will flash to inform driver of a problem. See DTC IDENTIFICATION table. CHECK TRANS light is located in instrument cluster.

DTCs may be retrieved to determine transmission problem area. For information on retrieving DTCs, see SELF-DIAGNOSTIC SYSTEM. The PCM contains a fail-safe system. When a certain failure or problem is present in the transmission electronic control system, the PCM may go into back-up mode using pre-programmed values, allowing vehicle to be driven. The CHECK TRANS light may flash to inform driver of a problem. See DTC IDENTIFICATION table.

Vehicle can be driven in back-up mode, but shifting must be done manually. When manually shifting transmission, if gearshift lever is placed in "D" or "3" position, transmission remains in 4th gear. If gearshift lever is placed in "2" position, transmission remains in 3rd gear. If gearshift lever is placed in "L" position, transmission remains in 1st gear. If gearshift lever is placed in "R" position, transmission will shift into reverse. Back-up mode may be cleared by turning ignition off, then back on again.

For additional information on the self-diagnostic system, see SELF-DIAGNOSTIC SYSTEM. The PCM is located below center of instrument panel. *See Fig. 2.*

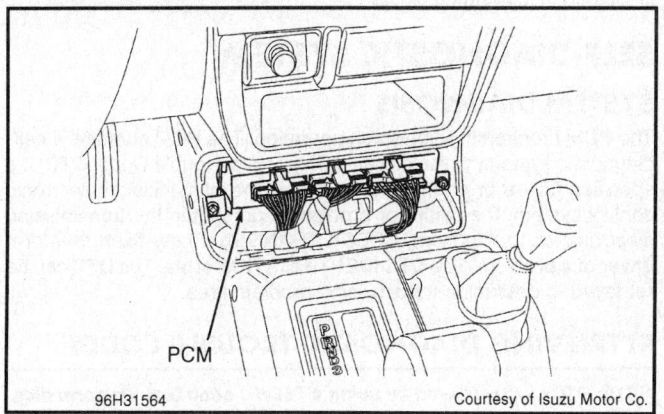

96H31564   Courtesy of Isuzu Motor Co.

Fig. 2: Locating PCM

PCM INPUT DEVICES

A/C Signal – The A/C compressor relay delivers an input signal to PCM to indicate A/C operation. The A/C compressor relay is located in fuse/relay box at passenger's side front corner of engine compartment.

Brakelight Switch – Brakelight switch delivers an input signal to PCM to indicate vehicle braking. Brakelight switch is located near brake pedal. Brakelight switch may be referred to as brake switch.

Cruise Control Signal – Transmission will downshift when an overdrive OFF signal is received from cruise control unit. Cruise control unit is located behind passenger's side kick panel. Cruise control unit may also be referred to as cruise control module.

Diagnostic Connector – Diagnostic connector will deliver an input signal to display a Diagnostic Trouble Code (DTC) using CHECK TRANS light on instrument panel. Diagnostic connector may be referred to as Data Link Connector (DLC). *See Fig. 3.*

Engine Coolant Temperature (ECT) Sensor – ECT sensor delivers an input signal to PCM to indicate engine coolant temperature. ECT sensor is located on coolant pipe at rear of cylinder head.

Engine Speed Or RPM Signal – An engine speed or RPM signal is delivered to PCM from ignition control module, located below ignition coils.

Kickdown Switch – Kickdown switch delivers an input signal to PCM to indicate if accelerator pedal is fully depressed. Kickdown switch is located on accelerator pedal.

96I31565   Courtesy of Isuzu Motor Co.

Fig. 3: Locating Data Link Connector (DLC)

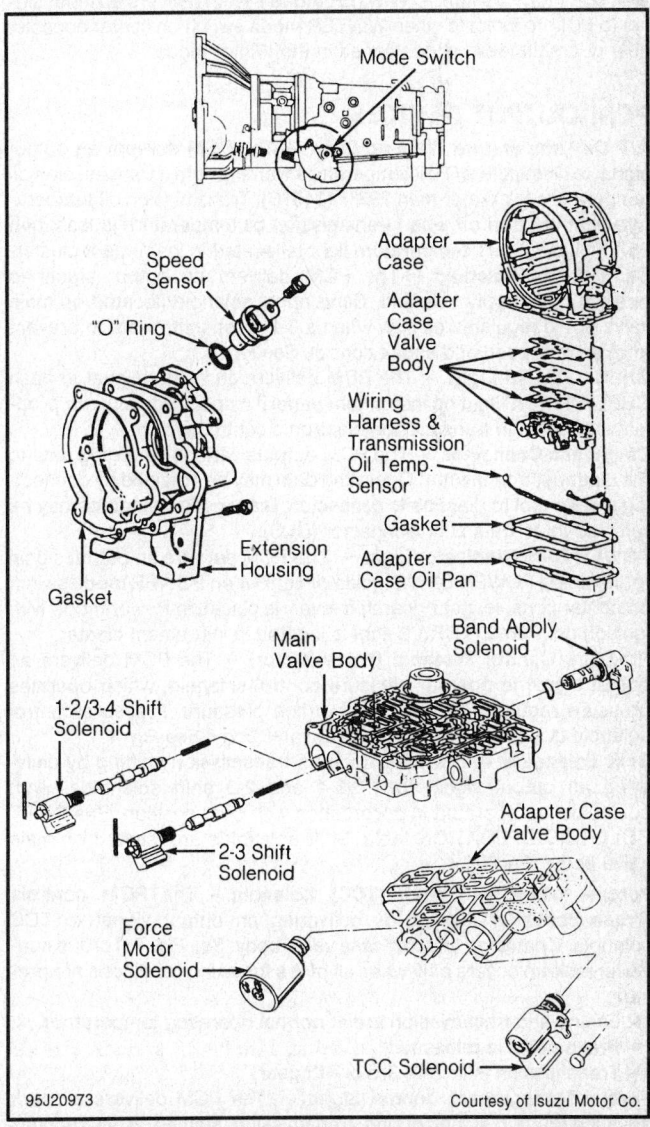

95J20973   Courtesy of Isuzu Motor Co.

Fig. 4: Identifying Mode Switch, Speed Sensor, Transmission Oil Temperature Sensor, Shift Solenoids & TCC Solenoid

3-696

AUTOMATIC TRANSMISSIONS
1996 Hydra-Matic 4L30-E Electronic Controls
Honda Passport & Isuzu Rodeo (Cont.)

Mode Switch – Mode switch delivers an input signal to PCM to indicate shift lever position. Mode switch is located on side of transmission. *See Fig. 4.*

POWER Mode Switch – POWER mode switch delivers an input signal to PCM to indicate when POWER mode switch is positioned in the Power mode. POWER mode switch is located on center console, near gearshift lever.

Speed Sensor – Speed sensor delivers an input signal to PCM to indicate transmission output shaft speed. Speed sensor is located on extension housing on rear of transmission. *See Fig. 4.* Speed sensor may be referred to as magnetic sensor.

Throttle Position (TP) Sensor – The TP sensor delivers an input signal to PCM to indicate throttle position. The TP sensor is mounted on side of throttle body.

Transmission Oil Temperature Sensor – Transmission oil temperature sensor delivers an input signal to PCM to indicate transmission oil temperature. The PCM uses this input signal for controlling the Winter shift mode. The PCM also uses input signal for controlling the torque converter clutch and A/T oil temperature warning light. Transmission oil temperature sensor is located on wiring harness in adapter case oil pan. *See Fig. 4.*

WINTER Mode Switch – WINTER mode switch delivers an input signal to PCM to indicate when WINTER mode switch on center console, near gearshift lever, is positioned in the Winter mode.

PCM OUTPUT DEVICES

A/T Oil Temperature Warning Light – The PCM delivers an output signal to illuminate A/T oil temperature warning light if transmission oil temperature is greater than 293°F (145°C). Transmission oil temperature light will turn off when transmission oil temperature is less than 257°F (125°C). A/T temperature light is located in instrument cluster.

Band Apply Solenoid – The PCM delivers an output signal to operate band apply solenoid. Band apply solenoid (located on main valve body) regulates oil flow when a 3-2 downshift exists to prevent engine overspeed and shock control. *See Fig. 4.*

CHECK TRANS Light – The PCM delivers an output signal to flash CHECK TRANS light on instrument panel if a specified failure or problem is present in transmission electronic control system.

Diagnostic Connector – The PCM outputs various operating data to the diagnostic connector. Operating data may be obtained by connecting a scan tool to diagnostic connector. Diagnostic connector may be referred to as Data Link Connector (DLC).

POWER DRIVE Indicator Light – The PCM delivers an output signal to illuminate POWER DRIVE indicator light when POWER mode switch on center console, near gearshift lever, is placed in Power mode with ignition on. POWER DRIVE light is located in instrument cluster.

Pressure Control Solenoid (Force Motor) – The PCM delivers an output signal to operate pressure control solenoid, which operates pressure regulator valve to control line pressure. Pressure control solenoid is located on adapter case valve body. *See Fig. 4.*

Shift Solenoids – The PCM controls transmission shifting by delivering an output signal to 1-2/3-4 and 2-3 shift solenoids. Shift solenoids are operated in accordance with gear position. See SHIFT SOLENOID OPERATION table. Shift solenoids are located on main valve body. *See Fig. 4.*

Torque Converter Clutch (TCC) Solenoid – The PCM controls torque converter lock-up by delivering an output signal to TCC solenoid, located on adapter case valve body. *See Fig. 4.* Torque converter lock-up occurs only when all of the following conditions are present.

- Engine and transmission are at normal operating temperature.
- Brake pedal is released.
- Transmission is in 2nd, 3rd or 4th gear.

Torque Management Control Signal – The PCM delivers a spark advance output signal during transmission shifting. This reduces engagement shock caused by a change in vehicle speed.

SHIFT SOLENOID OPERATION

Gearshift Lever Position	1-2/3-4 Solenoid	2-3 Solenoid
"P" Or "N"	Off	On
"R"	Off	On
"D"		
1st Gear	Off	On
2nd Gear	On	On
3rd Gear	On	Off
4th Gear	Off	Off
"3"		
1st Gear	Off	On
2nd Gear	On	On
3rd Gear	On	Off
"2"		
1st Gear	Off	On
2nd Gear	On	On
"L"		
1st Gear	Off	On

WINTER DRIVE Indicator Light – The PCM delivers an output signal to illuminate WINTER DRIVE indicator light on instrument panel when WINTER mode switch on center console, near gearshift lever, is placed in Winter mode with ignition on. WINTER DRIVE indicator light is located in instrument cluster.

SELF-DIAGNOSTIC SYSTEM

SYSTEM DIAGNOSIS

The PCM monitors transmission operation. The PCM contains a self-diagnostic system, which stores a Diagnostic Trouble Code (DTC) if a specified failure or problem is present in the transmission electronic control system. If a failure or problem is present in the transmission electronic control system, CHECK TRANS light may flash to inform driver of a problem. See DTC IDENTIFICATION table. The DTC can be retrieved to determine transmission problem area.

RETRIEVING DIAGNOSTIC TROUBLE CODES

NOTE: DTCs are retrieved by using a TECH 1 scan tool. Perform diagnostic circuit check to ensure proper operation of CHECK TRANS light before attempting to retrieve DTCs. When using TECH 1 scan tool, different modes may be used. Follow scan tool manufacturer's instructions.

Diagnostic Circuit Check – **1)** Turn ignition on. CHECK TRANS light should illuminate for 2-3 seconds, then go off, indicating light circuit is operating properly.

2) If CHECK TRANS light functions as specified, DTCs can be retrieved. See PCM DIAGNOSTIC TROUBLE CODES. If CHECK TRANS light is flashing with ignition on, proceed to PCM DIAGNOSTIC TROUBLE CODES.

3) If CHECK TRANS light does not illuminate as specified, or remains off, proceed to CHECK TRANS LIGHT TEST under TROUBLE SHOOTING.

PCM Diagnostic Trouble Codes – **1)** Ensure ignition is off. Connect Adapter Cable (3000081) and scan tool to DLC. Connect scan tool to battery voltage (if required). Go to next step.

2) Turn ignition on. Using scan tool, note DTC displays on scan tool following scan tool manufacturer's instructions. Go to next step.

3) Once DTC is obtained, determine probable cause and symptom. See DTC IDENTIFICATION table. For trouble shooting of DTCs, see appropriate DTC test under DIAGNOSTIC TESTS. Turn ignition off. Remove scan tool.

AUTOMATIC TRANSMISSIONS
1996 Hydra-Matic 4L30-E Electronic Controls
Honda Passport & Isuzu Rodeo (Cont.)

3-697

DTC IDENTIFICATION

DTC	Description
P0218	Transmission Fluid Over-Temperature
P0560	System Voltage Malfunction
P0705	Transmission Range Switch (Mode Switch) Illegal Position
P0706	Transmission Range Switch (Mode Switch) Performance
P0712	Transmission Fluid Temperature (TFT) Sensor Circuit (Low Input)
P0713	Transmission Fluid Temperature (TFT) Sensor Circuit (High Input)
P0719	TCC Brake Switch Circuit High (Stuck On)
P0722	Transmission Output Speed Sensor (OSS) (Low Input)
P0723	Transmission Output Speed Sensor (OSS) (Intermittent)
P0724	TCC Brake Switch Circuit Low (Stuck Off)
P0730	Transmission Incorrect Gear Ratio
P0742	TCC Circuit Stuck On
P0748	Pressure Control Solenoid (Force Motor) (Circuit Electrical)
P0751	Shift Solenoid "A" Performance (Without Input Speed)
P0753	Shift Solenoid "A" Electrical
P0756	Shift Solenoid "B" Performance (Without Input Speed)
P0758	Shift Solenoid "B" Electrical
P1790	ROM Transmission Side Bad Check Sum
P1792	EEPROM Transmission Side Bad Check Sum
P1835	Kickdown Switch Always On
P1850	Brake Band Apply Solenoid Malfunction
P1860	TCC PWM Solenoid Electrical
P1870	Transmission Component Slipping

CLEARING DIAGNOSTIC TROUBLE CODES

1) Using TECH 1 scan tool, use F4: Clear Code mode from main menu to clear DTC from PCM memory using scan tool manufacturer's instructions.
2) If DTC cannot be cleared from PCM memory, or if TECH 1 scan tool is not available, remove ECM fuse (15-amp) from instrument panel fuse box for at least 10 seconds.

TROUBLE SHOOTING

CHECK TRANS LIGHT TEST

NOTE: Perform this test if CHECK TRANS light is on steady at all times with ignition on and no diagnostic trouble codes are stored, or CHECK TRANS light remains off when ignition is first turned on.

Description – When ignition is turned on, CHECK TRANS light on instrument panel should come on for about 2-3 seconds while PCM is performing a self-test of the circuit and components, then light should go off. When ignition is on and PCM detects an electrical failure in the transmission electronic control system, the PCM will flash CHECK TRANS light and may store a diagnostic trouble code in memory.
CHECK TRANS Light Is On Steady With Ignition On – **1)** This condition may be caused by a short circuit to ground between CHECK TRANS light and PCM. Check wiring between PCM and CHECK TRANS light on instrument panel for a short circuit to ground.
2) If no short circuit to ground is present in the wiring, replace PCM. See PCM under REMOVAL & INSTALLATION.
CHECK TRANS Light Remains Off – **1)** This condition may be caused by an open circuit or short to power between CHECK TRANS light and PCM. Check wiring between PCM and CHECK TRANS light on instrument panel for an open circuit or short to power.
2) Ensure battery voltage is present between fuse in fuse box and CHECK TRANS light. Check fuse and all connections as necessary.
3) If battery voltage is present as specified and no open short circuit is present between CHECK TRANS light and PCM, replace PCM. See PCM under REMOVAL & INSTALLATION.

INTERMITTENT CONDITIONS

If TECH 1 scan tool displays DTC as intermittent, or if after a test drive a DTC does not reappear though the detection conditions for the DTC, problem is most likely a faulty electrical connection or loose wiring. Intermittent problems are rarely present in electronic components such as the PCM, but rather in electrical connections or ground circuits. When an intermittent condition is present, perform the following procedure.

1) Check for loose connections at electrical terminal connectors. Check for improperly seated electrical connectors or damaged electrical terminals.
2) Check for loose or corroded ground connections. Check for pinched or damaged wiring. Check for improperly routed wiring which may cause electro-magnetic interference from spark plug wires, distributor wires, ignition coil and alternator.
3) Use F3: Snapshot mode to isolate the cause of an intermittent condition following scan tool manufacturer's instructions. Set Snapshot mode to trigger on suspected DTC, or if you notice the reported symptom during test drive, manually trigger Snapshot mode.
4) After Snapshot mode is triggered, command scan tool to play back flow of data recorded from each of the various sensors. Signs of an intermittent condition in a sensor circuit may cause a sudden jump in data values out of normal range.

SYSTEM TESTING

KEY LOCK SYSTEM

NOTE: Shift lock cable is connected between gearshift lever and ignition switch. When gearshift lever is placed in "P" position, shift lock cable moves lock on ignition switch so ignition switch may be placed in LOCK position.

1) To check system operation, ensure gearshift lever cannot be moved from "P" position with ignition switch in LOCK position.
2) Ensure ignition switch can be turned to LOCK position only when gearshift lever is in "P" position. If operation is not as specified, adjust shift lock cable. See SHIFT LOCK CABLE ADJUSTMENT under ON-VEHICLE SERVICE in appropriate overhaul article.

DIAGNOSTIC TESTS

NOTE: Perform ON-BOARD DIAGNOSTIC (OBD) SYSTEM CHECK before proceeding with diagnostic tests. See appropriate BASIC DIAGNOSTIC PROCEDURES article in ENGINE PERFORMANCE in appropriate MITCHELL® manual.

NOTE: See appropriate wiring diagram under WIRING DIAGRAMS to aid in component location, wire color and terminal identification.

DTC P0218:
TRANSMISSION FLUID OVER-TEMPERATURE

Conditions For Setting DTC:
- DTCs P0712 and P0713 are not present.
- Transmission fluid temperature is greater than 284°F (140°C).
- Conditions must be present for 21 seconds.

Diagnosis – **1)** Ensure engine is mechanically in good condition, and not cause of a transmission overheating problem. Ensure transmission fluid is at proper level. See CHECKING FLUID LEVEL under LUBRICATION in appropriate AUTOMATIC TRANSMISSION SERVICING article. Repair as necessary. Go to next step.
2) Install scan tool. Turn ignition on. Using scan tool, record DTC FAILURE RECORDS. Observe Transmission Fluid Temperature (TFT) sensor voltage reading on scan tool. If TFT sensor reading is less than .33 volt, go to next step. If reading is not as specified, see DIAGNOSTIC AIDS.

3-698

AUTOMATIC TRANSMISSIONS
1996 Hydra-Matic 4L30-E Electronic Controls
Honda Passport & Isuzu Rodeo (Cont.)

3) Turn ignition off. Disconnect transmission harness connector H-12 (16-pin Blue connector). Turn ignition on. If TFT sensor signal voltage reading is greater than 4.92 volts, check for faulty wiring harness. If reading is not as specified, go to next step.

4) Check Green/Red wire between PCM and TFT sensor for a short to ground. Repair as necessary and go to step **6)**. If no problem is found, go to next step.

5) Inspect PCM for poor harness connections. Repair as necessary. If no problem is found, replace PCM and go to next step.

6) Using scan tool, select DTC, then CLEAR INFO function. Ensure transmission fluid temperature is less than 266°F (130°C) for at least 10 seconds. Review DTC INFO. If last test failed, or DTC P0218 is present, repeat step **1)**. If last test passed and no DTCs are present, testing is complete.

Diagnostic Aids – Inspect for poor harness connections and improper wire harness routing. An intermittent condition may be caused by a wire which is broken inside its insulation, or shorted to an additional circuit or chassis ground. Check harness connectors for damaged, corroded or backed-out terminal pins. Repair as necessary. Check for possible torque converter stator problem. Verify vehicle owners driving habits, trailer towing, etc.

DTC P0560: SYSTEM VOLTAGE MALFUNCTION

Conditions For Setting DTC (System Voltage Low):
- Engine speed is greater than 1000 RPM.
- System voltage is less than 10 volts at a maximum transmission temperature of 302°F (150°C).
- System voltage is less than 7.3 volts at a minimum transmission temperature of –40°F (–40°C).
- Conditions must be present for 4 seconds.

Conditions For Setting DTC (System Voltage High):
- System voltage is greater than 16 volts for 2 seconds.

Diagnosis – **1)** Install scan tool. Turn ignition on. Using scan tool, record DTC FAILURE RECORDS. Using a DVOM, measure voltage between battery terminals. Note reading for future reference. If reading is greater than 10.5 volts, go to next step. If reading is not as specified, charge or replace battery.

2) Start engine and allow it to reach normal operating temperature. Observe generator/check engine light. If light is illuminated, inspect and repair faulty charging system. If light is not illuminated, go to next step.

3) Increase engine speed to 1000-1500 RPM. Observe scan tool system voltage. If reading is within 13-15 volts, go to next step. If reading is not as specified, inspect and repair faulty charging system.

4) Turn ignition off. Disconnect PCM harness connectors A-36 (Red) and A-38 (Blue). Turn ignition on. Using a DVOM, measure voltage between ground and PCM harness connector A-36, terminal A4 (Red/White wire), then between ground and PCM harness connector A-38, terminal E16 (Red/Blue wire). Compare voltage readings with that of reading noted in step **1)**. If difference in voltage reading is greater than .5 volt, go to next step. If difference in voltage is not as specified, go to step **6)**.

5) Repair Red/White wire between PCM and battery for high resistance. Go to step **10)**.

6) Using a DVOM, measure voltage between ground and PCM harness connector A-38, terminal E16 (Red/Blue wire), then between ground and PCM harness connector A-38, terminal F16 (Red/Blue wire). Compare voltage readings with that of reading noted in step **1)**. If difference in voltage reading is greater than .5 volt, go to next step. If difference in voltage is not as specified, go to step **8)**.

7) Repair Red/Blue wire between PCM and PCM relay for high resistance. Go to step **10)**.

8) Check PCM harness connector A-36, terminal A4 (Red/White wire); harness connector A-38, terminal E16 (Red/Blue wire); and harness connector A-38, terminal F16 (Red/Blue wire) for damaged, corroded, or backed-out terminal pins. Repair as necessary and go to step **10)**. If no problem is found, go to next step.

9) Replace PCM. Go to next step.

10) Using scan tool, select DTC, then CLEAR INFO function. Start engine and allow it to reach normal operating temperature. PCM must see a system voltage of 10-16 volts. Review DTC INFO. If last test failed, or DTC P0560 is present, repeat step **1)**. If last test passed and no DTCs are present, testing is complete.

Diagnostic Aids – Inspect for poor harness connections and improper wire harness routing. An intermittent condition may be caused by a wire which is broken inside its insulation, or shorted to an additional circuit or chassis ground. Check harness connectors for damaged, corroded or backed-out terminal pins. Repair as necessary. Check for proper belt tension. Charging battery or jump starting may set DTC P0560.

DTC P0705: TRANSMISSION RANGE SWITCH (MODE SWITCH) ILLEGAL POSITION

Conditions For Setting DTC:
- Illegal range position detected for 5 seconds.

Diagnosis – **1)** Ensure transmission linkage between gearshift lever and manual valve is adjusted properly. Check diagnostic circuit. See RETRIEVING DIAGNOSTIC TROUBLE CODES under SELF-DIAGNOSTIC SYSTEM. Go to next step.

2) Install scan tool. Turn ignition on. Using scan tool, record DTC FREEZE FRAME and FAILURE RECORDS. Observe scan tool while moving gearshift lever through all gear ranges. If scan tool display coincides with actual gear range selected, go to DIAGNOSTIC AIDS. If operation is not as specified, go to next step.

3) Turn ignition off. Disconnect mode switch harness connector A-32 (8-pin Black connector). Turn ignition on. Using a DVOM, measure voltage between ground and mode switch harness connector A-32, terminals No. 6 (Pink/Black wire), No. 3 (Blue/White wire), No. 2 (Pink wire), then No. 1 (Pink/Blue wire). If battery voltage is present at all circuits, go to step **5)**. If battery voltage is not present at all circuits, go to next step.

4) Check for an open or short to ground in any circuit which did not indicate battery voltage. Repair as necessary and go to step **8)**. If no problem is found, go to step **6)**.

5) Ensure circuits checked in step **3)** are not shorted together. To check, apply ground to each circuit while monitoring range switch display on scan tool. If more than one gear range is displayed at one time, go to step **7)**. If no problem is found, refer to RANGE SWITCH LOGIC TABLE. See Fig. 5.

6) Check PCM for poor harness connections. Repair a necessary. If no problem is found, replace PCM. Go to step **8)**.

7) Repair appropriate wire as necessary. Go to next step.

8) Using scan tool, select DTC, then CLEAR INFO function. Road test vehicle. Review DTC INFO. If last test failed, or DTC P0705 is present, repeat step **1)**. If last test passed and no DTCs are present, testing is complete.

Diagnostic Aids – Inspect for poor harness connections and improper wire harness routing. An intermittent condition may be caused by a wire which is broken inside its insulation, or shorted to an additional circuit or chassis ground. Check harness connectors for damaged, corroded or backed-out terminal pins. Repair as necessary. Refer to RANGE SWITCH LOGIC TABLE for additional information. See Fig. 5.

Range Position	Range Switch Pin No.			
	8	7	6	3
Park	ON	OFF	OFF	ON
Reverse	ON	ON	OFF	OFF
Neutral	OFF	ON	OFF	ON
D4	OFF	ON	ON	OFF
D3	ON	ON	ON	ON
"2"	ON	OFF	ON	OFF
"L"	OFF	OFF	ON	ON
Illegal	OFF	OFF	OFF	OFF
Illegal	OFF	OFF	OFF	ON

96J31566   Courtesy of Isuzu Motor Co.

Fig. 5: Range Switch Logic Table

DTC P0706: TRANSMISSION RANGE SWITCH (MODE SWITCH) PERFORMANCE

Conditions For Setting DTC ("R" Bad Position):
- Engine is running.
- DTCs P0722 and P0723 are not present.
- Output speed greater than 3000 RPM.
- Range switch indicates "R".
- Conditions must be met for 4 seconds.

Conditions For Setting DTC ("P" Or "N" Bad Position):
- Engine is running.
- No TP sensor DTCs.
- Engine speed is less than 3000 RPM.
- TP sensor angle is greater than 20 percent.
- Range switch indicates "P" or "N".
- Conditions must be met for 4 seconds.

Diagnosis – 1) Ensure transmission linkage between gearshift lever and manual valve is adjusted properly. Check diagnostic circuit. See RETRIEVING DIAGNOSTIC TROUBLE CODES under SELF-DIAGNOSTIC SYSTEM. Go to next step.
2) Install scan tool. Turn ignition on. Using scan tool, record DTC FREEZE FRAME and FAILURE RECORDS. Observe scan tool while moving gearshift lever through all gear ranges. If scan tool display coincides with actual gear range selected, go to DIAGNOSTIC AIDS. If operation is not as specified, go to next step.
3) Turn ignition off. Disconnect mode switch harness connector A-32 (8-pin Black connector). Turn ignition on. Using a DVOM, measure voltage between ground and mode switch harness connector A-32, terminals No. 6 (Pink/Black wire), No. 3 (Blue/White wire), No. 2 (Pink wire), then No. 1 (Pink/Blue wire). If battery voltage is present at all circuits, go to step 5). If battery voltage is not present at all circuits, go to next step.
4) Check for an open or short to ground in any circuit which did not indicate battery voltage. Repair as necessary and go to step 8). If no problem is found, go to step 6).
5) Ensure circuits checked in step 3) are not shorted together. To check, apply ground to each circuit while monitoring range switch display on scan tool. If more than one gear range is displayed at one time, go to step 7). If no problem is found, refer to RANGE SWITCH LOGIC TABLE. See Fig. 5.
6) Check PCM for poor harness connections. Repair a necessary. If no problem is found, replace PCM. Go to step 8).
7) Repair appropriate wire as necessary. Go to next step.

8) Using scan tool, select DTC, then CLEAR INFO function. Road test vehicle. Review DTC INFO. If last test failed, or DTC P0705 is present, repeat step 1). If last test passed and no DTCs are present, testing is complete.

Diagnostic Aids – Inspect for poor harness connections and improper wire harness routing. An intermittent condition may be caused by a wire which is broken inside its insulation, or shorted to an additional circuit or chassis ground. Check harness connectors for damaged, corroded or backed-out terminal pins. Repair as necessary. Refer to RANGE SWITCH LOGIC TABLE for additional information. See Fig. 5.

DTC P0712: TRANS. FLUID TEMP. (TFT) SENSOR CIRCUIT LOW INPUT

Conditions For Setting DTC:
- DTC P0560 is not present.
- Ignition is on.
- TFT sensor indicates a voltage less than .4 volt.
- Conditions must be present for 20 seconds.

Diagnosis – 1) Perform transmission fluid checking procedure. See CHECKING FLUID LEVEL under LUBRICATION in appropriate AUTOMATIC TRANSMISSION SERVICING article. Fill if necessary and go to next step.
2) Install scan tool. Turn ignition on. Using scan tool, record DTC FREEZE FRAME and FAILURE RECORDS. If scan tool displays TFT sensor voltage less than .4 volt, go to next step. If reading is not as specified, go to DIAGNOSTIC AIDS.
3) Turn ignition off. Disconnect transmission harness connector H-12 (16-pin Blue connector). Turn ignition on. If TFT sensor voltage rises to 4.92 volts, go to next step. If reading is not as specified, go to step 9).
4) Turn ignition off. Using a DVOM, measure resistance between TFT sensor harness connector terminals (Gray wire and Green/Red wire). Compare resistance readings with table. See TFT SENSOR RESISTANCE table. If resistance is within specification, go to DIAGNOSTIC AIDS. If resistance is not within specification, go to next step.

TFT SENSOR RESISTANCE

Temperature °F (°C)	Resistance (Ohms)
–40 (–40)	672,000
32 (0)	65,000
68 (20)	25,000
176 (80)	2,500
248 (120)	780
302 (150)	370

3-700

AUTOMATIC TRANSMISSIONS
1996 Hydra-Matic 4L30-E Electronic Controls
Honda Passport & Isuzu Rodeo (Cont.)

5) Disconnect transmission harness connector M-6 (5-pin Black connector). Using a DVOM, measure resistance between TFT sensor terminals (Gray wire and Green/Red wire). Compare resistance readings with table. See TFT SENSOR RESISTANCE table. If resistance is within specification, go to DIAGNOSTIC AIDS. If resistance is not within specification, go to next step.

6) Remove transmission oil pan. Inspect internal wiring harness for a short to ground. If a short to ground is found, go to step 8). If no problem is found, go to next step.

7) Disconnect internal wiring harness at TFT sensor. Using a DVOM, measure resistance of TFT sensor. Compare resistance readings with table. See TFT SENSOR RESISTANCE table. If resistance is within specification, go to DIAGNOSTIC AIDS. If resistance is not within specification, go to next step.

8) Replace TFT sensor. Go to step 12).

9) Check Green/Red wire between TFT sensor and PCM for a short to ground. Repair as necessary and go to step 12). If no problem is found, go to next step.

10) Check PCM for poor harness connections. Repair as necessary and go to step 12). If no problem is found, go to next step.

11) Replace PCM. Go to next step.

12) Using scan tool, select DTC, then CLEAR INFO function. Ensure TFT sensor indicates a voltage greater than .33 volt for 2 seconds. Review DTC INFO. If last test failed, or DTC P0712 is present, repeat step 1). If last test passed and no DTCs are present, testing is complete.

Diagnostic Aids – Inspect for poor harness connections and improper wire harness routing. An intermittent condition may be caused by a wire which is broken inside its insulation, or shorted to an additional circuit or chassis ground. Check harness connectors for damaged, corroded or backed-out terminal pins. Repair as necessary. A scan tool which displays a TFT sensor temperature value at 212°F (100°C), may indicate a short to ground in Green/Red wire between TFT sensor and PCM.

DTC P0713: TRANS. FLUID TEMP. (TFT) SENSOR CIRCUIT HIGH INPUT

Conditions For Setting DTC:
- DTC P0560 is not present.
- Ignition is on.
- TFT sensor indicates a voltage greater than 4.86 volts.
- Conditions must be present for 20 seconds.

Diagnosis – 1) Perform transmission fluid checking procedure. See CHECKING FLUID LEVEL under LUBRICATION in appropriate AUTOMATIC TRANSMISSION SERVICING article. Fill if necessary and go to next step.

2) Install scan tool. Turn ignition on. Using scan tool, record DTC FREEZE FRAME and FAILURE RECORDS. If scan tool displays TFT sensor voltage greater than 4.86 volts, go to next step. If reading is not as specified, go to DIAGNOSTIC AIDS.

3) Turn ignition off. Disconnect transmission harness connector H-12 (16-pin Blue connector). Using a fused jumper wire, jumper Gray wire and Green/Red wire together (engine harness side). Turn ignition on. If TFT sensor voltage drops to less than .4 volt, go to next step. If voltage does not drop as specified, go to step 9).

4) Turn ignition off. Using a DVOM, measure resistance between TFT sensor harness connector terminals (Gray wire and Green/Red wire). Compare resistance readings with table. See TFT SENSOR RESISTANCE table. If resistance is within specification, go to DIAGNOSTIC AIDS. If resistance is not within specification, go to next step.

TFT SENSOR RESISTANCE

Temperature °F (°C)	Resistance (Ohms)
-40 (-40)	672,000
32 (0)	65,000
68 (20)	25,000
176 (80)	2,500
248 (120)	780
302 (150)	370

5) Disconnect transmission harness connector M-6 (5-pin Black connector). Using a DVOM, measure resistance between TFT sensor terminals (Gray wire and Green/Red wire). Compare resistance readings with table. See TFT SENSOR RESISTANCE table. If resistance is within specification, go to DIAGNOSTIC AIDS. If resistance is not within specification, go to next step.

6) Remove transmission oil pan. Inspect internal wiring harness for an open. Repair as necessary and go to step 13). If no problem is found, go to next step.

7) Disconnect internal wiring harness at TFT sensor. Using a DVOM, measure resistance of TFT sensor. Compare resistance readings with table. See TFT SENSOR RESISTANCE table. If resistance is within specification, go to DIAGNOSTIC AIDS. If resistance is not within specification, go to next step.

8) Replace TFT sensor. Go to step 13).

9) Check Green/Red wire between TFT sensor and PCM for a short to power. Repair as necessary and go to step 13). If no problem is found, go to next step.

10) Check Green wire between TFT sensor and PCM for an open. Repair as necessary and go to step 13). If no problem is found, go to next step.

11) Check PCM for poor harness connections. Repair as necessary and go to step 13). If no problem is found, go to next step.

12) Replace PCM. Go to next step.

13) Using scan tool, select DTC, then CLEAR INFO function. Ensure TFT sensor indicates a voltage less than 4.92 volts for 2 seconds. Review DTC INFO. If last test failed, or DTC P0713 is present, repeat step 1). If last test passed and no DTCs are present, testing is complete.

Diagnostic Aids – Inspect for poor harness connections and improper wire harness routing. An intermittent condition may be caused by a wire which is broken inside its insulation, or shorted to an additional circuit or chassis ground. Check harness connectors for damaged, corroded or backed-out terminal pins. Repair as necessary. After transmission is operating, TFT sensor temperature value on scan tool should rise steadily to about 212°F (100°C), then stabilize.

DTC P0719: TCC BRAKE SWITCH CIRCUIT HIGH (STUCK ON)

Conditions For Setting DTC:
- DTCs P0722 and P0723 are not present.
- PCM detects a closed brake switch/circuit (12 volts) for 2 seconds, and the following events occur 7 consecutive times: vehicle speed is less than 5 MPH, then between 5 MPH and 20 MPH for 4 seconds; then vehicle speed is greater than 20 MPH for 4 seconds.

Diagnosis – 1) Install scan tool. Turn ignition on. If an ABS DTC is set, check appropriate fuse. Using scan tool, record DTC FREEZE FRAME and FAILURE RECORDS. Apply, then release brake pedal. If scan tool displays TCC brake switch as CLOSED with brake pedal applied, then OPEN when released, go to DIAGNOSTIC AIDS. If scan tool display is not as specified, go to next step.

2) Using a test light connected to ground, backprobe ignition feed circuit (Green wire) at brake switch. If test light illuminates, go to next step. If test light does not illuminate, go to step 4).

3) Using a test light connected to ground, backprobe Red wire at brake switch. If test light does not illuminate, go to step 7). If test light illuminates, leave test light connected and go to step 5).

4) Check fuse CB-13 (15-amp) in instrument panel fuse box. If fuse is blown, check for a short to ground. Repair as necessary. If fuse is okay, repair open in ignition feed circuit (Green wire) between brake switch and instrument panel fuse box. Go to step 13).

5) Disconnect brake switch harness connector. If test light remains illuminated, go to step 8). If test light is not illuminated, go to next step.

6) Using a DVOM, check for continuity between brake switch terminals. If continuity is present, go to step 9). If continuity is not present, go to step 10).

AUTOMATIC TRANSMISSIONS
1996 Hydra-Matic 4L30-E Electronic Controls
Honda Passport & Isuzu Rodeo (Cont.)

3-701

7) Disconnect brake switch harness connector. Ensure ignition is on. Using a test light connected to ground, probe Red wire terminal (harness side). If test light illuminates, leave test light connected and go to next step. If test light does not illuminate, go to step **10)**.

8) Turn ignition off. Disconnect PCM harness connector A-38 (Blue). Turn ignition on. If test light illuminates, check Red wire between brake switch and PCM for a short to power. Repair as necessary and go to step **13)**. If no problem is found, go to step **10)**.

9) Replace brake switch. Go to step **13)**.

10) Turn ignition off. Reconnect PCM harness connector A-38 (Blue) if disconnected. Turn ignition on. Observe scan tool. If display shows TCC brake switch as OPEN, with brake pedal applied, then CLOSED with brake pedal released, go to DIAGNOSTIC AIDS. If scan tool display is not as specified, go to next step.

11) Check PCM for poor harness connections. Repair as necessary and go to step **13)**. If no problem is found, go to next step.

12) Replace PCM. Go to next step.

13) Using scan tool, select DTC, then CLEAR INFO function. Ensure PCM brake switch signal indicates zero volts for at least one second with brake pedal applied. Review DTC INFO. If last test failed, or DTC P0719 is present, repeat step **1)**. If last test passed and no DTCs are present, testing is complete.

Diagnostic Aids – Inspect for poor harness connections and improper wire harness routing. An intermittent condition may be caused by a wire which is broken inside its insulation, or shorted to an additional circuit or chassis ground. Check harness connectors for damaged, corroded or backed-out terminal pins. Repair as necessary. Check brake switch for proper mounting and adjustment.

DTC P0722: TRANSMISSION OUTPUT SPEED SENSOR (OSS) LOW INPUT

Conditions For Setting DTC:
- DTCs P0107, P0108, P0106, P1106, P1107, P0122 and P0123 are not present.
- Not in Park or Neutral.
- TP sensor angle is greater than 10 percent.
- Engine vacuum is between zero and 10.2 in. Hg.
- Engine speed is between 3000 RPM and 5000 RPM.
- Transmission speed is less than zero RPM.
- All conditions must be present for 5 seconds.

Diagnosis – 1) Install scan tool. Turn ignition on. Using scan tool, record DTC FREEZE FRAME and FAILURE RECORDS. Raise and support vehicle. Start engine. Place gearshift lever in any drive range. Observe TRANS OUTPUT SPEED parameter on scan tool. If scan tool indicates that transmission output speed increases as wheel speed increases, go to DIAGNOSTIC AIDS. If transmission output speed does not change as specified, go to next step.

2) Check speedometer operation. If operation is okay, go to next step. If operation is not okay, go to step **4)**.

3) Check for proper speedometer calibration. If calibration is okay, go to step **16)**. If calibration is not okay, go to next step.

4) Turn ignition off. Disconnect PCM harness connector A-38 (Blue). Using a DVOM, measure resistance between PCM harness connector terminal E1 (Yellow wire), and terminal E2 (Brown wire). If resistance is 3000 ohms, go to next step. If resistance is not as specified, go to step **6)**.

5) Using a DVOM, select AC volts. Turn driveshaft by rotating a rear wheel by hand. If reading is greater than .5 volt, go to step **7)**. If reading is not as specified, go to step **8)**.

6) Inspect Yellow wire and Brown wire between OSS and PCM for an open or poor connection. Repair as necessary and go to step **17)**. If no problem is found, go to step **8)**.

7) Reconnect PCM harness connector. Disconnect OSS harness connector. Turn ignition on. Using a DVOM, measure voltage between OSS Harness connector terminals. If reading is 4.0-5.1 volts, go to step **16)**. If reading is not a specified, go to step **10)**.

8) Remove OSS. Check output shaft speed sensor rotor for damage or misalignment. Repair as necessary and go to step **17)**. If no problem is found, go to next step.

9) Replace OSS. Go to step **17)**.

10) If reading in step **7)** was less than 4.0 volts, go to step **12)**. If reading was not less than 4.0 volts in step **7)**, go to next step.

11) If reading in step **7)** was greater than 5.1 volts, go to step **15)**.

12) Using a DVOM, measure voltage between ground and Yellow wire at OSS harness connector. If reading is 4.0-5.1 volts, go to next step. If reading is not as specified, go to step **14)**.

13) Repair open in Brown wire between OSS and PCM. Go to step **17)**.

14) Check Yellow wire between OSS and PCM for an open or short to ground. Repair as necessary and go to step **17)**. If no problem is found, go to step **16)**.

15) Repair short to power in Yellow wire between OSS and PCM. Go to step **17)**.

16) Replace PCM. Go to next step.

17) Using scan tool, select DTC, then CLEAR INFO function. Operate vehicle so scan tool indicates a transmission output speed greater than 101 RPM for 3 seconds. Review DTC INFO. If last test failed, or DTC P0722 is present, repeat step **1)**. If last test passed and no DTCs are present, testing is complete.

Diagnostic Aids – DTC P0722 will set when no output speed is detected at start-off. Inspect for poor harness connections and improper wire harness routing. An intermittent condition may be caused by a wire which is broken inside its insulation, or shorted to an additional circuit or chassis ground. Check harness connectors for damaged, corroded or backed-out terminal pins. Repair as necessary.

DTC P0723: TRANSMISSION OUTPUT SPEED SENSOR (OSS) INTERMITTENT

Conditions For Setting DTC (In Park Or Neutral):
- Transmission output speed change is greater than 7000 RPM.
- Condition is present for 6 seconds.
- Engine running time is greater than 2 seconds.

Conditions For Setting DTC (Not In Park Or Neutral):
- Transmission output speed change is greater than 512 RPM.
- Condition is present for .1 second.
- Engine running time is greater than 2 seconds.

Diagnosis – 1) Install scan tool. Turn ignition on. Using scan tool, record DTC FREEZE FRAME and FAILURE RECORDS. Raise and support vehicle. Start engine. Place gearshift lever in any drive range. Observe TRANS OUTPUT SPEED parameter on scan tool. If scan tool indicates that transmission output speed increases as wheel speed increases, go to DIAGNOSTIC AIDS. If transmission output speed does not change as specified, go to next step.

2) Check speedometer operation. If operation is okay, go to next step. If operation is not okay, go to step **4)**.

3) Check for proper speedometer calibration. If calibration is okay, go to step **16)**. If calibration is not okay, go to next step.

4) Turn ignition off. Disconnect PCM harness connector A-38 (Blue). Using a DVOM, measure resistance between PCM harness connector terminal E1 (Yellow wire), and terminal E2 (Brown wire). If resistance is 3000 ohms, go to next step. If resistance is not as specified, go to step **6)**.

5) Using a DVOM, select AC volts. Turn driveshaft by rotating a rear wheel by hand. If reading is greater than .5 volt, go to step **7)**. If reading is not as specified, go to step **8)**.

6) Inspect Yellow wire and Brown wire between OSS and PCM for an open or poor connection. Repair as necessary and go to step **17)**. If no problem is found, go to step **8)**.

7) Reconnect PCM harness connector. Disconnect OSS harness connector. Turn ignition on. Using a DVOM, measure voltage between OSS harness connector terminals. If reading is 4.0-5.1 volts, go to step **16)**. If reading is not a specified, go to step **10)**.

3-702

AUTOMATIC TRANSMISSIONS
1996 Hydra-Matic 4L30-E Electronic Controls
Honda Passport & Isuzu Rodeo (Cont.)

8) Remove OSS. Check output shaft speed sensor rotor for damage or misalignment. Repair as necessary and go to step **17)**. If no problem is found, go to next step.

9) Replace OSS. Go to step **17)**.

10) If reading in step **7)** was less than 4.0 volts, go to step **12)**. If reading was not less than 4.0 volts in step **7)**, go to next step.

11) If reading in step **7)** was greater than 5.1 volts, go to step **15)**.

12) Using a DVOM, measure voltage between ground and Yellow wire at OSS harness connector. If reading is 4.0-5.1 volts, go to next step. If reading is not as specified, go to step **14)**.

13) Repair open in Brown wire between OSS and PCM. Go to step **17)**.

14) Check Yellow wire between OSS and PCM for an open or short to ground. Repair as necessary and go to step **17)**. If no problem is found, go to step **16)**.

15) Repair short to power in Yellow wire between OSS and PCM. Go to step **17)**.

16) Replace PCM. Go to next step.

17) Using scan tool, select DTC, then CLEAR INFO function. Operate vehicle so scan tool indicates a transmission output speed greater than 101 RPM for 3 seconds. Review DTC INFO. If last test failed, or DTC P0723 is present, repeat step **1)**. If last test passed and no DTCs are present, testing is complete.

Diagnostic Aids – DTC P0723 will set when output speed has been detected, then lost. Inspect for poor harness connections and improper wire harness routing. An intermittent condition may be caused by wire which is broken inside its insulation, or shorted to an additional circuit or chassis ground. Check harness connectors for damaged, corroded or backed-out terminal pins. Repair as necessary.

DTC P0724:
TCC BRAKE SWITCH CIRCUIT LOW (STUCK OFF)
Conditions For Setting DTC:
- DTCs P0722 or P0723 are not present.
- PCM detects an open brake switch/circuit (zero volts) during decelerations, and the following events occur 7 consecutive times: vehicle speed is greater than 20 MPH for 4 seconds, then between 5 MPH and 20 MPH for 4 seconds; then vehicle speed is less than 5 MPH.

Diagnosis – **1)** Install scan tool. Turn ignition on. Using scan tool, record DTC FAILURE RECORDS. Apply, then release brake pedal. If scan tool displays TCC brake switch as CLOSED with brake pedal applied, then OPEN when released, go to DIAGNOSTIC AIDS. If scan tool display is not as specified, go to next step.

2) Using a test light connected to ground, backprobe ignition feed circuit (Green wire) at brake switch. If test light illuminates, go to next step. If test light does not illuminate, go to step **4)**.

3) Using a test light connected to ground, backprobe Red wire at brake switch. Apply brake pedal. If test light illuminates, go to step **6)**. If test light does not illuminate, go to next step.

4) Check fuse CB-13 (15-amp) in instrument panel fuse box. If fuse is blown, check for a short to ground. Repair as necessary. If fuse is okay, repair open in ignition feed circuit (Green wire) between brake switch and instrument panel fuse box. Go to step **10)**.

5) Disconnect brake switch electrical connector. Using a DVOM, measure resistance between terminals No. 2 and 3 of brake switch. Apply brake pedal. If resistance is zero ohms, go to next step. If resistance is not as specified, go to step **7)**.

6) Check Red wire between PCM and brake switch for an open. Repair as necessary and go to step **10)**. If no problem is found, go to step **8)**.

7) Replace brake switch. Go to step **10)**.

8) Check for poor PCM harness connections. Repair as necessary and go to step **10)**. If no problem is found, go to next step.

9) Replace PCM. Go to next step.

10) Using scan tool, select DTC, then CLEAR INFO function. Ensure PCM brake switch signal indicates 12 volts for at least one second with brake pedal released. Review DTC INFO. If last test failed, or DTC P0724 is present, repeat step **1)**. If last test passed and no DTCs are present, testing is complete.

Diagnostic Aids – Inspect for poor harness connections and improper wire harness routing. An intermittent condition may be caused by a wire which is broken inside its insulation, or shorted to an additional circuit or chassis ground. Check harness connectors for damaged, corroded or backed-out terminal pins. Repair as necessary. Check brake switch for proper mounting and adjustment.

DTC P0730:
TRANSMISSION INCORRECT GEAR RATIO
Conditions For Setting DTC:
- DTCs P0722 and P0723 are not present.
- Not in Park, Neutral or Reverse.
- Engine speed is greater than 3500 RPM.
- Three seconds since up-shift.
- Three seconds since garage shift ("N" to "D").
- One of the following occurs: slip is greater than 595 RPM in 1st gear, greater than 556 RPM in 2nd gear, greater than 536 RPM in 3rd gear or greater than 528 RPM in 4th gear.
- Conditions must be present for 5.5 seconds.

Diagnosis – **1)** Inspect cooling system for leaks. Repair as necessary and go to step **6)**. If no problem is found, go to next step.

2) Perform transmission fluid checking procedure. See CHECKING FLUID LEVEL under LUBRICATION in appropriate AUTOMATIC TRANSMISSION SERVICING article. Fill if necessary and go to next step.

3) Install scan tool. Turn ignition on. Using scan tool, record DTC FAILURE RECORDS. Test drive vehicle in 1st, 2nd, 3rd and "D" with engine speed greater than 3500 RPM for 5.5 seconds. Using scan tool in SNAPSHOT mode, record each gear ratio. Compare recorded value with GEAR RATIO SPECIFICATION table. If gear ratios match, go to DIAGNOSTIC AIDS. If gear ratios do not match, go to next step.

GEAR RATIO SPECIFICATION

Gear Range	Ratio
1st	2.73-2.99
2nd	1.54-1.71
3rd	0.93-1.05
4th	0.66-0.78

4) Perform hydraulic pressure test. See TRANSMISSION TESTING in appropriate overhaul article. Repair as necessary and go to step **6)**. If no problem is found, go to next step.

5) Check for possible clutch slippage. See TROUBLE SHOOTING in appropriate overhaul article. Repair as necessary and go to next step.

6) Using scan tool, select DTC, then CLEAR INFO function. Select SPECIFIC DTC, then enter DTC P1871. Test drive vehicle in D4 with engine speed greater than 3500 RPM to obtain any of the following gear ratios for 7 seconds:
- 1st 1:2.73-1:2.99
- 2nd 1:1.54-1:1.71
- 3rd 1:0.93-1:1.05
- 4th 1:0.66-1:0.78

If last test failed, or DTC P0730 is present, repeat step **1)**. If last test passed and no DTCs are present, testing is complete.

Diagnostic Aids – Check for intermittent output speed sensor circuit problems. Check for possible incorrect calibration (PCM part number, tire size or rear axle ratio).

DTC P0742: TORQUE CONVERTER CLUTCH (TCC) CIRCUIT STUCK ON
Conditions For Setting DTC:
- DTCs P0122, P0123, P0722, P0723 and P1860 are not present.
- TP angel is greater than 20 percent.
- Engine speed is greater than 500 RPM and less than 3000 RPM.
- Engine vacuum is between zero and 10.2 in. Hg.
- Commanded gear is not 1st.
- Gear range is D4.
- TCC is commanded OFF.

AUTOMATIC TRANSMISSIONS

3-703

1996 Hydra-Matic 4L30-E Electronic Controls
Honda Passport & Isuzu Rodeo (Cont.)

- TCC slip speed is between –30 and 30 RPM for 4 seconds.
- Vehicle speed is greater than 15 MPH, and less than 75 MPH.
- Speed ratio is greater than .9 and less than 1.8.

Diagnosis – 1) Install scan tool. Turn ignition on. Using scan tool, record DTC FREEZE FRAME and FAILURE RECORDS. Verify TP sensor operation. If TP sensor value is .6-5.0 volts, go to next step. If TP sensor value is not as specified, go to DIAGNOSTIC AIDS.

2) Test drive vehicle in D4 range in 4th gear under steady acceleration, with TP sensor angle greater than 20 percent. Using scan tool, observe TCC SLIP SPEED parameter. If display indicates –30 to 30 RPM while TCC solenoid state is OFF, go to next step. If display is not as specified, go to DIAGNOSTIC AIDS.

3) TCC solenoid is mechanically stuck on. Check for the following:
- Clogged TCC solenoid exhaust orifice.
- TCC apply valve stuck in apply position.
- Misaligned or damaged valve body gaskets.
- Restricted release passage.

Repair as necessary and go to next step.

4) Using scan tool, select DTC, then CLEAR INFO function. Ensure TCC slip is between 200 and 2500 RPM for 4 seconds. Review DTC INFO. If last test failed, or DTC P0742 is present, repeat step **1)**. If last test passed and no DTCs are present, testing is complete.

Diagnostic Aids – If TCC is mechanically stuck on with parking brake applied and any gear range selected, TCC fluid will mechanically apply TCC, possibly causing engine to stall.

DTC P0748: PRESSURE CONTROL SOLENOID (FORCE MOTOR) CIRCUIT ELECTRICAL

Conditions For Setting DTC:
- DTC P0560 is not present.
- PCM detects that pressure control solenoid has reached its electrical high or low limit.

Diagnosis – 1) Install scan tool. Turn ignition on. Using scan tool, record DTC FAILURE RECORDS. Start engine. Ensure gearshift lever is in "P" position. Using scan tool, apply .1 amp through 1.0 amp while observing PC REF. CURRENT and PC ACT. CURRENT. If PC ACT. CURRENT is always within .16 amp, go to DIAGNOSTIC AIDS. If PC ACT. CURRENT is not as specified, go to next step.

2) Turn ignition off. Disconnect transmission harness connector M-6 (5-pin Black connector). Using a DVOM, measure resistance between terminals of pressure control solenoid (Red/Black wire and Red/Green wire). If resistance is 3-7 ohms, go to step **6)**. If resistance is not as specified, go to next step.

3) Remove transmission oil pan. Disconnect internal wiring harness. Using a DVOM, measure resistance of pressure control solenoid. If resistance is 3-7 ohms, go to step **5)**. If resistance is not as specified, go to next step.

4) Replace pressure control solenoid. Go to step **8)**.

5) Repair open in internal wiring harness. Go to step **8)**.

6) Inspect pressure control solenoid circuit for an open, short or poor connection. Repair as necessary and go to step **8)**. If no problem is found, go to next step.

7) Replace PCM. Go to next step.

8) Using scan tool, select DTC, then CLEAR INFO function. Ensure pressure control solenoid duty cycle is not at its electrical high or low limit. Review DTC INFO. If last test failed, or DTC P0748 is present, repeat step **1)**. If last test passed and no DTCs are present, testing is complete.

Diagnostic Aids – Inspect for poor harness connections and improper wire harness routing. An intermittent condition may be caused by a wire which is broken inside its insulation, or shorted to an additional circuit or chassis ground. Check harness connectors for damaged, corroded or backed-out terminal pins. Repair as necessary.

DTC P0751: SHIFT SOLENOID "A" PERFORMANCE (WITHOUT INPUT SPEED)

NOTE: Shift solenoid "A" may also be known as 1-2/3-4 shift solenoid. Shift solenoid "B" may also be known as 2-3 shift solenoid.

Conditions For Setting DTC:
- DTCs P0122, P0123, P0722, P0723, P0742, P1860, P0753 and P0758 are not present.
- Gear range is D4.
- Vehicle speed is greater than 6.25 MPH.
- Transmission fluid temperature is 68-266°F (20-130°C).

All conditions above must be met, and the combination of conditions No. 1, 2, 3 and 4, or 1, 2, 3 and 5 occur 2 consecutive times.

Condition No. 1:
- Commanded 1-2 shift.
- TP angle is between 10 and 60 percent.
- TP angle is constant within plus or minus 5 percent.
- Vehicle speed is between 11 and 31 MPH.
- Within 2.2 seconds, engine speed in 2nd gear must be 100 RPM greater than last speed in 1st gear.

Condition No. 2:
- Commanded 2-3 shift.
- TP angle is between 15 and 60 percent.
- TP angle is constant within plus or minus 5 percent.
- Vehicle speed is between 20 and 45 MPH.
- Within 2.2 seconds, engine speed in 3rd gear must be 64 RPM less than last speed in 2nd gear.

Condition No. 3:
- Commanded 3-4 shift.
- TP angle is between 23 and 60 percent.
- TP angle is constant within plus or minus 5 percent.
- Vehicle speed is between 31 and 87 MPH.
- Within 2.2 seconds, engine speed in 4th gear must not be greater than last speed in 3rd gear.

Condition No. 4:
- Commanded 4th gear.
- TCC is ON.
- TP angle is between 15 and 60 percent.
- Speed ratio is between .85 and 1.2 (speed ratio = engine speed divided by output speed).
- TCC slip speed is between 100 and 2000 RPM for 3 seconds.

Condition No. 5:
- Commanded 4th gear.
- TCC is ON.
- TP angle is between 15 and 60 percent.
- Speed ratio is between .5 and .85.
- TCC slip speed is between –50 and 500 RPM for 3 seconds.

Diagnosis – 1) Install scan tool. Turn ignition on. Using scan tool, record DTC FREEZE FRAME and FAILURE RECORDS. Start engine. Apply brake pedal. Observe scan tool while moving gearshift lever through all gear ranges. If scan tool display coincides with actual gear range selected, go to next step. If operation is not as specified, go to RANGE SWITCH LOGIC TABLE. *See Fig. 5.*

2) Raise and support vehicle. With engine running, place gearshift lever in D4. Using scan tool, command 1st, 2nd, 3rd and 4th gears while accelerating vehicle. If 2-3 or 1-4 shift patterns are detected only, go to next step. If all shift patterns are detected, go to DIAGNOSTIC AIDS.

3) Check shift solenoid/hydraulic circuit for the following:
- Internal malfunction in one or both shift solenoids.
- Contamination in one or both shift solenoids.
- Damaged seals on one or both shift solenoids.

Repair as necessary and go to next step. If no problem is found, go to DIAGNOSTIC AIDS.

AUTOMATIC TRANSMISSIONS
1996 Hydra-Matic 4L30-E Electronic Controls
Honda Passport & Isuzu Rodeo (Cont.)

3-704

4) Using scan tool, select DTC, then CLEAR INFO function. Road test vehicle. Review DTC INFO. If last test failed, or DTC P0751 is present, repeat step **1)**. If last test passed and no DTCs are present, testing is complete.

Diagnostic Aids – Verify transmission shift speeds are correct. See TRANSMISSION TESTING in appropriate overhaul article. Other transmission internal failures may cause more than one shift to occur. A shift solenoid "A" performance problem may set a shift solenoid "B" DTC P0756 or a transmission component slipping DTC P1870.

DTC P0753: SHIFT SOLENOID "A" ELECTRICAL

NOTE: Shift solenoid "A" may also be known as 1-2/3-4 shift solenoid. Shift solenoid "B" may also be known as 2-3 shift solenoid.

Conditions For Setting DTC:
- Ignition on.
- DTC P0560 is not present.
- PCM commands solenoid on and voltage remains high (battery voltage).
- PCM commands solenoid off and voltage remains low (zero voltage).
- Conditions must be present for .275 second.

Diagnosis – 1) Install scan tool. Turn ignition on. Using scan tool, record DTC FREEZE FRAME and FAILURE RECORDS. If DTCs P0753, P0758 and P1860 are set, go to next step. If specified, DTCs are not set, go to DIAGNOSTIC AIDS.

2) Ensure ignition is on. Using a DVOM, measure voltage (backprobe) between ground and PCM harness connector A-38 (Blue), terminal E14 (Brown/White wire). If reading is 10-12 volts, go to next step. If reading is not as specified, go to step **4)**.

3) Turn ignition off. Disconnect PCM harness connector A-38. Turn ignition on. Using a DVOM, measure voltage between ground and PCM harness connector A-38, terminal F14 (Yellow/Green wire). If reading is 10-14 volts, go to step **10)**. If reading is not as specified, go to next step.

4) Turn ignition off. Using a DVOM, measure resistance between PCM harness connector A-38, terminal E14 (Brown/White wire) and terminal F14 (Yellow/Green wire). If resistance is 18-20 ohms, go to next step. If resistance is not as specified, go to step **6)**.

5) Disconnect PCM harness connectors A-36 (Red) and A-37 (White). Using a DVOM, check for continuity between ground and PCM harness connector A-38, terminal F14 (Yellow/Green wire). If continuity is present, go to step **11)**. If no continuity is present, go to step **7)**.

6) Disconnect transmission harness connector H12 (16-pin Blue connector). Using a DVOM, measure resistance between terminals No. 5 (Yellow/Green wire) and No. 12 (Brown/White wire). If resistance is 18-20 ohms, go to step **13)**. If resistance is not as specified, go to step **8)**.

7) Using a DVOM, measure continuity between ground and PCM harness connector A-38 (Blue), terminal E14 (Brown/White wire). If continuity is present, go to step **12)**. If continuity is not present, go to step **9)**.

8) Disconnect transmission harness connector M-7 (4-pin Black connector). Using a DVOM, measure resistance between harness connector M-7, terminals No. 3 (Yellow/Green wire) and No. 4 (Brown/White wire). If resistance is 18-20 ohms, go to step **14)**. If resistance is not as specified, go to step **15)**.

9) Check all PCM harness connections. If a problem is found, go to step **17)**. If no problem is found, go to step **16)**.

10) Repair Yellow/Green wire between PCM harness connector A-38 (Blue) and shift solenoid "A" for a short to power. Go to step **18)**.

11) Repair Yellow/Green wire between PCM harness connector A-38 (Blue) and shift solenoid "A" for a short to ground. Go to step **18)**.

12) Repair Brown/White wire between PCM harness connector A-38 (Blue) and shift solenoid "A" for a short to ground. Go to step **18)**.

13) Repair wiring harness between transmission harness connector H-12 (16-pin Blue connector) and PCM harness connector A-38 (Blue) for an open or poor connection. Go to step **18)**.

14) Repair open or poor connection in wiring harness between transmission harness connector H-12 (16-pin Blue connector) and transmission harness connector M-7 (4-pin Black connector). Go to step **18)**.

15) Replace shift solenoid "A". Go to step **18)**.

16) Replace PCM. Go to step **18)**.

17) Repair PCM harness connections. Go to next step.

18) Using scan tool, select DTC, then CLEAR INFO function. Operate vehicle and ensure that when shift solenoid "A" is commanded on, voltage drops to zero, then increases to battery voltage when commanded off. Review DTC INFO. If last test failed, or DTC P0753 is present, repeat step **1)**. If last test passed and no DTCs are present, testing is complete.

Diagnostic Aids – Inspect for poor harness connections and improper wire harness routing. An intermittent condition may be caused by a wire which is broken inside its insulation, or shorted to an additional circuit or chassis ground. Check harness connectors for damaged, corroded or backed-out terminal pins. Repair as necessary. An open ignition feed circuit can cause multiple DTCs to set. A shift solenoid "B" DTC P0756 may also set with a shift solenoid "A" failure.

DTC P0756: SHIFT SOLENOID "B" PERFORMANCE (WITHOUT INPUT SPEED)

NOTE: Shift solenoid "A" may also be known as 1-2/3-4 shift solenoid. Shift solenoid "B" may also be known as 2-3 shift solenoid.

Conditions For Setting DTC:
- DTCs P0122, P0123, P0722, P0723, P0742, P1860, P0753, P0758, P0106, P1106, P0107, P1107 and P0108 are not present.
- Vehicle speed is greater than 6.25 MPH.
- Gear range is D4.
- Engine vacuum is between zero and 10.2 in. Hg.
- Engine speed is less than 6000 RPM.
- Transmission temperature is 68-266°F (20-130°C).
- TCC is off.

All conditions above must be met, and either one of the following fail conditions occurs:

Condition No. 1:
- TP angle is greater than 45 percent.
- 1st gear is commanded for 3 seconds.
- Speed ratio is between .5 and 2.65 (speed ratio = engine speed divided by output speed).
- Transmission output speed is between 320 and 2000 RPM.
- TCC slip speed is between –200 and –4000 RPM for 1.8 seconds.

Condition No. 2:
- Not used.

Condition No. 3:
- Commanded 2-3 shift.
- TP angle is between 10 and 60 percent.
- TP angle is within plus or minus 5 percent.
- 3rd gear is commanded for 2 seconds.
- 3rd gear speed ratio is higher than the last 2nd gear speed ratio minus .3 (scan tool value is numerically greater in 3rd gear).
- 3rd gear TCC slip speed is greater than or equal to last 2nd gear TCC slip speed plus 520 RPM for 2.1 seconds.
- Discontinue test if time since last commanded 2-3 shift is 6 seconds.

Condition No. 4:
- TP angle is greater than 10 percent.
- 4th gear is commanded for one second.
- Speed ratio is between 2.0 and 4.0.
- Transmission output speed is between zero and 8192 RPM.

Diagnosis – 1) Install scan tool. Turn ignition on. Using scan tool, record DTC FREEZE FRAME and FAILURE RECORDS. Start engine. Apply brake pedal. Observe scan tool while moving gearshift lever through all gear ranges. If scan tool display coincides with actual gear range selected, go to next step. If operation is not as specified, go to RANGE SWITCH LOGIC TABLE. *See Fig. 5.*

AUTOMATIC TRANSMISSIONS
1996 Hydra-Matic 4L30-E Electronic Controls
Honda Passport & Isuzu Rodeo (Cont.)

3-705

2) Raise and support vehicle. With engine running, place gearshift lever in D4. Using scan tool, command 1st, 2nd, 3rd and 4th gears while accelerating vehicle. If 1st gear was commanded and not achieved, or 4th gear was commanded and a gear range other than 4th occurred, go to next step. If all shift patterns are detected, go to DIAGNOSTIC AIDS.

3) Check shift solenoid/hydraulic circuit for the following:
- Internal malfunction in one or both shift solenoids.
- Contamination in one or both shift solenoids.
- Damaged seals on one or both shift solenoids.

Repair as necessary and go to next step. If no problem is found, go to DIAGNOSTIC AIDS.

4) Using scan tool, select DTC, then CLEAR INFO function. Road test vehicle. Review DTC INFO. If last test failed, or DTC P0756 is present, repeat step **1)**. If last test passed and no DTCs are present, testing is complete.

Diagnostic Aids – A shift solenoid "A" electrical failure can also set a shift solenoid "B" performance DTC P0756. A shift solenoid "B" electrical failure can also set a shift solenoid "B" performance DTC P0756.

DTC P0758: SHIFT SOLENOID "B" ELECTRICAL

NOTE: Shift solenoid "A" may also be known as 1-2/3-4 shift solenoid. Shift solenoid "B" may also be known as 2-3 shift solenoid.

Conditions For Setting DTC:
- Ignition on.
- DTC P0560 is not present.
- PCM commands solenoid on and voltage remains high (battery voltage).
- PCM commands solenoid off and voltage remains low (zero voltage).
- Conditions must be present for .275 second.

Diagnosis – **1)** Install scan tool. Turn ignition on. Using scan tool, record DTC FREEZE FRAME and FAILURE RECORDS. If DTCs P0753, P0758 and P1860 are set, go to step **3)**. If specified, DTCs are not set, go to next step.

2) With engine running, apply brake pedal and place gearshift lever in "D" position. Press WINTER switch to select Winter mode. If scan tool displays DTC P0758 at 3rd gear, go to step **7)**. If display is not as specified, go to DIAGNOSTIC AIDS.

3) Turn ignition off. Disconnect PCM harness connectors A-37 (White) and A-38 (Blue). Turn ignition on. Using a DVOM, measure voltage between PCM harness connector A-37, terminal C2 (Brown/Black wire) and terminal C8 (Black/Red wire). If reading is 10-12 volts, go to step **14)**. If reading is not as specified, go to next step.

4) Turn ignition off. Using a DVOM, measure resistance between PCM harness connector A-37, terminal C2 (Brown/Black wire) and PCM harness connector A-28, terminal E-14 (Brown/White wire). If resistance is 18-20 ohms, go to step **15)**. If resistance is not as specified, go to next step.

5) Disconnect transmission harness connector H-12 (16-pin Blue connector). Using a DVOM, measure resistance between transmission harness connector H-12, terminals No. 7 (Brown/Black wire) and No. 12 (Brown/White wire). If resistance is 18-20 ohms, go to step **16)**. If resistance is not as specified, go to next step.

6) Disconnect transmission harness connector M-7 (4-pin Black connector). Using a DVOM, measure resistance between transmission harness connector M-7, terminals No. 1 (Brown/Black wire) and No. 4 (Brown/White wire). If resistance is 18-20 ohms, go to step **17)**. If resistance is not as specified, go to step **18)**.

7) Turn ignition off. Disconnect PCM harness connectors A-37 (White) and A-38 (Blue). Using a DVOM, measure resistance between PCM harness connector A-37, terminal C2 (Brown/Black wire) and PCM harness connector A-38, terminal E14 (Brown/white wire). If resistance is between 18-20 ohms, go to next step. If resistance is not as specified, go to step **9)**.

8) Using a DVOM, check for continuity between PCM harness connector A-37, terminal C2 (Brown/Black wire) and ground. If continuity is present, go to step **19)**. If no continuity is present, go to step **10)**.

9) Disconnect transmission harness connector H-12 (16-pin Blue connector). Using a DVOM, measure resistance between transmission harness connector H-12, terminals No. 7 (Brown/Black wire) and No. 12 (Brown/White wire). If resistance is 18-20 ohms, go to step **20)**. If resistance is not as specified, go to step **11)**.

10) Using a DVOM, check for continuity between ground and PCM harness connector A-38, terminal E14 (Brown/White wire). If continuity is present, go to step **21)**. If no continuity is present, go to step **12)**.

11) Disconnect transmission harness connector M-7 (4-pin Black connector). Using a DVOM, measure resistance between harness connector M-7, terminals No. 1 (Brown/Black wire) and No. 4 (Brown/White wire). If resistance is 18-20 ohms, go to step **22)**. If resistance is not as specified, go to step **23)**.

12) Check all connections at PCM and transmission harness connector H-12. repair as necessary and go to step **25)**. If no problem is found, go to next step.

13) Reconnect PCM harness connectors A-37 and A-38. Start engine and repeat step **2)**. If scan tool displays DTC P0758 at 3rd gear, go to step **24)**. If display is not as specified, go to DIAGNOSTIC AIDS.

14) Repair Brown/Black wire between PCM harness connector A-37 and transmission harness connector M-7 for a short to power. Go to step **25)**.

15) PCM harness connector A-37, internal terminal C2 (Brown/Black wire) is shorted to power. Replace PCM. Go to step **25)**.

16) Repair wire harness between PCM and transmission harness connector H-12 for a short circuit. Go to step **25)**.

17) Repair wire harness between transmission harness connector H-12 and transmission harness connectors M-6 or M-7 for a short circuit. Go to step **25)**.

18) Shift solenoid "B" or its internal wiring harness is faulty. Repair as necessary. Go to step **25)**.

19) Repair Brown/Black wire between PCM harness connector A-37 and transmission harness connector M-7 for a short to ground. Go to step **25)**.

20) Brown/Black wire between PCM harness connector A-37 and transmission harness connector H-12 is open, or Brown/White wire between PCM harness connector A-38 and transmission harness connector H-12 is open. Repair as necessary. Go to step **25)**.

21) Repair Brown/White wire between PCM harness connector A-38 and transmission harness connector M-7 for a short to ground. Go to step **25)**.

22) Brown/Black wire between transmission harness connector H-12 and transmission harness connector M-7 is open, or Brown/White wire between transmission harness connector H-12 and transmission harness connector M-7 is open. Repair as necessary. Go to step **25)**.

23) Shift solenoid "B" or its internal wiring harness is faulty. Repair as necessary. Go to step **25)**.

24) Replace PCM. Go to next step.

25) Using scan tool, select DTC, then CLEAR INFO function. Operate vehicle and ensure that when shift solenoid "B" is commanded on, voltage drops to zero, then increases to battery voltage when commanded off. Review DTC INFO. If last test failed, or DTC P0758 is present, repeat step **1)**. If last test passed and no DTCs are present, testing is complete.

Diagnostic Aids – Inspect for poor harness connections and improper wire harness routing. An intermittent condition may be caused by a wire which is broken inside its insulation, or shorted to an additional circuit or chassis ground. Check harness connectors for damaged, corroded or backed-out terminal pins. Repair as necessary.

3-706

AUTOMATIC TRANSMISSIONS
1996 Hydra-Matic 4L30-E Electronic Controls
Honda Passport & Isuzu Rodeo (Cont.)

DTC P1790:
ROM TRANSMISSION SIDE BAD CHECK SUM
DTC P1792:
EEPROM TRANSMISSION SIDE BAD CHECK SUM

Conditions For Setting DTC:
- Check Sum (CSUM) error detected for one second.

Diagnosis – 1) Install scan tool. Turn ignition on. Using scan tool, record DTC FAILURE RECORDS. If DTC P1790 is set, go to step **4)**. If DTC P1790 is not set, go to next step.
2) If DTC P1792 is set, go to next step.
3) Remove PCM. Using Service Programming System (T-6), reprogram transmission EEPROM. Go to step **5)**.
4) Replace PCM. Go to next step.
5) Using scan tool, select DTC, then CLEAR INFO function. Road test vehicle. Review DTC INFO. If last test failed, or DTCs P1790 or P1792 are present, repeat step **1)**. If last test passed and no DTCs are present, testing is complete.

DTC P1835: KICKDOWN SWITCH ALWAYS ON

Conditions For Setting DTC:
- DTCs P0122 and P0123 are not set.
- TP angle is lees than 70 percent.
- Kickdown switch is on.
- Conditions must be present for one second.

Diagnosis – 1) Install scan tool. Turn ignition on. Using scan tool, record DTC FAILURE RECORDS. If scan tool displays KICKDOWN SWITCH LOW (closed), go to next step. If display is not as specified, go to step **3)**.
2) Turn ignition off. Disconnect PCM harness connector A-38 (Blue). Using a DVOM, check for continuity between ground and PCM harness connector A-38, terminal F11 (Light Blue wire). If continuity is present, go to step **4)**. If no continuity is present, go to step **7)**.
3) If scan tool displays kickdown switch ON when TP angle is less than 70 percent, go to step **5)**. If display is not as specified, go to DIAGNOSTIC AIDS.
4) Disconnect kickdown switch electrical connector. Using a DVOM, check for continuity between kickdown switch terminals. If continuity is present, go to step **6)**. If no continuity is present, go to step **8)**.
5) Adjust kickdown switch. If scan tool should display kickdown switch ON when TP angle is greater than 95 percent. Go to step **9)**.
6) Replace kickdown switch. Go to step **9)**.
7) Replace PCM. Go to step **9)**.
8) Repair Light Blue wire between PCM and kickdown switch for a short to ground. Go to next step.
9) Using scan tool, select DTC, then CLEAR INFO function. Ensure torque converter stator temperature switch circuit does not indicate a hot mode when transmission fluid temperature is less than 140°F (60°C) for at least 5 seconds. Review DTC INFO. If last test failed, or DTC P1835 is present, repeat step **1)**. If last test passed and no DTCs are present, testing is complete.

Diagnostic Aids – Check wire harness for a short to ground between PCM and kickdown switch. Check for misadjusted or faulty kickdown switch.

DTC P1850:
BRAKE BAND APPLY SOLENOID MALFUNCTION

Conditions For Setting DTC:
- DTC P0560 is not present.
- Ignition on.
- PCM commands solenoid on, and voltage remains high (battery voltage).
- PCM commands solenoid off, and voltage remains low (zero voltage).
- Conditions met in 1.3 seconds.

Diagnosis – 1) Install scan tool. Turn ignition on. Using scan tool, record DTC FREEZE FRAME and FAILURE RECORDS. If DTCs P0753 and P0758 are set, go to next step. If specified DTCs are not present, go to step **3)**.
2) Using a DVOM, measure voltage (backprobe) between PCM harness connector A-37 (White), terminal C8 (Black/Red wire) and PCM harness connector A-38 (Blue), terminal E14 (Brown/White wire). If reading is 10-12 volts, go to step **4)**. If reading is not as specified, go to step **5)**.
3) Turn ignition off. Disconnect PCM harness connectors A-36 (Red) and A-38 (Blue). Using a DVOM, measure resistance between PCM harness connector A-36, terminal A16 (Yellow/Black wire) and PCM harness connector A-38, terminal E14 (Brown/White wire). If resistance is 10-12 ohms, go to step **11)**. If resistance is not as specified, go to step **12)**.
4) Using a DVOM, measure voltage (backprobe) between PCM harness connector A-36, terminal A16 (Yellow/Black wire) and PCM harness connector A-37, terminal C8 (Black/Red wire). If reading is 10-12 volts, go to step **25)**. If reading is not as specified, go to step **3)**.
5) Turn ignition off. Disconnect PCM harness connectors A-36 (Red) and A-38 (Blue). Using a DVOM, check for continuity between ground and PCM harness connector A-38, terminal E14 (Brown/white wire). If continuity is present, go to next step. If no continuity is present, go to step **8)**.
6) Disconnect transmission harness connector H-12 (16-pin Blue connector). Using a DVOM, check for continuity between ground and transmission harness connector H-12, terminal No. 6 (Yellow/Black wire). If continuity is present, go to next step. If no continuity is present, go to step **16)**.
7) Disconnect transmission harness connector M-7 (4-pin Black connector). Using a DVOM, check for continuity between ground and transmission harness connector M-7, terminal No. 2 (Yellow/Black wire). If continuity is present, go to step **17)**. If no continuity is present, go to step **18)**.
8) Disconnect PCM harness connector A-36 (Red). Using a DVOM, measure resistance between PCM harness connector A-36, terminal A16 (Yellow/Black wire) and PCM harness connector A-38, terminal E14 (Brown/White wire). If resistance is 10-12 ohms, go to step **25)**. If resistance is not as specified, go to next step.
9) Disconnect transmission harness connector H-12 (16-pin Blue connector. Using a DVOM, measure resistance between transmission harness connector H-12, terminals No. 6 (Yellow/Black wire) and No. 12 (Brown/White wire). If resistance is 10-12 ohms, go to step **16)**. If resistance is not as specified, go to next step.
10) Disconnect transmission harness connector M-7 (4-pin Black connector). Using a DVOM, measure resistance between transmission harness connector M-7, terminals No. 2 (Yellow/Black wire) and No. 4 (Brown/White wire). If resistance is 10-12 ohms, go to step **19)**. If resistance is not as specified, go to step **20)**.
11) Using a DVOM, check for continuity between ground and PCM harness connector A-36, terminal A-16 (Yellow/Black wire). If continuity is present, go to step **13)**. If continuity is not present, go to step **25)**.
12) Disconnect transmission harness connector H-12 (16-pin Blue connector). Using a DVOM, measure resistance between transmission harness connector H-12, terminals No. 6 (Yellow/Black wire) and No. 12 (Brown/White wire). If resistance is 10-12 ohms, go to step **23)**. If resistance is not as specified, go to step **14)**.
13) Disconnect transmission harness connector H-12 (16-pin Blue connector). Using a DVOM, check for continuity between ground and transmission harness connector H-12, terminal No. 6 (Yellow/Black wire). If continuity is present, go to step **15)**. If no continuity is present, go to step **21)**.
14) Disconnect transmission harness connector M-7 (4-pin Black connector). Using a DVOM, measure resistance between transmission harness connector M-7, terminals No. 2 (Yellow/Black wire) and No. 4 (Brown/White wire). If resistance is 10-12 ohms, go to step **24)**. If resistance is not as specified, go to step **20)**.

AUTOMATIC TRANSMISSIONS
1996 Hydra-Matic 4L30-E Electronic Controls
Honda Passport & Isuzu Rodeo (Cont.)

3-707

15) Disconnect transmission harness connector M-7 (4-pin Black connector). Using a DVOM, check for continuity between ground and transmission harness connector M-7, terminal No. 2 (Yellow/Black wire). If continuity is present, go to step **17)**. If no continuity is present, go to step **22)**.

16) Repair open in Brown/White wire between PCM harness connector A-38 and transmission harness connector H-12. Go to step **26)**.

17) Brake band apply solenoid is faulty, or its internal wiring harness is shorted to ground. Repair as necessary. Go to step **26)**.

18) Repair short to ground in Brown/White wire between transmission harness connector M-7 and transmission harness connector H-12. Go to step **26)**.

19) Repair open in Brown/White wire between transmission harness connector M-7 and transmission harness connector H-12. Go to step **26)**.

20) Brake band apply solenoid is faulty, or its internal wiring harness is open. Repair as necessary. Go to step **26)**.

21) Repair short to ground in Yellow/Black wire between PCM harness connector A-36 and transmission harness connector H-12. Go to step **26)**.

22) Repair short to ground in Yellow/Black wire between transmission harness connector M-7 and transmission harness connector H-12. Go to step **26)**.

23) Repair open in Yellow/Black wire between PCM harness connector A-36 and transmission harness connector H-12. Go to step **26)**.

24) Repair open in Yellow/Black wire between transmission harness connector M-7 and transmission harness connector H-12. Go to step **26)**.

25) Check PCM harness connections. Repair as necessary. If connections are okay, replace PCM. Go to next step.

26) Using scan tool, select DTC, then CLEAR INFO function. Ensure that when 3-2 control solenoid is commanded on, voltage drops to zero, and when commanded off, voltage increases to battery voltage. Review DTC INFO. If last test failed, or DTC P1850 is present, repeat step **1)**. If last test passed and no DTCs are present, testing is complete.

Diagnostic Aids – Inspect for poor harness connections and improper wire harness routing. An intermittent condition may be caused by a wire which is broken inside its insulation, or shorted to an additional circuit or chassis ground. Check harness connectors for damaged, corroded or backed-out terminal pins. Repair as necessary.

DTC P1860: TCC PWM SOLENOID ELECTRICAL

Conditions For Setting DTC:
- DTCs P0560, P0751, P0753, P0756 and P0758 are not present.
- Ignition on.
- PCM commands solenoid on, and voltage remains low (zero voltage).
- PCM commands solenoid off, and voltage remains high (battery voltage).
- Conditions present for .15 second.

Diagnosis – 1) Install scan tool. Turn ignition on. Using scan tool, record DTC FREEZE FRAME and FAILURE RECORDS. If DTC P1860 is set, go to next step. If DTC P1860 is not present, go to step **3)**.

2) Using a DVOM, measure voltage (backprobe) between PCM harness connector A-37 (White), terminal D2 (Red/Yellow wire) and terminal C8 (Black/Red wire). If reading is zero volts, go to step **4)**. If reading is not as specified, go to step **5)**.

3) Apply brake pedal and place gearshift lever in "D" position. Road test vehicle and increase vehicle speed until TCC shows ON in 4th gear. If scan tool displays DTC P1860 with TCC on, go to step **9)**. If DTC P1860 is not displayed, go to DIAGNOSTIC AIDS.

4) Turn ignition off. Disconnect PCM harness connector A-37 (White). Using a DVOM, measure resistance between PCM harness connector A-37, terminal D2 (Red/Yellow wire) and terminal C8 (Black/Red wire). If resistance is 18-20 ohms, go to step **6)**. If resistance is not as specified, go to step **7)**.

5) Check Red/Yellow wire for a short to power between PCM harness connector A-37 and transmission harness connector M-6 (5-pin Black connector). Repair as necessary and go to step **18)**. If no problem is found, go to step **19)**.

6) Possible intermittent condition. Check wiring harness and terminals between PCM harness connector A-37 and transmission harness connector M-6. Repair as necessary and go to step **18)**. If no problem is found, go to step **19)**.

7) Disconnect transmission harness connector H-12 (16-pin Blue connector). Using a DVOM, measure resistance between ground and transmission harness connector H-12, terminal No. 4 (Red/Yellow wire). If resistance is 18-20 ohms, go to step **15)**. If resistance is not as specified, go to next step.

8) Disconnect transmission harness connector M-6 (5-pin Black connector. Using a DVOM, measure resistance between ground and transmission harness connector M-6, terminal No. 4 (Red/Yellow wire). If resistance is 18-20 ohms, go to step **16)**. If resistance is not as specified, go to step **17)**.

9) Turn ignition off. Disconnect PCM harness connector A-37 (White). Using a DVOM, measure resistance between PCM harness connector A-37, terminal D2 (Red/Yellow wire) and terminal C8 (Black/Red wire). If resistance is 18-20 ohms, go to step **18)**. If resistance is not as specified, go to next step.

10) Disconnect transmission harness connector H-12 (16-pin Blue connector). Using a DVOM, measure resistance between ground and transmission harness connector H-12, terminal No. 4 (Red/Yellow wire). If resistance is 18-20 ohms, go to step **12)**. If resistance is not as specified, go to next step.

11) Disconnect transmission harness connector M-6 (5-pin Black connector. Using a DVOM, measure resistance between ground and transmission harness connector M-6, terminal No. 4 (Red/Yellow wire). If resistance is 18-20 ohms, go to step **13)**. If resistance is not as specified, go to step **14)**.

12) Repair Red/Yellow wire for a short to ground between PCM harness connector A-37 and transmission harness connector H-12. Go to step **20)**.

13) Repair wiring harness for a short to ground between transmission harness connector H-12 and transmission harness connector M-6. Go to step **20)**.

14) TCC PWM solenoid is faulty, or its internal wiring harness is shorted to ground. Repair as necessary. Go to step **20)**.

15) Repair open in Red/Yellow wire between PCM harness connector A-37 and transmission harness connector H-12. Go to step **20)**.

16) Repair open in wiring harness between transmission harness connector H-12 and transmission harness connector M-6. Go to step **20)**.

17) TCC PWM solenoid is faulty, or its internal wiring harness is open. Repair as necessary. Go to step **20)**.

18) Check PCM harness connections. Repair as necessary. If connections are okay, replace PCM. Go to step **20)**.

19) Check Red/Yellow wire connections at PCM harness connector A-37 and transmission harness connectors H-12 and M-6. Repair as necessary and go to next step.

20) Using scan tool, select DTC, then CLEAR INFO function. Ensure that when TCC PWM solenoid is commanded on, voltage increases to battery voltage, and when commanded off, voltage decreases to zero volts. Review DTC INFO. If last test failed, or DTC P1860 is present, repeat step **1)**. If last test passed and no DTCs are present, testing is complete.

Diagnostic Aids – Inspect for poor harness connections and improper wire harness routing. An intermittent condition may be caused by a wire which is broke inside its insulation, or shorted to an additional circuit or chassis ground. Check harness connectors for damaged, corroded or backed-out terminal pins. Repair as necessary.

3-708

AUTOMATIC TRANSMISSIONS
1996 Hydra-Matic 4L30-E Electronic Controls
Honda Passport & Isuzu Rodeo (Cont.)

DTC P1870:
TRANSMISSION COMPONENT SLIPPING

Conditions For Setting DTC:
The following conditions must be met for 3 TCC cycles with excessive TCC slip conditions.

- DTCs P0106, P1106, P0107, P1107, P0108, P0122, P0123, P0722, P0723, P0751, P0753, P0756, P0758, P1860 and P0742 are not present.
- Engine speed is between 800 and 3360 RPM.
- Engine vacuum is between zero and 10.2 in. Hg.
- Gear range is D4.
- TP angle is between 12 and 70 percent.
- TFT is between 68-286°F (20-141°C).
- TCC is on for 3 seconds.
- TCC slip speed is between 300 and 800 RPM for 10 seconds.
- Vehicle speed is between 24 and 69 MPH.
- Speed ratio is between .5 and .95.

Diagnosis – 1) Install scan tool. Turn ignition on. Using scan tool, record DTC FREEZE FRAME and FAILURE RECORDS. Apply brake pedal. Observe scan tool while moving gearshift lever through all gear ranges. If scan tool display matches each gear range selected, go to next step. If operation is not as specified, go to RANGE SWITCH LOGIC TABLE. *See Fig. 5.*
2) Road test vehicle in 4th gear with TCC engaged. Observe scan tool. If TCC SLIP SPEED is greater than 130 RPM for 8 seconds at any time with TCC engaged, see TROUBLE SHOOTING in appropriate overhaul article. If TCC SLIP SPEED never exceeds 130 RPM for 8 seconds, go to DIAGNOSTIC AIDS.

Diagnostic Aids – A malfunctioning range switch, faulty shift solenoids, faulty TCC solenoid or faulty TCC PWM solenoid may set DTC P1870. An internal transmission failure or incorrect engine speed may also set DTC P1870.

COMPONENT TESTING

A/C COMPRESSOR RELAY

1) Remove A/C compressor relay from fuse/relay box at passenger's side front corner of engine compartment. Note A/C compressor terminal identification. *See Fig. 6.*
2) Using a DVOM, ensure continuity is present between terminals No. 3 and 5. Continuity should not be present between terminals No. 1 and 5.
3) Apply battery voltage to terminals No. 2 and 4. Ensure continuity is now present between terminals No. 1 and 5, and continuity is not present between terminals No. 3 and 5. Replace A/C compressor relay if defective.

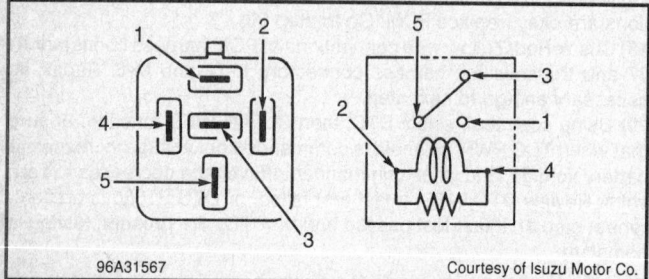

96A31567   Courtesy of Isuzu Motor Co.

Fig. 6: Identifying A/C Compressor Relay Terminals

BAND APPLY SOLENOID

Band apply solenoid is located on main valve body. *See Fig. 4.* Component testing information is not available from manufacturer.

BRAKELIGHT SWITCH

Without Cruise Control – 1) Disconnect electrical connector from brakelight switch. Brakelight switch is located near brake pedal.
2) Using a DVOM, ensure continuity is present between terminals on brakelight switch only when brake pedal is depressed.
3) If continuity is not as specified, ensure brake pedal is properly adjusted so brakelight switch can obtain proper travel for switch operation. If brakelight switch travel is okay, replace brakelight switch.
With Cruise Control – 1) Disconnect electrical connector from brakelight switch and note terminal identification. *See Fig. 7.* Brakelight switch is located near brake pedal.
2) Using a DVOM, ensure continuity is present between specified terminals in relation to brake pedal position. See BRAKELIGHT SWITCH CONTINUITY SPECIFICATIONS table.
3) If continuity is not as specified, ensure brake pedal is properly adjusted so brakelight switch can obtain proper travel for switch operation. If brakelight switch travel is okay, replace brakelight switch.

BRAKELIGHT SWITCH CONTINUITY SPECIFICATIONS

Condition	Continuity Between Terminals No.
Brake Pedal Released	1 & 4
Brake Pedal Depressed	2 & 3

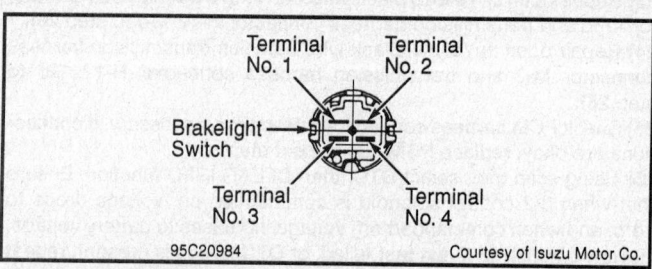

95C20984   Courtesy of Isuzu Motor Co.

Fig. 7: Identifying Brakelight Switch Terminals

ENGINE COOLANT TEMPERATURE (ECT) SENSOR

ECT sensor is located on coolant pipe at rear of cylinder head. ECT sensor contains a Blue/Red wire and Blue/Yellow wire in harness connector. Component testing information is not available from manufacturer.

KICKDOWN SWITCH

Kickdown switch is located on accelerator pedal. Component testing information is not available from manufacturer.

MODE SWITCH

1) Mode switch is located on side of transmission. *See Fig. 4.* Remove necessary covers for access to mode switch electrical connector. Disconnect mode switch electrical connector and note terminal identification. *See Fig. 8.*
2) Using a DVOM, check for continuity between specified terminals in relation to shift lever position. See MODE SWITCH CONTINUITY table. If continuity is not as specified, mode switch may require adjustment. See MODE SWITCH under REMOVAL & INSTALLATION. Replace mode switch if specified continuity cannot be obtained by adjusting.

MODE SWITCH CONTINUITY

Shift Lever Position	Continuity Between Terminals No.
"P"	3, 5 & 8
"R"	5, 7 & 8
"N"	3, 5 & 7
"D"	5, 6 & 7
"3"	3, 5, 6, 7 & 8
"2"	5, 6 & 8
"L"	3, 5 & 6

AUTOMATIC TRANSMISSIONS
1996 Hydra-Matic 4L30-E Electronic Controls
Honda Passport & Isuzu Rodeo (Cont.)

3-709

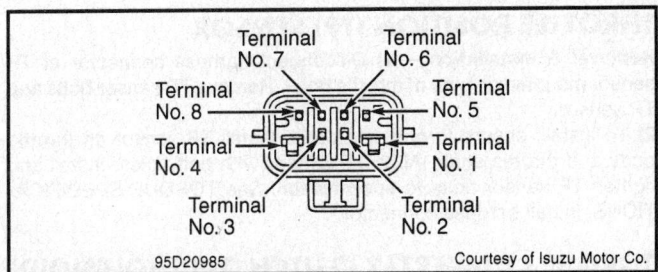

Fig. 8: Identifying Mode Switch Terminals

POWER MODE SWITCH

POWER mode switch is located on center console, near gearshift lever. Component testing information is not available from manufacturer.

PRESSURE CONTROL SOLENOID (FORCE MOTOR)

Force motor solenoid is located on adapter case valve body. See Fig. 4. Component testing information is not available from manufacturer.

SHIFT SOLENOID

NOTE: *Shift solenoid "A" may also be known as 1-2/3-4 shift solenoid. Shift solenoid "B" may also be known as 2-3 shift solenoid.*

Shift solenoids "A" and "B" are located on main valve body. See Fig. 4. Component testing information is not available from manufacturer.

SPEED SENSOR

Speed sensor is located on extension housing on rear of transmission. See Fig. 4. Speed sensor may be referred to as magnetic sensor. Component testing information is not available from manufacturer.

THROTTLE POSITION (TP) SENSOR

The TP sensor is mounted on side of throttle body. Component testing information is not available from manufacturer.

TORQUE CONVERTER CLUTCH (TCC) SOLENOID

Torque Converter Clutch (TCC) solenoid is located on adapter case valve body. See Fig. 4. Component testing information is not available from manufacturer.

TRANSMISSION OIL TEMPERATURE SENSOR

Transmission oil temperature sensor is located on wiring harness in adapter case oil pan. See Fig. 4. Component testing information is not available from manufacturer.

WINTER MODE SWITCH

WINTER mode switch is mounted on center console, near gearshift lever. Component testing information is not available from manufacturer.

REMOVAL & INSTALLATION

A/C COMPRESSOR RELAY

Removal & Installation – Remove A/C compressor relay from fuse/relay box at passenger's side front corner of engine compartment. To install, reverse removal procedure.

BAND APPLY SOLENOID

Removal – 1) Band apply solenoid is located on main valve body. See Fig. 4. Disconnect negative battery cable. Remove exhaust pipe (if necessary) to access main case oil pan. Remove bolts, main case oil pan, magnet and gasket. Remove bolts and oil filter. Disconnect electrical connectors at band apply solenoid.

2) Remove spring pin used to retain band apply solenoid in main valve body. Remove band apply solenoid and gasket from main valve body by pulling on metal tip. DO NOT pull on electrical connector housing on band apply solenoid.

Installation – To install, reverse removal procedure using NEW gaskets and oil filter. Ensure spring pin is fully seated in main valve body. Install and tighten oil filter and main case oil pan bolts to specification. See TORQUE SPECIFICATIONS. Fill transmission with Dexron-III ATF.

BRAKELIGHT SWITCH

Removal & Installation – 1) Disconnect electrical connector from brakelight switch located near brake pedal. Remove lock nut. Unscrew brakelight switch.

2) To install, screw brakelight switch inward until clearance between threaded end on brakelight switch and pedal is .020-.040" (.51-1.02 mm). Install and tighten lock nut. Connect electrical connector. Ensure brakelights and cruise control operate properly.

ENGINE COOLANT TEMPERATURE (ECT) SENSOR

Removal – 1) ECT sensor is located on coolant pipe at rear of cylinder head, and contains a Blue/Red wire and a Blue/Yellow wire in electrical connector.

2) Disconnect negative battery cable. Drain cooling system. It may be necessary to remove fuel inlet manifold for access to ECT sensor. Remove ECT sensor.

Installation – Apply thread sealant to threads of ECT sensor. Install and tighten ECT sensor to specification. See TORQUE SPECIFICATIONS. Fill cooling system.

KICKDOWN SWITCH

Removal & Installation – Kickdown switch is located on accelerator pedal. Replacement information is not available from manufacturer.

MODE SWITCH

Removal – 1) Disconnect negative battery cable. Apply parking brake. Place gearshift lever in "N" position. Remove mode switch cover to access mode switch located on side of transmission. See Fig. 4. Remove shift lever nut and disconnect shift lever from mode switch.

2) Remove bolts and heat protector from torque converter housing for access to wiring and mode switch. Remove air cleaner assembly. Disconnect mode switch harness connector. Remove clips for mode switch wiring. Remove mode switch retaining bolts and mode switch.

Installation – 1) Install mode switch with retaining bolts. DO NOT tighten mode switch retaining bolts at this time. Mode switch must be adjusted. To adjust mode switch, rotate mode switch until slot in housing on mode switch aligns with selector shaft bushing. Insert a 3/32" punch into slot. See Fig. 9.

2) Tighten mode switch retaining bolts to specification. See TORQUE SPECIFICATIONS. Install shift lever on mode switch and tighten shift lever nut to specification. Install mode switch cover on mode switch. Install heat protector. Install and tighten bolts to specification. Install air cleaner assembly.

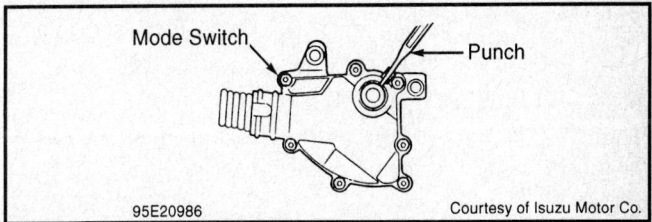

Fig. 9: Adjusting Mode Switch

3-710

AUTOMATIC TRANSMISSIONS
1996 Hydra-Matic 4L30-E Electronic Controls
Honda Passport & Isuzu Rodeo (Cont.)

PCM

Removal & Installation – Ensure ignition is off. Disconnect negative battery cable. Remove front console. Disconnect PCM harness connectors. Remove PCM and brackets. To install, reverse removal procedure.

POWER MODE SWITCH

Removal & Installation – POWER mode switch is located on center console, near gearshift lever. Replacement information is not available from manufacturer.

PRESSURE CONTROL SOLENOID (FORCE MOTOR)

Removal – 1) Pressure control solenoid is located on adapter case valve body. See Fig. 4. Disconnect negative battery cable.
2) Remove exhaust pipe (if necessary) for access to adapter case oil pan. Remove bolts, adapter case oil pan and gasket. Disconnect electrical connectors at pressure control solenoid. Remove bolt and pressure control solenoid.
Installation – 1) Install pressure control solenoid on adapter case valve body. Ensure pressure control solenoid is installed with electrical connector terminals facing upward, toward transmission.
2) Install and tighten pressure control solenoid bolt to specification. See TORQUE SPECIFICATIONS. Using a NEW gasket, install adapter case oil pan. Install and tighten bolts to specification. To install remaining components, reverse removal procedure. Fill transmission with Dexron-III ATF.

SHIFT SOLENOID

NOTE: Shift solenoid "A" may also be known as 1-2/3-4 shift solenoid. Shift solenoid "B" may also be known as 2-3 shift solenoid.

Removal – 1) Shift solenoids "A" and "B" are located on main valve body. See Fig. 4. Disconnect negative battery cable. Remove exhaust pipe (if necessary) to access main case oil pan. Remove bolts, main case oil pan, magnet and gasket. Remove bolts and oil filter. Disconnect electrical connectors at appropriate shift solenoid.
2) Remove spring pin used to retain shift solenoid in main valve body. Remove shift solenoid and gasket from main valve body by pulling on metal tip. DO NOT pull on electrical connector housing on shift solenoid.
Installation – To install, reverse removal procedure using NEW gaskets and oil filter. Ensure spring pin is fully seated in main valve body. Install and tighten oil filter and main case oil pan bolts to specification. See TORQUE SPECIFICATIONS. Fill transmission with Dexron-III ATF.

SPEED SENSOR

Removal & Installation – 1) Disconnect electrical connector at speed sensor located on rear of transmission. See Fig. 4. Remove speed sensor bolt, speed sensor and "O" ring.
2) To install, reverse removal procedure using a NEW "O" ring. Install and tighten speed sensor bolt to specification. See TORQUE SPECIFICATIONS.

THROTTLE POSITION (TP) SENSOR

Removal & Installation – 1) Disconnect harness connector at TP sensor mounted on side of throttle body. Remove TP sensor bolts and TP sensor.
2) To install, ensure throttle is closed. Install TP sensor on throttle body and throttle shaft. Align TP sensor with bolt holes. Install and tighten TP sensor bolts to specification. See TORQUE SPECIFICATIONS. Install harness connector.

TORQUE CONVERTER CLUTCH (TCC) SOLENOID

Removal – 1) The TCC solenoid is located on adapter case valve body. See Fig. 4. Disconnect negative battery cable.
2) Remove exhaust pipe (if necessary) to access adapter case oil pan. Remove bolts, adapter case oil pan and gasket. Disconnect electrical connector at TCC solenoid. Remove bolt, TCC solenoid and "O" ring.
Installation – 1) Using a NEW "O" ring, install TCC solenoid on adapter case valve body. Install and tighten TCC solenoid bolt to specification. See TORQUE SPECIFICATIONS.
2) Using a NEW gasket, install adapter case oil pan. Install and tighten bolts to specification. To install remaining components, reverse removal procedure. Fill transmission with Dexron-III ATF.

TRANSMISSION OIL TEMPERATURE SENSOR

Removal & Installation – Transmission oil temperature sensor is located on wiring harness in adapter case oil pan. See Fig. 4. Replacement information is not available from manufacturer.

WINTER MODE SWITCH

Removal & Installation – WINTER mode switch is located on center console, near gearshift lever. Replacement information is not available from manufacturer.

TORQUE SPECIFICATIONS
TORQUE SPECIFICATIONS

Application	Ft. Lbs. (N.m)
ECT Sensor	22 (30)
Oil Filter Bolt	15 (20)
Shift Lever Nut	17 (23)

	INCH Lbs. (N.m)
Adapter Case Oil Pan Bolt	96 (10.8)
Heat Protector Bolt	52 (5.9)
Main Case Oil Pan Bolt	96 (10.8)
Mode Switch Retaining Bolt	113 (12.8)
Pressure Control Solenoid Bolt	87 (9.8)
Speed Sensor Bolt	78 (8.8)
TCC Solenoid Bolt	87 (9.8)
TP Sensor Bolt	18 (2.0)

AUTOMATIC TRANSMISSIONS
1996 Hydra-Matic 4L30-E Electronic Controls
Honda Passport & Isuzu Rodeo (Cont.)

3-711

WIRING DIAGRAMS

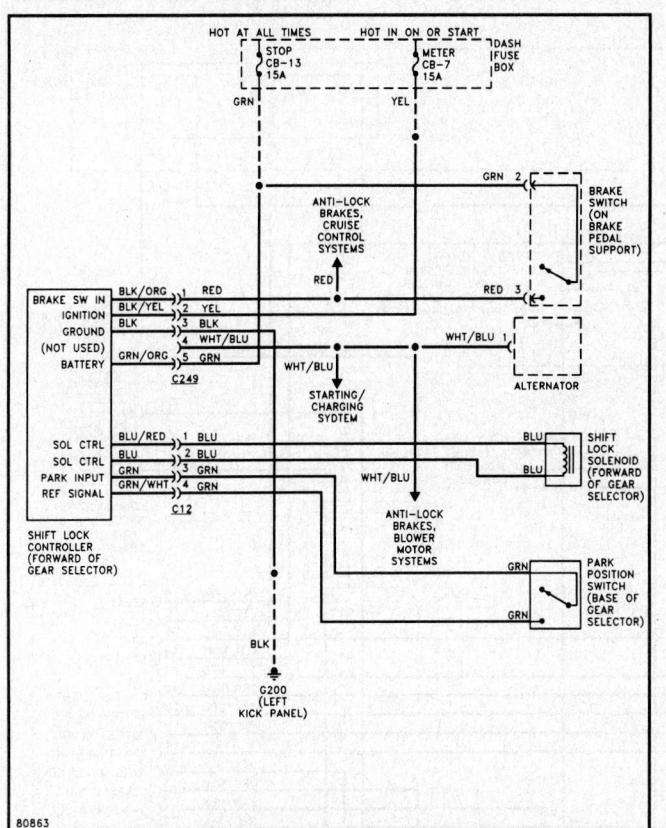

Fig. 10: Shift Lock System Wiring Diagram (1996 Passport)

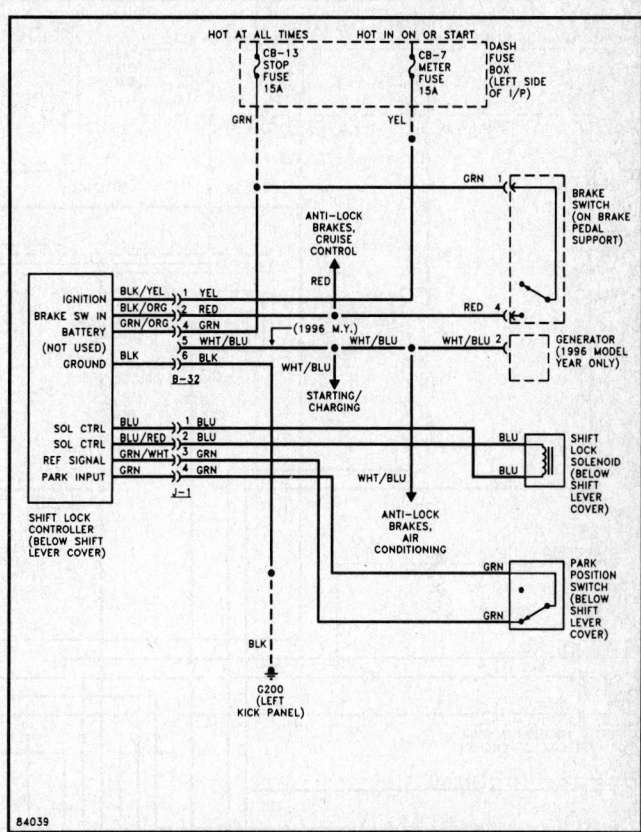

Fig. 11: Shift Lock System Wiring Diagram (1996 Rodeo)

3-712

AUTOMATIC TRANSMISSIONS
1996 Hydra-Matic 4L30-E Electronic Controls
Honda Passport & Isuzu Rodeo (Cont.)

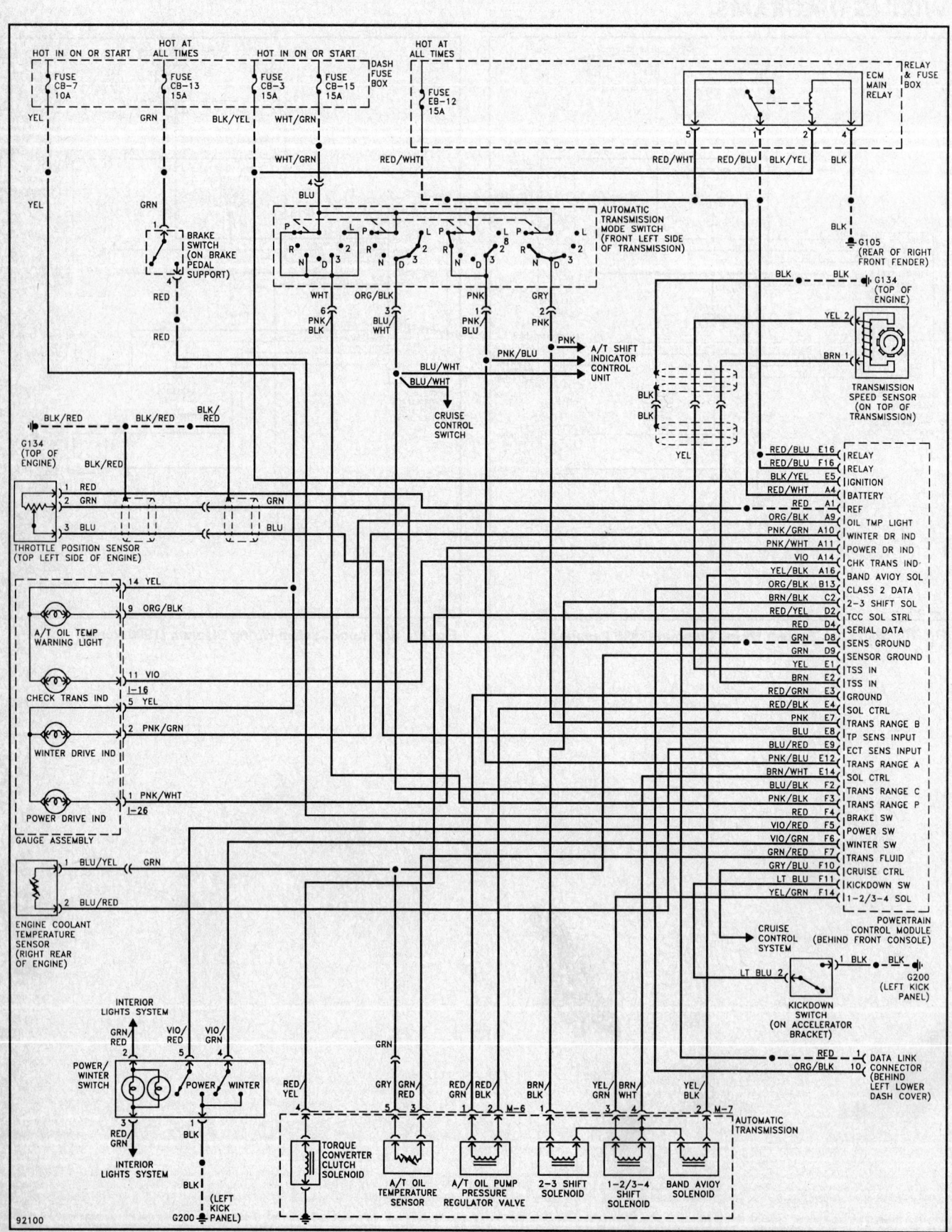

Fig. 12: 4L30-E Transmission Wiring Diagram (1996 Passport & Rodeo)

Accent, Elantra & Scoupe

APPLICATION & LABOR TIMES

APPLICATION & LABOR TIMES

Vehicle Application	Labor Times ¹ R & I	² Overhaul	Trans. Model
Hyundai			
Accent	3.8	8.9	A4AF2
Elantra (1996)	4.3	9.0	A4BF1
Scoupe	3.8	8.9	A4AF

¹ – Removal and installation of transmission from vehicle chassis.

² – Bench overhaul time for transmission and differential. DOES NOT include removal and installation.

IDENTIFICATION

Transaxle identification number is stamped on transaxle housing. *See Fig. 1.* First digit, letter "G", indicates transaxle model. Second digit indicates model year, as letter "S" indicates 1995 models and letter "T" indicates 1996 models. Third digit, letter "T" indicates final gear ratio of 4.029. Fourth digit letter indicates transaxle vehicle application. Fifth digit is not used. Remaining digits are the transaxle serial number. Transaxle model and serial number may be required when ordering replacement components.

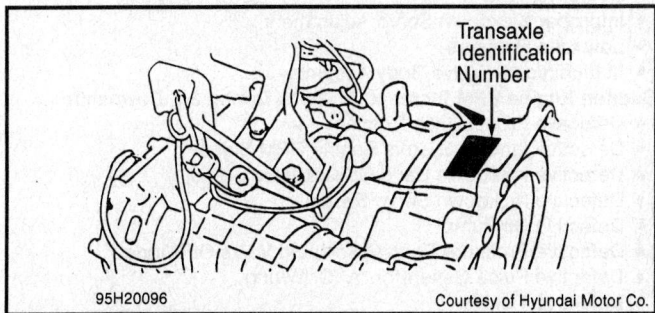

Transaxle Identification Number

95H20096   Courtesy of Hyundai Motor Co.

Fig. 1: Locating Transaxle Identification Number

DESCRIPTION

Automatic transaxle is electronically controlled and has 4 forward speeds and one reverse speed. Transaxle shifting and damper clutch lock-up (torque converter lock-up) are controlled by Transmission Control Module (TCM).

Electronic control system contains a fail-safe system in the event that an electronic component should malfunction. Fail-safe system will provide transaxle operation until malfunction is repaired. If failures exists in certain electronic components for a repeated number of times, transaxle may lock-up and remain in 2nd or 3rd gear. For more information on fail-safe system, see HYUNDAI A4AF & A4BF ELECTRONIC CONTROLS article.

OPERATION

Shift lever has 6 positions. Shift lever controls manual valve. Shift lever also controls input signal of range switch which is mounted on transaxle. Transaxle range switch delivers an input signal to TCM to indicate shift lever position. The TCM uses input signal and operates shift control solenoid valves to control transaxle shifting.

The TCM controls transaxle shift points and hydraulic pressure to various friction elements. The TCM calculates shift points from input devices and transmits electrical signal to appropriate Shift Control Solenoid Valves (SCSV) and Pressure Control Solenoid Valve (PCSV), mounted on valve body assembly to control transaxle shifting. The TCM controls damper clutch (torque converter lock-up) by operating Damper Clutch Control Solenoid Valve (DCCSV), located on valve body assembly.

An overdrive switch is mounted on driver's side of shift lever. When overdrive switch is depressed to the ON position, transaxle will automatically upshift to overdrive and O/D OFF indicator light on instrument panel will be off.

When overdrive switch is released to the OFF position, transaxle will not upshift to overdrive and O/D OFF indicator light on instrument panel will come on.

A range switch is located on passenger's side of shift lever, near console. On Accent and Scoupe, range switch contains an ECON (economy) mode and NORM (normal) mode. When range switch is depressed to the NORM (normal) mode, an input signal is delivered to TCM, and TCM changes shift points to provide maximum performance. When range switch is released to the ECON (economy) mode, an input signal is delivered to TCM, and TCM changes shift points to provide maximum fuel economy.

On Elantra (1996), range switch contains a NORM (normal) mode and PWR (power) mode. When range switch is depressed to the PWR (power) mode, an input signal is delivered to TCM, and TCM changes shift points to provide maximum performance. When range switch is released to the NORM (normal) mode, an input signal is delivered to TCM, and TCM changes shift points to provide maximum fuel economy.

NOTE: On Accent and Scoupe, if engine coolant temperature is less than 68°F (20°C), transaxle will remain in ECON mode (NORM mode on Elantra) even if range switch is in NORM mode (PWR mode on Elantra). When range switch is in ECON mode (NORM mode on Elantra) and vehicle speed exceeds 60 MPH, transaxle will not downshift when accelerator pedal is depressed. Range switch must be in NORM mode (PWR mode on Elantra) for transaxle to downshift.

The TCM contains self-diagnostic system, which stores fault code if failure or problem exists in transaxle electronic control system. Fault codes may be retrieved to determine transaxle problem area. Fault code may be referred to as Diagnostic Trouble Code (DTC). For information on electronic transaxle components, see HYUNDAI A4AF & A4BF ELECTRONIC CONTROLS article.

Transaxle is equipped with shift and key interlock systems. Shift interlock system prevents shift lever from being moved from Park position unless brake pedal is depressed, ignition is on and release button on side of shift lever is depressed.

The key interlock system prevents ignition key from being turned to LOCK position unless shift lever is in Park position. For additional information on shift and key interlock systems, see HYUNDAI A4AF & A4BF ELECTRONIC CONTROLS article.

LUBRICATION & ADJUSTMENTS

See appropriate AUTOMATIC TRANSMISSION SERVICING article in TRANSMISSION SERVICING section.

TROUBLE SHOOTING

TRANSAXLE ELECTRONIC CONTROL SYSTEM

See HYUNDAI A4AF & A4BF ELECTRONIC CONTROLS article.

TROUBLE SHOOTING

SYMPTOM DIAGNOSIS

Transaxle malfunctions may be caused by poor engine performance, improper adjustments or failure of hydraulic, mechanical or electronic components. Always begin by checking fluid level, fluid condition and cable adjustments. Perform road test to determine if problem has been corrected. If problem still exists, perform several tests on transaxle. See TESTING.

Damper Clutch Inoperative
- Defective Accelerator Switch Or Improper Switch Adjustment
- Defective Damper Clutch Control Solenoid Valve Or Wiring

- Defective Ignition System Engine RPM Signal
- Defective Oil Temperature Sensor
- Defective Pulse Generator "A", "B" Or Wiring
- Defective TCM
- Defective Throttle Position Sensor Or Improper Adjustment
- Defective Torque Converter
- Malfunction In Valve Body Assembly

Engine Stalls With Transaxle In Neutral, Drive Or Reverse
- Incorrect Idle Speed
- Poor Engine Performance
- Defective Damper Clutch Control Solenoid Valve Or Wiring
- Malfunction In Valve Body Assembly

Excessive Vibration & Shock During All Upshifts
- Defective Front Clutch Or Piston
- Defective Ignition System Engine RPM Signal
- Defective Pulse Generator "A" Or Wiring
- Defective TCM
- Defective Throttle Position Sensor Or Improper Adjustment
- Malfunction In Valve Body Assembly
- Poor Engine Performance

Excessive Vibration & Shock During 1-2 Or 3-4 Upshift
- Defective End Clutch Or Piston
- Defective Ignition System Engine RPM Signal
- Defective Kickdown Band Or Kickdown Servo
- Defective Kickdown Servo Switch
- Defective Pulse Generator "A" Or Wiring
- Defective TCM
- Defective Throttle Position Sensor Or Improper Adjustment
- Improper Kickdown Servo Adjustment
- Malfunction In Valve Body Assembly
- Poor Engine Performance

Excessive Vibration & Shock During 2-3 Upshift Or 4-3 Downshift
- Defective Front Clutch Or Piston
- Defective Ignition System Engine RPM Signal
- Defective Pulse Generator "A" Or Wiring
- Defective TCM
- Defective Throttle Position Sensor Or Improper Adjustment
- Malfunction In Valve Body Assembly
- Poor Engine Performance

Excessive Vibration & Shock When Shifting From Drive To 2nd Gear Position
- Defective Ignition System Engine RPM Signal
- Defective Low-Reverse Brake Or Piston
- Defective Pulse Generator "A" Or Wiring
- Defective TCM
- Defective Throttle Position Sensor Or Improper Adjustment
- Malfunction In Valve Body Assembly
- Poor Engine Performance

Excessive Vibration & Shock When Shifting Into Any Forward Gear Or Reverse
- Defective Accelerator Switch Or Improper Switch Adjustment
- Defective Front Clutch, Rear Clutch Or Piston
- Defective Low-Reverse Brake Or Piston
- Defective Or Improperly Adjusted Shift Cable
- Defective TCM
- Defective Throttle Position Sensor Or Improper Adjustment
- Defective Wiring, Transaxle Range Switch Or Switch Adjustment
- Incorrect Idle Speed
- Malfunction In Valve Body Assembly

Improper Shift Speeds
- Defective Pulse Generator "B" Or Wiring
- Defective TCM
- Defective Throttle Position Sensor Or Improper Adjustment
- Malfunction In Valve Body Assembly

Slips In Drive
- Defective Oil Pump
- Defective Overrunning Clutch
- Defective Or Improperly Adjusted Shift Cable
- Defective Pressure Control Solenoid Valve Or Wiring

- Defective Rear Clutch Or Piston
- Low Fluid Level
- Low Line Pressure
- Malfunction In Valve Body Assembly

Slips In Reverse
- Defective Front Clutch Or Piston
- Defective Front Clutch Retainer
- Defective Low-Reverse Brake Or Piston
- Defective Oil Pump
- Defective Or Improperly Adjusted Shift Cable
- Defective Pressure Control Solenoid Valve Or Wiring
- Low Fluid Level
- Low Line Pressure
- Malfunction In Valve Body Assembly
- "O" Ring Missing Between Valve Body Assembly & Transaxle Housing

Sudden Engine RPM Increase During Upshift
- Defective End Clutch Or Piston
- Defective Front Clutch Or Piston
- Defective Front Clutch Retainer
- Defective Ignition System Engine RPM Signal
- Defective Kickdown Band Or Kickdown Servo
- Defective Pressure Control Solenoid Valve Or Wiring
- Defective Pulse Generator "A" Or Wiring
- Defective Throttle Position Sensor Or Improper Adjustment
- Defective TCM
- Improper Kickdown Servo Adjustment
- Low Line Pressure
- Malfunction In Valve Body Assembly

Sudden Engine RPM Increase & Shock During 3-2 Downshift
- Defective Front Clutch Retainer
- Defective Ignition System Engine RPM Signal
- Defective Kickdown Band Or Kickdown Servo
- Defective Kickdown Servo Switch
- Defective Oil Pump
- Defective Pressure Control Solenoid Valve Or Wiring
- Defective Pulse Generator "A" Or Wiring
- Defective TCM
- Defective Throttle Position Sensor Or Improper Adjustment
- Improper Kickdown Servo Adjustment
- Low Fluid Level
- Low Line Pressure
- Malfunction In Valve Body Assembly

Vehicle Moves In Neutral
- Defective Or Improperly Adjusted Shift Cable
- Defective Parking Mechanism
- Malfunction In Valve Body Assembly
- Defective Wiring, Transaxle Range Switch Or Switch Adjustment

Vehicle Starts Off Other Than 1st Gear
- Defective Accelerator Switch Or Improper Switch Adjustment
- Defective Or Improperly Adjusted Shift Cable
- Defective TCM
- Defective Wiring, Transaxle Range Switch Or Switch Adjustment
- Malfunction In Valve Body Assembly

Vehicle Will Not Move
- Defective Low-Reverse Brake Or Piston
- Defective Oil Pump
- Defective Or Improperly Adjusted Shift Cable
- Defective Pressure Control Solenoid Valve Or Wiring
- Defective Torque Converter
- Low Fluid Level
- Low Line Pressure
- Malfunction In Valve Body Assembly

Vehicle Will Not Move In Any Forward Gear
- Defective Oil Pump
- Defective Overrunning Clutch
- Defective Or Improperly Adjusted Shift Cable
- Defective Pressure Control Solenoid Valve Or Wiring
- Defective Rear Clutch Or Piston
- Defective Torque Converter

- Low Fluid Level
- Low Line Pressure
- Malfunction In Valve Body Assembly

Vehicle Will Not Move In Reverse

- Defective Front Clutch Or Piston
- Defective Front Clutch Retainer
- Defective Low-Reverse Brake Or Piston
- Defective Oil Pump
- Defective Or Improperly Adjusted Shift Cable
- Defective Pressure Control Solenoid Valve Or Wiring
- Defective Pulse Generator "B" Or Wiring
- Defective Torque Converter
- Low Fluid Level
- Low Line Pressure
- Malfunction In Valve Body Assembly
- "O" Ring Missing Between Valve Body Assembly & Transaxle Housing

Will Not Shift Into 4th Gear

- Defective End Clutch Or Piston
- Defective Front Clutch Retainer
- Defective Overdrive Switch
- Defective Pressure Control Solenoid Valve Or Wiring
- Defective TCM
- Defective Wiring, Transaxle Range Switch Or Switch Adjustment

Will Not Upshift From 2nd To 3rd Gear

- Defective Front Clutch Or Piston
- Defective Front Clutch Retainer
- Defective Pressure Control Solenoid Valve Or Wiring
- Defective TCM
- Malfunction In Valve Body Assembly

TESTING

ROAD TEST

1) Before road testing vehicle, ensure transaxle fluid level, fluid condition and shift cable adjustments have been checked and corrected (as necessary).

2) Road test vehicle and check for abnormal noise and clutch slippage. Specified clutch and brake are applied in designated gear. See CLUTCH & BRAKE APPLICATION table.

3) Ensure upshift and downshift speeds are correct in relation to throttle opening, vehicle speed and position of range switch and overdrive switch. *See Figs. 2-5.* Range switch is located on center console, near passenger's side of shift lever. Overdrive switch is mounted on driver's side of shift lever.

4) Various test procedures given can be used to detect any slipping component and confirm proper operation of good components. Malfunction may be caused by leaking hydraulic circuits or sticking valves.

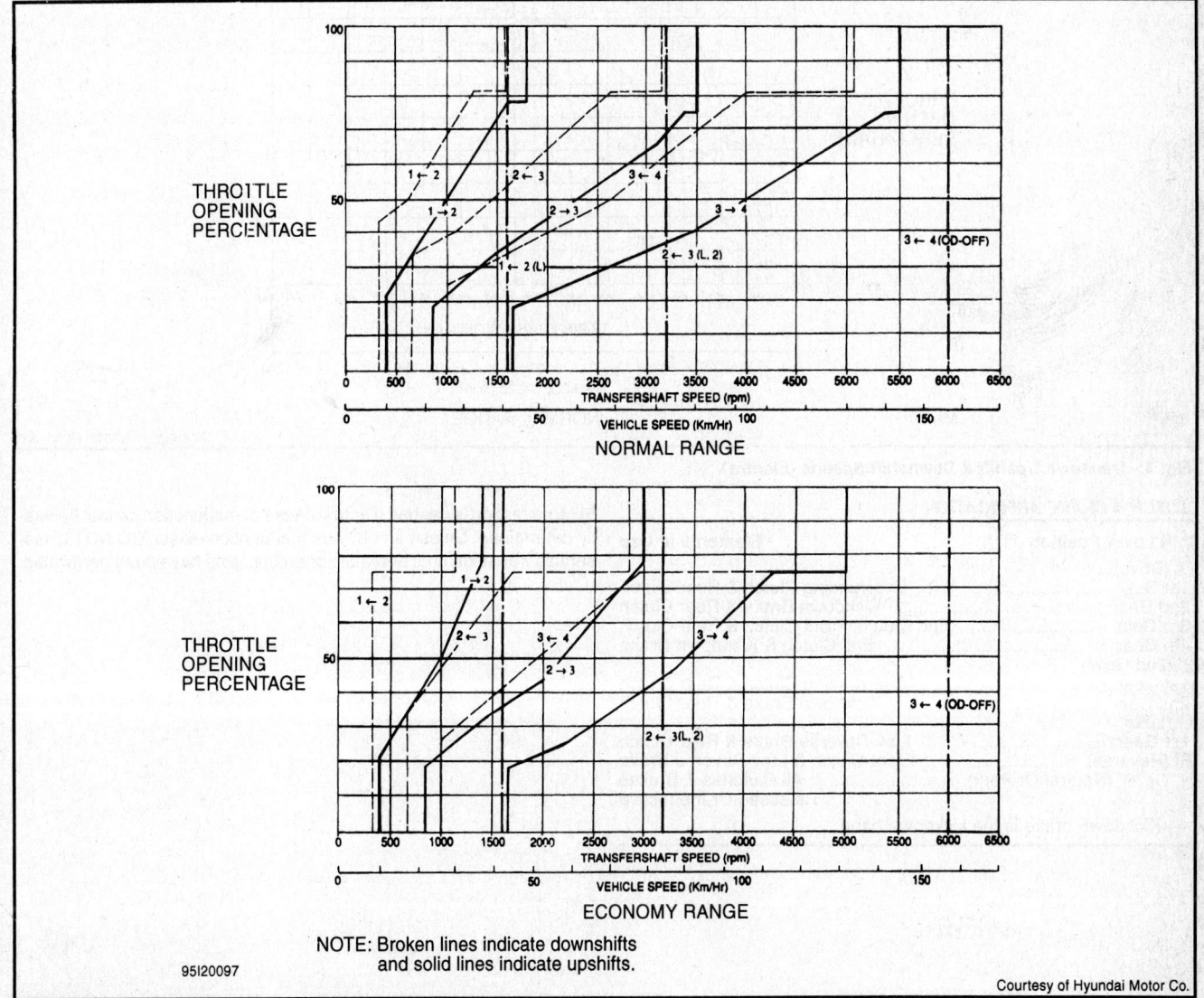

NOTE: Broken lines indicate downshifts and solid lines indicate upshifts.

95120097

Courtesy of Hyundai Motor Co.

Fig. 2: Transaxle Upshift & Downshift Speeds (Scoupe)

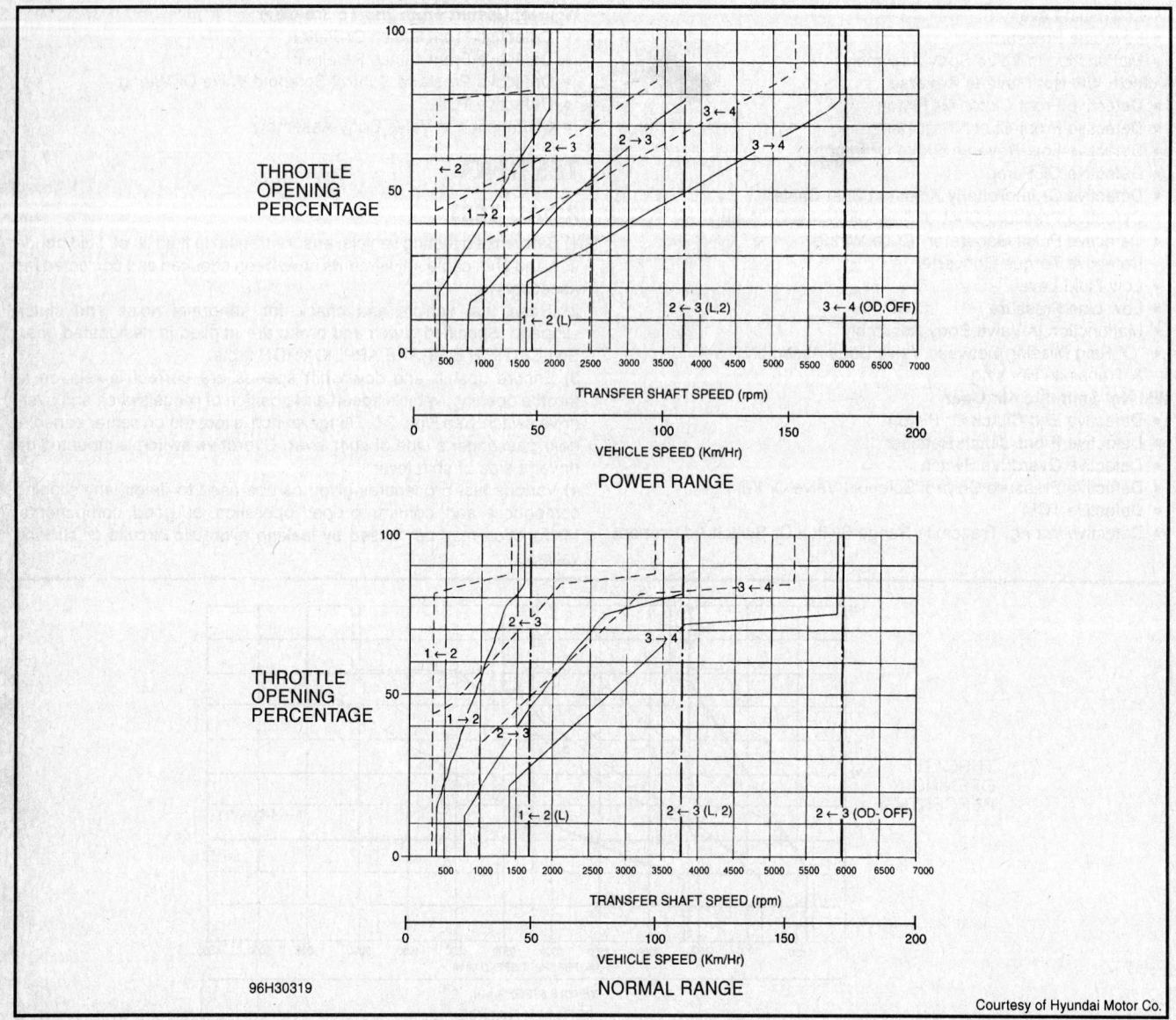

96H30319

Fig. 3: Transaxle Upshift & Downshift Speeds (Elantra)

Courtesy of Hyundai Motor Co.

CLUTCH & BRAKE APPLICATION

Shift Lever Position .... [1] **Elements In Use**

"D" (Drive)
1st Gear .... Overrunning Clutch & Rear Clutch
2nd Gear .... Kickdown Brake & Rear Clutch
3rd Gear .... End Clutch, Front Clutch & Rear Clutch
4th Gear .... End Clutch & Kickdown Brake
"2" (2nd Gear)
1st Gear .... Overrunning Clutch & Rear Clutch
2nd Gear .... Kickdown Brake & Rear Clutch
"L" (Low)
1st Gear .... Low-Reverse Brake & Rear Clutch
"R" (Reverse) .... Front Clutch & Low-Reverse Brake
"N" Or "P" (Neutral Or Park) .... All Clutches & Brakes
Released Or Ineffective

[1] – Kickdown brake is the kickdown band.

5) More testing is needed if actual cause of malfunction cannot be easily determined. Unless an obvious malfunction exists, DO NOT disassemble transaxle until hydraulic pressure tests have been performed.

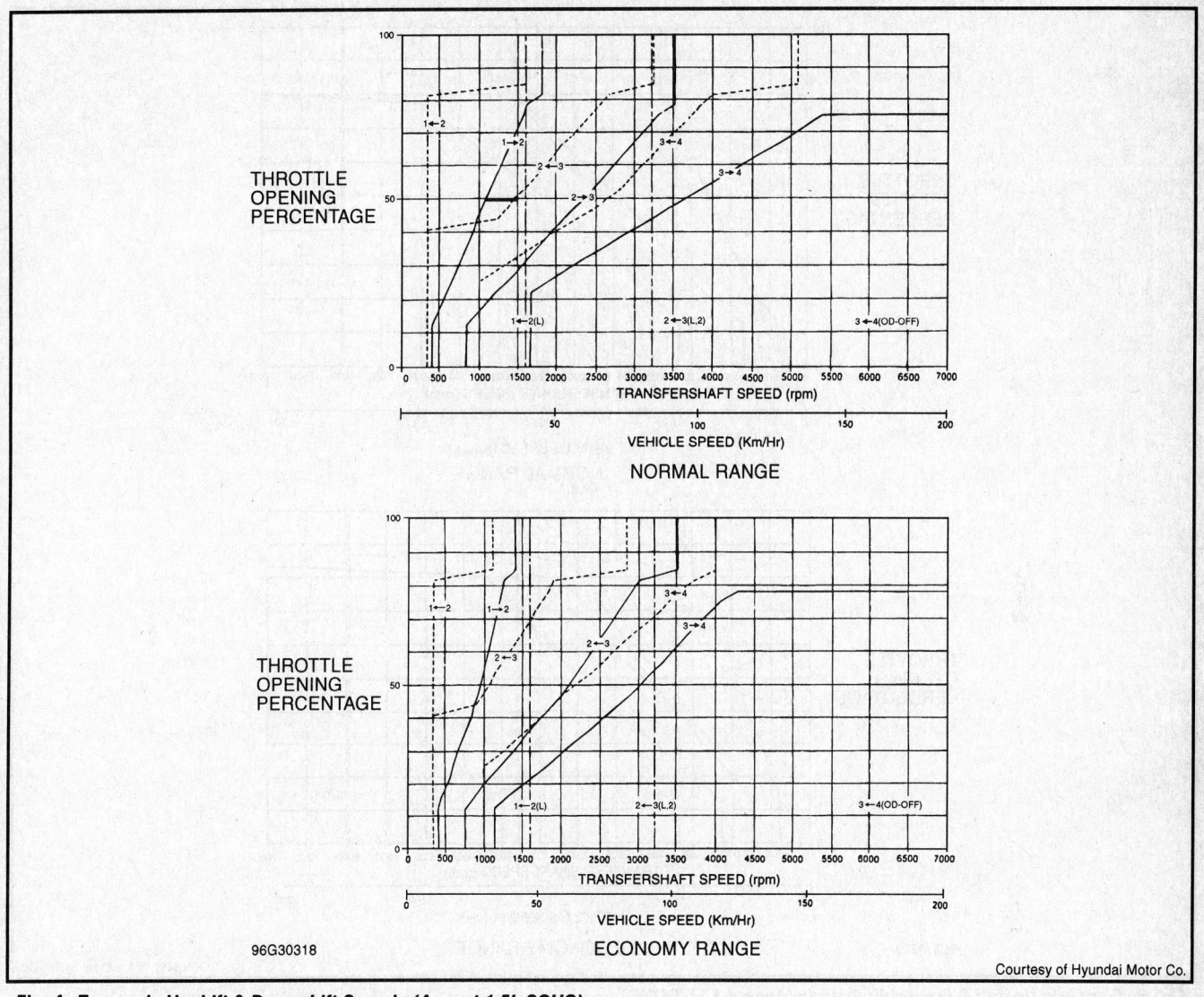

96G30318

Courtesy of Hyundai Motor Co.

Fig. 4: Transaxle Upshift & Downshift Speeds (Accent 1.5L SOHC)

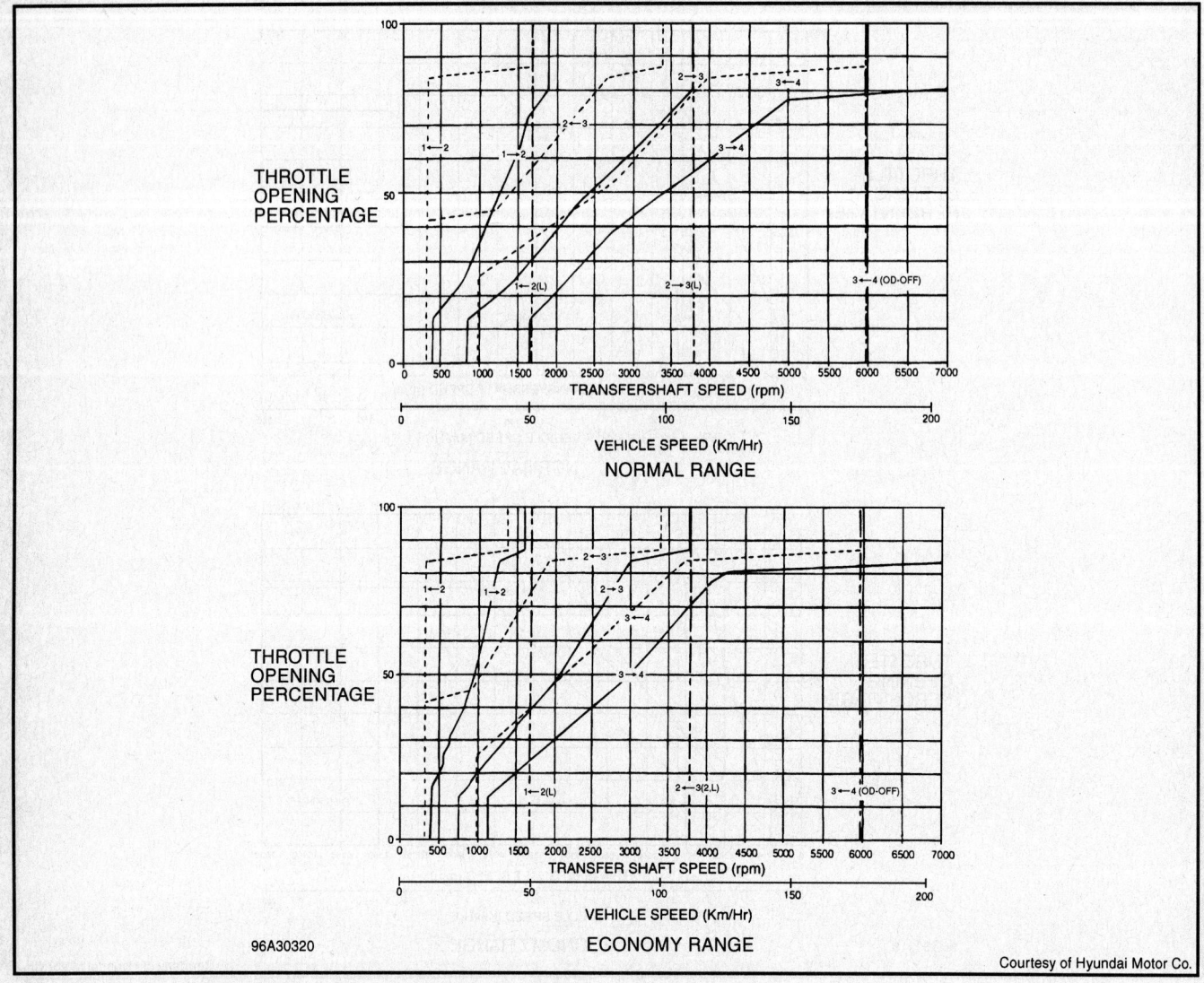

96A30320

Courtesy of Hyundai Motor Co.

Fig. 5: Transaxle Upshift & Downshift Speeds (Accent 1.5L DOHC)

TORQUE CONVERTER STALL SPEED TEST

CAUTION: DO NOT perform torque converter stall speed test for more than 5 seconds or transaxle may be damaged. If performing more than one torque converter stall speed test, place shift lever in Neutral position. Operate engine at 1000 RPM for at least 2 minutes to cool transaxle before performing next test.

1) Apply parking brake. Block all wheels. Connect tachometer and start engine. Warm engine to normal operating temperature. Ensure transaxle fluid level is correct.
2) Place shift lever in "D" position. Fully depress brake pedal. Fully depress accelerator for no more than 5 seconds and note maximum engine speed. This is the torque converter stall speed.
3) Place shift lever in "N" position. Operate engine at 1000 RPM for at least 2 minutes to cool transaxle. Repeat test procedure with shift lever in "R" position.
4) On Scoupe, ensure torque converter stall speed is 2500-2900 RPM. On Accent and Elantra (1996), ensure torque converter stall speed is 2300-2700 RPM. If torque converter stall speed is not within specification, see TORQUE CONVERTER STALL SPEED TROUBLE SHOOTING table for possible causes.
5) If torque converter stall speed exceeds specification, perform hydraulic pressure tests. See HYDRAULIC PRESSURE TEST under TESTING.

TORQUE CONVERTER STALL SPEED TROUBLE SHOOTING

Torque Converter Stall Speed Test Results	Probable Cause
Stall Speed RPM High In "D"	Slipping Rear Clutch Or Overrunning Clutch
Stall Speed RPM High In "R"	Slipping Front Clutch Or Low-Reverse Brake
Stall Speed RPM Low In "D" & "R"	Engine Output Low Or Defective Torque Converter

HYDRAULIC PRESSURE TEST

1) Install tachometer. Warm engine to normal operating temperature. Ensure transaxle fluid level is correct. Apply parking brake. Block rear wheels. Raise and support vehicle so front wheels can rotate.
2) Reducing pressure, kickdown brake pressure, front clutch, rear clutch, end clutch, low-reverse brake and torque converter pressure are checked at specified pressure taps on transaxle. See Fig. 8.
3) Remove pressure tap plug. Install pressure gauge at appropriate pressure tap. Start and operate engine at specified RPM with shift lever in position for pressure being tested. See Fig. 6 or 7. Pressure should be within specification.
4) If pressure is not within specification, see HYDRAULIC PRESSURE TEST TROUBLE SHOOTING table. If kickdown brake pressure or any clutch pressure is less than specified, line pressure adjustment may be required. See LINE PRESSURE ADJUSTMENT under ON-VEHICLE SERVICE.

| No. | CONDITIONS | | | | STANDARD OIL PRESSURE (PSI) | | | | | | |
	Selector Lever Position	Engine Speed RPM	Shift Position	1 Reducing Pressure	2 Kickdown Brake Pressure (application)	3 Kickdown Brake Pressure (release)	4 Front Clutch Pressure	5 Rear Clutch Pressure	6 End Clutch Pressure	7 Low Reverse Brake Pressure	8 Torque Converter Pressure
1	N	Idle	Neutral	51-68	----	----	----	----	----	----	*
2	D	Idle	2nd	51-68	14-30	----	----	104-118	----	----	*
3	D (OD SW On)	Approx. 2,500	4th	51-68	118-128	----	----	----	118-128	----	64-92
4	D (OD SW Off)	Approx. 2,500	3rd	51-68	118-128	118-128	118-128	118-128	118-128	----	64-92
5	2	Approx. 2,500	2nd	51-68	118-128	----	----	118-128	----	----	64-92
6	L	Approx. 1,000	1st	51-68	----	----	----	118-128	----	43-64	*
7	R	Approx 2,500 ---------- 1,000	Reverse	51-68	----	233-318 -------- 213 or more	233-318 -------- 213 or more	----	----	233-319 --------- 213 or more	64-92

NOTE: - Indicates pressure is less than 1.4 psi.
OD SW-ON: Overdrive switch is in ON position.
OD SW-OFF: Overdrive switch is in OFF position.
* - Pressure is not standard.

95A20099

Courtesy of Hyundai Motor Co.

Fig. 6: Hydraulic Pressure Test Specifications (Scoupe)

| No. | Conditions | | | | Standard oil pressure (psi) | | | | | | | |
	Selector lever position	(Reference) vehicle speed mph	Engine speed rpm	Shift position	1 Reducing pressure	2 Kickdown brake pressure (application)	3 Kickdown brake pressure (release)	4 End clutch presure	5 Low-reverse brake pressure	6 Torque-converter pressure	7 Damper clutch release pressure	8 Rear clutch pressure
1	N	0	Idling	Neutral	55-67	-	-	-	-	*	*	-
2	D	0	Approx	2nd gear	55-67	13-43	-	-	-	*	*	*
3	D (OD SW-ON)	68	2,500 Approx	4th gear	55-67	122-131	-	122-131	-	71-114	-	122-131
4	D (OD SW-OFF)	47	2,500 Approx	3rd gear	55-67	122-131	122-131	122-131	-	71-114	-	122-131
5	2	31	2,500 Approx	2nd gear	55-67	122-131	-	-	-	71-114	-	122-131
6	L	0	1,000 Approx	1st gear	55-67	-	-	-	73-91	*	59-73	122-131
7	R	22	2,500 Approx	Reverse	55-67		254-297		254-297	39-49	61-73	
		0	1,000 Approx			-	65 or more		65 or more	*	*	-

NOTE: -Indicates pressure is less than 1.4 psi.
OD SW-ON: Overdrive switch is in ON position.
OD SW-OFF: Overdrive switch is in OFF position.
* - Pressure is not standard.

96B19316

Courtesy of Hyundai Motor Co.

Fig. 7: Hydraulic Pressure Test Specifications (Accent & Elantra)

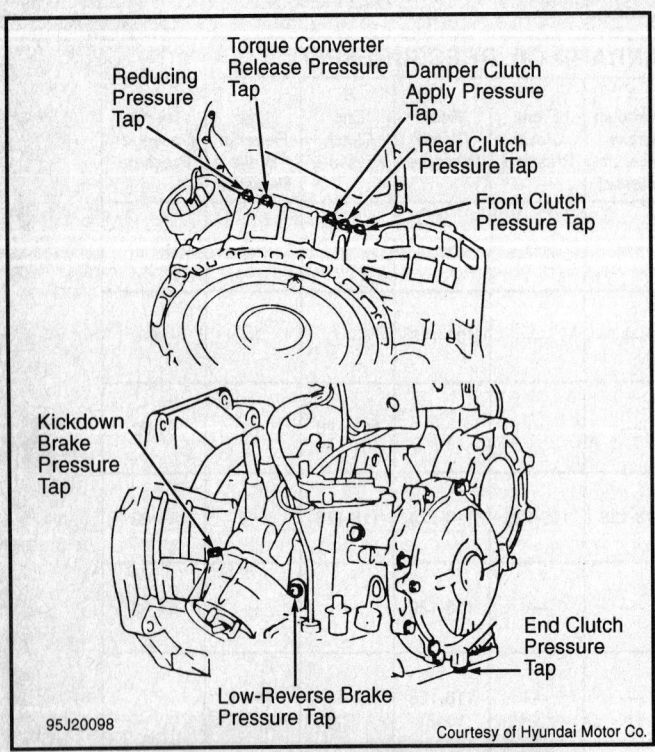

Fig. 8: Identifying Transaxle Pressure Taps

5) If reducing pressure is not within specification, reducing pressure adjustment may be required. See REDUCING PRESSURE ADJUSTMENT under ON-VEHICLE SERVICE.

6) Shut engine off. Remove pressure gauge. Install and tighten pressure tap plug to specification. See TORQUE SPECIFICATIONS.

HYDRAULIC PRESSURE TEST TROUBLE SHOOTING

Application	Probable Cause
All Pressures Are Low Or High	Restricted Main Oil Filter On Valve Body, Improper Line Pressure Adjustment, Sticking Regulator Valve In Valve Body, Loose Valve Body Bolts, Defective Oil Pump
Improper Reducing Pressure	Improper Line Pressure Adjustment, Restricted "L" Shaped Oil Filter On Intermediate Plate In Valve Body, Improper Reducing Pressure Adjustment, Sticking Reducing Valve In Valve Body, Loose Valve Body Bolts
Improper Kickdown Brake Pressure	Defective "D" Rings Or Seal Rings On Kickdown Servo Piston Or Sleeve, Loose Valve Body Bolts, Defective Valve Body
Improper Front Clutch Pressure	Defective "D" Rings Or Seal Rings On Kickdown Servo Piston Or Sleeve, Loose Valve Body Bolts, Defective Valve Body, Defective Front Clutch Components
Improper End Clutch Pressure	Defective "D" Rings Or Seal Rings On End Clutch, Loose Valve Body Bolts, Defective Valve Body
Improper Low-Reverse Brake Pressure	"O" Ring Between Valve Body & Transaxle Housing Is Missing, Loose Valve Body Bolts, Defective Valve Body, Defective "O" Rings On Low-Reverse Brake Piston
Improper Torque Converter Pressure	Sticking Damper Clutch Control Solenoid Valve, Restricted Or Leaking Oil Cooler, Defective Seal Rings On Input Shaft, Defective Torque Converter

ON-VEHICLE SERVICE

AXLE SHAFTS

See appropriate AXLE SHAFTS article in AXLE SHAFTS & TRANSFER CASES section.

LINE PRESSURE ADJUSTMENT

NOTE: Manufacturer specifies Mopar Plus-Type 7176 ATF for use in this transaxle. This fluid should also be used for assembly lubrication.

1) Remove valve body assembly. See VALVE BODY ASSEMBLY under REMOVAL & INSTALLATION.

2) Rotate line pressure adjusting screw at regulator valve on valve body assembly to adjust line pressure. See Fig. 9.

3) Rotating line pressure adjusting screw clockwise one revolution decreases line pressure approximately 5.5 psi (.39 kg/cm²). Rotating line pressure adjusting screw counterclockwise one revolution increases line pressure approximately 5.5 psi (.39 kg/cm²). Standard line pressure is 124.7-130.5 psi (8.77-9.18 kg/cm²).

4) Install valve body assembly using proper procedure. See VALVE BODY ASSEMBLY under REMOVAL & INSTALLATION. Fill transaxle with ATF. Recheck line pressure and adjust (if necessary).

REDUCING PRESSURE ADJUSTMENT

1) Valve body assembly removal is not required for reducing pressure adjustment. Drain transaxle fluid. Remove bolts, oil pan, gasket and oil filter.

2) Rotating reducing pressure adjusting screw clockwise one revolution decreases reducing pressure approximately 4.3 psi (.3 kg/cm²). See Fig. 9. Rotating reducing pressure adjusting screw counterclockwise one revolution increases reducing pressure approximately 4.3 psi (.3 kg/cm²). Standard reducing pressure is 59-62 psi (4.2-4.4 kg/cm²).

3) Install oil filter. Tighten oil filter bolts to specification. Using NEW gasket, install oil pan. Install and tighten oil pan bolts to specification.

4) Fill transaxle with ATF. Recheck reducing pressure and adjust (if necessary).

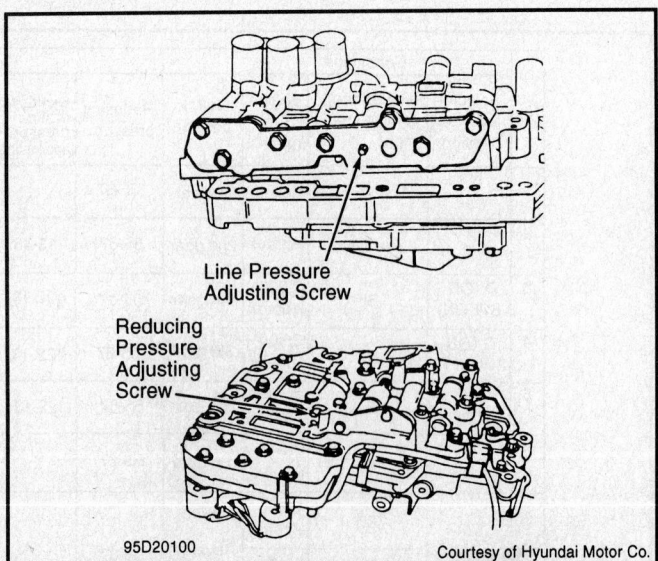

Fig. 9: Identifying Line Pressure & Reducing Pressure Adjusting Screws

KICKDOWN SERVO ADJUSTMENT

1) Note location of kickdown servo adjusting screw on top of transaxle. See Fig. 10. Ensure area around kickdown servo adjusting screw is clean.

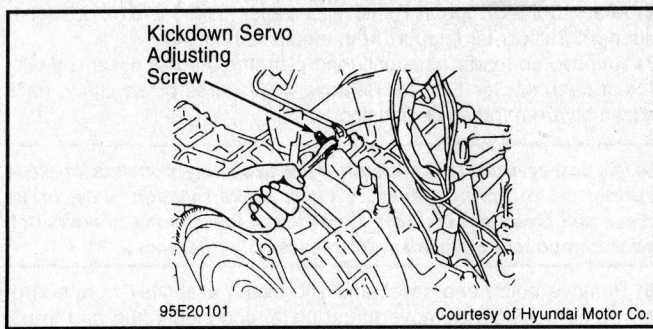

Fig. 10: Identifying Kickdown Servo Adjusting Screw

2) Loosen kickdown servo lock nut on kickdown servo adjusting screw. Loosen kickdown servo adjusting screw. Using INCH-lb. torque wrench, tighten kickdown servo adjusting screw to 44 INCH. lbs. (5.0 N.m).

3) Loosen kickdown servo adjusting screw and then retighten to 44 INCH. lbs. (5.0 N.m) again. Loosen kickdown servo adjusting screw 3 to 3 1/3 turns.

4) Apply Sealant (DC780) on threads of kickdown servo adjusting screw. Hold kickdown adjusting screw and tighten kickdown servo lock nut to specification. See TORQUE SPECIFICATIONS.

VALVE BODY ASSEMBLY

Valve body assembly may be serviced on the vehicle. See VALVE BODY ASSEMBLY under REMOVAL & INSTALLATION.

REMOVAL & INSTALLATION

ELECTRICAL COMPONENTS

See HYUNDAI A4AF & A4BF ELECTRONIC CONTROLS article.

TRANSAXLE

See appropriate AUTOMATIC TRANSMISSION REMOVAL article in TRANSMISSION SERVICING section.

VALVE BODY ASSEMBLY

Removal – 1) Drain transaxle fluid. Remove bolts, oil pan, gasket and oil filter. Remove oil temperature sensor, located on bottom of valve body assembly. *See Fig. 11.*

2) Push tab inward on solenoid valve electrical connector grommet, located on transaxle housing, above oil pan area. Push solenoid valve electrical connector grommet out of transaxle housing so valve body assembly can be removed.

3) Note location of valve body assembly-to-transaxle housing bolts. Remove valve body assembly-to-transaxle housing bolts. Remove valve body assembly, using care not to allow manual valve to fall from valve body assembly.

NOTE: Manufacturer specifies Mopar Plus-Type 7176 ATF for use in this transaxle. This fluid should also be used for assembly lubrication.

Installation – 1) Install NEW "O" ring on upper surface of valve body assembly, where valve body seals against transaxle housing.

2) Install NEW "O" ring on solenoid valve electrical connector grommet where it seals against transaxle housing. Install valve body assembly and solenoid valve electrical connector grommet.

3) Ensure notch on solenoid valve electrical connector grommet is toward front of transaxle housing and wiring is properly routed.

4) Install valve body assembly-to-transaxle housing bolts. Ensure proper length bolt is installed in correct location. *See Fig. 12.*

5) Tighten valve body assembly-to-transaxle housing bolts to specification. See TORQUE SPECIFICATIONS. Install oil temperature sensor and oil filter. Tighten oil filter bolts to specification.

6) Ensure 5 magnets are installed in 5 depression areas on oil pan. Using NEW gasket, install oil pan. Install and tighten oil pan bolts to specification. Fill transaxle with ATF.

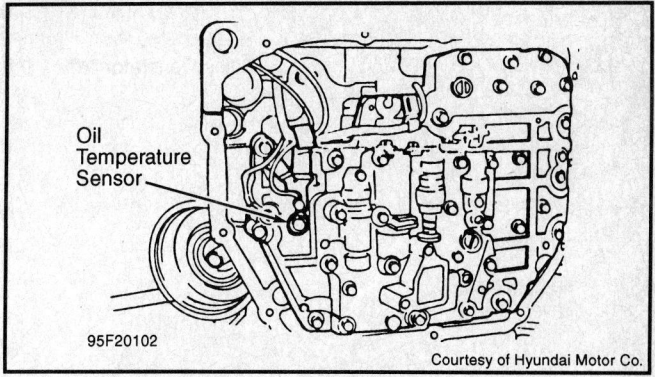

Fig. 11: Identifying Oil Temperature Sensor

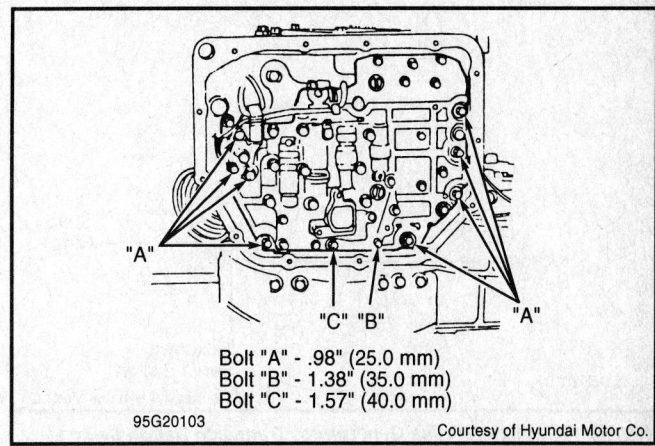

Bolt "A" - .98" (25.0 mm)
Bolt "B" - 1.38" (35.0 mm)
Bolt "C" - 1.57" (40.0 mm)

Fig. 12: Identifying Valve Body Assembly-To-Transaxle Housing Bolt Locations

TORQUE CONVERTER

NOTE: Torque converter is a sealed unit and cannot be disassembled. Replace torque converter if defective.

NOTE: For torque converter stall speed test, see TORQUE CONVERTER STALL SPEED TEST under TESTING.

TRANSAXLE DISASSEMBLY

VALVE BODY ASSEMBLY & INTERNAL COMPONENTS

1) Remove torque converter. Using dial indicator, measure input shaft end play for reassembly reference. Input shaft end play should be .012-.039" (.30-1.00 mm). This will indicate if thrust washer change is required.

2) Remove pulse generators, manual control lever and transaxle range switch from transaxle housing. *See Fig. 13.* Remove snap ring and kickdown servo switch.

3) Remove oil pump-to-transaxle housing bolts. Thread 2 pull-out bolts in oil pump and evenly tighten to pull oil pump from transaxle housing. *See Fig. 14.* Lightly tap on oil pump with soft-faced hammer while tightening pull-out bolts during oil pump removal.

4) Remove fiber thrust washer from front of input shaft. Lift upward on input shaft to remove front and rear clutch assemblies from transaxle housing.

5) Remove thrust bearing, located on front side of clutch hub. Remove clutch hub, thrust race and bearing. Remove kickdown drum and kickdown band. From inside transaxle, remove snap ring that retains center support in transaxle housing.

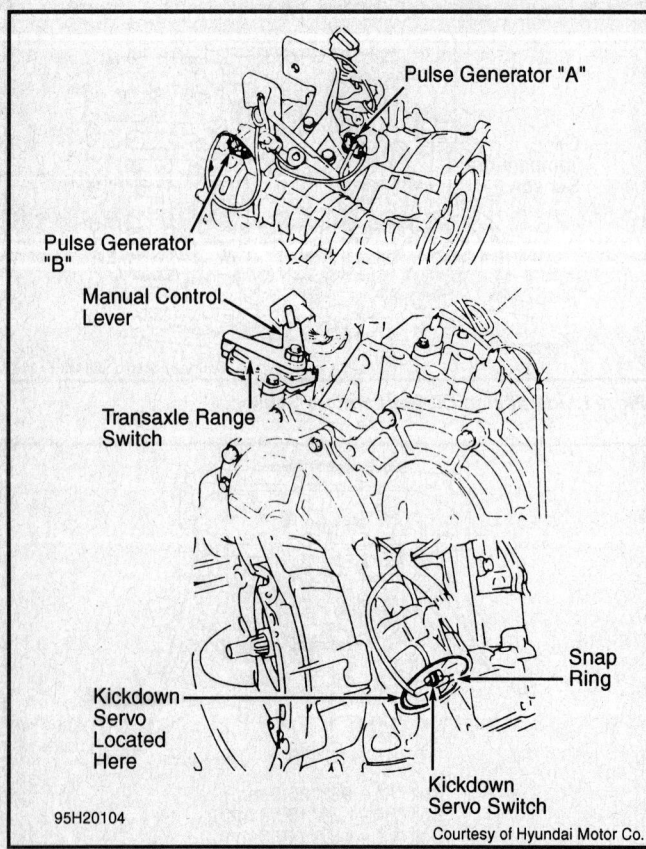

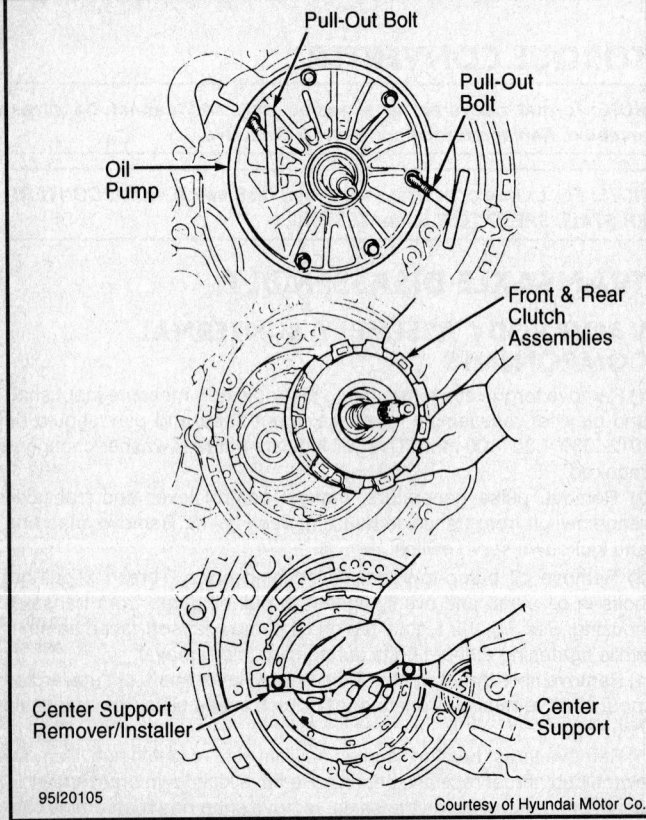

Fig. 13: Identifying Pulse Generators, Transaxle Range Switch, Kickdown Servo Switch & Kickdown Servo Location

Fig. 14: Identifying Oil Pump, Front & Rear Clutch Assemblies & Center Support

6) Attach Center Support Remover/Installer (09453-21310) on center support. Pull center support from transaxle housing.

7) Remove sun gear assembly and planetary carrier assembly with thrust bearing. *See Fig. 15.* Remove low-reverse brake clutch pack assembly from transaxle housing.

NOTE: Low-reverse brake clutch pack assembly consists of wave spring, return spring, pressure plate, brake reaction plate, brake discs and brake plates. Note sequence of low-reverse brake clutch pack component installation for reassembly reference.

---

8) Remove bolts, end cover and end clutch assembly from end of transaxle housing. Remove thrust plate, end clutch hub and thrust bearing from end of transaxle housing. Remove end clutch shaft.

9) Remove bolts, oil pan, gasket and oil filter. Remove oil temperature sensor, located on bottom of valve body assembly. *See Fig. 11.*

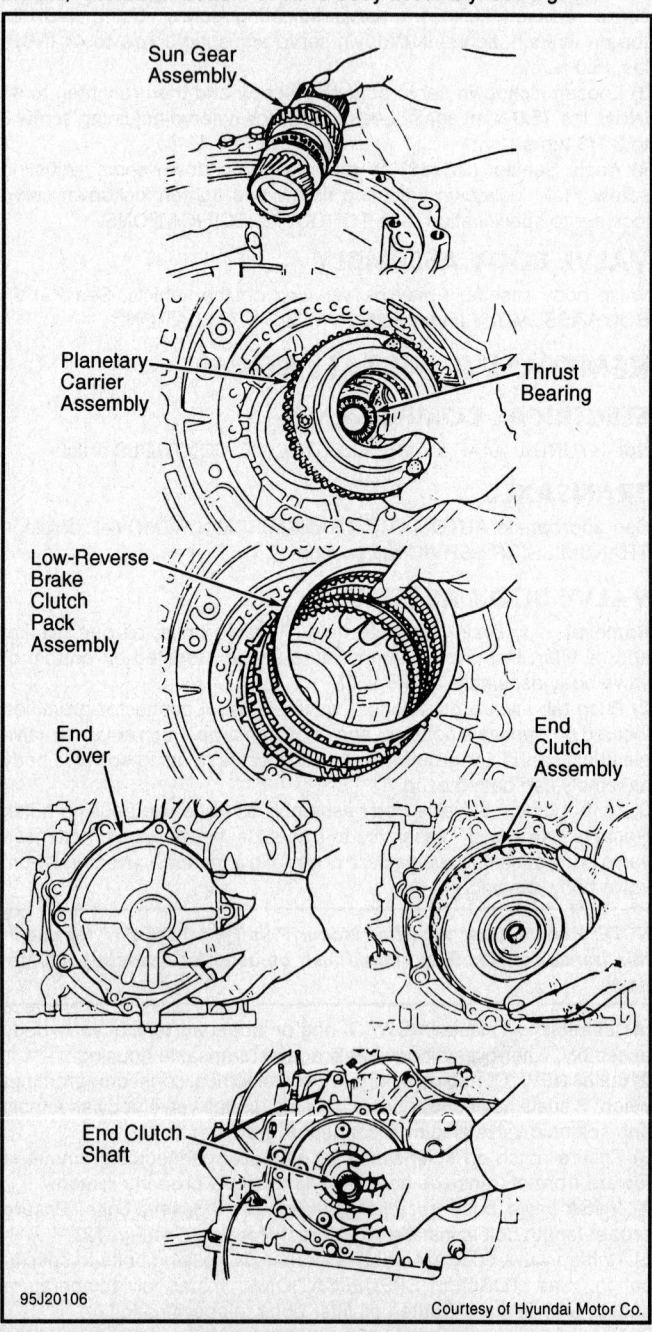

Fig. 15: Removing & Installing Sun Gear Assembly, Planetary Carrier Assembly, Clutch Pack Assembly, End Cover, End Clutch Assembly & End Clutch Shaft

10) Push tab inward on solenoid valve electrical connector grommet, located on transaxle housing, above oil pan area. Push solenoid valve electrical connector grommet out of transaxle housing so valve body assembly can be removed.

11) Note location of valve body assembly-to-transaxle housing bolts. Remove valve body assembly-to-transaxle housing bolts. Remove valve body assembly, using care not to allow manual valve to fall from valve body assembly.

12) Remove screws and bearing retainer. *See Fig. 16.* Remove snap ring from rear bearing. Remove rear cover. Using hammer and chisel, loosen staked area on transfer shaft lock nut.

13) Place shift lever on transaxle in Park position. Remove transfer shaft lock nut from transfer shaft. Using puller, remove transfer driven gear from transfer shaft.

14) Remove bearing outer race for transfer shaft from transaxle housing. Remove snap ring from inside of transaxle housing, near transfer shaft. Remove transfer shaft with bearing.

15) Place shift lever on transaxle in Neutral position. Remove stopper plate, located on top of rear bearing.

16) Using press, press output flange from transfer drive gear. *See Fig. 16.* Remove output flange and transfer drive gear from transaxle housing. Remove speedometer drive gear assembly. Speedometer drive gear assembly is located on transaxle housing, near differential cover. Remove bolts, differential cover and gasket.

17) Remove bolts from differential bearing retainer. Screw bolts into differential bearing retainer to press differential bearing retainer from transaxle housing. *See Fig. 17.* Remove bolts, differential bearing cap and differential assembly.

18) Remove bolts, parking brake rod support and parking brake rod. Remove set screw, manual control shaft, detent ball, seat and spring from transaxle housing.

19) Remove snap ring and kickdown servo piston assembly from side of transaxle housing. *See Fig. 13.*

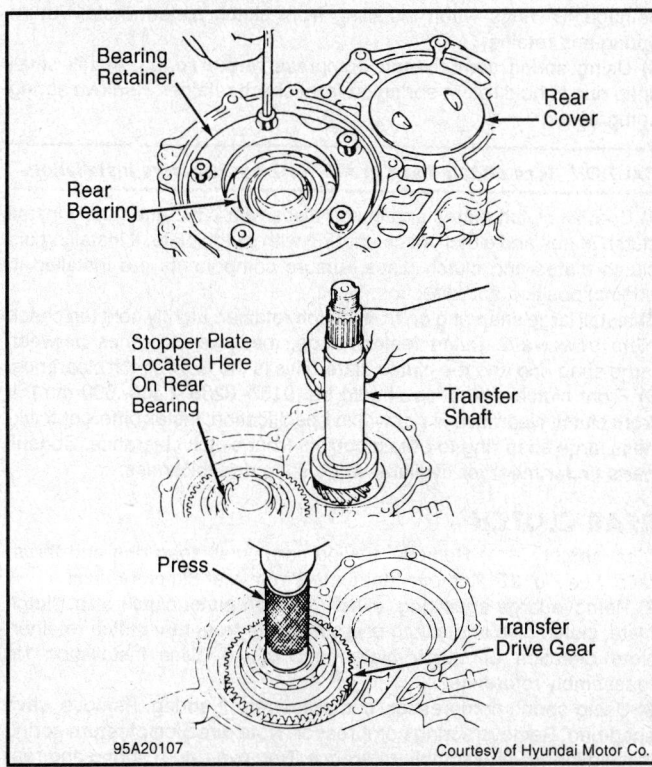

Fig. 16: *Identifying Bearing Retainer, Rear Cover, Stopper Plate & Output Flange With Transfer Drive Gear*

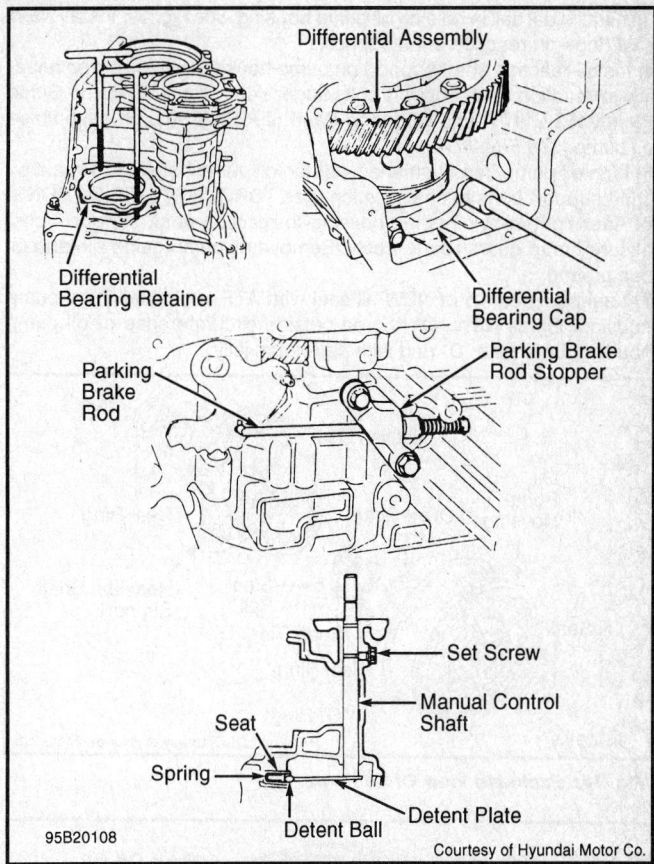

Fig. 17: *Identifying Differential Bearing Retainer, Differential Bearing Cap, Differential Assembly, Manual Control Shaft Assembly & Parking Brake Rod*

COMPONENT DISASSEMBLY & REASSEMBLY

OIL PUMP

Disassembly – 1) Place oil pump on torque converter with reaction shaft support facing upward. Remove seal rings and "O" ring from oil pump.

2) Remove oil pump housing-to-reaction shaft support bolts. Remove reaction shaft support from oil pump housing. *See Fig. 18.* Remove oil pump housing from torque converter.

3) Place reference marks on drive and driven gears for reassembly reference to ensure gears are installed in original direction. Remove drive and driven gears from oil pump housing.

4) Remove steel ball from oil pump housing. Remove snap ring and seal ring from drive gear. Pry oil seal from oil pump housing.

Cleaning & Inspection – 1) Clean components with solvent and dry with compressed air. Inspect components for damage or signs of wear.

2) Install drive and driven gears in oil pump housing. Ensure gears rotate smoothly. Place straightedge on oil pump housing, above both gears.

3) Using feeler gauge, measure oil pump gear side clearance between each gear and the straightedge. Replace oil pump if oil pump gear side clearance exceeds .0008-.0019" (.020-.048 mm).

4) Measure inside diameter of oil pump housing bushing. Replace oil pump housing if bushing inside diameter exceeds 1.690" (43.01 mm).

Reassembly – 1) Install NEW seal ring in drive gear. Install snap ring in drive gear. Coat all components with ATF.

2) Install drive and driven gears in oil pump housing. If installing original gears, ensure gears are installed in original positions using reference marks made during disassembly.

3) Install steel ball in hole on oil pump housing. *See Fig. 19.* Install NEW seal rings on reaction shaft support.

4) Install reaction shaft support on pump housing with oil pump housing-to-reaction shaft support bolts finger tight. Install Oil Pump Guide Pin (09452-21401) and Oil Pump Band (09452-21301) on assembled oil pump. *See Fig. 20.*

5) With oil pump band tightened, tighten oil pump housing-to-reaction shaft support bolts to specification. See TORQUE SPECIFICATIONS.

6) After tightening oil pump housing-to-reaction shaft support bolts, ensure pump gears rotate freely. Remove oil pump guide pin and oil pump band.

7) Lubricate seal lip of NEW oil seal with ATF and install in oil pump housing. Install NEW "O" ring on outside circumference of oil pump housing. Lubricate "O" ring with petroleum jelly.

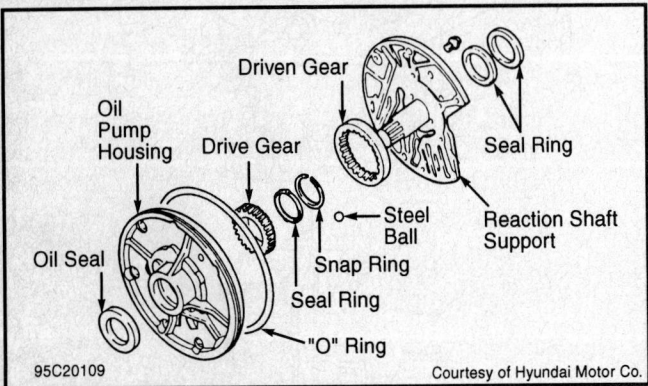

Fig. 18: *Exploded View Of Oil Pump*

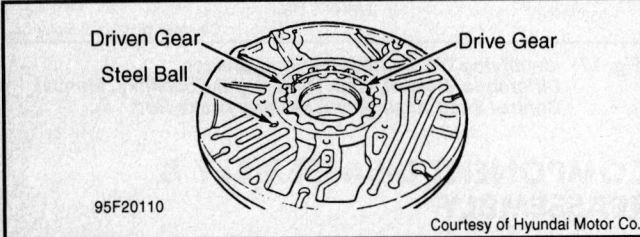

Fig. 19: *Installing Steel Ball In Oil Pump Housing*

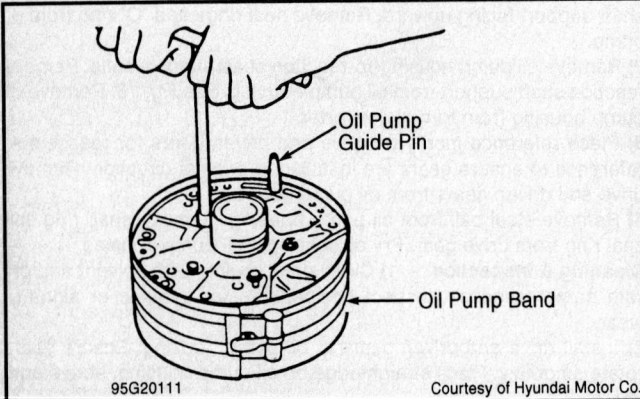

Fig. 20: *Assembling Oil Pump*

FRONT CLUTCH

Disassembly – 1) Remove large snap ring, clutch plates and clutch discs from front clutch retainer. *See Fig. 21.* Note direction of clutch plates and clutch discs installation for reassembly reference.

2) Using spring compressor, compress return spring. Remove small snap ring from front clutch retainer. Remove spring compressor. Remove return spring and retainer.

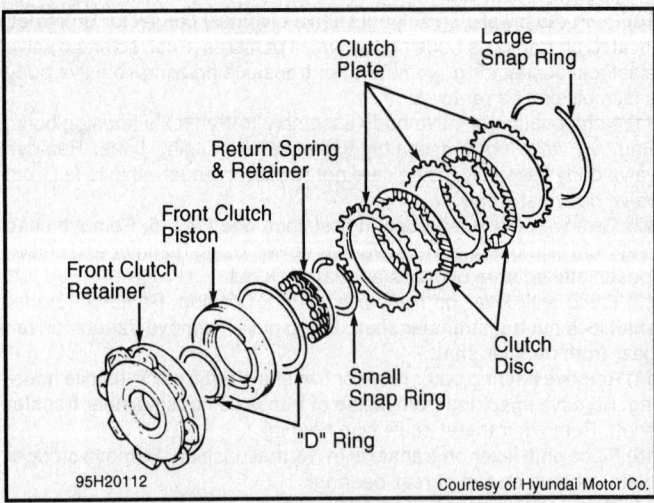

Fig. 21: *Exploded View Of Front Clutch*

3) Remove front clutch piston from front clutch retainer. Remove "D" rings from clutch piston and front clutch retainer.

Cleaning & Inspection – Clean metal components with solvent and dry with compressed air. Shake front clutch piston to ensure check ball located in front clutch piston moves freely. Inspect components for damage and replace if necessary. Ensure no rough edges exist in "D" ring sealing areas.

Reassembly – 1) Install NEW "D" ring on front clutch piston and front clutch retainer with rounded side of "D" ring facing outward, away from front clutch piston or front clutch retainer. Lubricate "D" rings with ATF.

2) Install front clutch piston in front clutch retainer. Use care not to damage "D" rings when installing front clutch piston. Install return spring and retainer.

3) Using spring compressor, compress return spring. Install small snap ring to hold return spring on front clutch retainer. Remove spring compressor.

CAUTION: Soak clutch discs in ATF for 2 hours before installation.

---

4) Coat all clutch plates and clutch discs with ATF. Alternately install clutch plates and clutch discs starting with clutch plate. If installing old clutch plates and clutch discs, ensure components are installed in original position and direction.

5) Install large snap ring on front clutch retainer. Lightly hold top clutch plate downward. Using feeler gauge, measure clearance between large snap ring and top clutch plate. This is the front clutch clearance.

6) Front clutch clearance should be .0157-.0236" (.400-.600 mm). If front clutch clearance is not within specification, install different thickness large snap ring to obtain correct front clutch clearance. Consult parts department for available large snap ring thickness.

REAR CLUTCH

Disassembly – 1) Remove sealing cap, small snap ring and thrust race. *See Fig. 22.* Remove input shaft from rear clutch retainer.

2) Remove large snap ring, clutch reaction plate, clutch disc, clutch plate, clutch disc and clutch pressure plate from rear clutch retainer. Note direction of clutch plates and clutch discs installation for reassembly reference.

3) Using spring compressor, compress return spring. Remove wave snap ring. Remove spring compressor. Note direction of return spring installation for reassembly reference. Remove return spring and rear clutch piston. Remove "D" rings from rear clutch piston.

Cleaning & Inspection – Clean metal components with solvent and dry with compressed air. Inspect components for damage. Replace components as required. Ensure no rough edges exist in "D" ring sealing areas.

Reassembly – 1) Install NEW "D" rings on rear clutch piston with rounded side of "D" ring facing outward, away from rear clutch piston. Lubricate "D" rings with ATF.

2) Install rear clutch piston in rear clutch retainer. Use care not to damage "D" rings when installing rear clutch piston. Install return spring on rear clutch piston. Ensure return spring is facing correct direction. *See Fig. 22.*

3) Compress return spring. Install wave snap ring. Ensure wave snap ring is fully seated in groove on rear clutch retainer.

CAUTION: Soak clutch discs in ATF for 2 hours before installation.

---

4) Coat all clutch plates and clutch discs with ATF. Install clutch pressure plate, clutch disc, clutch plate, clutch disc and clutch reaction plate in rear clutch retainer.

5) If installing old clutch plates and clutch discs, ensure components are installed in original position and direction. Install large snap ring on rear clutch retainer.

6) Lightly hold clutch reaction plate downward. Using feeler gauge, measure clearance between large snap ring and clutch reaction plate. This is the rear clutch clearance.

7) Rear clutch clearance should be .0118-.0197" (.300-.500 mm). If rear clutch clearance is not within specification, install different thickness large snap ring to obtain correct rear clutch clearance. Consult parts department for available large snap ring thickness.

8) Install input shaft in rear clutch retainer. Install thrust race, small snap ring and sealing cap. Install NEW sealing rings on input shaft.

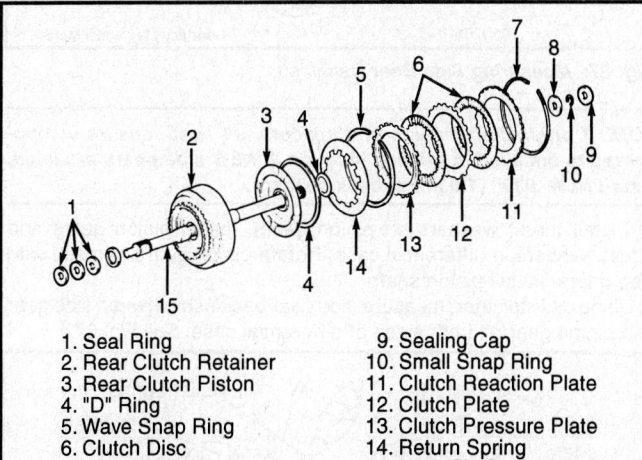

1. Seal Ring
2. Rear Clutch Retainer
3. Rear Clutch Piston
4. "D" Ring
5. Wave Snap Ring
6. Clutch Disc
7. Large Snap Ring
8. Thrust Race
9. Sealing Cap
10. Small Snap Ring
11. Clutch Reaction Plate
12. Clutch Plate
13. Clutch Pressure Plate
14. Return Spring
15. Input Shaft

95I20113 Courtesy of Hyundai Motor Co.

Fig. 22: Exploded View Of Rear Clutch

END CLUTCH

Disassembly – 1) Remove large snap ring, clutch reaction plate, clutch discs and clutch plates from end clutch retainer. *See Fig. 23.* Note direction of clutch plates and clutch discs installation for reassembly reference.

2) Remove small snap ring and washer from inside of end clutch retainer. Note direction of return spring installation for reassembly reference. Remove return spring.

3) Remove end clutch piston from end clutch retainer. It may be necessary to apply air pressure to oil passage on rear side of end clutch retainer for removal of end clutch piston.

4) Remove "D" rings and oil seal from end clutch piston. Remove seal ring and oil seal from end clutch retainer.

Cleaning & Inspection – Clean metal components with solvent and dry with compressed air. Inspect components for damage. Replace components as required. Ensure no rough edges exist in "D" ring or oil seal sealing areas.

Reassembly – 1) Install NEW "D" rings and oil seal on end clutch piston. Ensure rounded side of "D" ring is facing outward, away from end clutch piston. Install NEW seal ring and oil seal on end clutch retainer.

2) Lubricate "D" ring, oil seals and seal ring with ATF. Install end clutch piston in end clutch retainer. Use care not to damage "D" rings when installing end clutch piston.

3) Install return spring and washer on end clutch piston. Ensure return spring is facing correct direction. *See Fig. 23.*

4) Compress return spring. Install NEW small snap ring. Ensure small snap ring is fully seated in groove on end clutch retainer.

CAUTION: Soak clutch discs in ATF for 2 hours before installation.

---

5) Coat all clutch plates and clutch discs with ATF. Alternately install clutch plates and clutch discs starting with clutch plate. If installing old clutch plates and clutch discs, ensure components are installed in original position and direction.

6) Install clutch reaction plate in end clutch retainer. Install large snap ring on end clutch retainer.

7) Lightly hold clutch reaction plate downward. Using feeler gauge, measure clearance between large snap ring and clutch reaction plate. This is the end clutch clearance.

8) End clutch clearance should be .0157-.0260" (.400-.650 mm). If end clutch clearance is not within specification, install different thickness large snap ring to obtain correct end clutch clearance. Consult parts department for available large snap ring thickness.

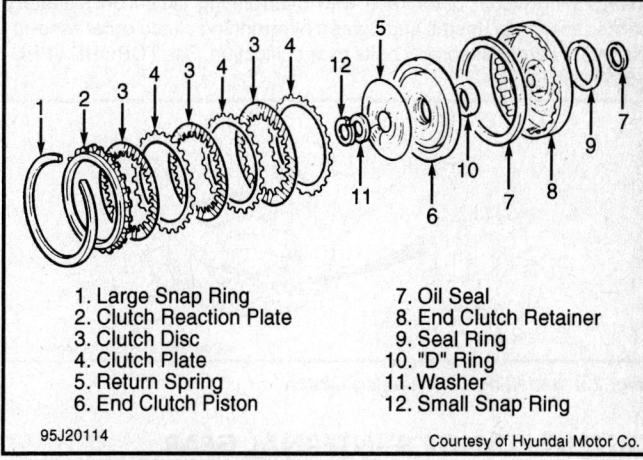

1. Large Snap Ring
2. Clutch Reaction Plate
3. Clutch Disc
4. Clutch Plate
5. Return Spring
6. End Clutch Piston
7. Oil Seal
8. End Clutch Retainer
9. Seal Ring
10. "D" Ring
11. Washer
12. Small Snap Ring

95J20114 Courtesy of Hyundai Motor Co.

Fig. 23: Exploded View Of End Clutch

PLANETARY CARRIER ASSEMBLY

Disassembly – 1) Remove overrunning clutch outer race-to-planetary carrier assembly bolts. Remove overrunning clutch outer race with overrunning clutch from planetary carrier assembly. *See Fig. 24.*

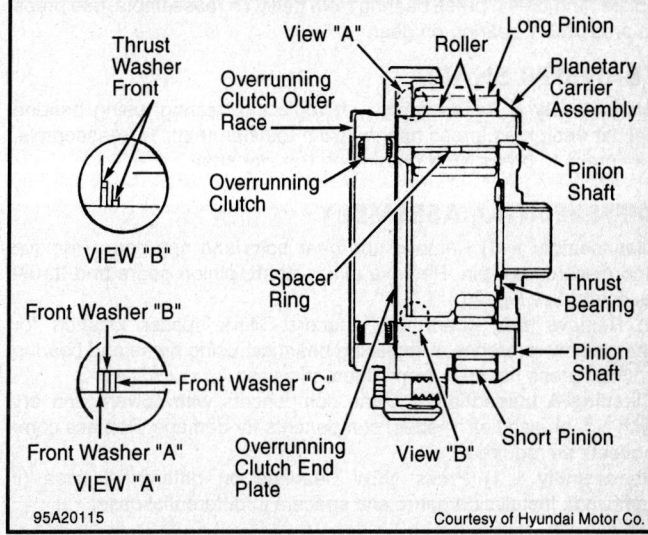

95A20115 Courtesy of Hyundai Motor Co.

Fig. 24: Cross-Section View Of Planetary Carrier Assembly

2) Remove overrunning clutch end plate. Remove pinion shaft from one short pinion. Remove short pinion with spacer bushing and washers. DO NOT allow rollers to fall from short pinion during removal.

3) Remove thrust bearing from center of planetary carrier assembly. Note direction of overrunning clutch installation in overrunning clutch outer race. Remove overrunning clutch from overrunning clutch outer race, by pressing on overrunning clutch.

Cleaning & Inspection – Clean components with solvent and dry with compressed air. Inspect components for damage. Replace components as required.

Reassembly – **1)** Install thrust bearing in center of planetary carrier assembly. Ensure thrust bearing is installed in correct direction and fully seated in planetary carrier assembly. *See Fig. 24.*

2) Apply petroleum jelly on inside of short pinion to hold rollers in place. Install short pinion, spacer bushing and washers in planetary carrier assembly. Ensure rollers do not fall from short pinion.

3) Install pinion shaft in short pinion and washers. Ensure flat side of pinion shaft aligns with flat area on rear washer.

4) Install end plate on inside of overrunning clutch outer race. Press overrunning clutch into overrunning clutch outer race. Ensure arrow mark on outside of overrunning clutch is pointing upward. *See Fig. 25.*

5) Apply petroleum jelly on overrunning clutch end plate. Install overrunning clutch end plate on inside of overrunning clutch. Install overrunning clutch outer race with overrunning clutch on planetary carrier assembly. Install and tighten overrunning clutch outer race-to-planetary carrier assembly bolts to specification. See TORQUE SPECIFICATIONS.

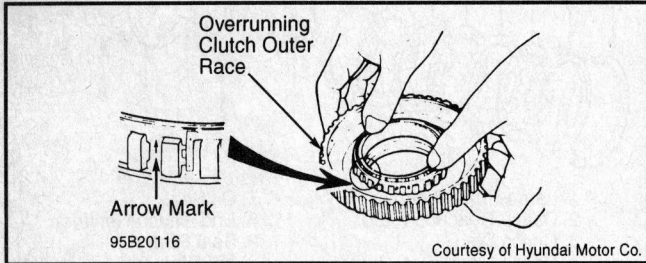

Fig. 25: *Installing Overrunning Clutch*

OUTPUT FLANGE & INTERNAL GEAR

Disassembly & Reassembly – Remove snap ring from rear of output flange. Separate gear from output flange. To reassemble, reverse disassembly procedure.

TRANSFER DRIVE & DRIVEN GEARS

Disassembly & Reassembly – If replacing bearing, using bearing splitter and press, press bearing from gear. To reassemble, use press to press NEW bearing on gear.

TRANSFER SHAFT

Disassembly & Reassembly – If replacing bearing, using bearing splitter and press, press bearing from transfer shaft. To reassemble, use press to press NEW bearing on transfer shaft.

DIFFERENTIAL ASSEMBLY

Disassembly – **1)** Remove ring gear bolts and ring gear. Remove and discard lock pin. Remove pinion shaft, pinion gears and thrust washers. *See Fig. 26.*

2) Remove side gears and spacers. Mark spacer location for reassembly reference. If replacing bearings, using press and bearing splitter, press bearings from differential case.

Cleaning & Inspection – Clean components with solvent and dry with compressed air. Inspect components for damage. Replace components as required.

Reassembly – **1)** Press NEW bearings on differential case (if removed). Install side gears and spacers in differential case.

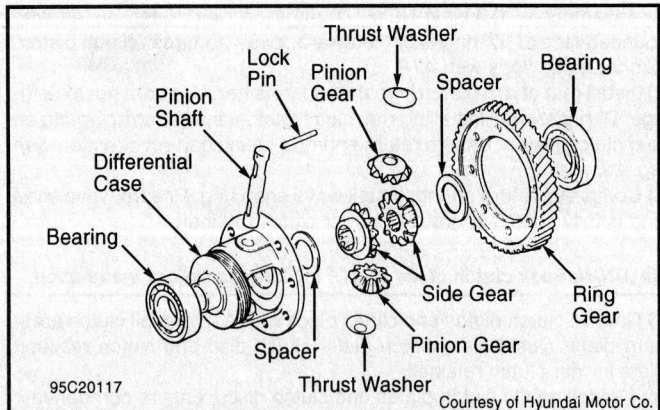

Fig. 26: *Exploded View Of Differential Assembly*

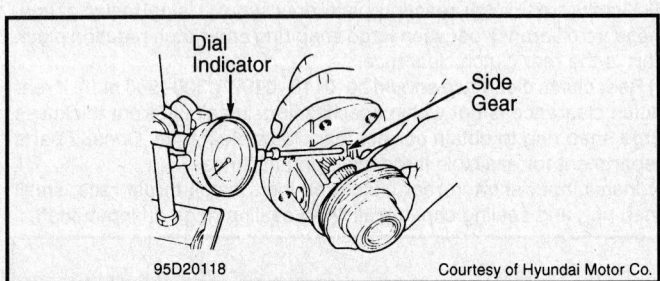

Fig. 27: *Measuring Side Gear Backlash*

NOTE: If original side gears and spacers are used, ensure components are installed in original location. If NEW side gears are used, install NEW .039" (1.00 mm) thick spacers.

2) Install thrust washers on pinion gears. Install pinion gears and thrust washers in differential case. Rotate pinion gears to mesh with side gears. Install pinion shaft.

3) Using dial indicator, measure side gear backlash between side gear and pinion gear on both sides of differential case. *See Fig. 27.*

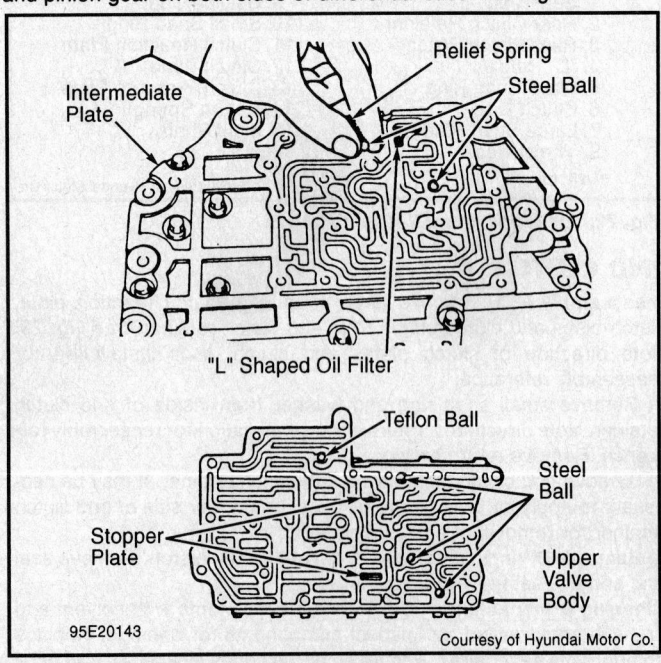

Fig. 28: *Identifying Relief Spring, Steel Balls, Teflon Ball & "L" Shaped Oil Filter Locations*

4) Side gear backlash should be .0010-.0059" (.025-.150 mm) and should be the same on both sides. If side gear backlash is not within specification, install different thickness spacers on side gears.

5) Once correct side gear backlash is obtained, install NEW lock pin in differential case. After installing lock pin, ensure distance from end of lock pin to surface on differential case is less than .118" (3.00 mm). This ensures full installation of lock pin.

6) Install ring gear on differential case. Lubricate threads of ring gear bolts with ATF. Install and tighten ring gear bolts in a crisscross pattern to specification. See TORQUE SPECIFICATIONS.

VALVE BODY ASSEMBLY

CAUTION: When disassembling valve body assembly, place components in order and mark spring locations for reassembly reference. DO NOT use force to remove components.

Disassembly – 1) Remove oil temperature sensor bracket and all solenoid valves from valve body assembly. Remove manual valve from valve body assembly. *See Fig. 29.*

2) Remove valve stopper and clamp. Place valve body assembly with lower valve body facing upward. Remove bolts, lower valve body and lower separator plate from intermediate plate.

3) Remove relief spring, steel balls and "L" shaped oil filter from intermediate plate. Remove bolts, intermediate plate and upper separator plate from upper valve body.

4) Remove block and upper separator plate from intermediate plate. Note location of Teflon ball, steel balls and stopper plates in upper valve body. *See Fig. 28.*

5) Remove Teflon ball, steel balls and stopper plates from upper valve body. Disassemble components from upper and lower valve bodies. *See Fig. 29.*

6) Ensure front end cover on upper valve body is held downward when removing bolts to prevent line pressure adjusting screw and spring from popping out of upper valve body. Use care when removing components from valve bodies, as components may be under spring tension.

Cleaning & Inspection – Clean components with solvent and dry with compressed air. Ensure all valves slide freely in bore.

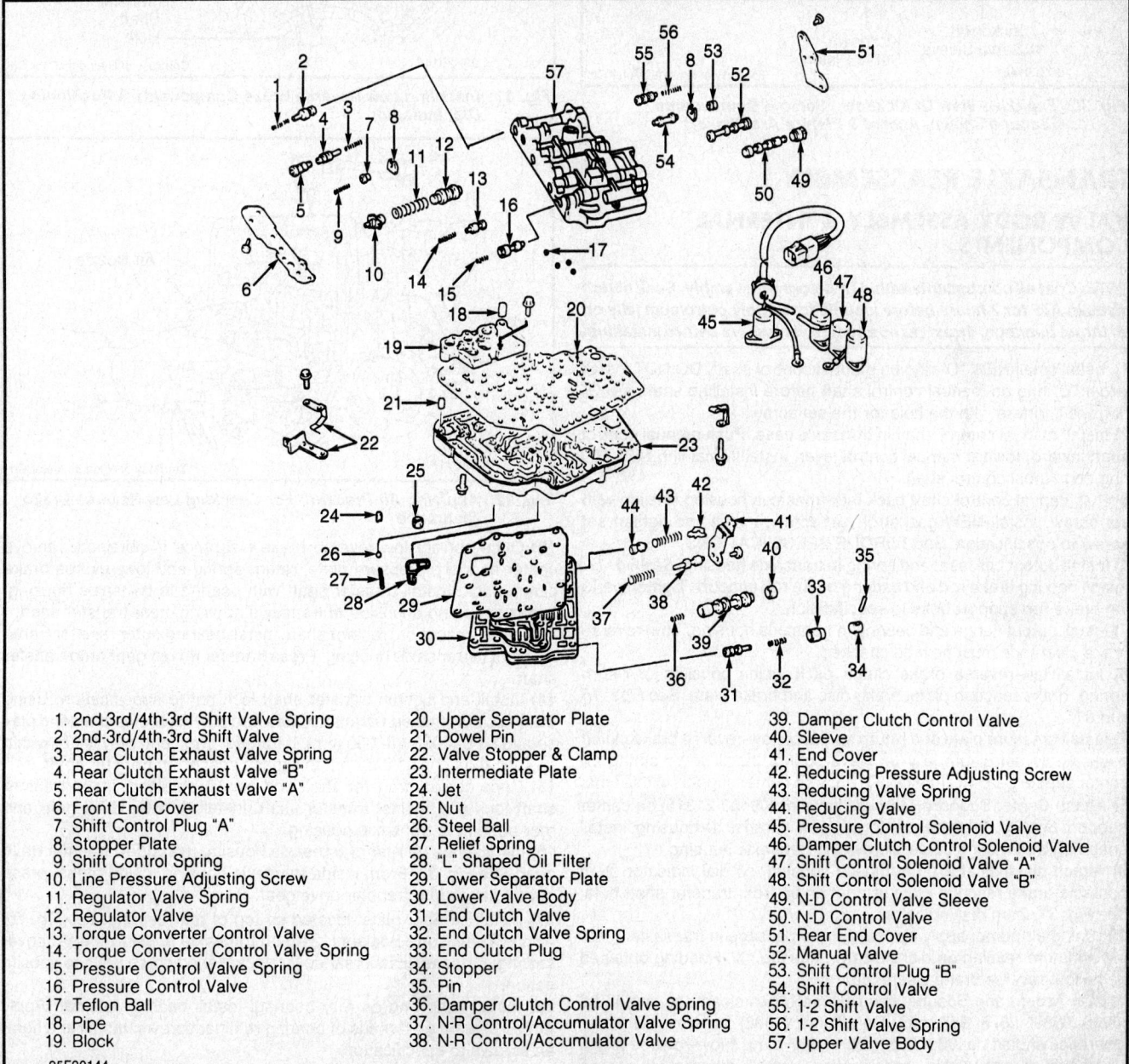

1. 2nd-3rd/4th-3rd Shift Valve Spring	20. Upper Separator Plate	39. Damper Clutch Control Valve
2. 2nd-3rd/4th-3rd Shift Valve	21. Dowel Pin	40. Sleeve
3. Rear Clutch Exhaust Valve Spring	22. Valve Stopper & Clamp	41. End Cover
4. Rear Clutch Exhaust Valve "B"	23. Intermediate Plate	42. Reducing Pressure Adjusting Screw
5. Rear Clutch Exhaust Valve "A"	24. Jet	43. Reducing Valve Spring
6. Front End Cover	25. Nut	44. Reducing Valve
7. Shift Control Plug "A"	26. Steel Ball	45. Pressure Control Solenoid Valve
8. Stopper Plate	27. Relief Spring	46. Damper Clutch Control Solenoid Valve
9. Shift Control Spring	28. "L" Shaped Oil Filter	47. Shift Control Solenoid Valve "A"
10. Line Pressure Adjusting Screw	29. Lower Separator Plate	48. Shift Control Solenoid Valve "B"
11. Regulator Valve Spring	30. Lower Valve Body	49. N-D Control Valve Sleeve
12. Regulator Valve	31. End Clutch Valve	50. N-D Control Valve
13. Torque Converter Control Valve	32. End Clutch Valve Spring	51. Rear End Cover
14. Torque Converter Control Valve Spring	33. End Clutch Plug	52. Manual Valve
15. Pressure Control Valve Spring	34. Stopper	53. Shift Control Plug "B"
16. Pressure Control Valve	35. Pin	54. Shift Control Valve
17. Teflon Ball	36. Damper Clutch Control Valve Spring	55. 1-2 Shift Valve
18. Pipe	37. N-R Control/Accumulator Valve Spring	56. 1-2 Shift Valve Spring
19. Block	38. N-R Control/Accumulator Valve	57. Upper Valve Body

95F20144

Courtesy of Hyundai Motor Co.

Fig. 29: Exploded View Of Valve Body Assembly

Reassembly – 1) To reassemble, reverse disassembly procedure. Ensure all steel balls, Teflon ball, relief spring and "L" shaped oil filter are installed in correct location. *See Fig. 28.*

2) Use guide studs when assembling valve body assembly to ensure correct alignment of valve bodies. Tighten valve body bolts and end cover bolts to specification. See TORQUE SPECIFICATIONS.

KICKDOWN SERVO

Disassembly & Reassembly – Disassemble kickdown servo components. *See Fig. 30.* To reassemble, reverse disassembly procedure use NEW "O" ring and "D" rings. Coat "O" ring and "D" rings with ATF.

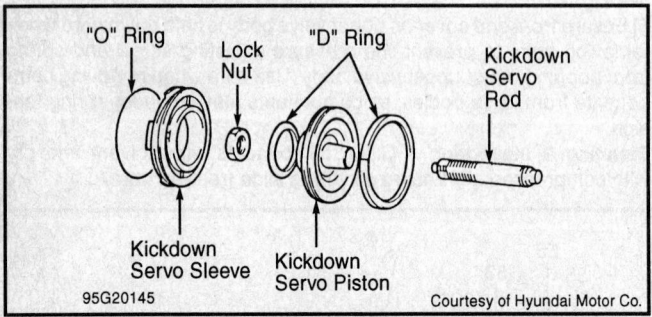

Fig. 30: Exploded View Of Kickdown Servo & Components (Scoupe Shown; Accent & Elantra Are Similar)

TRANSAXLE REASSEMBLY

VALVE BODY ASSEMBLY & INTERNAL COMPONENTS

NOTE: Coat all components with ATF before reassembly. Soak clutch discs in ATF for 2 hours before installation. Apply petroleum jelly on all thrust bearings, thrust races and thrust washers before installing.

1) Install small NEW "O" ring on manual control shaft. DO NOT install larger "O" ring on manual control shaft before installing shaft, as "O" ring will interfere with the hole for the set screw.

2) Install manual control shaft in transaxle case. Push manual control shaft inward, toward manual control lever. Install remaining NEW "O" ring on manual control shaft.

3) Pull manual control shaft back into transaxle housing to align with set screw. Install NEW gasket on set screw. Install and tighten set screw to specification. See TORQUE SPECIFICATIONS.

4) Install detent ball, seat and spring in transaxle housing. *See Fig. 17.* Install parking brake rod and parking brake rod support. Tighten parking brake rod support bolts to specification.

5) Install output flange and bearing in transaxle housing. Low-reverse brake clearance must now be checked.

6) Install low-reverse brake clutch pack which consists of return spring, brake reaction plate, brake disc and brake plate. *See Figs. 15 and 31.*

7) Install pressure plate and return spring on low-reverse brake clutch pack. Apply petroleum jelly on wave spring. Install wave spring on center support. DO NOT install "O" rings on center support at this time.

8) Attach Center Support Remover/Installer (09453-21310) on center support. *See Fig. 14.* Install center support in transaxle housing. Install snap ring that retains center support in transaxle housing.

9) Attach dial indicator on transaxle housing, so dial indicator stem contacts brake reaction plate at right angle from transfer shaft hole. *See Fig. 31.* Zero dial indicator.

10) Using air pump, apply air pressure to passage in transaxle housing and note reading on dial indicator. *See Fig. 32.* Reading obtained is the low-reverse brake clearance.

11) On Accent and Scoupe, low-reverse brake clearance should be .0266-.0389" (.675-.987 mm). On Elantra (1996), low-reverse brake clearance should be .038-.051" (.987-1.287 mm). If low-reverse brake clearance is not within specification, install different thickness pressure plate to obtain correct clearance. Remove dial indicator.

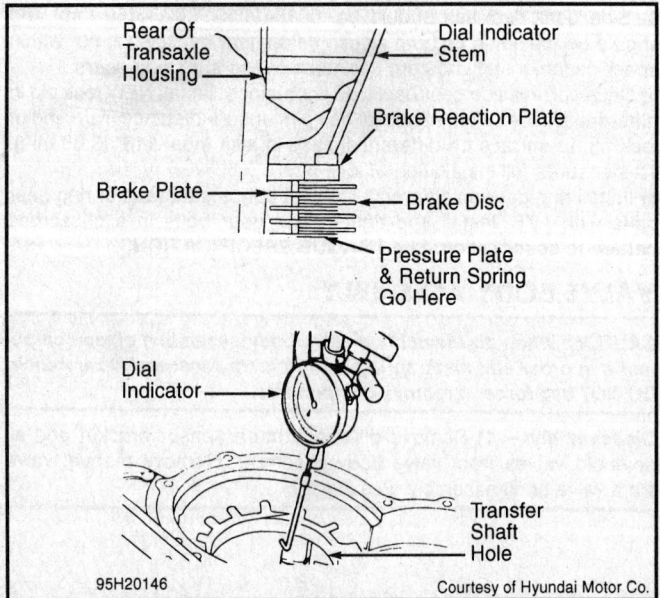

Fig. 31: Installing Low-Reverse Brake Components & Positioning Dial Indicator

Fig. 32: Applying Air Pressure For Checking Low-Reverse Brake Clearance

12) Once correct low-reverse brake clearance is obtained, remove center support, pressure plate, return spring and low-reverse brake clutch pack. Install transfer shaft with bearing in transaxle housing. Install snap ring on inside of transaxle housing, near transfer shaft.

13) Install spacer on transfer shaft. Install bearing outer race for transfer shaft in transaxle housing. Press transfer driven gear onto transfer shaft.

14) Install and tighten transfer shaft lock nut to specification. Using dial indicator, measure transfer shaft end play. Transfer shaft end play should be 0-.0023" (0-.060 mm). If transfer shaft end play is not within specification, install different thickness spacer on transfer shaft.

15) Once correct transfer shaft end play is obtained, stake transfer shaft lock nut against transfer shaft. Install transfer drive gear and rear bearing in transaxle housing.

16) Install plate on rear of transaxle housing to support transfer drive gear. *See Fig. 33.* From inside transaxle housing, using press, press output flange into transfer drive gear.

17) Install stopper plate, located on top of rear bearing. *See Fig. 16.* Apply Three Bond Sealant (1216) on transaxle housing-to-rear cover sealing surfaces. Install rear cover. Install and tighten bolts to specification.

18) Install snap ring on rear bearing. Install bearing retainer. Apply thread sealant on threads of bearing retainer screws. Install and tighten screws to specification.

19) Install thrust bearing No. 12 on rear of planetary carrier assembly. Ensure thrust bearing is installed in correct direction. *See Fig. 34.*

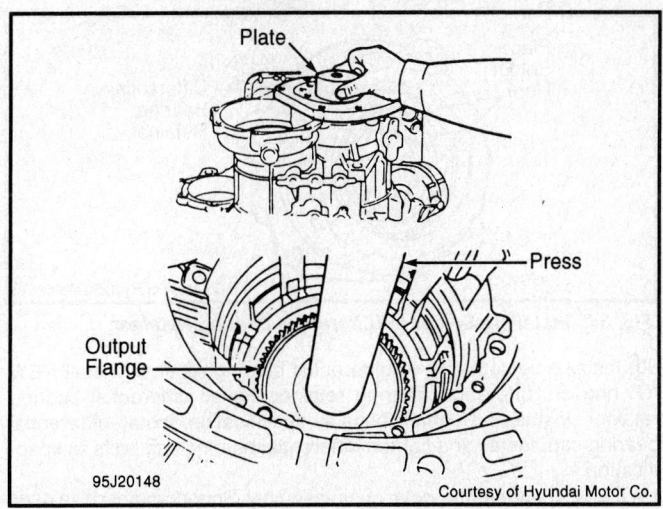

Fig. 33: Installing Output Flange On Transfer Drive Gear

20) Install planetary carrier assembly into transaxle housing. If assembling sun gear assembly, squeeze ends of seal ring together before installing on sun gear assembly. Install seal ring and snap ring on sun gear assembly.

21) Install thrust bearing No. 9 and thrust race No. 10 on reverse sun gear. *See Fig. 35.* Assemble reverse sun gear and forward sun gear.

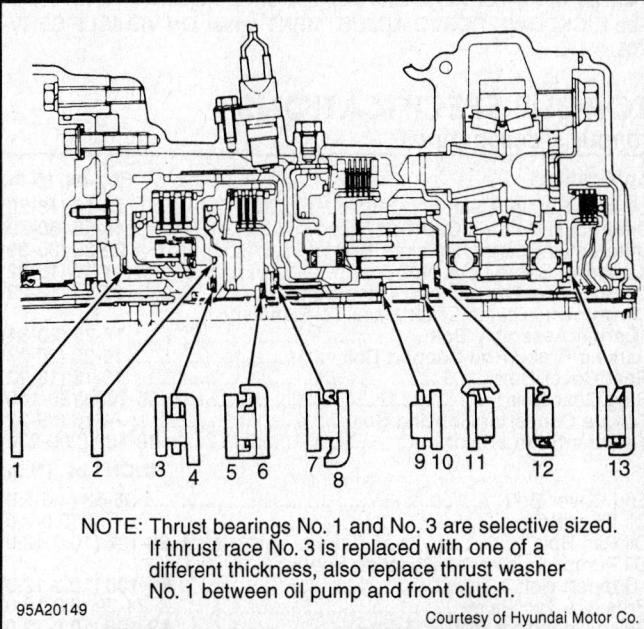

NOTE: Thrust bearings No. 1 and No. 3 are selective sized. If thrust race No. 3 is replaced with one of a different thickness, also replace thrust washer No. 1 between oil pump and front clutch.

Fig. 34: Identifying Thrust Bearing, Thrust Race & Thrust Washer Locations

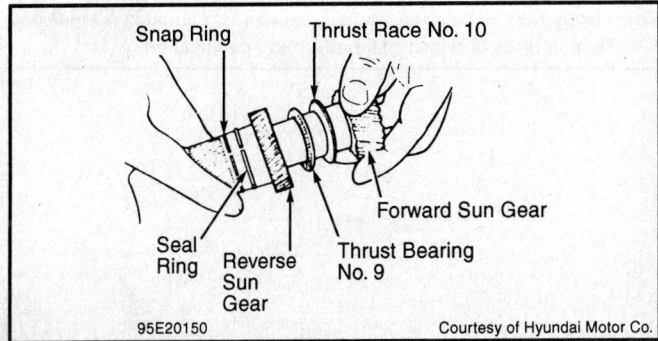

Fig. 35: Assembling Sun Gear Assembly

22) Install sun gear assembly in planetary carrier assembly. *See Fig. 15.* Install low-reverse brake clutch pack, pressure plate and return spring.

23) Apply petroleum jelly on wave spring. Install wave spring on center support. Install NEW "O" rings on center support. Coat "O" rings with ATF.

24) Install center support in transaxle housing. Ensure wave spring stays properly positioned on center support. Install snap ring that retains center support in transaxle housing so ends of snap ring align with hole in transaxle case for pulse generator "A". *See Fig. 36.*

CAUTION: Ensure ends of snap ring align with hole in transaxle case for pulse generator "A".

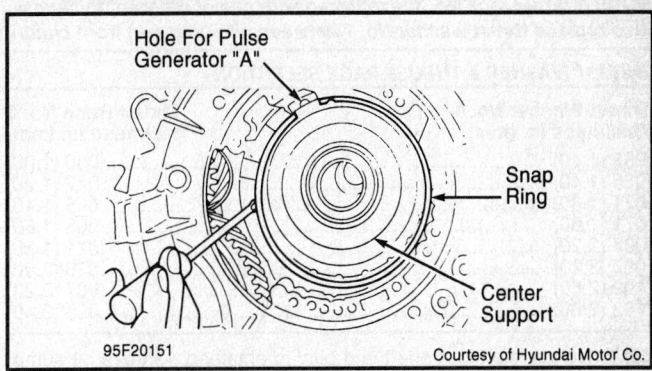

Fig. 36: Installing Snap Ring For Center Support

25) Install NEW "O" ring and NEW "D" rings on kickdown servo assembly. *See Fig. 30.* Install kickdown servo assembly with spring in transaxle housing.

26) Using spring compressor, depress kickdown servo and install snap ring. Remove spring compressor. Install end clutch shaft with long splines on the shaft toward oil pump end of transaxle housing. *See Fig. 15.*

CAUTION: Ensure long splines on end clutch shaft are toward oil pump end of transaxle housing. Short splines should be toward rear of transaxle housing.

---

27) Install thrust washer on end clutch assembly so thrust washer faces the return spring on end clutch assembly. Install end clutch hub in end clutch assembly. Ensure end clutch hub aligns with splines on clutch discs on end clutch assembly.

28) Install thrust bearing No. 13 on end clutch hub. Ensure thrust bearing is installed in correct direction. *See Fig. 34.* Install end clutch assembly.

29) Install NEW "O" ring and NEW "D" ring on end cover. Coat "O" ring and "D" rings with ATF. Ensure "O" ring and "D" ring are not twisted.

30) Align bolt holes in end cover with bolt holes in transaxle housing and install end cover. Bolt holes must be aligned before installing end cover. If end cover is rotated after installation, "O" ring or "D" ring may be damaged.

31) Install and tighten end cover bolts to specification. Install kickdown drum and kickdown band. Tighten kickdown servo adjusting screw to hold kickdown band in place. *See Fig. 10.*

32) Install thrust bearing No. 8 on center of kickdown drum. Ensure thrust bearing is installed in correct direction. *See Fig. 34.*

33) Install thrust race No. 7 on rear of clutch hub. Install clutch hub. Ensure clutch hub fully engages splines on sun gear assembly.

34) Install thrust bearing No. 6 on front of clutch hub. Install thrust washer No. 2 and thrust bearing No. 4 on shaft end at front side of rear clutch. Install rear clutch assembly on front clutch assembly. Ensure clutch assemblies are fully engaged.

35) Install front and rear clutch assemblies in transaxle housing. *See Fig. 14.* Install thrust race No. 3 (metal race) on front clutch assembly. Install thrust washer No. 1 (fiber washer) on rear of oil pump.

36) Install guide studs for oil pump alignment in transaxle case. Install NEW gasket for oil pump in transaxle housing. DO NOT install NEW "O" ring on outside of oil pump at this time.

37) Install oil pump. Ensure thrust washer No. 1 remains in place on oil pump during installation. Remove guide studs. Install and tighten oil pump-to-transaxle housing bolts to specification.

38) Using dial indicator, measure input shaft end play. Input shaft end play should be .012-.039" (.30-1.00 mm). If input shaft end play is not within specification, install different thickness thrust race No. 3. When selecting thrust race No. 3, select appropriate thrust washer No. 1 to be used with thrust race No. 3. See THRUST WASHER & THRUST RACE SELECTION table.

NOTE: If thrust race No. 3 is replaced with one of different thickness, also replace thrust washer No. 1 between oil pump and front clutch.

THRUST WASHER & THRUST RACE SELECTION

Thrust Washer No. 1 Thickness In. (mm)	Thrust Race No. 3 Thickness In. (mm)
.055 (1.40)	.039 (1.00)
.055 (1.40)	.047 (1.20)
.071 (1.80)	.055 (1.40)
.071 (1.80)	.063 (1.60)
.087 (2.20)	.071 (1.80)
.087 (2.20)	.079 (2.00)
.102 (2.60)	.087 (2.20)
.102 (2.60)	.095 (2.40)

39) Once correct input shaft end play is obtained, remove oil pump. Install NEW "O" ring on outside of oil pump. Reinstall oil pump. Tighten bolts to specifications.

40) Install NEW "O" ring on upper surface of valve body assembly, where valve body seals against transaxle housing. Install NEW "O" ring on solenoid valve electrical connector grommet where it seals against transaxle housing.

41) Install valve body assembly and solenoid valve electrical connector grommet on transaxle housing. Ensure notch on solenoid valve electrical connector grommet is toward front of transaxle housing and wiring is properly routed.

42) Install valve body assembly-to-transaxle housing bolts. Ensure proper length bolt is installed in correct location. *See Fig. 12.*

43) Tighten valve body assembly-to-transaxle housing bolts to specification. Install oil temperature sensor and oil filter. Tighten oil filter bolts to specification.

44) Ensure the 5 magnets are installed in 5 depression areas on oil pan. Using NEW gasket, install oil pan. Install and tighten oil pan bolts to specification.

45) Using NEW "D" ring, install kickdown servo switch and snap ring. *See Fig. 13.* Install transaxle range switch. For adjustment of transaxle range switch, see HYUNDAI A4AF & A4BF ELECTRONIC CONTROLS article.

46) Install pulse generators. Install and tighten pulse generator bolts to specification.

47) Install differential assembly with bearings in transaxle housing. Remove old spacer from inside of differential bearing retainer. Install 2 pieces of solder .39" (10.0 mm) long and .12" (3.0 mm) in diameter at 2 places on differential bearing retainer. *See Fig. 37.*

48) Install differential bearing retainer. Install and tighten differential bearing retainer bolts to specification. Remove bolts and differential bearing retainer. Remove solder. Using micrometer, measure thickness of solder.

49) To determine spacer thickness needed, use following formula:

Shim thickness = solder thickness + standard gasket thickness - differential end play.

"S" = "T" + .015" (.38 mm) - (Differential End Play)

Example:

Measured Solder Thickness	"T"
Standard Gasket Thickness	+ .015" (.38 mm)
Differential End Play Range	- 0-.006" (0-.15 mm)
Shim Thickness	= "S"

95G20152   Courtesy of Hyundai Motor Co.

Fig. 37: Installing Solder In Differential Bearing Retainer

50) Install selected shim in differential bearing retainer. Install NEW "O" ring on differential bearing retainer. Install differential bearing retainer. Install and tighten bolts to specification. Install differential bearing cap. Install and tighten differential bearing cap bolts to specification.

51) Install speedometer drive gear assembly. Speedometer drive gear assembly is located on transaxle housing, near differential cover.

52) Lubricate torque converter surface (where converter slides into oil pump) with ATF. Install torque converter.

53) To ensure torque converter is fully seated, measure distance from front of ring gear surface to mounting surface on torque converter housing. Distance should be approximately .472" (12.00 mm) if torque converter is fully seated.

54) If distance is incorrect, remove torque converter and check alignment of torque converter with oil pump drive. Adjust kickdown servo. See KICKDOWN SERVO ADJUSTMENT under ON-VEHICLE SERVICE.

TORQUE SPECIFICATIONS
TORQUE SPECIFICATIONS

Application	Ft. Lbs. (N.m)
Bearing Retainer Screw	13-16 (18-22)
Differential Bearing Cap Bolt	44-58 (60-79)
Differential Bearing Retainer Bolt	22-29 (30-39)
Kickdown Servo Lock Nut	11-16 (15-22)
Oil Pump-To-Transaxle Housing Bolt	13-16 (18-22)
Overrunning Clutch Outer Race-To-Planetary Carrier Assembly Bolt	17-25 (23-34)
Parking Brake Rod Support Bolt	15-20 (20-27)
Rear Cover Bolt	13-16 (18-22)
Ring Gear Bolt [1]	96-103 (130-140)
Torque Converter Housing Bolt	14-16 (19-22)
Transfer Shaft Lock Nut	148-169 (200-230)

	INCH Lbs. (N.m)
End Cover Bolt	35-53 (4.0-6.0)
Oil Filter Bolt	44-62 (5.0-7.0)
Oil Pan Bolt	89-106 (10.0-12.0)
Oil Pump Housing-To-Reaction Shaft Support Bolt	89-106 (10.0-12.0)
Pressure Tap Plug	71-89 (8.0-10.0)
Pulse Generator Bolt	89-106 (10.0-12.0)
Set Screw	71-89 (8.0-10.0)
Valve Body Assembly-To-Transaxle Housing Bolt	89-106 (10.0-12.0)
Valve Body Bolt	35-53 (4.0-6.0)

[1] – Tighten bolts in crisscross pattern to specification.

TRANSAXLE SPECIFICATIONS

TRANSAXLE SPECIFICATIONS

Application	In. (mm)
Clutch Clearances	
End Clutch	.0157-.0260 (.400-.650)
Front Clutch	.0157-.0236 (.400-.600)
Rear Clutch	.0118-.0197 (.300-.500)
Differential Side Gear Backlash	.0010-.0059 (.025-.150)
Input Shaft End Play	.012-.039 (.30-1.00)
Low-Reverse Brake Clearance	
Accent & Scoupe	.0266-.0389 (.675-.987)
Elantra	.038-.051 (.975-1.287)
Oil Pump Gear Side Clearance	.0008-.0019 (.020-.048)
Oil Pump Housing Bushing Maximum	
Inside Diameter	1.690 (43.01)
Transfer Shaft End Play	0-.0023 (0-.060)

WIRING DIAGRAMS

For appropriate wiring diagram, see HYUNDAI A4AF & A4BF ELECTRONIC CONTROLS article.

AUTOMATIC TRANSMISSIONS
Hyundai A4AF & A4BF Electronic Controls

Accent, Elantra & Scoupe

APPLICATION

APPLICATION

Vehicle	Transaxle Model
Accent	A4AF2
Elantra (1996)	A4BF1
Scoupe	A4AF

DESCRIPTION

Automatic transaxle is electronically controlled. Transaxle shifting and damper clutch lock-up (torque converter lock-up) are controlled by Transmission Control Module (TCM). The TCM receives information from input devices and transmits electrical signal to appropriate Shift Control Solenoid Valves (SCSV) and Pressure Control Solenoid Valve (PCSV), mounted on valve body assembly to control transaxle shifting. The TCM controls damper clutch (torque converter lock-up) by operating Damper Clutch Control Solenoid Valve (DCCSV), located on valve body.

An overdrive switch is mounted on driver's side of shift lever. When overdrive switch is depressed to the ON position, transaxle will automatically upshift to overdrive and O/D OFF indicator light on instrument panel will be off.

When overdrive switch is released to the OFF position, transaxle will not upshift to overdrive and O/D OFF indicator light on instrument panel will come on.

On Accent and Scoupe, a mode switch is located on passenger's side of shift lever, near console. Mode switch contains a ECON (economy) mode and NORM (normal) mode. On Elantra, mode switch contains a NORM (normal) mode and PWR (power) mode. When mode switch is depressed to the NORM mode (PWR mode on Elantra), an input signal is delivered to TCM, and TCM changes shift points to provide maximum performance. When Mode switch is released to ECON mode (NORM mode on Elantra), an input signal is delivered to TCM, and TCM changes shift points to provide maximum fuel economy.

NOTE: On Accent and Scoupe, if engine coolant temperature is less than 68°F (20°C), transaxle will remain in ECON mode (NORM mode on Elantra) even if range switch is in NORM mode (PWR mode on Elantra). When range switch is in ECON mode (NORM mode on Elantra) and vehicle speed exceeds 60 MPH, transaxle will not downshift when accelerator pedal is depressed. Range switch must be in NORM mode (PWR mode on Elantra) for transaxle to downshift.

The TCM contains self-diagnostic system, which stores fault code if failure or problem exists in transaxle electronic control system. Fault codes may be retrieved to determine transaxle problem area. Fault code may be referred to as Diagnostic Trouble Code (DTC). For information on self-diagnostic system, see SELF-DIAGNOSIS under SELF-DIAGNOSTIC SYSTEM.

Electronic control system contains a fail-safe system in the event that an electronic component should malfunction. The fail-safe system will control transaxle operation until the malfunction is repaired. If failures exists in certain electronic components for a repeated number of times, transaxle may remain in 2nd or 3rd gear. This is referred to as fail-safe mode. Park, Neutral and Reverse gears will operate in fail-safe mode, but only one forward gear will operate.

Transaxle is equipped with shift and key interlock systems. Shift interlock system prevents shift lever from being moved from Park position unless brake pedal is depressed, ignition is on and release button on side of shift lever is depressed. Key interlock system prevents ignition key from being turned to LOCK position unless shift lever is in Park position. For additional information, see SHIFT & KEY INTERLOCK SYSTEMS under OPERATION.

OPERATION

SHIFT & KEY INTERLOCK SYSTEMS

Shift and key interlock system prevents shift lever from being moved from Park position unless brake pedal is depressed, ignition is on and release button on side of shift lever is depressed. The shift and key interlock systems consists of A/T and key lock control unit, A/T shift lock solenoid, park position/key lock switch, key lock solenoid and brakelight switch.

The A/T and key lock control unit controls operation of A/T shift lock solenoid for shift lever operation. On Scoupe, A/T and key lock control unit is located behind passenger's side inner panel. On Accent, A/T and key lock control unit is located on right side of A/C blower motor assembly. On Elantra, A/T and key lock control unit is located next to TCM under left side of instrument panel. The A/T shift lock solenoid and park position/key lock switch are located on shift lever. Brakelight switch is mounted on brake pedal bracket. Key lock solenoid is located in ignition lock assembly on steering column.

The key interlock system prevents ignition key from being turned to LOCK position unless shift lever is in Park position. The A/T and key lock control unit controls operation of key lock solenoid.

TRANSMISSION CONTROL MODULE (TCM)

The TCM receives information from input devices and transmits electrical signal to appropriate Shift Control Solenoid Valves (SCSV) and Pressure Control Solenoid Valve (PCSV) to control transaxle shifting. Shift control and pressure control solenoid valves are mounted on valve body assembly. The TCM controls damper clutch (torque converter lock-up) by operating Damper Clutch Control Solenoid Valve (DCCSV), located on valve body assembly.

The TCM contains self-diagnostic system, which stores fault code if failure or problem exists in transaxle electronic control system. Fault code may be retrieved to determine transaxle problem area. Fault code may be referred to as Diagnostic Trouble Code (DTC). For information on self-diagnostic system, see SELF-DIAGNOSTIC SYSTEM. On Scoupe, the TCM is located below driver's seat. On Accent and Elantra, TCM is located under instrument panel, left of steering wheel.

TCM INPUT DEVICES

Accelerator Switch (Scoupe) – Accelerator switch is a contact-type switch, which opens when throttle is depressed and closes when throttle is released. Accelerator switch delivers input signal to TCM to indicate position of accelerator pedal. Accelerator switch is mounted above accelerator pedal. *See Fig. 1.*

Idle Switch (Accent & Elantra) – Idle switch is a contact-type switch, which opens when throttle is depressed and closes when throttle is released. Idle switch delivers input signal to TCM to indicate position of throttle valve. Idle switch is located on throttle body.

Kickdown Servo Switch – Kickdown servo switch delivers input signal to TCM to indicate kickdown servo position. Kickdown servo switch may also be referred to as kickdown switch. Kickdown servo switch is located on kickdown servo on transaxle. *See Fig. 1.*

Oil Temperature Sensor – Oil temperature sensor delivers input signal to TCM to indicate transaxle oil temperature. Oil temperature sensor is located on bottom of valve body assembly. *See Fig. 1.*

Overdrive Switch – Overdrive switch is switch is mounted on driver's side of shift lever. When overdrive switch is depressed to the ON position, transaxle will automatically upshift to overdrive and overdrive off indicator light on instrument panel will be off. When overdrive switch is released to the OFF position, transaxle will not upshift to overdrive and overdrive off indicator light on instrument panel will come on.

Pulse Generators "A" & "B" – Pulse generators "A" and "B" deliver input signals to TCM to indicate the speed of transaxle internal components. Pulse generators "A" and "B" are mounted on the transaxle. *See Fig. 1.*

Mode Switch – Mode switch is located on passenger's side of shift lever, near console. This switch may be also be referred to as Range switch or ECO/NORM mode (NORM/PWR mode on Elantra) switch in testing procedures, DO NOT confuse it with the transaxle mounted Transaxle Range Switch. On Accent and Scoupe, Mode switch contains a ECON (economy) mode and NORM (normal) mode. On Elantra, mode switch contains a NORM (normal) mode and PWR (power) mode. When Mode switch is depressed to the NORM mode (PWR mode on Elantra), an input signal is delivered to TCM, and TCM changes shift points to provide maximum performance. When Mode switch is released to ECON mode (NORM mode on Elantra), an input signal is delivered to TCM, and TCM changes shift points to provide maximum fuel economy. When engine coolant temperature is less than 68°F (20°C), transaxle will remain in ECON mode (NORM mode on Elantra) even if range switch is in NORM mode (PWR mode on Elantra).

Throttle Position Sensor (TPS) – Throttle position sensor delivers an input signal to TCM to indicate throttle position. Throttle position sensor is mounted on side of throttle body.

Transaxle Range Switch – When shift lever is moved, shift cable moves the manual control lever which operates the transaxle range switch. Transaxle range switch delivers an input signal to TCM to indicate shift lever position. The TCM uses input signal and operates shift control solenoid valves to control transaxle shifting. Transaxle range switch is mounted on transaxle. See Fig. 1. Transaxle range switch may also be referred to as inhibitor switch.

Vehicle Speed Sensor (VSS) – Vehicle speed sensor delivers an input signal to TCM to indicate the vehicle speed. Vehicle speed sensor is located on rear of speedometer on instrument panel gauge assembly. See Fig. 1. Vehicle speed sensor may also be referred to as vehicle speed reed switch.

TCM OUTPUT DEVICES

Damper Clutch Control Solenoid Valve (DCCSV) – The TCM controls damper clutch (torque converter lock-up) operation by delivering an output signal to damper clutch control solenoid valve. Damper clutch control solenoid valve is operated in accordance with gear position. See DAMPER CLUTCH CONTROL SOLENOID VALVE OPERATION table. The damper clutch control solenoid valve is located on valve body assembly. See Fig. 2.

DAMPER CLUTCH CONTROL SOLENOID VALVE OPERATION

Gear Position	Solenoid Operation
Park & Neutral	Off
Reverse	Off
1st Gear	Off
2nd Gear	On
3rd Gear	On
4th Gear	On
During Lock-Up	Off

Pressure Control Solenoid Valve (PCSV) – The TCM controls transaxle shifting by delivering an output signal to pressure control solenoid valve. Pressure control solenoid valve may also be referred to as oil pressure control solenoid valve. Pressure control solenoid valve is operated in accordance with gear position. See PRESSURE CONTROL SOLENOID VALVE OPERATION table. Pressure control solenoid valve is mounted on valve body assembly. See Fig. 2.

PRESSURE CONTROL SOLENOID VALVE OPERATION

Gear Position	Solenoid Operation
Park & Neutral	Off
Reverse	Off
1st Gear	On
2nd Gear	Off
3rd Gear	Off
4th Gear	Off
During Lock-Up	On

Shift Control Solenoid Valve (SCSV) – The TCM controls transaxle shifting by delivering an output signal to shift control solenoid valves "A" and "B". Shift control solenoid valves are operated in accordance with gear position. See SHIFT CONTROL SOLENOID VALVE OPERATION table. Shift control solenoid valves are located on valve body assembly. See Fig. 2.

SHIFT CONTROL SOLENOID VALVE OPERATION

Gear Position	SCSV "A"	SCSV "B"
Park & Neutral	Off	Off
Reverse	Off	Off
1st Gear	On	On
2nd Gear	Off	On
3rd Gear	Off	Off
4th Gear	On	Off
During Lock-Up	On	On

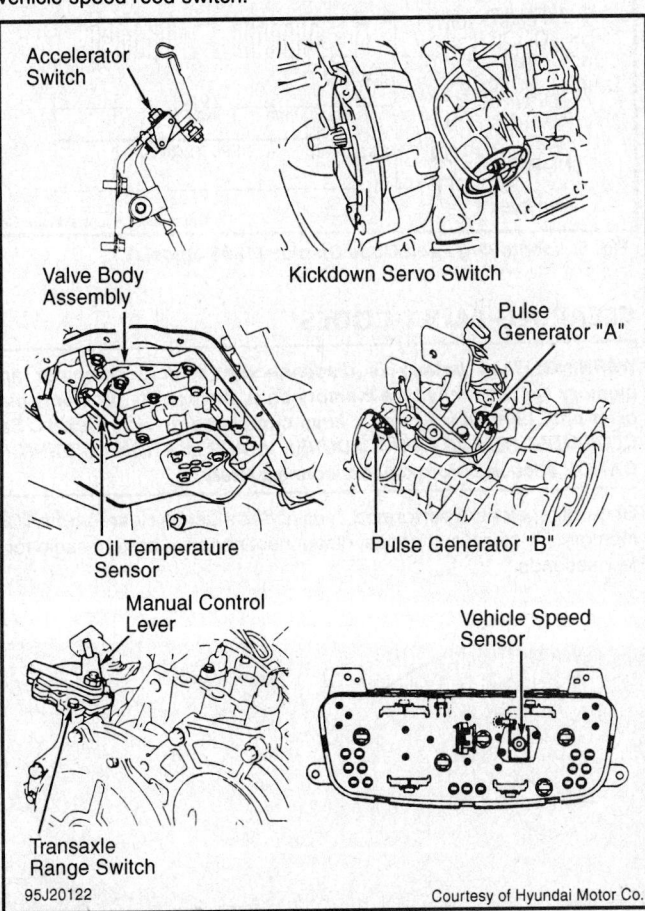

Fig. 1: Identifying TCM Input Device Locations

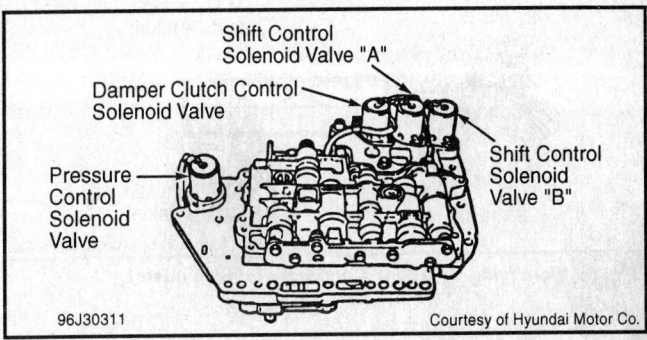

Fig. 2: Identifying Control Solenoid Valves & Wire Colors

SELF-DIAGNOSTIC SYSTEM

SYSTEM DIAGNOSIS

The TCM contains self-diagnostic system, which stores fault code in TCM memory if failure or problem exists in transaxle electronic control system. Fault code may be referred to as Diagnostic Trouble Code (DTC). Fault code can be retrieved for diagnosing transaxle electronic control system. See RETRIEVING FAULT CODES.

RETRIEVING FAULT CODES

NOTE: Fault codes may be retrieved using scan tester or voltmeter.

1) On Accent and Elantra, data link connector is located on lower left instrument panel. On Scoupe, data link connector is located on top of drivers kick panel fuse block. Identify data link connector terminals. *See Fig. 3 or 4.*

2) If using scan tester, connect scan tester to data link connector and cigarette lighter. If using voltmeter, connect voltmeter between ground terminal and diagnostic output terminal on data link connector. On 1996 models, data link connector terminal No. 15 must be grounded to retrieve diagnostic codes.

3) Turn ignition on. If using scan tester, note fault code displays on scan tester using scan tester manufacturer's instructions.

4) If using voltmeter, note fluctuations of voltmeter needle to indicate the fault code. Fault codes will be displayed by short and long fluctuations of voltmeter. The first fluctuation indicates first digit of fault code. Following fluctuations indicate second digit of fault code. *See Fig. 5 or 6.*

5) Record fault codes in the order they are displayed. If transaxle is not in fail-safe mode and does not remain in 2nd or 3rd gear, a maximum of 10 fault codes may be stored in the TCM memory. The same fault code may be stored only one time.

6) If number of stored fault codes exceeds the maximum of 10 fault codes, previously stored fault codes will be erased beginning with the oldest fault code.

7) If transaxle is in fail-safe mode and remains in 2nd or 3rd gear, a special fail-safe fault code will be stored in the TCM memory. Only 3 fail-safe mode fault codes may be stored in the TCM memory at one time.

8) When transaxle is in fail-safe mode and remains in 2nd or 3rd gear, fail safe-mode fault codes will be cancelled when ignition is turned off. Transaxle will no longer remain in 2nd or 3rd gear, but fail-safe mode fault code will be stored in the TCM memory.

9) To identify fault code and items to be checked or adjusted, see appropriate FAULT CODE IDENTIFICATION table. To check electrical system components, see ELECTRONIC SYSTEM COMPONENTS under ELECTRONIC TROUBLE SHOOTING.

10) Once all repairs are performed, ensure fault codes are cleared from the TCM memory. See CLEARING FAULT CODES under SELF-DIAGNOSTIC SYSTEM

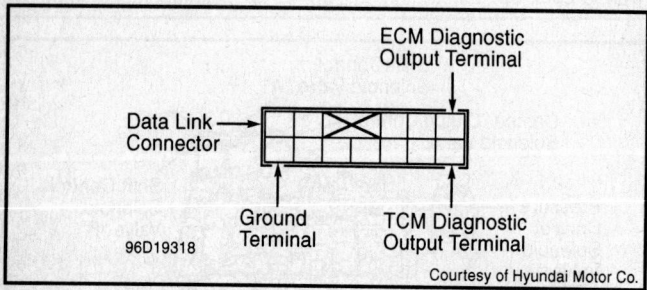

Fig. 3: Identifying Data Link Connector (1995 Models)

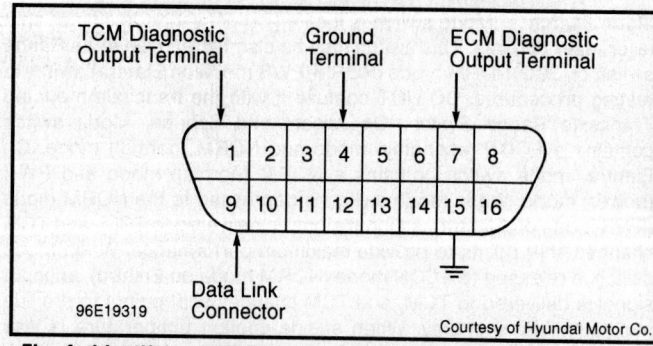

Fig. 4: Identifying Data Link Connector (1996 Models)

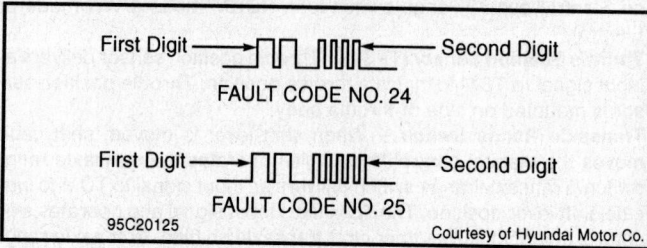

Fig. 5: Identifying Fault Code Display (1995 Models)

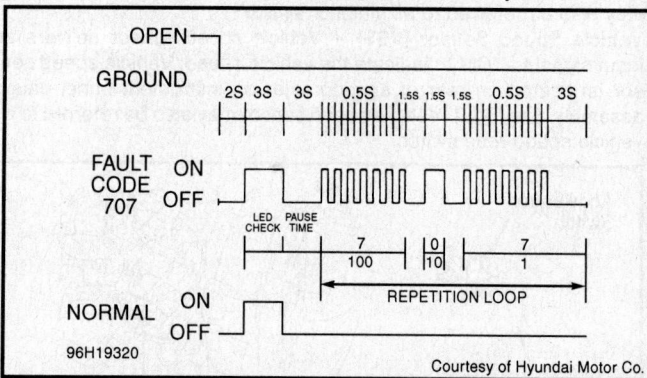

Fig. 6: Identifying Fault Code Display (1996 Models)

CLEARING FAULT CODES

WARNING: When battery is disconnected, vehicle computer and memory systems may lose memory data. Driveability problems may exist until computer systems have completed a relearn cycle. See COMPUTER RELEARN PROCEDURES in APPLICATIONS & IDENTIFICATION section before disconnecting battery.

Once all repairs are performed, fault codes must be cleared from TCM memory. To clear fault codes, disconnect negative battery cable for a few seconds.

FAULT CODE IDENTIFICATION (1995 MODELS)

Fault Code Number	Probable Cause	Fail-Safe Mode	[1] Items To Check Or Replace
11	High TPS Output	No	Check TPS Operation, Adjustment & Wiring Circuit, Check Accelerator Switch, Check For Fault Code No. 24
12	Low TPS Output	No	Check TPS Operation, Adjustment & Wiring Circuit, Check Accelerator Switch, Check For Fault Code No. 24
13	Defective TPS	No	Check TPS Operation, Adjustment & Wiring Circuit
14	Improperly Adjusted TPS	No	Check TPS Adjustment
15	Open Oil Temperature Sensor Circuit (Low Temperature Side)	No	Check Oil Temperature Sensor & Wiring Circuit
16	Shorted Oil Temperature Sensor Circuit (High Temperature Side)	No	Check Oil Temperature Sensor & Wiring Circuit
17	Oil Temperature Sensor Open Circuit (High Temperature Side) Or Shorted Circuit (Low Temperature Side)	No	Check Oil Temperature Sensor & Wiring Circuit
21	Open Kickdown Servo Switch Circuit	No	Check Kickdown Servo Switch & Wiring Circuit
22	Shorted Kickdown Servo Switch Circuit	No	Check Kickdown Servo Switch & Wiring Circuit
23	Ignition Pulse Signal Circuit	No	Check For Open Circuit To Pin No. 9 (White Wire) On 14-Pin Connector At TCM
24	Improperly Adjusted Accelerator Switch Or Open Wiring Circuit	No	Check Accelerator Switch Adjustment & Wiring Circuit
31	Pulse Generator "A" Circuit	No	Check Pulse Generator "A" & Wiring Circuit, Check Vehicle Speed Sensor
32	Pulse Generator "B" Circuit	No	Check Pulse Generator "B" & Wiring Circuit, Check Vehicle Speed Sensor
41	Open Shift Control Solenoid Valve "A" Circuit	No	Check Shift Control Solenoid Valve "A" & Wiring Circuit
42	Shorted Shift Control Solenoid Valve "A" Circuit	No	Check Shift Control Solenoid Valve "A" & Wiring Circuit
43	Open Shift Control Solenoid Valve "B" Circuit	No	Check Shift Control Solenoid Valve "B" & Wiring Circuit
44	Shorted Shift Control Solenoid Valve "B" Circuit	No	Check Shift Control Solenoid Valve "B" & Wiring Circuit
45	Open Pressure Control Solenoid Valve Circuit	No	Check Pressure Control Solenoid Valve & Wiring Circuit
46	Shorted Pressure Control Solenoid Valve Circuit	No	Check Pressure Control Solenoid Valve & Wiring Circuit
47	Open Damper Clutch Control Solenoid Valve Circuit	No	Check Damper Clutch Control Solenoid Valve & Wiring Circuit
48	Shorted Damper Clutch Control Solenoid Valve Circuit	No	Check Damper Clutch Control Solenoid Valve & Wiring Circuit
49	Defective Damper Clutch Control System	No	Check Damper Clutch Hydraulic Circuit, Check Damper Clutch Control Solenoid Valve, Defective TCM
51	Incorrect 1st Gear Shift [3]	No	Check Pulse Generators "A", "B" & Wiring Circuits, Rear Clutch Or Low-Reverse Brake Slipping
52	Incorrect 2nd Gear Shift [3]	No	Check Pulse Generator "A" & Wiring Circuit, Rear Clutch Or Kickdown Brake Slipping
53	Incorrect 3rd Gear Shift [3]	No	Check Pulse Generators "A", "B" & Wiring Circuits, Front, End Or Rear Clutch Slipping
54	Incorrect 4th Gear Shift [3]	No	Check Pulse Generator "A" & Wiring Circuit, End Clutch Or Kickdown Brake Slipping
81	Open Pulse Generator "A" Circuit	Yes	Check Pulse Generator "A" & Wiring Circuit, Check Vehicle Speed Sensor
82	Open Pulse Generator "B" Circuit	Yes	Check Pulse Generator "B" & Wiring Circuit, Check Vehicle Speed Sensor
83	Open Or Shorted Shift Control Solenoid Valve "A" Circuit	Yes	Check Shift Control Solenoid Valve "A" & Wiring Circuit
84	Open Or Shorted Shift Control Solenoid Valve "B" Circuit	Yes	Check Shift Control Solenoid Valve "B" & Wiring Circuit
85	Open Or Shorted Pressure Control Solenoid Valve	Yes	Check Pressure Control Solenoid Valve & Wiring Circuit
86	Transaxle Shifting Non-Synchronous	Yes	[2]

[1] – To check items listed, see ELECTRONIC TROUBLE SHOOTING or ELECTRONIC SYSTEM COMPONENT TESTING. For adjustment of components, see ADJUSTMENTS.

[2] – See Fault Codes No. 51, 52, 53 Or 54 for items to be checked in relation to improper gear operation.

[3] – Shift speed does not correspond to engine speed.

FAULT CODE IDENTIFICATION (1996 MODELS)

Fault Code Number	Probable Cause	Fail-Safe Mode	[1] Items To Check Or Replace
1701	Open In TPS Circuit	No	Check TPS Operation, Adjustment, Wiring Circuit & Idle Switch
1702	Short In TPS Circuit	No	Check TPS Operation, Adjustment, Wiring Circuit & Idle Switch
1704	Defective TPS	No	Check TPS Operation, Adjustment & Wiring Circuit
1709	Open Or Shorted Kickdown	No	Check Kickdown Servo Switch & Wiring Circuit
1714	Improperly Adjusted Idle Switch	No	Check Idle Switch Adjustment, Wiring Circuit & Idle Switch
0707	No Input Signal To TCM	No	Check Transaxle Range Switch & Wiring Circuit
0708	Too Many Input Signals To TCM	No	Check Transaxle Range Switch & Wiring Circuit
0712	Open Oil Temperature Sensor Circuit (Low Temperature Side)	No	Check Oil Temperature Sensor & Wiring Circuit
0713	Shorted Oil Temperature Sensor Circuit (High Temperature Side) Servo Switch Circuit	No	Check Oil Temperature Sensor & Wiring Circuit
0717	Pulse Generator "A" Circuit	Yes	Check Pulse Generator "A" & Wiring Circuit, Check Vehicle Speed Sensor
0722	Pulse Generator "B" Circuit	Yes	Check Pulse Generator "B" & Wiring Circuit, Check Vehicle Speed Sensor
0727	Open Ignition Pulse Signal Circuit	No	Check For Open Ignition Pulse Signal Circuit
0731	Incorrect 1st Gear Shift [2]	Yes	Check Pulse Generators "A", "B" & Wiring Circuits, Rear Clutch Or Low-Reverse Brake Slipping
0732	Incorrect 2nd Gear Shift [2]	Yes	Check Pulse Generator "A" & Wiring Circuit, Rear Clutch Or Kickdown Brake Slipping
0733	Incorrect 3rd Gear Shift [2]	Yes	Check Pulse Generators "A", "B" & Wiring Circuits, Front, End Or Rear Clutch Slipping
0734	Incorrect 4th Gear Shift [2]	Yes	Check Pulse Generator "A" & Wiring Circuit, End Clutch Or Kickdown Brake Slipping
0740	Defective Damper Clutch Control System	No	Check Damper Clutch Hydraulic Circuit, Check Damper Clutch Control Solenoid Valve, Defective TCM
0742	Shorted Damper Clutch Control Solenoid Valve Circuit	No	Check Damper Clutch Control Solenoid Valve & Wiring Circuit
0743	Open Damper Clutch Control Solenoid Valve Circuit	No	Check Damper Clutch Control Solenoid Valve & Wiring Circuit
0747	Open Pressure Control Solenoid Valve Circuit	Yes	Check Pressure Control Solenoid Valve & Wiring Circuit
0748	Shorted Pressure Control Solenoid Valve Circuit	Yes	Check Pressure Control Solenoid Valve & Wiring Circuit
0752	Open Shift Control Solenoid Valve "A" Circuit	Yes	Check Shift Control Solenoid Valve "A" & Wiring Circuit
0753	Shorted Shift Control Solenoid Valve "A" Circuit	Yes	Check Shift Control Solenoid Valve "A" & Wiring Circuit
0757	Open Shift Control Solenoid Valve "B" Circuit	Yes	Check Shift Control Solenoid Valve "B" & Wiring Circuit
0758	Shorted Shift Control Solenoid Valve "B" Circuit	Yes	Check Shift Control Solenoid Valve "B" & Wiring Circuit

[1] – To check items listed, see ELECTRONIC TROUBLE SHOOTING or ELECTRONIC SYSTEM COMPONENT TESTING. For adjustment of components, see ADJUSTMENTS.

[2] – Shift speed does not correspond to engine speed.

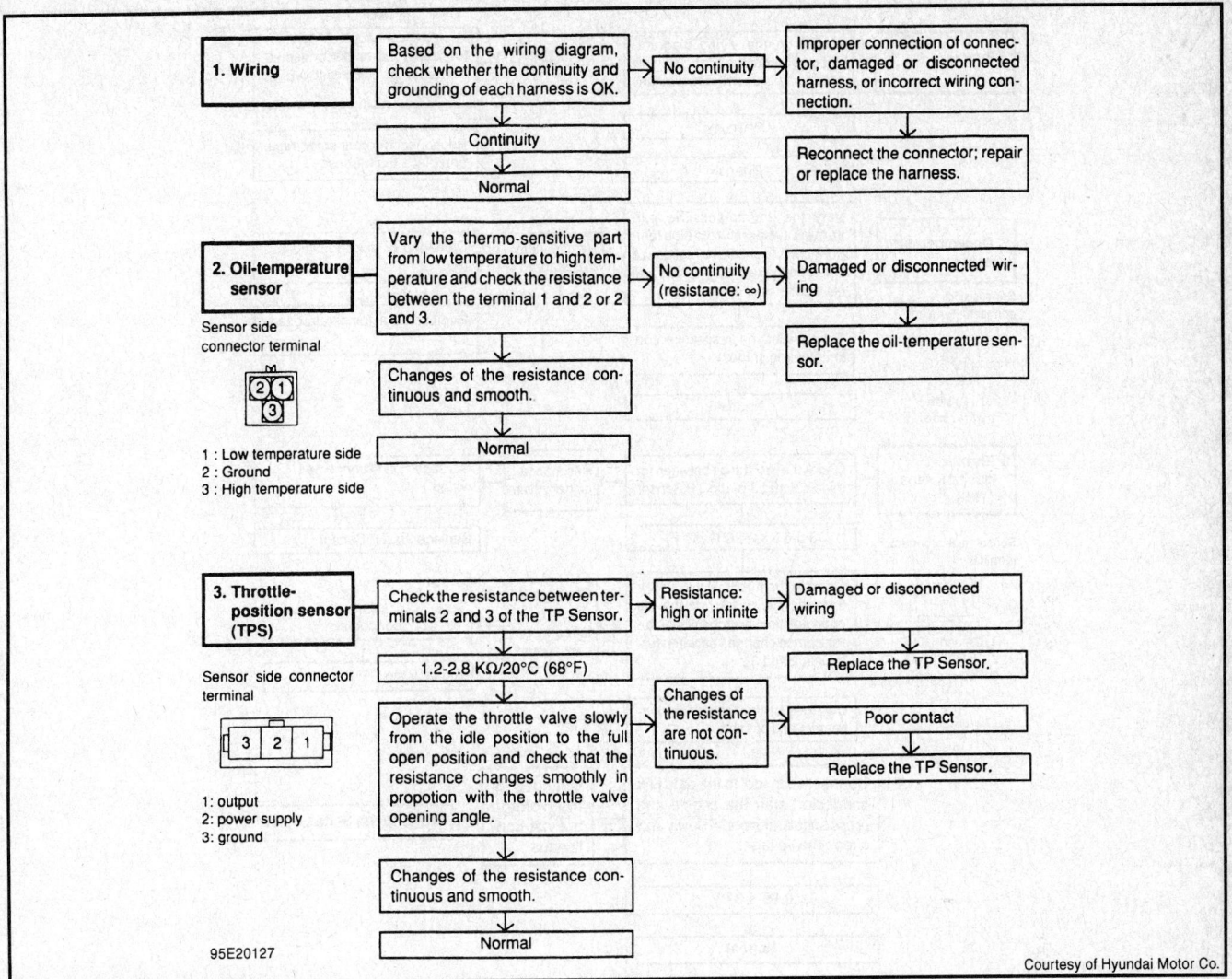

Fig. 7: Electronic Trouble Shooting

ELECTRONIC TROUBLE SHOOTING

ELECTRONIC SYSTEM COMPONENTS

Different electronic system components may be checked when performing electronic trouble shooting. *See Figs. 7-15*. For component, figure and step reference, see COMPONENT TESTING & FIGURE REFERENCE table.

COMPONENT TESTING & FIGURE REFERENCE

Component	Figure	Step
Accelerator Switch	12	10
Damper Clutch Control		
Solenoid Valve	10	9
Damper Clutch System	10	8
Idle Switch	11	10
Kickdown Servo Switch	12	12
Oil Temperature Sensor		
Accent & Elantra	8	2
Scoupe	7	2
Pressure Control Solenoid Valve	9	6
Pulse Generator Resistance	9	4
Pulse Generator		
(With Oscilloscope)	9	5
Shift Control Solenoid Valves	10	7
TCM	15	13
Throttle Position Sensor		
Accent & Elantra	8	3
Scoupe	7	3
Transaxle Range Switch		
Elantra	14	11
Accent & Scoupe	13	11

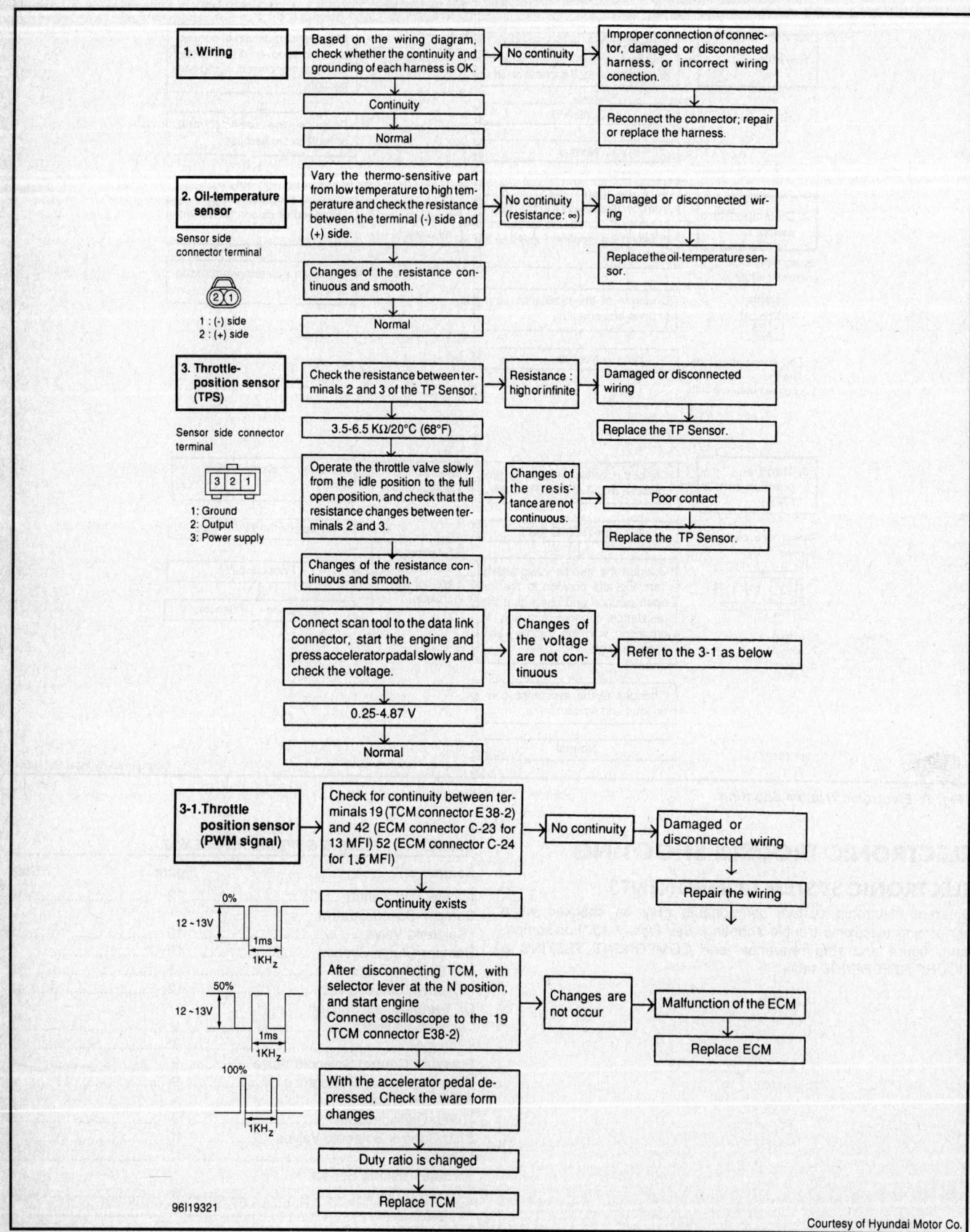

Fig. 8: Electronic Trouble Shooting

Courtesy of Hyundai Motor Co.

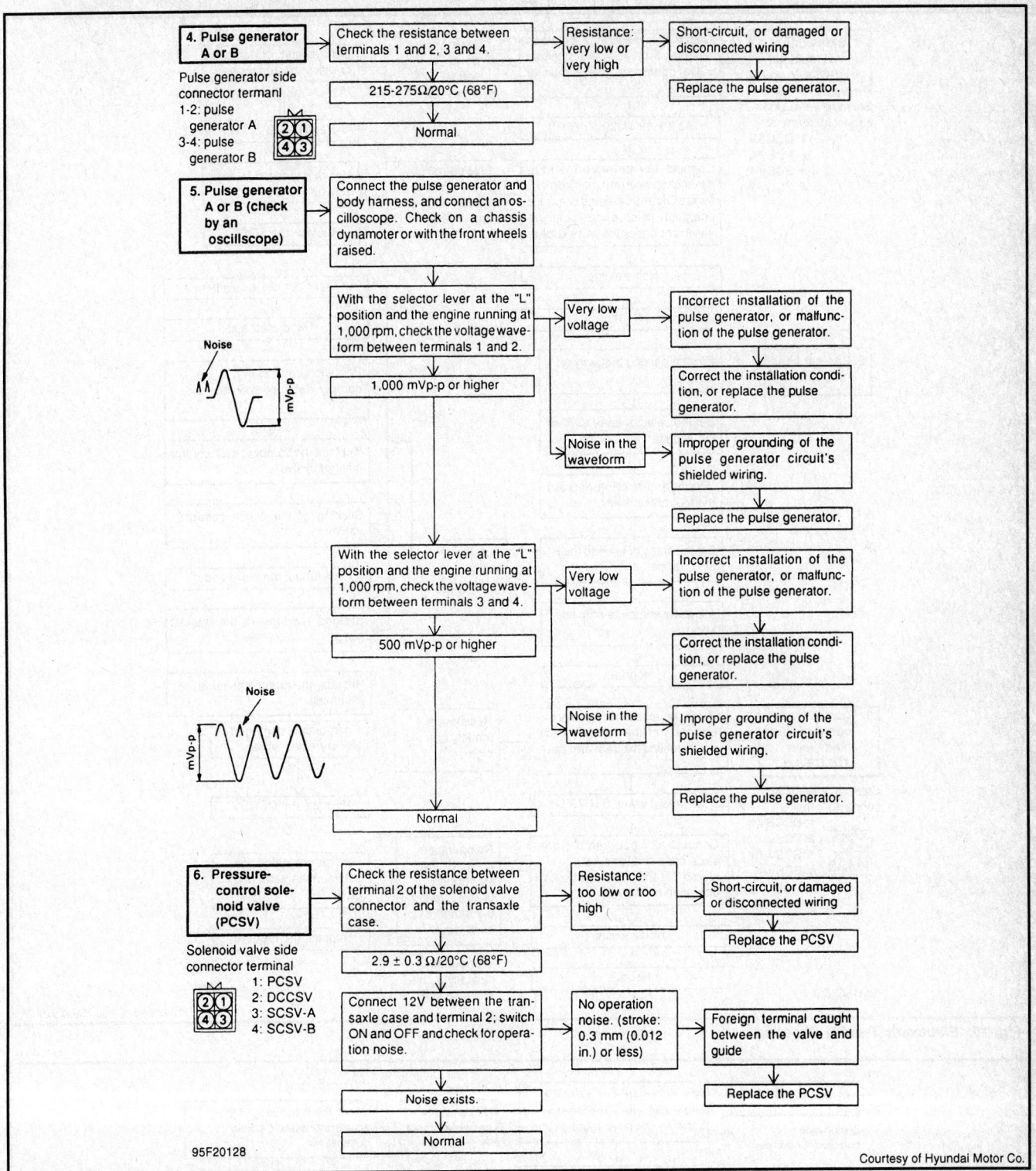

Fig. 9: Electronic Trouble Shooting

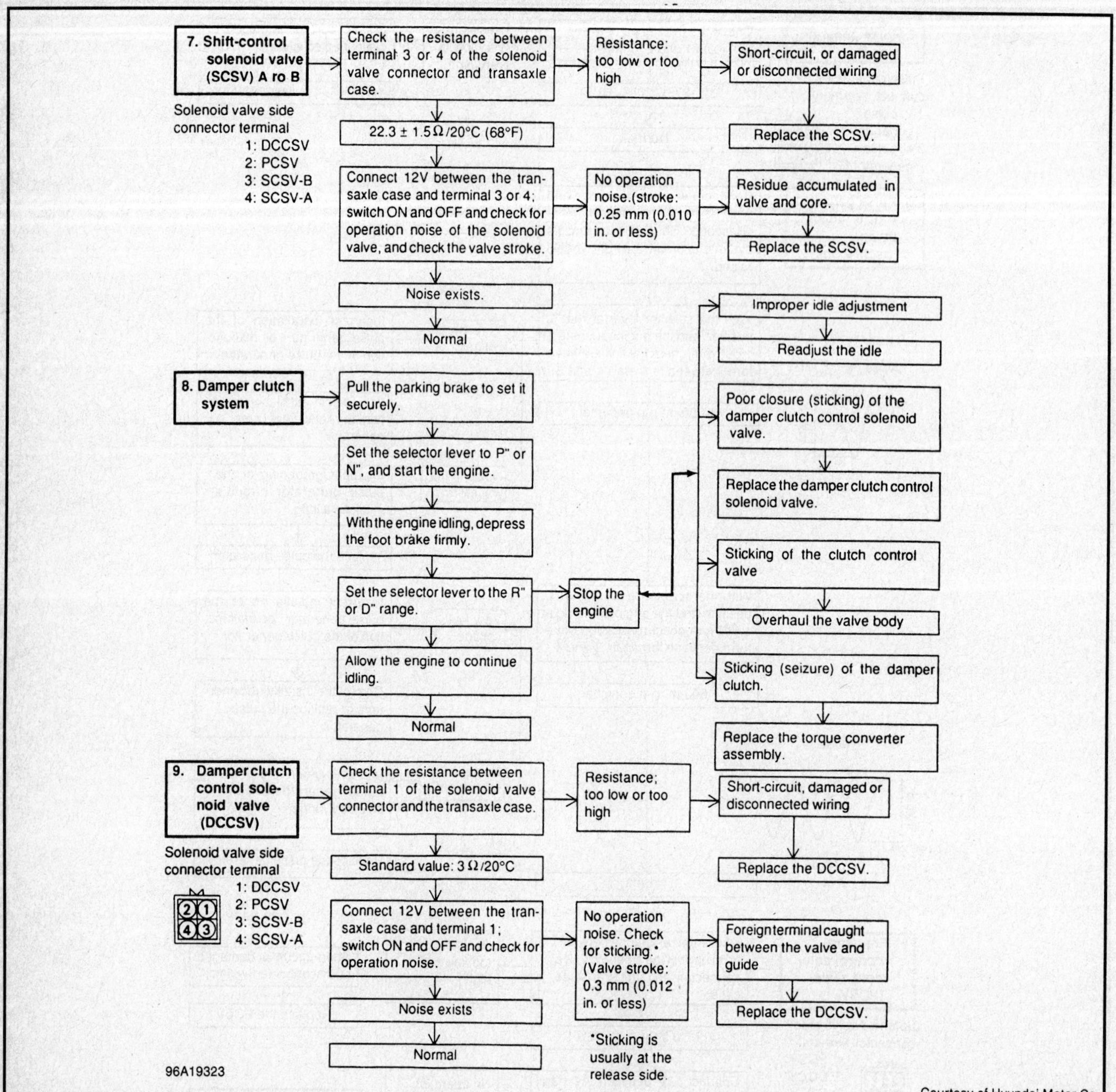

7. Shift-control solenoid valve (SCSV) A ro B

Solenoid valve side connector terminal
1: DCCSV
2: PCSV
3: SCSV-B
4: SCSV-A

Check the resistance between terminal 3 or 4 of the solenoid valve connector and transaxle case. → Resistance: too low or too high → Short-circuit, or damaged or disconnected wiring → Replace the SCSV.

22.3 ± 1.5 Ω /20°C (68°F)

Connect 12V between the transaxle case and terminal 3 or 4; switch ON and OFF and check for operation noise of the solenoid valve, and check the valve stroke. → No operation noise.(stroke: 0.25 mm (0.010 in. or less) → Residue accumulated in valve and core. → Replace the SCSV.

Noise exists.

Normal

8. Damper clutch system

Pull the parking brake to set it securely.

Set the selector lever to P" or N", and start the engine.

With the engine idling, depress the foot brake firmly.

Set the selector lever to the R" or D" range. → Stop the engine

Allow the engine to continue idling.

Normal

Improper idle adjustment → Readjust the idle

Poor closure (sticking) of the damper clutch control solenoid valve. → Replace the damper clutch control solenoid valve.

Sticking of the clutch control valve → Overhaul the valve body

Sticking (seizure) of the damper clutch. → Replace the torque converter assembly.

9. Damper clutch control solenoid valve (DCCSV)

Solenoid valve side connector terminal
1: DCCSV
2: PCSV
3: SCSV-B
4: SCSV-A

Check the resistance between terminal 1 of the solenoid valve connector and the transaxle case. → Resistance; too low or too high → Short-circuit, damaged or disconnected wiring → Replace the DCCSV.

Standard value: 3 Ω/20°C

Connect 12V between the transaxle case and terminal 1; switch ON and OFF and check for operation noise. → No operation noise. Check for sticking.* (Valve stroke: 0.3 mm (0.012 in. or less) → Foreign terminal caught between the valve and guide → Replace the DCCSV.

Noise exists

Normal

*Sticking is usually at the release side.

96A19323

Courtesy of Hyundai Motor Co.

Fig. 10: Electronic Trouble Shooting

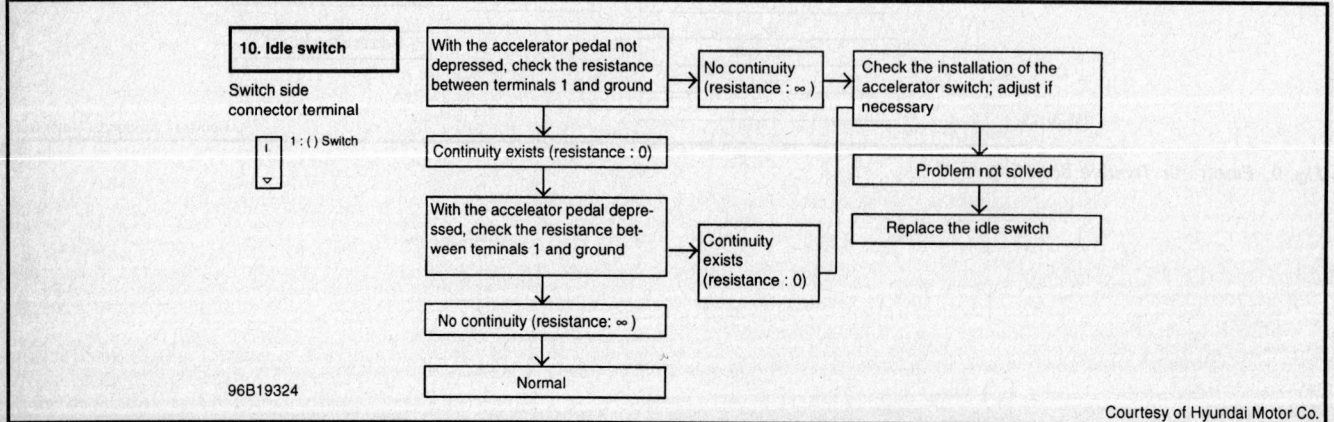

10. Idle switch

Switch side connector terminal
1: ( ) Switch

With the accelerator pedal not depressed, check the resistance between terminals 1 and ground → No continuity (resistance : ∞) → Check the installation of the accelerator switch; adjust if necessary

Continuity exists (resistance : 0)

With the acceleator pedal depressed, check the resistance between terminals 1 and ground → Continuity exists (resistance : 0)

No continuity (resistance: ∞)

Normal

Problem not solved → Replace the idle switch

96B19324

Courtesy of Hyundai Motor Co.

Fig. 11: Electronic Trouble Shooting

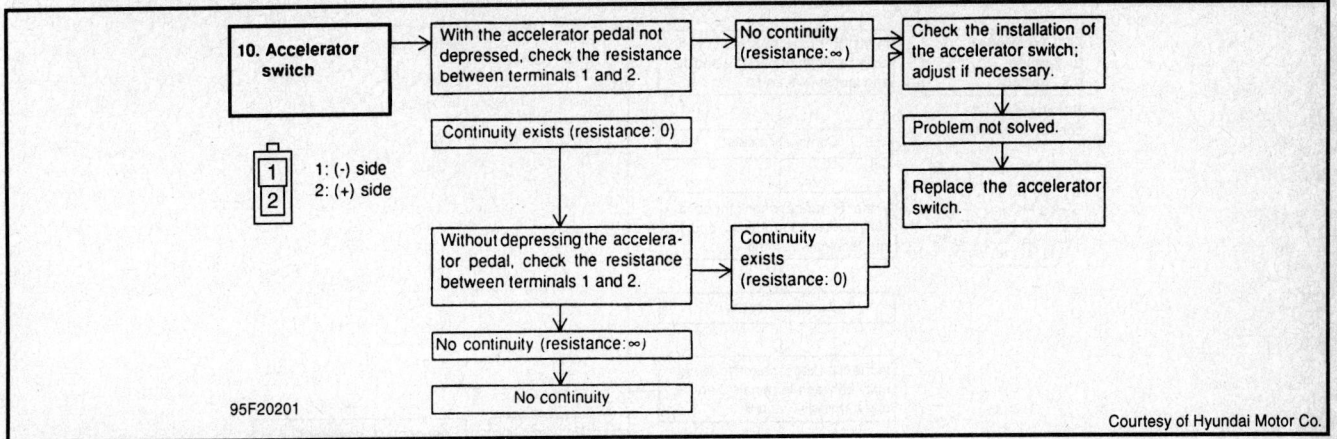

Fig. 12: Electronic Trouble Shooting

---

11. Transaxle range switch

Switch side connector terminal

```
6 5 4 3 2 1
12 11 10 9 8 7
```

In the "P" range, check for continuity between terminals 3 and 4, and terminals 10 and 11.
↓
Continuity exists
↓
In the "R" range, check for continuity between terminals 3 and 12, and terminals 9 and 8.
↓
Continuity exists
↓
In the "N" range, check for continuity between terminals 3 and 5, and terminals 10 and 11.
↓
Continuity exists
↓
In the "D" range, check for condinuity between terminals 3 and 1.
↓
Continuity exists
↓
In the "2" range, check for continuity between terminals 3 and 6.
↓
Continuity exists
↓
In the "L" range, check for continuity between terminals 3 and 2.
↓
Continuity exists
↓
Normal

No continuity
↓
Poor contact, damaged or disconnected wiring.
↓
Replace the transaxle range switch

95A20131

Courtesy of Hyundai Motor Co.

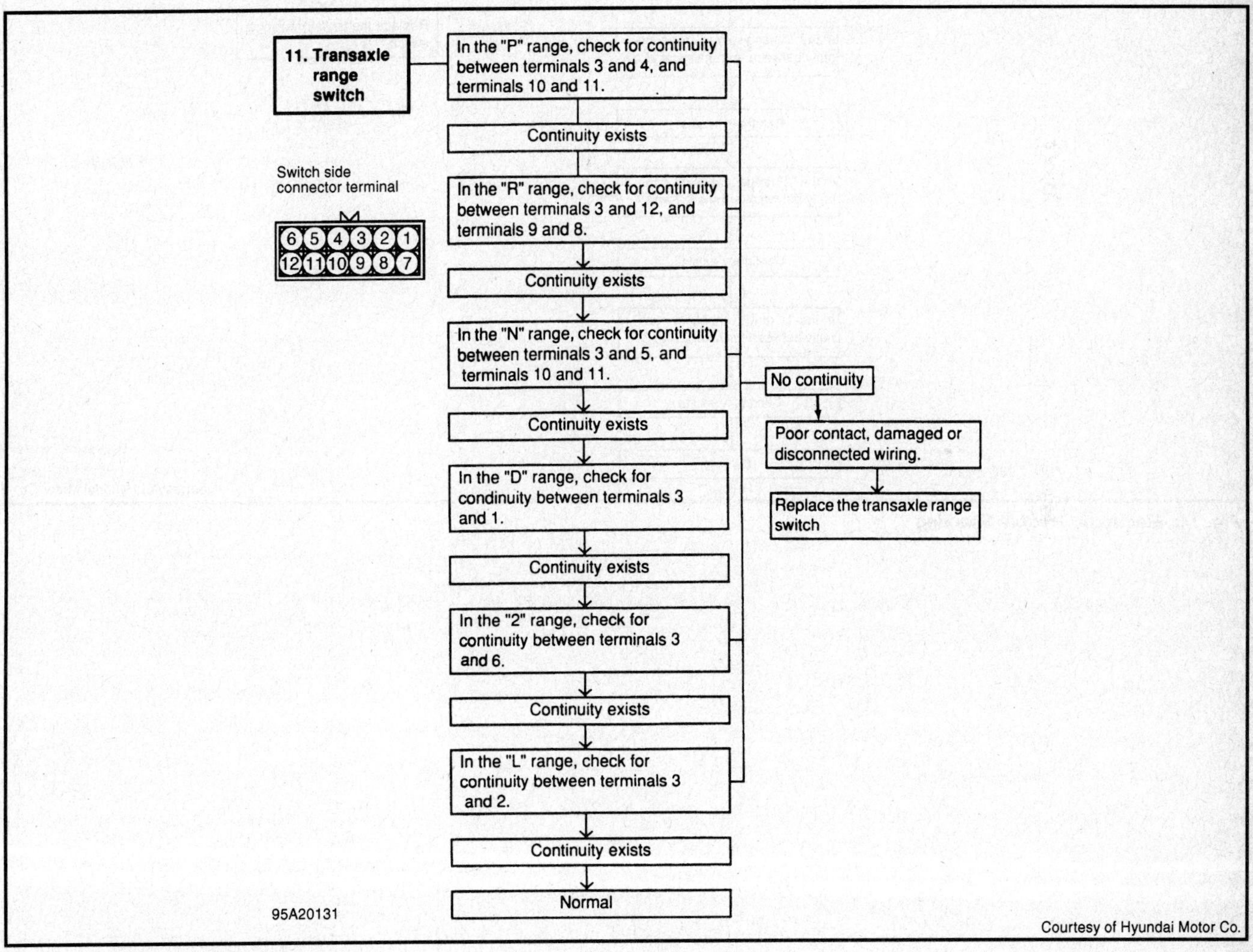

Fig. 13: Electronic Trouble Shooting

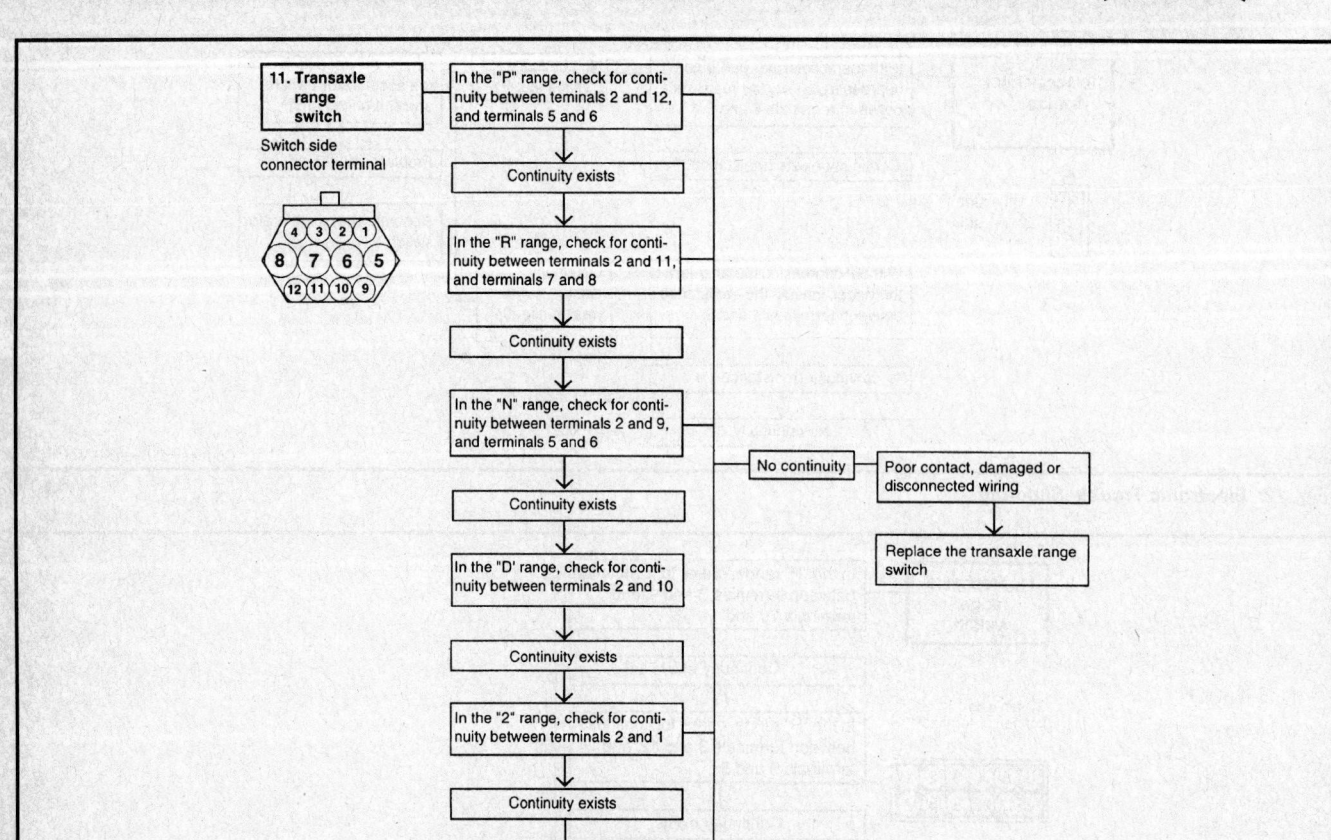

96C19325   Courtesy of Hyundai Motor Co.

Fig. 14: Electronic Trouble Shooting

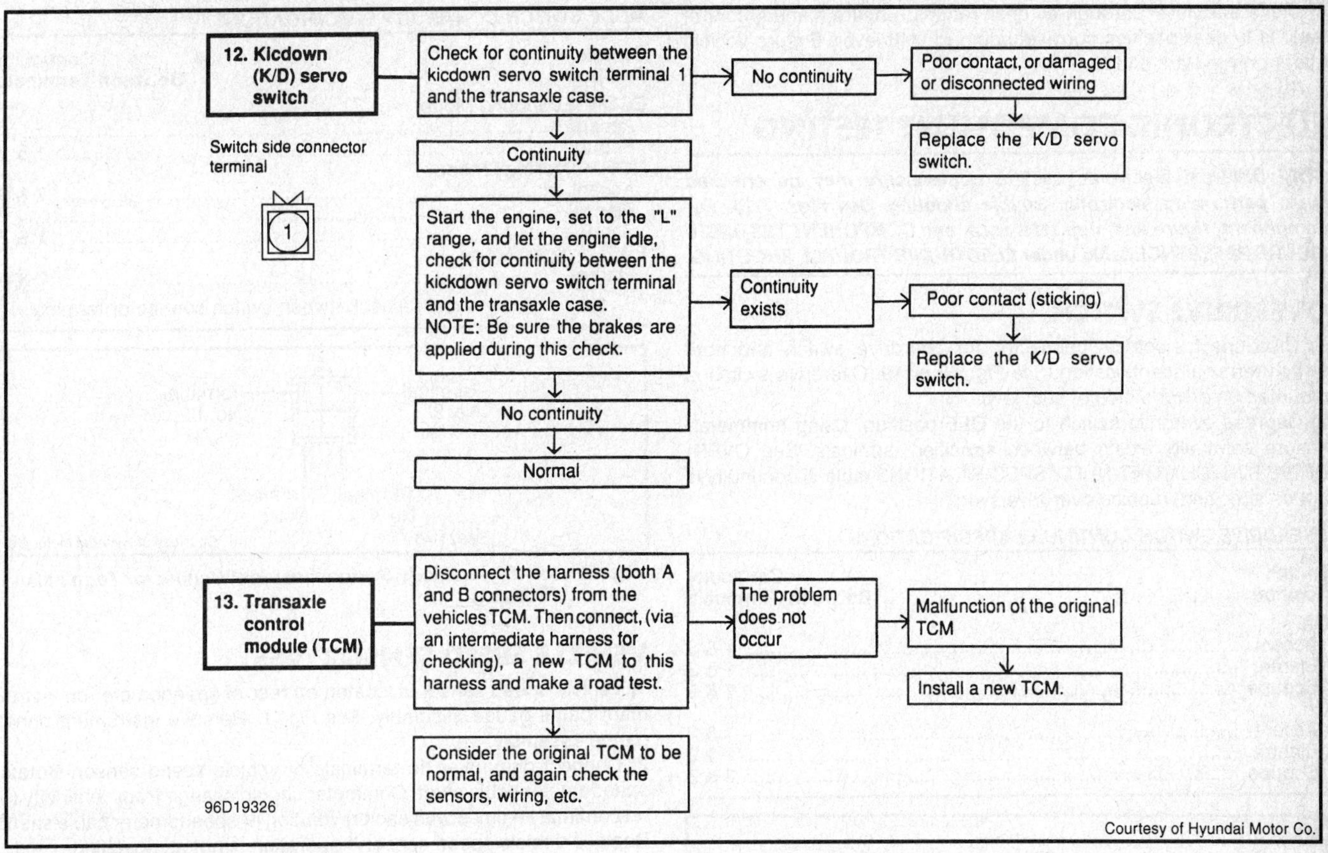

12. Kicdown (K/D) servo switch
Check for continuity between the kicdown servo switch terminal 1 and the transaxle case.
No continuity
Poor contact, or damaged or disconnected wiring
Replace the K/D servo switch.
Switch side connector terminal
1
Continuity
Start the engine, set to the "L" range, and let the engine idle, check for continuity between the kickdown servo switch terminal and the transaxle case. NOTE: Be sure the brakes are applied during this check.
Continuity exists
Poor contact (sticking)
Replace the K/D servo switch.
No continuity
Normal
13. Transaxle control module (TCM)
Disconnect the harness (both A and B connectors) from the vehicles TCM. Then connect, (via an intermediate harness for checking), a new TCM to this harness and make a road test.
The problem does not occur
Malfunction of the original TCM
Install a new TCM.
Consider the original TCM to be normal, and again check the sensors, wiring, etc.
96D19326
Courtesy of Hyundai Motor Co.

Fig. 15: Electronic Trouble Shooting

ADJUSTMENTS

ACCELERATOR SWITCH

1) Warm engine to normal operating temperature. Using voltmeter, measure voltage at Green wire on electrical connector on accelerator switch with accelerator pedal in idle (ON) position. Accelerator switch is mounted above accelerator pedal. *See Fig. 1.*

2) No voltage should exist with accelerator pedal in idle (switch on) position. Depress accelerator pedal approximately .16-.31" (4.0-8.0 mm) to the (switch off) position. Distance is measured at accelerator pedal. *See Fig. 16.*

3) Voltage should now be 12 volts. If voltage readings are not correct, adjust accelerator switch by loosening lock nut and rotating adjusting bolt until correct operation is obtained.

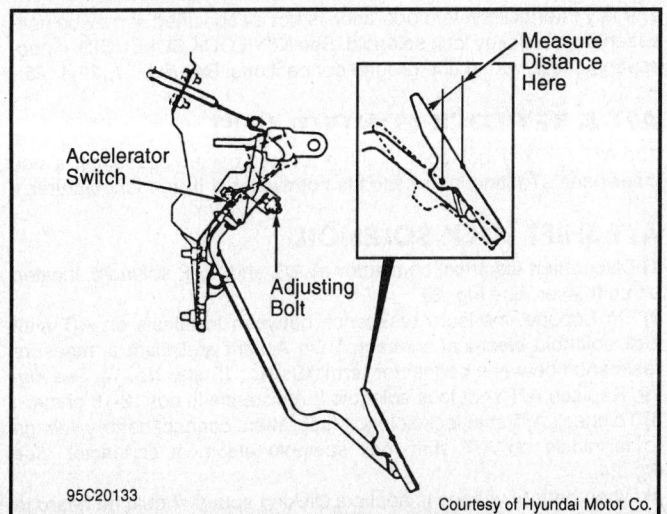

Measure Distance Here
Accelerator Switch
Adjusting Bolt
95C20133
Courtesy of Hyundai Motor Co.

Fig. 16: Checking & Adjusting Accelerator Switch

IDLE POSITION SWITCH

Run engine to normal operating temperature. With engine idling, check voltage at idle switch connector. Voltage should be zero volts. Voltage should be 12 volts above idle. If voltage is not as specified adjust and recheck.

THROTTLE POSITION SENSOR (TPS)

Throttle position sensor is not adjustable. To test TPS, See ELECTRONIC TROUBLE SHOOTING.

TRANSAXLE RANGE SWITCH

1) Transaxle range switch is mounted on transaxle. *See Fig. 1.* Place shift lever and manual control lever on transaxle in Neutral position.

2) Loosen transaxle range switch retaining bolts. Rotate transaxle range switch body until the .47" (12.0 mm) wide end of manual control lever aligns with wide flange area on transaxle range switch. *See Fig. 17.* Use care not to allow "O" ring to fall from transaxle range switch.

3) Tighten transaxle range switch retaining bolts to specification. See TORQUE SPECIFICATIONS. Remove any slack in shift cable by using adjusting nut located near end of shift cable at transaxle range switch.

Transaxle Range Switch
Manual Control Lever
Retaining Bolt
95E20135
Courtesy of Hyundai Motor Co.

Fig. 17: Adjusting Transaxle Range Switch

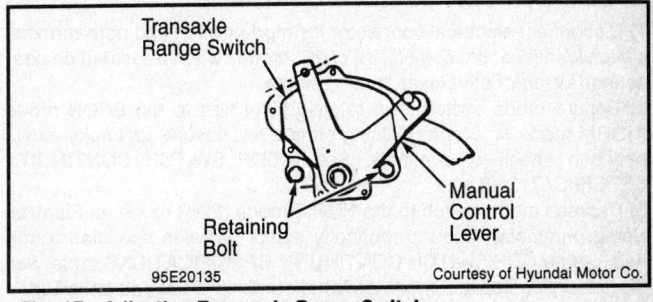

4) Move shift lever through all gear ranges. Ensure manual control lever is in gear position corresponding to shift lever. Ensure vehicle starts only in Park and Neutral.

ELECTRONIC COMPONENT TESTING

NOTE: Different electronic system components may be checked when performing electronic trouble shooting. See Figs. 7-15. For component, figure and step reference, see COMPONENT TESTING & FIGURE REFERENCE table under ELECTRONIC TROUBLE SHOOTING.

OVERDRIVE SWITCH

1) Disconnect electrical connector for overdrive switch and note switch terminal identification. *See Fig. 18 or 19.* Overdrive switch is mounted on driver's side of shift lever.
2) Depress overdrive switch to the OFF position. Using ohmmeter, ensure continuity exists between specified terminals. See OVERDRIVE SWITCH CONTINUITY SPECIFICATIONS table. If continuity is not as specified, replace overdrive switch.

OVERDRIVE SWITCH CONTINUITY SPECIFICATIONS

Switch Position	Continuity Between Terminals
Off	
Accent	1 & 3
Elantra	1 & 3
Scoupe	1 & 2
On	
Accent	1 & 2
Elantra	1 & 2
Scoupe	2 & 3

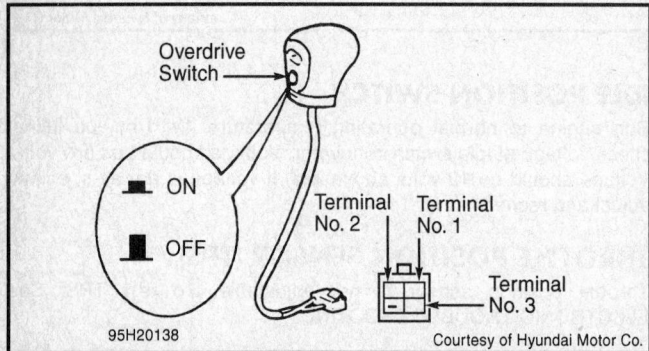

Fig. 18: Identifying Overdrive Switch Terminals (Scoupe)

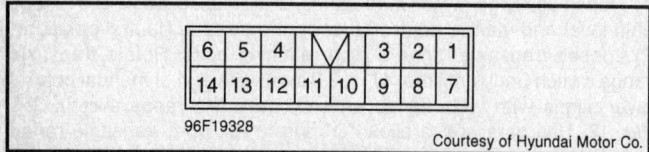

Fig. 19: Identifying Overdrive Switch, Mode Switch & A/T Shift Lock Solenoid Terminals (Accent & Elantra)

MODE SWITCH (RANGE SWITCH)

1) Disconnect electrical connector for mode switch and note terminal switch identification. *See Fig. 19 or 20.* Mode switch is located on passenger's side of shift lever, near console.
2) Ensure mode switch is in released position to the ECON mode (NORM mode on Elantra). Using ohmmeter, ensure continuity exists between specified terminals. See MODE SWITCH CONTINUITY SPECIFICATIONS.
3) Depress mode switch to the NORM mode (PWR mode on Elantra). Using ohmmeter, ensure continuity exists between specified terminals. See MODE SWITCH CONTINUITY SPECIFICATIONS table. *See Fig. 19 or 20.* Replace mode switch if continuity is not as specified.

MODE SWITCH CONTINUITY SPECIFICATIONS

Switch Position	Continuity Between Terminals
ECON (Economy) Mode	
Accent	[1]
Scoupe	1 & 4
NORM (Normal) Mode	
Accent	7 & 9
Elantra	[1]
Scoupe	1 & 2
PWR (Power) Mode	
Elantra	7 & 9

[1] – No continuity should exist between switch connector terminals.

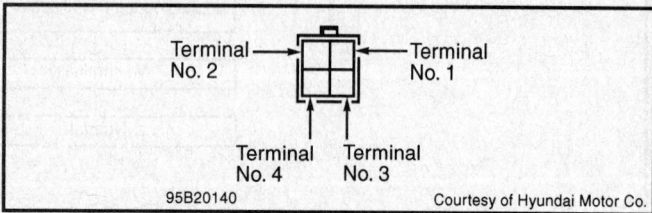

Fig. 20: Identifying Mode Switch Electrical Connector Terminals (Scoupe)

VEHICLE SPEED SENSOR (VSS)

1) Vehicle speed sensor is located on rear of speedometer on instrument panel gauge assembly. *See Fig. 1.* Remove instrument panel gauge assembly.
2) Connect ohmmeter on terminals of vehicle speed sensor. Rotate speedometer cable shaft. Ohmmeter should change from continuity to no continuity 4 times with each revolution of speedometer cable shaft. Replace vehicle speed sensor if operation is not as specified.

SHIFT & KEY INTERLOCK SYSTEMS

SYSTEM TESTS

Shift Interlock System – 1) To check system operation, turn ignition on. Depress release button on side of shift lever.
2) With brake pedal released, shift lever should not move from Park. Depress brake pedal. Shift lever should now move from Park.
3) If shift interlock system operation is not as specified, it may be necessary to check brakelight switch and A/T shift lock solenoid. See BRAKELIGHT SWITCH and A/T SHIFT LOCK SOLENOID. If necessary, check wiring and ground connections. *See Fig. 21, 22 or 23.*
Key Interlock System – 1) With shift lever in any gear position except Park, ensure ignition key cannot be turned to LOCK position. Place shift lever in Park. Ensure ignition key can now be turned to LOCK position.
2) If key interlock system operation is not as specified, it may be necessary to check key lock solenoid. See KEY LOCK SOLENOID. If necessary, check wiring and ground connections. *See Fig. 21, 22 or 23.*

A/T & KEY LOCK CONTROL UNIT

The A/T and key lock control unit is located behind passenger's side inner panel. Testing information is not available from manufacturer.

A/T SHIFT LOCK SOLENOID

1) Disconnect electrical connector at A/T shift lock solenoid, located on shift lever. *See Fig. 26.*
2) On Scoupe, measure resistance between terminals on A/T shift lock solenoid electrical connector. On Accent and Elantra, measure resistance between connector terminals No. 13 and No. 14. *See Fig. 19.* Replace A/T shift lock solenoid if resistance is not 12-16 ohms.
3) To check A/T shift lock solenoid operation, connect battery voltage to terminals on A/T shift lock solenoid electrical connector. *See Fig. 24.*
4) When battery voltage is applied, clicking sound should be heard to indicate solenoid operation. Replace A/T shift lock solenoid if solenoid fails to operate.

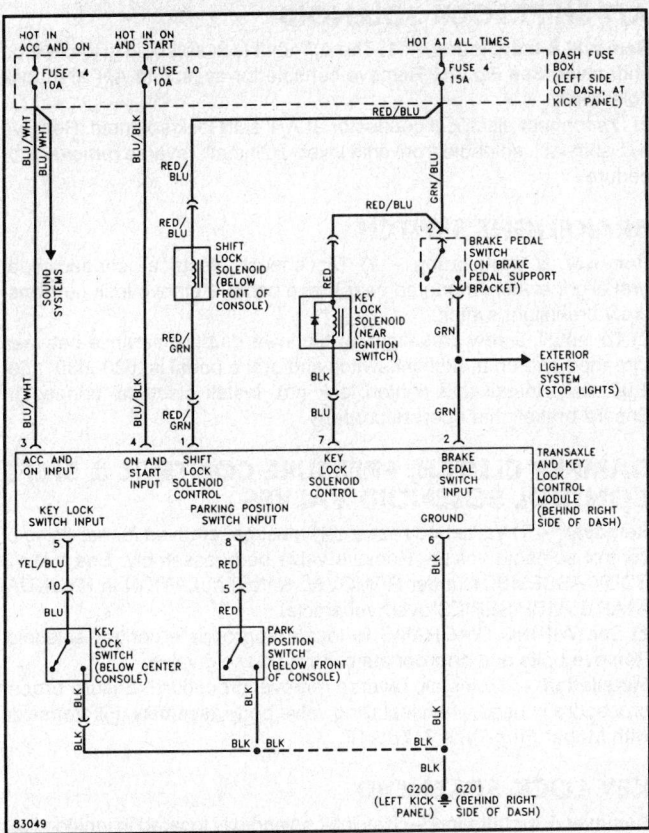

Fig. 21: Shift & Key Interlock System Wiring Schematic (Accent)

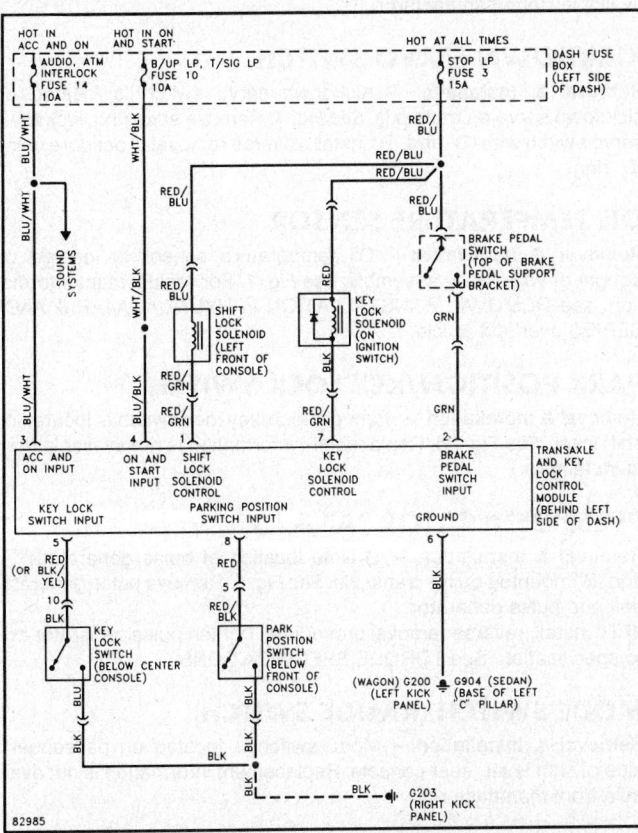

Fig. 22: Shift & Key Interlock System Wiring Schematic (Elantra)

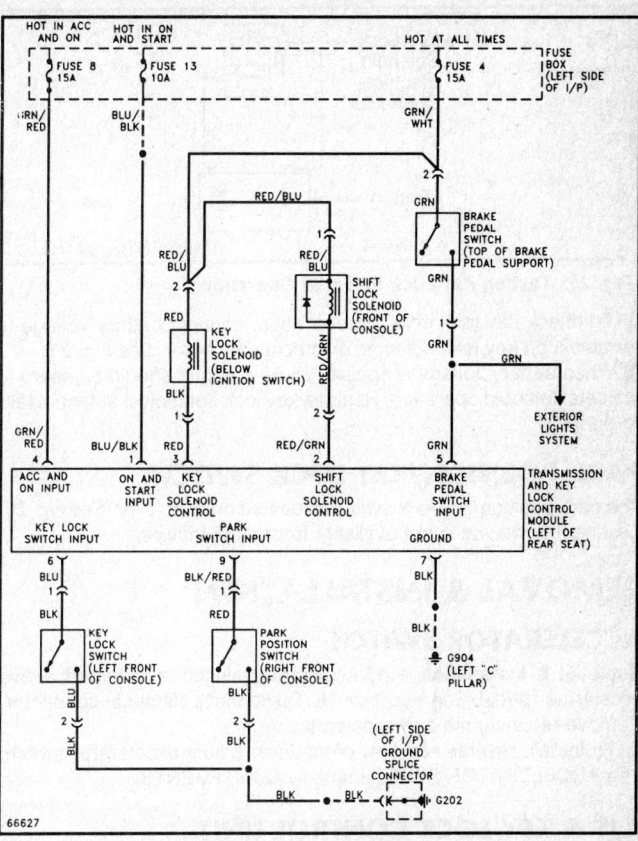

Fig. 23: Shift & Key Interlock System Wiring Schematic (Scoupe)

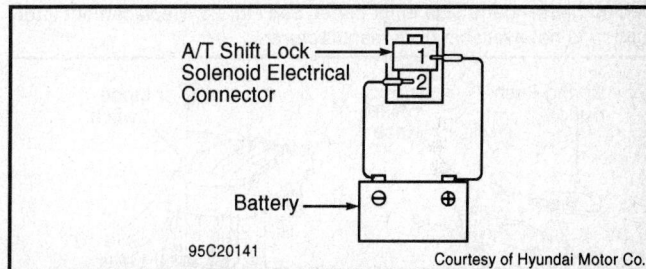

Fig. 24: Testing A/T Shift Lock Solenoid Operation (Scoupe)

BRAKELIGHT SWITCH

1) Disconnect brakelight switch electrical connector. Brakelight switch is mounted near brake pedal.

2) Using ohmmeter, check for continuity between electrical terminals on brakelight switch with brake pedal depressed. Continuity should exist.

3) Using ohmmeter, check for continuity between electrical terminals on brakelight switch with brake pedal released. Continuity should not exist.

4) If operation is not as specified, ensure brake pedal is properly adjusted so brakelight switch can obtain proper travel for switch operation. If proper brakelight switch travel exists, replace brakelight switch.

KEY LOCK SOLENOID

1) Disconnect electrical connector at key lock solenoid. Key lock solenoid is located in ignition lock assembly on steering column.

2) Using ohmmeter measure resistance between terminals on key lock solenoid electrical connector. Replace key lock solenoid if resistance is not 12.5-16.5 ohms.

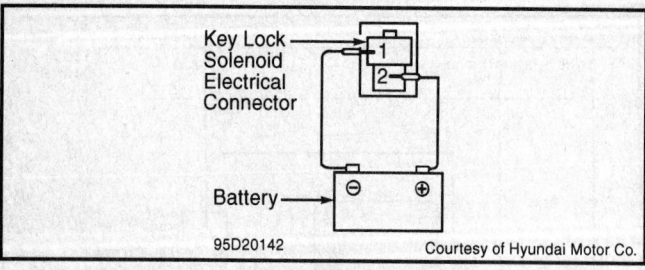

Fig. 25: Testing Key Lock Solenoid Operation

3) To check key lock solenoid operation, connect battery voltage to terminals on key lock solenoid electrical connector. *See Fig. 25.*
4) When battery voltage is applied, clicking sound should be heard to indicate solenoid operation. Replace key lock solenoid if solenoid fails to operate.

PARK POSITION/KEY LOCK SWITCH

The park position/key lock switch is located on shift lever. *See Fig. 26.* Testing information is not available from manufacturer.

REMOVAL & INSTALLATION

ACCELERATOR SWITCH

Removal & Installation – 1) Accelerator switch is mounted above accelerator pedal. *See Fig. 1 or 16.* Disconnect electrical connector. Remove retaining nut and accelerator switch.
2) To install, reverse removal procedure. Adjust accelerator switch. See ACCELERATOR SWITCH under ADJUSTMENTS.

A/T & KEY LOCK CONTROL UNIT

Removal & Installation – The A/T and key lock control unit is located behind passenger's side inner panel. *See Fig. 26.* Replacement information is not available from manufacturer.

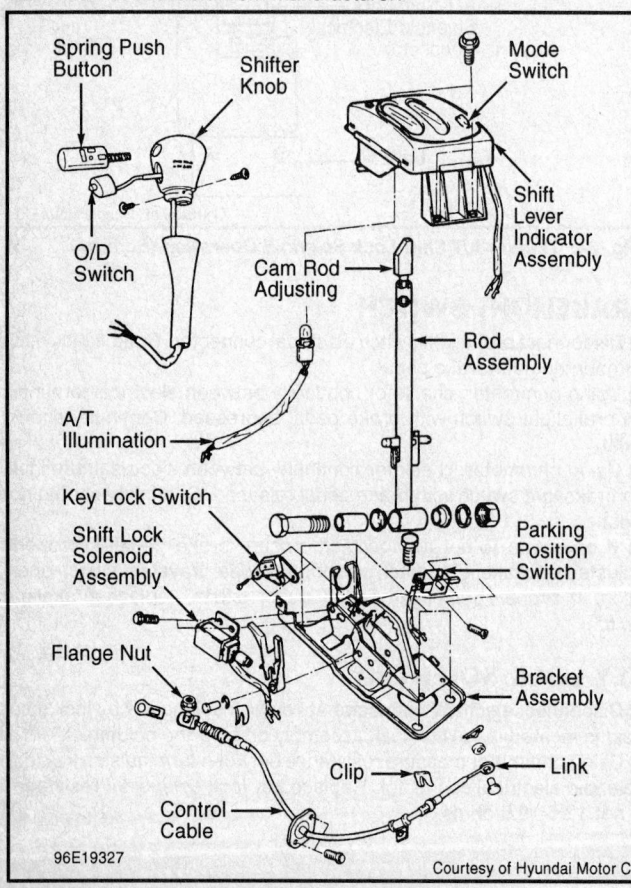

Fig. 26: Exploded View Of Shifter & Components

A/T SHIFT LOCK SOLENOID

Removal & Installation – 1) The A/T shift lock solenoid is located on shift lever. *See Fig. 26.* Remove console for access to A/T shift lock solenoid.
2) Disconnect electrical connector at A/T shift lock solenoid. Remove A/T shift lock solenoid from shift lever. To install, reverse removal procedure.

BRAKELIGHT SWITCH

Removal & Installation – 1) Disconnect electrical connector at brakelight switch, mounted near brake pedal. Remove lock nut. Unscrew brakelight switch.
2) To install, screw brakelight switch inward until clearance between threaded end on brakelight switch and brake pedal is .020-.039" (.50-1.00 mm). Install and tighten lock nut. Install electrical connector. Ensure brakelights operate properly.

DAMPER CLUTCH, PRESSURE CONTROL & SHIFT CONTROL SOLENOID VALVES

Removal – 1) Valve body assembly must be removed for servicing of control solenoid valves. Remove valve body assembly. See VALVE BODY ASSEMBLY under REMOVAL & INSTALLATION in HYUNDAI A4AF & A4BF SERIES overhaul article.
2) See WIRING DIAGRAMS to locate appropriate control solenoid. Remove bolts and appropriate control solenoid valve.
Installation – To install, reverse removal procedure. Ensure proper procedure is used when installing valve body assembly. Fill transaxle with Mopar Plus-Type 7176 ATF.

KEY LOCK SOLENOID

Removal & Installation – Key lock solenoid is located in ignition lock assembly on steering column. Replacement information is not available from manufacturer.

KICKDOWN SERVO SWITCH

Removal & Installation – Kickdown servo switch is located on kickdown servo on transaxle. *See Fig. 1.* Remove snap ring, kickdown servo switch with "D" ring. To install, reverse removal procedure using "D" ring.

OIL TEMPERATURE SENSOR

Removal & Installation – Oil temperature sensor is located on bottom of valve body assembly. *See Fig. 1.* For replacement information, see REMOVAL & INSTALLATION in HYUNDAI A4AF & A4BF SERIES overhaul article.

PARK POSITION/KEY LOCK SWITCH

Removal & Installation – Park position/key lock switch is located on shift lever. *See Fig. 26.* Replacement information is not available from manufacturer.

PULSE GENERATOR "A" & "B"

Removal & Installation – 1) Note location of pulse generators "A" and "B" mounted on the transaxle. *See Fig. 1.* Remove pulse generator bolt and pulse generator.
2) To install, reverse removal procedure. Tighten pulse generator bolt to specification. See TORQUE SPECIFICATIONS.

MODE SWITCH (RANGE SWITCH)

Removal & Installation – Mode switch is located on passenger's side of shift lever, near console. Replacement information is not available from manufacturer.

THROTTLE POSITION SENSOR (TPS)

Removal & Installation – 1) Disconnect electrical connector at throttle position sensor, mounted on side of throttle body. Remove bolts and throttle position sensor.

2) To install, reverse removal procedure. Tighten throttle position sensor bolts to specification. See TORQUE SPECIFICATIONS. Throttle position sensor adjustment is not available from manufacturer.

TRANSAXLE CONTROL MODULE (TCM)

Removal & Installation – The TCM is located below driver's seat. Replacement information is not available from manufacturer.

TRANSAXLE RANGE SWITCH

Removal & Installation – **1)** Transaxle range switch is mounted on transaxle. See Fig. 1. Disconnect shift cable and electrical connector at transaxle range switch.

2) Remove lock nut and manual control lever. Remove transaxle range switch retaining bolts and transaxle range switch.

3) To install, reverse removal procedure. DO NOT tighten transaxle range switch retaining bolts until switch is adjusted. Tighten manual control lever lock nut to specification.

4) Adjust transaxle range switch. See TRANSAXLE RANGE SWITCH under ADJUSTMENTS.

VEHICLE SPEED SENSOR (VSS)

Removal & Installation – Vehicle speed sensor is located on rear of speedometer on instrument panel gauge assembly. See Fig. 1. Replacement information is not available from manufacturer.

TORQUE SPECIFICATIONS
TORQUE SPECIFICATIONS

Application	Ft. Lbs. (N.m)
Manual Control Lever Lock Nut	12-15 (16-20)
	INCH Lbs. (N.m)
Pulse Generator Bolt	89-106 (10.0-12.0)
Throttle Position Sensor Bolt	27-35 (3.0-4.0)
Transaxle Range Switch Retaining Bolt	89-106 (10.0-12.0)

AUTOMATIC TRANSMISSIONS
Hyundai A4AF & A4BF Electronic Controls (Cont.)

WIRING DIAGRAMS

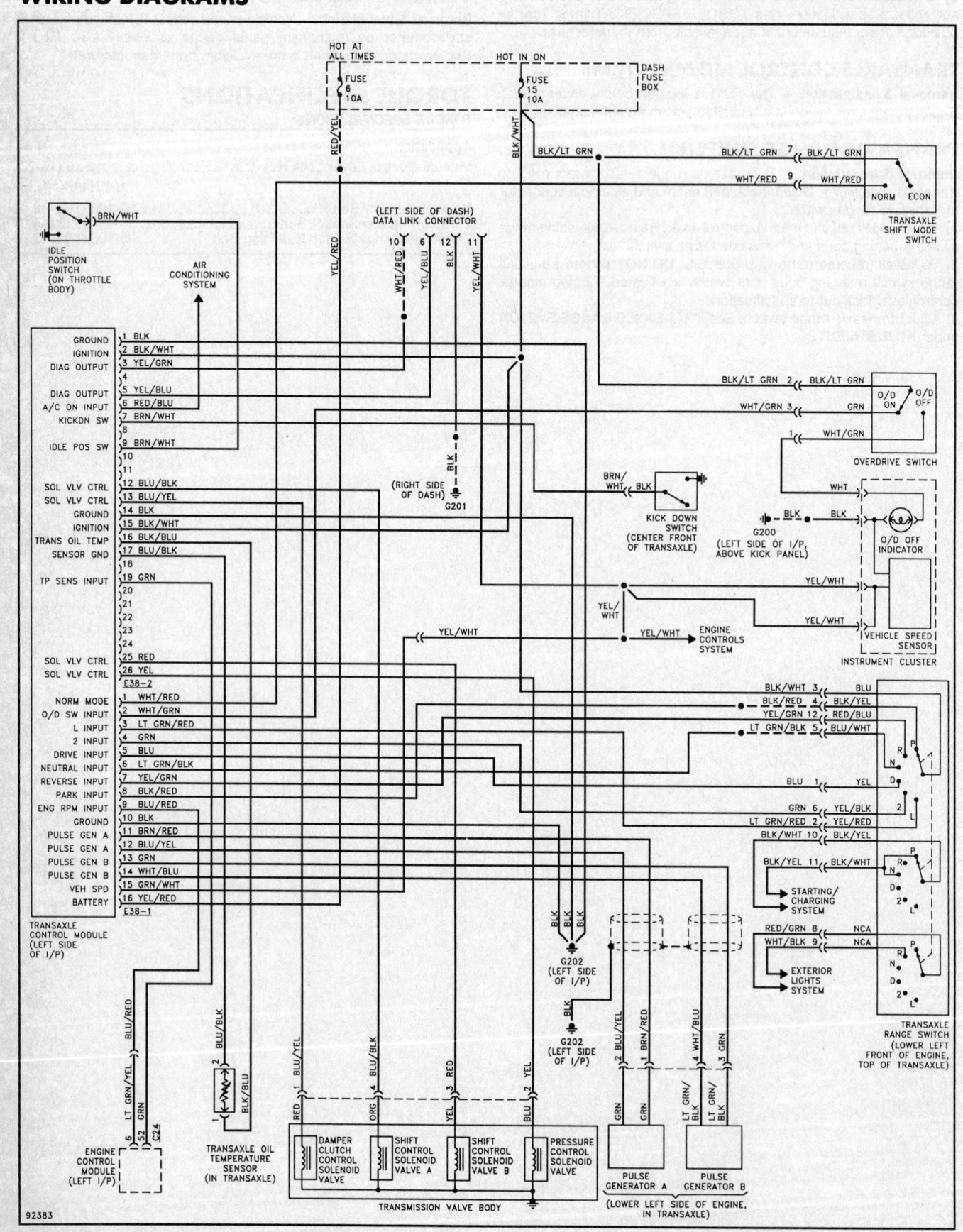

Fig. 27: Transaxle Wiring Diagram (1995 Accent)

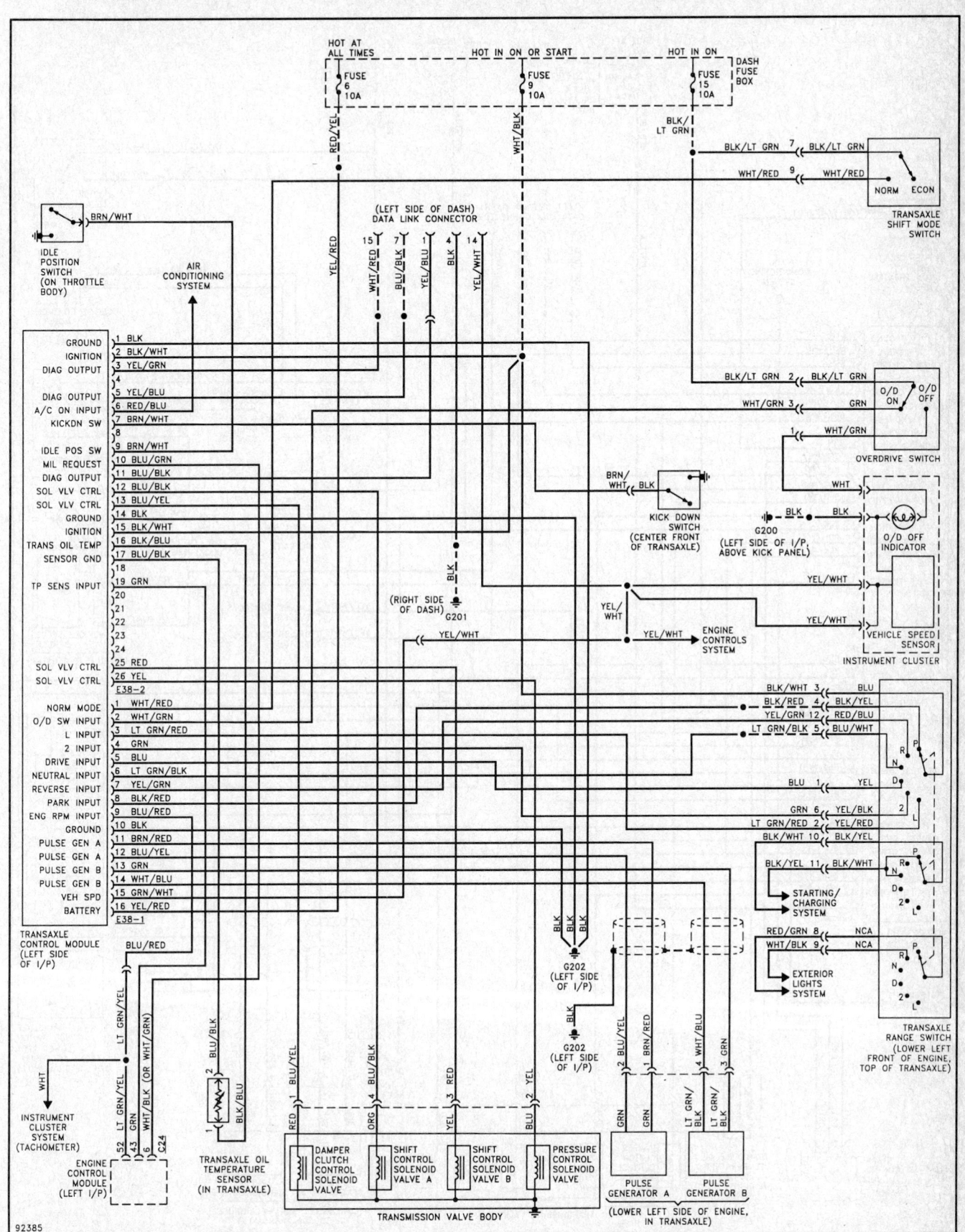

Fig. 28: Transaxle Wiring Diagram (1996 Accent)

AUTOMATIC TRANSMISSIONS
Hyundai A4AF & A4BF Electronic Controls (Cont.)

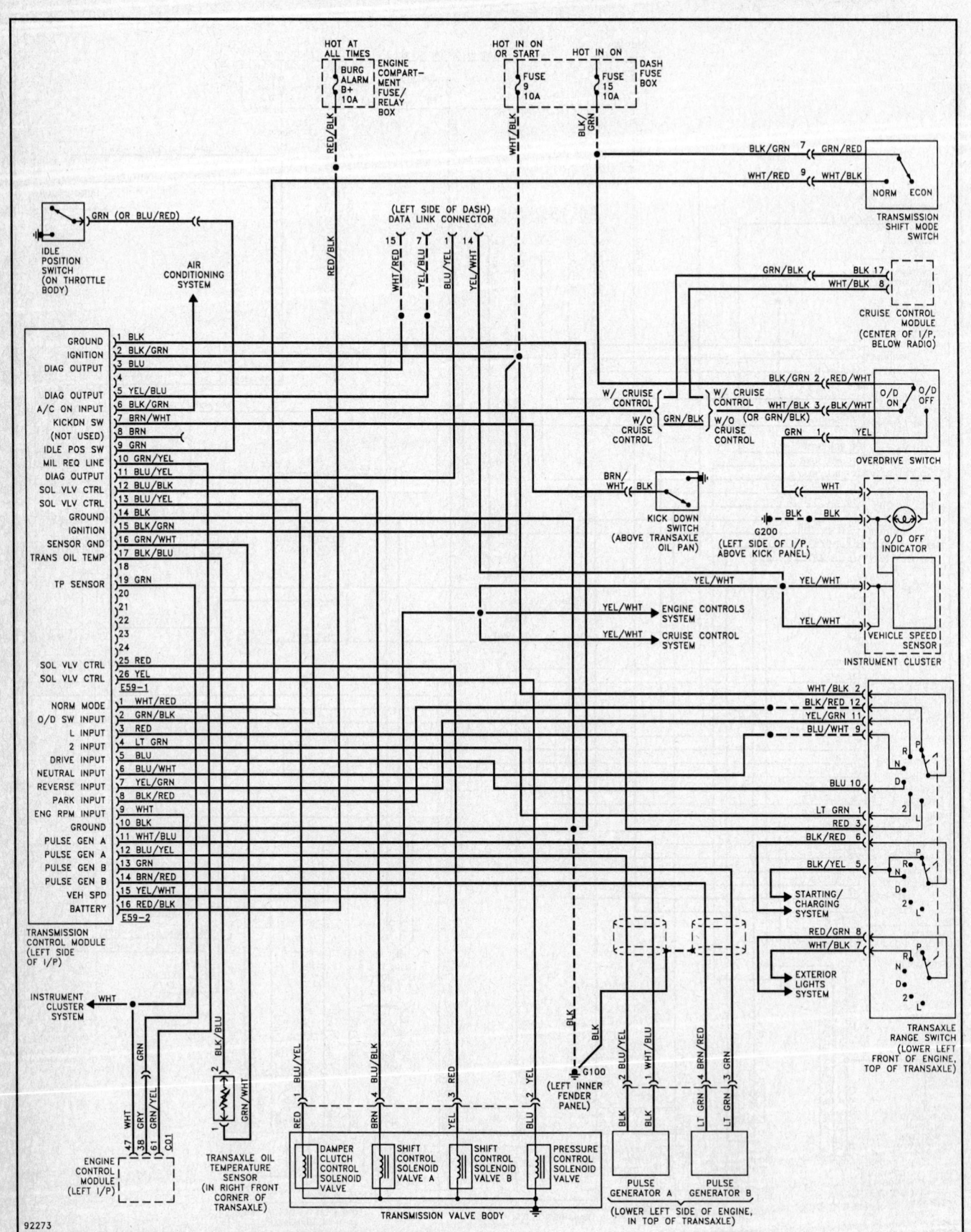

Fig. 29: Transaxle Wiring Diagram (1996 Elantra)

92273

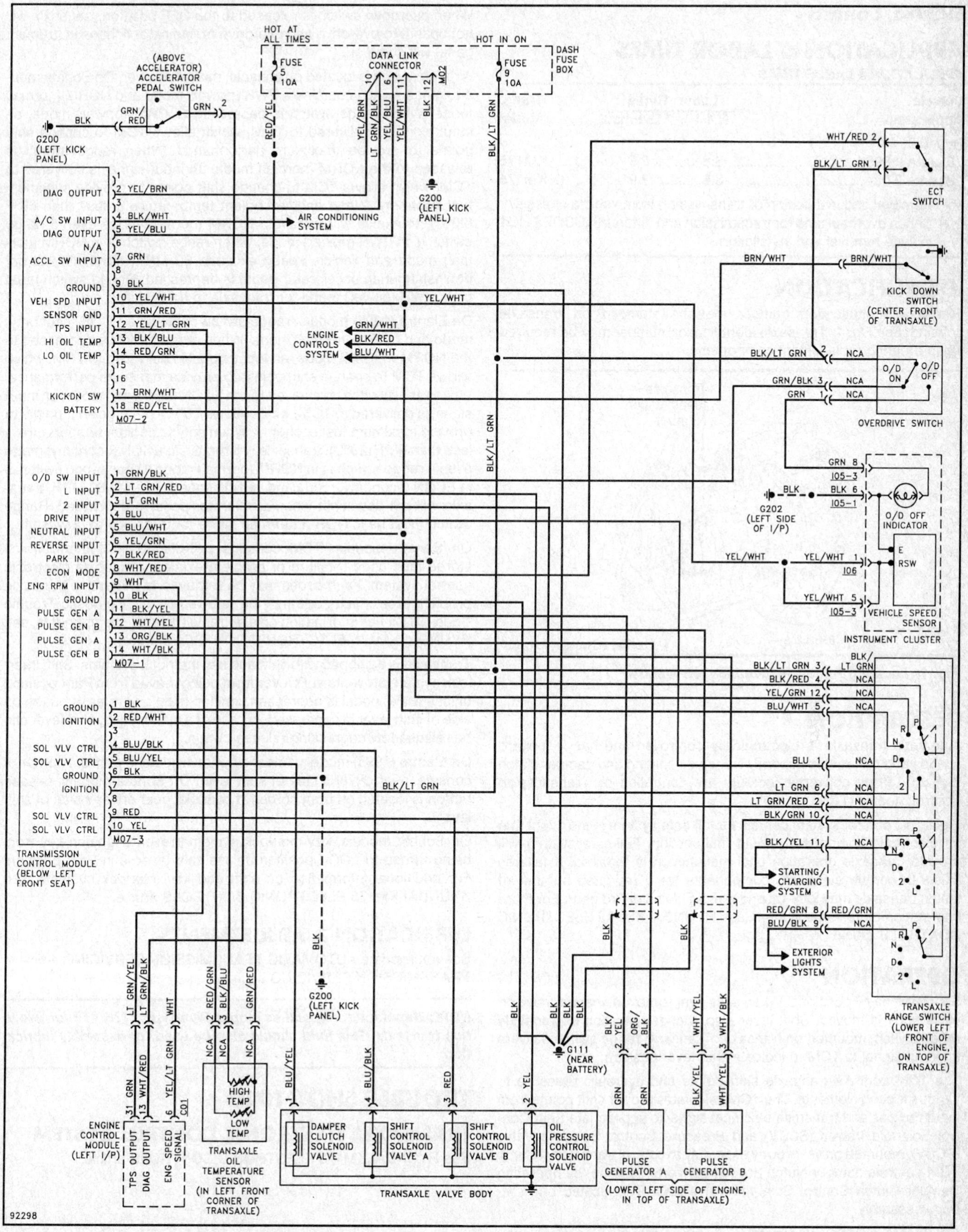

Fig. 30: Transaxle Wiring Diagram (1995 Scoupe)

92298

Elantra, Sonata

APPLICATION & LABOR TIMES

APPLICATION & LABOR TIMES

Vehicle Application	Labor Times		Trans. Model
	[1] R & I	[2] Overhaul	
Hyundai			
Elantra (1995)	3.8	8.9	KM175
Sonata 2.0L	3.8	8.9	KM175

[1] – Removal and installation of transmission from vehicle chassis.
[2] – Bench overhaul time for transmission and differential. DOES NOT include removal and installation.

IDENTIFICATION

Transaxle identification number may be stamped on transaxle housing. See Fig. 1. Transaxle identification number may be required when ordering replacement components.

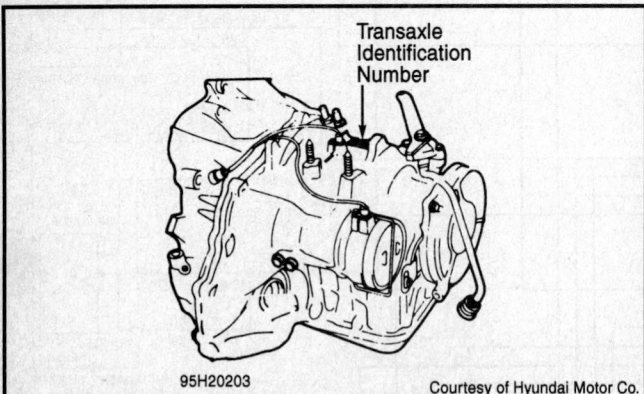

Transaxle
Identification
Number

95H20203   Courtesy of Hyundai Motor Co.

Fig. 1: Locating Transaxle Identification Number

DESCRIPTION

Automatic transaxle is electronically controlled and has 4 forward speeds and one reverse speed. Transaxle shifting and damper clutch lock-up (torque converter lock-up) are controlled by Transmission Control Module (TCM).

Electronic control system contains a fail-safe system in the event that an electronic component should malfunction. Fail-safe system will provide transaxle operation until malfunction is repaired. If failures exists in certain electronic components for a repeated number of times, transaxle may lock-up and remain in 2nd or 3rd gear. For more information on fail-safe system, see HYUNDAI KM175 ELECTRONIC CONTROLS article.

OPERATION

Shift lever has 6 positions. When shift lever is moved, manual valve on valve body is moved. Shift lever also changes position of transaxle range switch, mounted on transaxle. Transaxle range switch delivers an input signal to TCM to indicate shift lever position.

The TCM controls transaxle shift points and hydraulic pressure to various friction elements. The TCM calculates proper shift points from input devices and transmits electrical signal to appropriate Shift Control Solenoid Valves (SCSV) and Pressure Control Solenoid Valve (PCSV), mounted on valve body assembly to control transaxle shifting. TCM controls damper clutch (torque converter lock-up) by operating Damper Clutch Control Solenoid Valve (DCCSV), located on valve body assembly.

On Sonata models, an overdrive switch is mounted on shift lever. When overdrive switch is depressed to the ON position, transaxle will automatically upshift to overdrive and overdrive off indicator light on instrument panel will be off.

When overdrive switch is released to the OFF position, transaxle will not upshift to overdrive and overdrive off indicator light on instrument panel will come on.

A range switch is located on console, near shift lever. On Sonata models, range switch contains a PWR (power) mode and NORM (normal) mode. When range switch is depressed to PWR (power) mode, an input signal is delivered to TCM, which allows TCM to change shift points to provide maximum performance. When range switch is released to the NORM (normal) mode, an input signal is delivered to TCM, which allows TCM to change shift points to provide maximum fuel economy. When engine coolant temperature is less than 68°F (20°C), transaxle will remain in NORM (normal) mode even if range switch is in PWR (power) mode. When range switch is in NORM (normal) mode and vehicle speed exceeds 60 MPH, transaxle will not downshift when accelerator pedal is depressed. Range switch must be in PWR (power) mode for transaxle to downshift.

On Elantra (1995) models, range switch contains a ECON (economy) mode and NORM (normal) mode. When range switch is depressed to the NORM (normal) mode, an input signal is delivered to TCM, which allows TCM to change shift points to provide maximum performance. When range switch is released to the ECON (economy) mode, an input signal is delivered to TCM, which allows TCM to change shift points to provide maximum fuel economy. When engine coolant temperature is less than 68°F (20°C), transaxle will remain in ECON (economy) mode even if range switch is in NORM (normal) mode. When range switch is in ECON (economy) mode and vehicle speed exceeds 60 MPH, transaxle will not downshift when accelerator pedal is depressed. Range switch must be in NORM (normal) mode for transaxle to downshift.

On Sonata models, TCM contains self-diagnostic system, which stores fault code if failure or problem exists in transaxle electronic control system. Fault codes may be retrieved to determine transaxle problem area. Fault code may be referred to as Diagnostic Trouble Code (DTC). For information on electronic transaxle components, see HYUNDAI KM175 ELECTRONIC CONTROLS article.

Transaxle is equipped with shift and key interlock systems. Shift interlock system prevents shift lever from being moved from Park position unless brake pedal is depressed, ignition is on and release button on side of shift lever is depressed. In case of a malfunction, shift lever can be released by depressing release button.

On Elantra (1995) models, release button is located on front corner of console, near driver's side of shift lever. On Sonata models, release button is located on front corner of console, near driver's side of shift lever.

On Sonata models, key interlock system prevents ignition key from being turned to LOCK position unless shift lever is in Park position. For additional information on shift and key interlock systems, see HYUNDAI KM175 ELECTRONIC CONTROLS article.

LUBRICATION & ADJUSTMENTS

See appropriate AUTOMATIC TRANSMISSION SERVICING article in TRANSMISSION SERVICING section.

NOTE: Manufacturer specifies Mopar Plus-Type 7176 ATF for use in this transaxle. This fluid should also be used for assembly lubrication.

TROUBLE SHOOTING

TRANSAXLE ELECTRONIC CONTROL SYSTEM

See HYUNDAI KM175 ELECTRONIC CONTROLS article.

TROUBLE SHOOTING

SYMPTOM DIAGNOSIS

Transaxle malfunctions may be caused by poor engine performance, improper adjustments or failure of hydraulic, mechanical or electronic components. Always begin by checking fluid level, fluid condition and cable adjustments. Perform road test to determine if problem has been corrected. If problem still exists, perform several tests on transaxle. See TESTING.

Damper Clutch Inoperative
- Defective Accelerator Switch Or Improper Switch Adjustment
- Defective Damper Clutch Control Solenoid Valve Or Wiring
- Defective Ignition System Engine RPM Signal
- Defective Oil Temperature Sensor
- Defective Pulse Generator "A", "B" Or Wiring
- Defective TCM
- Defective Throttle Position Sensor Or Improper Adjustment
- Defective Torque Converter
- Malfunction In Valve Body Assembly

Engine Stalls With Transaxle In Neutral, Drive Or Reverse
- Incorrect Idle Speed
- Defective Damper Clutch Control Solenoid Valve Or Wiring
- Poor Engine Performance
- Malfunction In Valve Body Assembly

Excessive Vibration & Shock During All Upshifts
- Defective Front Clutch Or Piston
- Defective Ignition System Engine RPM Signal
- Defective Pulse Generator "A" Or Wiring
- Defective TCM
- Defective Throttle Position Sensor Or Improper Adjustment
- Malfunction In Valve Body Assembly
- Poor Engine Performance

Excessive Vibration & Shock During 1-2 Or 3-4 Upshift
- Defective End Clutch Or Piston
- Defective Ignition System Engine RPM Signal
- Defective Kickdown Band Or Kickdown Servo
- Defective Kickdown Servo Switch
- Defective Pulse Generator "A" Or Wiring
- Defective TCM
- Defective Throttle Position Sensor Or Improper Adjustment
- Improper Kickdown Servo Adjustment
- Malfunction In Valve Body Assembly
- Poor Engine Performance

Excessive Vibration & Shock During 2-3 Upshift Or 4-3 Downshift
- Defective Front Clutch Or Piston
- Defective Ignition System Engine RPM Signal
- Defective Pulse Generator "A" Or Wiring
- Defective TCM
- Defective Throttle Position Sensor Or Improper Adjustment
- Malfunction In Valve Body Assembly
- Poor Engine Performance

Excessive Vibration & Shock When Shifting From Drive To 2nd Gear Position
- Defective Ignition System Engine RPM Signal
- Defective Low-Reverse Brake Or Piston
- Defective Pulse Generator "A" Or Wiring
- Defective TCM
- Defective Throttle Position Sensor Or Improper Adjustment
- Malfunction In Valve Body Assembly
- Poor Engine Performance

Excessive Vibration & Shock When Shifting Into Any Forward Gear Or Reverse
- Defective Accelerator Switch Or Improper Switch Adjustment
- Defective Front Clutch, Rear Clutch Or Piston
- Defective Low-Reverse Brake Or Piston
- Defective Or Improperly Adjusted Shift Cable
- Defective TCM

- Defective Throttle Position Sensor Or Improper Adjustment
- Defective Wiring, Transaxle Range Switch Or Switch Adjustment
- Incorrect Idle Speed
- Malfunction In Valve Body Assembly

Improper Shift Speeds
- Defective Pulse Generator "B" Or Wiring
- Defective TCM
- Defective Throttle Position Sensor Or Improper Adjustment
- Malfunction In Valve Body Assembly

Slips In Drive
- Defective Oil Pump
- Defective Or Improperly Adjusted Shift Cable
- Defective Overrunning Clutch
- Defective Pressure Control Solenoid Valve Or Wiring
- Defective Rear Clutch Or Piston
- Low Fluid Level
- Low Line Pressure
- Malfunction In Valve Body Assembly

Slips In Reverse
- Defective Front Clutch Or Piston
- Defective Front Clutch Retainer
- Defective Low-Reverse Brake Or Piston
- Defective Oil Pump
- Defective Or Improperly Adjusted Shift Cable
- Defective Pressure Control Solenoid Valve Or Wiring
- Low Fluid Level
- Low Line Pressure
- Malfunction In Valve Body Assembly
- "O" Ring Missing Between Valve Body Assembly & Transaxle Housing

Sudden Engine RPM Increase During Upshift
- Defective End Clutch Or Piston
- Defective Front Clutch Or Piston
- Defective Front Clutch Retainer
- Defective Ignition System Engine RPM Signal
- Defective Kickdown Band Or Kickdown Servo
- Defective Pressure Control Solenoid Valve Or Wiring
- Defective Pulse Generator "A" Or Wiring
- Defective Throttle Position Sensor Or Improper Adjustment
- Defective TCM
- Improper Kickdown Servo Adjustment
- Low Line Pressure
- Malfunction In Valve Body Assembly

Sudden Engine RPM Increase & Vibration During 3-2 Downshift
- Defective Front Clutch Retainer
- Defective Ignition System Engine RPM Signal
- Defective Kickdown Band Or Kickdown Servo
- Defective Kickdown Servo Switch
- Defective Oil Pump
- Defective Pressure Control Solenoid Valve Or Wiring
- Defective Pulse Generator "A" Or Wiring
- Defective TCM
- Defective Throttle Position Sensor Or Improper Adjustment
- Improper Kickdown Servo Adjustment
- Low Fluid Level
- Low Line Pressure
- Malfunction In Valve Body Assembly

Vehicle Moves In Park Or Neutral
- Defective Or Improperly Adjusted Shift Cable
- Defective Parking Mechanism
- Malfunction In Valve Body Assembly
- Defective Wiring, Transaxle Range Switch Or Switch Adjustment

Vehicle Starts Off Other Than 1st Gear
- Defective Accelerator Switch Or Improper Switch Adjustment
- Defective Or Improperly Adjusted Shift Cable
- Defective TCM
- Defective Wiring, Transaxle Range Switch Or Switch Adjustment
- Malfunction In Valve Body Assembly

Vehicle Will Not Move
- Defective Low-Reverse Brake Or Piston
- Defective Oil Pump
- Defective Or Improperly Adjusted Shift Cable
- Defective Pressure Control Solenoid Valve Or Wiring
- Defective Torque Converter
- Low Fluid Level
- Low Line Pressure
- Malfunction In Valve Body Assembly

Vehicle Will Not Move In Any Forward Gear
- Defective Oil Pump
- Defective Overrunning Clutch
- Defective Or Improperly Adjusted Shift Cable
- Defective Pressure Control Solenoid Valve Or Wiring
- Defective Rear Clutch Or Piston
- Defective Torque Converter
- Low Fluid Level
- Low Line Pressure
- Malfunction In Valve Body Assembly

Vehicle Will Not Move In Reverse
- Defective Front Clutch Or Piston
- Defective Front Clutch Retainer
- Defective Low-Reverse Brake Or Piston
- Defective Oil Pump
- Defective Or Improperly Adjusted Shift Cable
- Defective Pressure Control Solenoid Valve Or Wiring
- Defective Pulse Generator "B" Or Wiring
- Defective Torque Converter
- Low Fluid Level
- Low Line Pressure
- Malfunction In Valve Body Assembly
- "O" Ring Missing Between Valve Body Assembly & Transaxle Housing

Will Not Shift Into 4th Gear
- Defective End Clutch Or Piston
- Defective Front Clutch Retainer
- Defective Overdrive Switch
- Defective Pressure Control Solenoid Valve Or Wiring
- Defective TCM
- Defective Wiring, Transaxle Range Switch Or Switch Adjustment

Will Not Upshift From 2nd To 3rd Gear
- Defective Front Clutch Or Piston
- Defective Front Clutch Retainer
- Defective Pressure Control Solenoid Valve Or Wiring
- Defective TCM
- Malfunction In Valve Body Assembly

TESTING

ROAD TEST

1) Before road testing vehicle, ensure transaxle fluid level, fluid condition and shift cable adjustments have been checked and corrected (as necessary).

2) Road test vehicle and check for abnormal noise and clutch slippage. Specified clutch and brake are applied in designated gear. See CLUTCH & BRAKE APPLICATION table.

3) Ensure upshift and downshift speeds are correct in relation to throttle opening, vehicle speed and position of range switch and overdrive switch. *See Figs. 2-4.* Range switch is located on console, near shift lever. Overdrive switch is mounted on shift lever.

4) Various test procedures given can be used to detect any slipping component and confirm proper operation of good components. Malfunction may be caused by leaking hydraulic circuits or sticking valves.

5) More testing is needed if actual cause of malfunction cannot be easily determined. Unless an obvious malfunction exists, DO NOT disassemble transaxle until hydraulic pressure tests have been performed.

CLUTCH & BRAKE APPLICATION

Shift Lever Position	[1] Elements In Use
"D" (Drive)	
1st Gear	Overrunning Clutch & Rear Clutch
2nd Gear	Kickdown Brake & Rear Clutch
3rd Gear	End Clutch, Front Clutch & Rear Clutch
4th Gear	End Clutch & Kickdown Brake
"2" (2nd Gear)	
1st Gear	Overrunning Clutch & Rear Clutch
2nd Gear	Kickdown Brake & Rear Clutch
"L" (Low)	
1st Gear	Low-Reverse Brake & Rear Clutch
"R" (Reverse)	Front Clutch & Low-Reverse Brake
"N" Or "P" (Neutral Or Park)	All Clutches & Brakes Released Or Ineffective

[1] – Kickdown brake is the kickdown band.

TORQUE CONVERTER STALL SPEED TEST

CAUTION: DO NOT perform torque converter stall speed test for more than 5 seconds or transaxle may be damaged. If performing more than one torque converter stall speed test, place shift lever in "N" position. Operate engine at 1000 RPM for at least 2 minutes to cool transaxle before performing next test.

1) Apply parking brake. Block all wheels. Connect tachometer and start engine. Warm engine to normal operating temperature. Ensure transaxle fluid level is correct.

2) Place shift lever in "D" position. Fully depress brake pedal. Fully depress accelerator for no more than 5 seconds and note maximum engine speed. This is the torque converter stall speed.

3) Place shift lever in "N" position. Operate engine at 1000 RPM for at least 2 minutes to cool transaxle. Repeat test procedure with shift lever in "R" position.

4) Ensure torque converter stall speed is within specification. See TORQUE CONVERTER STALL SPEED SPECIFICATIONS table.

5) If torque converter stall speed is not within specification, see TORQUE CONVERTER STALL SPEED TROUBLE SHOOTING table for possible causes.

6) If torque converter stall speed exceeds specification, perform hydraulic pressure tests on transaxle. See HYDRAULIC PRESSURE TEST under TESTING.

TORQUE CONVERTER STALL SPEED SPECIFICATIONS

Application	Stall Speed RPM
Elantra (1995)	1800-2200
Sonata 2.0L	2200-2800

TORQUE CONVERTER STALL SPEED TROUBLE SHOOTING

Torque Converter Stall Speed Test Results	Probable Cause
Stall Speed RPM High In "D"	Slipping Rear Clutch Or Overrunning Clutch
Stall Speed RPM High In "R"	Slipping Front Clutch Or Low-Reverse Brake
Stall Speed RPM Low In "D" & "R"	Engine Output Low Or Defective Torque Converter

HYDRAULIC PRESSURE TEST

1) Install tachometer. Warm engine to normal operating temperature. Ensure transaxle fluid level is correct. Apply parking brake. Block rear wheels. Raise and support vehicle.

2) Reducing pressure, kickdown brake pressure, front clutch, end clutch, low-reverse brake and torque converter pressure are checked at specified pressure taps on transaxle. See Fig. 5.

3) Remove pressure tap plug. Install pressure gauge at appropriate pressure tap. Start and operate engine at specified RPM with shift lever in proper position in accordance with pressure being tested. See Fig. 6. Pressure should be within specification.

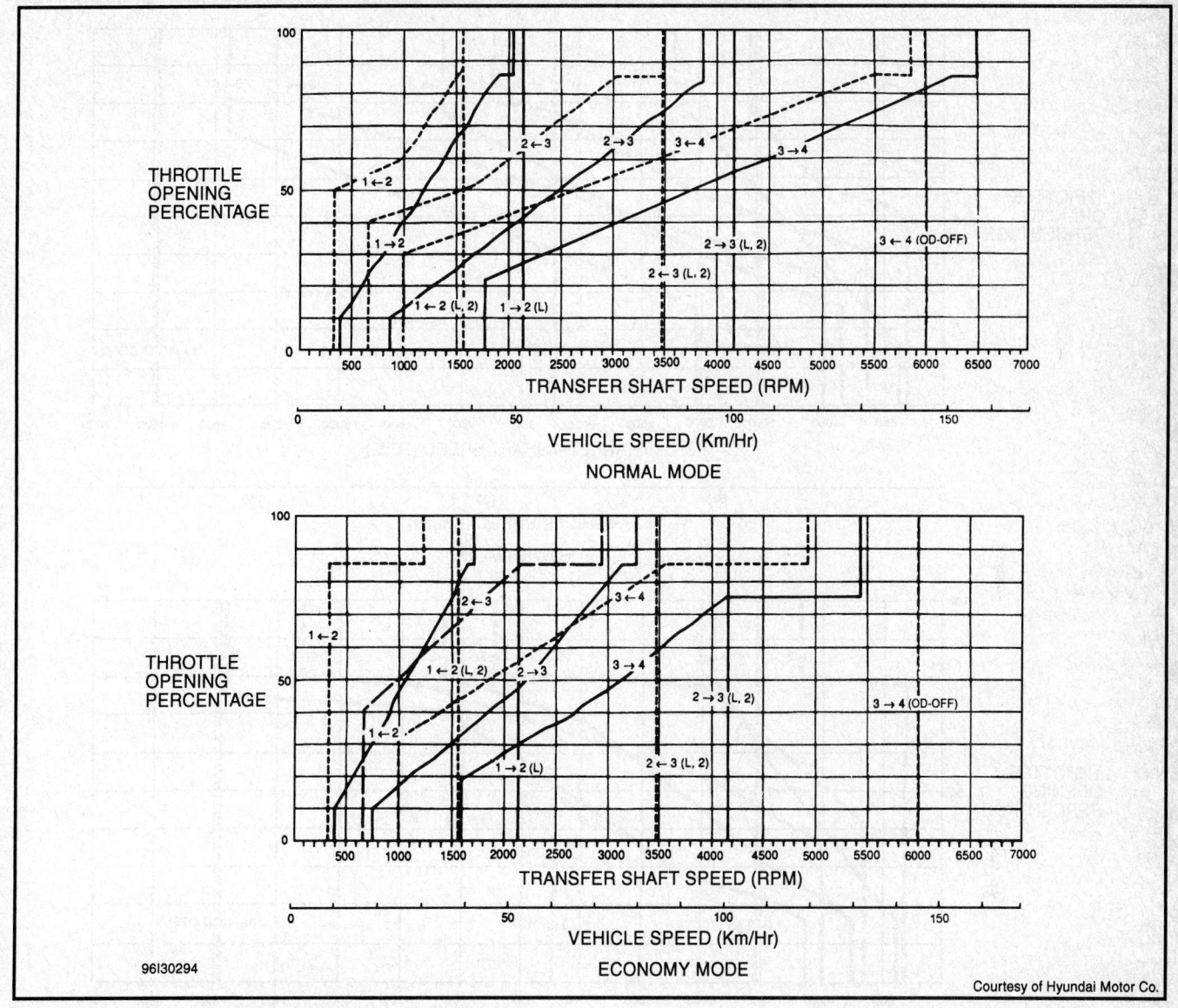

Fig. 2: Transaxle Upshift & Downshift Speeds (1995 Elantra)

4) If pressure is not within specification, see HYDRAULIC PRESSURE TEST TROUBLE SHOOTING table. If kickdown brake pressure or any clutch pressure is less than specified, line pressure adjustment may be required. See LINE PRESSURE ADJUSTMENT under ON-VEHICLE SERVICE.

5) If reducing pressure is not within specification, reducing pressure adjustment may be required. See REDUCING PRESSURE ADJUSTMENT under ON-VEHICLE SERVICE.

6) Shut engine off. Remove pressure gauge. Install and tighten pressure tap plug to specification. See TORQUE SPECIFICATIONS.

HYDRAULIC PRESSURE TEST TROUBLE SHOOTING

Application	Probable Cause
All Pressures Are Low Or High	Restricted Main Oil Filter On Valve Body, Improper Line Pressure Adjustment, Sticking Regulator Valve In Valve Body, Loose Valve Body Bolts, Defective Oil Pump
Improper Reducing Pressure	Improper Line Pressure Adjustment, Restricted "L" Shaped Oil Filter On Intermediate Plate In Valve Body, Improper Reducing Pressure Adjustment, Sticking Reducing Valve In Valve Body, Loose Valve Body Bolts

HYDRAULIC PRESSURE TEST TROUBLE SHOOTING (Cont.)

Application	Probable Cause
Improper Kickdown Brake Pressure	Defective "D" Rings Or Seal Rings On Kickdown Servo Piston Or Sleeve, Loose Valve Body Bolts, Defective Valve Body
Improper Front Clutch Pressure	Defective "D" Rings On Kickdown Servo Piston Or Sleeve, Loose Valve Body Bolts, Defective Valve Body, Defective Front Clutch Components
Improper End Clutch Pressure	Defective "D" Rings Or Seal Rings On End Clutch, Loose Valve Body Bolts, Defective Valve Body
Improper Low-Reverse Brake Pressure	"O" Ring Between Valve Body & Transaxle Housing Is Missing, Loose Valve Body Bolts, Defective Valve Body, Defective "O" Rings On Low-Reverse Brake Piston
Improper Torque Converter Pressure	Sticking Damper Clutch Control Solenoid Valve, Restricted Or Leaking Oil Cooler, Defective Seal Rings On Input Shaft, Defective Torque Converter

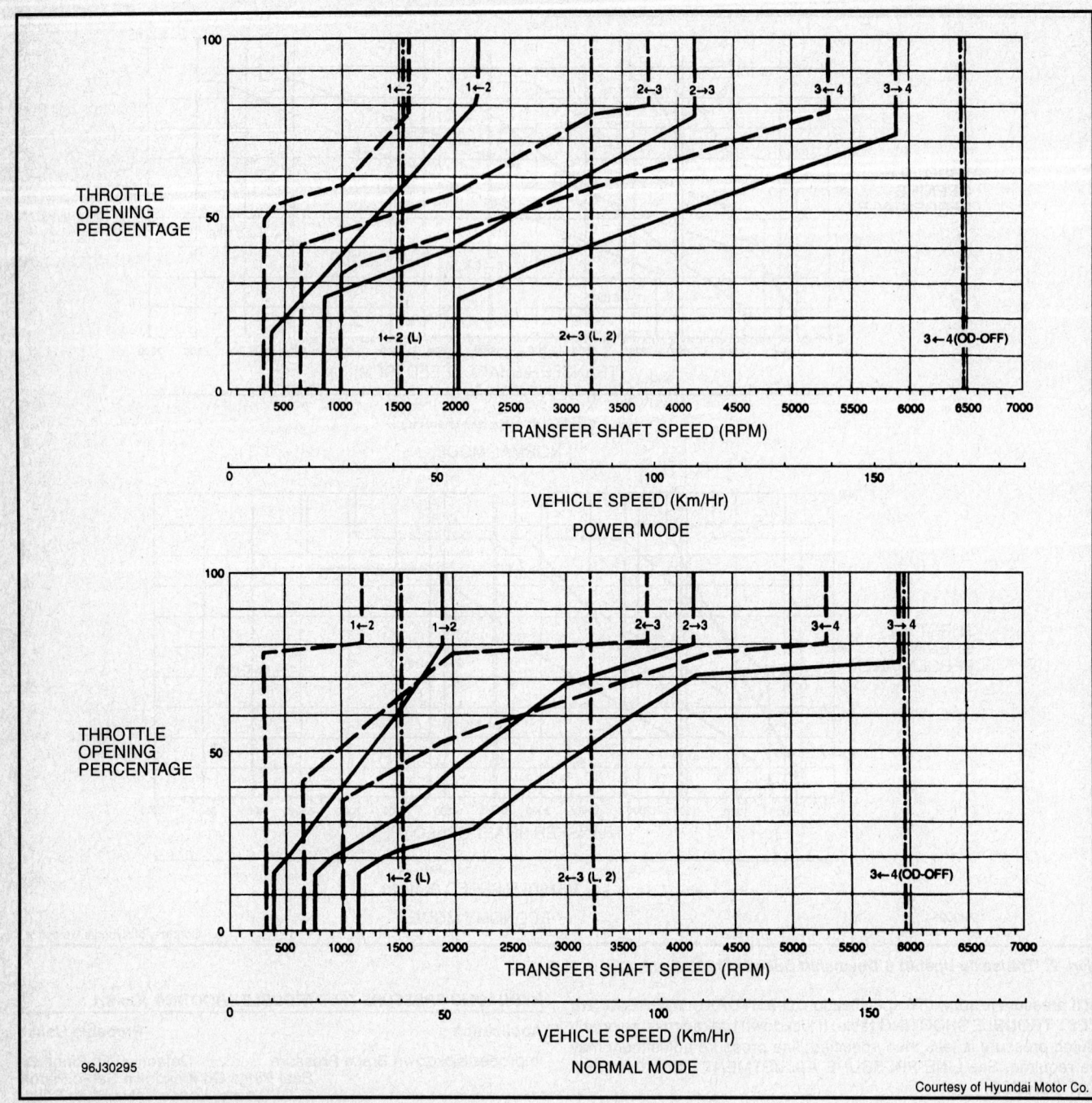

96J30295

Courtesy of Hyundai Motor Co.

Fig. 3: Transaxle Upshift & Downshift Speeds (1995 Sonata)

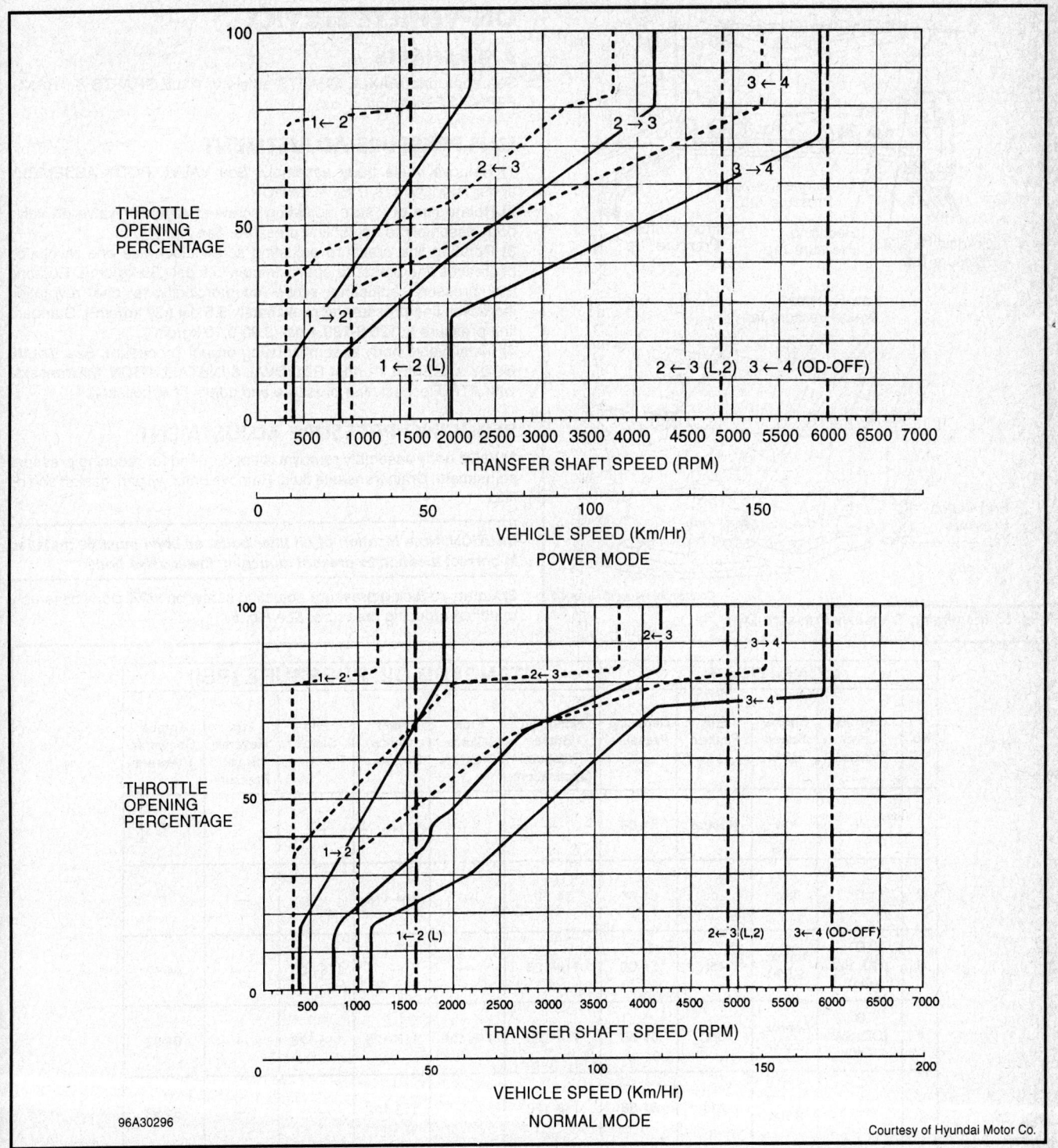

Fig. 4: Transaxle Upshift & Downshift Speeds (1996 Sonata)

Courtesy of Hyundai Motor Co.

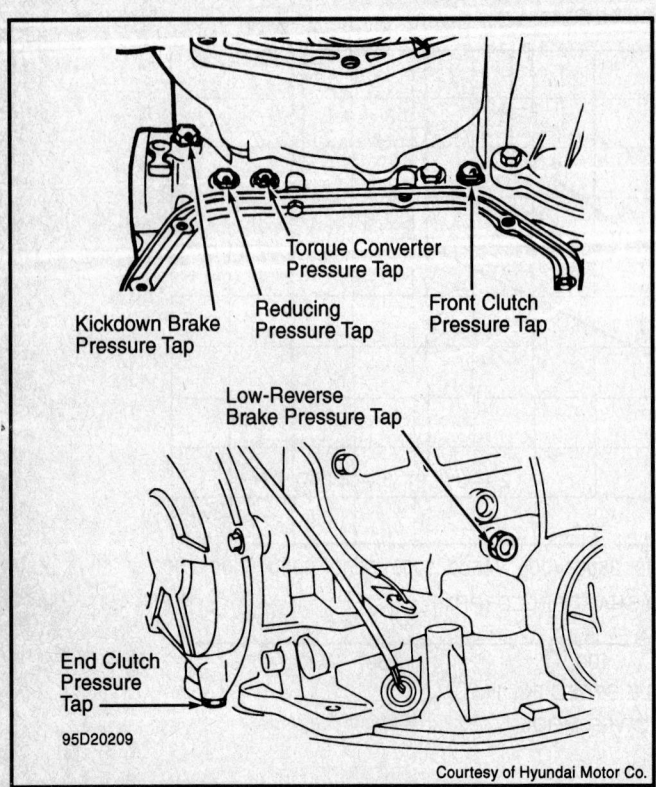

Torque Converter
Pressure Tap

Kickdown Brake
Pressure Tap

Reducing
Pressure Tap

Front Clutch
Pressure Tap

Low-Reverse
Brake Pressure Tap

End Clutch
Pressure
Tap

95D20209

Courtesy of Hyundai Motor Co.

Fig. 5: Identifying Transaxle Pressure Taps

ON-VEHICLE SERVICE

AXLE SHAFTS

See appropriate AXLE SHAFTS article in AXLE SHAFTS & TRANSFER CASES section.

LINE PRESSURE ADJUSTMENT

1) Remove valve body assembly. See VALVE BODY ASSEMBLY under REMOVAL & INSTALLATION.

2) Rotate line pressure adjusting screw at regulator valve on valve body assembly to adjust line pressure. *See Fig. 7.*

3) Rotating line pressure adjusting screw clockwise one revolution decreases line pressure approximately 5.5 psi (.39 kg/cm²). Rotating line pressure adjusting screw counterclockwise one revolution increases line pressure approximately 5.5 psi (.39 kg/cm²). Standard line pressure is 126.5-129.4 psi (8.90-9.10 kg/cm²).

4) Install valve body assembly using proper procedure. See VALVE BODY ASSEMBLY under REMOVAL & INSTALLATION. Fill transaxle with ATF. Recheck line pressure and adjust (if necessary).

REDUCING PRESSURE ADJUSTMENT

1) Valve body assembly removal is not required for reducing pressure adjustment. Drain transaxle fluid. Remove bolts, oil pan, gasket and oil filter.

CAUTION: Note location of oil filter bolts, as bolts must be installed in correct location to prevent damaging lower valve body.

2) Rotate reducing pressure adjusting screw on valve body assembly to adjust reducing pressure. *See Fig. 8.*

	CONDITIONS				STANDARD OIL PRESSURE (PSI)					
No.	Selector Lever Position	Engine Speed RPM	Shift Position	Reducing Pressure	Kickdown Brake Pressure (application)	Front Clutch Pressure	Rear Clutch Pressure	End Clutch Pressure	Low Reverse Brake Pressure	Torque Converter Pressure
1	N	Idle	Neutral	51-68	----	----	----	----	----	*
2	D	Idle	2nd	51-68	14-30	----	104-118	---	----	*
3	D (OD SW On)	Approx. 2.500	4th	51-68	118-128	----	----	118-128	----	64-92
4	D (OD SW Off)	Approx. 2.500	3rd	51-68	118-128	118-128	118-128	118-128	---	64-92
5	2	Approx. 2.500	2nd	51-68	118-128	----	118-128	----	----	64-92
6	L	Approx. 1.000	1st	51-68	----	----	118-128	----	43-64	*
7	R	Approx 2.500 --------- 1.000	Reverse	51-68	----	238-325 --------- 145 or more	----	----	238-325 --------- 145 or more	64-92

NOTE: – – Indicates pressure is less than 1.4 psi.
OD SW ON: Overdrive switch is in ON position.
OD SW OFF: Overdrive switch is in OFF position.
* - Pressure is not standard.

96B30297

Courtesy of Hyundai Motor Co.

Fig. 6: Hydraulic Pressure Test Specifications

3) Rotating reducing pressure adjusting screw clockwise one revolution decreases reducing pressure approximately 4.3 psi (.3 kg/cm²). Rotating reducing pressure adjusting screw counterclockwise one revolution increases reducing pressure approximately 4.3 psi (.3 kg/cm²). Standard reducing pressure is 59.7-62.5 psi (4.20-4.40 kg/cm²).
4) Install oil filter. Tighten oil filter bolts to specification. Using NEW gasket, install oil pan. Install and tighten oil pan bolts to specification.
5) Fill transaxle with ATF. Recheck reducing pressure and adjust (if necessary).

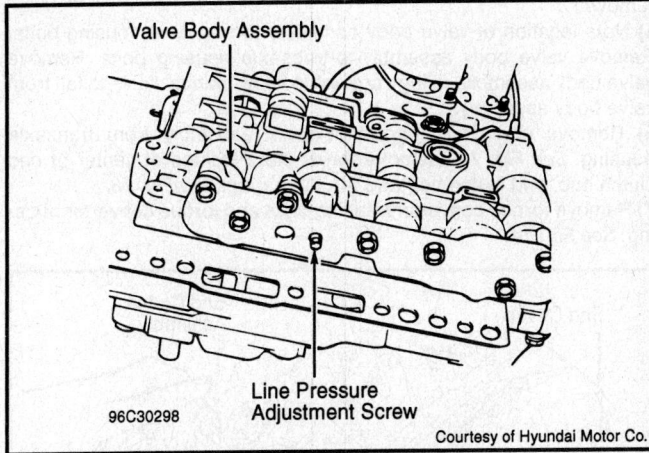

Fig. 7: Identifying Line Pressure Adjusting Screw

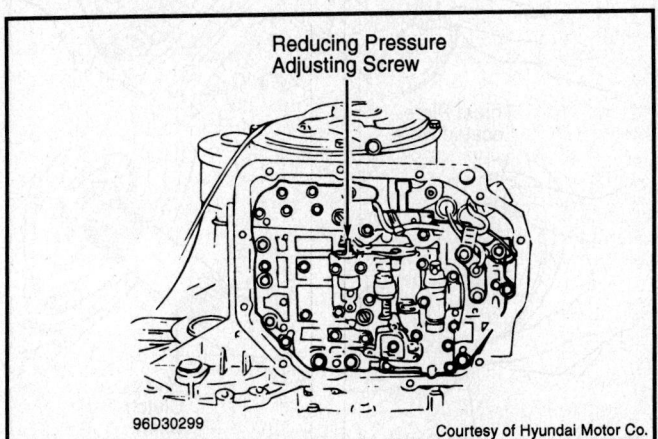

Fig. 8: Identifying Reducing Pressure Adjusting Screw

KICKDOWN SERVO ADJUSTMENT

1) Ensure area around kickdown servo area on side of transaxle is clean. See Fig. 9. Remove snap ring and kickdown servo switch.
2) Loosen kickdown servo lock nut on kickdown servo adjusting screw. Using Kickdown Servo Socket "A" (09454-33101A), hold kickdown servo piston from rotating. See Fig. 9.
3) Using INCH-lb. torque wrench and Kickdown Servo Socket "B" (09454-33101B), tighten kickdown servo adjusting screw to 89 INCH. lbs. (10.0 N.m).
4) Loosen kickdown servo adjusting screw 2 full turns. Tighten kickdown servo adjusting screw to 44 INCH lbs. (5.0 N.m).
5) Loosen kickdown servo adjusting screw 2 - 2 1/4 turns. Hold kickdown servo piston and adjusting screw from rotating. Tighten kickdown servo lock nut to specification. See TORQUE SPECIFICATIONS. Using NEW "O" ring, install kickdown servo switch and snap ring.

VALVE BODY ASSEMBLY

Valve body assembly may be serviced on the vehicle. See VALVE BODY ASSEMBLY under REMOVAL & INSTALLATION.

Fig. 9: Identifying & Adjusting Kickdown Servo

REMOVAL & INSTALLATION

ELECTRICAL COMPONENTS

See HYUNDAI KM175 ELECTRONIC CONTROLS article.

TRANSAXLE

See appropriate AUTOMATIC TRANSMISSION REMOVAL article in TRANSMISSION SERVICING section.

VALVE BODY ASSEMBLY

Removal – 1) Drain transaxle fluid. Remove bolts, oil pan, gasket and oil filter.

CAUTION: Note location of oil filter bolts, as bolts must be installed in correct location to prevent damaging lower valve body.

---

2) Remove oil temperature sensor, located on bottom of valve body assembly. See Fig. 10.

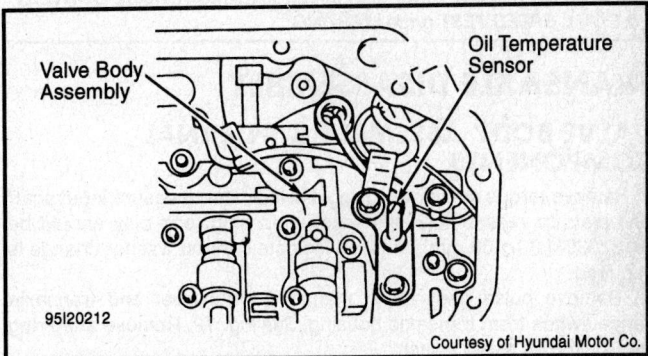

Fig. 10: Identifying Oil Temperature Sensor

3) Push tab inward on solenoid valve electrical connector grommet, located on transaxle housing, above oil pan area. Push solenoid valve electrical connector grommet out of transaxle housing so valve body assembly can be removed.
4) Note location of valve body assembly-to-transaxle housing bolts. Remove valve body assembly-to-transaxle housing bolts. Remove valve body assembly, using care not to allow manual valve to fall from valve body assembly.
Installation – 1) Install NEW "O" ring on upper surface of valve body assembly, where valve body seals against transaxle housing.
2) Install NEW "O" ring on solenoid valve electrical connector grommet where it seals against transaxle housing. Install valve body assembly and solenoid valve electrical connector grommet. Ensure pin on manual control shaft engages with manual valve on valve body assembly.
3) Ensure notch on solenoid valve electrical connector grommet is toward front of transaxle housing and wiring is properly routed.
4) Install oil temperature sensor and valve body assembly-to-transaxle housing bolts. Ensure proper length bolt is installed in correct location. See Fig. 11.

5) Tighten valve body assembly-to-transaxle housing bolts to specification. See TORQUE SPECIFICATIONS. Install oil filter. Tighten oil filter bolts to specification.

6) Ensure the 5 magnets are installed in 5 depression areas on oil pan. Using NEW gasket, install oil pan. Install and tighten oil pan bolts to specification. Fill transaxle with ATF.

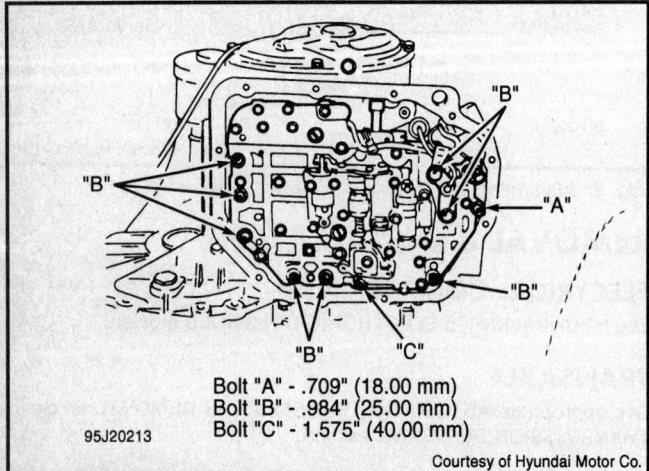

Bolt "A" - .709" (18.00 mm)
Bolt "B" - .984" (25.00 mm)
Bolt "C" - 1.575" (40.00 mm)

95J20213

Courtesy of Hyundai Motor Co.

Fig. 11: Identifying Valve Body Assembly-To-Transaxle Housing Bolt Locations

TORQUE CONVERTER

NOTE: Torque converter is a sealed unit and cannot be disassembled. Replace torque converter if defective.

NOTE: For torque converter stall speed test, see TORQUE CONVERTER STALL SPEED TEST under TESTING.

TRANSAXLE DISASSEMBLY

VALVE BODY ASSEMBLY & INTERNAL COMPONENTS

1) Remove torque converter. Using dial indicator, measure input shaft end play for reassembly reference. Input shaft end play should be .012-.039" (.30-1.00 mm). This will indicate if thrust washer change is required.

2) Remove pulse generators, manual control lever and transaxle range switch from transaxle housing. See Fig. 12. Remove snap ring and kickdown servo switch.

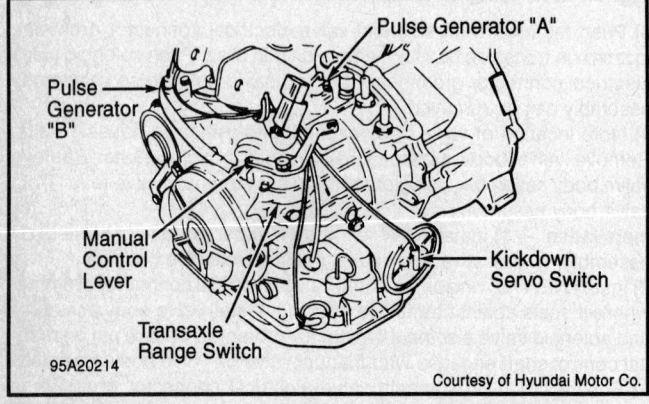

95A20214

Courtesy of Hyundai Motor Co.

Fig. 12: Identifying Pulse Generators, Manual Control Lever, Transaxle Range Switch, & Kickdown Servo Switch

CAUTION: Note location of oil filter bolts, as bolts must be installed in correct location to prevent damaging lower valve body.

3) Remove oil pan, oil pan gasket and oil filter. Remove oil temperature sensor, located on bottom of valve body assembly. See Fig. 10.

4) Push tabs inward on solenoid valve electrical connector grommet, located on transaxle housing. Push solenoid valve electrical connector grommet out of transaxle housing so valve body assembly can be removed.

5) Note location of valve body assembly-to-transaxle housing bolts. Remove valve body assembly-to-transaxle housing bolts. Remove valve body assembly, using care not to allow manual valve to fall from valve body assembly.

6) Remove end cover and end clutch assembly from transaxle housing. See Fig. 13. Remove thrust plate located at center of end clutch hub, end clutch hub and thrust bearing. See Fig. 13.

7) Remove torque converter housing bolts and torque converter housing. See Fig. 14.

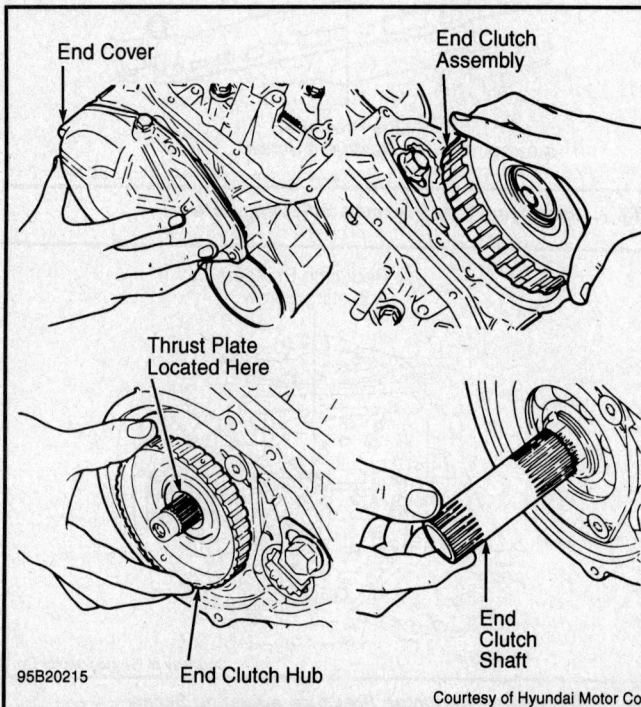

95B20215

Courtesy of Hyundai Motor Co.

Fig. 13: Removing & Installing End Cover, End Clutch Assembly Thrust Plate, End Clutch Hub & End Clutch Shaft

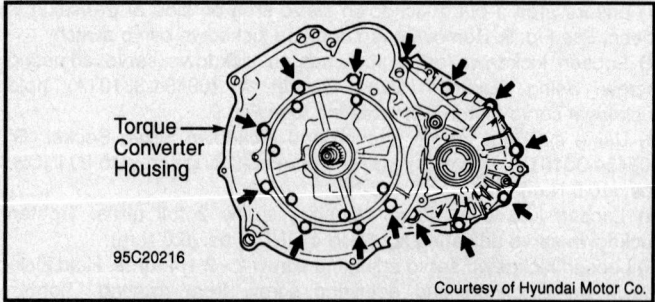

95C20216

Courtesy of Hyundai Motor Co.

Fig. 14: Identifying Torque Converter Housing Bolts & Torque Converter Housing

8) Remove oil pump-to-transaxle housing bolts. Thread 2 pull-out bolts in oil pump and gently tighten to press oil pump from transaxle housing. Lightly tap on oil pump with soft-faced hammer while tightening pull-out bolts during oil pump removal.

9) Remove spacer, differential assembly with bearings. Spacer fits on top of bearing on differential assembly. *See Fig. 15.*

10) Remove fiber thrust washer from front of input shaft. Lift upward on input shaft to remove front and rear clutch assemblies from transaxle housing.

11) Remove thrust bearing, located on front side of clutch hub. Remove clutch hub, thrust race and bearing. Remove kickdown drum and kickdown band.

12) Using spring compressor, compress kickdown servo spring on kickdown servo. Release and remove spring compressor. Remove kickdown servo piston and spring.

13) Remove anchor rod for kickdown band from inside of transaxle housing. *See Fig. 15.* Remove snap ring that retains center support in transaxle housing.

14) Attach Center Support Remover/Installer (09453-21310) on center support. Pull center support from transaxle housing.

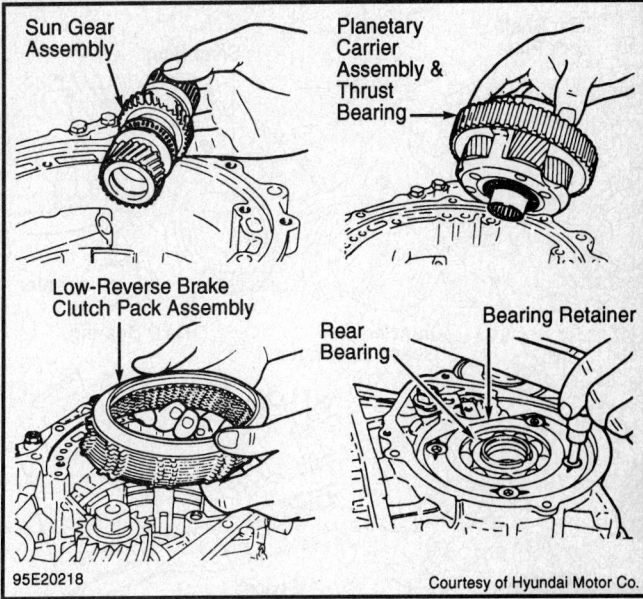

Fig. 16: *Removing & Installing Sun Gear Assembly, Planetary Carrier Assembly, Clutch Pack Assembly & Bearing Retainer*

17) Remove bolt and idler shaft lock plate. *See Fig. 17.* Using Adapter (09545-21100), loosen idler shaft. Remove idler shaft, transfer idler gear with bearings and spacer from transaxle housing.

18) Remove snap ring from rear bearing. Remove internal gear, output flange and transfer drive gear with rear bearing as an assembly.

19) Remove transfer shaft cover. Using hammer and chisel, loosen staked area on transfer shaft lock nut. Transfer shaft lock nut contains left-hand threads. Remove transfer shaft lock nut from transfer shaft.

20) Using hammer and brass drift, tap transfer shaft from transfer driven gear and transaxle housing. DO NOT lose spacer located on transfer shaft. Using press and bearing remover, press bearing from transfer shaft.

21) Remove bearing races for transfer shaft bearings from transaxle housing. Remove parking brake rod support and parking brake rod. *See Fig. 17.* Remove set screw, manual control shaft, detent ball, seat and spring from transaxle housing.

COMPONENT DISASSEMBLY & REASSEMBLY

NOTE: Manufacturer specifies Mopar Plus-Type 7176 ATF for use in this transaxle. This fluid should also be used for assembly lubrication.

OIL PUMP

Disassembly – 1) Remove "O" ring from oil pump housing. Remove oil pump housing-to-reaction shaft support bolts. Remove reaction shaft support from oil pump housing. *See Fig. 18.*

2) Place reference marks on drive and driven gears for reassembly reference to ensure gears are installed in original direction. Remove drive and driven gears from oil pump housing.

3) Remove steel ball from oil pump housing. Remove snap ring and seal ring from drive gear. Remove seal rings from reaction shaft support. Remove oil seal from oil pump housing.

Cleaning & Inspection – 1) Clean components with solvent and dry with compressed air. Inspect components for damage or signs of wear.

2) Install drive and driven gears in oil pump housing. Ensure gears rotate smoothly. Place straightedge on oil pump housing, above both gears.

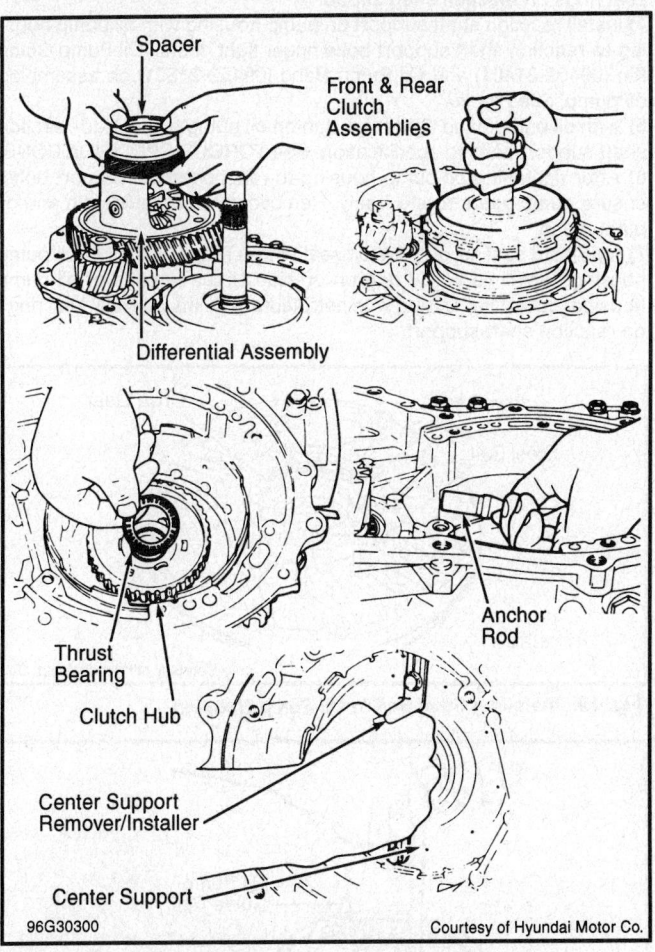

Fig. 15: *Removing & Installing Differential Assembly, Front & Rear Clutch, Clutch Hub, Thrust Bearing, Anchor Rod & Center Support*

15) Remove sun gear assembly and planetary carrier assembly with thrust bearing. *See Fig. 16.* Remove low-reverse brake clutch pack assembly from transaxle housing.

NOTE: Low-reverse brake clutch pack assembly consists of wave spring, return spring, pressure plate, brake reaction plate, brake discs and brake plates. Note sequence of low-reverse brake clutch pack component installation for reassembly reference.

16) Using hammer and punch, lightly tap on heads of retaining screws for bearing retainer to loosen thread sealant on retaining screws. *See Fig. 10.* Remove retaining screws and bearing retainer.

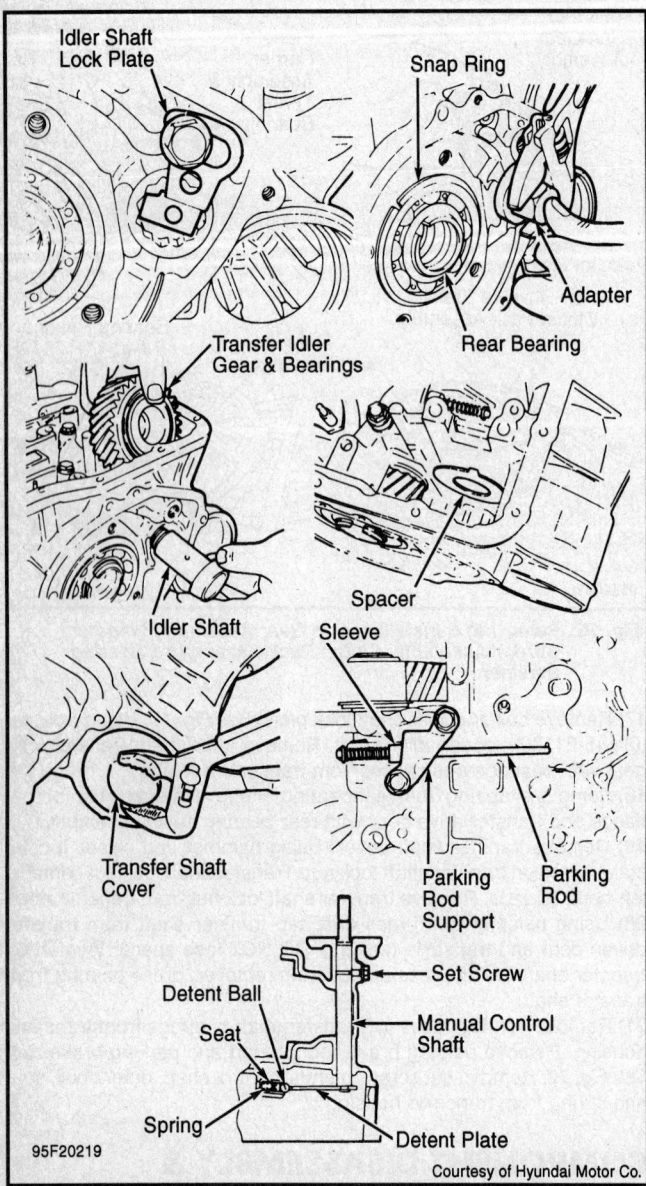

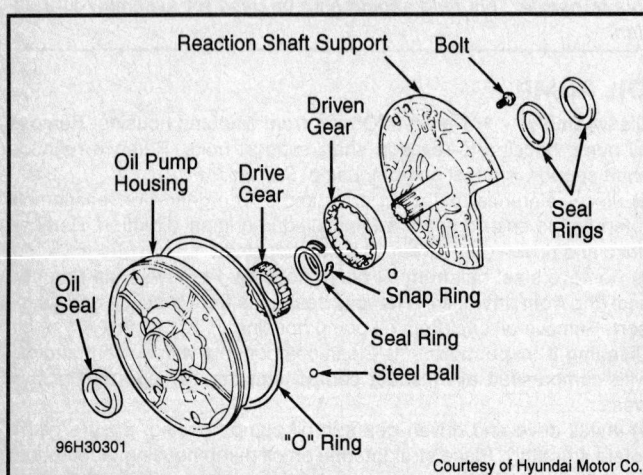

Fig. 17: Removing & Installing Idler Shaft, Transfer Idler Gear, Spacer, Rear Bearing Snap Ring, Transfer Shaft Cover, Parking Rod & Manual Control Shaft

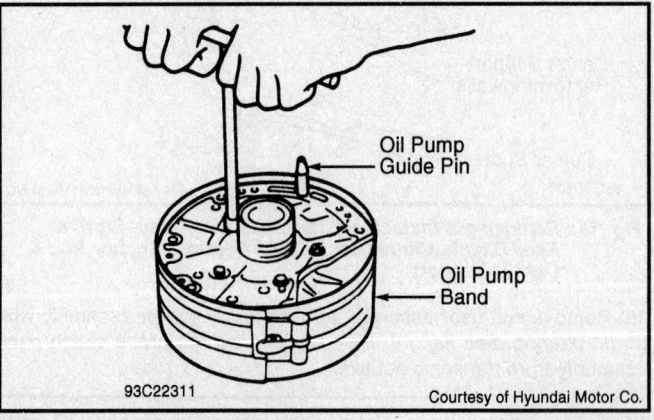

Fig. 18: Exploded View Of Oil Pump

3) Using feeler gauge, measure oil pump gear side clearance between each gear and straightedge. Replace oil pump if oil pump gear side clearance exceeds specification. See OIL PUMP SIDE GEAR CLEARANCE SPECIFICATIONS table.

OIL PUMP SIDE GEAR CLEARANCE SPECIFICATIONS

Application	In. (mm)
Elantra (1995)	.0012-.0020 (.030-.050)
Sonata	.0004-.0019 (.010-.048)

Reassembly – 1) Install NEW seal ring in drive gear. Install snap ring in drive gear. Coat all components with ATF.

2) Install drive and driven gears in oil pump housing. If installing original gears, ensure gears are installed in original positions using reference marks made during disassembly.

3) Install steel ball in hole on oil pump housing. See Fig. 19. Install NEW seal rings on reaction shaft support.

4) Install reaction shaft support on pump housing with oil pump housing-to-reaction shaft support bolts finger tight. Install Oil Pump Guide Pin (09452-21401) and Oil Pump Band (09452-21301) on assembled oil pump. See Fig. 20.

5) With oil pump band tightened, tighten oil pump housing-to-reaction shaft support bolts to specification. See TORQUE SPECIFICATIONS.

6) After tightening oil pump housing-to-reaction shaft support bolts, ensure pump gears rotate freely. Remove oil pump guide pin and oil pump band.

7) Lubricate seal lip of NEW oil seal with ATF and install in oil pump housing. Install NEW "O" ring on outside circumference of oil pump housing. Lubricate "O" ring with petroleum jelly. Install NEW seal rings on reaction shaft support.

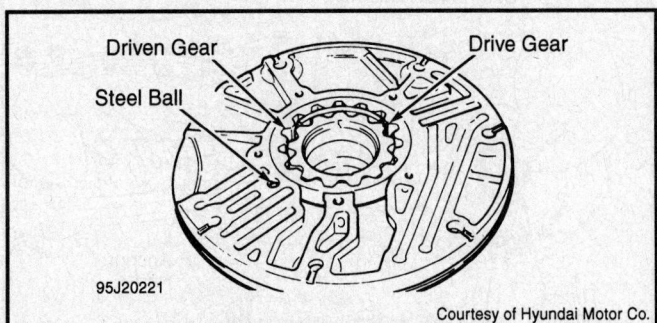

Fig. 19: Installing Steel Ball In Oil Pump Housing

Fig. 20: Assembling Oil Pump

FRONT CLUTCH

Disassembly – 1) Remove large snap ring, clutch plates and clutch discs from front clutch retainer. See Fig. 21. If clutch reaction plates are to be reused, note direction and order of clutch plates for reassembly reference.

2) Using spring compressor, compress return spring. Remove small snap ring from front clutch retainer. Remove spring compressor. Remove return spring and retainer.

3) Remove front clutch piston from front clutch retainer. Remove "D" rings from clutch piston and front clutch retainer.

Cleaning & Inspection – Clean metal components with solvent and dry with compressed air. Inspect components for damage and replace if necessary. Ensure no rough edges exist in "D" ring sealing areas.

Reassembly – **1)** Install NEW "D" ring on front clutch piston and front clutch retainer. Ensure rounded side of "D" ring is facing outward, away from front clutch piston or front clutch retainer. Lubricate "D" rings with ATF.

2) Install front clutch piston in front clutch retainer. Use care not to damage "D" rings when installing front clutch piston. Install return spring and retainer.

3) Using spring compressor, compress return spring. Install small snap ring to hold return spring on front clutch retainer. Remove spring compressor.

CAUTION: Soak clutch discs in ATF for 2 hours before installation.

---

4) Coat all clutch plates and clutch discs with ATF. Alternately install clutch plates and clutch discs starting with clutch plate. If installing old clutch plates and clutch discs, ensure components are installed in original position and direction. Ensure original number of components are installed.

5) Install large snap ring on front clutch retainer. Lightly hold top clutch plate downward. Using feeler gauge, measure clearance between large snap ring and top clutch plate. This is the front clutch clearance.

6) Front clutch clearance should be within specification. See FRONT CLUTCH CLEARANCE SPECIFICATIONS table. If front clutch clearance is not within specification, install different thickness large snap ring to obtain correct front clutch clearance.

FRONT CLUTCH CLEARANCE SPECIFICATIONS

Application	In. (mm)
Elantra (1995)	.016-.024 (.40-.60)
Sonata	.028-.035 (.70-.90)

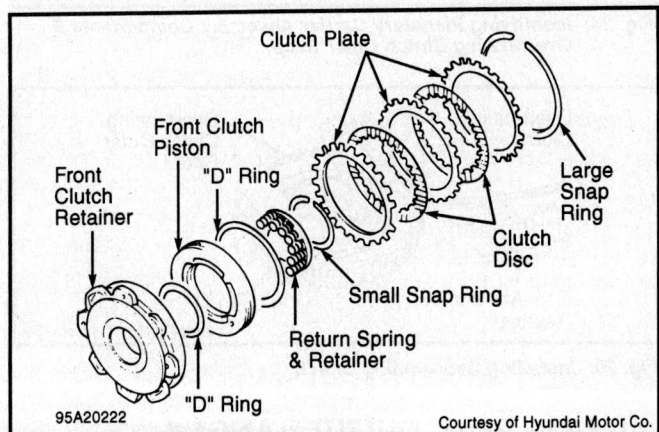

95A20222   Courtesy of Hyundai Motor Co.

Fig. 21: Exploded View Of Front Clutch

REAR CLUTCH

Disassembly – **1)** Remove small snap ring and thrust race. *See Fig. 22.* Remove input shaft from rear clutch retainer.

2) Remove large snap ring, clutch reaction plate, clutch discs, clutch plates and clutch pressure plate from rear clutch retainer. *See Fig. 22.* Note direction and order of clutch plates and clutch discs installation for reassembly reference.

3) Using spring compressor, compress return spring. Remove wave spring. Remove spring compressor. Note direction of return spring installation for reassembly reference. Remove return spring and rear clutch piston. Remove "D" rings from rear clutch piston.

Cleaning & Inspection – Clean metal components with solvent and dry with compressed air. Inspect components for damage. Replace components as required. Ensure no rough edges exist in "D" ring sealing areas.

Reassembly – **1)** Install NEW "D" rings on rear clutch piston. Ensure rounded side of "D" ring facing outward, away from rear clutch piston. Lubricate "D" rings with ATF.

2) Install rear clutch piston in rear clutch retainer. Use care not to damage "D" rings when installing rear clutch piston. Install return spring on rear clutch piston. Ensure return spring is facing correct direction. *See Fig. 22.*

3) Compress return spring. Install wave spring. Ensure wave spring is fully seated in groove on rear clutch retainer.

CAUTION: Soak clutch discs in ATF for 2 hours before installation.

---

4) Coat all clutch plates and clutch discs with ATF. Install clutch pressure plate, clutch discs, clutch plates and clutch reaction plate in rear clutch retainer.

5) If installing old clutch plates and clutch discs, ensure components are installed in original position and direction. Ensure original number of components are installed.

6) Install large snap ring on rear clutch retainer. Lightly hold clutch reaction plate downward. Using feeler gauge, measure clearance between large snap ring and clutch reaction plate. This is the rear clutch clearance.

7) Rear clutch clearance should be within specification. See REAR CLUTCH CLEARANCE SPECIFICATIONS table. If rear clutch clearance is not within specification, install different thickness large snap ring to obtain correct rear clutch clearance.

REAR CLUTCH CLEARANCE SPECIFICATIONS

Application	In. (mm)
Elantra (1995)	.012-.020 (.30-.50)
Sonata	.016-.024 (.40-.60)

8) Install input shaft in rear clutch retainer. Install thrust race and small snap ring. Install NEW sealing rings on input shaft.

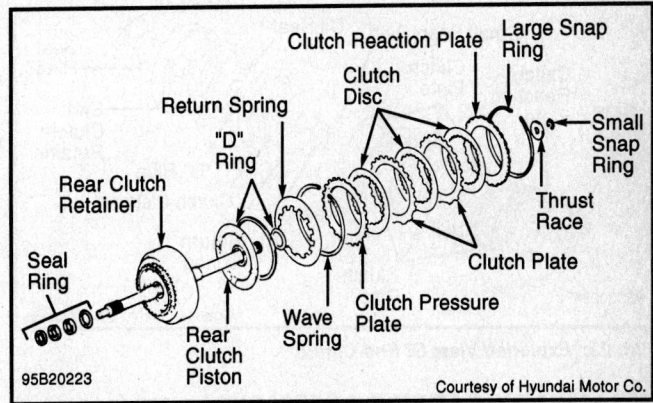

95B20223   Courtesy of Hyundai Motor Co.

Fig. 22: Exploded View Of Rear Clutch

END CLUTCH

Disassembly – **1)** Remove large snap ring, clutch reaction plate, clutch discs and clutch plates from end clutch retainer. *See Fig. 23.* Note direction and order of clutch plates and clutch discs installation for reassembly reference.

2) Remove small snap ring and washer from inside of end clutch retainer. Note direction of return spring installation for reassembly reference. Remove return spring.

3) Remove clutch piston from end clutch retainer. It may be necessary to apply air pressure to oil passage on rear side of end clutch retainer for removal of clutch piston.

4) Remove "D" rings and oil seal from clutch piston. Remove seal ring and oil seal from end clutch retainer.

Cleaning & Inspection – Clean metal components with solvent and dry with compressed air. Inspect components for damage. Replace components as required. Ensure no rough edges exist in "D" ring or oil seal sealing areas.

Reassembly – **1)** Install NEW "D" rings and oil seal on clutch piston. Ensure rounded side of "D" ring is facing outward, away from clutch piston. Install NEW seal ring and oil seal on end clutch retainer.

2) Lubricate "D" ring, oil seals and seal ring with ATF. Install clutch piston in end clutch retainer. Use care not to damage "D" rings when installing clutch piston.

3) Install return spring and washer on clutch piston. Ensure return spring is facing correct direction. *See Fig. 23.*

4) Compress return spring. Install NEW small snap ring. Ensure small snap ring is fully seated in groove on end clutch retainer.

CAUTION: Soak clutch discs in ATF for 2 hours before installation.

---

5) Coat all clutch plates and clutch discs with ATF. Alternately install clutch plates and clutch discs starting with clutch plate. If installing old clutch plates and clutch discs, ensure components are installed in original position and direction. Ensure original number of components are installed.

6) Install clutch reaction plate in end clutch retainer. Install large snap ring on end clutch retainer.

7) Lightly hold clutch reaction plate downward. Using feeler gauge, measure clearance between large snap ring and clutch reaction plate. This is the end clutch clearance.

8) End clutch clearance should be within specification. See END CLUTCH CLEARANCE SPECIFICATIONS table. If end clutch clearance is not within specification, install different thickness large snap ring to obtain correct end clutch clearance.

END CLUTCH CLEARANCE SPECIFICATIONS

Application	In. (mm)
Elantra (1995)	.016-.026 (.40-.65)
Sonata	.024-.033 (.60-.85)

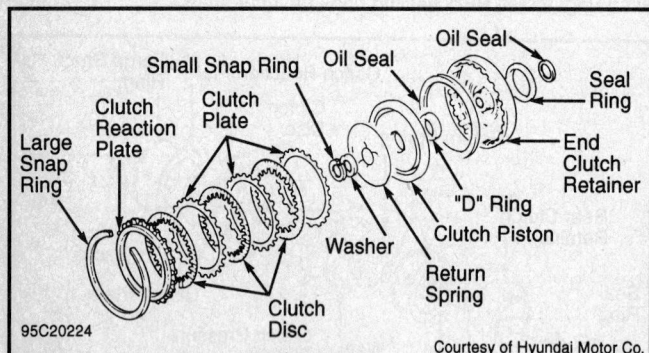

95C20224

Courtesy of Hyundai Motor Co.

Fig. 23: Exploded View Of End Clutch

PLANETARY CARRIER ASSEMBLY

Disassembly – **1)** Bend lock plate tabs away from bolt head on overrunning clutch outer race-to-planetary carrier assembly bolts. Remove overrunning clutch outer race-to-planetary carrier assembly bolts.

2) Remove overrunning clutch outer race with overrunning clutch from planetary carrier assembly. *See Fig. 24.*

3) Remove overrunning clutch end plate, located between overrunning clutch and planetary carrier assembly. Remove pinion shaft from one short pinion.

4) Remove short pinion with spacer bushing and thrust washers. DO NOT allow rollers to fall from short pinion during removal.

5) Remove thrust bearing from center of planetary carrier assembly. Note direction of overrunning clutch installation in overrunning clutch outer race.

6) Remove overrunning clutch from overrunning clutch outer race, by pressing on overrunning clutch. Remove overrunning clutch end plate from overrunning clutch outer race.

Cleaning & Inspection – Clean components with solvent and dry with compressed air. Inspect components for damage. Replace components as required.

Reassembly – **1)** Install thrust bearing in center of planetary carrier assembly. Ensure thrust bearing is installed with rollers on thrust bearing facing upward, toward overrunning clutch outer race surface on planetary carrier assembly. Flat side should be facing toward hub (rear) side of planetary carrier assembly.

2) Apply petroleum jelly on inside of short pinion to hold rollers in place. Install short pinion, spacer bushing and thrust washers in planetary carrier assembly. Ensure rollers do not fall from short pinion.

3) Install pinion shaft in short pinion and thrust washers. Ensure flat side of pinion shaft aligns with flat area on rear thrust washer.

4) Install overrunning clutch end plate on inside of overrunning clutch outer race. Press overrunning clutch into overrunning clutch outer race. Ensure arrow mark on outside of overrunning clutch is pointing upward. *See Fig. 25.*

5) Apply petroleum jelly on overrunning clutch end plate. Install overrunning clutch end plate on inside of overrunning clutch. Install overrunning clutch outer race with overrunning clutch on planetary carrier assembly.

6) Install overrunning clutch outer race-to-planetary carrier assembly bolts and tighten to specification. See TORQUE SPECIFICATIONS. Bend lock plate tabs against bolt head on overrunning clutch outer race-to planetary carrier assembly bolts.

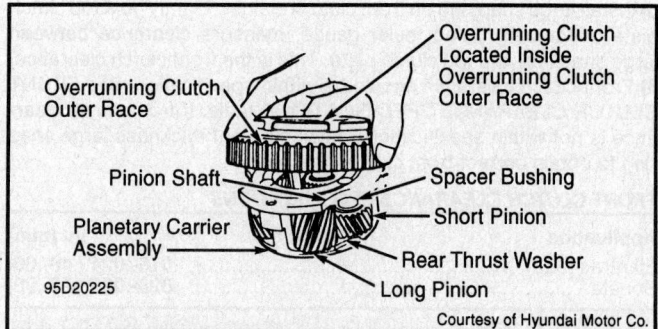

95D20225

Courtesy of Hyundai Motor Co.

Fig. 24: Identifying Planetary Carrier Assembly Components & Overrunning Clutch Outer Race

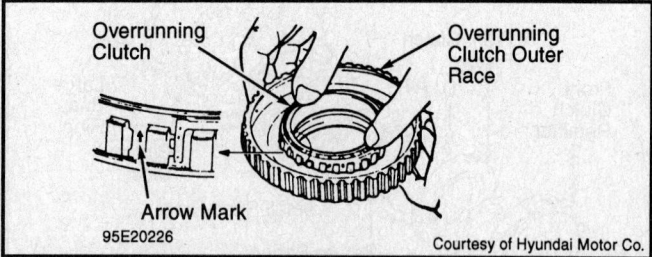

95E20226

Courtesy of Hyundai Motor Co.

Fig. 25: Installing Overrunning Clutch

INTERNAL GEAR, OUTPUT FLANGE & TRANSFER DRIVE GEAR

Disassembly – **1)** Remove small snap ring from rear of output flange. *See Fig. 26.* Using puller, pull outer bearing, transfer drive gear and inner bearing from output flange.

2) Remove large snap ring from internal gear. Separate output flange from internal gear.

Cleaning & Inspection – Clean components with solvent and dry with compressed air. Inspect components for damage. Replace components as required. Output flange and transfer drive gear must be replaced as a set if damaged.

Reassembly – **1)** Install inner bearing and transfer drive gear on output flange. Ensure transfer drive gear is installed with groove on edge of gear facing upward, away from output flange. *See Fig. 27.*

CAUTION: *Transfer drive gear must be installed with groove on edge of gear facing upward, away from output flange. See Fig. 29.*

2) Using hammer and bearing installer, drive inner bearing and transfer drive gear on output flange. Using hammer and bearing installer, drive outer bearing on output flange.

3) Install the thickest small snap ring possible on output flange. Install output flange on internal gear. Install large snap ring.

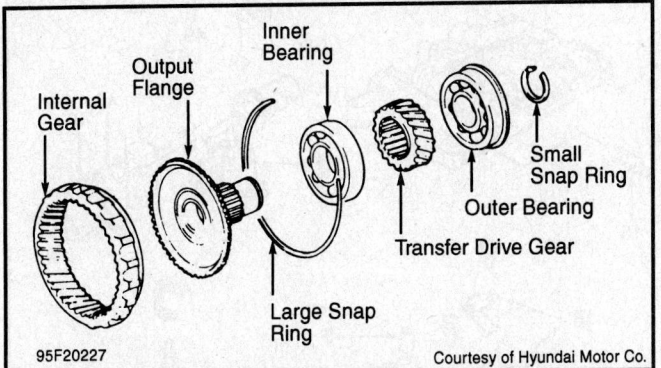

Fig. 26: *Exploded View Of Internal Gear, Output Flange & Transfer Drive Gear*

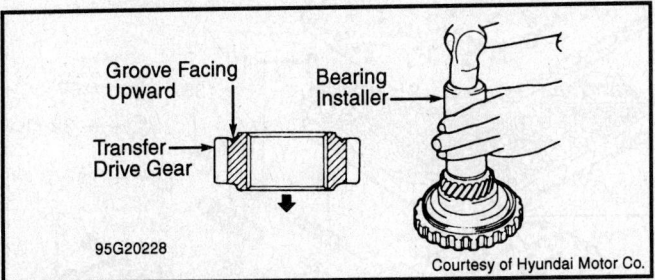

Fig. 27: *Installing Transfer Drive Gear*

TRANSFER SHAFT

Disassembly & Reassembly – If replacing bearing, using bearing splitter and press, press bearing from transfer shaft. To reassemble, use press to press NEW bearing on transfer shaft.

DIFFERENTIAL ASSEMBLY

Disassembly – 1) Remove ring gear bolts and ring gear. Remove and discard lock pin. Remove pinion shaft, pinion gears and thrust washers. *See Fig. 28.*

2) Remove side gears and spacers. Mark spacer location for reassembly reference. If replacing bearings, using press and bearing splitter, press bearings from differential case.

Cleaning & Inspection – Clean components with solvent and dry with compressed air. Inspect components for damage. Replace components as required.

Reassembly – 1) Using press, press NEW bearings on differential case (if removed). Install side gears and spacers in differential case.

NOTE: *If original side gears and spacers are used, ensure components are installed in original location. If NEW side gears are used, install NEW spacers with thickness of .039" (1.00 mm).*

2) Install thrust washers on pinion gears. Install pinion gears and thrust washers in differential case. Rotate pinion gears to mesh with side gears. Install pinion shaft.

3) Using dial indicator, measure side gear backlash between side gear and pinion gear on both sides of differential case. *See Fig. 29.*

4) Side gear backlash should be .0010-.0059" (.025-.150 mm) and should be the same on both sides. If side gear backlash is not within specification, install different thickness spacers on side gears.

5) Once correct side gear backlash is obtained, install NEW lock pin in differential case. After installing lock pin, ensure distance from end of lock pin to surface on differential case is less than .118" (3.00 mm). This ensures full installation of lock pin.

6) Install ring gear on differential case. Apply ATF on threads of ring gear bolts. Install and tighten ring gear bolts in a crisscross pattern to specification. See TORQUE SPECIFICATIONS.

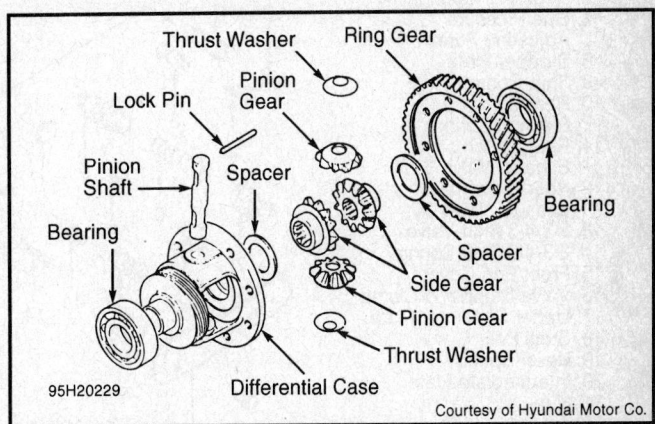

Fig. 28: *Exploded View Of Typical Differential Assembly*

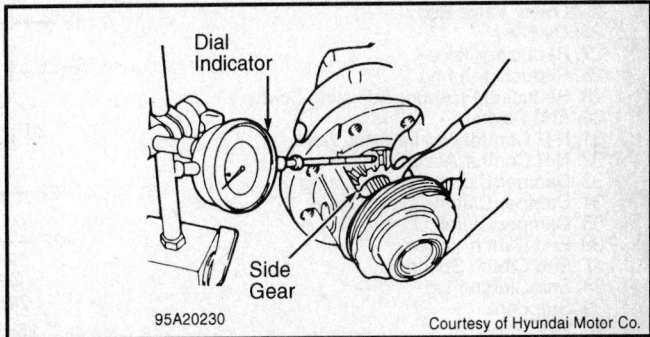

Fig. 29: *Measuring Side Gear Backlash*

VALVE BODY ASSEMBLY

CAUTION: *When disassembling valve body assembly, place components in order and mark spring locations for reassembly reference. DO NOT use force to remove components.*

Disassembly – 1) Remove bolts and all solenoid valves. *See Fig. 30.* Remove manual valve from valve body assembly.

2) Remove valve stopper and clamp. Place valve body assembly with lower valve body facing upward. Remove bolts, lower valve body and lower separator plate from intermediate plate.

3) Remove relief spring, steel balls and "L" shaped oil filter from intermediate plate. *See Fig. 31.* Remove bolts, intermediate plate and upper separator plate from upper valve body. *See Fig. 30.*

4) Remove block and upper separator plate from intermediate plate. Note location of Teflon ball, steel balls and stopper plates in upper valve body. *See Fig. 31.*

5) Remove Teflon ball, steel balls and stopper plates from upper valve body. Disassemble components from upper and lower valve bodies. *See Fig. 30.*

6) Ensure front end cover on upper valve body is held downward when removing bolts to prevent line pressure adjusting screw and spring from popping out of upper valve body. Use care when removing components from valve bodies, as components may be under spring tension.

Cleaning & Inspection – Clean components with solvent and dry with compressed air. Ensure all valves slide freely in bore.

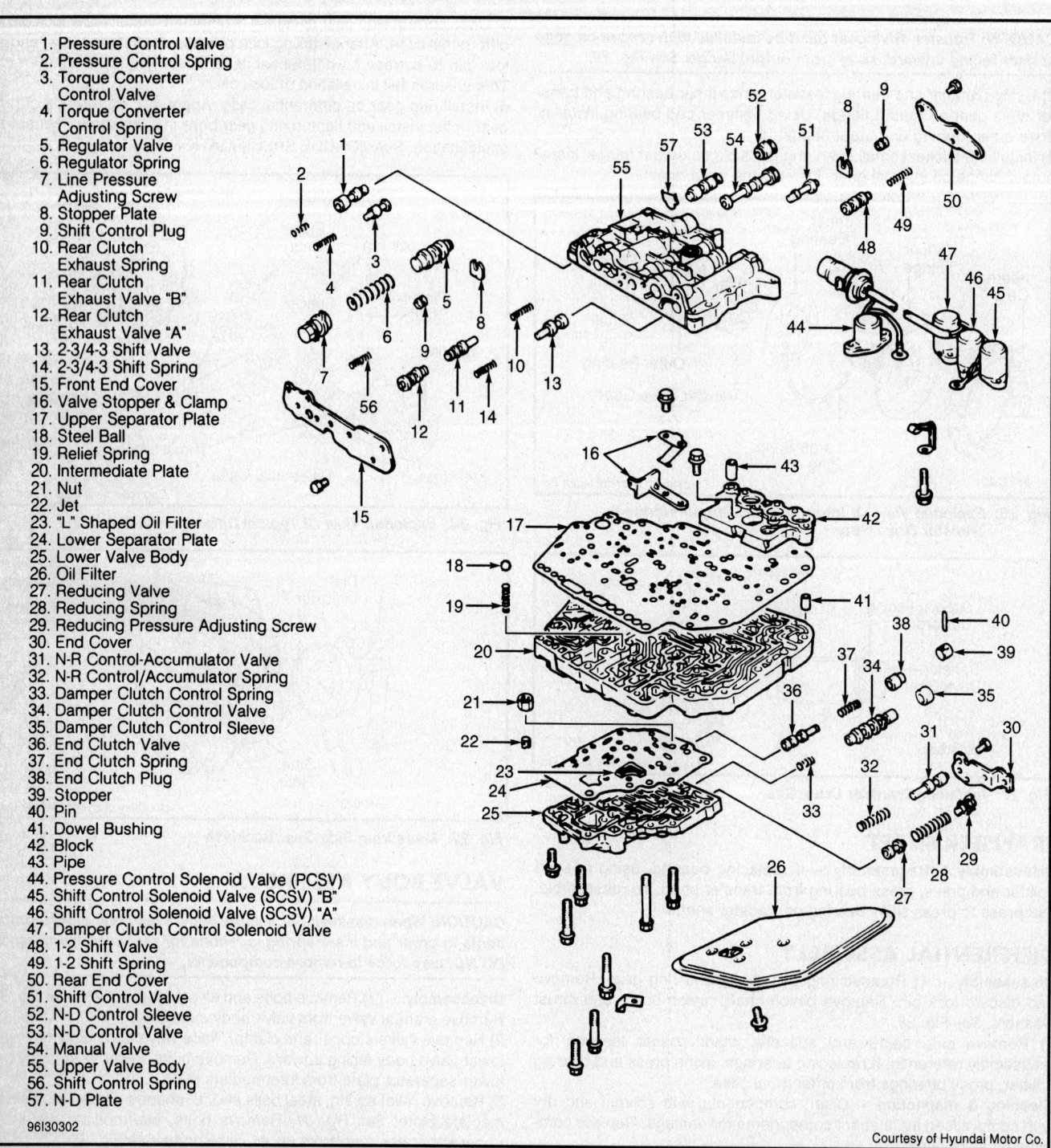

1. Pressure Control Valve
2. Pressure Control Spring
3. Torque Converter Control Valve
4. Torque Converter Control Spring
5. Regulator Valve
6. Regulator Spring
7. Line Pressure Adjusting Screw
8. Stopper Plate
9. Shift Control Plug
10. Rear Clutch Exhaust Spring
11. Rear Clutch Exhaust Valve "B"
12. Rear Clutch Exhaust Valve "A"
13. 2-3/4-3 Shift Valve
14. 2-3/4-3 Shift Spring
15. Front End Cover
16. Valve Stopper & Clamp
17. Upper Separator Plate
18. Steel Ball
19. Relief Spring
20. Intermediate Plate
21. Nut
22. Jet
23. "L" Shaped Oil Filter
24. Lower Separator Plate
25. Lower Valve Body
26. Oil Filter
27. Reducing Valve
28. Reducing Spring
29. Reducing Pressure Adjusting Screw
30. End Cover
31. N-R Control-Accumulator Valve
32. N-R Control/Accumulator Spring
33. Damper Clutch Control Spring
34. Damper Clutch Control Valve
35. Damper Clutch Control Sleeve
36. End Clutch Valve
37. End Clutch Spring
38. End Clutch Plug
39. Stopper
40. Pin
41. Dowel Bushing
42. Block
43. Pipe
44. Pressure Control Solenoid Valve (PCSV)
45. Shift Control Solenoid Valve (SCSV) "B"
46. Shift Control Solenoid Valve (SCSV) "A"
47. Damper Clutch Control Solenoid Valve
48. 1-2 Shift Valve
49. 1-2 Shift Spring
50. Rear End Cover
51. Shift Control Valve
52. N-D Control Sleeve
53. N-D Control Valve
54. Manual Valve
55. Upper Valve Body
56. Shift Control Spring
57. N-D Plate

96I30302

Courtesy of Hyundai Motor Co.

Fig. 30: Exploded View Of Valve Body Assembly

Reassembly – 1) To reassemble, reverse disassembly procedure. Ensure all steel balls, Teflon ball, relief spring and "L" shaped oil filter are installed in correct location. *See Fig. 31.*

2) Use guide studs when assembling valve body assembly to ensure correct alignment of valve bodies. Tighten valve body bolts to specification. See TORQUE SPECIFICATIONS.

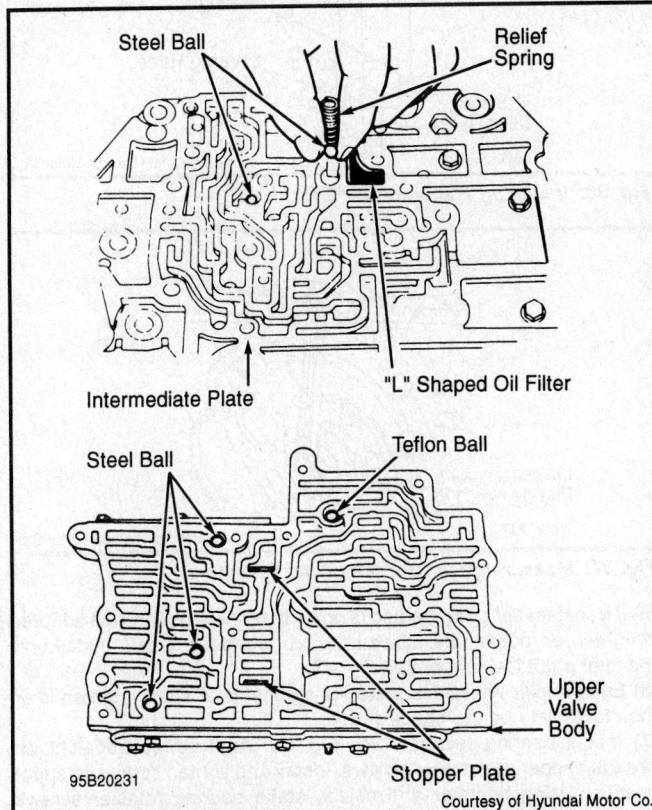

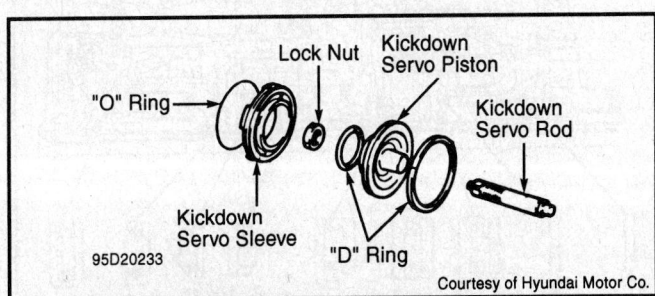

Fig. 31: Identifying Relief Spring, Steel Balls, Teflon Ball, "L" Shaped Oil Filter & Stopper Plate Locations

KICKDOWN SERVO

Disassembly & Reassembly – Disassemble kickdown servo components. *See Fig. 32.* To reassemble, reverse disassembly procedure using NEW "O" ring and NEW "D" rings. Coat "O" ring and "D" rings with ATF.

Fig. 32: Exploded View Of Kickdown Servo & Components

TRANSAXLE REASSEMBLY

VALVE BODY ASSEMBLY & INTERNAL COMPONENTS

NOTE: Manufacturer specifies Mopar Plus-Type 7176 ATF for use in this transaxle. This fluid should also be used for assembly lubrication.

NOTE: Coat all components with ATF before reassembly. New clutch discs must be soaked in ATF for at least 2 hours before installing. Apply petroleum jelly on all thrust bearings, thrust races and thrust washers before installing.

1) Low-reverse brake clearance must be checked first before assembly of transaxle. Install low-reverse brake clutch pack which consists of brake reaction plate, brake discs and brake plates in transaxle housing. *See Fig. 33.*

2) Install pressure plate and return spring on low-reverse brake clutch pack. Ensure return spring is installed facing correct direction.

3) Apply petroleum jelly on wave spring and install on center support. DO NOT install "O" rings on center support at this time.

4) Attach Center Support Remover/Installer (09453-21310) on center support. *See Fig. 15.* Install center support in transaxle housing. Install snap ring that retains center support in transaxle housing.

5) Attach dial indicator on transaxle housing, so dial indicator stem contacts brake reaction plate at right angle from transfer idler shaft hole. *See Fig. 33.* Zero dial indicator.

6) Using air pump, apply air pressure on passage in transaxle housing and note reading on dial indicator. *See Fig. 34.* Reading obtained is the low-reverse brake clearance.

7) Low-reverse brake clearance should be within specification. See LOW-REVERSE BRAKE CLEARANCE SPECIFICATIONS table.

LOW-REVERSE BRAKE CLEARANCE SPECIFICATIONS

Application	In. (mm)
Elantra (1995)	.0307-.0430 (.780-1.090)
Sonata	.0384-.0507 (.975-1.287)

8) If low-reverse brake clearance is not within specification, install different thickness pressure plate to obtain correct clearance. Consult parts department for available pressure plate thickness. Remove dial indicator.

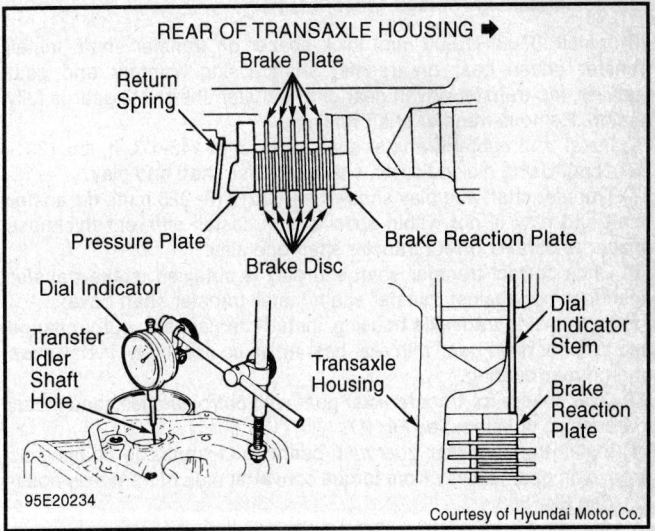

Fig. 33: Installing Low-Reverse Brake Components & Positioning Dial Indicator

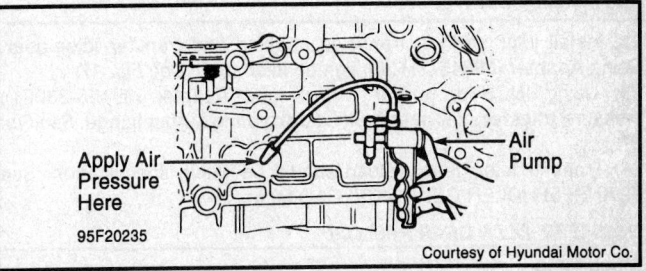

Fig. 34: Applying Air Pressure For Checking Low-Reverse Brake Clearance

9) Once correct low-reverse brake clearance is obtained, remove center support, pressure plate, return spring and low-reverse brake clutch pack. Using hammer and bearing race installer, install bearing races for transfer shaft bearing in transaxle housing (if removed).

10) Install small NEW "O" ring on manual control shaft. DO NOT install larger "O" ring on manual control shaft before installing shaft, as "O" ring will interfere with hole for the set screw.

11) Install manual control shaft in transaxle case. Push manual control shaft inward, toward manual control lever. Install remaining NEW "O" ring on manual control shaft.

12) Pull manual control shaft back into transaxle housing to align with set screw. Install NEW gasket on set screw. Install and tighten set screw to specification. See TORQUE SPECIFICATIONS.

13) Install detent ball, seat and spring in transaxle housing. See Fig. 17. Install parking brake rod and parking brake rod support. Tighten parking brake rod support bolts to specification.

14) Install transfer shaft with bearing in transaxle housing. Install Transfer Shaft Retainer (09455-21301) on transaxle housing to support transfer shaft. See Fig. 35.

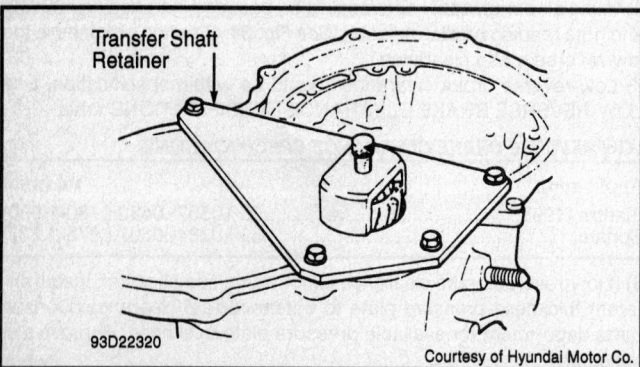

Fig. 35: Installing Transfer Shaft Retainer

15) Install .0709" (1.800 mm) thick spacer on transfer shaft. Install transfer driven gear on transfer shaft. Using hammer and gear installer, tap transfer driven gear onto transfer shaft until gear is fully seated. Remove transfer shaft retainer.

16) Install and tighten transfer shaft lock nut to 148-170 ft. lbs. (201-231 N.m). Using dial indicator, check transfer shaft end play.

17) Transfer shaft end play should be 0-.0010 (0-.025 mm). If transfer shaft end play is not within specification, install different thickness spacer to obtain correct transfer shaft end play.

18) Once correct transfer shaft end play is obtained, stake transfer shaft lock nut against transfer shaft. Install transfer shaft cover.

19) From inside transaxle housing, install internal gear, output flange and transfer drive gear with rear bearing as an assembly. Install snap ring on rear bearing.

20) Coat spacer for transfer idler gear with petroleum jelly and install in transaxle housing. See Fig. 17.

21) Install transfer idler gear with bearings in transaxle housing so groove on gear is away from torque converter side of transaxle housing. See Fig. 36.

CAUTION: Transfer idler gear must be installed in transaxle housing with groove on gear facing away from torque converter side of transaxle housing. See Fig. 38.

22) Install idler shaft in transaxle housing and transfer idler gear. Using Adapter (09545-21100), tighten idler shaft. See Fig. 17.

23) Using INCH-lb. torque wrench and Adapter (09458-33001), measure transfer idler gear preload by rotating output flange. See Fig. 37.

24) Transfer idler gear preload should be within specification. See TRANSFER IDLER GEAR PRELOAD table.

TRANSFER IDLER GEAR PRELOAD

Application	INCH lbs. (N.m)
Elantra (1995)	13 (1.5)
Sonata	7 (.8)

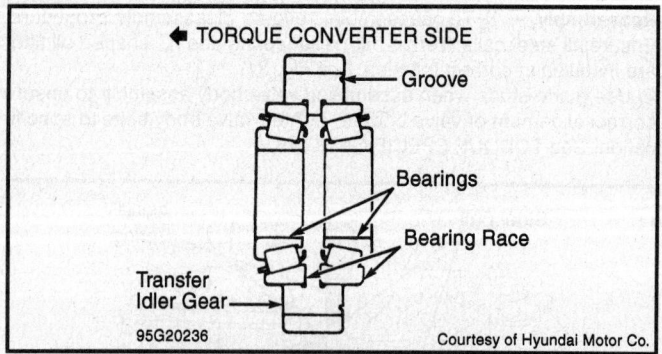

Fig. 36: Installing Transfer Idler Gear

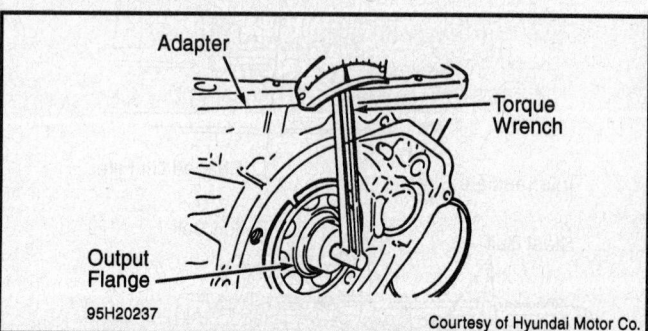

Fig. 37: Measuring Transfer Idler Gear Preload

25) If transfer idler gear preload is not within specification, use adapter to tighten or loosen idler shaft to obtain correct preload. Install bolt and idler shaft lock plate. See Fig. 17.

26) Ensure idler shaft lock plate fits against idler shaft. Tighten idler shaft lock plate bolt to specification.

27) Install bearing retainer. See Fig. 16. Apply thread sealant on threads of bearing retainer screws. Install and tighten screws to specification. Using hammer and chisel, stake bearing retainer screws against bearing retainer.

28) Install thrust bearing No. 12 on rear of planetary carrier assembly. Ensure thrust bearing is installed in correct direction. See Fig. 38.

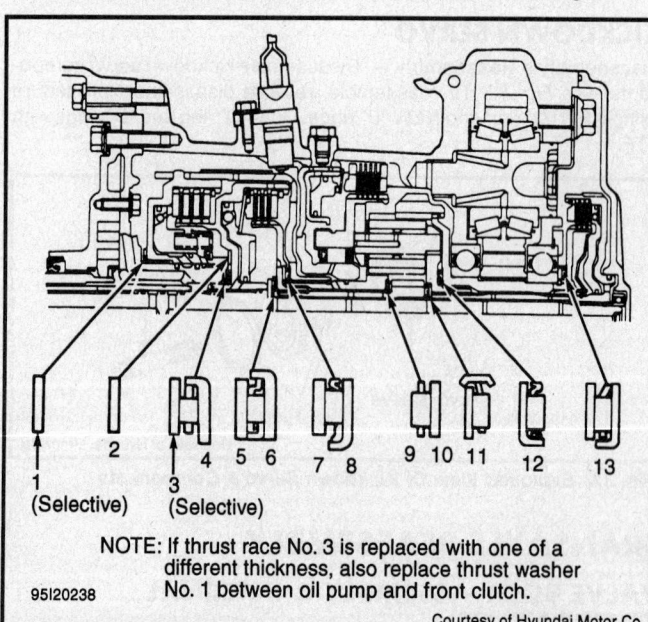

NOTE: If thrust race No. 3 is replaced with one of a different thickness, also replace thrust washer No. 1 between oil pump and front clutch.

Fig. 38: Identifying Thrust Bearing, Thrust Race & Thrust Washer Locations

29) Install planetary carrier assembly in transaxle housing. If assembling sun gear assembly, squeeze ends of seal ring together before installing on sun gear assembly. Install seal ring and snap ring on sun gear assembly.

30) Install thrust bearing No. 9 and thrust race No. 10 on forward sun gear. *See Fig. 39.* Assemble reverse sun gear and forward sun gear.

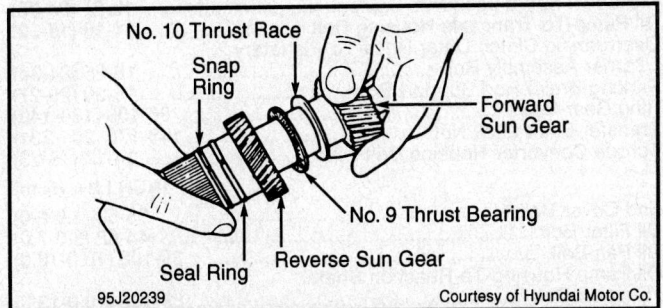

Fig. 39: Assembling Sun Gear Assembly

31) Install sun gear assembly in planetary carrier assembly. *See Fig. 16.* Install low-reverse brake clutch pack which consists of brake reaction plate, brake discs and brake plates in transaxle housing. *See Fig. 33.*

32) Install pressure plate and return spring on low-reverse brake clutch pack. Ensure return spring is installed facing correct direction.

33) Apply petroleum jelly on wave spring and install on center support. Install NEW "O" rings on center support. Coat "O" rings with ATF.

34) Using center support remover/installer, install center support in transaxle housing. Ensure wave spring stays properly positioned on center support.

35) Install snap ring that retains center support in transaxle housing so ends of snap ring align with hole in transaxle case for pulse generator "A". *See Fig. 40.*

CAUTION: Ensure ends of snap ring align with hole in transaxle case for pulse generator "A".

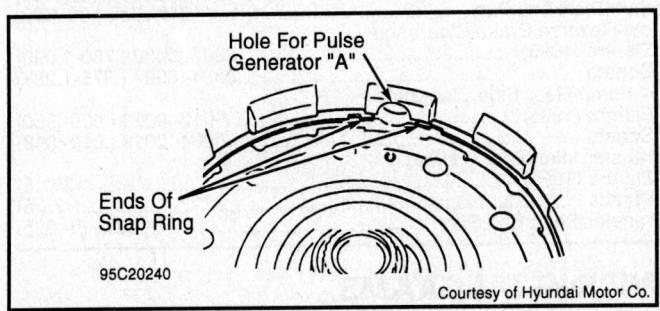

Fig. 40: Installing Snap Ring For Center Support

36) Install anchor rod for kickdown band in transaxle housing. *See Fig. 15.* Install NEW "O" ring and NEW "D" rings on kickdown servo assembly. *See Fig. 32.*

37) Install kickdown servo assembly with spring in transaxle housing. Using spring compressor, depress kickdown servo and install snap ring. Remove spring compressor.

38) Install kickdown band so end of band engages with anchor rod and kickdown servo rod on kickdown servo. Install kickdown drum so splines on drum engage with sun gear assembly.

39) Tighten kickdown servo adjusting screw to hold kickdown band in place. Install thrust bearing No. 8 on center of kickdown drum. Ensure thrust bearing is installed in correct direction. *See Fig. 38.*

40) Install thrust race No. 7 on rear of clutch hub. Install clutch hub. Ensure clutch hub fully engages splines on sun gear assembly.

41) Install thrust bearing No. 6 on front of clutch hub. *See Fig. 15.* Install thrust washer No. 2 and thrust bearing No. 4 on shaft end at front side of rear clutch. Install rear clutch assembly on front clutch assembly. Ensure clutch assemblies are fully engaged.

42) Install front and rear clutch assemblies in transaxle housing. Install differential assembly in transaxle housing.

43) Install thrust race No. 3 (metal race) on front clutch assembly. Install thrust washer No. 1 (fiber washer) on rear of oil pump.

44) Install guide studs for oil pump alignment in transaxle case. Install NEW gasket for oil pump in transaxle housing. DO NOT install NEW "O" ring on outside of oil pump housing at this time.

45) Install oil pump. Ensure thrust washer No. 1 remains in place on oil pump during installation. Remove guide studs. Install and tighten oil pump-to-transaxle housing bolts to specification.

46) Using dial indicator, measure input shaft end play. Input shaft end play should be .012-.039" (.30-1.00 mm). If input shaft end play is not within specification, install different thickness thrust race No. 3. When selecting thrust race No. 3, select appropriate thrust washer No. 1 to be used with thrust race No. 3. See THRUST WASHER & THRUST RACE SELECTION table.

NOTE: If thrust race No. 3 is replaced with one of different thickness, also replace thrust washer No. 1 between oil pump and front clutch to obtain correct input shaft end play.

THRUST WASHER & THRUST RACE SELECTION

Thrust Washer No. 1 Thickness In. (mm)	Thrust Race No. 3 Thickness In. (mm)
.055 (1.40)	.039 (1.00)
.055 (1.40)	.047 (1.20)
.071 (1.80)	.055 (1.40)
.071 (1.80)	.063 (1.60)
.087 (2.20)	.071 (1.80)
.087 (2.20)	.079 (2.00)
.102 (2.60)	.087 (2.20)
.102 (2.60)	.095 (2.40)

47) Once correct input shaft end play is obtained, remove oil pump. Install NEW "O" ring on outside of oil pump housing. Reinstall oil pump. Tighten bolts to specifications.

48) Place 2 pieces of solder .39" (10.0 mm) long and .12" (3.0 mm) in diameter at 2 places on bearing on differential assembly. *See Fig. 41.*

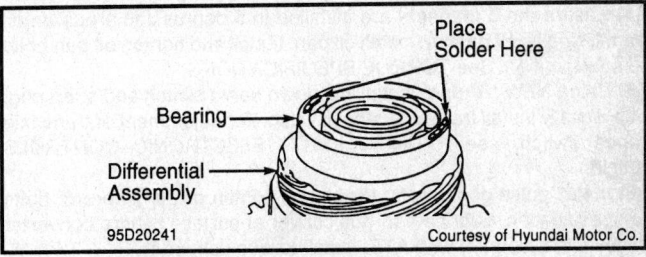

Fig. 41: Installing Solder To Check Differential Bearing Preload

49) Install NEW gasket on transaxle housing. Install torque converter housing on transaxle housing.

50) Install and tighten torque converter housing bolts to 14-17 ft. lbs. (19-23 N.m). Remove bolts, torque converter housing and gasket. Remove solder from bearing on differential assembly.

51) Using micrometer, measure thickness of solder. To determine spacer thickness needed, use following formula:

Shim thickness = solder thickness + standard gasket thickness - differential end play.

"S" = "T" + .015" (.38 mm) - (Differential End Play)

Example:

Measured Solder Thickness	"T"
Standard Gasket Thickness	+ .015" (.38 mm)
Differential End Play Range	- 0-.006" (0-.15 mm)
Shim Thickness	= "S"

52) Install selected spacer on bearing on differential assembly. *See Fig. 15.* Apply silicone sealant on torque converter housing-to-transaxle housing sealing surfaces.

53) Install NEW gasket on transaxle housing. Install torque converter housing on transaxle housing. Install and tighten torque converter housing bolts to specification. See TORQUE SPECIFICATIONS.

54) Install end clutch shaft with long splines on the shaft toward oil pump end of transaxle housing. *See Fig. 13.*

CAUTION: Ensure long splines on end clutch shaft are toward oil pump end of transaxle housing. Short splines should be toward rear of transaxle housing.

---

55) Install thrust washer on end clutch assembly so thrust washer faces the return spring on end clutch assembly. Install end clutch hub in end clutch assembly. Ensure end clutch hub aligns with splines on clutch discs on end clutch assembly.

56) Install thrust bearing No. 13 on rear of end clutch hub. Ensure thrust bearing is installed in correct direction. *See Fig. 38.* Install end clutch assembly.

57) Install NEW "O" ring and NEW "D" ring on end cover. Coat "O" ring and "D" rings with ATF. Ensure "O" ring and "D" ring are not twisted.

58) Align bolt holes in end cover with bolt holes in transaxle housing and install end cover. Bolt holes must be aligned before installing end cover. If end cover is rotated after installation, "O" ring or "D" ring may be damaged.

59) Install and tighten end cover bolts to specification. Install NEW "O" ring on upper surface of valve body assembly, where valve body seals against transaxle housing.

60) Install NEW "O" ring on solenoid valve electrical connector grommet where it seals against transaxle housing. Install valve body assembly and solenoid valve electrical connector grommet. Ensure pin on manual control shaft engages with manual valve on valve body assembly.

61) Ensure notch on solenoid valve electrical connector grommet is toward front of transaxle housing and wiring is properly routed.

62) Install oil temperature sensor and valve body assembly-to-transaxle housing bolts. Ensure proper length bolt is installed in correct location. *See Fig. 11.*

63) Tighten valve body assembly-to-transaxle housing bolts to specification. Install oil filter. Tighten oil filter bolts to specification.

64) Ensure the 5 magnets are installed in 5 depression areas on oil pan. Using NEW gasket, install oil pan. Install and tighten oil pan bolts to specification. See TORQUE SPECIFICATIONS.

65) Using NEW "D" ring, install kickdown servo switch and snap ring. *See Fig. 12.* Install transaxle range switch. For adjustment of transaxle range switch, see HYUNDAI KM175 ELECTRONIC CONTROLS article.

66) Install pulse generators. Install and tighten pulse generator bolts to specification. Lubricate torque converter surface (where converter slides into oil pump) with ATF. Install torque converter.

67) To ensure torque converter is fully seated, measure distance from front of ring gear surface to mounting surface on torque converter housing. Distance should be approximately .472" (12.00 mm) if torque converter is fully seated.

68) If distance is incorrect, remove torque converter and check alignment of torque converter with oil pump drive. Adjust kickdown servo. See KICKDOWN SERVO ADJUSTMENT under ON-VEHICLE SERVICE.

TORQUE SPECIFICATIONS
TORQUE SPECIFICATIONS

Application	Ft. Lbs. (N.m)
Bearing Retainer Screw	13-16 (18-22)
Drain Plug	22-26 (30-35)
Idler Shaft Lock Plate Bolt	35-44 (47-60)
Kickdown Servo Lock Nut	18-24 (24-33)
Oil Pump-To-Transaxle Housing Bolt	11-16 (15-22)
Overrunning Clutch Outer Race-To-Planetary Carrier Assembly Bolt	18-25 (24-34)
Parking Brake Rod Support Bolt	15-20 (20-27)
Ring Gear Bolt [1]	96-103 (130-140)
Transfer Shaft Lock Nut	148-170 (201-231)
Torque Converter Housing Bolt	14-17 (19-23)

Application	INCH Lbs. (N.m)
End Cover Bolt	35-53 (4.0-6.0)
Oil Filter Bolt	44-62 (5.0-7.0)
Oil Pan Bolt	89-106 (10.0-12.0)
Oil Pump Housing-To-Reaction Shaft Support Bolt	89-106 (10.0-12.0)
Pressure Tap Plug	71-89 (8.0-10.0)
Pulse Generator Bolt	89-106 (10.0-12.0)
Set Screw	71-89 (8.0-10.0)
Transaxle Range Switch Bolt	89-106 (10.0-12.0)
Valve Body Assembly-To-Transaxle Housing Bolt	89-106 (10.0-12.0)
Valve Body Bolt	35-53 (4.0-6.0)

[1] – Tighten bolts in crisscross pattern to specification.

TRANSAXLE SPECIFICATIONS
TRANSAXLE SPECIFICATIONS

Application	In. (mm)
Clutch Clearances	
End Clutch Clearance	.016-.026 (.40-.65)
Front Clutch Clearance	
Elantra (1995)	.016-.024 (.40-.60)
Sonata	.028-.035 (.70-.90)
Rear Clutch Clearance	
Elantra (1995)	.012-.020 (.30-.50)
Sonata	.016-.024 (.40-.60)
Differential Side Gear Backlash	.0010-.0059 (.025-.150)
Input Shaft End Play	.012-.039 (.30-1.00)
Low-Reverse Brake Clearance	
Elantra (1995)	.0307-.0430 (.780-1.090)
Sonata	.0384-.0507 (.975-1.287)
Oil Pump Gear Side Clearance	
Elantra (1995)	.0012-.0020 (.030-.050)
Sonata	.0004-.0019 (.010-.048)
Transfer Idler Gear Preload	
Elantra (1995)	13 (1.5)
Sonata	7 (.8)
Transfer Shaft End Play	0-.0010 (0-.025)

WIRING DIAGRAMS

For appropriate wiring diagram, see HYUNDAI KM175 ELECTRONIC CONTROLS article.

TECHNICAL SERVICE BULLETINS

HARSH COAST DOWNSHIFTS

ATRA Technical Service Bulletin 288 (1995) – Some vehicles with KM series transaxles may exhibit a harsh coast downshift. Harsh coast downshift may be caused by an improperly adjusted accelerator switch. For accelerator switch adjustment procedure, see HYUNDAI KM175 ELECTRONIC CONTROLS article.

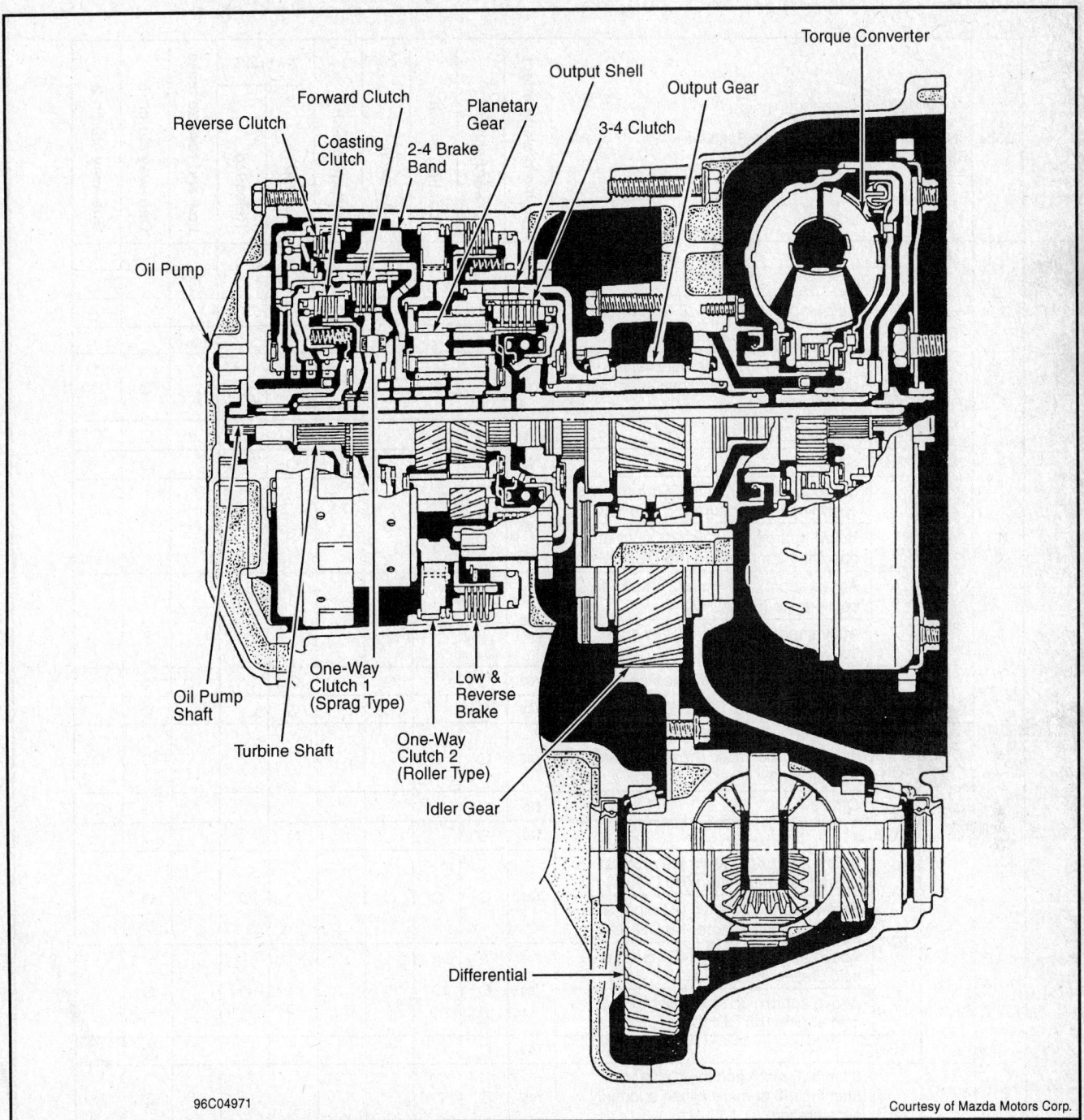

Fig. 1: Cut-Away View Of GF4A-EL (FA4A-EL Is Similar)

Transaxle Overheats – Possible causes: ATF level (low), internal component failure, torque converter clutch piston, shift solenoids, 3-2 timing solenoid, pressure control solenoid, throttle position sensor, turbine shaft speed sensor, vehicle speed sensor, engine speed input signal, transaxle fluid temperature sensor, TCM or PCM malfunction and fluid cooling system.

CLUTCH & BAND APPLICATION TABLES

NOTE: Clutch and band application table for Kia Sephia 1.6L SOHC is not available from manufacturer. Following tables are not model specific. Check vehicle to determine appropriate table.

AUTOMATIC TRANSMISSIONS
Mazda FA4A-EL & GF4A-EL (Cont.)

Mode	Posi-tion/ Range	Gear Position		Engine braking effect	Forward clutch	Coasting clutch	3-4 clutch	Reverse clutch	2-4 brake Applied	2-4 brake Released	Low and reverse brake	One-way clutch 1	One-way clutch 2
—	P	—		—									
	R	Reverse		Yes				○			○		
	N	—	Below approx. 4 km/h {2.5 mph}	—									
			Above approx. 5 km/h {3.1 mph}	—									
Non-HOLD	D	1GR	0 km/h {0 mph} and throttle valve opening 4/8 or more (when suddenly accelerating)	Yes	○	○						○	○
			Others	No	○							○	○
		2GR		No	○				○			○	
		3GR	Below approx. 33 km/h {20 mph} at operating temperature (B6 DOHC)	Yes	○	○	○			○		○	
			Below approx. 33 km/h {20 mph} at operating temperature (K8 DOHC)										
			Above approx. 34 km/h {21 mph} or cold engine (B6 DOHC)	Yes	○	○	○		⊗	○		○	
			Above approx. 35 km/h {22 mph} or cold engine (K8 DOHC)										
		4GR	Torque converter clutch non-operation	Yes	○		○		○			◎	
			Torque Converter Clutch ON	Yes	○		○		○			◎	
	S	1GR	0 km/h {0 mph} and throttle valve opening 4/8 or more (when suddenly accelerating)	Yes	○	○						○	○
			Others	No	○							○	○
		2GR		No	○				○			○	
		3GR	Below approx. 33 km/h {20 mph} at operating temperature (B6 DOHC)	Yes	○	○	○			○		○	
			Below approx. 33 km/h {20 mph} at operating temperature (K8 DOHC)										
			Above approx. 34 km/h {21 mph} or cold engine (B6 DOHC)	Yes	○	○	○		⊗	○		○	
			Above approx. 35 km/h {22 mph} or cold engine (K8 DOHC)										
		4GR		Yes	○		○		○			◎	
	L	1GR	0 km/h {0 mph} and throttle valve opening 4/8 or more (when suddenly accelerating)	Yes	○	○					○	○	○
			Others	No	○						○	○	○
		2GR	Below approx. 104 km/h {64 mph} (B6 DOHC)	Yes	○	○			○			○	
			Below approx. 99 km/h {61 mph} (K8 DOHC)										
			Above approx. 110 km/h {68 mph} (B6 DOHC)	Yes	○	○			○			○	
			Above approx. 105 km/h {65 mph} (K8 DOHC)										

96J04979

Courtesy of Mazda Motors Corp.

Fig. 2: Clutch & Band Application Table (HOLD Type Systems, 1 Of 2)

AUTOMATIC TRANSMISSIONS
Mazda FA4A-EL & GF4A-EL (Cont.)

Mode	Position/Range	Gear Position		Engine braking effect	Forward clutch	Coasting clutch	3–4 clutch	Reverse clutch	2-4 brake Applied	2-4 brake Released	Low and reverse brake	One–way clutch 1	One–way clutch 2
HOLD	D	1GR	0 km/h {0 mph} and throttle valve opening 4/8 or more (when suddenly accelerating)	Yes	○	○						○	○
			Others	No	○							○	○
		2GR	0 km/h {0 mph} and throttle valve opening 4/8 or more (when suddenly accelerating)	No	○	○			○			○	
			Others	No	○				○			○	
		3GR	Below approx. 33 km/h {20 mph} at operating temperature (B6 DOHC)	Yes	○	○	○			○		○	
			Below approx. 33 km/h {20 mph} at operating temperature (K8 DOHC)										
			Above approx. 34 km/h {21 mph} or cold engine (B6 DOHC)	Yes	○	○	○		⊗	○		○	
			Above approx. 35 km/h {22 mph} or cold engine (K8 DOHC)										
		4GR		Yes	○		○		○			◎	
	S	2GR		Yes	○	○			○			○	
		3GR	Below approx. 33 km/h {20 mph} at operating temperature (B6 DOHC)	Yes	○	○	○			○		○	
			Below approx. 33 km/h {20 mph} at operating temperature (K8 DOHC)										
			Above approx. 34 km/h {21 mph} or cold engine (B6 DOHC)	Yes	○	○	○		⊗	○		○	
			Above approx. 35 km/h {22 mph} or cold engine (K8 DOHC)										
		4GR		Yes	○		○		○			◎	
	L	1GR		Yes	○	○					○	○	○
		2GR	Below approx. 104 km/h {64 mph} (B6 DOHC)	Yes	○	○			○			○	
			Below approx. 99 km/h {61 mph} (K8 DOHC)										
			Above approx. 110 km/h {68 mph} (B6 DOHC)	Yes	○	○			○			○	
			Above approx. 105 km/h {65 mph} (K8 DOHC)										

⊗ : Fluid pressure to servo but band not applied due to pressure difference in servo.
◎ : Does not transmit power.

96B04980

Courtesy of Mazda Motors Corp.

Fig. 3: Clutch & Band Application Table (HOLD Type Systems, 2 Of 2)

Position/ Range	Mode	Gear		Engine braking effect	Forward clutch	Coasting clutch	3–4 clutch	Reverse clutch	2–4 brake Applied	2–4 brake Released	Low and reverse brake	One-way clutch 1 (Sprag type)	One-way clutch 2 (Roller type)
P	—	—		—									
R	—	Reverse	Below approx. 4 km/h {2.5 mph}	Yes				○			○		
		Reverse	Above approx. 5 km/h {3 mph}	Yes				○			○		
		—	Above approx. 30 km/h {19 mph}	No				○					
N	—	—	Below approx. 4 km/h {2.5 mph}	—									
			Above approx. 5 km/h {3 mph}	—									
D	☆ O/D OFF SW OFF POWER/ NORMAL		First gear	No	○							○	○
			Second gear	No	○				○			○	
			Third gear	Yes	○	○	○		⊗	○		○	
			Fourth gear	Yes	○		○		○				◎
	☆ O/D OFF SW ON POWER/ NORMAL	Second gear	Below approx. 14 km/h {8.7 mph}	Yes	○	○			○			○	
			Above approx. 17 km/h {10.5 mph}	No	○				○			○	
			Third gear	Yes	○	○	○		⊗	○		○	
			*Fourth gear	Yes	○		○		○				◎
2	—		Second gear	Yes	○	○			○			○	
			*Third gear	Yes	○	○	○		⊗	○		○	
			*Fourth gear	Yes	○		○		○				◎
1	—		First gear	Yes	○	○					○	○	○
			*Second gear	Yes	○	○			○			○	

○ Operating.
⊗ Operating but not contributing to the power transmission.
◎ POWER is not transmitted.
*   Engine overspeed protection.
☆ The powertrain control module automatically switches between POWER and NORMAL modes corresponding to the speed at which the accelerator pedal is depressed.

96A04970

Courtesy of Mazda Motors Corp.

Fig. 4: Clutch & Band Application Table (O/D OFF Type Systems)

TESTING

PRELIMINARY CHECKS

Before testing transaxle, ensure fluid level is correct and shift linkage, range switch and idle speed are adjusted correctly.

TIME LAG TEST

Preparation – Check and adjust coolant, engine oil and ATF levels. Warm engine and transaxle to normal operating temperature. Block front and rear wheels on both sides. Set parking brake. Ensure engine idle speed and ignition timing is correct. See appropriate ON-VEHICLE ADJUSTMENTS article in ENGINE PERFORMANCE in appropriate MITCHELL® manual.

This test measures time lag between selecting specific gear and actual transaxle shift. Test checks condition of the 1-2, N-R and N-D accumulators, forward and one-way clutches, 2-4 brake band and low-reverse brake.

Testing – Start engine and shift from "N" to "D", "N" to "2" and "N" to "R". Measure time interval from moving shift lever to when shift shock is felt. See TIME LAG TEST SPECIFICATIONS table and TIME LAG TEST EVALUATION table.

TIME LAG TEST SPECIFICATIONS

Application Range	Time Seconds
MX-3, Protege & Sephia	
"N"-"D"	0.5-0.6
"N"-"2"	0.5-0.7
"N"-"R"	0.6-0.7
Millenia, MX-6 & 626	
"N"-"D"	Less Than 0.9
"N"-"R"	Less Than 1.1

TIME LAG TEST EVALUATION

Application & Shift	Time	Possible Cause
"N"-"D"	More	Insufficient Line Pressure
		Forward Clutch Slipping
		One-Way Clutch No. 1 Slipping
		One-Way Clutch No. 2 Slipping
	Less	"N"-"D" Accumulator Not Operating Properly
		Excessive Line Pressure
"N"-"D" HOLD	More	Insufficient Line Pressure
		Forward Clutch Slipping
		2-4 Brake Band Slipping
		One-Way Clutch No. 1 Slipping
	Less	1-2 Accumulator Not Operating Properly
		Excessive Line Pressure
"N"-"R"	More	Insufficient Line Pressure
		Low-Reverse Brake Slipping
		Reverse Clutch Slipping
	Less	"N"-"R" Accumulator Not Operating Properly
		Excessive Line Pressure

ROAD TEST

1) Check for shift shock, positive shifts and shifting through all ranges. Ensure kickdown occurs within kickdown limits. See appropriate chart in ROAD TEST SPECIFICATIONS CHARTS. Manually shift from "D₃" to "D₂". Shift should take place immediately and engine braking should occur.

2) Manually shift from "D" to "2" to "L". Ensure appropriate downshift takes place with engine braking in 3rd and 2nd gear. With gear selector in "L", ensure transaxle does not upshift from "1". With gear selector in "2", ensure no upshift from "2" occurs.

3) On vehicles quipped with O/D OFF button, depress button while transaxle is in 4th gear. Transaxle should downshift to 3rd gear and upshift once button is released.

4) On vehicles equipped with HOLD switch, depress switch. HOLD function may be activated in "D", "S" or "L" gears. In "L" and "S" positions vehicle is held in these gears and no upshift or downshift takes place. In "D" position a 1-2 and 2-3 upshift is permitted when starting from a stop but after the 2-3 upshift the vehicle is locked in "D" until it comes to a complete stop. The 1-2 and 2-3 upshift pattern is changed to a "short shift" specification. Pushing HOLD button again deactivates system.

5) Ensure transaxle stays locked in "P". Compare actual shift speeds with appropriate ROAD TEST SPECIFICATIONS. *See Figs. 5-9.* If upshifts and downshifts are not as specified, see ROAD TEST EVALUATION table for possible cause.

ROAD TEST EVALUATION

Condition	Possible Cause
No 1-2 Shift	Stuck 1-2 Shift Solenoid Valve "A"
	Stuck 1-2 Shift Valve
No 2-3 Shift	Stuck 2-3 Shift Solenoid Valve "B"
	Stuck 2-3 Shift Valve
No 3-OD Shift	Stuck 3-4 Shift Solenoid Valve "C"
	Stuck 3-4 Shift Valve
No Lock-Up	Stuck TCC Lock-Up Solenoid Valve
	Stuck TCC Lock-Up Shift Valve
Incorrect Shift Point	Mis-Adjusted TPS
	Stuck Shift Valves
Excessive Shift Shock	Stuck Accumulators
	Stuck Or Missing One-Way Check Valve
	Worn Clutches, Brakes Or One-Way Clutch
No Engine Braking	Worn Clutches Or Brakes

AUTOMATIC TRANSMISSIONS
Mazda FA4A-EL & GF4A-EL (Cont.)

ROAD TEST SPECIFICATIONS

Range Mode		Throttle condition	Shift	Vehicle speed km/h {mph}	Turbine speed rpm
POWER	D	Wide open throttle	$D_1 \rightarrow D_2$	61—67 {38—41}	6100—6700
			$D_2 \rightarrow D_3$	106—113 {66—70}	5850—6200
			$D_3 \rightarrow D_4$	172—182 {107—112}	6150—6500
		Half throttle	$D_1 \rightarrow D_2$	42—51 {26—31}	4200—5100
			$D_2 \rightarrow D_3$	72—91 {45—56}	4000—5000
			$D_3 \rightarrow D_4$	119—145 {74—89}	4250—5150
		Closed throttle position	$D_4 \rightarrow D_3$	11—17 {7—10}	300—400
			$D_3 \rightarrow D_1$	29—35 {18—21}	1050—1250
		Kickdown (wide open throttle)	$D_4 \rightarrow D_3$	143—153 {89—94}	3600—3800
			$D_3 \rightarrow D_2$	91—99 {56—61}	3250—3500
			$D_2 \rightarrow D_1$	37—43 {23—26}	2050—2350
NORMAL		Wide open throttle	$D_1 \rightarrow D_2$	61—67 {38—41}	6100—6700
			$D_2 \rightarrow D_3$	106—113 {66—70}	5850—6200
			$D_3 \rightarrow D_4$	172—182 {107—112}	6150—6500
			TCC ON (D_4)	147—157 {91—97}	3700—3900
		Half throttle	$D_1 \rightarrow D_2$	33—42 {20—26}	3300—4200
			$D_2 \rightarrow D_3$	59—76 {37—47}	3250—4150
			$D_3 \rightarrow D_4$	96—124 {60—76}	3450—4400
			TCC ON (D_4)	127—150 {79—93}	3200—3750
		Closed throttle position	$D_4 \rightarrow D_3$	11—17 {7—10}	300—400
			$D_3 \rightarrow D_1$	29—35 {18—21}	1050—1250
		Kickdown (wide open throttle)	$D_4 \rightarrow D_3$	143—153 {89—94}	3600—3800
			$D_3 \rightarrow D_2$	91—99 {56—61}	3250—3500
			$D_2 \rightarrow D_1$	37—43 {23—26}	2050—2350
HOLD		—	$D_2 \rightarrow D_3$	15—25 {9—16}	850—1350
			TCC ON (D3)	105—115 {65—71}	3750—4100
			$D_4 \rightarrow D_3$	172—178 {100—104}	4300—4450
			$D_3 \rightarrow D_2$	7—13 {4—8}	250—450

96I04974

Courtesy of Mazda Motors Corp.

Fig. 5: Shift Speed Table (1995-96 Millenia)

Dial Indicator

93H23660 Courtesy of Toyota Motor Sales, U.S.A., Inc.

Fig. 9: Measuring Ring Gear Runout

Install transfer right case. Torque bolts to 33 ft. lbs. (44 N.m). Using pecial Tool (09318-20010), Adjust total preload by tightening ifferential bearing adjusting nut. While measuring preload, tighten djusting nut a little at a time. Using Special Tool (09326-20011) and pring tension gauge, measure total preload. Starting preload with ew bearing is driven pinion preload plus 2.1-3.1 lb. (1.3-1.4 kg). With used bearing, 1-2 lb. (.5-.9 kg). If total preload exceeds specification, move right transfer case, push in adjusting nut and outer race. eadjust total preload. See Fig. 7.

RIVEN PINION PRELOAD SPECIFICATIONS

Application	Lbs. (kg)
tarting Preload [1]	
New Bearing	2.1-3.1 (1.3-1.4)
Used Bearing	1-2 (.5-.9)

[1] – Plus driven pinion preload

Using dial indicator measure ring gear backlash. Backlash should e .005-.007" (.13-.18 mm). If backlash exceeds specification, select a ifferent plate washer to previously selected. Readjust backlash and otal preload. Check gear tooth contact. Coat 3 to 4 teeth at four differ- nt positions on ring gear with Prussian Blue. Rotate ring gear and spect ring gear tooth contact. See GEAR TOOTH CONTACT ATTERN article in APPLICATIONS & IDENTIFICATION section. hims for driven pinion cage are available in thicknesses of .0118" (.30 m) to .0224" (.57 mm) in .0022" (.03 mm) increments.

Remove ring gear mounting case assembly. Remove transfer inion bearing cage assembly. Coat "O" ring with gear oil, install on ransfer pinion bearing cage. Install transfer pinion bearing cage with reviously selected adjusting shim to transfer left case. Torque to pecifications. See TORQUE SPECIFICATIONS. Install ring gear nounting case assembly. Install adjusting nut lock plate. Install differ- ntial side gear shaft holder to right case. Install snap ring. Install ansfer right case oil seal. Coat lip of seal with MP grease.

OTE: This transmission does not use gaskets between major hous- gs. Use Three Bond (1281) sealant. Assemble housings or other omponents immediately after applying sealant and let cure for at ast 30 minutes before filling with oil.

Apply Three Bond to left case, apply sealant to bolt threads. Install ft and right case, torque bolts to 33 ft. lbs. (44 N.m). Check total pre- ad. See step 3). Install shift fork, shift fork shaft and lock sleeve. stall and torque bolt to 12 ft. lbs. (16 N.m). Apply Three Bond (1281) ealant to left transfer case inspection hole, install cover, torque bolts 12 ft. lbs. (16 N.m). Install and torque 10 mm plug and differential ck indicator switch. Apply sealant to 6 mm plug, install and torque to 8 ft. lbs. (25 N.m). Coat "O" ring with gear oil, install on extension ousing. Install housing to transfer pinion bearing cage, torque to 19 . lbs. (25 N.m). Install dynamic dampener, torque to 19 ft. lbs. (25 .m) Install dust boot. Apply Three Bond (1281) sealant to transfer ase housing and mount to transmission case assembly.

TORQUE SPECIFICATIONS
TORQUE SPECIFICATIONS

Application	Ft. Lbs. (N.m)
Driven Pinion Cage Bolt	29 (39)
Driven Pinion Lock Nut	70 (95)
Dynamic Dampener	19 (25)
Extension Housing Bolt	19 (25)
Indicator Switch	30 (40)
Inspection Cover Bolt	12 (16)
Large Plugs (2)	29 (39)
Right Case Bolt	32 (44)
Ring Gear-To-Mounting Case	71 (96)
Shift Lever Cover	13 (17)
Small Plug	18 (24)
Shift Fork Set Bolt	12 (16)
Stiffener Bracket	27 (37)
Transfer Case-To-Transaxle Case	51 (69)
Vacuum Actuator Bolt	27 (37)

WIRING DIAGRAMS

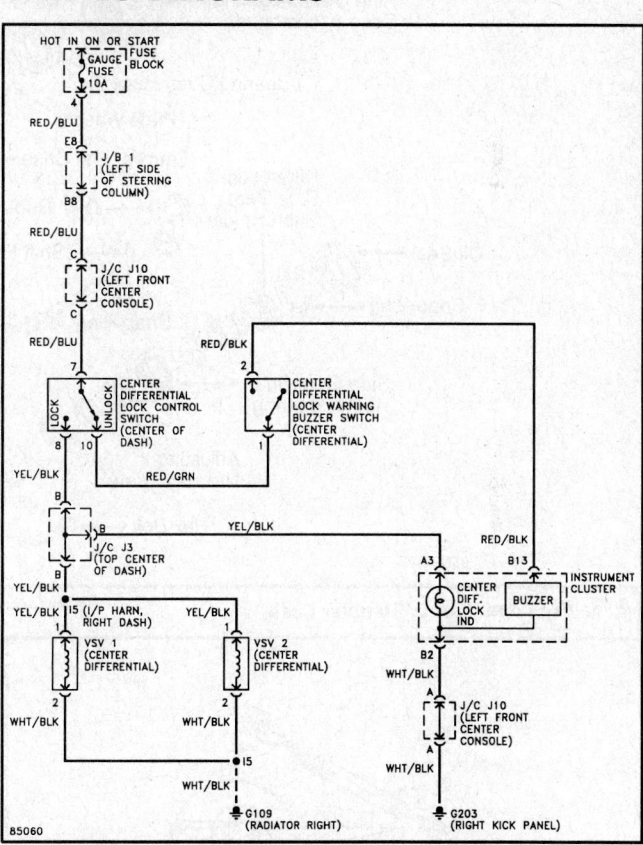

Fig. 10: Transfer Case Wiring Diagram (1996 RAV4 With Manual Transmission)

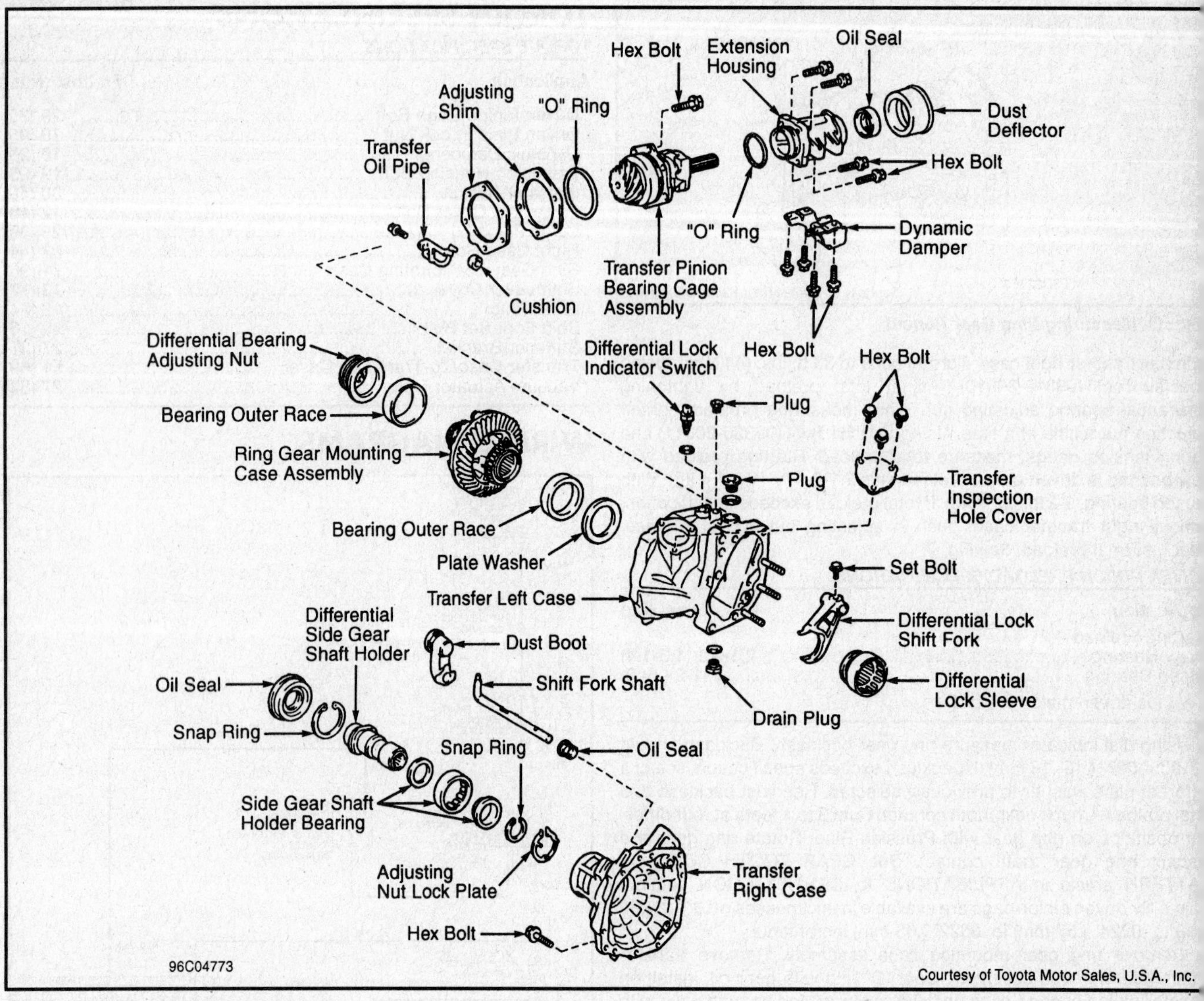

Hex Bolt

Extension Housing

Oil Seal

Dust Deflector

Adjusting Shim

"O" Ring

Hex Bolt

Transfer Oil Pipe

"O" Ring

Dynamic Damper

Transfer Pinion Bearing Cage Assembly

Hex Bolt

Cushion

Differential Lock Indicator Switch

Hex Bolt

Hex Bolt

Differential Bearing Adjusting Nut

Plug

Bearing Outer Race

Plug

Transfer Inspection Hole Cover

Ring Gear Mounting Case Assembly

Bearing Outer Race

Set Bolt

Plate Washer

Transfer Left Case

Differential Lock Shift Fork

Differential Side Gear Shaft Holder

Dust Boot

Differential Lock Sleeve

Oil Seal

Shift Fork Shaft

Snap Ring

Drain Plug

Side Gear Shaft Holder Bearing

Snap Ring

Oil Seal

Adjusting Nut Lock Plate

Transfer Right Case

Hex Bolt

96C04773

Courtesy of Toyota Motor Sales, U.S.A., Inc.

Fig. 6: Exploded View Of Transfer Case

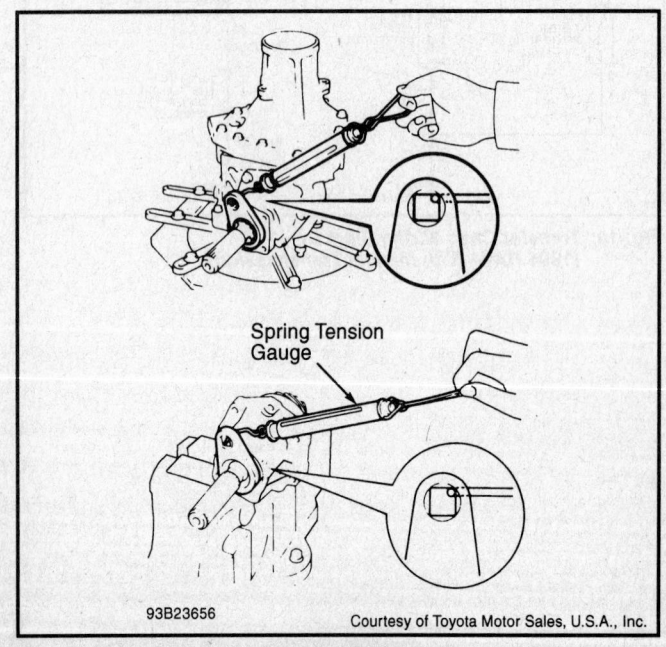

Spring Tension Gauge

93B23656

Courtesy of Toyota Motor Sales, U.S.A., Inc.

Fig. 7: Measuring Starting & Total Preload

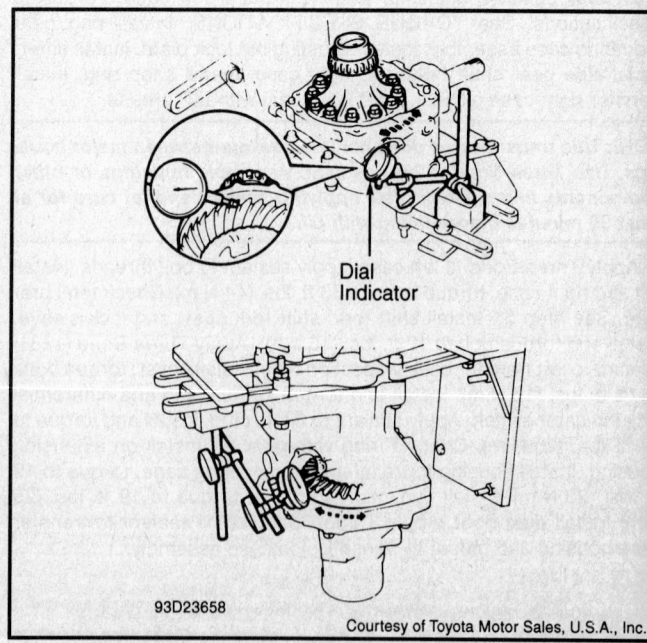

Dial Indicator

93D23658

Courtesy of Toyota Motor Sales, U.S.A., Inc.

Fig. 8: Measuring Backlash

Mode	Range	Throttle condition (throttle position sensor voltage)	Shift	Vehicle speed km/h {mph}	
				4 Cyl. DOHC	V6 DOHC
Non-HOLD	D	Wide open throttle (3.1–4.4 V)	D₁ → D₂	58–64 {36–40}	59–65 {37–40}
			D₂ → D₃	102–110 {63–68}	101–109 {62.7–67.5}
			D₃ → D₄	166–176 {103–109}	167–177 {104–109}
		Half throttle (1.7–2.7 V)	D₁ → D₂	34–43 {22–26}	39–48 {25–29}
			D₂ → D₃	60–77 {37–48}	70–88 {44–54}
			D₃ → D₄	104–130 {64–81}	127–153 {78.8–94.8}
			TCC operation {D₄}	99–124 {61–77}	127–153 {78.8–94.8}
		Closed throttle position (0.1–1.1 V)	D₄ → D₃	29–35 {18–22}	27–33 {17–20}
			D₃ → D₁	9–15 {5.6–9.3}	12–18 {7.5–11}
		Kickdown	D₄ → D₃	142–152 {88.1–94.2}	155–165 {96.1–102}
			D₃ → D₂	82–90 {51–55}	94–102 {59–63.2}
			D₂ → D₁	42–48 {27–29}	52–58 {33–35}
	S	Wide open throttle (3.1–4.4 V)	S₁ → S₂	58–64 {36–40}	59–65 {37–40}
			S₂ → S₃	102–110 {63–68}	101–109 {62.7–67.5}
		Half throttle (1.7–2.7 V)	S₁ → S₂	34–43 {22–26}	39–48 {25–29}
			S₂ → S₃	60–77 {37–48}	70–88 {44–54}
		Closed throttle position (0.1–1.1 V)	S₄ → S₃	166–172 {103–107}	167–173 {104–107}
			S₃ → S₁	9–15 {5.6–9.3}	12–18 {7.5–11}
		Kickdown	S₃ → S₂	82–90 {51–55}	94–102 {59–63.2}
			S₂ → S₁	42–48 {27–29}	52–58 {33–35}
	L	Wide open throttle (3.1–4.4 V)	L₁ → L₂	58–64 {36–40}	59–65 {37–40}
		Half throttle (1.7–2.7 V)	L₁ → L₂	34–43 {22–26}	39–48 {25–29}
		Closed throttle position (0.1–1.1 V)	L₂ → L₁	9–15 {6–9.3}	12–18 {7.5–11}
		Kickdown	L₂ → L₁	42–48 {27–29}	52–58 {33–35}
HOLD	D	—	D₁ → D₂	27–33 {17–20}	27–33 {17–20}
			D₂ → D₃	40–50 {25–31}	40–50 {25–31}
			D₄ → D₃	166–172 {103–107}	167–173 {104–107}
			D₃ → D₁	9–15 {6–9.3}	12–18 {7.5–11}
	S	—	S₄ → S₃	166–172 {103–107}	167–173 {104–107}
			S₃ → S₂	101–107 {62–66}	100–106 {62–65.7}
	L	—	L₂ → L₁	43–49 {27–30}	52–58 {33–35}

96E04972

Courtesy of Mazda Motors Corp.

Fig. 6: Shift Speed Table (1995 MX3)

AUTOMATIC TRANSMISSIONS
Mazda FA4A-EL & GF4A-EL (Cont.)

Range/Mode			Throttle condition (throttle position sensor voltage)	Shift	Vehicle speed km/h {mph}	Turbine speed (rpm)
D	O/D OFF switch OFF	POWER	Wide open throttle (3.0—4.4 V)	$D_1 \rightarrow D_2$	57—63 {36—39}	6,050—6,600
				$D_2 \rightarrow D_3$	99—107 {62—66}	5,750—6,200
				$D_3 \rightarrow D_4$	162—172 {101—106}	6,100—6,500
			Half throttle	$D_1 \rightarrow D_2$	39—49 {25—30}	4,150—5,150
				$D_2 \rightarrow D_3$	69—87 {43—53}	4,050—5,000
				$D_3 \rightarrow D_4$	114—138 {71—85}	4,300—5,150
			Closed throttle position (0.1—1.1 V)	$D_4 \rightarrow D_1$	11—17 {7—10}	300—400
			Kickdown	$D_4 \rightarrow D_3$	135—145 {84—89}	3,600—3,800
				$D_3 \rightarrow D_2$	86—94 {54—58}	3,250—3,500
				$D_2 \rightarrow D_1$	37—43 {23—26}	2,150—2,450
		NORMAL	Wide open throttle (3.0—4.4 V)	$D_1 \rightarrow D_2$	57—63 {36—39}	6,050—6,600
				$D_2 \rightarrow D_3$	99—107 {62—66}	5,750—6,200
				$D_3 \rightarrow D_4$	162—172 {101—106}	6,100—6,500
				TCC ON (D_4)	162—172 {101—106}	6,100—6,500
			Half throttle	$D_1 \rightarrow D_2$	32—40 {20—24}	3,400—4,200
				$D_2 \rightarrow D_3$	53—69 {33—42}	3,100—4,000
				$D_3 \rightarrow D_4$	92—119 {58—73}	3,500—4,450
				TCC ON (D_4)	124—148 {77—91}	3,300—3,900
			Closed throttle position (0.1—1.1 V)	$D_4 \rightarrow D_1$	11—17 {7—10}	300—400
			Kickdown	$D_4 \rightarrow D_3$	135—145 {84—89}	3,600—3,800
				$D_3 \rightarrow D_2$	86—94 {54—58}	3,250—3,500
				$D_2 \rightarrow D_1$	37—43 {23—26}	2,150—2,450
	O/D OFF switch ON	POWER	Wide open throttle (3.0—4.4 V)	$D_1 \rightarrow D_2$	57—63 {36—39}	6,050—6,600
				$D_2 \rightarrow D_3$	99—107 {62—66}	5,750—6,200
			Half throttle	$D_1 \rightarrow D_2$	39—49 {25—30}	4,150—5,150
				$D_2 \rightarrow D_3$	69—87 {43—53}	4,050—5,000
			Closed throttle position (0.1—1.1 V)	$D_3 \rightarrow D_1$	11—17 {7—10}	450—600
			Kickdown	$D_3 \rightarrow D_2$	86—94 {54—58}	3,250—3,500
				$D_2 \rightarrow D_1$	37—43 {23—26}	2,150—2,450
		NORMAL	Wide open throttle (3.0—4.4 V)	$D_1 \rightarrow D_2$	57—63 {36—39}	6,050—6,600
				$D_2 \rightarrow D_3$	99—107 {62—66}	5,750—6,200
			Half throttle	$D_1 \rightarrow D_2$	32—41 {20—25}	3,400—4,300
				$D_2 \rightarrow D_3$	53—69 {33—42}	3,100—4,000
			Closed throttle position (0.1—1.1 V)	$D_3 \rightarrow D_1$	11—17 {7—10}	450—600
			Kickdown	$D_3 \rightarrow D_2$	86—94 {54—58}	3,250—3,500
				$D_2 \rightarrow D_1$	37—43 {23—26}	2,150—2,450

96G04973

Courtesy of Mazda Motors Corp.

Fig. 7: Shift Speed Table (1995-96 MX6 & 626)

Range/Mode		Throttle condition	Shift	Vehicle speed (km/h { mph })		Turbine speed (rpm)	
				1.5L	1.8L	1.6L	1.8L
D	Except O/D OFF mode	Wide open throttle	1GR→2GR	52—58 { 32—36 }	53—59 { 33—36 }	5,600—6,200	5,300—5,850
			2GR→3GR	94—102 { 58—63 }	98—106 { 61—65 }	5,600—6,000	5,400—5,800
			3GR→4GR	149—159 { 92—99 }	162—172 { 101—106 }	5,750—6,100	5,800—6,100
		Half throttle	1GR→2GR	33—43 { 20—27 }	33—42 { 21—26 }	3,600—4,600	3,300—4,150
			2GR→3GR	64—84 { 40—52 }	66—85 { 41—52 }	3,800—4,950	3,650—4,650
			3GR→4GR	127—152 { 79—94 }	112—142 { 70—88 }	4,900—5,800	4,000—5,050
			TCC ON (4GR)	127—152 { 79—94 }	92—120 { 57—74 }	4,900—5,800	2,300—2,950
		Closed throttle position	4GR→3GR	27—33 { 17—20 }	33—39 { 21—24 }	750—850	850—950
			3GR→1GR	11—17 { 7—11 }	12—18 { 8—11 }	450—650	450—600
		Kickdown (wide open throttle)	4GR→3GR	143—153 { 87—95 }	151—161 { 94—99 }	3,850—4,100	3,800—4,000
			3GR→2GR	84—94 { 52—57 }	91—99 { 56—61 }	3,250—3,600	3,250—3,500
			2GR→1GR	42—48 { 27—29 }	44—50 { 27—31 }	2,500—2,800	2,450—2,700
	O/D OFF mode	Wide open throttle	1GR→2GR	52—58 { 32—36 }	53—59 { 33—36 }	5,600—6,200	5,300—5,850
			2GR→3GR	94—102 { 58—63 }	98—106 { 61—65 }	5,600—6,000	5,400—5,800
		Half throttle	1GR→2GR	33—42 { 20—27 }	32—41 { 20—25 }	3,600—4,600	3,200—4,050
			2GR→3GR	64—84 { 40—52 }	66—85 { 41—52 }	3,800—4,950	3,650—4,650
		Closed throttle position	4GR→3GR	149—155 { 92—96 }	162—168 { 100—104 }	4,050—4,150	4,050—4,150
			3GR→1GR	11—17 { 7—11 }	12—18 { 8—11 }	450—650	450—600
		Kickdown (wide open throttle)	3GR→2GR	84—92 { 52—57 }	91—99 { 57—61 }	3,250—3,600	3,250—3,500
			2GR→1GR	42—48 { 27—29 }	44—50 { 27—31 }	2,500—2,800	2,450—2,700

96D04976

Courtesy of Mazda Motors Corp.

Fig. 8: Shift Speed Table (1995-96 Protege)

Range		Throttle Condition	Shift	Vehicle Speed mph (km/h)
O/D Switch OFF	D	Wide open throttle	1GR→2GR	36 - 39 (57 - 63)
			2GR→3GR	61 - 65 (98 - 106)
			3GR→4GR	101 - 106 (165 - 172)
		Half throttle	1GR→2GR	21 - 26 (33 - 43)
			2GR→3GR	42 - 53 (67 - 86)
			3GR→4GR	70 - 88 (113 - 142)
			TCC ON (4GR)	58 - 74 (93 - 120)
		Closed throttle position	4GR→3GR	21 - 24 (33 - 39)
			3GR→1GR	8 - 11 (12 - 18)
		Kickdown (wide open throttle)	4GR→3GR	94 - 99 (151 - 161)
			3GR→2GR	57 - 61 (91 - 99)
			2GR→1GR	28 - 31 (44 - 50)
O/D Switch ON		Wide open throttle	1GR→2GR	36 - 39 (57 - 63)
			2GR→3GR	61 - 65 (98 - 106)
		Half throttle	1GR→2GR	21 - 26 (33 - 43)
			2GR→3GR	42 - 53 (67 - 86)
		Closed throttle position	4GR→3GR	100 - 104 (162 - 168)
			3GR→1GR	8 - 11 (12 - 18)
		Kickdown (wide open throttle)	3GR→2GR	57 - 61 (91 - 99)
			2GR→1GR	28 - 31 (44 - 50)

96B04975   Courtesy of Mazda Motors Corp.

Fig. 9: Shift Speed Table (1995-96 Sephia)

STALL SPEED TEST

Preparation – Check and adjust coolant, engine oil and ATF levels. Warm engine and transaxle to operating temperature. Block front and rear wheels on both sides. Set parking brake. Connect tachometer to engine. Ensure engine idle speed and ignition timing is correct. See appropriate ON-VEHICLE ADJUSTMENTS article in ENGINE PERFORMANCE in appropriate MITCHELL® manual.

CAUTION: Stall test generates high ATF temperatures. DO NOT hold throttle open at stall speed for more than 5 seconds. Allow engine to idle for at least one minute to cool fluid between each test.

Testing – Firmly depress brake pedal with engine running. Select "R" range and depress accelerator pedal to floor. When engine speed no longer increases, read RPM on tachometer and release accelerator pedal. Perform stall test in "R" , "D", "S" and "L". Compare RPM with STALL SPEED table.

NOTE: Stall speed specifications are approximate.

STALL SPEED

Application	RPM
MX-3	
4-Cylinder	2100-2400
V6	2450-2750
Millenia	2270-2500
MX-6 & 626	2270-2500
Protege	
1993-94	
1.5L (ZJ)	1950-2250
1.8L (BP)	2200-2500
Sephia	
1.6L (B6)	2200-2500
1.8L (BP)	2300-2600

STALL SPEED EVALUATION

High In "L", "S", "D" & "R" – Worn oil pump. Oil leakage from oil pump, control valve and/or transmission case. Stuck pressure regulator valve. Solenoid valve malfunction. Pressure modulator valve sticking.

High In "D", "S" & "L" – Forward clutch and/or one-way clutch No. 1 slipping.

High In "D" – One-way clutch No. 2 slipping.

High In "S" HOLD & "L" HOLD – Coasting clutch slipping.

High In "D" HOLD & "S" HOLD – 2-4 brake band slipping.

High In "R", "L" & "L" HOLD – Low-reverse brake slipping.

High In "R" – Low-reverse brake slipping. Reverse clutch slipping. Perform road test to determine whether problem is low-reverse brake or reverse clutch. If engine braking is okay in "L", problem is reverse clutch. If no engine braking is present in "L", problem is low-reverse brake.

Below Specifications – Engine out of tune. One-way clutch slipping within torque converter.

LINE PRESSURE TEST

Inspection of line pressure checks the condition of hydraulic components and ensures that no internal oil leaks exist.

Preparation – Follow stall speed test preparation. Connect line pressure gauge to line pressure test port. *See Fig. 10 or 11.* Place line pressure gauge where it can be read from driver seat. Ensure engine idle speed and ignition timing is correct. See appropriate ON-VEHICLE ADJUSTMENTS article in ENGINE PERFORMANCE in appropriate MITCHELL® manual.

Testing – Start engine, depress brake pedal firmly, shift selector to "D" and read line pressure at idle. Depress accelerator fully and read line pressure as soon as RPM becomes constant, then release accelerator pedal. Shift selector to "N" and idle engine for at least one minute, to cool fluid. Read line pressure at idle and stall speeds for each range in the same manner. Compare with LINE PRESSURE TEST SPECIFICATIONS table and LINE PRESSURE TEST EVALUATION.

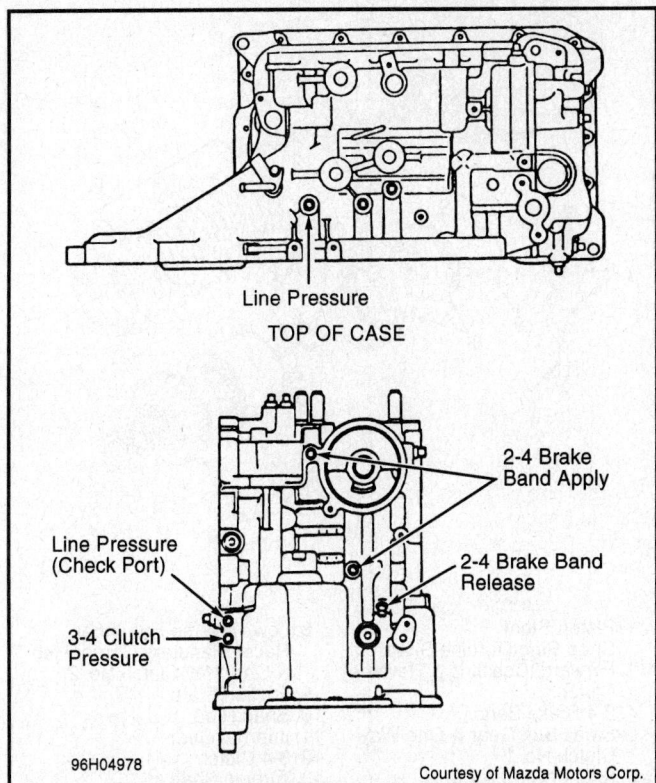

Fig. 10: Locating Line Pressure Test Port (FA4A-EL)

NOTE: Line pressure specifications are approximate.

LINE PRESSURE TEST SPECIFICATIONS

Application & Range	Idle Pressure psi (kPa)	Stall Pressure psi (kPa)
MX-3		
"D", "S" & "L"	62-79 (430-550)	133-151 (920-1040)
"R"	106-126 (730-870)	218-247 (1500-1700)
Millenia		
"D", "S" & "L"	60-79 (420-550)	160-170 (1100-1170)
"R"	106-146 (730-1010)	277-293 (1910-2020)
MX-6 & 626		
"D", "S" & "L"	61-77 (420-530)	160-170 (1100-1170)
"R"	106-146 (730-1010)	277-294 (1910-2030)
Protege		
"D", "S" & "L"	62-79 (430-550)	133-151 (920-1040)
"R"	106-126 (730-870)	218-247 (1500-1700)
Sephia		
"D", "S" & "L"	62-7981 (430-550)	133-151 (920-1040)
"R"	106-126 (730-870)	218-248 (1500-1710)

LINE PRESSURE TEST EVALUATION

Low In "D", "S", "L" & "R" – Worn oil pump. Fluid leaking from oil pump, control valve body or transaxle case. Pressure regulator valve stuck.

Low In "D" & "S" – Fluid leaking from hydraulic circuit of forward clutch.

Low In "R" – Fluid leaking from hydraulic circuit of low and reverse brake.

High In "D", "S", "L" & "R" – Throttle valve stuck. Throttle modulator valve stuck. Pressure regulator valve stuck.

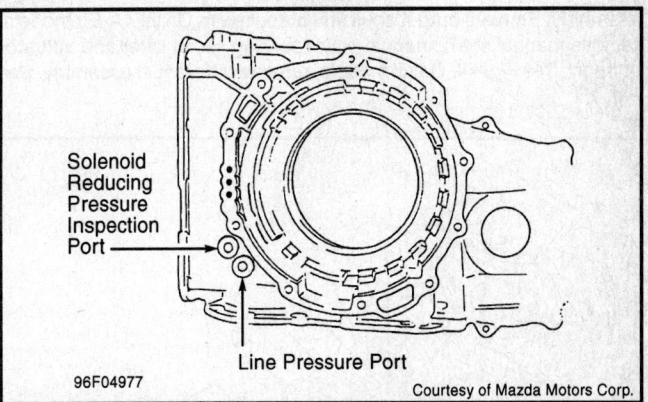

Fig. 11: Locating Line Pressure Test Port (GF4A-EL)

ON-VEHICLE SERVICE

See appropriate article in TRANSMISSION SERVICING section.

REMOVAL & INSTALLATION

For transmission removal and installation, see appropriate AUTOMATIC TRANSMISSION REMOVAL article in TRANSMISSION SERVICING section.

TORQUE CONVERTER

1) Torque converter is a sealed unit and cannot be disassembled for service. Inspect for damage and cracks. Replace torque converter if defective. Remove any rust from pilot hub and boss of converter. Replace torque converter if converter boss bushing inner diameter exceeds specification. Maximum bushing diameter on FA4A-EL converter is 2.090" (53.08 mm). Maximum bushing diameter on GF4A-EL converter is 2.0884" (53.045 mm).

2) Flush torque converter. After converter is removed from cleaner, thoroughly drain solvent through hub. Add about .53 qt. (.5L) clean ATF to converter. Agitate fluid by hand. Drain ATF from converter.

TRANSAXLE DISASSEMBLY

1) Mount transaxle on stand. Remove torque converter. Remove oil pump drive shaft. Remove dipstick tube. Remove range switch, turbine shaft speed sensor. Remove oil pipe, spring and ball next to range switch.

2) Remove oil pan and gasket. Remove oil strainer and "O" ring. On GF4A-EL models, remove valve body cover and gasket. On all models, remove valve body with electrical harness. On FA4A-EL models, remove throttle cable. Remove manual shaft, manual plate, parking assist lever and actuator support. Remove oil pipe at oil pump. On all models, remove oil pump and gasket.

3) Remove clutch assembly turbine shaft snap ring and remove clutch assembly. On FA4A-EL models, compress servo and remove retaining ring, servo and spring. Pull anchor shaft while holding strut and remove strut.

4) On all models, remove small sun gear and one-way clutch No. 1 assembly. See Fig. 12 or 13. Secure 2-4 band with wire to prevent stretching and remove 2-4 band. On GF4A-EL models, pull anchor shaft while holding strut and remove strut. Pull piston stem from 2-4 brake band servo. Remove snap ring, band servo and spring.

5) On all models, remove one-way clutch retaining snap ring, one-way clutch No. 2 and carrier hub assembly. Remove low and reverse brake snap ring, retaining plate, drive and driven plates.

6) Remove internal gear snap ring and remove internal gear from output shell. Remove "O" ring located on converter housing side of turbine shaft. Pull out turbine shaft with 3-4 clutch assembly.

7) Remove bolts from converter housing to transaxle. Tap lightly with a plastic hammer to remove transaxle case. Remove parking pawl assembly. Remove output shell and output gear. On GF4A-EL models, remove manual shaft, manual plate, parking assist lever and actuator support. *See Fig. 14.* On all models, remove differential assembly. *See Fig. 15.*

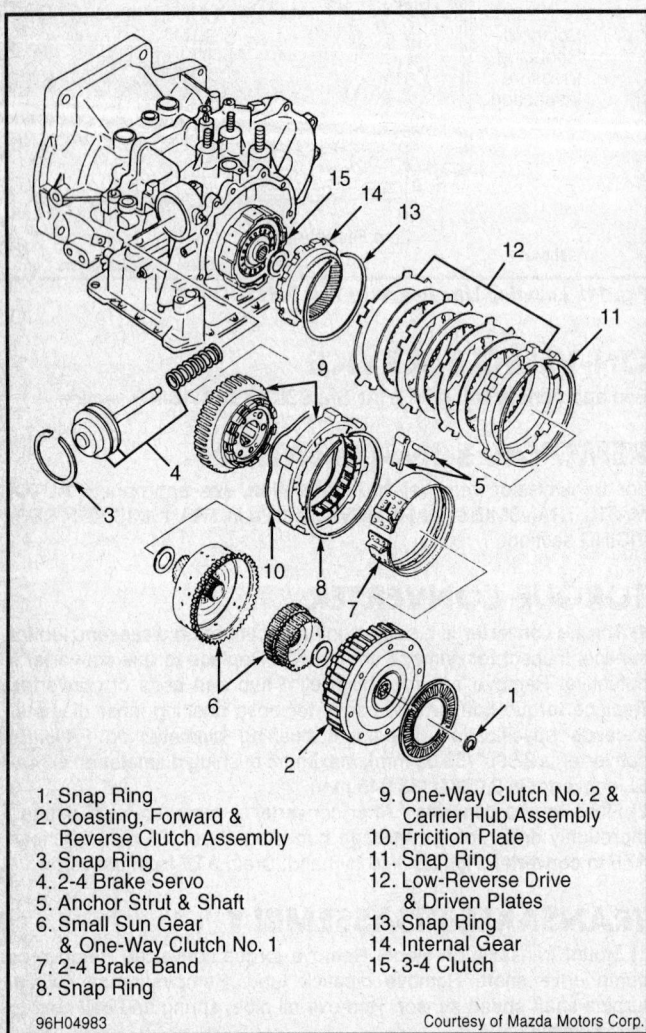

96H04983   Courtesy of Mazda Motors Corp.

1. Snap Ring
2. Coasting, Forward & Reverse Clutch Assembly
3. Snap Ring
4. 2-4 Brake Servo
5. Anchor Strut & Shaft
6. Small Sun Gear & One-Way Clutch No. 1
7. 2-4 Brake Band
8. Snap Ring
9. One-Way Clutch No. 2 & Carrier Hub Assembly
10. Friction Plate
11. Snap Ring
12. Low-Reverse Drive & Driven Plates
13. Snap Ring
14. Internal Gear
15. 3-4 Clutch

Fig. 12: Exploded View Of Internal Clutch Assemblies (FA4A-EL)

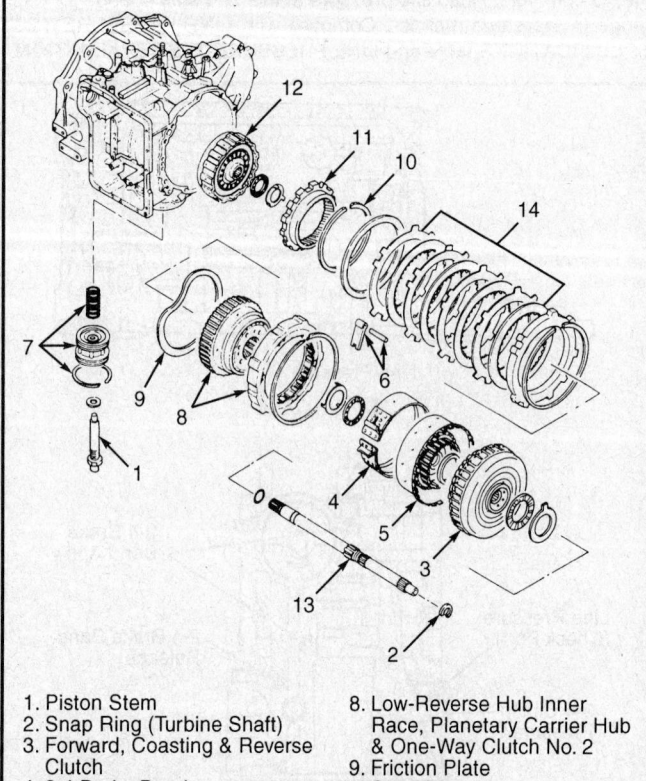

96J04984   Courtesy of Mazda Motors Corp.

1. Piston Stem
2. Snap Ring (Turbine Shaft)
3. Forward, Coasting & Reverse Clutch
4. 2-4 Brake Band
5. Small Sun Gear & One-Way Clutch No. 1
6. Anchor Strut & Pin
7. Servo
8. Low-Reverse Hub Inner Race, Planetary Carrier Hub & One-Way Clutch No. 2
9. Friction Plate
10. Snap Ring
11. Internal Gear
12. 3-4 Clutch
13. Turbine Shaft
14. Low-Reverse Clutch

Fig. 13: Exploded View Of Internal Clutch Assemblies (GF4A-EL)

8) On GF4A-EL models, remove 2-3 accumulator, orifice check valve spring and check valve. On all models, remove bolt in idler gear and output gear bearing housing to access roll pin in idler gear. Drive roll pin out with pin punch. *See Fig. 15.* Remove other bolts in idler gear and output gear housing.

9) Tap housing with plastic hammer lightly to remove. Tap out idler gear shaft from converter housing and remove idler gear with output gear. Remove bearing cover assembly. Remove converter housing from holding fixture. Press bearing race out of torque converter housing using step plate.

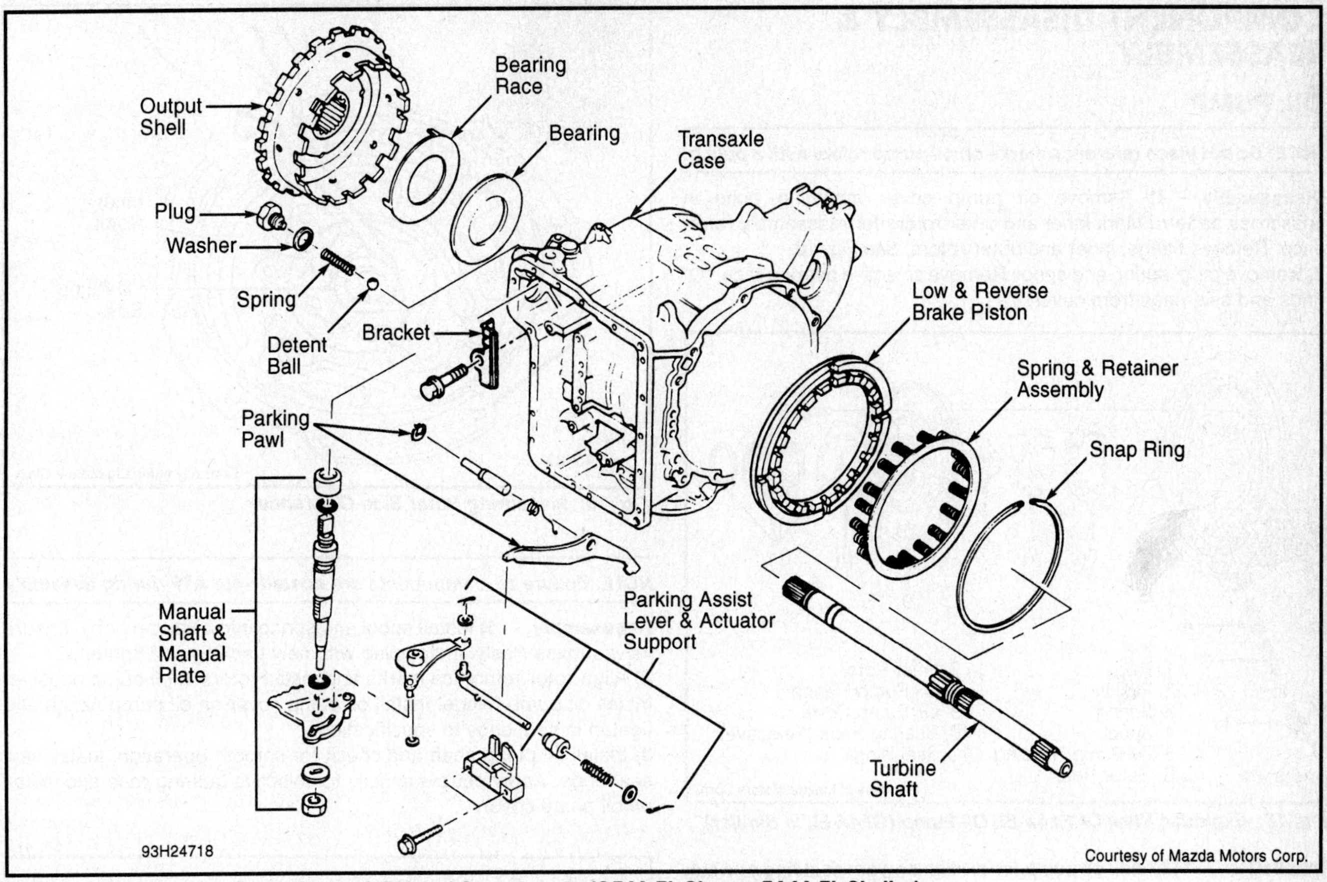

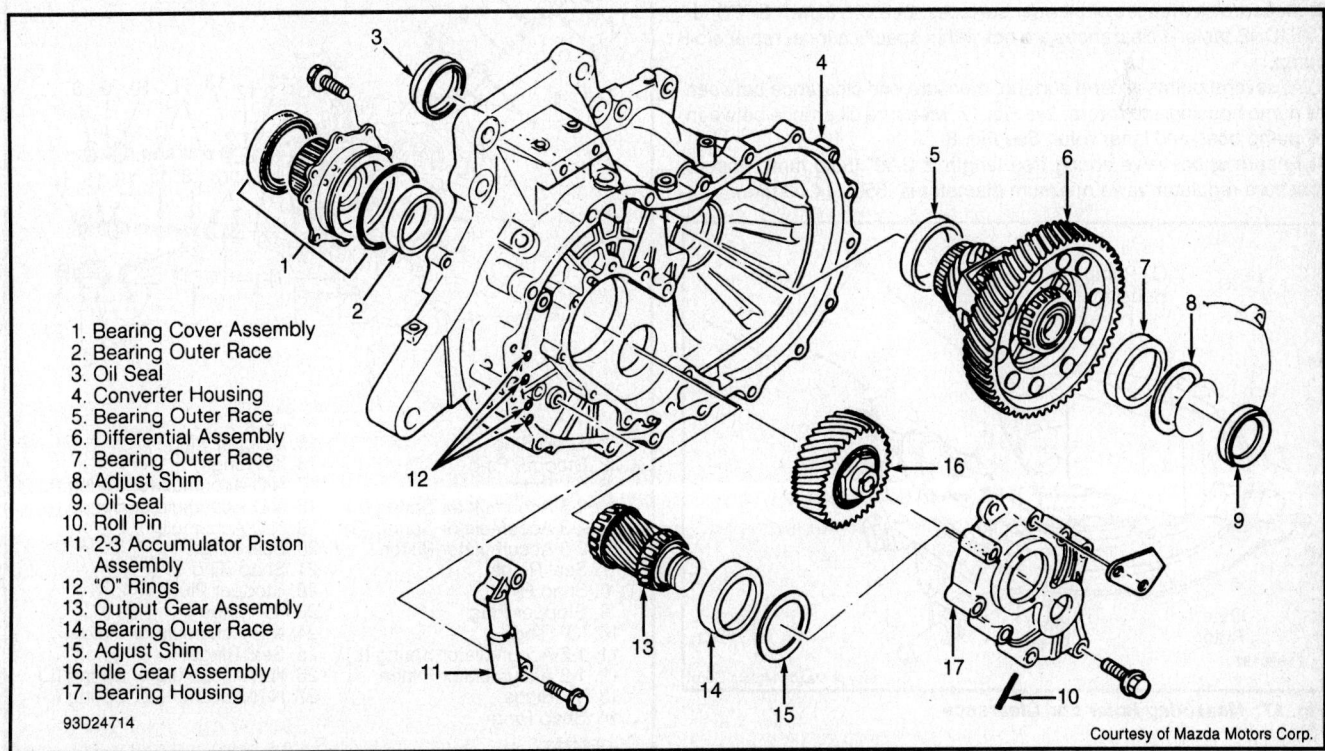

Fig. 14: Low & Reverse Brake Piston & Related Components (GF4A-EL Shown; FA4A-EL Similar)

1. Bearing Cover Assembly
2. Bearing Outer Race
3. Oil Seal
4. Converter Housing
5. Bearing Outer Race
6. Differential Assembly
7. Bearing Outer Race
8. Adjust Shim
9. Oil Seal
10. Roll Pin
11. 2-3 Accumulator Piston Assembly
12. "O" Rings
13. Output Gear Assembly
14. Bearing Outer Race
15. Adjust Shim
16. Idle Gear Assembly
17. Bearing Housing

93D24714

Courtesy of Mazda Motors Corp.

Fig. 15: Exploded View Of Idler & Differential Assembly (GF4A-EL Shown; FA4A-EL Similar)

COMPONENT DISASSEMBLY & REASSEMBLY

OIL PUMP

NOTE: Do not place reference marks on oil pump rotors with a punch.

Disassembly – 1) Remove oil pump cover mounting bolts in crisscross pattern. Mark inner and outer rotors for reassembly reference. Remove flange, inner and outer rotors. *See Fig. 16.*
2) Remove plug, spring and spool. Remove selective bearing race, "O" rings and seal rings from cover.

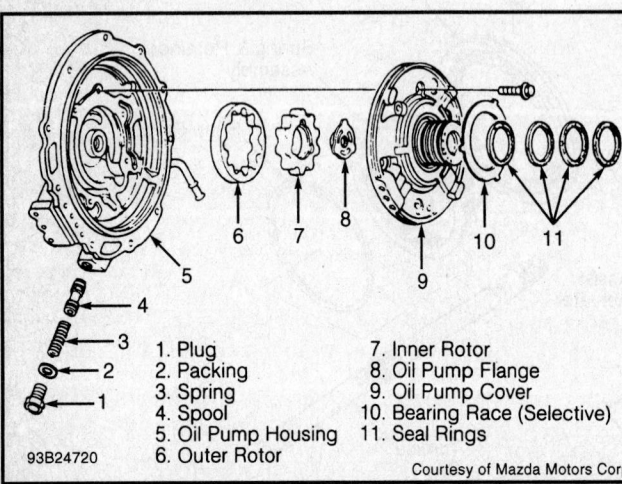

1. Plug	7. Inner Rotor
2. Packing	8. Oil Pump Flange
3. Spring	9. Oil Pump Cover
4. Spool	10. Bearing Race (Selective)
5. Oil Pump Housing	11. Seal Rings
6. Outer Rotor	

Courtesy of Mazda Motors Corp.

Fig. 16: Exploded View Of FA4A-EL Oil Pump (GF4A-EL Is Similar)

Inspection – 1) Check oil pump for broken or worn seal ring or weak springs. Check for damaged or worn sliding surfaces. Replace as required.
2) Measure clearances of all wear surfaces. See OIL PUMP SPECIFICATIONS table. If clearances are not within specifications, replace oil pump.
3) At several points around surface, measure end clearance between oil pump housing and rotors. *See Fig. 17.* Measure clearance between oil pump boss and inner rotor. *See Fig. 8.*
4) Ensure spool valve spring free length is 2.09" (53.0 mm). Ensure pressure regulator valve minimum diameter is .550" (14.00 mm).

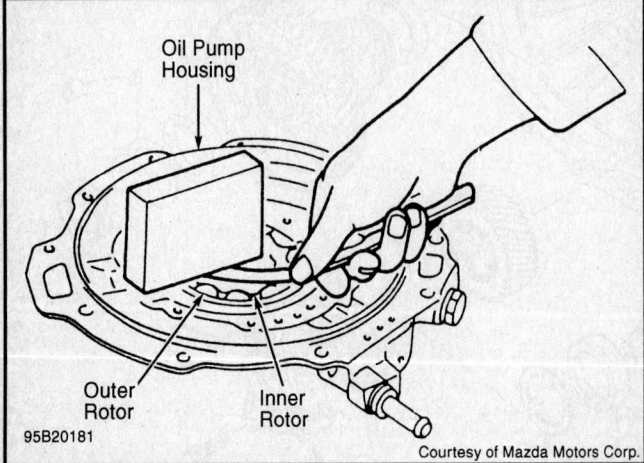

Fig. 17: Measuring Rotor End Clearance

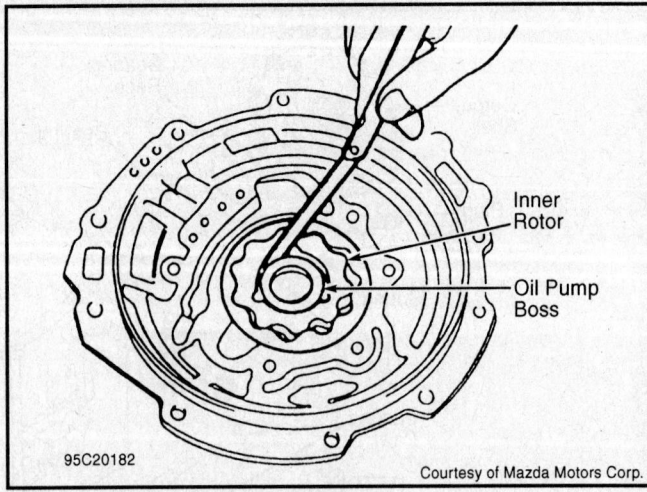

Fig. 18: Measuring Rotor Side Clearance

NOTE: Ensure all components are coated with ATF during assembly

Reassembly – 1) Install spool and spring into oil pump body. Ensure valve moves freely. Install plug with new packing and tighten.
2) Align rotor reference marks and install rotors in oil pump housing. Install oil pump flange. Install oil pump cover on oil pump flange and tighten in sequence to specification.
3) Install oil pump shaft and check for smooth operation. Install new seal rings. Apply petroleum jelly to selective bearing race and install on oil pump cover.

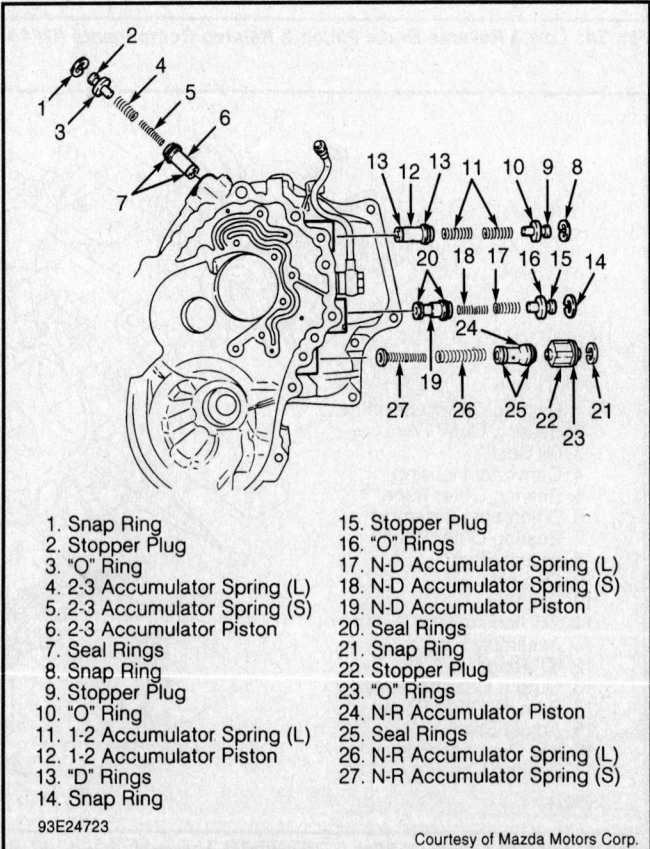

1. Snap Ring	15. Stopper Plug
2. Stopper Plug	16. "O" Rings
3. "O" Ring	17. N-D Accumulator Spring (L)
4. 2-3 Accumulator Spring (L)	18. N-D Accumulator Spring (S)
5. 2-3 Accumulator Spring (S)	19. N-D Accumulator Piston
6. 2-3 Accumulator Piston	20. Seal Rings
7. Seal Rings	21. Snap Ring
8. Snap Ring	22. Stopper Plug
9. Stopper Plug	23. "O" Rings
10. "O" Ring	24. N-R Accumulator Piston
11. 1-2 Accumulator Spring (L)	25. Seal Rings
12. 1-2 Accumulator Piston	26. N-R Accumulator Spring (L)
13. "D" Rings	27. N-R Accumulator Spring (S)
14. Snap Ring	

Courtesy of Mazda Motors Corp.

Fig. 19: Exploded View Of FA4A-EL Accumulators

OIL PUMP SPECIFICATIONS

Application	In. (mm)
Rotor End Clearance	.0008-.0016 (.020-.040)
Rotor Side Clearance	.0016-.005 (.040-.125)
Seal Ring Inner Diameter	
FA4A-EL	1.553 (39.45)
GF4A-EL	2.026 (51.45)

ACCUMULATORS

Disassembly (FA4A-EL) – **1)** Remove snap rings and stopper plugs. *See Fig. 19.* Remove accumulator pistons by applying air pressure to oil passages. *See Fig. 20.*
2) Measure spring free length. See FA4A-EL ACCUMULATOR SPRING SPECIFICATIONS table. If not within specifications, replace spring.

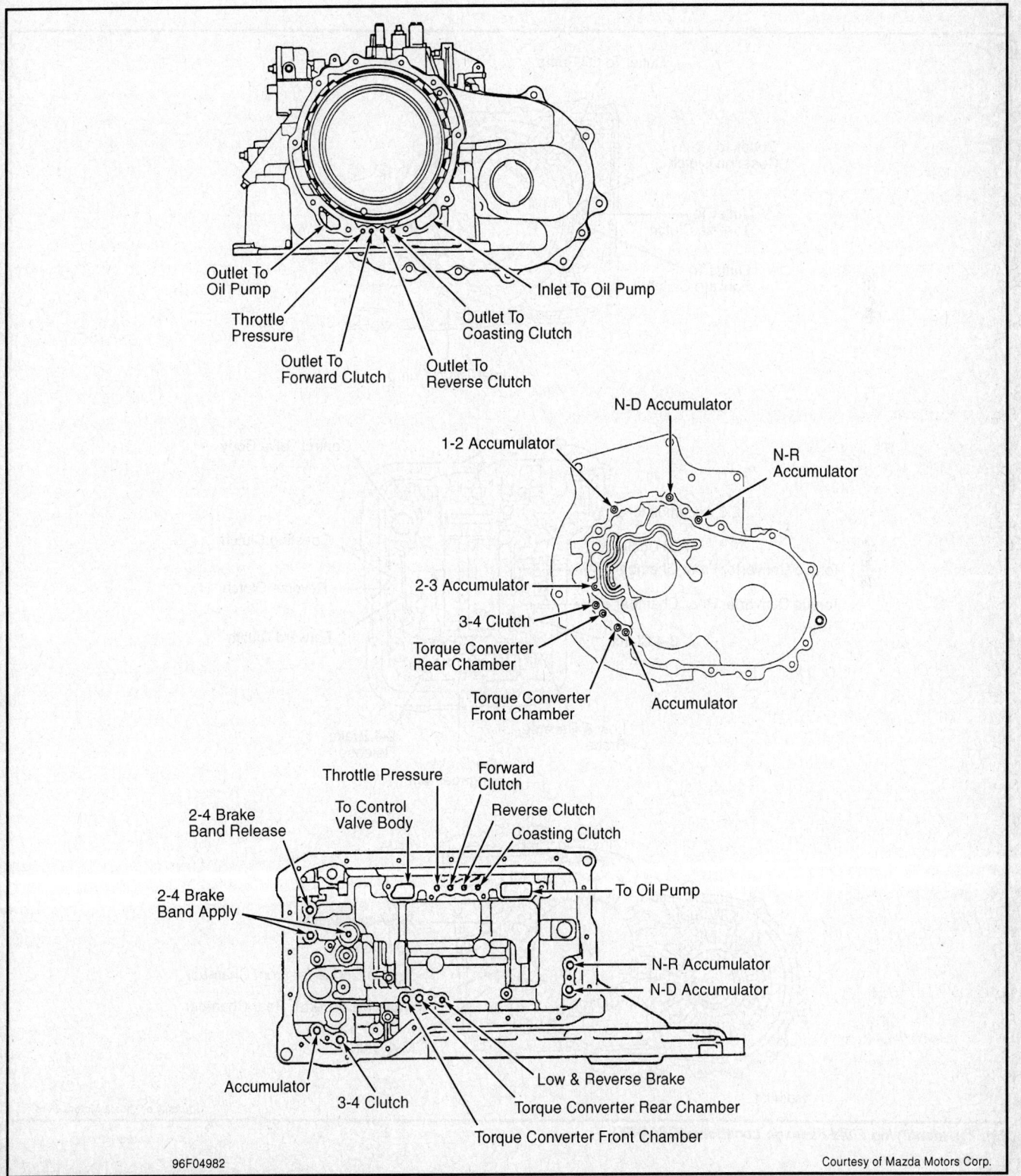

96F04982

Courtesy of Mazda Motors Corp.

Fig. 20: Identifying Fluid Passage Locations (FA4A-EL)

Reassembly – To reassemble, reverse disassembly procedure. Note location of piston and springs. See FA4A-EL ACCUMULATOR & SIZE chart. *See Fig. 19.*

Disassembly – 2-3 Accumulator (GF4A-EL) – Remove snap ring and stopper plug. *See Fig. 22.* Remove accumulator spring and piston. Remove orifice check valve and spring.

Inspection – Check spring free lengths and replace if not within specification. Ensure accumulator spring is 3.06" (77.7 mm) in length. Ensure orifice check valve spring is .512" (13.00 mm) in length.

Reassembly – Install "O" rings on accumulator using ATF. Install accumulator piston and spring. Install stopper plug and "O" ring. Install snap ring while applying pressure to stopper plug. For remainder of installation procedures, reverse disassembly procedures. Ensure snap ring is seated properly.

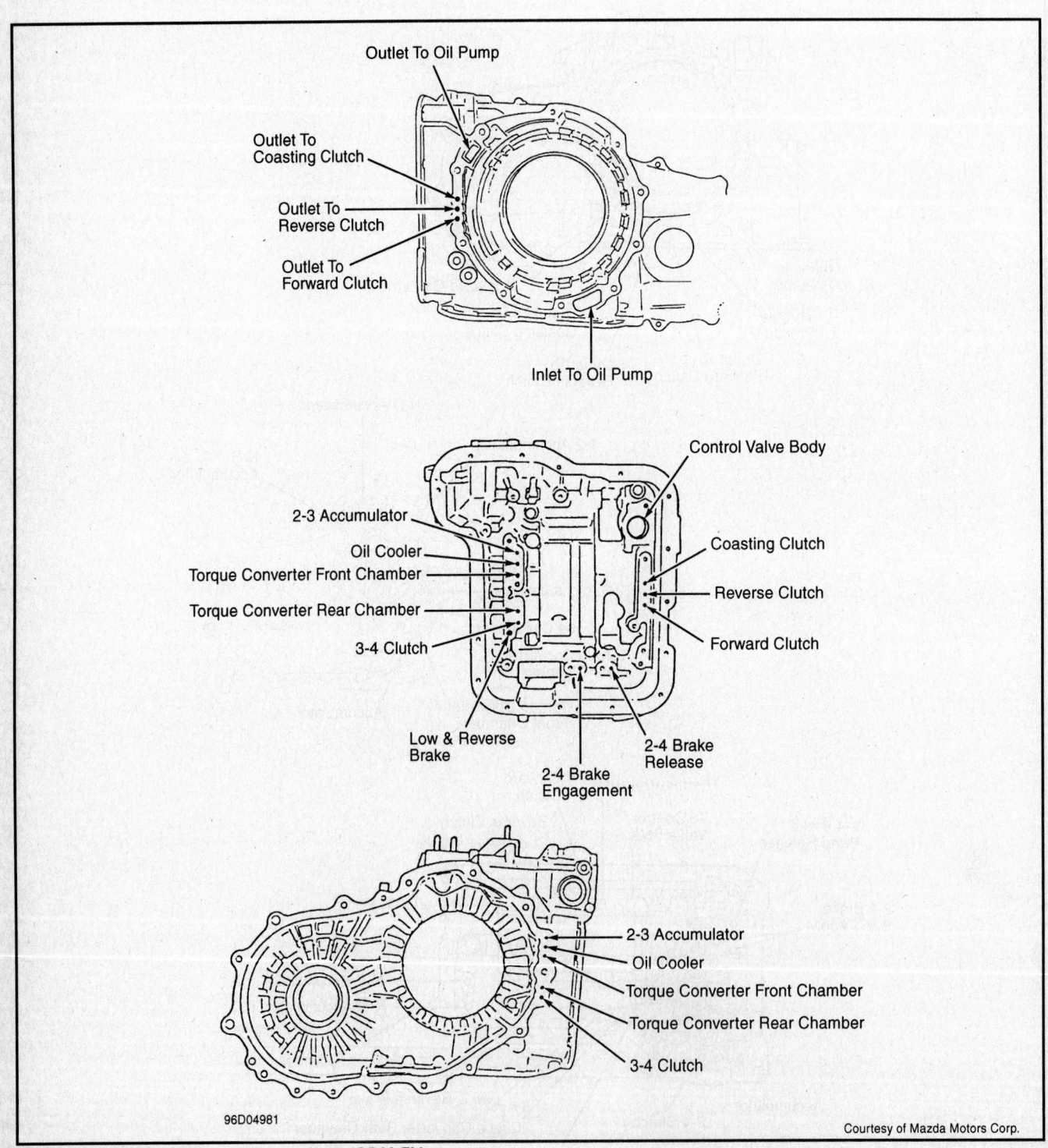

96D04981

Courtesy of Mazda Motors Corp.

Fig. 21: Identifying Fluid Passage Locations (GF4A-EL)

FA4A-EL ACCUMULATOR SPRING SPECIFICATIONS

Application	Spring Color	In. (mm)
N-D		
Small Spring	None	3.98 (101.2)
Large Spring	Red	3.71 (94.2)
N-R		
Small Spring	None	3.67 (93.2)
Large Spring	Orange	4.19 (106.5)
1-2		
Small Spring		
1.5L & 1.6L	Purple	3.34 (84.7)
1.8L & 2.5L V6	Red	3.22 (81.7)
Large Spring		
1.5L & 1.6L	Purple	3.34 (84.7)
1.8L & 2.5L V6	Yellow	3.23 (82.1)
2-3		
Small Spring		
1.5L & 1.6L	Pink	2.70 (67.8)
1.8L & 2.5L V6	Gray	2.35 (59.7)
Large Spring		
1.5L & 1.6L	Maroon	2.74 (69.5)
1.8L & 2.5L V6	Gray	2.83 (71.8)

FA4A-EL ACCUMULATOR & SIZE

Seal Ring & Piston Application	Large In. (mm)	Small In. (mm)
2-3 Accumulator [1]	1.176 (29.87)	.863 (21.91)
1-2 Accumulator [1]	.961 (24.40)	.657 (16.70)
N-D Accumulator [1]	1.176 (29.87)	.863 (21.91)
N-R Accumulator [1]	1.176 (29.87)	.866 (22.00)

[1] – For location on transaxle case, See Fig. 19.

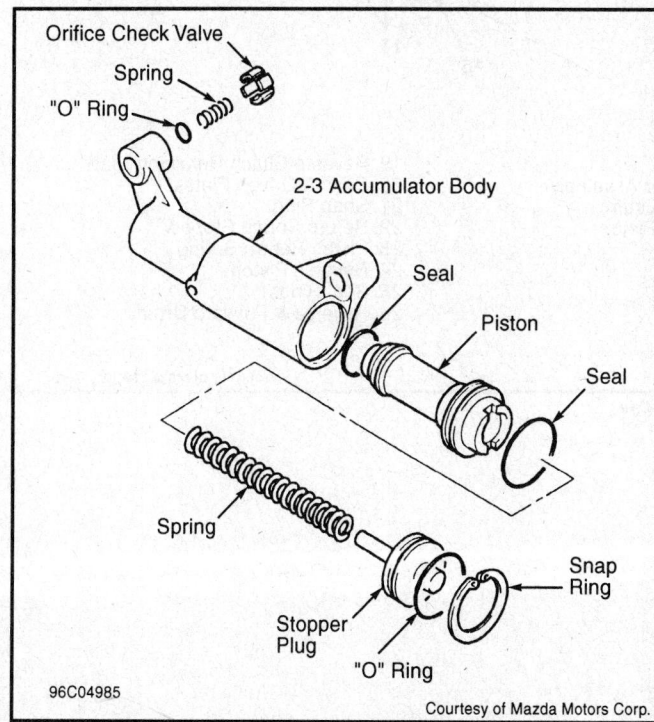

Fig. 22: Exploded View Of GF4A-EL 2-3 Accumulator

96C04985

Courtesy of Mazda Motors Corp.

FORWARD, COASTING & REVERSE CLUTCHES

Disassembly – 1) Remove snap ring, retainer plate, drive and driven plates and dished plate from forward clutch, coasting clutch and reverse clutch. See Fig. 23.

2) Compress coasting clutch spring and remove snap ring. Remove spring and retainer assembly. Remove coasting clutch drum from reverse and forward drum. Using air pressure, remove coasting clutch piston from coasting clutch drum. See Fig. 24.

3) Remove reverse clutch snap ring from reverse and forward drum. Place reverse and forward drum on oil pump. Use air pressure to remove reverse piston.

4) Check and repair or replace any faulty parts. Inspect piston check ball for leakage and sticking. Check for worn snap ring.

5) Check for broken or weak return springs. Check spring and retainer assembly for separation or deformation. Replace drive plates (friction discs) is thickness is less than .055" (1.40 mm). Measure spring and retainer free height. See Fig. 25. On FA4A-EL models, height should be .805" (20.45 mm). On GF4A-EL models, height should be 1.242" (31.54 mm).

Reassembly – 1) Apply ATF to all parts. Soak drive plates for at least 15 minutes. Install inner and outer seals on reverse piston. Install reverse piston into reverse clutch drum. Install piston return spring with tabs facing away from piston. Install return spring stop with step upward. Compress spring and retainer. Install snap ring.

2) Install reverse clutch dished plate with the dished side facing piston. Install drive and driven plates, retaining plate (step facing down) and snap rings. Measure clearance of reverse clutch between retaining plate and snap ring. See Fig. 26.

3) On FA4A-EL models, clearance should be .083-.094" (2.10-2.40 mm). Adjust clearance by installing selective snap ring. Snap rings range in thickness from .079" (2.0 mm) to .118" (3.00 mm) in .008" (.20 mm) increments.

4) On GF4A-EL models, clearance should be .059-.071" (1.50-1.80 mm). Adjust clearance by installing selective snap ring. Snap rings range in thickness from .079" (2.00) to .110" (2.80 mm) in .008" (.20 mm) increments.

5) Install inner and outer seals on coasting drum. Install drum into forward and reverse drum. Install seal rings onto coasting clutch piston. Install coasting clutch piston into coasting clutch drum. Install spring and retainer. Compress spring and retainer, and install snap ring.

6) Install dished plate with dished side facing upward. Install drive (friction) and driven plates, retaining plate and snap ring. See Fig. 23. Ensure coasting clutch snap ring opening is opposite of piston snap ring. Measure coasting clutch clearance. See Fig. 27. Clearance should be .039-.047" (1.00-1.20 mm).

7) Adjust clearance by installing selective snap ring. On FA4A-EL models, selective snap rings range in thickness from .063" (1.60 mm) to .104" (2.65 mm) in .006" (.15 mm) increments. On GF4A-EL models, selective snap rings range in thickness from .059" (1.50 mm) to .089" (2.25 mm) in increments of .006" (.15 mm).

8) Install forward clutch dished plate with dished side facing downward. Install drive (friction) and driven plates, retainer plate and snap ring. Check forward clutch clearance between retainer plate and snap ring. See Fig. 28. Clearance should be .039-.047" (1.00-1.20 mm).

9) Adjust clearance by installing selective snap ring. On FA4A-EL models, selective snap rings range in thickness from .063" (1.60 mm) to .104" (2.65 mm) in .006" (.15 mm) increments. On GF4A-EL models, selective snap rings range in thickness from .059" (1.50 mm) to .089" (2.25 mm) in increments of .006" (.15 mm).

10) Check operation of clutches by setting clutch assembly onto oil pump. Apply 57 psi (4 kg/cm²) air pressure to appropriate oil passage. See Fig. 24.

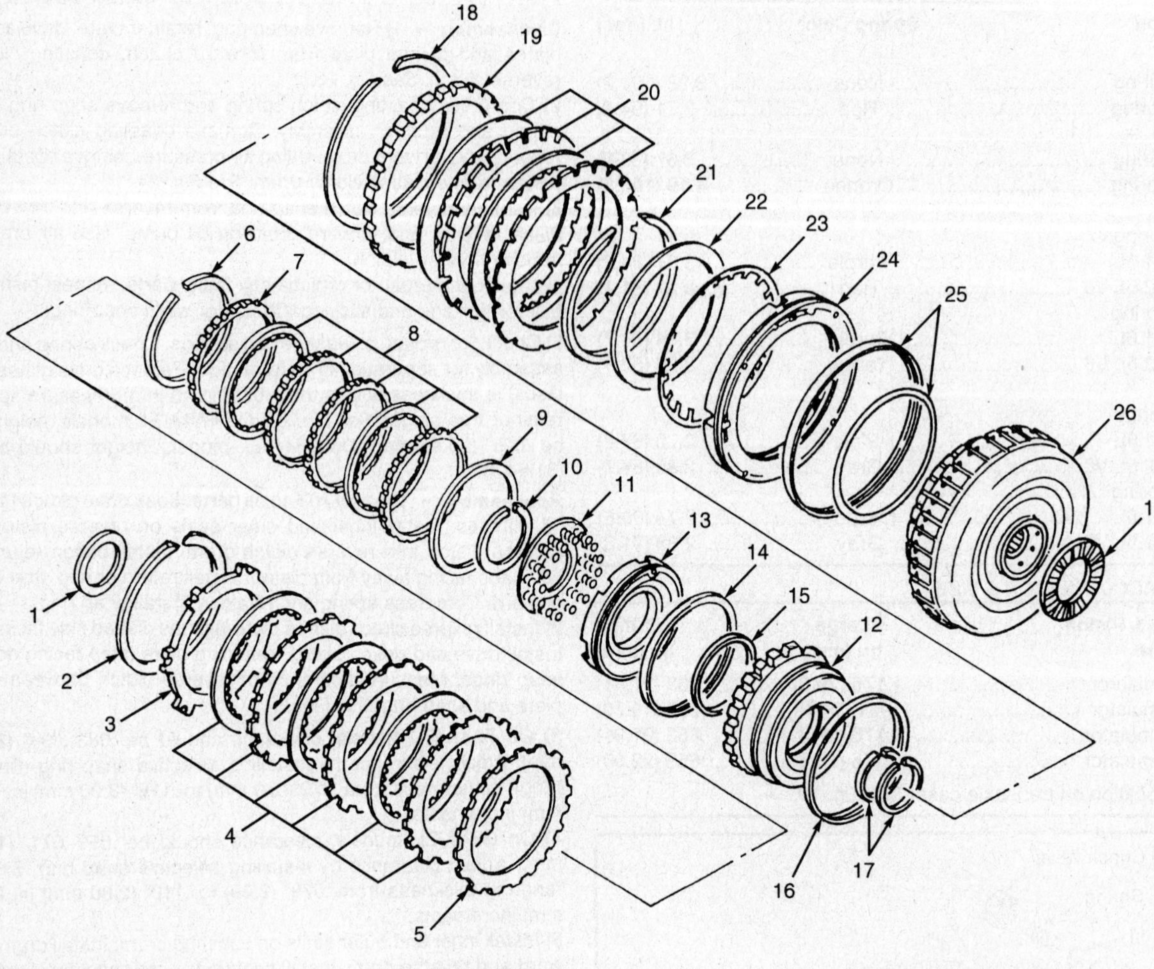

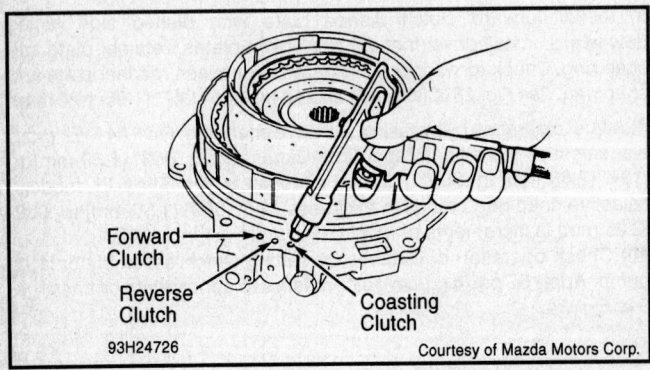

1. Thrust Bearing
2. Snap Ring
3. Forward Clutch Retaining Plate
4. Drive & Driven Plates
5. Forward Clutch Dished Plate
6. Snap Ring
7. Coasting Clutch Retaining Plate
8. Drive & Driven Plates
9. Coasting Clutch Dished Plate

10. Snap Ring
11. Spring & Retainer Assembly
12. Coasting Clutch Drum
13. Coasting Clutch Piston
14. Outer Seal
15. Inner Seal
16. Outer Seal
17. Seal Rings
18. Snap Ring

19. Reverse Clutch Retaining Plate
20. Drive & Driven Plates
21. Snap Ring
22. Return Spring Stopper
23. Piston Return Spring
24. Reverse Piston
25. Seal Rings
26. Reverse & Forward Drum

96E04986

Courtesy of Mazda Motors Corp.

Fig. 23: Exploded View Of Forward, Coasting & Reverse Clutch Assemblies

93H24726

Courtesy of Mazda Motors Corp.

Fig. 24: Removing Clutch Pistons & Air Checking Clutches

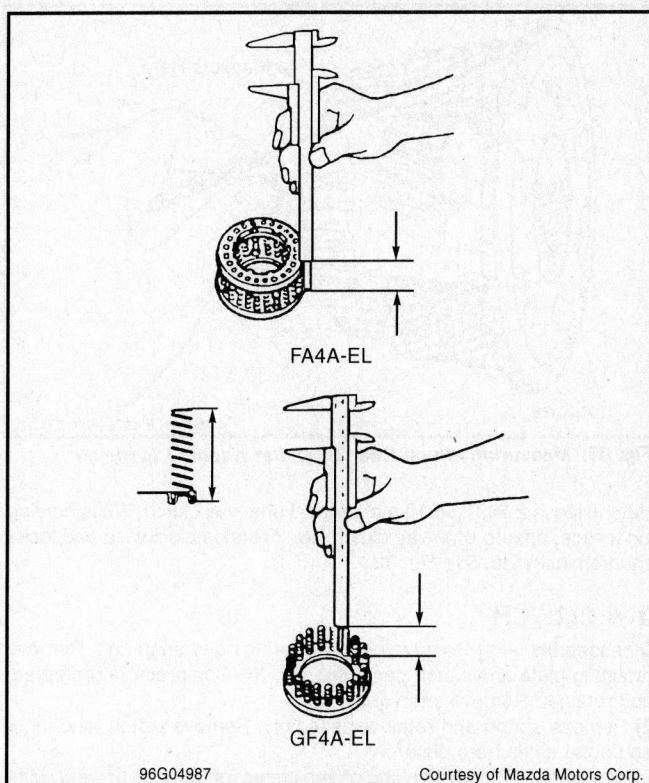

FA4A-EL

GF4A-EL

96G04987   Courtesy of Mazda Motors Corp.

Fig. 25: Measuring Clutch Spring & Retainer Height

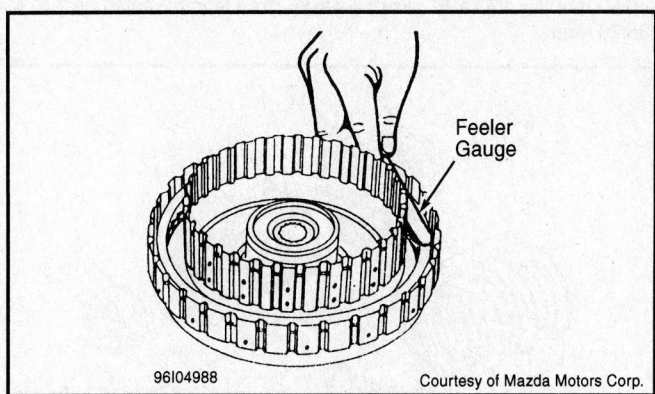

Feeler Gauge

96I04988   Courtesy of Mazda Motors Corp.

Fig. 26: Measuring Reverse Clutch Clearance

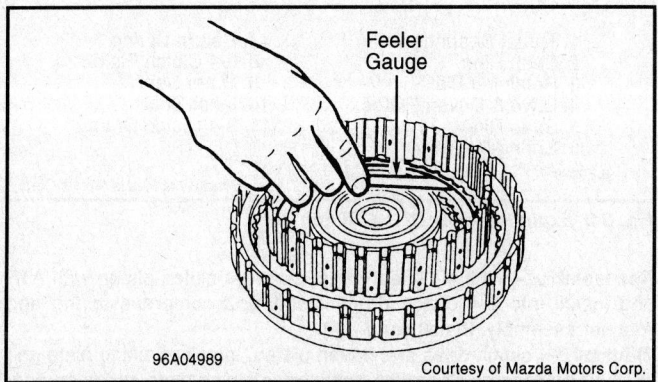

Feeler Gauge

96A04989   Courtesy of Mazda Motors Corp.

Fig. 27: Measuring Coasting Clutch Clearance

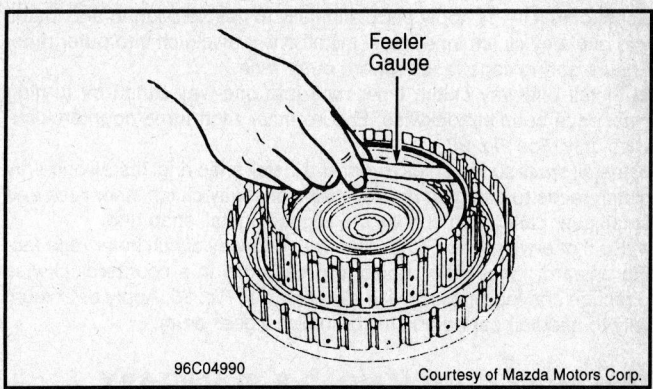

Feeler Gauge

96C04990   Courtesy of Mazda Motors Corp.

Fig. 28: Measuring Forward Clutch Clearance

SMALL SUN GEAR & ONE-WAY CLUTCH NO. 1

Disassembly – 1) Remove snap ring, one-way clutch inner race, snap ring, needle bearing, one-way clutch, one-way clutch outer race, needle bearing and small sun gear. *See Fig. 29.*

2) Measure bushing inside diameters. Maximum inside diameter of sun gear drum is 1.198" (30.42 mm) on FA4A-EL, or 1.316" (33.43 mm) on GF4A-EL. Maximum inside diameter of sun gear is .828" (21.20 mm) on FA4A-EL, or .945" (24.00 mm) on GF4A-EL. Check sun gear drum and small sun gear, inner and outer race, clutch hub, gear and needle bearings for damage or wear.

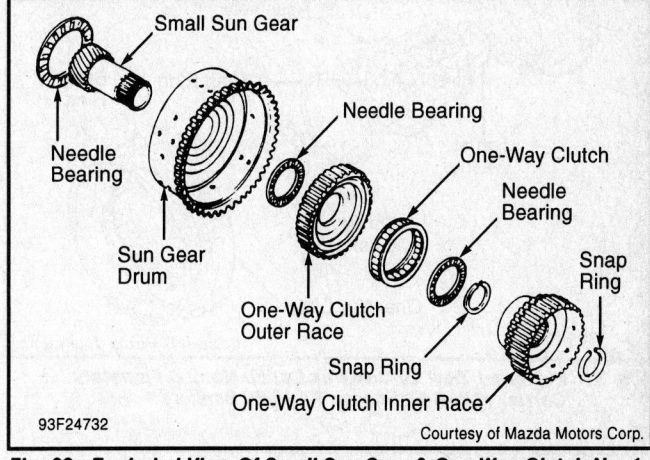

Small Sun Gear

Needle Bearing

Needle Bearing

One-Way Clutch

Needle Bearing

Snap Ring

Sun Gear Drum

One-Way Clutch Outer Race

Snap Ring

One-Way Clutch Inner Race

93F24732   Courtesy of Mazda Motors Corp.

Fig. 29: Exploded View Of Small Sun Gear & One-Way Clutch No. 1

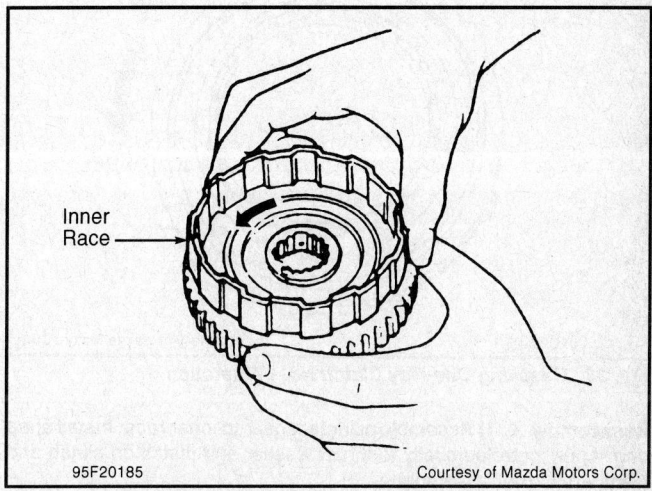

Inner Race

95F20185   Courtesy of Mazda Motors Corp.

Fig. 30: Checking One-Way Clutch No. 1 Operation

Reassembly – 1) Apply petroleum jelly to needle bearing and install into one-way clutch inner race. Install one-way clutch into outer race. Ensure spring cage faces toward outer race.

2) Install one-way clutch inner race into one-way clutch by turning inner race counterclockwise. Ensure inner race turns counterclockwise only. *See Fig. 30.*

3) Install small sun gear into drum and install snap ring. Install one-way clutch races to sun gear drum. Ensure one-way clutch inner race and small gear clutch hub splines are aligned. Install snap ring.

4) Hold one-way clutch outer race with one-way clutch inner race facing upward. Inner race should turn smoothly in a counterclockwise direction and lock in clockwise direction. *See Fig. 30.* Apply petroleum jelly to needle bearing and install into sun gear drum.

ONE-WAY CLUTCH NO. 2 & PLANETARY CARRIER

Disassembly – 1) Remove one-way clutch, thrust washers and snap ring. *See Fig. 31.* Remove planetary carrier assembly from inner race. Place one-way clutch on inner race. Holding inner race, ensure one-way clutch rotates smoothly in clockwise direction. *See Fig. 32.*

2) Inspect for damaged or worn parts. Ensure clearance between planetary pinion gear and washer is .008-.028" (.20-.70 mm). *See Fig. 33.*

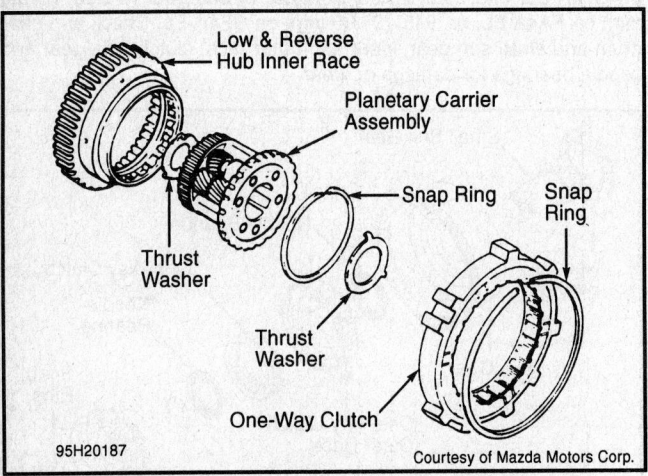

Fig. 31: Exploded View Of One-Way Clutch No. 2 & Planetary Carrier (GF4A-EL Shown, FA4A-EL Similar)

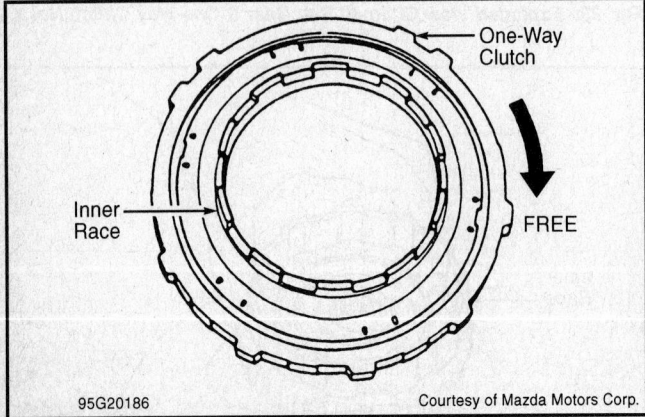

Fig. 32: Checking One-Way Clutch No. 2 Operation

Reassembly – 1) Assemble planetary gear to inner race. Install snap ring. Apply petroleum jelly to thrust washer and install on clutch and planetary carrier assembly.

2) Outer diameter of thrust washer for FA4A-EL is 3.307" (84.0 mm). Outer diameter of thrust washer for sun gear side of GF4A-EL planetary is 2.835" (72.00 mm). Outer diameter of thrust washer for 3-4

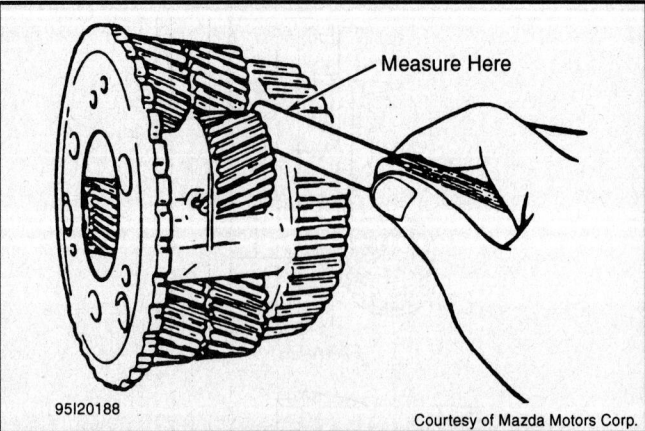

Fig. 33: Measuring Pinion Gear To Thrust Washer Clearance

clutch side is 2.209" (56.10 mm). Install one-way clutch. While holding inner race, ensure one-way clutch No. 2 rotates clockwise and locks counterclockwise. *See Fig. 32.*

3-4 CLUTCH

Disassembly – 1) Remove needle bearings and snap ring. Remove retaining plate and clutch pack. *See Fig. 34.* Compress return spring and retainer. Remove snap ring.

2) Remove spring and retainer assembly. Remove piston, and inner and outer seals from piston.

Inspection – Check drive and driven plates for damage or wear. Minimum thickness of drive (friction) plates is .055" (1.40 mm). Check return spring free length. Free length of springs should be 1.594" (40.50 mm) for FA4A-EL. For GF4A-EL, free length should be 1.524" (38.70 mm).

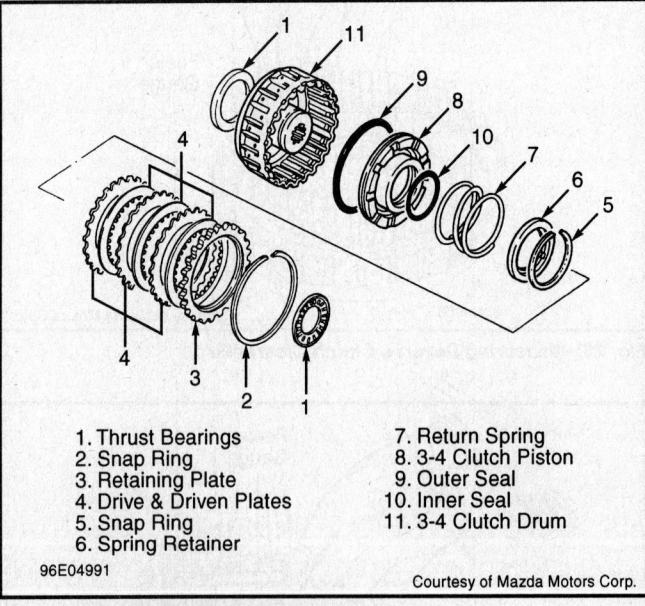

1. Thrust Bearings
2. Snap Ring
3. Retaining Plate
4. Drive & Driven Plates
5. Snap Ring
6. Spring Retainer
7. Return Spring
8. 3-4 Clutch Piston
9. Outer Seal
10. Inner Seal
11. 3-4 Clutch Drum

Fig. 34: Exploded View Of 3-4 Clutch

Reassembly – 1) Install seal rings. Coat 3-4 clutch piston with ATF and install into 3-4 clutch drum. Install and compress spring and retainer assembly. Install snap ring.

2) Install 3-4 clutch drive and driven plates. Install retaining plate and snap ring. Measure clearance between retaining plate and snap ring. On FA4A-EL models, clearance should be .051-.063" (1.30-1.60 mm). Adjust clearance by installing selective snap ring. Snap rings range in thickness from .055" (1.40 mm) to .094" (2.40 mm) in .008" (.20 mm) increments.

3) On GF4A-EL models, clearance should be .051-.059" (1.30-1.50 mm). Adjust clearance by installing selective retaining plate. Retaining plates range in thickness from .150" (3.80 mm) to .189" (4.80 mm) in .008" (.20 mm) increments.

4) Check clutch operation. Ensure clutch piston seal does not leak. Apply petroleum jelly to needle bearings and install on 3-4 clutch. Bearing outer diameter is 2.21" (56.1 mm) for carrier side and 2.84" (72.1 mm) for output shell side.

LOW & REVERSE BRAKE

Disassembly & Inspection – **1)** Use air pressure to remove low and reverse brake. See Fig. 20 or 21. Check for worn drive (friction) and driven plates. See Fig. 12 or 13. Drive plate minimum thickness is .055" (1.40 mm). Check snap ring for wear and cracks. Check for deformed or detached spring and retainer assembly. Check for broken or weak springs.

2) Check for spring free length of .563" (14.30 mm) for FA4A-EL, and .711" (18.07 mm) for GF4A-EL. Check piston for damage or wear and seal contact area in transaxle case for damage.

Reassembly – **1)** Install low and reverse brake piston. Install spring and retainer assembly. Compress spring and retainer assembly enough to install snap ring. Install clutches in order: driven, drive, driven, drive, driven, drive, driven and drive. Install retaining plate and snap ring.

2) Measure clearance between retaining plate and snap ring. See Fig. 35. Adjust clearance by selective snap rings or retainer plates. On FA4A-EL models, clearance should be .083-.094" (2.10-2.40 mm). Adjust clearance by installing selective snap ring. Snap rings range in thickness from .079" (2.0 mm) to .118" (3.0 mm) in .008" (.20 mm) increments.

3) On GF4A-EL models, clearance should be .059-.071" (1.50-1.80 mm). Adjust clearance by installing selective retaining plate. Retaining plates range in thickness from .276" (7.0 mm) to .291" (7.4 mm) in .008" (.20 mm) increments.

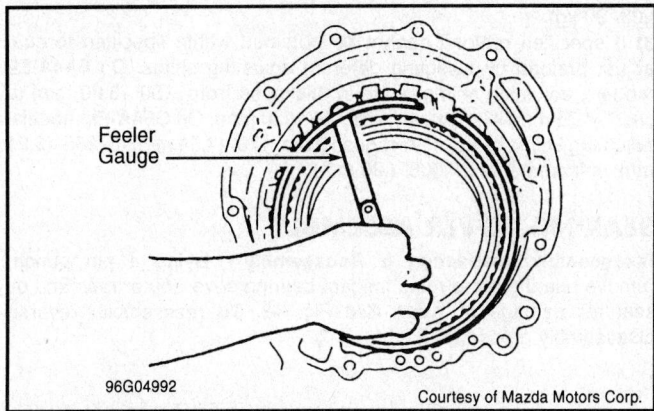

Fig. 35: Measuring Low & Reverse Clutch Clearance

2-4 BRAKE BAND SERVO

Disassembly (FA4A-EL) – Separate servo retainer from servo piston. See Fig. 12. Remove "O" rings, "D" rings, spring clip and piston stem.

Inspection – Check for damaged or worn piston and spring. Spring free length should be 1.703" (43.25 mm).

Reassembly – Install new "O" ring and "D" rings. Assemble servo piston to servo retainer. Install 2-4 brake band servo.

NOTE: Alternative method of adjustment for 2-4 servo is available. See appropriate AUTOMATIC TRANSMISSION SERVICING article in TRANSMISSION SERVICING section.

Adjustment (Without Transaxle Internal Components Installed) – Measure by marking piston stem at transmission case. Apply air pressure of 57 psi (393 kPa) or less to oil passage. See Fig. 36. Make sec-

ond mark on piston stem. Distance of stroke should be .039-.067" (1.00-1.70 mm). If not correct, install different piston stem. Selective piston stems are available in lengths from 3.74" (95.0 mm) to 3.90" (99.0 mm) in .020" (.50 mm) increments.

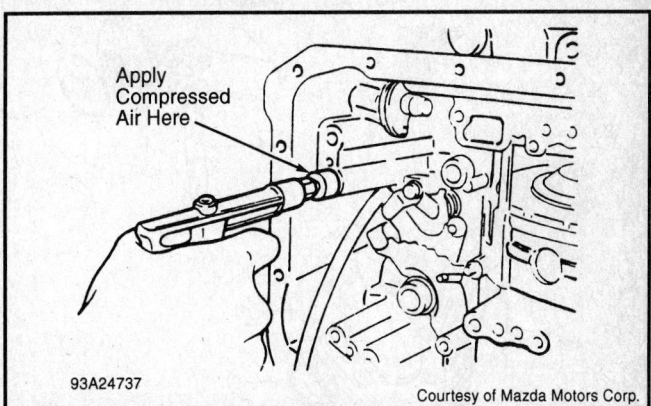

Fig. 36: Checking 2-4 Brake Band Servo

Disassembly (GF4A-EL) – Separate servo retainer from servo piston. See Fig. 13. Remove "O" rings, "D" rings, spring and piston stem.

Inspection – Check for damaged or worn piston and spring. Spring free length should be 1.703" (43.25 mm).

Reassembly – Install new "O" ring and "D" rings. Assemble servo piston to servo retainer. Install 2-4 brake band servo.

2-4 BRAKE BAND

After 2-4 brake band servo is removed, remove 2-4 brake band. If damaged or worn, replace 2-4 band.

DIFFERENTIAL ASSEMBLY

Pre-Disassembly Backlash Inspection – Install left and right axle shafts into differential. Support axle shafts on V-blocks. See Fig. 37. Measure backlash of both pinion gears. Backlash should be .002-.006" (.05-.15 mm). Maximum service limit is .020" (.50 mm). Rebuild or replace differential assembly if backlash is not as specified.

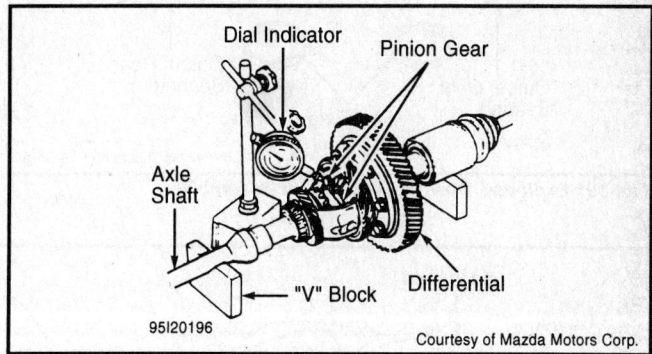

Fig. 37: Checking Pinion Gear Backlash

Disassembly – **1)** Remove roll pin and pinion shaft. See Fig. 38. Remove pinion gears and rotate thrust washers out of differential housing.

2) Remove side gears and thrust washers. Using appropriate bearing puller, remove side bearings. DO NOT remove speedometer drive gear unless damaged.

Reassembly – Install speedometer drive gear (if removed) and bearings. Install thrust washers, pinion gears and side gears. Install pinion shaft. Install and crimp roll pin.

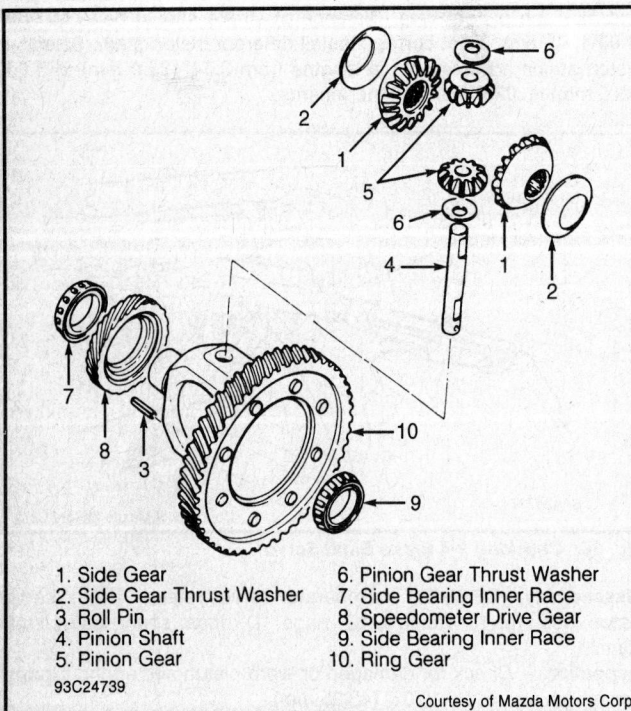

1. Side Gear
2. Side Gear Thrust Washer
3. Roll Pin
4. Pinion Shaft
5. Pinion Gear
6. Pinion Gear Thrust Washer
7. Side Bearing Inner Race
8. Speedometer Drive Gear
9. Side Bearing Inner Race
10. Ring Gear

93C24739

Courtesy of Mazda Motors Corp.

Fig. 38: Exploded View Of Differential

OUTPUT GEAR

Disassembly & Reassembly – Remove seal rings. Using bearing puller, remove bearings. To reassemble, reverse disassembly procedure. See Fig. 39.

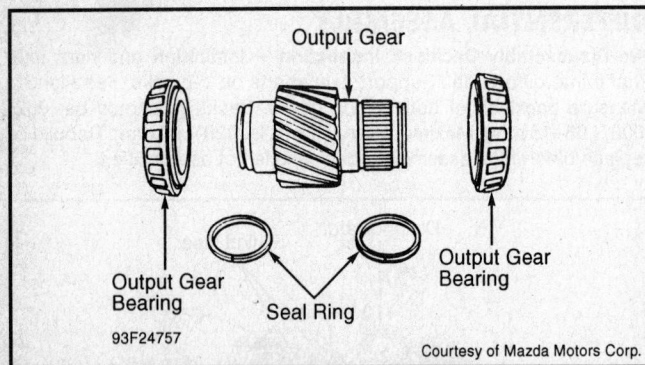

93F24757

Courtesy of Mazda Motors Corp.

Fig. 39: Exploded View Of Output Gear Assembly

IDLER GEAR ASSEMBLY

Disassembly – Using Holding Device (49G019013), mount idler gear shaft in vise. Remove lock nut from idler shaft. Remove both outer bearing races from idler gear. See Fig. 40.

Cleaning & Inspection – Inspect idler gear and bearings for damage or wear. Replace as needed.

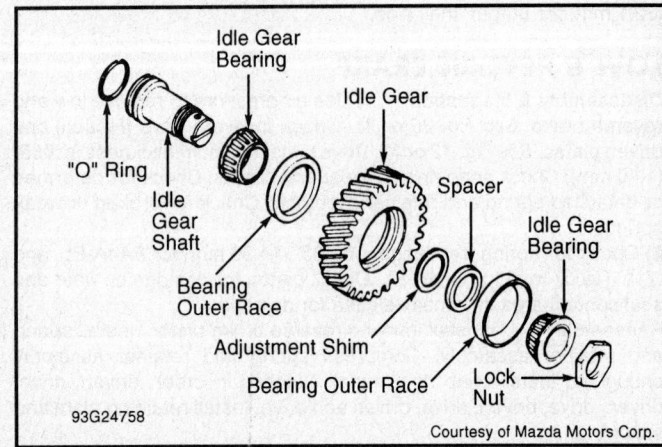

93G24758

Courtesy of Mazda Motors Corp.

Fig. 40: Exploded View Of Idler Gear Assembly

Reassembly – 1) Press both outer bearing races into idler gear. Assemble idler gear assembly. See Fig. 40. Using holding device, mount idler gear shaft in vise. Tighten lock nut to lower limit of torque specifications. See TORQUE SPECIFICATIONS.

2) Secure idle gear assembly in vise and measure bearing preload. See Fig. 41. Preload can be measured using a INCH Lb. torque wrench or pull scale. Using torque wrench, preload should be .22-6.2 INCH Lbs. (.03-.70 N.m). Using pull scale, preload should be .066-1.98 Lbs. (.03-.90 kg).

3) If specified preload cannot be obtained within specified torque, adjust preload by selecting different adjusting shims. On FA4A-EL models, adjusting shims range in thickness from .150" (3.80 mm) to .187" (4.75 mm) in increments of .008" (.20 mm). On GF4A-EL models, adjusting shims range in thickness from .179" (4.54 mm) to .205" (5.21 mm) in increments of .008" (.20 mm).

BEARING COVER ASSEMBLY

Disassembly, Inspection & Reassembly – Using a pin punch, remove bearing outer race. Inspect bearing cover, outer race and oil seal for damage or wear. See Fig. 42. To reassemble, reverse disassembly procedure.

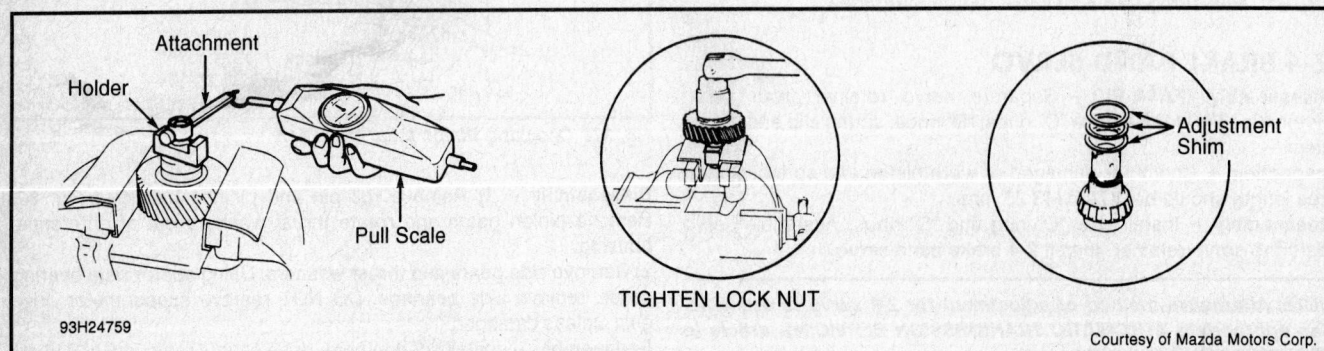

TIGHTEN LOCK NUT

93H24759

Courtesy of Mazda Motors Corp.

Fig. 41: Measuring Idler Gear Preload

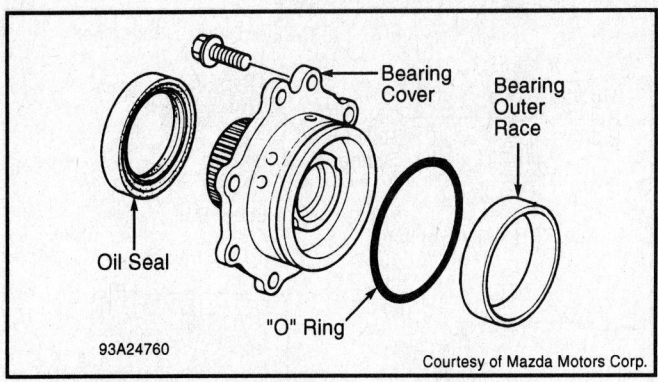

93A24760

Courtesy of Mazda Motors Corp.

Fig. 42: Bearing Cover Assembly

VALVE BODY ASSEMBLY

CAUTION: All valve body components must be installed in original location. Lay all components in sequence during removal for reassembly reference.

Disassembly (FA4A-EL) – 1) Remove solenoid valves, "O" rings, oil strainers and oil pipe assembly. Remove upper valve body, gasket "B", upper separator plate oil filter and gasket "A".

2) Remove throttle relief ball and spring from upper valve body. Remove main valve body, gasket "D", main separator plate and gasket "C". Remove rubber balls from main valve body.

3) Remove pre-main valve body. Remove oil strainer from pre-main valve body. Remove oil filter, gasket "E", lower separator plate and gasket "F". Remove oil strainer from lower valve body.

4) Disassemble pre-main body, main body and rear body valve assemblies. See Figs. 43, 45 and 49-51.

Disassembly (GF4A-EL) – 1) Remove sensors, solenoid valves and "O" rings. Remove front valve body, pre-main separator plate and pre-main separator plate gaskets. Remove front/pre-main gaskets, pre-main separator plate and pre-main separator plate gaskets. See Figs. 44 and 46

2) Locate and remove rubber balls from front and pre-main valve body. Remove pre-main valve body, main separator plate and main separator plate gaskets.

3) Remove pre-main/main gaskets and main separator plate from pre-main valve body. Remove jet orifices and nuts from main separator plate. Locate and remove rubber balls and oil strainer from pre-main valve body.

4) Locate and remove rubber balls and oil strainer from main valve body. Turn assembly over and remove oil pipe, baffle and shift solenoids. Remove rear separator plate and rear separator plate gaskets from main valve body.

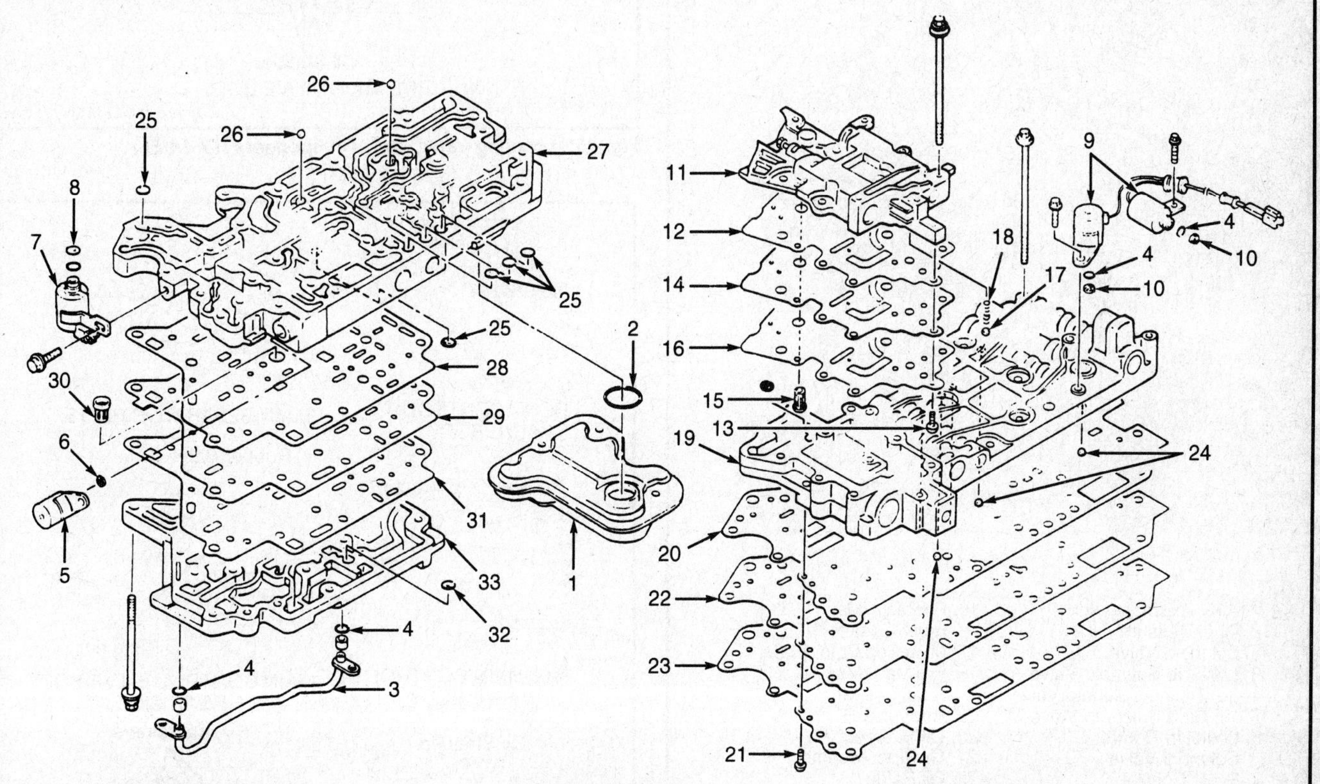

1. Oil Strainer Assembly	12. Gasket "B"	23. Gasket "C"
2. "O" Ring	13. Screws	24. Rubber Balls
3. Oil Pipe Assembly	14. Upper Separator Plate	25. Oil Strainers
4. "O" Rings	15. Oil Filter	26. Rubber Balls
5. 1-2 Solenoid Valve "A"	16. Gasket "A"	27. Pre-Main Control Valve Body
6. Oil Strainer	17. Throttle Relief Ball	28. Gasket "E"
7. Lock-Up Solenoid Valve	18. Throttle Relief Spring	29. Lower Separator Plate
8. Oil Strainer	19. Main Control Valve Body	30. Oil Filter
9. 2-3 & 3-4 Solenoid Valve "B" & "C"	20. Gasket "D"	31. Gasket "F"
10. Oil Strainers	21. Screws	32. Oil Strainer
11. Upper Control Valve Body	22. Main Separator Plate	33. Lower Control Valve Body

96I04969

Courtesy of Mazda Motors Corp.

Fig. 43: Exploded View Of Valve Body Assembly (FA4A-EL)

5) Remove main/rear gaskets and separator plate from rear valve body. Locate and remove rubber balls and oil strainer from rear valve body. Locate and remove rubber balls and oil strainer from main valve body.

6) Disassemble pre-main body, main body and rear body valve assemblies. See Figs. 47, 48 and 52.

Cleaning & Inspection – Inspect valve bodies for worn valves, damaged oil passages and cracks. Check operation of each valve in valve bore and valve spring free length. See VALVE BODY SPRING SPECIFICATIONS table.

Reassembly (FA4A-EL & GF4A-EL) – **1)** Reassemble valve bodies. Install check balls, oil strainers and jet orifices in correct location. See Figs. 43-46.

2) During assembly of valve body, ensure bolts are installed in correct location. See Fig. 55 or 56. Ensure valve body gaskets are installed in correct location. See Figs. 42-43. Tighten all bolts to specification. See TORQUE SPECIFICATIONS.

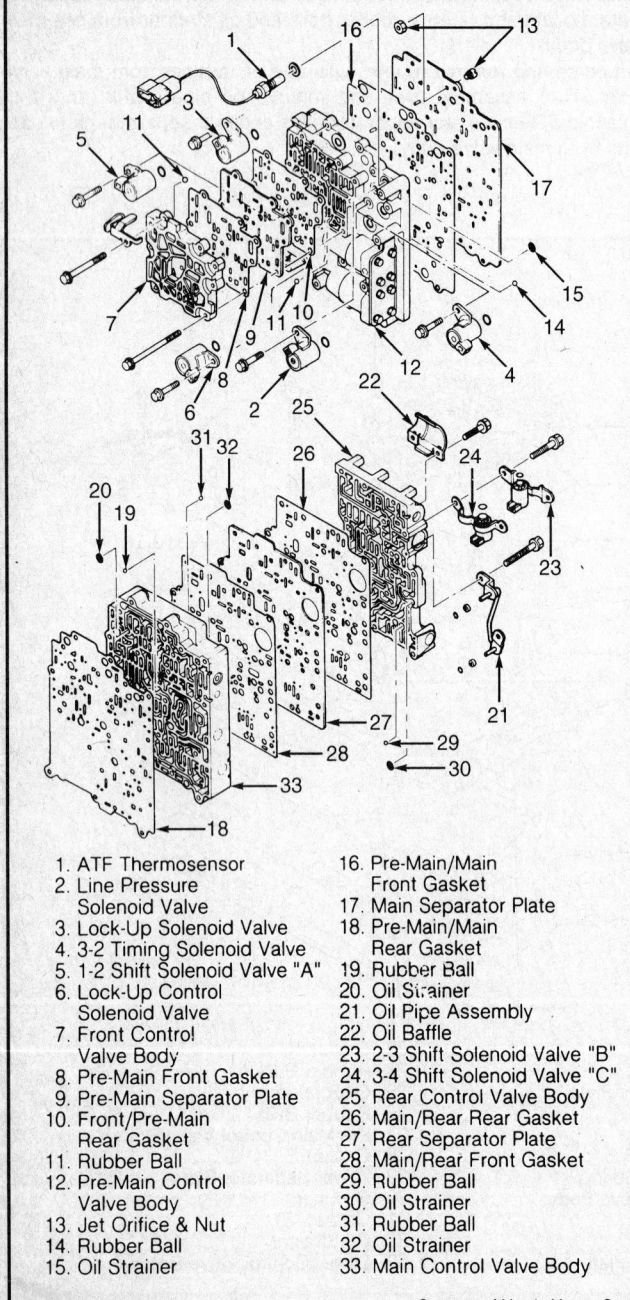

1. ATF Thermosensor
2. Line Pressure Solenoid Valve
3. Lock-Up Solenoid Valve
4. 3-2 Timing Solenoid Valve
5. 1-2 Shift Solenoid Valve "A"
6. Lock-Up Control Solenoid Valve
7. Front Control Valve Body
8. Pre-Main Front Gasket
9. Pre-Main Separator Plate
10. Front/Pre-Main Rear Gasket
11. Rubber Ball
12. Pre-Main Control Valve Body
13. Jet Orifice & Nut
14. Rubber Ball
15. Oil Strainer
16. Pre-Main/Main Front Gasket
17. Main Separator Plate
18. Pre-Main/Main Rear Gasket
19. Rubber Ball
20. Oil Strainer
21. Oil Pipe Assembly
22. Oil Baffle
23. 2-3 Shift Solenoid Valve "B"
24. 3-4 Shift Solenoid Valve "C"
25. Rear Control Valve Body
26. Main/Rear Rear Gasket
27. Rear Separator Plate
28. Main/Rear Front Gasket
29. Rubber Ball
30. Oil Strainer
31. Rubber Ball
32. Oil Strainer
33. Main Control Valve Body

96G29997   Courtesy of Mazda Motors Corp.

Fig. 44: Exploded View Of Valve Body Assembly (GF4A-EL)

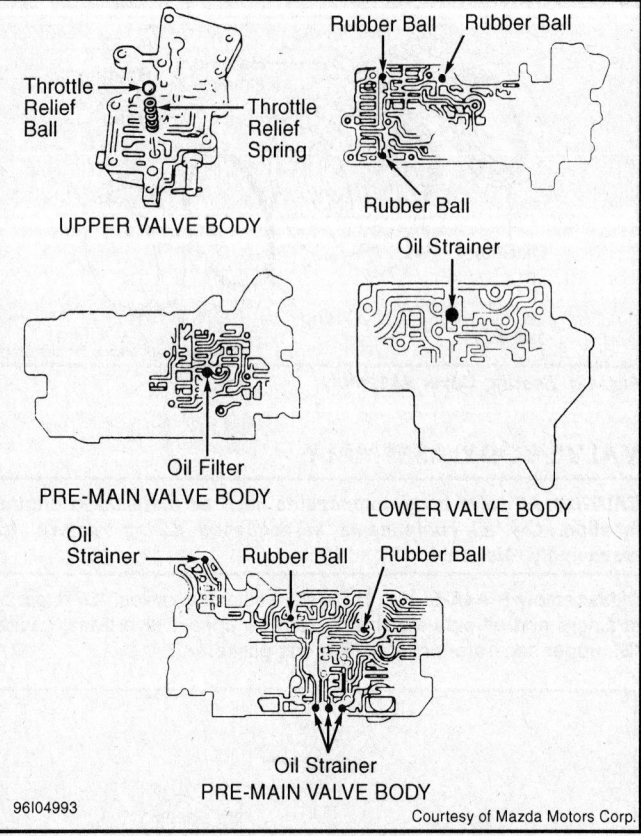

96I04993   Courtesy of Mazda Motors Corp.

Fig. 45: Locating Valve Body Components (FA4A-EL)

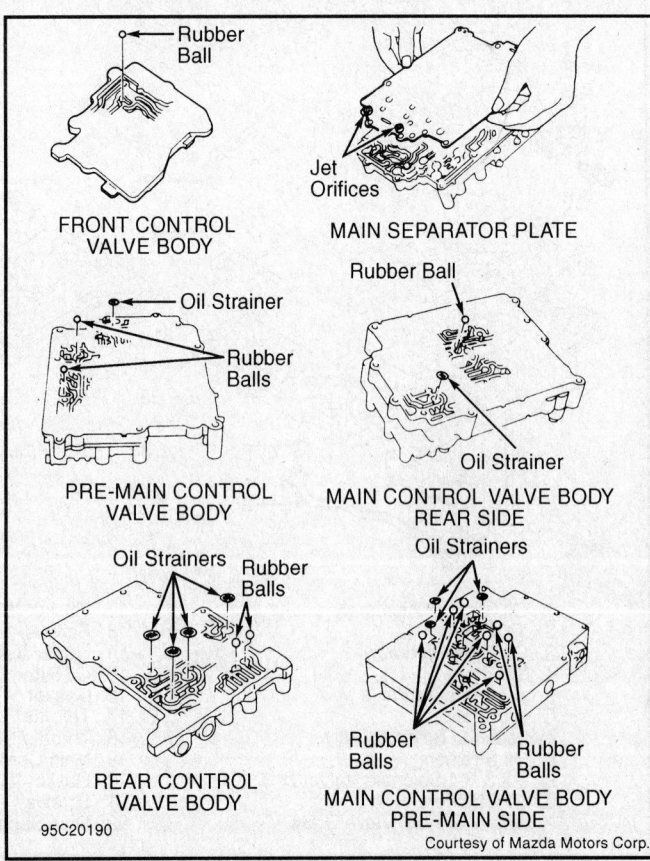

95C20190   Courtesy of Mazda Motors Corp.

Fig. 46: Locating Valve Components (GF4A-EL)

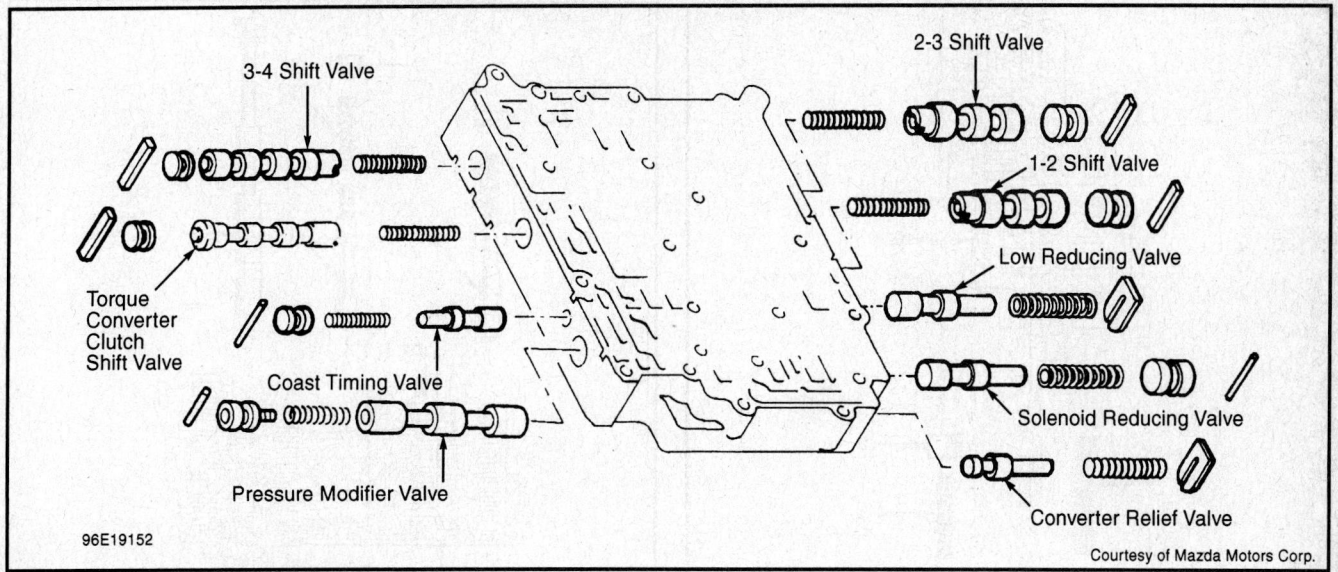

3-4 Shift Valve

2-3 Shift Valve

1-2 Shift Valve

Low Reducing Valve

Torque Converter Clutch Shift Valve

Coast Timing Valve

Solenoid Reducing Valve

Pressure Modifier Valve

Converter Relief Valve

96E19152

Courtesy of Mazda Motors Corp.

Fig. 47: Exploded View Of Main Valve Body (GF4A-EL)

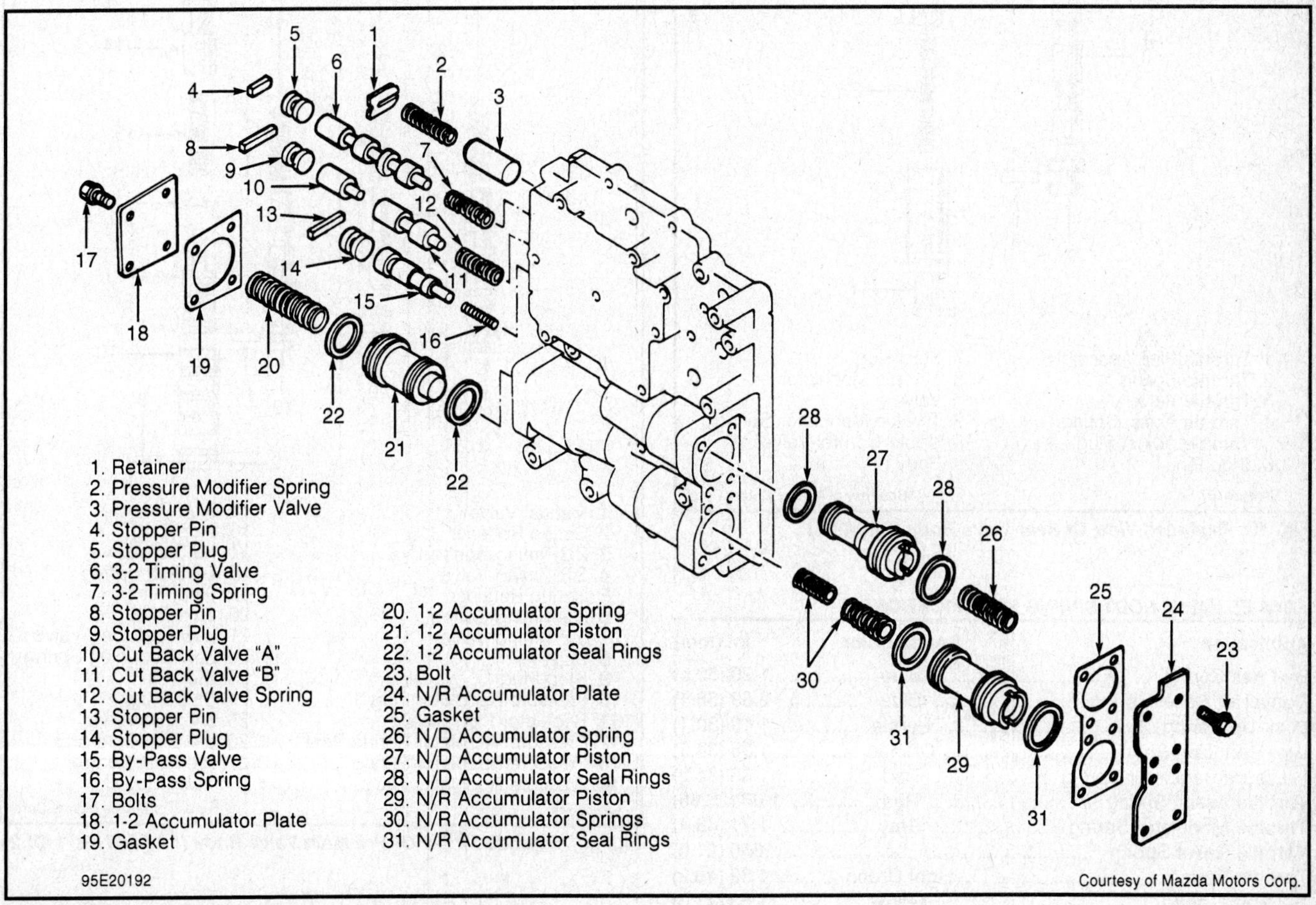

1. Retainer
2. Pressure Modifier Spring
3. Pressure Modifier Valve
4. Stopper Pin
5. Stopper Plug
6. 3-2 Timing Valve
7. 3-2 Timing Spring
8. Stopper Pin
9. Stopper Plug
10. Cut Back Valve "A"
11. Cut Back Valve "B"
12. Cut Back Valve Spring
13. Stopper Pin
14. Stopper Plug
15. By-Pass Valve
16. By-Pass Spring
17. Bolts
18. 1-2 Accumulator Plate
19. Gasket
20. 1-2 Accumulator Spring
21. 1-2 Accumulator Piston
22. 1-2 Accumulator Seal Rings
23. Bolt
24. N/R Accumulator Plate
25. Gasket
26. N/D Accumulator Spring
27. N/D Accumulator Piston
28. N/D Accumulator Seal Rings
29. N/R Accumulator Piston
30. N/R Accumulator Springs
31. N/R Accumulator Seal Rings

95E20192

Courtesy of Mazda Motors Corp.

Fig. 48: Exploded View Of Pre-Main Valve Body (GF4A-EL)

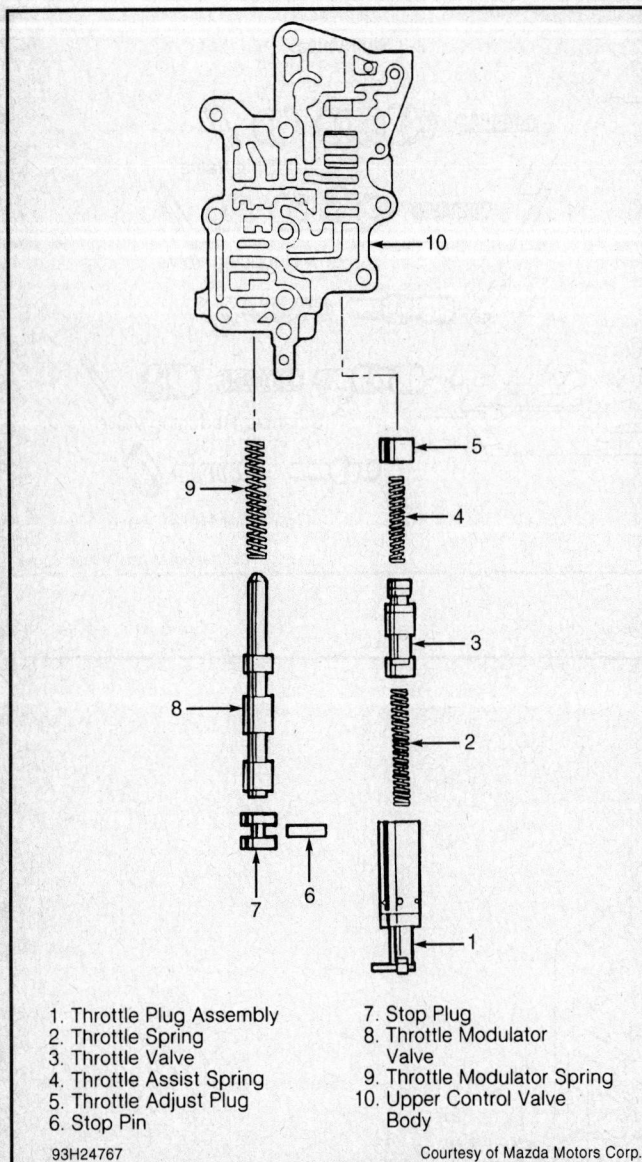

1. Throttle Plug Assembly
2. Throttle Spring
3. Throttle Valve
4. Throttle Assist Spring
5. Throttle Adjust Plug
6. Stop Pin
7. Stop Plug
8. Throttle Modulator Valve
9. Throttle Modulator Spring
10. Upper Control Valve Body

93H24767   Courtesy of Mazda Motors Corp.

Fig. 49: Exploded View Of Rear Valve Body (FA4A-EL)

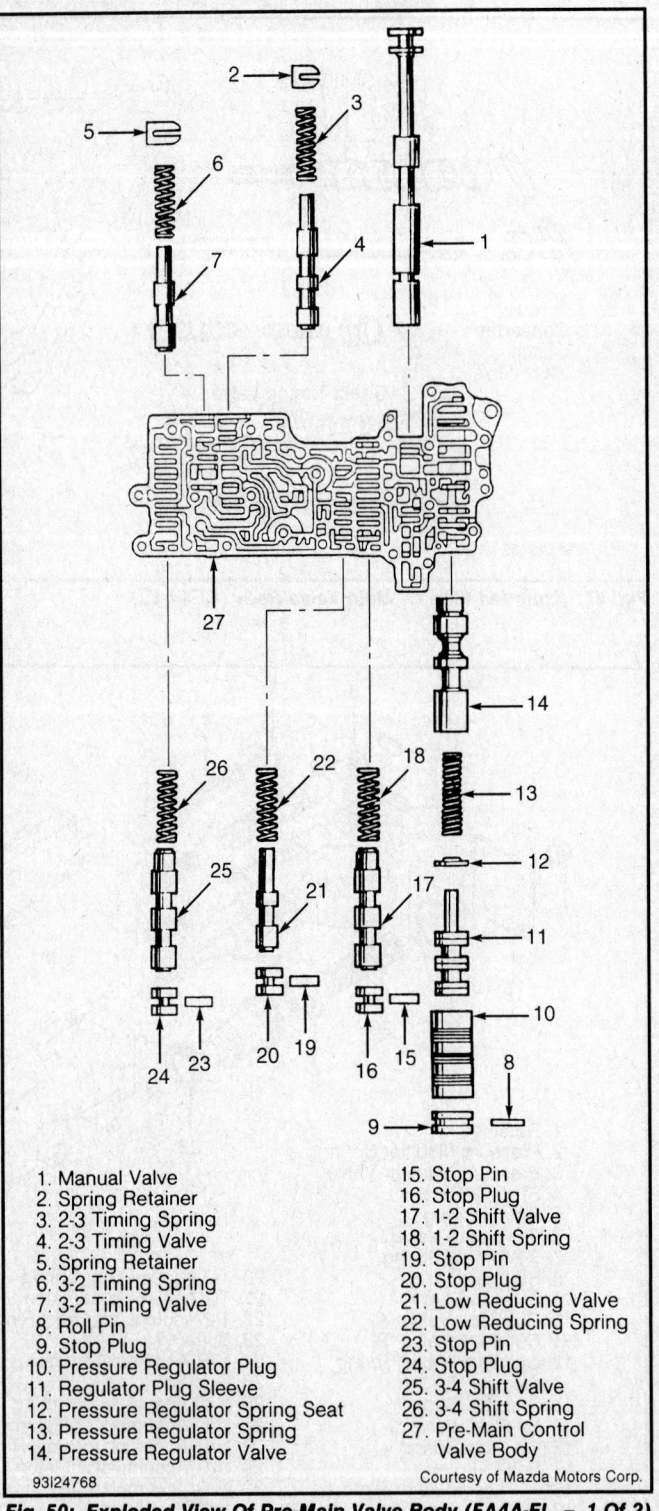

1. Manual Valve
2. Spring Retainer
3. 2-3 Timing Spring
4. 2-3 Timing Valve
5. Spring Retainer
6. 3-2 Timing Spring
7. 3-2 Timing Valve
8. Roll Pin
9. Stop Plug
10. Pressure Regulator Plug
11. Regulator Plug Sleeve
12. Pressure Regulator Spring Seat
13. Pressure Regulator Spring
14. Pressure Regulator Valve
15. Stop Pin
16. Stop Plug
17. 1-2 Shift Valve
18. 1-2 Shift Spring
19. Stop Pin
20. Stop Plug
21. Low Reducing Valve
22. Low Reducing Spring
23. Stop Pin
24. Stop Plug
25. 3-4 Shift Valve
26. 3-4 Shift Spring
27. Pre-Main Control Valve Body

93I24768   Courtesy of Mazda Motors Corp.

Fig. 50: Exploded View Of Pre-Main Valve Body (FA4A-EL – 1 Of 2)

FA4A-EL VALVE BODY SPRING SPECIFICATIONS

Application	Spring Color	In. (mm)
By-Pass Spring	Blue	1.20 (30.5)
Converter Relief Spring	Blue	2.69 (68.4)
Lock-Up Spring	Purple	1.19 (30.1)
Low Reducing Spring	Orange	1.36 (34.5)
Pressure Regulator Spring	Red	1.35 (34.2)
Throttle Assist Spring	Red	1.06 (26.88)
Throttle Modulator Spring	Gray	1.71 (43.4)
Throttle Relief Spring		.850 (21.6)
Throttle Spring	Light Green	1.82 (46.2)
1-2 Shift Spring	Yellow	1.63 (41.3)
2-3 Shift Spring	Yellow	1.63 (41.3)
3-4 Shift Spring	Yellow	1.63 (41.3)
3-2 Timing Spring	Blue	1.18 (30.0)

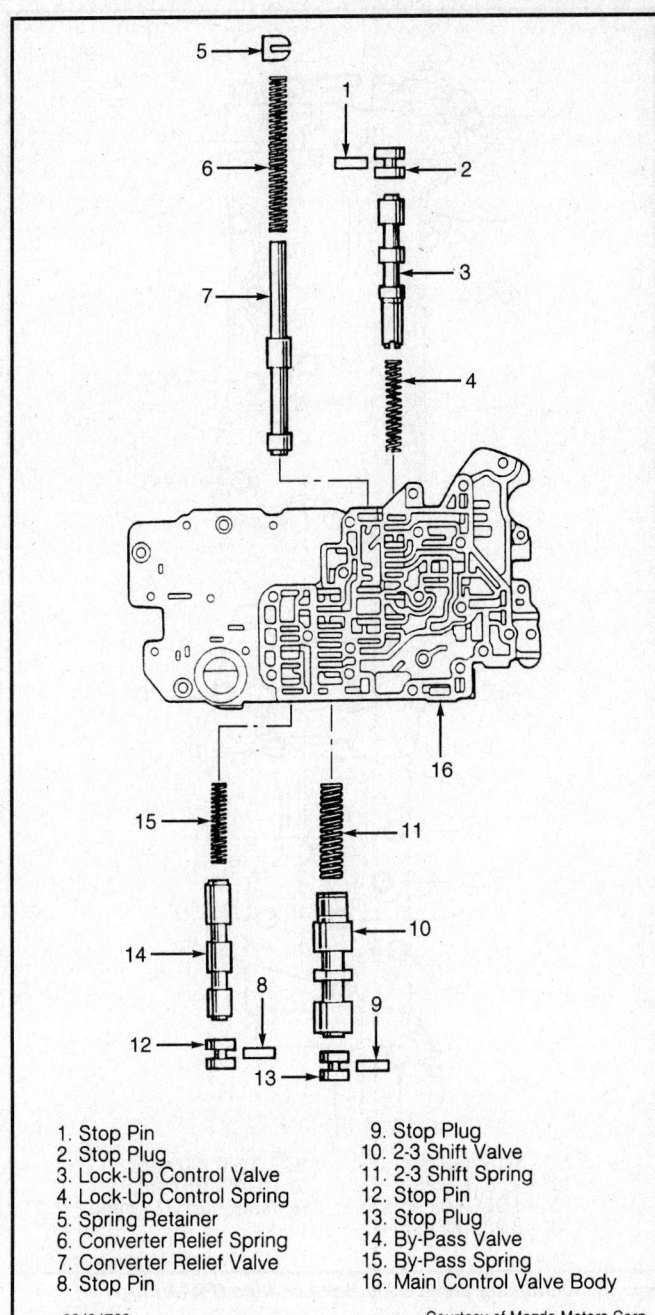

1. Stop Pin
2. Stop Plug
3. Lock-Up Control Valve
4. Lock-Up Control Spring
5. Spring Retainer
6. Converter Relief Spring
7. Converter Relief Valve
8. Stop Pin
9. Stop Plug
10. 2-3 Shift Valve
11. 2-3 Shift Spring
12. Stop Pin
13. Stop Plug
14. By-Pass Valve
15. By-Pass Spring
16. Main Control Valve Body

93J24769   Courtesy of Mazda Motors Corp.

Fig. 51: Exploded View Of Pre-Main Valve Body (FA4A-EL – 2 Of 2)

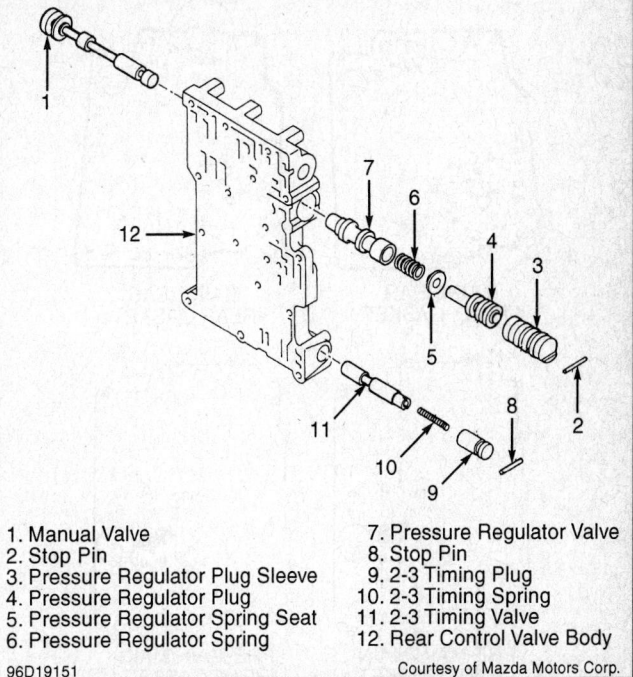

1. Manual Valve
2. Stop Pin
3. Pressure Regulator Plug Sleeve
4. Pressure Regulator Plug
5. Pressure Regulator Spring Seat
6. Pressure Regulator Spring
7. Pressure Regulator Valve
8. Stop Pin
9. 2-3 Timing Plug
10. 2-3 Timing Spring
11. 2-3 Timing Valve
12. Rear Control Valve Body

96D19151   Courtesy of Mazda Motors Corp.

Fig. 52: Exploded View Of Rear Valve Body (GF4A-EL)

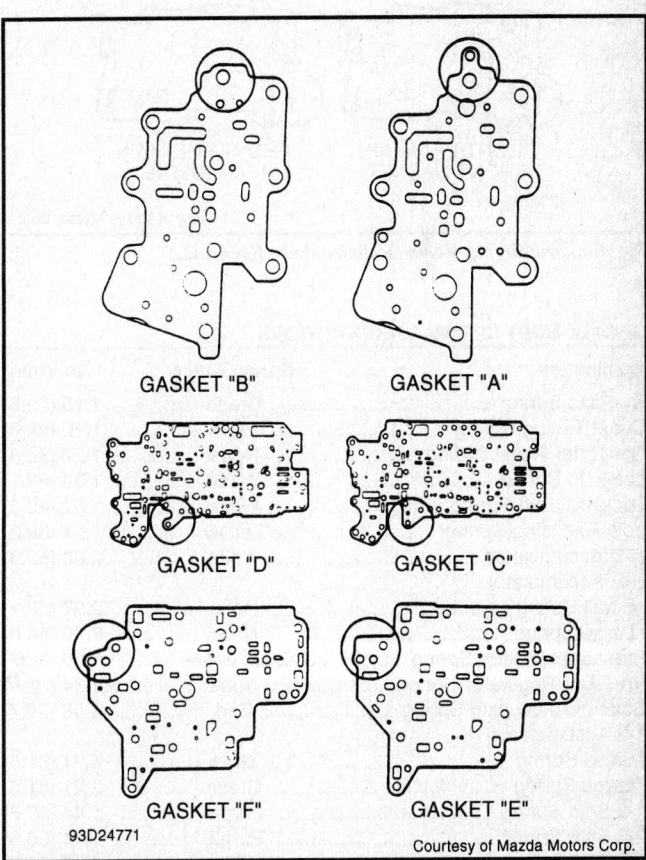

GASKET "B"   GASKET "A"

GASKET "D"   GASKET "C"

GASKET "F"   GASKET "E"

93D24771   Courtesy of Mazda Motors Corp.

Fig. 53: Identifying Valve Body Gaskets (FA4A-EL)

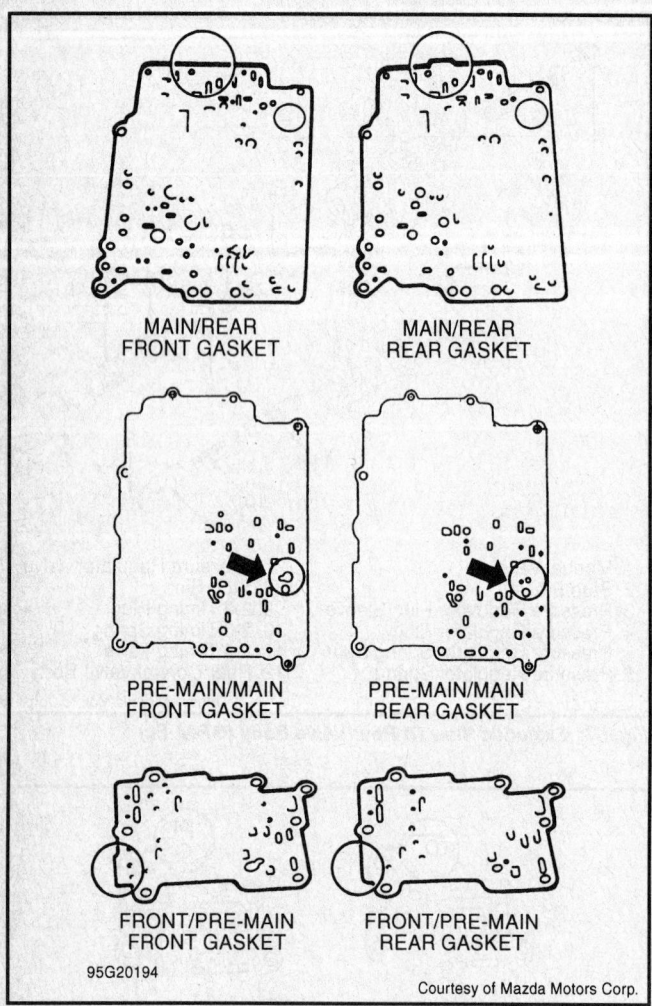

MAIN/REAR
FRONT GASKET

MAIN/REAR
REAR GASKET

PRE-MAIN/MAIN
FRONT GASKET

PRE-MAIN/MAIN
REAR GASKET

FRONT/PRE-MAIN
FRONT GASKET

FRONT/PRE-MAIN
REAR GASKET

95G20194

Courtesy of Mazda Motors Corp.

Fig. 54: Identifying Valve Body Gaskets (GF4A-EL)

GF4A-EL BODY SPRING SPECIFICATIONS

Application	Spring Color	In. (mm)
By-Pass Spring	Green	1.16 (29.5)
Coast Timing Spring	Blue	1.10 (28.0)
Converter Relief Spring	None	1.27 (32.3)
Lock-Up Spring	White	1.30 (33.1)
Lock-Up Shift Spring	White	1.57 (40.0)
Low Reducing Spring	Yellow	1.51 (38.3)
N-D Accumulator	White	2.08 (52.9)
N-R Accumulator		
Small Spring	None	2.37 (60.1)
Large Spring	None	2.20 (56.0)
Pressure Modifier Spring	Light Green	1.50 (38.2)
Pressure Regulator Spring	None	1.34 (33.9)
Solenoid Reducing Spring	Red	1.56 (39.7)
1-2 Accumulator		
Small Spring	Gray	3.21 (81.6)
Large Spring	Green	3.21 (81.6)
1-2 Shift Spring	Purple	1.44 (36.6)
2-3 Shift Spring	Purple	1.44 (36.6)
2-3 Timing Spring	White	0.88 (22.3)
3-4 Shift Spring	Purple	1.44 (36.6)
3-2 Timing Spring	Light Blue	1.39 (35.4)

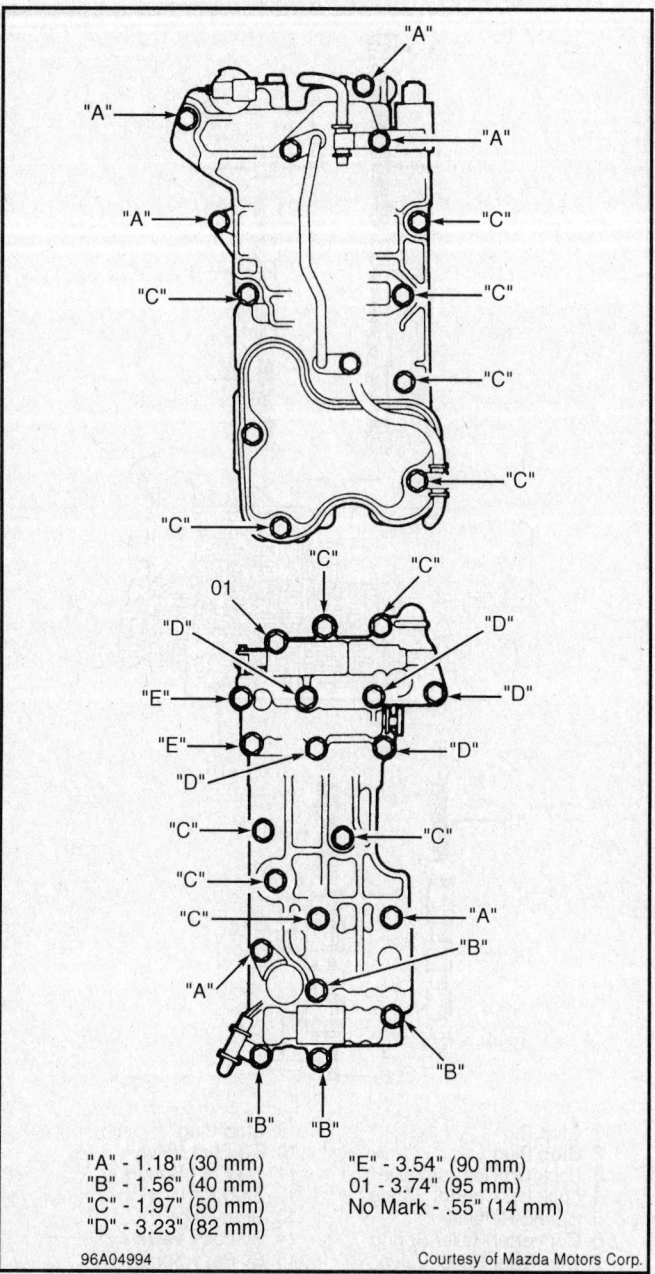

"A" - 1.18" (30 mm)   "E" - 3.54" (90 mm)
"B" - 1.56" (40 mm)   01 - 3.74" (95 mm)
"C" - 1.97" (50 mm)   No Mark - .55" (14 mm)
"D" - 3.23" (82 mm)

96A04994

Courtesy of Mazda Motors Corp.

Fig. 55: Identifying Valve Body Bolt Location (FA4A-EL)

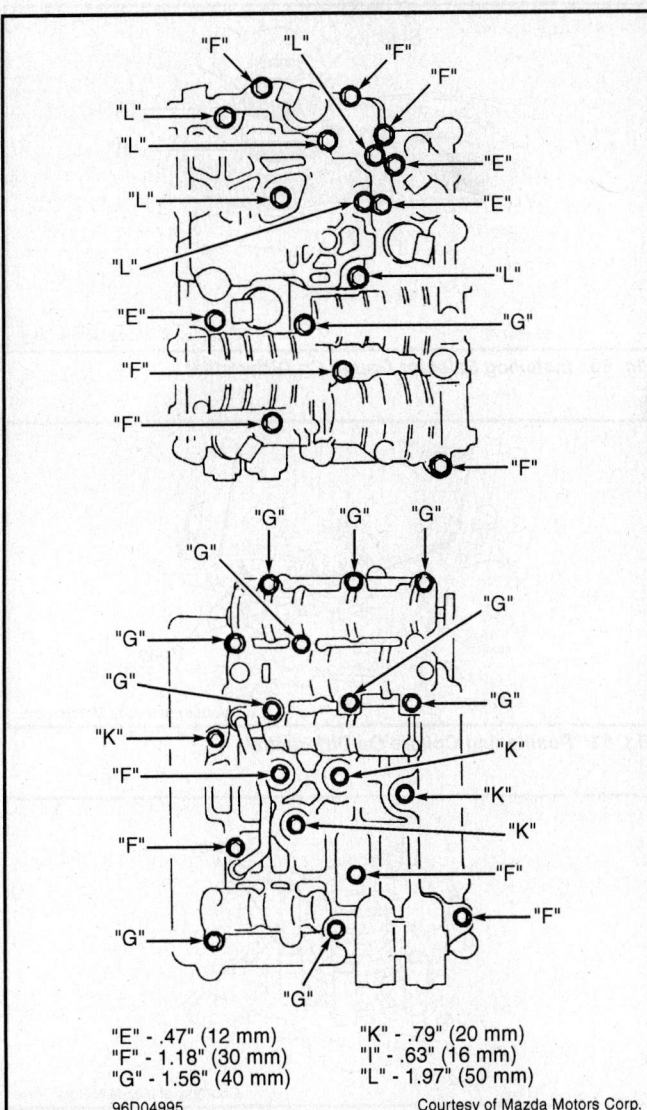

"E" - .47" (12 mm)   "K" - .79" (20 mm)
"F" - 1.18" (30 mm)   "I" - .63" (16 mm)
"G" - 1.56" (40 mm)   "L" - 1.97" (50 mm)

96D04995   Courtesy of Mazda Motors Corp.

Fig. 56: Identifying Valve Body Bolt Location (GF4A-EL)

TRANSAXLE REASSEMBLY

ADJUSTMENTS

Output Gear Bearing Preload – 1) Install bearing cover into converter housing. Before installing bearing housing, adjust output gear bearing preload.

2) Remove bearing outer race and adjustment shims from bearing housing. Reinstall bearing race into bearing housing. Mount output gear assembly on converter housing. Mount selector gauge (49 B019 0A0B-Selector Tool Set) on output gear assembly. Eliminate gap of selector gauge by turning collars "A" or "B" of selector gauge. See Fig. 57.

3) Mount bearing housing on selector gauge. Mount 4 collars between converter housing and bearing housing. Tighten bolts to 14-19 ft. lbs. (19-25 N.m). See Fig. 58.

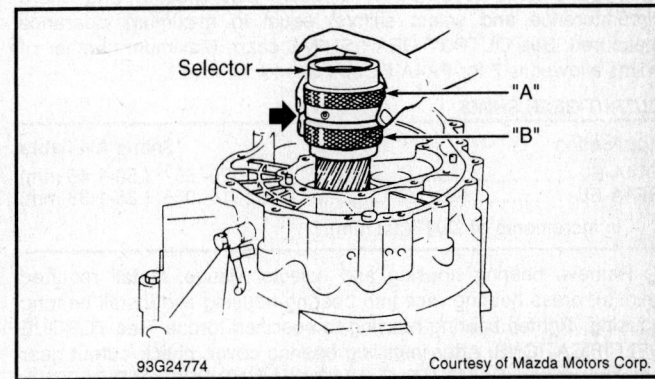

93G24774   Courtesy of Mazda Motors Corp.

Fig. 57: Installing Selector Gauge On Output Gear Assembly

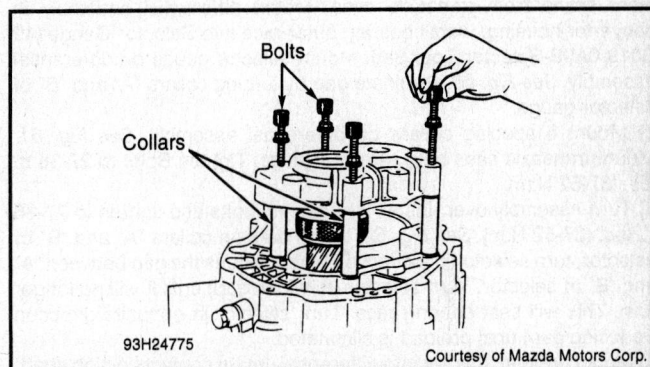

93H24775   Courtesy of Mazda Motors Corp.

Fig. 58: Mounting Bearing Housing On Selector Gauge

4) Turn selector in a direction which widens the gap between "A" and "B" of selector gauge until it will no longer turn. This will seat bearing race. Turn selector in opposite direction (reducing gap) until gap is eliminated.

5) Mount preload adapter to output gear. See Fig. 59. Measure preload with torque wrench or pull scale. Widen gap on selector gauge to obtain specified reading. See OUTPUT GEAR BEARING PRELOAD SPECIFICATION table.

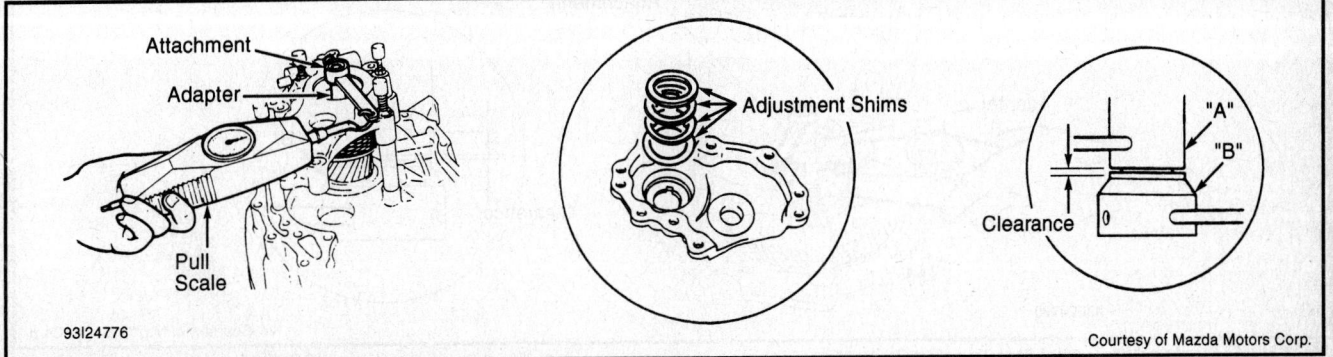

93I24776   Courtesy of Mazda Motors Corp.

Fig. 59: Measuring Output Gear Bearing Preload

OUTPUT GEAR BEARING PRELOAD SPECIFICATION

Measuring Tool	Specification
FA4A-EL	
Torque Wrench	8-15 INCH lbs. (.9-1.7 N.m)
Pull Scale	2.0-3.9 lbs. (9-17 N)
GF4A-EL	
Torque Wrench	10-17 INCH lbs. (1.1-1.9 N.m)
Pull Scale	2.5-4.4 lbs. (11-19 N)

6) Measure clearance between "A" and "B" of selector gauge when specified preload is obtained. Measure clearance around entire circumference and select shim(s) equal to maximum clearance measured. See OUTPUT GEAR SHIMS chart. Maximum number of shims allowed is 7 for FA4A-EL and one for GF4A-EL.

OUTPUT GEAR SHIMS

Application	¹Shims Available
FA4A-EL	.020-.057" (.50-1.45 mm)
GF4A-EL	.014-.055" (.35-1.38 mm)

¹ – In increments of .001" (.02 mm).

7) Remove bearing housing and selector gauge. Install required shim(s), press bearing race into bearing housing and install bearing housing. Tighten bearing housing to specified torque. See TORQUE SPECIFICATIONS. After installing bearing cover, check output gear bearing preload. See OUTPUT GEAR BEARING PRELOAD SPECIFICATION table.

Differential Assembly – 1) Remove bearing outer race and adjustment shims from transaxle case. Mount differential assembly in converter housing. Install bearing outer race into Selector Gauge (49 B019 0A0B-Selector Tool Set). Mount selector gauge on differential assembly. See Fig. 60. Eliminate gap by turning collars "A" and "B" of selector gauge.

2) Mount 6 spacing collars on differential assembly. See Fig. 61. Mount transaxle case onto selector gauge. Tighten Bolts to 27-38 ft. lbs. (37-52 N.m).

3) Turn assembly over. Install 2 remaining bolts and tighten to 27-38 ft. lbs. (37-52 N.m). See Fig. 62. Using bars on collars "A" and "B" of selector, turn selector in a direction which widens the gap between "A" and "B" of selector. Turn selector (to widen gap) until it will no longer turn. This will seat bearing race. Turn selector in opposite direction (reducing gap) until preload is eliminated.

4) Mount preload adapter into differential until in contacts pinion shaft. Measure preload with torque wrench or pull scale. See Fig. 63. Widen gap on selector gauge to obtain specified reading. See DIFFERENTIAL BEARING PRELOAD SPECIFICATION table.

5) Measure clearance between "A" and "B" of selector gauge when specified preload is obtained. Measure clearance around entire circumference and select shims equal to maximum clearance measured. Add .012" (.30 mm) to measured clearance. Maximum of 3 shims may be used. For available shims, see DIFFERENTIAL BEARING SHIM chart.

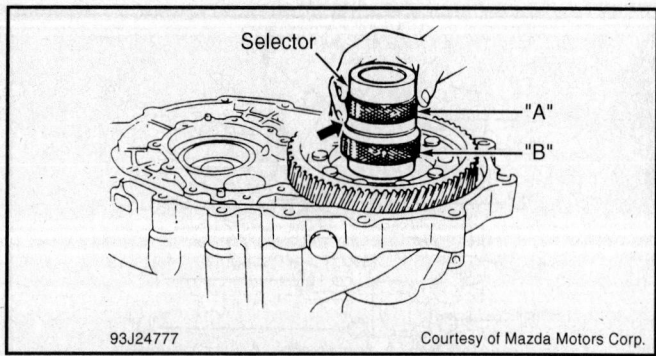

93J24777   Courtesy of Mazda Motors Corp.

Fig. 60: Installing Selector Gauge On Differential

93B24779   Courtesy of Mazda Motors Corp.

Fig. 61: Positioning Collars On Differential

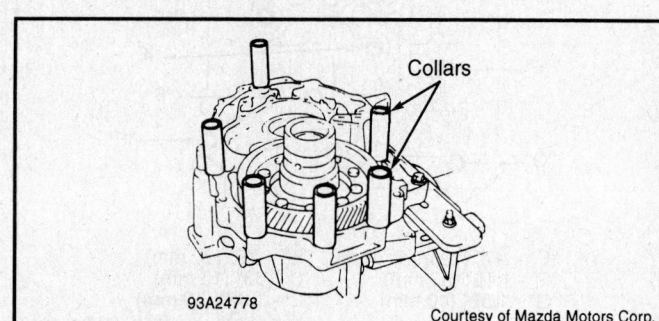

93A24778   Courtesy of Mazda Motors Corp.

Fig. 62: Installing Collar Bolts

DIFFERENTIAL BEARING PRELOAD SPECIFICATION

Measuring Tool	Specification
Torque Wrench	4.4 INCH lbs. (.5 N.m)
Pull Scale	1.1 lbs. (5.0 N)

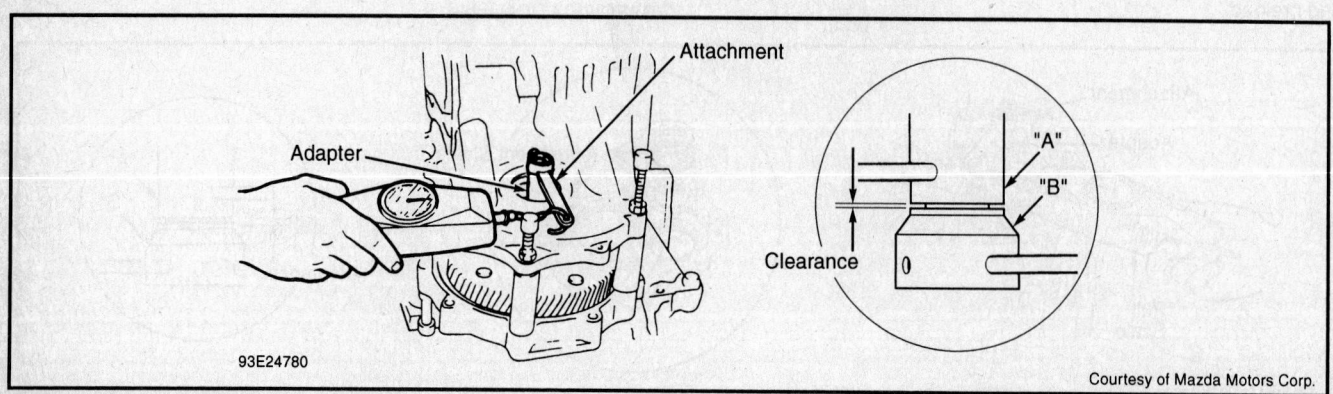

93E24780   Courtesy of Mazda Motors Corp.

Fig. 63: Measuring Differential Side Bearing Preload

DIFFERENTIAL BEARING SHIM

Application	Thickness of Shim
FA4A-EL	[1] .020-.057" (.50-1.45 mm)
GF4A-EL	[2] .004-.047" (.10-1.20 mm)

[1] – In increments of .001" (.02 mm).
[2] – In increments of .002" (.05 mm).

6) Remove transaxle case and selector. Install the required amount of shims and press bearing race into bearing housing. Install bearing housing. Check differential bearing preload. Using torque wrench, preload should be 26-35 INCH lbs. (2.9-3.9 N.m). Using pull scale, preload should be 6.6-8.8 lbs. (29-39 N). If preload is not within specification, repeat measuring and adjusting procedure (as necessary).

7) Remove transaxle case and bearing housing. Install output gear with idler gear. Tap idler gear in position with a plastic hammer. Install bearing housing. Align groove on idler shaft with matching mark on bearing housing and install roll pin. Install differential assembly. On GF4A-EL models, install 2-3 accumulator piston assembly.

FINAL ASSEMBLY

NOTE: Ensure all bearing preloads are set and appropriate shims are installed. See ADJUSTMENTS.

NOTE: For location of thrust bearings and races, see Fig. 64.

1) Install parking pawl. Assemble parking assist lever and actuator support, manual shaft and manual plate. See Fig. 14. Install detent ball, spring washer and plug. Manually check that parking pawl operates.

2) Install output shell to output gear. Ensure thrust bearing is installed on output shell. Apply a thin coat of sealant to contact surfaces of converter housing and transmission case. Install oil passage "O" rings in converter housing. Install transaxle case to converter housing. Install bolts and tighten to specifications. See TORQUE SPECIFICATIONS.

3) Install holding support to hold turbine shaft. Place turbine shaft through 3-4 clutch assembly. Install thrust bearings on both sides of 3-4 clutch assembly and install 3-4 clutch assembly with turbine shaft into transaxle case. Install internal gear to 3-4 clutch drum and install snap ring. See Fig. 12 or 13.

4) Install bearing race in carrier hub and hold turbine shaft to prevent it from turning while installing carrier hub assembly with a rotating motion into 3-4 clutch drum.

5) Install low-reverse brake drive and driven plates, retaining plate and snap ring. Check clearance with a feeler gauge between retaining plate and snap ring. See LOW & REVERSE BRAKE under COMPONENT DISASSEMBLY & REASSEMBLY. Check low-reverse brake operation by applying air pressure to low-reverse oil passage. See Fig. 20 or 21.

6) Hold one-way clutch horizontally while installing. Rotate carrier hub assembly counterclockwise and install snap ring. Install servo spring, servo assembly and snap ring. On GF4A-EL, install piston stem and hand tighten nut. On all models, install anchor strut with groove upward. Install 2-4 brake band in transaxle case, interlocking brake band into anchor strut.

7) Install bearing race on carrier hub and thrust bearing on small sun gear and one-way clutch. Install small sun gear and one-way clutch with rotating motion.

8) Install forward, coasting and reverse clutch assembly. Ensure thrust bearings are on both sides of clutch assembly. Measure the height of reverse, coasting and forward drum above transaxle case. See Fig. 65. On FA4A-EL, height should be .035" (.90 mm) or .028-.075" (.7-1.9 mm) on GF4A-EL. Install snap ring on turbine shaft bottom groove.

9) Remove bearing race and gasket from oil pump (if installed). Select a .087" (2.20 mm) bearing race and place on oil pump. Install oil pump on transaxle case. Measure with a feeler gauge between oil pump and transaxle case. See Fig. 66. Use clearance measured to select bearing race. See OIL PUMP BEARING RACE SELECTION table.

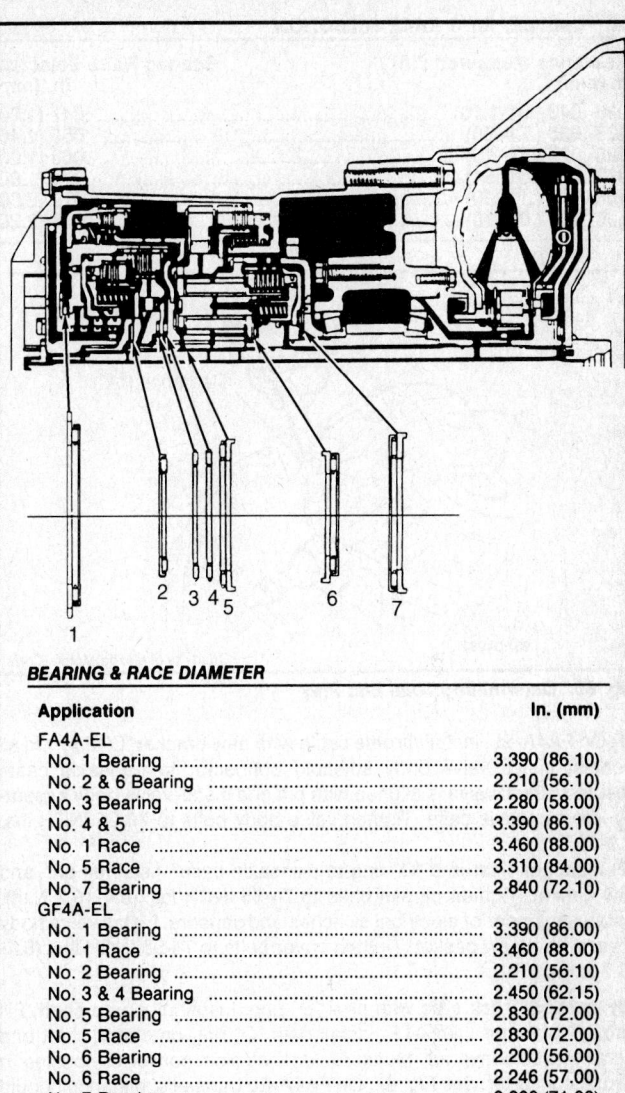

2 3 4 5 6 7
1

95H20195 — Courtesy of Mazda Motors Corp.

Fig. 64: Locating Thrust Bearings & Races

BEARING & RACE DIAMETER

Application	In. (mm)
FA4A-EL	
No. 1 Bearing	3.390 (86.10)
No. 2 & 6 Bearing	2.210 (56.10)
No. 3 Bearing	2.280 (58.00)
No. 4 & 5	3.390 (86.00)
No. 1 Race	3.460 (88.00)
No. 5 Race	3.310 (84.00)
No. 7 Bearing	2.840 (72.10)
GF4A-EL	
No. 1 Bearing	3.390 (86.00)
No. 1 Race	3.460 (88.00)
No. 2 Bearing	2.210 (56.10)
No. 3 & 4 Bearing	2.450 (62.15)
No. 5 Bearing	2.830 (72.00)
No. 5 Race	2.830 (72.00)
No. 6 Bearing	2.200 (56.00)
No. 6 Race	2.246 (57.00)
No. 7 Bearing	2.800 (71.00)
No. 7 Race	2.830 (72.00)

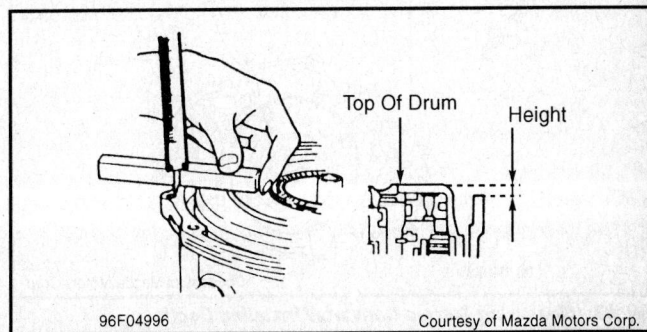

Top Of Drum   Height

96F04996 — Courtesy of Mazda Motors Corp.

Fig. 65: Checking Reverse, Coasting & Forward Drum Installation

10) Remove oil pump. Install selected bearing race and new gasket onto oil pump. Install oil pump onto reverse, coasting and forward drum. Install oil pipe. Tighten oil pump bolts to 14-19 ft. lbs. (19-26 N.m) in crisscross pattern. On GF4A-EL, install oil pipe. Tighten 2-4 brake band servo stem adjusting nut to 105-130 INCH lbs. (11.8-14.7 N.m), then loosen piston 1.5 turns. Tighten lock nut to 19-28 ft. lbs. (25-39 N.m).

OIL PUMP BEARING RACE SELECTION

Clearance Measured ("A") In. (mm)	Bearing Race Selection In. (mm)
.036-.043 (.91-1.10)	.047 (1.20)
.028-.035 (.71-.90)	.055 (1.40)
.020-.027 (.51-.70)	.063 (1.60)
.012-.020 (.31-.51)	.071 (1.80)
.004-.012 (.11-.30)	.079 (2.00)
.000-.004 (.00-.10)	.087 (2.20)

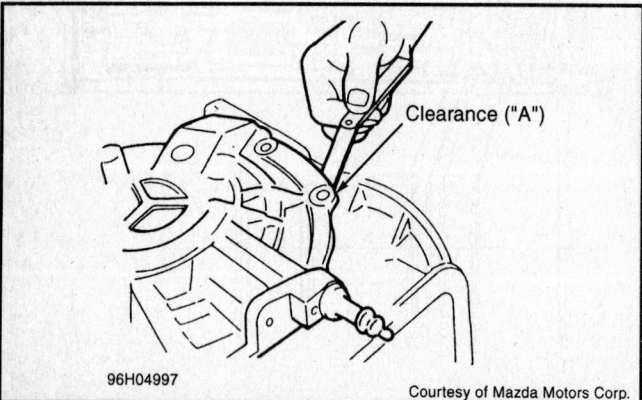

Clearance ("A")

96H04997   Courtesy of Mazda Motors Corp.

Fig. 66: Determining Total End Play

11) On FA4A-EL, install throttle cable with new bracket "O" ring. On all models, install valve body solenoid connector to transaxle case. Ensure manual valve is aligned with pin and install valve body assembly into transaxle case. Tighten valve body bolts to 70-95 INCH lbs. (7.9-10.7 N.m).

12) Install oil filter and "O" ring to transaxle case. Install oil pan and new gasket. Tighten oil pan bolts to 74-95 INCH lbs. (8.4-10.7 N.m). Install remainder of electrical switches and sensors. Install valve body cover with a new gasket. Tighten cover bolts to 74-95 INCH lbs. (8.4-10.7 N.m).

13) Install dipstick tube with new "O" ring. Install oil pump shaft. Fill torque converter with ATF. Install new "O" ring on stator shaft and install torque converter. Measure distance from converter housing to torque converter. *See Fig. 67.* On FA4A-EL transaxle, distance should be .54" (13.6 mm) and .61" (15.4 mm) on GF4A-EL transaxle.

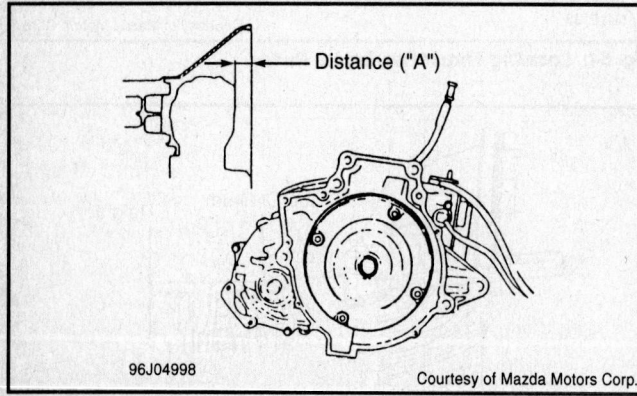

Distance ("A")

96J04998   Courtesy of Mazda Motors Corp.

Fig. 67: Measuring Torque Converter Installed Depth

TORQUE SPECIFICATIONS

TORQUE SPECIFICATIONS

Application	Ft. Lbs. (N.m)
Bearing Cover Bolts	
FA4A-EL	14-18 (19-25)
GF4A-EL	21-25 (28-34)
Converter Housing-To-Transaxle Case	27-38 (37-51)
Drive Plate Bolts	27-40 (37-54)
Idler Gear Nut	94-130 (128-177)

TORQUE SPECIFICATIONS (Cont.)

Application	Ft. Lbs. (N.m)
Manual Shaft (Large Nut)	31-40 (42-54)
Oil Pump-To-Transaxle Case Bolts	14-19 (19-26)
Oil Pump Spool Valve Plug	24-34 (32-47)
Output Gear Bearing Housing Bolt	21-25 (28-34)
2-4 Brake Band Lock Nut	18-29 (25-39)

Application	INCH Lbs. (N.m)
Detent Ball Plug	105-156 (12-18)
Dipstick Tube Bolt	61-86 (7-10)
Lever Holder Bolt	70-95 (8-11)
Manual Shaft (Small Nut)	70-95 (8-11)
N-R Accumulator Plate Bolts	58-69 (6-8)
Oil Filter Bolts	70-95 (8-11)
Oil Filter Pan Bolts	70-95 (8-11)
Oil Pump Cover-To-Pump Body Bolts	70-95 (8-11)
Solenoid Valves-To-Control Valve Body	58-69 (6-8)
Stopper Bolt	53-80 (6-9)
Transaxle Fluid Temperature Switch	70-95 (8-11)
Valve Body Bolts	53-69 (6-8)
Valve Body Pan Bolts	70-95 (8-11)
Valve Body-To-Case Bolts	97-130 (11-15)
1-2 Accumulator Plate Bolts	58-69 (6-8)
2-3 Accumulator Bolts	70-95 (8-11)
2-4 Brake Band Adjustment Bolt (GF4A-EL)	105-130 (12-15)

TRANSAXLE SPECIFICATIONS

TRANSAXLE SPECIFICATIONS (FA4A-EL)

Application	In. (mm)
Bushing Inside Diameter (Maximum)	
Torque Converter	2.090 (53.08)
Brake Snap Ring-To-Retaining Plate Clearance	
Low & Reverse Brake	.083-.094 (2.10-2.40)
Clutch Snap Ring-To-Retaining Plate Clearance	
Coasting Clutch	.039-.047 (1.00-1.20)
Forward Clutch	.039-.047 (1.00-1.20)
Reverse Clutch	.083-.094 (2.10-2.40)
3-4 Clutch	.051-.063 (1.30-1.60)
Clutch Drive Plate Minimum Thickness	
All Clutches	.055 (1.40)
Planetary Pinion Gear Clearance	.008-.028 (.20-.70)
Oil Pump	
Rotor End Clearance	.0008-.0016 (.020-.040)
Rotor Side Clearance	.0016-.005 (.040-.125)
Seal Ring Inner Diameter	1.553 (39.45)

Bearing Preload

Differential	
Torque Wrench	26-35 INCH Lbs. (2.9-3.9 N.m)
Pull Scale	6.6-8.8 Lbs. (29-39 N)
Output Gear	
Torque Wrench	8-15 INCH Lbs. (.9-1.7 N.m)
Pull Scale	2.0-3.9 Lbs. (9-17 N)

TRANSAXLE SPECIFICATIONS (GF4A-EL)

Application	In. (mm)
Bushing Inside Diameter (Maximum)	
Torque Converter	2.0884 (53.045)
Brake Snap Ring-To-Retaining Plate Clearance	
Low & Reverse Brake	.059-.071 (1.50-1.80)
Clutch Snap Ring-To-Retaining Plate Clearance	
Coasting Clutch	.039-.047 (1.00-1.20)
Forward Clutch	.039-.047 (1.00-1.20)
Reverse Clutch	.059-.071 (1.50-1.80)
3-4 Clutch	.051-.059 (1.30-1.50)
Clutch Drive Plate Minimum Thickness	
All Clutches	.055 (1.40)
Planetary Pinion Gear Clearance	.008-.028 (.20-.70)
Oil Pump	
Rotor End Clearance	.0008-.0016 (.020-.040)
Rotor Side Clearance	.0016-.005 (.040-.125)
Seal Ring Inner Diameter	2.026 (51.45)

Bearing Preload

Differential	
Torque Wrench	26-35 INCH Lbs. (2.9-3.9 N.m)
Pull Scale	6.6-8.8 Lbs. (29-39 N)
Output Gear	
Torque Wrench	10-17 INCH Lbs. (1.1-1.9 N.m)
Pull Scale	2.5-4.4 Lbs. (11-19 N)

AUTOMATIC TRANSMISSIONS
Mazda FA4A-EL & GF4A-EL Electronic Controls

Millenia, MX3, MX6, Protege, 626

APPLICATION

APPLICATION

Vehicle	Transmission Model
1995	
MX3	FA4A-EL
1995-96	
Millenia, MX6 & 626	GF4A-EL
Protege	FA4A-EL

CAUTION: Vehicle is equipped with Supplemental Restraint System (SRS). When servicing vehicle, use care to avoid accidental air bag deployment. SRS-related components are located in steering column, center console and instrument panel. DO NOT use electrical test equipment on these circuits. If necessary, deactivate SRS before servicing components. See AIR BAG SERVICING article in APPLICATIONS & IDENTIFICATIONS section.

DESCRIPTION

The FA4A-EL is a 4-speed electronically controlled automatic transaxle. Four solenoids that control shift changes are located in valve body. Solenoids are controlled by the Transmission Control Module (TCM) on MX3 or the Powertrain Control Module (PCM) for Protege.

The GF4A-EL is a 4-speed electronically controlled automatic transaxle. Seven solenoids that control shift changes and shift feel are located in valve body. Solenoids are controlled by the Transmission Control Module (TCM) for 1995 Millenia, MX6 and 626 or the Powertrain Control Module (PCM) for 1996 Millenia, MX6 and 626.

TCM or PCM for FA4A-EL models receives information from various input devices and uses this information to control shift solenoids for transaxle shifting and Torque Converter Clutch (TCC) solenoid for torque converter clutch lock-up. *See Fig. 1.*

NOTE: TCC solenoid is also known as lock-up solenoid or TCC lock-up solenoid.

TCM or PCM for GF4A-EL models receives information from various input devices. *See Fig. 2.* TCM or PCM uses this information to control following solenoids:

- Shift solenoids for transaxle shifting.
- Torque Converter Clutch (TCC) control solenoid for torque converter clutch lock-up.
- Torque Converter Clutch (TCC) solenoid for TCC apply rate (slip lock-up).
- 3-2 timing solenoid to reduce downshift shock.
- Pressure control solenoid to control line pressure.

On TCM equipped models (except 1995 MX6/626 models), a HOLD switch is mounted on the shift lever. HOLD function may be activated in "D", "S" or "L" gears by pressing HOLD button. In "L" and "S" positions, vehicle is held in selected gear and no upshift or downshift takes place. This function is used for driving up steep inclines or for engine braking assistance when descending steep grades. If activated in "D" position a 1-2 and 2-3 upshift is permitted when starting from a stop but after the 2-3 upshift the vehicle is locked in "D" until it comes to a complete stop. The 1-2 and 2-3 upshift pattern is changed to a "short shift" specification. This function is used for starting off or driving on slippery surfaces. Pushing HOLD button again deactivates system.

On PCM equipped vehicles (including 1995 MX6/626 models), an Overdrive OFF (O/D OFF) switch is mounted on the shift lever. When O/D OFF switch is released to ON position, transaxle will shift into 4th gear when shift lever is in "D" position. O/D OFF light on combination meter should not be illuminated. When O/D OFF switch is depressed to OFF position, transaxle will not shift into 4th gear. O/D OFF light will be illuminated.

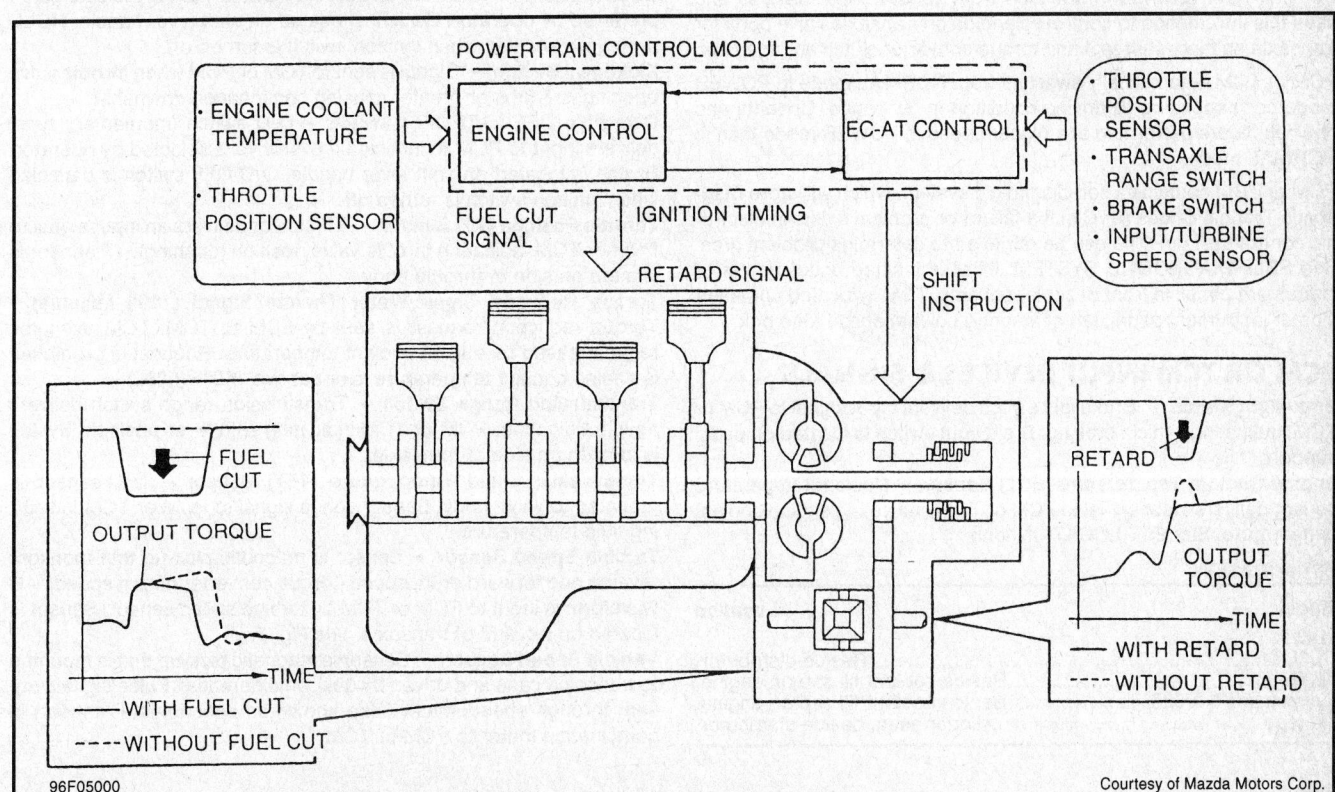

Courtesy of Mazda Motors Corp.

Fig. 1: Transaxle Control System Operational Overview (Protege Shown, MX3 Similar)

3-864

AUTOMATIC TRANSMISSIONS
Mazda FA4A-EL & GF4A-EL Electronic Controls (Cont.)

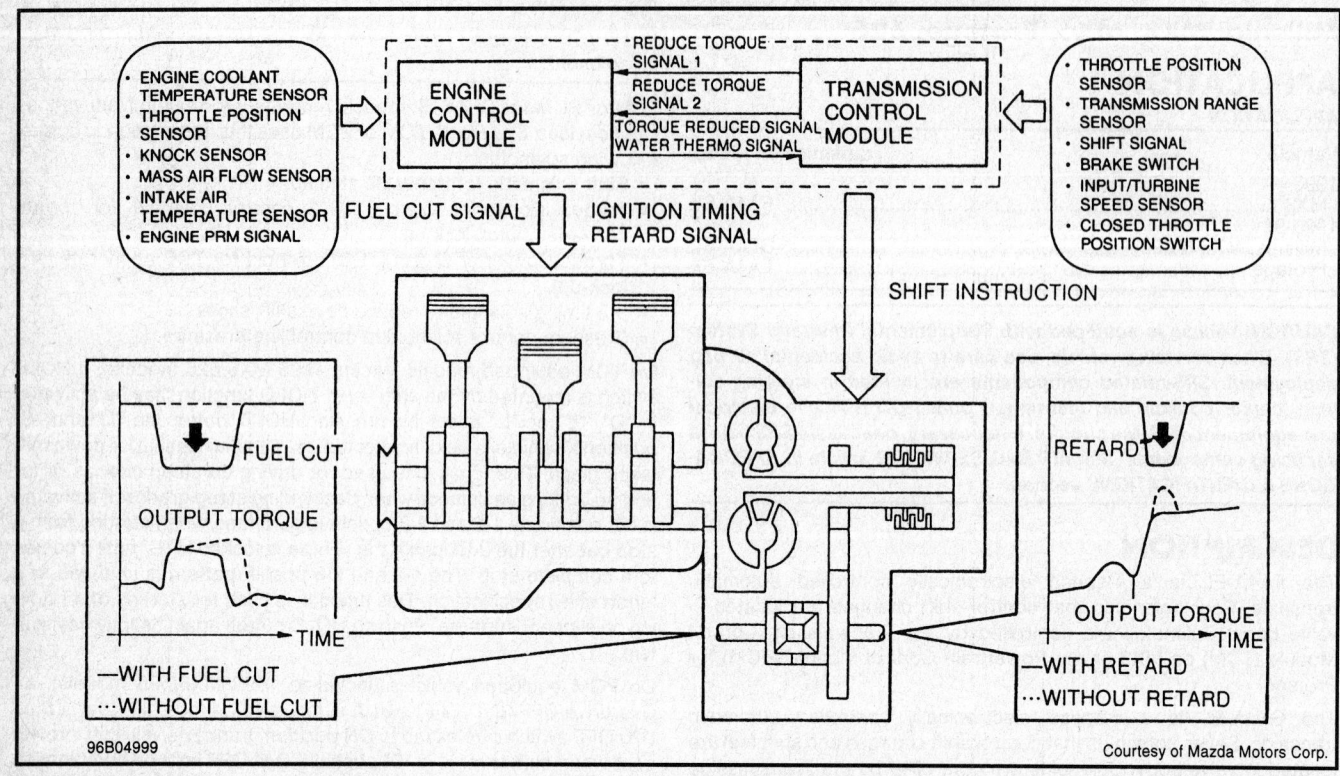

Fig. 2: Transaxle Control System Operational Overview (Millenia Shown, MX6 & 626 Similar)

OPERATION

PCM OR TCM

PCM or TCM receives information from various input devices and uses this information to control solenoids on transaxle valve body for transaxle shifting, shift feel and torque converter clutch engagement.

PCM or TCM automatically switches from NORMAL mode to POWER mode corresponding to driving condition in "D" range. Upshifts and downshifts are performed at a higher speed in POWER mode than in NORMAL mode.

PCM or TCM contains a self-diagnostic system, which will store Diagnostic Trouble Codes (DTC's) if a failure or problem exists in electronic control system. DTC can be retrieved to determine problem area. See SELF-DIAGNOSTIC SYSTEM. PCM is located under center of instrument panel, in front of center console. TCM is located under left side of instrument panel, left of steering column above fuse box.

PCM OR TCM INPUT DEVICES & SIGNALS

Brakelight Switch – Brakelight switch delivers input signal to PCM or TCM, indicating vehicle braking. Brakelight switch is located on pedal support.

Engine Coolant Temperature (ECT) Sensor – Coolant temperature sensor delivers input signal to PCM or TCM, indicating engine coolant temperature. See ECT LOCATION table.

ECT LOCATION

Model	Location
MX3	
1.6L	Beside distributor.
2.5L	Beside coolant fill cap on engine.
Millenia, MX6 & 626	Beside coolant fill cap on engine.
Protege	Back of cylinder head, beside distributor.

4th Gear Inhibit Signal – Signal is input to TCM or PCM when cruise control is on. Signal detects when difference between target speed and actual speed exceeds specification.

HOLD Switch – HOLD switch delivers input to TCM to indicate gears preferred by operator. Switch is located on shift lever handle. HOLD switch is canceled when ignition switch is turned off.

Kickdown Switch – Signal is sent to TCM or PCM when throttle valve opening is 7/8ths or greater causing commanded downshift.

Overdrive OFF (O/D OFF) Switch – O/D switch (momentary type) delivers input to PCM to inmicate if overdrive is selected by operator. Switch is located on shift lever handle. O/D OFF switch is canceled when ignition switch is turned off.

Throttle Position (TP) Sensor – TP sensor delivers an input signal to PCM or TCM indicating throttle valve position (opening). TP sensor is located on side of throttle body.

Torque Reduced Signal/Water Thermo Signal (1995 Millenia) – Torque reduction request is sent by ECM to TCM. TCM executes request based on engine coolant temperature. Request is prohibited is engine coolant temperature is not above 140°F (60°C).

Transmission Range Switch – Transmission range switch delivers an input signal to PCM or TCM indicating shift lever position. Switch is located on side of transaxle.

Transmission Fluid Temperature (TFT) Sensor – TFT sensor is mounted to valve body. Sensor sends signal to PCM or TCM indicating fluid temperature.

Turbine Speed Sensor – Sensor is magnetic pick-up that monitors reverse and forward drum speed (torque converter output speed). AC waveform is input to PCM or TCM by turbine speed sensor. Sensor is located on top end of transaxle. *See Fig. 3.*

Vehicle Speed Sensor – Sensor is magnetic pick-up that is mounted to transaxle case and driven by gear on differential. Pulse signals are sent through speedometer (also known as speedometer sensor) in combination meter to PCM or TCM.

AUTOMATIC TRANSMISSIONS
Mazda FA4A-EL & GF4A-EL Electronic Controls (Cont.)

3-865

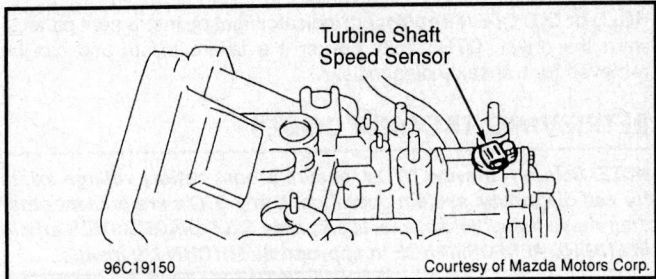

Fig. 3: Locating Turbine Speed Sensor (FA4A-EL Shown, GF4A-EL Similar)

PCM OR TCM OUTPUT DEVICES

NOTE: Shift solenoid operation table for GF4A-EL (O/D OFF) is not available from manufacturer.

Shift Solenoids "A", "B" & "C" – The PCM or TCM controls transaxle shifting by delivering an output signal to operate proper solenoid. See appropriate SOLENOID OPERATION table or *Fig. 4*. Solenoids are located on transaxle valve body. *See Fig. 5 or 6*.

FA4A-EL SOLENOID OPERATION (HOLD SYSTEM)

Shift Lever Position	Solenoid "A"	Solenoid "B"	Solenoid "C"
"D" (Drive)			
1st Gear	Off	On	On
2nd Gear	On	On	On
3rd Gear	On	Off	Off
4th Gear	On	Off	On
"2" (Second)			
1st Gear	Off	On	On
2nd Gear	On	On	On
"L" (Low)			
1st Gear	Off	On	On
"R" (Reverse)	On	Off	Off
"N" Or "P"	Off	OfF	On

FA4A-EL SOLENOID OPERATION (O/D OFF SYSTEM)

Shift Lever Position	Solenoid "A"	Solenoid "B"	Solenoid "C"
"D" (Drive)			
1st Gear	Off	On	On
2nd Gear	On	On	On
3rd Gear	On	Off	Off
4th Gear	On	Off	On
"2" (Second)			
2nd Gear	On	On	Off
"L" (Low)			
1st Gear	Off	On	Off
"R" (Reverse)	On	Off	Off
"N" Or "P"	Off	OfF	On

HOLD Indicator Light – Receives signal from TCM to indicate switch position.

Inhibitor Signal (1995 Millenia) – When shift selector lever is moved from Park or Neutral to another gear, signal is sent from TCM to ECM to regulate fuel injection volume for shift shock prevention.

O/D OFF Indicator Light – Receives signal from PCM to indicate switch position.

Pressure Control Solenoid – PCM or TCM controls pressure control solenoid to regulate modifier pressure based on signals received from TP sensor. Modifier pressure as a signal pressure controls pressure regulator valves to adjust hydraulic pressure discharged from oil pump to the optimum line pressure corresponding to driving conditions.

Range	Mode	Gear position		Engine braking effect	Shift solenoid A	Shift solenoid B	Shift solenoid C
P	—	—		—			○
R	—	Reve-rse	Below approx. 4 km/h {2.5 MPH}	Yes		○	○
			Above approx. 6 km/h {3 MPH}	Yes			
			Above approx. 30 km/h {19 MPH}	No	○		
N	—		Below approx. 4 km/h {2.5 MPH}	—			○
			Above approx. 6 km/h {3 MPH}	—	○		
D	★ POWER NORMAL (Except HOLD)		1st	No		○	○
			2nd	No	○	○	
			3GR	Yes	○		
			4GR	Yes	○		○
	HOLD	2nd	Below approx. 13 km/h {8.1 MPH}	Yes	○	○	
			Above approx. 17 km/h {10.5 MPH}	No	○	○	
			3GR	Yes	○		
			✵ 4GR	Yes	○		
S	Except HOLD		1st	No		○	○
			2nd	No	○	○	
			3GR	Yes	○		
			✵ 4GR	Yes	○		
	HOLD		2nd	Yes	○	○	
			✵ 3GR	Yes	○		
			✵ 4GR	Yes			○
L	Except HOLD		1st	No		○	○
			2nd	Yes	○	○	
	HOLD		1st	Yes		○	
			✵ 2nd	Yes	○	○	

○ : Operating
✵ : Engine overspeed protection.
★ : The transmission control module automatically switches between POWER and NORMAL modes corresponding to the speed at which the accelerator pedal is depressed.

Fig. 4: GF4A-EL Solenoid Operation (HOLD SYSTEM) Table

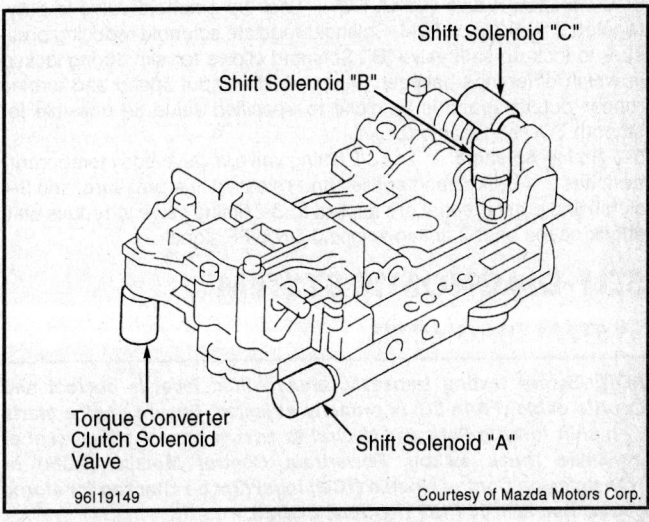

Fig. 5: Locating Transaxle Solenoids (FA4A-EL)

3-866

AUTOMATIC TRANSMISSIONS
Mazda FA4A-EL & GF4A-EL Electronic Controls (Cont.)

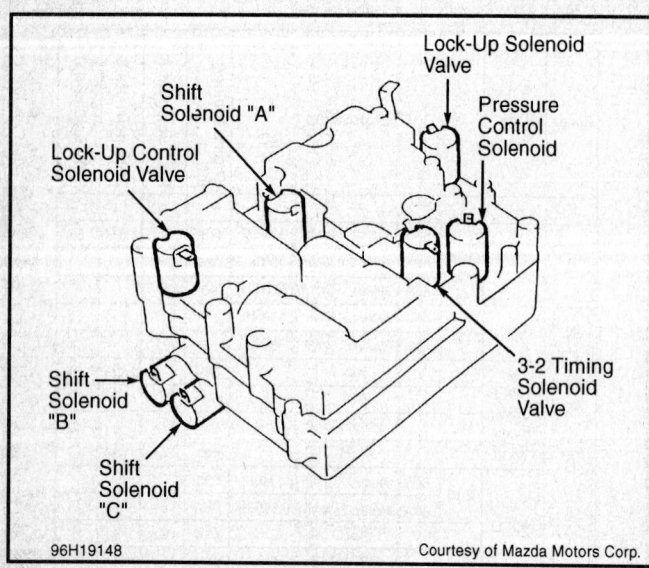

Fig. 6: *Locating Transaxle Solenoids (GF4A-EL)*

PCM or TCM detects engine load using TP sensor and adjusts line pressure to level required by clutch(s) in use. To reduce shift shock during shifting, line pressure characteristics are set to match engine driving force during shifting. Line pressure is also adjusted for ATF temperature, high engine torque and engine braking.

Reduce Torque Signal No. 1 (GF4A-EL With TCM) – TCM sends signal to ECM during upshifting when throttle valve opening angle is 3/8ths or greater. ECM reduces torque to decrease shift shock.

Reduce Torque Signal No. 2 (GF4A-EL With TCM) – TCM sends signal to ECM during downshifting. ECM reduces torque to decrease shift shock.

TCC Solenoid (FA4A-EL) – The PCM or TCM controls torque converter clutch lock-up by delivering an output signal to TCC solenoid. Solenoid is activated when shift lever is in "D", engine is normal operating temperature and vehicle is at specified speed. TCC solenoid is located on transaxle valve body. *See Fig. 5.*

TCC Control Solenoid Valve (GF4A-EL) – Solenoid valve is ON/OFF type controlled by PCM or TCM. Solenoid regulates line pressure to lock-up shift valve "A".

TCC Solenoid Valve (GF4A-EL) – Lock-up solenoid valve is duty-regulated by PCM or TCM. Solenoid regulate solenoid reducing pressure to lock-up shift valve "B". Solenoid allows for slip during lockup in which difference between pump impeller input speed and turbine runner output speed is as close to specified value as possible for smooth TCC engagement.

3-2 Timing Solenoid – The 3-2 timing valve in valve body temporarily switches 2-4 brake band applied and released line pressure, and 3-4 clutch line pressure that are applied to 3-2 timing valve to reduce shift shock based on 3-2 timing solenoid ON/OFF signal.

SELF-DIAGNOSTIC SYSTEM

SYSTEM DIAGNOSIS

NOTE: Before testing transaxle, ensure fluid level is correct and throttle cable (FA4A-EL) is properly adjusted. Ensure engine starts with shift lever in Park and Neutral to ensure proper adjustment of transaxle range switch. Powertrain Control Module (PCM) or Transmission Control Module (TCM) must first be checked for stored codes. See RETRIEVING TROUBLE CODES.

PCM or TCM (depending on model) monitors transaxle operation and contains a self-diagnostic system which stores a Diagnostic Trouble Code (DTC) if an electronic control system failure or component malfunction exists. If a problem exists in any of the solenoids or speed sensors and DTC is set, PCM or TCM will deliver a signal to blink the

HOLD or O/D OFF (as equipped) indicator light on instrument panel to warn the driver. DTC's may be set if a failure exists and can be retrieved for transaxle diagnosis.

RETRIEVING TROUBLE CODES

NOTE: Before retrieving DTC's, ensure proper battery voltage exists for self-diagnostic system operation. If any DTC's are present other than those listed below, see appropriate SELF-DIAGNOSTICS article in ENGINE PERFORMANCE in appropriate MITCHELL® manual.

Using HOLD or O/D OFF Indicator Light (1995 MX3, MX6 & 626 Models) – **1)** Raise hood and access Data Link Connector (DLC) on left side of engine compartment. *See Fig. 7.*

2) Connect jumper wire between TAT and GND terminals on DLC connector. *See Fig. 7.* Turn ignition switch to ON position. If DTC exists, HOLD or O/D OFF indicator light will flash every 4 seconds. Long (1.2 second duration) flash indicates first digit and short (.4 second duration) flash indicates second digit.

3) If more than one DTC exists, next code will be displayed after pause of 4 seconds. Lowest number code will be displayed first. DTC's will be repeated. Once DTC is obtained, determine probable cause and symptom. See DIAGNOSTIC TROUBLE CODE IDENTIFICATION (1995 MX3, MX6 & 626) table. For trouble shooting of DTC's, see DIAGNOSTIC TESTING. Turn ignition off and remove jumper wire.

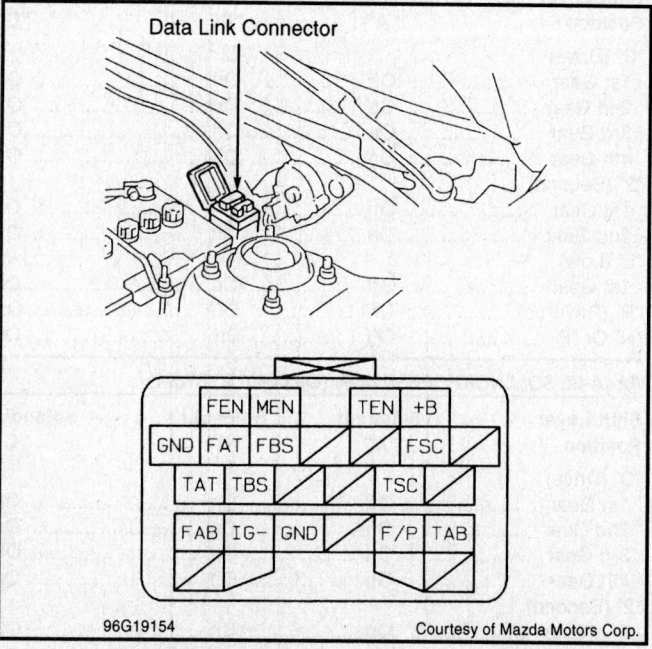

Fig. 7: *Locating DLC Connector & Identifying Terminals (MX3 Shown, 626 Similar)*

Using Scan Tool (Except 1995 MX3, MX6 & 626 Models) – Ensure ignition is in OFF position. Connect scan tool to Data Link Connector (DLC) located under left side of instrument panel, near center console. *See Fig. 8.* Turn ignition switch to ON position. Check for stored DTC's. See DIAGNOSTIC TROUBLE CODE IDENTIFICATION (1995-96 MILLENIA, PROTEGE & 1996 MX6, 626) table. For trouble shooting of codes, see DIAGNOSTIC TESTING.

NOTE: Once repairs have been performed, DTC's must be cleared from PCM or TCM memory and vehicle test driven. See CLEARING TROUBLE CODES. Accelerate vehicle to 31 MPH for 1 minute. Fully depress accelerator pedal to force downshift. Release accelerator pedal and slow vehicle to stop. Perform retrieval procedure to ensure DTC's have been cleared and no new DTC's exist.

AUTOMATIC TRANSMISSIONS
Mazda FA4A-EL & GF4A-EL Electronic Controls (Cont.)

3-867

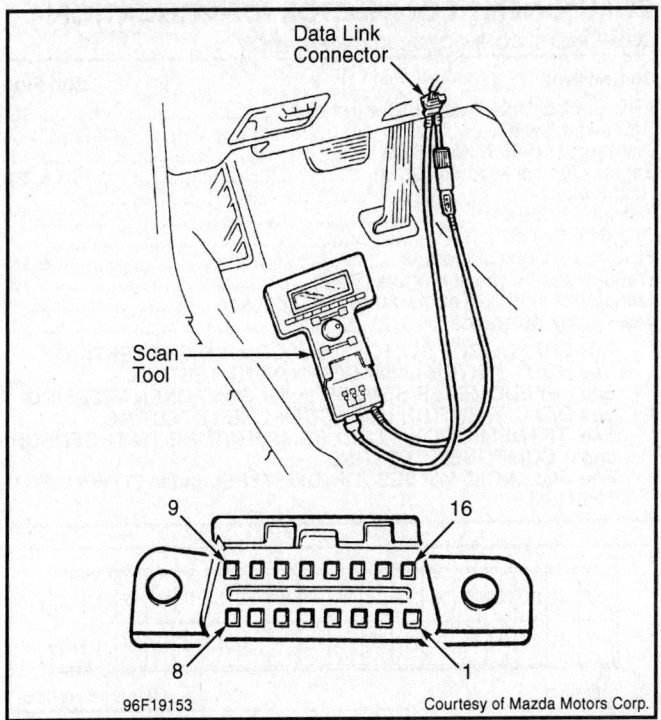

Fig. 8: Connecting Scan Tool

DIAGNOSTIC TROUBLE CODE IDENTIFICATION
(1995 MX3, MX6 & 626)

DTC No.	[1] Probable Cause
1	[2] Engine Speed Input Signal
6	Vehicle Speed Sensor
12	Throttle Position Sensor
14	[2] Baro Pressure Sensor
55	Turbine Speed Sensor
56	[3] TFT Sensor
57	Reduce Torque Signal No. 1
58	Reduce Torque Signal No. 2
59	[2] Torque Reduced/Coolant Temp Signal No. 2
60	Shift Solenoid "A"
61	Shift Solenoid "B"
62	Shift Solenoid "C"
63	TCC Control Solenoid Valve
64	[2] 3-2 Timing Solenoid Valve
65	[2] TCC Solenoid Valve
66	[2] Pressure Control Solenoid

[1] – Check listed component for probable cause. Also check wiring and connection of specified component.
[2] – MX6 & 626 models only.
[3] – Transaxle Fluid Temperature.

DIAGNOSTIC TROUBLE CODE IDENTIFICATION
(1995-96 MILLENIA, PROTEGE & 1996 MX6, 626)

DTC No.	[1] Probable Cause
P0705	Transaxle Range Switch
P0710	[2] TFT Sensor
P0715	Turbine Speed Sensor
P0725	Engine Speed Input Circuit Malfunction
P0730	[3] Incorrect Gear Ratio
P0731	Incorrect 1st Gear Ratio
P0732	Incorrect 2nd Gear Ratio
P0733	Incorrect 3rd Gear Ratio
P0734	Incorrect 4th Gear Ratio
P0740	TCC System Malfunction
P0745	Pressure Control Solenoid
P0750	Shift Solenoid "A"

[1] – Check listed component for probable cause. Also check wiring and connection of specified component.
[2] – Transaxle Fluid Temperature.
[3] – 1995 Millenia model only.

DIAGNOSTIC TROUBLE CODE IDENTIFICATION (Cont.)
(1995-96 MILLENIA, PROTEGE & 1996 MX6, 626)

DTC No.	[1] Probable Cause
P0755	Shift Solenoid "B"
P0760	Shift Solenoid "C"
P1720	[3] Speedometer Sensor
P1743	TCC Control Solenoid Valve
P1744	TCC Solenoid Valve
P1765	3-2 Timing Solenoid Valve
P1775	[3] Reduce Torque Signal No. 1
P1776	[3] Reduce Torque Signal No. 2
P1777	[3] Torque Reduced/Coolant Temp Signal
P1790	[3] Throttle Position Sensor
P1792	[3] Closed Throttle Position Switch
P1795	[3] EGR Boost Sensor

[1] – Check listed component for probable cause. Also check wiring and connection of specified component.
[2] – Transaxle Fluid Temperature.
[3] – 1995 Millenia model only.

CLEARING TROUBLE CODES

To clear DTC's stored in PCM or TCM, disconnect negative battery cable for at least 20 seconds.

COMPONENT LOCATION

COMPONENT LOCATION

Description	Location
Coolant Temperature Sensor	See PCM OR TCM INPUT DEVICES & SIGNALS.
ABS Control Unit/Traction Control Unit (1995 Millenia)	See Fig. 9
Engine Control Module	Located under center of instrument panel, forward of center console. See Fig. 10.
Powertrain Control Module	See Fig. 10.
Pressure Control Solenoid	See Fig. 6.
Solenoids "A", "B" & "C"	See Fig. 5 or 6.
TCC Solenoid	See Fig. 5 or 6.
TCC Control Solenoid	See Fig. 6.
3-2 Timing Solenoid	See Fig. 6.
Transmission Control Unit MX3	Behind center of instrument panel, forward of center console.
Millenia, MX6 & 626	Behind left side of instrument panel, next to relay block. See Fig. 10.
Turbine Speed Sensor	See Fig. 3.
Vehicle Speed Sensor	Mounted on transaxle, near differential.

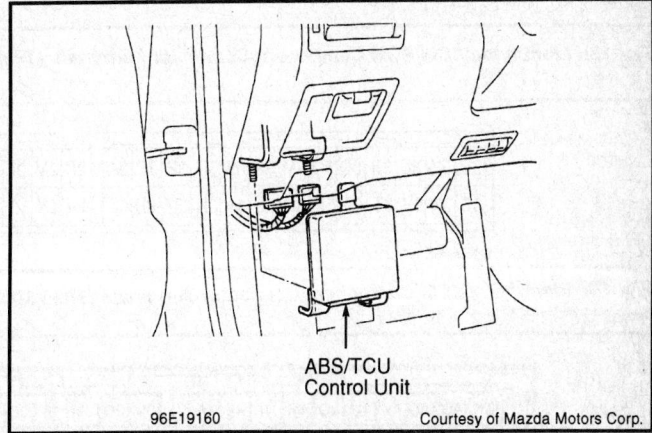

Fig. 9: Locating ABS/TCU Control Unit (1995 Millenia)

3-868

AUTOMATIC TRANSMISSIONS
Mazda FA4A-EL & GF4A-EL Electronic Controls (Cont.)

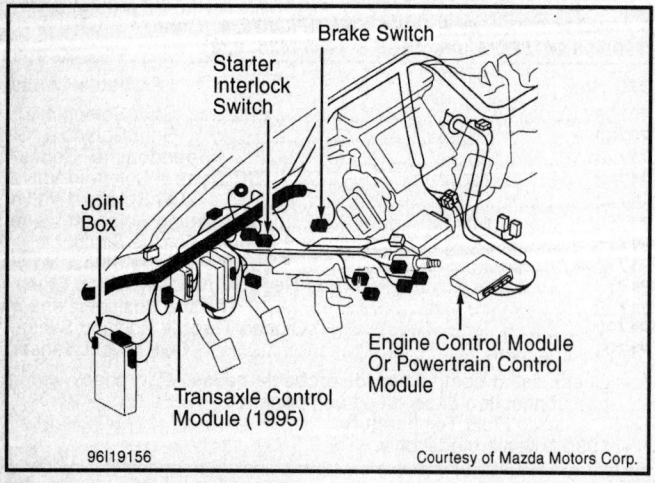

Fig. 10: Locating PCM & TCM

96I19156   Courtesy of Mazda Motors Corp.

COMPONENT CONNECTOR IDENTIFICATION
COMPONENT CONNECTOR IDENTIFICATION

Component	See Fig.
ABS Control Unit/Traction Control Unit	12
Brakelight Switch	1
Distributor (1995 MX6 & 626)	11
Engine Control Module (ECM)	13 & 14
Hold Switch	2
Instrument Cluster	3
O/D OFF Switch	4
Powertrain Control Module	13 & 15
Transmission Control Module (TCM)	16
Transmission Fluid Temperature (TFT) Sensor	5
Valve Body Solenoids	6

1 – See BRAKELIGHT SWITCH under COMPONENT TESTING.
2 – See HOLD SWITCH under COMPONENT TESTING.
3 – See SPEEDOMETER SENSOR under COMPONENT TESTING.
4 – See O/D OFF SWITCH under COMPONENT TESTING.
5 – See TRANSMISSION FLUID TEMPERATURE (TFT) SENSOR under COMPONENT TESTING.
6 – See SOLENOID VALVES (ON/OFF TYPE) under COMPONENT TESTING.

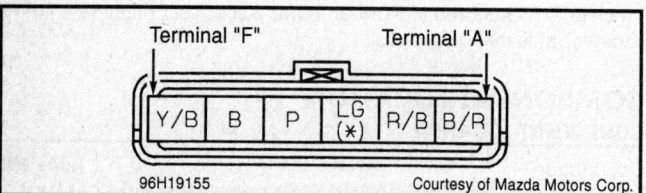

Fig. 11: Identifying Distributor Harness Connector Terminals & Wire Colors (1995 MX6 & 626)

96H19155   Courtesy of Mazda Motors Corp.

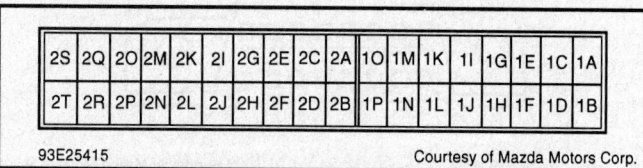

Fig. 16: Identifying TCM Component Connector Terminals (1995 Millenia, MX3, MX6 & 626)

93E25415   Courtesy of Mazda Motors Corp.

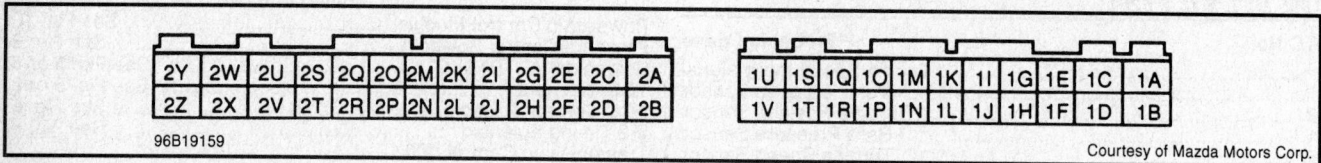

96B19159   Courtesy of Mazda Motors Corp.

Fig. 12: Identifying ABS Control Unit/Traction Control Unit Component Connector Terminals (1995 Millenia)

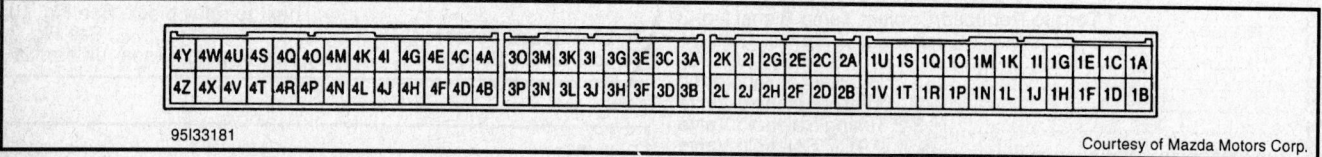

95I33181   Courtesy of Mazda Motors Corp.

Fig. 13: Identifying ECM/PCM Component Connector Terminals (1995 Millenia & 1995-96 Protege)

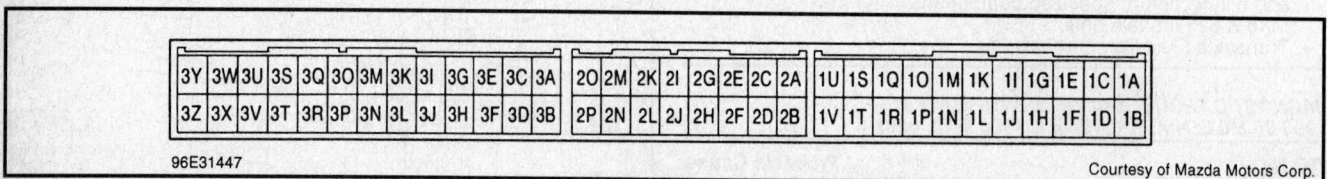

96E31447   Courtesy of Mazda Motors Corp.

Fig. 14: Identifying ECM Component Connector Terminals (1995 MX6 & 626)

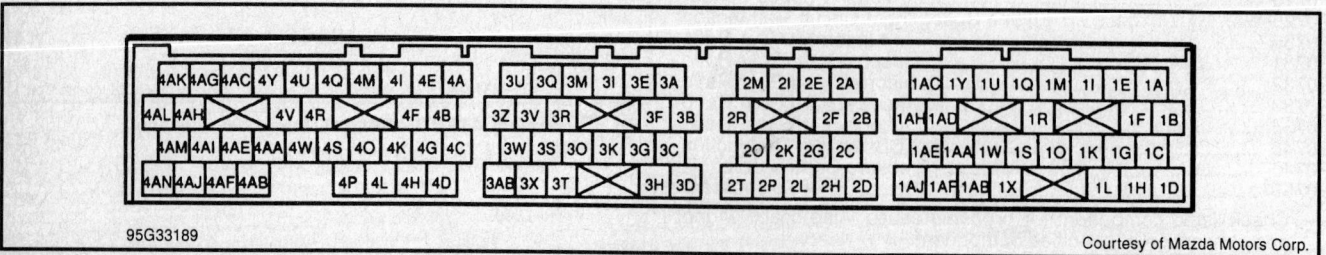

95G33189   Courtesy of Mazda Motors Corp.

Fig. 15: Identifying PCM Component Connector Terminals (1996 Millenia, MX6 & 626)

AUTOMATIC TRANSMISSIONS
Mazda FA4A-EL & GF4A-EL Electronic Controls (Cont.)

3-869

DIAGNOSTIC TESTS

NOTE: For connector terminal identification, see COMPONENT CONNECTOR IDENTIFICATION table. For circuit or wire color identification, see appropriate wiring diagram in WIRING DIAGRAMS.

DTC 1: ENGINE SPEED INPUT SIGNAL

Condition – No input signal from distributor with forward/reverse drum speed greater than 600 RPM. Shift selector in "D", "2" or "L" position. Possible causes are:
- Distributor connector.
- Circuit fault between ECM and TCM.

Diagnosis & Repair Procedure – **1)** Inspect harness connections at distributor and TCM. Repair as needed. Turn ignition on. Using voltmeter, backprobe TCM harness connector. Do not disconnect connector. Measure voltage between ground and terminal No. 1N (Light Green wire). If voltage is 4.5-5.5 volts with engine stopped or 2-3 volts with engine running, go to next step. If voltage is not 4.5-5.5 volts with engine stopped or 2-3 volts with engine running, repair Light Green wire between TCM and ECM for open or short.

2) Stop engine. Ensure ignition is on. Disconnect distributor harness connector. Backprobing TCM harness connector with voltmeter, measure voltage between ground and terminal No. 1N (Light Green wire) on TCM harness connector. If voltage is 4.5-5.5 volts, go to next step. If voltage is not 4.5-5.5 volts, see appropriate SELF-DIAGNOSTICS article in ENGINE PERFORMANCE in appropriate MITCHELL® manual for diagnostic information on circuits between distributor and ECM.

DTC 6: VEHICLE SPEED SENSOR (MX3)

Condition – No input signal from vehicle speed sensor with forward/reverse drum speed greater than 600 RPM. Shift selector in "D", "2" or "L" position. Possible causes are:
- Poor harness connection at vehicle speed sensor.
- Circuit fault between sensor and speedometer.
- Circuit fault between speedometer and TCM.
- Vehicle speed sensor.

Diagnosis & Repair Procedure – **1)** Inspect harness connections at TCM. Repair as needed. Turn ignition on. Backprobing TCM harness connector with voltmeter, measure voltage between ground and terminal No. 1P (Violet/Red wire). If voltage is 3-4 volts with vehicle moving, or 6-8 or zero volts with vehicle stopped, go to step **4)**. If voltage is not 3-4 volts with vehicle moving, or 6-8 or zero volts with vehicle stopped, go to next step.

2) Turn ignition off. Remove instrument cluster. Disconnect TCM harness connectors. Check continuity on Violet/Red wire between terminal No. 2D on instrument cluster harness connector and terminal No. 1P on TCM harness connector. Repair as needed. If continuity exists, go to next step.

3) Inspect vehicle speed sensor and related circuits. See VEHICLE SPEED SENSOR under COMPONENT TESTING. Repair as needed. If sensor and related circuits are okay, go to next step.

4) Disconnect negative battery cable for at least 20 seconds. Depress brake pedal. Reconnect negative battery cable. Road test vehicle. Retrieve DTC's. If DTC 6 is still present, replace TCM. If code is no longer present, problem may be caused by poor connection. Repair as needed.

DTC 6: VEHICLE SPEED SENSOR (MX6 & 626)

Condition – No input signal from vehicle speed sensor with forward/reverse drum speed greater than 600 RPM. Shift selector in "D", "2" or "L" position. Possible causes are:
- Poor harness connection at vehicle speed sensor.
- Circuit fault between sensor and speedometer.
- Circuit fault between speedometer and TCM.
- Vehicle speed sensor.

Diagnosis & Repair Procedure – **1)** Inspect harness connections at TCM. Repair as needed. Turn ignition on. Backprobing TCM harness connector with voltmeter, measure voltage between ground and terminal No. 1P (Green/Red wire). If voltage is 4.5-5.5 volts with vehicle moving or 2-3 volts with vehicle stopped, go to step **4)**. If voltage is not 4.5-5.5 volts with vehicle moving or 2-3 volts with vehicle stopped, go to next step.

2) Turn ignition off. Remove instrument cluster. Disconnect TCM harness connectors. Check continuity on Green/Red wire between terminal No. 1H on instrument cluster harness connector and terminal No. 1P on TCM harness connector. Repair as needed. If continuity exists, go to next step.

3) Inspect vehicle speed sensor and related circuits. See VEHICLE SPEED SENSOR under COMPONENT TESTING. Repair as needed. If sensor and related circuits are okay, go to next step.

4) Disconnect negative battery cable for at least 20 seconds. Depress brake pedal. Reconnect negative battery cable. Road test vehicle. Retrieve DTC's. If DTC 6 is still present, replace TCM. If code is no longer present, problem may be caused by poor connection. Repair as needed.

DTC 12: THROTTLE POSITION (TP) SENSOR

Condition – Open or short circuit. Possible causes are:
- Poor harness connection at TP sensor.
- Circuit fault between TP sensor and TCM.
- TP sensor.

Diagnosis & Repair Procedure – **1)** Turn ignition on. Using voltmeter, backprobe TCM harness connector. Do not disconnect connector. Measure voltage between ground and terminal No. 2T (Blue/White wire on MX3 or Pink/Green wire on MX6/626) on TCM connector. Slowly depress accelerator pedal while monitoring voltage. Go to next step.

2) If voltage changes as accelerator pedal is depressed, go to step **5)**. If voltage does not change as accelerator pedal is depressed, go to next step.

3) Measure voltage between ground and terminal No. 2A (Light Green/Red wire on MX3 or Green/Blue wire on MX6/626) on TCM connector. If 4.5-5.5 volts is present, go to next step. If 4.5-5.5 volts is not present, go to step **5)**.

4) Turn ignition switch to OFF position. Disconnect Throttle Position (TP) sensor harness connector. Measure resistance between specified component terminals. See appropriate SYSTEM & COMPONENT TESTING article in ENGINE PERFORMANCE of appropriate MITCHELL® manual. Replace as needed. If TP sensor is okay, go to next step.

5) Disconnect negative battery cable for at least 20 seconds. Depress brake pedal. Reconnect negative battery cable. Road test vehicle. Retrieve DTC's. If DTC 12 is still present, replace TCM. If code is no longer present, problem may be caused by poor connection. Repair as needed.

DTC 14: BAROMETRIC PRESSURE SENSOR

Condition – Open or short circuit. Possible causes are:
- Poor harness connection at barometric pressure sensor.
- Circuit fault between barometric pressure sensor and ECM.

Diagnosis & Repair Procedure – **1)** Turn ignition on. Using voltmeter, backprobe TCM harness connector. Do not disconnect connector. Measure voltage between ground and terminal No. 2R (Green/Orange wire) on TCM connector. Voltage should be about 3.5 volts or greater below 4900 ft. elevation or less than 3.5 volts above 4900 ft. elevation. If voltage is within specification, go to step **3)**. If voltage is not within specification, go to next step.

2) Turn ignition off. Disconnect ECM and TCM harness connectors. Check continuity of Green/Orange wire between terminal No. 2A on ECM harness connector and terminal No. 2R on TCM harness connector. Repair as needed. If circuit is okay, go to next step.

3) Disconnect negative battery cable for at least 20 seconds. Depress brake pedal. Reconnect negative battery cable. Road test vehicle. Retrieve DTC's. If DTC 14 is still present, replace ECM. If code is no longer present, problem may be caused by poor connection. Repair as needed.

3-870

AUTOMATIC TRANSMISSIONS
Mazda FA4A-EL & GF4A-EL Electronic Controls (Cont.)

DTC 55: TURBINE SPEED SENSOR

Condition – No input from turbine speed sensor while driving vehicle at 25 MPH or more. Shift selector is in "D", "2" or "L" position. Possible causes are:
- Poor harness connection at turbine speed sensor.
- Circuit fault between turbine speed sensor and TCM.
- Turbine speed sensor.

Diagnosis & Repair Procedure – **1)** Turn ignition on. Using voltmeter, backprobe TCM harness connector. Do not disconnect connector. Start and idle engine in Park (GF4A-EL) or Neutral (FA4A-EL). Measure AC voltage between terminals No. 2J (positive) and No. 2L (negative). If .1-1.0 volt is present, go to step **4)**. If .1-1.0 volt is not present, go to next step.

2) Turn ignition off. Disconnect TCM harness connector. Measure resistance between terminals No. 2J (White wire) and No. 2L (Red wire). Resistance should be 253-604 ohms for MX6/626 models or 200-400 ohms for MX3 models. If resistance is within specification, go to step **4)**. If resistance is not within specification, go to next step.

3) Inspect turbine speed sensor and related circuits. See TURBINE SPEED SENSOR under COMPONENT TESTING. Repair as needed. If sensor and related circuits are okay, go to next step.

4) Disconnect negative battery cable for at least 20 seconds. Depress brake pedal. Reconnect negative battery cable. Road test vehicle. Retrieve DTC's. If DTC 55 is still present, replace TCM. If code is no longer present, problem may be caused by poor connection. Repair as needed.

DTC 56: TRANSAXLE FLUID TEMPERATURE (TFT) SENSOR

Condition – Open or short circuit. Possible causes are:
- Poor harness connection at TFT sensor.
- Circuit fault between TFT sensor and TCM.
- TFT sensor.

Diagnosis & Repair Procedure – **1)** Turn ignition on. Using voltmeter, backprobe TCM harness connector. Do not disconnect connector. Start and idle engine in Park. Measure voltage between terminals No. 1G (positive) and No. 2P (negative). Voltage reading should decrease as fluid temperature increases. Voltage should be about 3.5 volts at 68°F (20°C) to .6 volts at 266°F (130°C). If voltage readings are within specification, go to step **4)**. If voltage readings are within not specification, go to next step.

2) Turn ignition off. Disconnect TCM harness connector. Measure resistance between terminals No. 1G (Gray wire) and No. 2P (Black/Red wire). Resistance reading should decrease as fluid temperature increases. Resistance should be about 2400 ohms at 68°F (20°C) to 360 ohms at 176°F (80°C). If resistance readings are within specification, go to step **4)**. If resistance readings are within not specification, go to next step.

3) Inspect TFT sensor and related circuits. See TRANSMISSION FLUID TEMPERATURE (TFT) SENSOR under COMPONENT TESTING. Repair as needed. If sensor and related circuits are okay, go to next step.

4) Disconnect negative battery cable for at least 20 seconds. Depress brake pedal. Reconnect negative battery cable. Road test vehicle. Retrieve DTC's. If DTC 56 is still present, replace TCM. If code is no longer present, problem may be caused by poor connection. Repair as needed.

DTC 57: REDUCE TORQUE SIGNAL NO. 1 (MX3)

Condition – Open or short in reduce torque signal No. 1 circuit. Possible causes are:
- Circuit fault between ECM and TCM.

Diagnosis & Repair Procedure – **1)** Turn ignition on. Using voltmeter, backprobe TCM harness connector. Do not disconnect connector. Test drive vehicle.

2) Measure voltage between ground and terminal No. 2M (Green/Black wire) on TCM harness connector. With transaxle in 1st gear, 2nd or during 2-3 shift with 3/4 throttle or greater, battery voltage should

exist. During any other operating condition, voltage should be 2.5 volts or less. If voltage is within specification, go to step **4)**. If voltage is not within specification, go to next step.

3) Turn ignition off. Disconnect TCM harness connector. Disconnect Electronic Control Module (ECM) harness connectors. Check continuity of Green/Black wire between terminal No. 1S on ECM harness connector and terminal No. 2M on TCM harness connector. Repair as needed. If continuity exists, go to next step.

4) Disconnect negative battery cable for at least 20 seconds. Depress brake pedal. Reconnect negative battery cable. Road test vehicle. Retrieve DTC's. If DTC 57 is still present, replace TCM. If code is no longer present, problem may be caused by poor connection. Repair as needed.

DTC 57: REDUCE TORQUE SIGNAL NO. 1 (MX6 & 626)

Condition – Open or short in reduce torque signal No. 1 circuit. Possible causes are:
- Circuit fault between ECM and TCM.

Diagnosis & Repair Procedure – **1)** Turn ignition on. Using voltmeter, backprobe TCM harness connector. Do not disconnect connector. Test drive vehicle.

2) Measure voltage between ground and terminal No. 1J (Brown/White wire) on TCM harness connector. During 1-2 or 2-3 shift, or with 1/2 throttle or greater voltage should be 1 volt or less. During any other operating condition, battery voltage should exist. If voltage is within specification, go to step **4)**. If voltage is not within specification, go to next step.

3) Turn ignition off. Disconnect TCM harness connector. Disconnect Electronic Control Module (ECM) harness connectors. Check continuity of Brown/White wire between terminal No. 1S on ECM harness connector and terminal No. 1J on TCM harness connector. Repair as needed. If continuity exists, go to next step.

4) Disconnect negative battery cable for at least 20 seconds. Depress brake pedal. Reconnect negative battery cable. Road test vehicle. Retrieve DTC's. If DTC 57 is still present, replace TCM. If code is no longer present, problem may be caused by poor connection. Repair as needed.

DTC 58: REDUCE TORQUE SIGNAL NO. 2 (MX3)

Condition – Open or short in reduce torque signal No. 2 circuit. Possible causes are:
- Circuit fault between ECM and TCM.

Diagnosis & Repair Procedure – **1)** Turn ignition on. Using voltmeter, backprobe TCM harness connector. Do not disconnect connector. Test drive vehicle.

2) Measure voltage between ground and terminal No. 1A (Light Green/Yellow wire) on TCM harness connector. During 4-2, 4-1, 3-2, 3-1 or 2-1 shift, or with 1/8 throttle or greater voltage should be 5 volts or less. During any other operating condition, battery voltage should exist. If voltage is within specification, go to step **5)**. If voltage is not within specification, go to next step.

3) Turn ignition off. Disconnect TCM harness connector. Disconnect Electronic Control Module (ECM) harness connectors. Check continuity of Light Green/Yellow wire between terminal No. 1V on ECM harness connector and terminal No. 1A on TCM harness connector. Repair as needed. If continuity exists, go to next step.

4) Check continuity of Red/Green wire between terminal No. 1I on ECM harness connector and terminal No. 1N on TCM harness connector. Repair as needed. If continuity exists, go to next step.

5) Disconnect negative battery cable for at least 20 seconds. Depress brake pedal. Reconnect negative battery cable. Road test vehicle. Retrieve DTC's. If DTC 58 is still present, replace ECM or TCM. If code is no longer present, problem may be caused by poor connection. Repair as needed.

AUTOMATIC TRANSMISSIONS
Mazda FA4A-EL & GF4A-EL Electronic Controls (Cont.)

3-871

DTC 58: REDUCE TORQUE SIGNAL NO. 2 (MX6 & 626)

Condition – Open or short in reduce torque signal No. 2 circuit. Possible causes are:
- Circuit fault between ECM and TCM.

Diagnosis & Repair Procedure – 1) Turn ignition on. Using voltmeter, backprobe TCM harness connector. Do not disconnect connector. Test drive vehicle.

2) Measure voltage between ground and terminal No. 1L (Blue wire) on TCM harness connector. During 4-2, 4-1, 3-2, 3-1 or 2-1 shift, or with 3/8 throttle or greater voltage should be 1 volt or less. During any other operating condition, battery voltage should exist. If voltage is within specification, go to step **4)**. If voltage is not within specification, go to next step.

3) Turn ignition off. Disconnect TCM harness connector. Disconnect Electronic Control Module (ECM) harness connectors. Check continuity of Blue wire between terminal No. 1V on ECM harness connector and terminal No. 1L on TCM harness connector. Repair as needed. If continuity exists, go to next step.

4) Disconnect negative battery cable for at least 20 seconds. Depress brake pedal. Reconnect negative battery cable. Road test vehicle. Retrieve DTC's. If DTC 58 is still present, replace TCM. If code is no longer present, problem may be caused by poor connection. Repair as needed.

DTC 59: TORQUE REDUCE SIGNAL/ENGINE COOLANT TEMPERATURE SIGNAL

Condition – Open or short in torque reduce signal/engine coolant temperature signal. Possible causes are:
- Circuit fault between ECM and TCM.

Diagnosis & Repair Procedure – 1) Turn ignition on. Using voltmeter, backprobe TCM harness connector. Do not disconnect connector. Start and idle engine.

2) Measure voltage between ground and terminal No. 1K (Yellow/Blue wire) on TCM harness connector. With engine coolant temperature of 140°F (60°C) or greater, battery voltage should exist. With engine coolant temperature less than 140°F (60°C), voltage should be 1 volt or less. If voltage is within specification, go to step **4)**. If voltage is not within specification, go to next step.

3) Turn ignition off. Disconnect TCM harness connector. Disconnect Electronic Control Module (ECM) harness connectors. Check continuity of Yellow/Blue wire between terminal No. 1K on ECM harness connector and terminal No. 1K on TCM harness connector. Repair as needed. If continuity exists, go to next step.

4) Disconnect negative battery cable for at least 20 seconds. Depress brake pedal. Reconnect negative battery cable. Road test vehicle. Retrieve DTC's. If DTC 59 is still present, replace TCM. If code is no longer present, problem may be caused by poor connection. Repair as needed.

DTC 60: SHIFT SOLENOID "A"

NOTE: Always check mechanical operation of solenoid. See COMPONENT TESTING. Replace as needed.

Condition – Open or short circuit of solenoid valve and/or harness. Possible causes are:
- Poor connection at solenoid harness connector.
- Circuit fault between solenoid and TCM.
- Malfunctioning solenoid valve.

Diagnosis & Repair Procedure – 1) Turn ignition on. Using voltmeter, backprobe TCM harness connector. Do not disconnect connector. Test drive vehicle.

2) Measure voltage between ground and terminal No. 2E on TCM harness connector. During test drive voltage should be less than 1 volt when solenoid is off and battery voltage when solenoid is on. See appropriate SOLENOID OPERATION TABLE under PCM OR TCM OUTPUT DEVICES. If voltage is within specification, go to step **5)**. If voltage is not within specification, go to next step.

3) Turn ignition off. Disconnect TCM harness connector. Measure resistance between ground and terminal No. 2E. If resistance is 11-27 ohms at 68°F (20°C), go to step **5)**. If resistance is not 11-27 ohms at 68°F (20°C), go to next step.

4) Inspect shift solenoid "A" and related circuits. See appropriate SOLENOID VALVES under COMPONENT TESTING. Repair as needed. If solenoid valve and related circuits are okay, go to next step.

5) Disconnect negative battery cable for at least 20 seconds. Depress brake pedal. Reconnect negative battery cable. Road test vehicle. Retrieve DTC's. If DTC 60 is still present, replace TCM. If code is no longer present, problem may be caused by poor connection. Repair as needed.

DTC 61: SHIFT SOLENOID "B"

NOTE: Always check mechanical operation of solenoid. See COMPONENT TESTING. Replace as needed.

Condition – Open or short circuit of solenoid valve and/or harness. Possible causes are:
- Poor connection at solenoid harness connector.
- Circuit fault between solenoid and TCM.
- Malfunctioning solenoid valve.

Diagnosis & Repair Procedure – 1) Turn ignition on. Using voltmeter, backprobe TCM harness connector. Do not disconnect connector. Test drive vehicle.

2) Measure voltage between ground and terminal No. 2G on TCM harness connector. During test drive voltage should be 0 volts when solenoid is off and battery voltage when solenoid is on. See appropriate SOLENOID OPERATION TABLE under PCM OR TCM OUTPUT DEVICES. If voltage is within specification, go to step **5)**. If voltage is not within specification, go to next step.

3) Turn ignition off. Disconnect TCM harness connector. Measure resistance between ground and terminal No. 2G. If resistance is 11-27 ohms at 68°F (20°C), go to step **5)**. If resistance is not 11-27 ohms at 68°F (20°C), go to next step.

4) Inspect shift solenoid "B" and related circuits. See appropriate SOLENOID VALVES under COMPONENT TESTING. Repair as needed. If solenoid valve and related circuits are okay, go to next step.

5) Disconnect negative battery cable for at least 20 seconds. Depress brake pedal. Reconnect negative battery cable. Road test vehicle. Retrieve DTC's. If DTC 61 is still present, replace TCM. If code is no longer present, problem may be caused by poor connection. Repair as needed.

DTC 62: SHIFT SOLENOID "C"

NOTE: Always check mechanical operation of solenoid. See COMPONENT TESTING. Replace as needed.

Condition – Open or short circuit of solenoid valve and/or harness. Possible causes are:
- Poor connection at solenoid harness connector.
- Circuit fault between solenoid and TCM.
- Malfunctioning solenoid valve.

Diagnosis & Repair Procedure – 1) Turn ignition on. Using voltmeter, backprobe TCM harness connector. Do not disconnect connector. Test drive vehicle.

2) Measure voltage between ground and terminal No. 2I on TCM harness connector. During test drive voltage should be 0 volts when solenoid is off and battery voltage when solenoid is on. See appropriate SOLENOID OPERATION TABLE under PCM OR TCM OUTPUT DEVICES. If voltage is within specification, go to step **5)**. If voltage is not within specification, go to next step.

3) Turn ignition off. Disconnect TCM harness connector. Measure resistance between ground and terminal No. 2I. If resistance is 11-27 ohms at 68°F (20°C), go to step **5)**. If resistance is not 11-27 ohms at 68°F (20°C), go to next step.

4) Inspect shift solenoid "C" and related circuits. See appropriate SOLENOID VALVES under COMPONENT TESTING. Repair as needed. If solenoid valve and related circuits are okay, go to next step.

3-872

AUTOMATIC TRANSMISSIONS
Mazda FA4A-EL & GF4A-EL Electronic Controls (Cont.)

5) Disconnect negative battery cable for at least 20 seconds. Depress brake pedal. Reconnect negative battery cable. Road test vehicle. Retrieve DTC's. If DTC 62 is still present, replace TCM. If code is no longer present, problem may be caused by poor connection. Repair as needed.

DTC 63: TCC CONTROL SOLENOID VALVE

NOTE: *Always check mechanical operation of solenoid. See COMPONENT TESTING. Replace as needed.*

Condition – Open or short circuit of solenoid valve and/or harness. Possible causes are:
- Poor connection at solenoid harness connector.
- Circuit fault between solenoid and TCM.
- Malfunctioning solenoid valve.

Diagnosis & Repair Procedure – 1) Turn ignition on. Using voltmeter, backprobe TCM harness connector. Do not disconnect connector. Test drive vehicle.
2) Measure voltage between ground and terminal No. 2K on TCM harness connector. During test drive, voltage should be less than 1 volt with TCC not engaged and battery voltage with TCC engaged. If voltage is within specification, go to step 5). If voltage is not within specification, go to next step.
3) Turn ignition off. Disconnect TCM harness connector. Measure resistance between ground and terminal No. 2K. If resistance is 11-27 ohms at 68°F (20°C), go to step 5). If resistance is not 11-27 ohms at 68°F (20°C), go to next step.
4) Inspect TCC control solenoid and related circuits. See appropriate SOLENOID VALVES under COMPONENT TESTING. Repair as needed. If solenoid valve and related circuits are okay, go to next step.
5) Disconnect negative battery cable for at least 20 seconds. Depress brake pedal. Reconnect negative battery cable. Road test vehicle. Retrieve DTC's. If DTC 63 is still present, replace TCM. If code is no longer present, problem may be caused by poor connection. Repair as needed.

DTC 64: 3-2 TIMING SOLENOID VALVE

NOTE: *Always check mechanical operation of solenoid. See COMPONENT TESTING. Replace as needed.*

Condition – Open or short circuit of solenoid valve and/or harness. Possible causes are:
- Poor connection at solenoid harness connector.
- Circuit fault between solenoid and TCM.
- Malfunctioning solenoid valve.

Diagnosis & Repair Procedure – 1) Turn ignition on. Using voltmeter, backprobe TCM harness connector. Do not disconnect connector. Test drive vehicle.
2) Measure voltage between ground and terminal No. 2M (Red/White wire) on TCM harness connector. During test drive voltage should be 0 volts in any forward gear and battery voltage during any upshift or downshift (except 4-3). If voltage is within specification, go to step 5). If voltage is not within specification, go to next step.
3) Turn ignition off. Disconnect TCM harness connector. Measure resistance between ground and terminal No. 2M (Red/White wire). If resistance is 11-27 ohms at 68°F (20°C), go to step 5). If resistance is not 11-27 ohms at 68°F (20°C), go to next step.
4) Inspect 3-2 timing solenoid and related circuits. See appropriate SOLENOID VALVES under COMPONENT TESTING. Repair as needed. If solenoid valve and related circuits are okay, go to next step.
5) Disconnect negative battery cable for at least 20 seconds. Depress brake pedal. Reconnect negative battery cable. Road test vehicle. Retrieve DTC's. If DTC 64 is still present, replace TCM. If code is no longer present, problem may be caused by poor connection. Repair as needed.

DTC 65: TCC SOLENOID VALVE

NOTE: *Always check mechanical operation of solenoid. See COMPONENT TESTING. Replace as needed.*

Condition – Open or short circuit of solenoid valve and/or harness. Possible causes are:
- Poor connection at solenoid harness connector.
- Circuit fault between solenoid and TCM.
- Malfunctioning solenoid valve.

Diagnosis & Repair Procedure – 1) Ensure ignition is off. Disconnect TCM harness connector. Measure resistance between ground and terminal No. 2C (White/Black wire). If resistance is 9-18 ohms at 68°F (20°C), go to step 3). If resistance is not 9-18 ohms at 68°F (20°C), go to next step.
2) Inspect TCC solenoid and related circuits. See appropriate SOLENOID VALVES under COMPONENT TESTING. Repair as needed. If solenoid valve and related circuits are okay, go to next step.
3) Disconnect negative battery cable for at least 20 seconds. Depress brake pedal. Reconnect negative battery cable. Road test vehicle. Retrieve DTC's. If DTC 65 is still present, replace TCM. If code is no longer present, problem may be caused by poor connection. Repair as needed.

DTC 66: PRESSURE CONTROL SOLENOID

NOTE: *Always check mechanical operation of solenoid. See COMPONENT TESTING. Replace as needed.*

Condition – Open or short circuit of solenoid valve and/or harness. Possible causes are:
- Poor connection at solenoid harness connector.
- Circuit fault between solenoid and TCM.
- Malfunctioning solenoid valve.

Diagnosis & Repair Procedure – 1) Ensure ignition is off. Disconnect TCM harness connector. Measure resistance between ground and terminal No. 2N (Red/Green wire). If resistance is 9-18 ohms at 68°F (20°C), go to step 4). If resistance is not 9-18 ohms at 68°F (20°C), go to next step.
2) Inspect pressure control solenoid and related circuits. See appropriate SOLENOID VALVES under COMPONENT TESTING. Repair as needed. If solenoid valve and related circuits are okay, go to next step.
3) Connect TCM harness connectors. Turn ignition on. Using dwell meter, backprobe TCM harness connector. Measure dwell between ground and terminal No. 2N (Red/Green wire) on TCM harness connector. With throttle fully closed, dwell should be about 67 degrees. With wide open throttle, dwell should be about 23 degrees. If dwell is within specification, go to step 4). If dwell is not within specification, go to next step.
4) Disconnect negative battery cable for at least 20 seconds. Depress brake pedal. Reconnect negative battery cable. Road test vehicle. Retrieve DTC's. If DTC 66 is still present, replace TCM. If code is no longer present, problem may be caused by poor connection. Repair as needed.

DTC P0705: TRANSAXLE RANGE SWITCH CIRCUIT MALFUNCTION

Condition – Engine speed is greater than 531 RPM and vehicle speed is more than 55 MPH. No signal is received from range switch. Vehicle speed is more than 12 MPH with "D" range and "N" position switches on. Possible causes for either condition are:
- Transaxle range switch malfunction.
- Damaged wiring or connectors between transaxle range switch and PCM or TCM.
- PCM or TCM malfunction.

AUTOMATIC TRANSMISSIONS
Mazda FA4A-EL & GF4A-EL Electronic Controls (Cont.)

3-873

Diagnosis & Repair Procedure – 1) Ensure all appropriate connections are clean and tight. Repair as needed. Turn ignition on. Using voltmeter, backprobe PCM or TCM connector (as applicable). Measure voltage between ground and specified terminal. See appropriate DTC P0705 TEST table. If all voltages are within specification, go to step 6). If any voltage is not within specification, go to next step.

DTC P0705 TEST (1996 MILLENIA, MX6 & 626 – PCM EQUIPPED)

PCM Terminal No.	Measured Voltage	Range Switch Position
1F	0	"P" Or "N"
1F	12-14	"R", "D", "2" Or "L"
2K	12-14	"R"
2K	0	All Except "R"
2I	12-14	"D"
2I	0	All Except "D"
2M	12-14	"2"
2M	0	All Except "2"
2R	12-14	"L"
2R	0	All Except "L"

DTC P0705 TEST (1995-96 PROTEGE – PCM EQUIPPED)

PCM Terminal No.	Measured Voltage	Range Switch Position
1L	0	"P" Or "N"
1L	12-14	"R", "D", "2" Or "L"
2F	12-14	"D"
2F	0	All Except "D"
2G	12-14	"2"
2G	0	All Except "2"
2H	12-14	"L"
2H	0	All Except "L"

DTC P0705 TEST (ALL TCM EQUIPPED MODELS)

TCM Terminal No.	Measured Voltage	Range Switch Position
12B	0	"P" Or "N"
12B	12-14	"R", "D", "2" Or "L"
1I	12-14	"R"
1I	0	All Except "R"
2D	12-14	"D"
2D	0	All Except "D"
2F	12-14	"S"
2F	0	All Except "S"
2H	12-14	"L"
2H	0	All Except "L"

2) Check continuity of circuits between transaxle range switch and PCM or TCM. See appropriate wiring diagram in WIRING DIAGRAMS. Repair as needed. If all circuits are okay, go to next step.

3) Disconnect negative battery cable. Disconnect transaxle range switch harness connector. Inspect continuity of transaxle range switch internal circuits. See appropriate TRANSMISSION RANGE SWITCH in COMPONENT TESTING. Replace as needed. If switch is okay, go to next step.

4) Leave negative battery cable disconnected. Check continuity of circuits between transaxle range switch and instrument cluster. See appropriate wiring diagram in WIRING DIAGRAMS. Repair as needed. If all circuits are okay, go to next step.

5) Reconnect negative battery cable. Turn ignition on. Measure voltage at terminal "A" (Black/Yellow wire) on transmission range switch harness connector. If battery voltage does not exist, repair Black/Yellow wire between switch and ignition switch. If battery voltage exists, go to next step.

6) Road test vehicle. Retrieve DTC's. If code P0705 is still present, replace PCM or TCM. If code is no longer present, problem may be caused by poor connection. Repair as needed.

DTC P0710: TRANSAXLE FLUID TEMPERATURE (TFT) SENSOR CIRCUIT MALFUNCTION (1995 MILLENIA)

Condition – Vehicle speed is more than 12 MPH and voltage input to TCM is less than .1 volts or greater than 4.9 volts. Possible causes for condition are:
- Transaxle fluid temperature sensor malfunction.
- Damaged wiring or connectors between transaxle fluid temperature sensor and TCM.

Diagnosis & Repair Procedure – 1) Ensure all appropriate connections are clean and tight. Repair as needed. Turn ignition on. Access TCM connectors. Using voltmeter, backprobe harness connectors. Do not disconnect connectors. Go to next step.

2) Measure voltage between ground and terminal No. 1G (Blue/Yellow wire) on TCM connector. Voltage should be about 3.5 volts at 68°F (20°C) or .6 volts at 256°F (130°C). If voltage is within specifications, go to step 6). If voltage is not within specifications, go to next step.

3) Turn ignition off. Disconnect TCM harness connector. Measure resistance between terminals No. 1G (Blue/Yellow wire) and No. 2P (Black/Red wire). See TFT SENSOR SPECIFICATIONS (1995 MILLENIA). If resistance is within specification, go to step 6). If resistance is not within specification, go to next step.

4) Inspect TFT sensor. See TRANSMISSION FLUID TEMPERATURE (TFT) SENSOR in COMPONENT TESTING. If resistance is within specification, go to step 6). If resistance is not within specification, replace TFT sensor.

5) Check continuity of circuits between TFT sensor and TCM. See appropriate wiring diagram in WIRING DIAGRAMS. Repair as needed. If circuit is okay, go to next step.

6) Reconnect all harness connectors. Road test vehicle. Retrieve DTC's. If code P0710 is still present, replace TCM. If code is no longer present, problem may be caused by poor connection. Repair as needed.

TFT SENSOR SPECIFICATIONS (1995 MILLENIA)

K/Ohms	Fluid Temperature
15.55-17.56	-20°F (-4°C)
5.83-6.45	0°F (32°C)
2.50-2.72	20°F (68°C)
1.19-1.28	40°F (104°C)
.622-.658	60°F (140°C)
.349-.366	80°F (176°C)
.209-.216	100°F (212°C)
.131-.135	120°F (248°C)
.109-.108	130°F (266°C)

DTC P0710: TRANSAXLE FLUID TEMPERATURE (TFT) SENSOR CIRCUIT MALFUNCTION (1996 MILLENIA, MX6 & 626)

Condition – Vehicle speed is more than 12 MPH and voltage input to PCM is less than .1 volts or greater than 4.9 volts. Possible causes for condition are:
- Transaxle fluid temperature sensor malfunction.
- Damaged wiring or connectors between transaxle fluid temperature sensor and PCM.

Diagnosis & Repair Procedure – 1) Ensure all appropriate connections are clean and tight. Repair as needed. Turn ignition on. Access PCM connectors. Using voltmeter, backprobe harness connectors. Do not disconnect connectors. Go to next step.

2) Measure voltage between ground and terminal No. 2O on PCM connector. Voltage should be about 3.5 volts at 68°F (20°C) or 1.3 volts at 176°F (80°C). If voltage is within specifications, go to step 6). If voltage is not within specifications, go to next step.

3) Turn ignition off. Disconnect PCM harness connector. Measure resistance between terminals No. 2O and No. 3AB. See TFT SENSOR SPECIFICATIONS (1996 MILLENIA, MX6 & 626). If resistance is within specification, go to step 6). If resistance is not within specification, go to next step.

3-874

AUTOMATIC TRANSMISSIONS
Mazda FA4A-EL & GF4A-EL Electronic Controls (Cont.)

4) Inspect TFT sensor. See TRANSMISSION FLUID TEMPERATURE (TFT) SENSOR in COMPONENT TESTING. If resistance is within specification, go to step **6)**. If resistance is not within specification, replace TFT sensor.

5) Check continuity of circuits between TFT sensor and PCM. See appropriate wiring diagram in WIRING DIAGRAMS. Repair as needed. If circuit is okay, go to next step.

6) Reconnect all harness connectors. Road test vehicle. Retrieve DTC's. If code P0710 is still present, replace PCM. If code is no longer present, problem may be caused by poor connection. Repair as needed.

TFT SENSOR SPECIFICATIONS (1996 MILLENIA, MX6 & 626)

K/Ohms	Fluid Temperature
15.55-17.56	-20°F (-4°C)
5.83-6.45	0°F (32°C)
2.50-2.72	20°F (68°C)
1.19-1.28	40°F (104°C)
.622-.658	60°F (140°C)
.349-.366	80°F (176°C)
.209-.216	100°F (212°C)
.131-.135	120°F (248°C)
.109-.108	130°F (266°C)

DTC P0710: TRANSAXLE FLUID TEMPERATURE (TFT) SENSOR CIRCUIT MALFUNCTION (1995-96 PROTEGE)

Condition – Vehicle speed is more than 12 MPH and voltage input to PCM is less than .1 volts or greater than 4.9 volts. Possible causes for condition are:

- Transaxle fluid temperature sensor malfunction.
- Damaged wiring or connectors between transaxle fluid temperature sensor and PCM.

Diagnosis & Repair Procedure – **1)** Ensure all appropriate connections are clean and tight. Repair as needed. Turn ignition on. Access PCM connectors. Using voltmeter, backprobe harness connectors. Do not disconnect connectors. Go to next step.

2) Measure voltage between ground and terminal No. 3E (White/Violet wire) on PCM connector. Voltage should be about 4.0 volts at 68°F (20°C) or 1.5 volts at 266°F (130°C). If voltage is within specifications, go to step **6)**. If voltage is not within specifications, go to next step.

3) Turn ignition off. Disconnect PCM harness connector. Measure resistance between terminals No. 3E and No. 3O. See TFT SENSOR SPECIFICATIONS (1995-96 PROTEGE). If resistance is within specification, go to step **6)**. If resistance is not within specification, go to next step.

4) Inspect TFT sensor. See appropriate TRANSMISSION FLUID TEMPERATURE (TFT) SENSOR in COMPONENT TESTING. If resistance is within specification, go to step **6)**. If resistance is not within specification, replace TFT sensor.

5) Check continuity of circuits between TFT sensor and PCM. See appropriate wiring diagram in WIRING DIAGRAMS. Repair as needed. If circuit is okay, go to next step.

6) Reconnect all harness connectors. Road test vehicle. Retrieve DTC's. If code P0710 is still present, replace PCM. If code is no longer present, problem may be caused by poor connection. Repair as needed.

TFT SENSOR SPECIFICATIONS (1995-96 PROTEGE)

K/Ohms	Fluid Temperature
21.0-25.0	20°F (68°C)
10.0-12.1	40°F (104°C)
5.4-6.3	60°F (140°C)
3.0-3.4	80°F (176°C)
1.7-2.0	100°F (212°C)
1.1-1.2	120°F (248°C)
.86-.92	130°F (266°C)

DTC P0715: TURBINE SPEED SENSOR (1995 MILLENIA)

Condition – Turbine speed sensor signal is not input to TCM when vehicle is above 25 MPH and shift lever is in "D", "S" or "L" position. Possible causes for condition are:

- Turbine speed sensor malfunction.
- Damaged wiring or connectors between turbine speed sensor and TCM.

Diagnosis & Repair Procedure – **1)** Ensure all appropriate connections are clean and tight. Repair as needed. Turn ignition on. Access TCM connectors. Using voltmeter, backprobe harness connectors. Do not disconnect connectors. Go to next step.

2) Start and idle engine in Park or Neutral. Measure AC voltage between terminals No. 2J (positive) and No. 2L (negative). If .1-1.0 volts is present, go to step **6)**. If .1-1.0 volts is not present, go to next step.

3) Turn ignition off. Disconnect TCM harness connector. Measure resistance between terminals No. 2J (White wire) and No. 2L (Red wire). Resistance should be 253-604 ohms. If resistance is within specification, go to step **6)**. If resistance is not within specification, go to next step.

4) Inspect turbine speed sensor. See TURBINE SPEED SENSOR under COMPONENT TESTING. Repair as needed. If sensor is okay, go to next step.

5) Check continuity of circuits between turbine speed sensor and TCM. See appropriate wiring diagram in WIRING DIAGRAMS. Repair as needed. If circuits are okay, go to next step.

6) Reconnect all harness connectors. Road test vehicle. Retrieve DTC's. If code P0715 is still present, replace PCM. If code is no longer present, problem may be caused by poor connection. Repair as needed.

DTC P0715: TURBINE SPEED SENSOR (1996 MILLENIA, MX6 & 626)

Condition – Turbine speed sensor signal is not input to PCM when vehicle is above 25 MPH and shift lever is in "D", "S" or "L" position. Possible causes for condition are:

- Turbine speed sensor malfunction.
- Damaged wiring or connectors between turbine speed sensor and PCM.

Diagnosis & Repair Procedure – **1)** Ensure all appropriate connections are clean and tight. Repair as needed. Turn ignition on. Access PCM connectors. Using voltmeter, backprobe harness connectors. Do not disconnect connectors. Go to next step.

2) Start and idle engine in Park or Neutral. Measure AC voltage between terminals No. 2P (positive) and No. 2T (negative). If .1-1.0 volts is present, go to step **6)**. If .1-1.0 volts is not present, go to next step.

3) Turn ignition off. Disconnect TCM harness connector. Measure resistance between terminals No. 2P (White wire) and No. 2T (Red wire). Resistance should be 253-604 ohms. If resistance is within specification, go to step **6)**. If resistance is not within specification, go to next step.

4) Inspect turbine speed sensor. See TURBINE SPEED SENSOR under COMPONENT TESTING. Repair as needed. If sensor is okay, go to next step.

5) Check continuity of circuits between turbine speed sensor and PCM. See appropriate wiring diagram in WIRING DIAGRAMS. Repair as needed. If circuits are okay, go to next step.

6) Reconnect all harness connectors. Road test vehicle. Retrieve DTC's. If code P0715 is still present, replace PCM. If code is no longer present, problem may be caused by poor connection. Repair as needed.

AUTOMATIC TRANSMISSIONS
Mazda FA4A-EL & GF4A-EL Electronic Controls (Cont.)

3-875

DTC P0715: TURBINE SPEED SENSOR (1995-96 PROTEGE)

Condition – Turbine speed sensor signal is not input to PCM when vehicle is above 25 MPH and shift lever is in "D", "S" or "L" position. Possible causes for condition are:

- Turbine speed sensor malfunction.
- Damaged wiring or connectors between turbine speed sensor and PCM.

Diagnosis & Repair Procedure – **1)** Ensure all appropriate connections are clean and tight. Repair as needed. Turn ignition on. Access PCM connectors. Using voltmeter, backprobe harness connectors. Do not disconnect connectors. Go to next step.

2) Start and idle engine in Park or Neutral. Measure AC voltage between terminals No. 2L (positive) and No. 2K (negative). If .1-1.1 volts is present, go to step **6)**. If .1-1.1 volts is not present, go to next step.

3) Turn ignition off. Disconnect TCM harness connector. Measure resistance between terminals No. 2L (White wire) and No. 2K (Red wire). Resistance should be 200-400 ohms. If resistance is within specification, go to step **6)**. If resistance is not within specification, go to next step.

4) Inspect turbine speed sensor. See TURBINE SPEED SENSOR under COMPONENT TESTING. Repair as needed. If sensor is okay, go to next step.

5) Check continuity of circuits between turbine speed sensor and PCM. See appropriate wiring diagram in WIRING DIAGRAMS. Repair as needed. If circuits are okay, go to next step.

6) Reconnect all harness connectors. Road test vehicle. Retrieve DTC's. If code P0715 is still present, replace PCM. If code is no longer present, problem may be caused by poor connection. Repair as needed.

DTC P0725: ENGINE SPEED INPUT CIRCUIT MALFUNCTION

Condition – Engine speed input signal is not input to TCM when reverse and forward drum speed is over 600 RPM. Shift selector in "D", "2" or "L" position. Possible causes are:

- Distributor malfunction.
- Damaged wiring or connectors between ECM and crankshaft position sensor.
- Damaged wiring or connectors between ECM and TCM.
- Damaged wiring or connectors between ECM and tachometer.

Diagnosis & Repair Procedure – **1)** Ensure all appropriate connections are clean and tight. Repair as needed. Turn ignition on. Using voltmeter, backprobe TCM harness connector. Do not disconnect connector.

2) Measure voltage between ground and terminal No. 1N (Green wire) on TCM harness connector. If voltage is 4.5-5.5 volts with engine stopped or 2-3 volts with engine running, go to next step. If voltage is not 4.5-5.5 volts with engine stopped or 2-3 volts with engine running, repair Green wire between TCM and ECM for open or short.

3) Using voltmeter, backprobe ECM harness connector. Measure voltage between ground and terminal No. 1T (Green wire). If voltage is 4.5-5.5 volts with engine stopped or 2-3 volts with engine running, go to next step. If voltage is not 4.5-5.5 volts with engine stopped or 2-3 volts with engine running, repair Green wire between ECM and crankshaft position sensor for open or short.

4) Using voltmeter, backprobe Anti-Lock Brake System (ABS) control unit harness connector. Measure voltage between ground and terminal No. 1D (Green wire). If voltage is 1-10 volts with engine running, go to next step. If voltage is not 1-10 volts with engine running, inspect ABS system operation. See appropriate ANTI-LOCK BRAKE article in BRAKES in appropriate MITCHELL® manual.

5) Turn ignition off. Disconnect negative battery cable. Disconnect TCM harness connectors. Measure resistance between terminals No. 1N and 2P on TCM harness connectors. If resistance is 7200-8000 ohms, go to next step. If resistance is not 7200-8000 ohms, replace TCM.

6) With TCM harness connector disconnected, measure resistance between terminals No. 1N (Green wire) and No. 2O (Blue/Red wire) on TCM harness connector. If infinite resistance is present, go to next step. If infinite resistance is not present, replace TCM.

7) Reconnect all harness connectors. Road test vehicle. Retrieve DTC's. If code P0725 is still present, replace PCM. If code is no longer present, problem may be caused by poor connection. Repair as needed.

DTC P0730: INCORRECT GEAR RATIO

Condition – Shift solenoids "A", "B", "C", speedometer sensor, turbine speed sensor and throttle position sensor function normally. Turbine speed sensor and speedometer sensor signals indicate that gear ratio is above set value. Possible causes are:

- Low ATF level.
- Low line pressure.
- Low solenoid reducing pressure.
- Control valve stuck.
- Solenoid valve malfunction.
- TCM malfunction.
- Forward clutch, 3-4 brake band, one-way clutch No. 1 slippage.

Diagnosis & Repair Procedure – **1)** Inspect ATF level and condition. Correct as needed. If fluid level and condition is okay, check line pressure. See TESTING in FA4A-EL & GF4A-EL overhaul article. Follow repair recommendations if line pressure is not within specifications. If line pressure is okay, go to next step.

2) Perform time lag test. See TESTING in FA4A-EL & GF4A-EL overhaul article. Follow repair recommendations if time lag is not within specifications. If time lag is okay, go to next step.

3) Perform road test. See TESTING in FA4A-EL & GF4A-EL overhaul article. Follow repair recommendations if transaxle shift speeds or shift feel is not as specified. If vehicle shifts at correct speeds and shift feel is acceptable, go to next step.

4) Clear DTC's. See CLEARING CODES. Retrieve DTC's. If code P0730 is still present, replace PCM. If code is no longer present, problem may be caused by intermittent clutch slippage. Further investigation may be required.

DTC P0731: INCORRECT 1ST GEAR RATIO

NOTE: If any of the following DTC's are also present, repair them first and then proceed with this test: DTC P0750, DTC P0755, DTC P0760.

Condition – Shift solenoids "A", "B", "C", vehicle speed sensor, turbine speed sensor and TFT sensor function normally and vehicle speed is 12-32 MPH in 1st gear. Turbine speed sensor and vehicle speed sensor signals indicate that gear ratio is above set value. Possible causes are:

- Low ATF level.
- Low line pressure.
- Control valve stuck.
- Solenoid valve malfunction.
- PCM malfunction.
- Forward clutch, 3-4 brake band, one-way clutch No. 1 slippage.

Diagnosis & Repair Procedure – **1)** Ensure ATF level and condition is okay. Refer to TESTING and COMPONENT TESTING in FA4A-EL & GF4A-EL overhaul article and perform the following tests, repair any components as necessary: Check line pressure, if line pressure is okay, go to next step.

2) Inspect turbine speed sensor. If sensor is okay, go to next step.

3) Perform stall speed test. If stall speed is okay, go to next step.

4) Perform time lag test. If time lag is okay, go to next step.

5) Perform road test. If vehicle shifts at correct speeds and shift feel is acceptable, go to next step.

6) Clear DTC's and retest. See CLEARING CODES. If code P0733 is still present, replace PCM. If code is no longer present, problem may be caused by intermittent clutch slippage. Further investigation may be required.

3-876

AUTOMATIC TRANSMISSIONS
Mazda FA4A-EL & GF4A-EL Electronic Controls (Cont.)

DTC P0732: INCORRECT 2ND GEAR RATIO

NOTE: If any of the following DTC's are also present, repair them first and then proceed with this test: DTC P0750, DTC P0755, DTC P0760.

Condition – Shift solenoids "A", "B", "C", vehicle speed sensor, turbine speed sensor and TFT sensor function normally and vehicle speed is 17-60 MPH in 2nd gear with 3/8ths throttle opening. Turbine speed sensor and vehicle speed sensor signals indicate that gear ratio is above set value. Possible causes are:

- Low ATF level.
- Low line pressure.
- Control valve stuck.
- Solenoid valve malfunction.
- PCM malfunction.
- Forward clutch, 2-4 brake band, one-way clutch No. 1 slippage.

Diagnosis & Repair Procedure – **1)** Ensure ATF level and condition is okay. Refer to TESTING and COMPONENT TESTING in FA4A-EL & GF4A-EL overhaul article and perform the following tests, repair any components as necessary: Check line pressure, if line pressure is okay, go to next step.
2) Inspect turbine speed sensor. If sensor is okay, go to next step.
3) Perform stall speed test. If stall speed is okay, go to next step.
4) Perform time lag test. If time lag is okay, go to next step.
5) Perform road test. If vehicle shifts at correct speeds and shift feel is acceptable, go to next step.
6) Clear DTC's and retest. See CLEARING CODES. If code P0733 is still present, replace PCM. If code is no longer present, problem may be caused by intermittent clutch slippage. Further investigation may be required.

DTC P0733: INCORRECT 3RD GEAR RATIO

NOTE: If any of the following DTC's are also present, repair them first and then proceed with this test: DTC P0750, DTC P0755, DTC P0760.

Condition – Shift solenoids "A", "B", "C", vehicle speed sensor, turbine speed sensor and TFT sensor function normally and vehicle speed is 19-32 MPH in 3rd gear. Turbine speed sensor and vehicle speed sensor signals indicate that gear ratio is above set value. Possible causes are:

- Low ATF level.
- Low line pressure.
- Control valve stuck.
- Solenoid valve malfunction.
- PCM malfunction.
- Forward clutch, 3-4 brake band, one-way clutch No. 1 slippage.

Diagnosis & Repair Procedure – **1)** Ensure ATF level and condition is okay. Refer to TESTING and COMPONENT TESTING in FA4A-EL & GF4A-EL overhaul article and perform the following tests, repair any components as necessary: Check line pressure, if line pressure is okay, go to next step.
2) Inspect turbine speed sensor. If sensor is okay, go to next step.
3) Perform stall speed test. If stall speed is okay, go to next step.
4) Perform time lag test. If time lag is okay, go to next step.
5) Perform road test. If vehicle shifts at correct speeds and shift feel is acceptable, go to next step.
6) Clear DTC's and retest. See CLEARING CODES. If code P0733 is still present, replace PCM. If code is no longer present, problem may be caused by intermittent clutch slippage. Further investigation may be required.

DTC P0734: INCORRECT 4TH GEAR RATIO

NOTE: If any of the following DTC's are also present, repair them first and then proceed with this test: DTC P0750, DTC P0755, DTC P0760.

Condition – Shift solenoids "A", "B", "C", vehicle speed sensor, turbine speed sensor and TFT sensor function normally and vehicle speed is 44-65 MPH in 4th gear. Turbine speed sensor and vehicle speed sensor signals indicate that gear ratio is above set value. Possible causes are:

- Low ATF level.
- Low line pressure.
- Control valve stuck.
- Solenoid valve malfunction.
- PCM malfunction.
- 2-4 brake band and 3-4 clutch slippage.

Diagnosis & Repair Procedure – **1)** Inspect ATF level and condition. Correct as needed. If fluid level and condition is okay, check line pressure. See TESTING in FA4A-EL & GF4A-EL overhaul article. Follow repair recommendations if line pressure is not within specifications. If line pressure is okay, go to next step.
2) Perform road test. See TESTING in FA4A-EL & GF4A-EL overhaul article. Follow repair recommendations if transaxle shift speeds or shift feel is not as specified. If vehicle shifts at correct speeds and shift feel is acceptable, go to next step.
3) Clear DTC's. See CLEARING CODES. Retrieve DTC's. If code P0734 is still present, replace PCM. If code is no longer present, problem may be caused by intermittent clutch slippage. Further investigation may be required.

DTC P0740: TORQUE CONVERTER CLUTCH MALFUNCTION

Condition – Shift solenoids "A", "B", "C", vehicle/speedometer speed sensor, turbine speed sensor and throttle position sensor function normally and vehicle speed is 44-65 MPH. There is a greater than 100 RPM difference between engine speed and reverse and forward drum speed with transaxle in 4th gear and TCC engaged. Possible causes are:

- Low ATF level.
- Low line pressure.
- Low solenoid reducing pressure.
- Torque converter slippage.
- Control valve stuck.
- TCC solenoid valve malfunction.
- PCM or TCM malfunction.

Diagnosis & Repair Procedure – **1)** Inspect ATF level and condition. Correct as needed. If fluid level and condition is okay, check line pressure. See TESTING in FA4A-EL & GF4A-EL overhaul article. Follow repair recommendations if line pressure is not within specifications. If line pressure is okay, go to next step.
2) Inspect TCC solenoid. See appropriate SOLENOID VALVES under COMPONENT TESTING. Repair as needed. If solenoid valve is okay, go to next step.
3) Inspect TCC control valve in valve body. See FA4A-EL & GF4A-EL overhaul article. Follow repair recommendations if valve operation is faulty. If valve is okay, go to next step.
4) Clear DTC's. See CLEARING CODES. Retrieve DTC's. If code P0740 is still present, replace PCM or TCM. If code is no longer present, problem may be caused by intermittent TCC slippage. Further investigation may be required.

DTC P0745: PRESSURE CONTROL SOLENOID MALFUNCTION (1995 MILLENIA)

Possible Causes:

- Open or short circuit.
- TCM malfunction.
- Pressue control solenoid malfunction.

Diagnosis & Repair Procedure – **1)** Ensure all appropriate connections are clean and tight. Repair as needed. Turn ignition on. Using voltmeter, backprobe TCM harness connector. Do not disconnect connector.
2) Measure voltage between ground and terminal No. 2N (Red/Green wire). Voltage should be battery voltage when driving and zero voltage with vehicle stopped. If voltage is within specifications, go to step **6)**. If voltage is not within specifications, go to next step.

AUTOMATIC TRANSMISSIONS
Mazda FA4A-EL & GF4A-EL Electronic Controls (Cont.)

3-877

3) Ensure ignition is off. Disconnect negative battery cable. Disconnect TCM harness connector. Measure resistance between ground and terminal No. 2N (Red/Green wire) on TCM harness connector. If resistance is 9-18 ohms at 68°F (20°C), go to step **6)**. If resistance is not 9-18 ohms at 68°F (20°C), go to next step.

4) Inspect pressure control solenoid. See appropriate SOLENOID VALVES under COMPONENT TESTING. Repair as needed. If solenoid valve is okay, go to next step.

5) Check continuity of circuits between pressure control solenoid and TCM. See appropriate wiring diagram in WIRING DIAGRAMS. Repair as needed. If circuits are okay, go to next step.

6) Disconnect negative battery cable for at least 20 seconds. Depress brake pedal. Reconnect negative battery cable. Road test vehicle. Retrieve DTC's. If DTC P0745 is still present, replace TCM. If code is no longer present, problem may be caused by poor connection. Repair as needed.

DTC P0745: PRESSURE CONTROL SOLENOID MALFUNCTION (1996 MILLENIA, MX6 & 626)

Possible Causes:
- Open or short circuit.
- PCM malfunction.
- Pressue control solenoid malfunction.

Diagnosis & Repair Procedure – **1)** Ensure all appropriate connections are clean and tight. Repair as needed. Turn ignition on. Using voltmeter, backprobe PCM harness connector. Do not disconnect connector.

2) Measure voltage between ground and terminal No. 2H (Red/Green wire). Voltage should be battery voltage when driving and zero voltage with vehicle stopped. If voltage is within specifications, go to step **6)**. If voltage is not within specifications, go to next step.

3) Ensure ignition is off. Disconnect negative battery cable. Disconnect PCM harness connector. Measure resistance between ground and terminal No. 2H (Red/Green wire) on PCM harness connector. If resistance is 9-18 ohms at 68°F (20°C), go to step **6)**. If resistance is not 9-18 ohms at 68°F (20°C), go to next step.

4) Inspect pressure control solenoid. See appropriate SOLENOID VALVES under COMPONENT TESTING. Repair as needed. If solenoid valve is okay, go to next step.

5) Check continuity of circuits between pressure control solenoid and PCM. See appropriate wiring diagram in WIRING DIAGRAMS. Repair as needed. If circuits are okay, go to next step.

6) Disconnect negative battery cable for at least 20 seconds. Depress brake pedal. Reconnect negative battery cable. Road test vehicle. Retrieve DTC's. If DTC P0745 is still present, replace TCM. If code is no longer present, problem may be caused by poor connection. Repair as needed.

DTC P0750: SHIFT SOLENOID "A" MALFUNCTION (1995 MILLENIA)

Possible Causes:
- Short or open circuit between PCM and solenoid.
- TCM malfunction.
- Shift solenoid malfunction.

Diagnosis & Repair Procedure – **1)** Ensure all appropriate connections are clean and tight. Repair as needed. Turn ignition on. Access TCM connectors. Using voltmeter, backprobe harness connectors. Do not disconnect connectors. Go to next step.

2) Measure voltage between ground and terminal No. 2E on TCM connector. During test drive, voltage should be less than one volt when solenoid is off and battery voltage when solenoid is on. See appropriate SOLENOID OPERATION TABLE under PCM OR TCM OUTPUT DEVICES. If voltage is within specification, go to step **5)**. If voltage is not within specification, go to next step.

3) Turn ignition off. Disconnect TCM harness connector. Measure resistance between ground and terminal No. 2E. If resistance is 11-27 ohms at 68°F (20°C), go to step **5)**. If resistance is not 11-27 ohms at 68°F (20°C), go to next step.

4) Inspect shift solenoid "A" and related circuits. See appropriate SOLENOID VALVES under COMPONENT TESTING. Repair as needed. If solenoid valve and related circuits are okay, go to next step.

5) Disconnect negative battery cable for at least 20 seconds. Depress brake pedal. Reconnect negative battery cable. Road test vehicle. Retrieve DTC's. If DTC P0750 is still present, replace TCM. If code is no longer present, problem may be caused by poor connection. Repair as needed.

DTC P0750: SHIFT SOLENOID "A" MALFUNCTION (1996 MILLENIA, MX6, 626 & 1995-96 PROTEGE)

Possible Causes:
- Short or open circuit between PCM and solenoid.
- PCM malfunction.
- Shift solenoid malfunction.

Diagnosis & Repair Procedure – **1)** Ensure all appropriate connections are clean and tight. Repair as needed. Turn ignition on. Access PCM connectors. Using voltmeter, backprobe harness connectors. Do not disconnect connectors. Go to next step.

2) Measure voltage between ground and terminal No. 2A on PCM connector. During test drive voltage should be less than one volt when solenoid is off and battery voltage when solenoid is on. See appropriate SOLENOID OPERATION TABLE under PCM OUTPUT DEVICES. If voltage is within specification, go to step **5)**. If voltage is not within specification, go to next step.

3) Turn ignition off. Disconnect PCM harness connector. Measure resistance between ground and terminal No. 2A. If resistance is 11-27 ohms at 68°F (20°C), go to step **5)**. If resistance is not 11-27 ohms at 68°F (20°C), go to next step.

4) Inspect shift solenoid "A" and related circuits. See appropriate SOLENOID VALVES under COMPONENT TESTING. Repair as needed. If solenoid valve and related circuits are okay, go to next step.

5) Disconnect negative battery cable for at least 20 seconds. Depress brake pedal. Reconnect negative battery cable. Road test vehicle. Retrieve DTC's. If DTC P0750 is still present, replace PCM. If code is no longer present, problem may be caused by poor connection. Repair as needed.

DTC P0755: SHIFT SOLENOID "B" MALFUNCTION (1995 MILLENIA)

Possible Causes:
- Short or open circuit between TCM and solenoid.
- PCM malfunction.
- Shift solenoid malfunction.

Diagnosis & Repair Procedure – **1)** Ensure all appropriate connections are clean and tight. Repair as needed. Turn ignition on. Using voltmeter, backprobe TCM harness connector. Do not disconnect connector. Test drive vehicle.

2) Measure voltage between ground and terminal No. 2G on TCM harness connector. During test drive voltage should be zero volts when solenoid is off and battery voltage when solenoid is on. See appropriate SOLENOID OPERATION TABLE under TCM OUTPUT DEVICES. If voltage is within specification, go to step **5)**. If voltage is not within specification, go to next step.

3) Turn ignition off. Disconnect TCM harness connector. Measure resistance between ground and terminal No. 2G. If resistance is 11-27 ohms at 68°F (20°C), go to step **5)**. If resistance is not 11-27 ohms at 68°F (20°C), go to next step.

4) Inspect shift solenoid "B" and related circuits. See appropriate SOLENOID VALVES under COMPONENT TESTING. Repair as needed. If solenoid valve and related circuits are okay, go to next step.

5) Disconnect negative battery cable for at least 20 seconds. Depress brake pedal. Reconnect negative battery cable. Road test vehicle. Retrieve DTC's. If DTC P0755 is still present, replace TCM. If code is no longer present, problem may be caused by poor connection. Repair as needed.

3-878

AUTOMATIC TRANSMISSIONS
Mazda FA4A-EL & GF4A-EL Electronic Controls (Cont.)

DTC P0755: SHIFT SOLENOID "B" MALFUNCTION (1996 MILLENIA, MX6, 626 & 1995-96 PROTEGE)

Possible Causes:
- Short or open circuit between PCM and solenoid.
- PCM malfunction.
- Shift solenoid malfunction.

Diagnosis & Repair Procedure – 1) Ensure all appropriate connections are clean and tight. Repair as needed. Turn ignition on. Using voltmeter, backprobe PCM harness connector. Do not disconnect connector. Test drive vehicle.

2) Measure voltage between ground and terminal No. 2B on PCM harness connector. During test drive voltage should be zero volts when solenoid is off and battery voltage when solenoid is on. See appropriate SOLENOID OPERATION TABLE under PCM OR TCM OUTPUT DEVICES. If voltage is within specification, go to step **5)**. If voltage is not within specification, go to next step.

3) Turn ignition off. Disconnect PCM harness connector. Measure resistance between ground and terminal No. 2B. If resistance is 11-27 ohms at 68°F (20°C), go to step **5)**. If resistance is not 11-27 ohms at 68°F (20°C), go to next step.

4) Inspect shift solenoid "B" and related circuits. See appropriate SOLENOID VALVES under COMPONENT TESTING. Repair as needed. If solenoid valve and related circuits are okay, go to next step.

5) Disconnect negative battery cable for at least 20 seconds. Depress brake pedal. Reconnect negative battery cable. Road test vehicle. Retrieve DTC's. If DTC P0755 is still present, replace PCM. If code is no longer present, problem may be caused by poor connection. Repair as needed.

DTC P0760: SHIFT SOLENOID "C" MALFUNCTION (1995 MILLENIA)

Possible Causes:
- Short or open circuit between TCM and solenoid.
- TCM malfunction.
- Shift solenoid malfunction.

Diagnosis & Repair Procedure – 1) Ensure all appropriate connections are clean and tight. Repair as needed. Turn ignition on. Using voltmeter, backprobe TCM harness connector. Do not disconnect connector. Test drive vehicle.

2) Measure voltage between ground and terminal No. 2I on TCM harness connector. During test drive voltage should be zero volts when solenoid is off and battery voltage when solenoid is on. See appropriate SOLENOID OPERATION TABLE under PCM OR TCM OUTPUT DEVICES. If voltage is within specification, go to step **5)**. If voltage is not within specification, go to next step.

3) Turn ignition off. Disconnect TCM harness connector. Measure resistance between ground and terminal No. 2I. If resistance is 11-27 ohms at 68°F (20°C), go to step **5)**. If resistance is not 11-27 ohms at 68°F (20°C), go to next step.

4) Inspect shift solenoid "C" and related circuits. See appropriate SOLENOID VALVES under COMPONENT TESTING. Repair as needed. If solenoid valve and related circuits are okay, go to next step.

5) Disconnect negative battery cable for at least 20 seconds. Depress brake pedal. Reconnect negative battery cable. Road test vehicle. Retrieve DTC's. If DTC P0760 is still present, replace TCM. If code is no longer present, problem may be caused by poor connection. Repair as needed.

DTC P0760: SHIFT SOLENOID "C" MALFUNCTION (1996 MILLENIA, MX6 & 626)

Possible Causes:
- Short or open circuit between PCM and solenoid.
- PCM malfunction.
- Shift solenoid malfunction.

Diagnosis & Repair Procedure – 1) Ensure all appropriate connections are clean and tight. Repair as needed. Turn ignition on. Using voltmeter, backprobe PCM harness connector. Do not disconnect connector. Test drive vehicle.

2) Measure voltage between ground and terminal No. 2F on PCM harness connector. During test drive voltage should be zero volts when solenoid is off and battery voltage when solenoid is on. See appropriate SOLENOID OPERATION TABLE under PCM OUTPUT DEVICES. If voltage is within specification, go to step **5)**. If voltage is not within specification, go to next step.

3) Turn ignition off. Disconnect PCM harness connector. Measure resistance between ground and terminal No. 2F. If resistance is 11-27 ohms at 68°F (20°C), go to step **5)**. If resistance is not 11-27 ohms at 68°F (20°C), go to next step.

4) Inspect shift solenoid "C" and related circuits. See appropriate SOLENOID VALVES under COMPONENT TESTING. Repair as needed. If solenoid valve and related circuits are okay, go to next step.

5) Disconnect negative battery cable for at least 20 seconds. Depress brake pedal. Reconnect negative battery cable. Road test vehicle. Retrieve DTC's. If DTC P0760 is still present, replace PCM. If code is no longer present, problem may be caused by poor connection. Repair as needed.

DTC P0760: SHIFT SOLENOID "C" MALFUNCTION (1995-96 PROTEGE)

Possible Causes:
- Short or open circuit between PCM and solenoid.
- PCM malfunction.
- Shift solenoid malfunction.

Diagnosis & Repair Procedure – 1) Ensure all appropriate connections are clean and tight. Repair as needed. Turn ignition on. Using voltmeter, backprobe PCM harness connector. Do not disconnect connector. Test drive vehicle.

2) Measure voltage between ground and terminal No. 2C (Orange wire) on PCM harness connector. During test drive voltage should be zero volts when solenoid is off and battery voltage when solenoid is on. See appropriate SOLENOID OPERATION TABLE under PCM OUTPUT DEVICES. If voltage is within specification, go to step **5)**. If voltage is not within specification, go to next step.

3) Turn ignition off. Disconnect PCM harness connector. Measure resistance between ground and terminal No. 2C. If resistance is 13-27 ohms at 68°F (20°C), go to step **5)**. If resistance is not 11-27 ohms at 68°F (20°C), go to next step.

4) Inspect shift solenoid "C" and related circuits. See appropriate SOLENOID VALVES under COMPONENT TESTING. Repair as needed. If solenoid valve and related circuits are okay, go to next step.

5) Disconnect negative battery cable for at least 20 seconds. Depress brake pedal. Reconnect negative battery cable. Road test vehicle. Retrieve DTC's. If DTC P0760 is still present, replace PCM. If code is no longer present, problem may be caused by poor connection. Repair as needed.

DTC P1720: SPEEDOMETER SENSOR MALFUNCTION

Condition – Speedometer sensor signal is not input to TCM when reverse and forward drum speed is over 600 RPM and shift selector is in "D", "S" or "L" position. Possible causes are:
- Speedometer sensor malfunction.
- Vehicle speed sensor malfunction.
- Damaged circuits or connectors between sensors and TCM.

Diagnosis & Repair – 1) Ensure all appropriate connections are clean and tight. Repair as needed. Turn ignition on. Using voltmeter, backprobe TCM harness connector. Do not disconnect connector. Test drive vehicle.

2) Measure voltage between ground and terminal No. 1P (Green/Red wire) on TCM harness connector. During test drive voltage should be 2-3 volts or 4-5 volts when parked. If voltage is within specifications, go to step **6)**. If voltage is not within specifications, go to next step.

3) Turn ignition off. Disconnect negative battery cable. Remove instrument cluter. Disconnect TCM harness connectors. Check continuity of Green/Red wire between terminal No. 1P on TCM connector and terminal No. 2K on instrument cluster harness center connector. Repair as needed. If continuity exists, go to next step.

AUTOMATIC TRANSMISSIONS
Mazda FA4A-EL & GF4A-EL Electronic Controls (Cont.)

3-879

4) Raise and support front of vehicle. Using voltmeter, measure voltage between terminals No. 2D (Blue/Red wire) and 2H (Red/Black wire) on instrument cluster center connector. Rotate front wheels. If voltage pulse is present, go to step **6)**. If voltage pulse is not present, go to next step.

5) Inspect vehicle speed sensor. See VEHICLE SPEED SENSOR under COMPONENT TESTING. Replace as needed. If vehicle speed sensor is okay, inspect circuits between vehicle speed sensor and instrument cluster. See appropriate wiring diagram under WIRING DIAGRAMS. Repair as needed. If circuits are okay between sensor and instrument cluster, replace insturment cluster.

6) Disconnect negative battery cable for at least 20 seconds. Depress brake pedal. Reconnect negative battery cable. Road test vehicle. Retrieve DTC's. If DTC P1720 is still present, replace TCM. If code is no longer present, problem may be caused by poor connection. Repair as needed.

DTC P1743: TORQUE CONVERTER CLUTCH (TCC) CONTROL SOLENOID MALFUNCTION (1995 MILLENIA)

Possible Causes:
- Short or open circuit between TCM and solenoid.
- TCM malfunction.
- TCC control solenoid malfunction.

Diagnosis & Repair Procedure – 1) Ensure all connections are clean and tight. Repair as needed. Turn ignition on. Access TCM connectors. Using voltmeter, backprobe harness connectors. Do not disconnect connectors. Go to next step.

2) Measure voltage between ground and terminal No. 2K. Battery voltage should be present with solenoid on and zero voltage with solenoid off. If voltage is within specifications, go to step **5)**. If voltage is not within specifications, go to next step.

3) Turn ignition off. Disconnect TCM harness connector. Measure resistance between ground and terminal No. 2K. If resistance is 11-27 ohms at 68°F (20°C), go to step **5)**. If resistance is not 11-27 ohms at 68°F (20°C), go to next step.

4) Inspect torque converter clutch solenoid and related circuits. See appropriate SOLENOID VALVES under COMPONENT TESTING. Repair as needed. If solenoid valve and related circuits are okay, go to next step.

5) Disconnect negative battery cable for at least 20 seconds. Depress brake pedal. Reconnect negative battery cable. Road test vehicle. Retrieve DTC's. If DTC P1743 is still present, replace TCM. If code is no longer present, problem may be caused by poor connection. Repair as needed.

DTC P1743: TORQUE CONVERTER CLUTCH (TCC) CONTROL SOLENOID MALFUNCTION (1996 MILLENIA, MX6 & 626)

Possible Causes:
- Short or open circuit between PCM and solenoid.
- PCM malfunction.
- TCC control solenoid malfunction.

Diagnosis & Repair Procedure – 1) Ensure all connections are clean and tight. Repair as needed. Turn ignition on. Access PCM connectors. Using voltmeter, backprobe harness connectors. Do not disconnect connectors. Go to next step.

2) Measure voltage between ground and terminal No. 2C (Blue/White wire). Battery voltage should be present with solenoid on and zero voltage with solenoid off. If voltage is within specifications, go to step **5)**. If voltage is not within specifications, go to next step.

3) Turn ignition off. Disconnect PCM harness connector. Measure resistance between ground and terminal No. 2C. If resistance is 11-27 ohms at 68°F (20°C), go to step **5)**. If resistance is not 11-27 ohms at 68°F (20°C), go to next step.

4) Inspect torque converter clutch solenoid and related circuits. See appropriate SOLENOID VALVES under COMPONENT TESTING. Repair as needed. If solenoid valve and related circuits are okay, go to next step.

5) Disconnect negative battery cable for at least 20 seconds. Depress brake pedal. Reconnect negative battery cable. Road test vehicle. Retrieve DTC's. If DTC P1743 is still present, replace PCM. If code is no longer present, problem may be caused by poor connection. Repair as needed.

DTC P1743: TORQUE CONVERTER CLUTCH (TCC) CONTROL SOLENOID MALFUNCTION (1995-96 PROTEGE)

Possible Causes:
- Short or open circuit between PCM and solenoid.
- PCM malfunction.
- TCC control solenoid malfunction.

Diagnosis & Repair Procedure – 1) Ensure all appropriate connections are clean and tight. Repair as needed. Turn ignition on. Access PCM connectors. Using voltmeter, backprobe harness connectors. Do not disconnect connectors. Go to next step.

2) Measure voltage between ground and terminal No. 2D (Brown/White wire). Battery voltage should be present with solenoid on and zero voltage with solenoid off. If voltage is within specifications, go to step **5)**. If voltage is not within specifications, go to next step.

3) Turn ignition off. Disconnect PCM harness connector. Measure resistance between ground and terminal No. 2C. If resistance is 13-27 ohms at 68°F (20°C), go to step **5)**. If resistance is not 11-27 ohms at 68°F (20°C), go to next step.

4) Inspect torque converter clutch solenoid and related circuits. See appropriate SOLENOID VALVES under COMPONENT TESTING. Repair as needed. If solenoid valve and related circuits are okay, go to next step.

5) Disconnect negative battery cable for at least 20 seconds. Depress brake pedal. Reconnect negative battery cable. Road test vehicle. Retrieve DTC's. If DTC P1743 is still present, replace PCM. If code is no longer present, problem may be caused by poor connection. Repair as needed.

DTC P1744: TORQUE CONVERTER CLUTCH (TCC) SOLENOID VALVE MALFUNCTION (1995 MILLENIA)

Possible Causes:
- Short or open circuit between TCM and solenoid.
- TCM malfunction.
- TCC solenoid valve malfunction.

Diagnosis & Repair Procedure – 1) Ensure all appropriate connections are clean and tight. Repair as needed. Turn ignition on. Access TCM connectors. Using voltmeter, backprobe harness connectors. Do not disconnect connectors. Go to next step.

2) Measure voltage between ground and terminal No. 2C. Battery voltage should be present with solenoid on and zero voltage with solenoid off. If voltage is within specifications, go to step **5)**. If voltage is not within specifications, go to next step.

3) Turn ignition off. Disconnect TCM harness connector. Measure resistance between ground and terminal No. 2C. If resistance is 9-18 ohms at 68°F (20°C), go to step **5)**. If resistance is not 9-18 ohms at 68°F (20°C), go to next step.

4) Inspect torque converter clutch solenoid and related circuits. See appropriate SOLENOID VALVES under COMPONENT TESTING. Repair as needed. If solenoid valve and related circuits are okay, go to next step.

5) Disconnect negative battery cable for at least 20 seconds. Depress brake pedal. Reconnect negative battery cable. Road test vehicle. Retrieve DTC's. If DTC P1744 is still present, replace TCM. If code is no longer present, problem may be caused by poor connection. Repair as needed.

3-880

AUTOMATIC TRANSMISSIONS
Mazda FA4A-EL & GF4A-EL Electronic Controls (Cont.)

DTC P1744: TORQUE CONVERTER CLUTCH (TCC) SOLENOID VALVE MALFUNCTION (1996 MILLENIA, MX6 & 626)

Possible Causes:
- Short or open circuit between PCM and solenoid.
- PCM malfunction.
- TCC solenoid valve malfunction.

Diagnosis & Repair Procedure – 1) Ensure all appropriate connections are clean and tight. Repair as needed. Turn ignition on. Access PCM connectors. Using voltmeter, backprobe harness connectors. Do not disconnect connectors. Go to next step.
2) Measure voltage between ground and terminal No. 2D. Battery voltage should be present with solenoid on and zero volts with solenoid off. If voltage is within specifications, go to step 5). If voltage is not within specifications, go to next step.
3) Turn ignition off. Disconnect PCM harness connector. Measure resistance between ground and terminal No. 2D. If resistance is 9-18 ohms at 68°F (20°C), go to step 5). If resistance is not 9-18 ohms at 68°F (20°C), go to next step.
4) Inspect torque converter clutch solenoid and related circuits. See appropriate SOLENOID VALVES under COMPONENT TESTING. Repair as needed. If solenoid valve and related circuits are okay, go to next step.
5) Disconnect negative battery cable for at least 20 seconds. Depress brake pedal. Reconnect negative battery cable. Road test vehicle. Retrieve DTC's. If DTC P1744 is still present, replace TCM. If code is no longer present, problem may be caused by poor connection. Repair as needed.

DTC P1765: 3-2 TIMING SOLENOID VALVE MALFUNCTION (1995 MILLENIA)

Possible Causes:
- Short or open circuit between PCM or TCM and solenoid.
- TCM malfunction.
- TCC control solenoid malfunction.

Diagnosis & Repair Procedure – 1) Ensure all appropriate connections are clean and tight. Repair as needed. Turn ignition on. Access TCM connectors. Using voltmeter, backprobe harness connectors. Do not disconnect connectors. Go to next step.
2) Measure voltage between ground and terminal No. 2M. Battery voltage should be present with solenoid on and zero volts with solenoid off. If voltage is within specifications, go to step 5). If voltage is not within specifications, go to next step.
3) Turn ignition off. Disconnect TCM harness connector. Measure resistance between ground and terminal No. 2M. If resistance is 11-27 ohms at 68°F (20°C), go to step 5). If resistance is not 11-27 ohms at 68°F (20°C), go to next step.
4) Inspect 3-2 timing solenoid and related circuits. See appropriate SOLENOID VALVES under COMPONENT TESTING. Repair as needed. If solenoid valve and related circuits are okay, go to next step.
5) Disconnect negative battery cable for at least 20 seconds. Depress brake pedal. Reconnect negative battery cable. Road test vehicle. Retrieve DTC's. If DTC P1765 is still present, replace TCM. If code is no longer present, problem may be caused by poor connection. Repair as needed.

DTC P1765: 3-2 TIMING SOLENOID VALVE MALFUNCTION (1996 MILLENIA, MX6 & 626)

Possible Causes:
- Short or open circuit between PCM and solenoid.
- PCM malfunction.
- 3-2 timing solenoid malfunction.

Diagnosis & Repair Procedure – 1) Ensure all appropriate connections are clean and tight. Repair as needed. Turn ignition on. Access PCM connectors. Using voltmeter, backprobe harness connectors. Do not disconnect connectors. Go to next step.
2) Measure voltage between ground and terminal No. 2G (Red/White wire). Battery voltage should be present with solenoid on and zero volts with solenoid off. If voltage is within specifications, go to step 5). If voltage is not within specifications, go to next step.
3) Turn ignition off. Disconnect PCM harness connector. Measure resistance between ground and terminal No. 2G. If resistance is 11-27 ohms at 68°F (20°C), go to step 5). If resistance is not 11-27 ohms at 68°F (20°C), go to next step.
4) Inspect 3-2 timing solenoid and related circuits. See appropriate SOLENOID VALVES under COMPONENT TESTING. Repair as needed. If solenoid valve and related circuits are okay, go to next step.
5) Disconnect negative battery cable for at least 20 seconds. Depress brake pedal. Reconnect negative battery cable. Road test vehicle. Retrieve DTC's. If DTC P1765 is still present, replace PCM. If code is no longer present, problem may be caused by poor connection. Repair as needed.

DTC P1775: REDUCE TORQUE SIGNAL NO. 1

Condition – Open or short in reduce torque signal No. 1 circuit. Possible causes are:
- Circuit fault between ECM and TCM.

Diagnosis & Repair Procedure – 1) Ensure all appropriate connections are clean and tight. Repair as needed. Turn ignition on. Access TCM connectors. Using voltmeter, backprobe harness connectors. Do not disconnect connectors. Go to next step.
2) Test drive vehicle. Measure voltage between ground and terminal No. 1J (Green/Yellow wire) on TCM harness connector. During 1-2 or 2-3 shift, or with 3/8 throttle or greater, voltage should be one volt or less. During any other operating condition, battery voltage should exist. If voltage is within specification, go to step 4). If voltage is not within specification, go to next step.
3) Turn ignition off. Disconnect TCM harness connector. Disconnect Electronic Control Module (ECM) harness connectors. Check continuity of Green/Yellow wire between terminal No. 1R on ECM harness connector and terminal No. 1J on TCM harness connector. Repair as needed. If continuity exists, go to next step.
4) Disconnect negative battery cable for at least 20 seconds. Depress brake pedal. Reconnect negative battery cable. Road test vehicle. Retrieve DTC's. If DTC P1775 is still present, replace TCM. If code is no longer present, problem may be caused by poor connection. Repair as needed.

DTC P1776: REDUCE TORQUE SIGNAL NO. 2

Condition – Open or short in reduce torque signal No. 2 circuit. Possible causes are:
- Circuit fault between ECM and TCM.

Diagnosis & Repair Procedure – 1) Ensure all appropriate connections are clean and tight. Repair as needed. Turn ignition on. Access TCM connectors. Using voltmeter, backprobe harness connectors. Do not disconnect connectors. Go to next step.
2) Test drive vehicle. Measure voltage between ground and terminal No. 1L (Orange/Black wire) on TCM harness connector. During 4-3, 4-2, 4-1, 3-2, 3-1 or 2-1 shift, or with 1/8 throttle or greater, voltage should be one volt or less. During any other operating condition, battery voltage should exist. If voltage is within specification, go to step 4). If voltage is not within specification, go to next step.
3) Turn ignition off. Disconnect TCM harness connector. Disconnect Electronic Control Module (ECM) harness connectors. Check continuity of Orange/Black wire between terminal No. 1S on ECM harness connector and terminal No. 1L on TCM harness connector. Repair as needed. If continuity exists, go to next step.
4) Disconnect negative battery cable for at least 20 seconds. Depress brake pedal. Reconnect negative battery cable. Road test vehicle. Retrieve DTC's. If DTC P1776 is still present, replace TCM. If code is no longer present, problem may be caused by poor connection. Repair as needed.

AUTOMATIC TRANSMISSIONS
Mazda FA4A-EL & GF4A-EL Electronic Controls (Cont.)

3-881

DTC P1777: TORQUE REDUCED/COOLANT TEMP SIGNAL

Condition – Open or short in torque reduce signal/engine coolant temperature signal. Possible causes are:
- Circuit fault between ECM and TCM.

Diagnosis & Repair Procedure – 1) Ensure all appropriate connections are clean and tight. Repair as needed. Turn ignition on. Access TCM connectors. Using voltmeter, backprobe harness connectors. Do not disconnect connectors. Go to next step. Start and idle engine.
2) Measure voltage between ground and terminal No. 1K (Yellow/Blue wire) on TCM harness connector. With engine coolant temperature of 140°F (60°C) or greater, battery voltage should exist. With engine coolant temperature of 140°F (60°C) or less, voltage should be one volt or less. If voltage is within specification, go to step 4). If voltage is not within specification, go to next step.
3) Turn ignition off. Disconnect TCM harness connector. Disconnect Electronic Control Module (ECM) harness connectors. Check continuity of Yellow/Blue wire between terminal No. 1K on ECM harness connector and terminal No. 1K on TCM harness connector. Repair as needed. If continuity exists, go to next step.
4) Disconnect negative battery cable for at least 20 seconds. Depress brake pedal. Reconnect negative battery cable. Road test vehicle. Retrieve DTC's. If DTC P1777 is still present, replace TCM. If code is no longer present, problem may be caused by poor connection. Repair as needed.

DTC P1790: THROTTLE POSITION SENSOR MALFUNCTION

Condition – Open or short circuit. Possible causes are:
- Poor harness connection at TP sensor.
- Circuit fault between TP sensor and TCM.
- TP sensor.

Diagnosis & Repair Procedure – 1) Ensure all appropriate connections are clean and tight. Repair as needed. Turn ignition on. Access TCM connectors. Using voltmeter, backprobe harness connectors. Do not disconnect connectors. Go to next step.
2) Measure voltage between ground and terminal No. 2T (Yellow wire) on TCM harness connector. With throttle closed, voltage should be .1-1.one volts. With wide open throttle, voltage should be 3.1-4.4 volts. If voltage is within specification, go to step 7). If voltage is not within specification, go to next step.
3) Measure voltage between ground and terminal No. 2A (Light Green/Red wire) on TCM harness connector. With ignition on, voltage should be 4.5-5.5 volts. With ignition off, voltage should be zero volts. If voltage is within specification, go to step 7). If voltage is not within specification, go to next step.
4) Access ECM connectors. Using voltmeter, backprobe harness connectors. Do not disconnect connectors. Measure voltage between ground and terminal No. 3I (Gray/Red wire) on ECM harness connector. With ignition on, voltage should be 4.5-5.5 volts. With ignition off, voltage should be zero volts. If voltage is within specification, go to step 7). If voltage is not within specification, go to next step.
5) Turn ignition switch to OFF position. Disconnect Throttle Position (TP) sensor harness connector. Measure resistance between specified component terminals. See appropriate SYSTEM & COMPONENT TESTING article in ENGINE PERFORMANCE of appropriate MITCHELL® manual. Replace as needed. If TP sensor is okay, go to next step.
6) Inspect circuits between TP sensor and TCM. See appropriate wiring diagram under WIRING DIAGRAMS. Repair as needed. If circuits are okay between sensor and TCM, go to next step.
7) Disconnect negative battery cable for at least 20 seconds. Depress brake pedal. Reconnect negative battery cable. Road test vehicle. Retrieve DTC's. If DTC P1790 is still present, replace TCM. If code is no longer present, problem may be caused by poor connection. Repair as needed.

DTC P1792: CLOSED THROTTLE POSITION SWITCH

Condition – Closed throttle position switch is on, voltage is more than 1.5 volts and Throttle Position (TP) sensor is functioning correctly. Possible causes are:
- Short circuit in TP sensor.
- Closed TP sensor malfunction.

Diagnosis & Repair Procedure – 1) Ensure all connections are clean and tight. Repair as needed. Turn ignition on. Access TCM connectors. Using voltmeter, backprobe harness connectors. Do not disconnect connectors. Go to next step.
2) Measure voltage between ground and terminal No. 1O (Brown wire) on TCM harness connector. With throttle closed, voltage should be zero volts. With wide open throttle, voltage should be battery volts. If voltage is within specification, go to step 6). If voltage is not within specification, go to next step.
3) Turn ignition off. Disconnect TCM harness connector. Check continuity between ground and terminal No. 1O (Brown wire) on TCM harness connector. With throttle closed, continuity should exist. With wide open throttle, continuity should not exist. If continuity is as specified, go to step 6). If continuity is not as specified, go to next step.
4) Turn ignition switch to OFF position. Disconnect Throttle Position (TP) sensor harness connector. Check continuity between specified component terminals. See appropriate SYSTEM & COMPONENT TESTING article in ENGINE PERFORMANCE of appropriate MITCHELL® manual. Replace as needed. If closed TP sensor is okay, go to next step.
5) Inspect circuits between TP sensor and TCM. See appropriate wiring diagram under WIRING DIAGRAMS. Repair as needed. If circuits are okay between sensor and TCM, go to next step.
6) Disconnect negative battery cable for at least 20 seconds. Depress brake pedal. Reconnect negative battery cable. Road test vehicle. Retrieve DTC's. If DTC P1792 is still present, replace TCM. If code is no longer present, problem may be caused by poor connection. Repair as needed.

DTC P1795: EGR BOOST SENSOR

Condition – Open or short circuit in system wiring. Possible causes are:
- ECM malfunction.
- TCM malfunction.
- Damaged wiring or connectors between ECM and TCM.

Diagnosis & Repair Procedure – 1) Ensure all appropriate connections are clean and tight. Repair as needed. Turn ignition on. Access TCM connectors. Using voltmeter, backprobe harness connectors. Do not disconnect connectors. Go to next step.
2) Measure voltage between ground and terminal No. 2R (Violet/Yellow wire) on TCM harness connector. With barometric pressure at 30 In. Hg (101 kPa), voltage should be about 4 volts. If voltage is within specification, go to step 6). If voltage is not within specification, go to next step.
3) Turn ignition off. Disconnect TCM harness connector. Disconnect Electronic Control Module (ECM) harness connectors. Check continuity of Violet/Yellow wire between terminal No. 3H on ECM harness connector and terminal No. 2R on TCM harness connector. Repair as needed. If continuity exists, go to next step.
4) Disconnect negative battery cable for at least 20 seconds. Depress brake pedal. Reconnect negative battery cable. Road test vehicle. Retrieve DTC's. If DTC P1795 is still present, replace TCM. If code is no longer present, problem may be caused by poor connection. Repair as needed.

COMPONENT TESTING

NOTE: For connector terminal identification, see COMPONENT CONNECTOR IDENTIFICATION table. For circuit or wire color identification, see appropriate wiring diagram in WIRING DIAGRAMS.

3-882

AUTOMATIC TRANSMISSIONS
Mazda FA4A-EL & GF4A-EL Electronic Controls (Cont.)

BRAKELIGHT SWITCH

MX6 & 626 – 1) Turn ignition on. Using voltmeter, backprobe brakelight switch connector. Measure voltage between ground and terminal "A" (White/Green wire). See Fig. 17. With brake pedal depressed, battery voltage should be present. With brake pedal released, zero voltage should be present. If voltage is not within specification, go to next step. If voltage is within specification, inspect circuit between brakelight switch and PCM or TCM.

2) Disconnect brakelight switch connector. Using an ohmmeter, check for continuity between brakelight switch terminals "A" and "B". Continuity should only exist with pedal depressed. Replace as needed. If switch tests okay, inspect power and ground circuits. Repair as needed.

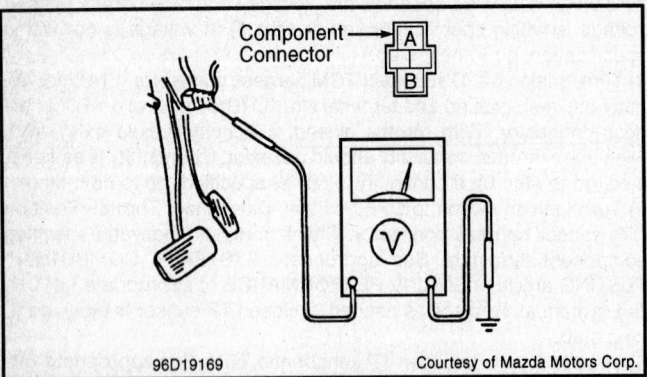

Fig. 17: Testing Brakelight Switch (MX6 & 626)

HOLD SWITCH

1) Turn ignition on. Ensure HOLD indicator illuminates with hold switch depressed. Ensure HOLD indicator is off when HOLD switch is released. If switch is not working as described, go to next step.

2) Remove center console to access switch connector. Disconnect connector. Check continuity between terminals "A" and "B". See Fig. 18 or 19. Continuity should exist when switch is depressed. When switch is released, continuity should not exist. Replace as needed. If HOLD switch system does not function correctly, inspect circuits between switch and TCM. See appropriate wiring diagram in WIRING DIAGRAMS.

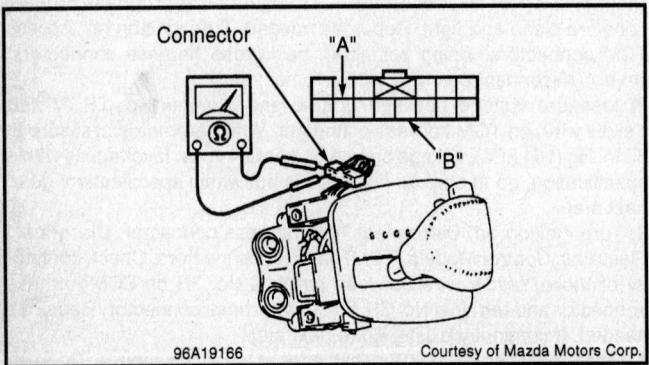

Fig. 18: Testing HOLD Or O/D OFF Switch (All Except MX3)

O/D OFF SWITCH

1) Remove center console to access switch connector. Turn ignition on. Using voltmeter, backprobe harness connector. With O/D OFF switch in released position, measure voltage between ground and terminal "A" (Brown/Black wire) on switch connector.

2) Battery voltage should be present. Depress switch. Zero volts should be present. If voltage is as specified, switch is functioning correctly. If voltage is not as specified, go to next step.

3) Turn ignition off. Disconnect O/D OFF switch harness connector. See Fig. 20. Check continuity between terminals "A" and "B" on switch connector. Continuity should exist with switch depressed. If continuity is as specified, switch is okay. Inspect circuits to ground and PCM or TCM. Repair as needed. If continuity is not as specified, replace switch.

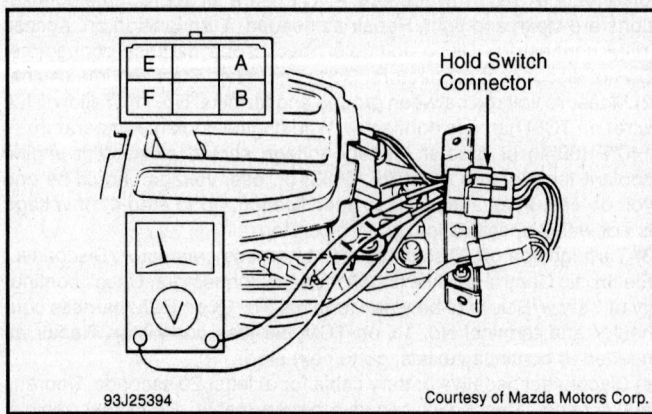

Fig. 19: Testing HOLD Switch (MX3)

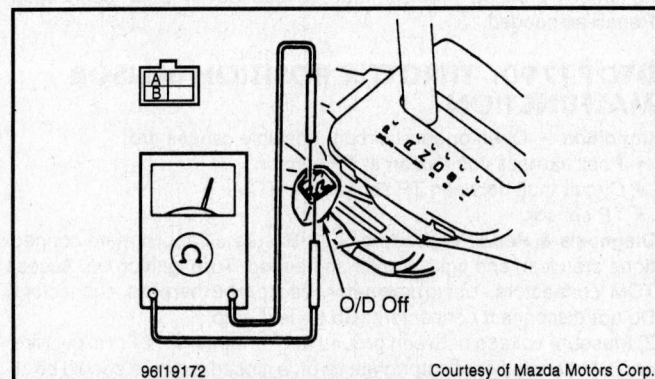

Fig. 20: Testing O/D OFF Switch (MX6, 626 & Protege)

SOLENOID VALVES (ON/OFF TYPE)

1) Disconnect negative battery cable. Disconnect transmission solenoid harness connector. Note that solenoids ground through transmission case. Check resistance between connector terminals and ground. See Fig. 21 or 22.

2) On FA4A-EL models, resistance should be 13-27 ohms at 68°F (20°C). On GF4A-EL models, resistance varies. See Fig. 22. Replace solenoids as necessary. Ensure transmission case is grounded. If resistance is okay on all solenoids, go to next step.

3) On all solenoids except TCC (Lockup) solenoid and pressure control solenoid, intermittently connect battery voltage to terminals of transmission solenoid harness connector and ground. An audible click should be heard from specified solenoid when voltage is applied. For TCC (Lockup) solenoid and pressure control solenoid, see SOLENOID VALVES (DUTY CYCLE TYPE).

SOLENOID VALVES (DUTY CYCLE TYPE)

Pressure Control Solenoid (Millenia, MX6 & 626) – 1) Backprobe TCM harness connector using dwell meter. Set dwell meter to 4-CYL position. Connect positive lead to terminal No. 2N (Red/Green wire) on 1995 model or terminal No. 2H (Red/Green wire) on 1996 model. Connect negative lead to ground.

2) Engage parking and service brakes. Start and idle engine. Place shift selector in "D". Verify duty ratio by depressing and releasing accelerator pedal. Dwell meter indicates OFF duty ratio. Dwell should

AUTOMATIC TRANSMISSIONS
Mazda FA4A-EL & GF4A-EL Electronic Controls (Cont.)

3-883

decrease as accelerator pedal is depressed (67 degress to about 23 degrees). If signal is as specified, check continuity of circuits between TCM and pressure control solenoid. Repair as needed. If circuits are okay, replace solenoid. If signal is not as specified, replace TCM.

TCC Lockup Solenoid (Millenia, MX6 & 626) – 1) Backprobe TCM harness connector using dwell meter. Set dwell meter to 4-CYL position. Connect positive lead to terminal No. 2C and negative lead to ground.

2) Test drive vehicle. Verify duty ratio by monitoring dwell meter during TCC engagement. Dwell meter indicates OFF duty ratio. Dwell should about 72 degrees when TCC lockup solenoid is operating (slip lockup). Once complete lockup is acheived, dwell should be zero.

3) If signal is as specified, check continuity of circuits between TCM and TCC lockup solenoid. Repair as needed. If circuits are okay, replace solenoid. If signal is not as specified, replace TCM.

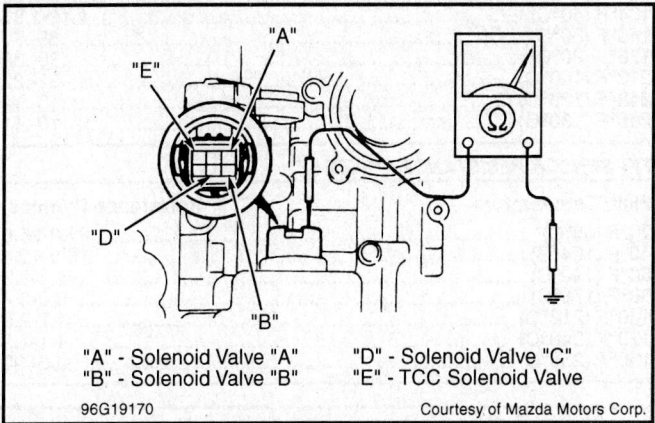

"A" - Solenoid Valve "A"   "D" - Solenoid Valve "C"
"B" - Solenoid Valve "B"   "E" - TCC Solenoid Valve

96G19170   Courtesy of Mazda Motors Corp.

Fig. 21: Identifying Solenoid Valve Terminals (FA4A-EL)

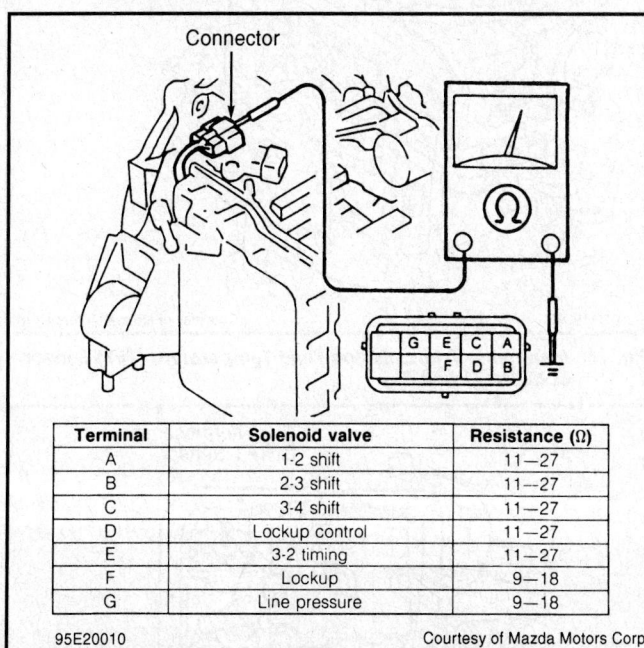

Terminal	Solenoid valve	Resistance (Ω)
A	1-2 shift	11—27
B	2-3 shift	11—27
C	3-4 shift	11—27
D	Lockup control	11—27
E	3-2 timing	11—27
F	Lockup	9—18
G	Line pressure	9—18

95E20010   Courtesy of Mazda Motors Corp.

Fig. 22: Identifying Solenoid Valve Terminals (GF4A-EL)

SPEEDOMETER SENSOR

1) Remove instrument cluster. Raise and support front of vehicle. Rotate front wheels. Measure voltage between specified terminals. See SPEEDOMETER SENSOR TERMINALS table.

2) Monitor voltage as wheels are rotated. If voltage pulse is present, go to next step. If voltage pulse is not present, inspect vehicle speed sensor. See VEHICLE SPEED SENSOR. Replace as needed. If vehicle

speed sensor is okay, repair circuits between vehicle speed sensor and speedometer sensor. Go to next step.

3) Ensure harness connector is connected to vehicle speed sensor. Turn ignition on. Rotate front wheels. Measure voltage between ground and specified terminal. See SPEEDOMETER OUTPUT CIRCUIT table. Monitor voltage as wheels are rotated. If voltage pulse is present, speedometer is currently functioning correctly. If voltage pulse is not present, replace combination meter or circuit board (as applicable).

SPEEDOMETER SENSOR TERMINALS

Model	Terminals
1995	
Millenia	[1] 2D & 2H
MX3	[2] 2I & 3G
MX6 & 626	[3] 1F & 1B
Protege	[2] 2G & 2J
1996	
Millenia	[1] 2D & 2H
MX6 & 626	[3] 1F & 1B
Protege	[2] 1F & 1B

[1] – See Fig. 23 for terminal locations.
[2] – See Fig. 24 for terminal locations.
[3] – See Fig. 25 for terminal locations.

SPEEDOMETER OUTPUT CIRCUIT

Model	TerminaL No.
1995	
Millenia	[1] 2K
MX3	[2] 2D
MX6 & 626	[3] 1H
Protege	[2] 2D
1996	
Millenia	[1] 2K
MX6 & 626	[3] 1H
Protege	[2] 2D

[1] – See Fig. 23 for terminal locations.
[2] – See Fig. 24 for terminal locations.
[3] – See Fig. 25 for terminal locations.

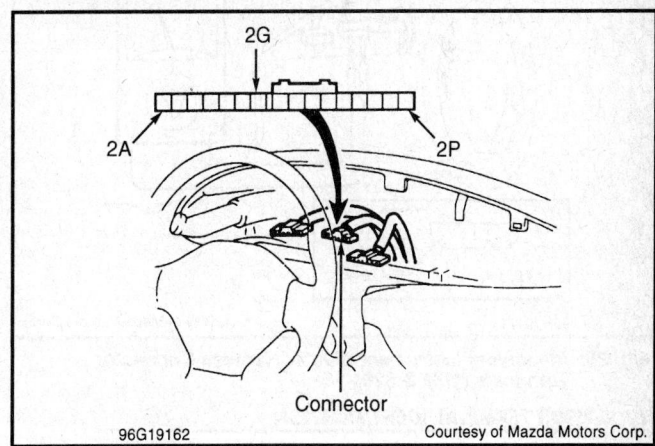

96G19162   Courtesy of Mazda Motors Corp.

Fig. 23: Identifying Instrument Cluster Harness Connector Terminals (Millenia)

TRANSMISSION FLUID TEMPERATURE (TFT) SENSOR

Remove valve body cover. Disconnect TFT sensor connector. Using appropriate sensor socket, remove TFT sensor. See Fig. 26 or 27. On 2-terminal connector, connect ohmmeter test leads to terminals. On multi-terminal connector, connect ohmmeter test leads to appropriate terminals. See TFT SENSOR TERMINAL IDENTIFICATION.

Place TFT sensor in container of ATF. Heat ATF and monitor ohmeter. Resistance should decrease as fluid temperature rises. See appropriate TFT SENSOR RESISTANCE table. If TFT sensor resistance is not within specification, replace TFT sensor.

3-884

AUTOMATIC TRANSMISSIONS
Mazda FA4A-EL & GF4A-EL Electronic Controls (Cont.)

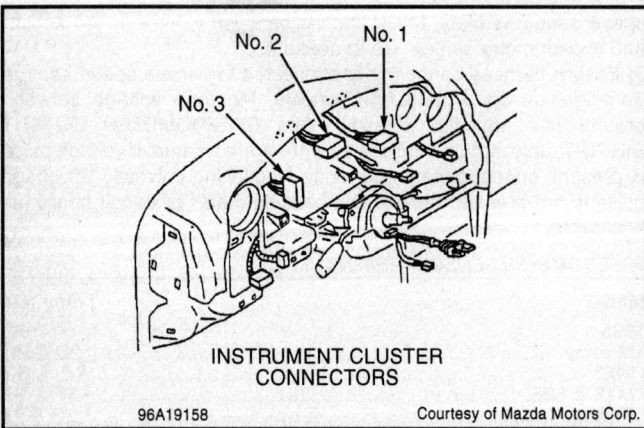

Fig. 24: Identifying Instrument Cluster Harness Connector Terminals (MX3 & Protege)

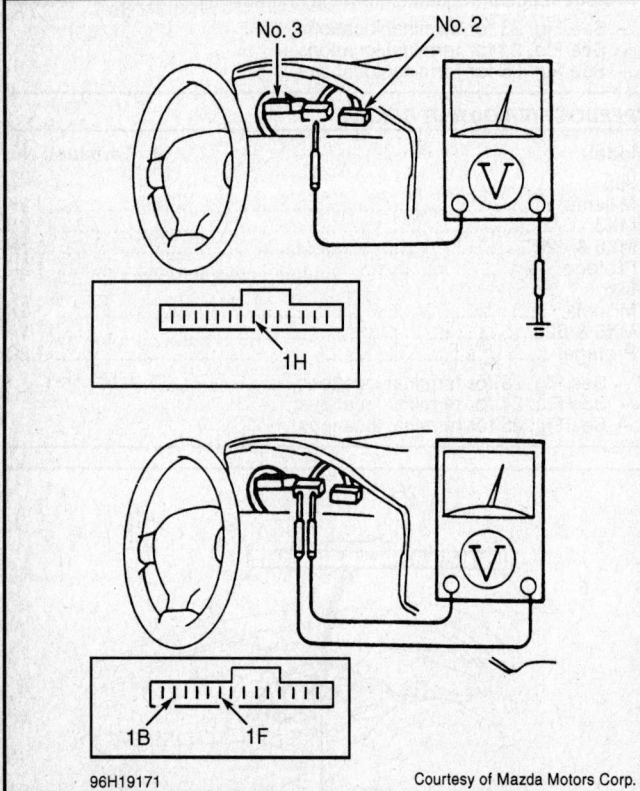

Fig. 25: Identifying Instrument Cluster Harness Connector Terminals (MX6 & 626)

TFT SENSOR TERMINAL IDENTIFICATION

Model	Terminals
MX-3 & Protege	[2] C & F
Millenia, MX-6 & 626	[1]

[1] – Uses a 2-pin connector. No identification is required.
[2] – See Fig. 28.

TFT SENSOR RESISTANCE (MX-3)

Fluid Temperature	Resistance (k/ohms)
-4°F (-20°C)	124.8-142.0
32°F (0°C)	52.0-57.4
68°F (20°C)	23.4-25.0
104°F (40°C)	11.1-12.1
140°F (60°C)	5.6-6.3
176°F (80°C)	3.0-3.4
212°F (100°C)	1.7-2.0
248°F (120°C)	1.1-1.2
266°F (130°C)	.86-.92

TFT SENSOR RESISTANCE (MILLENIA)

Fluid Temperature	Resistance (k/Ohms)
-20°F (-4°C)	15.55-17.56
0°F (32°C)	5.83-6.45
20°F (68°C)	2.50-2.72
40°F (104°C)	1.19-1.28
60°F (140°C)	.622-.658
80°F (176°C)	.349-.366
100°F (212°C)	.209-.216
120°F (248°C)	.131-.135
130°F (266°C)	.109-.108

TFT SENSOR RESISTANCE (MX-6 & 626)

Fluid Temperature	Resistance (k/ohms)
-4°F (-20°C)	13.47-17.17
32°F (0°C)	5.45-6.68
68°F (20°C)	2.44-2.89
104°F (40°C)	1.19-1.37
140°F (60°C)	.63-.70
176°F (80°C)	.35-.39
212°F (100°C)	.21-.22
248°F (120°C)	.13-.14
266°F (130°C)	.10-.11

TFT SENSOR RESISTANCE (PROTEGE)

Fluid Temperature	Resistance (k/ohms)
20°F (68°C)	21.0-25.0
40°F (104°C)	10.0-12.1
60°F (140°C)	5.4-6.3
80°F (176°C)	3.0-3.4
100°F (212°C)	1.7-2.0
120°F (248°C)	1.1-1.2
130°F (266°C)	.86-.92

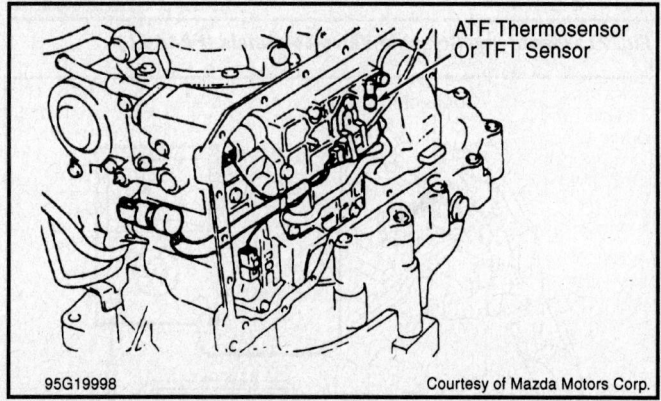

Fig. 26: Identifying Transmission Fluid Temperature (TFT) Sensor Location (FA4A-EL)

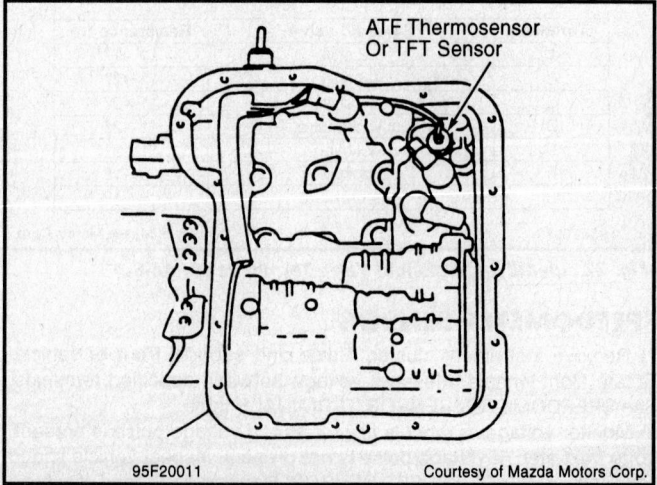

Fig. 27: Identifying Transmission Fluid Temperature (TFT) Sensor Location (GF4A-EL)

AUTOMATIC TRANSMISSIONS
Mazda FA4A-EL & GF4A-EL Electronic Controls (Cont.)

3-885

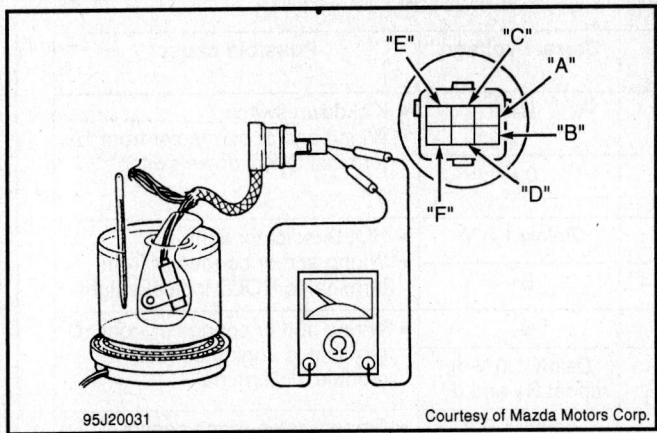

Fig. 28: Checking Transmission Fluid Temperature (TFT) Sensor

TRANSMISSION RANGE SWITCH

1) Check for starter operation with ignition switch in START position and selector lever in "P" and "N" position only. Ensure back-up lights illuminate with ignition in ON position and selector lever in "R". If any problems are found, go to next step.

2) Disconnect transmission range switch connector(s) and check continuity between specified terminals. See Fig. 29. If continuity is not as specified, replace switch.

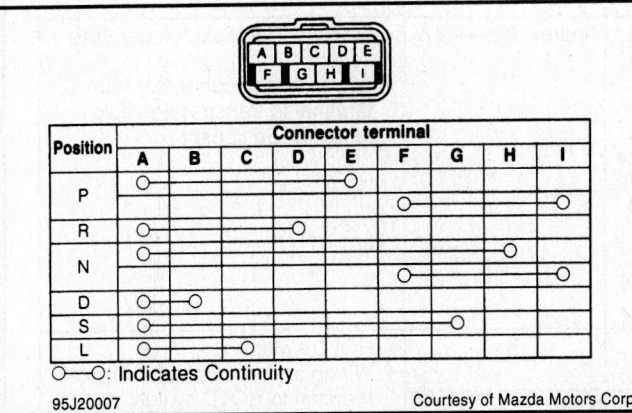

Fig. 29: Checking Transmission Range Switch

TURBINE SPEED SENSOR

1) Disconnect turbine speed sensor connector. Measure resistance between terminals. Resistance should be 253-604 ohms for Millenia, MX-6 and 626, and 200-400 ohms for MX3 and Protege. See Fig. 30. Replace as needed.

2) If lab ocilloscope is available, start and idle engine. Inspect turbine speed sensor waveform. See Fig. 30. Replace as needed.

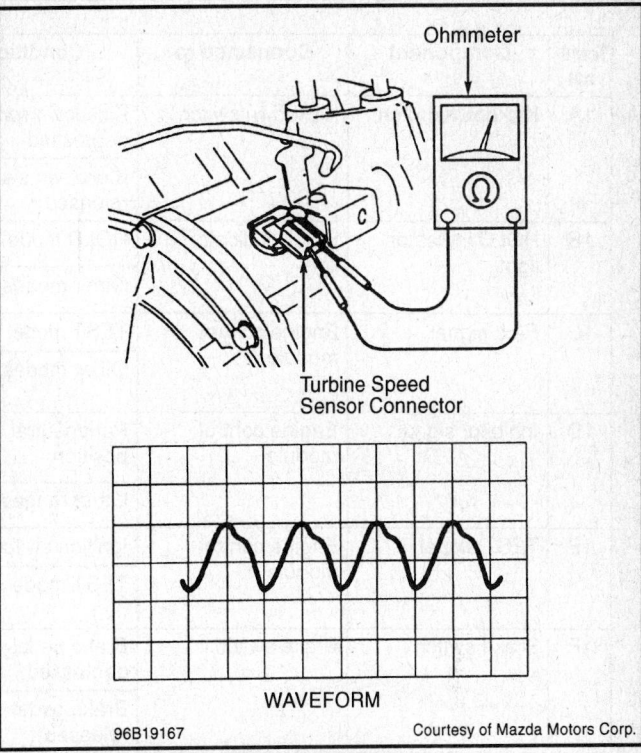

Fig. 30: Testing Turbine Speed Sensor (GF4A-EL Shown, FA4A-EL Similar)

VEHICLE SPEED SENSOR

NOTE: Vehicle speed sensor signal is input to speedometer sensor in combination meter than output to PCM or TCM (as applicable).

1) Disconnect negative battery cable. Disconnect vehicle speed sensor connector. Rotate front wheels and measure voltage between sensor terminals. See Fig. 31.

2) If voltmeter needle does not fluctuate, replace sensor. If voltmeter needle fluctuates, but signal to PCM or TCM is suspect, go to SPEEDOMETER SENSOR.

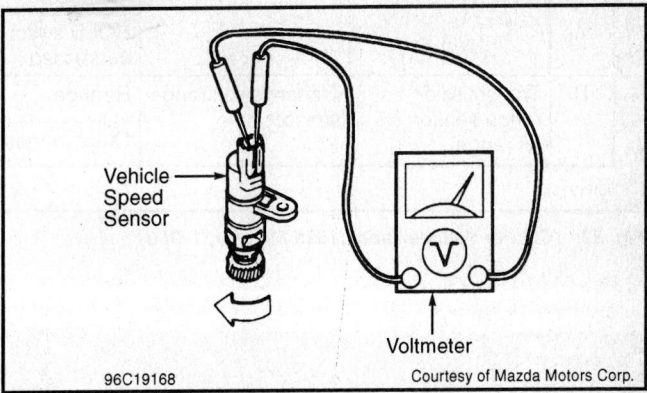

Fig. 31: Checking Speedometer Sensor

PCM & TCM TERMINAL VOLTAGE TESTS

Turn ignition switch to ON position. Access PCM or TCM. Do not disconnect harness connector. Using DVOM, measure voltage. See Figs. 32-46. After verifying that appropriate condition has been met, check voltage. If voltage is not within specification, replace PCM or TCM (as applicable).

3-886

AUTOMATIC TRANSMISSIONS
Mazda FA4A-EL & GF4A-EL Electronic Controls (Cont.)

Termi-nal	Component	Connected to	Condition	Correct voltage	Possible cause
1A	Kickdown switch	Kickdown switch	Kickdown switch depressed	B+	• Kickdown switch • Wiring and/or connector from 1A terminal to kickdown switch
			Kickdown switch released	0 V	
1B	HOLD indicator light	HOLD indicator light	HOLD mode	Below 1.0 V	• HOLD indicator light • Wiring and/or connector from terminal to HOLD indicator light
			Other modes	B+	
1C	FAIL signal	Engine control module	TEST mode	B+	• Wiring and/or connector from 1C terminal to engine control module 3E terminal
			Other modes	Below 1.0 V or repeat B+ and 0 V	
1D	Inhibitor signal	Engine control module	Park/neutral position	Below 1.0 V	• Transmission range sensor • Wiring and/or connector from 1L terminal to engine control module 1R terminal
			Other ranges	B+	
1E	TEST signal	Engine control module	Ignition switch ON	B+	• Wiring and/or connector from 1E terminal to engine control module 4M terminal
			TEST mode	Below 1.0 V or repeat B+ and 0 V	
1F	Brake switch	Brake switch	Brake pedal depressed	B+	• Brake switch • Wiring and/or connector from 1F terminal to brake switch
			Brake pedal released	0 V	
1G	Transmission fluid temperature sensor	Transmission fluid temperature sensor	Verify that voltage decreases according to ATF temperature rise For reference, if the ATF is 20°C {68°F} the voltage should be 3.5V. If the ATF is 130°C {260°F} the voltage should be 0.6V	Approx. 0.6—4.8 V	• Transmission fluid temperature sensor • Wiring and/or connector from 1G terminal to transmission fluid temperature sensor
1H	HOLD switch	HOLD switch	HOLD switch released	B+	• HOLD switch • Wiring and/or connector from 1H terminal to HOLD switch
			HOLD switch depressed	0 V	
1I	Transmission range sensor (R range)	Transmission range sensor	R range	B+	• Transmission range sensor
			Other ranges	0 V	

96H19163   Courtesy of Mazda Motors Corp.

Fig. 32: TCM Pin Voltage Table (1995 Millenia, 1 Of 3)

AUTOMATIC TRANSMISSIONS
Mazda FA4A-EL & GF4A-EL Electronic Controls (Cont.)

3-887

B+: Battery positive voltage

Terminal	Component	Connected to	Condition	Correct voltage	Possible cause
1J	Reduce torque signal 1	Engine control module	1→2, 2→3 shift, and throttle opening 3/8 or more	Below 1.0 V	• Wiring and/or connector from 1J terminal to engine control module 1R terminal • Engine control module
			Other than above	B+	
1K	Torque reduced signal/water thermo signal	transmission control module	Water temperature: More than 60°C {140°F}	B+	• Wiring and/or connector from 1K terminal to engine control module • Engine control module
			Water temperature: Less than 60°C {140°F} or torque control during shifting	Below 1.0 V	
1L	Reduce torque signal 2	Engine control module	4GR→3, 4GR→2, 4GR→1, 3→2, 3→1, 2→1 shift and throttle opening 1/8 or more	0 V	• Wiring and/or connector from 1L terminal to engine control module 1S terminal
			Other than above	B+	
1M	Fourth gear inhibit signal (auto speed control signal)	Cruise control unit	Ignition switch ON	B+	• Wiring and/or connector from terminal 1M to cruise control unit terminal 1G
			—	0 V	
1N	Engine speed input signal	Engine control module	Ignition switch ON	0 V or 4.5—5.5 V	• Engine control module • Wiring and/or connector from terminal 1T to engine control module
			Engine running at idle	2.0—3.0 V	
1O	Closed throttle position switch	Throttle position sensor	Accelerator pedal depressed	B+	• Throttle position sensor • Wiring and/or connector from terminal 1O to throttle position sensor
			Accelerator pedal released	0 V	
1P	Speedometer sensor	Speed sensor	Ignition switch ON	0 V or 4.0—5.0 V	• Vehicle speed sensor • Speedometer sensor • Wiring and/or connector from terminal 1P to vehicle speed sensor terminal
			Vehicle moving	2.0—3.0 V	
2A	Throttle position sensor (Vref)	Throttle position sensor	Ignition switch ON	4.5—5.5 V	• Throttle position sensor • Wiring and/or connector from terminal 2A to throttle position sensor • Engine control module
			Ignition switch OFF	0 V	
2B	Transmission range sensor (Park/neutral position)	Transmission range sensor	Park/neutral position	0 V	• Transmission range sensor • Wiring and/or connector from terminal 2B to transmission range sensor
			Other ranges	B+	
2C	Lockup solenoid valve	Lockup solenoid valve	Lockup	B+	• Lockup solenoid valve • Wiring and/or connector from terminal 2C to lockup solenoid valve
			Slip lockup	0 V	
2D	Transmission range sensor (D range)	Transmission range sensor	D range	B+	• Transmission range sensor • Wiring and/or connector from terminal 2D to transmission range sensor
			Other ranges	0 V	
2E	Shift solenoid A	Shift solenoid A	Solenoid valve ON	B+	• Shift solenoid A • Wiring and/or connector from terminal 2E to Shift solenoid A
			Solenoid valve OFF	0 V	

96I19164

Courtesy of Mazda Motors Corp.

Fig. 33: TCM Pin Voltage Table (1995 Millenia, 2 Of 3)

3-888

AUTOMATIC TRANSMISSIONS
Mazda FA4A-EL & GF4A-EL Electronic Controls (Cont.)

B+: Battery positive voltage

Terminal	Component	Connected to	Condition	Correct voltage	Possible cause
2F	Transmission range sensor (S range)	Transmission range sensor	S range	B+	• Transmission range sensor • Wiring and/or connector from terminal 2F to transmission range sensor
			Other ranges	0 V	
2G	Shift solenoid B	Shift solenoid B	Solenoid valve ON	B+	• Shift solenoid B • Wiring and/or connector from terminal 2G to shift solenoid B
			Solenoid valve OFF	0 V	
2H	Transmission range sensor (L range)	Transmission range sensor	L range	B+	• Transmission range sensor • Wiring and/or connector from terminal 2H to transmission range sensor
			Other ranges	0 V	
2I	Shift solenoid C	Shift solenoid C	Solenoid valve ON	B+	• Shift solenoid C • Wiring and/or connector from terminal 2I to shift solenoid C
			Solenoid valve OFF	0 V	
2J	Input/turbine speed sensor	Input/turbine speed sensor	Ignition switch ON	0 V	• Input/turbine speed sensor • Wiring and/or connector from terminal 2J to input/turbine speed sensor
			Engine running (N range)	0.1—1.0 V	
2K	Lockup control solenoid valve	Lockup control solenoid valve	Solenoid valve ON	B+	• Lockup control solenoid valve • Wiring and/or connector from terminal 2K to lockup control solenoid valve
			Solenoid valve OFF	0 V	
2L	Ground (Input/turbine speed sensor)	Input/turbine speed sensor	Constant	0 V	—
2M	3–2 timing solenoid valve	3–2 timing solenoid valve	Solenoid valve ON	B+	• 3–2 timing solenoid valve • Wiring and/or connector from terminal 2M to 3–2 timing solenoid valve
			Solenoid valve OFF	0 V	
2N	Pressure control solenoid	Pressure control solenoid	Throttle valve closed throttle position	8.0 V	• Pressure control solenoid • Wiring and/or connector from terminal 2N to pressure control solenoid
			Throttle valve wide open throttle	1.6 V	
2O	Battery (back-up)	Battery	Constant	B+	• Wiring and/or connector from terminal 2O to battery
2P	Ground (Transmission control module)	—	Constant	0 V	—
2Q	Battery	METER fuse	Ignition switch ON	B+	• METER fuse • Wiring and/or connector from terminal 2Q to METER fuse
			Ignition switch OFF	0 V	
2R	EGR boost sensor	EGR boost sensor	Ignition switch ON : 101 kPa {760 mmHg, 30.0 inHg}	Approx. 4.0 V	• Wiring and/or connector from terminal 2R to EGR boost sensor
2S	Battery	METER fuse	Ignition switch ON	B+	• METER fuse • Wiring and/or connector from terminal 2S to METER fuse
			Ignition switch OFF	0 V	
2T	Throttle position sensor (TVO)	Throttle position sensor	Throttle valve closed throttle position	0.1—1.1 V	• Throttle position sensor • Wiring and/or connector from terminal and/or connector from terminal 2T to throttle position sensor • Engine control module
			Throttle valve wide open throttle	3.1—4.4 V	

96J19165

Courtesy of Mazda Motors Corp.

Fig. 34: TCM Pin Voltage Table (1995 Millenia, 3 Of 3)

AUTOMATIC TRANSMISSIONS
Mazda FA4A-EL & GF4A-EL Electronic Controls (Cont.)

3-889

Terminal	Signal	Connected to	Test condition	Voltage (V)	Possible malfunction
2A	Shift solenoid A	Shift solenoid A	Solenoid valve ON	B+	• Shift solenoid A • Wiring and/or connector from terminal 2A to shift solenoid A
			Solenoid valve OFF	Below 1.0	
2B	Shift solenoid B	Shift solenoid B	Solenoid valve ON	B+	• Shift solenoid B • Wiring and/or connector from terminal 2B to shift solenoid B
			Solenoid valve OFF	Below 1.0	
2C	TCC* control solenoid valve	TCC control solenoid valve	TCC operation	B+	• TCC control solenoid valve • Wiring and/or connector from terminal 2C to TCC control solenoid valve
			TCC non operation	Below 1.0	
2D	TCC* solenoid valve	TCC solenoid valve	TCC slip operation→TCC operation	B+→Below 1.0	• TCC solenoid valve • Wiring and/or connector from terminal 2D to TCC solenoid valve
			TCC non operation	Below 1.0	
2E	HOLD indicator light	HOLD indicator light	HOLD mode	Below 1.0	• HOLD indicator light • Wiring and/or connector from terminal 2E to HOLD indicator light
			Except HOLD mode	B+	
2F	Shift solenoid C	Shift solenoid C	Solenoid valve ON	B+	• Shift solenoid C • Wiring and/or connector from terminal 2F to shift solenoid C
			Solenoid valve OFF	Below 1.0	
2G	3–2 timing solenoid valve	3–2 timing solenoid valve	Solenoid valve ON	B+	• 3–2 timing solenoid valve • Wiring and/or connector from terminal 2G to 3–2 timing solenoid valve
			Solenoid valve OFF	Below 1.0	
2H	Pressure control solenoid	Pressure control solenoid	Throttle valve closed throttle position	8.0	• Pressure control solenoid • Wiring and/or connector from terminal 2H to pressure control solenoid
			Throttle valve wide open throttle	1.6	
2I	Transaxle range switch (D range)	Transaxle range switch	D range	B+	• Transaxle range switch • Wiring and/or connector from terminal 2I to transaxle range switch
			Other ranges All positions	Below 1.0	
2J	—	—	—	—	—
2K	Transaxle range switch (R position)	Transaxle range switch	R position	B+	• Transaxle range switch • Wiring and/or connector from terminal 2K to transaxle range switch
			All ranges Other positions	Below 1.0	
2L	HOLD switch	HOLD switch	HOLD switch released	B+	• HOLD switch • Wiring and/or connector from terminal 2L to HOLD switch
			HOLD switch depressed	Below 1.0	

*: TCC = Torque converter clutch
B+: Battery positive voltage

96B19175

Courtesy of Mazda Motors Corp.

Fig. 35: PCM Pin Voltage Table (1996 Millenia, 1 Of 2)

3-890

AUTOMATIC TRANSMISSIONS
Mazda FA4A-EL & GF4A-EL Electronic Controls (Cont.)

Terminal	Signal	Connected to	Test condition	Voltage (V)	Possible malfunction
2M	Transaxle range switch (S range)	Transaxle range switch	S range	B+	• Transaxle range switch • Wiring and/or connector from terminal 2M to transaxle range switch
			Other ranges All positions	Below 1.0	
2N	—	—	—	—	—
2O	Transaxle fluid temperature sensor	Transaxle fluid temperature sensor	Verify that voltage decreases according to ATF temperature rise For reference, if the ATF is 20°C {68°F} the voltage should be 3.5 V If the ATF is 130°C {260°F} the voltage should be 0.6 V	Approx. 0.6—4.8	• Transaxle fluid temperature sensor • Wiring and/or connector from terminal 2O to transaxle fluid temperature sensor
2P	Input/turbine speed sensor	Input/turbine speed sensor	Ignition switch ON	Below 1.0	• Input/turbine speed sensor • Wiring and/or connector from terminal 2P to input/turbine speed sensor
			Engine running (P position)	0.1—1.0	
2Q	—	—	—	—	—
2R	Transaxle range switch (L range)	Transaxle range switch	L range	B+	• Transaxle range switch • Wiring and/or connector from terminal 2R to transaxle range switch
			Other ranges All positions	Below 1.0	
2S	—	—	—	—	—
2T	Ground (Input/turbine speed sensor)	Input/turbine speed sensor	Constant	Below 1.0	—

96A19174

Courtesy of Mazda Motors Corp.

Fig. 36: PCM Pin Voltage Table (1996 Millenia, 2 Of 2)

AUTOMATIC TRANSMISSIONS
Mazda FA4A-EL & GF4A-EL Electronic Controls (Cont.)

3-891

B+: Battery positive voltage

Terminal	Connected to	Voltmeter		Voltage	Condition
		+ terminal	–terminal		
1A (Output)	Engine control module (Reduce torque signal 2)	1A	Ground	Below 5 V	D, S, or L ranges and downshifting (except 4→3 shift) with throttle valve opening 1/8 or more
				B+	Others
1B (Output)	HOLD indicator light	1B	Ground	0 V	HOLD mode
				B+	NORMAL mode
1C (Output)	FAT terminal (Data link connector)	1C	Ground	0 V	HOLD mode
				B+	NORMAL mode
				0V or Approx. B+ (fluctuating)	If malfunction present
				Code signal	TAT terminal grounded
1D (Output)	Engine control module (Park / neutral position signal)	1D	Ground	Below 1.6 V	P or N position
				B+	R position, All ranges
1E (Input)	TAT terminal (Data link connector)	1E	Ground	B+	Normal
				0 V	TAT terminal grounded
1F (Input)	Brake switch	1F	Ground	B+	Brake pedal depressed
				0 V	Brake pedal released
1G (Input)	Transaxle fluid temperature sensor	1G	Ground	Approx. 4.95 V–1.12 V [ATF temp.–30°C {–20°F}–150°C {302°F}]	While warming-up ATF Note Approx. 4.6 V: ATF temp. 20°C {68°F} Approx. 1.5 V: ATF temp. 130°C {266°F}
1H (Input)	HOLD switch	1H	Ground	0 V	Switch depressed point
				B+	Switch released point
1I	—	—	—	—	—
1J (Ground)	Battery ground	1J	Ground	0 V	Constant
1K (Battery power)	Battery	1K	Ground	B+	Ignition switch ON
				0 V	Ignition switch OFF
1L	—	—	—	—	—
1M	—	—	—	—	—
1N (Input)	Engine control module (Torque reduced signal/ water thermo signal)	1N	Ground	B+	Above 60°C{140°F}
				0 V	Operate torque reduction
				0 V	Below 60°C{140°F}
1O (Input)	Closed throttle position switch	1O	Ground	0 V	Closed throttle position switch ON (Closed throttle position)
				B+	Closed throttle position switch OFF (Throttle valve open)
1P (Input)	Vehicle speed sensor	1P	Ground	3 V–4 V	While driving
				0 V or 6 V–8 V	Vehicle stopped

96C19176

Courtesy of Mazda Motors Corp.

Fig. 37: TCM Pin Voltage Table (1995 MX3, 1 Of 2)

3-892

AUTOMATIC TRANSMISSIONS
Mazda FA4A-EL & GF4A-EL Electronic Controls (Cont.)

Terminal	Connected to	Voltmeter		Voltage	Condition
		+ terminal	−terminal		
2A (Input)	Throttle position sensor(V_{REF})	2A	Ground	4.5 V–5.5 V	Ignition switch ON
				0 V	Ignition switch OFF
2B (Input)	Transaxle range switch (P or N position)	2B	Ground	0 V	P or N position
				B+	R position, All ranges
2C	—	—	—	—	—
2D (Input)	Transaxle range switch (D range)	2D	Ground	B+	D range
				0 V	Other ranges, All positions
2E (Output)	Shift solenoid A	2E	Ground	B+	Solenoid valve ON
				0 V	Solenoid valve OFF
2F (Input)	Transaxle range switch (S range)	2F	Ground	B+	S range
				0 V	Other ranges, All positions
2G (Output)	Shift solenoid B	2G	Ground	B+	Solenoid valve ON
				0 V	Solenoid valve OFF
2H (Input)	Transaxle range switch (L range)	2H	Ground	B+	L range
				0 V	Other ranges, All positions
2I (Output)	Shift solenoid C	2I	Ground	B+	Solenoid valve ON
				0 V	Solenoid valve OFF
2J (Input)	Input / turbine speed sensor *	2J	Ground	0 V	Engine stopped
				Approx. 0.5 V	Engine running (N position)
2K (Output)	Torque converter clutch solenoid valve	2K	Ground	B+	Solenoid valve ON
				0 V	Solenoid valve OFF
2L (Ground)	Input / turbine speed sensor	2L	Ground	0 V	Constant
2M (Output)	Engine control module (Reduce torque signal 1)	2M	Ground	B+	D, S, or L ranges and 1 2 or 2 3 upshifting with throttle valve opening 6/8 or more
				Below 2.5 V	Others
2N	—	—	—	—	—
2O (Memory power)	Battery	2O	Ground	B+	Constant
2P (Ground)	Battery ground	2P	Ground	0 V	Constant
2Q (Battery power)	Battery	2Q	Ground	B+	Ignition switch ON
				0 V	Ignition switch OFF
2R	—	—	—	—	—
2S	—	—	—	—	—
2T (Input)	Throttle position sensor (TVO)	2T	Ground	0.1 V–1.1 V	Closed throttle position
				3.1 V–4.4 V	Wide open throttle

* Checked in AC range

96D19177

Courtesy of Mazda Motors Corp.

Fig. 38: TCM Pin Voltage Table (1995 MX3, 2 Of 2)

AUTOMATIC TRANSMISSIONS
Mazda FA4A-EL & GF4A-EL Electronic Controls (Cont.)

3-893

B+: Battery positive voltage

Terminal	Component	Connected to	Voltmeter		Correct voltage	Condition	Possible cause
			+ terminal	– terminal			
1A	A/C signal	A/C switch	1A		Below 1.0 V	A/C switch ON	• A/C switch
					B+	A/C switch OFF	
1B	O/D OFF indicator light	Instrument cluster (O/D OFF indicator light)	1B		Below 1.0 V	O/D OFF mode	• Instrument cluster (O/D OFF indicator light)
					B+	Other modes	
1C	FAT terminal (data link connector)	FAT terminal (data link connector)	1C		Below 2.5 V	O/D OFF mode	• Wiring and/or connector from 1C terminal to data link connector FAT terminal
					B+	Other modes	
1D	Park/neutral position signal	Engine control module	1D	Ground	Below 1.0 V	P and N positions	• Wiring and/or connector from 1D terminal to engine control module 1R terminal
					B+	R position All ranges	
1E	TAT terminal (data link connector)	TAT terminal (data link connector)	1E		B+	Ignition switch ON (vehicle stopped)	• Wiring and/or connector from 1E terminal to data link connector TAT terminal
					0 V	TAT terminal grounded (vehicle stopped)	
1F	Brake switch	Brake switch	1F		B+	Brake pedal depressed	• Brake switch
					0 V	Brake pedal released	
1G	Transaxle fluid temperature sensor	Transaxle fluid temperature sensor	1G	2R	Approx. 0.6— 4.8 V	Verify that voltage decreases according to ATF temperature rise **Note** • For reference, if the ATF is 20°C {68°F} the voltage should be 3.5 V. If the ATF is 130°C {266°F} the voltage should be 0.6 V	• Transaxle fluid temperature sensor • Wiring and/or connector from 1G terminal to transaxle fluid temperature sensor

96E19178

Courtesy of Mazda Motors Corp.

Fig. 39: TCM Pin Voltage Table (1995 MX6 & 626, 1 Of 5)

3-894

AUTOMATIC TRANSMISSIONS
Mazda FA4A-EL & GF4A-EL Electronic Controls (Cont.)

B+: Battery positive voltage

Terminal	Component	Connected to	Voltmeter + terminal	Voltmeter – terminal	Correct voltage	Condition	Possible cause
1H	O/D OFF switch	O/D OFF switch	1H		B+	Switch released	• O/D OFF switch
					0 V	Switch depressed	
1I	Transaxle range switch (R position)	Transaxle range switch	1I		B+	R position	• Transaxle range switch • Wiring and/or connector from 1I terminal to transaxle range switch
					0 V	Other positions All ranges	
1J	Reduce torque signal 1	Engine control module	1J		Below 1.0 V	1→2, 2→3 shift, and throttle opening 4/8 or more	• Wiring and/or connector from 1J terminal to engine control module 1S terminal
					B+	Other than above	
1K	Torque reduced signal/engine coolant temperature signal	Engine control module	1K		B+	Water temperature: more than 60°C {140°F}	• Wiring and/or connector from 1K terminal to engine control module 1K terminal
					Below 1.0 V	Water temperature: less than 60°C {140°F} or torque control during shifting	
1L	Reduce torque signal 2	Engine control module	1L		Below 1.0 V	4→2, 4→1, 3→2, 3→1, 2→1 shift and throttle opening 3/8 or more	• Wiring and/or connector from 1L terminal to engine control module 1V terminal
					B+	Other than above	
1M	4GR inhibit signal (auto speed control signal)	Cruise control unit	1M	Ground	Below 1.0 V	The vehicle speed drops 8 km/h {5 mph} below the set speed or RESUME/ACCEL switch is operated during cruise control operation	• Wiring and/or connector from 1M terminal to cruise control unit 1G terminal
					B+	Other than above	
1N	Engine speed input signal	Distributor	1N		0 V or 4.5—5.5 V	Engine stopped (ignition switch ON)	• Wiring and/or connector from 1N terminal to distributor • Distributor
					2.0—3.0 V	Engine running at idle	
1O	Closed throttle position switch	Throttle position sensor	1O		B+	Accelerator pedal depressed	• Throttle position sensor • Wiring and/or connector from 1O terminal to throttle position sensor
					0 V	Accelerator pedal released	
1P	Vehicle speedometer sensor	Vehicle speed sensor	1P		0 V or 4.0—5.0 V	Vehicle stopped	• Vehicle speed sensor • Vehicle speedometer sensor
					2.0—3.0 V	Vehicle moving	

96F19179

Courtesy of Mazda Motors Corp.

Fig. 40: TCM Pin Voltage Table (1995 MX6 & 626, 2 Of 5)

AUTOMATIC TRANSMISSIONS
Mazda FA4A-EL & GF4A-EL Electronic Controls (Cont.)

3-895

B+: Battery positive voltage

Terminal	Component	Connected to	Voltmeter		Correct voltage	Condition	Possible cause
			+ terminal	– terminal			
2A	Throttle position sensor (VREF)	Throttle position sensor	2A	Ground	0 V	Ignition switch OFF	• Wiring and/or connector from 2A terminal to throttle position sensor
					4.5—5.5 V	Ignition switch ON	
2B	Transaxle range switch (P and N positions)	Transaxle range switch	2B		0 V	P and N positions	• Wiring and/or connector from 2B terminal to transaxle range switch • Wiring and/or connector from 2B terminal to ignition switch • Transaxle range switch • Ignition switch
					B+	R positions All ranges	
2C	Torque converter clutch solenoid valve	Torque converter clutch solenoid valve	2C		Below 1.0 V	TCC non operation	• Torque converter clutch solenoid valve • Wiring and/or connector from 2C terminal to torque converter clutch solenoid valve
					B+ → Below 1.0 V	Slip TCC operation → TCC operation	
2D	Transaxle range switch (D range)	Transaxle range switch	2D		B+	D range	• Transaxle range switch • Wiring and/or connector from 2D terminal to transaxle range switch
					0 V	Other ranges All positions	
2E	Shift solenoid A	Shift solenoid A	2E		B+	Solenoid valve ON	• Shift solenoid A • Wiring and/or connector from 2E terminal to shift solenoid A
					0 V	Solenoid valve OFF	
2F	Transaxle range switch (2 range)	Transaxle range switch	2F		B+	2 range	• Transaxle range switch • Wiring and/or connector from 2F terminal to transaxle range switch
					0 V	Other ranges All positions	
2G	Shift solenoid B	Shift solenoid B	2G		B+	Solenoid valve ON	• Shift solenoid B • Wiring and/or connector from 2G terminal to shift solenoid B
					0 V	Solenoid valve OFF	
2H	Transaxle range switch (1 range)	Transaxle range switch	2H		B+	1 range	• Transaxle range switch • Wiring and/or connector from 2H terminal to transaxle range switch
					0 V	Other ranges All positions	

96I19180

Courtesy of Mazda Motors Corp.

Fig. 41: TCM Pin Voltage Table (1995 MX6 & 626, 3 Of 5)

3-896

AUTOMATIC TRANSMISSIONS
Mazda FA4A-EL & GF4A-EL Electronic Controls (Cont.)

B+: Battery positive voltage

Terminal	Component	Connected to	Voltmeter + terminal	Voltmeter − terminal	Correct voltage	Condition	Possible cause
2I	Shift solenoid C	Shift solenoid C	2I	Ground	B+	Solenoid valve ON	• Shift solenoid C • Wiring and/or connector from 2I terminal to Shift solenoid C
					0 V	Solenoid valve OFF	
2J	Input/turbine speed sensor	Input/turbine speed sensor	2J*	2L	Approx. 0 V (AC)	Engine stopped	• Input/turbine speed sensor • Wiring and/or connector from 2J terminal to input/turbine speed sensor
					0.1—1.0 V (AC)	Engine running (P position)	
2K	Torque converter clutch control solenoid valve	Torque converter clutch control solenoid valve	2K	Ground	B+	TCC operation	• Torque converter clutch control solenoid valve • Wiring and/or connector from 2K terminal to torque converter clutch control solenoid valve
					0 V	TCC non operation	
2L	Ground (input/turbine speed sensor)	Input/turbine speed sensor	2L		0 V	Constant	• Input/turbine speed sensor • Wiring and/or connector from 2L terminal to input/turbine speed sensor
2M	3-2 timing solenoid valve	3-2 timing solenoid valve	2M		B+	1→2, 2→3, 3→4, 3→2, 3→1, 2→1 shift or select R position from other ranges	• 3-2 timing solenoid valve • Wiring and/or connector from 2M terminal to 3-2 timing solenoid valve
					0 V	Other than above	
2N	Pressure control solenoid	Pressure control solenoid	2N		Approx. 8.0 V	Throttle valve closed throttle position (engine running)	• Pressure control solenoid • Wiring and/or connector from 2N terminal to pressure control solenoid
					Approx. 1.6 V	Throttle valve wide open throttle (engine running)	
2O	Battery (backup)	ROOM fuse	2O		B+	Constant	• Wiring and/or connector from 2O terminal to ROOM fuse • ROOM fuse
2P	Ground (transaxle control module and transaxle fluid temperature sensor)	Transaxle fluid temperature sensor	2P		0 V	Constant	• Transaxle fluid temperature sensor • Wiring and/or connector from 2P terminal to transaxle fluid temperature sensor

* Check the 2J (input/turbine speed sensor) terminal voltage by using the AC range.

96E29961

Courtesy of Mazda Motors Corp.

Fig. 42: TCM Pin Voltage Table (1995 MX6 & 626, 4 Of 5)

AUTOMATIC TRANSMISSIONS
Mazda FA4A-EL & GF4A-EL Electronic Controls (Cont.)

3-897

B+: Battery positive voltage

Terminal	Component	Connected to	Voltmeter		Correct voltage	Condition	Possible cause
			+ terminal	– terminal			
2Q	Battery	METER fuse	2Q	Ground	B+	Ignition switch ON	• Wiring and/or connector from 2Q terminal to METER fuse • METER fuse
					0 V	Ignition switch OFF	
2R	Barometric pressure sensor	Engine control module	1R		Above approx. 3.5 V	Barometric pressure more than 89.6 kPa {672 mmHg, 26.5 inHg} (below approx. 1,500 m {4,921 ft})	• Wiring and/or connector from 1R terminal to engine control module 2A terminal
					Below approx. 3.5 V	Barometric pressure less than 89.6 kPa {672 mmHg, 26.5 inHg} (above approx. 1,500 m {4,921 ft})	
2S	Battery	METER fuse	2S		B+	Ignition switch ON	• Wiring and/or connector from 2S terminal to METER fuse • METER fuse
					0V	Ignition switch OFF	
2T	Throttle position sensor (TVO)	Throttle position sensor	2T		0.1—1.1 V	Throttle valve closed throttle position	• Wiring and/or connector from 2T terminal to throttle position sensor • Throttle position sensor
					3.1—4.4 V	Throttle valve wide open throttle	

96F29962

Courtesy of Mazda Motors Corp.

Fig. 43: TCM Pin Voltage Table (1995 MX6 & 626, 5 Of 5)

3-898

AUTOMATIC TRANSMISSIONS
Mazda FA4A-EL & GF4A-EL Electronic Controls (Cont.)

Terminal	Signal	Connected to	Test condition	Voltage (V)	Possible malfunction
2A	Shift solenoid A (ATX)	Shift solenoid A	Solenoid valve ON	B+	• Shift solenoid A • Wiring and/or connector from terminal 2A to shift solenoid A
			Solenoid valve OFF	Below 1.0	
2B	Shift solenoid B (ATX)	Shift solenoid B	Solenoid valve ON	B+	• Shift solenoid B • Wiring and/or connector from terminal 2B to shift solenoid B
			Solenoid valve OFF	Below 1.0	
2C	TCC* control solenoid valve (ATX)	TCC control solenoid valve	TCC operation	B+	• TCC control solenoid valve • Wiring and/or connector from terminal 2C to TCC control solenoid valve
			TCC non operation	Below 1.0	
2D	TCC* solenoid valve (ATX)	TCC solenoid valve	TCC slip operation→TCC operation	B+→ Below 1.0	• TCC solenoid valve • Wiring and/or connector from terminal 2D to TCC solenoid valve
			TCC non operation	Below 1.0	
2E	O/D OFF indicator light (ATX)	O/D OFF indicator light	O/D OFF mode	Below 1.0	• O/D OFF indicator light • Wiring and/or connector from terminal 2E to O/D OFF indicator light
			Except O/D OFF mode	B+	
2F	Shift solenoid C (ATX)	Shift solenoid C	Solenoid valve ON	B+	• Shift solenoid C • Wiring and/or connector from terminal 2F to shift solenoid C
			Solenoid valve OFF	Below 1.0	
2G	3–2 timing solenoid valve (ATX)	3–2 timing solenoid valve	Solenoid valve ON	B+	• 3–2 timing solenoid valve • Wiring and/or connector from terminal 2G to 3–2 timing solenoid valve
			Solenoid valve OFF	Below 1.0	
2H	Pressure control solenoid (ATX)	Pressure control solenoid	Throttle valve closed throttle position	8.0	• Pressure control solenoid • Wiring and/or connector from terminal 2H to pressure control solenoid
			Throttle valve wide open throttle	1.6	
2I	Transaxle range switch (D range) (ATX)	Transaxle range switch	D range	B+	• Transaxle range switch • Wiring and/or connector from terminal 2I to transaxle range switch
			Other ranges All positions	Below 1.0	
2J	—	—	—	—	
2K	Transaxle range switch (R position) (ATX)	Transaxle range switch	R position	B+	• Transaxle range switch • Wiring and/or connector from terminal 2K to transaxle range switch
			All ranges Other positions	Below 1.0	
2L	O/D OFF switch (ATX)	O/D OFF switch	O/D OFF switch released	B+	• O/D OFF switch • Wiring and/or connector from terminal 2L to O/D OFF switch
			O/D OFF switch depressed	Below 1.0	
2M	Transaxle range switch (S range) (ATX)	Transaxle range switch	S range	B+	• Transaxle range switch • Wiring and/or connector from terminal 2M to transaxle range switch
			Other ranges All positions	Below 1.0	
2N	—	—	—	—	

*: TCC = Torque converter clutch
B+: Battery positive voltage
96G29963

Courtesy of Mazda Motors Corp.

Fig. 44: PCM Pin Voltage Table (1996 MX6 & 626, 1 Of 2)

AUTOMATIC TRANSMISSIONS
Mazda FA4A-EL & GF4A-EL Electronic Controls (Cont.)

3-899

Terminal	Signal	Connected to	Test condition	Voltage (V)	Possible malfunction
2O	Transaxle fluid temperature sensor (ATX)	Transaxle fluid temperature sensor	Verify that voltage decreases according to ATF temperature rise. For reference, if the ATF is 20°C {68°F} the voltage should be 3.5 V. If the ATF is 130°C {260°F} the voltage should be 0.6 V	Approx. 0.6—4.8	• Transaxle fluid temperature sensor • Wiring and/or connector from terminal 2O to transaxle fluid temperature sensor
2P	Input/turbine speed sensor (ATX)	Input/turbine speed sensor	Ignition switch ON	Below 1.0	• Input/turbine speed sensor • Wiring and/or connector from terminal 2P to input/turbine speed sensor
			Engine running (P position)	0.1—1.0	
2Q	—	—	—	—	—
2R	Transaxle range switch (L range) (ATX)	Transaxle range switch	L range	B+	• Transaxle range switch • Wiring and/or connector from terminal 2R to transaxle range switch
			Other ranges All positions	Below 1.0	
2S	—	—	—	—	—
2T	Ground (Input/turbine speed sensor) (ATX)	Input/turbine speed sensor	Constant	Below 1.0	—

B+: Battery positive voltage

96H29964

Courtesy of Mazda Motors Corp.

Fig. 45: PCM Pin Voltage Table (1996 MX6 & 626, 2 Of 2)

3-900

AUTOMATIC TRANSMISSIONS
Mazda FA4A-EL & GF4A-EL Electronic Controls (Cont.)

Termi-nal	Signal	Connected to	Test condition		Voltage (V)	Possible malfunction
*²2A	Shift solenoid A control	Shift solenoid A	During shifting		B+	• Shift solenoid A
			Others		Below 1.0	
*²2B	Shift solenoid B control	Shift solenoid B	During shifting		B+	• Shift solenoid B
			Others		Below 1.0	
*²2C	Shift solenoid C control	Shift solenoid C	During shifting		B+	• Shift solenoid C
			Others		Below 1.0	
*²2D	Torque converter clutch solenoid valve control	Torque converter clutch solenoid valve	During shifting		B+	• Torque converter clutch solenoid valve
			Others		Below 1.0	
*²2E	O/D OFF indicator light control	O/D OFF indicator light	Ignition switch ON	O/D OFF mode	Below 2.0	• Instrument cluster (O/D OFF indicator)
				Others	B+	
*²2F	D range	Transaxle range switch (D range)	Idle	D range	B+	• Transaxle range switch
				Others	Below 1.0	
*²2G	2 range	Transaxle range switch (2 range)	Idle	2 range	B+	
				Others	Below 1.0	
*²2H	1 range	Transaxle range switch (1 range)	Idle	1 range	B+	
				Others	Below 1.0	
*²2I	O/D OFF switch	O/D OFF switch	Ignition switch ON	O/D OFF switch pressed	Below 1.0	• O/D OFF switch
				O/D OFF switch released	B+	
2J	—	—	—		—	—
*²2K	Input/turbine speed sensor	Input/turbine speed sensor (turbine)	Ignition switch ON		Approx. 1.0	• Input/turbine speed sensor
			Idle			
*²2L	Input/turbine speed sensor ground	Input/turbine speed sensor (ground)	Constant		Below 1.0	• PCM 2L terminal continuity harness

B+: Battery positive voltage
*¹: In data link connector
*²: ATX only
96J19173

Courtesy of Mazda Motors Corp.

Fig. 46: PCM Pin Voltage Table (Protege)

AUTOMATIC TRANSMISSIONS
Mazda FA4A-EL & GF4A-EL Electronic Controls (Cont.)

3-901

WIRING DIAGRAMS

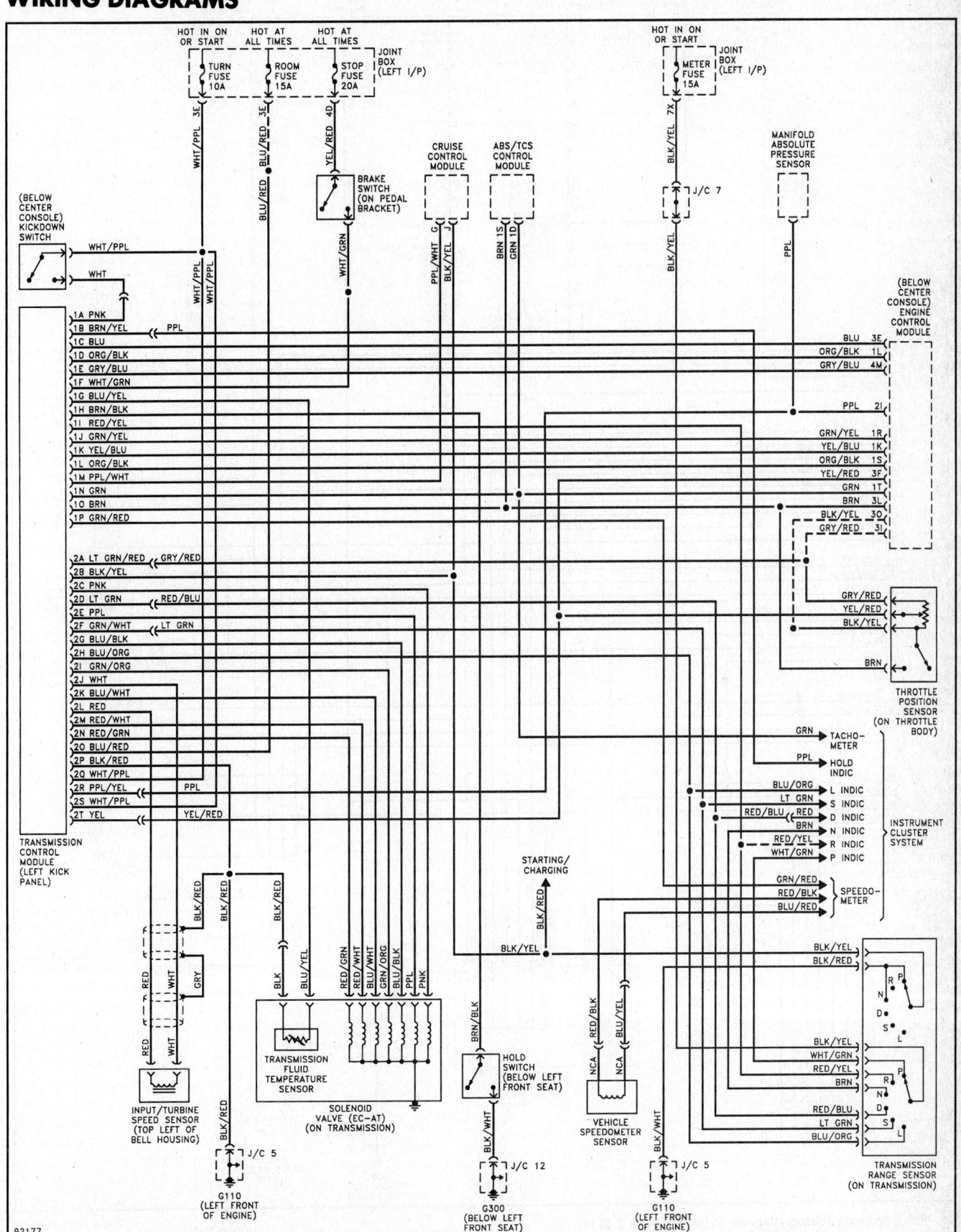

Fig. 47: Transaxle Wiring Diagram (1995 Millenia 2.5L)

3-902

AUTOMATIC TRANSMISSIONS
Mazda FA4A-EL & GF4A-EL Electronic Controls (Cont.)

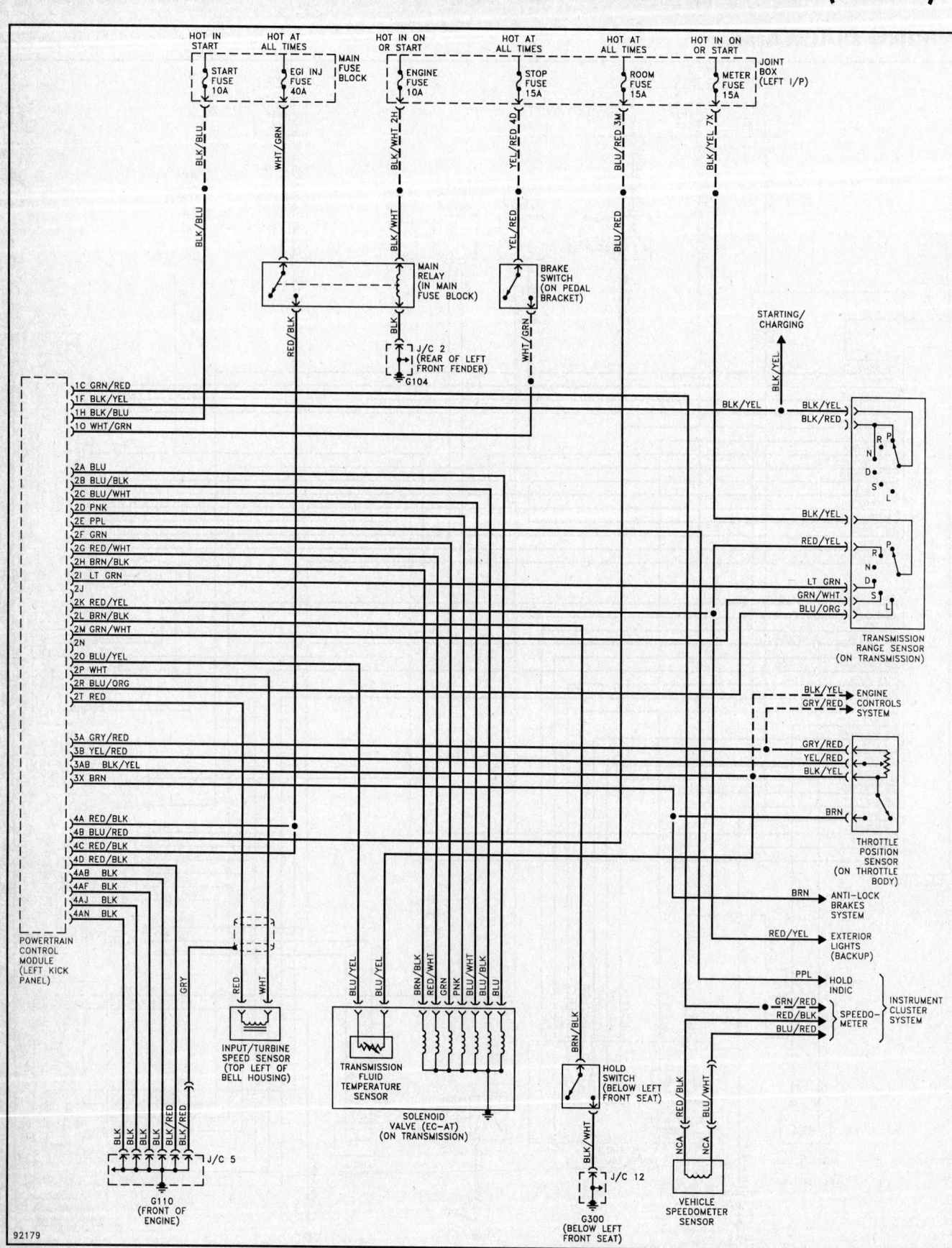

Fig. 48: Transaxle Wiring Diagram (1996 Millenia 2.5L)

AUTOMATIC TRANSMISSIONS
Mazda FA4A-EL & GFA4-EL Electronic Controls (Cont.)

3-903

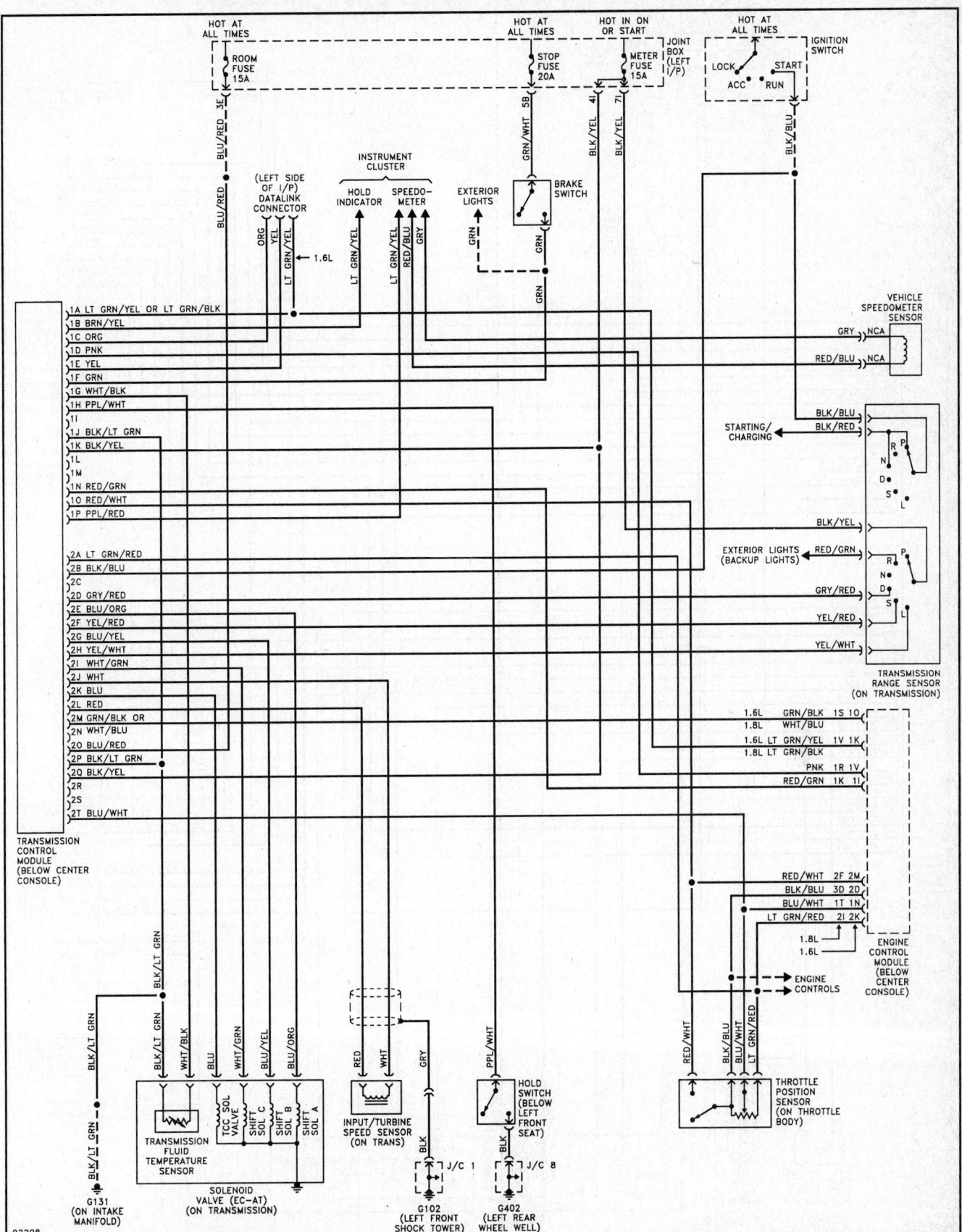

Fig. 49: Transaxle Wiring Diagram (1995 MX3)

3-904

AUTOMATIC TRANSMISSIONS
Mazda FA4A-EL & GFA4-EL Electronic Controls (Cont.)

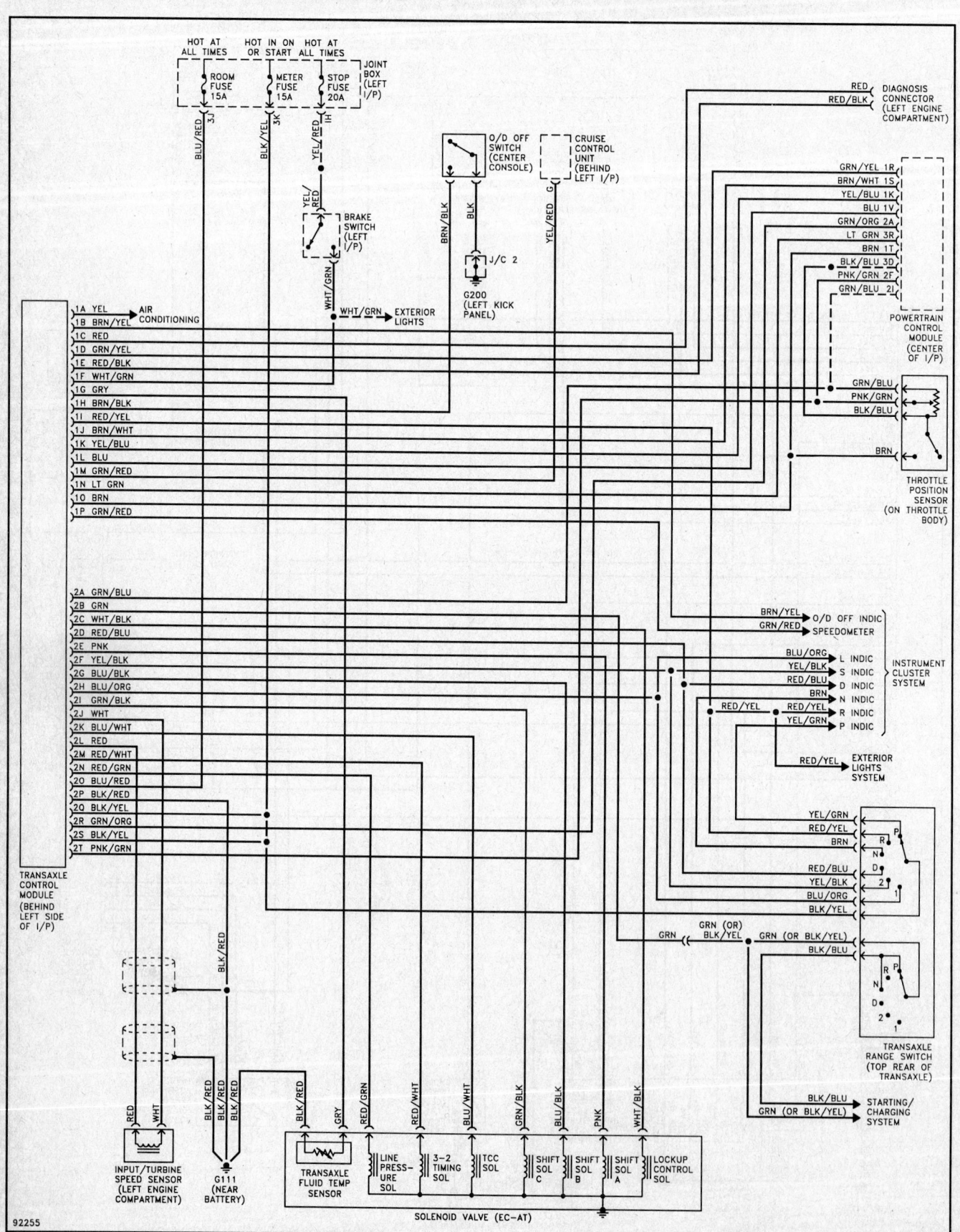

Fig. 50: Transaxle Wiring Diagram (1995 MX6 & 626 2.5L)

AUTOMATIC TRANSMISSIONS
Mazda FA4A-EL & GFA4-EL Electronic Controls (Cont.)

3-905

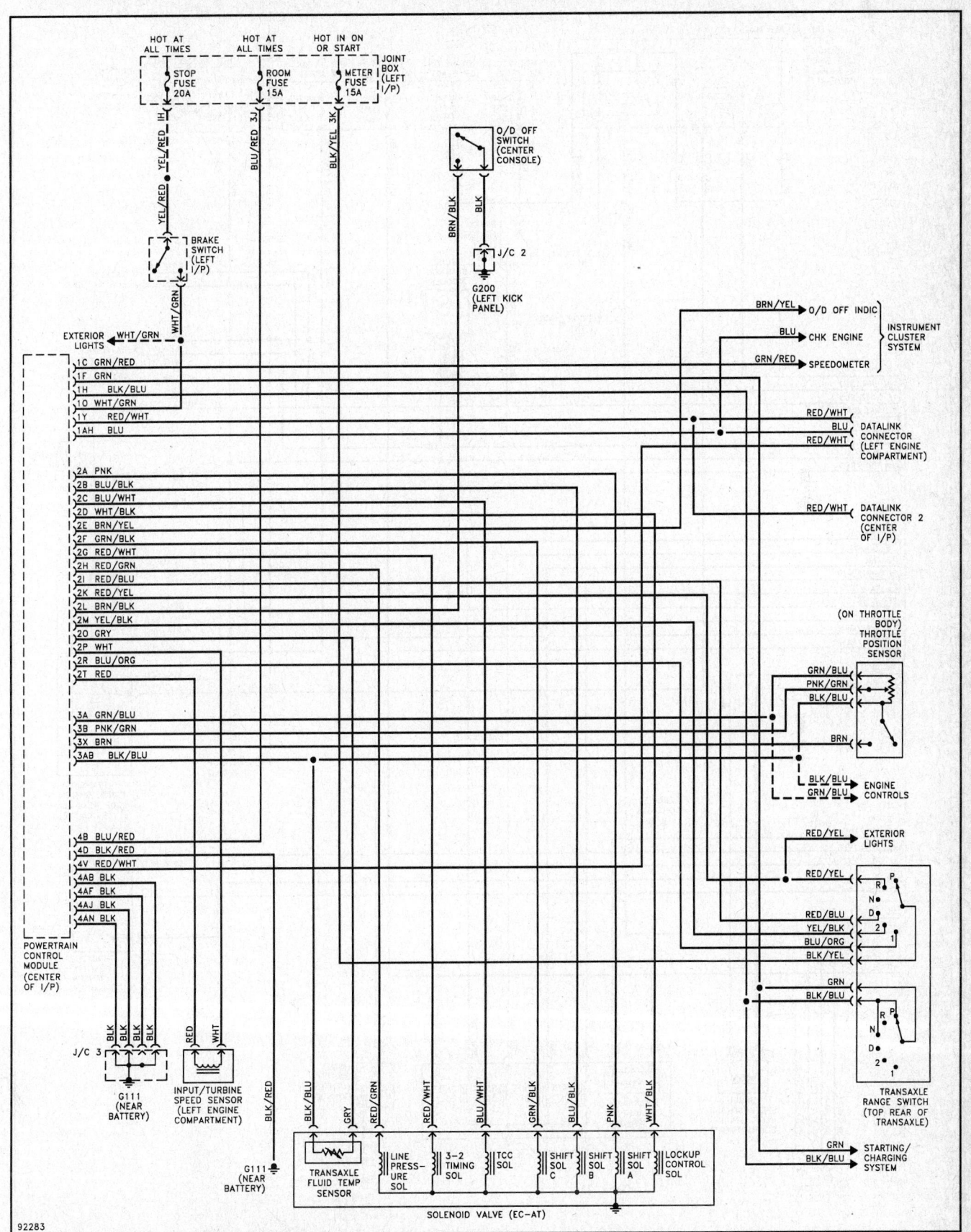

Fig. 51: Transaxle Wiring Diagram (1996 MX6 & 626 2.5L)

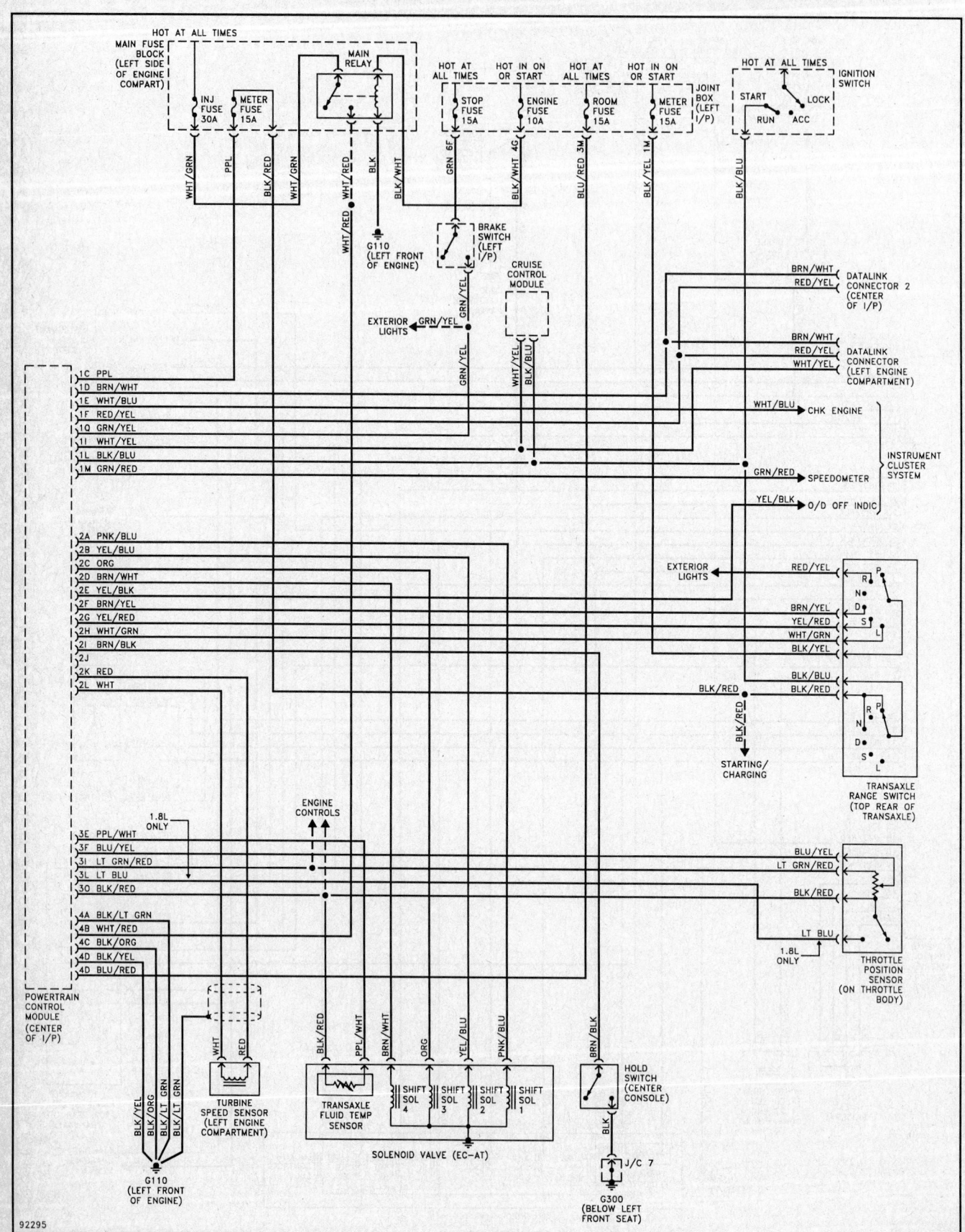

Fig. 52: Transaxle Wiring Diagram (1995 Protege)

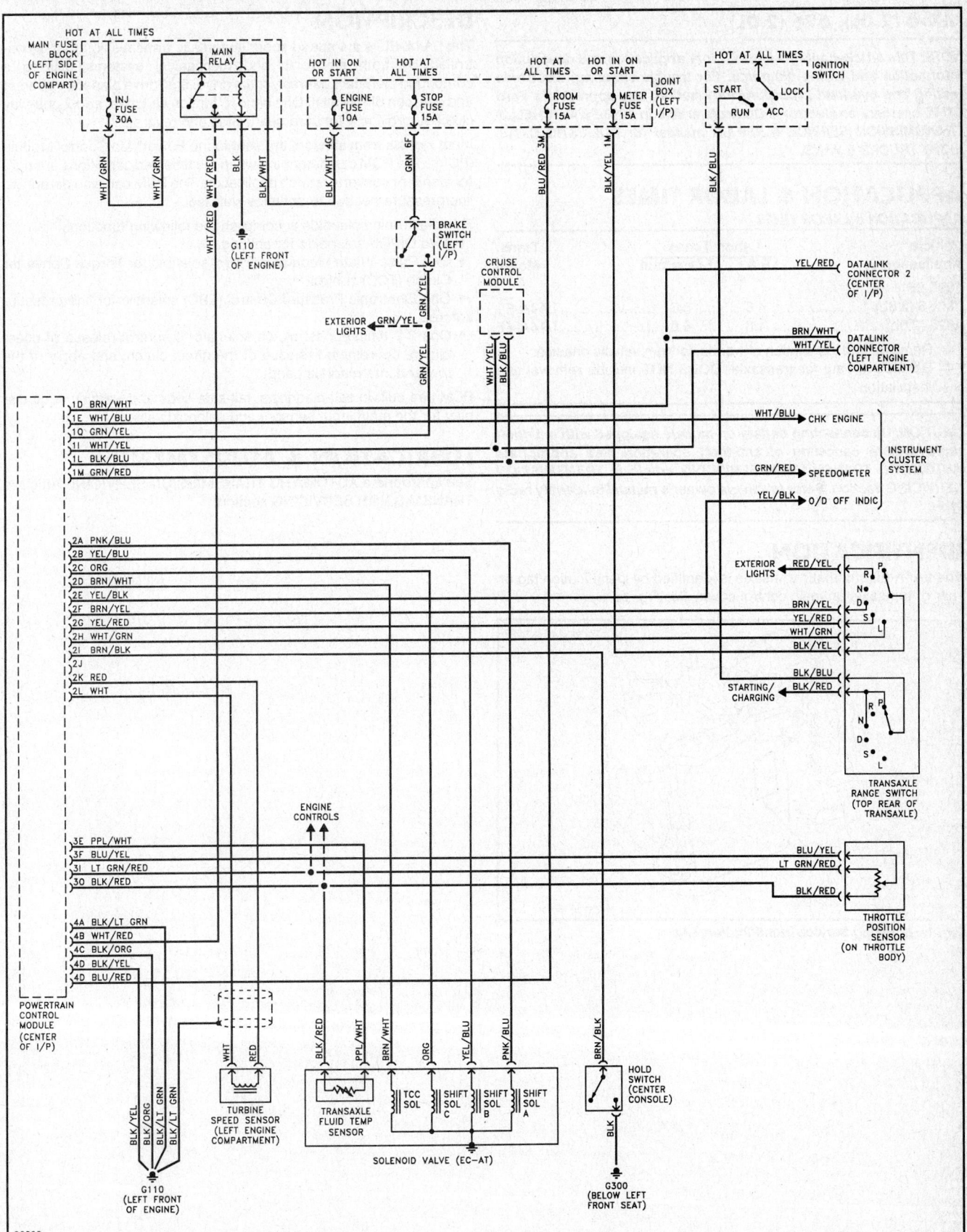

Fig. 53: Transaxle Wiring Diagram (1996 Protege)

92299

AUTOMATIC TRANSMISSIONS
Mazda LA4A-EL

MX-6 (2.0L), 626 (2.0L)

NOTE: This article contains introductory application and description information and wiring diagrams. For trouble shooting, electronic testing and overhaul procedure information, see appropriate Ford CD4E overhaul or Electronic Controls article in 1995-96 MITCHELL® TRANSMISSION SERVICE & REPAIR manual for DOMESTIC CARS, LIGHT TRUCKS & VANS.

APPLICATION & LABOR TIMES

APPLICATION & LABOR TIMES

Vehicle Application	Labor Times		Trans. Model
	[1] R & I	[2] Overhaul	
1995-96			
MX-6 (2.0L)	4.8	.... 8.6	.... LA4A-EL
626 (2.0L)	4.8	.... 8.6	.... LA4A-EL

[1] – Removal and installation of transaxle from vehicle chassis.

[2] – Bench overhaul for transaxle. DOES NOT include removal and installation.

CAUTION: Disconnecting battery on models equipped with anti-theft radio require canceling of anti-theft operation. See appropriate AUTOMATIC TRANSMISSION SERVICING article in TRANSMISSION SERVICING section. Refer to vehicle owner's manual to identify radio type.

IDENTIFICATION

The LA4A-EL automatic transaxle is identified by identification tag on rear of transaxle on main control cover. *See Fig. 1.*

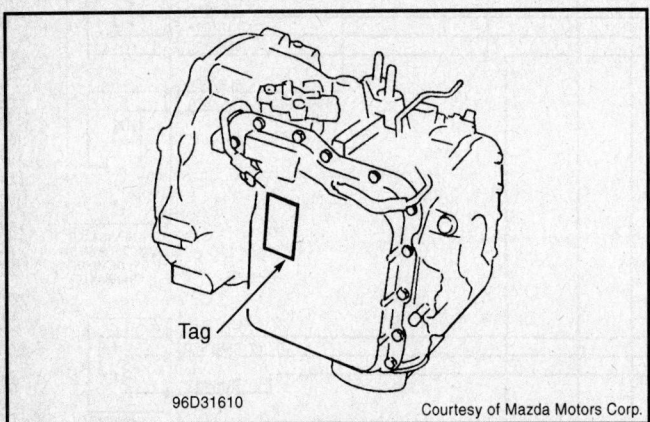

Tag

96D31610   Courtesy of Mazda Motors Corp.

Fig. 1: Locating Service Identification Tag

DESCRIPTION

The LA4A-EL is a 4-speed speed automatic transmission that is controlled by both electronic and mechanical systems utilizing a compound planetary gearset, chain drive, final drive planetary gearset and an open differential. One band, 5 friction clutches, and 2 one-way clutches provide 4 forward gear ratios and reverse.

Input signals from sensors are sent to the Powertrain Control Module (PCM). The PCM can determine when the time and conditions are right for a shift or converter clutch application. The PCM can also determine line pressure needed to optimize shift feel.

Five electronic solenoids accomplish the following functions:
- Two On/Off solenoids for shifting.
- One Pulse-Width Modulator (PWM) solenoid for Torque Converter Clutch (TCC) control.
- One Electronic Pressure Control (EPC) solenoid for line pressure control.
- One 3-2 timing/coast clutch solenoid to control release of coast clutch, coordinated release of the direct clutch, and apply of the low and intermediate band.

PCM has built-in self-diagnosis, fail-safe code and warning code display for the main input sensors and solenoid valves.

LUBRICATION & ADJUSTMENTS

See appropriate AUTOMATIC TRANSMISSION SERVICING article in TRANSMISSION SERVICING section.

WIRING DIAGRAMS

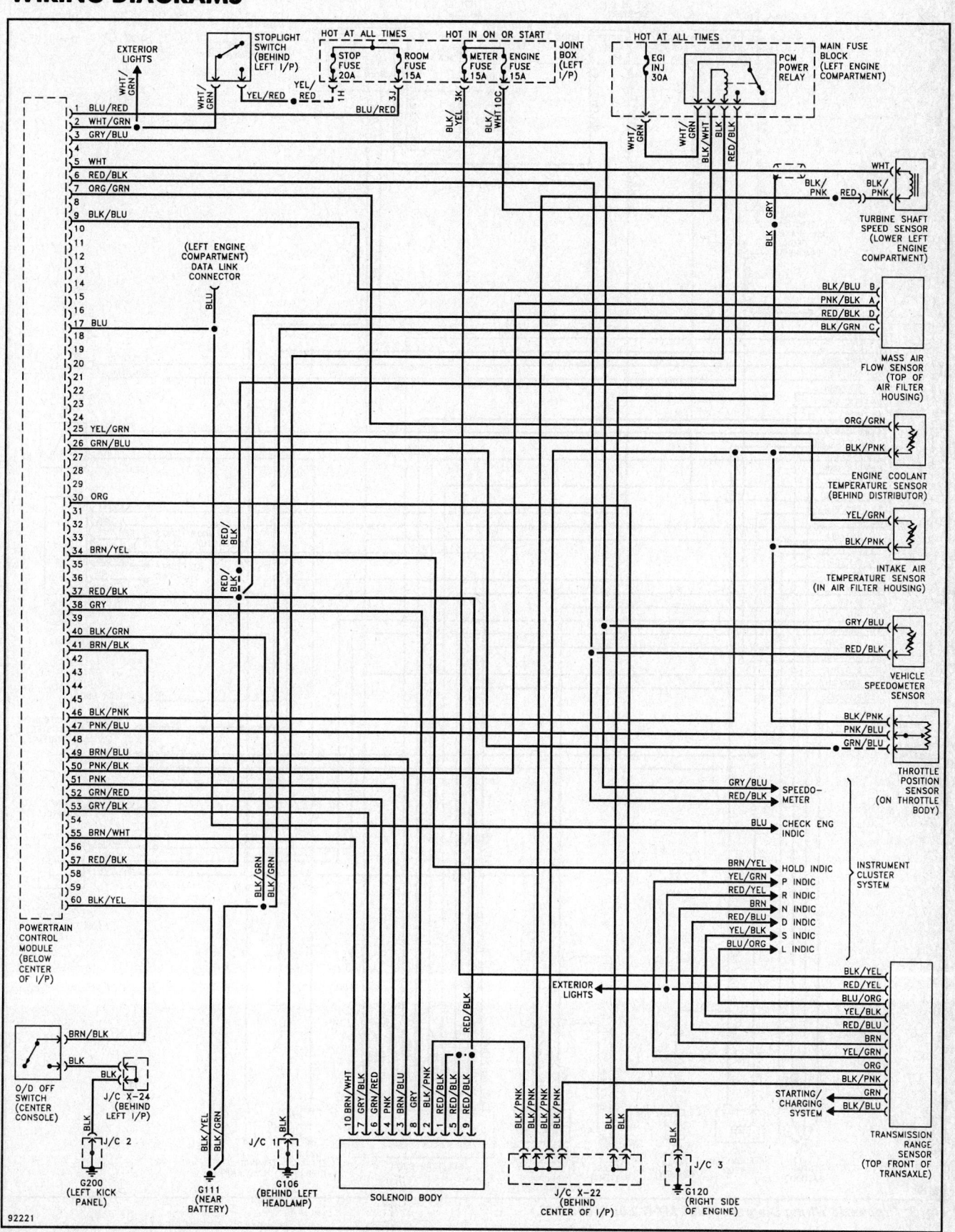

Fig. 2: Transaxle Wiring Diagram (1995 MX-6 2.0L & 626 2.0L)

92221

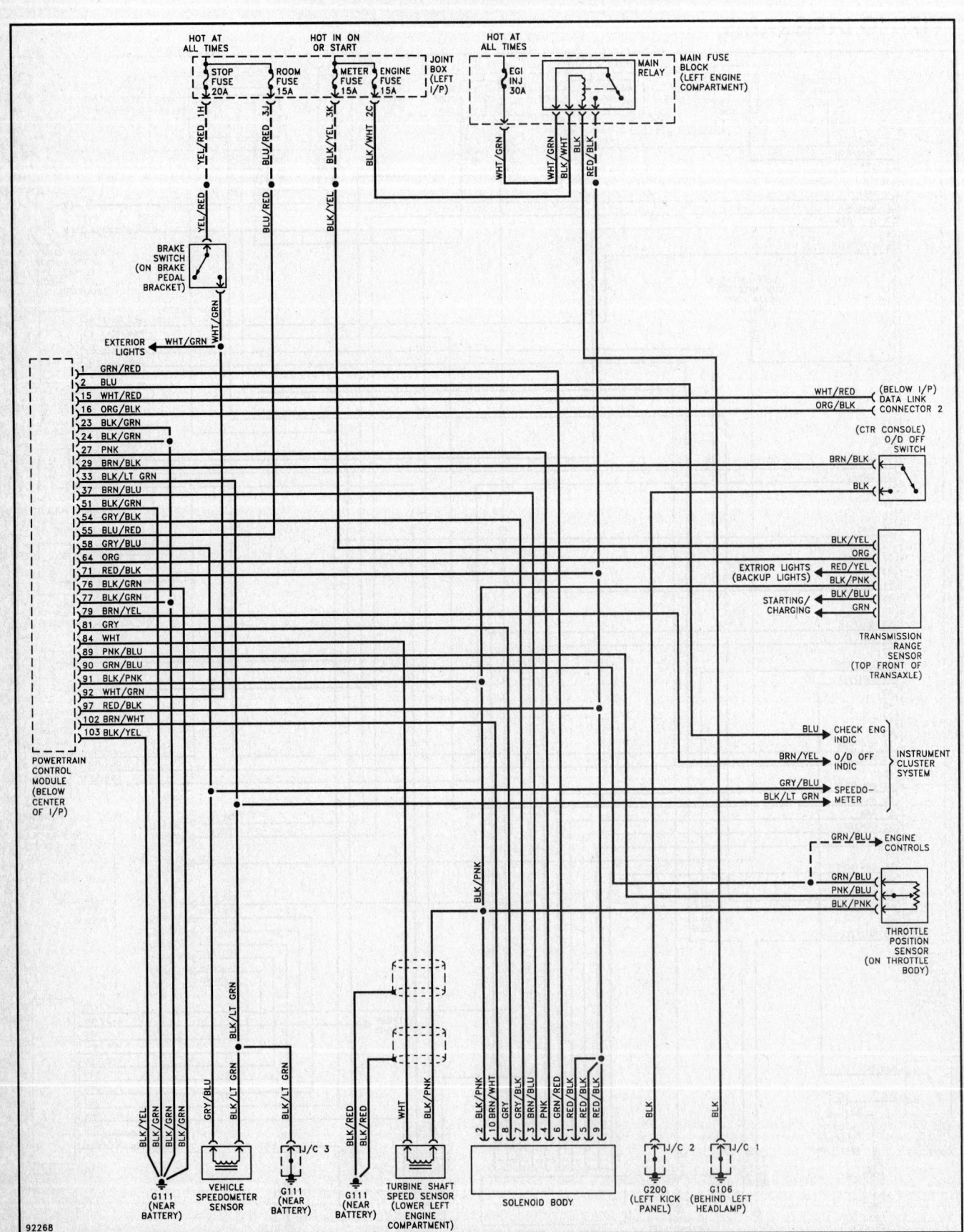

Fig. 3: *Transaxle Wiring Diagram (1996 MX-6 2.0L & 626 2.0L)*

Millenia

APPLICATION & LABOR TIMES

APPLICATION & LABOR TIMES

Vehicle Application	Labor Times [1] R & I	[2] Overhaul	Trans. Model
Millenia 2.3L	7.8	8.6	LJ4A-EL

[1] – Removal and installation of transmission from vehicle chassis.
[2] – On bench overhaul for transmission and differential. DOES NOT include removal and installation.

CAUTION: Disconnecting battery on models equipped with anti-theft radio requires canceling of anti-theft operation. See appropriate AUTOMATIC TRANSMISSION SERVICING article in TRANSMISSION SERVICING section. Refer to vehicle owner's manual to identify radio type.

IDENTIFICATION

Vehicle Identification Number (VIN) is used for correct application of component parts and assemblies. Number is on a plate located at top left of instrument panel and on transaxle flange (exhaust side of engine).

DESCRIPTION

The LJ4A-EL is a 4-speed electronically controlled automatic transaxle that incorporate 5 multi-disc hydraulic clutches, 2 one-way clutches (sprag type) and a friction lined brake band that prevents rotation of front sun gear drum. *See Fig. 1.*

ON/OFF and duty cycle solenoids control shift changes, line pressure and torque converter clutch lock-up. Solenoids are attached to valve body. Solenoids are operated by Transmission Control Module (TCM).

TCM receives information from various input devices and uses this information to control solenoids for transaxle shifting, line pressure, shift feel and torque converter clutch lock-up.

LUBRICATION & ADJUSTMENTS

See appropriate AUTOMATIC TRANSMISSION SERVICING article in TRANSMISSION SERVICING section.

TROUBLE SHOOTING

Preliminary Checks – Automatic transaxle malfunction can be caused by either engine or transaxle problems. Isolate malfunction to engine or transaxle before proceeding with trouble shooting. Prior to trouble shooting check and adjust shift linkage, range switch and idle speed as needed. Ensure fluid level is correct. Check tires for correct inflation.

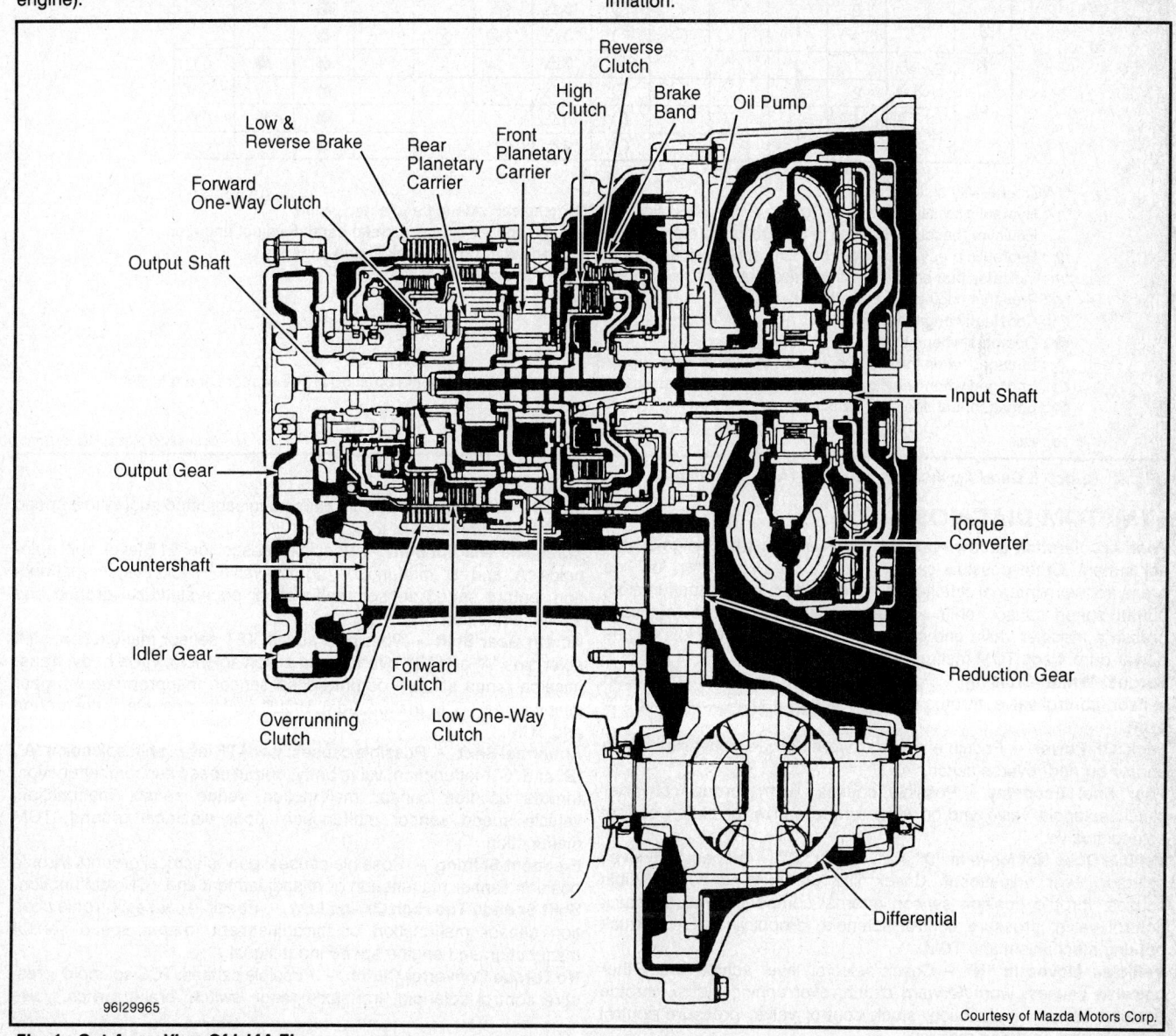

96129965

Courtesy of Mazda Motors Corp.

Fig. 1: Cut-Away View Of LJ4A-EL

CLUTCH & BAND APPLICATION TABLE

Range	Mode	Gear	Shift	Reverse clutch	High clutch	Forward clutch	Over-running clutch	Band servo piston 2nd applied	3GR released	4GR applied	Forward OWC	Low OWC	Low and reverse brake
P	—	—	—										
R	—	Reverse	—	O									O
N	—	—	—										
D	Except HOLD	1	↕			O					●	●	
		2	↕			O		O			●		
		3	↕		O	O		*1⊗	⊗		●		
		4	↕		O	⊗		*2⊗	⊗	O			
	HOLD	2	↕			O	*3◎	O			●		
		3	↕		O	O	*3◎	*1⊗	⊗		●		
		4	↑		O	⊗		*2⊗	⊗	O			
S	Except HOLD	1	↕			O					●	●	
		2	↕			O	*3△	O			●		
		3	↕		O	O	*3△	*1⊗	⊗		●		
	HOLD	2	↑			O	*3△	O			●		
		3	↕		O	O	*3△	*1⊗	⊗		●		
L	Except HOLD	1	↕			O	*3△				●	●	O
		2	↕			O	*3△	O			●		
	HOLD	1	↑			O	*3△				●	●	O
		2				O	*3△	O			●		

OWC: one-way clutch

*1 : Hydraulic pressure is applied to both 2nd applied side and 3GR released side of band servo piston.
However, because the area of 3GR released side is larger than 2nd applied side, the brake band does not engage.

*2 : Hydraulic pressure is applied to O/D applied side in the above conditions (*1) and brake band engages.

*3 : Indicates that engine braking is available as a result of operation of overrunning clutch.

*4 : Prevents engine overspeed.

O : Constantly engaged.

● : Operates when accelerated.

△ : Engaged when throttle opening is below approximately 5/8.

◎ : Engaged when vehicle speed is above approximately 10 km/h {6.2 MPH} and throttle opening is below approximately 5/8.

⊗ : Engaged, but does not transmit power.

96J29966

Courtesy of Mazda Motors Corp.

Fig. 2: Clutch & Band Application Table (LJ4A-EL Transaxle)

SYMPTOM DIAGNOSIS

Poor Acceleration & Low Maximum Speed – Inspect range switch adjustment. Other possible causes: worn torque converter, low line pressure, worn internal clutches, throttle position sensor malfunction, output speed sensor, shift solenoids, sticking pressure regulator, pressure modifier valve and or solenoid reducing valve, low engine power output and TCM malfunction.

Surges While Cruising – Possible causes: turbine shaft speed sensor, control valve, throttle position sensor, engine speed input to TCM.

Lack Of Power – Possible causes: worn torque converter clutch and/or burned reverse clutch.

Poor Fuel Economy – Possible causes: worn torque converter clutch solenoid valve and/or worn torque converter clutch control solenoid valve.

Vehicle Does Not Move In "D", "2", "1" Or "R" – Inspect ATF level, selector lever adjustment. Check line pressure. Other possible causes: throttle position sensor, internal component failure, stuck control valve, pressure control solenoid, dropping resistor, stuck parking mechanism and TCM.

Vehicles Moves In "N" – Check selector lever adjustment. Other possible causes: worn forward clutch, overrunning clutch, throttle position sensor malfunction, stuck control valve, pressure control solenoid and dropping resistor.

Excessive Creep – Possible causes: misadjusted engine idle speed or high line pressure at idle.

Transaxle Will Not Shift – Possible causes: low ATF level, shift solenoids "A" and "B" malfunction, control valve, HOLD system malfunction, output speed sensor malfunction, poor electrical ground and TCM malfunction.

No 4th Gear Shift – Possible causes: TFT sensor malfunction, shift solenoids "A" and "B", overrunning clutch solenoid, valve body, transmission range sensor, output speed sensor, inappropriate 4th gear inhibit signal (TCM malfunction), HOLD switch, poor electrical ground and TCM.

Abnormal Shift – Possible causes: low ATF level, shift solenoids "A", "B" and "C" malfunction, valve body, output speed sensor malfunction, throttle position sensor malfunction, range sensor malfunction, vehicle speed sensor malfunction, poor electrical ground, TCM malfunction.

Frequent Shifting – Possible causes: poor electrical ground, throttle position sensor malfunction or misadjustment and TCM malfunction.

Shift Speeds Too High Or Too Low – Possible causes: throttle position sensor malfunction or misadjustment, output speed sensor malfunction and engine speed input signal.

No Torque Converter Clutch – Possible causes: TCC solenoid, pressure control solenoid, transaxle range switch, brake switch, valve body, transaxle fluid temperature sensor, engine speed input signal to TCM, output speed sensor, vehicle speed sensor, TCM malfunction and torque converter.

No Kickdown – Possible causes: throttle position sensor, shift solenoids "A" and "B", HOLD switch, transaxle range switch, pressure control solenoid, output speed sensor, valve body and TCM malfunction.

Transaxle Shift Flare – Possible causes: ATF level (low), selector lever adjustment, throttle position sensor, line pressure (low), internal component failure, pressure control solenoid, valve body, output speed sensor, transaxle fluid temperature sensor and TCM malfunction.

Excessive Gear Engagement Shock – Possible causes: idle speed (high), throttle position sensor, line pressure (high), valve body, internal clutch slippage, pressure control solenoid, shift solenoids, transaxle fluid temperature sensor, N-D accumulator, transaxle range switch, output speed sensor and TCM malfunction.

Excessive Gear Shift Shock – Possible causes: ATF level (high), throttle position sensor, line pressure (high), valve body, internal clutch slippage, pressure control solenoid, shift solenoids, pressure control solenoid, output speed sensor, transaxle fluid temperature sensor and TCM malfunction.

No Engine Braking – Possible causes: ATF level (low), internal clutch slippage, valve body, shift solenoids "B" and/or "C" and TCM malfunction.

Transaxle Overheats – Possible causes: ATF level (low), internal component failure, torque converter clutch piston, shift solenoids, pressure control solenoid, throttle position sensor, output speed sensor, vehicle speed sensor, engine speed input signal, transaxle fluid temperature sensor, TCM malfunction and fluid cooling system.

TESTING

PRELIMINARY CHECKS

Before testing transaxle, ensure fluid level is correct and shift linkage, range switch and idle speed are adjusted correctly.

ROAD TEST SPECIFICATIONS

TIME LAG TEST

Preparation – Check and adjust coolant, engine oil and ATF levels. Warm engine and transaxle to normal operating temperature. Block front and rear wheels on both sides. Set parking brake. Ensure engine idle speed and ignition timing is correct. See appropriate ON-VEHICLE ADJUSTMENTS article in ENGINE PERFORMANCE in appropriate MITCHELL® manual.

This test measures time lag between selecting specific gear and actual transaxle shift. Test checks condition of the 1-2, 3-4/N-R and N-D accumulators, forward and one-way clutches, 2-4 brake band and low-reverse brake.

Testing – Start engine and shift from "N" to "D", "N" to "S" and "N" to "R". Measure time interval from moving shift lever to when shift shock is felt. See TIME LAG TEST SPECIFICATIONS table and TIME LAG TEST EVALUATION table.

TIME LAG TEST SPECIFICATIONS

Application Range	Time Seconds
"N" To "D"	Less Than 0.9
"N" To "R"	Less Than 1.1

TIME LAG TEST EVALUATION [1]

Application & Shift	Time	Possible Cause
"N" To "D", Then "N"-"D" HOLD		Insufficient Line Pressure
		Forward Clutch Slipping
		Forward One-Way Clutch Slipping
"N"-"D" HOLD		Insufficient Line Pressure
		1-2 Accumulator Not Operating Properly
"N"-"D"		Insufficient Line Pressure
		Low One-Way Clutch Slipping
		N-D Accumulator Not Operating Properly
"N"-"R"		Insufficient Line Pressure
		Low-Reverse Brake Slipping
Reverse Clutch Slipping		N-R Accumulator Not Operating Properly

[1] – Possible causes for time lag being above specification.

Range/Mode		Throttle condition (throttle position sensor voltage)	Shift	Vehicle speed km/h {mph}
D	Except HOLD	Wide open throttle	$D_1 \rightarrow D_2$	50—56 {31—34}
			$D_2 \rightarrow D_3$	92—100 {58—62}
			$D_3 \rightarrow D_4$	166—176 {103—109}
		Half throttle	$D_1 \rightarrow D_2$	42—48 {27—29}
			$D_2 \rightarrow D_3$	84—96 {52—59}
			$D_3 \rightarrow D_4$	146—164 {91—101}
			Lockup ON (D_3)	114—126 {71—78}
			Lockup ON (D_4)	146—164 {91—101}
		Closed throttle position	$D_4 \rightarrow D_3$	32—38 {20—23}
			$D_3 \rightarrow D_2$	5—11 {4—6}
			$D_2 \rightarrow D_1$	5—11 {4—6}
		Kickdown	$D_4 \rightarrow D_3$	147—157 {92—97}
			$D_3 \rightarrow D_2$	83—91 {52—56}
			$D_2 \rightarrow D_1$	30—37 {19—22}
	HOLD	—	$D_2 \rightarrow D_3$	15—25 {10—15}
			$D_4 \rightarrow D_3$	166—176 {103—109}
			$D_3 \rightarrow D_2$	7—13 {5—8}
			Lockup ON (D_3)	114—126 {71—78}

96A29967

Courtesy of Mazda Motors Corp.

Fig. 3: Shift Speed Table (1995-96 Millenia)

ROAD TEST

NOTE: Road test evaluation information is not available from manufacturer.

1) Check for shift shock, positive shifts and shifting through all ranges. Ensure kickdown occurs within kickdown limits. See appropriate chart in ROAD TEST SPECIFICATIONS CHARTS. Manually shift from "D" to "S". Shift should take place immediately and engine braking should occur.

2) Manually shift from "D" to "2" to "L". Ensure appropriate downshift takes place with engine braking in 3rd and 2nd gear. With gear selector in "L", ensure transaxle does not upshift from "1". With gear selector in "2", ensure no upshift from "2" occurs.

3) Depress HOLD switch. HOLD function may be activated in "D", "S" or "L" gears. In "L" and "S" positions vehicle is held in these gears and no upshift or downshift takes place. In "D" position a 1-2 and 2-3 upshift is permitted when starting from a stop but after the 2-3 upshift the vehicle is locked in "D" until it comes to a complete stop. The 1-2 and 2-3 upshift pattern is changed to a "short shift" specification. Pushing HOLD button again deactivates system.

4) Ensure transaxle stays locked in "P". Compare actual shift speeds with ROAD TEST SPECIFICATIONS. *See Figs. 3.* Road test evaluation information is not available from manufacturer if upshifts and downshifts are not as specified.

STALL SPEED TEST

Preparation – Check and adjust coolant, engine oil and ATF levels. Warm engine and transaxle to operating temperature. Block front and rear wheels on both sides. Set parking brake. Connect tachometer to engine. Ensure engine idle speed and ignition timing is correct. See appropriate ON-VEHICLE ADJUSTMENTS article in ENGINE PERFORMANCE in appropriate MITCHELL® manual.

CAUTION: Stall test generates high ATF temperatures. DO NOT hold throttle open at stall speed for more than 5 seconds. Allow engine to idle for at least one minute to cool fluid between each test.

Testing – Firmly depress brake pedal with engine running. Select "R" range and depress accelerator pedal to floor. When engine speed no longer increases, read RPM on tachometer and release accelerator pedal. Perform stall test in "R" , "D", "S" and "L". Compare RPM with STALL SPEED table.

NOTE: Stall speed specifications are approximate.

STALL SPEED

Gear Position	RPM
"D", "S" Or "L"	2150-2450
"R"	1950-2250

STALL SPEED EVALUATION

High In "L", "S", "D" & "R" – Worn oil pump. Oil leakage from oil pump, control valve and/or transmission case. Stuck pressure regulator valve.

High In "D" & "S" (HOLD Off) – Forward clutch, forward one-way clutch and/or low one-way clutch slipping.

High In "R" – Low-reverse brake slipping. Reverse clutch slipping. Perform road test to determine whether problem is low-reverse brake or reverse clutch. If engine braking is okay in "L", problem is reverse clutch. If no engine braking is present in "L", problem is low-reverse brake.

Below Specifications – Engine out of tune. One-way clutch slipping within torque converter.

LINE PRESSURE TEST

Inspection of line pressure checks the condition of hydraulic components and ensures that no internal oil leakages exist.

Preparation – Follow stall speed test preparation. Connect line pressure gauge to line pressure test port. *See Fig. 4.* Place line pressure gauge where it can be read from driver seat. Ensure engine idle speed and ignition timing is correct. See appropriate ON-VEHICLE ADJUSTMENTS article in ENGINE PERFORMANCE in appropriate MITCHELL® manual.

Testing – Start engine, depress brake pedal firmly, shift selector to "D" and read line pressure at idle. Depress accelerator fully and read line pressure as soon as RPM becomes constant, then release accelerator pedal. Shift selector to "N" and idle engine for at least one minute, to cool fluid. Read line pressure at idle and stall speeds for each range in the same manner. Compare with LINE PRESSURE TEST SPECIFICATIONS table and LINE PRESSURE TEST EVALUATION.

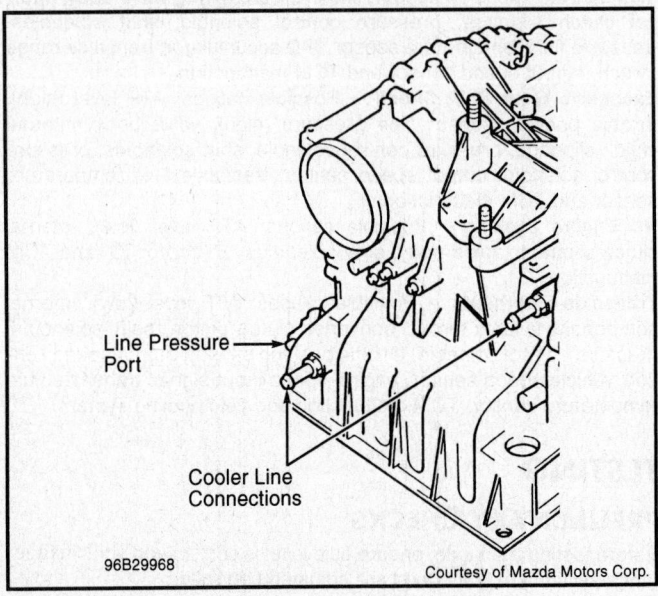

Line Pressure Port

Cooler Line Connections

96B29968   Courtesy of Mazda Motors Corp.

Fig. 4: Locating Line Pressure Test Port (LJ4A-EL)

LINE PRESSURE TEST SPECIFICATIONS

Application & Range	Idle Pressure psi (kPa)	Stall Pressure psi (kPa)
"D", "S" & "L"	64-69 (450-510)	175-186 (1210-1280)
"R"	80-91 (550-620)	234-244 (1610-1680)

LINE PRESSURE TEST EVALUATION

Low At Idle In "D", "S", "L" & "R" – Worn oil pump. Fluid leaking from oil pump, valve body or transaxle case. Pressure regulator valve stuck.

Low At Idle In "D", "S" & "L" – Fluid leaking from hydraulic circuit of forward clutch.

Low At Idle In "D" & "S" (HOLD On) – Fluid leaking from hydraulic circuit of band apply servo.

Low At Idle In "R" – Fluid leaking from hydraulic circuit of reverse brake.

Low At Idle In "L" & "R" – Fluid leaking from hydraulic circuit of low and reverse brake.

High At Idle In "D", "S", "L" & "R" – Throttle position sensor misadjusted. Pressure control solenoid sticking. Transmission fluid temperature sensor damaged. Pressure control solenoid short circuit. Throttle valve stuck. Pressure modulator valve stuck. Pressure regulator valve stuck.

Low At Stall Speed In "D", "S", "L" & "R" – Throttle position sensor misadjusted. Pressure control solenoid sticking. Pressure control solenoid short circuit. Throttle valve stuck. Pressure modulator valve stuck. Pressure regulator valve stuck. Pressure modifier valve sticking. Pilot valve sticking. Oil pump control piston damaged.

ON-VEHICLE SERVICE

See appropriate article in TRANSMISSION SERVICING section.

REMOVAL & INSTALLATION

For transmission removal and installation, see appropriate AUTOMATIC TRANSMISSION REMOVAL article in TRANSMISSION SERVICING section.

TORQUE CONVERTER

1) Torque converter is a sealed unit and cannot be disassembled for service. Inspect for damage and cracks. Replace torque converter if defective. Remove any rust from pilot hub and boss of converter.

2) Flush torque converter. After converter is removed from cleaner, thoroughly drain solvent through hub. Add about 2.1 qt. (2.0L) clean ATF to converter. Agitate fluid by hand. Drain ATF from converter.

TRANSAXLE DISASSEMBLY

1) Mount transaxle on stand. Remove torque converter. Remove manual rod and bracket. Remove transmission range switch. Remove output speed sensor. See Fig. 5. Remove vehicle speed sensor, located beside differential assembly.

2) Remove oil pan. Remove retaining clip from electrical harness on outside of case. Unbolt and remove valve body with electrical harness. Remove low and reverse brake sleeve. See Fig. 6. Remove 2-3 accumulator spring.

3) Unbolt and remove converter housing from transaxle case. Remove differential assembly. Remove oil pump and gasket. See Fig. 9. Loosen lock nut securing 2-4 brake band anchor end bolt. Remove anchor end bolt. Remove 2-4 brake band.

4) Pulling up on input shaft, remove reverse clutch, high clutch, high clutch hub and front sun gear as an assembly. Using appropriate compressor tool, compress brake band servo. See Fig. 7. Remove snap ring.

5) Remove servo retainer, servo piston and return springs. See Fig. 9. Remove snap ring retaining low one-way clutch. Remove clutch. Unbolt and remove transaxle case side cover. Remove output gear and thrust bearing.

6) Remove front planetary carrier and low and reverse brake piston. Remove snap ring. Pull out front planetary carrier and low and reverse brake piston retainer as an assembly. Remove low and reverse brake spring and retainer.

7) Remove rear sun gear and rear planetary carrier. Remove rear internal gear and forward clutch hub. Remove overrunning clutch hub. Remove thrust washer and bearing race from hub. See Fig. 9.

NOTE: *Do not remove idler gear unless necessary.*

Fig. 5: *Removing Output Speed Sensor*

8) Remove forward clutch drum. Move selector lever to Park position. Remove idler gear lock nut. Using press and appropriate adapter, press out idler gear from case. Remove reduction gear outer race (if necessary).

9) Remove parking lever and parking rod. See Fig. 8. Remove parking pawl, parking actuator support and spring. Remove drum support. See Fig. 9.

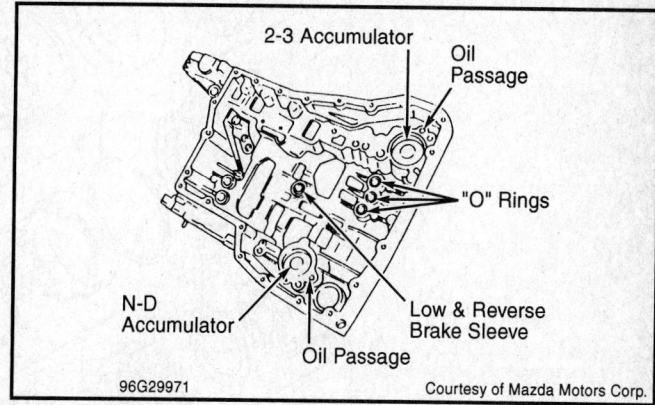

Fig. 6: *Locating Accumulators & Low & Reverse Brake Sleeve*

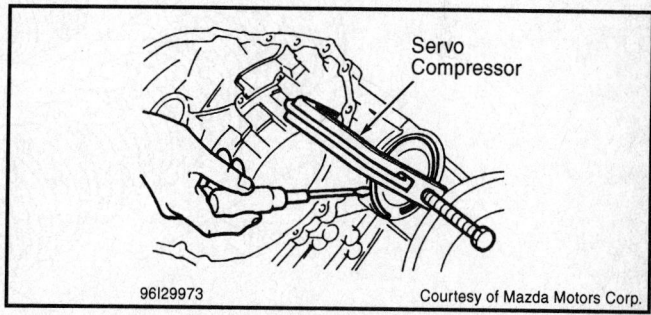

Fig. 7: *Removing 2-4 Brake Band Servo Snap Ring*

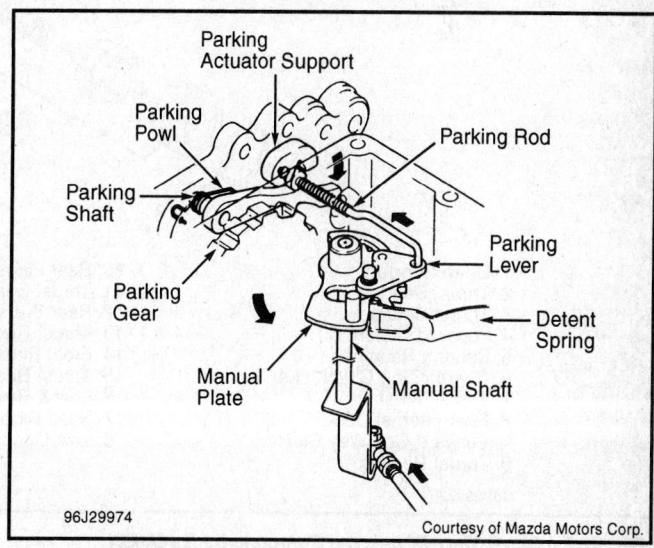

Fig. 8: *Identifying Parking Mechanism Components*

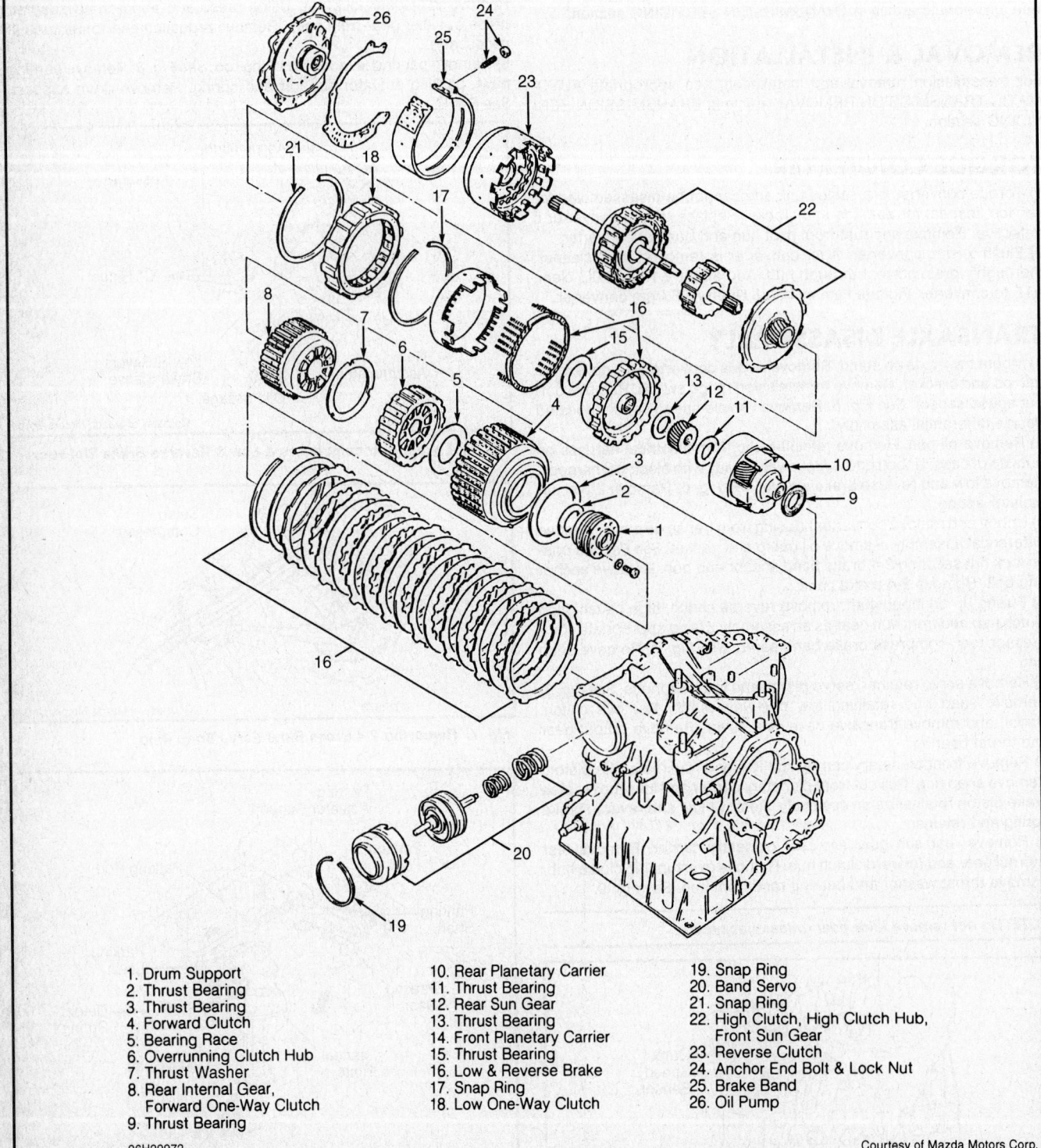

Fig. 9: Exploded View Of Internal Components (LJ4A-EL)

1. Drum Support
2. Thrust Bearing
3. Thrust Bearing
4. Forward Clutch
5. Bearing Race
6. Overrunning Clutch Hub
7. Thrust Washer
8. Rear Internal Gear, Forward One-Way Clutch
9. Thrust Bearing
10. Rear Planetary Carrier
11. Thrust Bearing
12. Rear Sun Gear
13. Thrust Bearing
14. Front Planetary Carrier
15. Thrust Bearing
16. Low & Reverse Brake
17. Snap Ring
18. Low One-Way Clutch
19. Snap Ring
20. Band Servo
21. Snap Ring
22. High Clutch, High Clutch Hub, Front Sun Gear
23. Reverse Clutch
24. Anchor End Bolt & Lock Nut
25. Brake Band
26. Oil Pump

96H29972

Courtesy of Mazda Motors Corp.

COMPONENT DISASSEMBLY & REASSEMBLY

ACCUMULATORS

Disassembly – Remove accumulator pistons by applying air pressure to oil passages. *See Fig. 6.* Measure spring free length. See LJ4A-EL ACCUMULATOR SPRING SPECIFICATIONS table. If not within specifications, replace spring.

Reassembly – To reassemble, reverse disassembly procedure. Note location of piston and springs. See LJ4A-EL ACCUMULATOR & SIZE chart.

LJ4A-EL ACCUMULATOR SPRING SPECIFICATIONS

Application	In. (mm)
N-D	1.79 (45.5)
2-3	2.07 (52.5)

LJ4A-EL ACCUMULATOR & SIZE

Seal Ring & Piston Application	Large In. (mm)	Small In. (mm)
N-D Accumulator [1]	1.772 (45.0)	1.142 (29.0)
2-3 Accumulator [1]	1.969 (50.0)	1.260 (32.0)

[1] – For location on transaxle case, See Fig. 6.

OIL PUMP

NOTE: Do not place reference marks on oil pump rotors with a punch.

Disassembly – Remove oil pump cover mounting bolts in crisscross pattern. Mark inner and outer rotors for reassembly reference. Remove flange, inner and outer rotors. See Fig. 10. Remove selective bearing race, "O" rings and seal rings from cover.

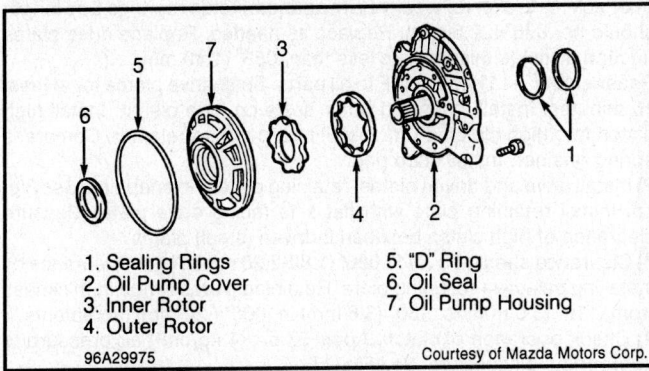

1. Sealing Rings	5. "D" Ring
2. Oil Pump Cover	6. Oil Seal
3. Inner Rotor	7. Oil Pump Housing
4. Outer Rotor	

96A29975   Courtesy of Mazda Motors Corp.

Fig. 10: Exploded View Of LJ4A-EL Oil Pump

Inspection – **1)** Check oil pump for broken or worn seal ring or weak springs. Check for damaged or worn sliding surfaces. Replace as required.
2) Measure clearances of all wear surfaces. See OIL PUMP SPECIFICATIONS table. If clearances are not within specifications, replace oil pump.
3) At several points around surface, measure end clearance between oil pump housing and rotors. See Fig. 11. Measure clearance between oil pump boss and inner rotor.

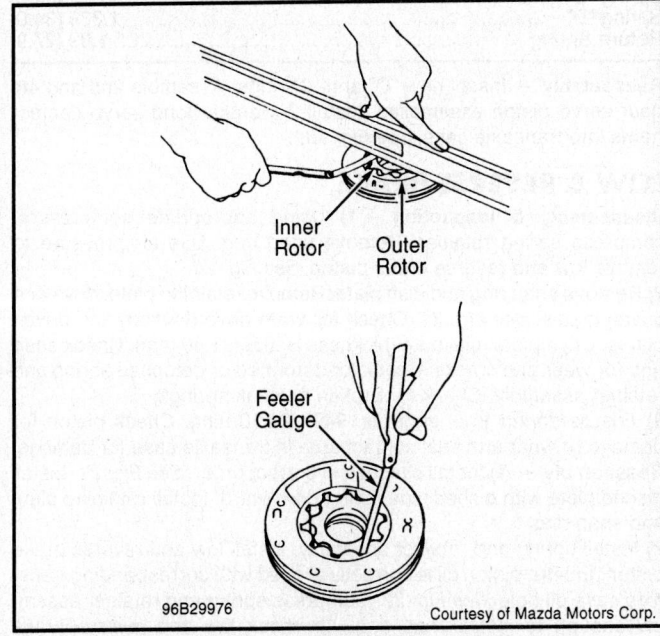

96B29976   Courtesy of Mazda Motors Corp.

Fig. 11: Measuring Oil Pump Rotor End & Side Clearance

NOTE: Ensure all components are coated with ATF during assembly

Reassembly – Align rotor reference marks and install rotors in oil pump housing. Install oil pump flange. Install oil pump cover on oil pump flange and tighten in crisscross pattern. Install new seal rings.

OIL PUMP SPECIFICATIONS

Application	In. (mm)
Rotor End Clearance	
Standard	.0008-.006 (.020-.15)
Service Limit	.006 (.15)
Rotor Side Clearance	
Standard	.0008-.0016 (.020-.040)
Service Limit	.0019 (.050)

REVERSE CLUTCH

Disassembly – **1)** Remove snap ring, retainer plate, drive and driven plates and dished plates from reverse clutch. See Fig. 12.
2) Compress return spring and remove snap ring. Remove return spring. Place reverse clutch drum on oil pump. Using air pressure, remove clutch piston from reverse clutch drum. See Fig. 13.
3) Check and repair or replace any faulty parts. Inspect piston check ball for leakage and sticking. Check for worn snap ring.
4) Check for broken or weak return spring. Replace drive plates (friction discs) is thickness is less than .055" (1.40 mm).

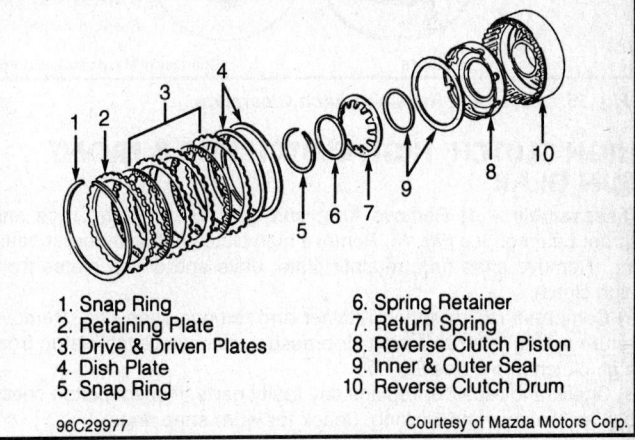

1. Snap Ring	6. Spring Retainer
2. Retaining Plate	7. Return Spring
3. Drive & Driven Plates	8. Reverse Clutch Piston
4. Dish Plate	9. Inner & Outer Seal
5. Snap Ring	10. Reverse Clutch Drum

96C29977   Courtesy of Mazda Motors Corp.

Fig. 12: Exploded View Of Reverse Clutch Assembly

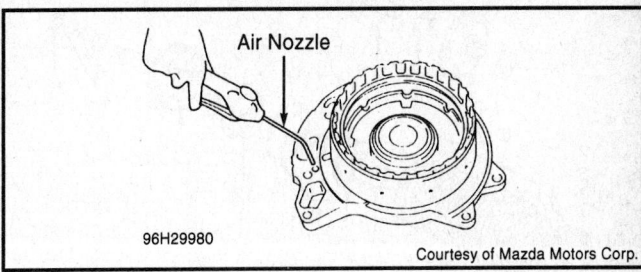

96H29980   Courtesy of Mazda Motors Corp.

Fig. 13: Removing Clutch Pistons & Air Checking Clutches

Reassembly – **1)** Apply ATF to all parts. Soak drive plates for at least 15 minutes. Install inner and outer seals on reverse piston. Install reverse piston into reverse clutch drum. Install piston return spring with tabs facing away from piston. Install return spring retainer. Compress spring and retainer. Install snap ring.
2) Install reverse clutch dished plates with dished sides facing each other. See Fig. 14. Install drive and driven plates, retaining plate and snap ring. Measure clearance of reverse clutch between retaining plate and snap ring. See Fig. 15.
3) Clearance should be .020-.031" (.50-.80 mm). Adjust clearance by installing selective retaining plate. Retaining plates range in thickness from .260" (6.6 mm) to .307" (7.8 mm) in .008" (.20 mm) increments.

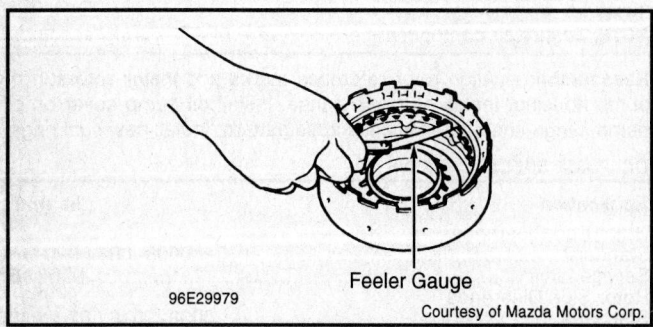

Fig. 14: Installing Reverse Clutch Dished Plates

4) Check operation of clutch by setting clutch assembly on oil pump. Apply 57 psi (4 kg/cm²) air pressure to appropriate oil passage. *See Fig. 13.*

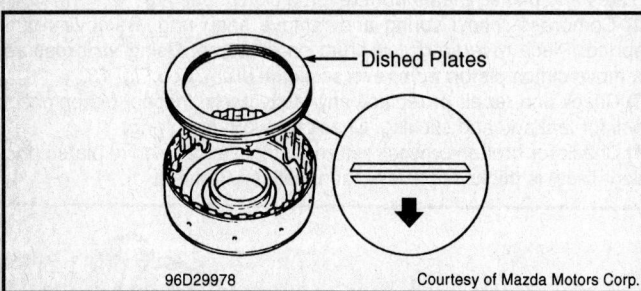

Fig. 15: Measuring Reverse Clutch Clearance

HIGH CLUTCH, HIGH CLUTCH HUB & FRONT SUN GEAR

Disassembly – 1) Remove front sun gear with bearing race and thrust bearing. *See Fig. 16.* Remove high clutch hub with thrust bearing. Remove snap ring, retainer plate, drive and driven plates from high clutch.

2) Compress return spring retainer and remove snap ring. Remove return spring retainer. Using air pressure, remove clutch piston from high clutch drum. *See Fig. 17.*

3) Check and repair or replace any faulty parts. Inspect piston check ball for leakage and sticking. Check for worn snap ring.

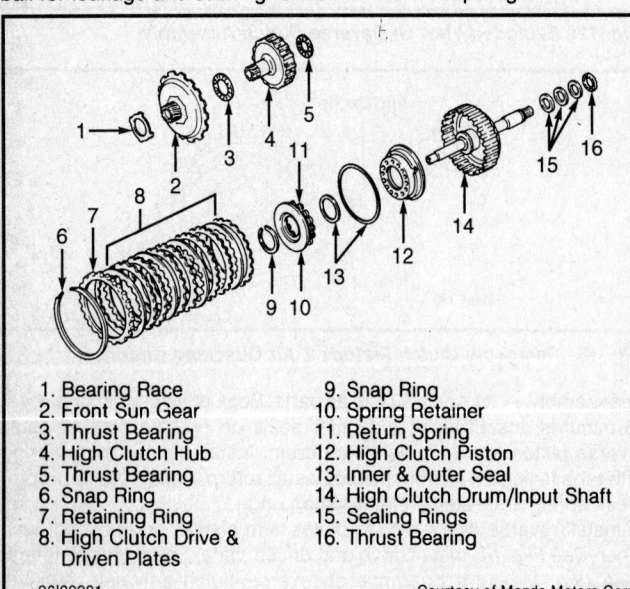

1. Bearing Race	9. Snap Ring
2. Front Sun Gear	10. Spring Retainer
3. Thrust Bearing	11. Return Spring
4. High Clutch Hub	12. High Clutch Piston
5. Thrust Bearing	13. Inner & Outer Seal
6. Snap Ring	14. High Clutch Drum/Input Shaft
7. Retaining Ring	15. Sealing Rings
8. High Clutch Drive & Driven Plates	16. Thrust Bearing

96I29981　　　　　Courtesy of Mazda Motors Corp.

Fig. 16: Exploded View Of High Clutch, High Clutch Hub & Front Sun Gear

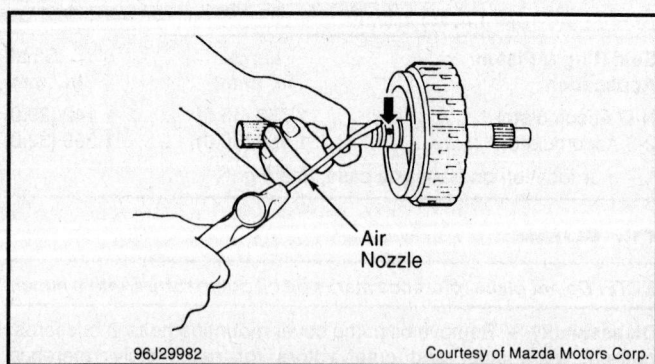

Fig. 17: Applying Air Pressure To High Clutch Assembly

4) Check for broken or weak return springs. Return springs free length should be .886" (22.5 mm). Replace as needed. Replace drive plates (friction discs) is thickness is less than .055" (1.40 mm).

Reassembly – 1) Apply ATF to all parts. Soak drive plates for at least 15 minutes. Install inner and outer seals on high piston. Install high piston into high clutch drum. Install return spring retainer. Compress spring retainer. Install snap ring.

2) Install drive and driven plates, retaining plate and snap ring. *See Fig. 16.* Install retaining plate with flat side facing drive plate. Measure clearance of high clutch between 2 driven (steel) plates.

3) Clearance should be .071-.086" (1.80-2.20 mm). Adjust clearance by installing selective retaining plate. Retaining plates range in thickness from .118" (3.0 mm) to .150" (3.8 mm) in .008" (.20 mm) increments.

4) Check operation of clutch. Apply 57 psi (4 kg/cm²) air pressure to appropriate oil passage. *See Fig. 17.*

2-4 BRAKE BAND SERVO

Disassembly – Separate servo retainer from servo piston. *See Fig. 18.* Disassemble 4th gear servo. Disassemble 2nd gear servo.

Inspection – Check for damaged or worn pistons and springs. See 2-4 BRAKE BAND SERVO SPRING SPECIFICATIONS.

2-4 BRAKE BAND SERVO SPRING SPECIFICATIONS

Application	Free Length In. (mm)
Spring "A"	1.508 (38.3)
Spring "B"	1.504 (38.2)
Spring "C"	1.339 (34.0)
Spring "D"	1.339 (34.0)
Return Spring	1.09 (27.9)

Reassembly – Install new "O" and "D" rings. Assemble 2nd and 4th gear servo piston assemblies. Install 2-4 brake band servo components into transaxle case. *See Fig. 18.* .

LOW & REVERSE BRAKE

Disassembly & Inspection – 1) Using appropriate compressor, compress spring retainer. Remove snap ring. Use air pressure to remove low and reverse brake piston. *See Fig. 20.*

2) Remove snap ring and dish plate. Remove retaining plate, drive and driven plates. *See Fig. 21.* Check for worn drive (friction) and driven plates. Drive plate minimum thickness is .055" (1.40 mm). Check snap ring for wear and cracks. Check for deformed or detached spring and retainer assembly. Check for broken or weak springs.

3) Ensure spring free length is .949" (24.10 mm). Check piston for damage or wear and seal contact area in transaxle case for damage.

Reassembly – 1) Install clutches in correct order. *See Fig. 21.* Install dished plate with dished side facing downward. Install retaining plate and snap ring.

2) Install spring and retainer assembly. Install low and reverse brake piston. Ensure piston oil is correctly aligned with corresponding transaxle case oil hole. *See Fig. 22.* Compress spring and retainer assembly enough to install snap ring. Air check low and reverse brake operation. *See Fig. 20.*

3) Measure clearance between transaxle case and driven plate. *See Fig. 23.* Clearance should be .067-.083" (1.70-2.10 mm). Adjust clearance by installing selective retainer plate. Retaining plates range in thickness from .079" (2.0 mm) to .134" (3.4 mm) in .008" (.20 mm) increments.

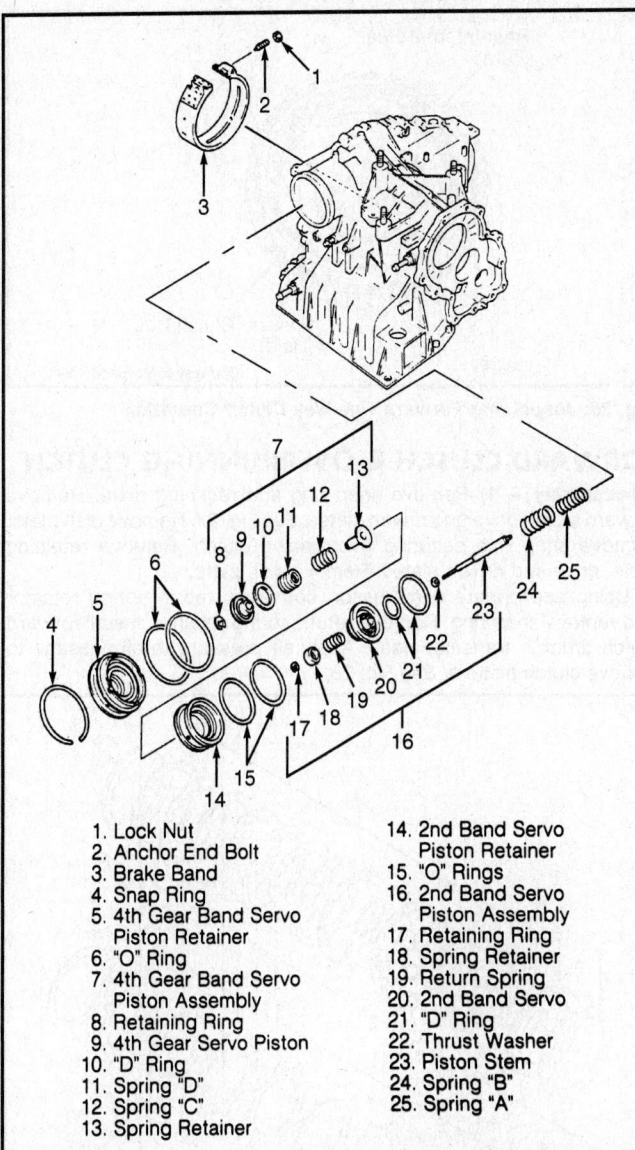

1. Lock Nut
2. Anchor End Bolt
3. Brake Band
4. Snap Ring
5. 4th Gear Band Servo Piston Retainer
6. "O" Ring
7. 4th Gear Band Servo Piston Assembly
8. Retaining Ring
9. 4th Gear Servo Piston
10. "D" Ring
11. Spring "D"
12. Spring "C"
13. Spring Retainer
14. 2nd Band Servo Piston Retainer
15. "O" Rings
16. 2nd Band Servo Piston Assembly
17. Retaining Ring
18. Spring Retainer
19. Return Spring
20. 2nd Band Servo
21. "D" Ring
22. Thrust Washer
23. Piston Stem
24. Spring "B"
25. Spring "A"

96B29984   Courtesy of Mazda Motors Corp.

Fig. 18: Exploded View Of 2-4 Brake Band Servo Assembly

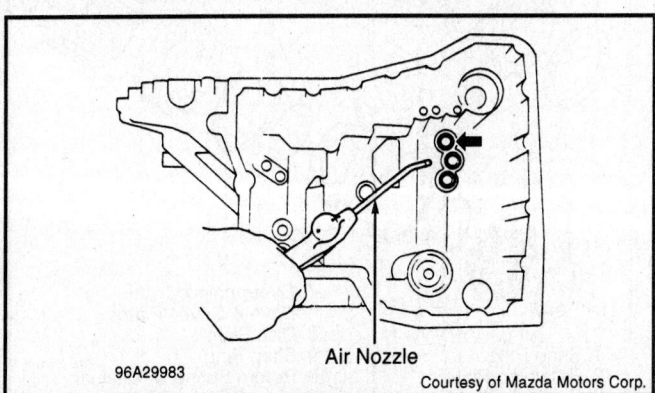

96A29983   Courtesy of Mazda Motors Corp.

Fig. 19: Checking 2-4 Brake Band Servo

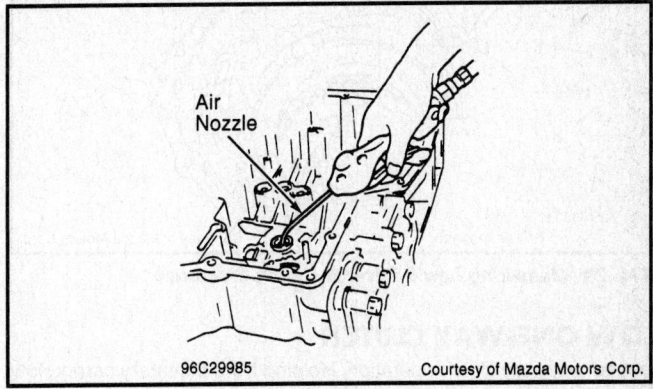

96C29985   Courtesy of Mazda Motors Corp.

Fig. 20: Applying Air Pressure To Low & Reverse Brake

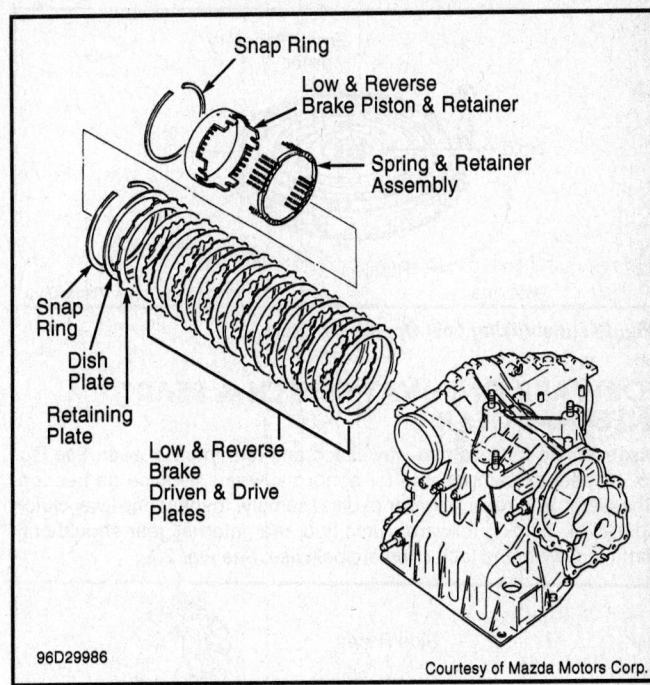

96D29986   Courtesy of Mazda Motors Corp.

Fig. 21: Exploded View Of Low & Reverse Brake

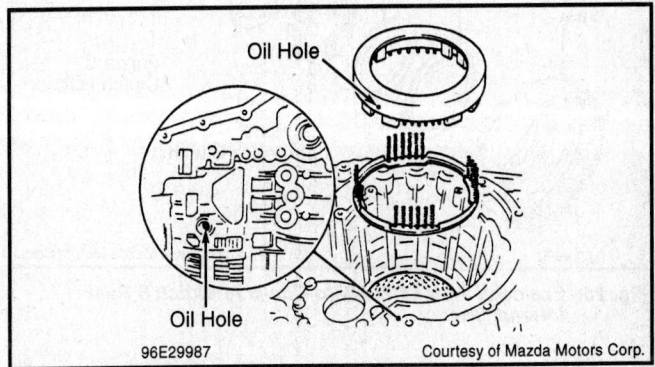

96E29987   Courtesy of Mazda Motors Corp.

Fig. 22: Locating Low & Reverse Oil Hole

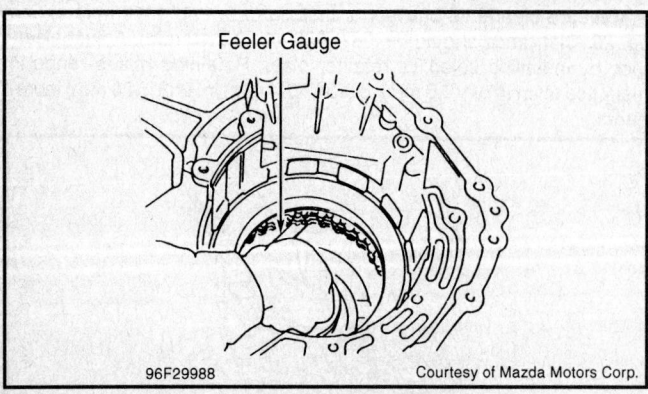

Fig. 23: Measuring Low & Reverse Clutch Clearance

LOW ONE-WAY CLUTCH

Inspect one-way clutch operation. Holding front planetary carrier, low one-way clutch should only rotate clockwise and lock when turned counterclockwise. See Fig. 24. Replace as needed.

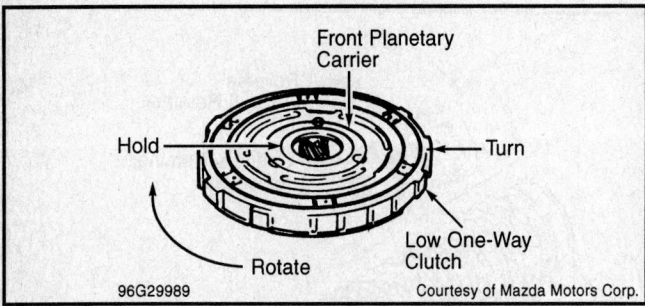

Fig. 24: Identifying Low One-Way Clutch

FORWARD ONE-WAY CLUTCH & REAR INTERNAL GEAR

Disassemble forward one-way clutch and rear internal gear. See Fig. 25. Inspect all components for abnormal wear. Replace as needed. Reassemble in reverse order of disassembly. Inspect one-way clutch operation. Holding forward clutch hub, rear internal gear should only turn clockwise and lock counterclockwise. See Fig. 26.

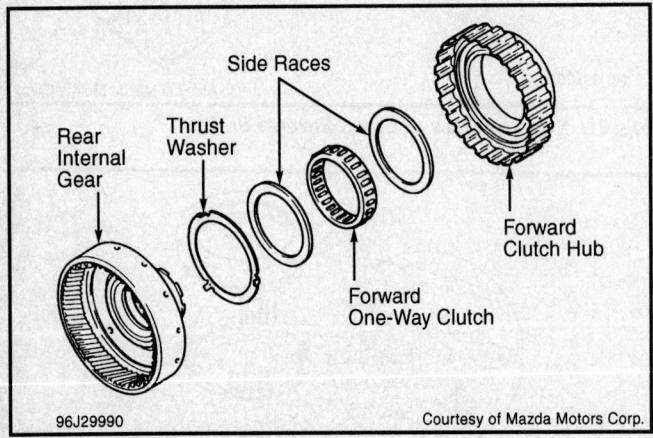

Fig. 25: Exploded View Of Forward One-Way Clutch & Rear Internal Gear

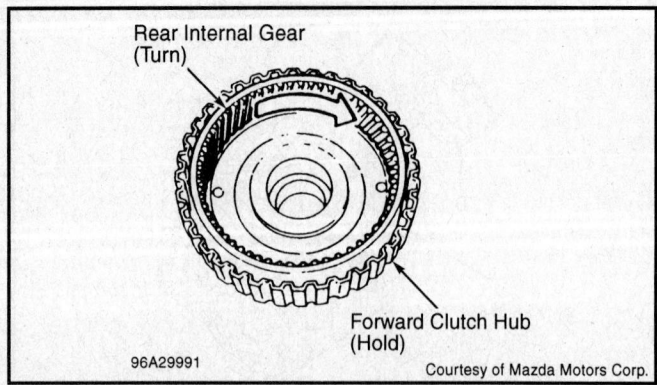

Fig. 26: Inspecting Forward One-Way Clutch Operation

FORWARD CLUTCH & OVERRUNNING CLUTCH

Disassembly – 1) Remove snap ring and retaining plate. Remove forward clutch drive and driven plates. See Fig. 27. Remove dish plate. Remove snap ring securing overrunning clutch. Remove retaining plate, drive and driven plates. Remove dish plate.

2) Using appropriate compressor, compress return spring retainer and remove snap ring. Remove return spring retainer. Install forward clutch drum in transaxle case. Apply air pressure to oil passage to remove clutch pistons. See Fig. 28.

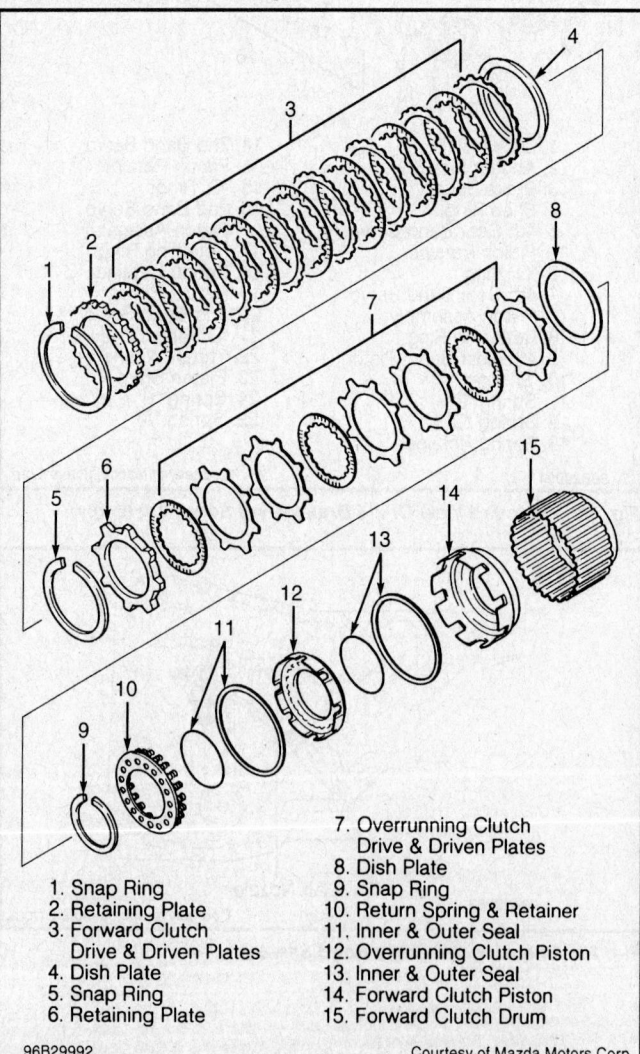

1. Snap Ring
2. Retaining Plate
3. Forward Clutch Drive & Driven Plates
4. Dish Plate
5. Snap Ring
6. Retaining Plate
7. Overrunning Clutch Drive & Driven Plates
8. Dish Plate
9. Snap Ring
10. Return Spring & Retainer
11. Inner & Outer Seal
12. Overrunning Clutch Piston
13. Inner & Outer Seal
14. Forward Clutch Piston
15. Forward Clutch Drum

Fig. 27: Exploded View Of Forward Clutch & Overrunning Clutch

3) Remove pistons from drum. Check for worn drive (friction) and driven plates. Drive plate minimum thickness for overrunning clutch is .055" (1.40 mm) or .071" (1.8 mm) for forward clutch. Check snap rings for wear and cracks. Check for deformed or detached spring and retainer assembly. Check for broken or weak springs.

4) Ensure spring free length is .841" (21.37 mm). Check piston for damage or wear and seal contact area in transaxle case for damage.
Reassembly – **1)** Apply ATF to all parts. Soak drive plates for at least 15 minutes. Install inner and outer seals on pistons. Install forward piston into clutch drum. Install overrunning piston. Install piston return spring with tabs facing away from piston. Install return spring retainer. Compress spring and retainer. Install snap ring.

2) Install dish plate with dished side facing upward. Install overrunning drive and driven clutch discs. Install retaining plate and snap ring.

3) Using feeler gauge, measure clearance of between drive and driven plates. See Fig. 29. Clearance should be .028-.043" (.70-1.10 mm). Adjust clearance by installing selective retaining plate. Retaining plates range in thickness from .118" (3.0 mm) to .150" (3.8 mm) in .008" (.20 mm) increments.

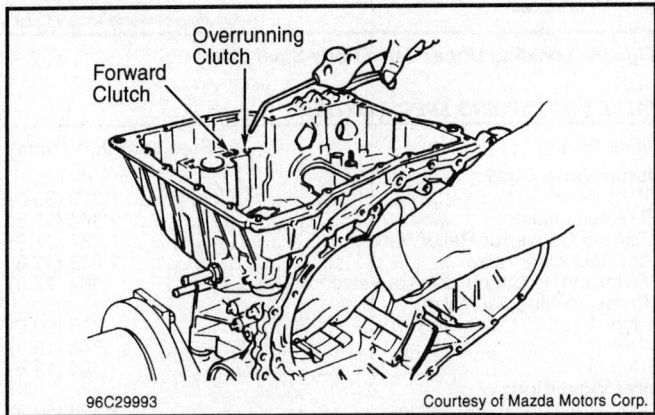

Fig. 28: **Air Checking Forward Clutch & Overrunning Clutch Operation**

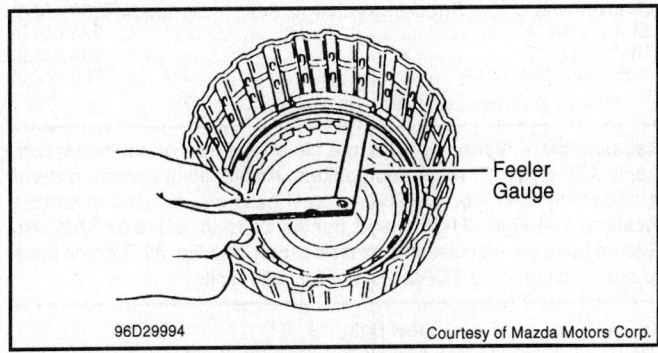

Fig. 29: **Measuring Overrunning Clutch Clearance**

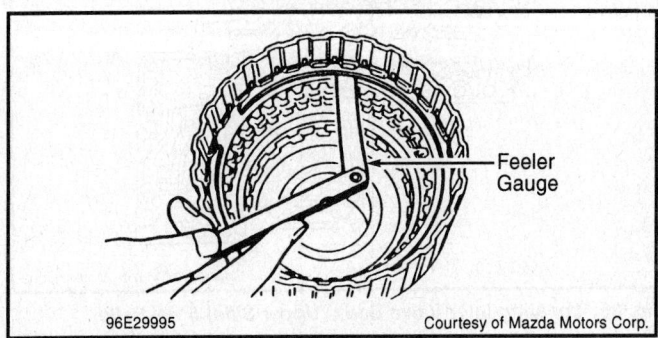

Fig. 30: **Measuring Forward Clutch Clearance**

4) Install forward clutch dish plate with dished side facing upward. Install forward drive and driven clutch discs. Install retaining plate and snap ring.

5) Using feeler gauge, measure clearance of between drive and driven plates. See Fig. 30. Clearance should be .018-.033" (.45-.85 mm). Adjust clearance by installing selective retaining plate. Retaining plates range in thickness from .150" (3.8 mm) to .197" (5.0 mm) in .008" (.20 mm) increments.

6) Install forward clutch drum in transaxle case. Apply air pressure to oil passage to check clutch operation. See Fig. 28.

DRUM SUPPORT

Disassemble drum support. See Fig. 31. Replace needle bearing as needed. Replace sealing rings. Apply petroleum jelly to thrust bearing.

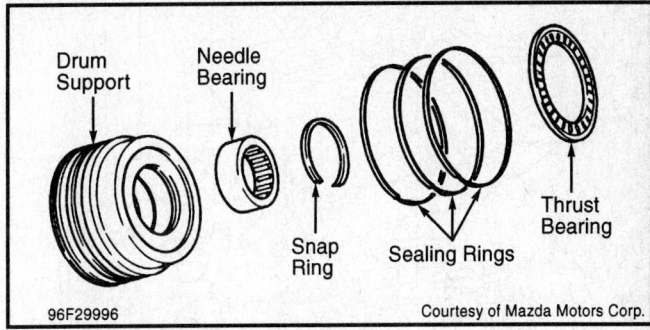

Fig. 31: **Exploded View Of Drum Support**

OUTPUT GEAR

Using appropriate puller, remove bearing as needed. Press on new bearing. Replace sealing rings. See Fig. 32. Apply petroleum jelly to thrust bearing.

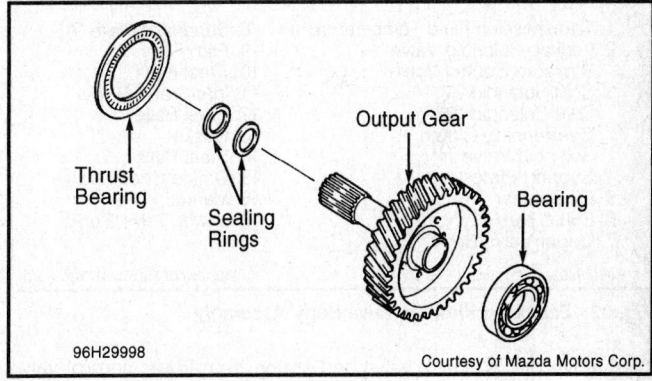

Fig. 32: **Exploded View Of Output Gear**

VALVE BODY

CAUTION: All valve body components must be installed in original location. Lay all components in sequence during removal for reassembly reference.

1) Remove Transmission Fluid Temperature (TFT) sensor from lower valve body. See Fig. 33. Remove lockup, pressure control solenoid valves from inter valve body. Remove remaining solenoid valves.

2) Remove bolts with support plates. Unbolt and remove oil strainer. Unbolt and remove upper valve body with separator plate "A" as an assembly to prevent loss of steel balls. Turn over upper valve body and remove steel balls. Remove pilot filter from separator plate "A". See Figs. 33 and 34.

3) Remove steel ball from upper side of inter valve body. See Fig. 35. Remove inter valve body with separator plate "B" as an assembly to prevent loss of steel balls. Turn over inter valve body and remove steel balls. See Fig. 36.

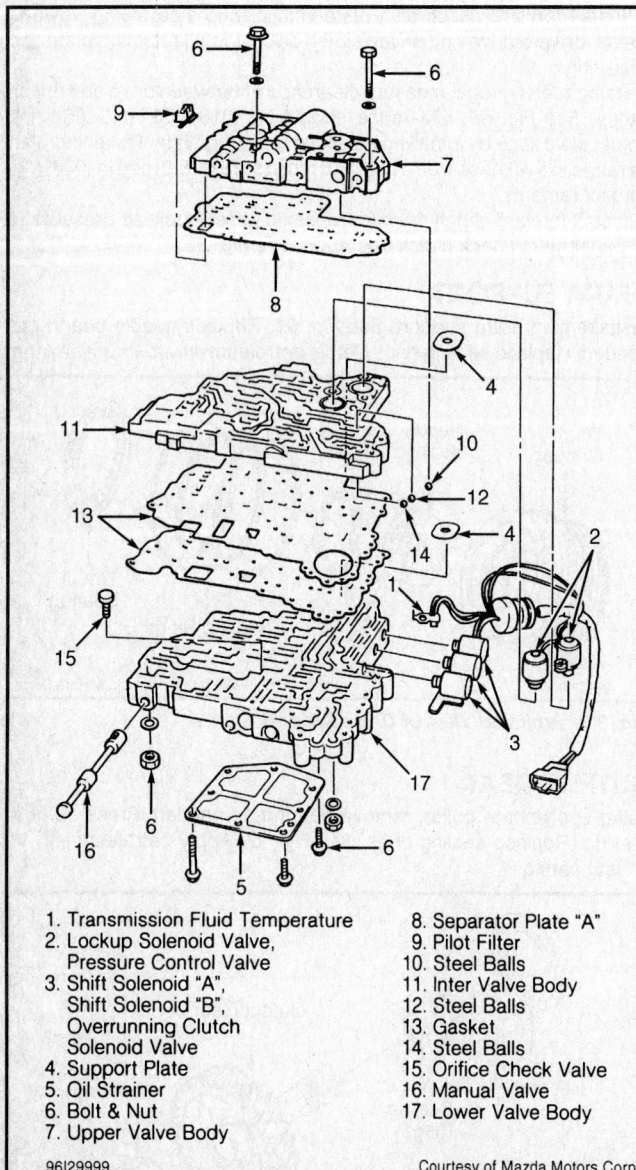

1. Transmission Fluid Temperature
2. Lockup Solenoid Valve, Pressure Control Valve
3. Shift Solenoid "A", Shift Solenoid "B", Overrunning Clutch Solenoid Valve
4. Support Plate
5. Oil Strainer
6. Bolt & Nut
7. Upper Valve Body
8. Separator Plate "A"
9. Pilot Filter
10. Steel Balls
11. Inter Valve Body
12. Steel Balls
13. Gasket
14. Steel Balls
15. Orifice Check Valve
16. Manual Valve
17. Lower Valve Body

96I29999   Courtesy of Mazda Motors Corp.

Fig. 33: Exploded View Of Valve Body Assembly

4) Remove orifice check valve and spring from lower control valve body. See Fig. 37. Remove manual valve.

Upper & Inter Valve Bodies – 1) Disassemble upper valve body in numbered order. See Fig. 38. Disassemble inter valve body in numbered order. See Fig. 40. If a valve does not slide out under its own weight, place valve body open side down and tap lightly with plastic hammer.

2) Clean all components in solvent. Dry with compressed air and immediately coat with ATF. Ensure all valve body passages are clear. Inspect valve for scoring or roughness. Ensure valves slide freely in bores.

3) Inspect valve springs for damage, squareness and collapsed coils. Measure spring free length. Replace spring if not within specification. See VALVE BODY SPRING SPECIFICATIONS table. Reassemble in reverse order of disassembly. Ensure all valves snap in place when moved.

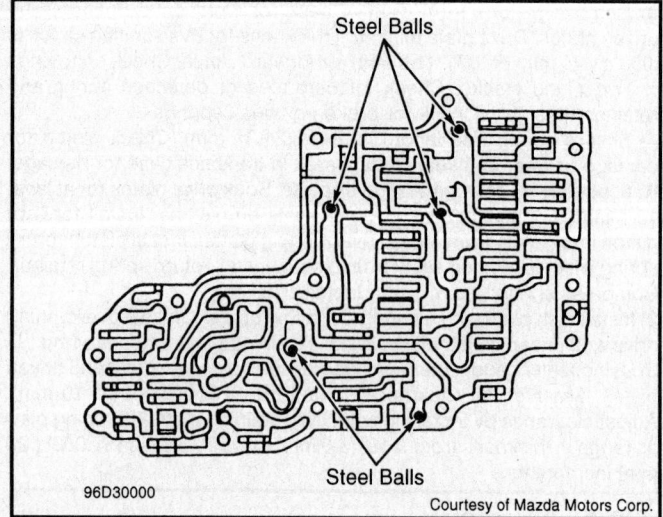

96D30000   Courtesy of Mazda Motors Corp.

Fig. 34: Locating Upper Valve Body Steel Balls

VALVE BODY SPRING SPECIFICATIONS

Valve Spring	Free Length In. (mm)
Upper Valve Body	
Pilot Valve	1.319 (33.5)
1-2 Accumulator	2.346 (59.6)
Torque Converter Relief Valve	1.087 (27.6)
1st Reducing Valve	1.008 (25.6)
Overrunning Clutch Control Valve	.984 (25.0)
Pressure Modifier Valve [1]	
No. 1	.795 (20.2)
No. 2	.748 (19.0)
No. 3	.764 (19.4)
Inter Valve Body	
Line Pressure Relief Valve	2.728 (69.3)
Pressure Regulator Valve	1.819 (46.2)
Pressure Regulator Plug	1.339 (34.0)
Lockup Control Valve	.984 (25.0)
Overrunning clutch Reducing Valve	1.280 (32.5)
Shift Valve "A"	.984 (25.0)
Shift Valve "B"	.984 (25.0)
4-2 Sequence Valve	.866 (22.0)

[1] – One of 3 valves listed may be installed.

Reassembly – Verify all parts are clean and free of contamination. Apply ATF to all "O" rings and gaskets. Assemble in reverse order if disassembly. See Fig. 33. Ensure steel balls are installed in correct location. See Figs. 34-36. Hand tighten bolts in crisscross pattern. Ensure bolts are installed in correct location. See Fig. 39. Tighten bolts to specification. See TORQUE SPECIFICATIONS.

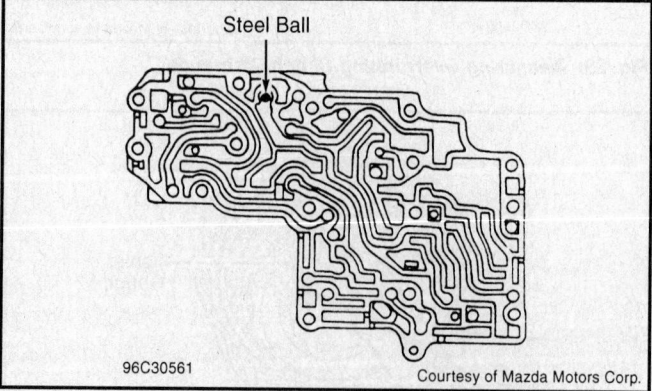

96C30561   Courtesy of Mazda Motors Corp.

Fig. 35: Locating Inter Valve Body (Upper Side) Steel Balls

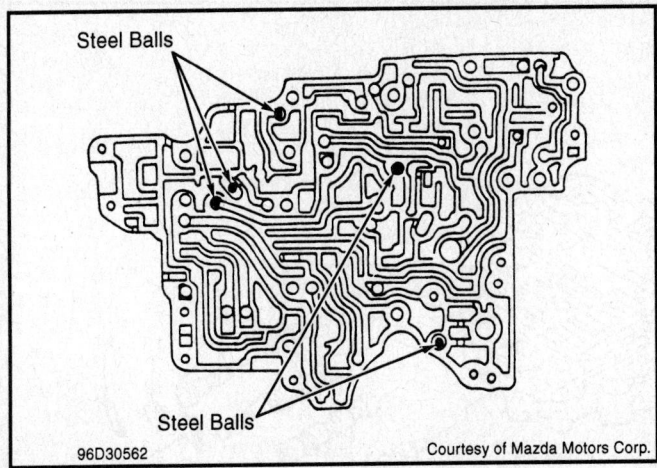

Fig. 36: Locating Inter Valve Body (Lower Side) Steel Balls

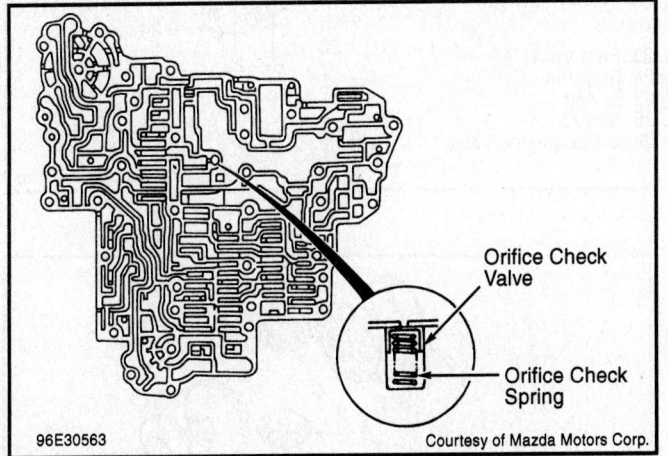

Fig. 37: Locating Lower Valve Body Orifice Check Valve

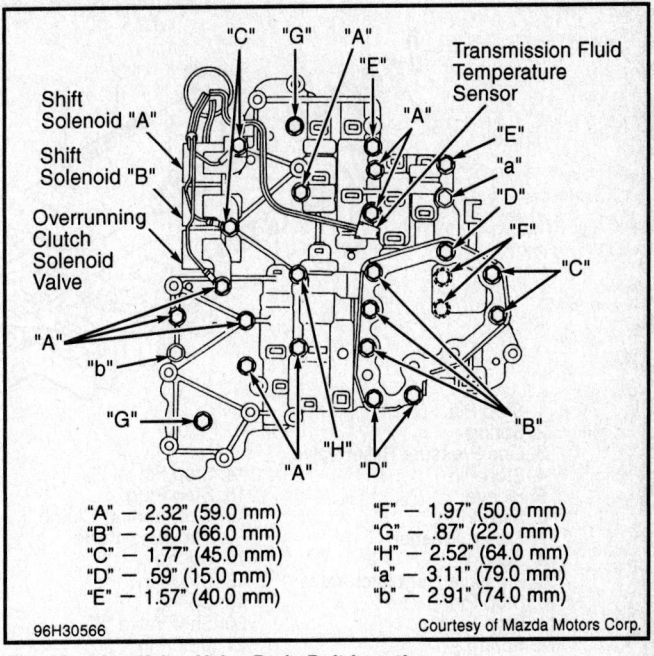

"A" — 2.32" (59.0 mm)	"F" — 1.97" (50.0 mm)
"B" — 2.60" (66.0 mm)	"G" — .87" (22.0 mm)
"C" — 1.77" (45.0 mm)	"H" — 2.52" (64.0 mm)
"D" — .59" (15.0 mm)	"a" — 3.11" (79.0 mm)
"E" — 1.57" (40.0 mm)	"b" — 2.91" (74.0 mm)

Fig. 39: Identifying Valve Body Bolt Location

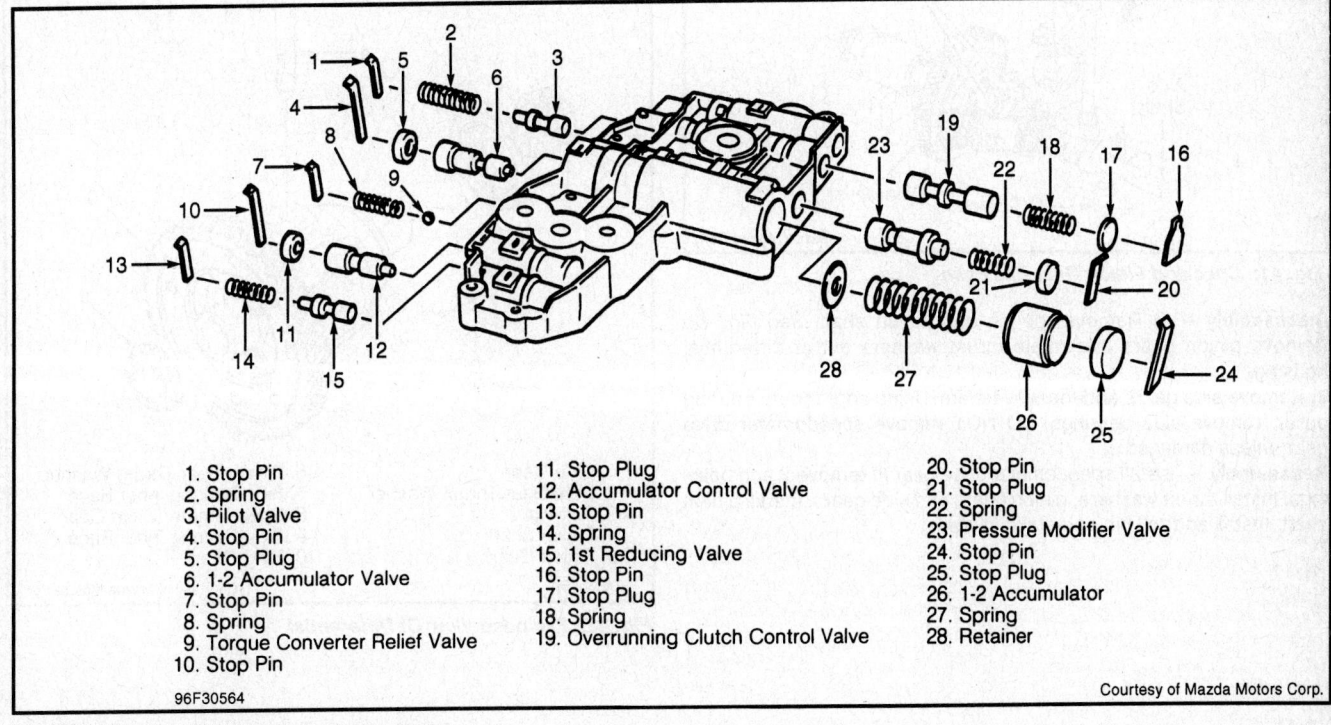

1. Stop Pin
2. Spring
3. Pilot Valve
4. Stop Pin
5. Stop Plug
6. 1-2 Accumulator Valve
7. Stop Pin
8. Spring
9. Torque Converter Relief Valve
10. Stop Pin
11. Stop Plug
12. Accumulator Control Valve
13. Stop Pin
14. Spring
15. 1st Reducing Valve
16. Stop Pin
17. Stop Plug
18. Spring
19. Overrunning Clutch Control Valve
20. Stop Pin
21. Stop Plug
22. Spring
23. Pressure Modifier Valve
24. Stop Pin
25. Stop Plug
26. 1-2 Accumulator
27. Spring
28. Retainer

Courtesy of Mazda Motors Corp.

Fig. 38: Exploded View Of Upper Valve Body

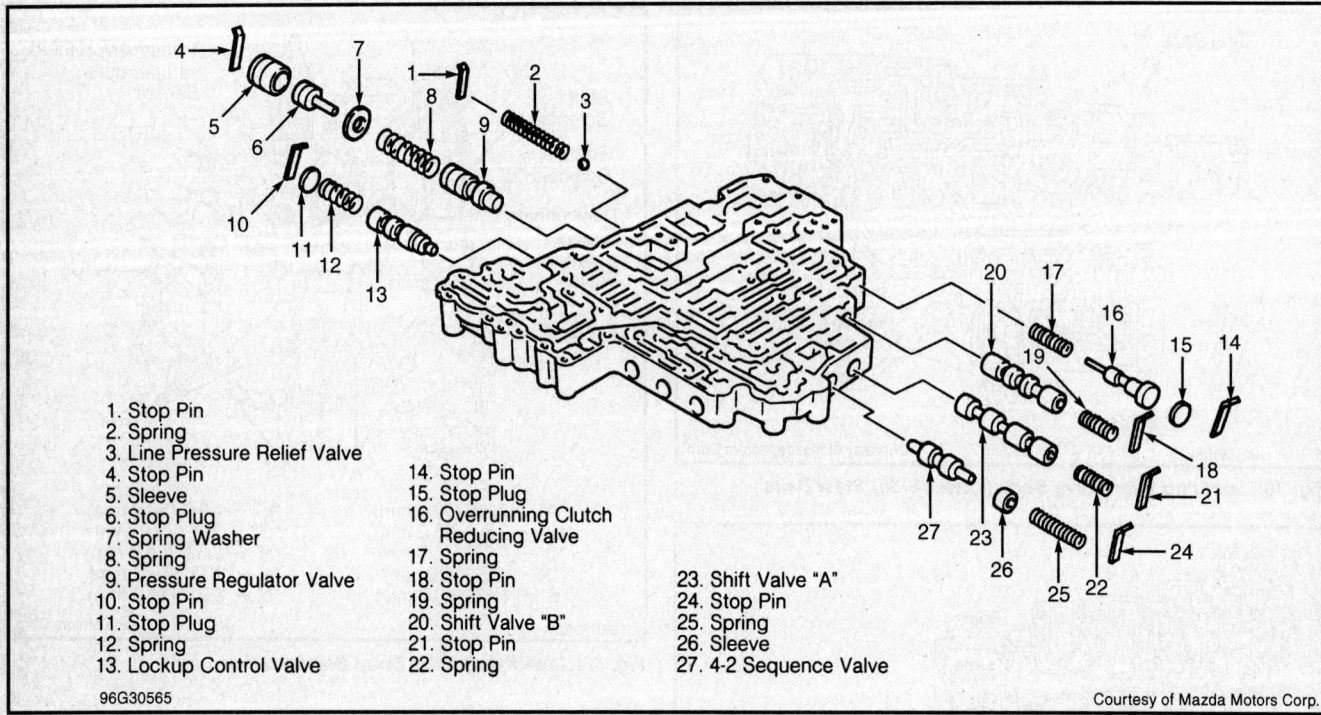

1. Stop Pin
2. Spring
3. Line Pressure Relief Valve
4. Stop Pin
5. Sleeve
6. Stop Plug
7. Spring Washer
8. Spring
9. Pressure Regulator Valve
10. Stop Pin
11. Stop Plug
12. Spring
13. Lockup Control Valve

14. Stop Pin
15. Stop Plug
16. Overrunning Clutch Reducing Valve
17. Spring
18. Stop Pin
19. Spring
20. Shift Valve "B"
21. Stop Pin
22. Spring

23. Shift Valve "A"
24. Stop Pin
25. Spring
26. Sleeve
27. 4-2 Sequence Valve

96G30565

Courtesy of Mazda Motors Corp.

Fig. 40: Exploded View Of Inter Valve Body

DIFFERENTIAL ASSEMBLY

Pre-Disassembly Backlash Inspection – Install left and right axle shafts into differential. Support axle shafts on V-blocks. See Fig. 41. Measure backlash of both pinion gears. Backlash should be .004-.008" (.10-.20 mm). Replace differential assembly if backlash is not as specified.

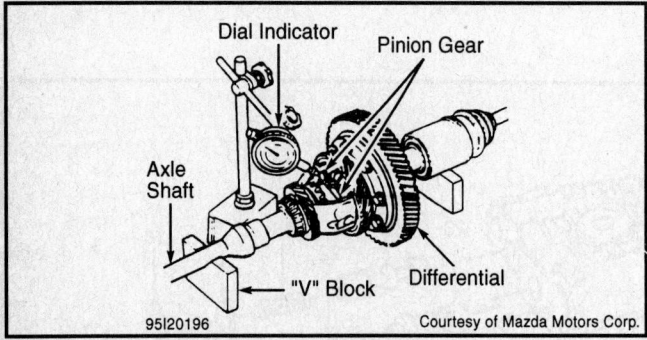

95I20196

Courtesy of Mazda Motors Corp.

Fig. 41: Checking Pinion Gear Backlash

Disassembly – 1) Remove roll pin and pinion shaft. See Fig. 42. Remove pinion gears and rotate thrust washers out of differential housing.

2) Remove side gears and thrust washers. Using appropriate bearing puller, remove side bearings. DO NOT remove speedometer drive gear unless damaged.

Reassembly – Install speedometer drive gear (if removed) and bearings. Install thrust washers, pinion gears and side gears. Install pinion shaft. Install and roll pin and stake in place.

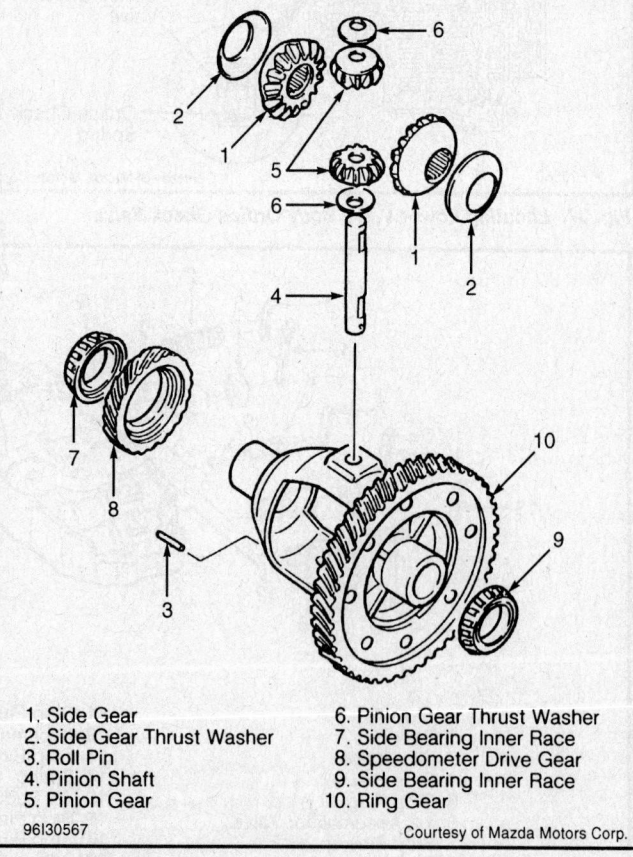

1. Side Gear
2. Side Gear Thrust Washer
3. Roll Pin
4. Pinion Shaft
5. Pinion Gear

6. Pinion Gear Thrust Washer
7. Side Bearing Inner Race
8. Speedometer Drive Gear
9. Side Bearing Inner Race
10. Ring Gear

96I30567

Courtesy of Mazda Motors Corp.

Fig. 42: Exploded View Of Differential

TRANSAXLE REASSEMBLY

ADJUSTMENTS

Differential Assembly – 1) Remove bearing outer race and adjustment shims from transaxle case. Mount differential assembly in converter housing. Install bearing outer race onto Selector Gauge (49 G019 0A5B-Selector Tool Set). Set selector gauge on transaxle case. Set differential on selector gauge. *See Fig. 43*. Eliminate gap on selector gauge by turning collars "A" and "B" of selector gauge.

2) Mount 6 spacing collars on transaxle case. Mount converter housing onto differential. Tighten bolts to 27-38 ft. lbs. (37-52 N.m).

3) Using rods on collars "A" and "B" of selector, turn selector in a direction which widens the gap between "A" and "B" of selector. *See Fig. 43*. Turn selector (to widen gap) until it will no longer turn. This will seat bearing race.

4) Using feeler gauge, measure clearance between collars "A" and "B" around entire circumference and add .006" (.15 mm) for total clearance. Select shims equal to clearance total. Maximum number of shims is 3. Shims range in thickness from .005" (.12 mm) to .048" (1.22 mm) in increments of .002" (.02 mm).

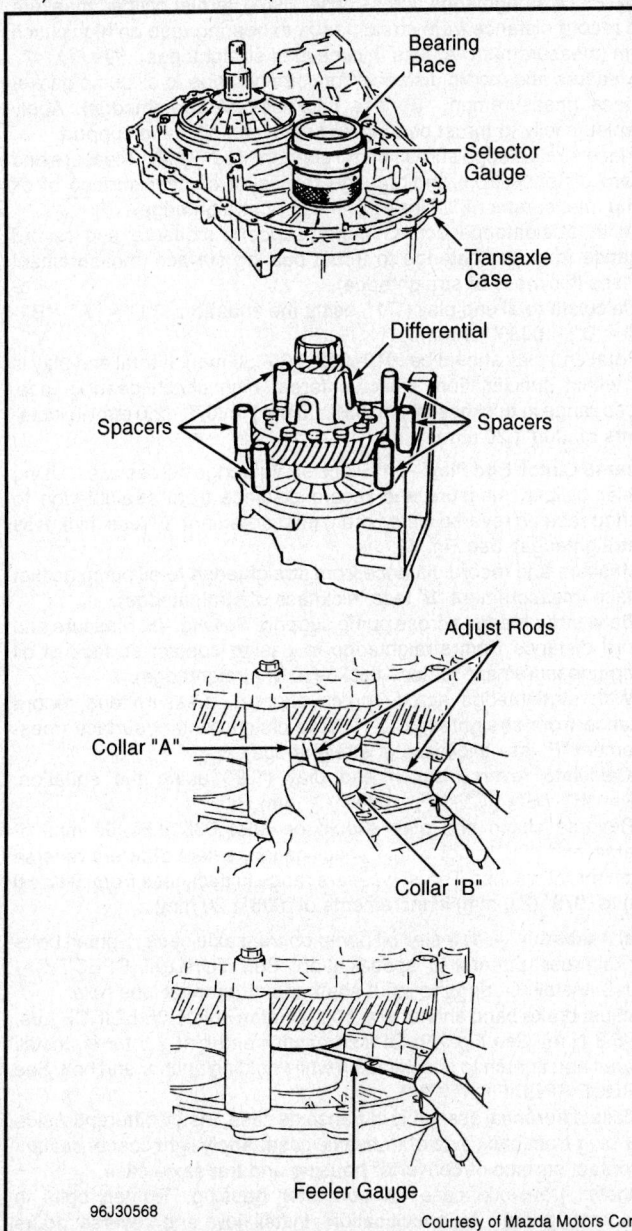

Fig. 43: Determining Differential Side Bearing Preload Shims

96J30568   Courtesy of Mazda Motors Corp.

5) Unbolt converter housing from transaxle case. Remove selector gauge. Install selected shims in transaxle case. Install bearing race. Set differential in transaxle case. Install converter housing. Tighten bolts to 21-22 ft. lbs. (27-30 N.m).

6) Mount preload adapter into differential until in contacts pinion shaft. Measure bearing preload with torque wrench. *See Fig. 44*. Differential bearing preload should be 70-104 INCH lbs. (7.9-11.7 N.m). If bearing preload is not within specification, repeat step 1) through 5).

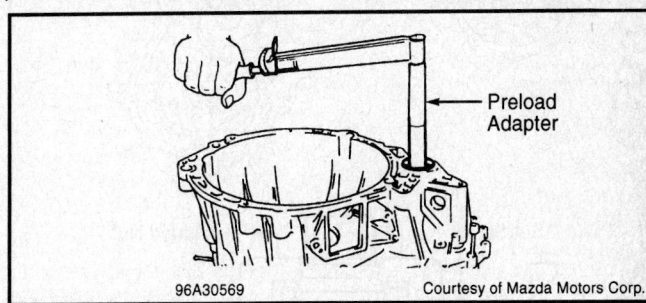

96A30569   Courtesy of Mazda Motors Corp.

Fig. 44: Measuring Differential Side Bearing Preload

IDLER GEAR

1) With counter shaft installed in transaxle case, measure distance between counter shaft and transaxle case. Install Collar (49 T019 009) onto countershaft. *See Fig. 45*. Place Measuring Cap (49 T019 008) over collar. Finger tighten Knurled Nut (49 T019 010) onto countershaft.

2) Tighten measuring cap set screws to secure collar. Remove knurled nut. Remove measuring cap with collar as an assembly. Using dial gauge, measure and record collar depth (measurement "a") from edge of measuring cap. *See Fig. 45*. Measure in 3 places and average measurements.

3) Place collar and measuring cap on idler gear. Tighten measuring cap set screws to secure collar. Remove measuring cap with collar as an assembly. Using dial gauge, measure and record collar depth (measurement "b") from edge of measuring cap. *See Fig. 45*. Measure in 3 places and average measurements.

4) To determine idler gear bearing preload shim thickness, compare measurement "a" to measurement "b". If "a" is less than "b", use equation "a" - "b" - .003" (.08 mm) = shim thickness.

5) If "b" is less than "a", use equation "a" + "b" - .003" (.08 mm) = shim thickness. Shims range in thickness from .006" (.16 mm) to .039" (.98 mm) in increments of .002" (.04 mm). Five additional shims are available in following thicknesses: .005" (.12 mm), .0055" (.14 mm), .057" (1.44 mm), .072" (1.82 mm) and .077" (1.96 mm).

FINAL ASSEMBLY

NOTE: For thrust bearing, race and washer dimensions and locations, see Fig. 46.

Pre-Assembly Precautions – Ensure adjustment shims for differential and idler gear have been selected. See ADJUSTMENTS. Soak brake band in ATF for 2 hours before installation. Apply ATF to all sealing rings, "O" rings and sliding parts before assembly. Ensure all "O" rings, seals and gaskets are replaced. Use petroleum jelly (or equivalent) to retain parts during assembly. If bushing replacement is necessary, replace bushing with appropriate component. Allow sealant to cure for at least one hour before filling transaxle with ATF.

Assembly Procedure – 1) Install parking pawl, parking actuator support and spring. Install parking lever and parking rod. *See Fig. 9*. Install selected idler gear bearing preload shim and bearing race into back of transaxle case.

2) Install selected differential bearing preload shim and bearing race into transaxle case (if applicable). Install countershaft into case. Press idler gear onto countershaft. Engage parking pawl to lock idler gear. Tighten lock nut to specification. See TORQUE SPECIFICATIONS. Ensure idler gear turns smoothly. Stake lock nut.

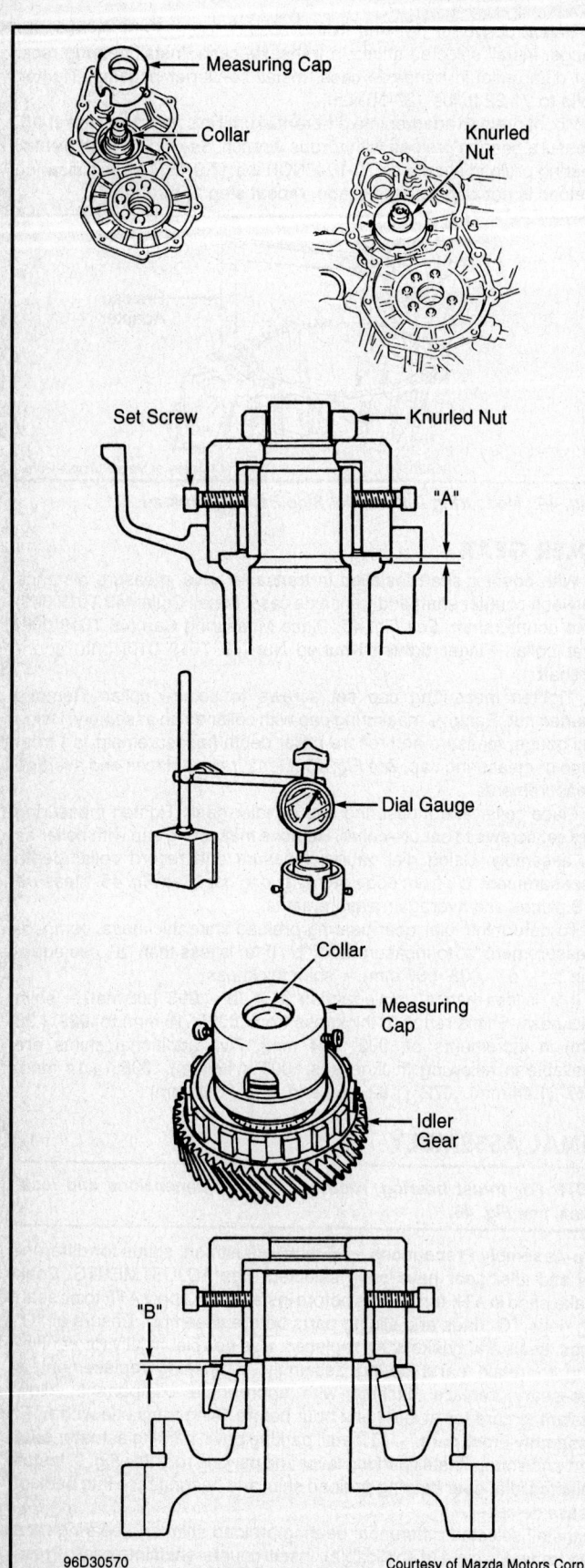

96D30570   Courtesy of Mazda Motors Corp.

Fig. 45: Determining Idler Gear Bearing Preload Shims

3) Install accumulators. *See Fig. 6.* Install drum support. Tighten screws to specification. Install forward clutch assembly with thrust bearing. *See Fig. 7.* Install overrunning clutch with thrust bearing and race into forward clutch.

4) Install rear internal gear and forward clutch hub into froward clutch drum. Install rear planetary carrier with thrust bearing into rear internal gear. Install rear sun gear into rear planetary gear.

5) Install front planetary carrier with thrust bearing to rear planetary carrier. Install low and reverse brake piston with spring retainer. *See Fig. 7.* Ensure piston oil hole is aligned with oil hole in case. *See Fig. 22.*

6) Using appropriate compressor, compress low and reverse piston and install snap ring. Remove compressor. Install low one-way clutch so that retaining clips are facing upward. Install snap ring.

7) Install brake band servo assembly in case. Using appropriate compressor tool, compress brake band servo. Install snap ring. Install reverse clutch, high clutch and front sun gear assembly with thrust bearing and bearing race. Install brake band. Install new anchor end bolt and loosely hand tighten.

Setting Total End Play – 1) Place new oil pump gaskets on transaxle case. Place straightedge across case. Using vernier caliper, measure and record distance from straightedge to bearing race on high clutch drum (measurement "A" less thickness of straightedge). *See Fig. 47.*

2) Measure and record distance from straightedge to oil pump gasket surface (measurement "B" less thickness of straightedge). Apply petroleum jelly to thrust bearing and install on oil pump support.

3) Place straightedge across pump support. *See Fig. 47.* Measure and record distance from straightedge to gasket contact surface of oil pump (measurement "C" less thickness of straightedge).

4) With straightedge across pump support, measure and record distance from straightedge to thrust bearing surface (measurement "D" less thickness of straightedge).

5) Calculate total end play ("T1") using the equation: "T1" = "A" - "B" - ("C" - "D") - .0039" (.1 mm).

6) Total end play should be .010-.022" (.25-.50 mm). If total end play is not within specification, select different high clutch bearing race. Races range in thickness from .031" (.8 mm) to .079" (2.0 mm) in increments of .008" (.20 mm).

Reverse Clutch End Play – 1) Place straightedge across case. Using vernier caliper, measure and record distance from straightedge to bearing race on reverse clutch drum (measurement "E" less thickness of straightedge). *See Fig. 48.*

2) Measure and record distance from straightedge to oil pump gasket surface (measurement "B" less thickness of straightedge).

3) Place straightedge across pump support. *See Fig. 48.* Measure and record distance from straightedge to gasket contact surface of oil pump (measurement "C" less thickness of straightedge).

4) With straightedge across pump support, measure and record distance from straightedge to reverse clutch contact surface (measurement "F" less thickness of straightedge).

5) Calculate reverse clutch end play ("T2") using the equation: "T2" = "E" - "B" - ("C" - "F") - .0039" (.1 mm).

6) Reverse clutch end play should be .022-.035" (.55-.90 mm). If reverse end play is not within specification, select different reverse clutch thrust washer. Thrust washers range in thickness from .031" (.8 mm) to .079" (2.0 mm) in increments of .008" (.20 mm).

Final Assembly – 1) Install oil pump on transaxle case. Tighten bolts in crisscross pattern to specification. See TORQUE SPECIFICATIONS. Install "O" rings to input shaft and differential lube hole.

2) Adjust brake band anchor end bolt. Tighten bolt to 35-52 INCH Lbs. (4.0-5.8 N.m). *See Fig. 49.* Loosen anchor end bolt 2.5 turns. Install lock nut and tighten to specification while holding anchor end bolt. See TORQUE SPECIFICATIONS.

3) Place differential assembly in transaxle case. Install differential side gear plug from back side of transaxle case. Apply light coat of sealant to contact surface of converter housing and transaxle case.

4) Install transaxle case on converter housing. Tighten bolts in crisscross pattern to specification. Install low and reverse brake sleeve. *See Fig. 6.* Install 2-3 accumulator return spring.

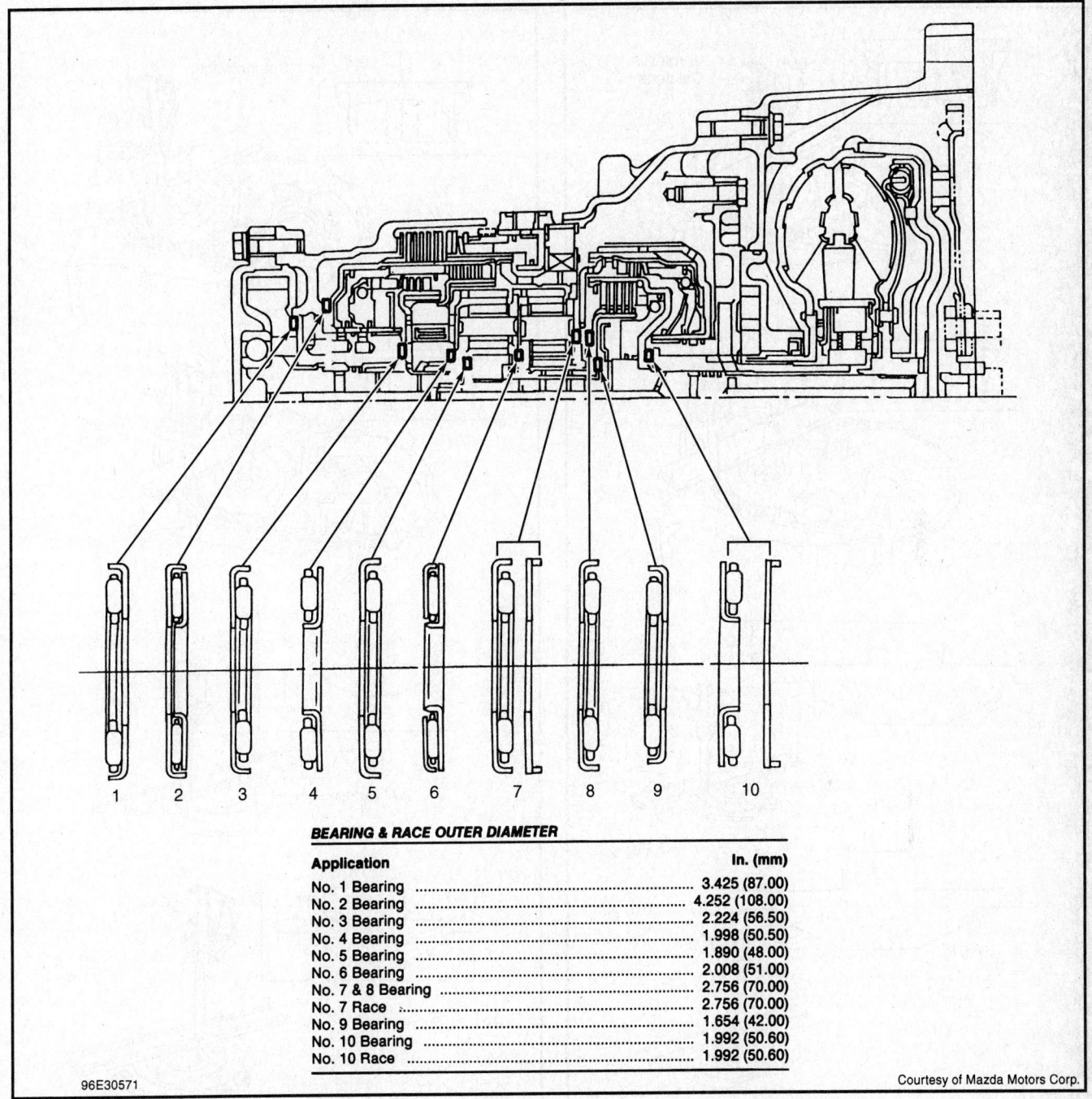

BEARING & RACE OUTER DIAMETER

Application	In. (mm)
No. 1 Bearing	3.425 (87.00)
No. 2 Bearing	4.252 (108.00)
No. 3 Bearing	2.224 (56.50)
No. 4 Bearing	1.998 (50.50)
No. 5 Bearing	1.890 (48.00)
No. 6 Bearing	2.008 (51.00)
No. 7 & 8 Bearing	2.756 (70.00)
No. 7 Race	2.756 (70.00)
No. 9 Bearing	1.654 (42.00)
No. 10 Bearing	1.992 (50.60)
No. 10 Race	1.992 (50.60)

96E30571   Courtesy of Mazda Motors Corp.

Fig. 46: Identifying Transaxle Thrust Bearings, Races & Washers

5) Align manual valve with pin on manual plate. Install valve body in transaxle case. Tighten bolts in crisscross pattern to specification. See TORQUE SPECIFICATIONS. Ensure valve body electrical harness is fully seated in transaxle case. Install retaining clip. Install oil pan and tighten bolts in crisscross pattern.

6) Install and adjust transmission range sensor. Ensure manual shaft is in "L" position (fully forward). Install range sensor. Turn manual shaft fully rearward. Return 2 notches to "N" position. Insert a .16" (4 mm) pin through holes of range sensor and manual shaft lever. See Fig. 50. Tighten retaining bolts. Remove pin.

7) Install output gear with thrust bearing into back of transaxle case. Apply sealant to contact surface of side cover and install cover. Tighten bolts in crisscross pattern to specification. Install output speed sensor. See Fig. 5.

8) Install vehicle speed sensor. Install shift control bracket onto transaxle case. Install control rod onto manual shaft. Fill torque converter with about 2.1 qt. (2.0L) of clean ATF. Install converter while rotating to align pump splines. Measure distance torque converter is set back from edge of converter housing (dimension "A") to verify converter installation. See Fig. 51. Torque converter should be inset .551" (14.0 mm).

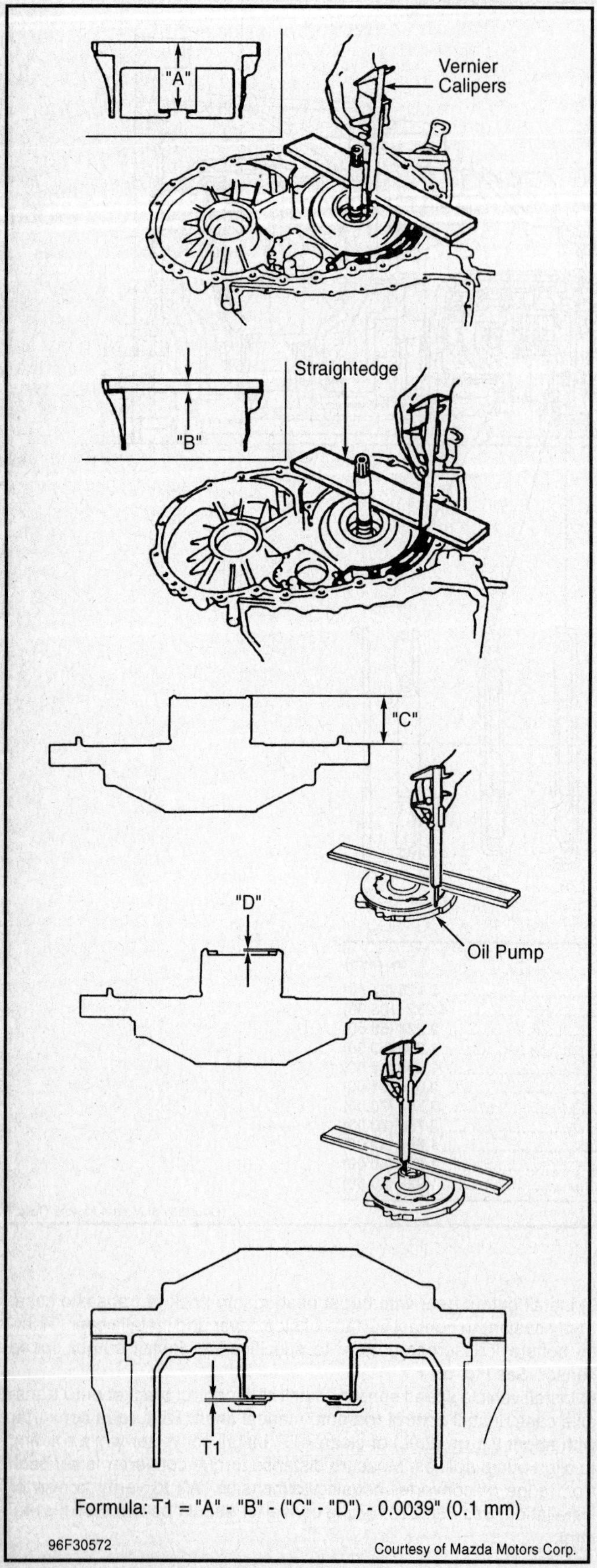

AUTOMATIC TRANSMISSIONS
Mazda LJ4A-EL (Cont.)

Formula: T1 = "A" - "B" - ("C" - "D") - 0.0039" (0.1 mm)

96F30572   Courtesy of Mazda Motors Corp.

Fig. 47: Measuring Transaxle Total End Play

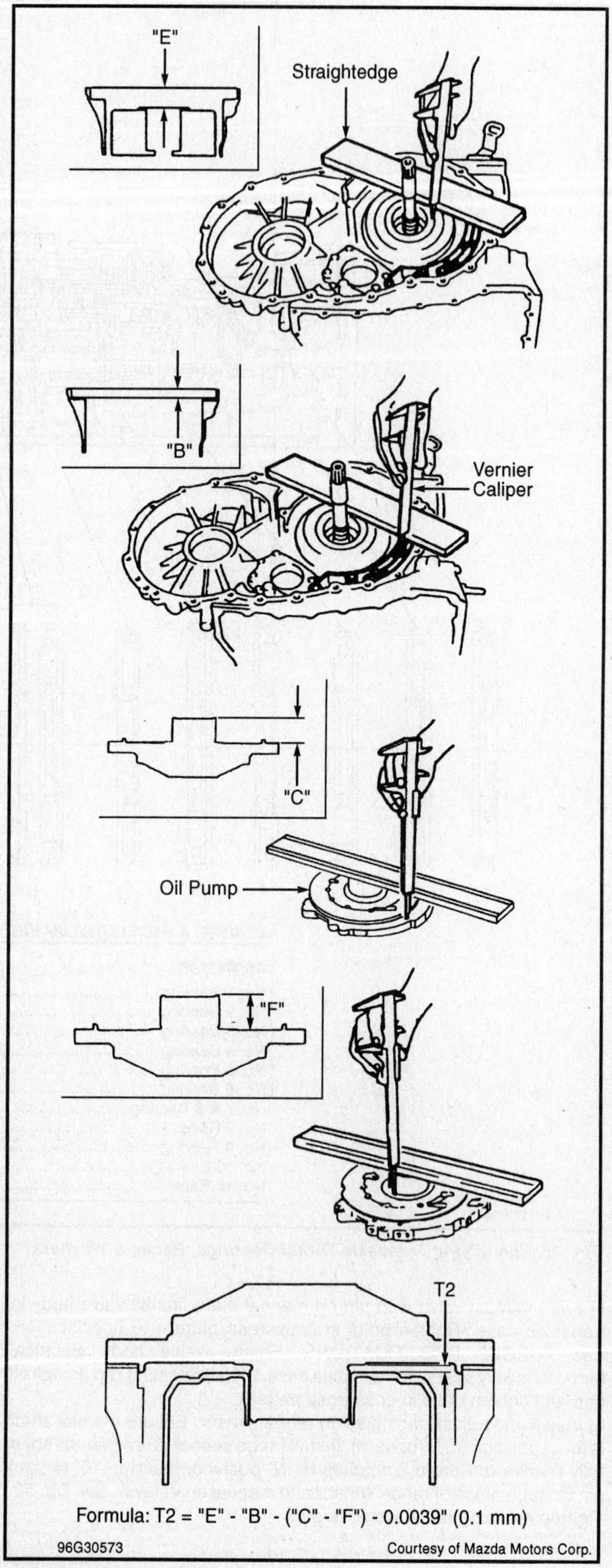

Formula: T2 = "E" - "B" - ("C" - "F") - 0.0039" (0.1 mm)

96G30573   Courtesy of Mazda Motors Corp.

Fig. 48: Measuring Reverse Clutch End Play

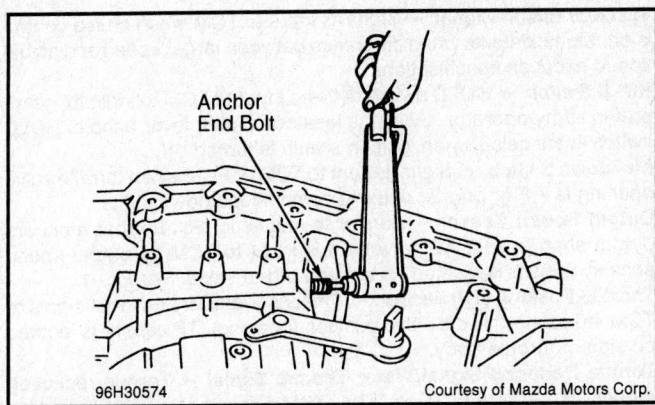

Fig. 49: Adjusting 2-4 Brake Band

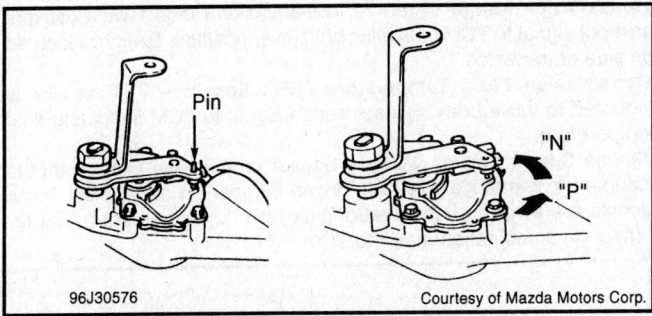

Fig. 50: Adjusting Transmission Range Sensor

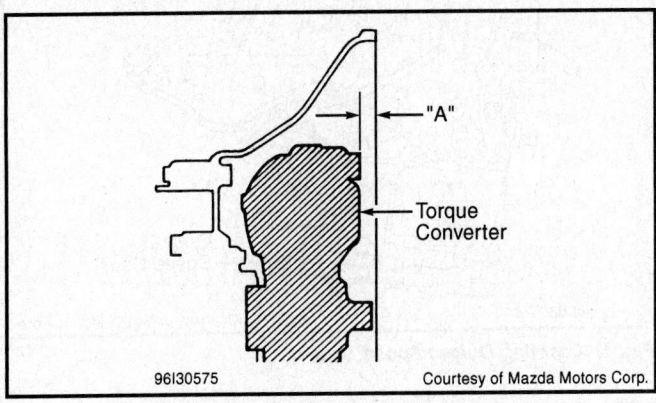

Fig. 51: Measuring Torque Converter Installed Depth

TORQUE SPECIFICATIONS
TORQUE SPECIFICATIONS

Application	Ft. Lbs. (N.m)
Converter Housing-To-Transaxle Case	20-22 (27-30)
Drum Support Bolt	12-15 (16-21)
Oil Pump Cover Bolt	18-20 (24-27)
Oil Pump-To-Transaxle Case Bolts	18-20 (24-27)
Output Gear Nut	145-180 (197-245)
Side Cover Bolt	14-15 (19-22)
2-4 Brake Band Lock Nut	24-31 (31-42)
	INCH Lbs. (N.m)
Oil Filter Bolts	61-80 (7-9)
Output Speed Sensor	44-62 (5-7)
Transmission Range Switch Bolt	61-80 (7-9)
Valve Body Bolts	61-80 (7-9)
Valve Body Pan Bolts	61-80 (7-9)
Valve Body-To-Case Bolts	61-80 (7-9)
Vehicle Speed Sensor Bolt	71-97 (8-11)

TRANSAXLE SPECIFICATIONS
TRANSAXLE SPECIFICATIONS

Application	In. (mm)
Bushing Inside Diameter (Maximum)	
Clutch Pack Clearances	
Forward Clutch	.018-.033 (.45-.85)
Reverse Clutch	.020-.031 (.50-.80)
Low & Reverse Clutch	.067-.083 (1.70-2.10)
High Clutch	.071-.086 (1.80-2.20)
Overrunning Clutch	.028-.043 (.70-1.10)
Clutch Drive Plate Minimum Thickness	
Forward Clutch	.071 (1.80)
All Except Clutches	.055 (1.40)
Oil Pump	
Rotor End Clearance	
Standard	.0008-.006 (.020-.15)
Service Limit	.006 (.15)
Rotor Side Clearance	
Standard	.0008-.0016 (.020-.040)
Service Limit	.0019 (.050)
Bearing Preload	
Differential	70-104 INCH lbs. (7.9-11.7 N.m)

Millenia

APPLICATION

APPLICATION

Vehicle	Transmission Model
1995-96	
Millenia (2.3L)	LJ4A-EL

CAUTION: Vehicle is equipped with Supplemental Restraint System (SRS). When servicing vehicle, use care to avoid accidental air bag deployment. SRS-related components are located in steering column, center console and instrument panel. DO NOT use electrical test equipment on these circuits. If necessary, deactivate SRS before servicing components. See AIR BAG SERVICING article in APPLICATIONS & IDENTIFICATIONS section.

DESCRIPTION

The LJ4A-EL is a 4-speed electronically controlled automatic transaxle. Five solenoids that control shift changes and shift feel are located on valve body. Solenoids are controlled by the Transmission Control Module (TCM).

NOTE: Lock-up solenoid is also known as Torque Converter Clutch (TCC) solenoid or TCC lock-up solenoid.

TCM receives information from various input devices. TCM uses this information to control following solenoids:
- Shift solenoids for transaxle shifting.
- Lock Up solenoid for torque converter clutch lock-up.
- Overrunning clutch solenoid to control overrunning clutch (engine braking).
- Pressure control solenoid to control line pressure.

A HOLD switch is mounted on the shift lever. HOLD function may be activated in "D", "S" or "L" gears by pressing HOLD button. In "L" and "S" positions, vehicle is held in selected gear and no upshift or downshift takes place. This function is used for driving up steep inclines or for engine braking assistance when descending steep grades. If activated in "D" position a 1-2 and 2-3 upshift is permitted when starting from a stop but after the 2-3 upshift the vehicle is locked in "D" until it comes to a complete stop. The 1-2 and 2-3 upshift pattern is changed to a "short shift" specification. This function is used for starting off or driving on slippery surfaces. Pushing HOLD button again deactivates system.

OPERATION

TCM

TCM receives information from various input devices and uses this information to control solenoids on transaxle valve body for transaxle shifting, shift feel and torque converter clutch engagement.

TCM automatically switches from NORMAL mode to POWER mode corresponding to driving condition in "D" range. Upshifts and downshifts are performed at a higher speed in POWER mode than in NORMAL mode.

TCM contains a self-diagnostic system, which will store Diagnostic Trouble Codes (DTC's) if a failure or problem exists in electronic control system. DTC can be retrieved to determine problem area. See SELF-DIAGNOSTIC SYSTEM. PCM is located under center of instrument panel, in front of center console. TCM is located under left side of instrument panel, left of steering column above fuse box.

TCM INPUT DEVICES & SIGNALS

Brakelight Switch – Brakelight switch delivers input signal to TCM, indicating vehicle braking. Brakelight switch is located on pedal support.

4th Gear Inhibit Signal – Signal is input to TCM when cruise control is on. Signal detects when difference between target speed and actual speed exceeds specification.

HOLD Switch – HOLD switch delivers input to TCM to indicate gears preferred by operator. Switch is located on shift lever handle. HOLD switch is canceled when ignition switch is turned off.

Kickdown Switch – Signal is sent to TCM or PCM when throttle valve opening is 7/8 or greater causing commanded downshift.

Output Speed Sensor – Sensor is magnetic pick-up that monitors output shaft speed. AC waveform is input to TCM by output speed sensor. Sensor is located on top end of transaxle. See Fig. 1.

Throttle Position (TP) Sensor – TP sensor delivers an input signal to TCM indicating throttle valve position (opening). TP sensor is located on side of throttle body.

Torque Reduced Signal/Water Thermo Signal – Torque reduction request is sent by ECM to TCM. TCM executes request based on engine coolant temperature. Request is prohibited if engine coolant temperature is not above 140°F (60°C).

Transmission Range Switch – Transmission range switch delivers an input signal to TCM indicating shift lever position. Switch is located on side of transaxle.

Transmission Fluid Temperature (TFT) Sensor – TFT sensor is mounted to valve body. Sensor sends signal to TCM indicating fluid temperature.

Vehicle Speed Sensor (VSS) – Sensor is magnetic pick-up that is mounted to transaxle case and driven by gear on differential. Pulse signals are sent through speedometer (also known as speedometer sensor) in combination meter to TCM.

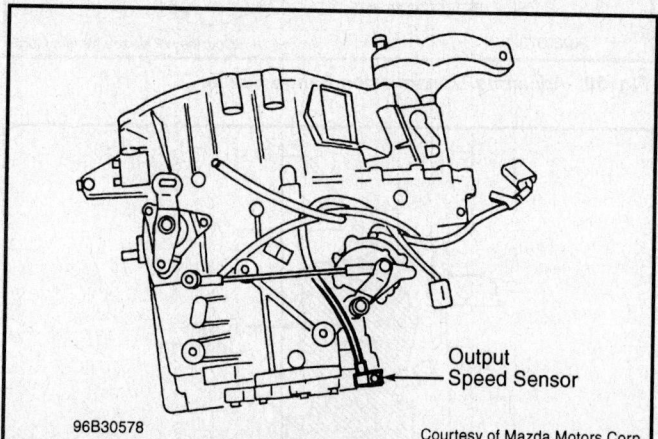

96B30578   Courtesy of Mazda Motors Corp.

Fig. 1: Locating Output Speed Sensor

TCM OUTPUT DEVICES

Shift Solenoids "A" & "B" – The TCM controls transaxle shifting by delivering an output signal to operate proper solenoid. See LJ4A-EL SOLENOID OPERATION table. Solenoids are located on transaxle valve body. See Fig. 2.

LJ4A-EL SOLENOID OPERATION

Shift Lever Position	Solenoid "A"	Solenoid "B"
"D" (Drive)		
1st Gear	On	On
2nd Gear	Off	On
3rd Gear	Off	Off
4th Gear	On	Off
"2" (Second)		
1st Gear	On	On
2nd Gear	Off	On
"L" (Low)		
1st Gear	On	On
"R" (Reverse)	On	On
"N" Or "P"	On	On

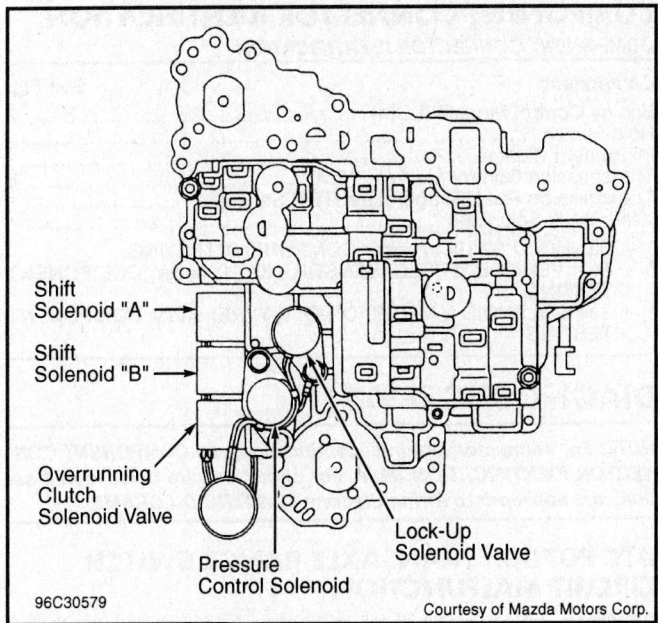

Fig. 2: Locating Transaxle Solenoids

HOLD Indicator Light – Receives signal from TCM to indicate switch position.

Inhibitor Signal – When shift selector lever is moved from Park or Neutral to another gear, signal is sent from TCM to ECM to regulate fuel injection volume for shift shock prevention.

Lock-Up Solenoid – The TCM controls torque converter clutch lock-up by delivering an output signal to lock up solenoid. Solenoid is activated when shift lever is in "D", engine is at normal operating temperature and vehicle is at specified speed. Lock up solenoid is located on transaxle valve body. See Fig. 2.

Pressure Control Solenoid – TCM controls pressure control solenoid to regulate modifier pressure based on signals received from TP sensor. Modifier pressure as a signal pressure controls pressure regulator valves to adjust hydraulic pressure discharged from oil pump to the optimum line pressure corresponding to driving conditions. TCM detects engine load using TP sensor and adjusts line pressure to level required by clutch(s) in use. To reduce shift shock during shifting, line pressure characteristics are set to match engine driving force during shifting. Line pressure is also adjusted for ATF temperature, high engine torque and engine braking.

SELF-DIAGNOSTIC SYSTEM

SYSTEM DIAGNOSIS

NOTE: Before testing transaxle, ensure fluid level is correct. Ensure engine starts with shift lever in Park and Neutral to ensure proper adjustment of transaxle range switch. Transmission Control Module (TCM) must first be checked for stored codes. See RETRIEVING TROUBLE CODES.

TCM monitors transaxle operation and contains a self-diagnostic system which stores a Diagnostic Trouble Code (DTC) if an electronic control system failure or component malfunction exists. If a problem exists in any of the solenoids or speed sensors and DTC is set, TCM will deliver a signal to blink the HOLD indicator light on instrument panel to warn the driver. DTC's may be set if a failure exists and can be retrieved for transaxle diagnosis.

RETRIEVING TROUBLE CODES

NOTE: Before retrieving DTC's, ensure proper battery voltage exists for self-diagnostic system operation. If any DTC's are present other than those listed below, see appropriate SELF-DIAGNOSTICS article in ENGINE PERFORMANCE in appropriate MITCHELL® manual.

Using Scan Tool – Ensure ignition is in OFF position. Connect scan tool to Data Link Connector (DLC) located under left side of instrument panel, near center console. See Fig. 3. Turn ignition switch to ON position. Check for stored DTC's. See DIAGNOSTIC TROUBLE CODE IDENTIFICATION table. For trouble shooting of codes, see DIAGNOSTIC TESTING.

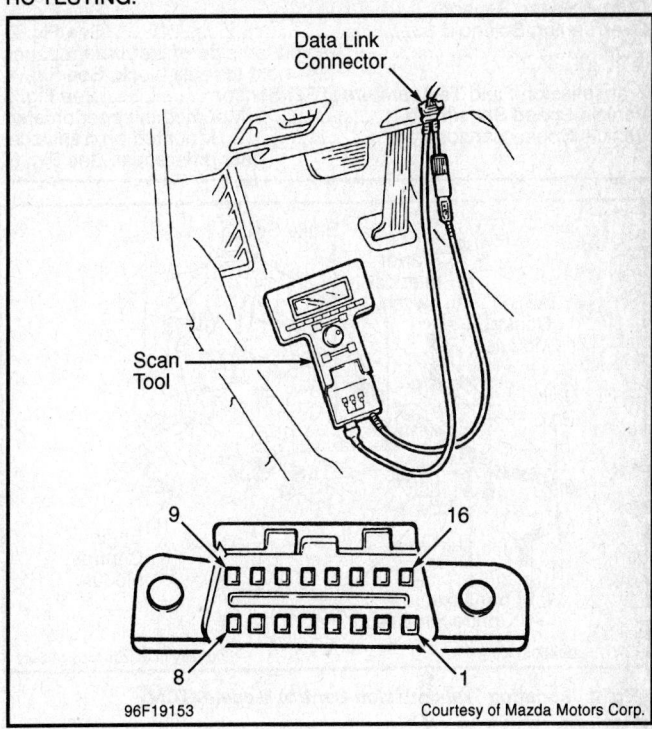

Fig. 3: Connecting Scan Tool

NOTE: Once repairs have been performed, DTC's must be cleared from TCM memory and vehicle test driven. See CLEARING TROUBLE CODES. Accelerate vehicle to 31 MPH for 1 minute. Fully depress accelerator pedal to force downshift. Release accelerator pedal and slow vehicle to stop. Perform retrieval procedure to ensure DTC's have been cleared and no new DTC's exist.

DIAGNOSTIC TROUBLE CODE IDENTIFICATION

DTC No.	[1] Probable Cause
P0705	Transaxle Range Switch
P0710	[2] TFT Sensor
P0720	Output Speed Sensor
P0725	Engine Speed Input Circuit Malfunction
P0731	Incorrect 1st Gear Ratio
P0732	Incorrect 2nd Gear Ratio
P0733	Incorrect 3rd Gear Ratio
P0734	Incorrect 4th Gear Ratio
P0740	TCC System Malfunction
P0745	Pressure Control Solenoid
P0750	Shift Solenoid "A"
P0755	Shift Solenoid "B"
P1720	Speedometer Sensor No. 2
P1743	Lock-Up Solenoid Valve
P1770	Overrunning Clutch Solenoid Valve
P1790	Throttle Position Sensor

[1] – Check listed component for probable cause. Also check wiring and connection of specified component.
[2] – Transaxle Fluid Temperature.

CLEARING TROUBLE CODES

To clear DTC's stored in TCM, disconnect negative battery cable for at least 20 seconds.

COMPONENT LOCATION

COMPONENT LOCATION

Description	Location
ECM	Located under center of instrument panel, forward of center console. See Fig. 4.
Pressure Control Solenoid	See Fig. 2.
Solenoids "A" & "B"	See Fig. 2.
Lock-up Solenoid	See Fig. 2.
Output Speed Sensor	See Fig. 1.
Overrunning Solenoid	See Fig. 2.
TCM	Behind left side of instrument panel, next to relay block. See Fig. 4.
Transmission Fluid Temperature (TFT) Sensor	See Fig. 5
Vehicle Speed Sensor No. 1	Mounted in speedometer.
Vehicle Speed Sensor No. 2	Mounted on transaxle, near differential. See Fig. 6.

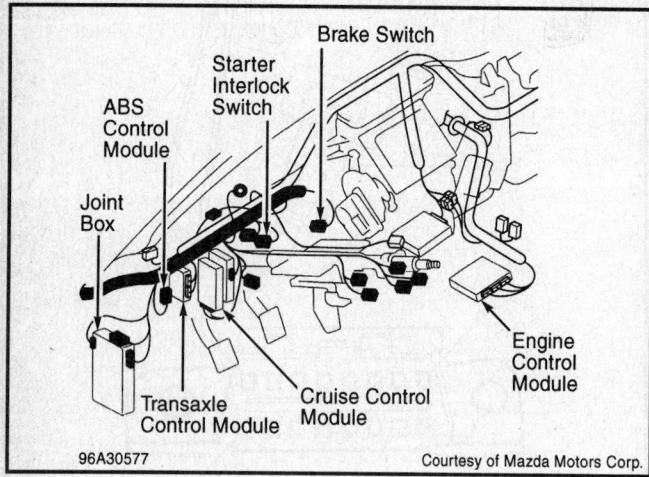

96A30577   Courtesy of Mazda Motors Corp.

Fig. 4: Locating Transmission Control Module (TCM)

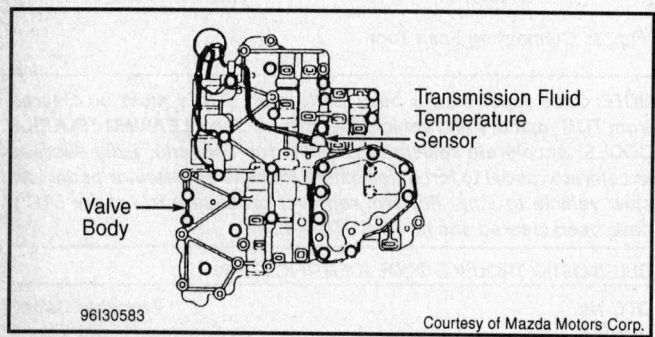

96I30583   Courtesy of Mazda Motors Corp.

Fig. 5: Locating TFT Sensor

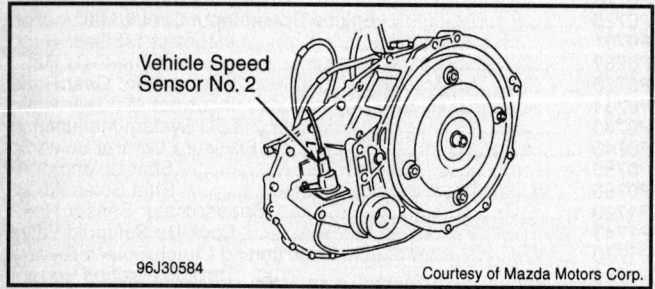

96J30584   Courtesy of Mazda Motors Corp.

Fig. 6: Locating Vehicle Speed Sensor No. 1

COMPONENT CONNECTOR IDENTIFICATION

COMPONENT CONNECTOR IDENTIFICATION

Component	See Fig.
Engine Control Module (ECM)	7
Hold Switch	1
Instrument Cluster	2
Transmission Control Module (TCM)	8
Transmission Fluid Temperature (TFT) Sensor	3
Valve Body Solenoids	4

1 – See HOLD SWITCH under COMPONENT TESTING.
2 – See VEHICLE SPEED SENSOR NO. 1 under COMPONENT TESTING.
3 – See SOLENOID VALVES (ON/OFF TYPE) under COMPONENT TESTING.

DIAGNOSTIC TESTS

NOTE: For connector terminal identification, see COMPONENT CONNECTOR IDENTIFICATION table. For circuit or wire color identification, see appropriate wiring diagram in WIRING DIAGRAMS.

DTC P0705: TRANSAXLE RANGE SWITCH CIRCUIT MALFUNCTION

Condition – No signal is received from range switch or more than 2 signals are received at one time. Possible causes for either condition are:

- Transaxle range switch malfunction.
- Damaged wiring or connectors between transaxle range switch and TCM.
- TCM malfunction.

Diagnosis & Repair Procedure – **1)** Ensure all connections are clean and tight. Repair as needed. Turn ignition on. Using voltmeter, backprobe TCM connector (as applicable). Measure voltage between ground and specified terminal. See appropriate DTC P0705 VOLTAGE TEST table. If all voltages are within specification, go to step **5)**. If any voltage is not within specification, go to next step.

DTC P0705 VOLTAGE TEST

TCM Terminal No.	Measured Voltage	Range Switch Position
2D	0	"P" Or "N"
2D	10-14	"R", "D", "S" Or "L"
1E	10-14	"R"
1E	0	All Except "R"
2B	10-14	"D"
2B	0	All Except "D"
2S	10-14	"S"
2S	0	All Except "S"
2Q	10-14	"L"
2Q	0	All Except "L"

2) Check continuity of circuits between transaxle range switch and TCM. See appropriate wiring diagram in WIRING DIAGRAMS. Repair as needed. If all circuits are okay, go to next step.

3) Disconnect negative battery cable. Disconnect transaxle range switch harness connector. Inspect continuity of transaxle range switch internal circuits. See TRANSMISSION RANGE SWITCH in COMPONENT TESTING. Replace as needed. If switch is okay, go to next step.

4) Reconnect negative battery cable. Turn ignition on. Measure voltage at terminal "I" (Black/Yellow wire) on transmission range switch harness connector. If battery voltage does not exist, repair Black/Yellow wire between switch and ignition switch. If battery voltage exists, go to next step.

5) Road test vehicle. Retrieve DTC's. If code P0705 is still present, replace TCM. If code is no longer present, system is okay.

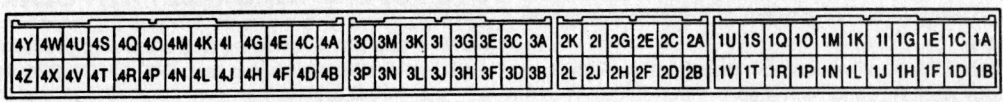

95I33181

Courtesy of Mazda Motors Corp.

Fig. 7: Identifying ECM Component Connector Terminals

2S	2Q	2O	2M	2K	2I	2G	2E	2C	2A	1O	1M	1K	1I	1G	1E	1C	1A
2T	2R	2P	2N	2L	2J	2H	2F	2D	2B	1P	1N	1L	1J	1H	1F	1D	1B

93E25415

Courtesy of Mazda Motors Corp.

Fig. 8: Identifying TCM Component Connector Terminals

DTC P0710: TRANSAXLE FLUID TEMPERATURE (TFT) SENSOR CIRCUIT MALFUNCTION

Condition – Voltage input to TCM is less than .1 volt or greater than 4.9 volts. Possible causes for condition are:
- Transaxle fluid temperature sensor malfunction.
- Damaged wiring or connectors between transaxle fluid temperature sensor and TCM.

Diagnosis & Repair Procedure – **1)** Ensure all connections are clean and tight. Repair as needed. Turn ignition on. Access TCM connectors. Using voltmeter, backprobe harness connectors. Do not disconnect connectors. Go to next step.

2) Measure voltage between terminal No. 2R (Blue/Yellow wire) and No. 2L (Red wire) on TCM connector. Voltage should be about 1.1 volts at 104°F (40°C) or .4 volt at 176°F (80°C). If voltage is within specifications, go to step **6)**. If voltage is not within specifications, go to next step.

3) Turn ignition off. Disconnect TCM harness connector. Measure resistance between terminals No. 2R (Blue/Yellow wire) and No. 2L (Red wire). See TFT SENSOR SPECIFICATIONS. If resistance is within specification, go to step **6)**. If resistance is not within specification, go to next step.

4) Inspect TFT sensor. Disconnect solenoid valve connector. Measure resistance between terminals "D" and "F". See TFT SENSOR SPECIFICATIONS. If resistance is within specification, go to step **6)**. If resistance is not within specification, replace TFT sensor.

5) Check continuity of circuits between TFT sensor and TCM. See appropriate wiring diagram in WIRING DIAGRAMS. Repair as needed. If circuit is okay, go to next step.

6) Reconnect all harness connectors. Road test vehicle. Retrieve DTC's. If code P0710 is still present, replace TCM. If code is no longer present, system is okay.

TFT SENSOR SPECIFICATIONS

K/Ohms	Fluid Temperature
13.8	50°F (10°C)
1.2	104°F (40°C)
.3	176°F (80°C)

DTC P0720: OUTPUT SPEED SENSOR

Condition – Output speed sensor signal is not input to TCM when vehicle is above 25 MPH and shift lever is in "D", "S" or "L" position. Possible causes for condition are:
- Output speed sensor malfunction.
- Damaged wiring or connectors between turbine speed sensor and TCM.

Diagnosis & Repair Procedure – **1)** Ensure all connections are clean and tight. Repair as needed. Turn ignition on. Access TCM connectors. Using voltmeter, backprobe harness connectors. Do not disconnect connectors. Go to next step.

2) Start and idle engine in Park or Neutral. Measure AC voltage between terminals No. 2J (positive) and No. 2L (negative). Test drive vehicle. Voltage should be zero when idling and about one volt above 25 MPH. If voltage is within specification, go to step **6)**. If voltage is not within specification, go to next step.

3) Turn ignition off. Disconnect TCM harness connector. Measure resistance between terminals No. 2J (White wire) and No. 2L (Red wire). Resistance should be 500-1000 ohms. If resistance is within specification, go to step **6)**. If resistance is not within specification, go to next step.

4) Inspect output speed sensor. See OUTPUT SPEED SENSOR under COMPONENT TESTING. Repair as needed. If sensor is okay, go to next step.

5) Check continuity of circuits between output speed sensor and TCM. See appropriate wiring diagram in WIRING DIAGRAMS. Repair as needed. If circuits are okay, go to next step.

6) Reconnect all harness connectors. Road test vehicle. Retrieve DTC's. If code P0720 is still present, replace PCM. If code is no longer present, system is okay.

DTC P0725: ENGINE SPEED INPUT CIRCUIT MALFUNCTION

Condition – Engine speed input signal is not input to TCM. Possible causes are:
- Crankshaft position sensor malfunction.
- Damaged wiring or connectors between ECM and crankshaft position sensor.
- Damaged wiring or connectors between ECM and TCM.
- TCM malfunction.

Diagnosis & Repair Procedure – **1)** Ensure all connections are clean and tight. Repair as needed. Turn ignition on. Using voltmeter, backprobe TCM harness connector. Do not disconnect connector.

2) Measure voltage between ground and terminal No. 1G (Green wire) on TCM harness connector. If voltage is 5-6 volts with engine stopped or battery voltage with engine running, go to next step. If voltage is not 5-6 volts with engine stopped or battery voltage with engine running, repair Green wire between TCM and ECM for open or short.

3) Using voltmeter, backprobe ECM harness connector. Measure voltage between ground and terminal No. 2O (Green wire). If voltage is 5-6 volts with engine stopped or battery voltage with engine running, go to step **5)**. If voltage is not 5-6 volts with engine stopped or battery voltage with engine running, go to next step.

4) Inspect crankshaft position sensor. See appropriate SYSTEM & COMPONENT TESTING article in ENGINE PERFORMANCE in appropriate MITCHELL® manual. Replace as needed. If sensor is okay, go to next step.

5) Reconnect all harness connectors. Road test vehicle. Retrieve DTC's. If code P0725 is still present, replace PCM. If code is no longer present, system is okay.

DTC P0731: INCORRECT 1ST GEAR RATIO

NOTE: If any of the following DTC's are also present, repair them first and then proceed with this test: DTC P0750, DTC P0755.

Condition – TCM outputs solenoid pattern of 1st gear when gear ratio is other than 1st gear. Possible causes are:
- Low ATF level.
- Low line pressure.
- Control valve stuck.
- Solenoid valve malfunction.
- TCM malfunction.

Diagnosis & Repair Procedure – **1)** Ensure ATF level and condition is okay. Refer to TESTING and COMPONENT TESTING in MAZDA LJ4A-EL overhaul article and perform the following tests, repair any components as necessary: Check line pressure, if line pressure is okay, go to next step.

2) Perform stall speed test. If stall speed is okay, go to next step.

3) Inspect solenoid valves "A" and "B". See SOLENOID VALVES under COMPONENT TESTING. Repair as needed. If solenoid valves are okay, go to next step.

4) Inspect valve body. Ensure all valves operate smoothly. Repair as needed. If valve body is okay, go to next step.

5) Clear DTC's and retest. See CLEARING CODES. If code P0733 is still present, replace PCM. If code is no longer present and symptom still exists, problem may be caused by intermittent clutch slippage. Further investigation may be required. See MAZDA LJ4A-EL overhaul article.

DTC P0732: INCORRECT 2ND GEAR RATIO

NOTE: If any of the following DTC's are also present, repair them first and then proceed with this test: DTC P0750, DTC P0755.

Condition – TCM outputs solenoid pattern of 2nd gear when gear ratio is other than 2nd gear. Possible causes are:
• Low ATF level.
• Forward clutch slippage.
• Forward one-way clutch slippage.
• Faulty band servo.
• Low line pressure.
• Control valve stuck.
• Solenoid valve malfunction.
• TCM malfunction.

Diagnosis & Repair Procedure – 1) Ensure ATF level and condition is okay. Refer to TESTING and COMPONENT TESTING in MAZDA LJ4A-EL overhaul article and perform the following tests, repair any components as necessary: Check line pressure, if line pressure is okay, go to next step.

2) Perform stall speed test. If stall speed is okay, go to next step.

3) Inspect solenoid valves "A" and "B". See SOLENOID VALVES under COMPONENT TESTING. Repair as needed. If solenoid valves are okay, go to next step.

4) Inspect valve body. Ensure all valves operate smoothly. Repair as needed. If valve body is okay, go to next step.

5) Clear DTC's and retest. See CLEARING CODES. If code P0732 is still present, replace PCM. If code is no longer present and symptom still exists, problem may be caused by intermittent clutch slippage. Further investigation may be required. See MAZDA LJ4A-EL overhaul article.

DTC P0733: INCORRECT 3RD GEAR RATIO

NOTE: If any of the following DTC's are also present, repair them first and then proceed with this test: DTC P0750, DTC P0755.

Condition – TCM outputs solenoid pattern of 3rd gear when gear ratio is other than 3rd gear. Possible causes are:
• Low ATF level.
• Forward clutch slippage.
• Forward one-way clutch slippage.
• High clutch slippage.
• Low line pressure.
• Control valve stuck.
• Solenoid valve malfunction.
• TCM malfunction.

Diagnosis & Repair Procedure – 1) Ensure ATF level and condition is okay. Refer to TESTING and COMPONENT TESTING in MAZDA LJ4A-EL overhaul article and perform the following tests, repair any components as necessary: Check line pressure, if line pressure is okay, go to next step.

2) Inspect solenoid valves "A" and "B". See SOLENOID VALVES under COMPONENT TESTING. Repair as needed. If solenoid valves are okay, go to next step.

3) Inspect valve body. Ensure all valves operate smoothly. Repair as needed. If valve body is okay, go to next step.

4) Clear DTC's and retest. See CLEARING CODES. If code P0733 is still present, replace PCM. If code is no longer present and symptom still exists, problem may be caused by intermittent clutch slippage. Further investigation may be required. See MAZDA LJ4A-EL overhaul article.

DTC P0734: INCORRECT 4TH GEAR RATIO

NOTE: If any of the following DTC's are also present, repair them first and then proceed with this test: DTC P0750, DTC P0755.

Condition – TCM outputs solenoid pattern of 3rd gear when gear ratio is other than 3rd gear. Possible causes are:
• Low ATF level.
• Band servo slippage.
• High clutch slippage.
• Low line pressure.
• Control valve stuck.
• Solenoid valve malfunction.
• TCM malfunction.

Diagnosis & Repair Procedure – 1) Ensure ATF level and condition is okay. Refer to TESTING and COMPONENT TESTING in MAZDA LJ4A-EL overhaul article and perform the following tests, repair any components as necessary: Check line pressure, if line pressure is okay, go to next step.

2) Inspect solenoid valves "A" and "B". See SOLENOID VALVES under COMPONENT TESTING. Repair as needed. If solenoid valves are okay, go to next step.

3) Inspect valve body. Ensure all valves operate smoothly. Repair as needed. If valve body is okay, go to next step.

4) Clear DTC's and retest. See CLEARING CODES. If code P0734 is still present, replace PCM. If code is no longer present and symptom still exists, problem may be caused by intermittent clutch slippage. Further investigation may be required. See MAZDA LJ4A-EL overhaul article.

DTC P0740: TORQUE CONVERTER CLUTCH MALFUNCTION

Condition – Shift solenoids "A", "B", vehicle speed sensor signal, output speed sensor and throttle position sensor function normally and vehicle speed is 44-65 MPH. There is a greater than 100 RPM difference between engine speed and idler gear speed with transaxle in 4th gear and TCC engaged. Possible causes are:
• Low ATF level.
• Low line pressure.
• Torque converter slippage.
• Control valve stuck.
• Lock-up solenoid valve malfunction.
• TCM malfunction.

Diagnosis & Repair Procedure – 1) Inspect ATF level and condition. Correct as needed. If fluid level and condition is okay, check line pressure. See TESTING in MAZDA LJ4A-EL overhaul article. Follow repair recommendations if line pressure is not within specifications. If line pressure is okay, go to next step.

2) Inspect lock-up solenoid. See SOLENOID VALVES (DUTY CYCLE TYPE) under COMPONENT TESTING. Repair as needed. If solenoid valve is okay, go to next step.

3) Inspect lock-up control valve in valve body. If valve is okay, go to next step.

4) Clear DTC's. See CLEARING CODES. Retrieve DTC's. If code P0740 is still present, replace TCM. If code is no longer present and symptom still exists, problem may be caused by intermittent TCC slippage. Further investigation may be required. See MAZDA LJ4A-EL overhaul article.

DTC P0745: PRESSURE CONTROL SOLENOID MALFUNCTION

Possible Causes:
• Open or short circuit.
• TCM malfunction.
• Pressure control solenoid malfunction.

Diagnosis & Repair Procedure – 1) Ensure all connections are clean and tight. Repair as needed. Turn ignition on. Using voltmeter, backprobe TCM harness connector. Do not disconnect connector.

2) Measure voltage between ground and terminal No. 1F (Violet wire). Voltage should be battery voltage when driving and zero voltage with vehicle stopped. If voltage is within specifications, go to step 6). If voltage is not within specifications, go to next step.

3) Ensure ignition is off. Disconnect negative battery cable. Disconnect TCM harness connector. Measure resistance between ground and terminal No. 1F (Violet wire) on TCM harness connector. If resistance is 2-6 ohms at 68°F (20°C), go to step **6)**. If resistance is not 2-6 ohms at 68°F (20°C), go to next step.

4) Inspect pressure control solenoid. See appropriate SOLENOID VALVES (DUTY CYCLE TYPE) under COMPONENT TESTING. Repair as needed. If solenoid valve is okay, go to next step.

5) Check continuity of circuits between pressure control solenoid and TCM. See appropriate wiring diagram in WIRING DIAGRAMS. Repair as needed. If circuits are okay, go to next step.

6) Disconnect negative battery cable for at least 20 seconds. Depress brake pedal. Reconnect negative battery cable. Road test vehicle. Retrieve DTC's. If DTC P0745 is still present, replace TCM. If code is no longer present, system is okay.

DTC P0750: SHIFT SOLENOID "A" MALFUNCTION

Possible Causes:
- Short or open circuit between TCM and solenoid.
- TCM malfunction.
- Shift solenoid malfunction.

Diagnosis & Repair Procedure – 1) Ensure all connections are clean and tight. Repair as needed. Turn ignition on. Access TCM connectors. Using voltmeter, backprobe harness connectors. Do not disconnect connectors. Go to next step.

2) Measure voltage between ground and terminal No. 1D (Red/White wire) on TCM connector. During test drive, voltage should be less than one volt when solenoid is off and battery voltage when solenoid is on. See SOLENOID OPERATION TABLE under TCM OUTPUT DEVICES. If voltage is within specification, go to step **5)**. If voltage is not within specification, go to next step.

3) Turn ignition off. Disconnect TCM harness connector. Measure resistance between ground and terminal No. 1D. If resistance is 20-40 ohms at 68°F (20°C), go to step **5)**. If resistance is not 20-40 ohms at 68°F (20°C), go to next step.

4) Inspect shift solenoid "A" and related circuits. See SOLENOID VALVES (ON/OFF TYPE) under COMPONENT TESTING. Repair as needed. If solenoid valve and related circuits are okay, go to next step.

5) Disconnect negative battery cable for at least 20 seconds. Depress brake pedal. Reconnect negative battery cable. Road test vehicle. Retrieve DTC's. If DTC P0750 is still present, replace TCM. If code is no longer present, system is okay.

DTC P0755: SHIFT SOLENOID "B" MALFUNCTION

Possible Causes::
- Short or open circuit between TCM and solenoid.
- PCM malfunction.
- Shift solenoid malfunction.

Diagnosis & Repair Procedure – 1) Ensure all connections are clean and tight. Repair as needed. Turn ignition on. Access TCM connectors. Using voltmeter, backprobe harness connectors. Do not disconnect connectors. Go to next step.

2) Measure voltage between ground and terminal No. 1B (Blue/White wire) on TCM connector. During test drive, voltage should be less than one volt when solenoid is off and battery voltage when solenoid is on. See SOLENOID OPERATION TABLE under TCM OUTPUT DEVICES. If voltage is within specification, go to step **5)**. If voltage is not within specification, go to next step.

3) Turn ignition off. Disconnect TCM harness connector. Measure resistance between ground and terminal No. 1B. If resistance is 20-40 ohms at 68°F (20°C), go to step **5)**. If resistance is not 20-40 ohms at 68°F (20°C), go to next step.

4) Inspect shift solenoid "B" and related circuits. See SOLENOID VALVES (ON/OFF TYPE) under COMPONENT TESTING. Repair as needed. If solenoid valve and related circuits are okay, go to next step.

5) Disconnect negative battery cable for at least 20 seconds. Depress brake pedal. Reconnect negative battery cable. Road test vehicle. Retrieve DTC's. If DTC P0755 is still present, replace TCM. If code is no longer present, problem may be caused by poor connection. Repair as needed.

DTC P1720: VEHICLE SPEED SENSOR (VSS) NO. 2 MALFUNCTION

Condition – Vehicle speed sensor No. 2 signal is not input to TCM when shift selector is in "D", "S" or "L" position. Possible causes are:
- Vehicle speed sensor No. 2 malfunction.
- Vehicle speed sensor No. 1 malfunction.
- Damaged circuits or connectors between sensors and TCM.

Diagnosis & Repair – 1) Ensure all connections are clean and tight. Repair as needed. Turn ignition on. Using voltmeter, backprobe TCM harness connector. Do not disconnect connector. Test drive vehicle.

2) Measure voltage between ground and terminal No. 1I (Green/Red wire) on TCM harness connector. During test drive voltage should be 2-3 volts or, 0 or 4-5 volts when parked. If voltage is within specifications, go to step **6)**. If voltage is not within specifications, go to next step.

3) Turn ignition off. Disconnect negative battery cable. Remove instrument cluster. Disconnect TCM harness connectors. Check continuity of Green/Red wire between terminal No. 1I on TCM connector and terminal No. 2K on instrument cluster harness center connector. Repair as needed. If continuity exists, go to next step.

4) Raise and support front of vehicle. Using voltmeter, measure voltage between terminals No. 2D (Blue/Red wire) and 2H (Red/Black wire) on instrument cluster center connector. Rotate front wheels. If voltage pulse is present, go to step **6)**. If voltage pulse is not present, go to next step.

5) Inspect VSS. See VEHICLE SPEED SENSOR under COMPONENT TESTING. Replace as needed. If VSS is okay, inspect circuits between VSS and instrument cluster. See appropriate wiring diagram under WIRING DIAGRAMS. Repair as needed. If circuits are okay between sensor and instrument cluster, replace instrument cluster.

6) Disconnect negative battery cable for at least 20 seconds. Depress brake pedal. Reconnect negative battery cable. Road test vehicle. Retrieve DTC's. If DTC P1720 is still present, replace TCM. If code is no longer present, problem may be caused by poor connection. Repair as needed.

DTC P1743: LOCK-UP SOLENOID MALFUNCTION

Possible Causes:
- Short or open circuit between TCM and solenoid.
- TCM malfunction.
- Lock-up solenoid malfunction.

Diagnosis & Repair Procedure – 1) Ensure all connections are clean and tight. Repair as needed. Turn ignition on. Access TCM connectors. Using voltmeter, backprobe harness connectors. Do not disconnect connectors. Go to next step.

2) Measure voltage between ground and terminal No. 1M. Battery voltage should be present with solenoid on and zero voltage with solenoid off. If voltage is within specifications, go to step **5)**. If voltage is not within specifications, go to next step.

3) Turn ignition off. Disconnect TCM harness connector. Measure resistance between ground and terminal No. 1M. If resistance is 10-20 ohms at 68°F (20°C), go to step **5)**. If resistance is not 10-20 ohms at 68°F (20°C), go to next step.

4) Inspect lock-up solenoid and related circuits. See SOLENOID VALVES (DUTY CYCLE TYPE) under COMPONENT TESTING. Repair as needed. If solenoid valve and related circuits are okay, go to next step.

5) Disconnect negative battery cable for at least 20 seconds. Depress brake pedal. Reconnect negative battery cable. Road test vehicle. Retrieve DTCs. If DTC P1743 is still present, replace TCM. If code is no longer present, problem may be caused by poor connection. Repair as needed.

DTC P1770: OVERRUNNING CLUTCH SOLENOID VALVE MALFUNCTION

Possible Causes:
- Short or open circuit between TCM and solenoid.
- TCM malfunction.
- Overrunning clutch solenoid malfunction.

Diagnosis & Repair Procedure – **1)** Ensure all connections are clean and tight. Repair as needed. Turn ignition on. Access TCM connectors. Using voltmeter, backprobe harness connectors. Do not disconnect connectors. Go to next step.

2) Measure voltage between ground and terminal No. 1O (Green/Orange wire). Battery voltage should be present with solenoid on and zero volts with solenoid off. If voltage is within specifications, go to step 5). If voltage is not within specifications, go to next step.

3) Turn ignition off. Disconnect TCM harness connector. Measure resistance between ground and terminal No. 1O. If resistance is 20-40 ohms at 68°F (20°C), go to step 5). If resistance is not 20-40 ohms at 68°F (20°C), go to next step.

4) Inspect overrunning clutch solenoid and related circuits. See SOLENOID VALVES (ON/OFF TYPE) under COMPONENT TESTING. Repair as needed. If solenoid valve and related circuits are okay, go to next step.

5) Disconnect negative battery cable for at least 20 seconds. Depress brake pedal. Reconnect negative battery cable. Road test vehicle. Retrieve DTC's. If DTC P1770 is still present, replace TCM. If code is no longer present, problem may be caused by poor connection. Repair as needed.

DTC P1790: THROTTLE POSITION (TP) SENSOR MALFUNCTION

Condition – TP sensor voltage is less than one volt or more than 4.9 volts. Possible causes are:
- Poor harness connection at TP sensor.
- Circuit fault between TP sensor and TCM.
- TP sensor.

Diagnosis & Repair Procedure – **1)** Ensure all connections are clean and tight. Repair as needed. Turn ignition on. Access TCM connectors. Using voltmeter, backprobe harness connectors. Do not disconnect connectors. Go to next step.

2) Measure voltage between ground and terminal No. 2T (Yellow wire) on TCM harness connector. With throttle closed, voltage should be .1-1.2 volts. With wide open throttle, voltage should be 3.5-4.0 volts. If voltage is within specification, go to step 7). If voltage is not within specification, go to next step.

3) Measure voltage between ground and terminal No. 2A (Light Green/Red wire) on TCM harness connector. With ignition on, voltage should be 4.5-5.5 volts. With ignition off, voltage should be zero volts. If voltage is within specification, go to step 7). If voltage is not within specification, go to next step.

4) Access ECM connectors. Using voltmeter, backprobe harness connectors. Do not disconnect connectors. Measure voltage between ground and terminal No. 3A (Light Green/Red wire) on ECM harness connector. With ignition on, voltage should be 4.5-5.5 volts. With ignition off, voltage should be zero volts. If voltage is within specification, go to step 7). If voltage is not within specification, go to next step.

5) Turn ignition switch to OFF position. Disconnect Throttle Position (TP) sensor harness connector. Measure resistance between specified component terminals. See appropriate SYSTEM & COMPONENT TESTING article in ENGINE PERFORMANCE of appropriate MITCHELL® manual. Replace as needed. If TP sensor is okay, go to next step.

6) Inspect circuits between TP sensor and TCM. See appropriate wiring diagram under WIRING DIAGRAMS. Repair as needed. If circuits are okay between sensor and TCM, go to next step.

7) Disconnect negative battery cable for at least 20 seconds. Depress brake pedal. Reconnect negative battery cable. Road test vehicle. Retrieve DTC's. If DTC P1790 is still present, replace TCM. If code is no longer present, problem may be caused by poor connection. Repair as needed.

COMPONENT TESTING

NOTE: For connector terminal identification, see COMPONENT CONNECTOR IDENTIFICATION table. For circuit or wire color identification, see appropriate wiring diagram in WIRING DIAGRAMS.

HOLD SWITCH

1) Turn ignition on. Ensure HOLD indicator illuminates with hold switch depressed. Ensure HOLD indicator is off when HOLD switch is released. If switch is not working as described, go to next step.

2) Remove center console to access switch connector. Disconnect connector. Check continuity between terminals "A" and "B". See Fig. 9. Continuity should exist when switch is depressed. When switch is released, continuity should not exist. Replace as needed. If HOLD switch system does not function correctly, inspect circuits between switch and TCM. See appropriate wiring diagram in WIRING DIAGRAMS.

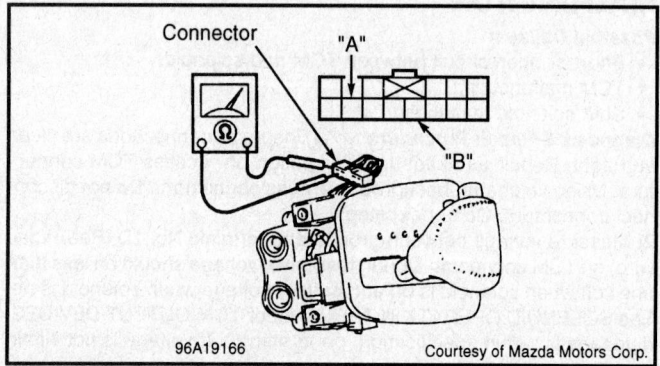

Fig. 9: Testing HOLD Switch

OUTPUT SPEED SENSOR

Disconnect output speed sensor connector. Measure resistance between terminals. Resistance should be 500-1000 ohms. See Fig. 10. Replace as needed.

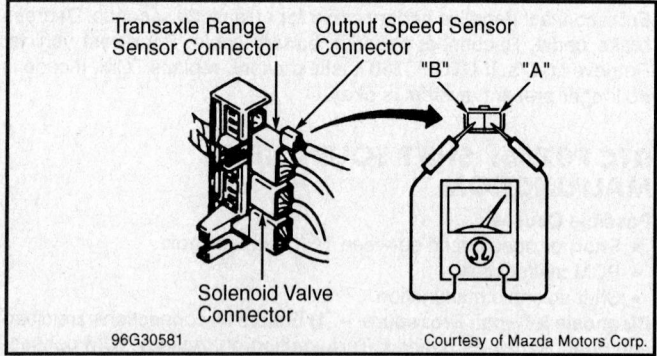

Fig. 10: Testing Output Speed Sensor & Locating Transaxle Component Connectors

SOLENOID VALVES (ON/OFF TYPE)

1) Disconnect negative battery cable. Disconnect transmission solenoid harness connector. See Fig. 10. Note that solenoids ground through transmission case. Check resistance between connector terminals and ground. See Fig. 11.

2) Resistance should be 20-40 ohms at 68°F (20°C). Replace solenoids as necessary. Ensure transmission case is grounded. If resistance is okay on all solenoids, go to next step.

3) On all solenoids except lock-up solenoid and pressure control solenoid, intermittently connect battery voltage to terminals of transmission solenoid harness connector and ground. An audible click should be heard from specified solenoid when voltage is applied. For lock-up solenoid and pressure control solenoid, see SOLENOID VALVES (DUTY CYCLE TYPE).

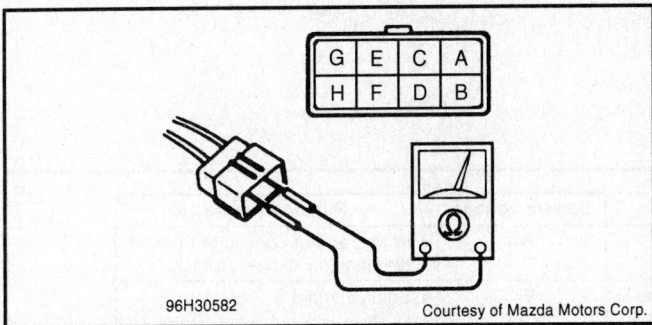

Fig. 11: *Identifying Solenoid Valve Terminals*

SOLENOID VALVES (DUTY CYCLE TYPE)

Pressure Control Solenoid – 1) Backprobe TCM harness connector using dwell meter. Set dwell meter to 4-CYL position. Connect positive lead to terminal No. 1F (Violet wire). Connect negative lead to ground. **2)** Engage parking and service brakes. Start and idle engine. Place shift selector in "D". Verify duty cycle ratio by depressing and releasing accelerator pedal. Dwell meter indicates OFF duty cycle ratio. Dwell should decrease as accelerator pedal is depressed. If signal is as specified, check continuity of circuits between TCM and pressure control solenoid. Repair as needed. If circuits are okay, replace solenoid. If signal is not as specified, replace TCM.

Lock-Up Solenoid – 1) Backprobe TCM harness connector using dwell meter. Set dwell meter to 4-CYL position. Connect positive lead to terminal No. 1M (Blue/Black wire) and negative lead to ground. **2)** Test drive vehicle. Verify duty cycle ratio by monitoring dwell meter during TCC engagement. Dwell meter indicates OFF duty cycle ratio. Dwell should about 95 degrees when TCC lockup solenoid is operating (slip lockup). Once complete lockup is achieved, dwell should be zero. **3)** If signal is as specified, check continuity of circuits between TCM and lock-up solenoid. Repair as needed. If circuits are okay, replace solenoid. If signal is not as specified, replace TCM.

VEHICLE SPEED SENSOR (VSS) NO. 1

NOTE: *Vehicle speed sensor No. 1 is part of speedometer in combination meter.*

1) Remove instrument cluster. Raise and support front of vehicle. Rotate front wheels. Measure voltage between terminals No. 2D and 2H. See Fig. 12.

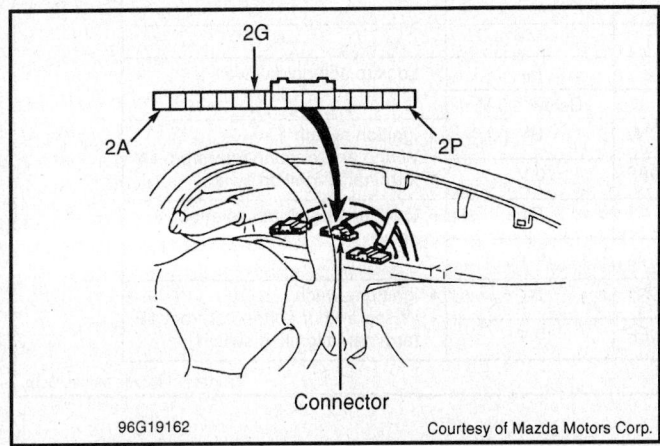

Fig. 12: *Identifying Instrument Cluster Harness Connector Terminals*

2) Monitor voltage as wheels are rotated. If voltage pulse is present, go to next step. If voltage pulse is not present, inspect vehicle speed sensor No. 1. See VEHICLE SPEED SENSOR NO. 2. Replace as needed. If vehicle speed sensor is okay, repair circuits between vehicle speed sensor No. 1 and vehicle speed sensor No. 2. Go to next step.

3) Ensure harness connector is connected to vehicle speed sensor No. 1. Turn ignition on. Rotate front wheels. Measure voltage between ground and terminal No. 2K. Monitor voltage as wheels are rotated. If voltage pulse is present, vehicle speed sensor No. 1 is currently functioning correctly. If voltage pulse is not present, replace combination meter or circuit board (as applicable).

VEHICLE SPEED SENSOR (VSS) NO. 2

NOTE: *Vehicle speed sensor signal is input to vehicle speed sensor No. 1 in combination meter than output to TCM (as applicable).*

1) Disconnect negative battery cable. Disconnect vehicle speed sensor connector. Rotate front wheels and measure voltage between sensor terminals. See Fig. 13.

2) If voltmeter needle does not fluctuate, replace sensor. If voltmeter needle fluctuates, but signal to TCM is suspect, go to VEHICLE SPEED SENSOR NO. 1.

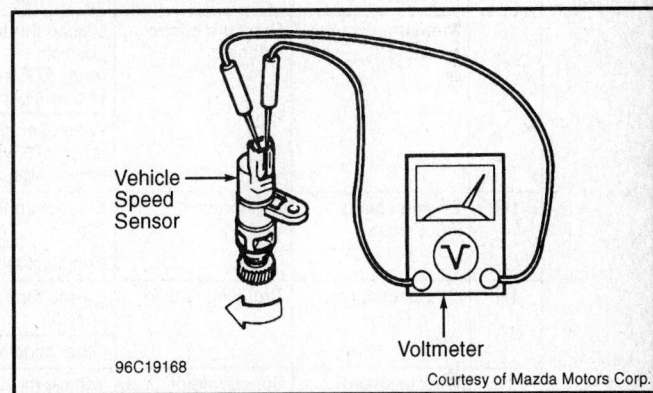

Fig. 13: *Checking Vehicle Speed Sensor No. 2*

TRANSMISSION RANGE (TR) SWITCH

1) Check for starter operation with ignition switch in START position and selector lever in "P" and "N" position only. Ensure back-up lights illuminate with ignition in ON position and selector lever in "R". If any problems are found, go to next step.

2) Disconnect TR switch connector. See Fig. 10. Check continuity between specified terminals. See Fig. 14. If continuity is not as specified, replace switch.

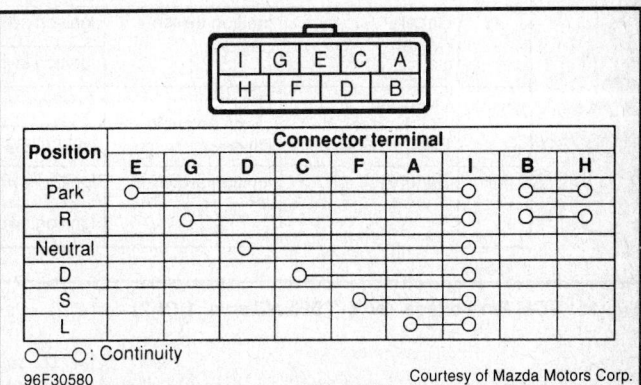

Position	Connector terminal								
	E	G	D	C	F	A	I	B	H
Park	O						O	O—O	
R		O					O	O—O	
Neutral			O				O		
D				O			O		
S					O		O		
L						O	O		

O——O: Continuity

Fig. 14: *Checking Transmission Range Switch*

AUTOMATIC TRANSMISSIONS
Mazda LJ4A-EL Electronic Controls (Cont.)

PCM & TCM TERMINAL VOLTAGE TESTS

Turn ignition switch to ON position. Access TCM. Do not disconnect harness connector. Using DVOM, measure voltage. *See Figs. 15-18.* After verifying that appropriate condition has been met, check voltage. If voltage is not within specification, replace TCM (as applicable).

Terminal	Component	Connected to	Condition	Correct voltage	Possible cause
1A	Battery (Back-up)	Battery	Constant	B+	• Wiring and/or connector from 1A terminal to kickdown switch
1B	Shift solenoid B	Shift solenoid B	Park, neutral and R ranges or 1st and 2nd gear	B+	• Shift solenoid B
			Third and fourth gear	Below 1.0 V	
1C	—	—	—	—	—
1D	Shift solenoid A	Shift solenoid A	Park, neutral and R ranges or 1st and fourth gear	B+	• Shift solenoid A
			2nd and Third gear	Below 1.0 V	
1E	Transmission range sensor (R range)	Transmission range sensor	R range	B+	• Transmission range sensor
			Other ranges	0 V	
1F	Pressure control solenoid	Pressure control solenoid	Closed throttle position (after ATF warm, engine stopped)	Above 2.0 V	• Pressure control solenoid and/or dropping resistor
			Wide open throttle (after ATF warm, engine stopped)	Below 1.0 V	
1G	Engine speed input signal	Distributor	Engine running at idle	5.0—6.0 V	• Distributor
			Engine stopped	0 V or B+	
1H	Dropping resistor	Dropping resistor	Closed throttle position	B+	• Dropping resistor and/or pressure control solenoid
			Other condition	Below 1.0 V	
1I	Vehicle speed sensor 2 (speedometer sensor)	Speedometer	Vehicle moving	2.0—3.0 V	• Vehicle speed sensor 2 and/or combination meter
			Vehicle stopped	0 V or 4.5—5.5 V	
1J	Ground	—	Constant	0 V	• Wiring from 1J terminal to ground
1K	HOLD indicator light	Combination meter (HOLD indicator light)	HOLD mode	Below 1.0 V	• combination meter
			Other modes	B+	
1L	—	—	—	—	—
1M	Lockup solenoid valve	Lockup solenoid valve	Lockup	B+	• Lockup solenoid valve
			No lockup	Below 1.0 V	
1N	Battery (Main)	Ignition switch	Ignition switch ON	B+	• Ignition switch • Wiring and/or connector from 1N terminal to ignition switch
			Ignition switch OFF	0 V	
1O	Overrunning clutch solenoid valve	Overrunning clutch solenoid valve	Driving	B+	• Overrunning clutch solenoid valve
			Not driving	0 V	
1P	Battery	Ignition switch	Ignition switch ON	B+	• Ignition switch • Wiring and/or connector from 1P terminal to ignition switch
			Ignition switch OFF	0 V	

96A30585 Courtesy of Mazda Motors Corp.

Fig. 15: *TCM Pin Voltage Table (1995 Millenia, 1 Of 2)*

Terminal	Component	Connected to	Condition	Correct voltage	Possible cause
2A	Throttle position sensor (V$_{RFE}$)	Throttle position sensor	Ignition switch ON	4.5—5.5 V	• Engine control module • Wiring and/or connector from 2A terminal to engine control module
			Ignition switch OFF	0 V	
2B	Transmission range sensor (D range)	Transmission range sensor	D range	B+	• Transmission range sensor
			Other ranges	0 V	
2C	—	—	—	—	—
2D	Transmission range sensor (Park and neutral position)	Transmission range sensor	Park and neutral position	0 V	• Transmission range sensor
			Other ranges	B+	
2E	—	—	—	—	—
2F	—	—	—	—	—
2G	4GR inhibit signal (auto speed control signal)	Cruise control unit	Ignition switch ON	B+	• Wiring and/or connector from 2G terminal to cruise control unit
				6.0 V	
				Below 1.0 V	
2H	Kickdown switch	Kickdown switch	Wide open throttle	B+	• Kickdown switch
			Throttle valve opening below 7/8		
2I	HOLD switch	HOLD switch	Switch depressed	0 V	• HOLD switch
			Switch released	B+	
2J	Output speed sensor	Output speed sensor	Vehicle speed above 25km/h {16mph}	Above 1.0 V	• Output speed sensor
			Vehicle stopped	0 V	
2K	ECM/TCM communication signal	Engine control module	Serial communication	5.0 V	• Wiring and/or connector from 2K terminal to engine control module
2L	Ground (Input signals)	—	Constant	0 V	• wiring from 2L terminal to ground
2M	Idle switch	Throttle position sensor	Throttle valve open	B+	• Wiring from 2M terminal to throttle sensor
			Throttle valve fully closed	0 V	
2N	ECM/TCM communication signal	Engine control module	Serial communication	5.0 V	• Wiring and/r connector from 2N terminal to engine control module
2O	—	—	—	—	—
2P	—	—	—	—	—
2Q	Transmission range sensor (L range)	Transmission range sensor	L range	B+	• Transmission range sensor
			Other ranges	0 V	
2R	Transmission fluid temperature sensor	Transmission fluid temperature sensor	While warming up ATF Note • 1.8V: ATF temperature 10°C {50°F} • 1.1V: ATF temperature 40°C {104°F}	0.1—2.4 V	• Transmission fluid temperature sensor
2S	Transmission range sensor (S range)	Transmission range sensor	S range	B+	• Transmission range sensor
			Other ranges	0 V	
2T	Throttle position sensor (TVO)	Throttle position sensor	Closed throttle position	0.1—1.2 V	• Throttle position sensor • Wiring and/or connector from 2T terminal to throttle position sensor
			Wide open throttle	3.5—4.0 V	

96B30586

Courtesy of Mazda Motors Corp.

Fig. 16: TCM Pin Voltage Table (1995 Millenia, 2 Of 2)

AUTOMATIC TRANSMISSIONS
Mazda LJ4A-EL Electronic Controls (Cont.)

Terminal	Component	Connected to	Condition	Correct voltage	Possible cause
1A	Battery (Back-up)	Battery	Constant	B+	• Wiring and/or connector from 1A terminal to battery
1B	Shift solenoid B	Shift solenoid B	P, N and R positions or 1GR and 2GR	B+	• Shift solenoid B and/or wiring
			3GR and 4GR	Below 1.0 V	
1C	—	—	—	—	—
1D	Shift solenoid A	Shift solenoid A	P, N, and R positions or 1GR and 4GR	B+	• Shift solenoid A and/or wiring
			2GR and 3GR	Below 1.0 V	
1E	Transaxle range switch (R position)	Transaxle range switch	R position	B+	• Transaxle range switch and/or wiring
			Other positions, all ranges	0 V	
1F	Pressure control solenoid	Pressure control solenoid	Closed throttle position (after ATF warm, engine stopped)	Above 2.0 V	• Pressure control solenoid and/or dropping resistor
			Wide open throttle (after ATF warm, engine stopped)	Below 1.0 V	
1G	Engine speed input signal	Engine control module	Engine running at idle	5.0—6.0 V	• Engine control module and/or wiring
			Engine stopped	0 V or B+	
1H	Dropping resistor	Dropping resistor	Closed throttle position	B+	• Dropping resistor and/or pressure control solenoid
			Other conditions	Below 1.0 V	
1I	Vehicle speedometer sensor	Speedometer	Vehicle moving	2.0—3.0 V	• Vehicle speedometer sensor and/or speed sensor
			Vehicle stopped	0 V or 4.5—5.5 V	
1J	Ground	—	Constant	0 V	• Wiring from 1J terminal to ground
1K	HOLD indicator light	Combination meter (HOLD indicator light)	HOLD mode	Below 1.0 V	• Combination meter
			Except HOLD mode	B+	
1L	—	—	—	—	—
1M	TCC solenoid valve	TCC solenoid valve	TCC operation	B+	• TCC solenoid valve and/or wiring
			TCC non-operation	Below 1.0 V	
1N	Battery (Main)	Ignition switch	Ignition switch ON	B+	• Ignition switch • Wiring and/or connector from 1N terminal to ignition switch
			Ignition switch OFF	0 V	
1O	Overrunning clutch solenoid valve	Overrunning clutch solenoid valve	Driving	B+	• Overrunning clutch solenoid valve and/or wiring
			Not driving	0 V	
1P	Battery	Ignition switch	Ignition switch ON	B+	• Ignition switch • Wiring and/or connector from 1P terminal to ignition switch
			Ignition switch OFF	0 V	
2A	Throttle position sensor (Vref)	Throttle position sensor	Ignition switch ON	4.5—5.5 V	• Engine control module • Wiring and/or connector from 2A terminal to engine control module
			Ignition switch OFF	0 V	

96C30587   Courtesy of Mazda Motors Corp.

Fig. 17: PCM Pin Voltage Table (1996 Millenia, 1 Of 2)

Terminal	Component	Connected to	Condition	Correct voltage	Possible cause
2B	Transaxle range switch (D range)	Transaxle range switch	D range	B+	• Transaxle range switch and/or wiring
			Other ranges, all positions	0 V	
2C	—	—	—	—	—
2D	Transaxle range switch (P and N position)	Transaxle range switch	P and N position	0 V	• Transaxle range switch and/or wiring
			Other positions, all ranges	B+	
2E	—	—	—	—	—
2F	—	—	—	—	—
2G	4GR inhibit signal (auto speed control signal)	Cruise control module	Ignition switch ON	B+	• Wiring and/or connector from 2G terminal to cruise control module
			When 4GR inhibit signal is not input	6.0 V	
			When 4GR inhibit signal is input	Below 1.0 V	
2H	Battery	Ignition switch	Ignition switch ON	B+	• Ignition switch • Wiring and/or connector from terminal 2H to ignition switch
			Ignition switch OFF	0 V	
2I	HOLD switch	HOLD switch	Switch depressed	0 V	• HOLD switch and/or wiring
			Switch released	B+	
2J	Output speed sensor	Output speed sensor	Vehicle speed above 25km/h {16mph}	Above 1.0 V	• Output speed sensor and/or wiring
			Vehicle stopped	0 V	
2K	ECM/TCM communication signal	Engine control module	Serial communication (Refer to section F2)	5.0 V	• Wiring and/or connector from 2K terminal to engine control module
2L	Ground (Input signals)	—	Constant	0 V	• Wiring from 2L terminal to ground
2M	Closed throttle position switch	Throttle position sensor	Throttle valve open	B+	• Wiring from 2M terminal to throttle position sensor
			Throttle valve closed throttle position	0 V	
2N	ECM/TCM communication signal	Engine control module	Serial communication (Refer to section F2)	5.0 V	• Wiring and/or connector from 2N terminal to engine control module
2O	—	—	—	—	—
2P	—	—	—	—	—
2Q	Transaxle range switch (L range)	Transaxle range switch	L range	B+	• Transaxle range switch and/or wiring
			Other ranges, all positions	0 V	
2R	Transaxle fluid temperature sensor	Transaxle fluid temperature sensor	While warming up ATF Note • 1.8V: ATF temperature 10°C {50°F} • 1.1V: ATF temperature 40°C {104°F}	0.1—2.4 V	• Transaxle fluid temperature sensor and/or wiring
2S	Transaxle range switch (S range)	Transaxle range switch	S range	B+	• Transaxle range switch and/or wiring
			Other ranges, all positions	0 V	
2T	Throttle position sensor (TVO)	Throttle position sensor	Closed throttle position	0.1—1.2 V	• Throttle position sensor • Wiring and/or connector from 2T terminal to throttle position sensor
			Wide open throttle	3.5—4.0 V	

96D30588

Courtesy of Mazda Motors Corp.

Fig. 18: PCM Pin Voltage Table (1996 Millenia, 2 Of 2)

WIRING DIAGRAMS

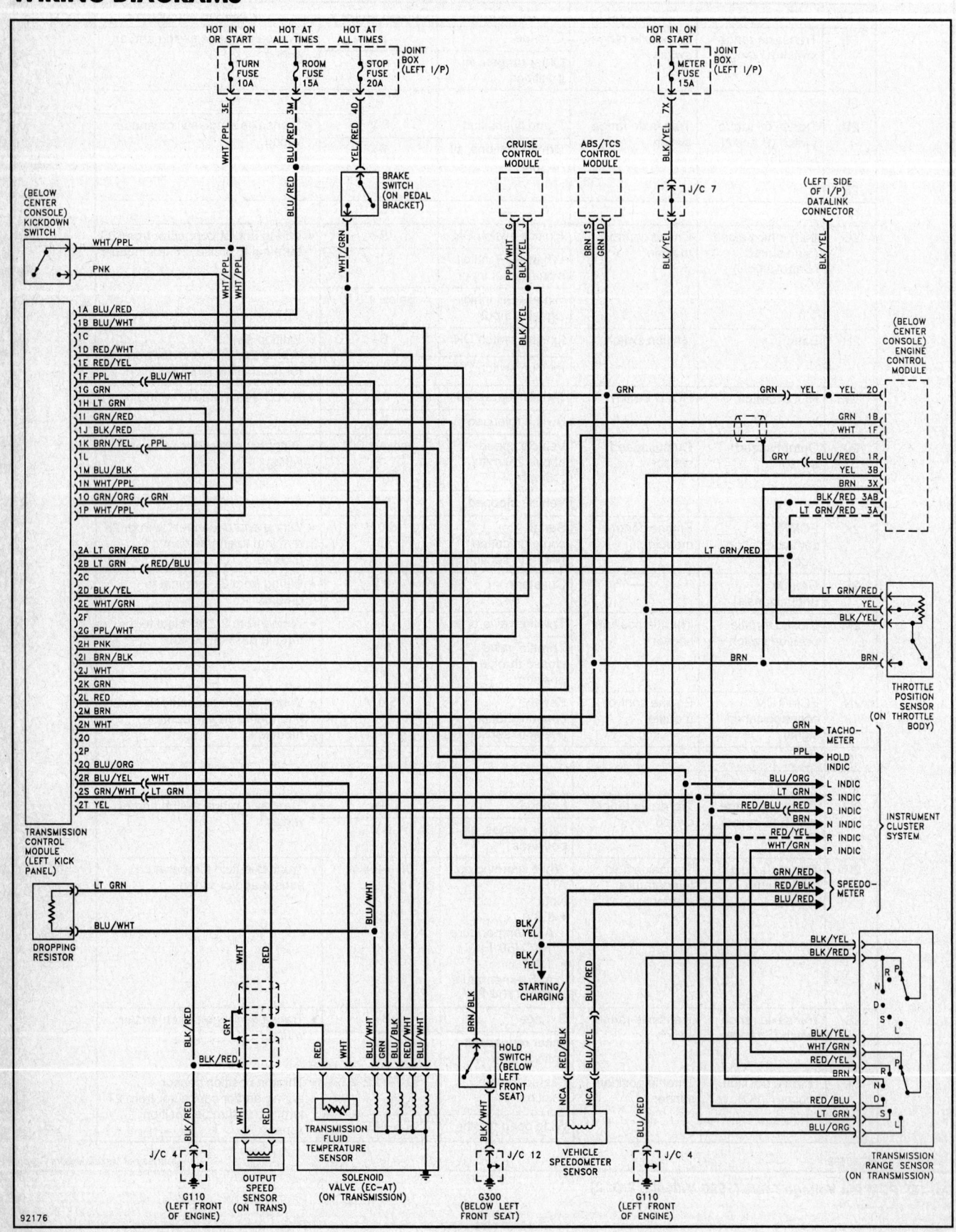

Fig. 19: Transaxle Wiring Diagram (1995 Millenia 2.3L)

92176

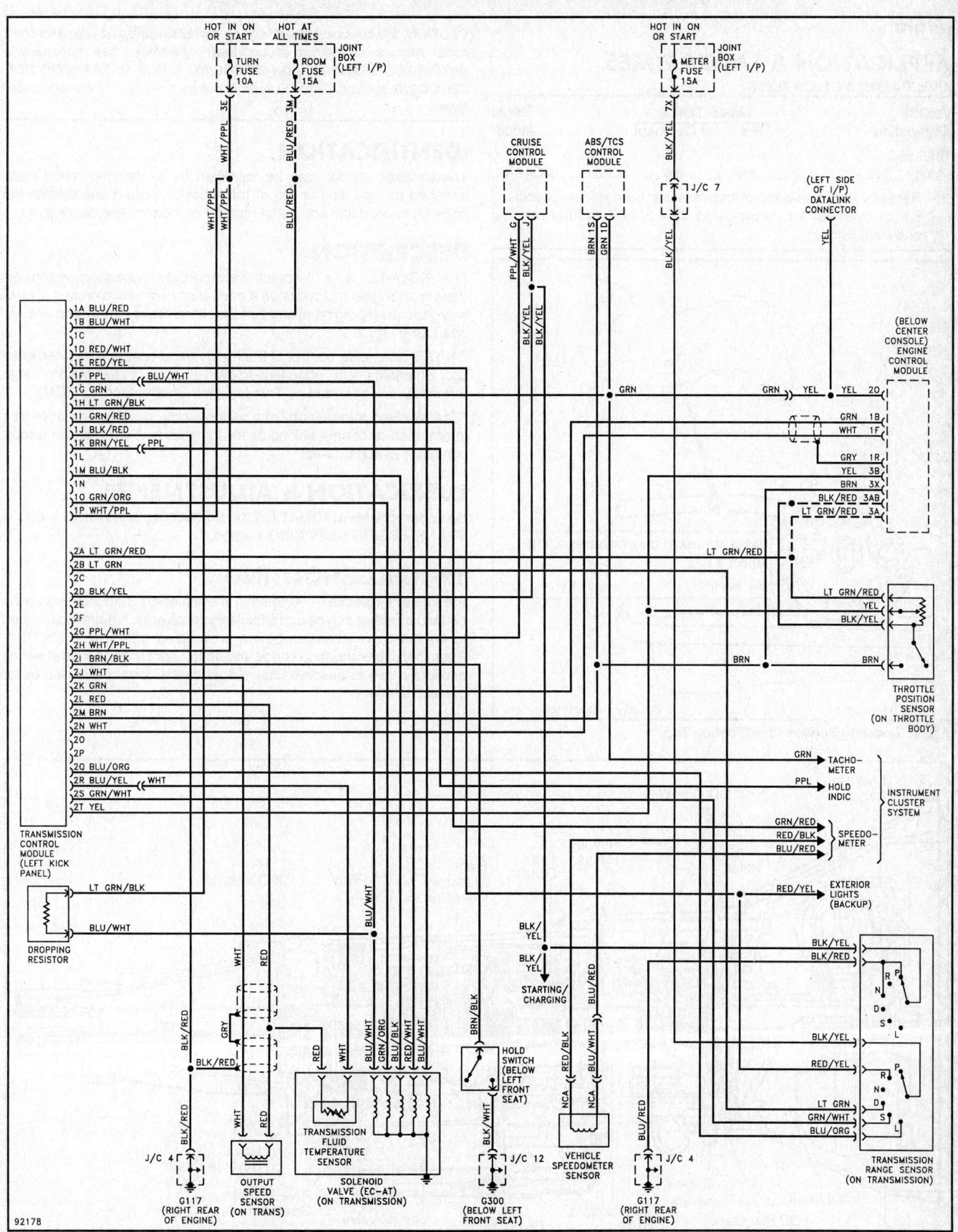

Fig. 20: Transaxle Wiring Diagram (1996 Millenia 2.3L)

AUTOMATIC TRANSMISSIONS
Mazda NC4A-EL

Miata

APPLICATION & LABOR TIMES

APPLICATION & LABOR TIMES

Vehicle Application	Labor Times [1] R & I	[2] Overhaul	Trans. Model
1995-96			
Miata	4.9	8.6	NC4A-EL

[1] – Removal and installation of transmission from vehicle chassis.

[2] – Bench overhaul for transmission. DOES NOT include removal and installation.

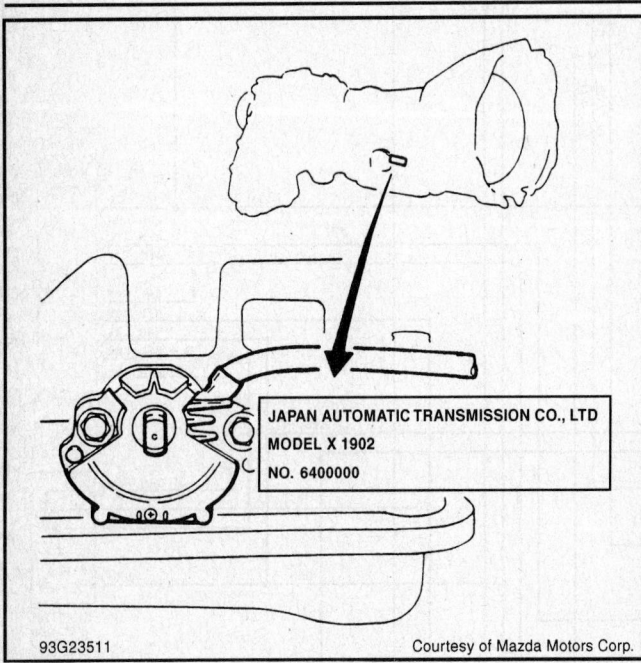

93G23511   Courtesy of Mazda Motors Corp.

Fig. 1: Locating Service Identification Tag

CAUTION: Disconnecting battery on models equipped with anti-theft radio require canceling of anti-theft operation. See appropriate AUTOMATIC TRANSMISSION SERVICING article in TRANSMISSION SERVICING section. Refer to vehicle owner's manual to identify radio type.

IDENTIFICATION

Transmission model may be identified by a stamped metal plate attached to right side or top of transmission case. Plate lists model code on second line and serial number on bottom line. *See Fig. 1.*

DESCRIPTION

The NC4A-EL is a 4-speed electronically controlled automatic transmission that incorporates 4 multi-disc hydraulic clutches, 2 one-way clutches (sprag type) and 2 friction lined brake bands (2nd and 4th gear). *See Fig. 2.*

ON/OFF solenoids control shift changes and torque converter lock-up. Solenoids are attached to valve body transmission case. Solenoids are operated by Transmission Control Module (TCM).

TCM receives information from various input devices and uses this information to control solenoids for transmission shifting and torque converter clutch lock-up.

LUBRICATION & ADJUSTMENTS

See appropriate AUTOMATIC TRANSMISSION SERVICING article in TRANSMISSION SERVICING section.

TROUBLE SHOOTING

Preliminary Checks – Automatic transmission malfunction can be caused by either engine or transmission problems. Isolate malfunction to engine or transmission before proceeding with trouble shooting. Prior to trouble shooting check and adjust shift linkage, range switch and idle speed as needed. Ensure fluid level is correct. Check tires for correct inflation.

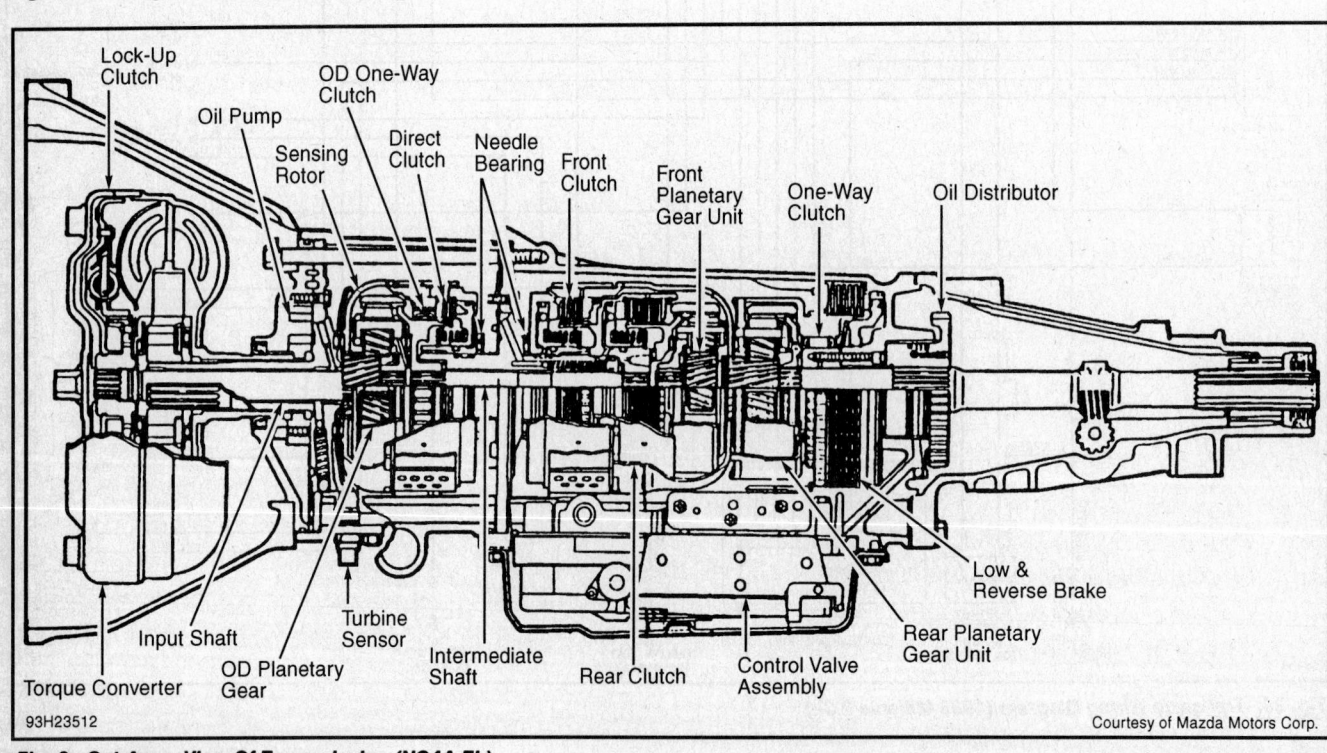

93H23512   Courtesy of Mazda Motors Corp.

Fig. 2: Cut-Away View Of Transmission (NC4A-EL)

SYMPTOM DIAGNOSIS

NOTE: See NC4A-EL ELECTRONIC CONTROLS article for electronic component testing.

Vehicle Does Not Move In Any Gear – Possible causes; ATF fluid level and condition, selector lever adjustment, valve body, oil pump, torque converter, direct clutch, front clutch, rear clutch, low & reverse brake and/or one-way clutch.

Vehicle Moves In "N" Position – Possible causes; selector lever adjustment and/or valve body.

Excessive Creep – Possible causes; high idle speed, ignition timing and/or torque converter clutch.

Transmission Does Not Shift – Possible causes; ATF fluid level and condition, selector lever adjustment, valve body, oil pump, transmission range switch, HOLD switch, shift solenoids and/or 3-2 control solenoid.

Abnormal Shift Sequence – Possible causes; ATF fluid level and condition, selector lever adjustment, valve body, 4th gear brake band/servo, front clutch, 2nd gear brake band/servo, transmission range switch, HOLD switch, cruise control switch, shift solenoids, 3-2 control solenoid, TP sensor and/or input/turbine speed sensor.

Frequent Shifting – Possible causes; valve body, transmission range switch, cruise control switch, TP sensor and/or input/turbine speed sensor.

Excessively High Or Low Shift Point – Possible causes; selector lever adjustment, valve body, transmission range switch, HOLD switch, shift solenoids, 3-2 control solenoid, TP sensor and/or input/turbine speed sensor.

No Torque Converter Clutch Engagement – Possible causes; selector lever adjustment, valve body, torque converter, cruise control switch, shift solenoids, 3-2 control solenoid, TP sensor, input/turbine speed sensor and/or TCC control solenoid.

No Kickdown – Possible causes; selector lever adjustment, TP sensor, transmission range switch and/or HOLD switch.

Transmission Flare When Starting From Stop – Possible causes; check ATF fluid level and condition, valve body, oil pump, direct clutch, 2nd gear brake band/servo, rear clutch, low and reverse brake, one-way clutch and/or transmission range switch.

Transmission Flare During Shifts – Possible causes; ATF fluid level and condition, valve body, oil pump, direct clutch, 4th gear brake band/servo, 4th gear one-way clutch, front clutch 2nd gear brake band/servo and/or rear clutch.

Excessive N-D Or N-R Shift Shock – Possible causes; high idle speed, ignition timing, valve body, accumulator, transmission range switch, vehicle speed sensor and/or input/turbine speed sensor.

Excessive Upshift Or Downshift Shift Shock – Possible causes; valve body, accumulator, 4th gear brake band/servo and/or 2nd gear brake band/servo.

No Engine Braking – Possible causes; ATF fluid level and condition, selector lever adjustment, valve body, oil pump, torque converter, direct clutch, front clutch, 2nd gear brake band/servo, rear clutch, low and reverse brake, 4th gear brake band/servo, shift solenoids and/or 3-2 control solenoid.

Transmission Overheats – Possible causes; check ATF fluid level and condition, selector lever adjustment, valve body, oil pump, torque converter, oil cooler and/or TCC control solenoid.

HOLD Indicator Light Flashes – Possible causes; vehicle speed sensor, TP sensor, shift solenoids, 3-2 control solenoid, input/turbine speed sensor and/or TCC control solenoid.

TESTING

Before testing transmission, ensure fluid level is correct and shift linkage, range switch and idle speed are adjusted correctly.

TIME LAG

With engine at idle, shift selector from "N" to "D", "N" to "D" HOLD and "N" to "R". Time lag for transmission to engage should be less than 1.5 seconds for "N" to "D" or "N" to "D" HOLD and less than 1.7 seconds for "N" to "R".

TIME LAG RESULTS

Longer Than Specified In "N" To "D" – Low line pressure. Rear clutch slipping. One-way clutch slipping.

Longer Than Specified In "N" To "D" HOLD – Low line pressure. Rear clutch slipping. 2nd gear brake band slipping.

Longer Than Specified In "N" To "R" – Low line pressure. Front clutch slipping. Low and reverse brake slipping.

CLUTCH & BAND APPLICATIONS

Position/ Range	Gear position	D/C	4GR Brk. Apl.	4GR Brk. Rel.	4GR OWC	R/C	F/C	2GR Brk. Apl.	2GR Brk. Rel.	L & R Brk.	OWC	A	B	C
P	—	○	⊗	○						○		○	○	○
R	—	○	⊗	○	○		○		○	○				○
N	Below 7 km/h { 4.34 mph }	○	⊗	○								○	○	○
N	Above 9 km/h { 5.58 mph }	○	⊗	○										○
D	1GR	○	⊗	○	○	○					○	○	○	○
D	2GR	○	⊗	○	○	○		○					○	○
D	3GR	○	⊗	○	○	○	○	⊗	○					○
D	4GR		○			○	○	⊗	○					○
S	1GR	○	⊗	○	○	○					○	○	○	○
S	2GR	○	⊗	○	○	○		○					○	○
S	3GR	○	⊗	○	○	○	○	⊗	○					○
L	1GR	○	⊗	○	○	○				○		○	○	○
L	2GR	○	⊗	○	○	○		○					○	○

○ Operating

⊗ indicates operation although the band servo remains deactivated due to the large area of the release pressure side.

The torque converter clutch control solenoid valve operates only during torque converter clutch operation.

The 3-2 control solenoid valve operates momentarily during 3-2 downshift.

The fourth gear one-way clutch operates momentarily during 4-3 downshift.

96H30814

Courtesy of Mazda Motors Corp.

Fig. 3: Clutch & Band Application Chart (NC4A-EL)

AUTOMATIC TRANSMISSIONS
Mazda NC4A-EL (Cont.)

Shorter Than Specified In "N" To "D" – N-D accumulator not operating properly. Excessive line pressure.
Shorter Than Specified In "N" To "D" HOLD – 1-2 accumulator not operating properly. Excessive line pressure.
Shorter Than Specified In "N" To "R" – N-R/2-3 accumulator not operating properly. Excessive line pressure.

ROAD TEST

Preparation – Check all fluid levels and correct if necessary. Warm engine and transmission to operating temperature.

Range	Mode	Throttle condition	Shift	Vehicle speed km/h { mph }	Turbine speed rpm
D	NORMAL	Wide open throttle	D₁→D₂	58—64 { 36—39 }	5600—6150
			D₂→D₃	100—108 { 62—66 }	5700—6150
			D₃ TCC operation	98—106 { 61—65 }	3850—4150
			D₃→D₄	152—162 { 95—100 }	5950—6350
		Half throttle	D₁→D₂	33—46 { 21—28 }	3150—4400
			D₂→D₃	58—76 { 36—47 }	3300—4300
			D₃→D₄	82—110 { 51—68 }	3200—4300
			D₄ TCC operation	74—100 { 46—62 }	2100—2800
		Closed throttle position	D₄→D₃	28—34 { 17—21 }	800—950
			D₃→D₁	11—17 { 7—10 }	430—650
		Kickdown (Wide open throttle)	D₄→D₃	140—150 { 87—93 }	3950—4200
			D₃→D₂	92—100 { 57—62 }	3600—3900
			D₂→D₁	42—48 { 26—29 }	2400—2700
	POWER	Wide open throttle	D₁→D₂	58—64 { 36—39 }	5600—6150
			D₂→D₃	100—108 { 62—66 }	5700—6150
			D₃ TCC operation	98—106 { 61—65 }	3850—4150
			D₃→D₄	152—162 { 95—100 }	5950—6350
		Half throttle	D₁→D₂	44—55 { 28—34 }	4250—5300
			D₂→D₃	99—108 { 56—66 }	5650—6150
			D₃ TCC operation	98—106 { 61—65 }	3850—4150
			D₃→D₄	140—164 { 87—101 }	5500—6400
		Closed throttle position	D₄→D₃	28—34 { 17—21 }	800—950
			D₃→D₁	11—17 { 7—10 }	430—650
		Kickdown (Wide open throttle)	D₄→D₃	140—150 { 87—93 }	3950—4200
			D₃→D₂	92—100 { 57—62 }	3600—3900
			D₂→D₁	42—48 { 26—29 }	2400—2700
	HOLD	All positions	D₁→D₂	27—33 { 17—20 }	2600—3150
			D₂→D₃	35—45 { 22—27 }	2000—2550
			D₄→D₃	152—158 { 94—97 }	4300—4450
			D₃→D₁	12—18 { 8—11 }	500—700
			D₃ TCC operation	95—105 { 59—65 }	3700—4100
S	Except HOLD	Wide open throttle	S₁→S₂	58—64 { 36—39 }	5600—6150
			S₂→S₃	100—108 { 62—66 }	5700—6150
			S₃ TCC operation	98—105 { 61—65 }	3850—4100
		Half throttle	S₁→S₂	44—55 { 28—34 }	4250—5300
			S₂→S₃	90—108 { 56—67 }	5150—6150
			S₃ TCC operation	94—106 { 58—66 }	3700—4150
		Closed throttle position	S₃→S₁	11—17 { 7—10 }	430—650
		Kickdown (Wide open throttle)	S₃→S₂	92—100 { 57—62 }	3600—3900
			S₂→S₁	42—48 { 26—29 }	2400—2700
	HOLD	All positions	S₃→S₂	99—105 { 61—65 }	3900—4100
			S₃ TCC operation	95—105 { 59—65 }	3700—4100
L	Except HOLD	Wide open throttle	L₁→L₂	56—62 { 35—38 }	5400—5950
		Half throttle	L₁→L₂	44—55 { 27—34 }	4250—5300
		Closed throttle position	L₃→L₂	96—104 { 60—64 }	3750—4050
			L₂→L₁	11—17 { 7—10 }	650—950
		Kickdown (Wide open throttle)	L₃→L₂	99—105 { 61—65 }	3900—4100
			L₂→L₁	42—48 { 26—29 }	2400—2700
	HOLD	All positions	L₂→L₁	35—41 { 21—25 }	2000—2300
			L₃ TCC operation	95—105 { 59—65 }	3700—4100

96I30815

Courtesy of Mazda Motors Corp.

Fig. 4: Shift Speed Chart (1995-96 Miata)

"D" RANGE

Inspection – **1)** Check shift point, shift pattern and shift shock. Shift selector to "D" range. Accelerate vehicle at half and full throttle, ensure 1-2, 2-3 and 3-OD upshifts, downshifts and lock-up are obtained. Note speed and compare with SHIFT SPEED CHART. See Fig. 4. Note upshifts for shift shock and slippage.

2) Select HOLD mode. Check for 2-3 upshifts and downshifts. Check for lock-up and no 1st or "OD".

3) Decelerate vehicle. Check for engine braking in 3rd and 2nd gears when throttle is open 1/8 or less.

4) Drive in 3rd and 4th gear to ensure no unusual noise or vibration. Check torque converter, driveshaft and differential for source of unusual noise. Ensure kickdown operates properly and shift points match SHIFT SPEED CHART.

NOTE: POWER or NORMAL driving mode is automatically selected according to throttle opening. TCC lock-up does not operate when throttle is closed with vehicle below 74 MPH or when ATF is below 104°F (40°C).

"D" RANGE RESULTS & POSSIBLE CAUSES

No 1-2 Or 2-1 Shift – Shift solenoid "A" stuck and/or 1-2 shift valve stuck.

No 2-3 Or 3-2 Shift – Shift solenoid "B" stuck and/or 2-3 shift valve stuck.

No 3-4 Or 4-3 Shift – Shift solenoid "C" stuck and/or 3-4 shift valve stuck.

No TCC Operation – TCC Shift solenoid stuck and/or TCC shift valve stuck.

Incorrect Shift Point – TP sensor misadjusted and/or sticking shift valves.

Excessive Shift Shock Or Slippage – Stuck accumulators, stuck or no one-way check orifice, 3-2 control solenoid valve stuck, 3-2 control valve stuck, worn internal clutches and/or one-way clutch.

No Engine Braking – Worn internal clutches and/or brake bands.

STALL SPEED

CAUTION: Stall and line pressure tests generate high engine and transmission temperatures. DO NOT hold throttle open more than 5 seconds. Allow engine to idle in "P" or "N" for at least one minute between tests.

Preparation – Check all fluid levels and correct if necessary. Warm engine and transmission to operating temperature. Prior to performing stall test, block front and rear wheels and set parking brake.

Connect tachometer to engine. Ensure engine idle speed and ignition timing is correct. See appropriate ON-VEHICLE ADJUSTMENTS article in ENGINE PERFORMANCE in appropriate MITCHELL© manual. Apply foot brake firmly and shift selector to "D" range. Press accelerator pedal to floor and note maximum RPM. Select "S", "R" and "L" ranges and repeat. Stall speed should be 1900-2100 RPM.

STALL SPEED RESULTS

Above Specification In All Ranges – Insufficient line pressure, worn oil pump. Oil leakage from oil pump, control valve and/or transmission case. Stuck pressure regulator. Slipping direct clutch and overdrive one-way clutch.

Above Specification In "D" & "L" – Rear clutch slipping.

Above Specification In "D" – One-way clutch slipping.

Above Specification In "R" Range – Low and reverse brake slipping. Front clutch slipping. Perform road test to see if low and/or reverse brake or front clutch is at fault. Results indicate the following:
- Engine braking in "L" range, front clutch faulty.
- No engine braking in "L" range, low and/or reverse brake faulty.

Below Specification In All Ranges – Low engine output. One-way clutch in torque converter slipping.

LINE PRESSURE TEST

1) Connect gauge to line pressure inspection port. See Fig. 5 Connect tachometer to engine. Ensure engine idle speed and ignition timing is correct. See appropriate ON-VEHICLE ADJUSTMENTS article in ENGINE PERFORMANCE in appropriate MITCHELL© manual. Apply foot brake firmly and shift selector to "D" range.

2) Press accelerator pedal to floor and note pressure gauge. Release throttle to read pressure at idle. Select "S", "R" and "L" ranges and repeat. Compare with LINE PRESSURE SPECIFICATIONS table.

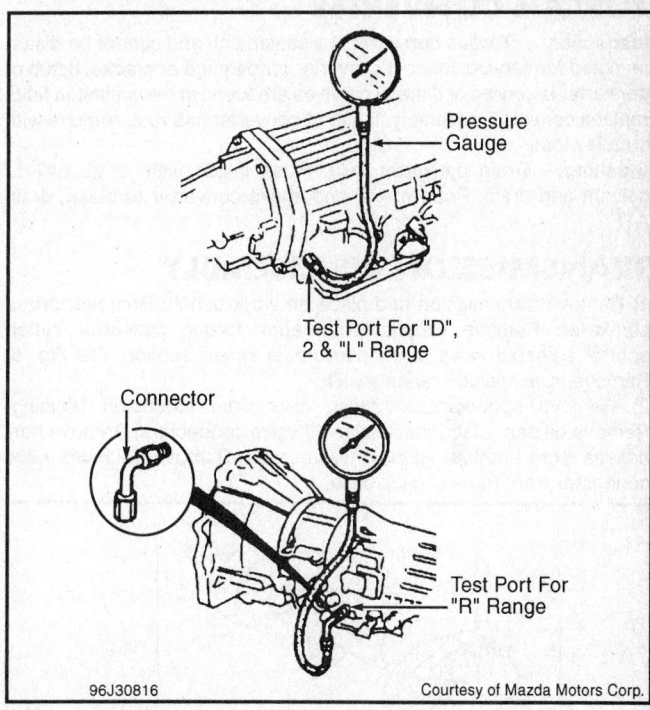

Fig. 5: *Identifying Transmission Fluid Pressure Ports*

LINE PRESSURE SPECIFICATIONS

Range	Idle psi (kPa)	Stall psi (kPa)
"D"	42-52 (285-362)	116-132 (795-912)
"S"	114-133 (785-921)	116-132 (795-912)
"L"	43-56 (295-392)	128-156 (883-1078)
"R"	57-71 (392-490)	273-300 (1884-2069)

LINE PRESSURE RESULTS

Low Pressure At Idle (All Ranges) – Worn oil pump. Damaged control piston in oil pump. Pressure regulator valve or plug sticking. Damaged pressure regulator valve spring. Fluid leakage between oil strainer and pressure regulator valve.

Low At Idle In "D", "S" Or "L" – Fluid leakage from hydraulic circuit of rear clutch.

Low At Idle In "D" HOLD & "S" Mode – Fluid leakage from hydraulic circuit of band servo 2nd apply side.

Low At Idle In "R" – Fluid leakage from hydraulic circuit of front clutch.

Low At Idle In "R" & "L" – Fluid leakage from hydraulic circuit of low and reverse brake.

High At Idle – Pressure modifier valve stuck. Backup control valve stuck.

AUTOMATIC TRANSMISSIONS
Mazda NC4A-EL (Cont.)

ON-VEHICLE SERVICE

See appropriate AUTOMATIC TRANSMISSION SERVICING article in TRANSMISSION SERVICING section.

REMOVAL & INSTALLATION

See appropriate AUTOMATIC TRANSMISSION REMOVAL article in TRANSMISSION SERVICING section.

TORQUE CONVERTER

Inspection – Torque converter is a sealed unit and cannot be disassembled for service. Inspect converter for damage or cracks. If hub of converter is scored or if metal particles are found in transmission fluid, replace converter assembly. If hub of converter has rust, remove with crocus cloth.

Cleaning – Drain converter fluid. Flush inside with .5 qt. (.47 L) solvent and drain. Pour in ATF and shake converter to clean, drain ATF.

TRANSMISSION DISASSEMBLY

1) Remove transmission and place on work bench. Remove torque converter. Remove vacuum diaphragm, torque converter clutch control solenoid valve and input/turbine speed sensor. *See Fig. 6.* Remove transmission range switch.

2) Remove speedometer driven gear from extension housing. Remove oil pan. Disconnect solenoid valve connectors. Remove harnesses from bracket. Remove valve body. Remove solenoid valve connector from transmission case.

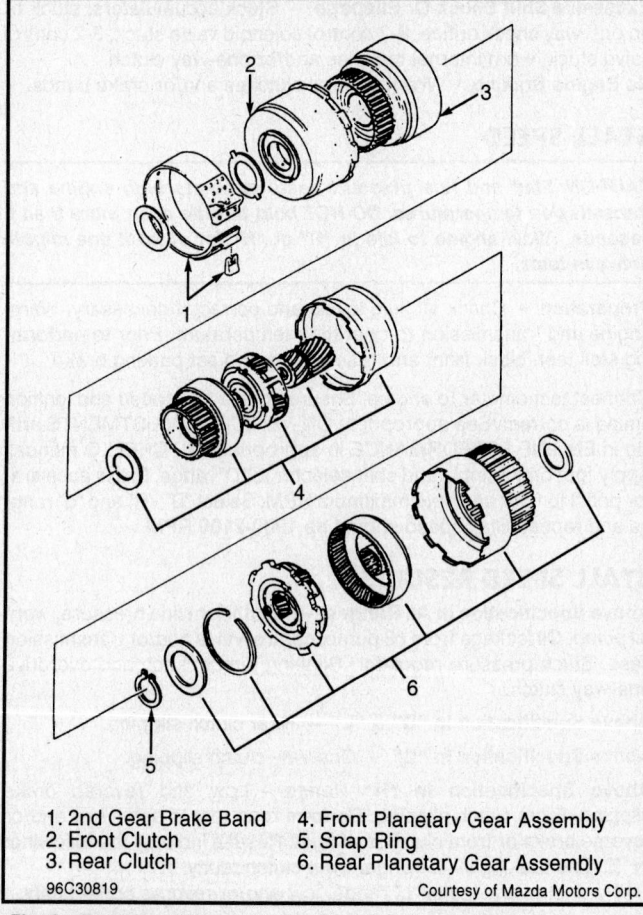

1. Oil Pump
2. 4th Gear Planetary Gear Assembly
3. Direct Clutch
4. 4th Gear Brake Band Strut
5. 4th Gear Case
6. 4th Gear Band Servo
7. Intermediate Shaft

96B30818   Courtesy of Mazda Motors Corp.

Fig. 7: Exploded View Of NC4A-EL 4th Gear Components

3) Place marks on converter housing, 4th gear case and transmission case for reassembly reference. Remove converter housing from 4th gear case. *See Fig. 6.* Remove 4th gear band servo cover.

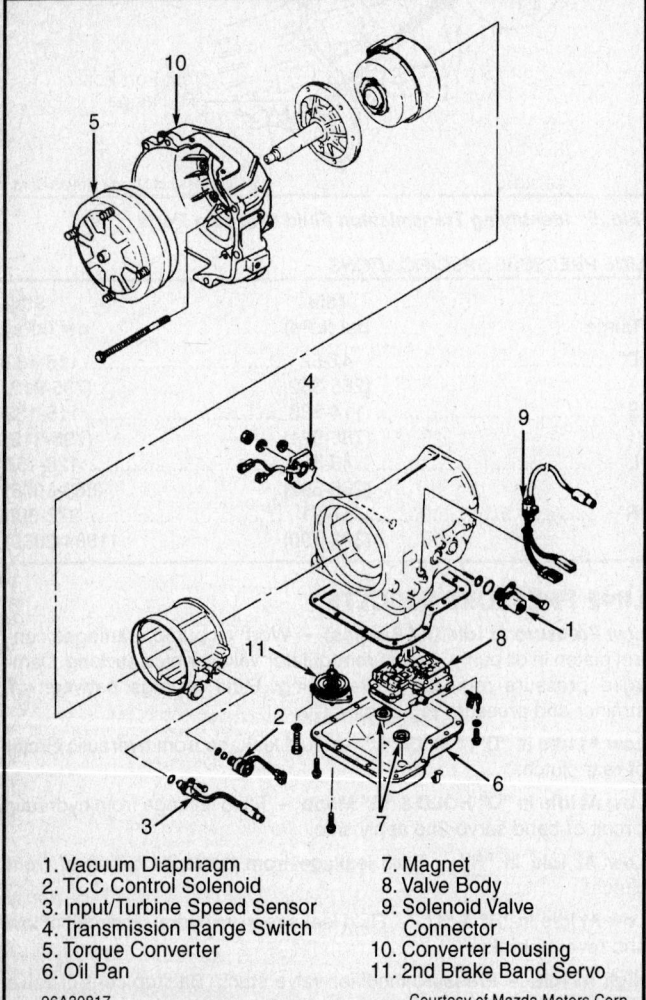

1. Vacuum Diaphragm
2. TCC Control Solenoid
3. Input/Turbine Speed Sensor
4. Transmission Range Switch
5. Torque Converter
6. Oil Pan
7. Magnet
8. Valve Body
9. Solenoid Valve Connector
10. Converter Housing
11. 2nd Brake Band Servo

96A30817   Courtesy of Mazda Motors Corp.

Fig. 6: Identifying NC4A-EL External Components

1. 2nd Gear Brake Band
2. Front Clutch
3. Rear Clutch
4. Front Planetary Gear Assembly
5. Snap Ring
6. Rear Planetary Gear Assembly

96C30819   Courtesy of Mazda Motors Corp.

Fig. 8: Exploded View Of NC4A-EL 1st, 2nd & 3rd Gear Components

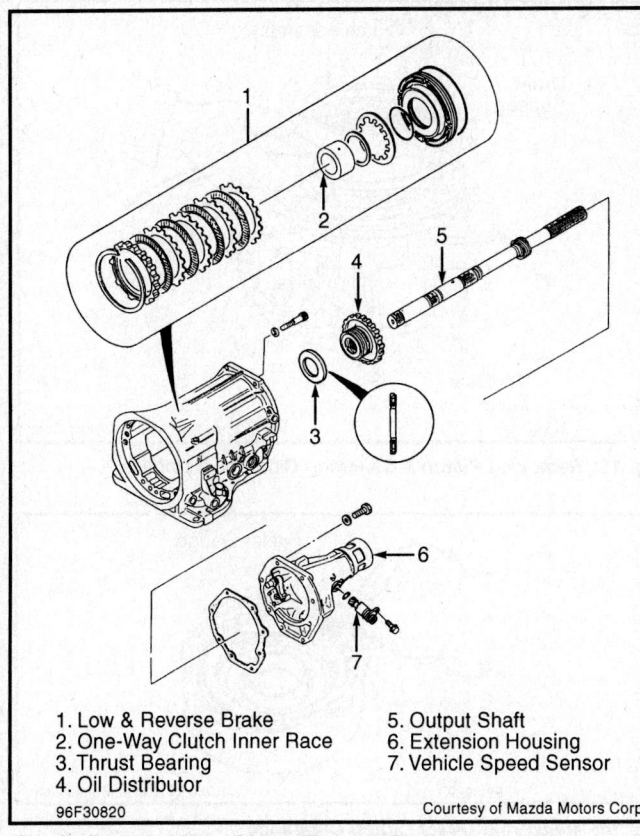

1. Low & Reverse Brake
2. One-Way Clutch Inner Race
3. Thrust Bearing
4. Oil Distributor
5. Output Shaft
6. Extension Housing
7. Vehicle Speed Sensor

96F30820   Courtesy of Mazda Motors Corp.

Fig. 9: Exploded View Of Low/Reverse Brake

4) Loosen 4th gear band servo lock nut and tighten piston stem. Place reference marks on 4th gear case and oil pump. Using 2 slide hammers, remove oil pump from transmission case. Loosen 4th gear band servo piston stem. Remove 4th gear connecting shell and 4th gear planetary gear unit. See Fig. 7.

5) Remove direct clutch. Remove 4th gear band. Secure band with wire to maintain shape. Remove band strut. Remove thrust bearing. Remove intermediate shaft. Loosen 2nd gear band servo locknut and tighten piston stem.

6) Separate drum support, accumulator and 4th gear case from transmission case. Remove thrust bearing from drum support, accumulator and 4th gear case. See Fig. 7. Loosen 2nd gear band servo piston stem and remove 2nd gear band strut. Secure band with wire to maintain shape. Remove band strut.

7) Remove bearing race, front clutch, rear clutch, connecting shell and front planetary gear unit. See Fig. 8. Remove extension housing. See Fig. 9. Remove snap ring from output shaft. Remove rear planetary gear unit. Pull out output shaft. Remove oil distributor and bearing.

COMPONENT DISASSEMBLY & REASSEMBLY

OIL PUMP

Disassembly & Reassembly – Remove snap ring from input shaft. Remove sensing rotor and input shaft. See Fig. 10. Remove oil pump bolts and separate pump cover and pump housing. Place match marks on oil pump gears with appropriate marker. DO NOT use a punch. Remove roll pin and remove lock-up control valve components (if necessary). To reassemble, reverse disassembly procedure. Tighten mounting bolts in star pattern.

Inspection – Measure outer gear-to-crescent clearance. Measure outer gear-to-housing clearance. Using a straightedge and feeler gauge, measure clearance between gears and pump cover. Measure lock-up control valve spring free length. Replace components if not within specification. See OIL PUMP SPECIFICATIONS table.

OIL PUMP SPECIFICATIONS

Application	In. (mm)
Outer Gear-To-Crescent Clearance	
Standard	.006-.008 (.14-.20)
Limit	.010 (.25)
Outer Gear-To-Housing Clearance	
Standard	.002-.008 (.05-.20)
Limit	.010 (.25)
Oil Pump Gear-To-Cover Clearance	
Standard	.001-.002 (.02-.04)
Limit	.003 (.07)
Lock-up Control Valve Spring Free Length	1.012 (25.70)

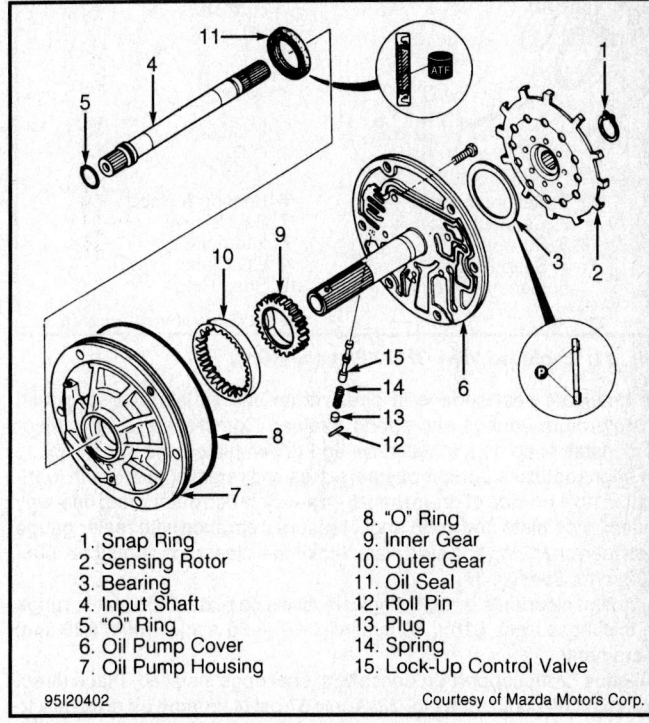

1. Snap Ring
2. Sensing Rotor
3. Bearing
4. Input Shaft
5. "O" Ring
6. Oil Pump Cover
7. Oil Pump Housing
8. "O" Ring
9. Inner Gear
10. Outer Gear
11. Oil Seal
12. Roll Pin
13. Plug
14. Spring
15. Lock-Up Control Valve

95I20402   Courtesy of Mazda Motors Corp.

Fig. 10: Exploded View Of Oil Pump Assembly

4TH GEAR PLANETARY GEAR

Disassembly, Inspection & Reassembly – Disassemble in numbered sequence. See Fig. 11. To reassemble, reverse disassembly procedure. Check clearance between pinion gear washer and planetary carrier housing. See PLANETARY GEAR SPECIFICATIONS table. Replace as needed.

PLANETARY GEAR SPECIFICATIONS

Application	In. (mm)
Pinion Gear Washer-To-Housing Clearance	
Standard	.008-.028 (.20-.70)
Service Limit	.0315 (.800)

DIRECT CLUTCH

Disassembly – Remove snap ring, side plate, one-way clutch assembly and retaining plate. See Fig. 12. Remove snap ring, drive and driven plates. Compress spring retainer, and remove snap ring. Remove spring retainer and springs. Mount direct clutch drum on drum support. Apply air pressure to remove piston. See Figs. 13 and 16.

Inspection – Replace drive plates (friction discs) is thickness is less than .055" (1.4 mm). Check for broken or weak return springs. Check spring and retainer assembly for separation or deformation. Measure return spring free length. Length should be 1.20" (30.5 mm). Ensure check ball in clutch piston allows air to flow in one direction only.

Reassembly – **1)** Install NEW "O" ring into piston groove. Install NEW seal ring on piston. Soak NEW friction discs in ATF prior to assembly.

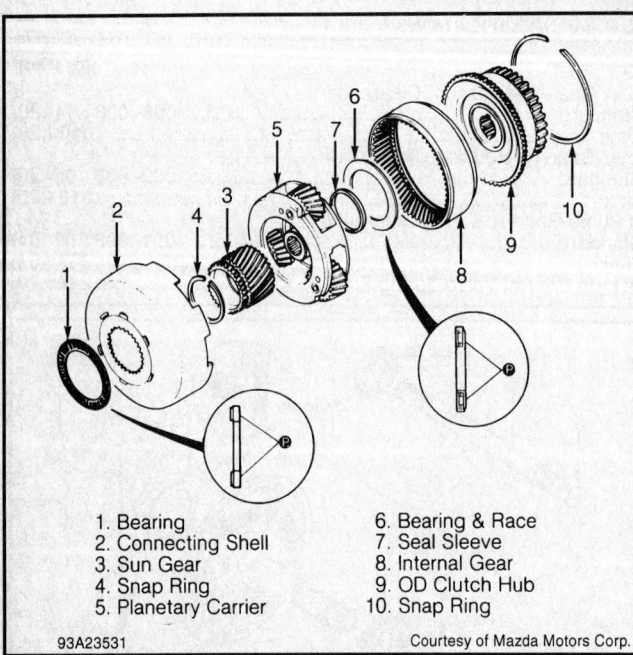

Fig. 11: Exploded View Of OD Planetary Gear

1. Bearing
2. Connecting Shell
3. Sun Gear
4. Snap Ring
5. Planetary Carrier
6. Bearing & Race
7. Seal Sleeve
8. Internal Gear
9. OD Clutch Hub
10. Snap Ring

93A23531   Courtesy of Mazda Motors Corp.

2) Lubricate seal surface in direct drum and install reverse clutch. Install return springs and spring retainer. Compress spring retainer and install snap ring. Install drive and driven plates and snap ring.

3) Align toothless portion of steel plates and retaining plate with lubrication hole on side of drum. Install one-way clutch outer race, one-way clutch, side plate and snap ring. Measure clearance with feeler gauge between snap ring and side plate. Maximum clearance should be .008" (.02 mm). See Fig. 14.

4) Adjust clearance by installing selective side plate. Side plates range in thickness from .016" (.40 mm) to .047" (5.80 mm) in .008" (.20 mm) increments.

5) Place drum support on bench with seal rings installed. Place direct clutch on oil pump. See Fig. 13. Apply 57 psi (4 kg/cm²) air pressure to appropriate oil passage and check clutch operation. See Fig. 16.

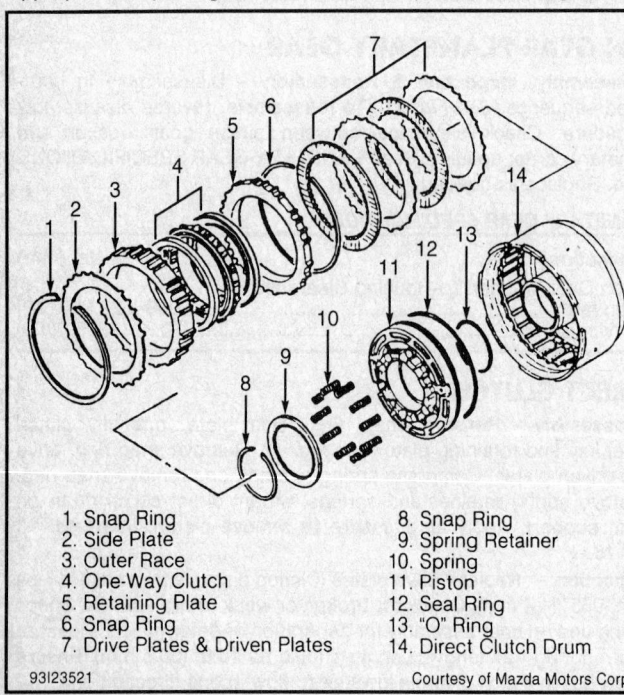

Fig. 12: Exploded View Of Direct Clutch

1. Snap Ring
2. Side Plate
3. Outer Race
4. One-Way Clutch
5. Retaining Plate
6. Snap Ring
7. Drive Plates & Driven Plates
8. Snap Ring
9. Spring Retainer
10. Spring
11. Piston
12. Seal Ring
13. "O" Ring
14. Direct Clutch Drum

93I23521   Courtesy of Mazda Motors Corp.

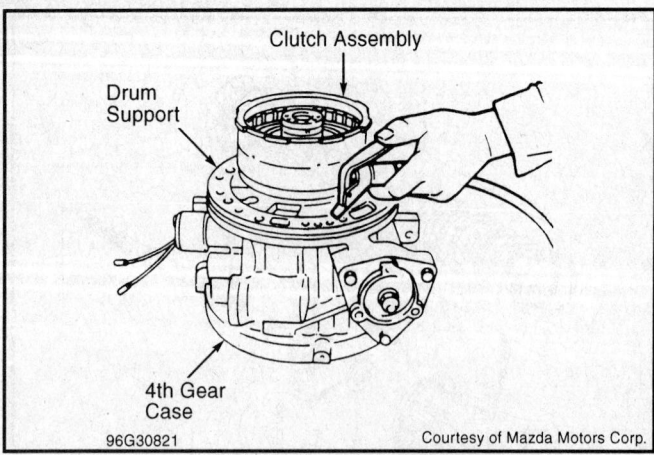

96G30821   Courtesy of Mazda Motors Corp.

Fig. 13: Removing Piston & Checking Clutch Assemblies

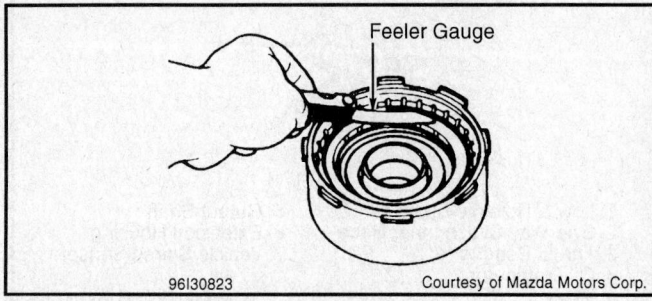

96I30823   Courtesy of Mazda Motors Corp.

Fig. 14: Measuring Direct Clutch Clearance

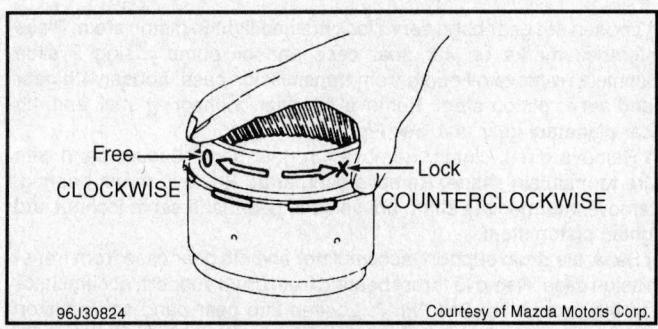

96J30824   Courtesy of Mazda Motors Corp.

Fig. 15: Checking One-Way Clutch Operation

6) Insert 4th gear clutch hub on top of direct clutch and ensure 4th gear clutch hub rotate smoothly in clockwise direction and locks in counterclockwise direction. See Fig. 15.

4TH GEAR BRAKE BAND

Disassembly & Reassembly – Disassemble servo in numbered order. See Fig. 17. Remove 3 bolts and remove cover. Remove servo body bolts. Apply air pressure to 4th gear case oil passage to remove servo body. Apply air pressure to oil hole in servo body to remove piston.

Inspection – Inspect all parts, and repair or replace as necessary. Check spring free length. Free length should be 1.850" (47 mm). Replace as needed.

Reassembly – To reassemble, reverse disassembly procedure. Lubricate NEW "O" rings and sealing rings with ATF. Install piston by applying even pressure on perimeter of piston. Tighten bolts on body and cover to specification. See TORQUE SPECIFICATIONS. Check operation by applying air pressure to oil hole. See Fig. 16.

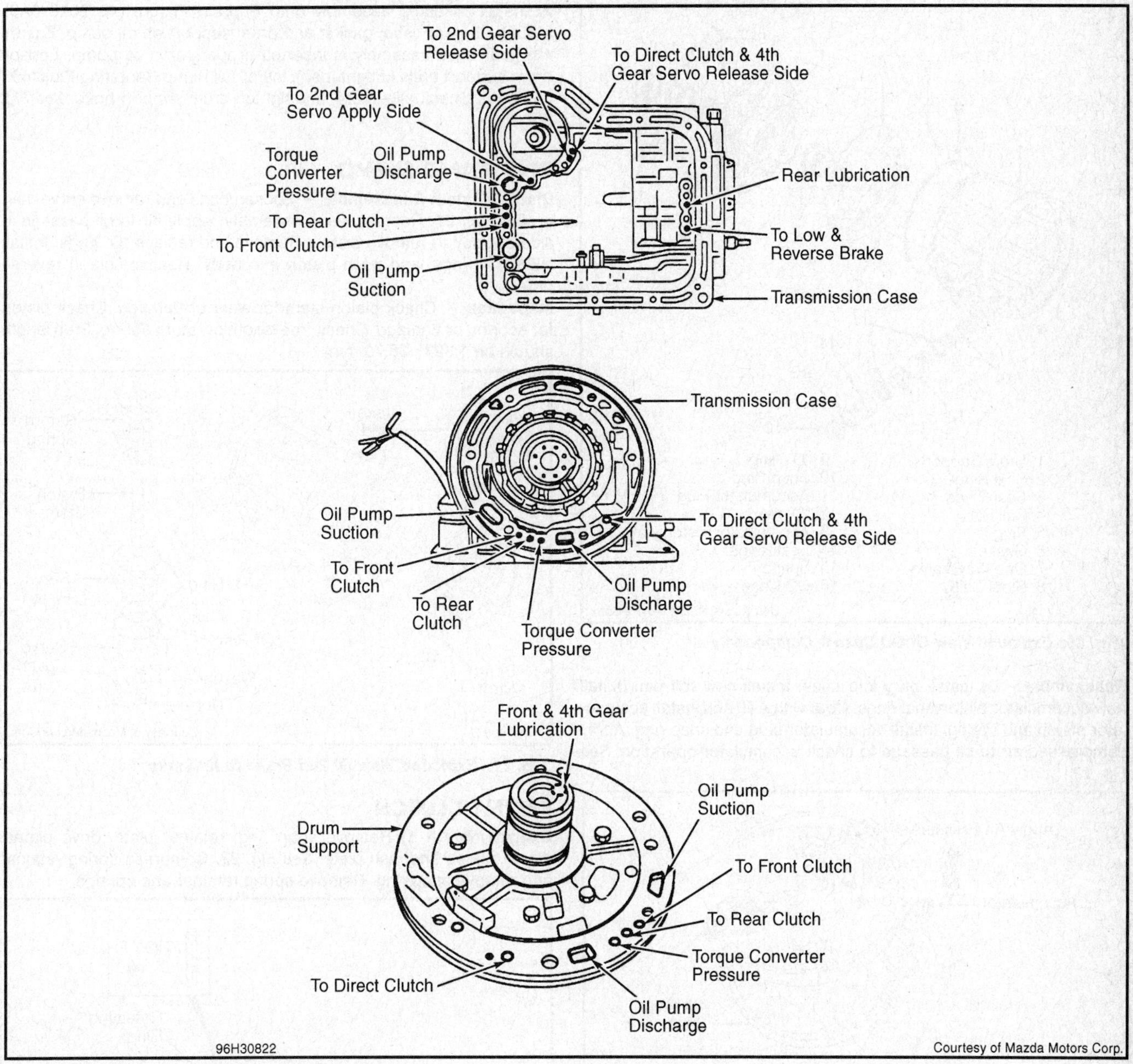

To 2nd Gear Servo
Release Side

To Direct Clutch & 4th
Gear Servo Release Side

To 2nd Gear
Servo Apply Side

Torque
Converter
Pressure

Oil Pump
Discharge

Rear Lubrication

To Rear Clutch

To Front Clutch

To Low &
Reverse Brake

Oil Pump
Suction

Transmission Case

Transmission Case

Oil Pump
Suction

To Direct Clutch & 4th
Gear Servo Release Side

To Front
Clutch

To Rear
Clutch

Oil Pump
Discharge

Torque Converter
Pressure

Front & 4th Gear
Lubrication

Oil Pump
Suction

Drum
Support

To Front Clutch

To Rear Clutch

Torque Converter
Pressure

To Direct Clutch

Oil Pump
Discharge

96H30822

Courtesy of Mazda Motors Corp.

Fig. 16: Identifying Transmission Fluid Passages

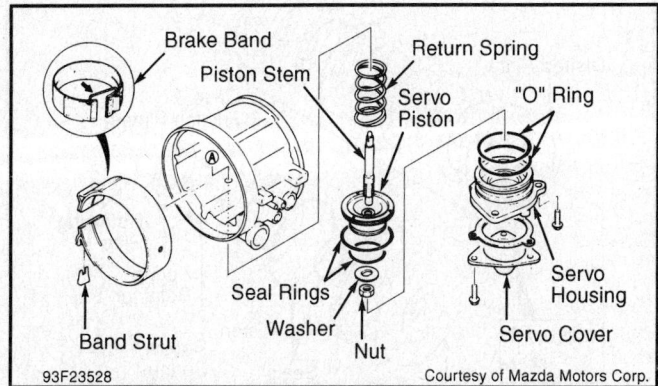

Brake Band

Return Spring

Piston Stem

Servo
Piston

"O" Ring

Seal Rings

Servo
Housing

Washer

Band Strut

Nut

Servo Cover

93F23528

Courtesy of Mazda Motors Corp.

Fig. 17: Exploded View Of 4th Gear Band Servo

4TH GEAR CASE & DRUM SUPPORT

Disassembly – 1) Place match marks on OD case to drum support for reassembly reference. Remove bolts retaining drum support to 4th gear case. Remove drum support. See Fig. 18. Using a punch, remove plug roll pin. Tap pin out from side opposite contacting face. Remove plug.

2) Remove accumulator snap ring. Apply compressed air to oil passage and remove accumulator plug, piston and spring. See Fig. 19. Ensure accumulator spring free length is about 1.59" (40.4 mm).

Inspection – Measure clearance between seal ring and groove. See DRUM SUPPORT RING-TO-GROOVE CLEARANCE table. Replace ring if not within specification. Check plug. Ensure it moves freely in bore.

DRUM SUPPORT RING-TO-GROOVE CLEARANCE

Clearance	In. (mm)
Standard	002-.006 (.04-.16)
Service Limit	.016 (.40)

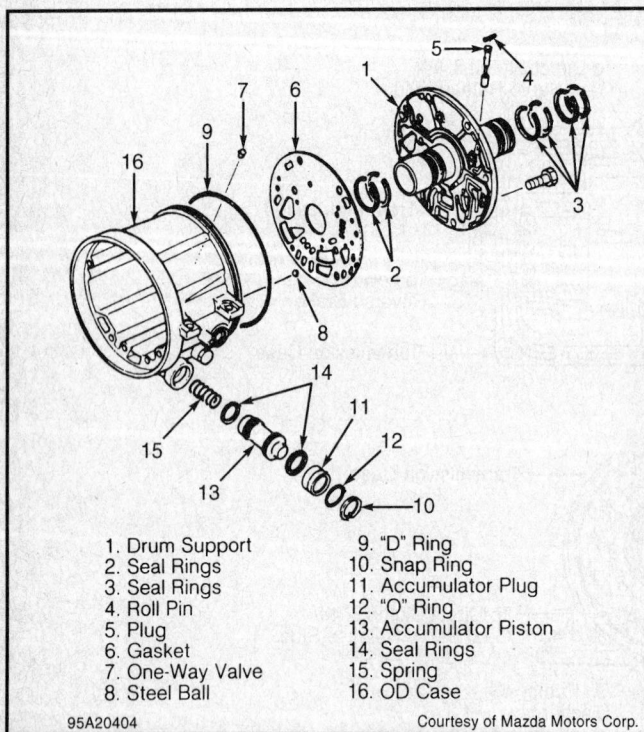

1. Drum Support
2. Seal Rings
3. Seal Rings
4. Roll Pin
5. Plug
6. Gasket
7. One-Way Valve
8. Steel Ball
9. "D" Ring
10. Snap Ring
11. Accumulator Plug
12. "O" Ring
13. Accumulator Piston
14. Seal Rings
15. Spring
16. OD Case

95A20404   Courtesy of Mazda Motors Corp.

Fig. 18: Exploded View Of OD Case & Components

Reassembly – 1) Install plug into case. Install new roll pin. Install new accumulator piston seal rings. Coat with ATF and install accumulator piston and spring. Install accumulator plug and snap ring. Apply compressed air to oil passage to check accumulator operation. *See Fig. 12.*

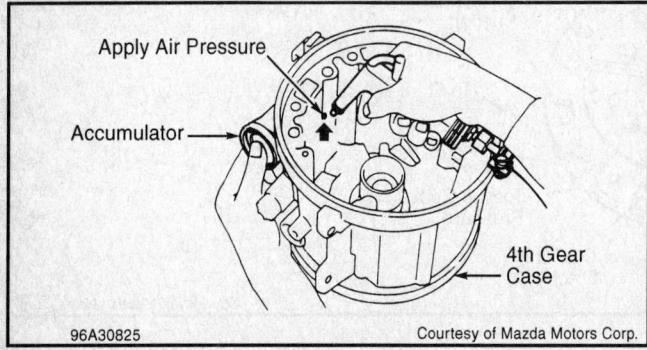

96A30825   Courtesy of Mazda Motors Corp.

Fig. 19: Removing Accumulator Assembly

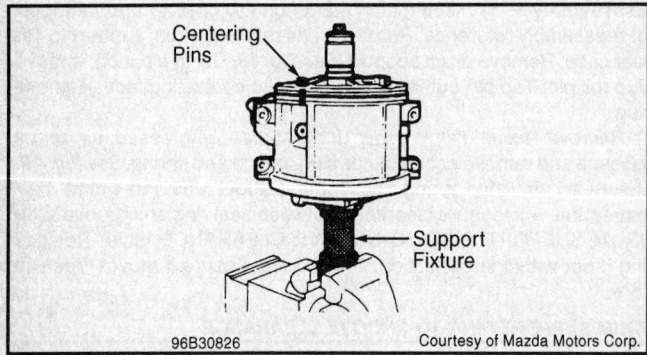

96B30826   Courtesy of Mazda Motors Corp.

Fig. 20: Aligning Drum Support

2) Install oil pump assembly onto Support Fixture (49 S019 0A0). Mount 4th gear case, gasket and drum support on oil pump. Ensure 4th gear case assembly is inserted properly into oil pump. Loosen drum support bolts (if tightened). Install Oil Pump Centering Pins (49S 019 004). Check alignment, and tighten drum support bolts. *See Fig. 20.*

2ND BAND SERVO

Disassembly & Reassembly – Loosen bolts and remove servo cover. *See Fig. 21.* Remove servo assembly. Apply air to oil passage in side of body to remove piston. Remove and replace "O" rings. Install NEW "O" rings, and push piston into body. Reassemble in reverse order.

Inspection – Check piston stem for wear or damage. Check piston for scoring or damage. Check free length of return spring. Free length should be 1.523" (38.70 mm).

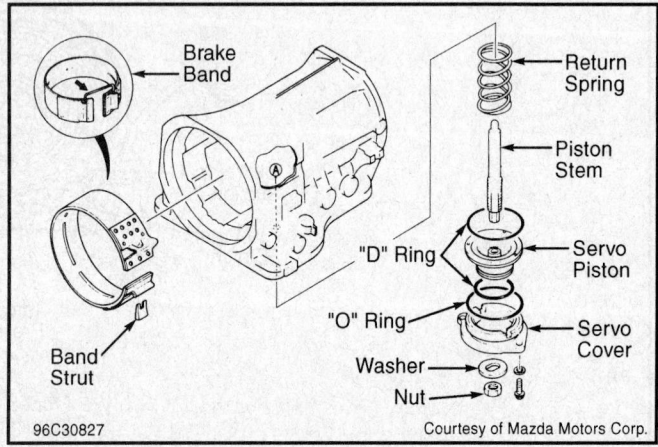

96C30827   Courtesy of Mazda Motors Corp.

Fig. 21: Exploded View Of 2nd Brake Band Servo

FRONT CLUTCH

Disassembly – 1) Remove snap ring, retainer plate, drive plates, driven plates and dish plate. *See Fig. 22.* Compress spring retainer and remove snap ring. Remove spring retainer and springs.

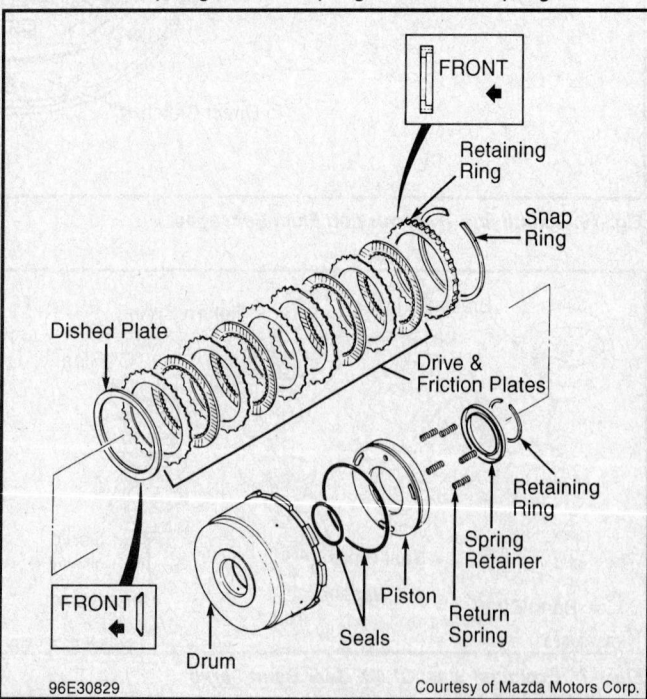

96E30829   Courtesy of Mazda Motors Corp.

Fig. 22: Exploded View Of Front Clutch

2) Place front clutch drum on drum support. *See Fig. 13*. Apply air pressure to oil passage to remove front clutch piston. *See Fig. 16*. Remove and discard "O" ring and seal on piston.

Inspection – Replace drive plates (friction discs) if thickness is less than .055" (1.4 mm). Check for broken or weak return springs. Check spring and retainer assembly for separation or deformation. Measure return spring free length. Length should be 1.20" (30.5 mm). Ensure check ball in clutch piston allows air to flow in one direction only.

Reassembly – **1)** Install NEW "O" ring into piston groove. Install NEW seal ring on piston. Soak NEW friction discs in ATF prior to assembly.

2) Lubricate seal surface in front drum and install piston. Install return springs and spring retainer. Compress spring retainer and install snap ring.

3) Install dished plate. *See Fig. 22*. Install drive and driven plates, retaining plate and snap ring. Measure clearance with feeler gauge between snap ring and retaining plate. Clearance should be .036-.043" (.90-1.10 mm). *See Fig. 23*.

4) Adjust clearance by installing selective retaining plate. Retaining plates range in thickness from .228" (5.80 mm) to .276" (7.0 mm) in .008" (.20 mm) increments.

5) Place front clutch on drum support. *See Fig. 13*. Apply 57 psi (4 kg/cm²) air pressure to appropriate oil passage and check clutch operation. *See Fig. 16*.

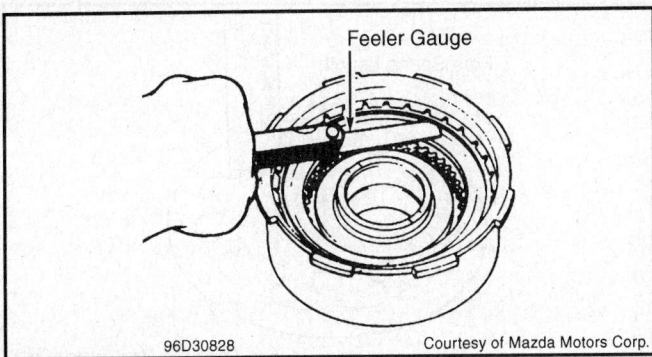

Fig. 23: *Measure Front Clutch Clearance*

REAR CLUTCH

Disassembly – **1)** Remove snap ring, retainer plate, drive plates, driven plates and dish plate. *See Fig. 24*. Compress spring retainer and remove snap ring. Remove spring retainer and springs.

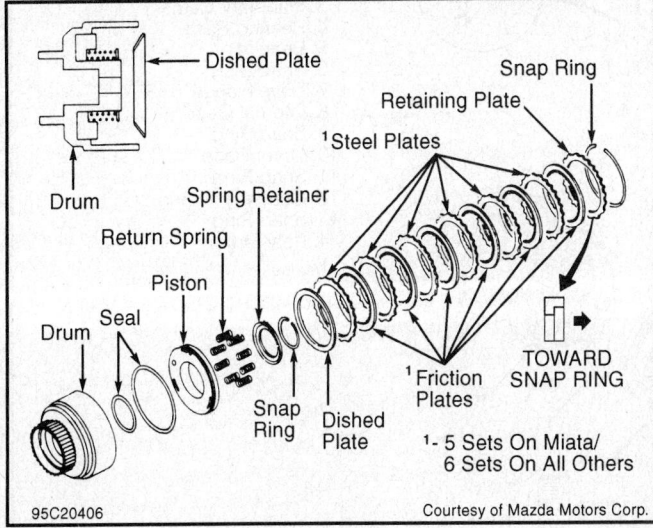

Fig. 24: *Exploded View Of Rear Clutch*

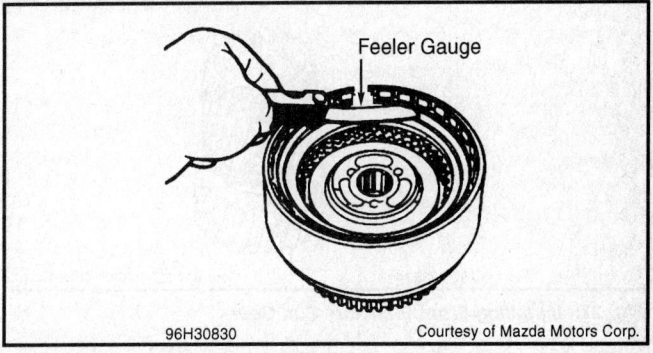

Fig. 25: *Measuring Rear Clutch Clearance*

2) Place rear clutch drum on drum support. *See Fig. 13*. Apply air pressure to oil passage to remove front clutch piston. *See Fig. 16*. Remove and discard "O" ring and seal on piston.

Inspection – Replace drive plates (friction discs) is thickness is less than .055" (1.4 mm). Check for broken or weak return springs. Check spring and retainer assembly for separation or deformation. Measure return spring free length. Length should be 1.20" (30.5 mm). Ensure check ball in clutch piston allows air to flow in one direction only.

Reassembly – **1)** Install NEW "O" ring into piston groove. Install NEW seal ring on piston. Soak NEW friction discs in ATF prior to assembly.

2) Lubricate seal surface in rear drum and install piston. Install return springs and spring retainer. Compress spring retainer and install snap ring.

3) Install dished plate. *See Fig. 24*. Install drive and driven plates, retaining plate and snap ring. Measure clearance with feeler gauge between snap ring and retaining plate. Clearance should be .032-.039" (.80-1.00 mm). *See Fig. 25*.

4) Adjust clearance by installing selective retaining plate. Retaining plates range in thickness from .370" (9.40 mm) to .417" (10.60 mm) in .008" (.20 mm) increments.

5) Place rear clutch on drum support. *See Fig. 13*. Apply 57 psi (4 kg/cm²) air pressure to appropriate oil passage and check clutch operation. *See Fig. 16*.

FRONT PLANETARY GEAR ASSEMBLY

Disassembly, Inspection & Reassembly – Disassemble front planetary gear assembly in numbered order. *See Fig. 26*. Check clearance between pinion gear washer and planetary carrier housing. Clearance should be .008-.028" (.20-.70 mm). Ensure sun gear is installed in proper direction. *See Fig. 27*. To reassemble, reverse disassembly procedure.

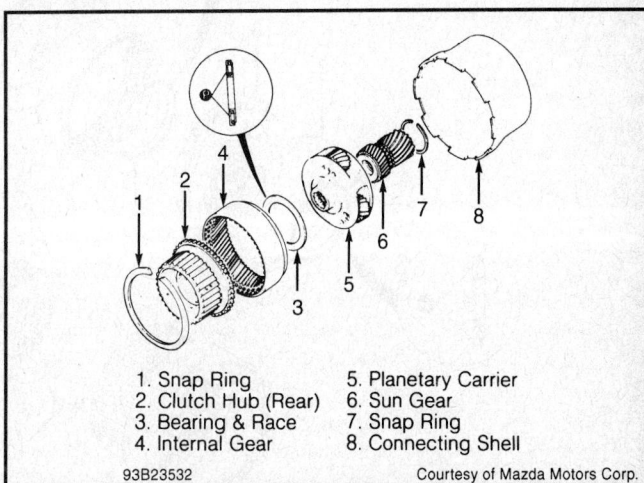

1. Snap Ring
2. Clutch Hub (Rear)
3. Bearing & Race
4. Internal Gear
5. Planetary Carrier
6. Sun Gear
7. Snap Ring
8. Connecting Shell

Fig. 26: *Exploded View Of Front Planetary Gear Assembly*

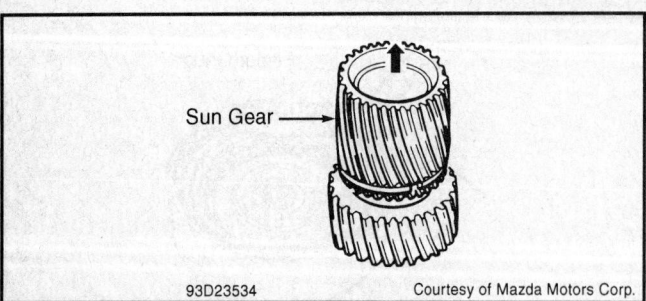

Fig. 27: Installing Front Planetary Sun Gear

REAR PLANETARY GEAR ASSEMBLY

Disassembly, Inspection & Reassembly – 1) Disassemble rear planetary gear assembly in numbered order. See Fig. 29. Check clearance between pinion gear washer and planetary carrier housing. Clearance should be .008-.028" (.20-.70 mm). To reassemble, reverse disassembly procedure.

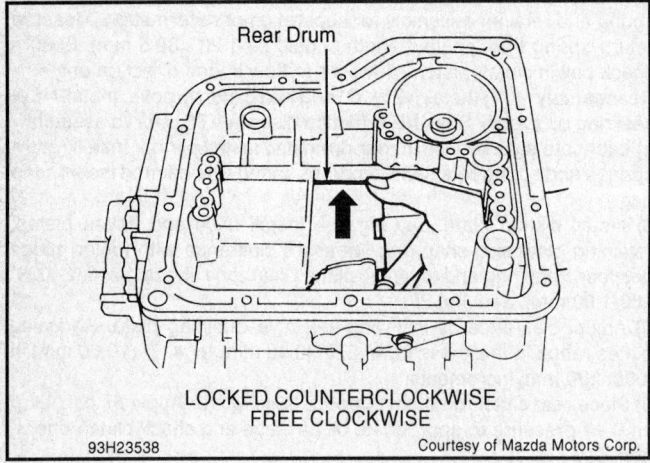

Fig. 28: Checking Operation Of One-Way Clutch

2) Check rotation of one-way clutch. Install rear planetary gear assembly into transmission case. Ensure one-way clutch rotates smoothly in clockwise direction only. See Fig. 28. Check installation of one-way clutch if it does not function as described.

LOW & REVERSE BRAKE

Disassembly – 1) Remove snap ring, retainer plate, drive and driven plates. See Fig. 9.

2) Using an Allen wrench, remove bolts holding one-way clutch inner race to rear case. Hold inner race and return springs while removing last 2 bolts. Remove retainer and spring. Apply air to oil passage to remove low and reverse brake piston. See Fig. 16.

Inspection – 1) Check for broken or weak return spring. Replace drive plates (friction discs) if thickness is less than .071" (1.80 mm). Measure return spring free length. See Fig. 30. Length should be .233-.244" (5.90-6.2 mm).

2) Inspect low and reverse piston check ball. Ensure air flows from spring-seat side of piston. Air should not flow in reverse direction.

Reassembly – 1) Install "O" ring to inside channel of low and reverse piston. Install seal ring to outer channel of low and reverse piston with lip of seal facing away from spring side.

2) Install low and reverse piston in case. Apply petroleum jelly to seal rings. Install seal rings to low and reverse piston.

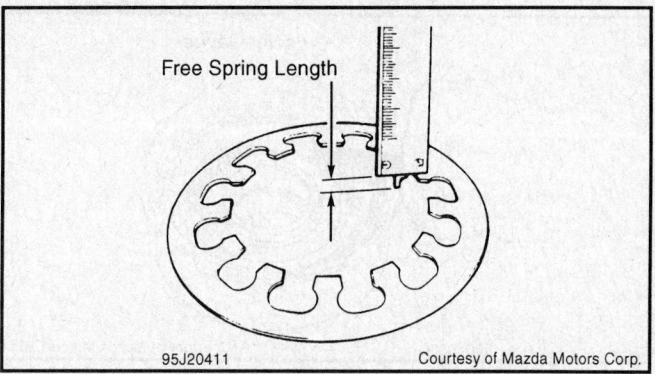

Fig. 30: Checking Low & Reverse Return Spring Free Length

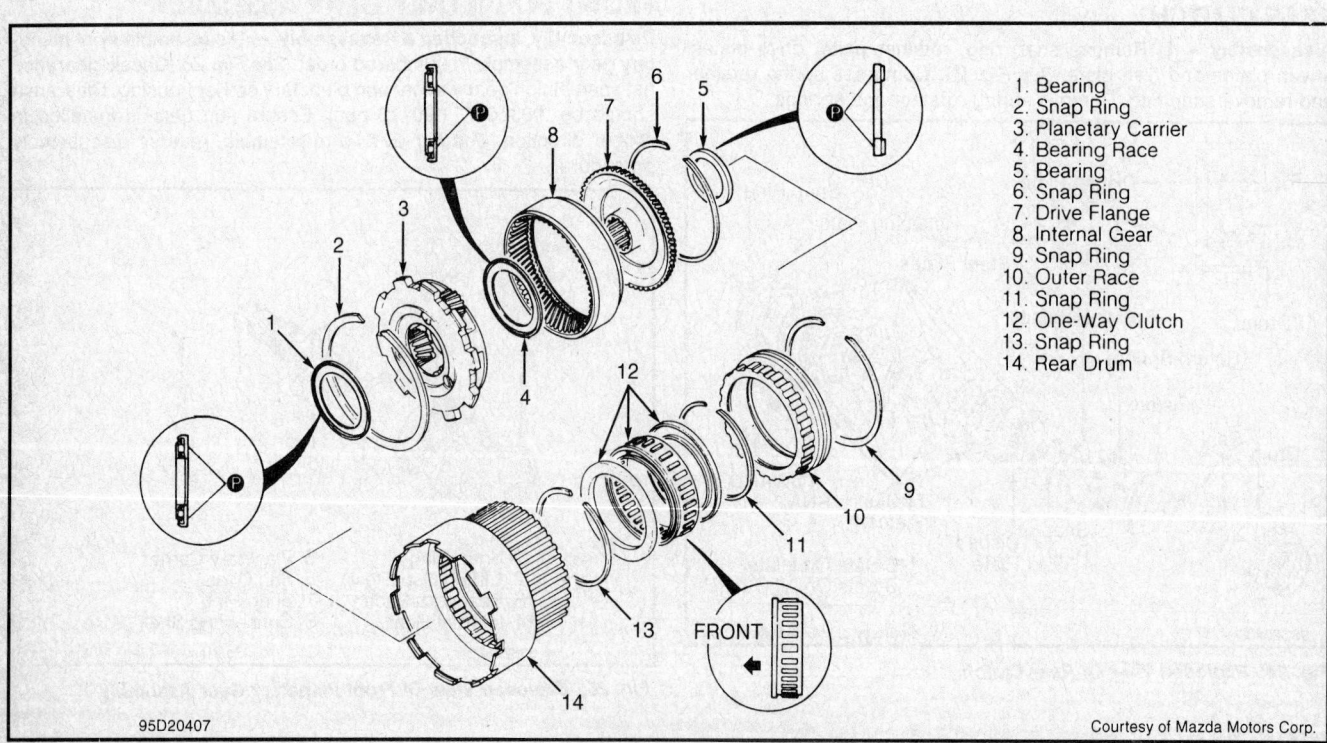

1. Bearing
2. Snap Ring
3. Planetary Carrier
4. Bearing Race
5. Bearing
6. Snap Ring
7. Drive Flange
8. Internal Gear
9. Snap Ring
10. Outer Race
11. Snap Ring
12. One-Way Clutch
13. Snap Ring
14. Rear Drum

Fig. 29: Exploded View Of Rear Planetary Gear

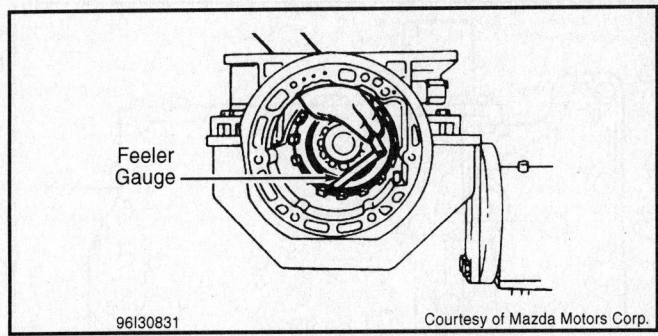

96I30831

Courtesy of Mazda Motors Corp.

Fig. 31: Measuring Low & Reverse Brake Clearance

3) Position case with piston facing upward and set return spring in proper location. Install spring retainer with low one-way clutch inner race centered in spring retainer.

4) Ensure spring retainer remains over spring and is centered on low one-way clutch inner race. Install and tighten bolts in crisscross pattern to specification. See TORQUE SPECIFICATIONS.

5) Soak friction discs in ATF prior to installation. Install drive and driven plates, retainer and snap ring. *See Fig. 9.* Using feeler gauge, measure clearance between snap ring and retainer plate. *See Fig. 31.*

6) Clearance should be .032-.041" (.80-1.05 mm). Adjust clearance with selective retainer plates. Retaining plates range in thickness from .465" (11.80 mm) to .504" (12.80 mm) in .008" (.20 mm) increments. Apply 57 psi (4 kg/cm²) air pressure to oil passage and check low and reverse clutch operation. *See Fig. 16.*

VALVE BODY ASSEMBLY

CAUTION: All valve body components must be installed in original location. Lay all components in sequence during removal for reassembly reference. Clean all parts with solvent and dry with compressed air. Clean all holes and passages and blow dry with compressed air. DO NOT wipe parts with shop towel.

Disassembly & Reassembly – 1) Remove oil strainer. Remove bolts retaining upper body, lower body and valve body cover. *See Fig. 32.* Remove upper body. Remove separator plate. Note location of check valves, springs and relief balls.

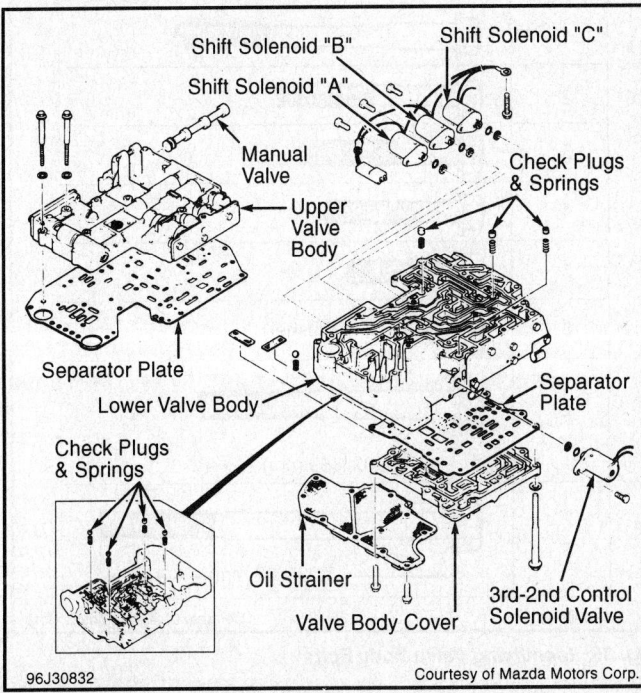

96J30832

Courtesy of Mazda Motors Corp.

Fig. 32: Exploded View Of Valve Body

2) Remove shift solenoids. Disassemble lower and upper valve body. Remove side plates and valve components. *See Figs. 33 and 34.*

Inspection – Inspect all parts for scratches and free movement in bores; valves should slide out on their own weight. Check spring free length. See VALVE BODY SPRING SPECIFICATIONS table. Replace parts as necessary. Replace all "O" rings on solenoid valves.

Reassembly – To reassemble, reverse disassembly procedure. Ensure all parts are installed correctly. *See Figs. 33 and 34.* Ensure orifice check valves are installed in correct location. *See Fig. 35.* During assembly of valve body, ensure bolts are installed in correct location. *See Fig. 36.* Tighten bolts to specification. See TORQUE SPECIFICATIONS.

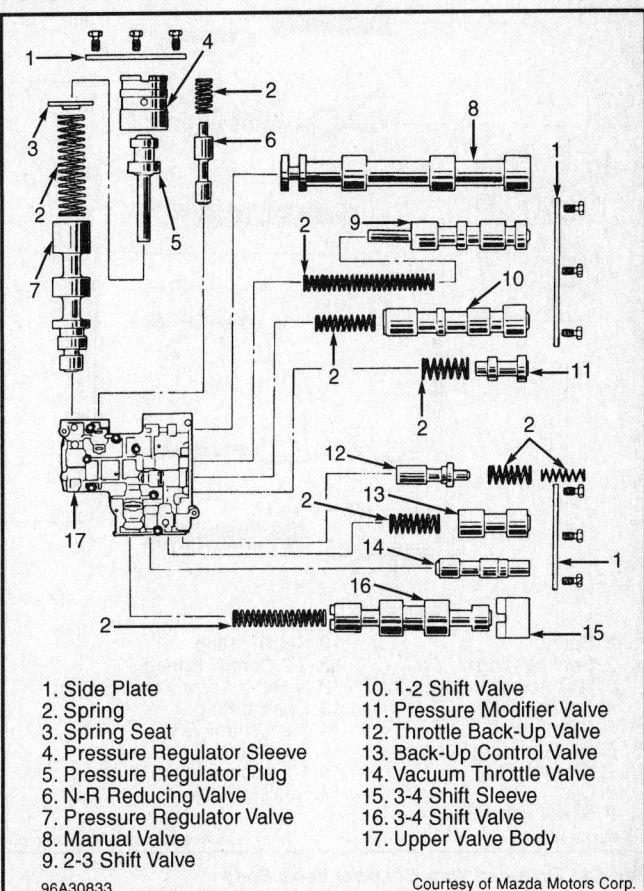

1. Side Plate	10. 1-2 Shift Valve
2. Spring	11. Pressure Modifier Valve
3. Spring Seat	12. Throttle Back-Up Valve
4. Pressure Regulator Sleeve	13. Back-Up Control Valve
5. Pressure Regulator Plug	14. Vacuum Throttle Valve
6. N-R Reducing Valve	15. 3-4 Shift Sleeve
7. Pressure Regulator Valve	16. 3-4 Shift Valve
8. Manual Valve	17. Upper Valve Body
9. 2-3 Shift Valve	

96A30833

Courtesy of Mazda Motors Corp.

Fig. 33: Exploded View Of Upper Valve Body

VALVE BODY SPRING SPECIFICATIONS

Application	Free Length In. (mm)
Lower Valve Body	
N-D Accumulator Valve	1.709 (43.40)
N-R/2-3 Accumulator Valve	3.248 (82.50)
Orifice Check Valve	.610 (15.49)
Throttle Relief Check Valve	1.055 (26.80)
1-2 Accumulator Valve	2.441 (62.00)
1-2 Reducing Valve	.768 (19.50)
3-2 Control Valve	1.555 (39.50)
3-4 Shift Valve	1.583 (40.20)
Upper Valve Body	
Back-Up Control Valve	.839 (21.30)
N-R Reducing Valve	.571 (14.50)
Pressure Modifier Valve	.780 (19.80)
Pressure Regulator Valve	1.693 (43.00)
Throttle Back-Up Valve	.689 (17.50)
1-2 Shift Valve	1.039 (26.40)
2-3 Shift Valve	1.969 (50.00)

ORIFICE CHECK VALVE ¹ SPECIFICATIONS

Check Valve	In. (mm)
A	.071 (1.80)
B	.087 (2.20)
C	.059 (1.50)
D	.047 (1.20)
E	.039 (1.00)

¹ – See Fig. 35 for check valve location.

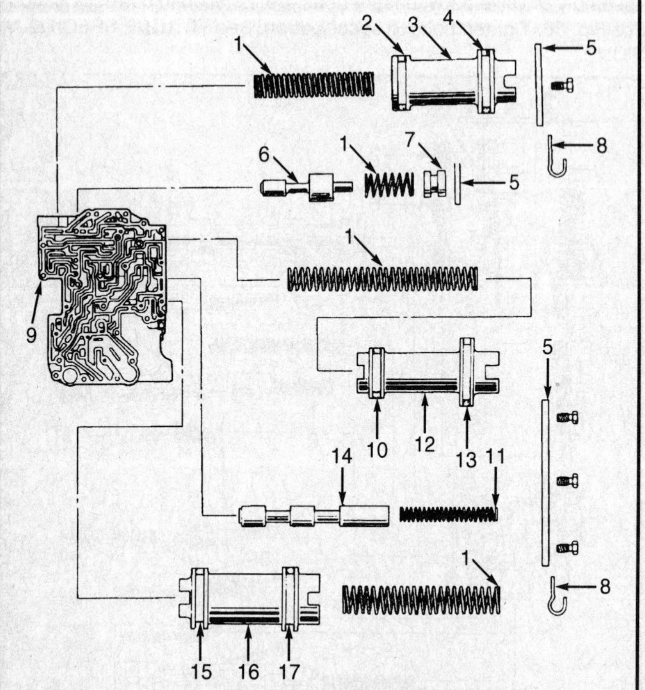

1. Spring
2. Sealing Ring
3. N-D Accumulator Piston
4. Sealing Ring
5. Side Plate
6. 1-2 Reducing Valve
7. Stopper Plug
8. Clip
9. Lower Valve Body
10. Sealing Ring
11. 3-2 Control Spring
12. N-R/2-3 Accumulator Spring
13. Sealing Ring
14. 3-2 Control Valve
15. Sealing Ring
16. 1-2 Accumulator Piston
17. Sealing Ring

96B30834

Courtesy of Mazda Motors Corp.

Fig. 34: Exploded View Of Lower Valve Body

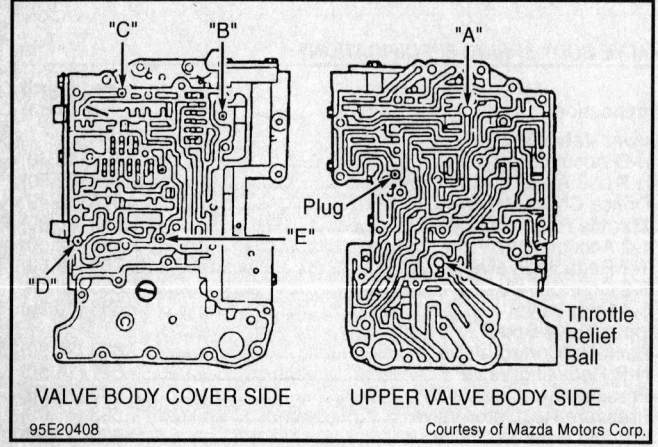

"C" "B" "A"

Plug

"E"

"D"

Throttle
Relief
Ball

VALVE BODY COVER SIDE   UPPER VALVE BODY SIDE

95E20408

Courtesy of Mazda Motors Corp.

Fig. 35: Locating Orifice Check Valves

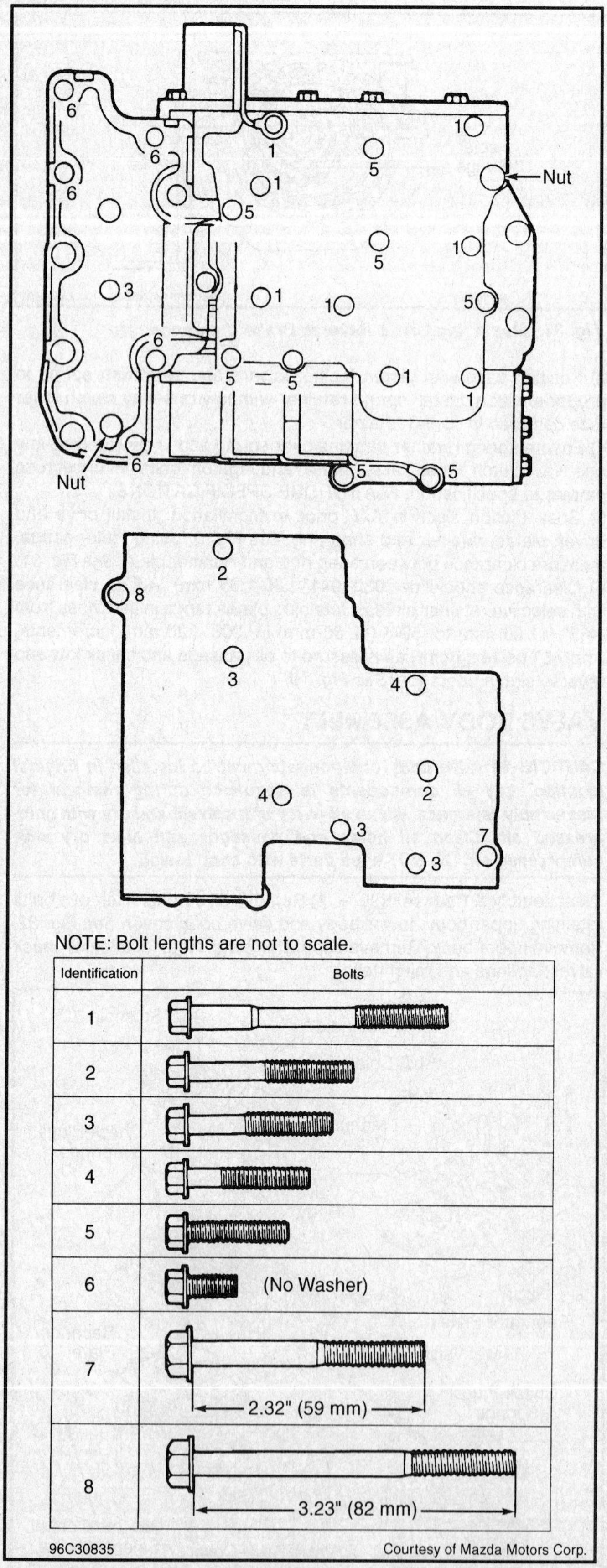

Nut

Nut

NOTE: Bolt lengths are not to scale.

Identification	Bolts
1	
2	
3	
4	
5	
6	(No Washer)
7	2.32" (59 mm)
8	3.23" (82 mm)

96C30835

Courtesy of Mazda Motors Corp.

Fig. 36: Identifying Valve Body Bolts

TRANSMISSION REASSEMBLY

Preparation – Apply ATF to all parts except where noted. Use petroleum jelly to lubricate and retain bushings and bearings. Assemble parts within 10 minutes after applying sealant and allow to cure 30 minutes before filling transmission with fluid. Locate thrust washers, bearings and races in proper location and direction. *See Fig. 37.*

Reassembly Procedure – 1) Attach thrust bearing to rear of transmission case with Black surface facing outward. Install oil distributor in case. Insert output shaft. *See Fig. 9.* Install rear planetary gear assembly. Install new snap ring onto front of output shaft.

2) Install extension housing. Tighten bolts to specification. Lock output shaft with manual lever in "P" position. Set rear clutch assembly on top of front clutch assembly. Install connecting shell and front planetary gear unit onto rear clutch assembly.

3) Install assembled unit with thrust bearing and races into transmission case. *See Fig. 8.* Place new gasket into front of case. Check rear clutch total end play. Place drum support bearing and race on rear clutch.

4) Using appropriate depth gauge, measure distance "A" between drum support mounting surface (including gasket) and drum support bearing race surface on rear clutch assembly. *See Fig. 38.*

5) Measure distance "B" between drum support bearing race contact surface and drum support gasket contact surface. Calculate rear clutch total end play using the equation: "A" - "B" - .0039" (.1 mm).

6) Rear clutch total end play should be .010-.020" (.25-.50 mm). If end play is not within specification, select different bearing race. Races range in thickness from .047" (1.2 mm) to .087" (2.2 mm) in increments of .008" (.20 mm).

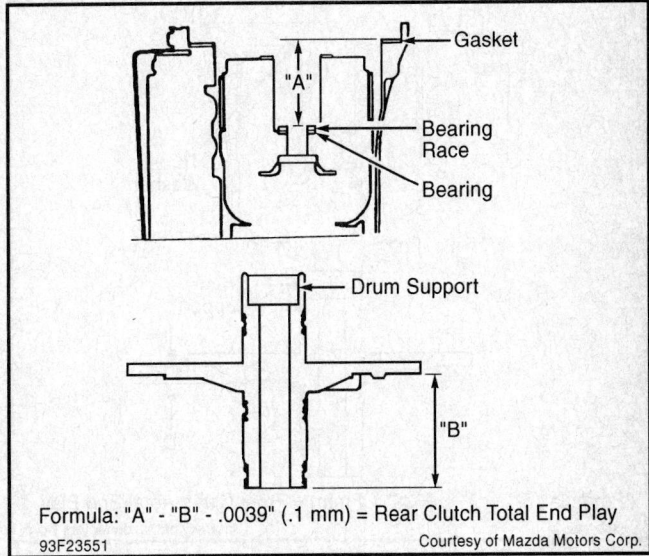

Formula: "A" - "B" - .0039" (.1 mm) = Rear Clutch Total End Play

93F23551   Courtesy of Mazda Motors Corp.

Fig. 38: Measuring Rear Clutch Total End Play

Fig. 37: Locating Thrust Washers, Bearings & Races

93I23547   Courtesy of Mazda Motors Corp.

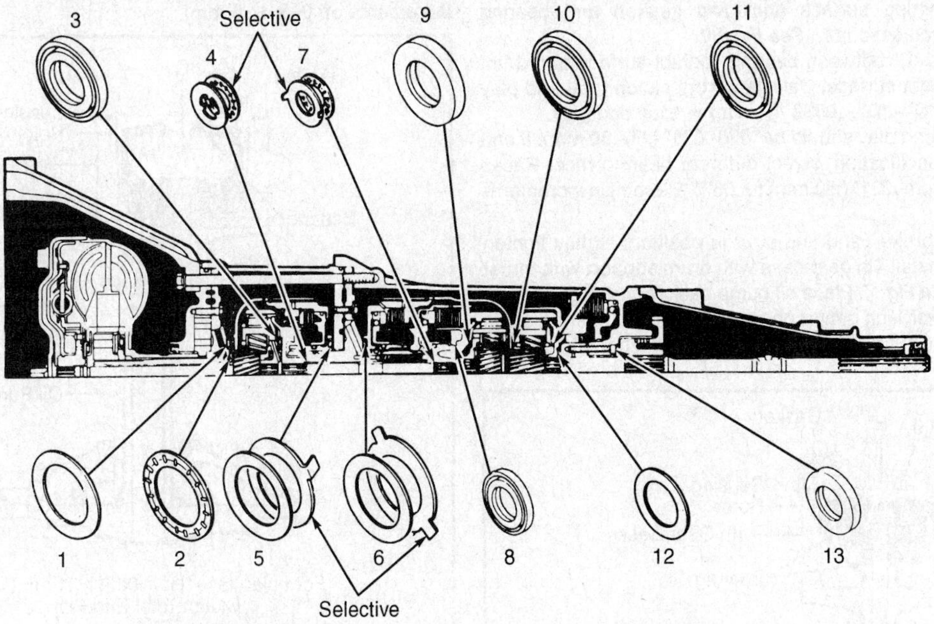

OUTER DIAMETER

Application (Location)	In. (mm)
1, 2, 3, 9, 10, & 11	
Bearing	2.756 (70.00)
5	
Bearing	2.756 (70.00)
Race	2.756 (70.00)
4 & 7	
Bearing	1.378 (35.00)
Race	1.299 (33.00)
6	
Bearing	2.756 (70.00)
Race	2.992 (76.0)
8, 12 & 13	
Bearing	2.087 (53.00)

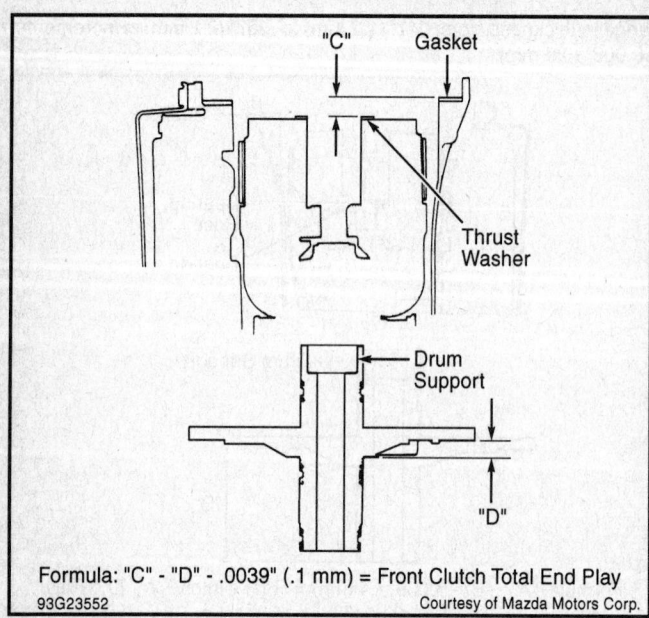

Formula: "C" - "D" - .0039" (.1 mm) = Front Clutch Total End Play

93G23552   Courtesy of Mazda Motors Corp.

Fig. 39: Measuring Front Clutch Total End Play

7) Check front clutch total end play. Place bearing and race on front clutch. Using appropriate depth gauge, measure distance "C" between drum support mounting surface (including gasket) and bearing surface on front clutch assembly. See Fig. 39.

8) Measure distance "D" between bearing contact surface and drum support gasket contact surface. Calculate front clutch total end play using the equation: "C" - "D" - .0039" (.1 mm) = total end play.

9) Front clutch total end play should be .020-.031" (.50-.80 mm). If end play is not within specification, select different bearing race. Races range in thickness from .031" (.80 mm) to .087" (2.2 mm) in increments of .008" (.20 mm).

10) Place 2nd gear brake band and strut in position. Lightly tighten servo piston stem. Install 4th gear case with drum support with thrust bearing and race. See Fig. 7. Place oil pump gasket on 4th gear case. Install planetary carrier, sun gear, connecting shell and bearing as an assembly. Install sensing rotor (part of oil pump) and bearing on connecting shell.

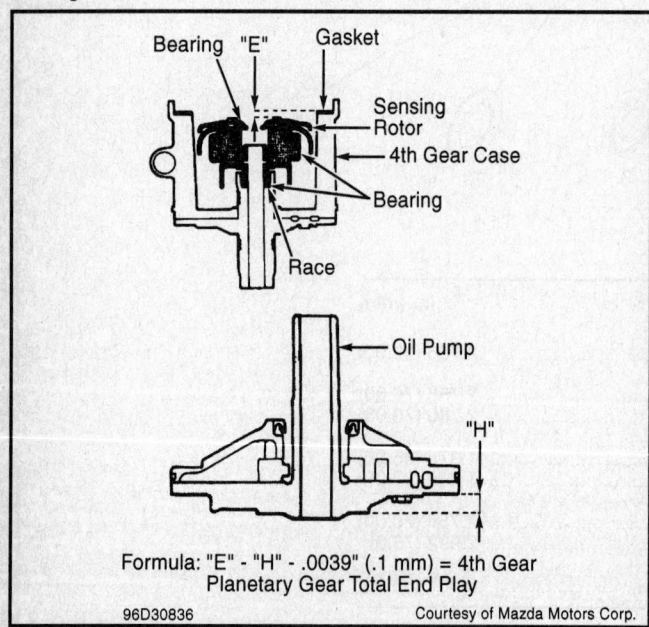

Formula: "E" - "H" - .0039" (.1 mm) = 4th Gear Planetary Gear Total End Play

96D30836   Courtesy of Mazda Motors Corp.

Fig. 40: Measuring 4th Gear Planetary Gear Assembly Total End Play

11) Check 4th gear planetary gear assembly total end play. Place bearing race on drum support. Using appropriate depth gauge, measure distance "E" between oil pump mounting surface (including gasket) and sensing rotor bearing surface. See Fig. 40.

12) Measure distance "H" between oil pump side sensing rotor bearing contact surface and oil pump gasket contact surface. Calculate 4th gear planetary gear total end play using the equation: "E" - "H" - .0039" (.1 mm) = total end play.

13) 4th gear planetary gear clutch total end play should be .010-.020" (.25-.50 mm). If end play is not within specification, select different bearing race. Races range in thickness from .047" (1.2 mm) to .087" (2.2 mm) in increments of .008" (.20 mm).

14) Remove 4th gear planetary gear assembly with connecting shell. Assemble connecting shell, sun gear and 4th gear clutch hub with direct clutch drum. See Fig. 7. 4th gear planetary is not used to determine direct clutch total end play. Install assemble components in 4th gear case with bearing race. Install sensing rotor and thrust bearing on connecting shell.

15) Check direct clutch total end play. Using appropriate depth gauge, measure distance "G" between oil pump mounting surface (including gasket) and sensing rotor bearing surface. See Fig. 41.

16) Measure distance "H" between oil pump side sensing rotor bearing contact surface and oil pump gasket contact surface. Calculate direct clutch total end play using the equation: "G" - "H" - .0039" (.1 mm) = total end play.

17) Direct clutch total end play should be .020-.031" (.50-.80 mm). If end play is not within specification, select different bearing race. Races range in thickness from .031" (.80 mm) to .087" (2.2 mm) in increments of .008" (.20 mm).

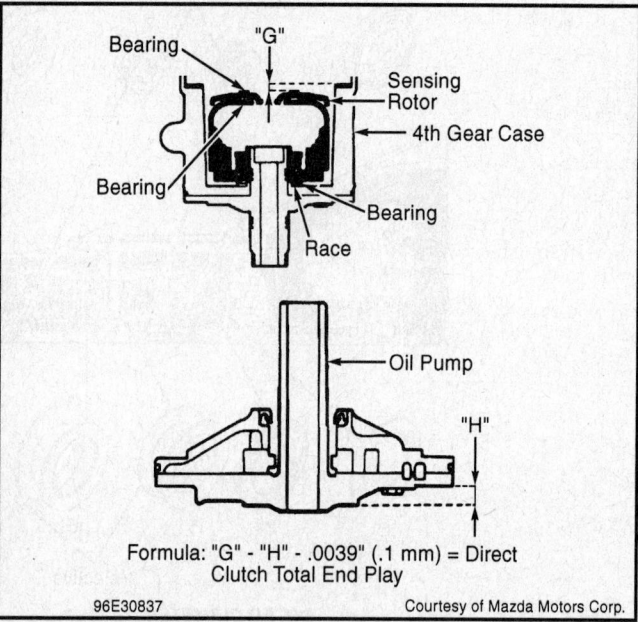

Formula: "G" - "H" - .0039" (.1 mm) = Direct Clutch Total End Play

96E30837   Courtesy of Mazda Motors Corp.

Fig. 41: Measuring Direct Clutch Total End Play

18) Install intermediate shaft with long splines facing forward. Install 2.756" (70 mm) bearing race into 4th gear case. See Fig. 7. Install thrust bearing and race. Install 4th gear brake band and strut. Install 4th gear connecting shell 4th gear planetary gear assembly onto direct clutch.

19) Install assembly into 4th gear case. Using 2 converter housing bolts as guides, install oil pump. Remove bolts. Apply sealant to contact surface of converter housing and oil pump and install housing. Install bolts with sealant and tighten to specification in crisscross pattern. See TORQUE SPECIFICATIONS.

20) Adjust 2nd gear brake band. Ensure lock nut is loosened. Tighten piston stem to 106-130 INCH lbs. (12-15 N.m). Loosen piston stem 2 1/2 turns. Tighten lock nut to 11-29 ft. lbs. (15-39 N.m) while holding stem stationary. Apply air pressure to servo apply and release passages to check servo operation. See Fig. 16.

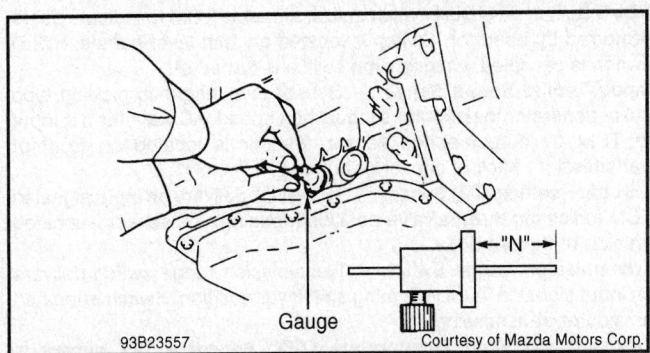

Fig. 42: Measuring Vacuum Throttle Valve Depth

21) Adjust 4th gear brake band. Ensure lock nut is loosened. Tighten piston stem to 106-130 INCH lbs. (12-15 N.m). Loosen piston stem 2 turns. Tighten lock nut to 11-29 ft. lbs. (15-39 N.m) while holding stem stationary. Apply air pressure to servo apply passages to check servo operation. *See Fig. 16.*

22) Install 4th gear band servo cover. Install solenoid valve connector in transmission case. *See Fig. 6.* Set valve body assembly in position, and align manual plate and manual valve. Install bolts and tighten to specification. See TORQUE SPECIFICATIONS. Connect solenoid valve connectors.

23) Using depth gauge, measure depth "N" of vacuum throttle valve. *See Fig. 42.* Determine correct length of vacuum diaphragm rod. See VACUUM DIAPHRAGM SELECTIVE ROD table. Install vacuum diaphragm rod, "O" ring and vacuum diaphragm in transmission case. *See Fig. 43.*

VACUUM DIAPHRAGM ROD

Measured Depth "N" In. (mm)	Install Rod In. (mm)
Less Than 1.010 (25.65)	1.14 (29.00)
1.010-1.019 (25.65-25.90)	1.16 (29.50)
1.020-1.039 (25.91-26.40)	1.17 (29.75)
1.040-1.049 (26.41-26.65)	1.18 (30.00)
1.050-1.069 (26.66-27.15)	1.20 (30.50)
More Than 1.069 (27.16)	1.22 (31.00)

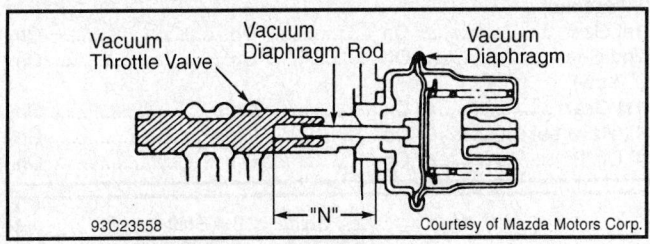

Fig. 43: Installing Vacuum Diaphragm

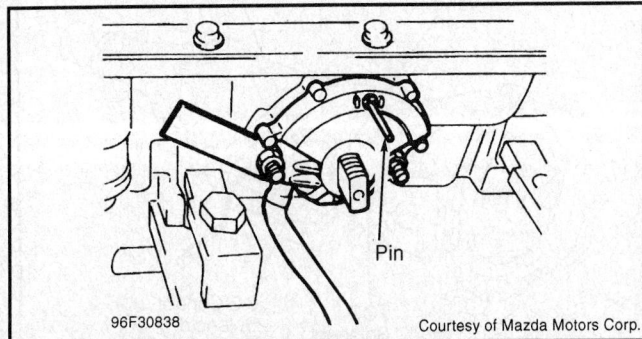

Fig. 44: Aligning Transmission Range Switch

24) Place magnets in oil pan and install pan on transmission. Install input/turbine speed sensor. *See Fig. 6.* Install torque converter clutch control solenoid.

25) Rotate manual shaft fully rearward. Return shaft 2 notches to "N" position. Hand tighten transmission range switch nuts. Remove screw on switch body and move switch so that screw hole on switch body is aligned with small hole inside switch. *See Fig. 44.* Install alignment pin into hole. Tighten switch nuts.

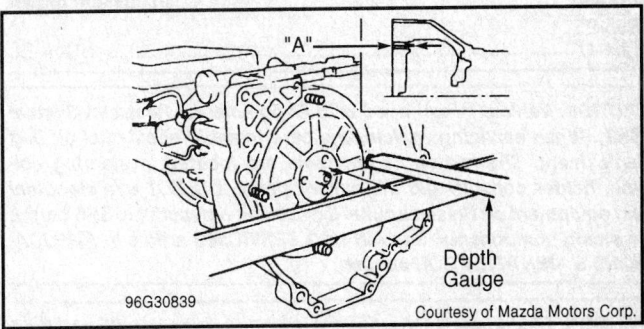

Fig. 45: Measuring Torque Converter Installed Depth

26) Set torque converter with hub up and fill with ATF. Install torque converter on input shaft. Ensure torque converter engages notches in oil pump. Measure depth of torque converter housing to stud on torque converter. Depth should be .89" (22.5 mm). *See Fig. 45.* If not, recheck torque converter installation.

TRANSMISSION SPECIFICATIONS

TRANSMISSION SPECIFICATIONS

Application	In. (mm)
Brake Snap Ring-To-Retaining Plate Clearance	
Low & Reverse Brake	.032-.041 (.80-1.05)
Clutch Snap Ring-To-Retaining Plate Maximum Clearance	
Front Clutch	.036-.043 (.90-1.10)
Direct Clutch	.008 (.20)
Rear Clutch	.032-.039 (.80-1.00)
Clutch Drive Plate Minimum Thickness	
All Except Low/Reverse Brake	.055 (1.40)
Low/Reverse Brake	.071 (1.80)
Planetary Pinion Gear Clearance	.008-.028 (.20-.70)
Oil Pump	
Outer Gear-To-Crescent Clearance	
Standard	.006-.008 (.14-.20)
Limit	.010 (.25)
Outer Gear-To-Housing Clearance	
Standard	.002-.008 (.05-.20)
Limit	.010 (.25)
Oil Pump Gear-To-Cover Clearance	
Standard	.001-.002 (.02-.04)
Limit	.003 (.07)
Torque Converter Installed Depth	.89 (22.5)

TORQUE SPECIFICATIONS

TORQUE SPECIFICATIONS

Application	Ft. Lbs. (N.m)
Band Piston Stem Lock Nut	11-29 (15-39)
Extension Housing Bolt	15-18 (20-24)
Manual Shaft Lock Nut	22-29 (30-39)
Oil Pump Bolt	12-15 (16-20)
Torque Converter Housing Bolts	44-50 (59-68)
One-Way Clutch Hub Bolt	10-13 (13-18)
Torque Converter Housing Bolt	43-51 (58-69)

	INCH Lbs. (N.m)
Drum Support Bolt	61-78 (6.9-8.8)
Input/Turbine Speed Sensor Bolt	70-95 (7.9-10.7)
Line Pressure Test Plugs	43-86 (4.9-9.7)
OD Servo Case	43-61 (4.9-6.9)
Oil Pan-To-Transmission Case	48-65 (5.9-7.4)
Oil Screen-To-Valve Body Bolt	26-35 (3.0-3.9)
Transmission Range Switch	44-60 (5.0-6.8)
Vacuum Diaphragm Bolt	70-95 (7.9-10.7)
Valve Body Bolt	96-130 (10.8-14.7)
2nd Servo-To-Transmission Case	60-78 (6.9-8.8)
4th Gear Band Servo Cover Bolt	44-60 (5.0-6.8)

Miata

APPLICATION

APPLICATION

Vehicle	Transmission Model
1995-96	
Miata	NC4A-EL

CAUTION: Vehicle is equipped with Supplemental Restraint System (SRS). When servicing vehicle, use care to avoid accidental air bag deployment. SRS-related components are located in steering column, center console and instrument panel. DO NOT use electrical test equipment on these circuits. If necessary, deactivate SRS before servicing components. See AIR BAG SERVICING article in APPLICATIONS & IDENTIFICATION section.

CAUTION: Disconnecting battery on models equipped with anti-theft radio require canceling of anti-theft operation. See appropriate AUTOMATIC TRANSMISSION SERVICING article in TRANSMISSION SERVICING section. Refer to vehicle owner's manual to identify radio type.

DESCRIPTION

The NC4A-EL series is a 4-speed electronically controlled automatic transmission. Five solenoids attached to valve body control shift changes. Solenoids are controlled by the Transmission Control Module (TCM).

NOTE: Torque Converter Clutch (TCC) solenoid is also known as lock-up solenoid, TCC lock-up or 4th gear solenoid.

The TCM receives information from various input devices. The TCM uses this information to control following solenoids:
- Shift solenoids for transmission shifting.
- Torque Converter Clutch (TCC) solenoid for torque converter clutch lock-up.
- 3-2 control solenoid for downshift timing control.

A HOLD switch is mounted on the shift lever. HOLD function may be activated in "D", "S" or "L" gears by pressing HOLD button. In "L" and "S" positions, vehicle is held in selected gear and no upshift or downshift takes place. This function is used for driving up steep inclines or for engine braking assistance when descending steep grades. If activated in "D" position a 1-2 and 2-3 upshift is permitted when starting from a stop, but after the 2-3 upshift the vehicle is locked in "D" until it comes to a complete stop. The 1-2 and 2-3 upshift pattern is changed to a "short shift" specification. This function is used for starting off or driving on slippery surfaces. Pushing HOLD button again deactivates system.

OPERATION

TCM

TCM receives information from various input devices and uses this information to control solenoids on transmission valve body for transmission shifting and torque converter clutch engagement.

TCM automatically switches from NORMAL mode to POWER mode corresponding to driving condition in "D" range. Upshifts and downshifts are performed at a higher speed in POWER mode than in NORMAL mode.

TCM contains a self-diagnostic system, which will store Diagnostic Trouble Codes (DTC's) if a failure or problem exists in electronic control system. DTC can be retrieved to determine problem area. See SELF-DIAGNOSTIC SYSTEM. TCM is located under left side of instrument panel, above fuse block.

TCM INPUT DEVICES & SIGNALS

4th Gear Inhibit Signal – Signal is input to TCM when cruise control is on. Signal detects when difference between target speed and actual speed exceeds specification.

HOLD Switch – HOLD switch delivers input to TCM to indicate gears preferred by operator. Switch is located on shift lever handle. HOLD switch is canceled when ignition switch is turned off.

Input/Turbine Speed Sensor – Sensor is a magnetic pick-up type pulse generator that monitors input shaft speed. AC waveform is input to TCM by output speed sensor. Sensor is located on front of transmission, back of converter housing.

Throttle Position (TP) Sensor – TP sensor delivers an input signal to TCM indicating throttle valve position (opening). TP sensor is located on side of throttle body.

Transmission Range Switch – Transmission range switch delivers an input signal to TCM indicating shift lever position. Switch is located on side of transmission.

Transmission Fluid Temperature (TFT) Sensor – TFT sensor is threaded into cooler line banjo mounting on side of transmission case. Sensor sends signal to TCM indicating fluid temperature.

Vehicle Speed Sensor – Sensor is a cable driven pulse generator that is part of speedometer. Pulse signals are sent to TCM.

TCM OUTPUT DEVICES

HOLD Indicator Light – Receives signal from TCM to indicate switch position.

Inhibitor Signal – When shift selector lever is moved from Park or Neutral to another gear, signal is sent from TCM to ECM to regulate fuel injection volume for shift shock prevention.

Shift Solenoids "A", "B", "C", 3-2 Control – The TCM controls transmission shifting by delivering an output signal to operate proper solenoid. 3-2 control solenoid affects downshift timing. See SOLENOID OPERATION table. Hydraulic pressure is retained when solenoid is off and drained when solenoid is on. Solenoids are located on transmission valve body. See Fig. 1.

SOLENOID OPERATION

Shift Lever Position	Solenoid "A"	Solenoid "B"	Solenoid "C"
"D" (Drive)			
1st Gear	On	On	On
2nd Gear	Off	On	On
3rd Gear	Off	Off	On
4th Gear	Off	Off	Off
"2" (Second)			
1st Gear	On	On	On
2nd Gear	Off	On	On
"L" (Low)			
1st Gear	On	On	On
"R" (Reverse)	Off	Off	On
"N" Or "P"	On	On	On

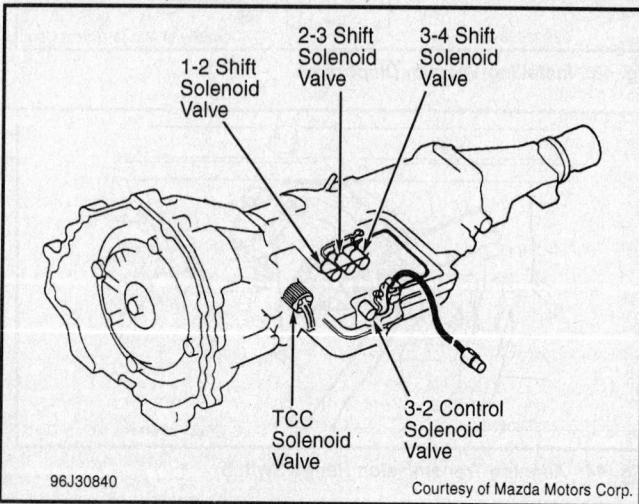

Fig. 1: Locating Solenoid Valves

Courtesy of Mazda Motors Corp.

96J30840

TCC Solenoid Valve – Solenoid valve is ON/OFF type controlled by TCM. Solenoid regulates pilot pressure to applied to lock-up control plug. Hydraulic pressure is retained when solenoid is on and drained when solenoid is off. Solenoid is located on side of case. *See Fig. 1.*

SELF-DIAGNOSTIC SYSTEM

SYSTEM DIAGNOSIS

NOTE: Before testing transmission, ensure fluid level is correct. Ensure engine starts with shift lever in Park and Neutral to ensure proper adjustment of transmission range switch. Transmission Control Module (TCM) must first be checked for stored codes. See RETRIEVING TROUBLE CODES.

TCM monitors transmission operation and contains a self-diagnostic system which stores a Diagnostic Trouble Code (DTC) if an electronic control system failure or component malfunction exists. If a problem exists in any of the solenoids or speed sensors and DTC is set, TCM will deliver a signal to blink the HOLD indicator light on instrument panel to warn the driver. DTC's may be set if a failure exists and can be retrieved for transmission diagnosis.

RETRIEVING TROUBLE CODES

NOTE: Before retrieving DTC's, ensure proper battery voltage exists for self-diagnostic system operation. If any DTC's are present other than those listed below, see appropriate SELF-DIAGNOSTICS article in ENGINE PERFORMANCE in appropriate MITCHELL® manual.

Using Scan Tool (1996 Miata) – Ensure ignition is in OFF position. Connect scan tool to Data Link Connector (DLC) located under left side of instrument panel, near center console. Turn ignition switch to ON position. Check for stored DTC's. See DIAGNOSTIC TROUBLE CODE IDENTIFICATION (1996 MIATA) table. For trouble shooting of codes, see DIAGNOSTIC TESTS.

Using HOLD Indicator Light (1995 Miata) – 1) Raise hood and access Data Link Connector (DLC) on left side of engine compartment. *See Fig. 2.*

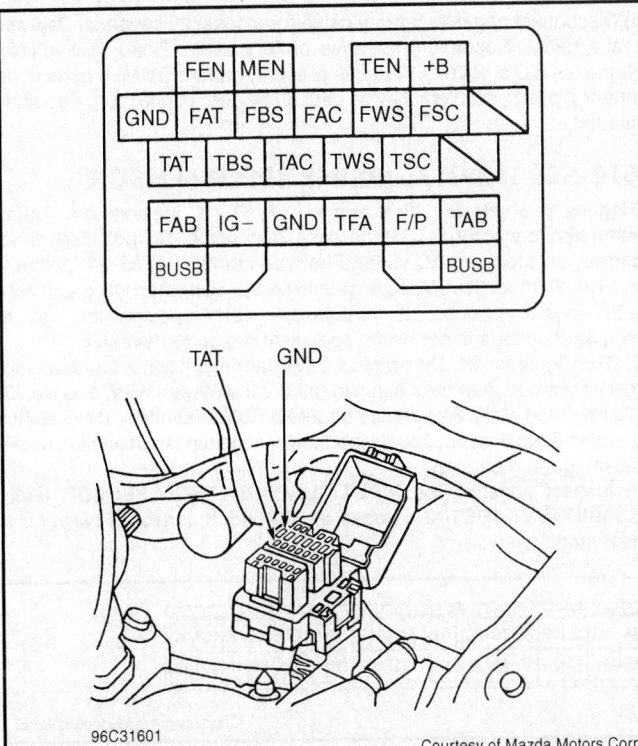

96C31601   Courtesy of Mazda Motors Corp.

Fig. 2: Locating DLC Connector & Identifying DLC Terminals

2) Connect jumper wire between TAT and GND terminals on DLC connector. *See Fig. 2.* Turn ignition switch to ON position. If DTC exists, HOLD indicator light will flash every 4 seconds. Long (1.2 second duration) flash indicates first digit and short (.4 second duration) flash indicates second digit.

3) If more than one DTC exists, next code will be displayed after pause of 4 seconds. Lowest number code will be displayed first. DTC's will be repeated. Once DTC is obtained, determine probable cause and symptom. See DIAGNOSTIC TROUBLE CODE IDENTIFICATION (1995 MIATA) table. For trouble shooting of DTC's, see DIAGNOSTIC TESTS. Turn ignition off and remove jumper wire.

NOTE: Once repairs have been performed, DTC's must be cleared from TCM memory and vehicle test driven. See CLEARING CODES. Accelerate vehicle to 31 MPH for 1 minute. Fully depress accelerator pedal to force downshift. Release accelerator pedal and slow vehicle to stop. Perform retrieval procedure to ensure DTC's have been cleared and no new DTC's exist.

DIAGNOSTIC TROUBLE CODE IDENTIFICATION (1995 MIATA)

DTC No.	[1] Probable Cause
6	Vehicle Speed Sensor
12	Throttle Position Sensor
55	Input/Turbine Speed Sensor
60	Shift Solenoid "A"
61	Shift Solenoid "B"
62	Shift Solenoid "C"
63	TCC Solenoid Valve
64	3-2 Control Solenoid

[1] – Check listed component for probable cause. Also check wiring and connection of specified component.

DIAGNOSTIC TROUBLE CODE IDENTIFICATION (1996 MIATA)

DTC No.	[1] Probable Cause
P0705	Transmission Range Switch
P0710	[2] TFT Sensor
P0715	Input/Turbine Speed Sensor
P0725	Engine Speed Input Circuit Malfunction
P0731	Incorrect 1st Gear Ratio
P0732	Incorrect 2nd Gear Ratio
P0733	Incorrect 3rd Gear Ratio
P0734	Incorrect 4th Gear Ratio
P0740	TCC System Malfunction
P0750	Shift Solenoid "A"
P0755	Shift Solenoid "B"
P0760	Shift Solenoid "C"
P1720	Vehicle Speed Sensor
P1743	Lock-Up Solenoid Valve
P1765	3-2 Timing Control Solenoid Valve
P1790	Throttle Position Sensor

[1] – Check listed component for probable cause. Also check wiring and connection of specified component.
[2] – Transmission Fluid Temperature.

CLEARING CODES

To clear DTC's stored in TCM, disconnect negative battery cable for at least 20 seconds. Depress brake pedal to bleed off any residual voltage. Reconnect negative battery cable. Road test vehicle.

COMPONENT LOCATION

COMPONENT LOCATION

Description	Location
Engine Control Module	Behind Passenger Seat.
Input/Turbine Speed Sensor	Mounted To 4th Gear Case.
Solenoids "A", "B" & "C"	See Fig. 1.
TCC Lock-up Solenoid	See Fig. 1.
Transmission Control Unit	Above Fuse Box.
3-2 Control Valve	See Fig. 1.
TFT Sensor	Mounted In-Line To Cooler Line.
Vehicle Speed Sensor	Mounted In Speedometer.

COMPONENT CONNECTOR IDENTIFICATION
COMPONENT CONNECTOR IDENTIFICATION [1]

Component	See Fig.
Engine Control Module (ECM)	5
Hold Switch	2
Instrument Cluster	3
Transmission Control Module (TCM)	4
Valve Body Solenoids	4

[1] – For connector location see Fig. 3.
[2] – See HOLD SWITCH under COMPONENT TESTING.
[3] – See SPEEDOMETER SENSOR under COMPONENT TESTING.
[4] – See SOLENOID VALVES under COMPONENT TESTING.

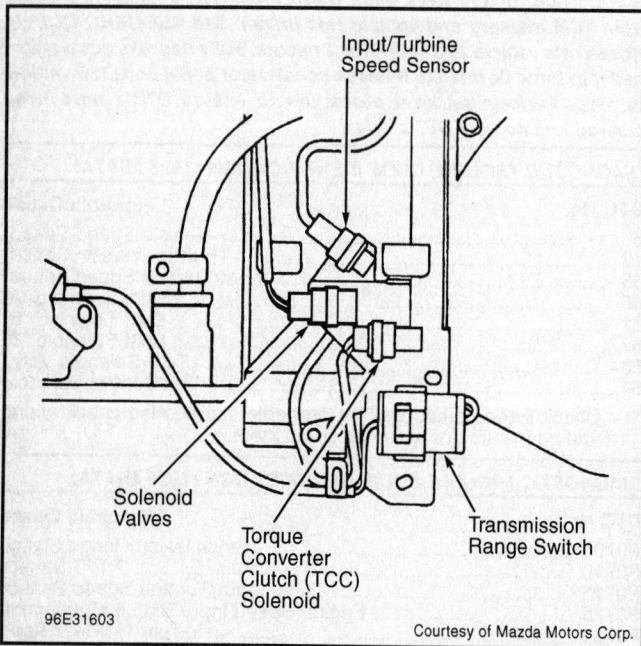

Input/Turbine
Speed Sensor

Solenoid
Valves

Torque
Converter
Clutch (TCC)
Solenoid

Transmission
Range Switch

96E31603

Courtesy of Mazda Motors Corp.

Fig. 3: Locating Transmission Component Connectors

2S	2Q	2O	2M	2K	2I	2G	2E	2C	2A	1O	1M	1K	1I	1G	1E	1C	1A
2T	2R	2P	2N	2L	2J	2H	2F	2D	2B	1P	1N	1L	1J	1H	1F	1D	1B

93E25415

Courtesy of Mazda Motors Corp.

Fig. 4: Identifying TCM Component Connector Terminals

DIAGNOSTIC TESTS

NOTE: For connector terminal identification, see COMPONENT CON-
NECTOR IDENTIFICATION table. For circuit or wire color identification, see appropriate wiring diagram in WIRING DIAGRAMS.

DTC 6: VEHICLE SPEED SENSOR (VSS)

Diagnosis & Repair Procedure – 1) Ensure all connections are clean
and tight. Repair as needed. Turn ignition on. Using voltmeter,
backprobe TCM harness connector. Do not disconnect connector.
Test drive vehicle.

2) Measure voltage between ground and terminal No. 1P (Green/Red
wire) on TCM harness connector. During test drive voltage should be
about 4 volts or, less than 1.5 or 7-9 volts when parked. If voltage is
within specifications, go to step **5)**. If voltage is not within specifications, go to next step.

3) Turn ignition off. Disconnect negative battery cable. Remove instrument cluster. Disconnect TCM harness connectors. Check continuity
of Green/Red wire between terminal No. 1P on TCM connector and
terminal No. 2F on instrument cluster harness center connector.
Repair as needed. If continuity exists, go to next step.

4) With combination removed, measure voltage between terminals No.
2F and 2D on combination meter connector using analog voltmeter.
Raise and support vehicle. Rotate rear wheels. If voltage pulse is present, go to next step. If voltage pulse is not present, replace combination meter or circuit board (as applicable).

5) Disconnect negative battery cable for at least 20 seconds. Depress
brake pedal. Reconnect negative battery cable. Road test vehicle.
Retrieve DTC's. If DTC 6 is still present, replace TCM. If code is no
longer present, problem may be caused by poor connection. Repair as
needed.

DTC 12: THROTTLE POSITION (TP) SENSOR

Diagnosis & Repair Procedure – 1) Turn ignition on. Using
voltmeter, backprobe TCM harness connector. Do not disconnect
connector. Measure voltage between ground and terminal No. 2T
(Red/Black wire) on TCM connector. Slowly depress accelerator pedal while monitoring voltage. Go to next step.

2) If voltage changes as accelerator pedal is depressed, go to step **5)**.
If voltage does not change as accelerator pedal is depressed, go to
next step.

3) Measure voltage between ground and terminal No. 2A (Light Green/
White wire) on TCM connector. If 4.5-5.5 volts is present, go to next
step. If 4.5-5.5 volts is not present, go to step **5)**.

4) Turn ignition switch to OFF position. Disconnect Throttle Position
(TP) sensor harness connector. Measure resistance between speci-
fied component terminals. See appropriate SYSTEM & COMPONENT
TESTING article in ENGINE PERFORMANCE of appropriate MITCH-
ELL® manual. Replace as needed. If TP sensor is okay, go to next
step.

5) Disconnect negative battery cable for at least 20 seconds. Depress
brake pedal. Reconnect negative battery cable. Road test vehicle.
Retrieve DTC's. If DTC 12 is still present, replace TCM. If code is no
longer present, problem may be caused by poor connection. Repair as
needed.

DTC 55: INPUT/TURBINE SPEED SENSOR

Diagnosis & Repair Procedure – 1) Turn ignition on. Using
voltmeter, backprobe TCM harness connector. Do not disconnect
connector. Measure AC voltage between terminals No. 2J (positive)
and No. 2L (negative). Voltage should be 0-.1 volt when idling and zero
with engine stopped. If voltage is within specification, go to
step **5)**. If voltage is not within specification, go to next step.

2) Turn ignition off. Disconnect TCM harness connector. Measure
resistance between terminals No. 2J (Yellow/Green wire) and No. 2L
(Yellow/Blue wire). Resistance should be 200-400 ohms. If resistance
is within specification, go to step **5)**. If resistance is not within specification, go to next step.

3) Inspect sensor. See INPUT/TURBINE SPEED SENSOR under
COMPONENT TESTING. Repair as needed. If sensor is okay, go to
next step.

4Y	4W	4U	4S	4Q	4O	4M	4K	4I	4G	4E	4C	4A	3O	3M	3K	3I	3G	3E	3C	3A	2K	2I	2G	2E	2C	2A	1U	1S	1Q	1O	1M	1K	1I	1G	1E	1C	1A
4Z	4X	4V	4T	4R	4P	4N	4L	4J	4H	4F	4D	4B	3P	3N	3L	3J	3H	3F	3D	3B	2L	2J	2H	2F	2D	2B	1V	1T	1R	1P	1N	1L	1J	1H	1F	1D	1B

95I33181

Courtesy of Mazda Motors Corp.

Fig. 5: Identifying ECM Component Connector Terminals

4) Check continuity of circuits between input/turbine speed sensor and TCM. See appropriate wiring diagram in WIRING DIAGRAMS. Repair as needed. If circuits are okay, go to next step.

5) Reconnect all harness connectors. Road test vehicle. Retrieve DTC's. If DTC 55 is still present, replace PCM. If code is no longer present, system is okay.

DTC 60: SHIFT SOLENOID "A"

NOTE: *Always check mechanical operation of solenoid. See COMPONENT TESTING. Replace as needed.*

Diagnosis & Repair Procedure – 1) Turn ignition on. Using voltmeter, backprobe TCM harness connector. Do not disconnect connector. Test drive vehicle.

2) Measure voltage between ground and terminal No. 2E (Blue/Yellow wire) on TCM harness connector. During test drive voltage should be less than 1 volt when solenoid is off and battery voltage when solenoid is on. See SOLENOID OPERATION TABLE under TCM OUTPUT DEVICES. If voltage is within specification, go to step **5)**. If voltage is not within specification, go to next step.

3) Turn ignition off. Disconnect TCM harness connector. Measure resistance between ground and terminal No. 2E. If resistance is 13-27 ohms at 68°F (20°C), go to step **5)**. If resistance is not 13-27 ohms at 68°F (20°C), go to next step.

4) Inspect shift solenoid "A" and related circuits. See SOLENOID VALVES under COMPONENT TESTING. Repair as needed. If solenoid valve and related circuits are okay, go to next step.

5) Disconnect negative battery cable for at least 20 seconds. Depress brake pedal. Reconnect negative battery cable. Road test vehicle. Retrieve DTC's. If DTC 60 is still present, replace TCM. If code is no longer present, problem may be caused by poor connection. Repair as needed.

DTC 61: SHIFT SOLENOID "B"

NOTE: *Always check mechanical operation of solenoid. See COMPONENT TESTING. Replace as needed.*

Diagnosis & Repair Procedure – 1) Turn ignition on. Using voltmeter, backprobe TCM harness connector. Do not disconnect connector. Test drive vehicle.

2) Measure voltage between ground and terminal No. 2G (Orange wire) on TCM harness connector. During test drive voltage should be 0 volts when solenoid is off and battery voltage when solenoid is on. See SOLENOID OPERATION TABLE under TCM OUTPUT DEVICES. If voltage is within specification, go to step **5)**. If voltage is not within specification, go to next step.

3) Turn ignition off. Disconnect TCM harness connector. Measure resistance between ground and terminal No. 2G. If resistance is 13-27 ohms at 68°F (20°C), go to step **5)**. If resistance is not 13-27 ohms at 68°F (20°C), go to next step.

4) Inspect shift solenoid "B" and related circuits. See SOLENOID VALVES under COMPONENT TESTING. Repair as needed. If solenoid valve and related circuits are okay, go to next step.

5) Disconnect negative battery cable for at least 20 seconds. Depress brake pedal. Reconnect negative battery cable. Road test vehicle. Retrieve DTC's. If DTC 61 is still present, replace TCM. If code is no longer present, problem may be caused by poor connection. Repair as needed.

DTC 62: SHIFT SOLENOID "C"

NOTE: *Always check mechanical operation of solenoid. See COMPONENT TESTING. Replace as needed.*

Diagnosis & Repair Procedure – 1) Turn ignition on. Using voltmeter, backprobe TCM harness connector. Do not disconnect connector. Test drive vehicle.

2) Measure voltage between ground and terminal No. 2I (Blue wire) on TCM harness connector. During test drive voltage should be 0 volts when solenoid is off and battery voltage when solenoid is on. See SOLENOID OPERATION TABLE under TCM OUTPUT DEVICES. If voltage is within specification, go to step **5)**. If voltage is not within specification, go to next step.

3) Turn ignition off. Disconnect TCM harness connector. Measure resistance between ground and terminal No. 2I. If resistance is 13-27 ohms at 68°F (20°C), go to step **5)**. If resistance is not 13-27 ohms at 68°F (20°C), go to next step.

4) Inspect shift solenoid "C" and related circuits. See SOLENOID VALVES under COMPONENT TESTING. Repair as needed. If solenoid valve and related circuits are okay, go to next step.

5) Disconnect negative battery cable for at least 20 seconds. Depress brake pedal. Reconnect negative battery cable. Road test vehicle. Retrieve DTC's. If DTC 61 is still present, replace TCM. If code is no longer present, problem may be caused by poor connection. Repair as needed.

DTC 63: TCC SOLENOID VALVE

NOTE: *Always check mechanical operation of solenoid. See COMPONENT TESTING. Replace as needed.*

Diagnosis & Repair Procedure – 1) Turn ignition on. Using voltmeter, backprobe TCM harness connector. Do not disconnect connector. Test drive vehicle.

2) Measure voltage between ground and terminal No. 2K (Yellow/Black wire) on TCM harness connector. During test drive voltage should be 0 volts when TCC is not engaged and battery voltage when TCC is engaged. If voltage is within specification, go to step **5)**. If voltage is not within specification, go to next step.

3) Turn ignition off. Disconnect TCM harness connector. Measure resistance between ground and terminal No. 2K. If resistance is 13-27 ohms at 68°F (20°C), go to step **5)**. If resistance is not 13-27 ohms at 68°F (20°C), go to next step.

4) Inspect TCC solenoid and related circuits. See SOLENOID VALVES under COMPONENT TESTING. Repair as needed. If solenoid valve and related circuits are okay, go to next step.

5) Disconnect negative battery cable for at least 20 seconds. Depress brake pedal. Reconnect negative battery cable. Road test vehicle. Retrieve DTC's. If DTC 63 is still present, replace TCM. If code is no longer present, problem may be caused by poor connection. Repair as needed.

DTC 64: 3-2 CONTROL SOLENOID VALVE

NOTE: *Always check mechanical operation of solenoid. See COMPONENT TESTING. Replace as needed.*

Diagnosis & Repair Procedure – 1) Turn ignition on. Using voltmeter, backprobe TCM harness connector. Do not disconnect connector. Test drive vehicle.

2) Measure voltage between ground and terminal No. 2M (Blue/Orange wire) on TCM harness connector. During test drive voltage should be battery voltage during 4-2 or 3-2 shift or zero voltage during any other condition. If voltage is within specification, go to step **5)**. If voltage is not within specification, go to next step.

3) Turn ignition off. Disconnect TCM harness connector. Measure resistance between ground and terminal No. 2M. If resistance is 13-27 ohms at 68°F (20°C), go to step **5)**. If resistance is not 13-27 ohms at 68°F (20°C), go to next step.

4) Inspect 3-3 control solenoid and related circuits. See SOLENOID VALVES under COMPONENT TESTING. Repair as needed. If solenoid valve and related circuits are okay, go to next step.

5) Disconnect negative battery cable for at least 20 seconds. Depress brake pedal. Reconnect negative battery cable. Road test vehicle. Retrieve DTC's. If DTC 64 is still present, replace TCM. If code is no longer present, problem may be caused by poor connection. Repair as needed.

DTC P0705: TRANSMISSION RANGE SWITCH CIRCUIT MALFUNCTION

Condition – No signal is received from range switch or more than 2 signals are received at one time. Possible causes for either condition are:

- Transmission range switch malfunction.
- Damaged wiring or connectors between transmission range switch and TCM.
- TCM malfunction.

Diagnosis & Repair Procedure – **1)** Ensure all connections are clean and tight. Repair as needed. Turn ignition on. Using voltmeter, backprobe TCM connector (as applicable). Measure voltage between ground and specified terminal. See DTC P0705 VOLTAGE TEST table. If all voltages are within specification, go to step **5)**. If any voltage is not within specification, go to next step.

DTC P0705 VOLTAGE TEST

TCM Terminal No.	Measured Voltage	Range Switch Position
2Q	10-14	"P" Or "N"
2Q	0	"R", "D", "S" Or "L"
2D	10-14	"D"
2D	0	All Except "D"
2F	10-14	"S"
2F	0	All Except "S"
2H	10-14	"L"
2H	0	All Except "L"

2) Check continuity of circuits between transmission range switch and TCM. See appropriate wiring diagram in WIRING DIAGRAMS. Repair as needed. If all circuits are okay, go to next step.
3) Disconnect negative battery cable. Disconnect transmission range switch harness connector. Inspect continuity of transmission range switch internal circuits. See TRANSMISSION RANGE SWITCH in COMPONENT TESTING. Replace as needed. If switch is okay, go to next step.
4) Reconnect negative battery cable. Turn ignition on. Measure voltage at terminal "I" (Black/Blue wire) on transmission range switch harness connector. If battery voltage does not exist, repair Black/Blue wire between switch and ignition switch. If battery voltage exists, go to next step.
5) Road test vehicle. Retrieve DTC's. If code P0705 is still present, replace TCM. If code is no longer present, system is okay.

DTC P0710: TRANSMISSION FLUID TEMPERATURE (TFT) SENSOR CIRCUIT MALFUNCTION

Condition – Voltage input to TCM is less than .1 volt or greater than 5.0 volts. Possible causes for condition are:
- Transmission fluid temperature sensor malfunction.
- Damaged wiring or connectors between transmission fluid temperature sensor and TCM.

Diagnosis & Repair Procedure – **1)** Ensure all connections are clean and tight. Repair as needed. Turn ignition on. Access TCM connectors. Using voltmeter, backprobe harness connectors. Do not disconnect. Go to next step.
2) Measure voltage between terminal No. 1G (Green wire) and No. 2P (Black/Light Blue wire) on TCM connector. Voltage should be about 3.3 volts at 77°F (25°C). If voltage is within specifications, go to step **6)**. If voltage is not within specifications, go to next step.
3) Turn ignition off. Disconnect TCM harness connector. Measure resistance between terminals No. 1G and No. 2P. See TFT SENSOR SPECIFICATIONS. If resistance is within specification, go to step **6)**. If resistance is not within specification, go to next step.
4) Inspect TFT sensor. Disconnect TFT sensor harness connector. Measure resistance between connector terminals. See TFT SENSOR SPECIFICATIONS. If resistance is within specification, go to step **6)**. If resistance is not within specification, replace TFT sensor.

5) Check continuity of circuits between TFT sensor and TCM. See appropriate wiring diagram in WIRING DIAGRAMS. Repair as needed. If circuit is okay, go to next step.
6) Reconnect all harness connectors. Road test vehicle. Retrieve DTC's. If code P0710 is still present, replace TCM. If code is no longer present, system is okay.

TFT SENSOR SPECIFICATIONS

Fluid Temperature	K/Ohms
68°F (20°C)	12.5
140°F (60°C)	.6
176°F (80°C)	.3

DTC P0715: INPUT/TURBINE SPEED SENSOR

Condition – Input/Turbine speed sensor signal is not input to TCM when vehicle is moving. Possible causes for condition are:
- Input/Turbine speed sensor malfunction.
- Damaged wiring or connectors between turbine speed sensor and TCM.
- TCM malfunction.

Diagnosis & Repair Procedure – **1)** Turn ignition on. Using voltmeter, backprobe TCM harness connector. Do not disconnect connector. Measure AC voltage between terminals No. 2J (positive) and No. 2L (negative). Voltage should be 0-.1 volts when idling and zero with engine stopped. If voltage is within specification, go to step **5)**. If voltage is not within specification, go to next step.
2) Turn ignition off. Disconnect TCM harness connector. Measure resistance between terminals No. 2J (Yellow/Green wire) and No. 2L (Yellow/Blue wire). Resistance should be 200-400 ohms. If resistance is within specification, go to step **5)**. If resistance is not within specification, go to next step.
3) Inspect sensor. See INPUT/TURBINE SPEED SENSOR under COMPONENT TESTING. Repair as needed. If sensor is okay, go to next step.
4) Check continuity of circuits between input/turbine speed sensor and TCM. See appropriate wiring diagram in WIRING DIAGRAMS. Repair as needed. If circuits are okay, go to next step.
5) Reconnect all harness connectors. Road test vehicle. Retrieve DTC's. If code P0715 is still present, replace PCM. If code is no longer present, system is okay.

DTC P0725: ENGINE SPEED INPUT CIRCUIT MALFUNCTION

Condition – Engine speed input signal is not input to TCM. Possible causes are:
- Crankshaft position sensor malfunction.
- Damaged wiring or connectors between ECM and TCM.
- ECM malfunction.
- TCM malfunction.

Diagnosis & Repair Procedure – **1)** Ensure all connections are clean and tight. Repair as needed. Turn ignition on. Using voltmeter, backprobe TCM harness connector. Do not disconnect connector.
2) Measure voltage between ground and terminal No. 1N (White wire) on TCM harness connector. Voltage should be zero or 4.5-5.5 volts with engine stopped or 2-3 volts with engine idling. If voltage is within specifications, go to step **5)**. If voltage is not within specifications, go to next step.
3) Using voltmeter, backprobe ECM harness connector. Measure voltage between ground and terminal No. 4H (Yellow/White wire). Voltage should be less than one volt with engine stopped or greater than one volt with engine idling. If voltage is within specifications, go to step **5)**. If voltage is not within specifications, go to next step.
4) Inspect crankshaft position sensor. See appropriate SYSTEM & COMPONENT TESTING article in ENGINE PERFORMANCE in appropriate MITCHELL® manual. Replace as needed. If sensor is okay, go to next step.
5) Turn ignition off. Using ohmmeter, backprobe TCM harness connector. Do not disconnect connector. Measure resistance

between terminals 1N (White wire) and 2P (Black/Light Green wire). If resistance is 7.2-8.0 ohms, go to next step. If resistance is not 7.2-8.0 ohms, replace TCM.

6) Reconnect all harness connectors. Road test vehicle. Retrieve DTC's. If code P0725 is still present, replace PCM. If code is no longer present, system is okay.

DTC P0731: INCORRECT 1ST GEAR RATIO

NOTE: *If any of the following DTC's are also present, repair them first and then proceed with this test: DTC P0750, P0755, P0760.*

Condition – TCM outputs solenoid pattern of 1st gear when gear ratio is other than 1st gear. Possible causes are:
- Low ATF level.
- Low line pressure.
- Control valve stuck.
- Solenoid valve malfunction.
- TCM malfunction.

Diagnosis & Repair Procedure – 1) Ensure ATF level and condition is okay. Refer to TESTING and COMPONENT TESTING in MAZDA NC4A-EL overhaul article and perform the following tests, repair any components as necessary: Check line pressure, if line pressure is okay, go to next step.
2) Perform stall speed test. If stall speed is okay, go to next step.
3) Inspect solenoid valves "A", "B" and "C". See SOLENOID VALVES under COMPONENT TESTING. Repair as needed. If solenoid valves are okay, go to next step.
4) Inspect valve body. Ensure all valves operate smoothly. Repair as needed. If valve body is okay, go to next step.
5) Clear DTC's and retest. See CLEARING CODES. If code P0731 is still present, replace PCM. If code is no longer present and symptom still exists, problem may be caused by intermittent clutch slippage. Further investigation may be required. See MAZDA NC4A-EL overhaul article.

DTC P0732: INCORRECT 2ND GEAR RATIO

Condition – TCM outputs solenoid pattern of 2nd gear when gear ratio is other than 2nd gear. Possible causes are:
- Low ATF level.
- Direct clutch slippage.
- One-way clutch slippage.
- Faulty band servo.
- Low line pressure.
- Control valve stuck.
- Solenoid valve malfunction.
- TCM malfunction.

Diagnosis & Repair Procedure – 1) Ensure ATF level and condition is okay. Refer to TESTING and COMPONENT TESTING in MAZDA NC4A-EL overhaul article and perform the following tests, repair any components as necessary: Check line pressure, if line pressure is okay, go to next step.
2) Perform stall speed test. If stall speed is okay, go to next step.
3) Inspect solenoid valves "A", "B" and "C". See SOLENOID VALVES under COMPONENT TESTING. Repair as needed. If solenoid valves are okay, go to next step.
4) Inspect valve body. Ensure all valves operate smoothly. Repair as needed. If valve body is okay, go to next step.
5) Clear DTC's and retest. See CLEARING CODES. If code P0732 is still present, replace PCM. If code is no longer present and symptom still exists, problem may be caused by intermittent clutch slippage. Further investigation may be required. See MAZDA NC4A-EL overhaul article.

DTC P0733: INCORRECT 3RD GEAR RATIO

NOTE: *If any of the following DTC's are also present, repair them first and then proceed with this test: DTC P0750, P0755, P0760.*

Condition – TCM outputs solenoid pattern of 3rd gear when gear ratio is other than 3rd gear. Possible causes are:
- Low ATF level.
- Direct clutch slippage.
- One-way clutch slippage.
- Front clutch slippage.
- Low line pressure.
- Control valve stuck.
- Solenoid valve malfunction.
- TCM malfunction.

Diagnosis & Repair Procedure – 1) Ensure ATF level and condition is okay. Refer to TESTING and COMPONENT TESTING in MAZDA NC4A-EL overhaul article and perform the following tests, repair any components as necessary: Check line pressure, if line pressure is okay, go to next step.
2) Perform stall speed test. If stall speed is okay, go to next step.
3) Inspect solenoid valves "A", "B" and "C". See SOLENOID VALVES under COMPONENT TESTING. Repair as needed. If solenoid valves are okay, go to next step.
4) Inspect valve body. Ensure all valves operate smoothly. Repair as needed. If valve body is okay, go to next step.
5) Clear DTC's and retest. See CLEARING CODES. If code P0733 is still present, replace PCM. If code is no longer present and symptom still exists, problem may be caused by intermittent clutch slippage. Further investigation may be required. See MAZDA NC4A-EL overhaul article.

DTC P0734: INCORRECT 4TH GEAR RATIO

NOTE: *If any of the following DTC's are also present, repair them first and then proceed with this test: DTC P0750, P0755, P0760.*

Condition – TCM outputs solenoid pattern of 3rd gear when gear ratio is other than 3rd gear. Possible causes are:
- Low ATF level.
- Band servo slippage.
- Front clutch slippage.
- Low line pressure.
- Control valve stuck.
- Solenoid valve malfunction.
- TCM malfunction.

Diagnosis & Repair Procedure – 1) Ensure ATF level and condition is okay. Refer to TESTING and COMPONENT TESTING in MAZDA NC4A-EL overhaul article and perform the following tests, repair any components as necessary: Check line pressure, if line pressure is okay, go to next step.
2) Inspect solenoid valves "A", "B" and "C". See SOLENOID VALVES under COMPONENT TESTING. Repair as needed. If solenoid valves are okay, go to next step.
3) Inspect valve body. Ensure all valves operate smoothly. Repair as needed. If valve body is okay, go to next step.
4) Clear DTC's and retest. See CLEARING CODES. If code P0734 is still present, replace PCM. If code is no longer present and symptom still exists, problem may be caused by intermittent clutch slippage. Further investigation may be required. See MAZDA NC4A-EL overhaul article.

DTC P0740: TORQUE CONVERTER CLUTCH MALFUNCTION

Condition – TCM outputs TCC signal, but TCC does not operate. Possible causes are:
- Low ATF level.
- Low line pressure.
- Torque converter slippage.
- Control valve stuck.
- Lock-up solenoid valve malfunction.
- TCM malfunction.

Diagnosis & Repair Procedure – 1) Inspect ATF level and condition. Correct as needed. If fluid level and condition is okay, check line pressure. See TESTING in MAZDA NC4A-EL overhaul article. Follow repair recommendations if line pressure is not within specifications. If line pressure is okay, go to next step.

2) Inspect lock-up solenoid. See SOLENOID VALVES under COMPONENT TESTING. Repair as needed. If solenoid valve is okay, go to next step.

3) Inspect lock-up control valve in valve body. If valve is okay, go to next step.

4) Clear DTC's. See CLEARING CODES. Retrieve DTC's. If code P0740 is still present, replace TCM. If code is no longer present and symptom still exists, problem may be caused by intermittent TCC slippage. Further investigation may be required. See MAZDA NC4A-EL overhaul article.

DTC P0750: SHIFT SOLENOID "A" MALFUNCTION

Possible Causes:
- Short or open circuit between TCM and solenoid.
- TCM malfunction.
- Shift solenoid malfunction.

Diagnosis & Repair Procedure – 1) Ensure all connections are clean and tight. Repair as needed. Turn ignition on. Access TCM connectors. Using voltmeter, backprobe harness connectors. Do not disconnect connectors. Go to next step.

2) Measure voltage between ground and terminal No. 2E (Blue/Yellow wire) on TCM connector. During test drive, voltage should be less than one volt when solenoid is off and battery voltage when solenoid is on. See SOLENOID OPERATION TABLE under TCM OUTPUT DEVICES. If voltage is within specification, go to step **5)**. If voltage is not within specification, go to next step.

3) Turn ignition off. Disconnect TCM harness connector. Measure resistance between ground and terminal No. 2E. If resistance is 13-27 ohms at 68°F (20°C), go to step **5)**. If resistance is not 13-27 ohms at 68°F (20°C), go to next step.

4) Inspect shift solenoid "A" and related circuits. See SOLENOID VALVES under COMPONENT TESTING. Repair as needed. If solenoid valve and related circuits are okay, go to next step.

5) Disconnect negative battery cable for at least 20 seconds. Depress brake pedal. Reconnect negative battery cable. Road test vehicle. Retrieve DTC's. If DTC P0750 is still present, replace TCM. If code is no longer present, system is okay.

DTC P0755: SHIFT SOLENOID "B" MALFUNCTION

Possible Causes:
- Short or open circuit between TCM and solenoid.
- TCM malfunction.
- Shift solenoid malfunction.

Diagnosis & Repair Procedure – 1) Ensure all connections are clean and tight. Repair as needed. Turn ignition on. Access TCM connectors. Using voltmeter, backprobe harness connectors. Do not disconnect connectors. Go to next step.

2) Measure voltage between ground and terminal No. 2G (Orange wire) on TCM connector. During test drive, voltage should be less than one volt when solenoid is off and battery voltage when solenoid is on. See SOLENOID OPERATION TABLE under TCM OUTPUT DEVICES. If voltage is within specification, go to step **5)**. If voltage is not within specification, go to next step.

3) Turn ignition off. Disconnect TCM harness connector. Measure resistance between ground and terminal No. 2G. If resistance is 13-27 ohms at 68°F (20°C), go to step **5)**. If resistance is not 13-27 ohms at 68°F (20°C), go to next step.

4) Inspect shift solenoid "B" and related circuits. See SOLENOID VALVES under COMPONENT TESTING. Repair as needed. If solenoid valve and related circuits are okay, go to next step.

5) Disconnect negative battery cable for at least 20 seconds. Depress brake pedal. Reconnect negative battery cable. Road test vehicle. Retrieve DTC's. If DTC P0755 is still present, replace TCM. If code is no longer present, system is okay.

DTC P0760: SHIFT SOLENOID "C" MALFUNCTION

Possible Causes:
- Short or open circuit between TCM and solenoid.
- TCM malfunction.
- Shift solenoid malfunction.

Diagnosis & Repair Procedure – 1) Ensure all connections are clean and tight. Repair as needed. Turn ignition on. Access TCM connectors. Using voltmeter, backprobe harness connectors. Do not disconnect connectors. Go to next step.

2) Measure voltage between ground and terminal No. 2I (Blue wire) on TCM connector. During test drive, voltage should be less than one volt when solenoid is off and battery voltage when solenoid is on. See SOLENOID OPERATION TABLE under TCM OUTPUT DEVICES. If voltage is within specification, go to step **5)**. If voltage is not within specification, go to next step.

3) Turn ignition off. Disconnect TCM harness connector. Measure resistance between ground and terminal No. 2E. If resistance is 13-27 ohms at 68°F (20°C), go to step **5)**. If resistance is not 13-27 ohms at 68°F (20°C), go to next step.

4) Inspect shift solenoid "C" and related circuits. See SOLENOID VALVES under COMPONENT TESTING. Repair as needed. If solenoid valve and related circuits are okay, go to next step.

5) Disconnect negative battery cable for at least 20 seconds. Depress brake pedal. Reconnect negative battery cable. Road test vehicle. Retrieve DTC's. If DTC P0760 is still present, replace TCM. If code is no longer present, system is okay.

DTC P1720: VEHICLE SPEED SENSOR MALFUNCTION

Condition – Vehicle speed sensor signal is not input to TCM. Possible causes are:
- Vehicle speed sensor malfunction.
- Damaged circuits or connectors between sensor and TCM.

Diagnosis & Repair Procedure – 1) Ensure all connections are clean and tight. Repair as needed. Turn ignition on. Using voltmeter, backprobe TCM harness connector. Do not disconnect connector. Test drive vehicle.

2) Measure voltage between ground and terminal No. 1P (Green/Red wire) on TCM harness connector. During test drive voltage should be about 4 volts or, less than 1.5 or 7-9 volts when parked. If voltage is within specifications, go to step **5)**. If voltage is not within specifications, go to next step.

3) Turn ignition off. Disconnect negative battery cable. Remove instrument cluster. Disconnect TCM harness connectors. Check continuity of Green/Red wire between terminal No. 1P on TCM connector and terminal No. 2F on instrument cluster harness left connector. Repair as needed. If continuity exists, go to next step.

4) With combination meter removed, measure voltage between terminals No. 2F and 2D on combination meter connector using analog voltmeter. Raise and support vehicle. Rotate rear wheels. If voltage pulse is present, go to next step. If voltage pulse is not present, inspect speedometer cable. Replace as needed. If cable is okay, replace combination meter or circuit board (as applicable).

5) Disconnect negative battery cable for at least 20 seconds. Depress brake pedal. Reconnect negative battery cable. Road test vehicle. Retrieve DTC's. If DTC 6 is still present, replace TCM. If code is no longer present, problem may be caused by poor connection. Repair as needed.

DTC P1743: TORQUE CONVERTER CLUTCH (TCC) SOLENOID MALFUNCTION

Possible Causes:
- Short or open circuit between TCM and solenoid.
- TCM malfunction.
- Lock-up solenoid malfunction.

Diagnosis & Repair Procedure – 1) Ensure all connections are clean and tight. Repair as needed. Turn ignition on. Access TCM connectors. Using voltmeter, backprobe harness connectors. Do not disconnect connectors. Go to next step.

2) Measure voltage between ground and terminal No. 2K (Yellow/Black wire). Battery voltage should be present with solenoid on and zero volts with solenoid off. If voltage is within specifications, go to step **5)**. If voltage is not within specifications, go to next step.

3) Turn ignition off. Disconnect TCM harness connector. Measure resistance between ground and terminal No. 2K. If resistance is 13-25 ohms at 68°F (20°C), go to step **5)**. If resistance is not 13-25 ohms at 68°F (20°C), go to next step.

4) Inspect lock-up solenoid and related circuits. See SOLENOID VALVES under COMPONENT TESTING. Repair as needed. If solenoid valve and related circuits are okay, go to next step.

5) Disconnect negative battery cable for at least 20 seconds. Depress brake pedal. Reconnect negative battery cable. Road test vehicle. Retrieve DTC's. If DTC P1743 is still present, replace TCM. If code is no longer present, problem may be caused by poor connection. Repair as needed.

DTC P1765: 3-2 CONTROL SOLENOID VALVE MALFUNCTION

Possible Causes:
- Short or open circuit between TCM and solenoid.
- TCM malfunction.
- 3-2 control solenoid malfunction.

Diagnosis & Repair Procedure – 1) Ensure all connections are clean and tight. Repair as needed. Turn ignition on. Access TCM connectors. Using voltmeter, backprobe harness connectors. Do not disconnect connectors. Go to next step.

2) Measure voltage between ground and terminal No. 2M (Blue/Orange wire). Battery voltage should be present with solenoid on and zero volts with solenoid off. If voltage is within specifications, go to step **5)**. If voltage is not within specifications, go to next step.

3) Turn ignition off. Disconnect TCM harness connector. Measure resistance between ground and terminal No. 2M. If resistance is 13-27 ohms at 68°F (20°C), go to step **5)**. If resistance is not 13-27 ohms at 68°F (20°C), go to next step.

4) Inspect 3-2 control clutch solenoid and related circuits. See SOLENOID VALVES under COMPONENT TESTING. Repair as needed. If solenoid valve and related circuits are okay, go to next step.

5) Disconnect negative battery cable for at least 20 seconds. Depress brake pedal. Reconnect negative battery cable. Road test vehicle. Retrieve DTC's. If DTC P1765 is still present, replace TCM. If code is no longer present, problem may be caused by poor connection. Repair as needed.

DTC P1790: THROTTLE POSITION (TP) SENSOR MALFUNCTION

Condition – TP sensor voltage is less than one volt or more than 4.9 volts. Possible causes are:
- Poor harness connection at TP sensor.
- Circuit fault between TP sensor and TCM.
- TP sensor.

Diagnosis & Repair Procedure – 1) Ensure all connections are clean and tight. Repair as needed. Turn ignition on. Access TCM connectors. Using voltmeter, backprobe harness connectors. Do not disconnect connectors. Go to next step.

2) Measure voltage between ground and terminal No. 2T (Red/Blue wire) on TCM harness connector. With throttle closed, voltage should be .1-1.1 volts. With wide open throttle, voltage should be 3.1-4.4 volts. If voltage is within specification, go to step **5)**. If voltage is not within specification, go to next step.

3) Measure voltage between ground and terminal No. 2A (Light Green/White wire) on TCM harness connector. With ignition on, voltage should be 4.5-5.5 volts. With ignition off, voltage should be zero volts. If voltage is within specification, go to step **5)**. If voltage is not within specification, go to next step.

4) Inspect circuits between TP sensor and TCM. See appropriate wiring diagram under WIRING DIAGRAMS. Repair as needed. If circuits are okay between sensor and TCM, go to next step.

5) Disconnect negative battery cable for at least 20 seconds. Depress brake pedal. Reconnect negative battery cable. Road test vehicle. Retrieve DTC's. If DTC P1790 is still present, replace TCM. If code is no longer present, system is okay.

COMPONENT TESTING

NOTE: For connector terminal identification, see COMPONENT CONNECTOR IDENTIFICATION table. For circuit or wire color identification, see appropriate wiring diagram in WIRING DIAGRAMS.

HOLD SWITCH

1) Turn ignition on. Ensure HOLD indicator illuminates with switch depressed. Ensure indicator light is not illuminated when switch is released. If switch is not working as described, go to next step.

2) Access switch connector under center console. Disconnect connector. Check continuity between terminals "A" and "B". *See Fig. 6.* Continuity should exist when switch is depressed. When switch is released, continuity should not exist. Replace as needed. If HOLD switch system does not function correctly, inspect circuits between switch and TCM. See appropriate wiring diagram in WIRING DIAGRAMS.

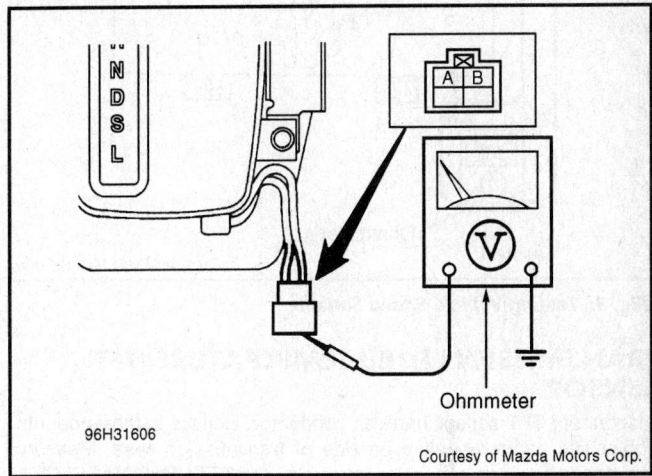

Ohmmeter

96H31606

Courtesy of Mazda Motors Corp.

Fig. 6: Testing HOLD Switch

INPUT/TURBINE SPEED SENSOR

Disconnect output speed sensor connector. *See Fig. 3.* Measure resistance between terminals. Resistance should be 245 ohms. Replace as needed.

SOLENOID VALVES (EXCEPT TCC SOLENOID)

Disconnect negative battery cable. Disconnect transmission solenoid harness connector. *See Fig. 3.* Note that solenoids ground through transmission case. Check resistance between connector terminals and ground. *See Fig. 7.* Resistance should be 13-27 ohms. Replace solenoids as necessary. Ensure transmission case is grounded.

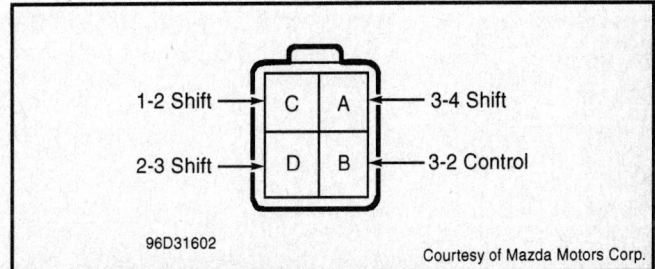

| 1-2 Shift | C | A | 3-4 Shift |
| 2-3 Shift | D | B | 3-2 Control |

96D31602

Courtesy of Mazda Motors Corp.

Fig. 7: Identifying Solenoid Valve Terminals

TCC SOLENOID

Disconnect negative battery cable. Disconnect TCC solenoid harness connector. See Fig. 3. Check resistance between connector terminals and ground. Resistance should be 13-25 ohms. Replace solenoids as necessary. Ensure transmission case is grounded.

VEHICLE SPEED SENSOR (VSS)

NOTE: Vehicle speed sensor signal is input to TCM from combination meter driven by speedometer cable.

Disconnect negative battery cable. Remove combination meter. Disconnect harness connectors and speedometer cable. Connect analog voltmeter leads to meter terminals No. 2D and 2F. See Fig. 8. Using appropriate screwdriver, rotate speedometer cable shaft. If voltmeter needle does not fluctuate, replace sensor.

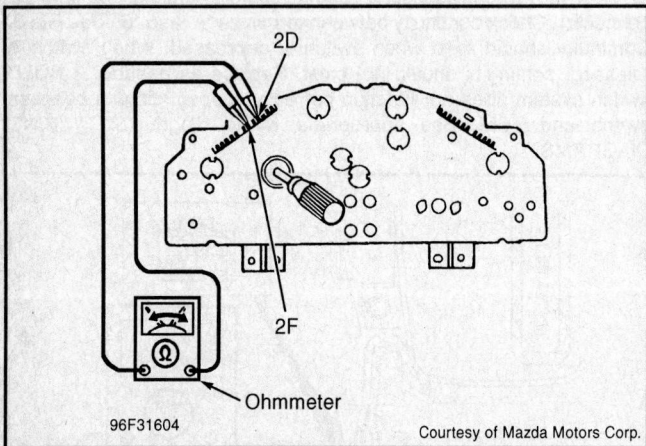

Fig. 8: Testing Vehicle Speed Sensor

TRANSMISSION FLUID TEMPERATURE (TFT) SENSOR

Disconnect TFT sensor harness connector. Sensor is threaded into cooler line banjo mounting on side of transmission case. Measure resistance between connector terminals. See TFT SENSOR SPECIFICATIONS.

TFT SENSOR SPECIFICATIONS

Fluid Temperature	K/Ohms
68°F (20°C)	12.5
140°F (60°C)	.6
176°F (80°C)	.3

TRANSMISSION RANGE SWITCH

1) Check for starter operation with ignition switch in START position and selector lever in "P" and "N" position only. Ensure back-up lights illuminate with ignition in ON position and selector lever in "R". If any problems are found, go to next step.

2) Disconnect transmission range switch connector. See Fig. 3. Check continuity between specified terminals. See Fig. 9. If continuity is not as specified, replace switch.

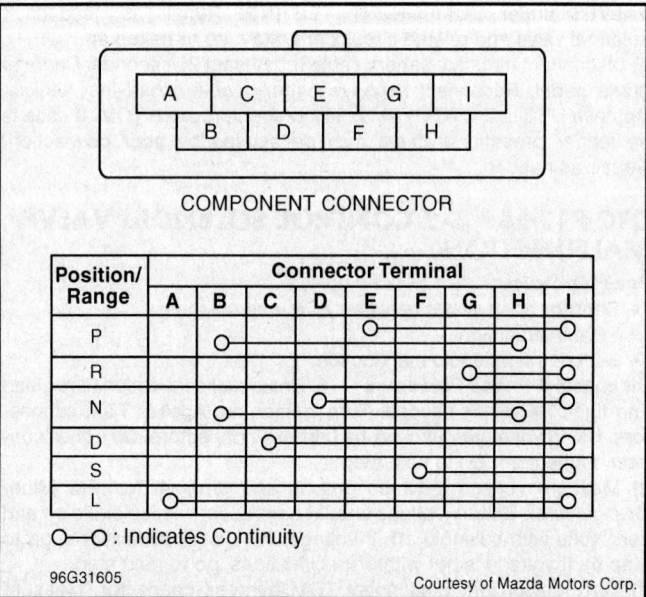

COMPONENT CONNECTOR

Position/ Range	Connector Terminal								
	A	B	C	D	E	F	G	H	I
P		O			O			O	O
R							O		O
N		O		O				O	O
D			O						O
S						O			O
L	O								O

O—O : Indicates Continuity

96G31605   Courtesy of Mazda Motors Corp.

Fig. 9: Checking Transmission Range Switch

TCM TERMINAL VOLTAGE TESTS

Turn ignition switch to ON position. Access TCM. TCM is mounted under left corner of dash, above fuse box. Do not disconnect harness connector. Using DVOM, measure voltage. See Figs. 10-11. After verifying that appropriate condition has been met, check voltage. If voltage is not within specification, inspect component or appropriate circuit. If voltage is within specification, replace TCM.

B+: Battery positive voltage

Terminal	Connected to	Voltmeter + terminal	Voltmeter – terminal	Voltage	Condition
1A	—	—	—	—	—
1B (Output)	HOLD indicator light	1B	Ground	B+	Non-HOLD mode
				Below 1.5 V	HOLD mode
1C (Output)	FAT terminal (data link connector)	1C	Ground	B+	Normal
				Below 1.5 V or B+ (fluctuating)	If malfunction present
				Code Signal	TAT terminal grounded
1D (Output)	Engine control module (terminal R)	1D	Ground	Below 2.5 V	N or P position
				B+	All ranges R position
1E (Input)	TAT terminal (data link connector)	1E	Ground	B+	—
1F	—	—	—	—	—
1G	Transmission fluid temperature sensor	1G	Ground	3.3 V	ATF temperature 25 °C { 77 °F }
1H (Input)	HOLD switch	1H	Ground	B+	Switch depressed
				0 V	Switch released
1I	—	—	—	—	—
1J	—	—	—	—	—
1K	—	—	—	—	—
1L	—	—	—	—	—
1M (Input)	Cruise control unit	1M	Ground	B+	Normal conditions
				Below 1.5 V	Set or Resume switch ON or vehicle speed 8 km/h { 5 MPH } lower than preset speed (Driving vehicle cruise control operation)
1N (Input)	Engine control module (terminal 3M)	1N	Ground	Below 1.5 V	Water temperature below 50 °C { 122 °F }
				B+	Water temperature above 60 °C { 140 °F }
1O	Closed throttle position switch	1O	Ground	0 V	Accelerator pedal depressed
				B+	Accelerator pedal released
1P (Input)	Vehicle speed sensor	1P	Ground	Approx. 4 V	While driving
				Approx. 7—9 V or Below 1.5 V	Vehicle stopped
2A (Input)	Throttle position sensor	2A	Ground	Approx. 4.4—5.5 V	Ignition switch ON
				0 V	Ignition switch OFF
2B (Input)	Transmission range switch (N and P position)	2B	Ground	0 V	N or P position
				B+	All ranges R position
2C	—	—	—	—	—

96I31607

Courtesy of Mazda Motors Corp.

Fig. 10: TCM Pin Voltage Table (Miata, 1 Of 2)

Terminal	Connected to	Voltmeter + terminal	Voltmeter – terminal	Voltage	Condition
2D (Input)	Transmission range switch (D range)	2D	Ground	B+	D range
				0 V	Other ranges All positions
2E (Output)	Shift solenoid A	2E		B+	Solenoid ON in following condition: • 1GR position
				0 V	Solenoid OFF in following condition: • 2GR, 3GR, and 4GR positions
2F (Input)	Transmission range switch (S range)	2F		B+	S range
				0 V	Other ranges All positions
2G (Output)	Shift solenoid B	2G		B+	Solenoid ON in following condition: • 1GR and 2GR gear positions
				0 V	Solenoid OFF in following condition: • 3GR, and 4GR positions
2H (Input)	Transmission range switch (L range)	2H		B+	L range
				0 V	Other ranges All positions
2I (Output)	Shift solenoid C	2I		B+	Solenoid ON in following condition: • 1GR, 2GR and 3GR positions
				0 V	Solenoid OFF in following condition: • 4GR position
2J (Input)*	Input/turbin speed sensor	2J	Ground	0—0.1 V (AC)	Engine running
				0 V (AC)	Engine stopped
2K (Output)	TCC control solenoid valve	2K		B+	Solenoid ON, TCC operation
				0 V	Solenoid OFF, TCC non-operation
2L (Ground)*	Input/turbin speed sensor	2L		Blow 1.5 V	—
2M (Output)	3–2 control solenoid valve	2M		B+	3–2 or 4–2 downshift
				0 V	Other conditions
2N	—	—	—	—	—
2O (Memory power)	Battery	2O	Ground	B+	Constant
2P (Ground)	—	2P		0 V	—
2Q (Battery power)	Battery	2Q		B+	Ignition switch ON
				0 V	Ignition switch OFF
2R	—	—	—	—	—
2S (Battery power)	Battery	2S	Ground	B+	Ignition switch ON
				0 V	Ignition switch OFF
2T (Input)	Throttle position sensor	2T		Approx. 0.4—4.1 V	Closed throttle position to wide open throttle

*: Checked with AC range

96J31608

Courtesy of Mazda Motors Corp.

Fig. 11: TCM Pin Voltage Table (Miata, 2 Of 2)

WIRING DIAGRAMS

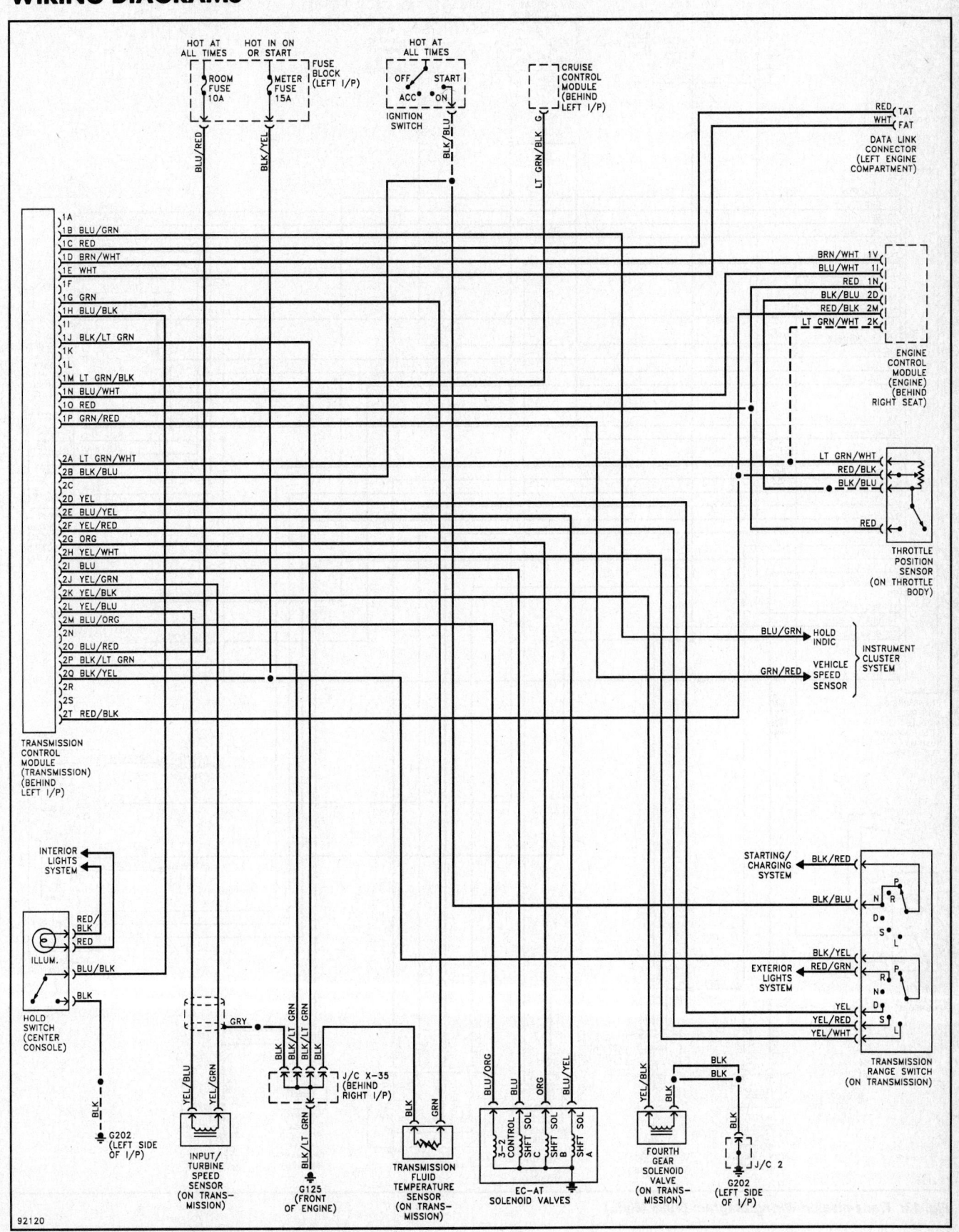

Fig. 12: *Transmission Wiring Diagram (1995 Miata)*

92120

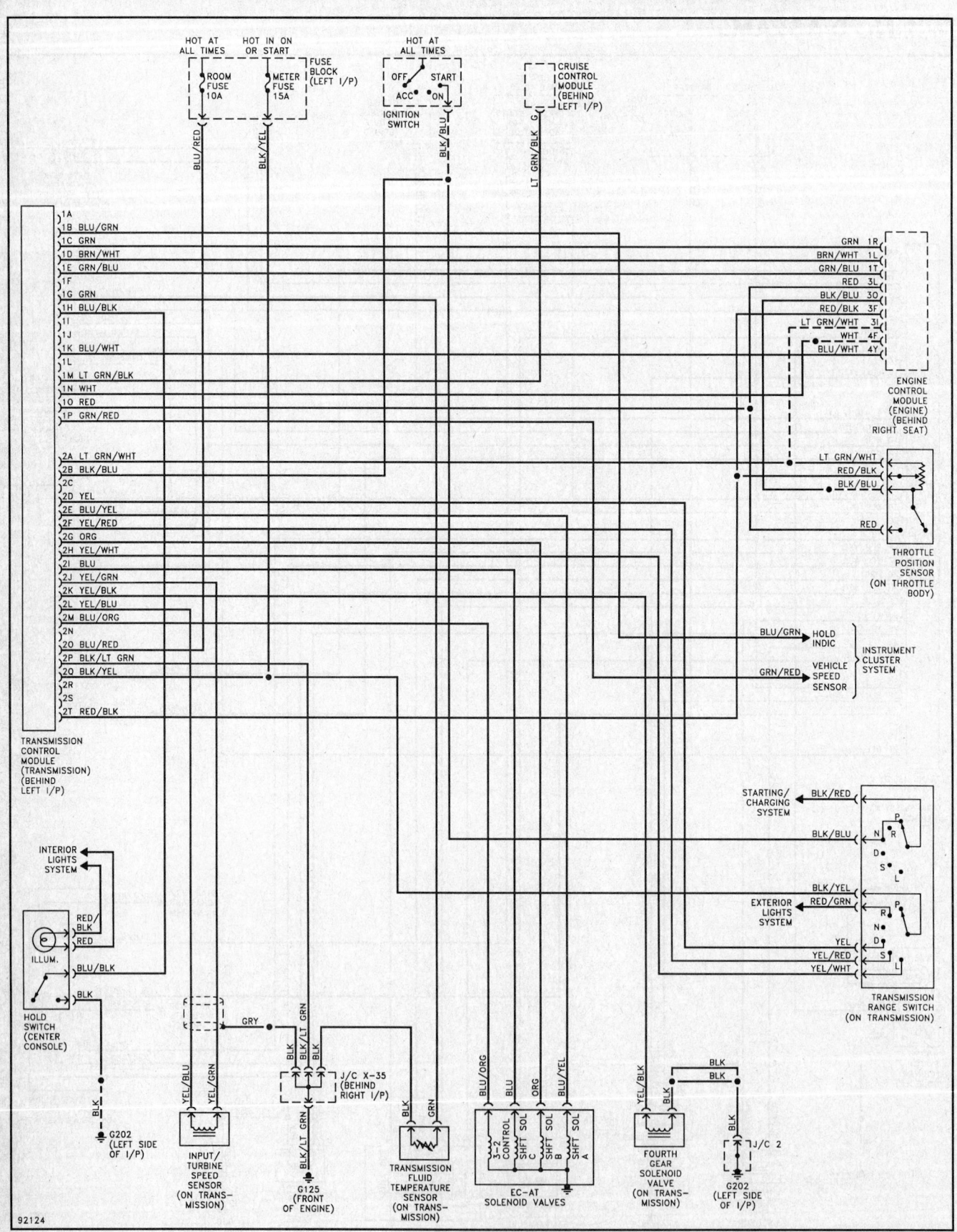

Fig. 13: Transmission Wiring Diagram (1996 Miata)

Mazda RA4A-EL, RA4AX-EL & RB4A-EL

MPV, RX7, 929

APPLICATION & LABOR TIMES

APPLICATION & LABOR TIMES

Vehicle Application	Labor Times		Trans. Model
	[1] R & I	[2] Overhaul	
MPV			
2WD	3.4	8.6	RA4A-EL
4WD	5.6	8.6	RA4AX-EL
RX7 (1995 Only)	4.4	8.6	RB4A-EL
929 (1995 Only)	4.4	8.6	RA4A-EL

[1] – Removal and installation of transmission from vehicle chassis.

[2] – On bench overhaul for transmission. DOES NOT include removal and installation.

CAUTION: Disconnecting battery on models equipped with anti-theft radio require canceling of anti-theft operation. See appropriate AUTOMATIC TRANSMISSION SERVICING article in TRANSMISSION SERVICING section. Refer to vehicle owner's manual to identify radio type.

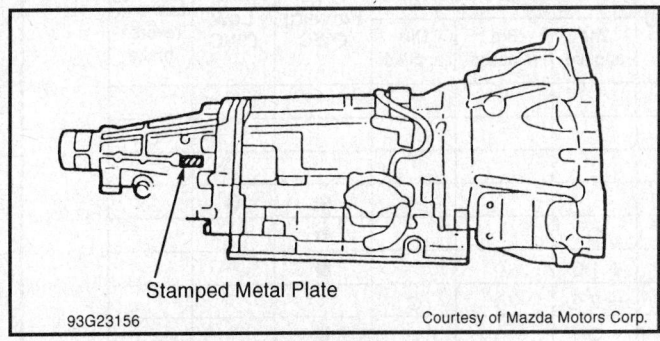

Stamped Metal Plate

93G23156

Courtesy of Mazda Motors Corp.

Fig. 1: Locating Transmission Identification Number (929 Shown, MPV & RX7 Similar)

IDENTIFICATION

Transmission model number is identified by a stamped metal plate attached to left or right side of rear transmission housing. *See Fig. 1.*

DESCRIPTION & OPERATION

The RA4A-EL, RA4AX-EL and RB4A-EL are 4-speed electronically controlled automatic transmissions that incorporate 5 multi-disc hydraulic clutches, 2 one-way clutches (sprag type) and a friction lined brake band that prevents rotation of rear sun gear drum. *See Fig. 2.*

ON/OFF and duty cycle solenoids control shift changes, line pressure and torque converter lock-up. Solenoids are attached to valve body. Solenoids are operated by Transmission Control Module (PCM).

TCM receives information from various input devices and uses this information to control solenoids for transmission shifting, line pressure, shift feel and torque converter clutch lock-up.

LUBRICATION & ADJUSTMENTS

See appropriate AUTOMATIC TRANSMISSION SERVICING article in TRANSMISSION SERVICING section.

TROUBLE SHOOTING

Preliminary Checks – Automatic transmission malfunction can be caused by either engine or transmission problems. Isolate malfunction to engine or transmission before proceeding with trouble shooting. Prior to trouble shooting check and adjust shift linkage, range switch and idle speed as needed. Ensure fluid level is correct. Check tires for correct inflation.

SYMPTOM DIAGNOSIS

Vehicle Does Not Move In Forward Or Reverse – Possible causes: low ATF level, selector lever adjustment, faulty or misadjusted TP sensor, low line pressure, internal transmission slippage, faulty valve body, faulty pressure control solenoid, faulty dropping resistor and/or worn parking mechanism.

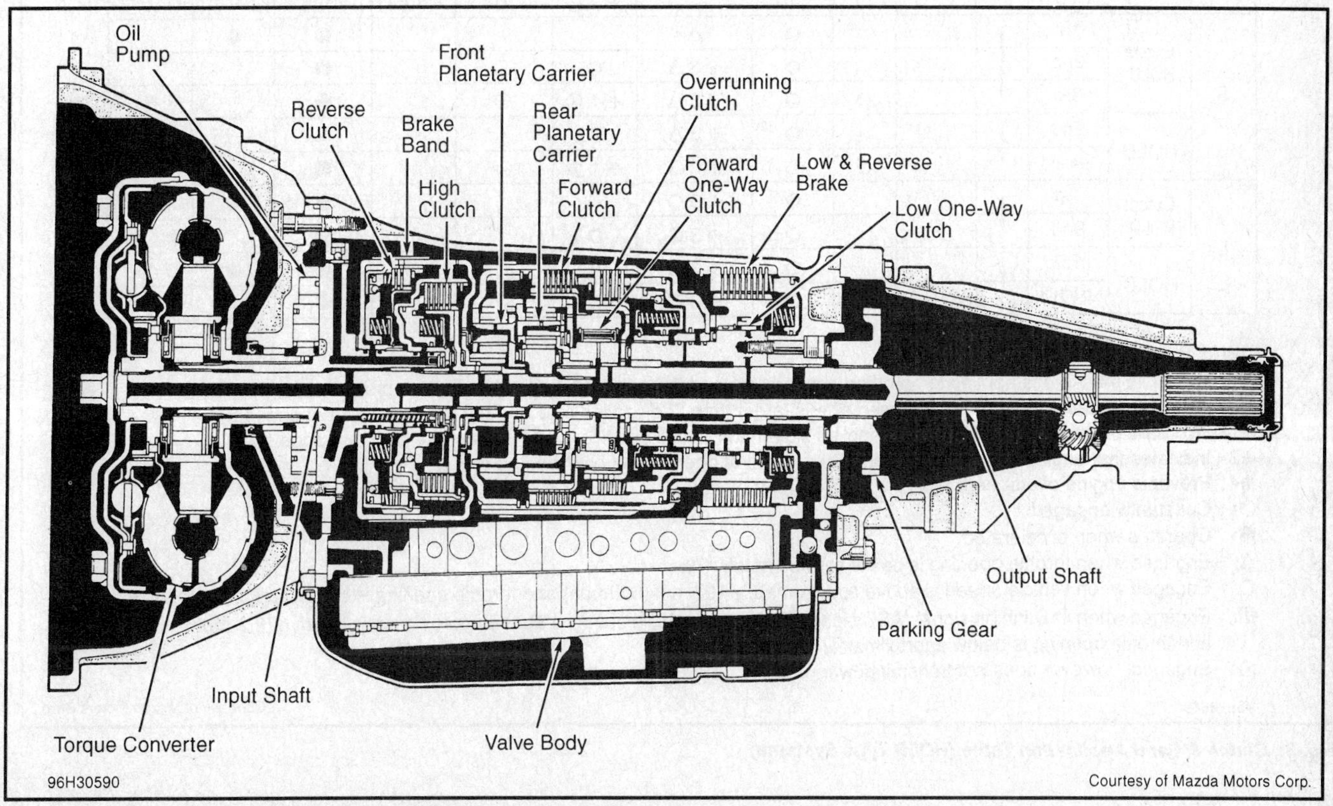

Oil Pump
Reverse Clutch
Brake Band
High Clutch
Front Planetary Carrier
Rear Planetary Carrier
Forward Clutch
Overrunning Clutch
Forward One-Way Clutch
Low & Reverse Brake
Low One-Way Clutch
Output Shaft
Parking Gear
Valve Body
Input Shaft
Torque Converter

96H30590

Courtesy of Mazda Motors Corp.

Fig. 2: Cut-Away View Of RA4A-EL Shown (RA4AX-EL & RB4A-EL Similar)

3-974

AUTOMATIC TRANSMISSIONS
Mazda RA4A-EL, RA4AX-EL & RB4A-EL (Cont.)

Vehicle Moves In "N" Position – Possible causes: selector lever adjustment, faulty or misadjusted TP sensor, internal transmission slippage, faulty manual valve, faulty pressure control solenoid and/or faulty dropping resistor.

Excessive Vehicle Movement At Idle – Possible causes: high idle speed and/or high line pressure.

Low Maximum Speed & Poor Acceleration – Possible causes: low ATF level, selector lever adjustment, faulty or misadjusted TP sensor, low line pressure, internal transmission slippage, faulty valve body, faulty pressure control solenoid, faulty dropping resistor, worn shift solenoids "A" and/or "B", misadjusted transmission range switch, faulty HOLD switch, faulty output speed sensor, worn torque converter and/or low engine output.

No Shifting – Possible causes: worn shift solenoids "A" and/or "B", misadjusted transmission range switch, faulty HOLD switch, faulty output speed sensor, faulty valve body, poor ground and/or faulty TCM.

Transmission Does Not Shift To 4th Gear – Possible causes: faulty TFT sensor, worn shift solenoids "A" and/or "B", worn overrunning clutch solenoid, faulty valve body, misadjusted transmission range switch, faulty output speed sensor, faulty 4th gear inhibit signal, shorted DLC connector TAT terminal, faulty HOLD switch, poor ground and/or faulty TCM.

Abnormal Shift – Possible causes: low ATF level, poor ground, misadjusted TP sensor, faulty output speed sensor, faulty TCM and/or faulty valve body.

Frequent Shifting – Possible causes: misadjusted TP sensor, poor ground and/or faulty TCM.

Shift Point High Or Low – Possible causes: misadjusted TP sensor, faulty engine RPM signal, faulty output speed sensor and/or faulty A/C signal.

Torque Converter Clutch (TCC) Non-Operation – Possible causes: worn TCC solenoid, worn TCC control solenoid, faulty valve body, faulty TFT sensor, misadjusted TP sensor, faulty closed throttle position switch, faulty engine RPM signal, faulty output speed sensor and/or faulty transmission range sensor.

CLUTCH & BAND APPLICATION TABLES

Range	Mode	Gear	Shift	Reverse clutch	High clutch	Forward clutch	Overrunning clutch	Band servo piston			Forward OWC	Low OWC	Low and reverse brake
								2nd applied	3rd released	O/D applied			
P	–	–	–										
R	–	Reverse	–	O									O
N	–	–	–										
D	Except HOLD	1st	↑↓			O	■				●	●	
		2nd	↑↓			O	✳3 ■	O			●		
		3rd	↑↓		O	O	✳3 ■	✳1 ⊗	⊗		●		
		O/D	↓		O	⊗		✳2 ⊗	⊗	O			
	HOLD	2nd	↑↓			O	✳3 ◎	O			●		
		3rd	↑↓		O	O	✳3 ◎	✳1 ⊗	⊗		●		
		✳4 O/D	↑		O	⊗		✳2 ⊗	⊗	O			
S	Except HOLD	1st	↑			O	Δ				●	●	
		2nd	↑↓			O	✳3 Δ	O			●		
		3rd	↓		O	O	✳3 Δ	✳1 ⊗	⊗		●		
	HOLD	2nd	↑↓			O	✳3 Δ	O			●		
		✳4 3rd			O	O	✳3 Δ	✳1 O	⊗		●		
L	Except HOLD	1st	↑			O	✳3 O				●	●	O
		2nd	↓			O	✳3 O	O			●		
	HOLD	1st	↑			O	✳3 O				●	●	O
		✳4 2nd				O	✳3 O				●		

OWC: one-way clutch

✳1: Hydraulic pressure is applied to both 2nd applied side and 3rd released side of band servo piston. However, because area of 3rd released side is larger than 2nd applied side, the brake band does not engage.

✳2: Hydraulic pressure is applied to O/D applied side in the above conditions (✳1) and brake band engages.

✳3: Indicates that engine braking is available as a result of operation of overrunning clutch.

✳4: Prevents engine overspeed.

O: Constantly engaged.

● : Operates when accelerated.

Δ: Engaged when throttle opening is below approximately 1/8.

◎: Engaged when vehicle speed is above approximately 10 km/h {6.2 mph} and throttle opening is below approximately 1/8.

■: Engaged when O/D inhibit signal (ASC signal) is ON and vehicle speed is above approximately 10 km/h {6.2 mph} and throttle opening is below approximately 1/8.

⊗: Engaged, however does not transmit power.

95E20648

Courtesy of Mazda Motors Corp.

Fig. 3: Clutch & Band Application Table (HOLD Type Systems)

AUTOMATIC TRANSMISSIONS
Mazda RA4A-EL, RA4AX-EL & RB4A-EL (Cont.)

3-975

No Kickdown – Possible causes: faulty or misadjusted TP sensor, faulty valve body, faulty HOLD switch and/or faulty output speed sensor.

Transmission Shift Flare Under Acceleration – Possible causes: low ATF level, selector lever adjustment, faulty or misadjusted TP sensor, low line pressure, internal transmission slippage, faulty valve body, faulty pressure control solenoid and/or faulty dropping resistor.

Transmission Shift Flare Or Slipping Shift During Upshifts Or Downshifts – Possible causes: low ATF level, selector lever adjustment, faulty or misadjusted TP sensor, low line pressure, internal transmission slippage, faulty valve body, faulty pressure control solenoid, faulty dropping resistor, faulty input/turbine speed sensor, faulty output speed sensor and/or faulty MAP sensor.

Harsh (Shudder) TCC Engagement – Possible causes: misadjusted ignition timing, low ATF level, worn TCC solenoid, worn TCC control solenoid, faulty valve body, misadjusted TP sensor, faulty closed throttle position switch, faulty engine RPM signal, faulty output speed sensor, low line pressure, faulty dropping resistor and/or faulty pressure control solenoid.

Excessive "N" To "D" Or "N" To "R" Shift Shock – Possible causes: low ATF lever, high idle speed, faulty TP sensor, high line pressure, faulty valve body, internal clutch slippage, worn pressure control solenoid, faulty dropping resistor, worn N-D or 3-4/N-R accumulator, faulty or misadjusted transmission range switch and/or faulty input/turbine speed sensor.

Excessive Shift Shock During Upshifts Or Downshifts – Possible causes: low ATF lever, faulty TP sensor, high line pressure, faulty valve body, internal clutch slippage, worn pressure control solenoid, faulty dropping resistor, faulty closed throttle position switch, faulty TFT sensor, faulty input/turbine speed sensor, faulty output speed sensor and/or faulty MAP sensor.

No Engine Braking – Possible causes: low ATF lever, internal clutch slippage, faulty valve body, worn overrunning clutch, faulty or misadjusted TP sensor, faulty 4th gear inhibit signal and/or faulty or misadjusted transmission range switch.

Transaxle Overheats – Possible causes: low ATF level, internal component failure, faulty pressure control solenoid, faulty or misadjusted TP sensor, faulty dropping resistor, worn TCC solenoid, worn TCC control solenoid and/or fluid cooling system.

Engine Stalls When Shifted Into Forward Or Reverse Gears – Possible causes: low idle speed, faulty valve body, faulty PNP switch signal, faulty or misadjusted transmission range switch, faulty input/turbine speed sensor and/or faulty output speed sensor.

Mode	Range	Gear	Reverse clutch	High clutch	Forward clutch	Overrunning clutch	Brake band 2nd applied	Brake band 3rd released	Brake band OD applied	Forward one-way clutch	Low one-way clutch	Low and reverse brake
ECONOMY/POWER	P	—										
	R	Reverse	O									O
	N	—										
	D	1st			·O	■				●	●	
	D	2nd			O	□	O			●		
	D	3rd		O	O	□	⊗*1	⊗		●		
	D	OD		O	⊗		⊗*2	⊗	O			
	S	1st			O	★				●	●	
	S	2nd			O	◎	O			●		
	S	3rd		O	O	◎	⊗*1	⊗		●		
	L	1st			O	O				●		O
	L	2nd			O	O	O			●		
HOLD	D	2nd			O	◎	O			●		
	D	3rd		O	O	◎	⊗*1	⊗		●		
	S	2nd			O	◎	O			●		
	L	1st		O	O					●		O

*1 : Hydraulic pressure is applied to both 2nd applied side and 3rd released side of band servo piston. However, because the area of the 3rd released side is larger than the 2nd applied side, the brake band does not operate.

*2 : Hydraulic pressure is applied to OD applied side, plus condition *1 above. Brake band is applied.

O : Operates.

◎ : Operates when throttle opening is less than 1/8. Engine braking effect available.

★ : Operates when throttle opening is less than 1/8. Engine braking effect not available.

□ : Operates when the EC-AT control unit recive OD inhibit signal from the cruise control unit and throttle opening less than 1/8. Engine braking effect available.

■ : Operates when the EC-AT control unit recive OD inhibit signal from the cruise control unit and throttle opening less than 1/8. Engine braking effect not available.

⊗ : Operates but does not transmit power.

● : Operates during acceleration and cruising.

95D20647

Courtesy of Mazda Motors Corp.

Fig. 4: Clutch & Band Application Table (HOLD Type Systems With Power/Economy Switch)

AUTOMATIC TRANSMISSIONS
Mazda RA4A-EL, RA4AX-EL & RB4A-EL (Cont.)

Position/Range	Mode	Gear	Reverse clutch	High clutch	Forward clutch	Over-running clutch	Brake band 2GR applied	Brake band 3GR released	Brake band 4GR applied	Forward one-way clutch	Low one-way clutch	Low and reverse brake
P	—	—										
R	—	Reverse	○									○
N	—	—										
D	Except O/D OFF	1			○	■				●	●	
		2			○	□	○			●		
		3		○	○	□	⊗*1	⊗		●		
		4		○	⊗		⊗*2	⊗	○			
	O/D OFF	1			○	■				●	●	
		2			○	◎	○			●		
		3		○	○	◎	⊗*1	⊗		●		
2	—	2			○	◎	○			●		
1	—	1			○	○				●		○

*1 : Hydraulic pressure is applied to both second gear applied side and third gear released side of band servo piston. However, because the area of the third gear released side is larger than the second gear applied side, the brake band does not operate.

*2 : Hydraulic pressure is applied to fourth gear applied side, plus condition *1 above. Brake band is applied.

○ : Operates.

◎ : Operates when throttle opening is less than 1/8. Engine braking effect available.

□ : Operates when the engine control module receives 4GR inhibit signal from the cruise control module and throttle opening is less than 1/8. Engine braking effect available.

■ : Operates when the engine control module receives 4GR inhibit signal from the cruise control module and throttle opening is less than 1/8. Engine braking effect not available.

⊗ : Operates but does not transmit power.

● : Operates during acceleration and cruising.

96I30591

Courtesy of Mazda Motors Corp.

Fig. 5: Clutch & Band Application Table (O/D OFF Type Systems)

TESTING
Before testing transmission, ensure fluid level is correct and shift linkage, range switch and idle speed are adjusted correctly.

TIME LAG
With engine at idle, shift selector from "N" to "D", "N" to "D" HOLD or O/D OFF (as equipped) and "N" to "R". Time lag for transmission to engage should be less than one second for "N" to "D" and less than 1.2 seconds for "N" to "R".

TIME LAG RESULTS
Longer Than Specified In "N" To "D" & "N" To "D" HOLD Or O/D OFF – Low line pressure. Forward clutch slipping. Forward one-way clutch slipping.

Longer Than Specified In "N" To "D" – Low line pressure. Low one-way clutch slipping. N-D accumulator not operating properly.

Longer Than Specified In "N" To "D" HOLD – Low line pressure. Brake band slipping. 1-2 accumulator not operating properly.

Longer Than Specified In "N" To "R" – Low line pressure. Reverse clutch slipping. Low and reverse brake slipping. 3-4/N-R accumulator not operating properly.

ROAD TEST
Preparation – Check all fluid levels and correct if necessary. Warm engine and transmission to operating temperature. If any problems occur during road test, see ROAD TEST RESULTS.

NOTE: On MPV (1995 4WD and 1996 All), RX7 and 929, the NORMAL/POWER mode feature is controlled by TCM.

Test Procedure – 1) Check for shift point, shift pattern and shift shock. Shift selector to "D" range (MPV (1995 4WD and 1996 All), RX7 and 929), "D" range ECONOMY mode (1995 MPV 2WD). Accelerate vehicle at half and full throttle, ensure 1-2, 2-3 and 3-OD upshifts, downshifts and lock-up are obtained. Note speed and compare with appropriate SHIFT SPEED CHART. *See Figs. 6-10.* Note upshifts for shift shock and slippage.

2) On 1995 MPV 2WD, select POWER mode. Note shift points, and any shock and slippage.

3) On all models, when driving in OD, shift to "S" and check that OD-3 downshift occurs immediately.

4) Select HOLD mode. Check for 2-3 upshifts and downshifts. Check for lock-up and no 1st or "OD".

5) Decelerate vehicle. Check for engine braking in 3rd and 2nd gears when throttle is open 1/8 or less.

6) Drive in 3rd and 4th gear to ensure no unusual noise or vibration is heard. Check torque converter, driveshaft(s) and differential for source of unusual noise. Ensure kickdown operates properly and shift points match appropriate SHIFT SPEED CHART.

NOTE: POWER or NORMAL driving mode is automatically selected according to throttle opening. O/D does not operate when ATF temperature is below 50°F (10°C) or when cruise control is operating with a 5 MPH difference between preset cruise speed and vehicle speed. TCC lock-up does not operate when throttle is closed with vehicle below 74 MPH or when ATF is below 104°F (40°C).

AUTOMATIC TRANSMISSIONS
Mazda RA4A-EL, RA4AX-EL & RB4A-EL (Cont.)

3-977

Mode	Range	Throttle condition (Throttle sensor voltage)	Shift	Vehicle speed km/h {mph}
Power	D	Fully opened (4.3 volt)	$D_1 \to D_2$	50—54 {31—33}
			$D_2 \to D_3$	99—107 {61—66}
			$D_3 \to OD$	157—167 {97—104}
		Half throttle (1.6—2.2 volt)	$D_1 \to D_2$	42—46 {26—29}
			$D_2 \to D_3$	66—72 {41—45}
			Lockup ON (D_3)	96—104 {60—64}
			$D_3 \to OD$	113—121 {70—75}
			Lockup ON (OD)	136—144 {84—89}
			Lockup OFF (OD)	126—134 {78—83}
			$OD \to D_3$	79—87 {49—54}
			Lockup OFF (D_3)	86—94 {53—58}
			$D_3 \to D_2$	43—49 {27—30}
		Kickdown	$OD \to D_3$	149—159 {92—99}
			$OD \to D_2$	87—95 {54—59}
			$OD \to D_1$	43—47 {27—29}
			$D_3 \to D_2$	87—95 {54—59}
			$D_3 \to D_1$	43—47 {27—29}
			$D_2 \to D_1$	43—47 {27—29}
Economy		Fully opened (4.3 volt)	$D_1 \to D_2$	50—54 {31—33}
			$D_2 \to D_3$	99—107 {61—66}
			$D_3 \to OD$	157—167 {97—104}
		Half throttle (1.6—2.2 volt)	$D_1 \to D_2$	31—35 {19—22}
			$D_2 \to D_3$	56—62 {35—38}
			$D_3 \to OD$	79—87 {49—54}
			Lockup ON (OD)	79—87 {49—54}
			Lockup OFF (OD)	74—82 {46—51}
			$OD \to D_3$	50—58 {31—36}
			$D_3 \to D_2$	22—28 {14—17}
		Kickdown	$OD \to D_3$	126—136 {78—84}
			$OD \to D_2$	81—89 {50—55}
			$OD \to D_1$	43—47 {27—29}
			$D_3 \to D_2$	81—89 {50—55}
			$D_3 \to D_1$	43—47 {27—29}
			$D_2 \to D_1$	43—47 {27—29}
Economy/Power	S	Fully opened (4.3 volt)	$S_1 \to S_2$	49—53 {30—33}
			$S_2 \to S_3$	95—103 {59—64}
			$S_3 \to S_2$	88—94 {55—58}
			$S_2 \to S_1$	43—47 {27—29}
		Half throttle (1.6—2.2 volt)	$S_1 \to S_2$	42—46 {26—29}
			$S_2 \to S_3$	68—74 {42—46}
			$S_3 \to S_2$	43—49 {27—30}
Economy/ Power	L	Fully opened (4.3 volt)	$L_1 \to L_2$	49—53 {30—33}
			$L_2 \to L_1$	43—47 {27—29}
		Half throttle (1.6—2.2 volt)	$L_1 \to L_2$	42—46 {26—29}
HOLD	D	—	$D_2 \to D_3$	18—22 {11—14}
			$D_3 \to D_2$	7—13 {4—8}
	S	Fully closed (0.5 volt)	$OD \to D_3$	157—167 {97—104}
			$S_3 \to S_2$	99—107 {61—66}
	L		$L_2 \to L_1$	44—48 {27—30}

95B20629

Courtesy of Mazda Motors Corp.

Fig. 6: 1995 MPV 2WD Shift Speed Chart

3-978

AUTOMATIC TRANSMISSIONS
Mazda RA4A-EL, RA4AX-EL & RB4A-EL (Cont.)

Mode	Range	Throttle condition (Throttle sensor voltage)	Shift	Vehicle speed km/h {mph}
Normal	D	Fully opened (4.3 volt)	$D_1 \rightarrow D_2$	53—57 {33—35}
			$D_2 \rightarrow D_3$	100—108 {62—67}
			$D_3 \rightarrow OD$	153—163 {95—101}
		Half throttle (1.6—2.2 volt)	$D_1 \rightarrow D_2$	32—36 {20—22}
			$D_2 \rightarrow D_3$	59—65 {37—40}
			$D_3 \rightarrow OD$	80—88 {50—55}
			Lockup ON (OD)	80—88 {50—55}
			Lockup OFF (OD)	74—82 {46—51}
			$OD \rightarrow D_3$	50—58 {31—36}
			$D_3 \rightarrow D_2$	22—28 {14—17}
		Kickdown	$OD \rightarrow D_3$	145—155 {90—96}
			$OD \rightarrow D_2$	92—100 {57—62}
			$OD \rightarrow D_1$	43—47 {27—29}
			$D_3 \rightarrow D_2$	92—100 {57—62}
			$D_3 \rightarrow D_1$	43—47 {27—29}
			$D_2 \rightarrow D_1$	43—47 {27—29}
	S	Fully opened (4.3 volt)	$S_1 \rightarrow S_2$	53—57 {33—35}
			$S_2 \rightarrow S_3$	100—108 {62—67}
			$S_3 \rightarrow S_2$	93—99 {58—61}
			$S_2 \rightarrow S_1$	43—47 {27—29}
		Half throttle (1.6—2.2 volt)	$S_1 \rightarrow S_2$	32—36 {20—22}
			$S_2 \rightarrow S_3$	59—65 {37—40}
			$S_3 \rightarrow S_2$	23—27 {14—17}
	L	Fully opened (4.3 volt)	$L_1 \rightarrow L_2$	53—57 {33—35}
			$L_2 \rightarrow L_1$	43—47 {27—29}
		Half throttle (1.6—2.2 volt)	$L_1 \rightarrow L_2$	32—36 {20—22}
Hold	D	—	$D_2 \rightarrow D_3$	18—22 {11—14}
			$D_3 \rightarrow D_2$	7—13 {4—8}
	S	Fully closed (0.5 volt)	$OD \rightarrow D_3$	153—163 {95—101}
			$S_3 \rightarrow S_2$	100—108 {62—67}
	L		$L_2 \rightarrow L_1$	43—47 {27—29}

95E20630

Courtesy of Mazda Motors Corp.

Fig. 7: 1995 MPV 4WD Shift Speed Chart

AUTOMATIC TRANSMISSIONS
Mazda RA4A-EL, RA4AX-EL & RB4A-EL (Cont.)

3-979

Range	Mode		Throttle condition (Throttle position sensor voltage)	Shift	Vehicle speed km/h { mph }	
					2WD	4WD
D	Except O/D OFF	POWER	Wide open throttle	$D_1 \rightarrow D_2$	51—57 { 32—35 }	54—60 { 34—37 }
				$D_2 \rightarrow D_3$	101—109 { 63—67 }	102—110 { 64—68 }
				TCC ON (D_3)	98—106 { 61—65 }	98—106 { 61—65 }
				$D_3 \rightarrow D_4$	159—169 { 99—104 }	155—165 { 97—102 }
			Half throttle	$D_1 \rightarrow D_2$	39—49 { 25—30 }	39—49 { 25—30 }
				$D_2 \rightarrow D_3$	62—79 { 39—48 }	63—81 { 40—50 }
				TCC ON (D_3)	94—106 { 59—65 }	94—106 { 59—65 }
				$D_3 \rightarrow D_4$	102—131 { 64—81 }	102—131 { 64—81 }
				TCC ON (D_4)	126—154 { 79—95 }	126—154 { 79—95 }
			Closed throttle position	$D_4 \rightarrow D_3$	44—50 { 28—31 }	44—50 { 28—31 }
				$D_3 \rightarrow D_2$	22—28 { 14—17 }	22—28 { 14—17 }
				$D_2 \rightarrow D_1$	6—12 { 4—7 }	6—12 { 4—7 }
			Kickdown	$D_4 \rightarrow D_3$	149—159 { 93—98 }	145—155 { 90—96 }
				$D_3 \rightarrow D_2$	87—95 { 54—58 }	92—100 { 58—62 }
				$D_2 \rightarrow D_1$	42—48 { 27—29 }	42—48 { 27—29 }
		NORMAL	Wide open throttle	$D_1 \rightarrow D_2$	51—57 { 32—35 }	54—60 { 34—37 }
				$D_2 \rightarrow D_3$	101—109 { 63—67 }	102—110 { 64—68 }
				TCC ON (D_3)	98—106 { 61—65 }	98—106 { 61—65 }
				$D_3 \rightarrow D_4$	159—169 { 99—104 }	155—165 { 97—102 }
			Half throttle	$D_1 \rightarrow D_2$	28—36 { 18—22 }	29—38 { 18—23 }
				$D_2 \rightarrow D_3$	54—70 { 34—43 }	52—69 { 33—42 }
				TCC ON (D_3)	94—106 { 59—65 }	94—106 { 59—65 }
				$D_3 \rightarrow D_4$	70—98 { 44—60 }	69—96 { 43—59 }
				TCC ON (D_4)	70—97 { 44—60 }	70—96 { 44—59 }
			Closed throttle position	$D_4 \rightarrow D_3$	22—28 { 14—17 }	22—28 { 14—17 }
				$D_3 \rightarrow D_2$	11—19 { 7—11 }	12—18 { 8—11 }
				$D_2 \rightarrow D_1$	6—12 { 4—7 }	6—12 { 4—7 }
			Kickdown	$D_4 \rightarrow D_3$	126—136 { 79—84 }	145—155 { 90—96 }
				$D_3 \rightarrow D_2$	81—89 { 51—55 }	92—100 { 58—62 }
				$D_2 \rightarrow D_1$	42—48 { 27—29 }	42—48 { 27—29 }
	O/D OFF	POWER	Wide open throttle	$D_1 \rightarrow D_2$	51—57 { 32—35 }	54—60 { 34—37 }
				$D_2 \rightarrow D_3$	101—109 { 63—67 }	102—110 { 64—68 }
				TCC ON (D_3)	98—106 { 61—65 }	98—106 { 61—65 }
			Half throttle	$D_1 \rightarrow D_2$	39—49 { 25—30 }	39—49 { 25—30 }
				$D_2 \rightarrow D_3$	62—79 { 39—48 }	63—81 { 40—50 }
				TCC ON (D_3)	94—106 { 59—65 }	94—106 { 59—65 }
			Closed throttle position	$D_3 \rightarrow D_2$	22—28 { 14—17 }	22—28 { 14—17 }
				$D_2 \rightarrow D_1$	6—12 { 4—7 }	6—12 { 4—7 }
			Kickdown	$D_3 \rightarrow D_2$	87—95 { 54—58 }	92—100 { 58—62 }
				$D_2 \rightarrow D_1$	42—48 { 27—29 }	42—48 { 27—29 }
		NORMAL	Wide open throttle	$D_1 \rightarrow D_2$	51—57 { 32—35 }	54—60 { 34—37 }
				$D_2 \rightarrow D_3$	101—109 { 63—67 }	102—110 { 64—68 }
				TCC ON (D_3)	98—106 { 61—65 }	98—106 { 61—65 }
			Half throttle	$D_1 \rightarrow D_2$	28—36 { 18—22 }	29—38 { 18—23 }
				$D_2 \rightarrow D_3$	54—70 { 34—43 }	52—69 { 33—42 }
				TCC ON (D_3)	94—106 { 59—65 }	94—106 { 59—65 }
			Closed throttle position	$D_3 \rightarrow D_2$	11—19 { 7—11 }	12—18 { 8—11 }
				$D_2 \rightarrow D_1$	6—12 { 4—7 }	6—12 { 4—7 }
			Kickdown	$D_3 \rightarrow D_2$	81—89 { 51—55 }	92—100 { 58—62 }
				$D_2 \rightarrow D_1$	42—48 { 27—29 }	42—48 { 27—29 }

96J30592

Courtesy of Mazda Motors Corp.

Fig. 8: 1995-96 MPV Shift Speed Chart

3-980

AUTOMATIC TRANSMISSIONS
Mazda RA4A-EL, RA4AX-EL & RB4A-EL (Cont.)

Range	Mode	Throttle condition (throttle sensor voltage)	Shift	Vehicle speed km/h {MPH}
D	POWER	Fully open (4.0–4.5V)	D₁ → D₂	50–56 {31–35}
			D₂ → D₃	103–111 {64–69}
			D₃ → O/D	178–188 {111–117}
		Half throttle	D₁ → D₂	35–41 {22–25}
			D₂ → D₃	81–93 {50–58}
			D₃ → O/D	126–144 {78–89}
			Lockup ON (D₃)	94–106 {58–66} (81–93 {50–58})
			Lockup ON (O/D)	174–192 {108–119} (126–144 {78–89})
		Fully closed (0.1–1.1V)	O/D → D₃	39–45 {24–28}
			D₃ → D₂	13–19 {8–12}
			D₂ → D₁	5–11 {3–7}
		Kickdown	O/D → D₃	142–152 {88–94}
			D₃ → D₂	91–99 {57–62}
			D₂ → D₁	38–44 {24–27}
	NORMAL A/C ON	Fully open (4.0–4.5V)	D₁ → D₂	50–56 {31–35}
			D₂ → D₃	103–111 {64–69}
			D₃ → O/D	178–188 {111–117}
		Half throttle	D₁ → D₂	32–38 {20–24}
			D₂ → D₃	80–92 {50–57}
			D₃ → O/D	126–144 {78–89}
			Lockup ON (D₃)	94–106 {58–66} (80–92 {50–57})
			Lockup ON (O/D)	174–192 {108–119} (126–144 {78–89})
		Fully closed (0.1–1.1V)	O/D → D₃	39–45 {24–28}
			D₃ → D₂	13–19 {8–12}
			D₂ → D₁	5–11 {3–7}
		Kickdown	O/D → D₃	142–152 {88–94}
			D₃ → D₂	91–99 {57–62}
			D₂ → D₁	38–44 {24–27}
	NORMAL A/C OFF	Fully open (4.0–4.5V)	D₁ → D₂	50–56 {31–35}
			D₂ → D₃	103–111 {64–69}
			D₃ → O/D	178–188 {111–117}
		Half throttle	D₁ → D₂	32–38 {20–24}
			D₂ → D₃	80–92 {50–57}
			D₃ → O/D	126–144 {78–89}
			Lockup ON (D₃)	94–106 {58–66} (80–92 {50–57})
			Lockup ON (O/D)	174–192 {108–119} (126–144 {78–89})
		Fully closed (0.1–1.1V)	O/D → D₃	32–38 {20–24}
			D₃ → D₂	13–19 {8–12}
			D₂ → D₁	5–11 {3–7}
		Kickdown	O/D → D₃	142–152 {88–94}
			D₃ → D₂	91–99 {57–62}
			D₂ → D₁	38–44 {24–27}
D	HOLD	–	O/D → D₃	180–186 {112–116}
			D₃ → D₂	7–13 {4–8}
			D₂ → D₃	15–25 {9–16}
			Lockup ON (D₃)	94–106 {58–66} (39–51 {24–32})
S	EXCEPT HOLD	Fully open (4.0–4.5V)	S₁ → S₂	50–56 {31–35}
			S₂ → S₃	103–111 {64–69}
		Half throttle	S₁ → S₂	35–41 {22–25}
			S₂ → S₃	81–93 {50–58}
			Lockup ON (S₃)	94–106 {58–66} (81–93 {50–58})
		Fully closed (0.1–1.1V)	S₃ → S₂	13–19 {8–12}
			S₂ → S₁	5–11 {3–7}
		Kickdown	S₃ → S₂	91–99 {57–62}
			S₂ → S₁	38–44 {24–27}
	HOLD	–	S₃ → S₂	112–118 {70–73}
L	EXCEPT HOLD	Fully open (4.0–4.5V)	L₁ → L₂	50–56 {31–35}
		Half throttle	L₁ → L₂	35–41 {22–25}
		Fully closed (0.1–1.1V)	L₂ → L₁	5–11 {3–7}
		Kickdown	L₂ → L₁	38–44 {24–27}
	HOLD	–	L₂ → L₁	45–51 {28–32}

95F20631

Courtesy of Mazda Motors Corp.

Fig. 9: RX7 Shift Speed Chart

AUTOMATIC TRANSMISSIONS
Mazda RA4A-EL, RA4AX-EL & RB4A-EL (Cont.)

3-981

Range	Mode	Throttle condition (throttle position sensor voltage)	Shift	Vehicle speed km/h {mph}
D	POWER	Fully open (3.0—4.3V)	D₁→D₂	49—55 {30—34}
			D₂→D₃	94—102 {58—63}
			D₃→O/D	152—162 {94—100}
		Half throttle (1.7—2.7V)	D₁→D₂	40—46 {25—29}
			D₂→D₃	79—91 {49—56}
			D₃→O/D	133—151 {82—94}
			Lockup ON (D₃)	94—106 {58—66}
			Lockup ON (O/D)	144—162 {89—100}
		Fully closed (0.1—1.1V)	O/D→D₃	24—30 {15—19}
			D₃→D₂	12—18 {7—11}
			D₂→D₁	5—11 {3—7}
		Kickdown	O/D→D₃	142—152 {88—94}
			D₃→D₂	87—95 {54—59}
			D₂→D₁	43—49 {27—30}
	NORMAL A/C ON	Fully open (3.0—4.3V)	D₁→D₂	49—55 {30—34}
			D₂→D₃	94—102 {58—63}
			D₃→O/D	152—162 {94—100}
		Half throttle (1.7—2.7V)	D₁→D₂	40—46 {25—29}
			D₂→D₃	79—91 {49—56}
			D₃→O/D	129—147 {80—91}
			Lockup ON (D₃)	94—106 {58—66}
			Lockup ON (O/D)	144—162 {89—100}
		Fully closed (0.1—1.1V)	O/D→D₃	24—30 {15—19}
			D₃→D₂	12—18 {7—11}
			D₂→D₁	5—11 {3—7}
		Kickdown	O/D→D₃	142—152 {88—94}
			D₃→D₂	87—95 {54—59}
			D₂→D₁	43—49 {27—30}
	NORMAL A/C OFF	Fully open (3.0—4.3V)	D₁→D₂	49—55 {30—34}
			D₂→D₃	94—102 {58—63}
			D₃→O/D	152—162 {94—100}
		Half throttle (1.7—2.7V)	D₁→D₂	40—46 {25—29}
			D₂→D₃	79—91 {49—56}
			D₃→O/D	129—147 {80—91}
			Lockup ON (D₃)	94—106 {58—66}
			Lockup ON (O/D)	144—162 {89—100}
		Fully closed (0.1—1.1V)	O/D→D₃	24—30 {15—19}
			D₃→D₂	12—18 {7—11}
			D₂→D₁	5—11 {3—7}
		Kickdown	O/D→D₃	142—152 {88—94}
			D₃→D₂	87—95 {54—59}
			D₂→D₁	43—49 {27—30}
D	HOLD	—	O/D→D₃	154—160 {95—99}
			D₃→D₂	7—13 {4—8}
			D₂→D₃	15—25 {9—16}
			Lockup ON (D₃)	94—106 {58—66}
S	NORMAL	Fully open (3.0—4.3V)	S₁→S₂	49—55 {30—34}
			S₂→S₃	94—102 {58—63}
		Half throttle (1.7—2.7V)	S₁→S₂	40—46 {25—29}
			S₂→S₃	79—91 {49—56}
			Lockup ON (S₃)	94—106 {58—66}
		Fully closed (0.1—1.1V)	S₃→S₂	12—18 {7—11}
			S₂→S₁	5—11 {3—7}
		Kickdown	S₃→S₂	87—95 {54—59}
			S₂→S₁	43—49 {27—30}
	HOLD	—	S₃→S₂	95—101 {59—63}
L	NORMAL	Fully open (3.0—4.3V)	L₁→L₂	49—55 {30—34}
		Half throttle (1.7—2.7V)	L₁→L₂	40—46 {25—29}
		Fully closed (0.1—1.1V)	L₂→L₁	5—11 {3—7}
		Kickdown	L₂→L₁	43—49 {27—30}
	HOLD	—	L₂→L₁	45—51 {28—32}

95G20632

Courtesy of Mazda Motors Corp.

Fig. 10: 929 Shift Speed Chart

3-982

AUTOMATIC TRANSMISSIONS
Mazda RA4A-EL, RA4AX-EL & RB4A-EL (Cont.)

ROAD TEST RESULTS

Starts In "S" Or Shifts Directly From "L" To "OD" – Stuck shift solenoid "A". Stuck shift valve "A".

Starts In "OD" – Stuck shift valve "B". Stuck shift solenoid "B".

No Shift – Stuck shift solenoid "A" and/or "B", or stuck shift valve "A" and/or "B".

Incorrect Shift Points – TP sensor out of adjustment. Output speed sensor not operating properly.

Shift Shock Or Slipping Is Felt – Stuck line pressure solenoid. Accumulators not operating properly. TP sensor out of adjustment. Output speed sensor not operating properly. TFT sensor not operating properly. Worn clutches, one-way clutches and/or brakes.

No Engine Braking – Stuck overrunning clutch solenoid. Worn clutches and/or brakes.

No Lock-Up Shift – Stuck lock-up solenoid. Stuck lock-up control valve.

STALL SPEED

CAUTION: Stall and line pressure tests generate high engine and transmission temperatures. DO NOT hold throttle open more than 5 seconds. Allow engine to idle in "P" or "N" for at least one minute between tests.

Preparation – Check all fluid levels and correct if necessary. Warm engine and transmission to operating temperature. Prior to performing stall test, block front and rear wheels and set parking brake.

Connect tachometer to engine. Ensure engine idle speed and ignition timing is correct. See appropriate ON-VEHICLE ADJUSTMENTS article in ENGINE PERFORMANCE in appropriate MITCHELL© manual. Apply foot brake firmly and shift selector to "D" range. Press accelerator pedal to floor and note maximum RPM. Select "S", "R" and "L" ranges and repeat. Compare with STALL SPEED SPECIFICATIONS table.

STALL SPEED SPECIFICATIONS

Application	Stall RPM
1995	
MPV	2300-2500
RX7	3000-3300
929	1950-2250
1996	
MPV	2300-2600

STALL SPEED RESULTS

Above Specification In All Ranges – Insufficient line pressure, worn oil pump. Oil leakage from oil pump, control valve and/or transmission case. Stuck pressure regulator.

Above Specification In "D" & "S" – Forward clutch slipping. Forward one-way clutch slipping. Low one-way clutch slipping.

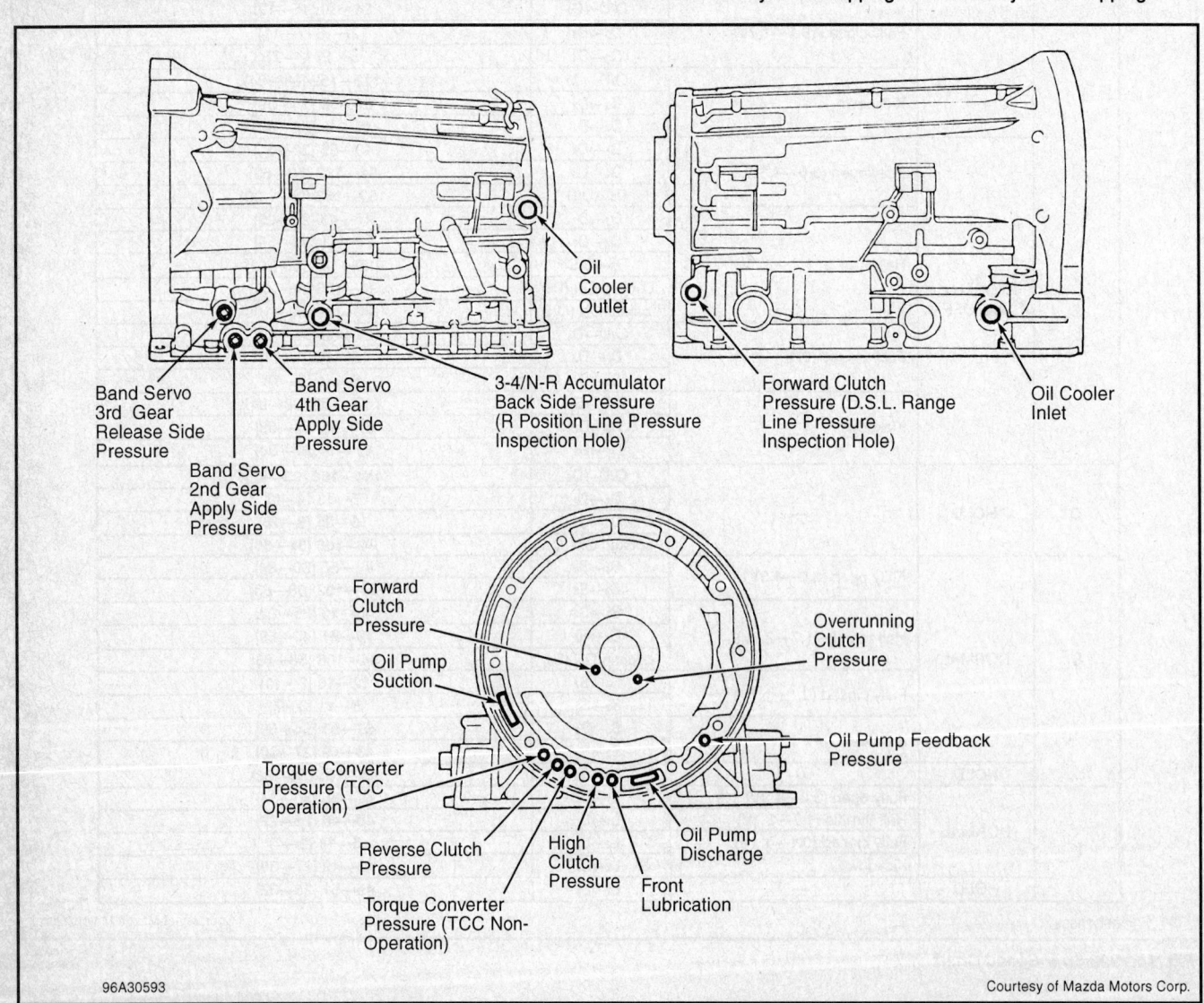

96A30593

Courtesy of Mazda Motors Corp.

Fig. 11: Identifying Transmission Fluid Passages

AUTOMATIC TRANSMISSIONS
Mazda RA4A-EL, RA4AX-EL & RB4A-EL (Cont.)

3-983

Above Specification In "R" Range – Low and reverse brake slipping. Reverse clutch slipping. Perform road test to see if low and/ or reverse brake or reverse clutch is at fault. Results indicate the following:

- Engine braking in "L" range, reverse clutch faulty.
- No engine braking in "L" range, low and/or reverse brake faulty.

Below Specification In All Ranges – Low engine output. One-way clutch in torque converter slipping.

LINE PRESSURE TEST

1) Connect gauges to appropriate line pressure inspection ports. *See Fig. 11.* Connect tachometer to engine. Ensure engine idle speed and ignition timing is correct. See appropriate ON-VEHICLE ADJUSTMENTS article in ENGINE PERFORMANCE in appropriate MITCHELL© manual. Apply foot brake firmly and shift selector to "D" range.

2) Press accelerator pedal to floor and note pressure gauge. Release throttle to read pressure at idle. Select "S", "R" and "L" ranges and repeat. Compare with LINE PRESSURE SPECIFICATIONS table.

LINE PRESSURE SPECIFICATIONS

Application	Range	Idle psi (kPa)	Stall psi (kPa)
MPV (2WD)	"D", "S", "L"	71-77 (490-531)	174-185 (1200-1276)
	"R"	89-95 (614-655)	217-229 (1496-1579)
MPV (4WD) & 929	"D", "S", "L"	63-68 (432-470)	151-162 (1040-1118)
	"R"	87-92 (600-638)	210-222 (1452-1530)
RX7	"D", "S", "L"	72-76 (496-524)	174-184 (1200-1269)
	"R"	90-95 (621-655)	218-228 (1503-1572)

LINE PRESSURE RESULTS

Low Pressure At Idle (All Ranges) – Worn oil pump. Damaged control piston in oil pump. Pressure regulator valve or plug sticking. Damaged pressure regulator valve spring. Fluid leakage between oil strainer and pressure regulator valve.

Low At Idle In "D", "S" Or "L" – Fluid leakage from hydraulic circuit of forward clutch.

Low At Idle In "D" & "S" HOLD Mode – Fluid leakage from hydraulic circuit of band servo 2nd apply side.

Low At Idle In "R" – Fluid leakage from hydraulic circuit of reverse clutch.

Low At Idle In "R" & "L" – Fluid leakage from hydraulic circuit of low and reverse brake.

High At Idle – Throttle sensor out of adjustment. Damaged thermosensor. Line pressure solenoid sticking. Short circuit of line pressure solenoid circuit. Pressure modifier valve sticking. Pressure regulator valve or plug sticking.

Low At Stall Speed – Throttle sensor out of adjustment. Damaged control piston in oil pump. Line pressure solenoid sticking. Short circuit of line pressure solenoid circuit. Pressure regulator valve or plug sticking. Pressure modifier valve sticking. Pilot valve sticking.

ON-VEHICLE SERVICE

See appropriate article in TRANSMISSION SERVICING section.

REMOVAL & INSTALLATION

See appropriate AUTOMATIC TRANSMISSION REMOVAL article in TRANSMISSION SERVICING section.

TORQUE CONVERTER

Inspection – The torque converter is a sealed unit and cannot be disassembled for service. Remove any rust from pilot hub and boss of converter. If hub of converter is scored or if metal particles are found in transmission fluid, replace torque converter.

Cleaning – Flush inside of converter first with solvent and then ATF.

TRANSMISSION DISASSEMBLY

1) Remove torque converter. Remove transfer case on 4WD and adaptor housing. Remove transmission range switch and vehicle speed sensor. Unbolt harness connector bracket (if applicable). Remove oil pan. *See Fig. 12.* Remove output speed sensor. Remove bolts from extension housing. Note location and length of bolts.

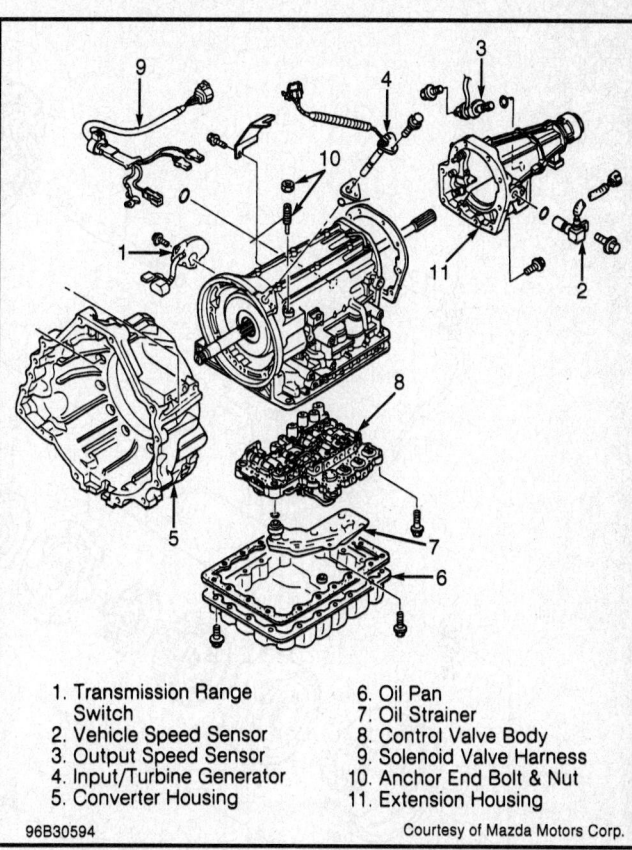

1. Transmission Range Switch
2. Vehicle Speed Sensor
3. Output Speed Sensor
4. Input/Turbine Generator
5. Converter Housing
6. Oil Pan
7. Oil Strainer
8. Control Valve Body
9. Solenoid Valve Harness
10. Anchor End Bolt & Nut
11. Extension Housing

96B30594   Courtesy of Mazda Motors Corp.

Fig. 12: Exploded View Of Transmission External Components & Valve Body (RX7 & 929 Shown, MPV Similar)

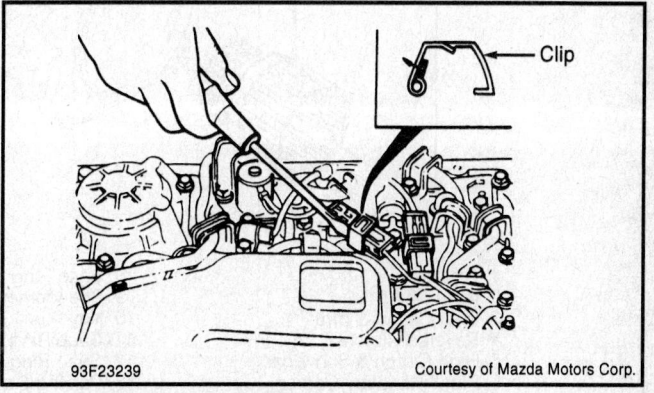

93F23239   Courtesy of Mazda Motors Corp.

Fig. 13: Disconnecting Solenoid Valve & TFT Sensor Harness Connector Clip

3-984

AUTOMATIC TRANSMISSIONS
Mazda RA4A-EL, RA4AX-EL & RB4A-EL (Cont.)

2) Remove input/turbine speed sensor. Remove clip from solenoid valve and TFT sensor harness connector. *See Fig. 13.* Remove TFT sensor. Remove oil strainer and "O" ring. Remove solenoid harness from clips. Remove valve body with oil pipes. Remove accumulator springs. Remove solenoid connector from transmission case. Remove converter housing and "O" rings from transmission case. Remove "O" ring from input shaft.

3) Install 2 slide hammers into oil pump housing and applying even pressure on both slide hammers, remove oil pump. Pull out input shaft while holding reverse drum. Loosen anchor end bolt lock nut and remove anchor end bolt. Do not reuse anchor end bolt. Remove brake band with strut and secure OD band with a wire clip.

4) Remove reverse clutch, high clutch and front sun gear as an assembly. *See Fig. 14.* Remove front planetary carrier, bearings and rear sun gear. Remove snap ring and speedometer drive gear with key or steel ball (as applicable). Remove front snap ring. Remove snap ring from output shaft and remove parking gear with bearing. Pushing output shaft forward, remove front snap ring from output shaft. Remove output shaft.

5) Remove front internal gear with rear planetary carrier, rear internal gear, forward clutch hub and overrunning clutch as an assembly. *See Fig. 14.* Remove forward clutch drum (forward clutch, overrunning clutch, low one-way clutch) from case.

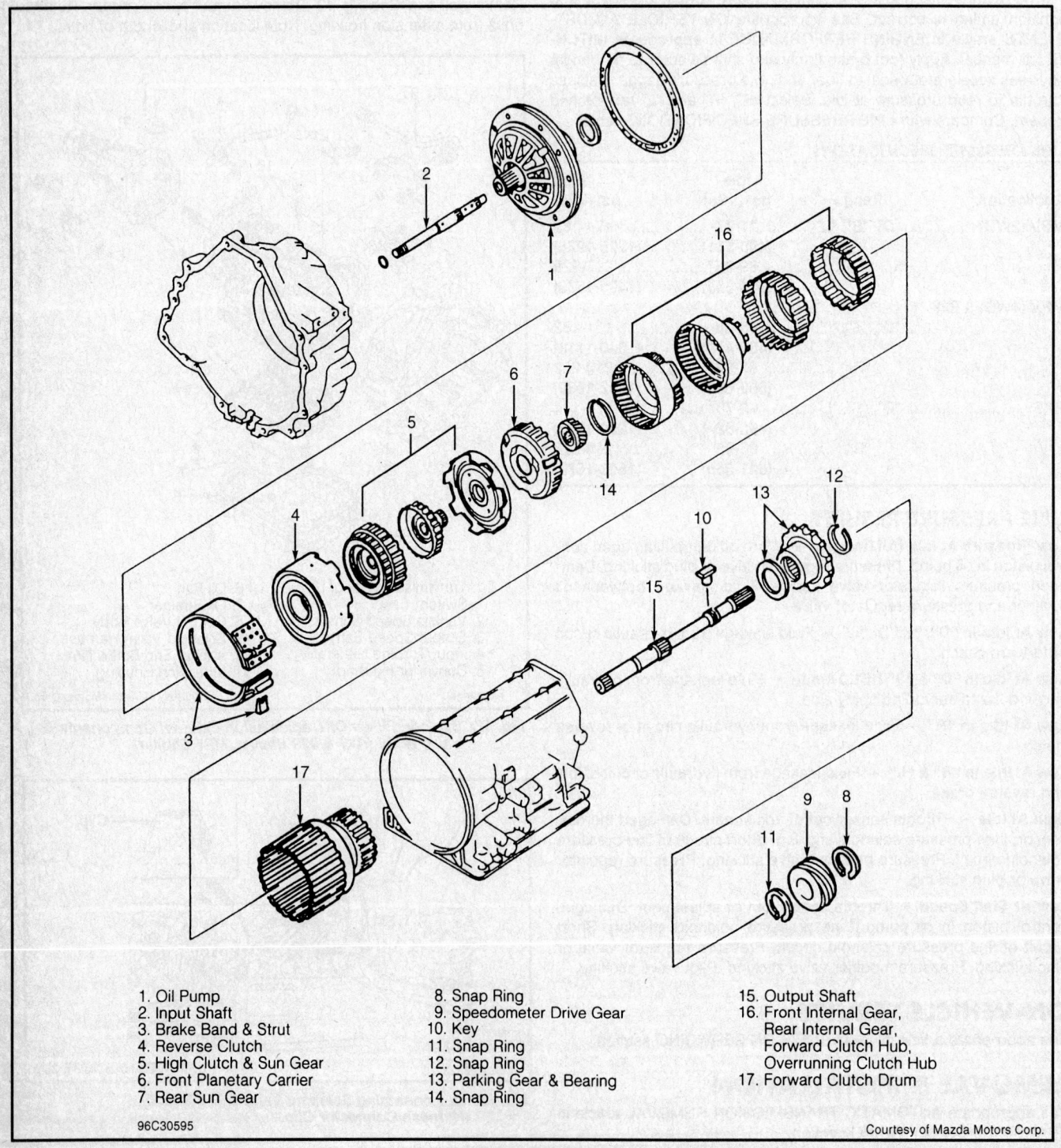

1. Oil Pump	8. Snap Ring	15. Output Shaft
2. Input Shaft	9. Speedometer Drive Gear	16. Front Internal Gear,
3. Brake Band & Strut	10. Key	Rear Internal Gear,
4. Reverse Clutch	11. Snap Ring	Forward Clutch Hub,
5. High Clutch & Sun Gear	12. Snap Ring	Overrunning Clutch Hub
6. Front Planetary Carrier	13. Parking Gear & Bearing	17. Forward Clutch Drum
7. Rear Sun Gear	14. Snap Ring	

96C30595

Courtesy of Mazda Motors Corp.

Fig. 14: Exploded View Of R4A-EL Series Transmission Internal Components

AUTOMATIC TRANSMISSIONS
Mazda RA4A-EL, RA4AX-EL & RB4A-EL (Cont.)

3-985

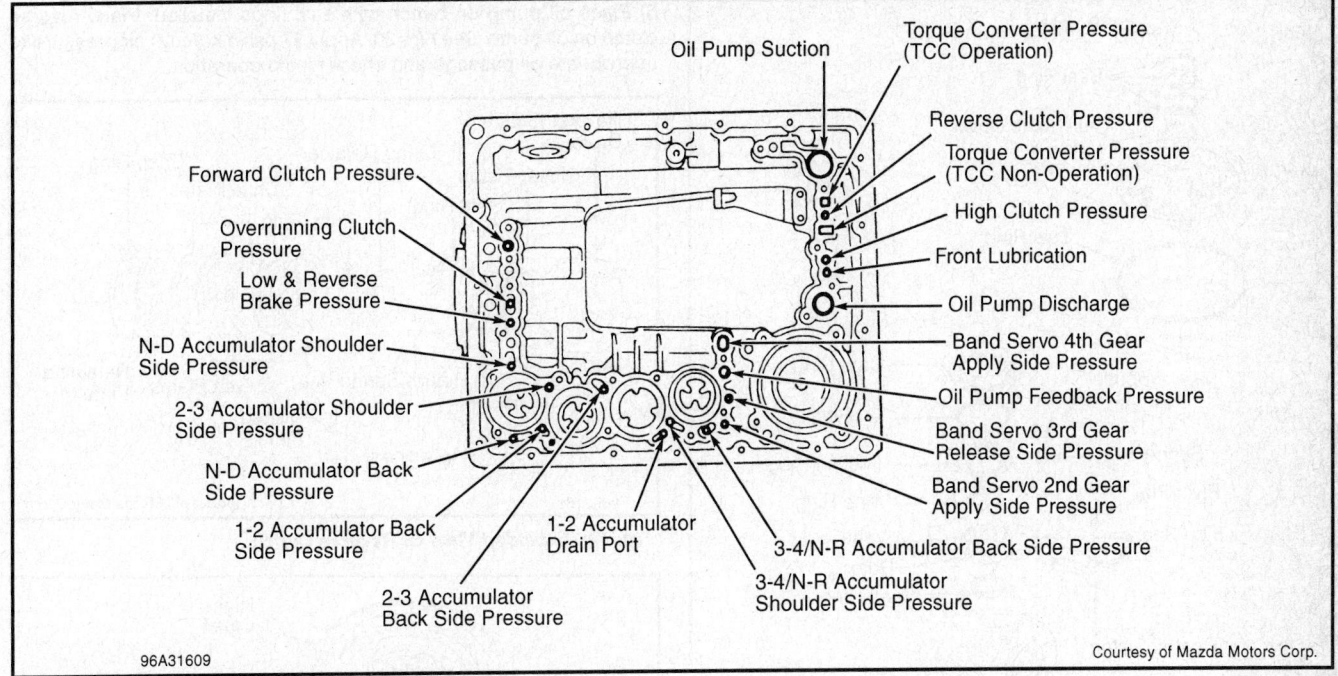

96A31609

Courtesy of Mazda Motors Corp.

Fig. 15: Identifying Transmission Fluid Passages

COMPONENT DISASSEMBLY & REASSEMBLY

ACCUMULATORS

Disassembly – Remove accumulator pistons by applying air pressure through oil passages. See Fig. 15. Remove "O" rings from pistons, clean grooves, check spring free length. See ACCUMULATOR SPRING FREE LENGTH table.

Reassembly – Install "O" rings on accumulator pistons. Place N-D accumulator spring in case and install pistons. See Fig. 16. Match springs to correct pistons.

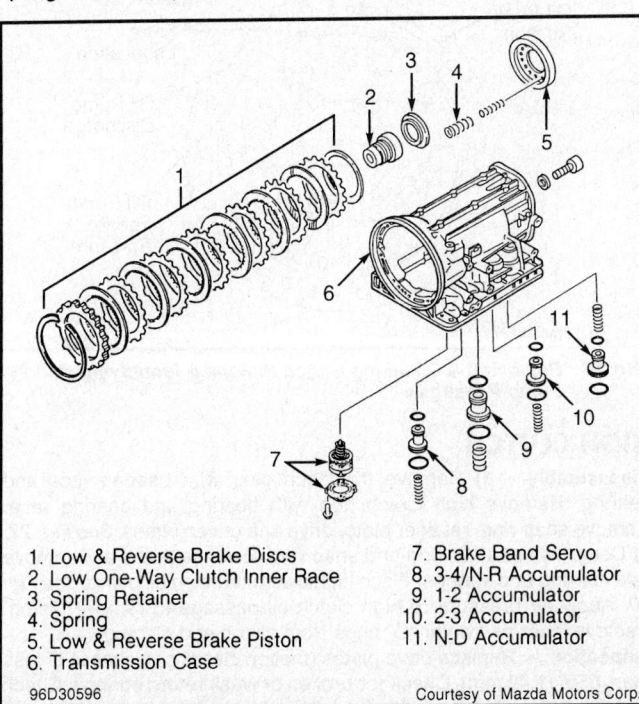

1. Low & Reverse Brake Discs
2. Low One-Way Clutch Inner Race
3. Spring Retainer
4. Spring
5. Low & Reverse Brake Piston
6. Transmission Case
7. Brake Band Servo
8. 3-4/N-R Accumulator
9. 1-2 Accumulator
10. 2-3 Accumulator
11. N-D Accumulator

96D30596

Courtesy of Mazda Motors Corp.

Fig. 16: Exploded View Of Low & Reverse Brake & Accumulators

ACCUMULATOR SPRING FREE LENGTH

Location	Free Length In. (mm)	Outer Diameter In. (mm)
RX7		
N-D	0.709 (18.00)	1.693 (43.00)
1-2	1.154 (29.30)	1.772 (45.00)
2-3	0.767 (19.50)	2.598 (66.00)
3-4/N-R	0.709 (18.00)	1.693 (43.00)
All Others		
N-D	0.709 (18.00)	1.693 (43.00)
1-2	1.154 (29.30)	1.772 (45.00)
2-3	0.787 (20.00)	2.598 (66.00)
3-4/N-R	0.681 (17.30)	2.299 (58.40)

OIL PUMP

Disassembly – Remove oil seal, loosen oil pump cover bolts evenly in sequence. See Fig. 17. Remove oil pump cover, mark rotor and cam ring. Do not use punch to mark parts. Separate rotor, vane ring and vanes. Wrap screwdriver tip with tape. On spring side of cam ring, push cam ring towards spring. Remove pivot pin. Holding spring, remove screwdriver and cam ring.

Inspection – **1)** Install NEW seal ring and ensure clearance between seal ring and ring groove is .004-.010" (.10-.25 mm). If not within specification, replace oil pump as an assembly.

2) Install cam ring vanes, rotor and control piston. DO NOT install friction ring, "O" ring, control piston side seals, or cam ring spring. Measure clearance between oil pump surface to cam ring, rotor, vanes and control piston in 4 places around oil pump. See Fig. 18. See OIL PUMP SPECIFICATIONS table. Cam ring spring free length should be 1.57" (39.8 mm).

Reassembly – Install oil seal in oil pump housing. To reassemble, reverse disassembly procedure. Tighten mounting bolts evenly in criss-cross pattern to specification. See TORQUE SPECIFICATIONS.

OIL PUMP SPECIFICATIONS

Component	Clearance – In. (mm)
Cam Ring	.0004-.0009 (.010-.024)
Rotor, Vane & Control Piston	.0012-.0017 (.030-.044)

3-986

AUTOMATIC TRANSMISSIONS
Mazda RA4A-EL, RA4AX-EL & RB4A-EL (Cont.)

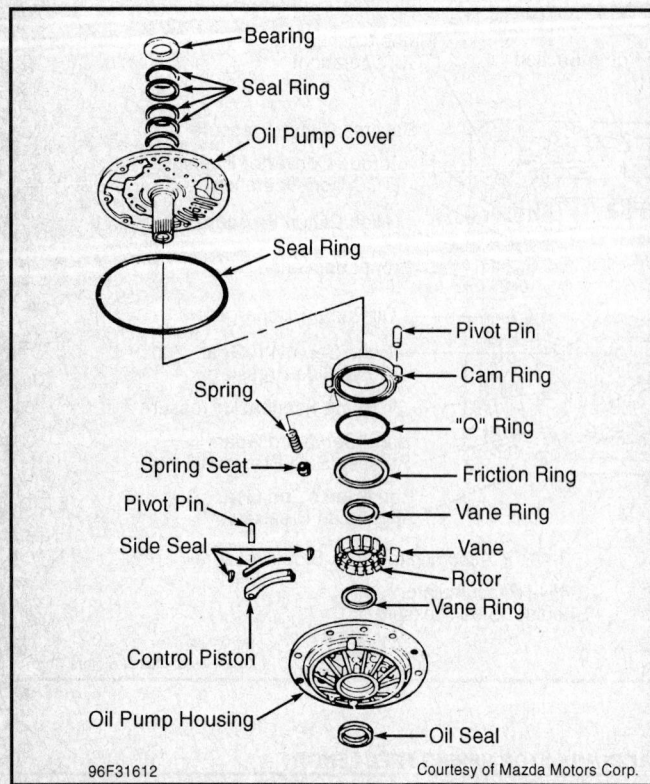

Fig. 17: Exploded View Of Oil Pump

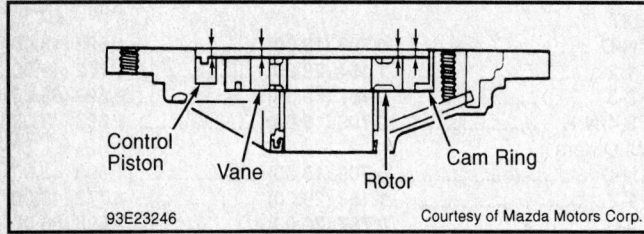

Fig. 18: Checking Oil Pump Clearance

REVERSE CLUTCH

Disassembly – 1) Remove snap ring, retainer plate, drive plates, driven plates and dish plate. *See Fig. 19.* Compress spring retainer and remove snap ring. Remove spring retainer and springs.

2) Place reverse clutch hub on oil pump hub support, apply air pressure to reverse clutch pressure oil passage to remove reverse clutch piston. *See Fig. 20.* Remove and discard "O" ring and seal on piston.

Inspection – Replace drive plates (friction discs) is thickness iF less than .071" (1.8 mm). Check for broken or weak return springs. Check spring and retainer assembly for separation or deformation. Measure return spring free length. Length should be .78" (19.7 mm). Ensure check ball in clutch piston allows air to flow in one direction only.

Reassembly – 1) Install NEW "D" ring into piston groove. Install NEW seal ring on piston. Ensure lip of seal faces away from spring side. Soak NEW friction discs in ATF prior to assembly.

2) Lubricate seal surface in reverse drum and install reverse clutch. Install return springs and spring retainer. Compress spring retainer and install snap ring.

3) Install dished plate. *See Fig. 19.* Install drive and driven plates, retaining plate and snap ring. Measure clearance with feeler gauge between snap ring and retaining plate. Clearance should be .020-.047" (.50-1.20 mm). *See Fig. 21.*

4) Adjust clearance by installing selective retaining plate. Retaining plates range in thickness from .185" (4.60 mm) to .228" (5.80 mm) in .008" (.20 mm) increments.

5) Place oil pump on bench with seal rings installed. Place reverse clutch on oil pump. *See Fig. 20.* Apply 57 psi (4 kg/cm²) air pressure to appropriate oil passage and check clutch operation.

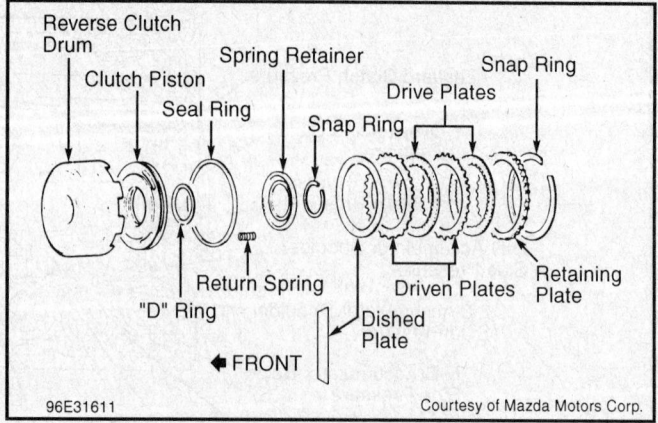

Fig. 19: Exploded View Of Reverse Clutch

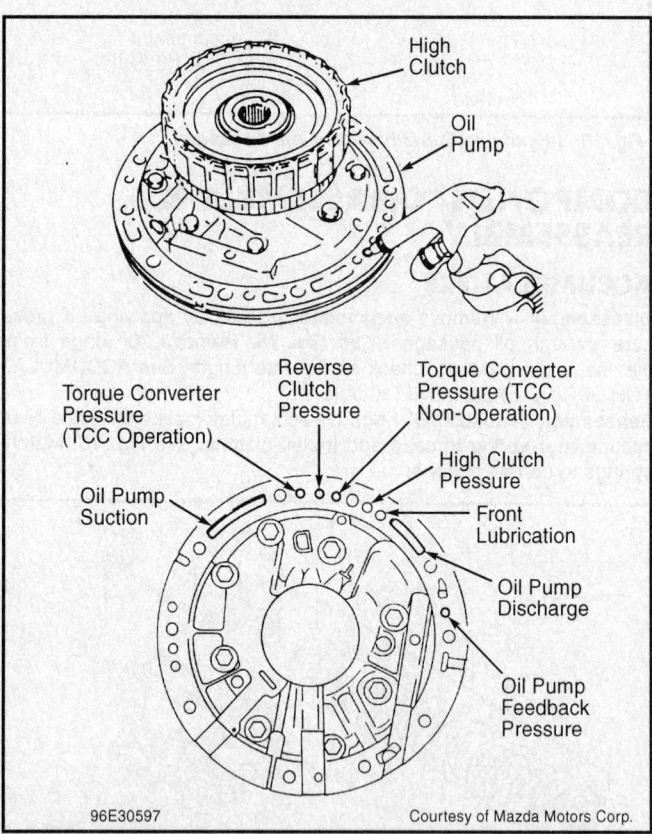

Fig. 20: Removing & Checking Clutch Pistons & Identifying Oil Pump Passages

HIGH CLUTCH

Disassembly – 1) Remove front sun gear with bearing race and bearing. Remove high clutch hub with bearing and bearing race. Remove snap ring, retainer plate, drive and driven plates. *See Fig. 22.*

2) Compress retainer ring and snap ring. Release press and remove retainer ring and springs. Place high clutch drum on oil pump. *See Fig. 20.* Apply air pressure to high clutch oil passage to remove piston. Remove inner and outer "D" rings from piston and discard.

Inspection – Replace drive plates (friction discs) is thickness iF less than .055" (1.40 mm). Check for broken or weak return springs. Check spring and retainer assembly for separation or deformation. Measure return spring free length. Length should be .87" (22.1 mm). Ensure check ball in clutch piston allows air to flow in one direction only.

AUTOMATIC TRANSMISSIONS
Mazda RA4A-EL, RA4AX-EL & RB4A-EL (Cont.)

3-987

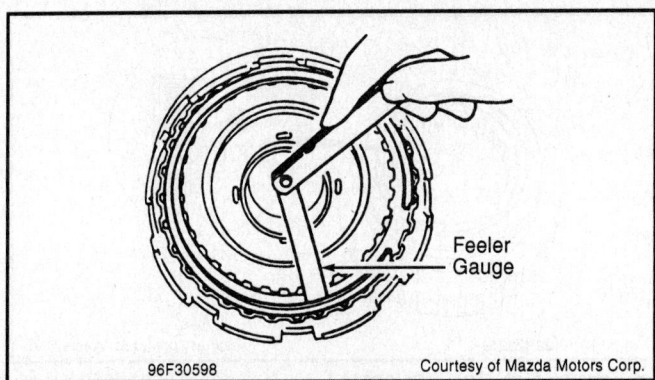

Fig. 21: *Measure Reverse Clutch Clearance*

Reassembly – **1)** Install NEW "D" rings on piston and install piston in drum. Install return springs and spring retainer. Compress spring retainer and install snap ring. DO NOT align snap ring gap with spring retainer stop.

2) Install drive and driven clutches into high clutch drum. *See Fig. 22.* Install retaining plate and snap ring. Measure clearance between snap ring and retaining plate. *See Fig. 23.* Clearance should be .071-.118" (1.80-3.00 mm). *See Fig. 21.*

3) Adjust clearance by installing selective retaining plate. Retaining plates range in thickness from .118" (3.00 mm) to .189" (4.80 mm) in .008" (.20 mm) increments.

4) Place high clutch on oil pump. Apply 57 psi (4 kg/cm²) air pressure to appropriate oil passage and check clutch operation. *See Fig. 20.*

5) Apply petroleum jelly to front and rear bearing races and install in high clutch hub. Apply petroleum jelly to needle bearing and install in high clutch hub. *See Fig. 22.*

6) Install high clutch hub into high clutch by turning to align clutch driven plates. Apply petroleum jelly on needle bearing and bearing race for front sun gear. Install needle bearing inside front sun gear. Install bearing race over front sun gear. Install front sun gear on high clutch hub.

Fig. 23: *Measuring High Clutch Clearance*

BRAKE BAND SERVO

Disassembly – **1)** Remove 4 cap screws from band servo retainer and remove cover. See Fig. 24. Apply air pressure to cover to remove piston.

2) Apply air pressure in 2nd gear servo oil passage to remove band servo piston and retainer. See Fig. 15. Remove retaining ring from piston stem. Remove spring retainer and return spring "C".

3) Separate servo piston retainer from band servo piston. Remove larger retaining ring from piston stem. Remove piston stem from servo cushion retainer and band servo piston from servo cushion retainer. See Fig. 24. Remove and discard all "O" rings and "D" rings.

Inspection – Inspect all parts, and repair or replace as necessary. Check spring free length. See RETURN SPRING FREE LENGTH table.

Reassembly – To reassemble, reverse disassembly procedure. Lubricate NEW "O" rings and "D" rings with ATF. Install pistons by applying even pressure on perimeter of piston. Torque OD band servo retainer bolts to specification. See TORQUE SPECIFICATIONS. Check operation by applying air pressure to oil holes. See Fig. 11.

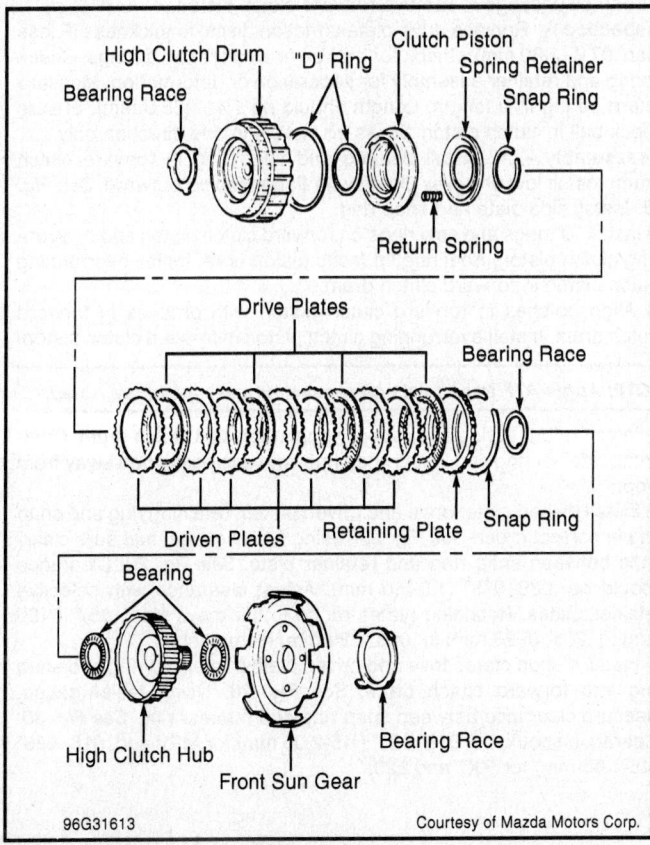

Fig. 22: *Exploded View Of High Clutch*

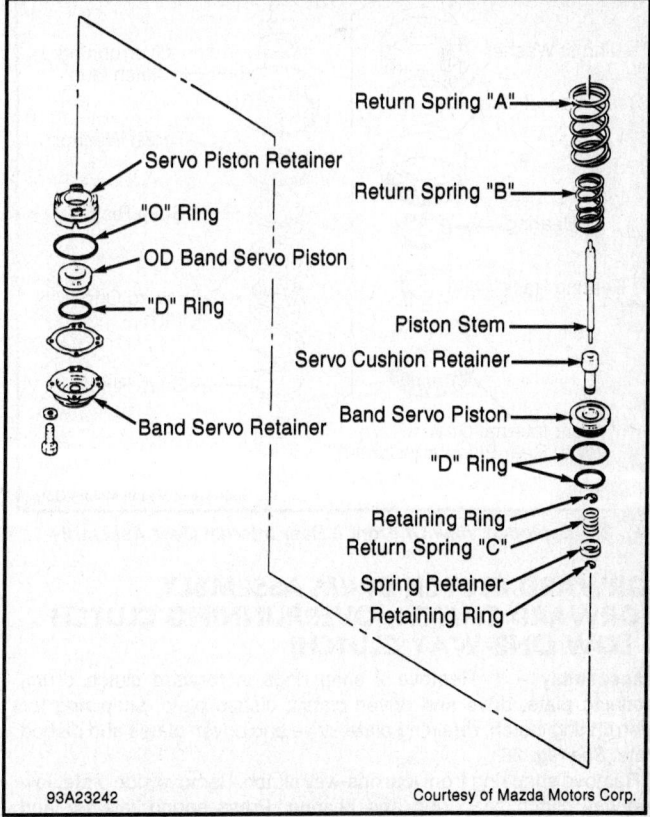

Fig. 24: *Exploded View Of Brake Band Servo*

3-988

AUTOMATIC TRANSMISSIONS
Mazda RA4A-EL, RA4AX-EL & RB4A-EL (Cont.)

RETURN SPRING FREE LENGTH

Application	Outer Diameter In. (mm)	Free Length In. (mm)
A	1.587 (40.30)	2.118 (53.80)
B	1.350 (34.30)	1.795 (45.60)
C	1.087 (27.60)	1.169 (29.70)

FRONT & REAR INTERNAL GEARS, FORWARD CLUTCH HUB & OVERRUNNING CLUTCH HUB

Disassembly – Remove front internal gear, bearing race, bearing, rear internal gear, thrust washer, bearing, overrunning clutch hub, thrust washer, snap ring and forward one-way clutch assembly. See Fig. 25.

Inspection – Inspect gear teeth for damage, wear or cracks, and rotation of pinion gears. Inspect bearing races and bearings for smooth rotation, damage, scoring and scratches.

Reassembly – 1) Install one-way clutch in forward clutch hub with arrow pointing forward. Install one-way clutch snap ring. See Fig. 26. Apply petroleum jelly to thrust washer and place on rear internal gear.

2) Install rear internal gear on forward clutch hub and one-way clutch assembly by turning it clockwise. Check one-way clutch rotation. Holding forward clutch hub, rear internal gear should rotate clockwise only and lock counterclockwise. See Fig. 27.

3) Apply petroleum jelly to bearing and install in rear internal gear. Apply petroleum jelly to thrust washer and set it in overrunning clutch hub, ensure tabs of thrust washer seat in holes in forward clutch hub. Install overrunning clutch hub on rear internal gear.

4) Apply petroleum jelly on bearing and set it on overrunning clutch hub. Apply petroleum jelly to bearing race and place on front internal gear pinion carrier side.

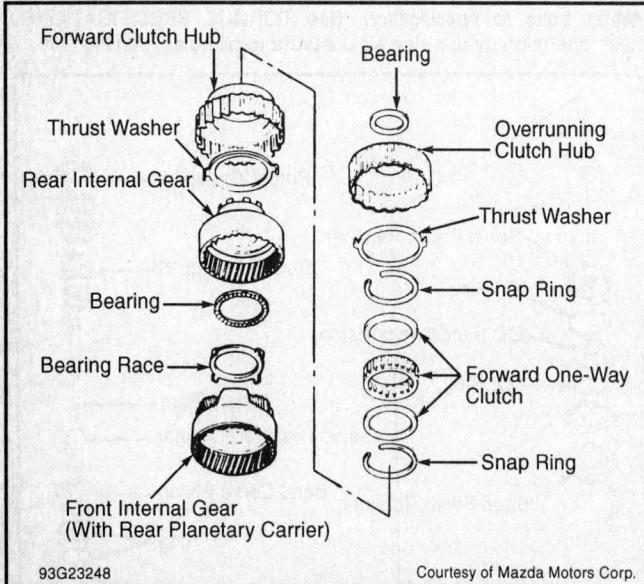

Fig. 25: Exploded View Of Front & Rear Internal Gear Assembly

Forward Clutch Hub
Bearing
Thrust Washer
Rear Internal Gear
Overrunning Clutch Hub
Thrust Washer
Bearing
Snap Ring
Bearing Race
Forward One-Way Clutch
Snap Ring
Front Internal Gear (With Rear Planetary Carrier)
93G23248   Courtesy of Mazda Motors Corp.

FORWARD CLUTCH DRUM ASSEMBLY (FORWARD CLUTCH, OVERRUNNING CLUTCH & LOW ONE-WAY CLUTCH)

Disassembly – 1) Remove 2 snap rings in forward clutch drum, retaining plate, drive and driven plates, dished plate, snap ring for overrunning clutch, retaining plate, drive and driven plates and dished plate. See Fig. 28.

2) Remove snap ring from low one-way clutch. Remove side plate, low one-way clutch snap ring and bearing. Press spring retainer and remove snap ring.

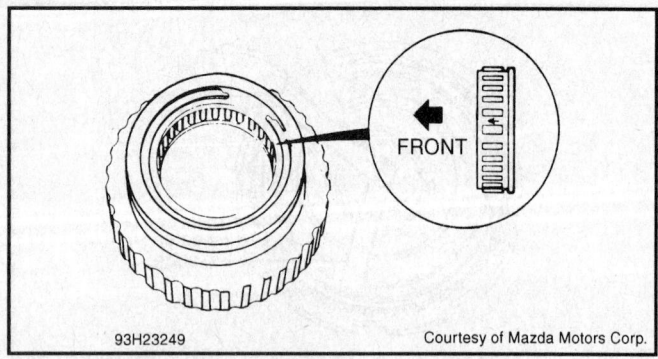

93H23249   Courtesy of Mazda Motors Corp.

Fig. 26: Installing One-Way Clutch

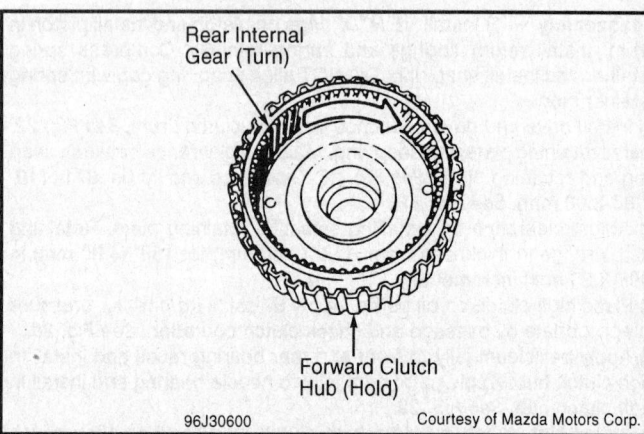

Rear Internal Gear (Turn)

Forward Clutch Hub (Hold)

96J30600   Courtesy of Mazda Motors Corp.

Fig. 27: Checking Forward One-Way Clutch Operation

3) Place forward clutch drum in transmission case. Apply air to oil passage to remove overrunning clutch piston. See Fig. 15. Apply air pressure to oil passage to remove forward clutch piston.

Inspection – Replace drive plates (friction discs) is thickness iF less than .071" (1.80 mm). Check for broken or weak return springs. Check spring and retainer assembly for separation or deformation. Measure return spring free length. Length should be 1.41" (35.8 mm). Ensure check ball in clutch piston allows air to flow in one direction only.

Reassembly – 1) Install bearing and snap ring in forward clutch drum. Install low one-way clutch with flange facing outward. See Fig. 28. Install side plate and snap ring.

2) Install "D" rings and seal rings on forward clutch piston and overrunning clutch piston. Seal ring lip faces piston bore. Install overrunning clutch piston in forward clutch drum.

3) Align notches in forward clutch piston with grooves in forward clutch drum. Install overrunning clutch piston in forward clutch piston.

NOTE: Apply ATF to all parts on reassembly except where noted.

4) Install return spring and retainer ring in forward clutch drum. Compress retainer ring and install snap ring with gap positioned away from stop.

5) Install dished plate, drive and driven plates, retaining ring and snap ring in correct order. See Fig. 28. Using feeler gauge, measure clearance between snap ring and retainer plate. See Fig. 29. Clearance should be .039-.079" (1.0-2.0 mm). Adjust clearance with selective retainer plates. Retaining plates range in thickness from .157" (4.00 mm) to .205" (5.20 mm) in .008" (.20 mm) increments.

6) Install dished plate, drive and driven plates, retaining ring and snap ring into forward clutch drum. See Fig. 28. Using feeler gauge, measure clearance between snap ring and retainer ring. See Fig. 30. Clearance should be .018-.081" (.45-2.05 mm) for MPV and .018-.073" (.45-1.85 mm) for RX7 and 929.

AUTOMATIC TRANSMISSIONS
Mazda RA4A-EL, RA4AX-EL & RB4A-EL (Cont.)

3-989

7) Adjust clearance with selective retainer plates. On MPV, retaining plates range in thickness from .157" (4.00 mm) to .205" (5.20 mm) in .008" (.20 mm) increments. On RX7 and 929, retaining plates range in thickness from .315" (8.00 mm) to .362" (9.20 mm) in .008" (.20 mm) increments.

8) Install forward clutch drum in transmission case. Apply 57 psi (4 kg/cm²) air pressure to forward and overrunning clutch oil passages. *See Fig. 15.* Check low one-way clutch operation. Forward clutch drum should turn clockwise only and lock counterclockwise. *See Fig. 31.*

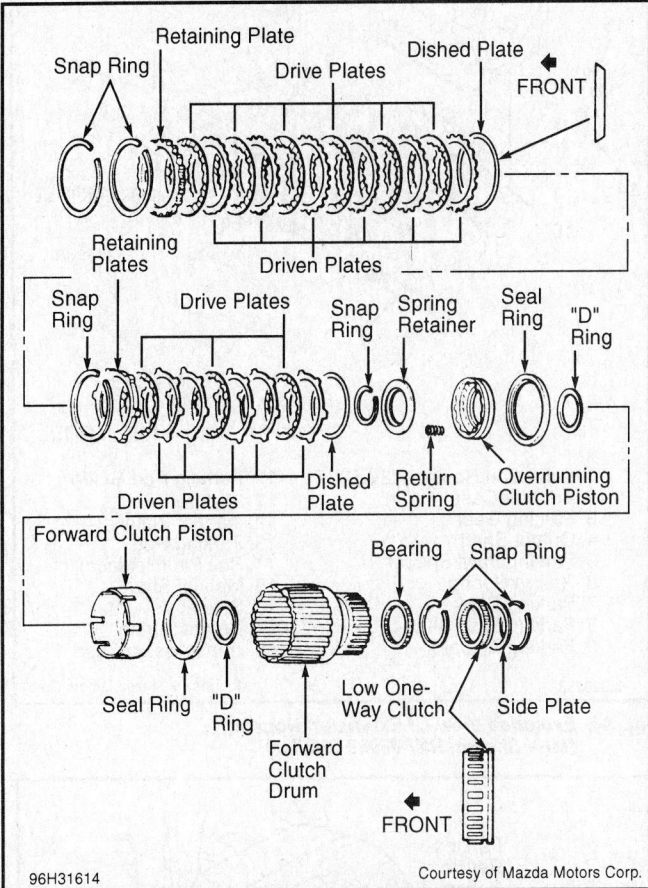

last 2 bolts. Remove retainer and springs. Apply air to oil passage to remove low and reverse brake piston. *See Fig. 15.*

Inspection – 1) Check for broken or weak return springs. Check spring and retainer assembly for separation or deformation. Replace drive plates (friction discs) is thickness if less than .071" (1.80 mm). Measure spring free length. Length should be .933" (23.70 mm) on MPV and .878" (22.30 mm) on RX7 and 929.

2) Inspect low and reverse piston check ball. Ensure air flows from spring-seat side of piston. Air should not flow in reverse direction. Inspect bearings for damage and roughness. Replace as necessary.

Reassembly – 1) Install "D" ring to inside channel of low and reverse piston. Install seal ring to outer channel of low and reverse piston with lip of seal facing away from spring side.

2) Install low and reverse piston in case. Apply petroleum jelly to seal rings. Install seal rings to low and reverse piston.

3) Position case with piston facing upward and set return springs in proper location. Install spring retainer with low one-way clutch inner race centered in spring retainer.

4) Ensure spring retainer remains over springs and is centered on low one-way clutch inner race. Install and tighten bolts in crisscross pattern to specification. See TORQUE SPECIFICATIONS.

5) Install drive and driven plates, retainer and snap ring. *See Fig. 32.* Using feeler gauge, measure clearance between snap ring and retainer plate. *See Fig. 33.*

6) Clearance should be .028-.091" (.70-2.30 mm) for MPV, .031-.102" (.80-2.60 mm) for RX7 or .031-.094" (.80-2.40 mm) for 929.

7) Adjust clearance with selective retainer plates. On RX7, retaining plates range in thickness from .244" (6.20 mm) to .315" (8.00 mm) in .008" (.20 mm) increments. On MPV and 929, retaining plates range in thickness from .354" (9.00 mm) to .394" (10.00 mm) in .008" (.20 mm) increments. Apply 57 psi (4 kg/cm²) air pressure to oil passage and check low and reverse clutch operation. *See Fig. 15.*

Fig. 28: Exploded View Of Forward Clutch Drum Assembly

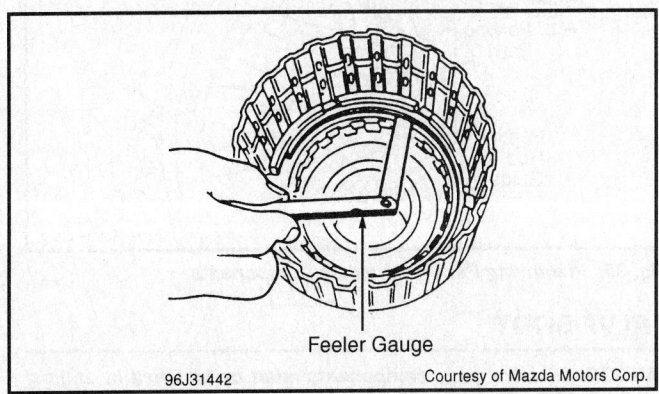

Fig. 29: Measuring Overrunning Clutch Clearance

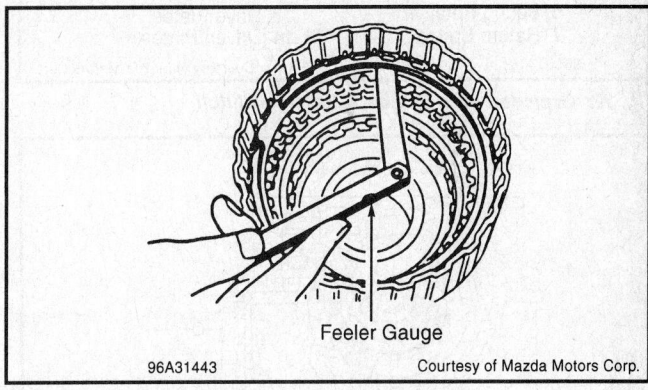

Fig. 30: Measure Forward Clutch Clearance

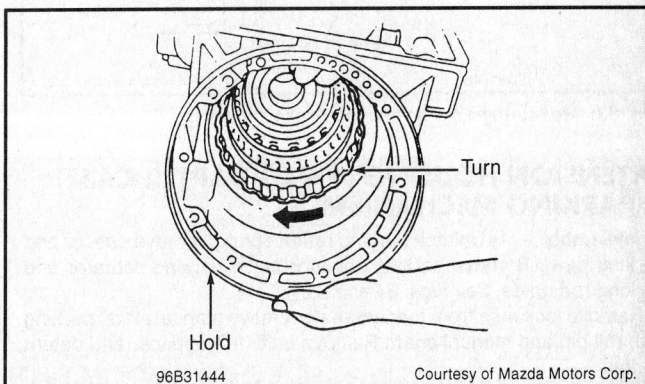

Fig. 31: Checking Low One-Way Clutch Operation

LOW & REVERSE BRAKE

Disassembly – 1) Remove snap ring, retainer plate, drive and driven plates. *See Fig. 32.*

2) Using an Allen wrench, remove 4 bolts holding one-way clutch inner race to rear case. Hold inner race and return springs while removing

AUTOMATIC TRANSMISSIONS
Mazda RA4A-EL, RA4AX-EL & RB4A-EL (Cont.)

3-990

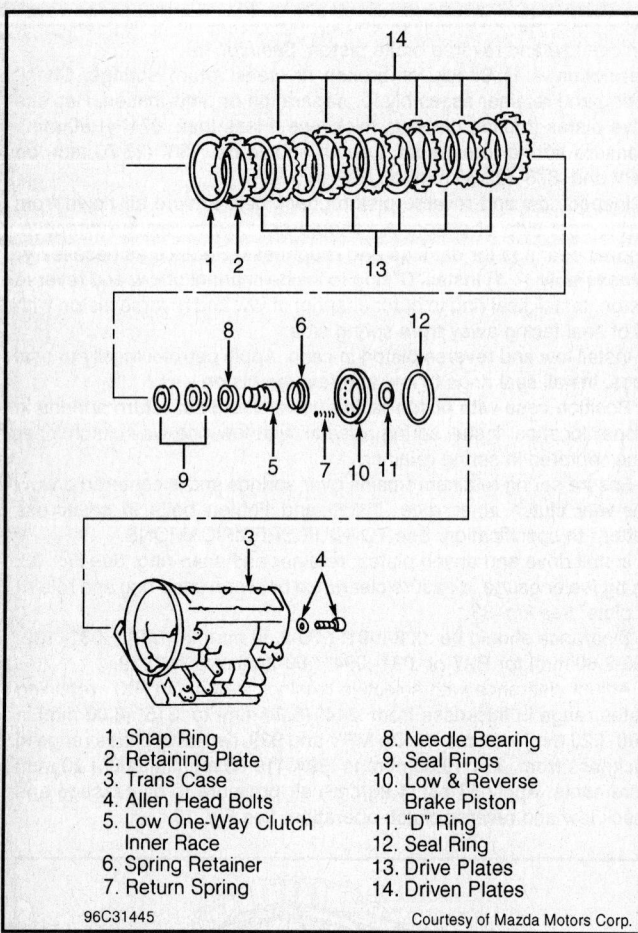

1. Snap Ring
2. Retaining Plate
3. Trans Case
4. Allen Head Bolts
5. Low One-Way Clutch Inner Race
6. Spring Retainer
7. Return Spring
8. Needle Bearing
9. Seal Rings
10. Low & Reverse Brake Piston
11. "D" Ring
12. Seal Ring
13. Drive Plates
14. Driven Plates

96C31445   Courtesy of Mazda Motors Corp.

Fig. 32: Exploded View Of Low & Reverse Clutch

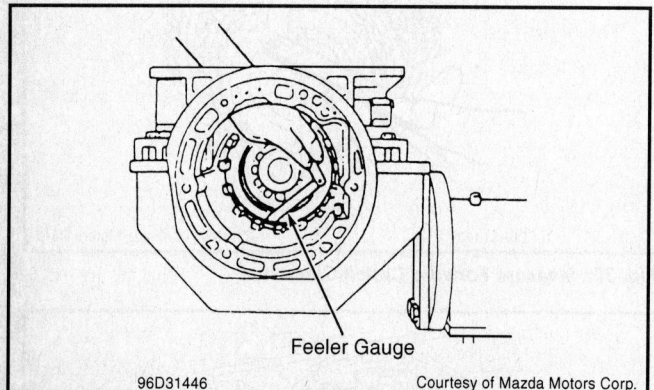

Feeler Gauge

96D31446   Courtesy of Mazda Motors Corp.

Fig. 33: Measuring Low & Reverse Brake Clearance

EXTENSION HOUSING (4WD ADAPTER CASE) & PARKING MECHANISM

Disassembly – **1)** Unlatch parking return spring, remove spacer and parking pawl. Remove parking actuator bolts, parking actuator and parking rod guide. *See Figs. 34 and 35.*

2) Remove lock nuts from manual shaft, remove manual plate, parking rod, roll pin and manual shaft. Remove bolts from spacer and detent spring.

3) Remove oil seals from transmission case for manual shaft and from extension housing or adaptor case.

Inspection – Check parking gear for teeth damage or wear. Check output shaft splines for wear or damage. Check detent spring for fracture or wear. Check transmission inner bearing for damage or rough rotation.

Reassembly – Install output shaft oil seal. Wrap tape around manual shaft threads and install manual shaft. Seat manual shaft seal into case and remove tape from manual shaft. Install roll pin to an installed height of .20" (5.0 mm). To reassemble, reverse disassembly procedure.

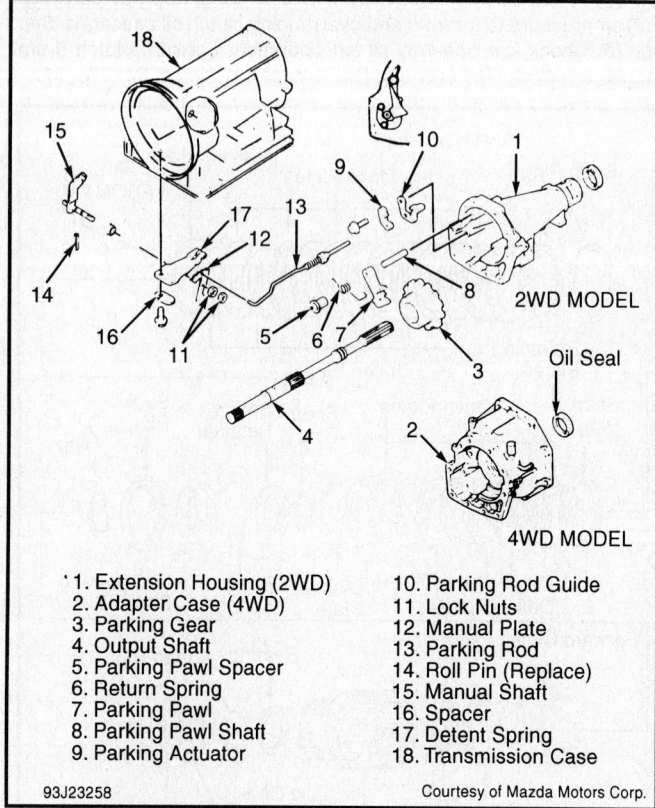

2WD MODEL

Oil Seal

4WD MODEL

1. Extension Housing (2WD)
2. Adapter Case (4WD)
3. Parking Gear
4. Output Shaft
5. Parking Pawl Spacer
6. Return Spring
7. Parking Pawl
8. Parking Pawl Shaft
9. Parking Actuator
10. Parking Rod Guide
11. Lock Nuts
12. Manual Plate
13. Parking Rod
14. Roll Pin (Replace)
15. Manual Shaft
16. Spacer
17. Detent Spring
18. Transmission Case

93J23258   Courtesy of Mazda Motors Corp.

Fig. 34: Exploded View Of Extension Housing (MPV Shown, RX7 & 929 Similar)

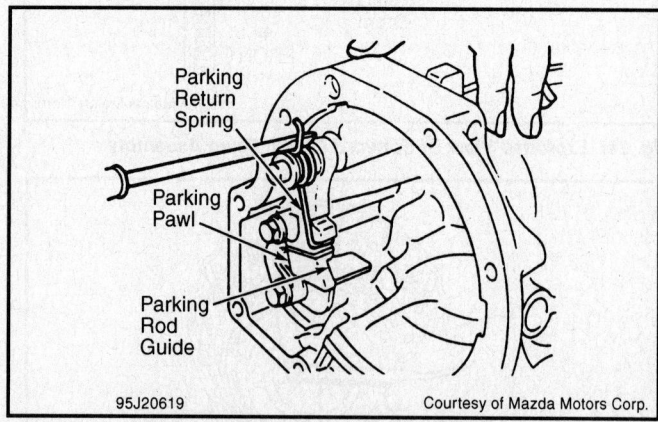

Parking Return Spring

Parking Pawl

Parking Rod Guide

95J20619   Courtesy of Mazda Motors Corp.

Fig. 35: Identifying Park Mechanism Components

VALVE BODY

CAUTION: All valve body components must be installed in original location. Lay all components in sequence during removal for reassembly reference. Clean all parts with solvent and dry with compressed air. Clean all holes and passages and blow dry with compressed air. DO NOT wipe parts with shop towel.

Disassembly – Remove all solenoids. Remove retaining bolts and nuts, brackets, lower valve body, steel balls, upper gasket, separator plate, lower gasket, orifice check valve with spring, pilot filter and manual valve. *See Figs. 36 and 37.* Disassemble lower and upper valve body. *See Figs. 38-41.*

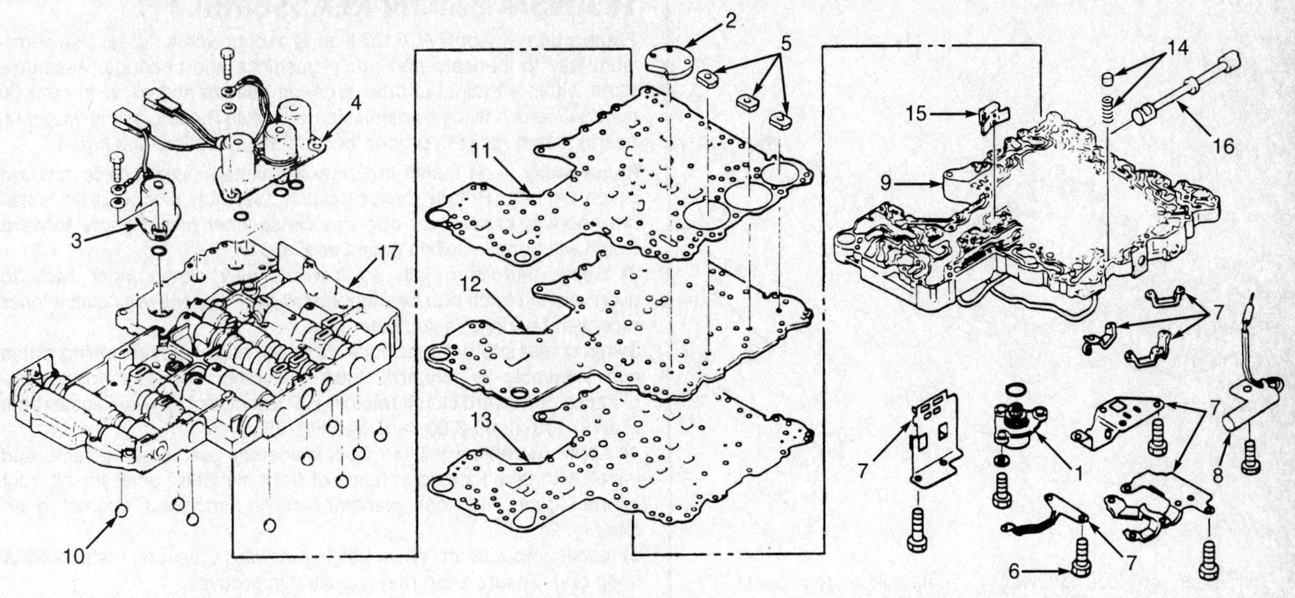

AUTOMATIC TRANSMISSIONS
Mazda RA4A-EL, RA4AX-EL & RB4A-EL (Cont.)

3-991

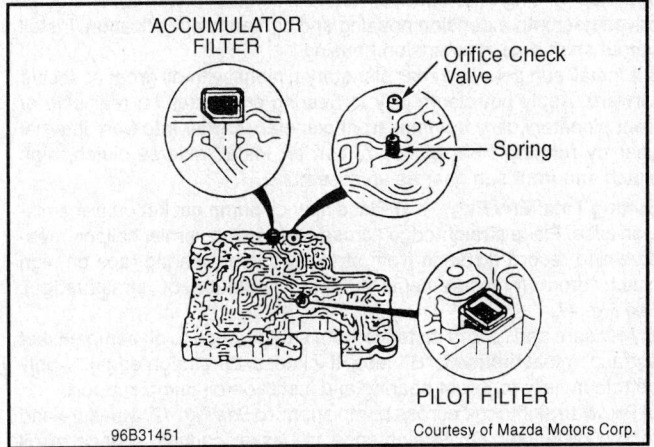

1. Lock-Up Solenoid
2. Side Plate
3. Line Pressure Solenoid
4. Overrunning Clutch Solenoid & Shift Solenoid "A"
5. Support Plate
6. Retaining Bolts & Nuts
7. Brackets
8. TFT Sensor
9. Lower Valve Body
10. Steel Ball
11. Upper Gasket
12. Separate Plate
13. Lower Gasket
14. Orifice Check Valve & Spring
15. Pilot Filter
16. Manual Valve
17. Upper Valve Body

96A31450

Courtesy of Mazda Motors Corp.

Fig. 36: Exploded View Of Valve Body

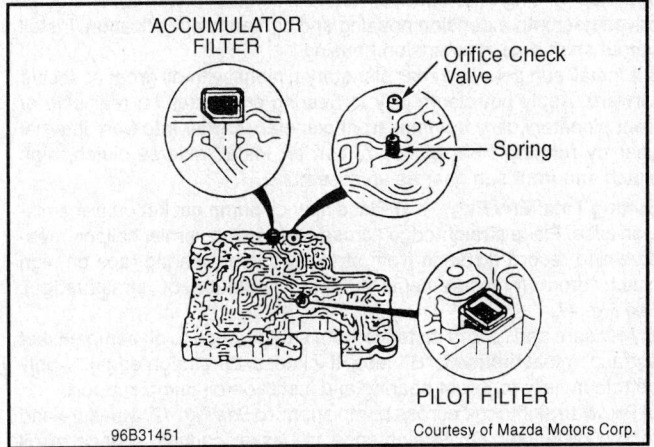

96B31451

Courtesy of Mazda Motors Corp.

Fig. 37: Identifying Lower Valve Body Filters

Inspection – Inspect all parts for scratches and free movement in bores; valves should slide out on their own weight. Check spring free length. See VALVE BODY SPRING SPECIFICATIONS table. Replace parts as necessary. Replace all "O" rings on solenoid valves.

Reassembly – To reassemble, reverse disassembly procedure. Ensure all parts are installed correctly. See Figs. 36-41. Ensure check balls are installed in correct location. During assembly of valve body, ensure bolts are installed in correct location. See Fig. 43. Tighten bolts to specification. See TORQUE SPECIFICATIONS.

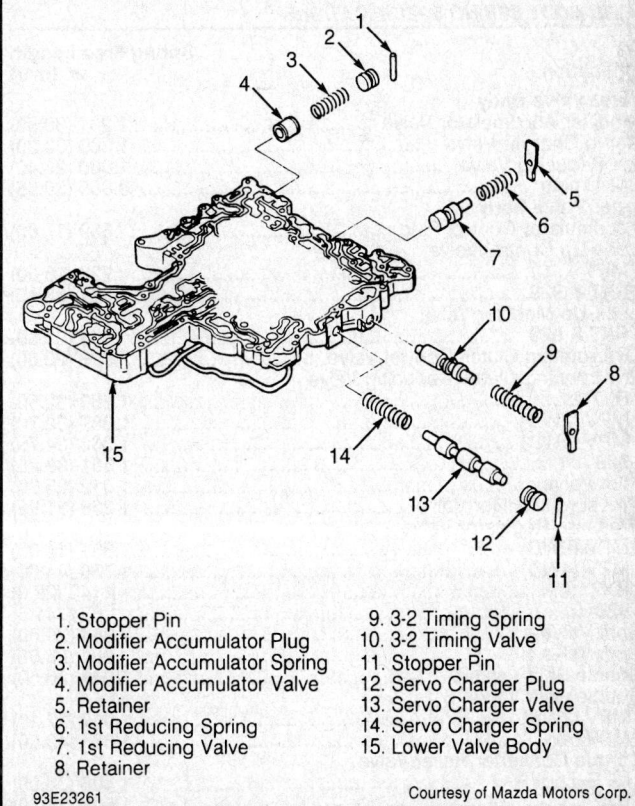

1. Stopper Pin
2. Modifier Accumulator Plug
3. Modifier Accumulator Spring
4. Modifier Accumulator Valve
5. Retainer
6. 1st Reducing Spring
7. 1st Reducing Valve
8. Retainer
9. 3-2 Timing Spring
10. 3-2 Timing Valve
11. Stopper Pin
12. Servo Charger Plug
13. Servo Charger Valve
14. Servo Charger Spring
15. Lower Valve Body

93E23261

Courtesy of Mazda Motors Corp.

Fig. 38: Exploded View Of Lower Valve Body (MPV)

3-992

AUTOMATIC TRANSMISSIONS
Mazda RA4A-EL, RA4AX-EL & RB4A-EL (Cont.)

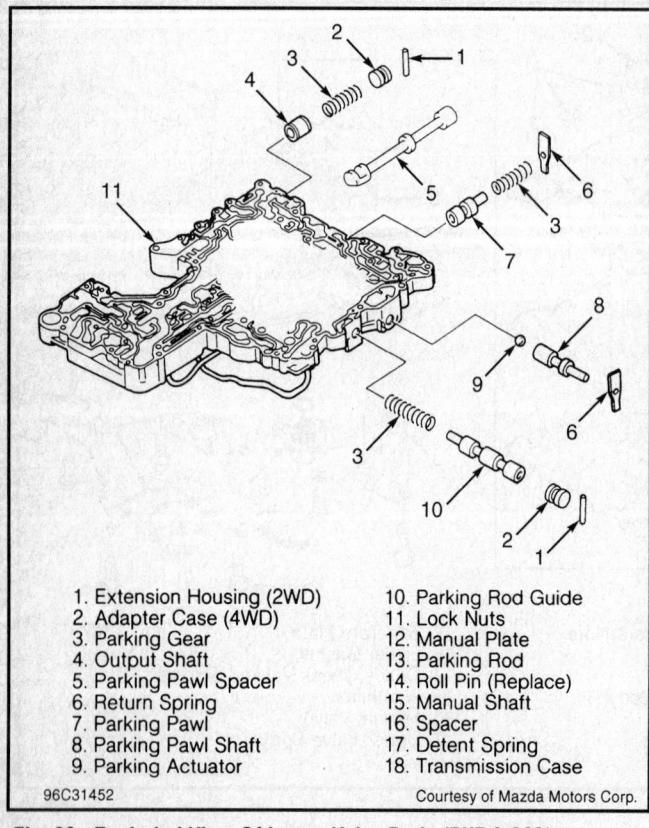

1. Extension Housing (2WD)
2. Adapter Case (4WD)
3. Parking Gear
4. Output Shaft
5. Parking Pawl Spacer
6. Return Spring
7. Parking Pawl
8. Parking Pawl Shaft
9. Parking Actuator
10. Parking Rod Guide
11. Lock Nuts
12. Manual Plate
13. Parking Rod
14. Roll Pin (Replace)
15. Manual Shaft
16. Spacer
17. Detent Spring
18. Transmission Case

96C31452   Courtesy of Mazda Motors Corp.

Fig. 39: Exploded View Of Lower Valve Body (RX7 & 929)

VALVE BODY SPRING SPECIFICATIONS

Application	Spring Free Length In. (mm)
Lower Valve Body	
Modifier Accumulator Valve	1.201 (30.50)
Servo Charger Valve	1.300 (33.20)
1st Reducing Valve	1.000 (25.40)
3-2 Timing	0.809 (20.55)
Upper Valve Body	
Accumulator Control Plug	.669 (17.00)
Lock-Up Control Valve	
MPV	.728 (18.50)
RX7 & 929	.921 (23.40)
Lock-Up Modifier Valve	
RX7 & 929	.846 (21.50)
Overrunning Clutch Control Valve	.929 (23.60)
Overrunning Clutch Reducing Valve	
RX7	1.280 (32.50)
MPV (2WD)	1.287 (32.70)
MPV (4WD)	1.366 (34.70)
929	1.531 (38.90)
Pilot Valve	1.012 (25.70)
Pressure Modifier Valve	1.258 (31.95)
Pressure Regulator Valve	
MPV (2WD)	.551 (14.00)
MPV (4WD)	1.730 (44.00)
RX7	1.142 (29.0)
929	1.634 (41.5)
Shift Valve A	.984 (25.00)
Shift Valve B	.984 (25.00)
Shuttle Shift Valve D	1.043 (26.50)
Shuttle Shift Valve "S"	
MPV (2WD)	1.067 (27.10)
MPV (4WD)	1.693 (43.00)
Torque Converter Relief Valve	
All Except RX7	1.496 (38.00)
RX7	1.508 (38.30)
4-2 Relay Valve	1.146 (29.10)
4-2 Sequence Valve	1.146 (29.10)

TRANSMISSION REASSEMBLY

Preparation – Apply ATF to all parts except where noted. Use petroleum jelly to lubricate and retain bushings and bearings. Assemble parts within 10 minutes after applying sealant and allow to cure 30 minutes before filling transmission with fluid. Locate thrust washers, bearings and races in proper location and direction. See Fig. 44.

Reassembly – 1) Install low one-way clutch inner race to forward clutch bearing. Rotate forward clutch assembly clockwise to install low one-way clutch over one-way clutch inner race. Ensure forward clutch will turn clockwise only. See Fig. 31.

2) Apply petroleum jelly to low one-way clutch inner race to overrunning clutch hub bearing. Install over low one-way clutch inner race with bearings facing inner race.

3) Install rear internal gear, forward clutch hub and overrunning clutch hub assembly to forward clutch assembly. See Fig. 15. Ensure distance of forward clutch retaining plate to top of forward clutch drum is .079-.118" (2.00-3.00 mm). See Fig. 45.

4) Apply petroleum jelly to front planetary gear bearing race, and install with tabs located in holes of front planetary gear. Install front internal gear and rear planetary carrier into rear internal gear. See Fig. 25.

5) Install output shaft. While holding forward pressure, install a NEW snap ring. Ensure snap ring is seated in groove.

6) Apply petroleum jelly to rear internal gear bearing. Install bearing, with Black side facing rearward, in rear internal gear with rollers facing out.

7) Apply petroleum jelly on parking gear to case bearing. Install parking gear and snap ring. Install front snap ring and speedometer drive gear with key or steel ball (as applicable). Install snap ring.

8) Install extension housing with gasket. Ensure bolt location is correct. See Fig. 46. Tighten bolts to specification. See TORQUE SPECIFICATIONS.

9) Install "O" ring onto speedometer driven gear, install speedometer driven gear into extension housing and tighten to specification. Install output shaft seal in extension housing.

10) Install sun gear into rear planetary pinions with oil grooves facing forward. Apply petroleum jelly to bearing and install on rear side of front planetary carrier. Install front planetary carrier into front internal gear by rotating front planetary carrier. Install reverse clutch, high clutch and front sun gear as an assembly.

Setting Total End Play – 1) Place new oil pump gasket on transmission case. Place straightedge across case. Using vernier caliper, measure and record distance from straightedge to bearing race on high clutch drum (measurement "A" less thickness of straightedge). See Fig. 47.

2) Measure and record distance from straightedge to oil pump gasket surface (measurement "B" less thickness of straightedge). Apply petroleum jelly to thrust bearing and install on oil pump support.

3) Place straightedge across pump support. See Fig. 47. Measure and record distance from straightedge to gasket contact surface of oil pump (measurement "C" less thickness of straightedge).

4) Calculate total end play ("T1") using following equation:
"T1" = "A" - "B" - "C" - .0039" (.1 mm).

5) Total end play should be .010-.022" (.25-.50 mm). If total end play is not within specification, select different high clutch bearing race. Races range in thickness from .031" (.8 mm) to .079" (2.0 mm) in increments of .008" (.20 mm).

Reverse Clutch End Play – 1) Install Black thrust washer on reverse clutch. Place straightedge across case. Using vernier caliper, measure and record distance from straightedge to bearing race on reverse clutch drum (measurement "E" less thickness of straightedge). See Fig. 48.

2) Measure and record distance from straightedge to oil pump gasket surface (measurement "B" less thickness of straightedge).

3) With straightedge across reverse clutch thrust washer contact surface on oil pump, measure and record distance from straightedge to oil pump gasket surface (measurement "F" less thickness of straightedge).

AUTOMATIC TRANSMISSIONS
Mazda RA4A-EL, RA4AX-EL & RB4A-EL (Cont.)

3-993

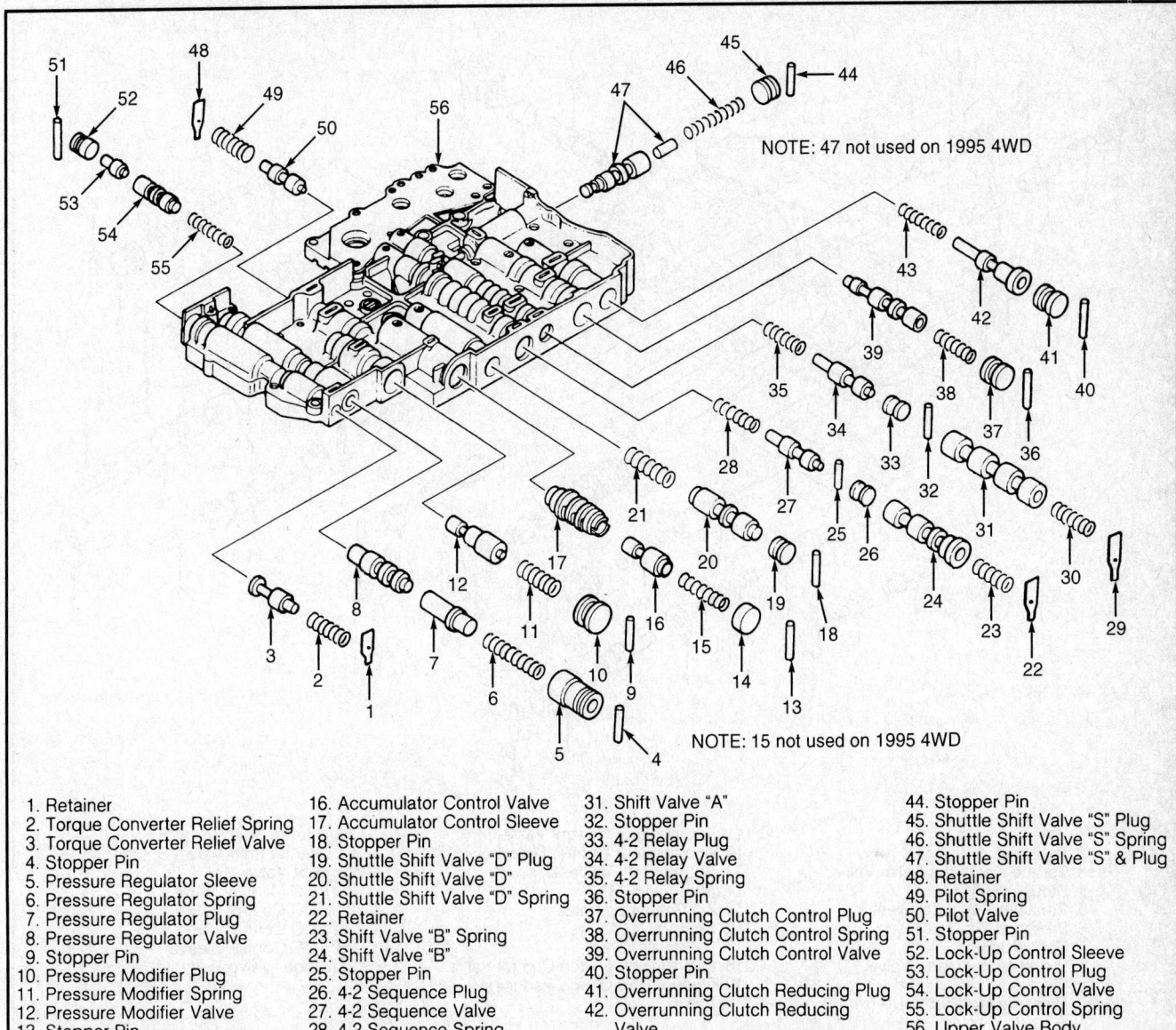

NOTE: 47 not used on 1995 4WD

NOTE: 15 not used on 1995 4WD

1. Retainer
2. Torque Converter Relief Spring
3. Torque Converter Relief Valve
4. Stopper Pin
5. Pressure Regulator Sleeve
6. Pressure Regulator Spring
7. Pressure Regulator Plug
8. Pressure Regulator Valve
9. Stopper Pin
10. Pressure Modifier Plug
11. Pressure Modifier Spring
12. Pressure Modifier Valve
13. Stopper Pin
14. Accumulator Control Plug
15. Accumulator Control Spring

16. Accumulator Control Valve
17. Accumulator Control Sleeve
18. Stopper Pin
19. Shuttle Shift Valve "D" Plug
20. Shuttle Shift Valve "D"
21. Shuttle Shift Valve "D" Spring
22. Retainer
23. Shift Valve "B" Spring
24. Shift Valve "B"
25. Stopper Pin
26. 4-2 Sequence Plug
27. 4-2 Sequence Valve
28. 4-2 Sequence Spring
29. Retainer
30. Shift Valve "A" Spring

31. Shift Valve "A"
32. Stopper Pin
33. 4-2 Relay Plug
34. 4-2 Relay Valve
35. 4-2 Relay Spring
36. Stopper Pin
37. Overrunning Clutch Control Plug
38. Overrunning Clutch Control Spring
39. Overrunning Clutch Control Valve
40. Stopper Pin
41. Overrunning Clutch Reducing Plug
42. Overrunning Clutch Reducing Valve
43. Overrunning Clutch Reducing Spring

44. Stopper Pin
45. Shuttle Shift Valve "S" Plug
46. Shuttle Shift Valve "S" Spring
47. Shuttle Shift Valve "S" & Plug
48. Retainer
49. Pilot Spring
50. Pilot Valve
51. Stopper Pin
52. Lock-Up Control Sleeve
53. Lock-Up Control Plug
54. Lock-Up Control Valve
55. Lock-Up Control Spring
56. Upper Valve Body

96G31449

Courtesy of Mazda Motors Corp.

Fig. 40: Exploded View Of Upper Valve Body (MPV)

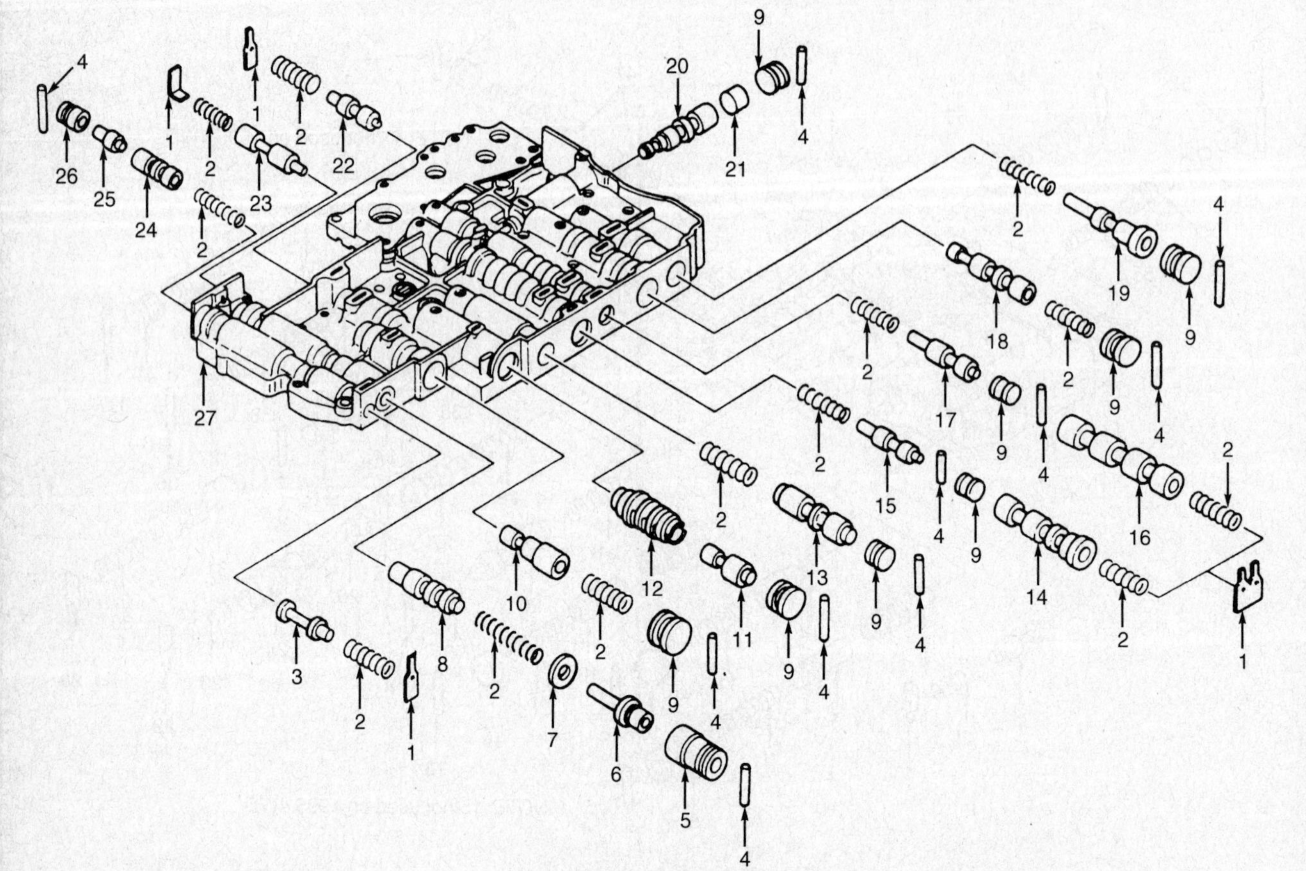

3-994

AUTOMATIC TRANSMISSIONS
Mazda RA4A-EL, RA4AX-EL & RB4A-EL (Cont.)

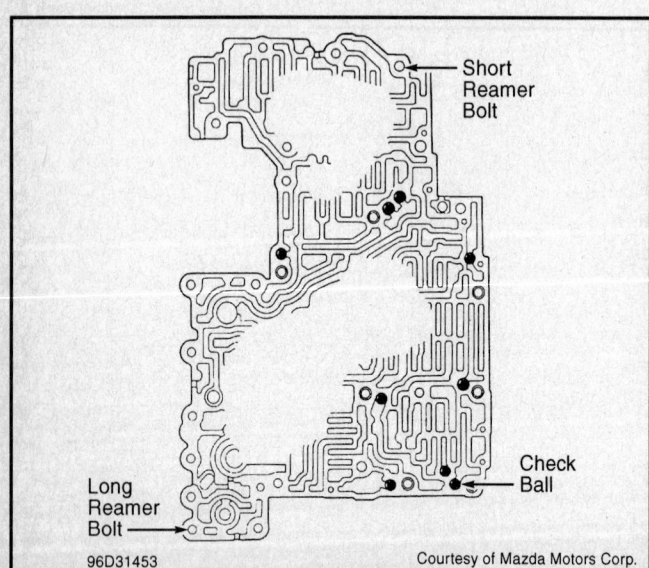

1. Retainer
2. Spring
3. Torque Converter Relief Valve
4. Stopper Pin
5. Pressure Regulator Sleeve
6. Pressure Regulator Plug
7. Spring Seat
8. Pressure Regulator Valve
9. Plug
10. Pressure Modifier Valve
11. Accumulator Control Valve
12. Accumulator Control Sleeve
13. Shuttle Shift Valve "D"
14. Shift Valve "B"
15. 4-2 Sequence Tralve
16. Shift Valve "A"
17. 4-2 Relay Valve
18. Overrunning Clutch Control Valve
19. Overrunning Clutch Reducing Valve
20. Shuttle Shift Valve "S"
21. Shuttle Shift Valve "S" Plug
22. Pilot Valve
23. TCC Modifier Valve
24. TCC Control Valve
25. TCC Control Plug
26. TCC Control Sleeve
27. Upper Valve Body

96F31448

Courtesy of Mazda Motors Corp.

Fig. 41: Exploded View Of Upper Valve Body (RX7 & 929)

96D31453   Courtesy of Mazda Motors Corp.

Fig. 42: Locating Lower Valve Body Check Balls

4) Calculate reverse clutch end play ("T2") using following equation: "T2" = "E" - "B" - "F" - .0039" (.1 mm).

5) Reverse clutch end play should be .022-.035" (.55-.90 mm). If reverse end play is not within specification, select different reverse clutch thrust washer. Thrust washers range in thickness from .028" (.7 mm) to .075" (1.9 mm) in increments of .008" (.20 mm).

Final Assembly – 1) Install brake band with strut and NEW anchor end bolt. Install input shaft. Apply petroleum jelly to large oil pump "O" ring and install on oil pump. Install oil pump.

2) Measure from transmission case to oil pump surface. *See Fig. 49.* Ensure height is about .004" (1.0 mm). Install "O" ring on input shaft.

3) Install "O" rings on converter housing and apply a small amount of sealer around "O" rings and bolt holes on both sides of torque converter housing. Install torque converter housing. Tighten bolts in a crisscross pattern to specification. See TORQUE SPECIFICATIONS.

4) Install input/turbine speed sensor. Tighten brake band anchor end bolt to 35-52 INCH lbs. (3.9-5.9 N.m) and back off 2 1/2 turns. Install lock nut and tighten to specification.

5) Install NEW "O" ring and install vehicle speed sensor. Install output speed sensor. Install "O" ring and install solenoid connector to transmission case.

AUTOMATIC TRANSMISSIONS
Mazda RA4A-EL, RA4AX-EL & RB4A-EL (Cont.)

3-995

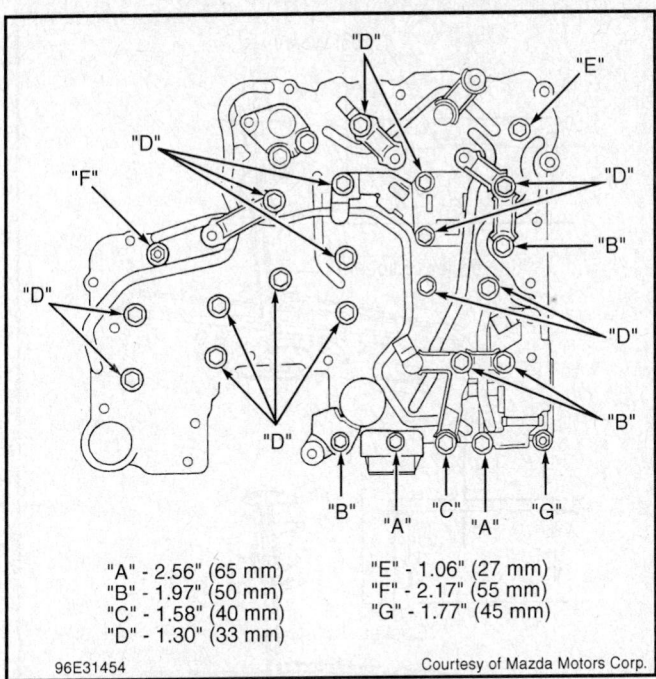

"A" - 2.56" (65 mm)
"B" - 1.97" (50 mm)
"C" - 1.58" (40 mm)
"D" - 1.30" (33 mm)

"E" - 1.06" (27 mm)
"F" - 2.17" (55 mm)
"G" - 1.77" (45 mm)

96E31454   Courtesy of Mazda Motors Corp.

Fig. 43: Identifying Valve Body Bolt Location

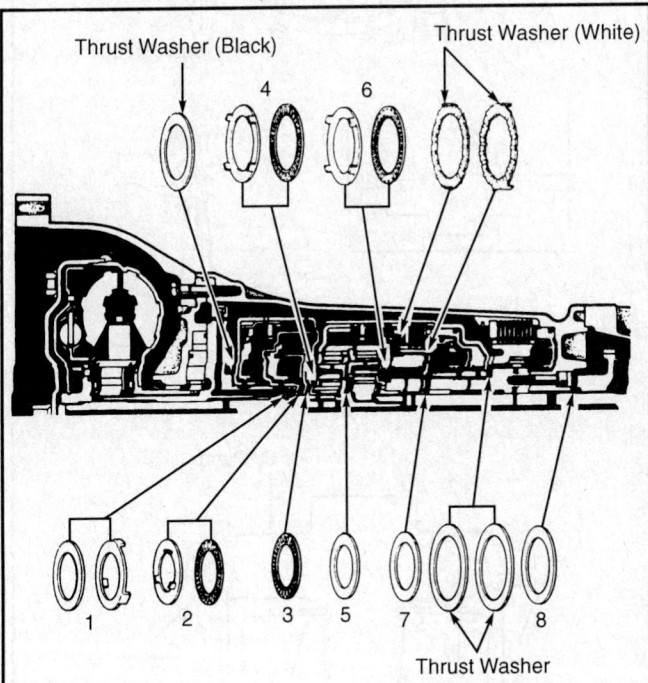

	1 In. (mm)	2 In. (mm)	3&5 In. (mm)	4&6 In. (mm)
Bearing	1.850 (47.00)	2.087 (53.00)	2.087 (53.00)	3.071 (78.00)
Race	1.713 (43.50)	2.028 (51.50)	–	2.953 (75.00)
	7 In. (mm)	8 In. (mm)		
Bearing	2.323 (59.00)	2.520 (64.00)		
Race	–	–		

95C20620   Courtesy of Mazda Motors Corp.

Fig. 44: Locating Thrust Washers, Bearings & Races

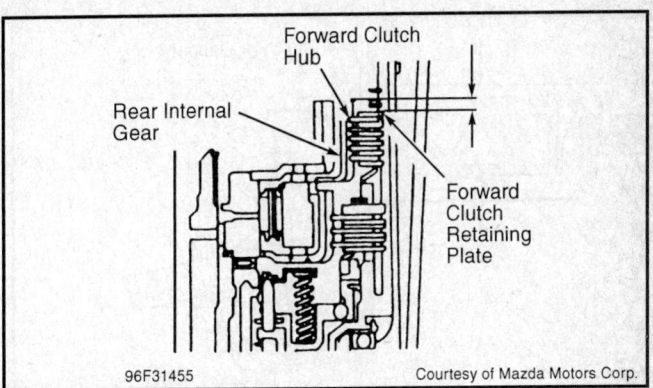

96F31455   Courtesy of Mazda Motors Corp.

Fig. 45: Checking Forward Clutch Hub Height

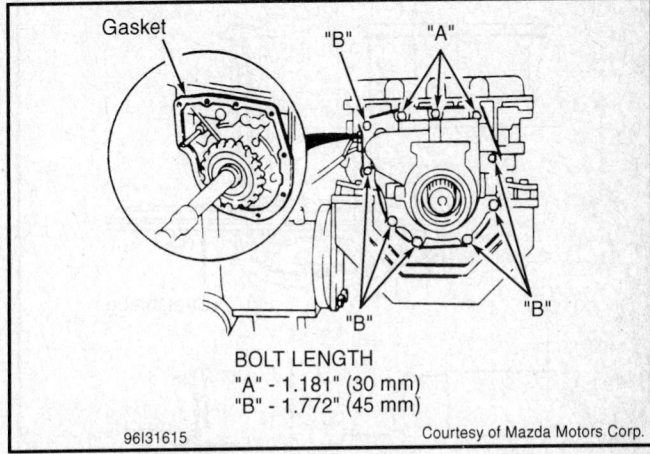

BOLT LENGTH
"A" - 1.181" (30 mm)
"B" - 1.772" (45 mm)

96I31615   Courtesy of Mazda Motors Corp.

Fig. 46: Locating Extension Housing Bolts

6) Install accumulator springs in correct location. *See Fig. 16.* See ACCUMULATORS under COMPONENT DISASSEMBLY & REASSEMBLY for spring dimensions. Install valve body assembly. Ensure manual valve engages manual shaft. Install retaining bolts. Ensure correct position of bolts. *See Fig 50.* Tighten bolts to specification. See TORQUE SPECIFICATIONS.

7) Install new "O" ring on oil strainer and install oil strainer into transmission. Install TFT sensor. *See Fig. 51.* Tighten bolts to specification. Mount solenoid wire harness with clips.

8) Place magnet in oil pan. Install oil pan gasket, oil pan and oil pan bolts. Install harness connector bracket (if applicable). Install transmission range switch over manual shaft. Move manual shaft fully rearward. Move manual shaft 2 notches forward ("N" position).

9) Insert a .157" (4.00 mm) pin through holes of manual shaft lever and transmission range switch for alignment. *See Fig. 52.* Tighten switch bolts to specification. See TORQUE SPECIFICATIONS. Remove alignment pin.

10) Set torque converter with hub up and fill with ATF. Install torque converter on input shaft. Ensure torque converter engages notches in oil pump. Measure depth of torque converter housing to threaded boss on torque converter. Depth should be 1.161" (29.50 mm). *See Fig. 53* If not, recheck torque converter installation.

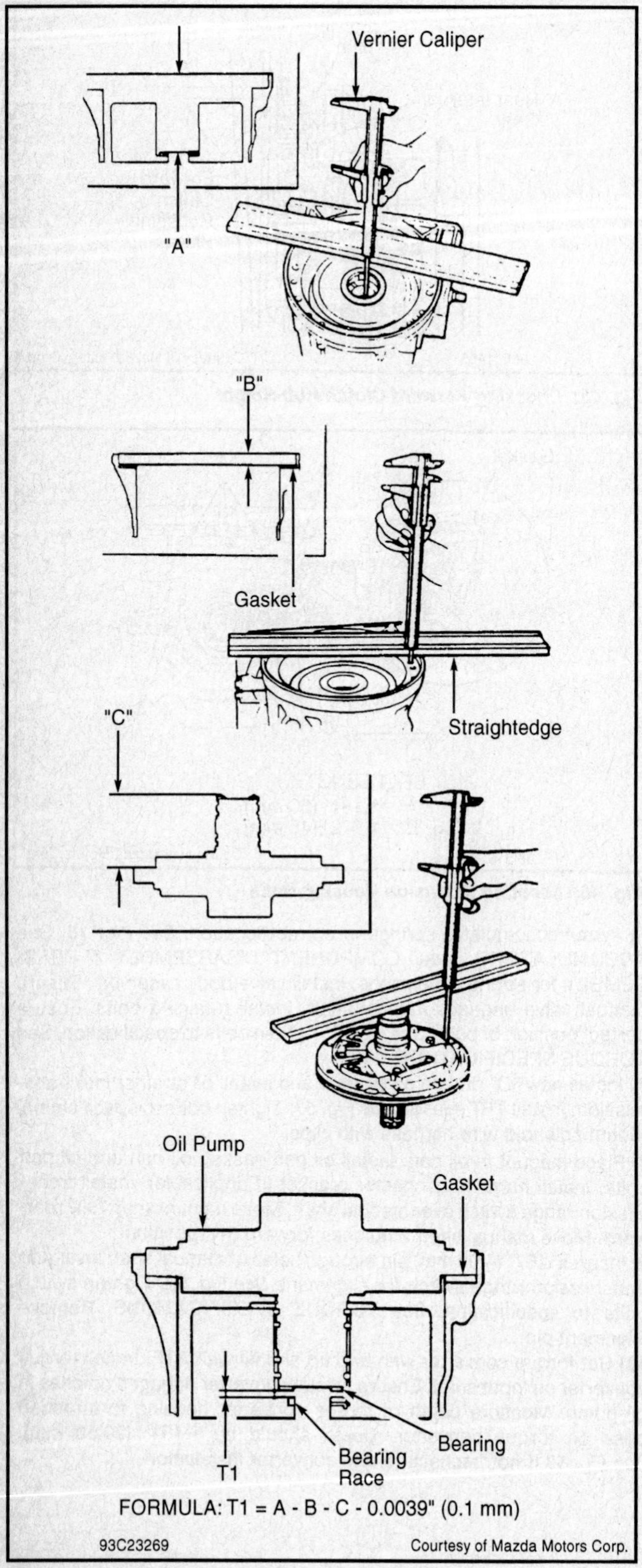

3-996

AUTOMATIC TRANSMISSIONS
Mazda RA4A-EL, RA4AX-EL & RB4A-EL (Cont.)

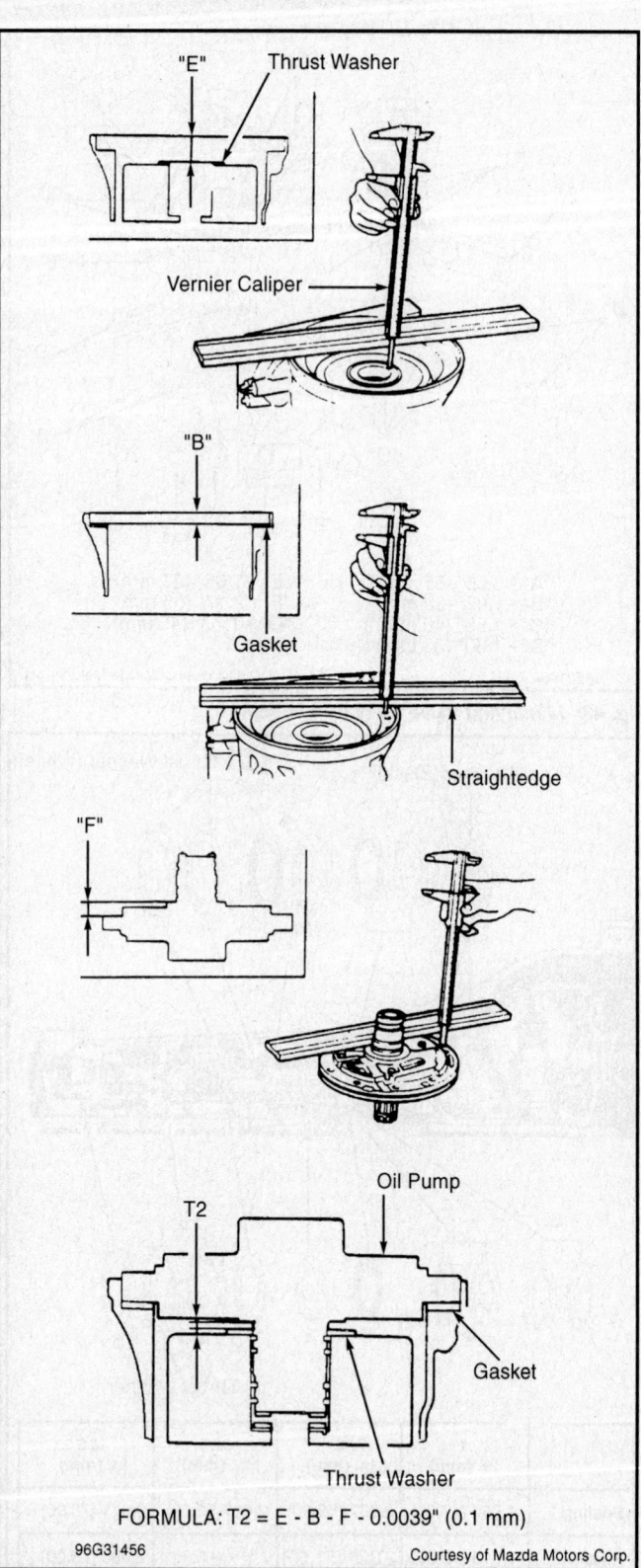

FORMULA: T1 = A - B - C - 0.0039" (0.1 mm)

93C23269   Courtesy of Mazda Motors Corp.

Fig. 47: Measuring Transmission Total End Play

FORMULA: T2 = E - B - F - 0.0039" (0.1 mm)

96G31456   Courtesy of Mazda Motors Corp.

Fig. 48: Measuring Reverse Clutch End Play

AUTOMATIC TRANSMISSIONS
Mazda RA4A-EL, RA4AX-EL & RB4A-EL (Cont.)

3-997

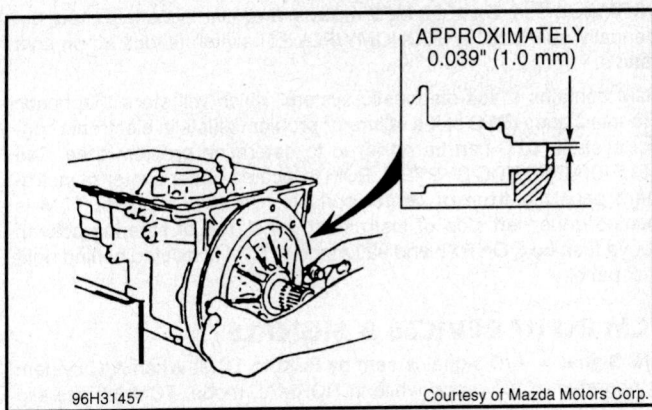

Fig. 49: Measuring Oil Pump Installed Depth

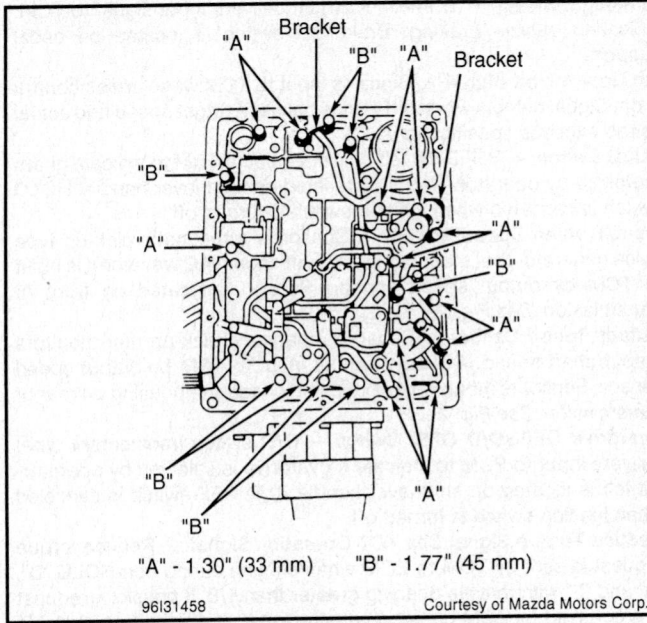

Fig. 50: Locating Valve Body Bolts

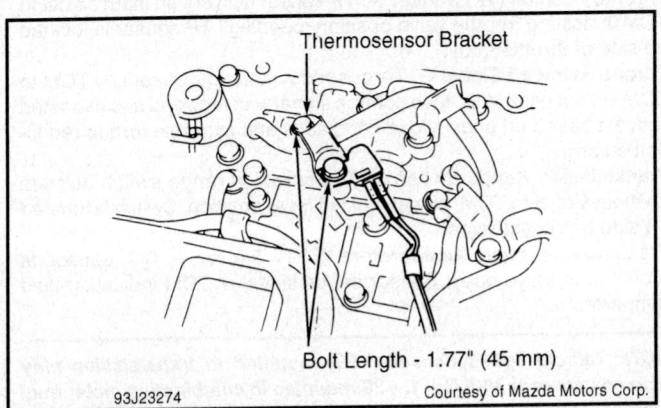

Fig. 51: Locating TFT Sensor

Fig. 52: Aligning Transmission Range Switch

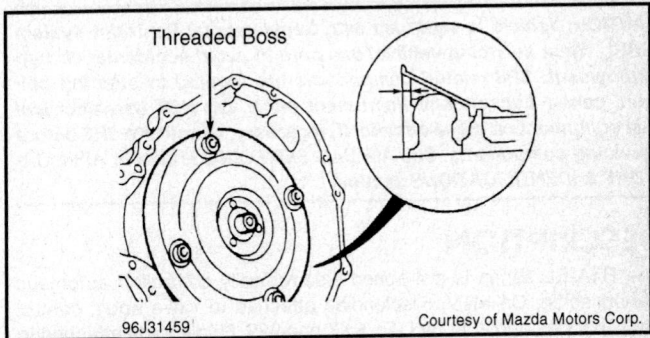

Fig. 53: Measuring Torque Converter Installed Depth

TORQUE SPECIFICATIONS
TORQUE SPECIFICATIONS

Application	Ft. Lbs. (N.m)
Anchor End Bolt Lock Nut	23-31 (31-42)
Extension Housing Bolt	15-20 (20-27)
Low One-Way Clutch Inner Race Bolt	15-20 (20-27)
Manual Shaft Lock Nut	22-29 (30-39)
Oil Pump Bolts	12-15 (16-20)
Torque Converter Housing Bolts	45-47 (61-64)

	INCH Lbs. (N.m)
Brake Band Servo Cover	61-78 (6.9-8.8)
Detent Spring	35-52 (3.9-5.9)
Oil Strainer	61-78 (6.9-8.8)
Oil Pan	43-70 (4.9-7.9)
Line Pressure Solenoid	61-87 (6.9-9.8)
Lock-Up Solenoid	61-87 (6.9-9.8)
Overrunning Clutch Solenoid	61-87 (6.9-9.8)
Speedometer Driven Gear Retainer	43-61 (4.9-6.9)
Valve Body (Upper-To-Lower)	61-78 (6.9-8.8)
Valve Body-To-Transmission	61-78 (6.9-8.8)
Vehicle Speed Sensor	43-61 (4.9-6.9)
Transmission Range Switch	22-35 (2.5-3.9)

TRANSMISSION SPECIFICATIONS
TRANSMISSION SPECIFICATIONS

Application	In. (mm)
Brake Snap Ring-To-Retaining Plate Clearance	
Low & Reverse Brake	
MPV	.028-.091 (.70-2.30)
RX7	.031-.102 (.80-2.60)
929	.031-.094 (.80-2.40)
Clutch Snap Ring-To-Retaining Plate Clearance	
Forward Clutch	
MPV	.018-.081 (.45-2.05)
RX7 & 929	.018-.073 (.45-1.85)
High Clutch	.071-.118 (1.80-3.00)
Overrunning Clutch	.039-.079 (1.00-2.00)
Reverse Clutch	.020-.047 (.50-1.20)
Clutch Drive Plate Minimum Thickness	
High Clutch	.055 (1.40)
All Except High Clutch	.071 (1.80)
Planetary Pinion Gear Clearance	.008-.028 (.20-.70)
Oil Pump	
Cam Ring	.0004-.0009 (.010-.024)
Rotor, Vane & Control Piston	.0012-.0017 (.030-.044)

MPV, RX7, 929

APPLICATION

TRANSMISSION APPLICATION

Vehicle	Transmission Model
MPV	
2WD	RA4A-EL
4WD	RA4AX-EL
RX-7	RB4A-EL
929	RA4A-EL

CAUTION: Vehicle is equipped with Supplemental Restraint System (SRS). When servicing vehicle, use care to avoid accidental air bag deployment. SRS-related components are located in steering column, center console and instrument panel. DO NOT use electrical test equipment on these circuits. If necessary, deactivate SRS before servicing components. See AIR BAG SERVICING article in APPLICATIONS & IDENTIFICATIONS section.

DESCRIPTION

The R4A-EL series is a 4-speed electronically controlled automatic transmission. On MPV, 5 solenoids attached to valve body, control shift changes and shift feel. On RX7 and 929, 6 solenoids attached to valve body, control shift changes and shift feel. Solenoids are controlled by the Transmission Control Module (TCM).

NOTE: TCC solenoid is also known as lock-up solenoid or TCC lock-up solenoid.

The TCM receives information from various input devices. *See Fig. 1.* The TCM uses the following information to control following solenoids:

- Shift solenoids for transmission shifting.
- Torque Converter Clutch (TCC) control solenoid for torque converter clutch lock-up.
- Torque Converter Clutch (TCC) solenoid for TCC apply rate (slip lock-up) on RX7 and 929 only.
- Overrunning clutch solenoid to control overrunning clutch (engine braking).
- Pressure control solenoid to control line pressure.

On all models except 1996 MPV, a HOLD switch is mounted on the shift lever. HOLD function may be activated in "D", "S" or "L" gears by pressing HOLD button. In "L" and "S" positions, vehicle is held in selected gear and no upshift or downshift takes place. This function is used for driving up steep inclines or for engine braking assistance when descending steep grades. If activated in "D" position a 1-2 and 2-3 upshift is permitted when starting from a stop, but after the 2-3 upshift the vehicle is locked in "D" until it comes to a complete stop. The 1-2 and 2-3 upshift pattern is changed to a "short shift" specification. This function is used for starting off or driving on slippery surfaces. Pushing HOLD button again deactivates system.

On 1996 MPV, an Overdrive OFF (O/D OFF) switch is mounted on the shift lever. When O/D OFF switch is released to ON position, transmission will shift into 4th gear when shift lever is in "D" position. O/D OFF light on combination meter should not be illuminated. When O/D OFF switch is depressed to OFF position, transmission will not shift into 4th gear. O/D OFF light will be illuminated.

OPERATION

TCM

TCM receives information from various input devices and uses this information to control solenoids on transmission valve body for transmission shifting, shift feel and torque converter clutch engagement.

TCM automatically switches from NORMAL mode to POWER mode corresponding to driving condition in "D" range. Upshifts and downshifts are performed at a higher speed in POWER mode than in NORMAL mode. On 1995 MPV models, a similar system is used, but manually operated. A ECONOMY/POWER switch is located on shift handle.

TCM contains a self-diagnostic system, which will store Diagnostic Trouble Codes (DTC's) if a failure or problem exists in electronic control system. DTC can be retrieved to determine problem area. See SELF-DIAGNOSTIC SYSTEM. PCM is located under center of instrument panel, in front of center console. On MPV models, TCM is located under left side of instrument panel, left of steering column above fuse box. On RX7 and 929 models, TCM is located behind right kick panel.

TCM INPUT DEVICES & SIGNALS

A/C Signal – A/C signal is sent by ECM to TCM. When A/C system is operated in "D" range while in NORMAL mode, TCM inhibits slip TCC lock-up and move shift points to higher speed to improve driveability.

Brakelight Switch – Brakelight switch delivers input signal to TCM, indicating vehicle braking. Brakelight switch is located on pedal support.

4th Gear Inhibit Signal – Signal is input to TCM when cruise control is on. Signal detects when difference between target speed and actual speed exceeds specification.

HOLD Switch – HOLD switch delivers input to TCM to indicate gears preferred by operator. Switch is located on shift lever handle. HOLD switch is canceled when ignition switch is turned off.

Input/Turbine Speed Sensor – Sensor is a magnetic pick-up type pulse generator that monitors input shaft speed. AC waveform is input to TCM by output speed sensor. Sensor is located on front of transmission. *See Fig. 2.*

Output Speed Sensor – Sensor is magnetic pick-up that monitors output shaft speed. AC waveform is input to TCM by output speed sensor. Sensor is mounted to extension or adapter housing on rear of transmission. *See Fig. 2.*

Overdrive OFF (O/D OFF) Switch – O/D switch (momentary type) delivers input to PCM to indicate if overdrive is selected by operator. Switch is located on shift lever handle. O/D OFF switch is canceled when ignition switch is turned off.

Reduce Torque Signal/Slip TCC Operation Signal – Reduce torque request is sent by TCM to ECM when shifting during non-HOLD "D", "S" and "L" with throttle opening greater than 1/8. If possible, request is processed by ECM based on engine load conditions and available torque reduction control.

Throttle Position (TP) Sensor – TP sensor delivers an input signal to TCM indicating throttle valve position (opening). TP sensor is located on side of throttle body.

Torque Reduced Signal – Torque reduction request sent by TCM to ECM is sent back to TCM to confirm signal was received and executed request based on engine load conditions and available torque reduction control.

Transmission Range Switch – Transmission range switch delivers an input signal to TCM indicating shift lever position. Switch is located on side of transmission.

Transmission Fluid Temperature (TFT) Sensor – TFT sensor is mounted to valve body. Sensor sends signal to TCM indicating fluid temperature.

NOTE: Vehicle Speed Sensor (VSS) mounted to transmission may also be known as VSS No. 1. VSS mounted in combination meter may also be known as VSS No. 2 or speedometer sensor.

Vehicle Speed Sensor (MPV) – Sensor is a cable driven pulse generator that is part of speedometer. Pulse signals are sent to TCM.

Vehicle Speed Sensors (RX-7 & 929) – Sensor is magnetic pick-up that is mounted to transmission case and driven by gear on output shaft. *See Fig. 2.* Pulse signals are sent through speedometer (also known as speedometer sensor or VSS No. 2) in combination meter to TCM.

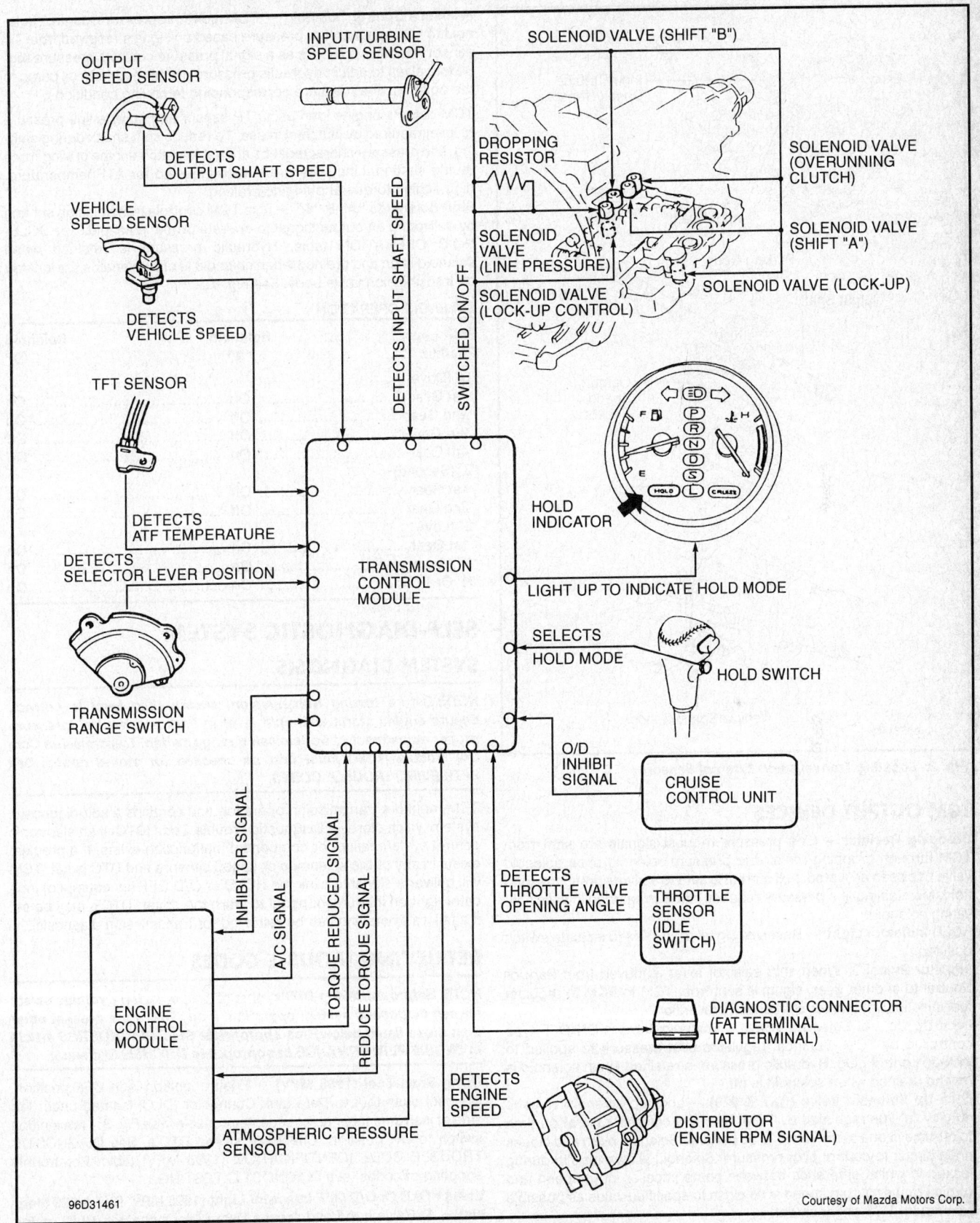

Fig. 1: Transmission Control System Operational Overview (929 Shown, MPV & RX7 Similar)

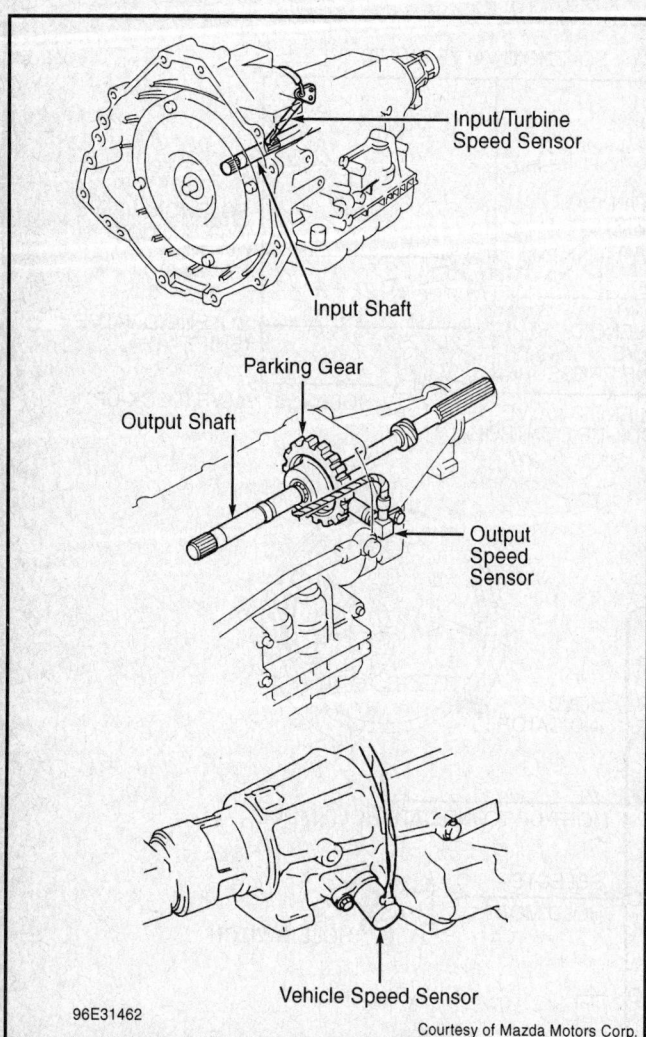

96E31462

Courtesy of Mazda Motors Corp.

Fig. 2: Locating Transmission External Sensors

TCM OUTPUT DEVICES

Dropping Resistor – Line pressure request signals are sent from TCM through dropping resistor to pressure solenoid once solenoid valve has been activated. Full current is sent to activate pressure solenoid. Maintaining line pressure requires less current than initially activating solenoid.

HOLD Indicator Light – Receives signal from TCM to indicate switch position.

Inhibitor Signal – When shift selector lever is moved from Park or Neutral to another gear, signal is sent from TCM to ECM to regulate fuel injection volume for shift shock prevention.

Lock-Up Control Solenoid Valve – Solenoid valve is ON/OFF type controlled by TCM. Solenoid regulates pilot pressure to applied to lock-up control plug. Hydraulic pressure is retained when solenoid is on and drained when solenoid is off.

Lock-Up Solenoid Valve (RX7 & 929) – Lock-up solenoid valve is duty-cycle type regulated by TCM. Solenoid controls ratio of on-time to off-time in one cycle from 5 to 95 percent. Solenoid open and closes drain circuit to control pilot pressure. Solenoid allows for slip during lockup in which difference between pump impeller input speed and turbine runner output speed is as close to specified value as possible for smooth TCC engagement.

Overrunning Solenoid – TCM controls overrunning solenoid to control overrunning clutch (engine braking). Hydraulic pressure is retained when solenoid is on and drained when solenoid is off.

Pressure Control Solenoid – TCM controls pressure control solenoid to regulate modifier pressure based on signals received from TP sensor. Modifier pressure as a signal pressure controls pressure regulator valves to adjust hydraulic pressure discharged from oil pump to the optimum line pressure corresponding to driving conditions.

TCM detects engine load using TP sensor and adjusts line pressure to level required by clutch(s) in use. To reduce shift shock during shifting, line pressure characteristics are set to match engine driving force during shifting. Line pressure is also adjusted for ATF temperature, high engine torque and engine braking.

Shift Solenoids "A" & "B" – The TCM controls transmission shifting by delivering an output signal to operate proper solenoid. See SOLENOID OPERATION table. Hydraulic pressure is retained when solenoid is on and drained when solenoid is off. Solenoids are located on transmission valve body. *See Fig. 1.*

SOLENOID OPERATION

Shift Lever Position	Solenoid "A"	Solenoid "B"
"D" (Drive)		
1st Gear	On	On
2nd Gear	Off	On
3rd Gear	Off	Off
4th Gear	On	Off
"2" (Second)		
1st Gear	On	On
2nd Gear	Off	On
"L" (Low)		
1st Gear	On	On
"R" (Reverse)	On	On
"N" Or "P"	On	On

SELF-DIAGNOSTIC SYSTEM

SYSTEM DIAGNOSIS

NOTE: Before testing transmission, ensure fluid level is correct. Ensure engine starts with shift lever in Park and Neutral to ensure proper adjustment of transmission range switch. Transmission Control Module (TCM) must first be checked for stored codes. See RETRIEVING TROUBLE CODES.

TCM monitors transmission operation and contains a self-diagnostic system which stores a Diagnostic Trouble Code (DTC) if an electronic control system failure or component malfunction exists. If a problem exists in any of the solenoids or speed sensors and DTC is set, TCM will deliver a signal to blink the HOLD or O/D OFF (as equipped) indicator light on instrument panel to warn the driver. DTC's may be set if a failure exists and can be retrieved for transmission diagnosis.

RETRIEVING TROUBLE CODES

NOTE: Before retrieving DTC's, ensure proper battery voltage exists for self-diagnostic system operation. If any DTC's are present other than those listed below, see appropriate SELF-DIAGNOSTICS article in ENGINE PERFORMANCE in appropriate MITCHELL® manual.

Using Scan Tool (1996 MPV) – Ensure ignition is in OFF position. Connect scan tool to Data Link Connector (DLC) located under left side of instrument panel, near center console. *See Fig. 3.* Turn ignition switch to ON position. Check for stored DTC's. See DIAGNOSTIC TROUBLE CODE IDENTIFICATION (1996 MPV) table. For trouble shooting of codes, see DIAGNOSTIC TESTING.

Using HOLD Or O/D OFF Indicator Light (1995 MPV, RX7 & 929 Models) – **1)** Raise hood and access Data Link Connector (DLC) on left side of engine compartment. On MPV and 929, DLC is mounted next to air cleaner housing. On RX7, DLC is mounted to relay box, beside battery.

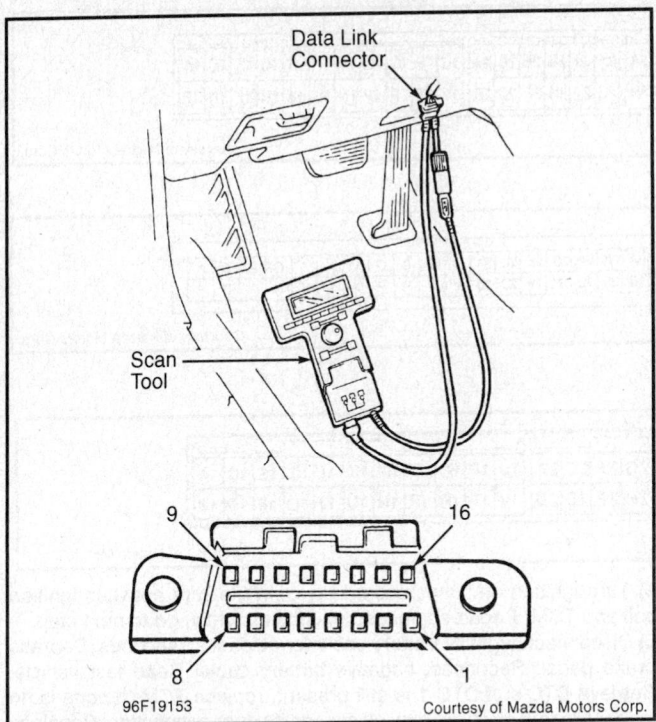

Fig. 3: Connecting Scan Tool

2) Connect jumper wire between TAT and GND terminals on DLC connector. *See Fig. 4.* Turn ignition switch to ON position. If DTC exists, HOLD or O/D OFF indicator light will flash every 4 seconds. Long (1.2 second duration) flash indicates first digit and short (.4 second duration) flash indicates second digit.

3) If more than one DTC exists, next code will be displayed after pause of 4 seconds. Lowest number code will be displayed first. DTC's will be repeated. Once DTC is obtained, determine probable cause and symptom. See DIAGNOSTIC TROUBLE CODE IDENTIFICATION (Except 1996 MPV) table. For trouble shooting of DTC's, see DIAGNOSTIC TESTING. Turn ignition off and remove jumper wire.

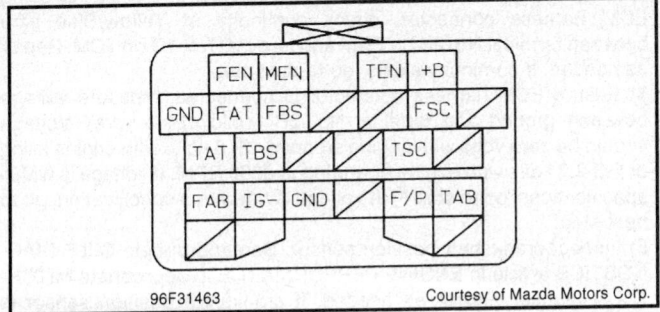

Fig. 4: Identifying DLC Terminals

NOTE: *Once repairs have been performed, DTC's must be cleared from TCM memory and vehicle test driven. See CLEARING TROUBLE CODES. Accelerate vehicle to 31 MPH for 1 minute. Fully depress accelerator pedal to force downshift. Release accelerator pedal and slow vehicle to stop. Perform retrieval procedure to ensure DTC's have been cleared and no new DTC's exist.*

DIAGNOSTIC TROUBLE CODE IDENTIFICATION (1996 MPV)

DTC No.	[1] Probable Cause
P0705	Transmission Range Switch
P0710	[2] TFT Sensor
P0720	Output Speed Sensor
P0725	Engine Speed Input Circuit Malfunction
P0731	Incorrect 1st Gear Ratio
P0732	Incorrect 2nd Gear Ratio
P0733	Incorrect 3rd Gear Ratio
P0734	Incorrect 4th Gear Ratio
P0740	TCC System Malfunction
P0745	Pressure Control Solenoid
P0750	Shift Solenoid "A"
P0755	Shift Solenoid "B"
P1720	Vehicle Speed Sensor
P1743	Lock-Up Solenoid Valve
P1770	Overrunning Clutch Solenoid Valve
P1790	Throttle Position Sensor
P1792	Barometric Pressure Sensor

[1] – Check listed component for probable cause. Also check wiring and connection of specified component.
[2] – Transmission Fluid Temperature.

DIAGNOSTIC TROUBLE CODE IDENTIFICATION (EXCEPT 1996 MPV)

DTC No.	[1] Probable Cause
1	Engine Speed Input Signal
6	Output Speed Sensor
7	Vehicle Speed Sensor
12	Throttle Position Sensor
55	Input/Turbine Speed Sensor
56	[3] TFT Sensor
57	Reduce Torque Signal
58	Barometric Pressure Sensor
60	Shift Solenoid "A"
61	Shift Solenoid "B"
62	Overrunning Clutch Solenoid
63	TCC Solenoid Valve
64	Pressure Control Solenoid
65	TCC Control Solenoid Valve

[1] – Check listed component for probable cause. Also check wiring and connection of specified component.
[2] – Transmission Fluid Temperature.

CLEARING TROUBLE CODES

To clear DTC's stored in TCM, disconnect negative battery cable for at least 20 seconds.

COMPONENT LOCATION
COMPONENT LOCATION

Description	Location
Engine Control Module	
MPV	Located under right side of instrument panel
RX7 & 929	Behind right kick panel
Pressure Control Solenoid	See Fig. 1.
Solenoids "A" & "B"	See Fig. 1.
Input/Turbine Speed Sensor	See Fig. 2.
Output Speed Sensor	See Fig. 2.
Overrunning Clutch Solenoid	See Fig. 1.
Speedometer Sensor	Mounted in speedometer.
TCC Lock-up Solenoid	See Fig. 1.
TCC Lock-up Control Solenoid	See Fig. 1.
Transmission Control Module	
MPV	Behind left side of instrument panel, next to relay block.
RX7 & 929	Behind right kick panel
Transmission Fluid Temperature (TFT) Sensor	Mounted to valve body.
Vehicle Speed Sensor	See Fig. 2.

| 4Y | 4W | 4U | 4S | 4Q | 4O | 4M | 4K | 4I | 4G | 4E | 4C | 4A | 3O | 3M | 3K | 3I | 3G | 3E | 3C | 3A | 2K | 2I | 2G | 2E | 2C | 2A | 1U | 1S | 1Q | 1O | 1M | 1K | 1I | 1G | 1E | 1C | 1A |
| 4Z | 4X | 4V | 4T | 4R | 4P | 4N | 4L | 4J | 4H | 4F | 4D | 4B | 3P | 3N | 3L | 3J | 3H | 3F | 3D | 3B | 2L | 2J | 2H | 2F | 2D | 2B | 1V | 1T | 1R | 1P | 1N | 1L | 1J | 1H | 1F | 1D | 1B |

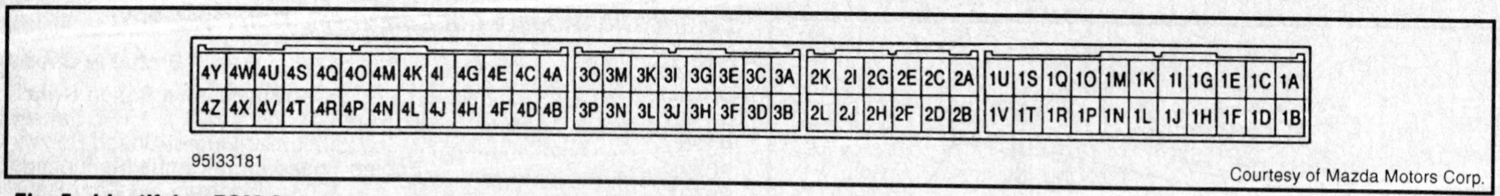

95I33181

Courtesy of Mazda Motors Corp.

Fig. 5: Identifying ECM Component Connector Terminals (MPV)

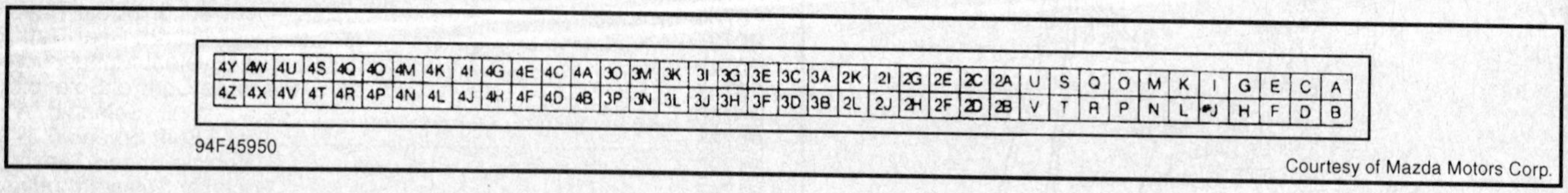

| 4Y | 4W | 4U | 4S | 4Q | 4O | 4M | 4K | 4I | 4G | 4E | 4C | 4A | 3O | 3M | 3K | 3I | 3G | 3E | 3C | 3A | 2K | 2I | 2G | 2E | 2C | 2A | U | S | Q | O | M | K | I | G | E | C | A |
| 4Z | 4X | 4V | 4T | 4R | 4P | 4N | 4L | 4J | 4H | 4F | 4D | 4B | 3P | 3N | 3L | 3J | 3H | 3F | 3D | 3B | 2L | 2J | 2H | 2F | 2D | 2B | V | T | R | P | N | L | •J | H | F | D | B |

94F45950

Courtesy of Mazda Motors Corp.

Fig. 6: Identifying ECM Component Connector Terminals (RX7)

| 3Y | 3W | 3U | 3S | 3Q | 3O | 3M | 3K | 3I | 3G | 3E | 3C | 3A | 2O | 2M | 2K | 2I | 2G | 2E | 2C | 2A | 1U | 1S | 1Q | 1O | 1M | 1K | 1I | 1G | 1E | 1C | 1A |
| 3Z | 3X | 3V | 3T | 3R | 3P | 3N | 3L | 3J | 3H | 3F | 3D | 3B | 2P | 2N | 2L | 2J | 2H | 2F | 2D | 2B | 1V | 1T | 1R | 1P | 1N | 1L | 1J | 1H | 1F | 1D | 1B |

95A33290

Courtesy of Mazda Motors Corp.

Fig. 7: Identifying ECM Component Connector Terminals (929)

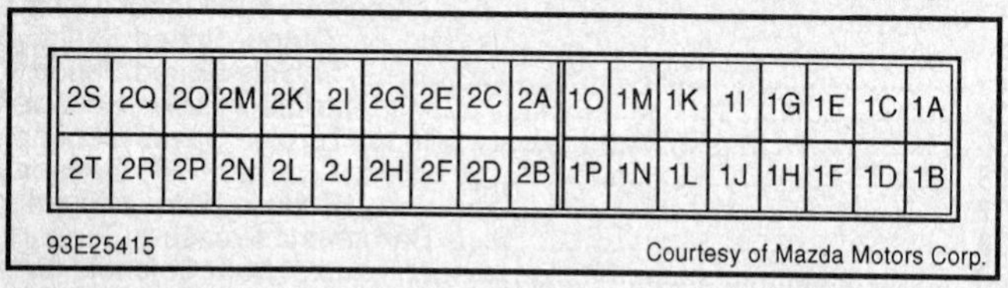

| 2S | 2Q | 2O | 2M | 2K | 2I | 2G | 2E | 2C | 2A | 1O | 1M | 1K | 1I | 1G | 1E | 1C | 1A |
| 2T | 2R | 2P | 2N | 2L | 2J | 2H | 2F | 2D | 2B | 1P | 1N | 1L | 1J | 1H | 1F | 1D | 1B |

93E25415

Courtesy of Mazda Motors Corp.

Fig. 8: Identifying TCM Component Connector Terminals

COMPONENT CONNECTOR IDENTIFICATION

COMPONENT CONNECTOR IDENTIFICATION

Component	See Fig.
Engine Control Module (ECM)	7
Hold Switch	2
Instrument Cluster	3
Transmission Control Module (TCM)	18
Transmission Fluid Temperature (TFT) Sensor	4
Valve Body Solenoids	4

1 – See BRAKELIGHT SWITCH under COMPONENT TESTING.
2 – See HOLD SWITCH under COMPONENT TESTING.
3 – See SPEEDOMETER SENSOR under COMPONENT TESTING.
4 – See SOLENOID VALVES under COMPONENT TESTING.

DIAGNOSTIC TESTS

NOTE: For connector terminal identification, see COMPONENT CONNECTOR IDENTIFICATION table. For circuit or wire color identification, see appropriate wiring diagram in WIRING DIAGRAMS.

DTC 1: ENGINE SPEED INPUT SIGNAL (1995 MPV)

Diagnosis & Repair Procedure – **1)** Inspect harness connections at distributor and TCM. Repair as needed. Turn ignition on. Using voltmeter, backprobe TCM harness connector. Do not disconnect connector.

2) Measure voltage between ground and terminal No. 1G (Green/ White wire). Voltage should be below .5 volt with engine stopped, or greater than one volt with engine running. If voltage is within specifications, go to step **4)**. If voltage is not within specification, go to next step.

3) Inspect ignition coil and related circuits. See appropriate BASIC DIAGNOSTIC PROCEDURES article in ENGINE PERFORMANCE in appropriate MITCHELL® manual. Repair as needed. If ignition coil and related circuits are okay, go to next step.

4) Turn ignition off. Check continuity of White wire between ignition coil and TCM. Repair as needed. If circuit is okay, go to next step.

5) Disconnect negative battery cable for at least 20 seconds. Depress brake pedal. Reconnect negative battery cable. Road test vehicle. Retrieve DTC's. If DTC 1 is still present, replace TCM. If code is no longer present, problem may be caused by poor connection. Repair as needed.

DTC 1: ENGINE SPEED INPUT SIGNAL (RX7)

Diagnosis & Repair Procedure – **1)** Inspect harness connections at distributor and TCM. Repair as needed. Turn ignition on. Using voltmeter, backprobe TCM harness connector. Do not disconnect connector. Go to next step.

2) Measure voltage between ground and terminal No. 1G (Green/ White wire). Voltage should be zero volts with engine stopped, .3-.8 volts with engine idling or 1.8-2.2 volts with engine operating at 3000 RPM. If voltage is within specifications, go to step **6)**. If voltage is not within specification, go to next step.

3) Disconnect TCM connector. Ensure ignition is off. Backprobing ECM harness connector, check continuity of Yellow/Blue wire between terminal No. 2B on ECM and terminal No. 1G on TCM. Repair as needed. If continuity exists, go to next step.

4) Ensure ECM harness connector is connected. Measure voltage between ground and terminal No. 2B (Yellow/Blue wire). Voltage should be zero volts with engine stopped, .3-.8 volts with engine idling or 1.8-2.2 volts with engine operating at 3000 RPM. If voltage is within specifications, go to step **6)**. If voltage is not within specification, go to next step.

5) Inspect crankshaft position sensor. See appropriate SELF-DIAGNOSTICS article in ENGINE PERFORMANCE in appropriate MITCHELL® manual. Repair as needed. If crankshaft position sensor is okay, replace ECM.

6) Disconnect negative battery cable for at least 20 seconds. Depress brake pedal. Reconnect negative battery cable. Road test vehicle. Retrieve DTC's. If DTC 1 is still present, replace TCM. If code is no longer present, problem may be caused by poor connection. Repair as needed.

DTC 1: ENGINE SPEED INPUT SIGNAL (929)

Diagnosis & Repair Procedure – **1)** Inspect harness connections at distributor and TCM. Repair as needed. Turn ignition on. Using voltmeter, backprobe TCM harness connector. Do not disconnect connector.

2) Measure voltage between ground and terminal No. 1G (Green/White wire). Voltage should be zero or 4.5-5.5 volts with engine stopped, or 2-3 volts with engine running. If voltage is within specifications, go to next step. If voltage is not within specification, repair Green/White wire circuit between TCM and distributor for open or short.

3) Disconnect distributor connector. Turn ignition on. Backprobing ECM harness connector, measure voltage between ground and terminal No. 3E (Green/White wire). If voltage is 4.5-5.5 volts, go to next step. If voltage is not 4.5-5.5 volts, replace TCM.

4) Ensure ignition is on. Measure voltage between ground and terminal No. 2 (Green/White wire) on distributor harness connector. If voltage is 4.5-5.5 volts, replace distributor. If voltage is not 4.5-5.5 volts, go to next step.

5) Turn ignition off. Check continuity of Green/White wire between distributor and ECM. Repair as needed. If circuit is okay, go to next step.

6) Disconnect negative battery cable for at least 20 seconds. Depress brake pedal. Reconnect negative battery cable. Road test vehicle. Retrieve DTC's. If DTC 1 is still present, replace TCM. If code is no longer present, problem may be caused by poor connection. Repair as needed.

DTC 6: OUTPUT SPEED SENSOR

Diagnosis & Repair Procedure – 1) Ensure all connections are clean and tight. Repair as needed. Turn ignition on. Access TCM connectors. Using voltmeter, backprobe harness connectors. Do not disconnect connectors. Go to next step.

2) Start and idle engine in Park or Neutral. Measure AC voltage between terminals No. 2J (positive) and No. 2L (negative). Test drive vehicle. Voltage should be zero when idling and more than one volt above 25 MPH. If voltage is within specification, go to step 6). If voltage is not within specification, go to next step.

3) Turn ignition off. Disconnect TCM harness connector. Measure resistance between terminals No. 2J and No. 2L. Resistance should be 504-616 ohms on MPV and 500-1000 ohms on RX7 and 929. If resistance is within specification, go to step 6). If resistance is not within specification, go to next step.

4) Inspect output speed sensor. See OUTPUT SPEED SENSOR under COMPONENT TESTING. Repair as needed. If sensor is okay, go to next step.

5) Check continuity of circuits between output speed sensor and TCM. See appropriate wiring diagram in WIRING DIAGRAMS. Repair as needed. If circuits are okay, go to next step.

6) Reconnect all harness connectors. Road test vehicle. Retrieve DTC's. If DTC 6 is still present, replace PCM. If code is no longer present, system is okay.

DTC 7: VEHICLE SPEED SENSOR (MPV)

Diagnosis & Repair Procedure – 1) Ensure all connections are clean and tight. Repair as needed. Turn ignition on. Using voltmeter, backprobe TCM harness connector. Do not disconnect connector. Test drive vehicle.

2) Measure voltage between ground and terminal No. 1I (Green/Red wire) on TCM harness connector. During test drive voltage should be 2-3 volts or, 0 or 4-5 volts when parked. If voltage is within specifications, go to step 5). If voltage is not within specifications, go to next step.

3) Turn ignition off. Disconnect negative battery cable. Remove instrument cluster. Disconnect TCM harness connectors. Check continuity of Green/Red wire between terminal No. 1I on TCM connector and terminal No. 1J on instrument cluster harness center connector. Repair as needed. If continuity exists, go to next step.

4) With combination removed, check continuity between terminals No. 1J and 2B on combination meter connectors. If continuity exists, go to next step. If continuity does not exist, replace combination meter or circuit board (as applicable).

5) Disconnect negative battery cable for at least 20 seconds. Depress brake pedal. Reconnect negative battery cable. Road test vehicle. Retrieve DTC's. If DTC 7 is still present, replace TCM. If code is no longer present, problem may be caused by poor connection. Repair as needed.

DTC 7: VEHICLE SPEED SENSOR (RX7 & 929)

Diagnosis & Repair Procedure – 1) Inspect harness connections at TCM. Repair as needed. Turn ignition on. Backprobing TCM harness connector with voltmeter, measure voltage between ground and terminal No. 1I (Green/Red wire). Voltage should be zero or 4.5-5.5 volts with vehicle stopped, or 2-3 volts with vehicle moving. If voltage is within specification, go to step 6). If voltage is not within specification, go to next step.

2) Turn ignition off. Remove instrument cluster. Disconnect TCM harness connectors. On RX7, check continuity of Green/Red wire between terminal No. 1M on instrument cluster harness connector and terminal No. 1I on TCM harness connector. Repair as needed. If continuity exists, go to step 4).

3) Turn ignition off. Remove instrument cluster. Disconnect TCM harness connectors. On 929, check continuity of Green/Red wire between terminal No. 3E on instrument cluster harness connector and terminal No. 1I on TCM harness connector. Repair as needed. If continuity exists, go to next step.

4) Inspect vehicle speed sensor and related circuits. See VEHICLE SPEED SENSOR under COMPONENT TESTING. Repair as needed. If sensor and related circuits are okay, go to next step.

5) Disconnect negative battery cable for at least 20 seconds. Depress brake pedal. Reconnect negative battery cable. Road test vehicle. Retrieve DTC's. If DTC 7 is still present, replace TCM. If code is no longer present, problem may be caused by poor connection. Repair as needed.

DTC 12: THROTTLE POSITION (TP) SENSOR

Diagnosis & Repair Procedure – 1) Turn ignition on. Using voltmeter, backprobe TCM harness connector. Do not disconnect connector. Measure voltage between ground and terminal No. 2T on TCM connector. Slowly depress accelerator pedal while monitoring voltage. Go to next step.

2) If voltage changes as accelerator pedal is depressed, go to step 5). If voltage does not change as accelerator pedal is depressed, go to next step.

3) Measure voltage between ground and terminal No. 2A on TCM connector. If 4.5-5.5 volts is present, go to next step. If 4.5-5.5 volts is not present, go to step 5).

4) Turn ignition switch to OFF position. Disconnect Throttle Position (TP) sensor harness connector. Measure resistance between specified component terminals. See appropriate SYSTEM & COMPONENT TESTING article in ENGINE PERFORMANCE of appropriate MITCHELL® manual. Replace as needed. If TP sensor is okay, go to next step.

5) Disconnect negative battery cable for at least 20 seconds. Depress brake pedal. Reconnect negative battery cable. Road test vehicle. Retrieve DTC's. If DTC 12 is still present, replace TCM. If code is no longer present, problem may be caused by poor connection. Repair as needed.

DTC 55: INPUT/TURBINE SPEED SENSOR

Diagnosis & Repair Procedure – 1) Turn ignition on. Using voltmeter, backprobe TCM harness connector. Do not disconnect connector.

2) Measure AC voltage between terminals No. 2E (positive) and No. 2L (negative). Voltage should be zero when idling and more than .5 volt above 25 MPH. If voltage is within specification, go to step 6). If voltage is not within specification, go to next step.

3) Turn ignition off. Disconnect TCM harness connector. Measure resistance between terminals No. 2E and No. 2L. Resistance should be 2200-3500 ohms. If resistance is within specification, go to step 6). If resistance is not within specification, go to next step.

4) Inspect output speed sensor. See INPUT/TURBINE SPEED SENSOR under COMPONENT TESTING. Repair as needed. If sensor is okay, go to next step.

5) Check continuity of circuits between input/turbine speed sensor and TCM. See appropriate wiring diagram in WIRING DIAGRAMS. Repair as needed. If circuits are okay, go to next step.

6) Reconnect all harness connectors. Road test vehicle. Retrieve DTC's. If DTC 55 is still present, replace PCM. If code is no longer present, system is okay.

DTC 56: TRANSMISSION FLUID TEMPERATURE (TFT) SENSOR

Condition – Open or short circuit. Possible causes are:
- Poor harness connection at TFT sensor.
- Circuit fault between TFT sensor and TCM.
- TFT sensor.

Diagnosis & Repair Procedure – 1) Turn ignition on. Using voltmeter, backprobe TCM harness connector. Do not disconnect connector. Start and idle engine in Park. Measure voltage between terminals No. 2R (positive) and No. 2L (negative). Voltage reading should decrease as fluid temperature increases. Voltage should be about 1.8 volts at 50°F (10°C) to .4 volt at 176°F (80°C). If voltage readings are within specification, go to step **4)**. If voltage readings are not within specification, go to next step.

2) Turn ignition off. Disconnect TCM harness connector. Measure resistance between terminals No. 2R and No. 2L. Resistance reading should decrease as fluid temperature increases. Resistance should be about 3800 ohms at 50°F (10°C) to 300 ohms at 176°F (80°C). If resistance readings are within specification, go to step **4)**. If resistance readings are not within specification, go to next step.

3) Inspect TFT sensor and related circuits. See TRANSMISSION FLUID TEMPERATURE (TFT) SENSOR under COMPONENT TESTING. Repair as needed. If sensor and related circuits are okay, go to next step.

4) Disconnect negative battery cable for at least 20 seconds. Depress brake pedal. Reconnect negative battery cable. Road test vehicle. Retrieve DTC's. If DTC 56 is still present, replace TCM. If code is no longer present, problem may be caused by poor connection. Repair as needed.

DTC 57: REDUCE TORQUE SIGNAL (RX7)

NOTE: Voltage output period is very short. Monitor voltmeter accordingly.

Diagnosis & Repair Procedure – 1) Turn ignition on. Using voltmeter, backprobe TCM harness connector. Do not disconnect connector. Test drive vehicle.

2) Measure voltage between ground and terminal No. 2H (Blue/Green wire) on TCM harness connector. With engine idling and at normal operating temperature, battery voltage should exist. With throttle opening 1/8 or greater and engine temperature less than 104°F (40°C), voltage should be one volt or less. If voltage is within specification, go to step **6)**. If voltage is not within specification, go to next step.

3) Turn ignition off. Disconnect TCM harness connector. Disconnect Electronic Control Module (ECM) harness connectors. Check continuity of Blue/Green wire between terminal No. 2G on ECM harness connector and terminal No. 2H on TCM harness connector. Repair as needed. If continuity exists, go to next step.

4) Reconnect ECM and TCM harness connectors. Turn ignition on. Measure voltage between ground and terminal No. 2P (Green/White wire) on TCM harness connector. With engine idling, battery voltage should be present. Test drive vehicle. Monitor voltage during 1-2 or 2-3 shift with throttle opening of 5/8 or greater, or slip TCC operation with throttle opening of less than 5/8. Voltage should be less than one volt. If voltage is within specification, go to step **6)**. If voltage is not within specification, go to next step.

5) Turn ignition off. Disconnect TCM harness connector. Disconnect Electronic Control Module (ECM) harness connectors. Check continuity of Green/White wire between terminal No. 1G on ECM harness connector and terminal No. 2P on TCM harness connector. Repair as needed. If continuity exists, go to next step.

6) Disconnect negative battery cable for at least 20 seconds. Depress brake pedal. Reconnect negative battery cable. Road test vehicle. Retrieve DTC's. If DTC 57 is still present, replace TCM. If code is no longer present, problem may be caused by poor connection. Repair as needed.

DTC 57: REDUCE TORQUE SIGNAL (929)

NOTE: Voltage output period is very short. Monitor voltmeter accordingly.

Diagnosis & Repair Procedure – 1) Turn ignition on. Using voltmeter, backprobe TCM harness connector. Do not disconnect connector. Test drive vehicle.

2) Measure voltage between ground and terminal No. 2H (Gray wire) on TCM harness connector. With engine idling and at normal operating temperature, battery voltage should exist. With throttle opening 1/8 or greater and engine temperature less than 104°F (40°C), voltage should be one volt or less. If voltage is within specification, go to step **6)**. If voltage is not within specification, go to next step.

3) Turn ignition off. Disconnect TCM harness connector. Disconnect Electronic Control Module (ECM) harness connectors. Check continuity of Blue/Green wire between terminal No. 2P on ECM harness connector and terminal No. 2H on TCM harness connector. Repair as needed. If continuity exists, go to next step.

4) Reconnect ECM and TCM harness connectors. Turn ignition on. Measure voltage between ground and terminal No. 2P (Gray/Blue wire) on TCM harness connector. With engine idling, battery voltage should be present. Test drive vehicle. Monitor voltage during 1-2 or 2-3 shift with throttle opening of 5/8 or greater, or slip TCC operation with throttle opening of less than 5/8. Voltage should be less than one volt. If voltage is within specification, go to step **6)**. If voltage is not within specification, go to next step.

5) Turn ignition off. Disconnect TCM harness connector. Disconnect Electronic Control Module (ECM) harness connectors. Check continuity of Gray/Blue wire between terminal No. 1S on ECM harness connector and terminal No. 2P on TCM harness connector. Repair as needed. If continuity exists, go to next step.

6) Disconnect negative battery cable for at least 20 seconds. Depress brake pedal. Reconnect negative battery cable. Road test vehicle. Retrieve DTC's. If DTC 57 is still present, replace TCM. If code is no longer present, problem may be caused by poor connection. Repair as needed.

DTC 58: BAROMETRIC PRESSURE SENSOR

Diagnosis & Repair Procedure – 1) Turn ignition on. Using voltmeter, backprobe TCM harness connector. Do not disconnect connector. Measure voltage between ground and terminal No. 2C (Green/Yellow wire) on TCM connector. Voltage should be about 2-4.5 volts with ignition on or zero volts with ignition off. If voltage is within specification, go to step **4)**. If voltage is not within specification, go to next step.

2) Turn ignition off. Disconnect ECM and TCM harness connectors. Check continuity of Green/Yellow wire between terminal No. 2D on ECM harness connector and terminal No. 2C on TCM harness connector. Repair as needed. If circuit is okay, go to next step.

3) Connect ECM and TCM connectors. Turn ignition on. Using voltmeter, backprobe ECM harness connector. Measure voltage between ground and terminal No. 2D (Green/Yellow wire) on TCM connector. Voltage should be about 2-4.5 volts with ignition on or zero volts with ignition off. If voltage is within specification, go to step **4)**. If voltage is not within specification, go to next step.

4) Disconnect negative battery cable for at least 20 seconds. Depress brake pedal. Reconnect negative battery cable. Road test vehicle. Retrieve DTC's. If DTC 58 is still present, replace ECM. If code is no longer present, problem may be caused by poor connection. Repair as needed.

DTC 60: SHIFT SOLENOID "A"

NOTE: Always check mechanical operation of solenoid. See COMPONENT TESTING. Replace as needed.

Diagnosis & Repair Procedure – 1) Turn ignition on. Using voltmeter, backprobe TCM harness connector. Do not disconnect connector. Test drive vehicle.

2) Measure voltage between ground and terminal No. 1D on TCM harness connector. During test drive voltage should be less than one volt when solenoid is off and battery voltage when solenoid is on. See SOLENOID OPERATION TABLE under TCM OUTPUT DEVICES. If voltage is within specification, go to step **5)**. If voltage is not within specification, go to next step.

3) Turn ignition off. Disconnect TCM harness connector. Measure resistance between ground and terminal No. 1D. If resistance is 20-40 ohms at 68°F (20°C), go to step **5)**. If resistance is not 20-40 ohms at 68°F (20°C), go to next step.

4) Inspect shift solenoid "A" and related circuits. See SOLENOID VALVES under COMPONENT TESTING. Repair as needed. If solenoid valve and related circuits are okay, go to next step.

5) Disconnect negative battery cable for at least 20 seconds. Depress brake pedal. Reconnect negative battery cable. Road test vehicle. Retrieve DTC's. If DTC 60 is still present, replace TCM. If code is no longer present, problem may be caused by poor connection. Repair as needed.

DTC 61: SHIFT SOLENOID "B"

NOTE: Always check mechanical operation of solenoid. See COMPONENT TESTING. Replace as needed.

Diagnosis & Repair Procedure – 1) Turn ignition on. Using voltmeter, backprobe TCM harness connector. Do not disconnect connector. Test drive vehicle.

2) Measure voltage between ground and terminal No. 1B on TCM harness connector. During test drive voltage should be zero volts when solenoid is off and battery voltage when solenoid is on. See SOLENOID OPERATION TABLE under TCM OUTPUT DEVICES. If voltage is within specification, go to step **5)**. If voltage is not within specification, go to next step.

3) Turn ignition off. Disconnect TCM harness connector. Measure resistance between ground and terminal No. 2G. If resistance is 20-40 ohms at 68°F (20°C), go to step **5)**. If resistance is not 20-40 ohms at 68°F (20°C), go to next step.

4) Inspect shift solenoid "B" and related circuits. See SOLENOID VALVES under COMPONENT TESTING. Repair as needed. If solenoid valve and related circuits are okay, go to next step.

5) Disconnect negative battery cable for at least 20 seconds. Depress brake pedal. Reconnect negative battery cable. Road test vehicle. Retrieve DTC's. If DTC 61 is still present, replace TCM. If code is no longer present, problem may be caused by poor connection. Repair as needed.

DTC 62: OVERRUNNING CLUTCH SOLENOID

NOTE: Always check mechanical operation of solenoid. See COMPONENT TESTING. Replace as needed.

Diagnosis & Repair Procedure – 1) Turn ignition on. Using voltmeter, backprobe TCM harness connector. Do not disconnect connector. Test drive vehicle.

2) Measure voltage between ground and terminal No. 1O on TCM harness connector. During test drive voltage should be zero volts when solenoid is off and battery voltage when solenoid is on (engine braking). If voltage is within specification, go to step **5)**. If voltage is not within specification, go to next step.

3) Turn ignition off. Disconnect TCM harness connector. Measure resistance between ground and terminal No. 1O. If resistance is 20-40 ohms at 68°F (20°C), go to step **5)**. If resistance is not 20-40 ohms at 68°F (20°C), go to next step.

4) Inspect overrunning clutch solenoid and related circuits. See SOLENOID VALVES under COMPONENT TESTING. Repair as needed. If solenoid valve and related circuits are okay, go to next step.

5) Disconnect negative battery cable for at least 20 seconds. Depress brake pedal. Reconnect negative battery cable. Road test vehicle. Retrieve DTC's. If DTC 62 is still present, replace TCM. If code is no longer present, problem may be caused by poor connection. Repair as needed.

DTC 63: TCC SOLENOID VALVE

NOTE: Always check mechanical operation of solenoid. See COMPONENT TESTING. Replace as needed.

Diagnosis & Repair Procedure – 1) Ensure ignition is off. Disconnect TCM harness connector. Measure resistance between ground and terminal No. 1M. If resistance is 10-20 ohms at 68°F (20°C), go to step **3)**. If resistance is not 10-20 ohms at 68°F (20°C), go to next step.

2) Inspect TCC solenoid and related circuits. See SOLENOID VALVES under COMPONENT TESTING. Repair as needed. If solenoid valve and related circuits are okay, go to next step.

3) Disconnect negative battery cable for at least 20 seconds. Depress brake pedal. Reconnect negative battery cable. Road test vehicle. Retrieve DTC's. If DTC 63 is still present, replace TCM. If code is no longer present, problem may be caused by poor connection. Repair as needed.

DTC 64: PRESSURE CONTROL SOLENOID

NOTE: Always check mechanical operation of solenoid. See COMPONENT TESTING. Replace as needed.

Diagnosis & Repair Procedure – 1) Ensure ignition is off. Disconnect TCM harness connector. Measure resistance between ground and terminal No. 1F. If resistance is 2-5 ohms at 68°F (20°C), go to step **4)**. If resistance is not 2-5 ohms at 68°F (20°C), go to next step.

2) Measure resistance between ground and terminal No. 1H. If resistance is 12.5-19.0 ohms at 68°F (20°C), go to step **4)**. If resistance is not 12.5-19.0 ohms at 68°F (20°C), go to next step.

3) Disconnect solenoid harness connector. Measure resistance between ground and terminal "E". If resistance is 2-5 ohms at 68°F (20°C), go to step **4)**. If resistance is not 2-5 ohms at 68°F (20°C), go to next step.

4) Inspect pressure control solenoid and related circuits. See SOLENOID VALVES under COMPONENT TESTING. Repair as needed. If solenoid valve and related circuits are okay, go to next step.

5) Check continuity of circuits between pressure control solenoid and TCM. See appropriate wiring diagram in WIRING DIAGRAMS. Repair as needed. If circuits are okay, go to next step.

6) Measure resistance between dropping resistor terminals. Dropping resistor is located in left rear corner or engine compartment. *See Fig. 9 or 10.* If resistance is 10-14 ohms, go to next step. If resistance is not 10-14 ohms, replace resistor.

7) Disconnect negative battery cable for at least 20 seconds. Depress brake pedal. Reconnect negative battery cable. Road test vehicle. Retrieve DTC's. If DTC 64 is still present, replace TCM. If code is no longer present, problem may be caused by poor connection. Repair as needed.

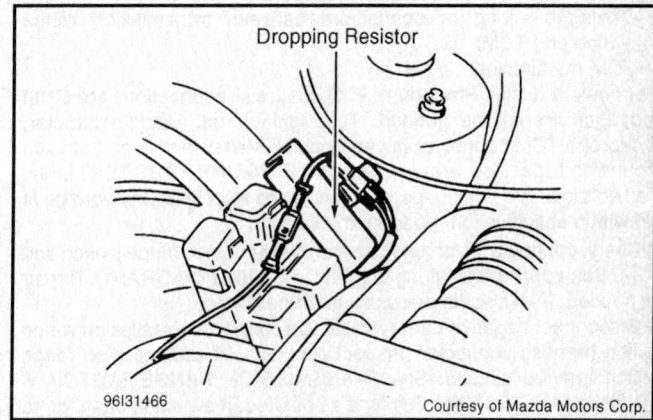

96I31466   Courtesy of Mazda Motors Corp.

Fig. 9: Locating Dropping Resistor (RX7)

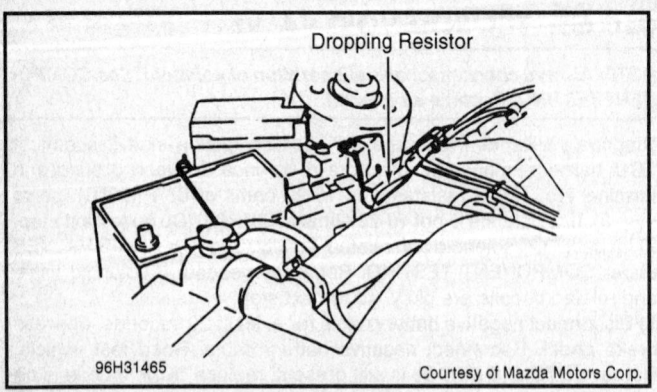

Fig. 10: Locating Dropping Resistor (929)

DTC 65: TCC CONTROL SOLENOID VALVE

NOTE: Always check mechanical operation of solenoid. See COMPONENT TESTING. Replace as needed.

1) Turn ignition on. Using voltmeter, backprobe TCM harness connector. Do not disconnect connector. Test drive vehicle.

2) Measure voltage between ground and terminal No. 2F on TCM harness connector. During test drive voltage should be zero volts when solenoid is off and battery voltage when solenoid is on. If voltage is within specification, go to step 5). If voltage is not within specification, go to next step.

3) Turn ignition off. Disconnect TCM harness connector. Measure resistance between ground and terminal No. 2F. If resistance is 20-40 ohms at 68°F (20°C), go to step 5). If resistance is not 20-40 ohms at 68°F (20°C), go to next step.

4) Inspect TCC control solenoid and related circuits. See SOLENOID VALVES under COMPONENT TESTING. Repair as needed. If solenoid valve and related circuits are okay, go to next step.

5) Disconnect negative battery cable for at least 20 seconds. Depress brake pedal. Reconnect negative battery cable. Road test vehicle. Retrieve DTC's. If DTC 65 is still present, replace TCM. If code is no longer present, problem may be caused by poor connection. Repair as needed.

DTC P0705: TRANSMISSION RANGE SWITCH CIRCUIT MALFUNCTION

Condition – No signal is received from range switch or more than 2 signals are received at one time. Possible causes for either condition are:

- Transmission range switch malfunction.
- Damaged wiring or connectors between transmission range switch and TCM.
- TCM malfunction.

Diagnosis & Repair Procedure – 1) Ensure all connections are clean and tight. Repair as needed. Turn ignition on. Using voltmeter, backprobe TCM connector (as applicable). Measure voltage between ground and specified terminal. See DTC P0705 VOLTAGE TEST table. If all voltages are within specification, go to step 5). If any voltage is not within specification, go to next step.

2) Check continuity of circuits between transmission range switch and TCM. See appropriate wiring diagram in WIRING DIAGRAMS. Repair as needed. If all circuits are okay, go to next step.

3) Disconnect negative battery cable. Disconnect transmission range switch harness connector. Inspect continuity of transmission range switch internal circuits. See TRANSMISSION RANGE SWITCH in COMPONENT TESTING. Replace as needed. If switch is okay, go to next step.

4) Reconnect negative battery cable. Turn ignition on. Measure voltage at terminal "I" (Blue/Black wire) on transmission range switch harness connector. If battery voltage does not exist, repair Blue/Black wire between switch and ignition switch. If battery voltage exists, go to next step.

DTC P0705 VOLTAGE TEST

TCM Terminal No.	Measured Voltage	Range Switch Position
2D	10-14	"P" Or "N"
2D	0	"R", "D", "S" Or "L"
1E	10-14	"R"
1E	0	All Except "R"
2B	10-14	"D"
2B	0	All Except "D"
2S	10-14	"S"
2S	0	All Except "S"
2Q	10-14	"L"
2Q	0	All Except "L"

5) Road test vehicle. Retrieve DTC's. If code P0705 is still present, replace TCM. If code is no longer present, system is okay.

DTC P0710: TRANSMISSION FLUID TEMPERATURE (TFT) SENSOR CIRCUIT MALFUNCTION

Condition – Voltage input to TCM is less than .1 volt or greater than 5.0 volts. Possible causes for condition are:

- Transmission fluid temperature sensor malfunction.
- Damaged wiring or connectors between transmission fluid temperature sensor and TCM.

Diagnosis & Repair Procedure – 1) Ensure all connections are clean and tight. Repair as needed. Turn ignition on. Access TCM connectors. Using voltmeter, backprobe harness connectors. Do not disconnect connectors. Go to next step.

2) Measure voltage between terminal No. 2R (Green/Black wire) and No. 2L (Blue wire) on TCM connector. Voltage should be about 1.8 volts at 50°F (10°C) or 1.1 volts at 104°F (40°C). If voltage is within specifications, go to step 6). If voltage is not within specifications, go to next step.

3) Turn ignition off. Disconnect TCM harness connector. Measure resistance between terminals No. 2R (Green/Black wire) and No. 2L (Blue wire). See TFT SENSOR SPECIFICATIONS. If resistance is within specification, go to step 6). If resistance is not within specification, go to next step.

4) Inspect TFT sensor. Disconnect TFT sensor harness connector. Measure resistance between connector terminals. See TFT SENSOR SPECIFICATIONS. If resistance is within specification, go to step 6). If resistance is not within specification, replace TFT sensor.

5) Check continuity of circuits between TFT sensor and TCM. See appropriate wiring diagram in WIRING DIAGRAMS. Repair as needed. If circuit is okay, go to next step.

6) Reconnect all harness connectors. Road test vehicle. Retrieve DTC's. If code P0710 is still present, replace TCM. If code is no longer present, system is okay.

TFT SENSOR SPECIFICATIONS

K/Ohms	Fluid Temperature
68°F (20°C)	12.5
176°F (80°C)	.3

DTC P0720: OUTPUT SPEED SENSOR

Condition – Output speed sensor signal is not input to TCM when vehicle is above 25 MPH and shift lever is in "D", "S" or "L" position. Possible causes for condition are:

- Output speed sensor malfunction.
- Damaged wiring or connectors between turbine speed sensor and TCM.
- TCM malfunction.

Diagnosis & Repair Procedure – 1) Ensure all connections are clean and tight. Repair as needed. Turn ignition on. Access TCM connectors. Using voltmeter, backprobe harness connectors. Do not disconnect connectors. Go to next step.

2) Start and idle engine in Park or Neutral. Measure AC voltage between terminals No. 2J (positive) and No. 2L (negative). Test drive

vehicle. Voltage should be zero when idling and more than one volt above 25 MPH. If voltage is within specification, go to step 6). If voltage is not within specification, go to next step.

3) Turn ignition off. Disconnect TCM harness connector. Measure resistance between terminals No. 2J (Red/White wire) and No. 2L (Blue wire). Resistance should be 504-616 ohms. If resistance is within specification, go to step 6). If resistance is not within specification, go to next step.

4) Inspect output speed sensor. See OUTPUT SPEED SENSOR under COMPONENT TESTING. Repair as needed. If sensor is okay, go to next step.

5) Check continuity of circuits between output speed sensor and TCM. See appropriate wiring diagram in WIRING DIAGRAMS. Repair as needed. If circuits are okay, go to next step.

6) Reconnect all harness connectors. Road test vehicle. Retrieve DTC's. If code P0720 is still present, replace PCM. If code is no longer present, system is okay.

DTC P0725: ENGINE SPEED INPUT CIRCUIT MALFUNCTION

Condition – Engine speed input signal is not input to TCM. Possible causes are:
- Crankshaft position sensor malfunction.
- Damaged wiring or connectors between ECM and TCM.
- ECM malfunction.
- TCM malfunction.

Diagnosis & Repair Procedure – 1) Ensure all connections are clean and tight. Repair as needed. Turn ignition on. Using voltmeter, backprobe TCM harness connector. Do not disconnect connector.

2) Measure voltage between ground and terminal No. 1G (Red/Yellow wire) on TCM harness connector. If voltage is 5-6 volts with engine stopped or battery voltage with engine running, go to next step. If voltage is not 5-6 volts with engine stopped or battery voltage with engine running, repair Red/Yellow wire between TCM and ECM for open or short.

3) Using voltmeter, backprobe ECM harness connector. Measure voltage between ground and terminal No. 4R (Red/Yellow wire). If voltage is 5-6 volts with engine stopped or battery voltage with engine running, go to step 5). If voltage is not 5-6 volts with engine stopped or battery voltage with engine running, go to next step.

4) Inspect crankshaft position sensor. See appropriate SYSTEM & COMPONENT TESTING article in ENGINE PERFORMANCE in appropriate MITCHELL® manual. Replace as needed. If sensor is okay, go to next step.

5) Reconnect all harness connectors. Road test vehicle. Retrieve DTC's. If code P0725 is still present, replace PCM. If code is no longer present, system is okay.

DTC P0731: INCORRECT 1ST GEAR RATIO

NOTE: If any of the following DTC's are also present, repair them first and then proceed with this test: DTC P0750, DTC P0755.

Condition – TCM outputs solenoid pattern of 1st gear when gear ratio is other than 1st gear. Possible causes are:
- Low ATF level.
- Low line pressure.
- Control valve stuck.
- Solenoid valve malfunction.
- TCM malfunction.

Diagnosis & Repair Procedure – 1) Ensure ATF level and condition is okay. Refer to TESTING and COMPONENT TESTING in MAZDA RA4A-EL, RA4AX-EL & RB4A-EL overhaul article and perform the following tests, repair any components as necessary: Check line pressure, if line pressure is okay, go to next step.

2) Perform stall speed test. If stall speed is okay, go to next step.

3) Inspect solenoid valves "A" and "B". See SOLENOID VALVES under COMPONENT TESTING. Repair as needed. If solenoid valves are okay, go to next step.

4) Inspect valve body. Ensure all valves operate smoothly. Repair as needed. If valve body is okay, go to next step.

5) Clear DTC's and retest. See CLEARING CODES. If code P0731 is still present, replace PCM. If code is no longer present and symptom still exists, problem may be caused by intermittent clutch slippage. Further investigation may be required. See MAZDA RA4A-EL, RA4AX-EL & RB4A-EL overhaul article.

DTC P0732: INCORRECT 2ND GEAR RATIO

NOTE: If any of the following DTC's are also present, repair them first and then proceed with this test: DTC P0750, DTC P0755.

Condition – TCM outputs solenoid pattern of 2nd gear when gear ratio is other than 2nd gear. Possible causes are:
- Low ATF level.
- Forward clutch slippage.
- Forward one-way clutch slippage.
- Faulty band servo.
- Low line pressure.
- Control valve stuck.
- Solenoid valve malfunction.
- TCM malfunction.

Diagnosis & Repair Procedure – 1) Ensure ATF level and condition is okay. Refer to TESTING and COMPONENT TESTING in MAZDA RA4A-EL, RA4AX-EL & RB4A-EL overhaul article and perform the following tests, repair any components as necessary: Check line pressure, if line pressure is okay, go to next step.

2) Perform stall speed test. If stall speed is okay, go to next step.

3) Inspect solenoid valves "A" and "B". See SOLENOID VALVES under COMPONENT TESTING. Repair as needed. If solenoid valves are okay, go to next step.

4) Inspect valve body. Ensure all valves operate smoothly. Repair as needed. If valve body is okay, go to next step.

5) Clear DTC's and retest. See CLEARING CODES. If code P0732 is still present, replace PCM. If code is no longer present and symptom still exists, problem may be caused by intermittent clutch slippage. Further investigation may be required. See MAZDA RA4A-EL, RA4AX-EL & RB4A-EL overhaul article.

DTC P0733: INCORRECT 3RD GEAR RATIO

NOTE: If any of the following DTC's are also present, repair them first and then proceed with this test: DTC P0750, DTC P0755.

Condition – TCM outputs solenoid pattern of 3rd gear when gear ratio is other than 3rd gear. Possible causes are:
- Low ATF level.
- Forward clutch slippage.
- Forward one-way clutch slippage.
- High clutch slippage.
- Low line pressure.
- Control valve stuck.
- Solenoid valve malfunction.
- TCM malfunction.

Diagnosis & Repair Procedure – 1) Ensure ATF level and condition is okay. Refer to TESTING and COMPONENT TESTING in MAZDA RA4A-EL, RA4AX-EL & RB4A-EL overhaul article and perform the following tests, repair any components as necessary: Check line pressure, if line pressure is okay, go to next step.

2) Inspect solenoid valves "A" and "B". See SOLENOID VALVES under COMPONENT TESTING. Repair as needed. If solenoid valves are okay, go to next step.

3) Inspect valve body. Ensure all valves operate smoothly. Repair as needed. If valve body is okay, go to next step.

4) Clear DTC's and retest. See CLEARING CODES. If code P0733 is still present, replace PCM. If code is no longer present and symptom still exists, problem may be caused by intermittent clutch slippage. Further investigation may be required. See MAZDA RA4A-EL, RA4AX-EL & RB4A-EL overhaul article.

DTC P0734: INCORRECT 4TH GEAR RATIO

NOTE: If any of the following DTC's are also present, repair them first and then proceed with this test: DTC P0750, DTC P0755.

Condition – TCM outputs solenoid pattern of 3rd gear when gear ratio is other than 3rd gear. Possible causes are:

- Low ATF level.
- Band servo slippage.
- High clutch slippage.
- Low line pressure.
- Control valve stuck.
- Solenoid valve malfunction.
- TCM malfunction.

Diagnosis & Repair Procedure – **1)** Ensure ATF level and condition is okay. Refer to TESTING and COMPONENT TESTING in MAZDA RA4A-EL, RA4AX-EL & RB4A-EL overhaul article and perform the following tests, repair any components as necessary: Check line pressure, if line pressure is okay, go to next step.

2) Inspect solenoid valves "A" and "B". See SOLENOID VALVES under COMPONENT TESTING. Repair as needed. If solenoid valves are okay, go to next step.

3) Inspect valve body. Ensure all valves operate smoothly. Repair as needed. If valve body is okay, go to next step.

4) Clear DTC's and retest. See CLEARING CODES. If code P0734 is still present, replace PCM. If code is no longer present and symptom still exists, problem may be caused by intermittent clutch slippage. Further investigation may be required. See MAZDA RA4A-EL, RA4AX-EL & RB4A-EL overhaul article.

DTC P0740: TORQUE CONVERTER CLUTCH MALFUNCTION

Condition – Shift solenoids "A", "B", vehicle speed sensor signal, output speed sensor and throttle position sensor function normally and vehicle speed is 44-65 MPH. There is a greater than 100 RPM difference between engine speed and idler gear speed with transmission in 4th gear and TCC engaged. Possible causes are:

- Low ATF level.
- Low line pressure.
- Torque converter slippage.
- Control valve stuck.
- Lock-up solenoid valve malfunction.
- TCM malfunction.

Diagnosis & Repair Procedure – **1)** Inspect ATF level and condition. Correct as needed. If fluid level and condition is okay, check line pressure. See TESTING in MAZDA RA4A-EL, RA4AX-EL & RB4A-EL overhaul article. Follow repair recommendations if line pressure is not within specifications. If line pressure is okay, go to next step.

2) Inspect lock-up solenoid. See SOLENOID VALVES under COMPONENT TESTING. Repair as needed. If solenoid valve is okay, go to next step.

3) Inspect lock-up control valve in valve body. If valve is okay, go to next step.

4) Clear DTC's. See CLEARING CODES. Retrieve DTC's. If code P0740 is still present, replace TCM. If code is no longer present and symptom still exists, problem may be caused by intermittent TCC slippage. Further investigation may be required. See MAZDA RA4A-EL, RA4AX-EL & RB4A-EL overhaul article.

DTC P0745: PRESSURE CONTROL SOLENOID MALFUNCTION

Possible Causes:
- Open or short circuit.
- TCM malfunction.
- Pressure control solenoid malfunction.

Diagnosis & Repair Procedure – **1)** Ensure all connections are clean and tight. Repair as needed. Turn ignition on. Using voltmeter, backprobe TCM harness connector. Do not disconnect connector.

2) Measure voltage between ground and terminal No. 1F (Violet wire). Battery voltage should be present when driving vehicle and zero voltage should be present with vehicle stopped. If voltage is within specifications, go to step **8)**. If voltage is not within specifications, go to next step.

3) Ensure ignition is off. Disconnect negative battery cable. Disconnect TCM harness connector. Measure resistance between ground and terminal No. 1F (Violet wire) on TCM harness connector. If resistance is 2.5-5 ohms at 68°F (20°C), go to step **8)**. If resistance is not 2.5-5 ohms at 68°F (20°C), go to next step.

4) Inspect pressure control solenoid. See SOLENOID VALVES under COMPONENT TESTING. Repair as needed. If solenoid valve is okay, go to next step.

5) Check continuity of circuits between pressure control solenoid and TCM. See appropriate wiring diagram in WIRING DIAGRAMS. Repair as needed. If circuits are okay, go to next step.

6) Measure resistance between dropping resistor terminals. Dropping resistor is located in left rear corner or engine compartment. *See Fig. 11.* If resistance is 10-14 ohms, go to next step. If resistance is not 10-14 ohms, replace resistor.

7) Check continuity of circuit between pressure control solenoid and dropping resistor. See appropriate wiring diagram in WIRING DIAGRAMS. Repair as needed. If circuit is okay, go to next step.

8) Disconnect negative battery cable for at least 20 seconds. Depress brake pedal. Reconnect negative battery cable. Road test vehicle. Retrieve DTC's. If DTC P0745 is still present, replace TCM. If code is no longer present, system is okay.

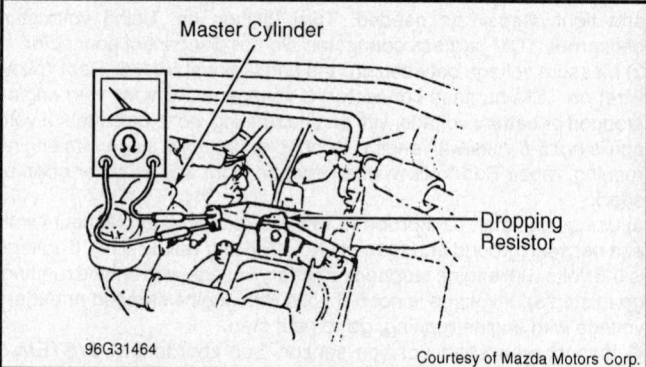

Fig. 11: Locating Dropping Resistor

DTC P0750: SHIFT SOLENOID "A" MALFUNCTION

Possible Causes:
- Short or open circuit between TCM and solenoid.
- TCM malfunction.
- Shift solenoid malfunction.

Diagnosis & Repair Procedure – **1)** Ensure all connections are clean and tight. Repair as needed. Turn ignition on. Access TCM connectors. Using voltmeter, backprobe harness connectors. Do not disconnect connectors. Go to next step.

2) Measure voltage between ground and terminal No. 1D (Pink/Black wire) on TCM connector. During test drive, voltage should be less than one volt when solenoid is off and battery voltage when solenoid is on. See SOLENOID OPERATION TABLE under TCM OUTPUT DEVICES. If voltage is within specification, go to step **5)**. If voltage is not within specification, go to next step.

3) Turn ignition off. Disconnect TCM harness connector. Measure resistance between ground and terminal No. 1D. If resistance is 20-40 ohms at 68°F (20°C), go to step **5)**. If resistance is not 20-40 ohms at 68°F (20°C), go to next step.

4) Inspect shift solenoid "A" and related circuits. See SOLENOID VALVES under COMPONENT TESTING. Repair as needed. If solenoid valve and related circuits are okay, go to next step.

5) Disconnect negative battery cable for at least 20 seconds. Depress brake pedal. Reconnect negative battery cable. Road test vehicle. Retrieve DTC's. If DTC P0750 is still present, replace TCM. If code is no longer present, system is okay.

DTC P0755: SHIFT SOLENOID "B" MALFUNCTION

Possible Causes:
- Short or open circuit between TCM and solenoid.
- PCM malfunction.
- Shift solenoid malfunction.

Diagnosis & Repair Procedure – **1)** Ensure all connections are clean and tight. Repair as needed. Turn ignition on. Access TCM connectors. Using voltmeter, backprobe harness connectors. Do not disconnect connectors. Go to next step.

2) Measure voltage between ground and terminal No. 1B (White/Red wire) on TCM connector. During test drive, voltage should be less than one volt when solenoid is off and battery voltage when solenoid is on. See SOLENOID OPERATION TABLE under TCM OUTPUT DEVICES. If voltage is within specification, go to step **5)**. If voltage is not within specification, go to next step.

3) Turn ignition off. Disconnect TCM harness connector. Measure resistance between ground and terminal No. 1B. If resistance is 20-40 ohms at 68°F (20°C), go to step **5)**. If resistance is not 20-40 ohms at 68°F (20°C), go to next step.

4) Inspect shift solenoid "B" and related circuits. See SOLENOID VALVES (ON/OFF TYPE) under COMPONENT TESTING. Repair as needed. If solenoid valve and related circuits are okay, go to next step.

5) Disconnect negative battery cable for at least 20 seconds. Depress brake pedal. Reconnect negative battery cable. Road test vehicle. Retrieve DTC's. If DTC P0755 is still present, replace TCM. If code is no longer present, problem may be caused by poor connection. Repair as needed.

DTC P1720: VEHICLE SPEED SENSOR MALFUNCTION

Condition – Vehicle speed sensor signal is not input to TCM when shift selector is in "D", "S" or "L" position. Possible causes are:
- Vehicle speed sensor malfunction.
- Damaged circuits or connectors between sensors and TCM.

Diagnosis & Repair Procedure – **1)** Ensure all connections are clean and tight. Repair as needed. Turn ignition on. Using voltmeter, backprobe TCM harness connector. Do not disconnect connector. Test drive vehicle.

2) Measure voltage between ground and terminal No. 1I (Green/Red wire) on TCM harness connector. During test drive voltage should be 2-3 volts or, 0 or 4-5 volts when parked. If voltage is within specifications, go to step **5)**. If voltage is not within specifications, go to next step.

3) Turn ignition off. Disconnect negative battery cable. Remove instrument cluter. Disconnect TCM harness connectors. Check continuity of Green/Red wire between terminal No. 1I on TCM connector and terminal No. 1G on instrument cluster harness center connector. Repair as needed. If continuity exists, go to next step.

4) With combination removed, check continuity between terminals No. 1G and 1H on combination meter center connector. If continuity exists, go to next step. If continuity does not exist, replace combination meter or circuit board (as applicable).

5) Disconnect negative battery cable for at least 20 seconds. Depress brake pedal. Reconnect negative battery cable. Road test vehicle. Retrieve DTC's. If DTC P1720 is still present, replace TCM. If code is no longer present, problem may be caused by poor connection. Repair as needed.

DTC P1743: TORQUE CONVERTER CLUTCH (TCC) CONTROL SOLENOID MALFUNCTION

Possible Causes:
- Short or open circuit between TCM and solenoid.

- TCM malfunction.
- Lock-up solenoid malfunction.

Diagnosis & Repair Procedure – **1)** Ensure all connections are clean and tight. Repair as needed. Turn ignition on. Access TCM connectors. Using voltmeter, backprobe harness connectors. Do not disconnect connectors. Go to next step.

2) Measure voltage between ground and terminal No. 1M (White wire). Battery voltage should be present with solenoid on and zero voltage with solenoid off. If voltage is within specifications, go to step **5)**. If voltage is not within specifications, go to next step.

3) Turn ignition off. Disconnect TCM harness connector. Measure resistance between ground and terminal No. 1M. If resistance is 10-20 ohms at 68°F (20°C), go to step **5)**. If resistance is not 10-20 ohms at 68°F (20°C), go to next step.

4) Inspect lock-up solenoid and related circuits. See SOLENOID VALVES under COMPONENT TESTING. Repair as needed. If solenoid valve and related circuits are okay, go to next step.

5) Disconnect negative battery cable for at least 20 seconds. Depress brake pedal. Reconnect negative battery cable. Road test vehicle. Retrieve DTC's. If DTC P1743 is still present, replace TCM. If code is no longer present, problem may be caused by poor connection. Repair as needed.

DTC P1770: OVERRUNNING CLUTCH SOLENOID VALVE MALFUNCTION

Possible Causes:
- Short or open circuit between TCM and solenoid.
- TCM malfunction.
- Overrunning clutch solenoid malfunction.

Diagnosis & Repair Procedure – **1)** Ensure all connections are clean and tight. Repair as needed. Turn ignition on. Access TCM connectors. Using voltmeter, backprobe harness connectors. Do not disconnect connectors. Go to next step.

2) Measure voltage between ground and terminal No. 1O (Pink wire). Battery voltage should be present with solenoid on and zero volts with solenoid off. If voltage is within specifications, go to step **5)**. If voltage is not within specifications, go to next step.

3) Turn ignition off. Disconnect TCM harness connector. Measure resistance between ground and terminal No. 1O. If resistance is 20-40 ohms at 68°F (20°C), go to step **5)**. If resistance is not 20-40 ohms at 68°F (20°C), go to next step.

4) Inspect overrunning clutch solenoid and related circuits. See SOLENOID VALVES under COMPONENT TESTING. Repair as needed. If solenoid valve and related circuits are okay, go to next step.

5) Disconnect negative battery cable for at least 20 seconds. Depress brake pedal. Reconnect negative battery cable. Road test vehicle. Retrieve DTC's. If DTC P1770 is still present, replace TCM. If code is no longer present, problem may be caused by poor connection. Repair as needed.

DTC P1790: THROTTLE POSITION (TP) SENSOR MALFUNCTION

Condition – TP sensor voltage is less than one volt or more than 4.9 volts. Possible causes are:
- Poor harness connection at TP sensor.
- Circuit fault between TP sensor and TCM.
- TP sensor.

Diagnosis & Repair Procedure – **1)** Ensure all connections are clean and tight. Repair as needed. Turn ignition on. Access TCM connectors. Using voltmeter, backprobe harness connectors. Do not disconnect connectors. Go to next step.

2) Measure voltage between ground and terminal No. 2T (Red/Blue wire) on TCM harness connector. With throttle closed, voltage should be .1-1.1 volts. With wide open throttle, voltage should be 3.1-4.4 volts. If voltage is within specification, go to step **5)**. If voltage is not within specification, go to next step.

3) Measure voltage between ground and terminal No. 2A (Brown/White wire) on TCM harness connector. With ignition on, voltage should be 4.5-5.5 volts. With ignition off, voltage should be zero volts. If voltage is within specification, go to step 5). If voltage is not within specification, go to next step.

4) Inspect circuits between TP sensor and TCM. See appropriate wiring diagram under WIRING DIAGRAMS. Repair as needed. If circuits are okay between sensor and TCM, go to next step.

5) Disconnect negative battery cable for at least 20 seconds. Depress brake pedal. Reconnect negative battery cable. Road test vehicle. Retrieve DTC's. If DTC P1790 is still present, replace TCM. If code is no longer present, problem may be caused by poor connection. Repair as needed.

DTC P1792: BAROMETRIC PRESSURE SENSOR

Condition – Open or short circuit. Possible causes are:
- Poor harness connection at barometric pressure sensor.
- Circuit fault between barometric pressure sensor and ECM.

Diagnosis & Repair Procedure – **1)** Turn ignition on. Using voltmeter, backprobe TCM harness connector. Do not disconnect connector. Measure voltage between ground and terminal No. 2G (Gray wire) on TCM connector. Voltage should be about 3.5 volts or greater below 4900 ft. elevation or less than 3.5 volts above 4900 ft. elevation. If voltage is within specification, go to step 3). If voltage is not within specification, go to next step.

2) Turn ignition off. Disconnect ECM and TCM harness connectors. Check continuity of Green/Orange wire between terminal No. 1K on ECM harness connector and terminal No. 2G on TCM harness connector. Repair as needed. If circuit is okay, go to next step.

3) Disconnect negative battery cable for at least 20 seconds. Depress brake pedal. Reconnect negative battery cable. Road test vehicle. Retrieve DTC's. If DTC P1792 is still present, replace ECM. If code is no longer present, problem may be caused by poor connection. Repair as needed.

COMPONENT TESTING

NOTE: For connector terminal identification, see COMPONENT CONNECTOR IDENTIFICATION table. For circuit or wire color identification, see appropriate wiring diagram in WIRING DIAGRAMS.

HOLD SWITCH OR O/D OFF SWITCH (MPV)

1) Turn ignition on. Ensure HOLD or O/D OFF indicator illuminates with switch depressed. Ensure indicator light is not illuminated when switch is released. If switch is not working as described, go to next step.

2) Access switch connector under driver's dash. Disconnect connector. Check continuity between ground and terminal "A". *See Fig. 12.* Continuity should exist when switch is released. When switch is depressed, continuity should not exist. Replace as needed. If HOLD or O/D OFF switch system does not function correctly, inspect circuits between switch and TCM. See appropriate wiring diagram in WIRING DIAGRAMS.

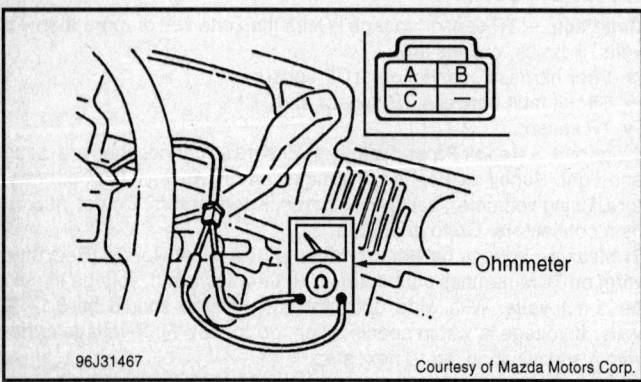

96J31467   Courtesy of Mazda Motors Corp.

Fig. 12: Testing HOLD Or O/D OFF Switch (MPV)

HOLD SWITCH (RX7)

1) Turn ignition on. Ensure HOLD indicator illuminates with switch depressed. Ensure indicator light is not illuminated when switch is released. If switch is not working as described, go to next step.

2) Access switch connector under center console. Disconnect connector. Check continuity between terminals "D" and "F". *See Fig. 13.* Continuity should exist when switch is released. When switch is depressed, continuity should not exist. Replace as needed. If HOLD switch system does not function correctly, inspect circuits between switch and TCM. See appropriate wiring diagram in WIRING DIAGRAMS.

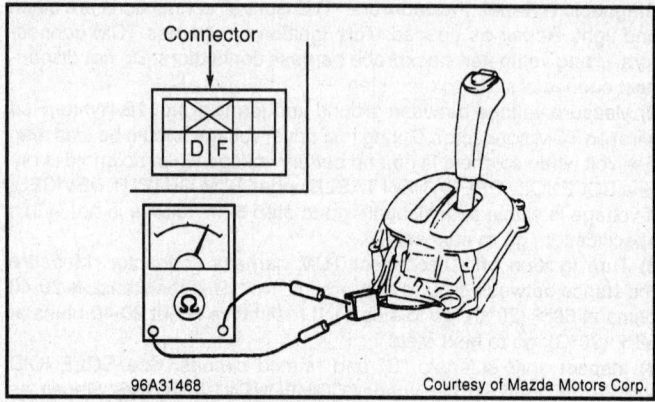

96A31468   Courtesy of Mazda Motors Corp.

Fig. 13: Testing HOLD Switch (RX7)

HOLD SWITCH (929)

1) Turn ignition on. Ensure HOLD indicator illuminates with switch depressed. Ensure indicator light is not illuminated when switch is released. If switch is not working as described, go to next step.

2) Access switch connector under center console. Disconnect connector. Check continuity between terminals "A" and "B". *See Fig. 14.* Continuity should exist when switch is released. When switch is depressed, continuity should not exist. Replace as needed. If HOLD switch system does not function correctly, inspect circuits between switch and TCM. See appropriate wiring diagram in WIRING DIAGRAMS.

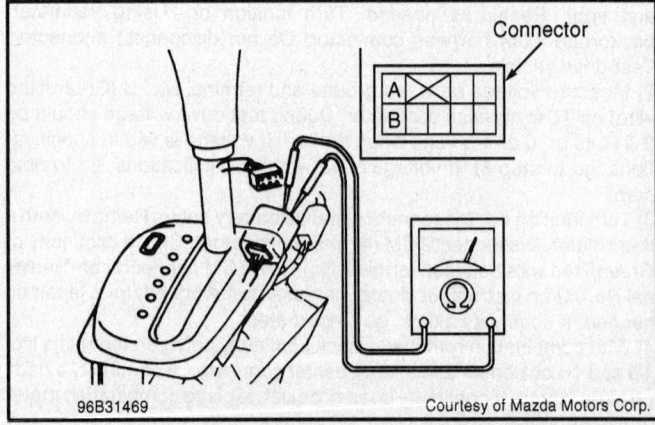

96B31469   Courtesy of Mazda Motors Corp.

Fig. 14: Testing HOLD Switch (929)

INPUT/TURBINE SPEED SENSOR (RX7 & 929)

Disconnect output speed sensor connector. Measure resistance between terminals. Resistance should be 500-1000 ohms between terminals "A" and "B" and infinite resistance between all other terminal pairings. Replace as needed. *See Fig. 15.*

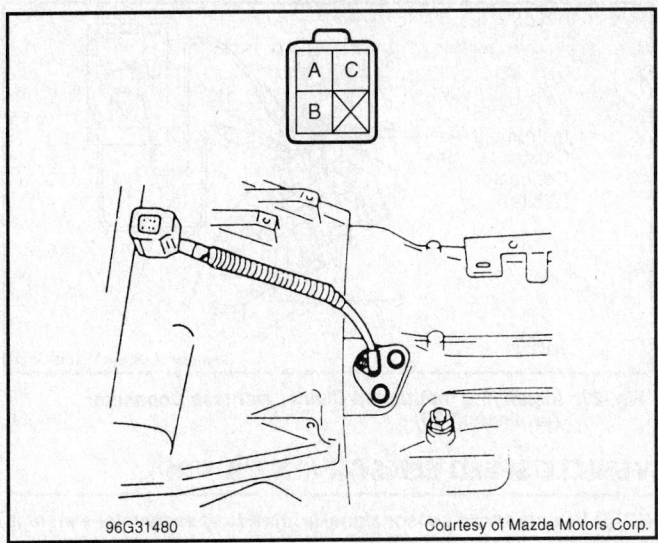

Fig. 15: Locating Input/Turbine Speed Sensor

OUTPUT SPEED SENSOR (MPV)

Disconnect output speed sensor connector. Measure resistance between terminals. Resistance should be 504-616 ohms between terminals "A" and "B" and infinite resistance between all other terminal pairings. *See Fig. 16.* Replace as needed.

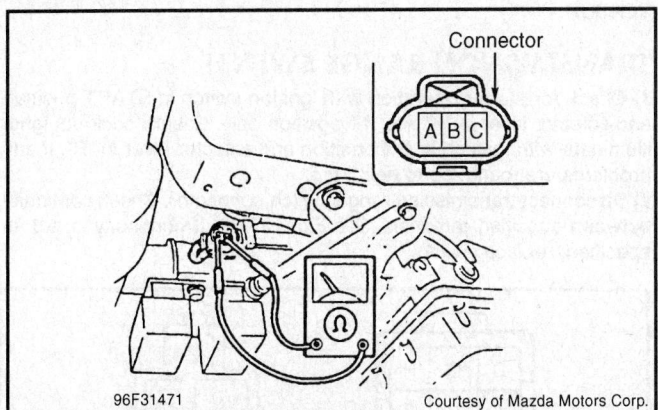

Fig. 16: Testing Output Speed Sensor & Locating Transaxle Component Connectors

OUTPUT SPEED SENSOR (RX7 & 929)

Disconnect output speed sensor connector. Measure resistance between terminals. *See Fig. 17.* Resistance should be 500-1000 ohms between terminals "A" and "B" and infinite resistance between all other terminal pairings. Replace as needed.

SOLENOID VALVES

Disconnect negative battery cable. Disconnect transmission solenoid harness connector. *See Figs. 18 and 19.* Note that solenoids ground through transmission case. Check resistance between connector terminals and ground. Replace solenoids as necessary. Ensure transmission case is grounded.

NOTE: *Information for vehicle speed sensor on MPV is not available from manufacturer.*

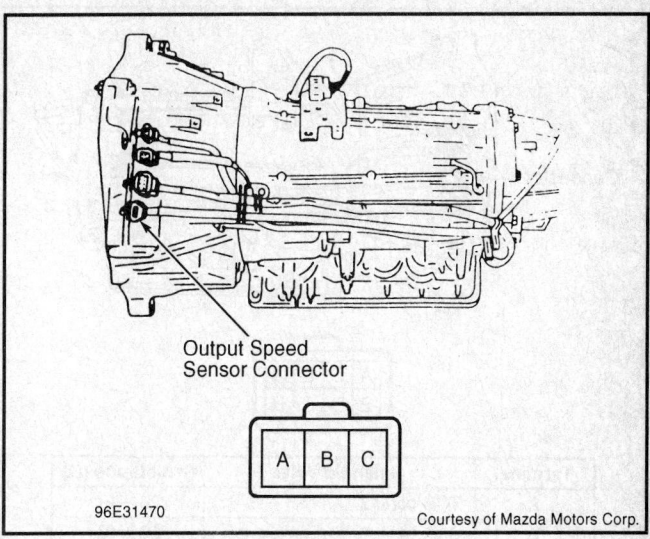

Fig. 17: Locating Output Speed Sensor & Identifying Connector Terminals

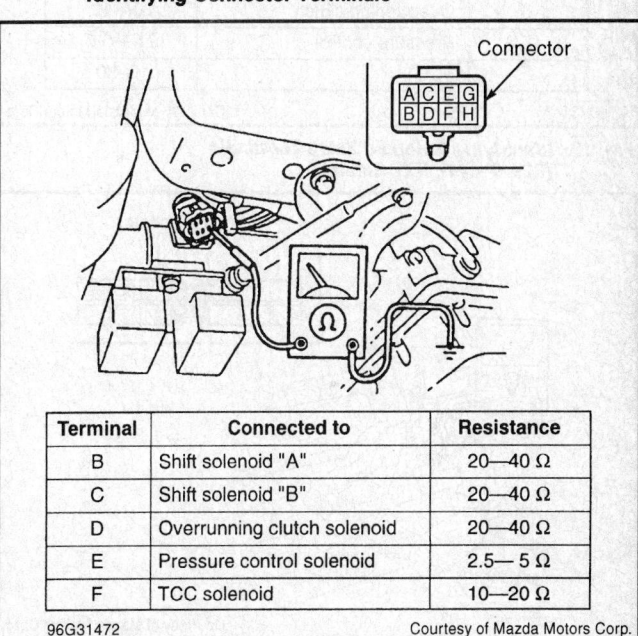

Terminal	Connected to	Resistance
B	Shift solenoid "A"	20—40 Ω
C	Shift solenoid "B"	20—40 Ω
D	Overrunning clutch solenoid	20—40 Ω
E	Pressure control solenoid	2.5— 5 Ω
F	TCC solenoid	10—20 Ω

Fig. 18: Identifying Solenoid Valve Terminals (MPV)

SPEEDOMETER SENSOR (RX7)

NOTE: *Speedometer sensor is part of speedometer in combination meter.*

1) Remove instrument cluster. Raise and support rear of vehicle. Rotate rear wheels. Measure voltage between terminals No. 3A (Yellow/White wire) and 3C (Yellow/Red wire). *See Fig. 20.*
2) Monitor voltage as wheels are rotated. If voltage pulse is present, go to next step. If voltage pulse is not present, inspect vehicle speed sensor. See VEHICLE SPEED SENSOR (RX7 & 929). Replace as needed. If vehicle speed sensor is okay, repair circuits between vehicle speed sensor and speedometer sensor. Go to next step.
3) Ensure harness connector is connected to speedmeter sensor. Turn ignition on. Rotate rear wheels. Measure voltage between ground and terminal No. 3E. Monitor voltage as wheels are rotated. If voltage pulse is present, speedometer sensor is currently functioning correctly. If voltage pulse is not present, replace combination meter or circuit board (as applicable).

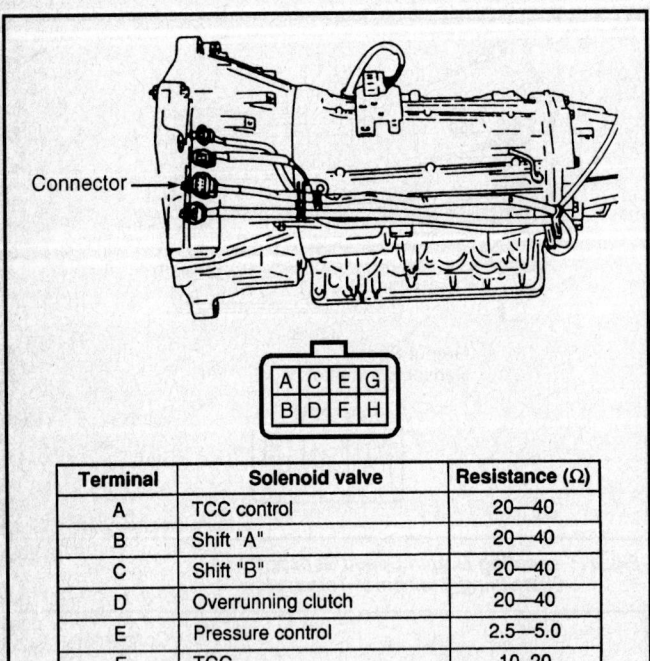

Terminal	Solenoid valve	Resistance (Ω)
A	TCC control	20—40
B	Shift "A"	20—40
C	Shift "B"	20—40
D	Overrunning clutch	20—40
E	Pressure control	2.5—5.0
F	TCC	10—20

96H31473   Courtesy of Mazda Motors Corp.

Fig. 19: Identifying Solenoid Valve Terminals (929 Shown, RX7 Similar)

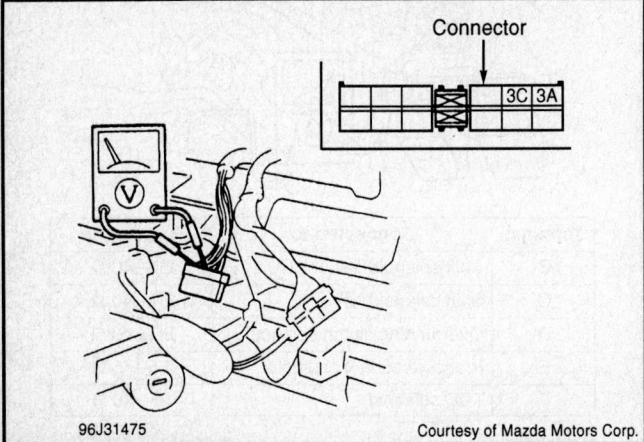

96J31475   Courtesy of Mazda Motors Corp.

Fig. 20: Identifying Instrument Cluster Harness Connector Terminals (RX7)

SPEEDOMETER SENSOR (929)

NOTE: Speedometer sensor is part of speedometer in combination meter.

1) Remove instrument cluster. Raise and support rear of vehicle. Rotate rear wheels. Measure voltage between terminals No. 1K (Blue/White wire) and 1L (Blue/Yellow wire). See Fig. 21.
2) Monitor voltage as wheels are rotated. If voltage pulse is present, go to next step. If voltage pulse is not present, inspect vehicle speed sensor. See VEHICLE SPEED SENSOR (RX7 & 929). Replace as needed. If vehicle speed sensor is okay, repair circuits between vehicle speed sensor and speedometer sensor. Go to next step.
3) Ensure harness connector is connected to speedmeter sensor. Turn ignition on. Rotate rear wheels. Measure voltage between ground and terminal No. 1M (Green/Red wire). Monitor voltage as wheels are rotated. If voltage pulse is present, speedometer sensor is currently functioning correctly. If voltage pulse is not present, replace combination meter or circuit board (as applicable).

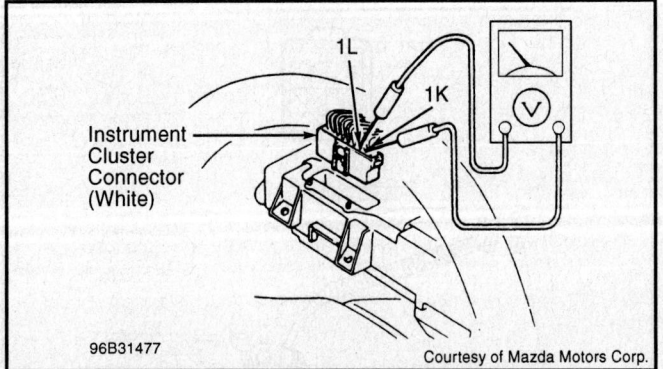

96B31477   Courtesy of Mazda Motors Corp.

Fig. 21: Identifying Instrument Cluster Harness Connector Terminals (929)

VEHICLE SPEED SENSOR (RX7 & 929)

NOTE: Vehicle speed sensor signal is input to speedometer sensor in combination meter than output to TCM (as applicable).

1) Disconnect negative battery cable. Disconnect vehicle speed sensor connector. Measure resistance between sensor connector terminals. If resistance is 290 ohms, go to next step. If resistance is not 290 ohms, replace sensor.
2) Rotate rear wheels and measure voltage between sensor terminals. If voltmeter needle does not fluctuate, replace sensor. If voltmeter needle fluctuates, but signal to TCM is suspect, go to SPEEDOMETER SENSOR.

TRANSMISSION RANGE SWITCH

1) Check for starter operation with ignition switch in START position and selector lever in "P" and "N" position only. Ensure back-up lights illuminate with ignition in ON position and selector lever in "R". If any problems are found, go to next step.
2) Disconnect transmission range switch connector. Check continuity between specified terminals. See Figs. 22-24. If continuity is not as specified, replace switch.

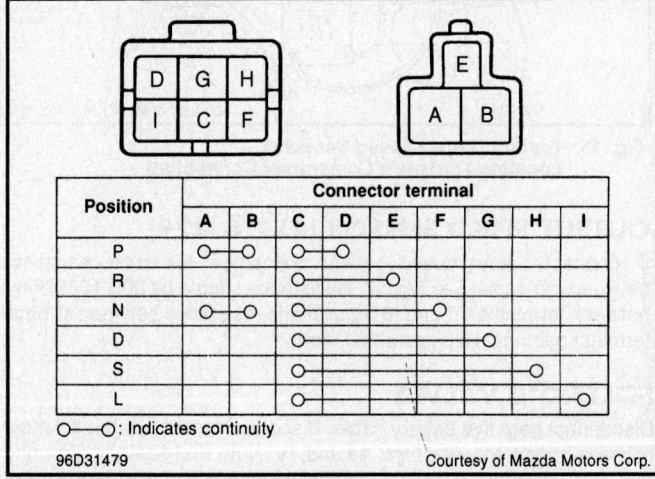

Position	Connector terminal								
	A	B	C	D	E	F	G	H	I
P	O—O		O—O						
R			O			O			
N	O—O		O				O		
D			O					O	
S			O						O
L			O						O

O—O : Indicates continuity

96D31479   Courtesy of Mazda Motors Corp.

Fig. 22: Checking Transmission Range Switch (1995 MPV)

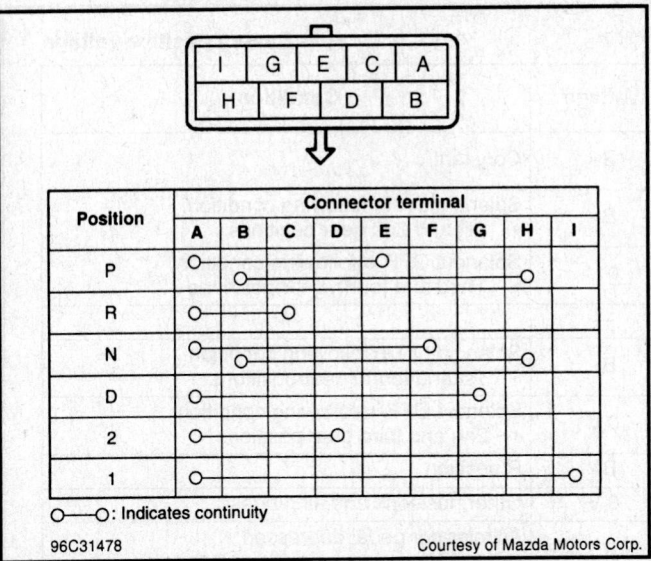

Fig. 23: Checking Transmission Range Switch (1996 MPV)

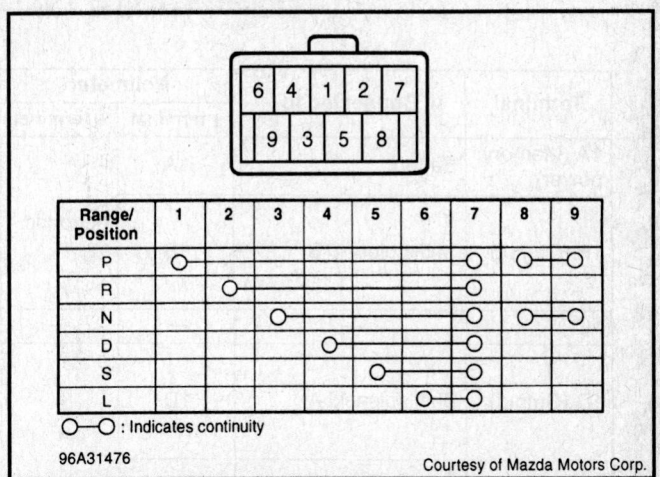

Fig. 24: Checking Transmission Range Switch (RX7 & 929)

TCM TERMINAL VOLTAGE TESTS

Turn ignition switch to ON position. Access TCM. Do not disconnect harness connector. Using DVOM, measure voltage. *See Figs. 25-37.* After verifying that appropriate condition has been met, check voltage. If voltage is not within specification, replace TCM (as applicable).

AUTOMATIC TRANSMISSIONS
Mazda R4A-EL Series Electronic Controls (Cont.)

B+: Battery positive voltage

Terminal	Connected to	Voltmeter		Voltage	Condition
		+ terminal	– terminal		
1A (Memory power)	Battery	1A	Ground	B+	Constant
1B (Output)	Shift solenoid B	1B		B+	Solenoid ON in following condition: • 1st and 2nd gear positions
				0 V	Solenoid OFF in following condition: • Third and fourth gear positions
1C	—	—	—	—	—
1D (Output)	Shift solenoid A	1D		B+	Solenoid ON in following condition: • 1st and fourth gear positions
				0 V	Solenoid OFF in following condition: • 2nd and third gear positions
1E (Input)	Transmission range switch (R position)	1E		B+	R position
				0 V	Other positions and all ranges
1F (Output)	Pressure control solenoid	1F		Below 1.5 V	Accelerator pedal depressed (After ATF warm, engine stopped)
				1.7—4.5 V	Accelerator pedal fully released (After ATF warm, engine stopped)
1G (Input)	Engine rpm sensor*	1G		Above 1 V (AC)	Engine running
				Below 0.5 V (AC)	Engine stopped
1H (Output)	Dropping resistor	1H		B+	Accelerator pedal fully released (After ATF warm, engine stopped)
				Below 1.5 V	Accelerator pedal depressed (After ATF warm, engine stopped)
1I (Input)	Vehicle speed sensor	1I	Ground	2—3 V	While driving
				0 V or 4.5—5.5 V	Vehicle stopped
1J (Ground)	—	1J		0 V	Constant
1K (Output)	Hold indicator light	1K		B+	POWER or ECONOMY mode
				0 V	HOLD mode
1L (Ground)	—	1L		0 V	Constant
1M (Output)	TCC solenoid	1M		B+	Solenoid ON, TCC operation
				Below 1.5 V	Solenoid OFF, TCC non-operation
1N (Battery power)	Battery	1N		B+	Ignition switch ON
				0 V	Ignition switch OFF
1O (Output)	Overrunning clutch solenoid	1O		B+	Solenoid ON in following condition: • D range (Engine stopped)
				0 V	Solenoid OFF in following condition: • Except D range (Engine stopped)
1P (Battery power)	Battery	1P		B+	Ignition switch ON
				0 V	Ignition switch OFF

* Checked with AC range

96C30801

Courtesy of Mazda Motors Corp.

Fig. 25: TCM Pin Voltage Table (1995 MPV, 1 Of 2)

B+: Battery positive voltage

Terminal	Connected to	Voltmeter		Voltage	Condition
2A (Input)	Throttle position sensor	2A	2L	4.5—5.5 V	Ignition switch ON
				0 V	Ignition switch OFF
2B (Input)	Transmission range switch (D range)	2B	Ground	B+	D range
				0 V	Other ranges and all positions
2C (Input)	Mode switch (2WD)	2C		Above 6 V	Switch released (Right position)
				0 V	Switch held to left
2D (Input)	Transmission range switch (N and P positions)	2D		B+	R position and all ranges
				0 V	P or N position
				Below 7 V	P or N position and engine crank
2E (Input)	Cruise control module	2E		Above 6 V	Normal conditions
				Below 1.5 V	Set or Resume switch ON or vehicle speed 8 km/h (5 mph) lower than preset speed (Driving vehicle cruise control operation)
2F (Output)	Mode indicator (2WD)	2F		B+	HOLD or ECONOMY mode
				0 V	POWER mode
2G (Input)	Engine control module	2G		Above 6 V	Normal condition
				Below 1.5 V	Atmospheric pressure below 89.5 kPa { 672 mmHg , 26.4 inHg } which is approximately at 1,500 m { 4,921 ft }
2H	—	—	—	—	—
2I (Input)	Hold switch	2I	Ground	Above 6 V	Switch released
				0 V	Switch depressed
2J (Input)	Output speed sensor	2J		Above 1 V (AC)	Vehicle speed above 25 km/h { 16 mph }
				Approx. 0 V (AC)	Vehicle stopped
2K (Input)	TAT terminal (Data link connector)	2K		Above 6 V	Normal
				0 V	TAT terminal grounded
2L (Ground)	Ground (For sensors)	2L		0 V	Constant
2M (Input)	Closed throttle position switch	2M		B+	Closed throttle position switch OFF (Throttle valve open)
				0 V	Closed throttle position switch ON (Throttle valve wide open throttle)
2N (Output)	FAT terminal (Data link connector)	2N		0 V	HOLD mode
				B+	Other modes
				Code signal	TAT terminal grounded
2O	—	—	—	—	—
2P	—	—	—	—	—
2Q (Input)	Transmission range switch (L range)	2Q	Ground	B+	L range
				0 V	Other ranges and all positions
2R (Input)	Transmission fluid temparature sensor	2R	2L	Approx. 2.4—0.4 V	While warming up ATF Note Approx. 1.8 V: ATF temp. 10 °C { 50 °F } Approx. 1.1 V: ATF temp. 40 °C { 104 °F }
2S (Input)	Transmission range switch (S range)	2S	Ground	B+	S range
				0 V	Other ranges and all positions
2T (Input)	Throttle position sensor	2T	2L	Approx. 0.4—4.4 V	Throttle valve closed throttle position to wide open throttle

* Checked with AC range

96D30802

Courtesy of Mazda Motors Corp.

Fig. 26: TCM Pin Voltage Table (1995 MPV, 2 Of 2)

AUTOMATIC TRANSMISSIONS
Mazda R4A-EL Series Electronic Controls (Cont.)

B+: Battery positive voltage

Terminal	Connected to	Voltmeter		Voltage	Condition
		+ terminal	− terminal		
1A	Battery	1A	Ground	B+	Constant
1B	Shift solenoid B	1B		B+	Solenoid ON in following condition: • 1GR and 2GR positions
				0 V	Solenoid OFF in following condition: • 3GR and 4GR positions
1C	—	—	—	—	—
1D	Shift solenoid A	1D		B+	Solenoid ON in following condition: • 1GR and 4GR positions
				0 V	Solenoid OFF in following condition: • 2GR and 3GR positions
1E	Transmission range switch (R position)	1E		B+	R position
				0 V	Other positions and all ranges
1F	Pressure control solenoid	1F		Below 1.5 V	Accelerator pedal depressed (After ATF warm, engine stopped)
				1.7—4.5 V	Accelerator pedal fully released (After ATF warm, engine stopped)
1G	Engine speed input signal*	1G	Ground	Above 1 V (AC)	Engine running
				Below 0.5 V (AC)	Engine stopped
1H	Dropping resistor	1H		B+	Accelerator pedal fully released (After ATF warm, engine stopped)
				Below 1.5 V	Accelerator pedal depressed (After ATF warm, engine stopped)
1I	Vehicle speed sensor	1I		2—3 V	While driving
				0 V or 4.5—5.5 V	Vehicle stopped
1J	—	1J		0 V	Constant
1K	O/D OFF indicator light	1K		B+	Except O/D OFF mode
				0 V	O/D OFF mode
1L	—	1L		0 V	Constant
1M	TCC solenoid	1M		B+	Solenoid ON, TCC operation
				Below 1.5 V	Solenoid OFF, TCC non-operation
1N	—	—	—	—	—
1O	Overrunning clutch solenoid	1O	Ground	B+	Solenoid ON in following condition: • D range (Engine stopped)
				0 V	Solenoid OFF in following condition: • Except D range (Engine stopped)
1P	Battery	1P		B+	Ignition switch ON
				0 V	Ignition switch OFF

* Checked with AC range

96E30803

Courtesy of Mazda Motors Corp.

Fig. 27: TCM Pin Voltage Table (1996 MPV, 1 Of 2)

B+: Battery positive voltage

Terminal	Connected to	Voltmeter		Voltage	Condition
		+ terminal	– terminal		
2A	Throttle position sensor	2A	2L	4.5—5.5 V	Ignition switch ON
				0 V	Ignition switch OFF
2B	Transmission range switch (D range)	2B	Ground	B+	D range
				0 V	Other ranges and all positions
2C	—	—	—	—	—
2D	Transmission range switch (N and P positions)	2D	Ground	B+	R position and all ranges
				0 V	P or N position
				Below 7 V	P or N position and engine crank
2E	Cruise control module	2E		Above 6 V	Normal conditions
				Below 1.5 V	Set or resume switch ON or vehicle speed 8 km/h (5 mph) lower than preset speed (Driving vehicle cruise control operation)
2F	—	—	—	—	—
2G	Engine control module	2G	Ground	Above 6 V	Normal condition
				Below 1.5 V	Atmospheric pressure below 89.5 kPa { 672 mmHg , 26.4 inHg } at 1,500 m { 4,921 ft }
2H	—	—	—	—	—
2I	O/D OFF switch	2I		Above 6 V	Switch released
				0 V	Switch depressed
2J	Output speed sensor	2J		Above 1 V (AC)	Vehicle speed above 25 km/h { 16 mph }
				Approx. 0 V (AC)	Vehicle stopped
2K	TEST signal	2K	Ground	B+	Ignition switch ON
				Below 1.0 V or repeat B+ and 0 V	TEST mode
2L	Ground (For sensors)	2L		0 V	Constant
2M	Closed throttle position switch	2M		B+	Closed throttle position switch OFF (Throttle valve open)
				0 V	Closed throttle position switch ON (Throttle valve wide open throttle)
2N	FAIL signal	2N		Below 1.0 V or repeat B+ and 0 V	Other modes
				B+	TEST mode
2O	—	—	—	—	—
2P	—	—	—	—	—
2Q	Transmission range switch (L range)	2Q	Ground	B+	L range
				0 V	Other ranges and all positions
2R	Transmission fluid temperature sensor	2R	2L	Approx. 2.4—0.4 V	While warming up ATF Note Approx. 1.8 V: ATF temp. 10 °C { 50 °F } Approx. 1.1 V: ATF temp. 40 °C { 104 °F }
2S	Transmission range switch (S range)	2S	Ground	B+	S range
				0 V	Other ranges and all positions
2T	Throttle position sensor	2T	2L	Approx. 0.4—4.4 V	Throttle valve moved from closed throttle position to wide open throttle

* Checked with AC range

96F30804

Courtesy of Mazda Motors Corp.

Fig. 28: TCM Pin Voltage Table (1996 MPV, 2 Of 2)

Mazda R4A-EL Series Electronic Controls (Cont.)

B+: Battery positive voltage

Terminal	Color	Component	Connected to	Voltmeter (+) terminal	Voltmeter (–) terminal	Correct voltage	Condition	Check area
1A	L/R	Battery (backup)	Battery	1A	Ground	B+	Constant	• Wiring and/or connector from terminal 1A to battery
1B (Output)	W/G	Shift solenoid B	Solenoid valve	1B	Ground	B+	All positions or 1GR and 2GR positions	• Shift solenoid B • Wiring and/or connector from 1B terminal to shift solenoid B
						Below 1.0V	4GR and 3GR positions	
1C (Output)	Y	Park/neutral position signal	Engine control module	1C	Ground	Below 1.0V	P and N positions	• Transmission range switch, input/turbine speed sensor and/or engine control module • Wiring and/or connector from terminal 1C to engine control module terminal 1R
						B+	R position and all ranges	
1D (Output)	W/R	Shift solenoid A	Solenoid valve	1D	Ground	B+	All positions or 1GR and 4GR positions.	• Shift solenoid A • Wiring and/or connector from terminal 1D to shift solenoid A
						Below 1.0V	2GR and 3GR positions	
1E (Input)	R	Transmission range switch (R position)	Transmission range switch	1E	Ground	B+	R position	• Transmission range switch • Wiring and/or connector from terminal 1E to transmission range switch
						0V	Except R position and all ranges	
1F (Output)	W/L	Pressure control solenoid	Solenoid valve	1F	Ground	Above 1.5V	Throttle valve closed throttle position	• Pressure control solenoid • Wiring and/or connector from terminal 1F to pressure control solenoid
						Below 1.0V	Throttle valve wide opened throttle	
1G (Input)	Y/L	Engine rpm signal	Engine control module	1G	Ground	0.3–0.8V	Engine running at idle	• Wiring and/or connector from terminal 1G to engine control module terminal 2B • Engine control module
						0V	Engine stopped	
						1.8–2.2V	Engine running at 3,000 rpm (no load)	
1H (Output)	B/LG	Dropping resistor	Dropping resistor	1H	Ground	B+	Throttle valve closed throttle position	• Dropping resistor and/or pressure control solenoid • Wiring and/or connector between terminal 1H, dropping resistor, and solenoid valve.
						Below 1.0V	Throttle valve wide opened throttle	

Terminal 1D voltage (shift solenoid A) is below 1.0V when in HOLD mode in P, R, and N positions.

96G30805

Courtesy of Mazda Motors Corp.

Fig. 29: PCM Pin Voltage Table (1995 RX7, 1 Of 5)

B+: Battery positive voltage

Terminal	Color	Component	Connected to	Voltmeter (+) terminal	Voltmeter (−) terminal	Correct voltage	Condition	Check area
1I (Input)	G/R	Vehicle speedometer sensor	Speedometer	1I		2–3V	Vehicle moving	• Vehicle speedometer sensor and/or speedometer
						0V or 4.5–5.5V	Vehicle stopped	• Wiring and/or connector between terminal 1I speedometer, and vehicle speedometer sensor.
1J (Ground)	B/L	Ground (Transmission control module)	—	1J		0V	Constant	• Wiring condition.
1K (Output)	Y	HOLD indicator light / FAT terminal (data link connector)	Combination meter (HOLD indicator light) and FAT terminal (data link connector)	1K		Below 1.0V	HOLD mode	• Wiring and/or connector from terminal 1K to HOLD indicator light (combination meter)
						B+	Non-HOLD mode	• HOLD indicator light
1L (Input)	V/P	A/C signal	A/C relay	1L		Below 3.0V	A/C ON	• Engine control module and/or A/C switch
						B+	A/C OFF	• Wiring and/or connector from terminal 1L to A/C switch
1M (Output)	W	TCC solenoid valve	Solenoid valve	1M	Ground	B+	TCC operation	• TCC solenoid valve • Wiring and/or connector from terminal 1M to TCC solenoid valve
						Below 1.0V	TCC non-operation	
1N	B/Y	Battery (main)	Ignition switch	1N		B+	Ignition switch ON	• Meter fuse and/or ignition switch
						0V	Ignition switch OFF	• Wiring and/or connector from terminal 1N to ignition switch (IG1)
1O (Output)	W/Y	Overrunning clutch solenoid valve	Solenoid valve	1O		Below 1.0V	Throttle valve wide opened throttle (D range)	• Overrunning clutch solenoid valve • Wiring and/or connector from terminal 1O to overrunning clutch solenoid valve
						B+	Throttle valve closed (D range)	
1P	B/Y	Battery (main)	Ignition switch	1P		B+	Ignition switch ON	• Meter fuse and/or ignition switch
						0V	Ignition switch OFF	• Wiring and/or connector from terminal 1P to ignition switch (IG1)
2A (Input)	BR/W	Throttle sensor (V$_{REF}$)	Throttle position sensor	2A		4.5–5.5V	Ignition switch ON	• Wiring and/or connector from terminal 2A to engine control module terminal 3I
						0V	Ignition switch OFF	• Throttle position sensor

96H30806

Courtesy of Mazda Motors Corp.

Fig. 30: PCM Pin Voltage Table (1995 RX7, 2 Of 5)

AUTOMATIC TRANSMISSIONS
Mazda R4A-EL Series Electronic Controls (Cont.)

B+: Battery positive voltage

Terminal	Color	Component	Connected to	Voltmeter		Correct voltage	Condition	Check area
				(+) terminal	(−) terminal			
2B (Input)	Y/G	Transmission range switch (D range)	Transmission range switch	2B	Ground	B+	D range	• Transmission range switch • Wiring and/or connector from terminal 2B to transmission range switch
						0V	Excect D range and all positions	
2C (Input)	G/Y	Barometric pressure sensor	Engine control module	2C		2.0–4.5V	Ignition switch ON	• Wiring and/or connector from terminal 2C to engine control module terminal 2D
						0V	Ignition switch OFF	
2D (Input)	L/Y	Transmission range switch (P and N positions)	Transmission range switch	2D	Ground	0V	P and N positions	• Transmission range switch and/or ignition switch • Wiring and/or connector between terminal 2D to transmission range switch, and ignition switch (STA)
						B+	Except P and N positions and all ranges	
2E (Input)	O	Input/turbine speed sensor	Input/turbine speed sensor	2E*¹	2L	Approx. above 0.5V AC	Vehicle speed above 25 km/h {16 MPH}	• Input/turbine speed sensor • Wiring and/or connector from terminal 2E to input/turbine speed sensor
						Approx. 0V (AC)	Vehicle stopped (Ignition switch ON)	
2F (Output)	W/R	TCC control solenoid valve	Solenoid valve	2F		B+	TCC operation	• TCC control solenoid valve • Wiring and/or connector from terminal 2F to TCC control solenoid valve
						Below 1.0V	TCC non-operation	
2G (Input)	G/R	Slip TCC OFF signal	Engine control module	2G		Below 1.0V	Engine running at 3.000 rpm	• Wiring and/or connector from terminal 2G to engine control module terminal 2C • Engine control module
						B+	Engine running at idle	
2H (Input)	L/G	Torque reduced signal	Engine control module	2H*²	Ground	B+	Engine running at idle	• Wiring and/or connector from terminal 2H to engine control module terminal 2G • Throttle position sensor, vehicle speed sensor input/turbine speed sensor, and/or engine control module
						Below 1.0V	Throttle opening above 1/8 (Engine coolant temp. below 40°C {104°F})	
2I (Input)	W/Y	HOLD switch	HOLD switch	2I		B+	Switch depressed	• HOLD switch • Wiring and/or connector from terminal 2I to HOLD switch
						0V	Switch released	

*1 Check terminal 2E (input/turbine speed sensor) voltage by using the AC range.
*2 2H (Torque reduced signal) : Some kinds of testers may give incorrect values. This is because the voltage output period is very short.

96I30807

Courtesy of Mazda Motors Corp.

Fig. 31: PCM Pin Voltage Table (1995 RX7, 3 Of 5)

B+: Battery positive voltage

Terminal	Color	Component	Connected to	Voltmeter		Correct voltage	Condition	Check area
				(+) terminal	(−) terminal			
2J (Input)	Y/G	Output speed sensor	Output speed sensor	2J*	2L	Approx. above 1.0V (AC)	Vehicle speed above 25 km/h {16 MPH}	• Output speed sensor • Wiring and/or connector from terminal 2J to output speed sensor
						Approx. 0V (AC)	Vehicle stopped	
2K	L/W	TAT terminal (data link connector) / 4GR inhibit signal (auto speed control signal)	TAT terminal (data link connector) and cruise control unit	2K	Ground	4.5–5.5	Ignition switch ON	• Terminal 1N and 1P voltage • Wiring and/or connector from terminal 2K to data link connector TAT terminal • Wiring and/or connector from terminal 2K to cruise control unit terminal G
						0V	TAT terminal grounded	
2L (Ground)	W	Ground (input signals)	—	2L		0V	Constant	• Wiring condition
2M (Input)	R/W	Idle signal	Engine control module	2M	Ground	4.5–5.5V	Throttle valve opened	• Throttle position sensor and/or engine control module • Wiring and/or connector from terminal 2M to engine control module terminal 2E
						Below 1.0V	Throttle valve closed throttle position	
2N (Input)	B	Water thermoswitch / mileage switch	Water thermoswitch and mileage switch	2N		0V	Engine coolant temp. above 115°C {239°F} or vehicle total mileage above 625 km {388 miles} and vehicle stopped	• Water thermoswitch and/or mileage switch • Wiring and/or connector from terminal 2N to water thermoswitch
						B+	Engine coolant temp. below 110°C {230°F} or vehicle total mileage below 625 km {388 miles} and vehicle stopped	
2O (Input)	LG/R	Brake switch	Brake switch	2O		B+	Brake pedal depressed	• Brake switch • Wiring and/or connector from terminal 2O to brake switch
						0V	Brake pedal released	

* Check terminal 2J (output speed sensor) voltage by using the AC range.

96J30808

Courtesy of Mazda Motors Corp.

Fig. 32: PCM Pin Voltage Table (1995 RX7, 4 Of 5)

B+: Battery positive voltage

Terminal	Color	Component	Connected to	Voltmeter (+) terminal	Voltmeter (−) terminal	Correct voltage	Condition	Check area
2P (Output)	G/W	Reduce torque signal / slip TCC signal	Engine control module	2P*	Ground	Below 1.0V	When shifting from 1GR to 2GR or from 2GR to Third with the throttle opening above 1.5/8. When slipTCC operation with the throttle opening below 0.5/8.	• Wiring and/or connector from terminal 2P to engine control module terminal 1Q • Throttle position sensor, vehicle speed sensor, input/turbine speed sensor TCC solenoid valve, TCC control solenoid valve, and/or engine control module
						B+	Engine running at idle	
2Q (Input)	BR/W	Transmission range switch (L range)	Transmission range switch	2Q		B+	L range	• Transmission range switch • Wiring and/or connector from terminal 2Q to transmission range switch
						0V	Except L range and all positions	
2R (Input)	R	Transmission fluid temperature sensor	Transmission fluid temperature sensor	2R	2L	Approx. 2.4–0.4V	While warming up ATF Note • Approx. 1.8V: ATF temperature 10°C {50°F} • Approx. 1.1V: ATF temperature 40°C {104°F}	• Transmission fluid temperature sensor • Wiring and/or connector from terminal 2R to transmission fluid temperature sensor
2S (Input)	L/R	Transmission range switch (S range)	Transmission range switch	2S	Ground	B+	S range	• Transmission range switch • Wiring and/or connector from terminal 2S to transmission range switch
						0V	Except S range and all positions	
2T (Input)	B/G	Throttle position sensor (TVO)	Throttle position sensor	2T		0.1–1.1V	Throttle valve closed throttle position	• Throttle position sensor • Wiring and/or connector from terminal 2T to throttle position sensor
						4.0–4.5V	Throttle valve wide opened throttle	

* 2P (Reduce torque signal/ torque converter clutch signal): Some kinds of testers may give incorrect values. This is because the voltage output period is very short.

96A30809

Courtesy of Mazda Motors Corp.

Fig. 33: PCM Pin Voltage Table (1995 RX7, 5 Of 5)

AUTOMATIC TRANSMISSIONS
Mazda R4A-EL Series Electronic Controls (Cont.)

B+: Battery positive voltage

Terminal	Component	Connection to	Voltmeter		Correct voltage	Condition	Possible cause
			(+) terminal	(−) terminal			
1A	Battery (back up)	Battery	1A		B+	Constant	• Wiring and/or connector from terminal 1A to battery
1B (Output)	Shift solenoid B	Solenoid valve	1B		B+	P, R, and N position or first and second gear positions	• Shift solenoid B
					Below 1.0V	Third and fourth gear positions	
1C (Output)	Park/Neutral signal position	ECM	1C		Below 1.0V	P and N position	• Transmission range switch and/or input/turbine speed sensor
					B+	Other positions, All ranges	
1D (Output)	Shift solenoid A	Solenoid valve	1D		B+	P, R, and N position or first and fourth gear positions	• Shift solenoid A
					Below 1.0V	Second and third gear positions	
1E (Input)	Transmission range switch (R position)	Transmission range switch	1E	Ground	B+	R position	• Transmission range switch
					0V	Other positions, All ranges	
1F (Output)	Pressure control solenoid	Solenoid valve	1F		Above 2.0V	Throttle valve closed throttle position (after ATF warm, engine stopped)	• Pressure control solenoid and/ or dropping resistor
					Below 1.0V	Throttle valve wide open throttle (after ATF warm, engine stopped)	
1G (Input)	Engine rpm signal (SGT signal)	Distributor	1G		2—3V	Engine running at idle	• Distributor
					0V or 4.5—5.5V	Engine stopped	
1H (Output)	Dropping resistor	Dropping resistor	1H		B+	Throttle valve closed throttle position	• Dropping resistor and/or pressure control solenoid
					Below 1.0V	Throttle valve wide open throttle	

The terminal 1D voltage (shift solenoid A) is below 1.0V when in HOLD mode in P, R, and N positions.

96D30810

Courtesy of Mazda Motors Corp.

Fig. 34: PCM Pin Voltage Table (1995 929, 1 Of 4)

AUTOMATIC TRANSMISSIONS
Mazda R4A-EL Series Electronic Controls (Cont.)

B+: Battery positive voltage

Terminal	Component	Connection to	Voltmeter		Correct voltage	Condition	Possible cause
			(+) terminal	(−) terminal			
1I (Input)	Vehicle speedometer sensor	Speedometer	1I		2—3V	Vehicle moving	• Vehicle speedometer sensor and/or combination meter
					0V or 4.5—5.5V	Vehicle stopped	
1J (Ground)	Ground (transmission control module)	—	1J		0V	Constant	• Wiring from terminal 1J to ground
1K (Output)	HOLD indicator light	Combination meter (HOLD indicator light)	1K		Below 1.0V	Hold mode	• Combination meter
					B+	Other modes	
1L (Input)	A/C signal	ECM	1L		B+	A/C ON	• ECM and/or A/C system components
					Below 1.0V	A/C OFF	
1M (Output)	TCC solenoid valve	Solenoid valve	1M		B+	TCC operation	• TCC solenoid valve
					Below 1.0V	No TCC operation	
1N	Battery (main)	Main relay	1N		B+	Ignition switch ON	• Main relay • Wiring and/or connector from terminal 1N to main relay
					0V	Ignition switch OFF	
1O (Output)	Overrunning clutch solenoid valve	Solenoid valve	1O	Ground	Below 1.0V	Throttle valve open (D range)	• Overrunning clutch solenoid valve
					B+	Throttle valve closed throttle position (D range)	
1P	Battery (main)	Main relay	1P		B+	Ignition switch ON	• Main relay • Wiring and/or connector from terminal 1P to main relay
					0V	Ignition switch OFF	
2A (Input)	Throttle position sensor	Throttle position sensor	2A		4.5—5.5V	Ignition switch ON	• Main relay • ECM terminal 1B
					0V	Ignition switch OFF	
2B (Input)	Transmission range switch (D range)	Transmission range switch	2B		B+	D range	• Transmission range switch
					0V	All positions, Other ranges	
2C (Input)	Barometric pressure sensor	ECM	2C		Approx. above 3.8V	Atmospheric pressure above 96.6 kPa {725 mmHg, 28.5 inHg} (approx. below 400 m {1,312 ft})	• ECM • Wiring from terminal 2C to ECM terminal 2G
					Approx. below 3.3V	Atmospheric pressure below 88.0 kPa {660 mmHg, 26.0 inHg} (approx. above 1,200 m {3,937 ft})	

96E30811

Courtesy of Mazda Motors Corp.

Fig. 35: PCM Pin Voltage Table (1995 929, 2 Of 4)

AUTOMATIC TRANSMISSIONS
Mazda R4A-EL Series Electronic Controls (Cont.)

B+: Battery positive voltage

Terminal	Component	Connection to	Voltmeter (+) terminal	Voltmeter (–) terminal	Correct voltage	Condition	Possible cause
2D (Input)	Transmission range switch (P and N positions)	Transmission range switch	2D	Ground	0V	P and N positions	• Transmission range switch
					B+	Other positions, All ranges	
2E (Input)	Input/turbine speed sensor	Input/turbine speed sensor	2E*1	2L	Approx. above 0.5V (AC)	Vehicle speed above 25 km/h {16 mph}	• Input/turbine speed sensor
					Approx. 0V(AC)	Engine stopped (ignition switch ON)	
2F (Output)	TCC control solenoid valve	Solenoid valve	2F	Ground	B+	TCC operation	• TCC control solenoid valve
					Below 1.0V	No TCC operation	
2H (Input)	Torque reduced signal	ECM	2H*2	Ground	B+	After engine warm-up	• Wiring and/or connector from terminal 2H to ECM terminal 2P • Input/turbine speed sensor
					Below 1.0V	Cold engine	
2I (Input)	Hold switch	Hold switch	2I	Ground	0V	Switch depressed	• Hold switch
					B+	Switch released	
2J (Input)	Output speed sensor	Output speed sensor	2J*1	2L	Approx. above 1.0V(AC)	Vehicle speed above 25 km/h {16 mph}	• Output speed sensor
					Approx. 0V(AC)	Vehicle stopped	
2K	TAT terminal (data link connector) and O/D inhibit signal (auto speed control signal)	TAT terminal (data link connector) and cruise control unit	2K	Ground	B+	Ignition switch ON (vehicle stopped)	• Main relay • terminals 1N and 1P voltage • Wiring and/or connector from terminal 2K to data link connector TAT terminal • Wiring and/or connector from terminal 2K to cruise control unit terminal 1G
					0V	TAT terminal grounded (vehicle stopped)	
2L (Ground)	Ground (Input signals)	—	2L	Ground	0V	Constant	• Wiring from terminal 2L to ground

*1 Check the 2E (input/turbine speed sensor) and the 2J (output speed sensor) terminals voltage by using the AC range.
*2 2H (Torque reduced signal): Some kinds of testers may give incorrect values. This is because the voltage output period is very short.

96F30812

Courtesy of Mazda Motors Corp.

Fig. 36: PCM Pin Voltage Table (1995 929, 3 Of 4)

AUTOMATIC TRANSMISSIONS
Mazda R4A-EL Series Electronic Controls (Cont.)

B+: Battery positive voltage

Terminal	Component	Connection to	Voltmeter (+) terminal	Voltmeter (−) terminal	Correct voltage	Condition	Possible cause
2M (Input)	Closed throttle position switch	Throttle position sensor	2M	Ground	B+	Throttle valve open	• Throttle position sensor
					0V	Throttle valve closed throttle position	• Wiring and/or connector from terminal 2M to throttle position sensor
2N (Output)	FAT terminal (data link connector)	FAT terminal (data link connector)	2N		0V	Hold mode	• Main relay • terminals 1N and 1P voltage
					B+	Other modes	• Wiring and/or connector from terminal 2N to data link connector FAT terminal
2P (Output)	Reduce torque signal	ECM	2P		Below 1.0V	When shifting	• Wiring and/or connector from terminal 2P to ECM terminal 1S
					B+	Other condition	
2Q (Input)	Transmission range switch (L range)	Transmission range switch	2Q		B+	L range	• Transmission range switch
					0V	All positions, Other ranges	
2R (Input)	Transmission fluid temperature sensor	Transmission fluid temperature sensor	2R	2L	Approx. 2.4—0.4V	While warming up ATF Note • Approx. 1.8V: ATF temperature 10°C {50°F} • Approx. 1.1V: ATF temperature 40°C {104°F}	• Transmission fluid temperature sensor
2S (Input)	Transmission range switch (S range)	Transmission range switch	2S		B+	S range	• Transmission range switch
					0V	All positions, Other ranges	
2T (Input)	Throttle position sensor	Throttle position sensor	2T	Ground	Approx. 0.1—1.1V	Throttle valve closed throttle position	• Throttle position sensor • ECM terminal 2I voltage
					3.0—4.3V	Throttle valve wide open throttle	• Wiring and/or connector from terminal 2T to throttle position sensor

*2P (Reduced torque signal): Some kinds of testers may give incorrect values. This is because the voltage output period is very short.

96G30813

Courtesy of Mazda Motors Corp.

Fig. 37: PCM Pin Voltage Table (1995 929, 4 Of 4)

WIRING DIAGRAMS

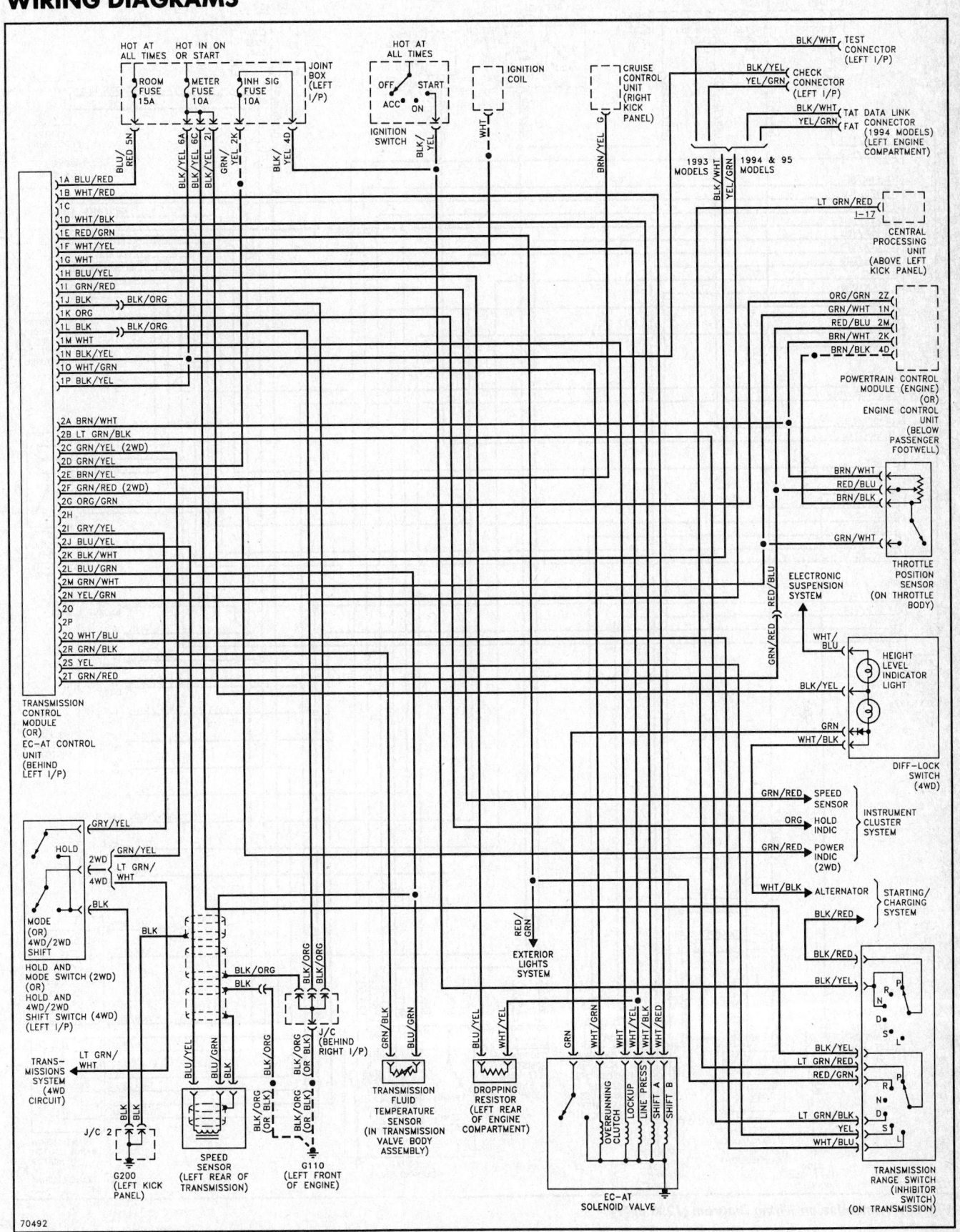

Fig. 38: Transmission Wiring Diagram (1995 MPV)

70492

AUTOMATIC TRANSMISSIONS
Mazda R4A-EL Series Electronic Controls (Cont.)

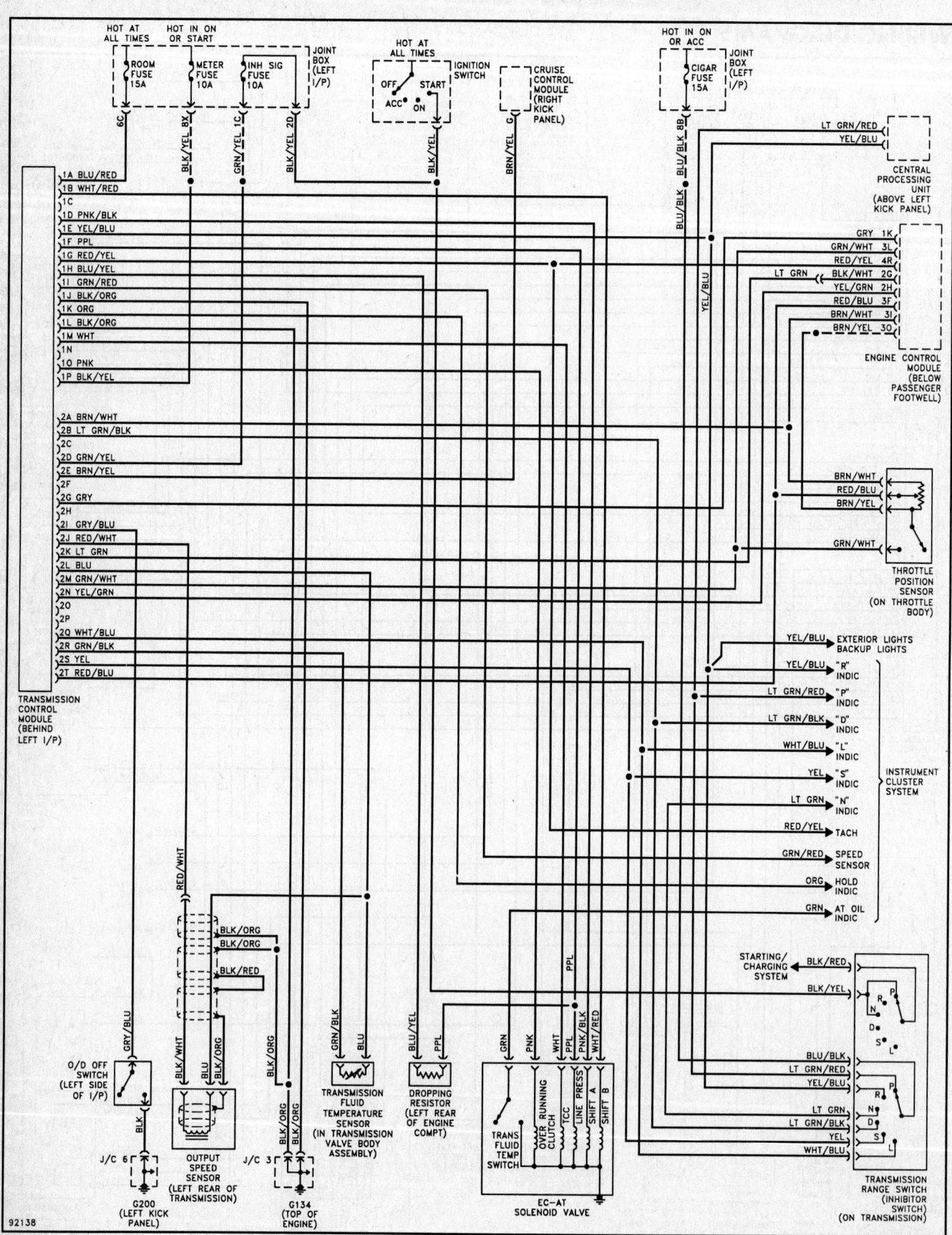

Fig. 39: Transmission Wiring Diagram (1996 MPV)

92138

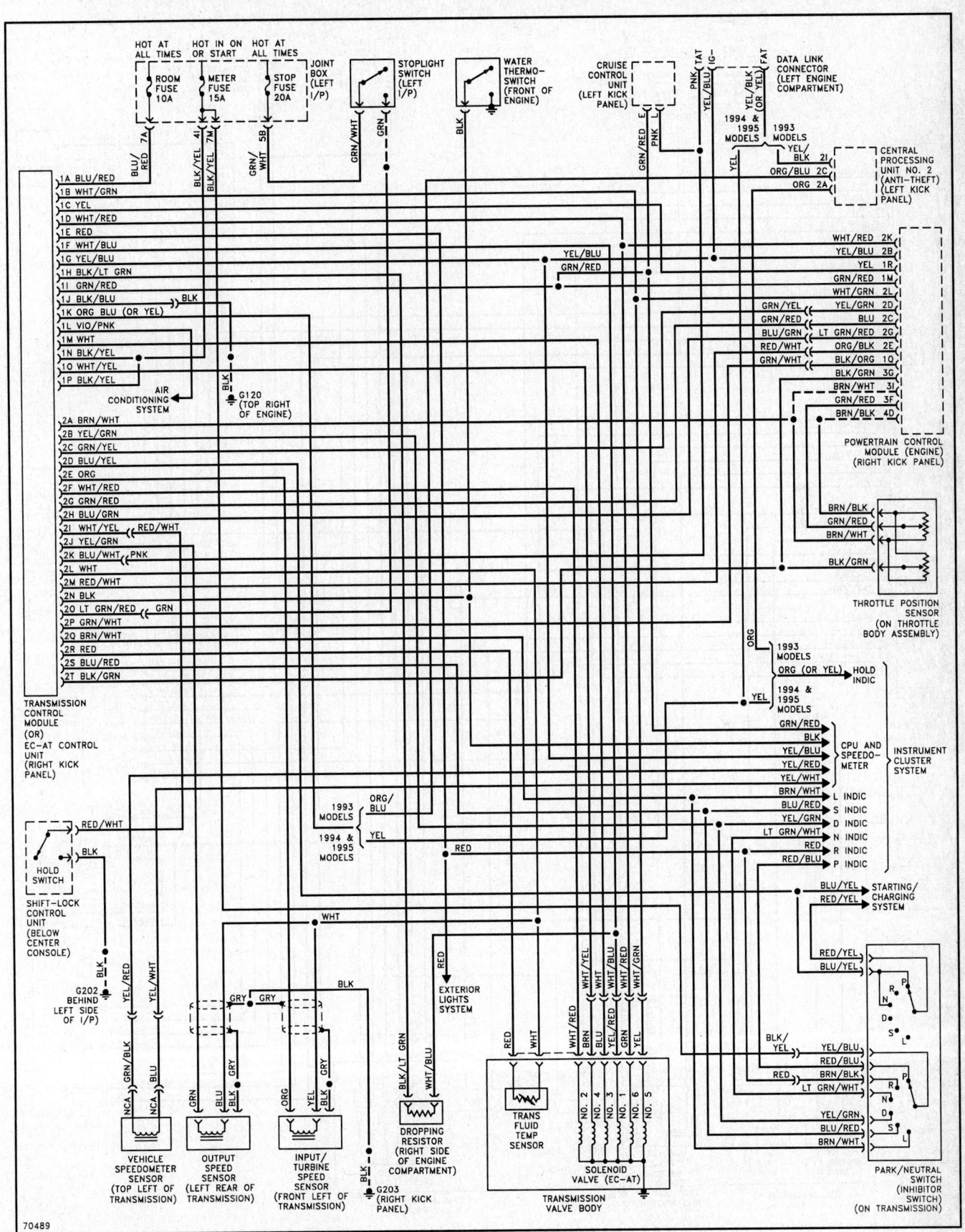

Fig. 40: Transmission Wiring Diagram (1995 RX7)

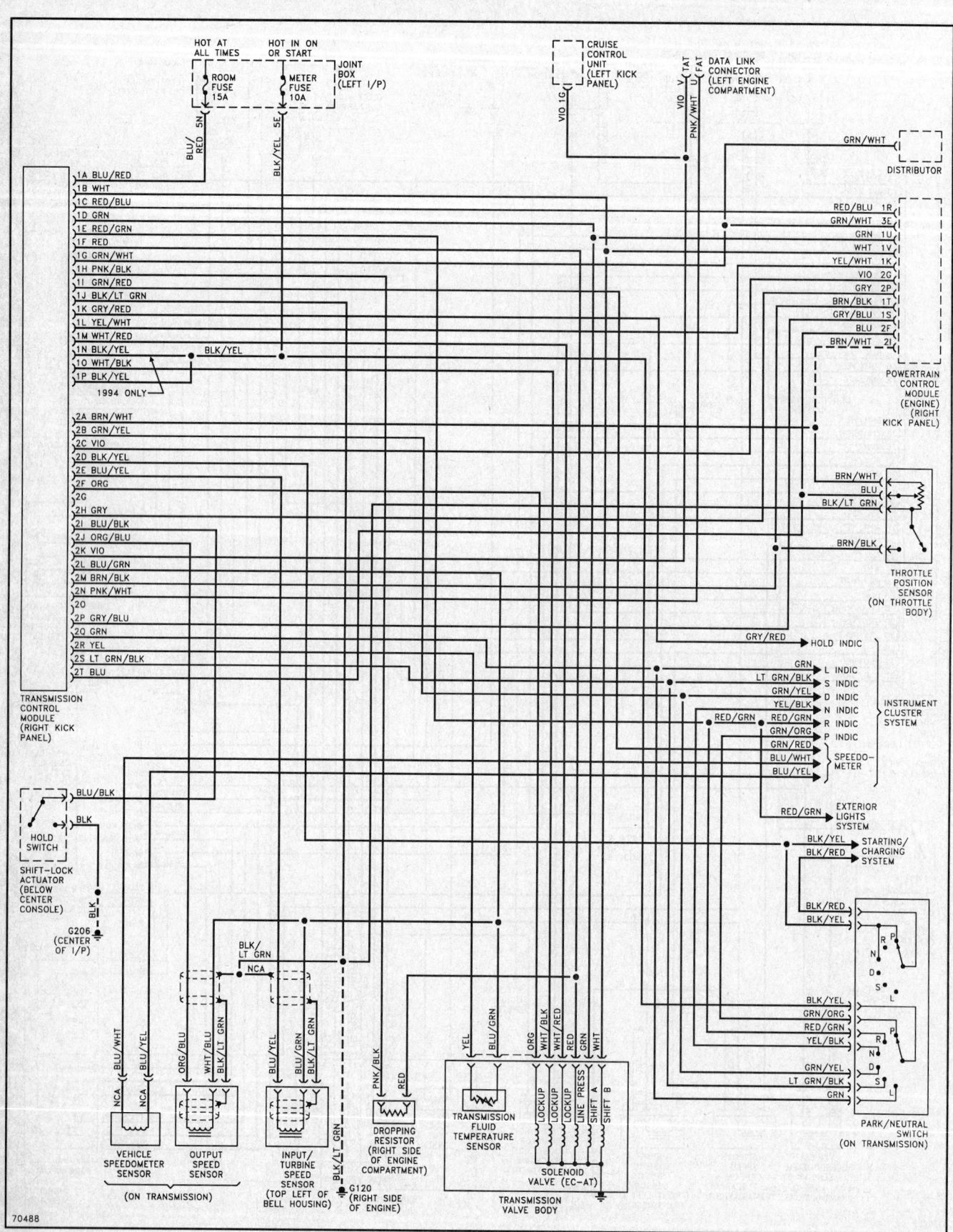

Fig. 41: *Transmission Wiring Diagram (1995 929)*

70488

B2300, B3000, B4000

NOTE: This article contains introductory application and description information and wiring diagrams. For trouble shooting, electronic testing and overhaul procedure information, see appropriate Ford 4R44E & 4R55E overhaul or Electronic Controls article in 1995-96 MITCHELL® TRANSMISSION SERVICE & REPAIR manual for DOMESTIC CARS, LIGHT TRUCKS & VANS.

APPLICATION & LABOR TIMES

APPLICATION & LABOR TIMES

Vehicle Application	Labor Times		Trans. Model
	¹ R & I	² Overhaul	
1995			
B2300 2WD	3.2	8.6	4R44E
B3000 2WD	3.2	8.6	4R44E
B4000 2WD	3.2	8.6	4R55E
B4000 4WD	5.8	8.6	4R55E
1996			
B2300 2WD	3.2	8.6	4R44E
B3000 2WD	3.2	8.6	4R44E
B4000 2WD	3.2	8.6	4R55E
B3000 4WD	5.2	8.6	4R44E
B4000 4WD	5.8	8.6	4R55E

¹ – Removal and installation of transmission from vehicle chassis.

² – Bench overhaul for transmission. DOES NOT include removal and installation.

IDENTIFICATION

The 4R44E/4R55E 4-speed automatic transmission can be identified by service identification tags affixed to unit. *See Fig. 1.* Bar code identification label is located on fluid pan. Metal tag is attached to extension housing bolt. Top line of tag shows transmission model number and line shift code. Bottom line on tag shows build date code.

DESCRIPTION

The 4R44E/4R55E is a 4-speed automatic overdrive transmission with lock-up type torque converter and electronic controls. The 4R44E is used with 2.3L and 3.0L engine applications. The 4R55E is used with 4.0L engine applications. Transmission consists of torque converter, 3 compound planetary gearsets, 3 multiple disc clutch packs, 3 bands and 2 one-way clutches.

Shift control solenoids control gear selection and are operated by the EEC-IV (1995) or EEC-V (1996) microprocessor. For additional information on the EEC-IV or EEC-V system, refer to appropriate SELF-DIAGNOSTICS article in ENGINE PERFORMANCE of appropriate MITCHELL® manual.

Input signals from sensors are sent to the Powertrain Control Module (PCM). The PCM can determine when the time and conditions are right for a shift or converter clutch application. The PCM can also determine line pressure needed to optimize shift feel.

Six electronic solenoids accomplish the following functions:
- Three On/Off solenoids for shifting.
- One Pulse-Width Modulator (PWM) solenoid for Torque Converter Clutch (TCC) control.
- One Electronic Pressure Control (EPC) solenoid for line pressure control.

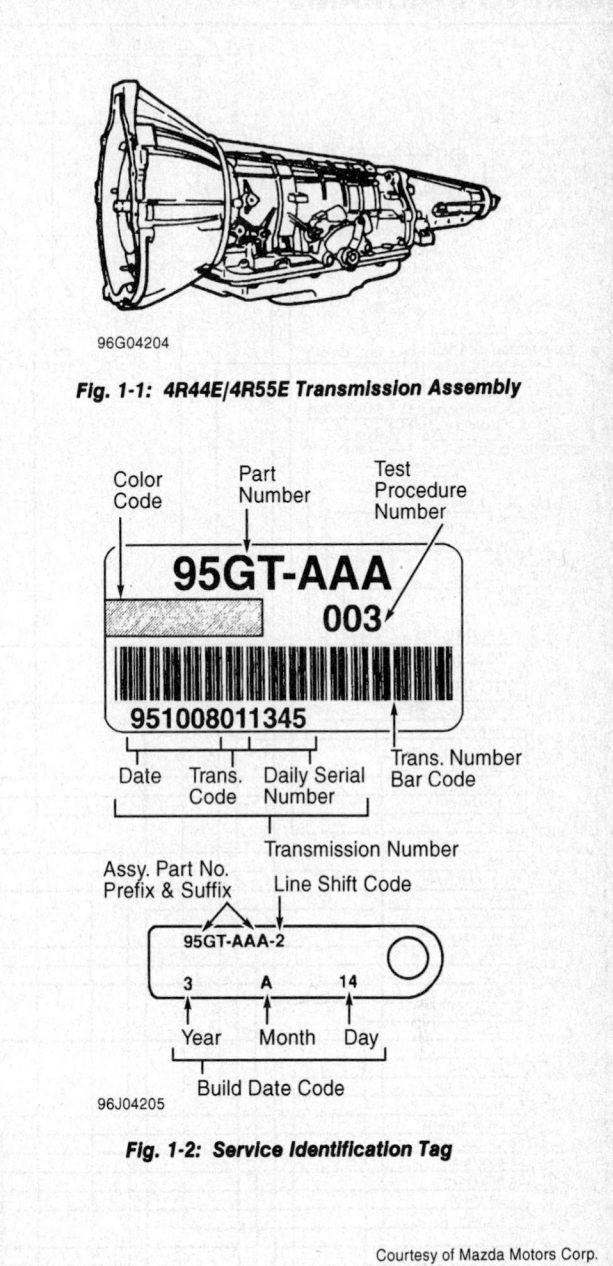

96G04204

Fig. 1-1: 4R44E/4R55E Transmission Assembly

Color Code — Part Number — Test Procedure Number

95GT-AAA
003

951008011345

Date — Trans. Code — Daily Serial Number — Trans. Number Bar Code

Transmission Number

Assy. Part No. Prefix & Suffix — Line Shift Code

95GT-AAA-2

3 — A — 14

Year — Month — Day

Build Date Code

96J04205

Fig. 1-2: Service Identification Tag

Courtesy of Mazda Motors Corp.

Fig. 1: Identifying 4R44E/4R55E Transmission

- One 3-2 timing/coast clutch solenoid to control release of coast clutch, coordinated release of the direct clutch, and apply of the low and intermediate band.

PCM has built-in self-diagnosis, fail-safe code and warning code display for the main input sensors and solenoid valves.

LUBRICATION & ADJUSTMENTS

See appropriate AUTOMATIC TRANSMISSION SERVICING article in TRANSMISSION SERVICING section.

AUTOMATIC TRANSMISSIONS
Mazda 4R44E & 4R55E (Cont.)

WIRING DIAGRAMS

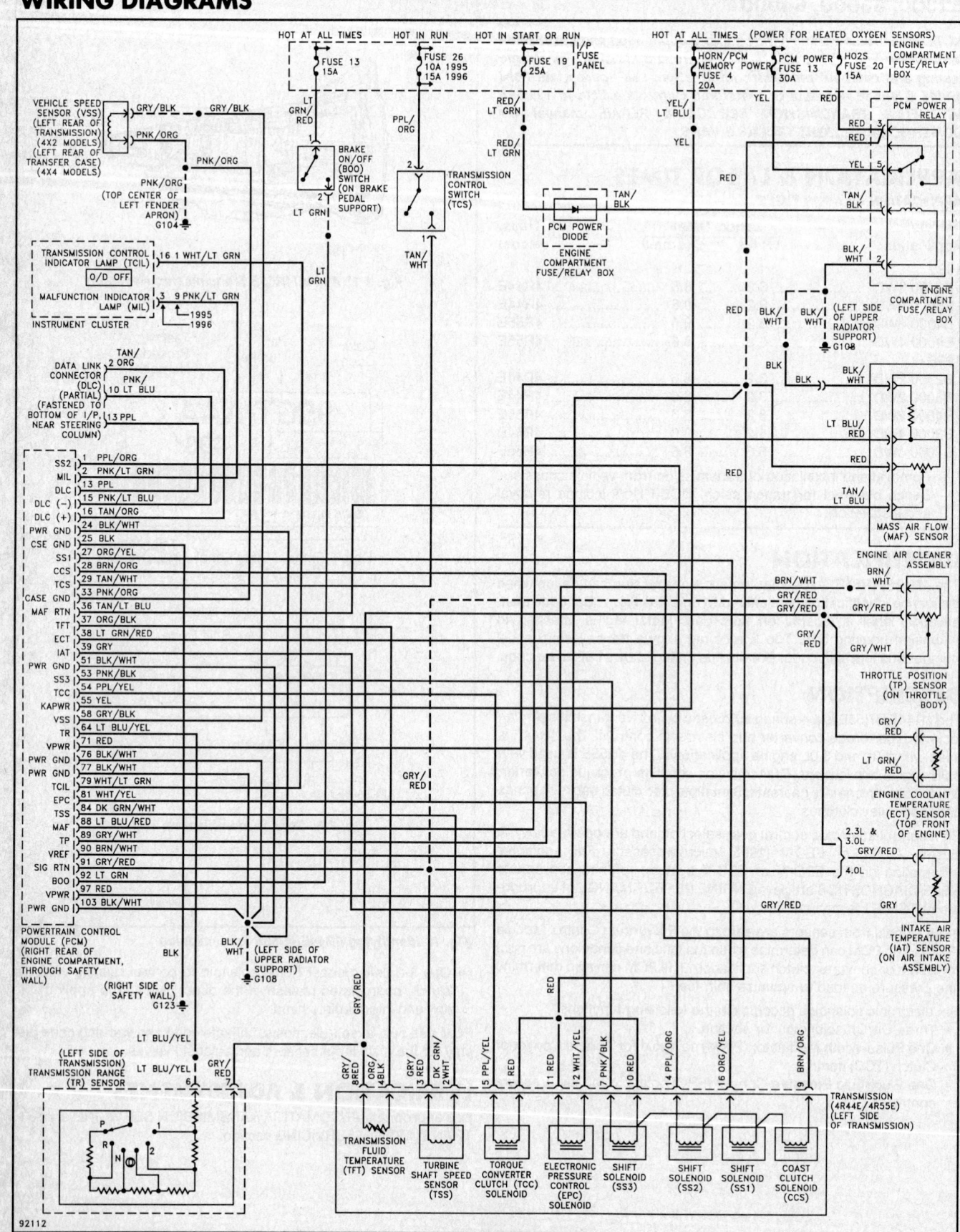

Fig. 2: 4R44E & 4R55E Transmission Wiring Diagram (1995-96 B2300, B3000 & B4000)

Miata, Millenia, MPV, MX-3, MX-6, Protege, RX7, 626, 929

CAUTION: Disconnecting battery on models equipped with anti-theft radio require cancelling of anti-theft operation. See CANCELLING ANTI-THEFT RADIO OPERATION in AUTOMATIC TRANSMISSION SERVICING.

DESCRIPTION

Vehicle is equipped with a electronically controlled shift lock system. *See Fig. 1.* Shift lock system prevents shift lever from being moved from Park unless brake pedal is depressed. In case of a malfunction, shift lever can be released by depressing shift lock emergency override button, located near shift lever. System consists of brakelight switch, shift lock actuator, park position switch and shift lock override button. System is controlled by shift lock control unit incorporated within shift lock actuator except on RX7. RX7 uses a separate control unit.

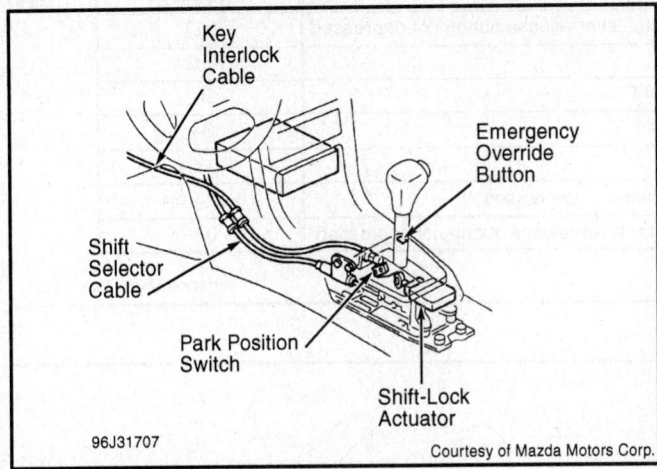

Fig. 1: Identifying Shift Lock System (Typical)

OPERATION

SHIFT LOCK SYSTEM

With ignition on, when brake pedal is depressed, park position switch on, an input signal is sent from brakelight switch to the actuator. The shift lock actuator then operates the lock lever (release position), so shift lever can be moved in Park.

FUNCTIONAL CHECK

1) With ignition key removed, ensure gear selector cannot be moved from Park. Insert key in ignition switch.
2) Turn ignition on. Ensure gear selector can only be moved with brake pedal pressed down. Move gear selector to Reverse.
3) Ensure ignition key cannot be removed, Move gear selector to Park. Ensure it is not possible to remove ignition key.
4) If shift lock system does not operate as described, check gear selector, shift lock solenoid and control cable.
5) On MPV, place gear selector in Park, depress and hold emergency override link. *See Fig. 2.* On all other models, place gear selector in Park. Using a screwdriver, push down emergency override button on shifter console and verify gear selector can be moved from Park position. *See Fig. 3.* On all models, if gear selector cannot be moved out of Park, adjust or replace shift lock actuator.

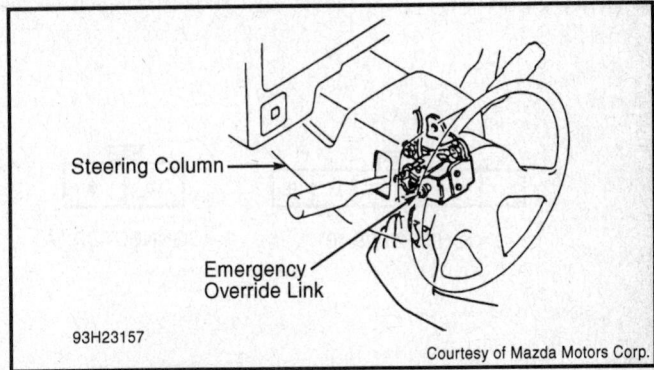

Fig. 2: Locating Emergency Link Override (MPV)

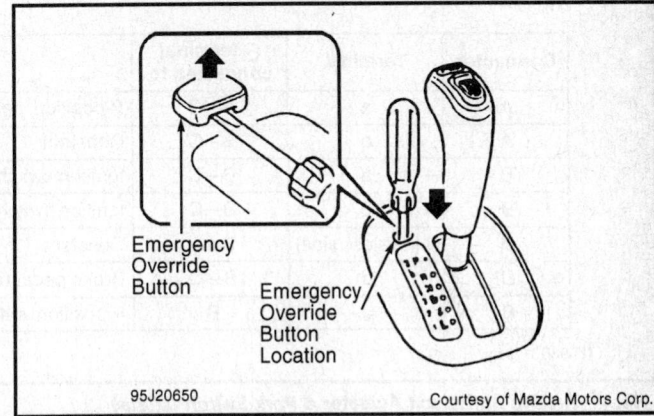

Fig. 3: Locating Emergency Override Button (All Models Except MPV)

TESTING

PARK POSITION SWITCH

Miata – Disconnect negative battery cable. Remove rear console. Remove indicator screws and lift up panel. Disconnect park position switch. Check continuity between connector terminals. *See Fig. 4.* Continuity should exist with switch released. Continuity should not exist with switch depressed. Replace as needed.

Millenia – Disconnect negative battery cable. Remove rear console and center panel. Remove indicator screws and lift up panel. Disconnect park position switch. Check continuity between terminals "k" and "h". *See Fig. 5.* Continuity should exist with switch released. Continuity should not exist with switch depressed. Replace as needed.

MX-3, MX-6, Protege & 626 – Disconnect negative battery cable. Remove rear ashtray, rear console and front console. Remove indicator screws and lift up panel. Disconnect park position switch. Check continuity between connector terminals. *See Fig. 6.* Continuity should exist with switch released. Continuity should not exist with switch depressed. Replace as needed.

RX7 – See SHIFT LOCK ACTUATOR.

929 – Disconnect negative battery cable. Remove front and rear console. Remove indicator screws and lift up panel. Disconnect park position switch. Check continuity between connector terminals. *See Fig. 7.* Continuity should exist with switch released. Continuity should not exist with switch depressed. Replace as needed.

SHIFT LOCK ACTUATOR

Miata – **1)** Remove rear console. Remove selector knob and indicator panel screws. Lift up selector lever, selector sleeve and indicator. Disconnect HOLD switch connector. Ensure selector lever is in Park position.

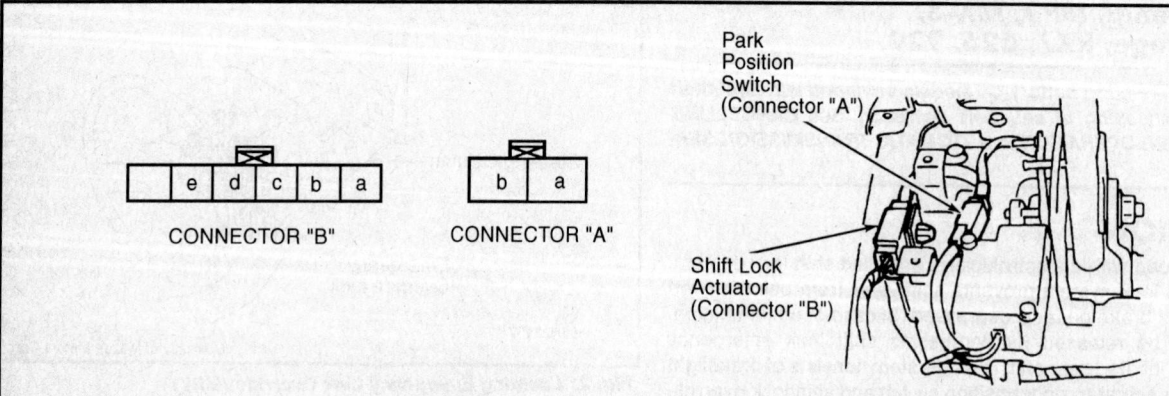

B+: Battery positive voltage

Connector	Terminal	⊖ terminal connected to	Condition	Correct measurement value
A	a	B—C	P position, selector lever release button not depressed	0 Ω
A	b	B—C	Constant	0 Ω
B	a	B—C	Ignition switch OFF	B+
B	b	B—C	Ignition switch ON	B+
B	C (harness side)	Body	Constant	0 Ω
B	d	B—C	Brake pedal released → depressed	0 V → B+
B	e	B	P position, selector lever release button not depressed	0 V

96D31701

Courtesy of Mazda Motors Corp.

Fig. 4: Testing Shift Lock Actuator & Park Switch (Miata)

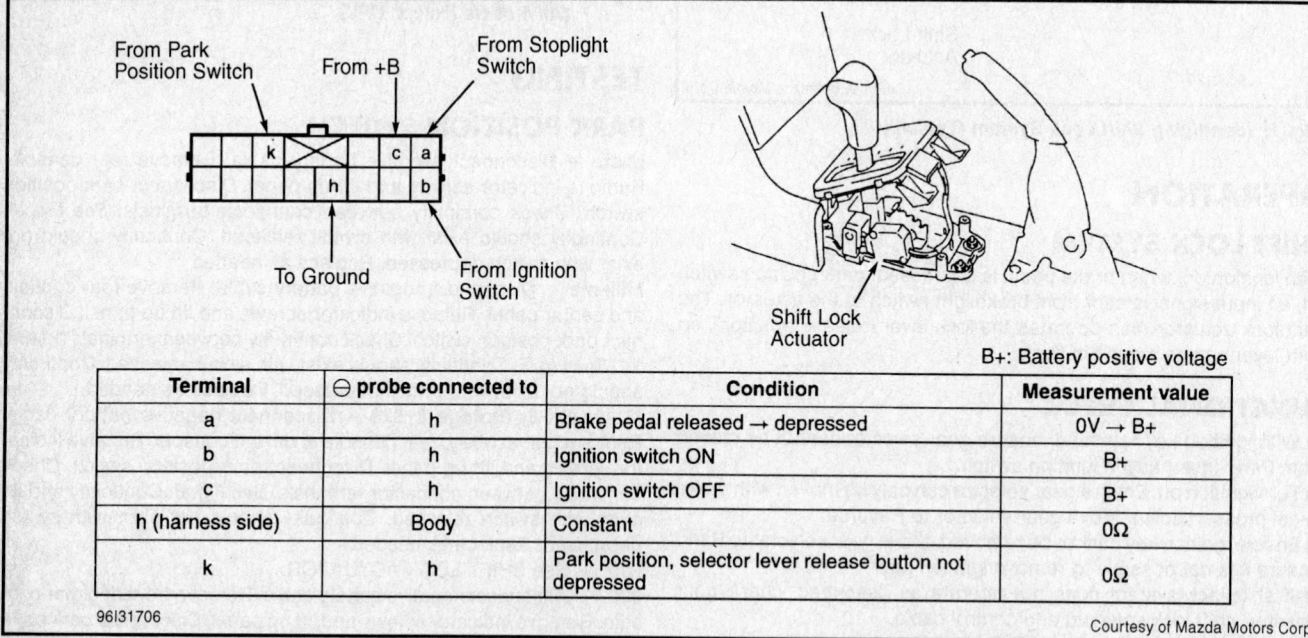

B+: Battery positive voltage

Terminal	⊖ probe connected to	Condition	Measurement value
a	h	Brake pedal released → depressed	0V → B+
b	h	Ignition switch ON	B+
c	h	Ignition switch OFF	B+
h (harness side)	Body	Constant	0Ω
k	h	Park position, selector lever release button not depressed	0Ω

96I31706

Courtesy of Mazda Motors Corp.

Fig. 5: Testing Shift Lock Actuator & Park Switch (Millenia)

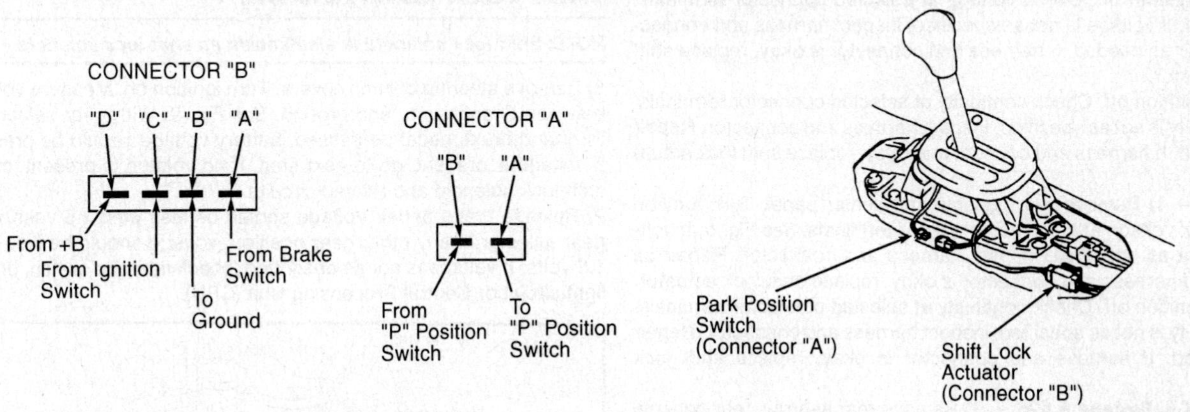

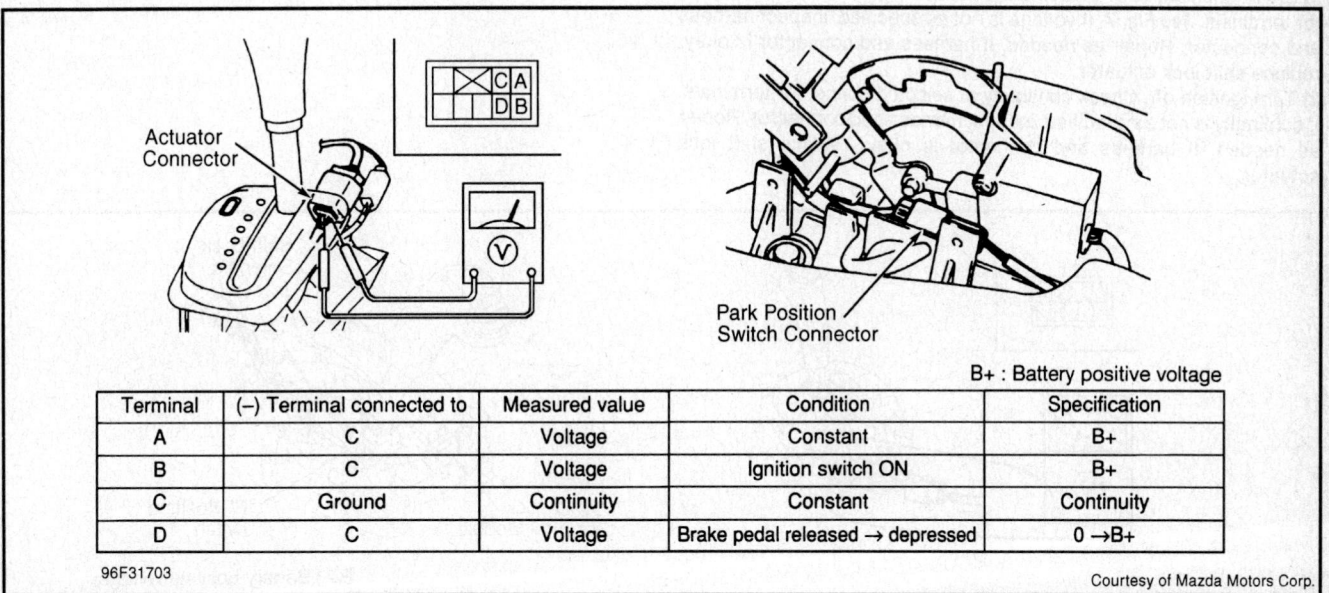

CONNECTOR "B"

"D" "C" "B" "A"

From +B
From Ignition Switch
To Ground
From Brake Switch

CONNECTOR "A"

"B" "A"

From "P" Position Switch
To "P" Position Switch

Park Position Switch (Connector "A")

Shift Lock Actuator (Connector "B")

B+ : Battery positive voltage

Check terminal		○ probe connected to		Measurement type	Condition	Measurement value
Connector	Terminal	Connector	Terminal			
A	A	B	B	Continuity	P position selector lever release button not depressed	Continuity
A	B	B	B	Continuity	Constant	Continuity
B	A	B	B	Voltage (V)	Brake pedal released → depressed	0 → B+
B	B	Body		Continuity	Constant	Continuity
B	C	B	B	Voltage (V)	Ignition switch ON	B+
B	D	B	B	Voltage (V)	Ignition switch OFF	B+

96E31702

Courtesy of Mazda Motors Corp.

Fig. 6: Testing Shift Lock Actuator & Park Switch (MX-3, MX-6, Protege & 626)

Actuator Connector

Park Position Switch Connector

B+ : Battery positive voltage

Terminal	(−) Terminal connected to	Measured value	Condition	Specification
A	C	Voltage	Constant	B+
B	C	Voltage	Ignition switch ON	B+
C	Ground	Continuity	Constant	Continuity
D	C	Voltage	Brake pedal released → depressed	0 → B+

96F31703

Courtesy of Mazda Motors Corp.

Fig. 7: Testing Shift Lock Actuator & Park Switch (929)

2) Turn ignition on. Check voltage at selected connector terminals. *See Fig. 4.* If voltage is not as specified, inspect harness and connector. Repair as needed. If harness and connector is okay, replace shift lock actuator.
3) Turn ignition off. Check continuity at selected connector terminals. If continuity is not as specified, inspect harness and connector. Repair as needed. If harness and connector is okay, replace shift lock actuator.
Millenia – 1) Remove rear console and center panel. Turn ignition on. Check voltage at selected connector terminals. *See Fig. 5.* If voltage is not as specified, inspect harness and connector. Repair as needed. If harness and connector is okay, replace shift lock actuator.
2) Turn ignition off. Check continuity at selected connector terminals. If continuity is not as specified, inspect harness and connector. Repair as needed. If harness and connector is okay, replace shift lock actuator.
MX-3, MX-6, Protege & 626 – 1) Remove rear ashtray, rear console and front console. Turn ignition on. Check voltage at selected connector terminals. *See Fig. 6.* If voltage is not as specified, inspect harness and connector. Repair as needed. If harness and connector is okay, replace shift lock actuator.
2) Turn ignition off. Check continuity at selected connector terminals. If continuity is not as specified, inspect harness and connector. Repair as needed. If harness and connector is okay, replace shift lock actuator.
RX7 – 1) Remove console panel. Shift selector lever to Park. Turn ignition on. Check voltage at selected connector terminals. *See Fig. 8.* If voltage is not as specified, inspect harness and connector. Repair as needed. If harness and connector is okay, go to next step.
2) Turn ignition off. Check continuity at selected connector terminals. If continuity is not as specified, inspect harness and connector. Repair as needed. If harness and connector is okay, replace park position switch, shift lock solenoid and/or shift lock control module.
929 – 1) Remove rear console and front console. Shift selector lever to PARK position. Turn ignition on. Check voltage at selected connector terminals. *See Fig. 7.* If voltage is not as specified, inspect harness and connector. Repair as needed. If harness and connector is okay, replace shift lock actuator.
2) Turn ignition off. Check continuity at selected connector terminals. If continuity is not as specified, inspect harness and connector. Repair as needed. If harness and connector is okay, replace shift lock actuator.

SHIFT LOCK SOLENOID (MPV)

NOTE: Shift lock solenoid is also known as shift lock solenoid valve.

1) Remove steering column covers. Turn ignition on. Measure voltage between Orange wire and ground. *See Fig. 9.* With gear selector in Park and brake pedal depressed, battery voltage should be present. If voltage is present, go to next step. If no voltage is present, check shift lock solenoid and related circuits.
2) Release brake pedal. Voltage should be less than 1.5 volts. With gear selector in any other gear position, voltage should be less than 1.5 volts. If voltage is not as described, check inhibitor switch, brake-light circuit or Central Processing Unit (CPU).

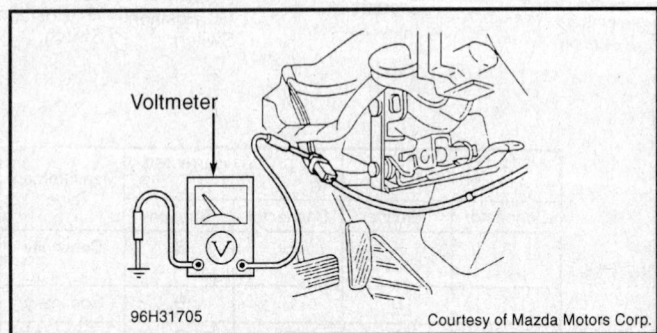

96H31705   Courtesy of Mazda Motors Corp.

Fig. 9: *Testing Shift Lock Solenoid*

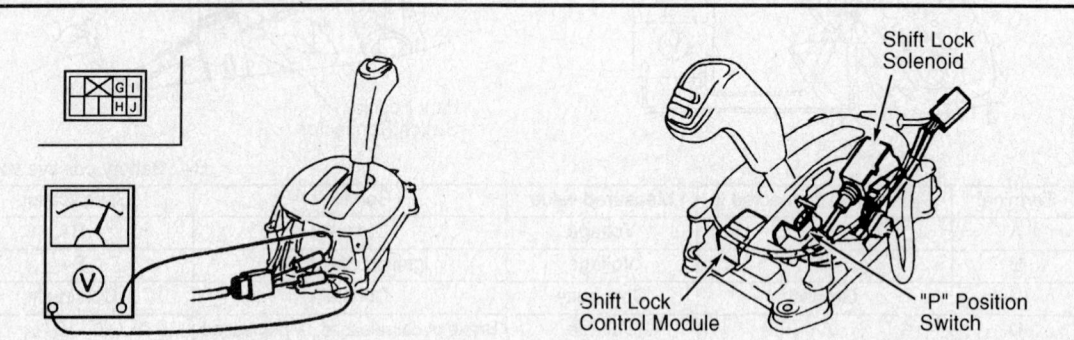

B+ : Battery positive voltage

Terminal	(–) terminal connected to	Measured value	Condition		Specification
G	Ground	Voltage	Brake pedal released → depressed		0V → B+
H	J	Continuity	P position	Selector lever push button released	No
				Selector lever push button depressed	Yes
			Except P position		Yes
I	Ground	Voltage	Ignition switch OFF → ON		0V → B+
J	Ground	Continuitiy	Constant		Yes

96G31704   Courtesy of Mazda Motors Corp.

Fig. 8: *Testing Shift Lock Actuator & Park Switch (RX7)*

WIRING DIAGRAMS

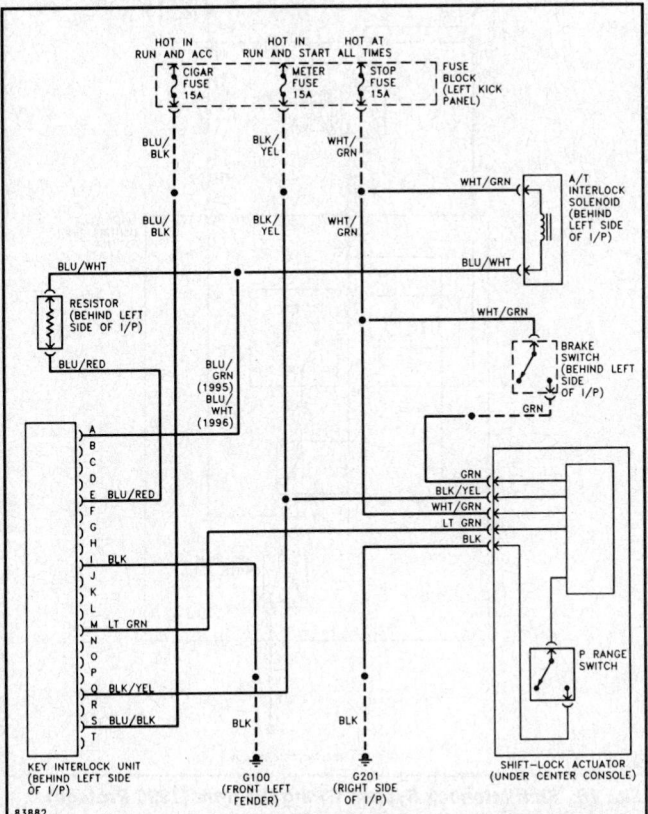

Fig. 10: Shift Interlock System Wiring Diagram (1995-96 Miata)

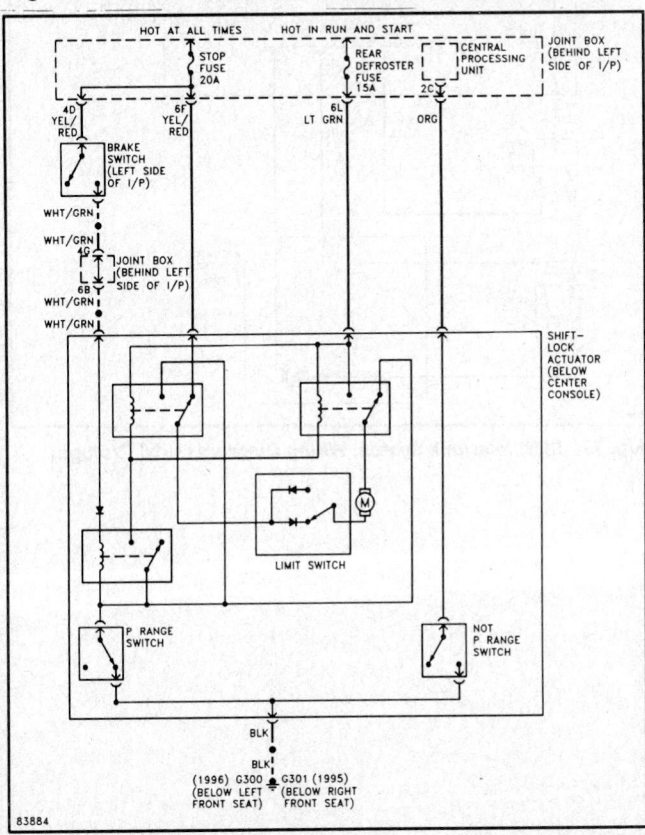

Fig. 11: Shift Interlock System Wiring Diagram (1995-96 Millenia)

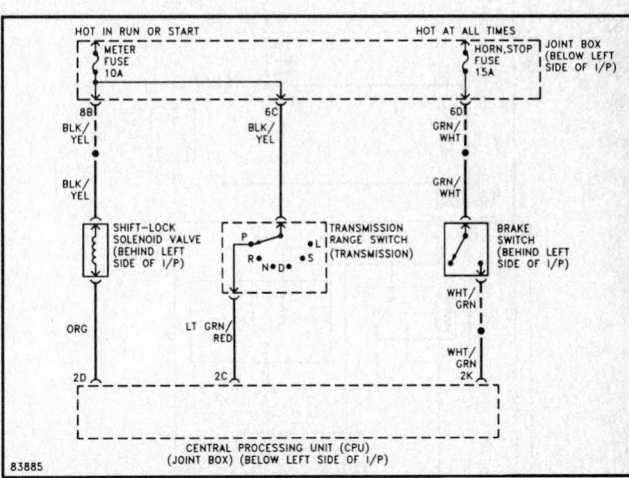

Fig. 12: Shift Interlock System Wiring Diagram (1995 MPV)

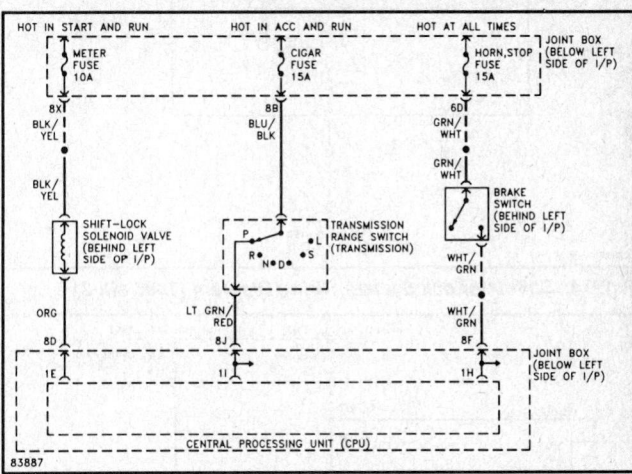

Fig. 13: Shift Interlock System Wiring Diagram (1996 MPV)

AUTOMATIC TRANSMISSIONS
Mazda Shift Lock System (Cont.)

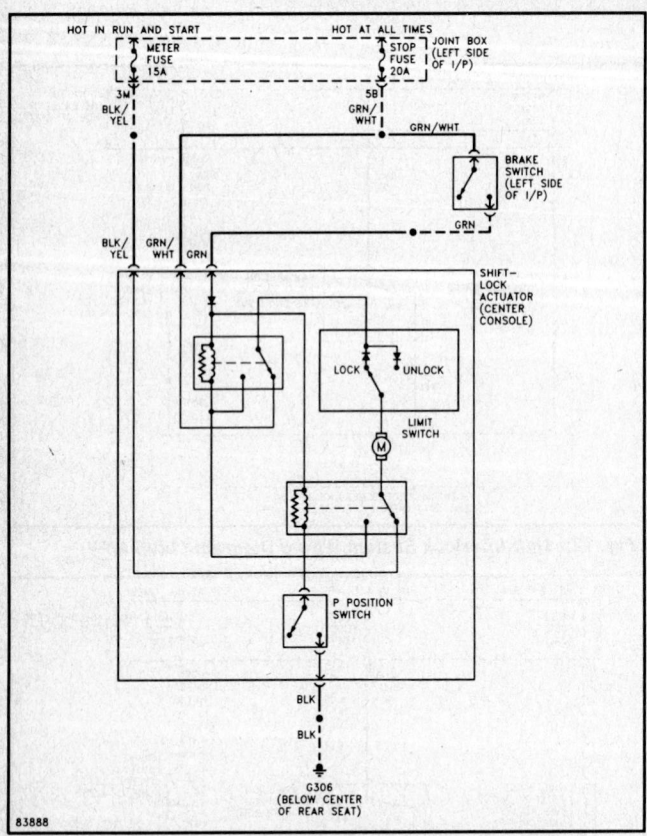

Fig. 14: Shift Interlock System Wiring Diagram (1995 MX-3)

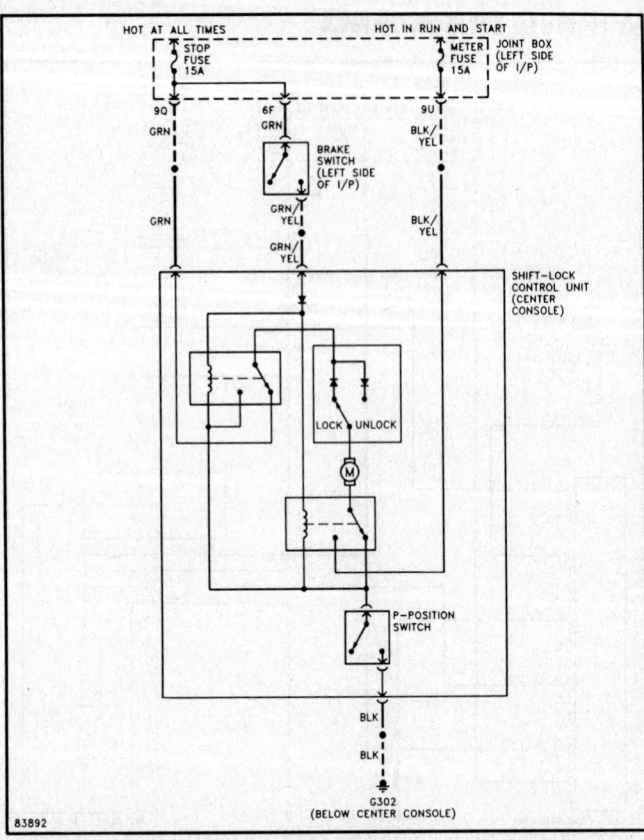

Fig. 16: Shift Interlock System Wiring Diagram (1995 Protege)

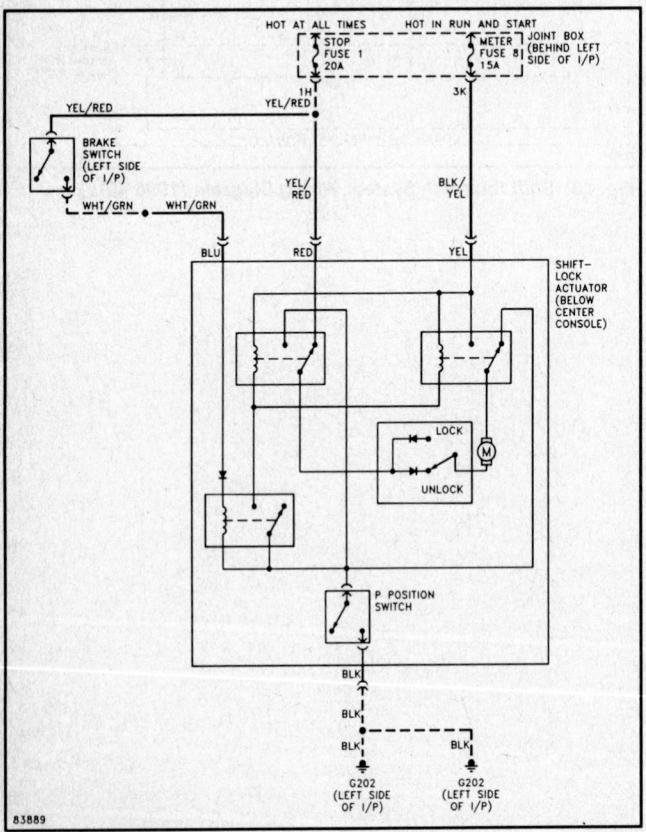

Fig. 15: Shift Interlock System Wiring Diagram (1995-96 MX-6 & 626)

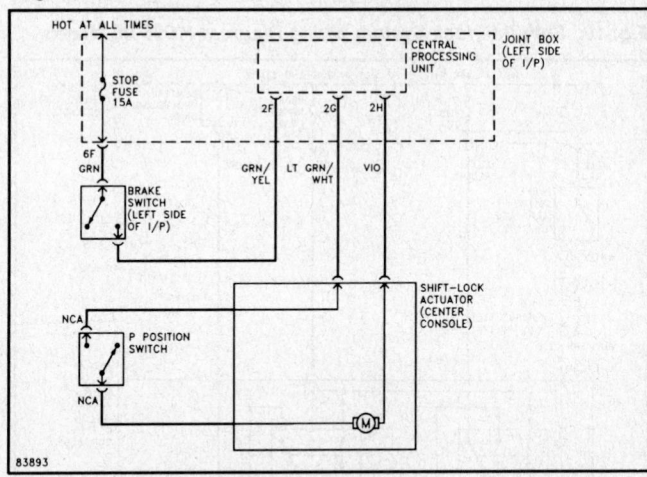

Fig. 17: Shift Interlock System Wiring Diagram (1996 Protege)

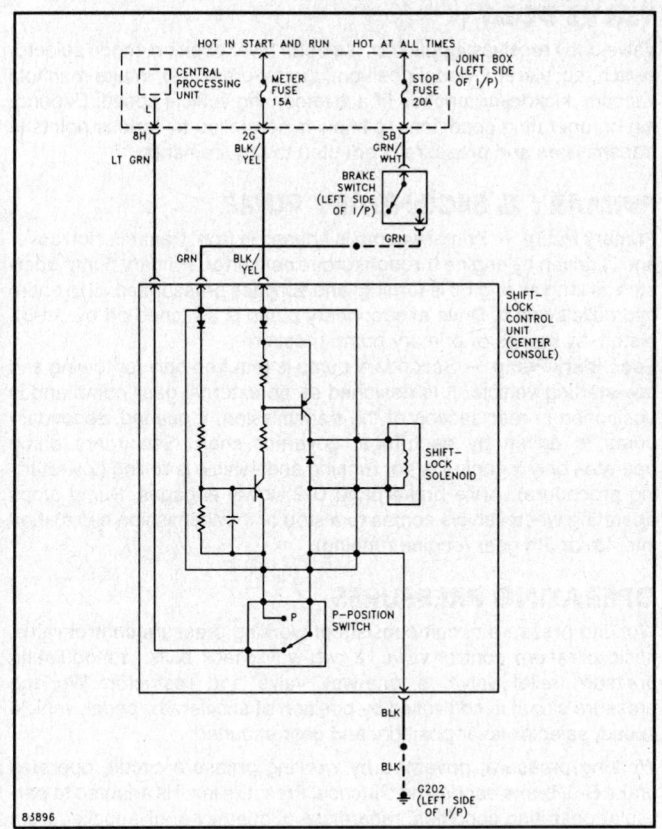

Fig. 18: Shift Interlock System Wiring Diagram (1995 RX7)

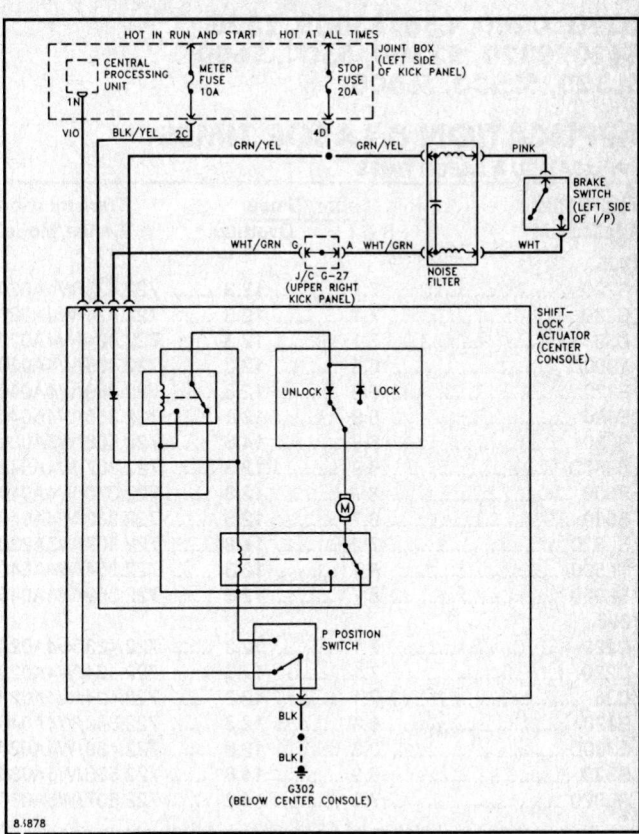

Fig. 19: Shift Interlock System Wiring Diagram (1995 929)

AUTOMATIC TRANSMISSIONS
Mercedes-Benz 722 Series

C220, C280, C36, E300D, E320
E420, S320, S350D, S500, S600
SL320, SL500, SL600

APPLICATION & LABOR TIMES

APPLICATION & LABOR TIMES

Year/Vehicle Application	Labor Times R & I [1]	Overhaul [2]	Transmission Series/Model
1995			
C220	7.1	12.3	722.423/W4A020
C280	7.1	12.3	722.424/W4A020
C36	7.1	12.3	722.424/W4A020
E300D	6.3	12.3	722.435/W4A020
E320	6.9	12.3	722.369/W4A040
E420	6.9	12.3	722.366/W4A040
S320	6.9	14.8	722.508/W5A030
S350D	6.9	12.3	722.367/W4A040
S500	8.7	12.3	722.370/W4A040
S600	8.7	12.3	722.362/W4A040
SL320	7.2	14.8	722.507/W5A030
SL500	8.7	12.3	722.364/W4A040
SL600	8.7	12.3	722.362/W4A040
1996			
C220	7.1	12.3	722.423/W4A020
C280	7.1	12.3	722.424/W4A020
C36	7.1	12.3	722.424/W4A020
E320	6.3	12.3	722.369/W4A040
E300D	6.3	12.3	722.438/W4A020
S320	6.9	14.8	722.508/W5A030
SL320	7.2	14.8	722.507/W5A030

[1] – Removal and installation of transmission from vehicle chassis.
[2] – Bench overhaul time for transmission. DOES NOT include removal and installation.

IDENTIFICATION

Identification code is stamped on identification plate on transmission housing. Use identification code when ordering parts.

DESCRIPTION

TRANSMISSION

Transmissions are fully automatic 4 or 5-speed consisting of a 3-element welded torque converter, 2 or 3 compound planetary gear sets, 2 or 3 multiple-disc clutches, one overrunning clutch and 3 brake bands. See Figs. 1 and 2. Brake bands control function of planetary gear sets. A hydraulic system, pressurized by a primary gear type pump and a secondary piston type pump provide working pressure required to operate friction elements and automatic controls.

1st Gear – In 1st gear, brake band B-2 is applied and one-way converter clutch is locked. In selector lever position "2", clutch K-2 is also engaged. Both planetary gear sets are involved in gear reduction.
2nd Gear – In 2nd gear, brake band B-1 and brake band B-2 are applied. Both planetary gear sets are involved in gear reduction.
3rd Gear – In 3rd gear, brake band B-2 is applied and clutch K-1 is engaged. Only rear planetary gear set is involved in gear reduction.
4th Gear – In 4th gear, clutch K-1 and clutch K-2 are applied. Both planetary gear sets rotate as a locked unit.
5th Gear – On 722.5 Series models, clutch K-1, clutch K-2 and overdrive brake are applied in 5th gear. Overdrive clutch and 2nd one-way clutch are also applied in all forward gears.
Reverse Gear – In reverse, brake B-3 is applied, one-way converter clutch is locked, and clutch K-2 is engaged. Both planetary gear sets are involved in gear reduction.

VALVE BODY

Valve body receives inputs from selector lever position, mode selector switch, accelerator pedal position (control pressure), intake manifold vacuum, kickdown function (if activated) and vehicle speed. Depending on operating conditions, oil flow is controlled to various points in transmission and pressure is adapted to requirements.

PRIMARY & SECONDARY PUMP

Primary Pump – Primary pump is housed in front transmission cover and is driven by engine through torque converter. Primary pump operates as long as engine is turning, and supplies pressurized oil to entire hydraulic system. Drive of secondary pump is switched off by cut-off piston, by means of primary pump pressure.
Secondary Pump – Secondary pump is required only for towing and tow-starting vehicle. It is designed as an external gear pump and is positioned in rear section of the transmission. If needed, secondary pump is driven by centrifugal governor shaft. Secondary pump operates only if engine is not running and vehicle is rolling (tow-starting procedure), while brake band B-2 slowly engages. Pump stops operating when vehicle comes to a stop or if transmission has shifted into 4th or 5th gear (engine running).

OPERATING PRESSURES

Working pressure circuit consists of working pressure control valve, basic working pressure control valve, 2 two-way check balls, a modulating pressure relief valve, a one-way valve and restrictor. Working pressure circuit is controlled by position of accelerator pedal, vehicle speed, selector lever position, and gear engaged.

Working pressure, governed by working pressure circuit, operates brake B-3, brake bands and clutches. Pressure level is adapted to particular operating condition, regardless of quantity of oil supplied from primary pump or secondary pump. This enables primary pump capacity to be kept as low as possible and the transmission to achieve high efficiency.

Working pressure is always the highest pressure in hydraulic system. All other operating pressures are derived from this pressure and reduced by control valves to a lower pressure level. The following governed pressures control hydraulic system and operate shift element.
- Reduced Operating Pressure
- Governor Pressure
- Lubricating Pressure
- Modulating Pressure (Vacuum Controlled)
- Modulating Pressure (Governor Controlled)
- Full Throttle Pressure
- Load Dependent Control Pressure
- Kickdown Control Pressure
- Boosted Governor Pressure
- Shift Pressure

DAMPER SYSTEM

Principal task of hydraulic circuits is to control working pressure during gear shifts. During each gear shift transition, engine speed increases (during a downshift) or decreases (during an upshift). In order to provide a smooth transition between gear shifts, 4 independent damper circuits are used.

Clutch K-1 damper circuit controls clutch K-1 during 2nd to 3rd gear downshifts or upshifts. Clutch K-2 damper circuit controls clutch K-2 during 3rd to 4th gear downshifts or upshifts. Brake band B-1 damper circuit controls brake band B-1 during 1st to 2nd gear downshifts or upshifts.

The "engaging" damper circuit controls engagement of clutches or brake bands, depending on selector lever position. When selector lever is moved from "N" position to "D" position or "3" position, brake bands B-1 and B-2 are controlled. When selector lever is moved from

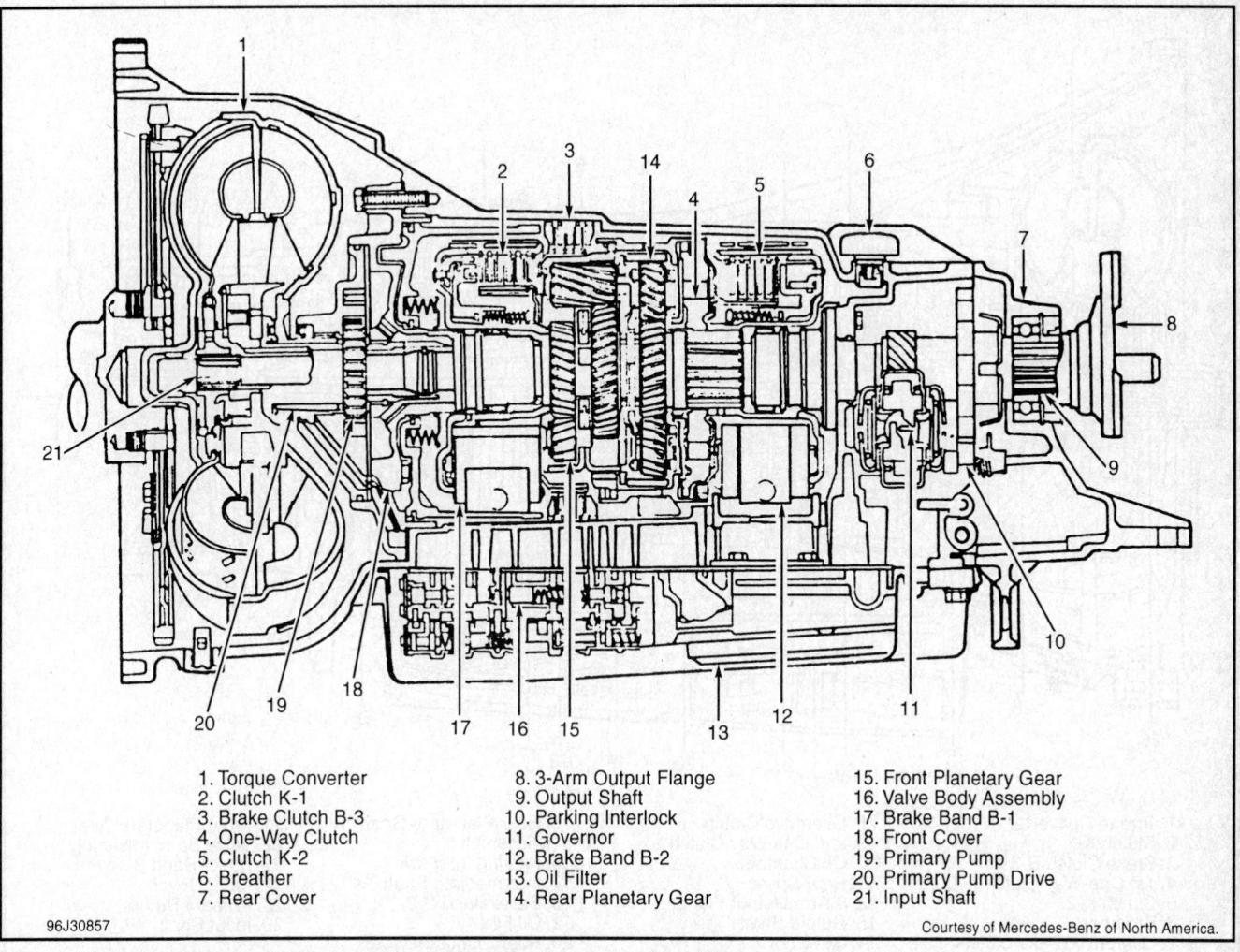

1. Torque Converter	8. 3-Arm Output Flange	15. Front Planetary Gear
2. Clutch K-1	9. Output Shaft	16. Valve Body Assembly
3. Brake Clutch B-3	10. Parking Interlock	17. Brake Band B-1
4. One-Way Clutch	11. Governor	18. Front Cover
5. Clutch K-2	12. Brake Band B-2	19. Primary Pump
6. Breather	13. Oil Filter	20. Primary Pump Drive
7. Rear Cover	14. Rear Planetary Gear	21. Input Shaft

96J30857 — Courtesy of Mercedes-Benz of North America.

Fig. 1: Identifying Transmission Components (722.3 & 722.4 Series Transmissions)

"N" position to "2" position, clutch K-2 and brake band B-2 are controlled. When selector lever is moved from "N" position to "R" position, clutch K-2 and disc brake B-3 are controlled. The "engaging" damper controls working pressure pattern after drive positions "R", "D", "3" and "2" are engaged.

TRANSMISSION SHIFT POINT DELAY

The 2nd to 3rd gear upshift on some models is delayed 60-80 seconds to enable catalytic converter to reach its operating temperature quicker. Shift point retard solenoid is energized by CIS-E control unit or air mass sensor control unit through transmission shift point (upshift) retard relay.

Governor pressure is lowered through hydraulic line which is bolted to governor pressure test port. See Fig. 3. Under certain operating conditions (coolant temperature, vehicle speed and time), solenoid valve is de-energized and governor pressure is dumped. The 2-3 upshift is delayed only when coolant temperature is 0-140°F (0-60°C). Operating time is dependent on coolant temperature when engine is started, and is longest when coolant temperature is 68-86°F (20-30°C).

LUBRICATION & ADJUSTMENTS

NOTE: See appropriate AUTOMATIC TRANSMISSION SERVICING article in TRANSMISSION SERVICING section.

TROUBLE SHOOTING

Transmission Slips In All Gears – Incorrect modulating pressure. Modulating pressure control valve or pressure relief valve is dirty or sticking. Vacuum line to transmission vacuum capsule clogged or leaking. Working pressure control valve dirty or sticking. Low working pressure. Defective primary pump.

Transmission Slips When Starting Off In 1st Or 2nd (Reverse Is Okay) – Band B-2 shift valve sticking. Band B-2 piston worn or damaged. Band B-2 adjusted incorrectly or worn or damaged. Adjust brake band B-2 by installing a longer thrust pin (if necessary). If transmission operates properly with selector lever in "2", but not in "3" or "D" position, one-way clutch may be slipping.

Transmission Slips In 2nd Gear Or Shifts From 1st To 3rd Gear – Check control valve B-1 for ease of operation. Replace valve body (if necessary). Remove and install brake band piston B-1, check sealing ring and replace (if necessary). Replace brake band B-1 and thrust body for B-1. Command valve binding.

Transmission Slips During 2-3 Upshift Or Slips Initially, Then Grabs Hold – Check modulating pressure and adjust (if necessary). Check for temperature throttle installation (if equipped). Valve body worn or damaged. Replace valve body (if necessary). Replace inner plates of clutch K-1 or recondition clutch (if necessary). Check front cover Teflon ring.

Transmission Slips During 3-4 Upshift – Check and adjust modulating pressure. Governor damaged or working pressure incorrect. Valve body worn or damaged. Replace valve body (if necessary). Check Teflon rings supporting clutch K-2. Replace inner plates of clutch K-2 or recondition clutch (if necessary).

AUTOMATIC TRANSMISSIONS
Mercedes-Benz 722 Series (Cont.)

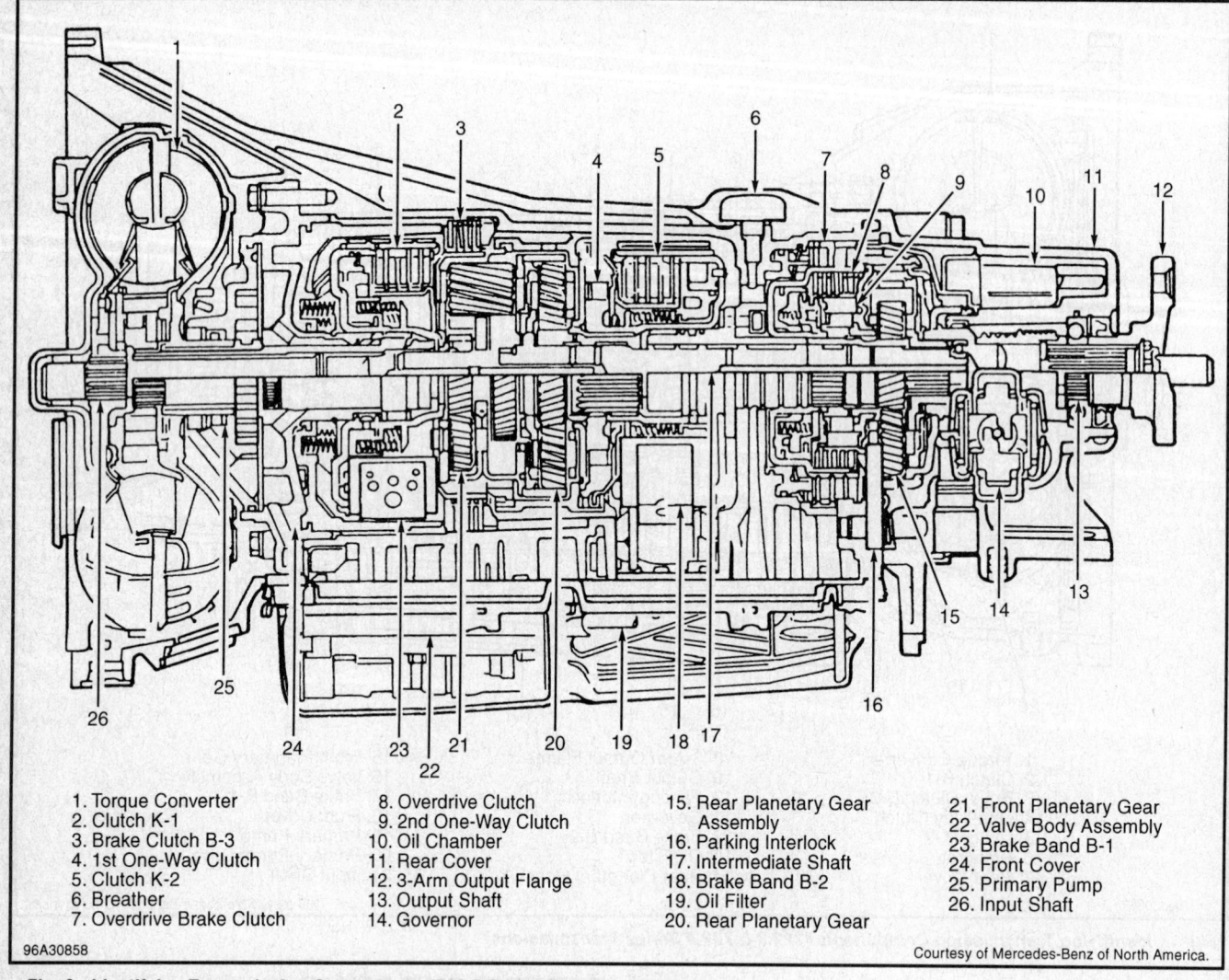

1. Torque Converter
2. Clutch K-1
3. Brake Clutch B-3
4. 1st One-Way Clutch
5. Clutch K-2
6. Breather
7. Overdrive Brake Clutch
8. Overdrive Clutch
9. 2nd One-Way Clutch
10. Oil Chamber
11. Rear Cover
12. 3-Arm Output Flange
13. Output Shaft
14. Governor
15. Rear Planetary Gear Assembly
16. Parking Interlock
17. Intermediate Shaft
18. Brake Band B-2
19. Oil Filter
20. Rear Planetary Gear
21. Front Planetary Gear
22. Valve Body Assembly
23. Brake Band B-1
24. Front Cover
25. Primary Pump
26. Input Shaft

96A30858

Courtesy of Mercedes-Benz of North America.

Fig. 2: Identifying Transmission Components (722.5 Series Transmission)

Intermittent No 5th Gear – Check loose connections at throttle valve switch. Check for poor or loose wiring connections between TCM and transmission. See WIRING DIAGRAMS. Ensure proper TCM is installed.

No 5th Gear Or Transmission Shifts To 5th Under Load – Check and repair vacuum line between intake manifold and ignition control unit.

No Positive Engagement In Reverse – Check plates and sealing rings on brake B-3 piston. Replace if necessary.

Harsh Engagement When Shifting Gears – Incorrect working pressure. Check and adjust modulating pressure. Check vacuum line and connections for leaks. On vehicles equipped with diesel engines, check vacuum control valve. Coolant entering transmission oil cooler and contaminating transmission fluid. Replace radiator. If necessary, replace all friction linings and/or replace transmission.

Harsh Engagement When Selecting "D" Or "R" – Idle speed too high. Check pressure receiving (pick-up) piston in valve body for ease of operation and correct installation. Replace valve body (if necessary).

NOTE: Pressure pick-up requires a running period of approximately 2 seconds. Harsh engagement may occur during repeated shifts between "N" and "D". If harshness takes place within 2 seconds, condition is considered normal.

Harshness On 4-3 Downshift – Sealing ring on release end of band B-2 worn or damaged. Band B-2 piston worn or damaged. Band B-2 thrust body damaged.

Chatter During Upshift – Valve body malfunction. Check and repair or replace valve body.

Will Not Upshift – Incorrect governor pressure. Defective governor assembly. Check for stuck kickdown solenoid or for constant voltage to solenoid caused by a defective fuel pump relay or sticking kickdown switch. Valve body dirty or valves sticking. Repair or replace valve body.

Upshifts At Higher Speeds Than Specified – Check pressure control cable engagement, condition and adjustment. Check for stuck kickdown solenoid or for constant voltage to solenoid caused by a defective fuel pump relay or sticking kickdown switch. Check governor pressure. If regulator pressure is too low, replace centrifugal governor. Ensure control pressure regulating valve is operable.

Upshifts At Lower Speeds Than Specified – Check pressure control cable engagement, condition and adjustment. Check full throttle stop by accelerating engine and ensuring throttle valve rests against full throttle stop. Readjust throttle stop (if necessary). Check governor pressure. If governor pressure is too high, replace centrifugal governor. Repair or replace valve body.

No Kickdown – Check throttle control and pressure control cable engagement, condition and adjustment. Connect kickdown solenoid to battery and check for proper operation. Replace solenoid (if necessary). Check kickdown valve in valve body. Replace valve body (if necessary).

No 4-3 Or 3-2 Downshift – Control pressure cable out of adjustment. Leaking vacuum hoses and/or connections. Ensure brake shaft piston is operable. Replace valve body (if necessary).

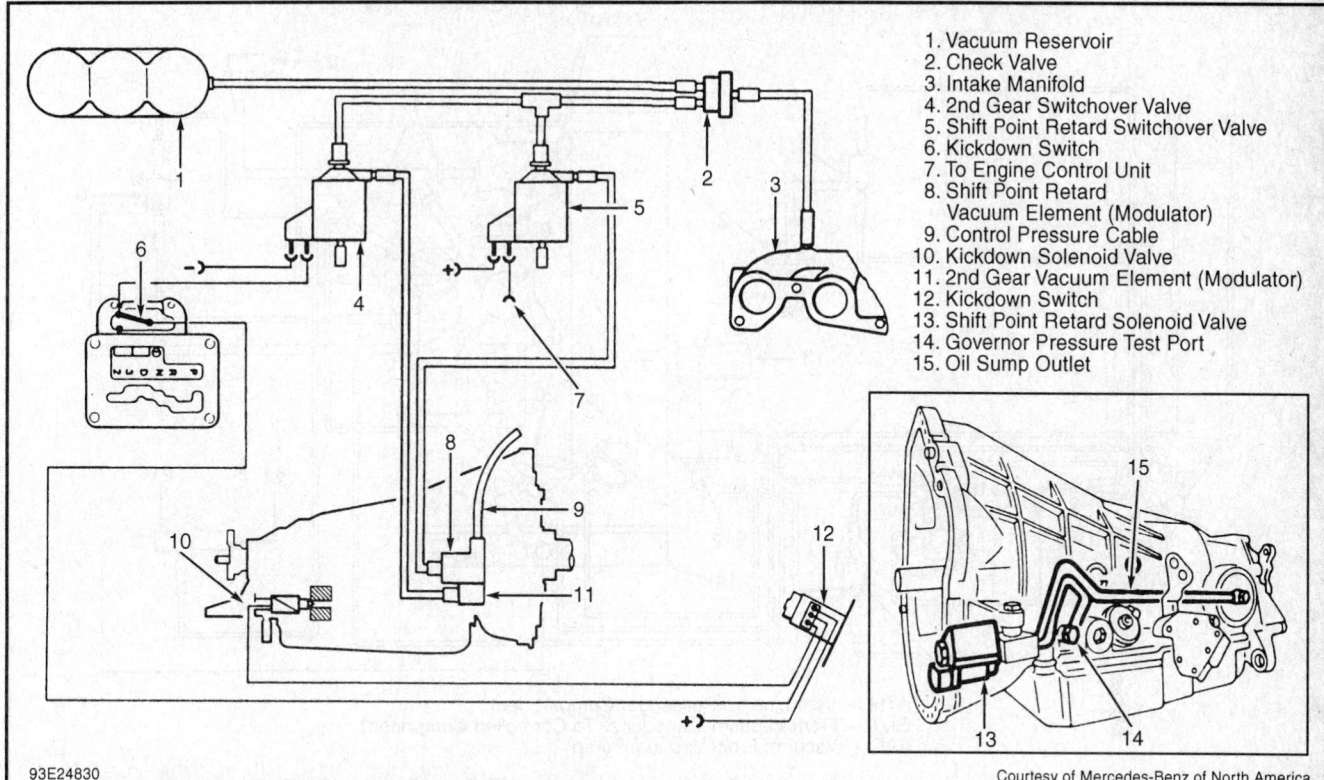

1. Vacuum Reservoir
2. Check Valve
3. Intake Manifold
4. 2nd Gear Switchover Valve
5. Shift Point Retard Switchover Valve
6. Kickdown Switch
7. To Engine Control Unit
8. Shift Point Retard
   Vacuum Element (Modulator)
9. Control Pressure Cable
10. Kickdown Solenoid Valve
11. 2nd Gear Vacuum Element (Modulator)
12. Kickdown Switch
13. Shift Point Retard Solenoid Valve
14. Governor Pressure Test Port
15. Oil Sump Outlet

93E24830

Courtesy of Mercedes-Benz of North America.

Fig. 3: Identifying Transmission Shift Point Delay Components

Uncontrolled Downshifts Outside Range Of Kickdown Switch – Remove kickdown solenoid. Check "O" ring on kickdown solenoid for damage. Check kickdown switch for sticking in pushed-in position. Replace switch (if necessary). Check for kickdown solenoid stuck in opened position. Replace kickdown solenoid (if necessary).

Poor Acceleration From Stopped Position – Check stall speed. If stall speed is 400-700 RPM less than specified value, one-way clutch in torque converter is slipping. Replace torque converter (if necessary).

Parking Pawl Will Not Engage – Check rear engine mount. Replace engine mount (if necessary). Check adjustment of selector rod. Adjust selector rod (if necessary).

Selector Lever Does Not Engage In "R" Or "P" – With engine running, clean centrifugal governor and ensure correct operation. With engine not running, check operation of detent piston in lower cover.

Engine Will Not Start In "P" Or "N" Position – Adjust shift rod and starter lock-out switch. Replace starter lock-out switch (if necessary).

Smoke In Exhaust (Fluid Loss) – Diaphragm in vacuum control unit defective. Transmission oil is being drawn from engine through vacuum line. Replace vacuum control unit (if necessary).

Fluid Loss Between Torque Converter & Primary Pump – Seal torque converter oil drain plug. If leak continues, replace radial sealing ring and "O" ring on primary pump. Check primary pump "O" ring groove for porosity. Replace primary pump (if necessary).

Howling Noise When Changing Gears (Under Full Load) – Replace transmission oil filter.

Howling Noise Which Increases As Engine RPM Increases – Check primary pump and replace if necessary.

1st Gear & Reverse Too Loud – Replace front planetary gear set. Reverse and 1st gear are louder than forward (driving) gears due to gear reduction. If noise seems too loud, or if in doubt, a similar vehicle should be used for comparison.

3rd Gear Too Loud – Replace rear planetary gear set.

Rattling Noise At 1500 RPM In All Positions Except "R" – Brake B-3 plates are vibrating in transmission housing. Replace brake B-3 plates, install damper spring and set release clearance to minimum value.

Light Grinding Noise In "P" & "N" Positions – This condition is normal if a "rolling" noise of front planetary gear set is heard. If noise seems too loud, or if in doubt, a similar vehicle should be used for comparison.

"Rolling" Noises When Driving In Reverse – Disc brake B-3 release clearance too great. Adjust release clearance to .06-.08" (1.5-2.0 mm) or replace disc brake plates. Outside plate carrier of clutch K-1 contacts piston.

Primary Pump Bushing Loosens After A Short Operating Period – Dowel pins for centering transmission to engine are not in place.

TESTING

VACUUM CONTROL CIRCUIT

Vacuum Control Valve (E300D & S350D) – **1)** Ensure engine is at normal operating temperature and throttle linkage is adjusted properly. Disconnect Black/White vacuum hose and connect vacuum/pressure tester.

2) Start engine and check vacuum at idle. Vacuum should be 11.6-13.2 in. Hg (395-445 mbar) with Red or Blue colored cap; 10.6-12.1 in. Hg (360-410 mbar) with Black colored cap. Stop engine and place throttle linkage at full throttle stop. Vacuum reading should be zero.

3) If vacuum readings are correct, vacuum control valve is okay. If readings are not correct, check vacuum hose routing. See Fig. 4. If routing is correct, check vacuum pump. If pump is okay, adjust vacuum control valve and replace (if necessary).

Vacuum Amplifier (E300D & S350D) – **1)** Disconnect vacuum hose and damper at vacuum control valve. Plug vacuum control valve opening. Disconnect pressure hose running from aneroid compensator (ALDA) to vacuum amplifier, and connect tester to overpressure side of detached hose.

2) If vehicle has only one hose at aneroid compensator, connect test hose directly to vacuum amplifier PRE (boost pressure) connection. Simulate boost pressure of 21.9 in. Hg (740 mbar). Replace vacuum transducer if leak is present.

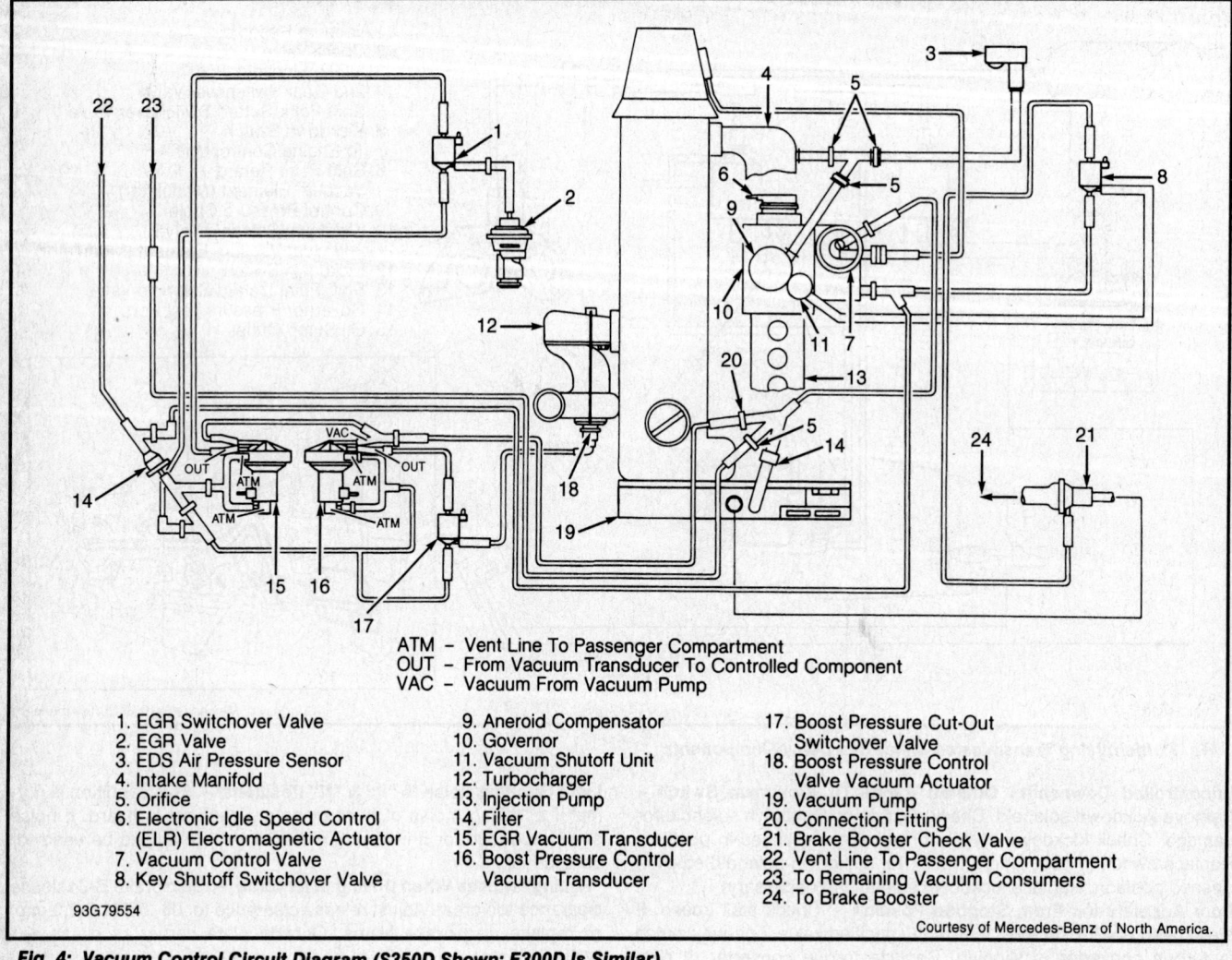

ATM – Vent Line To Passenger Compartment
OUT – From Vacuum Transducer To Controlled Component
VAC – Vacuum From Vacuum Pump

1. EGR Switchover Valve
2. EGR Valve
3. EDS Air Pressure Sensor
4. Intake Manifold
5. Orifice
6. Electronic Idle Speed Control (ELR) Electromagnetic Actuator
7. Vacuum Control Valve
8. Key Shutoff Switchover Valve
9. Aneroid Compensator
10. Governor
11. Vacuum Shutoff Unit
12. Turbocharger
13. Injection Pump
14. Filter
15. EGR Vacuum Transducer
16. Boost Pressure Control Vacuum Transducer
17. Boost Pressure Cut-Out Switchover Valve
18. Boost Pressure Control Valve Vacuum Actuator
19. Vacuum Pump
20. Connection Fitting
21. Brake Booster Check Valve
22. Vent Line To Passenger Compartment
23. To Remaining Vacuum Consumers
24. To Brake Booster

93G79554

Courtesy of Mercedes-Benz of North America.

Fig. 4: Vacuum Control Circuit Diagram (S350D Shown; E300D Is Similar)

3) Using a "T" fitting, connect tester at vacuum end of vacuum transducer connection TRA (transmission). Start engine and check vacuum at idle. Vacuum should be .59-1.8 in. Hg (20-60 mbar). If vacuum readings are correct, vacuum amplifier is okay. If readings are not correct, check vacuum hose routing. If routing is correct, replace vacuum amplifier.

ROAD TEST

NOTE: Before road testing, check transmission fluid level, idle speed and control pressure cable adjustment. See appropriate AUTOMATIC TRANSMISSION SERVICING article in TRANSMISSION SERVICING section.

1) During road test, transmission should upshift and downshift at approximate speeds shown in appropriate SHIFT SPEEDS table. All shifts may vary somewhat due to production tolerances or tire size. The important factor is quality of shifts. All shifts should be smooth, responsive and with no engine speed flare-up.

NOTE: If transmission shift point delay feature is used (see Fig. 3), the 2-3 upshift under light throttle (partially depressed accelerator pedal) will be higher with engine cold.

2) Slipping or engine RPM flare-up usually indicates clutch or band problems. Slipping clutch or band in particular gear can usually be identified by noting transmission operation in all gear positions and comparing which internal units are applied in those positions. See CLUTCH & BAND APPLICATION CHART.

3) This process of elimination can be used to detect any unit which slips and to test proper operation of good units. Cause of malfunction usually cannot be decided. Most conditions may be caused by leaking hydraulic circuits or sticking valves. Unless an obvious condition exists, transmission should never be disassembled until hydraulic pressure tests have been performed.

CLUTCH & BAND APPLICATION CHART

Selector Lever Position	Elements In Use [1]
"D"	
1st Gear	B-2 Brake & One-Way Clutch
2nd Gear	B-1 Brake & B-2 Brake
3rd Gear	B-2 Brake & K-1 Clutch
4th Gear	K-1 Clutch & K-2 Clutch
5th Gear	K-1 Clutch, K-2 Clutch & Overdrive Brake
"3"	
1st Gear	B-2 Brake & One-Way Clutch
2nd Gear	B-1 Brake & B-2 Brake
3rd Gear	B-2 Brake & K-1 Clutch
"2"	
1st Gear	B-2 Brake, [2] K-2 Clutch & One-Way Clutch,
2nd Gear	B-1 Brake & B-2 Brake
"R"	B-3 Brake, [2] K-2 Clutch & One-Way Clutch
"N" & "P"	All Clutches & Bands Released

[1] – Overdrive clutch and 2nd one-way clutch are also in effect on 722.5 series transmissions.

[2] – Applied but not effective. K-2 clutch provides engine braking in Reverse and manual low.

C220 SHIFT SPEEDS – SHIFT LEVER IN "D"

Application	MPH
Full Throttle	
1-2 Upshift	27
2-3 Upshift	48
3-4 Upshift	80
4-3 Downshift	67
3-2 Downshift	29
2-1 Downshift	10
Kickdown	
1-2 Upshift	30
2-3 Upshift	53
3-4 Upshift	83
4-3 Downshift	75
3-2 Downshift	45
2-1 Downshift	17

C280 SHIFT SPEEDS – SHIFT LEVER IN "D"

Application	MPH
Full Throttle	
1-2 Upshift	29
2-3 Upshift	58
3-4 Upshift	99
4-3 Downshift	70
3-2 Downshift	28
2-1 Downshift	11
Kickdown	
1-2 Upshift	37
2-3 Upshift	64
3-4 Upshift	103
4-3 Downshift	92
3-2 Downshift	54
2-1 Downshift	23

E300D SHIFT SPEEDS – SHIFT LEVER IN "D"

Application	MPH
Full Throttle	
1-2 Upshift	26
2-3 Upshift	48
3-4 Upshift	81
4-3 Downshift	50
3-2 Downshift	26
2-1 Downshift	15
Kickdown	
1-2 Upshift	29
2-3 Upshift	51
3-4 Upshift	82
4-3 Downshift	72
3-2 Downshift	41
2-1 Downshift	23

E320 SHIFT SPEEDS – SHIFT LEVER IN "D"

Application	MPH
Full Throttle	
1-2 Upshift	36
2-3 Upshift	68
3-4 Upshift	110
4-3 Downshift	77
3-2 Downshift	35
2-1 Downshift	14
Kickdown	
1-2 Upshift	44
2-3 Upshift	74
3-4 Upshift	115
4-3 Downshift	102
3-2 Downshift	63
2-1 Downshift	26

E420 SHIFT SPEEDS – SHIFT LEVER IN "D"

Application	MPH
Full Throttle	
1-2 Upshift	42
2-3 Upshift	78
3-4 Upshift	125
4-3 Downshift	91
3-2 Downshift	35
2-1 Downshift	19

E420 SHIFT SPEEDS – SHIFT LEVER IN "D" (Cont.)

Application	MPH
Kickdown	
1-2 Upshift	49
2-3 Upshift	85
3-4 Upshift	131
4-3 Downshift	118
3-2 Downshift	69
2-1 Downshift	35

S320 SHIFT SPEEDS – SHIFT LEVER IN "D"

Application [1]	MPH
Full Throttle	
1-2 Upshift	30
2-3 Upshift	56
3-4 Upshift	89
4-5 Upshift	136
Kickdown	
1-2 Upshift	35
2-3 Upshift	61
3-4 Upshift	94
4-5 Upshift	136

[1] – Downshift speed specification for 722.5 series are not available.

S350 SHIFT SPEEDS – SHIFT LEVER IN "D"

Application	MPH
Full Throttle	
1-2 Upshift	23
2-3 Upshift	47
3-4 Upshift	75
4-3 Downshift	53
3-2 Downshift	29
2-1 Downshift	13
Kickdown	
1-2 Upshift	30
2-3 Upshift	52
3-4 Upshift	80
4-3 Downshift	72
3-2 Downshift	45
2-1 Downshift	19

S420 SHIFT SPEEDS – SHIFT LEVER IN "D"

Application	MPH
Full Throttle	
1-2 Upshift	30
2-3 Upshift	67
3-4 Upshift	107
4-3 Downshift	75
3-2 Downshift	26
2-1 Downshift	15
Kickdown	
1-2 Upshift	44
2-3 Upshift	73
3-4 Upshift	111
4-3 Downshift	100
3-2 Downshift	60
2-1 Downshift	25

S500 & SL500 SHIFT SPEEDS – SHIFT LEVER IN "D"

Application	MPH
Full Throttle	
1-2 Upshift	32
2-3 Upshift	72
3-4 Upshift	113
4-3 Downshift	80
3-2 Downshift	27
2-1 Downshift	17
Kickdown	
1-2 Upshift	46
2-3 Upshift	78
3-4 Upshift	117
4-3 Downshift	106
3-2 Downshift	63
2-1 Downshift	27

SL320 SHIFT SPEEDS – SHIFT LEVER IN "D"

Application [1]	MPH
Full Throttle	
1-2 Upshift	27
2-3 Upshift	51
3-4 Upshift	81
4-5 Upshift	123
Kickdown	
1-2 Upshift	32
2-3 Upshift	55
3-4 Upshift	86
4-5 Upshift	123

[1] – Downshift speed specification for 722.5 series are not available.

HYDRAULIC PRESSURE TEST

NOTE: Working pressure specification for 722.5 series transmission is not available.

Preliminary Test – 1) Before performing tests, check fluid level and condition, throttle linkage, EGR system and neutral safety switch. Correct as necessary. Connect pressure gauge to appropriate pressure port on transmission. See Fig. 5.
2) Attach pressure gauge to inside mirror in such a manner that it can be easily read from driver's seat. Run pressure hoses through passenger window.
3) Ensure pressure hoses do not drag on pavement or contact exhaust system. After test, run engine and check pressure ports for leaks.

Modulating Pressure Test – 1) Remove vacuum line and holder from vacuum control unit (modulator). Place transmission in "D" position and drive vehicle on road or on dynamometer at 31 MPH. Apply full throttle and maintain speed at 31 MPH by lightly applying brakes.
2) Read resulting pressure on gauge attached to modulating pressure port on transmission. Pressure should be as shown in MODULATING PRESSURE table.
3) If necessary, adjust modulating pressure. Modulator pressure port is next to vacuum control unit at 4 o'clock position. Disconnect vacuum hose and remove rubber cap from vacuum control unit. Pull "T" handle out of locking slots to permit rotation. Turning "T" handle one rotation in vacuum control unit results in pressure change of about 6 psi (.422 kg/cm²). Adjust to correct value. See MODULATING PRESSURE table.
4) After adjusting pressure, push "T" handle back into locking slots. Put rubber cap back on vacuum control unit. Connect vacuum hose, and check modulating pressure.

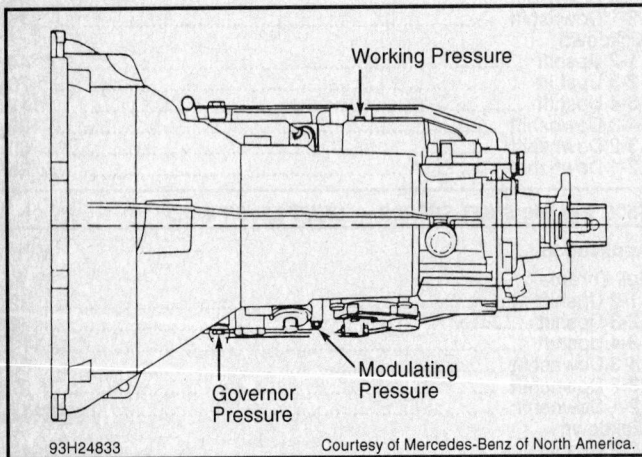

93H24833   Courtesy of Mercedes-Benz of North America.

Fig. 5: Locating Pressure Test Ports

MODULATING PRESSURE

Model	[1] psi (kPa)
C220	53.7 (370)
C280	56.6 (390)
E300D	47.1 (325)
E320	60.9 (420)
S350D	44.9 (310)
E420	55.1 (380)
S320	58.0 (400)
S420	55.1 (380)
S500	58.0 (400)
SL320	58.0 (400)

[1] – Measure pressure in "D" position at 31 MPH.

NOTE: Modulating pressure must be measured and adjusted before performing working pressure and governor pressure tests.

Working Pressure Test – 1) Disconnect vacuum line from vacuum control unit (modulator). Start and run engine at 1000 RPM while reading pressure. Pressure should be as shown in WORKING PRESSURE table.
2) Working pressure is not adjustable. Measurement simply provides information concerning operation of working pressure regulator valve in valve housing.

WORKING PRESSURE

Model	[1] psi (kPa)
C220, C280 & C36	[2]
E300D	212-239 (1460-1660)
E320	174-203 (1200-1400)
S350D	213-242 (1470-1670)
E420 & S420	160-174 (1100-1200)
S320 & SL320	[2]
S500 & SL500	186-215 (1280-1480)

[1] – Measure pressure in "D" position with vehicle stationary.
[2] – Information not available.

Governor Pressure – Drive vehicle on road or on dynamometer at speeds indicated in GOVERNOR PRESSURE table. Compare pressures noted on gauge with pressures given in table.

NOTE: Governor pressure is a part of working pressure and is controlled by governor assembly on output shaft. If values are not within specifications, disassemble and clean governor assembly.

GOVERNOR PRESSURE

Model	psi (kPa) @ 19 MPH	psi (kPa) @ 56 MPH
C220, C280 & C36	[1]	[1]
E300D & S350D	11.6 (80)	37.7 (260)
E320	11.6 (80)	37.7 (260)
E420 & S420	10.2 (70)	30.5 (210)
S320 & SL320	[1]	[1]
S500 & SL500	8.7 (60)	29.0 (200)

[1] – Information not available.

STALL TEST

Information not available.

ON-VEHICLE SERVICE

The following components may be removed from transmission without removing transmission from vehicle: oil pan and gasket, valve body, vacuum control unit, speedometer driven gear assembly, secondary pump assembly, extension housing, pressure receiving piston, modulating pressure housing and bimetallic spring, speedometer drive gear, secondary pump eccentric, governor assembly, parking pawl and parking linkage. For removal and installation procedures for these components, see TRANSMISSION DISASSEMBLY and TRANSMISSION REASSEMBLY.

AUTOMATIC TRANSMISSIONS
Mercedes-Benz 722 Series (Cont.)

REMOVAL & INSTALLATION

See appropriate AUTOMATIC TRANSMISSION REMOVAL article in TRANSMISSION SERVICING section.

TORQUE CONVERTER

NOTE: Torque converter is a sealed unit and cannot be disassembled for service. If hub of converter is scored or if metallic particles are found in transmission fluid, replace torque converter.

TRANSMISSION DISASSEMBLY

722.3 & 722.4 SERIES

1) Remove control pressure cable sleeve by pressing tab inward, turning cable counterclockwise 90 degrees, and pulling sleeve upward. Detach selector lever cable by releasing locking device with a screwdriver. Position transmission in holding fixture and mounting plate with oil pan facing upward.

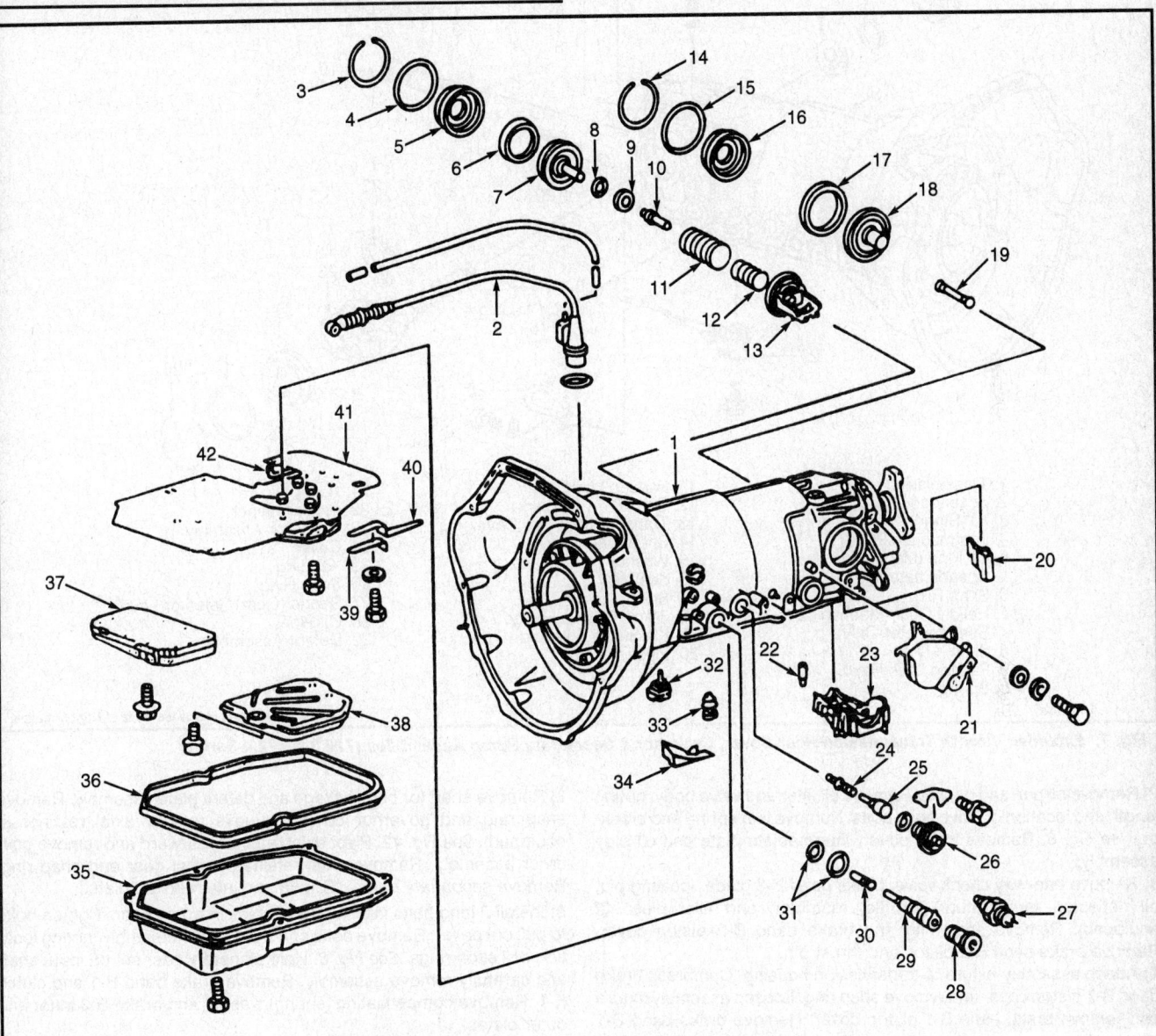

1. Transmission
2. Control Pressure Cable
3. Snap Ring
4. "O" Ring
5. Brake Band B-1 Piston Cover
6. Lip Sealing Ring
7. Brake Band B-1 Piston
8. Shim(s)
9. Shim(s)
10. Thrust Pin
11. Return Spring
12. Return Spring
13. Brake Band B-1 Guide
14. Snap Ring
15. "O" Ring
16. Brake Band B-2 Piston Cover
17. Lip Sealing Ring
18. Brake Band B-2 Piston
19. Thrust Pin
20. Filler Piece (If Equipped)
21. Starter Lock-Out Switch
22. Locating Pin
23. Brake Band B-3 Guide
24. Modulating Pressure Control Valve
25. Heat Expansion Pin
26. Vacuum Control Unit (Modulator)
27. Transmission Overload Protection Switch (If Equipped)
28. Screw-On Plug (If Equipped)
29. Brake Band B-1 Thrust Element Of Thrust Bearing
30. Thrust Pin
31. "O" Rings
32. Temperature Throttle
33. One-Way Check Valve
34. Oil Deflector
35. Oil Pan
36. Gasket
37. Valve Body
38. Oil Filter
39. Bracket
40. Leaf Spring
41. Intermediate Plate
42. Oil Pipe

Courtesy of Mercedes-Benz of North America.

93I24834

Fig. 6: Exploded View Of Transmission Case External Components (722.3 & 722.4 Series)

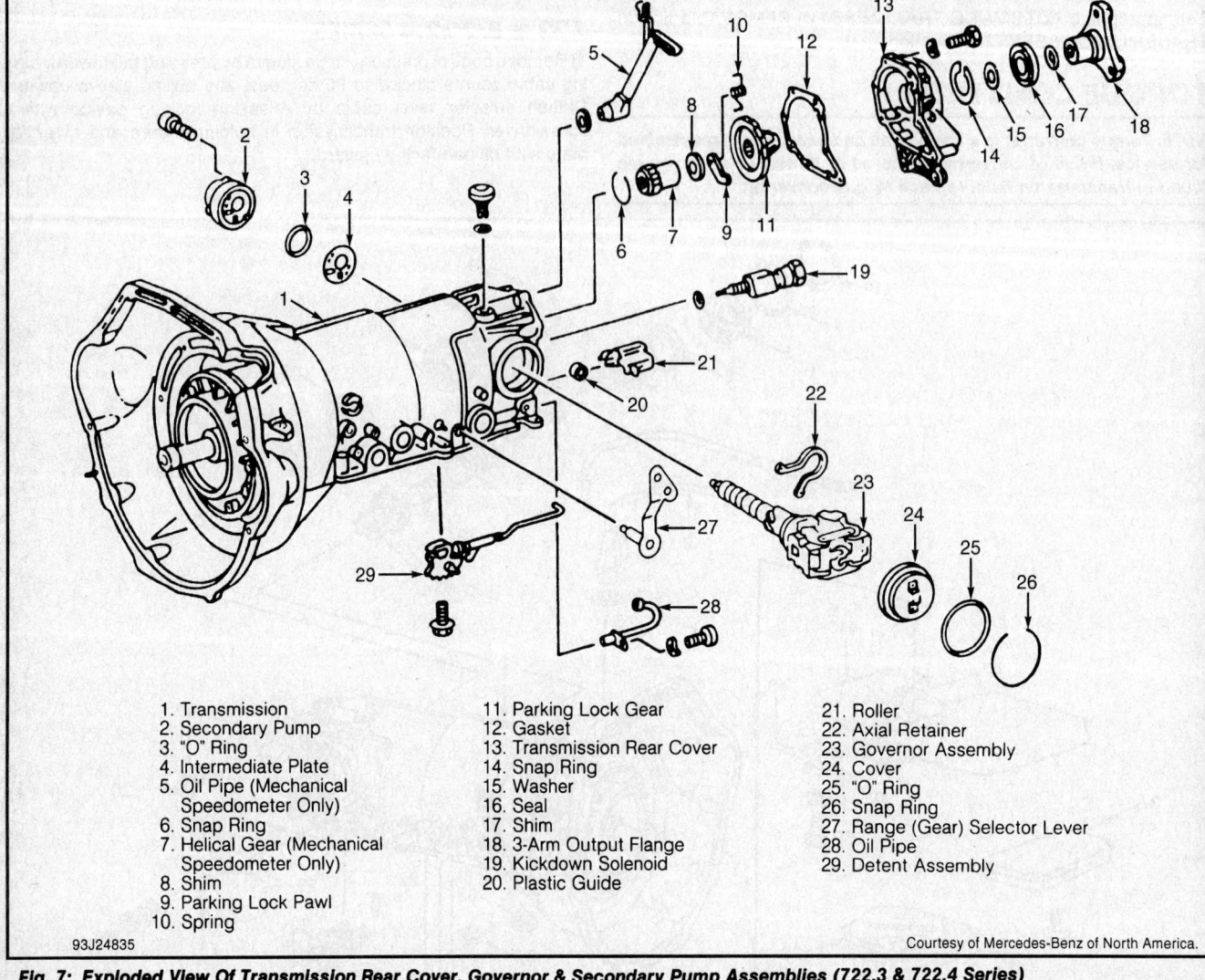

1. Transmission
2. Secondary Pump
3. "O" Ring
4. Intermediate Plate
5. Oil Pipe (Mechanical Speedometer Only)
6. Snap Ring
7. Helical Gear (Mechanical Speedometer Only)
8. Shim
9. Parking Lock Pawl
10. Spring
11. Parking Lock Gear
12. Gasket
13. Transmission Rear Cover
14. Snap Ring
15. Washer
16. Seal
17. Shim
18. 3-Arm Output Flange
19. Kickdown Solenoid
20. Plastic Guide
21. Roller
22. Axial Retainer
23. Governor Assembly
24. Cover
25. "O" Ring
26. Snap Ring
27. Range (Gear) Selector Lever
28. Oil Pipe
29. Detent Assembly

93J24835

Courtesy of Mercedes-Benz of North America.

Fig. 7: Exploded View Of Transmission Rear Cover, Governor & Secondary Pump Assemblies (722.3 & 722.4 Series)

2) Remove oil pan and gasket. Remove oil filter and valve body, noting length and location of valve body bolts. Remove leaf spring and bracket. *See Fig. 6*. Remove lower cover, intermediate plate and oil pipe assembly.

3) Remove one-way check valve, brake band B-3 guide, locating pin, oil deflector, temperature (throttle) restrictor, and filler piece (if equipped). Remove snap ring and brake band B-2 piston cover. Remove brake band B-2 piston and thrust pin.

4) Attach assembly fixture to transmission housing. Compress brake band B-1 piston cover and remove snap ring. Loosen assembly fixture and remove brake band B-1 piston cover. Remove brake band B-1 piston, thrust pin and return springs. Remove brake band B-1 guide.

5) Remove transmission overload protection switch or screw-on plug for brake band B-1 thrust element and thrust pin. Remove gear selector lever and starter lock-out switch. Remove vacuum control unit (modulator) and retaining plate. Remove modulating pressure control valve and heat expansion pin.

6) Remove kickdown solenoid. Remove output shaft nut. Remove 3-arm output flange and washer. *See Fig. 7*. Remove shift point retard switchover valve and oil sump drain tube (if equipped). Remove transmission rear cover.

7) Remove mechanical speedometer drive oil pipe (if equipped). Remove parking lock gear, parking lock pawl, spring and shim(s) from output shaft. Pull out plastic guide, roller, bolt and oil pipe (if equipped).

8) Remove shaft (or bolt), linkage and detent plate assembly. Remove snap ring and governor cover. Remove nut for axial retainer (if equipped). *See Fig. 42*. Pivot axial retainer rearward and remove governor assembly. Remove axial retainer, helical gear and snap ring. Remove secondary pump, "O" ring and intermediate plate.

9) Install 2 long bolts into threaded holes in front cover. Tighten bolts to pull out cover. Remove bolts and front cover assembly, noting location of Teflon rings. *See Fig. 8*. Hold planetary gear set on input shaft and carefully remove assembly. Remove brake band B-1 and clutch K-1. Remove compensating (spring) washer and brake B-3 inner and outer plates.

10) Remove brake band B-2 damping spring, thrust pin, and clutch K-2. *See Fig. 8*. Remove thrust washer from support flange. Remove support flange, "O" ring and Teflon rings.

11) Compress brake band B-2 as much as possible and remove snap ring. Remove brake band piston. Remove brake band B-2 thrust element. Remove "O" rings, sealing rings, and aluminum sealing rings from transmission housing.

722.5 SERIES

1) Remove control pressure cable sleeve by pressing tab inward, turning cable counterclockwise 90 degrees, and pulling sleeve upward. Detach selector lever cable by releasing locking device with a screwdriver. Remove shift point retard switchover valve from transmission.

1. Transmission
2. Lip Sealing Ring
3. Guide Ring
4. "O" Ring
5. "O" Ring
6. Sealing Ring
7. "O" Ring
8. Support Flange
9. Teflon Rings
10. Brake Band B-2 Thrust Element
11. Thrust Pin
12. Support Flange Disc
13. Brake Band B-2
14. Clutch K-2
15. Brake Band B-1
16. Compensating (Spring) Washer
17. Brake B-3 Outer Plate
18. Brake B-3 Inner Plate
19. Damping Spring
20. Brake B-3 Outer Plate
21. Input Shaft
22. Lubricating Thrust Ring
23. Planetary Gear Set Assembly
24. Output Shaft
25. Front Cover & Primary Pump Assembly
26. Gasket
27. Bearing
28. Thrust Washer
29. Shim
30. Clutch K-1

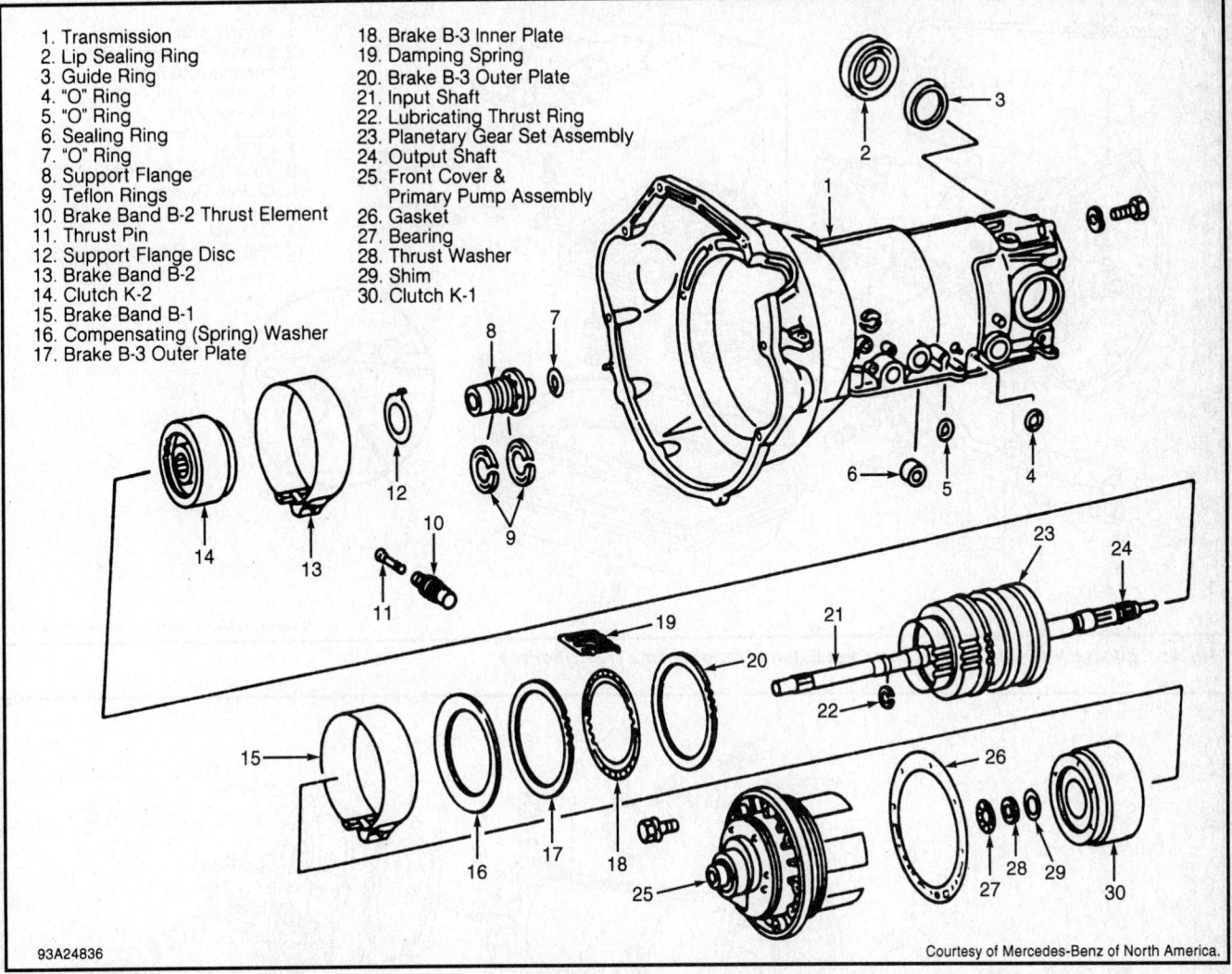

93A24836

Courtesy of Mercedes-Benz of North America.

Fig. 8: Exploded View Of Front Cover, Planetary Gear Set, Clutch & Brake Band Assemblies (722.3 & 722.4 Series)

2) Position transmission in holding fixture and mounting plate with oil pan facing upward. Remove oil pan and gasket. Remove oil filter and valve body, noting length and location of valve body bolts. Remove leaf spring and bracket. See Fig. 9. Remove lower cover, intermediate plate and oil pipe assembly.

3) Remove vacuum modulator valve securing bracket bolts and vacuum modulator valve. See Fig. 10. Remove starter lock-out switch. Remove secondary pump and transmission vent. Install 2 long bolts into threaded holes in front cover. Tighten bolts to pull out cover. Remove bolts and front cover assembly.

4) Engage parking lock mechanism and remove output shaft nut. Remove 3-arm flange from output shaft. Remove locking ring, governor cover, and governor assembly. Attach assembly fixture to transmission housing. Remove rear cover.

CAUTION: Do not face torque converter housing downwards while removing overdrive brake and overdrive clutch. Components will fall out causing damage to components.

5) Remove spring and parking lock pawl. See Fig. 11. Remove plastic parking lock pawl guide and detent assembly. Remove electrical connector for kick-down solenoid valve. Remove snap ring and output shaft with planetary gear set. Remove 2nd one-way clutch and overdrive clutch assemblies.

6) Remove snap ring securing overdrive brake assembly. Remove friction and steel plates. Remove overdrive brake piston and damper spring. Remove overload switch (or bolt if not equipped with overload switch) and remove brake band thrust pin.

7) Compress brake band B-1 piston cover and remove snap ring. See Fig. 12. Loosen assembly fixture and remove brake band B-1 piston cover. Remove brake band B-1 piston and return springs. Remove brake band B-1 guide. Remove input shaft with brake band B-1, clutch K-1 and brake B-1 assembly attached.

8) Remove damper spring. Compress brake band B-2 as much as possible and remove snap ring. Remove brake band piston. Remove brake band B-2 thrust element. Remove "O" rings, sealing rings, and aluminum sealing rings from transmission housing.

9) Remove clutch K-2 and brake band B-2 from transmission housing. Remove plastic ring guide and seal. Remove thrust washers from support flange. Remove securing bolts and support flange.

COMPONENT DISASSEMBLY & REASSEMBLY

VALVE BODY

Disassembly – **1)** Remove 2 screws at arrows, plate check valve and strainer. See Fig. 13. Hold damper housing and valve body together and turn over. Carefully remove damper housing and intermediate plate from valve body. Note direction and location of retainers, springs and check valves.

AUTOMATIC TRANSMISSIONS
Mercedes-Benz 722 Series (Cont.)

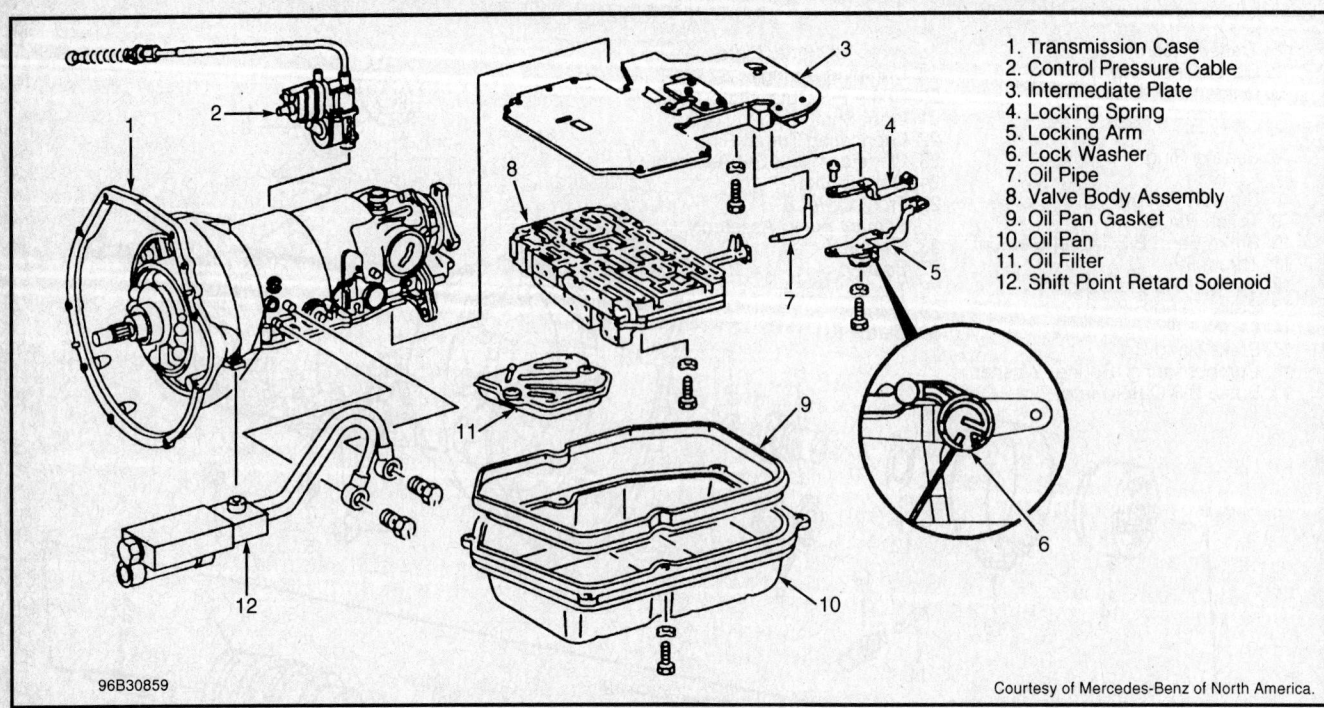

1. Transmission Case
2. Control Pressure Cable
3. Intermediate Plate
4. Locking Spring
5. Locking Arm
6. Lock Washer
7. Oil Pipe
8. Valve Body Assembly
9. Oil Pan Gasket
10. Oil Pan
11. Oil Filter
12. Shift Point Retard Solenoid

96B30859

Courtesy of Mercedes-Benz of North America.

Fig. 9: Exploded View Of Transmission Case External Components (722.5 Series)

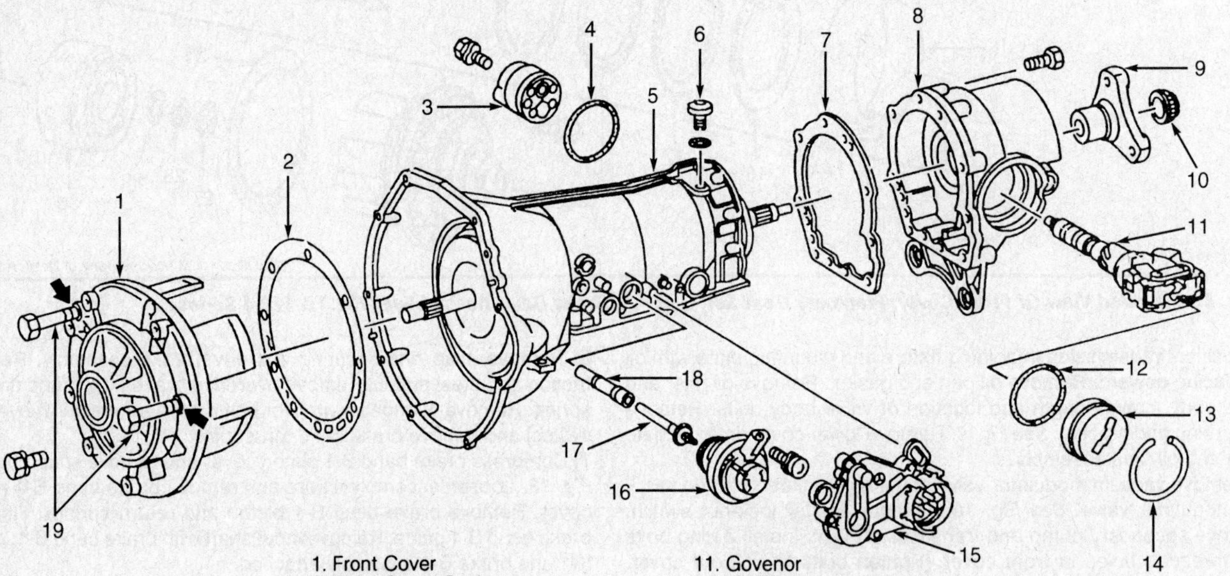

1. Front Cover
2. Front Cover Gasket
3. Secondary Pump
4. "O" Ring
5. Transmission Case
6. Breather
7. Rear Cover Gasket
8. Rear Cover
9. 3-Arm Output Flange
10. Output Flange Nut
11. Govenor
12. "O" Ring
13. Govenor Cover
14. Snap Ring
15. Starter Lock-Out Switch
16. Modulator Valve
17. Pressure Pin
18. Modulator Valve Pin
19. Front Cover Removal Bolt

96E30860

Courtesy of Mercedes-Benz of North America.

Fig. 10: Exploded View Of Transmission Rear Cover, Governor & Secondary Pump Assemblies (722.5 Series)

2) Remove check balls from valve body, noting number (18 or 19), type, size and location for reassembly reference. *See Fig. 14.* Remove side covers, control valves, pistons and springs. *See Figs. 15 and 16.*

Inspection – 1) Wash all parts in clean solvent and blow dry with compressed air. Closely inspect valve body and pick-up housing passages for obstructions or defects.

2) Inspect intermediate plate for damage. Inspect check balls for damage. If internal valve body problems are found or suspected, valve body must be replaced as an assembly.

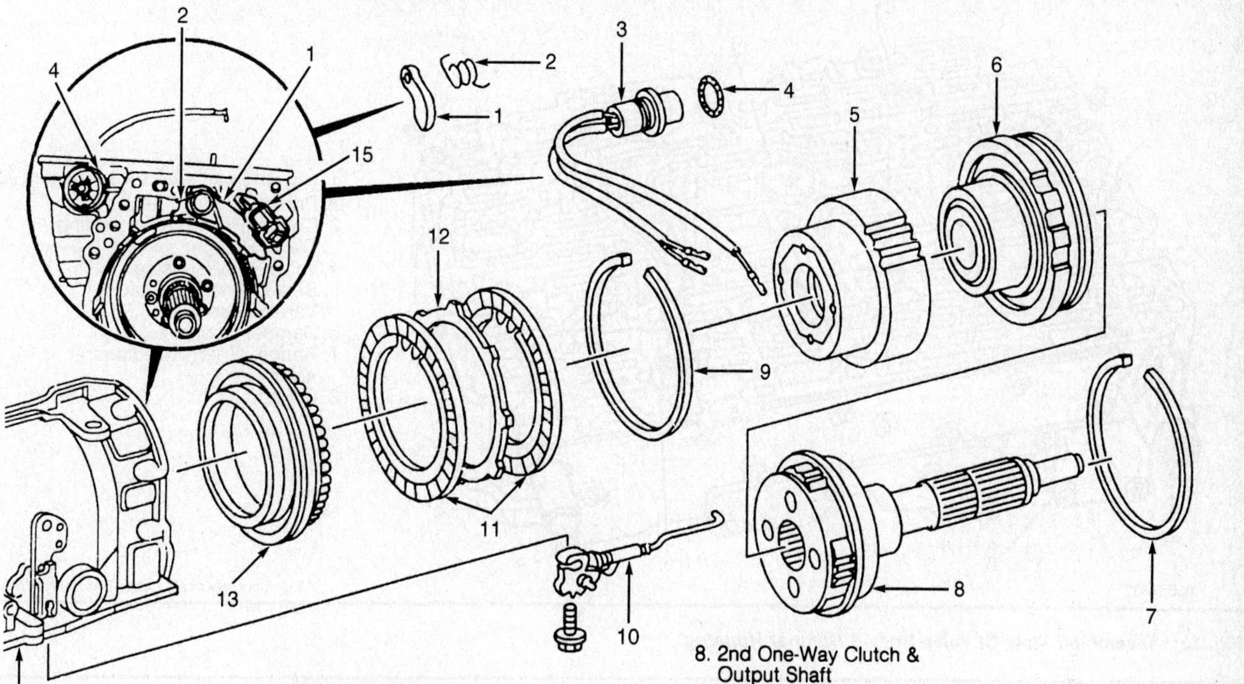

1. Parking Pawl
2. Parking Pawl Spring
3. Solenoid Valve Connector
4. "O" Ring
5. Overdrive Clutch Assembly
6. 2nd One-Way Clutch Hub
7. Snap Ring

8. 2nd One-Way Clutch & Output Shaft
9. Snap Ring
10. Detent Assembly
11. Friction Plates
12. Steel Plates
13. Overdrive Brake Piston
14. Transmission Case
15. Plastic Parking Pawl Guide

96F30861

Courtesy of Mercedes-Benz of North America.

Fig. 11: Exploded View Of Overdrive Clutch & Brake Band Assemblies (722.5 Series)

Reassembly – To reassemble valve body, reverse order of disassembly. Check ball rests on a conical spring. See Fig. 14. Tighten valve body screws at arrows so damper housing and valve body may be shifted in relation to each other. Rotating full throttle pressure adjustment screw clockwise produces earlier full throttle or kickdown upshifts; counterclockwise rotation of screw delays upshifts. See Fig. 14.

LOWER COVER

NOTE: If installed, note location of temperature restrictor, deflector piece, and locating pin after removing lower cover and intermediate plate. An auxiliary restrictor may also be installed.

Disassembly – 1) Remove valve body and oil filter (if installed). Remove leaf spring and bracket. See Figs. 17 and 18. Remove lower cover, intermediate plate and oil pipe as an assembly.

2) Press injector tabs inward and remove injector. Pull out oil tube. Remove cover plate and intermediate plate. Remove gasket from intermediate plate. Remove "E" ring, plug, spring and secondary pump shift valve. Remove "E" clip, bushing, spring, pin and shutoff valve.

Inspection – Ensure cover and intermediate plates are not plugged or distorted. Inspect secondary pump shift valve, shutoff valve and springs for damage.

Reassembly – To reassemble lower cover, reverse order of disassembly. Ensure locating pin for detent spring bracket is correctly inserted. Ensure temperature restrictor, deflector piece, locating pin and auxiliary restrictor are properly installed.

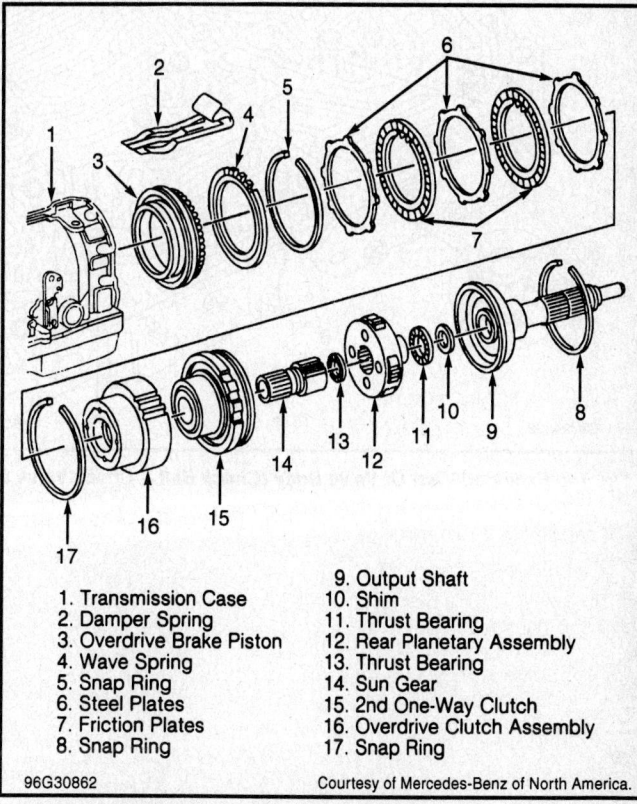

1. Transmission Case
2. Damper Spring
3. Overdrive Brake Piston
4. Wave Spring
5. Snap Ring
6. Steel Plates
7. Friction Plates
8. Snap Ring

9. Output Shaft
10. Shim
11. Thrust Bearing
12. Rear Planetary Assembly
13. Thrust Bearing
14. Sun Gear
15. 2nd One-Way Clutch
16. Overdrive Clutch Assembly
17. Snap Ring

96G30862

Courtesy of Mercedes-Benz of North America.

Fig. 12: Exploded View Of Overdrive Brake & 2nd One-Way Clutch (722.5 Series)

AUTOMATIC TRANSMISSIONS
Mercedes-Benz 722 Series (Cont.)

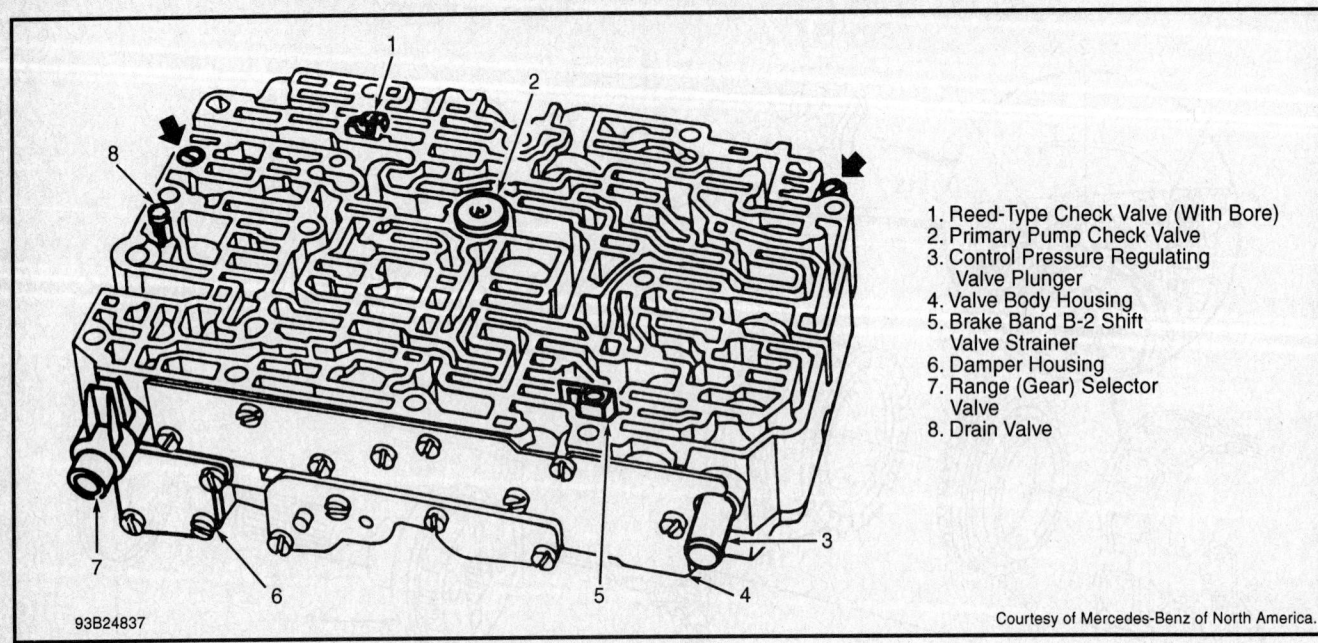

1. Reed-Type Check Valve (With Bore)
2. Primary Pump Check Valve
3. Control Pressure Regulating Valve Plunger
4. Valve Body Housing
5. Brake Band B-2 Shift Valve Strainer
6. Damper Housing
7. Range (Gear) Selector Valve
8. Drain Valve

93B24837

Courtesy of Mercedes-Benz of North America.

Fig. 13: Assembled View Of Valve Body & Damper Housing

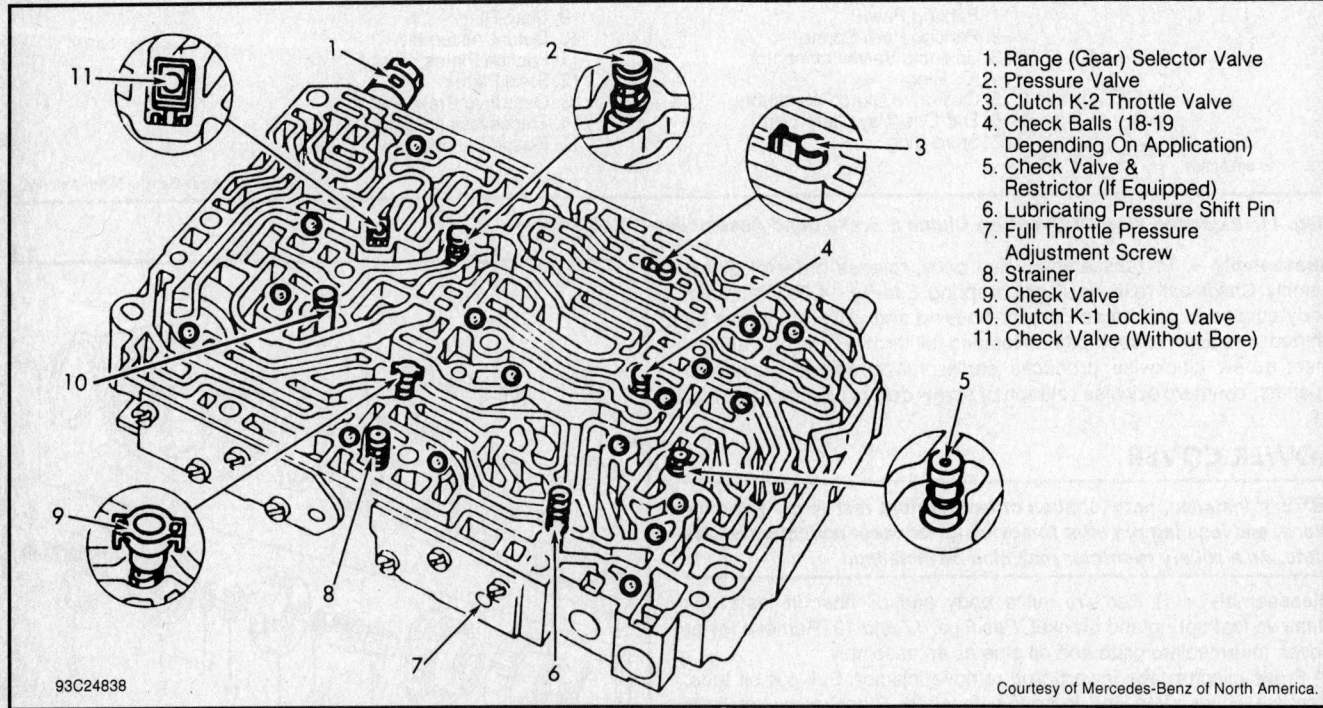

1. Range (Gear) Selector Valve
2. Pressure Valve
3. Clutch K-2 Throttle Valve
4. Check Balls (18-19 Depending On Application)
5. Check Valve & Restrictor (If Equipped)
6. Lubricating Pressure Shift Pin
7. Full Throttle Pressure Adjustment Screw
8. Strainer
9. Check Valve
10. Clutch K-1 Locking Valve
11. Check Valve (Without Bore)

93C24838

Courtesy of Mercedes-Benz of North America.

Fig. 14: Exploded View Of Valve Body (Check Ball & Check Valve Locations)

1. Clutch K-1 Locking Valve
2. Range (Gear) Selector Valve
3. Torque Converter Control Valve
4. 3-4 Command Valve Piston
5. 3-4 Command Valve
6. 1-2 Command Valve
7. 1-2 Command Valve Sleeve
8. 1-2 Command Valve Piston
9. Lock-Up Clutch Shift Valve
10. Kickdown Shift Valve
11. Brake Band B-2 Shift Valve
12. Governor Pressure Shift Valve
13. Controlled Pressure Control Valve
14. Controlled Pressure Control Valve Piston
15. Lubricating Pressure Shift Pin

16. Governor Pressure Booster Valve
17. Brake Band B-1 Control Valve
18. Brake Band B-1 Control Valve Piston
19. Throttle Control Valve
20. Working Pressure Control Valve
21. Basic Pressure Control Valve
22. Brake Band B-1 Shift Valve
23. 2-3 Command Valve Piston
24. 2-3 Command Valve

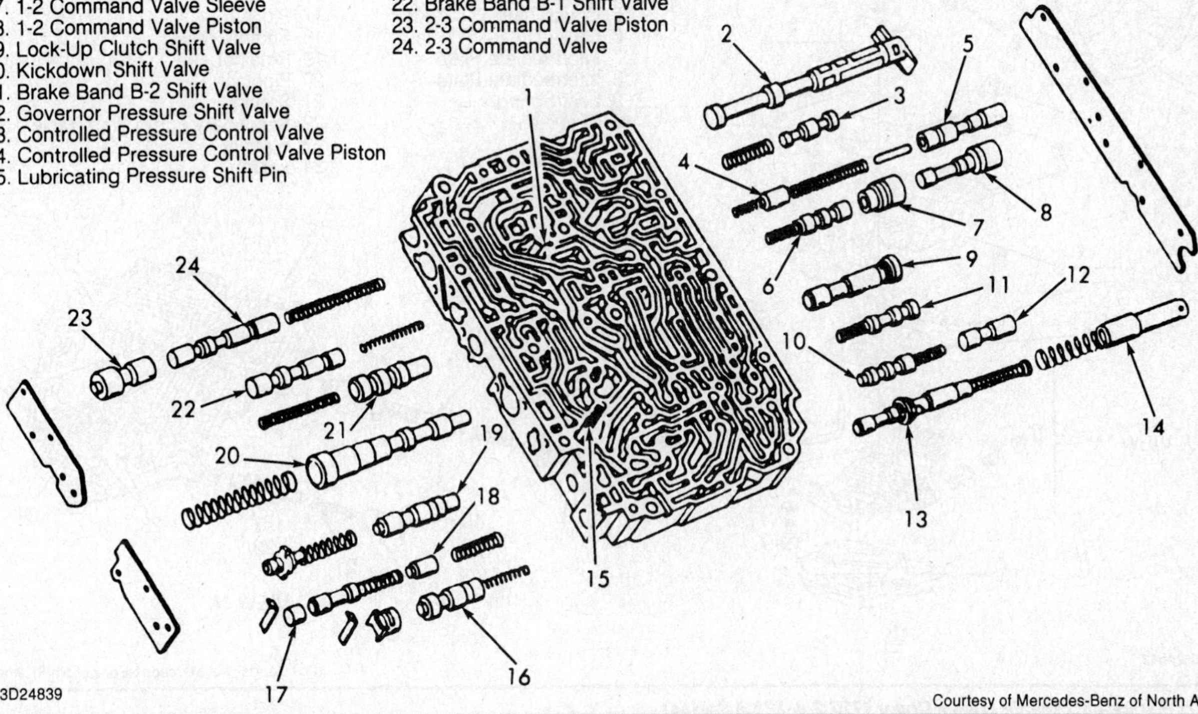

93D24839

Courtesy of Mercedes-Benz of North America.

Fig. 15: Exploded View Of Valve Body

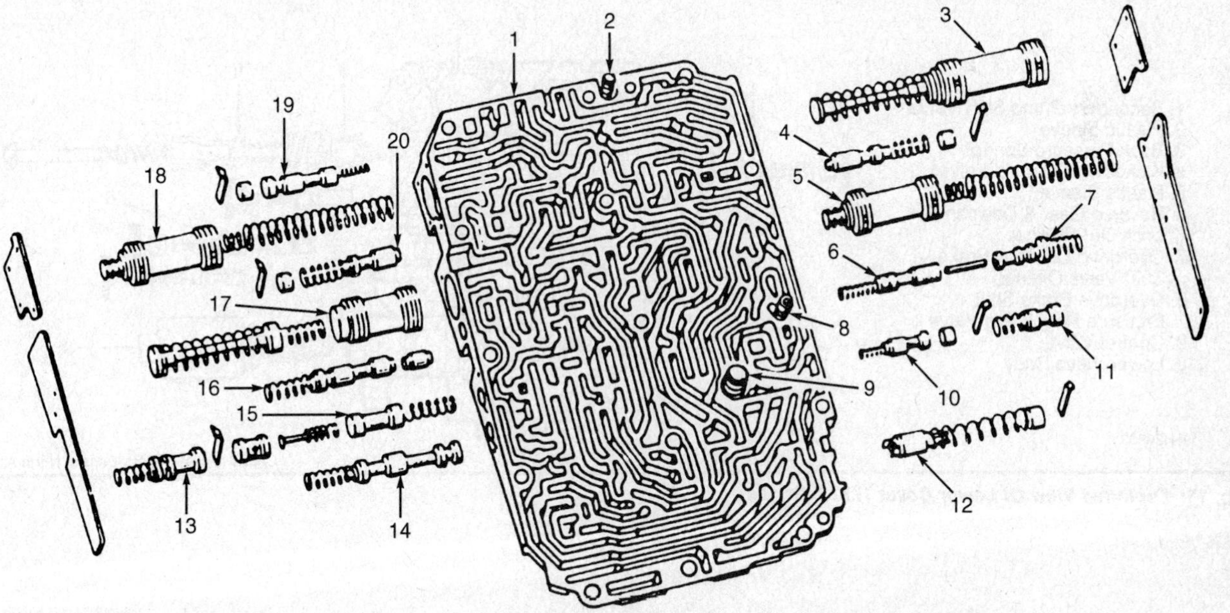

1. Damper Housing
2. Pressure Limiting Valve
3. Clutch K-1 Damper
4. Clutch K-1 Damper Control Valve
5. Brake Band B-1 Damper
6. Brake Band B-1 Damper Control Valve
7. Deceleration (Fuel Cut-Off) Shift Valve

8. Modulating Pressure Valve
9. Lubricating Pressure Valve
10. Reverse (RV1) Shut-Off Valve
11. Braking Shift Shut-Off Valve
12. Kickdown Damper
13. Clutch K-2 Shift Valve
14. Brake Band B-2 Detent Valve

15. Damper (Cut-In) Switching Control Valve
16. Reverse (RV2) Shut-Off Valve
17. Damper (Cut-In) Switching Valve
18. Clutch K-2 Damper
19. Shift Pressure Control Valve
20. Clutch K-2 Damper Control Valve

93G24840

Courtesy of Mercedes-Benz of North America.

Fig. 16: Exploded View Of Damper Housing

AUTOMATIC TRANSMISSIONS
Mercedes-Benz 722 Series (Cont.)

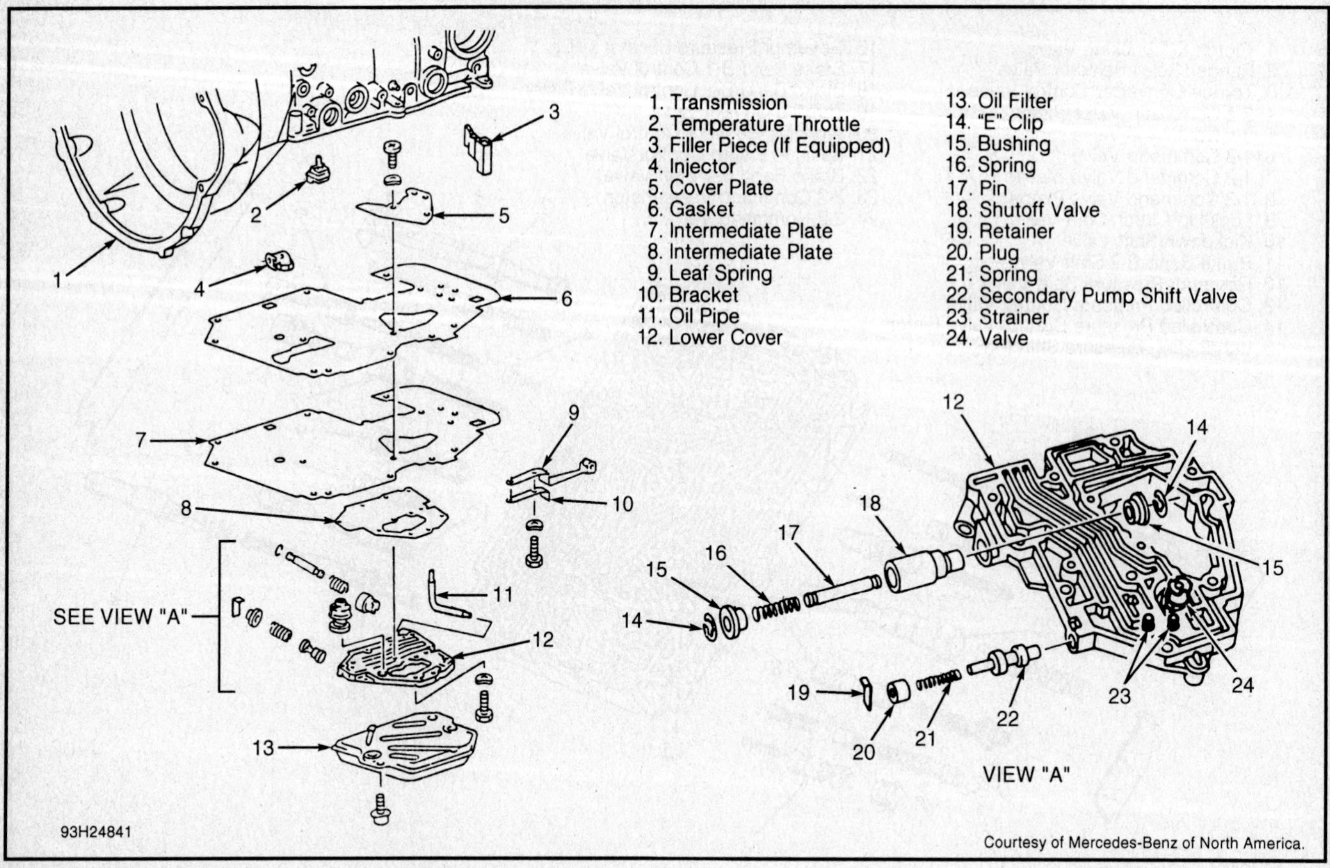

1. Transmission
2. Temperature Throttle
3. Filler Piece (If Equipped)
4. Injector
5. Cover Plate
6. Gasket
7. Intermediate Plate
8. Intermediate Plate
9. Leaf Spring
10. Bracket
11. Oil Pipe
12. Lower Cover
13. Oil Filter
14. "E" Clip
15. Bushing
16. Spring
17. Pin
18. Shutoff Valve
19. Retainer
20. Plug
21. Spring
22. Secondary Pump Shift Valve
23. Strainer
24. Valve

SEE VIEW "A"

VIEW "A"

93H24841

Courtesy of Mercedes-Benz of North America.

Fig. 17: Exploded View Of Lower Cover (722.3 & 722.4 Series)

1. Secondary Pump Shift Valve
2. Plastic Sleeve
3. Back Pressure Spring
4. Kickdown Solenoid Valve
5. Plastic Sleeve
6. Reverse Gear & Downshift Lock-Out Plunger
7. Overdrive Clutch & Brake Shift Valve Overlap
8. Overdrive Brake Shift Pressure Regulating Valve
9. Control Valve
10. Lower Valve Body

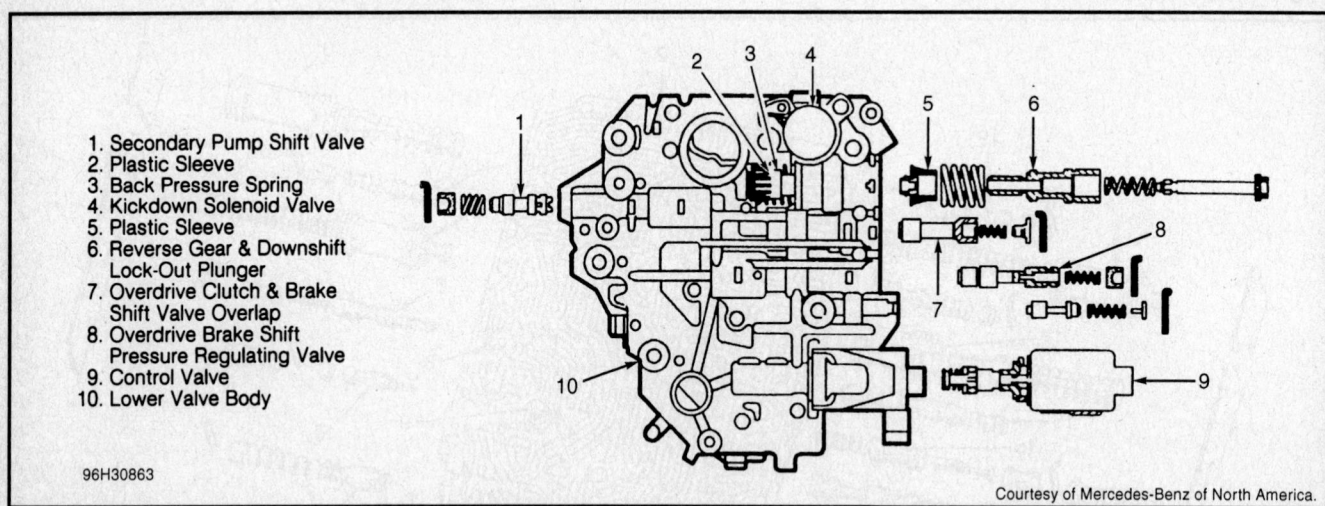

96H30863

Courtesy of Mercedes-Benz of North America.

Fig. 18: Exploded View Of Lower Cover (722.5 Series)

REAR COVER

Disassembly & Reassembly – 1) Pry out rear cover seal. Remove snap ring and press out bearing. Using drift pin, drive speedometer gear and shaft from rear cover. Screw 12-mm bolt into radial seal ring. Using a plastic hammer, apply light blows to bolt to remove radial seal ring. Remove oil accumulator from rear cover.

2) To reassemble, reverse disassembly procedure. Using a .004" (.10 mm) feeler gauge, measure clearance between snap ring and bearing. There should be no play between snap ring and bearing.

3) Snap ring is available in thicknesses of .079-.090" (2.00-2.30 mm) in increments of .004" (.10 mm). When inserting replacement snap ring, ensure it is correctly seated in groove. If snap ring cannot be inserted, use a thinner snap ring.

SECONDARY PUMP

Disassembly – Remove gears from pump housing. *See Fig. 19.* Remove shutoff piston cover retaining ring and cover. Remove shutoff piston, compression spring and spring retainer from pump housing.

Inspection – Check gears and pump housing for damage or unusual wear. Check compression spring for distortion. Check shutoff piston and Teflon ring for damage, and replace as necessary.

Reassembly – Install "O" ring in pump housing. Install Teflon ring on shutoff piston. Install shutoff piston into pump housing. Install compression spring and spring retainer into shutoff piston. Install piston cover and piston cover retaining ring. Lubricate gears and place in pump housing.

PRIMARY PUMP

Disassembly – 1) Remove 2 Teflon seals from stator shaft. Using appropriate spring compressor, compress spring retainer and remove snap ring. Remove spring retainer and springs for brake B-3 piston.

2) Remove brake B-3 piston. Remove pump housing bolts and lift primary pump from transmission front cover. Remove gears from pump housing. *See Fig. 20.*

Inspection – Check bearing for scoring or damage. Check seal for damage. Check "O" ring for correct installation in groove. Check pump gears for scoring or damage.

Reassembly – 1) Lubricate and install gears into pump housing. Ensure chamfered edge of driven gear faces down in pump housing. *See Fig. 21.*

2) Install intermediate plate on primary pump assembly. Install primary pump housing onto pump cover, being careful not to damage bearing on stator shaft. Install primary pump bolts.

3) Install sealing rings on brake B-3 piston, with lip of sealing rings facing downward. Place Insertion Sleeve (126589041400) on pump cover. Lubricate sealing rings. Install piston over insertion sleeve with pin on piston lining up with bore in pump cover. Carefully install brake B-3 piston. *See Fig. 20.*

4) Install springs and spring retainer. Slide snap ring over insertion sleeve. Hold snap ring at bottom of sleeve and remove sleeve. Using appropriate spring compressor, compress spring retainer and install snap ring. Ensure snap ring seats in groove. Install Teflon seals on stator shaft.

PLANETARY GEAR SET

Disassembly – 1) Position assembly fixture with plate facing upward. Place planetary gear set on assembly fixture with input shaft pointing upward. Remove lubrication thrust ring(s). *See Fig. 22.* Remove snap ring retaining front planetary gear set. Lift front planetary gear set off input shaft.

2) Remove axial bearing and input shaft. Remove radial bearing and axial bearing. Remove output shaft. Remove axial bearing and sun gear. *See Fig. 22.* Remove snap ring retaining clutch K-2 in plate carrier.

3) Remove inner plate carrier with one-way clutch from connecting carrier. Remove support disc, compensating ring and "O" ring from one-way clutch. Rotate inner race of one-way clutch in counterclockwise direction and pull out inner race. Remove one-way clutch and rollers.

Inspection – Check bearing surfaces and bearing races for scoring or damage. Check one-way clutch roller bearings for scoring, roundness and wear. If one-way clutch rollers are damaged, replace one-way clutch as an assembly. Lubricate bearings with ATF during assembly.

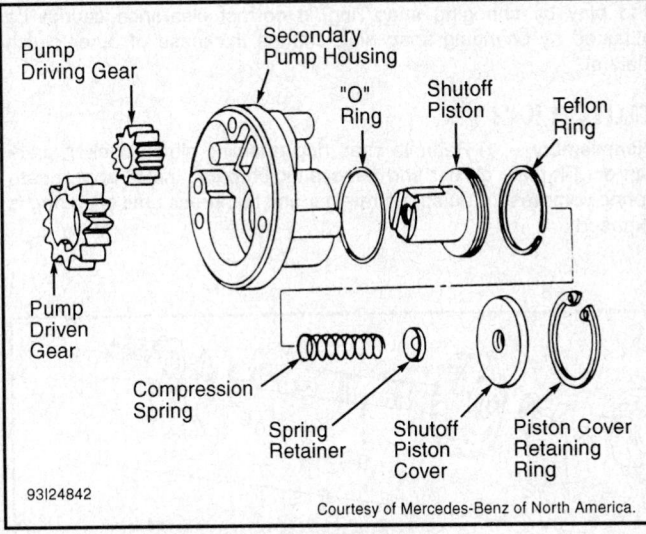

93I24842

Courtesy of Mercedes-Benz of North America.

Fig. 19: Exploded View Of Secondary Pump

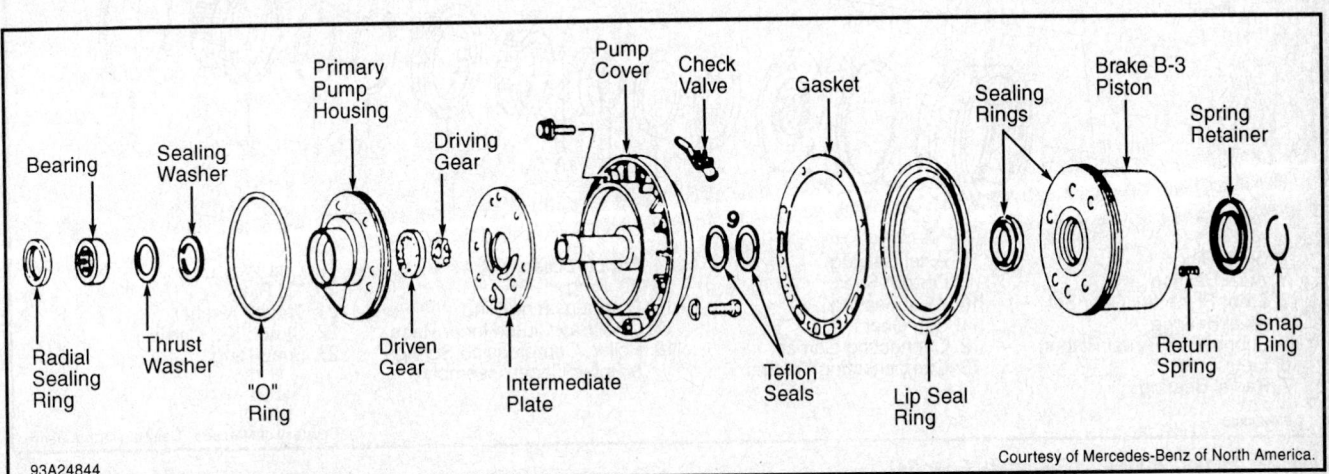

93A24844

Courtesy of Mercedes-Benz of North America.

Fig. 20: Exploded View Of Primary Pump

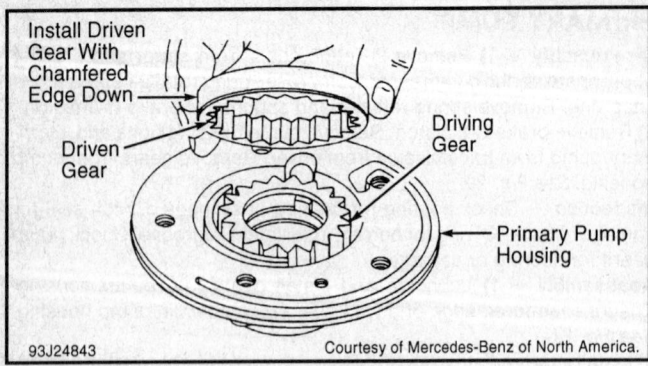

Install Driven Gear With Chamfered Edge Down

Driven Gear

Driving Gear

Primary Pump Housing

93J24843

Courtesy of Mercedes-Benz of North America.

Fig. 21: Installing Primary Pump Driven Gear

Reassembly – 1) To reassemble planetary gear set, reverse order of disassembly. Install one-way clutch outer race on inner plate carrier and insert roller cage. Press rollers against compression springs and insert retainer plates with rounded edge pointing outward. See Fig. 23.

2) Install one-way clutch inner race while rotating counterclockwise. Pull out retainer plates. Install compensating ring. Install support disc so pin enters bore of one-way clutch outer race. See Fig. 24.

3) Install compensating ring into connecting carrier. Hold one-way clutch together and place assembly into connecting carrier. Install snap ring and push into groove with screwdriver.

4) With one-way clutch "O" ring removed, check clearance between one-way clutch and connecting carrier. See Fig. 25. Clearance should be .002-.008" (.05-.20 mm). If clearance is incorrect, add or remove compensating shim(s) until clearance is within specifications. If clearance is correct, install one-way clutch "O" ring.

5) Insert sun gear into one-way clutch assembly. One-way clutch should lock when sun gear is rotated in clockwise direction. Install axial bearing on sun gear. Place one-way clutch on assembly fixture and install output shaft. Install axial and radial bearings on output shaft.

6) Install input shaft and axial bearing. Install front planetary gear set and secure by pushing snap ring into groove. Install lubrication thrust ring(s) into groove. Remove planetary gear set from assembly fixture.

CLUTCH K-1

Disassembly – 1) Remove snap ring retaining clutch pack in plate carrier. Remove clutch pack and spring washer. Install appropriate spring compressor on spring retainer and compress until snap ring is exposed. Remove snap ring.

2) Release pressure from spring compressor and remove. Remove spring retainer and compression springs. Remove piston from plate carrier. See Fig. 26. Remove snap ring, piston guide and "O" ring (if equipped).

Reassembly – 1) Install NEW sealing rings on piston with lip of sealing rings pointing toward flat surface of piston. Place Installation Sleeves (126589021400 and 126589031400) on plate carrier.

2) Lubricate installation sleeves and sealing rings with ATF. Install piston into plate carrier. Ensure piston is centered in carrier. Remove installation sleeves.

3) Install compression springs into piston. Install spring retainer. Ensure each compression spring is centered by a guide pin. Install spring compressor and compress springs. Install snap ring and release compressor. Ensure snap ring is properly seated in groove. Remove spring compressor.

4) Soak inner clutch plates in ATF for at least one hour. Install clutch plates in plate carrier. See Fig. 28. Install snap ring. Ensure snap ring is fully seated in groove.

5) With a screwdriver on top outer plate, force snap ring upward along entire circumference of plate carrier. Check clutch pack end play between top outer plate and snap ring.

6) End play should be .028-.051" (.70-1.30 mm). If necessary, adjust end play by changing snap ring. If correct clearance cannot be obtained by changing snap ring, change thickness of outer clutch plate(s).

CLUTCH K-2

Disassembly – 1) Remove snap ring retaining clutch pack in plate carrier. Tilt plate carrier and remove clutch pack. Install appropriate spring compressor on spring retainer and compress until snap ring is exposed.

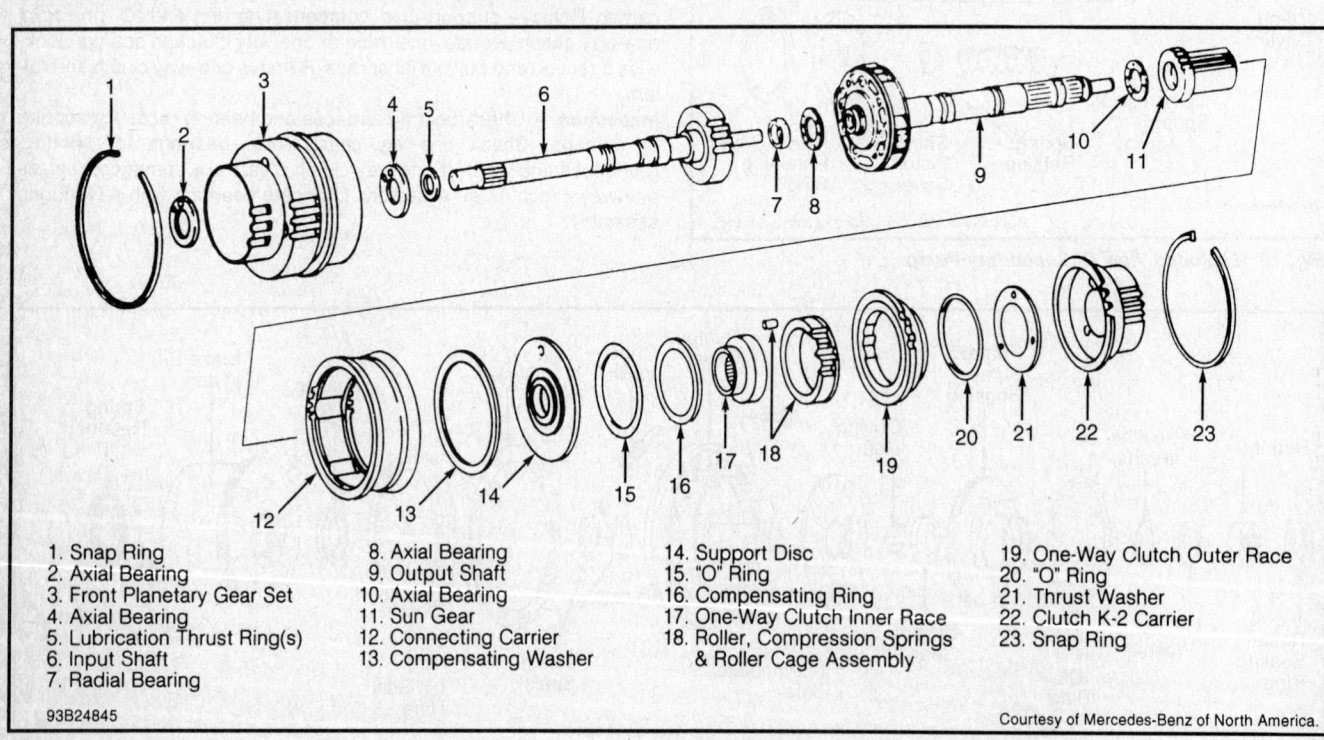

1. Snap Ring
2. Axial Bearing
3. Front Planetary Gear Set
4. Axial Bearing
5. Lubrication Thrust Ring(s)
6. Input Shaft
7. Radial Bearing
8. Axial Bearing
9. Output Shaft
10. Axial Bearing
11. Sun Gear
12. Connecting Carrier
13. Compensating Washer
14. Support Disc
15. "O" Ring
16. Compensating Ring
17. One-Way Clutch Inner Race
18. Roller, Compression Springs & Roller Cage Assembly
19. One-Way Clutch Outer Race
20. "O" Ring
21. Thrust Washer
22. Clutch K-2 Carrier
23. Snap Ring

93B24845

Courtesy of Mercedes-Benz of North America.

Fig. 22: Exploded View Of Planetary Gear Set

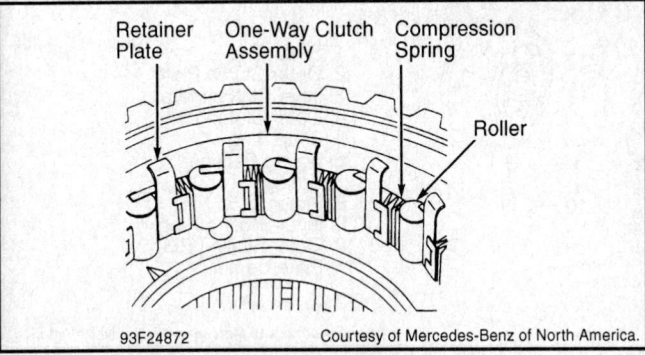

Retainer Plate · One-Way Clutch Assembly · Compression Spring · Roller

93F24872 · Courtesy of Mercedes-Benz of North America.

Fig. 23: Installing One-Way Clutch Rollers

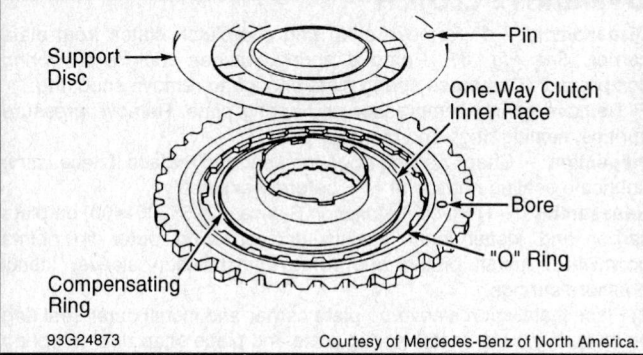

Support Disc · Pin · One-Way Clutch Inner Race · Bore · "O" Ring · Compensating Ring

93G24873 · Courtesy of Mercedes-Benz of North America.

Fig. 24: Installing One-Way Clutch Support Disc

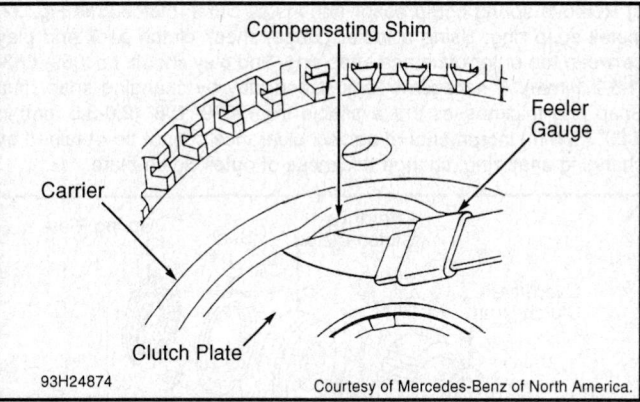

Compensating Shim · Feeler Gauge · Carrier · Clutch Plate

93H24874 · Courtesy of Mercedes-Benz of North America.

Fig. 25: Measuring One-Way Clutch Clearance

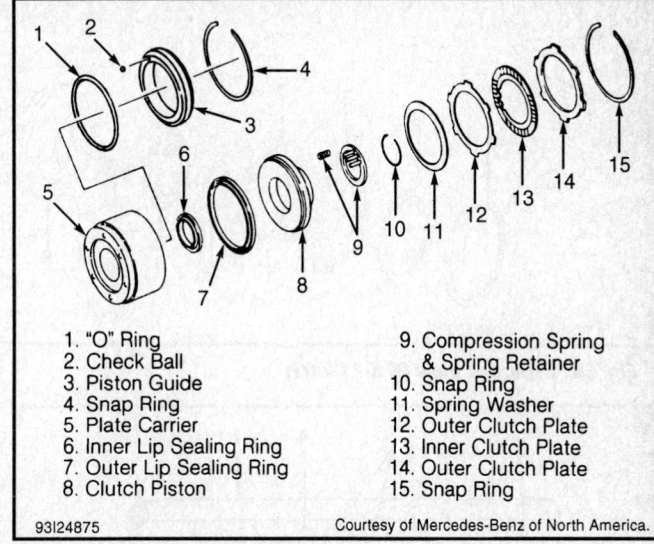

1. "O" Ring
2. Check Ball
3. Piston Guide
4. Snap Ring
5. Plate Carrier
6. Inner Lip Sealing Ring
7. Outer Lip Sealing Ring
8. Clutch Piston
9. Compression Spring & Spring Retainer
10. Snap Ring
11. Spring Washer
12. Outer Clutch Plate
13. Inner Clutch Plate
14. Outer Clutch Plate
15. Snap Ring

93I24875 · Courtesy of Mercedes-Benz of North America.

Fig. 26: Exploded View Of K-1 Clutch

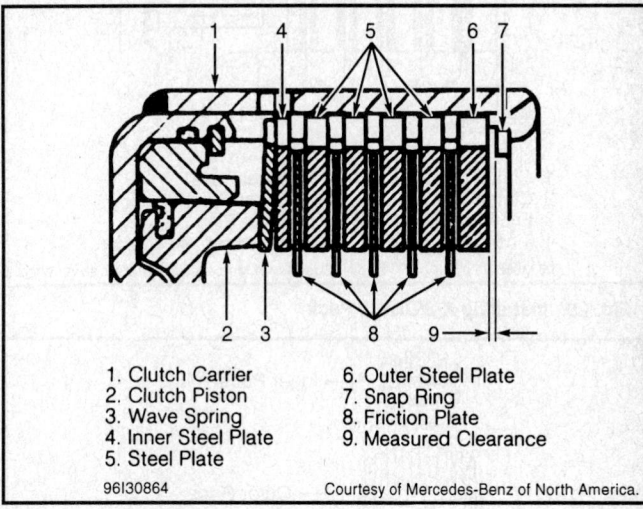

1. Clutch Carrier
2. Clutch Piston
3. Wave Spring
4. Inner Steel Plate
5. Steel Plate
6. Outer Steel Plate
7. Snap Ring
8. Friction Plate
9. Measured Clearance

96I30864 · Courtesy of Mercedes-Benz of North America.

Fig. 27: Installing K-1 Clutch Pack

5) With a screwdriver against top outer plate, force snap ring upward along entire circumference of plate carrier. Using a feeler gauge, check clutch pack end play between top outer plate and snap ring.
6) End play should be .028-.051" (.70-1.30 mm). If necessary, adjust end play by changing snap ring. If correct clearance cannot be obtained by changing snap ring, change thickness of outer clutch plate(s).

2ND ONE-WAY CLUTCH

Disassembly – Remove snap ring and one-way clutch from clutch hub. See Fig. 30. Remove inner snap ring, support disc and "O" ring. Separate inner race from roller cage and remove roller cage.
Inspection – Check all components for wear or damage and replace as necessary.
Reassembly – To reassemble, reverse disassembly procedure. Ensure rollers do not fall out of cage assembly during reassembly. Install inner race into roller cage. Using a plate approximately 2 3/16" (55 mm) square, turn roller cage while pressing down on outer race assembly. An additional person may be required to assemble. Ensure "O" ring seats correctly in groove.

2) Remove snap ring. Release pressure from spring compressor and remove. Remove spring retainer and compression springs. Remove piston from plate carrier. See Fig. 28.
Reassembly – 1) Install NEW sealing rings on piston with lip of sealing rings pointing downward (away from piston flange). On 722.3 Series transmissions, place Installation Sleeve (126589021400) on center hub of plate carrier. On 722.4 and 722.5 Series transmissions, place Installation Sleeve (140589001400) on center hub of plate carrier.
2) On all models, lubricate installation sleeve (if used) and clutch piston sealing rings with ATF. Carefully place clutch piston over installation sleeve and slide piston onto plate carrier. Ensure piston is centered in carrier. Remove installation sleeve.
3) Install compression springs on clutch piston. Install spring retainer with spring centered by guide pin. Install spring compressor on spring retainer. Compress spring retainer and install snap ring. Ensure snap ring is fully seated in groove.
4) Remove compressor. Soak inner clutch plates in ATF for at least one hour. Install clutch plates in plate carrier. See Fig. 29. Install snap ring. Ensure snap ring is fully seated in groove.

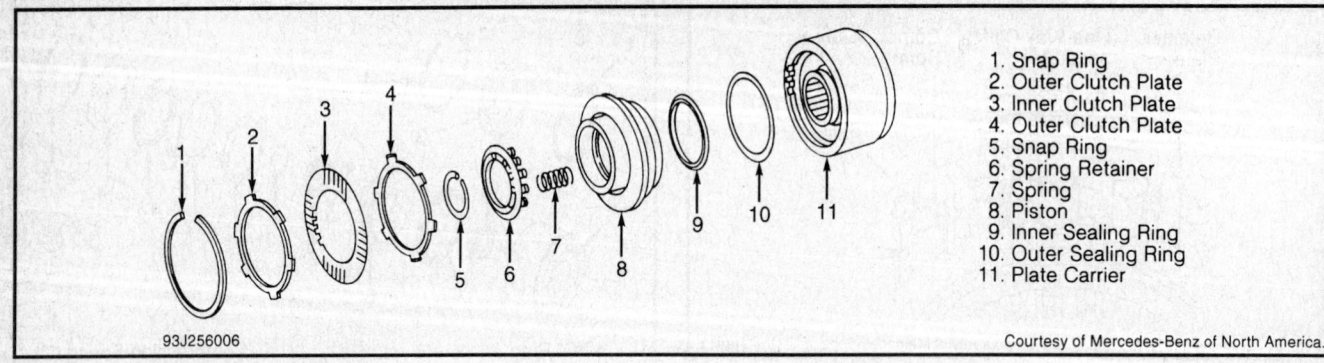

1. Snap Ring
2. Outer Clutch Plate
3. Inner Clutch Plate
4. Outer Clutch Plate
5. Snap Ring
6. Spring Retainer
7. Spring
8. Piston
9. Inner Sealing Ring
10. Outer Sealing Ring
11. Plate Carrier

93J256006   Courtesy of Mercedes-Benz of North America.

Fig. 28: Exploded View Of K-2 Clutch

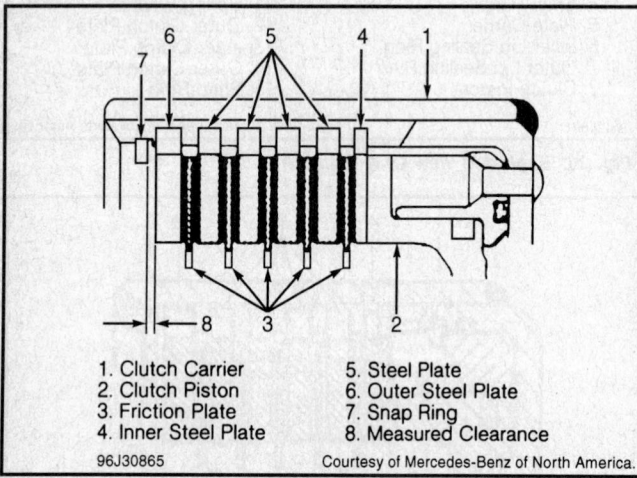

1. Clutch Carrier
2. Clutch Piston
3. Friction Plate
4. Inner Steel Plate
5. Steel Plate
6. Outer Steel Plate
7. Snap Ring
8. Measured Clearance

96J30865   Courtesy of Mercedes-Benz of North America.

Fig. 29: Installing K-2 Clutch Pack

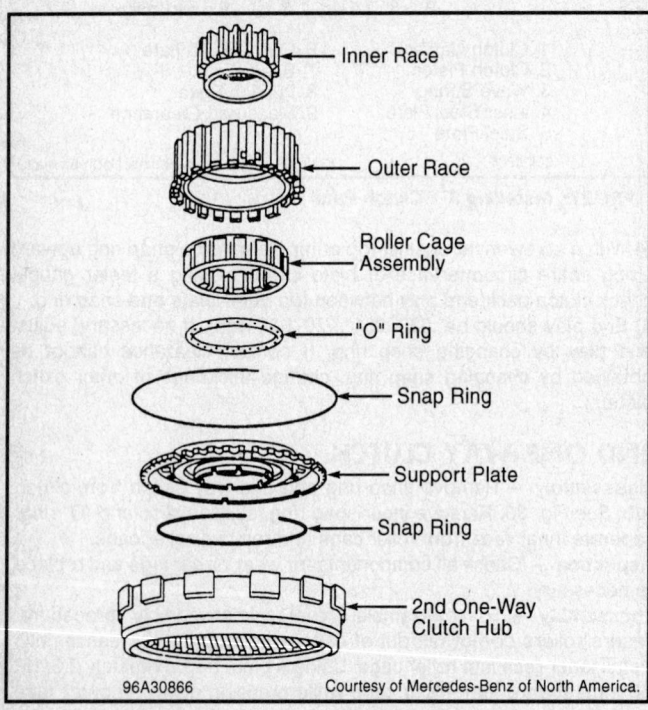

Inner Race
Outer Race
Roller Cage Assembly
"O" Ring
Snap Ring
Support Plate
Snap Ring
2nd One-Way Clutch Hub

96A30866   Courtesy of Mercedes-Benz of North America.

Fig. 30: Exploded View Of 2nd One-Way Clutch

OVERDRIVE CLUTCH

Disassembly – 1) Remove snap ring and clutch plates from plate carrier. See Fig. 31. Remove spring washer and install spring compressor. Compress spring plate enough to remove snap ring.

2) Remove spring compressor and spring plate. Remove pressure springs, sealing rings and piston.

Inspection – Check sealing rings for wear and replace if necessary. Lubricate sealing rings with ATF before reassembly.

Reassembly – 1) Place Installation Sleeve (129589001400) on plate carrier and install inner sealing ring ensuring outer lip points downward. Install piston and remove installation sleeve. Install pressure springs.

2) Place installation sleeve on plate carrier and install outer seal ring on to spring plate. Install spring plate and place snap ring on spring plate. Remove installation sleeve. Install spring compressor and compress spring plate. Insert snap ring into groove securing spring plate.

3) Remove spring compressor and install clutch plates. See Fig. 32. Install snap ring. Using a feeler gauge, check clutch pack end play between top outer plate and snap ring. End play should be .059-.083" (1.5-2.1 mm). If necessary, adjust end play by changing snap ring. Snap ring thicknesses are available from .079-.138" (2.0-3.5 mm) in .020" (.5 mm) increments. If correct clearance cannot be obtained by changing snap ring, change thickness of outer clutch plate.

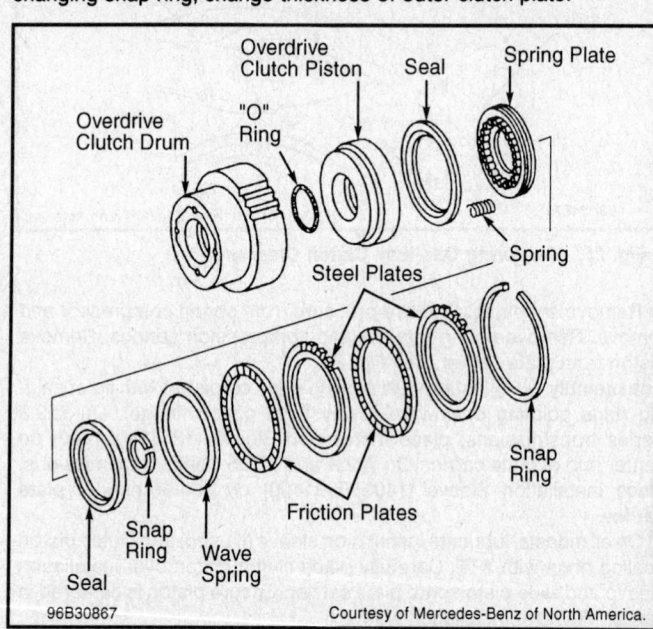

Overdrive Clutch Drum
"O" Ring
Overdrive Clutch Piston
Seal
Spring Plate
Spring
Steel Plates
Snap Ring
Seal
Snap Ring
Wave Spring
Friction Plates

96B30867   Courtesy of Mercedes-Benz of North America.

Fig. 31: Exploded View Of Overdrive Clutch Assembly

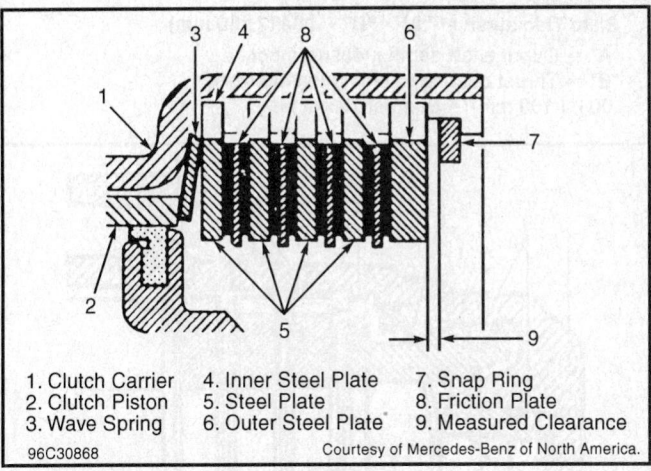

1. Clutch Carrier
2. Clutch Piston
3. Wave Spring
4. Inner Steel Plate
5. Steel Plate
6. Outer Steel Plate
7. Snap Ring
8. Friction Plate
9. Measured Clearance

96C30868 Courtesy of Mercedes-Benz of North America.

Fig. 32: Installing Overdrive Clutch Plates

TRANSMISSION REASSEMBLY

NOTE: During reassembly, lubricate bearing and valve body sliding surfaces with ATF. Soak new brake bands and clutch inner plates in ATF for at least one hour prior to installation.

1) Place transmission case in holding fixture. Install guide ring and sealing ring in transmission housing. Sealing lip should face direction of brake band piston cover. Install "O" ring and radial sealing ring into selector lever shaft bores.

2) Install screw-on plug and aluminum sealing ring. Install "O" ring in support flange bore of transmission case. Install Teflon rings on clutch K-2 support flange. Install support flange and tighten bolts to specifications. See TORQUE SPECIFICATIONS.

NOTE: With brake band B-2 thrust element removed, the bore and tab on thrust element must align. With thrust element installed, one spring winding must be visible through the bore for lower cover oil pipe.

3) Install brake band B-2 thrust element with tab in upward direction. Install thrust element on support flange so that tab engages housing. Ensure Teflon rings on support flange are still in their grooves.

4) Compress brake band B-2 by support tabs as much as possible and install. Brake band may be held in place with a snap ring. Install clutch K-2 on planetary gear set. While rotating input shaft, install planetary gear set assembly into case.

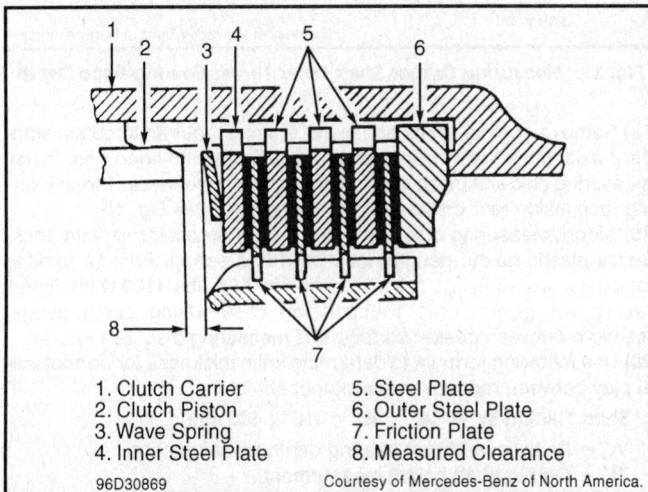

1. Clutch Carrier
2. Clutch Piston
3. Wave Spring
4. Inner Steel Plate
5. Steel Plate
6. Outer Steel Plate
7. Friction Plate
8. Measured Clearance

96D30869 Courtesy of Mercedes-Benz of North America.

Fig. 33: Installing Brake B-3 Clutch Pack

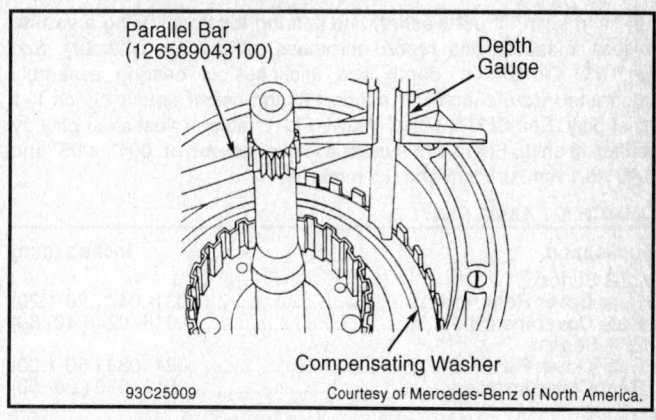

93C25009 Courtesy of Mercedes-Benz of North America.

Fig. 34: Measuring Brake B-3 Clutch Pack Depth

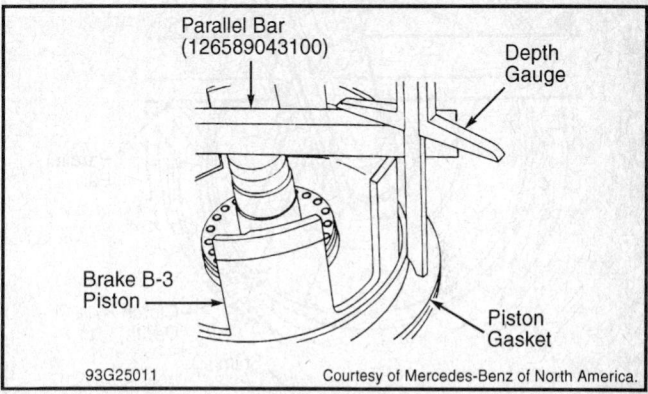

93G25011 Courtesy of Mercedes-Benz of North America.

Fig. 35: Measuring Brake B-3 Piston Height

5) Place transmission in a vertical position with input shaft pointing upward. Ensure planetary gear set is properly installed. Planetary gear set is properly installed when upper edge of connecting carrier is lower than supporting surface of brake B-3 outside plate. Install damping spring.

6) Install brake B-3 clutch plates and compensating (spring) washer. *See Fig. 33.* Place Parallel Bar (126589043100) on machined surface of transmission case. Place top of depth gauge on bar and tip of depth gauge on compensating (spring) washer. *See Fig. 34.* Measure and record distance.

7) Install gasket on front cover. Place parallel bar on top of brake B-3 piston. Place top of depth gauge on parallel bar and tip of depth gauge on gasket. *See Fig. 35.* Measure and record distance.

8) Difference between clutch pack depth measurement and piston height measurement is brake B-3 release clearance. Clearance should be .059-.079" (1.50-2.00 mm). Adjust clearance by changing thickness of brake B-3 outside plate(s).

9) Coat groove(s) in input shaft with grease and install lubrication thrust ring(s). Diagonal cut on ring(s) must be held closed by grease. Install clutch K-1 while rotating it, so that splines engage. Engage lock assembly on brake band B-1. Install brake band B-1 with pin of lock assembly facing toward brake band B-1 thrust element.

10) Install thrust pin and "O" rings into B-1 thrust element. Install thrust element and plug or overload protection switch into transmission case. Install brake band B-1 guide into transmission case bore. Ensure locating lugs engage in housing.

11) On 722.3 and 722.4 Series transmissions, install gasket on front cover. Place parallel bar on clutch K-1 support flange. Place top of depth gauge on bar and tip of depth gauge on front cover gasket. Measure and record distance.

12) Place parallel bar on machined surface of transmission case. Place top of depth gauge on bar and tip of depth gauge on clutch K-1 surface. *See Fig. 36.* Measure and record distance.

13) Hold shim, thrust washer, and bearing together. Using a vernier caliper, measure and record thickness of bearing assembly. See Fig. 36. Clutch K-1 depth and thickness of bearing assembly subtracted from clutch K-1 support flange height equals clutch K-1 axial play. See CLUTCH K-1 AXIAL PLAY table. Adjust axial play by replacing shim. Shims are available in thicknesses of .004", .008" and .020" (0.1 mm, 0.2 mm and 0.5 mm).

CLUTCH K-1 AXIAL PLAY

Application	Inches (mm)
722.3 Series	
Rear Cover Removed	.031-.047 (.80-1.20)
Rear Cover Installed	.016-.024 (.40-.60)
722.4 Series	
Rear Cover Removed	.024-.039 (.60-1.00)
Rear Cover Installed	.012-.020 (.30-.50)

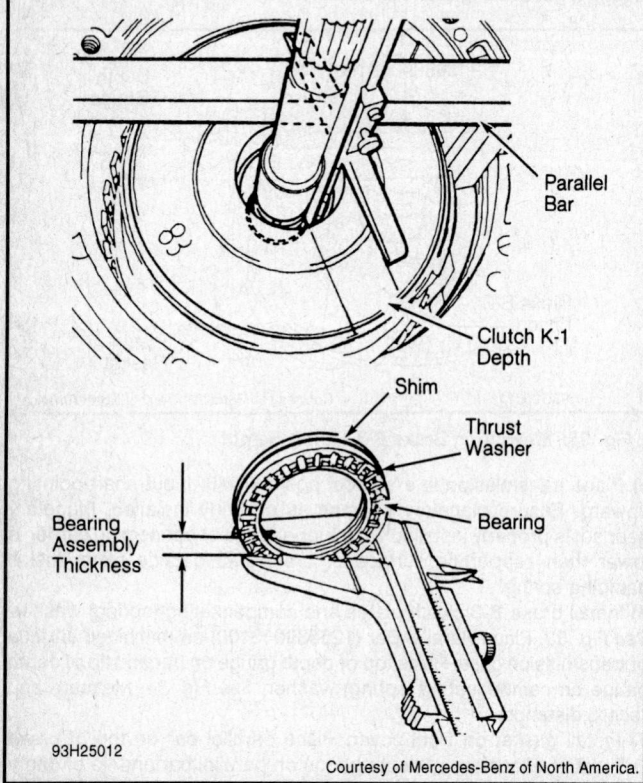

Fig. 36: **Measuring Clutch K-1 Axial Play (722.3 & 722.4 Series)**

14) On 722.3 or 722.4 Series transmissions, go to step **22)**. On 722.5 Series transmissions, ensure lubricating nozzle is installed and install thrust bearing. Lubricate overdrive brake piston "O" rings with ATF and press piston into transmission case. Install Teflon rings until seated into grooves. Install wave spring and overdrive brake piston snap ring.

15) Install overdrive brake clutch plates and snap ring. Using feeler guage, measure overdrive brake clutch plate clearance between top plate and snap ring. See Fig. 37. Clearance should be .020-.043" (0.5-1.1 mm). Replace snap ring to obtain proper clearance.

16) Place overdrive clutch assembly inside overdrive brake clutch plates. Install overdrive brake hub and sun gear. Install planet carrier gear with thrust bearing in place. Ensure thrust bearing does not move. Install original shims onto thrust bearing.

17) Using depth guage, measure distance between output shaft thrust bearing race and inner thrust bearing race. See Fig. 38. Measure depth between shims and thrust bearing. See Fig. 39. Using following formula determine shim thickness for correct axial play:

Shim Thickness = "A" - "B" - .004" (.100 mm)

"A" = Ouput shaft depth measurement.
"B" = Thrust bearing to shim measurement.
.004" (.100 mm) = Standard axial play.

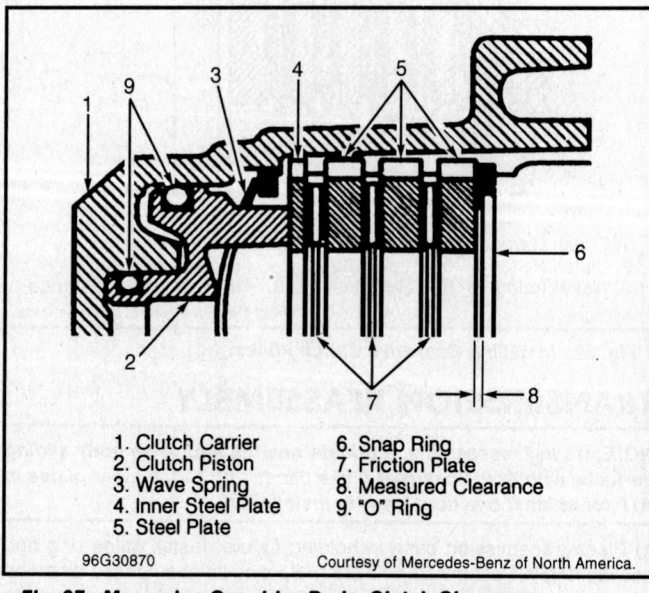

1. Clutch Carrier	6. Snap Ring
2. Clutch Piston	7. Friction Plate
3. Wave Spring	8. Measured Clearance
4. Inner Steel Plate	9. "O" Ring
5. Steel Plate	

Fig. 37: **Measuring Overdrive Brake Clutch Clearance**

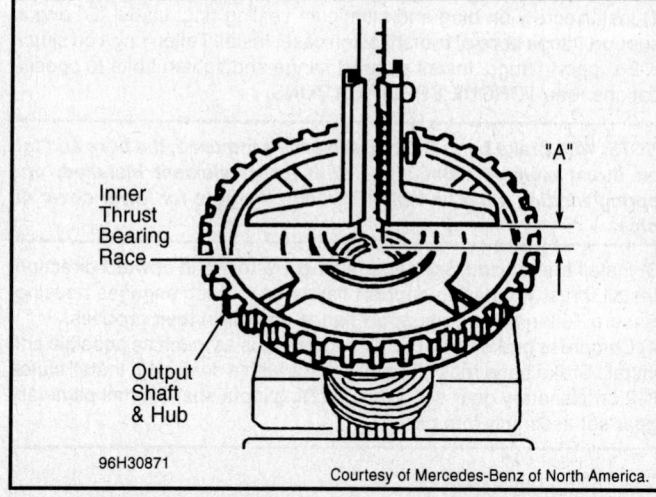

Fig. 38: **Measuring Output Shaft Inner Thrust Bearing Race Depth**

18) Remove original shims and install shim(s) required to obtain standard axial play. Install ouput shaft and secure with snap ring. Install measuring disc and using depth gauge, measure between thrust bearing race inside rear cover and measuring disc. See Fig. 40.

19) Mount measuring disc and 3-arm flange onto intermediate shaft. Install plastic guide, parking lock pawl and spring. Engage parking lock pawl. Install flange nut and torque to 74 ft. lbs. (100 N.m). Install rear cover gasket onto transmission case. Using depth gauge, measure between gasket surface and measuring disc. See Fig. 41.

20) Use following formula to determine shim thickness for correct axial play between rear cover and output shaft:

Shim Thickness = "A" - "B" - .016" (.400 mm)

"A" = Rear cover thrust bearing depth measurement.
"B" = Output shaft height measurment.
.016" (.400 mm) = Standard axial play.

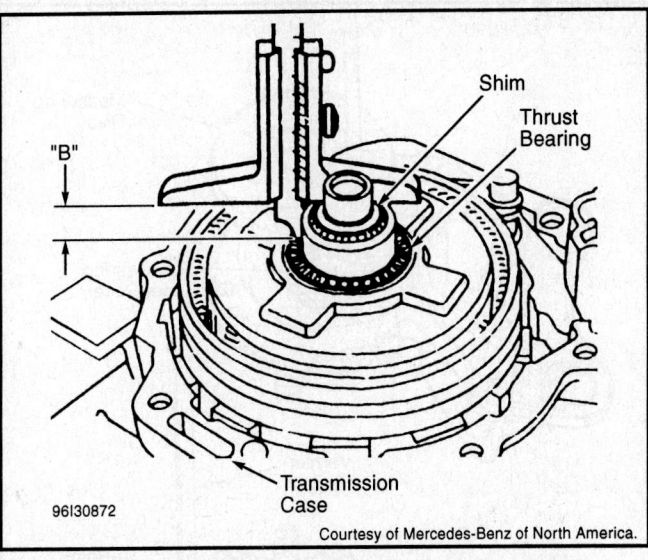

Fig. 39: *Measuring Intermediate Shaft Thrust Bearing Height*

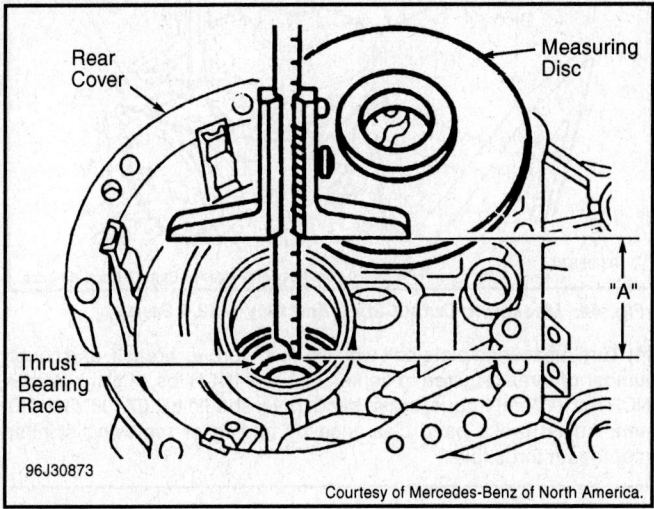

Fig. 40: *Measuring Rear Cover Inner Thrust Bearing Race Depth*

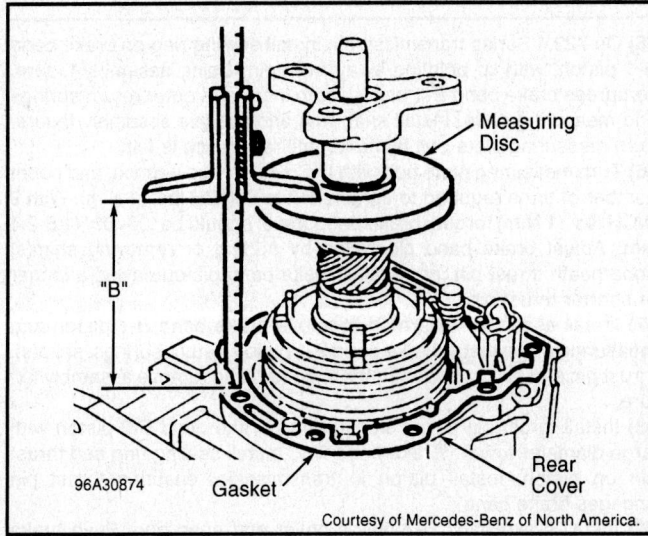

Fig. 41: *Measuring Output Shaft Height*

21) Remove flange nut, 3-arm flange and measuring disc. Replace shim with shim(s) required to obtain standard axial play. Install electrical plug for solenoid valves. Install rear cover, 3-arm flange and torque all bolts to specifications. See TORQUE SPECIFICATIONS.

22) On all transmissions, coat Teflon rings on front cover with grease. Diagonal cut on rings must be held closed by grease. If necessary, remove rings and shape to a smaller diameter. Install front cover and gasket. Coat front cover bolt with non-hardening sealant and install.

23) Rotate transmission so output shaft is pointing upward. Install snap ring on groove of output shaft. Install helical gear on output shaft (722.3 Series transmissions only). Install governor axial retainer. Install "O" ring and governor. Swivel axial retainer (if equipped) toward governor so it will enter groove of governor shaft. Install governor cover and snap ring. Pull cover out so it rests on snap ring.

24) Install intermediate plate, "O" ring, and secondary pump. *See Fig. 7.* Ensure governor axial retainer is properly seated and install nut. *See Fig. 42.* Install oil pipe and bolt (if equipped).

25) Install detent plate, linkage and shaft (or bolt). Mount roller on linkage and install plastic guide over roller. On 722.3 and 722.4 Series transmissions, install shim(s) on helical gear. Mount parking lock pawl, insert spring, and attach spring to pawl. Install parking lock gear.

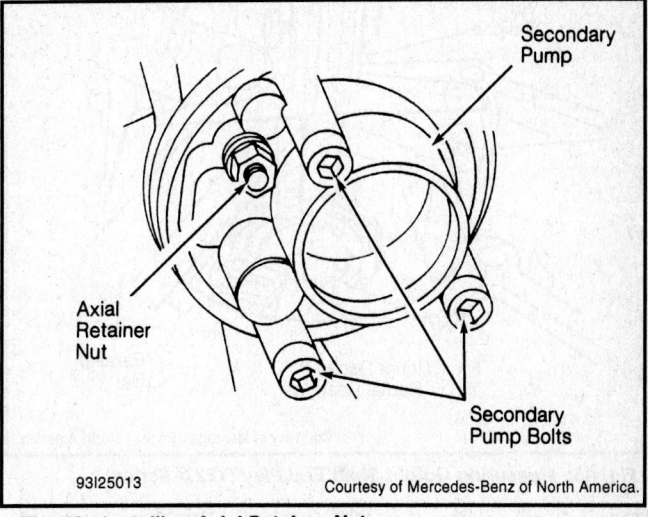

Fig. 42: *Installing Axial Retainer Nut*

NOTE: On 722.3 Series transmissions, use steps 26) through 28) to adjust output shaft end play. On 722.4 Series transmissions, use steps 29) and 30) to adjust output shaft end play.

---

26) On 722.3 Series transmissions, install Measuring Sleeve (126589061400) over output shaft. Tighten output shaft nut to 74 ft. lbs. (100 N.m), engaging parking lock pawl to keep assembly from turning. Install rear cover gasket.

27) Place parallel bar across rear cover gasket surface. Measure from top of parallel bar to flange of measuring sleeve. *See Fig. 43.* Add .59" (15.0 mm) to measurement to compensate for parallel bar height and lip of measuring sleeve. Record measurement.

28) Assemble rear cover. Measure distance from rear cover sealing surface to inner race of radial bearing. Subtract this measurement from measurement made in step 27) to obtain output shaft end play. End play should be .011-.020" (.30-.50 mm). Adjust end play by adding or removing shims under parking lock pawl.

29) On 722.4 Series transmissions, place Measuring Disc (129589062300) on rear cover surface. *See Fig. 44.* Measure and record distance between measuring disc and ball bearing inner race. Install measuring disc and output shaft flange over output shaft. Tighten output shaft nut to 74 ft. lbs. (100 N.m), engaging parking lock pawl to keep assembly from turning.

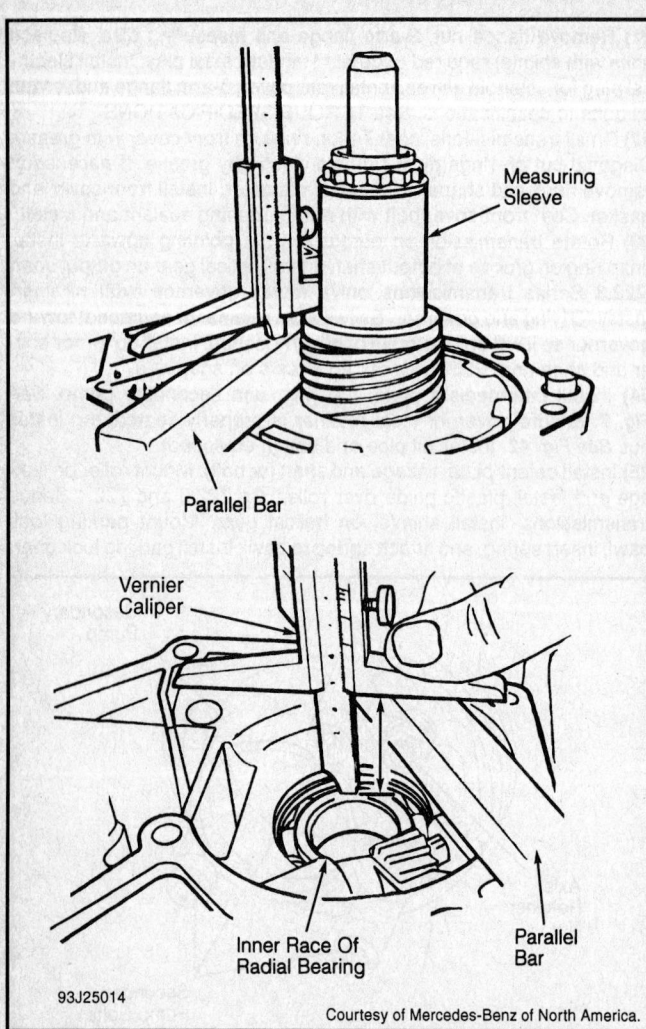

Fig. 43: *Measuring Output Shaft End Play (722.3 Series)*

30) Install rear cover gasket. Measure and record distance between measuring disc and rear cover gasket. Difference between measurements is equal to output shaft end play. End play should be .008-.016" (.20-.40 mm). Adjust end play by adding or removing shims under parking lock pawl. Install helical gear on output shaft.

31) On all transmissions, install mechanical speedometer oil pipe (if equipped). Install rear cover and washer on output shaft. Install "O" ring in output flange. Install output flange and tighten output shaft nut to specification. See TORQUE SPECIFICATIONS. Using a drift, stake collar of output shaft nut into groove of output shaft.

32) Install kickdown solenoid. Install modulating pressure control valve and thrust pin. Install vacuum control unit (modulator) and retaining plate. Install starter lock-out switch, but DO NOT tighten screws at this time.

NOTE: Some models may have a modified vacuum modulator (identified by its plastic cover). If a customer complains of harsh upshifts, it is possible to reduce modulator pressure by 2.9 psi (.2 bar) by turning modulator cover counterclockwise all the way to end stop.

33) On 722.3 Series transmissions, install sealing ring on brake band B-1 piston, with lip pointing away from pin. Using assembly fixture, compress brake band B-1 piston, outer return spring and measuring plate. Install snap ring and remove assembly fixture. Turn measuring plate bolt by hand until resistance is felt.

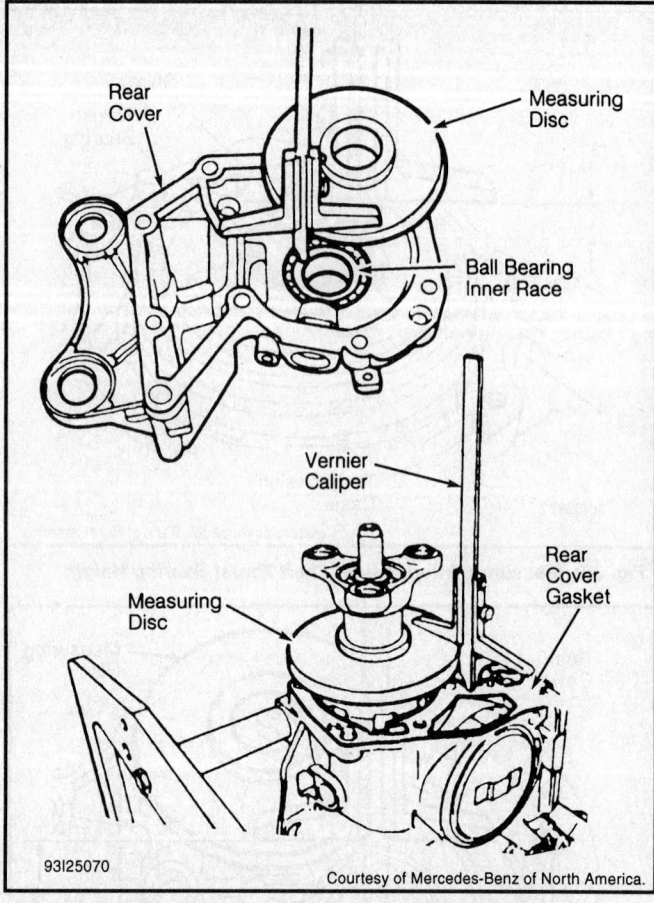

Fig. 44: *Measuring Output Shaft End Play (722.4 Series)*

34) Turn measuring plate bolt with INCH-lb. torque wrench, and count number of turns required to tighten bolt to 9 INCH lbs. (1 N.m). With 9 INCH lbs. (1 N.m) torque, brake band travel should be .07-.08" (1.8-2.0 mm). Adjust brake band clearance by adding or removing shim(s) underneath thrust pin.

NOTE: Measuring plate and screw have a 1-mm thread pitch, one turn on screw equals 1 mm of travel. For brake band pistons with removable thrust pin, use a bolt without measuring tip.

35) On 722.4 Series transmissions, install sealing ring on brake band B-1 piston, with lip pointing away from pin. Using assembly fixture, compress brake band B-1 piston, both inner and outer return springs and measuring plate. Install snap ring and remove assembly fixture. Turn measuring plate bolt by hand until resistance is felt.

36) Turn measuring plate bolt with INCH-lb. torque wrench, and count number of turns required to tighten bolt to 9 INCH lbs. (1 N.m). With 9 INCH lbs. (1 N.m) torque, brake band travel should be .07-.09" (1.8-2.4 mm) Adjust brake band clearance by adding or removing shim(s) underneath thrust pin, or install a brake band piston having a longer or shorter thrust pin.

37) Install assembly fixture and remove brake band B-1 piston and measuring plate. Install brake band B-1 piston, return springs, shim(s), thrust pin and piston cover. Install snap ring and remove assembly fixture.

38) Install thrust pin thrust element into brake band B-2 piston with large diameter toward brake band B-2. Install sealing ring and thrust pin on piston. Install piston in transmission, ensuring thrust pin engages brake band.

39) Install brake band B-2 piston cover and snap ring. Push brake band support lug in direction of brake band piston until piston rests against piston cover. *See Fig. 45.* Using vernier caliper, measure and record distance between support lug and brake band end.

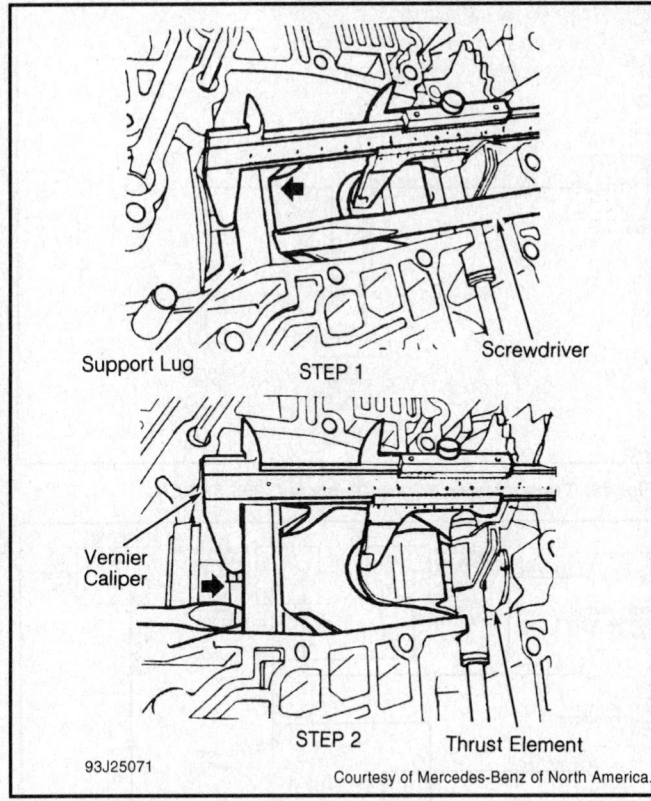

Fig. 45: Measuring Brake Band B-2 Free Play

Support Lug — STEP 1 — Screwdriver

Vernier Caliper

STEP 2 — Thrust Element

93J25071

Courtesy of Mercedes-Benz of North America.

40) On 722.3 and 722.4 Series transmissions, push brake band support lug toward thrust element. Measure and record distance between support lug and brake band end. Brake band B-2 clearance should be .216-.220" (5.5-5.6 mm). Adjust clearance by changing thrust pin. Thrust pin is available in lengths of 1.85-1.95" (47.2-49.6 mm) in increments of .030" (.8 mm).

41) On all transmissions, insert brake band B-2 guide, one-way check valve, locating pin, temperature (throttle) restrictor, oil deflector, and filler piece (if equipped). Assemble lower cover and intermediate plate.

42) Install lower cover and intermediate plate, ensuring oil pipe is positioned in bore. Center intermediate plate by means of 2 corner screws. Install and tighten remaining screws. Install leaf spring with bracket and tighten bolt.

43) Install range selector lever, bolt and nut. Move range selector lever into Neutral and insert a .160" (4.0 mm) adjustment pin through range selector lever and into bore of starter lock-out switch. Tighten starter lock-out switch screws. Remove adjustment pin.

44) Install valve body, ensuring range selector valve engages detent plate. Install and tighten valve body bolts. Install oil filter and attaching bolts. Install oil pan with NEW gasket.

45) With selector lever in "N" position, check clearance between detent piston and stop on shift linkage. Adjust clearance to .016-.039" (.40-1.0 mm) by means of plastic clip. Plastic clip is available in 2 thicknesses.

46) Check "O" ring on control pressure cable and replace (if necessary). Engage control pressure cable in connecting rod. Insert limiting rod into transmission housing and insert control pressure cable. Turn cable clockwise until it locks into place. Press sleeve of control pressure cable into housing. Turn sleeve clockwise until tab engages housing.

TORQUE SPECIFICATIONS

TORQUE SPECIFICATIONS

Application	Ft. Lbs. (N.m)
Brake Band B-1 Thrust Element Plug	52 (70)
Converter Drain Plug	10 (13)
Converter-To-Drive Plate Bolt	31 (42)
Drive Shaft Clamping Nut	22 (30)
Front Cover-To-Case Bolts	10 (13)
Kickdown Solenoid	15 (20)
Oil Drain Plug	10 (13)
Pressure Test Port Plug	10 (13)
Primary Pump-To-Front Cover Bolts	15 (20)
Rear Cover Bolts	10 (13)
Transmission-To-Engine	
M10 Bolts	41 (55)
M12 Bolts	48 (65)
3-Arm Output Flange Nut	89 (120)

	INCH Lbs. (N.m)
Axial Retainer Nut	71 (8)
Clutch K-2 Support Flange Bolts	97 (11)
Detent Plate Bolt	71 (8)
Intermediate Plate Bolts	71 (8)
Leaf Spring Bracket Bolt	71 (8)
Lower Cover-To-Case Bolts	71 (8)
Oil Filter-To-Valve Body Bolts	35 (4)
Oil Pan Bolts	71 (8)
Oil Pipe Bolt	71 (8)
Range Selector Lever Nut	71 (8)
Secondary Pump Bolts	71 (8)
Starter Lock-Out Switch Screw	71 (8)
Vacuum Unit (Modulator) Bolts	71 (8)
Valve Body-To-Case Bolts	71 (8)

WIRING DIAGRAMS

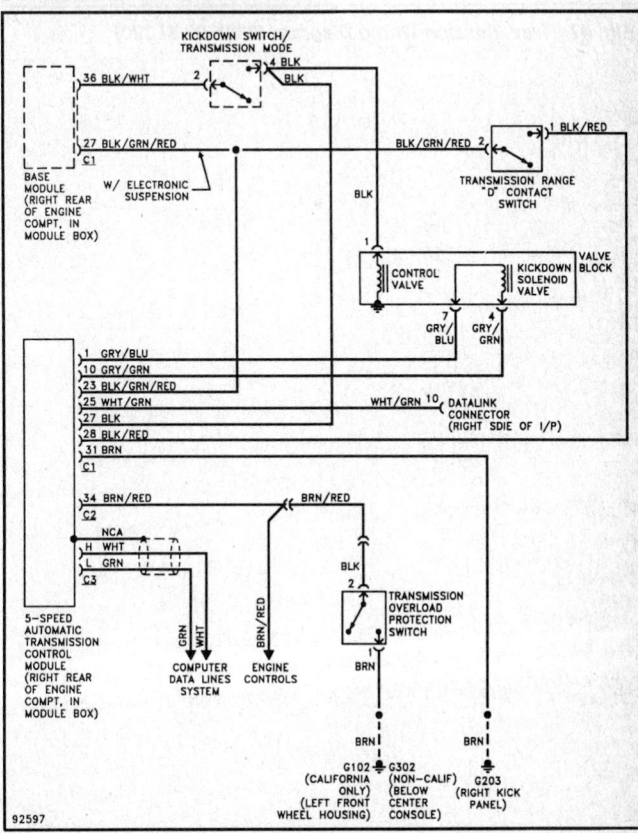

Fig. 46: Transmission Wiring Diagram (1995-96 S320)

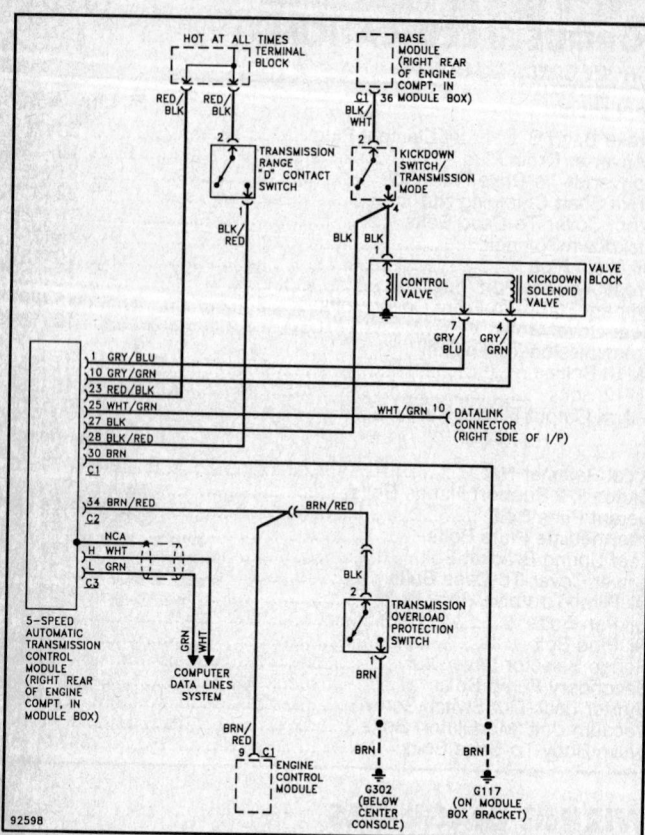

Fig. 47: Transmission Wiring Diagram (1995-96 SL320)

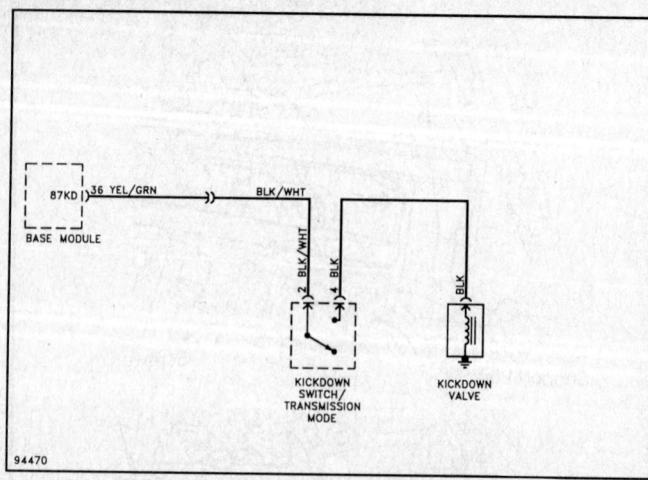

Fig. 48: Transmission Wiring Diagram (1995 S350D)

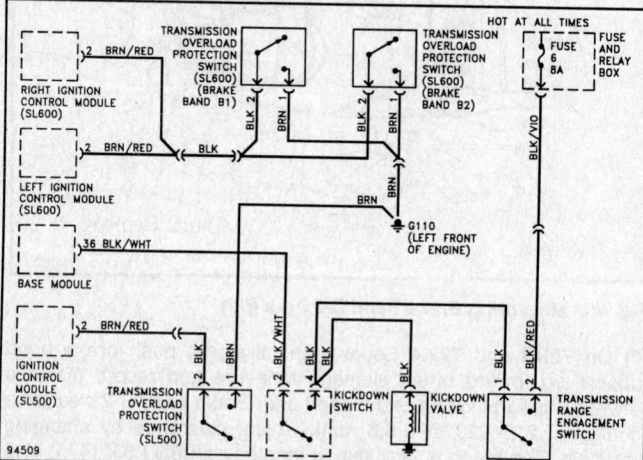

Fig. 49: Transmission Wiring Diagram (1995 SL500 & SL600)

AUTOMATIC TRANSMISSIONS
Mitsubishi F3A20 & F4A20 Series

Eclipse, Expo, Galant, Mirage

APPLICATION & LABOR TIMES

APPLICATION & LABOR TIMES

Vehicle Application	Labor Times		Transaxle Series
	¹ R & I	² Overhaul	
Eclipse			
2.4L	6.8	8.9	F4A23
Expo FWD			
1.8L	4.6	8.9	F4A22
2.4L	4.6	8.9	F4A23
Galant ³	5.9	8.9	F4A23
Mirage			
1.5L	4.6	8.9	F3A21
1.8L	4.6	8.9	F4A22

¹ – Removal and installation of transmission from vehicle chassis.
² – Bench overhaul time for transmission. DOES NOT include removal and installation.
³ – If equipped with Electronically Controlled Suspension, add .2 hr.

IDENTIFICATION

Vehicle information code plate is riveted to firewall in engine compartment area. Plate contains transaxle identification information. Identification numbers are also stamped on transaxle bell housing. *See Fig. 1.*

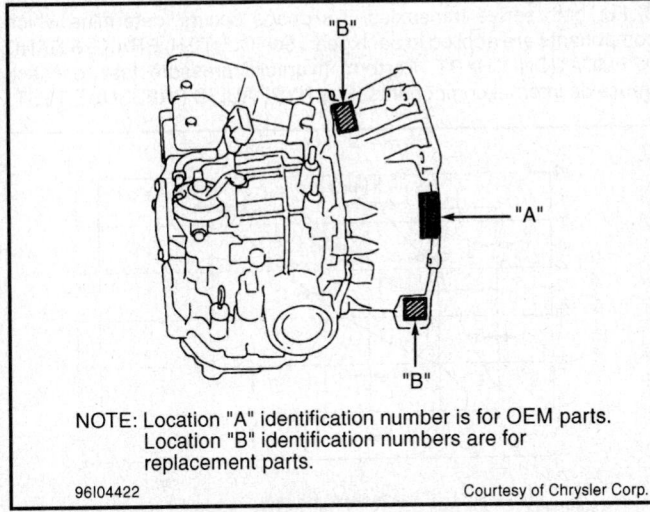

NOTE: Location "A" identification number is for OEM parts. Location "B" identification numbers are for replacement parts.

Courtesy of Chrysler Corp.

Fig. 1: Locating Transaxle Identification Numbers

DESCRIPTION

Transaxles consist of torque converter, transfer assembly and differential. The F3A21 is an automatic 3-speed unit which is not electronically controlled. The F4A20 series is an electronically controlled automatic 4-speed unit. Internal components for both transaxles are basically identical, with exception of an overdrive 4th gear on F4A20 series transaxle.

Transaxles consist of a 3-element torque converter with governor assembly (F3A20 series), torque converter clutch (F4A20 series), one planetary gear set, one brake band, 3 multiple-disc clutch assemblies for the F3A20 series, and 4 clutch assemblies for the F4A20 series. *See Figs. 2 and 3.*

On F4A40 series, transaxle shifting points are controlled by the Transmission Control Module (TCM). TCM receives information from various inputs and controls solenoids on the valve body for different gear operation. Overdrive or 4th gear operation is controlled by a manually operated overdrive control switch. Transaxle will not shift into overdrive unless overdrive control switch is in ON position.

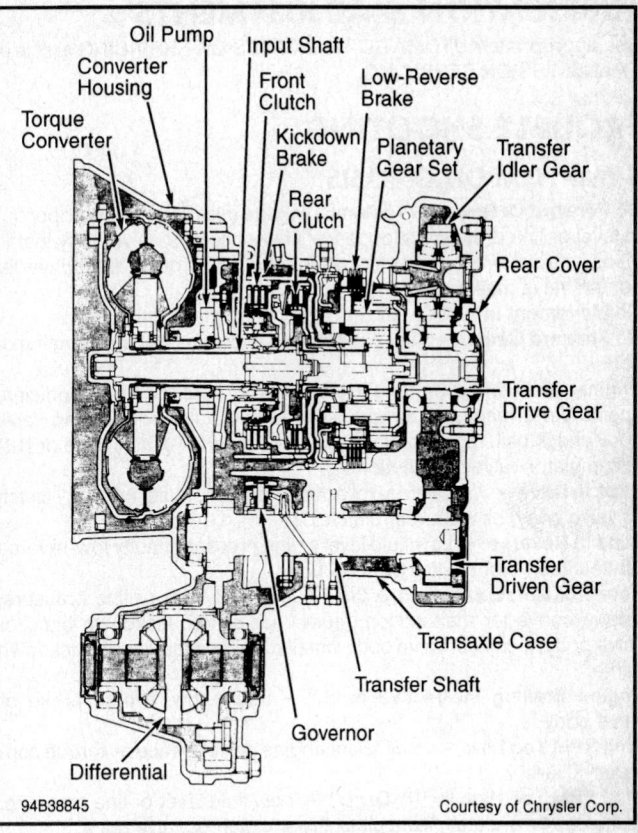

Courtesy of Chrysler Corp.

Fig. 2: Identifying Transaxle Components (F3A21)

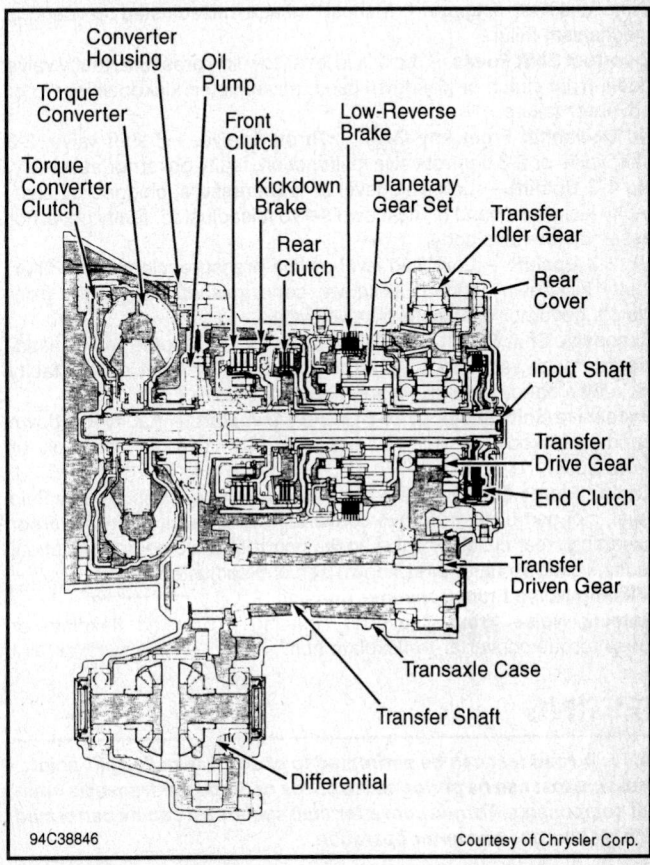

Courtesy of Chrysler Corp.

Fig. 3: Identifying Transaxle Components (F4A20 Series)

LUBRICATION & ADJUSTMENTS

See appropriate AUTOMATIC TRANSMISSION SERVICING article in TRANSMISSION SERVICING.

TROUBLE SHOOTING

SYMPTOM DIAGNOSIS

No Forward Or Reverse – Manual linkage misadjusted, improper fluid level or line pressure, clogged oil filter, incorrect valve body installation, regulator valve, line pressure relief valve or torque converter control valve malfunction.

No Movement In "D" Or "2" – Front clutch malfunction.

No Forward Gears – Rear clutch or N-D accumulator valve malfunction.

Engine Stalls When Shifting From "N" To "D" Or "R" – Insufficient engine performance, incorrect valve body installation, sticking valve body check ball, regulator valve, torque converter clutch valve or N-D accumulator valve malfunction.

Slips In Drive – Low fluid level or line pressure, faulty one-way clutch or valve body, or worn rear clutch.

Slips In Reverse – Low fluid level or line pressure, faulty low-reverse brake circuit, front clutch or valve body.

Poor Acceleration In 2nd & 3rd – Low fluid level or line pressure, torque converter malfunction, faulty rear clutch, kickdown band or valve body, incorrect valve body installation, or misadjusted kickdown servo.

Engine Braking Ineffective In "L" – Faulty low-reverse brake or valve body.

Stall RPM Too Low – Insufficient engine performance or torque converter failure.

Stall RPM Too High In "R" Or "D" – Low fluid lever or line pressure, faulty one-way clutch, front clutch, rear clutch or valve body.

Vehicle Creeps In "N" – Front or rear clutch malfunction.

Park Will Not Engage – Manual linkage misadjusted or parking mechanism failure.

Incorrect Shift Points – Low fluid level, low line pressure, faulty valve body, front clutch or kickdown band, misadjusted kickdown servo or governor failure.

No Downshift From Any Gear – Throttle valve, 1-2 shift valve, 2-3 shift valve or 2-3 control valve malfunction, faulty governor assembly.

No 1-2 Upshift – Low fluid level or line pressure, clogged oil filter, faulty kickdown band or kickdown servo misadjusted, faulty governor assembly or valve body.

No 2-3 Upshift – Low fluid level or line pressure, clogged oil filter, faulty kickdown band or kickdown servo misadjusted, faulty front clutch, governor assembly or valve body.

Excessive Shift Shock On 1-2 Or 2-3 Upshift – Throttle cable misadjusted, faulty valve body, governor assembly or front clutch, faulty kickdown band or kickdown servo misadjusted.

Excessive Shift Shock On 2-1 Or 3-2 Downshift – Faulty kickdown band or kickdown servo misadjusted, faulty governor assembly or valve body.

Engine Flares On 1-2 Or 2-3 Upshift – Low line pressure, low fluid level, clogged oil filter, torque converter malfunction, faulty governor assembly, rear clutch or valve body, incorrect valve body installation, faulty kickdown band or kickdown servo misadjusted.

Whining Noise From Converter Housing – Oil pump failure.

Rattling Noise From Converter Housing – Cracked flexplate or loose torque converter-to-flexplate bolt.

TESTING

NOTE: A road test can be performed to check transaxle shift points. Pressure test can be performed to check operation of transaxle internal components. Torque converter stall speed test can be performed to check torque converter operation.

CLUTCH, BRAKE & BAND APPLICATION CHART

Selector Lever Position	Elements In Use
"D" (Drive)	
1st Gear	Rear Clutch & One-Way Clutch
2nd Gear	Rear Clutch & Kickdown Band
3rd Gear	Front Clutch, Rear Clutch & [1] End Clutch
4th Gear [1]	End Clutch & Kickdown Band
"2" (Second)	
1st Gear	Rear Clutch & One-Way Clutch
2nd Gear	Rear Clutch & Kickdown Band
"1" (Low)	
1st Gear	Rear Clutch & Low-Reverse Brake
"R" (Reverse)	Front Clutch & Low-Reverse Brake
"N" Or "P" (Neutral Or Park)	All Clutches, Brakes & Bands Released Or Ineffective

[1] – F4A20 series only.

ROAD TEST

NOTE: Perform road test to ensure transaxle shift points are at specified speeds. See Figs. 4-6. Broken lines in shift point charts indicate downshifts, and solid lines indicate upshifts.

1) Ensure shift cable is properly adjusted, and fluid level and condition are okay. Add fluid and adjust shift cable if necessary. Road test vehicle, and check if shift points are at specified speeds. See Figs. 4-6.
2) If shift points are not as specified, see TROUBLE SHOOTING. Check for stored diagnostic trouble codes. See MITSUBISHI F4A20, F4A30 & W4A30 SERIES ELECTRONIC CONTROLS article.
3) For both series transaxles, if slippage occurs, determine which components are applied in each gear. See CLUTCH, BRAKE & BAND APPLICATION CHART. Perform hydraulic pressure test to check transaxle internal components. See HYDRAULIC PRESSURE TEST.

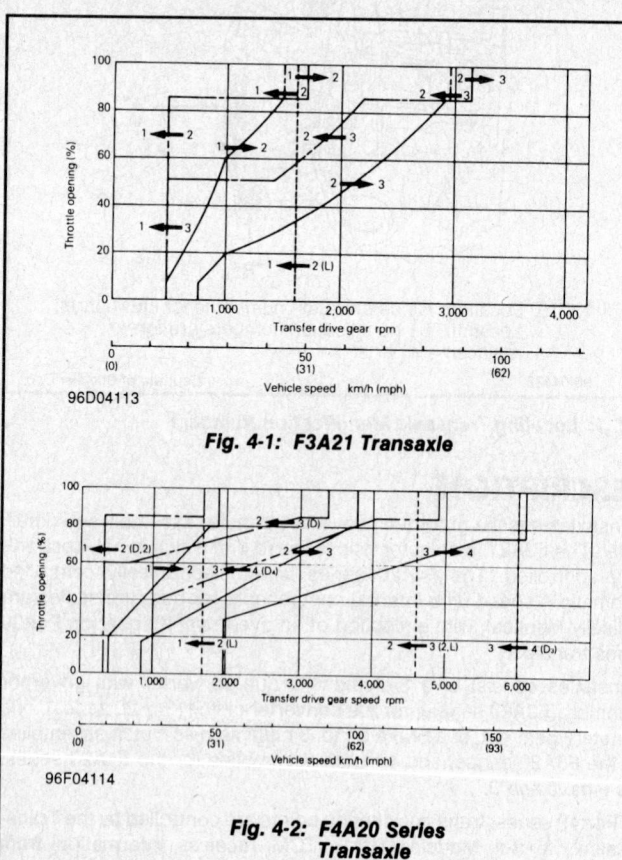

96D04113

Fig. 4-1: F3A21 Transaxle

96F04114

Fig. 4-2: F4A20 Series Transaxle

Courtesy of Chrysler Corp.

Fig. 4: Identifying Transaxle Shift Points (Mirage)

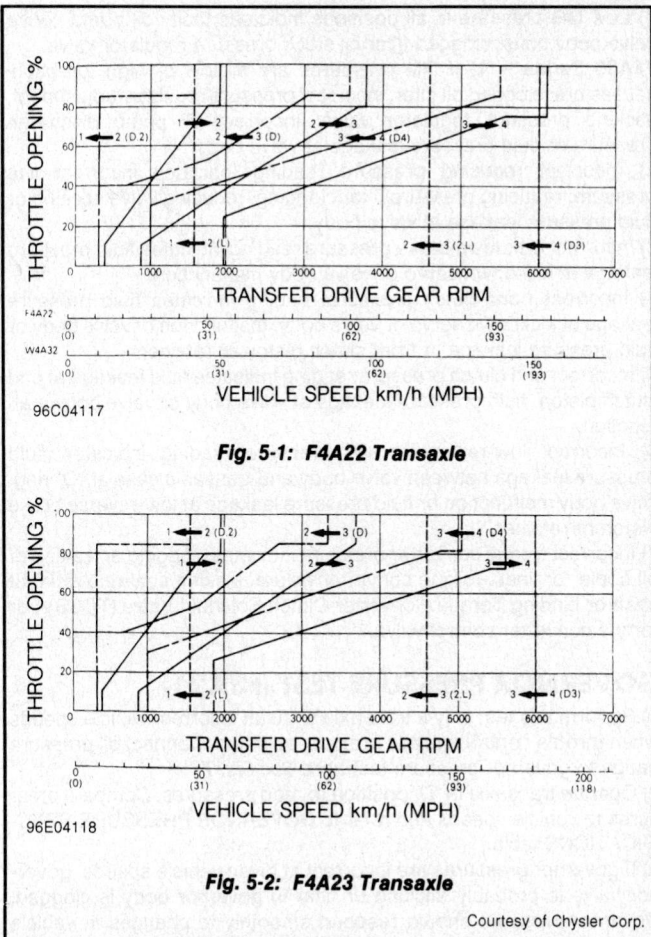

Fig. 5-1: F4A22 Transaxle

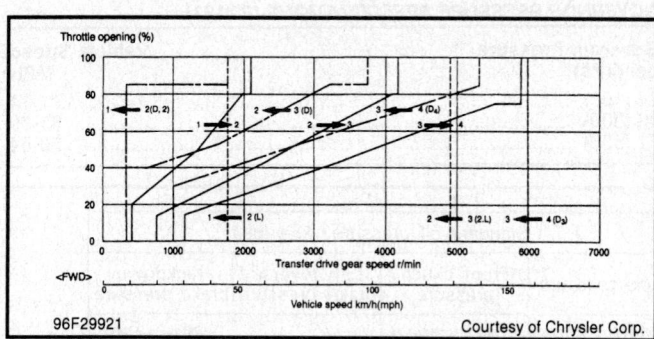

Fig. 5-2: F4A23 Transaxle

Courtesy of Chysler Corp.

Fig. 5: Identifying Transaxle Shift Points (Expo & Galant)

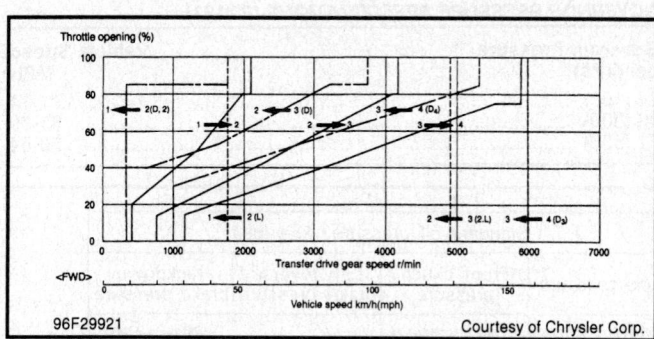

96F29921   Courtesy of Chrysler Corp.

Fig. 6: Identifying Transaxle Shift Points (Eclipse)

The TCM contains a self-diagnostic system, which stores a Diagnostic Trouble Code (DTC) if a transaxle fault exists. DTC can be retrieved to determine the transaxle problem area.

NOTE: Electronic trouble shooting for F3A20 & F4A20 series transaxles are not covered in this article. For electronic trouble shooting, see MITSUBISHI F4A20, F4A30 & W4A30 SERIES ELECTRONIC CONTROLS article.

CAUTION: A 400-psi (28 kg/cm²) pressure gauge is required for checking certain pressures. See Figs. 9 or 10 to determine when this gauge should be used in accordance with hydraulic pressure specification.

HYDRAULIC PRESSURE TESTS

NOTE: In the following test procedures, an additional person may be necessary to activate the transaxle throttle control cable. Before performing pressure tests ensure fluid level and condition are acceptable.

1) Ensure transaxle is at normal operating temperature and fluid level is correct. Raise and support vehicle so drive wheels rotate freely. Install tachometer, and position so driver can view it.
2) Note locations of hydraulic pressure taps on side of transaxle case and near oil pan. *See Figs. 7 and 8.* Remove plug, and install adapter and pressure gauge to each pressure tap.

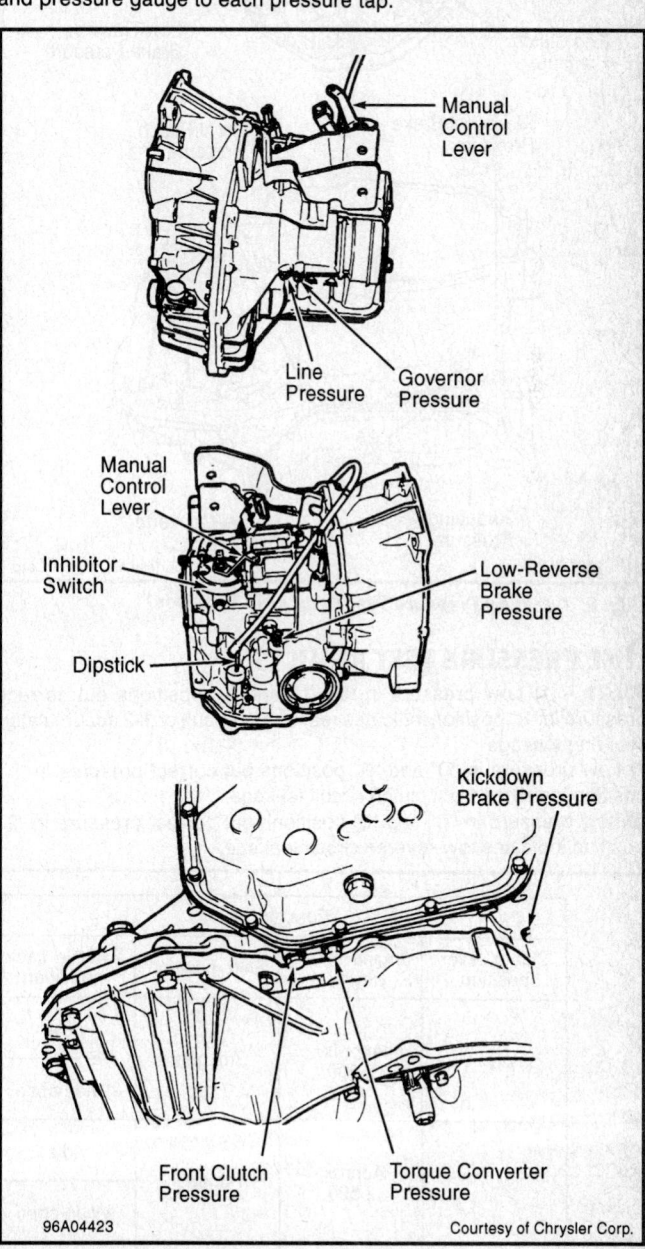

96A04423   Courtesy of Chrysler Corp.

Fig. 7: Locating Pressure Test Ports (F3A21)

3) Measure hydraulic pressure at various specified engine RPM and transaxle gears. *See Figs. 9 or 10.* Ensure pressure is within specification. If proper line pressure cannot be obtained, check for proper adjustment. See LINE PRESSURE under ADJUSTMENTS.
4) If proper line pressure cannot be obtained, check for probable defective components. See LINE PRESSURE TEST RESULTS. Remove pressure gauge. Install and tighten plug to specification. See TORQUE SPECIFICATIONS.

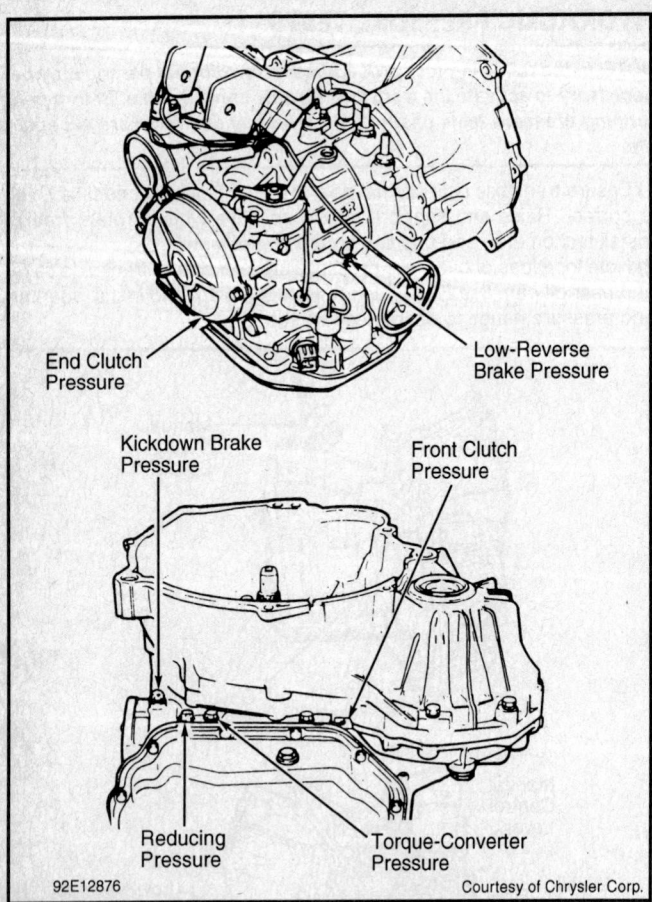

End Clutch Pressure

Low-Reverse Brake Pressure

Kickdown Brake Pressure

Front Clutch Pressure

Reducing Pressure

Torque-Converter Pressure

92E12876

Courtesy of Chrysler Corp.

Fig. 8: Locating Pressure Test Ports (F4A20 Series)

LINE PRESSURE TEST RESULTS

F3A21 – 1) Low pressure in "D", "L" and "2" positions but correct pressure in "R" position indicates rear clutch circuit or 1-2 accumulator seal ring leakage.
2) Low pressure in "D" and "R" positions but correct pressure in "L" position indicates front clutch circuit leakage.
3) Low pressure in "D" and "L" positions but correct pressure in "2" position indicates low-reverse circuit leakage.

4) Low line pressure in all positions indicates faulty oil pump, loose valve body bolts, clogged filter or stuck pressure regulator valve.
F4A20 Series – 1) If line pressures are all low or high, probable causes are: clogged oil filter, incorrect pressure regulator adjustment, sticking pressure regulator valve, incorrect oil pump discharge pressure or fluid pressure leakage at valve body.
2) Incorrect reducing pressure reading indicates incorrect line pressure, reducing pressure filter clogging, reducing valve sticking or fluid pressure leakage at valve body.
3) Incorrect kickdown brake pressure reading indicates fluid pressure leakage at kickdown servo or valve body malfunction.
4) Incorrect front clutch pressure reading indicates fluid pressure leakage at kickdown servo or valve body, malfunction of valve body or fluid pressure leakage at front clutch piston or retainer.
5) Incorrect end clutch pressure reading indicates fluid leakage at end clutch piston, fluid pressure leakage at valve body or valve body malfunction.
6) Incorrect low-reverse brake pressure reading indicates fluid pressure leakage between valve body and transaxle case at "O" ring, valve body malfunction or fluid pressure leakage at low-reverse brake piston or retainer.
7) Incorrect torque converter pressure indicates clogging or leaking of oil cooler or lines, torque converter failure, leaking seal ring at input shaft or binding Torque Converter Clutch Solenoid Valve (TCCSV) or torque converter control valve.

GOVERNOR PRESSURE TEST (F3A21)

1) Perform this test only if transaxle shifts at incorrect vehicle speeds when throttle control cable is properly adjusted. Connect oil pressure gauge to governor pressure test port. *See Fig. 7.*
2) Operate transaxle in "D" position to read pressures. Compare pressures to vehicle speeds and refer to GOVERNOR PRESSURE SPECIFICATIONS table.
3) If governor pressures are incorrect at given vehicle speeds, governor valve is probably sticking or filter in governor body is clogged. Governor pressure should respond smoothly to changes in vehicle speed and should return to 0-2.8 psi (0-20 kPa) when vehicle is stopped.

GOVERNOR PRESSURE SPECIFICATIONS (F3A21)

Governor Pressure psi (kPa)	Vehicle Speed MPH
14 (100)	14
43 (300)	35-39
71 (500)	50-54

Conditions				Standard oil pressure kPa (psi)			
Select lever position	Engine speed (rpm)	Shift position	Throttle cable condition	Line pressure	Front clutch pressure	Low-reverse brake pressure	Kickdown brake pressure
D	Approx. 2,500	3rd gear	Idle	360 – 420 (51 – 60)	360 – 420 (51 – 60)	–	360 – 420 (51 – 60)
			Wide-open	690 – 710 (98 – 101)	690 – 710 (98 – 101)	–	690 – 710 (98 – 101)
L	Approx. 2,500	1st gear	Idle	360 – 420 (51 – 60)		360 – 420 (51 – 60)	
			Wide-open	690 – 710 (98 – 101)		690 – 710 (98 – 101)	
2	Approx. 2,500	2nd gear	Idle	360 – 420 (51 – 60)	–	–	360 – 420 (51 – 60)
			Wide-open	690 – 710 (98 – 101)	–	–	690 – 710 (98 – 101)
R	Approx. 2,500	Reverse	–	1,400 – 2,000 (200 – 284)	1,400 – 2,000 (200 – 284)		–

94E38855

Courtesy of Chrysler Corp.

Fig. 9: Transaxle Hydraulic Pressure Specifications (F3A21)

No.	Conditions			Standard oil pressure kPa (psi)					
	Select lever position	Engine speed rpm	Shift position	① Reducing pressure	② Kickdown brake pressure	③ Front clutch pressure	④ End clutch pressure	⑤ Low-reverse brake pressure	⑥ Torque-converter pressure
1	N	Idling	Neutral	360–490 (51–70)	–	–	–	–	☆
2	D	Idling	2nd gear	360–490 (51–70)	100–210 (14–30)	–	–	–	☆
3	D (SW-ON)	Approx. 2,500	4th gear	360–490 (51–70)	830–900 (118–128)	–	830–900 (118–128)	–	450-650 (64-92)
4	D (SW-OFF)	Approx. 2,500	3rd gear	360–490 (51–70)	830–900 (118–128)	830–900 (118–128)	830–900 (118–128)	–	450-650 (64-92)
5	2	Approx. 2,500	2nd gear	360–490 (51–70)	830–900 (118–128)	–	–	–	450-650 (64-92)
6	L	Approx. 1,000	1st gear	360–490 (51–70)	–	–	–	300–420 (43–60)	☆
7	R	Approx. 2,500	Reverse	360–490 (51–70)	–	1,640–2,240 (233–319)	–	1,640–2,240 (233–319)	450-650 (64-92)
		Approx. 1,000				1,000 (142) or more		1,000 (142) or more	

NOTE
– must be 10 kPa (1.4 psi) or less.
SW-ON: Switch ON the overdrive control switch
SW-OFF: Switch OFF the overdrive control switch
☆: Hydraulic pressure is generated, but not the standard value.

94F38856

Courtesy of Chysler Corp.

Fig. 10: Transaxle Hydraulic Pressure Specifications (F4A20 Series)

TORQUE CONVERTER STALL SPEED TEST

CAUTION: DO NOT allow anyone to stand in front of or behind vehicle while performing stall speed test. Always block both rear wheels and apply parking and service brakes fully.

Stall Speed Test Procedure – 1) Check transaxle fluid level. Fluid should be at normal operating temperature of 160-180°F (70-80°C). Engine coolant should also be at normal operating temperature of 180-190°F (60-90°C).
2) Block both rear wheels. Install engine tachometer to be seen from driver's seat. Apply parking and service brakes fully. Start engine and move gear selector to "D" position.
3) With brakes fully applied, depress accelerator pedal fully to read maximum engine RPM. See STALL SPEED SPECIFICATIONS table.

NOTE: DO NOT hold wide open throttle for longer than 5 seconds at a time. If more than one stall speed test is required, operate engine at approximately 1000 RPM in Neutral for 2 minutes to cool transaxle fluid.

4) Move gear selector to "R" position and repeat stall speed test procedure. See STALL SPEED SPECIFICATIONS table.
Stall Speed Test Results – 1) If stall speed is above specification in "D" position, rear clutch or one-way clutch is slipping. HYDRAULIC PRESSURE TESTS can be performed to isolate problem.

STALL SPEED SPECIFICATIONS

Application	Stall Speed RPM
F3A21	
Mirage	1000-2200
F4A20 Series	
Eclipse & Galant	2100-2600
Expo	1800-3200
Mirage	2500-3000

2) If stall speed is above specification in "R" position, front clutch or low-reverse brake is slipping. HYDRAULIC PRESSURE TESTS can be performed to isolate problem.
3) If stall speed is below specification in "R" and "D" positions, insufficient engine performance or faulty torque converter are probable causes.

ON-VEHICLE SERVICE

NEUTRAL SAFETY SWITCH & CONTROL CABLE ADJUSTMENTS

See appropriate AUTOMATIC TRANSMISSION SERVICING article in TRANSMISSION SERVICING.

THROTTLE CONTROL CABLE ADJUSTMENT

See appropriate AUTOMATIC TRANSMISSION SERVICING article in TRANSMISSION SERVICING.

ADJUSTMENTS

KICKDOWN SERVO ADJUSTMENT (F4A20 SERIES)

1) Thoroughly clean area around kickdown servo switch. Remove snap ring. Remove kickdown servo switch. Using kickdown servo wrench and wrench adapter, secure kickdown servo piston from turning. *See Fig. 11.*

CAUTION: DO NOT press piston inward while engaging wrench in piston. Tighten wrench adapter by hand.

2) Loosen lock nut back to "V" groove in adjusting rod. *See Fig. 12.* Thread inner half of Kickdown Servo Socket Wrench Set (MD998916) onto adjusting rod, and tighten it until it contacts lock nut. *See Fig. 13.* Place outer half of wrench set onto lock nut. Tighten inner and outer halves together using open end wrenches.

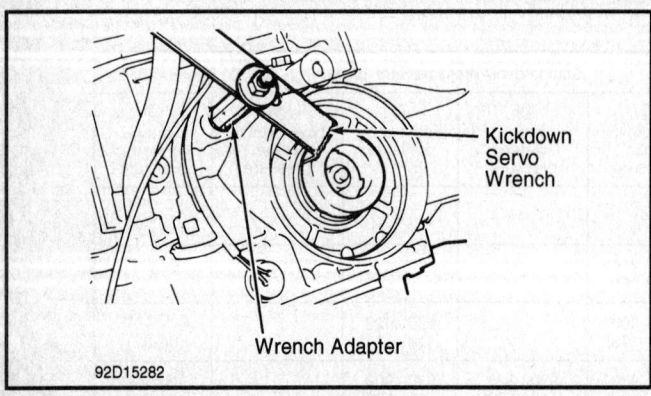

Fig. 11: Installing Kickdown Servo Wrench

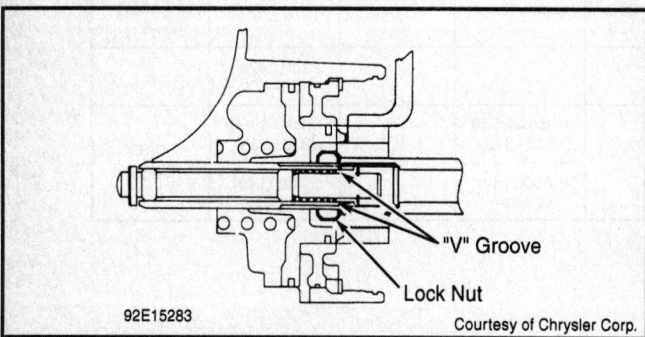

Fig. 12: Sectional View Of Kickdown Servo Adjustment Mechanism

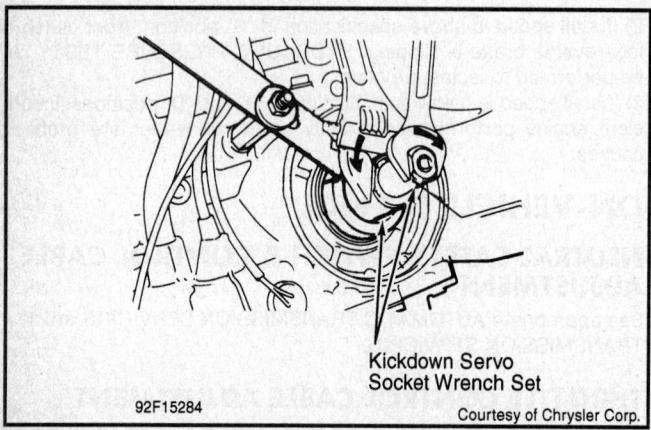

Fig. 13: Locking Servo Wrench To Adjusting Rod

3) Remove outer half of wrench set. Using a torque wrench, tighten inner half of wrench set to 89 INCH lbs. (10 N.m). *See Fig. 14.* Back off wrench and repeat tightening to specified torque. Back off wrench once again then tighten to 44 INCH lbs (5 N.m). When specified torque is reached, back off wrench 2-2 1/4 turns.

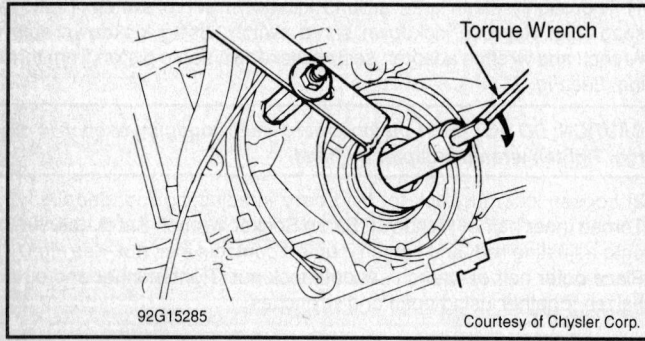

Fig. 14: Adjusting Kickdown Servo

4) Unlock inner half of wrench set from kickdown servo lock nut. Tighten lock nut by hand until it contacts kickdown servo piston. Tighten servo lock nut to 18-23 Ft. Lbs. (25-32 N.m).

NOTE: Ensure adjusting rod DOES NOT turn while tightening lock nut.

LINE PRESSURE

NOTE: Since valve body must be removed for adjustment, check line pressure before attempting to adjust line pressure.

F3A21 – 1) Remove valve body. See VALVE BODY under REMOVAL & INSTALLATION. Note location of line pressure adjusting screw. *See Fig. 15.*
2) To adjust line pressure, rotate line pressure adjusting screw at regulator valve. Rotate line pressure adjusting screw clockwise to decrease line pressure and counterclockwise to increase line pressure.
3) Rotating line pressure adjusting screw one revolution will change line pressure approximately 3.7 psi (26 kPa). The standard adjusting value for line pressure is 51-60 psi (360-420 kPa) at idle and 98-101 psi (690-710 kPa) at WOT. For hydraulic pressure specifications, *see Fig. 9.* Reinstall valve body. Fill transaxle with Mopar ATF Plus-Type 7176, and check line pressure.

F4A20 Series – 1) Remove valve body. See VALVE BODY under REMOVAL & INSTALLATION. Note location of line pressure adjusting screw. *See Fig. 15.*
2) To adjust line pressure, rotate line pressure adjusting screw at regulator valve. Rotate line pressure adjusting screw clockwise to decrease line pressure and counterclockwise to increase line pressure.
3) Rotating line pressure adjusting screw one revolution will change line pressure approximately 5.4 psi (38 kPa). The standard adjusting value for line pressure is 124-127 psi (870-890 kPa). For hydraulic pressure specifications, *See Fig. 11.* Reinstall valve body. Fill transaxle with Mopar ATF Plus-Type 7176, and check line pressure.

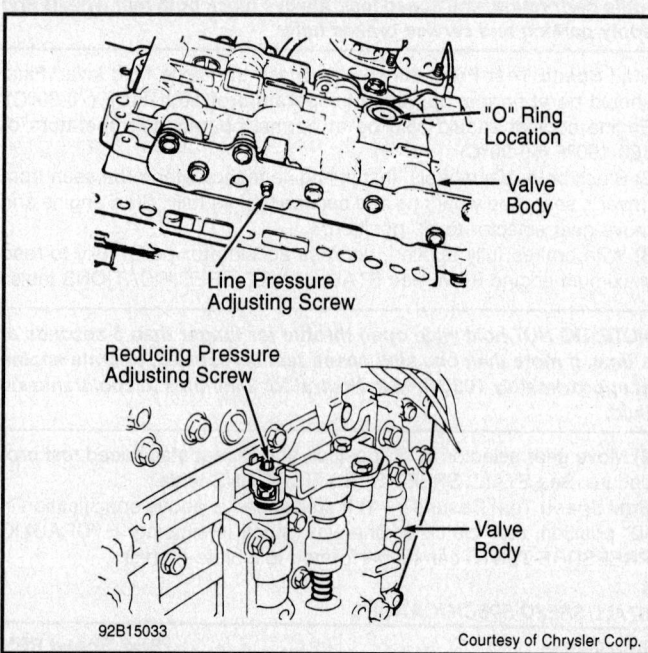

Fig. 15: Identifying Line Pressure & Reducing Pressure Adjusting Screws

REDUCING PRESSURE (F4A20 SERIES)

NOTE: Since valve body must be removed for adjustment, check reducing pressure before attempting to adjust reducing pressure.

REMOVAL & INSTALLATION

AXLE SHAFTS

See appropriate AXLE SHAFTS article in AXLE SHAFTS & TRANSFER CASES section.

TRANSAXLE ASSEMBLY

See appropriate AUTOMATIC TRANSMISSION REMOVAL article in TRANSMISSION SERVICING section.

VALVE BODY

Removal – Raise and support vehicle. Drain transaxle fluid. Remove retaining bolts, oil pan, gasket, oil filter and oil temperature sensor. Press solenoid valve wiring harness grommet and connector into transaxle case. Remove valve body bolts. Note bolt length and location for reassembly reference. See Fig. 49. Remove valve body.

CAUTION: DO NOT allow manual valve to fall from valve body during removal. Ensure "O" ring, located between valve body and transaxle case, is removed. See Fig. 15.

Installation – **1)** Always install NEW "O" ring between valve body and transaxle case and on solenoid valve wiring harness. Ensure "O" ring is seated on top of valve body. See Fig. 15.
2) Install valve body. Ensure detent plate pin engages groove on manual valve. Install retaining bolts, ensuring proper length bolt is installed in designated area. See Fig. 49. Tighten valve body bolts to specification. See TORQUE SPECIFICATIONS. Install oil temperature sensor and solenoid valve wiring harness.

CAUTION: Position wiring so it does not contact detent plate. Ensure park rod is properly retained in the clamps.

3) Install oil filter, magnet, gasket and oil pan. Tighten bolts to specification. See TORQUE SPECIFICATIONS. Fill transaxle with Mopar ATF Plus-Type 7176.

TORQUE CONVERTER

Torque converter is a sealed unit and cannot be disassembled for service. Replace unit if damaged or contaminated. For stall speed test, see TORQUE CONVERTER STALL SPEED TEST under TESTING.

TRANSAXLE DISASSEMBLY

F3A21 – 1) Prior to disassembling unit, plug all openings and thoroughly clean exterior. Remove torque converter and position transaxle with oil pan down.
2) Measure input shaft end play before disassembling transaxle. See Fig. 16. This will indicate when a thrust washer change is required (except when major parts are replaced). Record dial indicator reading for later use.
3) Remove transfer shaft cover and measure transfer shaft end play. See Fig. 17. Record dial indicator reading for use when reassembling transaxle. Remove inhibitor switch. Remove oil pan, gasket and filter. See Fig. 18. Remove valve body assembly after throttle cable has been disconnected. Remove accumulator piston and springs.
4) Remove converter housing, oil pump assembly and thrust washer. See Fig. 18. Remove differential assembly with spacer. Remove input shaft with front and rear clutch assemblies as a unit.
5) Remove thrust bearing and clutch hub. Remove thrust washer and bearing. Remove kickdown drum and band. Remove kickdown servo snap ring, piston, spring and anchor rod. Remove snap ring and center support. Remove reverse and forward sun gears. Remove planetary gear set. See Fig. 21.
6) Remove wave spring, return spring, pressure plate, brake discs, brake plates and reaction plate. Note direction of return spring for reassembly reference. Remove transfer idler gear shaft lock plate and

bolt. Remove transfer idler gear shaft using Wrench Adapter (MD998344). Remove transfer idler gear bearing inner races (2) and spacer. See Fig. 18.
7) Remove output flange bearing retainer and "O" ring. Remove snap ring from outer race of bearing. Remove internal gear, output flange, transfer drive gear and bearing as an assembly.
8) Remove snap ring at rear end of transfer shaft. Using brass drift on rear end of transfer shaft, drive shaft toward engine mounting surface. Transfer driven gear will come off. Remove snap ring, then tapered roller bearing inner and outer races (if necessary). Remove sprag rod support then manual control shaft, steel ball and spring.

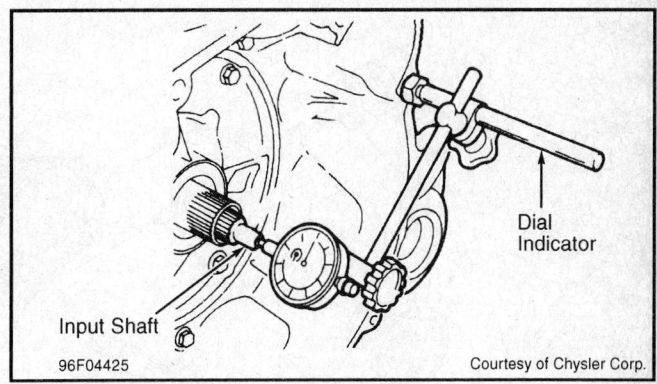

Fig. 16: Measuring Input Shaft End Play

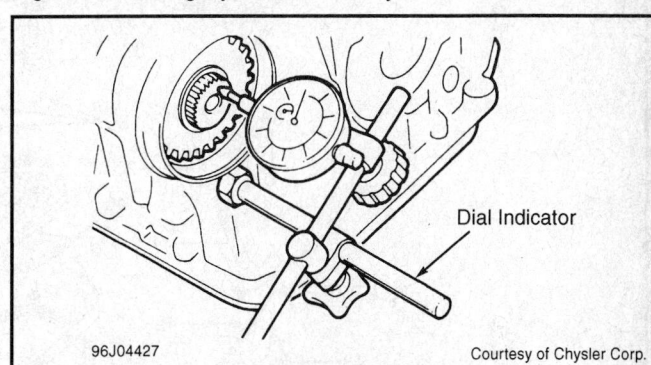

Fig. 17: Measuring Transfer Shaft End Play
(F3A21 Shown, F4A20 Series Is Similar)

F4A20 Series – 1) Prior to disassembly, plug all openings and thoroughly clean exterior of transaxle. Remove torque converter and measure input shaft end play. See Fig. 16. This will indicate when a thrust washer change is required (except when major parts are replaced). Record dial indicator reading for later use.
2) Remove pulse generators "A" and "B" and neutral safety switch. See Fig. 19. Remove kickdown servo switch. Remove oil pan, gasket and filter. Remove oil temperature sensor. See Fig. 20.
3) Remove solenoid valve connector and valve body. Remove end clutch cover and end clutch assembly. Remove end clutch hub, thrust bearing and end clutch shaft.
4) Remove converter housing, oil pump assembly and thrust washer. Remove differential assembly and spacer. Remove input shaft with front and rear clutch assemblies. Remove thrust bearing and clutch hub. Remove thrust race and bearing. Remove kickdown drum and band. See Fig. 21.
5) Remove kickdown servo retainer, piston and spring. Remove anchor rod. Remove snap ring and center support. Remove reverse and forward sun gears. Remove planetary carrier assembly and thrust bearing. Remove wave spring, return spring, pressure plate, brake discs, brake plates and reaction plate. See Fig. 21. Note direction of return spring for reassembly reference. Remove end bearing retainer. Use impact driver if necessary.

AUTOMATIC TRANSMISSIONS
Mitsubishi F3A20 & F4A20 Series (Cont.)

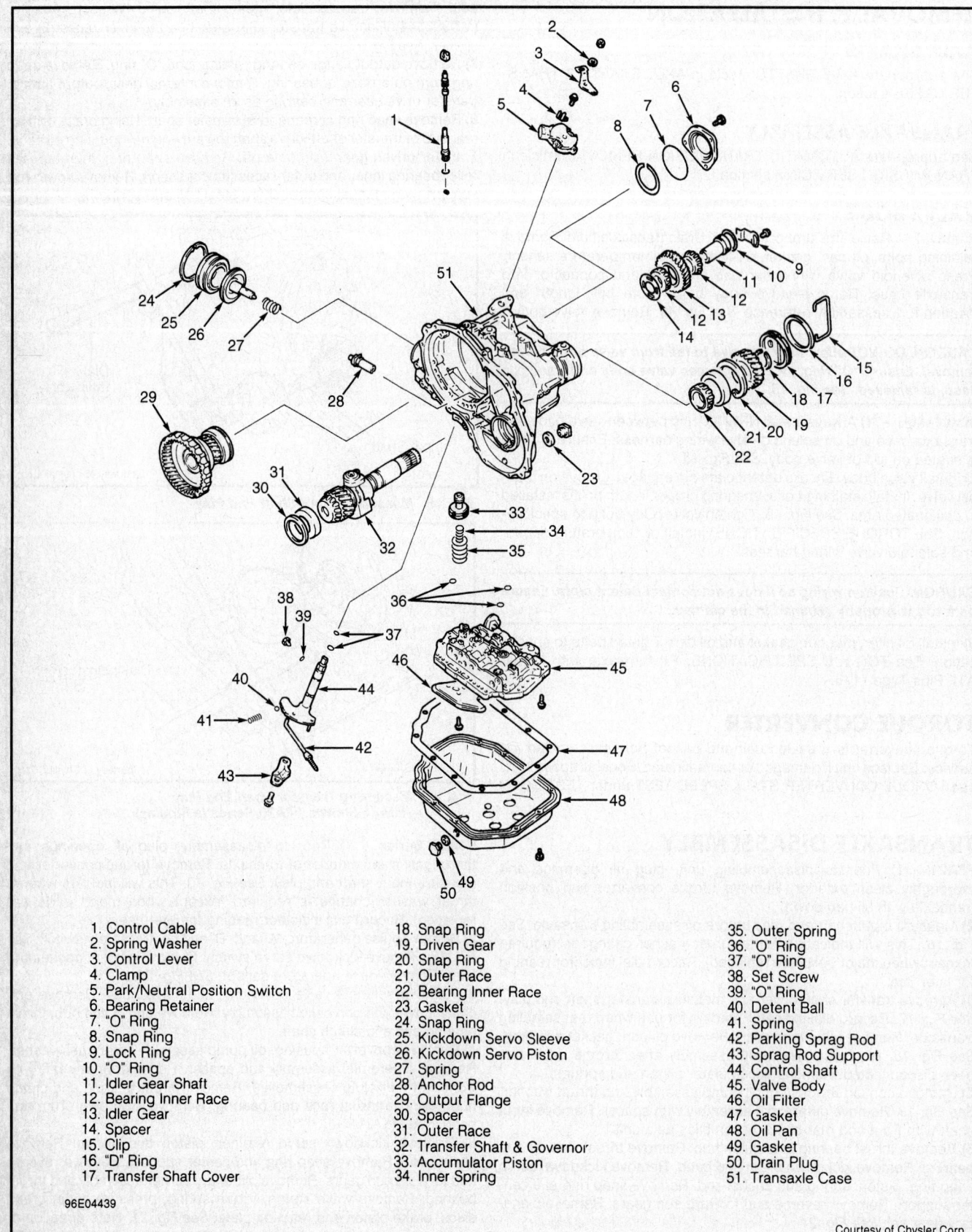

96E04439

1. Control Cable	18. Snap Ring	35. Outer Spring
2. Spring Washer	19. Driven Gear	36. "O" Ring
3. Control Lever	20. Snap Ring	37. "O" Ring
4. Clamp	21. Outer Race	38. Set Screw
5. Park/Neutral Position Switch	22. Bearing Inner Race	39. "O" Ring
6. Bearing Retainer	23. Gasket	40. Detent Ball
7. "O" Ring	24. Snap Ring	41. Spring
8. Snap Ring	25. Kickdown Servo Sleeve	42. Parking Sprag Rod
9. Lock Ring	26. Kickdown Servo Piston	43. Sprag Rod Support
10. "O" Ring	27. Spring	44. Control Shaft
11. Idler Gear Shaft	28. Anchor Rod	45. Valve Body
12. Bearing Inner Race	29. Output Flange	46. Oil Filter
13. Idler Gear	30. Spacer	47. Gasket
14. Spacer	31. Outer Race	48. Oil Pan
15. Clip	32. Transfer Shaft & Governor	49. Gasket
16. "D" Ring	33. Accumulator Piston	50. Drain Plug
17. Transfer Shaft Cover	34. Inner Spring	51. Transaxle Case

Courtesy of Chysler Corp.

Fig. 18: Exploded View Of Transaxle Assembly (F3A21)

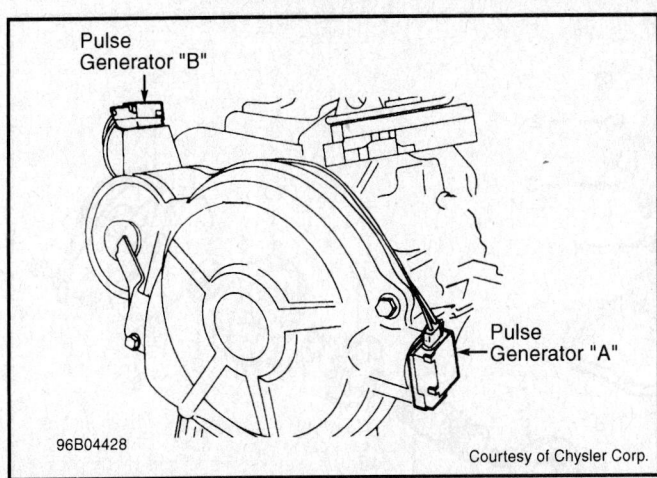

96B04428

Courtesy of Chysler Corp.

Fig. 19: Identifying Pulse Generators

6) Remove idler gear shaft lock bolt and plate. Remove transfer idler shaft with Wrench Adapter (MD998344). Pull out transfer idler shaft and remove transfer idler gear bearing inner races (2) and spacer.

7) Remove snap ring from end bearing. Remove internal gear, output flange, transfer drive gear and bearing as an assembly from case. Remove transfer shaft cover.

8) Remove transfer shaft LEFT-HAND threaded lock nut. Remove transfer shaft with a press. Remove transfer shaft bearing using a bearing splitter. Remove set screw and manual control shaft with sprag rod support.

COMPONENT DISASSEMBLY & REASSEMBLY

OIL PUMP

Disassembly – 1) Remove "O" ring from oil pump housing. Place reassembly reference mark on oil pump housing and reaction shaft support. Remove 5 retaining bolts and reaction shaft support from housing. Place reassembly reference marks on drive and driven gears.

2) Remove oil pump drive and driven gears from housing. *See Fig. 22.* Remove check ball from housing. Remove snap ring and oil seal from oil pump drive gear. Remove 2 seal rings from reaction shaft support.

Inspection – 1) Using a straightedge, check oil pump gear side clearance. Clearance should be .001-.002" (.03-.05 mm). If clearance is not within specification, replace oil pump as an assembly.

2) Check reaction shaft support surface in contact with oil pump gear for evidence of interference and replace oil pump assembly if necessary.

Reassembly – 1) Fit oil seal and snap ring to oil pump drive gear. After immersing drive and driven gears in ATF, install gears in pump housing. Align reference marks made during disassembly.

2) Install check ball in pump housing. *See Fig. 23.* Install 2 seal rings to reaction shaft support. Install NEW "O" ring to pump housing, and lubricate with ATF.

3) Install reaction shaft support to oil pump housing and tighten 5 bolts finger tight. Using guide pin and support band, align reaction shaft support with oil pump housing. *See Fig. 24.* Install oil pump bolts. Tighten bolts to specification. See TORQUE SPECIFICATIONS. Ensure oil pump gears turn freely.

FRONT CLUTCH

Disassembly – 1) Remove snap ring from clutch retainer. Remove clutch reaction plates and clutch discs. Note number of plates and discs removed.

NOTE: If clutch reaction plates and clutch discs are to be reused, DO NOT change the installation order or direction. Soak NEW clutch discs in ATF for 2 hours prior to installation.

2) Compress return spring and remove snap ring, retainer and return spring. Remove piston from retainer and "D" rings from piston and retainer.

Reassembly – 1) Install "D" rings in piston and retainer with round side out. Apply ATF to outside surface of "D" rings and install piston in front clutch retainer by pushing with hand. Install return spring and spring retainer. *See Fig. 25.* Compress return spring and install snap ring.

2) Apply ATF and install clutch reaction plates and clutch discs. Install snap ring. Using a feeler gauge, check clearance between snap ring and clutch reaction plate. For clearance specifications, see TRANSAXLE SPECIFICATIONS table. If clearance is not as specified, replace snap ring. Selective snap rings are available in thicknesses of .063-.118" (1.6-3.0 mm), in increments of .004" (.10 mm).

REAR CLUTCH

Disassembly – 1) Remove snap ring and thrust race. Remove input shaft from rear clutch retainer. Remove snap ring from rear clutch retainer.

2) Remove clutch reaction plate, clutch plates, clutch discs and clutch pressure plate from retainer. Note number of plates and discs removed. *See Fig. 26.* Compress return spring and remove wave spring. Remove spring and piston. Remove "D" rings from piston.

NOTE: If clutch reaction plates and clutch discs are to be reused, DO NOT change the installation order or direction. Soak NEW clutch discs in ATF for 2 hours prior to installation.

Reassembly – 1) Install "D" rings in clutch piston. Apply ATF to outside surfaces of "D" rings and install piston in clutch retainer by pushing with hand.

2) Install return spring on piston. Compress return spring and install wave spring. Install clutch pressure plate, clutch discs, clutch plates and clutch reaction plate in rear clutch retainer. *See Fig. 26.* Apply ATF to plates and NEW discs and install snap ring.

3) Using a feeler gauge, check clearance between snap ring and clutch reaction plate with spring compressed. For clearance specifications, see TRANSAXLE SPECIFICATIONS table. If clearance is not as specified, replace snap ring. Selective snap rings are available in thicknesses of .063-.118" (1.6-3.0 mm), in increments of .004" (.10 mm).

4) Insert input shaft with one oil groove aligned with reference mark or oil hole on rear clutch retainer. *See Fig. 27.* Install thrust race, snap ring and 3 seal rings on input shaft.

END CLUTCH (F4A20 SERIES ONLY)

Disassembly – Remove snap ring, washer and return spring. Remove large snap ring, clutch reaction plate, clutch discs and clutch plates. Note number of plates and discs removed. Remove clutch piston. Use compressed air if necessary. Remove seal ring from clutch retainer and 2 "D" rings from clutch piston.

NOTE: If clutch reaction plates and clutch discs are to be reused, DO NOT change the installation order or direction. Soak NEW clutch discs in ATF for 2 hours prior to installation.

Reassembly – 1) Install "D" rings in piston. Apply ATF to outer surfaces of "D" rings, and install clutch piston in end clutch retainer by pushing by hand.

2) Install return spring, washer and NEW snap ring. *See Fig. 28.* Install clutch plates, clutch discs and reaction plate in end clutch retainer. Install snap ring.

3) Using a feeler gauge, check clearance between snap ring and clutch reaction plate while compressed. For clearance specifications, see TRANSAXLE SPECIFICATIONS table. If clearance is not as specified, replace snap ring. Selective snap rings are available in thicknesses of .041-.081" (1.05-2.05 mm) in increments of .010" (.25 mm).

AUTOMATIC TRANSMISSIONS
Mitsubishi F3A20 & F4A20 Series (Cont.)

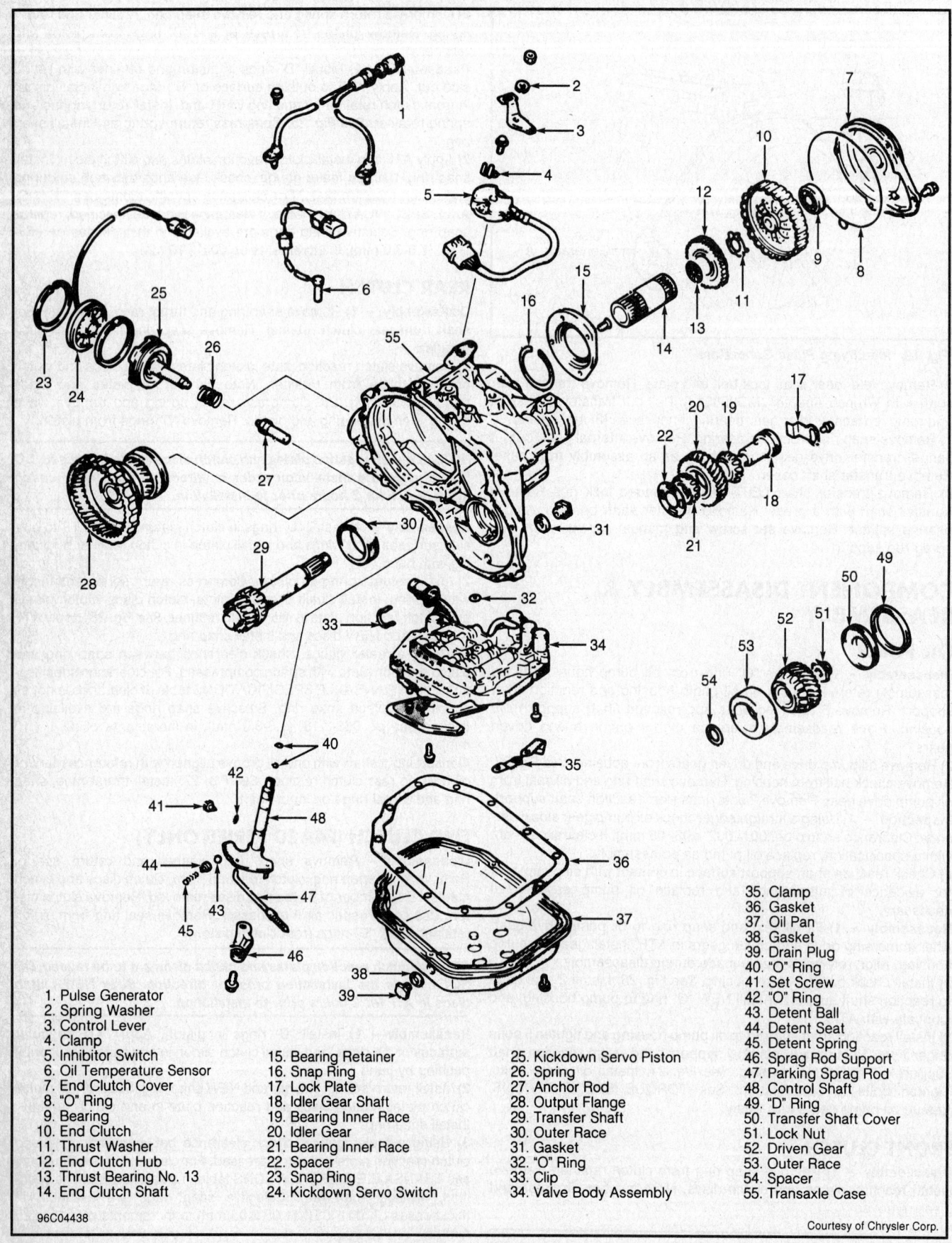

1. Pulse Generator
2. Spring Washer
3. Control Lever
4. Clamp
5. Inhibitor Switch
6. Oil Temperature Sensor
7. End Clutch Cover
8. "O" Ring
9. Bearing
10. End Clutch
11. Thrust Washer
12. End Clutch Hub
13. Thrust Bearing No. 13
14. End Clutch Shaft
15. Bearing Retainer
16. Snap Ring
17. Lock Plate
18. Idler Gear Shaft
19. Bearing Inner Race
20. Idler Gear
21. Bearing Inner Race
22. Spacer
23. Snap Ring
24. Kickdown Servo Switch
25. Kickdown Servo Piston
26. Spring
27. Anchor Rod
28. Output Flange
29. Transfer Shaft
30. Outer Race
31. Gasket
32. "O" Ring
33. Clip
34. Valve Body Assembly
35. Clamp
36. Gasket
37. Oil Pan
38. Gasket
39. Drain Plug
40. "O" Ring
41. Set Screw
42. "O" Ring
43. Detent Ball
44. Detent Seat
45. Detent Spring
46. Sprag Rod Support
47. Parking Sprag Rod
48. Control Shaft
49. "D" Ring
50. Transfer Shaft Cover
51. Lock Nut
52. Driven Gear
53. Outer Race
54. Spacer
55. Transaxle Case

96C04438

Courtesy of Chrysler Corp.

Fig. 20: Exploded View Of Transaxle Assembly (F4A20 Series)

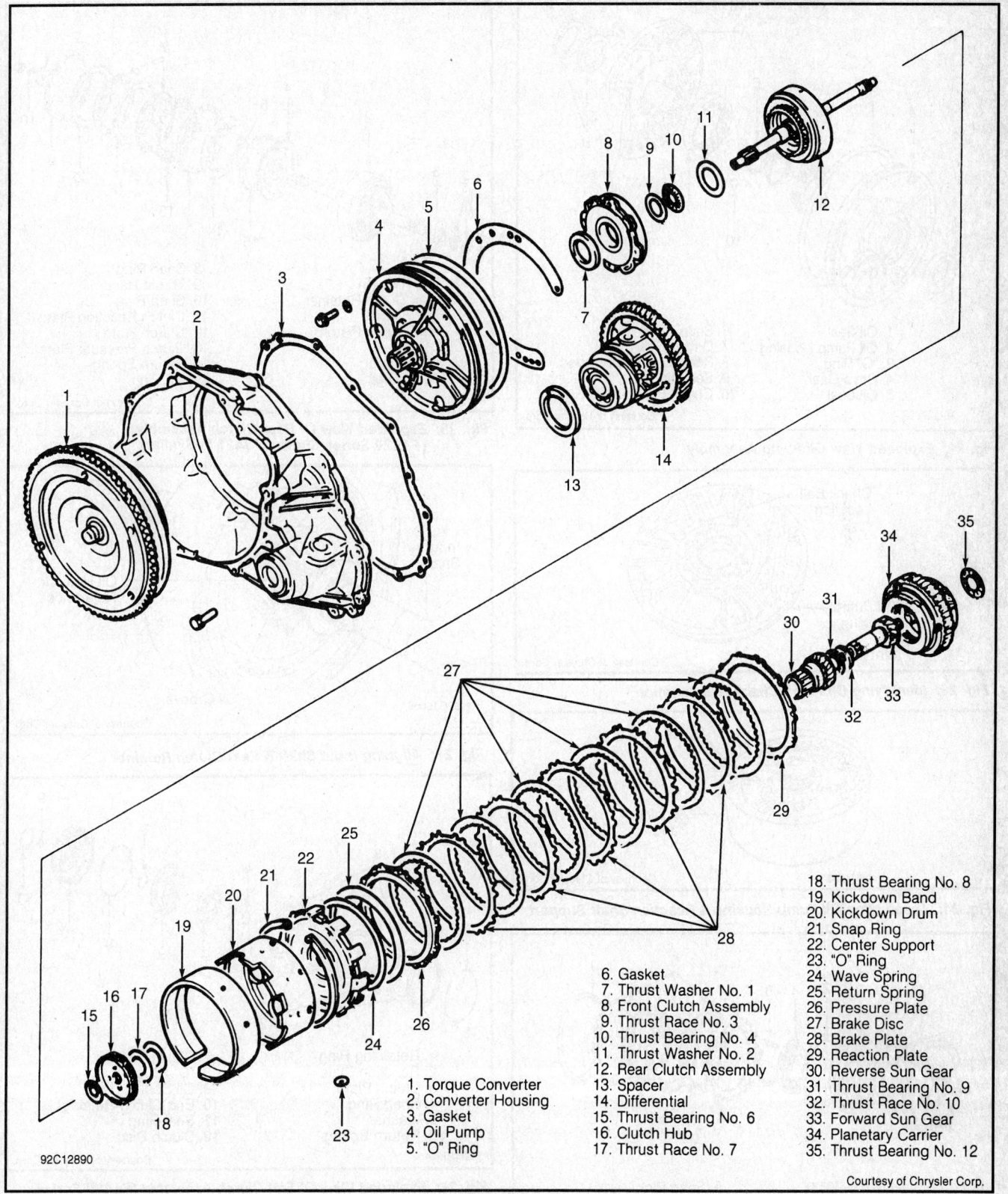

18. Thrust Bearing No. 8
19. Kickdown Band
20. Kickdown Drum
21. Snap Ring
22. Center Support
23. "O" Ring
24. Wave Spring
25. Return Spring
26. Pressure Plate
27. Brake Disc
28. Brake Plate
29. Reaction Plate
30. Reverse Sun Gear
31. Thrust Bearing No. 9
32. Thrust Race No. 10
33. Forward Sun Gear
34. Planetary Carrier
35. Thrust Bearing No. 12

6. Gasket
7. Thrust Washer No. 1
8. Front Clutch Assembly
9. Thrust Race No. 3
10. Thrust Bearing No. 4
11. Thrust Washer No. 2
12. Rear Clutch Assembly
13. Spacer
14. Differential
15. Thrust Bearing No. 6
16. Clutch Hub
17. Thrust Race No. 7

1. Torque Converter
2. Converter Housing
3. Gasket
4. Oil Pump
5. "O" Ring

92C12890

Courtesy of Chrysler Corp.

Fig. 21: Exploded View Of Transaxle Internal Components (F4A20 Series Shown, F3A21 Is Similar)

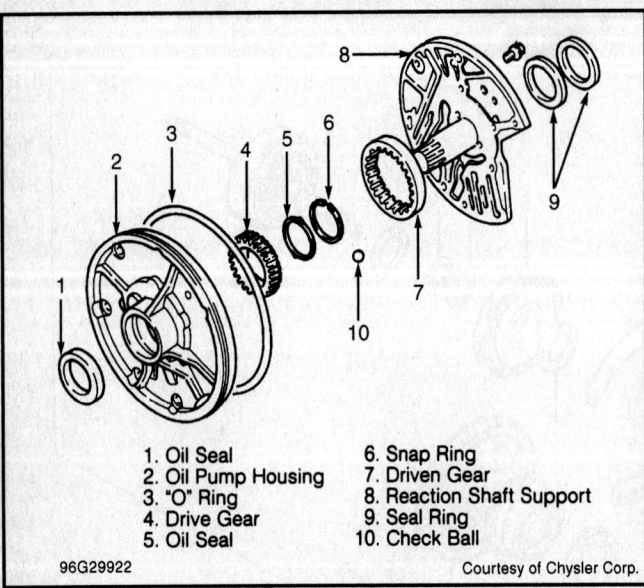

1. Oil Seal
2. Oil Pump Housing
3. "O" Ring
4. Drive Gear
5. Oil Seal
6. Snap Ring
7. Driven Gear
8. Reaction Shaft Support
9. Seal Ring
10. Check Ball

96G29922   Courtesy of Chysler Corp.

Fig. 22: Exploded View Oil Pump Assembly

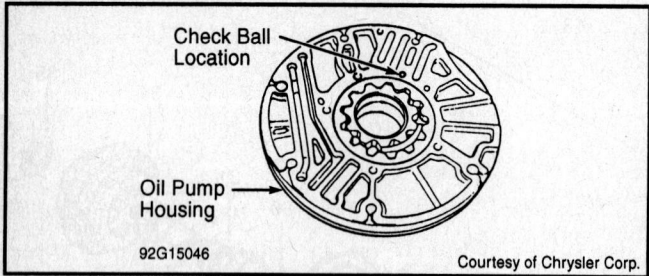

Check Ball Location

Oil Pump Housing

92G15046   Courtesy of Chrysler Corp.

Fig. 23: Identifying Oil Pump Check Ball Location

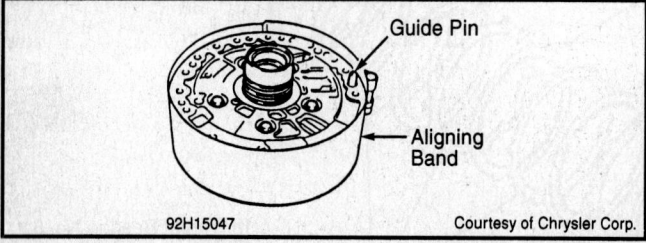

Guide Pin

Aligning Band

92H15047   Courtesy of Chrysler Corp.

Fig. 24: Assembling Oil Pump Housing & Reaction Shaft Support

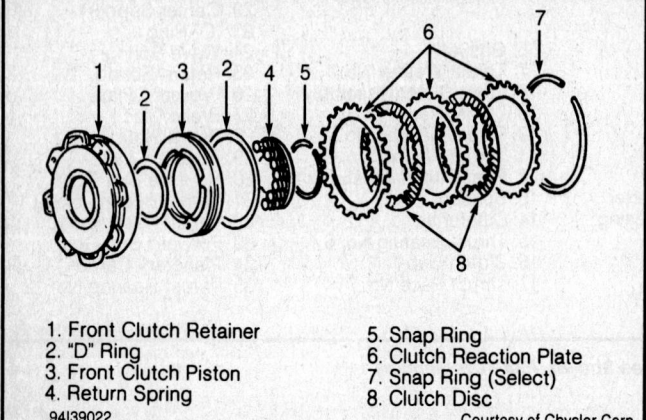

1. Front Clutch Retainer
2. "D" Ring
3. Front Clutch Piston
4. Return Spring
5. Snap Ring
6. Clutch Reaction Plate
7. Snap Ring (Select)
8. Clutch Disc

94I39022   Courtesy of Chysler Corp.

Fig. 25: Exploded View Of Front Clutch Assembly

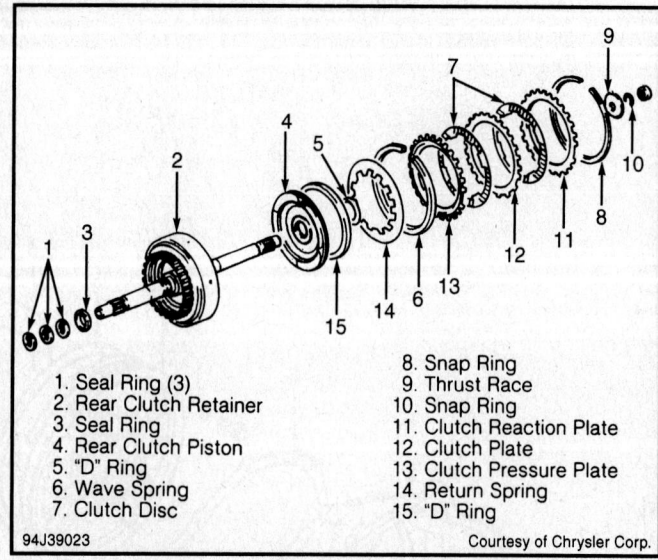

1. Seal Ring (3)
2. Rear Clutch Retainer
3. Seal Ring
4. Rear Clutch Piston
5. "D" Ring
6. Wave Spring
7. Clutch Disc
8. Snap Ring
9. Thrust Race
10. Snap Ring
11. Clutch Reaction Plate
12. Clutch Plate
13. Clutch Pressure Plate
14. Return Spring
15. "D" Ring

94J39023   Courtesy of Chrysler Corp.

Fig. 26: Exploded View Of Rear Clutch Assembly (F4A20 Series Shown, F3A21 Is Similar)

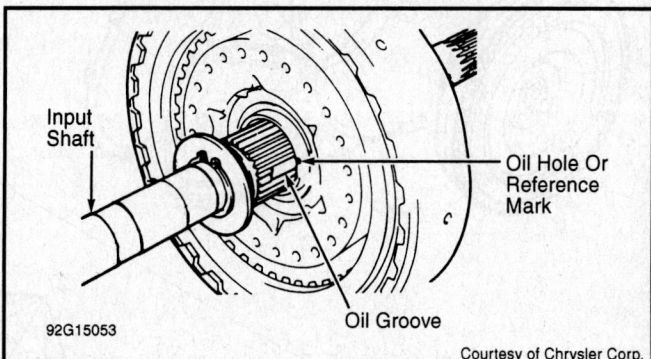

Input Shaft

Oil Hole Or Reference Mark

Oil Groove

92G15053   Courtesy of Chrysler Corp.

Fig. 27: Aligning Input Shaft & Rear Clutch Retainer

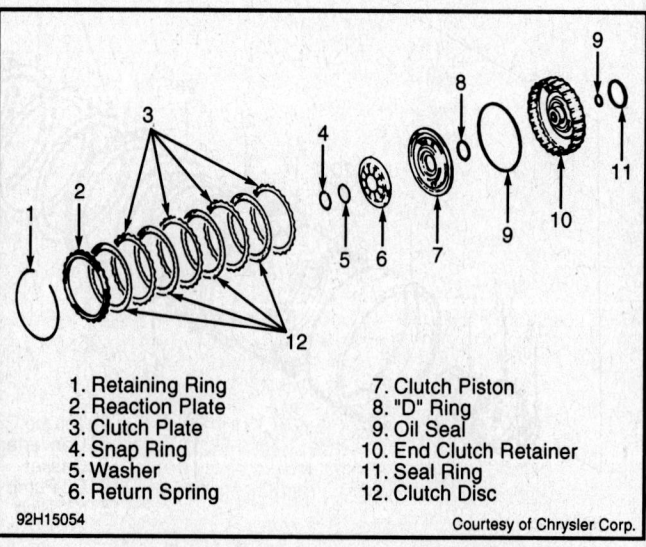

1. Retaining Ring
2. Reaction Plate
3. Clutch Plate
4. Snap Ring
5. Washer
6. Return Spring
7. Clutch Piston
8. "D" Ring
9. Oil Seal
10. End Clutch Retainer
11. Seal Ring
12. Clutch Disc

92H15054   Courtesy of Chrysler Corp.

Fig. 28: Exploded View Of End Clutch Assembly (F4A20 Series)

LOW & REVERSE BRAKE

Disassembly & Reassembly – Remove piston using compressed air. Remove "D" ring from piston. Fit NEW "D" ring in piston and apply ATF. Press piston in center support by hand.

PLANETARY GEAR SET

Disassembly – 1) Remove 3 bolts retaining one-way clutch outer race assembly. Remove one-way clutch outer race assembly and one-way clutch end plate. Remove short pinion shaft, spacer bushing and front thrust washers. *See Fig. 29.*

2) Remove only one short pinion using care not to lose 17 needle rollers in short pinion. Remove thrust bearing from pinion carrier. Remove one-way clutch by pushing outer race out using fingers.

Reassembly – 1) Install NEW thrust bearing in pinion carrier and ensure correct fit. Apply generous amount of petroleum jelly to inside diameter of short pinion and install 17 rollers.

2) Align holes in front and rear thrusts with shaft hole of carrier. Install short pinion, spacer bushing and 2 front thrust washers and align holes. Insert pinion shaft. Install end plate in one-way clutch outer race. Push one-way clutch in outer race. Ensure one-way clutch is installed in proper direction. *See Fig. 30.*

3) Apply petroleum jelly and install one-way clutch end plate. Install one-way clutch assembly to carrier and align bolt holes. Tighten bolts to specification. See TORQUE SPECIFICATIONS.

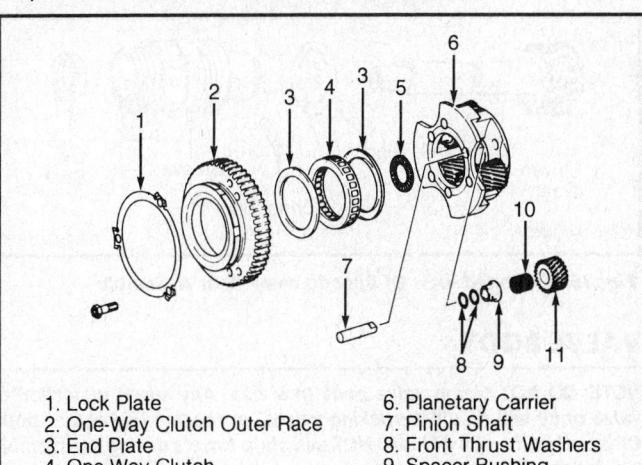

1. Lock Plate	6. Planetary Carrier
2. One-Way Clutch Outer Race	7. Pinion Shaft
3. End Plate	8. Front Thrust Washers
4. One-Way Clutch	9. Spacer Bushing
5. Thrust Bearing	10. Short Pinion
	11. Roller

94A39024　　　　　　　　　　Courtesy of Chrysler Corp.

Fig. 29: Exploded View Of Planetary Gear Set

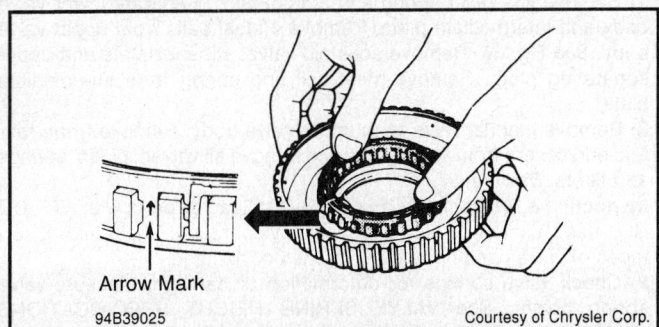

94B39025　　　　　　　　　　Courtesy of Chrysler Corp.

Fig. 30: Installing One-Way Clutch Into Outer Race

INTERNAL GEAR & TRANSFER DRIVE GEAR SET

Disassembly – Remove snap ring from rear end of output flange. Using a puller, remove bearings (2) and transfer drive gear from output flange. Remove large snap ring, and separate internal gear from output flange.

NOTE: If replacing output flange or transfer drive gear, service as a set only.

Reassembly – Press transfer drive gear and bearings on output flange. Ensure transfer drive gear is installed in proper direction. *See Fig. 31.* Install output flange selective snap ring. Use thickest one that can be installed in groove. Standard value for snap ring is 0-.0024" (0-.06 mm).

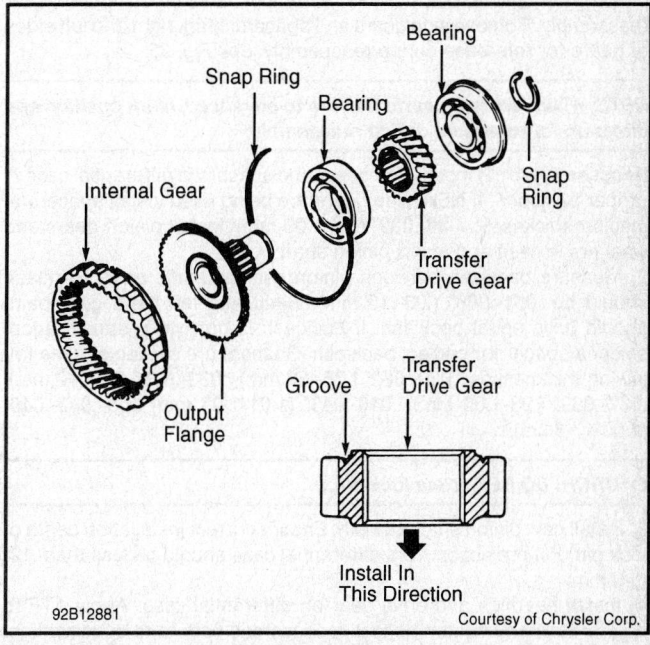

92B12881　　　　　　　　　　Courtesy of Chrysler Corp.

Fig. 31: Exploded View Of Internal & Transfer Gear

TRANSFER SHAFT & GOVERNOR ASSEMBLY (F3A21)

Disassembly – Remove seal rings from transfer shaft. Loosen governor set screw and remove governor assembly. Remove snap ring and disassemble governor. *See Fig. 32.* Remove governor filter. Clean or replace as necessary. Press bearing off transfer shaft.

Reassembly – 1) Install bearing on transfer shaft. Install governor valve, spring, spring retainer and governor weight in governor body, then install snap ring.

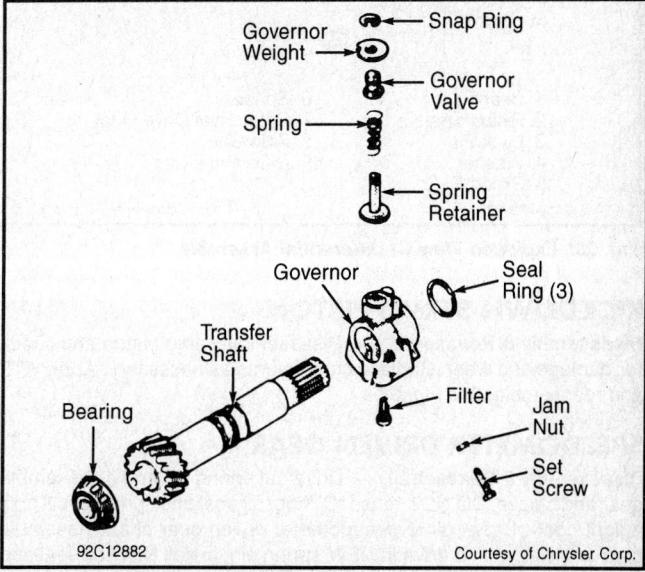

92C12882　　　　　　　　　　Courtesy of Chrysler Corp.

Fig. 32: Exploded View Of Transfer Shaft & Governor (F3A21)

2) Install governor filter. Assemble governor assembly with transfer shaft. Tighten set screw and jam nut to specification. See TORQUE SPECIFICATIONS.

DIFFERENTIAL

Disassembly – Remove drive gear and bolts from differential case. Inspect bearings for wear or damage. Using puller, remove bearings (if necessary). Drive out lock pin with punch. Remove pinion shaft, pinion gears and washers. Make reference marks on components for reassembly. Remove side gears and spacers. Mark right and left sides of gears for reference during reassembly. *See Fig. 33.*

NOTE: When removing parts that are to be reused, mark position and direction for reference during reassembly.

Reassembly – **1)** Install side gears and spacers in differential case in proper positions. If NEW side gears are being used install spacers of medium thickness, .036-.039" (.93-1.00 mm). Install pinion gears and washers in case and insert pinion shaft.
2) Measure backlash between pinion gear and side gear. Backlash should be .001-.006" (.03-.15 mm). Right and left hand gear pairs should have equal backlash. If backlash is not within specification, select a spacer for correct backlash. Spacers are available in the following thicknesses: .030-.032" (.75-.82 mm), .033-.036" (.83-.92 mm), .037-.039" (.93-1.00 mm), .040-.043" (1.01-1.08 mm) and .043-.046" (1.09-1.16mm).

CAUTION: DO NOT reuse lock pin.

3) Install new pinion shaft lock pin. Ensure correct installation depth of lock pin. Pin projection from differential case should be less than .12" (3.0 mm).
4) Install bearings and drive gear on differential case. Apply ATF to bolt threads and tighten bolts in a crisscross pattern to specification. See TORQUE SPECIFICATIONS.

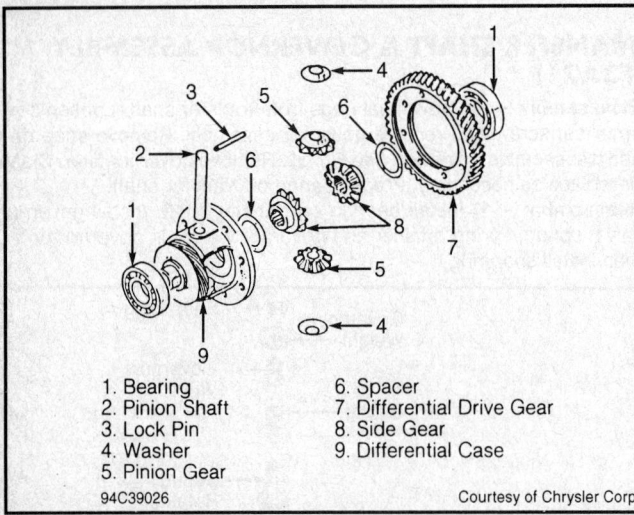

1. Bearing
2. Pinion Shaft
3. Lock Pin
4. Washer
5. Pinion Gear
6. Spacer
7. Differential Drive Gear
8. Side Gear
9. Differential Case

94C39026   Courtesy of Chrysler Corp.

Fig. 33: Exploded View Of Differential Assembly

KICKDOWN SERVO PISTON

Disassembly & Reassembly – Disassemble servo piston and check for damage and wear. Replace components as necessary. Apply ATF and reassemble. *See Fig. 34.*

SPEEDOMETER DRIVEN GEAR

Disassembly & Reassembly – Drive out spring pin and disassemble gear and sleeve. DO NOT reuse "O" ring, oil seal and spring pin. Apply a light coat of gear oil to speedometer driven gear shaft. Assemble gear and sleeve and drive in NEW spring pin. Install NEW oil seal and "O" ring. *See Fig. 35.*

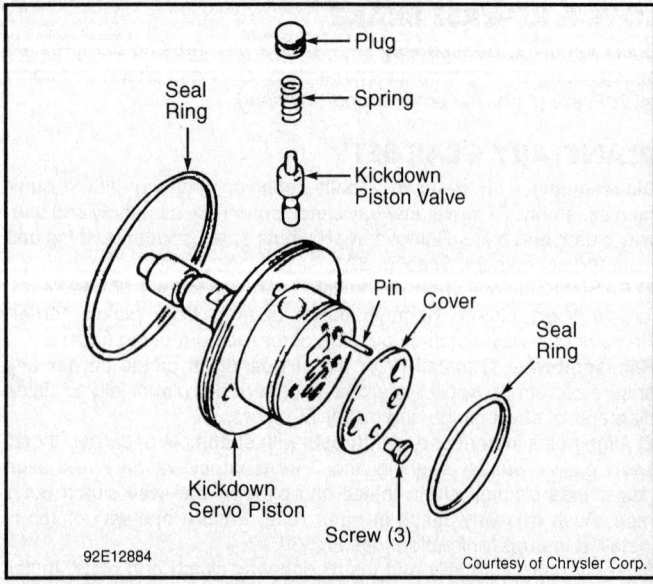

92E12884   Courtesy of Chrysler Corp.

Fig. 34: Exploded View Of Kickdown Servo Piston Assembly (F3A21 Is Shown, F4A20 Series Similar)

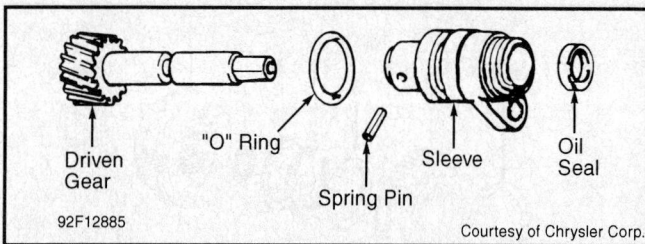

92F12885   Courtesy of Chrysler Corp.

Fig. 35: Exploded View Of Speedometer Gear Assembly

VALVE BODY

NOTE: DO NOT clamp valve body in a vise. Any slight distortion of valve body will result in sticking valves, excessive leakage or both. Clean all parts with ATF. DO NOT use shop towels during reassembly operation.

Disassembly (F3A21) – **1)** Remove throttle cam assembly from valve body. Remove 13 valve body bolts. Remove lower valve body and lower separator plate.
2) Remove line relief spring and 3 steel balls. Separate lower valve body and intermediate plate. Remove 4 steel balls from upper valve body. *See Fig. 36.* Remove solenoid valve, stiffener plate and upper separating plate. Remove steel ball and spring from intermediate plate.
3) Remove manual valve from upper valve body. Remove front, rear and end covers from valve body, and remove all valves, plugs, springs and filters. *See Fig. 37.*

Inspection & Reassembly (F3A21) – **1)** Clean all parts with ATF. DO NOT use shop towels during reassembly operation. Check sliding surfaces of valves and body for scratches or damage.
2) Check valve springs for deformation or damage. Measure valve spring height. See VALVE SPRING HEIGHT SPECIFICATIONS (F3A21) table. Replace as necessary. Lubricate with ATF and install valves, springs and plugs. *See Fig. 37.*
3) Tighten all valve body bolts to specification. See TORQUE SPECIFICATIONS. When assembling upper and lower bodies use guide pins at locations shown in *Fig. 36.* Ensure steel balls are properly positioned.

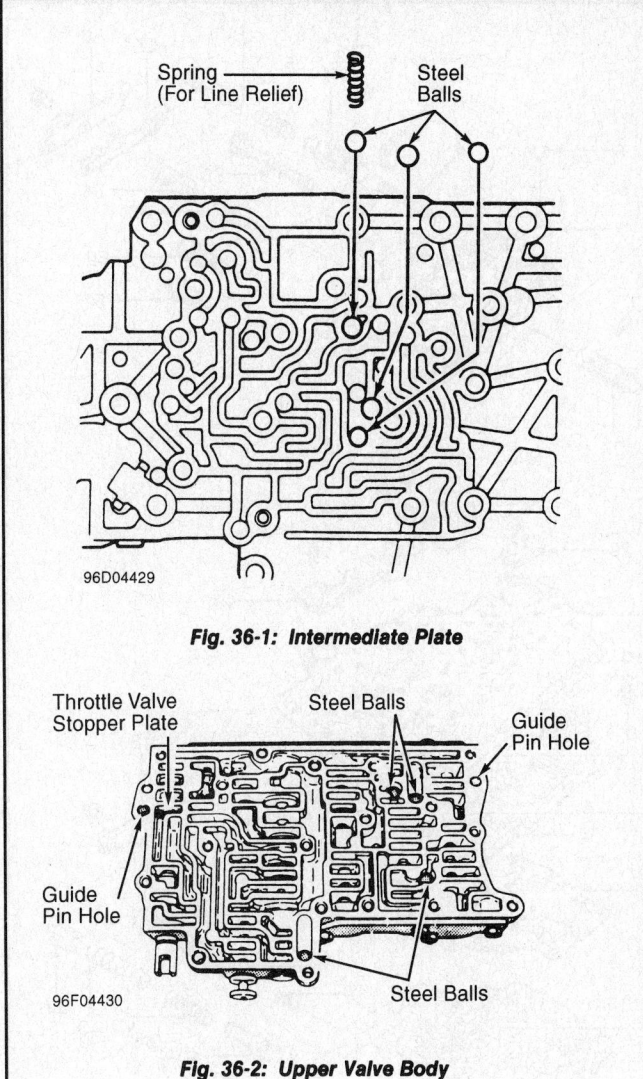

Fig. 36-1: Intermediate Plate

Fig. 36-2: Upper Valve Body

Courtesy of Chrysler Corp.

Fig. 36: Locating Steel Balls (F3A21)

Disassembly (F4A20 Series) – **1)** Remove solenoid valves and manual valve. Remove valve stopper and clamp. Remove 13 bolts and remove lower valve body.

2) Remove separator plate from intermediate plate. Remove relief spring, 2 steel balls and oil filter from intermediate plate. *See Fig. 39.* Remove 8 bolts, and remove intermediate plate and upper separating plate.

3) Remove 3 steel balls, Teflon ball and 2 stopper plates from upper valve body. *See Fig. 39.* Remove valves, springs and plugs as shown in *Fig. 38.*

Inspection & Reassembly (F4A20 Series) – **1)** Clean all parts with ATF. DO NOT use shop towels during reassembly operation. Check sliding surfaces of oil valves and valve body for scratches or damage. Check valve springs for deformation or damage.

2) Measure valve spring height. See VALVE SPRING HEIGHT SPECIFICATIONS (F4A20 SERIES) table. Replace as necessary. Lubricate with ATF and install valves, springs and plugs. *See Fig. 38.*

VALVE SPRING HEIGHT SPECIFICATIONS (F3A21)

Application	In. (mm)
Kickdown Valve	1.029 (26.14)
Line Relief	.681 (17.30)
Low Relief	.491 (12.46)
N-D Accumulator	2.044 (51.92)
N-D Accumulator Plug	1.472 (37.39)
Range Control Valve	.923 (23.44)
Regulator Valve	2.024 (51.40)
Throttle Valve	1.262 (32.05)
Torque Converter Control Valve	1.039 (26.40)
1-2 Shift Valve	1.232 (31.30)
2-3 Control Valve	2.000 (50.80)
2-3 Shift Valve	.933 (23.71)

VALVE SPRING HEIGHT SPECIFICATIONS (F4A20 SERIES)

Application	In. (mm)
End Clutch Valve	.961 (24.40)
N-R Control Valve	1.264 (32.10)
Pressure Control Valve	.839 (21.30)
Shift Control Valve	1.055 (26.80)
Rear Clutch Exhaust Valve	1.079 (27.41)
Reducing Valve	1.315 (33.40)
Regulator Valve	2.047 (52.00)
Relief Valve	.681 (17.30)
Torque Converter Clutch Control Valve	
F4A22	.618 (15.70)
F4A23	.559 (14.20)
Torque Converter Control Valve	.890 (22.60)
1-2 Shift Valve	1.047 (26.60)
2-3 Shift Valve	1.083 (27.50)

TRANSAXLE REASSEMBLY

NOTE: Lubricate all components with ATF. Apply petroleum jelly on "O" rings and seal rings. Use petroleum jelly to hold thrust bearings, thrust races and thrust washers in position. Ensure thrust bearings, thrust races and thrust washers are installed in original location and proper direction. See Fig. 48.

F3A21 – **1)** Prior to reassembly, measure low-reverse brake clearance and select appropriate pressure plate to obtain specified clearance.

2) Install brake reaction plate, brake plates and brake discs in transaxle case. *See Fig. 21.* Install a pressure plate with adequate size. Install return spring. Ensure return spring is installed in proper direction.

3) Apply petroleum jelly to wave spring and attach it to the center support. Install center support and snap ring in case. Check low-reverse brake clearance by mounting a dial indicator on rear of transaxle case. *See Fig. 40.* Install dial indicator through transfer idler shaft hole so its feeler is held perpendicular to brake reaction plate.

4) Using a hand pump, feed air into low-reverse brake and read dial indicator deflection. *See Fig. 40.* Select a pressure plate to obtain specified clearance. Clearance for F3A20 series transaxle is .032-.039" (.80-1.00 mm). Remove all previously installed components.

5) Place transaxle case on work bench with valve body mounting surface facing upward. Insert output flange in case. *See Fig. 18.* Secure output flange bearing with snap ring from outside of transaxle case. Install transfer idler gear spacer in case.

6) Install transfer idler gear and shaft. Tighten idler shaft with Wrench Adapter (MD998344). *See Fig. 42.* Insert Socket (MD998343) into output flange. *See Fig. 43.* Using INCH lb. torque wrench, measure output flange turning torque. Turning torque should be .6 ft. lbs. (.8 N.m). Adjust turning torque by tightening or loosening transfer idler gear shaft.

7) Once preload adjustment is completed, install idler shaft lock plate. Install bearing retainer. Insert transfer shaft. Mount transfer shaft Alignment Tool (MD998319). *See Fig. 44.*

8) Using driver, install bearing on transfer shaft. Using driver, install transfer shaft outer race in case. Install transfer shaft driven gear. Install snap ring on end of transfer shaft.

AUTOMATIC TRANSMISSIONS
Mitsubishi F3A20 & F4A20 Series (Cont.)

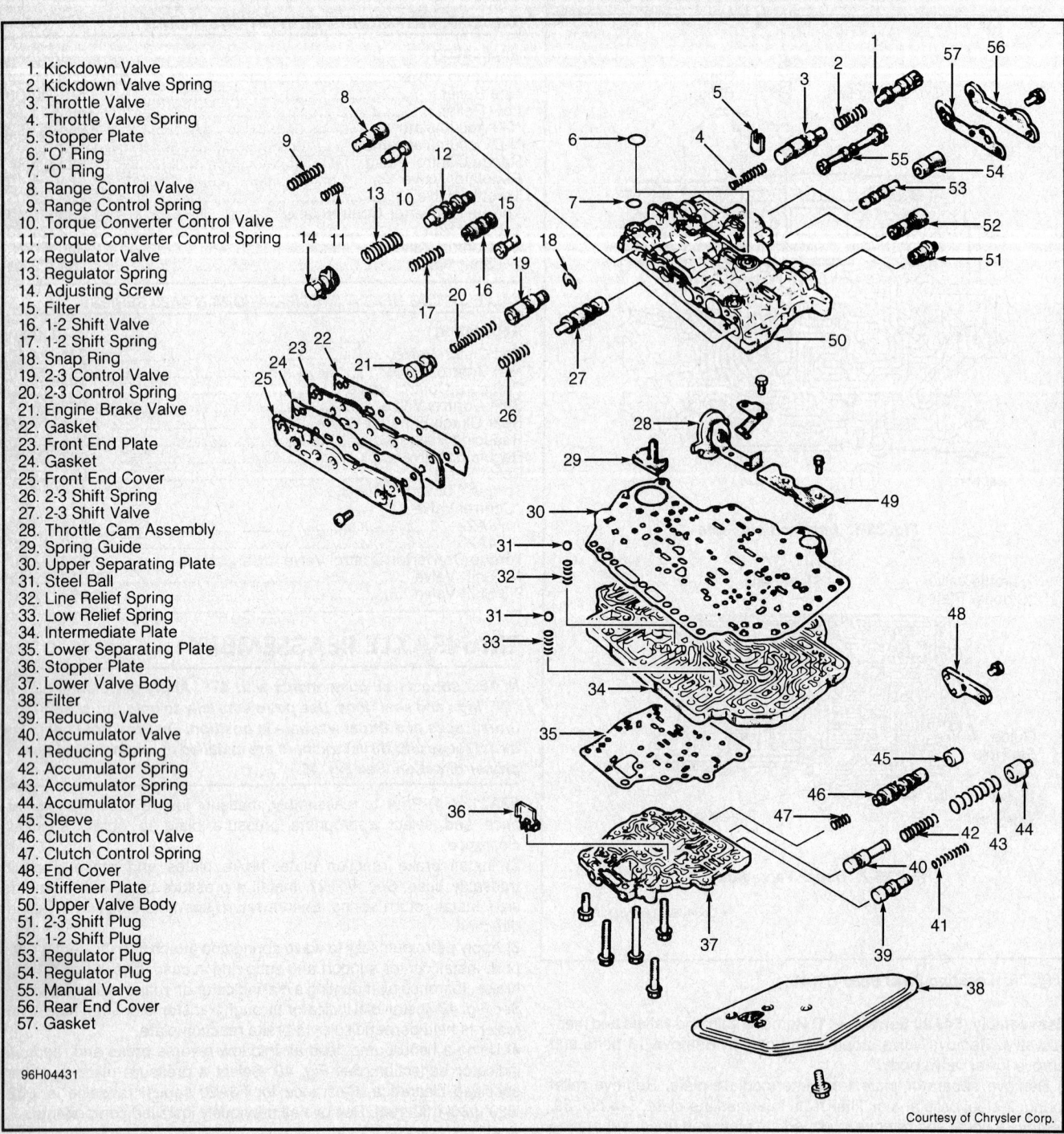

1. Kickdown Valve
2. Kickdown Valve Spring
3. Throttle Valve
4. Throttle Valve Spring
5. Stopper Plate
6. "O" Ring
7. "O" Ring
8. Range Control Valve
9. Range Control Spring
10. Torque Converter Control Valve
11. Torque Converter Control Spring
12. Regulator Valve
13. Regulator Spring
14. Adjusting Screw
15. Filter
16. 1-2 Shift Valve
17. 1-2 Shift Spring
18. Snap Ring
19. 2-3 Control Valve
20. 2-3 Control Spring
21. Engine Brake Valve
22. Gasket
23. Front End Plate
24. Gasket
25. Front End Cover
26. 2-3 Shift Spring
27. 2-3 Shift Valve
28. Throttle Cam Assembly
29. Spring Guide
30. Upper Separating Plate
31. Steel Ball
32. Line Relief Spring
33. Low Relief Spring
34. Intermediate Plate
35. Lower Separating Plate
36. Stopper Plate
37. Lower Valve Body
38. Filter
39. Reducing Valve
40. Accumulator Valve
41. Reducing Spring
42. Accumulator Spring
43. Accumulator Spring
44. Accumulator Plug
45. Sleeve
46. Clutch Control Valve
47. Clutch Control Spring
48. End Cover
49. Stiffener Plate
50. Upper Valve Body
51. 2-3 Shift Plug
52. 1-2 Shift Plug
53. Regulator Plug
54. Regulator Plug
55. Manual Valve
56. Rear End Cover
57. Gasket

96H04431

Courtesy of Chrysler Corp.

Fig. 37: Exploded View Of Valve Body Assembly (F3A21)

9) Place thrust race No. 13 on output flange. Install planetary carrier with thrust bearing No. 12 in place, in transaxle case. Assemble reverse sun gear and forward sun gear and install in planetary carrier. *See Fig. 45.*

10) Install low-reverse brake assembly with pressure plate selected previously. Install return spring. Apply petroleum jelly to wave spring and attach it to center support.

11) Install 2 NEW "O" rings to hydraulic holes of center support. *See Fig. 46.* Apply ATF to "O" rings.

12) Install center support ensuring 2 NEW "O" rings are properly positioned on center support. Ensure wave spring does not shift out of position. Install center support snap ring.

13) Install kickdown band anchor rod. Install kickdown servo assembly with new sealing rings. Install NEW "O" ring on inner edge of servo sleeve. Install NEW "D" ring on outer edge of servo sleeve. Install sleeve in transaxle case with snap ring. Install kickdown band and attach ends to anchor rod and servo piston rod.

14) Install kickdown drum and position band on drum. Apply petroleum jelly to thrust bearing No. 8 and attach it to kickdown drum. Apply petroleum jelly to thrust race No. 7 and attach it to rear clutch hub.

15) Install rear clutch hub to sun gear splines and attach thrust bearing No. 6 to outer side of clutch hub. Install thrust washer No. 2 and thrust bearing No. 4 on rear clutch assembly. Assemble front and rear clutch assemblies and install in transaxle case. Install differential assembly.

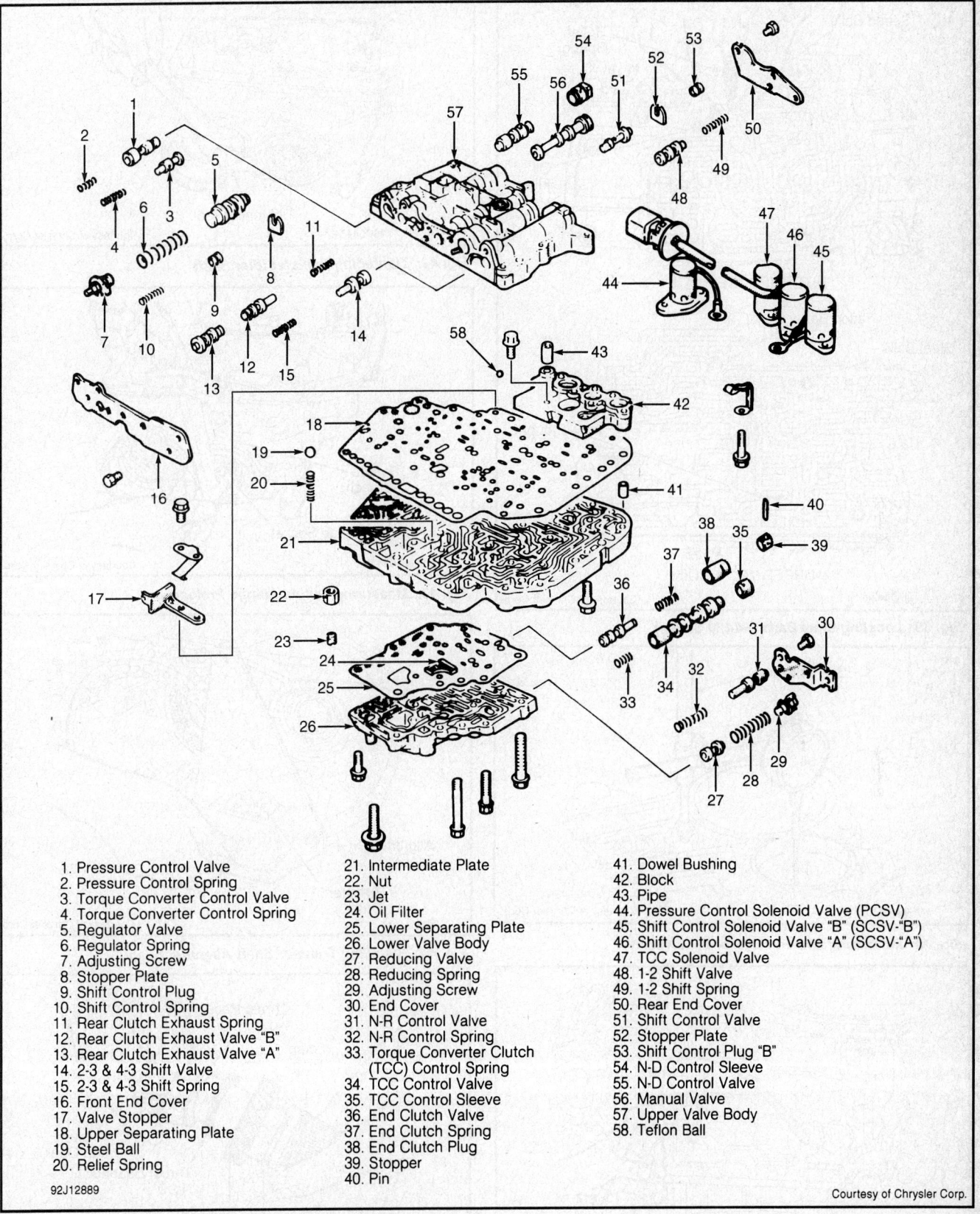

Courtesy of Chrysler Corp.

1. Pressure Control Valve
2. Pressure Control Spring
3. Torque Converter Control Valve
4. Torque Converter Control Spring
5. Regulator Valve
6. Regulator Spring
7. Adjusting Screw
8. Stopper Plate
9. Shift Control Plug
10. Shift Control Spring
11. Rear Clutch Exhaust Spring
12. Rear Clutch Exhaust Valve "B"
13. Rear Clutch Exhaust Valve "A"
14. 2-3 & 4-3 Shift Valve
15. 2-3 & 4-3 Shift Spring
16. Front End Cover
17. Valve Stopper
18. Upper Separating Plate
19. Steel Ball
20. Relief Spring

21. Intermediate Plate
22. Nut
23. Jet
24. Oil Filter
25. Lower Separating Plate
26. Lower Valve Body
27. Reducing Valve
28. Reducing Spring
29. Adjusting Screw
30. End Cover
31. N-R Control Valve
32. N-R Control Spring
33. Torque Converter Clutch (TCC) Control Spring
34. TCC Control Valve
35. TCC Control Sleeve
36. End Clutch Valve
37. End Clutch Spring
38. End Clutch Plug
39. Stopper
40. Pin

41. Dowel Bushing
42. Block
43. Pipe
44. Pressure Control Solenoid Valve (PCSV)
45. Shift Control Solenoid Valve "B" (SCSV-"B")
46. Shift Control Solenoid Valve "A" (SCSV-"A")
47. TCC Solenoid Valve
48. 1-2 Shift Valve
49. 1-2 Shift Spring
50. Rear End Cover
51. Shift Control Valve
52. Stopper Plate
53. Shift Control Plug "B"
54. N-D Control Sleeve
55. N-D Control Valve
56. Manual Valve
57. Upper Valve Body
58. Teflon Ball

92J12889

Fig. 38: Exploded View Of Valve Body Assembly (F4A20 Series)

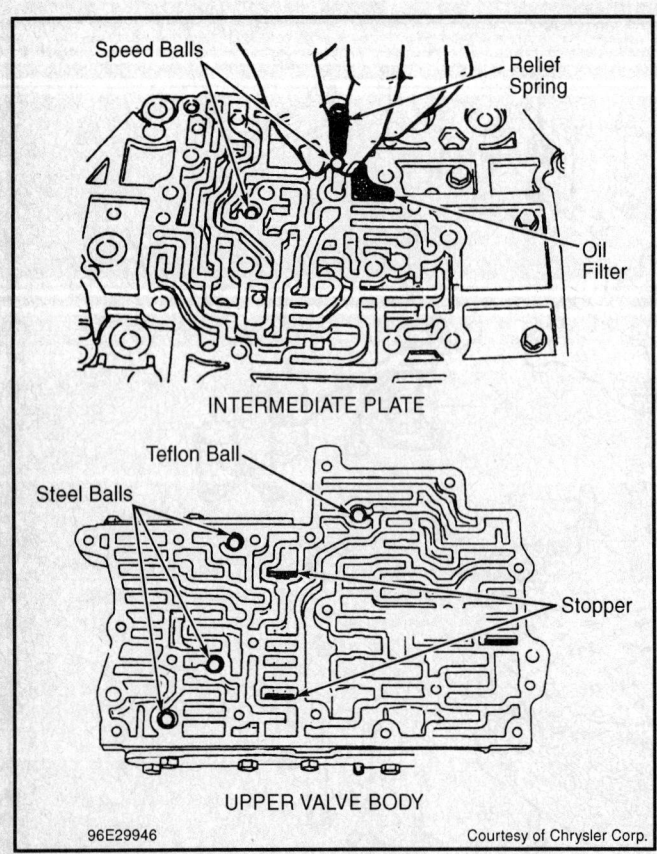

INTERMEDIATE PLATE

UPPER VALVE BODY

96E29946
Courtesy of Chrysler Corp.

Fig. 39: Locating Steel Balls (F4A20 Series)

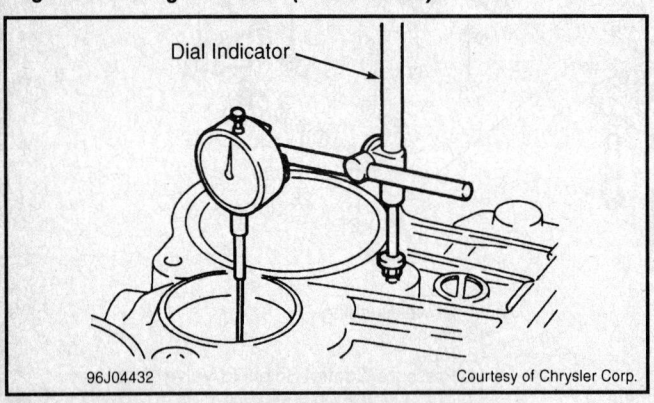

96J04432
Courtesy of Chrysler Corp.

Fig. 40: Measuring Low-Reverse Brake Clearance

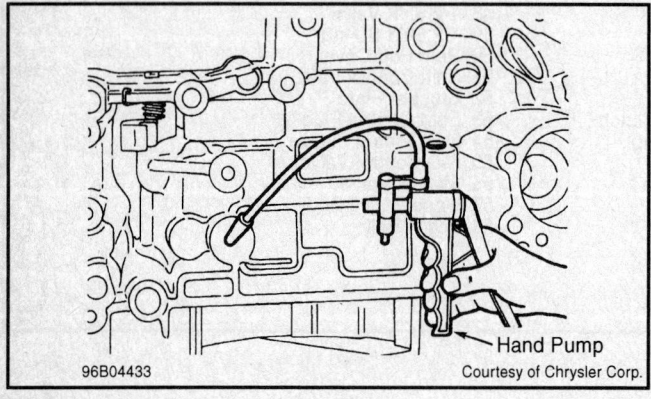

96B04433
Courtesy of Chrysler Corp.

Fig. 41: Actuating Low-Reverse Brake

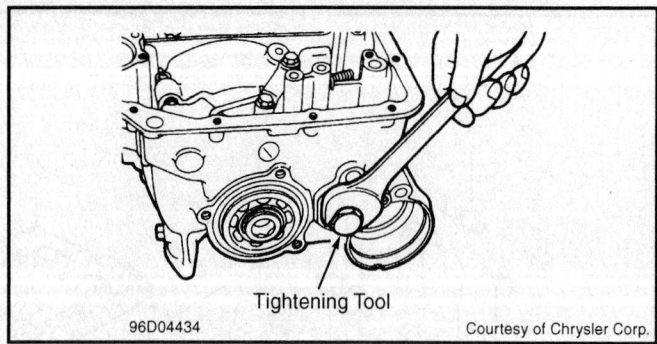

96D04434
Courtesy of Chrysler Corp.

Fig. 42: Tightening Transfer Idler Shaft

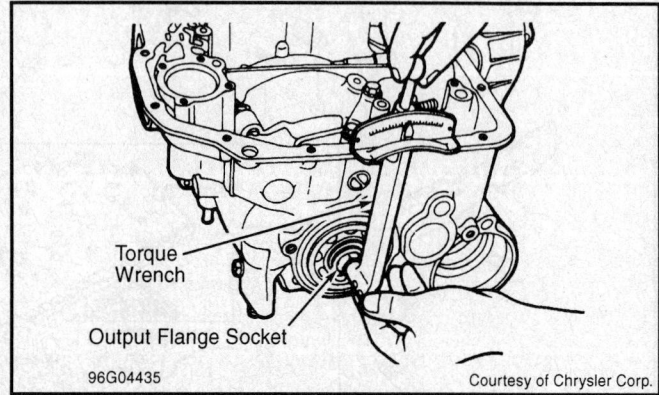

96G04435
Courtesy of Chrysler Corp.

Fig. 43: Measuring Output Flange Preload

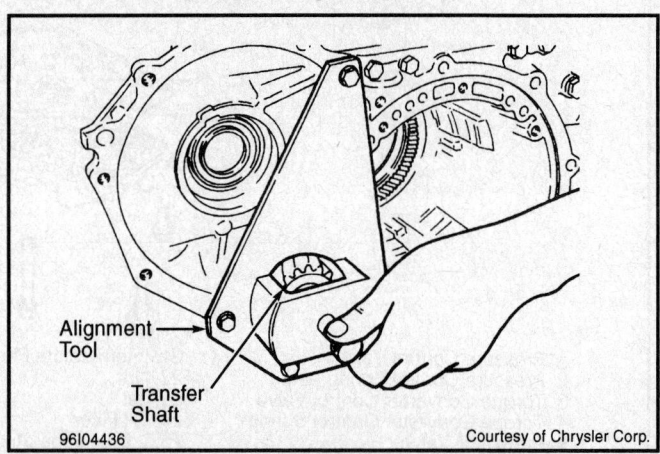

96I04436
Courtesy of Chrysler Corp.

Fig. 44: Installing Transfer Shaft Alignment Tool

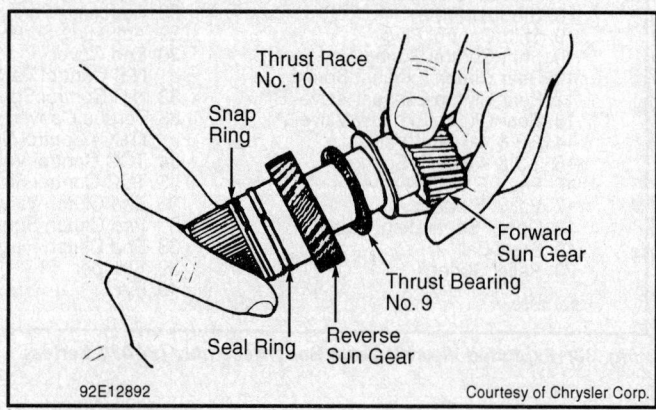

92E12892
Courtesy of Chrysler Corp.

Fig. 45: Assembling Sun Gears

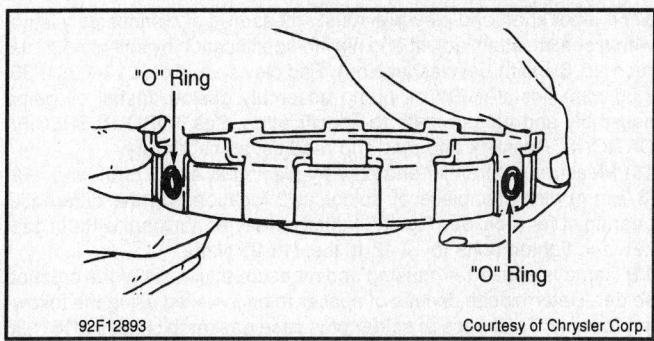

Fig. 46: Positioning "O" Rings On Center Support

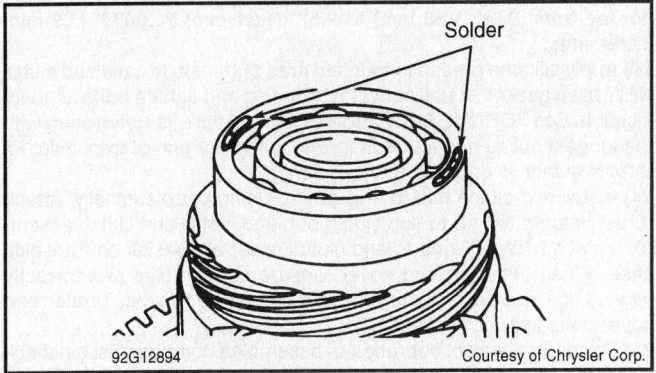

Fig. 47: Locating Solder On Differential Bearing

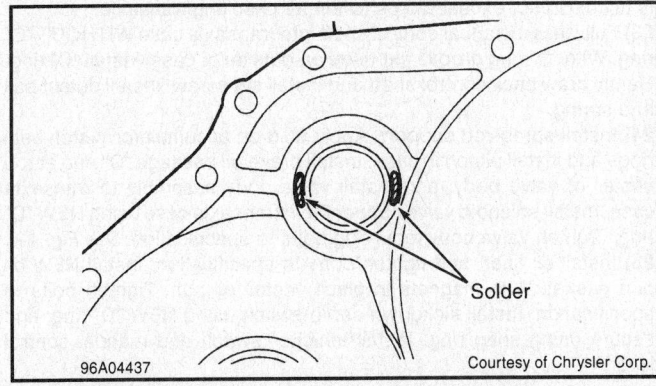

Fig. 48: Locating Solder On Transfer Shaft Race Bore

16) If input shaft end play previously measured at disassembly is not within specification, adjust end play to specification by selecting thrust race No. 3 and thrust washer No. 1. End play should be .012-.039" (.30-1.00 mm). Install NEW oil pump assembly gasket. Install oil pump assembly and tighten bolts to specification. See TORQUE SPECIFICATIONS. Recheck end play and readjust as necessary. See Fig. 16.

17) Place a .40" (10 mm) long, .12" (3 mm) diameter piece of solder at 2 locations on the differential bearing outer race. See Fig. 47. Place a .40" (10 mm) long, .12" (3 mm) diameter piece of solder at 2 locations on converter housing at transfer shaft outer race location. Install bearing race in converter housing. See Fig. 48.

18) Install converter housing, without gasket, and tighten bolts to 14-17 ft. lbs. (19-23 N.m). Remove converter housing and measure thickness of crushed solder. Determine thickness of differential spacer to be installed using the following formula:

Solder thickness plus case gasket thickness .015" (.38 mm), minus end play at differential. End play should be 0-.006" (0-.15 mm).

19) Determine thickness of transfer shaft spacer to be installed using the following formula:

Solder thickness plus case gasket thickness .015" (.38 mm), plus preload at transfer shaft bearing. Preload should be .004-.006" (.10-.15 mm).

20) Install appropriate spacer in converter housing for transfer shaft bearing preload. Spacers are available in thicknesses from .032" (.82 mm) to .067" (1.69 mm) in .0012" (.03 mm) increments. Install transfer shaft bearing race. Install appropriate spacer on differential bearing. Spacers are available in thicknesses from .052" (1.31 mm) to .084" (1.12 mm).

21) Apply silicone grease to hatched area of transaxle case and install NEW case gasket. Install converter housing and tighten bolts to specification. See TORQUE SPECIFICATIONS. Fully insert manual control shaft into transaxle case WITHOUT "O" ring. With "O" ring groove exposed on outside of case, install "O" ring. Gently draw back control shaft and install set screw.

22) Install sprag rod support. Install oil passage "O" rings (3) on valve body. Apply fluid on accumulator piston seal rings and install piston in case. See Fig. 18. Install valve body assembly to transaxle case. Ensure manual control shaft pin is in slot of manual valve. Tighten valve body mounting bolts to specification. See Fig. 49.

23) Install oil filter, and tighten bolts to specification. Install NEW oil pan gasket. With magnets in place, install oil pan. Tighten bolts to specification. Apply ATF to torque converter sealing area, and install torque converter. Measure distance between ring gear end and converter housing end. Installed depth should be approximately .47" (12.0 mm).

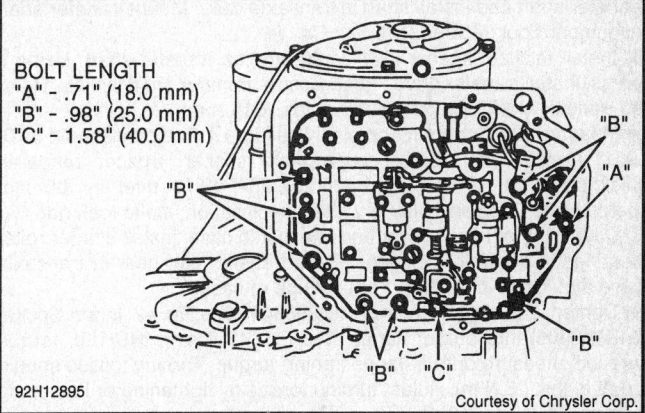

Fig. 49: Locating Valve Body Bolts

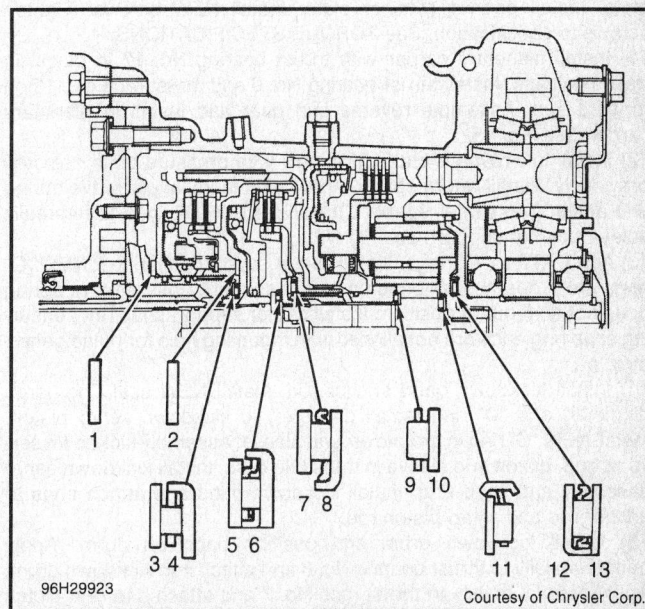

Fig. 50: Identifying Thrust Bearing, Thrust Race & Thrust Washer Locations (F3A21)

NOTE: Lubricate all components with ATF. Apply petroleum jelly on "O" rings and seal rings. Use petroleum jelly to hold thrust bearings, thrust races and thrust washers in position. Ensure thrust bearings, thrust races and thrust washers are installed in original location and proper direction. See Fig. 51.

F4A20 Series – **1)** Prior to reassembly, measure low-reverse brake clearance and select appropriate pressure plate to obtain specified clearance.

2) Install brake reaction plate, brake plates and brake discs in transaxle case. *See Fig. 21.* Install a pressure plate with adequate size. Install return spring. Ensure return spring is installed in proper direction.

3) Apply petroleum jelly to wave spring and attach it to the center support. Install center support and snap ring in case. Check low-reverse brake clearance by mounting a dial indicator on rear of transaxle case. *See Fig. 40.* Install dial indicator through transfer idler shaft hole so its feeler is held perpendicular to brake reaction plate.

4) Using a hand pump, feed air into low-reverse brake and read dial indicator deflection. *See Fig. 41.* Select a pressure plate to obtain specified clearance. Clearance for F4A20 transaxles is .039-.047" (1.00-1.20 mm). Remove all previously install components.

5) Install transfer shaft bearing outer race in case. Install bearings on transfer shaft and install shaft in transaxle case. Mount transfer shaft Alignment Tool (MD998319). *See Fig. 44.*

6) Install thickest spacer .071" (1.80 mm) on transfer shaft. Using a press, install transfer driven gear. Secure transfer shaft in vise. Tighten transfer shaft lock nut to 156 ft. lbs. (215 N.m).

7) Measure transfer shaft end play. *See Fig. 17.* End play should be 0-.001" (0-.025 mm). Select appropriate spacer. Spacer range in thickness from .072" (1.82 mm) to .084" (2.12 mm) in .06 mm increments. Once end play is within specification, stake lock nut.

8) Coat transfer idler spacer and attach it to case. Install 2 taper roller bearings in transfer idler gear. Place transfer idler gear in transaxle case and insert idler shaft from outside of case.

9) Tighten idler shaft with Tool (MD998344). *See Fig. 42.* Insert Socket (MD998906) into output flange. *See Fig. 43.* Using INCH lb. torque wrench, measure output flange turning torque. Turning torque should be .6 ft. lbs. (.8 N.m). Adjust turning torque by tightening or loosening transfer idler gear shaft.

10) Once preload adjustment is completed, install idler shaft lock plate. Install bearing retainer plate. Install NEW screws. Tighten screws to specification. See TORQUE SPECIFICATIONS.

11) Install planetary carrier with thrust bearing No. 12 in place, in transaxle case. Install thrust bearing No. 9 and thrust race No. 10 on forward sun. Assemble reverse sun gear and install in planetary carrier. *See Fig. 45.*

12) Install low-reverse brake assembly with pressure plate selected previously. Install return spring. Apply petroleum jelly to wave spring and attach it to center support. Install 2 NEW "O" rings to hydraulic holes of center support. *See Fig. 46.*

13) Apply ATF to "O" rings. Install center support ensuring 2 NEW "O" rings are properly positioned on center support. Ensure wave spring does not shift out of position. Install center support snap ring, ensuring snap ring ends are not aligned with mounting hole for pulse generator "A".

14) Install kickdown band anchor rod. Install NEW seal ring (large diameter) and "D" ring (small diameter) to kickdown servo piston. Install NEW "O" ring in groove around sleeve. Assembly kickdown servo spring, piston and sleeve in transaxle case. Install kickdown servo assembly and snap ring. Install kickdown band and attach ends to anchor rod and servo piston rod.

15) Install kickdown drum and position band on drum. Apply petroleum jelly to thrust bearing No. 8 and attach it to kickdown drum. Apply petroleum jelly to thrust race No. 7 and attach it to rear clutch hub.

16) Install clutch hub to sun gear splines and attach thrust bearing No. 6 to outer side of clutch hub. Install thrust washer No. 2 and thrust bearing No. 4 on rear clutch assembly. Assemble front and rear clutch assemblies and install in transaxle case. Install differential assembly.

17) If input shaft end play previously measured at disassembly is not within specification, adjust end play to specification by selecting thrust race No. 3 and thrust washer No. 1. End play should be .012-.039" (.30-1.00 mm). Install NEW oil pump assembly gasket. Install oil pump assembly and tighten bolts to specification. See TORQUE SPECIFICATIONS. Recheck end play and readjust as necessary.

18) Measure differential end play by placing a .4" (10 mm) long, .12" (3.0 mm) diameter piece of solder at 2 locations on the differential bearing outer race. *See Fig. 47.* Install converter housing, without gasket, and tighten bolts to 14-17 ft. lbs. (19-23 N.m).

19) Remove converter housing and measure thickness of the crushed solder. Determine thickness of spacer to be installed using the following formula: Thickness of solder plus case gasket thickness .015" (.38 mm) minus end play at differential 0-.006" (0-.15 mm) Install appropriate spacer on differential bearing. Spacers are available in thicknesses from .073" (1.85 mm) to 2.57" (1.01 mm) in .0035" (.09 mm) increments.

20) Apply silicone grease to hatched area of transaxle case and install NEW case gasket. Install converter housing and tighten bolts to specification. See TORQUE SPECIFICATIONS. Install end clutch shaft with the longest spline end towards torque converter end of transaxle. Fit thrust washer to end clutch return spring.

21) Install end clutch hub to end clutch. Using petroleum jelly, attach thrust bearing No. 13 to end clutch hub and install end clutch assembly. Attach NEW "O" ring to end clutch cover and install on transaxle case. When installing end cover, ensure screw holes are correctly aligned. If aligned after installing, "O" ring may be twisted. Tighten end cover bolts to specification.

22) To confirm correct operation of assembled components, air check transaxle. Using air nozzle with rubber tip, apply air to specific ports and observe operation of clutch. *See Fig. 52.* Ensure moisture free air is used. Do not exceed 25 psi when air checking transaxle.

23) Fully insert manual control shaft into transaxle case WITHOUT "O" ring. With "O" ring groove exposed on outside of case, install "O" ring. Gently draw back control shaft and install set screw. Install detent ball and spring.

24) Install sprag rod support. Apply fluid on accumulator piston seal rings and install piston in case. Install brake oil passage "O" ring at top center of valve body, and install valve body assembly to transaxle case. Install solenoid valve connector in transaxle case using NEW "O" ring. Tighten valve body mounting bolts to specification. *See Fig. 49.*

25) Install oil filter, and tighten bolts to specification. Install NEW oil pan gasket. With magnets in place, install oil pan. Tighten bolts to specification. Install kickdown servo switch using NEW "D" ring, and secure using snap ring. Install inhibitor switch and manual control lever.

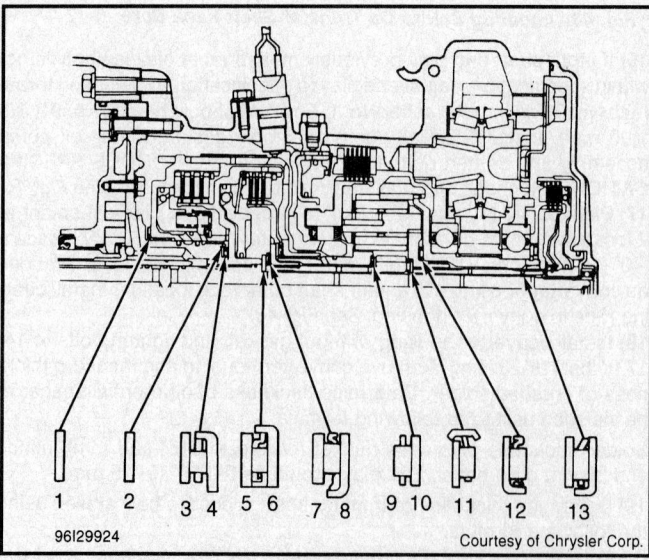

96l29924   Courtesy of Chrysler Corp.

Fig. 51: Identifying Thrust Bearing, Thrust Race & Thrust Washer Locations (F4A20 Series)

26) Adjust inhibitor switch. Install pulse generators "A" and "B". *See Fig. 19.* Apply ATF to torque converter sealing area, and install torque converter. Measure distance between ring gear end and converter housing end. Installed depth should be approximately .47" (12.0 mm).

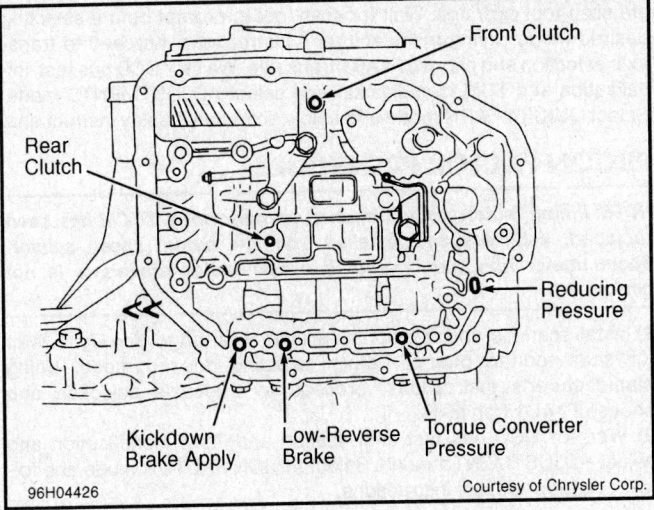

Fig. 52: *Identifying Clutch Fluid Passages (F4A20 Series)*

TORQUE SPECIFICATIONS
TORQUE SPECIFICATIONS

Application	Ft. Lbs. (N.m)
Bearing Retainer Bolt	13-16 (17-22)
Converter Housing Bolt	14-17 (19-23)
Differential Drive Gear Bolt	96-103 (130-140)
Drive Plate-To-Converter Bolt	34-39 (46-53)
Idler Shaft Lock Plate Bolt	35-43 (47-58)
Manual Control Lever Nut	13-16 (17-22)
Oil Pump Bolt	11-15 (15-20)
Planetary Carrier-To-One-Way Clutch	26-33 (35-45)
Sprag Rod Support Bolt	15-20 (20-27)
Transfer Shaft Lock Nut	148-170 (200-230)

Application	INCH Lbs. (N.m)
End Clutch Cover Bolt	53-71 (6-8)
Governor Set Screw	71-89 (8-10)
Inhibitor Switch Bolt	89-106 (10-12)
Manual Control Lever Set Screw	71-89 (8-10)
Oil Filter Bolt	44-62 (5-7)
Oil Pan Bolt	89-106 (10-12)
Pulse Generator Bolt	89-106 (10-12)
Reaction Shaft Support-To-Oil Pump Housing Bolt	89-106 (10-12)
Valve Body Bolt	35-53 (4-6)
Valve Body-To-Case Bolt	89-106 (10-12)

TRANSAXLE SPECIFICATIONS
TRANSAXLE SPECIFICATIONS

Application	In. (mm)
Clearances	
End Clutch	
F4A22	.016-.026 (.40-.65)
F4A23	.024-.031 (.60-.85)
Front Clutch	
F3A21	.016-.023 (.40-.60)
F4A20 Series	.028-.035 (.70-.90)
Low-Reverse Brake	
F3A21	.032-.039 (.08-1.00)
F4A20 Series	.039-.047 (1.00-1.20)
Rear Clutch	
F3A21	.012-.020 (.30-.50)
F4A20	.016-.023 (.40-.60)
Oil Pump	.001-.002 (.03-.05)
Differential Backlash	.001-.006 (.03-.15)
End Play	
Differential Case	0-0.006 (0-0.15)
Input Shaft	.012-.039 (0.30-1.00)
Output Flange Bearing	0-.002 (0-.06)
Transfer Shaft	0-0.0010 (0-0.025)

AUTOMATIC TRANSMISSIONS
Mitsubishi F4AC1 Electronic Controls

Eclipse

APPLICATION & LABOR TIMES

APPLICATION & LABOR TIMES

Vehicle Application	Labor Times		Transaxle Series
	[1] R & I	[2] Overhaul	
Eclipse			
2.0L Non-Turbo	6.8	8.9	F4AC1

[1] – Removal and installation of transmission from vehicle chassis.

[2] – Bench overhaul time for transmission. DOES NOT include removal and installation.

NOTE: This article contains electronic controls diagnostic, testing and repair information only. For overhaul procedures, transaxle tests and specification information, see CHRYSLER 41TE/AE article in 1995-96 MITCHELL® TRANSMISSION SERVICE & REPAIR manual for DOMESTIC CARS, LIGHT TRUCKS & VANS.

IDENTIFICATION

Vehicle information code plate is riveted to firewall in engine compartment area. Plate contains transaxle identification information.

DESCRIPTION

The F4AC1 is an electronically-controlled 4-speed transaxle. Transaxle uses hydraulically operated clutches controlled by the Transaxle Control Module (TCM).

The TCM is considered a fully adaptive control module. Adaptive controls perform function based on real-time sensor feedback information. Transaxle consists of 3 multiple-disc input clutches, 2 multiple-disc holding clutches, accumulators and 2 planetary gear sets to provide 4 forward speeds and a reverse gear.

ADJUSTMENTS

NOTE: See appropriate AUTOMATIC TRANSMISSION SERVICING article in TRANSMISSION SERVICING section for procedures not covered in this article.

QUICK LEARN PROCEDURE

1) Quick learn procedure must be performed if any of the following repairs or services occur:
- Transaxle Assembly Replacement
- TCM Replacement
- Solenoid And Pressure Switch Assembly Replacement
- Clutch Plate Or Seal Replacement
- Valve Body Replacement Or Recondition

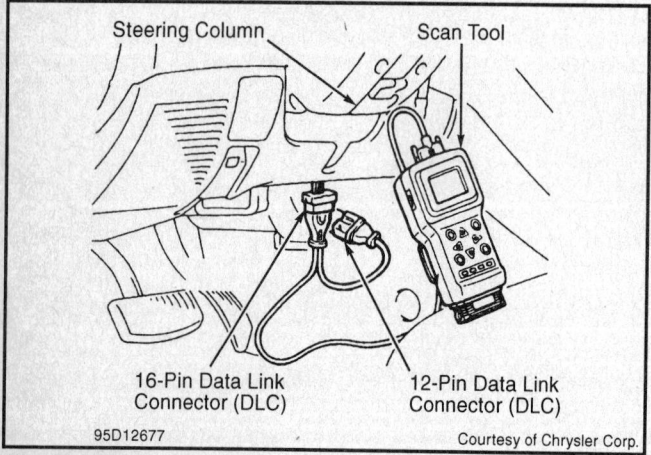

Steering Column   Scan Tool

16-Pin Data Link Connector (DLC)   12-Pin Data Link Connector (DLC)

95D12677   Courtesy of Chrysler Corp.

Fig. 1: Installing Scan Tool

2) Before performing quick learn procedure, ensure transaxle fluid temperature is 60-200°F (15.5-93.3°C), selector lever in "D" position, overdrive switch on, throttle angle less than 3 degrees open, engine speed is more than 500 RPM and brake pedal is applied.

3) Install scan tool to data link connector. *See Fig. 1.* Install appropriate scan tool cartridge. Wait for scan tool to prompt before selecting desired mode. Using manufacturer's instructions, proceed to transaxle selection and choose F4AC1 transaxle. Wait for CCD bus test, initialization and TCM identification and select ADJUSTMENTS mode. Select QUICK LEARN mode and follow scan tool display instructions.

PINION FACTOR PROCEDURE

NOTE: Pinion factor procedure must be performed if TCM has been replaced. Vehicle speed is taken from the output speed sensor. Speedometer may not operate if pinion factor procedure is not performed.

1) Install scan tool and appropriate scan tool cartridge. *See Fig. 1.* Wait for scan tool to prompt before selecting desired mode. Using manufacturer's instructions, proceed to transaxle selection and choose F4AC1 transaxle.

2) Wait for CCD bus test, initialization and TCM identification and select ADJUSTMENTS mode. Select PINION FACTOR mode and follow scan tool display instructions.

TORQUE CONVERTER CLUTCH (TCC) BREAK-IN PROCEDURE

NOTE: Torque converter clutch break-in procedure must be performed if torque converter or TCM is replaced. Transaxle may shudder during partial TCC operation if TCC break-in procedure is not performed.

1) Install scan tool and appropriate scan tool cartridge. *See Fig. 1.* Wait for scan tool to prompt before selecting desired mode. Using manufacturer's instructions, proceed to transaxle selection and choose F4AC1 transaxle.

2) Wait for CCD bus test, initialization and TCM identification and select ADJUSTMENTS mode. Select RESET LU CLUTCH mode and follow maufacturer's instructions for reseting TCC.

LUBRICATION

NOTE: See appropriate AUTOMATIC TRANSMISSION SERVICING article in TRANSMISSION SERVICING section.

OPERATION

FAIL-SAFE MODE

NOTE: Transaxle will enter fail safe mode when certain codes are set. See DIAGNOSTIC TROUBLE CODE (DTC) IDENTIFICATION table.

The TCM monitors transaxle for electrical or internal problems. If battery voltage is lost, or TCM senses a transaxle failure and diagnostic trouble code is set, the TCM de-energizes the transaxle control relay which then de-energizes the solenoid assembly. Transaxle then enters fail-safe mode. In fail-safe mode, only Park, Neutral, Reverse and 3rd gears function. Transaxle will not upshift or downshift. Vehicle can be operated, but performance will be reduced.

When ignition is turned off and then back on again, the TCM will reset for normal operation. If circuit failure is sensed by TCM, transaxle will then enter fail-safe mode.

TCM

NOTE: If TCM is replaced, a quick learn procedure and pinion factor procedure must be performed to ensure proper shift sequence occurs. See QUICK LEARN PROCEDURE and PINION FACTOR PROCEDURE under ADJUSTMENTS.

The TCM recieves information from various input devices and uses this information to control No. 1 and No. 2 shift solenoids on transmission valve body for transmission shifting and Torque Converter Clutch (TCC) solenoid for torque converter lock-up.

The TCM contains a self-diagnostic system, which will store trouble codes if failure or problems exist in electronic control system. Trouble codes can be retrieved to determine problem area. See SELF-DIAGNOSTIC SYSTEM.

TCM INPUT DEVICES

Engine Speed Signal – The TCM uses a direct signal from distributior pick-up coil or crank shaft position sensor to determine engine RPM. The TCM uses the direct signal and compares it to the engine speed received from the Engine Control Module (PCM) by the CCD bus to confirm that direct engine speed signal is valid.

Ignition Signal – When ignition is turned to OFF, ON or START position, the TCM checks the incoming voltage. If voltage is less than specified or exceeds specified voltage, TCM will cause transaxle to enter fail-safe mode to prevent damage to electrical components.

When ignition is turned on, TCM performs a series of circuit and relay checks. If no problem exists, TCM provides voltage to transaxle control relay, causing contacts to close, supplying voltage to solenoid assembly and TCM. Voltage supplied to TCM is referred to as switched battery voltage. If provlem exists, TCM turns off power supply to transaxle control relay, which causes transaxle to enter fail-safe mode.

Input Speed Sensor – Input speed sensor uses a magnetic pick-up coil to generate an AC voltage input signal when trigger teeth on input clutch assembly pass magnetic pick-up coil. The TCM uses input signal to determine input shaft speed. See Figs. 2 or 3.

Neutral Safety Switch & Transaxle Range Switch – TCM uses input signals from neutral safety switch and transaxle range switch to determine gear position selected. On 1995 models, transaxle uses 2 separate switches. On 1996 models, neutral safety and transaxle range switches are incorporated into one transaxle range switch. See Figs. 2 or 3. Switches are located on side of transaxle. Switches are also used to activate starter relay, Reverse lights and prevent starter engagement in any gear except Park or Neutral.

Low-Reverse, Overdrive (OD) & 2-4 Pressure Switches – Pressure switches are located in solenoid and pressure switch assembly. See Figs. 2 or 3. Switches provide input information to TCM, indicating whether pressure exists in a specified hydraulic circuit. The TCM uses this information to verify solenoid assembly operation.

Oil Temperature Sensor (1996 Models) – Oil temperature sensor supplies TCM with transaxle fluid temperature information. Oil temperature sensor is located in transaxle range switch. See Fig. 3.

Overdrive Switch – An overdrive switch is located on shift lever. Overdrive switch delivers an input signal to TCM to prevent transaxle from shifting into overdrive.

Output Speed Sensor Signal – Output speed sensor uses a magnetic pick-up coil to generate an AC voltage input signal when trigger teeth on output shaft pass the magnetic pick-up coil. The TCM uses input signal to determine output shaft speed. The TCM compares output speed sensor signal against the input speed sensor signal to determine gear ratio and clutch slippage. Output speed sesor signal is also compared to throttle position sensor signal to determine transaxle shift points. See Figs. 2 or 3.

Output speed sensor signal is also used for determining vehicle speed. Vehicle speed signal is delivered from TCM to Engine Control Module (ECM). The ECM delivers vehicle speed signal on CCD bus for use by Body Control Module (BCM) if equipped and other vehicle control modules.

Throttle Position Sensor (TPS) – The TPS uses a 5-volt input voltage supplied by ECM. A shared TPS return wire is connected to TCM and ECM. The TCM uses TPS reference signal to determine throttle position for controlling shift points, shift quality and torque converter clutch operation for lock-up.

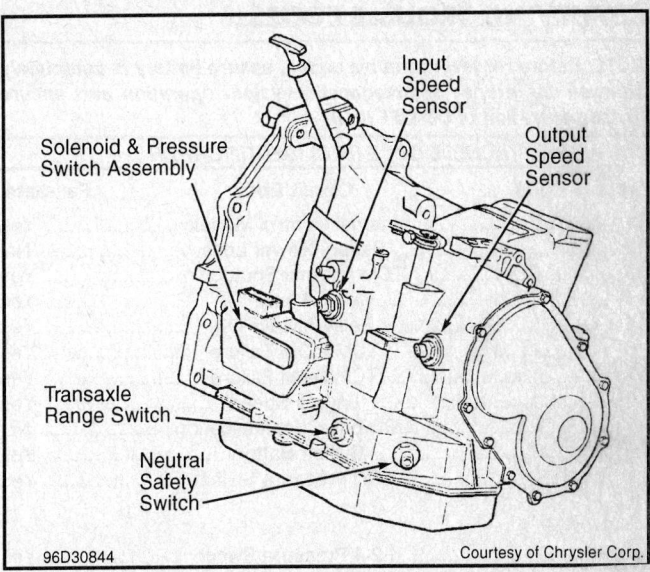

Fig. 2: Locating Transaxle Components (1995 Models)

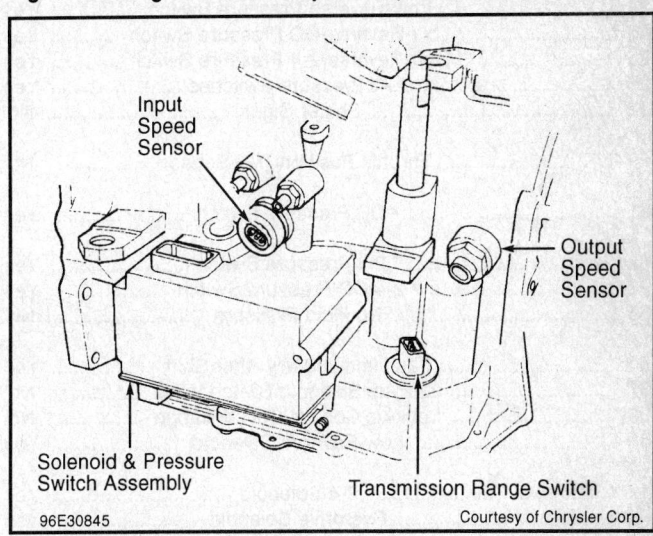

Fig. 3: Locating Transaxle Components (1996 Models)

SELF-DIAGNOSTIC SYSTEM

SYSTEM DIAGNOSIS

NOTE: Before testing transmission, ensure fluid level is correct and throttle and shift cables are properly adjusted. Ensure engine starts with shift lever in Park and Neutral to ensure proper adjustment of neutral safety switch. Transmission must first be tested by checking for stored codes. See RETRIEVING TROUBLE CODES.

TCM monitors transmission operation and contains a self-diagnostic system which stores a trouble code if an electronic control system failure or problem exists. If a problem exists in any of the solenoids or speed sensors and a trouble code is set, TCM delivers a signal to blink OD OFF light on instrument panel to warn the driver. Trouble codes may be set if a failure exists and can be retrieved for transaxle diagnosis.

AUTOMATIC TRANSMISSIONS
Mitsubishi F4AC1 Electronic Controls (Cont.)

RETRIEVING TROUBLE CODES

NOTE: Before retrieving trouble codes, ensure battery is completely charged for proper self-diagnostic system operation and ensure proper operation of OD OFF light.

Install scan tool to data link connector and turn ignition on. See Fig. 1. Follow manufacturer's instructions while using scan tool. Identify and record all trouble codes before clearing TCM memory. See DIAGNOSTIC TROUBLE CODE (DTC) IDENTIFICATION table.

DIAGNOSTIC TROUBLE CODE (DTC) IDENTIFICATION

Trouble Code	Circuit Error	Fail-Safe Mode	Probable Cause
11	Internal Control Module	Yes	TCM Failure
12	Battery Power Loss	No	Battery Disconnected
13	TCM Internal Shutdown	Yes	TCM Failure
14	Relay Always On	Yes	Relay Failure, Short To Power, TCM Relay Driver
15	Relay Always Off	Yes	Relay Failure, Relay Power Or Ground Loss
16	TCM ROM Failure	Yes	TCM Failure
17	TCM RAM Failure	Yes	TCM Failure
18	Engine Speed	Yes	Crankshaft Position Sensor Failure, TCM Failure
19	CCD Bus Communication	No	CCD Bus Short Circuit
20	Switch Battery	Yes	Relay Or Circuit Failure
21	[1] OD Pressure Switch	Yes	High Or Low Fluid Level, Pressure Switch Failure, Open Or Short In Switch Harness, TCM Failure, Internal Transaxle Failure
22	[1] 2-4 Pressure Switch	Yes	See DTC 21
23	[1] 2-4/OD Pressure Switch	Yes	See DTC 21
24	[1] Low-Reverse Pressure Switch	Yes	See DTC 21
25	[1] Low-Reverse/OD Pressure Switch	Yes	See DTC 21
26	[1] Low-Reverse/2-4 Pressure Switch	Yes	See DTC 21
27	[1] All Pressure Switches	Yes	See DTC 21
28	Shifter Signal	No	Transaxle Range Sensor Failure, Neutral Safety Switch Failure, Open Or Short In Switch Wire Harness, TCM Failure
29	Throttle Position (TP) Sensor	No	TP Sensor Failure, Open Or Short In Sensor Wire Harness TCM Or ECM Failure
31	[2] OD Pressure Switch	Yes	High Or Low Fluid Level, OD Pressure Switch Failure, Internal Transaxle Failure
32	[2] 2-4 Pressure Switch	Yes	See DTC 31
33	[2] 2-4/OD Pressure Switch	Yes	See DTC 31
35	No Fluid Pressure	No	High Or Low Fluid Level, Oil Filter Damaged, Oil Filter "O" Ring Missing, Oil Cooler Failure
36	Fault Immediately After Shift	Yes	Internal Transaxle Failure
37	Lock-up Solenoid Switch Valve	No	Internal Transaxle Failure
38	Lock-up Control Out Of Range	No	High Or Low Fluid Level, Internal Transaxle Failure
41	Low-Reverse Solenoid	Yes	Pressure Switch Failure, Open Or Shorted Low-Reverse Solenoid Harness, Open TCM Ground Circuit, TCM Failure
42	2-4 Solenoid	Yes	See DTC 41
43	Overdrive Solenoid	Yes	See DTC 41
44	Underdrive Solenoid	Yes	See DTC 41
45	Internal Conrol Module	No	TCM Failure
46	Underdrive Hydraulic Failure	Nc	Internal Transaxle Failure
47	Solenoid Switch Valve	Yes	Internal Transaxle Failure
48	TRD Communication Failure	No	CCD Bus Failure, TP Sensor, Open Or Short In TCM To ECM Harness
50	Reverse Gear Ratio Incorrect	Yes	Input Or Ouput Speed Sensor Failure, Open Or Short In Input Or Output Speed Sensor To TCM Harness, TCM Failure, Internal Transaxle Failure
51	1st Gear Ratio Incorrect	Yes	See DTC 50
52	2nd Gear Ratio Incorrect	Yes	See DTC 50
53	3rd Gear Ratio Incorrect	Yes	See DTC 50
54	4th Gear Ratio Incorrect	Yes	See DTC 50
56	Input Speed Sensor Failure	Yes	Input Speed Sensor Failure, Open Or Short In Input Speed Sensor Harness, TCM Failure
57	Output Speed Sensor Failure	Yes	Output Speed Sensor Failure, Open Or Short In Output Speed Sensor Harness, TCM Failure
58	Speed Sensor Ground	Yes	Open Input Or Output Speed Sensor Ground, TCM Failure
60	Low-Reverse Clutch Failing	No	Internal Transaxle Failure
61	2-4 Clutch Failing	No	Internal Transaxle Failure
62	OD Clutch Failing	No	Internal Transaxle Failure
73	Fluid Worn Out Or Burnt	No	Transaxle Fluid Worn Out Or Burnt, Wheels Out Of Allignment, TCM Failure
74	Oil Temperature Sensor Failure	No	Oil Temperature Sensor Failure, Open Or Short In Transaxle Range Switch, TCM Failure

[1] – Trouble code is set when an electronic failure is detected.
[2] – Trouble code is set when a mechanical failure is detected.

CLEARING TROUBLE CODES

After repairs have been performed, use scan tool and manufacturer's instructions to clear or erase DTC from TCM memory.

DTC 11, 13, 16, 17 & 45: TCM FAILURE

If DTC 11, 13, 16, 17 or 45 are present, record all DTCs and clear trouble codes. If DTC 11, 13, 16, 17 or 45 reoccur, replace TCM. Retest system and ensure DTC 11, 13, 16, 17 or 45 do not reoccur.

DTC 12: BATTERY POWER LOSS

TCM is equipped with a back-up battery power pack. If vehicles' battery is disconnected, DTC 12 will be set.

DTC 14: TRANSAXLE RELAY ALWAYS ON

1) Turn ignition on and off several times and listen for transaxle relay engaging. If relay engages, go to next step. If relay does not engage, remove and test transaxle relay. See TRANSAXLE RELAY under COMPONENT TESTING. If relay is okay, go to step 6).

2) Measure voltage between transaxle relay connector terminal No. 4 and ground. See Fig. 4. If voltage is less than one volt, go to next step. If voltage is more than one volt, check and repair wiring harness between TCM and transaxle relay connector for a short to power. See WIRING DIAGRAMS. If wiring harness is okay, recheck trouble codes. If DTC 14 reoccurs, replace TCM.

3) Disconnect TCM connector. Connect voltmeter between TCM connector terminal No. 56 and ground. See Fig. 5. Turn ignition on. If voltage is less than one volt, go to next step. If voltage is more than one volt, check wiring harness for short to power between transaxle relay and TCM connector terminal No. 56. See WIRING DIAGRAMS.

4) Turn ignition off. Connect voltmeter between TCM connector terminal No. 57 and ground. Turn ignition on. If voltage is less than one volt, go to next step. If voltage is more than one volt, check wiring harness for short to power between solenoid and pressure switch assembly and TCM connector. See WIRING DIAGRAMS.

5) Turn ignition off. Reconnect TCM connector. Turn ignition on and measure voltage between TCM connector terminal No. 8 and ground. If voltage is more than 3 volts, replace TCM. If voltage is less than 3 volts, replace transaxle relay.

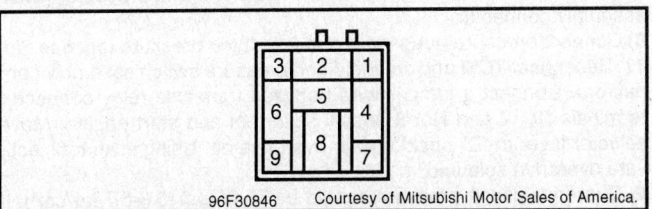

96F30846   Courtesy of Mitsubishi Motor Sales of America.

Fig. 4: Identifying Transaxle Relay Connector Terminals

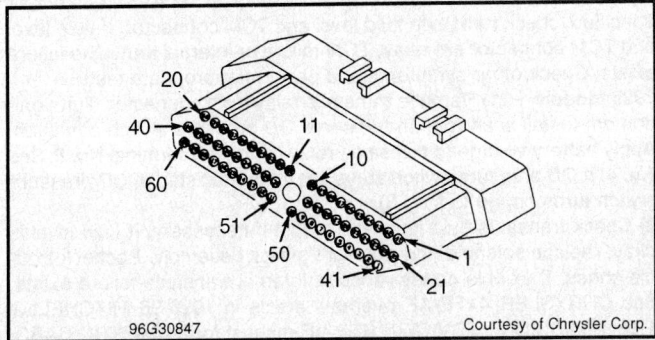

96G30847   Courtesy of Chrysler Corp.

Fig. 5: Identifying TCM Connector Terminals

6) Measure continuity between transaxle relay connector terminal No. 6 and ground. See Fig. 4. If continuity exists, go to next step. If continuity does not exist, repair wiring harness between transaxle relay connector terminal No. 6 and ground. See WIRING DIAGRAMS.

7) Turn ignition off. Measure voltage between transaxle relay connector terminal No. 4 and ground. If voltage is less than one volt, go to next step. If voltage is more than one volt, repair wiring harness between transaxle relay connector terminal No. 4 and TCM.

8) Check wiring harness and connectors between TCM and relay connector. See WIRING DIAGRAMS. If wiring harness and connectors are okay, replace TCM.

DTC 15: TRANSAXLE RELAY ALWAYS OFF

1) Turn ignition on and off several times and listen for transaxle relay engaging. If relay engages, go to next step. If relay does not engage, remove and test transaxle relay. See TRANSAXLE RELAY under COMPONENT TESTING. If relay is okay, go to step 4).

2) Measure voltage between transaxle relay connector terminal No. 8 and ground. See Fig. 4. If battery voltage is present, go to next step. If battery voltage is not present, check wiring harness for open circuit between battery and transaxle relay connector.

3) Check and repair wiring harness for short to power between TCM connector terminal No. 56 and transaxle relay connector. See WIRING DIAGRAMS. Also check and repair Red wire for short to power between TCM and solenoid and pressure switch assembly. If wiring harness and connectors are okay, recheck trouble codes. If trouble code still exists, replace TCM.

4) Measure continuity between transaxle relay connector terminal No. 6 and ground. See Fig. 4. If continuity exists, go to next step. If continuity does not exist, repair wiring harness between transaxle relay connector terminal No. 6 and ground. See WIRING DIAGRAMS.

5) Turn ignition on. Measure voltage between transaxle relay connector terminal No. 4 and ground. If battery voltage is present, go to next step. If battery voltage is not present, repair wiring harness between transaxle relay connector terminal No. 4 and TCM.

6) Check TCM and transaxle relay connectors. If connectors are okay, recheck trouble code. If trouble code still exists, replace TCM.

DTC 18: ENGINE SPEED SENSOR

1) Using scan tool, start engine and observe engine RPM. If engine speed is more than 400 RPM, go to next step. If engine speed is less than 400 RPM, go to step 4).

2) Turn ignition off. Disconnect TCM connector. Check continuity between terminals No. 13, 17 and ground. See Fig. 5. If continuity is okay, go to next step. If continuity does not exist between either terminal, repair open circuit and reconnect TCM connector.

3) Retest vehicle for abnormal operation. If operation is normal and no trouble codes are set, system is okay at this time. If operation is abnormal and no trouble codes are set, check symptoms. If operation is abnormal and trouble codes are set, recheck trouble codes.

4) Turn ignition off. Disconnect TCM connector. Connect voltmeter between TCM connector terminal No. 46 and ground. Start engine and observe voltage reading. If voltage is .3-3.0 volts, go to next step. If voltage is not .3-3.0 volts, check and repair CCD bus harness and engine speed sensor connectors.

5) Check TCM connector and repair as necessary. If TCM connector is okay, recheck trouble codes. If trouble code reoccurs, replace TCM.

DTC 19: CCD BUS COMMUNICATION

1) Disconnect ECM harness connectors. Measure resistance between ECM connector terminal No. 60 and data link connector terminal No. 28. See Figs. 6 and 7. If resistance is less than 5 ohms, go to next step. If resistance is more than 5 ohms, check and repair wiring harness between ECM connector and data link connector. See WIRING DIAGRAMS.

AUTOMATIC TRANSMISSIONS
Mitsubishi F4AC1 Electronic Controls (Cont.)

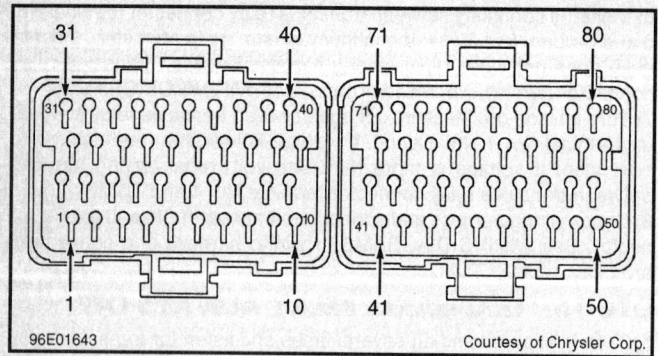

Fig. 6: Identifying ECM Connector Terminals

2) Measure resistance between ECM connector terminal No. 59 and data link connector terminal No. 27. If resistance is less than 5 ohms, go to next step. If resistance is more than 5 ohms, check and repair wiring harness between ECM connector and data link connector.

3) Measure resistance between TCM connector terminal No. 44 and data link connector terminal No. 28. See Figs. 5 and 7. If resistance is less than 5 ohms, go to next step. If resistance is more than 5 ohms, check and repair wiring harness between TCM connector and data link connector.

4) Measure resistance between TCM connector terminal No. 3 and data link connector terminal No. 27. If resistance is less than 5 ohms, go to next step. If resistance is more than 5 ohms, check and repair wiring harness between TCM connector and data link connector.

5) Check TCM and ECM harness connectors and repair as necessary. If connectors are okay, replace TCM. Recheck trouble codes. If trouble codes reoccur, replace ECM.

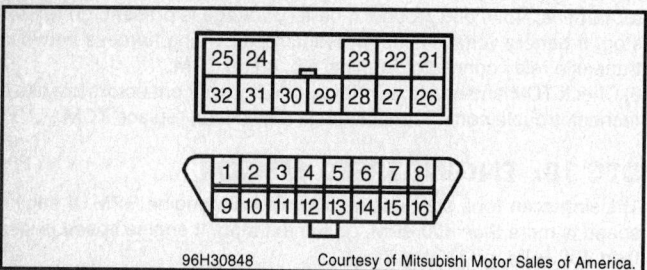

Fig. 7: Identifying Data Link Connector Terminals

DTC 20: SWITCHED BATTERY

1) Disconnect solenoid and pressure switch assembly connector. Turn ignition on. Measure voltage between solenoid and pressure switch terminals No. 1, 2, 5 and ground. See Fig. 8. Voltage should be zero at each terminal. If specified voltage exists, go to next step. If voltage is not as specified, check and repair short to power between transaxle relay connector and solenoid and pressure switch assembly connector. See WIRING DIAGRAMS. Recheck trouble codes. If trouble code reoccurs, replace TCM.

2) Turn ignition off. Disconnect TCM connector. Turn ignition on. Measure voltage between TCM connector terminals No. 7, 10, 49 and ground. See Fig. 5. Voltage should be zero volts for each terminal. If specified voltage exists, go to next step. If voltage is not as specified, check and repair short to power between TCM connector and solenoid and pressure switch assembly connector. See WIRING DIAGRAMS. Recheck trouble codes. If trouble code reoccurs, replace TCM.

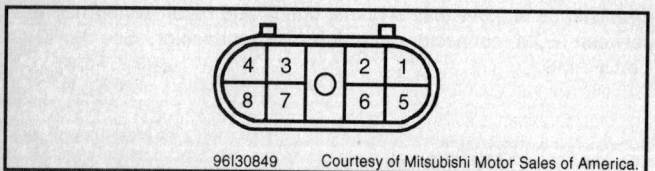

Fig. 8: Identifying Solenoid & Pressure Switch Connector Terminals

3) Check wiring harness between TCM connector and transaxle relay connector. See WIRING DIAGRAMS. Repair wiring harness as necessary.

DTC 21: OD PRESSURE SWITCH

1995 Models – 1) Disconnect solenoid and pressure switch assembly connector. Measure resistance between solenoid and pressure switch assembly connector terminal No. 8 and ground. See Fig. 8. If resistance is more than 500 ohms, go to step 4). If resistance is less than 500 ohms, disconnect TCM connector.

2) Measure resistance between TCM connector terminal No. 20 and ground. See Fig. 5. If resistance is more than 5 ohms, go to next step. If resistance is less than 5 ohms, check wiring harness between TCM connector and solenoid and pressure switch assembly connector for short to ground.

3) Measure resistance between TCM connector terminal No. 20 and solenoid and pressure switch assembly connector terminal No. 8. See Figs. 5 and 8. If resistance is less than 5 ohms, check and repair TCM connector. If TCM connector is okay, replace TCM. If resistance is more than 5 ohms, check and repair wiring harness and connectors between TCM and solenoid and pressure switch assembly.

4) Install scan tool. Turn ignition on. Connect jumper wire between battery positive voltage and solenoid and pressure switch assembly connector terminal No. 8. See Fig. 8. While monitoring overdrive solenoid with scan tool, connect and disconnect jumper wire several times and note scan tool display.

5) If scan tool display changes with jumper wire, go to step 7). If scan tool display does not change with jumper wire, disconnect TCM connector. Connect jumper wire between battery positive voltage and solenoid and pressure switch assembly connector terminal No. 8.

6) Measure voltage between TCM connector terminal No. 20 and ground. See Fig. 5. If battery voltage exists, check and repair TCM connector. If TCM connector is okay, replace TCM. If battery voltage does not exist, check and repair wiring harness and connectors between TCM and solenoid and pressure switch assembly.

7) Disconnect TCM connector. Measure resistance between TCM connector terminal No. 56 and solenoid and pressure switch assembly connector terminal No. 6. If resistance is less than 5 ohms, go to next step. If resistance is more than 5 ohms, check and repair wiring harness between TCM connector and solenoid and pressure switch assembly connector.

8) Connect pressure guage to overdrive clutch pressure tap. See Fig. 11. Reconnect TCM and solenoid and pressure switch assembly connectors. Connect a jumper wire between transaxle relay connector terminals No. 2 and No. 8. Install scan tool and start engine. Move selector lever to "D" position with overdrive on. Using scan tool, activate overdrive solenoid.

9) Overdrive clutch pressure should be 75-95 psi (5.3-6.7 kg/cm²). If pressure is as specified, replace solenoid and pressure switch assembly. If pressure is not as specified but is more than 5 psi (.4 kg/cm²), replace solenoid and pressure switch assembly. If pressure is not as specified, check transaxle fluid level and TCM connector. If fluid level and TCM connector are okay, TCM failure or internal transaxle failure exists. Check other symptoms and perform appropriate tests.

1996 Models – 1) Remove transaxle relay from connector. Turn ignition on. Install scan tool and observe OD pressure switch condition. Apply battery voltage to transaxle relay connector terminal No. 8. See Fig. 4. If OD pressure switch stays off, go to next step. If OD pressure switch turns on, go to step 3).

2) Check transaxle fluid level and adjust if necessary. If fluid level is okay, replace solenoid and pressure switch assembly. Recheck trouble codes. If trouble codes reoccur, internal transaxle failure exists. See CHRYSLER 41TE/AE overhaul article in 1995-96 MITCHELL® TRANSMISSION SERVICE & REPAIR manual for DOMESTIC CARS, LIGHT TRUCKS & VANS.

3) Check and repair wiring harness between transaxle relay connector and solenoid and pressure switch assembly connector. If wiring harness is okay, check Light Green wire between TCM connector terminal No. 49 and solenoid and pressure switch assembly. See WIRING DIAGRAMS.

4) If Light Green wire is okay, check TCM and solenoid and pressure switch assembly connectors. Repair connectors as necessary. If connectors are okay, recheck trouble codes. If trouble code reoccurs, replace solenoid and pressure switch assembly. Recheck trouble codes. If trouble code reoccurs, replace TCM.

DTC 22: 2-4 PRESSURE SWITCH

1995 Models – 1) Disconnect solenoid and pressure switch assembly connector. Measure resistance between solenoid and pressure switch assembly connector terminal No. 3 and ground. See Fig. 8. If resistance is more than 500 ohms, go to next step. If resistance is less than 500 ohms, check and repair wiring harness between solenoid pressure switch assembly and TCM.

2) Install scan tool. See Fig. 1. Turn ignition on. Connect jumper wire between battery positive voltage and solenoid and pressure switch assembly connector terminal No. 3. While monitoring 2-4 solenoid with scan tool, connect and disconnect jumper wire several times and note scan tool display.

3) If scan tool display changes with jumper wire, go to step **5)**. If scan tool display does not change with jumper wire, disconnect TCM connector. Connect jumper wire between battery positive voltage and solenoid and pressure switch connector terminal No. 3.

4) Measure voltage between TCM connector terminal No. 59 and ground. See Fig. 5. If battery voltage exists, check and repair TCM connector. If TCM connector is okay, replace TCM. If battery voltage does not exist, check and repair wiring harness and connectors between TCM and solenoid and pressure switch assembly.

5) Disconnect TCM connector. Measure resistance between TCM connector terminal No. 56 and solenoid and pressure switch assembly connector terminal No. 6. See Figs. 5 and 8. If resistance is less than 5 ohms, go to next step. If resistance is more than 5 ohms, check and repair wiring harness between TCM connector and solenoid and pressure switch assembly connector.

6) Connect pressure guage to overdrive clutch pressure tap. See Fig. 11. Reconnect TCM and solenoid and pressure switch assembly connectors. Connect a jumper wire between transaxle relay connector terminals No. 2 and No. 8. Install scan tool and start engine. Move selector lever to "D" position with overdrive on. Using scan tool, activate 2-4 solenoid.

7) 2-4 clutch pressure should be 120-150 psi (8.4-10.5 kg/cm²). If 2-4 clutch pressure is not as specified, go to next step. If 2-4 clutch pressure is as specified, replace solenoid and pressure switch assembly.

8) If 2-4 clutch pressure test is more than 100 psi (7.0 kg/cm²), replace solenoid and pressure switch assembly and retest system. If 2-4 clutch pressure test is less than 100 psi (7.0 kg/cm²), check transaxle fluid level and TCM connector and repair as necessary. If fluid level and TCM connector are okay, TCM failure or internal transaxle failure exists. Check other symptoms and perform appropriate tests.

1996 Models – 1) Remove transaxle relay from connector. Turn ignition on. Install scan tool and observe 2-4 pressure switch condition. Apply battery voltage to transaxle relay connector terminal No. 8. See Fig. 4. If 2-4 pressure switch stays off, go to next step. If 2-4 pressure switch turns on, go to step **4)**.

2) Raise vehicle enough to allow drive wheels to spin freely. Test 2-4 clutch hydraulic pressure. See HYDRAULIC PRESSURE TESTS under TESTING. If 2-4 clutch pressure test is not within specification, internal transaxle failure exists. If 2-4 clutch pressure test is within specification, observe scan tool.

3) If 2-4 pressure switch turns on, trouble code is intermittent. Check wire harnesses and connectors for damage or poor connection. If 2-4 pressure switch does not turn on, replace solenoid and pressure switch assembly. Recheck trouble codes. If trouble code reoccurs, replace TCM.

4) Check and repair wiring harness between transaxle relay connector and solenoid and pressure switch assembly connector. If wiring harness is okay, check Green wire between TCM connector terminal No. 7 and solenoid and pressure switch assembly. See WIRING DIAGRAMS.

5) If Green wire is okay, check TCM and solenoid and pressure switch assembly connectors. Repair connectors as necessary. If connectors are okay, recheck trouble codes. If trouble code reoccurs, replace solenoid and pressure switch assembly. Recheck trouble codes. If trouble code reoccurs, replace TCM.

DTC 23: 2-4/OD PRESSURE SWITCH

1995 Models – To test circuit for DTC 23, perform DTC 22: 2-4 PRESSURE SWITCH circuit tests.
1996 Models – To test circuit for DTC 23, perform DTC 21: OD PRESSURE SWITCH and DTC 22: 2-4 PRESSURE SWITCH circuit tests.

DTC 24: LOW-REVERSE PRESSURE SWITCH

1995 Models – 1) Disconnect solenoid and pressure switch assembly connector. Turn ignition on. Measure resistance between solenoid and pressure switch assembly connector terminal No. 4 and ground. See Fig. 8. If resistance is more than 500 ohms, go to next step. If resistance is less than 500 ohms, check and repair wiring harness between solenoid pressure switch assembly and TCM.

2) Install scan tool. See Fig. 1. Connect jumper wire between battery positive voltage and solenoid and pressure switch assembly connector terminal No. 4. While monitoring 2-4 solenoid with scan tool, connect and disconnect jumper wire several times and note scan tool display.

3) If scan tool display changes with jumper wire, go to step **5)**. If scan tool display does not change with jumper wire, disconnect TCM connector. Connect jumper wire between battery positive voltage and solenoid and pressure switch connector terminal No. 4.

4) Measure voltage between TCM connector terminal No. 59 and ground. See Fig. 5. If battery voltage exists, check and repair TCM connector. If TCM connector is okay, replace TCM. If battery voltage does not exist, check and repair wiring harness and connectors between TCM and solenoid and pressure switch assembly.

5) Disconnect TCM connector. Measure resistance between TCM connector terminal No. 56 and solenoid and pressure switch assembly connector terminal No. 6. See Figs. 5 and 8. If resistance is less than 5 ohms, go to next step. If resistance is more than 5 ohms, check and repair wiring harness between TCM connector and solenoid and pressure switch assembly connector.

6) Turn ignition on and put selector lever in "2" position. With TCM connector connected, measure voltage between TCM connector terminal No. 41 and ground. If voltage is zero volts, go to step **11)**. If voltage is not zero volts, disconnect transaxle range switch connector.

7) Install scan tool. Using scan tool manufacturer's instructions, proceed to Data List 01: Transaxle Range Switch "B". Move selector lever to "R" position. While monitoring scan tool display, connect a jumper wire between transaxle range switch connector terminal No. 3 and ground. See Fig. 9.

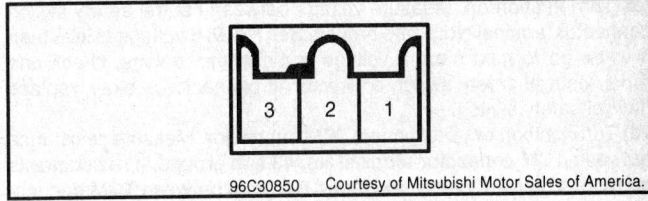

96C30850   Courtesy of Mitsubishi Motor Sales of America.

Fig. 9: Identifying Transaxle Range Switch & Neutral Safety Switch Connector Terminals (1995 Models)

8) If battery voltage is displayed, go to step **10)**. If battery voltage is not displayed, check and repair TCM connector. If connector is okay, measure resistance between TCM connector terminals No. 13, No. 17 and ground.

9) If resistance is more than 5 ohms, check wiring harness between TCM connector and ground. If resistance is less than 5 ohms, measure resistance between TCM connector terminal No. 41 and transaxle range switch connector terminal No. 3. See Figs. 5 and 9. If resistance is less than 5 ohms, replace TCM. If resistance is more than 5 ohms, check and repair wiring harness between TCM connector and transaxle range switch connector.

10) Remove jumper wire. Measure resistance between transaxle range switch connector terminal No. 1 and ground. If resistance is more than 5 ohms, check and repair Black wire between transaxle range switch connector and ground. If resistance is less than 5 ohms, check and repair transaxle range switch connector. If connector is okay, replace transaxle range switch.

11) Move selector lever to "L" position. Measure voltage between TCM connector terminal No. 41 and ground. If battery voltage exists, go to step 14). If battery voltage does not exist, move selector lever to "P" position, turn ignition off and disconnect transaxle range switch connector.

12) Turn ignition on. Measure voltage between transaxle range switch connector terminal No. 3 and ground. If voltage is less than 5 volts, go to next step. If voltage is more than 5 volts, check and repair transaxle range switch connector. If connector is okay, replace transaxle range switch.

13) Disconnect TCM connector. Measure resistance between transaxle range switch connector terminal No. 3 and ground. If resistance is more than 5 ohms, check and repair Yellow/Green wire between TCM connector and transaxle range switch connector. If resistance is less than 5 ohms, check TCM connector. If connector is okay, replace TCM.

14) Move selector lever to "R" position. Measure voltage between TCM connector terminal No. 43 and ground. If battery voltage exists, go to step 18). If battery voltage does not exist, move selector lever to "R" position, turn ignition off and disconnect neutral safety switch connector.

15) Connect a jumper wire between neutral safety switch connector terminals No. 1 and No. 3. See Fig. 9. Turn ignition on. Measure voltage between neutral safety switch connector terminal No. 3 and ground. If battery voltage does not exist, check and repair Black/White wire between neutral safety switch and ignition switch. If battery voltage exists, check and repair neutral safety switch connector. If connector is okay, go to next step.

16) With selector lever in "R" position, measure continuity between neutral safety switch connector terminals No. 1 and No. 3. If continuity does not exist, replace neutral safety switch. If continuity exists, disconnect TCM connector. Measure continuity between TCM connector terminal No. 43 and neutral safety switch connector terminal No. 1.

17) If continuity does not exist, check and repair Red wire between TCM and neutral safety switch. If continuity exists, check and repair TCM connector. If connector is okay, replace TCM.

18) Move selector lever to "P" position. Measure voltage between TCM connector terminal No. 43 and ground. If voltage is zero volts, go to step 21). If voltage is not zero volts, move selector lever to "P" position, turn ignition off and disconnect neutral safety switch connector.

19) Turn ignition on. Measure voltage between neutral safety switch connector terminal No. 1 and ground. See Fig. 9. If voltage is less than 5 volts, go to next step. If voltage is more than 5 volts, check and repair neutral safety switch connector. If connector is okay, replace neutral safety switch.

20) Turn ignition off. Disconnect TCM connector. Measure resistance between TCM connector terminal No. 43 and ground. If resistance is more than 5 ohms, check and repair Red wire between TCM connector and neutral safety switch connector. If resistance is less than 5 ohms, check and repair TCM connector. If connector is okay, replace TCM.

21) Check and adjust selector lever linkage. If selector lever linkage is okay, disconnect TCM and transaxle range switch connectors. Measure resistance between TCM connector terminal No. 41 and transaxle range switch connector terminal No. 3. See Figs. 5 and 9. If resistance is less than 5 ohms, go to next step. If resistance is more than 5 ohms, check and repair wiring harness between TCM connector and transaxle range switch connector.

22) Check and repair TCM and transaxle range switch connectors. If connectors are okay, replace transaxle range switch. Retest system. If trouble code reoccurs, disconnect TCM and neutral safety switch connectors. Measure resistance between TCM connector terminal No. 1 and neutral safety switch connector terminal No. 2.

23) If resistance is more than 5 ohms, check and repair wiring harness between TCM connector and neutral safety switch connector. If resistance is less than 5 ohms, check and repair TCM and neutral safety switch connectors. If connectors are okay, replace neutral safety switch. Retest system. If trouble code reoccurs, replace TCM.

1996 Models – 1) Remove transaxle relay from connector. Turn ignition on. Install scan tool and observe Low-Reverse pressure switch condition. Apply battery voltage to transaxle relay connector terminal No. 8. See Fig. 4. If Low-Reverse pressure switch stays off, go to next step. If Low-Reverse pressure switch turns on, go to step 4).

2) Raise vehicle enough to allow drive wheels to spin freely. Test Low-Reverse clutch hydraulic pressure. See HYDRAULIC PRESSURE TESTS under TESTING. If Low-Reverse clutch pressure test is not within specification, internal transaxle failure exists. If Low-Reverse clutch pressure test is within specification, observe scan tool.

3) If Low-Reverse pressure switch turns on, trouble code is intermittent. Check wire harnesses and connectors for damage or poor connection. If Low-Reverse pressure switch does not turn on, replace solenoid and pressure switch assembly. Recheck trouble codes. If trouble code reoccurs, replace TCM.

4) Check and repair wiring harness between transaxle relay connector and solenoid and pressure switch assembly connector. If wiring harness is okay, check Green/Red wire between TCM connector terminal No. 10 and solenoid and pressure switch assembly. See WIRING DIAGRAMS.

5) If Green/Red wire is okay, check TCM and solenoid and pressure switch assembly connectors. Repair connectors as necessary. If connectors are okay, recheck trouble codes. If trouble code reoccurs, replace solenoid and pressure switch assembly. Recheck trouble codes. If trouble code reoccurs, replace TCM.

DTC 25: LOW-REVERSE/OD PRESSURE SWITCH

1995 Models – To test circuit for DTC 25, perform DTC 24: LOW-REVERSE PRESSURE SWITCH circuit test.

1996 Models – To test circuit for DTC 25, perform DTC 21: OD PRESSURE SWITCH and DTC 24: LOW-REVERSE PRESSURE SWITCH circuit tests.

DTC 26: LOW-REVERSE/2-4 PRESSURE SWITCH

1995 Models – To test circuit for DTC 26, perform DTC 24: LOW-REVERSE PRESSURE SWITCH circuit test.

1996 Models – To test circuit for DTC 26, perform DTC 22: 2-4 PRESSURE SWITCH and DTC 24: LOW-REVERSE PRESSURE SWITCH circuit tests.

DTC 27: ALL PRESSURE SWITCHES

1995 Models – To test circuit for DTC 27, perform DTC 22: 2-4 PRESSURE SWITCH circuit tests.

1996 Models – To test circuit for DTC 27, perform DTC 21: OD PRESSURE SWITCH, DTC 22: 2-4 PRESSURE SWITCH and DTC 24: LOW-REVERSE PRESSURE SWITCH circuit tests.

DTC 28: SHIFTER SIGNAL

1995 Models – 1) Turn ignition on and put selector lever in "P" position. With TCM connector connected, measure voltage between TCM connector terminal No. 2 and ground. See Fig. 5. If voltage is zero volts, go to step 5). If voltage is not zero volts, turn ignition off. Disconnect TCM and transaxle range switch connectors.

2) Measure resistance between TCM connector terminal No. 41 and transaxle range switch connector terminal No. 3. See Figs. 5 and 9. If resistance is less than 5 ohms, go to next step. If resistance is more than 5 ohms, check and repair Yellow/Green wire between TCM connector and transaxle range switch connector.

3) Check and repair TCM and transaxle range switch connectors. If connectors are okay, connect transaxle range switch connector and turn ignition on. Measure voltage between TCM connector terminal No. 2 and ground. If voltage is zero volts, go to next step. If voltage is not zero volts, check and repair Red/Green wire between TCM connector and transaxle range switch connector.

4) Turn ignition off. Connect TCM connector. Disconnect transaxle range switch connector. Turn ignition on. Measure voltage between transaxle range switch connector terminal No. 2 and ground. If voltage is zero volts, replace TCM. If voltage is not zero volts, replace transaxle range switch.

5) Move selector lever to "R" position. Measure voltage between TCM connector terminal No. 2 and ground. If battery voltage exists, go to step **8)**. If battery voltage does not exist, move selector lever to "P" position, turn ignition off and disconnect transaxle range switch connector.

6) Turn ignition on. Measure voltage between transaxle range switch connector terminal No. 2 and ground. If voltage is less than 10 volts, go to next step. If voltage is more than 10 volts, check and repair transaxle range switch connector. If connector is okay, replace transaxle range switch.

7) Disconnect TCM connector. Measure resistance between TCM connector terminal No. 2 and ground. If resistance is more than 5 ohms, check and repair Red/Green wire between TCM connector and transaxle range switch connector. If resistance is less than 5 ohms, check TCM connector. If connector is okay, replace TCM.

8) Move selector lever to "N" position. Measure voltage between TCM connector terminal No. 1 and ground. If voltage is zero volts, go to step **12)**. If voltage is not zero volts, move selector lever to "P" position, turn ignition off and disconnect TCM and neutral safety switch connectors.

9) Turn ignition on. Measure voltage between TCM connector terminal No. 1 and neutral safety switch connector terminal No. 2. *See Figs. 5 and 9.* If voltage is zero volts, go to next step. If voltage is not zero volts, check and repair Black/Yellow wire between TCM connector and neutral safety switch connector.

10) Turn ignition off. Measure resistance between neutral safety switch connector terminal No. 2 and ground. If resistance is more than 5 ohms, go to next step. If resistance is less than 5 ohms, check and repair Black/Yellow wire between TCM connector and neutral safety switch connector.

11) If resistance is more than 5 ohms and less than 50 ohms, check and repair TCM connector. If connector is okay, replace TCM. If resistance is more than 50 ohms, check and repair transaxle range switch connector. If connector is okay, replace transaxle range switch.

12) Move selector lever to "D" position. Measure voltage between TCM connector terminal No. 1 and ground. If battery voltage exists, go to step **15)**. If battery voltage does not exist, move selector lever to "P" position, turn ignition off and disconnect neutral safety switch connector.

13) Turn ignition on. Measure voltage between neutral safety switch connector terminal No. 2 and ground. *See Fig. 9.* If voltage is less than 10 volts, go to next step. If voltage is more than 10 volts, check and repair neutral safety switch connector. If connector is okay, replace neutral safety switch.

14) Turn ignition off. Disconnect TCM connector. Measure resistance between TCM connector terminal No. 1 and ground. If resistance is more than 5 ohms, check and repair Blue/Yellow wire between TCM connector and neutral safety switch connector. If resistance is less than 5 ohms, check and repair TCM connector. If connector is okay, replace TCM.

15) Connect pressure gauge to Low-Reverse clutch pressure tap. *See Fig. 11.* Remove transaxle relay from connector. Connect a jumper wire between transaxle relay connector terminals No. 2 and No. 8. *See Fig. 4.* Start engine and move selector lever to "D" position with overdrive on.

16) Using scan tool, activate Low-Reverse solenoid. Hydraulic pressure should be 120-150 psi (8.4-10.5 kg/cm²). If Low-Reverse clutch pressure is not as specified, go to next step. If Low-Reverse clutch pressure is as specified, replace solenoid and pressure switch assembly.

17) If Low-Reverse clutch pressure test is more than 100 psi (7.0 kg/cm²), replace solenoid and pressure switch assembly and retest system. If Low-Reverse clutch pressure test is less than 100 psi (7.0 kg/cm²), check transaxle fluid level and TCM connector and repair as necessary. If fluid level and TCM connector are okay, TCM failure or internal transaxle failure exists. Check other symptoms and perform appropriate tests.

1996 Models – **1)** Using scan tool, scroll through appropriate Data List numbers and observe transaxle range output for different shift lever positions. See TRANSAXLE RANGE SWITCH SPECIFICATIONS table.

TRANSAXLE RANGE SWITCH SPECIFICATIONS

Data List No.	[1] Selector Lever Position
24	"P" & "N"
25	"P", "R", "N" & "L"
26	"P", 2 & "L"
27	"N", "D" & "L"

[1] – Scan tool should display transaxle range switch "ON" in only listed selector lever positions.

2) If transaxle range switch is not within specifications, test transaxle range switch. See TRANSAXLE RANGE SWITCH under COMPONENT TESTING. If transaxle range switch is okay, check and repair TCM and transaxle range switch connectors. If connectors are okay, check wire harness for short to power between TCM and transaxle range switch. See WIRING DIAGRAMS.

DTC 29: TP SENSOR SIGNAL

1) Start engine and note MIL. If MIL is on, perform engine diagnostics before transaxle diagnostics. See appropriate SELF-DIAGNOSTICS article in ENGINE PERFORMANCE in appropriate MITCHELL® manual. If MIL is not on, turn engine off and install scan tool. *See Fig. 1.*

2) Disconnect TP sensor connector and turn ignition on. Scan tool TP sensor display voltage should be more than 4.0 volts. If voltage is within specification, go to step **4)**. If voltage is not within specification, check TCM connector and engine ground for damage or poor connection. If connections are okay, retest vehicle for abnormal operation.

3) If operation is normal and no trouble codes are set, system is okay at this time. If operation is abnormal and no trouble codes are set, check symptoms. If operation is abnormal and trouble codes are set, recheck trouble codes.

4) Disconnect TCM connector. Measure voltage between TCM connector terminal No. 52 and ground. *See Fig. 5.* If voltage is more than 4.0 volts, go to next step. If voltage is less than 4.0 volts, check and repair wiring harness and connectors between ECM and TP sensor.

5) Measure resistance between TCM connector terminal No. 11 and TP sensor Black/Green wire. If resistance is more than 5 ohms, check and repair Black/Green wire and connectors between TCM and TP sensor. If resistance is less than 5 ohms, check and repair TCM connector. If connector is okay, replace TCM.

DTC 31: OD PRESSURE SWITCH

1) Perform a hydraulic pressure test of OD clutch system before proceeding with electrical tests. See HYDRAULIC PRESSURE TESTS under TESTING. If hydraulic pressure test is okay, check and repair solenoid and pressure switch assembly wiring harness and connector. If wiring harness and connector is okay, replace solenoid and pressure switch assembly.

2) If hydraulic pressure test is not okay, check transaxle fluid level. Adjust fluid level to proper level if necessary. If fluid level is okay, internal transaxle failure exists. See CHRYSLER 41TE/AE overhaul article in 1995-96 MITCHELL® TRANSMISSION SERVICE & REPAIR manual for DOMESTIC CARS, LIGHT TRUCKS & VANS.

DTC 32: 2-4 PRESSURE SWITCH

1) Perform a hydraulic pressure test of 2-4 clutch system before proceeding with electrical tests. See HYDRAULIC PRESSURE TESTS under TESTING. If hydraulic pressure test is okay, check and repair solenoid and pressure switch assembly wiring harness and connector. If wiring harness and connector is okay, replace solenoid and pressure switch assembly.

2) If hydraulic pressure test is not okay, check transaxle fluid level. Adjust fluid level to proper level if necessary. If fluid level is okay, internal transaxle failure exists. See CHRYSLER 41TE/AE overhaul article in 1995-96 MITCHELL® TRANSMISSION SERVICE & REPAIR manual for DOMESTIC CARS, LIGHT TRUCKS & VANS.

DTC 33: 2-4/OD PRESSURE SWITCH

To test circuit for DTC 33, perform DTC 31: OD PRESSURE SWITCH and DTC 32: 2-4 PRESSURE SWITCH circuit tests.

DTC 35: NO FLUID PRESSURE

DTC 35 occurs when TCM does not detect fluid pressure for any component. Check fluid level, oil filter failure, missing oil filter "O" ring or transaxle fluid cooler failure.

DTC 36: FAULT IMMEDIATELY AFTER SHIFT

DTC 36 sets when a problem occurs 1.3 seconds after a shift. This trouble code is not stored alone. One or more of trouble codes 50 through 58 will also be set. Internal transaxle problem may exist. Check symptoms and other trouble codes for diagnostic procedures.

DTC 37: LOCK-UP SOLENOID SWITCH VALVE

DTC 37 sets when 3 unsuccessful attempts to shift into 1st gear occur. Internal transaxle failure may exist. See CHRYSLER 41TE/AE overhaul article in 1995-96 MITCHELL® TRANSMISSION SERVICE & REPAIR manual for DOMESTIC CARS, LIGHT TRUCKS & VANS.

DTC 38: LOCK-UP CONTROL OUT OF RANGE

1) Operate vehicle in overdrive until transaxle is at normal operating temperature. Operate transaxle for at least 10 seconds at 50 MPH (80 km/h) and TP sensor open more than 6 degrees.

2) Perform torque converter clutch off hydraulic pressure test. See HYDRAULIC PRESSURE TEST under TESTING. If hydraulic pressure test is okay, install scan tool, go to next step. If hydraulic pressure test is not okay, valve body operation problem exists. See CHRYSLER 41TE/AE overhaul article in 1995-96 MITCHELL® TRANSMISSION SERVICE & REPAIR manual for DOMESTIC CARS, LIGHT TRUCKS & VANS.

3) Erase trouble codes and road test vehicle. If DTC 38 resets, replace torque converter and flush transaxle fluid cooler. If DTC 38 does not reset, check transaxle fluid level and adjust if necessary. If fluid level is okay, internal transaxle failure exists. See CHRYSLER 41TE/AE overhaul article in 1995-96 MITCHELL® TRANSMISSION SERVICE & REPAIR manual for DOMESTIC CARS, LIGHT TRUCKS & VANS.

DTC 41: LOW-REVERSE SOLENOID

1) Disconnect TCM connector. Using ohmmeter, measure resistance between TCM connector terminal No. 60 and ground. See Fig. 5. If resistance is more than 10,000 ohms, go to step **4)**. If resistance if less than 10,000 ohms, disconnect solenoid and pressure switch assembly connector.

2) Measure resistance between solenoid and pressure switch assembly connector terminal No. 4 and ground. See Fig. 8. If resistance is less than 10,000 ohms, go to next step. If resistance is more than 10,000 ohms, check and repair solenoid and pressure switch assembly. If connector is okay, replace solenoid and pressure switch assembly.

3) Check wiring harness between TCM connector and solenoid and pressure switch assembly connector. If wiring harness is okay, recheck trouble codes. If trouble code resets, replace TCM.

4) Measure resistance between TCM connector terminals No. 56 and No. 60. If resistance is not 1.0-3.0 ohms, go to next step. If resistance is 1.0-3.0 ohms, measure resistance between TCM connector terminals No. 13 and No. 17. If resistance is more than 5 ohms, check

wiring harness between TCM connector and ground. If resistance is less than 5 ohms, check TCM connector. If connector is okay, replace TCM.

5) Disconnect solenoid and pressure switch assembly connector. Measure resistance between TCM connector terminal No. 60 and solenoid and pressure switch assembly connector terminal No. 4. See Figs. 5 and 8. If resistance is less than 5 ohms, go to next step. If resistance is more than 5 ohms, check and repair wiring harness between TCM connector and solenoid and pressure switch assembly connector.

6) Remove transaxle relay from connector. Measure resistance between transaxle relay connector terminal No. 8 and solenoid and pressure switch assembly connector terminal No. 6. If resistance is more than 5 ohms, check and repair wiring harness between transaxle relay connector and solenoid and pressure switch assembly connector. If resistance is less than 5 ohms, replace solenoid and pressure switch assembly.

DTC 42: 2-4 SOLENOID

1) Disconnect TCM connector. Using ohmmeter, measure resistance between TCM connector terminal No. 59 and ground. See Fig. 5. If resistance is more than 10,000 ohms, go to step **4)**. If resistance if less than 10,000 ohms, disconnect solenoid and pressure switch assembly connector.

2) Measure resistance between solenoid and pressure switch assembly connector terminal No. 3 and ground. See Fig. 8. If resistance is less than 10,000 ohms, go to next step. If resistance is more than 10,000 ohms, check and repair solenoid and pressure switch assembly connector. If connector is okay, replace solenoid and pressure switch assembly.

3) Check wiring harness between TCM connector and solenoid and pressure switch assembly connector. If wiring harness is okay, recheck trouble codes. If trouble code resets, replace TCM.

4) Measure resistance between TCM connector terminals No. 56 and No. 59. If resistance not 1.0-3.0 ohms, go to next step. If resistance is 1.0-3.0 ohms, measure resistance between TCM connector terminals No. 13 and No. 17. If resistance is more than 5 ohms, check wiring harness between TCM connector and ground. If resistance is less than 5 ohms, check TCM connector. If connector is okay, replace TCM.

5) Disconnect solenoid and pressure switch assembly connector. Measure resistance between TCM connector terminal No. 59 and solenoid and pressure switch assembly connector terminal No. 3. See Figs. 5 and 8. If resistance is less than 5 ohms, go to next step. If resistance is more than 5 ohms, check and repair wiring harness between TCM connector and solenoid and pressure switch assembly connector.

6) Remove transaxle relay from connector. Measure resistance between transaxle relay connector terminal No. 8 and solenoid and pressure switch assembly connector terminal No. 6. See Figs. 4 and 8. If resistance is more than 5 ohms, check and repair wiring harness between transaxle relay connector and solenoid and pressure switch assembly connector. If resistance is less than 5 ohms, replace solenoid and pressure switch assembly.

DTC 43: OVERDRIVE SOLENOID

1) Disconnect TCM connector. Using ohmmeter, measure resistance between TCM connector terminal No. 20 and ground. See Fig. 5. If resistance is more than 10,000 ohms, go to step **4)**. If resistance if less than 10,000 ohms, disconnect solenoid and pressure switch assembly connector.

2) Measure resistance between solenoid and pressure switch assembly connector terminal No. 8 and ground. See Fig. 8. If resistance is less than 10,000 ohms, go to next step. If resistance is more than 10,000 ohms, check and repair solenoid and pressure switch assembly connector. If connector is okay, replace solenoid and pressure switch assembly.

3) Check wiring harness between TCM connector and solenoid and pressure switch assembly connector. If wiring harness is okay, recheck trouble codes. If trouble code resets, replace TCM.

4) Measure resistance between TCM connector terminals No. 56 and No. 20. If resistance is not 1.0-3.0 ohms, go to next step. If resistance is 1.0-3.0 ohms, measure resistance between TCM connector terminals No. 13 and No. 17. If resistance is more than 5 ohms, check wiring harness between TCM connector and ground. If resistance is less than 5 ohms, check TCM connector. If connector is okay, replace TCM.

5) Disconnect solenoid and pressure switch assembly connector. Measure resistance between TCM connector terminal No. 20 and solenoid and pressure switch assembly connector terminal No. 8. *See Figs. 5 and 8.* If resistance is less than 5 ohms, go to next step. If resistance is more than 5 ohms, check and repair wiring harness between TCM connector and solenoid and pressure switch assembly connector.

6) Remove transaxle relay from connector. Measure resistance between transaxle relay connector terminal No. 8 and solenoid and pressure switch assembly connector terminal No. 6. *See Figs. 4 and 8.* If resistance is more than 5 ohms, check and repair wiring harness between transaxle relay connector and solenoid and pressure switch assembly connector. If resistance is less than 5 ohms, replace solenoid and pressure switch assembly.

DTC 44: UNDERDRIVE SOLENOID

1) Disconnect TCM connector. Using ohmmeter, measure resistance between TCM connector terminal No. 19 and ground. *See Fig. 5.* If resistance is more than 10,000 ohms, go to step **4)**. If resistance if less than 10,000 ohms, disconnect solenoid and pressure switch assembly connector.

2) Measure resistance between solenoid and pressure switch assembly connector terminal No. 7 and ground. *See Fig. 8.* If resistance is less than 10,000 ohms, go to next step. If resistance is more than 10,000 ohms, check and repair solenoid and pressure switch assembly connector. If connector is okay, replace solenoid and pressure switch assembly.

3) Check wiring harness between TCM connector and solenoid and pressure switch assembly connector. If wiring harness is okay, recheck trouble codes. If trouble code resets, replace TCM.

4) Measure resistance between TCM connector terminals No. 56 and No. 19. If resistance not 1.0-3.0 ohms, go to next step. If resistance is 1.0-3.0 ohms, measure resistance between TCM connector terminals No. 13 and No. 17. If resistance is more than 5 ohms, check wiring harness between TCM connector and ground. If resistance is less than 5 ohms, check TCM connector. If connector is okay, replace TCM.

5) Disconnect solenoid and pressure switch assembly connector. Measure resistance between TCM connector terminal No. 19 and solenoid and pressure switch assembly connector terminal No. 7. *See Figs. 5 and 8.* If resistance is less than 5 ohms, go to next step. If resistance is more than 5 ohms, check and repair wiring harness between TCM connector and solenoid and pressure switch assembly connector.

6) Remove transaxle relay from connector. Measure resistance between transaxle relay connector terminal No. 8 and solenoid and pressure switch assembly connector terminal No. 6. *See Figs. 4 and 8.* If resistance is more than 5 ohms, check and repair wiring harness between transaxle relay connector and solenoid and pressure switch assembly connector. If resistance is less than 5 ohms, replace solenoid and pressure switch assembly.

DTC 46: UNDERDRIVE HYDRAULIC FAILURE

1) Install scan tool and turn ignition on. *See Fig. 1.* Scroll through appropriate scan tool data list numbers and observe appropriate clutch volume index. See HYDRAULIC CLUTCH CIRCUIT VOLUME SPECIFICATIONS table.

HYDRAULIC CLUTCH CIRCUIT VOLUME SPECIFICATIONS

Data List No./Circuit	Volume Index Range
51/Low-Reverse	35-85
52/2-4	20-77
53/Overdrive	75-100
54/Underdrive	24-70

2) If volume specifications are okay for all hydraulic circuits, check and repair wiring harness and connectors for the following components: TCM, Input Speed Sensor, Output Speed Sensor and Junction Connector 4. See WIRING DIAGRAMS. If volume specifications are not okay, internal transaxle failure exists. See CHRYSLER 41TE/AE overhaul article in 1995-96 MITCHELL® TRANSMISSION SERVICE & REPAIR manual for DOMESTIC CARS, LIGHT TRUCKS & VANS.

DTC 47: LOW-REVERSE SWITCH VALVE

DTC 47 sets when Low-Reverse solenoid switch valve pressure is high for second time. Internal transaxle failure may exist. See CHRYSLER 41TE/AE overhaul article in 1995-96 MITCHELL® TRANSMISSION SERVICE & REPAIR manual for DOMESTIC CARS, LIGHT TRUCKS & VANS.

DTC 48: TRD COMMUNICATION FAILURE

1) Check TP sensor for proper operation. See appropriate SELF-DIAGNOSTICS article in ENGINE PERFORMANCE in appropriate MITCHELL® manual. If TP sensor is okay, check and repair CCD bus communication. See DTC 19: CCD BUS COMMUNICATION circuit test. If CCD bus communication is okay, check TCM and ECM connectors.

2) If connectors are okay, recheck symptom. If trouble code still exists, check and repair Orange/Black wire between TCM connector terminal No. 50 and ECM connector terminal No. 63. *See Figs. 5 and 6.*

DTC 50: REVERSE GEAR RATIO INCORRECT
DTC 51: 1ST GEAR RATIO INCORRECT
DTC 52: 2ND GEAR RATIO INCORRECT
DTC 53: 3RD GEAR RATIO INCORRECT
DTC 54: 4TH GEAR RATIO INCORRECT

1) Check and repair input and output speed sensors for correct installation. If speed sensors are okay, check speed sensor connectors. If speed sensor connectors are okay, install scan tool and start engine.

2) Move shifter selector lever to "D" position. Observe scan tool data list No. 44 and No. 45. Scan tool display should show engine speed is more than zero RPM. If engine speed is as specified, go to next step. If engine speed is not as specified, perform DTC 56: INPUT SPEED SENSOR FAILURE circuit test.

3) Check transaxle fluid level and adjust as necessary. If fluid level is okay, raise and support vehicle to allow drive wheels to spin freely. Start engine, apply brakes and move selector lever to "R" position.

4) Using scan tool, open throttle to 30 percent and monitor input speed sensor RPM for 5 seconds. Bring engine back to idle. Scan tool display should show zero RPM for input speed sensor. If sensor RPM is not okay, 2-4 clutch or Underdrive clutch may be slipping. If sensor RPM is okay, move selector lever to "R" position.

5) Using scan tool, open throttle to 30 percent and monitor input speed sensor RPM for 5 seconds. Bring engine back to idle. Scan tool display should show zero RPM for input speed sensor. If sensor RPM is okay, go to next step. If sensor RPM is not okay, Reverse clutch or Low-Reverse clutch may be slipping. See CHRYSLER 41TE/AE overhaul article in 1995-96 MITCHELL® TRANSMISSION SERVICE & REPAIR manual for DOMESTIC CARS, LIGHT TRUCKS & VANS.

6) Check symptoms and verify a clutch slip is occurring. Check appropriate trouble code for specific clutch. Ensure problem is internal before removing and repairing transaxle. See INTERNAL CLUTCH FAULT IDENTIFICATION table.

INTERNAL CLUTCH FAULT IDENTIFICATION

DTC No.	Problem Clutch
50	Reverse Or Low-Reverse
51	Underdrive
52	2-4 Or Underdrive
53	Overdrive
54	Overdrive

7) If transaxle does not indicate signs of clutch slippage, check TCM connector for poor connection. If connection is okay, replace TCM with known good unit and retest system.

DTC 56: INPUT SPEED SENSOR FAILURE

1) Using scan tool, monitor data list No. 45 output speed sensor. Start engine, apply brakes and move selector lever to "D" position. Scan tool display should show zero RPM for output speed sensor. If sensor RPM is not okay, perform DTC 57: OUTPUT SPEED SENSOR FAILURE test. If sensor RPM is okay, disconnect TCM connector.

2) Measure resistance between TCM connector terminal No. 12 and ground. See Fig. 5. If resistance is more than 10,000 ohms, go to next step. If resistance is less than 10,000 ohms, check and repair wiring harness between TCM and input speed sensor. If wiring harness is okay, replace input speed sensor.

3) Measure resistance between TCM connector terminal No. 12 and No. 53. If resistance is not 300-1200 ohms, go to next step. If resistance check and repair TCM connector. If connector is okay, replace TCM.

4) Measure resistance between TCM connector terminal No. 12 and input speed sensor White/Green wire terminal. If resistance is less than 5 ohms, go to next step. If resistance is more than 5 ohms, check and repair White/Green wire between TCM connector and input speed sensor.

5) Measure resistance between TCM connector terminal No. 53 and input speed sensor Gray/Blue wire terminal. If resistance is less than 5 ohms, replace input speed sensor. If resistance is more than 5 ohms, check and repair Gray/Blue wire between TCM connector and input speed sensor connector.

DTC 57: OUTPUT SPEED SENSOR FAILURE

1) Disconnect TCM connector. Measure resistance between TCM connector terminal No. 54 and ground. See Fig. 5. If resistance is more than 10,000 ohms, go to next step. If resistance is less than 10,000 ohms, check and repair wiring harness between TCM and output speed sensor. If wiring harness is okay, replace output speed sensor.

2) Measure resistance between TCM connector terminal No. 53 and No. 54. If resistance is not 300-1200 ohms, go to next step. If resistance check and repair TCM connector. If connector is okay, replace TCM.

3) Measure resistance between TCM connector terminal No. 53 and output speed sensor Gray/Blue wire terminal. If resistance is less than 5 ohms, go to next step. If resistance is more than 5 ohms, check and repair Gray/Blue wire between TCM connector and output speed sensor.

4) Measure resistance between TCM connector terminal No. 54 and output speed sensor White/Yellow wire terminal. If resistance is less than 5 ohms, replace output speed sensor. If resistance is more than 5 ohms, check and repair White/Yellow wire between TCM connector and output speed sensor connector.

DTC 58: SPEED SENSOR GROUND

1) Disconnect TCM connector. Measure resistance between TCM connector terminals No. 12 and No. 53 and terminals No. 53 and No. 54. See Fig. 5. If resistance is 300-1200 ohms, check and repair TCM connector. If TCM connector is okay, replace TCM. If resistance is less than 300 ohms, check wiring harness between TCM connector, input and output speed sensor connectors. See WIRING DIAGRAMS.

2) If resistance is more than 1200 ohms, check and repair junction connector No. 4. See WIRING DIAGRAMS. If junction connector No. 4 is okay, check wiring harness between TCM connector, input and output speed sensor connectors.

DTC 60: LOW-REVERSE CLUTCH FAILING
DTC 61: 2-4 CLUTCH FAILING
DTC 62: OD CLUTCH FAILING

Using scan tool, monitor individual clutch volume needed to engage clutch. See CLUTCH VOLUME SPECIFICATIONS table. If clutch volume is not as specified, clutch may be damaged or failing. See CHRYSLER 41TE/AE overhaul article in 1995-96 MITCHELL® TRANSMISSION SERVICE & REPAIR manual for DOMESTIC CARS, LIGHT TRUCKS & VANS.

CLUTCH VOLUME SPECIFICATIONS

Clutch	Displayed Volume
Low-Reverse	35-83
Overdrive	75-150
2-4	20-77
Underdrive	24-70

DTC 73: FLUID WORN OUT OR BURNT

Check transaxle fluid and replace if necessary. If transaxle fluid is okay, internal transaxle failure exists. See CHRYSLER 41TE/AE overhaul article in 1995-96 MITCHELL® TRANSMISSION SERVICE & REPAIR manual for DOMESTIC CARS, LIGHT TRUCKS & VANS.

DTC 74: OIL TEMPERTURE SENSOR FAILURE

1) Check oil temperature sensor. See OIL TEMPERATURE SENSOR under COMPONENT TESTING. If oil temperature sensor is okay, disconnect transaxle range switch connector. Turn ignition on. Measure voltage between transaxle range switch connector terminal No. 4 and ground. See Fig. 10.

2) If voltage is more than 6 volts, go to next step. If voltage is less than 6 volts, check and repair TCM connector. If connector is okay, recheck trouble code. If code resets, go to next step.

3) Measure resistance between TCM connector terminal No. 3 and ground. See Fig. 5. If resistance is more than 5 ohms, go to next step. If resistance is less than 5 ohms, check wiring harness between TCM connector and transaxle range switch connector for short to ground. If wiring harness is okay, replace TCM.

4) Check TCM and transaxle range switch connectors for damage or poor connection. Recheck trouble code. If trouble code resets, check and repair wiring harness between TCM connector and transaxle range switch connector.

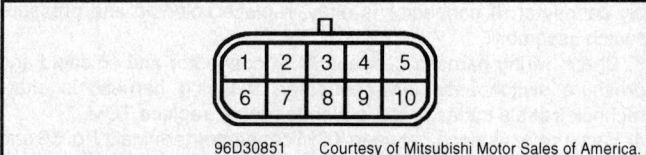

96D30851   Courtesy of Mitsubishi Motor Sales of America.

Fig. 10: Identifying Transaxle Range Switch & Oil Temperature Sensor Connector Terminals (1996 Models)

TESTING

HYDRAULIC PRESSURE TESTS

Pressure Test Preparation – 1) Ensure shift linkage or cable is properly adjusted, and that fluid level and condition are okay. Add fluid and adjust shift linkage or control cable as needed.

2) Ensure fluid is at normal operating temperature of 150-200°F (66-93°C). Install tachometer. Raise and support vehicle on hoist, allowing front wheels to rotate freely.

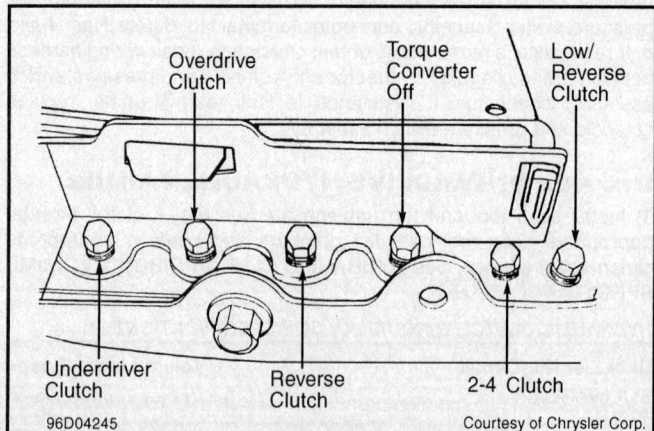

96D04245   Courtesy of Chrysler Corp.

Fig. 11: Identifying Hydraulic Clutch Pressure Taps

NOTE: A 150 psi (11 kg/cm²) pressure gauge is used for checking all clutches except reverse clutch. A 300 psi (21 kg/cm²) pressure gauge is used for checking reverse clutch.

Low-Reverse Clutch Pressure Test – 1) Remove plug and install pressure gauge in low-reverse clutch pressure tap. *See Fig. 11.*

2) Place gearshift in "L" position. Allowing front wheels to rotate, accelerate until vehicle speed indicates 20 MPH (32 km/h).

3) Low-Reverse clutch pressure should be 115-145 psi (8.0-10.1 kg/cm²). This pressure test checks oil pump output, pressure regulation and low-reverse clutch hydraulic circuit and shift schedule. Remove pressure gauge. Install and tighten pressure tap plug to specification. See TORQUE SPECIFICATIONS.

Underdrive Clutch Pressure Test – 1) Remove plug and install pressure gauge in underdrive clutch pressure tap. *See Fig. 11.*

2) Place gearshift in "D" or "2" position. Allowing front wheels to rotate, accelerate until vehicle speed indicates 30 MPH (48 km/h).

3) Underdrive clutch pressure should be 110-145 psi (7.7-10.1 kg/cm²). This pressure test checks underdrive clutch hydraulic circuit and shift schedule. Remove pressure gauge. Install and tighten pressure tap plug to specification. See TORQUE SPECIFICATIONS.

Overdrive Clutch Pressure Test – 1) Remove plug and install pressure gauge in overdrive clutch pressure tap. *See Fig. 11.*

2) Place gearshift in "OD" or "D" (Overdrive switch released) position. Allowing front wheels to rotate, accelerate until vehicle speed indicates 20 MPH (32 km/h).

3) Overdrive clutch pressure should be 74-95 psi (5.3-6.7 kg/cm²). Place gearshift in "2" position and increase vehicle speed to 30 MPH (48 km/h).

4) Transaxle should be in 2nd gear and overdrive clutch pressure should now be less than 5 psi (.35 kg/cm²). This pressure test checks overdrive clutch hydraulic cicuit and shift schedule. Remove pressure gauge. Install and tighten pressure tap plug to specification. See TORQUE SPECIFICATIONS.

Torque Converter Clutch Off Pressure Test – 1) Remove plug and install pressure gauge in torque converrter clutch off pressure tap. *See Fig. 11.* Allowing front wheels to rotate, accelerate until vehicle speed indicates 50 MPH (80 km/h).

2) Torque converter clutch off pressure should be less than 5 psi (.35 kg/cm²). This pressure test checks torque converter clutch hydraulic circuit. Remove pressure gauge. Install and tighten pressure tap plug to specification. See TORQUE SPECIFICATIONS.

Reverse Clutch Pressure Test – 1) Remove plug and install pressure gauge in reverse clutch pressure tap. *See Fig. 11.* Place gearshift in Reverse.

2) Accelerate until engine speed is 1500 RPM and note reverse clutch pressure. Reverse clutch pressure should be 165-235 psi (11.6-16.5 kg/cm²). This pressure test checks reverse clutch hydraulic circuit.

3) Remove pressure gauge. Install and tighten pressure tap plug to specification. See TORQUE SPECIFICATIONS.

Pressure Test Result Indications – 1) If proper hydraulic pressure exists in any one pressure test, oil pump and pressure regulator valve are operating properly. Various clutch operating hydraulic pressures exist depending on gearshift position.

2) Low hydraulic pressure in any or all positions indicates a defective oil pump, restricted oil filter or stuck pressure regulator valve. If hydraulic pressure is not within specification, clutch hydraulic circuit is leaking.

3) If overdrive clutch hydraulic pressure exceeds 5 psi (.35 kg/cm²) in step **4)** of OVERDRIVE CLUTCH PRESSURE TEST, a worn reaction shaft seal ring is indicated.

TCM VOLTAGES

Access TCM. *See Fig. 12 or 13.* Turn ignition on. Using voltmeter, backprobe TCM connector. *See Fig. 5.* Check voltage between designated TCM connector terminals and ground. Voltage should be as specified. See TCM TERMINAL VOLTAGE SPECIFICATIONS table.

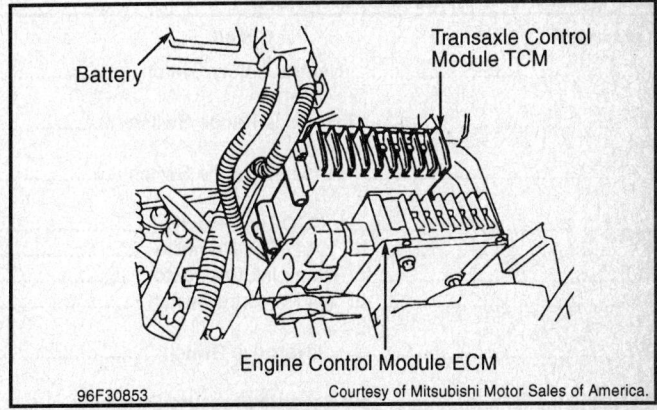

Fig. 12: Locating TCM (1995 Models)

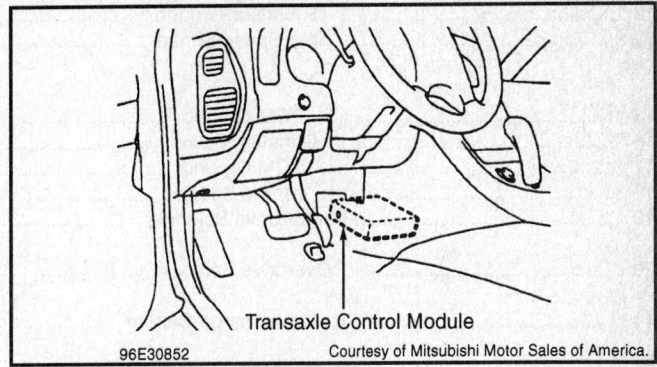

Fig. 13: Locating TCM (1996 Models)

COMPONENT TESTING

INPUT & OUTPUT SPEED SENSORS

Disconnect appropriate speed sensor harness connector. *See Figs. 2 or 3.* Measure resistance between speed sensor terminals. If resistance is not 300-1200 ohms, replace speed sensor.

OIL TEMPERATURE SENSOR

Disconnect transaxle range switch harness connector. Measure resistance between terminals No. 2 and No. 3. *See Fig. 10.* With oil temperature at 32°F (0°C), resistance should be 29,330-35,990 ohms. With oil temperature at 212°F (100°C), resistance should be 640-720 ohms. If resistance is not as specified, replace transaxle range switch.

NEUTRAL SAFETY SWITCH

Disconnect neutral safety switch harness connector. *See Fig. 2.* Move selector lever to each gear position and test continuity between specified terminals. See NEUTRAL SAFETY SWITCH SPECIFICATION table. *See Fig. 9.* If continuity is not as specified, replace transaxle range switch.

NEUTRAL SAFETY SWITCH SPECIFICATION

Selector Position	Continuity Between Terminals
"P"	1 & 3
"R"	2 & Ground
"N"	1 & 3
"D"	2 & Ground
"2"	1
"L"	1

1 – Continuity should not exist between any terminals.

AUTOMATIC TRANSMISSIONS
Mitsubishi F4AC1 Electronic Controls (Cont.)

TCM TERMINAL VOLTAGE SPECIFICATIONS

Terminal No.	Circuit	[1] Conditions	Voltage
1	Neutral Safety Switch	"R", "D", "2" & "L" Selector Positions	Battery Voltage
		"P" & "N" Selector Positions	0
2 [2]	Transaxle Range Switch	"R", "N", "D" & "2" Selector Positions	Battery Voltage
		"P" & "L" Selector Positions	0
2 [3]	Transaxle Range Switch	"D" & "2" Selector Positions	Battery Voltage
		"P", "R", "N" & "L" Selector Positions	0
3	CCD Bus Positive	Ignition Off	2.5
4 [2]	CCD Bus Negative	Ignition Off	2.5
6	Data Link Connector	Ignition Off	5
7	2-4 Pressure Switch	Transaxle In 2nd Or 4th Gear	0
		In Any Other Gear	Battery Voltage
9	Overdrive Switch	Overdrive Switch On	Battery Voltage
		Overdrive Switch Off	0
10	Low-Reverse Pressure Switch	Transaxle In "N" Or 1 Gear	0
		Transaxle In Any Other Gear	Battery Voltage
11	TP Sensor Ground	Ignition On	0
12	Input Speed Sensor	Measure Between Terminals 12 & 53	2.6
		Engine @ 3000 RPM, "D" Selector Position	
		Transaxle In 3rd Gear	
13	TCM Ground	Ignition On	0
16	Constant Power	Ignition Off	Battery Voltage
17	TCM Ground	Ignition On	0
18	Vehicle Speed	Vehicle Moving Slowly	0-4
19	Underdrive Solenoid	Transaxle In 1st, 2nd Or 3rd Gear	Battery Voltage
		Transaxle In Any Other Gear	10
20	Overdrive Solenoid	Transaxle In 3rd Or 4th Gear	10
		Transaxle In Any Other Gear	Battery Voltage
41 [2]	Transaxle Range Sensor	"P", "R" & "L" Selector Position	Battery Voltage
		"R", "N" & "2" Selector Position	0
41 [3]	Transaxle Range Sensor	"P", "R" & "2" Selector Position	Battery Voltage
		"R", "N" & "L" Selector Position	0
42 [2]	Reverse Light Relay Coil	"D" Selector Position	Battery Voltage
		All Other Selector Positions	0
43	Transaxle Range Sensor	"N", "D" & "L" Selector Position	0
44	CCD Bus Negative	Ignition Off	2.5
45 [2]	CCD Bus Positive	Ignition Off	2.5
46	Crank Signal	Engine Idling	1.5
48	Ignition Ground	"P" & "N" Selector Position	0
		All Other Selector Positions	Battery Voltage
49	Overdrive Pressure Switch	Transaxle In 3rd Or 4th Gear	Battery Voltage
		Transaxle In Any Other Gear	0
51	Power Feed	Ignition On	Battery Voltage
		Ignition Off	0
52	TP Sensor	Accelerator Fully Released	0
		Accelerator Fully Depressed	3.8
53	Speed Sensor Ground	Ignition On	0
54	Output Speed Sensor	Measure Between Terminals 12 & 53	2.6
		Engine @ 3000 RPM, "D" Selector Position	
		Transaxle In 3rd Gear	
55	Transaxle Relay	Ignition On	Battery Voltage
		Ignition Off	0
56	Switched Battery	Ignition On	Battery Voltage
		Ignition Off	0
57	Switched Battery	Ignition On	Battery Voltage
		Ignition Off	0
59	2-4 Solenoid	Transaxle In 2nd Or 4th Gear	Battery Voltage
		Transaxle In Any Other Gear	10
60	Low-Reverse Solenoid	Transaxle In "N" Or 1st	10
		Transaxle In Any Other Gear	Battery Voltage

[1] – Ignition is considered to be on unless otherwise noted.
[2] – Applies to 1995 models only.
[3] – Applies to 1996 models only.

SOLENOIDS

Low-Reverse Solenoid – Disconnect solenoid and pressure switch harness connector. *See Figs. 2 or 3.* Measure resistance between solenoid and pressure switch terminals No. 4 and No. 6. *See Fig. 8.* If resistance is not one ohm at 68°F (20°C), replace solenoid and pressure switch assembly.

2-4 Solenoid – Disconnect solenoid and pressure switch harness connector. Measure resistance between solenoid and pressure switch terminals No. 3 and No. 6. *See Fig. 8.* If resistance is not one ohm at 68°F (20°C), replace solenoid and pressure switch assembly.

Overdrive Solenoid – Disconnect solenoid and pressure switch harness connector. Measure resistance between solenoid and pressure switch terminals No. 6 and No. 8. *See Fig. 8.* If resistance is not one ohm at 68°F (20°C), replace solenoid and pressure switch assembly.

Underdrive Solenoid – Disconnect solenoid and pressure switch harness connector. Measure resistance between solenoid and pressure switch terminals No. 6 and No. 7. *See Fig. 8.* If resistance is not one ohm at 68°F (20°C), replace solenoid and pressure switch assembly.

TRANSAXLE RANGE SWITCH

Disconnect transaxle range switch harness connector. Move selector lever to each gear position and test continuity between specified terminals. See appropriate TRANSAXLE RANGE SWITCH SPECIFICATION table. *See Figs. 9 and 10.* If continuity is not as specified, replace transaxle range switch.

TRANSAXLE RANGE SWITCH SPECIFICATION (1995 MODELS)

Selector Position	Continuity Between Terminals
"P"	1 & 3
"R"	2 & Ground
"N"	2 & Ground
"D"	[1]
"2"	2 & Ground
"L"	1 & 3

[1] – Continuity should not exist between any terminals.

TRANSAXLE RANGE SWITCH SPECIFICATION (1996 MODELS)

Selector Position	[1] Continuity
"P"	1, 6, 7 & 8
"R"	[2] 7
"N"	1, 6, 7 & 9
"D"	9
"2"	8
"L"	7, 8 & 9

[1] – Measure continuity between specified terminal and ground.
[2] – Continuity should also exist between terminals 5 & 10.

TRANSAXLE RELAY

NOTE: Transaxle relay may also be referred to as the EATX relay.

1) Disconnect transaxle relay harness connector and remove relay from firewall bracket. *See Fig. 16.* Measure continuity between transaxle relay terminals No. 4 and No. 6. *See Fig. 4.* If continuity exists, go to next step. If continuity does not exist, replace transaxle relay.

2) Connect negative battery terminal to transaxle relay terminal No. 6. Connect positive relay terminal No. 4. Measure continuity between transaxle relay terminals No. 2 and No. 8. If continuity is not as specified, replace transaxle relay.

REMOVAL & INSTALLATION

INPUT & OUTPUT SPEED SENSOR

Locate appropriate speed sensor to be removed. *See Fig. 2 or 3.* Disconnect speed sensor connector. Using appropriate wrench, unscrew speed sensor from transaxle. To install, reverse removal procedure.

NEUTRAL SAFETY SWITCH

Locate neutral safety switch. *See Fig. 2 or 3.* Disconnect switch connector. Unscrew switch from transaxle. To install, reverse removal procedure.

OVERDRIVE SWITCH

1) Remove selector knob cover. Remove shift indicator upper and lower covers. Disconnect overdrive switch and position indicator light connector.

2) Using flat blade screwdriver, remove overdrive switch button. Remove screw and overdrive switch from selector lever knob. Remove overdrive switch wires from connector and pull through selector lever knob. To install, reverse removal procedure.

SOLENOID & PRESSURE SWITCH ASSEMBLY

1) Disconnect input speed sensor connector. *See Fig. 2 or 3.* Remove input speed sensor. Disconnect solenoid and pressure switch assembly connector. Remove sound cover from solenoid and pressure switch assembly.

2) Remove 3 solenoid and pressure switch assembly retaining bolts. *See Fig. 14.* Remove sound cover attaching plate and gaskets. To install, reverse removal procedure. Before installing sound cover, clean sound cover and sound cover-to-transaxle mating surface.

NOTE: DO NOT use solvents or petroleum based cleaners on sound cover. Solvents may deteriorate sound cover or electrical components.

3) Apply a bead of RTV sealant to sound cover-to-transaxle mating surface and install sound cover. Failure to apply sealant will cause a racheting noise from sound cover vibration.

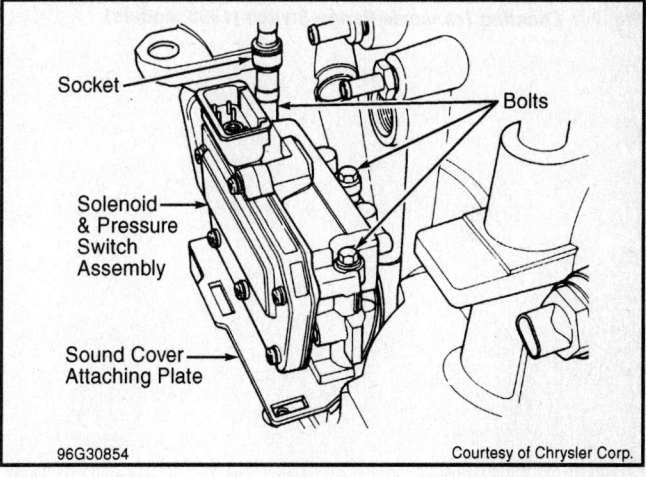

Fig. 14: Removing Solenoid & Pressure Switch Assembly

TCM

On 1995 models, TCM is located next to battery in engine compartment. On 1996 models, TCM is located inside center console. *See Fig. 12 or 13.* Disconnect TCM connector. Remove 3 TCM securing bolts and TCM. To install, reverse removal procedure. After installing TCM perform quick learn, pinion factor and torque converter clutch break-in procedures. See ADJUSTMENTS.

TRANSAXLE RANGE SWITCH

1995 Models – Locate transaxle range switch. *See Fig. 2.* Disconnect transaxle range switch connector. Using appropriate wrench, unscrew transaxle range switch from transaxle. To install, reverse removal procedure.

1996 Models – 1) Transaxle range switch is located on valve body. *See Fig. 3.* Disconnect battery negative cable. Remove air cleaner. Remove gearshift cable and manual lever. Disconnect transaxle range switch connector. Raise and support vehicle.

2) Remove transaxle oil pan and carefully drain fluid. Remove oil filter and allow transaxle to drain fully. Remove valve body retaining bolts. Remove parking rod from guide bracket and remove valve body assembly. *See Fig. 15.*

3) Place valve body assembly on workbench. Remove transaxle range switch retaining bolt and slide transaxle range switch off of manual shaft. To install, reverse removal procedure. Torque transaxle range switch, oil pan and valve body bolts to specifications. See TORQUE SPECIFICATIONS table. Refill transaxle with ATF.

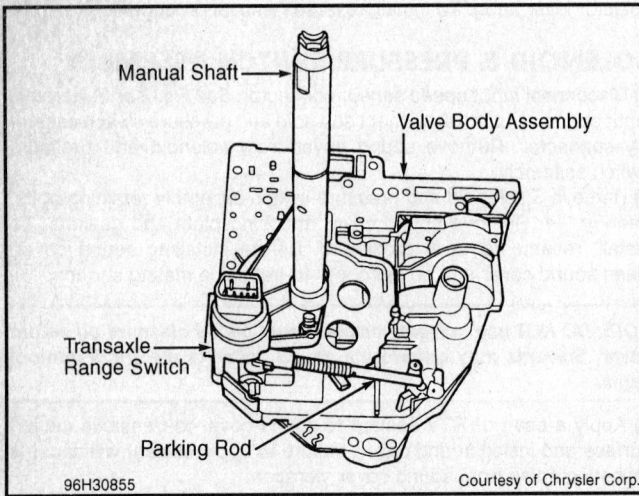

Fig. 15: Locating Transaxle Range Switch (1996 Models)

TRANSAXLE RELAY

Locate transaxle relay. *See Fig. 16.* Disconnect transaxle relay connector. Remove transaxle relay from relay bracket. To install, reverse removal procedure.

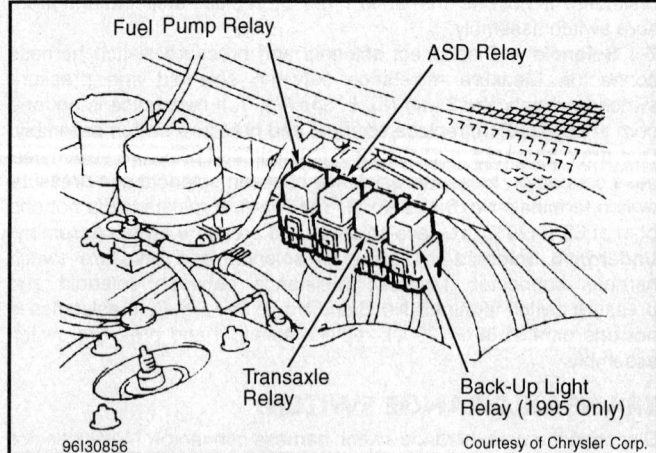

Fig. 16: Locating Transaxle Relay

TORQUE SPECIFICATIONS
TORQUE SPECIFICATIONS

Application	Ft. Lbs. (N.m)
Input Speed Sensor	20 (27)
Output Speed Sensor	20 (27)
Neutral Safety Switch	20 (27)
Transaxle Oil Pan	14 (19)
Transaxle Range Switch (1995)	20 (27)
	INCH Lbs. (N.m)
Solenoid & Pressure Switch Assembly Connector	35 (4)
Solenoid & Pressure Switch Assembly	106 (12)
TCM Connector	35 (4)
Transaxle Range Switch (1996)	44 (5)
Valve Body Assembly	106 (12)

WIRING DIAGRAMS

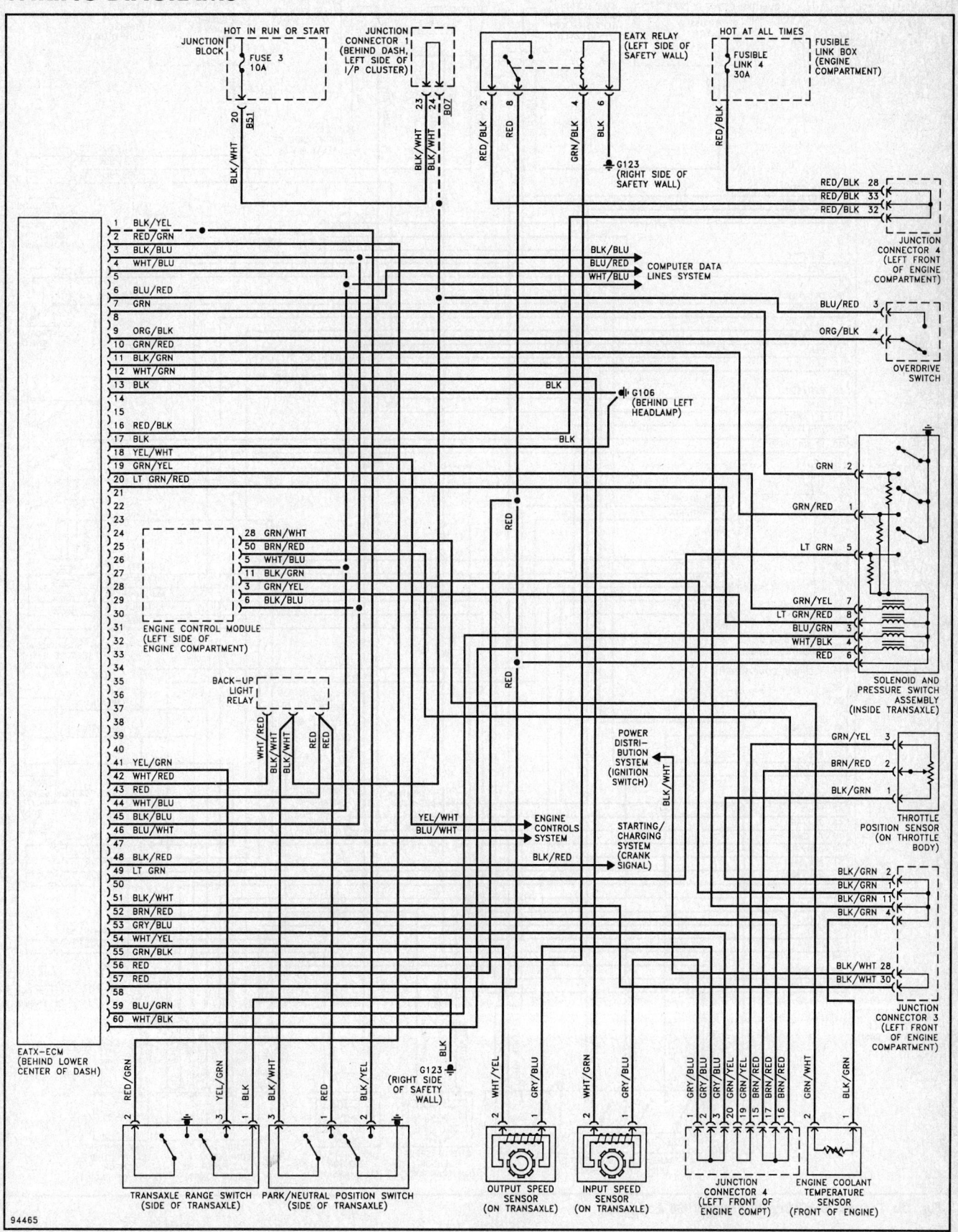

Fig. 17: *Transaxle Wiring Diagram (1995 Eclipse)*

94465

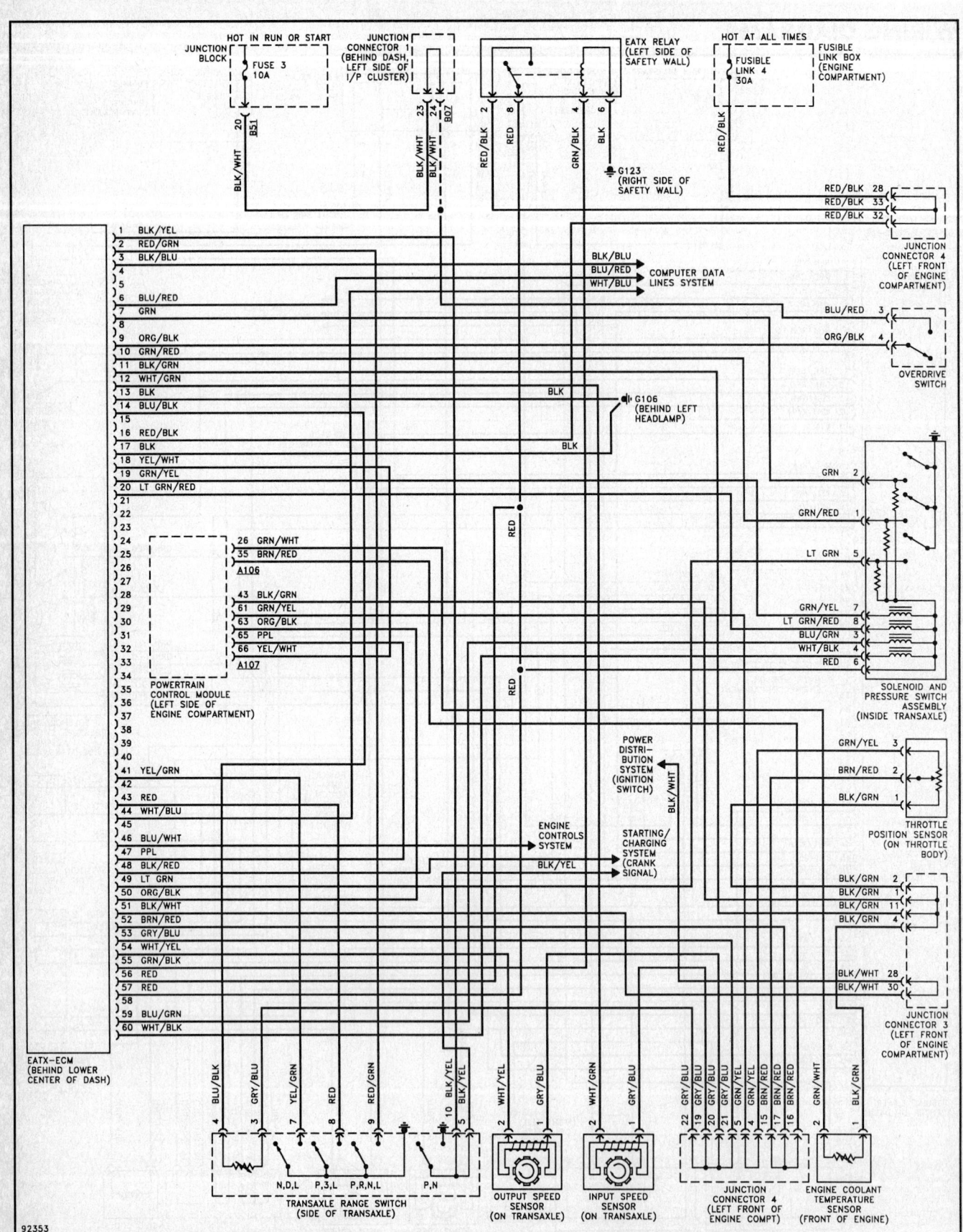

Fig. 18: Transaxle Wiring Diagram (1996 Eclipse)

Hyundai: Sonata
Mitsubishi: Diamante, Eclipse, Expo, 3000GT

APPLICATION & LABOR TIMES

APPLICATION & LABOR TIMES

Vehicle Application	Labor Times [1] R & I	[2] Overhaul	Transaxle Series
Hyundai			
Sonata 3.0L	4.6	8.9	F4A33
Mitsubishi			
Diamante [3]	5.1	8.9	F4A33
Eclipse			
2.0L Turbo			
AWD	7.4	8.9	W4A33
FWD	6.8	8.9	F4A33
Expo			
AWD	7.4	8.9	W4A32
3000GT	4.6	8.9	F4A33

[1] – Removal and installation of transmission from vehicle chassis.

[2] – Bench overhaul time for transmission. DOES NOT include removal and installation.

[3] – If equipped with Electronically Controlled Suspension, add .2 hr.

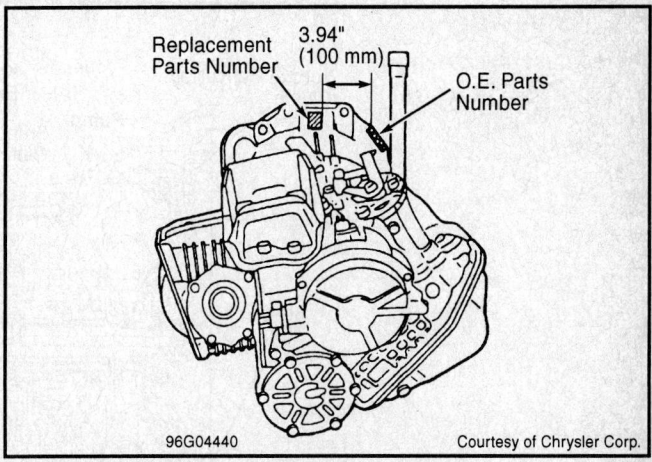

96G04440   Courtesy of Chrysler Corp.

Fig. 1: Locating Transaxle Identification Numbers

IDENTIFICATION

Transaxle model can be identified on metal tag attached to center of firewall. For parts replacement, identification is stamped on transaxle case on top of transaxle converter housing. *See Fig. 1.*

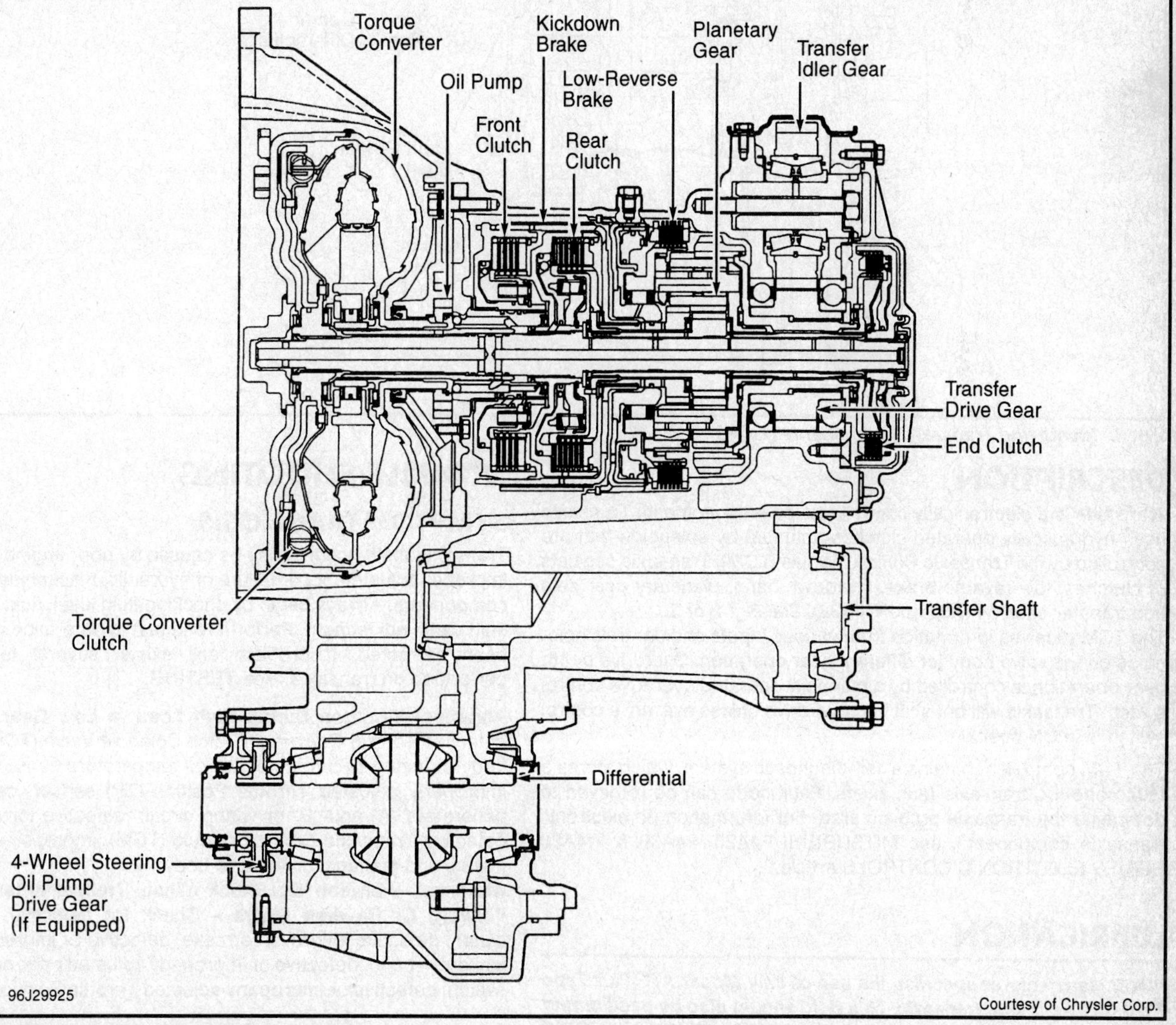

96J29925   Courtesy of Chrysler Corp.

Fig. 2: Identifying Transaxle Components (F4A33)

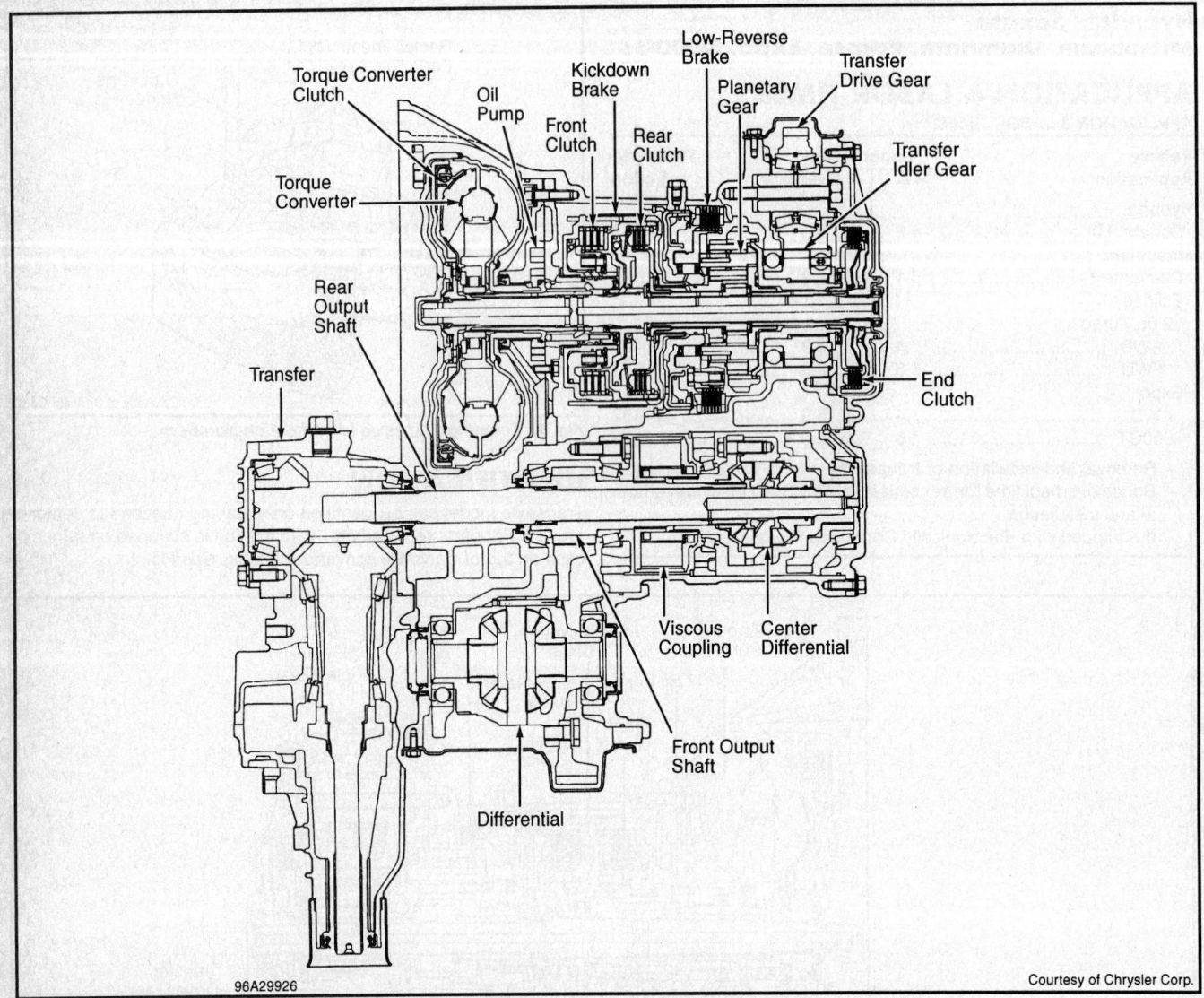

Courtesy of Chrysler Corp.

Fig. 3: Identifying Transaxle Components (W4A32 & W4A33)

DESCRIPTION

Transaxle is a electronically controlled 4-speed automatic. Transaxle uses hydraulically operated clutches actuated by solenoids that are controlled by the Transaxle Control Module (TCM). Transaxle consists of clutches, low-reverse brake, kickdown band, planetary gear sets and transfer case (W4A32 and W4A33). See Fig. 2 or 3.

The TCM receives information from various inputs and controls solenoids on the valve body for different gear operation. Overdrive or 4th gear operation is controlled by a manually operated overdrive control switch. Transaxle will not shift into overdrive unless overdrive control switch is in ON position.

The TCM controller contains a self-diagnostic system, which stores a fault code if a transaxle fault exists. Fault code can be retrieved to determine the transaxle problem area. For information on electronic transaxle components, see MITSUBISHI F4A20, F4A30 & W4A30 SERIES ELECTRONIC CONTROLS article.

LUBRICATION

NOTE: Manufacturer specifies the use of only Mopar ATF Plus-Type 7176 for use in this transaxle. This fluid should also be used during assembly. See appropriate AUTOMATIC TRANSMISSION SERVICING article in TRANSMISSION SERVICING for additional information and draining and refilling procedures.

TROUBLE SHOOTING

SYMPTOM DIAGNOSIS

Transaxle malfunctions may be caused by poor engine performance, improper adjustments or failure of hydraulic, mechanical or electronic components. Always begin by checking fluid level, fluid condition and shift cable adjustment. Perform road test to determine if problem has been corrected. If problem still exists, several tests must be performed on transaxle. See TESTING.

Abnormal Vibration During High Load In Low Gear – Check for defective Torque Converter Clutch Solenoid Valve (TCCSV) on valve body or wiring circuit, defective oil temperature sensor, defective or improperly adjusted Throttle Position (TP) sensor, defective pulse generators "A" and "B" or wiring circuit, defective torque converter, defective Transaxle Control Module (TCM), improper engine performance and malfunction in valve body.

Abnormal Vibration Or Shock When Transaxle Is Shifted Into Forward Or Reverse Gears – Check for defective front or rear clutch, defective low-reverse brake, defective or improperly adjusted kickdown band, defective or improperly adjusted park/neutral position switch, defective or improperly adjusted Throttle Position (TP) sensor, defective Pressure Control Solenoid Valve (PCSV) on valve body or wiring circuit, defective Transaxle Control Module (TCM), improper engine idle speed, improper shift cable adjustment and malfunction in valve body.

Clutch Slips In Drive & Torque Converter Stall Speed Is Excessive – Check for defective oil pump, defective one-way clutch, defective torque converter, defective Pressure Control Solenoid Valve (PCSV) on valve body or wiring circuit, defective Torque Converter Clutch Solenoid Valve (TCCSV) on valve body or wiring circuit, defective rear clutch, improper shift cable adjustment, low fluid level, low line pressure and malfunction in valve body.

Clutch Slips In Reverse & Torque Converter Stall Speed Is Excessive – Check for defective front clutch or retainer, defective low-reverse brake, defective torque converter, defective oil pump, defective Pressure Control Solenoid Valve (PCSV) on valve body or wiring circuit, improper shift cable adjustment, low fluid level, low line pressure, malfunction in valve body and 'O' ring for low-reverse brake circuit not installed between valve body and transaxle case.

Torque Converter Clutch Inoperative – Check for defective Torque Converter Clutch Solenoid Valve (TCCSV) on valve body or wiring circuit, defective oil temperature sensor, defective or improperly adjusted Throttle Position (TP) sensor, defective pulse generators "A" and "B" or wiring circuit, defective torque converter, defective Transaxle Control Module (TCM), malfunction in ignition signal system and malfunction in valve body.

Engine Stalls When Shifted From Neutral To Drive Or Reverse – Check for defective Torque Converter Clutch Solenoid Valve (TCCSV) on valve body or wiring circuit, improper engine idle speed or performance, defective torque converter and malfunction in valve body.

Engine Starts, Or Vehicle Moves Between Neutral & Reverse Or Neutral & Drive – Check for defective or improperly adjusted park/neutral position switch, improper shift cable adjustment and malfunction in valve body.

Excessive Creeping Or Idling Vibration – Check for defective or improperly adjusted accelerator switch, defective Transaxle Control Models (TCM) and improper engine idle speed.

Excessive Vibration During All Upshifts – Check for defective front clutch, defective or improperly adjusted Throttle Position (TP) sensor, defective pulse generator "A" or wiring circuit, defective Transaxle Control Model (TCM), improper engine performance, malfunction in ignition signal system and malfunction in valve body.

Excessive Vibration During D-2 Downshift – Check for defective low-reverse brake, defective kickdown band or piston, defective kickdown servo switch, defective or improperly adjusted Throttle Position (TP) sensor, defective pulse generator "A" or wiring circuit, defective Transaxle Control Module (TCM), improper engine performance, malfunction in ignition signal system and malfunction in valve body.

Excessive Vibration During 1-2 Or 3-4 Upshift – Check for defective end clutch, defective kickdown band or piston, defective kickdown servo switch, defective or improperly adjusted Throttle Position (TP) sensor, defective pulse generator "A" or wiring circuit, defective Transaxle Control Module (TCM), improper engine performance, improper kickdown servo adjustment, malfunction in ignition signal system and malfunction in valve body.

Excessive Vibration During 2-3 Or 4-3 Shift – Check for defective front clutch, defective or improperly adjusted Throttle Position (TP) sensor, defective pulse generator "A" or wiring circuit, defective Transaxle Control Module (TCM), improper engine performance, malfunction in ignition signal system and malfunction in valve body.

Excessive Vibration When Cold – Check for improper engine performance and malfunction in valve body.

Overdrive Control Switch Will Not Operate – Check for defective overdrive control switch or wiring circuit and defective Transaxle Control Module (TCM).

Sudden Engine RPM Increase During Upshift – Check for low fluid level, defective end clutch, defective oil pump, defective front clutch or retainer, defective kickdown band, defective or improperly adjusted Throttle Position (TP) sensor, defective Pressure Control Solenoid Valve (PCSV) on valve body or wiring circuit, defective pulse generator "A" or wiring circuit, defective Transaxle Control Module (TCM),

improper kickdown servo adjustment, low line pressure, malfunction in ignition signal system and malfunction in valve body.

Sudden Engine RPM Increase During 3-2 Shift With Excessive Vibration – Check for defective front clutch retainer, defective kickdown band, defective kickdown servo switch, defective oil pump, defective or improperly adjusted Throttle Position (TP) sensor, defective Pressure Control Solenoid Valve (PCSV) on valve body, defective pulse generator "A" or wiring circuit, defective Transaxle Control Module (TCM), improper kickdown servo adjustment, low fluid level, low line pressure, malfunction in ignition signal system and malfunction in valve body.

Torque Converter Stall Speed Is Low – Check for defective torque converter and improper engine performance.

Transaxle Remains In 3rd Gear – Check for defective contacts at ignition switch, defective Torque Converter Clutch Solenoid Valve (TCCSV) on valve body or wiring circuit, defective end clutch, defective front clutch retainer, defective front or rear clutch, defective kickdown band, defective kickdown servo switch, defective low-reverse brake, defective or improperly adjusted park/neutral position switch, defective Pressure Control Solenoid Valve (PCSV) on valve body or wiring circuit, defective pulse generator "B" or wiring circuit, defective Shift Control Solenoid Valve (SCSV) "A" or "B" on valve body or wiring circuit, defective Transaxle Control Module (TCM), improper shift cable adjustment, low fluid level, low line pressure, malfunction in valve body and "O" Ring for low-reverse brake circuit not installed between valve body and transaxle case.

Transaxle Shifts But Not Within Specified Range – Check for defective connection at ignition switch, defective or improperly adjusted Throttle Position (TP) sensor, defective pulse generator "B" or wiring circuit, defective Transaxle Control Module (TCM) and malfunction in valve body.

Transaxle Starts Off From 2nd Gear – Check for defective or improperly adjusted accelerator switch, defective or improperly adjusted park/neutral position switch, defective Transaxle Control Module (TCM), defective torque converter, improper engine performance, improper shift cable adjustment and malfunction in valve body.

Transaxle Will Not Upshift From 2nd To 3rd Gear – Check for defective front clutch or retainer, defective Pressure Control Solenoid Valve (PCSV) on valve body or wiring circuit, defective Transaxle Control Module (TCM), defective or improperly adjusted park/neutral position switch, defective torque converter and malfunction in valve body.

Transaxle Will Not Upshift Into 4th Gear – Check for defective end clutch, defective front clutch retainer, defective or improperly adjusted park/neutral position switch, defective overdrive control switch, defective Transaxle Control Module (TCM), improper shift cable adjustment and malfunction in valve body.

Vehicle Moves In Park Or Neutral – Check for defective or improperly adjusted park/neutral position switch, defective parking mechanism, defective rear clutch, improper shift cable adjustment and malfunction in valve body.

Vehicle Will Not Hold In Park – Check for defective parking mechanism and improper shift cable adjustment.

Vehicle Will Not Move Forward – Check for defective oil pump, defective one-way clutch, defective Pressure Control Solenoid Valve (PCSV) on valve body or wiring circuit, defective rear clutch, defective torque converter, improper shift cable adjustment, low fluid level, low line pressure and malfunction in valve body.

Vehicle Will Not Move Forward Or Backward – Check for defective low-reverse brake, defective oil pump, defective Pressure Control Solenoid Valve (PCSV) on valve body or wiring circuit, defective torque converter, defective torque converter drive plate, improper shift cable adjustment, low fluid level, low line pressure and malfunction in valve body.

Vehicle Will Not Move In Reverse – Check for defective front clutch or retainer, defective low-reverse brake, defective oil pump, defective Pressure Control Solenoid Valve (PCSV) on valve body or wiring circuit, defective pulse generator "B" or wiring circuit, defective torque converter, improper shift cable adjustment, low fluid level, low line pressure, malfunction in valve body and "O" Ring for low-reverse brake circuit not installed between valve body and transaxle case.

CLUTCH, BRAKE & BAND APPLICATION CHART

Selector Lever Position	Elements In Use
"D" (Drive)	
1st Gear	Rear Clutch & One-Way Clutch
2nd Gear	Rear Clutch & Kickdown Band
3rd Gear	Front Clutch, Rear Clutch & End Clutch
4th Gear	End Clutch & Kickdown Band
"2" (Second)	
1st Gear	Rear Clutch & One-Way Clutch
2nd Gear	Rear Clutch & Kickdown Band
"1" (Low)	
1st Gear	Rear Clutch & Low-Reverse Brake
"R" (Reverse)	Front Clutch & Low-Reverse Brake
"N" Or "P" (Neutral Or Park)	All Clutches, Brakes & Bands Released Or Ineffective

TESTING

NOTE: A road test can be performed to check transaxle shift points. Pressure test can be performed to check operation of transaxle internal components. Torque converter stall speed test can be performed to check torque converter operation.

ROAD TEST

NOTE: Perform road test to ensure transaxle shift points are at specified speeds. See Figs. 4-7. Shift point information is not available for Sonata 3.0L.

1) Ensure shift cable is properly adjusted, and fluid level and condition are okay. Add fluid and adjust shift cable if necessary. Road test vehicle, and check if shift points are at specified speeds. *See Figs. 4-7.*

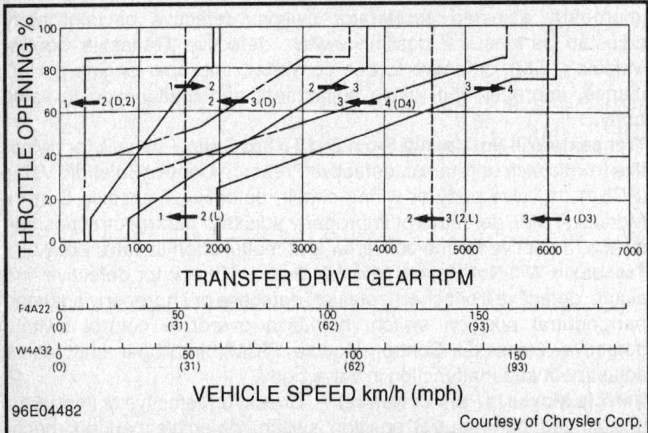

Courtesy of Chrysler Corp.

Fig. 4: Identifying Transaxle Shift Points (Expo)

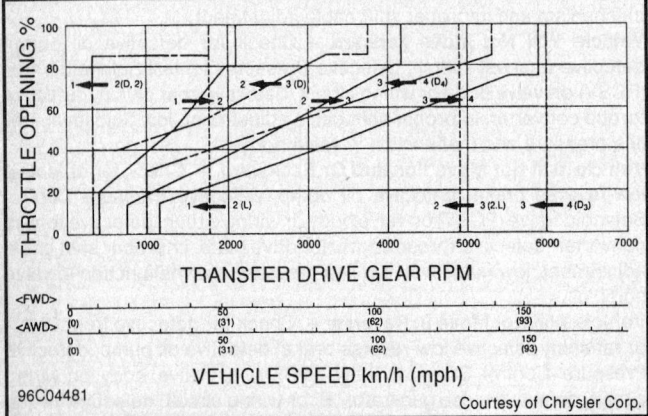

Courtesy of Chrysler Corp.

Fig. 5: Identifying Transaxle Shift Points (Eclipse)

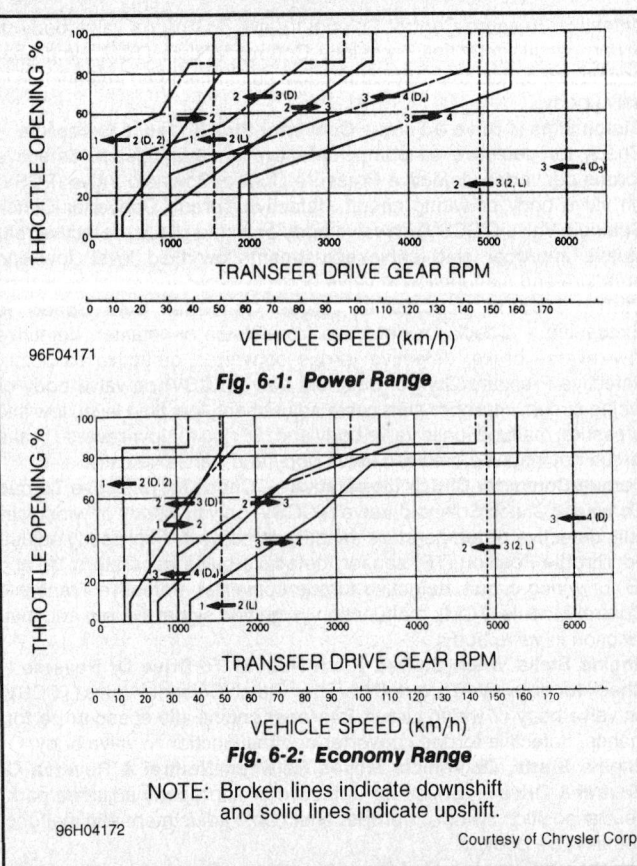

Fig. 6-1: Power Range

Fig. 6-2: Economy Range

NOTE: Broken lines indicate downshift and solid lines indicate upshift.

Courtesy of Chrysler Corp.

Fig. 6: Identifying Transaxle Shift Points (Diamante & 3000GT SOHC)

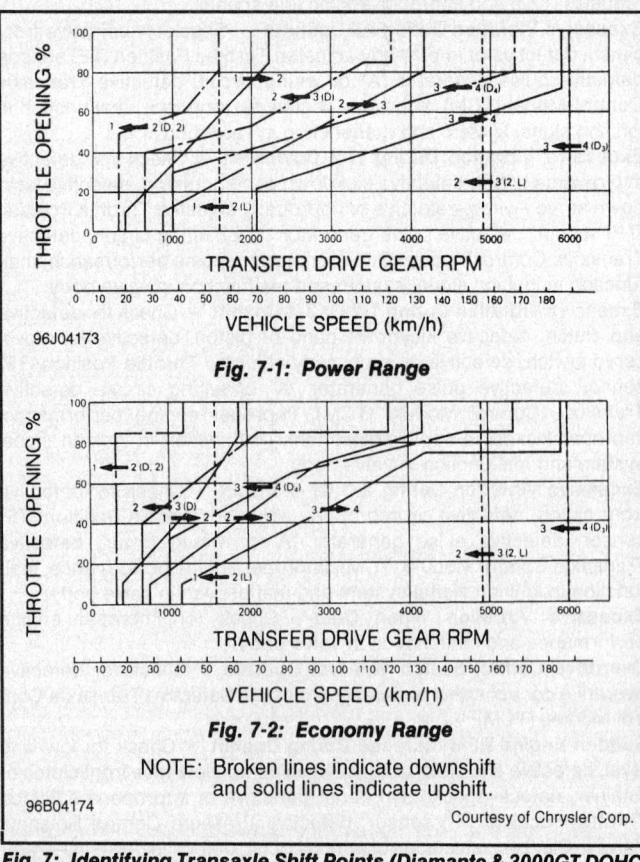

Fig. 7-1: Power Range

Fig. 7-2: Economy Range

NOTE: Broken lines indicate downshift and solid lines indicate upshift.

Courtesy of Chrysler Corp.

Fig. 7: Identifying Transaxle Shift Points (Diamante & 3000GT DOHC)

2) If shift points are not as specified, check for stored fault codes. See MITSUBISHI F4A20, F4A30 & W4A30 SERIES ELECTRONIC CONTROLS article. If slippage occurs, determine which components are applied in each gear. See CLUTCH, BRAKE & BAND APPLICATION CHART table. Perform hydraulic pressure test to check transaxle internal components. See HYDRAULIC PRESSURE TEST under TESTING.

TORQUE CONVERTER STALL SPEED TEST

Stall Speed Test Procedure – 1) Install tachometer. Ensure transaxle fluid level is correct. Start engine, and operate it until transaxle fluid is at normal operating temperature. Ensure engine operating temperature is approximately 180-190°F (80-90°C).
2) Block rear wheels. Apply parking and service brakes. Place transaxle in Drive, and open throttle to wide open position. Note maximum engine RPM. This is torque converter stall speed. Repeat procedure with transaxle in Reverse.

CAUTION: DO NOT open throttle to wide open position for more than 5 seconds, or transaxle damage may occur. If performing more than one torque converter stall speed test, operate engine at 1000 RPM in Neutral for at least 2 minutes to cool transaxle fluid before performing next stall speed test.

3) Stall speed should be within specification. See STALL SPEED SPECIFICATIONS table. Once stall speed is obtained, place transaxle in Neutral. Operate engine, allowing transaxle to cool. Stop engine and place transaxle in Park. Remove tachometer.

STALL SPEED SPECIFICATIONS

Application	Stall Speed Engine RPM
Eclipse	3300-3800
Expo	1800-3200
Diamante & 3000GT	
DOHC	2200-3200
SOHC	1800-2800
Sonata	2200-2500

NOTE: Use the following symptoms for trouble shooting results of stall speed tests.

Stall Speed Exceeds Specification – If stall speed exceeds specification in Drive, rear clutch or one-way clutch is slipping. If stall speed exceeds specification in Reverse, front clutch or low-reverse brake is slipping. Perform hydraulic pressure test to find problem area. See HYDRAULIC PRESSURE TEST under TESTING.

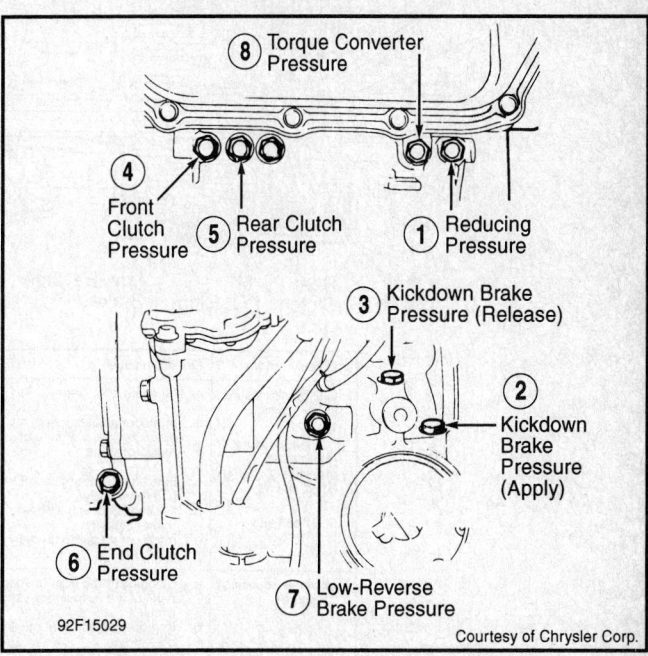

Fig. 9: Identifying Transaxle Hydraulic Pressure Taps

No.	Conditions			Standard oil pressure kPa (psi)							
	Select lever position	Engine speed rpm	Shift position	① Reducing pressure	② Kickdown brake pressure (Apply)	③ Kickdown brake pressure (Release)	④ Front clutch pressure	⑤ Rear clutch pressure	⑥ End clutch pressure	⑦ Low-reverse brake pressure	⑧ Torque-converter pressure
1	N	Idling	Neutral	360–480 (51–68)	–	–	–	–	–	–	*
2	D	Idling	2nd gear	360–480 (51–68)	100–210 (14–30)	–	–	730–830 (104–118)	–	–	*
3	D (SW-ON)	Approx. 2,500	4th gear	360–480 (51–68)	830–900 (118–128)	–	–	–	830–900 (118–128)	–	450–650 (64–92)
4	D (SW-OFF)	Approx. 2,500	3rd gear	360–480 (51–68)	830–900 (118–128)	830–900 (118–128)	830–900 (118–128)	830–900 (118–128)	830–900 (118–128)	–	450–650 (64–92)
5	2	Approx. 2,500	2nd gear	360–480 (51–68)	830–900 (118–128)	–	–	830–900 (118–128)	–	–	450–650 (64–92)
6	L	Approx. 1,000	1st gear	360–480 (51–68)	–	–	–	830–900 (118–128)	–	300–450 (43–64)	*
7	R	Approx. 2,500	Reverse	360–480 (51–68)	1,640–2,240 (233–319)	1,640–2,240 (233–319)	–	–	–	1,640–2,240 (233–319)	450–650 (64–92)
		Approx. 1,000	Reverse		①	①	–	–	–	①	

NOTE: – Must be 10 kPa (1.4 psi) or less.
    SW-ON – This indicates overdrive control switch must be in ON position.
    SW-OFF – This indicates overdrive control switch must be in OFF position.
    ✱ – Hydraulic pressure is generated, but no standard value exists.
    ① – On all models, pressure should be 1000 kPa (142 psi) or more.

92I15030

Courtesy of Chrysler Corp.

Fig. 8: Testing Transaxle Hydraulic Pressures

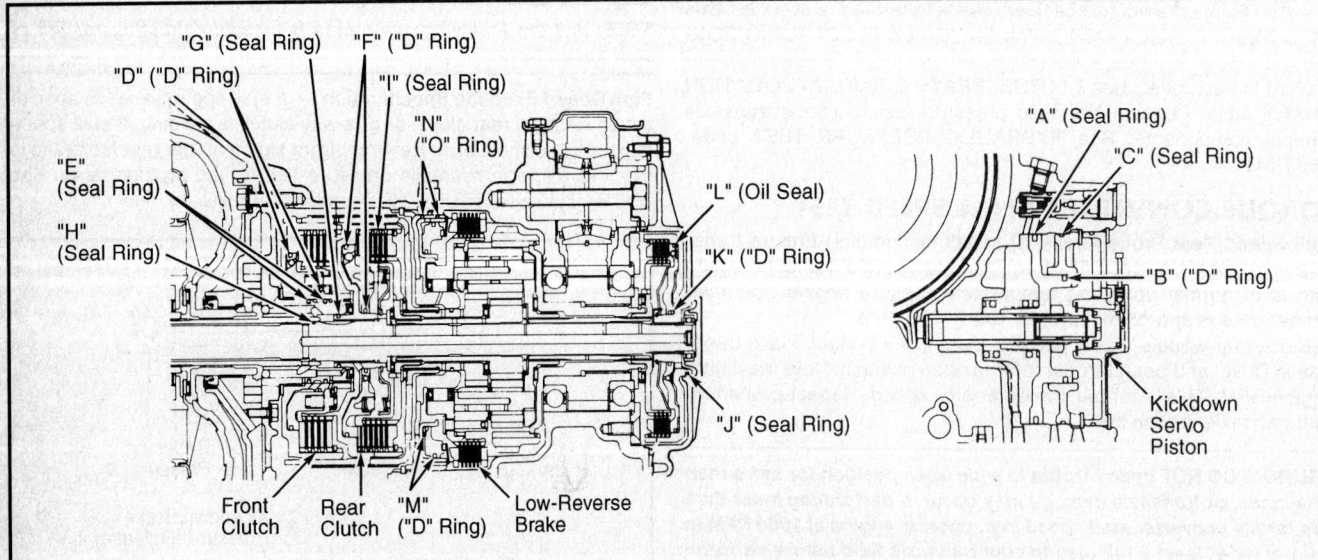

Trouble symptom	Probable cause	Remedy
1. Line pressures are all low (or high). NOTE • "Line pressures" refers to oil pressure ②, ③, ④, ⑤, ⑥ and ⑦. See Fig. 9	a. Clogging of oil filter	a. Visually inspect the oil filter; replace the oil filter if it is clogged.
	b. Improper adjustment of oil pressure (line pressure of regulator valve	b. Measure line pressure ② (kickdown brake pressure); if the pressure is not the standard value, readjust the line pressure, or, if necessary, replace the valve body assembly.
	c. Functional malfunction of valve body assembly	c. Replace the valve body assembly.
	d. Looseness of valve body tightening part	d. Tighten the valve body tightening bolt and installation bolt.
	e. Improper oil pump discharge pressure	e. Check the side clearance of the oil pump gear; replace the oil pump assembly if necessary.
2. Improper reducing pressure	a. Clogging of the filter (L-shaped type) of the reducing-pressure circuit	a. Disassemble the valve body assembly and check the filter; replace the filter if it is clogged.
	b. Improper adjustment of oil pressure	b. Measure the ① reducing pressure; if it is not the standard value, readjust, or replace the valve body assembly.
	c. Functional malfunction of the valve body assembly	c. Replace the valve body assembly.
3. Improper kickdown brake pressure (Apply)	a. Malfunction of the seal ring Ⓐ, D-ring Ⓑ or seal ring Ⓒ of the sleeve of the kickdown servo piston.	a. Disassemble the kickdown servo and check whether the seal ring or D-ring is damaged. If it is cut or has scratches, replace the seal ring or D-ring.
	b. Functional malfunction of the valve body assembly	b. Replace the valve body assembly.
4. Improper kickdown brake pressure (Release)	a. Malfunction of the seal ring Ⓐ, D-ring Ⓑ or seal ring Ⓒ of the sleeve of the kickdown servo piston.	a. Disassemble the kickdown servo and check whether the seal ring or D-ring is damaged. If it is cut or has scratches, replace the seal ring or D-ring.
	b. Functional malfunction of the valve body assembly	b. Replace the valve body assembly.
5. Improper front clutch pressure	a. Malfunction of the seal ring Ⓐ, D-ring Ⓑ or seal ring Ⓒ of the sleeve of the kickdown servo piston.	a. Disassemble the kickdown servo and check whether the seal ring or D-ring is damaged. If it is cut or has scratches, replace the seal ring or D-ring.
	b. Functional malfunction of the valve body assembly	b. Replace the valve body assembly.
	c. Wear of the front clutch piston or retainer, or malfunction of the D-ring Ⓓ or seal ring Ⓔ.	c. Disassemble the transaxle itself and check whether or not there is wear of the front clutch piston and retainer inner circumference, or damage of the D-ring and/or seal ring. If there is any wear or damage, replace the piston, retainer, D-ring and/or seal ring.
6. Improper rear clutch pressure	a. Malfunction of D-ring Ⓕ of rear clutch piston, retainer seal ring Ⓖ and seal rings Ⓗ and Ⓘ of input shaft.	a. Disassemble the rear clutch, check input shaft seal ring, retainer seal ring, piston D ring, etc. and replace broken or damaged parts.
	b. Functional malfunction of the valve body assembly	b. Replace the valve body assembly.
7. Improper end clutch pressure	a. Malfunction of seal ring Ⓙ or the D-ring Ⓚ and/or oil seal Ⓛ of end clutch.	a. Disassemble the end clutch and check the oil seal or D-ring of the piston, seal ring of the retainer, etc.; replace if there are cuts, scars, scratches or damage.
	b. Functional malfunction of the valve body assembly	b. Replace the valve body assembly.
8. Improper low-reverse brake pressure	a. O-ring between valve body and transaxle damaged or missing	a. Remove the valve body assembly and check to be sure that the O-ring at the upper surface of the upper valve body is not missing or damaged; install or replace the O-ring if necessary.
	b. Functional malfunction of the valve body assembly	b. Replace the valve body assembly.
	c. Malfunction of the D-ring Ⓜ of the low-reverse brake piston or the O-ring Ⓝ of the retainer	c. Disassemble the transaxle itself and check the D-ring and O-ring for damage; replace if there are cuts, scars, scratches or damage.
9. Improper torque converter pressure	a. Clogging or leaking of the oil cooler and/or piping	a. Repair or replace, as necessary, the cooler and/or piping.
	b. Malfunction of the torque converter	b. Replace the torque converter.

96G04483

Courtesy of Chrysler Corp.

Fig. 10: *Analyzing Hydraulic Pressure Test Results*

Stall Speed Is Less Than Specification In Drive & Reverse – If stall speed is less than specified, either engine performance is poor or torque converter is defective. If engine operates correctly, torque converter is defective.

HYDRAULIC PRESSURE TEST

1) Ensure transaxle is at normal operating temperature and fluid level is correct. Raise and support vehicle so drive wheels rotate freely. Install tachometer, and position it so driver can view it.

2) Note locations of hydraulic pressure taps on side of transaxle case and near oil pan. *See Fig. 9.* Remove plug, and install adapter and pressure gauge to each pressure tap.

CAUTION: A 400 psi (28 kg/cm²) pressure gauge is required for checking certain pressures. See Fig. 8 to determine when this gauge should be used in accordance with hydraulic pressure specification.

3) Measure hydraulic pressure at various specified engine RPM and transaxle gears. *See Fig. 8.* Ensure pressure is within specification. If proper line pressure or reducing pressure cannot be obtained, check for proper adjustment. See LINE PRESSURE or REDUCING PRESSURE under ADJUSTMENTS.

4) If proper pressure cannot be obtained, check for probable defective components. *See Fig. 10.* Remove pressure gauge. Install and tighten plug to specification. See TORQUE SPECIFICATIONS table.

ADJUSTMENTS

KICKDOWN SERVO

1) Ensure area around kickdown servo switch is clean. Remove snap ring and kickdown servo switch. To prevent rotation of kickdown servo piston, engage pawl of Kickdown Servo Wrench (MD998918) in notch on kickdown servo piston. *See STEP 1 in Fig. 11.*

2) Remove plug, and install adapter between kickdown servo wrench and transaxle case in low-reverse hydraulic pressure tap port. Tighten adapter by hand only.

CAUTION: DO NOT press kickdown servo piston inward with kickdown servo wrench. Tighten adapter on transaxle case by hand only to prevent damage to transaxle case.

3) Loosen lock nut located before "V" groove on adjusting rod. *See STEP 2 in Fig. 11.* Install and tighten inner portion of socket wrench until it contacts the lock nut. Engage outer portion of socket wrench with lock nut.

4) Rotate outer portion of socket wrench counterclockwise and inner portion of socket wrench clockwise to secure lock nut and inner portion of socket wrench. *See STEP 3 in Fig. 11.*

5) Attach INCH lb. torque wrench on inner portion of socket wrench. *See STEP 4 in Fig. 11.* Tighten inner portion of socket wrench to 86 INCH lbs. (10 N.m), and then loosen lock nut at least 2 turns.

6) Tighten inner portion of socket wrench to 43 INCH lbs. (5 N.m). Back off inner portion of socket wrench 2-2 1/4 revolutions. Engage outer portion of socket wrench with lock nut.

7) Rotate outer portion of socket wrench clockwise and inner portion of socket wrench counterclockwise to release lock nut and inner portion of socket wrench. *See STEP 5 in Fig. 11.*

8) Tighten lock nut by hand until it contacts kickdown servo piston. Using torque wrench, tighten lock nut to specification. *See STEP 6 in Fig. 11.* See TORQUE SPECIFICATIONS table.

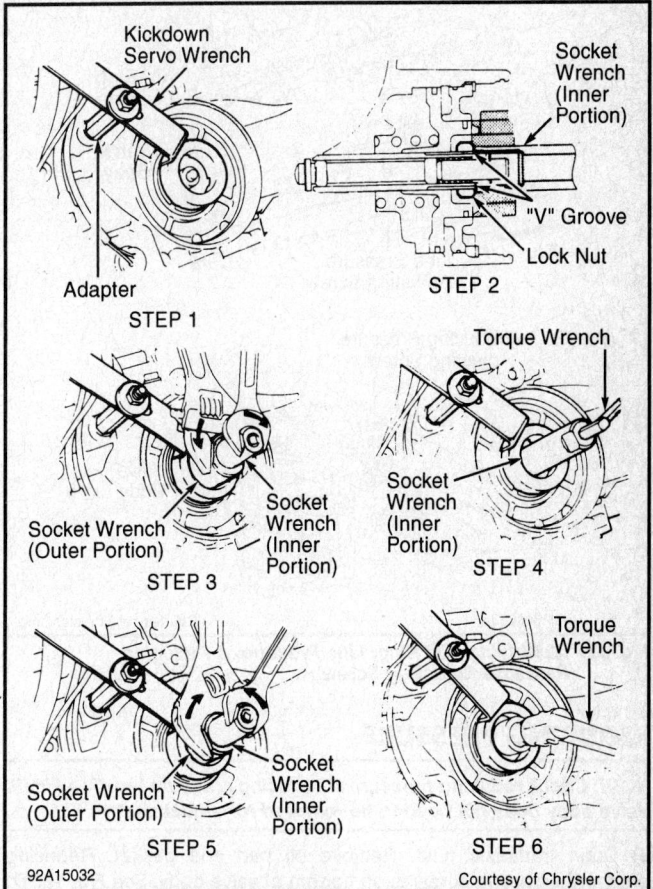

Fig. 11: Adjusting Kickdown Servo

CAUTION: Tighten lock nut by hand first to prevent lock nut and adjusting rod from rotating together.

9) Remove kickdown servo wrench and adapter. Install plug in low-reverse pressure tap and tighten to specification. See TORQUE SPECIFICATIONS table. Install kickdown servo switch and snap ring.

LINE PRESSURE

NOTE: Line pressure should be checked at kickdown brake pressure (apply) tap. See Fig. 9. Since valve body must be removed for adjustment, check line pressure before attempting to adjust line pressure.

1) Remove valve body. See VALVE BODY under REMOVAL & INSTALLATION. Note location of line pressure adjusting screw. *See Fig. 12.*

2) To adjust line pressure, rotate line pressure adjusting screw. Rotate line pressure adjusting screw clockwise to decrease line pressure and counterclockwise to increase line pressure.

3) Rotating line pressure adjusting screw one revolution will change line pressure approximately 5.4 psi (3.8 kPa). The standard adjusting value for line pressure should be 124-127 psi (870-890 kPa). Reinstall valve body. Fill transaxle with ATF, and recheck line pressure.

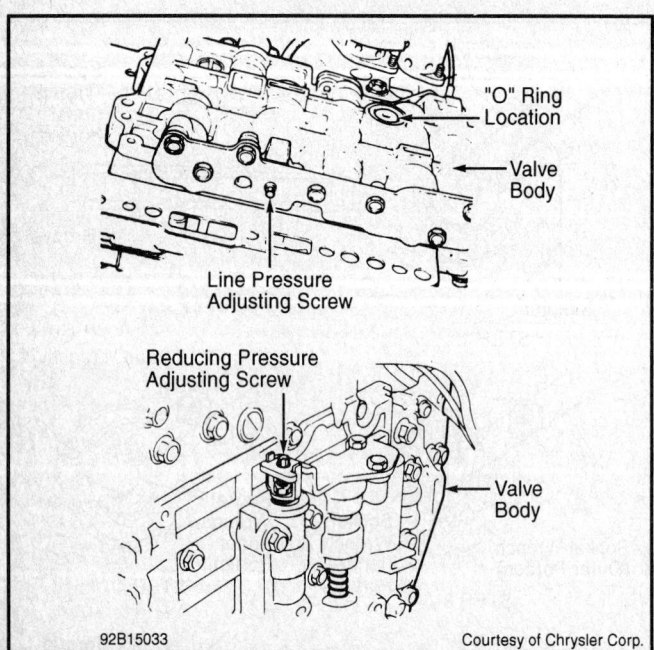

Fig. 12: Identifying "O" Ring, Line Pressure & Reducing Pressure Adjusting Screw

REDUCING PRESSURE

NOTE: Check reducing pressure at reducing pressure tap. See Fig. 9. Valve body does not need to be removed for adjustment.

1) Drain transaxle fluid. Remove oil pan and gasket. Reducing pressure adjusting screw is on bottom of valve body. *See Fig. 12.* To adjust reducing pressure, rotate reducing pressure adjusting screw. Rotate reducing pressure adjusting screw inward (clockwise) to decrease reducing pressure and outward (counterclockwise) to increase reducing pressure.
2) Rotating reducing pressure adjusting screw one revolution will change reducing pressure approximately 6.4 psi (45 kPa). The standard adjusting value for reducing pressure is 59-61 psi (415-435 kPa). Reinstall gasket and oil pan. Tighten oil pan bolts to specification. See TORQUE SPECIFICATIONS table. Fill transaxle with ATF, and recheck reducing pressure.

TORQUE CONVERTER

CAUTION: Torque converter is a welded assembly and is not service-able. If a malfunction occurs or torque converter becomes contaminated with foreign material, it MUST be replaced. Torque converter cannot be flushed or repaired.

NOTE: For torque converter stall speed test, see TORQUE CONVERTER STALL SPEED TEST under TESTING.

ON-VEHICLE SERVICE

Valve body can be serviced on vehicle. See VALVE BODY under REMOVAL & INSTALLATION.

REMOVAL & INSTALLATION

AXLE SHAFTS

See appropriate AXLE SHAFTS article in AXLE SHAFTS & TRANSFER CASES.

TRANSFER CASE

AWD – See appropriate TRANSFER CASE article in AXLE SHAFTS & TRANSFER CASES.

TRANSAXLE ASSEMBLY

See appropriate AUTOMATIC TRANSMISSION REMOVAL article in TRANSMISSION SERVICING.

VALVE BODY

Removal – Raise and support vehicle. Drain transaxle fluid. Remove retaining bolts, oil pan, gasket, oil filter and oil temperature sensor. Press solenoid valve wiring harness grommet and connector into transaxle case. Remove valve body bolts. Note bolt length and location for reassembly reference. *See Fig. 13.* Remove valve body.

CAUTION: DO NOT allow manual valve to fall from valve body during removal. Ensure "O" ring, located between valve body and transaxle case, is removed. See Fig. 12.

Installation – **1)** Always install NEW "O" ring between valve body and transaxle case and on solenoid valve wiring harness. Ensure "O" ring is seated on top of valve body. *See Fig. 12.*
2) Install valve body. Ensure detent plate pin engages groove on manual valve. Install retaining bolts, ensuring proper length bolt is installed in designated area. *See Fig. 13.* Tighten valve body bolts to specification. See TORQUE SPECIFICATIONS table. Install oil temperature sensor and solenoid valve wiring harness.

CAUTION: Position wiring so it does not contact detent plate. Ensure park rod is properly retained in the clamps. See Fig. 13.

3) Install oil filter, magnet, gasket and oil pan. Tighten bolts to specification. See TORQUE SPECIFICATIONS table. Fill transaxle with ATF.

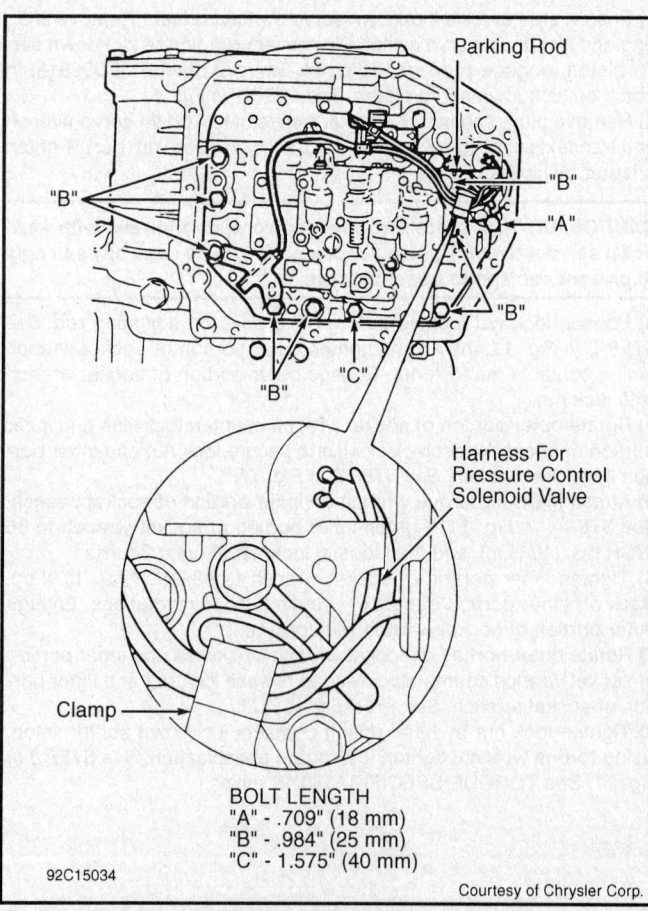

BOLT LENGTH
"A" - .709" (18 mm)
"B" - .984" (25 mm)
"C" - 1.575" (40 mm)

92C15034   Courtesy of Chrysler Corp.

Fig. 13: Identifying Valve Body Bolt Length, Location & Wire Routing

TRANSAXLE DISASSEMBLY

VALVE BODY & COMPONENTS

CAUTION: Note locations of all thrust bearings, thrust races and thrust washers for reassembly reference. See Figs. 14 and 51.

1) Remove torque converter. Using dial indicator, check input shaft end play for reassembly reference. Record result. *See Fig. 17.* Remove dipstick and dipstick tube. Remove pulse generators. *See Fig. 18.* Remove manual control lever and park/neutral position switch. *See Fig. 15 or 16.*

2) Remove retaining bolt, sleeve and speedometer driven gear assembly from transaxle case. Remove retaining bolts, oil pan, gasket and oil filter. Press solenoid valve wiring harness grommet and connector into transaxle case.

3) Remove valve body bolts. Note bolt length and location for reassembly reference. Remove valve body and oil temperature sensor.

CAUTION: DO NOT allow manual valve to fall from valve body during removal. Ensure "O" ring, located between valve body and transaxle case, is removed. See Fig. 12.

4) Remove parking roller support, located on bottom of transaxle case, above valve body area. *See Fig. 15 or 16.* Remove manual control shaft retaining set screw, located near top of manual control shaft area, on transaxle case. Remove manual control shaft and detent.

5) Remove retaining bolts, differential cover, gasket and differential bearing cap. Remove retaining bolts and differential bearing retainer.

6) Remove differential assembly. Remove end clutch cover, "O" ring, end clutch assembly and thrust washer. Remove end clutch hub and No. 11 thrust bearing. Remove end clutch shaft.

7) Remove retaining bolts, idler gear cover and gasket. Bend lock tabs, and remove lock bolt for idler shaft. Using appropriate puller, pull idler shaft from transaxle case.

8) Remove idler gear and spacer. Remove oil pump retaining bolts. Install puller into threaded holes on oil pump. Pull oil pump and gasket from transaxle case.

9) Remove No. 1 thrust washer and No. 3 thrust race from rear of oil pump. *See Fig. 14.* Holding input shaft, remove front and rear clutch assembly. Remove No. 5 thrust bearing.

10) Remove rear clutch hub, No. 6 thrust race and No. 7 thrust bearing. Remove kickdown drum and kickdown band. Remove snap ring and kickdown servo switch. *See Fig. 15 or 16.*

11) Using cup, adapter and compressor, depress kickdown servo piston. *See Fig. 19.* Remove snap ring. Remove compressor, adapter, cup, kickdown servo piston and anchor rod.

12) Remove plug and air exhaust plug. *See Fig. 20.* Remove snap ring from inside transaxle case, located above center support. Secure handle on center support, and remove center support. *See Fig. 21.*

13) Remove reverse sun gear, forward sun gear and planetary carrier assembly. *See Fig. 14.* Remove wave spring, return spring, pressure plate, clutch plates and clutch discs.

CAUTION: Note number of components and sequence of clutch plates and clutch discs installation for reassembly reference.

14) Remove retaining bolts and bearing retainer. Bearing retainer is located on transaxle case, near end clutch hub area.

15) Remove snap ring and output flange. *See Fig. 14.* Remove retaining bolts and output bearing retainer and outer bearing race. *See Fig. 15 or 16.* On F4A33 models, remove transfer shaft. *See Fig. 15.* Remove bearing race and oil seal from transaxle case.

16) On W4A32 and W4A33 models, insert a .31" (8 mm) diameter rod, 7.87" (199.9 mm) long, through hole in center differential assembly. *See Fig. 22.* Tap on rod to remove rear output shaft.

17) Thread puller into hole in end of center differential assembly. Remove center differential assembly. Install bolt in threaded areas on center bearing retainer. Hold bolts, and remove center bearing retainer from transaxle case. *See Fig. 16.*

18) Remove center bearing stopper bolt. *See Fig. 23.* Remove stopper ring. *See Fig. 16.* Place bearing puller across groove in viscous coupling unit, and remove viscous coupling unit. *See Fig. 24.* Remove bearing race and oil seal from transaxle case. Remove front output shaft.

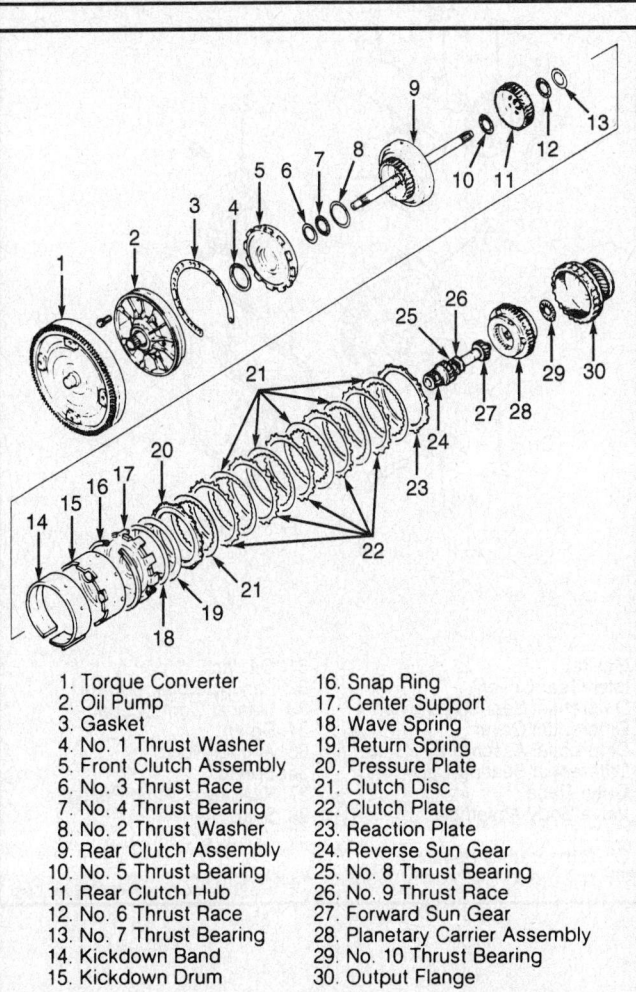

1. Torque Converter	16. Snap Ring
2. Oil Pump	17. Center Support
3. Gasket	18. Wave Spring
4. No. 1 Thrust Washer	19. Return Spring
5. Front Clutch Assembly	20. Pressure Plate
6. No. 3 Thrust Race	21. Clutch Disc
7. No. 4 Thrust Bearing	22. Clutch Plate
8. No. 2 Thrust Washer	23. Reaction Plate
9. Rear Clutch Assembly	24. Reverse Sun Gear
10. No. 5 Thrust Bearing	25. No. 8 Thrust Bearing
11. Rear Clutch Hub	26. No. 9 Thrust Race
12. No. 6 Thrust Race	27. Forward Sun Gear
13. No. 7 Thrust Bearing	28. Planetary Carrier Assembly
14. Kickdown Band	29. No. 10 Thrust Bearing
15. Kickdown Drum	30. Output Flange

92D15035   Courtesy of Chrysler Corp.

Fig. 14: *Exploded View Of Transaxle Internal Components*

AUTOMATIC TRANSMISSIONS
Mitsubishi F4A33, W4A32 & W4A33 (Cont.)

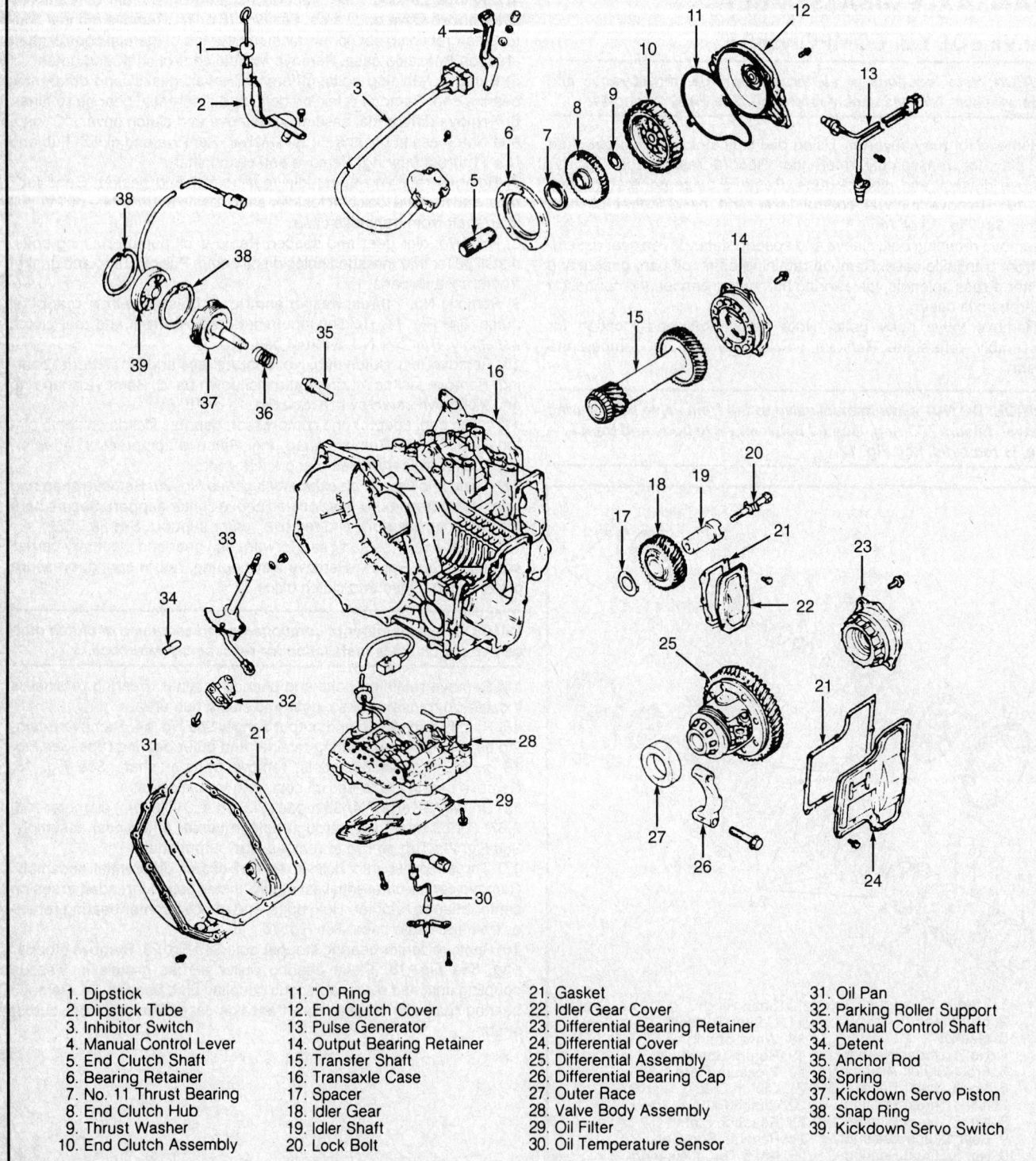

1. Dipstick	11. "O" Ring	21. Gasket	31. Oil Pan
2. Dipstick Tube	12. End Clutch Cover	22. Idler Gear Cover	32. Parking Roller Support
3. Inhibitor Switch	13. Pulse Generator	23. Differential Bearing Retainer	33. Manual Control Shaft
4. Manual Control Lever	14. Output Bearing Retainer	24. Differential Cover	34. Detent
5. End Clutch Shaft	15. Transfer Shaft	25. Differential Assembly	35. Anchor Rod
6. Bearing Retainer	16. Transaxle Case	26. Differential Bearing Cap	36. Spring
7. No. 11 Thrust Bearing	17. Spacer	27. Outer Race	37. Kickdown Servo Piston
8. End Clutch Hub	18. Idler Gear	28. Valve Body Assembly	38. Snap Ring
9. Thrust Washer	19. Idler Shaft	29. Oil Filter	39. Kickdown Servo Switch
10. End Clutch Assembly	20. Lock Bolt	30. Oil Temperature Sensor	

92E15036   Courtesy of Chrysler Corp.

Fig. 15: Exploded View Of Transaxle Case & Components (F4A33)

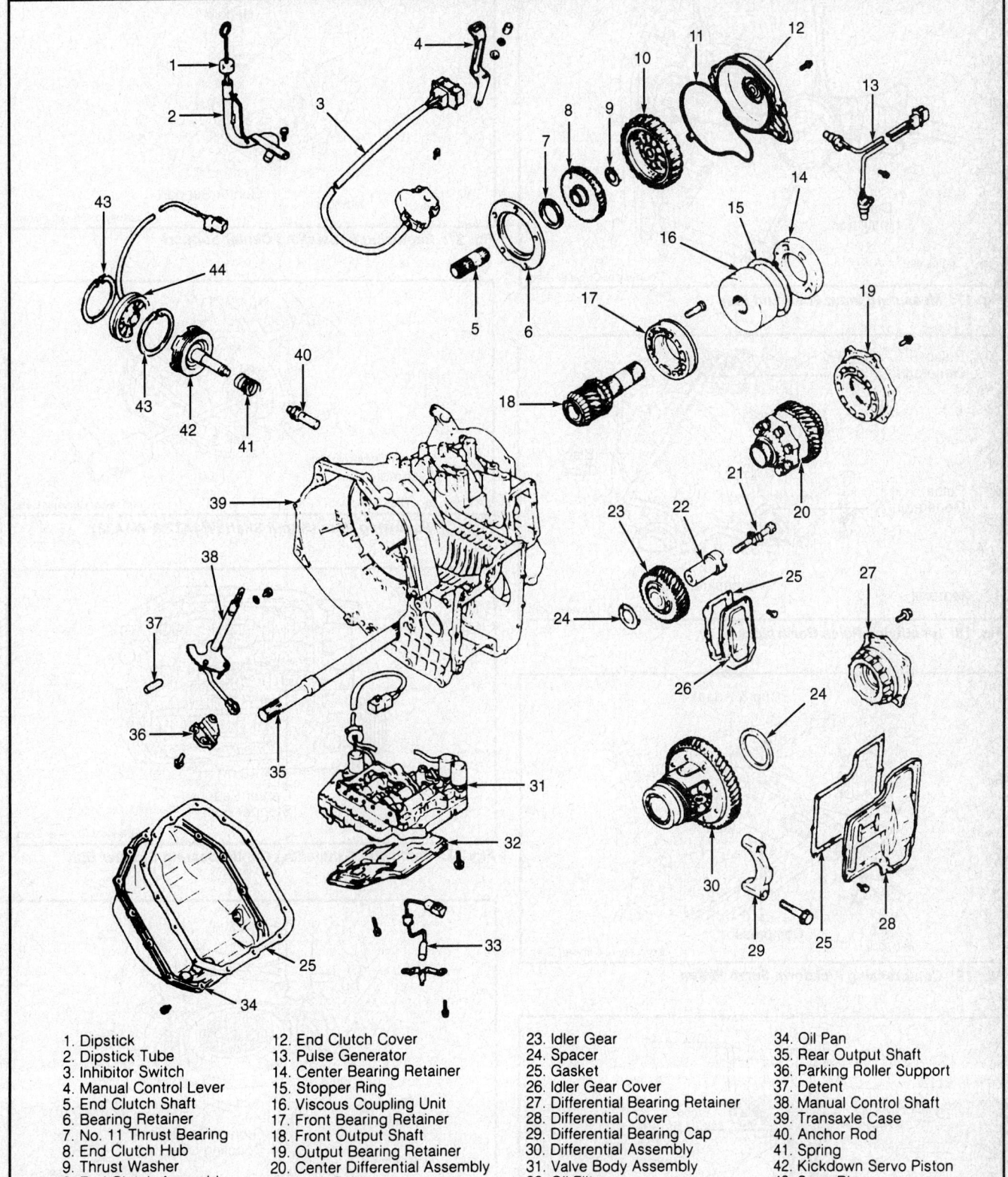

1. Dipstick
2. Dipstick Tube
3. Inhibitor Switch
4. Manual Control Lever
5. End Clutch Shaft
6. Bearing Retainer
7. No. 11 Thrust Bearing
8. End Clutch Hub
9. Thrust Washer
10. End Clutch Assembly
11. "O" Ring
12. End Clutch Cover
13. Pulse Generator
14. Center Bearing Retainer
15. Stopper Ring
16. Viscous Coupling Unit
17. Front Bearing Retainer
18. Front Output Shaft
19. Output Bearing Retainer
20. Center Differential Assembly
21. Lock Bolt
22. Idler Shaft
23. Idler Gear
24. Spacer
25. Gasket
26. Idler Gear Cover
27. Differential Bearing Retainer
28. Differential Cover
29. Differential Bearing Cap
30. Differential Assembly
31. Valve Body Assembly
32. Oil Filter
33. Oil Temperature Sensor
34. Oil Pan
35. Rear Output Shaft
36. Parking Roller Support
37. Detent
38. Manual Control Shaft
39. Transaxle Case
40. Anchor Rod
41. Spring
42. Kickdown Servo Piston
43. Snap Ring
44. Kickdown Servo Switch

92F15037

Courtesy of Chrysler Corp.

Fig. 16: *Exploded View Of Transaxle Case & Components (W4A32 & W4A33)*

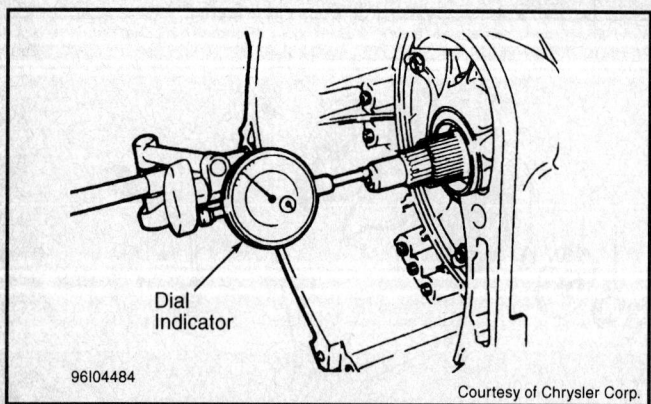

Fig. 17: Measuring Input Shaft End Play

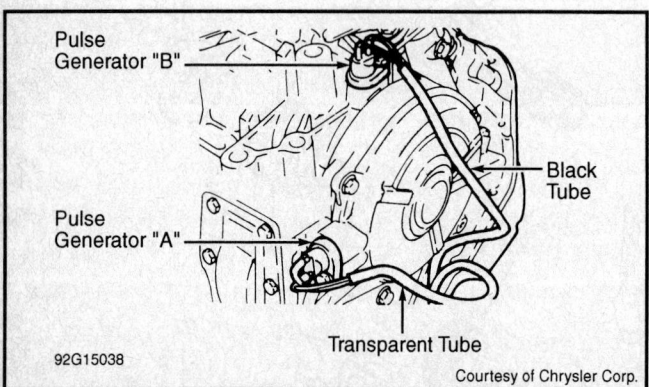

Fig. 18: Identifying Pulse Generators

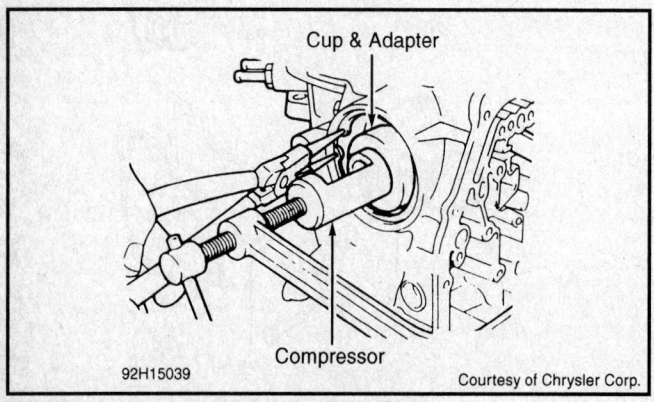

Fig. 19: Compressing Kickdown Servo Piston

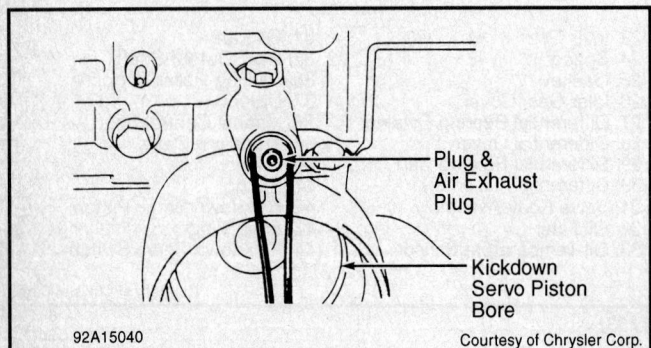

Fig. 20: Identifying Air Exhaust Plug

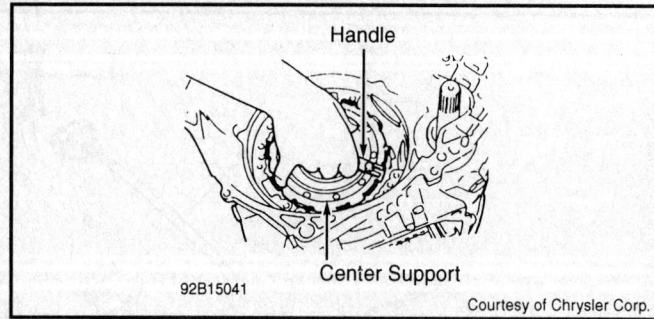

Fig. 21: Removing & Installing Center Support

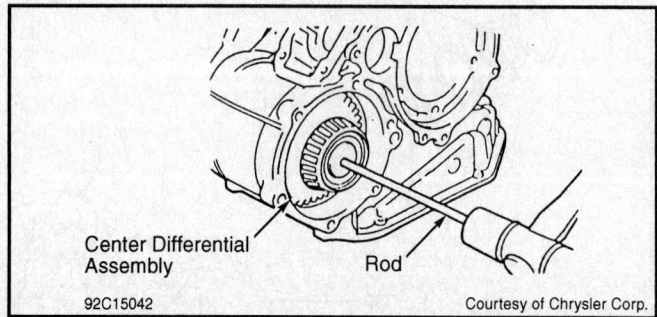

Fig. 22: Removing Rear Output Shaft (W4A32 & W4A33)

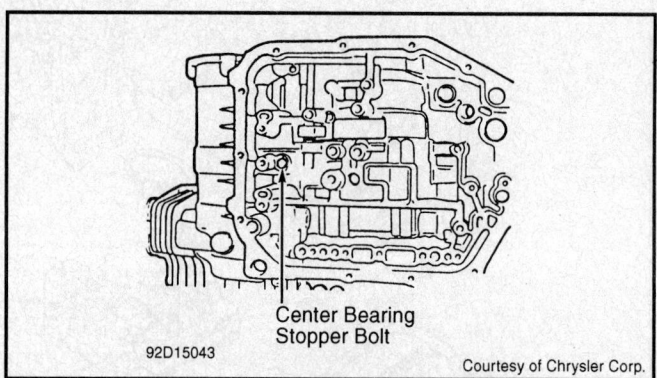

Fig. 23: Removing & Installing Center Bearing Stopper Bolt

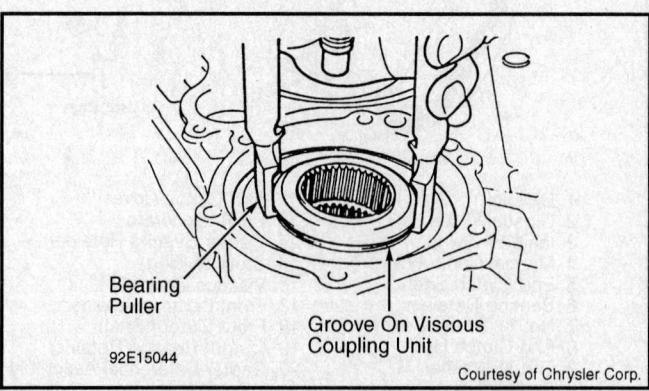

Fig. 24: Removing & Installing Viscous Coupling Module

COMPONENT DISASSEMBLY & REASSEMBLY

NOTE: Manufacturer specifies the use of only Mopar ATF Plus-Type 7176 for use in this transaxle. This fluid should also be used during assembly. See appropriate AUTOMATIC TRANSMISSION SERVICING article in TRANSMISSION SERVICING for additional information and draining and refilling procedures.

OIL PUMP

Disassembly – 1) Remove "O" ring from outer diameter of oil pump housing. Place reference mark on oil pump housing and reaction shaft support. Remove retaining bolts, and separate reaction shaft support from oil pump housing. *See Fig. 25.*

2) Remove check ball. Place reference mark on drive and driven gears for direction of installation. Remove drive and driven gears. Remove snap ring and oil seal from inside oil pump housing. Remove seal rings from reaction shaft support. Using hammer and punch, tap oil seal from front of oil pump housing.

Cleaning & Inspection – Clean and inspect components for damage. Inspect all machined surfaces for pitting or damage. Install drive and driven gears in oil pump housing. Place straightedge on oil pump housing, above gears. Using feeler gauge, measure gear end clearance between each gear and straightedge. Replace gears or oil pump assembly if gear end clearance is not .0012-.0020" (.03-.05 mm).

Reassembly – 1) Lubricate drive and driven gears with ATF and install in oil pump housing. Ensure reference marks align. Install check ball in oil pump housing. *See Fig. 26.*

2) Install reaction shaft support on oil pump housing, and finger tighten retaining bolts. DO NOT tighten bolts to specification at this time. Install guide pin in hole of reaction shaft support and oil pump housing. *See Fig. 27.*

3) Install aligning band on outer diameter of reaction shaft support and oil pump housing, and tighten aligning band. Tighten reaction shaft retaining bolts to specification. See TORQUE SPECIFICATIONS.

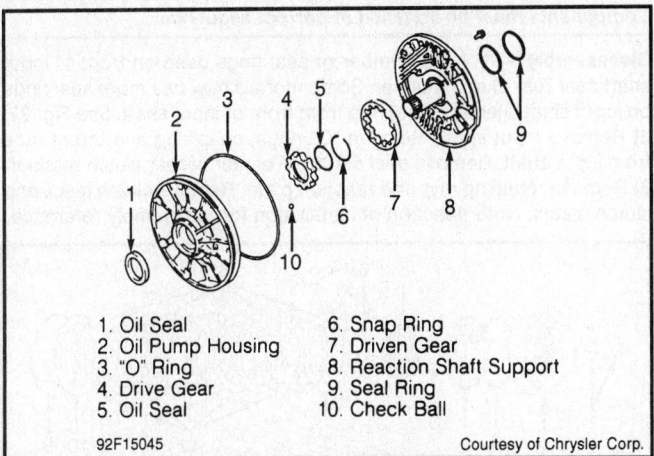

1. Oil Seal
2. Oil Pump Housing
3. "O" Ring
4. Drive Gear
5. Oil Seal
6. Snap Ring
7. Driven Gear
8. Reaction Shaft Support
9. Seal Ring
10. Check Ball

92F15045   Courtesy of Chrysler Corp.

Fig. 25: Exploded View Of Oil Pump & Components

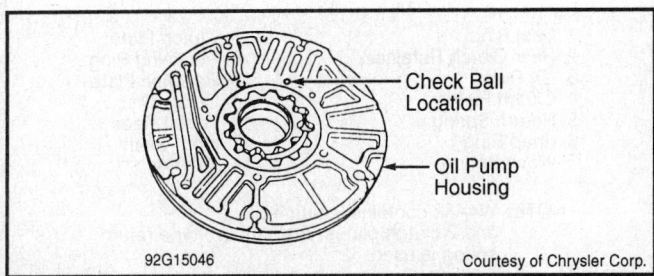

92G15046   Courtesy of Chrysler Corp.

Fig. 26: Identifying Oil Pump Check Ball Location

4) Ensure gears rotate freely in oil pump. Install NEW "O" ring on oil pump housing and lubricate with petroleum jelly. Install seal rings on reaction shaft support.

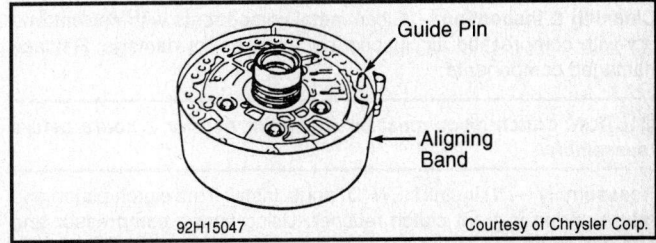

92H15047   Courtesy of Chrysler Corp.

Fig. 27: Assembling Oil Pump Housing & Reaction Shaft Support

TRANSFER SHAFT (F4A33)

Disassembly & Reassembly – Using bearing puller, remove bearings from transfer shaft (if necessary). Using bearing installer and adapter, install bearing on front side (small gear end) of transfer shaft. Using bearing installer and adapter, install bearing on rear side (large gear end) of transfer shaft.

FRONT CLUTCH

CAUTION: Note direction of clutch discs and clutch plates for reassembly reference. Also note number of each component, as some models may contain different number of clutch components. Components must be installed in correct sequence.

Disassembly – 1) Remove retaining ring and reaction plate. *See Fig. 28.* Remove clutch discs and clutch plates. Note direction of installation for reassembly reference. Remove pressure plate.

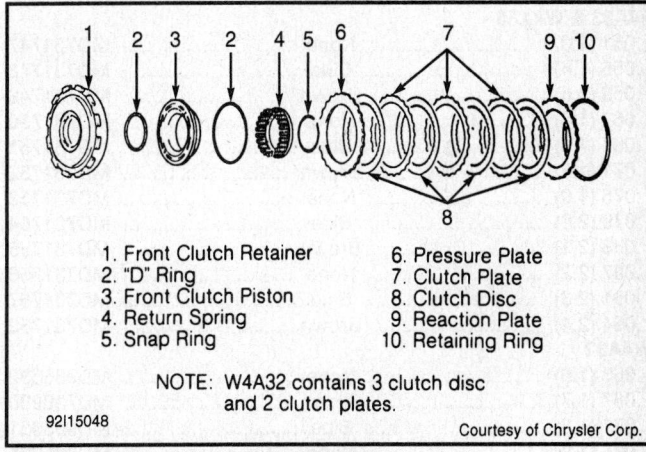

1. Front Clutch Retainer
2. "D" Ring
3. Front Clutch Piston
4. Return Spring
5. Snap Ring
6. Pressure Plate
7. Clutch Plate
8. Clutch Disc
9. Reaction Plate
10. Retaining Ring

NOTE: W4A32 contains 3 clutch disc and 2 clutch plates.

92I15048   Courtesy of Chrysler Corp.

Fig. 28: Exploded View Of Front Clutch (F4A33 & W4A33 Shown; W4A32 Is Similar)

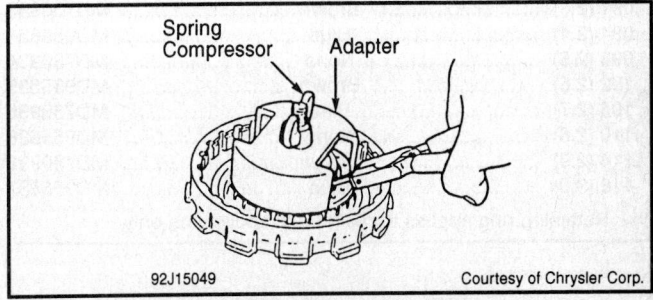

92J15049   Courtesy of Chrysler Corp.

Fig. 29: Compressing Clutch Piston Return Spring (Front Clutch Application Shown; Rear Clutch Is Similar)

2) Using spring compressor and adapter, compress return spring. *See Fig. 29.* Remove snap ring. Release and remove spring compressor. Remove return spring, front clutch piston and "D" rings from front clutch retainer.

Cleaning & Inspection – Clean metal components with solvent and dry with compressed air. Inspect components for damage. Replace damaged components.

CAUTION: Clutch discs must be soaked in ATF for 2 hours before reassembly.

Reassembly – **1)** Install NEW "D" rings. Install front clutch piston and return spring in front clutch retainer. Using spring compressor and adapter, compress return spring and install snap ring. Install pressure plate, clutch discs, clutch plates and reaction plate.

CAUTION: Align missing tooth area on pressure plate, clutch plates and reaction plate before installing. See Fig. 30. This aids in cooling of clutch plates. Ensure pressure plate, clutch plates and reaction plate are installed with beveled side toward front clutch retainer. See Fig. 31.

2) Install retaining ring. To check front clutch clearance, hold entire circumference of reaction plate downward. Using feeler gauge, measure clearance between retaining ring and reaction plate.

3) Front clutch clearance should be .028-.035" (.71-.89 mm) on W4A32 models and .031-.039" (.81-.99 mm) on all others. If front clutch clearance is not within specification, select different thickness retaining ring to obtain correct clearance. See FRONT & REAR CLUTCH RETAINING RING IDENTIFICATION table.

FRONT & REAR CLUTCH RETAINING RING IDENTIFICATION

Ring Thickness In. (mm)	Identification Mark	Part Number
F4A33 & W4A33		
.051 (1.3) [1]	None	MD731747
.055 (1.4) [1]	Blue	MD731748
.059 (1.5)	Brown	MD731749
.063 (1.6)	None	MD731750
.067 (1.7)	Blue	MD731751
.071 (1.8)	Brown	MD731752
.075 (1.9)	None	MD731753
.079 (2.0)	Blue	MD731754
.083 (2.1)	Brown	MD731755
.087 (2.2)	None	MD731756
.091 (2.3)	Blue	MD731757
.094 (2.4)	Brown	MD731758
W4A32		
.063 (1.6)	None	MD955630
.067 (1.7)	Brown	MD730930
.071 (1.8)	Blue	MD955631
.075 (1.9)	None	MD730931
.079 (2.0)	Brown	MD955632
.083 (2.1)	Blue	MD730932
.087 (2.2)	None	MD955633
.091 (2.3)	Brown	MD730933
.094 (2.4)	Blue	MD955634
.098 (2.5)	None	MD730934
.102 (2.6)	Brown	MD955635
.106 (2.7)	Blue	MD730935
.110 (2.8)	None	MD955636
.114 (2.9)	Brown	MD730936
.118 (3.0)	Blue	MD955637

[1] – Retaining ring applies to rear clutch application only.

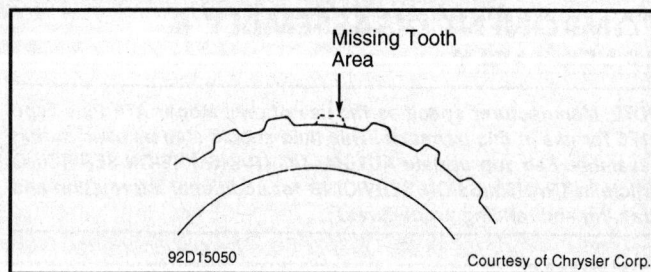

Fig. 30: Identifying Pressure Plate, Clutch Plate & Reaction Plate Missing Tooth Area

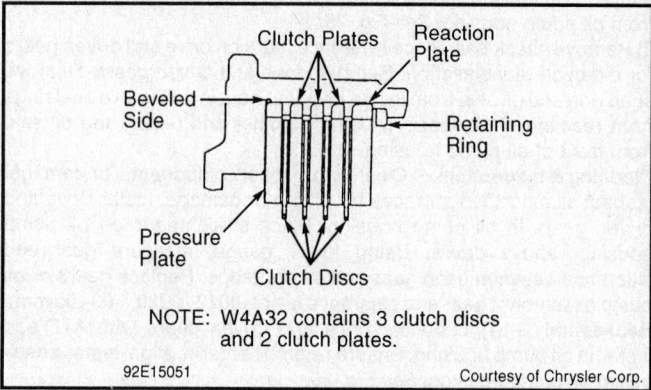

NOTE: W4A32 contains 3 clutch discs and 2 clutch plates.

Fig. 31: Assembling Front Clutch Components

REAR CLUTCH

CAUTION: Note direction of clutch discs and clutch plates for reassembly reference. Also note number of each component, as some models may contain different number of clutch components. Components must be installed in correct sequence.

Disassembly – **1)** Note number of seal rings used on front of input shaft near rear clutch retainer. Some models may use more seal rings on input shaft. Remove seal ring from front of input shaft. *See Fig. 32.*

2) Remove input shaft. Remove "O" rings, snap ring and thrust race from input shaft. Remove seal ring from center of rear clutch retainer.

3) Remove retaining ring and reaction plate. Remove clutch discs and clutch plates. Note direction of installation for reassembly reference.

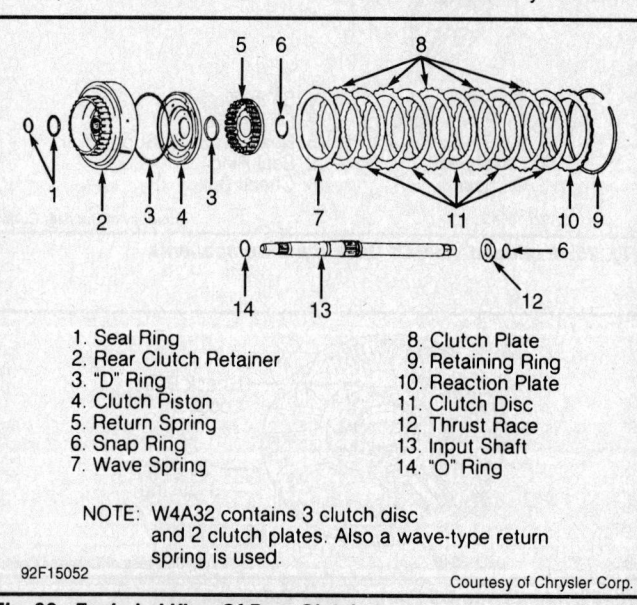

1. Seal Ring
2. Rear Clutch Retainer
3. "D" Ring
4. Clutch Piston
5. Return Spring
6. Snap Ring
7. Wave Spring
8. Clutch Plate
9. Retaining Ring
10. Reaction Plate
11. Clutch Disc
12. Thrust Race
13. Input Shaft
14. "O" Ring

NOTE: W4A32 contains 3 clutch disc and 2 clutch plates. Also a wave-type return spring is used.

Fig. 32: Exploded View Of Rear Clutch (F4A33 & W4A33 Shown; W4A32 Is Similar)

4) Remove wave spring. Using spring compressor and adapter, compress return spring. See Fig. 29. Remove snap ring. Release and remove spring compressor. Remove return spring, rear clutch piston and "D" rings from rear clutch retainer.

Cleaning & Inspection – Clean metal components with solvent and dry with compressed air. Inspect components for damage. Replace damaged components.

CAUTION: Clutch discs must be soaked in ATF for 2 hours before reassembly.

Reassembly – **1)** Install NEW "D" rings. Install rear clutch piston and return spring in rear clutch retainer. Using spring compressor and adapter, compress return spring, and install snap ring. Install wave spring, clutch discs, clutch plates and reaction plate.

CAUTION: Align missing tooth area on clutch plates and reaction plate before installing. See Fig. 30. This aids in cooling of clutch plates. On W4A32 models, ensure reaction plate is installed with beveled edge toward clutch piston.

2) Install retaining ring. To check rear clutch clearance, hold entire circumference of reaction plate downward. Using feeler gauge, measure clearance between retaining ring and reaction plate.

3) Rear clutch clearance should be .016-.024" (.41-.61 mm) on W4A32 models and .039-.047" (.99-1.19 mm) on all others. If rear clutch clearance is not within specification, select different thickness retaining ring to obtain correct clearance. See FRONT & REAR CLUTCH RETAINING RING IDENTIFICATION table.

4) Install NEW seal ring in rear clutch retainer. Install thrust race, snap ring and "O" ring on input shaft. Install input shaft in rear clutch retainer, aligning oil groove on input shaft with reference mark or oil hole on rear clutch retainer. See Fig. 33. Install seal ring on input shaft.

CAUTION: Ensure oil groove on input shaft aligns with reference mark or oil hole on rear clutch retainer. See Fig. 33.

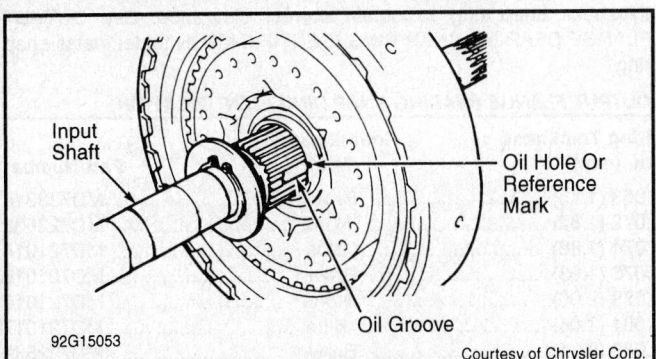

Fig. 33: Aligning Input Shaft & Rear Clutch Retainer

END CLUTCH

CAUTION: Note direction of clutch discs and clutch plates for reassembly reference. Also note number of each component, as some models may contain different number of clutch components. Components must be installed in correct sequence.

Disassembly – **1)** Remove seal ring from rear of end clutch retainer. Remove retaining ring, reaction plate, clutch discs and clutch plates. Note direction of installation for reassembly reference. See Fig. 34. Remove snap ring, washer and return spring.

2) Remove clutch piston from end clutch retainer. If necessary, place end clutch retainer on workbench with clutch piston facing downward, and apply low air pressure on oil passage on rear of end clutch retainer to remove clutch piston. Remove oil seal from clutch piston. Remove "D" ring and remaining oil seal. See Fig. 34.

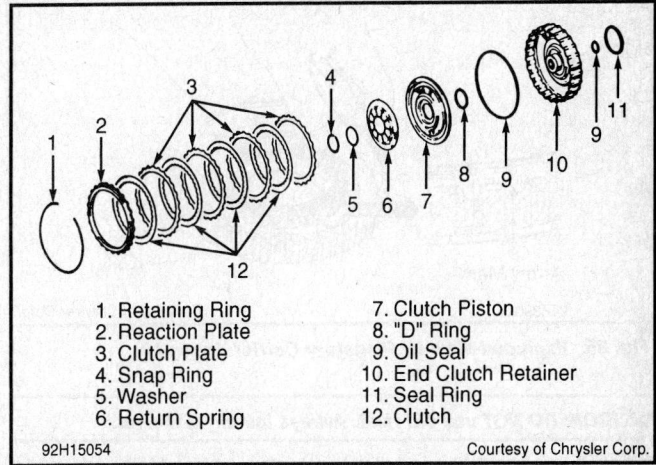

1. Retaining Ring	7. Clutch Piston
2. Reaction Plate	8. "D" Ring
3. Clutch Plate	9. Oil Seal
4. Snap Ring	10. End Clutch Retainer
5. Washer	11. Seal Ring
6. Return Spring	12. Clutch

92H15054   Courtesy of Chrysler Corp.

Fig. 34: Exploded View Of End Clutch

Cleaning & Inspection – Clean metal components with solvent and dry with compressed air. Inspect components for damage. Replace damaged components.

CAUTION: Clutch discs must be soaked in ATF for 2 hours before reassembly.

Reassembly – **1)** Install NEW oil seals and "D" ring. Install clutch piston in end clutch retainer. Install return spring and washer. Install snap ring on end clutch retainer. Using snap ring installer, press snap ring onto end clutch retainer until it seats in groove. Ensure snap ring is fully seated.

2) Install clutch discs, clutch plates and reaction plate. See Fig. 34. Install retaining ring. To check end clutch clearance, hold entire circumference of reaction plate downward. Using feeler gauge, measure clearance between retaining ring and reaction plate.

3) End clutch clearance should be .024-.033" (.61-.84 mm). If end clutch clearance is not within specification, select different thickness retaining ring to obtain correct clearance. See END CLUTCH RETAINING RING IDENTIFICATION table. Install seal ring on rear of end clutch retainer.

END CLUTCH RETAINING RING IDENTIFICATION

Ring Thickness In. (mm)	Identification Mark	Part Number
.047 (1.20)	Purple	MD757421
.051 (1.30)	Yellow	MD756034
.055 (1.40)	Brown	MD758167
.061 (1.55)	None	MD756035
.065 (1.65)	Gray	MD757424
.071 (1.80)	Green	MD756036
.077 (1.95)	Red	MD757544

PLANETARY CARRIER ASSEMBLY

Disassembly – Remove thrust bearing. See Fig. 35. Position stopper plate on one-way clutch outer race so it does not contact rivet. Using punch and hammer, drive out rivet. See Fig. 36. Remove waved washer, one-way clutch outer race and end plate. See Fig. 35. Remove one-way clutch and end plate from planetary carrier.

Cleaning & Inspection – Clean components with solvent and dry with compressed air. Inspect components for damage. Replace damaged components.

Reassembly – **1)** Install end plate on one-way clutch outer race. Install one-way clutch so flange side is upward (away from one-way clutch outer race). See Fig. 37.

2) Install end plate. Install one-way clutch outer race on planetary carrier. Install waved washer on NEW rivet. Ensure concave side of wave washer faces away from rivet head. See Fig. 36.

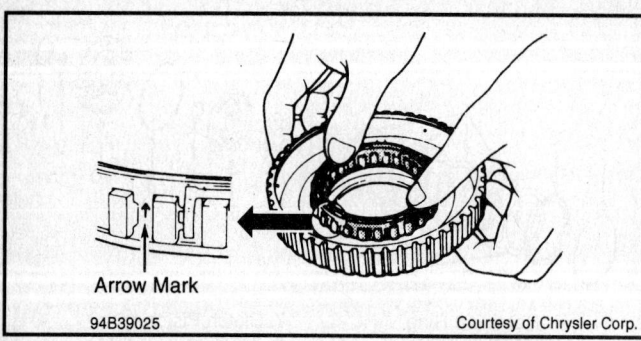

Fig. 35: Exploded View Of Planetary Carrier Assembly

CAUTION: DO NOT use old rivet. Always install NEW rivet.

---

3) Install waved washer and rivet in planetary carrier. Using press and punch with 60 degree angle tip, stake rivet. Apply 2425-2866 lbs. of pressure on press when staking rivet. Install thrust bearing.

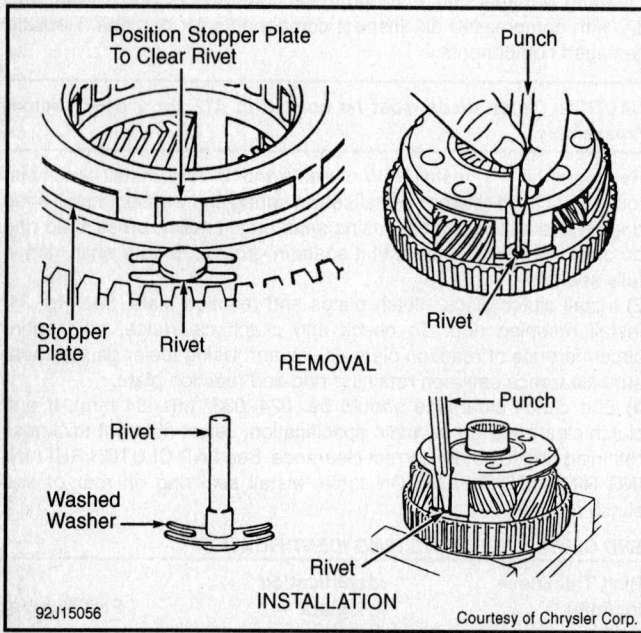

Fig. 36: Removing & Installing Planetary Carrier Assembly Rivet

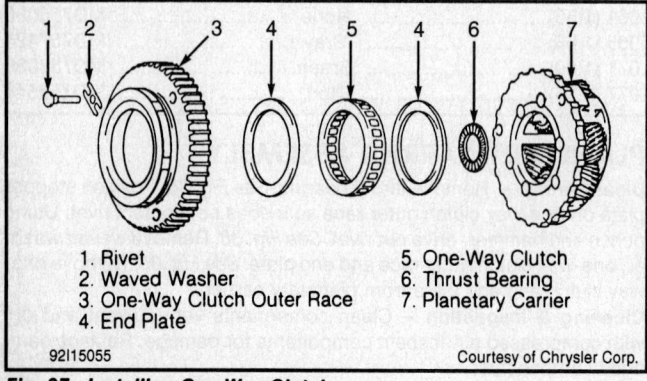

1. Rivet
2. Waved Washer
3. One-Way Clutch Outer Race
4. End Plate
5. One-Way Clutch
6. Thrust Bearing
7. Planetary Carrier

Fig. 37: Installing One-Way Clutch

OUTPUT FLANGE & TRANSFER DRIVE GEAR

Disassembly – 1) Remove snap ring and stopper plate from end of transfer drive gear. *See Fig. 38.* Place bearing remover between output flange and bearing. Using press, remove bearings and transfer drive gear as a unit from output flange.

2) Using press and bearing remover, remove bearings from transfer drive gear (if necessary). Remove snap ring and output flange from annulus gear. *See Fig. 38.*

Cleaning & Inspection – Clean components with solvent and dry with compressed air. Inspect components for damage. Replace damaged components.

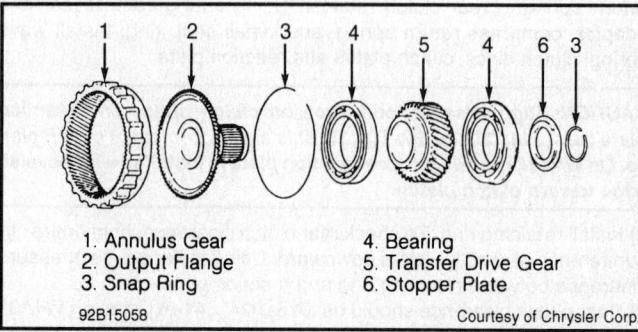

1. Annulus Gear
2. Output Flange
3. Snap Ring
4. Bearing
5. Transfer Drive Gear
6. Stopper Plate

Fig. 38: Exploded View Of Output Flange & Transfer Drive Gear

---

Reassembly – 1) Install output flange and snap ring in annulus gear. *See Fig. 38.* Press NEW bearings on transfer drive gear. Using adapter, bearing installer and press, install transfer drive gear and bearings on output flange.

2) Install stopper plate. Using feeler gauge, measure output flange bearing end play between groove on output flange and stopper plate surface. *See Fig. 39.*

3) Output flange end play should be 0-.0035" (0-.089 mm). If output flange bearing end play is not within specification, select different thickness snap ring to obtain correct clearance. See OUTPUT FLANGE BEARING SNAP RING IDENTIFICATION table. Install snap ring.

OUTPUT FLANGE BEARING SNAP RING IDENTIFICATION

Ring Thickness In. (mm)	Identification Mark	Part Number
.069 (1.75)	Brown	MD733314
.072 (1.82)	None	MD722538
.074 (1.88)	Blue	MD721014
.076 (1.93)	Brown	MD721015
.079 (2.00)	None	MD721016
.081 (2.06)	Blue	MD721017
.083 (2.11)	Brown	MD722539
.086 (2.18)	None	MD733315

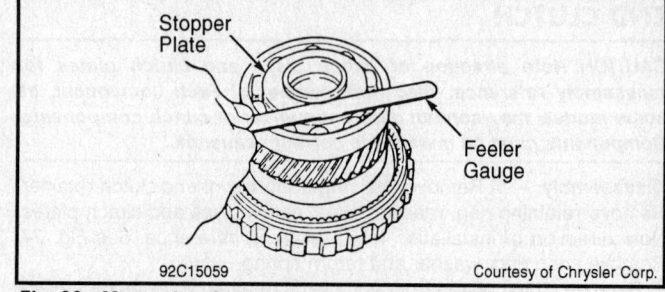

Fig. 39: Measuring Output Flange Bearing End Play

DIFFERENTIAL ASSEMBLY

Disassembly – 1) Remove retaining bolts and ring gear. Remove tapered or ball bearings from differential case if replacement is required. See Fig. 40.

2) Using hammer and punch, drive roll pin toward ring gear side of differential case. Remove pinion shaft, pinion gears, thrust washers, side gears and spacers from differential case.

Cleaning & Inspection – Clean components with solvent and dry with compressed air. Inspect components for damage. Replace damaged components.

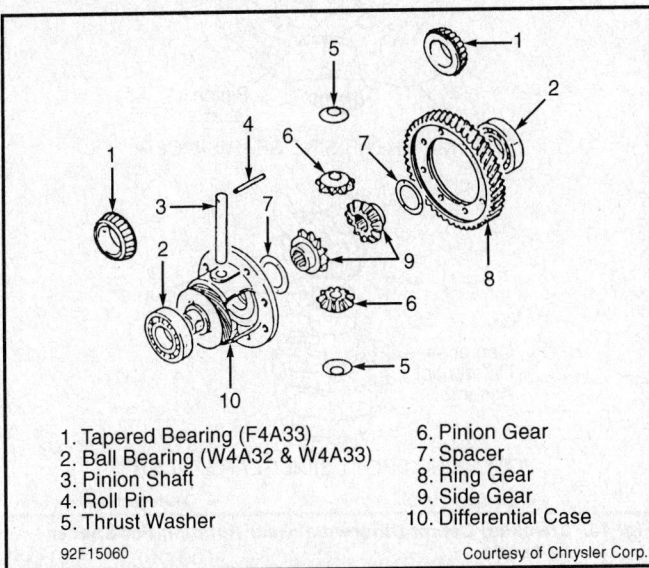

1. Tapered Bearing (F4A33)
2. Ball Bearing (W4A32 & W4A33)
3. Pinion Shaft
4. Roll Pin
5. Thrust Washer
6. Pinion Gear
7. Spacer
8. Ring Gear
9. Side Gear
10. Differential Case

92F15060   Courtesy of Chrysler Corp.

Fig. 40: Exploded View Of Differential Assembly

Reassembly – 1) Place spacer on side gear. Install side gear in differential case. Install thrust washers on pinion gears. Place pinion gears in differential case.

2) Rotate side gears and pinion gears until they align with pinion shaft opening. Install pinion shaft. Position dial indicator so stem rests against side gear. See Fig. 41. Rotate pinion gear, and note side gear-to-pinion gear backlash. Check backlash on both side gears.

3) Side gear-to-pinion gear backlash should be .0010-.0059" (.025-.150 mm). If side gear-to-pinion gear backlash is not within specification, select different thickness side gear spacer. See SIDE GEAR SPACER IDENTIFICATION table.

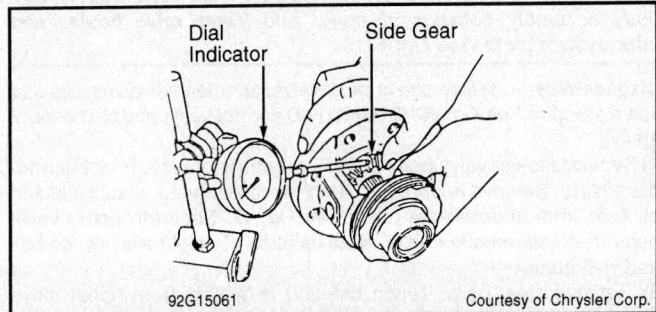

92G15061   Courtesy of Chrysler Corp.

Fig. 41: Checking Side Gear-To-Pinion Gear Backlash

SIDE GEAR SPACER IDENTIFICATION

Spacer Thickness In. (mm)	Part Number
.0295-.0323 (.749-.820)	MD722986
.0327-.0362 (.830-.919)	MD722985
.0366-.0394 (.930-1.001)	MD722984
.0398-.0425 (1.011-1.080)	MD722983
.0429-.0457 (1.090-1.161)	MD722982

4) Once proper spacers are installed, install NEW roll pin from ring gear side of differential case.

CAUTION: Always install NEW roll pin. DO NOT reuse roll pin. Ensure roll pin is positioned below surface of differential case.

5) Press tapered or ball bearings on differential case (if removed). Install ring gear on differential case.

CAUTION: On F4A33 and W4A33 models, coat ring gear retaining bolts with ATF. On W4A32 models, coat retaining bolts with thread sealant.

6) Install and tighten ring gear retaining bolts to specification in a crisscross pattern. See TORQUE SPECIFICATIONS.

CAUTION: Ensure ring gear retaining bolts are tightened to specification in a crisscross pattern to prevent damage to ring gear and differential case.

KICKDOWN SERVO

Disassembly & Reassembly – Remove "O" ring, kickdown servo, "D" ring and seal ring. See Fig. 42. Remove lock nut. Separate servo rod from kickdown servo piston. To reassemble, reverse disassembly procedure using NEW "O" ring, seal ring and "D" ring. Tighten lock nut to specification. See TORQUE SPECIFICATIONS.

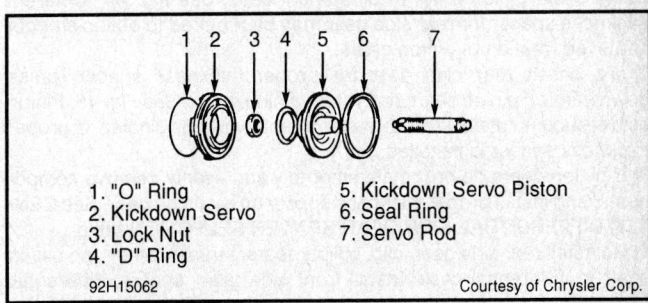

1. "O" Ring
2. Kickdown Servo
3. Lock Nut
4. "D" Ring
5. Kickdown Servo Piston
6. Seal Ring
7. Servo Rod

92H15062   Courtesy of Chrysler Corp.

Fig. 42: Exploded View Of Kickdown Servo

LOW-REVERSE BRAKE

Disassembly & Reassembly – Remove low-reverse brake piston from center support. See Fig. 43. Remove "D" rings from low-reverse brake piston. To reassemble, reverse disassembly procedure using NEW "D" rings.

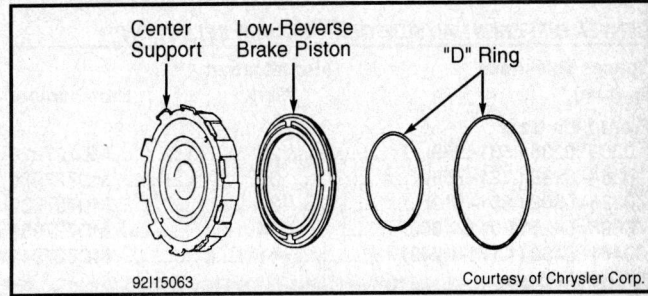

Center Support   Low-Reverse Brake Piston   "D" Ring

92I15063   Courtesy of Chrysler Corp.

Fig. 43: Exploded View Of Low-Reverse Brake

CENTER DIFFERENTIAL ASSEMBLY (W4A32 & W4A33)

Disassembly – 1) Install bearing remover between transfer driven gear and differential case. See Fig. 44. Using press, press differential case from transfer driven gear. Tapered bearing is removed along with transfer driven gear.

2) Using press and bearing remover, remove tapered bearings from transfer driven gear, and differential case if replacement is required. Remove retaining bolts. Separate differential flange from differential

case. *See Fig. 44.* Remove spacers, front and rear side gears, pinion shaft, pinion gears, thrust washers and clip from differential case.
Cleaning & Inspection – Clean components with solvent and dry with compressed air. Inspect components for damage. Replace damaged components.

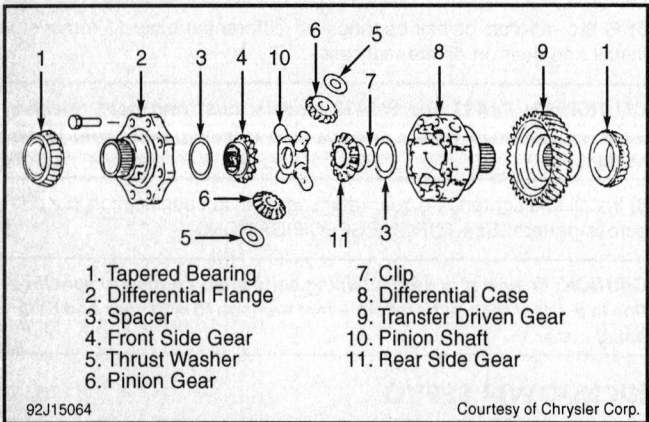

1. Tapered Bearing
2. Differential Flange
3. Spacer
4. Front Side Gear
5. Thrust Washer
6. Pinion Gear
7. Clip
8. Differential Case
9. Transfer Driven Gear
10. Pinion Shaft
11. Rear Side Gear

92J15064   Courtesy of Chrysler Corp.

Fig. 44: Exploded View Of Center Differential Assembly (W4A32 & W4A33)

Reassembly – 1) Install spacer, rear side gear, pinion gears, thrust washer and pinion shaft in differential case. *See Fig. 44.* Different thickness spacer for rear side gear may be required to obtain smooth and even rotation of pinion gears.
2) To check rear side gear for proper thickness spacer, press downward on pinion shaft, and rotate pinion gears. *See Fig. 45.* Pinion gears should rotate smoothly and evenly without binding if proper thickness spacer is installed.
3) If pinion gears do not rotate smoothly and evenly, remove components, and install proper thickness spacer on rear side gear. See CENTER DIFFERENTIAL SIDE GEAR SPACER SELECTION table.
4) Reinstall rear side gear, clip, pinion gears, thrust washer and pinion shaft in differential case. Install front side gear, spacer, differential flange and retaining bolts.
5) Tighten retaining bolts to specification in a crisscross pattern. See TORQUE SPECIFICATIONS. To check front side gear for proper thickness spacer, insert front output shaft into front side gear and, rotate front side gear. *See Fig. 45.*
6) Front side gear should rotate smoothly and evenly without binding if proper thickness spacer is installed. If front side gear does not rotate smoothly and evenly, install proper thickness spacer. See CENTER DIFFERENTIAL SIDE GEAR SPACER SELECTION table.

CENTER DIFFERENTIAL SIDE GEAR SPACER SELECTION

Spacer Thickness In. (mm)	Identification Mark	Part Number
Front Side Gear		
.0209-.0236 (.531-.599)	28	MD727928
.0284-.0299 (.721-.759)	30	MD727930
.0335-.0362 (.851-.919)	32	MD727932
.0398-.0425 (1.011-1.080)	34	MD727934
.0461-.0489 (1.171-1.242)	41	MD727941
Rear Side Gear		
.0232-.0260 (.589-.660)	73	MD724973
.0295-.0323 (.749-.820)	46	MD724946
.0366-.0394 (.930-1.001)	81	MD724981
.0429-.0457 (1.090-1.161)	43	MD724943
.0492-.0520 (1.249-1.321)	72	MD724972

7) Once proper spacers are installed, remove differential flange retaining bolts. Apply thread sealant to bolt threads. Install retaining bolts and tighten in a crisscross pattern to specification. See TORQUE SPECIFICATIONS.

8) Using press, bearing installer and adapter, press tapered bearing on differential flange (if removed). Using press, bearing installer and adapter, press tapered bearing on transfer driven gear (if removed). Press transfer driven gear on differential case.

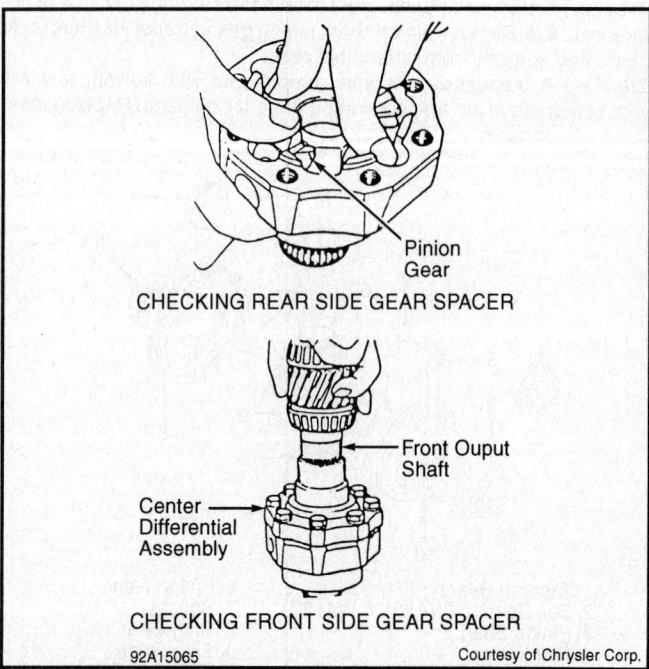

CHECKING REAR SIDE GEAR SPACER

CHECKING FRONT SIDE GEAR SPACER

92A15065   Courtesy of Chrysler Corp.

Fig. 45: Checking Center Differential Gear Rotation For Spacer Selection

FRONT OUTPUT SHAFT (W4A32 & W4A33)
Disassembly & Reassembly – Using press and bearing remover, remove tapered bearings from output shaft if replacement is required. To reassemble, using press, bearing installer and adapters, install tapered bearing on long end of front output shaft. Use bearing installer and adapter to install tapered bearing on short end of front output shaft.

VALVE BODY

CAUTION: When disassembling valve body, place valve body components in order, and mark spring locations for reassembly reference. DO NOT use force to remove components from valve body. Valve body assembly consists of upper and lower valve bodies and intermediate plate. See Fig. 46.

Disassembly – 1) Remove manual valve, all solenoid valves, clip and valve stopper. *See Fig. 46.* Remove N-D control valve and N-D control sleeve.
2) Separate lower valve body and lower separator plate from intermediate plate. Remove nut and jet. Remove relief spring, steel balls and oil filter from intermediate plate. *See Fig. 47.* Separate upper valve body from intermediate plate. Note location of steel balls, Teflon ball and N-D plate.
3) Remove steel balls, Teflon ball and N-D plate from upper valve body. Remove block and upper separator plate. Remove remaining components from upper and lower valve bodies. *See Figs. 48 and 49.*
Cleaning & Inspection – 1) Clean components with solvent and dry with compressed air. DO NOT use shop towels to dry components. Ensure all components slide freely in housing bores, and bores are not scored. Inspect machined surfaces for nicks, burrs or distortion.
2) Inspect valve and plugs for burrs or scratches. Ensure all fluid passages are open. Inspect transfer plate and separator plates for distortion. Inspect steel balls, Teflon ball and seats for damage.

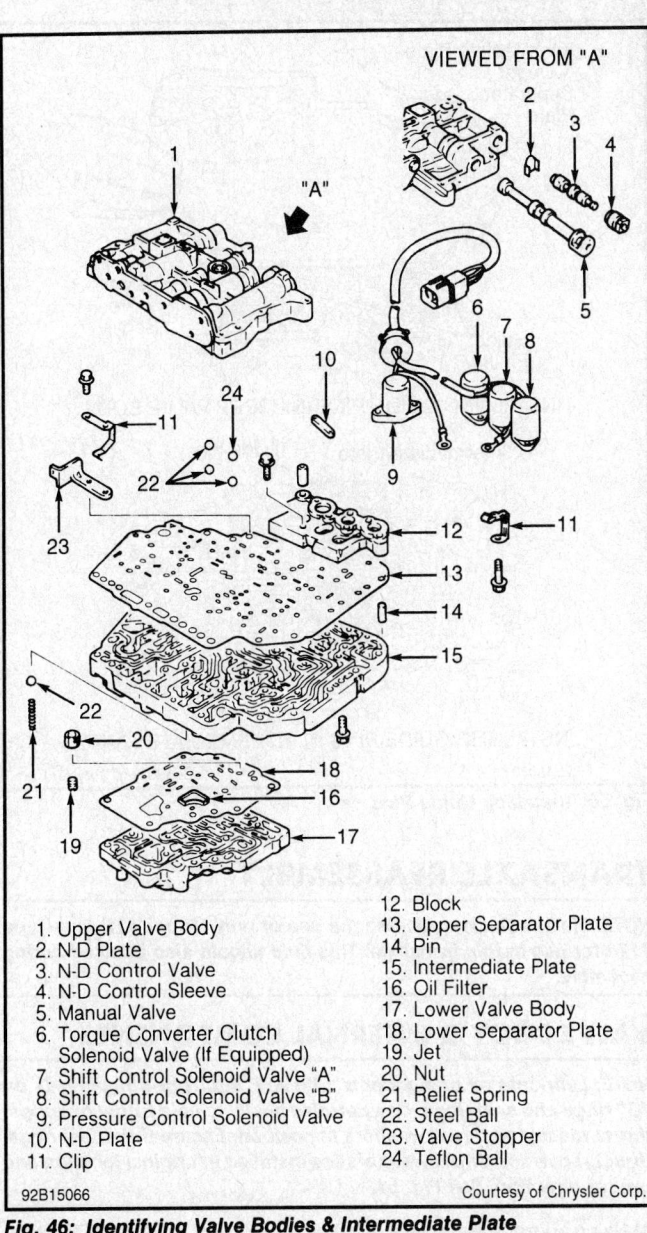

1. Upper Valve Body
2. N-D Plate
3. N-D Control Valve
4. N-D Control Sleeve
5. Manual Valve
6. Torque Converter Clutch Solenoid Valve (If Equipped)
7. Shift Control Solenoid Valve "A"
8. Shift Control Solenoid Valve "B"
9. Pressure Control Solenoid Valve
10. N-D Plate
11. Clip
12. Block
13. Upper Separator Plate
14. Pin
15. Intermediate Plate
16. Oil Filter
17. Lower Valve Body
18. Lower Separator Plate
19. Jet
20. Nut
21. Relief Spring
22. Steel Ball
23. Valve Stopper
24. Teflon Ball

92B15066   Courtesy of Chrysler Corp.

Fig. 46: Identifying Valve Bodies & Intermediate Plate

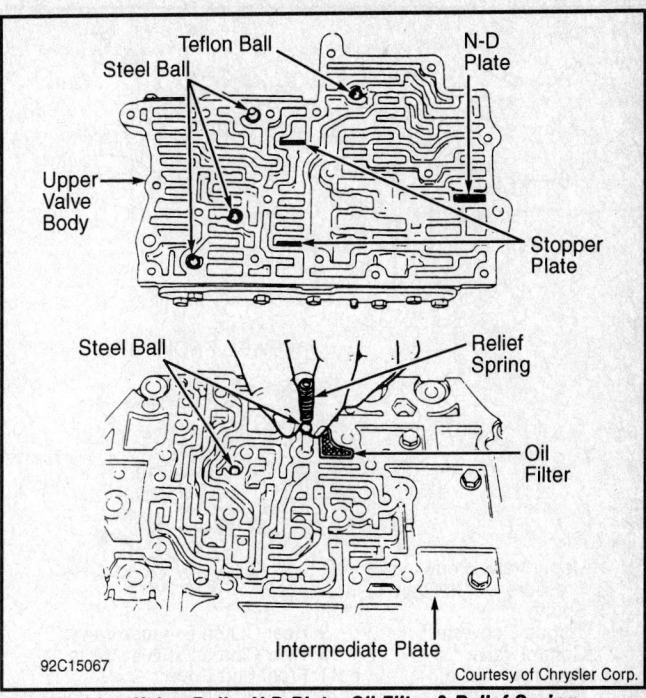

92C15067   Courtesy of Chrysler Corp.

Fig. 47: Identifying Balls, N-D Plate, Oil Filter & Relief Spring

Reassembly – 1) Lubricate all components and fluid passages with ATF. Install upper and lower valve body components in original location. See Figs. 48 and 49. To verify proper valve body spring application, see VALVE BODY SPRING SPECIFICATIONS.

2) Install upper separator plate and block on intermediate plate. See Fig. 46. Install steel balls, Teflon ball and N-D plate in upper valve body. See Fig. 47. Install guide pins in upper valve body. See Fig. 50. Install intermediate plate and upper separator plate on upper valve body.

3) Install valve body bolts to retain upper valve body on intermediate plate. Tighten bolts to specification. See TORQUE SPECIFICATIONS. Remove guide pins.

4) Install steel balls, relief spring and oil filter in intermediate plate. See Fig. 47. Install guide pins in intermediate plate. See Fig. 50. Install lower separator plate on intermediate plate.

5) Install lower valve body on intermediate plate. Install valve body bolts to retain lower valve body on intermediate plate. Tighten bolts to specification. See TORQUE SPECIFICATIONS. Remove guide pins.

6) To reassemble remaining components, reverse disassembly procedure. Ensure all solenoids valves are installed in proper location. See Fig. 46. Solenoid valves can be identified by wire color. See SOLENOID VALVE IDENTIFICATION table.

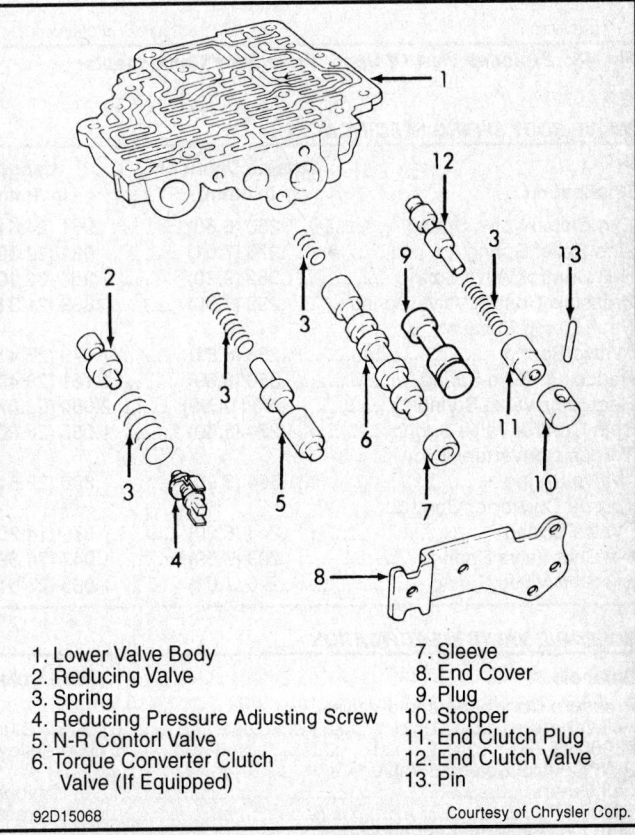

1. Lower Valve Body
2. Reducing Valve
3. Spring
4. Reducing Pressure Adjusting Screw
5. N-R Contorl Valve
6. Torque Converter Clutch Valve (If Equipped)
7. Sleeve
8. End Cover
9. Plug
10. Stopper
11. End Clutch Plug
12. End Clutch Valve
13. Pin

92D15068   Courtesy of Chrysler Corp.

Fig. 48: Exploded View Of Lower Valve Body Components

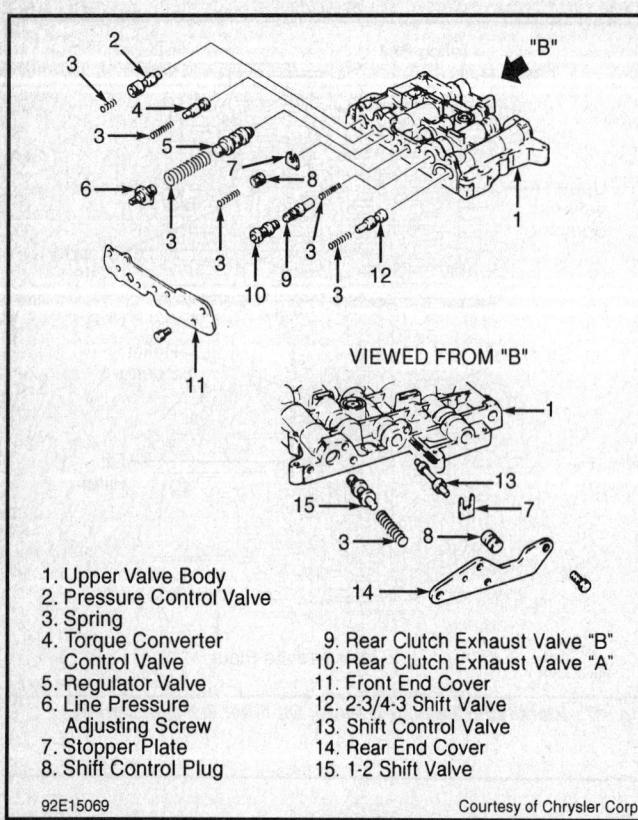

1. Upper Valve Body
2. Pressure Control Valve
3. Spring
4. Torque Converter
   Control Valve
5. Regulator Valve
6. Line Pressure
   Adjusting Screw
7. Stopper Plate
8. Shift Control Plug
9. Rear Clutch Exhaust Valve "B"
10. Rear Clutch Exhaust Valve "A"
11. Front End Cover
12. 2-3/4-3 Shift Valve
13. Shift Control Valve
14. Rear End Cover
15. 1-2 Shift Valve

92E15069   Courtesy of Chrysler Corp.

Fig. 49: Exploded View Of Upper Valve Body Components

VALVE BODY SPRING SPECIFICATIONS

Application	Outside Diameter In. (mm)	Length In. (mm)
End Clutch Valve Spring	.260 (6.60)	.961 (24.41)
Line Relief Spring	.276 (7.01)	.681 (17.30)
N-R Control Valve Spring	.362 (9.20)	1.264 (32.10)
Pressure Control Valve Spring	.299 (7.59)	.839 (21.31)
Rear Clutch Exhaust Valve Spring	.268 (6.81)	1.079 (27.41)
Reducing Valve Spring	.350 (8.89)	1.161 (29.49)
Regulator Valve Spring	.590 (14.99)	2.050 (52.07)
Shift Control Valve Spring	.224 (5.69)	1.055 (26.80)
Torque Converter Clutch Valve Spring	.354 (8.99)	.890 (22.61)
Torque Converter Control Valve Spring	.244 (6.20)	.559 (14.20)
1-2 Shift Valve Spring	.299 (7.59)	1.047 (26.59)
2-3 Shift Valve Spring	.276 (7.01)	1.083 (27.51)

SOLENOID VALVE IDENTIFICATION

Solenoid	Wire Color
Pressure Control Solenoid Valve	
All Others	Blue
3000GT	Blue/Yellow
Shift Control Solenoid Valve "A"	
All Others	Orange
3000GT	Green
Shift Control Solenoid Valve "B"	
All Others	Yellow
3000GT	Orange
Torque Converter Clutch Solenoid Valve	Red

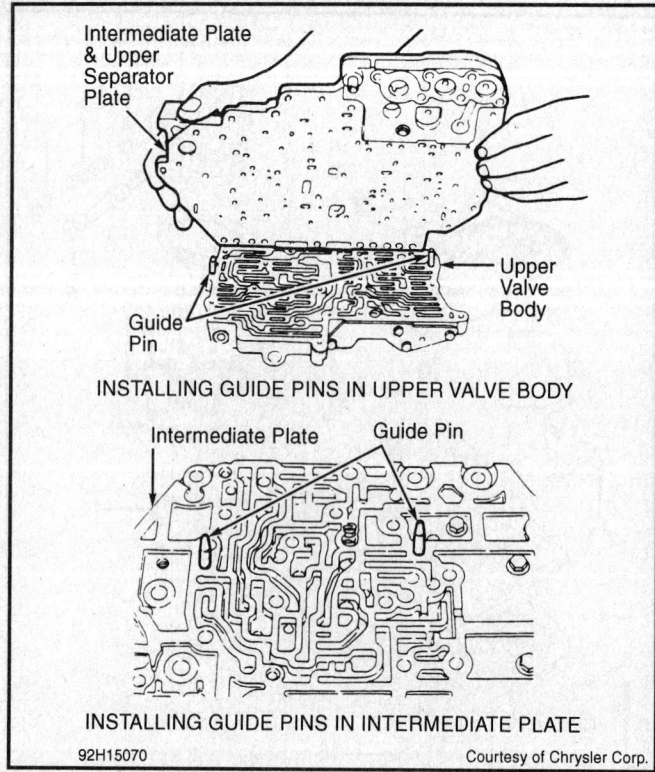

INSTALLING GUIDE PINS IN UPPER VALVE BODY

INSTALLING GUIDE PINS IN INTERMEDIATE PLATE

92H15070   Courtesy of Chrysler Corp.

Fig. 50: Installing Guide Pins

TRANSAXLE REASSEMBLY

NOTE: Manufacturer specifies the use of only Mopar ATF Plus-Type 7176 for use in this transaxle. This fluid should also be used during assembly.

VALVE BODY & INTERNAL COMPONENTS

NOTE: Lubricate all components with ATF. Apply petroleum jelly on "O" rings and seal rings. Use petroleum jelly to hold thrust bearings, thrust races and thrust washers in position. Ensure thrust bearings, thrust races and thrust washers are installed in original location and proper direction. See Fig. 51.

1) Using appropriate oil seal installer, install NEW drive shaft oil seals. On W4A32 and W4A33 models, align drive shaft oil seal with transaxle case positioning boss. Ensure drive shaft oil seal flange pieces are toward top of transaxle when installed.
2) On all models, use handle and bearing race installer to install bearing race in transaxle case. On F4A33 models, proceed to step 9).
3) On W4A32 and W4A33 models, use oil seal installer to install rear output shaft oil seal. Install front output shaft. Place a piece of solder, .06" (1.5 mm) diameter by .40" (10.1 mm) long, on each side of front bearing retainer. See Fig. 52. Install outer race.

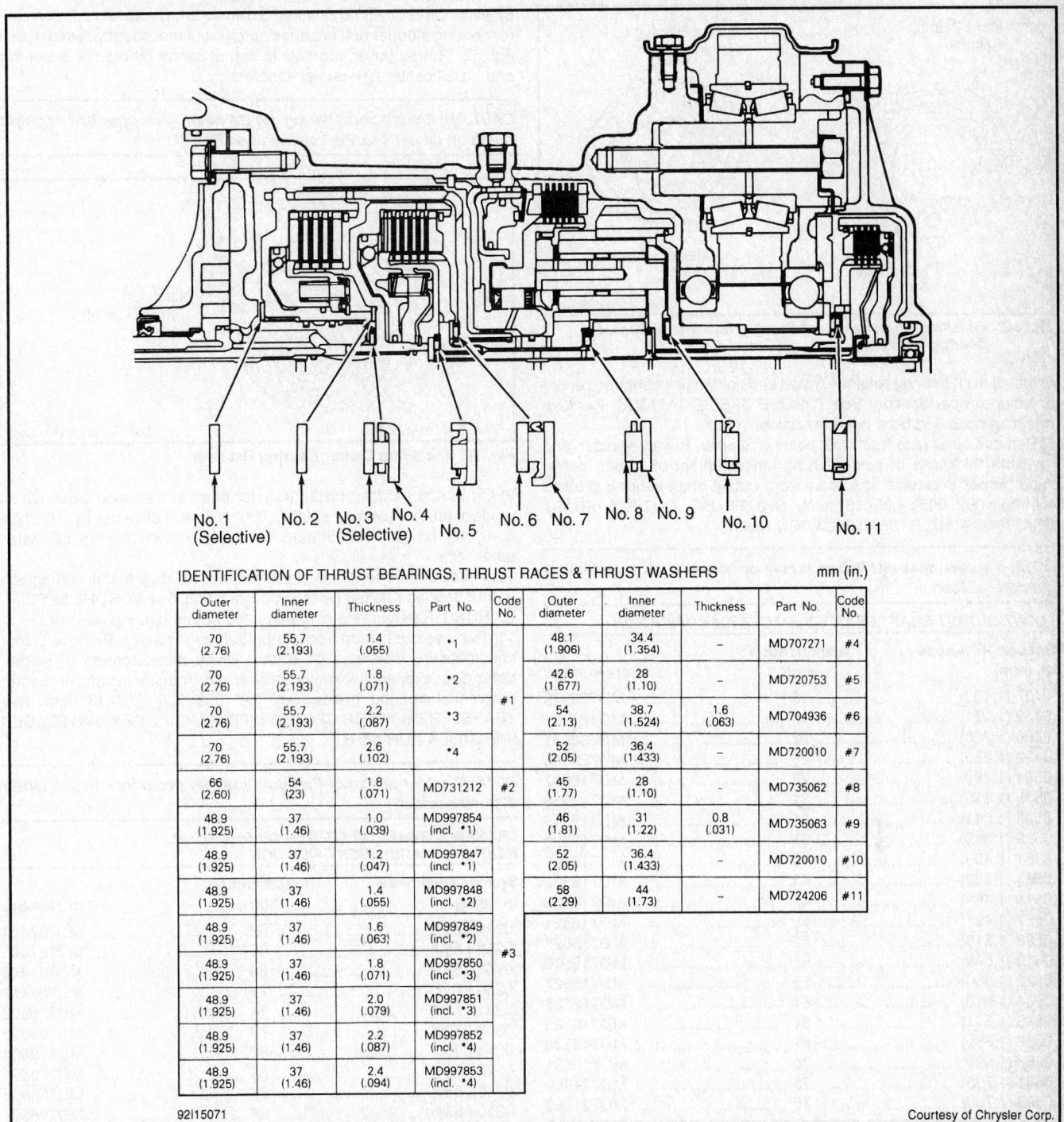

IDENTIFICATION OF THRUST BEARINGS, THRUST RACES & THRUST WASHERS   mm (in.)

Outer diameter	Inner diameter	Thickness	Part No.	Code No.	Outer diameter	Inner diameter	Thickness	Part No.	Code No.
70 (2.76)	55.7 (2.193)	1.4 (.055)	*1		48.1 (1.906)	34.4 (1.354)	–	MD707271	#4
70 (2.76)	55.7 (2.193)	1.8 (.071)	*2		42.6 (1.677)	28 (1.10)	–	MD720753	#5
70 (2.76)	55.7 (2.193)	2.2 (.087)	*3	#1	54 (2.13)	38.7 (1.524)	1.6 (.063)	MD704936	#6
70 (2.76)	55.7 (2.193)	2.6 (.102)	*4		52 (2.05)	36.4 (1.433)	–	MD720010	#7
66 (2.60)	54 (23)	1.8 (.071)	MD731212	#2	45 (1.77)	28 (1.10)	–	MD735062	#8
48.9 (1.925)	37 (1.46)	1.0 (.039)	MD997854 (incl. *1)		46 (1.81)	31 (1.22)	0.8 (.031)	MD735063	#9
48.9 (1.925)	37 (1.46)	1.2 (.047)	MD997847 (incl. *1)		52 (2.05)	36.4 (1.433)	–	MD720010	#10
48.9 (1.925)	37 (1.46)	1.4 (.055)	MD997848 (incl. *2)		58 (2.29)	44 (1.73)	–	MD724206	#11
48.9 (1.925)	37 (1.46)	1.6 (.063)	MD997849 (incl. *2)	#3					
48.9 (1.925)	37 (1.46)	1.8 (.071)	MD997850 (incl. *3)						
48.9 (1.925)	37 (1.46)	2.0 (.079)	MD997851 (incl. *3)						
48.9 (1.925)	37 (1.46)	2.2 (.087)	MD997852 (incl. *4)						
48.9 (1.925)	37 (1.46)	2.4 (.094)	MD997853 (incl. *4)						

92I15071   Courtesy of Chrysler Corp.

Fig. 51: Identifying Thrust Bearing, Thrust Race & Thrust Washer Locations

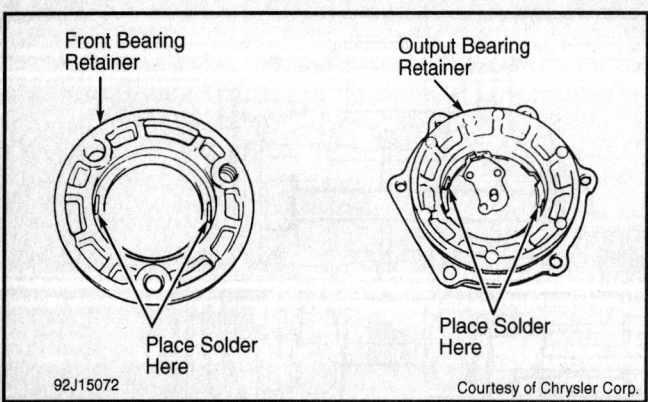

Fig. 52: Installing Solder In Front Bearing Retainer & Output Bearing Retainer

4) Install front bearing retainer. Install and tighten front bearing retainer bolts to specification. See TORQUE SPECIFICATIONS. Remove retaining bolts and front bearing retainer.

5) Remove outer race from front bearing retainer. Remove solder, and measure thickness of solder. Using measurement of solder, determine proper thickness spacer so front output shaft bearing preload will be .002-.005" (.05-.13 mm). See FRONT OUTPUT SHAFT BEARING SPACER IDENTIFICATION table.

NOTE: If solder does not flatten, it may be necessary to use a larger diameter solder.

FRONT OUTPUT SHAFT BEARING SPACER IDENTIFICATION

Spacer Thickness In. (mm)	Identification Mark	Part Number
.0457 (1.160)	16	MD736929
.0469 (1.191)	19	MD736751
.0480 (1.220)	22	MD736931
.0492 (1.250)	25	MD726166
.0504 (1.280)	28	MD718517
.0516 (1.310)	31	MD718518
.0528 (1.341)	34	MD718519
.0539 (1.369)	37	MD718520
.0551 (1.400)	40	MD718521
.0563 (1.430)	43	MD718522
.0575 (1.461)	46	MD718523
.0587 (1.491)	49	MD718524
.0598 (1.519)	52	MD718525
.0610 (1.549)	55	MD718526
.0622 (1.580)	58	MD718527
.0634 (1.610)	61	MD718528
.0646 (1.641)	64	MD718529
.0657 (1.669)	67	MD718530
.0669 (1.690)	70	MD718531
.0681 (1.730)	73	MD721959
.0693 (1.760)	76	MD721960

6) Install proper spacer and outer race in front bearing retainer. Install front bearing retainer. Apply thread sealant to front bearing retainer bolts. Install and tighten front bearing retainer bolts to specification.

CAUTION: Ensure thread sealant is applied to front bearing retainer bolts.

7) Using bearing puller installed in grooves, install viscous coupling unit. See Fig. 24. Install stopper ring. See Fig. 16. Using handle and bearing race installer, install bearing race in center bearing retainer. Install center bearing stopper bolt. See Fig. 23. Tighten center bearing stopper bolt to specification.

8) Install center bearing retainer in transaxle case so shoulder on center bearing stopper bolt engages notch on center bearing retainer. See Fig. 53. Thread puller into hole in end of center differential assembly and install center differential assembly.

CAUTION: Ensure shoulder on center bearing stopper bolt engages notch on center bearing retainer. See Fig. 51.

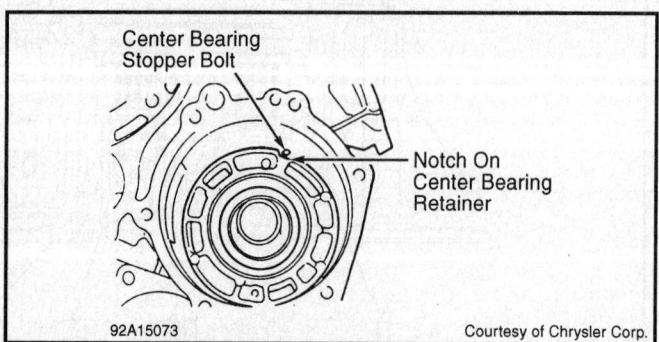

Fig. 53: Installing Center Bearing Retainer

9) On F4A33 models, install transfer shaft in transaxle case. On all models, place a piece of solder, .060" (1.5 mm) diameter by .40" (10.1 mm) long, on each side of output bearing retainer. See Fig. 52. Install outer race.

10) Install output bearing retainer without "O" ring. Install and tighten output bearing retainer bolts to specification. See TORQUE SPECIFICATIONS. Remove retaining bolts and output bearing retainer.

11) Remove outer race from output bearing retainer. Remove solder and measure thickness of solder. Using measurement of solder, determine proper thickness spacer so transfer shaft or center differential bearing preload will be .003-.005" (.07-.13 mm). See TRANSFER SHAFT OR CENTER DIFFERENTIAL BEARING SPACER IDENTIFICATION table.

NOTE: If solder does not flatten, it may be necessary to use larger diameter solder.

TRANSFER SHAFT OR CENTER DIFFERENTIAL BEARING SPACER IDENTIFICATION

Spacer Thickness In. (mm)	Identification Mark	Part Number
.0244 (.620)	62	MD737444
.0256 (.650)	65	MD737445
.0268 (.681)	68	MD737446
.0280 (.711)	71	MD737447
.0291 (.739)	74	MD728802
.0303 (.770)	77	MD728803
.0315 (.800)	80	MD728804
.0327 (.831)	83	MD728805
.0339 (.861)	86	MD728806
.0350 (.889)	89	MD728807
.0362 (.919)	92	MD728808
.0374 (.950)	95	MD728809
.0386 (.980)	98	MD728810
.0398 (1.010)	01	MD728811
.0409 (1.039)	04	MD728812
.0421 (1.069)	07	MD728813
.0433 (1.100)	10	MD728814
.0445 (1.130)	13	MD728815
.0457 (1.161)	16	MD728816
.0469 (1.191)	19	MD728817
.0480 (1.220)	22	MD728818
.0492 (1.250)	25	MD728819
.0504 (1.280)	28	MD728820
.0516 (1.311)	31	MD728821

12) Install proper spacer and outer race in output bearing retainer. Install NEW "O" ring on output bearing retainer. Lubricate "O" ring with ATF.

13) Install output bearing retainer. Install and tighten output bearing retainer bolts to specification. See TORQUE SPECIFICATIONS. Install output flange in transaxle case. Install snap ring in bearing outer circumference.

14) Install bearing retainer and NEW retaining bolts. Tighten retaining bolts to specification. Stake heads of bearing retainer bolts against bearing retainer.

CAUTION: Always install NEW retaining bolts for bearing retainer. Ensure retaining bolts are staked against bearing retainer.

---

15) Coat No. 10 thrust bearing with petroleum jelly and install on rear of planetary carrier assembly. See Fig. 14. Install planetary carrier assembly in transaxle case.

16) Assemble forward sun gear, No. 9 thrust race, No. 8 thrust bearing and reverse sun gear. See Fig. 54. Install forward and reverse sun gear assembly in planetary carrier assembly.

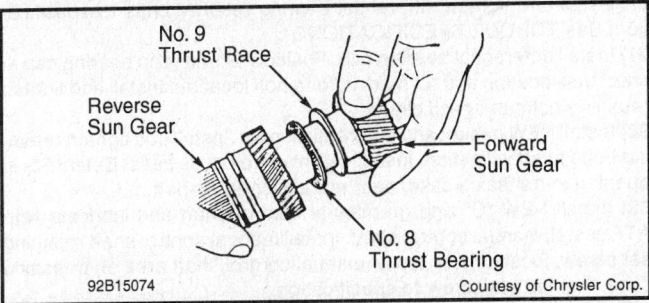

No. 9 Thrust Race

Reverse Sun Gear

Forward Sun Gear

No. 8 Thrust Bearing

92B15074   Courtesy of Chrysler Corp.

Fig. 54: Assembling Forward & Reverse Sun Gear

17) Ensure clutch discs have been soaked in ATF for at least 2 hours. Install reaction plate, clutch discs, clutch plates and pressure plate in transaxle case. See Fig. 14. Install return spring with raised side away from pressure plate. See Fig. 55.

18) Coat wave spring with petroleum jelly and install on center support. Using handle, install center support and 2 "O" rings in transaxle case.

CAUTION: Ensure center support aligns with oil hole and wave spring is aligned.

---

19) Install snap ring to retain center support in transaxle case. Using feeler gauge, measure low-reverse brake clearance. See Fig. 56. Low-reverse brake clearance should be .039-.047" (.99-1.19 mm).

20) If low-reverse brake clearance is not within specification, select different thickness pressure plate to obtain correct clearance. See PRESSURE PLATE IDENTIFICATION table.

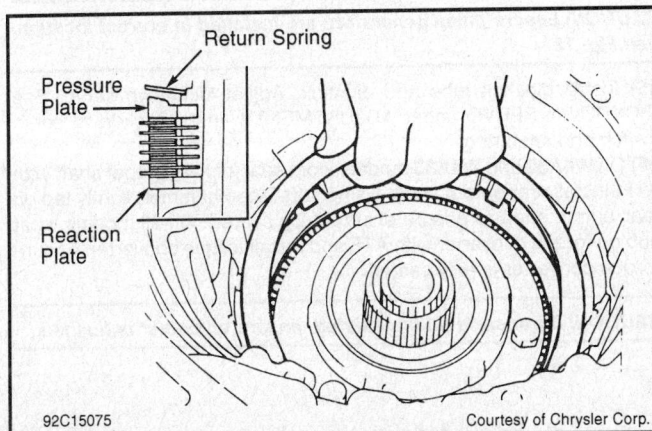

Return Spring

Pressure Plate

Reaction Plate

92C15075   Courtesy of Chrysler Corp.

Fig. 55: Installing Pressure Plate & Return Spring

PRESSURE PLATE IDENTIFICATION

Plate Thickness In. (mm)	Identification Mark	Part Number
F4A33 & W4A33		
.232 (5.89)	A	MD731736
.236 (5.99)	0	MD731737
.240 (6.10)	1	MD731738
.244 (6.20)	2	MD731739
.248 (6.30)	3	MD731740
.252 (6.40)	4	MD731588
.256 (6.50)	5	MD731741
.260 (6.60)	6	MD731742
.264 (6.71)	7	MD731743
.268 (6.81)	8	MD731744
.272 (6.91)	9	MD731745
W4A32		
.220 (5.59)	Y	MD731720
.224 (5.69)	Z	MD731721
.228 (5.79)	8	MD727801
.232 (5.89)	9	MD731000
.236 (5.99)	0	MD727802
.240 (6.10)	1	MD731001
.244 (6.20)	2	MD727803
.248 (6.30)	3	MD731002
.252 (6.40)	4	MD727804
.256 (6.50)	5	MD731003
.260 (6.60)	6	MD727805
.264 (6.71)	7	MD731004
.268 (6.81)	X	MD731005
.272 (6.91)	A	MD734766
.276 (7.01)	B	MD734767

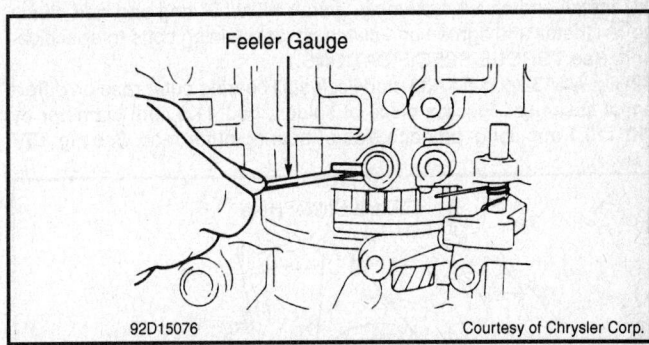

Feeler Gauge

92D15076   Courtesy of Chrysler Corp.

Fig. 56: Measuring Low-Reverse Brake Clearance

21) Install air exhaust plug and plug. See Fig. 20. Tighten plug to specification. See TORQUE SPECIFICATIONS. Install anchor rod, spring and kickdown servo piston.

CAUTION: Ensure ends of seal rings on kickdown servo piston DO NOT align with oil supply passages in kickdown servo bore on transaxle case.

---

22) Using cup, adapter and compressor, depress kickdown servo piston. See Fig. 19. Install snap ring. Remove cup, adapter and compressor. Install kickdown band with arrow on kickdown band pointing toward oil pump end of transaxle.

23) Install No. 4 thrust bearing and No. 2 thrust washer on rear clutch assembly. See Fig. 14. Assemble front and rear clutch assembly. Install No. 5 thrust bearing in rear clutch hub. See Fig. 15. Install rear clutch hub in rear clutch. Install No. 6 thrust race on end of rear clutch hub.

24) Install No. 7 thrust bearing in kickdown drum. See Fig. 15. Install front and rear clutch assembly in kickdown drum. Install front and rear clutch assembly with kickdown drum in transaxle case.

25) Coat No. 1 thrust washer and No. 3 thrust race with petroleum jelly and install on rear of oil pump. *See Fig. 13.* Install NEW gasket and install oil pump in transaxle case. Install and tighten oil pump retaining bolts to specification. See TORQUE SPECIFICATIONS.

26) Using dial indicator, check input shaft end play. *See Fig. 17.* Input shaft end play should be .012-.039" (.3-1.0 mm). If input shaft end play is not within specification, replace No. 1 thrust washer and No. 3 thrust race as a set to obtain correct end play. See NO. 1 THRUST WASHER & NO. 3 THRUST RACE SPECIFICATIONS.

NO. 1 THRUST WASHER & NO. 3 THRUST RACE SPECIFICATIONS

Thickness In. (mm)	Part Number
.040-.055 (1.01-1.40)	MD997854
.047-.055 (1.19-1.40)	MD997847
.055-.071 (1.40-1.80)	MD997848
.063-.071 (1.60-1.80)	MD997849
.071-.087 (1.80-2.21)	MD997850
.079-.087 (2.01-2.21)	MD997851
.087-.102 (2.21-2.59)	MD997852
.095-1.02 (2.41-2.59)	MD997853

27) Install spacer, idler gear, bearing and idler shaft. *See Fig. 15 or 16.* Ensure idle gear is installed so identification groove on end of idler gear faces rear of transaxle (away from oil pump).

28) Install NEW lock plate on lock bolt for idler gear shaft. Install lock bolt and tighten to specification. Bend lock tabs over on lock plate.

29) Install NEW idler gear cover gasket. Install idler gear cover and retaining bolts. Tighten retaining bolts to specification. See TORQUE SPECIFICATIONS. Install end clutch shaft with long splined area toward transaxle.

30) Install thrust washer on end clutch assembly. Install end clutch hub in end clutch assembly. *See Fig. 15 or 16.* Coat No. 11 thrust bearing with petroleum jelly and install on end clutch hub.

31) Install end clutch assembly. Install NEW "O" ring and end clutch cover. Install and tighten end clutch cover retaining bolts to specification. See TORQUE SPECIFICATIONS.

32) On W4A32 and W4A33 models, install bearing outer race on differential assembly. Place a piece of solder, .060" (1.5 mm) diameter by .40" (10.1 mm) long, on each side of bearing outer race. *See Fig. 57.*

33) On F4A33 models, place a piece of solder, .060" (1.5 mm) diameter by .40" (10.1 mm) long, on each side of differential bearing retainer. *See Fig. 57.* Install outer race.

34) On all models, install differential bearing retainer without "O" ring. Install and tighten differential bearing retainer bolts to specification. See TORQUE SPECIFICATIONS. Remove retaining bolts and differential bearing retainer.

35) On F4A33 models, remove outer race from differential bearing retainer. On all models, remove solder and measure thickness of the solder. Using measurement of solder, determine proper thickness spacer so differential assembly end play. End play should be .0030-.0053" (.076-.135 mm). If end play is not within specifications, replace differential assembly spacer. SEE DIFFERENTIAL ASSEMBLY SPACER IDENTIFICATION table.

NOTE: If solder does not flatten, it may be necessary to use a larger diameter solder.

36) Install proper spacer. Install NEW "O" ring on differential bearing retainer. Lubricate "O" ring with ATF. Install differential bearing retainer. Install and tighten differential bearing retainer bolts to specification. See TORQUE SPECIFICATIONS.

37) Install differential bearing cap. Position "S" mark on bearing cap at short bolt location and "L" mark at long bolt location. Install and tighten retaining bolts to specification.

38) Install NEW gasket and differential cover. Install and tighten retaining bolts to specification. Install detent in transaxle case. Detent fits in opening in transaxle case, near manual control shaft.

39) Install NEW "O" ring on manual control shaft and lubricate with ATF. Install manual control shaft. Install manual control shaft retaining set screw, located near top of manual control shaft area on transaxle case. Tighten set screw to specification.

40) Install parking roller support and retaining bolts. Tighten retaining bolts to specification. Install oil temperature sensor in transaxle case.

41) Install NEW "O" ring on solenoid valve wiring harness and in groove on top of valve body. *See Fig. 11.* Install solenoid valve wiring harness connector from inside transaxle case, and install grommet.

42) Install valve body. Ensure detent plate pin engages with groove on manual valve. Install retaining bolts, ensuring proper length bolt is installed in designated area. *See Fig. 13.* Tighten valve body bolts to specification. See TORQUE SPECIFICATIONS.

CAUTION: Position wiring so it does not contact detent plate. Ensure parking rod is properly retained in clamps. See Fig. 13.

43) Install oil filter, magnet, gasket, oil pan, park/neutral position switch, manual control lever and speedometer gear assembly. Tighten bolts to specification.

44) Note color of tubes on pulse generators. Install pulse generators in proper location according to color of tubes. *See Fig. 18.* Tighten bolts to specification.

CAUTION: Ensure pulse generators are installed in correct location. See Fig. 18.

45) Install dipstick tube and dipstick. Adjust kickdown servo. See KICKDOWN SERVO under ADJUSTMENTS. Install kickdown servo switch and snap ring.

46) On W4A32 and W4A33 models, coat seal for rear output shaft with ATF. Install rear output shaft. Using soft-faced hammer, lightly tap on rear output shaft to ensure shaft is fully seated. On all models, coat hub on torque converter with ATF and install torque converter. Ensure torque converter is fully seated.

CAUTION: If transaxle failure existed, ensure oil cooler is flushed.

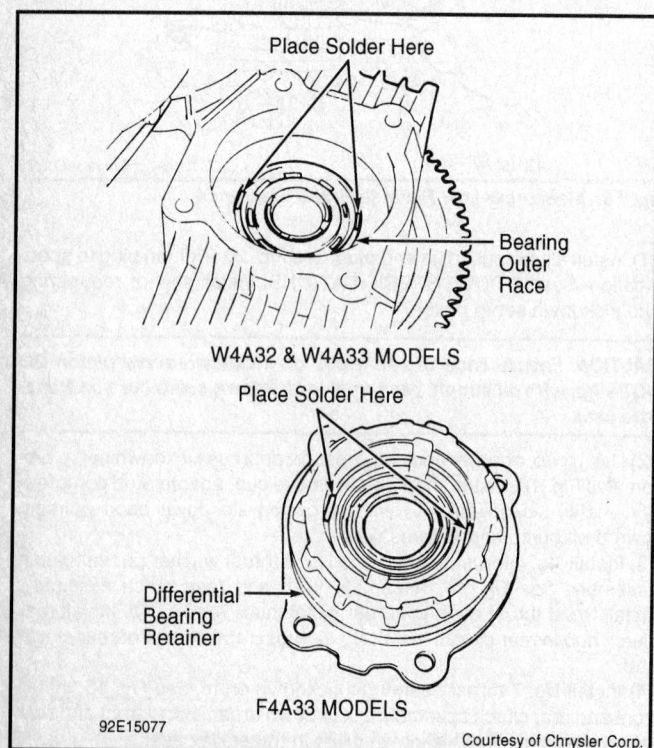

Place Solder Here

Bearing Outer Race

W4A32 & W4A33 MODELS

Place Solder Here

Differential Bearing Retainer

F4A33 MODELS

92E15077

Courtesy of Chrysler Corp.

Fig. 57: *Installing Solder On Outer Race Or In Differential Bearing Retainer*

DIFFERENTIAL ASSEMBLY SPACER IDENTIFICATION

Spacer Thickness In. (mm)	Identification Mark	Part Number
F4A33		
Eclipse		
.0279 (.710)	71	MD754475
.0291 (.740)	74	MD727660
.0303 (.770)	77	MD754476
.0315 (.800)	80	MD727661
.0327 (.831)	83	MD720937
.0339 (.861)	86	MD720938
.0350 (.889)	89	MD720939
.0362 (.919)	92	MD720940
.0374 (.950)	95	MD720941
.0386 (.980)	98	MD720942
.0409 (1.039)	04	MD720944
.0421 (1.069)	07	MD720945
.0445 (1.130)	D	MD700270
.0457 (1.161)	K	MD710455
.0469 (1.190)	L	MD710456
.0480 (1.219)	G	MD700271
.0492 (1.250)	M	MD710457
.0504 (1.280)	N	MD710458
.0516 (1.311)	E	MD706574
.0528 (1.341)	O	MD710459
.0539 (1.369)	P	MD710460
3000GT		
.0280 (.711)	71	MD754446
.0291 (.741)	74	MD754447
.0303 (.771)	77	MD754448
.0315 (.801)	80	MD754449
.0327 (.831)	83	MD740846
.0339 (.861)	86	MD740847
.0350 (.889)	89	MD740848
.0362 (.919)	92	MD740849
.0374 (.950)	95	MD740850
.0386 (.980)	98	MD740851
.0398 (1.011)	01	MD740852
.0409 (1.039)	04	MD740853
.0421 (1.069)	07	MD740854
.0433 (1.100)	10	MD740855
.0445 (1.130)	13	MD740856
.0457 (1.161)	16	MD740857
.0469 (1.191)	19	MD740858
.0480 (1.219)	22	MD740859
.0492 (1.250)	25	MD740860
.0504 (1.280)	28	MD740861
.0516 (1.311)	31	MD740862
.0528 (1.341)	34	MD740863
.0539 (1.369)	37	MD740864
W4A32 & W4A33		
.0398 (1.011)	01	MD720943
.0433 (1.100)	J	MD710454
.0469 (1.191)	L	MD710456
.0504 (1.280)	N	MD710458

TORQUE SPECIFICATIONS
TORQUE SPECIFICATIONS

Application	Ft. Lbs. (N.m)
Air Exhaust Plug	22-25 (30-34)
Bearing Retainer Bolt	13-14 (18-19)
Differential Bearing Cap Bolt	43-58 (58-79)
Differential Bearing Retainer Bolt	22-28 (30-38)
Differential Flange-To-Differential Case Bolt	51-57 (69-77)
Front Bearing Retainer Bolt	32-39 (43-53)
Idler Gear Lock Bolt	22-32 (30-43)
Kickdown Servo Lock Nut	18-23 (24-31)
Manual Control Lever Bolt	12-15 (16-20)
Oil Pump-To-Transaxle Case Bolt	14-16 (19-22)
Output Bearing Retainer Bolt	15-19 (20-26)
Parking Roller Support Bolt	15-19 (20-26)
Ring Gear Bolt	94-101 (127-137)

Application	INCH Lbs. (N.m)
Center Bearing Stopper Bolt	36-48 (4.1-5.4)
Differential Cover Bolt	89-102 (10.1-11.5)
End Clutch Cover Bolt	89-102 (10.1-11.5)
Hydraulic Pressure Tap Plug	36-48 (4.1-5.4)
Idler Gear Cover Bolt	89-102 (10.1-11.5)
Inhibitor Switch Bolt	89-102 (10.1-11.5)
Manual Control Shaft Set Screw	72-84 (8.1-9.5)
Oil Filter Bolt	48-60 (5.4-6.8)
Oil Pan Bolt	89-102 (10.1-11.5)
Pulse Generator Bolt	89-102 (10.1-11.5)
Reaction Shaft Support Bolt	84-108 (9.5-12.2)
Speedometer Gear Assembly Bolt	36-48 (4.1-5.4)
Valve Body Bolt	
Valve Body-To-Transaxle Case Bolt	89-102 (10.1-11.5)
Upper & Lower Valve Body Bolt	36-48 (4.1-5.4)

TRANSAXLE SPECIFICATIONS
TRANSAXLE SPECIFICATIONS

Application	In. (mm)
Differential Assembly End Play & Preload	.0030-.0053 (.076-.135)
Differential Side Gear-To-Pinion	
Gear Backlash	.0010-.0059 (.025-.150)
End Clutch Clearance	.024-.033 (.61-.84)
Front Clutch Clearance	
F4A33 & W4A33	.032-.039 (.81-.99)
W4A32	.028-.035 (.71-.89)
Front Output Shaft Bearing Preload	.002-.005 (.05-.13)
Input Shaft End Play	.012-.039 (.30-.99)
Low-Reverse Brake Clearance	.039-.047 (.99-1.19)
Oil Pump Gear End Clearance	.001-.002 (.03-.05)
Output Flange End Play	0-.0035 (0-.089)
Rear Clutch Clearance	
F4A33 & W4A33	.039-.047 (.99-1.19)
W4A32	.016-.024 (.41-.61)
Transfer Shaft Or Center Differential	
Bearing Preload	.003-.005 (.07-.13)

AUTOMATIC TRANSMISSIONS
Mitsubishi F4A20, F4A30 & W4A30 Series
Electronic Controls

Hyundai: Sonata
Mitsubishi: Diamante, Eclipse, Expo
 Galant, Mirage, 3000GT

APPLICATION

TRANSAXLE APPLICATIONS

Vehicle & Model	Transaxle Model
Hyundai	
Sonata (3.0L)	F4A33
Mitsubishi	
Diamante	F4A33
Eclipse	
2.0L Turbo	
AWD	W4A33
FWD	F4A33
2.4L	F4A23
Expo	
AWD	W4A32
FWD	
1.8L	F4A22
2.4L	F4A23
Galant	F4A23
Mirage	F4A22
3000GT	F4A33

INTRODUCTION

The first step in diagnosing any driveability problem is verifying the customer's complaint with a test drive under the conditions the problem reportedly occurred. Before entering self-diagnostics, perform a careful and complete visual inspection. Most transmission control problems result from mechanical breakdowns or poor electrical connections.

DESCRIPTION

The transaxle electronic control system controls transaxle shift points and torque converter clutch control for torque converter lock-up. Transaxle uses hydraulically operated clutches controlled by the Transaxle Control Module (TCM). Overdrive or 4th gear operation is controlled by a manually operated overdrive control switch. Transaxle will not shift into overdrive unless overdrive control switch is in the ON position.

OPERATION

TRANSAXLE CONTROL MODULE (TCM)

The TCM receives information from various input devices and controls various output devices for different gear operation. The TCM is located behind instrument panel, near center of console, and contains a 42-pin connector. *See Figs. 1-4.*

On Diamante and 3000GT models, a POWER/ECONOMY switch, located on center of console, is used to change shift patterns. The preset shift patterns are controlled by the TCM.

The TCM controller contains a self-diagnostic system which stores a Diagnostic Trouble Code (DTC) if a transaxle fault exists. Trouble code can be retrieved to determine transaxle problem area. See SELF-DIAGNOSTIC SYSTEM. The TCM contains a fail-safe mode. If certain trouble codes are set, transaxle will enter fail-safe mode. When in fail-safe mode, transaxle will remain in 2nd or 3rd gear with no upshifts or downshifts. Transaxle will also function in Park, Neutral and Reverse when in fail-safe mode.

TCM works in conjunction with the Engine Control Module (ECM) for receiving information for transaxle control. *See Figs. 1-4.*

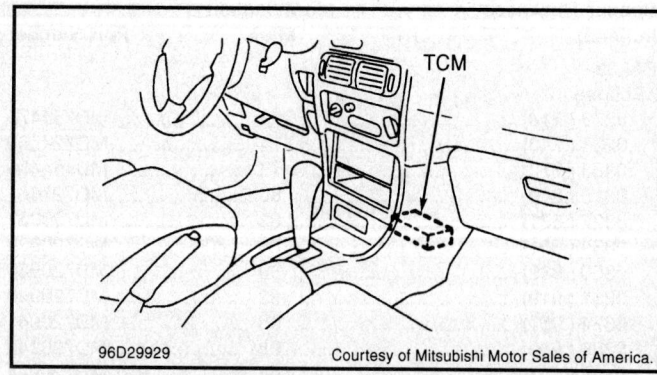

96D29929 Courtesy of Mitsubishi Motor Sales of America.

Fig. 1: Locating TCM (Mirage)

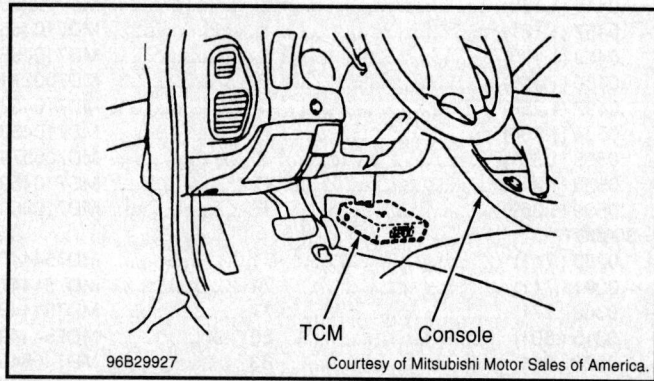

96B29927 Courtesy of Mitsubishi Motor Sales of America.

Fig. 2: Locating TCM (Eclipse)

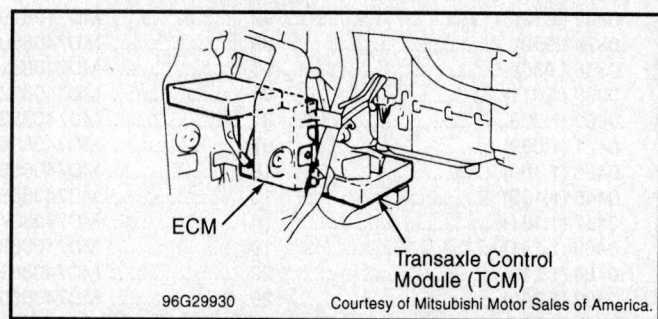

96G29930 Courtesy of Mitsubishi Motor Sales of America.

Fig. 3: Locating TCM (3000GT)

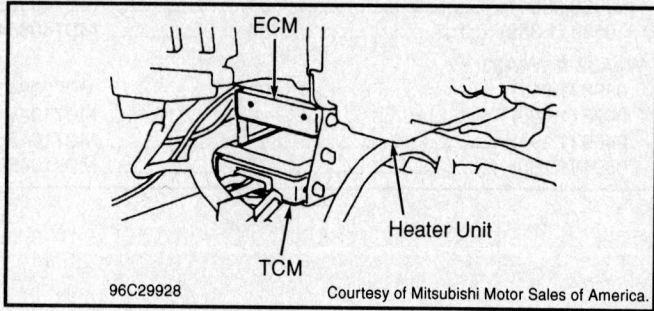

96C29928 Courtesy of Mitsubishi Motor Sales of America.

Fig. 4: Locating TCM (Galant & Sonata)

AUTOMATIC TRANSMISSIONS
Mitsubishi F4A20, F4A30 & W4A30 Series
Electronic Controls (Cont.)

3-1129

INPUT DEVICES

Neutral Safety Switch – Neutral Safety switch is an input device mounted on the transaxle manual control shaft. *See Fig. 5*. Neutral Safety switch delivers an input signal to TCM, indicating transaxle manual valve gear position.

Kickdown Servo Switch – Kickdown servo switch is an input device mounted on the side of transaxle case. *See Fig. 5*. Kickdown servo switch delivers an input signal to the TCM to indicate kickdown servo operation.

Oil Temperature Sensor – Oil temperature sensor is an input device mounted inside the transaxle case. *See Fig. 5*. Oil temperature sensor delivers an input signal to the TCM to indicate the fluid temperature.

NOTE: Oil temperature sensor may also be referred to as fluid temperature sensor. It may be necessary to identify wire color to oil temperature sensor for proper identification. See appropriate wiring diagram under WIRING DIAGRAMS.

Overdrive Control Switch – Overdrive control switch, located on gear selector lever, delivers an input signal to the TCM. Transaxle will not shift into overdrive unless overdrive control switch is in the ON position.

POWER/ECONOMY Switch (Diamante & 3000GT) – The POWER/ECONOMY switch, located on center of console, delivers an input signal to the TCM. The TCM uses this signal to change shift patterns.

Pulse Generators – Pulse generators are mounted on transaxle case. *See Figs. 5 or 6*. Pulse generators indicate transfer shaft speed and end clutch speed. Signals are input to the TCM for transaxle control.

Throttle Position (TP) Sensor – The TP sensor, mounted on the throttle body, determines throttle position and inputs a signal to the TCM. The TCM uses signal to control transaxle upshifts.

Vehicle Speed Sensor (VSS) – Vehicle speed sensor inputs signal to the TCM to indicate vehicle speed. Vehicle speed sensor is mounted on rear of instrument cluster.

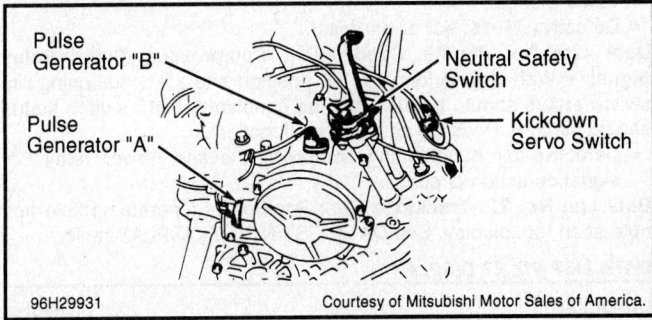

96H29931   Courtesy of Mitsubishi Motor Sales of America.

Fig. 5: Locating Neutral Safety Switch, Kickdown Servo Switch & Pulse Generators (AWD)

OUTPUT DEVICES

NOTE: For solenoid valve wire color identification, see WIRING DIAGRAMS.

Pressure Control Solenoid Valve (PCSV) – The PCSV is located on the valve body. *See Fig. 7*. The TCM operates the PCSV for controlling transaxle shifts.

Shift Control Solenoid Valve (SCSV) – The SCSV "A" or "B" are located on the valve body. *See Fig. 7*. The TCM operates SCSV for controlling transaxle shifts.

Torque Converter Clutch Solenoid Valve (TCCSV) – The TCCSV is located on the valve body. *See Fig. 7*. The TCM operates the TCCSV for torque converter clutch control of torque converter lock-up.

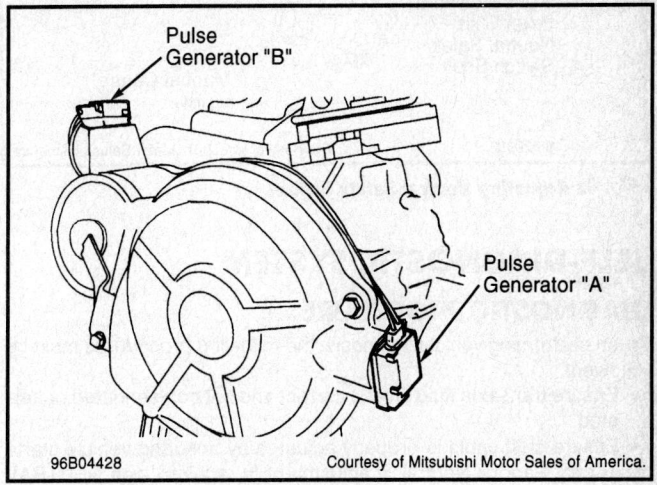

96B04428   Courtesy of Mitsubishi Motor Sales of America.

Fig. 6: Locating Pulse Generators (FWD)

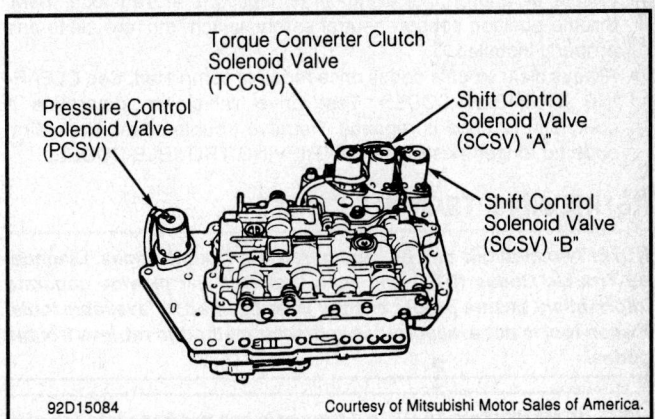

92D15084   Courtesy of Mitsubishi Motor Sales of America.

Fig. 7: Identifying Solenoid Valves

ADJUSTMENTS

NEUTRAL SAFETY SWITCH

1) Place gear selector lever and manual control lever on transaxle in Neutral position. Loosen neutral safety switch retaining screws. Rotate neutral safety switch body so hole in manual control lever aligns with hole on neutral safety switch body. *See Fig. 8*. Tighten neutral safety switch retaining screws to specification. See TORQUE SPECIFICATIONS.

2) Loosen shift control cable lock nut at shift control cable-to-manual control lever. Pull end of shift control cable toward manual control lever. Tighten shift control cable lock nut to specification. See TORQUE SPECIFICATIONS.

3) Move gear selector lever through all gear ranges. Ensure manual control lever is in gear position corresponding to gear selector lever. Ensure vehicle starts only in Park and Neutral.

3-1130

AUTOMATIC TRANSMISSIONS
Mitsubishi F4A20, F4A30 & W4A30 Series
Electronic Controls (Cont.)

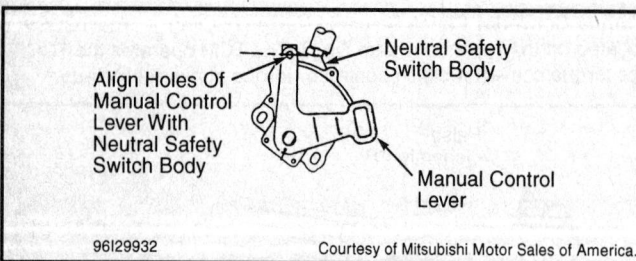

Fig. 8: Adjusting Neutral Safety Switch

96I29932   Courtesy of Mitsubishi Motor Sales of America.

SELF-DIAGNOSTIC SYSTEM

DIAGNOSTIC PROCEDURE

When performing vehicle diagnosis, the following procedures must be followed:

- Ensure transaxle fluid level is correct and not contaminated or aerated.
- Ensure shift cable is properly adjusted by ensuring vehicle starts in only Park or Neutral. If adjustment is required, see NEUTRAL SAFETY SWITCH under ADJUSTMENTS.
- Ensure all appropriate electrical connections at transaxle, TCM, throttle position sensor, neutral safety switch, etc. are clean and properly installed.
- Always clear trouble codes once repair is completed. See CLEARING TROUBLE CODES. Test drive vehicle to determine if complaint or code is repaired. Retrieve trouble codes to confirm code no longer exists. See RETRIEVING TROUBLE CODES.

RETRIEVING TROUBLE CODES

NOTE: Two methods can be used to retrieve trouble codes. Diagnostic Trouble Codes (DTC) and scan tool data list provide separate information. Ensure proper method is being used for available tools. If scan tool is not available, use voltmeter method to retrieve trouble codes.

NOTE: TCM will store 10 DTCs if transaxle has not gone into fail-safe mode. Only 3 DTCs will be stored if transaxle goes into fail-safe mode. See DTC IDENTIFICATION table for fail-safe mode trouble codes.

Scan Tool Method – Locate diagnostic connector below instrument panel. On Eclipse, Galant and 3000GT models, diagnostic connector is located to the right side of steering wheel under the instrument panel. On all other models, diagnostic connector is located next to left kick-panel fuse box. Connect scan tool and follow manufacturer's instructions. Check scan tool data list for system failure and test probable cause.

SCAN TOOL DATA LIST IDENTIFICATION

Data List No.	Circuit
11	TP Sensor
15	Oil Temperature Sensor
21	Kickdown Servo Switch
23	Ignition Pulse Signal
25	Closed TP Switch
26	A/C Compressor Clutch Relay Signal
27	Transaxle Gear Position
31	Pulse Generator "A"
32	Pulse Generator "B"
35	Overdrive Switch
36	Power/Economy Switch
37	Neutral Safety Switch
38	Vehicle Speed Sensor
45	PCSV Duty Solenoid
47	Torque Converter Clutch Slippage
49	Torque Converter Clutch Solenoid Duty

Data List No. 11: Throttle Position (TP) Sensor – With accelerator pedal released, voltage should be .4-1.0 volts. Voltage should increase smoothly as accelerator is depressed to Wide Open Throttle (WOT). Voltage should be 4.5-5.0 volts at WOT. Possible causes of malfunction are:

- Incorrectly adjusted TP sensor. See appropriate SELF-DIAGNOSTICS article in ENGINE PERFORMANCE in appropriate MITCHELL® manual.
- TP sensor or harness malfunction.
- Defective throttle cable.

Data List No. 15: Oil Temperature Sensor – For cold engine, scan tool temperature should equal outside ambient temperature. Start and run vehicle engine. Temperature should gradually increase to 176-230°F (80-110°C) degrees. Possible cause of malfunction is:

- Defective oil temperature sensor or harness.

Data List No. 21: Kickdown Servo Switch – With engine idling and transaxle in "L" position, switch status should be ON. Test drive vehicle in "D" position. Switch status should be ON in 1st or 3rd gear. Switch status should be OFF in 2nd or 4th gear. Possible causes of malfunction are:

- Incorrectly adjusted kickdown servo.
- Defective kickdown servo switch or harness.
- Defective kickdown servo.

Data List No. 23: Ignition Pulse Signal – With engine idling in neutral, engine speed should be 650-900 RPM. Using vehicles tachometer, increase engine speed to 2500 RPM. Scan tool should display 2400-2600 RPM. Possible causes of malfunction are:

- Defective ignition system.
- Defective ignition signal pickup circuit harness.

Data List No. 25: Closed Throttle Position Switch – With accelerator pedal fully released, switch status should be ON. With accelerator pedal slightly depressed, switch status should be OFF. Possible causes of malfunction are:

- Incorrectly adjusted TP sensor. See appropriate SELF-DIAGNOSTICS article in ENGINE PERFORMANCE in appropriate MITCHELL® manual.
- Defective TP sensor or harness.

Data List No. 26: Air Conditioning Compressor Clutch Relay Signal – With engine idling in "D" position and air conditioning on, switch status should be ON. With air conditioning off, switch status should be OFF. Possible cause of malfunction is:

- Defective air conditioning compressor clutch power relay ON signal detection circuit.

Data List No. 27: Transaxle Gear Position – Operate vehicle and note scan tool display. See DATA LIST NO. 27 DISPLAY table.

DATA LIST NO. 27 DISPLAY

Condition	Display
"D" Range, Idling	C
"L" Range, Idling	1ST
"2" Range, 2nd Gear	2ND
"D" Range, O/D Off, 3rd Gear	3RD
"D" Range, O/D On, 4th Gear	4TH

Possible causes for malfunction are:

- Defective TCM.
- Defective TP sensor.
- Defective neutral safety switch.

Data List No. 31: Pulse Generator "A" – Operate vehicle and note scan tool display. See DATA LIST NO. 31 DISPLAY table.

DATA LIST NO. 31 DISPLAY

Condition	Display RPM
"D" Range, Stopped	0
"D" Range, 3rd Gear, 31 MPH	1600-2200
"D" Range, 4th Gear, 31 MPH	1100-1600

AUTOMATIC TRANSMISSIONS
Mitsubishi F4A20, F4A30 & W4A30 Series
Electronic Controls (Cont.)

3-1131

Possible causes of malfunction are:
- Defective pulse generator "A" or harness.
- Defective pulse generator "A" shielded wire.
- External noise interference.

Data List No. 32: Pulse Generator "B" – Operate vehicle and note scan tool display. See DATA LIST NO. 32 DISPLAY table.

DATA LIST NO. 32 DISPLAY

Condition	Display RPM
"D" Range, Stopped	0
"D" Range, 3rd Gear, 31 MPH	1600-2000
"D" Range, 4th Gear, 31 MPH	1600-2000

Possible causes of malfunction are:
- Defective pulse generator "B" or harness.
- Defective pulse generator "B" shielded wire.
- External noise interference.

Data List No. 35: Overdrive Switch – Scan tool display should match overdrive switch position. Possible cause of malfunction is:
- Defective OD switch or harness.

Data List No. 36: Power/Economy Switch – Scan tool display should match power/economy switch position. Possible cause of malfunction is:
- Defective power/economy switch or harness.

Data List No. 37: Neutral Safety Switch – Operate shift lever and note scan tool display. Display should match neutral safety switch position. Possible cause of malfunction is:
- Incorrectly adjusted neutral safety switch.
- Defective neutral safety switch or harness.
- Defective manual control cable.

Data List No. 38: Vehicle Speed Sensor (VSS) – Test drive vehicle. Scan tool display should match speedometer reading. Possible cause of malfunction is:
- Vehicle speed sensor or harness is defective.

Data List No. 45: PCSV Duty Solenoid – Operate vehicle and note scan tool display. See DATA LIST NO. 45 DISPLAY table.

DATA LIST NO. 45 DISPLAY

Condition	Display
"D" Range, Idling	50-70%
"D" Range, 1st Gear	100%
"D" Range, Transaxle Shifting	Variable

Possible causes of malfunction are:
- Defective TCM.
- Defective TP sensor.

Data List No. 47: Torque Converter Clutch Slipage – Operate vehicle and note scan tool display. See DATA LIST NO. 47 DISPLAY table.

DATA LIST NO. 47 DISPLAY

Condition	Display
"D" Range, 3rd Gear, 1500 RPM	100-300 RPM
"D" Range, 3rd Gear, 3500 RPM	0 RPM

Possible causes of malfunction are:
- Defective torque converter clutch.
- Defective ignition signal line or pulse generator "B" circuit.
- Incorrect transmission fluid pressure.
- Defective TCC solenoid.

Data List No. 49: TCC Solenoid Duty – Operate vehicle and note scan tool display. See DATA LIST NO. 49 DISPLAY table.

DATA LIST NO. 49 DISPLAY

Condition	Display
"D" Range, 3rd Gear, 1500 RPM	0%
"D" Range, 3rd Gear, 3500 RPM	Variable

Possible causes of malfunction are:
- Defective TCM.
- Defective TP sensor circuit.
- Defective pulse generator "B" circuit.

Voltmeter Method – **1)** Locate diagnostic connector below instrument panel. On Eclipse, Galant and 3000GT models, diagnostic connector is located to the right side of steering wheel under the instrument panel. On all other models, diagnostic connector is located next to left kick-panel fuse box. Install voltmeter between ground terminal No. 4 or No. 5 and diagnostic output terminal No. 6. *See Fig. 9.*
2) Turn ignition on. Note fluctuations of voltmeter needle to indicate DTC. The first fluctuation indicates first digit of DTC. Following fluctuations indicate the second digit of DTC. *See Fig. 10.* Record DTC's in order displayed. To identify DTC and items to be checked or adjusted, see DTC IDENTIFICATION table.

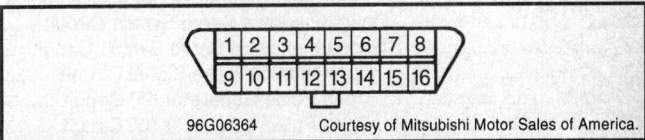

96G06364   Courtesy of Mitsubishi Motor Sales of America.

Fig. 9: Identifying Data Link Connector Terminals

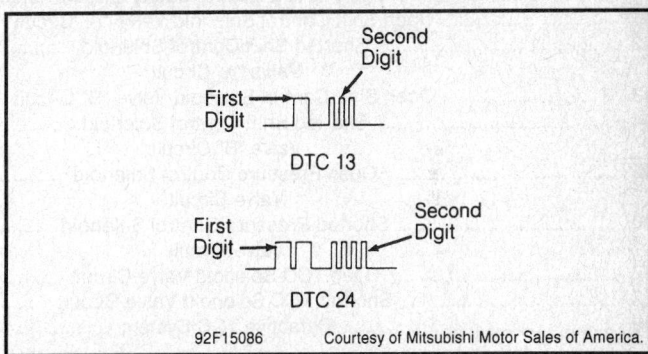

92F15086   Courtesy of Mitsubishi Motor Sales of America.

Fig. 10: Identifying Voltmeter Trouble Code Display

CLEARING TROUBLE CODES

Trouble codes can be cleared from TCM memory by disconnecting negative battery cable for more than 10 seconds. Ensure trouble codes are cleared after performing repairs.

WARNING: When battery is disconnected, vehicle computer and memory systems may lose memory data. Driveability problems may exist until computer systems have completed a relearn cycle. See COMPUTER RELEARN PROCEDURES in APPLICATIONS & IDENTIFICATION section before disconnecting battery.

DIAGNOSTIC TESTING

NOTE: For engine-related DTCs, see appropriate SELF-DIAGNOSTICS article in ENGINE PERFORMANCE in appropriate MITCHELL® manual. These DTCs apply to engine performance and must be repaired first, as engine performance and related component signals will affect transmission operation and diagnosis.

DTC 11, 12, 13 & 14: THROTTLE POSITION (TP) SENSOR MALFUNCTION

1) Inspect TP sensor. See appropriate SELF-DIAGNOSTICS article in ENGINE PERFORMANCE in appropriate MITCHELL® manual. Replace as needed and go to next step. If TP sensor is okay, inspect TP sensor connector and TCM connector. Repair as needed and go to next step.
2) Clear DTC's. See CLEARING TROUBLE CODES (DTC). Operate vehicle and check if DTC resets. If DTC is not present, vehicle is currently operating correctly. If DTC is reset, turn ignition off. Inspect continuity of circuits between TCM and TP sensor. See WIRING DIAGRAMS. Repair as needed. If circuit(s) are okay, replace TCM.

AUTOMATIC TRANSMISSIONS
Mitsubishi F4A20, F4A30 & W4A30 Series
Electronic Controls (Cont.)

DTC IDENTIFICATION

DIAGNOSTIC TROUBLE CODE (DTC) IDENTIFICATION

DTC Number	Probable Cause	[1] Items To Check
11	High TPS Output	Check TPS Operation, Adjustment & Connector, Check Accelerator Switch
12	Low TPS Output	Check TPS Operation, Adjustment & Connector, Check Accelerator Switch
13	Defective Or Improperly Adjusted TPS	Check TPS Operation & Adjustment
14	Improperly Adjusted TPS	Check TPS Adjustment
15	Open Oil Temperature Sensor Circuit	Check Oil Temperature Sensor & Connector
16	Shorted Oil Temperature Sensor Circuit	Check Oil Temperature Sensor Wiring Harness
21	Open Kickdown Servo Switch Circuit	Check Kickdown Servo Switch & Connector
22	Shorted Kickdown Servo Switch Circuit	Check Kickdown Servo Switch & Connector
23	Open Ignition Pulse Signal Circuit	Check For Open Circuit To Pins No. 46 Or 63 At TCM
31	Open Pulse Generator "A" Circuit	Check Pulse Generator, Check Vehicle Speed Sensor
32	Open Pulse Generator "B" Circuit	Check Pulse Generator, Check Vehicle Speed Sensor
36	Short Circuit Neutral Safety Switch	Check Neutral Safety Switch
37	Open Circuit Neutral Safety Switch	Check Neutral Safety Switch
41	Open Shift Control Solenoid Valve "A" Circuit	Check Shift Control Solenoid Valve & Connector
42	Shorted Shift Control Solenoid Valve "A" Circuit	Check Shift Control Solenoid Valve & Connector
43	Open Shift Control Solenoid Valve "B" Circuit	Check Shift Control Solenoid Valve & Connector
44	Shorted Shift Control Solenoid Valve "B" Circuit	Check Shift Control Solenoid Valve & Connector
45	Open Pressure Control Solenoid Valve Circuit	Check Pressure Control Solenoid Valve & Connector
46	Shorted Pressure Control Solenoid Valve Circuit	Check Pressure Control Solenoid Valve & Connector
47	Open TCC Solenoid Valve Circuit	Check TCC Solenoid Valve & Connector
48	Shorted TCC Solenoid Valve Circuit	Check TCC Solenoid Valve & Connector
49	Defective TCC System	Check TCC Hydraulic Circuit, Check TCC Solenoid Valve, Defective TCM
51	Incorrect Or No Upshift From 1st Gear	Check Pulse Generators "A" & "B" Or Connectors, Rear Clutch Slipping
52	Incorrect Or No Upshift From 2nd Gear	Check Pulse Generators "A" & "B" Or Connectors, Rear Clutch Slipping, Kickdown Band Slipping
53	Incorrect Or No Upshift From 3rd Gear	Check Pulse Generators "A" & "B" Or Connectors, Front Or Rear Clutch Slipping
54	Incorrect Or No Upshift From 4th Gear	Check Pulse Generators "A" & "B" Or Connectors, End Clutch Slipping, Kickdown Band Slipping
59	Abnormal Vibration	Check Pulse Generator "A" Or Connector, Replace ATF
61 [2]	Shorted Torque Reduction Request Signal Line Or Open Torque Converter Reduction Execution Signal Line	Check Torque Reduction Request Or Execution Signal Line
62 [2]	Open Circuit On Torque Reduction Request Signal Line	Check Torque Reduction Request Signal Line
63 [2]	Shorted Circuit On Torque Reduction Execution Signal Line	Check Torque Reduction Execution Signal Line
81 [3]	Open Pulse Generator "A" Circuit	See DTC No. 31
82 [3]	Open Pulse Generator "B" Circuit	See DTC No. 32
83 [3]	Open Or Shorted Shift Control Solenoid Valve "A" Circuit	See DTC No. 41 & 42
84 [3]	Open Or Shorted Shift Control Solenoid Valve "B"	See DTC No. 43 & 44
85 [3]	Open Or Shorted Pressure Control Solenoid Valve	See DTC No. 45 & 46
86 [3]	Incorrect Or No Upshift	See DTC No. 51, 52, 53 & 54

[1] – To check items listed, see DIAGNOSTIC TESTING or COMPONENT TESTING.
[2] – Applies to Diamante, Eclipse and 3000GT models only.
[3] – Trouble code is set in fail-safe mode only.

AUTOMATIC TRANSMISSIONS
Mitsubishi F4A20, F4A30 & W4A30 Series
Electronic Controls (Cont.)

3-1133

DTC 15 & 16: OIL TEMPERATURE SENSOR

1) Inspect oil temperature sensor. See COMPONENT TESTING. Replace as needed. With sensor connector disconnected, turn ignition on. Using voltmeter, measure voltage between sensor harness connector terminal No. 1 and ground. *See Fig. 11.* If voltage is not 4.8-5.2 volts, go to next step. If voltage is 4.8-5.2 volts, go to step **4)**.

2) Turn ignition off. Using ohmmeter, check continuity between ground and terminal No. 2 on sensor harness connector. If continuity does not exist, go to next step. If continuity exists, go to step **4)**.

3) Turn ignition off. Disconnect TCM connector. Inspect connector and repair as needed. Using ohmmeter, check continuity of circuits between TCM and oil temperature sensor harness connectors. See WIRING DIAGRAMS. Repair as needed. If circuit is okay, replace TCM.

4) Turn ignition off. Disconnect TCM connector(s). Inspect connector and repair as needed. Clear DTC. See CLEARING TROUBLE CODES. Operate vehicle and recheck DTC. If DTC is not present, vehicle is currently operating correctly. If DTC resets, repeat step **1)**.

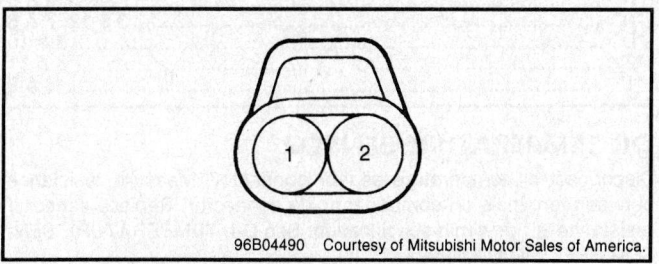

96B04490   Courtesy of Mitsubishi Motor Sales of America.

Fig. 11: *Identifying Oil Temperature Sensor Terminals*

DTC 21 & 22: KICKDOWN SERVO SWITCH

1) Inspect kickdown servo switch. See COMPONENT TESTING. Replace as needed. With switch connector disconnected, turn ignition on. Using voltmeter, measure voltage at harness connector terminal. If battery voltage does not exist, go to next step. If battery voltage exists, go to step **3)**.

2) Turn ignition off. Disconnect TCM connector. Inspect connector and repair as needed. Using ohmmeter, check continuity between TCM and kickdown servo switch harness connectors. See WIRING DIAGRAMS. Repair as needed. If circuit is okay, replace TCM.

3) Turn ignition off. Disconnect TCM connector. Inspect connector and repair as needed. Clear DTC's. See CLEARING TROUBLE CODES. Operate vehicle and recheck DTC. If DTC is not present, vehicle is currently operating correctly. If DTC resets, repeat step **1)**.

DTC 23: IGNITION SIGNAL

1) If ignition pulses are not input to TCM while engine is idling, an open circuit in ignition signal line to TCM exists. Inspect appropriate connectors and repair as needed. See WIRING DIAGRAMS.

2) If vehicle's tachometer is not functioning correctly, inspect ignition circuit system. See appropriate SELF-DIAGNOSTICS article in ENGINE PERFORMANCE in appropriate MITCHELL® manual. Possible causes of trouble code are ignition coil or power transistor malfunction. If tachometer is functioning correctly, replace TCM.

DTC 31 & 81: PULSE GENERATOR "A"

1) Inspect pulse generator "A". See COMPONENT TESTING. Replace as needed. If pulse generator is okay, inspect harness and connector. Repair as needed. Check continuity of circuit(s) between pulse generator "A" and TCM. See WIRING DIAGRAMS. Repair as needed.

2) Inspect end clutch retainer for damage. See appropriate overhaul article. Replace as needed. If end clutch retainer is okay, replace TCM.

DTC 32 & 82: PULSE GENERATOR "B"

1) Inspect pulse generator "B". See COMPONENT TESTING. Replace as needed. If pulse generator is okay, inspect harness and connector.

Repair as needed. Check continuity between pulse generator "B" and TCM. See WIRING DIAGRAMS. Repair as needed.

2) Inspect end clutch retainer for damage. See appropriate overhaul article. Replace as needed. If end clutch retainer is okay, replace TCM.

DTC 36 & 37: NEUTRAL SAFETY SWITCH

1) Inspect neutral safety switch. See COMPONENT TESTING. Replace as needed. If switch is okay, disconnect connector. Turn ignition on. Using voltmeter, measure voltage between neutral safety switch connector terminal No. 3 or No. 4 and ground. *See Fig. 12.* See WIRING DIAGRAMS. If battery voltage exists, go to next step. If battery voltage does not exist, repair circuit and recheck DTC.

2) Turn ignition off. Disconnect TCM connector. Using ohmmeter, check continuity of circuits between neutral safety switch and TCM. Repair as needed. If all circuits are okay, replace TCM.

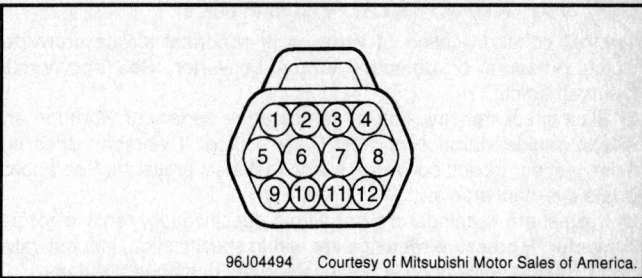

96J04494   Courtesy of Mitsubishi Motor Sales of America.

Fig. 12: *Identifying Neutral Safety Switch Connector Terminals*

DTC 41, 42 & 83: SHIFT CONTROL SOLENOID VALVE "A" (SCSV-A)

Inspect SCSV-A. See COMPONENT TESTING. Replace as needed. If shift solenoid is okay, disconnect TCM connector. Using ohmmeter, check continuity between SCSV-A and TCM. See WIRING DIAGRAMS. Repair as needed. If circuit is okay, replace TCM.

DTC 43, 44 & 84: SHIFT CONTROL SOLENOID VALVE "B" (SCSV-B)

Inspect SCSV-B. See COMPONENT TESTING. Replace as needed. If shift solenoid is okay, disconnect TCM connector. Using ohmmeter, check continuity between SCSV-B and TCM. See WIRING DIAGRAMS. Repair as needed. If circuit is okay, replace TCM.

DTC 45, 46 & 85: PRESSURE CONTROL SOLENOID VALVE (PCSV)

Inspect PCSV. See COMPONENT TESTING. Replace as needed. If shift solenoid is okay, disconnect TCM connector. Using ohmmeter, check continuity between PCSV and TCM. See WIRING DIAGRAMS. Repair as needed. If circuit is okay, replace TCM.

DTC 47, 48 & 49: TORQUE CONVERTER CLUTCH (TCC) SOLENOID

Inspect TCC solenoid. See COMPONENT TESTING. Replace as needed. If shift solenoid is okay, disconnect TCM connector. Using ohmmeter, check continuity between TCC solenoid and TCM. See WIRING DIAGRAMS. Repair as needed. If circuit is okay, replace TCM.

DTC 51 & 86: 1ST GEAR RATIO INCORRECT

If code 31 is output, see DTC 31 & 81: PULSE GENERATOR "A". If code 32 is output, see DTC 32 & 82: PULSE GENERATOR "B". If neither code is output, inspect wiring harness to both pulse generators on transmission for damage. Noise interference may cause a trouble code to set. If wiring harness is okay, inspect transfer driven gear, end clutch retainer and rear clutch. See appropriate overhaul article.

3-1134

AUTOMATIC TRANSMISSIONS
Mitsubishi F4A20, F4A30 & W4A30 Series
Electronic Controls (Cont.)

DTC 52 & 86: 2ND GEAR RATIO INCORRECT

If code 51 is output, see DTC 51 & 86: 1ST GEAR RATIO INCORRECT. If code 51 is not output, replace kickdown brake. See appropriate overhaul article.

DTC 53 & 86: 3RD GEAR RATIO INCORRECT

If code 51 is output, see DTC 51 & 86: 1ST GEAR RATIO INCORRECT. If code 51 is not output, replace front clutch. See appropriate overhaul article.

DTC 54 & 86: 4TH GEAR RATIO INCORRECT

If code 52 is output, see DTC 52 & 86: 2ND GEAR RATIO INCORRECT. If code 52 is not output, replace end clutch. See appropriate overhaul article.

DTC 59: ABNORMAL VIBRATION

1) Most common cause of vibration is abnormal torque converter clutch pressure or defective torque converter. See appropriate overhaul article.

2) Disconnect transmission oil temperature sensor. If vibration still exists, engine vibration is most likely source. If vibration does not exist, inspect torque converter clutch hydraulic pressure. See appropriate overhaul article.

3) If pressure readings are not within specification, replace torque converter. If pressure readings are within specification, inspect valve body. Ensure valve body is not loose or has damaged "O" rings.

DTC 61, 62 & 63: TORQUE REDUCTION REQUEST & EXECUTION SIGNAL LINES

1) Code(s) are normally set due to poor connection, open circuit or, TCM or ECM malfunction. Ensure ignition is off. Disconnect ECM harness connector. Turn ignition on. Using voltmeter, measure voltage between ground and terminal No. 7 on ECM connector. *See Fig. 13.* If voltage is not 4.8-5.2 volts, go to next step. If voltage is 4.8-5.2 volts, substitute ECM with known good unit and retest.

2) Turn ignition off. Disconnect TCM connector. Using ohmmeter, check continuity of torque reduction request circuit between TCM and ECM. Repair as needed. If circuit is okay, replace TCM.

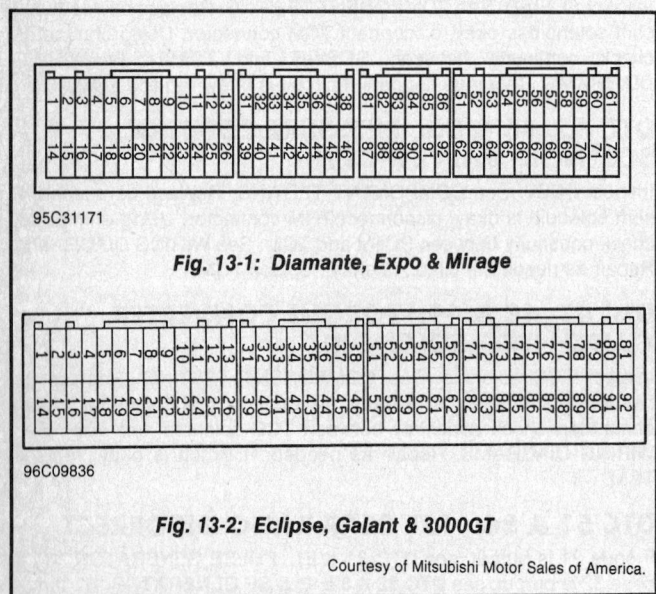

95C31171

Fig. 13-1: Diamante, Expo & Mirage

96C09836

Fig. 13-2: Eclipse, Galant & 3000GT

Courtesy of Mitsubishi Motor Sales of America.

Fig. 13: Identifying ECM Connector Terminals

COMPONENT TESTING
NEUTRAL SAFETY SWITCH

Disconnect harness connector. Using ohmmeter, check continuity between specified terminals in each gear position. *See Fig. 12.* See NEUTRAL SAFETY SWITCH CONTINUITY SPECIFICATIONS table. If continuity is not as specified, replace switch.

NEUTRAL SAFETY SWITCH CONTINUITY SPECIFICATIONS

Application & Switch Position	Continuity Between Terminals
Expo (FWD), Galant & Mirage	
"P"	1 & 4, 5 & 8
"R"	4 & 10, 6 & 7
"N"	2 & 4, 5 & 8
"D"	4 & 9
"2"	3 & 4
"1"	4 & 11
Diamante, Eclipse, Expo (AWD), Sonata & 3000GT	
"P"	3 & 4, 7 & 8
"R"	2 & 3, 5 & 6
"N"	3 & 12, 7 & 8
"D"	3 & 10
"2"	3 & 11
"1"	3 & 9

OIL TEMPERATURE SENSOR

Disconnect oil temperature sensor connector. Measure resistance between terminals on component side connector. Replace sensor if resistance is not within specification. See OIL TEMPERATURE SENSOR SPECIFICATION table.

OIL TEMPERATURE SENSOR SPECIFICATION

Oil Temperature °F (°C)	Resistance-Ohms
32 (0)	16,700-20,500
212 (100)	570-690

OVERDRIVE CONTROL SWITCH

Disconnect electrical connector from overdrive control switch. Using ohmmeter, check continuity between specified wire terminals at switch connector. *See Figs. 14-16.* See OVERDRIVE CONTROL SWITCH CONTINUITY SPECIFICATIONS table. Replace overdrive control switch if defective.

OVERDRIVE CONTROL SWITCH CONTINUITY SPECIFICATIONS

Application & Switch Position	Continuity Between Terminals
Diamante, Eclipse, Galant & Mirage	
ON	3 & 4
OFF	3 & 5
Expo	
ON	3 & 5
OFF	3 & 4
Sonata	
ON	2 & 5
OFF	1 & 2
3000GT	
ON	5 & 6
OFF	4 & 6

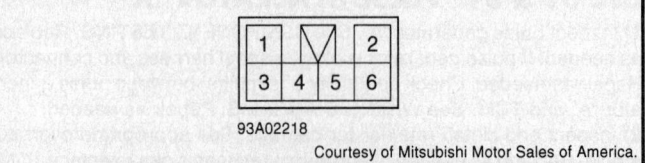

93A02218

Courtesy of Mitsubishi Motor Sales of America.

Fig. 14: Identifying Overdrive Switch Connector Terminals (All Models Except Sonata & 3000GT)

AUTOMATIC TRANSMISSIONS
Mitsubishi F4A20, F4A30 & W4A30 Series
Electronic Controls (Cont.)

3-1135

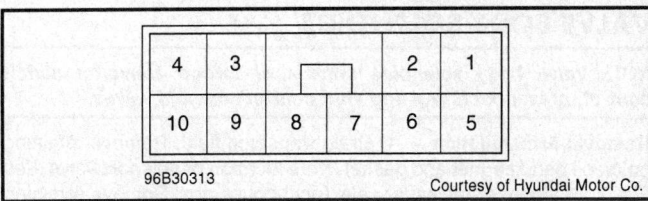

Fig. 15: Identifying Overdrive Switch Connector Terminals (Sonata)

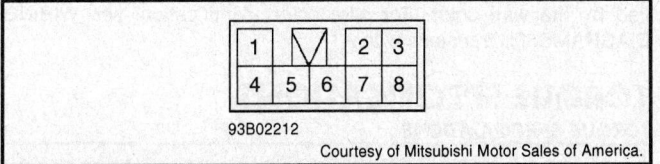

Fig. 16: Identifying Overdrive Switch & Power/Economy Switch Connector Terminals (3000GT)

POWER/ECONOMY SWITCH

On Diamante models, remove power/economy switch from console. On 3000GT models, disconnect power/economy and overdrive switch connector. Measure continuity between specified terminals. See POWER/ECONOMY SWITCH CONTINUITY SPECIFICATIONS table. See Fig. 16 or 17.

POWER/ECONOMY SWITCH CONTINUITY SPECIFICATIONS

Application & Condition	Continuity Between Terminals
Diamante	
Power Mode	4 & 5
Economy Mode	3 & 5
Sonata [1]	
Power Mode	3 & 5
Economy Mode	3 & 6
3000GT	
Power Mode	1 & 2
Economy Mode	[2]

[1] – Use Fig. 14 to identify Power/Economy switch connector terminals for Sonata.

[2] – Continuity should not exist between any terminals in Economy mode. Continuity exists between terminals 2 & 3 in Hold mode.

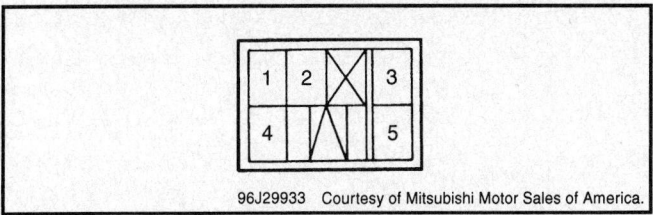

Fig. 17: Identifying Power/Economy Switch Terminals (Diamante)

PULSE GENERATORS

Disconnect pulse generator harness connector. Measure resistance between terminals No. 1 or No. 2 for generator "A" or terminals No. 3 and No. 4 for generator "B". See Fig. 18. Replace pulse generator if resistance is not 215-275 ohms at 68°F (20°C).

Fig. 18: Identifying Pulse Generator Or Solenoid Connector Terminals

SOLENOIDS

NOTE: All solenoids can be operated by applying 12 volts to specific connector terminal and solenoid case. See Fig. 18. See SOLENOID CONNECTOR TERMINAL IDENTIFICATION table.

Disconnect solenoid connector. Measure resistance between ground and appropriate terminal at component side of solenoid connector. See Fig. 18. See SOLENOID CONNECTOR TERMINAL IDENTIFICATION table. If solenoid does not test as specified, replace and retest system.

SOLENOID CONNECTOR TERMINAL IDENTIFICATION

Solenoid	Terminal No.	[1] Ohms
PCSV	1	2.6-3.2
SCSV "A"	3	20.8-23.8
SCSV "B"	4	20.8-23.8
TCC	2	13

[1] – Test solenoid resistance with ambient temperature at 68°F (20°C).

REMOVAL & INSTALLATION

NEUTRAL SAFETY SWITCH

Removal & Installation – 1) Disconnect shift control cable. Remove retaining bolt and manual control lever. Remove retaining screws and neutral safety switch.

2) To install, reverse removal procedure. DO NOT tighten neutral safety switch retaining screws at this time. Tighten manual control lever retaining bolt to specification. See TORQUE SPECIFICATIONS. Adjust neutral safety switch. See NEUTRAL SAFETY SWITCH under ADJUSTMENTS.

KICKDOWN SERVO SWITCH

Removal & Installation – Disconnect electrical connector. Remove snap ring and kickdown servo switch. To install, reverse removal procedure.

OIL TEMPERATURE SENSOR

Removal & Installation – Oil temperature sensor is mounted inside transaxle case. See Fig. 19. Drain transaxle fluid. Remove oil pan bolts and oil pan. Remove bolts securing oil temperature sensor to valve body. To install, reverse removal procedure.

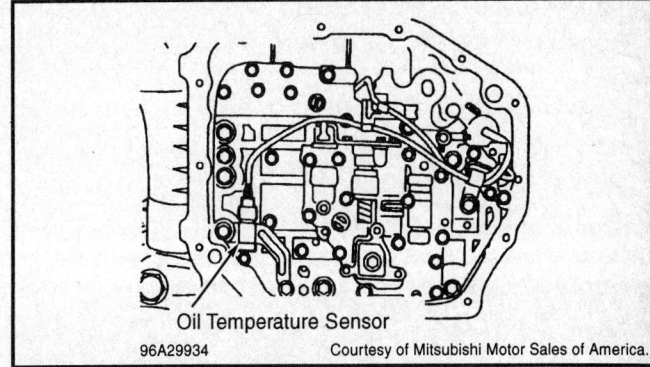

Fig. 19: Locating Oil Temperature Sensor

OVERDRIVE CONTROL SWITCH

Removal & Installation – Remove cover plate on inside of gear selector lever. Remove screw securing overdrive switch to lever. Remove overdrive control switch from side of gear selector lever. To install, reverse removal procedure.

3-1136

AUTOMATIC TRANSMISSIONS
Mitsubishi F4A20, F4A30 & W4A30 Series
Electronic Controls (Cont.)

POWER/ECONOMY SWITCH

Removal & Installation (Diamante & 3000GT) – Slide flat tipped screw driver down each side of switch to unlatch tabs. Remove power/economy switch from center console. To install, reverse removal procedure.

PULSE GENERATORS

Removal & Installation – 1) Note location of pulse generators "A" and "B" for reassembly reference. Pulse generator "A" wires are wrapped in a transparent tube and "B" wires are wrapped in a Black tube. See Fig. 5.
2) Remove retaining bolt and pulse generator. To install, reverse removal procedure. Tighten retaining bolt to specification. See TORQUE SPECIFICATIONS.

TRANSAXLE CONTROL MODULE (TCM)

Removal & Installation – The TCM is located behind instrument panel, near center of console. See Figs. 1-4. Manufacturer does not give specific information on TCM removal.

VALVE BODY SOLENOIDS

NOTE: Valve body solenoids consist of torque converter clutch control, pressure control and shift control solenoid valves.

Removal & Installation – 1) Drain transaxle fluid. Remove retaining bolts, oil pan, magnet and gasket. Note location of solenoid valve. See Fig. 7. Disconnect necessary electrical connector. Remove retaining bolt and solenoid valve.
2) To install, reverse removal procedure. Ensure solenoid valve is installed in proper location. See Fig. 7. Solenoid valves can be identified by the wire color. For wire color identification, see WIRING DIAGRAMS. Fill transaxle with ATF.

TORQUE SPECIFICATIONS
TORQUE SPECIFICATIONS

Application	Ft. Lbs. (N.m)
Manual Control Lever Bolt	13-15 (18-20)

	INCH Lbs. (N.m)
Neutral Safety Switch Bolt	89-102 (10.1-11.5)
Oil Filter Bolt	48-60 (5.4-6.8)
Oil Pan Bolt	48-60 (5.4-6.8)
Pulse Generator Bolt	89-102 (10.1-11.5)
Shift Control Cable Lock Nut	108 (12.2)
TP Sensor Retaining Screw	17 (1.9)

AUTOMATIC TRANSMISSIONS
Mitsubishi F4A20, F4A30 & W4A30 Series
Electronic Controls (Cont.)

3-1137

WIRING DIAGRAMS

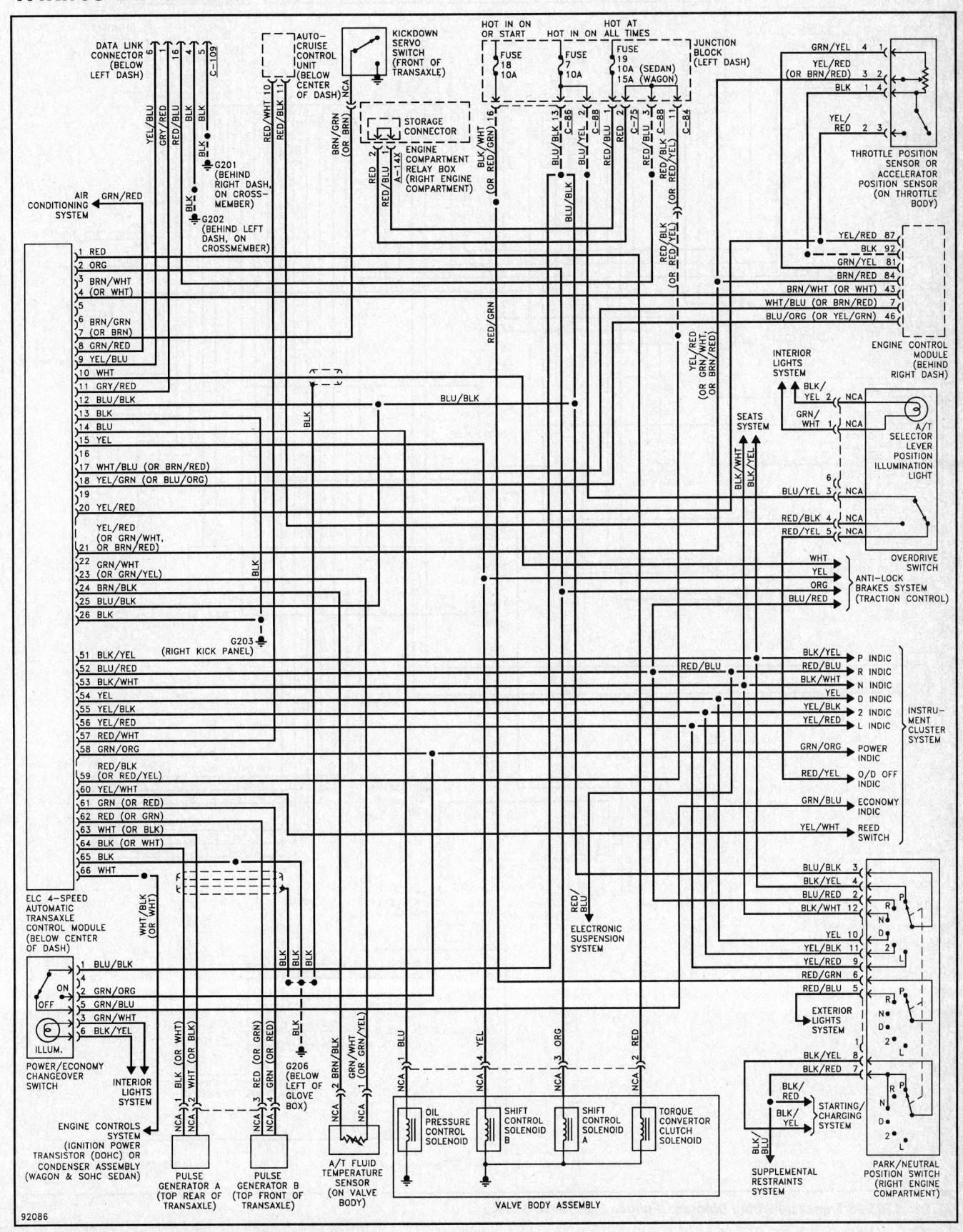

Fig. 20: 1995-96 Transaxle Wiring Diagram (Diamante)

92086

AUTOMATIC TRANSMISSIONS
Mitsubishi F4A20, F4A30 & W4A30 Series
Electronic Controls (Cont.)

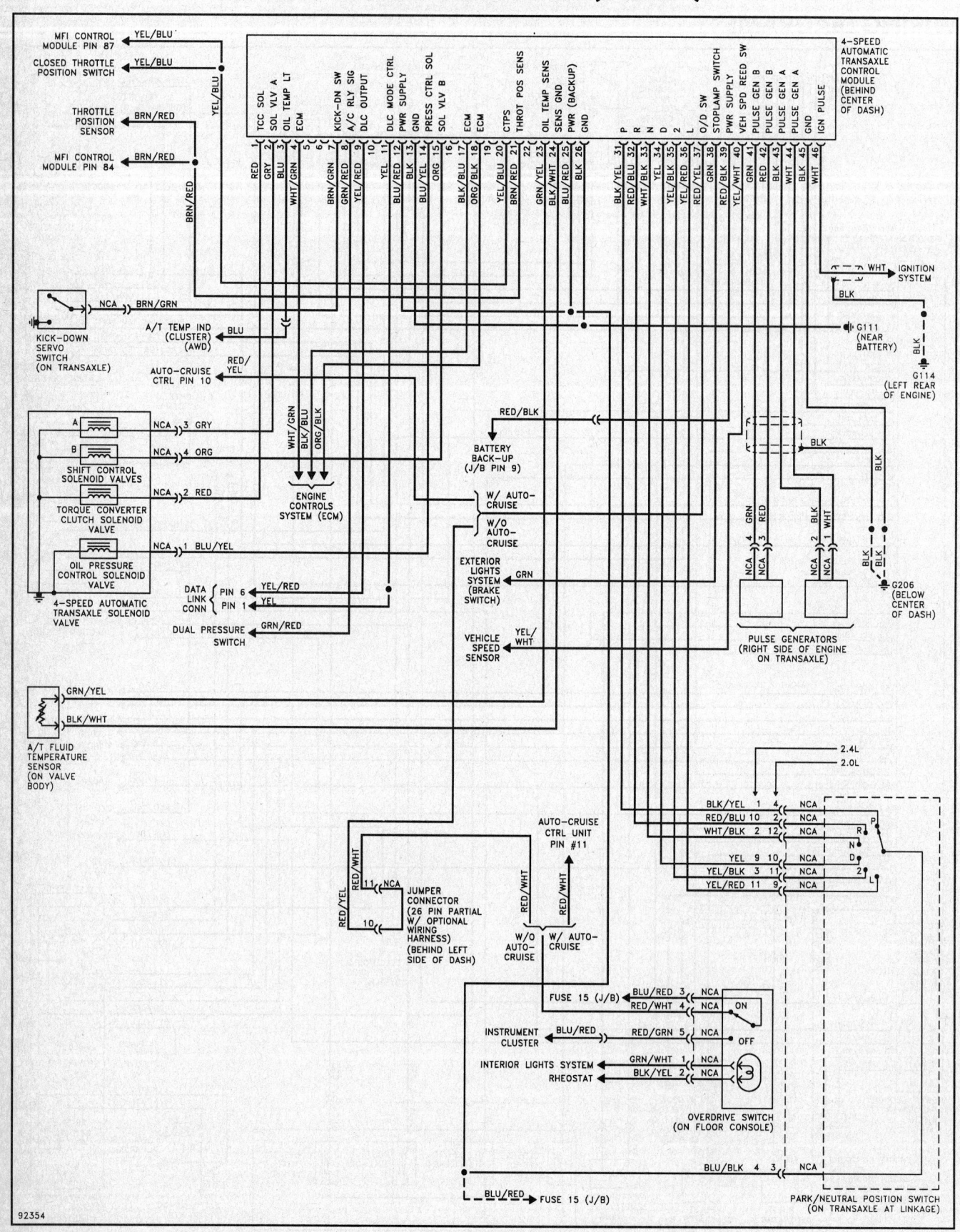

Fig. 21: 1995-96 Transaxle Wiring Diagram (Eclipse 2.0L Turbo & 2.4L)

92354

AUTOMATIC TRANSMISSIONS
Mitsubishi F4A20, F4A30 & W4A30 Series
Electronic Controls (Cont.)

3-1139

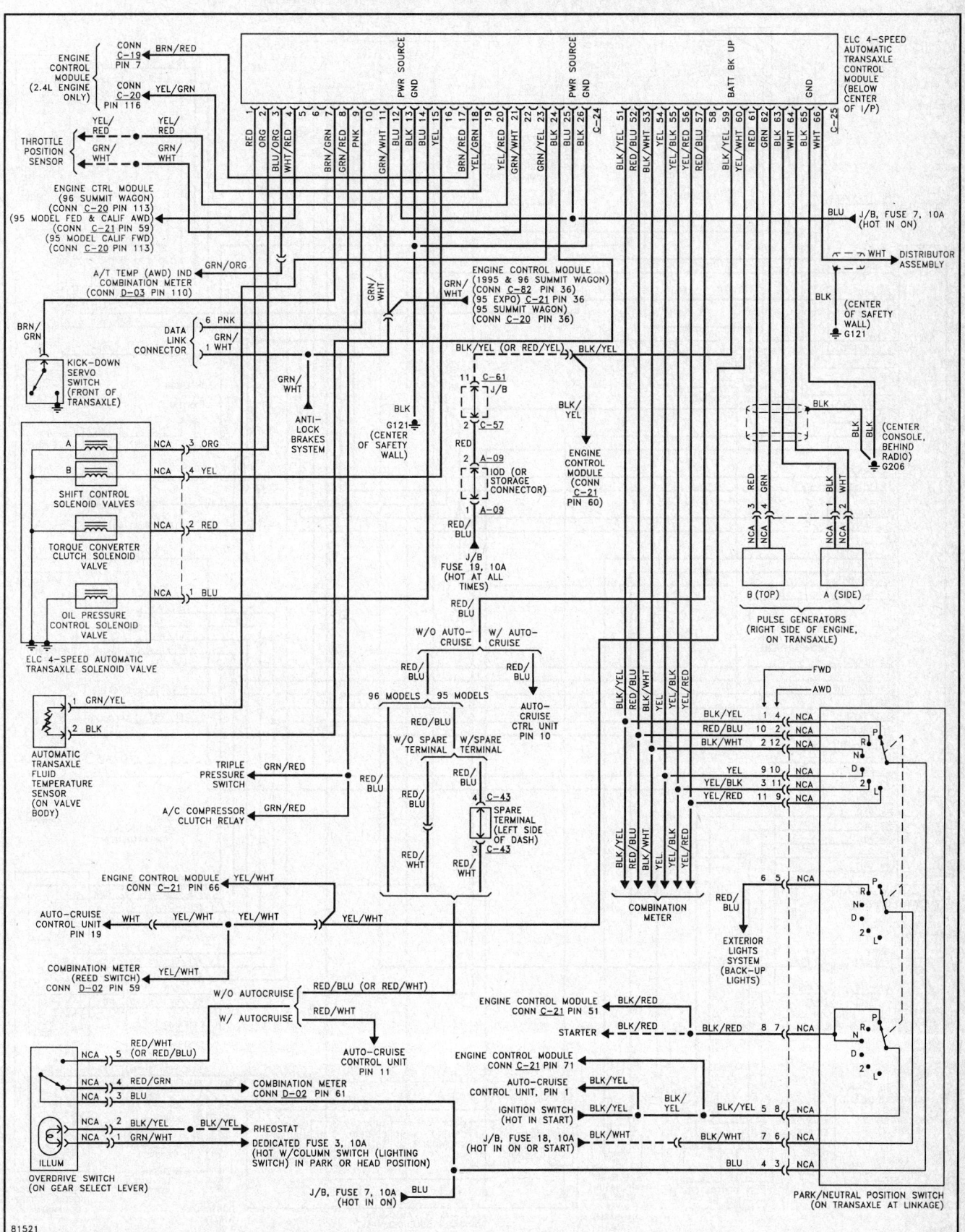

Fig. 22: 1995-96 Transaxle Wiring Diagram (Expo)

81521

AUTOMATIC TRANSMISSIONS
Mitsubishi F4A20, F4A30 & W4A30 Series
Electronic Controls (Cont.)

3-1140

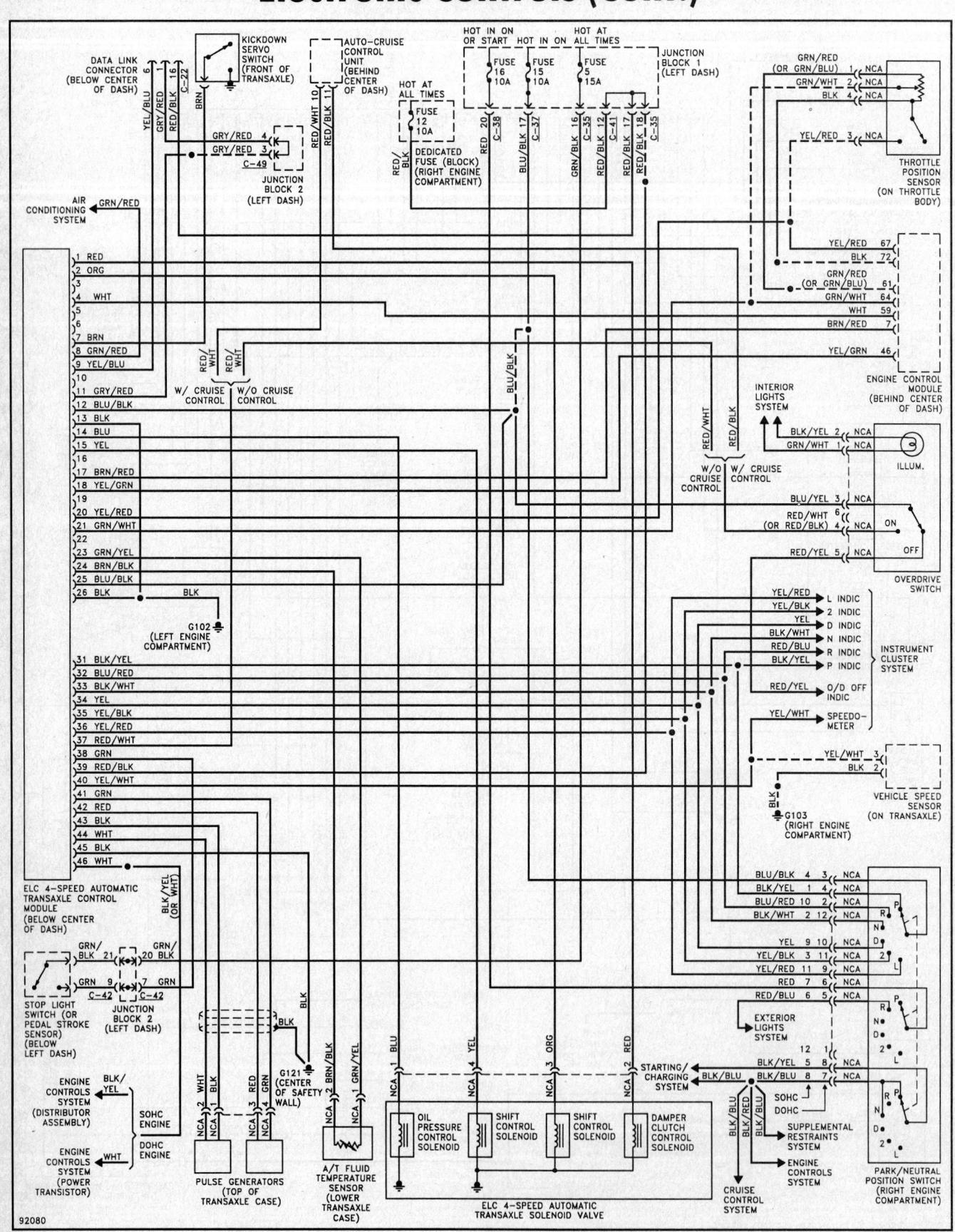

Fig. 23: 1995 Transaxle Wiring Diagram (Galant)

AUTOMATIC TRANSMISSIONS
Mitsubishi F4A20, F4A30 & W4A30 Series
Electronic Controls (Cont.)

3-1141

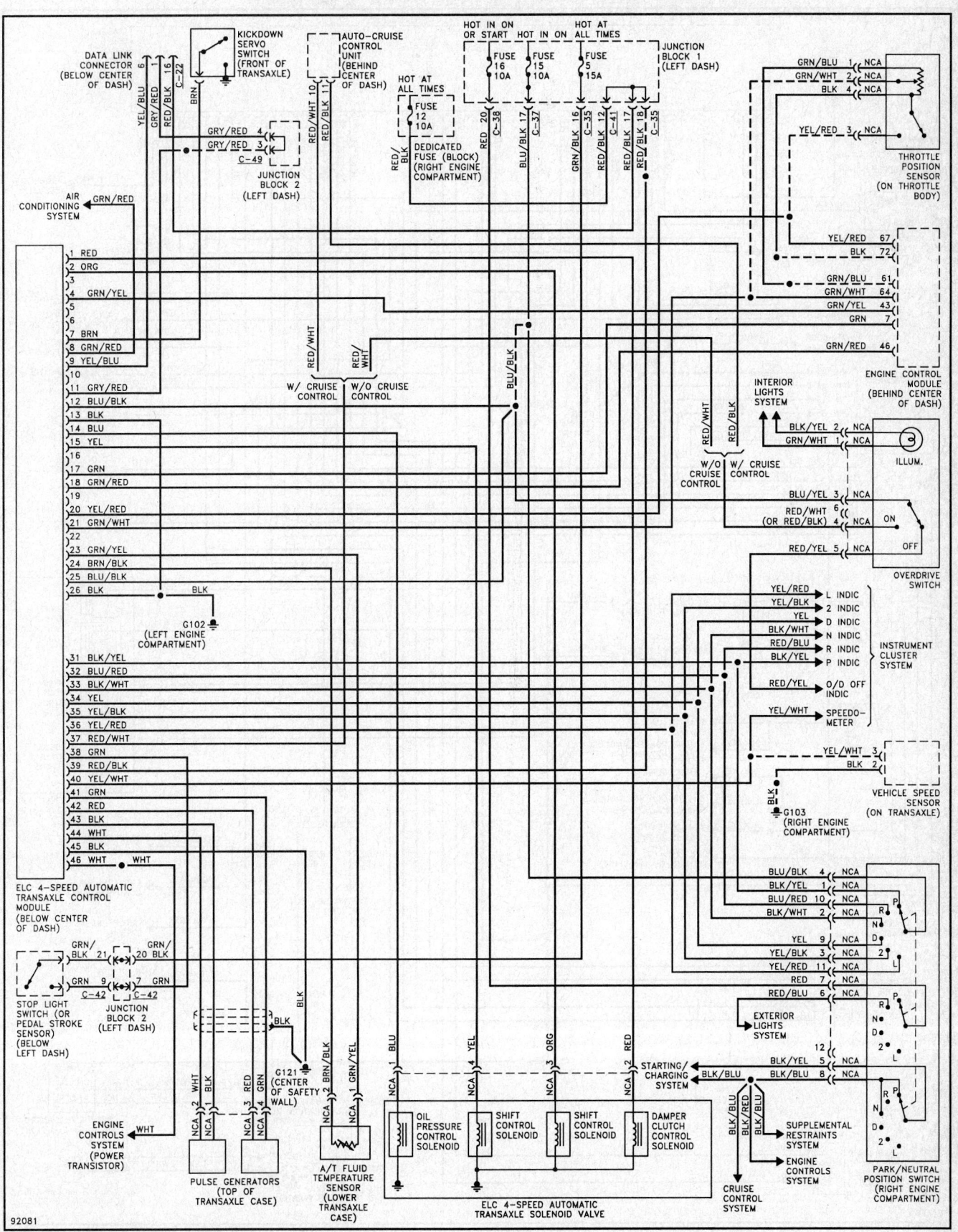

Fig. 24: 1996 Transaxle Wiring Diagram (Galant)

3-1142

AUTOMATIC TRANSMISSIONS
Mitsubishi F4A20, F4A30 & W4A30 Series
Electronic Controls (Cont.)

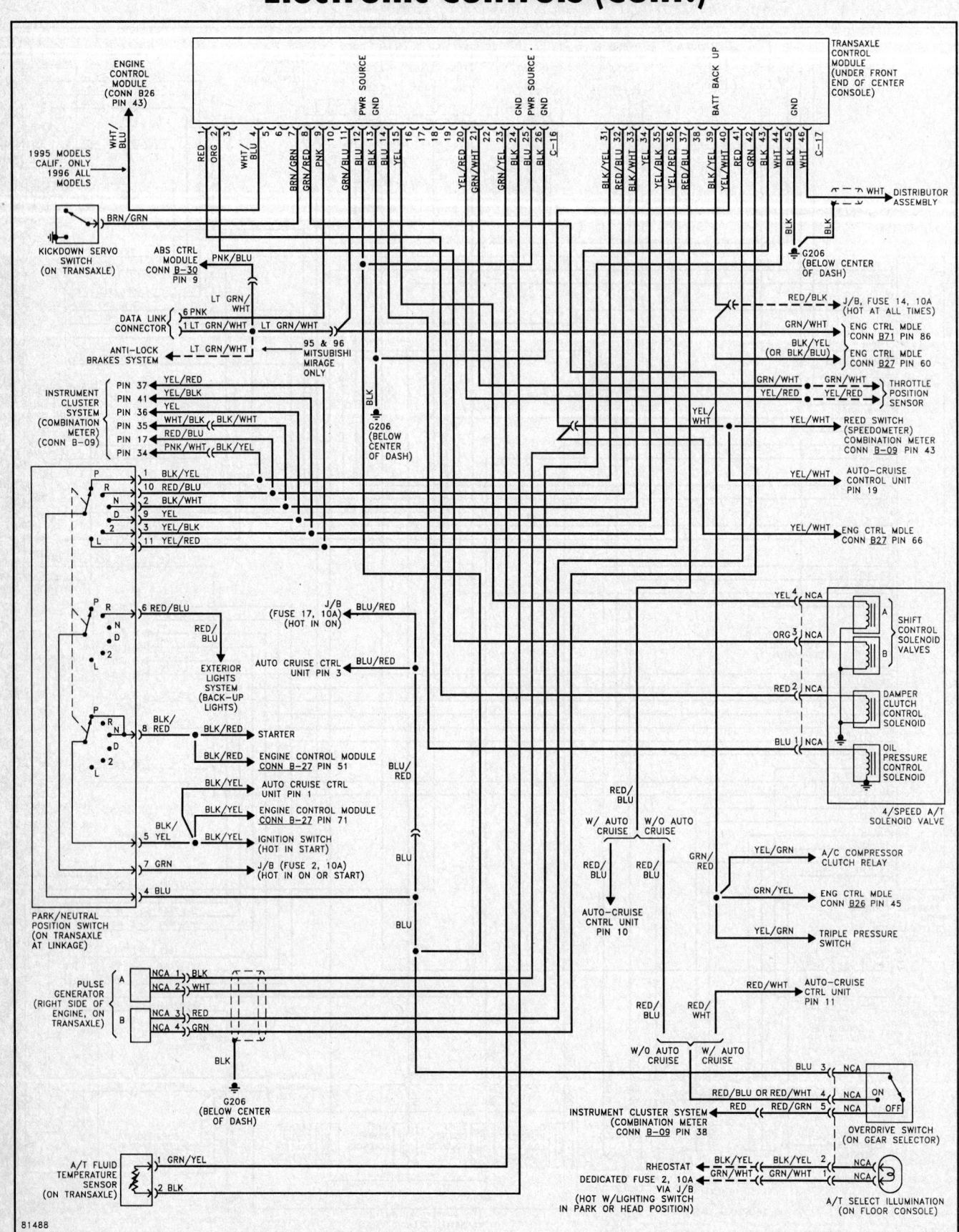

Fig. 25: 1995-96 Transaxle Wiring Diagram (Mirage)

AUTOMATIC TRANSMISSIONS
Mitsubishi F4A20, F4A30 & W4A30 Series
Electronic Controls (Cont.)

3-1143

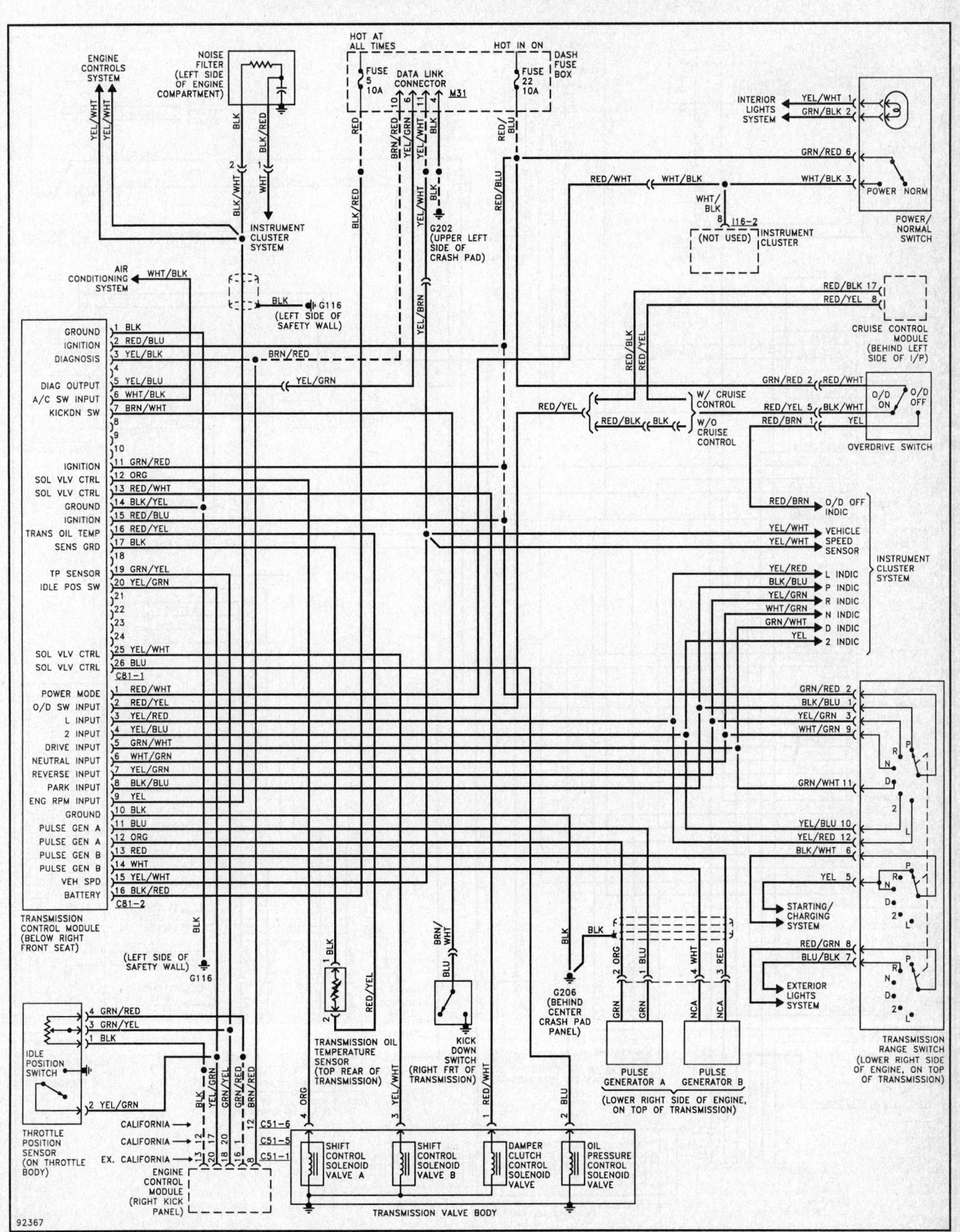

Fig. 26: 1995 Transaxle Wiring Diagram (Sonata 3.0L)

92367

AUTOMATIC TRANSMISSIONS
Mitsubishi F4A20, F4A30 & W4A30 Series
Electronic Controls (Cont.)

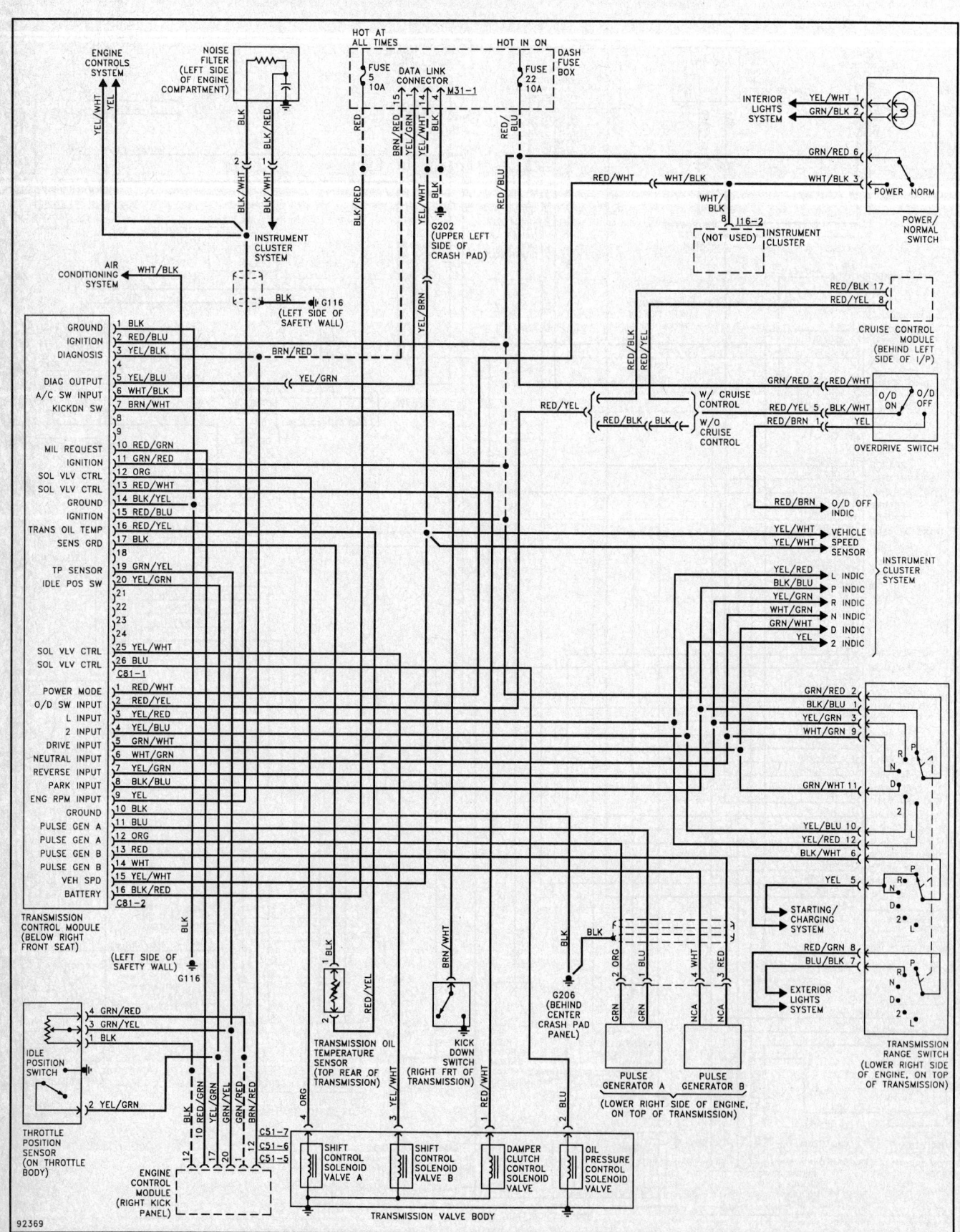

Fig. 27: 1996 Transaxle Wiring Diagram (Sonata 3.0L)

92369

AUTOMATIC TRANSMISSIONS
Mitsubishi F4A20, F4A30 & W4A30 Series
Electronic Controls (Cont.)

3-1145

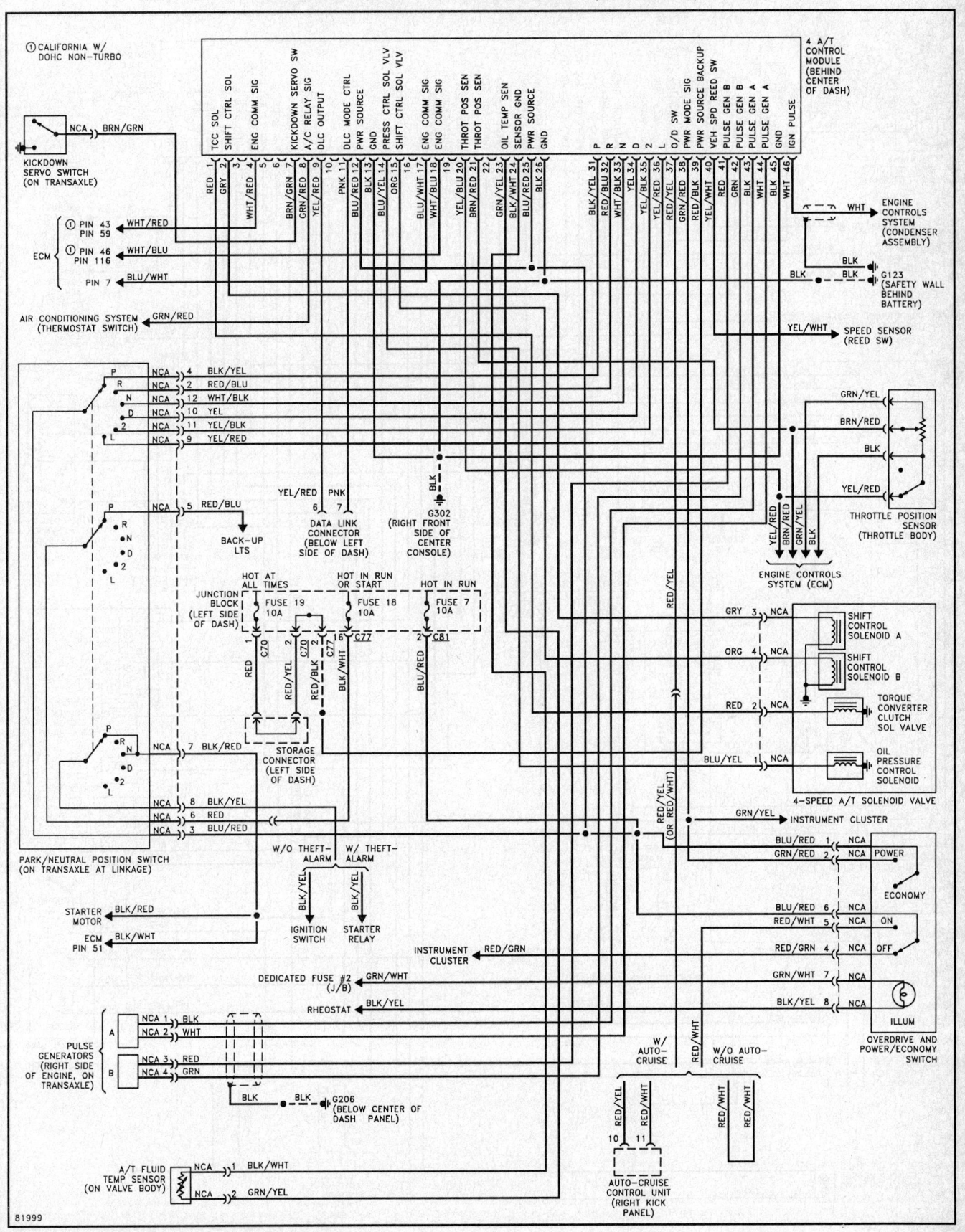

Fig. 28: 1995 Transaxle Wiring Diagram (3000GT)

81999

3-1146

AUTOMATIC TRANSMISSIONS
Mitsubishi F4A20, F4A30 & W4A30 Series
Electronic Controls (Cont.)

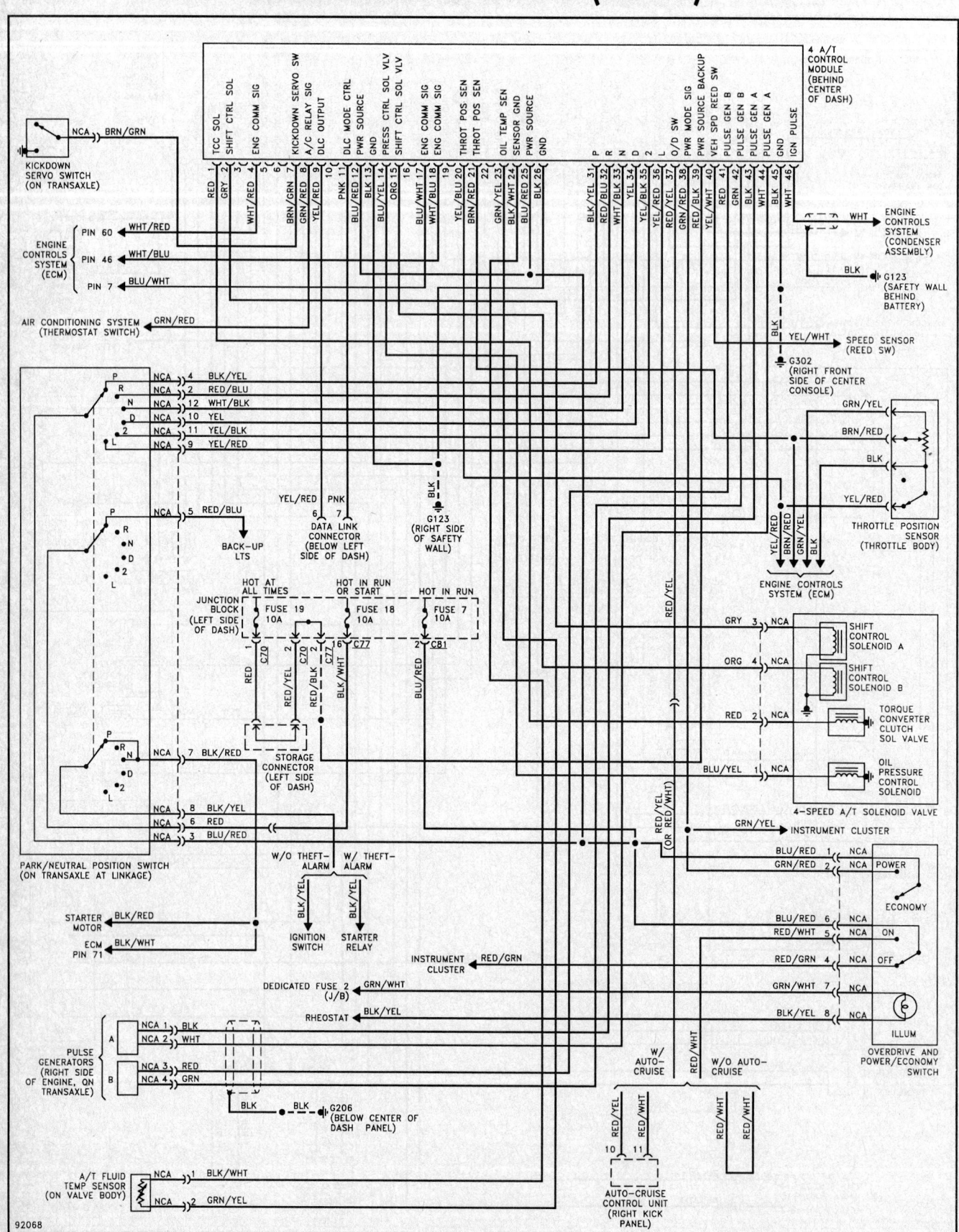

Fig. 29: 1996 Transaxle Wiring Diagram (3000GT)

Montero

APPLICATION & LABOR TIMES

APPLICATION & LABOR TIMES

Vehicle Application	Labor Times [1] R & I	[2] Overhaul	Trans. Model
Montero 3.0L	8.8	8.5	V4AW2

[1] – Removal and installation of transmission from vehicle chassis.

[2] – Bench overhaul time for transmission. DOES NOT include removal and installation.

IDENTIFICATION

Transmission model number is stamped on Vehicle Information Code Plate attached to the firewall in engine compartment. *See Fig. 1.*

DESCRIPTION

Transmission has 4 forward speeds (4th is overdrive) and reverse. Gearshifts are determined by engine load, selector lever position, throttle valve position and output shaft speed. Components include a governor, torque converter, forward clutch, direct clutch, overdrive (OD) clutch, planetary gears and transfer case. *See Fig. 2.* For transfer case overhaul information, see appropriate article in AXLE SHAFTS & TRANSFER CASES section.

An Overdrive (OD) switch is mounted on the shift lever. When OD switch is depressed to ON position, transmission will shift into 4th gear when shift lever is in "D" position, and OD OFF light on instrument panel will go off. When OD switch is released to OFF position, transmission will shift into 3rd gear, and OD OFF light on instrument panel will illuminate.

A pattern select switch (if equipped) is located near shift lever on center console. Pattern select switch contains a POWER (PWR) and a HOLD operating position. When pattern select switch is depressed (PWR position), transmission upshifts and downshifts will occur at a higher vehicle speed than with switch released. An indicator light on instrument panel indicates pattern select switch is in PWR (on) position.

Transmission is equipped with a shift lock and key interlock system. Shift lock system prevents shift lever from being moved from Park unless brake pedal is depressed. Key interlock system prevents ignition key from being moved from ACC to LOCK position on ignition switch unless shift lever is in Park.

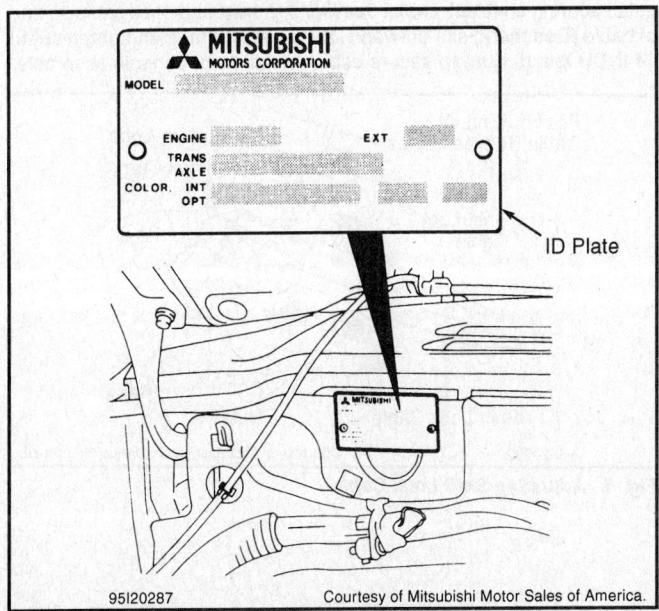

Fig. 1: Locating Vehicle Identification Code Plate

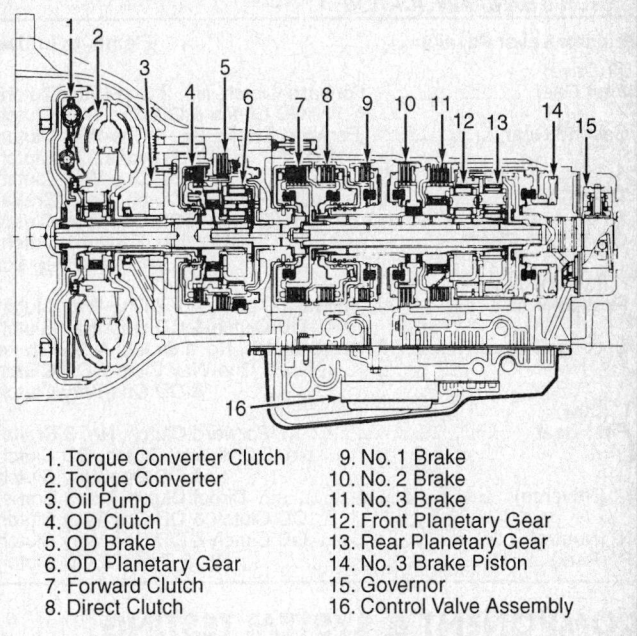

1. Torque Converter Clutch
2. Torque Converter
3. Oil Pump
4. OD Clutch
5. OD Brake
6. OD Planetary Gear
7. Forward Clutch
8. Direct Clutch
9. No. 1 Brake
10. No. 2 Brake
11. No. 3 Brake
12. Front Planetary Gear
13. Rear Planetary Gear
14. No. 3 Brake Piston
15. Governor
16. Control Valve Assembly

95J20288   Courtesy of Mitsubishi Motor Sales of America.

Fig. 2: Identifying Transmission Component Locations

LUBRICATION

NOTE: See appropriate AUTOMATIC TRANSMISSION SERVICING article in TRANSMISSION SERVICING section.

TROUBLE SHOOTING

SYMPTOM DIAGNOSIS

Preliminary Checks – Ensure fluid level is correct. Inspect and adjust throttle cable, shift linkage and neutral safety switch (if necessary). Check engine idle speed and adjust as necessary.

Fluid Discolored Or Smells Burnt – Fluid contaminated, damaged torque converter or transmission assembly.

No Movement In Any Gear Position – Manual shift linkage or cable out of adjustment. Faulty valve body, primary regulator valve, parking lock pawl or torque converter. Damaged or broken converter drive plate or restricted oil filter.

Selector Lever Position Incorrect – Manual shift linkage or cable out of adjustment. Faulty manual valve and lever.

Harsh Engagement Into Any Forward Gear Position – Throttle cable out of adjustment. Faulty valve body, primary regulator valve, accumulator pistons or transmission assembly.

Delayed Upshifts Or Downshifts From OD-3 Or 3-2, Then Back To OD – Throttle cable or cam faulty or out of adjustment. Faulty governor, OD solenoid valve or valve body.

Slips On Upshift, Or Slips Or Shudders On Acceleration – Manual shift linkage, cable or throttle cable out of adjustment. Faulty valve body, OD solenoid valve or transmission assembly.

Drag Or Binding On Upshifts – Manual shift linkage or cable out of adjustment. Faulty valve body or transmission assembly.

Lock-Up Does Not Occur – Faulty valve body, OD solenoid valve, torque converter or transmission assembly.

Harsh Downshift – Throttle cable or cam faulty or out of adjustment. Faulty accumulator pistons, valve body or transmission assembly.

No Downshift When Coasting – Faulty governor, valve body, OD switch or OD solenoid valve.

No OD-3, 3-2 Or 2-1 Kickdown – Throttle cable out of adjustment. Faulty governor, valve body or OD solenoid valve.

No Engine Braking In 2nd Or "L" Position – Faulty valve body, OD solenoid valve or transmission assembly.

Vehicle Does Not Hold In "P" Position – Manual shift linkage or cable out of adjustment. Faulty parking lock pawl and spring.

CLUTCH & BAND APPLICATION

Selector Lever Position	Elements In Use
"D" (Drive)	
First Gear	Forward Clutch, No. 2 One-Way Clutch, OD Clutch & OD One-Way Clutch
Second Gear	Forward Clutch, No. 1 One-Way Clutch No. 2 Brake, OD Clutch & OD One-Way Clutch
Third Gear	Direct Clutch, Forward Clutch, No. 2 Brake, OD Clutch & OD One-Way Clutch
OD (Fourth Gear)	Direct Clutch, Forward Clutch, No. 2 Brake & OD Brake
"2" (Intermediate)	
First Gear	Forward Clutch, No. 2 One-Way Clutch OD Clutch & OD One-Way Clutch
Second Gear	Forward Clutch, No. 1 Brake, No. 2 Brake No. 1 One-Way Clutch, OD Clutch & OD One-Way Clutch
"1" (Low)	
First Gear	Forward Clutch, No. 3 Brake, No. 2 One-Way Clutch, OD Clutch & OD One Way Clutch
"R" (Reverse)	Direct Clutch, No. 3 Brake, OD Clutch & OD One-Way Clutch
"N" (Neutral)	OD Clutch & OD One-Way Clutch
"P" (Park)	No. 3 Brake & OD Clutch

COMPONENT & SYSTEM TESTING

A/T FLUID TEMPERATURE SWITCH

1) Remove fluid temperature switch, located to rear of neutral safety switch. Immerse switch in container of ATF up to top threaded portion of switch. Using a DVOM, check continuity between switch terminals. Continuity should not exist when fluid temperature is 257°F (125°C) or less.

2) When fluid is heated to 289-304°F (143-151°C), continuity should exist. Replace switch if necessary. Apply thread sealant to fluid temperature switch threads and install in transmission.

OVERDRIVE SOLENOID VALVE

Normal condition exists when ohmmeter indicates continuity between terminal and ground. Ensure operating noise (click) is heard when ignition switch is turned to ON position.

OVERDRIVE SWITCH

Using a screwdriver, remove overdrive switch from selector lever, located below selector lever button. Using a DVOM, check continuity between overdrive switch terminals No. 3 and 5 with switch in ON position. Continuity should exist. With switch in OFF position, check continuity between terminals No. 3 and 4. Continuity should exist. If continuity is not as specified, replace switch. See Fig. 3.

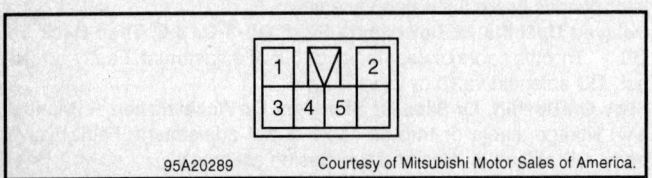

95A20289   Courtesy of Mitsubishi Motor Sales of America.

Fig. 3: Identifying Overdrive Switch Terminals

KEY INTERLOCK SYSTEM

1) With ignition switch in LOCK position and brake pedal depressed, ensure selector lever cannot be moved from Park to any other position. Ensure selector lever button cannot be pushed. With ignition switch in ACC position, brake pedal depressed and selector lever button pushed, ensure selector lever can be moved from Park position to any other position. Ensure selector lever moves smoothly.

2) Ensure ignition key cannot be turned to LOCK position from any selector lever positions other than Park. Ensure ignition key turns smoothly to LOCK position when selector lever is set to Park and

selector lever button is released. If key interlock system is not as specified, adjust key interlock cable. See KEY INTERLOCK CABLE under ADJUSTMENTS.

SHIFT LOCK SYSTEM

1) With ignition switch in ACC position, brake pedal released and selector lever button pushed, ensure selector lever cannot be moved from Park to any other position. With ignition switch in ACC position, brake pedal depressed and selector lever button pushed, ensure selector lever can be moved from Park position to any other position.

2) With selector lever in Reverse, ignition switch in ACC position, brake pedal released and selector button pushed, ensure selector lever can be moved from Reverse to Park position. If shift lock system is not as specified, adjust shift lock cable. See SHIFT LOCK CABLE under ADJUSTMENTS.

ADJUSTMENTS

KEY INTERLOCK CABLE

Remove front console assembly. Move selector lever to Park. Turn ignition switch to LOCK position. Loosen nut securing key interlock cable. See Fig. 4. Gently push lock cam until pin stops in direction of arrow, then tighten nut to 106 INCH lbs. (12 N.m) to secure cable. Install front console assembly.

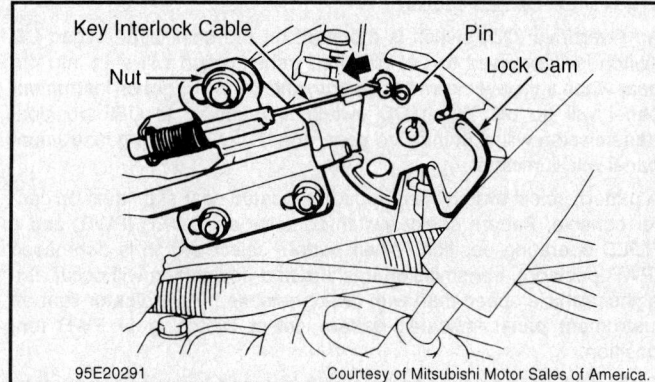

95E20291   Courtesy of Mitsubishi Motor Sales of America.

Fig. 4: Adjusting Key Interlock Cable

SHIFT LOCK CABLE

Remove front console assembly. Move selector lever to Park. Loosen nuts securing shift lock cable. See Fig. 5. Adjust shift lock cable so end of cable (Red mark) sits between lobe of lock cam, then tighten nut to 44 INCH lbs. (5 N.m) to secure cable. Install front console assembly.

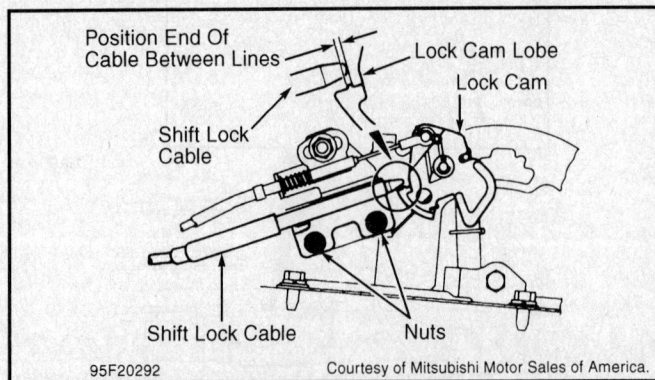

95F20292   Courtesy of Mitsubishi Motor Sales of America.

Fig. 5: Adjusting Shift Lock Cable

TESTING

ROAD TEST

NOTE: Perform road test to ensure transmission shift points are at specified speeds. See Fig. 6. Broken lines in shift point chart indicates downshifts, and solid lines indicate upshifts.

"D" Position Test – 1) Engine and transmission must be at normal operating temperature. Shift transmission into "D" position with OD switch in ON position. Ensure transfer case is in 2H (2WD-High) position. Depress accelerator pedal to full throttle. Ensure all upshifts and downshifts occur at specified points. *See Fig. 6.*
2) Ensure lock-up occurs at appropriate speeds. Lightly depress accelerator pedal. If excessive increase in engine RPM exists, lock-up did not occur.

NOTE: A 3-OD upshift will not occur with a throttle valve opening greater than 86 percent or if coolant temperature is below 122°F (50°C). A OD-3 kickdown is always possible with throttle valve opening of 86 percent or greater. Lock-up does not occur at coolant temperatures below 158°F (70°C).

3) Check for shock and slippage during all upshifts. Drive vehicle in 3rd and OD. Check for abnormal noise and vibration. While driving in OD, "D", 3rd and 2nd gear, ensure kickdown speeds in 2-1, 3-2 and OD-3 are within specification. Check for shock and slippage during kickdown.
"D" Position Test Results
- **No 1-2 Upshift:** Defective governor or stuck 1-2 shift valve.
- **No 2-3 Upshift:** Defective governor or stuck 2-3 shift valve.
- **No 3-OD Upshift With Throttle Opening Less Than 86 Percent:** Stuck 3-OD shift valve. If shift point is not within specification, check for misadjusted throttle cable or defective throttle valve, governor, OD switch or solenoid valve.
- **Lock-Up Does Not Occur:** Stuck OD solenoid valve.
- **Excessive Shock & Slippage:** High line pressure, defective accumulator or check balls. Abnormal noise and vibration may be caused by unbalance in drive shaft, differential, tires or torque converter.

"2" Position Test – Shift transmission to "2" position. With accelerator pedal held at full throttle, check for proper 1-2 upshift at specified throttle positions. *See Fig. 6.* While driving vehicle in 2nd gear, release accelerator and check engine braking effect. If engine braking does not exist, No. 1 brake is defective.
"L" Position Test – While driving vehicle in "L" position, check for failure to upshift to 2nd gear. Check engine braking effect when accelerator is released. If engine braking does not exist, No. 3 brake is defective.
"R" Position Test – Shift vehicle to "R" position. Accelerate vehicle and check for transmission slippage.
"P" Position Test – Stop vehicle on incline of 5 degrees or steeper. Shift vehicle to "P" position and release parking brake. Ensure parking lock pawl prevents vehicle from moving.

STALL SPEED TEST

1) Operate engine and transmission at normal operating temperature. Connect tachometer to vehicle and ensure it is visible to driver. Apply parking brake and block front wheels.

CAUTION: DO NOT maintain stall speed RPM for more than 5 seconds. If performing more than one stall speed test, operate engine at about 1000 RPM in Neutral for 2 minutes to cool transmission fluid before performing next test.

2) Start engine, apply brakes and place transmission in "D" position. Depress accelerator to full throttle and note maximum RPM obtained. Repeat test in "R" position. Stall speed should be 2100-2400 RPM.
Stall Speed Test Results
- **Stall Speed Is Same In Both Positions, But Less Than Specified:** Engine output may be insufficient or defective stator one-way clutch.

NOTE: If stall speed RPM is greater than 600 RPM lower than specification, torque converter may be faulty.

- **Stall Speed High In "D" Position:** Low line pressure, slipping forward clutch or defective No. 2 or OD one-way clutch.
- **Stall Speed High In "R" Position:** Low line pressure, direct clutch slipping, No. 3 brake slipping or defective OD one-way clutch.
- **Stall Speed High In Both Positions:** Low line pressure, improper fluid level or defective OD one-way clutch.

HYDRAULIC PRESSURE TESTS

NOTE: Hydraulic pressure tests should be performed with transmission fluid at normal operating temperature of 158-176°F (70-80°C).

Line Pressure Test – 1) Ensure transmission fluid is at normal operating temperature. Connect pressure gauge to line pressure test port on transmission. *See Fig. 7.*
2) Connect tachometer to vehicle and ensure it is visible to driver. Block all 4 wheels and fully apply parking brake. Start engine and ensure idle speed is adjusted to specification.
3) Apply service brake and shift transmission to "D" position. Check line pressure at idle and record pressure reading. Accelerate vehicle to stall speed and record line pressure reading.
4) Repeat test procedure in "R" position. If line pressures are not as specified, check throttle cable adjustment. Adjust throttle cable (if necessary), and repeat test procedure and record pressure readings. Compare all readings to specification. See LINE PRESSURE SPECIFICATIONS table.

LINE PRESSURE SPECIFICATIONS

Engine Speed	"D" Position psi (kPa)	"R" Position psi (kPa)
Idle Speed	75-87 (520-600)	115-132 (790-910)
Stall Speed	160-189 (1100-1300)	232-290 (1600-2000)

Line Pressure Test Results
- **Line Pressure High In Both Positions:** Defective regulator valve or throttle valve, or throttle cable out of adjustment.
- **Line Pressure Low In Both Positions:** Defective oil pump, regulator valve, throttle valve or OD clutch, or throttle cable out of adjustment.
- **Line Pressure Low In "D" Position Only:** Defective forward clutch, OD clutch or fluid leak in "D" position circuit.
- **Line Pressure Low In "R" Position Only:** Defective direct clutch, OD clutch, No. 3 brake or fluid leak in "R" position circuit.

Governor Pressure Test – 1) Install pressure gauge to governor pressure test port on transmission. *See Fig. 7.* Start engine and release parking brake. With transmission in "D" position, slowly depress accelerator and check governor pressure at specified speed. See GOVERNOR PRESSURE SPECIFICATIONS table.

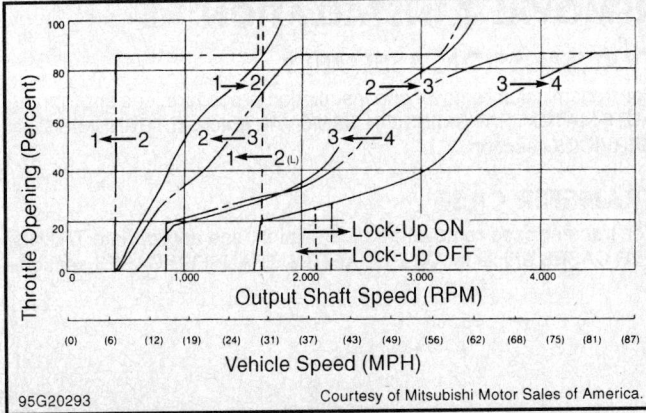

95G20293   Courtesy of Mitsubishi Motor Sales of America.

Fig. 6: *Identifying Transmission Shift Points*

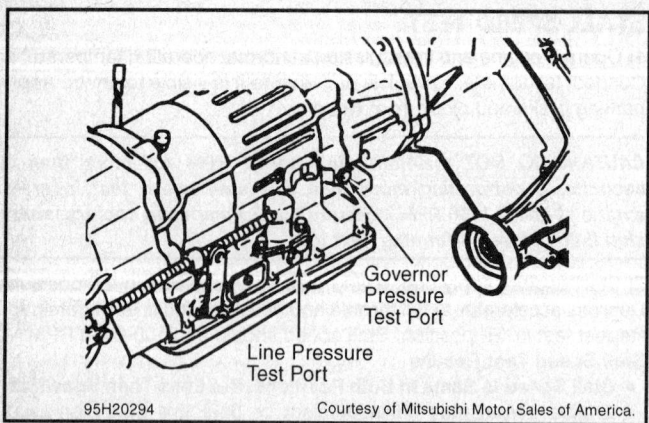

95H20294   Courtesy of Mitsubishi Motor Sales of America.

Fig. 7: Identifying Transmission Hydraulic Pressure Test Ports

CAUTION: Road test vehicle or use chassis dynamometer to check governor pressures exceeding minimum vehicle speed specification.

2) If governor pressures are incorrect, possible causes are: incorrect line pressure, fluid leakage in governor pressure circuit or defective governor.

GOVERNOR PRESSURE SPECIFICATIONS

Vehicle Speed MPH (kmp/h)	Output Shaft RPM	Pressure psi (kPa)
17 (27)	1000	20-25 (140-170)
35 (56)	2000	36-42 (250-290)
56 (90)	3200	59-68 (410-470)

ON-VEHICLE SERVICE

CONTROL VALVE ASSEMBLY

Removal – 1) Remove drain plug and drain ATF. Remove oil pan and gasket. Remove magnets from oil pan. Note location of oil tubes. Using screwdrivers, pry at both ends of oil tubes and remove oil tubes.
2) Remove oil strainer and gasket. Remove control valve assembly retaining bolts. *See Fig. 8.* Note bolt location and length for installation reference. Slightly lower control valve assembly and disconnect throttle cable from throttle cam. Remove control valve assembly.
Installation – To install, reverse removal procedure. Ensure manual shift lever in transmission case aligns with manual valve of control valve assembly. Connect throttle cable to throttle cam. Tighten control valve assembly bolts to 89 INCH lbs. (10 N.m). Tighten oil pan bolts to 40 INCH lbs. (4.5 N.m). Fill transmission with ATF to proper fluid level.

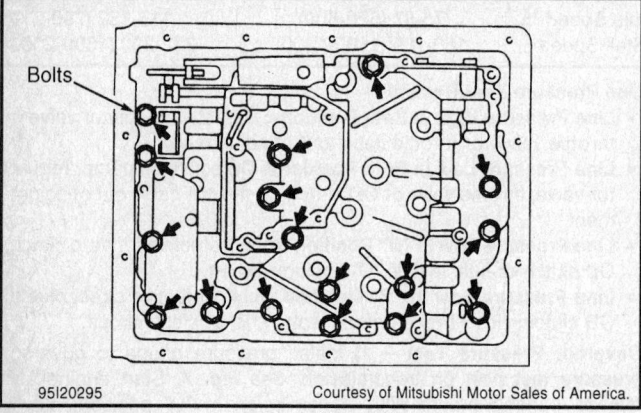

95I20295   Courtesy of Mitsubishi Motor Sales of America.

Fig. 8: Identifying Control Valve Assembly Bolt Locations

PARKING LOCK PAWL

Removal & Installation – 1) Remove control valve assembly. Remove parking lock pawl bolts and bracket. Remove parking pawl torsion spring. Pull out pivot pin and remove parking lock pawl. Remove parking lock rod from manual valve lever. *See Fig. 9.*
2) To install, reverse removal procedures. Prior to installing parking lock pawl bracket bolts, push lock rod forward. Finger tighten bolts and ensure parking lock pawl operates smoothly. Tighten bracket bolts to 65 INCH lbs. (7.4 N.m).

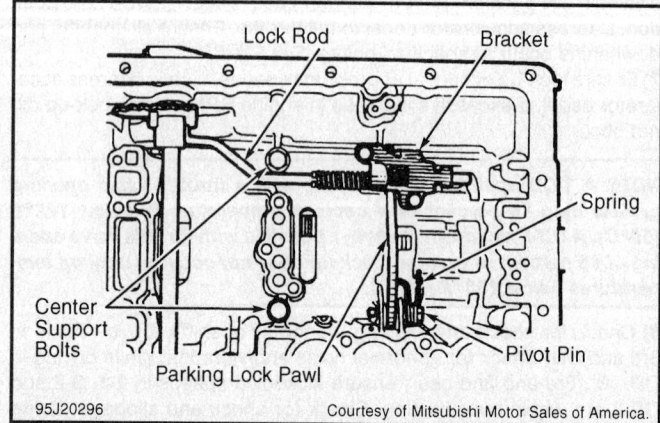

95J20296   Courtesy of Mitsubishi Motor Sales of America.

Fig. 9: Removing Parking Lock Pawl Components

REAR OIL SEAL

Removal & Installation – 1) Raise and support vehicle. Place reference marks on drive shaft and companion flange. Remove drive shaft. Clean seal surrounding areas. Using appropriate seal remover, remove oil seal from extension housing. Note direction of seal installation.
2) Using appropriate seal installer, install seal in extension housing until seal bottoms. To complete installation, reverse removal procedure. Fill transmission to proper level.

NEUTRAL SAFETY SWITCH

For neutral safety switch adjustment, see appropriate AUTOMATIC TRANSMISSION SERVICING article in TRANSMISSION SERVICING section.

SHIFT LINKAGE

For shift linkage adjustment, see appropriate AUTOMATIC TRANSMISSION SERVICING article in TRANSMISSION SERVICING section.

THROTTLE CABLE

For throttle cable adjustment, see appropriate AUTOMATIC TRANSMISSION SERVICING article in TRANSMISSION SERVICING section.

REMOVAL & INSTALLATION

TRANSMISSION ASSEMBLY

For transmission removal and installation procedure, see appropriate AUTOMATIC TRANSMISSION REMOVAL article in TRANSMISSION SERVICING section.

TRANSFER CASE

For transfer case removal and installation, see appropriate TRANSFER CASES article in AXLE SHAFTS & TRANSFER CASES section.

TORQUE CONVERTER

CAUTION: Torque converter is a welded assembly and is not service-able. If a malfunction occurs or torque converter becomes contaminated with foreign material, it MUST be replaced. Torque converter cannot be flushed or repaired.

NOTE: For torque converter stall speed test, see STALL SPEED TEST under TESTING.

TRANSMISSION DISASSEMBLY

1) Ensure transmission case is clean of dirt and grease prior to disassembly. Remove transfer case. See appropriate article in AXLE SHAFTS & TRANSFER CASES section. Remove torque converter. Remove OD solenoid valve and neutral safety switch. Remove governor mounting bolt.

2) Remove governor retaining ring and governor. Remove oil pan bolts and oil pan. Carefully remove oil pipe. Remove oil screen and spacer from valve body. Remove valve body assembly bolts. Lift valve body assembly and remove throttle inner cable from throttle cam. Remove valve body.

3) Remove throttle cable from transmission case. Remove bracket, parking lock pawl spring, pivot pin and parking lock pawl. *See Fig. 9.* Remove lock rod. Using screwdriver, move manual valve lever cover outward. Remove spring pin, shaft and manual valve lever. *See Fig. 10.* Remove oil seal from manual valve shaft.

4) Place shop cloth over accumulator pistons. Using compressed air, remove accumulator pistons and springs from transmission case. *See Fig. 11.* Note location of springs and pistons for reassembly reference.

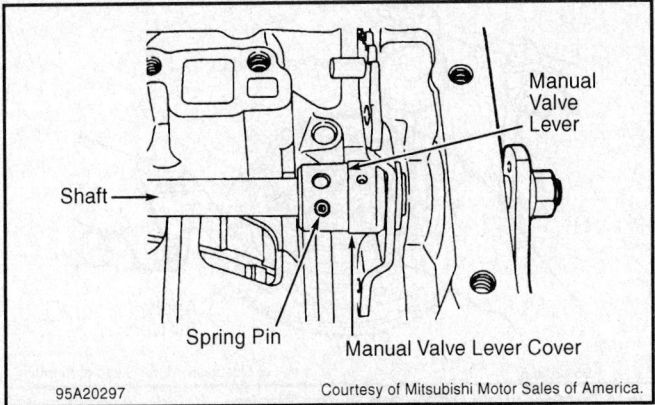

Fig. 10: Removing Manual Valve Shaft & Lever

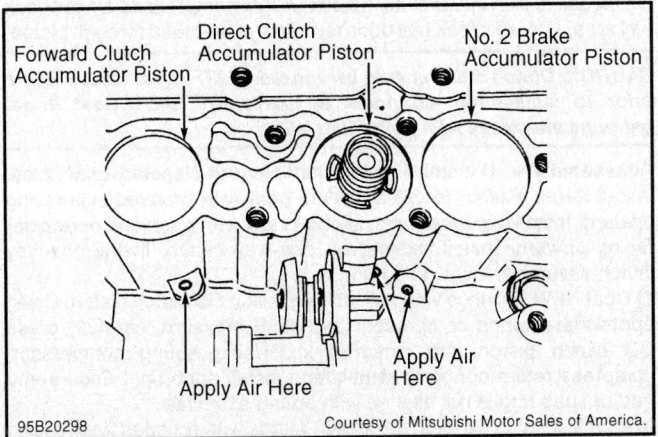

Fig. 11: Removing Accumulator Pistons

5) Remove oil pump bolts and oil pump from case. Remove torque converter housing bolts and housing. Remove input shaft, OD planetary gear and OD clutch as an assembly from transmission case. Remove OD case, forward clutch and direct clutch. Remove 2 center support bolts. *See Fig. 9.*

6) Remove center support and sun gear as an assembly. Remove snap ring securing planetary assembly in transmission case. Remove intermediate shaft, clutch plates and planetary assembly from transmission case. Remove output shaft from transmission case. Remove No. 3 brake apply tube.

7) Remove output shaft thrust bearing race No. 19 and thrust bearing No. 18 from transmission case. Remove rear cover and gasket. Remove case filter. *See Fig. 12.*

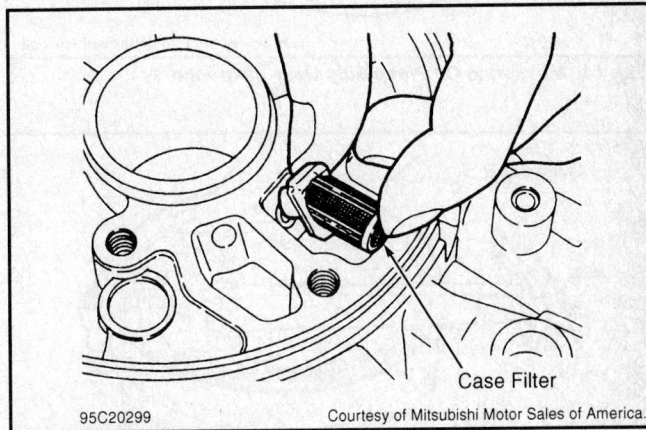

Fig. 12: Removing Case Filter

COMPONENT DISASSEMBLY & REASSEMBLY

OIL PUMP

Disassembly – Remove "O" ring from oil pump housing. Remove stator support bolts. Remove stator support from oil pump housing. Place reference marks on drive and driven gears for reassembly reference. Remove gears. Remove seal rings from stator support. Pry oil seal from oil pump housing. *See Fig. 13.*

Inspection – Clean all components in solvent. Dry with compressed air. Inspect all components for damage or wear. Using feeler gauge and straightedge, measure side gear clearance between pump housing face and top of gears. *See Fig. 14.* Clearance should be .0008-.0020" (.020-.050 mm), with a limit of .004" (.10 mm). If clearance is not as specified, replace components as necessary.

Reassembly – **1)** Coat all components with ATF. Align reference marks on drive and driven gears during reassembly. Install stator support on oil pump housing and align bolt holes. Install but do not tighten stator support bolts.

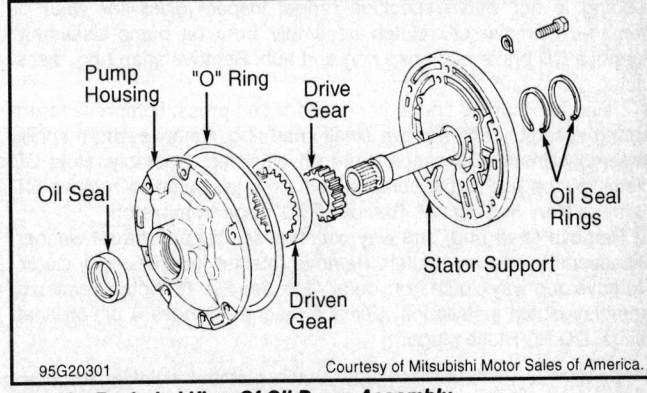

Fig. 13: Exploded View Of Oil Pump Assembly

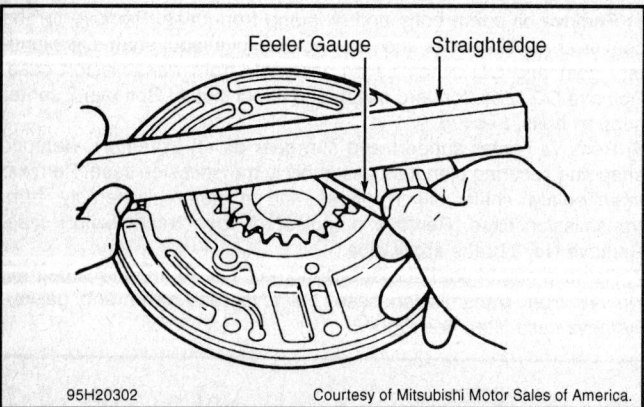

95H20302   Courtesy of Mitsubishi Motor Sales of America.

Fig. 14: Measuring Oil Pump Side Gear Clearance

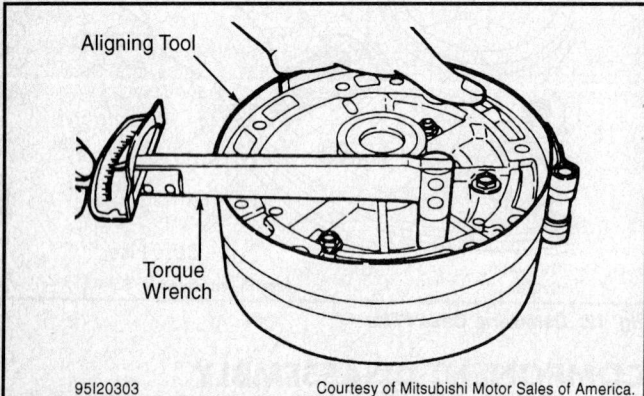

95I20303   Courtesy of Mitsubishi Motor Sales of America.

Fig. 15: Aligning Oil Pump Housing & Stator Support

2) Install Oil Pump Aligning Tool (MD998335) around outside of oil pump housing to align pump housing and stator support. See Fig. 15. Tighten stator support bolts to 53-71 INCH lbs. (6-8 N.m). Remove aligning tool. Install seal rings. DO NOT spread seal ring ends more than necessary for installation. Ensure seal rings move smoothly after installation. Ensure oil pump drive gear rotates smoothly. Lubricate and install "O" ring on oil pump housing.

OD PLANETARY GEAR, OD CLUTCH & OD ONE-WAY CLUTCH

Disassembly – 1) Remove OD clutch drum from OD planetary gear. Remove No. 3 thrust bearing from planetary gear. See Fig. 16. Place OD clutch assembly on oil pump assembly. Using a dial indicator, measure OD clutch piston stroke, while applying 57-114 psi (4-8 kg/cm²) to oil pump port. See Fig. 17.

2) Piston stroke should be .076-.104" (1.92-2.64 mm). If dial indicator reading is not within specified range, inspect discs for wear or damage. Remove OD clutch assembly from oil pump assembly. Remove OD brake hub snap ring and hub. Remove snap ring, discs, clutch plates and cushion plate.

3) Using appropriate spring compressor and press, compress return spring assembly and remove small snap ring. Remove return spring assembly. Install OD clutch drum on oil pump assembly. Hold OD clutch piston and apply compressed air to oil pump to remove OD clutch piston. See Fig. 17. Remove 2 "O" rings from piston.

4) Remove snap ring, one-way clutch assembly and thrust washer. Disassemble one-way clutch. Remove retainer from one-way clutch. Remove one-way clutch from outer race. See Fig. 16. Note direction of one-way clutch installation. Using a magnet, remove 4 pinion shaft plugs. DO NOT lose plugs.

Inspection – Inspect discs and clutch plates for flaking or burnt areas. If disc lining is peeling or discolored, replace discs. Inspect return springs for wear, damage and collapsed coils. Clean all compo-

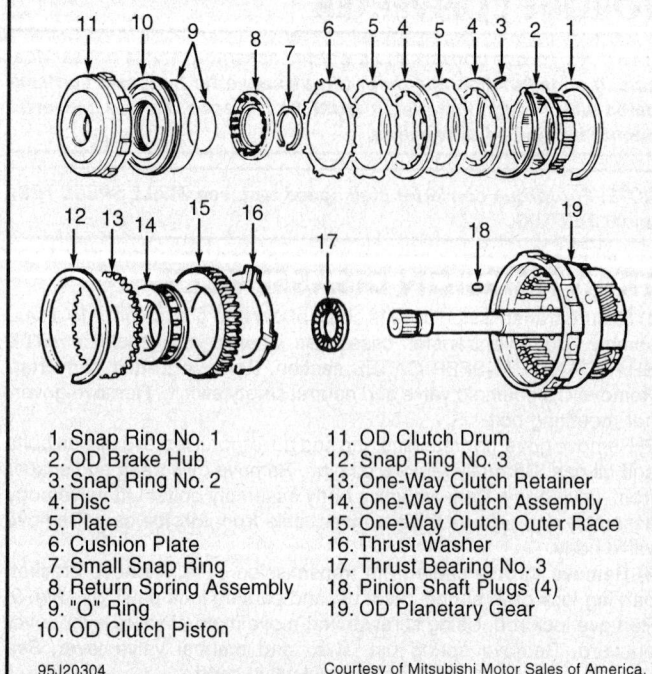

1. Snap Ring No. 1
2. OD Brake Hub
3. Snap Ring No. 2
4. Disc
5. Plate
6. Cushion Plate
7. Small Snap Ring
8. Return Spring Assembly
9. "O" Ring
10. OD Clutch Piston
11. OD Clutch Drum
12. Snap Ring No. 3
13. One-Way Clutch Retainer
14. One-Way Clutch Assembly
15. One-Way Clutch Outer Race
16. Thrust Washer
17. Thrust Bearing No. 3
18. Pinion Shaft Plugs (4)
19. OD Planetary Gear

95J20304   Courtesy of Mitsubishi Motor Sales of America.

Fig. 16: Exploded View Of OD Planetary Gear, OD Clutch & OD One-Way Clutch

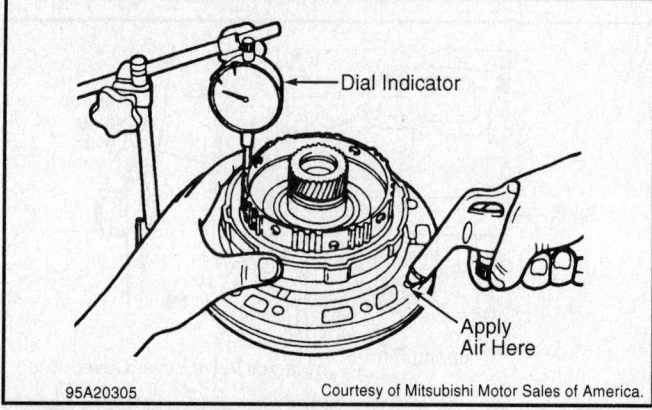

95A20305   Courtesy of Mitsubishi Motor Sales of America.

Fig. 17: Measuring OD Clutch Piston Stroke

nents (except disc) with solvent. Dry with compressed air. Ensure check ball is free in OD clutch piston. Apply compressed air to check ball area. Ensure check ball does not allow air to bleed through piston.

CAUTION: Clutch discs should be soaked in ATF for at least 2 hours prior to installation. Lubricate all parts with ATF. Coat thrust bearings and races with petroleum jelly.

Reassembly – 1) Install 4 pinion shaft plugs in planetary gear holes. Install thrust washer to OD planetary gear with grooved side facing upward. Install one-way clutch in outer race with open end of retainer facing upward. Install retainer on one-way clutch. Install one-way clutch assembly. Install snap ring.

2) Coat NEW "O" rings with ATF and install on OD clutch piston. Using appropriate spring compressor and hand pressure, carefully press OD clutch piston into clutch drum. Using spring compressor, compress return spring assembly and install snap ring. Ensure end gap of snap ring is not aligned with spring seat claw.

3) Install cushion plate. Install clutch plates with rounded edge facing upward. Install clutch discs and snap ring. Ensure end gap of snap ring is not aligned with cutout portion of clutch drum. Install OD brake hub and snap ring. Ensure end gap of snap ring is not aligned with cut-out portion of drum.

4) Recheck piston stroke of OD clutch. If piston stroke is less than specified, check for incorrect reassembly of components. Install thrust bearing No. 3 on OD planetary gear. Install OD clutch assembly on OD planetary gear.

5) Rotate and push OD planetary gear to mesh splines of planetary gear with flukes of discs. Check one-way clutch operation. Hold OD clutch drum and rotate input shaft. Input shaft should rotate freely in clockwise direction and lock in counterclockwise direction. See Fig. 18.

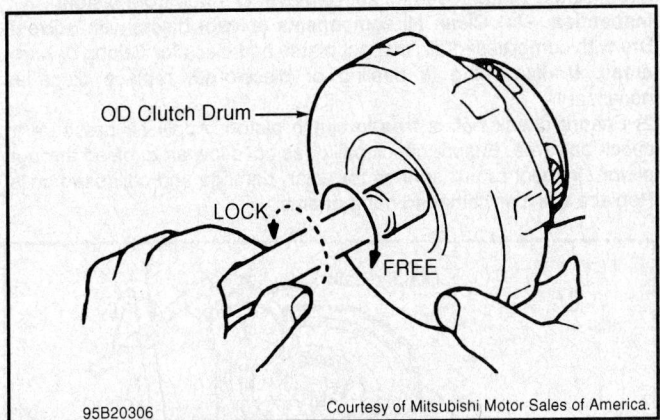

Fig. 18: Checking OD One-Way Clutch Operation

OVERDRIVE BRAKE

Disassembly – 1) Prior to disassembly, check OD brake clearance. Using a feeler gauge, measure clearance between snap ring and flange. Standard clearance should be .026-.087" (.65-2.21 mm). Remove snap ring from OD case. Remove flange, discs, plates and cushion plate. Note location and number of components.

2) Remove OD planetary ring gear, thrust bearing and races from OD case. Remove snap ring, spring retainer and return springs. See Fig. 19. Remove brake piston by applying air pressure to OD case. See Fig. 20. Remove oil seal rings from OD case and "O" rings from piston.

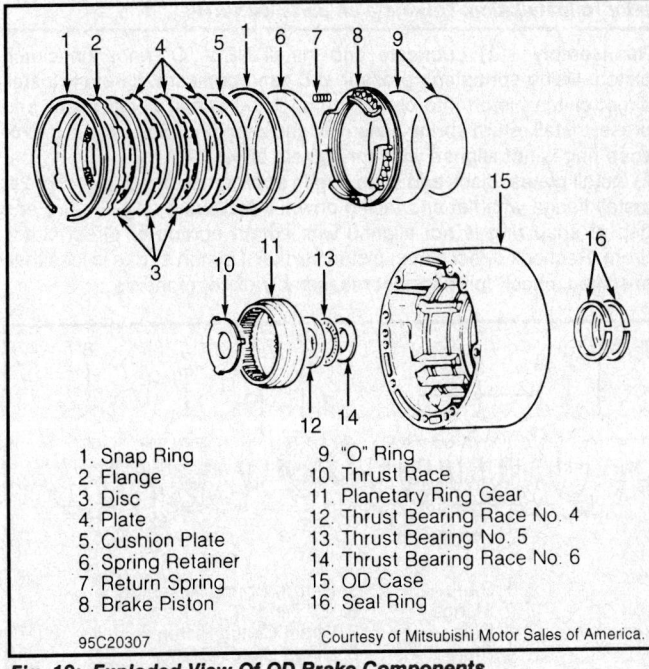

1. Snap Ring	9. "O" Ring
2. Flange	10. Thrust Race
3. Disc	11. Planetary Ring Gear
4. Plate	12. Thrust Bearing Race No. 4
5. Cushion Plate	13. Thrust Bearing No. 5
6. Spring Retainer	14. Thrust Bearing Race No. 6
7. Return Spring	15. OD Case
8. Brake Piston	16. Seal Ring

95C20307   Courtesy of Mitsubishi Motor Sales of America.

Fig. 19: Exploded View Of OD Brake Components

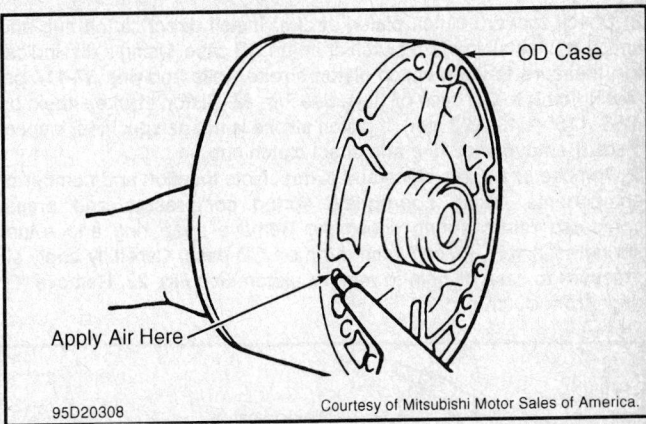

95D20308   Courtesy of Mitsubishi Motor Sales of America.

Fig. 20: Removing OD Brake Piston

Inspection – Clean all components (except discs) with solvent. Dry with compressed air. Inspect flange, discs and plates for flaking or burnt areas. If disc lining is peeling or discolored, replace discs as necessary. Inspect return springs for wear, damage and collapsed coils.

CAUTION: Clutch discs should be soaked in ATF for at least 2 hours prior to installation. Lubricate all parts with ATF. Coat thrust bearing and races with petroleum jelly.

Reassembly – 1) Lubricate and install oil seal rings on OD case. Ensure rings rotate smoothly after installation. Install NEW "O" rings on brake piston. Using hand pressure, carefully install brake piston into OD case.

2) Install return springs into OD case. Install spring retainer and snap ring. Ensure end gap of snap ring is not aligned with cutout portion of OD case. Ensure snap ring is inserted in its groove.

3) Install No. 6 bearing race, No. 5 thrust bearing and No. 4 bearing race on OD planetary ring gear. Install OD planetary ring gear assembly into OD case.

4) Install cushion plate into OD case with rounded side inward. Install discs and plates in appropriate order. Install flange with rounded edge facing upward. Install snap ring. Ensure end gap of snap ring is not aligned with cutout portion of OD case. Recheck OD brake clearance. If measurement is not as specified, check for incorrect reassembly of components.

FORWARD CLUTCH

Disassembly – 1) Prior to disassembly, check forward clutch piston stroke. Install forward clutch assembly to OD case. Remove snap ring. Remove direct and forward clutch hubs. Remove thrust bearing and races from clutch drum, noting component direction prior to removal. See Fig. 21.

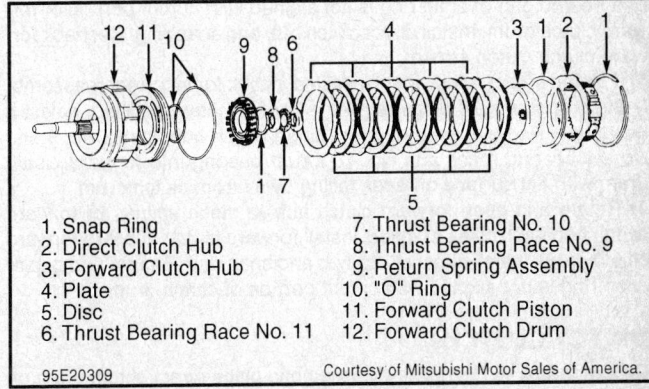

1. Snap Ring	7. Thrust Bearing No. 10
2. Direct Clutch Hub	8. Thrust Bearing Race No. 9
3. Forward Clutch Hub	9. Return Spring Assembly
4. Plate	10. "O" Ring
5. Disc	11. Forward Clutch Piston
6. Thrust Bearing Race No. 11	12. Forward Clutch Drum

95E20309   Courtesy of Mitsubishi Motor Sales of America.

Fig. 21: Exploded View Of Forward Clutch Components

2) Check forward clutch piston stroke. Install direct clutch hub and snap ring. Install forward clutch drum on OD case. Using a dial indicator, measure forward clutch piston stroke while applying 57-114 psi (4-8 kg/cm²) to OD case oil hole. *See Fig. 22.* Piston stroke should be .056-.115" (1.43-2.93 mm). If piston stroke is not as specified, inspect discs. Remove snap ring and direct clutch hub.

3) Remove snap ring, discs and plates. Note location and number of components. Using appropriate spring compressor and press, compress return spring assembly. Remove snap ring and return spring assembly. Place clutch drum on OD case. Carefully apply air pressure to case oil hole to remove piston. *See Fig. 22.* Remove "O" rings from clutch piston.

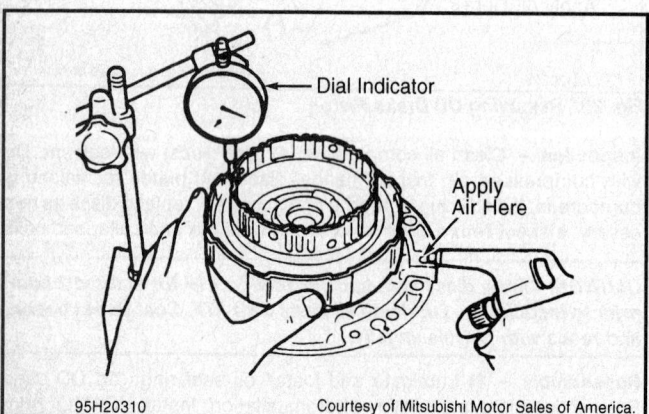

Fig. 22: Measuring Forward Clutch Piston Stroke

Inspection – 1) Clean all components (except discs) with solvent. Dry with compressed air. Inspect plates and discs for flaking or burnt areas. If disc lining is peeling or discolored, replace discs as necessary.

2) Ensure check ball is free in clutch piston. Apply air pressure to check ball area. Ensure check ball does not allow air to bleed through piston. Inspect return spring assembly for wear, damage and collapsed coils. Replace worn or damaged components.

CAUTION: Clutch discs should be soaked in ATF for at least 2 hours prior to installation. Lubricate all parts with ATF. Coat thrust bearing and races with petroleum jelly.

Reassembly – 1) Lubricate and install NEW "O" rings onto clutch piston. Using appropriate spring compressor and hand pressure, carefully install forward clutch piston into clutch drum. Install return spring assembly. Using spring compressor and appropriate press, compress return spring assembly and install snap ring. Ensure end gap of snap ring is not aligned with claw area on spring seat.

2) Install plates, discs and snap ring in appropriate order. *See Fig. 21.* Ensure end gap of snap ring is not aligned with cutout portion of forward clutch drum. Install direct clutch hub and snap ring. Recheck forward clutch piston stroke.

3) If piston stroke is less than specified, check for incorrect reassembly of components. If piston stroke is greater than specified, select a new plate. Remove snap ring and direct clutch hub. Install No. 9 and No. 11 bearing races and No. 10 thrust bearing into forward clutch drum with flat surface of races facing away from clutch drum.

4) Rotate and push forward clutch hub to mesh splines of forward clutch hub with flukes of discs. Install forward clutch hub into forward clutch drum. Install direct clutch hub and snap ring. Ensure end gap of snap ring is not aligned with cutout portion of clutch drum.

DIRECT CLUTCH

Disassembly – 1) Prior to disassembly, place direct clutch drum on center support. Using a dial indicator and compressed air, measure direct clutch piston stroke while applying 57-114 psi (4-8 kg/cm²) to center support oil hole. *See Fig. 23.* Piston stroke should be .036-.078" (.91-1.99 mm). If piston stroke is not as specified, inspect discs. Remove direct clutch from center support.

2) Remove snap ring, flange, discs and plates. Note location and number of components. Using appropriate spring compressor and press, compress return spring assembly and remove snap ring. Remove return spring assembly.

3) Place direct clutch drum on center support. Hold direct clutch piston with hand, and apply compressed air to center support to remove direct clutch piston. *See Fig. 23.* Remove "O" rings from piston.

Inspection – 1) Clean all components (except discs) with solvent. Dry with compressed air. Inspect plates and discs for flaking or burnt areas. If disc lining is peeling or discolored, replace discs as necessary.

2) Ensure check ball is free in clutch piston. Apply air pressure to check ball area. Ensure check ball does not allow air to bleed through piston. Inspect return springs for wear, damage and collapsed coils. Replace worn or damaged components.

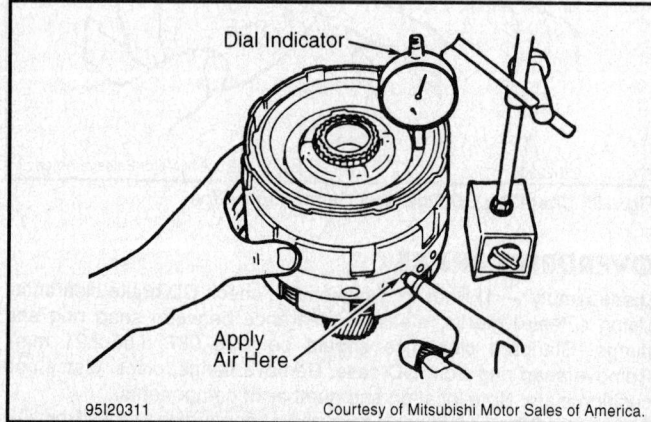

Fig. 23: Measuring Direct Clutch Piston Stroke

CAUTION: Clutch discs should be soaked in ATF for at least 2 hours prior to installation. Lubricate all parts with ATF.

Reassembly – 1) Lubricate and install NEW "O" rings on clutch piston. Using spring compressor and hand pressure, carefully install direct clutch piston into clutch drum. Using spring compressor and press, install return spring assembly and snap ring. Ensure end gap of snap ring is not aligned with spring seat claw.

2) Install plates, discs and snap ring in appropriate order. *See Fig. 24.* Install flange with flat end facing down. Install snap ring. Ensure end gap of snap ring is not aligned with cutout portion of direct clutch drum. Recheck direct clutch piston stroke. If piston stroke is less than specified, check for incorrect reassembly of components.

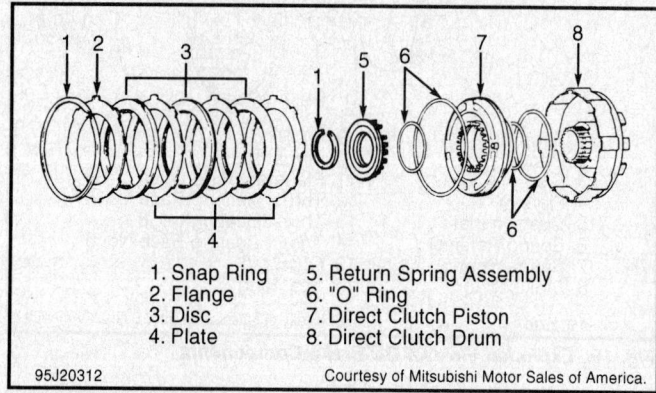

1. Snap Ring
2. Flange
3. Disc
4. Plate
5. Return Spring Assembly
6. "O" Ring
7. Direct Clutch Piston
8. Direct Clutch Drum

Fig. 24: Exploded View Of Direct Clutch Components

CENTER SUPPORT ASSEMBLY

Disassembly – 1) Remove snap ring from end of sun gear shaft. Remove planetary sun gear with No. 1 one-way clutch from center support. Repeat procedure used in direct clutch disassembly to check No. 1 brake piston stroke. Piston stroke should be .031-.068" (.78-1.73 mm). If piston stroke is not as specified, inspect discs. *See Fig. 25.*

2) Remove snap ring from front of center support. Remove flange, discs and plates. *See Fig. 26.* Using appropriate spring compressor and press, compress return spring assembly. Remove snap ring. Remove return spring assembly.

3) Hold No. 1 brake piston and apply air pressure to center support oil hole to remove No. 1 brake piston. *See Fig. 25.* Remove "O" rings and oil seal rings. Turn center support over.

4) Check No. 2 brake piston stroke. Repeat test procedure used previously for checking piston stroke on No. 1 brake piston. *See Fig. 27.* Piston stroke should be .040-.089" (1.01-2.25 mm). If piston stroke is not as specified, inspect discs. Remove rear snap ring, flange, discs and plates. Note location and number of components. *See Fig. 26.*

5) Using appropriate spring compressor and press, compress return spring assembly. Remove snap ring. Remove return spring assembly. Hold No. 2 brake piston and apply air pressure to center support oil hole to remove No. 2 brake piston. *See Fig. 27.* Remove "O" rings.

6) Hold No. 1 one-way clutch and rotate planetary sun gear. Sun gear should rotate freely in counterclockwise direction and lock in clockwise direction. *See Fig. 28.* If component does not test as

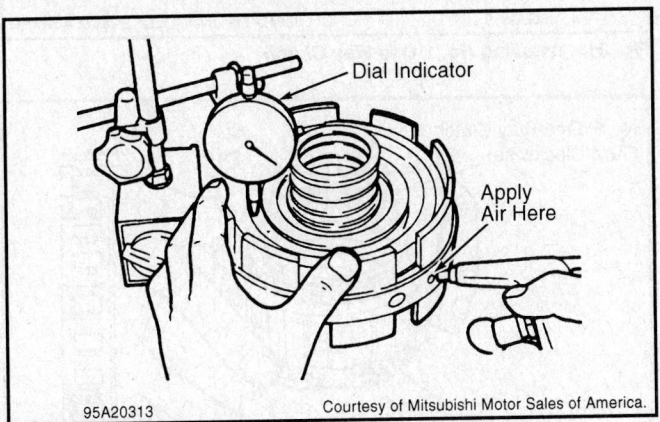

Fig. 25: Measuring No. 1 Brake Piston Stroke

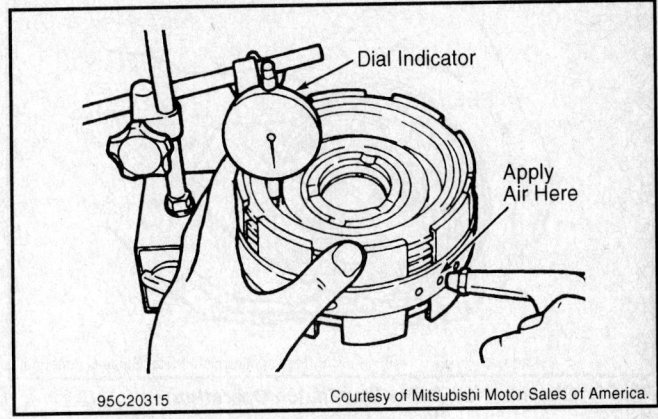

Fig. 27: Measuring No. 2 Brake Piston Stroke

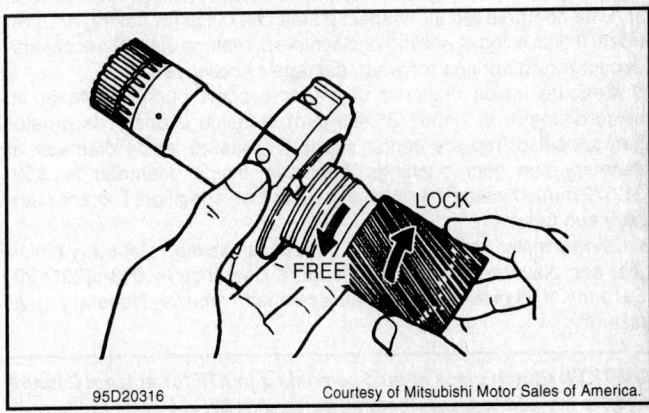

Fig. 28: Checking No. 1 One-Way Clutch Operation

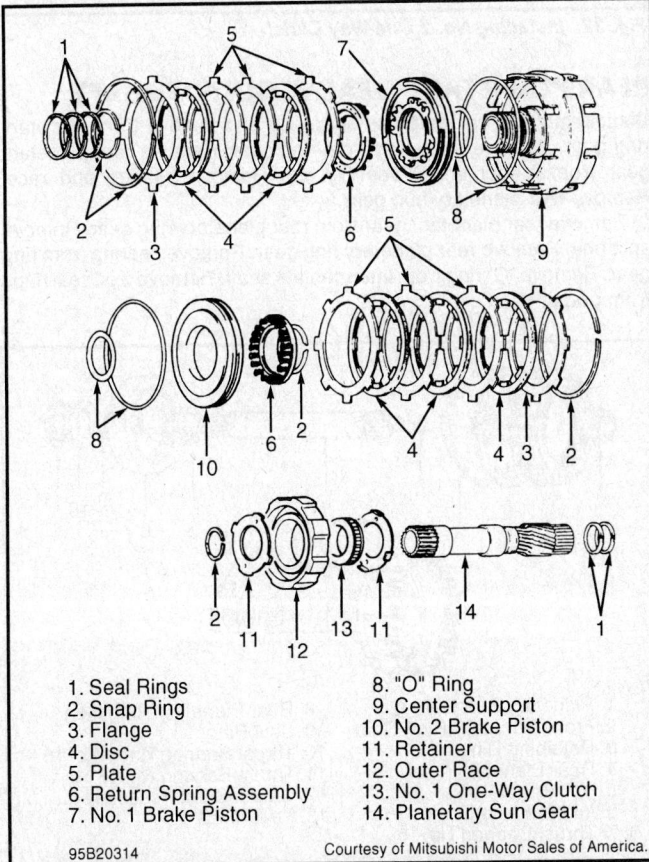

1. Seal Rings
2. Snap Ring
3. Flange
4. Disc
5. Plate
6. Return Spring Assembly
7. No. 1 Brake Piston
8. "O" Ring
9. Center Support
10. No. 2 Brake Piston
11. Retainer
12. Outer Race
13. No. 1 One-Way Clutch
14. Planetary Sun Gear

Fig. 26: Exploded View Of Center Support Assembly Components

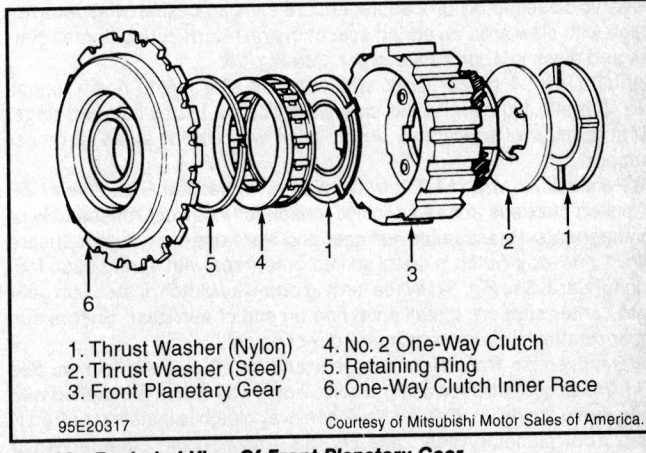

1. Thrust Washer (Nylon)
2. Thrust Washer (Steel)
3. Front Planetary Gear
4. No. 2 One-Way Clutch
5. Retaining Ring
6. One-Way Clutch Inner Race

Fig. 29: Exploded View Of Front Planetary Gear & No. 2 One-Way Clutch

described, one-way clutch requires replacement. Loosen staked part of rear side retainer. Remove No. 1 one-way clutch and 2 retainers from outer race. See Fig. 26. Using a pin punch and hammer, remove front side retainer. Remove oil seal rings from sun gear.

7) Remove thrust washers from front planetary gear. See Fig. 29. Hold one-way clutch inner race and rotate planetary gear. Planetary gear should rotate freely in counterclockwise direction and lock in clockwise direction. See Fig. 30. Remove one-way clutch inner race. Remove retaining ring, one-way clutch and nylon thrust washer. See Fig. 29.

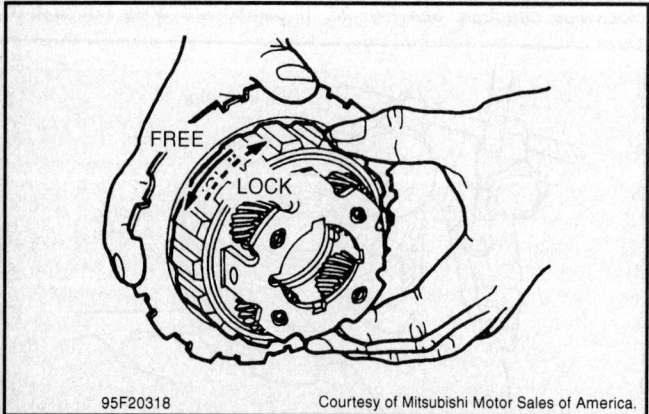

Fig. 30: Checking No. 2 One-Way Clutch Operation

Inspection – 1) Clean all components (except discs) with solvent. Dry with compressed air. Inspect plates and discs for flaking or burnt areas. If disc lining is peeling or discolored, replace disc as necessary. Inspect return springs for wear, damage or collapsed coils.

2) Measure inside diameter of center support bushing. Maximum inside diameter is 1.435" (36.495 mm). If inside diameter is greater than specified, replace center support. Measure inside diameter of planetary sun gear bushings. Maximum inside deameter is .850" (21.577 mm). If inside diameter is greater than specified, replace planetary sun gear.

3) Using a feeler gauge, measure clearance between planetary pinion gear and planetary gear case. Standard clearance is .008-.020" (.20-.50 mm). If clearance is not as specified, replace planetary gear assembly.

CAUTION: Clutch discs should be soaked in ATF for at least 2 hours prior to installation. Lubricate all parts with ATF.

Reassembly – 1) Lubricate "O" rings with ATF. To reassemble, reverse disassembly procedure. Ensure end gap of snap ring does not align with claw area on spring seat of piston return spring. Install plates and discs in appropriate order. See Fig. 26.

2) Install No. 1 brake flange with rounded side facing down. Install No. 2 brake flange with flat side facing down. Install all snap rings. Ensure ends of snap rings do not align with cutout areas of center support.

3) Recheck No. 1 and No. 2 brake piston stroke. See Figs. 25 and 27. If piston stroke is not as specified, check for incorrect reassembly of components. Reassemble sun gear and No. 1 one-way clutch. Ensure No. 1 one-way clutch is installed into outer race with spring cage facing forward. See Fig. 31. While turning one-way clutch, install sun gear into center support. Install snap ring on end of sun gear. Ensure sun gear rotates in counterclockwise direction only.

4) Reassemble front planetary gear and No. 2 one-way clutch. See Fig. 29. Ensure thrust washer for No. 2 one-way clutch is installed with oil groove facing up. Ensure No. 2 one-way clutch is installed correctly into front planetary gear. See Fig. 32. Ensure front planetary gear rotates in counterclockwise direction only.

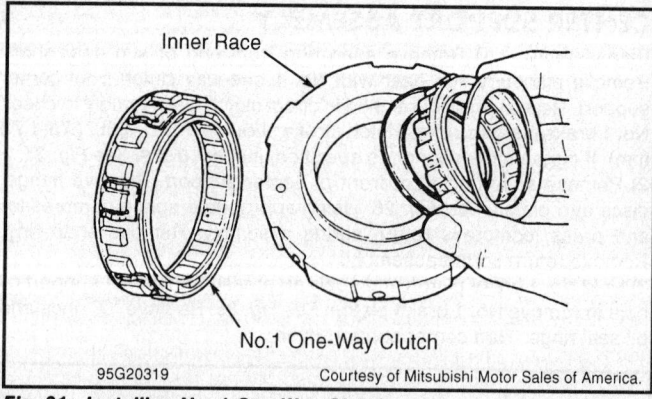

Fig. 31: Installing No. 1 One-Way Clutch

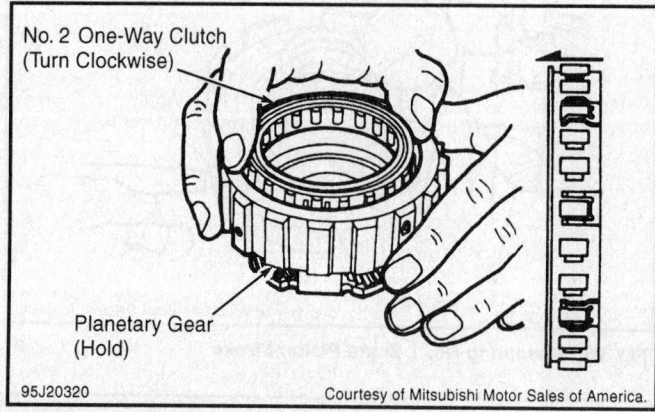

Fig. 32: Installing No. 2 One-Way Clutch

REAR PLANETARY GEAR & OUTPUT SHAFT

Disassembly – 1) Compress snap ring and remove front planetary ring gear. Remove snap ring from ring gear. Remove rear planetary gear from output shaft. See Fig. 33. Remove bearing and race. Remove rear planetary sun gear.

2) Remove rear planetary gear from rear planetary ring gear. Remove split ring. Remove rear planetary ring gear. Remove bearing from ring gear. Remove "O" ring from intermediate shaft. Remove 3 oil seal rings from output shaft.

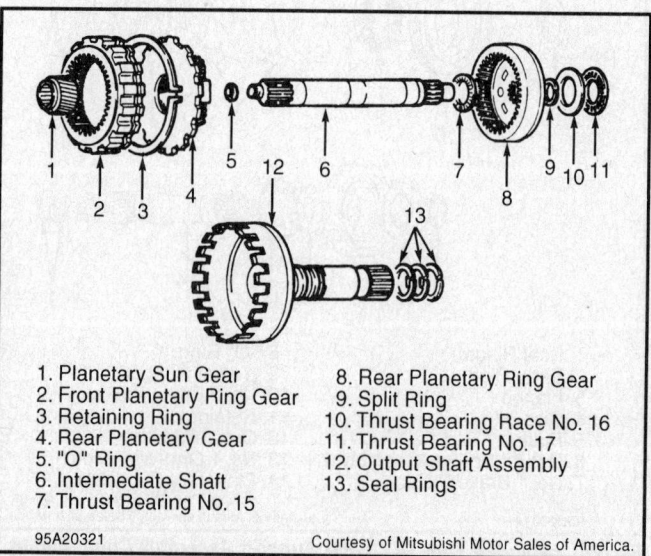

1. Planetary Sun Gear
2. Front Planetary Ring Gear
3. Retaining Ring
4. Rear Planetary Gear
5. "O" Ring
6. Intermediate Shaft
7. Thrust Bearing No. 15
8. Rear Planetary Ring Gear
9. Split Ring
10. Thrust Bearing Race No. 16
11. Thrust Bearing No. 17
12. Output Shaft Assembly
13. Seal Rings

Fig. 33: Exploded View Of Rear Planetary Gear & Output Shaft

Inspection – 1) Clean all components with solvent. Dry with compressed air. Inspect all components for wear or damage. Measure inside diameter of output shaft bushing. Maximum inside diameter is .712" (18.076 mm). If inside diameter is greater than specified, replace output shaft.

2) Using a feeler gauge, measure clearance between rear planetary carrier pinion gear and carrier case. Standard clearance should be .008-.020" (.20-.50 mm). If clearance is not as specified, inspect rear planetary carrier thrust washer. If necessary, replace rear planetary carrier assembly.

Reassembly – 1) Lubricate oil seal rings with ATF. Install oil seal rings on output shaft. Ensure rings rotate smoothly after installation. Lubricate and install NEW "O" ring on intermediate shaft. Ensure ring rotates smoothly. Apply petroleum jelly to thrust bearing No. 15 and install bearing on intermediate shaft with flat surface away from shaft.

2) Install rear planetary ring gear on intermediate shaft. Install split ring. Install rear planetary gear to planetary ring gear. Install rear planetary sun gear. Apply petroleum jelly to thrust bearing No. 17 and bearing race No. 16, and install on rear planetary ring gear. Install rear planetary gear assembly to output shaft. Install front planetary ring gear. See Fig. 33. Ensure snap ring is installed in groove of output shaft. Align snap ring end with wide cutout portion of output shaft.

NO. 3 BRAKE PISTON

Disassembly – 1) Using appropriate spring compressor, compress return spring assembly and remove snap ring. Remove return spring assembly. See Fig. 34. Position transmission with front opening facing upward.

2) Place shop towels under case to prevent piston damage. Apply air pressure to case passages to remove No. 3 brake primary piston, reaction sleeve and No. 3 brake secondary piston. See Fig. 35. It may be necessary to use long hooks to remove sleeve and secondary piston. Using screwdriver, pry manual valve lever shaft seals from case if replacement is required.

Inspection – Clean all parts (except discs) in solvent. Dry with compressed air. Inspect pistons and sleeve for scoring, wear or damage. Check return spring assembly for cracked or broken coils. If disc lining is peeled or discolored, replace discs as necessary. Replace damaged components as necessary.

Reassembly – 1) Using appropriate installer, install manual valve lever shaft seals if removed. Lubricate and install all NEW "O" rings. Thin "O" ring goes on outside of reaction sleeve. Soak discs in ATF for 2 hours prior to installation. Install No. 3 brake discs and plates.

2) Using calipers, measure pack clearance of No. 3 brake between disc and transmission case. See Fig. 36. Pack clearance should be .024-.1039" (.61-2.640 mm). If clearance is not as specified, inspect disc installation. If disc installation is okay, check pressure plate thickness and replace as necessary.

3) Check No. 3 brake operation. See Fig. 35. Measure inside diameter of transmission case rear bushing. Replace transmission case if bushing diameter exceeds 1.504" (38.19 mm).

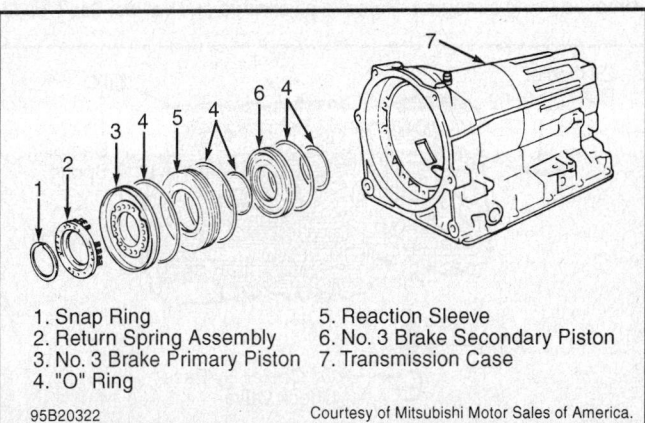

1. Snap Ring
2. Return Spring Assembly
3. No. 3 Brake Primary Piston
4. "O" Ring
5. Reaction Sleeve
6. No. 3 Brake Secondary Piston
7. Transmission Case

95B20322   Courtesy of Mitsubishi Motor Sales of America.

Fig. 34: Exploded View Of No. 3 Brake Components

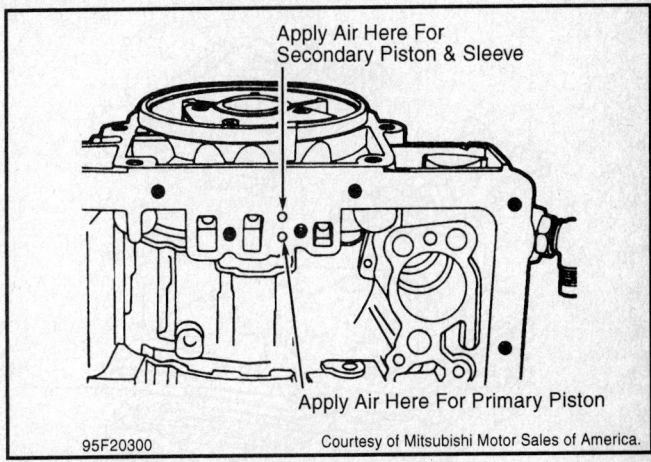

Apply Air Here For Secondary Piston & Sleeve

Apply Air Here For Primary Piston

95F20300   Courtesy of Mitsubishi Motor Sales of America.

Fig. 35: Removing No. 3 Brake Pistons & Sleeve

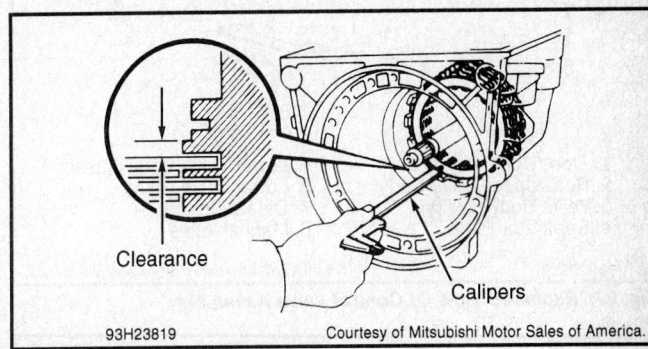

Clearance

Calipers

93H23819   Courtesy of Mitsubishi Motor Sales of America.

Fig. 36: Measuring No. 3 Brake Pack Clearance

CONTROL VALVE ASSEMBLY

CAUTION: All valve body components must be installed in original location. Lay all components in sequence during removal for reassembly reference.

Disassembly – 1) Remove detent spring and manual valve. See Fig. 37. Remove 3 lower valve body bolts securing front upper valve body. See Fig. 38. Invert control valve assembly and remove 5 bolts securing front upper valve body. See Fig. 39.

2) Remove front upper valve body. Remove 5 rear upper valve body bolts. See Fig. 40. Invert control valve assembly and remove 3 bolts securing rear upper valve body. See Fig. 41. Remove rear upper valve body. Remove valve body gasket, separator plate and lower valve body gasket. See Fig. 37. DO NOT drop check valve and ball.

Reassembly – 1) Install and align NEW valve body gasket on rear upper valve body. Ensure NEW gasket matches old gasket. Install lower valve body with separator plate and lower valve body gasket on rear upper valve body. Install and loosely tighten 3 lower valve body bolts. Length of bolt "A" is 2.047" (52.00 mm). Length of bolt "B" is 1.102" (28.00 mm). See Fig. 41.

2) Turn control valve assembly over. Ensure gasket is aligned. Install and tighten 5 rear upper valve body bolts. See Fig. 40. Length of bolt "A" is 1.378" (35.00 mm). Length of bolt "B" is 1.102" (28.00 mm). Install front upper valve body onto lower valve body. Install 3 lower valve body bolts to secure front upper valve body. Length of bolt "A" is .866" (22.00 mm). Length of bolt "B" is 1.102" (28.00 mm). Length of bolt "C" is 2.047" (52.00 mm). See Fig. 38.

3) Install 5 front upper valve body bolts. Length of bolt "A" is .709" (18.00 mm). Length of bolt "B" is .866" (22.00 mm). See Fig. 39. Ensure gaskets are properly aligned. Tighten front and rear upper valve body bolts to 48 INCH lbs. (5.4 N.m). Turn control valve assembly over and tighten lower valve body bolts to same specification. Insert manual valve into valve body. Install detent spring and bolt.

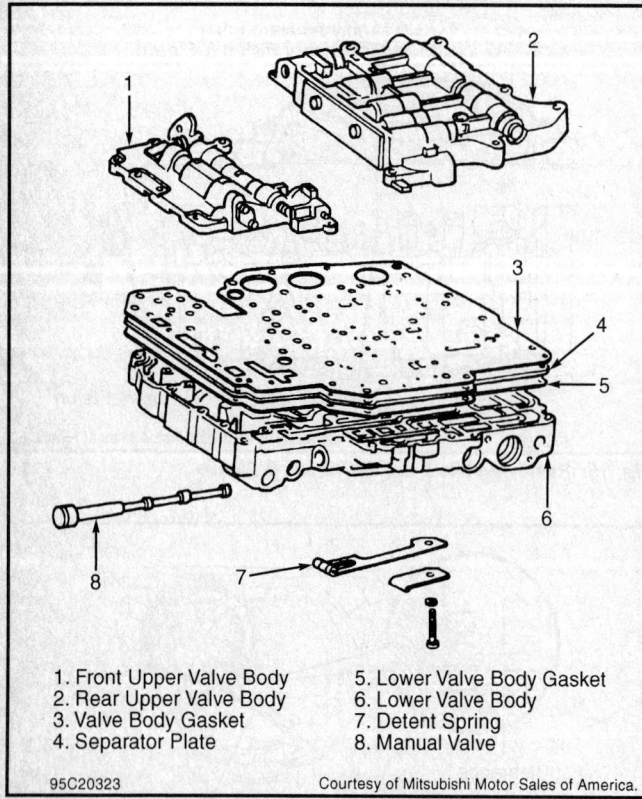

1. Front Upper Valve Body
2. Rear Upper Valve Body
3. Valve Body Gasket
4. Separator Plate
5. Lower Valve Body Gasket
6. Lower Valve Body
7. Detent Spring
8. Manual Valve

95C20323   Courtesy of Mitsubishi Motor Sales of America.

Fig. 37: Exploded View Of Control Valve Assembly

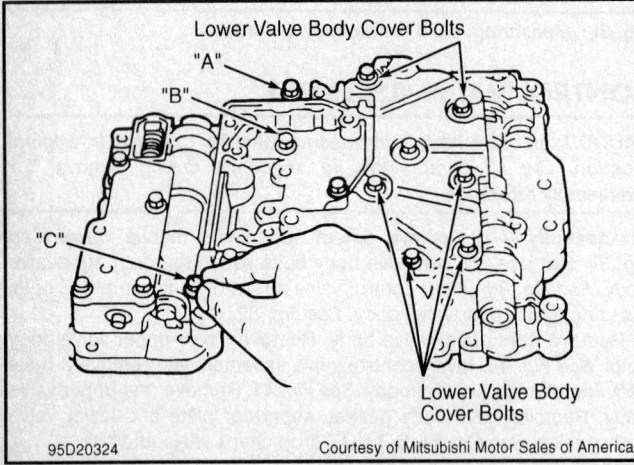

Lower Valve Body Cover Bolts

Lower Valve Body Cover Bolts

95D20324   Courtesy of Mitsubishi Motor Sales of America.

Fig. 38: Identifying Lower Valve Body-To-Front Upper Valve Body Bolts

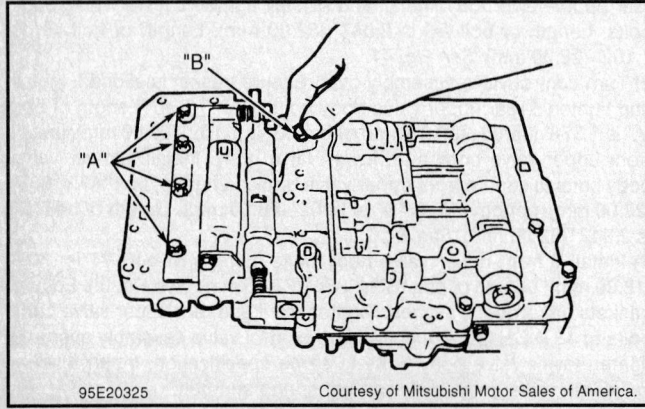

95E20325   Courtesy of Mitsubishi Motor Sales of America.

Fig. 39: Identifying Front Upper Valve Body Bolts

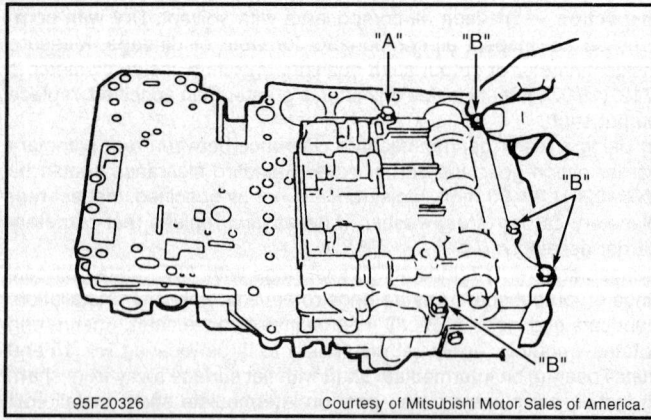

95F20326   Courtesy of Mitsubishi Motor Sales of America.

Fig. 40: Identifying Rear Upper Valve Body Bolts

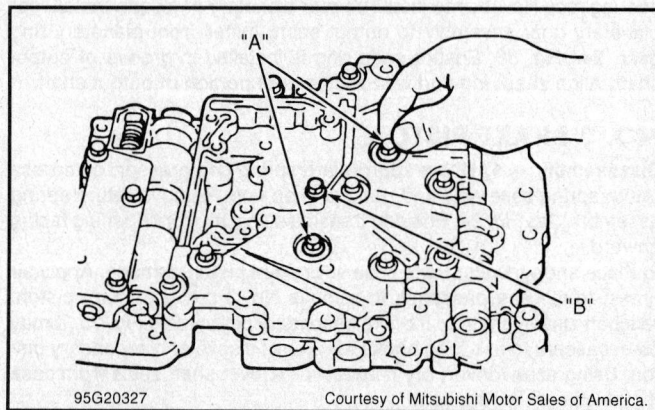

95G20327   Courtesy of Mitsubishi Motor Sales of America.

Fig. 41: Identifying Lower Valve Body-To-Rear Upper Valve Body Bolts

LOWER VALVE BODY

CAUTION: All valve body components must be installed in original location. Lay all components in sequence during removal for reassembly reference.

Disassembly – 1) Remove upper valve bodies from lower valve body. See CONTROL VALVE ASSEMBLY. Remove check balls, damping check ball and spring, oil cooler return check ball and spring, oil cooler bypass check valve and spring. *See Fig. 42.* Remove 6 lower valve body cover bolts. *See Fig. 38.* Remove cover, gaskets and plate.
2) Remove 4 check balls, noting location and diameter for reassembly reference. Push inward on sleeves or plugs to remove all pins and retainers. Note location of pins and retainers. Retainers may be removed using a magnet. Remove all springs and valves. *See Fig. 43.*

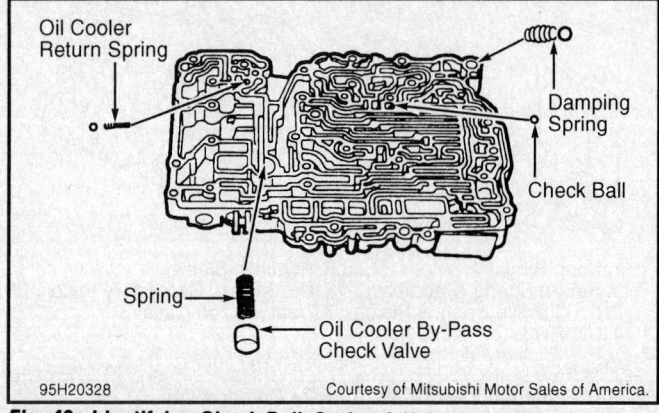

Oil Cooler Return Spring

Damping Spring

Check Ball

Spring

Oil Cooler By-Pass Check Valve

95H20328   Courtesy of Mitsubishi Motor Sales of America.

Fig. 42: Identifying Check Ball, Spring & Valve Locations

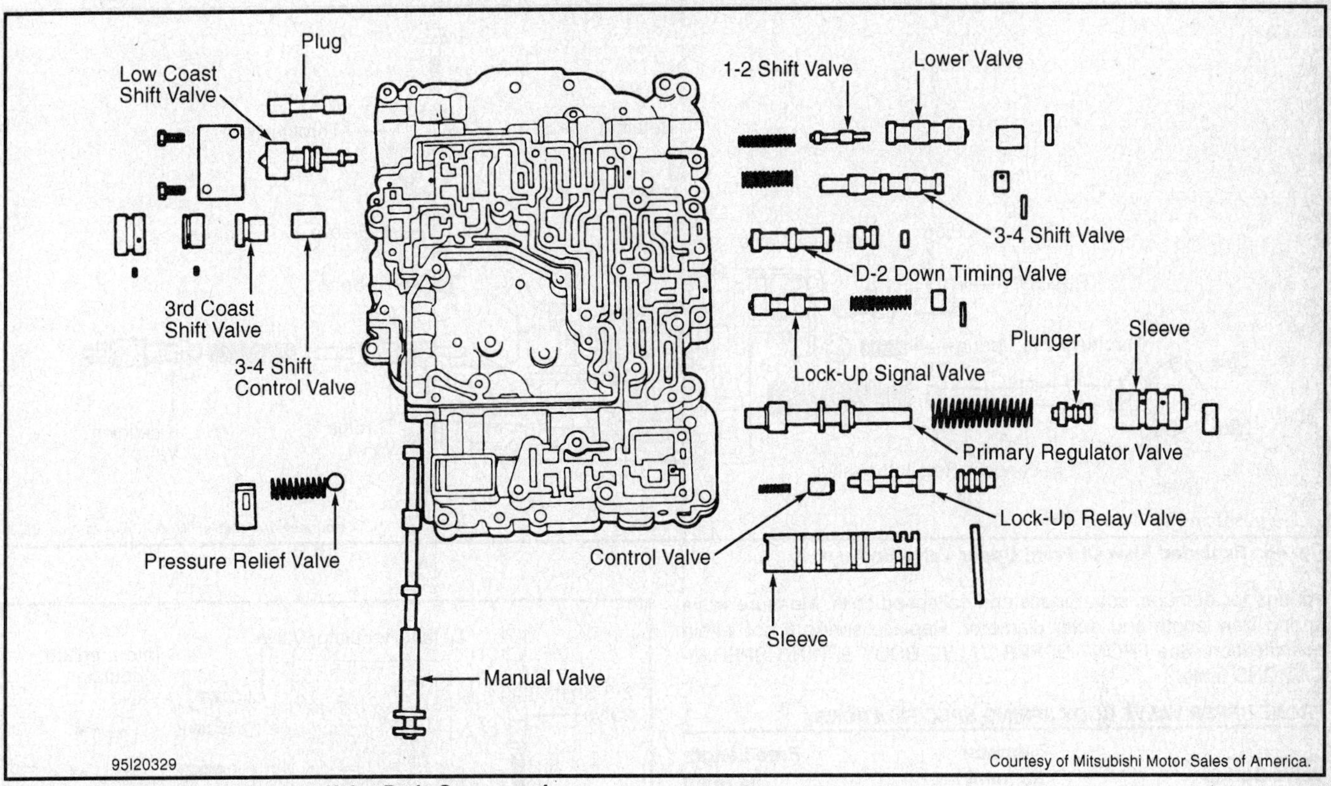

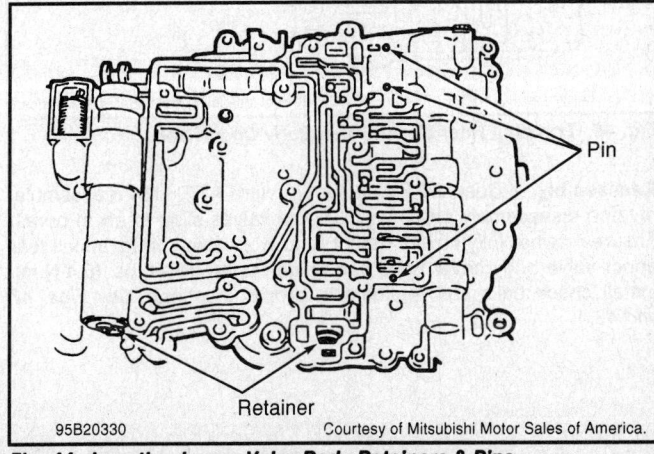

Fig. 43: Exploded View Of Lower Valve Body Components

Inspection – Clean all parts in solvent. Dry with compressed air. Ensure all valve body passages are clear. Inspect valves for scoring or roughness. Ensure valves slide freely in bores. Inspect valve springs for damage, squareness and collapsed coils. Measure spring free length and outer diameter. Replace spring if not within specification. See LOWER VALVE BODY SPRING SPECIFICATIONS table.

LOWER VALVE BODY SPRING SPECIFICATIONS [1]

Valve Spring	Diameter In. (mm)	Free Length In. (mm)
Damping	.196 (4.97)	.787 (20.00)
Lock-Up Relay	.205 (5.20)	.728 (18.50)
Lock-Up Signal	.382 (9.70)	1.811 (46.00)
Oil Cooler By-Pass	.543 (13.80)	1.138 (28.90)
Pressure Relief	.517 (13.14)	1.265 (32.14)
Primary Regulator	.670 (17.02)	2.346 (59.59)
1-2 Shift	.298 (7.56)	1.363 (34.62)
3-4 Shift	.417 (10.60)	.1.385 (35.18)

[1] – For spring locations, See Figs. 42 and 43.

Reassembly – Coat all components with ATF. To reassemble, reverse disassembly procedure. Ensure primary regulator valve plunger is fully recessed in sleeve. Ensure valves slide freely in bores. Ensure retainers, pins and check balls are located in correct locations. See Figs. 44 and 45. Install plate, cover and NEW gaskets. Ensure all holes in gaskets and components are aligned.

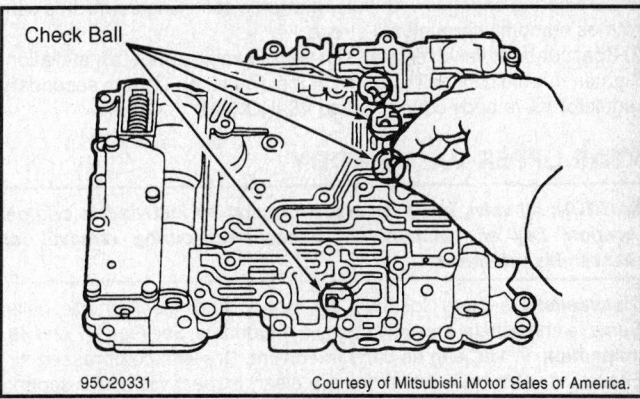

Fig. 45: Locating Lower Valve Body Check Balls

FRONT UPPER VALVE BODY

CAUTION: All valve body components must be installed in original location. Lay all components in sequence during removal for reassembly reference.

Disassembly – Remove valve body components. When removing secondary regulator valve, use care as valve is under spring pressure. See Fig. 46.

Inspection – Clean all parts in solvent. Dry with compressed air. Ensure all valve body passages are clear. Inspect valves for scoring or roughness. Ensure valves slide freely in bores. Inspect valve

Fig. 44: Locating Lower Valve Body Retainers & Pins

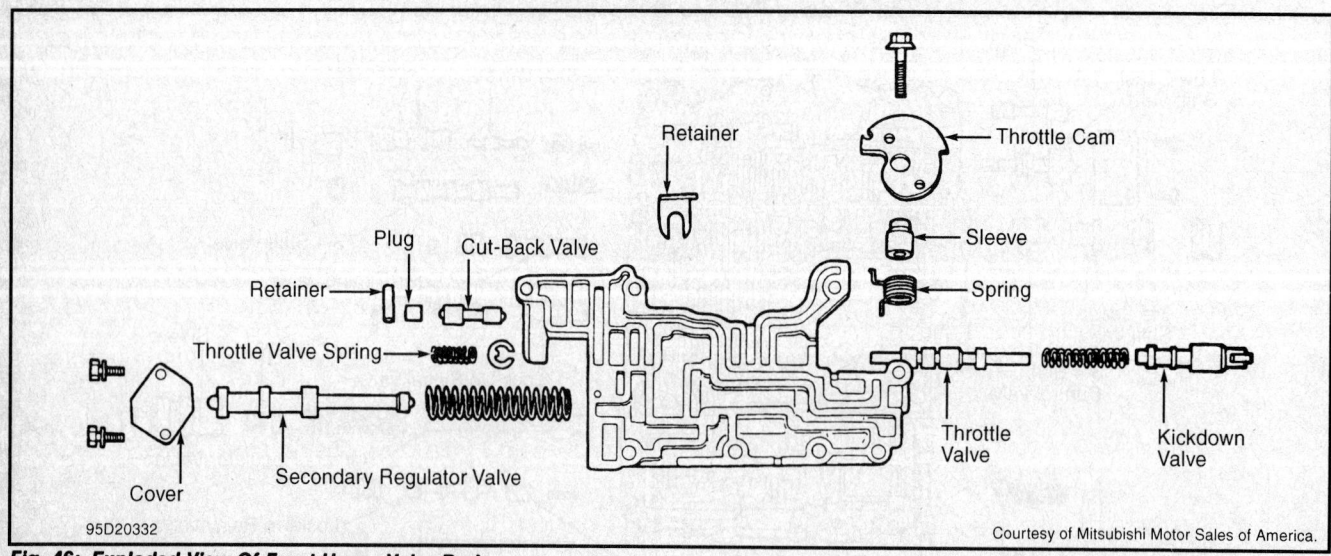

95D20332   Courtesy of Mitsubishi Motor Sales of America.

Fig. 46: Exploded View Of Front Upper Valve Body

springs for damage, squareness and collapsed coils. Measure valve spring free length and outer diameter. Replace spring if not within specification. See FRONT UPPER VALVE BODY SPRING SPECIFICATIONS table.

FRONT UPPER VALVE BODY SPRING SPECIFICATIONS [1]

Valve Spring	Diameter In. (mm)	Free Length In. (mm)
Kickdown	.426 (10.83)	1.565 (39.76)
Secondary Regulator	.686 (17.43)	2.806 (71.27)
Throttle	.338 (8.58)	.864 (21.94)

[1] – For spring locations, *See Fig. 46.*

Reassembly – 1) Coat all components with ATF. To reassemble, reverse disassembly procedure. Ensure valves slide freely in bores. Ensure spring engages with hole of throttle cam. Ensure throttle cam rotates smoothly through full stroke.
2) Coat cut-back valve retainer with petroleum jelly prior to installation. Tighten throttle cam bolt to 65 INCH lbs. (7.4 N.m). Tighten secondary regulator valve body cover bolts to 48 INCH lbs. (5.4 N.m).

REAR UPPER VALVE BODY

CAUTION: All valve body components must be installed in original location. Lay all components in sequence during removal for reassembly reference.

Disassembly – Note location of rubber and steel check balls. Remove check balls and valve body components. *See Figs. 47 and 48.*
Inspection – 1) Clean all parts in solvent. Dry with compressed air. Ensure all valve body passages are clear. Inspect valves for scoring or roughness.
2) Ensure valves slide freely in bores. Inspect valve springs for damage, squareness and collapsed coils. Measure spring free length and outer diameter. Replace spring if not with specification. See REAR UPPER VALVE BODY SPRING SPECIFICATIONS table.

REAR UPPER VALVE BODY SPRING SPECIFICATIONS [1]

Valve Spring	Diameter In. (mm)	Free Length In. (mm)
Detent Regulator	.348 (8.85)	1.236 (31.39)
Intermediate Modulator	.346 (8.80)	1.395 (35.43)
Low Coast Modulator	.364 (9.24)	1.667 (42.35)
Reverse Clutch Sequence	.362 (9.20)	1.478 (37.55)
2-3 Shift	.353 (8.96)	1.382 (35.10)

[1] – For spring location, *See Fig. 47.*

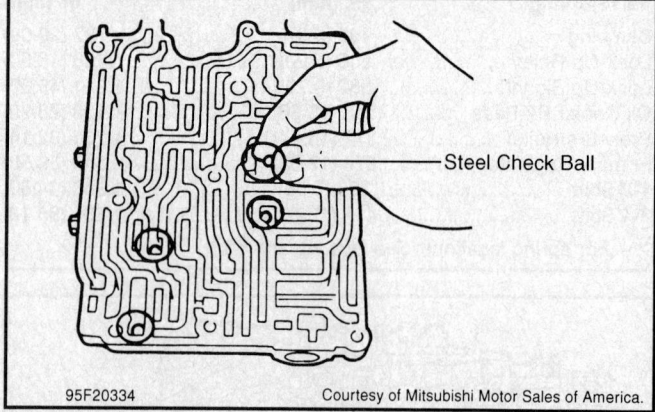

95E20333   Courtesy of Mitsubishi Motor Sales of America.

Fig. 47: Exploded View Of Rear Upper Valve Body

95F20334   Courtesy of Mitsubishi Motor Sales of America.

Fig. 48: Locating Rear Upper Valve Body Check Balls

Reassembly – Coat all components with ATF. To reassemble, reverse disassembly procedure. Ensure valves slide freely in bores. Ensure retainer fully covers detent regulator valve spring. Install rear upper valve body cover bolts and tighten to 48 INCH lbs. (5.4 N.m). Install check balls and retainers in proper locations. *See Figs. 47 and 48.*

GOVERNOR ASSEMBLY

Disassembly & Reassembly – Remove retaining ring (if necessary). Push downward on governor valve shaft. Remove "E" ring and governor components. *See Fig. 49.* Inspect all parts for wear and damage. Insert valve shaft into body. Ensure valve slides smoothly. Check oil passage for restrictions. To reassemble, reverse disassembly procedure. Ensure "E" ring is fully seated.

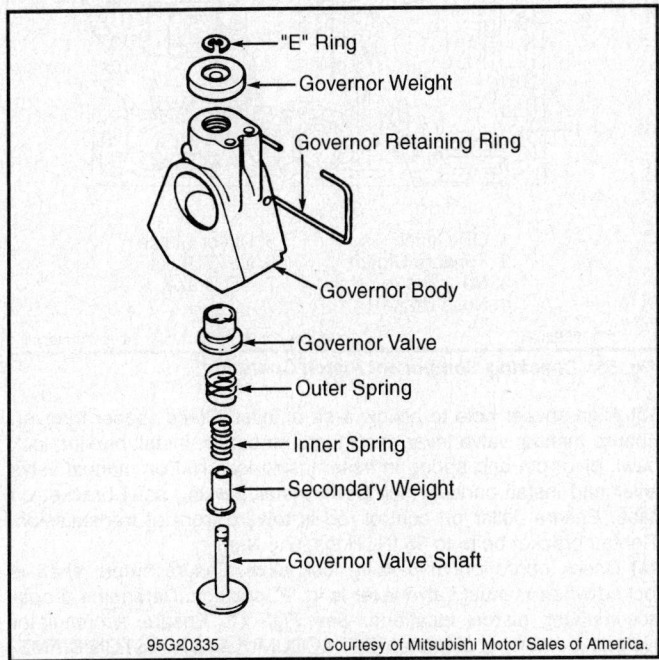

Fig. 49: *Exploded View Of Governor Assembly*

TRANSMISSION REASSEMBLY

NOTE: For bearing race and thrust bearing locations and installation direction, See Fig. 56.

CAUTION: Lubricate all components with ATF. Clutch disc should be soaked in ATF for 2 hours prior to installation. Coat thrust bearings and races with petroleum jelly. Ensure ends of snap rings are not aligned with cutout area of case.

1) Position transmission case with front facing upward. Assemble No. 3 brake secondary piston, reaction sleeve and primary piston. Press assembled pistons into case with hand pressure. Using appropriate spring compressor, install return spring assembly on primary piston. Install snap ring. Ensure No. 3 brake piston moves smoothly when compressed air is applied. *See Fig. 35.*

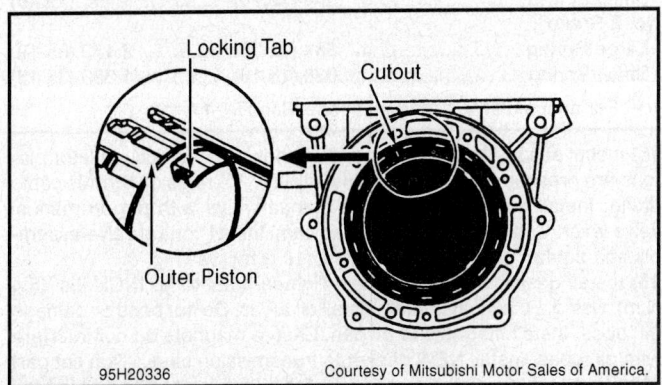

Fig. 50: *Installing Brake Apply Tube*

2) Install bearing race No. 19. Install output shaft thrust bearing No. 18 into case. Install brake apply tube into transmission case, aligning locking tab with cutout in valve body side of transmission case. Ensure lips of tube end are completely inserted onto outer piston. *See Fig. 51.* Install rear planetary gear and output shaft into case.

3) Install pressure plate, with flat surface facing forward. Install discs and plates, starting with a disc and alternating each component. Measure No. 3 brake clutch pack clearance. *See Fig. 36.* Clearance should be .024-.104" (.61-2.64 mm).

4) Remove one-way clutch inner race from planetary gear assembly. Install front planetary gear. Mesh splines of planetary gear with flukes of discs by rotating and pushing planetary gear. Position one-way clutch inner race with notched tooth "A" toward valve body side of case. *See Fig. 51.* Push plate into place. Install snap ring. Ensure snap ring is fully seated.

5) Align oil hole and bolt hole of center support toward valve body side. Align center support bolt holes with case holes and install. Install bolts with wave washers. Tighten bolt on accumulator piston side first to 18 ft. lbs. (25 N.m). Install direct clutch assembly while rotating to align with center support.

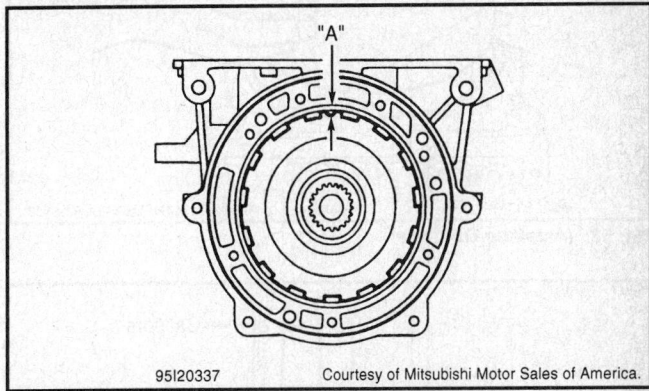

Fig. 51: *Positioning One-Way Clutch Inner Race*

6) If fully installed, splined center of clutch will be even with end of sun gear shaft. Install bearing race No. 12, thrust bearing No. 13 and bearing race No. 14 over splined end of forward clutch. *See Fig. 56.* Install forward clutch. Rotate and push forward clutch to mesh splines of front clutch with flukes of discs.

7) Using calipers and Clutch Drum Thrust Plate Gauge (MD998217), measure distance between top of case and forward clutch drum. Measured value minus thickness of plate gauge equals forward clutch installation height. *See Fig. 52.* Distance should be .059" (1.5 mm). If distance is not as specified, check installation of previously installed components. Install thrust bearing No. 8 and bearing race No. 7 to forward clutch. Install Guide Rods (MD998412) finger tight in front case bolt holes.

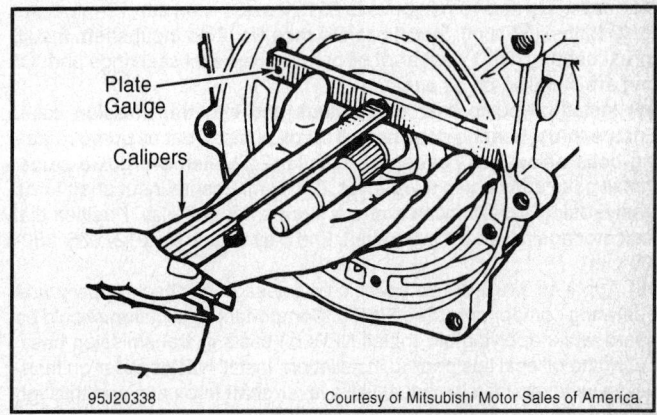

Fig. 52: *Measuring Forward Clutch Installed Height*

8) Install OD case over guide pins with notch area toward valve body side of case. *See Fig. 53.* Install thrust washer on OD case and OD planetary gear. Ensure washer lugs align with holes in OD case and planetary gear assembly.

9) Install OD planetary gear assembly with OD clutch and one-way clutch. Rotate and push OD planetary gear to mesh splines with flukes of discs. Ensure thrust washer does not fall during installation. Using calipers and Clutch Drum Thrust Plate Gauge (MD998217), measure distance between top of case and OD clutch drum. Measured value minus thickness of plate gauge equals OD clutch installation height. *See Fig. 54.* Distance should be .08" (2.0 mm). If distance is not as specified, check installation of previously installed components.

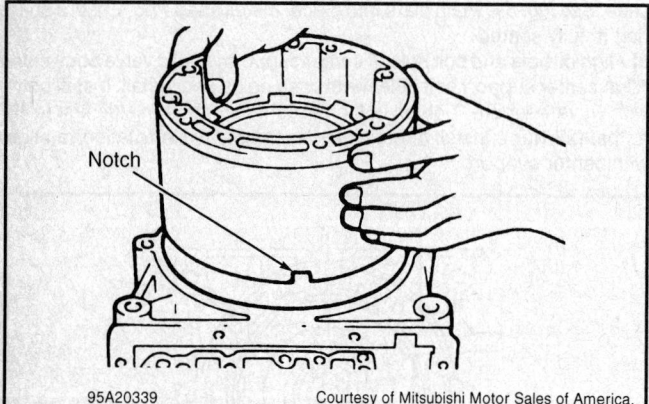

Fig. 53: Installing OD Case

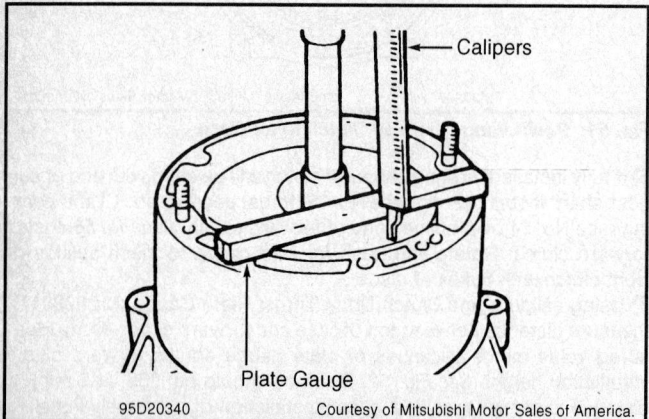

Fig. 54: Measuring OD Clutch Installed Height

10) Install "O" ring on OD case. Install converter housing to transmission case. Tighten 10-mm bolts to 25 ft. lbs. (34 N.m) and 12-mm bolts to 42 ft. lbs. (57 N.m). Install bearing race No. 2 on input shaft. Install thrust bearing No. 1 on rear of oil pump. Ensure oil seal rings and "O" ring are installed on oil pump.

11) Install oil pump over guide studs and into transmission case. Ensure thrust bearing does not fall off oil pump. Coat oil pump retaining bolts below bolt heads with Loctite (242). Remove guide studs. Install bolts and tighten to 16 ft. lbs. (21 N.m). Ensure input shaft turns freely. Using a dial indicator, check input shaft end play. Position dial indicator against end of input shaft. End play should be .012-.035" (.30-.90 mm).

12) Apply air pressure to specific oil passage to check appropriate operating components. *See Fig. 55.* Component application should be heard while applying air. Install NEW oil seals in transmission case. Lubricate oil seal lips prior to installation. Install NEW spacer on manual valve lever. Install manual valve lever shaft into case and through manual valve lever. Install NEW spring pin with slot at right angle to shaft.

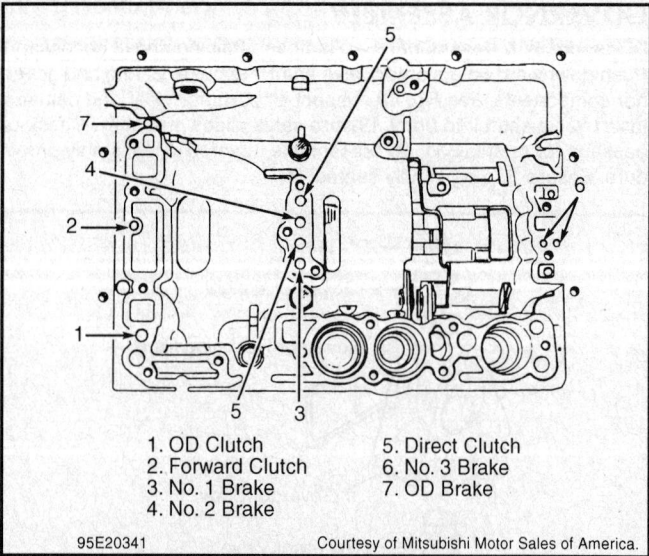

1. OD Clutch
2. Forward Clutch
3. No. 1 Brake
4. No. 2 Brake
5. Direct Clutch
6. No. 3 Brake
7. OD Brake

95E20341   Courtesy of Mitsubishi Motor Sales of America.

Fig. 55: Checking Component Piston Operation

13) Align spacer hole to hollow area of lever. Stake spacer to lever. Ensure manual valve lever shaft turns smoothly. Install parking lock pawl, pivot pin and spring in case. Install lock rod on manual valve lever and install parking lock pawl. Install parking pawl bracket on case. Ensure collar on control rod is toward front of transmission. Tighten bracket bolts to 65 INCH lbs. (7.4 N.m).

14) Check operation of parking lock pawl. Ensure output shaft is locked when manual valve lever is in "P" position. Determine proper accumulator piston locations. *See Fig. 11.* Ensure accumulator pistons are correct diameter. See ACCUMULATOR PISTON DIAMETER table. Determine proper spring free length and outer diameter for accumulator piston application. See ACCUMULATOR SPRING SPECIFICATIONS table.

ACCUMULATOR PISTON DIAMETER

Application	In. (mm)
Forward & Direct Clutch	1.252 (31.80)
No. 2 Brake	1.370 (34.80)

[1] – For accumulator piston locations, *See Fig. 11.*

ACCUMULATOR SPRING SPECIFICATIONS [1]

Application	Diameter In. (mm)	Free Length In. (mm)
Direct Clutch		
Large Spring	.610 (15.50)	1.181 (30.00)
Small Spring	.563 (14.30)	1.715 (43.56)
Forward Clutch		
Large Spring	.689 (17.50)	2.252 (57.20)
Small Spring	.500 (12.70)	1.157 (29.40)
No. 2 Brake		
Large Spring	.881 (22.39)	2.172 (55.18)
Small Spring	.636 (16.16)	1.383 (35.13)

[1] – For accumulator spring locations, *See Fig. 11.*

15) Install accumulator pistons and springs. Ensure accumulator pistons are pressed fully into bore. Install NEW "O" rings on throttle cable fitting. Install throttle cable. Align manual valve with pin on manual valve lever. Connect throttle cable to cam. Install control valve assembly and tighten bolts to 89 INCH lbs. (10 N.m). *See Fig. 8.*

16) Install gasket and oil strainer. Tighten bolts to 48 INCH lbs. (5.4 N.m). Using a plastic hammer, install oil tubes. Do not bend or damage oil tubes. Install magnets in oil pan. Ensure magnets do not interfere with oil tubes. Install NEW gasket to transmission case. Align cut part of gasket and transmission case. Install oil pan and bolts and tighten to 39 INCH lbs. (4.4 N.m).

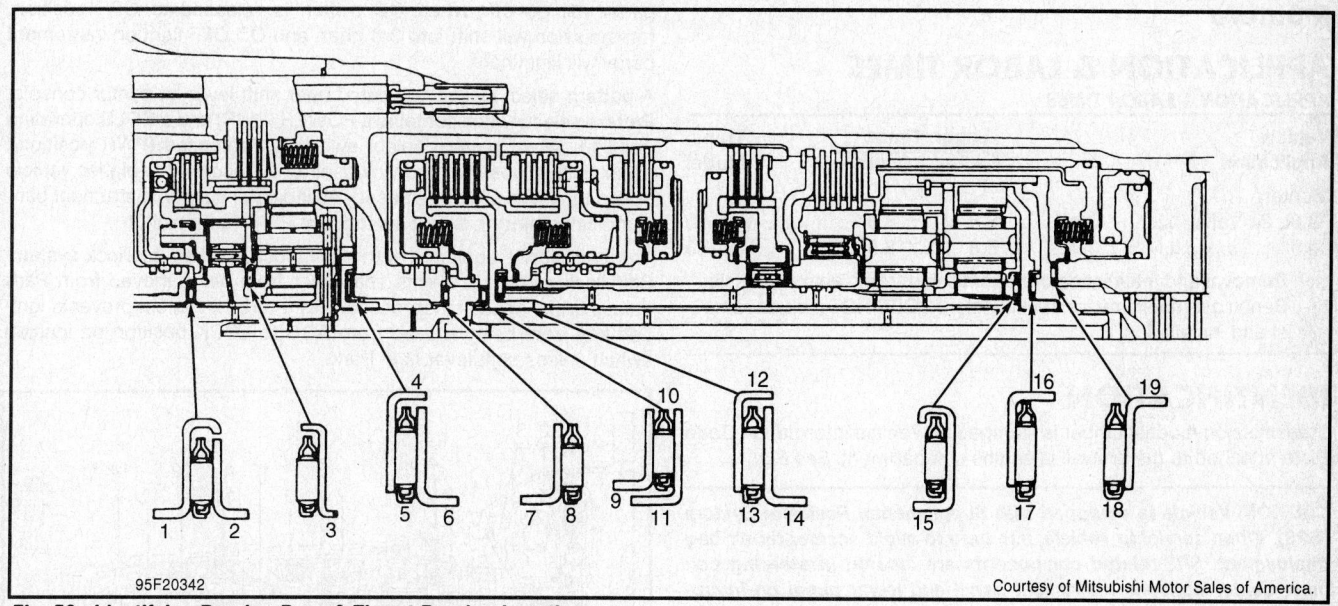

95F20342

Courtesy of Mitsubishi Motor Sales of America.

Fig. 56: Identifying Bearing Race & Thrust Bearing Locations

17) Lift governor retaining clip with screwdriver. Slide governor onto output shaft. Install retaining clip into hole on output shaft. Install lock plate and bolt. Tighten bolt to 35 INCH lbs. (3.9 N.m). Stake lock plate in place.

18) Install snap ring, lock ball, speedometer drive gear and retaining snap rings. Install overdrive solenoid. Tighten bolts to 115 INCH lbs. (13 N.m). Insert neutral safety switch on manual valve lever shaft and temporarily tighten adjusting bolt. Install grommet and NEW lock washer. Install and tighten nut to 35 INCH lbs. (3.9 N.m). Align neutral safety switch basic line and switch groove. Tighten adjusting bolt to 48 INCH lbs. (5.4 N.m). Bend over at least 2 washer tabs.

19) Install control shaft lever with spring washer and nut. Tighten nut to 61 INCH lbs. (6.9 N.m). Install wire harness and throttle cable clamp. Install torque converter. Ensure torque converter is installed correctly.

TORQUE SPECIFICATIONS
TORQUE SPECIFICATIONS

Application	Ft. Lbs. (N.m)
Center Support-To-Case Bolt	18 (25)
Converter-To-Drive Plate Bolt	20 (27)
Oil Pump-To-Case Bolt	15 (21)
Transmission Case-To-Converter Housing Bolt	
10-mm	25 (34)
12-mm	42 (57)

Application	INCH Lbs. (N.m)
Control Shaft Lever Bolt	61 (6.9)
Governor Lock Plate Bolt	35 (3.9)
Hydraulic Test Plug	65 (7.4)
Lock Pawl Bracket Bolt	65 (7.4)
Neutral Safety Switch	
Adjusting Bolt	48 (5.4)
Mounting Nut	35 (3.9)
Oil Pan Bolt	39 (4.4)
Oil Pump Housing Bolt	65 (7.4)
Oil Strainer Bolt	48 (5.4)
Overdrive Solenoid Bolt	115 (13)
Throttle Cam Bolt	65 (7.4)
Upper Valve Body-To-Lower	
Valve Body Bolt	48 (5.4)
Valve Assembly-To-Case Bolt	89 (10)

TRANSMISSION SPECIFICATIONS
TRANSMISSION SPECIFICATIONS

Application	In. (mm)
Center Support Bushing Inside Diameter	1.435 (36.46)
Direct Clutch Piston Stroke	.036-.78 (.91-1.99)
Extension Housing Bushing Inside Diameter	1.563 (39.71)
Forward Clutch Piston Stroke	.059-.115 (1.43-2.92)
Input Shaft End Play	.012-.035 (.30-.90)
No. 1 Brake Piston Stroke	.032-.068 (.80-1.73)
No. 2 Brake Piston Stroke	.040-.089 (1.01-2.25)
No. 3 Brake Pack Clearance	.024-.104 (.61-2.64)
OD Brake Piston Stroke	.026-.087 (.65-2.21)
OD Brake Snap Ring-To-Flange	
Standard Clearance	.026-.087 (.065-2.21)
OD Clutch Piston Stroke	.076-.104 (1.92-2.64)
OD Clutch Drum Bushing Inside Diameter	.911 (23.14)
OD Planetary Gear Bushing Inside Diameter	.444 (11.27)
Oil Pump Side Gear Clearance	.0008-.0020 (.020-.050)
Output Shaft Bushing Inside Diameter	.712 (18.08)
Planetary Pinion Gear Clearance	.008-.020 (.20-.50)

AUTOMATIC TRANSMISSIONS
Mitsubishi V4AW3

Montero

APPLICATION & LABOR TIMES

APPLICATION & LABOR TIMES

Vehicle Application	Labor Times [1] R & I	[2] Overhaul	Trans. Model
Montero			
3.0L 24-Valve	8.8	8.5	V4AW3
3.5L	8.8	8.5	V4AW3

[1] – Removal and installation of transmission from vehicle chassis.
[2] – Bench overhaul time for transmission. DOES NOT include removal and installation.

IDENTIFICATION

Transmission model number is stamped on Vehicle Information Code Plate attached to the firewall in engine compartment. *See Fig. 1.*

CAUTION: Vehicle is equipped with Supplemental Restraint System (SRS). When servicing vehicle, use care to avoid accidental air bag deployment. SRS-related components are located in steering column, center console, instrument panel and lower panel on instrument panel. DO NOT use electrical test equipment on these circuits. If necessary, deactivate SRS before servicing components. See AIR BAG SERVICING article in APPLICATIONS & IDENTIFICATION section.

DESCRIPTION

Automatic transmission is a 4-speed electronically controlled transmission. Solenoids that control shift changes are located in valve body. Transmission consists of lock-up torque converter, overdrive (OD) clutch, direct clutch, forward clutch, 3 planetary gears, hydraulic control system and electronic control system. *See Fig. 2.*

Solenoids are controlled by a Transmission Control Module (TCM). For electronic diagnosis, see appropriate ELECTRONIC CONTROLS article. The TCM receives information from various input devices and uses this information to control shift solenoids for transmission shifting and lock-up solenoid for torque converter lock-up.

An Overdrive (OD) switch is mounted on the shift lever. When OD switch is depressed to ON position, transmission will shift into 4th gear when shift lever is in "D" position, and OD OFF light on instrument

panel will go off. When OD switch is released to OFF position, transmission will shift into 3rd gear, and OD OFF light on instrument panel will illuminate.

A pattern select switch is located near shift lever on center console. Pattern select switch contains a POWER (PWR) and a HOLD operating position. When pattern select switch is depressed (PWR position), transmission upshifts and downshifts will occur at a higher vehicle speed than with switch released. An indicator light on instrument panel indicates pattern select switch is in PWR (on) position.

Transmission is equipped with a shift lock and key interlock system. Shift lock system prevents shift lever from being moved from Park unless brake pedal is depressed. Key interlock system prevents ignition key from being moved from ACC to LOCK position on ignition switch unless shift lever is in Park.

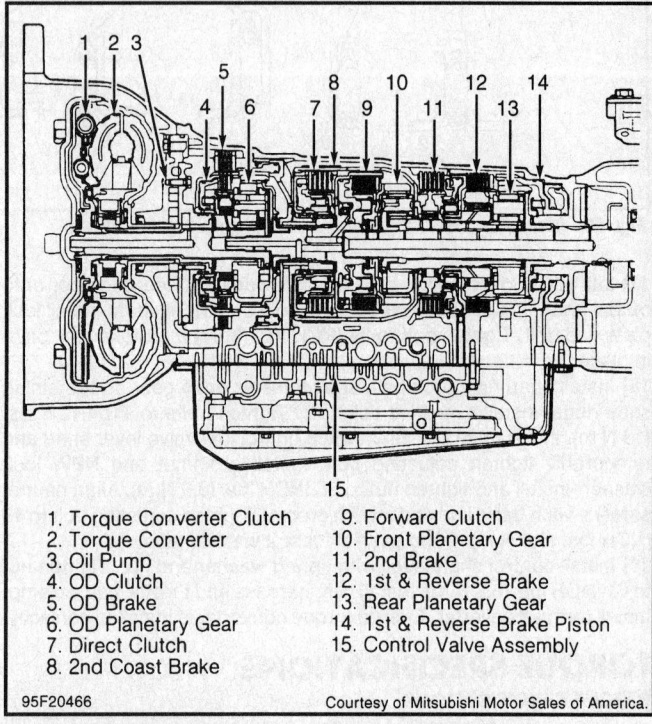

1. Torque Converter Clutch
2. Torque Converter
3. Oil Pump
4. OD Clutch
5. OD Brake
6. OD Planetary Gear
7. Direct Clutch
8. 2nd Coast Brake
9. Forward Clutch
10. Front Planetary Gear
11. 2nd Brake
12. 1st & Reverse Brake
13. Rear Planetary Gear
14. 1st & Reverse Brake Piston
15. Control Valve Assembly

95F20466   Courtesy of Mitsubishi Motor Sales of America.

Fig. 2: Identifying Transmission Component Locations

LUBRICATION & ADJUSTMENTS

NOTE: See appropriate AUTOMATIC TRANSMISSION SERVICING article in TRANSMISSION SERVICING section.

TROUBLE SHOOTING

NOTE: See MITSUBISHI V4AW3 – ELECTRONIC CONTROLS article for trouble shooting solenoids, sensors and control module. Ensure transmission fluid level is correct before diagnosing transmission.

Preliminary Checks – Ensure fluid level is correct. Inspect and adjust throttle cable, shift linkage and neutral safety switch (if necessary). Check idle speed RPM and adjust as necessary.

SYMPTOM DIAGNOSIS

Fluid Discolored Or Smells Burnt – Fluid contaminated. Faulty torque converter or transmission.
No Movement In Any Gear – Manual linkage out of adjustment. Faulty valve body, primary regulator, parking lock pawl, torque converter, OD one-way clutch, OD brake, OD clutch or OD planetary gear. Defective TCM. Converter drive plate damaged or broken. Oil pump intake screen blocked. Control shaft lever out of adjustment.

MITSUBISHI
MOTORS CORPORATION

MODEL

ENGINE   EXT
TRANS
AXLE
COLOR. INT
       OPT

95I20287   Courtesy of Mitsubishi Motor Sales of America.

Fig. 1: Locating Vehicle Identification Code Plate

Selector Lever Position Incorrect – Manual linkage out of adjustment. Faulty manual valve and lever.

Harsh Engagement Into Any Drive Position – Throttle cable out of adjustment. Faulty valve body, primary regulator, accumulator pistons, OD brake, OD clutch, OD planetary gear, torque converter, 1st and reverse brake, direct clutch or forward clutch.

Delayed 1-2, 2-3 Or 3-OD Upshifts, Or Downshifts From OD-3 Or 3-2, Then Changes Back To OD Or 3rd – Faulty valve body or solenoid valve. Defective TCM.

Slips On Any Upshift Or Slips Or Shudders On Acceleration – Manual linkage or throttle cable out of adjustment. Faulty valve body or solenoid valve.

Drag Or Binding On Upshifts – Manual linkage out of adjustment or faulty valve body.

No Lock-Up In 2nd, 3rd Or OD – Faulty valve body or solenoid valve. Defective TCM.

Harsh Downshift – Throttle cable out of adjustment or faulty accumulator pistons or valve body.

No Downshift When Coasting – Faulty valve body, electronic control or solenoid valve.

Downshifts Too Soon Or Late When Coasting – Throttle cable out of adjustment or faulty valve body, electronic control or solenoid valve.

No OD-3, 3-2 Or 2-1 Kickdown – Faulty valve body, electronic control or solenoid valve.

No Engine Braking In "2" Or "L" Position – Faulty valve body, electronic control or solenoid valve.

Vehicle Does Not Move In "R" Position – Faulty 2nd coast brake, front and rear planetary gear, direct clutch, 1st and reverse brake or OD clutch.

Vehicle Does Not Move In "D", "2" Or "L" Position – Faulty forward clutch, No. 2 one-way clutch, 2nd brake, 1st and reverse brake, 2nd coast brake or direct clutch.

No 1-2, 2-3 Or 3-OD Upshift – Faulty 2nd brake, No. 1 one-way clutch, direct clutch or OD brake.

No 2-1 Downshift – Faulty 2nd coast brake or 2nd brake.

No Lock-Up – Faulty torque converter or solenoid.

Slip Or Shudder In Any Gear – Faulty torque converter, OD one-way clutch, OD clutch, 1st and reverse brake, direct clutch, forward clutch, No. 2 one-way clutch, 2nd brake, 2nd coast brake, No. 1 one-way clutch or OD brake.

CLUTCH & BAND APPLICATION CHART

Selector Lever Position	Elements In Use
"D" (Drive)	
1st Gear	Forward Clutch, No. 2 One-Way Clutch & OD Clutch
2nd Gear	Forward Clutch, No. 1 One-Way Clutch, OD Clutch, OD One-Way Clutch & 2nd Brake
3rd Gear	Direct Clutch, Forward Clutch, OD Clutch, OD One-Way Clutch & 2nd Brake
OD (4th Gear)	Direct Clutch, Forward Clutch, OD Brake & 2nd Brake
"2" (Intermediate)	
1st Gear	Forward Clutch, No. 2 One-Way Clutch OD Clutch & OD One-Way Clutch
2nd Gear	Forward Clutch, No. 1 One-Way Clutch, OD Clutch, OD One-Way Clutch, 2nd Brake & 2nd Coast Brake
3rd Gear	Direct Clutch, Forward Clutch, OD Clutch, OD One-Way Clutch & 2nd Brake
"L" (Low)	
1st Gear	Forward Clutch, No. 2 One-Way Clutch, OD One-Way Clutch, OD Clutch & 1st & Reverse Brake
2nd Gear [1]	Forward Clutch, No. 1 One-Way Clutch, OD Clutch, OD One-Way Clutch, 2nd Brake & 2nd Coast Brake
"R" (Reverse)	Direct Clutch, OD Clutch, OD One-Way Clutch & 1st & Reverse Brake
"N" (Neutral)	OD Clutch
"P" (Park)	OD Clutch

[1] – Downshift only in "L" position and 2nd gear. No upshift.

Poor Acceleration – Faulty torque converter, OD clutch, OD planetary gear, OD brake, 2nd coast brake, direct clutch, 2nd brake, 1st and reverse brake or forward clutch.

Engine Stalls When Starting Off Or Stopping – Faulty torque converter.

Vehicle Does Not Hold In "P" Position – Manual linkage faulty or out of adjustment. Defective parking lock pawl assembly.

TESTING

ELECTRICAL TESTING

Electrical tests should be performed prior to hydraulic testing to ensure problem is not in electrical circuit. See MITSUBISHI V4AW3 – ELECTRONIC CONTROLS article.

PRELIMINARY CHECKS

Before testing transmission, perform following procedures:
- Ensure fluid level is correct.
- Inspect and adjust throttle cable.
- Ensure battery is fully charged for accurate testing.
- Adjust shift linkage.
- Adjust neutral safety switch.
- Inspect idle speed RPM.

COMPONENT & SYSTEM TESTING

A/T FLUID TEMPERATURE SWITCH

1) Remove fluid temperature switch, located to rear of neutral safety switch. Immerse switch in container of ATF up to top threaded portion of switch. Using a DVOM, check continuity between switch terminals. Continuity should not exist when fluid temperature is 257°F (125°C) or less.

2) When fluid is heated to 289-304°F (143-151°C), continuity should exist. Replace switch if necessary. Apply thread sealant to fluid temperature switch threads and install in transmission.

OVERDRIVE SWITCH

Using a screwdriver, remove overdrive switch from selector lever, located below selector lever button. Using a DVOM, check continuity between overdrive switch terminals No. 3 and 5 with switch in ON position. Continuity should exist. With switch in OFF position, check continuity between terminals No. 3 and 4. Continuity should exist. If continuity is not as specified, replace switch. See Fig. 3.

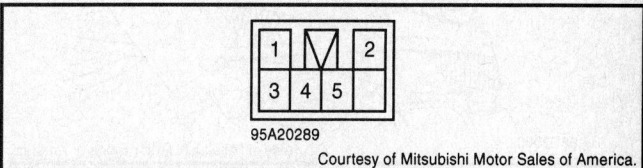

95A20289

Courtesy of Mitsubishi Motor Sales of America.

Fig. 3: Identifying Overdrive Switch Terminals

PATTERN SELECT SWITCH

Using a screwdriver, remove pattern select switch from console. Switch is located at rear of selector lever, to right of emergency brake handle. Using a DVOM, check continuity between pattern select switch terminals No. 1 and 2, with switch in HOLD position. Continuity should exist. With switch in POWER position, check continuity between terminals No. 1 and 6. Continuity should exist. If continuity is not as specified, replace switch. See Fig. 4.

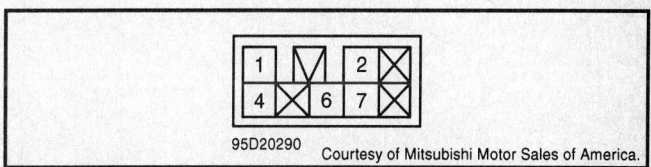

95D20290

Courtesy of Mitsubishi Motor Sales of America.

Fig. 4: Identifying Pattern Select Switch Terminals

KEY INTERLOCK SYSTEM

1) With ignition switch in LOCK position and brake pedal depressed, ensure selector lever cannot be moved from "P" to any other position. Ensure selector lever button cannot be pushed. With ignition switch in ACC position, brake pedal depressed and selector lever button pushed, ensure selector lever can be moved from "P" position to any other position. Ensure selector lever moves smoothly.

2) Ensure ignition key cannot be turned to LOCK position at all selector lever positions other than "P". Ensure ignition key turns smoothly to LOCK position when selector lever is set to "P" and selector lever button is released. If key interlock system is not as specified, adjust key interlock cable. See KEY INTERLOCK CABLE under ADJUSTMENTS.

SHIFT LOCK SYSTEM

1) With ignition switch in ACC position, brake pedal released and selector lever button pushed, ensure selector lever cannot be moved from "P" to any other position. With ignition switch in ACC position, brake pedal depressed and selector lever button pushed, ensure selector lever can be moved from "P" position to any other position.

2) With selector lever in "R" position, ignition switch in ACC position, brake pedal released and selector button pushed, ensure selector lever can be moved from "R" to "P" position. If shift lock system is not as specified, adjust shift lock cable. See SHIFT LOCK CABLE under ADJUSTMENTS.

ADJUSTMENTS

KEY INTERLOCK CABLE

Remove front console assembly. Move selector lever to "P". Turn ignition switch to LOCK position. Loosen nut securing key interlock cable. *See Fig. 5.* Gently push lock cam until pin stops in direction of arrow, then tighten nut to 106 INCH lbs. (12 N.m) to secure cable. Install front console assembly.

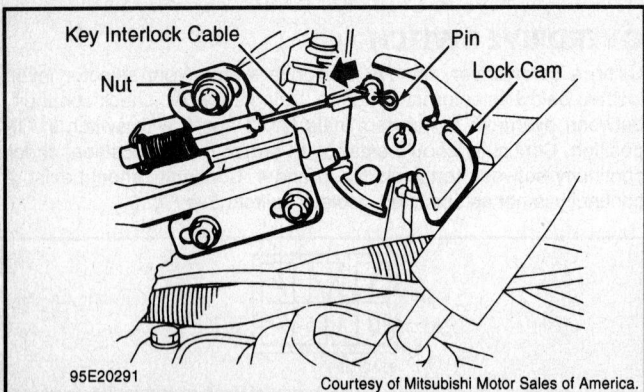

95E20291   Courtesy of Mitsubishi Motor Sales of America.

Fig. 5: Adjusting Key Interlock Cable

SHIFT LOCK CABLE

Remove front console assembly. Move selector lever to "P". Loosen nuts securing shift lock cable. *See Fig. 6.* Adjust shift lock cable so end of cable (Red mark) sits between lobe of lock cam, then tighten nut to 44 INCH lbs. (5 N.m) to secure cable. Install front console assembly.

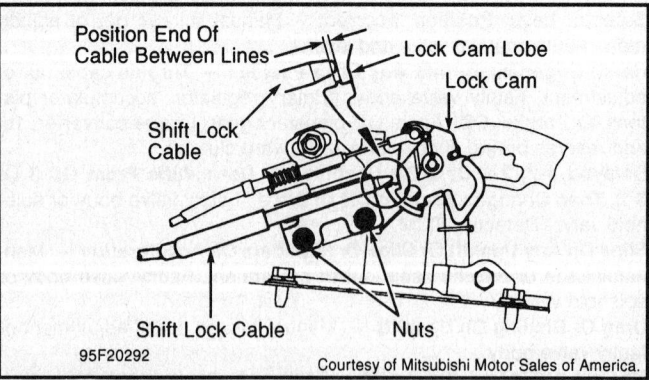

95F20292   Courtesy of Mitsubishi Motor Sales of America.

Fig. 6: Adjusting Shift Lock Cable

TESTING
ROAD TEST

NOTE: Perform road test to ensure transmission shift points are at specified speeds. See Fig. 7. Broken lines in shift point chart indicates downshifts, and solid lines indicate upshifts.

"D" Position Test – 1) Engine and transmission must be at normal operating temperature. Shift transmission into "D" position with OD switch in ON position. Ensure transfer case is in 2H (2WD-High) position. Depress accelerator pedal to full throttle. Ensure all upshifts and downshifts occur at specified points. *See Fig. 7.*

2) Ensure lock-up occurs. Lightly depress accelerator pedal. If excessive increase in engine RPM exists, lock-up did not occur.

NOTE: A 3-OD upshift will not occur with a throttle valve opening greater than 86 percent or if coolant temperature is below 122°F (50°C). A OD-3 kickdown is always possible with throttle valve opening of 86 percent or greater. Lock-up does not occur at coolant temperatures below 158°F (70°C).

3) Check for shift shock and slippage during all upshifts. Drive vehicle in "D" and OD. Check for abnormal noise and vibration. While driving in OD, "D" and 2nd gear, ensure kickdown speeds in 2-1, 3-2 and OD-3 are within specification. Check for shock and slippage during kickdown.

"D" Position Test Results

- **No 1-2 Upshift:** Defective No. 2 solenoid or stuck 1-2 shift valve.
- **No 2-3 Upshift:** Defective No. 1 solenoid or stuck 2-3 shift valve.
- **No 3-OD Upshift With Throttle Opening Less Than 86 Percent:** Stuck 3-4 shift valve. If shift point is not within specification, check for misadjusted throttle cable or defective throttle valve, OD switch or solenoid valve.
- **Lock-Up Does Not Occur:** Stuck lock-up solenoid valve.
- **Excessive Shock & Slippage:** High line pressure, defective accumulator or check balls. Abnormal noise and vibration may be caused by unbalance in drive shaft, differential, tires or torque converter.

"2" Position Test – Shift transmission to "2" position. With accelerator pedal held at full throttle, check for proper 1-2 upshift at specified throttle positions. *See Fig. 7.* While driving vehicle in 2nd gear, release accelerator and check engine braking effect. If engine braking does not exist, 2nd coast brake is defective.

"L" Position Test – While driving vehicle in "L" position, check for failure to upshift to 2nd gear. Check engine braking effect when accelerator is released. If engine braking does not exist, 1st and reverse brake is defective.

"R" Position Test – Shift vehicle to "R" position. Accelerate vehicle and check for transmission slippage.

"P" Position Test – Stop vehicle on incline of 5 degrees or steeper. Shift vehicle to "P" position and release parking brake. Ensure parking lock pawl prevents vehicle from moving.

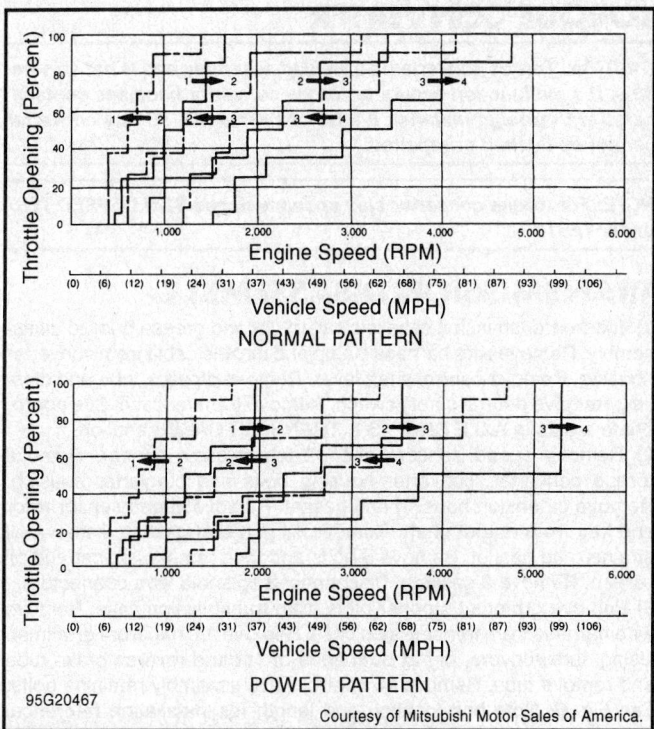

Fig. 7: *Identifying Transmission Shift Points*

STALL SPEED TEST

1) Operate engine and transmission at normal operating temperature. Connect tachometer to vehicle and ensure it is visible to driver. Apply parking brake and block front wheels.

CAUTION: DO NOT maintain stall speed RPM for more than 5 seconds. If performing more than one stall speed test, operate engine at about 1000 RPM in Neutral for 2 minutes to cool transmission fluid before performing next test.

---

2) Start engine, apply brakes and place transmission in "D" position. Depress accelerator to full throttle and note maximum RPM obtained. Repeat test in "R" position. Stall speed should be 2100-2600 RPM.

Stall Speed Test Results

- **Stall Speed Is Same In Both Positions, But Less Than Specified:** Engine output may be insufficient or defective stator one-way clutch. Throttle valve is not opening fully.

NOTE: If stall speed RPM is greater than 600 RPM lower than specification, torque converter may be faulty.

- **Stall Speed High In "D" Position:** Low line pressure, slipping forward clutch or defective No. 2 or OD one-way clutch.
- **Stall Speed High In "R" Position:** Low line pressure, direct clutch slipping, 1st and reverse brake slipping or defective OD one-way clutch.
- **Stall Speed High In Both Positions:** Low line pressure, improper fluid level or defective OD one-way clutch.

HYDRAULIC PRESSURE TEST

NOTE: Hydraulic pressure test should be performed with transmission fluid at normal operating temperature of 158-176°F (70-80°C).

Line Pressure Test – 1) Ensure transmission fluid is at normal operating temperature. Connect pressure gauge to line pressure test port on transmission. See Fig. 8.

2) Connect tachometer to vehicle and ensure it is visible to driver. Block all 4 wheels and fully apply parking brake. Start engine and ensure idle speed is adjusted to specification.

3) Apply service brake and shift transmission to "D" position. Check line pressure at idle and record pressure reading. Accelerate vehicle to stall speed and record line pressure reading.

4) Repeat test procedure in "R" position. If line pressures are not as specified, check throttle cable adjustment. Adjust throttle cable (if necessary), and repeat test procedure and record pressure readings. Compare all readings to specification. See LINE PRESSURE SPECIFICATIONS table.

LINE PRESSURE SPECIFICATIONS

Engine Speed	"D" Position psi (kPa)	"R" Position psi (kPa)
Idle Speed	62-71 (430-490)	75-90 (520-620)
Stall Speed	165-202 (1140-1390)	203-254 (1400-1750)

Line Pressure Test Results

- **Line Pressure High In Both Positions:** Defective regulator valve or throttle valve, or throttle cable out of adjustment.
- **Line Pressure Low In Both Positions:** Defective oil pump, regulator valve, throttle valve or OD clutch, or throttle cable out of adjustment.
- **Line Pressure Low In "D" Position Only:** Defective forward clutch, OD clutch or fluid leak in "D" position circuit.
- **Line Pressure Low In "R" Position Only:** Defective direct clutch, OD clutch, 1st and reverse brake or fluid leak in "R" position circuit.

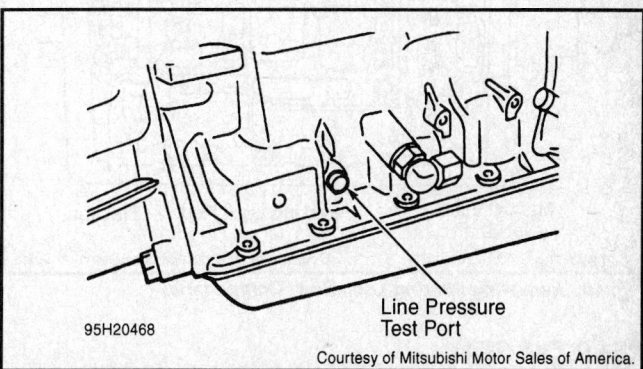

Line Pressure Test Port

Fig. 8: *Identifying Transmission Hydraulic Pressure Test Port*

ON-VEHICLE SERVICE

CONTROL VALVE ASSEMBLY

Removal – 1) Remove drain plug and drain ATF. Remove oil pan and gasket. Remove oil strainer and gasket. Remove 5 bolts and then remove spacer and oil screen. Remove 2 gaskets. Disconnect 3 solenoid wire connectors.

2) Remove grommet stopper plate from transmission case. Remove wire harness from transmission case. Using screwdrivers, pry at both ends of 1st and reverse brake tube and remove tube. Remove 16 control valve assembly retaining bolts. See Fig. 9. Note bolt location and

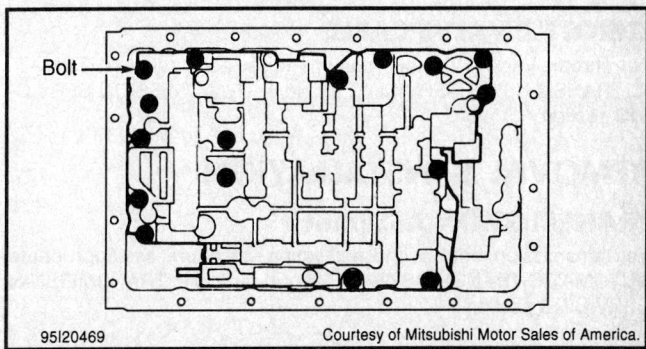

Bolt

Fig. 9: *Identifying Control Valve Assembly Bolt Locations*

length for installation reference. Slightly lower control valve assembly and disconnect throttle cable from throttle cam. Remove control valve assembly.

Installation – To install, reverse removal procedure. Ensure manual shift lever in transmission case aligns with manual valve of control valve assembly. Connect throttle cable to throttle cam. Tighten control valve assembly bolts to 89 INCH lbs. (10 N.m). Tighten oil pan bolts to 71 INCH lbs. (8 N.m). Fill transmission with ATF to proper fluid level.

PARKING LOCK PAWL

Removal & Installation – 1) Remove control valve assembly. Remove parking lock pawl bolts and bracket. Remove parking lock rod from manual valve lever. Remove parking pawl torsion spring. Pull out pivot pin and remove parking lock pawl. See Fig. 10.

2) To install, reverse removal procedures. Prior to installing parking lock pawl bracket bolts, push lock rod forward. Finger tighten bolts and ensure parking lock pawl operates smoothly. Tighten bracket bolts to 65 INCH lbs. (7.4 N.m).

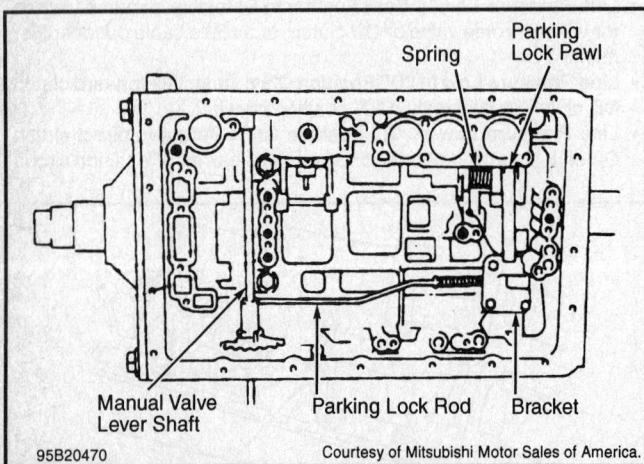

Fig. 10: Removing Parking Lock Pawl Components

REAR OIL SEAL

Removal & Installation – 1) Raise and support vehicle. Place reference marks on drive shaft and companion flange. Remove drive shaft. Clean seal surrounding areas. Using appropriate seal remover, remove oil seal from extension housing. Note direction of seal installation.

2) Using appropriate seal installer, install seal in extension housing until seal bottoms. To complete installation, reverse removal procedure. Fill transmission to proper level.

NEUTRAL SAFETY SWITCH

For neutral safety switch adjustment, see appropriate AUTOMATIC TRANSMISSION SERVICING article in TRANSMISSION SERVICING section.

THROTTLE VALVE CABLE

For Throttle Valve (TV) cable adjustment, see appropriate AUTOMATIC TRANSMISSION SERVICING article in TRANSMISSION SERVICING section.

REMOVAL & INSTALLATION

TRANSMISSION ASSEMBLY

For transmission removal and installation procedure, see appropriate AUTOMATIC TRANSMISSION REMOVAL article in TRANSMISSION SERVICING section.

TRANSFER CASE

For transfer case removal and installation, see appropriate TRANSFER CASES article in AXLE SHAFTS & TRANSFER CASES section.

TORQUE CONVERTER

CAUTION: Torque converter is a welded assembly and is not serviceable. If a malfunction occurs or torque converter becomes contaminated with foreign material, it MUST be replaced. Torque converter cannot be flushed or repaired.

NOTE: For torque converter stall speed test, see STALL SPEED TEST under TESTING.

TRANSMISSION DISASSEMBLY

1) Ensure transmission case is clean of dirt and grease prior to disassembly. Remove wire harness clamp and throttle cable from converter housing. Remove control shaft lever. Remove dipstick tube and dipstick. Remove neutral safety switch. Remove transfer case. See appropriate article in AXLE SHAFTS & TRANSFER CASES section.

2) Remove speed sensors and oil temperature sensor. Remove torque converter, converter housing bolts and converter housing. Remove extension housing and gasket. Remove speed sensor rotor and key from output shaft. Remove oil pan and gasket. Remove oil strainer and gasket. Remove 5 bolts and then remove spacer and oil screen. Remove 2 gaskets. Disconnect 3 solenoid wire connectors.

3) Remove grommet stopper plate from transmission case. Remove wire harness from transmission case. Remove "O" ring from grommet. Using screwdrivers, pry at both ends of 1st and reverse brake tube and remove tube. Remove 16 control valve assembly retaining bolts. See Fig. 9. Note bolt location and length for installation reference. Slightly lower control valve assembly and disconnect throttle valve cable from throttle cam. Remove control valve assembly.

4) Place shop cloth over accumulator pistons. Using compressed air, remove accumulator pistons and springs from transmission case. See Figs. 11-13. Note location of springs and pistons for reassembly reference.

5) Remove throttle valve cable from transmission case. Remove parking lock pawl bracket. Disconnect parking rod from manual valve lever. Remove "E" ring from shaft. Carefully remove lock pawl, spring and shaft. Drive out roll pin. Remove manual valve lever shaft through transmission case. Remove manual valve lever. See Fig. 10.

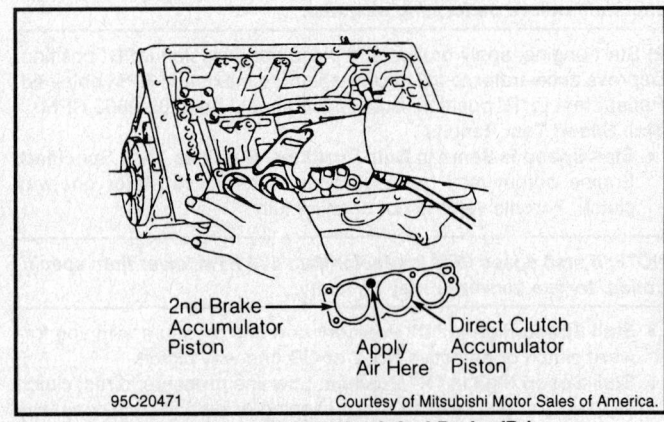

Fig. 11: Removing Direct Clutch (C₂) & 2nd Brake (B₂) Accumulator Pistons & Springs

6) Remove oil pump from transmission case using appropriate puller. While holding input shaft, remove OD planetary gear with OD clutch from case. Remove bearing and race. Remove OD planetary ring gear. Remove bearing and race.

7) Check OD brake piston stroke. Install dial indicator on OD brake piston. Measure stroke by applying 57-114 psi (4-8 kg/cm²) compressed air to opening in case. See Fig. 14. Piston stroke should be .055-.067" (1.40-1.70 mm). If piston stroke is not within specifications, inspect discs.

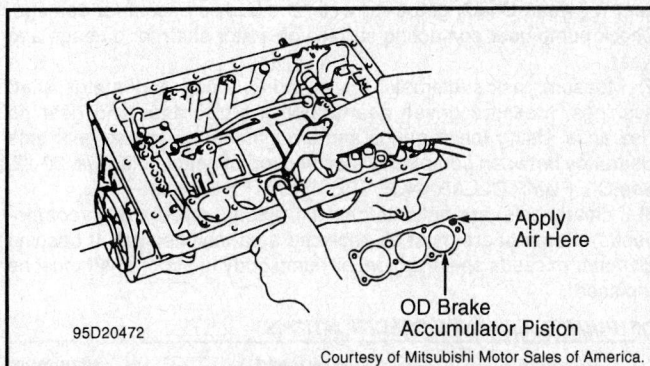

95D20472

Apply Air Here

OD Brake Accumulator Piston

Courtesy of Mitsubishi Motor Sales of America.

Fig. 12: Removing OD Brake (B₀) Accumulator Piston & Springs

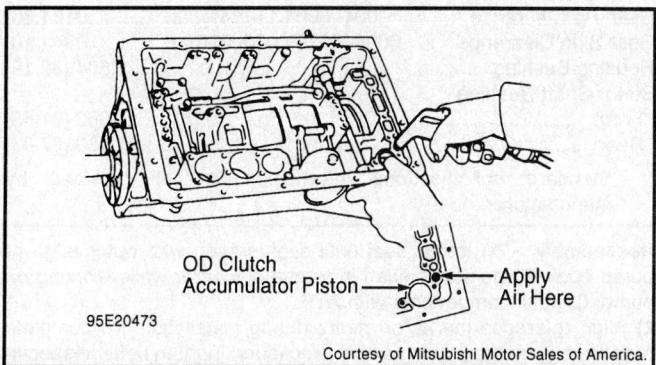

OD Clutch Accumulator Piston — Apply Air Here

95E20473

Courtesy of Mitsubishi Motor Sales of America.

Fig. 13: Removing OD Clutch (C₀) Accumulator Piston & Springs

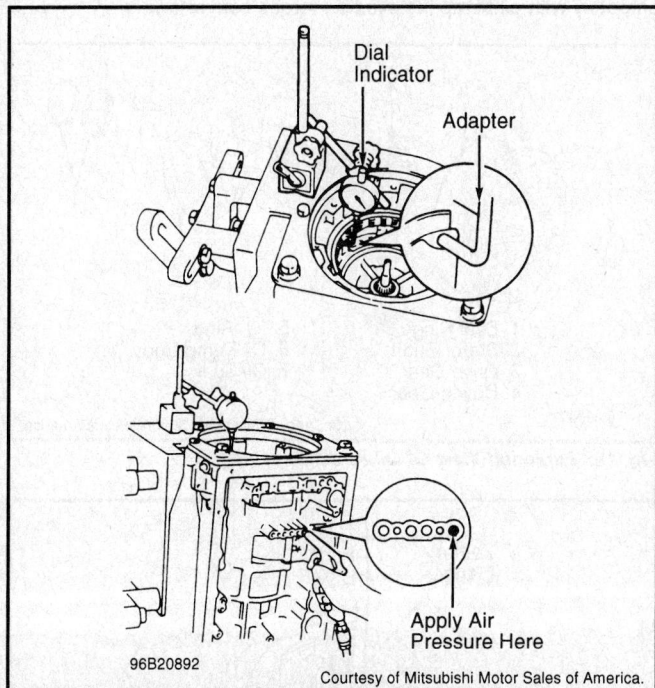

Dial Indicator

Adapter

Apply Air Pressure Here

96B20892

Courtesy of Mitsubishi Motor Sales of America.

Fig. 14: Measuring OD Brake Piston Stroke

8) Remove snap ring. Remove OD brake clutch pack flanges, plates and discs. Note number and location of all components. Place reference mark on 2nd coast brake piston rod. Apply 57-114 psi (4.8 kg/cm²) of air at opening of transmission case. Using wire gauge, measure clearance between reference mark and case. *See Fig. 15.* Stroke should be .059-.118" (1.49-3.00 mm). If stroke is not within specification, inspect brake band.

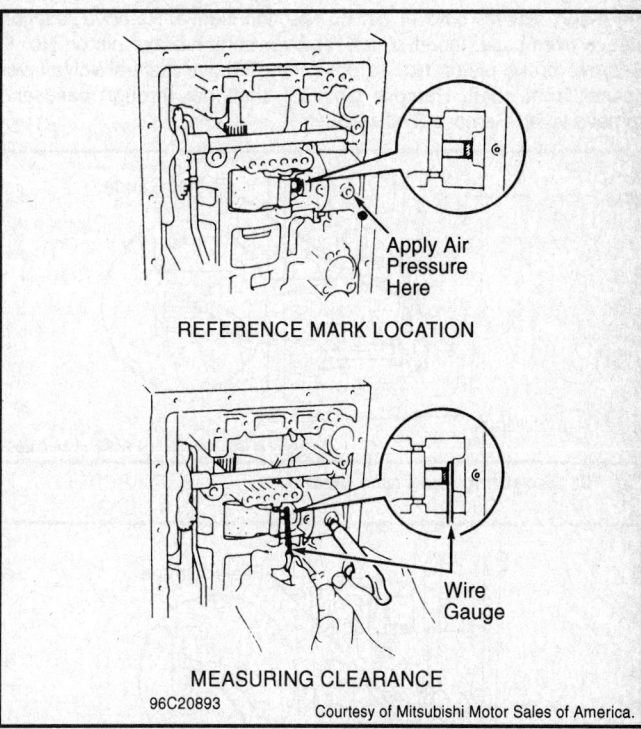

Apply Air Pressure Here

REFERENCE MARK LOCATION

Wire Gauge

MEASURING CLEARANCE

96C20893

Courtesy of Mitsubishi Motor Sales of America.

Fig. 15: Measuring 2nd Coast Brake Piston Stroke

9) Remove 2nd coast brake cover snap ring. Carefully apply air pressure to oil hole as in previous step to remove cover, piston and spring. Remove thrust bearing and race from OD support assembly. Remove OD support-to-case bolts. Remove snap ring. Using appropriate puller, remove OD support assembly. Remove race from rear of support assembly. Remove direct clutch with forward clutch from case. Remove bearings and race from forward clutch assembly.

10) Remove "E" ring from 2nd coast brake band pin and remove pin. Remove 2nd coast brake band. Remove race from front planetary ring gear. Remove front planetary ring gear. Remove thrust bearing and race from inside ring gear. Remove race from front planetary gear. Place transmission on end and support output shaft on wooden blocks. Remove snap ring located above front planetary gear. Remove front planetary gear.

11) Remove sun gear drum and one-way clutch. Check clutch pack clearance of second brake. *See Fig. 16.* Clearance should be .024-.078" (.62-1.98 mm). If clearance is not within specifications, inspect condition of clutch discs. Remove flange snap ring. Remove flange, plates and discs. Note number and location of all components.

12) Remove 3 bolts and then remove parking lock pawl bracket. Remove parking lock rod, spring, shaft and pawl. Check clutch pack clearance of 1st and reverse brake. *See Fig. 17.* Clearance should be .028-.048" (.70-1.22 mm). If clearance is not within specifications, inspect condition of discs.

13) Remove 2nd brake piston sleeve. Remove rear planetary gear snap ring. Remove rear planetary gear, 2nd brake drum, 1st and reverse brake pack and output shaft as an assembly. Remove thrust bearing and race from case. Remove 2nd brake drum assembly.

14) Remove 1st and reverse brake cushion plate, flange, plates and discs. Note number and location of all components. Remove leaf spring from case. Remove brake drum gasket from case.

15) Ensure 1st and reverse brake pistons move smoothly when applying compressed air into case. *See Fig. 18.* Disassemble 1st and reverse brake piston. Install appropriate compressor on spring retainer and compress return spring assembly. Remove snap ring. Remove return spring assembly. Using compressed air, remove 1st and reverse brake piston No. 2. *See Fig. 18.*

16) Insert sleeve remover behind reaction sleeve. Remove reaction sleeve from case. Insert piston remover behind brake piston No. 1. Remove brake piston No. 1 from case. Remove manual valve lever spacer from shaft. Remove pin. Pull shaft out through case and remove lever. Remove 2 oil seals.

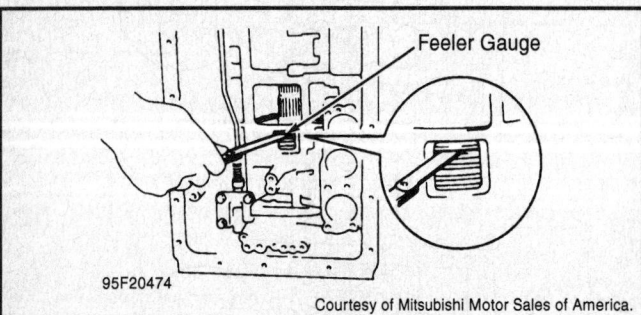

95F20474

Courtesy of Mitsubishi Motor Sales of America.

Fig. 16: Measuring 2nd Brake Clearance

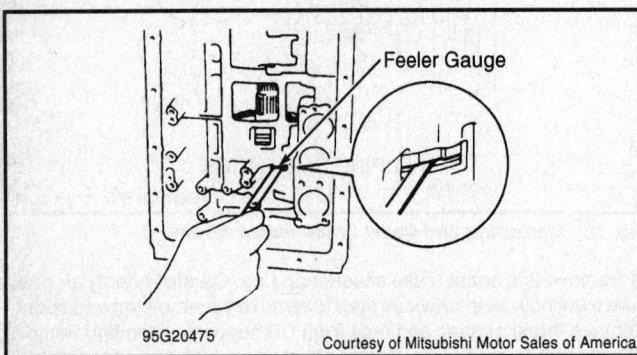

95G20475

Courtesy of Mitsubishi Motor Sales of America.

Fig. 17: Measuring 1st & Reverse Brake Clearance

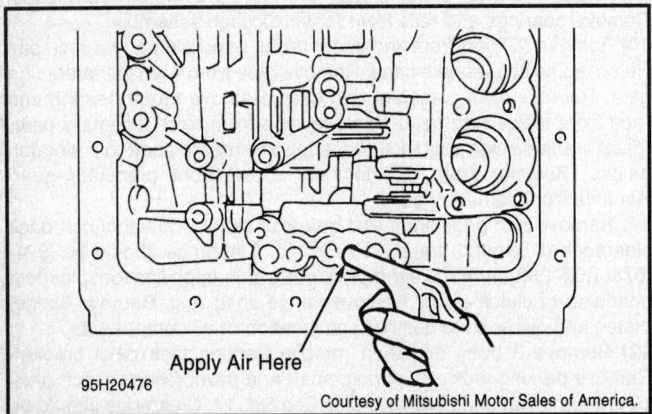

Apply Air Here

95H20476

Courtesy of Mitsubishi Motor Sales of America.

Fig. 18: Checking & Removing 1st & Reverse Brake Pistons

COMPONENT DISASSEMBLY & REASSEMBLY

OIL PUMP

Disassembly – 1) Remove seal rings from rear of stator shaft. Remove bolts from rear of pump assembly. Remove stator shaft from pump body. See Fig. 19.

2) Place reference mark on drive and driven gears for reassembly reference and remove from pump body. If oil seal requires replacement, pry seal from body.

Cleaning & Inspection – 1) Clean all components in solvent. Dry with compressed air. Inspect contacting surfaces between body and driven gear for wear. Check gears for wear and body crescent for damage. Check pump gear contacting surface on stator shaft for damage and wear.

2) Measure inside diameter of oil pump body and stator shaft bushings. Measure driven gear-to-housing clearance and gear tip clearance. Using feeler gauge and straightedge, measure gear side clearance between pump body face and top of gears. See Figs. 20-22. See OIL PUMP CLEARANCE SPECIFICATIONS table.

3) If clearance(s) are not within specifications, replace worn component(s). Pump gears must be replaced as a matched set. If bushing diameter exceeds specification, oil pump body or stator shaft must be replaced.

OIL PUMP CLEARANCE SPECIFICATIONS

Application	Standard In. (mm)	Maximum In. (mm)
Gear-To-Body	.003-.006 (.07-.15)	.012 (.30)
Gear Tip Clearance	.004-.006 (.11-.14)	.012 (.30)
Gear Side Clearance	.0008-.0020 (.020-.050)	.004 (.10)
Housing Bushing	[1]	1.504 (38.19)
Stator Shaft Bushing		
Front	[1]	.850 (21.58)
Rear	[1]	1.066 (27.08)

[1] – Standard specifications information is not provided by manufacturer.

Reassembly – 1) Install seal until seal is even with outer edge of pump body. Place stator shaft in torque converter while working on pump. Coat all components with ATF.

2) Align reference marks on gears during installation. To complete reassembly, reverse disassembly procedure. Tighten bolts to specification. DO NOT over expand seal rings during installation. Ensure seal rings move smoothly after installation. Ensure drive gear rotates smoothly with oil pump installed on torque converter.

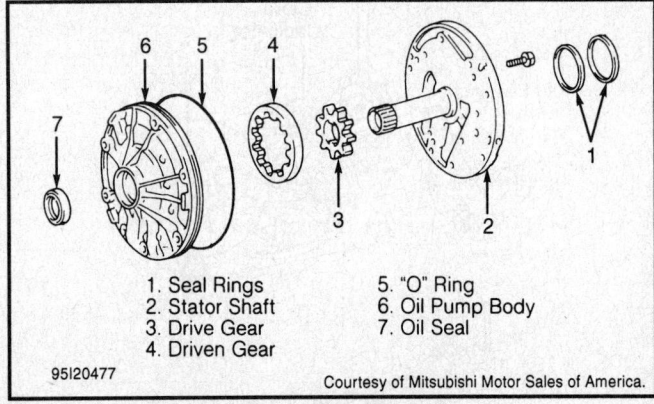

1. Seal Rings
2. Stator Shaft
3. Drive Gear
4. Driven Gear
5. "O" Ring
6. Oil Pump Body
7. Oil Seal

95I20477

Courtesy of Mitsubishi Motor Sales of America.

Fig. 19: Exploded View Of Oil Pump Assembly

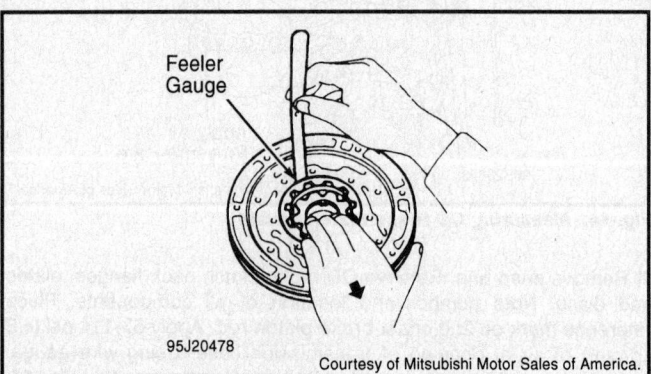

Feeler Gauge

95J20478

Courtesy of Mitsubishi Motor Sales of America.

Fig. 20: Measuring Oil Pump Gear-To-Body Clearance

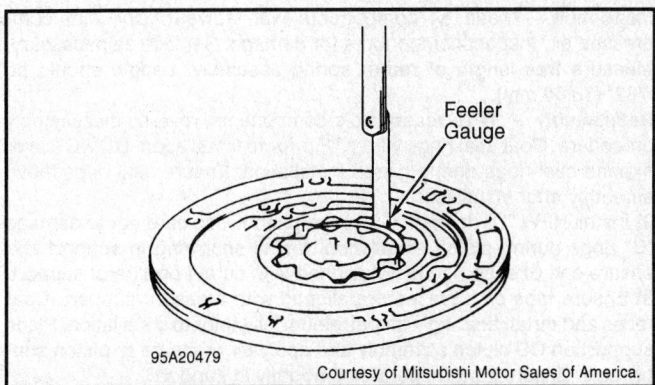

95A20479

Courtesy of Mitsubishi Motor Sales of America.

Fig. 21: Measuring Oil Pump Gear Tip Clearance

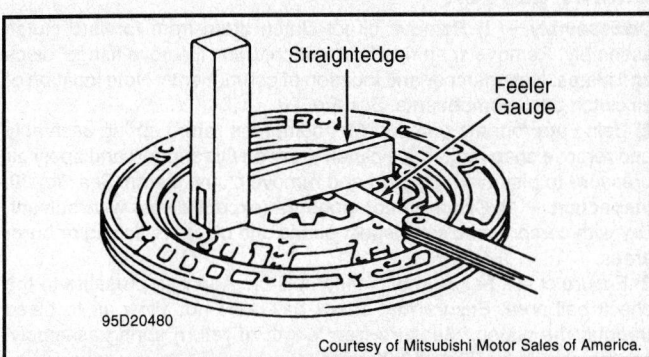

95D20480

Courtesy of Mitsubishi Motor Sales of America.

Fig. 22: Measuring Oil Pump Gear Side Clearance

OD PLANETARY GEAR, OD CLUTCH & OD ONE-WAY CLUTCH

Disassembly – 1) One-way clutch operation should be checked prior to disassembly. Hold clutch drum and rotate input shaft clockwise. See Fig. 23. Input shaft should rotate freely clockwise and lock counterclockwise.

2) Remove clutch drum from planetary gear. Remove thrust bearing and race from clutch drum. Remove snap ring, flange, discs and plates from clutch drum. Note number and location of components. See Fig. 24.

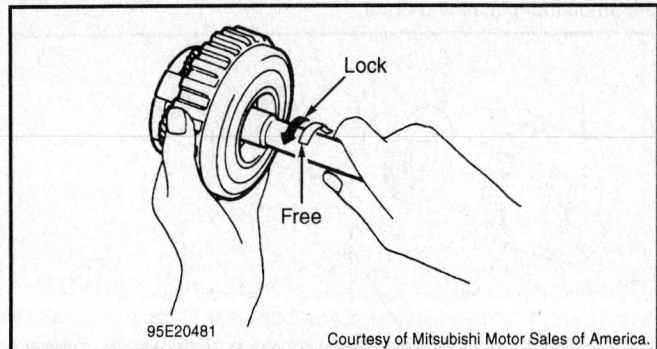

95E20481

Courtesy of Mitsubishi Motor Sales of America.

Fig. 23: Checking OD One-Way Clutch Operation

3) Using appropriate compressor, compress return spring assembly and remove snap ring. Release compressor and remove return spring assembly. Place oil pump on torque converter. Place clutch drum on oil pump. Hold clutch piston and carefully apply air pressure to oil pump port. See Fig. 25. Remove OD clutch piston.

4) Remove snap ring and ring gear flange from planetary ring gear. Remove bearing races and thrust bearing from rear of planetary gear. Remove snap ring, retaining plate, one-way clutch assembly and thrust washer from planetary gear. Remove one-way clutch from outer race.

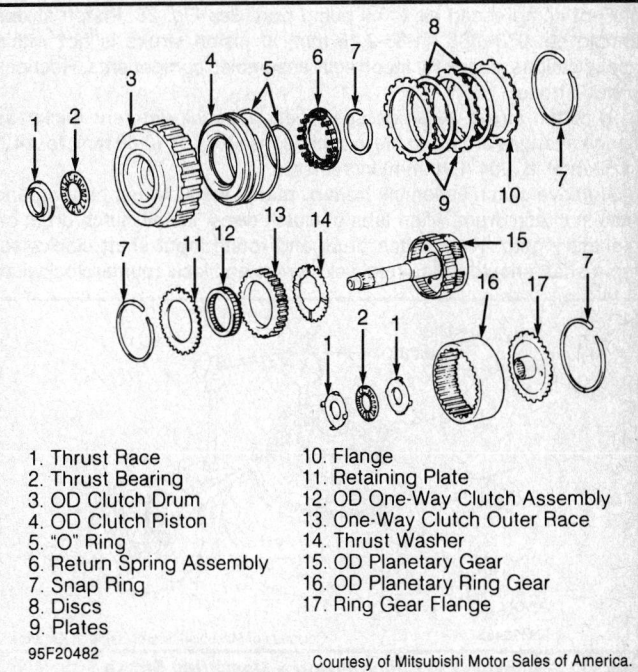

1. Thrust Race
2. Thrust Bearing
3. OD Clutch Drum
4. OD Clutch Piston
5. "O" Ring
6. Return Spring Assembly
7. Snap Ring
8. Discs
9. Plates
10. Flange
11. Retaining Plate
12. OD One-Way Clutch Assembly
13. One-Way Clutch Outer Race
14. Thrust Washer
15. OD Planetary Gear
16. OD Planetary Ring Gear
17. Ring Gear Flange

95F20482

Courtesy of Mitsubishi Motor Sales of America.

Fig. 24: Exploded View Of OD Planetary Gear & OD Clutch Assembly

Inspection – 1) Clean all components (except discs) with solvent. Dry with compressed air. Inspect plates and discs for flaking or burnt areas. Ensure check ball does not allow air to bleed through piston.

2) Measure inside diameter of clutch drum bushing and planetary gear bushing. Maximum diameter for OD clutch drum bushing is 1.067" (27.11 mm). Maximum diameter for OD planetary gear bushing is .444" (11.27 mm). Replace components if damaged or not within specifications.

3) Measure planetary pinion gear thrust clearance. Standard clearance should be .008-.024" (.20-.60 mm). Maximum clearance is .039" (1.00 mm). If clearance is not within specifications, replace planetary gear assembly. Check OD clutch return spring free length. Include spring seat in measurement. Standard free length is .622" (15.80 mm).

4) Measure OD clutch disc thickness at several points. Average OD clutch disc thickness limit is .072" (1.83 mm).

CAUTION: Clutch discs should be soaked in ATF for 2 hours prior to installation. Coat all parts with ATF prior to installation. Coat thrust bearings and races with petroleum jelly prior to installation.

Reassembly – 1) Position planetary gear with input shaft pointing upward. Install thrust washer in planetary gear with grooved side facing upward. Install one-way clutch into outer race with flanged side facing upward. See Fig. 26.

2) Install one-way clutch assembly on planetary gear. Install retaining plate and snap ring. Install race on back of planetary gear. Race tabs must be engaged in planetary gear.

3) Install ring gear flange and snap ring. Install thrust bearing and race in planetary ring gear. Race tabs must be engaged in ring gear. Coat "O" rings with ATF and install on clutch piston. Carefully install clutch piston in clutch drum. Install return spring assembly. Using appropriate compressor, compress return spring assembly and install snap ring. Ensure ring is fully seated.

CAUTION: Ensure ends of snap ring do not align with claw area on spring retainer of return spring assembly.

4) With clutch drum open area facing upward, install plates and discs, starting with plate. Install flange with flat end facing toward disc. Install snap ring. Place oil pump on torque converter. Place clutch drum on oil pump. Measure piston stroke while applying 57-114 psi (4-8 kg/

cm²) of compressed air to oil pump port. *See Fig. 25*. Piston stroke should be .073-.085" (1.85-2.15 mm). If piston stroke is not within specifications, check for incorrectly assembled components. Recheck piston stroke.

5) If piston stroke exceeds specification, install different thickness flange. Flanges are available in thicknesses of .122" (3.09 mm) to .142" (3.60 mm) in .004" (.10 mm) increments.

6) Remove clutch assembly from oil pump. Install thrust bearing and race in clutch drum. Align tabs of clutch discs. Install clutch drum on planetary gear. Hold clutch drum and rotate input shaft clockwise. Input shaft should rotate freely clockwise and lock counterclockwise.

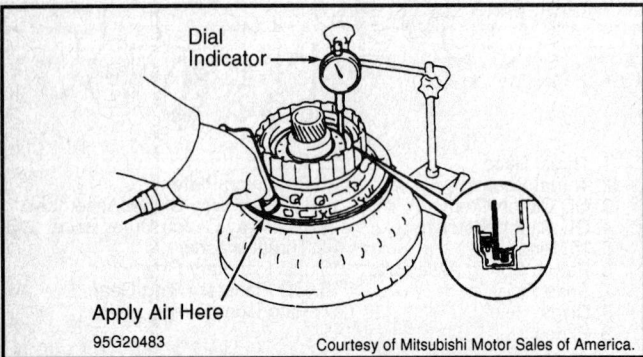

Fig. 25: *Removing OD Clutch Piston & Measuring Stroke*

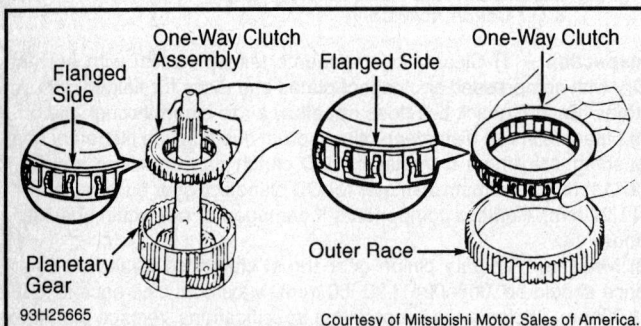

Fig. 26: *Installing Overdrive One-Way Clutch*

OD SUPPORT & BRAKE ASSEMBLY

Disassembly – Remove thrust bearing, thrust washer and bearing races from OD support. Using appropriate compressor, compress return spring assembly and remove snap ring. Place support on OD clutch assembly. Hold brake piston in a level position. Carefully apply air pressure to piston supply port and remove piston. Remove oil seal rings from rear of support. *See Fig. 27*.

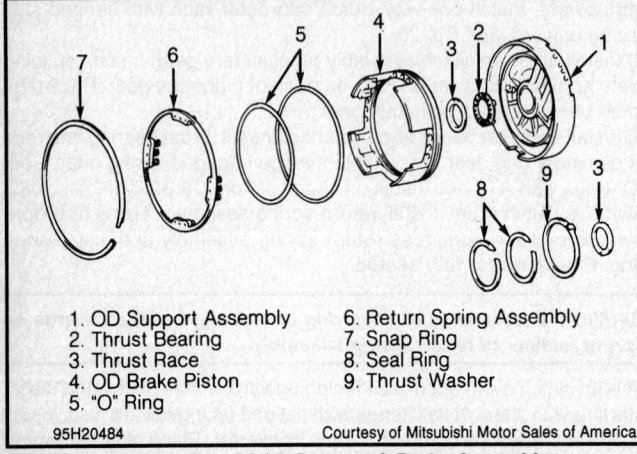

1. OD Support Assembly
2. Thrust Bearing
3. Thrust Race
4. OD Brake Piston
5. "O" Ring
6. Return Spring Assembly
7. Snap Ring
8. Seal Ring
9. Thrust Washer

95H20484

Courtesy of Mitsubishi Motor Sales of America.

Fig. 27: *Exploded View Of OD Support & Brake Assembly*

Inspection – Clean all components with solvent. Dry with compressed air. Inspect components for damage. Replace as necessary. Measure free length of return spring assembly. Length should be .732" (18.60 mm).

Reassembly – 1) To reassemble components, reverse disassembly procedure. Coat seal rings with ATF prior to installation. DO NOT over expand seal rings during piston installation. Ensure seal rings move smoothly after installation.

2) Install NEW "O" rings on OD brake piston. Use care not to damage "O" rings during piston installation. Install snap ring in support and ensure end of snap ring is not aligned with cutout portion of support.

3) Ensure tabs on all races are aligned with areas on support. Coat races and thrust bearing with petroleum jelly prior to installation. Place support on OD clutch assembly and apply air pressure to piston supply port. Ensure piston operates smoothly in support.

DIRECT CLUTCH

Disassembly – 1) Remove direct clutch drum from forward clutch assembly. Remove snap ring from clutch drum. Remove flange, discs and plates. Note number and location of components. Note location of all clutch pack components. *See Fig. 28*.

2) Using appropriate compressor, compress return spring assembly and remove snap ring. Place clutch drum on OD support and apply air pressure to piston supply port and remove clutch piston. *See Fig. 29*.

Inspection – 1) Clean all components (except discs) with solvent. Dry with compressed air. Inspect plates and discs for flaking or burnt areas.

2) Ensure check ball is free in clutch piston. Apply air pressure to the check ball area. Ensure that check ball does not allow air to bleed through the piston. Measure free length of return spring assembly. Length should be .780" (19.80 mm).

3) Measure the inside diameter of the clutch drum bushing. Inside bushing diameter should be 2.124" (53.97 mm). Replace clutch drum if bushing diameter exceeds specification.

CAUTION: Clutch discs should be soaked in ATF for 2 hours prior to installation.

Reassembly – 1) Coat "O" rings with ATF. To reassembly components, reverse disassembly procedure. Ensure return spring assembly snap ring is fully seated and ring ends do not align with claw area on spring retainer of return spring assembly.

2) With clutch drum open area facing upward, install plates and discs, starting with a plate and then alternating with a disc. Install appropriate amount of plates and discs.

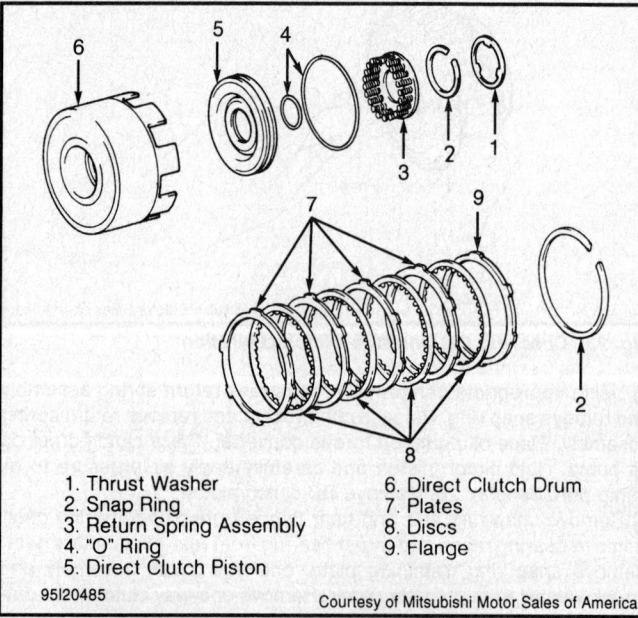

1. Thrust Washer
2. Snap Ring
3. Return Spring Assembly
4. "O" Ring
5. Direct Clutch Piston
6. Direct Clutch Drum
7. Plates
8. Discs
9. Flange

95I20485

Courtesy of Mitsubishi Motor Sales of America.

Fig. 28: *Exploded View Of Direct Clutch Assembly*

3) Install flange with flat end facing toward disc. Place clutch drum on OD support. Measure piston stroke with a dial indicator while applying 57-114 psi (4-8 kg/cm²) of compressed air to piston supply port. See Fig. 29.

4) Piston stroke should be .054-.066" (1.37-1.67 mm). If piston stroke is not within specifications, check for incorrectly assembled components. Recheck piston stroke measurement.

5) If piston stroke is not within specifications, install different thickness flange. Flanges are available in thicknesses of .118" (2.99 mm) to .146" (3.70 mm) in .004" (.10 mm) increments.

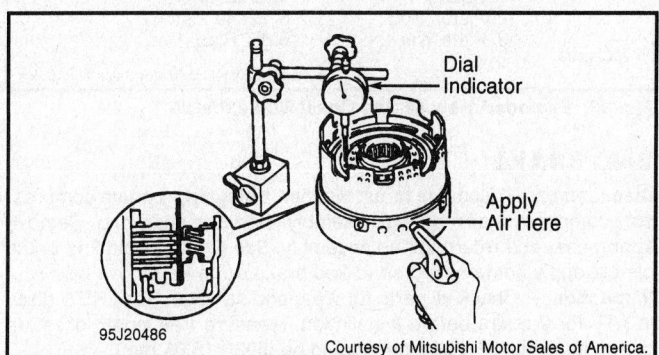

95J20486

Courtesy of Mitsubishi Motor Sales of America.

Fig. 29: Removing Direct Clutch Piston & Measuring Stroke

FORWARD CLUTCH

Disassembly – 1) Separate forward clutch assembly from direct clutch. Remove thrust bearings and race from forward clutch drum. Remove snap ring from clutch drum. Remove flange, discs, plates and cushion plate. See Fig. 30. Note number and location of components.

2) Using appropriate compressor, compress return spring assembly and remove snap ring. Place OD support on wooden blocks and install forward clutch in OD support. Apply air pressure to piston supply port and remove clutch piston. See Fig. 31. Remove "O" rings from clutch piston. Remove oil seal rings.

Inspection – Clean all components (except discs) with solvent. Dry with compressed air. Inspect plates and discs for flaking or burnt areas. Ensure check ball is free in clutch piston. Apply air pressure to check ball area. Ensure check ball does not allow air to bleed through piston. Measure inside diameter of clutch drum bushing. Replace clutch drum if bushing diameter exceeds .948" (24.08 mm). Measure free length of return spring assembly. Length should be .455" (11.55 mm).

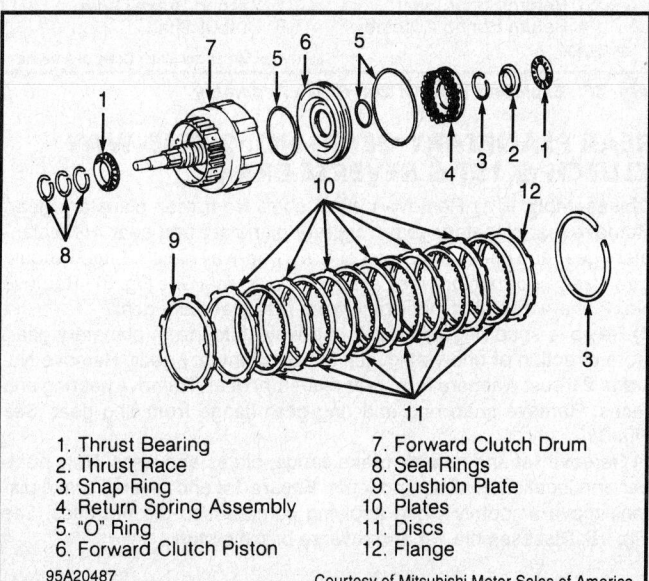

1. Thrust Bearing
2. Thrust Race
3. Snap Ring
4. Return Spring Assembly
5. "O" Ring
6. Forward Clutch Piston
7. Forward Clutch Drum
8. Seal Rings
9. Cushion Plate
10. Plates
11. Discs
12. Flange

95A20487

Courtesy of Mitsubishi Motor Sales of America.

Fig. 30: Exploded View Of Forward Clutch

CAUTION: Clutch disc should be soaked in ATF for 2 hours prior to installation.

Reassembly – 1) Coat "O" rings with ATF. To reassemble components, reverse disassembly procedure. Ensure return spring assembly snap ring is fully seated and ends do not align with claw area on spring retainer of return spring assembly.

2) Install cushion plate with rounded end toward inside of clutch drum. Install plates and discs, starting with a plate. Install appropriate amount of plates and discs. See Fig. 30.

3) Install flange with rounded edge toward disc. Install snap ring. Ensure end gap of snap ring is not aligned with forward clutch drum cut out portion. Place clutch drum on overdrive support. Measure piston stroke while applying 57-114 psi (4-8 kg/cm²) of compressed air to piston supply port. See Fig. 31.

4) Piston stroke should be .114-.169" (2.90-4.29 mm). If piston stroke is not within specifications, install different thickness flange. Install thrust bearing and race. Align tabs of clutch discs.

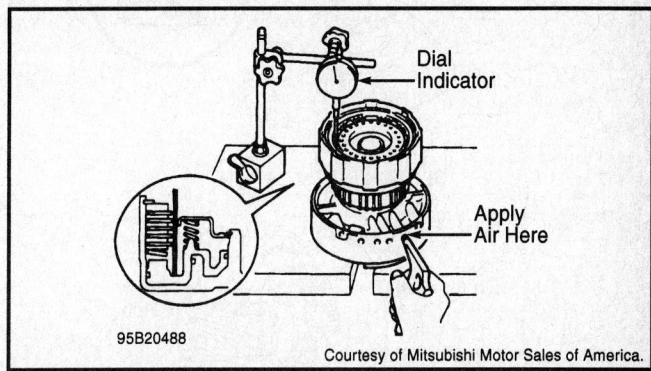

95B20488

Courtesy of Mitsubishi Motor Sales of America.

Fig. 31: Removing Forward Clutch Piston & Measuring Stroke

FRONT PLANETARY GEAR

Disassembly & Inspection – Remove thrust bearings and races from planetary gear and front planetary ring gear. See Fig. 32. Note direction of race installation. Measure front planetary ring gear bushing inside diameter. Replace planetary ring gear if bushing diameter exceeds .948" (24.08 mm). Measure planetary pinion gear thrust clearance. Clearance should be .008-.024" (.20-.60 mm). Maximum clearance is .039" (1.00 mm). If clearance is not within specifications, replace planetary gear assembly.

Reassembly – Coat thrust bearings and races with petroleum jelly. Install thrust bearings and races, ensuring tabs on race align with planetary gear. Install races in planetary ring gear and planetary gear with the flat side against the gear surface. See Fig. 32.

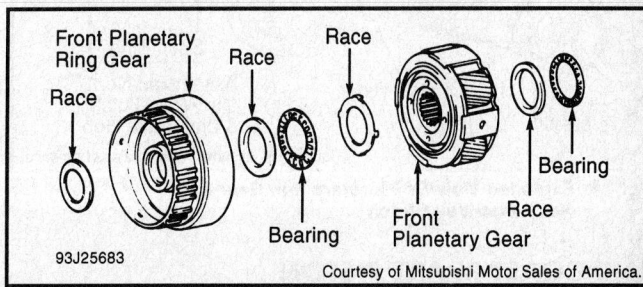

93J25683

Courtesy of Mitsubishi Motor Sales of America.

Fig. 32: Exploded View Of Front Planetary Gear

PLANETARY SUN GEAR & NO. 1 ONE-WAY CLUTCH

Disassembly – 1) Hold sun gear drum and check rotation of one-way clutch. Clutch should turn freely clockwise and lock counterclockwise. See Fig. 33. Remove one-way clutch assembly. Note direction of clutch installation.

2) Remove thrust washer and oil seal rings from sun gear drum and sun gear. Support sun gear drum on wooden block and remove snap ring from sun gear. Separate sun gear from sun gear drum. See Fig. 34.

Inspection – Clean components in solvent. Dry with compressed air. Measure inside diameter of sun gear bushing. Replace sun gear if diameter exceeds .948 (24.08 mm).

Reassembly – To reassemble components, reverse disassembly procedure. See Fig. 34. Ensure ends of oil seal rings are properly locked together and seal rings move smoothly. Install one-way clutch assembly in proper direction. Check one-way clutch operation. See Fig. 33.

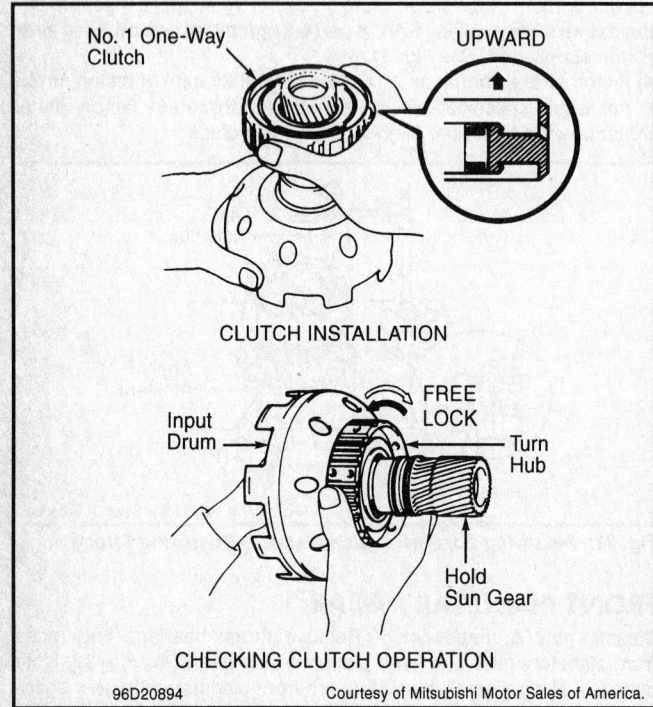

CLUTCH INSTALLATION

CHECKING CLUTCH OPERATION

96D20894   Courtesy of Mitsubishi Motor Sales of America.

Fig. 33: Installing & Checking No. 1 One-Way Clutch

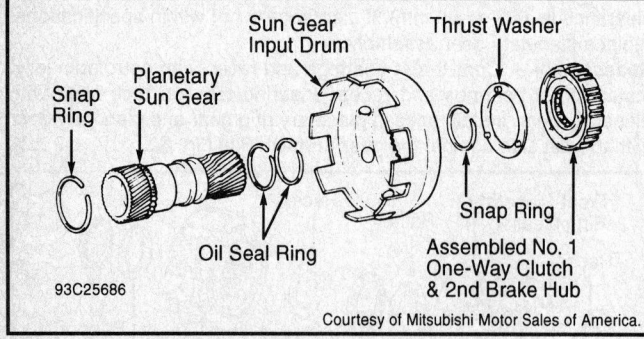

93C25686   Courtesy of Mitsubishi Motor Sales of America.

Fig. 34: Exploded View Of Planetary Sun Gear & No. 1 One-Way Clutch

2ND COAST BRAKE PISTON

Disassembly – Remove "E" ring from piston rod. Remove 2nd coast brake piston, spring and retainer from piston rod. Remove oil seal ring. See Fig. 35.

Inspection – Replace brake band if lining is peeled off or discolored or printed numbers are defaced. Before assembling NEW band, soak band in ATF for at least 2 hours. If brake band is serviceable but piston rod stroke is not within specification, select replacement piston rod.

Reassembly – Install oil seal ring on piston. Install retainer, spring and piston to piston rod. Install "E" ring. See Fig. 35.

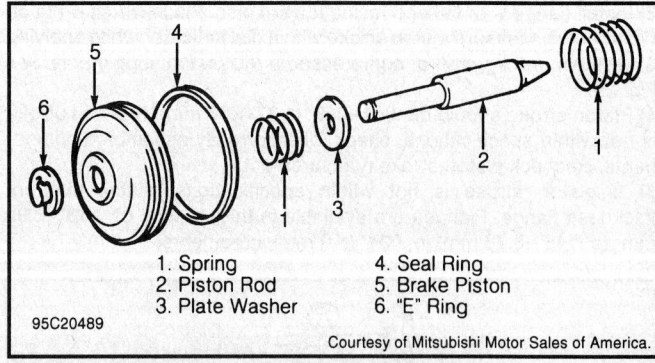

1. Spring	4. Seal Ring
2. Piston Rod	5. Brake Piston
3. Plate Washer	6. "E" Ring

95C20489   Courtesy of Mitsubishi Motor Sales of America.

Fig. 35: Exploded View Of 2nd Coast Brake Piston

2ND BRAKE

Disassembly – Remove thrust washer. Using appropriate compressor, compress return spring assembly. Remove snap ring. Remove spring seat and return spring assembly. See Fig. 36. Hold 2nd brake piston, apply compressed air to 2nd brake drum to remove piston.

Inspection – Check all parts for wear and damage. Soak NEW discs in ATF for 2 hours before installation. Measure free length of return spring assembly. Free length should be .593" (15.05 mm).

Reassembly – Coat NEW "O" rings with ATF and install. Carefully press 2nd brake piston into 2nd brake drum. Install return spring assembly and spring seat. See Fig. 36. Compress return spring assembly and install snap ring. Apply compressed air to 2nd brake drum. Ensure 2nd brake piston moves smoothly. Install thrust washer. Ensure cutout portions of thrust washer match teeth of spring retainer.

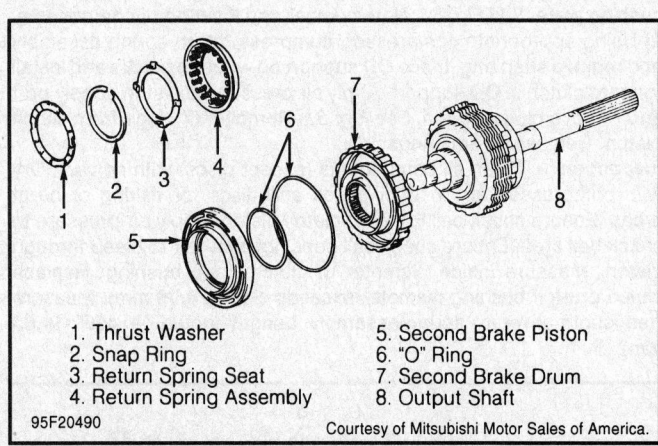

1. Thrust Washer	5. Second Brake Piston
2. Snap Ring	6. "O" Ring
3. Return Spring Seat	7. Second Brake Drum
4. Return Spring Assembly	8. Output Shaft

95F20490   Courtesy of Mitsubishi Motor Sales of America.

Fig. 36: Exploded View Of 2nd Brake Assembly

REAR PLANETARY GEAR, NO. 2 ONE-WAY CLUTCH & 1ST & REVERSE BRAKE

Disassembly – **1)** Remove output shaft from rear planetary gear. Remove rear planetary gear from rear planetary ring gear. Hold planetary gear and check operation of No. 2 one-way clutch. Clutch should turn freely counterclockwise and lock clockwise. See Fig. 37. Remove No. 2 one-way clutch inner race from rear planetary gear.

2) Remove snap ring and No. 2 one-way clutch from planetary gear. Note direction of one-way clutch in rear planetary gear. Remove No. 1 and 2 thrust washers from rear planetary gear. Remove bearing and races. Remove snap ring and ring gear flange from ring gear. See Fig. 38.

3) Remove 1st and reverse brake flange, plates and discs. Note number and location of all components. Ensure 1st and reverse brake pistons move smoothly when applying compressed air into case. See Fig. 18. Disassemble 1st and reverse brake piston.

4) Install appropriate compressor on spring retainer, and compress return spring assembly. Remove snap ring. Remove return spring assembly. Using compressed air, remove 1st and reverse brake piston No. 2. *See Fig. 18.* Insert appropriate sleeve remover behind reaction sleeve. Remove reaction sleeve from case. Using compressed air, remove brake piston No. 1 from case.

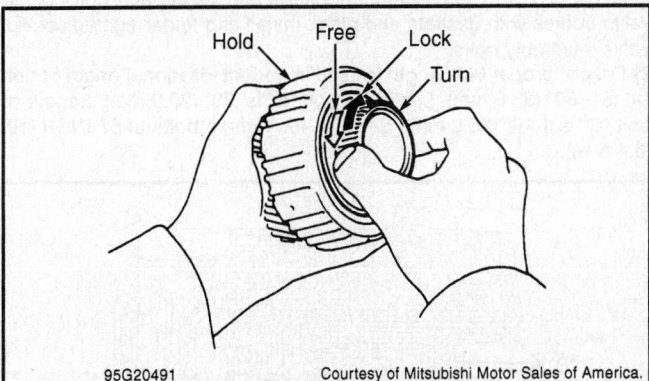

Fig. 37: *Checking No. 2 One-Way Clutch Operation*

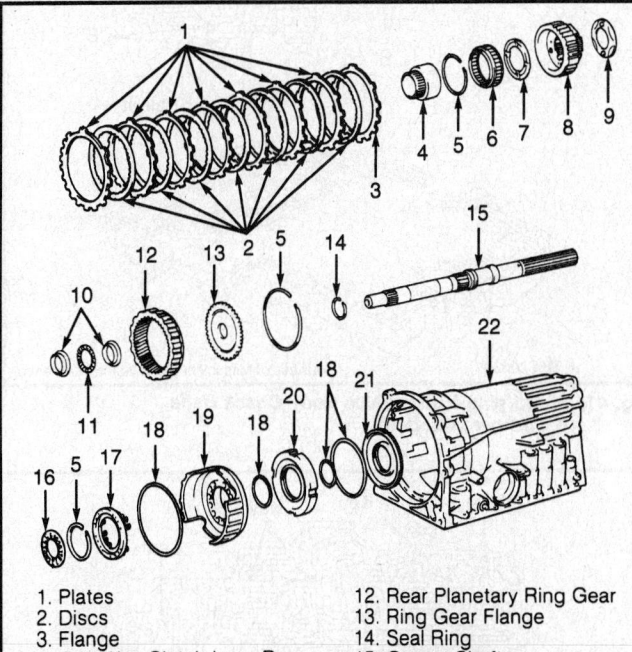

1. Plates
2. Discs
3. Flange
4. One-Way Clutch Inner Race
5. Snap Ring
6. No. 2 One-Way Clutch
7. Thrust Washer No. 2
8. Rear Planetary Gear
9. Thrust Washer No. 1
10. Thrust Race
11. Thrust Bearing
12. Rear Planetary Ring Gear
13. Ring Gear Flange
14. Seal Ring
15. Output Shaft
16. Thrust Bearing With Race
17. Return Spring Assembly
18. "O" Ring
19. Brake Piston No. 2
20. Brake Reaction Sleeve
21. Brake Piston No. 1
22. Transmission Case

95H20492

Courtesy of Mitsubishi Motor Sales of America.

Fig. 38: *Exploded View Of Rear Planetary Gear & 1st & Reverse Brake Components*

Inspection – Clean all components with solvent. Dry with compressed air. Inspect all components for damage. Replace if necessary. Measure planetary pinion gear thrust clearance. Standard clearance should be .008-.024" (.20-.60 mm). Maximum clearance is .039" (1.00 mm). If clearance is not within specifications, replace planetary gear assembly. Measure free length of return spring assembly. Include spring seat in measurement. Free length should be .515" (13.09 mm).

Reassembly – **1)** To reassemble, reverse disassembly procedure. Coat all thrust bearings and races with petroleum jelly. When installing thrust bearings and races in ring gear, flat side of race must be placed against ring gear.

2) Install 1st and reverse brake piston No. 1 to reaction sleeve. Install piston No. 1 with reaction sleeve on piston No. 2. Align piston No. 2 teeth into proper grooves. Carefully press brake pistons No. 1 and No. 2 into case. Position return spring assembly on piston No. 2. Using appropriate spring compressor, compress return spring assembly.

3) Install snap ring. Ensure snap ring end-gap is not aligned with spring retainer claw. Ensure 1st and reverse brake pistons move smoothly by applying compressed air to case. *See Fig. 18.*

4) Ensure No. 1 and 2 thrust washer tangs align with cutout area of planetary gear. Install No. 2 one-way clutch with the open ends facing upward.

5) Rotate one-way clutch inner race counterclockwise during installation into rear planetary gear. Ensure No. 2 one-way clutch turns freely counterclockwise and locks clockwise. *See Fig. 37.*

6) Install rear planetary gear on rear planetary ring gear. Install oil seal ring. DO NOT spread oil seal ring too much. After installing oil seal ring, ensure seal ring rotates smoothly. Install output shaft into rear planetary gear assembly.

CONTROL VALVE ASSEMBLY

CAUTION: All valve body components must be installed in original location. Lay all components in sequence during removal for reassembly reference. Note diameter and ball location. Throttle pressure is changed according to number of adjusting rings. When assembling valve body, install same number of adjusting rings as removed.

Disassembly & Reassembly – **1)** Remove detent spring cover, detent spring and manual valve from control valve assembly. *See Fig. 39.* Remove 25 lower valve body-to upper valve body bolts. *See Fig. 40.* Note bolt length and location for reassembly reference.

2) Separate upper valve body and valve body plate from lower valve body. Remove gaskets. *See Fig. 39.* To reassemble valve assembly, reverse disassembly procedure.

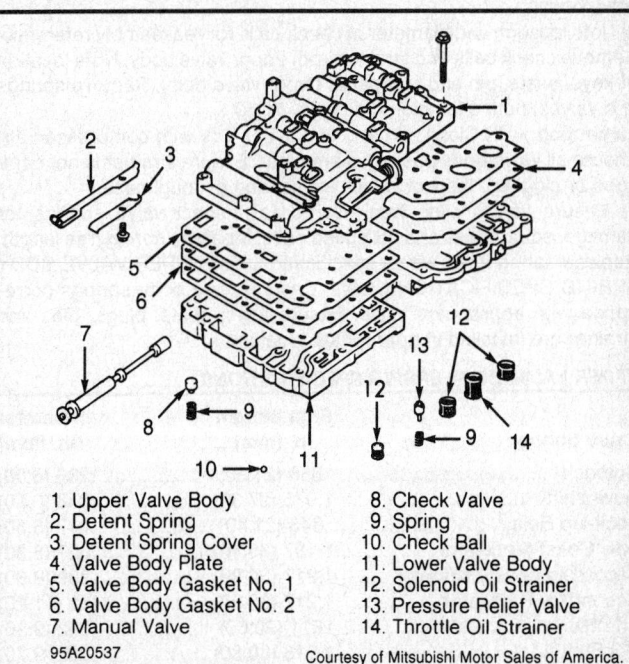

1. Upper Valve Body
2. Detent Spring
3. Detent Spring Cover
4. Valve Body Plate
5. Valve Body Gasket No. 1
6. Valve Body Gasket No. 2
7. Manual Valve
8. Check Valve
9. Spring
10. Check Ball
11. Lower Valve Body
12. Solenoid Oil Strainer
13. Pressure Relief Valve
14. Throttle Oil Strainer

95A20537

Courtesy of Mitsubishi Motor Sales of America.

Fig. 39: *Exploded View Of Control Valve Assembly*

3) Ensure proper bolt length is used in correct location. Length of bolt "A" is 1.50" (38.0 mm). Length of bolt "B" is .79" (20.0 mm). Length of bolt "C" is 1.10" (28.0 mm). *See Fig. 40.* Tighten bolts to 57 INCH lbs. (6.4 N.m).

CAUTION: DO NOT allow valve body plate to separate from upper valve body during removal or check balls and strainers may fall out.

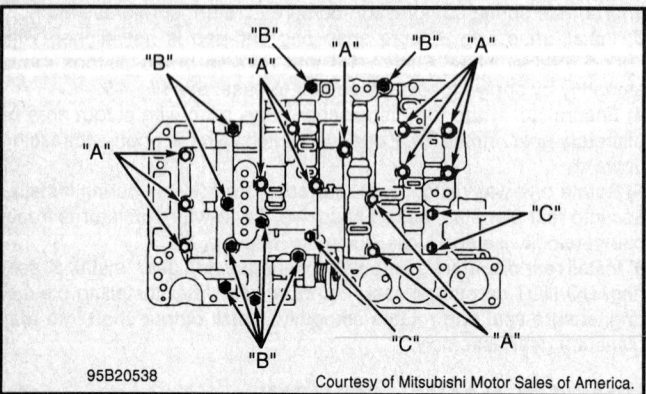

95B20538   Courtesy of Mitsubishi Motor Sales of America.

Fig. 40: Identifying Control Valve Assembly Bolt Length

UPPER VALVE BODY

CAUTION: All valve body components must be installed in original location. Lay all components in sequence during removal for reassembly reference. Note diameter and check ball location.

NOTE: Valves may be held in with keys, seats, plugs or pins. Remove components and note locations. Arrange parts in order for reassembly reference.

Disassembly – 1) Remove upper valve body from lower valve body. See DISASSEMBLY & REASSEMBLY under CONTROL VALVE ASSEMBLY. Remove 2 valve body gaskets and plate from upper valve body.

2) Note location and diameter of check balls for reassembly reference. Remove check balls and strainer from upper valve body. Note location of keys, seats, pin and stopper in upper valve body. Remove springs and valves, noting location. *See Figs. 41-43.*

Inspection – 1) Clean all parts in solvent. Dry with compressed air. Ensure all valve body passages are clear. Ensure strainer is not damaged or clogged. Inspect valves for scoring or roughness.

2) Ensure valves slide freely in bores. Inspect valve springs for damage, squareness and collapsed coils. Measure spring free length. Replace spring if not within specification. See UPPER VALVE BODY SPRING SPECIFICATIONS table. Ensure valve body springs correspond with appropriate valve. Ensure keys, seats, plugs, pins and strainer are installed in appropriate locations.

UPPER VALVE BODY SPRING SPECIFICATIONS

Valve Spring [1]	Free Length In. (mm)	Diameter In. (mm)
Cutback	.858 (21.80)	.236 (6.00)
Downshift	1.075 (27.30)	.343 (8.70)
Lock-Up Relay	.843 (21.40)	.217 (5.50)
Low Coast Modulator	1.197 (30.40)	.327 (8.30)
Secondary Coast Modulator	1.217 (30.90)	.339 (8.60)
Secondary Regulator	1.217 (30.90)	.441 (11.20)
Throttle	.811 (20.60)	.362 (9.20)
2-3 Shift	1.213 (30.80)	.382 (9.70)
3-4 Shift	1.213 (30.80)	.382 (9.70)

[1] – For valve spring locations, *see Fig. 43.*

Reassembly – 1) Coat all components with ATF. To reassemble, reverse disassembly procedure. Ensure check balls are installed correctly. Diameter of "A" check ball is .250" (6.35 mm). Diameter of "B" check balls is .219" (5.56 mm). *See Fig. 41.*

2) Position NEW No. 1 gasket, plate and NEW No. 2 gasket on upper valve body. Place lower valve body on upper valve body with plate and gaskets. DO NOT let components separate. Align each bolt hole in valve bodies with gaskets and plate. Install and finger tighten control valve assembly bolts.

3) Ensure proper bolt length is used in correct location. Length of bolt "A" is 1.50" (38.0 mm). Length of bolt "B" is .79" (20.0 mm). Length of bolt "C" is 1.10" (28.0 mm). *See Fig. 40.* Tighten bolts to 57 INCH lbs. (6.4 N.m).

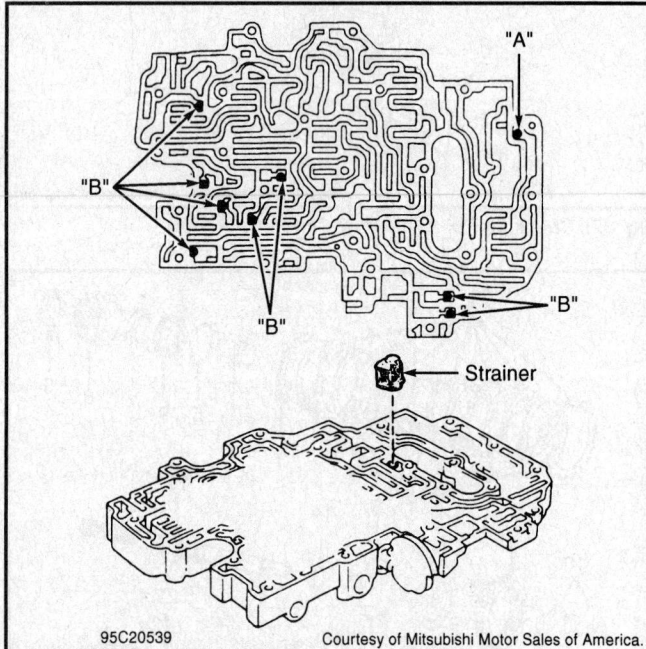

95C20539   Courtesy of Mitsubishi Motor Sales of America.

Fig. 41: Identifying Upper Valve Body Check Balls & Strainer Locations

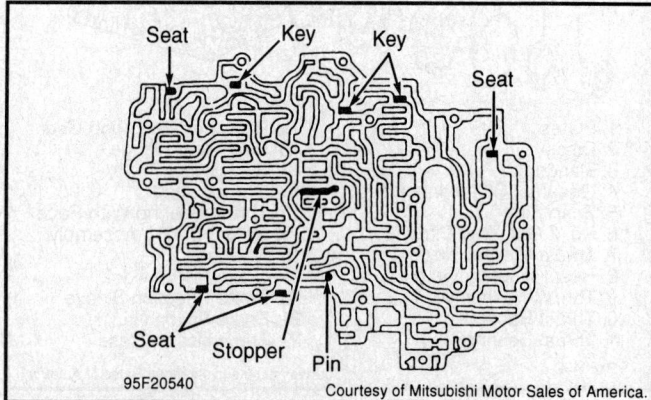

95F20540   Courtesy of Mitsubishi Motor Sales of America.

Fig. 42: Identifying Upper Valve Body Keys, Seats, Pin & Stopper Locations

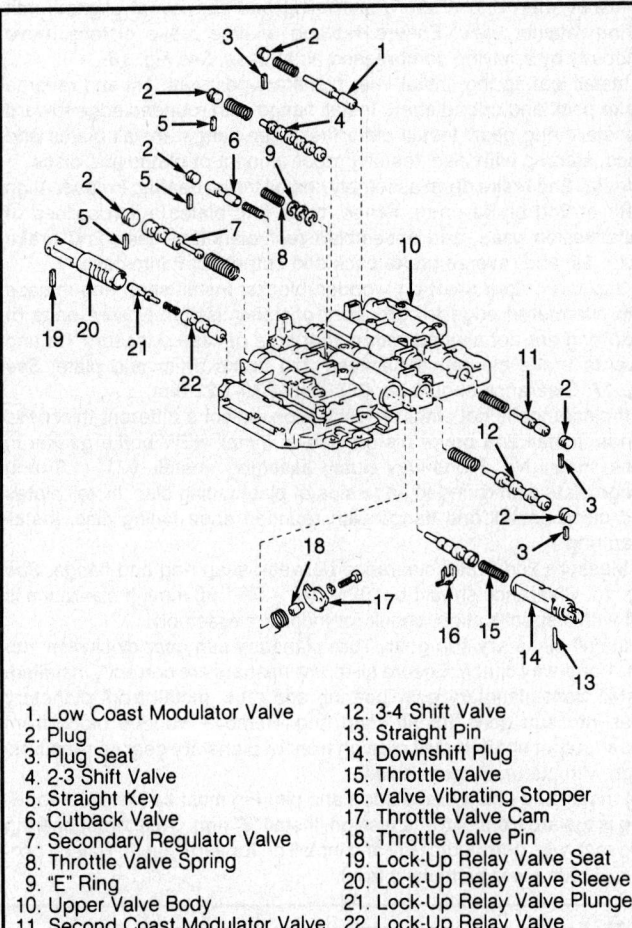

1. Low Coast Modulator Valve
2. Plug
3. Plug Seat
4. 2-3 Shift Valve
5. Straight Key
6. Cutback Valve
7. Secondary Regulator Valve
8. Throttle Valve Spring
9. "E" Ring
10. Upper Valve Body
11. Second Coast Modulator Valve
12. 3-4 Shift Valve
13. Straight Pin
14. Downshift Plug
15. Throttle Valve
16. Valve Vibrating Stopper
17. Throttle Valve Cam
18. Throttle Valve Pin
19. Lock-Up Relay Valve Seat
20. Lock-Up Relay Valve Sleeve
21. Lock-Up Relay Valve Plunger
22. Lock-Up Relay Valve

95G20541

Courtesy of Mitsubishi Motor Sales of America.

Fig. 43: Exploded View Of Upper Valve Body

LOWER VALVE BODY

CAUTION: All valve body components must be installed in original location. Lay all components in sequence during removal for reassembly reference. Note diameter and check ball location.

NOTE: Valves may be held in with pins, seats or plugs. Remove components and note locations. Arrange parts in order for reassembly reference.

Disassembly – Remove upper valve body from lower valve body. See DISASSEMBLY & REASSEMBLY under CONTROL VALVE ASSEMBLY. Remove No. 1, No. 2 and lock-up solenoids. Remove check valve, pressure relief valve and springs. Remove 3 oil strainers from lower valve body. Note location of seats, clip and pin in lower valve body. Remove springs and valves, noting location. See Figs. 44-48.

Inspection – **1)** Clean all parts in solvent. Dry with compressed air. Ensure all valve body passages are clear. Ensure strainers are not damaged or clogged. Inspect valves for scoring or roughness.

2) Ensure valves slide freely in bores. Inspect valve springs for damage, squareness and collapsed coils. Measure spring free length. Replace spring if not within specification. See LOWER VALVE BODY SPRING SPECIFICATIONS table. Ensure valve body springs correspond with appropriate valve. Ensure seats, clip and pin are installed in appropriate locations.

LOWER VALVE BODY SPRING SPECIFICATIONS

Valve Spring [1]	Free Length In. (mm)	Diameter In. (mm)
Accumulator Control	1.335 (33.90)	.346 (8.80)
Check	.795 (20.20)	.476 (12.10)
Primary Regulator	2.453 (62.30)	.732 (18.60)
Pressure Relief	.441 (11.20)	.252 (6.40)
1-2 Shift	1.213 (30.80)	.382 (9.70)

[1] – For valve spring locations, see Figs. 45 and 48.

Reassembly – **1)** Coat all components with ATF. To reassemble, reverse disassembly procedure. Place lower valve body on upper valve body with plate and gaskets. DO NOT let components separate. Align each bolt hole in valve bodies with gaskets and plate. Install and finger tighten control valve assembly bolts.

2) Ensure proper bolt length is used in correct location. Length of bolt "A" is 1.50" (38.0 mm). Length of bolt "B" is .79" (20.0 mm). Length of bolt "C" is 1.10" (28.0 mm). See Fig. 40. Tighten bolts to 57 INCH lbs. (6.4 N.m).

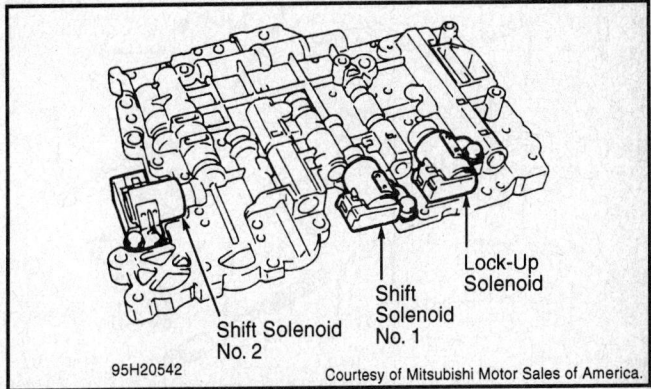

95H20542

Courtesy of Mitsubishi Motor Sales of America.

Fig. 44: Identifying Solenoid Locations

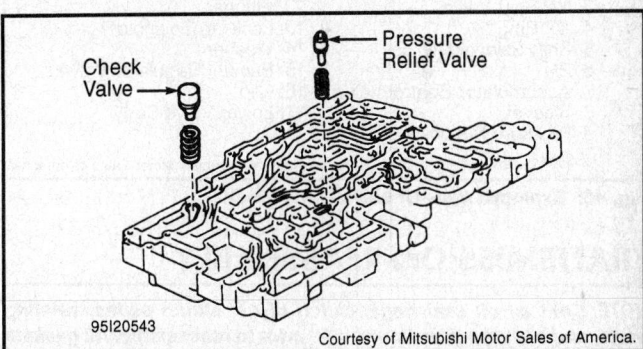

95I20543

Courtesy of Mitsubishi Motor Sales of America.

Fig. 45: Identifying Check Valve, Pressure Relief Valve & Spring Locations

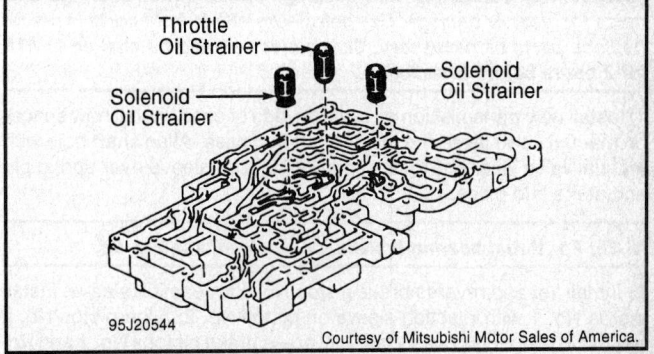

95J20544

Courtesy of Mitsubishi Motor Sales of America.

Fig. 46: Identifying Oil Strainer Locations

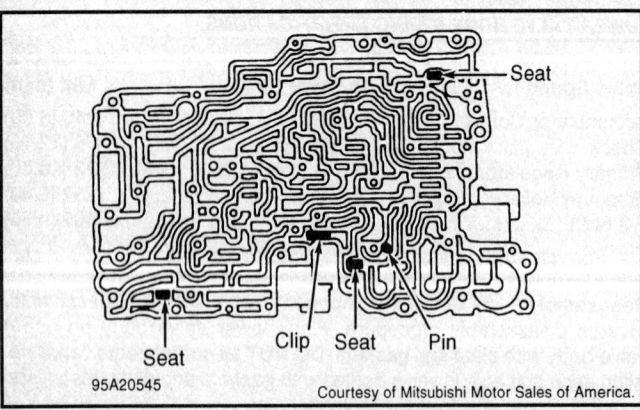

Fig. 47: Identifying Lower Valve Body Seats, Clip & Pin Locations

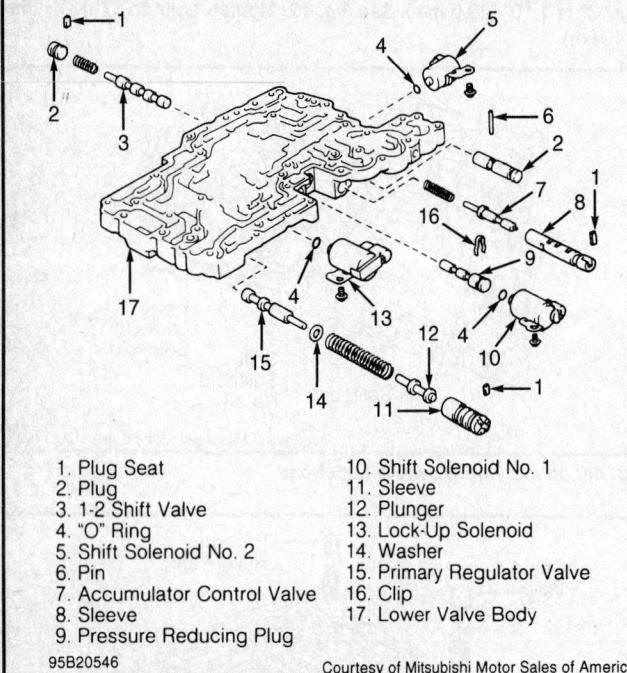

1. Plug Seat
2. Plug
3. 1-2 Shift Valve
4. "O" Ring
5. Shift Solenoid No. 2
6. Pin
7. Accumulator Control Valve
8. Sleeve
9. Pressure Reducing Plug
10. Shift Solenoid No. 1
11. Sleeve
12. Plunger
13. Lock-Up Solenoid
14. Washer
15. Primary Regulator Valve
16. Clip
17. Lower Valve Body

95B20546   Courtesy of Mitsubishi Motor Sales of America.

Fig. 48: Exploded View Of Lower Valve Body

TRANSMISSION REASSEMBLY

NOTE: Coat all oil seal rings, clutch discs, clutch plates, rotating parts, and sliding surfaces with ATF prior to reassembly. All gaskets and rubber "O" rings should be replaced. Ensure ends of snap rings are not aligned with cut-outs and are installed correctly in groove. If a worn bushing is to be replaced, replacement must be made with subassembly containing that bushing. Check thrust bearings and races for wear or damage. Use petroleum jelly to hold parts in place. Replace parts as necessary. Clutch discs should be soaked in ATF for 2 hours before installation.

1) Install new transmission oil seals on side of case. Install new spacer on manual valve lever and install shaft into case. Align shaft hole with manual valve lever and install spring pin. Slide sleeve over spring pin and stake into place.

NOTE: For thrust bearing installation position, see Fig. 54.

2) Install 1st and reverse brake piston No. 1 to reaction sleeve. Install piston No. 1 with reaction sleeve on piston No. 2. Align piston No. 2 teeth into proper grooves. Carefully press brake pistons No. 1 and No. 2 into case. Position return spring assembly on piston No. 2. Using spring compressor, compress return spring assembly.

3) Install snap ring. Ensure snap ring end-gap is not aligned with spring retainer claw. Ensure 1st and reverse brake pistons move smoothly by applying compressed air to case. *See Fig. 18.*

4) Install leaf spring. Install rear planetary gear with 1st and reverse brake pack and output shaft. Install flange with rounded edge toward planetary ring gear. Install plate first, then flange. Install plates and discs, starting with disc. Install proper amount of plates and discs.

5) Install 2nd brake drum assembly. Install thrust bearing in case. Align teeth of 2nd brake drum, flange, discs and plates. Align splines of transmission case, and assembled rear planetary gear, 2nd brake drum, 1st and reverse brake pack and output shaft into case.

6) Support output shaft on wooden blocks. Install snap ring in case with chamfered edge toward front of transmission. Ensure ends of snap ring are not aligned with cutout area of case. Measure 1st and reverse brake clearance between 2nd brake drum and plate. *See Fig. 17.* Clearance should be .028-.048" (.70-1.22 mm)

7) If clearance is not within specification, select a different thickness flange. Install 2nd brake piston sleeve. Install NEW brake gasket in case. Install No. 1 one-way clutch assembly. Install .071" (1.8 mm) flange plate with rounded edge side of plate facing disc. Install plates and discs. Install end flange with rounded edge facing disc. Install snap ring.

8) Measure 2nd brake clearance between snap ring and flange. *See Fig. 16.* Clearance should be .024-.078" (.62-1.98 mm). If clearance is not within specification, check for incorrect assembly.

9) Install planetary sun gear. Turn planetary sun gear clockwise into No. 1 one-way clutch. Ensure all thrust washers are correctly installed. Install front planetary gear bearing and race. Install front planetary gear into sun gear. Install snap ring. Remove wooden block from under output shaft. Install race on front of planetary gear so race tabs align with planetary gear holes.

10) Install 2nd coast brake band and pin. Pin must be installed so "E" ring is toward front of transmission. Install "E" ring. Coat thrust bearing and race with petroleum jelly and install on forward clutch. Raised portion of race must be toward front.

NOTE: For thrust bearing installation position, see Fig. 54.

11) Install race on front planetary ring gear. Smooth flat surface must be toward front. Align disc tabs of forward clutch. Install front planetary ring gear in forward clutch. Ensure gear is aligned with all clutch discs.

12) Install bearing race and thrust bearing on ring gear. Raised portion of race must be toward rear. Install forward and direct clutch assembly and front planetary ring gear in transmission case. Measure distance between sun gear input drum and direct clutch drum. *See Fig. 49.* Clearance should be .210-.290" (5.30-7.30 mm). If clearance is not within specifications, check for incorrect installation.

13) Install thrust bearing and race on forward clutch assembly with flat side toward the clutch assembly. Install NEW "O" ring on 2nd coast brake cover. Install spring, 2nd coast brake piston assembly and cover to case. Install snap ring.

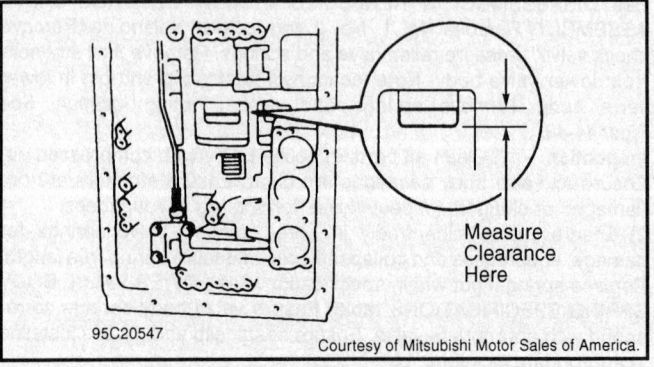

Fig. 49: Measuring Input Drum & Direct Clutch Drum Clearance

14) Place reference mark on 2nd coast brake piston rod. Apply 57-114 psi (4.8 kg/cm²) of air at opening of transmission case. Using wire gauge, measure clearance between reference mark and case. Clearance should be .059-.118" (1.49-3.00 mm). *See Fig. 15.*

15) If stroke is not within specification, install replacement piston rod. Rods are available in lengths of 2.78" (70.7 mm), 2.81" (71.4 mm), 2.84" (72.2 mm) and 2.870" (72.9 mm). If stroke is not within specification, install NEW brake band. Install race on OD support. Align bolt and oil holes of OD support toward valve body side and bolt hole of case and install support.

16) Ensure support is properly aligned. Install support snap ring with chamfered edge toward front of transmission. End of snap ring must be positioned to valve body side of case within .55-1.34" (14-34 mm) from center line of valve body as viewed from front of transmission.

17) Using dial indicator, check output shaft end play. *See Fig. 50.* End play should be 011-.034" (.27-.86 mm). If end play is not within specifications, check for incorrect assembly. Ensure output shaft rotates smoothly.

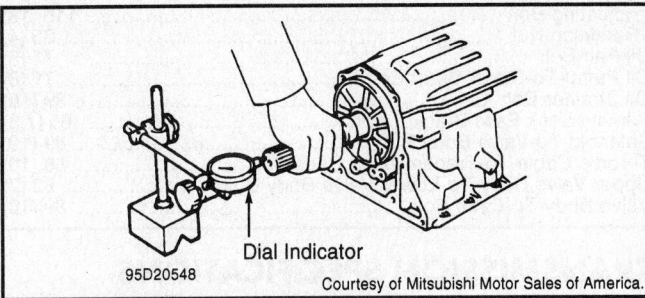

Dial Indicator

95D20548   Courtesy of Mitsubishi Motor Sales of America.

Fig. 50: Measuring Output Shaft End Play

18) Install a .157" (4.00 mm) thick flange with rounded edge facing disc. Install correct amount of discs and plates, beginning with plate. Install end flange (stepped ring) with flat side toward disc. Install snap ring. Ensure ends of snap ring are not located at cutout areas of case.

19) Install dial indicator on case and measure piston stroke. Apply 57-114 psi (4-8 kg/cm²) at opening of transmission case and note piston stroke. *See Fig. 14.* Piston stroke should be .055-.067 (1.40-1.70).

20) If piston stroke is not within specifications, check for incorrect installation. Recheck piston stroke. If piston stroke is not within specifications, install different thickness flange. Flanges are available in thicknesses of .130" (3.3 mm) to .157" (4.0 mm) in .008" (.20 mm) increments.

21) Install thrust bearing and races on OD support. Ensure race tabs align with hole support. Install OD planetary ring gear. Install thrust bearing and race in ring gear. Install race on rear of OD planetary gear, aligning race tabs with holes of gear. Install OD planetary gear with OD clutch and one-way clutch. Install thrust bearing and race onto OD clutch with race flat side toward OD clutch.

22) Install race on rear of oil pump with raised side toward oil pump. Install NEW "O" ring on outer diameter of oil pump. Ensure seal rings are installed on rear of oil pump. Align holes of oil pump and case. Install oil pump while holding input shaft and lightly pressing on oil pump.

CAUTION: DO NOT apply excessive pressure on oil pump during installation or seal rings will stick to the direct clutch drum.

23) Install oil pump bolts. Ensure input shaft rotates smoothly. Install throttle cable. Apply air pressure to specified oil passage to check operating components. *See Fig. 51.* When air checking the OD clutch, OD accumulator piston hole must be plugged.

24) Install speed sensor rotor and key on output shaft. Install "E" ring, parking lock pawl, shaft and spring. Connect parking lock rod to manual valve lever. Position parking lock pawl, shaft and spring. Connect parking lock rod to manual valve lever. Position parking lock pawl bracket on case and install. *See Fig. 10.*

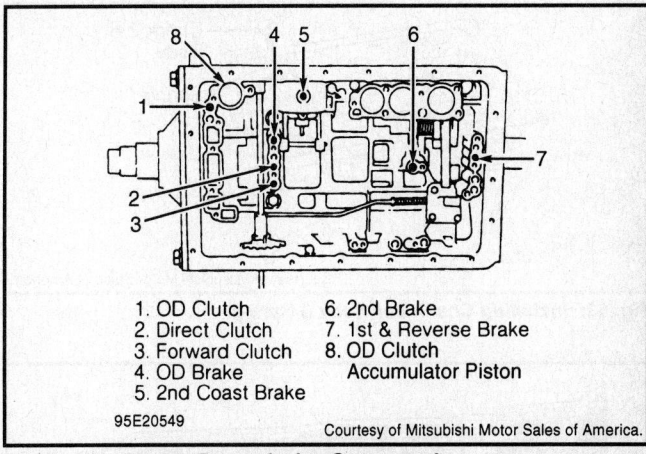

1. OD Clutch
2. Direct Clutch
3. Forward Clutch
4. OD Brake
5. 2nd Coast Brake
6. 2nd Brake
7. 1st & Reverse Brake
8. OD Clutch Accumulator Piston

95E20549   Courtesy of Mitsubishi Motor Sales of America.

Fig. 51: Air Testing Transmission Components

25) Install accumulator pistons with NEW "O" rings. Install accumulator springs. *See Fig. 52.* Accumulator pistons and springs must be proper diameter and height. Accumulator pistons are stamped with identification codes. For accumulator piston locations, *see Figs. 11-13.* Determine proper spring free length. See ACCUMULATOR SPRING SPECIFICATIONS table.

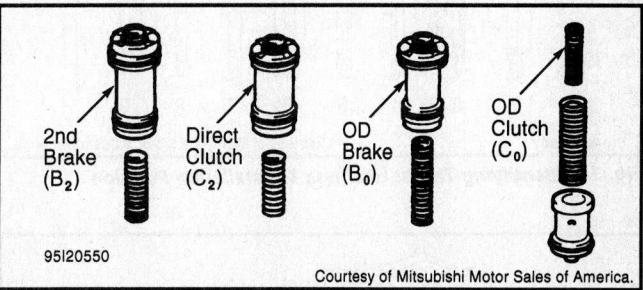

2nd Brake (B₂)   Direct Clutch (C₂)   OD Brake (B₀)   OD Clutch (C₀)

95I20550   Courtesy of Mitsubishi Motor Sales of America.

Fig. 52: Identifying Accumulator Piston Assemblies

ACCUMULATOR SPRING SPECIFICATIONS

Piston Spring (ID Code)	Free Length In. (mm)	Diameter In. (mm)
2nd Brake (B_2)		
Inner	2.858 (72.60)	.626 (15.90)
Outer	.866 (22.00)	.551 (14.00)
Direct Clutch (C_2)		
Inner	2.764 (70.20)	.795 (20.20)
Outer	.787 (20.00)	.476 (12.10)
OD Brake (B_0)		
Inner	2.441 (62.00)	.630 (16.00)
Outer	.571 (14.50)	.512 (13.00)
OD Clutch (C_0)		
Inner	1.811 (46.00)	.551 (14.00)
Outer	2.937 (74.60)	.823 (20.90)

26) Install check ball body and spring. *See Fig. 53.* Install valve body. See CONTROL VALVE ASSEMBLY under ON-VEHICLE SERVICE Install speedometer drive gear and lock ball and snap ring on output shaft. Install extension housing and NEW gasket. Shorter mounting bolts go to bottom of extension housing.

27) Install transmission housing. Install speed sensor and speedometer driven gear. Install front and rear cooler line unions. Install transmission oil temperature sensor. Install neutral safety switch. Tighten nut to 35 INCH lbs. (4 N.m). Align neutral basic line and switch groove. Bend at least 2 lock washer tabs.

28) Install control shaft lever. If throttle cable is new, stake stopper on inner cable. Install wire harness and throttle cable clamp. Install torque converter. Using straightedge and depth gauge, measure distance from front of torque converter to front mounting surface of transmission housing. Distance should be 1.22" (31.1 mm). *See Fig. 55.*

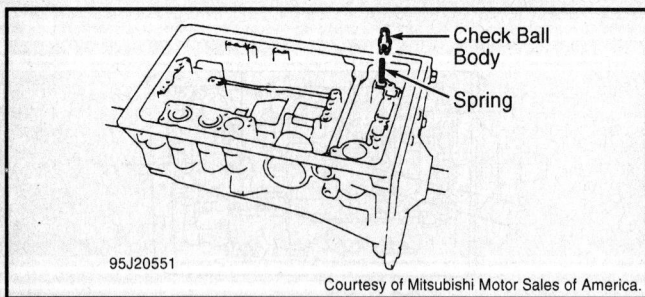

95J20551

Courtesy of Mitsubishi Motor Sales of America.

Fig. 53: Installing Check Ball Body & Spring

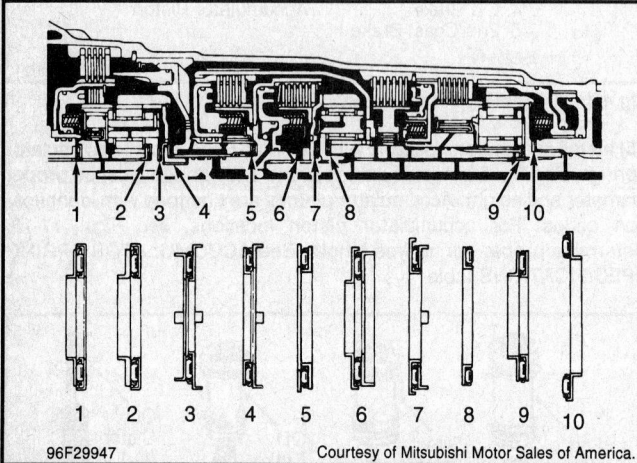

96F29947

Courtesy of Mitsubishi Motor Sales of America.

Fig. 54: Identifying Thrust Bearings & Installation Position

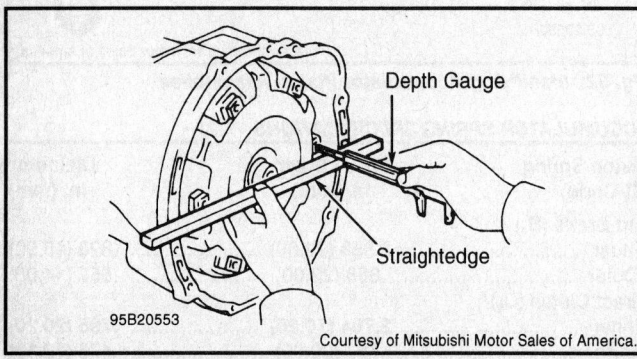

95B20553

Courtesy of Mitsubishi Motor Sales of America.

Fig. 55: Measuring Torque Converter Depth

TORQUE SPECIFICATIONS
TORQUE SPECIFICATIONS

Application	Ft. Lbs. (N.m)
Cooler Union	21 (29)
Extension Housing Bolt	27 (36)
Oil Temperature Sensor	11 (15)
Oil Cooler Pipe Union Nut	25 (34)
Oil Pump-To-Case Bolt	16 (22)
Overdrive-To-Case Bolt	18 (25)
Rear Mounting-To-Extension Housing Bolt	18 (25)
Shift Lever Nut	12 (16)
Speed Sensor Bolt	12 (16)
Speedometer Driven Gear Bolt	12 (16)
Torque Converter-To-Drive Plate Bolt	30 (41)
Transmission Housing Bolt	
10 mm	25 (34)
12 mm	42 (57)

Application	INCH Lbs. (N.m)
Detent Spring Bolt	89 (10)
Neutral Safety Switch	
Adjusting Bolt	115 (13)
Retaining Nut	35 (4)
Oil Pan Bolt	71 (8)
Oil Pump-To-Stator Shaft Bolt	71 (8)
Oil Strainer Bolt	89 (10)
Parking Lock Pawl Bracket Bolt	65 (7.3)
Solenoid-To-Valve Body Bolt	89 (10)
Throttle Cable-To-Transmission Case Bolt	89 (10)
Upper Valve Body-To-Lower Valve Body Bolt	62 (7)
Valve Body-To-Case Bolt	89 (10)

TRANSMISSION SPECIFICATIONS
TRANSMISSION SPECIFICATIONS

Application	In. (mm)
Bushing Diameter (Maximum)	
Direct Clutch Drum	2.126 (53.97)
Extension Housing	1.578 (40.09)
Forward Clutch Drum	.948 (24.08)
Front Planetary Ring Gear	.948 (24.08)
OD Clutch Drum	1.067 (27.11)
OD Planetary Gear	.444 (11.27)
Oil Pump Body	1.504 (38.19)
Oil Pump Stator Shaft	
Front	.850 (38.19)
Rear	1.066 (27.08)
Sun Gear Bushing	.948 (24.8)
Transmission Case	1.504 (38.19)
Clutch Pack Clearance	
1st & Reverse Brake Pack	.028-.048 (.70-1.22)
2nd Brake Clutch	.024-.078 (.62-1.98)
Oil Pump Clearance	
Gear Tip	
Standard	.004-.006 (.11-.14)
Maximum	.012 (.30)
Gear-To-Body	
Standard	.003-.006 (.07-.15)
Maximum	.012 (.30)
Side Gear	
Standard	.0008-.0020 (.020-.050)
Maximum	.004 (.10)
Output Shaft End Play	.011-.034 (.27-.86)
Piston Stroke	
Direct Clutch	.054-.066 (1.37-1.67)
Forward Clutch	.114-.169 (2.90-4.29)
OD Brake	.055-.067 (1.40-1.70)
OD Clutch	.073-.085 (1.85-2.15)
2nd Brake	.024-.078 (.62-1.98)
2nd Coast Brake	.059-.118 (1.49-3.00)
Planetary Pinion Gear Clearance	.008-.024 (.20-.60)
Torque Converter Depth	1.22 (31.1)

Montero

APPLICATION

APPLICATION

Vehicle	Transmission Model
1995-96 Montero	V4AW3

CAUTION: Vehicle is equipped with Supplemental Restraint System (SRS). When servicing vehicle, use care to avoid accidental air bag deployment. SRS-related components are located in steering column, center console, instrument panel and lower panel on instrument panel. DO NOT use electrical test equipment on these circuits. If necessary, deactivate SRS before servicing components. See AIR BAG SERVICING article in APPLICATIONS & IDENTIFICATION section.

DESCRIPTION

Automatic transmission is a 4-speed electronically controlled transmission. Solenoids that control shift changes are located in valve body. Solenoids are controlled by a Transmission Control Module (TCM). TCM receives information from various input devices and uses this information to control shift solenoids for transmission shifting and lock-up solenoid for torque converter lock-up.

An Overdrive (OD) switch is mounted on the shift lever. When OD switch is depressed to ON position, transmission will shift into 4th gear when shift lever is in "D" position, and OD OFF light on instrument panel will go off. When OD switch is released to OFF position, transmission will shift into 3rd gear, and OD OFF light on instrument panel will illuminate.

A pattern select switch is located near shift lever on center console. Pattern select switch contains a POWER (PWR) and a HOLD operating position. When pattern select switch is depressed (PWR position), transmission upshifts and downshifts will occur at a higher vehicle speed than with switch released. An indicator light on instrument panel indicates pattern select switch is in PWR (on) position.

Transmission is equipped with a shift lock and key interlock system. Shift lock system prevents shift lever from being moved from Park unless brake pedal is depressed. Key interlock system prevents ignition key from being moved from ACC to LOCK position on ignition switch unless shift lever is in Park.

NOTE: For shift lock and key interlock system testing and adjustments, see MITSUBISHI V4AW3 overhaul article.

OPERATION

TCM

TCM receives information from various input devices and uses this information to control solenoids on transmission valve body. TCM controls transmission shifting, shift feel, line pressure and torque converter lock-up.

TCM contains a self-diagnostic system, which will store trouble code(s) if failure or problem exists in electronic control system. DTC can be retrieved to determine problem area. See SELF-DIAGNOSTIC SYSTEM. TCM is located under left side of instrument panel, left of steering column. *See Fig. 1.*

TCM INPUT DEVICES

Brakelight Switch Signal – Brakelight switch delivers input signal to TCM, indicating vehicle braking. Brakelight switch is located on brake pedal support.

Engine Coolant Temperature Sensor (ECT) Signal – Engine coolant temperature sensor delivers input signal to TCM, indicating engine coolant temperature. Coolant temperature sensor is located on engine. *See Fig. 2.*

Cruise Control Electronic Control Unit (ECU) – Cruise control ECU delivers an input signal to control overdrive operation in accordance with vehicle speed when cruise control is operating. When in overdrive with cruise control on, if vehicle speed drops 2 MPH less than the set speed, overdrive is released to prevent reduction in vehicle speed. Once vehicle speed is more than the set speed, overdrive function is resumed. If coolant temperature is low, transmission will not shift into overdrive. Cruise control ECU is located below center A/C vent, behind temperature control panel.

OD Switch Signal – The OD switch provides an input signal to TCM to indicate when overdrive is selected by operator. When OD switch is depressed to ON position, transmission will shift into 4th gear when shift lever is in "D" position, and OD OFF light on instrument panel will go off. When OD switch is released to OFF position, transmission will shift into 3rd gear, and OD OFF light on instrument panel will come on. The OD switch is mounted on shift lever.

Oil Temperature Sensor Signal – Oil temperature sensor provides TCM with ATF temperature values. TCM uses this information to control shift points for maximum performance. If transmission oil temperature exceeds standard values, instrument panel ATF - TEMP light will come on.

Neutral Safety Switch Signal – Neutral safety switch delivers an input signal to TCM indicating shift lever position. Switch is located on side of transmission.

Throttle Position (TP) Sensor Signal – TP sensor delivers closed throttle and variable throttle position input signals to TCM. TP sensor is located on side of throttle body.

Vehicle Speed Sensor Signal – Vehicle speed signal is delivered to TCM by No. 1 and No. 2 speed sensors.

4WD Low Range Detection Switch – On 1996 models only, 4WD low range detection switch provides information to TCM when transfer case is in 4WD low-lock range.

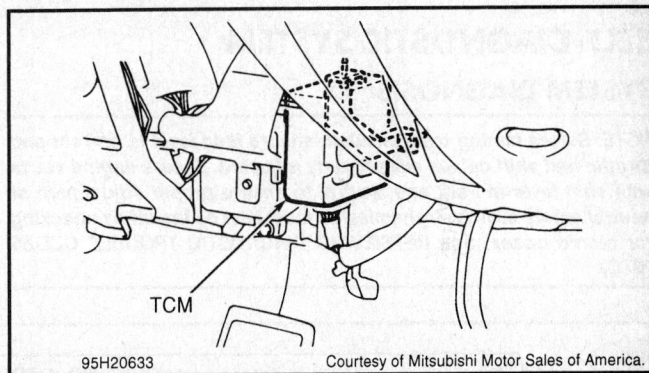

95H20633   Courtesy of Mitsubishi Motor Sales of America.

Fig. 1: Locating Transmission Control Module (TCM)

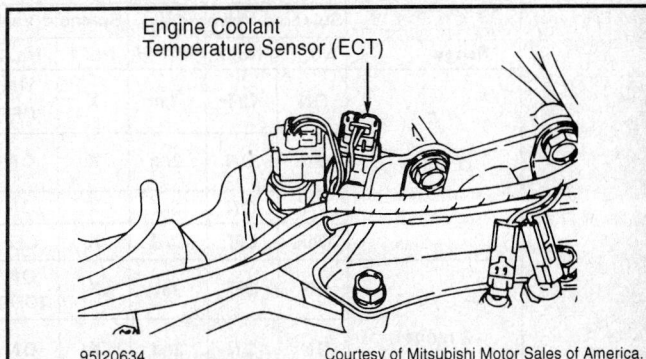

95I20634   Courtesy of Mitsubishi Motor Sales of America.

Fig. 2: Locating Coolant Temperature Sensor (CTS)

TCM OUTPUT DEVICES

Shift Solenoids No. 1 & No. 2 – TCM controls transmission shifting by delivering an output signal to operate proper solenoid. Solenoids

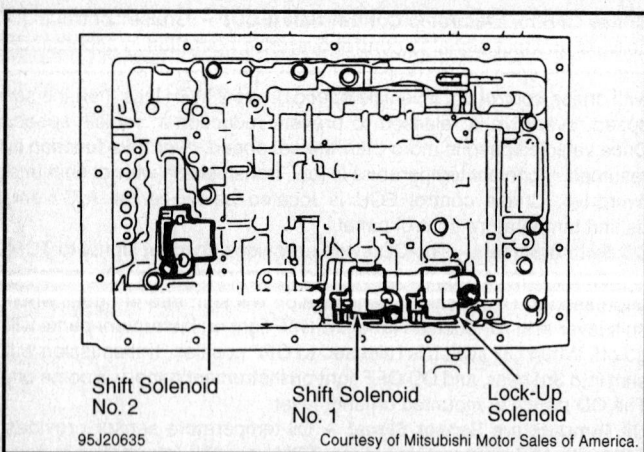

Fig. 3: Locating Lock-Up & Shift Solenoids

are located on transmission valve body. *See Fig. 3.* Solenoids are operated in accordance with shift lever range. If a solenoid malfunctions, TCM may select a preselected gear. *See Fig. 4.*

NOTE: *TCM provides a fail-safe system which will place transmission in preselected gear depending on solenoid failure. In other gears, fail-safe system will not be activated and transmission will be placed in a specified gear. See Fig. 4.*

Lock-Up Solenoid – TCM controls torque converter lock-up by delivering an output signal to lock-up solenoid. Lock-up solenoid is activated when shift lever is in "D" position and vehicle is at specified speed. Solenoid is located on transmission valve body. *See Fig. 3.*

SELF-DIAGNOSTIC SYSTEM

SYSTEM DIAGNOSIS

NOTE: *Before testing transmission, ensure fluid level is correct and throttle and shift cables are properly adjusted. Ensure engine starts with shift lever in Park and Neutral to ensure proper adjustment of neutral safety switch. Transmission must first be tested by checking for stored codes. See RETRIEVING DIAGNOSTIC TROUBLE CODES (DTC).*

TCM monitors transmission operation and contains a self-diagnostic system which stores a DTC if an electronic control system failure or problem exists. If a problem exists in any of the solenoids or speed sensors and a DTC is set, TCM delivers a signal to blink the ATF TEMP light on instrument panel to warn the driver. DTCs may be set if a failure exists and can be retrieved for transmission diagnosis.

RETRIEVING DIAGNOSTIC TROUBLE CODES (DTC)

NOTE: *Before retrieving DTC, ensure proper battery voltage exists for proper self-diagnosis system operation. DO NOT disconnect battery or ECM connectors before retrieving DTCs.*

Retrieving Codes Using Scan Tool – Ensure ignition switch is in OFF position. Connect scan tool to Data Link Connector (DLC). *See Fig. 5.* Turn ignition switch to ON position. Check for stored DTCs and record code(s). See DIAGNOSTIC TROUBLE CODE IDENTIFICATION table.

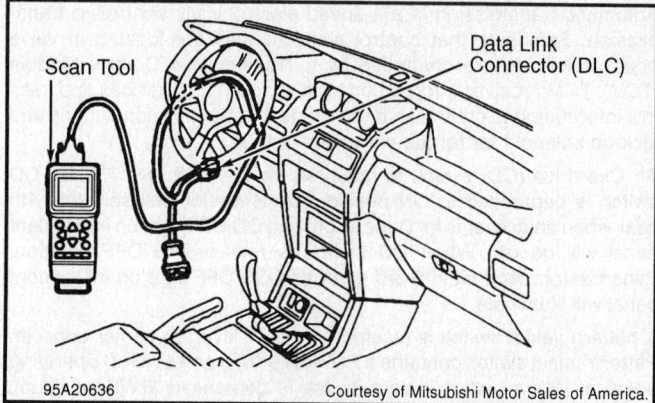

Fig. 5: Retrieving Codes Using Scan Tool

Retrieving Codes Using Oil Temperature Warning Light – **1)** Using jumper wire, ground DLC terminal No. 1. *See Fig. 6.* Note number of flashes from oil temperature warning light on instrument panel. *See Fig. 7.* If normal system operation exists, oil temperature warning light will blink 2 times per second. *See Fig. 8.*
2) If system is operating correctly and no DTC exists, turn ignition off and remove jumper wire. If DTC exists, oil temperature warning light

Range	NORMAL			NO. 1 SOLENOID MALFUNCTIONING			NO. 2 SOLENOID MALFUNCTIONING			BOTH SOLENOIDS MALFUNCTIONING		
	Solenoid Valve		Gear Position	Solenoid Valve		Gear Position	Solenoid Valve		Gear Position	Solenoid Valve		Gear Position
	No. 1	No. 2		No. 1	No. 2		No. 1	No. 2		No. 1	No. 2	
D range	ON	OFF	1st	X	ON (OFF)	3rd (O/D)	ON	X	1st	X	X	O/D
	ON	ON	2nd	X	ON	3rd	OFF (ON)	X	O/D (1st)	X	X	O/D
	OFF	ON	3rd	X	ON	3rd	OFF	X	O/D	X	X	O/D
	OFF	OFF	O/D	X	OFF	O/D	OFF	X	O/D	X	X	O/D
2 range	ON	OFF	1st	X	ON (OFF)	3rd (O/D)	ON	X	1st	X	X	3rd
	ON	ON	2nd	X	ON	3rd	OFF (ON)	X	3rd (1st)	X	X	3rd
	OFF	ON	3rd	X	ON	3rd	OFF	x	3rd	X	X	3rd
L range	ON	OFF	1st	X	OFF	1st	ON	X	1st	X	X	1st
	ON	ON	2nd	X	ON	2nd	ON	X	1st	X	X	1st

( ): No fail-safe function   X: Malfunctions

93E25019   Courtesy of Mitsubishi Motor Sales of America.

Fig. 4: Checking Operation Of Shift Solenoids No. 1 & No. 2

will flash once every 2 seconds. The number of flashes will equal first digit of DTC. After a pause of 2 seconds, second digit will be displayed. Oil temperature warning light will flash once every half second for second digit. *See Fig. 8.*

3) If more than one DTC exists, next DTC will be displayed after pause of 3 seconds. Smallest DTC number will be first. DTCs will be repeated.

4) Once DTC is obtained, determine probable cause and symptom. See appropriate DIAGNOSTIC TROUBLE CODE IDENTIFICATION table. To trouble shoot DTC, see DIAGNOSTIC TESTING. Turn ignition off and remove jumper wire.

NOTE: Once repairs have been performed, DTCs must be cleared from TCM memory. See CLEARING DIAGNOSTIC TROUBLE CODES (DTC).

DIAGNOSTIC TROUBLE CODE IDENTIFICATION (1995 MODELS)

DTC No.	[1] Probable Cause
11	Defective TP Sensor Or TP Sensor Circuit
32	Open No. 1 Speed Sensor Circuit
38	Open No. 2 Speed Sensor Circuit
41	Open Solenoid No. 1 Circuit
42	Short Solenoid No. 1 Circuit
43	Open Solenoid No. 2 Circuit
44	Short Solenoid No. 2 Circuit
47	Open Lock-Up Solenoid Circuit
48	Short Lock-up Solenoid Circuit

[1] – Check listed fault code and component for probable cause. See appropriate fault code listing under DIAGNOSTIC TESTING. Also check wiring and connections of specified component.

DIAGNOSTIC TROUBLE CODE IDENTIFICATION (1996 MODELS)

DTC No.	[1] Probable Cause
11	Defective TP Sensor Or TP Sensor Circuit
15	Open Oil Temperature Sensor Circuit
16	Short Oil Temperature Sensor Circuit
21	Short Ignition Signal Circuit
22	Open Ignition Signal Circuit
29	Short Neutral Safety Switch Circuit
30	Open Neutral Safety Switch Circuit
31	Open No. 2 Speed Sensor Circuit
32	Open No. 1 Speed Sensor Circuit
41	Open Solenoid No. 1 Circuit
42	Short Solenoid No. 1 Circuit
43	Open Solenoid No. 2 Circuit
44	Short Solenoid No. 2 Circuit
47	Open Lock-Up Solenoid Circuit
48	Short Lock-up Solenoid Circuit
49	[2] Torque Converter Clutch Engagement Malfunction
50	[2] Torque Converter Clutch Disengagement Malfunction
51	1st Gear Ratio Signal Incorrect
52	2nd Gear Ratio Signal Incorrect
53	3rd Gear Ratio Signal Incorrect
54	4th Gear Ratio Signal Incorrect

[1] – Check listed fault code and component for probable cause. See appropriate fault code listing under DIAGNOSTIC TESTING. Also check wiring and connections of specified component.

[2] – Scan tool is required for testing malfunctioning circuit.

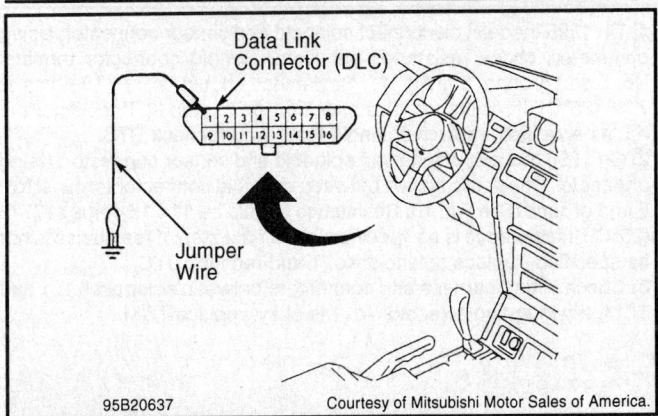

95B20637   Courtesy of Mitsubishi Motor Sales of America.

Fig. 6: Identifying Data Link Connector (DLC) Terminals

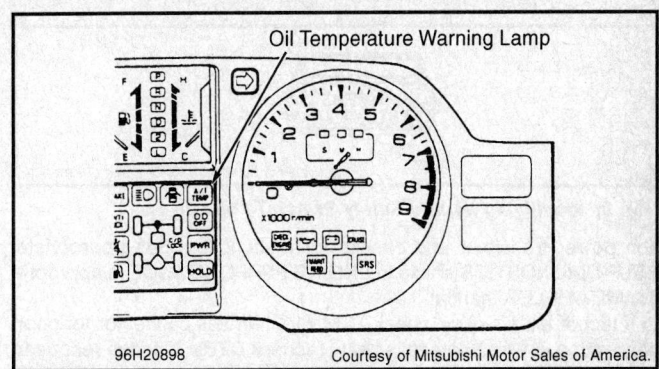

96H20898   Courtesy of Mitsubishi Motor Sales of America.

Fig. 7: Locating A/T Temperature Warning Light

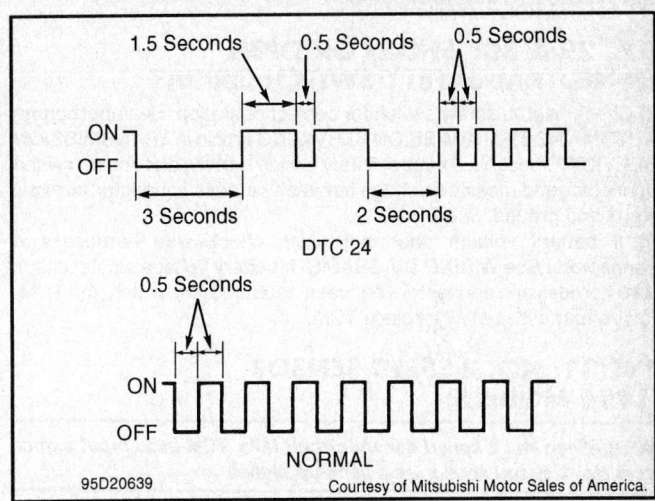

95D20639   Courtesy of Mitsubishi Motor Sales of America.

Fig. 8: Identifying DTC Displays

CLEARING DIAGNOSTIC TROUBLE CODES (DTC)

Once repairs have been performed, DTCs must be cleared from TCM memory. DTCs may be cleared by disconnecting negative battery cable for 10 seconds or more. Reconnect cable and ensure DTCs have been cleared. Start engine and warm to normal operating temperature. Run engine at idle for 10 minutes. DTCs may also be cleared using scan tool. Refer to manufacturer's instruction manual.

DIAGNOSTIC TESTING

DTC 11: THROTTLE POSITION (TP) SENSOR

For diagnosis and testing information, see appropriate SELF-DIAGNOSTICS article in ENGINE PERFORMANCE in appropriate MITCHELL® manual. If TP sensor is okay, check wiring harness and connectors between TP sensor and TCM. Repair if necessary. If wiring harness and connectors are okay, replace TCM.

DTC 15 & 16: OPEN OR SHORT IN OIL TEMPERATURE SENSOR CIRCUIT

1) Test oil temperature for proper operation. See OIL TEMPERATURE SENSOR under COMPONENT TESTING. If oil temperature sensor is okay, check wire harness, connectors and ground circuit for poor connections or damage. Go to next step.

2) If wire harness and connectors are okay, check DTCs again and verify code No. 15 or No. 16 still exists. If either code still exists, replace TCM.

DTC 21 & 22: SHORT OR OPEN IN IGNITION SIGNAL CIRCUIT

1) Using an external tachometer, verify vehicles' tachometer is operating accurately. If tachometer is incorrect, check ignition coil and igni-

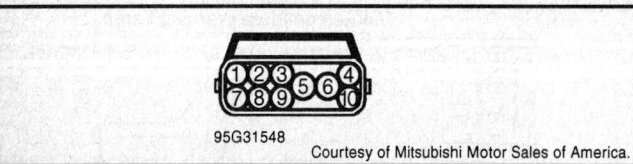

95G31548

Courtesy of Mitsubishi Motor Sales of America.

Fig. 9: Identifying Neutral Safety Switch Terminals

tion power transistor and circuits for malfunction. See appropriate SELF-DIAGNOSTICS article in ENGINE PERFORMANCE in appropriate MITCHELL® manual.

2) If tachometer is okay, check TCM wire harness connector for poor connection. If wire harness is okay, recheck DTCs. If codes reappear check wire harness between ignition power transistor and TCM. If wire harness is okay, replace TCM.

DTC 29 & 30: SHORT OR OPEN IN NEUTRAL SAFETY SWITCH CIRCUIT

1) Check neutral safety switch for correct operation. See appropriate AUTOMATIC TRANSMISSION SERVICING article in TRANSMISSION SERVICING section. If neutral safety switch is okay, disconnect switch connector and measure voltage between harness connector terminal No. 1 and ground. *See Fig. 9.*

2) If battery voltage does not exist, check wire harness and connectors. See WIRING DIAGRAMS. If battery voltage exists, check wire harness and connectors between neutral safety switch and TCM. If wire harness is okay, replace TCM.

DTC 31: NO. 2 SPEED SENSOR (1996 MODELS)

NOTE: When No. 2 speed sensor circuit fails, TCM uses input signal from No. 1 speed sensor as a back-up signal.

1) Check No. 2 speed sensor. See NO. 2 SPEED SENSOR (1996 MODELS) under COMPONENT TESTING. If resistance is as specified, reconnect speed sensor connector and go to next step. If resistance is not as specified replace No. 2 speed sensor and recheck DTCs.

2) Connect voltmeter between solenoid and sensor connector terminals No. 9 and No. 10. *See Fig. 10.* Lift and support vehicle to allow drive wheels to spin freely. With transmission in "D" position, engine at 1000 RPM and wheel speed at 19 mph (30 km/h). Measured voltage should be .3 - 2.5 volts.

3) If voltage is as specified, go to next step. If voltage is not as specified, replace the No. 2 speed sensor. If DTC still exists, check speed sensor rotor. See MITSUBISHI V4AW3 overhaul article. If DTC still exists after speed sensor rotor is replaced, check for noise interference and repair.

4) Check and repair wiring harness and connectors between No. 2 speed sensor and TCM. If wiring is okay, recheck DTC. If DTC still exists, replace TCM.

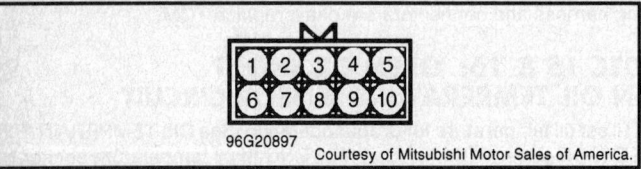

96G20897

Courtesy of Mitsubishi Motor Sales of America.

Fig. 10: Identifying Sensor & Solenoid Connector Terminals (1996 Models)

DTC 32: NO. 1 SPEED SENSOR (1995-96 MODELS)

1) Check No. 1 speed sensor. See NO. 1 SPEED SENSOR under COMPONENT TESTING. If resistance is as specified, reconnect speed sensor connector and go to next step. If resistance is not as specified replace No. 1 speed sensor and recheck DTCs.

2) On 1995 models, connect voltmeter between solenoid and sensor connector terminals No. 3 and No. 4. *See Fig. 11.* On 1996 models, connect voltmeter between solenoid and sensor connector terminals No. 9 and No. 10. *See Fig. 10.* Lift and support vehicle to allow drive wheels to spin freely. With transmission in "D" position, engine at 1000 RPM and wheel speed at 19 mph (30 km/h). Measured voltage should be .3 - 2.5 volts.

3) If voltage is as specified, go to next step. If voltage is not as specified, replace the No. 1 speed sensor. If DTC still exists, check speed sensor rotor. See MITSUBISHI V4AW3 overhaul article. If DTC exists after speed sensor rotor is replaced, check for noise interference and repair.

4) Check and repair wiring harness and connectors between No. 1 speed sensor and TCM. If wiring is okay, recheck DTCs. If DTCs still exists, replace TCM.

96H09829

Courtesy of Mitsubishi Motor Sales of America.

Fig. 11: Identifying Sensor & Solenoid Connector Terminals (1995 Models)

DTC 38: NO. 2 SPEED SENSOR (1995 MODELS)

1) Test drive vehicle and check operation of speedometer. If speedometer is functioning properly, go to next step. If speedometer is not functioning properly, check No. 2 speed sensor. See NO. 2 SPEED SENSOR (1995 MODELS) under COMPONENT TESTING. If resistance is as specified, reconnect speed sensor connector and go to step 3). If resistance is not as specified replace No. 2 speed sensor and recheck DTCs.

2) Check speedometer circuit and speedometer. See appropriate INSTRUMENT PANELS article in ACCESSORIES & EQUIPMENT in appropriate MITCHELL® manual. Replace as necessary.

3) Lift and support vehicle to allow drive wheels to spin freely. Allow engine to idle with transmission in "D" position. Using voltmeter, measure voltage between TCM connector terminal No. 9 and ground. *See Fig. 12.* Voltage should alternate between 0 - 5 volts. If voltage is as specified, go to next step. If voltage is not as specified, recheck DTC. If DTC still exists, replace TCM.

4) Check and repair wiring harness and connectors between ECM and TCM. If wiring is okay, recheck DTC.

DTC 41 & 42: OPEN OR SHORT IN SOLENOID NO. 1 CIRCUIT

NOTE: A stuck solenoid will not set a DTC. DTCs are only set for circuit malfunctions, not mechanical failures.

1) On 1995 models, disconnect solenoid and sensor connector. Using ohmmeter, check resistance between solenoid connector terminal No. 5 and ground. *See Fig. 11.* Resistance should be 11 - 15 ohms at 77°F (25°C). If resistance is as specified, go to step 3). If resistance is not as specified, replace solenoid No. 1 and recheck DTC.

2) On 1996 models, disconnect solenoid and sensor connector. Using ohmmeter, check resistance between solenoid connector terminal No. 6 and ground. *See Fig. 10.* Resistance should be 11 - 15 ohms at 77°F (25°C). If resistance is as specified, go to next step. If resistance is not as specified, replace solenoid No. 1 and recheck DTC.

3) Check wiring harness and connectors between solenoid No. 1 and TCM. If wiring and solenoid No. 1 is okay, replace TCM.

DTC 43 & 44: OPEN OR SHORT IN SOLENOID NO. 2 CIRCUIT

NOTE: A stuck solenoid will not set a DTC. DTCs are only set for circuit malfunctions, not mechanical failures.

1) On 1995 models, disconnect solenoid and sensor connector. Using ohmmeter, check resistance between solenoid connector terminal No. 6 and ground. See Fig. 11. Resistance should be 11 - 15 ohms at 77°F (25°C). If resistance is as specified, go to step 3). If resistance is not as specified, replace solenoid No. 2 and recheck DTC.
2) On 1996 models, disconnect solenoid and sensor connector. Using ohmmeter, check resistance between solenoid connector terminal No. 7 and ground. See Fig. 10. Resistance should be 11 - 15 ohms at 77°F (25°C). If resistance is as specified, go to next step. If resistance is not as specified, replace solenoid No. 2 and recheck DTC.
3) Check wiring harness and connectors between solenoid No. 2 and TCM. If wiring and solenoid No. 2 is okay, replace TCM.

DTC 47 & 48: OPEN OR SHORT IN LOCK-UP SOLENOID CIRCUIT

NOTE: A stuck solenoid will not set a DTC. DTCs are only set for circuit malfunctions, not mechanical failures.

1) On 1995 models, disconnect solenoid and sensor connector. Using ohmmeter, check resistance between solenoid connector terminal No. 7 and ground. See Fig. 11. Resistance should be 11 - 15 ohms at 77°F (25°C). If resistance is as specified, go to step 3). If resistance is not as specified, replace lock-up solenoid and recheck DTC.
2) On 1996 models, disconnect solenoid and sensor connector. Using ohmmeter, check resistance between solenoid connector terminal No. 8 and ground. See Fig. 10. Resistance should be 11 - 15 ohms at 77°F (25°C). If resistance is as specified, go to next step. If resistance is not as specified, replace lock-up solenoid and recheck DTC.
3) Check wiring harness and connectors between lock-up solenoid and TCM. If wiring and lock-up solenoid is okay, replace TCM.

DTC 49: TORQUE CONVERTER CLUTCH (TCC) ENGAGEMENT MALFUNCTION

1) Using scan tool, verify vehicle tachometer and scan tool vehicle rpm values are identical. If tachometer values are identical, go to next step. If tachometer values are different, test ignition signal circuit. See DTC 21 & 22: SHORT OR OPEN IN IGNITION SIGNAL CIRCUIT.
2) Lift and support vehicle to allow drive wheels to spin freely. With transmission in "D" position, run engine to 1300 - 1900 rpm. Verify scan tool and speedometer read 31 mph (50 km/h). If values are identical, go to next step. If values are different, test No. 2 speed sensor. See DTC 31: NO. 2 SPEED SENSOR (1996 MODELS).
3) Check lock-up solenoid for proper operation. See LOCK-UP SOLENOID under COMPONENT TESTING. If lock-up solenoid is okay, go to next step. If lock-up solenoid is bad, replace and retest system.
4) Check wiring harness and connectors between lock-up solenoid and TCM. If wiring harness and connectors are okay, check TCC engagement hydraulic pressure, valve body malfunction or TCC slipping.

DTC 50: TORQUE CONVERTER CLUTCH (TCC) DISENGAGEMENT MALFUNCTION

1) Using scan tool, verify vehicle tachometer and scan tool vehicle rpm values are identical. If tachometer values are identical, go to next step. If tachometer values are different, test ignition signal circuit. See DTC 21 & 22: SHORT OR OPEN IN IGNITION SIGNAL CIRCUIT.
2) Lift and support vehicle to allow drive wheels to spin freely. With transmission in "D" position, run engine to 1300 - 1900 rpm. Verify scan tool and speedometer read 31 mph (50 km/h). If values are identical, go to next step. If values are different, test No. 2 speed sensor. See DTC 31: NO. 2 SPEED SENSOR (1996 MODELS).
3) Check lock-up solenoid for proper operation. See LOCK-UP SOLENOID under COMPONENT TESTING. If lock-up solenoid is okay, go to next step. If lock-up solenoid is bad, replace and retest system.
4) Check wiring harness and connectors between lock-up solenoid and TCM. If wiring harness and connectors are okay, check valve body malfunction or TCC sticking.

DTC 51: 1ST GEAR RATIO SIGNAL INCORRECT

1) If DTC 31 is set, go to DTC 31: NO. 2 SPEED SENSOR (1996 MODELS). If DTC 31 is not set and DTC 32 is set, go to DTC 32: NO. 1 SPEED SENSOR. If neither DTC 31 nor DTC 32 is set, go to next step.
2) Test No. 2 speed sensor. See NO. 2 SPEED SENSOR (1996 MODELS) under COMPONENT TESTING. If resistance is as specified, go to next step. If resistance is not as specified, replace No. 2 speed sensor and recheck DTC. If DTC still exists, go to step 5).
3) Test No. 1 speed sensor. See NO. 1 SPEED SENSOR under COMPONENT TESTING. If resistance is as specified, go to next step. If resistance is not as specified, replace No. 1 speed sensor and recheck DTC. If DTC still exists, go to step 5).
4) If referenced from another DTC, go back to referenced DTC. Check No. 2 one-way clutch system. See NO. 2 ONE-WAY CLUTCH in MITSUBISHI V4AW3 overhaul article.
5) Check No. 1 speed sensor and No. 2 speed sensor shielding wire. Repair as necessary. If shielding wire is okay, recheck DTC. If DTC still exists, replace sensor rotor. If DTC still exists after sensor rotor is replaced, check for interference noise and repair.

DTC 52: 2ND GEAR RATIO SIGNAL INCORRECT

If DTC 51 is set also, go to DTC 51: 1ST GEAR RATIO SIGNAL INCORRECT test. If DTC 51 is not set, check 2nd brake and No. 1 one-way clutch systems for a mechanical failure. See 2ND BRAKE and NO. 1 ONE-WAY CLUTCH in MITSUBISHI V4AW3 overhaul article.

DTC 53: 3RD GEAR RATIO SIGNAL INCORRECT

If DTC 51 is set also, go to DTC 51: 1ST GEAR RATIO SIGNAL INCORRECT test. If DTC 51 is not set, check direct clutch system for a mechanical failure. See DIRECT CLUTCH in MITSUBISHI V4AW3 overhaul article.

DTC 54: 4TH GEAR RATIO SIGNAL INCORRECT

If DTC 51 is set also, go to DTC 51: 1ST GEAR RATIO SIGNAL INCORRECT test. If DTC 51 is not set, check overdrive brake system for a mechanical failure. See OVERDRIVE BRAKE in MITSUBISHI V4AW3 overhaul article.

SYSTEM TROUBLE SHOOTING

NOTE: Check system using appropriate scan tool. See WIRING DIAGRAMS, ELECTRICAL TESTING and COMPONENT TESTING for further information when trouble shooting system problems.

Communication With Scan Tool Not Possible – If scan tool cannot communicate with TCM, check proper connection with DLC. Check TCM power circuits, TCM ground circuits and malfunctioning TCM.
Shift Points Incorrect – If shift points are incorrect, check for DTCs. If no DTC is present, check oil temperature sensor, pattern select switch, 4WD low range detection switch and TCM for proper operation.
Upshifts Occur Spontaneously – If upshifting occurs spontaneously, check neutral safety switch, overdrive switch and TCM for proper operation.
TCC Lock-up Malfunctioning – If TCC lock-up system is not operating properly, check torque converter, valve body, lock-up switch and oil temperature switch.

ELECTRICAL TESTING

THROTTLE POSITION (TP) SENSOR SIGNAL

For diagnostic and testing information, see appropriate SELF-DIAG-NOSTICS article in ENGINE PERFORMANCE in appropriate MITCH-ELL® manual.

TCM VOLTAGES

Access TCM. *See Fig. 1.* Turn ignition on. Using DVOM, backprobe TCM connector. *See Fig. 12 or 13.* Check voltage between designated terminals on TCM connector and ground. See appropriate TCM TERMINAL VOLTAGE SPECIFICATIONS table. Voltage should be as specified.

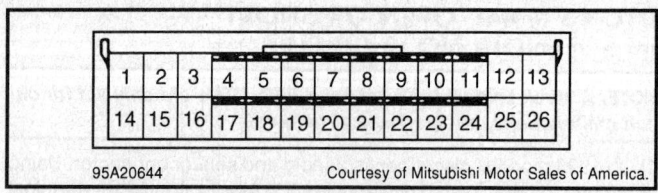

95A20644   Courtesy of Mitsubishi Motor Sales of America.

Fig. 12: Identifying TCM Terminals (1995)

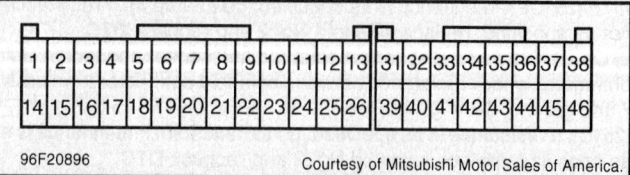

96F20896   Courtesy of Mitsubishi Motor Sales of America.

Fig. 13: Identifying TCM Terminals (1996)

TCM TERMINAL VOLTAGE SPECIFICATIONS (1995 MODELS)

Terminal No.	Circuit	Condition	Voltage
1	No. 1 Shift Solenoid	Transmission In 1st Or 2nd Gear	Battery Voltage
		Transmission In 3rd Or 4th Gear	0
2	No. 2 Shift Solenoid	Transmission In 2nd Or 3rd Gear	Battery Voltage
		Transmission In 1st Or 4th Gear	0
3	Lock-Up Solenoid	Lock-Up Clutch Engaged	Battery Voltage
		Lock-Up Clutch Disengaged	0
4	No. 1 Speed Sensor Ground	Ignition Off	0
		Ignition On	2.5
5	Neutral Safety Switch	Transmission In "N" Position	Battery Voltage
		Transmission Not In "N" Position	0
6	Diagnostic Output Terminal	Scan Tool Not Connected	Battery Voltage
7	HOLD Mode	HOLD Mode Selected	Battery Voltage
		HOLD Mode Not Selected	0
8	Overdrive Switch	Overdrive ON	0
		Overdrive OFF	Battery Voltage
9	No. 2 Speed Sensor	Vehicle Moving	0 - 5 Alternating
10	No. 1 Speed Sensor Output	Vehicle Stopped	About 2.5
		Vehicle Moving	Other Than 2.5
11	Cruise Control Switch	Cruise Control ON	0
		Cruise Control OFF	Battery Voltage
12	Oil Temperature Sensor	Oil Temperature @ 248°F (120°C)	About 1.9
		Oil Temperature @ 302°F (150°C)	About 1.1
13	Diagnostic Test Mode Terminal	Manufacturer Does Not Specify	Not Specified
14	Power Supply	Ignition ON	Battery Voltage
		Ignition OFF	0
15	Back-Up Power Supply	At All Times	Battery Voltage
16	Ground	Engine Idling	0
17	Brakelight Switch	Brake Pedal Depressed	0
		Brake Pedal Released	Battery Voltage
18	Neutral Safety Switch	Transmission In "2" Position	Battery Voltage
		Transmission Not In "2" Position	0
19	Neutral Safety Switch	Transmission In "L" Position	Battery Voltage
		Transmission Not In "L" Position	0
20	Oil Temperature Warning Light	Normal Temperature Range	0
		For 5 Seconds After Ignition Is Turned ON	Battery Voltage
21	Power Mode	Power Mode Selected	Battery Voltage
		Power Mode Not Selected	0
24	Engine Coolant Temperature Sensor	Coolant Temperature @ 86°F (30°C)	Battery Voltage
		Coolant Temperature @ 176°F (80°C)	0
26	Throttle Position Sensor	Throttle Closed (At Idle)	.3 - 1.0
		Throttle Wide Open	4.4 - 5.0

TCM TERMINAL VOLTAGE SPECIFICATIONS (1996 MODELS)

Terminal No.	Circuit	Condition	Voltage
1	Lock-Up Solenoid	Lock-Up Clutch Engaged	Battery Voltage
		Lock-Up Clutch Disengaged	0
2	Back-Up Power Supply	At All Times	Battery Voltage
5	Brakelight Switch	Brake Pedal Depressed	0
		Brake Pedal Released	Battery Voltage
8	Throttle Position Sensor	Throttle Closed (At Idle)	.3 - 1.0
		Throttle Wide Open	4.4 - 5.0
11	Neutral Safety Switch	Transmission In "P" Position	Battery Voltage
		Transmission Not In "P" Position	0
12	Ground	Engine Idling	0
14	No. 1 Shift Solenoid	Transmission In 1st Or 2nd Gear	Battery Voltage
		Transmission In 3rd Or 4th Gear	0
15	Power Supply	Ignition ON	Battery Voltage
16	No. 2 Shift Solenoid	Transmission In 2nd Or 3rd Gear	Battery Voltage
		Transmission In 1st Or 4th Gear	0
17	Diagnostic Test Mode Terminal	Manufacturer Does Not Specify	Not Specified
		Ignition OFF	0
18	Diagnostic Output Terminal	Scan Tool Not Connected	Battery Voltage
21	Oil Temperature Warning Light	Normal Temperature Range	0
		For 5 Seconds After Ignition Is Turned ON	Battery Voltage
22	Oil Temperature Sensor	Oil Temperature @ 248°F (120°C)	About 1.9
		Oil Temperature @ 302°F (150°C)	About 1.1
23	4WD Low Range Detection Switch	Transfer Lever In 4H-Lock	Battery Voltage
		Transfer Lever In 4L-Lock	0
24	Neutral Safety Switch	Transmission In "R" Position	Battery Voltage
		Transmission Not In "R" Position	0
25 & 26	Ground	Engine Idling	0
31	Neutral Safety Switch	Transmission In "L" Position	Battery Voltage
		Transmission Not In "L" Position	0
32	Neutral Safety Switch	Transmission In "N" Position	Battery Voltage
		Transmission Not In "N" Position	0
34	Power Mode	Power Mode Selected	Battery Voltage
		Power Mode Not Selected	0
35	No. 1 Speed Sensor Ground	Ignition Off	0
		Ignition On	2.5
36	No. 2 Speed Sensor Ground	Ignition Off	0
		Ignition On	2.5
37	Overdrive OFF Signal	[1] Steady Driving @ 31 mph (50 km/h)	Battery Voltage
		[1] Climbing Hill @ 31 mph (50 km/h)	0 - 1
38	Engine Ignition Signal	Engine @ 3000 RPM	.3 - 3.0
39	Neutral Safety Switch	Transmission In "D" Position	Battery Voltage
		Transmission Not In "D" Position	0
40	Neutral Safety Switch	Transmission In "2" Position	Battery Voltage
		Transmission Not In "2" Position	0
41	HOLD Mode	HOLD Mode Selected	Battery Voltage
		HOLD Mode Not Selected	0
42	Overdrive Switch	Overdrive ON	0
		Overdrive OFF	Battery Voltage
43	No. 1 Speed Sensor Output	Vehicle Stopped	About 2.5
		Vehicle Moving	Other Than 2.5
44	No. 1 Speed Sensor Output	Vehicle Stopped	About 2.5
		Vehicle Moving	Other Than 2.5
45	Engine Coolant Temperature Sensor	Coolant Temperature @ 86°F (30°C)	0
		Coolant Temperature @ 176°F (80°C)	2.5
46	MIL Signal	Ignition ON	.5 - 4.5

[1] – Test circuit with transmission in "D" position, mode selector normal and cruise control on.

COMPONENT TESTING

BRAKELIGHT SWITCH

1) Disconnect electrical connector from brakelight switch, located near brake pedal. Using ohmmeter, ensure continuity exists between terminal No. 2 (White/Red wire) and terminal No. 3 (Green wire) with brake pedal released. Replace brakelight switch if continuity does not exist. Continuity should not exist between terminals No. 2 and No. 3 with brake pedal depressed.

2) If continuity does not exist, ensure brake pedal is properly adjusted so brakelight switch has proper travel for switch operation. If proper brakelight switch travel exists, replace brakelight switch.

COOLANT TEMPERATURE SENSOR

Disconnect electrical connector from coolant temperature sensor. See Fig. 2. Using ohmmeter, check resistance between terminals of coolant temperature sensor. Resistance should be as specified in accordance with TEMPERATURE-TO-RESISTANCE VALUES table. Replace coolant temperature if resistance is not within specification.

TEMPERATURE-TO-RESISTANCE VALUES

Temperature °F (°C)	Ohms
32 (0)	5.8
68 (20)	2.4
104 (40)	1.1
176 (80)	0.3

NEUTRAL SAFETY SWITCH

For neutral safety switch testing procedure, see appropriate AUTOMATIC TRANSMISSION SERVICING article in TRANSMISSION SERVICING section.

OIL TEMPERATURE SENSOR

Disconnect solenoid and sensor connector. Using ohmmeter, check resistance between sensor connector terminals No. 1 and No. 2. See Fig. 10 or 11. Resistance should be 10k/ohms when oil temperature is 77°F (25°C). With oil temperature at 248°F (120°C), resistance should be 615 ohms. If resistance is not as specified, replace oil temperature sensor.

SOLENOIDS

For solenoid testing, see appropriate DTC under DIAGNOSTIC TESTING. To check solenoid operation, apply battery voltage to appropriate terminal of TCM connector and ground. Ensure operating sound can be heard when battery voltage is connected. Replace solenoid if operating sound cannot be heard.

THROTTLE POSITION (TP) SENSOR

For diagnostic and testing information, see appropriate SELF-DIAGNOSTICS article in ENGINE PERFORMANCE in appropriate MITCHELL® manual.

NO. 1 SPEED SENSOR

Disconnect solenoid and sensor connector. Using ohmmeter, measure resistance between terminals No. 3 and No. 4. See Fig. 10 or 11. Resistance should be 560-680 ohms at 68°F (20°C). If resistance is not as specified, replace No. 1 speed sensor.

NO. 2 SPEED SENSOR (1995 MODELS)

1) Lift and support vehicle. Disconnect solenoid and sensor connector. Remove No. 2 speed sensor from transmission. See Fig. 16. Connect jumper wire from negative battery terminal to speed sensor terminal No. 2. See Fig. 14. Connect jumper wire from positive battery terminal to speed sensor terminal No. 1. Connect a 3000-10,000 ohm resistor as shown in illustration.

2) Connect a voltmeter to speed sensor terminals No. 2 and No. 3. Ensure voltage is present while rotating speed sensor shaft clockwise. Voltage should fluctuate 4 pulses per revolution. If sensor does not test as specified, replace No. 2 speed sensor.

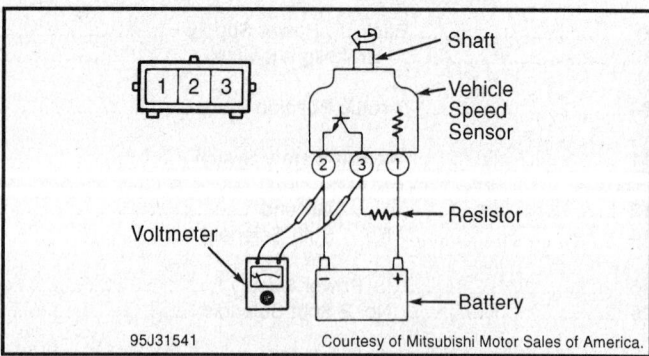

95J31541   Courtesy of Mitsubishi Motor Sales of America.

Fig. 14: Testing No. 2 Speed Sensor (1995 Models)

NO. 2 SPEED SENSOR (1996 MODELS)

Disconnect solenoid and sensor connector. Using ohmmeter, measure resistance between terminals No. 9 and No. 10. See Fig. 10. Resistance should be 560-680 ohms at 68°F (20°C). If resistance is not as specified, replace No. 2 speed sensor.

4WD LOW RANGE DETECTION SWITCH

For location and testing information on 4WD low range detection switch, see MITSUBISHI article in AXLE SHAFTS & TRANSFER CASES section.

REMOVAL & INSTALLATION

BRAKELIGHT SWITCH

Removal & Installation – 1) Disconnect electrical connector. Remove lock nut, and unscrew brakelight switch. To install, screw brakelight switch inward until brakelight plunger contacts brake pedal.

2) Loosen brakelight switch 1/2 to one turn. Install and tighten lock nut on brakelight switch. Install electrical connector. Ensure brakelights and cruise control operate properly.

OIL TEMPERATURE SENSOR

Removal & Installation – Sensor is located on transmission, near neutral safety switch. Disconnect electrical connector. Remove oil temperature sensor from transmission. To install, reverse removal procedure using NEW gasket.

NEUTRAL SAFETY SWITCH

Removal – Switch is located on side of transmission. Remove manual lever from control shaft on transmission. Bend up tabs on lock washer. Remove lock nut, lock washer and seal from control shaft. Remove retaining bolt and neutral safety switch.

Installation – 1) Install switch on control shaft. Loosely install switch retaining bolt. Install seal and lock washer. Install lock nut and tighten to specification. See TORQUE SPECIFICATIONS.

2) Switch must be adjusted. Ensure parking brake is applied. Temporarily install manual lever on control shaft. Place shift lever in Neutral. Remove manual lever. Rotate switch and align reference mark on switch with groove.

3) Hold switch in this position. Tighten retaining bolt to specification. Bend tabs on lock washer over against lock nut. To install remaining components, reverse removal procedure.

SOLENOIDS

Removal & Installation – Solenoids are located on transmission valve body. See Fig. 3. Remove bolt, solenoid and gasket from valve body. To install, reverse removal procedure.

THROTTLE POSITION SENSOR

For removal and installation information, see appropriate SELF-DIAG-NOSTICS article in ENGINE PERFORMANCE in appropriate MITCH-ELL® manual.

NO. 1 SPEED SENSOR

Removal & Installation – Disconnect electrical connector from No. 1 speed sensor. *See Fig. 15.* Remove bolt and No. 1 speed sensor. To install, reverse removal procedure.

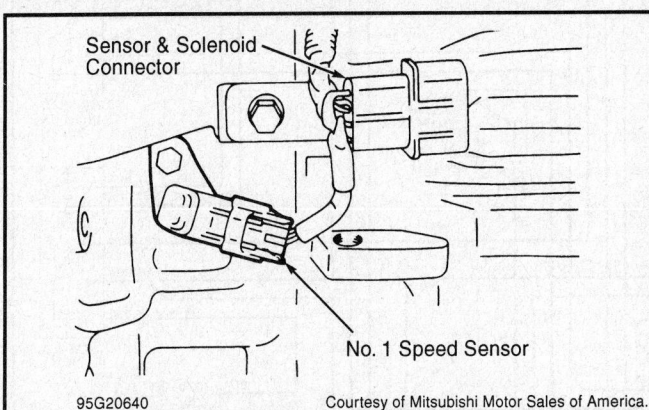

95G20640   Courtesy of Mitsubishi Motor Sales of America.

Fig. 15: Locating No. 1 Speed Sensor & Connector

NO. 2 SPEED SENSOR

Removal & Installation – Disconnect electrical connector. On 1996 models, remove bolt securing sensor to transmission. On 1995 models, unscrew sensor. On all models, remove No. 2 speed sensor from transmission. *See Fig. 16 or 17.* To install, reverse removal procedure.

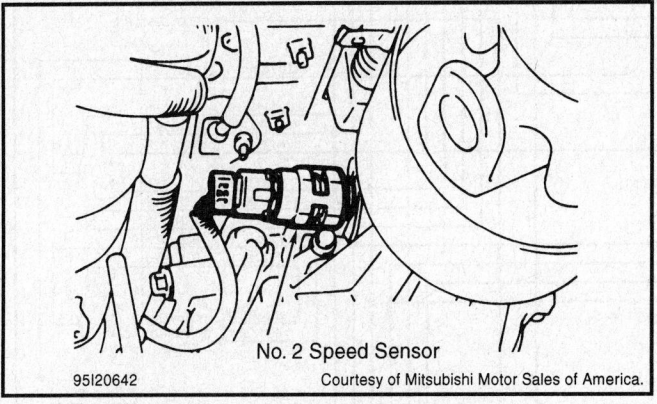

95I20642   Courtesy of Mitsubishi Motor Sales of America.

Fig. 16: Locating No. 2 Speed Sensor (1995 Models)

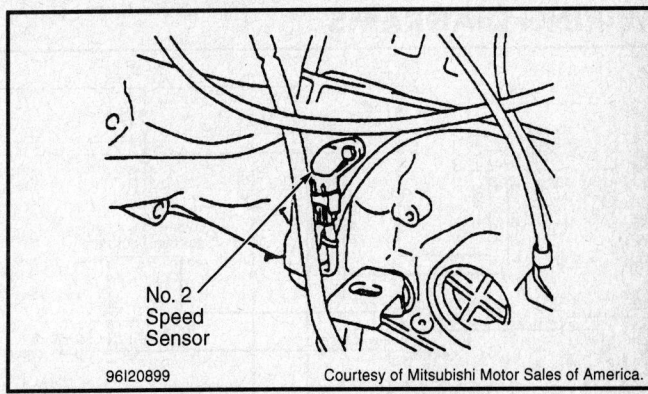

96I20899   Courtesy of Mitsubishi Motor Sales of America.

Fig. 17: Locating No. 2 Speed Sensor (1996 Models)

TORQUE SPECIFICATIONS

TORQUE SPECIFICATIONS

Application	INCH Lbs. (N.m)
Neutral Safety Switch Bolt	48 (5.4)
Neutral Safety Switch Lock Nut	35 (4.0)

AUTOMATIC TRANSMISSIONS
Mitsubishi V4AW3 — Electronic Controls (Cont.)

WIRING DIAGRAMS

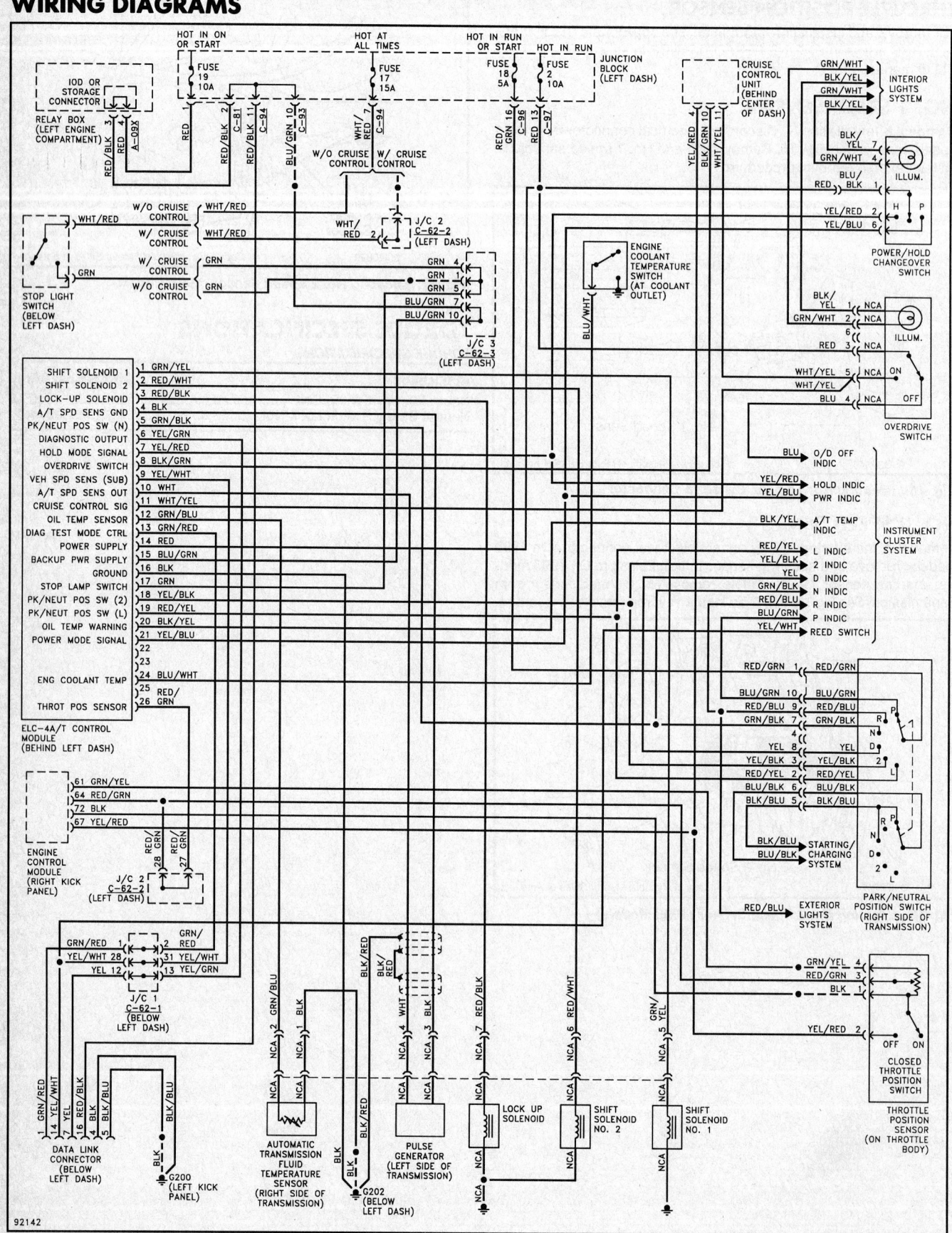

Fig. 18: Transmission Wiring Diagram (Montero 1995)

92142

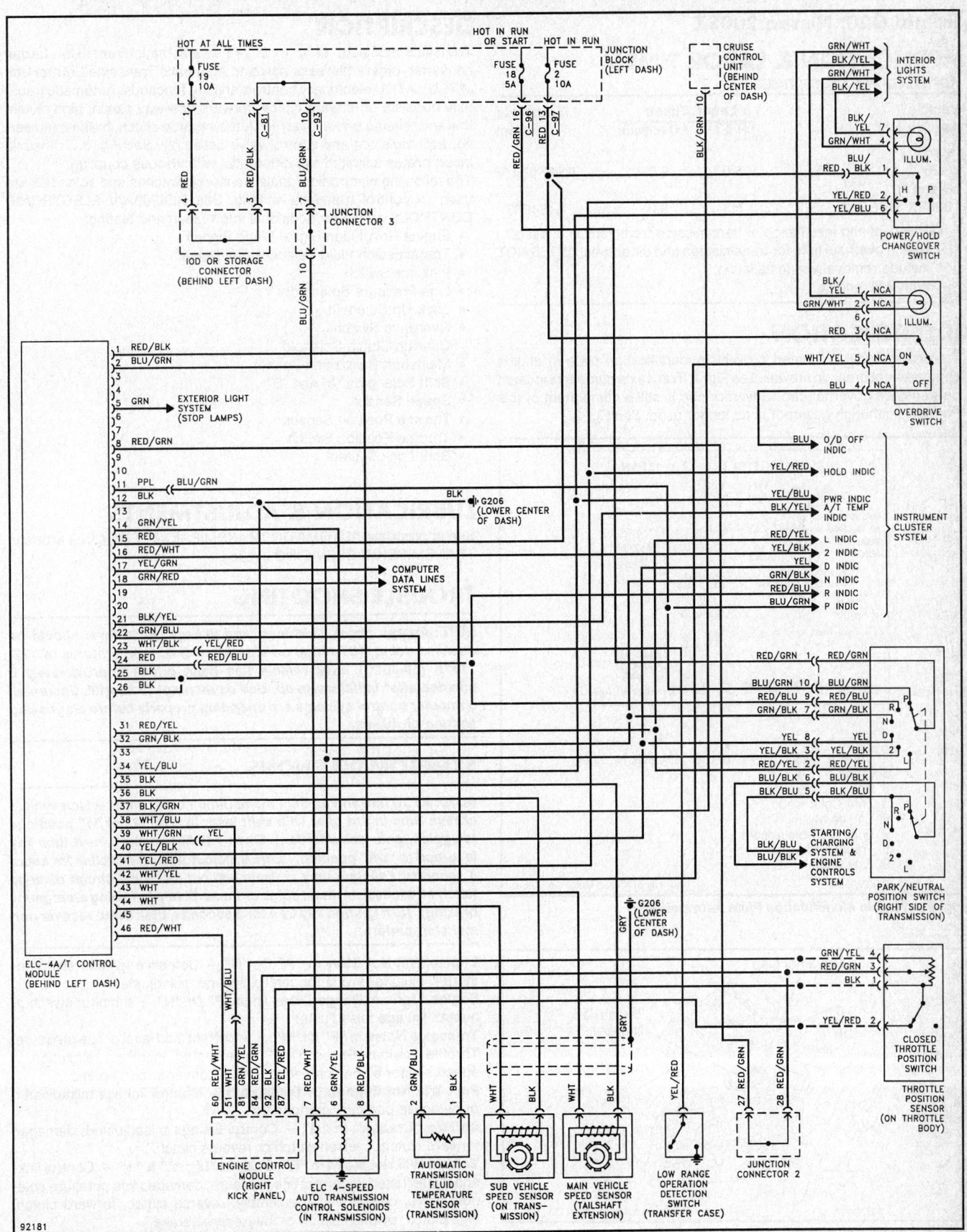

Fig. 19: Transmission Wiring Diagram (Montero 1996)

AUTOMATIC TRANSMISSIONS
Nissan RE4F03A/V

Infiniti G20, Nissan 200SX

APPLICATION & LABOR TIMES

APPLICATION & LABOR TIMES

Vehicle Application	Labor Times [1] R & I	[2] Overhaul	Transaxle Model
Infiniti [3]			
G20	5.0	9.0	RE4F03A/V
Nissan [3]			
200SX SE-R	5.3	9.0	RE4F03V

[1] – Removal and installation of transmission from vehicle chassis.
[2] – Bench overhaul time for transmission and differential. DOES NOT include removal and installation.
[3] – With 2.0L engine.

IDENTIFICATION

Transaxle model is located on vehicle identification plate in engine compartment area, on firewall. See Fig. 1. Transaxle number is located on transaxle governor cap. Governor cap is still a component of this transaxle although governor is no longer used. See Fig. 2.

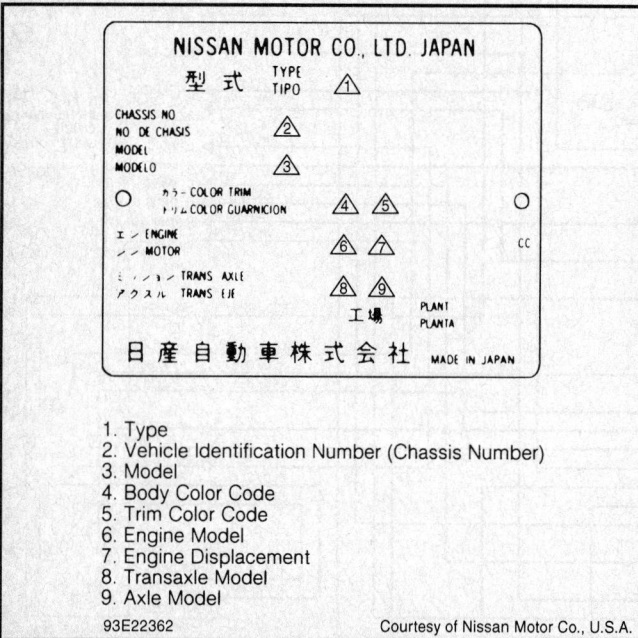

1. Type
2. Vehicle Identification Number (Chassis Number)
3. Model
4. Body Color Code
5. Trim Color Code
6. Engine Model
7. Engine Displacement
8. Transaxle Model
9. Axle Model

93E22362   Courtesy of Nissan Motor Co., U.S.A.

Fig. 1: Vehicle Identification Plate Information

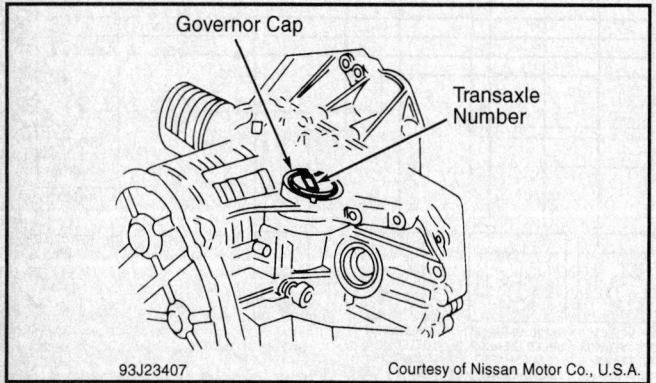

93J23407   Courtesy of Nissan Motor Co., U.S.A.

Fig. 2: Locating Automatic Transaxle Model Number

DESCRIPTION

Transaxle consists of 4 main units: automatic transaxle, torque converter, differential assembly and Automatic Transaxle Control Unit (ATCU). ATCU electrically controls shifting functions. Automatic transaxle consists of forward clutch, forward one-way clutch, high clutch, low and reverse brake, overrun clutch, reverse clutch, brake band servo, accumulators and control valve assembly. See Fig. 3. Transaxle incorporates a limited slip differential with viscous coupling.

The following electronic signals, sensors, switches and solenoids are used to control transaxle shifting. See RE4F03A/V ELECTRONIC CONTROLS article for additional information and testing:

- Engine Revolution Signal (Tach Signal)
- Transmission Fluid Temperature Sensor
- Inhibitor Switch
- Line Pressure Solenoid
- Lock-Up Solenoid
- Overdrive Switch
- Overrun Clutch Solenoid
- Mainshaft Revolution Sensor
- Shift Solenoids "A" and "B"
- Speed Sensor
- Throttle Position Sensor
- Throttle Position Switch
- Shift Lock System

LUBRICATION & ADJUSTMENTS

See appropriate AUTOMATIC TRANSMISSION SERVICING article in TRANSMISSION SERVICING section.

TROUBLE SHOOTING

NOTE: Always check fluid level and linkage. Fluid level should be checked using HOT range on dipstick at fluid temperatures of 122-176°F (50-80°C) after vehicle has been driven approximately 5 minutes after initial warm-up. Use caution not to overfill. Ensure all computer control systems are operating properly before diagnosing shifting problems.

SYMPTOM DIAGNOSIS

NOTE: ATCU has an Fail-Safe mode (limp home) under which vehicle always runs in 3rd gear with shift lever in "D", "2" or "1" positions (sluggish, poor acceleration). When Fail-Safe occurs, next time key is turned to "ON" position, POWER indicator lamp will blink for about 8 seconds. Fail-Safe may activate without electrical circuit damage (such as excessive wheel spins or immediately following emergency braking). Turn ignition key OFF for 5 seconds, then ON to recover normal shift pattern.

Engine Will Not Start In "P" Or "N" – Defective ignition switch or starter. Inhibitor switch or control linkage misadjusted.

Engine Starts In Range Other Than "P" Or "N" – Inhibitor switch or control linkage misadjusted.

Transaxle Noise In "P" Or "N" – Incorrect fluid level or line pressure, Throttle Position Sensor (TPS) misadjusted, incorrect revolution or speed sensor signal, damaged torque converter or oil pump.

Park Will Not Engage Or Disengage – Control linkage misadjusted or defective parking components.

Vehicle "Creeps" In "N" – Control linkage misadjusted, damaged forward clutch, overrun clutch or reverse clutch.

Vehicle Will Not Move In "R"; Okay In "D", "2" & "1" – Control linkage misadjusted, incorrect line pressure, damaged line pressure solenoid valve, control valve assembly, reverse clutch, forward clutch, high clutch, overrun clutch or low/reverse brake.

Vehicle Brakes When Shifted To "R" – Incorrect fluid level or line pressure, control linkage misadjusted, damaged line pressure solenoid valve, control valve assembly, high clutch, forward clutch, overrun clutch or brake band.

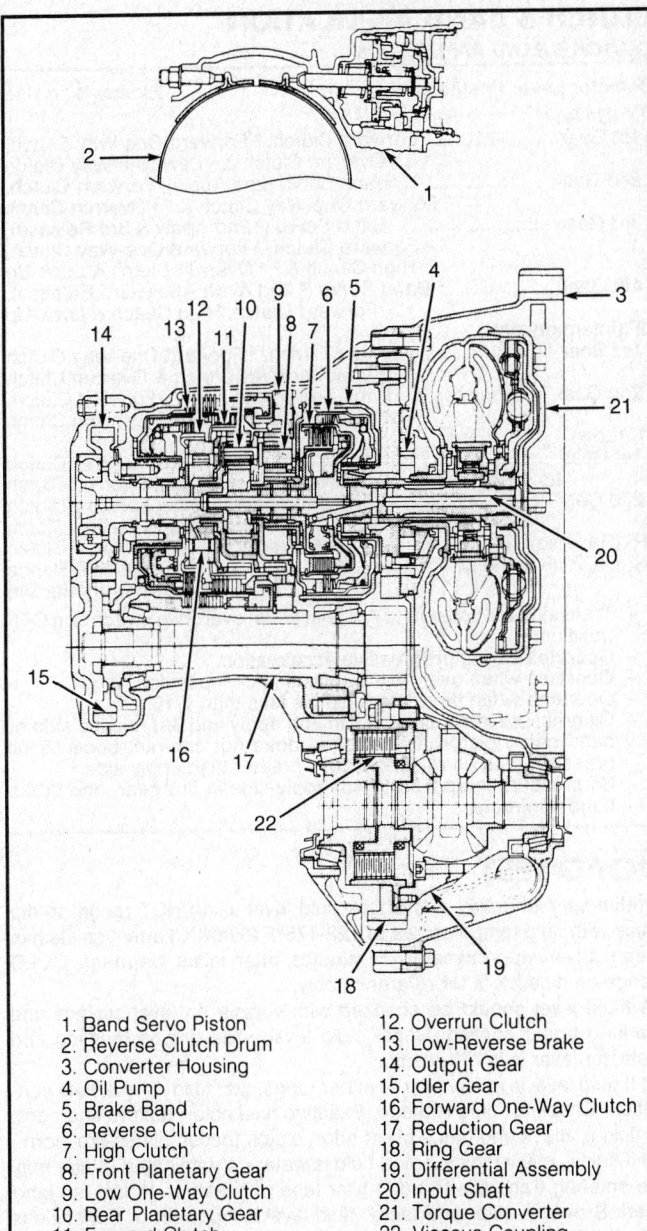

1. Band Servo Piston
2. Reverse Clutch Drum
3. Converter Housing
4. Oil Pump
5. Brake Band
6. Reverse Clutch
7. High Clutch
8. Front Planetary Gear
9. Low One-Way Clutch
10. Rear Planetary Gear
11. Forward Clutch
12. Overrun Clutch
13. Low-Reverse Brake
14. Output Gear
15. Idler Gear
16. Forward One-Way Clutch
17. Reduction Gear
18. Ring Gear
19. Differential Assembly
20. Input Shaft
21. Torque Converter
22. Viscous Coupling

93B23581   Courtesy of Nissan Motor Co., U.S.A.

Fig. 3: Identifying Transaxle Component Locations (RE4F03V Shown, RE4F03A Similar)

Excessive Shift Shock From "N" To "D" – Engine idle RPM or TPS misadjusted, incorrect line pressure, fluid temperature or engine RPM signal, line pressure solenoid valve, damaged N-D accumulator or forward clutch.

Vehicle Will Not Move In "D" & "2"; Okay In "1" & "R" – Control linkage misadjusted, damaged low one-way clutch.

Vehicle Will Not Move Or Slips In "D", "1" & "2"; Okay in "R" – Incorrect fluid level or line pressure, damaged line pressure solenoid valve, control valve assembly, N-D accumulator, reverse clutch, high clutch, forward clutch or low one-way clutch. See CLUTCH & BAND APPLICATION table.

Slips On Acceleration – Incorrect fluid level or line pressure, control linkage or TPS misadjusted, damaged line pressure solenoid valve, control valve assembly, forward clutch, reverse clutch, N-D accumulator, low/reverse brake, torque converter or oil pump.

Excessive "Creep" – Incorrect engine idle RPM.

No "Creep" – Incorrect fluid level or line pressure, damaged control valve assembly, torque converter, oil pump or forward clutch.

No 1-2 Upshift – Inhibitor switch or control linkage misadjusted, damaged control valve assembly, brake band or shift solenoid "A", incorrect revolution or speed sensor signal.

No 2-3 Upshift – Inhibitor switch or control linkage misadjusted, incorrect revolution or speed sensor signal, damaged control valve assembly, shift solenoid "B", high clutch or brake band.

No 3-4 Upshift – Inhibitor switch or control linkage misadjusted, incorrect revolution, speed or fluid temperature sensor signal, damaged shift solenoid "A" or brake band.

Upshift Points Too High In All Gears – TPS misadjusted, incorrect revolution or speed sensor signal, damaged shift solenoid "A" or "B".

Shifts From 1st To 3rd; Skips 2nd – Incorrect fluid level, damaged brake band or leaking accumulator servo release.

Shifting Into "R", "D", "2", Or "1" Kills Engine – Incorrect engine idle RPM or line pressure, damaged control valve assembly, lock-up solenoid or torque converter.

Excessive Shock During 1-2 Upshift – Incorrect line pressure, TPS misadjusted, incorrect revolution or fluid temperature sensor signal, damaged shift solenoid "A", control valve assembly or brake band, binding or leaking accumulator servo release.

Excessive Shock During 2-3 Upshift – Incorrect line pressure, TPS misadjusted, damaged high clutch, brake band, control valve assembly or shift solenoid "A".

Excessive Shock During 3-4 Upshift – Incorrect line pressure, TPS misadjusted, damaged control valve assembly, brake band or overrun clutch.

Slips During 1-2 Upshift – Incorrect fluid level or line pressure, TPS misadjusted, damaged control valve assembly, accumulator servo release or brake band.

Slips During 2-3 Or 3-4 Upshift – Incorrect fluid level or line pressure, TPS misadjusted, damaged control valve assembly, high clutch or brake band.

Vehicle Brakes During 1-2 Upshift – Incorrect fluid level, low reverse brake, damaged reverse or high clutch or low one-way clutch.

Vehicle Brakes During 2-3 Upshift – Incorrect fluid level or damaged brake band.

Vehicle Brakes During 3-4 Upshift – Incorrect fluid level, damaged reverse clutch, one-way clutch or overrun clutch.

Acceleration Poor; Maximum Speed Unattainable – Incorrect fluid level, misadjusted inhibitor switch, damaged shift solenoids "A" or "B", control valve assembly, reverse or high clutch, low/reverse brake, brake band, torque convertor or oil pump.

No 4-3 Downshift – Incorrect fluid level, TPS misadjusted, damaged overrun clutch solenoid valve, control valve assembly, shift solenoid valve "A", line pressure solenoid valve, low/reverse band or brake band.

No 3-2 Or 4-2 Downshift – incorrect fluid level, TPS misadjusted, damaged shift solenoid valves "A" or "B", control valve assembly, high clutch or brake band.

No 2-1 Or 3-1 Downshift – Incorrect fluid level, TPS misadjusted, damaged shift solenoids "A" or "B", control valve assembly, low one way clutch brake, brake band or high clutch.

Shift Shock Felt During Deceleration When Accelerator Released – TPS misadjusted, line pressure, damaged overrun clutch solenoid or control valve assembly.

Shift Point Too High From 4-3, 3-2, 2-1 – TPS misadjusted, damaged revolution or speed sensor, overrun clutch solenoid valve or control valve assembly.

No Kickdown From 4th Gear Within Kickdown Range Or Kickdown Or Engine Overruns When Accelerator Pedal Depressed In 4th Gear Beyond Kickdown Range – Damaged or TPS misadjusted, revolution or speed sensor, shift solenoid valves "A" or "B".

Engine Races Or Slips From 4-3 When Accelerator Pedal Depressed – Incorrect fluid level or line pressure, misadjusted throttle fluid level, line pressure solenoid valve, control valve assembly, forward or high clutch.

Engine Races Or Slips From 4-2 When Depressing Accelerator Pedal – Incorrect fluid level or line pressure, TPS misadjusted, damaged line pressure solenoid valve, shift solenoid valve "A", control valve assembly, forward clutch or brake band.

Engine Races Or Slips From 3-2 When Depressing Accelerator Pedal – Incorrect fluid level or line pressure, TPS misadjusted, damaged line pressure solenoid valve, control valve assembly, fluid temperature sensor, brake band, forward or high clutch.

Engine Races Or Slips From 4th Gear Or 3-1 When Depressing Accelerator Pedal – Incorrect fluid level or line pressure, TPS misadjusted, damaged line pressure solenoid valve, control valve assembly, forward or forward one-way clutch or low one-way clutch.

Vehicle Will Not Run In Any Position – Incorrect fluid level or line pressure, control linkage, damaged line pressure solenoid valve, control valve assembly, fluid temperature assembly, brake band, high of forward clutch.

Transaxle Noise In "D", "2", "1" & "R" Positions – Incorrect fluid level or damaged fluid level.

Will Not Shift 3-2 When Changing Lever Into "2" Position – Inhibitor switch, TPS misadjusted, overrun clutch solenoid valve, shift solenoids "A" or "B", control valve assembly, control linkage, brake band or overrun clutch.

2-3 Upshift In "2" Position – Misadjusted or damaged inhibitor switch.

No Engine Braking In "1" Position – Misadjusted or damaged inhibitor switch, control linkage, TPS misadjusted, damaged engine revolution and speed sensor, shift solenoid "A", control valve assembly, overrun clutch solenoid valve, overrun clutch or low/reverse brake.

1-2 Upshift In "1" Position – Misadjusted or damaged inhibitor switch or control linkage.

No 2-1 Downshift When Shifted To "1" Position — Misadjusted or damaged inhibitor switch, engine revolution or speed sensor, shift solenoid "A", damaged control valve assembly, overrun clutch solenoid valve, overrun clutch or low/reverse brake.

Heavy Shift Shock Shifting From 2-1 In "1" Position – Damaged or defective control valve assembly or low/reverse brake.

Transaxle Overheats – Incorrect fluid level or line pressure, Engine idling RPM, TPS misadjusted, damaged line pressure solenoid valve, control valve assembly, reverse, high or forward clutch, oil pump, torque converter, overrun clutch, low/reverse brake or brake band.

ATF Shoots Out From Relief Valve &/Or Filler Tube; White Smoke From Tailpipe – Incorrect fluid level, damaged overrun, reverse, high, forward or low one-way clutches, brake band or low/reverse brake.

Offensive Odor At Filler Tube – Incorrect fluid level, damaged torque converter, oil pump, reverse, high, overrun or forward clutches, brake band or low/reverse brake.

No Lock-Up Occurs – TPS misadjusted, damaged engine revolution or speed sensor, inhibitor switch, fluid temperature sensor, line pressure, torque converter clutch solenoid, control valve assembly or torque converter.

Extremely High Or Low Lock-Up – TPS misadjusted, incorrect revolution or speed sensor signal, damaged control valve assembly or lock-up solenoid.

No 3-4 Upshift With OD Switch On – TPS misadjusted, damaged inhibitor switch, engine revolution or speed sensor, shift solenoid "A", overrun solenoid valve, control valve assembly, fluid temperature sensor, line pressure, brake band or overrun clutch.

Engine Stalls In "R", "D", "2" & "1" Positions – Incorrect fluid level, torque converter clutch solenoid valve, shift solenoid valves "A" or "B", or control valve assembly.

Vehicle Will Not Move In Any Range – Incorrect fluid level or line pressure, control linkage misadjusted, damaged line pressure solenoid, torque converter, oil pump, high clutch, low/reverse brake, brake band or parking components. See CLUTCH & BAND APPLICATION table.

CLUTCH & BAND APPLICATION
CLUTCH & BAND APPLICATION

Selector Lever Position	Elements In Use
"D" (Drive) [1]	
1st Gear	Forward Clutch, [2] Forward One-Way Clutch, [3][4] Overrun Clutch & [2] Low One-Way Clutch
2nd Gear	Band Servo (2nd Apply), Forward Clutch, [2] Forward One-Way Clutch & [3][4] Overrun Clutch
3rd Gear	Band Servo ([5] 2nd Apply & 3rd Release), Forward Clutch, [2] Forward One-Way Clutch, High Clutch & [3][4] Overrun Clutch & Lock-Up
4th Gear	Band Servo ([6] 2nd & 4th Apply, 3rd Release), Forward Clutch, High Clutch & Lock-Up
"2" (Intermediate)	
1st Gear	Forward Clutch, [2] Forward One-Way Clutch, [2] Low One-Way Clutch & Overrun Clutch
2nd Gear	Band Servo (2nd Apply), Forward Clutch, [2] Forward One-Way Clutch & Overrun Clutch
"1" (Low)	
1st Gear	Forward Clutch, [2] Forward One-Way Clutch, Low-Reverse Brake, Low One-Way Clutch, Overrun Clutch
2nd Gear	Band Servo (2nd Apply), Forward Clutch, [2] Forward One-Way Clutch & Overrun Clutch
"R" (Reverse)	Low-Reverse Brake & Reverse Clutch
"N" Or "P" (Neutral Or Park)	All Clutches & Bands Released Or Ineffective

[1] – Transaxle will not shift to 4th gear when overdrive switch is in OFF position.

[2] – Operates during progressive acceleration.

[3] – Operates when overdrive switch is in OFF position.

[4] – Operates when throttle opening is less than 1/16.

[5] – Oil pressure is applied to both 2nd apply and 3rd release side of band servo piston. Brake band does not contract because oil pressure area on release side is greater than apply side.

[6] – Oil pressure is applied to 4th apply side in 3rd gear, and brake band contracts.

ROAD TEST

Preliminary Checks – **1)** Check fluid level using HOT range on dip stick with fluid temperatures of 122-176°F (50-80°C) after vehicle has been driven approximately 5 minutes after initial warm-up. COLD range on dipstick is for reference only.

2) Fluid level should be checked with vehicle on level surface and parking brake applied. Check fluid level while engine is idling and selector lever is in "P" position.

3) If fluid level is at low side of either range, add fluid. Check fluid condition. Check for fluid leakage. Examine fluid color, texture and odor. If fluid is Black and has a burnt odor, clutch friction plates are worn.

4) If fluid is milky Pink in color, fluid is water-contaminated. Water may be entering transaxle through filler tube or breather. If fluid is Light/Dark Brown in color and tacky, fluid level is incorrect or transaxle is overheating.

Check Before Engine Is Started – **1)** Park vehicle on flat surface. Set transmission mode switch (G20) to AUTO position, move selector lever to "P" position. Turn ignition switch to ON position. Power indicator light should come on for about 2 seconds.

2) Set transmission mode switch to POWER position. POWER indicator light should come on. Set transmission mode switch to COMFORT position. COMFORT indicator light should come on. Set overdrive switch to OFF position. Overdrive OFF indicator light should come on.

3) Move selector lever to "D" position and depress and release accelerator pedal quickly. POWER indicator light should come on for about 3 seconds.

Check With Engine Idling – **1)** Ensure engine starts with selector lever in "P" position. Turn ignition switch to "ACC", move selector to "D", "2", "1", or "R" position. Ensure engine will not start in these positions. With selector lever in "P" position, parking brake off, verify PARK engagement by pushing vehicle backward or forward. Apply parking brake. Move selector to "N" position. Vehicle should not roll.

2) Apply foot brake. Move selector lever to "R" position. Release parking brake for several seconds. Vehicle should creep backward with parking brake released. Repeat to verify operation of forward gear positions.

Road Test Procedure – **1)** Park vehicle on flat surface and set transmission mode switch to AUTO position (G20). Set overdrive switch to ON position. Move selector lever to "P" position and start engine.

2) Move selector lever to "D" position. Depress accelerator pedal halfway. Vehicle should start from 1st gear. Verify 1-2, 2-3 and 3-4 upshifts occur at specified speed. Refer to SHIFT SPEED SPECIFICATIONS tables.

3) Lock-up occurs at speeds relative to throttle opening in 4th gear. To verify lock-up speeds, see LOCK-UP SPEED SPECIFICATIONS table. Lock-up condition should be maintained for more than 30 seconds. Lock-up state is released upon deceleration. Confirm transmission mode switch is in AUTO position, overdrive switch is in ON position and selector lever is in "D" position.

4) Accelerate vehicle to approximately 12 MPH using light-throttle. Release accelerator pedal and then quickly depress pedal to floor. Transaxle should downshift from 4th to 2nd. Release accelerator and verify 2-3, and 3-4 upshifts. Check shift points and specified speeds. Refer to SHIFT SPEED SPECIFICATIONS (COMFORT PATTERN) tables.

5) Confirm transmission mode switch is in AUTO position, overdrive switch is in ON position and selector lever is in "D" position. Accelerate vehicle to 4th gear using half-throttle. Release accelerator and switch overdrive to OFF position. Verify 4-3 downshift.

6) While still in 3rd gear, move selector lever from "D" to "2" position. Downshift should occur and deceleration should occur by engine braking. While still in 2nd gear, move selector lever from "2" to "1" position. Downshift should occur and deceleration should occur by engine braking.

LOCK-UP SPEED SPECIFICATIONS [1]

Application	MPH
Comfort Pattern	
Lock-Up ON in 4th	50-55
Lock-Up OFF in 4th	38-43
Power Pattern	
Lock-Up ON in 3rd	53-58
Lock-Up OFF in 3rd	52-57

[1] – With 1/4 throttle opening.

SHIFT SPEED SPECIFICATIONS (COMFORT PATTERN)

Application	Full Throttle MPH	Half Throttle MPH
1st-2nd	35-40	18-24
2nd-3rd	63-71	39-45
3rd-4th	101-110	61-73
4th-3rd	98-108	39-51
3rd-2nd	57-65	23-30
2nd-1st	29-34	6-11

STALL SPEED TEST

Stall Speed Test Procedure – **1)** Check engine and transaxle fluid levels. Ensure engine and transaxle are at normal operating temperatures. Set parking brake and block wheels.

2) Install tachometer so it is visible to driver. Start engine, apply foot brake and move selector lever to "D" position. Gradually depress accelerator pedal to wide-open throttle position while applying foot brake. Note engine stall speed and release accelerator pedal immediately. Stall speed should be 1900-2200 RPM.

3) Place selector lever in "N" position and run engine at idle for one minute to allow transaxle to cool. Repeat stall speed test procedure in "2", "1" and "R" positions, allowing transaxle to cool between each test.

CAUTION: DO NOT hold wide-open throttle for more than 5 seconds during test.

Stall Speed Test Results

- **Stall Speed Low In All Positions** – Insufficient engine performance or faulty torque converter one-way clutch.
- **Stall Speed High In All Positions** – Low/reverse brake slipping, faulty forward one-way clutch, forward clutch, overrun clutch or hydraulic circuit for line pressure control.
- **Stall Speed High In "R" Position Only** – Reverse clutch slipping or low/reverse brake slipping.
- **Stall Speed High In "D", "2" & "R" Positions, Okay In "1" Position** – Defective reverse clutch, forward clutch, forward clutch or low one-way clutch.
- **Stall Speed High In "D", "2" & "1" Positions, Okay In "R" Position** – Defective forward clutch, overrun clutch or forward one-way clutch.
- **Stall Speed High In "D" & "2" Positions, Okay In "1" & "R" Positions** – Defective forward clutch, low one-way clutch and overrun clutch.

NOTE: Condition of high clutch and brake band cannot be confirmed by stall speed test.

HYDRAULIC PRESSURE TESTS

NOTE: Always replace pressure plug. Plug is self-sealing type.

Line Pressure Test Procedure – **1)** Warm engine and transaxle to normal operating temperature. Check engine and transaxle fluid levels and add fluid as necessary. Install pressure gauge to line pressure port. *See Fig. 4.*

2) Set parking brake and block wheels. Apply foot brake fully while line pressure test at stall speed is performed. Start engine and measure line pressure at idle and stall speed in "D", "2", "1" and "R" positions. When measuring line pressure at stall speed, follow stall speed test procedure. Note pressure readings and refer to LINE PRESSURE SPECIFICATIONS table.

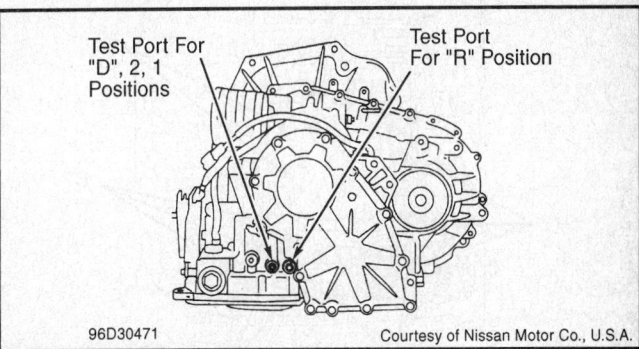

Test Port For "D", 2, 1 Positions

Test Port For "R" Position

96D30471 Courtesy of Nissan Motor Co., U.S.A.

Fig. 4: Identifying Hydraulic Pressure Test Port

LINE PRESSURE SPECIFICATIONS

Application	psi (kPa)
At Idle	
In "D", "2" & "1"	73 (500)
In "R"	124 (853)
At Stall Speed	
In "D", "1" & "2"	159 (1098)
In "R"	270 (1863)

Line Pressure Test Results – If line pressure is low at idle in all positions, possible causes are: Oil pump wear, control piston damage, pressure regulator valve or plug sticking, spring for pressure regulator valve damaged, fluid pressure leakage between strainer and pressure regulator valve.

2) If line pressure is low at idle in a particular shift position, possible causes are: fluid pressure leakage between manual valve and a particular clutch. If line pressure is low in "R" and "1" position, but is normal in "D" and "2" position, fluid leakage exists at or around low-reverse brake circuit.

3) If line pressure is high at idle, possible causes are: TPS misadjusted, fluid temperature sensor damaged, line pressure solenoid sticking or shorted, pressure regulator or plug, or modifier valve sticking. Open in dropping resistor.

4) If line pressure is low at stall speed, possible causes are: TPS misadjusted, line pressure solenoid valve sticking or shorted, pressure regulator or plug sticking, modifier valve or pilot valve sticking.

ON-VEHICLE SERVICE

CONTROL VALVE ASSEMBLY

Removal & Installation – **1)** Remove drain plug. Drain fluid. Remove oil pan and gasket. Remove oil strainer. Remove control valve assembly by removing bolts and disconnecting wiring harness connector. See CONTROL VALVE ASSEMBLY BOLT IDENTIFICATION table. *See Fig. 5.* Remove accumulators by applying compressed air (if necessary).

2) To install control valve assembly, set manual valve in Neutral position and align with manual plate. Install control valve assembly and tighten bolts to 62-80 INCH lbs (7-9 N.m). To complete installation, reverse removal procedure. Fill transaxle to appropriate fluid level.

CONTROL VALVE ASSEMBLY BOLT IDENTIFICATION [1]

Identification	In. (mm)
A	1.713 (43.50)
B	1.30 (33.00)
C	1.57 (40.00)

[1] – See Fig. 5 for control valve bolt locations.

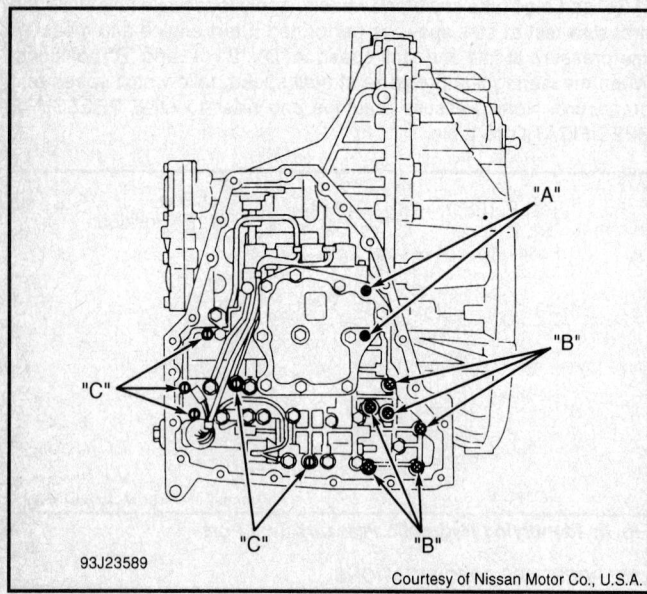

93J23589

Courtesy of Nissan Motor Co., U.S.A.

Fig. 5: Removing & Installing Control Valve Assembly

INHIBITOR SWITCH ADJUSTMENT

See appropriate AUTOMATIC TRANSMISSION SERVICING article in TRANSMISSION SERVICING section.

OIL COOLER FLUSHING PROCEDURE

Vehicles with tube type transaxle fluid cooler may be cleaned using cleaning solvent and compressed air. Cooler lines must also be flushed to remove any foreign material. Vehicles with fin type transaxle fluid cooler cannot be cleaned. Replace radiator (radiator incorporates transaxle cooler) and flush cooler lines to remove any foreign material.

REMOVAL & INSTALLATION

See appropriate AUTOMATIC TRANSMISSION REMOVAL article in TRANSMISSION SERVICING section.

TORQUE CONVERTER

1) Torque converter is a sealed unit and cannot be disassembled for service. Replace torque converter if damaged. Check converter one-way clutch using flat-blade screwdriver and suitable wire. *See Fig. 6.*
2) Hook wire into groove of bearing support unitized with one-way clutch outer race. While holding bearing support with wire, rotate one-way clutch spline using screwdriver. Ensure inner race rotates clockwise only. If inner race rotates in both directions, replace torque converter.

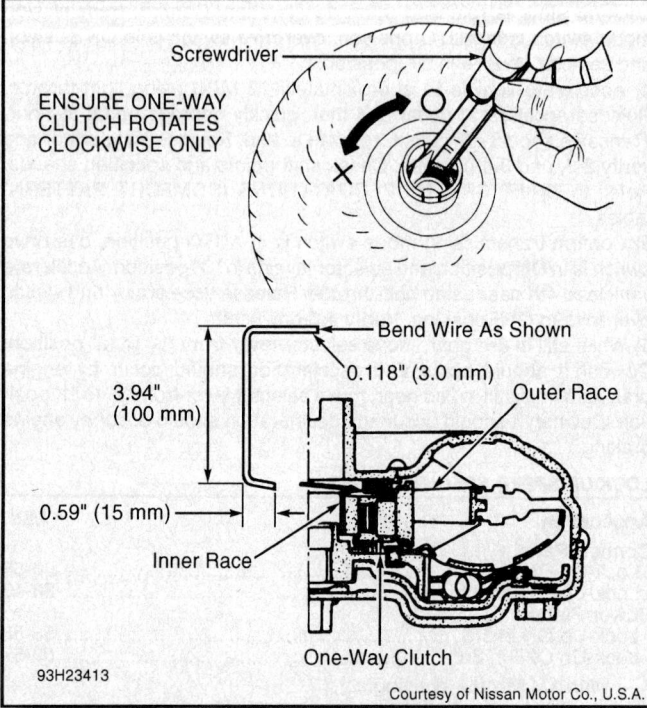

93H23413

Courtesy of Nissan Motor Co., U.S.A.

Fig. 6: Checking Torque Converter One-Way Clutch

TRANSAXLE DISASSEMBLY

1) Remove drain plug and drain fluid. Remove torque converter. Check torque converter one-way clutch. See TORQUE CONVERTER. Remove dipstick and dipstick tube. Remove oil cooler tube. Set manual lever to "P" position. Remove inhibitor switch. Remove oil pan and gasket. *See Fig. 7.* DO NOT reuse oil pan bolts.
2) Remove control valve assembly bolts. *See Fig. 5.* Remove clip from terminal body. Push terminal body into transaxle case and remove solenoid harness. Remove manual valve from control valve assembly. Remove return spring from servo release accumulator piston. Using compressed air, remove servo release accumulator piston. *See Fig. 11.*
3) Remove "O" rings from servo release accumulator piston. Using compressed air, remove N-D accumulator piston and return spring. *See Fig. 8.* Remove "O" rings from N-D accumulator piston. Check accumulator pistons and contact surface of transaxle case for damage. Check accumulator return springs free length and diameter. See ACCUMULATOR SPRING SPECIFICATIONS table.

ACCUMULATOR SPRING SPECIFICATIONS

Application	In. (mm)
N-D Accumulator Spring	
Free Length	1.772 (45.0)
Outer Diameter	1.087 (27.6)
Servo Release Accumulator	
Inner Spring	
Free Length	2.047 (52.00)
Outer Diameter	.516 (13.10)
Outer Spring	
Free Length	2.067 (52.50)
Outer Diameter	.831 (21.10)

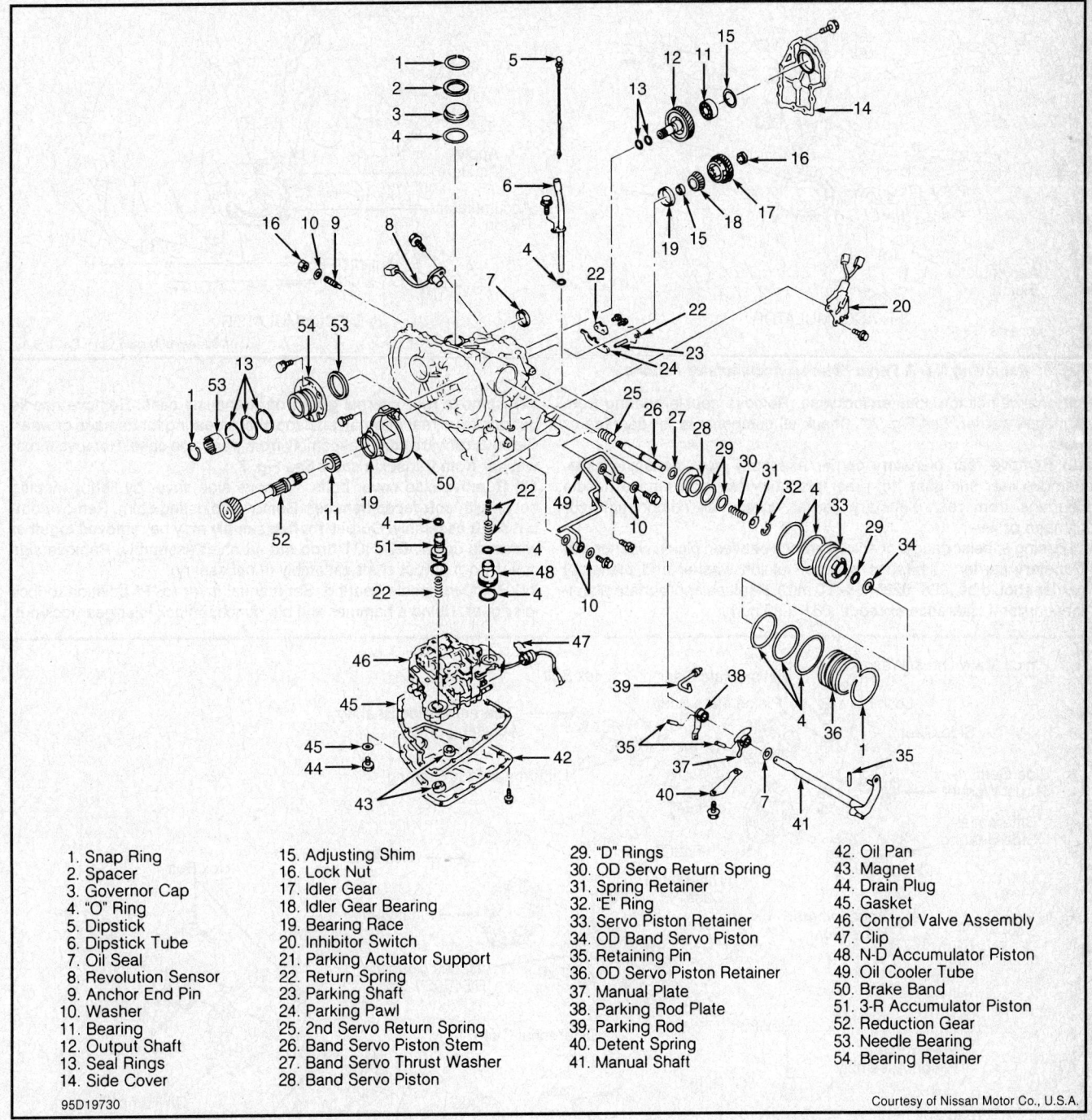

Fig. 7: Exploded View Of Transaxle Case Components

95D19730

Courtesy of Nissan Motor Co., U.S.A.

1. Snap Ring	15. Adjusting Shim	29. "D" Rings	42. Oil Pan
2. Spacer	16. Lock Nut	30. OD Servo Return Spring	43. Magnet
3. Governor Cap	17. Idler Gear	31. Spring Retainer	44. Drain Plug
4. "O" Ring	18. Idler Gear Bearing	32. "E" Ring	45. Gasket
5. Dipstick	19. Bearing Race	33. Servo Piston Retainer	46. Control Valve Assembly
6. Dipstick Tube	20. Inhibitor Switch	34. OD Band Servo Piston	47. Clip
7. Oil Seal	21. Parking Actuator Support	35. Retaining Pin	48. N-D Accumulator Piston
8. Revolution Sensor	22. Return Spring	36. OD Servo Piston Retainer	49. Oil Cooler Tube
9. Anchor End Pin	23. Parking Shaft	37. Manual Plate	50. Brake Band
10. Washer	24. Parking Pawl	38. Parking Rod Plate	51. 3-R Accumulator Piston
11. Bearing	25. 2nd Servo Return Spring	39. Parking Rod	52. Reduction Gear
12. Output Shaft	26. Band Servo Piston Stem	40. Detent Spring	53. Needle Bearing
13. Seal Rings	27. Band Servo Thrust Washer	41. Manual Shaft	54. Bearing Retainer
14. Side Cover	28. Band Servo Piston		

4) Remove lip seals from band servo oil port. Remove converter housing bolts and remove converter housing by tapping housing with soft-faced hammer. Remove "O" ring from differential oil port.

5) Remove differential assembly from transaxle case. Use appropriate puller to remove differential side bearing outer race from transaxle case and converter housing. Remove differential side bearing adjustment shim from transaxle case.

6) Using a hammer and screwdriver, remove oil seal from converter housing, being careful not to damage converter housing. Remove oil tube from converter housing. Remove "O" ring from input shaft. *See Fig. 9.* Remove oil pump assembly bolts and remove oil pump assembly from transaxle case. Remove thrust washer and bearing race from oil pump assembly. Loosen anchor end pin lock nut, then back off anchor end pin.

7) Remove brake band from transaxle case. When removing brake band, insert wire clip into brake band ends for support. To prevent brake lining from cracking or peeling, DO NOT stretch brake band. Check brake band facing for damage, cracks, wear or burns. Remove high clutch (with input shaft assembly) and reverse clutch assemblies. Remove high clutch from reverse clutch. *See Fig. 10.*

8) Remove needle bearing from high clutch drum. Remove high clutch hub and needle bearing from transaxle case. Remove front sun gear and needle bearings from transaxle case. Check all components for damage or wear.

9) Remove snap ring and front planetary carrier assembly with low one-way clutch. Ensure low one-way clutch rotates counterclockwise only. Remove low one-way clutch from front planetary carrier by rotat-

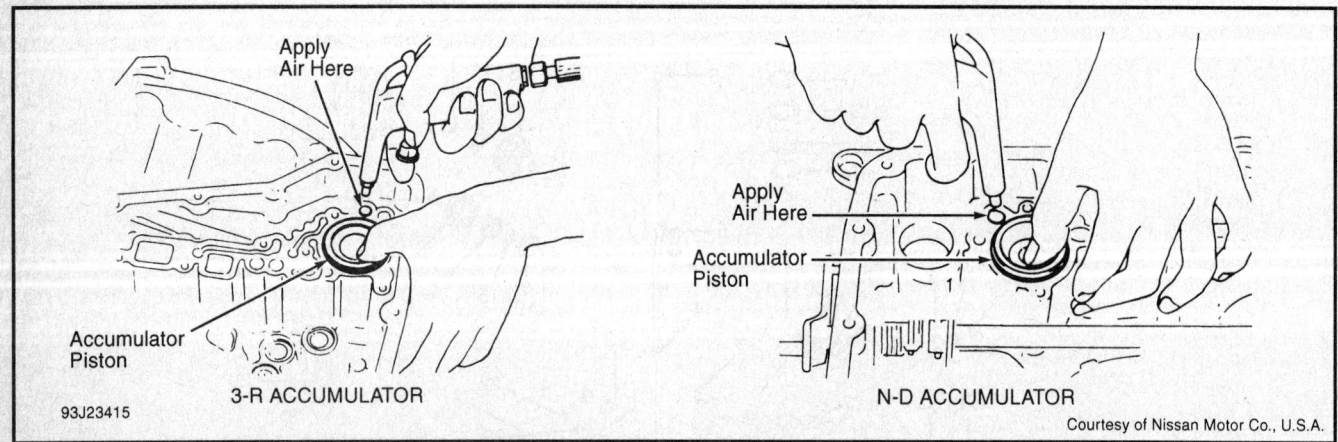

93J23415

Courtesy of Nissan Motor Co., U.S.A.

Fig. 8: Removing N-D & Servo Release Accumulator Pistons

ing one-way clutch counterclockwise. Remove needle bearing from planetary carrier. *See Fig. 10.* Check all components for damage or wear.

10) Remove rear planetary carrier assembly from transaxle case. Remove rear sun gear from rear planetary carrier. Remove needle bearings from rear planetary carrier. Check all components for damage or wear.

11) Using a feeler gauge, check clearance between pinion washer and planetary carrier. Clearance between pinion washer and planetary carrier should be .006-.028" (.15-.70 mm). Replace appropriate planetary carrier if clearance exceeds .031" (.80 mm).

12) Remove rear internal gear from transaxle case. Remove needle bearing from rear internal gear and check bearing for damage or wear. Remove forward clutch assembly from transaxle case. Remove thrust washer from transaxle case. *See Fig. 7.*

13) Remove side cover bolts. Remove side cover by lightly tapping cover with soft-faced hammer. Remove adjusting shim. Remove output shaft assembly. Output shaft assembly may be removed together with side cover. DO NOT drop output shaft assembly. Remove side cover from output shaft assembly (if necessary).

14) Remove needle bearing. Set manual lever to "P" position to lock idler gear. Using a hammer and pin punch, unlock idler gear lock nut.

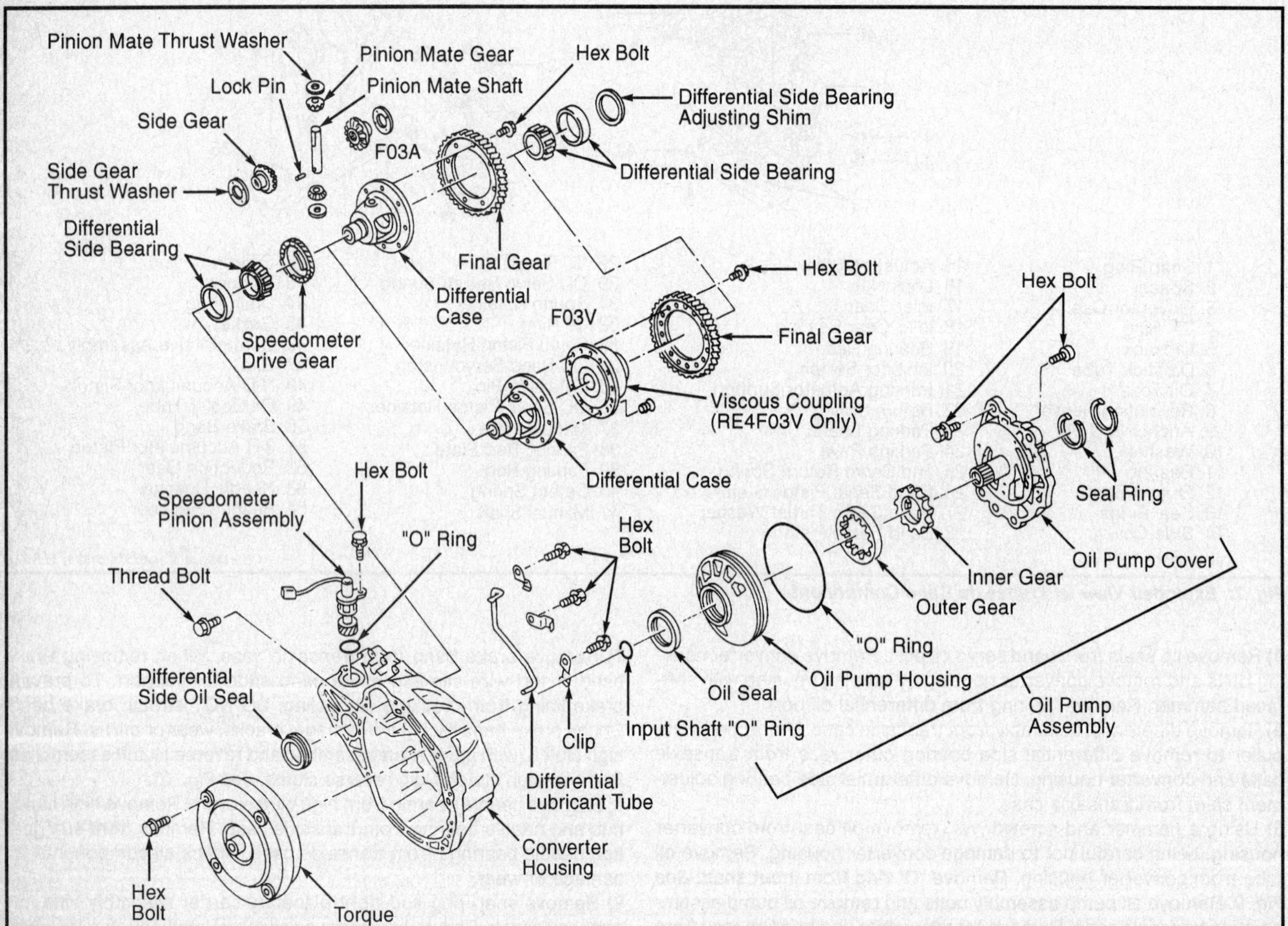

96I30476

Courtesy of Nissan Motor Co., U.S.A.

Fig. 9: Exploded View Of Torque Converter Housing & Differential Components

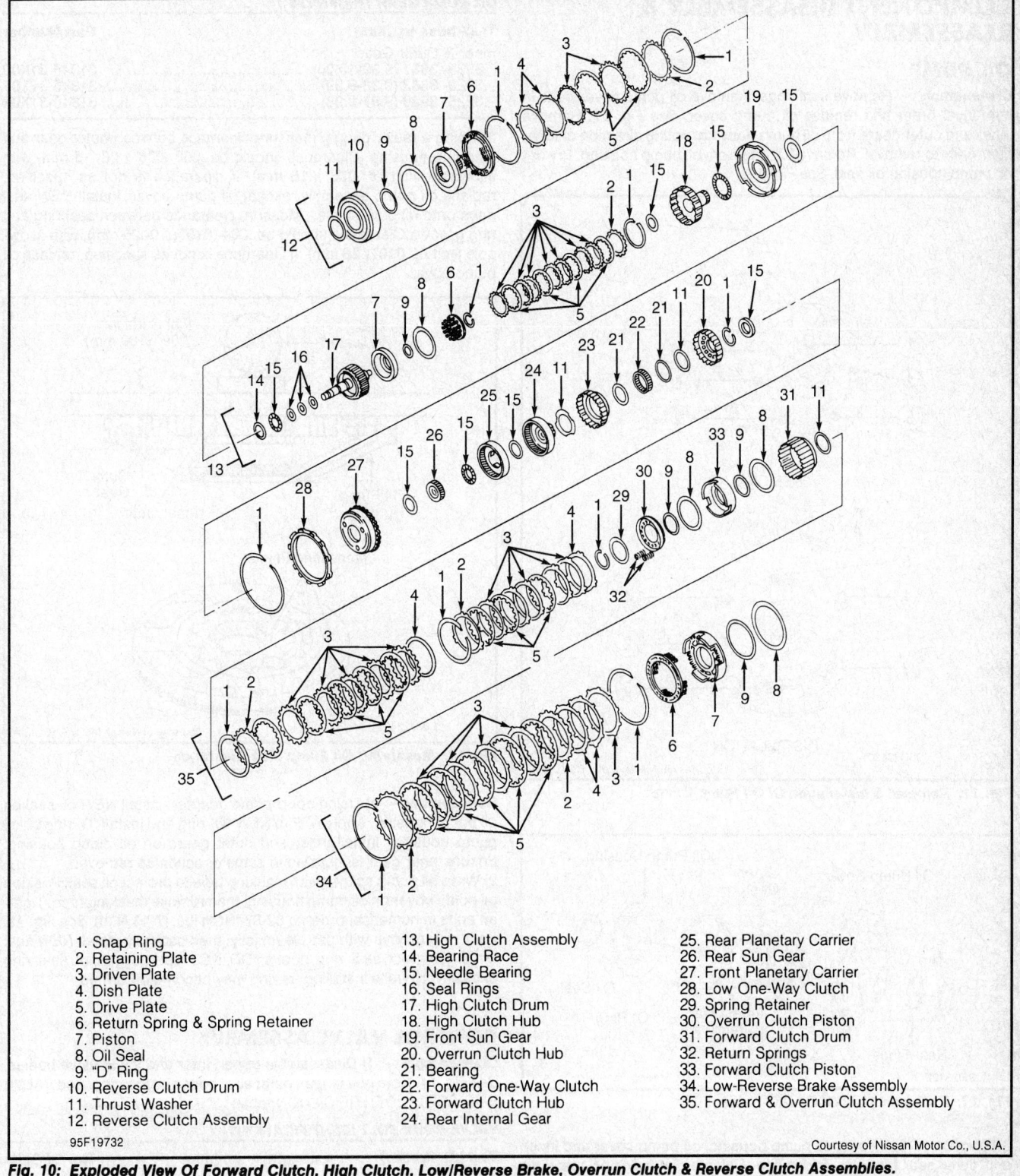

Fig. 10: Exploded View Of Forward Clutch, High Clutch, Low/Reverse Brake, Overrun Clutch & Reverse Clutch Assemblies.

1. Snap Ring	13. High Clutch Assembly	25. Rear Planetary Carrier
2. Retaining Plate	14. Bearing Race	26. Rear Sun Gear
3. Driven Plate	15. Needle Bearing	27. Front Planetary Carrier
4. Dish Plate	16. Seal Rings	28. Low One-Way Clutch
5. Drive Plate	17. High Clutch Drum	29. Spring Retainer
6. Return Spring & Spring Retainer	18. High Clutch Hub	30. Overrun Clutch Piston
7. Piston	19. Front Sun Gear	31. Forward Clutch Drum
8. Oil Seal	20. Overrun Clutch Hub	32. Return Springs
9. "D" Ring	21. Bearing	33. Forward Clutch Piston
10. Reverse Clutch Drum	22. Forward One-Way Clutch	34. Low-Reverse Brake Assembly
11. Thrust Washer	23. Forward Clutch Hub	35. Forward & Overrun Clutch Assembly
12. Reverse Clutch Assembly	24. Rear Internal Gear	

95F19732

Courtesy of Nissan Motor Co., U.S.A.

Remove idler gear lock nut. Use appropriate puller to remove idler gear. Remove reduction gear. Remove adjusting shim from reduction gear.

15) Remove return spring from parking shaft. Remove parking shaft and parking pawl from transaxle case. Check parking shaft and pawl for wear or damage. Note direction of parking actuator support and remove actuator support from transaxle case. Inspect actuator support for wear or damage. Remove revolution sensor from transaxle. *See Fig. 7.*

16) Remove manual shaft and throttle lever components. See MANUAL SHAFT & THROTTLE LEVER under COMPONENT DISASSEMBLY & REASSEMBLY.

COMPONENT DISASSEMBLY & REASSEMBLY

OIL PUMP

Disassembly – Remove seal rings. Remove oil pump cover bolts in numerical order and remove oil pump cover. *See Fig. 11*. Remove inner and outer gears from oil pump housing, noting direction of inner gear prior to removal. Remove "O" ring from oil pump housing. Pry out oil pump housing oil seal. *See Fig. 12*.

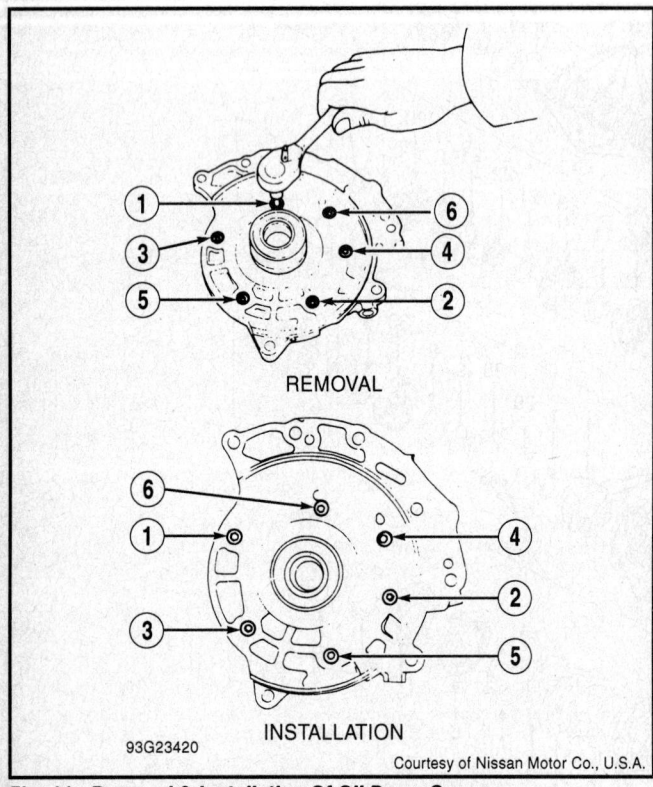

Fig. 11: *Removal & Installation Of Oil Pump Cover*

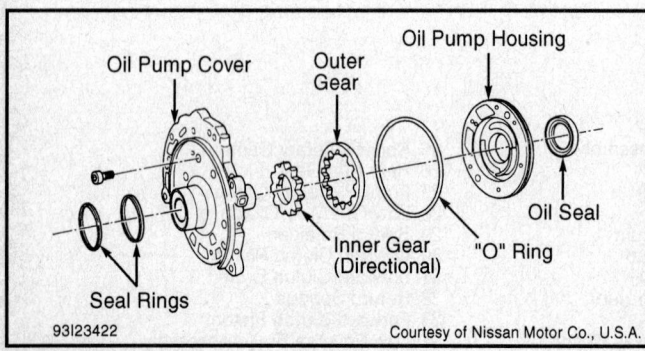

Fig. 12: *Exploded View Of Oil Pump Assembly*

Inspection – 1) Inspect oil pump housing, oil pump cover and inner and outer gear for wear or damage. Using a dial indicator, measure side clearance between end of oil pump housing and inner and outer gears in at least 4 places along their circumferences. Clearance should be .0008-.0016" (.02-.04 mm). *See Fig. 13*.
2) If clearance is less then specified, replace inner and outer gears as a set. Note direction of gears for installation. Ensure clearance is as specified. Gears are available in varied thicknesses. See OIL PUMP GEAR THICKNESS table. If clearance is greater than specified, replace oil pump assembly, except oil pump cover.

OIL PUMP GEAR THICKNESS

Thickness In. (mm)	Part Number
Inner & Outer Gear	
.3933-.3937 (9.99-10.00)	31346-31X00
.3929-.3933 (9.98-9.99)	31346-31X01
.3925-.3929 (9.97-9.98)	31346-31X02

3) Using a feeler gauge, measure clearance between outer gear and oil pump housing. Clearance should be .003-.006" (.08-.15 mm) with allowable limit of .006" (.15 mm). If clearance is not as specified, replace oil pump assembly, except oil pump cover. Install NEW seal rings onto oil pump cover. Measure clearance between seal ring and ring groove. Clearance should be .004-.010" (.10-.25 mm), with allowable limit of .010" (.25 mm). If clearance is not as specified, replace oil pump cover.

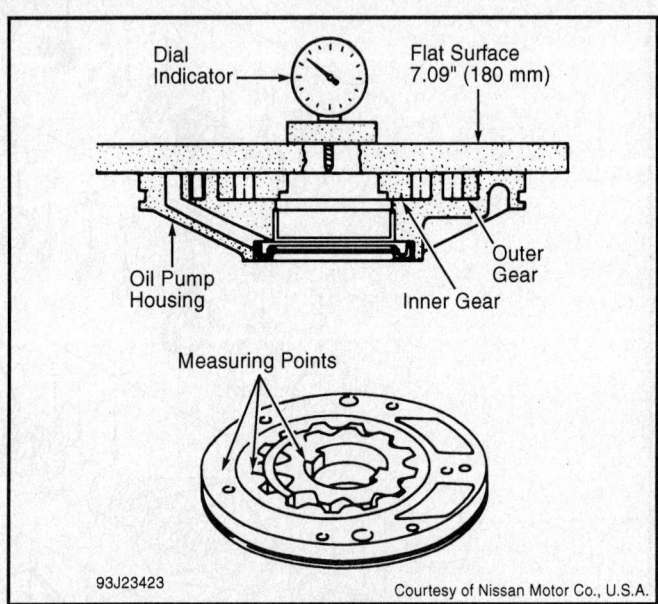

Fig. 13: *Measuring Oil Pump Side Clearance*

Reassembly – 1) Using appropriate adapter, install NEW oil seal on oil pump housing. Apply ATF to NEW "O" ring and install "O" ring on oil pump housing. Install inner and outer gears on oil pump housing. Ensure inner gear is installed in same direction as removed.
2) Wrap oil pump splines with masking tape to protect oil seal. Position oil pump cover on oil pump housing, then remove masking tape. Tighten bolts in numerical order to 62-97 INCH lbs. (7-11 N.m). *See Fig. 11*. Pack ring groove with petroleum jelly, then carefully install NEW seal rings. Connect seal ring hooks. DO NOT spread gap of seal ring excessively while installing as ring may become deformed.

CONTROL VALVE ASSEMBLY

Disassembly – 1) Disassemble upper, inter and lower valve bodies. *See Fig. 14*. Note bolt length, number of bolts and location. See VALVE BODY BOLT IDENTIFICATION table.

VALVE BODY BOLT IDENTIFICATION [1]

Bolt I.D. (Letter)	Length – In. (mm)	No. Of Bolts
A	.53 (13.5)	6
B	2.28 (58.0)	3
C	1.57 (40.0)	6
D	2.60 (66.0)	11
E	1.30 (33.0)	2
F	3.07 (78.0)	2

[1] – *See Fig. 15 for bolt location.*

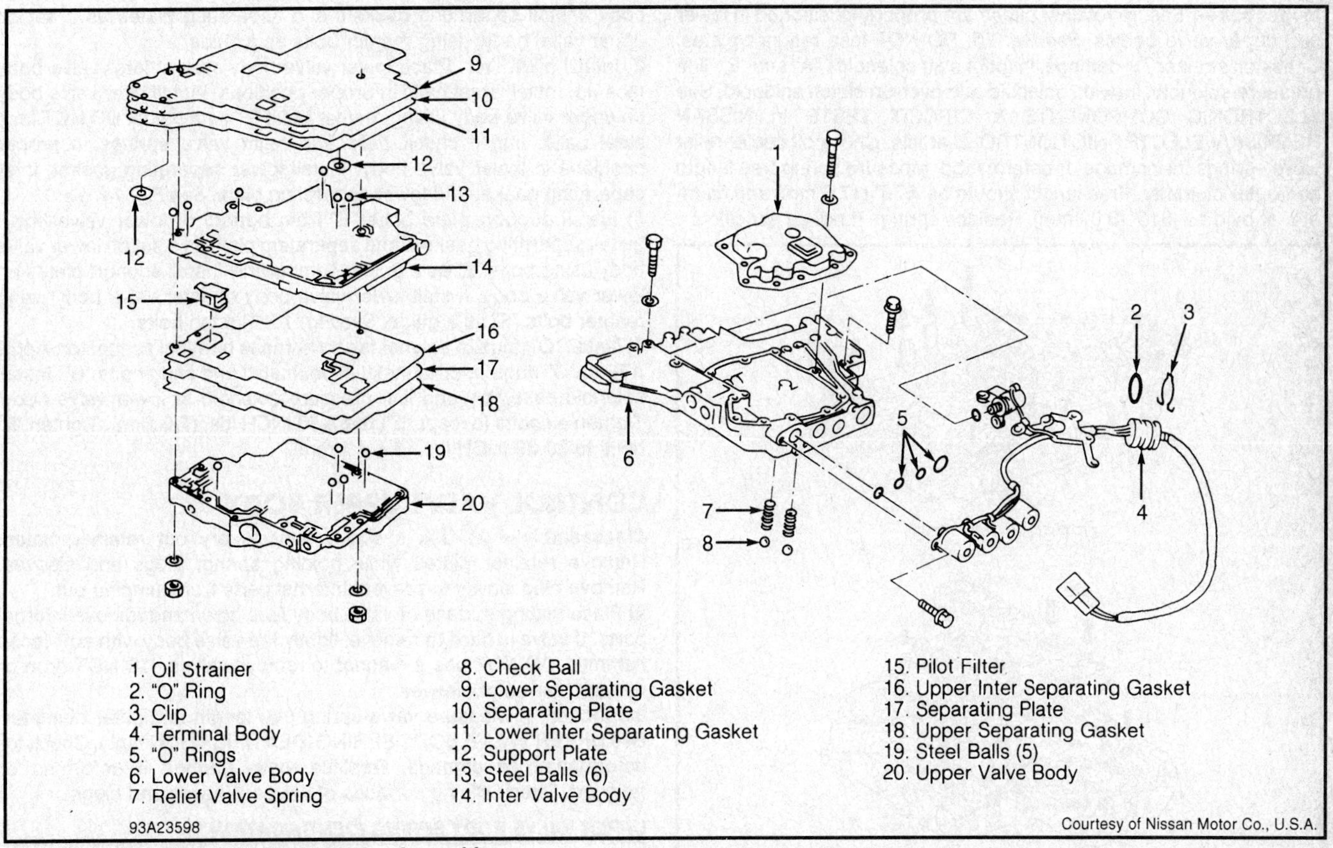

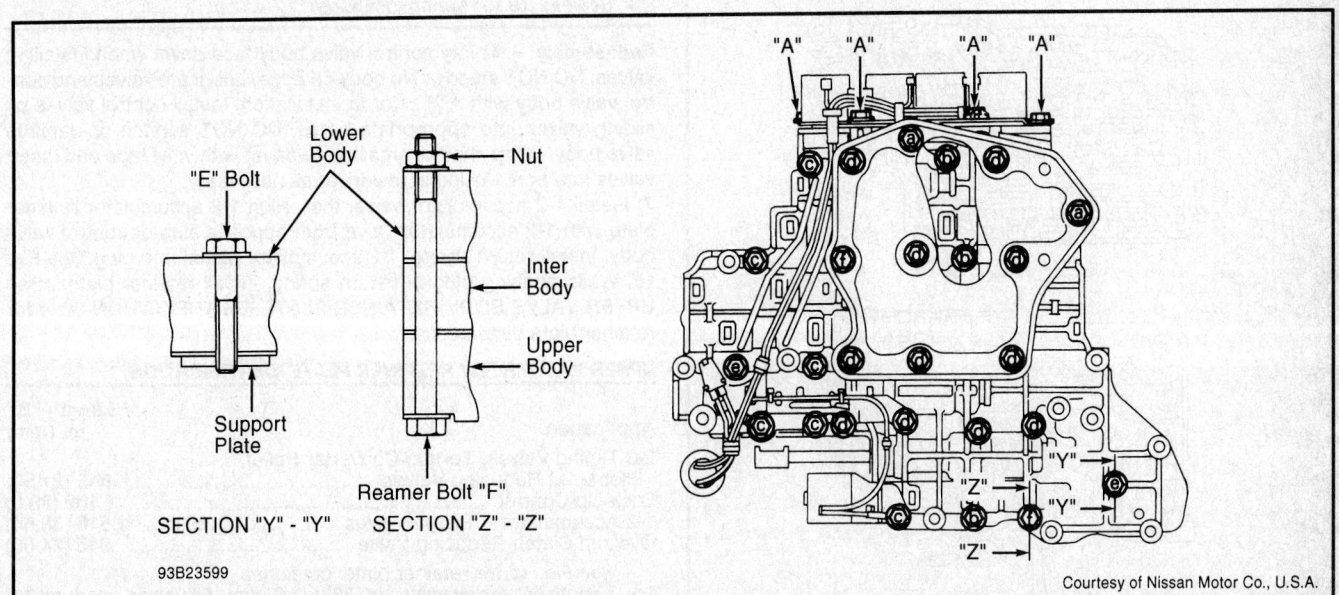

Fig. 14: **Exploded View Of Control Valve Assembly**

1. Oil Strainer
2. "O" Ring
3. Clip
4. Terminal Body
5. "O" Rings
6. Lower Valve Body
7. Relief Valve Spring
8. Check Ball
9. Lower Separating Gasket
10. Separating Plate
11. Lower Inter Separating Gasket
12. Support Plate
13. Steel Balls (6)
14. Inter Valve Body
15. Pilot Filter
16. Upper Inter Separating Gasket
17. Separating Plate
18. Upper Separating Gasket
19. Steel Balls (5)
20. Upper Valve Body

93A23598

Courtesy of Nissan Motor Co., U.S.A.

2) Remove bolts "A", "D" and "F", and remove oil strainer from control valve assembly. Remove solenoid assembly and line pressure solenoid from control valve assembly. Remove "O" rings from solenoids and harness terminal body. Place upper valve body face down. Remove bolts "B", "C" and "F".

3) Remove inter valve body from lower valve body. Turn lower valve body over and remove accumulator support plate. Remove bolts "E",

separating plate and separating gasket from lower valve body. *See Fig. 14.* Remove check balls and relief valve springs from lower valve body. DO NOT lose check balls or relief valve springs.

4) Remove inter valve body with separating plate and separating gasket from upper valve body. Ensure steel balls are properly positioned in upper and inter valve bodies, then remove balls from valve bodies. DO NOT lose steel balls.

Fig. 15: **Identifying Control Valve Assembly Bolt Locations**

Inspection – Ensure retainer plates are properly positioned in lower and upper valve bodies. *See Fig. 16.* DO NOT lose retainer plates. Check oil strainer for damage. Inspect shift solenoids "A" and "B", line pressure solenoid, lock-up solenoid and overrun clutch solenoid. See ELECTRONIC COMPONENTS & CIRCUIT TESTS in NISSAN RE4F03A/V ELECTRONIC CONTROLS article. Check oil cooler relief valve springs for damage or deformation. Measure spring free length and outer diameter. Free length should be .670" (17.0 mm) and diameter should be .315" (8.00 mm). Replace springs if not as specified.

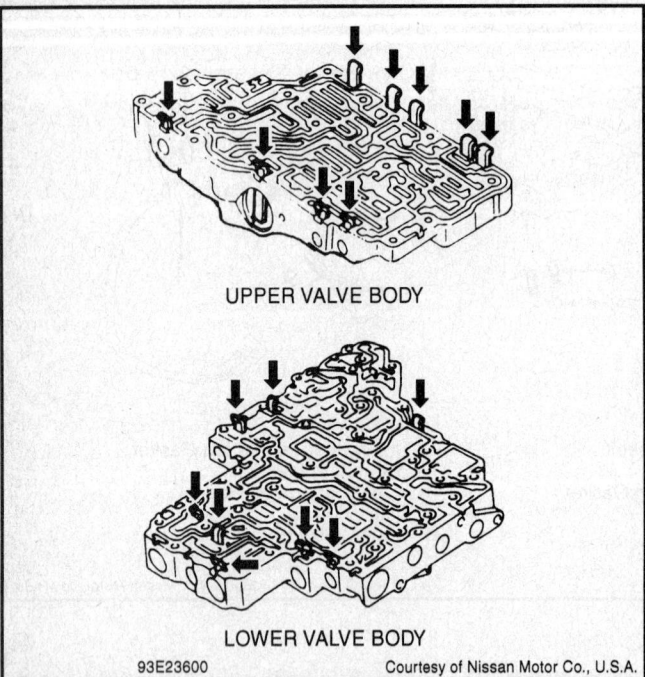

UPPER VALVE BODY

LOWER VALVE BODY

93E23600   Courtesy of Nissan Motor Co., U.S.A.

Fig. 16: Identifying Retainer Plate Locations

Reassembly – **1)** Place oil circuit of upper valve body face up. Install steel balls in proper positions. *See Fig. 17.* Using NEW gaskets, install upper separating gasket, upper inter separating gasket and upper separating plate. Install reamer bolts "F" from bottom of upper valve

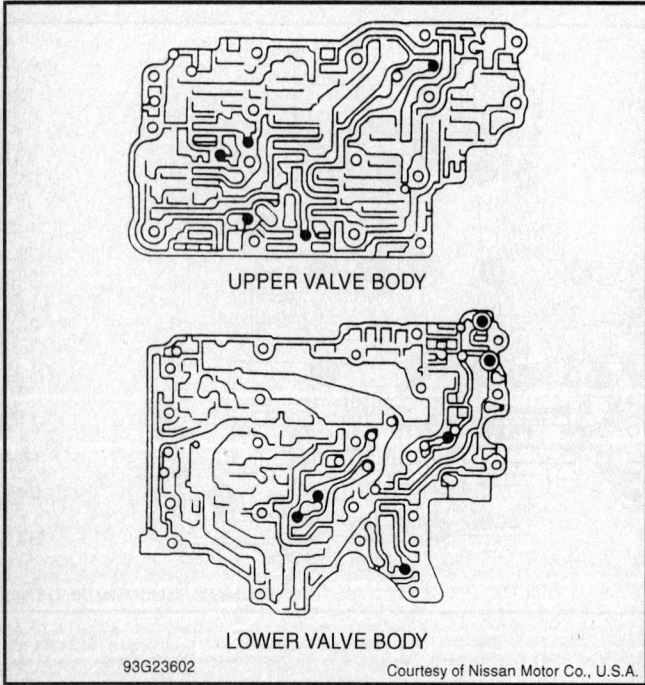

UPPER VALVE BODY

LOWER VALVE BODY

93G23602   Courtesy of Nissan Motor Co., U.S.A.

Fig. 17: Identifying Steel Ball Locations

body. Install separating gaskets and separating plates as a set on upper valve body, using reamer bolts as a guide.
2) Install pilot filter. Place lower valve body side of inter valve body face up. Install steel balls in proper positions. Install inter valve body on upper valve body, using reamer bolts "F" as a guide. DO NOT lose steel balls. Install check balls and relief valve springs in proper positions in lower valve body. Install lower separating gasket, inter separating gasket and lower separating plate. *See Fig. 14.*
3) Install support plate bolts "E" from bottom of lower valve body. Install separating gaskets and separating plate as a set on lower valve body using bolts "E" as a guide. Temporarily install support plates on lower valve body. Install lower valve body on inter valve body using reamer bolts "F" as a guide. *See Fig. 15.* Tighten bolts.
4) Install "O" rings to solenoids and harness terminal connector. Apply ATF to "O" rings prior to installation. Install and snug bolts "B". Install solenoid assembly and line pressure solenoid to lower valve body. Tighten all bolts (except "E") to 62-80 INCH lbs. (7-9 N.m). Tighten "E" bolts to 30-39 INCH lbs. (3.4-4.4 mm).

CONTROL VALVE UPPER BODY

Disassembly – **1)** Use a screwdriver to pry out retainer plates. Remove retainer plates while holding spring, plugs and sleeves. Remove plug slowly to prevent internal parts from jumping out.
2) Place mating surface of valve body face down and remove internal parts. If valve is hard to remove, lightly tap valve body with soft-faced hammer. DO NOT use a magnet to remove valves. DO NOT drop or damage valves or sleeves.
Inspection – Measure valve spring free length and outer diameter. See UPPER VALVE BODY SPRING IDENTIFICATION table. Check for deformation or damage. Replace valve springs if deformed or fatigued. Check sliding surfaces of valves, sleeves and plugs.

UPPER VALVE BODY SPRING IDENTIFICATION [1]

Spring No.	Length In. (mm)	Diameter In. (mm)
1	.48 (37.5)	.28 (7.00)
2	1.22 (31.0)	.35 (8.9)
3	1.56 (39.5)	.43 (11.0)
4	.81 (20.5)	.28 (7.00)
5	1.42 (36.0)	.32 (8.1)
6	1.92 (48.8)	.77 (19.6)
7	1.06 (27.0)	.28 (7.00)

[1] – See Fig. 18 for spring locations.

Reassembly – **1)** Lay control valve body face down when installing valves. DO NOT stand valve body on edge. Lubricate valves and control valve body with ATF prior to installation. Install control valves by sliding valves into appropriate bores. DO NOT scratch or damage valve body. Wrap shaft of small screwdriver with vinyl tape and insert valves into bores using screwdriver as necessary.
2) Install 1-2 accumulator valve, then align 1-2 accumulator retainer plate with 1-2 accumulator valve from opposite side of control valve body. Install return spring, 1-2 accumulator piston and plug. *See Fig. 18.* While pushing plug or return spring, install retainer plates. See UPPER VALVE BODY RETAINER PLATE IDENTIFICATION table for retainer plate dimensions.

UPPER VALVE BODY RETAINER PLATE IDENTIFICATION [1]

Application	[2] Length "B" In. (mm)
2-3 Timing Valves, Torque Converter Relief, Pilot & 1st Reducing Valves	.846 (21.50)
Lock-Up Control	1.102 (28.0)
1-2 Accumulator & Piston Valves	1.516 (38.50)
Overrun Clutch Reducing Valve	.945 (24.00)

[1] – See Fig. 16 for retainer plate locations.
[2] – Length "A" for all valves is .236" (6.0 mm). All valves use type "A" retainer plate. *See Fig. 19.*

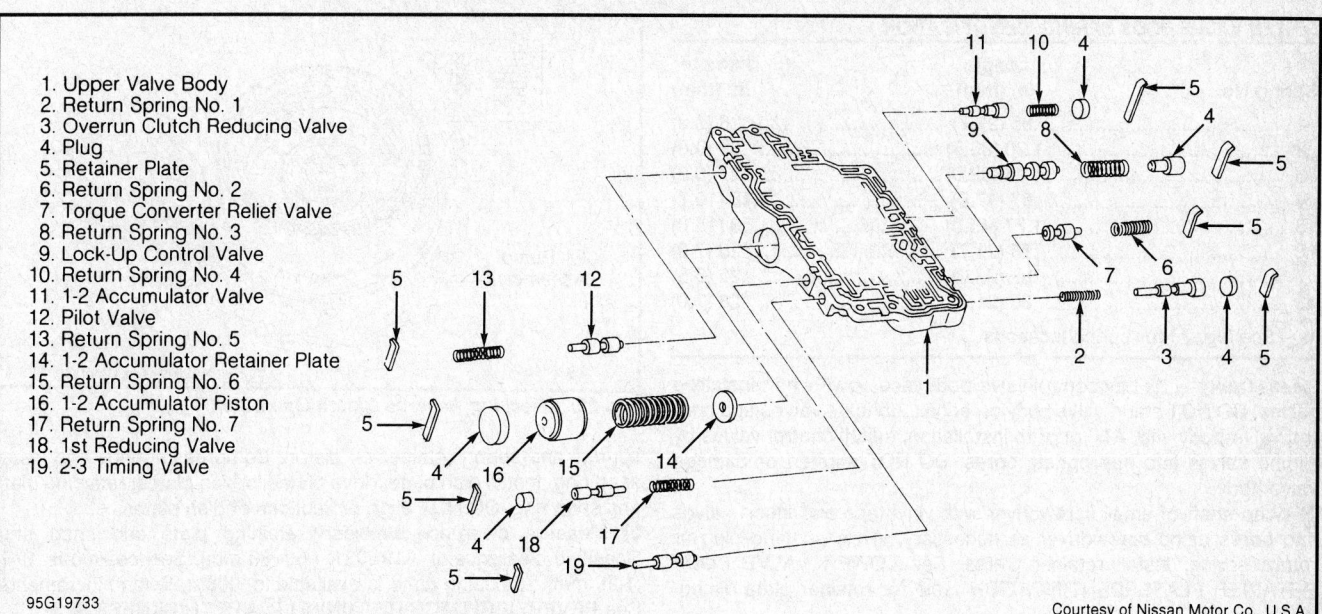

1. Upper Valve Body
2. Return Spring No. 1
3. Overrun Clutch Reducing Valve
4. Plug
5. Retainer Plate
6. Return Spring No. 2
7. Torque Converter Relief Valve
8. Return Spring No. 3
9. Lock-Up Control Valve
10. Return Spring No. 4
11. 1-2 Accumulator Valve
12. Pilot Valve
13. Return Spring No. 5
14. 1-2 Accumulator Retainer Plate
15. Return Spring No. 6
16. 1-2 Accumulator Piston
17. Return Spring No. 7
18. 1st Reducing Valve
19. 2-3 Timing Valve

95G19733

Courtesy of Nissan Motor Co., U.S.A.

Fig. 18: Exploded View Of Control Valve Upper Body

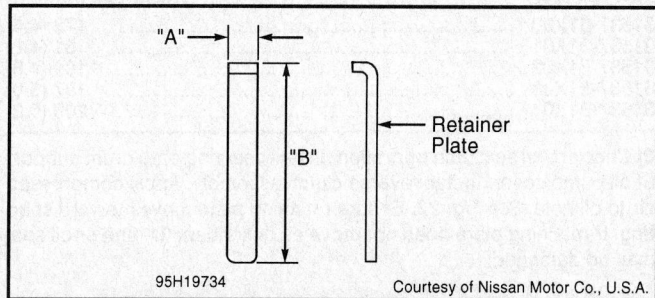

95H19734

Courtesy of Nissan Motor Co., U.S.A.

Fig. 19: Measuring Retainer Plate Dimensions (Upper Valve Body)

CONTROL VALVE LOWER BODY

Disassembly – Use a screwdriver to pry out retainer plates. Remove retainer plates while holding spring, plugs and sleeves. Remove plug slowly to prevent internal parts from jumping out. Place mating surface of valve body face down and remove internal parts. If valve is hard to remove, lightly tap valve body with soft-faced hammer. DO NOT use a magnet to remove valves. DO NOT drop or damage valves or sleeves.

Inspection – Measure spring free length and outer diameter. See LOWER VALVE BODY SPRING IDENTIFICATION table. Check for deformation or damage. Replace valve springs if deformed or fatigued. Check sliding surfaces of valves, sleeves and plugs.

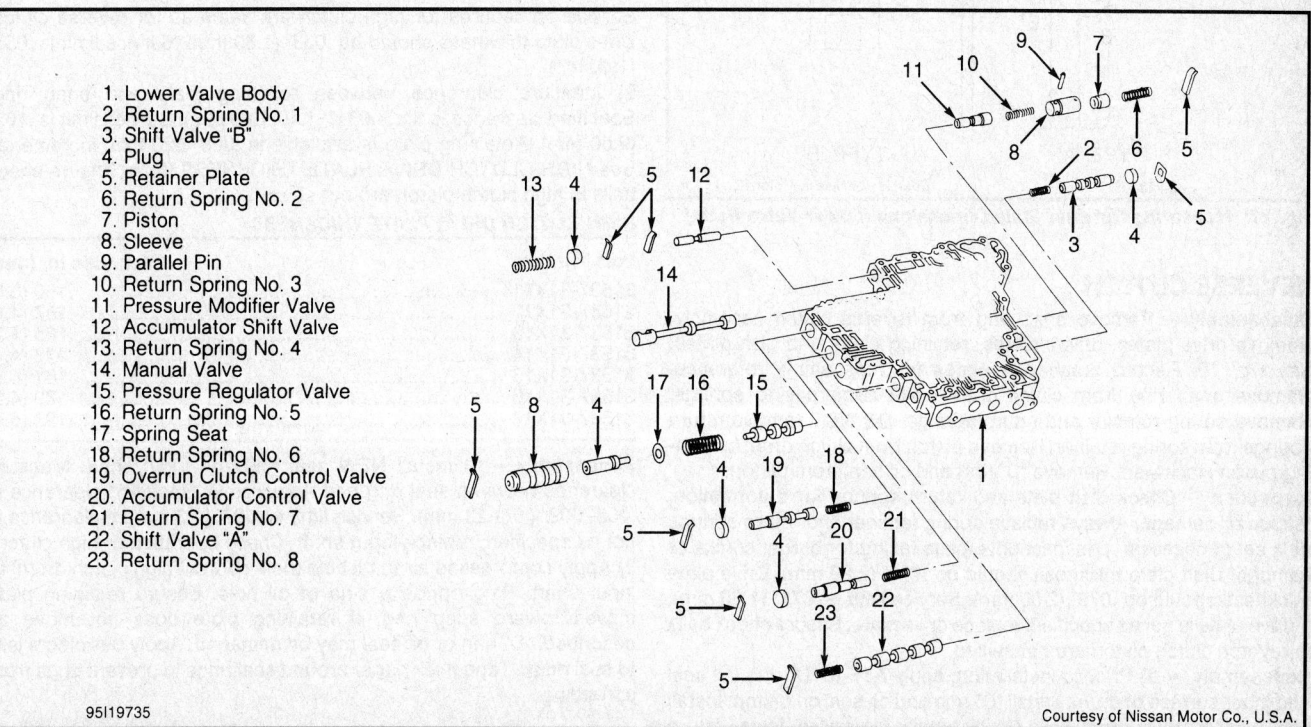

1. Lower Valve Body
2. Return Spring No. 1
3. Shift Valve "B"
4. Plug
5. Retainer Plate
6. Return Spring No. 2
7. Piston
8. Sleeve
9. Parallel Pin
10. Return Spring No. 3
11. Pressure Modifier Valve
12. Accumulator Shift Valve
13. Return Spring No. 4
14. Manual Valve
15. Pressure Regulator Valve
16. Return Spring No. 5
17. Spring Seat
18. Return Spring No. 6
19. Overrun Clutch Control Valve
20. Accumulator Control Valve
21. Return Spring No. 7
22. Shift Valve "A"
23. Return Spring No. 8

95I19735

Courtesy of Nissan Motor Co., U.S.A.

Fig. 20: Exploded View Of Control Valve Lower Body (RE4F03V Shown)

LOWER VALVE BODY SPRING IDENTIFICATION [1]

Spring No.	Length In. (mm)	Diameter In. (mm)
1	.85 (21.7)	.28 (7.0)
2	1.20 (30.5)	.39 (9.8)
3	1.26 (32.0)	.27 (6.9)
4	.67 (17.0)	.42 (10.7)
5	1.77 (45.0)	.59 (15.0)
6	.85 (21.7)	.28 (7.0)
7	.87 (22.0)	.26 (6.5)
8	.85 (21.7)	.28 (7.0)

[1] – See Fig. 20 for spring locations.

Reassembly – 1) Lay control valve body face down when installing valves. DO NOT stand valve body on edge. Lubricate valves and control valve body with ATF prior to installation. Install control valves by sliding valves into appropriate bores. DO NOT scratch or damage valve body.

2) Wrap shaft of small screwdriver with vinyl tape and insert valves into bores using screwdriver as necessary. While pushing plug or return spring, install retainer plates. See LOWER VALVE BODY RETAINER PLATE IDENTIFICATION table for retainer plate dimensions.

LOWER VALVE BODY RETAINER PLATE IDENTIFICATION [1]

Application	Length "A" In. (mm)	Length "B" In. (mm)
Accumulator Shift Valve	.236 (6.00)	.768 (19.50)
All Other Valves [2]	.236 (6.00)	1.106 (27.00)

[1] – See Fig. 16 for retainer plate locations.

[2] – Shift Valve "B" not applicable. All valves use type "A" retainer plate except shift valve "B" (Type "B"). See Fig. 21.

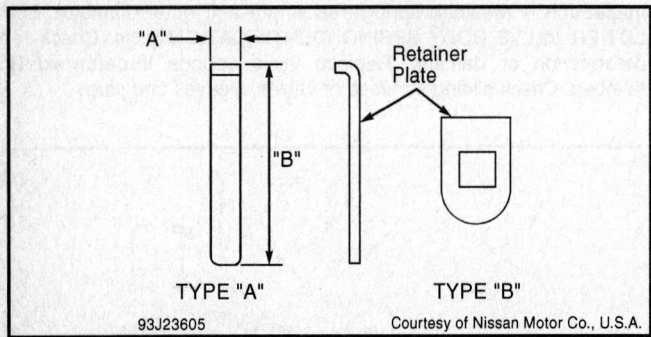

Fig. 21: Measuring Retainer Plate Dimensions (Lower Valve Body)

REVERSE CLUTCH

Disassembly – Remove snap ring from reverse clutch assembly. Remove drive plates, driven plates, retaining plate, and dish plates. See Fig. 10. Record number of plates for reassembly reference. Remove snap ring from clutch drum while compressing springs. Remove spring retainer and return springs. DO NOT remove return springs from spring retainer. Remove piston from clutch drum by turning piston clockwise. Remove "D" ring and oil seal from piston.

Inspection – Check dish plate and return springs for deformation, fatigue or damage. Always replace spring retainer and return springs as a set (if necessary). Inspect drive plate facing for burns, cracks or damage. Dish plate thickness should be .110" (2.80 mm). Drive plate thickness should be .079" (2.00 mm). Service limit is .071" (1.80 mm). If drive plate is not as specified, replace drive plate. Ensure check balls in reverse clutch piston are not seized.

Reassembly – 1) Prior to installation, apply ATF to "D" ring, oil seal and inner surface of drum. Install "D" ring and oil seal on piston. Install piston assembly in drum while slowly turning clockwise. Install return

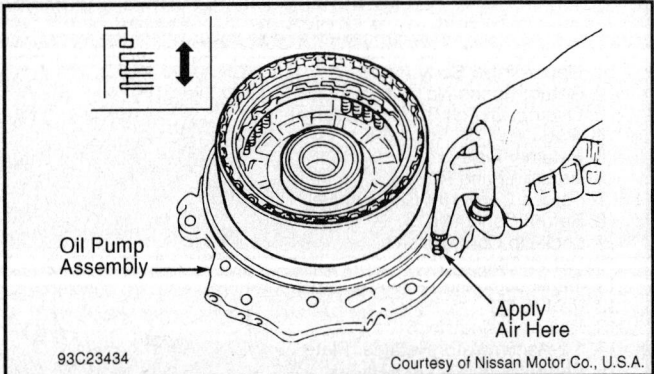

Fig. 22: Checking Reverse Clutch Operation

springs and spring retainer on piston. Compress springs and install snap ring. Install dish plate, drive plates, driven plates, retaining plate and snap ring. DO NOT align projections of dish plates.

2) Measure clearance between retaining plate and snap ring. Specified clearance is .019-.031" (.50-.80 mm). Service limit is .047" (1.20 mm). Retaining plate is available in .008" (.20 mm) increments. See REVERSE CLUTCH RETAINING PLATE THICKNESS table.

REVERSE CLUTCH RETAINING PLATE THICKNESS

Part Number	Thickness In. (mm)
31537-31X00	.173 (4.4)
31537-31X01	.181 (4.6)
31537-31X02	.189 (4.8)
31537-31X03	.197 (5.0)
31537-31X04	.205 (5.2)

3) Check reverse clutch operation. Install seal ring onto drum support of oil pump cover. Install reverse clutch assembly. Apply compressed air to oil hole. See Fig. 22. Ensure retaining plate moves toward snap ring. If retaining plate does not move as described, "D" ring or oil seal may be damaged.

HIGH CLUTCH

Disassembly & Inspection – 1) Remove seal rings from input shaft. Service procedures for high clutch are same as for reverse clutch. Drive plate thickness should be .063" (1.60 mm). Service limit is .055" (1.40 mm).

2) Measure clearance between retaining plate and snap ring. Specified clearance is .055-.071" (1.40-1.80 mm). Service limit is .102" (2.60 mm). Retaining plate is available in .008" (.20 mm) increments. See HIGH CLUTCH DRIVE PLATE THICKNESS table. Ensure check balls in high clutch piston are not seized.

HIGH CLUTCH DRIVE PLATE THICKNESS

Part Number	Thickness In. (mm)
31537-31X11	.150 (3.8)
31537-31X12	.157 (4.0)
31537-31X13	.165 (4.2)
31537-31X14	.173 (4.4)
31537-31X15	.181 (4.6)
31537-31X16	.189 (4.8)
31537-31X17	.197 (5.0)

Reassembly – 1) Install NEW seal rings on input shaft. Measure clearance between seal ring and ring groove. Specified clearance is .003-.009" (.08-.23 mm). Service limit is .009" (.23 mm). If clearance is not as specified, replace input shaft. Check operation of high clutch.

2) Apply compressed air to oil hole (hole nearest high clutch drum) of input shaft. Plug opposite side of oil hole. Ensure retaining plate moves toward snap ring. If retaining plate does not move as described, "D" ring or oil seal may be damaged. Apply petroleum jelly to seal rings. Tape thick paper around seal rings to prevent rings from spreading.

FORWARD & OVERRUN CLUTCHES

Disassembly – Service procedures for forward clutch and overrun clutch are same as for reverse clutch. *See Fig. 10.*

Inspection – Check forward clutch and overrun clutch return springs for deformation or damage. Check spring free length and outer diameter. Inner spring free length should be 1.035" (26.30 mm). Inner spring diameter should be .30" (7.7). Outer spring free length should be 1.047" (26.60 mm). Outer spring diameter should be .417" (10.60 mm). Inspect drive plate facing for burns, cracks or damage. Ensure check balls in forward clutch and overrun clutch pistons are not seized.

Reassembly – **1)** Reassembly procedures for forward and overrun clutches are same as for reverse clutch. Dish plate thickness for forward clutch should be .098" (2.50 mm). Dish plate thickness for overrun clutch should be .085" (2.15 mm). Drive plate thickness for forward clutch should be .071" (1.80 mm). Service limit is .063" (1.60 mm). Drive plate thickness for overrun clutch should be .063" (1.60 mm). Service limit is .055" (1.40 mm).

2) Measure clearance between retaining plate and snap ring. Specified clearance for forward clutch is .018-.034" (.45-.85 mm). Service limit is .073" (1.85 mm). Specified clearance for overrun clutch is .039-.055" (1.00-1.40 mm). Service limit is .079" (2.00 mm).

3) Forward clutch retaining plate is available in .008" (.20 mm) increments. Overrun clutch retaining plate is available in .008" (.20 mm) increments. See FORWARD CLUTCH RETAINING PLATE THICKNESS and OVERRUN CLUTCH RETAINING PLATE THICKNESS tables.

FORWARD CLUTCH RETAINING PLATE THICKNESS

Part Number	Thickness In. (mm)
31537-31X60	.142 (3.6)
31537-31X61	.150 (3.8)
31537-31X62	.157 (4.0)
31537-31X63	.165 (4.2)
31537-31X64	.173 (4.4)
31537-31X65	.181 (4.6)

OVERRUN CLUTCH RETAINING PLATE THICKNESS

Part Number	Thickness In. (mm)
31567-31X72	.142 (3.6)
31567-31X73	.150 (3.8)
31567-31X74	.157 (4.0)
31567-31X75	.165 (4.2)
31567-31X76	.173 (4.4)

4) Check forward and overrun clutch operation. Install bearing retainer on forward clutch drum. Apply compressed air to appropriate oil hole of forward clutch drum. *See Fig. 23.* Ensure retaining plate moves toward snap ring. If retaining plate does not move as described, "D" ring or oil seal may be damaged.

LOW- REVERSE BRAKE

Disassembly – Position transaxle case to obtain access to low-reverse brake snap ring. Remove snap ring. Remove drive plates, driven plates and retaining plate from transaxle case. *See Fig. 10.* Record number of plates for reassembly reference. Compress return springs and remove snap ring. Remove spring retainer and return springs from transaxle case. DO NOT remove return springs from spring retainer. Apply compressed air to oil hole in transaxle case and remove piston. *See Fig. 24.* Remove "D" ring and oil seal from piston.

Inspection – Check low-reverse brake snap ring, springs and retainer for deformation or damage. Always replace spring retainer and return springs as a set (if necessary). Check low-reverse drive plates for burns, cracks or damage.

Reassembly – **1)** Reassembly procedures for low-reverse brake are same as for reverse clutch. Drive plate thickness should be .079" (2.00 mm). Service limit is .070" (1.80 mm). Specified clearance is .055-.071" (1.40-1.80 mm). Service limit is .110" (2.80 mm). Retaining plate is available in increments of .008" (.20 mm). See LOW-REVERSE BRAKE RETAINING PLATE THICKNESS table.

LOW-REVERSE BRAKE RETAINING PLATE THICKNESS

Part Number	Thickness In. (mm)
31667-31X16	.142 (3.6)
31667-31X17	.150 (3.8)
31667-31X18	.157 (4.0)
31667-31X19	.165 (4.2)
31667-31X20	.173 (4.4)
31667-31X21	.181 (4.6)

2) Check low-reverse brake operation. Apply compressed air to oil hole in transaxle case. *See Fig. 25.* Ensure retaining plate moves toward snap ring. If retaining plate does not move, "D" ring or oil seal may be damaged.

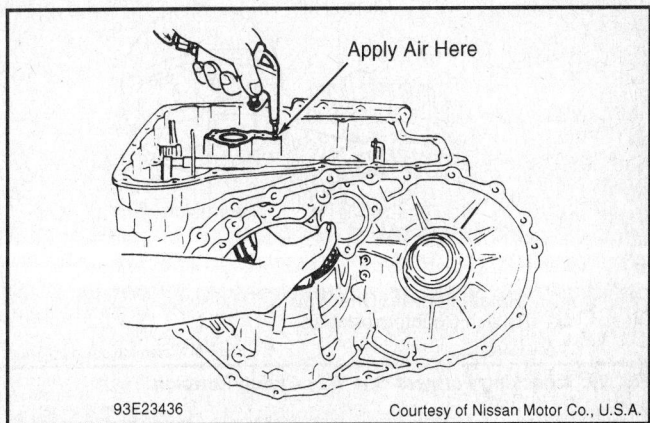

93E23436

Courtesy of Nissan Motor Co., U.S.A.

Fig. 24: Removing Low-Reverse Brake Piston

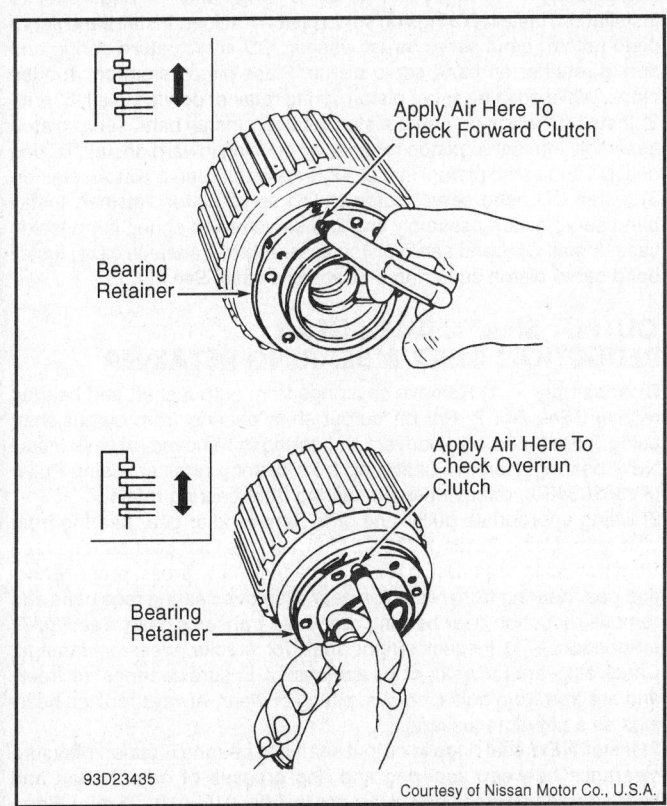

Apply Air Here To Check Forward Clutch

Bearing Retainer

Apply Air Here To Check Overrun Clutch

Bearing Retainer

93D23435

Courtesy of Nissan Motor Co., U.S.A.

Fig. 23: Checking Forward & Overrun Clutch Operation

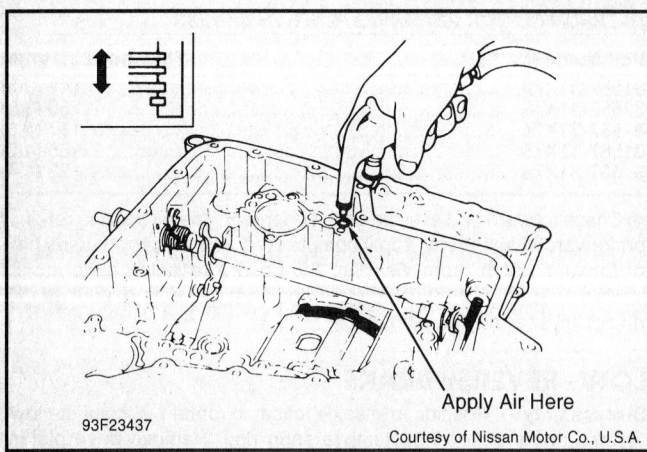

Fig. 25: *Checking Low & Reverse Operation*

REAR INTERNAL GEAR, FORWARD CLUTCH HUB & OVERRUN CLUTCH HUB

Disassembly – Remove snap ring from overrun clutch hub. Remove overrun clutch hub from forward clutch hub. *See Fig. 10.* Remove thrust washer from forward clutch hub. Remove forward clutch hub from rear internal gear. Remove end bearing from rear internal gear. Remove thrust washer from rear internal gear. Remove end bearing from forward one-way clutch. Remove one-way clutch from forward clutch hub.

Inspection – Check frictional surfaces for wear or damage. Check forward one-way clutch, end bearing and snap ring for wear or damage.

Reassembly – 1) Install forward one-way clutch on forward clutch hub with arrow facing forward. *See Fig. 26.* Apply petroleum jelly to end bearings and thrust washers. Install end bearing on forward one-way clutch.

2) Install thrust washer on rear internal gear. Align pawls of thrust washer with holes in rear internal gear. Install end bearing on rear internal gear. Install forward clutch hub on rear internal gear. Ensure forward clutch hub rotates counterclockwise only.

3) Install thrust washer on overrun clutch hub. Align pawls of thrust washer with holes in overrun clutch hub. Install overrun clutch hub on rear internal gear. Align projections of rear internal gear with holes in overrun clutch hub. Install snap ring to rear internal gear.

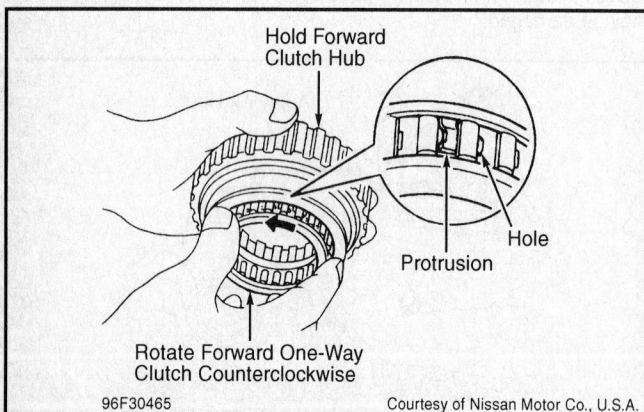

Fig. 26: *Checking Forward One-Way Clutch Rotation*

BAND SERVO PISTON ASSEMBLY

Disassembly – 1) Use appropriate puller to compress servo piston. Remove band servo piston snap ring. Apply compressed air to oil hole in transaxle case to remove OD servo piston retainer and band servo piston assembly. *See Fig. 27.*

2) Apply compressed air to oil hole in servo piston retainer to remove OD band servo piston from retainer. Secure OD band servo piston while applying compressed air. Remove "D" ring from OD band servo piston. Remove "O" rings from OD servo piston retainer. *See Fig. 10.*

3) Remove band servo piston assembly from servo piston retainer by pushing forward. Place piston stem end on wooden block. While pushing servo piston spring retainer down, remove "E" ring. Remove OD servo retainer spring, band servo thrust washer and band servo piston stem from band servo piston. Remove "O" rings from servo piston retainer. Remove "D" rings from band servo piston.

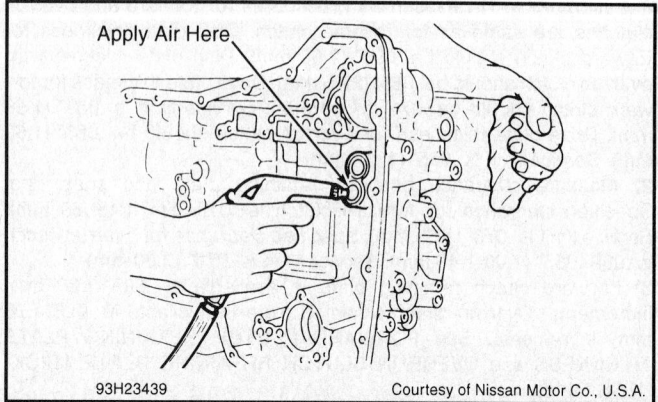

Fig. 27: *Removing OD Piston Retainer & Band Servo Piston*

Inspection – Check frictional surfaces for abnormal wear or damage. Check return springs for deformation or damage. Check spring free length and outer diameter. Free length of 2nd servo return spring should be 1.28" (32.5 mm), diameter should be 1.020" (25.90 mm). Free length of OD servo return spring should be 1.220" (31.00 mm), diameter should be .854" (21.70 mm). Replace spring(s) if not as specified.

Reassembly – 1) Apply ATF to all "D" rings and "O" rings prior to installation. Install "D" rings on servo piston retainer. Install band servo piston stem, band servo thrust washer, OD servo return spring and spring retainer on band servo piston. Place piston stem on wooden block. While pushing servo piston spring retainer down, install "E" ring.

2) Install "O" rings on servo piston retainer. Install band servo piston assembly into servo piston retainer by pushing inward. Install "D" ring on OD band servo piston. Install "O" rings on OD servo piston retainer.

3) Install OD band servo piston to OD servo piston retainer. Install band servo piston assembly and 2nd servo return spring in transaxle case. Install OD band servo piston assembly to transaxle case. Install band servo piston snap ring on transaxle case. *See Fig. 7.*

OUTPUT SHAFT, IDLER GEAR, REDUCTION GEAR & BEARING RETAINER

Disassembly – 1) Remove seal rings from output shaft and bearing retainer. *See Fig. 7.* Pry off output shaft bearing from output shaft using 2 flat-blade screwdrivers. If bearing is removed, always install NEW bearing. Remove snap ring from bearing retainer. Using Puller (KV381054S0), remove needle bearing from bearing retainer.

2) Using appropriate puller and drift, remove idler gear bearing from idler gear. Using Puller (KV381054S0), remove idler gear bearing race from transaxle case. Using appropriate puller and press, press reduction gear bearing from reduction gear. Remove bearing race bolts and remove reduction gear bearing race from transaxle case. *See Fig. 7.*

Inspection – 1) Inspect output shaft for cracks, wear or damage. Check all gears for wear, chips and cracks. Ensure bearings roll freely and are free from noise, cracks, pitting or wear. Always replace bearings as a set (if necessary).

2) Install NEW seal rings to output shaft and bearing retainer. Measure clearance between seal ring and ring grooves of output shaft and bearing retainer. Specified clearance is .004-.010" (.10-.25 mm). Service limit is .010" (.25 mm). If clearance is not as specified, replace output shaft or bearing retainer as necessary.

Reassembly – To reassemble, reverse disassembly procedure. Tighten reduction gear bearing race bolts to 46-49 ft. lbs. (63-67 N.m). Apply petroleum jelly to NEW seal rings and install seal rings on output shaft and bearing retainer. Tape thick paper around seal rings to prevent rings from spreading.

MANUAL SHAFT & THROTTLE LEVER

Disassembly – **1)** Remove detent spring from transaxle case. Drive out manual plate retaining pin. Drive and pull out parking rod plate retaining pin. Remove parking rod plate from manual shaft. See Fig. 7.

2) Remove parking rod from transaxle case. Pull out manual shaft retaining pin. Remove manual shaft and manual plate from transaxle case. Remove manual shaft oil seal. Inspect all components for wear or damage.

Reassembly – To reassemble, reverse disassembly procedure. Apply ATF to outer surface of oil seal prior to installation. Manual plate and parking rod plate retaining pins should extend .20-.24" (5.00-6.00 mm) outside of shaft. Tighten detent spring bolt to 57-66 INCH lbs. (6.4-7.5 N.m).

DIFFERENTIAL ASSEMBLY

Disassembly – Remove ring gear. Using appropriate puller, adapter and drift, remove differential side bearings. Remove viscous coupling (RE4F03V). Remove speedometer drive gear. Drive out pinion shaft retaining pin. Remove pinion shaft from differential case. Remove pinion gears and side gears. See Fig. 9.

Inspection – Check mating surfaces of differential case, side gears and pinion gears for wear, scoring or damage. Check washers for wear or damage. Ensure bearings roll freely and are free from cracks, pitting or wear. Inspect viscous coupling case for cracks or silicone oil leakage.

Reassembly – **1)** Install side gears and thrust washers in differential case. Install pinion gears and thrust washers in case by rotating gears. Apply ATF to all components. Using a dial indicator and Adapter (KV38105710) on RE4F03A, Adapter (KV38107700) on RE4F03V, measure clearance on differential case side, between side gear thrust washer and differential case. Move side gear up and down to measure deflection. Always measure deflection on both side gears. See Fig. 28.

2) Specified clearance is .004-.008" (.10-.20 mm). If clearance is not as specified, adjust clearance by changing thickness of side gear thrust washers. Washers are available in increments of .002" (.05 mm). See DIFFERENTIAL SIDE GEAR THRUST WASHER THICKNESS tables.

DIFFERENTIAL SIDE GEAR THRUST WASHER THICKNESS (RE4F03A)

Part Number	Thickness In. (mm)
38424-D2111	.0295-.0315 (.75-.80)
38424-D2112	.0315-.0335 (.80-.85)
38424-D2113	.0335-.0354 (.85-.90)
38424-D2114	.0354-.0374 (.90-.95)
38424-D2115	.0374-.0394 (.95-1.00)

DIFFERENTIAL SIDE GEAR THRUST WASHER THICKNESS (RE4F03V)

Part Number	Thickness In. (mm)
38424-D2110	.0276-.0295 (.70-.75)
38424-D2111[1]	.0295-.0315 (.75-.80)
38424-D2112[1]	.0315-.0335 (.80-.85)
38424-D2113[1]	.0335-.0354 (.85-.90)
38424-D2114[1]	.0354-.0374 (.90-.95)
38424-D2115[1]	.0374-.0394 (.95-1.00)
38424-D2116	.0394-.0413 (1.00-1.05)
38424-D2117	.0413-.0433 (1.05-1.10)
38424-D2118	.0433-.0453 (1.10-1.15)
38424-D2119	.0453-.0472 (1.15-1.20)
38424-D2120	.0472-.0492 (1.20-1.25)
38424-D2121	.0492-.0512 (1.25-1.30)
38424-D2122	.0512-.0531 (1.30-1.35)

[1] – Part numbers used on differential case side. (All shims may be used on viscous coupling side).

3) Place side gear and thrust washer on pinion gears installed on viscous coupling side of differential. Using a height gauge, measure dimension "X" of differential case and dimension "Y" of viscous coupling in at least 2 places. See Fig. 29.

4) Clearance between side gear and viscous coupling is determined by using the following equation:

$$X + Y - 2A = \text{CLEARANCE}$$

(Dimension A = height of gauge spacer).

5) Specified clearance is .004-.008" (.10-.20 mm). If clearance is not as specified, adjust clearance by changing thickness of side gear thrust washers. Washers are available in increments of .002" (.05 mm). See DIFFERENTIAL SIDE GEAR THRUST WASHER THICKNESS (RE4F03V) table.

6) Install retaining pin. Ensure retaining pin is flush with case. Install side gear (viscous coupling side), on differential case, then install viscous coupling. Install speedometer drive gear in differential case. Align projections of speedometer drive gear with groove in differential case. See Fig. 30.

7) Press differential side bearings on differential case. Install ring gear and tighten bolts in numerical order. See Fig. 31. Tighten bolts to 39-50 ft. lbs. (53-68 N.m).

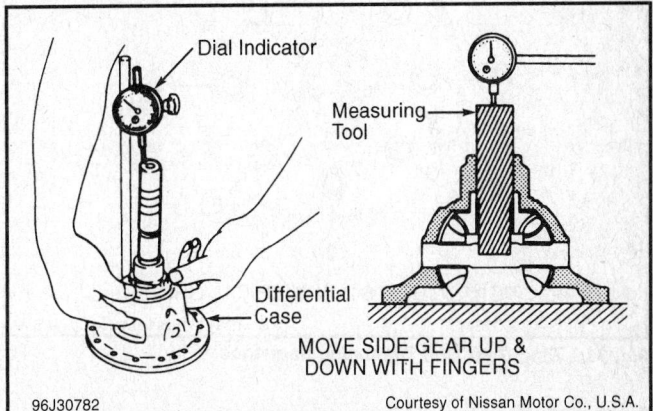

Fig. 28: Measuring Side Gear-To-Differential Case Clearance

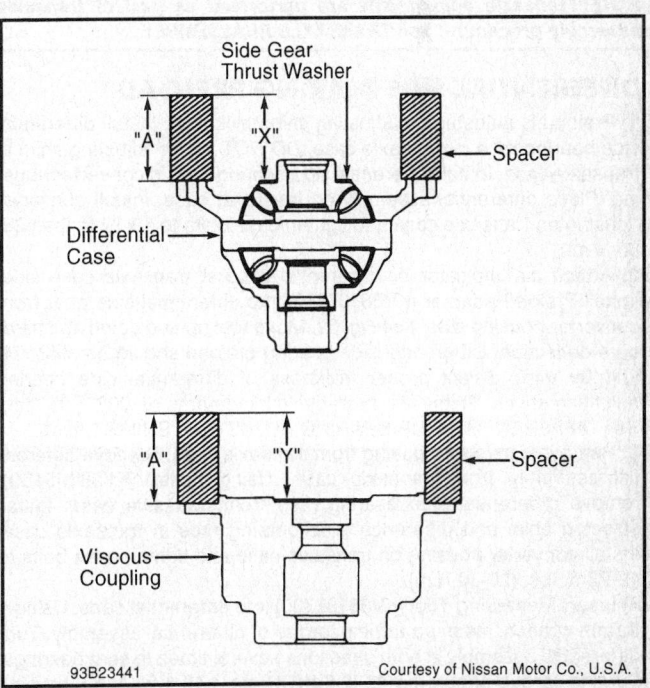

Fig. 29: Measuring Side Gear-To-Viscous Coupling Clearance

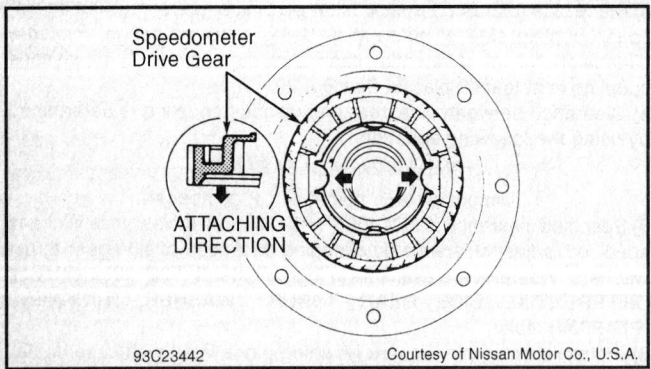

Fig. 30: Installing Speedometer Drive Gear

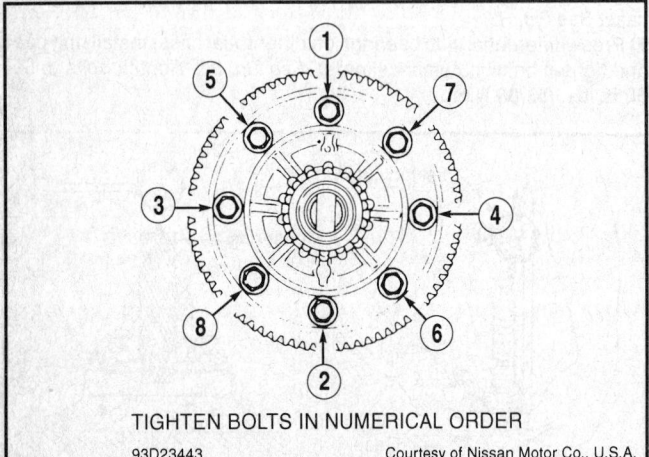

TIGHTEN BOLTS IN NUMERICAL ORDER

Fig. 31: Ring Gear Bolt Tightening Sequence

TRANSAXLE ADJUSTMENTS

NOTE: Transaxle adjustments are performed as part of transaxle assembly procedure. See TRANSAXLE REASSEMBLY.

DIFFERENTIAL SIDE BEARING PRELOAD

1) Preload is adjusted by adjusting shim thickness. Install differential side bearing race in transaxle case. DO NOT install adjusting shim in transaxle case. Install differential side bearing race in converter housing. Place differential assembly on transaxle case. Install converter housing on transaxle case and tighten case bolts to 19-22 ft. lbs. (26-30 N.m).

2) Attach dial indicator on differential case at transaxle case side. Install Preload Adapter (KV38107700) into differential side gear from converter housing side. *See Fig. 32.* Move tool up and down and measure deflection. Differential side bearing preload should be .002-.04" (.04-.09 mm). Select proper thickness of differential side bearing adjusting shims. Shims are available in increments of .002" (.05 mm). See DIFFERENTIAL SIDE BEARING ADJUSTING SHIMS tables.

3) Remove converter housing from transaxle case. Remove differential assembly from transaxle case. Using Puller (KV381054S0), remove differential side bearing race from transaxle case. Install selected shim and differential side bearing race in transaxle case. Install converter housing on transaxle case and tighten case bolts to 19-22 ft. lbs. (26-30 N.m).

4) Insert Measuring Tool (KV38107700) into differential case. Using a torque wrench, measure turning torque of differential assembly. Turn differential assembly in both directions several times to seat bearings. Turning torque should be 4.3-9.6 INCH lbs. (.49-1.08 N.m). If using original bearings, turning torque will be slightly less then specified. Ensure turning torque is within specified range.

DIFFERENTIAL SIDE BEARING ADJUSTING SHIMS (RE4F03A)

Part Number	Thickness In. (mm)
31499-21X07	.0157 (.40)
31499-21X08	.0173 (.44)
31499-21X09	.0189 (.48)
31499-21X10	.0205 (.52)
31499-21X11	.0220 (.56)
31499-21X12	.0236 (.60)
31499-21X13	.0252 (.64)
31499-21X14	.0268 (.68)
31499-21X15	.0283 (.72)
31499-21X16	.0299 (.76)
31499-21X17	.0315 (.80)
31499-21X18	.0331 (.84)
31499-21X19	.0346 (.88)
31499-21X20	.0362 (.92)
31499-21X21	.0567 (1.44)

DIFFERENTIAL SIDE BEARING ADJUSTING SHIMS (RE4F03V)

Part Number	Thickness In. (mm)
31439-31X00	.0110 (.28)
31439-31X01	.0126 (.32)
31439-31X02	.0142 (.36)
31439-31X03	.0157 (.40)
31439-31X04	.0173 (.44)
31439-31X05	.0189 (.48)
31439-31X06	.0205 (.52)
31439-31X07	.0220 (.56)
31439-31X08	.0236 (.60)
31439-31X09	.0252 (.64)
31439-31X10	.0268 (.68)
31439-31X11	.0283 (.72)
31439-31X12	.0299 (.76)
31439-31X13	.0315 (.80)
31439-31X14	.0331 (.84)
31439-31X15	.0346 (.88)
31439-31X16	.0362 (.92)
31439-31X17	.0378 (.96)
31439-31X18	.0567 (1.44)

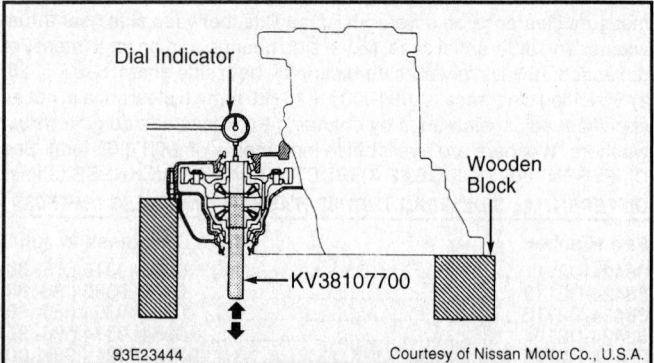

Fig. 32: Measuring Differential Side Bearing Preload

REDUCTION GEAR BEARING PRELOAD

1) Preload is adjusted by adjusting shim thickness. Remove converter housing and differential assembly from transaxle case (if necessary). Install reduction gear and idler gear in transaxle case. Using a depth gauge and straightedge, measure distance between end of reduction gear and surface of transaxle case in at least 2 places (dimension "B"). *See Fig. 33.* Measure distance between surface of idler gear bearing and surface of transaxle case in at least 2 places (dimension "C").

2) Measure distance between end of reduction gear and adjusting shim mating surface of reduction gear in at least 2 places (dimension "D"). Dimension "A" (distance between surface of idler gear bearing and adjusting shim mating surface of reduction pinion gear). To determine dimension "A" use the following equation:

$$A = D - (B + C)$$

3) For example, dimension "D" is .24" (6.0 mm). Dimension "B" is .08" (2.0 mm) and dimension "C" is .04" (1.0 mm). Total dimension "A" would be .12" (3.0 mm). *See Fig. 33.*

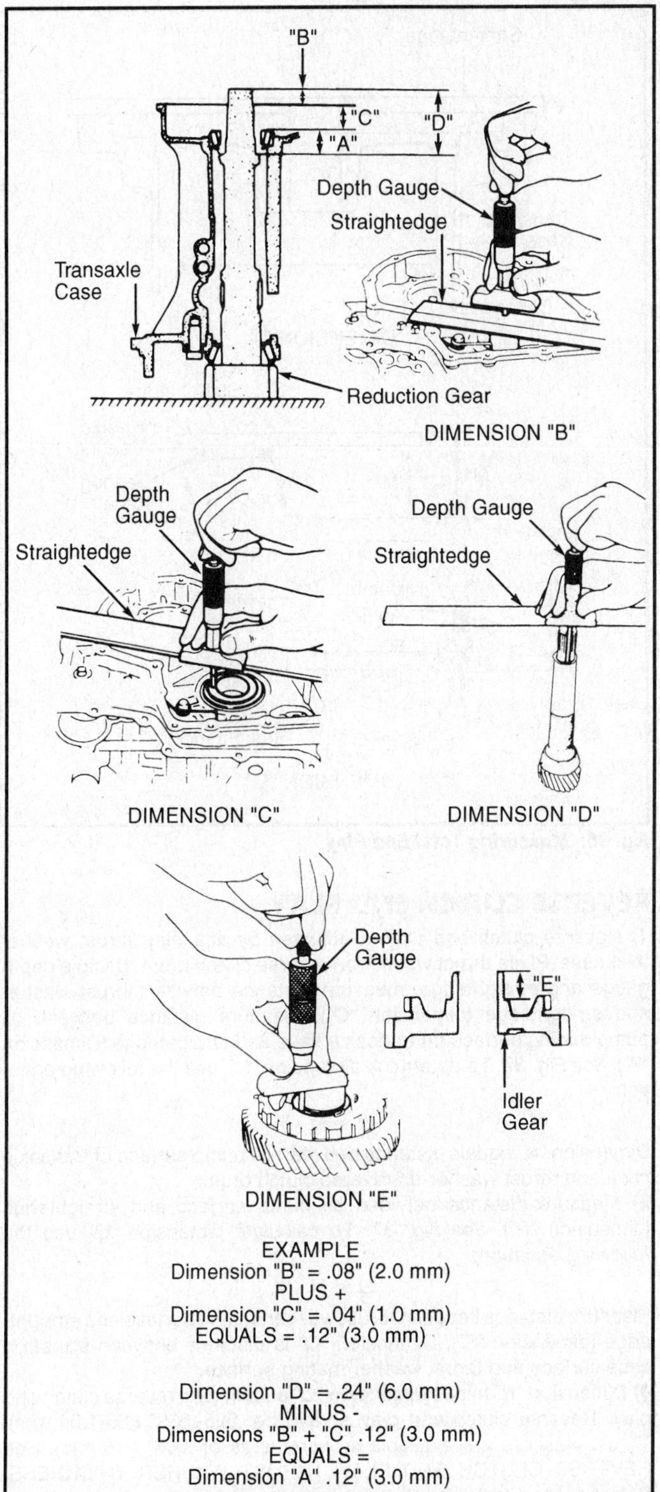

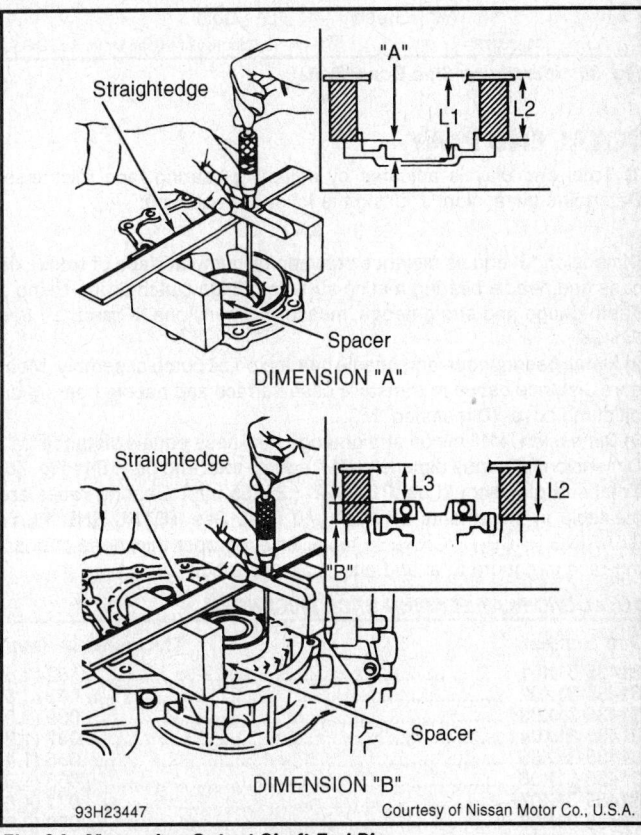

4) Measure distance between end of idler gear and idler gear bearing mating surface of idler gear in at least 2 places (dimension "E"). Reduction gear bearing preload should be .002" (.05 mm).

5) Select proper thickness of reduction gear bearing adjusting shim by subtracting dimension "E" from dimension "A". Shims are available in thicknesses of .0685-.1047" (1.74-2.66 mm), in increments of .002" (.04 mm). If total dimension is .045-.046" (1.13-1.17 mm), required shim thickness is .043" (1.10 mm). For each .002" (.04 mm) dimension increase, shim thickness will increase same amount up to .112-.114" (2.85-2.89 mm).

6) Install selected adjusting shim. Press idler gear bearing on idler gear. Press idler gear on reduction gear. Ensure idler gear locks on parking pawl. Lock idler gear with parking pawl and tighten idler gear lock nut to 181-203 ft. lbs. (245-275 N.m).

7) Turn reduction gear in both directions several times to seat bearings. Using a torque wrench and appropriate socket, measure reduction gear turning torque. Turning torque should be .95-6.08 INCH Lbs. (.10-.70 N.m). After adjusting turning torque, stake lock nut to ensure nut will not loosen.

OUTPUT SHAFT END PLAY

1) Output shaft end play is adjusted by adjusting output shaft shim thickness. Install output shaft bearing retainer. Tighten bolts to 12-15 ft. lbs. (16-21 N.m). Install output shaft thrust needle bearing on bearing retainer with smooth side down.

2) Install output shaft in transaxle case. Using a depth gauge and straightedge, measure dimensions "L1" and "L2" at side cover in at least 2 places. See Fig. 34. Determine dimension "A" using the following equation:

$$A = L1 - L2$$

Dimension "A" equals distance between transaxle case surface and adjusting shim mating surface. "L2" = height of gauge.

3) Determine dimension "B" using the following equation:

$$B = L2 - L3$$

"B"
"C"
"A"
"D"

Depth Gauge
Straightedge

Transaxle Case

Reduction Gear

DIMENSION "B"

Depth Gauge

Straightedge

DIMENSION "C"

Depth Gauge

Straightedge

DIMENSION "D"

Depth Gauge

"E"

Idler Gear

DIMENSION "E"

EXAMPLE
Dimension "B" = .08" (2.0 mm)
PLUS +
Dimension "C" = .04" (1.0 mm)
EQUALS = .12" (3.0 mm)

Dimension "D" = .24" (6.0 mm)
MINUS -
Dimensions "B" + "C" .12" (3.0 mm)
EQUALS =
Dimension "A" .12" (3.0 mm)

Dimension "A" .12" (3.0 mm)
MINUS -
Dimension "E"
EQUALS =
Thickness Of Thrust Shim

95G19691   Courtesy of Nissan Motor Co., U.S.A.

Fig. 33: Measuring Reduction Gear Bearing Preload

Straightedge

"A"
L1
L2

Spacer

DIMENSION "A"

Straightedge

L3
L2

"B"

Spacer

DIMENSION "B"

93H23447   Courtesy of Nissan Motor Co., U.S.A.

Fig. 34: Measuring Output Shaft End Play

Measure Dimensions "L2" and "L3" in at least 2 places. Dimension "B" equals distance between end of output shaft bearing race and side cover surface of transaxle case. Specified output shaft end play ("A" - "B") should be 0-0.02" (0-.5 mm). Select proper thickness of adjusting shim to ensure output shaft end play is within specification. Adjusting shims are available in 3 thicknesses. See OUTPUT SHAFT ADJUSTING SHIM THICKNESS table.

OUTPUT SHAFT ADJUSTING SHIM THICKNESS

Part Number	Thickness In. (mm)
31438-31X46	.0220 (.56)
31438-31X47	.0378 (.96)
31438-31X48	.0535 (1.236)

4) Install selected adjusting shim on output shaft bearing. Apply a bead of liquid gasket .06" (1.5 mm) in diameter on inside edge of side cover surface of transaxle case. Install side cover on transaxle case and tighten bolts to 19-22 ft. lbs. (26-30 N.m). See Fig. 35. Always replace bolts "A". Bolts have Green threads and are self-sealing.

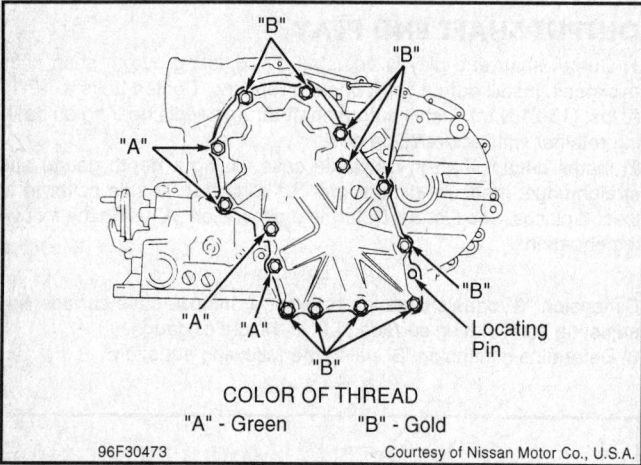

COLOR OF THREAD
"A" - Green   "B" - Gold

96F30473   Courtesy of Nissan Motor Co., U.S.A.

Fig. 35: Identifying Side Cover Bolts

TOTAL END PLAY

1) Total end play is adjusted by adjusting bearing race thickness. Determine dimension "J" using the following equation:

$$J = K - L$$

Dimension "J" equals distance between oil pump surface of transaxle case and needle bearing mating surface of high clutch drum. Using a depth gauge and straightedge, measure dimensions "K" and "L". See Fig. 36.

2) Install bearing race and needle bearing on oil pump assembly. Measure distance between transaxle case surface and needle bearing on oil pump cover (Dimension "M").

3) Dimension "M1" minus straightedge thickness equals distance "M". Dimension "J" minus dimension "M" equals total end play. See Fig. 36. Total end play should be .010-.022" (.25-.55 mm). Bearing races are available in increments of .015" (.40 mm). See TOTAL END PLAY BEARING RACE THICKNESS table. Select proper thickness of bearing race to ensure total end play is as specified.

TOTAL END PLAY BEARING RACE THICKNESS

Part Number	Thickness In. (mm)
31435-31X01	.024 (.6)
31435-31X02	.031 (.8)
31435-31X03	.039 (1.0)
31435-31X04	.047 (1.2)
31435-31X05	.055 (1.4)
31435-31X06	.063 (1.6)
31435-31X07	.071 (1.8)
31435-31X08	.079 (2.0)

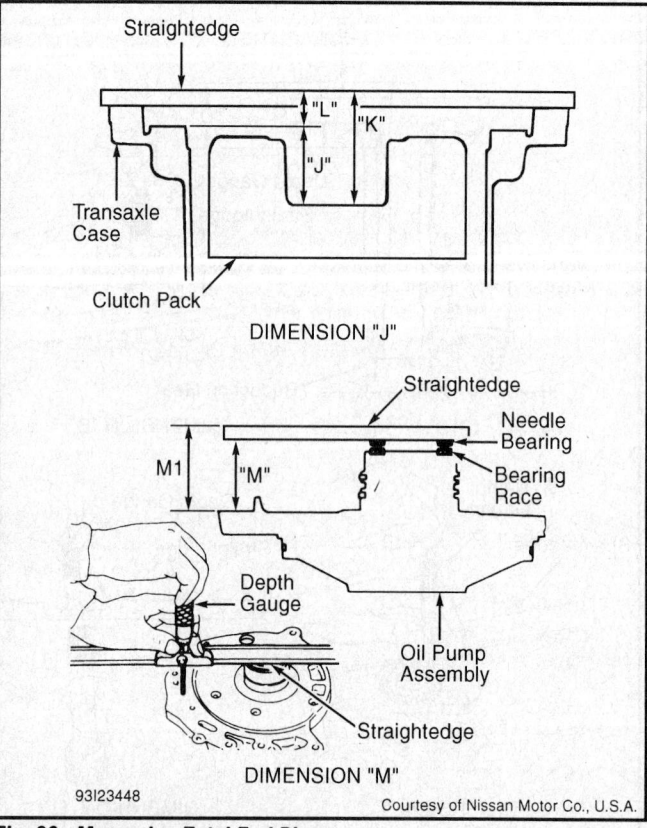

93123448   Courtesy of Nissan Motor Co., U.S.A.

Fig. 36: Measuring Total End Play

REVERSE CLUTCH END PLAY

1) Reverse clutch end play is adjusted by adjusting thrust washer thickness. Place thrust washer on reverse clutch drum. Using a depth gauge and straightedge, measure distance between thrust washer and straightedge (dimension "O"). Measure distance between oil pump mating surface on transaxle case and straightedge (Dimension "P"). See Fig. 37. To determine dimension "N", use the following equation:

$$N = O - P$$

Dimension "N" equals distance between oil pump surface of transaxle case and thrust washer on reverse clutch drum.

2) Measure distance between oil pump surface and straightedge (dimension "R"). See Fig. 37. To calculate dimension "Q" use the following equation:

$$Q = R - S$$

Measure distance between thrust washer mating surface and straightedge (dimension "S"). Dimension "Q" is distance between transaxle case surface and thrust washer mating surface.

3) Dimension "N" minus dimension "Q" equals total reverse clutch end play. Reverse clutch end play should be .026-.039" (.65-1.00 mm). Thrust washers are available in increments of .006" (.15 mm). See REVERSE CLUTCH END PLAY THRUST WASHER THICKNESS. Select proper thickness thrust washer to ensure reverse clutch end play is as specified.

REVERSE CLUTCH END PLAY THRUST WASHER THICKNESS

Part Number	Thickness In. (mm)
31508-31X00	.0256 (.65)
31508-31X01	.0315 (.80)
31508-31X02	.0374 (.95)
31508-31X03	.0433 (1.10)
31508-31X04	.0492 (1.25)
31508-31X05	.0551 (1.40)

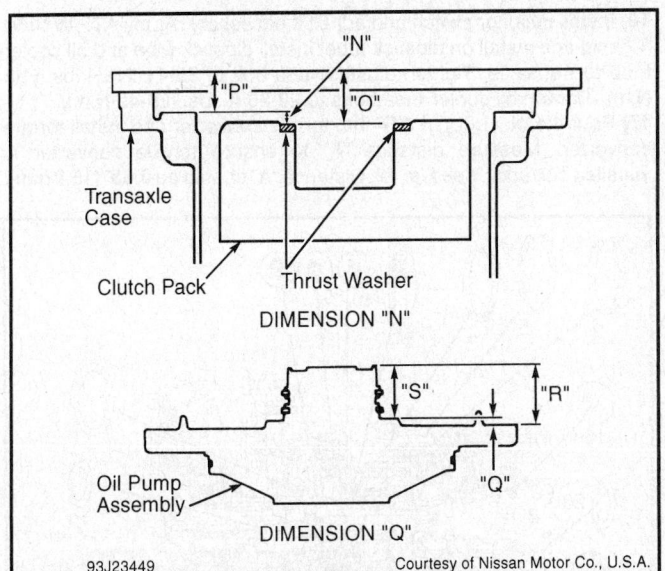

Fig. 37: Measuring Reverse Clutch End Play

TRANSAXLE REASSEMBLY

NOTE: See NEEDLE BEARING, SNAP RING, THRUST WASHER & SHIM IDENTIFICATIONS table for component locations. See Fig. 41.

1) Install revolution sensor into transaxle case. Install differential side oil seals in converter housing ensure that "A" and "B" are within specifications. See Fig. 38. Dimension "A" should be .217-.256" (5.50-6.50 mm) of seal recessed from housing. Dimension "B" should be .020 (.5 mm) of oil seal protruding from housing. See Fig. 38

2) Install parking actuator support to transaxle case with beveled edge inward. Install parking pawl on transaxle case and secure with parking shaft. Install return spring. See Fig. 7. Perform DIFFERENTIAL SIDE BEARING PRELOAD, REDUCTION GEAR BEARING PRELOAD and OUTPUT SHAFT END PLAY adjustment procedures. See TRANSAXLE ADJUSTMENTS.

3) Remove paper from bearing retainer. Apply petroleum jelly to thrust washers, bearing races and needle bearings. Install thrust washer on bearing retainer. Ensure bearing retainer seal rings are not spread. Align teeth of low-reverse brake drive plates. Install forward clutch assembly. Install thrust needle bearing race on bearing retainer. Install bearing on rear internal gear with smooth side down.

4) Hold forward clutch hub and turn overrun clutch hub. Ensure overrun clutch hub rotates counterclockwise and does not rotate clockwise. If overrun clutch hub does not operate as described, check installed direction of forward one-way clutch. Align forward clutch and overrun clutch drive plate teeth and install rear internal gear assembly. See Fig. 10.

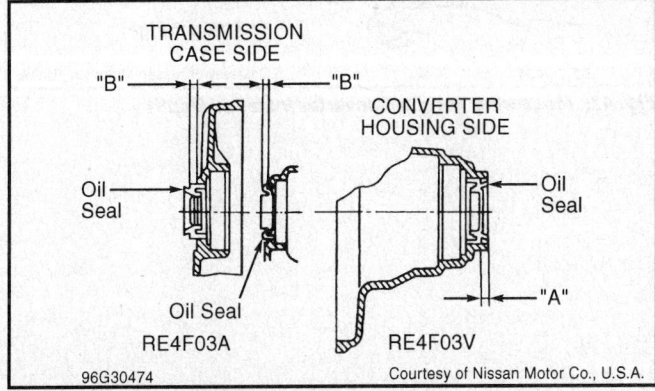

Fig. 38: Installing Differential Side Oil Seals

5) Apply petroleum jelly to needle bearing and install needle bearing with smooth side down on rear planetary carrier. Install rear sun gear on rear planetary carrier with grooved side facing out. Install rear planetary carrier in transaxle case. Apply petroleum jelly to thrust needle bearing and install bearing on front planetary carrier with grooved side down.

6) Install low one-way clutch to front planetary carrier by rotating clutch counterclockwise. Ensure low one-way clutch does not rotate in clockwise direction. Install front planetary carrier assembly in transaxle case. Install snap ring.

NOTE: Snap ring will not fit in groove of transaxle case if forward clutch and bearings are not installed correctly.

7) Apply petroleum jelly to thrust needle bearing and needle bearings. Install thrust needle bearing on front sun gear with flat side down. Install front sun gear on front planetary carrier. Install needle bearing on front sun gear with smooth side down. Install high clutch hub on front sun gear. Install needle bearing on high clutch hub with smooth side up. See Fig. 10.

8) Remove paper from input shaft. Align teeth of high clutch drive plates and install input shaft assembly. Align teeth of reverse clutch drive plates. Apply petroleum jelly to needle bearing and install needle bearing on high clutch assembly with smooth side down.

9) Install reverse clutch assembly. Install anchor end pin, washer and lock nut on transaxle case. Place brake band on reverse clutch drum. Tighten anchor end pin enough that brake band is on reverse drum evenly.

10) Apply petroleum jelly on bearing race selected in TOTAL END PLAY adjustment procedure. See TRANSAXLE ADJUSTMENTS. Install bearing race on oil pump cover. Apply petroleum jelly on thrust washer selected in REVERSE CLUTCH END PLAY adjustment procedure. See TRANSAXLE ADJUSTMENTS. Install thrust washer on reverse clutch drum. Install oil pump assembly on transaxle case.

11) Tighten oil pump bolts to 62-97 INCH lbs. (7-11 N.m). Apply ATF to input shaft "O" ring and install "O" ring on input shaft. Adjust brake band. Tighten anchor end pin to 35-53 INCH lbs. (4-6 N.m). Back off anchor end pin 2 1/2 turns. While holding anchor end pin, tighten lock nut. Apply compressed air to oil holes in transaxle case to ensure correct brake band operation. See Fig. 39.

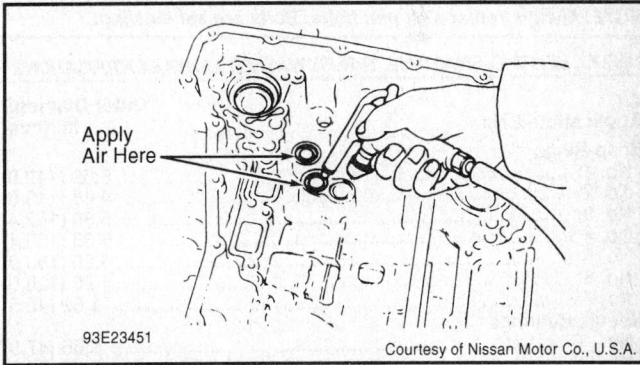

Fig. 39: Checking Brake Band Operation

12) Install differential assembly on transaxle case. Install oil tube on converter housing and tighten bolts to 35-43 INCH lbs. (4-5 N.m). Install "O" ring on differential oil port of transaxle case. Apply a bead of liquid gasket .060" (1.5 mm) in diameter on inside edge of converter housing mating surface. Install converter housing on transaxle case. Tighten bolts ("A" and "B", see BOLT LENGTH table) to 19-22 ft. lbs. (26-30 N.m). See Fig. 40.

BOLT LENGTH

Bolt	Length In. (mm)
A	1.18 (30)
B	1.57 (40)

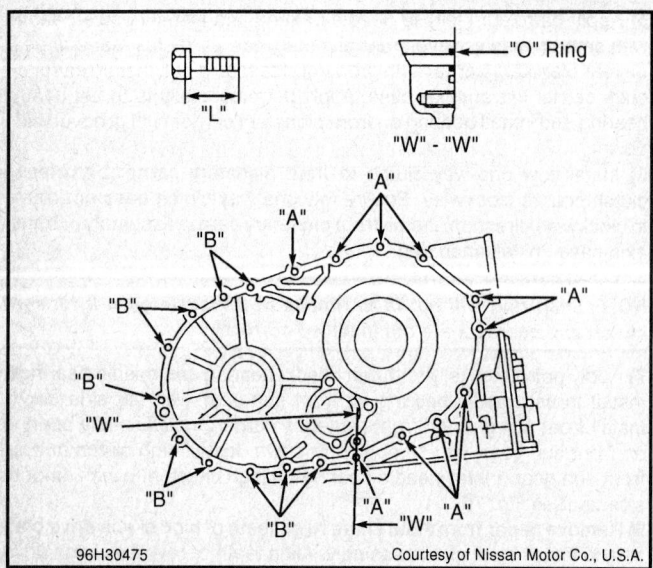

Fig. 40: *Identifying Converter Housing Bolt Length & Location*

13) Check contact surface of accumulator piston for damage. Apply ATF to "O" rings and install on accumulator piston. Install accumulator pistons and return springs in transaxle case. Apply petroleum jelly to lip seals for band servo oil holes and install in transaxle case.

14) Apply ATF to manual valve and insert valve into control valve assembly. Set manual shaft in Neutral position. Install control valve assembly on transaxle case while aligning manual valve with manual plate and detent valve with throttle lever.

15) Put solenoid harness into transaxle case and push terminal body onto transaxle case. Install clip to terminal body. Install and tighten control valve assembly bolts to 62-80 INCH lbs. (7-9 N.m). See Fig. 5. Attach magnet to oil pan. Install NEW oil pan gasket and install oil pan. Tighten NEW pan bolts in a crisscross pattern to 44-62 INCH lbs. (5-7 N.m). Install drain plug (if necessary) and tighten to 22-29 ft. lbs. (29-39 N.m).

NOTE: *Always replace oil pan bolts. Bolts are self-sealing.*

16) Install inhibitor switch and adjust if necessary. Apply ATF to NEW "O" ring and install on dipstick tube. Install dipstick tube and oil cooler tube to transaxle. Tighten dipstick tube bolt to 35-44 INCH lbs. (4-5 N.m). Tighten oil cooler tube bolts to 22-36 ft. lbs. (29-49 N.m).

17) Pour 1.1 qt. (1.0L) of ATF into torque converter and install torque converter. Measure distance "A" to ensure torque converter is installed correctly. *See Fig. 42*. Distance "A" should be 0.63" (15.9 mm).

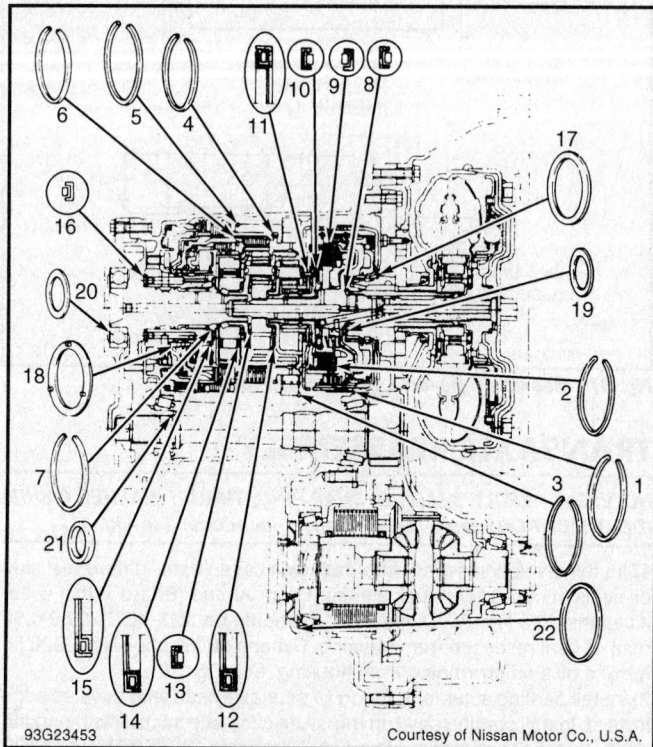

Fig. 41: *Identifying Needle Bearing, Snap Ring, Thrust Washer & Selective Shim Locations*

NEEDLE BEARING, SNAP RING, THRUST WASHER & SHIM IDENTIFICATIONS [1]

Application & No.	Outer Diameter In. (mm)
Snap Rings	
No. 1	5.59 (142.0)
No. 2	4.45 (113.0)
No. 3	6.39 (162.4)
No. 4	5.33 (135.4)
No. 5	6.26 (159.0)
No. 6	4.96 (126.0)
No. 7	1.59 (40.5)
Needle Bearings	
No. 8	1.85 (47.0)
No. 9	1.38 (35.0)
No. 10	2.36 (60.0)
No. 11	2.36 (60.0)
No. 12	1.85 (47.0)
No. 13	1.68 (42.6)
No. 14	1.89 (48.0)
No. 15	2.16 (55.0)
No. 16	2.36 (60.0)
Thrust Washers	
No. 17 (Selective)	2.84 (72.0)
No. 18	3.09 (78.5)
Race & Shims (Selective)	
No. 19	1.89 (48.0)
No. 20	2.83 (72.0)
No. 21	1.36 (34.5)
No. 22	4.13 (105.0)

[1] – See Fig. 41 for component locations.

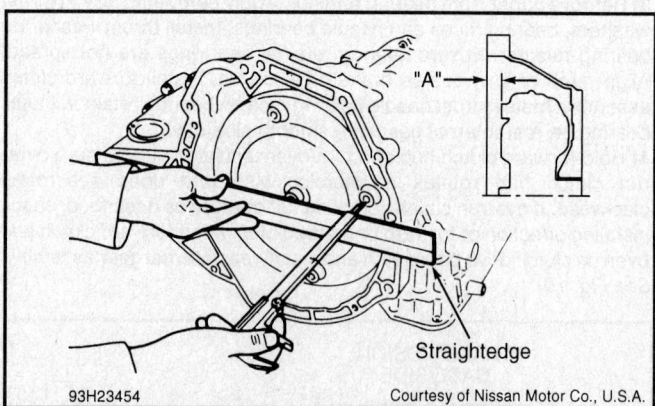

Fig. 42: *Measuring Torque Converter Installed Depth*

TORQUE SPECIFICATIONS

TORQUE SPECIFICATIONS

Application	Ft. Lbs. (N.m)
Anchor End Pin Lock Nut	23-27 (31-36)
Bearing Retainer	12-15 (16-21)
Converter Housing Bolt	19-22 (26-30)
Idler Gear Lock Nut	181-203 (245-275)
Oil Cooler Tube Bolt	22-36 (29-49)
Oil Pan Drain Plug	22-29 (29-39)
Oil Pump-To-Converter Housing Bolt	19-22 (26-30)
Output Gear Lock Nut	181-203 (245-275)
Output Shaft Bearing Retainer Bolt	12-15 (16-21)
Parking Actuator Support Bolt	15-18 (21-24)
Reduction Gear Bearing	
Race Bolt	46-49 (63-67)
Ring Gear Bolt	
Infiniti	
F03A	55-65 (74-88)
F03V	39-50 (53-68)
Nissan	
F03V	39-50 (53-68)
Side Cover Bolt	19-22 (26-30)
	INCH Lbs. (N.m)
Control Valve Assembly Bolt (All Exect "E")	62-80 (7-9)
Control Valve Body Bolt "E"	44-62 (5-7)
Detent Spring Bolt	57-66 (6.4-7.5)
Dipstick Tube	35-44 (4-5)
Inhibitor Switch Bolt	18-22 (2-2.5)
Oil Pan Bolt	62-80 (7-9)
Oil Pump Cover-To-Housing Bolt	62-97 (7-11)
Oil Tube	35-43 (4-5)
Revolution Sensor	44-62 (5-7)
Speedometer Pinion Bolt	33-44 (3.7-5)
Viscous Coupling to Differential Case	33-52 (3.7-5.9)

TRANSAXLE SPECIFICATIONS

TRANSAXLE SPECIFICATIONS

Application	In. (mm)
Differential Assembly	
Side Gear-To-Differential Case	
Specified Clearance	.004-.008 (0.10-0.20)
Differential End Play	0-.006 (0-.15)
Differential Side Bearing Preload	.002-.004 (.04-.010)
Forward & Overrun Clutches	
Dish Plate Thickness	
Forward Clutch	.098 (2.50)
Overrun Clutch	.085 (2.15)
Drive Plate Thickness (Forward Clutch)	.071 (1.80)
Allowable Limit	.063 (1.60)
Drive Plate Thickness (Overrun Clutch)	.063 (1.60)
Allowable Limit	.055 (1.40)
Retaining Plate-To-Snap Ring	
Specified Clearance (Forward Clutch)	.018-.0335 (.45-.85)
Specified Clearance (Overrun Clutch)	.039-.055 (1.00-1.40)
Allowable Limit (Forward Clutch)	.073 (1.85)
Allowable Limit (Overrun Clutch)	.079 (2.00)
High Clutch	
Drive Plate Thickness	.063 (1.60)
Allowable Limit	.055 (1.40)
Retaining Plate-To-Snap Ring	
Specified Clearance	.055-.071 (1.40-1.80)
Allowable Limit	.102 (2.60)
Input Shaft Seal Ring-To-Ring Groove	
Specified Clearance	.003-.009 (.08-.23)
Allowable Limit	.009 (.23)
Low-Reverse Brake	
Drive Plate Thickness	.079 (2.00)
Allowable Limit	.071 (1.80)
Specified Clearance	.055-.071 (1.40-1.80)
Allowable Limit	.110 (2.80)
Oil Pump Seal Ring-To-Ring Groove	
Specified Clearance	.004-.010 (.10-.25)
Allowable Limit	.010 (.25)
Oil Pump Side Clearance	.0008-.0016 (.020-.040)
Output Shaft End Play	0-.02 (0-.5)
Output Shaft Seal Ring-To-Ring Groove	
Specified Clearance	.004-.010 (.10-.25)
Allowable Limit	.010 (.25)
Pinion Washer-To-Planetary Gear	
Specified Clearance	.006-.028 (.15-.70)
Allowable Limit	.031 (.80)
Reverse Clutch	
Dish Plate Thickness	.110 (2.80)
Drive Plate Thickness	.079 (2.00)
Allowable Limit	.071 (1.80)
Retaining Plate-To-Snap Ring	
Specified Clearance	.020-.031 (.50-.80)
Allowable Limit	.047 (1.20)
Reduction Gear Bearing Preload	.002 (.05)
Reverse Clutch End Play	.026-.039 (.65-1.00)
Total End Play	.010-.022 (.25-.55)

AUTOMATIC TRANSMISSIONS
RE4F03A/V Electronic Controls

Infiniti G20, Nissan 200SX

APPLICATION

APPLICATION

Vehicle	Transaxle Model
Infiniti G20 (2.0L)	RE4F03A/V
Nissan 200SX SE-R (2.0L)	RE4F03V

DESCRIPTION

Automatic transaxle is electronically controlled. Transaxle shifting and lock-up is controlled by Automatic Transaxle Control Unit (ATCU) for optimal performance. The ATCU receives information from various input devices and uses this information to control shift and lock-up solenoid valves.

The following electronic signals, sensors, switches and solenoids are used to control transaxle shifting. See ELECTRONIC COMPONENT & CIRCUIT TESTS for additional information and testing:

- Engine Revolution Signal (Tach Signal)
- Transmission Fluid Temperature Sensor
- Inhibitor Switch
- Line Pressure Solenoid
- Lock-Up Solenoid
- Overdrive Switch
- Overrun Clutch Solenoid
- Mainshaft Revolution Sensor
- Shift Solenoids "A" and "B"
- Speed Sensor
- Throttle Position Sensor
- Throttle Position Switch
- Shift Lock System

ELECTRONIC SELF-DIAGNOSTICS

NOTE: Driveability problems that may appear to be transmission related may be caused by a faulty engine component. Engine related fault codes MUST be repaired before diagnosing transmission. See ENGINE PERFORMANCE in appropriate MITCHELL© repair manual. Failure to diagnose and repair engine fault codes prior to transmission diagnosis may result in incorrect diagnosis or component repair.

SELF-DIAGNOSTIC PROCEDURE

NOTE: Perform self-diagnosis and code retrieval procedures with engine at normal operating temperature.

There are 3 ways to retrieve DTCs. They are displayed in different formats and by different indicators. Retrieve the codes and refer to the DTC DESCRIPTIONS table.

Scan Tool (OBD-II) – OBD-II codes must be retrieved using a scan tool connected to the OBD-II connector. Follow the scan tool manufacturer's procedure to connect and operate the scan tool.

MIL Light (MIL) – MIL light will illuminate when ignition switch is turned to ON position (engine not running). This is a bulb check. When engine is started, MIL light should turn OFF. If light remains ON, on-board diagnostics has detected an engine or transmission system fault. A/T self-diagnosis is performed by A/T Control Unit (ATCU) in combination with ECM. Self-diagnosis codes indicated by MIL are stored in both ATCU and ECM memory. Codes may be retrieved from vehicles equipped with a MIL light by using the following procedure:

1) Ensure ignition is in ON position and engine is off (KOEO). Turn diagnostic test mode selector, (located on side of ECM), fully clockwise. Wait 2 seconds, and turn diagnostic test mode selector fully counterclockwise. This puts ECM into Diagnostic Test Mode II (code retrieval mode).
2) DTCs are indicated by the MIL light "blinking" sequence. A sequence of LONG (MIL light ON for .6 second) blinks indicates the first and second digits of the DTC.

3) The third and fourth digits are indicated by a sequence of SHORT (MIL light ON for .3 second) blinks. Example: MIL blinks 10 times for 6 seconds (.6 x 10 times), and then blinks 3 times for about one second (.3 x 3 times). This indicates MIL DTC 1003.
4) ECM will not switch to Diagnostic Test Mode II when engine is running. When engine is turned off after code retrieval, power to ECM is lost after 5 seconds. Turn ECM switch to full counterclockwise position. This returns system to Diagnostic Test Mode I which provides bulb test and system monitoring functions.

OD OFF/POWER Light (Flash) – Flash codes are also referred to by the manufacturer as "Judgement Flickers". To retrieve Flash codes using the OD OFF/POWER indicator light use the following procedure:
1) Turn ignition switch to OFF position, then to ACC position. Set transmission mode switch to AUTO position, overdrive switch to OFF position, and selector lever to "D" position. Turn ignition switch to ON position. OD OFF (Nissan) or POWER (Infiniti) indicator light should come on for 2 seconds.
2) Move selector lever to "2" position. Set overdrive switch to ON position. Move selector lever to "1" position. Set overdrive switch to OFF position. Depress accelerator pedal to floor and release pedal. Record OD OFF/POWER indicator light flashes. Where the LONG light flash appears in the flash sequence (1st, 2nd, 3rd etc.) indicates the code. Refer to DTC DESCRIPTIONS table.

NOTE: Codes are displayed in the following order in tables and in DTC TESTING: OBD-II Code/MIL Code/Flash.

DTC DESCRIPTIONS

OBD-II/MIL/Flash [1]	DTC Description
P0000/0505/All Flashes Same	No Codes In System
P0705/1003 Or 1101/No Flash	Inhibitor, TP Or OD Switch Circuit
P0710/1208/8th	Fluid Temp Sensor/ATCU Power Source Circuit
P0720/1102/1st	Vehicle Speed Sensor (A/T Revolution) Circuit
[3] / [2]/2nd	Vehicle Speed Sensor/MTR (At Speedometer)
P0725/1207/9th	Engine Speed Signal Circuit
P0731/1103/N/A [2]	A/T 1st Signal
P0732/1104/N/A [2]	A/T 2nd Signal
P0733/1105/N/A [2]	A/T 3rd Signal
P0734/1106/N/A [2]	A/T 4th Signal Or TCC
P0740/1204/7th	Torque Converter Solenoid Valve
P0745/1205/10th	Line Pressure Solenoid Valve
P0750/1108/4th	Shift Solenoid Valve "A"
P0755/1201/5th	Shift Solenoid Valve "B"
P1705/1206/3rd	Throttle Position Sensor Or Switch
P1760/1203/6th	Overrun Clutch Solenoid Valve

[1] – Indicated by long flash (Judgement Flicker) of OD OFF (Nissan) or POWER (Infiniti) indicator light in self diagnostic check. See SELF-DIAGNOSTIC PROCEDURE.
[2] – Malfunction cannot be displayed by MIL if another malfunction is assigned to OD OFF/POWER light.
[3] – OBD-II code number is not available.

DTC TESTING

NOTE: For additional wiring diagram information, See WIRING DIAGRAMS.

NOTE: Codes are indicated as follows: DTC OBD-II/MIL/Flash.

DTC P0705/1101/NO FLASH: INHIBITOR, TP OR OD SWITCH CIRCUIT

Circuit Description – Inhibitor switch detects selector lever position and sends a signal to ATCU. OD switch sends ON or OFF signal to ATCU. Throttle Position Switch consist of a wide open throttle switch which sends a signal to ATCU when throttle valve is open 50 percent and a closed throttle position switch which indicates when throttle valve is fully closed. Code is set when ATCU receives an excessively low or high voltage from sensor.

Diagnosis & Repair – 1) Check inhibitor switch. See appropriate test under ELECTRONIC COMPONENT & CIRCUIT TESTS.

2) Check harness and connectors for open or short between ignition switch and inhibitor switch and between inhibitor switch and ATCU. If continuity exists for all circuits, go to next step. If continuity does not exist for any circuit inspect and repair circuit(s) as needed.

OD Switch – With KOEO, check voltage between ATCU terminal No. 30 and ground. With OD switch in ON position, battery voltage should be present. With OD switch in OFF position, voltage should be one volt maximum. If voltage is not as specified, check OD switch see appropriate test in ELECTRONIC COMPONENT & CIRCUIT TEST. Check harness for open or short between ATCU and OD switch and ground circuit for OD switch. If continuity exists for all circuits, go to next test.

Throttle Position Switch – 1) Start and warm engine. With KOEO, check voltage between ATCU terminals No. 14, No. 21 and ground while depressing and releasing accelerator pedal slowly. See THROTTLE POSITION VOLTAGE TEST table.

THROTTLE POSITION VOLTAGE TEST

Accelerator Pedal	Voltage
Released	
Terminal No. 14	Battery Voltage
Terminal No. 21	One Volt Maximum
Fully Depressed	
Terminal No. 14	One Volt Maximum
Terminal No. 21	Battery Voltage

2) If voltage is not as specified, check throttle position switch. See appropriate test under ELECTRONIC COMPONENT & CIRCUIT TESTING. Check harness for open or short between ignition switch and ATCU to throttle position switch. If within specifications, perform self-diagnosis again after test driving vehicle.

DTC P0710/1208/8TH: FLUID TEMPERATURE SENSOR/ATCU

Circuit Description – Fluid temperature sensor detects ATF temperature and sends a signal to ATCU. Code is set when ATCU receives an excessively low or high voltage from sensor.

Diagnosis & Repair – 1) Check ATCU power source. With KOEO, check voltage between ATCU terminals No. 4, No. 9 and ground. Battery voltage should exist. If battery voltage does not exist, check harness for short or open between ignition switch and ATCU and between ignition switch and fuse.

2) Check fluid temperature sensor with terminal cord assembly. See FLUID TEMPERATURE SENSOR TEST in ELECTRONIC COMPONENT & CIRCUIT TESTS. If resistance values are not within specifications, remove oil pan and check harness for open or short.

DTC P0720/1102/1ST: A/T REVOLUTION SENSOR

Circuit Description – Revolution sensor detects revolution of the idler gear parking pawl lock gear and emits a pulse signal. Pulse signal is sent to ATCU which converts it into vehicle speed. Code is set when ATCU does not receive proper voltage signal from sensor.

Diagnosis & Repair – 1) Start engine. Check voltage between ATCU terminal No. 25 and ground while driving. With voltmeter in AC range, voltage at zero MPH should be 0 volts. Voltage at 19 MPH should be one volt. Voltage should rise gradually in response to vehicle speed.

2) If voltage is not within specifications, check harness between ATCU and revolution sensor and between revolution sensor and ECM for open or short. See ENGINE PERFORMANCE in appropriate MITCHELL© repair manual.

DTC – / – /2ND: VEHICLE SPEED SENSOR/MTR

Circuit Description – Vehicle speed sensor/MTR is built into speedometer assembly. It functions as an auxiliary device for the revolution sensor when it is malfunctioning. ATCU will then use a signal sent from vehicle speed sensor/MTR. Code is set when ATCU does not receive proper voltage signal from sensor.

Diagnosis & Repair – For sensor testing, see SPEED SENSOR CIRCUIT TEST (VEHICLE SPEED SENSOR/MTR) in ELECTRONIC COMPONENT & CIRCUIT TESTS.

DTC P0725/1207/9TH: ENGINE SPEED SIGNAL

Circuit Description – Engine speed signal (tach signal) is sent from ECM to ACTU. Code is set when ATCU does not receive proper voltage signal from ECM.

Diagnosis & Repair – For sensor testing, see ENGINE REVOLUTION SIGNAL CIRCUIT TEST (TACH SIGNAL) in ELECTRONIC COMPONENT & CIRCUIT TESTS.

DTC P0731, P0732, P0733/1103, 1104, 1105/NO FLASH: A/T 1ST SIGNAL, 2ND SIGNAL, 3RD SIGNAL

Circuit Description – When vehicle is being driven in any gear other than 1st (P0731)/2nd (P0732)/3rd (P0733), ATCU is signals A/T to shift to 1st/2nd/3rd gear. A/T 1st/2nd/3rd signal is not determined as a fault unless ATCU self diagnosis system is in "No Failure" condition. When A/T 1st/2nd/3rd code is displayed, it indicates that the gears are not properly shifted. Problem is NOT caused by electrical failure of A/T circuits but by mechanical failure (control valve sticking, improper solenoid valve operation, etc).

Diagnosis & Repair – 1) Remove control valve assembly. See CONTROL VALVE ASSEMBLY in ON VEHICLE SERVICE. Check shift solenoid valve "A" and "B" operation. See appropriate tests in ELECTRONIC COMPONENT & CIRCUIT TESTS. Repair or replace shift solenoid valve assembly as needed.

2) Check control valve. Disassemble control valve assembly. See CONTROL VALVE ASSEMBLY in overhaul article. Ensure that valves, sleeve and plug slide along valve bore under their own weight, and are free of burrs, dents and scratches. Ensure control valve springs are free from damage deformation and fatigue. Ensure hydraulic line is free from obstacles. Repair control valve assembly as needed and recheck.

DTC P0734/1106/NO FLASH: A/T 4TH SIGNAL OR TCC SIGNAL

Circuit Description – Improper shifting to 4th gear position or improper torque converter clutch operation. When vehicle is being driven in any gear other than 4th ATCU signals A/T to shift to 4th gear. Also indicated when vehicle is being driven at any gear position without TCC lock-up and ATCU is signaling A/T to lock-up torque converter. A/T 4th or TCC is not determined as a fault unless ATCU self-diagnosis system is in "No Failure" condition. When A/T 4th or TCC Signal is displayed, it indicates that the gears are not properly shifted. Problem is NOT caused by electrical failure of A/T circuits but by mechanical failure. Control valve sticking, improper solenoid valve operation, malfunctioning oil pump or torque converter clutch etc.

Diagnosis & Repair – 1) If during road test transaxle did NOT shift from 3rd to 4th at specified speed, go to step 2). If shift from 3rd to 4th gear is at specified speed and lock-up did NOT occur at specified speed, go to step 5).

2) Perform pressure test. See HYDRAULIC PRESSURE TESTS in overhaul article. If pressure is not within specification go to step 6). If okay, check solenoid valves. Remove control valve assembly. See CONTROL VALVE ASSEMBLY in overhaul article. Check solenoid valve assembly operation. Repair or replace as needed.

3) Check control valve. Disassemble control valve assembly. See CONTROL VALVE ASSEMBLY in overhaul article. Ensure valves, sleeve and plug slide along valve bore under their own weight, and are free of burrs, dents and scratches. Ensure control valve springs are free from damage deformation and fatigue. Ensure hydraulic line is free from obstacles. Repair control valve assembly as needed and recheck.

4) Road test vehicle. Ensure vehicle shifts from 3-4 at specified speed and lock-up occurs properly.

5) Check TCC solenoid valve. Remove control valve assembly. See CONTROL VALVE ASSEMBLY in ON-VEHICLE SERVICE. Check TCC solenoid valve assembly. See LOCK-UP SOLENOID TEST (TCC) in ELECTRONIC COMPONENT & CIRCUIT TESTS. Replace or repair

as necessary. Check TCC control valve and TCC relief valve for sticking. Repair as needed. Road test vehicle, ensure A/T performs lock up at specific speed. See LOCK-UP SPEED SPECIFICATIONS table in overhaul article. If okay, ensure symptoms from circuit description are no longer present.

6) Remove control valve assembly. See CONTROL VALVE ASSEMBLY in ON-VEHICLE SERVICE in overhaul article. Check line pressure solenoid. See LINE PRESSURE SOLENOID TEST in ELECTRONIC COMPONENT & CIRCUIT TESTS in this article. Repair or replace solenoid valve assembly as needed. If okay, remove and disassemble control valve assembly. See CONTROL VALVE ASSEMBLY in overhaul article. Check pressure regulator, pilot and pressure modifier valves for sticking. Repair as needed.

7) Road test vehicle, ensure 3-4 shift and lock-up occurs at specified speed.

DTC P0740/1204/7TH:
TORQUE CONVERTER CLUTCH VALVE

Circuit Description – Torque converter clutch solenoid valve circuit check. TCC solenoid valve is activated, in 4th gear, by ATCU in response to signals sent from vehicle speed and throttle position sensors. Lock-up piston will then be controlled. Lock-up is prohibited when ATF temperature is too low.

Diagnosis & Repair – 1) Check ground circuit. With ignition switch OFF, disconnect terminal cord assembly connector in engine compartment. Check resistance between terminal No. 5 and ground. Resistance should be 10-16 ohms. If resistance is within specifications, go to next step. If not within specifications, remove oil pan, check harness for open or short and TCC solenoid valve. See LOCK-UP SOLENOID (TCC) TEST in ELECTRONIC COMPONENT & CIRCUIT TESTS.

2) With ignition in OFF position, disconnect ATCU connector. Check resistance between connector terminal No. 5 and ATCU terminal No. 5. Resistance should be zero ohms. Repair or replace as needed. Reinstall any part removed.

3) Road test and perform self-diagnosis. If unable to obtain ATCU feedback, check ATCU input/output signal. See ATCU POWER SOURCE TEST in ELECTRONIC COMPONENT & CIRCUIT TESTS. If not within specifications, recheck ATCU pin terminals for damage or loose connections.

DTC P0745/1205/10TH:
LINE PRESSURE SOLENOID VALVE

Circuit Description – Line pressure solenoid valve circuit check. Line pressure solenoid valve regulates oil pump discharge pressure to suit driving conditions in response to a signal sent from ATCU.

Diagnosis & Repair – 1) Check line pressure solenoid valve circuit. See LINE PRESSURE SOLENOID TEST in ELECTRONIC COMPONENT & CIRCUIT TESTS. If resistance is not as specified, remove control valve assembly. See CONTROL VALVE ASSEMBLY in overhaul article. Inspect line pressure solenoid, see appropriate solenoid test under ELECTRONIC COMPONENT & CIRCUIT TESTS. Inspect harness for short or open of terminal cord assembly.

2) If resistance is okay, check power source circuit. Using ohmmeter, check resistance between terminal No. 1 and ATCU terminal No. 2. Resistance should be 11.2-12.8 ohms. If resistance is not as specified, check dropping resistor. See appropriate test under ELECTRONIC COMPONENT & CIRCUIT TESTS. Inspect harness for open or short between ATCU terminal No. 2 and terminal cord assembly.

3) If resistance is okay, with ignition in OFF position, check resistance between connector terminal No. 1 and ATCU terminal No. 1. Resistance should be zero ohms. If not as specified, repair or replace harness between ATCU and terminal cord assembly.

4) If resistance is as specified, road test vehicle and perform self-diagnosis. If unable to obtain ATCU feedback, recheck ATCU input/output signal inspection. If not as specified, check ATCU pin terminals for damage or loose connection with harness connector.

DTC P0750/1108/4TH:
SHIFT SOLENOID VALVE "A"

Circuit Description – Shift solenoid valves "A" and "B" are turned ON and OFF by ATCU in response to output signal from the inhibitor switch, vehicle speed sensor and throttle position sensors. A voltage drop not within specifications during solenoid operation will set code. Shift solenoid "A" is normally ON in 1st and 4th gear. Shift solenoid "B" is normally ON in 1st and 2nd gear.

Diagnosis & Repair – 1) With ignition switch OFF, disconnect terminal cord assembly in engine compartment. Check resistance between terminal No. 6 and ground. Resistance should be 20-30 ohms.

2) If resistance is not within specifications, remove control valve assembly. See CONTROL VALVE ASSEMBLY in overhaul article. Check solenoid valve "A", see appropriate test under ELECTRONIC COMPONENT & CIRCUIT TESTS. Check wiring harness and connectors for open or short.

3) If resistance is within specifications, check power source circuit. With ignition OFF, disconnect ATCU harness connector. Check resistance between connector terminal No. 6 and ATCU terminal No. 6. Resistance should be zero ohms. If resistance is as specified, reconnect connectors.

4) If resistance is NOT as specified, repair or replace harness between ATCU and terminal cord assembly. Road test and perform self diagnosis. If unable to obtain ATCU feedback, recheck ATCU input/output signal inspection. If not as specified, check ATCU pin terminals for damage or loose connection with harness connector.

DTC P0755/1201/5TH:
SHIFT SOLENOID VALVE "B"

Circuit Description – Shift solenoid valves "A" and "B" are turned ON and OFF by ATCU in response to output from the inhibitor switch, vehicle speed sensor and throttle position sensors. Information received determines best possible gear choice. Code is set when ATCU detects improper voltage drop during operation of solenoid valve. Shift solenoid "A" is normally ON in 1st and 4th gear. Shift solenoid "B" is normally ON in 1st and 2nd gear.

Diagnosis & Repair – 1) With ignition switch OFF, disconnect harness connector in engine compartment. Check resistance between terminal No. 6 and ground. Resistance should be 20-30 ohms.

2) If resistance is not within specifications, remove control valve assembly. See CONTROL VALVE ASSEMBLY in overhaul article. Check solenoid valve "A", see appropriate test under ELECTRONIC COMPONENT & CIRCUIT TESTS. Check wiring harness and connectors for open or short.

3) If resistance is within specifications, check power source circuit. With ignition OFF, disconnect ATCU harness connector. Check resistance between connector terminal No. 7 and ATCU terminal No. 7. Resistance should be zero ohms. If resistance is as specified, reconnect connectors.

4) If resistance is NOT as specified, repair or replace harness between ATCU and terminal cord assembly. Road test and perform self-diagnosis. If unable to obtain ATCU feedback, recheck ATCU input/output signal inspection. If not as specified, check ATCU pin terminals for damage or loose connection with harness connector.

DTC P1705/1206/3RD:
THROTTLE POSITION (TP) SENSOR

Circuit Description – TP sensor relays throttle valve position to ATCU. A code is set when ATCU receives an excessively high or low voltage from TP sensor.

Diagnosis & Repair – 1) Check TP sensor circuit for engine control. Refer to SELF-DIAGNOSTICS in ENGINE PERFORMANCE in appropriate MITCHELL® repair manual for TP sensor fault code test (DTC/P0120 MIL/0403). If engine control test okay, go to next step.

2) Check TP sensor input signal. See appropriate test under ELECTRONIC COMPONENT & CIRCUIT TESTS. Refer to DTC P0705/1003 OR 1101/NO FLASH: INHIBITOR, TP OR OD SWITCH CIRCUIT. If voltage is NOT as specified, check harness for open or short between ECM and ATCU. If results are as specified, check throttle position switch. Repair or replace damaged parts. Road test and perform self diagnosis. If unable to obtain ATCU feedback, recheck ATCU input/output signal inspection. If not as specified, check ATCU pin terminals for damage or loose connection with harness connector.

DTC P1760/1203/6TH: OVERRUN CLUTCH SOLENOID VALVE

Circuit Description – Overrun clutch solenoid valve is activated by ATCU in response to signals sent from inhibitor switch, OD switch, vehicle speed and throttle position sensors. Overrun clutch operation is controlled by outputs from the sensors. If ATCU detects unspecified voltage drops when it tries to operate overrun clutch solenoid valve.

Diagnosis & Repair – **1)** Check ground circuit. With KOEO, disconnect solenoid wiring harness assembly connector in engine compartment. Check resistance between terminal No. 8 and ground. Resistance should be 20-30 ohms. If resistance is not as specified, remove control valve. See CONTROL VALVE ASSEMBLY in overhaul article. Check overrun clutch solenoid valve, See appropriate test under ELECTRONIC COMPONENT & CIRCUIT TESTS. Check harness for open or short of terminal cord assembly.

2) If resistance is within specifications, Check power source. With ignition OFF, disconnect ATCU harness connector. Check resistance between solenoid wiring harness connector terminal No. 8 and ATCU harness terminal No. 8. Resistance should be zero ohms. Repair or replace harness between ATCU and solenoid wiring harness assembly if not as specified. Road test and perform self diagnosis. If unable to obtain ATCU feedback, recheck ATCU input/output signal inspection. If not as specified, check ATCU pin terminals for damage or loose connection with harness connector.

ELECTRONIC COMPONENT & CIRCUIT TESTS

NOTE: If the following circuit tests do not give results as described, check wiring circuit between specified components to correct circuit malfunction. Repair as necessary. For wiring diagram information, see WIRING DIAGRAMS.

ATCU POWER SOURCE TEST

1) With ignition switch in ON position, and engine off, check voltage between ATCU terminals No. 4, 9 and ground. Battery voltage should be present. If voltage is not as specified, repair circuit(s) as necessary. Ensure ground resistance between ATCU terminals No. 15 and 48 is zero ohms. If not, check harness for short or open between ATCU and ground. If okay, check light circuit.

2) With Ignition in OFF position, check resistance between ATCU terminals No. 3 and 4. Resistance should be 50-100 ohms. If not as specified, check power indicator light (Infiniti). Check harness for open or short between ignition switch and POWER indicator light or between indicator light and ATCU.

ENGINE REVOLUTION SIGNAL CIRCUIT TEST (TACH SIGNAL)

Start engine, check voltage between ATCU terminal No. 24 and ground. Voltage should vary from .9-4.5 volts.

FLUID TEMPERATURE SENSOR TEST

1) Check resistance between fluid temperature sensor terminals. Resistance should be 2500 ohms at 68°F (20°C), and 300 ohms at 176°F (80°C). If resistance is not as specified, replace sensor.

2) Disconnect solenoid harness connector in engine compartment. Check resistance between terminals No. 33 and 35 when transaxle is cold. See FLUID TEMPERATURE SENSOR DIAGNOSIS table. Check voltage between ATCU terminal No. 33 and ground, while warming up transaxle. If resistance and voltage is not as specified, repair circuit as necessary. See Fig. 1.

FLUID TEMPERATURE SENSOR DIAGNOSIS

Terminal No.	Transaxle Temperature	Resistance	Voltage
33 To 35	Cold [1]	2500 Ohms	1.5
33 To 35	Warming Up [2]	.3 Ohms	.5

[1] – Cold 68°F (20°C).
[2] – Cold 68°F (20°C); Hot 176°F (80°C).

INHIBITOR SWITCH CIRCUIT TEST

1) Check inhibitor switch for continuity while moving lever through each position. See INHIBITOR SWITCH CONTINUITY TEST table. *See Fig. 3.*

INHIBITOR SWITCH CONTINUITY TEST

Selector Position	Continuity Between Pins No.
"P"	1 & 2, 3 & 4
"R"	3 & 5, 10 & 9
"N"	1 & 2, 3 & 6
"D"	3 & 7
"2"	3 & 8
"1"	3 & 9

2) Check voltage between ATCU terminals No. 16, 17, 18, 19, 20 and ground, while moving selector lever through each gear position. Battery voltage should be present at specified terminal when selector lever is in specified position. See INHIBITOR SWITCH VOLTAGE table.

INHIBITOR SWITCH VOLTAGE

Position	Terminal No.
"P" & "N"	19
"R"	20
"D"	18
"2"	17
"1"	16

LINE PRESSURE SOLENOID TEST

1) With ignition switch in OFF position, disconnect solenoid harness connector in engine compartment. Check resistance between solenoid harness connector terminal No. 1 and ground. Resistance should be 2.5-5 ohms. If resistance is not as specified, repair circuit as necessary. *See Fig. 3.*

2) Disconnect ATCU connector and check resistance between solenoid harness connector terminal No. 1 and ATCU terminal No. 2. Resistance should be 11.2-12.8 ohms. If resistance is not as specified, disconnect dropping resistor connector, check resistance of dropping resistor, located on left front fender, near air cleaner. Resistance should be 11.2-12.8 ohms. Replace resistor as necessary.

3) Check resistance between solenoid harness connector terminal No. 1 and ATCU terminal No. 1. Resistance should be approximately zero ohms. If resistance is not as specified, repair circuit as necessary.

LOCK-UP SOLENOID TEST (TCC)

1) Check resistance between solenoid assembly connector terminal No. 5 (Blue wire) and ground. Resistance should be 10-16 ohms. If resistance is not as specified, replace solenoid. *See Fig. 2.*

2) Check operation of solenoid valve by listening for its operating sound while applying battery voltage to terminal No. 5 and ground (bracket).

3) Disconnect ATCU connector and check resistance between ATCU terminal No. 5 and solenoid harness connector terminal No. 5. Resistance should be approximately zero ohms. If resistance is not as specified, repair circuit as necessary.

OVERDRIVE SWITCH TEST

1) Check continuity between terminal No. 1 (Black/Yellow wire) and terminal No. 2 (Black wire) at overdrive switch. Continuity should exist with switch in OFF position. Continuity should not exist with switch in ON position. Replace switch as necessary.

2) Turn ignition switch to ON position. Check voltage between ATCU terminal No. 39 and ground while overdrive switch is in ON position. Battery voltage should be present. With overdrive switch in OFF position, one volt or less should be present. If voltage is not as specified, repair circuit as necessary.

OVERRUN CLUTCH SOLENOID TEST

1) With ignition switch in OFF position, disconnect solenoid harness connector in engine compartment. Check resistance between solenoid terminal No. 8 and ground. Resistance should be 20-30 ohms. If resistance is not as specified, repair circuit as necessary. See Fig. 2.
2) Disconnect ATCU connector. Check resistance between terminal No. 8 of sensor harness connector and ATCU terminal No. 8. Resistance should be approximately zero ohms. If resistance is not as specified, repair circuit as necessary.

REVOLUTION SENSOR TEST (TRANSMISSION MAINSHAFT)

1) Check resistance between White and Black wire terminals at revolution sensor. Resistance should be 500-650 ohms. If resistance is not as specified, replace sensor.
2) Revolution sensor is a voltage generating sensor and should be tested using a voltmeter set on AC scale. Check voltage between ATCU terminal No. 25 and ground while driving vehicle. Voltage should rise gradually relative to vehicle speed. At zero MPH, voltage should not be present. If voltage does not rise when vehicle is driven, repair circuit as necessary.

SHIFT SOLENOID "A" TEST

1) Check resistance between solenoid assembly connector terminal No. 6 and ground. Resistance should be 20-30 ohms. If resistance is not as specified, replace solenoid. See Fig. 2.
2) With ignition switch in OFF position, disconnect solenoid harness connector in engine compartment. Check resistance between solenoid harness connector terminal No. 6 and ground. Resistance should be 20-30 ohms. If resistance is not as specified, repair circuit as necessary.
3) Disconnect ATCU connector. Check resistance between terminal No. 6 of sensor harness connector and ATCU terminal No. 6. Resistance should be approximately zero ohms. If resistance is not as specified, repair circuit as necessary. See Fig. 2.

SHIFT SOLENOID "B" TEST

1) Check resistance between solenoid assembly connector terminal No. 7 and ground. Resistance should be 20-30 ohms. If resistance is not as specified, replace solenoid. See Fig. 2.
2) With ignition switch in OFF position, disconnect solenoid harness connector in engine compartment. Check resistance between solenoid harness connector terminal No. 7 and ground. Resistance should be 20-30 ohms. If resistance is not as specified, repair circuit as necessary.
3) Disconnect ATCU connector. Check resistance between terminal No. 7 of sensor harness connector and ATCU terminal No. 7. Resistance should be approximately zero ohms. If resistance is not as specified, repair circuit as necessary. See Figs. 1 and 2.

SPEED SENSOR CIRCUIT TEST (VEHICLE SPEED SENSOR/MTR)

Check voltage between ATCU terminal No. 27 and ground while driving 1-2 MPH for 3 ft. (1m) or more. Voltage should vary from 0-5 volts. If voltage is not as described, check for continuity in wiring harness between ATCU and speed sensor. Check for poor ground circuit. See Fig. 1.

THROTTLE SENSOR (TP) CIRCUIT TEST

Check voltage between ATCU terminals No. 34 and 35 while depressing accelerator pedal slowly. At closed throttle, approximately .5 volt should be present. At wide open throttle, approximately 4 volts should be present. Voltage rises relative to throttle valve opening. See Fig. 1.

THROTTLE POSITION SWITCH CIRCUIT

Checking Idle Switch Circuit – Check voltage between ATCU terminal No. 14 and ground while depressing accelerator slowly. When depressing accelerator pedal to wide open throttle, one volt or less should be present. When releasing accelerator pedal, 8-15 volts should be present. See Fig. 1.
Checking Full Throttle Switch Circuit – Check voltage between ATCU terminal No. 21 and ground while depressing accelerator slowly. When depressing accelerator pedal to wide open throttle, 8-15 volts should be present. When releasing accelerator pedal, one volt or less should be present.

DROPPING RESISTOR

Check resistance between 2 terminals. Resistance should be 11.2-12.8 ohms.

A/T MODE SWITCH (INFINITI)

1) Check voltage between ATCU and terminal No. 42. With KOEO, switch in "COMFORT" position, battery voltage should be present. In any other position, one volt maximum should be present. See Fig. 1.
2) Check continuity between A/T mode switch terminals. See A/T MODE SWITCH CONTINUITY TEST table.

A/T MODE SWITCH CONTINUITY TEST

Switch Position	Continuity Between Pins No.
"Power"	2 & 3
"Auto"	No Continuity
"Comfort"	1 & 26

KEY INTERLOCK CABLE

NOTE: Ensure key interlock cable is installed without sharp bends, twists or interference with adjacent parts. Ensure casing cap and bracket are secured firmly. If casing cap can be remove with a load of less than 8.8 lbs (39.2 N), replace key interlock cable. See Fig. 4.

Removal – Unlock slider from adjuster holder. Remove rod from cable. Remove lock plate (at ignition switch), pull out key interlock cable.
Installation – Install key interlock cable to steering lock assembly and install lock plate. Clamp cable to steering column. Place selector lever in "P" position. Install interlock rod into adjuster holder. Install casing cap to bracket. Move slider in order to fix adjuster holder to interlock rod.

SHIFT LOCK SYSTEM TESTING

NOTE: Terminal numbers are identified for both models. Infiniti G20 is listed first and Nissan Sentra second. Example: No. 2/5 (G20/Sentra). Single numbers apply to both models.

Ignition Signal – **1)** Turn ignition switch to OFF position. Check voltage between harness terminal No. 2/6 and ground. Battery voltage should exist.
2) Check for ignition signal. With key off, check voltage between control harness terminal No. 1 and ground. Voltage should be zero. With KOEO, check voltage between control unit harness terminal No. 1 and ground. Battery voltage should exist. If voltage is not as specified, check ignition switch, fuse and/or harness for open or short. See Fig. 1.
Control Unit Circuit – Turn ignition switch "OFF". Disconnect control unit harness connector. Continuity should exist between control unit harness terminal No. 8/7 and ground. If continuity is not as specified, repair harness or connector.
Park Position Switch – **1)** Reconnect control unit harness connector. Check input signal. With KOEO, selector lever in "P" position, release

selector lever button. Disconnect control unit harness connector. Continuity should NOT exist between control harness terminal No. 6/5 and ground.

2) Check voltage between control unit harness terminal No. 6/5 and ground. Check with brake pedal depressed and selector lever button pushed. Voltage should be zero.

3) Check control unit harness terminal No. 6/5 and ground with selector lever set in any position except "P". Battery voltage should exist. If voltage is not as specified, check harness for open or short between terminal No. 6/5 and park position switch harness terminal No. 6/5 or between harness terminal No. 6/5 and ground. Check park position switch. Ensure continuity exists between terminals No. 6/5 and No. 11/1 in all positions except "P" position with select lever button released. See Fig. 2.

Stop Light Switch – 1) Check stop light switch input signal. With KOEO, check voltage between control harness terminal No. 5/8 and ground. With brake pedal depressed, battery voltage should be present. With brake pedal released, zero volts should be present.

2) If voltage is not as specified, check harness for open or short between control unit harness terminal No. 5/8 and stop light switch harness terminal No. 2/2. and between stop light harness terminal No. 5/1 and fuse. Ensure continuity exists between terminals No. 2/1 and No. 5/2 of stop light switch harness connector only when brake pedal is depressed.

Shift Lock Solenoid – 1) Check shift lock solenoid output signal. With KOEO and selector lever in "P" position, check voltage between shift lock harness connector terminal No. 4 and body ground. With brake pedal depressed, battery voltage should be present. With brake pedal released, voltage should be zero.

2) With ignition key in OFF position, check voltage between shift lock harness connector terminal No. 4 with brake pedal depressed. Voltage should be zero. If voltage readings are not as specified, check harness for short or open between control unit harness terminal No. 4/4 and shift lock solenoid harness terminal No. 4/7.

3) Ensure continuity exists between shift lock harness terminal No. 9 and ground. If continuity is not present, repair harness or connector.

4) Check operation of shift lock solenoid by applying battery voltage to shift lock harness connector. See Fig. 1.

Shift Lock Control Unit – Measure voltage between each terminal and terminal No. 8/7. See SHIFT LOCK CONTROL UNIT INSPECTION table. See Fig. 1.

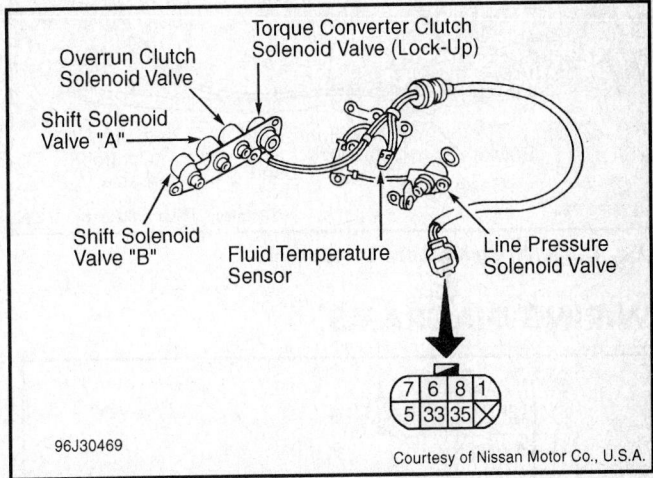

Fig. 2: Identifying Terminal Connector Pins

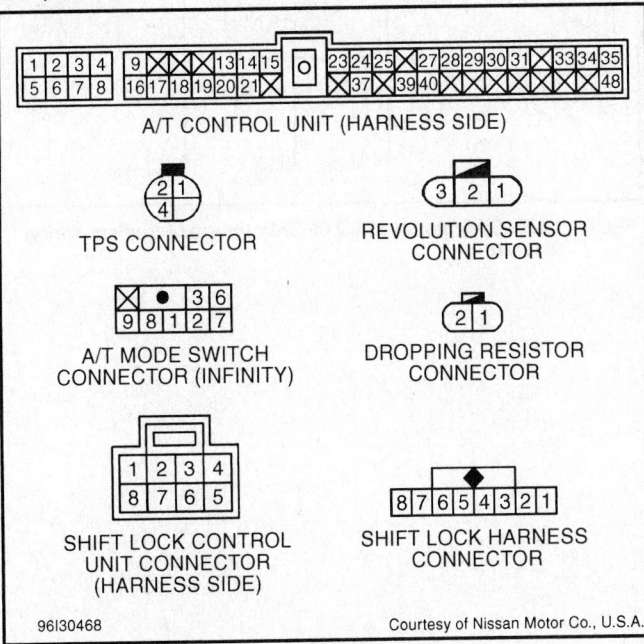

Fig. 1: Identifying Terminal Connector Pins

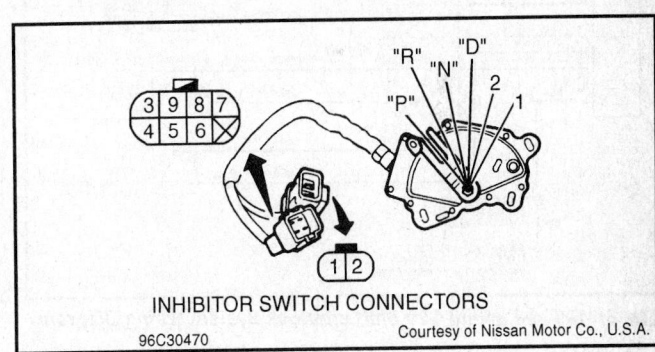

Fig. 3: Identifying Inhibitor Switch Terminal Connector Pins

SHIFT LOCK CONTROL UNIT INSPECTION

Terminal No.[1]	Item	Condition	Standard
1 & 8/7	Ignition Signal	Ignition Switch "ON" Position	Battery Voltage
		Any Position Except "ON" Position	0 Volts
2/6 & 8/7	Power Source	Any condition	Battery Voltage
4 & 8/7	Shift Lock Signal	Ignition Switch to "ON" Position, Selector Lever In "P" Position, Brake Pedal Depressed	Battery Voltage
		Except As Above	0 Volts
5/8 & 8/7	Stop Lamp Switch	Brake Pedal Depressed	Battery Voltage
		Brake Pedal Released	0 Volts
6/5 & 8/7	Park Position Switch	Ignition Key In Key Cylinder, Selector Lever In "P" Position, Selector Lever In Any Position & Button Pushed	Battery Voltage
		Except As Above	0 Volts

[1] – Terminal numbers are identified for both models. Infiniti G20 is listed first and Nissan 200SX second. Example: No. 2/5 (G20/200SX). Single numbers apply to both models.

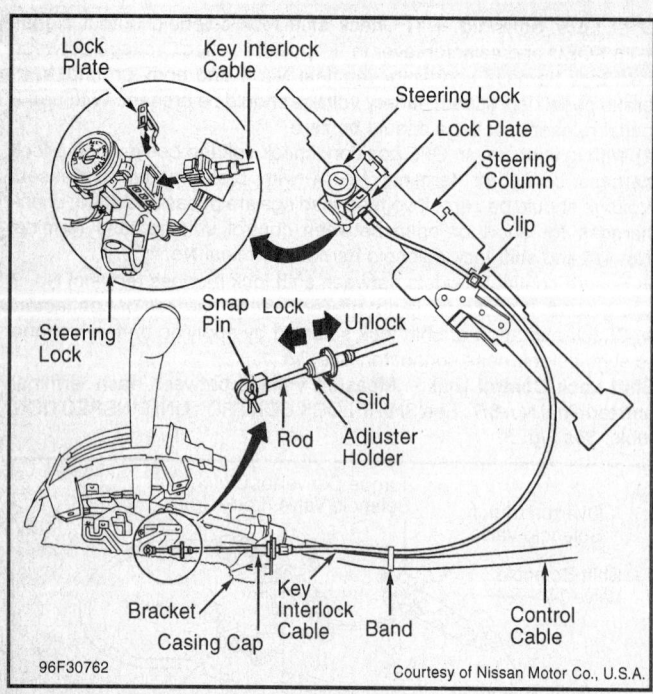

Fig. 4: Identifying Key Lock Components

WIRING DIAGRAMS

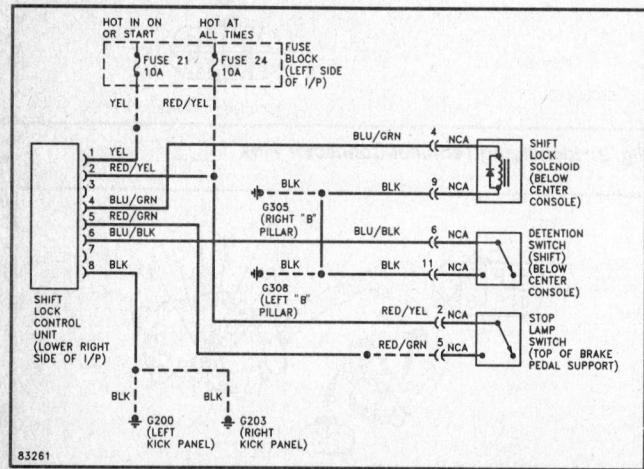

Fig. 5: 1995-96 Infiniti G20 Shift Interlock System Wiring Diagram

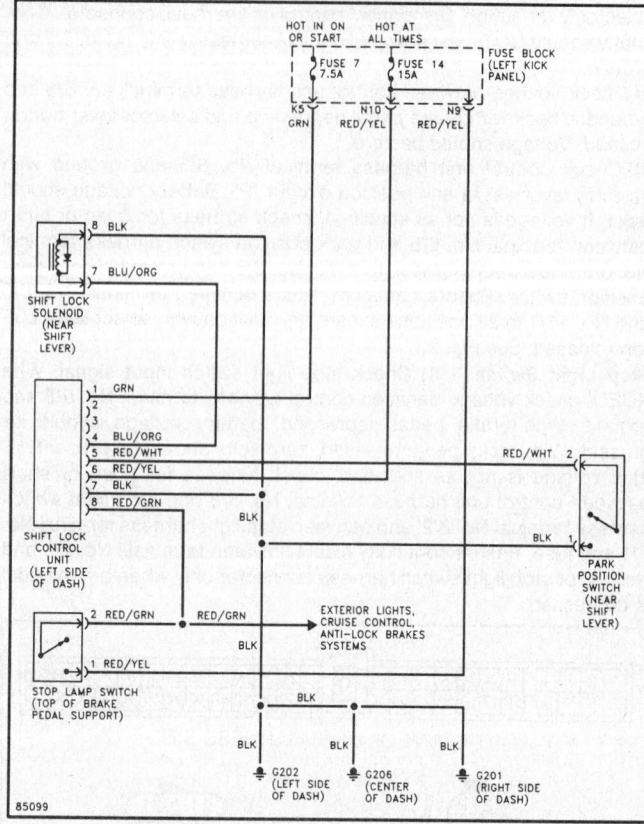

Fig. 6: 1995-96 Nissan 200SX 2.0L Shift Interlock System Wiring Diagram

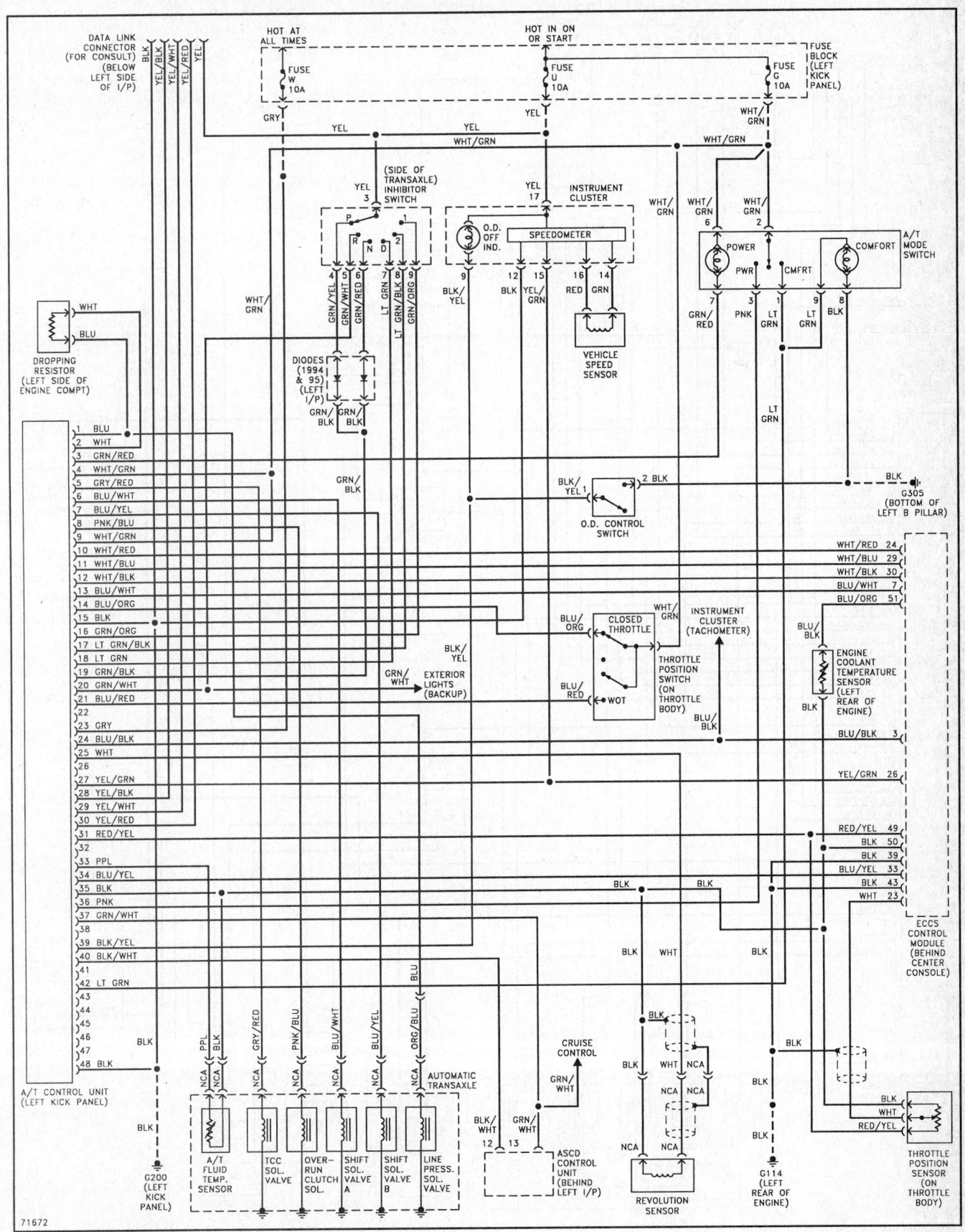

Fig. 7: 1995-96 Infiniti G20 Transaxle Wiring Diagram

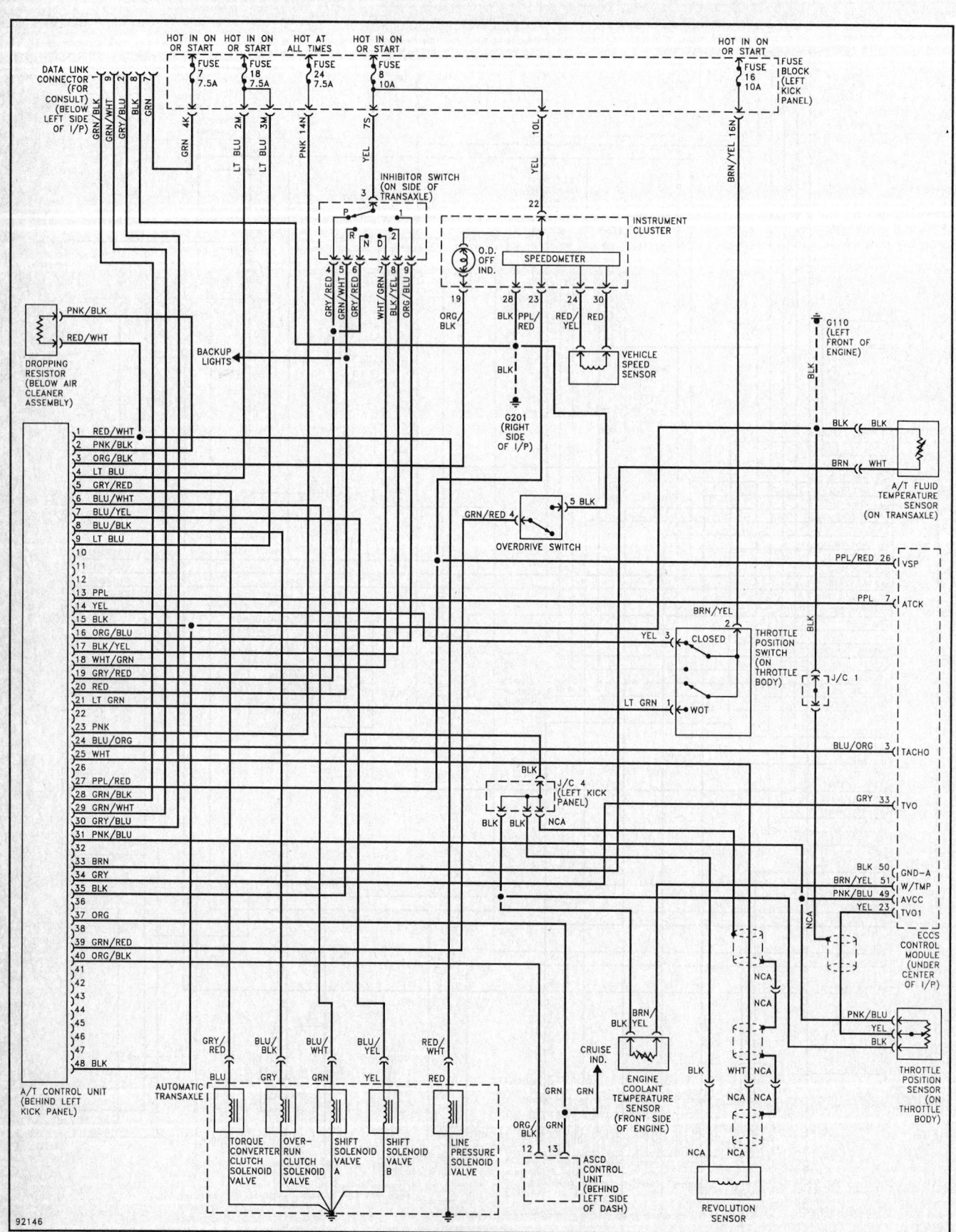

Fig. 8: 1995-96 Nissan 200SX 2.0L Transaxle Wiring Diagram

AUTOMATIC TRANSMISSIONS
Nissan RE4F04A & RE4F04V

Infiniti: I30
Mercury: Villager
Nissan: Altima, Maxima, Quest

APPLICATION & LABOR TIMES

APPLICATION & LABOR TIMES

Vehicle	Labor Times		Transaxle
Application	[1] R & I	[2] Overhaul	Model
Nissan			
Altima	6.6	9.0	RE4F04A/V
Maxima	6.8	9.0	RE4F04A/V
Quest	4.6	9.0	RE4F04A
Infiniti			
I30	6.8	9.0	RE4F04A/V
Mercury			
Villager	4.6	9.0	[3] 4F20E

[1] – Removal and installation of transmission from vehicle chassis.

[2] – Bench overhaul time for transmission and differential. DOES NOT include removal and installation.

[3] – For additional information, see appropriate 4F20E article in MITCHELL® 1995-96 TRANSMISSION SERVICE & REPAIR manual for DOMESTIC CARS, LIGHT TRUCKS & VANS.

IDENTIFICATION

Transaxle model is located on vehicle identification plate in engine compartment area. *See Fig. 1.* On Maxima and I30, transaxle number is stamped on transaxle above axle shaft. *See Fig. 2.* On Altima, Quest and Villager, label is located on transaxle side cover.

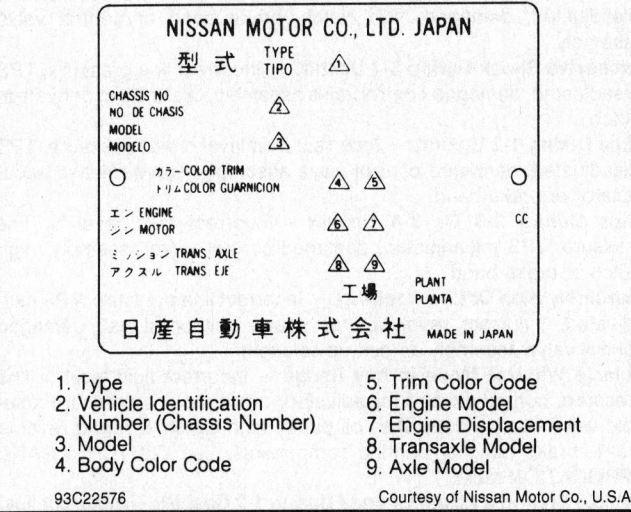

1. Type
2. Vehicle Identification Number (Chassis Number)
3. Model
4. Body Color Code
5. Trim Color Code
6. Engine Model
7. Engine Displacement
8. Transaxle Model
9. Axle Model

93C22576   Courtesy of Nissan Motor Co., U.S.A.

Fig. 1: Identification Plate Information

DESCRIPTION

Transaxle consists of 4 main units: automatic transaxle, torque converter, differential assembly and Automatic Transaxle Control Unit (ATCU). ATCU electrically controls shifting functions. Automatic transaxle consists of forward clutch, forward one-way clutch, high clutch, low and reverse brake, overrun clutch, reverse clutch, brake band servo, accumulators and control valve assembly. *See Fig. 3.* Transaxle incorporates a limited slip differential with viscous coupling.

LUBRICATION & ADJUSTMENTS

See appropriate AUTOMATIC TRANSMISSION SERVICING article in TRANSMISSION SERVICING section.

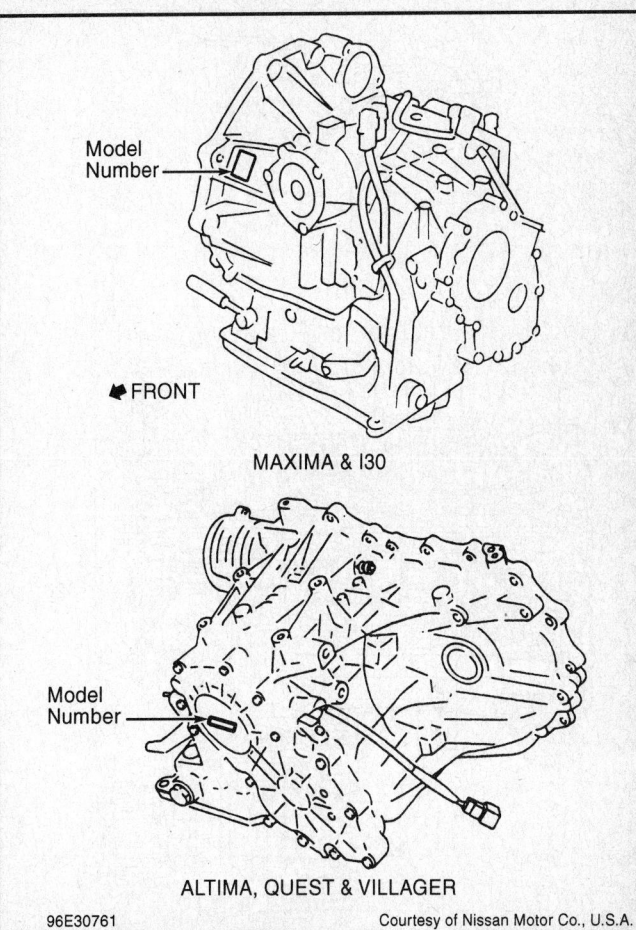

MAXIMA & I30

ALTIMA, QUEST & VILLAGER

96E30761   Courtesy of Nissan Motor Co., U.S.A.

Fig. 2: Locating Transaxle Number

TROUBLE SHOOTING

NOTE: Always check fluid level and linkage. Fluid level should be checked using HOT range on dipstick at fluid temperatures of 122-176°F (50-80°C) after vehicle has been driven approximately 5 minutes after initial warm-up. Use caution not to overfill. Ensure all computer control systems are operating properly before diagnosing shifting problems.

SYMPTOM DIAGNOSIS

NOTE: ATCU has an Fail-Safe mode (limp home) under which vehicle always runs in 3rd gear with shift lever in "D", "2" or "1" positions (sluggish, poor acceleration). When Fail-Safe occurs, next time key is turned to "ON" position, POWER indicator lamp will blink for about 8 seconds. Fail-Safe may activate without electrical circuit damage (such as excessive wheel spins and emergency braking immediately afterwards). In this case turn ignition key OFF for 5 seconds, then ON to recover normal shift pattern.

Engine Will Not Start In "P" Or "N" – Defective ignition switch or starter. Inhibitor switch or control linkage misadjusted.

Engine Starts In Range Other Than "P" Or "N" – Inhibitor switch or control linkage misadjusted.

Transaxle Noise In "P" Or "N" – Incorrect fluid level or line pressure, Throttle Position Sensor (TPS) misadjusted, incorrect revolution or speed sensor signal, damaged torque converter or oil pump.

Park Will Not Engage Or Disengage – Control linkage misadjusted or defective parking components.

Vehicle "Creeps" In "N" – Control linkage misadjusted, damaged forward clutch, overrun clutch or reverse clutch.

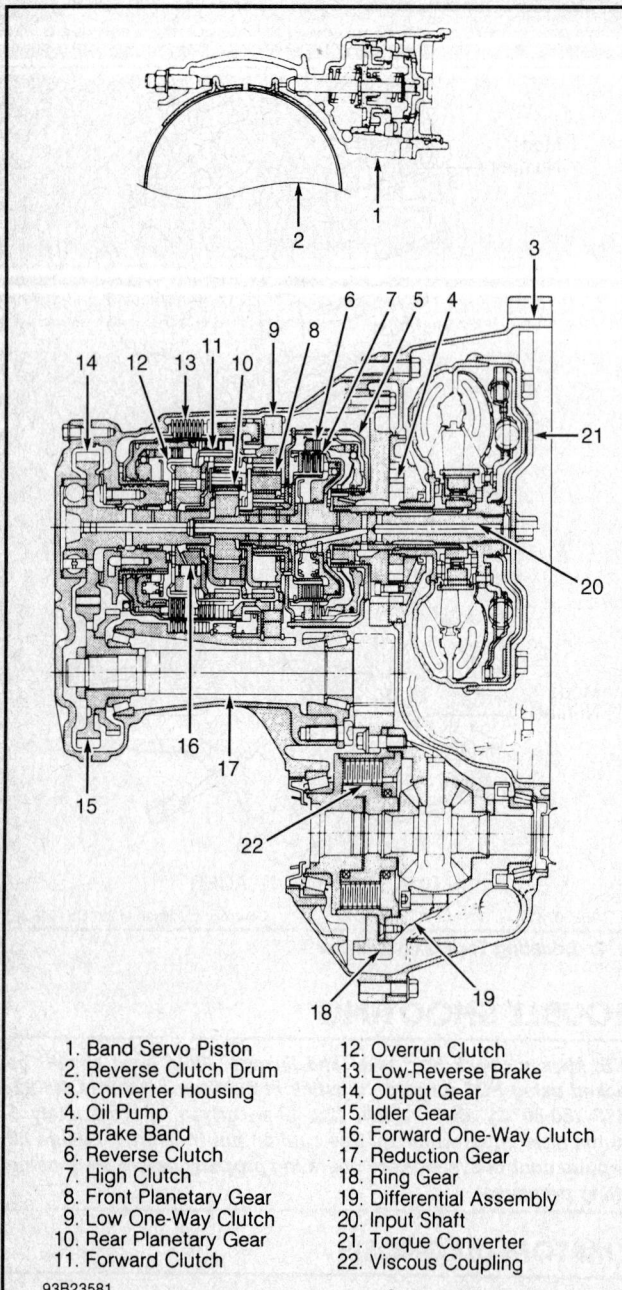

1. Band Servo Piston
2. Reverse Clutch Drum
3. Converter Housing
4. Oil Pump
5. Brake Band
6. Reverse Clutch
7. High Clutch
8. Front Planetary Gear
9. Low One-Way Clutch
10. Rear Planetary Gear
11. Forward Clutch
12. Overrun Clutch
13. Low-Reverse Brake
14. Output Gear
15. Idler Gear
16. Forward One-Way Clutch
17. Reduction Gear
18. Ring Gear
19. Differential Assembly
20. Input Shaft
21. Torque Converter
22. Viscous Coupling

93B23581   Courtesy of Nissan Motor Co., U.S.A.

**Fig. 3: Identifying Transaxle Component Locations
(RE4F04V Shown)**

Vehicle Will Not Move In "R"; Okay In "D", "2" & "1" – Control linkage misadjusted, incorrect line pressure, damaged line pressure solenoid, control valve assembly, reverse clutch, forward clutch, high clutch, overrun clutch or low and reverse brake.

Vehicle Brakes When Shifted To "R" – Incorrect fluid level or line pressure, control linkage misadjusted, damaged line pressure solenoid, control valve assembly, high clutch, forward clutch, overrun clutch or brake band.

Excessive Shift Shock From "N" To "D" – Engine idle RPM or TPS misadjusted, incorrect line pressure, fluid temperature or engine RPM signal, control valve assembly, damaged N-D accumulator or forward clutch.

Vehicle Will Not Move In "D" & "2"; Okay In "1" & "R" – Control linkage misadjusted, damaged low one-way clutch.

Vehicle Will Not Move Or Slips In "D", "1" & "2"; Okay In "R" –Incorrect fluid level or line pressure, damaged line pressure solenoid, control valve assembly, N-D accumulator, reverse clutch, high clutch, forward clutch low one way or forward one-way clutch. See CLUTCH & BAND APPLICATION table.

Slips On Acceleration – Incorrect fluid level or line pressure, control linkage or TPS misadjusted, damaged line pressure solenoid, control valve assembly, forward clutch, reverse clutch, N-D accumulator, low and reverse brake, torque converter or oil pump.

Excessive "Creep" – Incorrect engine idle RPM.

No "Creep" – Incorrect fluid level or line pressure, damaged control valve assembly, torque converter, oil pump or forward clutch.

No 1-2 Upshift – Inhibitor switch or control linkage misadjusted, damaged control valve assembly, brake band or shift solenoid "A", incorrect revolution or speed sensor signal.

No 2-3 Upshift – Inhibitor switch or control linkage misadjusted, incorrect revolution or speed sensor signal, damaged control valve assembly, shift solenoid "B", high clutch or brake band.

No 3-4 Upshift – Inhibitor switch or control linkage misadjusted, incorrect revolution, speed or fluid temperature sensor signal, damaged shift solenoid "A" or brake band.

Upshift Points Too High In All Gears – TPS misadjusted, incorrect revolution or speed sensor signal, damaged shift solenoid "A" or "B".

Shifts From 1st To 3rd; Skips 2nd – Incorrect fluid level, damaged brake band or leaking servo release accumulator.

Shifting Into "R", "D", "2", Or "1" Kills Engine – Incorrect engine idle RPM or line pressure, damaged control valve assembly, lock-up solenoid or torque converter.

Excessive Shock During 1-2 Upshift – Incorrect line pressure, TPS misadjusted, incorrect revolution or fluid temperature sensor signal, control valve assembly or brake band, binding or leaking servo release accumulator .

Excessive Shock During 2-3 Upshift – Incorrect line pressure, TPS misadjusted, damaged high clutch, brake band or control valve assembly.

Excessive Shock During 3-4 Upshift – Incorrect line pressure, TPS misadjusted, damaged control valve assembly, brake band or overrun clutch.

Slips During 1-2 Upshift – Incorrect fluid level or line pressure, TPS misadjusted, damaged control valve assembly, servo release accumulator or brake band.

Slips During 2-3 Or 3-4 Upshift – Incorrect fluid level or line pressure, TPS misadjusted, damaged control valve assembly, high clutch or brake band.

Extremely High Or Low Lock-Up – Incorrect line pressure, TPS misadjusted, incorrect revolution or speed sensor signal, damaged control valve assembly or lock-up solenoid.

Vehicle Will Not Move In Any Range – Incorrect fluid level or line pressure, control linkage misadjusted, damaged line pressure solenoid valve, torque converter, oil pump, high clutch, low and reverse brake, brake band or parking components. See CLUTCH & BAND APPLICATION table.

Vehicle Braked By Gear Change During 1-2 Upshift – Incorrect fluid level, damaged high clutch, low/reverse brake or low one-way clutch.

Vehicle Braked By Gear Change During 2-3 Upshift – Incorrect fluid level, damaged brake band.

Vehicle Braked By Gear Change During 3-4 Upshift – Incorrect fluid level, damaged overrun clutch, forward clutch forward/one-way clutch or reverse clutch.

Poor Acceleration, Unable To Obtain Maximum Speed – Incorrect fluid level, misadjusted inhibitor switch, damaged shift solenoid "A" or "B", control valve assembly, reverse clutch, high clutch, brake band, low/reverse brake, oil pump or torque converter.

No 4-3 Downshift – Incorrect fluid level, Misadjusted TPS, damaged overrun clutch solenoid valve, shift solenoid valve "A", line pressure solenoid valve, control valve solenoid, low/reverse brake or overrun clutch.

No 3-2 Or 4-2 Downshift – Incorrect fluid level, misadjusted TPS, damaged shift solenoid valve "A" or "B", control valve assembly, high clutch or brake band.

No 2-1 Or 3-1 Downshift – Incorrect fluid level, misadjusted TPS, damaged shift solenoid valve "A" or "B", control valve assembly, low one-way clutch, high clutch or brake band

Excessive Gear Change Shock During Deceleration With Release Of Accelerator Pedal – Misadjusted TPS, incorrect line pressure, damaged overrun clutch solenoid valve or control valve assembly.

Shift Points From 4-3, 3-2, 2-1 Too High – Misadjusted or damaged TPS, revolution sensor or speed sensor.

No Kickdown From 4th Gear Within Kickdown Speed – Misadjusted or damaged TPS, revolution sensor or speed sensor, shift solenoid "A" or "B".

Kickdown Operates Or Engine Overruns In 4th Gear When Depressing Pedal Beyond Kickdown Speed – Misadjusted or damaged TPS, revolution sensor or speed sensor, shift solenoid "A" or "B".

Slips Or Engine Races Changing From 4-3 When Depressing Pedal – Incorrect fluid level or line pressure, misadjusted TPS, damaged line pressure solenoid valve, control valve assembly, high clutch or forward clutch.

Slips Or Engine Races Changing From 4-2 When Depressing Pedal – Incorrect fluid level or line pressure, misadjusted TPS, damaged line pressure solenoid valve, control valve assembly, shift solenoid valve "A", forward clutch or brake band.

Slips Or Engine Races Changing From 3-2 When Depressing Pedal – Incorrect fluid level or line pressure, misadjusted TPS, damaged line pressure solenoid valve, control valve assembly, A/T fluid temperature sensor, brake band, forward clutch or high clutch.

Slips Or Engine Races Changing From 4-1 Or 3-1 When Depressing Pedal – Incorrect fluid level or line pressure, misadjusted TPS, damaged line pressure solenoid valve, control valve assembly, forward clutch, forward one-way clutch or low one-way clutch.

Transaxle Noise In "D", "2", "1" & "R" Positions – Incorrect fluid level or damaged torque converter.

Will Not Change From 3-2 When Shifting Into "2" Position – Damaged or misadjusted inhibitor switch or TPS, damaged overrun clutch solenoid, shift solenoid valves "A" or "B", control valve assembly, overrun clutch or brake band.

Gear Change From 2-3 With Selector In "2" Position – Damaged or misadjusted inhibitor switch.

Engine Brake Does Not Operate In "1" Position – Misadjusted inhibitor switch, control linkage or TPS, damaged revolution sensor or speed sensor, shift solenoid valve "A", control valve assembly, overrun clutch solenoid valve, overrun clutch or low/reverse brake.

Gear Change From 1-2 In "1" Position – Damaged or misadjusted inhibitor switch or control linkage.

Will Not Change From 2-1 In "1" Position – Damaged or misadjusted inhibitor switch, damaged shift solenoid valve "A", control valve assembly, overrun clutch solenoid valve, overrun clutch or low/reverse brake.

Excessive Shock When Shifting From 2-1 In "1" Position – Damaged control valve assembly or low/reverse brake.

Transaxle Overheats – Incorrect fluid level or line pressure, misadjusted TPS, engine idle RPM, damaged control valve assembly, oil pump, reverse clutch, high clutch, brake band, low/reverse brake, overrun clutch, forward clutch or torque converter.

ATF Shoots Out During Operation, White Smoke Emitted From Exhaust – Incorrect fluid level, damaged reverse clutch, high clutch, brake band, forward clutch, overrun clutch or low/reverse brake.

Offensive Smell At Oil Filler Pipe – Incorrect fluid level, damaged torque converter, oil pump, reverse clutch, high clutch, brake band, forward clutch, one-way clutch, overrun clutch or low/reverse clutch.

Torque Converter Will Not Lock Up – Misadjusted TPS, damaged revolution sensor or speed sensor, inhibitor switch, engine speed signal, A/T fluid temperature sensor, incorrect line pressure, torque converter clutch solenoid valve, control valve assembly or torque converter.

Torque Converter Clutch Piston Slip – Incorrect fluid level or fluid pressure, misadjusted TPS, torque converter solenoid valve, line pressure solenoid valve, control valve assembly or torque converter.

A/T Will Not Shift To 4th Gear When Driving With OD Switch "ON" – Misadjusted TPS, damaged inhibitor switch, revolution sensor or speed sensor, shift solenoid valve "A", overrun clutch solenoid

valve, control valve assembly, A/T fluid temperature sensor, incorrect line pressure, brake band or overrun clutch.

Engine Stalls In "R", "D", "2" & "1" Positions – Incorrect fluid level, damaged torque converter lock up solenoid valve, shift solenoid valves "A" or "B" or control valve assembly.

CLUTCH & BAND APPLICATION
CLUTCH & BAND APPLICATION

Selector Lever Position	Elements In Use
"D" (Drive) [1]	
First Gear	Forward Clutch, [2] Forward One-Way Clutch [3][4] Overrun Clutch & [2] Low One-Way Clutch
Second Gear	Band Servo (2nd Apply), Forward Clutch, [2] Forward One-Way Clutch & [3][4] Overrun Clutch
Third Gear	Band Servo ([5] 2nd Apply & 3rd Release), Forward Clutch, [2] Forward One-Way Clutch, High Clutch & [3][4] Overrun Clutch
Fourth Gear	Band Servo ([6] 2nd & 4th Apply, 3rd Release), Forward Clutch, High Clutch & Lock-up
"2" (Intermediate)	
First Gear	Forward Clutch, [2] Forward One-Way Clutch [2] Low One-Way Clutch & Overrun Clutch
Second Gear	Band Servo (2nd Apply), Forward Clutch, [2] Forward One-Way Clutch & Overrun Clutch
"1" (Low)	
First Gear	Forward Clutch, [2] Forward One-Way Clutch Low-Reverse Brake, Low One-Way, Overrun Clutch
Second Gear	Band Servo (2nd Apply), Forward Clutch [2] Forward One-Way Clutch & Overrun Clutch
"R" (Reverse)	Low-Reverse Brake & Reverse Clutch
"N" Or "P" (Neutral Or Park)	All Clutches & Bands Released Or Ineffective

[1] – Transaxle will not shift to 4th gear when overdrive switch is in OFF position.
[2] – Operates during progressive acceleration.
[3] – Operates when overdrive switch is in OFF position.
[4] – Operates when throttle opening is less than 1/16.
[5] – Oil pressure is applied to both 2nd apply and 3rd release side of band servo piston. Brake band does not contract because oil pressure area on release side is greater than apply side.
[6] – Oil pressure is applied to 4th apply side in 3rd gear, and brake band contracts.

ROAD TEST

Preliminary Checks – Fluid level should be checked using HOT range on dipstick at fluid temperatures of 122-176°F (50-80°C) after vehicle has been driven approximately 5 minutes after initial warm-up. COLD range on dipstick is for reference only. Fluid level must be checked and adjusted using HOT range. Ensure the following procedures are followed:
- Check fluid level with vehicle on level surface and parking brake set.
- Check fluid level with engine running and selector lever in PARK.
- If fluid level is at low side of either range, add fluid.
- Check fluid condition.
- Check for fluid leakage at cases, pan, etc.

Check Before Engine Is Started – 1) Park vehicle on flat surface. Turn ignition to OFF position. Move selector lever to "P" position. Set OD switch to ON position. Turn ignition switch to ON position. OD OFF indicator light should come on for about 2 seconds.

2) If light flickers for about 8 seconds, see appropriate NISSAN ELECTRONIC CONTROLS article for testing procedure. Turn ignition switch to OFF position. With parking brake off, verify PARK engagement by pushing vehicle backward or forward. Ensure vehicle starts only in "P" and "N".

Check With Engine Idling – 1) Start engine. Apply parking brake. Move selector to "N" position. Vehicle should not roll.

2) Apply foot brake. Move selector lever to "R" position. Release parking brake for several seconds. Vehicle should creep backward with parking brake released. Repeat to verify operation of forward gear positions.

Road Test Procedure – 1) Park vehicle on flat surface and set OD switch to ON position. Move selector lever to "P" position and start engine.

2) Move selector lever to "D" position. Slowly depress accelerator pedal halfway. Vehicle should start from 1st gear. Verify 1-2, 2-3 and 3-4 upshifts occur at specified speed. Refer to SHIFT SPEED SPECIFICATIONS tables.

3) Lock-up occurs at speeds relative to throttle opening in D_4. To verify lock-up speeds, see LOCK-UP SPEED SPECIFICATIONS table. Lock-up condition should be maintained for more than 30 seconds. Lock-up condition is released upon deceleration. Confirm transmission OD switch is in ON position and selector lever is in "D" position.

4) Accelerate vehicle to approximately 25 MPH using half-throttle. Release accelerator pedal and then quickly depress pedal to floor. Transaxle should downshift from 4th to 2nd. Release accelerator and verify 2-3, and 3-4 upshifts. Check shift points and specified speeds. Refer to SHIFT SPEED SPECIFICATIONS tables.

5) Confirm transmission mode switch is in AUTO position, overdrive switch is in ON position and selector lever is in "D" position. Accelerate vehicle to 4th gear using half-throttle. Release accelerator and switch overdrive to OFF position. Verify 4-3 downshift.

6) While still in 3rd gear, move selector lever from "D" to "2" position. Downshift should occur and deceleration should occur by engine braking. While still in 2nd gear, move selector lever from "2" to "1" position. Downshift should occur and deceleration should occur by engine braking.

LOCK-UP SPEED SPECIFICATIONS [1]

Application	OD Switch	MPH
Altima		
Comfort (Normal) Pattern		
Lock-Up ON in 4th	ON	65-70
Lock-Up OFF in 4th	ON	33-38
Comfort Pattern		
Lock-Up ON in 3rd	OFF	53-58
Lock-Up OFF in 3rd	OFF	52-57
Maxima		
Comfort Pattern		
Lock-Up ON in 4th	ON	63-68
Lock-Up OFF in 4th	ON	56-61
Lock-Up ON in 3rd	OFF	53-58
Lock-Up OFF in 3rd	OFF	52-57
Auto Power Pattern		
Lock-Up ON in 4th	ON	63-68
Lock-Up OFF in 4th	ON	56-61
Lock-Up ON in 3rd	OFF	53-58
Lock-Up OFF in 3rd	OFF	52-57
Quest & Villager		
Comfort Pattern		
Lock-Up ON in 4th	ON	41-48
Lock-Up OFF in 4th	ON	39-44
Lock-Up ON in 3rd	OFF	53-58
lock-Up OFF in 3rd	OFF	52-57
I30		
Comfort Pattern		
Lock-Up ON in 4th	ON	30-40

[1] – With 1/4 throttle opening.

ALTIMA SHIFT SPEED SPECIFICATIONS (COMFORT PATTERN)

Application	Full Throttle – MPH	Half Throttle – MPH
1st-2nd	39-43	26-31
2nd-3rd	71-76	48-53
3rd-4th	111-116	77-82
4th-3rd	109-114	47-52
3rd-2nd	65-70	25-30
2nd-1st	25-30	3-8

MAXIMA SHIFT SPEED SPECIFICATIONS (COMFORT PATTERN)

Application	Full Throttle – MPH	Half Throttle – MPH
1st-2nd	38-43	24-29
2nd-3rd	70-75	45-50
3rd-4th	110-115	70-75
4th-3rd	108-112	49-54
3rd-2nd	64-69	22-27
2nd-1st	34-39	3-8

MAXIMA SHIFT SPEED SPECIFICATIONS (AUTO POWER PATTERN)

Application	Full Throttle – MPH	Half Throttle – MPH
1st-2nd	38-43	29-34
2nd-3rd	70-76	53-58
3rd-4th	110-115	83-88
4th-3rd	108-112	53-58
3rd-2nd	64-69	32-37
2nd-1st	34-39	3-8

QUEST & VILLAGER SHIFT SPEED SPECIFICATIONS (COMFORT PATTERN)

Application	Full Throttle – MPH	Half Throttle – MPH
1st-2nd	35-40	22-27
2nd-3rd	62-67	39-44
3rd-4th	103-108	63-68
4th-3rd	98-103	40-45
3rd-2nd	56-61	22-27
2nd-1st	26-31	5-10

I30 SHIFT SPEED SPECIFICATIONS (COMFORT, NORMAL PATTERN)

Application	Full Throttle – MPH	Half Throttle – MPH
1st-2nd	38-43	24-29
2nd-3rd	70-75	45-50
3rd-4th	110-115	70-75
4th-3rd	108-112	49-54
3rd-2nd	64-69	22-27
2nd-1st	34-39	3-8

I30 SHIFT SPEED SPECIFICATIONS (AUTO POWER PATTERN)

Application	Full Throttle – MPH	Half Throttle – MPH
1st-2nd	38-43	29-34
2nd-3rd	70-75	53-58
3rd-4th	110-115	83-88
4th-3rd	108-112	53-58
3rd-2nd	64-69	32-37
2nd-1st	34-39	3-8

STALL SPEED TEST

Stall Speed Test Procedure – 1) Check engine and transaxle fluid levels. Ensure engine and transaxle are at normal operating temperatures. Set parking brake and block wheels.

2) Install tachometer so it is visible to driver. Start engine, apply foot brake and move selector lever to "D" position. Accelerate to wide-open throttle gradually while applying foot brake. Note engine stall speed and release accelerator pedal immediately. See STALL SPEED SPECIFICATIONS table.

3) Place selector lever in "N" position and run engine at idle for one minute to allow transaxle to cool. Repeat stall speed test procedure in "2", "1" and "R" positions, allowing transaxle to cool between each test.

CAUTION: DO NOT hold wide-open throttle for more than 5 seconds during test.

Stall Speed Test Results – 1) If stall speed is low in all positions, possible causes are: insufficient engine performance or faulty torque converter one-way clutch.

2) If stall speed is high in all positions, possible causes are: low and reverse brake slipping, faulty low one-way clutch or hydraulic circuit for line pressure control.

3) If stall speed is high in "R" position only, possible causes are: reverse clutch slipping or low and reverse brake slipping.

4) If stall speed is high in "D", "2" and "R" positions, but okay in "1" position, possible causes are: reverse clutch, low and reverse clutch, forward clutch, forward one-way clutch or low one-way clutch.

5) If stall speed is high in "D", "2" and "1" positions, but okay in "R" position, possible causes are: forward clutch, low-one way clutch or forward one-way clutch.

6) If stall speed is high in "D" and "2" positions, but okay in "1" and "R" positions, possible causes are: forward clutch, low one-way clutch and overrun clutch.

NOTE: Condition of high clutch and brake band cannot be confirmed by stall speed test.

STALL SPEED SPECIFICATIONS

Application	Stall Speed
Altima	2150-2450
Maxima	2000-2300
Quest & Villager	1800-2100
I30	1800-2100

HYDRAULIC PRESSURE TESTS

NOTE: Always replace pressure plugs. Plugs are self-sealing type.

Line Pressure Test – 1) Check transaxle and engine fluid levels. Warm engine and transaxle to operating temperature. Drive vehicle approximately 10 minutes before testing.

2) Install pressure gauge to line pressure port. *See Fig. 4.* Set parking brake and block wheels. Continue to press brake fully while line pressure and stall speed tests are performed. Start engine and measure line pressure at idle and stall speed. See LINE PRESSURE SPECIFICATIONS table.

NOTE: When measuring line pressure at stall speed, follow stall speed test procedure.

LINE PRESSURE SPECIFICATIONS

Application	psi (kg/cm²)
Altima, Maxima & I30	
At Idle	
In "D", "2" & "1"	72 (5.1)
In "R"	124 (8.7)
At Stall Speed	
In "D", "2" & "1"	159 (11.2)
In "R"	270 (19)
In "D" (1995)	146 (10.3)
In "R" (1995)	249 (17.5)
Quest	
At Idle	
In "D", "2" & "1"	72 (5.1)
In "R"	124 (8.7)
At Stall Speed	
In "D", "2" & "1"	159 (11.2)
In "R"	270 (19)
Villager	
At Idle	
In "D", "2" & "1"	72 (5.1)
In "R"	124 (8.7)
In "D", "2" & "1" (1995)	72 (5.1)
In "R" (1995)	113 (7.9)
At Stall Speed	
In "D", "2" & "1"	159 (11.2)
In "R"	270 (19)
In "D", "2" & "1" (1995)	176 (12.4)
In "R" (1995)	284 (20)

Line Pressure Test Results – 1) If line pressure is low at idle in all positions, possible causes are: oil pump wear, control piston damage, pressure regulator valve or plug sticking, spring for pressure regulator

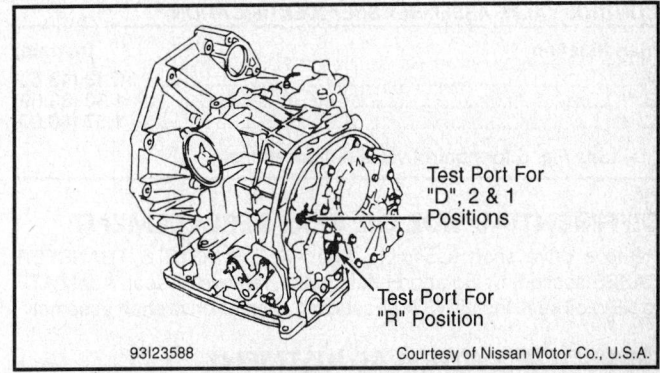

93I23588   Courtesy of Nissan Motor Co., U.S.A.

Test Port For "D", 2 & 1 Positions

Test Port For "R" Position

Fig. 4: Identifying Hydraulic Pressure Test Ports

valve damaged, clogged oil strainer, fluid pressure leakage between oil strainer and pressure regulator valve.

2) If line pressure is low at idle in a particular shift position, possible causes are: fluid pressure leakage between manual valve and a particular clutch. If line pressure is low in "R" and "1" position, but is normal in "D" and "2" position, fluid leakage exists at or around low-reverse brake circuit.

3) If line pressure is high at idle, possible causes are: TPS misadjusted, fluid temperature sensor damaged, line pressure solenoid sticking or shorted, pressure regulator or plug, or modifier valve sticking.

4) If line pressure is low at stall speed, possible causes are: TPS misadjusted, line pressure solenoid sticking or shorted, pressure regulator or plug, modifier valve or pilot valve sticking.

ON-VEHICLE SERVICE
CONTROL VALVE ASSEMBLY

Removal & Installation – 1) Drain ATF. Remove oil pan and gasket. Remove oil strainer. Remove control valve assembly by removing bolts and disconnecting wiring harness connector. *See Fig. 5.* Accumulators may be removed by applying compressed air (if necessary).

2) To install, set manual valve in neutral position and align with manual plate. Install control valve assembly and tighten bolts to 62-80 INCH lbs (7-9 N.m). Ensure bolts are installed in correct locations. See CONTROL VALVE ASSEMBLY BOLT IDENTIFICATION table. To complete installation, reverse removal procedure.

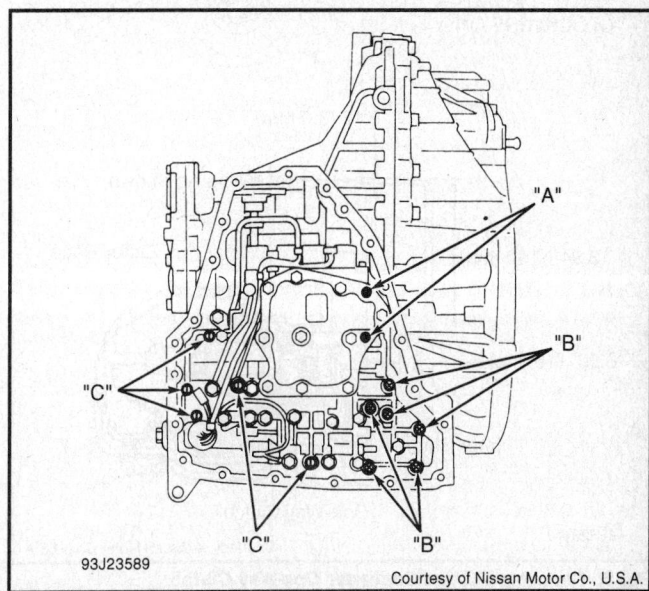

93J23589   Courtesy of Nissan Motor Co., U.S.A.

Fig. 5: Removing & Installing Control Valve Assembly

Identification	In. (mm)
A	1.713 (43.50)
B	1.30 (33.00)
C	1.57 (40.00)

[1] – *See Fig. 5 for control valve bolt locations.*

DIFFERENTIAL SIDE OIL SEAL REPLACEMENT

Remove drive shaft assembly. See AXLE SHAFTS & TRANSFER CASES section. Using appropriate puller, remove oil seal. Apply ATF to NEW oil seal. Install NEW oil seal and reinstall drive shaft assembly.

INHIBITOR SWITCH ADJUSTMENT

Remove control cable from manual shaft. Set manual shaft in "N" position. Loosen inhibitor switch attaching bolts. Insert .16" (4 mm) pin vertically into adjustment holes and tighten attaching bolts. Reattach control cable.

OIL COOLER FLUSHING PROCEDURE

Vehicles with tube type transaxle fluid cooler may be cleaned by using cleaning solvent and compressed air. Cooler lines must also be flushed to remove any foreign material. Vehicles with fin type transaxle fluid cooler cannot be cleaned. Replace radiator (radiator incorporates transaxle cooler), and flush cooler lines to remove any foreign material.

REMOVAL & INSTALLATION

See appropriate AUTOMATIC TRANSMISSION REMOVAL article in TRANSMISSION SERVICING section.

TORQUE CONVERTER

1) Torque converter is a sealed unit and cannot be disassembled for service. Replace torque converter if damaged. Check converter one-way clutch using flat-blade screwdriver and suitable wire. *See Fig. 6.*

2) Hook wire into groove of bearing support unitized with one-way clutch outer race. While holding bearing support with wire, rotate one-way clutch spline using screwdriver. Ensure inner race rotates clockwise only. If inner race rotates in both directions, replace torque converter.

TRANSAXLE DISASSEMBLY

1) Remove drain plug and drain fluid. Remove torque converter. Check torque converter one-way clutch. Remove dipstick and dipstick tube. Remove oil cooler tube. Set manual lever to "P" position. Remove inhibitor switch. Remove oil pan and gasket. *See Fig. 8.* DO NOT reuse oil pan bolts.

2) Remove control valve assembly bolts. *See Fig. 5.* Remove clip from terminal body. Push terminal body into transaxle case and remove solenoid harness. Remove manual valve from control valve assembly. Remove return spring from servo release accumulator piston. Using compressed air, remove servo release accumulator piston. *See Fig. 7.*

3) Remove "O" rings from servo release accumulator piston. Using compressed air, remove N-D accumulator piston and return spring. *See Fig. 7.* Remove "O" rings from N-D accumulator piston. Check accumulator pistons and contact surface of transaxle case for damage. Check accumulator return springs free length and diameter. See ACCUMULATOR SPRING SPECIFICATIONS table.

ACCUMULATOR SPRING SPECIFICATIONS

Application	In. (mm)
N-D Accumulator Spring	
Free Length	1.713 (43.50)
Outer Diameter	1.163 (27.00)
Servo Release Accumulator Spring	
Free Length	2.067 (52.50)
Outer Diameter	.803 (20.40)

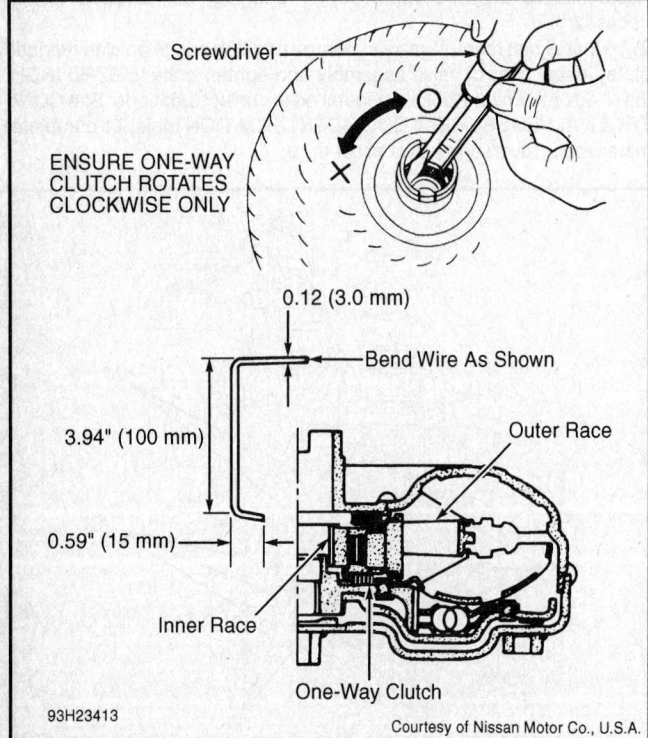

Fig. 6: *Checking Torque Converter One-Way Clutch*

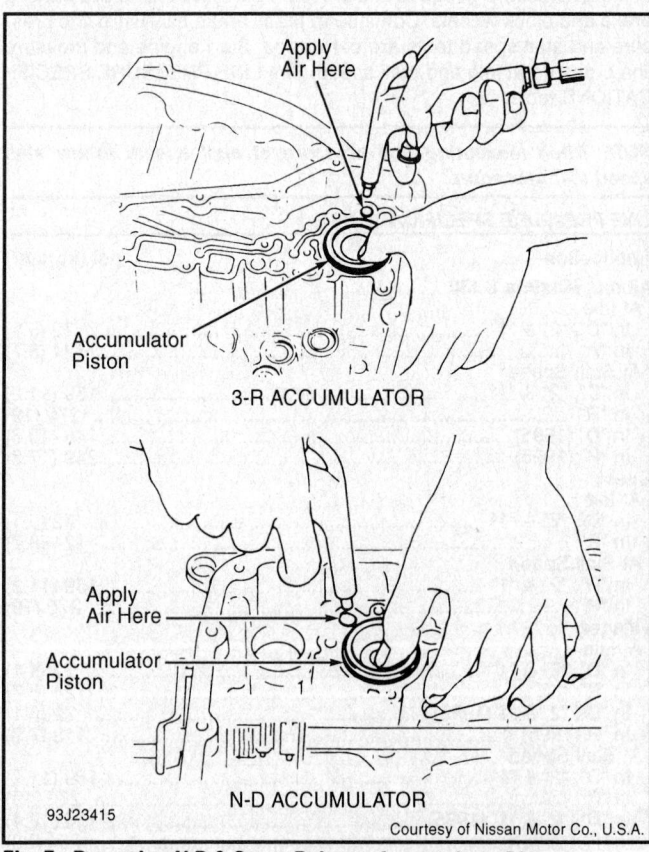

Fig. 7: *Removing N-D & Servo Release Accumulator Pistons*

4) Remove 4 lip seals from transaxle case. Remove Low and Reverse oil tube and sleeve. Remove converter housing bolts. Remove converter housing by tapping housing with soft-faced hammer. Remove "O" ring from differential oil port.

5) Remove differential assembly from transaxle case. Use appropriate puller to remove differential side bearing outer race from transaxle case and converter housing. Remove differential side bearing adjustment shim from transaxle case.

6) Using a hammer and screwdriver, remove oil seal from converter housing, being careful not to damage converter housing. Remove oil tube from converter housing. Remove "O" ring from input shaft. *See Fig. 9.* Remove oil pump assembly bolts and remove oil pump assembly, baffle and gasket from transaxle case. Remove thrust washer and bearing race from oil pump assembly. Loosen anchor end pin lock nut, then back off anchor end pin.

7) Remove brake band and strut from transaxle case. When removing brake band, insert wire clip into brake band ends for support. To prevent brake lining from cracking or peeling, DO NOT stretch brake band. Check brake band facing for damage, cracks, wear or burns. Remove high clutch (with input shaft assembly), reverse clutch. Remove high clutch from reverse clutch. *See Fig. 12.*

8) Remove needle bearing from high clutch drum. Remove high clutch hub and front sun gear. Remove needle bearing from high clutch drum. Remove front sun gear and needle bearing from high clutch drum. Remove bearing race from front sun gear. Check all components for damage or wear.

9) Remove needle bearing from transaxle case. Apply compressed air to transaxle case to check low and reverse brake operation. *See Fig. 10.* Remove snap ring. Using a bent wire, remove low one-way clutch from transaxle case. *See Fig. 11.* Remove snap ring and front planetary carrier with low-reverse brake piston and spring retainer.

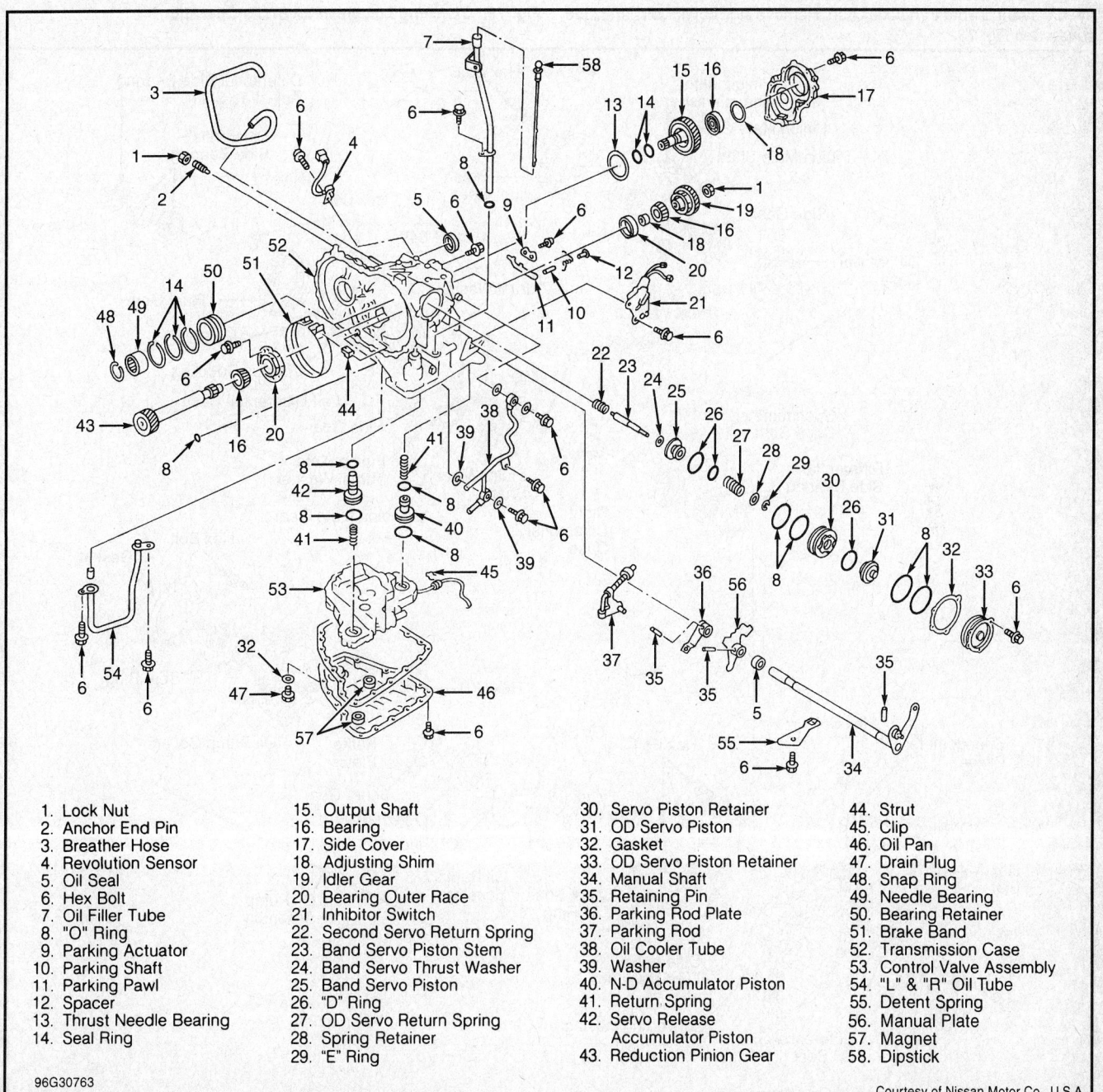

1. Lock Nut	15. Output Shaft	30. Servo Piston Retainer	44. Strut
2. Anchor End Pin	16. Bearing	31. OD Servo Piston	45. Clip
3. Breather Hose	17. Side Cover	32. Gasket	46. Oil Pan
4. Revolution Sensor	18. Adjusting Shim	33. OD Servo Piston Retainer	47. Drain Plug
5. Oil Seal	19. Idler Gear	34. Manual Shaft	48. Snap Ring
6. Hex Bolt	20. Bearing Outer Race	35. Retaining Pin	49. Needle Bearing
7. Oil Filler Tube	21. Inhibitor Switch	36. Parking Rod Plate	50. Bearing Retainer
8. "O" Ring	22. Second Servo Return Spring	37. Parking Rod	51. Brake Band
9. Parking Actuator	23. Band Servo Piston Stem	38. Oil Cooler Tube	52. Transmission Case
10. Parking Shaft	24. Band Servo Thrust Washer	39. Washer	53. Control Valve Assembly
11. Parking Pawl	25. Band Servo Piston	40. N-D Accumulator Piston	54. "L" & "R" Oil Tube
12. Spacer	26. "D" Ring	41. Return Spring	55. Detent Spring
13. Thrust Needle Bearing	27. OD Servo Return Spring	42. Servo Release Accumulator Piston	56. Manual Plate
14. Seal Ring	28. Spring Retainer	43. Reduction Pinion Gear	57. Magnet
	29. "E" Ring		58. Dipstick

96G30763

Courtesy of Nissan Motor Co., U.S.A.

Fig. 8: Exploded View Of Transaxle Case Components

AUTOMATIC TRANSMISSIONS
Nissan RE4F04A & RE4F04V (Cont.)

10) Remove low and reverse brake spring retainer. Ensure low one-way clutch rotates counterclockwise only. Remove needle bearing, low and reverse brake piston and spring retainer from front planetary carrier. See Fig. 10. Check all components for damage or wear.

11) Remove rear planetary carrier from transaxle case. Remove rear sun gear from rear planetary carrier. Note direction of rear sun gear prior to removal. Remove needle bearings from rear planetary carrier. Check all components for damage or wear.

12) Using a feeler gauge, check clearance between pinion washer and appropriate planetary carrier. Clearance between pinion washer and planetary carrier should be .008-.027" (.20-.70 mm), with allowable limit of .031" (.80 mm). If clearance is not as specified, replace appropriate planetary carrier.

13) Remove rear internal gear and forward clutch hub from transaxle case. Remove overrun clutch hub from transaxle case. Remove needle bearing from overrun clutch hub and check bearing for damage or wear. Remove forward clutch assembly from transaxle case. Remove needle bearing from transaxle case. Remove side cover bolts and side cover. See Fig. 13.

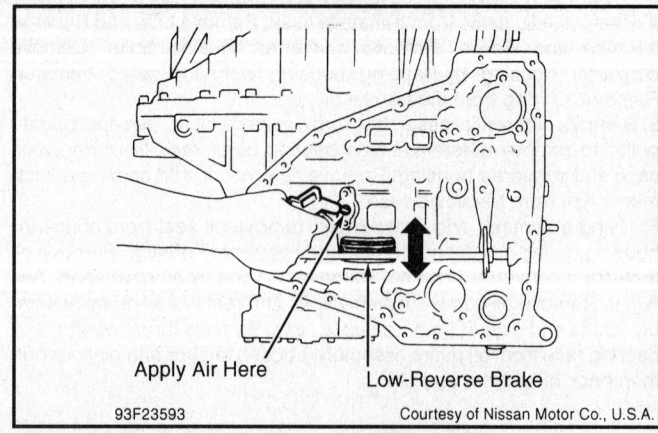

Apply Air Here   Low-Reverse Brake

93F23593   Courtesy of Nissan Motor Co., U.S.A.

Fig. 10: Checking Low-Reverse Brake Operation

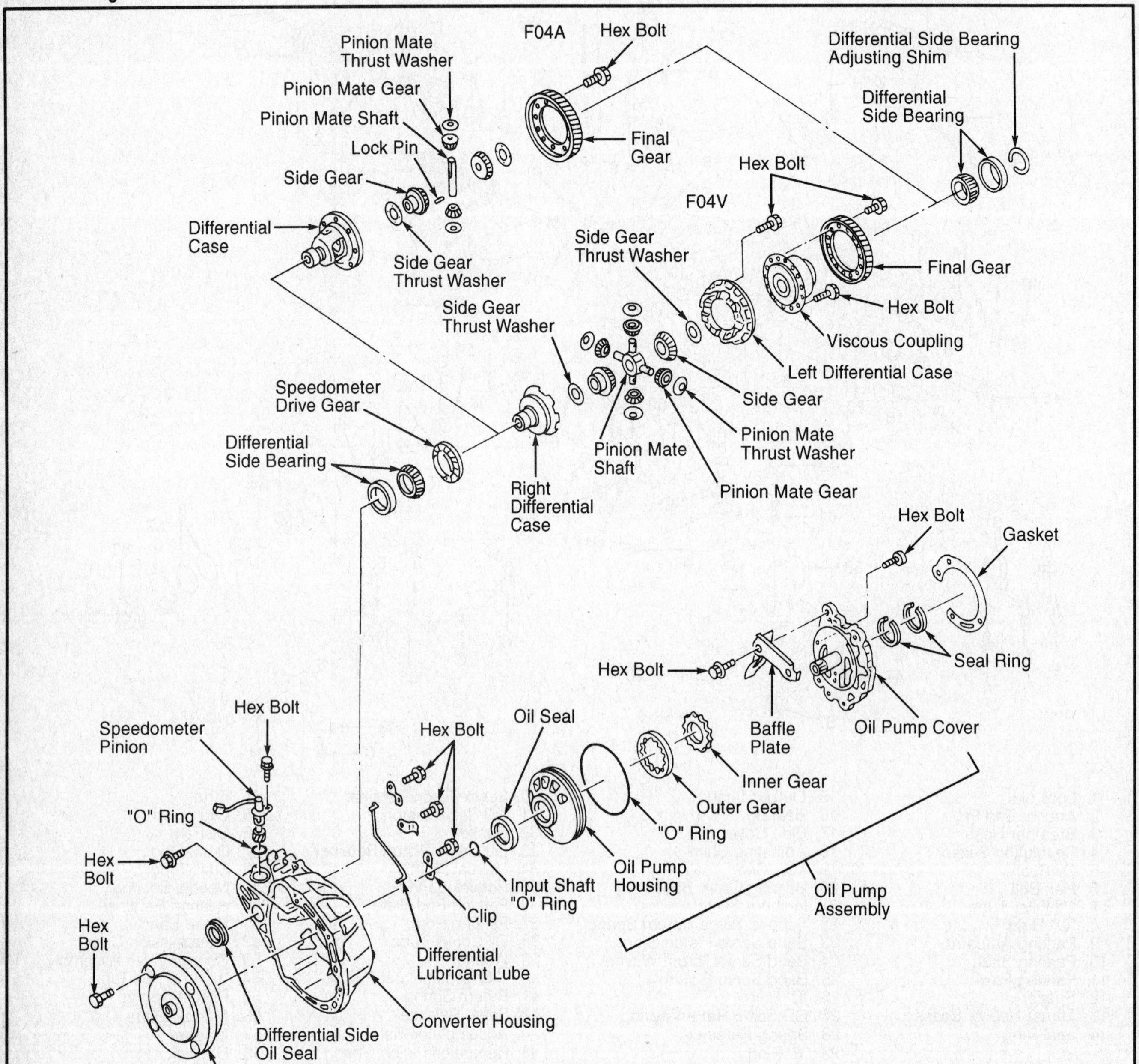

Pinion Mate Thrust Washer
Pinion Mate Gear
Pinion Mate Shaft
Lock Pin
Side Gear
Differential Case
Side Gear Thrust Washer
Side Gear Thrust Washer
Speedometer Drive Gear
Differential Side Bearing
Right Differential Case
Pinion Mate Shaft
Side Gear Thrust Washer
Side Gear
Pinion Mate Thrust Washer
Pinion Mate Gear
Left Differential Case
Viscous Coupling
Hex Bolt
Final Gear
Differential Side Bearing
Differential Side Bearing Adjusting Shim
Hex Bolt
Final Gear
F04A
F04V
Hex Bolt

Hex Bolt
Gasket
Seal Ring
Oil Pump Cover
Baffle Plate
Inner Gear
Outer Gear
"O" Ring
Oil Pump Housing
Oil Pump Assembly
Oil Seal
Hex Bolt

Speedometer Pinion
Hex Bolt
"O" Ring
Hex Bolt
Hex Bolt
Hex Bolt
Clip
Input Shaft "O" Ring
Differential Lubricant Lube
Differential Side Oil Seal
Converter Housing
Torque Converter

96H30764   Courtesy of Nissan Motor Co., U.S.A.

Fig. 9: Exploded View Of Torque Converter Housing & Differential Components (RE4F04V Is Shown; RE4F04A Is Similar)

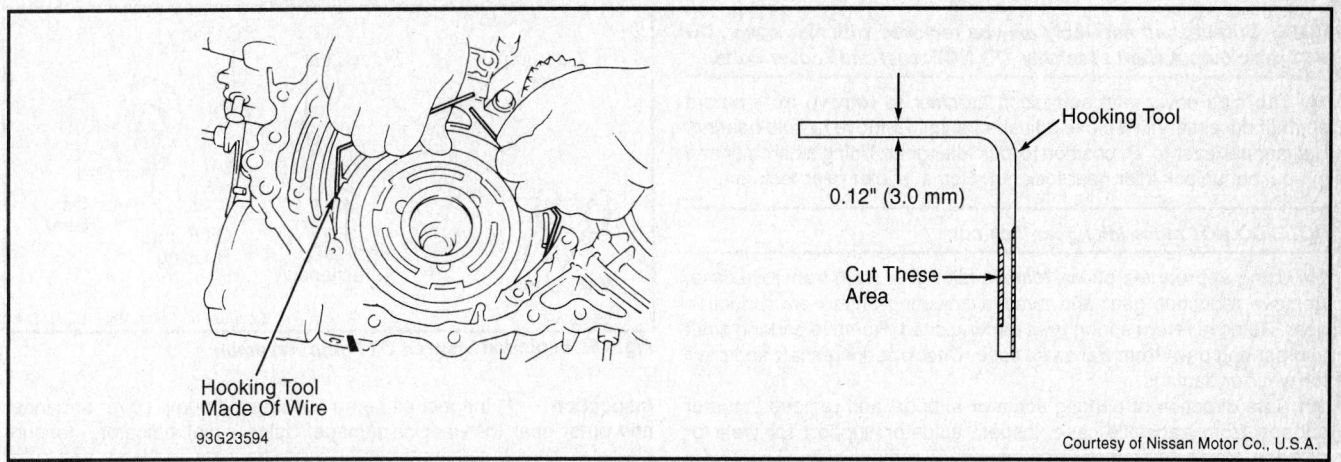

Hooking Tool

0.12" (3.0 mm)

Hooking Tool
Made Of Wire

Cut These
Area

93G23594

Courtesy of Nissan Motor Co., U.S.A.

Fig. 11: Removing Low-One Way Clutch

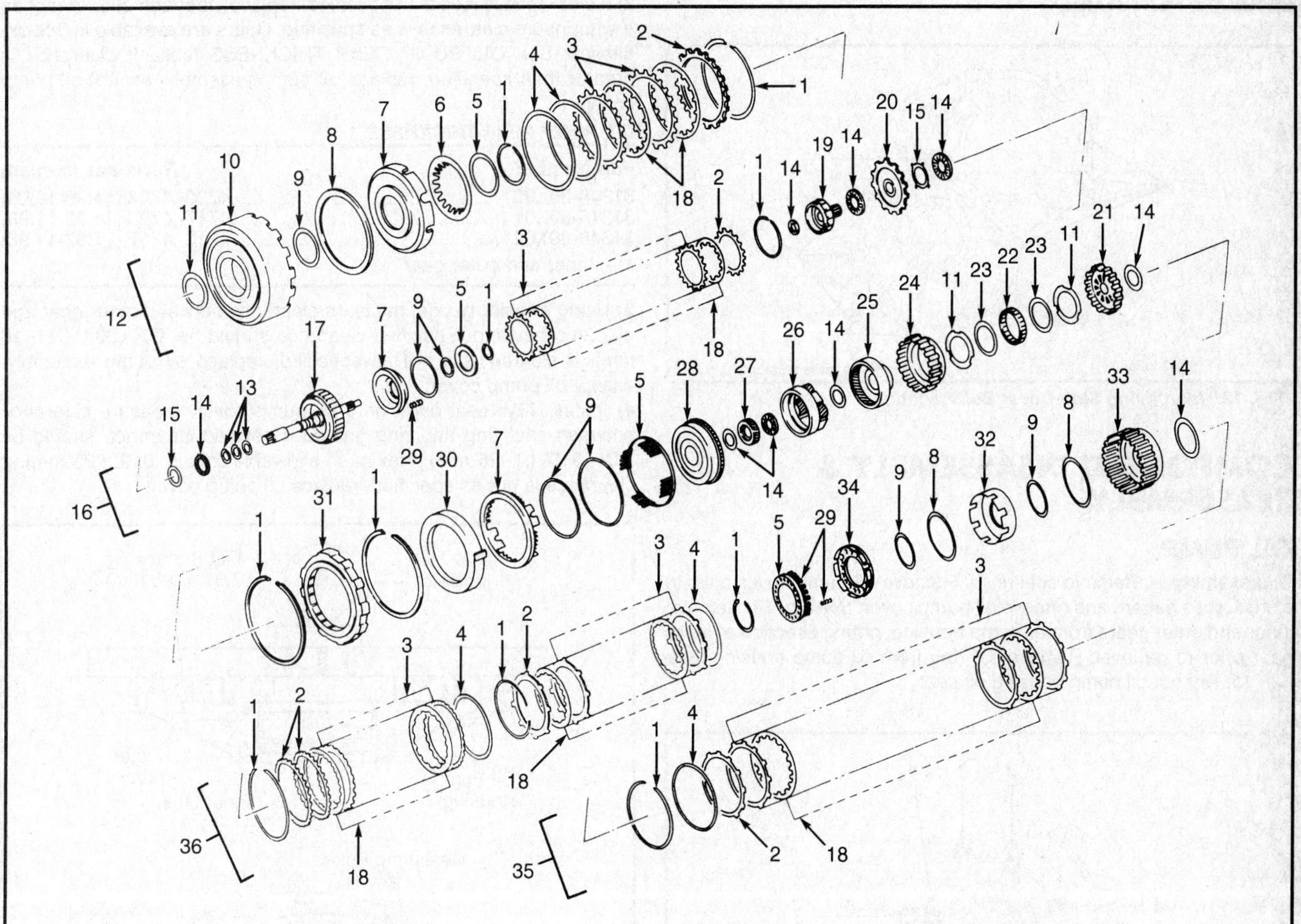

93E23592

Courtesy of Nissan Motor Co., U.S.A.

1. Snap Ring
2. Retaining Plate
3. Driven Plate
4. Dish Plate
5. Spring Retainer
6. Retainer Spring
7. Piston
8. Oil Seal
9. "D" Ring
10. Reverse Clutch Drum
11. Thrust Washer
12. Reverse Clutch Assembly
13. Seal Ring
14. Needle Bearing
15. Bearing Race
16. High Clutch Assembly
17. High Clutch Drum
18. Drive Plate
19. High Clutch Hub
20. Front Sun Gear
21. Overrun Clutch Hub
22. Forward One-Way Clutch
23. End Bearing
24. Forward Clutch Hub
25. Rear Internal Gear
26. Rear Planetary Carrier
27. Rear Sun Gear
28. Front Planetary Carrier
29. Return Spring
30. Retainer
31. Low One-Way Clutch
32. Forward Clutch Piston
33. Forward Clutch Drum
34. Overrun Clutch Piston
35. Low & Reverse Brake Assembly
36. Forward & Overrun Clutch Assembly

Fig. 12: Exploded View Of Forward Clutch, High Clutch, Low-Reverse Brake, Overrun Clutch & Reverse Clutch Assemblies

NOTE: *Output shaft assembly may be removed with side cover. DO NOT drop output shaft assembly. DO NOT reuse side cover bolts.*

14) Tap side cover with soft-faced hammer to remove from output shaft (if necessary). Remove adjusting shim. Remove needle bearing. Set manual lever to "P" position to lock idler gear. Using a hammer and pin punch, unlock idler gear lock nut. Remove idler gear lock nut.

NOTE: *DO NOT reuse idler gear lock nut.*

15) Using appropriate puller, remove idler gear from transaxle case. Remove reduction gear and remove adjusting shim from reduction gear. Remove return spring from parking shaft. Remove parking shaft and parking pawl from transaxle case. Check parking shaft and pawl for wear or damage.

16) Note direction of parking actuator support and remove actuator support from transaxle case. Inspect actuator support for wear or damage. Using a hammer and screwdriver, remove side oil seal from transaxle case. Remove manual shaft components from transaxle case. See MANUAL SHAFT ASSEMBLY under COMPONENT DISASSEMBLY & REASSEMBLY.

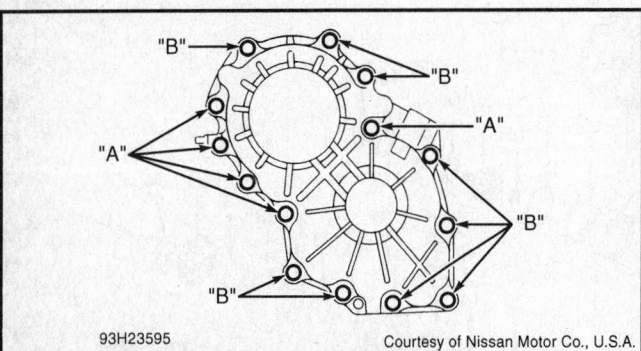

Fig. 13: Identifying Side Cover Bolt Locations

COMPONENT DISASSEMBLY & REASSEMBLY

OIL PUMP

Disassembly – Remove seal rings. Remove oil pump cover bolts in a crisscross pattern and remove oil pump cover. *See Fig. 14.* Remove inner and outer gears from oil pump housing, noting direction of inner gear prior to removal. Remove "O" ring from oil pump housing. *See Fig. 15.* Pry out oil pump housing oil seal.

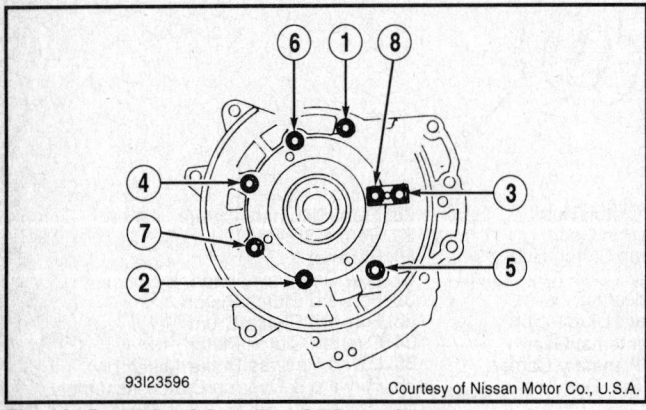

Fig. 14: Removing & Installing Oil Pump Cover

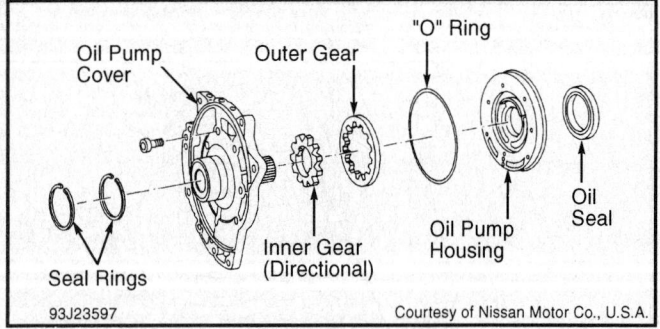

Fig. 15: Exploded View Of Oil Pump Assembly

Inspection – **1)** Inspect oil pump housing, oil pump cover and inner and outer gear for wear or damage. Using a dial indicator, measure side clearance between end of oil pump housing and inner and outer gears in at least 4 places along their circumferences. Specified clearance should be .001-.002" (.03-.05 mm). *See Fig. 16.*

2) If clearance is less then specified, replace inner and outer gears as a set. Ensure clearance is as specified. Gears are available in 3 thicknesses. See OIL PUMP GEAR THICKNESS table. If clearance is greater than specified, replace oil pump assembly, except oil pump cover.

OIL PUMP GEAR THICKNESS [1]

Part Number	Thickness In. (mm)
31346-80X00	.4720-.4724 (11.99-12.00)
31346-80X01	.4717-.4720 (11.98-11.99)
31346-80X02	.4713-.4717 (11.97-11.98)

[1] – Inner and outer gear

3) Using a feeler gauge, measure clearance between outer gear and oil pump housing. Specified clearance should be .004-.007" (.11-.18 mm). If clearance is not as specified, replace oil pump assembly, except oil pump cover.

4) Install NEW seal rings onto oil pump cover. Measure clearance between seal ring and ring groove. Specified clearance should be .004-.010" (.1-.25 mm). Maximum allowable limit is .010" (.25 mm). If clearance is not as specified, replace oil pump cover.

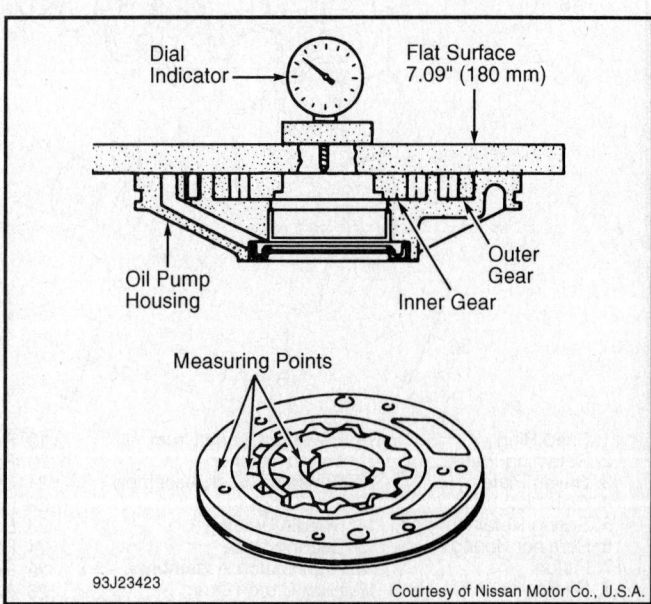

Fig. 16: Measuring Oil Pump Side Clearance

Reassembly – 1) Using appropriate adapter, install NEW oil seal on oil pump housing. Apply ATF to NEW "O" ring and install "O" ring on oil pump housing. Install inner and outer gears on oil pump housing. Ensure inner gear is installed in same direction as removed.

2) Wrap oil pump splines with masking tape to protect oil seal. Position oil pump cover on oil pump housing, then remove masking tape. Tighten bolts in a crisscross pattern to 62-97 INCH lbs. (7-11 N.m). *See Fig. 14.*

3) Pack ring groove with petroleum jelly, then carefully install NEW seal rings (if necessary). Connect seal ring hooks. DO NOT spread gap of seal ring excessively while installing as ring may become deformed.

CONTROL VALVE ASSEMBLY

Disassembly – 1) Disassemble upper, inter and lower valve bodies. *See Fig. 17.* Note bolt length, number of bolts and location. See VALVE BODY BOLT IDENTIFICATION table.

VALVE BODY BOLT IDENTIFICATION [1]

Identification	Length – In. (mm)	No. Of Bolts
A	.531 (13.50)	6
B	2.283 (58.00)	3
C	1.575 (40.00)	6
D	2.598 (66.00)	11
E	1.299 (33.00)	2
F	3.071 (78.00)	2

[1] – See Fig. 18 for bolt location.

2) Remove bolts "A", "D" and nut "F", and remove oil strainer from control valve assembly. Remove solenoid assembly and line pressure solenoid from control valve assembly. Remove "O" rings from solenoids and harness terminal body. Place upper valve body face down. Remove bolts "B", "C" and "F".

3) Remove inter valve body from lower valve body. Turn lower valve body over and remove accumulator support plate. Remove bolts "E", separating plate and separating gasket from lower valve body. *See Fig. 17.* Remove check balls and relief valve springs from lower valve body. DO NOT lose check balls or relief valve springs.

4) Remove inter valve body with separating plate and separating gasket from upper valve body. Ensure steel balls are properly positioned in upper and inter valve bodies, then remove balls from valve bodies. DO NOT lose steel balls.

Inspection – Ensure retainer plates are properly positioned in lower and upper valve bodies. *See Fig. 19.* DO NOT lose retainer plates. Check oil strainer for damage. Inspect shift solenoids "A" and "B", line pressure solenoid, lock-up solenoid and overrun clutch solenoid. Check oil cooler relief valve springs for damage or deformation. Measure spring free length and outer diameter. Free length should be .670" (17.02 mm), and diameter should be .315" (8.00 mm). Replace springs if not as specified.

Reassembly – 1) Place oil circuit of upper valve body face up. Install steel balls in proper positions. *See Fig. 20.* Install upper separating plate gasket, upper inter separating plate gasket and upper separating plate. Install reamer bolts "F" from bottom of upper valve body. Install separating gaskets and separating plates as a set on upper valve body, using reamer bolts as a guide.

2) Install pilot filter. Place lower valve body with inter valve body side face up. Install steel balls in proper positions. *See Fig. 20.* Install inter valve body on upper valve body, using reamer bolts "F" as a guide. DO NOT lose steel balls. Install check balls and relief valve springs in proper positions in lower valve body. Install lower separating plate gasket, inter separating plate gasket and lower separating plate. *See Fig. 17.*

3) Install support plate bolts "E" from bottom of lower valve body. Install separating plate gaskets and separating plate as a set on lower valve body using bolts "E" as a guide. Temporarily install support plates on lower valve body. Install lower valve body on inter valve body using reamer bolts "F" as a guide. *See Fig. 18.* Tighten bolts snug.

4) Install "O" rings on solenoids and harness terminal connector. Apply ATF to "O" rings prior to installation. Install and snug bolts "B". Install solenoid assembly and line pressure solenoid to lower valve body. Install oil strainer. Tighten all bolts to 62-80 INCH lbs. (7-9 N.m).

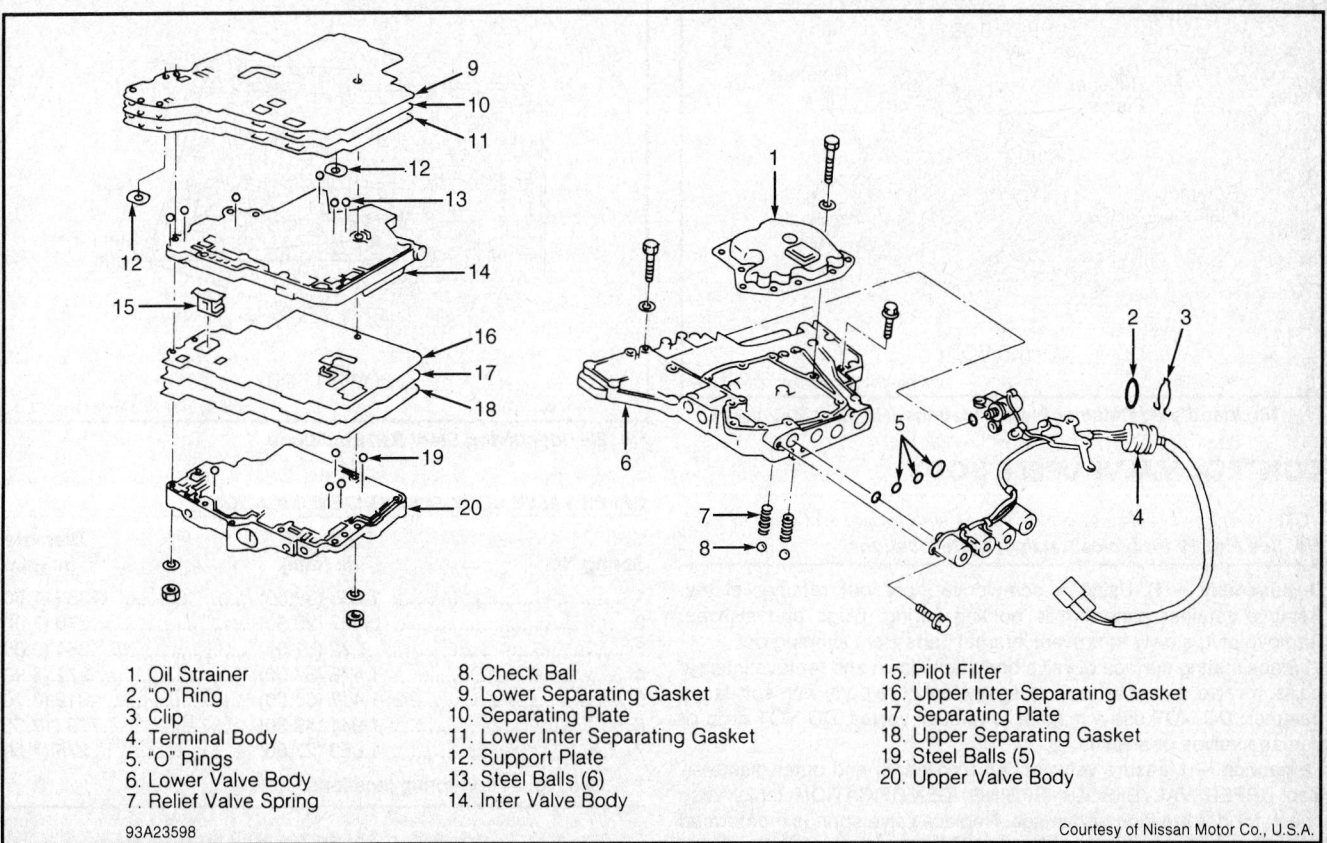

1. Oil Strainer	8. Check Ball	15. Pilot Filter
2. "O" Ring	9. Lower Separating Gasket	16. Upper Inter Separating Gasket
3. Clip	10. Separating Plate	17. Separating Plate
4. Terminal Body	11. Lower Inter Separating Gasket	18. Upper Separating Gasket
5. "O" Rings	12. Support Plate	19. Steel Balls (5)
6. Lower Valve Body	13. Steel Balls (6)	20. Upper Valve Body
7. Relief Valve Spring	14. Inter Valve Body	

93A23598   Courtesy of Nissan Motor Co., U.S.A.

Fig. 17: Exploded View Of Control Valve Assembly

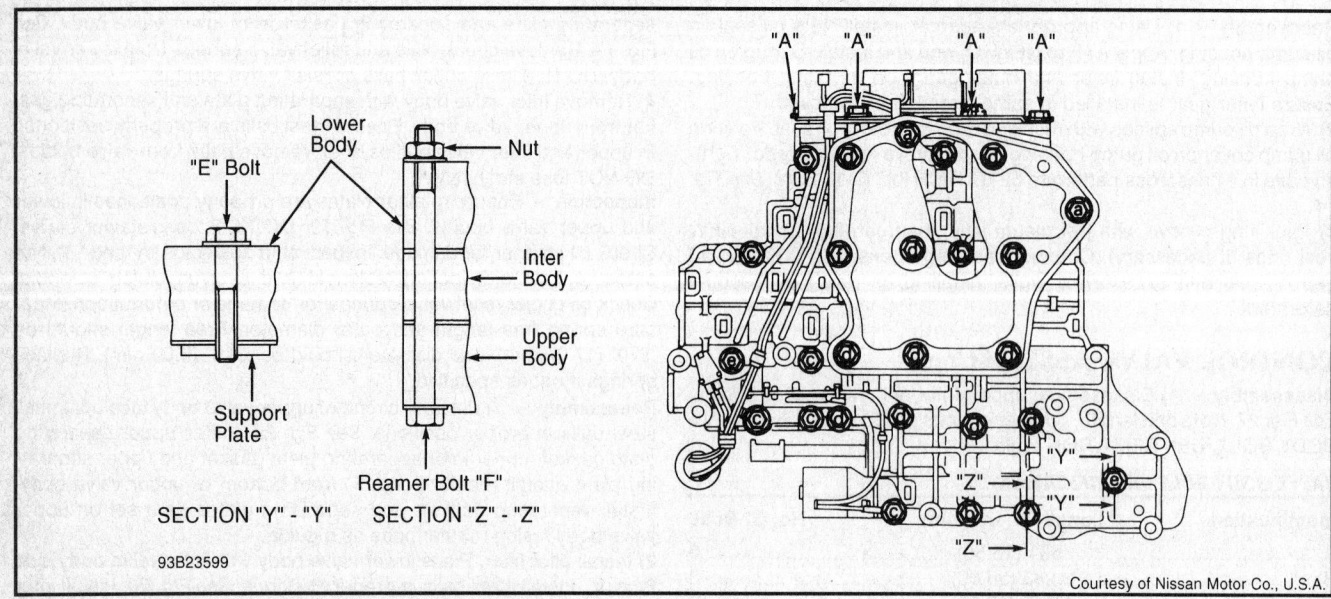

Fig. 18: Identifying Control Valve Assembly Bolt Locations

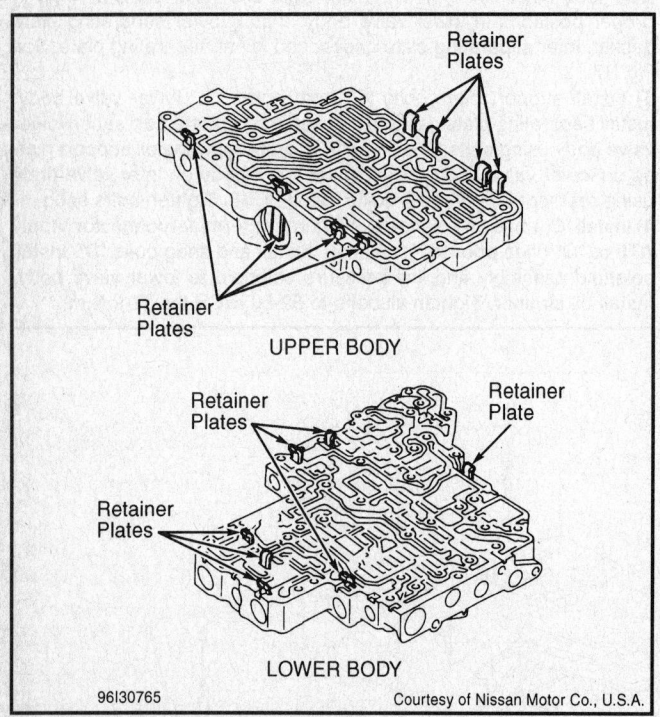

Fig. 19: Identifying Retainer Plate Locations (Number May Vary)

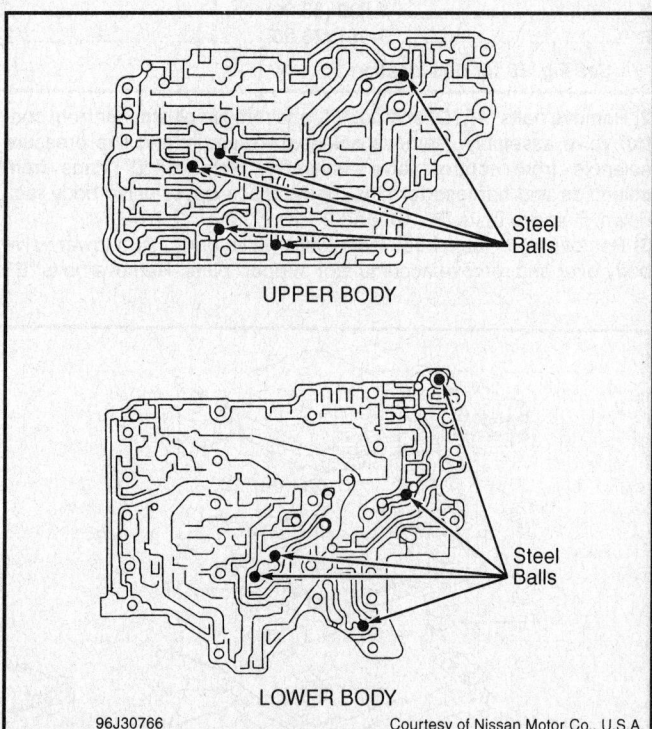

Fig. 20: Identifying Steel Ball Locations

CONTROL VALVE UPPER BODY

NOTE: Number of retainer plates varies with model and year of vehicle. See Fig. 19 for typical retainer plate locations.

Disassembly – 1) Using a screwdriver, pry out retainer plates. Remove retainer plates while holding spring, plugs and sleeves. Remove plug slowly to prevent internal parts from jumping out.

2) Place mating surface of valve body face down and remove internal parts. If valve is hard to remove, lightly tap valve body with soft-faced hammer. DO NOT use a magnet to remove valves. DO NOT drop or damage valves or sleeves.

Inspection – Measure valve spring free length and outer diameter. See UPPER VALVE BODY SPRING IDENTIFICATION table. Also check for deformation or damage. Replace valve springs if deformed or fatigued. Check sliding surfaces of valves, sleeves and plugs.

UPPER VALVE BODY SPRING IDENTIFICATION [1]

Spring No.	Length In. (mm)	Diameter In. (mm)
1	1.555 (39.50)	.433 (11.00)
2	0.807 (20.50)	.276 (7.00)
3	1.22 (31.0)	.354 (9.00)
4	1.476 (37.50)	.272 (6.90)
5	1.417 (36.00)	.319 (8.10)
6	1.941 (49.30)	.772 (19.60)
7	1.063 (27.00)	.276 (7.00)

[1] – See Fig. 21 for spring locations.

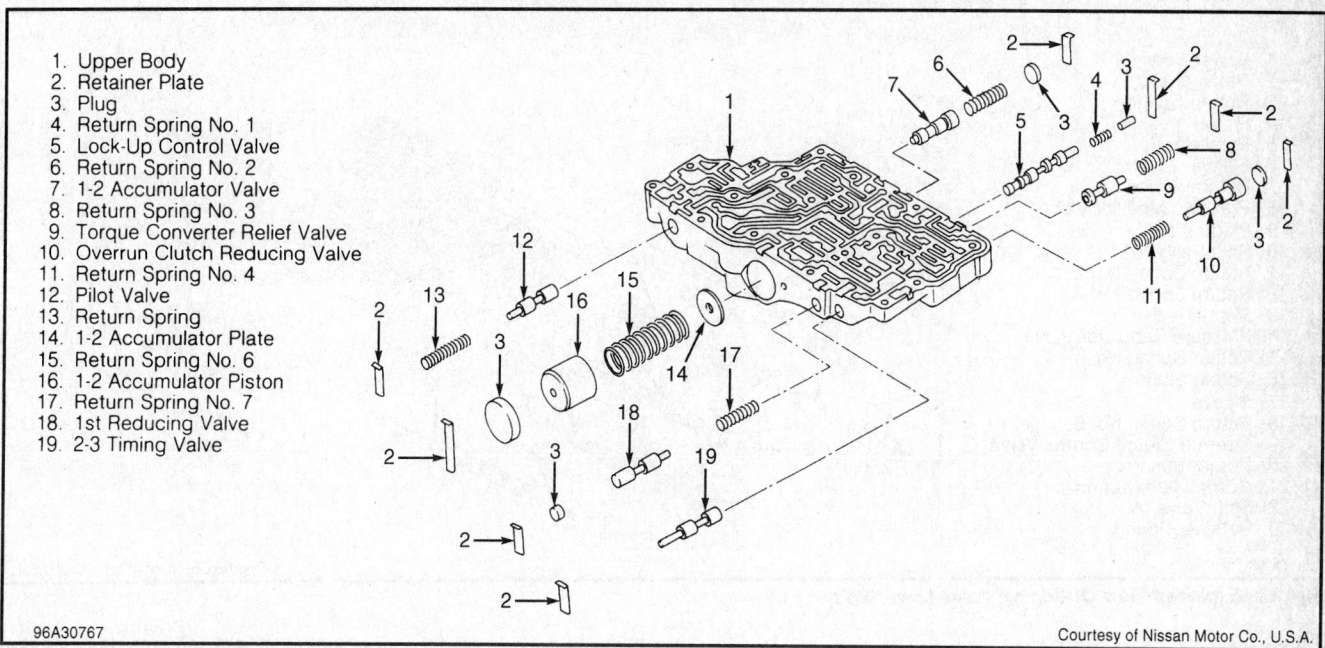

1. Upper Body
2. Retainer Plate
3. Plug
4. Return Spring No. 1
5. Lock-Up Control Valve
6. Return Spring No. 2
7. 1-2 Accumulator Valve
8. Return Spring No. 3
9. Torque Converter Relief Valve
10. Overrun Clutch Reducing Valve
11. Return Spring No. 4
12. Pilot Valve
13. Return Spring
14. 1-2 Accumulator Plate
15. Return Spring No. 6
16. 1-2 Accumulator Piston
17. Return Spring No. 7
18. 1st Reducing Valve
19. 2-3 Timing Valve

96A30767

Courtesy of Nissan Motor Co., U.S.A.

Fig. 21: Exploded View Of Control Valve Upper Body

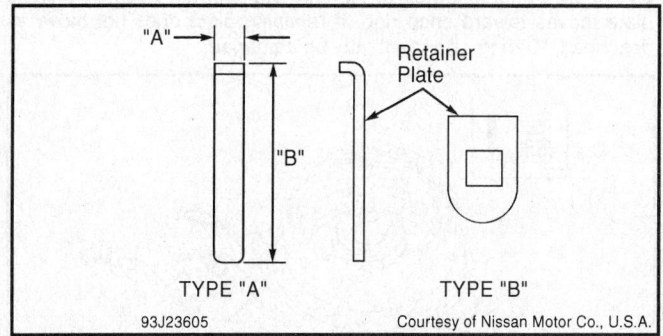

93J23605   Courtesy of Nissan Motor Co., U.S.A.

Fig. 22: Measuring Retainer Plate Dimensions

Reassembly – 1) Lay control valve body face down when installing valves. DO NOT stand valve body on edge. Lubricate valves and control valve body with ATF prior to installation. Install control valves by sliding valves into appropriate bores. DO NOT scratch or damage valve body. Wrap shaft of small screwdriver with vinyl tape and insert valves into their bores using screwdriver as necessary.

2) Install 1-2 accumulator valve, then align 1-2 accumulator retainer plate with 1-2 accumulator valve from opposite side of control valve body. Install return spring, 1-2 accumulator piston and plug. See Fig. 21. While pushing plug or return spring, install retainer plates. See RETAINER PLATE IDENTIFICATION table for retainer plate dimensions.

RETAINER PLATE IDENTIFICATION [1]

Application	[2] Length "B" In. (mm)
Lock-Up Control	1.102 (28.00)
Torque Converter Relief, Pilot, 1st Reducing	.846 (21.50)
1-2 Accumulator & Piston Valves, 1-2 Accumulator valve	1.516 (38.50)
Overrun Clutch Reducing Valve	.945 (24.00)

[1] – See Fig. 19 for retainer plate locations.
[2] – Length "A" for all valves is .236" (6.0 mm). All valves use type "A" retainer plate. See Fig. 22.

CONTROL VALVE LOWER BODY

NOTE: Number of retainer plates varies with model and year of vehicle. See Fig. 19 for typical retainer plate locations.

Disassembly – Using a screwdriver, pry out retainer plates. Remove retainer plates while holding spring, plugs and sleeves. Remove plug slowly to prevent internal parts from jumping out. Place mating surface of valve body face down and remove internal parts. If valve is hard to remove, lightly tap body with soft-faced hammer. DO NOT use a magnet to remove valves. DO NOT drop or damage valves or sleeves.

Inspection – Measure valve spring free length and outer diameter. See LOWER VALVE BODY SPRING IDENTIFICATION table. Also check for deformation or damage. Replace valve springs if deformed or fatigued. Check sliding surfaces of valves, sleeves and plugs.

LOWER VALVE BODY SPRING IDENTIFICATION [1]

Spring No.	Length In. (mm)	Diameter In. (mm)
1	1.201 (30.50)	.386 (9.80)
2	1.26 (32.00)	.272 (6.91)
3, 6 & 8	.854 (21.70)	.276 (7.00)
4	.669 (17.00)	.421 (10.70)
5	1.772 (45.00)	.591 (15.01)
7	.866 (22.00)	.256 (6.50)

[1] – See Fig. 23 for spring locations.

Reassembly – 1) Lay control valve body face down when installing valves. DO NOT stand valve body on edge. Lubricate valves and control valve body with ATF prior to installation. Install control valves by sliding valve into appropriate bore. DO NOT scratch or damage valve body.

2) Wrap shaft of small screwdriver with vinyl tape and insert valves into their bores using screwdriver as necessary. While pushing plug or return spring, install retainer plates. See RETAINER PLATE IDENTIFICATION table for retainer plate dimensions.

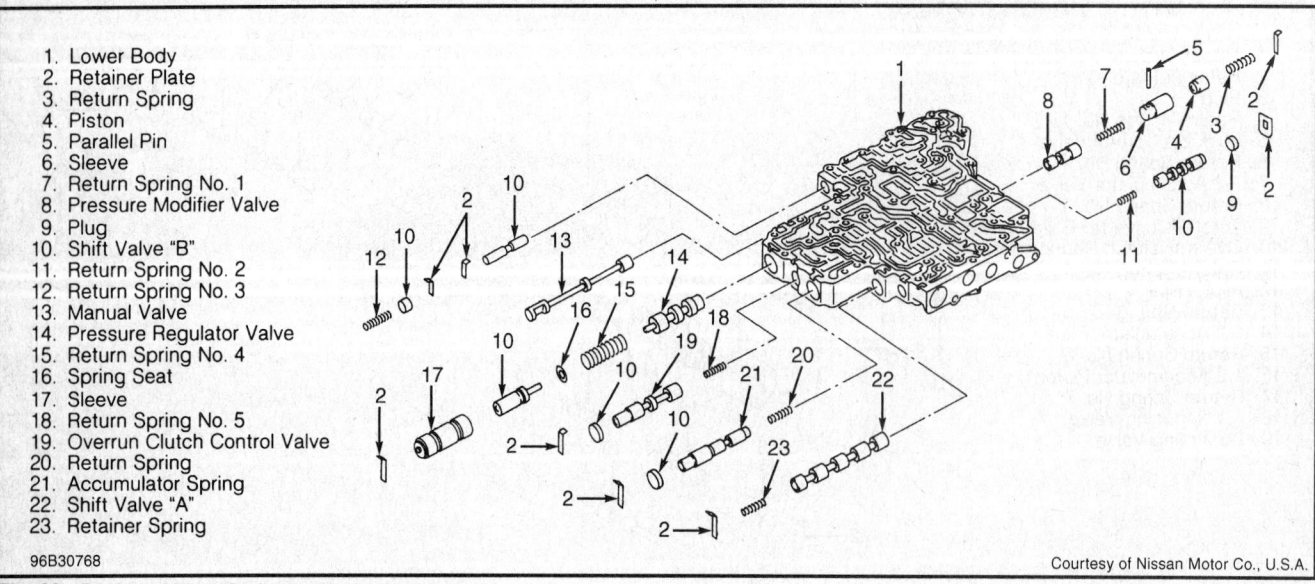

1. Lower Body
2. Retainer Plate
3. Return Spring
4. Piston
5. Parallel Pin
6. Sleeve
7. Return Spring No. 1
8. Pressure Modifier Valve
9. Plug
10. Shift Valve "B"
11. Return Spring No. 2
12. Return Spring No. 3
13. Manual Valve
14. Pressure Regulator Valve
15. Return Spring No. 4
16. Spring Seat
17. Sleeve
18. Return Spring No. 5
19. Overrun Clutch Control Valve
20. Return Spring
21. Accumulator Spring
22. Shift Valve "A"
23. Retainer Spring

96B30768   Courtesy of Nissan Motor Co., U.S.A.

Fig. 23: Exploded View Of Control Valve Lower Body

RETAINER PLATE IDENTIFICATION [1]

Application	Length [1] "B" In. (mm)
Plug	.768 (19.50)
All Other Valves [2]	1.102 (28.00)

[1] – See Fig. 19 for retainer plate locations.
[2] – Shift Valve "B" not applicable. All valves use type "A" retainer plate except shift valve "B" (Type "B"). See Fig. 22.

REVERSE CLUTCH

Disassembly – Remove snap ring from reverse clutch assembly. Remove drive plates, driven plates, retaining plate, and dish plates. See Fig. 12. Record number of plates for reassembly reference. Remove snap ring from reverse clutch drum while compressing springs. Remove spring retainer and return spring. Remove piston from reverse clutch drum by turning piston clockwise. Remove "D" ring and oil seal from piston.

Inspection – Check dish plate and return springs for deformation, fatigue or damage. Inspect drive plate facing for burns, cracks or damage. Dish plate thickness should be .121" (3.08 mm). On all models, drive plate thickness should be .063" (1.60 mm), with allowable limit of .055" (1.40 mm). On all models, if drive plate thickness is not as specified, replace drive plate. Ensure check balls in reverse clutch piston are not seized.

Reassembly – **1)** Prior to installation, apply ATF to "D" ring, oil seal and inner surface of drum. Install "D" ring and oil seal on piston. Install piston assembly in clutch drum while slowly turning clockwise. Install return spring and spring retainer on piston. Compress springs and install snap ring. Install drive plates, driven plates, retaining plate, dish plates and snap ring.

2) Measure clearance between retaining plate and snap ring. Specified clearance is .020-.031" (.50-.80 mm), with allowable limit of .047" (1.20 mm). Retaining plate is available in .008" (.20 mm) increments. See REVERSE CLUTCH RETAINING PLATE THICKNESS table.

REVERSE CLUTCH RETAINING PLATE THICKNESS

Part No.	Thickness In. (mm)
31537-80X05	.260 (6.60)
31537-80X06	.268 (6.80)
31537-80X07	.276 (7.01)
31537-80X08	.283 (7.20)
31537-80X09	.291 (7.40)
31537-80X20	.299 (7.60)
31537-80X21	.307 (7.80)

3) Check reverse clutch operation. Install seal ring onto drum support of oil pump cover. Install reverse clutch assembly on oil pump assembly. Apply compressed air to oil hole. See Fig. 24. Ensure retaining plate moves toward snap ring. If retaining plate does not move as described, "D" ring or oil seal may be damaged.

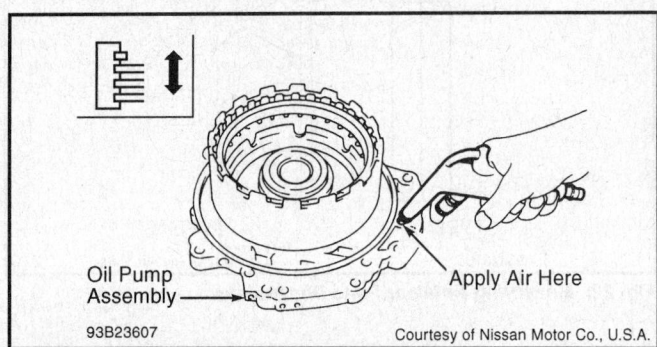

Oil Pump Assembly   Apply Air Here

93B23607   Courtesy of Nissan Motor Co., U.S.A.

Fig. 24: Checking Reverse Clutch Operation

HIGH CLUTCH

Disassembly & Inspection – **1)** Remove seal rings from input shaft. Service procedures for high clutch are same as for reverse clutch. Drive plate thickness should be .063" (1.60 mm), with allowable limit of .055" (1.40 mm).

2) Measure clearance between retaining plate and snap ring. Specified clearance is .071-.087" (1.80-2.20 mm), with allowable limit of .12" (3.0 mm).

3) Retaining plate is available in .008" (.20 mm) increments. See HIGH CLUTCH RETAINING PLATE THICKNESS table. Ensure check balls in high clutch piston are not seized.

HIGH CLUTCH RETAINING PLATE THICKNESS

Part No.	Thickness In. (mm)
31537-80X10	.118 (3.00)
31537-80X11	.126 (3.20)
31537-80X12	.134 (3.40)
31537-80X13	.142 (3.60)
31537-80X14	.150 (3.81)
31537-80X16 [1]	.126 (3.20)
31537-80X17 [1]	.134 (3.40)
31537-80X18 [1]	.142 (3.60)
31537-80X19 [1]	.150 (3.81)
31537-80X20 [1]	.157 (4.00)

[1] – Part numbers for 1995 Altima (RE4F04A)

Reassembly – 1) Always replace spring retainer and return springs as a set (if necessary). Do not align snap ring gap with spring retainer stopper. Install NEW seal rings on input shaft. Measure clearance between seal ring and ring groove. Specified clearance is .003-.009" (.08-.23 mm) with maximum allowable limit of .009". (.23 mm). If clearance is not as specified, replace input shaft. Check high clutch operation.

2) Apply compressed air to oil hole (hole nearest high clutch drum) of input shaft. Plug opposite side of oil hole. Ensure retaining plate moves toward snap ring. If retaining plate does not move as described, "D" ring or oil seal may be damaged. Apply petroleum jelly to seal rings. Tape thick paper around seal rings to prevent rings from spreading.

FORWARD & OVERRUN CLUTCHES

Disassembly – Service procedures for forward clutch and overrun clutch are same as for reverse clutch. See Fig. 12.

Inspection – Check forward clutch and overrun clutch return springs for deformation or damage. Always replace spring retainer and return springs as a set (if necessary). Inspect drive plate facing for burns, cracks or damage. Ensure check balls in forward clutch and overrun clutch pistons are not seized.

Reassembly – 1) Reassembly procedures for forward and overrun clutches are same as for reverse clutch. Dish plate thickness for forward and overrun clutch should be .106" (2.70 mm). Drive plate thickness for forward and overrun clutch should be .063" (1.60 mm), with allowable limit of .055" (1.40 mm).

2) Lubricate "D" rings and oil seals with ATF, and install on forward and overrun clutch pistons. Ensure "D" rings and oil seals are installed in correct direction. See Fig. 25. Align triangle mark on spring retainer with check ball in overrun clutch piston. Do not align snap ring gap with spring retainer stopper.

3) Measure clearance between retaining plate and snap ring. Specified clearance for forward clutch is .018-.033" (.45-.85 mm), with allowable limit of .073" (1.85 mm).

4) Forward clutch retaining plate is available in .008" (.20 mm) increments. See FORWARD CLUTCH RETAINING PLATE THICKNESS table. Overrun clutch retaining plate is available in .008" (.20 mm) increments. See OVERRUN CLUTCH RETAINING PLATE THICKNESS table.

5) Check forward and overrun clutch operation. Install bearing retainer on forward clutch drum. Apply compressed air to appropriate oil hole of forward clutch drum. See Fig. 26. Ensure retaining plate moves toward snap ring. If retaining plate does not move as described, "D" ring or oil seal may be damaged.

FORWARD CLUTCH RETAINING PLATE THICKNESS

Part No.	Thickness In. (mm)
31537-80X70	.142 (3.60)
31537-80X71	.150 (3.81)
31537-80X72	.157 (4.00)
31537-80X73	.165 (4.20)
31537-80X74	.173 (4.40)
31537-80X75	.134 (3.40)
31537-80X76	.126 (3.20)

OVERRUN CLUTCH RETAINING PLATE THICKNESS

Part No.	Thickness In. (mm)
31537-80X65 (60) [1]	.118 (3.00)
31537-80X66 (61) [1]	.126 (3.20)
31537-80X67 (62) [1]	.134 (3.40)
31537-80X68 (63) [1]	.142 (3.60)
31537-80X69 (64) [1]	.150 (3.81)

[1] – 1995 Part Numbers

LOW & REVERSE BRAKE

Disassembly – Position transaxle case to obtain access to low and reverse brake snap ring. Remove snap ring. Remove dish plate, retaining plate, drive plates and driven plates from transaxle case. See Fig. 12. Record number of plates for reassembly reference. Apply compressed air to oil hole of piston retainer to remove piston. Remove "D" rings from piston.

Inspection – Check low and reverse brake snap ring, springs and retainer for deformation or damage. Always replace spring retainer and return springs as a set (if necessary). Check low and reverse drive plates for burns, cracks or damage.

Reassembly – 1) Reassembly procedures for low and reverse brake are same as for reverse clutch. Drive plate thickness should be .071" (1.80 mm), with allowable minimum limit of .063" (1.60 mm). Specified clearance is .067-.083" (1.70-2.10 mm), with allowable minimum limit of .138" (3.50 mm). Retaining plate is available in increments of .008" (.20 mm). See LOW & REVERSE BRAKE RETAINING PLATE THICKNESS table.

2) Lubricate "D" rings with ATF, and install on low-reverse brake piston. Ensure "D" rings are installed in correct direction. See Fig. 27. Ensure piston bracket is aligned with retainer bracket. See Fig. 28. Check low and reverse brake operation. Apply compressed air to oil hole in transaxle case. See Fig. 10.

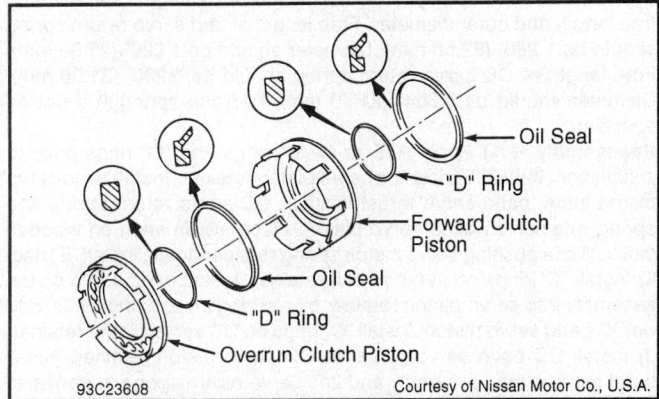

93C23608   Courtesy of Nissan Motor Co., U.S.A.

Fig. 25: Installing Forward & Overrun Clutch "D" Rings & Oil Seals

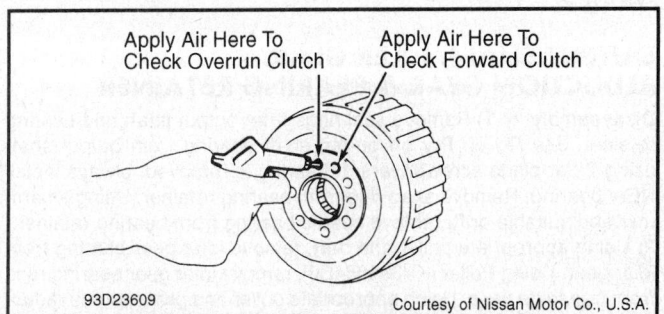

93D23609   Courtesy of Nissan Motor Co., U.S.A.

Fig. 26: Checking Forward & Overrun Clutch Operation

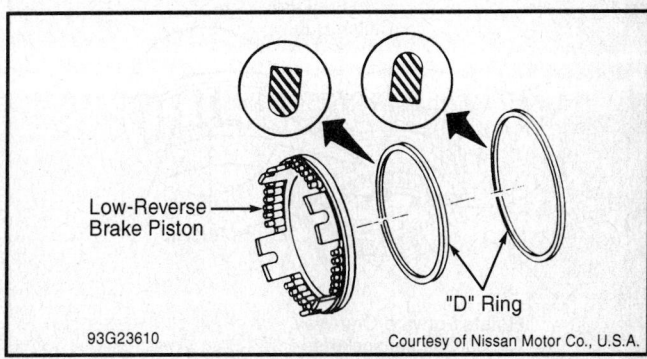

93G23610   Courtesy of Nissan Motor Co., U.S.A.

Fig. 27: Installing Low-Reverse Brake "D" Rings

LOW & REVERSE RETAINING PLATE THICKNESS

Part No.	Thickness In. (mm)
31667-80X00	.079 (2.00)
31667-80X01	.087 (2.21)
31667-80X02	.094 (2.40)
31667-80X03	.102 (2.60)
31667-80X04	.110 (2.80)
31667-80X05	.118 (3.00)
31667-80X06	.126 (3.20)
31667-80X07	.134 (3.40)
31667-80X09	.354 (9.00)

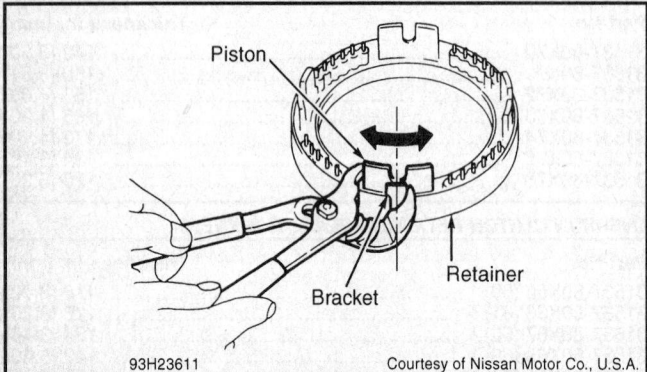

93H23611   Courtesy of Nissan Motor Co., U.S.A.

Fig. 28: Aligning Brake Piston With Spring Retainer

REAR INTERNAL GEAR, FORWARD CLUTCH HUB & OVERRUN CLUTCH HUB

Disassembly – Remove overrun clutch hub and thrust washer from forward clutch hub. See Fig. 12. Remove forward clutch hub from rear internal gear. Remove end bearing from rear internal gear. Remove thrust washer from rear internal gear. Remove end bearing from forward one-way clutch. Remove forward one-way clutch from forward clutch hub.

Inspection – Check rear internal gear, forward clutch hub and overrun clutch hub frictional surfaces for wear or damage. Check forward one-way clutch and end bearings for wear or damage.

Reassembly – 1) Install forward one-way clutch on forward clutch hub. See Fig. 29. Apply petroleum jelly to end bearings and thrust washers. Install end bearing on forward one-way clutch with smooth side up.

2) Install thrust washer on rear internal gear. Install end bearing on rear internal gear with smooth side down. Install forward clutch hub on rear internal gear. Ensure forward clutch hub rotates counterclockwise only.

3) Install thrust washer on overrun clutch hub. Align pawls of thrust washer with holes in overrun clutch hub. Install overrun clutch hub on rear internal gear. Align projections of rear internal gear with holes in overrun clutch hub.

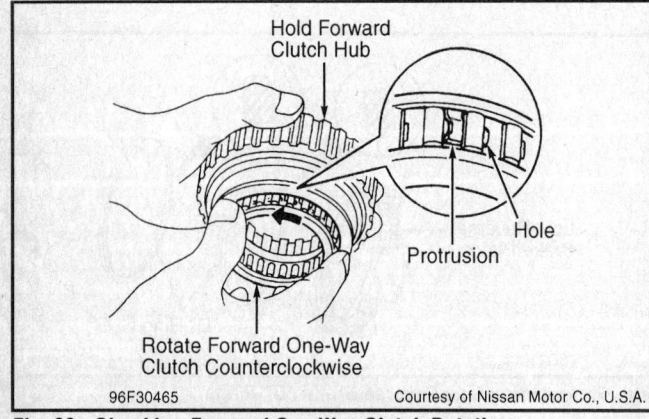

96F30465   Courtesy of Nissan Motor Co., U.S.A.

Fig. 29: Checking Forward One-Way Clutch Rotation

BAND SERVO PISTON ASSEMBLY

Disassembly – 1) Use appropriate puller to compress servo piston (if necessary). Remove band servo piston retainer bolts. Apply compressed air to oil hole in transaxle case to remove OD servo piston retainer and band servo piston assembly. See Fig. 30.

2) Apply compressed air to oil hole in servo piston retainer to remove OD band servo piston from retainer. Secure OD band servo piston while applying compressed air. Remove "D" ring from OD band servo piston. Remove "E" ring, cushion servo return spring and spring retainer from OD band servo piston. On all models, remove "O" rings from OD servo piston retainer. See Fig. 8.

3) Remove band servo piston assembly from servo piston retainer by pushing forward. Place piston stem end on wooden block. While pushing servo piston spring retainer down, remove "E" ring. Remove OD servo return spring, band servo thrust washer and band servo piston stem from band servo piston. Remove "O" rings from servo piston retainer. Remove "D" rings from band servo piston.

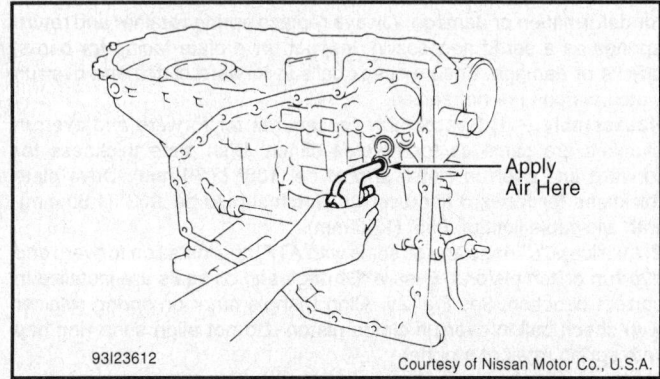

93I23612   Courtesy of Nissan Motor Co., U.S.A.

Fig. 30: Removing OD Piston Retainer & Band Servo Piston

Inspection – Check frictional surfaces for abnormal wear or damage. Check return springs for deformation or damage. Check spring free length and outer diameter. Free length of 2nd servo return spring should be 1.280" (32.50 mm). Diameter should be 1.020" (25.90 mm). Free length of OD servo return spring should be 1.220" (31.00 mm). Diameter should be 0.854" (21.70 mm). Replace spring(s) if not as specified.

Reassembly – 1) Apply ATF to all "D" rings and "O" rings prior to installation. Install "D" rings on servo piston retainer. Install band servo piston stem, band servo thrust washer, OD servo return spring and spring retainer on band servo piston. Place piston stem on wooden block. While pushing servo piston spring retainer down, install "E" ring.

2) Install "O" rings on servo piston retainer. Install band servo piston assembly into servo piston retainer by pushing inward. Install "D" ring on OD band servo piston. Install "O" rings on OD servo piston retainer.

3) Install OD band servo piston to OD servo piston retainer. Install band servo piston assembly and 2nd servo return spring in transaxle case. Install OD band servo piston assembly in transaxle case. Install band servo piston retainer and snap ring or bolts on transaxle case. See Fig. 8.

OUTPUT SHAFT, IDLER GEAR, REDUCTION GEAR & BEARING RETAINER

Disassembly – 1) Remove seal rings from output shaft and bearing retainer. See Fig. 8. Pry off output shaft bearing from output shaft using 2 flat-blade screwdrivers. If bearing is removed, always install NEW bearing. Remove snap ring from bearing retainer. Using a hammer and suitable drift, remove needle bearing from bearing retainer.

2) Using appropriate puller and drift, remove idler gear bearing from idler gear. Using Puller (KV381054S0), remove idler gear bearing race from transaxle case. Using appropriate puller and press, press reduction gear bearing from reduction gear. Remove bearing race bolts and remove reduction gear bearing race from transaxle case. See Fig. 8.

Inspection – 1) Inspect output shaft for cracks, wear or damage. Check all gears for wear, chips and cracks. Ensure bearings roll freely and are free from noise, cracks, pitting or wear. Always replace bearings as a set (if necessary).

2) Install NEW seal rings to output shaft and bearing retainer. Measure clearance between seal ring and ring grooves of output shaft. Specified clearance is .004-.010" (.10-.25 mm). If clearance is not as specified, replace output shaft.

3) Measure clearance between seal ring and ring grooves of bearing retainer. Specified clearance is .004-.012" (.10-.30 mm). If clearance is not as specified, replace bearing retainer.

Reassembly – To reassemble, reverse disassembly procedure. Tighten reduction gear bearing race bolts to 80-90 ft. lbs. (109-123 N.m). Apply petroleum jelly to NEW seal rings installed on output shaft and bearing retainer. Tape thick paper around seal rings to prevent rings from spreading.

MANUAL SHAFT ASSEMBLY

Disassembly & Reassembly – **1)** Remove detent spring from transaxle case. Drive out manual plate retaining pin. Drive and pull out parking rod plate retaining pin. Remove parking rod plate from manual shaft. See Fig. 8. Remove parking rod from transaxle case.

2) Pull out manual shaft retaining pin. Remove manual shaft and manual plate from transaxle case. Remove manual shaft oil seal. Inspect all components for wear or damage. To reassemble, reverse disassembly procedure. Apply ATF to outer surface of oil seal prior to installation. Both ends of manual plate and parking rod plate retaining pins should protrude evenly, .12" (3.0 mm) outside of shaft. Tighten detent spring bolt to 57-66 INCH lbs. (6.4-7.5 N.m).

DIFFERENTIAL ASSEMBLY

Disassembly – Remove ring gear. Using appropriate puller and adapter, remove differential side bearings noting location for reassembly reference. Using appropriate puller and Adapter (KV381054S0), remove differential side bearing race and adjusting shim from transaxle case. Remove speedometer drive gear. Remove viscous coupling (if equipped). Mark differential case halves for reassembly reference. Remove differential case bolts and separate differential case. Remove pinion shaft from differential case. Remove pinion shaft and gears from differential case. See Fig. 9.

Inspection – Check mating surfaces of differential case, gears and pinion shaft for wear, scoring or damage. Check thrust washers for wear or damage. Ensure bearings roll freely and are free from cracks, pitting or wear. Check viscous coupling case for cracks or silicone oil leakage (if equipped). Replace bearings as a set (if necessary).

Reassembly – **1)** Install Gauge Set (J34291) on differential case (speedometer drive gear side) and lock gauging cylinder in place (STEP "A"). See Fig. 31. Install Gauging Plunger (J34290-6) into gauging cylinder. Install pinion and side gears with thrust washers in viscous coupling half of differential case. Install gauge set on case and allow gauging plunger to rest on side gear thrust washer.

2) Using a feeler gauge, measure gap between gauging plunger and gauging cylinder (STEP "B"). See Fig. 31. Specified clearance is .004-.008" (0.1-0.2 mm). If clearance is not as specified, adjust clearance by changing thrust washer thickness. Thrust washers are available in increments of .002" (.05 mm). See DIFFERENTIAL SIDE GEAR THRUST WASHER THICKNESS table.

3) Install Gauge Set (J34291) on differential case side of viscous coupling and lock gauging cylinder in place. Remove gauging cylinder. Install speedometer drive gear side of differential case to viscous coupling side of differential case, matching marks made during disassembly. Tighten case bolts to 27-30 ft. lbs. (36-40 N.m). Install gauge set on viscous coupling side of differential case and allow gauging plunger to rest on thrust washer. See Fig. 31.

4) Using a feeler gauge, measure gap between gauging plunger and gauging cylinder (STEP "C"). See Fig. 31. Measurement should be exact clearance between side gear thrust washer and differential case. Specified clearance is .004-.008" (0.10-0.20 mm).

5) If clearance is not as specified, adjust clearance by changing thrust washer thickness. Thrust washers are available in increments of .008" (.02 mm). See DIFFERENTIAL SIDE GEAR THRUST WASHER THICKNESS table.

DIFFERENTIAL SIDE GEAR THRUST WASHER THICKNESS

Part No.	Thickness In. (mm)
RE4F04A	
38424-81X00	.295 (.75)
38424-81X01	.315 (.80)
38424-81X02	.335 (.85)
38424-81X03	.354 (.90)
38424-81X04	.374 (.95)
RE4F04V	
Viscous Coupling Side	
38424-51E10	.0169-.0177 (.43-.45)
38424-51E11	.0205-.0213 (.52-.54)
38424-51E12	.0240-.0248 (.61-.63)
38424-51E13	.0276-.0283 (.70-.72)
38424-51E14	.0311-.0319 (.70-.81)
Differential Side	
38424-E3000[1]	.0295-.0315 (.75-.80)
38424-E3001[1]	.0315-.0335 (.80-.85)
38424-E3002[1]	.0335-.0354 (.85-.90)
38424-E3003[1]	.0354-.0374 (.90-.95)

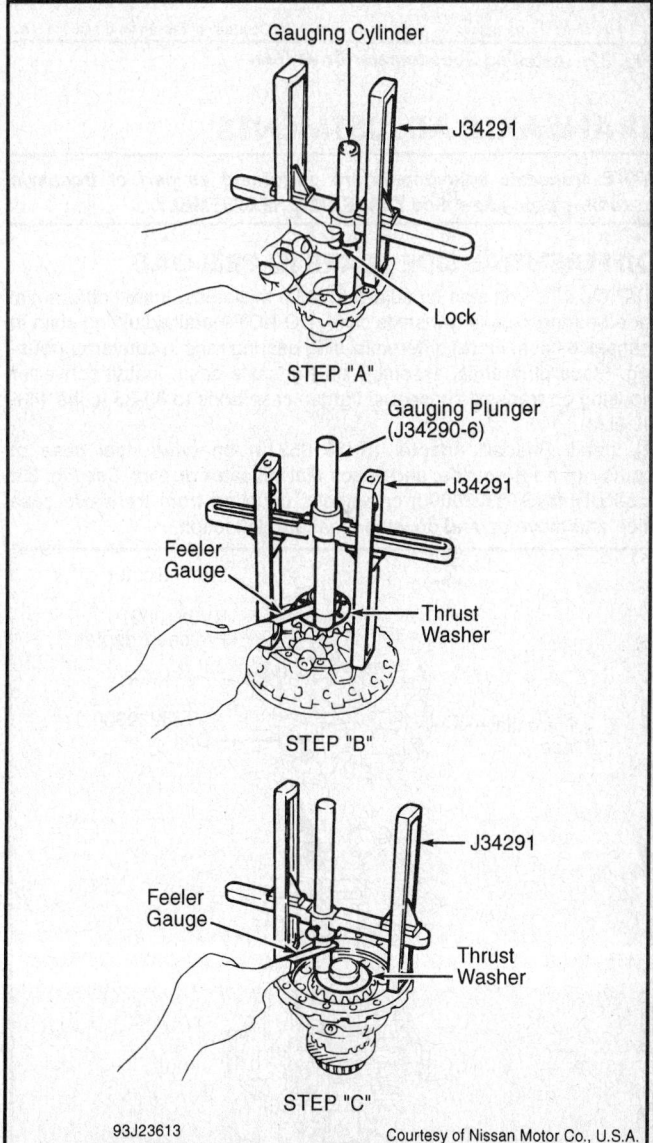

93J23613 Courtesy of Nissan Motor Co., U.S.A.

Fig. 31: Measuring Side Gear-To-Differential Case Clearance (With Viscous Coupling)

6) Install viscous coupling onto differential case (if equipped). Tighten bolts to 33-52 INCH lbs. (3.7-5.9 N.m). Install speedometer drive gear in differential case. Align projections of speedometer drive gear with groove in differential case. *See Fig. 32.* Press differential side bearings on differential case. Install ring gear and tighten bolts in crisscross pattern to 65-76 ft. lbs. (88-103 N.m).

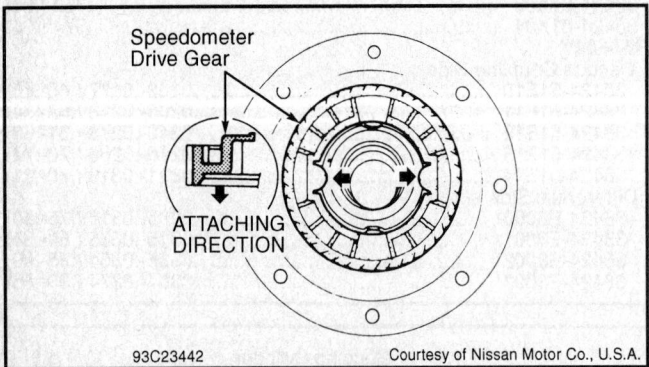

Fig. 32: Installing Speedometer Drive Gear

TRANSAXLE ADJUSTMENTS

NOTE: Transaxle adjustments are performed as part of transaxle assembly procedure. See TRANSAXLE REASSEMBLY.

DIFFERENTIAL SIDE BEARING PRELOAD

1) Preload is adjusted by adjusting shim thickness. Install differential side bearing race in transaxle case. DO NOT install adjusting shim in transaxle case. Install differential side bearing race in converter housing. Place differential assembly on transaxle case. Install converter housing on transaxle case and tighten case bolts to 30-35 ft. lbs. (43-47 N.m).

2) Install Preload Adapter (KV38105210) on differential case at converter housing side, and attach dial indicator on tool. *See Fig. 33.* Insert Drift (ST33220000) on viscous coupling from transaxle case side and move up and down to measure deflection.

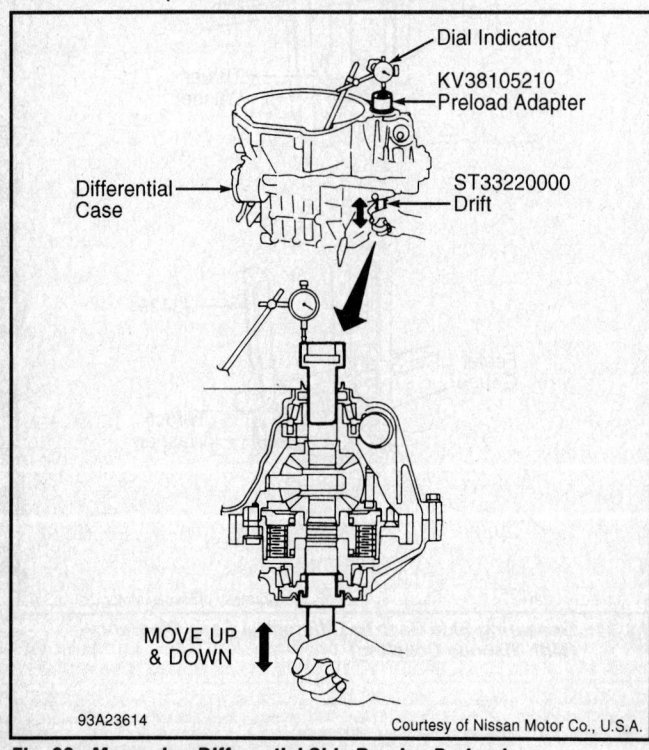

Fig. 33: Measuring Differential Side Bearing Preload

3) Determine shim thickness by adding dial indicator reading to bearing preload specification. Differential side bearing preload dimension should be .002-.003" (.05-.09 mm). Select proper thickness of differential side bearing adjusting shim. Shims are available in thicknesses of .0142-.0362" (.36-.92 mm), in increments of .002" (.04 mm).

4) Remove converter housing from transaxle case. Remove differential assembly from transaxle case. Using Puller (KV381054S0), remove differential side bearing race from transaxle case. Install selected shim and differential side bearing race in transaxle case. Install converter housing on transaxle case and tighten case bolts to 30-35 ft. lbs. (43-47 N.m).

5) Insert Preload Adapter (KV38105210) into viscous coupling. Using a torque wrench, measure turning torque of differential assembly. Turn differential assembly in both directions several times to seat bearings. Turning torque should be 6.9-12.2 INCH lbs. (.78-1.37 N.m). If using original bearings, turning torque will be slightly less then specified. Ensure turning torque is within specified range.

REDUCTION GEAR BEARING PRELOAD

1) Preload is adjusted by adjusting shim thickness between adjusting gear and bearing. Remove converter housing and differential assembly from transaxle case (if necessary). Install reduction gear and idler gear in transaxle case. Using a depth gauge and straightedge, measure distance between end of reduction gear and surface of transaxle case in at least 2 places (Dimension "B"). *See Fig. 34.* Measure distance between surface of idler gear bearing and surface of transaxle case in at least 2 places (Dimension "C").

2) Measure distance between end of reduction gear and adjusting shim mating surface of reduction gear in at least 2 places (Dimension "D"). To determine Dimension "A", use the following equation:

$$A = D - (B + C)$$

"A" = Distance between surface of idler gear bearing inner race and adjusting shim mating surface of reduction pinion gear. *See Fig. 34 for example.*

3) Measure distance between end of idler gear and idler gear bearing mating surface of idler gear in at least 2 places (Dimension "E"). Reduction gear bearing preload should be .002" (.05 mm).

4) Select proper thickness of reduction gear bearing adjusting shim by using the following equation:

$$\text{Proper shim thickness} = A - E - .0020" (.5 \text{ mm})^*$$

*(.0020" (.5 mm) equals bearing preload)

Shims are available in thicknesses of .2008-.2598" (5.10-6.60 mm), in increments of .0008" (.02 mm).

5) Install reduction gear and selected adjusting shim. Press idler gear bearing on idler gear. Press idler gear on reduction gear, ensuring idler gear fully contacts adjusting shim. Lock idler gear with parking pawl and tighten idler gear lock nut to 217-239 ft. lbs (294-324 N.m).

6) Turn reduction gear in both directions several times to seat bearings. Using a torque wrench and appropriate socket, measure reduction gear turning torque. Turning torque should be .44-3.45 INCH lbs. (.05-.39 N.m). After adjusting turning torque, stake lock nut to ensure nut will not loosen.

OUTPUT SHAFT END PLAY

1) Output shaft end play is adjusted by adjusting output shaft shim thickness. Install output shaft bearing retainer. Install output shaft thrust needle bearing on bearing retainer with smooth side down.

2) Install output shaft in transaxle case. Using a depth gauge and straightedge, measure Dimensions "L1" and "L2" at side cover in at least 2 places. *See Fig. 35.* Use the following equation to determine distance between transaxle case surface and adjusting shim mating surface (Dimension "A"):

$$A = L1 - L2$$

(L2 equals height of gauge)

3) Measure Dimensions "L2" and "L3" in at least 2 places. Use the following equation to determine distance between end of output shaft

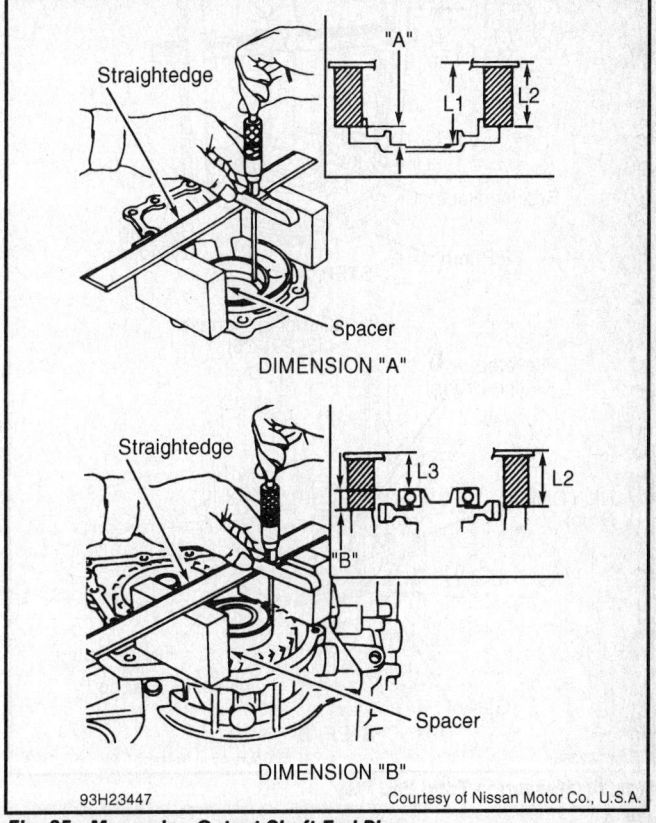

bearing race and side cover surface of transaxle case (Dimension "B"):

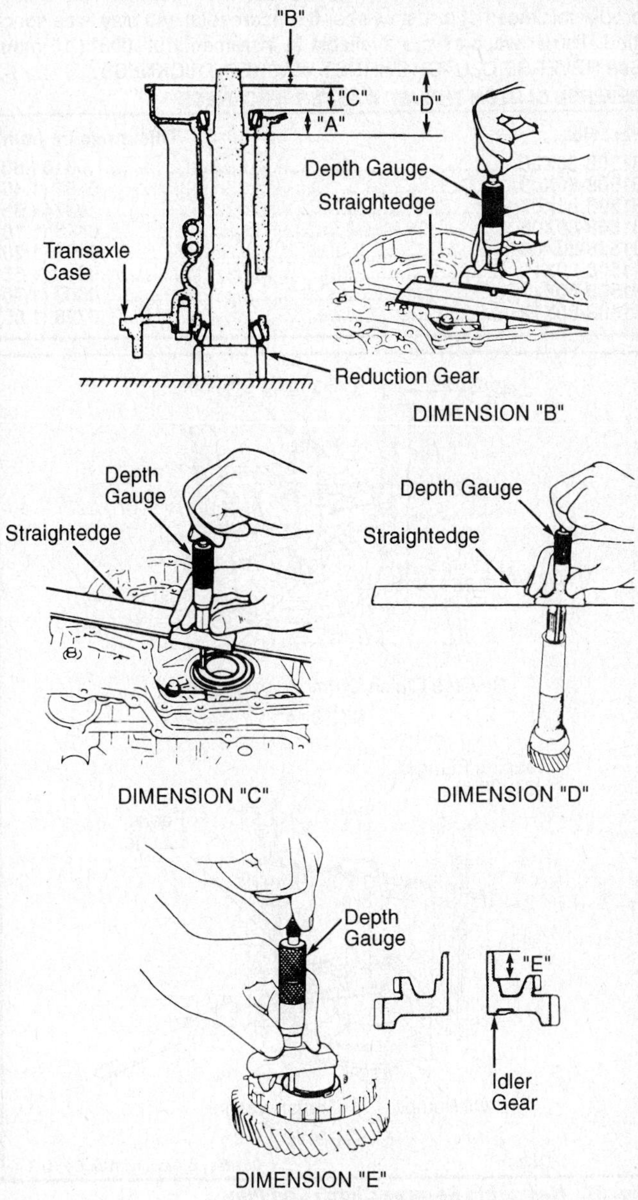

$$B = L2 - L3$$

(L2 equals height of gauge)

Specified output shaft end play should be 0-0.006" (0-.15 mm). Select proper thickness of adjusting shim to ensure output shaft end play is within specification. Adjusting shims are available in increments of .002" (.04 mm). See OUTPUT SHAFT ADJUSTING SHIM THICKNESS table.

OUTPUT SHAFT ADJUSTING SHIM THICKNESS

Part No.	Thickness In. (mm)
31438-80X60	.0315 (.80)
31438-80X61	.0331 (.84)
31438-80X62	.0346 (.88)
31438-80X63	.0362 (.92)
31438-80X64	.0378 (.96)
31438-80X65	.0394 (1.00)
31438-80X66	.0409 (1.04)
31438-80X68	.0425 (1.08)
31438-80X69	.0457 (1.16)
31438-80X70	.0472 (1.20)

4) Install selected adjusting shim on output shaft bearing. Apply a bead of liquid gasket .059" (1.50 mm) in diameter on inside edge of side cover surface of transaxle case. Install side cover on transaxle case and tighten bolts to 20-22 ft. lbs. (26-30 N.m). *See Fig. 13.* Always replace bolts "A". Bolts are self-sealing.

Straightedge
Spacer
DIMENSION "A"

Straightedge
Spacer
DIMENSION "B"

93H23447   Courtesy of Nissan Motor Co., U.S.A.

Fig. 35: Measuring Output Shaft End Play

TOTAL END PLAY

1) Total end play is adjusted by adjusting bearing race thickness. With original bearing race installed on oil pump, place Gauge Set (J34291) onto oil pump. Long ends of gauge set legs should be placed firmly on machined surface of oil pump assembly, and gauging cylinder should rest on top of bearing race. Lock gauging cylinder in place (STEP "A"). *See Fig. 36.* Remove gauging cylinder. Install Gauging Plunger (J34291-25) into gauging cylinder.

"B"
"C"
"A"
"D"
Depth Gauge
Straightedge
Transaxle Case
Reduction Gear
DIMENSION "B"

Depth Gauge
Straightedge
DIMENSION "C"

Depth Gauge
Straightedge
DIMENSION "D"

Depth Gauge
"E"
Idler Gear
DIMENSION "E"

EXAMPLE
Dimension "B" = .08" (2.0 mm)
PLUS +
Dimension "C" = .04" (1.0 mm)
EQUALS = .12" (3.0 mm)

Dimension "D" = .24" (6.0 mm)
MINUS -
Dimensions "B" + "C" .12" (3.0 mm)
EQUALS =
Dimension "A" .12" (3.0 mm)

Dimension "A" .12" (3.0 mm)
MINUS -
Dimension "E"
EQUALS =
Thickness Of Thrust Shim

95G19691   Courtesy of Nissan Motor Co., U.S.A.

Fig. 34: Measuring Reduction Gear Bearing Preload

2) With needle bearing installed on high clutch drum, place gauge set legs on machined surface of transaxle case (with gasket), and allow plunger to rest on needle bearing (STEP "B"). *See Fig. 36.* Using a feeler gauge, measure gap between gauging cylinder and gauging plunger. Measurement should give exact total end play. Total end play should be .010-.022" (.25-.55 mm). Select proper thickness of bearing race to ensure total end play is as specified. Bearing race are available in increments of .008" (.20 mm). See TOTAL END PLAY BEARING RACE THICKNESS table.

TOTAL END PLAY BEARING RACE THICKNESS

Part No.	Thickness In. (mm)
31435-80X00	.031 (.80)
31435-80X01	.039 (1.00)
31435-80X02	.047 (1.20)
31435-80X03	.055 (1.40)
31435-80X04	.063 (1.60)
31435-80X05	.071 (1.80)
31435-80X06	.079 (2.00)
31435-80X09	.035 (.90)
31435-80X10	.043 (1.10)
31435-80X11	.051 (1.30)
31435-80X12	.059 (1.50)
31435-80X13	.067 (1.70)
31435-80X14	.075 (1.90)

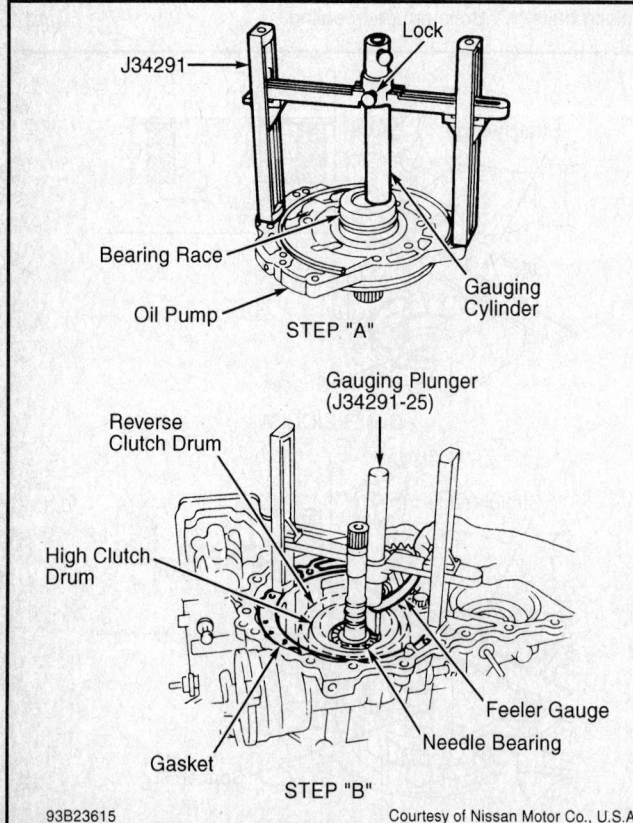

Fig. 36: Measuring Total End Play

REVERSE CLUTCH END PLAY

1) Reverse clutch end play is adjusted by adjusting thrust washer thickness. Place Gauge Set (J34291) on machined surface of transaxle case (with gasket), and allow gauging cylinder to rest on reverse clutch drum. Lock cylinder in place. Remove gauging cylinder. Install Gauging Plunger (J344290-6) into gauging cylinder. *See Fig. 37.*
2) With original thrust washer installed on oil pump, place gauge set legs onto machined surface of oil pump assembly, and allow plunger to rest on thrust washer. Using a feeler gauge, measure gap between gauging cylinder and gauging plunger. Measurement should give exact reverse clutch end play.

3) Reverse clutch end play should be .022-.035" (.55-.90 mm). Select proper thickness of thrust washer to ensure total end play is as specified. Thrust washers are available in increments of .006" (.15 mm). See REVERSE CLUTCH THRUST WASHER THICKNESS.

REVERSE CLUTCH THRUST WASHER THICKNESS

Part No.	Thickness In. (mm)
31508-80X00	.0315 (.80)
31508-80X03	.0551 (1.40)
31508-80X07	.0374 (.95)
31508-80X08	.0443 (1.10)
31508-80X09	.0492 (1.25)
31508-80X10	.0610 (1.55)
31508-80X11	.0669 (1.70)
31508-80X12	.0728 (1.85)

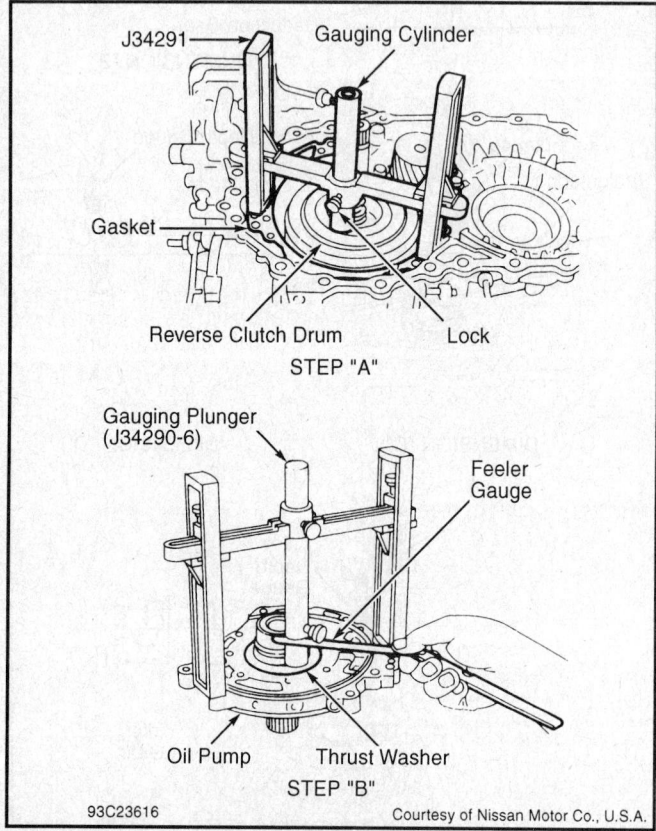

Fig. 37: Measuring Reverse Clutch End Play

TRANSAXLE REASSEMBLY

NOTE: For needle bearing, snap ring and thrust washer locations, See Fig. 12.

1) Install differential side oil seals in converter housing and transaxle case. Install parking actuator support to transaxle case with beveled edge inward. Install parking pawl on transaxle case and secure with parking shaft. Install return spring. *See Fig. 7.*
2) Perform DIFFERENTIAL SIDE BEARING PRELOAD, REDUCTION GEAR BEARING PRELOAD and OUTPUT SHAFT END PLAY adjustment procedures. See TRANSAXLE ADJUSTMENTS.
3) Remove paper from bearing retainer. Apply petroleum jelly to thrust washer. Install thrust washer on bearing retainer with Black side facing up. Ensure bearing retainer seal rings are not spread. Align teeth of low and reverse brake drive plates. Install forward clutch assembly. Forward clutch is installed correctly if bearing retainer and edge of forward clutch drum are near same level.
4) Apply petroleum jelly to thrust needle bearing. Install thrust needle bearing on bearing retainer with flat side down. Align teeth of overrun clutch drive plates. Install overrun clutch hub. Apply petroleum jelly to thrust washer and install thrust washer on overrun clutch hub.

5) Hold forward clutch hub and turn rear internal gear. Ensure overrun clutch hub rotates clockwise and does not rotate counterclockwise. If overrun clutch hub does operate as described, check installed direction of forward one-way clutch. Align forward clutch hub drive plate teeth and install forward clutch hub and rear internal gear assembly. Ensure thrust washer hooks are aligned on forward clutch hub.

6) Apply petroleum jelly to needle bearings. Install one needle bearing in rear planetary carrier with Black side down. Install other needle bearing on opposite side of rear planetary carrier with smooth side of bearing toward planetary carrier.

7) Install rear sun gear on rear planetary carrier with grooved side facing up. Install rear planetary carrier in transaxle case. Apply petroleum jelly to thrust needle bearing and install bearing on front planetary carrier with Black side up.

8) Align return springs to transaxle case gutters. See Fig. 38. Align brake piston with spring retainer. See Fig. 38. Install piston and retainer assembly in transaxle case. Align bracket with gutter and band servo piston stem. See Fig. 39.

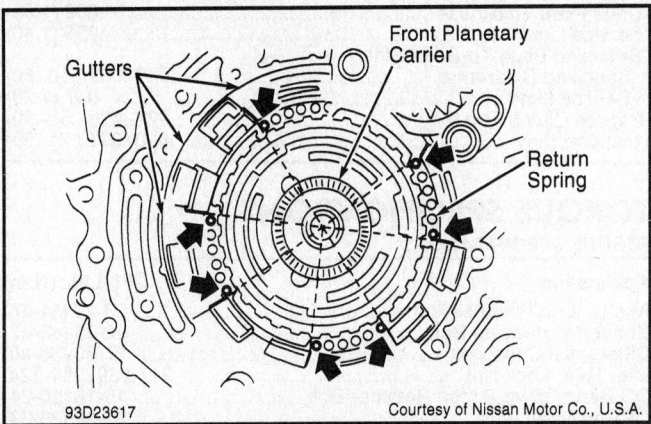

Fig. 38: **Aligning Return Springs-To-Case Gutters**

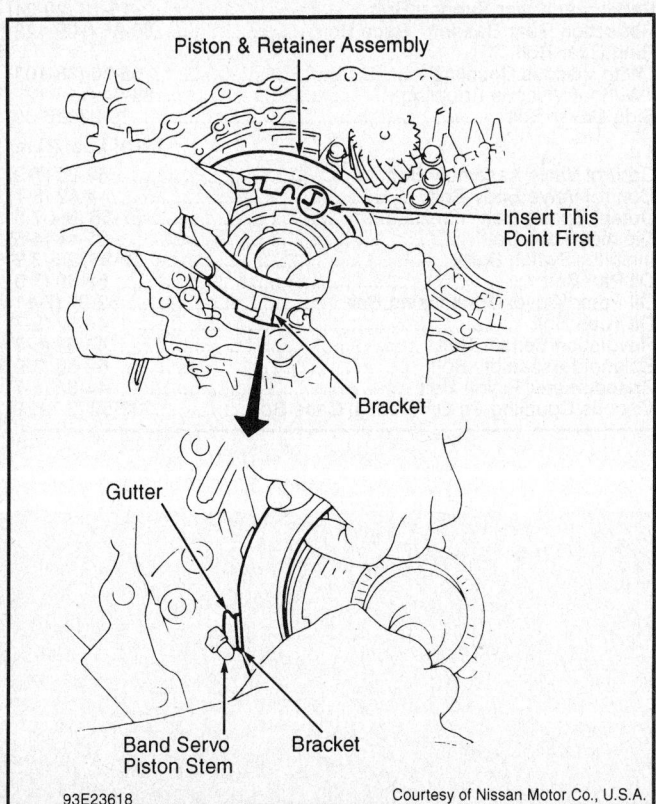

Fig. 39: **Aligning Bracket-To-Case Gutter**

9) Ensure each protrusion of piston is correctly set to corresponding return spring. Push piston and retainer assembly evenly and confirm smooth movement. If smooth movement does not occur, remove piston and retainer assembly and align return springs. See Fig. 38.

10) Using Tool (KV31102400), compress piston and retainer assembly and install snap ring. Install low one-way clutch to front planetary carrier by rotating carrier clockwise. Install snap ring.

11) Apply petroleum jelly to needle bearings and bearing race. Install needle bearing on front planetary carrier with flat side down. Install bearing race on front sun gear. Install needle bearing on high clutch hub with flat side facing front sun gear.

12) Install high clutch hub on front sun gear. Install needle bearing on high clutch drum side of high clutch hub. Install high clutch drum on high clutch hub. Install needle bearing on high clutch drum with flat side down. See Fig. 6.

13) Remove paper from input shaft. Align teeth of reverse clutch drive plates and install input shaft assembly. Align teeth of high clutch drive plates and install reverse clutch assembly.

14) Install anchor end pin, washer and lock nut on transaxle case. Place brake band and strut on reverse clutch drum. Tighten anchor end pin until brake band is on reverse drum evenly.

15) Apply petroleum jelly on bearing race selected in TOTAL END PLAY adjustment procedure. See TRANSAXLE ADJUSTMENTS. Install bearing race on oil pump cover. Apply petroleum jelly on thrust washer selected in REVERSE CLUTCH END PLAY adjustment procedure. See TRANSAXLE ADJUSTMENTS. Install thrust washer on reverse clutch drum.

16) Install oil pump assembly, baffle plate and gasket on transaxle case. Tighten oil pump bolts to 13-15 ft. lbs. (18-21 N.m). Apply ATF to input shaft "O" ring and install "O" ring on input shaft. Adjust brake band. Tighten anchor end pin to 35-53 INCH lbs. (4-6 N.m). Back off anchor end pin 2 1/2 turns. While holding anchor end pin, tighten lock nut. Apply compressed air to oil holes in transaxle case to ensure correct brake band operation. See Fig. 40.

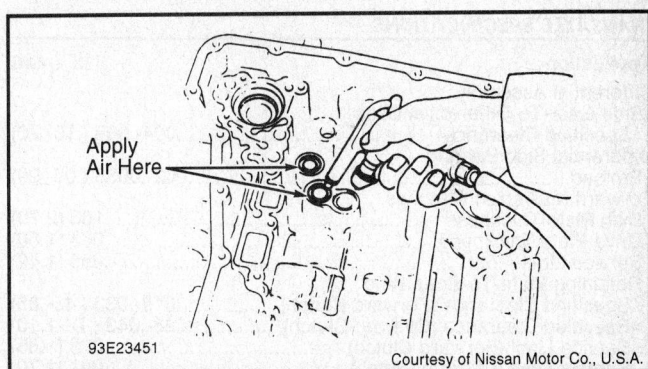

Fig. 40: **Checking Brake Band Operation**

17) Install differential assembly on transaxle case. Install oil tube on converter housing and tighten bolts to 44-62 INCH lbs. (5-7 N.m). Install "O" ring on differential oil port of transaxle case. Apply a .059" (1.50 mm) bead of liquid gasket on inside edge of converter housing mating surface. Install converter housing on transaxle case. Tighten bolts to 32-35 ft. lbs. (43-47 N.m).

18) Check contact surface of accumulator piston for damage. Apply ATF to "O" rings and install on accumulator piston. Install accumulator pistons and return springs in transaxle case. Apply petroleum jelly to lip seals for band servo oil holes and install in transaxle case. Install tube and sleeve.

19) Apply ATF to manual valve and insert valve into control valve assembly. Set manual shaft in Neutral position. Install control valve assembly on transaxle case while aligning manual valve with manual plate.

20) Put solenoid harness into transaxle case and push terminal body onto transaxle case. Install clip to terminal body. Install and tighten control valve assembly bolts to 44-62 INCH lbs. (5-7 N.m). See Fig. 5. Attach magnet to oil pan. Install NEW oil pan gasket and install oil pan.

Tighten NEW pan bolts in a crisscross pattern to 62-80 INCH lbs. (7-9 N.m). Install drain plug (if necessary) and tighten to 22-29 ft. lbs. (29-39 N.m) .

NOTE: Always replace oil pan bolts. Bolts are self-sealing.

21) Install inhibitor switch and adjust if necessary. Apply ATF to NEW "O" ring and install on dipstick tube. Install dipstick tube and oil cooler tube to transaxle. Tighten dipstick tube bolt to 35-44 INCH lbs. (4-5 N.m). Tighten oil cooler tube bolts to 22-36 ft. lbs. (29-49 N.m).

22) Pour 1.1 qt. (1.0L) of ATF into torque converter and install torque converter. Measure distance "A" to ensure torque converter is installed correctly. See Fig. 41. Distance "A" should be .55" (14 mm) on I30, Maxima, Quest and Villager. For Altima, distance "A" should be .75" (19 mm).

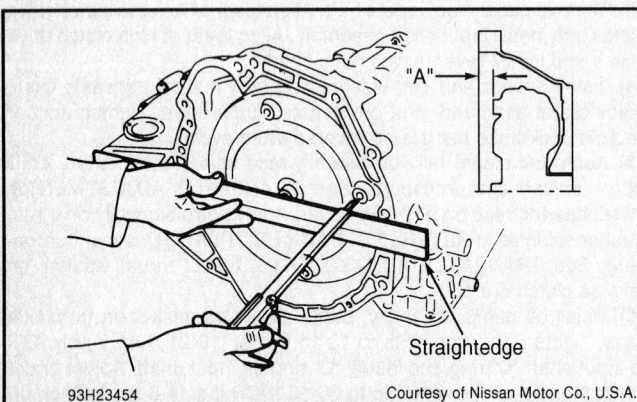

93H23454   Courtesy of Nissan Motor Co., U.S.A.

Fig. 41: Measuring Converter Installed Depth

TRANSAXLE SPECIFICATIONS

TRANSAXLE SPECIFICATIONS

Application	In. (mm)
Differential Assembly	
Side Gear-To-Differential Case	
Specified Clearance	.004-.008 (.10-.20)
Differential Side Bearing	
Preload	.002-.0035 (.05-.09)
Forward & Overrun Clutches	
Dish Plate Thickness	.106 (2.70)
Drive Plate Thickness	.063 (1.60)
Service Limit	.055 (1.40)
Retaining Plate-To-Snap Ring	
Specified Clearance (Forward Clutch)	.018-.033 (.45-.85)
Specified Clearance (Overrun Clutch)	.028-.043 (.70-1.10)
Service Limit (Forward Clutch)	.073 (1.85)
Service Limit (Overrun Clutch)	.067 (1.70)
High Clutch	
Drive Plate Thickness	.063 (1.60)
Service Limit	.055 (1.40)
Retaining Plate-To-Snap Ring	
Specified Clearance	.071-.087 (1.80-2.20)
Service Limit	.118 (3.00)
Input Shaft Seal Ring-To-Ring Groove	
Specified Clearance	.003-.009 (.08-.23)
Service Limit	.009 (.23)

TRANSAXLE SPECIFICATIONS (Cont.)

Application	In. (mm)
Low & Reverse Brake	
Drive Plate Thickness	.071 (1.80)
Service Limit	.063 (1.60)
Specified Clearance	.067-.083 (1.70-2.10)
Service Limit	.138 (3.50)
Oil Pump Seal Ring-To-Ring Groove	
Specified Clearance	.0039-.0098 (.10-.25)
Service Limit	.0098 (.25)
Oil Pump Side Clearance	.001-.002 (.03-.05)
Oil Pump Outer	
Gear-To-Housing Clearance	.004-.007 (.10-.18)
Output Shaft End Play	0-.0059 (0-.15)
Output Shaft Seal Ring-To-Ring Groove	
Specified Clearance	.004-.010 (.10-.25)
Service Limit	.010 (.25)
Pinion Washer-To-Planetary Gear	
Specified Clearance	.008-.028 (.20-.70)
Service Limit	.031 (.80)
Reverse Clutch	
Dish Plate Thickness	.121 (3.08)
Drive Plate Thickness	.063 (1.60)
Service Limit	.055 (1.40)
Retaining Plate-To-Snap Ring	
Specified Clearance	.020-.031 (.50-.80)
Service Limit	.047 (1.20)
Reverse Clutch End Play	.022-.035 (.55-.90)
Total End Play	.010-.022 (.25-.55)

TORQUE SPECIFICATIONS

TORQUE SPECIFICATIONS

Application	Ft. Lbs. (N.m)
Anchor End Pin Lock Nut	23-27 (31-36)
Converter Housing Bolt	32-35 (43-47)
Differential Case Bolt	27-30 (36-40)
Idler Gear Lock Nut	217-239 (294-324)
OD Band Servo Piston Retainer Bolt	15-18 (20-24)
Oil Pan Drain Plug	21-29 (29-39)
Oil Cooler Tube Bolt	21-36 (29-49)
Oil Pump-To-Transaxle Case Bolt	13-15 (18-21)
Parking Actuator Support Bolt	15-18 (20-24)
Reduction Gear Bearing Race Bolt	80-91 (109-123)
Ring Gear Bolt	
With Viscous Coupling	65-76 (88-103)
Without Viscous Coupling	83-94 (113-127)
Side Cover Bolt	19-22 (26-30)

Application	INCH Lbs. (N.m)
Control Valve Assembly Bolt	62-80 (7-9)
Control Valve Body Bolt	44-62 (5-7)
Detent Spring Bolt	57-66 (6.4-7.5)
Dipstick Tube Bolt	35-44 (4-5)
Inhibitor Switch Bolt	22-35 (2.5-3.9)
Oil Pan Bolt	62-80 (7-9)
Oil Pump Cover-To-Housing Bolt	62-97 (7-11)
Oil Tube Bolt	44-62 (5-7)
Revolution Sensor Bolt	44-62 (5-7)
Solenoid Assembly Bolt	62-80 (7-9)
Speedometer Pinion Bolt	44-62 (5-7)
Viscous Coupling-To-Differential Case Bolt	33-52 (3.7-5.9)

TECHNICAL SERVICE BULLETINS

OVERDRIVE GEAR WHINE

1993-95 Quest (Nissan TSB NTB95-061a) – 1) Vehicles may exhibit gear whine between 32-45 MPH, when transaxle is in overdrive and under light throttle pressure.

2) To determine cause of condition, operate vehicle between 32-45 MPH with overdrive engaged. Accelerator must be depressed slightly to avoid shifting out of overdrive. If gear whine is heard, press overdrive switch to disengage overdrive. Overdrive OFF indicator light should come on.

3) This gear whine will NOT be heard when overdrive switch is turned off (in 3rd gear at any speed). To correct this situation, replace front sun gear, front planetary carrier, oil pan gasket, oil pump gasket and 21 oil pan bolts. If gear whine is not reduced significantly, refer to appropriate NISSAN ELECTRONIC CONTROLS article for further diagnosis.

1995-96 MAXIMA A/T KEY INTERLOCK CABLE

1995-96 Maxima With RE4F04A Transmissions (Nissan TSB No. NTB95-095 – 1) Shift lever cannot be moved from "P" position under hot ambient conditions. Problem may occur more frequently when vehicle is parked in direct sunlight. A NEW A/T interlock cable has been developed to reduce internal friction under hot ambient conditions.

2) If able to duplicate incident, isolate whether shifter or cable is at fault. Disconnect cable at selector lever. Ensure shifter solenoid operates properly. Inspect for bent or broken parts and evidence of liquid spills. Repair or clean components as necessary and recheck operation. Disconnect interlock cable at key. Ensure cable moves freely.

3) If any binding or friction is felt, replace cable with part number 34908-40U00. Use caution not to twist the adjuster holder when performing cable adjustment. After installation, ensure that shifter lever cannot be moved after key has been removed from ignition. If shifter can be moved, lengthen cable and recheck.

AUTOMATIC TRANSMISSIONS
RE4F04A/V Electronic Controls

Infiniti: I30
Nissan: Altima, Maxima, Quest

NOTE: This transaxle is also used in the Mercury Villager and is identified as a Ford 4F20E. For additional information see appropriate 4F20E article in MITCHELL® 1995-96 TRANSMISSION SERVICE & REPAIR manual for DOMESTIC CARS, LIGHT TRUCKS & VANS.

APPLICATION

APPLICATION

Vehicle	Transaxle Model
Nissan	
Altima	RE4F04A/V
Maxima	RE4F04A/V
Quest	RE4F04A
Infiniti	
I30	RE4F04A/V
Mercury	
Villager	4F20E

DESCRIPTION

Automatic transaxle is electronically controlled. Transaxle shifting and lock-up is controlled by Automatic Transaxle Control Unit (ATCU) for optimal performance. The ATCU receives information from various electronic sensors, switches and solenoids and uses this information to control shift and lock-up solenoid valves. For additional information and testing of these components, see COMPONENT TESTING & CIRCUIT TESTS.

ELECTRONIC SELF-DIAGNOSTICS

NOTE: Driveability problems that may appear to be transmission related may be caused by a faulty engine component. Engine related fault codes MUST be repaired before diagnosing transmission. See ENGINE PERFORMANCE in appropriate MITCHELL® repair manual. Failure to diagnose and repair engine fault codes prior to transmission diagnosis may result in incorrect diagnosis or component repair.

SELF-DIAGNOSTIC PROCEDURE

NOTE: Perform self-diagnosis and code retrieval procedures with engine at normal operating temperature.

There are 3 ways to retrieve DTCs. They are displayed in different formats and by different indicators. Retrieve the codes and refer to the DTC DESCRIPTIONS table.
Scan Tool (OBD-II) – OBD-II codes must be retrieved using a scan tool connected to the OBD-II connector. Follow the scan tool manufacturer's procedure to connect and operate the scan tool.
MIL Light (MIL) – MIL light will illuminate when ignition switch is turned to ON position (engine not running). This is a bulb check. When engine is started, MIL light should turn OFF. If light remains ON, on-board diagnostics has detected an engine or transmission system fault. A/T self-diagnosis is performed by A/T Control Unit (ATCU) in combination with ECM. Self-diagnosis codes indicated by MIL are stored in both ATCU and ECM memory. Codes may be retrieved from vehicles equipped with a MIL light by using the following procedure:
1) Ensure ignition is in ON position and engine is off (KOEO). Turn diagnostic test mode selector, (located on side of ECM), fully clockwise. Wait 2 seconds, and turn diagnostic test mode selector fully counterclockwise. This puts ECM into Diagnostic Test Mode II (code retrieval mode).
2) DTCs are indicated by the MIL light "blinking" sequence. A sequence of LONG (MIL light ON for .6 second) blinks indicates the first and second digits of the DTC.

3) The third and fourth digits are indicated by a sequence of SHORT (MIL light ON for .3 second) blinks. Example: MIL blinks 10 times for 6 seconds (.6 x 10 times), and then blinks 3 times for about 1 second (.3 x 3 times). This indicates MIL DTC 1003.
4) ECM will not switch to Diagnostic Test Mode II when engine is running. When engine is turned off after code retrieval, power to ECM is lost after 5 seconds. Turn ECM switch to full counterclockwise position. This returns system to Diagnostic Test Mode I which provides bulb test and system monitoring functions.

OD OFF/POWER Light (Flash) – Flash codes are also referred to by the manufacturer as "Judgement Flickers". To retrieve Flash codes using the OD OFF/POWER indicator light use the following procedure:
1) Ensure engine is at normal operating temperature. Turn ignition switch to OFF position for at least 5 seconds. Turn ignition switch to "ACC" position. Set overdrive switch to "ON" position, and selector lever to "P" position. Turn ignition switch to "ON" position, but DO NOT start engine. OD OFF indicator light should come on for 2 seconds.
2) Turn ignition switch to "OFF" position. Move selector lever to "D" position. OD switch to off. Turn ignition switch to "ON" position, but DO NOT start engine. Wait for 2 seconds, move selector lever to "2" position. Set OD switch to ON position, move selector lever to "1" position, and set OD switch to OFF position.
3) Depress accelerator pedal to floor and release pedal. Record OD OFF indicator light flashes and refer to DTC DESCRIPTIONS table.

NOTE: The term "Judgement Flicker" refers to light flashes of the OD OFF indicator light. For additional wiring diagram information, See WIRING DIAGRAMS.

NOTE: Codes are displayed in the following order in tables and in DTC TESTING: OBD-II Code/MIL Code/Flash.

DTC DESCRIPTIONS

OBD-II/MIL/Flash [1]	DTC Description
P0000/0505/All Flashes Same	No Codes In System
P0705/1003 Or	
1101/No Flash	Inhibitor, TP Or OD Switch Circuit
P0710/1208/8th	Fluid Temp Sensor/ATCU Power Source Circuit
P0720/1102/1st	Vehicle Speed Sensor (A/T Revolution) Circuit
[3] / [2]/2nd	Vehicle Speed Sensor/MTR (At Speedometer)
P0725/1207/9th	Engine Speed Signal Circuit
P0731/1103/N/A [2]	A/T 1st Signal
P0732/1104/N/A [2]	A/T 2nd Signal
P0733/1105/N/A [2]	A/T 3rd Signal
P0734/1106/N/A [2]	A/T 4th Signal Or TCC
P0740/1204/7th	Torque Converter Solenoid Valve
P0745/1205/10th	Line Pressure Solenoid Valve
P0750/1108/4th	Shift Solenoid Valve "A"
P0755/1201/5th	Shift Solenoid Valve "B"
P1705/1206/3rd	Throttle Position Sensor Or Switch
P1760/1203/6th	Overrun Clutch Solenoid Valve

[1] – Indicated by long flash (Judgement Flicker) of OD OFF indicator light in self diagnostic check. See SELF-DIAGNOSTIC PROCEDURE.
[2] – Malfunction cannot be displayed by MIL if another malfunction is assigned to OD OFF light.
[3] – OBD-II code number is not available.

DTC TESTING

NOTE: For additional wiring diagram information, See WIRING DIAGRAMS.

NOTE: Codes are indicated as follows: DTC OBD-II/MIL/Flash.

DTC P0705/1003 OR 1101/NO FLASH: INHIBITOR, TP OR OD SWITCH

Circuit Description – Inhibitor switch detects selector lever position and sends a signal to ATCU. OD switch sends ON or OFF signal to ATCU. Throttle Position Switch consist of a wide open throttle switch which sends a signal to ATCU when throttle valve is open 50 percent and a closed throttle position switch which indicates when throttle valve is fully closed. Code is set when ATCU receives an excessively low or high voltage from sensor.

Diagnosis & Repair – 1) Check inhibitor switch. See appropriate test under COMPONENT TESTING & CIRCUIT TESTS.

2) Check harness and connectors for open or short between ignition switch and inhibitor switch and between inhibitor switch and ATCU. If continuity exists for all circuits, go to next step. If continuity does not exist for any circuit inspect and repair circuit(s) as needed.

OD Switch – With KOEO, check voltage between ATCU terminal No. 39 and ground. With OD switch in ON position, battery voltage should be present. With OD switch in OFF position, voltage should be one volt maximum. If voltage is not as specified, check OD switch. See appropriate test in COMPONENT TESTING & CIRCUIT TESTS. Check harness for open or short between ATCU and OD switch and ground circuit for OD switch. If continuity exists for all circuits, go to next test.

Throttle Position Switch – 1) Start and warm engine. With KOEO, check voltage between ATCU terminals No. 14, No. 21 and ground while depressing and releasing accelerator pedal slowly. See THROTTLE POSITION VOLTAGE TEST table.

THROTTLE POSITION VOLTAGE TEST

Accelerator Pedal	Voltage
Released	
Terminal No. 14 .... Battery Voltage	
Terminal No. 21 .... One Volt Maximum	
Fully Depressed	
Terminal No. 14 .... One Volt Maximum	
Terminal No. 21 .... Battery Voltage	

2) If voltage is not as specified, check throttle position switch. See appropriate test under COMPONENT TESTING & CIRCUIT TESTS. Check harness for open or short between ignition switch and ATCU to throttle position switch. If within specifications, perform self-diagnosis again after test driving vehicle.

DTC P0710/1208/8TH: FLUID TEMPERATURE SENSOR/ATCU POWER

Circuit Description – Fluid temperature sensor detects ATF temperature and sends a signal to ATCU. Code is set when ATCU receives an excessively low or high voltage from sensor.

Diagnosis & Repair – 1) Check ATCU power source. With KOEO, check voltage between ATCU terminals No. 4, No. 9 and ground. Battery voltage should exist. If battery voltage does not exist, check harness for short or open between ignition switch and ATCU and between ignition switch and fuse.

2) Check fluid temperature sensor through terminal cord (sub-harness) assembly. See FLUID TEMPERATURE SENSOR TEST in COMPONENT TESTING & CIRCUIT TESTS. If resistance values are not within specifications, remove oil pan and check harness for open or short.

DTC P0720/1102/1ST: REVOLUTION SENSOR

Circuit Description – Revolution sensor detects revolution of the idler gear parking pawl lock gear and emits a pulse signal. Pulse signal is sent to ATCU which converts it into vehicle speed. Code is set when ATCU does not receive proper voltage signal from sensor.

Diagnosis & Repair – 1) Start engine. Check voltage between ATCU terminal No. 25 and ground while driving. With voltmeter in AC range, voltage at zero MPH should be zero volts. Voltage at 19 MPH should be one volt. Voltage should rise gradually in response to vehicle speed.

2) If voltage is not within specifications, check harness between ATCU and revolution sensor and between revolution sensor and ECM for open or short. See appropriate SELF-DIAGNOSTICS article in ENGINE PERFORMANCE of appropriate MITCHELL® manual.

DTC – / – /2ND: VEHICLE SPEED SENSOR/MTR

Circuit Description – Vehicle speed sensor/MTR is built into speedometer assembly. It functions as an auxiliary device for the revolution sensor when it is malfunctioning. ATCU will then use a signal sent from vehicle speed sensor/MTR. Code is set when ATCU does not receive proper voltage signal from sensor.

Diagnosis & Repair – For sensor testing, see SPEED SENSOR CIRCUIT TEST in COMPONENT TESTING & CIRCUIT TESTS.

DTC P0725/1207/9TH: ENGINE SPEED SIGNAL

Circuit Description – Engine speed signal (tach signal) is sent from ECM to ACTU. Code is set when ATCU does not receive proper voltage signal from ECM.

Diagnosis & Repair – For sensor testing, see ENGINE REVOLUTION SIGNAL CIRCUIT TEST in COMPONENT TESTING & CIRCUIT TESTS.

DTC P0731, P0732, P0733/1103, 1104, 1105/NO FLASH: A/T 1ST SIGNAL, 2ND SIGNAL, 3RD SIGNAL

Circuit Description – When vehicle is being driven in any gear other than 1st (P0731)/2nd (P0732)/3rd (P07033), ATCU is signals A/T to shift to 1st/2nd/3rd gear. A/T 1st/2nd/3rd signal is not determined as a fault unless ATCU self diagnosis system is in "No Failure" condition. When A/T 1st/2nd/3rd code is displayed, it indicates that the gears are not properly shifted. Problem is NOT caused by electrical failure of A/T circuits but by mechanical failure (control valve sticking, improper solenoid valve operation, etc).

Diagnosis & Repair – 1) Remove control valve assembly. See CONTROL VALVE ASSEMBLY in ON VEHICLE SERVICE in overhaul article. Check shift solenoid valve "A" and "B" operation. See appropriate tests in COMPONENT TESTING & CIRCUIT TESTS. Repair or replace shift solenoid valve assembly as needed.

2) Check control valve. Disassemble control valve assembly. See CONTROL VALVE ASSEMBLY in overhaul article. Ensure that valves, sleeve and plug slide along valve bore under their own weight, and are free of burrs, dents and scratches. Ensure control valve springs are free from damage deformation and fatigue. Ensure hydraulic line is free from obstacles. Repair control valve assembly as needed and recheck.

A/T 4TH SIGNAL OR TCC SIGNAL

Circuit Description – Improper shifting to 4th gear position or improper torque converter clutch operation. When vehicle is being driven in any gear other than 4th, ATCU signals A/T to shift to 4th gear. Also may be indicated when vehicle is being driven at any gear position without TCC lock-up and ATCU is signaling A/T to lock-up torque converter. A/T 4th or TCC is not determined as a fault unless ATCU self-diagnosis system is in "No Failure" condition. When A/T 4th or TCC Signal is displayed, it indicates that the gears are not properly shifted. Problem is NOT caused by electrical failure of A/T circuits but by mechanical failure. Control valve sticking, improper solenoid valve operation, malfunctioning oil pump or torque converter clutch etc.

Diagnosis & Repair – **1)** If during road test transaxle did NOT shift from 3rd to 4th at specified speed, go to step **2)**. If shift from 3rd to 4th gear is at specified speed and lock-up did NOT occur at specified speed, go to step **5)**.

2) Perform pressure test. See HYDRAULIC PRESSURE TESTS in overhaul article. If pressure is not within specification go to step **6)**. If okay, check solenoid valves. Remove control valve assembly. See CONTROL VALVE ASSEMBLY in overhaul article. Check solenoid valve assembly operation. Repair or replace as needed.

3) Check control valve. Disassemble control valve assembly. See CONTROL VALVE ASSEMBLY in overhaul article. Ensure valves, sleeve and plug slide along valve bore under their own weight, and are free of burrs, dents and scratches. Ensure control valve springs are free from damage deformation and fatigue. Ensure hydraulic line is free from obstacles. Repair control valve assembly as needed and recheck.

4) Road test vehicle. Ensure vehicle shifts from 3-4 at specified speed and lock-up occurs properly.

5) Check TCC solenoid valve. Remove control valve assembly. See CONTROL VALVE ASSEMBLY in overhaul article. Check TCC solenoid valve assembly. See LOCK-UP SOLENOID TEST in COMPONENT TESTING & CIRCUIT TESTS. Replace or repair as necessary. Check TCC control valve and TCC relief valve for sticking. Repair as needed. Road test vehicle, ensure A/T performs lock up at specific speed. See LOCK-UP SPEED SPECIFICATIONS table in overhaul article. If okay, ensure symptoms from circuit description are no longer present.

6) Remove control valve assembly. See CONTROL VALVE ASSEMBLY in ON-VEHICLE SERVICE in overhaul article. Check line pressure solenoid. See LINE PRESSURE SOLENOID TEST in COMPONENT TESTING & CIRCUIT TESTS. Repair or replace solenoid assembly as needed. If okay, remove and disassemble control valve assembly. See CONTROL VALVE ASSEMBLY in overhaul article. Check pressure regulator, pilot and pressure modifier valves for sticking. Repair as needed.

7) Road test vehicle, ensure 3-4 shift and lock-up occurs at specified speed.

DTC P0740/1204/7TH:
TORQUE CONVERTER CLUTCH VALVE

Circuit Description – Torque converter clutch solenoid valve circuit check. TCC solenoid valve is activated, in 4th gear, by ATCU in response to signals sent from vehicle speed and throttle position sensors. Lock-up piston will then be controlled. Lock-up is prohibited when ATF temperature is too low.

Diagnosis & Repair – **1)** Check ground circuit. With ignition switch OFF, disconnect terminal cord assembly (sub-harness) connector in engine compartment. Check resistance between terminal No. 5 and ground. Resistance should be 10-16 ohms. If resistance is within specifications, go to next step. If not within specifications, remove oil pan, check harness for open or short and TCC solenoid valve. See LOCK-UP SOLENOID TEST in COMPONENT TESTING & CIRCUIT TESTS.

2) With ignition in OFF position, disconnect ATCU connector. Check resistance between connector terminal No. 5 and ATCU terminal No. 5. Resistance should be zero ohms. Repair or replace as needed. Reinstall any part removed.

3) Road test and perform self-diagnosis. If unable to obtain ATCU feedback, check ATCU input/output signal. See ATCU POWER SOURCE TEST in COMPONENT TESTING & CIRCUIT TESTS. If not within specifications, recheck ATCU pin terminals for damage or loose connections.

DTC P0745/1205/10TH:
LINE PRESSURE SOLENOID VALVE

Circuit Description – Line pressure solenoid valve circuit check. Line pressure solenoid valve regulates oil pump discharge pressure to suit driving conditions in response to a signal sent from ATCU.

Diagnosis & Repair – **1)** With Ignition OFF, Disconnect solenoid harness connector in engine compartment. Check resistance between terminal No. 4 (Maxima and I30), No. 1 (Altima and Quest) and ground. Resistance should be 2.5-5 ohms. If resistance is not within specifications, check line pressure solenoid valve circuit. See LINE PRESSURE SOLENOID TEST in COMPONENT TESTING & CIRCUIT TESTS. If resistance is not as specified, remove control valve assembly. See CONTROL VALVE ASSEMBLY in overhaul article. Inspect line pressure solenoid, see appropriate solenoid test under COMPONENT TESTING & CIRCUIT TESTS. Inspect sub harness for short or open of solenoid wiring assembly.

2) If resistance is okay, check power source circuit. Using ohmmeter, check resistance between terminal No. 4 (Maxima and I30), No. 1 (Altima and Quest) and ATCU connector terminal No. 2. Resistance should be 11.2-12.8 ohms. If resistance is not as specified, check dropping resistor. See appropriate test under COMPONENT TESTING & CIRCUIT TESTS. Inspect harness for open or short between ATCU terminal No. 2 and terminal cord assembly.

3) If resistance is okay, with ignition in OFF position, check resistance between connector terminal No. 1 and ATCU terminal No. 1. Resistance should be zero ohms. If not as specified, repair or replace harness between ATCU and terminal cord assembly.

4) If resistance is as specified, road test vehicle and perform self-diagnosis. If unable to obtain ATCU feedback, recheck ATCU input/output signal inspection. If not as specified, check ATCU pin terminals for damage or loose connection with harness connector.

DTC P0750/1108/4TH:
SHIFT SOLENOID VALVE "A"

Circuit Description – Shift solenoid valves "A" and "B" are turned ON and OFF by ATCU in response to output signal from the inhibitor switch, vehicle speed sensor and throttle position sensors. A voltage drop not within specifications during solenoid operation will set code. Shift solenoid "A" is normally ON in 1st and 4th gear. Shift solenoid "B" is normally ON in 1st and 2nd gear.

Diagnosis & Repair – **1)** Check ground circuit. With ignition switch OFF, disconnect wiring sub-assembly in engine compartment. Check resistance between sub assembly terminal No. 2 (I30 and Maxima), No. 6 (Altima and Quest) and ground. Resistance should be 20-30 ohms.

2) If resistance is not within specifications, remove control valve assembly. See CONTROL VALVE ASSEMBLY in overhaul article. Check solenoid valve "A", see appropriate test under COMPONENT TESTING & CIRCUIT TESTS. Check wiring harness and connectors for open or short.

3) If resistance is within specifications, check power source circuit. With ignition OFF, disconnect ATCU harness connector. Check resistance between connector terminal No. 2 (I30 and Maxima), No. 6 (Altima and Quest) and ATCU terminal No. 6. Resistance should be zero ohms. If resistance is as specified, reconnect connectors.

4) If resistance is NOT as specified, repair or replace harness between ATCU and terminal cord assembly. Road test and perform self diagnosis. If unable to obtain ATCU feedback, recheck ATCU input/output signal inspection. If not as specified, check ATCU pin terminals for damage or loose connection with harness connector.

DTC P0755/1201/5TH:
SHIFT SOLENOID VALVE "B"

Circuit Description – Shift solenoid valves "A" and "B" are turned ON and OFF by ATCU in response to output from the inhibitor switch, vehicle speed sensor and throttle position sensors. Information received determines best possible gear choice. Code is set when ATCU detects improper voltage drop during operation of solenoid valve. Shift solenoid "A" is normally ON in 1st and 4th gear. Shift solenoid "B" is normally ON in 1st and 2nd gear.

Diagnosis & Repair – 1) With ignition switch OFF, disconnect harness connector in engine compartment. Check resistance between terminal No. 1 (I30 & Maxima), No. 7 (Altima and, Quest) and ground. Resistance should be 20-30 ohms.

2) If resistance is not within specifications, remove control valve assembly. See CONTROL VALVE ASSEMBLY in overhaul article. Check solenoid valve "A", see appropriate test under COMPONENT TESTING & CIRCUIT TESTS. Check wiring harness and connectors for open or short.

3) If resistance is within specifications, check power source circuit. With ignition OFF, disconnect ATCU harness connector. Check resistance between connector terminal No. 1 (I30 and Maxima) No. 7 (Altima and Quest) and ATCU terminal No. 7. Resistance should be zero ohms. If resistance is as specified, reconnect connectors.

4) If resistance is NOT as specified, repair or replace harness between ATCU and terminal cord assembly. Road test and perform self-diagnosis. If unable to obtain ATCU feedback, recheck ATCU input/output signal inspection. If not as specified, check ATCU pin terminals for damage or loose connection with harness connector.

DTC P1705/1206/3RD:
THROTTLE POSITION SENSOR

Circuit Description – TPS relays throttle valve position to ATCU. A code is set when ATCU receives an excessively high or low voltage from TPS.

Diagnosis & Repair – 1) Check TP sensor circuit for engine control. Refer to appropriate SELF-DIAGNOSTICS article in ENGINE PERFORMANCE in appropriate MITCHELL® manual for TP sensor fault code test (DTC/P0120 MIL/0403). If engine control test okay, go to next step.

2) Check throttle valve switch input signal. See appropriate test under COMPONENT TESTING & CIRCUIT TESTS. Refer to DTC P0705/1003 OR 1101/NO FLASH: INHIBITOR, TP OR OD SWITCH CIRCUIT. If voltage is NOT as specified, check harness for open or short between ECM and ATCU. If results are as specified, check throttle position switch. Repair or replace damaged parts. Road test and perform self diagnosis. If unable to obtain ATCU feedback, recheck ATCU input/output signal inspection. If not as specified, check ATCU pin terminals for damage or loose connection with harness connector.

DTC P1760/1203/6TH:
OVERRUN CLUTCH SOLENOID VALVE

Circuit Description – Overrun clutch solenoid valve is activated by ATCU in response to signals sent from inhibitor switch, OD switch, vehicle speed and throttle position sensors. Overrun clutch operation is controlled by outputs from the sensors. If ATCU detects unspecified voltage drops when it tries to operate overrun clutch solenoid valve.

Diagnosis & Repair – 1) Check ground circuit. With KOEO, disconnect solenoid wiring harness assembly connector in engine compartment. Check resistance between terminal No. 3 (I30 and Maxima) No. 8 (Altima and, Quest) and ground. Resistance should be 20-30 ohms.

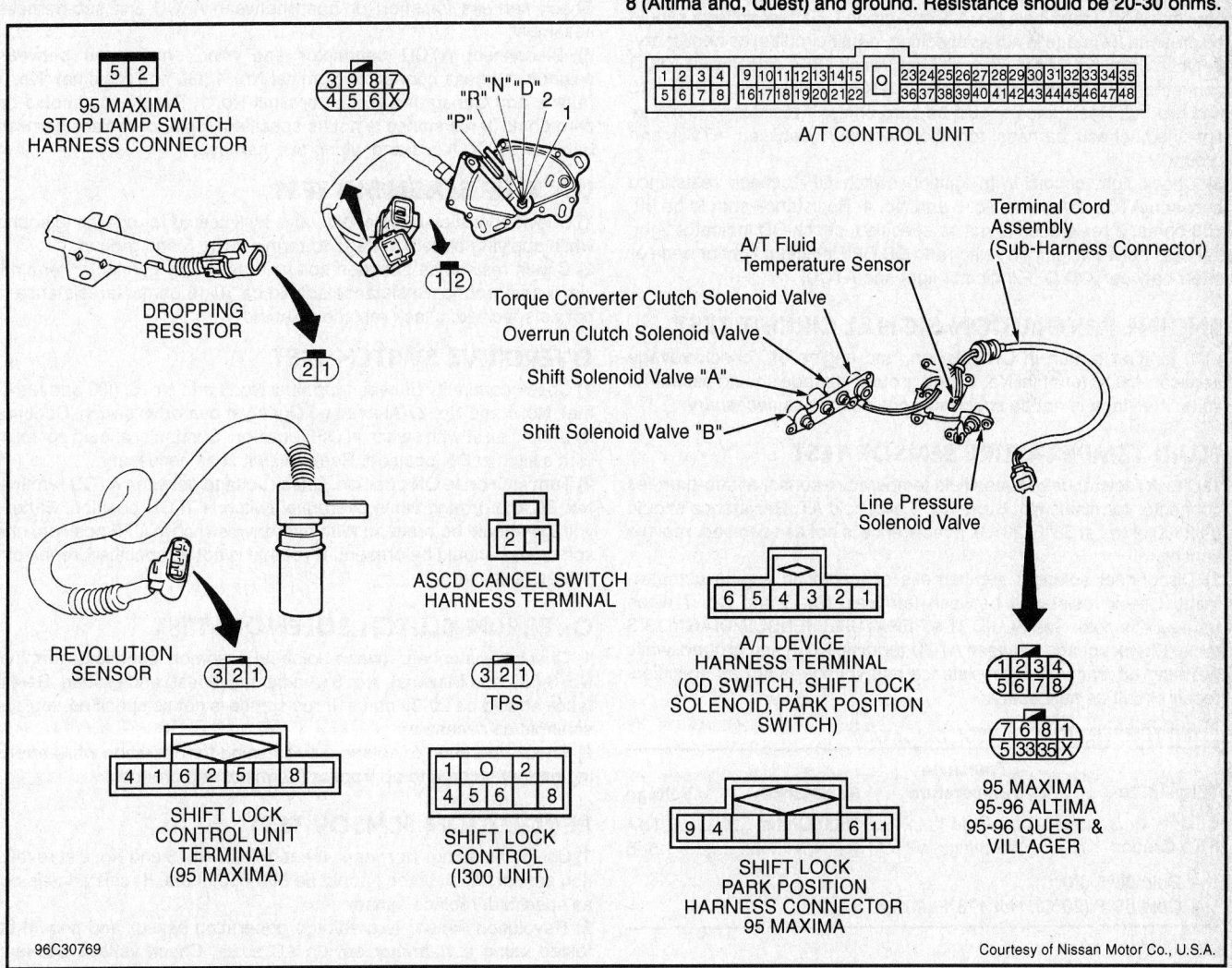

Fig. 1: Identifying Terminal Pins & Connectors

96C30769

Courtesy of Nissan Motor Co., U.S.A.

If resistance is not as specified, remove control valve. See CONTROL VALVE ASSEMBLY in overhaul article. Check overrun clutch solenoid valve, See appropriate test under COMPONENT TESTING & CIRCUIT TESTS. Check harness for open or short of terminal cord assembly.

2) If resistance is within specifications, Check power source. With ignition OFF, disconnect ATCU harness connector. Check resistance between solenoid wiring harness connector terminal No. 3 (I30 and Maxima), No. 8 (Altima and Quest) and ATCU harness terminal No. 8. Resistance should be zero ohms. Repair or replace harness between ATCU and solenoid wiring harness assembly if not as specified. Road test and perform self diagnosis. If unable to obtain ATCU feedback, recheck ATCU input/output signal inspection. If not as specified, check ATCU pin terminals for damage or loose connection with harness connector.

COMPONENT TESTING & CIRCUIT TESTS

NOTE: Refer to Fig. 1 for terminal pin and connector identification. If the following circuit tests do not give results as described, check wiring circuit between specified components to correct circuit malfunction. Repair as necessary. For wiring diagram information, see WIRING DIAGRAMS.

ATCU POWER SOURCE TEST

1) With ignition switch in ON position, and engine off, check voltage between ATCU terminals No. 4, 9 and ground. Battery voltage should be present. If voltage is not as specified, repair circuit(s) as necessary.
2) Check ground circuit. With ignition switch OFF, disconnect ATCU connector. Check resistance between ATCU terminals No. 15, No. 48 and ground. Resistance should be zero ohms. If resistance is not as specified, check harness for short or open between ATCU and ground.
3) Check light circuit. With ignition switch OFF, check resistance between ATCU terminals No. 3 and No. 4. Resistance should be 50-100 ohms. If resistance is not as specified, check OD indicator light, harness between ignition switch and OD OFF indicator light or open or short between OD OFF indicator light and ATCU.

ENGINE REVOLUTION SIGNAL CIRCUIT TEST

With ignition switch in ON position, and engine off, check voltage between ATCU terminal No. 25 and ground. Voltage should be 0.9-4.5 volts. If voltage is not as specified, repair circuit as necessary.

FLUID TEMPERATURE SENSOR TEST

1) Check resistance between fluid temperature sensor at sub-harness connector terminals No. 6 and No. 7 with cold AT. Resistance should be 2500 ohms at 68°F (20°C). If resistance is not as specified, replace sensor.
2) Disconnect solenoid sub-harness connector in engine compartment. Check resistance between terminals No. 6 and No. 7 when transaxle is cold. See FLUID TEMPERATURE SENSOR DIAGNOSIS table. Check voltage between ATCU terminal No. 6 and ground, while warming up transaxle. If resistance and voltage is not as specified, repair circuit as necessary.

FLUID TEMPERATURE SENSOR DIAGNOSIS

Terminal No.	Transaxle Temperature	Resistance	Voltage
6 To 7 .... Cold [1]		.... 2500 Ohms	.... N/A
6 To Ground .... Warming Up [2]		.... N/A	.... 1.5-.5

[1] – Cold 68°F (20°C).
[2] – Cold 68°F (20°C); Hot 176°F (80°C).

INHIBITOR SWITCH CIRCUIT TEST

Check voltage between ATCU terminals No. 16, 17, 18, 19, 20 and ground, while moving selector lever through each gear position. Battery voltage should be present at specified terminal when selector lever is in specified position. See INHIBITOR SWITCH VOLTAGE table.

INHIBITOR SWITCH VOLTAGE

Gear Position	Terminal No.
"P" & "N"	19
"R"	20
"D"	18
"2"	17
"1"	16

LINE PRESSURE SOLENOID TEST

1) Check ground circuit. Check resistance between solenoid assembly connector terminal No. 4 (I30 and Maxima), No. 1 (Altima and Quest) and ground. Solenoid resistance should be 2.5-5 ohms. If resistance is not as specified, replace solenoid.
2) Check power source circuit. With ignition switch in OFF position, disconnect ATCU harness connector. Check resistance between ATCU connector terminal No. 4 (I30 and Maxima), No. 1 (Altima and Quest) and terminal No. 2. Resistance should be 11.2-12.8 ohms. If resistance is not as specified, check resistance of dropping resistor. Check harness for short or open between ATCU and sub-harness assembly.
3) Disconnect ATCU connector and check resistance between solenoid harness connector terminal No. 4 (I30 and Maxima), No. 1 (Altima and Quest) and ATCU terminal No. 1. Resistance should be zero ohms. If resistance is not as specified, repair or replace harness between ATCU No. 1 and wiring sub-harness.

LOCK-UP SOLENOID TEST

1) Check operation of solenoid valve by listening for operating sound while applying battery voltage to terminal No. 5 and ground.
2) Check resistance between solenoid assembly connector terminal No. 5 and ground. Resistance should be 10-16 ohms. If resistance is not as specified, check replace solenoid.

OVERDRIVE SWITCH TEST

1) Check continuity between terminal No. 5 and No. 6, (I30 and Maxima), No. 1 and No. 2, (Altima and Quest) at overdrive switch. Continuity should exist with switch in OFF position. Continuity should not exist with switch in ON position. Replace switch as necessary.
2) Turn ignition to ON position. Check voltage between ATCU terminal No. 39 and ground while overdrive switch is in ON position. Battery voltage should be present. With overdrive switch in OFF position, one volt or less should be present. If voltage is not as specified, repair circuit as necessary.

OVERRUN CLUTCH SOLENOID TEST

1) Check resistance between solenoid assembly connector terminal No. 3 (I30 and Maxima), No. 8 (Altima and Quest) and ground. Resistance should be 20-30 ohms. If resistance is not as specified, replace solenoid as necessary.
2) Check operation of solenoid by listening for operation while applying battery voltage to appropriate terminal and ground.

REVOLUTION SENSOR TEST

1) Check resistance between wire terminals No. 3 and No. 2 at revolution sensor. Resistance should be 500-650 ohms. If resistance is not as specified, replace sensor.
2) Revolution sensor is a voltage generating sensor and should be tested using a voltmeter set on AC scale. Check voltage between ATCU terminal No. 25 and ground while driving vehicle. Voltage should rise gradually relative to vehicle speed. At zero MPH, voltage should not be present. If voltage is not as specified, repair circuit as necessary.

SHIFT SOLENOID "A" TEST

1) Check resistance between solenoid assembly connector terminal No. 2 (I30 and Maxima), No. 6 (Altima and Quest) and ground. Resistance should be 20-30 ohms. If resistance is not as specified, replace solenoid.
2) Check operation of solenoid by listening for operation while applying battery voltage to appropriate terminal and ground.

SHIFT SOLENOID "B" TEST

1) Check resistance between solenoid assembly connector terminal No. 1 (I30 and Maxima), No. 7 (Altima and Quest) and ground. Resistance should be 20-30 ohms. If resistance is not as specified, replace solenoid.
2) Check operation of solenoid by listening for operation while applying battery voltage to appropriate terminal and ground.

SPEED SENSOR CIRCUIT TEST

Check voltage between ATCU terminal No. 28 (I30 and Maxima), No. 27 (Altima and Quest) and ground while driving 1-2 MPH for 3 ft. (1m) or more. Voltage should vary from 0-5 volts. If voltage is not as described, check for continuity in wiring harness between ATCU and speed sensor. Check for poor ground circuit.

THROTTLE SENSOR CIRCUIT TEST

Check voltage between ATCU terminals No. 34 and 35 while depressing accelerator pedal slowly. At closed throttle, .2-.6 volt should be present. At wide open throttle, 2.9-3.9 volts should be present. Voltage rises relative to throttle valve opening.

THROTTLE VALVE SWITCH CIRCUIT

Checking Idle Switch Circuit – Check continuity between TVS terminal No. 2 and No. 3 with accelerator released, continuity should exist. With accelerator pedal depressed, no continuity should exist. At terminals No. 1 and No. 2, when depressing accelerator pedal to wide open throttle, continuity should be present. With accelerator pedal released, no continuity should exist.

SHIFT LOCK SOLENOID

Check operation of solenoid by listening for operation while applying battery voltage to shift lock harness connector terminals. Apply voltage to terminals and listen for operation. See SHIFT LOCK SOLENOID OPERATION TEST table for model identification and terminal numbers.

SHIFT LOCK SOLENOID OPERATION TEST

Model	Voltage Between Terminals
1995 Altima	8 & 9
1996 Altima	5 & 1
1995 Maxima	9 & 4
1996 Maxima, 1995 & 96 I30, Quest	2 & 2

PARK POSITION SWITCH

Continuity should exist at all times EXCEPT when selector lever is in "P" position with selector lever button released. See PARK POSITION SWITCH CONTINUITY TEST table for terminal identification.

PARK POSITION SWITCH CONTINUITY TEST [1]

Model	Continuity Between Terminals
1995 Altima	6 & 11
1996 Altima	6 & 1
1995 Maxima	6 & 7
1996 Maxima, 1995 & 96 I30, Quest	1 & 2

[1] – Continuity should exist at all times EXCEPT when selector lever is in "P" position with selector lever button released.

STOP LIGHT SWITCH

Maxima – Check for continuity between terminals No. 2 (1996 Maxima) and No. 5 (1995 Maxima) of stop light switch harness connector. With brake pedal depressed, continuity should exist. No continuity should exist with brake pedal released.

ASCD CANCEL OR A/T SHIFT LOCK SWITCH

Check for continuity between terminals No. 2 and No. 5 (1995 Maxima), No. 1 and No. 2 (all other models). Continuity should exist only with brake pedal released.

KEY INTERLOCK CABLE

NOTE: Ensure key interlock cable is installed without sharp bends, twists or interference with adjacent parts. Ensure casing cap and bracket are secured firmly. If casing cap can be remove with a load of less than 8.8 lbs (39.2 N), replace key interlock cable. See Fig. 2.

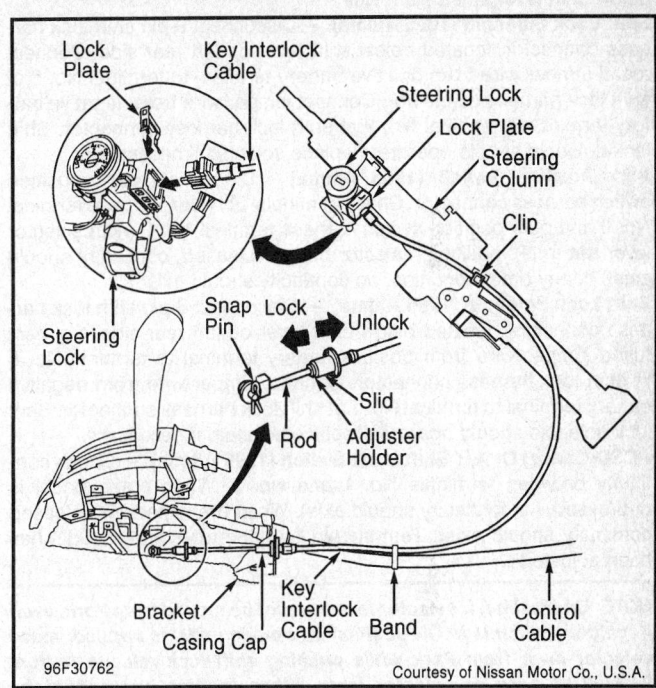

Fig. 2: Identifying Key Interlock Components

Removal – Unlock slider from adjuster holder. Remove rod from cable. Remove lock plate (at ignition switch), pull out key interlock cable.
Installation – Install key interlock cable to steering lock assembly and install lock plate. Clamp cable to steering column. Place selector lever in "P" position. Install interlock rod into adjuster holder. Install casing cap to bracket. Move slider in order to fix adjuster holder to interlock rod.

SHIFT LOCK SYSTEM TESTING

Shift Lock Control Unit (1995 Altima & Maxima) – Measure voltage between each terminal and terminal No. 8. See SHIFT LOCK CONTROL UNIT INSPECTION table. *See Fig. 1.*

Park Position Switch (1995 Altima) – 1) Disconnect 9-pin shift lock harness connector, located below shift lever on left rear side. Check for continuity between shift lock harness connector terminal No. 5 and terminal No. 6.

SHIFT LOCK CONTROL UNIT INSPECTION

Terminal No.	Item	Condition	Standard
1 & 8	Ignition Signal	Ignition Switch "ON" Position	Battery Voltage
		Any Position Except "ON" Position	0 Volts
2 & 8	Power Source	Any Condition	Battery Voltage
4 & 8	Shift Lock Signal	Ignition Switch to "ON" Position, Selector Lever In "P" Position, Brake Pedal Depressed	Battery Voltage
		Except As Above	0 Volts
5 & 8	Stop Lamp Switch	Brake Pedal Depressed	Battery Voltage
		Brake Pedal Released	0 Volts
6 & 8	Park Position Switch	Ignition Key In Key Cylinder, Selector Lever In "P" Position, Selector Lever In Any Position & Button Pushed	Battery Voltage
		Except As Above	0 Volts

2) When selector lever is in Park and selector lever button is released, continuity should not exist. Continuity should exist for all other conditions. If continuity is not as specified, replace detention switch, located below shift lever at left front side.

Shift Lock Solenoid (1995 Altima) – Disconnect 9-pin shift lock harness connector, located below shift lever on left rear side. Connect fused jumper wire from positive battery terminal to terminal No. 8 at shift lock harness connector. Connect jumper wire from negative battery terminal to terminal No. 9 at shift lock harness connector. Shift lock solenoid should operate. Replace solenoid if necessary.

Park Position Switch (1996 Altima) – Disconnect park position switch harness connector. Check continuity between harness terminal No. 6 and park position switch harness terminal No. 1. With selector lever set in "P" position, selector button released, continuity should exist. In any other condition, no continuity should exist.

Shift Lock Solenoid (1996 Altima) – Disconnect 6-pin shift lock harness connector, located below shift lever on left rear side. Connect fused jumper wire from positive battery terminal to terminal No. 5 at shift lock harness connector. Connect jumper wire from negative battery terminal to terminal No. 1 at shift lock harness connector. Shift lock solenoid should operate. Replace solenoid if necessary.

ACSD Cancel Or A/T Shift Lock Switch (1996 Altima) – Check continuity between terminals No. 1 and No. 2. When brake pedal is depressed, no continuity should exist. When brake pedal is released continuity should exist. Test should be done after brake pedal has been adjusted.

NOTE: On Maxima, if selector lever cannot be moved from Park, even if ignition switch is in ON position and brake pedal is applied, move selector lever from Park while pushing shift lock release button, located at base of selector lever. When ignition key cannot be removed, even if selector lever is in Park, push emergency button, located at ignition switch, to remove key.

Shift Lock Control Unit - SLCU (1995 Maxima) – **1)** Ensure battery voltage exists at control unit terminal No. 2 and ground at all times. Terminal No. 1 should have battery voltage only with ignition switch in ON position. Disconnect 8-pin SLCU harness connector, check for continuity between SLCU harness connector terminal No. 8 and ground. Reconnect SLCU connector.

2) If continuity is not as specified, inspect wiring harness for open or short, connectors for poor contacts, fuse or ignition switch.

Park Position Switch – **1)** Check input signal. With KOEO, set select lever in "P" position, selector lever button released. Disconnect SLCU harness connector. Ensure no continuity exists between control unit harness connector No. 6 and ground. If not as specified, check park position switch. See PARK POSITION SWITCH in COMPONENT TESTING & CIRCUIT TESTS.

2) With KOEO, check voltage between SLCU harness terminal No. 6 and ground. Check with brake pedal depressed and selector lever button pushed. Zero volts should exist. Check voltage at SLCU harness connector terminal No. 6 and ground with selector lever in any position except "P". Battery voltage should exist. If not as specified, check harness continuity between SLCU terminal No. 6 and park position switch harness terminal and to ground. Check park position switch. See PARK POSITION SWITCH in COMPONENT TESTING & CIRCUIT TESTS.

Stop Light Switch (1995 Maxima) – Check voltage between SLCU harness terminal No. 5 and ground. With brake pedal depressed, battery voltage should exist. With brake pedal released, no voltage should exist. If not as specified, check continuity in harness between SLCU terminal No. 5 and stop light switch harness terminal No. 2. Check stop light switch. See STOP LIGHT SWITCH in COMPONENT TESTING & CIRCUIT TESTS.

Shift Lock Solenoid (1995 Maxima) – With KOEO, check voltage between shift lock harness connector terminal No. 4 and body ground. With brake pedal depressed, battery voltage should be present. With brake pedal released, zero voltage should be present. With ignition in OFF position, check voltage between shift lock harness connector terminal No. 4 and ground with brake pedal depressed. Zero voltage should exist. If voltages are not as specified, check continuity of harness between SLCU terminal No. 4 and shift lock harness terminal No. 4. Ensure continuity exists between shift lock harness terminal No. 9 and ground.

Shift Lock System (1996 Maxima & I30) – **1)** Ensure key lock cable is not kinked or damaged. Check selector lever position for damage. Check power source. With KOEO, check voltage between ASCD cancel switch harness terminal No. 1 and ground. Battery voltage should be present. If voltage is not as specified, check harness for open or short between battery and ASCD cancel switch harness terminal No. 1. Check fuse and ignition switch.

2) Check ASCD cancel switch input signal. With KOEO, check voltage between A/T device harness No. 2 and ground. With brake pedal depressed, zero volts should be present. With brake pedal released battery voltage should be present. If voltage is not as specified, check harness for open or short between A/T device harness connector and ASCD harness connector No. 2. Check ASCD cancel switch. See COMPONENT TESTING & CIRCUIT TESTS.

3) Check ground circuit. With ignition switch in OFF position. Disconnect A/T device harness connector. Check for continuity between A/T device harness terminal No. 1 and ground. If no continuity exists, repair or replace harness or connector. Check park position switch and shift lock solenoid. See appropriate tests in COMPONENT TESTING & CIRCUIT TESTS.

Shift Lock System (Quest) – **1)** Check power source. With KOEO, check voltage between ASCD cancel switch harness terminal No. 1 and ground. Battery voltage should be present. If no voltage is present, check harness for open or short, fuse and ignition switch.

2) Check ASCD cancel switch. With KOEO, check voltage between shift lock solenoid and park position switch harness terminal No. 2 and ground. With brake pedal depressed, zero volts should be present. With brake pedal released, battery voltage should be present. If voltage is not as specified, check harness for open or short between shift lock solenoid and park position switch harness connector No. 2 and ASCD cancel switch harness connector No. 2.

3) Check ground circuit. With ignition in OFF position. Disconnect shift lock solenoid and park position switch harness connector. Check continuity between shift lock solenoid and park position switch harness terminal No. 1 and ground. If no continuity exists, repair or replace harness or connector.

4) Check park position switch and shift lock solenoid. See appropriate tests in COMPONENT TESTING & CIRCUIT TESTS. Reconnect shift lock solenoid and park position switch harness connector. With KOEO, recheck shift lock operation.

SHIFT LOCK ROD

Removal (Quest) – Turn ignition key to ACC position. Unlock slider by squeezing lock tabs. Remove shift lock rod from key interlock rod.

Installation – Place selector lever in "P" position. Turn ignition key to ACC position. Insert shift lock rod into slider. Push key interlock rod toward shift lock rod to adjust. DO NOT hold shift lock rod. Lock slider into position. Test shift lock operation.

WIRING DIAGRAMS

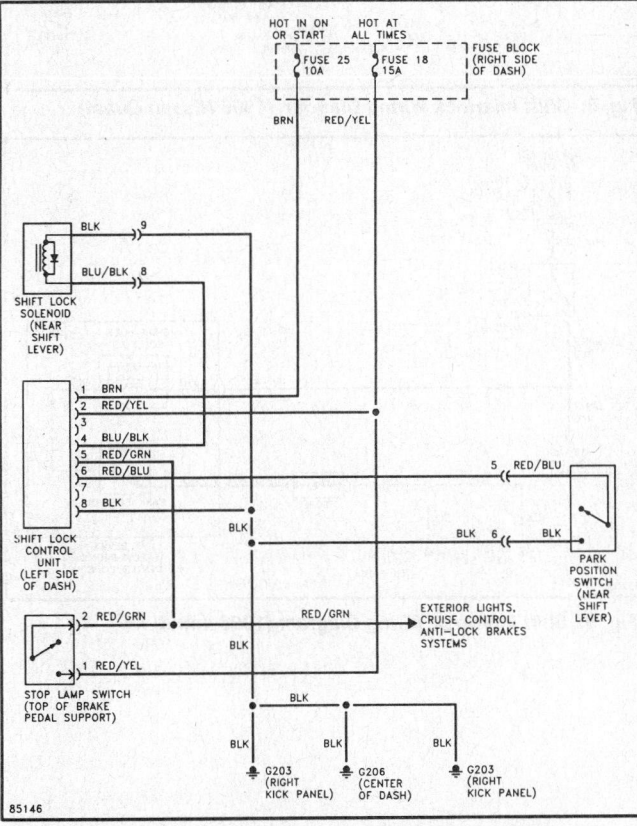

Fig. 3: Shift Interlock Wiring Diagram (1995 Nissan Altima)

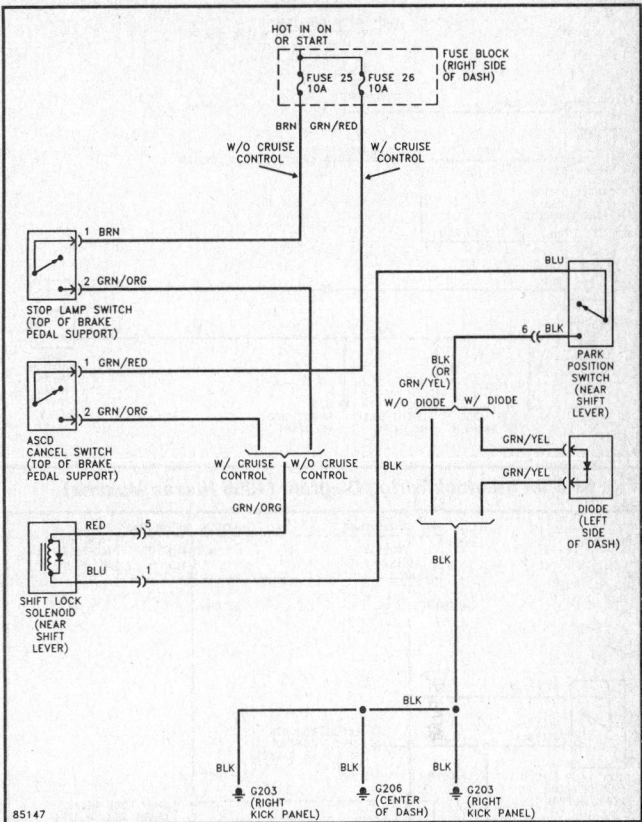

Fig. 4: Shift Interlock Wiring Diagram (1996 Nissan Altima)

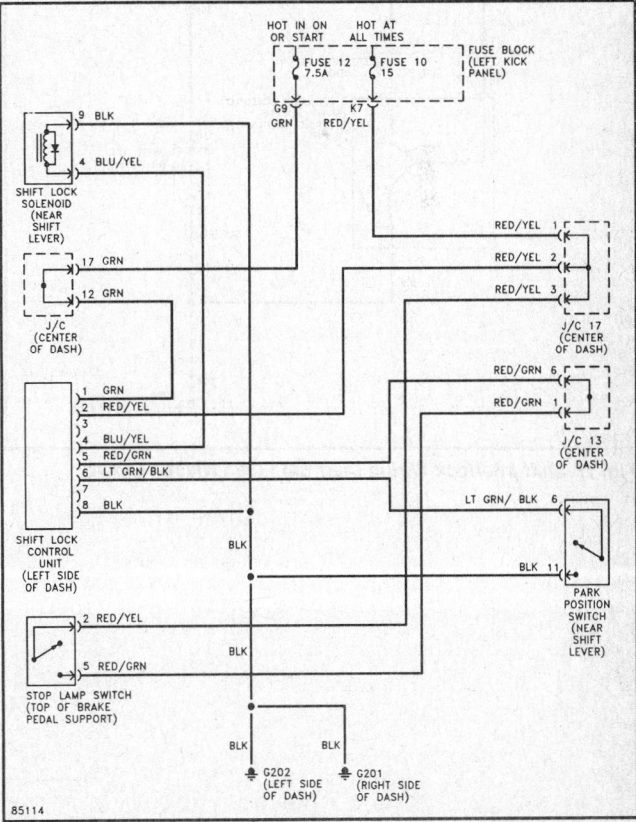

Fig. 5: Shift Interlock Wiring Diagram (1995 Nissan Maxima)

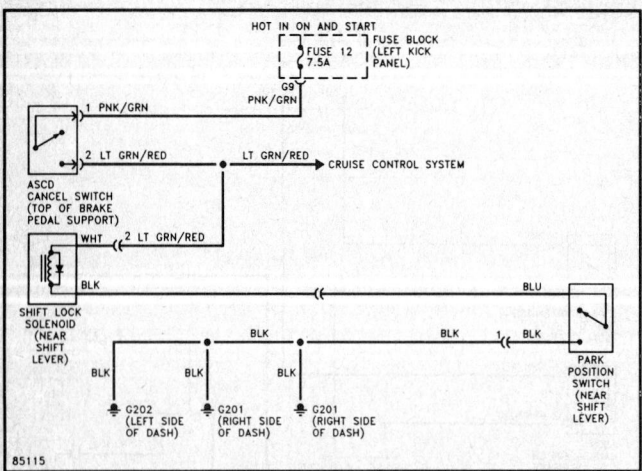

Fig. 6: Shift Interlock Wiring Diagram (1996 Nissan Maxima)

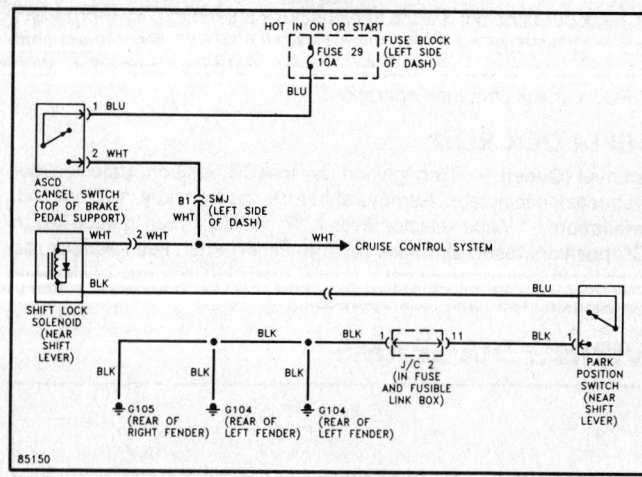

Fig. 8: Shift Interlock Wiring Diagram (1996 Nissan Quest)

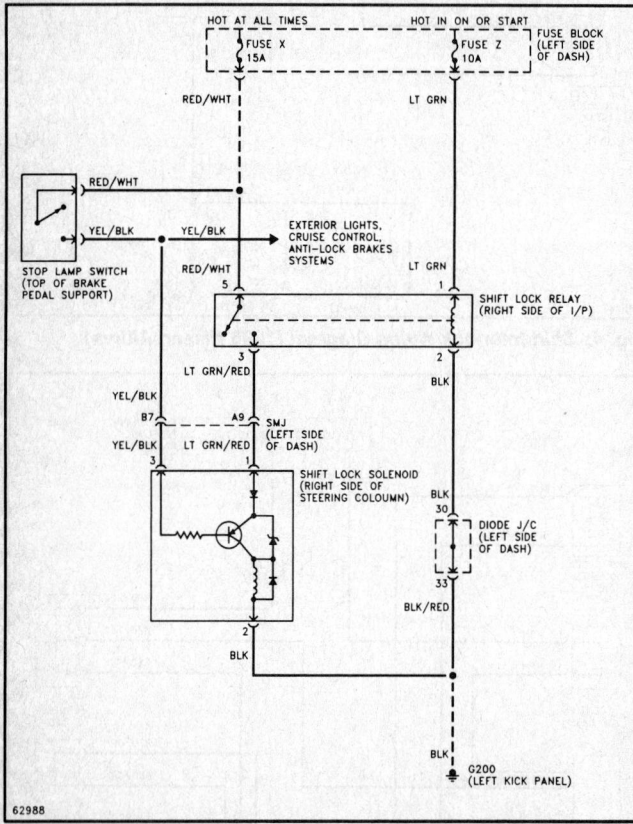

Fig. 7: Shift Interlock Wiring Diagram (1995 Nissan Quest)

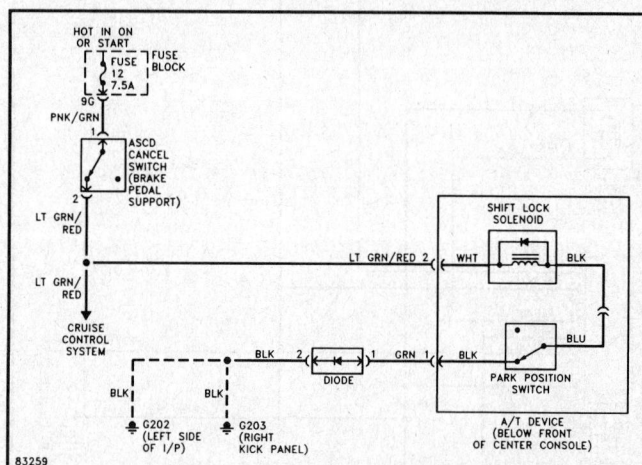

Fig. 9: Shift Interlock Wiring Diagram (1996 Infiniti I30)

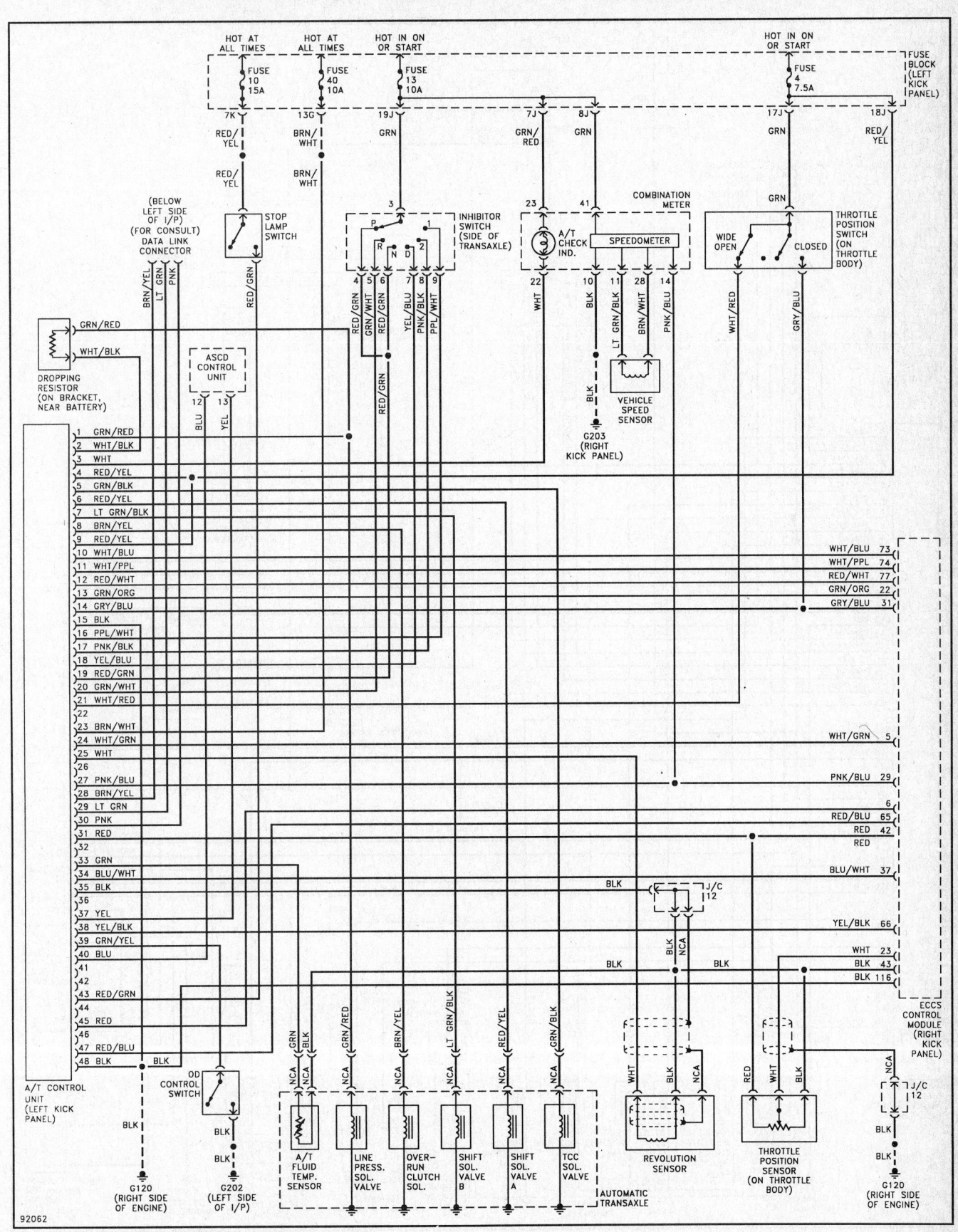

Fig. 10: Transaxle Wiring Diagram (1996 Infiniti I30)

AUTOMATIC TRANSMISSIONS
RE4F04A/V Electronic Controls (Cont.)

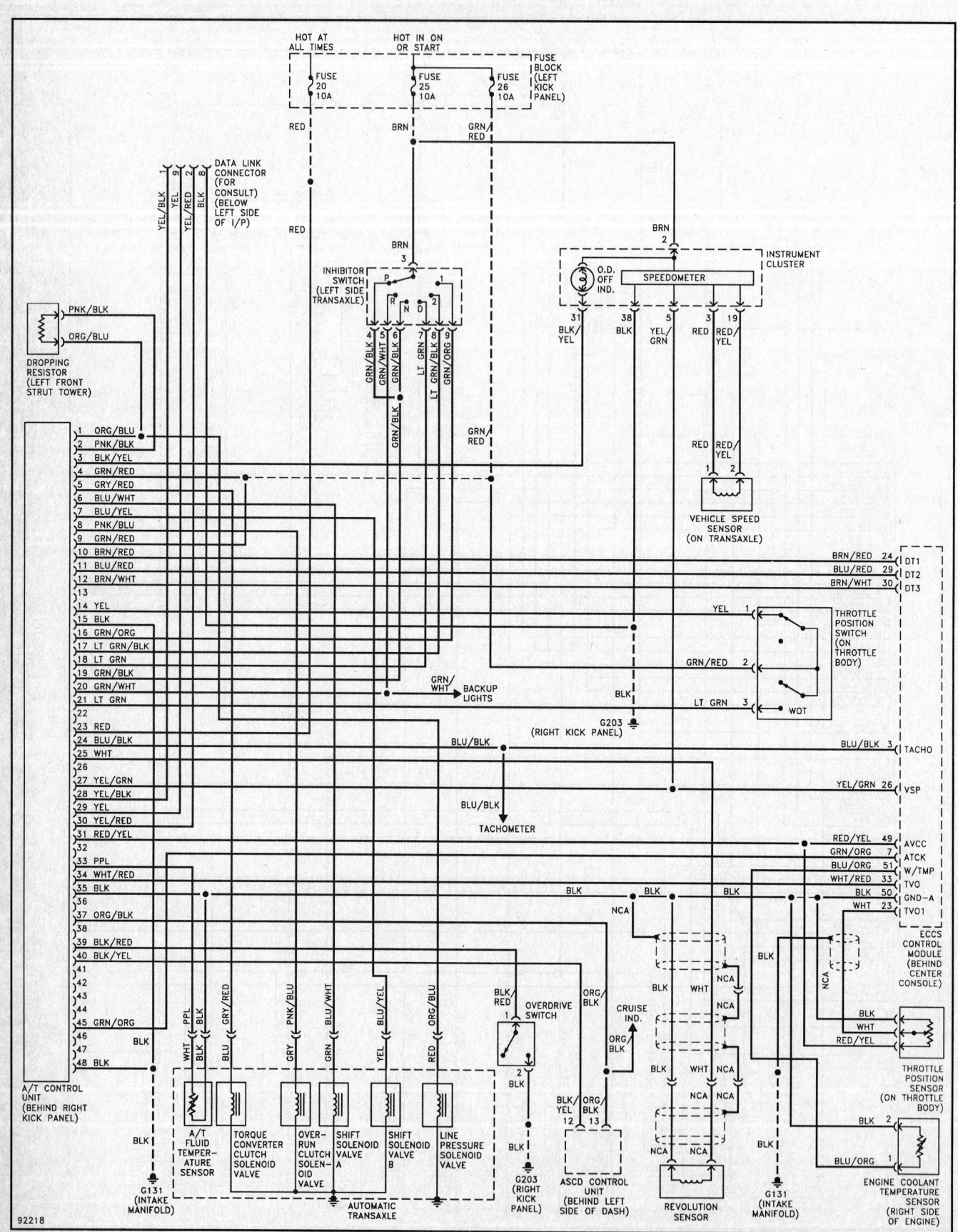

Fig. 11: Transaxle Wiring Diagram (1995-96 Nissan Altima)

92218

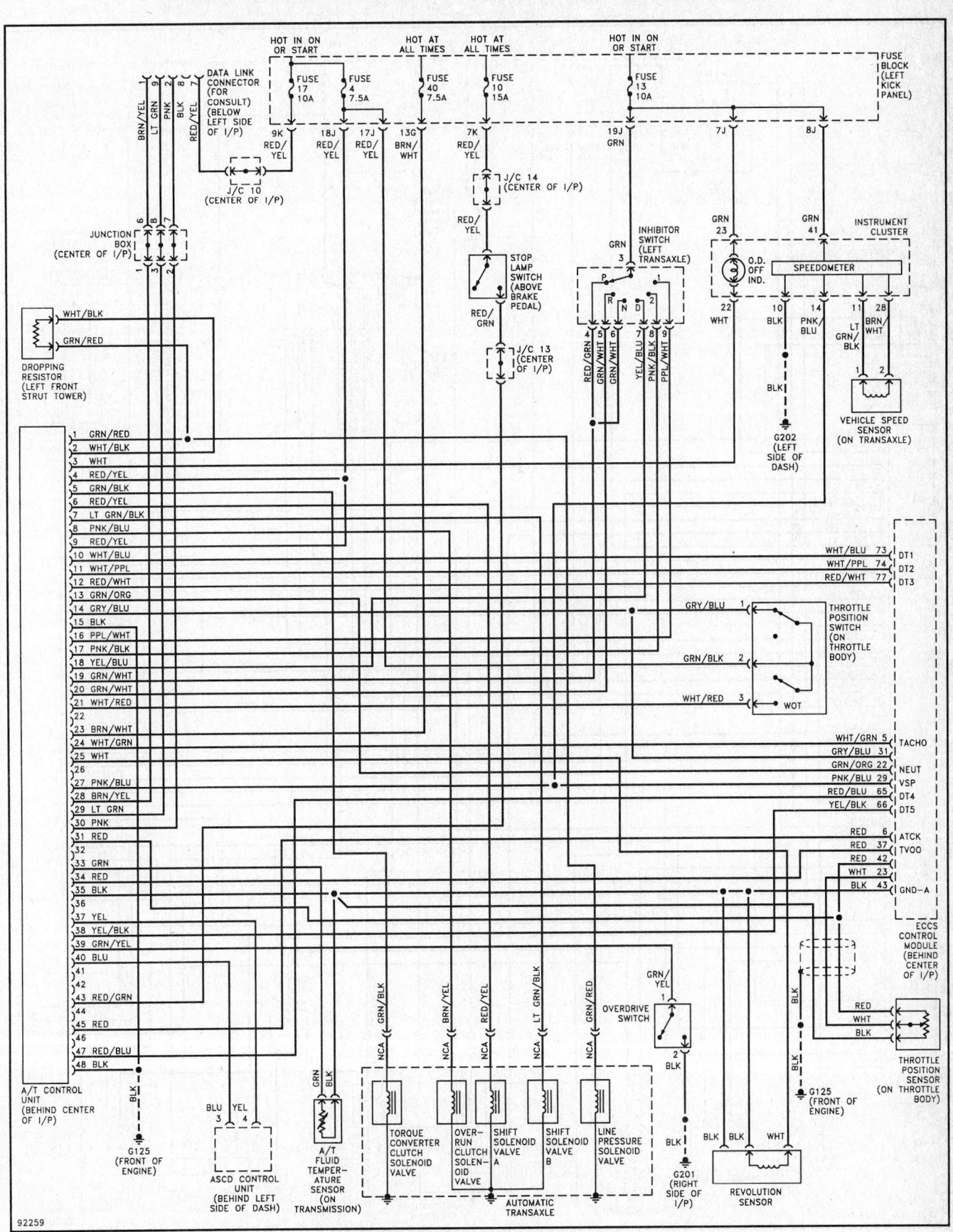

Fig. 12: Transaxle Wiring Diagram (1995 Nissan Maxima)

92259

AUTOMATIC TRANSMISSIONS
RE4F04A/V Electronic Controls (Cont.)

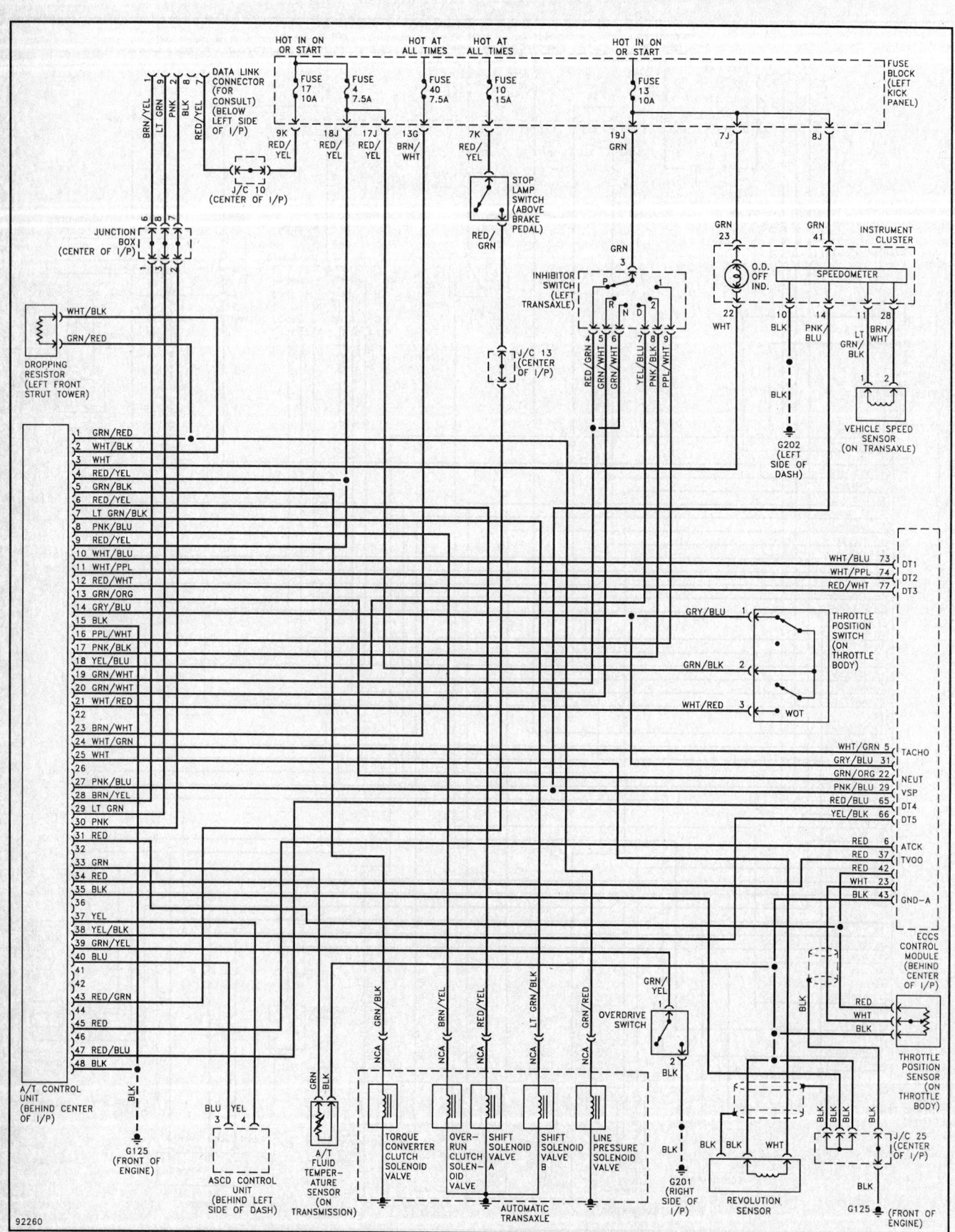

Fig. 13: Transaxle Wiring Diagram (1996 Nissan Maxima)

92260

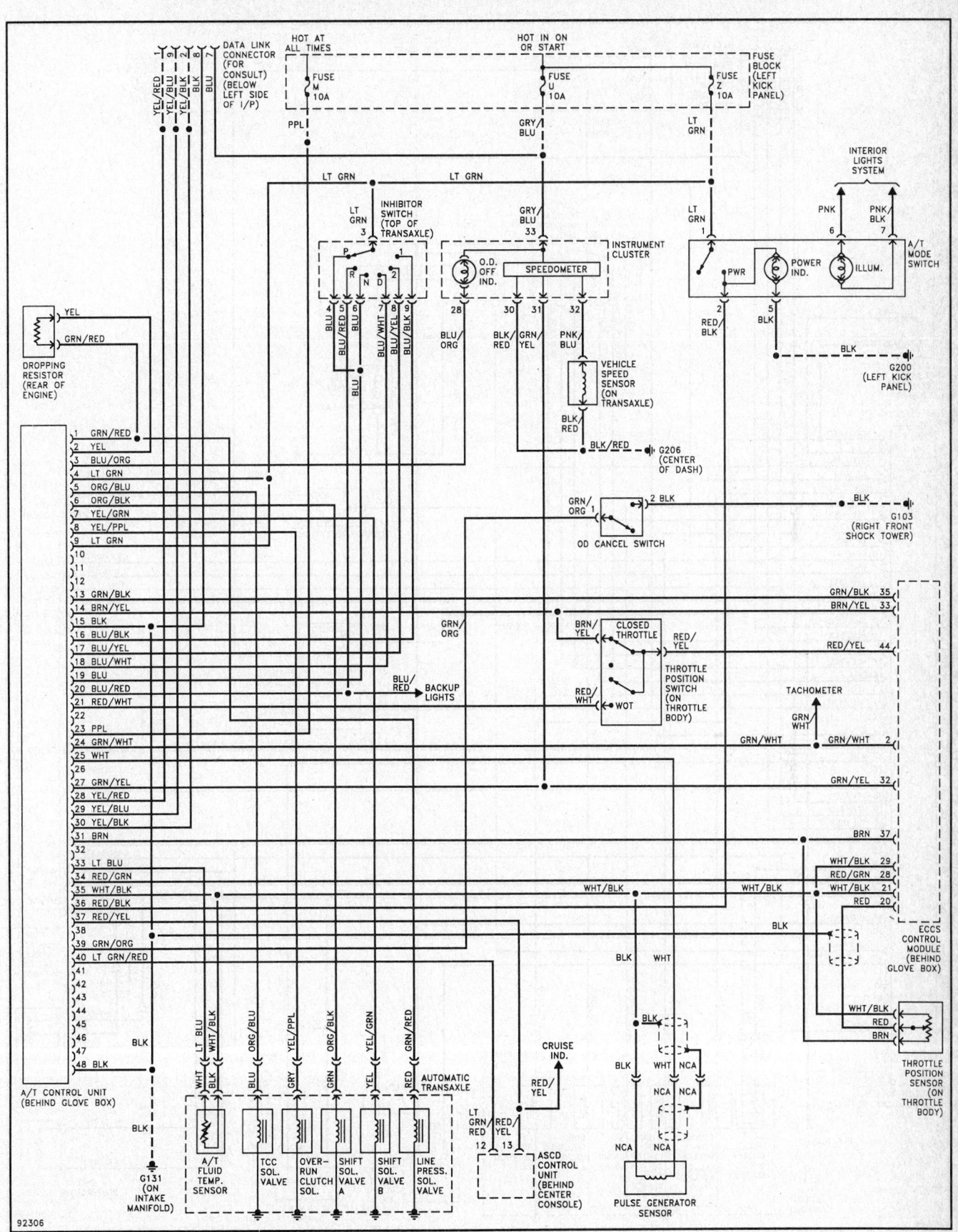

Fig. 14: Transaxle Wiring Diagram (1995 Nissan Quest)

AUTOMATIC TRANSMISSIONS
RE4F04A/V Electronic Controls (Cont.)

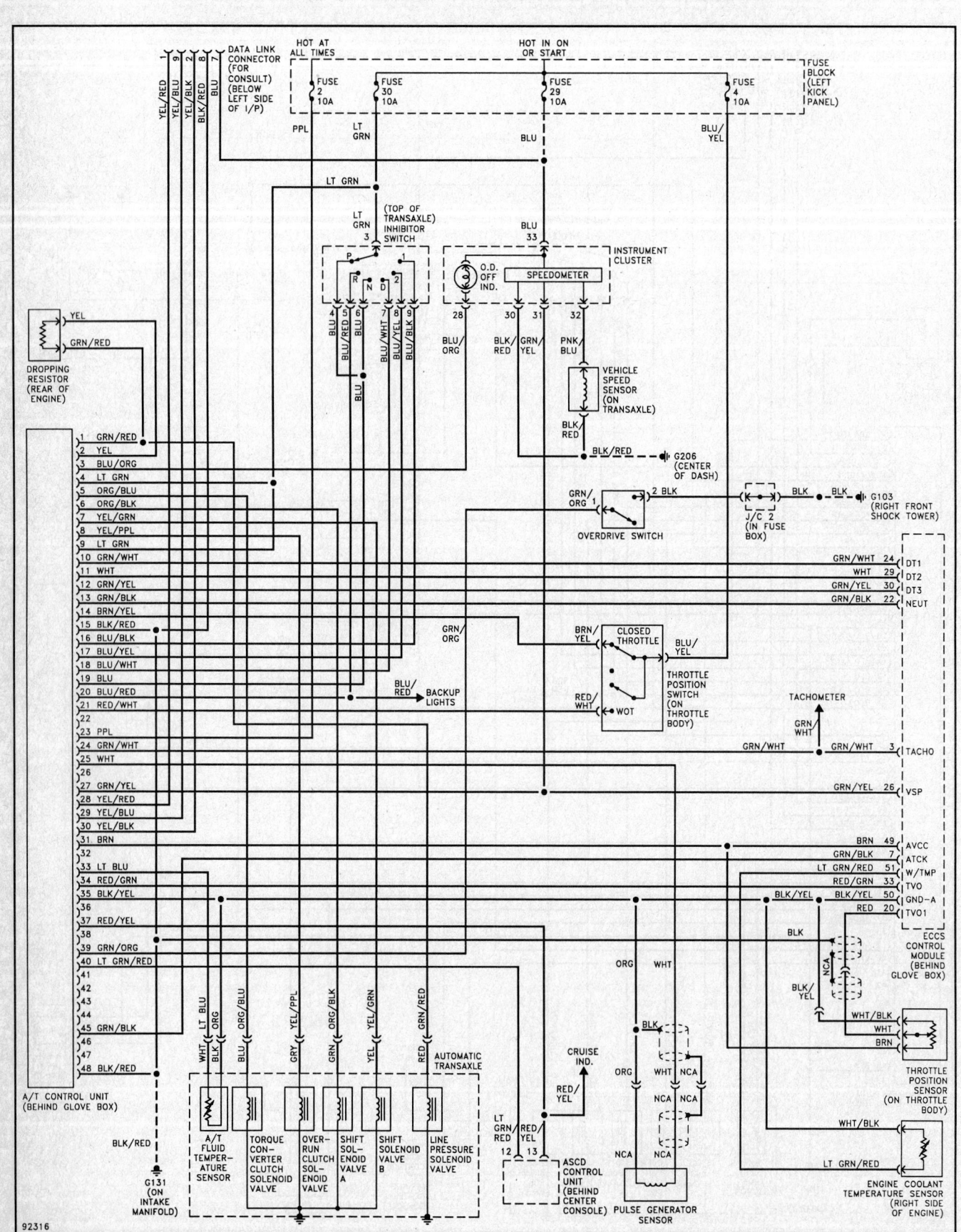

Fig. 15: *Transaxle Wiring Diagram (1996 Nissan Quest)*

AUTOMATIC TRANSMISSIONS
Nissan RE4R01A, RE4R03A & RL4R01A

Infiniti: J30, Q45
Nissan: Pathfinder, Pickup, 240SX, 300ZX

APPLICATION & LABOR TIMES

APPLICATION & LABOR TIMES

Vehicle Application	[1] R & I	[2] Overhaul	Trans. Model
Infiniti			
J30	4.8	9.5	RE4R01A
Q45	7.0	9.5	RE4R03A
Nissan			
Pathfinder			
2WD	4.3	9.5	RE4R01A
4WD	7.8	9.5	RE4R01A
Pickup			
2WD (4-Cyl)	3.9	9.5	RL4R01A
4WD (V6)	7.5	9.5	RE4R01A
240SX	4.5	9.5	RE4R01A
300ZX			
Non-Turbo	4.0	9.5	RE4R01A
Turbo	4.3	9.5	RE4R03A

[1] – Removal and installation of transmission from vehicle chassis.
[2] – Bench overhaul time for transmission and differential. DOES NOT include removal and installation.

IDENTIFICATION

Transmission model is identified by vehicle identification plate located in engine compartment. See Fig. 1. Transmission number is located on right side of transmission rear extension. See Fig. 2.

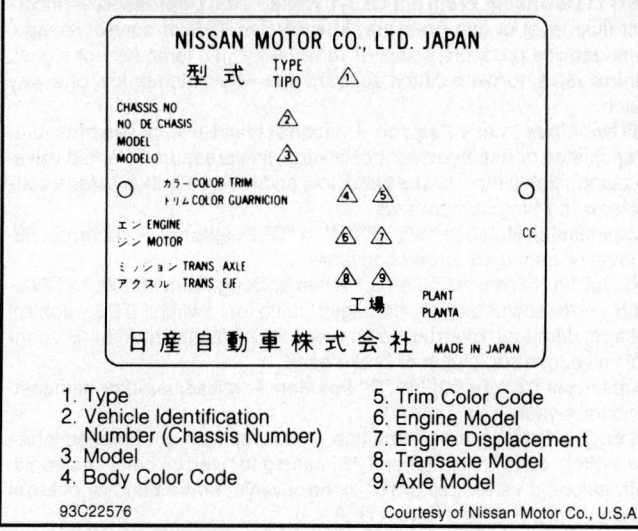

NISSAN MOTOR CO., LTD. JAPAN

型式 TYPE / TIPO ⚠1

CHASSIS NO / NO DE CHASIS ⚠2
MODEL / MODELO ⚠3

○ カラ—COLOR TRIM / トリム COLOR GUARNICION ⚠4 ⚠5 ○

エン ENGINE / ジン MOTOR ⚠6 ⚠7 CC

ミッション TRANS AXLE / アクスル TRANS EJE ⚠8 ⚠9 PLANT / PLANTA 工場

日産自動車株式会社 MADE IN JAPAN

1. Type
2. Vehicle Identification Number (Chassis Number)
3. Model
4. Body Color Code
5. Trim Color Code
6. Engine Model
7. Engine Displacement
8. Transaxle Model
9. Axle Model

93C22576 — Courtesy of Nissan Motor Co., U.S.A.

Fig. 1: Identifying Transmission Model

LUBRICATION & ADJUSTMENTS

See appropriate AUTOMATIC TRANSMISSION SERVICING article in TRANSMISSION SERVICING section.

NOTE: Fluid level should be checked using HOT range on dipstick at fluid temperatures of 122-176°F (50-80°C) after vehicle has been driven approximately 5 minutes after initial warm-up. DO NOT overfill. Ensure computer control systems are operating properly before diagnosing shifting problems.

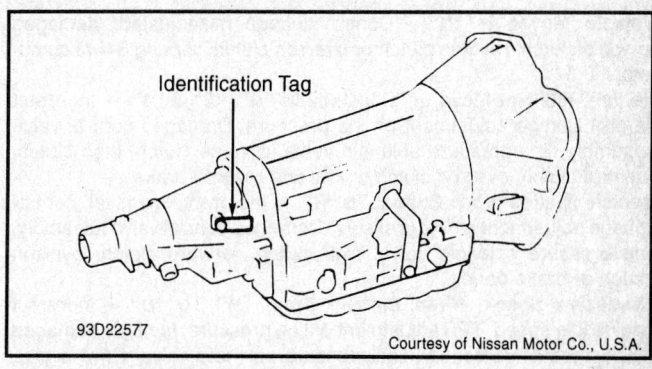

Identification Tag

93D22577 — Courtesy of Nissan Motor Co., U.S.A.

Fig. 2: Locating Transmission Number (RL4R01A Shown; Others Are Similar)

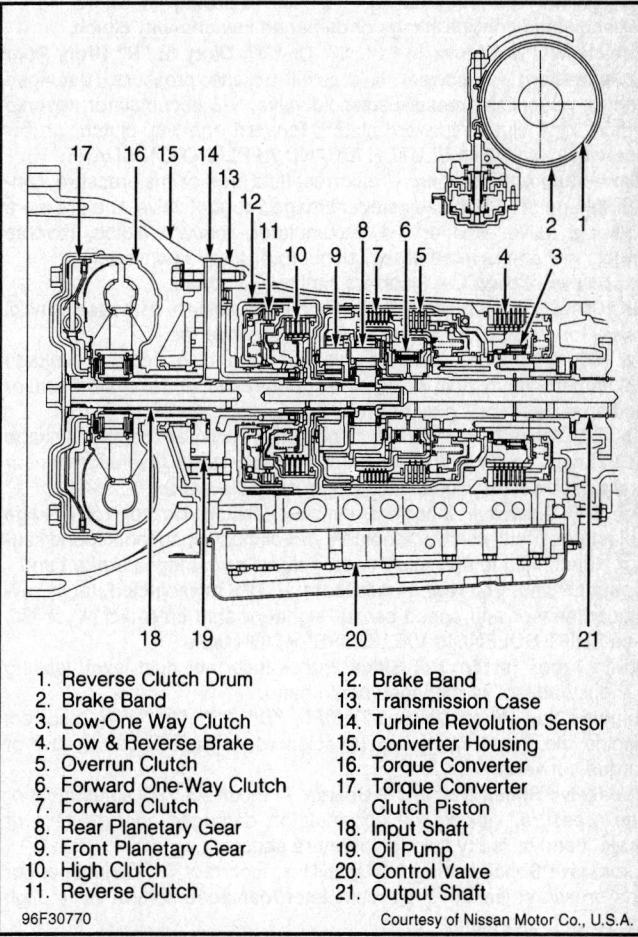

1. Reverse Clutch Drum
2. Brake Band
3. Low-One Way Clutch
4. Low & Reverse Brake
5. Overrun Clutch
6. Forward One-Way Clutch
7. Forward Clutch
8. Rear Planetary Gear
9. Front Planetary Gear
10. High Clutch
11. Reverse Clutch
12. Brake Band
13. Transmission Case
14. Turbine Revolution Sensor
15. Converter Housing
16. Torque Converter
17. Torque Converter Clutch Piston
18. Input Shaft
19. Oil Pump
20. Control Valve
21. Output Shaft

96F30770 — Courtesy of Nissan Motor Co., U.S.A.

Fig. 3: Identifying Transmission Component Locations (RE4R03A Shown, Others Are Similar)

TROUBLE SHOOTING

SYMPTOM DIAGNOSIS

Engine Will Not Start In "P" Or "N" – Inhibitor switch, control linkage, ignition switch or starter malfunction.

Engine Will Start In "D", "2", "1" Or "R" – Inhibitor switch or control linkage misadjusted.

Transmission Noise In "P" & "N" – Incorrect fluid level or line pressure, TPS misadjusted, faulty revolution sensor or speed sensor signal, damaged oil pump or torque converter.

Parking Gear Will Not Engage; Or Parking Gear Will Not Disengage – Control linkage misadjusted or defective parking components.

Vehicle Moves In "N" – Control linkage misadjusted, damaged forward clutch, reverse clutch or overrun clutch, leaking 3-4 accumulator.

Vehicle Will Not Move In "R"; Okay In "D", "2" & "1" – Incorrect control linkage adjustment or line pressure. Damaged control valve assembly, line pressure solenoid valve, reverse clutch, high clutch, forward clutch, overrun clutch or low and reverse brake.

Vehicle Brakes When Shifted To "R" – Incorrect fluid level, control linkage adjustment or line pressure. Damaged control valve assembly, line pressure solenoid valve, high clutch, forward clutch, overrun clutch or brake band.

Excessive Shock When Shifting From "N" To "D" – Incorrect engine idle speed, TPS adjustment or line pressure, faulty or damaged fluid temperature sensor, line pressure solenoid valve, RPM signal, control valve assembly, N-D accumulator, turbine revolution sensor or forward clutch.

Vehicle Will Not Move In "D", "2" Or "3"; Okay In "1" & "R" – Misadjusted control linkage or damaged low one-way clutch.

Vehicle Will Not Move In "1", "2" Or "D"; Okay In "R" (Very Poor Acceleration) – Incorrect fluid level or line pressure, damaged control valve, line pressure solenoid valve, N-D accumulator, reverse clutch, high clutch, forward clutch, forward one-way clutch, or low one-way clutch. See CLUTCH & BAND APPLICATION CHART.

Slips When Accelerating – Incorrect fluid level or line pressure, control linkage or TPS misadjusted, damaged control valve, line pressure solenoid valve, N-D or 3-4 accumulator, forward clutch, reverse clutch, low and reverse brake, oil pump or torque converter.

Excessive "Creep" – Incorrect engine idle speed.

No "Creep" – Incorrect fluid level or line pressure, damaged control valve, forward clutch, oil pump or torque converter.

No 1-2 Upshift – Incorrect inhibitor switch or control linkage adjustment, faulty shift solenoid "A", control valve, revolution sensor and speed sensor signal or brake band.

No 2-3 Upshift – Incorrect inhibitor switch or control linkage adjustment, faulty shift solenoid "B", control valve, revolution sensor and speed sensor signal, high clutch or brake band.

No 3-4 Upshift – Incorrect inhibitor switch or control linkage adjustment, faulty shift solenoid "A", revolution sensor and speed sensor signal, fluid temperature sensor signal or damaged brake band.

Upshift Points Too High In All Gears – TPS misadjusted, faulty revolution sensor and speed sensor signal or shift solenoid "A" or "B". See SHIFT SOLENOID VALVE OPERATION table.

Shifts From 1st To 3rd; Skips 2nd – Incorrect fluid level, leaking 1-2 accumulator or damaged brake band.

Engine Dies When Shifted To "R", "D", "2" Or "1" – Incorrect engine idle speed, faulty lock-up solenoid, damaged control valve or torque converter.

Excessive Shock During 1-2 Upshift – Incorrect TPS adjustment or line pressure, leaking 1-2 accumulator, damaged control valve or brake band or faulty fluid temperature sensor.

Excessive Shock During 2-3 Upshift – Incorrect TPS adjustment or line pressure, leaking 2-3 accumulator, damaged control valve, high clutch or brake band.

Excessive Shock During 3-4 Upshift – Incorrect TPS adjustment or line pressure, leaking 3-4 accumulator, damaged control valve, overrun clutch or brake band.

Slips During 1-2 Upshift – Incorrect fluid level, TPS adjustment or line pressure, damaged control valve, 1-2 accumulator or brake band.

Slips During 2-3 Upshift – Incorrect fluid level, TPS adjustment or line pressure, damaged control valve, 2-3 accumulator, high clutch or brake band.

Slips During 3-4 Upshift – Incorrect fluid level, TPS adjustment or line pressure, damaged control valve, 3-4 accumulator, high clutch or brake band.

Vehicle Brakes During 1-2 Upshift – Incorrect fluid level, damaged reverse clutch, low and reverse clutch, high clutch or low one-way clutch.

Vehicle Brakes During 2-3 Upshift – Incorrect fluid level or damaged brake band.

Vehicle Brakes During 3-4 Upshift – Incorrect fluid level, damaged overrun clutch, forward one-way clutch or reverse clutch.

Poor Acceleration, Cannot Achieve Maximum Speed – Incorrect fluid level, incorrect inhibitor adjustment, damaged shift solenoid valve "A" or "B", control valve, reverse clutch, high clutch, brake band, low and reverse brake, oil pump or torque converter.

Will Not Shift From 4-3 – Incorrect fluid level, misadjusted TPS, damaged overrun clutch solenoid, shift solenoid valve "A", line pressure solenoid valve, control valve, low and reverse brake or overrun clutch.

Will Not Shift 3-2, 4-2 Or 2-1 Or 3-1 – Incorrect fluid level, misadjusted TPS, damaged shift solenoid valves "A" or "B", control valve, high clutch, low one-way clutch or brake band.

Release Of Acceleration Pedal Causes Excessive Gear Change Shock During Deceleration – Misadjusted TPS, incorrect line pressure, damaged overrun clutch solenoid or control valve.

Shift Points, 4-3, 3-2, 2-1 Too High – Misadjusted TPS or faulty revolution or vehicle speed sensor.

No Kickdown From 4th While Depressing Pedal Within Kickdown Vehicle Speed Or Kickdown Operates While Depressing Pedal In 4th Beyond Kickdown Limit – Misadjusted TPS, faulty revolution or vehicle speed sensor, damaged shift solenoid "A" or "B".

Slips In Downshift From 4-3 While Pedal Depressed – Incorrect fluid level or line pressure, Misadjusted TPS, damaged line pressure solenoid valve, control valve, high clutch or forward clutch.

Slips In Downshift From 4-2 While Pedal Depressed – Incorrect fluid level or line pressure, Misadjusted TPS, damaged line pressure solenoid valve, shift solenoid valve "A", control valve, high clutch or brake band.

Slips In Downshift From 3-2 While Pedal Depressed – Incorrect fluid level or line pressure, Misadjusted TPS, faulty fluid temp sensor signal, damaged line pressure solenoid valve, control valve, brake band, forward clutch or high clutch.

Slips In Downshift From 4-1 Or 3-1 While Pedal Depressed – Incorrect fluid level or line pressure, Misadjusted TPS or control linkage, damaged line pressure solenoid valve faulty fluid temp sensor signal, control valve, forward clutch, forward one-way clutch or low one-way clutch.

Will Not Move In Any Position – Incorrect fluid level or line pressure, Misadjusted or damaged control linkage, line pressure solenoid valve, oil pump, high clutch, brake band, low and reverse brake, torque converter or parking components.

Transmission Noise In "D", "2", "1" & "R" Positions. – Incorrect fluid level or damaged torque converter.

Will Not Shift From "D3" To "2₂" When Shifting From "D" To "2" Position — Misadjusted or damaged inhibitor switch, TPS, control linkage, damaged overrun clutch solenoid, shift valves "A" or "B", control valve, overrun clutch or brake band.

Shifts From "2₂" To "D₃" In "2" Position – Misadjusted or damaged inhibitor switch.

No Engine Braking In "1" Position – Misadjusted or damaged inhibitor switch, control linkage or TPS, damaged overrun clutch solenoid, shift solenoid valves,"A" or "B", control valve, brake band or overrun clutch.

Shifts From "1₁" To "1₂" In "1" Position – Misadjusted or damaged inhibitor switch.

No Shift From "1₂" To "1₁" In "1" Position – Damaged control valve assembly or low and reverse brake.

Transmission Overheats – Incorrect fluid level, idle RPM, line pressure. Misadjusted TPS. Damaged line pressure solenoid, control valve, oil pump, reverse clutch, high clutch, brake band, forward clutch, overrun clutch, low and reverse brake or torque converter.

ATF Shoots Out, White Smoke From Tailpipe – Incorrect fluid level, damaged reverse clutch, high clutch, brake band, forward clutch, overrun clutch or low and reverse brake.

Offensive Smell At Filler Tube – Incorrect fluid level, damaged torque converter, oil pump, reverse clutch, high clutch, brake band, forward clutch, overrun clutch or low and reverse brake.

Converter Does Not Lock Up – Incorrect TPS or inhibitor switch adjustment, line pressure or engine RPM signal, faulty revolution sensor or speed sensor, lock-up solenoid, fluid temperature sensor, control valve assembly or torque converter.

Torque Converter Clutch Piston Slip – Incorrect fluid level or line pressure, misadjusted TPS, damaged torque converter clutch solenoid valve, line pressure solenoid or control valve assembly.

Lock-Up Point Too High Or Low – Misadjusted TPS, faulty revolution or speed sensor signal or control valve assembly.

Will Not Shift To "D₄" With "OD" Switch On – Misadjusted TPS or inhibitor switch, incorrect line pressure, faulty revolution or speed sensor signal, damaged shift solenoid valve "A", overrun clutch solenoid, control valve, fluid temp sensor, brake band or overrun clutch.

Engine Stalls In "R", "D", "2" & "1" Positions – Incorrect fluid level, torque converter clutch solenoid, shift valves "A" or "B" or control valve assembly.

SHIFT SOLENOID VALVE OPERATION

Application	Solenoid "A"	Solenoid "B"
1st Gear	On	On
2nd Gear	Off	On
3rd Gear	Off	Off
4th Gear	On	Off

CLUTCH & BAND APPLICATION CHART

Selector Lever Position	Elements In Use
"D" (Drive) ¹	
First Gear	Forward Clutch, ² Forward One-Way Clutch ³ ⁴ Overrun Clutch & ² Low One-Way Clutch
Second Gear	Band Servo (2nd Apply), Forward Clutch, ² Forward One-Way Clutch & ³ ⁵ Overrun Clutch
Third Gear	Band Servo (⁶ 2nd Apply & 3rd Release), Forward Clutch, ² Forward One-Way Clutch, High Clutch & ³ ⁵ Overrun Clutch
Fourth Gear	Band Servo (⁷ 2nd & 4th Apply, 3rd Release), Forward Clutch, High Clutch & Lock-Up
"2" (Intermediate)	
First Gear	Forward Clutch, ² Forward One-Way Clutch ² Low One-Way Clutch & ⁴ Overrun Clutch
Second Gear	Band Servo (2nd Apply), Forward Clutch, ² Forward One-Way Clutch & ⁵ Overrun Clutch
Third (Q45)	Band Servo (2nd Apply & 3rd Release), Forward Clutch, ² Forward One-Way Clutch, High Clutch & ⁵ Overrun Clutch
"1" (Low)	
First Gear	Forward Clutch, ² Forward One-Way Clutch Low-Reverse Brake & Overrun Clutch
Second Gear	Band Servo (2nd Apply), Forward Clutch ² Forward One-Way Clutch & Overrun Clutch
"R" (Reverse)	Low-Reverse Brake & Reverse Clutch
"N" Or "P" (Neutral Or Park)	All Clutches & Bands Released Or Ineffective

¹ – Transmission will not shift to 4th gear when overdrive switch is in OFF position.
² – Operates during progressive acceleration.
³ – Operates when overdrive switch is in OFF position.
⁴ – Operates when throttle opening is less than 1/16. Does not effect engine braking.
⁵ – Operates when throttle opening is less than 1/16. Engine braking activated.
⁶ – Oil pressure is applied to both 2nd apply and 3rd release side of band servo piston. Brake band does not contract because oil pressure area on release side is greater than apply side.
⁷ – Oil pressure is applied to 4th apply side in 3rd gear, and brake band contracts.

ROAD TEST

Preliminary Checks – 1) Check fluid level using HOT range on dip stick at fluid temperatures of 122-176°F (50-80°C) after vehicle has been driven approximately 5 minutes after initial warm-up. COLD range on dipstick is for reference only.
2) Fluid level should be checked with vehicle on level surface and parking brake applied. Check fluid level while engine is idling and selector lever is in "P" position.

3) If fluid level is at low side of either range, add fluid. Check fluid condition. Check for fluid leakage. Examine fluid color, texture and odor. If fluid is Black and has a burnt odor, clutch friction plates are worn.
4) If fluid is milky Pink in color, fluid is water-contaminated. Water may be entering transmission through filler tube or breather. If fluid is Light/Dark Brown in color and tacky, fluid level is incorrect or transmission is overheating.

Check Before Engine Is Started – 1) Park vehicle on flat surface. Move selector lever to "P" position. Set power shift switch to AUTO position. Turn ignition switch to ON position. A/T check lamp should come on for about 2 seconds.
2) Verify engine starts in "P" or "N" only. Move selector lever to "P" position and release parking brake. Ensure park engagement by pushing vehicle forward or backward.

Check With Engine Idling – 1) Start engine and let idle. Release parking brake. Apply foot brake, move selector lever to "R" position. Vehicle should creep backwards after foot brake is released.
2) Move selector lever to "D", "2" and "1" positions. Vehicle should creep forward in all 3 positions. Move selector lever to "N" position. Vehicle should not roll forward or backward.

Road Test Procedure – 1) Park vehicle on flat surface. Set overdrive switch to ON position. Set power shift switch to AUTO position. Start engine. Move selector lever to "D" position and accelerate vehicle at half-throttle. Vehicle should start from 1st gear.
2) Refer to appropriate SHIFT SPEED SPECIFICATIONS table and verify upshifts occur at specified speeds. Accelerate vehicle to lock-up speeds and verify lock-up. See LOCK-UP SPEED SPECIFICATIONS table. Lock-up condition should be maintained for more than 30 seconds.
3) When accelerator pedal is released, lock-up is released. Confirm overdrive switch is in ON position and selector lever is in "D" position. Accelerate vehicle to 50 MPH at half-throttle. Release accelerator pedal then quickly depress pedal to floor. Transmission should downshift from 4th to 2nd gear.
4) Release accelerator pedal and verify 2-3 and 3-4 upshifts and shift points. Accelerate vehicle to 60 MPH at half-throttle. Release accelerator pedal and set overdrive switch to OFF position. Verify 4-3 downshift and vehicle deceleration by engine braking.
5) Move selector lever from "D" to "2" position. Verify 3-2 downshift and vehicle deceleration by engine braking. Move selector lever from "2" to "1" position. Verify 2-1 downshift and vehicle deceleration by engine braking.

LOCK-UP SPEED SPECIFICATIONS – INFINITI J30

	Full Throttle	Half Throttle
Application	MPH	MPH
OD ON		
Lock-Up ON in 4th	111-116	79-84
Lock-Up OFF in 4th	106-111	62-67

SHIFT SPEED SPECIFICATIONS – INFINITI J30

	Full Throttle	Half Throttle
Application	MPH	MPH
1st-2nd	37-40	29-32
2nd-3rd	71-76	54-58
3rd-4th	110-116	80-85
4th-3rd	105-111	42-47
3rd-2nd	63-68	21-25
2nd-1st	27-30	4-7

LOCK-UP SPEED SPECIFICATIONS – 1995 INFINITI Q45

	Full Throttle	Half Throttle
Application	MPH	MPH
OD ON		
Lock-Up ON in 4th	126-130	86-91
Lock-Up OFF in 4th	121-126	64-69
OD OFF		
Lock-Up ON in 3rd	71-76	67-72
Lock-Up OFF in 3rd	67-72	63-68

AUTOMATIC TRANSMISSIONS
Nissan RE4R01A, RE4R03A & RL4R01A (Cont.)

NOTE: Second gear starts in "D" range is normal A/T control unit strategy. ATCU will only command 1st gear when accelerator pedal is fully depressed or when in manual low position.

SHIFT SPEED SPECIFICATIONS – 1995 INFINITI Q45

Application	Full Throttle MPH	Half Throttle MPH
1st-2nd	48-51	8-11
2nd-3rd	84-89	32-35
3rd-4th	125-131	85-91
4th-3rd	121-127	49-55
3rd-2nd	78-83	14-17
2nd-1st	27-29	6-9

LOCK-UP SPEED SPECIFICATIONS – 1996 INFINITI Q45

Application	Full Throttle MPH	Half Throttle MPH
OD ON		
Lock-Up ON in 4th	116-121	86-91
Lock-Up OFF in 4th	111-116	68-73
Lock-Up ON in 3rd	71-76	67-72
Lock-Up OFF In 3rd	68-73	64-69

SHIFT SPEED SPECIFICATIONS – 1996 INFINITI Q45

Application	Full Throttle MPH	Half Throttle MPH
1st-2nd	42-44	29-31
2nd-3rd	77-82	59-63
3rd-4th	115-121	86-91
4th-3rd	111-117	50-55
3rd-2nd	71-76	17-21
2nd-1st	27-29	6-9

LOCK-UP SPEED SPECIFICATIONS – PATHFINDER

Application	Full Throttle MPH	Half Throttle MPH
2WD & 4WD [1]		
OD ON		
Lock-Up ON in 4th	93-98	88-93
Lock-Up OFF in 4th	88-93	53-58
Lock-Up On in 3rd	58-63	55-60
Lock-Up OFF in 3rd	46-51	44-49

[1] – 2WD Final Gear Ratio 4.363, 4WD Final Gear Ratio 4.636

SHIFT SPEED SPECIFICATIONS – PATHFINDER

Application	Full Throttle MPH	Half Throttle MPH
2WD & 4WD [1]		
1st-2nd	30-32	22-24
2nd-3rd	58-63	38-42
3rd-4th	92-98	52-58
4th-3rd	89-95	53-58
3rd-2nd	55-60	20-24
2nd-1st	27-29	6-9

[1] – 2WD Final Gear Ratio 4.363, 4WD Final Gear Ratio 4.636

LOCK-UP SPEED SPECIFICATIONS – PICKUP

Application	Full Throttle MPH	Half Throttle MPH
2WD & 4WD [1]		
OD ON		
Lock-Up ON in 4th	N/A	44-49
Lock-Up OFF in 4th	N/A	44-49

[1] – 2WD Final Gear Ratio 4.111, 4WD Final Gear Ratio 4.625

SHIFT SPEED SPECIFICATIONS – PICKUP

Application	Full Throttle MPH	Half Throttle MPH
2WD & 4WD [1]		
1st-2nd	33-35	20-22
2nd-3rd	62-67	35-40
3rd-4th	N/A	71-77
4th-3rd	91-98	40-47
3rd-2nd	57-62	17-22
2nd-1st	29-32	7-10

[1] – 2WD Final Gear Ratio 4.111, 4WD Final Gear Ratio 4.625

LOCK-UP SPEED SPECIFICATIONS – 240SX

Application	Full Throttle MPH	Half Throttle MPH
OD ON		
Lock-Up ON in 4th	93-98	70-75
Lock-Up OFF in 4th	89-94	66-71
OD OFF		
Lock-Up ON in 3rd	57-62	57-62
Lock-Up OFF in 3rd	53-58	53-58

SHIFT SPEED SPECIFICATIONS – 240SX

Application	Full Throttle MPH	Half Throttle MPH
1st-2nd	33-35	24-27
2nd-3rd	60-65	46-50
3rd-4th	93-94	70-75
4th-3rd	89-95	35-40
3rd-2nd	53-58	17-21
2nd-1st	25-27	6-9

LOCK-UP SPEED SPECIFICATIONS – 300ZX

Application	Full Throttle MPH	Half Throttle MPH
OD ON		
Lock-Up ON in 4th	104-109	74-79
Lock-Up OFF in 4th	100-105	52-57
OD OFF		
Lock-Up ON in 3rd	66-71	57-62
Lock-Up OFF in 3rd	60-65	53-58

SHIFT SPEED SPECIFICATIONS – 300ZX

Application	Full Throttle MPH	Half Throttle MPH
1st-2nd	37-40	28-30
2nd-3rd	66-71	51-56
3rd-4th	103-109	74-79
4th-3rd	99-106	50-55
3rd-2nd	60-65	20-25
2nd-1st	27-30	6-9

STALL SPEED TEST

Stall Speed Test Procedure – 1) Check engine and transmission fluid levels. Ensure engine and transmission are at normal operating temperatures. Set parking brake and block wheels.

2) Install tachometer so it is visible to driver. Start engine, apply foot brake and move selector lever to "D" position. Accelerate to wide-open throttle gradually while applying foot brake. Note engine stall speed and release accelerator pedal. See STALL SPEED SPECIFICATIONS table for stall speed specification.

NOTE: Never hold wide-open throttle for more than 5 seconds during test.

STALL SPEED SPECIFICATIONS

Application	RPM
Infiniti	
J30	2320-2720
Q45	2100-2300
Nissan	
Pickup (V6)	2260-2510
Pickup (4-Cyl.)	2100-2300
Pathfinder	2440-2690
240SX	2050-2250
300ZX	
1995	
RE4R01A	2450-2650
RE4R03A	2950-3200
1996	
RE4R01A	2300-2500
RE4R03A	2930-3180

3) Shift selector lever to "N" position. Run engine at idle for one minute or more to cool ATF. Repeat steps **1)** through **3)** with selector lever in "2", "1" and "R" positions respectively.

Stall Speed Test Results

- **Stall Speed Low In All Positions** – Insufficient engine performance or faulty torque converter one-way clutch.
- **Stall Speed High In All Positions** – Low and reverse brake slipping, faulty low one-way clutch or hydraulic circuit for line pressure control.
- **Stall Speed High In "R" Position Only** – Reverse clutch slipping or low and reverse brake slipping.
- **Stall Speed High In "D", "3", "2" & "R" Positions, Okay In "1" Position** – Reverse clutch, forward clutch, forward one-way clutch, overrun clutch or low one-way clutch.
- **Stall Speed High In "D", "3" & "2" Positions, Okay In "1" And "R" Position** – Forward clutch, forward one-way clutch, overrun
- **Stall Speed High In "D", "3", "2" & "1" Positions, Okay In "R" Position** – Forward clutch, overrun clutch or forward one-way clutch.

NOTE: Condition of high clutch and brake band cannot be confirmed by stall speed test.

HYDRAULIC PRESSURE TESTS

Line Pressure Test Procedure – **1)** Warm engine and transmission to normal operating temperature. Check engine and transmission fluid levels and add fluid as necessary. Install pressure gauge to line pressure port for "D", "2" and "1" positions. *See Fig. 4.*

2) Set parking brake and block wheels. Apply foot brake fully while line pressure test at stall speed is performed. Start engine and measure line pressure at idle and stall speed, in "D", "2", "1" and "R" positions. When measuring line pressure at stall speed, follow stall speed test procedure. Note pressure readings and refer to LINE PRESSURE SPECIFICATIONS table.

Line Pressure Test Results:

- **Line Pressure Low At Idle In All Positions** – Oil pump wear, control piston damage, pressure regulator valve or plug sticking, or fluid pressure leakage between oil strainer and pressure regulator.
- **Line Pressure Low At Idle In A Particular Position** – Check for fluid pressure leakage between manual valve and the particular clutch.
- **Line Pressure High At Idle** – Misadjusted TPS, fluid temperature sensor or line pressure solenoid damaged, pressure modifier valve sticking or pressure regulator valve sticking.
- **Line Pressure Low At Stall Speed** – Misadjusted TPS, control piston damaged, line pressure solenoid sticking, pressure regulator valve or plug sticking, pressure modifier valve or pilot valve sticking.

LINE PRESSURE SPECIFICATIONS

Application	Pressure psi (kPa)
Infiniti J30	
At idle	
"D", "3", "2" & "1" positions	61-67 (422-461)
"R" position	88-94 (608-647)
At stall speed	
"D", "3", "2" & "1" positions	148-159 (1020-1098)
"R" position	206-218 (1422-1500)
Infiniti Q45	
At idle	
"D", "3", "2" & "1" positions	65-71 (451-490)
"R" position	91-97 (627-667)
At stall speed	
"D", "3", "2" & "1" positions	148-159 (1020-1098)
"R" position	206-219 (1422-1501)
Pickup 4 Cylinder	
At idle	
"D", "2" & "1" positions	61-67 (422-461)
"R" position	97-102 (667-706)
At stall speed	
"D", "2" & "1" positions	128-139 (883-961)
"R" position	202-213 (1393-1471)
Pathfinder & 300ZX (1995)	
At idle	
"D", "2" & "1" positions	61-67 (422-461)
"R" position	97-102 (667-706)
At stall speed	
"D", "2" & "1" positions	148-159 (1020-1098)
"R" position	206-218 (1422-1500)
300ZX (1996)	
At idle	
"D", "2" & "1" positions	65-71 (451-490)
"R" position	91-97 (627-667)
At stall speed	
"D", "2" & "1" positions	148-159 (1020-1098)
"R" position	206-219 (1422-1501)
240SX	
At idle	
"D", "2" & "1" positions	62.6-68.3 (432-471)
"R" position	99.5-103.7 (686-715)
At stall speed	
"D", "2" & "1" positions	150.7-162.1 (1039-1118)
"R" position	214.6-225.9 (1480-1558)

Vehicle Will Not Move In "D", "3" Or "2"; Okay In "1" & "R" – Misadjusted control linkage or damaged low one-way clutch.

ON-VEHICLE SERVICE

CONTROL VALVE ASSEMBLY

Removal & Installation – **1)** Remove drain plug and drain ATF. Remove oil pan and gasket. Remove oil strainer. Remove control valve assembly by removing bolts and disconnecting wiring harness connector. *See Fig. 5.* Accumulators may be removed by applying compressed air (if necessary). *See Fig. 6.*

2) To install, set manual valve in Neutral position and align with manual plate. Install control valve assembly and tighten bolts to 62-80 INCH lbs (7-9 N.m). *See Fig. 5. See VALVE BODY BOLT LENGTH table.* To complete installation, reverse removal procedure.

VALVE BODY BOLT LENGTH

Application	Length In. (mm)
A	1.30 (33)
B	1.77 (45)

INHIBITOR SWITCH ADJUSTMENT

See appropriate AUTOMATIC TRANSMISSION SERVICING article in TRANSMISSION SERVICING section.

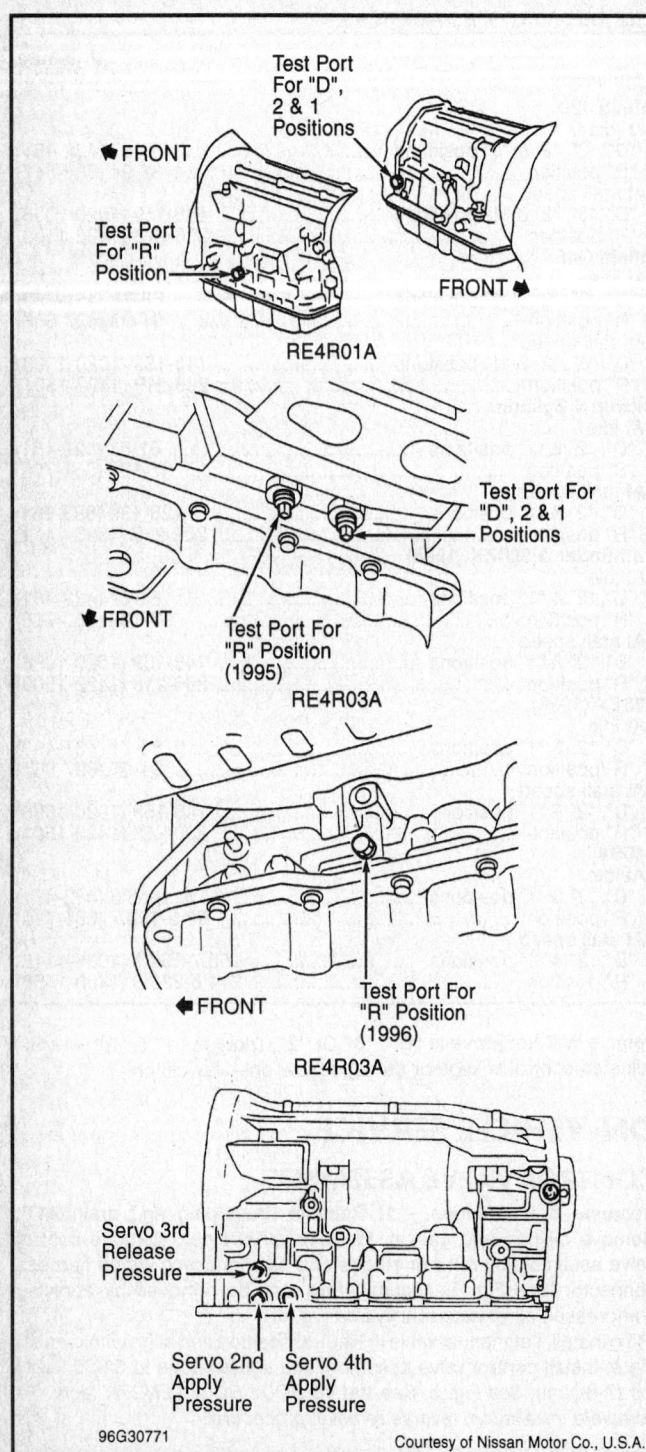

Fig. 4: Locating Pressure Test Ports

OIL COOLER FLUSHING PROCEDURE
Vehicles with tube type transmission fluid cooler may be cleaned using cleaning solvent and compressed air. Cooler lines must also be flushed to remove any foreign material. Vehicles with fin type transmission fluid cooler cannot be cleaned. Replace radiator (radiator incorporates transmission fluid cooler), and flush cooler lines to remove any foreign material.

MANUAL CONTROL LINKAGE ADJUSTMENT
See appropriate AUTOMATIC TRANSMISSION SERVICING article in TRANSMISSION SERVICING section.

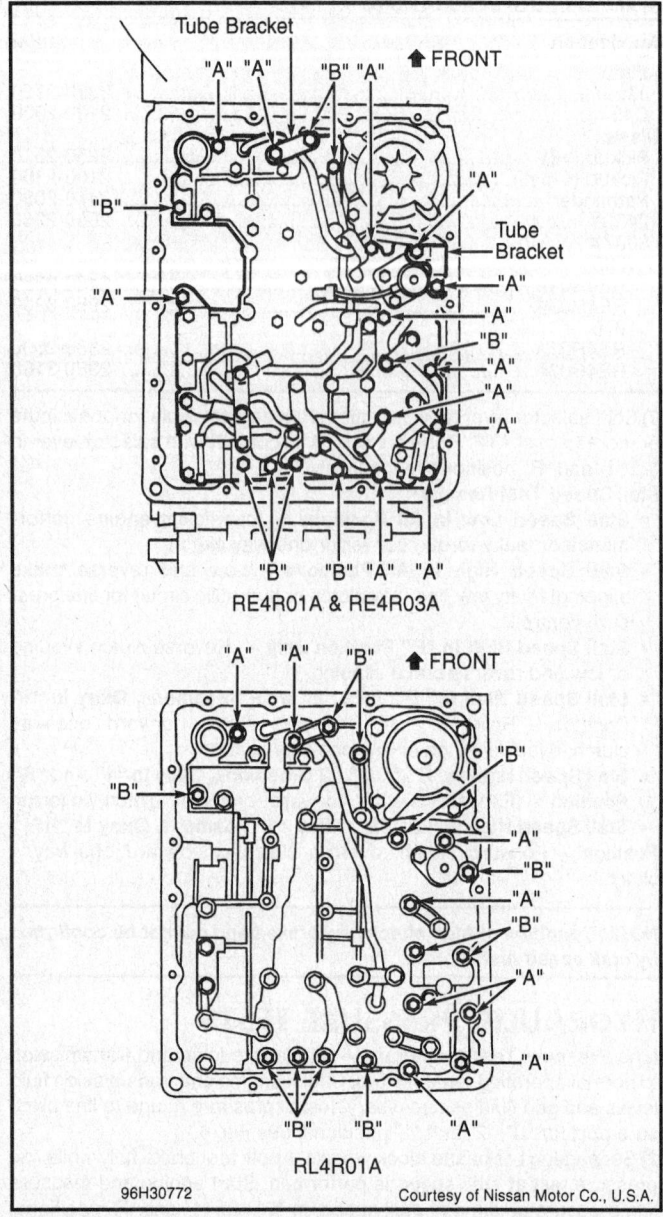

Fig. 5: Identifying Control Valve Assembly Bolt Location

REAR OIL SEAL REPLACEMENT
Removal & Installation – Mark drive shaft for reassembly reference. Remove drive shaft from vehicle. Remove rear oil seal. Apply ATF to NEW seal and install. Reinstall drive shaft. Check fluid level and fill as necessary.

REMOVAL & INSTALLATION
For transmission removal procedure, see appropriate AUTOMATIC TRANSMISSION REMOVAL article in TRANSMISSION SERVICING section.

TORQUE CONVERTER
1) Torque converter is a sealed unit and cannot be disassembled for service. Replace converter if damaged. Converter one-way clutch may be checked by inserting Splined Tool (KV31102100) into spline of one-way clutch inner race.
2) Hook bearing support unitized with one-way clutch outer race with suitable wire. See Fig. 7. Ensure one-way clutch inner race rotates clockwise only while holding bearing support with wire.

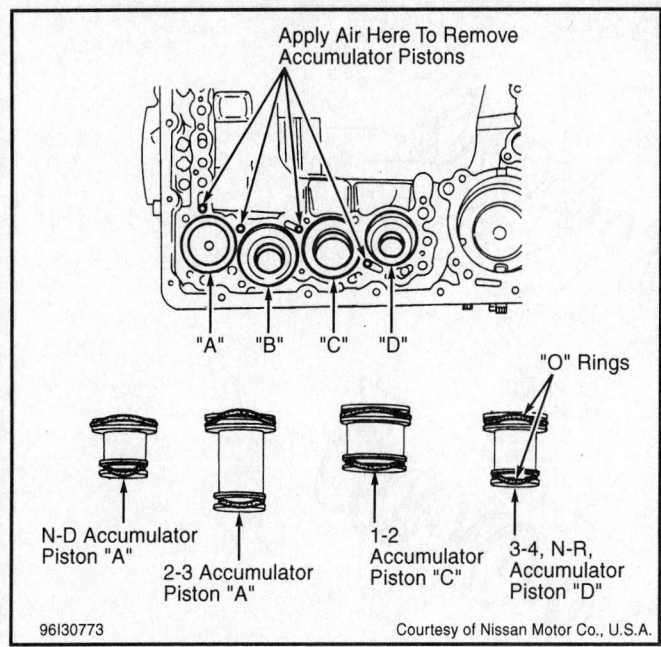

Fig. 6: Locating & Removing Accumulator Pistons

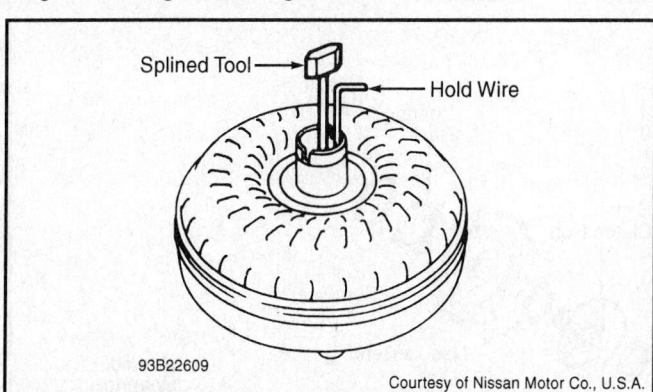

Fig. 7: Checking Torque Converter One-Way Clutch Rotation

TRANSMISSION DISASSEMBLY

1) Remove torque converter. Remove inhibitor switch. Remove drain plug and drain ATF. Remove inhibitor switch from transmission case. Remove oil pan and gasket. Check oil pan and oil strainer for accumulation of foreign material. If foreign material is present, replace torque converter and check transmission for cause of foreign material accumulation.

2) Remove lock-up solenoid and fluid temperature sensor connectors. Remove oil strainer and "O" ring from control valve. Remove control valve assembly. See Fig. 5. Remove solenoid wiring harness from transmission case.

3) Remove converter housing from transmission case. Remove "O" ring from input shaft. Using appropriate puller, remove oil pump assembly from transmission case. Remove oil pump "O" ring, needle bearing, thrust washer and oil pump gasket. See Fig. 8.

4) Remove input shaft. Loosen lock nut and remove band servo anchor end bolt from transmission case. Before removing brake band, secure band with wire clip placed into ends of band. Leave wire clip in position after removing band to prevent brake lining from cracking or peeling. DO NOT stretch brake band excessively. Remove brake band and strut.

5) Remove reverse clutch, high clutch and front sun gear from transmission case. Remove front and rear bearing race from clutch pack.

Remove front planetary carrier from transmission case. Remove front needle bearing and rear bearing from planetary carrier. Remove rear sun gear from transmission case. See Fig. 8. Remove rear extension housing and gasket from transmission case.

6) Remove revolution sensor and "O" ring from extension housing. Remove output shaft and parking gear by removing rear snap ring from output shaft and slowly push output shaft all the way forward. Remove snap ring from output shaft, then remove output shaft and parking gear as a unit. See Fig. 10.

7) Remove needle bearing from transmission case. Remove front internal gear and bearing race. Remove needle bearing from rear internal gear. Remove rear internal gear, forward clutch hub and overrun clutch hub as a set from transmission case.

8) Remove needle bearing from overrun clutch hub. Separate overrun clutch hub from rear internal gear and forward clutch hub. Remove thrust washer from overrun clutch hub. Remove forward clutch assembly from transmission case.

9) Remove band servo assembly from transmission case. Remove springs and accumulator pistons. See Figs. 6,9 And 10 Remove manual shaft (if necessary). Remove spacer and detent spring from transmission case. Remove manual shaft oil seal.

COMPONENT DISASSEMBLY & REASSEMBLY

OIL PUMP

Disassembly – **1)** Loosen bolts in numerical order and remove oil pump cover. See Fig. 12. Mark direction of rotor for reassembly reference. Remove rotor, vane rings and vanes. See Fig. 11.

2) Remove pivot pin while pushing on cam ring. DO NOT scratch oil pump housing. Remove cam ring and spring from oil pump housing. Remove pivot pin from control piston and remove control piston assembly. Remove oil seal from oil pump housing.

Inspection – **1)** To measure side clearances, ensure friction rings, "O" ring, control piston side seals and cam ring are removed. Measure side clearances between end of oil pump housing and cam ring, rotor, vanes and control piston in at least 4 places along circumferences. See Fig. 13.

2) Standard clearance for cam ring is .0004-.0009" (.010-.024 mm). Standard clearance for rotor, vanes and control piston is .0012-.0017" (.030-.044 mm). Measure clearance between seal rings and ring grooves. Standard clearance is .004-.010" (.10-.25 mm), with a wear limit of .010" (.25 mm). If clearance is not within wear limit, replace oil pump cover assembly.

Reassembly – **1)** Install oil seal in pump housing and lubricate with ATF. Install side seal on control piston with Black surface toward control piston. Use petroleum jelly to position side seal.

2) Install control piston on oil pump housing. Using petroleum jelly, install "O" ring and friction ring on cam ring. Assemble cam ring, spring and spring seat and install in pump housing. Install cam ring pivot pin.

3) Install rotor, vane and vane rings in oil pump housing. Ensure rotor is positioned in proper direction. Assemble oil pump housing and oil pump cover. Tighten bolts to 12-15 ft. lbs (16-21 N.m) in crisscross pattern. See Fig. 12. Pack ring grooves with petroleum jelly and install seal rings. Ensure 2 different diameter seal rings are in proper positions. Large diameter rings are installed near oil pump housing.

CONTROL VALVE ASSEMBLY

Disassembly – **1)** Remove lock-up solenoid, "O" ring and side plate from lower body. Remove line pressure solenoid and "O" ring from upper body. Remove 3-unit solenoid assembly from upper body. Place upper body face down and remove bolts, reamer bolts and support plates.

2) Remove lower body, separator plate and gasket as a unit from upper body. Place lower body face down and remove separator plate and gasket. Remove pilot filter, orifice check valve and orifice check spring. Ensure steel check balls are in proper positions and remove. See Fig. 14.

AUTOMATIC TRANSMISSIONS
Nissan RE4R01A, RE4R03A & RL4R01A (Cont.)

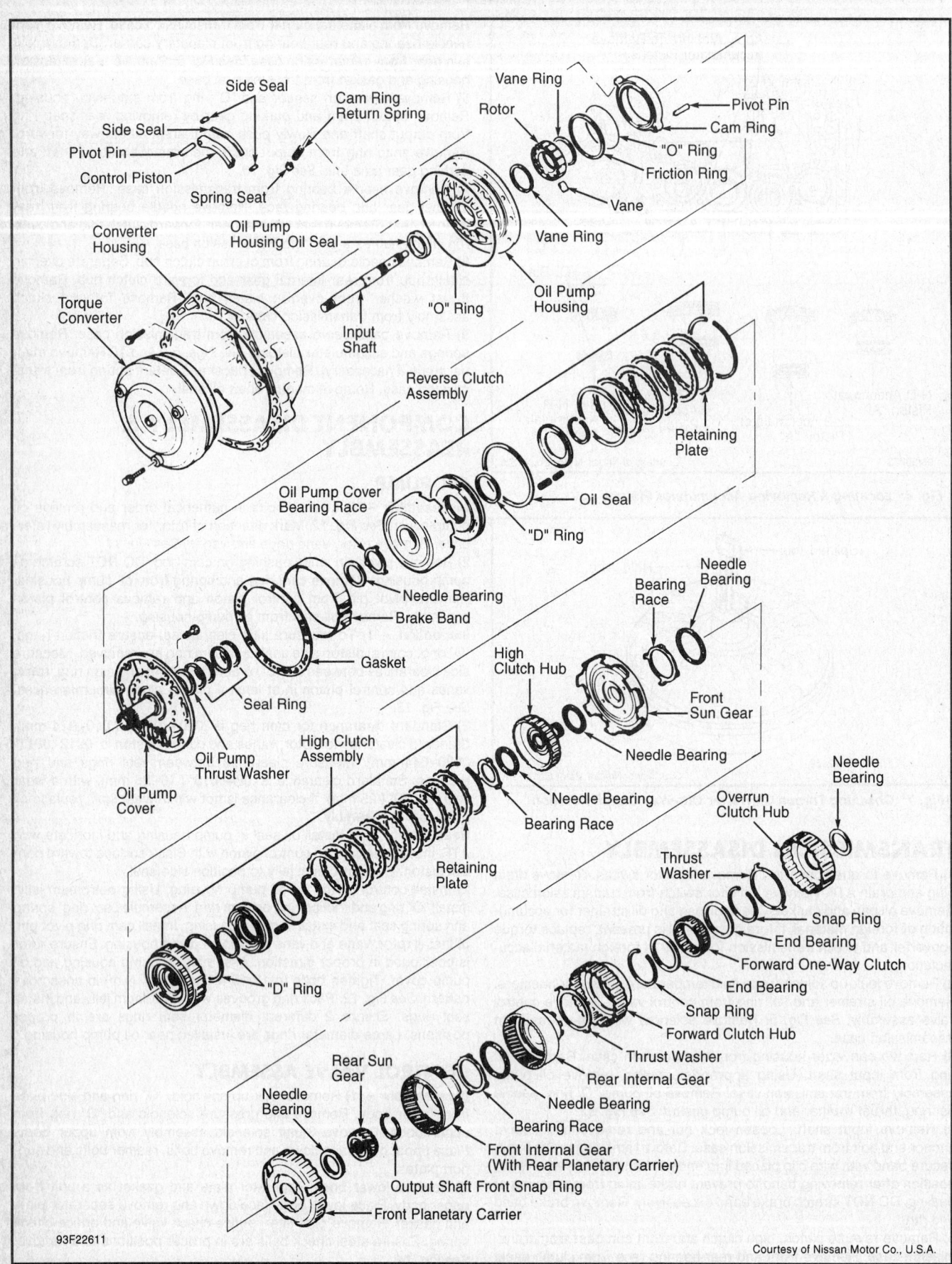

93F22611

Courtesy of Nissan Motor Co., U.S.A.

Fig. 8: Exploded View Of Transmission Components (RE4R01A, RE4R03A & RL4R01A)

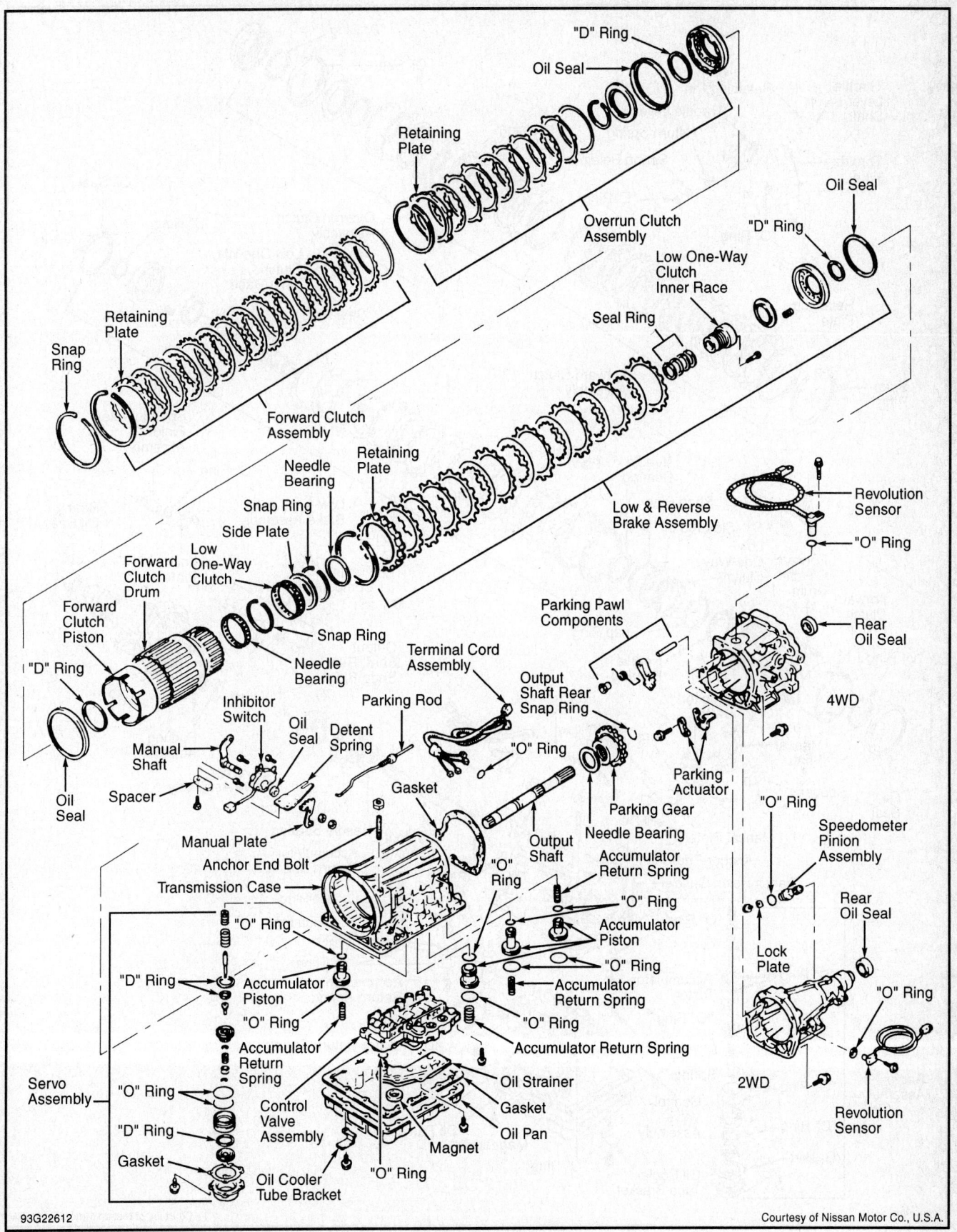

93G22612

Courtesy of Nissan Motor Co., U.S.A.

Fig. 9: Exploded View Of Transmission Case Components (RE4R01A & RE4R03A)

AUTOMATIC TRANSMISSIONS
Nissan RE4R01A, RE4R03A & RL4R01A (Cont.)

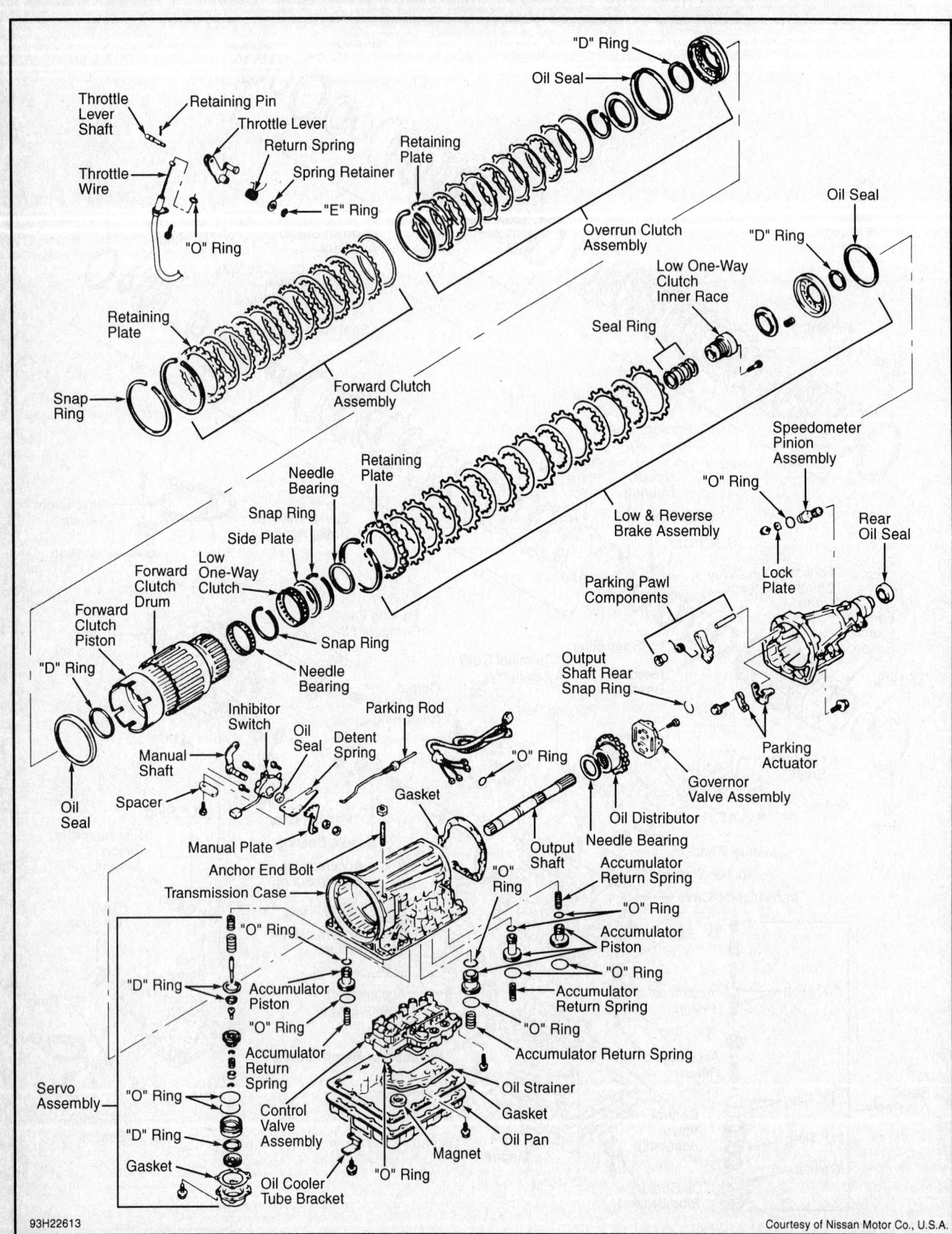

93H22613   Courtesy of Nissan Motor Co., U.S.A.

Fig. 10: Exploded View Of Transmission Case Components (RL4R01A)

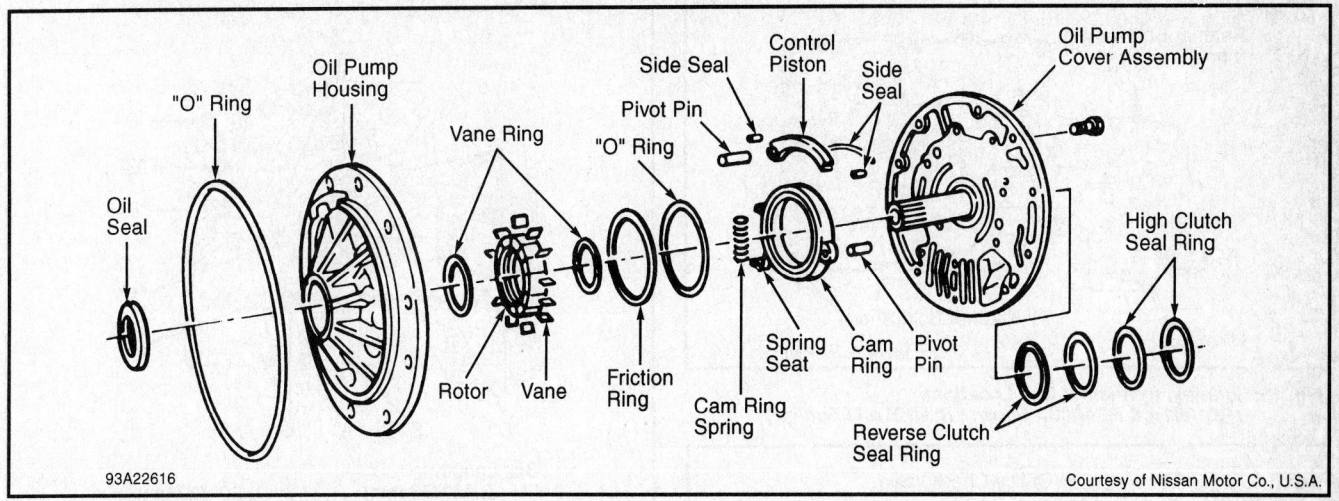

Fig. 11: Exploded View Of Oil Pump Assembly

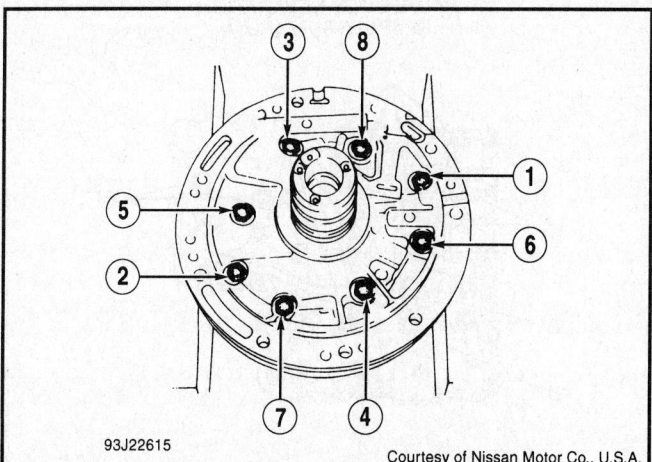

Fig. 12: Removing & Installing Oil Pump Bolts

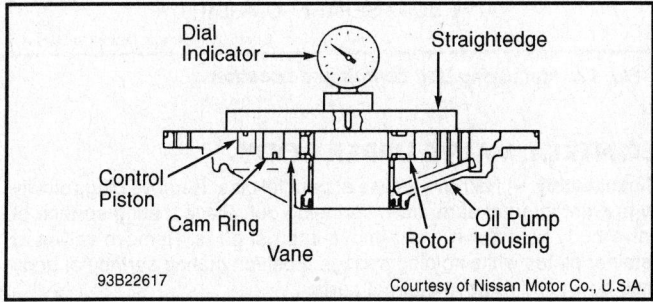

Fig. 13: Checking Oil Pump Side Clearances

Inspection – Ensure pins and retainer plates are in upper and lower bodies. Ensure oil circuits are clean and not damaged. Inspect tube brackets and tube connectors for damage. Inspect separator plates for damage, deformation and clean oil holes. Ensure pilot, lock-up solenoid and line pressure solenoid filters are clean.

Reassembly – **1)** Place oil circuit of upper body face up. Install steel check balls in proper locations. See Fig. 14. Install reamer bolts from bottom of upper body and install separator gasket. See Fig. 15.

2) Position oil circuit of lower body face up and install orifice check spring, orifice check valve and pilot filter. See Fig. 16. Install lower separator gasket and separator plate on lower body.

3) Install and temporarily tighten support plates, fluid temperature sensor and tube brackets. Ensure separator plate is installed correctly. Temporarily assemble upper and lower bodies using reamer bolts as a guide. Ensure steel check balls, orifice check valve and pilot filter are in proper positions.

4) Install and temporarily tighten bolts and tube brackets in the proper locations. For bolt location and length See Fig. 17. Attach "O" ring and install lock-up solenoid and side plate on lower body.

5) Attach "O" rings and install 3-unit solenoid assembly on upper body. Attach "O" ring and install line pressure solenoid on upper body. Tighten bolts and nuts to 45-58 INCH lbs. (5.1-6.5 N.m).

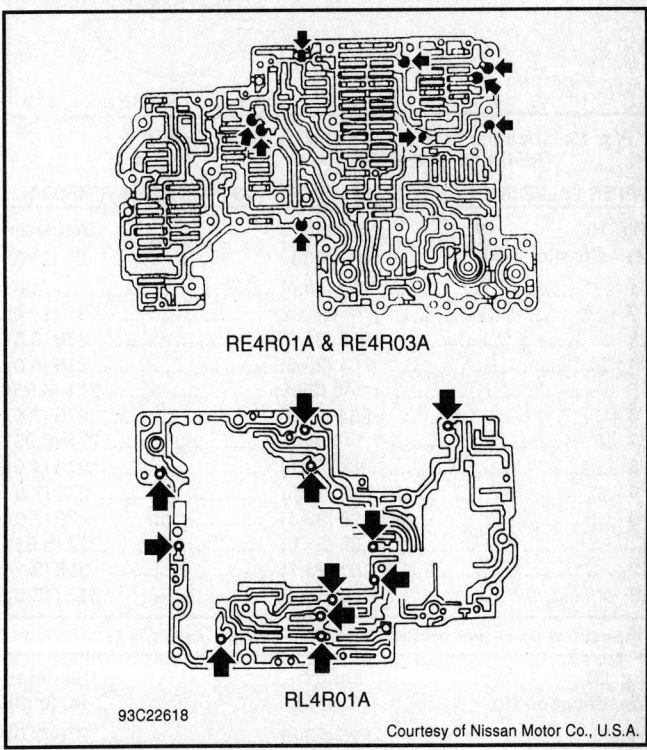

Fig. 14: Identifying Steel Check Ball Locations

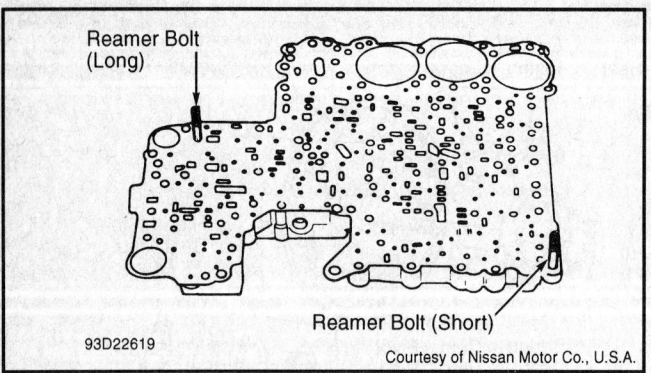

**Fig. 15: Identifying Reamer Bolt Locations
(RE4R01A & RE4R03A Shown; RL4R01A Is Similar)**

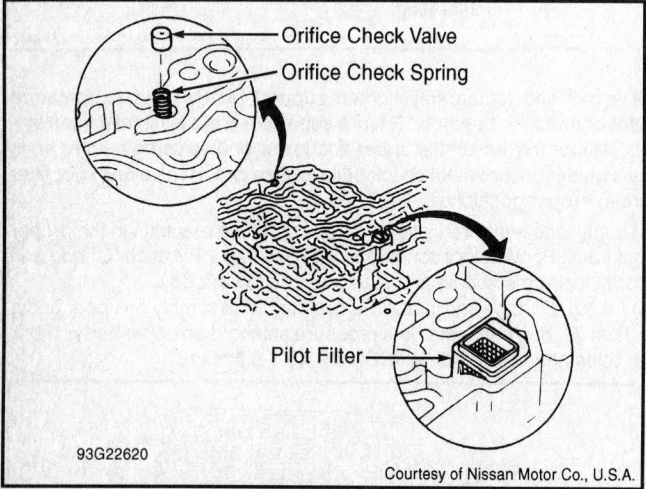

**Fig. 16: Locating Pilot Filter & Orifice Check Spring
(RE4R01A & RE4R03A)**

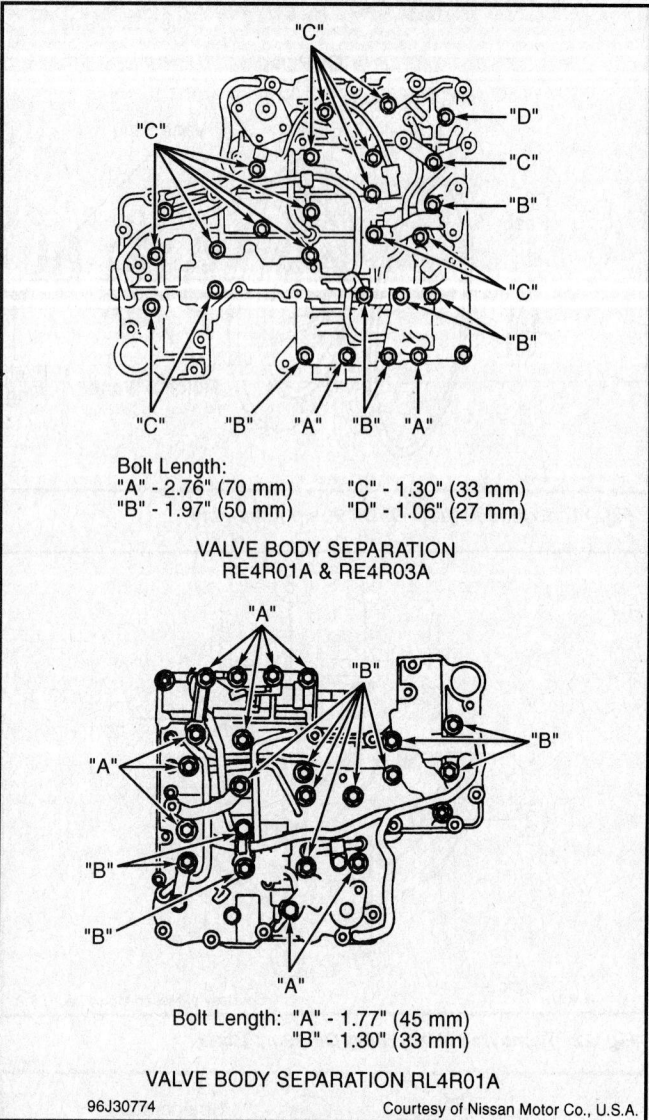

Bolt Length:
"A" - 2.76" (70 mm)   "C" - 1.30" (33 mm)
"B" - 1.97" (50 mm)   "D" - 1.06" (27 mm)

**VALVE BODY SEPARATION
RE4R01A & RE4R03A**

Bolt Length: "A" - 1.77" (45 mm)
              "B" - 1.30" (33 mm)

VALVE BODY SEPARATION RL4R01A

Fig. 17: Identifying Bolt Length and Location

UPPER VALVE BODY SPRING SPECIFICATIONS (RE4R01A & RE4R03A)

Fig. 18 Identification No.	Length In. (mm)	Diameter In. (mm)
1	1.50 (38.0)	.354 (9.0)
2	1.73 (44.02)	.551 (14.0)
3	1.258 (31.95)	.268 (6.8)
4	1.04 (26.5)	.236 (6.0)
5	1.146 (29.1)	.274 (6.95)
6	.984 (25.0)	.276 (7.0)
7	1.146 (29.1)	.274 (6.95)
8	.984 (25.0)	.276 (7.0)
9	.929 (23.6)	.276 (7.0)
10	1.28 (32.5)	.276 (7.0)
11	2.00 (51.0)	.222 (5.65)
12	1.01 (25.7)	.358 (9.1)
13	.728 (18.5)	.512 (13.0)

UPPER VALVE BODY SPRING SPECIFICATIONS (RL4R01A)

Fig. 20 Identification No.	Length In. (mm)	Diameter In. (mm)
1	.925 (23.5)	.276 (7.0)
2	1.909 (48.5)	.476 (12.1)
3	1.607 (40.83)	.315 (8.0)
4	1.709 (43.4)	.236 (6.0)
5	1.681 (42.7)	.354 (9.0)
6	1.733 (44.03)	.315 (8.0)
7	1.154 (29.3)	.315 (8.0)
8	1.299 (33.0)	.256 (6.5)
9	1.146 (29.1)	.274 (6.95)
10	.787 (20.0)	.215 (5.45)

CONTROL VALVE UPPER BODY

Disassembly – Remove valves at parallel pins. Remove plugs slowly to prevent internal parts from springing out. Place mating surface of valve body face down and remove internal parts. Remove valves at retainer plates while holding springs. Position mating surface of body face down and remove internal parts.

NOTE: Use suitable wire or paper clip to push parallel pins out. DO NOT use magnet for valve body repairs.

Inspection – Check valve springs for damage or deformation. Replace spring if specifications in UPPER VALVE BODY SPRING SPECIFICATIONS tables are exceeded. Inspect sliding surfaces of valves, sleeves and plugs for wear or damage.
Reassembly – Lubricate control valve body and all valves with ATF. Install control valves, plugs, sleeves, retainer plates and parallel pins. See Figs. 18 and 20.

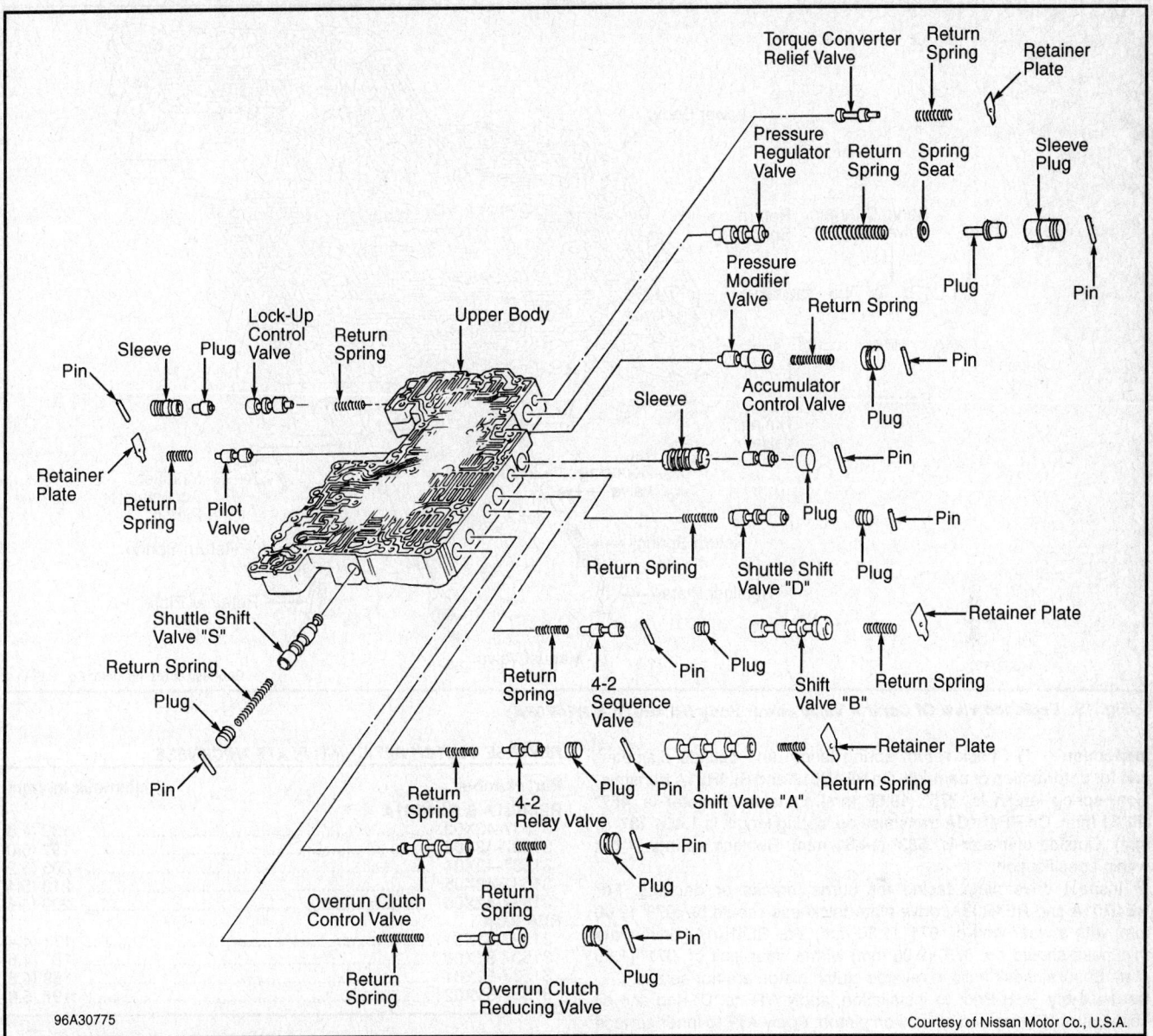

Fig. 18: Exploded View Of Control Valve Upper Body (RE4R01A & RE4R03A)

CONTROL VALVE LOWER BODY

Disassembly & Inspection – Remove valves at retainer plates and parallel pins. Check valve springs for damage or deformation. Replace spring if specifications in LOWER VALVE BODY SPRING SPECIFICATIONS tables are exceeded. Inspect sliding surfaces of valves, sleeves and plugs for wear or damage.

Reassembly – Lubricate control valve body and all valves with ATF. Install control valves, sleeves, retainer plates, plugs and pins. See Figs. 19 and 21.

LOWER VALVE BODY SPRING SPECIFICATIONS (RE4R01A & RE4R03A)

Fig. 19 Identification No.	Length In. (mm)	Diameter In. (mm)
1	1.236 (31.4)	.386 (9.8)
2	1.00 (25.4)	.266 (6.75)
3	.809 (20.55)	.266 (6.75)
4	.906 (23.0)	.264 (6.7)

LOWER VALVE BODY SPRING SPECIFICATIONS (RL4R01A)

Fig. 21 Identification No.	Length In. (mm)	Diameter In. (mm)
1	1.348 (34.23)	.433 (11.0)
2	1.783 (45.3)	.276 (7.0)
3	1.169 (29.7)	.283 (7.2)
4	1.307 (33.2)	.303 (7.7)
5	1.220 (31.0)	.205 (5.2)
6	.906 (23.0)	.276 (7.0)
7	1.496 (38.0)	.354 (9.0)
8	1.146 (29.1)	.274 (6.95)

REVERSE CLUTCH

Disassembly – Remove snap ring from reverse clutch assembly. Remove drive plates, driven plates, retaining plate and dish plate. Record number of plates for reassembly reference. See Fig. 8. Remove snap ring from clutch drum while compressing springs. Remove spring retainer and return springs. Install seal ring onto oil pump cover and install reverse clutch drum. Hold piston gradually apply air to oil hole to remove piston.

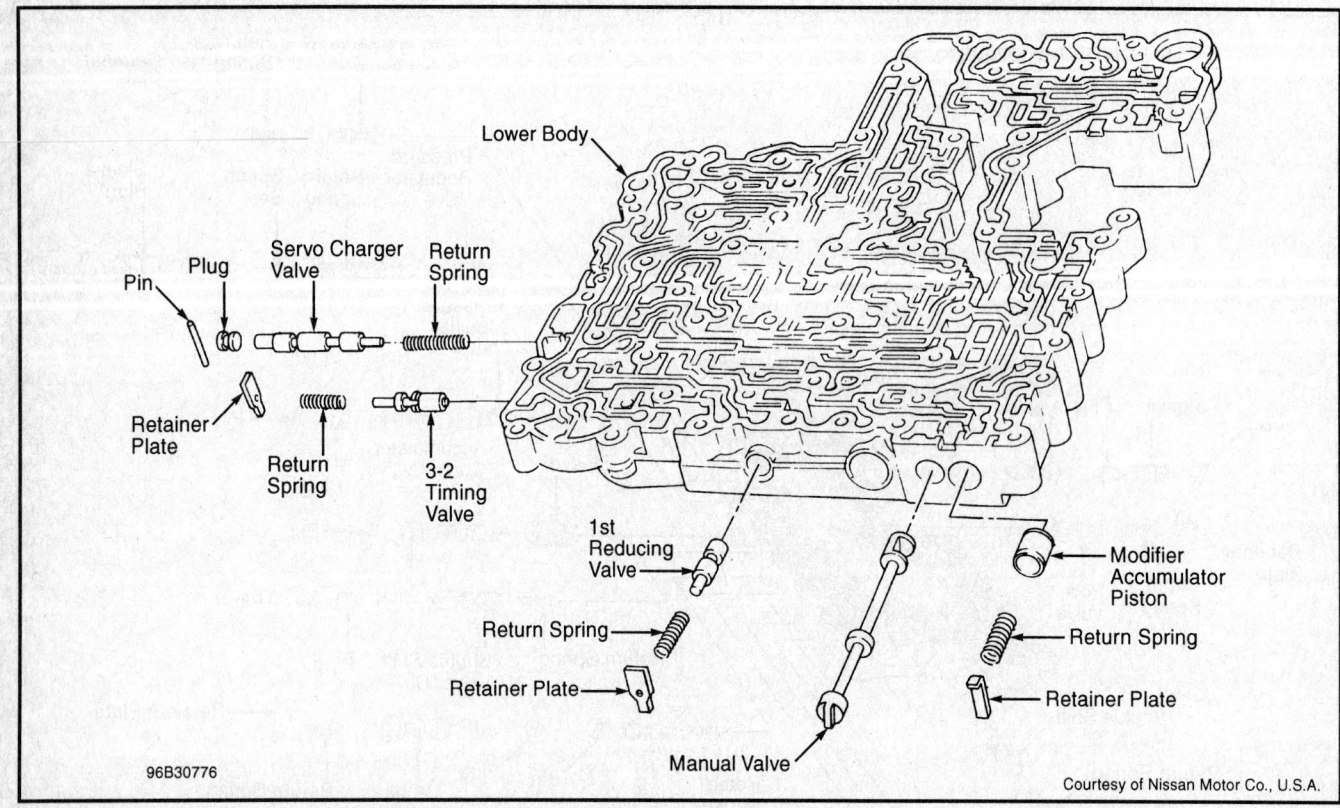

Fig. 19: Exploded View Of Control Valve Lower Body (RE4R01A & RE4R03A)

96B30776

Courtesy of Nissan Motor Co., U.S.A.

Inspection – 1) Check return spring length and outside diameter, and for deformation or damage. On RE4R01A and RL4R01A transmission, spring length is .775" (19.69 mm). Outside diameter is .457" (11.61 mm). On RE4R03A transmission, spring length is 1.464" (37.18 mm). Outside diameter is .583" (14.81 mm). Replace springs if not within specification.

2) Inspect drive plate facing for burns, cracks or damage. For RE4R01A and RE4R03A, drive plate thickness should be .079" (2.00 mm) with a wear limit of .071" (1.80 mm). For RL4R01A, drive plate thickness should be .075" (2.05 mm) with a wear limit of .071" (1.80 mm). Ensure check balls in reverse clutch piston are not seized.

Reassembly – 1) Prior to installation, apply ATF to "D" ring and oil seal. Install "D" ring and oil seal on piston. Apply ATF to inner surface of drum. Install piston assembly while turning slowly. Install return springs and retainer. Compress springs and install snap ring. Install drive plates, driven plates, retaining plate, dish plate and snap ring.

NOTE: DO NOT align snap ring gap with spring retainer stopper.

---

2) Measure clearance between retaining plate and snap ring. Specified clearance is .020-.031" (.50-.80 mm). Allowable limit is .055" (1.40 mm) for RE4R01A and RL4R01A, .024-.035" (.60-.90 mm) for RE4R03A. Allowable limit for all other models is .047" (1.20 mm). Retaining plate is available in .008" (.20 mm) increments. See REVERSE CLUTCH RETAINING PLATE THICKNESS tables.

3) Check reverse clutch operation. Install seal ring onto oil pump cover and install reverse clutch. Apply compressed air to oil hole. See Fig. 23. Ensure retaining plate moves toward snap ring. If retaining plate does not move as described, "D" ring or oil seal may be damaged, or fluid may be leaking at piston check ball.

REVERSE CLUTCH RETAINING PLATE THICKNESS

Part Number	Thickness In. (mm)
RE4R01A & RL4R01A	
31537-42X02	.189 (4.8)
31537-42X03	.197 (5.0)
31537-42X04	.205 (5.2)
31537-42X05	.213 (5.4)
31537-42X06	.220 (5.6)
RE4R03A	
31537-51X61	.173 (4.4)
31537-51X00	.181 (4.6)
31537-51X01	.189 (4.8)
31537-51X02	.197 (5.0)

HIGH CLUTCH

1) Service procedures for high clutch are the same as given for reverse clutch. For RE4R01A and RE4R03A, drive plate thickness is .063" (1.60 mm) with allowable limit of .055" (1.40 mm). For RL4R01A, drive plate thickness is .071-.087" (1.52-1.67 mm) with allowable limit of .055" (1.40 mm). Specified clearance is .071-.087" (1.80-2.20 mm). For allowable limit, see TRANSMISSION SPECIFICATIONS table. Retaining plate is available in .008" (.20 mm) increments. See HIGH CLUTCH RETAINING PLATE THICKNESS table.

2) Check high clutch operation. Install seal ring onto oil pump cover and install high clutch. Apply compressed air to oil hole. See Fig. 23. Ensure retaining plate moves toward snap ring. If retaining plate does not move as described, "D" ring or oil seal may be damaged, or fluid may be leaking at piston check ball.

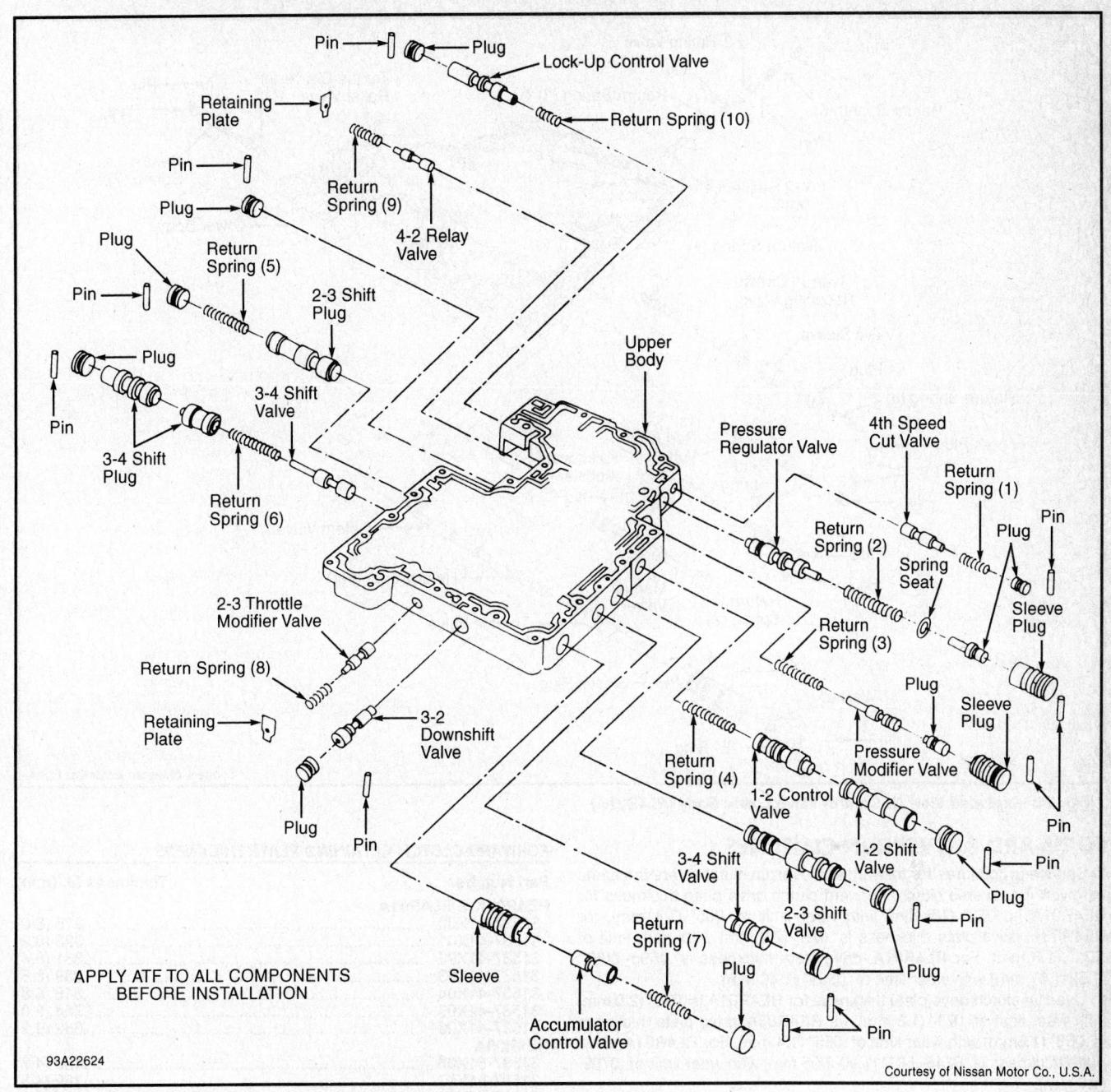

APPLY ATF TO ALL COMPONENTS
BEFORE INSTALLATION

93A22624

Courtesy of Nissan Motor Co., U.S.A.

Fig. 20: Exploded View Of Control Valve Upper Body (RL4R01A)

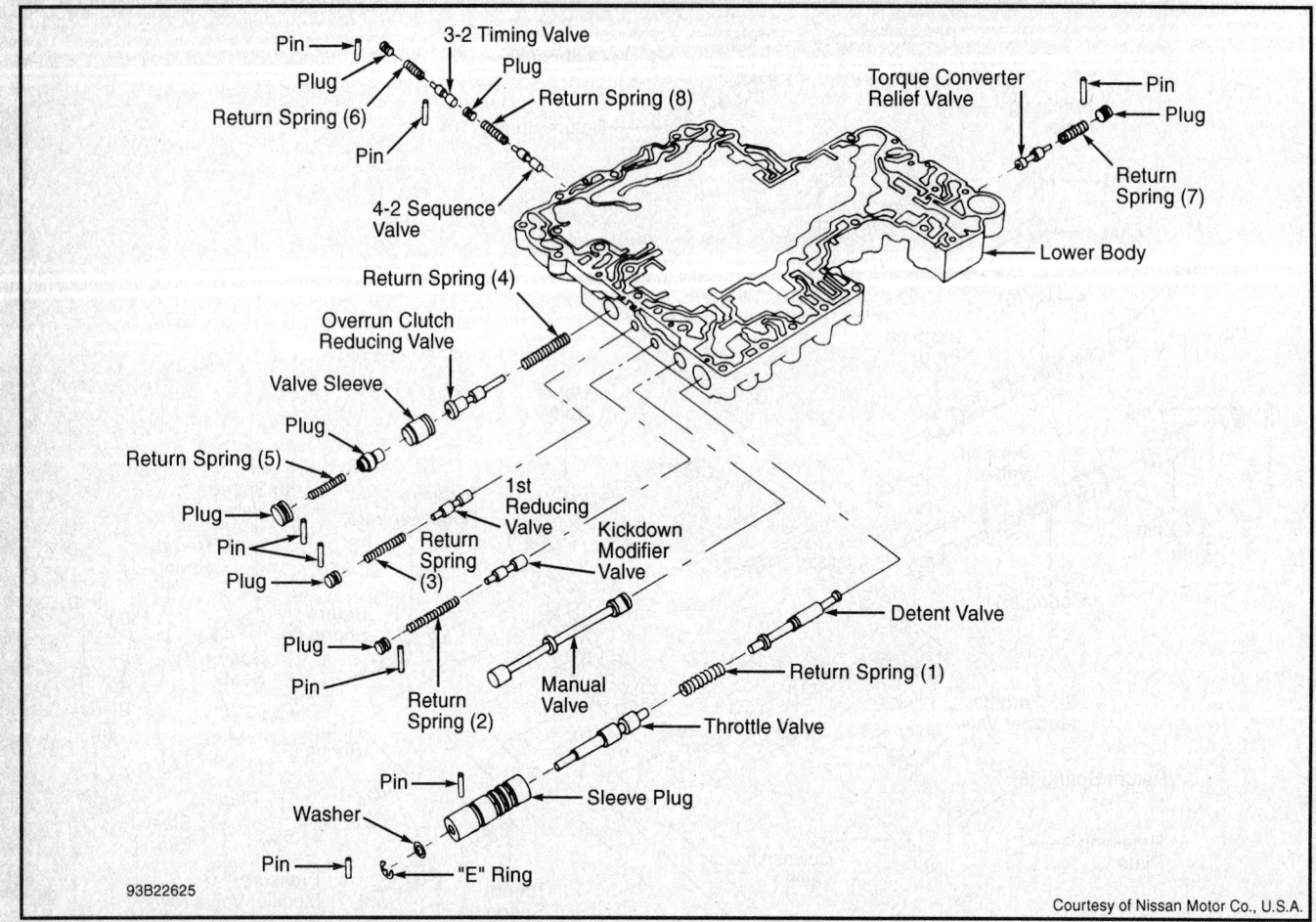

Fig. 21: Exploded View Of Control Valve Lower Body (RL4R01A)

FORWARD & OVERRUN CLUTCHES

1) Service procedures for forward and overrun clutches are the same as given for reverse clutch. Forward clutch drive plate thickness for RE4R01A is .063" (1.6 mm) with wear limit of .055" (1.4 mm), for RE4R03A, drive plate thickness is .079" (2.0 mm) with wear limit of .071" (1.8 mm). For RL4R01A, drive plate thickness is .0598-.0657" (1.52-1.67 mm) with wear limit of .0551" (1.40 mm).

2) Overrun clutch drive plate thickness for RE4R01A is .079" (2.0 mm) with wear limit of .071" (1.8 mm), for RE4R03A, drive plate thickness is .063" (1.6mm) with wear limit of .055" (1.4 mm). For RL4R01A, drive plate thickness is .0748-.807" (1.90-2.05 mm) with wear limit of .0709" (1.8 mm).

3) For all models specified clearance for forward clutch is .0138-.0295" (.35-.75 mm) for RE4R03A and RL4R01A, with allowable limit of .0965" (2.45 mm) for RE4R03A and .728" (1.85mm) for RL4R01A, .0177-.0335" (.45-.85 mm) with allowable limit of .0886" (2.25 mm) for RE4R01A.

4) For all models specified clearance for overrun clutch is .039-.055" (1.0-1.4 mm) with allowable limit of .079" (2.0 mm) for RE4R01A and RL4R01A, .087" (2.2 mm) for RE4R03A. To adjust clearance, retaining plate is available in .008" (.20 mm) increments. See FORWARD & OVERRUN CLUTCH RETAINING PLATE THICKNESS table.

5) Check return spring length and outside diameter, and for deformation or damage. On RE4R01A and RL4R01A transmission, spring length is 1.408" (35.77 mm). Outside diameter is .382" (9.70 mm). On RE4R03A transmission, spring length is 1.449" (36.80 mm). Outside diameter is .421" (10.70 mm). Replace springs if not within specification.

6) Check forward clutch and overrun clutch operation during reassembly procedure. Apply compressed air to appropriate hole in transmission case. See Fig. 24.

FORWARD CLUTCH RETAINING PLATE THICKNESS

Part Number	Thickness In. (mm)
RE4R01A & RL4R01A	
31537-41X00	.315 (8.0)
31537-41X01	.323 (8.2)
31537-41X02	.331 (8.4)
31537-41X03	.339 (8.6)
31537-41X04	.346 (8.8)
31537-41X05	.354 (9.0)
31537-41X06	.362 (9.2)
RE4R03A	
31537-51X06	.150 (4.6)
31537-51X07	.189 (4.8)
31537-51X08	.197 (5.0)
31537-51X09	.205 (5.2)
31537-51X10	.213 (5.4)
31537-51X69	.220 (5.6)

OVERRUN CLUTCH RETAINING PLATE THICKNESS

Part Number	Thickness In. (mm)
RE4R01A & RL4R01A	
31537-41X80	.165 (4.2)
31537-41X81	.173 (4.4)
31537-41X82	.181 (4.6)
31537-41X83	.189 (4.8)
31537-41X84	.197 (5.0)
RE4R03A	
31537-51X11	.150 (3.8)
31537-51X12	.157 (4.0)
31537-51X13	.165 (4.2)
31537-51X14	.173 (4.4)
31537-51X15	.181 (4.6)
31537-51X64	.189 (4.8)

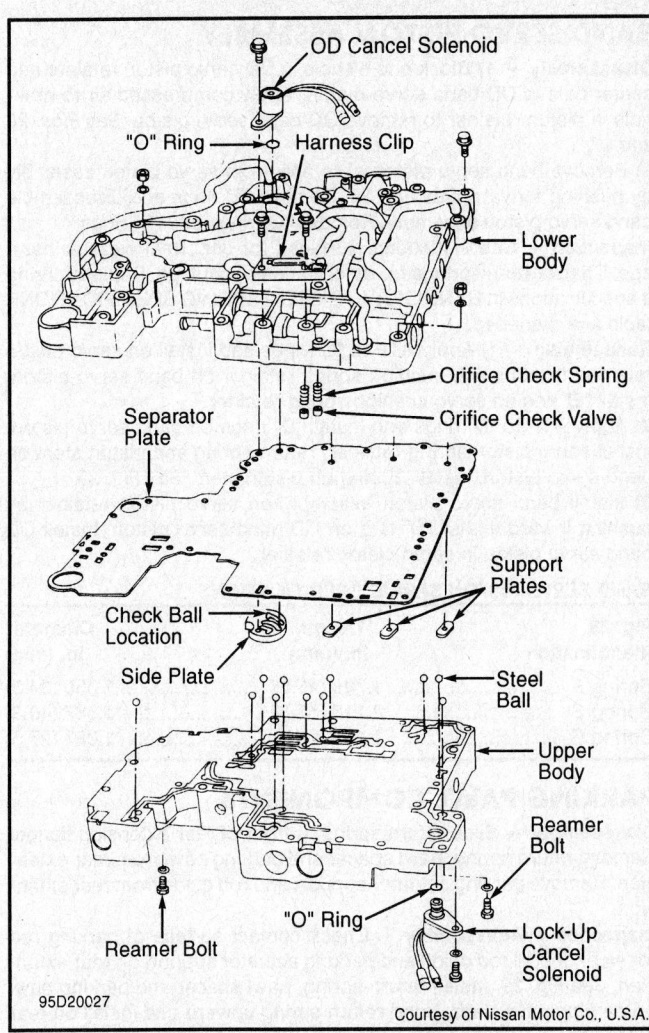

Fig. 22: **Exploded View Of Control Valve Assembly (RL4R01A Is Shown: Others Are Similar)**

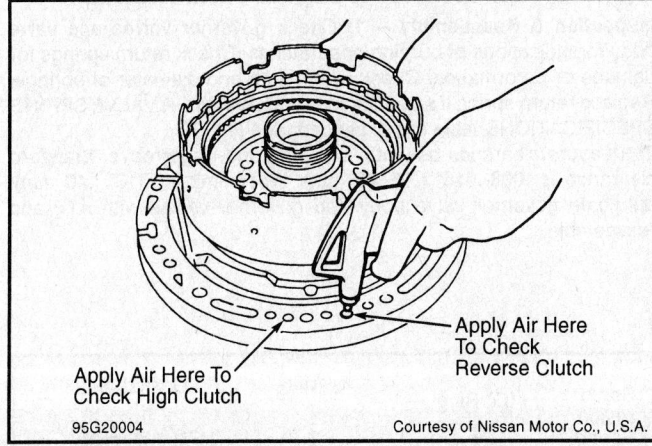

Fig. 23: **Checking Reverse & High Clutch Operation**

LOW & REVERSE BRAKE

Disassembly – 1) Remove snap ring, drive plates, driven plates and dish plate. Record number of plates for reassembly reference. Remove low one-way clutch inner race, spring retainer and return spring from transmission case.

2) Remove seal rings from low one-way clutch inner race. Remove thrust washers from low one-way clutch inner race. Remove low and reverse brake piston, oil seal and "D" ring.

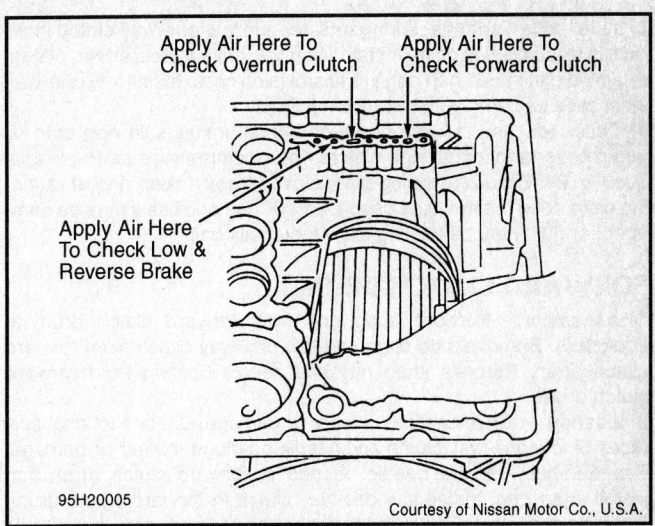

Fig. 24: **Checking Forward Clutch, Overrun Clutch & Low & Reverse Brake Operation**

Inspection – 1) Check low and reverse brake snap ring, springs and retainer for deformation or damage. Check spring length and outside diameter. On RE4R01A and RL4R01A transmission, spring length is .878" (22.30 mm). Outside diameter is .457" (11.60 mm). On RE4R03A transmission, inner spring length is .804" (20.43 mm). Outer spring length is .801" (20.35 mm). Outside diameter for inner spring is .406" (10.30 mm). Outside diameter for outer spring is .512" (13.00 mm). Replace springs if not within specification.

2) Check low and reverse drive plates for burns, cracks or damage. Check frictional surface of inner race for wear or damage. Install NEW seal rings on low one-way clutch inner race and measure ring groove clearance. Groove clearance should be .004-.010" (.10-.25 mm). Allowable limit is .010" (.25 mm). Standard drive plate thickness for RE4R01A is .079" (2.0 mm) with wear limit of .071" (1.8 mm), for RE4R03A drive plate thickness is .063" (.063) with wear limit of .055" (1.4 mm), for RL4R01A drive plate thickness is .0598-.0657" (1.52-1.67 mm). Retaining plate is available in .008" (.20 mm) increments. See LOW & REVERSE BRAKE RETAINING PLATE THICKNESS table.

LOW & REVERSE BRAKE RETAINING PLATE THICKNESS

Part Number	Thickness In. (mm)
RE4R01A & RL401A	
31667-41X12	.276 (7.0)
31667-41X13	.283 (7.2)
31667-41X14	.291 (7.4)
31667-41X07	.299 (7.6)
31667-41X08	.307 (7.8)
31667-41X00	.315 (8.0)
31667-41X01	.323 (8.2)
31667-41X02	.331 (8.4)
31667-41X03	.339 (8.6)
31667-41X04	.346 (8.8)
31667-41X05	.354 (9.0)
31667-41X06	.362 (9.2)
RE4R03A	
31667-51X11	.157 (4.0)
31667-51X10	.165 (4.2)
31667-51X00	.173 (4.4)
31667-51X01	.181 (4.6)
31667-51X02	.189 (4.8)
31667-51X03	.197 (5.0)
31667-51X04	.205 (5.2)
31667-51X05	.213 (5.4)
31667-51X06	.220 (5.6)
31667-51X07	.228 (5.8)
31667-51X08	.236 (6.0)
31667-51X09	.244 (6.2)

Reassembly – 1) Install bearing on one-way clutch inner race with Black surface to rear side. Install oil seal and "D" ring on piston. Install piston while rotating slowly.

2) Install return springs, spring retainer and low one-way clutch inner race in transmission case. Install dish plate, drive plates, driven plates, retaining plate and snap ring in transmission case. Install low one-way inner race seal ring with petroleum jelly.

3) Check low and reverse brake operation. Install seal ring onto oil pump cover and install high clutch. Apply compressed air to oil hole. *See Fig. 24.* Ensure retaining plate moves toward snap ring. If retaining plate does not move as described, "D" ring or oil seal may be damaged, or fluid may be leaking at piston check ball.

FORWARD CLUTCH DRUM

Disassembly – Remove snap ring from forward clutch drum (if equipped). Remove side plate and low one-way clutch from forward clutch drum. Remove snap ring and needle bearing from forward clutch drum.

Inspection – Check spline for wear or damage. Check frictional surfaces of low one-way clutch and needle bearing for wear or damage.

Reassembly – Install needle bearing in forward clutch drum and install snap ring. Install low one-way clutch in forward clutch drum. Install low one-way clutch with flange facing rearward. Install side plate and snap ring in forward clutch drum. *See Fig. 9.*

REAR INTERNAL GEAR & FORWARD CLUTCH HUB

Disassembly – Remove rear internal gear by pushing forward clutch hub forward. Remove thrust washer from rear internal gear. Remove snap ring from forward clutch hub. Remove forward one-way clutch and end bearing.

Inspection – Check gear for chips, cracks or excessive wear. Check frictional surfaces of forward one-way clutch and thrust washer for wear or damage. Check spline, end bearing and snap ring for wear or damage.

Reassembly – 1) Install snap ring and end bearing in forward clutch hub. Install forward one-way clutch in hub with flange facing rearward. Install end bearing and snap ring in forward clutch hub. *See Fig. 8.*

2) Install thrust washer on rear internal gear. Apply petroleum jelly to hold thrust washer in place. Position forward clutch hub in rear internal gear. Ensure forward clutch hub rotates clockwise only. *See Fig. 25.*

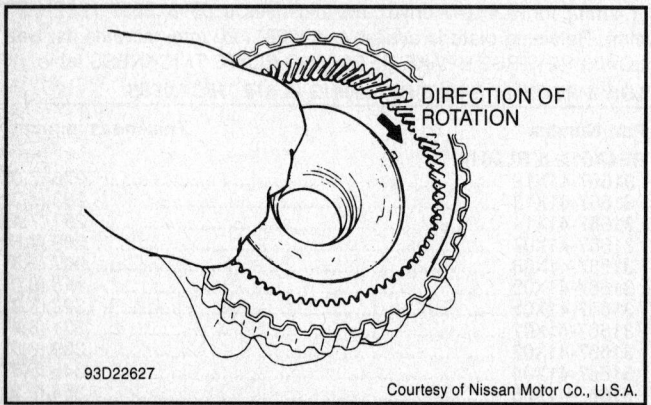

DIRECTION OF ROTATION

93D22627

Courtesy of Nissan Motor Co., U.S.A.

Fig. 25: Checking Forward Clutch Hub Rotation

BAND SERVO PISTON ASSEMBLY

Disassembly – 1) Block one oil hole in OD servo piston retainer and center hole in OD band servo piston. Apply compressed air to other hole in piston retainer to remove OD band servo piston. *See Figs. 26 and 27.*

2) Remove band servo piston assembly from servo piston assembly by pushing forward. *See Fig. 28.* Remove "E" rings and disassemble band servo piston assembly. Remove "O" rings and "D" rings.

Inspection – Check frictional surfaces for abnormal wear or damage. Check return springs for deformation or damage. Replace spring if specifications in BAND SERVO PISTON SPRING SPECIFICATIONS table are exceeded.

Reassembly – 1) Apply ATF to "O" rings and install on servo piston retainer. Install servo cushion spring retainer on band servo piston. Install "E" ring on servo cushion spring retainer.

2) Apply ATF to "D" rings and install "D" rings on band servo piston. Install servo piston spring retainer, return spring and piston stem on band servo piston. Install "E" ring on piston stem. *See Fig. 26.*

3) Install band servo piston assembly on servo piston retainer by pushing inward. Install "D" ring on OD band servo piston. Install OD band servo piston in servo piston retainer.

BAND SERVO PISTON SPRING SPECIFICATIONS

Identification	Length In. (mm)	Diameter In. (mm)
Spring A	1.795 (45.6)	1.350 (34.3)
Spring B	2.118 (53.8)	1.587 (40.3)
Spring C	1.169 (29.7)	1.087 (27.6)

PARKING PAWL COMPONENTS

Disassembly – Slide return spring to front of rear extension flange. Remove return spring, pawl spacer and parking pawl from rear extension. Remove parking actuator support and rod guide from rear extension.

Inspection & Reassembly – Check contact surface of parking rod for wear. Install rod guide and parking actuator support on rear extension. *See Fig. 29.* Install return spring, pawl spacer and parking pawl on parking pawl shaft. Bend return spring upward and install on rear extension.

GOVERNOR VALVE ASSEMBLY (RL4R01A)

Inspection & Reassembly – 1) Check governor valves and valve body for indications of burning or scratches. Check return springs for damage or deformation. Check free length and diameter of springs. Replace return spring if specifications in GOVERNOR VALVE SPRING SPECIFICATIONS table are exceeded. *See Fig. 30*

2) Measure clearance between seal ring and ring groove. Standard clearance is .006-.016" (.15-.40 mm). Wear limit is .016" (.40 mm). Lubricate governor valve body and governor valves with ATF and reassemble.

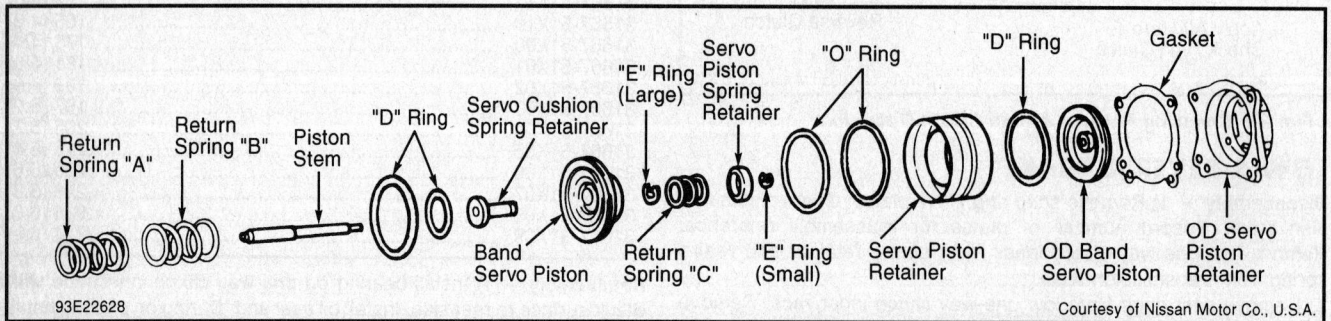

Return Spring "A" Return Spring "B" Piston Stem "D" Ring Servo Cushion Spring Retainer Band Servo Piston "E" Ring (Large) Return Spring "C" Servo Piston Spring Retainer "E" Ring (Small) "O" Ring Servo Piston Retainer "D" Ring OD Band Servo Piston Gasket OD Servo Piston Retainer

93E22628

Courtesy of Nissan Motor Co., U.S.A.

Fig. 26: Exploded View Of Band Servo Piston

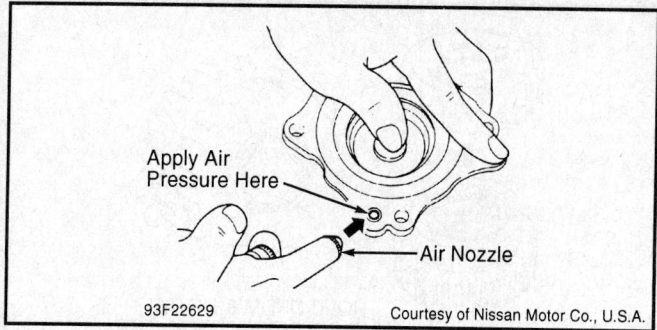

Fig. 27: Removing OD Band Servo Piston

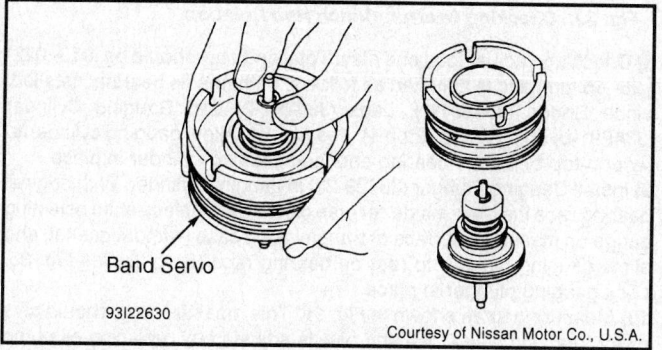

Fig. 28: Disassembling Band Servo Piston

GOVERNOR VALVE SPRING SPECIFICATIONS

Fig. 30 Identification No.	Length In. (mm)	Diameter In. (mm)
Spring No. 1	.752 (19.1)	.356 (9.05)
Spring No. 2	1.204 (30.58)	.362 (9.20)
Spring No. 3	.661 (16.80)	.354 (9.00)

TRANSMISSION REASSEMBLY

1) Install manual shaft and oil seal as a unit in transmission case. Align groove in shaft with drive pin hole. Drive pin into case as shown in *Fig. 31*. Install detent spring and spacer. While pushing detent spring down, install manual plate on manual shaft.

2) Install lock nuts on manual shaft. Install "O" rings on accumulator pistons. Apply ATF to transmission case and install accumulator pistons as shown in *Fig. 6*. Install band servo piston and return springs. Install band servo gasket and retainer on transmission case.

3) Place transmission case in vertical position. Slightly lift forward clutch drum assembly and slowly rotate clockwise until hub passes over one-way clutch inner race inside transmission case. *See Fig. 32*. Ensure forward clutch assembly rotates in clockwise direction only. Apply petroleum jelly to thrust washer and install on front of overrun clutch hub.

4) Install overrun clutch hub on rear internal gear assembly. Install needle bearing on rear of overrun clutch hub. Use petroleum jelly to hold needle bearing in place. Ensure overrun clutch hub rotates counterclockwise while holding forward clutch hub. *See Fig. 33*.

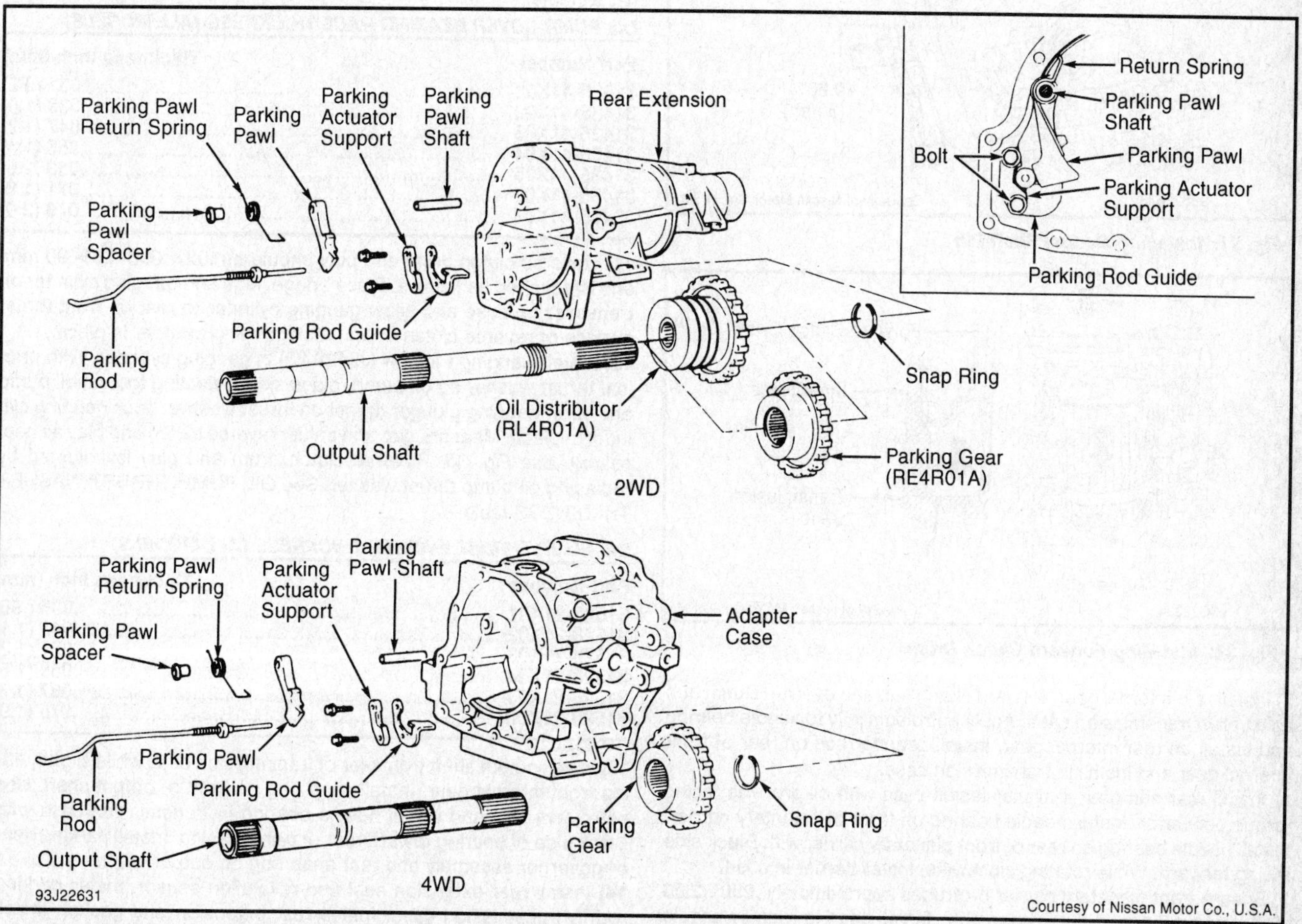

Fig. 29: Exploded View Of Parking Components (RE4R01A, RE4R03A & RL4R01A)

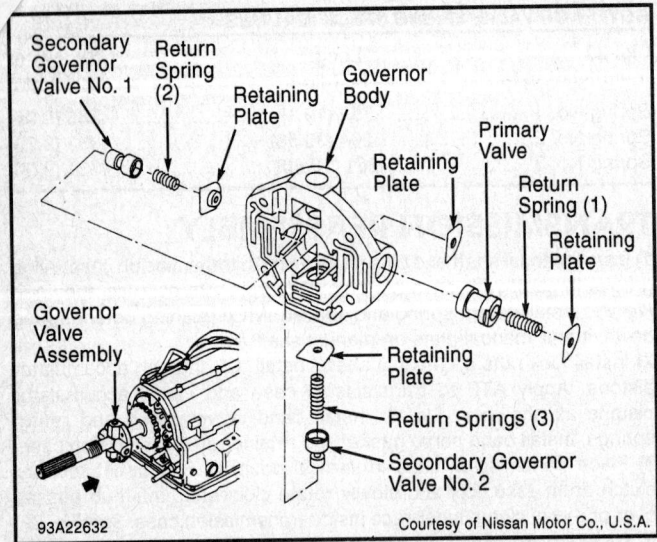

Fig. 30: Exploded View Of Governor Valve Assembly (RL4R01A)

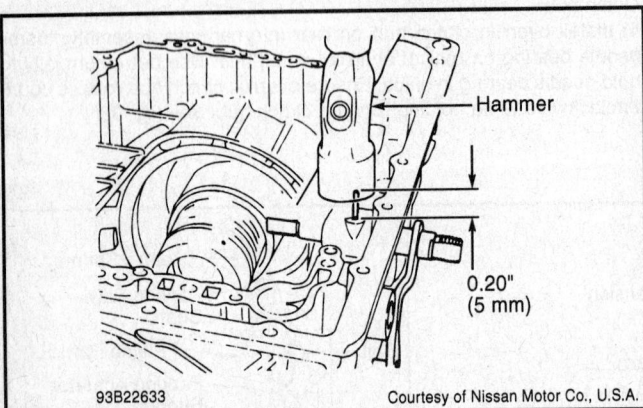

Fig. 31: Installing Manual Shaft Pin

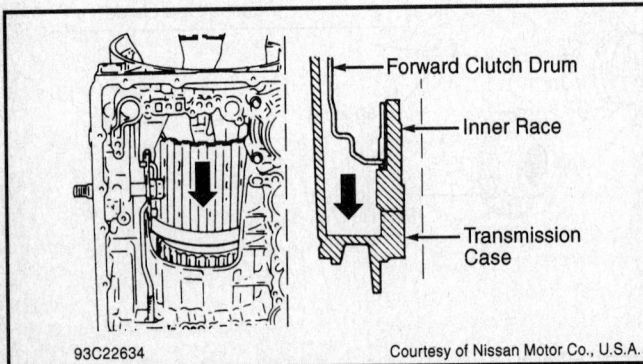

Fig. 32: Installing Forward Clutch Drum

5) Install rear internal gear, forward clutch hub and overrun clutch hub as a unit in transmission case. Apply petroleum jelly to needle bearing and install on rear internal gear. Install bearing race on rear of front internal gear and install in transmission case.

6) Install rear sun gear in transmission case with oil grooves facing torque converter. Install needle bearing on front of planetary carrier. Install needle bearing on rear of front planetary carrier with Black side facing forward. While rotating clockwise, install carrier in case.

7) Ensure front planetary carrier protrudes approximately .080" (2.00 mm) beyond forward clutch assembly. Install bearing race or needle bearing on rear of clutch pack assembly. With transmission in vertical position, install clutch pack assembly in transmission case.

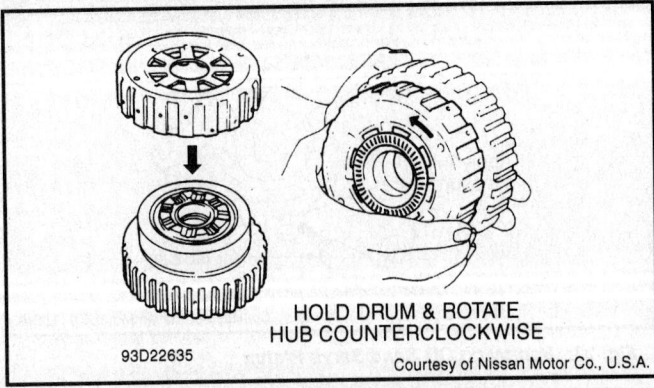

Fig. 33: Checking Overrun Clutch Hub Rotation

8) Check and adjust total end play. Total end play should be .010-.022" (.25-.55 mm) and is adjusted as follows: With needle bearing installed, place Bridge (J34291-1), Legs (J34291-2) and Gauging Cylinder (J34291-5) on oil pump (Step 1). See Fig. 34. Allow gauging cylinder to rest on top of needle bearing and lock gauging cylinder in place.

9) Install Gauging Plunger (J3429-23) in gauging cylinder. With original bearing race installed inside reverse clutch drum, place shim selecting gauge on machined surface of transmission case (without gasket) and allow gauging plunger to rest on bearing race (Step 2). See Fig. 35. Lock gauging plunger in place.

10) Measure gap as shown in Fig. 35. This measurement should give exact total end play. Total end play is adjusted by replacing oil pump cover bearing race. See OIL PUMP COVER BEARING RACE THICKNESS table.

OIL PUMP COVER BEARING RACE THICKNESS (ALL MODELS)

Part Number	Thickness Inch (mm)
31435-41X01	.031 (.80)
31435-41X02	.039 (1.0)
31435-41X03	.047 (1.2)
31435-41X04	.055 (1.4)
31435-41X05	.063 (1.6)
31435-41X06	.071 (1.8)
31435-41X07	.079 (2.0)

11) Reverse clutch drum end play should be .022-.035" (.55-.90 mm) and is adjusted as follows: Place bridge, legs and gauging cylinder on transmission case and allow gauging cylinder to rest on front thrust surface of reverse clutch drum. Lock gauging cylinder in place.

12) Install Gauging Plunger (J3429-23) in gauging cylinder. With original thrust washer on oil pump, place shim selecting tool on oil pump and allow gauging plunger to rest on thrust washer. Lock gauging cylinder in place. Measure gap and adjust reverse clutch end play as necessary. See Fig. 36. Reverse clutch drum end play is adjusted by replacing oil pump thrust washer. See OIL PUMP THRUST WASHER THICKNESS table

OIL PUMP THRUST WASHER THICKNESS (ALL MODELS)

Part Number	Thickness Inch (mm)
31528-21X01	.035 (.90)
31528-21X02	.043 (1.1)
31528-21X03	.051 (1.3)
31528-21X04	.059 (1.5)
31528-21X05	.067 (1.7)
31528-21X06	.075 (1.9)

13) Insert output shaft from rear of transmission case while slightly lifting front internal gear. Install snap ring on front of output shaft. Use petroleum jelly and install needle bearing in transmission case with Black side of bearing toward rear of transmission. Install parking gear or governor assembly and rear snap ring on output shaft.

14) Install rear extension seal and revolution sensor. Install parking rod in transmission case. Install rear extension and gasket. Install brake band and band strut. Install anchor end bolt in transmission case. Tighten anchor end bolt just enough so reverse clutch drum will not tilt forward.

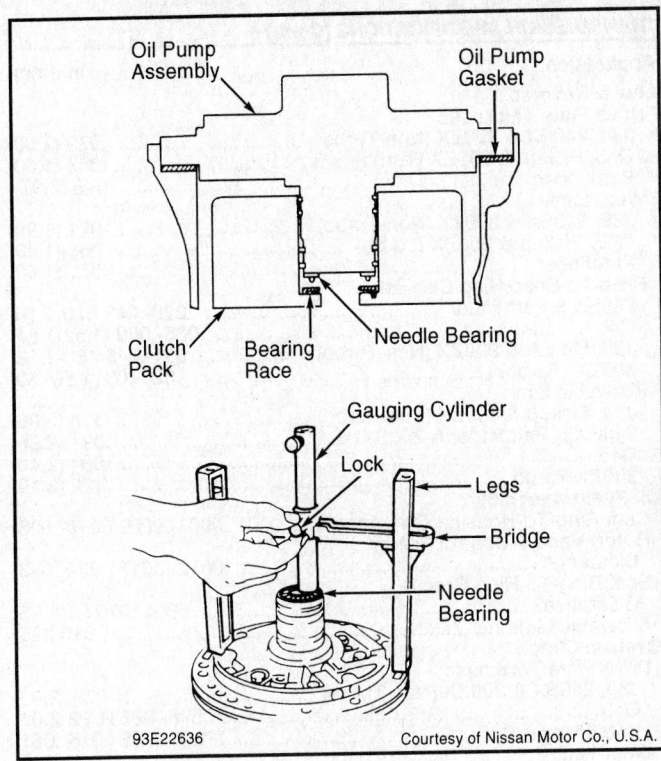

Fig. 34: Measuring Total End Play (Step 1)

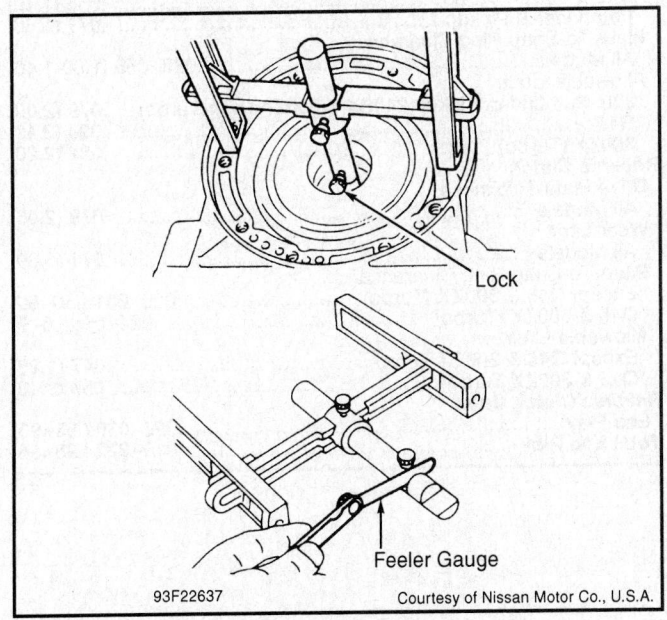

Fig. 35: Measuring Total End Play (Step 2)

15) Install input shaft in transmission case with "O" ring groove on shaft facing forward. Apply petroleum jelly to needle bearing, install needle bearing on oil pump assembly. Apply petroleum jelly to selected thrust washer to oil pump assembly. Install "O" ring on oil pump. Install oil pump gasket and oil pump. Install "O" ring to input shaft. Apply sealer to outer edge of bolt holes in converter housing. Apply sealant to seating surfaces of bolts securing converter housing. Install converter housing.

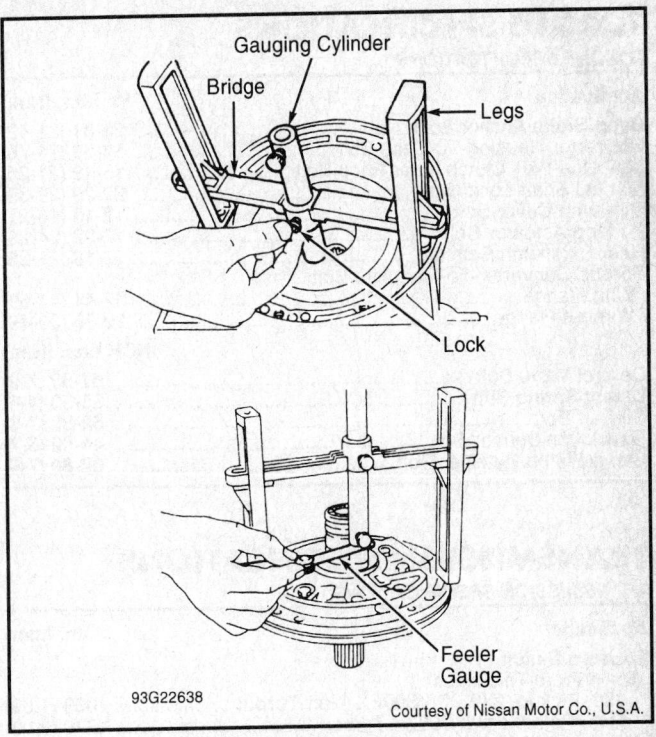

Fig. 36: Measuring Reverse Clutch Drum End Play

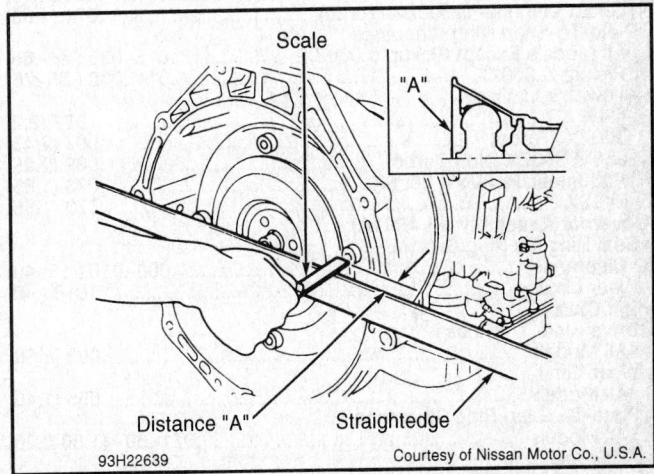

Fig. 37: Measuring Torque Converter Installed Depth

16) Adjust brake band by tightening anchor end bolt to 35-53 INCH lbs. (4-6 N.m), then back off anchor end bolt 2 1/2 turns. Hold anchor end bolt and tighten lock nut. Install solenoid harness assembly with "O" ring. Install accumulator piston return springs and control valve assembly. Connect solenoid wiring harness. Install oil strainer.

17) Install oil pan and inhibitor switch. Fill torque converter with 2.1 qts (2.0L) of ATF and install. To ensure torque converter is in proper position, measure distance from torque converter mounting holes to transmission converter surface using a straightedge. See Fig. 37. Distance should be 1.02" (26 mm) on RE4R01A and RL4R01A transmission, or .98" (25 mm) on RE4R03A transmission.

TORQUE SPECIFICATIONS
TORQUE SPECIFICATIONS

Application	Ft. Lbs. (N.m)
Band Brake Anchor Lock Nut	23-31 (31-42)
Converter Housing-To-Case Bolt	54-56 (74-76)
Low One-Way Clutch Inner Race Bolt	15-19 (21-26)
Manual Shaft Lock Nut	22-29 (29-39)
Oil Pump Cover Bolt	12-15 (16-21)
Parking Actuator Bolt	17-22 (24-29)
Rear Extension Bolt	15-18 (21-25)
Torque Converter-To-Flexplate Bolt	
With Flange	32-44 (44-59)
Without Flange	29-36 (39-49)

Application	INCH Lbs. (N.m)
Control Valve Bolt	62-80 (7-9)
Detent Spring Bolt	35-53 (4-6)
Oil Pan Bolt	62-80 (7-9)
Revolution Sensor Bolt	44-62 (5-7)
Servo Piston Retainer Bolt	62-80 (7-9)

TRANSMISSION SPECIFICATIONS
TRANSMISSION SPECIFICATIONS

Application	In. (mm)
Forward Clutch	
Drive Plate Thickness	
J30, Pickup, 240SX & 300ZX (Non-Turbo)	.063 (1.60)
Q45, Pathfinder & 300ZX Turbo	.079 (2.00)
Wear Limit	
J30, Pickup, 240SX & 300ZX (Non-Turbo)	.055 (1.40)
Q45, Pathfinder & 300ZX (Turbo)	.071 (1.80)
Plate-To-Snap Ring Clearance	
All Models Except Pickup & 300ZX	.018-.033 (.45-.85)
Pickup & 300ZX	.014-.030 (.35-.75)
Allowable Limit	
Q45	.087 (2.2)
300ZX (Turbo)	.097 (2.45)
J30 & 300ZX (Non-Turbo)	.089 (2.25)
Pathfinder/Pickup & 200SX	.073 (1.85)
240SX	.073 (1.85)
Governor Assembly (RL4R01A)	
Seal Ring-To-Ring Groove	
Clearance	.006-.016 (.15-.40)
Wear Limit	.016 (.40)
High Clutch	
Drive Plate Thickness	
All Models	.063 (1.60)
Wear Limit	
All Models	.055 (1.40)
Plate-To-Snap Ring Clearance	
All Models	.071-.087 (1.80-2.20)
Allowable Limit	
J30, & 300ZX (Non-Turbo)	.126 (3.20)
Pathfinder & Pickup	.110 (2.80)
Q45	.134 (3.40)
240SX & 300ZX (Turbo)	.118 (3.00)

TRANSMISSION SPECIFICATIONS (Cont.)

Application	In. (mm)
Low & Reverse	
Drive Plate Thickness	
J30, 240SX & 300ZX (Non-Turbo)	.079 (2.00)
Q45, Pickup & 300ZX (Turbo)	.063 (1.60)
Pathfinder	.078 (2.97)
Wear Limit	
J30, 240SX & 300ZX (Non-Turbo)	.071 (1.80)
Q45, Pickup & 300ZX (Turbo)	.055 (1.40)
Pathfinder	.071 (1.80)
Plate-To-Snap Ring Clearance	
240SX & Pathfinder	.028-.043 (.70-1.10)
Q45	.035-.066 (1.52-1.67)
J30, Pickup & 300ZX (Non-Turbo)	.031-.043 (.80-1.10)
300ZX (Turbo)	.020-.031 (.50-.80)
Allowable Limit	
J30, Pickup & 300ZX (Non-Turbo)	.114 (2.90)
240SX & Pathfinder & 240SX	.091 (2.30)
Q45	.094 (2.40)
300ZX Turbo	.122 (3.10)
Oil Pump Assembly	
Cam Ring-To-Housing Clearance	.0004-.0009 (.010-.023)
Rotor, Vane & Control Piston	
Clearance	.0012-.0017 (.030-.043)
Seal Ring-To-Ring Groove	
Clearance	.004-.010 (.10-.25)
Allowable Limit	.010 (.25)
Overrun Clutch	
Drive Plate Thickness	
J30, 240SX & 300ZX (Non-Turbo)	.079 (2.00)
Q45	.076-.082 (1.92-2.07)
Pathfinder & Pickup	1.90-2.05 (.075-.081)
Wear Limit	
J30, 240SX & 300ZX (Non-Turbo)	.071 (1.80)
Q45 & 300ZX Turbo	.055 (1.40)
Pathfinder & Pickup	.071 (1.80)
Plate-To-Snap Ring Clearance	
All Models	.039-.055 (1.00-1.40)
Allowable Limit	
J30, Pathfinder, Pickup,240SX & 300ZX (Non-Turbo)	.079 (2.00)
Q45	.094 (2.40)
300ZX (Turbo)	.087 (2.20)
Reverse Clutch	
Drive Plate Thickness	
All Models	.079 (2.00)
Wear Limit	
All Models	.071 (1.80)
Plate-To-Snap Ring Clearance	
Except Q45 & 300ZX (Turbo)	.020-.031 (.50-.80)
Q45 & 300ZX (Turbo)	.024-.035 (.6-.9)
Allowable Limit	
Except Q45 & 300ZX Turbo	.047 (1.20)
Q45 & 300ZX Turbo	.055 (1.40)
Reverse Clutch Drum	
End Play	.022-.035 (.55-.90)
Total End Play	.010-.022 (.25-.55)

Infiniti: J30, Q45
Nissan: Pathfinder, Pickup, 240SX, 300ZX

APPLICATION

APPLICATION

Vehicle Application	Trans. Model
Infiniti	
J30	RE4R01A
Q45	RE4R03A
Nissan	
Pathfinder	
2WD	RE4R01A
4WD	RE4R01A
Pickup	
2WD (4-Cyl)	RL4R01A
4WD (V6)	RE4R01A
240SX	RE4R01A
300ZX	
Non-Turbo	RE4R01A
Turbo	RE4R03A

DESCRIPTION & OPERATION

Automatic transaxle is electronically controlled. Transaxle shifting and lock-up is controlled by Automatic Transaxle Control Unit (ATCU) for optimal performance. The ATCU receives information from various input devices and uses this information to control shift and lock-up solenoid valves.

The following electronic signals, sensors, switches and solenoids are used to control transaxle shifting. See COMPONENT TESTING & CIRCUIT TESTS. for additional information and testing:

- Engine Revolution Signal (Tach Signal)
- Turbine Revolution Sensor (Q45)
- Transmission Fluid Temperature Sensor
- Inhibitor Switch
- Line Pressure Solenoid
- Lock-Up Solenoid
- Overdrive Switch
- Overrun Clutch Solenoid
- Mainshaft Revolution Sensor
- Shift Solenoids "A" and "B"
- Vehicle Speed Sensor
- Throttle Position Sensor
- Throttle Position Switch
- Shift Lock System

ELECTRONIC SELF-DIAGNOSTICS

NOTE: Driveability problems that may appear to be transmission related may be caused by a faulty engine component. Engine related fault codes MUST be repaired before diagnosing transmission. See ENGINE PERFORMANCE in appropriate MITCHELL® repair manual. Failure to diagnose and repair engine fault codes prior to transmission diagnosis may result in incorrect diagnosis or component repair.

SELF-DIAGNOSTIC PROCEDURE

NOTE: Perform self-diagnosis and code retrieval procedures with engine at normal operating temperature.

There are 4 ways to retrieve DTCs. They are displayed in different formats and by different indicators. Retrieve the codes and refer to the DTC DESCRIPTIONS table.

Scan Tool (OBD-II) – OBD-II codes must be retrieved using a scan tool connected to the OBD-II connector. Follow the scan tool manufacturer's procedure to connect and operate the scan tool.

MIL Light (MIL) – MIL light will illuminate when ignition switch is turned to ON position (engine not running). This is a bulb check. When engine is started, MIL light should turn OFF. If light remains ON, on-board diagnostics has detected an engine or transmission system fault. A/T self-diagnosis is performed by A/T Control Unit (ATCU) in combination with ECM. Self-diagnosis codes indicated by MIL are stored in both ATCU and ECM memory. Codes may be retrieved from vehicles equipped with a MIL light by using the following procedure:

1) Ensure ignition is in ON position and engine is off (KOEO). Turn diagnostic test mode selector, (located on side of ECM), fully clockwise. Wait 2 seconds, and turn diagnostic test mode selector fully counterclockwise. This puts ECM into Diagnostic Test Mode II (code retrieval mode).

2) DTCs are indicated by the MIL light "blinking" sequence. A sequence of LONG (MIL light ON for .6 second) blinks indicates the first and second digits of the DTC.

3) The third and fourth digits are indicated by a sequence of SHORT (MIL light ON for .3 second) blinks. Example: MIL blinks 10 times for 6 seconds (.6 x 10 times), and then blinks 3 times for about 1 second (.3 x 3 times). This indicates MIL DTC 1003.

4) ECM will not switch to Diagnostic Test Mode II when engine is running. When engine is turned off after code retrieval, power to ECM is lost after 5 seconds. Turn ECM switch to full counterclockwise position. This returns system to Diagnostic Test Mode I which provides bulb test and system monitoring functions.

Diagnostic Information Display (DID)/ OD OFF Light (Flash) – Flash codes are also referred to by the manufacturer as "Judgement Flickers". To retrieve Flash codes using the OD OFF indicator light or DID (Q45) use the following procedures:

Infiniti J30 – 1) Turn ignition switch to OFF position, then to ACC position. Wait at least 5 seconds. Move selector lever to "D" position. Turn ignition switch to ON position. A/T CHECK indicator light should come on for 2 seconds.

2) Move selector lever to "3" position. Depress accelerator pedal to floor and release pedal. Move selector to "2" position. Move selector lever to "1" position. Depress accelerator pedal to floor and release pedal. Record A/T CHECK indicator light flashes. Where the LONG light flash appears in the flash sequence (1st, 2nd, 3rd etc.) indicates the code. Refer to DTC DESCRIPTIONS table.

Nissan 300ZX – 1) Turn ignition switch to OFF. Wait 5 seconds. Turn ignition switch to ACC. Set OD switch in OFF position. Move selector lever to "D" position. Turn ignition switch to ON position. A/T CHECK light should come on for 2 seconds.

2) Move selector lever to "2" position. Set OD switch to ON position. Move selector lever to "1" position. Set OD switch to OFF position. Depress accelerator pedal to floor and release pedal. Record A/T CHECK indicator light flashes. Where the LONG light flash appears in the flash sequence (1st, 2nd, 3rd etc.) indicates the code. Refer to DTC DESCRIPTIONS table.

Nissan 240SX – 1) Turn ignition switch to OFF position. Wait 5 seconds. Turn ignition switch to ACC. Set OD switch in ON position. Move selector lever to "P" position. Turn ignition switch to ON position. OD OFF light should come on for 2 seconds.

2) Turn ignition switch to OFF position. Turn ignition switch to "ON" position. Move selector lever to "D" position. Turn ignition to OFF Position. Set OD switch to OFF position. Turn ignition switch to ON position. Wait 2 seconds minimum after ignition switch is ON. Move selector lever to "2" position. Set OD switch in "ON" position.

3) Move selector lever to "1" position. Set OD switch in OFF position. Depress accelerator pedal to floor and release pedal. Record A/T CHECK indicator light flashes. Where the LONG light flash appears in the flash sequence (1st, 2nd, 3rd etc.) indicates the code. Refer to DTC DESCRIPTIONS table.

Nissan Pathfinder – 1) Turn ignition switch to OFF position. Wait 5 seconds. Turn ignition switch to ACC. Set OD switch in ON position. Move selector lever to "P" position. Turn ignition switch to ON position. OD OFF light should come on for 2 seconds.

2) Turn ignition switch to OFF position. Turn ignition switch to ACC position. Move selector lever to "D" position. Set OD control switch to OFF position. Wait 2 seconds (minimum) after ignition switch is ON. Move selector position lever to "2" position. Set OD control switch in ON position.

3) Move selector lever to "1" position. Set OD switch in OFF. Depress accelerator pedal to floor and release pedal. Record A/T CHECK indicator light flashes. Where the LONG light flash appears in the flash sequence (1st, 2nd, 3rd etc.) indicates the code. Refer to DTC DESCRIPTIONS table.

Infiniti Q45 – 1) Turn ignition switch to OFF position. Using shift ock release knob, move selector lever to "D" position. Turn trip reset button counterclockwise and hold it. Turn ignition switch to ON position (Do not start engine). Diagnostic information display should A/T CHECK. If A/T CHECK does not appear, the "D" input of inhibitor switch or trip odometer button may be at fault.

2) Move selector lever to "3" position. Depress accelerator pedal to floor and release pedal. Move selector lever to "2" position. Move selector lever to "1" position. Depress accelerator pedal to floor and release pedal. Wait 30 seconds. Record diagnostic display information. Refer to DTC DESCRIPTIONS table.

NOTE: *Diagnostic information display will flash "OK" if system is normal. Diagnostic information display will flash corresponding number of judgement flicker. See Fig. 1. Also see appropriate wiring diagram for terminal and wire circuit identification. See WIRING DIAGRAMS.*

DTC TESTING

NOTE: *For additional wiring diagram information, See WIRING DIAGRAMS.*

DTC P0705/1101/1ST OR A/T CHECK: INHIBITOR SWITCH

Circuit Description – Inhibitor switch detects selector lever position and sends a signal to ATCU. 1st gear position switch holds selector lever in 1st speed position. Kickdown switch detects full-throttle position of the accelerator pedal when the TPS is malfunctioning. ATCU will then receive a signal from kickdown switch. Throttle Position Switch consist of a wide open throttle switch which sends a signal to

---

NOTE: *Codes are displayed in the following order in tables and in DTC TESTING: OBD-II Code/MIL Code/Flash.*

DTC DESCRIPTIONS (EXCEPT Q45)

OBD-II/MIL/Flash [1]

	DTC Description
P0000/0505/All Flashes Same	No Codes In System
P0705/1003 Or 1101/No Flash	Inhibitor, Kickdown switch or Throttle position switch circuit, 1 position switch, Or ATCU
P0710/1208/8th	Fluid Temp Sensor/ATCU Power Source Circuit
P0720/1102/1st	Vehicle Speed Sensor (A/T Revolution) Circuit
[3] / [2] /2nd	Vehicle Speed Sensor/MTR (At Speedometer)
P0725/1207/9th	Engine Speed Signal Circuit
P0731/1103/No Flash[2]	A/T First Signal
P0732/1104/No Flash[2]	A/T Second Signal
P0733/1105/No Flash[2]	A/T Third Signal
P0734/1106/No Flash[2]	A/T Fourth Signal Or TCC
P0740/1204/7th	Torque Converter Solenoid Valve
P0745/1205/11th	Line Pressure Solenoid Valve
P0750/1108/4th	Shift Solenoid Valve "A"
P0755/1201/5th	Shift Solenoid Valve "B"
P1705/1206/3rd	Throttle Position Sensor Or Switch
P1760/1203/6th	Overrun Clutch Solenoid Valve
[3] / [3] /10th	Turbine Revolution Sensor

[1] – Indicated by long flash (Judgement Flicker) of OD OFF indicator light in self diagnostic check. See Self-Diagnostic Procedure.
[2] – Malfunction cannot be displayed by MIL if another malfunction is assigned to OD OFF/ A/T CHECK light.
[3] – OBD-II code number is not available.

NOTE: *Codes are indicated as follows: DTC OBD-II/MIL/DID (Diagnostic Information Display).*

DTC DESCRIPTIONS (Q45)

OBD-II/MIL/DID [1]

	DTC Description
P0000/0505/OK	No Codes In System, Circuits OK
P0705/1003 Or 1101/ A/T Check	Inhibitor, Kickdown switch or Throttle position switch circuit, 1 position switch, Or ATCU
P0710/1208/8	Fluid Temp Sensor/ATCU Power Source Circuit
P0720/1102/1	Vehicle Speed Sensor (A/T Revolution) Circuit
[3] / [2] / 2nd	Vehicle Speed Sensor/MTR (At Speedometer)
P0725/1207/9	Engine Speed Signal Circuit
P0731/1103/N/A[2]	A/T First Signal
P0732/1104/N/A[2]	A/T Second Signal
P0733/1105/N/A[2]	A/T Third Signal
P0734/1106/N/A[2]	A/T Fourth Signal Or TCC
P0740/1204/7	Torque Converter Solenoid Valve
P0745/1205/B	Line Pressure Solenoid Valve
P0750/1108/4	Shift Solenoid Valve "A"
P0755/1201/5	Shift Solenoid Valve "B"
P1705/1206/3	Throttle Position Sensor Or Switch
P1760/1203/6	Overrun Clutch Solenoid Valve
[3] / [3] /A	Turbine Revolution Sensor Circuit
P1605/ [3] /C	Engine Control Circuit
[3] / [3] /D	Low Battery Power, Mis-connected Or Has Been Disconnected For Long Period Of Time

[1] – Indicated by digit(s) or letter(s) on diagnostic information display indicator in self diagnostic check. See SELF-DIAGNOSTIC PROCEDURE.
[2] – Malfunction cannot be displayed by MIL if another malfunction is assigned to Diagnostic Information Display (DID).
[3] – OBD-II/MIL code number is not available.

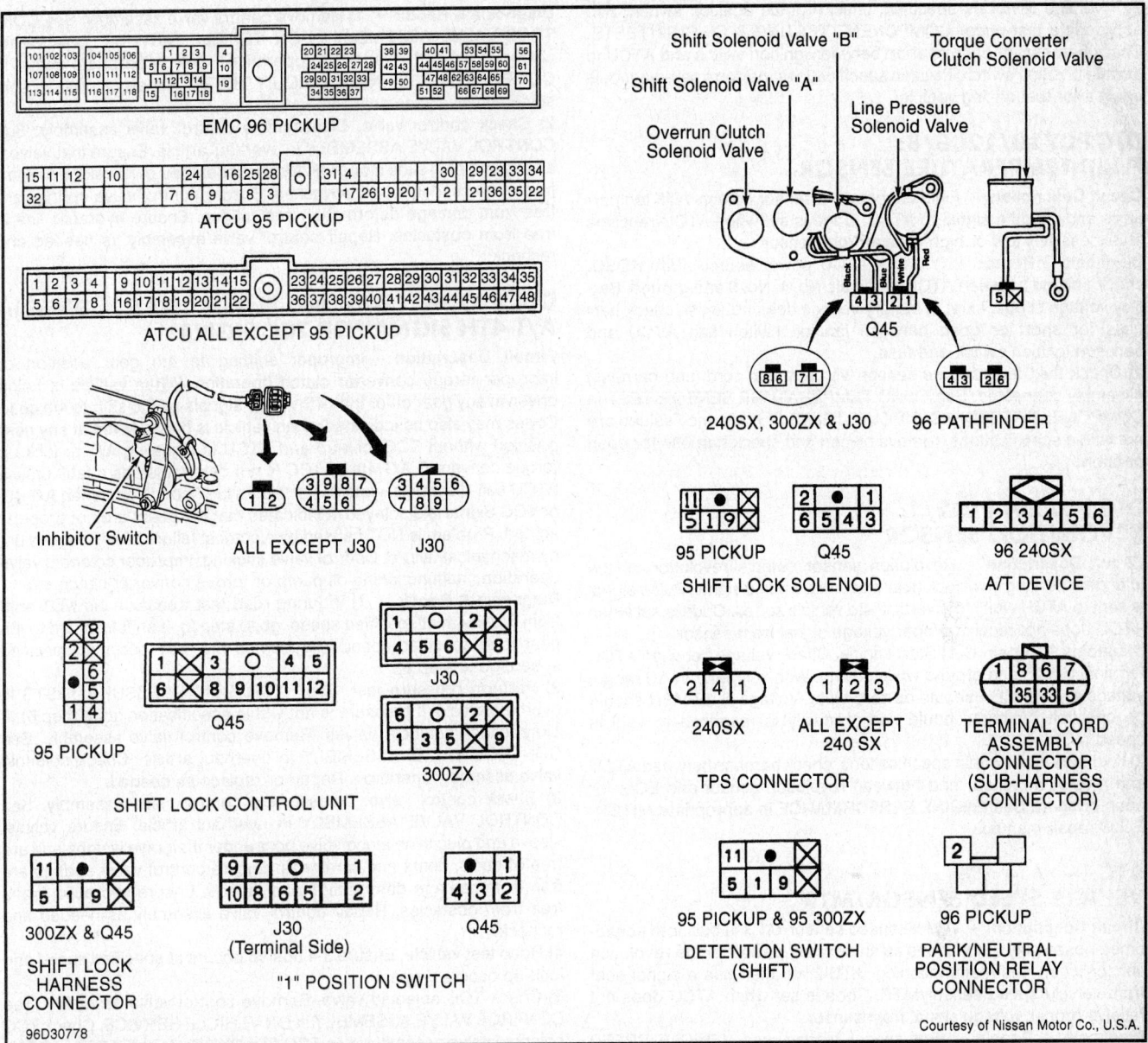

Fig. 1: Identifying Connector Terminal Pins

ATCU when throttle valve is open 50 percent and a closed throttle position switch which indicates when throttle valve is fully closed. Code is set when ATCU receives an excessively low or high voltage from sensor.

Diagnosis & Repair – 1) Check inhibitor switch. See appropriate test under COMPONENT TESTING & CIRCUIT TESTS.

2) Check harness and connectors for open or short between ignition switch and inhibitor switch and between inhibitor switch and ATCU. If continuity exists for all circuits, go to next step. If continuity does not exist for any circuit inspect and repair circuit(s) as needed.

1st gear ("1") Position Switch (Infiniti) – With KOEO, check voltage between ATCU terminal No. 39 and ground while moving selector lever to "1" position. Battery voltage should be present. If voltage is not as specified, check "1" position switch. See appropriate test in COMPONENT TESTING & CIRCUIT TESTS. Check harness for open or short between ATCU and "1" position switch and ground circuit for "1" position switch. If continuity exists for all circuits, go to next test.

OD Switch (Nissan) – With KOEO, check voltage between ATCU terminal No. 39 and ground with OD switch in ON and OFF position. Battery voltage should be present with OD switch in ON position. With OD switch OFF, voltage should be one volt maximum.

Kickdown Switch – With KOEO, check voltage between ATCU and terminal No. 41 and ground while depressing accelerator pedal slowly (engine warm). Voltage should be 3-8 volts when releasing pedal, one volt maximum with pedal fully depressed. If voltage is not as specified, check kickdown switch. See appropriate test in COMPONENT TESTING & CIRCUIT TESTS. Check harness for open or short between ATCU and kickdown switch and ground circuit for kickdown switch. If continuity exists for all circuits, go to next test.

Throttle Position Switch – 1) Start and warm engine. With KOEO, check voltage between ATCU terminals No. 14, No. 21 and ground while depressing and releasing accelerator pedal slowly. See THROTTLE POSITION VOLTAGE TEST table.

THROTTLE POSITION VOLTAGE TEST

Accelerator Pedal	Voltage
Released	
Terminal No. 14	Battery Voltage
Terminal No. 21	1 Volt Maximum
Fully Depressed	
Terminal No. 14	1 Volt Maximum
Terminal No. 21	Battery Voltage

2) If voltage is not as specified, check throttle position switch. See appropriate test under COMPONENT TESTING & CIRCUIT TESTS. Check harness for open or short between ignition switch and ATCU to throttle position switch. If within specifications, perform self-diagnosis again after test driving vehicle.

DTC P0710/1208/8:
FLUID TEMPERATURE SENSOR

Circuit Description – Fluid temperature sensor detects ATF temperature and sends a signal to ATCU. Code is set when ATCU receives an excessively low or high voltage from sensor.

Diagnosis & Repair – 1) Check ATCU power source. With KOEO, check voltage between ATCU terminals No. 4, No. 9 and ground. Battery voltage should exist. If battery voltage does not exist, check harness for short or open between ignition switch and ATCU and between ignition switch and fuse.

2) Check fluid temperature sensor with terminal cord (sub-harness) assembly connected. See FLUID TEMPERATURE SENSOR TEST in COMPONENT TESTING & CIRCUIT TESTS. If resistance values are not within specifications, remove oil pan and check harness for open or short.

DTC P0720/1102/1:
REVOLUTION SENSOR

Circuit Description – Revolution sensor detects revolution of the idler gear parking pawl lock gear and emits a pulse signal. Pulse signal is sent to ATCU which converts it into vehicle speed. Code is set when ATCU does not receive proper voltage signal from sensor.

Diagnosis & Repair – 1) Start engine. Check voltage between ATCU terminal No. 25 and ground while driving. With voltmeter in AC range, voltage at zero MPH should be zero volts. Voltage at 19 MPH should be one volt. Voltage should rise gradually in response to vehicle speed.

2) If voltage is not within specifications, check harness between ATCU and revolution sensor and between revolution sensor and ECM for open or short. See ENGINE PERFORMANCE in appropriate MITCHELL® repair manual.

DTC – / – /2:
VEHICLE SPEED SENSOR/MTR

Circuit Description – Vehicle speed sensor/MTR is built into speedometer assembly. It functions as an auxiliary device for the revolution sensor when it is malfunctioning. ATCU will then use a signal sent from vehicle speed sensor/MTR. Code is set when ATCU does not receive proper voltage signal from sensor.

Diagnosis & Repair – For sensor testing, see VEHICLE SPEED SENSOR/MTR in COMPONENT TESTING & CIRCUIT TESTS.

DTC P0725/1207/9:
ENGINE SPEED SIGNAL

Circuit Description – Engine speed signal (tach signal) is sent from ECM to ACTU. Code is set when ATCU does not receive proper voltage signal from ECM.

Diagnosis & Repair – For sensor testing, see ENGINE SPEED SENSOR (TACH SIGNAL) in COMPONENT TESTING & CIRCUIT TESTS.

DTC P0731, P0732, P07033/1103, 1104, 1105/ NO FLASH, (Q45 = Blank):
A/T 1ST SIGNAL, 2ND SIGNAL, 3RD SIGNAL

Circuit Description – When vehicle is being driven in any gear other than 1st (P0731),2nd (P0732),3rd (P07033), ATCU is signals A/T to shift to 1st/2nd/3rd gear. A/T 1st/2nd/3rd signal is not determined as a fault unless ATCU self diagnosis system is in "No Failure" condition. When A/T 1st/2nd/3rd code is displayed, it indicates that the gears are not properly shifted. Problem is NOT caused by electrical failure of A/T circuits but by mechanical failure (control valve sticking, improper solenoid valve operation, etc.).

Diagnosis & Repair – 1) Remove control valve assembly. See CONTROL VALVE ASSEMBLY in ON VEHICLE SERVICE. Check shift solenoid valve "A" and "B" operation. See appropriate tests in COMPONENT TESTING & CIRCUIT TESTS. Repair or replace shift solenoid valve assembly as needed.

2) Check control valve. Disassemble control valve assembly. See CONTROL VALVE ASSEMBLY in overhaul article. Ensure that valves, sleeve and plug slide along valve bore under their own weight, and are free of burrs, dents and scratches. Ensure control valve springs are free from damage deformation and fatigue. Ensure hydraulic line is free from obstacles. Repair control valve assembly as needed and recheck.

DTC P0734/1106/ NO FLASH, (Q45 = Blank):
A/T 4TH SIGNAL OR TCC SIGNAL

Circuit Description – Improper shifting to 4th gear position or improper torque converter clutch operation. When vehicle is being driven in any gear other than 4th ATCU signals A/T to shift to 4th gear. Codes may also be indicated when vehicle is being driven at any gear position without TCC lock-up and ATCU is signaling A/T to lock-up torque converter. A/T 4th or TCC is not determined as a fault unless ATCU self-diagnosis system is in "No Failure" condition. When A/T 4th or TCC Signal is displayed, it indicates that the gears are not properly shifted. Problem is NOT caused by electrical failure of A/T circuits but by mechanical failure. Control valve sticking, improper solenoid valve operation, malfunctioning oil pump or torque converter clutch etc.

Diagnosis & Repair – 1) If during road test transaxle did NOT shift from 3rd to 4th at specified speed, go to step **2)**. If shift from 3rd to 4th gear is at specified speed and lock-up did NOT occur at specified speed, go to step **5)**.

2) Perform pressure test. See HYDRAULIC PRESSURE TESTS in overhaul article. If pressure is not within specification go to step **6)**. If okay, check solenoid valves. Remove control valve assembly. See CONTROL VALVE ASSEMBLY in overhaul article. Check solenoid valve assembly operation. Repair or replace as needed.

3) Check control valve. Disassemble control valve assembly. See CONTROL VALVE ASSEMBLY in overhaul article. Ensure valves, sleeve and plug slide along valve bore under their own weight, and are free of burrs, dents and scratches. Ensure control valve springs are free from damage deformation and fatigue. Ensure hydraulic line is free from obstacles. Repair control valve assembly as needed and recheck.

4) Road test vehicle. Ensure 3-4 upshift occurs at specified speed and lock-up occurs properly.

5) Check TCC solenoid valve. Remove control valve assembly. See CONTROL VALVE ASSEMBLY in ON VEHICLE SERVICE. Check TCC solenoid valve assembly. See TCC SOLENOID VALVE TEST in COMPONENT TESTING & CIRCUIT TESTS. Replace or repair as necessary. Check TCC control valve and TCC relief valve for sticking. Repair as needed. Road test vehicle, ensure A/T performs lock up at specific speed. See LOCK-UP SPEED SPECIFICATIONS table in overhaul article. If okay, ensure symptoms from circuit description are no longer present.

6) Remove control valve assembly. See CONTROL VALVE ASSEMBLY in ON VEHICLE SERVICE. Check line pressure solenoid. See LINE PRESSURE SOLENOID TEST in COMPONENT TESTING & CIRCUIT TESTS. Repair or replace solenoid valve assembly as needed. If okay, remove and disassemble control valve assembly. See CONTROL VALVE ASSEMBLY in overhaul article. Check pressure regulator, pilot and pressure modifier valves for sticking. Repair as needed.

7) Road test vehicle, ensure 3-4 shift and lock-up occurs at specified speed.

DTC P0740/1204/7:
TORQUE CONVERTER CLUTCH VALVE

Circuit Description – Torque converter clutch solenoid valve circuit check. TCC solenoid valve is activated, in 4th gear, by ATCU in response to signals sent from vehicle speed and throttle position sensors. Lock-up piston will then be controlled. Lock-up is prohibited when ATF temperature is too low.

Diagnosis & Repair – 1) Check ground circuit. With ignition switch OFF, disconnect terminal cord assembly connector in engine compartment. Check resistance between terminal No. 5 (except Q45), No. 8 (Q45) and ground. Resistance should be 10-20 ohms. If resistance is within specifications, go to next step. If not within specifications, remove oil pan, check harness for open or short and TCC solenoid valve. See TORQUE CONVERTER CLUTCH SOLENOID VALVE TEST in COMPONENT TESTING & CIRCUIT TESTS.

2) With ignition in OFF position, disconnect ATCU connector. Check resistance between connector terminal No. 5 (except Q45), No. 8 (Q45) and ATCU terminal No. 5. Resistance should be zero ohms. Repair or replace as needed. Reinstall any part removed.

3) Road test and perform self-diagnosis. If unable to obtain ATCU feedback, check ATCU input/output signal. See ATCU POWER SOURCE TEST in COMPONENT TESTING & CIRCUIT TESTS. If not within specifications, recheck ATCU pin terminals for damage or loose connections.

DTC P0745/1205/11TH, (PATHFINDER = 10TH, Q45 = "B"):
LINE PRESSURE SOLENOID VALVE

Circuit Description – Line pressure solenoid valve circuit check. Line pressure solenoid valve regulates oil pump discharge pressure to suit driving conditions in response to a signal sent from ATCU.

Diagnosis & Repair – 1) Check line pressure solenoid valve circuit. See LINE PRESSURE SOLENOID VALVE TEST in COMPONENT TESTING & CIRCUIT TESTS. If resistance is not as specified, remove control valve assembly. See CONTROL VALVE ASSEMBLY in overhaul article. Inspect line pressure solenoid, see appropriate solenoid test under COMPONENT TESTING & CIRCUIT TESTS. Inspect harness for short or open of terminal cord assembly.

2) If resistance is okay, check power source circuit. Using ohmmeter, check resistance between terminal No. 1 and ATCU terminal No. 2. Resistance should be 11.2-12.8 ohms. If resistance is not as specified, check dropping resistor. See appropriate test under COMPONENT TESTING & CIRCUIT TESTS. Inspect harness for open or short between ATCU terminal No. 2 and terminal cord assembly.

3) If resistance is okay, with ignition in OFF position, check resistance between terminal cord assembly connector terminal No. 1 and ATCU terminal No. 1. Resistance should be zero ohms. If not as specified, repair or replace harness between ATCU and terminal cord assembly.

4) If resistance is as specified, road test vehicle and perform self-diagnosis. If unable to obtain ATCU feedback, recheck ATCU input/output signal inspection. If not as specified, check ATCU pin terminals for damage or loose connection with harness connector.

DTC P0750/1108/4:
SHIFT SOLENOID VALVE "A"

Circuit Description – Shift solenoid valves "A" and "B" are turned ON and OFF by ATCU in response to output signal from the inhibitor switch, vehicle speed sensor and throttle position sensors. A voltage drop not within specifications during solenoid operation will set code. Shift solenoid "A" is normally ON in 1st and 4th gear. Shift solenoid "B" is normally ON in 1st and 2nd gear.

Diagnosis & Repair – 1) With ignition off, disconnect terminal cord assembly in engine compartment. Check resistance between terminal No. 6 (except 300ZX and Q45), No 2 (300ZX), No. 3 (Q45) and ground. Resistance should be 20-40 ohms.

2) If resistance is not within specifications, remove control valve assembly. See CONTROL VALVE ASSEMBLY in overhaul article. Check solenoid valve "A", see appropriate test under COMPONENT TESTING & CIRCUIT TESTS. Check wiring harness and connectors for open or short.

3) If resistance is within specifications, check power source circuit. With ignition OFF, disconnect ATCU harness connector. Check resistance between connector terminal No. 6 (except 300ZX and Q45), No 2 (300ZX), No. 3 and ATCU terminal No. 6. Resistance should be zero ohms. If resistance is as specified, reconnect connectors.

4) If resistance is NOT as specified, repair or replace harness between ATCU and terminal cord assembly. Road test and perform self diagnosis. If unable to obtain ATCU feedback, recheck ATCU input/output signal inspection. If not as specified, check ATCU pin terminals for damage or loose connection with harness connector.

DTC P0755/1201/5:
SHIFT SOLENOID VALVE "B"

Circuit Description – Shift solenoid valves "A" and "B" are turned ON and OFF by ATCU in response to output from the inhibitor switch, vehicle speed sensor and throttle position sensors. Information received determines best possible gear choice. Code is set when ATCU detects improper voltage drop during operation of solenoid valve. Shift solenoid "A" is normally ON in 1st and 4th gear. Shift solenoid "B" is normally ON in 1st and 2nd gear. Code will set if ATCU detects improper voltage drop when it signals solenoid operation.

Diagnosis & Repair – 1) With ignition off, disconnect terminal cord assembly (sub-harness) connector in engine compartment. Check resistance between terminal No. 7 (except 300ZX and Q45), No. 1 (300ZX), No. 4 (Q45) and ground. Resistance should be 20-40 ohms.

2) If resistance is not within specifications, remove control valve assembly. See CONTROL VALVE ASSEMBLY in overhaul article. Check solenoid valve "B", see appropriate test under COMPONENT TESTING & CIRCUIT TESTS. Check wiring harness and connectors for open or short.

3) If resistance is within specifications, check power source circuit. With ignition OFF, disconnect ATCU harness connector. Check resistance between connector terminal No. 7 (except 300ZX and Q45), No. 1 (300ZX), No. 4 and ATCU terminal No. 7. Resistance should be zero ohms. If resistance is as specified, reconnect connectors.

4) If resistance is NOT as specified, repair or replace harness between ATCU and terminal cord assembly. Road test and perform self-diagnosis. If unable to obtain ATCU feedback, recheck ATCU input/output signal inspection. If not as specified, check ATCU pin terminals for damage or loose connection with harness connector.

DTC P1705/1206/3:
THROTTLE POSITION SENSOR

Circuit Description – TP sensor relays throttle valve position to ATCU. A code is set when ATCU receives an excessively high or low voltage from TP sensor.

Diagnosis & Repair – 1) Check TP sensor circuit for engine control. Refer to appropriate SELF-DIAGNOSTICS article in ENGINE PERFORMANCE of appropriate MITCHELL® manual for TP sensor DTC test (DTC P0120 or MIL 0403). If engine control test okay, go to next step.

2) Check idle switch input signal. See IDLE SWITCH circuit test under COMPONENT TESTING & CIRCUIT TESTS. Check terminals for damage or loose connection with harness connector. Repair as necessary.

DTC P1760/1203/6:
OVERRUN CLUTCH SOLENOID VALVE

Circuit Description – Overrun clutch solenoid valve is activated by ATCU in response to signals sent from inhibitor switch, OD switch, vehicle speed and throttle position sensors. Overrun clutch operation is controlled by outputs from the sensors. If ATCU detects unspecified voltage drops when it tries to operate overrun clutch solenoid valve.

Diagnosis & Repair – 1) Check ground circuit. With KOEO, disconnect terminal cord harness assembly connector in engine compartment. Check resistance between terminal No. 2 and ground. Resistance should be 20-40 ohms. If resistance is not as specified, remove control valve. See CONTROL VALVE ASSEMBLY in overhaul article. Check overrun clutch solenoid valve, See appropriate test under COMPONENT TESTING & CIRCUIT TESTS. Check harness for open or short of terminal cord assembly.

2) If resistance is within specifications, Check power source. With ignition OFF, disconnect ATCU harness connector. Check resistance between solenoid wiring harness connector terminal No. 2 and ATCU harness terminal No. 8. Resistance should be zero ohms. Repair or replace harness between ATCU and solenoid wiring harness assembly if not as specified. Road test and perform self diagnosis. If unable to obtain ATCU feedback, recheck ATCU input/output signal inspection. If not as specified, check ATCU pin terminals for damage or loose connection with harness connector.

DTC – / – /10TH (J30)- "A" (Q45): TURBINE REVOLUTION SENSOR

Circuit Description – Turbine revolution sensor detects input shaft RPM. Located on input side of transmission. Vehicle speed sensor (revolution sensor) is located on output side of transmission. Input and output shaft RPM are accurately detected between the 2 sensors, resulting in optimal shift timing during deceleration and improved shifting. Code is set when ATCU does not receive proper voltage signal from the sensor.

Diagnosis & Repair – 1) Check turbine revolution sensor. See appropriate test under COMPONENT TESTING & CIRCUIT TESTS. Check voltage between ATCU terminal No. 26 and No. 35 (J30) No. 26 and ground (Q45). Using voltmeter in AC range, voltage should be .3-4.5 volts. If voltage is not as specified, check harness for short or open between ATCU and turbine revolution sensor.

2) Repair or replace harness between ATCU and solenoid wiring harness assembly if not as specified. Road test and perform self diagnosis. If unable to obtain ATCU feedback, recheck ATCU input/output signal inspection. If not as specified, check ATCU pin terminals for damage or loose connection with harness connector.

DTC P1605 / – / "C" (Q45 ONLY): ENGINE CONTROL CIRCUIT

Circuit Description – ECM and ATCU provide mutual communication in relation to engine output control signal (ignition timing retard signal) during rapid standing starts/acceleration. Improved shifting is a result of this consistent real-time control. Code will set if ECM-ATCU communication is open or shorted.

Diagnosis & Repair – 1) With ignition OFF, check continuity between ATCU terminal No. 10 and ECM terminal No. 73 and between ATCU terminal No. 11 and ECM terminal No. 74. Continuity should exist. If continuity does NOT exist, repair or replace connector between ATCU and ECM.

2) If continuity exists, check ECM. Perform self-diagnosis for engine control. See appropriate SELF-DIAGNOSTICS article in ENGINE PERFORMANCE of appropriate MITCHELL® manual. If ECM is okay, perform DTC confirmation procedure. If DTC exists, recheck ATCU pin terminals for damage or loose connections.

COMPONENT TESTING & CIRCUIT TESTS

NOTE: If the following circuit test results are not as described, check wiring circuit between specified components to correct circuit malfunction. Repair as necessary. For wiring diagram information, see WIRING DIAGRAMS. Also See Fig. 1.

ATCU POWER SOURCE TEST

With ignition switch in ON position, and engine off, check voltage between ATCU terminals No. 4, 9 and ground. Battery voltage should be present. If voltage is not as specified, repair circuit(s) as necessary.

FLUID TEMPERATURE SENSOR TEST

1) Check resistance between fluid temperature sensor terminals. Resistance should be 2500 ohms at 68°F (20°C), and 300 ohms at 176°F (80°C). If resistance is not as specified, replace sensor.

2) Disconnect sensor harness connector in engine compartment. Check resistance between terminals No. 33 and 35 (Infiniti, Pathfinder (1996), 240SX and 300ZX), or terminals No. 12 and 15 (Pathfinder (1995) and Pickup) when transmission is cold. Resistance should be approximately 2500 ohms at 68°F (20°C).

3) Check voltage between ATCU terminal No. 33 and ground (Infiniti, Pathfinder (1996), 240SX and 300ZX) or ATCU terminal No. 12 and

ground (Pathfinder (1995) and Pickup), while warming up transmission from 68°F (20°C) to 176°F (80°C). Voltage should be approximately 1.5 volts at 68°F (20°C) and .5 volt at 176°F (80°C). If resistance and voltage is not as specified, repair circuit as necessary.

ENGINE REVOLUTION SENSOR

Circuit Test – With ignition switch in ON position, and engine off, measure voltage between ATCU terminal No. 24 and ground (Infiniti, Pathfinder (1996), 240SX and 300ZX) or ATCU terminal No. 25 and ground (Pathfinder (1995) and Pickup). Voltage should be .9-4.5 volts for Infiniti, 240SX and 300ZX, or 9.5-12 volts for Pathfinder and Pickup. If voltage is not as specified, repair circuit(s) as necessary.

Component Test – Check resistance between terminals No. 1, 2 and 3. See REVOLUTION SENSOR RESISTANCE TEST table.

REVOLUTION SENSOR RESISTANCE TEST

Terminal Number	Resistance
2 & 3	500-650
1 & 2	No Continuity
1 & 3	No Continuity

TURBINE REVOLUTION SENSOR

Check resistance between terminals No. 1, No. 2 and No. 3. See TURBINE REVOLUTION SENSOR RESISTANCE table

TURBINE REVOLUTION SENSOR RESISTANCE TEST

Terminal Number	Resistance
2 & 3	2200-2800
1 & 2	No Continuity
1 & 3	No Continuity

"1" POSITION SWITCH (INFINITI)

Check continuity between terminals No. 3 and No. 4 of "1" position switch harness connector. With selector lever is in "1" position, continuity should exist. With selector lever is in any position except "1", NO continuity should exist.

IDLE SWITCH

Circuit Test – With ignition switch in ON position, measure voltage between ATCU terminal No. 14 and ground (Infiniti, Pathfinder (1996), 240SX and 300ZX) or ATCU terminal No. 4 and ground (Pathfinder (1995) and Pickup), while depressing accelerator pedal slowly. When releasing accelerator pedal, voltage should be 8-15 volts. When depressing accelerator pedal fully, voltage should be one volt or less. If voltage is not as specified, repair circuit as necessary.

Component Test – 1) Check continuity between terminals No. 1 and No. 2. With accelerator pedal released (closed throttle position), continuity should exist. With pedal depressed, continuity should not exist.

2) Check continuity between terminals No. 2 and No. 3 with accelerator pedal depressed (wide open throttle position switch), continuity should exist. With pedal released, no continuity should exist.

INHIBITOR SWITCH CIRCUIT TEST

1) With ignition switch in ON position, measure voltage between appropriate ATCU terminal and ground, while moving selector lever through each position. Battery voltage should be present at specified terminal when selector lever is in specified position. See appropriate INHIBITOR SWITCH VOLTAGE table. If switch does not test as described, repair or replace switch.

INHIBITOR SWITCH VOLTAGE
(INFINITI J30, PATHFINDER (1996), 240SX & 300ZX)

Position	Battery Voltage At Terminal No.
"P" Or "N"	19
"R"	20
"D"	18
"2"	17
"1"	16

INHIBITOR SWITCH VOLTAGE (INFINITI Q45)

Position	Battery Voltage At Terminal No.
"P" Or "N"	19
"R"	20
"D"	18
"3"	17
"2" & "1"	16

INHIBITOR SWITCH VOLTAGE (PATHFINDER (1995) & PICKUP)

Position	Battery Voltage At Terminal No.
"P" Or "N"	19
"R"	26
"D"	20
"2"	1
"1"	2

2) Check continuity between terminals specified while moving selector lever through each position. See INHIBITOR SWITCH CONTINUITY TEST table. If continuity is not as specified, re-check again with manual control linkage disconnected from manual shaft of A/T assembly. If continuity is as specified, adjust manual control linkage. See ON VEHICLE SERVICE. If continuity is not as specified with manual control linkage disconnected, remove inhibitor switch from A/T and check continuity of inhibitor switch terminals. If not as specified, replace inhibitor switch. *See Fig. 1.*

INHIBITOR SWITCH CONTINUITY TEST

Selector Position	Continuity Between Pins No.
"P"	1 & 2, 3 & 4
"R"	3 & 5
"N"	1 & 2, 3 & 6
"D"	3 & 7
"2"	3 & 8
"1"	3 & 9

KICKDOWN SWITCH CIRCUIT TEST

1) With ignition switch in ON position, measure voltage between ATCU terminal No. 41 and ground (Infiniti, 240SX and 300ZX) or ATCU terminal No. 7 and ground (Pathfinder (1995) and Pickup), while depressing accelerator pedal slowly. When releasing accelerator pedal, voltage should be 3-8 volts. When depressing accelerator pedal fully, voltage should be one volt or less. If voltage is not as specified, repair circuit as necessary.

2) Check continuity between terminals No. 1 and No. 2. With accelerator pedal released, no continuity should exist. With pedal fully depressed, continuity should exist.

LINE PRESSURE SOLENOID CIRCUIT TEST

1) Check resistance between solenoid assembly connector terminal No. 1 and ground. Solenoid resistance should be 2.5-5 ohms. If resistance is not as specified, replace solenoid.

2) With ignition switch in OFF position, disconnect solenoid harness connector in engine compartment. Use an ohmmeter to measure resistance between solenoid harness connector terminal No. 1 and ground (Infiniti, Pathfinder (1996), 240SX and 300ZX) or terminal No. 34 and ground (Pathfinder (1995) and Pickup). Resistance should be 2.5-5.0 ohms. If resistance is not as specified, repair circuit as necessary.

3) Disconnect ATCU connector. Measure resistance between solenoid harness connector terminal No. 1 and ATCU terminal No. 2 (Infiniti, Pathfinder (1996), 240SX and 300ZX), or terminal No. 34 and ATCU terminal No. 33 (Pathfinder (1995) and Pickup). Resistance should be 11.2-12.8 ohms. If resistance is not as specified, check resistance of dropping resistor, located at right side fender panel. Resistance should be 11.2-12.8 ohms. Replace resistor as necessary.

4) Measure resistance between solenoid harness connector terminal No. 1 and ATCU terminal No. 1 (Infiniti, Pathfinder (1996), 240SX and 300ZX), or terminal No. 34 and ATCU terminal No. 34 (Pathfinder (1995) and Pickup). Resistance should be approximately zero ohms. If resistance is not as specified, repair circuit as necessary.

LOCK-UP SOLENOID CIRCUIT TEST

1) Check resistance between solenoid assembly connector terminal No. 5 and ground. Solenoid resistance should be 10-20 ohms. If resistance is not as specified, replace solenoid.

2) With ignition switch in OFF position, disconnect solenoid harness connector in engine compartment. Use an ohmmeter to measure resistance between solenoid harness connector terminal No. 5 and No. 5 of ATCU connector. (Infiniti, Pathfinder (1996), 240SX and 300ZX) or harness terminal connector No. 5 and ATCU terminal No. 22 (Pathfinder (1995) and Pickup). Resistance should be zero ohms. If resistance is not as specified, repair circuit as necessary.

3) Disconnect ATCU connector. Measure resistance between solenoid harness connector terminal No. 5 and ATCU terminal No. 5 (Infiniti, 240SX and 300ZX) or terminal No. 22 and ATCU terminal No. 22 (Pathfinder and Pickup). Resistance should be approximately zero ohms. If resistance is not as specified, repair circuit as necessary.

OVERDRIVE SWITCH CIRCUIT TEST

1) Disconnect overdrive switch connector. Check continuity between overdrive switch terminals. Continuity should exist with switch in OFF position. Continuity should not exist with switch in ON position. Replace switch as necessary.

2) With ignition switch in ON position, use a voltmeter to measure voltage between ATCU terminal No. 39 and ground (Infiniti, 240SX and 300ZX) or ATCU terminal No. 9 and ground (Pathfinder and Pickup). With ignition switch in ON position, battery voltage should be present. With ignition in OFF position, one volt or less should be present. If voltage is not as specified, repair circuit as necessary.

OVERRUN CLUTCH SOLENOID CIRCUIT TEST

1) Check resistance between solenoid assembly connector terminal No. 4 and ground. Solenoid resistance should be 20-40 ohms. If resistance is not as specified, replace solenoid.

2) With ignition switch in OFF position, disconnect solenoid harness connector in engine compartment. Use an ohmmeter to measure resistance between solenoid harness connector terminal No. 8 and ground (Infiniti, 240SX and 300ZX), or terminal No. 21 and ground (Pathfinder and Pickup). Resistance should be 20-40 ohms for Infiniti, 240SX and 300ZX, or 20-30 ohms for Pathfinder and Pickup. If resistance is not as specified, repair circuit as necessary.

3) Disconnect ATCU connector. Measure resistance between solenoid harness connector terminal No. 8 and ATCU terminal No. 8 (Infiniti, 240SX and 300ZX) or terminal No. 21 and ATCU terminal No. 21 (Pathfinder and Pickup). Resistance should be approximately zero ohms. If resistance is not as specified, repair circuit as necessary.

REVOLUTION SENSOR TEST

1) Check resistance between revolution sensor terminals. Resistance should be 500-650 ohms. If resistance is not as specified, replace sensor.

2) Revolution sensor is a voltage generating sensor and should be tested using a voltmeter set on AC scale. Check voltage between ATCU terminal No. 25 and ground (Infiniti, 240SX and 300ZX) or ATCU terminal No. 16 and ground (Pathfinder and Pickup), while driving vehicle. Voltage should rise gradually relative to vehicle speed. At zero MPH, voltage should not be present. If voltage does not rise gradually, repair circuit as necessary.

SHIFT SOLENOID "A" TEST

1) Check resistance between solenoid assembly connector terminal No. 3 (Blue wire) and ground. Solenoid resistance should be 20-40 ohms. If resistance is not as specified, replace solenoid.

2) With ignition switch in OFF position, disconnect solenoid harness connector in engine compartment. Use an ohmmeter to measure resistance between solenoid harness connector terminal No. 6 and ground (Infiniti, 240SX and 300ZX), or terminal No. 35 and ground (Pathfinder and Pickup). Resistance should be 20-40 ohms for Infiniti, 240SX and 300ZX, or 20-30 ohms for Pathfinder and Pickup. If resistance is not as specified, repair circuit as necessary.

3) Disconnect ATCU connector. Measure resistance between solenoid harness connector terminal No. 6 and ATCU terminal No. 6 (Infiniti, 240SX and 300ZX) or terminal No. 35 and ATCU terminal No. 35 (Pathfinder and Pickup). Resistance should be approximately zero ohms. If resistance is not as specified, repair circuit as necessary.

SHIFT SOLENOID "B" TEST

1) Check resistance between solenoid assembly connector terminal No. 2 and ground. Solenoid resistance should be 20-40 ohms. If resistance is not as specified, replace solenoid.

2) With ignition switch in OFF position, disconnect solenoid harness connector in engine compartment. Use an ohmmeter to measure resistance between solenoid harness connector terminal No. 7 and ground (Infiniti, 240SX and 300ZX), or terminal No. 36 and ground (Pathfinder and Pickup). Resistance should be 20-40 ohms for Infiniti, 240SX and 300ZX, or 20-30 ohms for Pathfinder and Pickup. If resistance is not as specified, repair circuit as necessary.

3) Disconnect ATCU connector. Measure resistance between solenoid harness connector terminal No. 7 and ATCU terminal No. 7 (Infiniti, 240SX and 300ZX) or terminal No. 36 and ATCU terminal No. 36 (Pathfinder and Pickup). Resistance should be approximately zero ohms. If resistance is not as specified, repair circuit as necessary.

SPEED SENSOR CIRCUIT TEST

While driving 1-2 MPH for 3 ft. or more, use a voltmeter to measure voltage between ATCU terminal No. 27 and ground (Infiniti, 240SX and 300ZX) or ATCU terminal No. 24 and ground (Pathfinder and Pickup). Voltage should be 0-5 volts. If voltage is not as specified, check for continuity in wiring harness between ATCU and speed sensor. Check for poor ground circuit.

THROTTLE SENSOR CIRCUIT TEST

1) Turn ignition switch to ON position. Depress accelerator pedal slowly. Use a voltmeter to measure voltage between ATCU terminals No. 34 and 35 (Infiniti, 240SX and 300ZX) or ATCU terminals No. 11 and 15 (1996 Pathfinder and Pickup). At closed throttle, voltage should be .5 volts.

2) At wide open throttle, voltage should be approximately 4 volts. Voltage increases relative to throttle valve opening. If voltage is not as specified, repair circuit as necessary.

TURBINE SHAFT REVOLUTION SENSOR CIRCUIT TEST

Infiniti Q45 – 1) With engine running, use a voltmeter to measure AC voltage between ATCU terminal No. 25 and ground (Q45), No. 26 and No. 35 (J30). Voltage should be .3-4.5 volts depending on engine speed.

2) With engine off, use an ohmmeter to measure resistance between sensor connector terminals No. 1, 2 and 3. Continuity should exist only between terminals No. 1 and 2. Resistance between terminals No. 1 and 2 should be 2200-2800 ohms. If resistance is not within specifications, replace sensor as necessary.

KEY INTERLOCK CABLE

Removal – At selector lever base, unlock slider from adjuster holder to remove rod from cable. At ignition key switch, remove lock plate and pull out cable.

Installation – To install, reverse removal procedure.

NOTE: Ensure key interlock cable is free of sharp bends, twists or interference with adjacent parts. Ensure casing cap and bracket are firmly secured. If casing cap can be removed with a load of less than 8.8 lbs., replace key interlock cable.

SHIFT LOCK SYSTEM TESTING

NOTE: For circuit diagrams and terminal locations, see CIRCUIT & WIRING DIAGRAMS and Fig. 1.

Description – Key interlock mechanism also operates as a shift lock. With key switch turned ON, selector lever cannot be shifted from "P" to any other position unless brake pedal is depressed. With key removed, selector lever cannot be shifted from "P" to any other position. Key cannot be removed unless selector lever is in "P" position. Shift lock and key interlock are controlled by ON-OFF operation of shift lock solenoid and by operation of rotator and slider located inside key cylinder.

Detention Switch (Key) – 1) Disconnect shift lock harness connector, located at base of shift lever. Check for continuity between shift lock harness connector terminals No. 2 and No. 3 (Q45 only).

2) When selector lever is in Park and selector lever button is released, continuity should not exist. Continuity should exist for all other conditions. If continuity is not as specified, replace detention switch, located below shift lever at left front side.

Detention Switch (Shift) – 1) Disconnect shift lock harness connector, located at base of shift lever. Check for continuity between shift lock harness connector, terminals No. 6 and 2 (Q45 only).

2) When selector lever is in Park and selector lever button is released, continuity should not exist. Continuity should exist for all other conditions. If continuity is not as specified, replace detention switch, located below shift lever at left front side.

Key Lock Solenoid – Disconnect key lock solenoid connector, located below ignition switch on steering column. Connect fused jumper wire from battery positive terminal to one terminal at key lock solenoid connector. Connect jumper wire from battery negative terminal to other terminal at key lock solenoid connector. Key lock solenoid should operate. Replace solenoid if necessary.

Key Switch – Disconnect key switch connector, located at base of steering column. Check for continuity between switch terminals. Continuity should exist when key is inserted into key cylinder. Continuity should not exist when key is removed from key cylinder. If continuity is not as specified, replace key switch.

Shift Lock Solenoid – Disconnect shift lock harness connector, located at base of shift lever. Apply battery voltage to shift lock harness connector terminal No. 4 and No. 5 (Q45), terminal No. 9 and No. 10 (J30), No. 2 and A/T device (shift lock solenoid and park position switch combination) connector terminal No. 5 (Pathfinder), terminal No. 2 and A/T device connector No. 2 (240SX), terminal No. 1 and No. 9 (300ZX) at shift lock harness connector.

Park Position Switch – Disconnect shift lock harness connector. Check continuity between terminals No. 1 and No. 2 (J30), 5 and No. 11 (300ZX) No. 2 and A/T device connector No. 6 (Pathfinder). When selector lever is in "P" position and selector lever button is released, continuity should NOT exist. In any other condition, continuity should exist.

Stop Light Switch – Check continuity between terminals No. 1 and No. 2 (J30 and Q45), No. 2 and No. 3 (300ZX) of stop light switch connector. When brake pedal is depressed continuity should exist. When brake pedal is released, NO continuity should exist.

ASCD Cancel Switch (Pathfinder) – Check continuity between ASCD cancel (shift lock brake) with harness connector terminals No. 1 and No. 2. Continuity should exist only when brake pedal is depressed.

Shift Lock Control Unit (Q45) – 1) Check voltage between specified terminals of 12-pin shift lock control unit connector, located to left of steering column, under dash. If voltage is not as specified, check appropriate component, connector or wiring harness and repair as necessary. See SHIFT LOCK CONTROL UNIT INSPECTION (Q45) table.

Shift Lock Control Module (J30) – 1) Check voltage at specified terminals of 8-pin shift lock control module connector, attached on bracket on steering column. If voltage is not as specified, check appropriate component, connector or wiring harness and repair as necessary. See SHIFT LOCK CONTROL UNIT INSPECTION (J30) table.

Shift Lock Control Unit (300ZX) – 1) Check voltage at specified terminals of 8-pin shift lock control module connector, attached on bracket on steering column. If voltage is not as specified, check appropriate component, connector or wiring harness and repair as necessary. See SHIFT LOCK CONTROL UNIT INSPECTION (300ZX) table.

SHIFT LOCK CONTROL UNIT INSPECTION (Q45)

Terminal No.	Item	Condition	Standard
1 & 9	Shift Lock Signal	Ignition Switch "ON" Position	Battery voltage
		Brake Pedal Depressed	Battery Voltage
		Any Position EXCEPT Above	0 Volts
3 & 9	Stop Light Switch	Brake Pedal Depressed	Battery Voltage
		Brake Pedal Released	0 Volts
4 & 9	Power Source	Key Off	Battery Voltage
5 & 9	Detention Switch (Shift)	Key In Cylinder, Selector Lever In "P", Selector Button Pushed Or Key In Cylinder, Selector In Any Position, Except "P", Selector Button Released	Battery Voltage
		Except As Above	0 Volts
6 & 9	Ignition Signal	Key On	Battery Voltage
8 & 10	Key Lock Signal	When Ignition Switch Turned From Lock, OFF, ACC to ON	Battery Voltage (For 0.1 Seconds)
10 & 8	Key Unlock Signal	Selector Lever In "P" Position With Button Released, Key Turned To Lock, OFF Or ACC to ON	Battery Voltage (For 0.1 Seconds)
11 & 9	Key Switch	When Key Inserted Into Key Cylinder	Battery Voltage
		When Key Removed From Cylinder	0 Volts
12 & 9	Detention Switch	With Key In Cylinder, Selector Lever In "P", Selector Lever Button pushed Or key In Cylinder, Selector Lever In Any Position Except "P" Selector Button Released	Battery Voltage
		Except As Above	0 Volts

SHIFT LOCK CONTROL UNIT INSPECTION (J30)

Terminal No.	Item	Condition	Standard
1 & 8	Ignition Signal	Ignition Switch "ON" Position	Battery voltage
		Any Position EXCEPT "ON" Position	0 Volts
2 & 8	Power Source	Any condition	Battery Voltage
4 & 8	Shift Lock Signal	Ignition Switch to "ON" Position, Selector Lever In "P" Position, Brake Pedal Depressed	Battery Voltage
		Except As Above	0 Volts
5 & 8	Stop Light Switch	Brake Pedal Depressed	Battery Voltage
		Brake Pedal Released	0 Volts
6 & 8	Park Position Switch	Ignition Key In Key Cylinder, Selector In "P" Position, Selector In Any Position And Button Pushed	Battery Voltage
		Except As Above	0 Volts

SHIFT LOCK CONTROL UNIT INSPECTION (300ZX)

Terminal No.	Item	Condition	Standard
1 & 9	Shift Lock Signal	Ignition Switch to "ON" Position, Selector Lever In "P" Position, Brake Pedal Depressed	Battery Voltage
		Except As Above	0 Volts
2 & 9	Power Source	Any condition	Battery Voltage
3 & 9	Stop Light Switch	Brake Pedal Depressed	Battery Voltage
		Brake Pedal Released	0 Volts
5 & 9	Park Position Switch	Ignition Key In Key Cylinder, Selector Lever In "P" Position, Selector Lever In Any Position And Button Pushed	Battery Voltage
		Except As Above	0 Volts
6 & 9	Ignition Signal	Ignition Switch "ON" Position	Battery voltage
		Any Position EXCEPT "ON" Position	0 Volts

Shift Lock System Diagnostic Procedure (Pathfinder, Pickup & 240SX) – 1) Check power source. With KOEO, check voltage between brake switch harness terminal No. 1 and ground (Pathfinder and 240SX), check voltage between ASCD cancel switch harness connector terminal No. 2 and ground. Battery voltage should be present. If voltage is not as specified, check harness for open or short between battery and brake switch harness terminal No. 1. Check fuse and ignition switch. If voltage is as specified, go to next step.

2) Check brake switch (Pathfinder and 240SX). Check ASCD cancel switch (Pickup). With KOEO, check voltage between A/T device harness terminal No. 5 (Pathfinder), No. 2 (240SX) and ground. With brake pedal depressed, zero volts should be present. With brake ped-

al released, battery voltage should be present. If voltage is not as specified, check harness for open or short between A/T device harness connector and brake switch harness connector terminal No. 5 (Pathfinder) No. 2 (240SX) and ground, terminal No. 5 and ASCD cancel switch terminal No. 1. Check brake light switch or ASCD cancel switch. See BRAKE LIGHT SWITCH or ASCD CANCEL SWITCH in SHIFT LOCK SYSTEM TESTING.

3) Check ground circuit. Turn ignition switch to OFF position. Disconnect A/T device harness connector. Check continuity between A/T device harness terminal No. 6 (Pathfinder and Pickup) No. 1 (240SX) and ground. With positive side of ohmmeter at terminal No. 6 (Pathfinder) No. 1 (240SX), continuity should NOT exist. With negative side of ohmmeter at terminal No. 6 (Pathfinder) No. 1 (240SX), continuity should exist. If not as specified, repair harness, connector or diode. If continuity results are as specified, go to next step.

4) Check park position switch. See PARK POSITION SWITCH in SHIFT LOCK SYSTEM TESTING. If okay, check shift lock solenoid. See SHIFT LOCK SOLENOID in SHIFT LOCK SYSTEM TESTING. If okay, reconnect shift lock harness connector. Turn ignition switch from OFF to ON position. Do not start engine. Recheck shift lock operation. If problem is present, perform A/T input/output signal check and harness connector connection.

WIRING DIAGRAMS

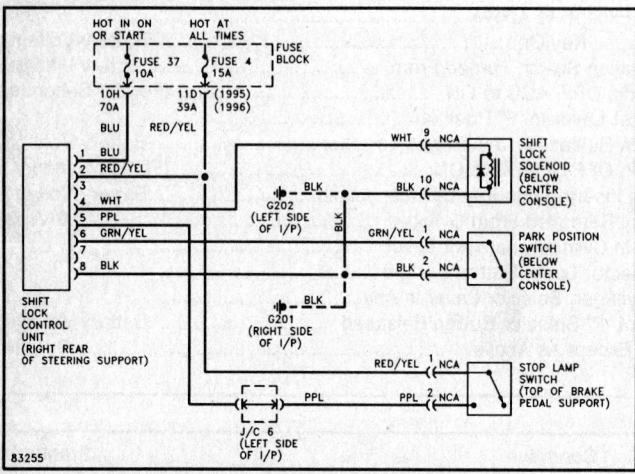

Fig. 2: Shift Interlock System Circuit Diagram (1995-96 Infiniti J30)

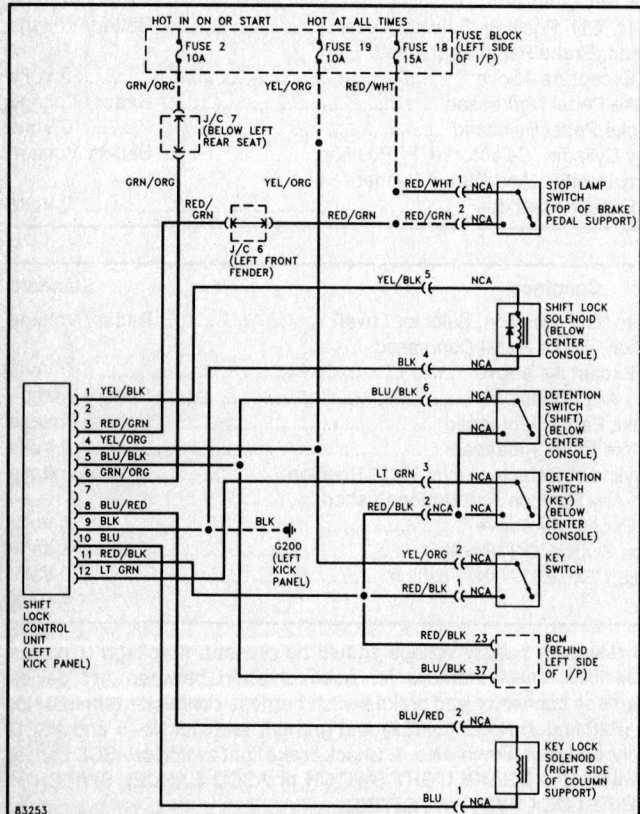

Fig. 3: Shift Lock System Circuit Diagram (1995-96 Infiniti Q45)

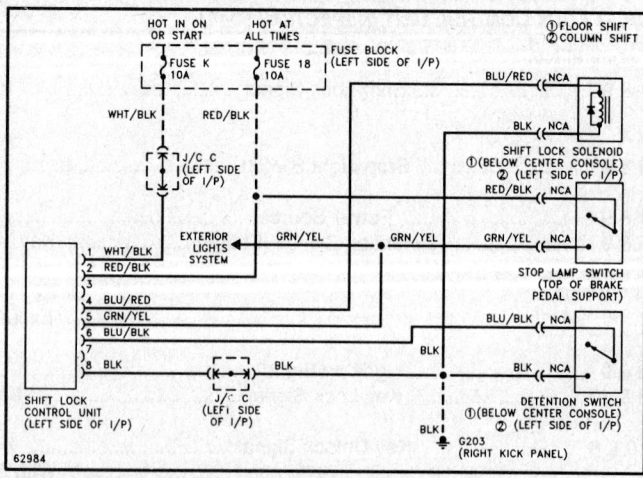

Fig. 4: Shift Lock System Circuit Diagram (1995 Pathfinder & Pickup)

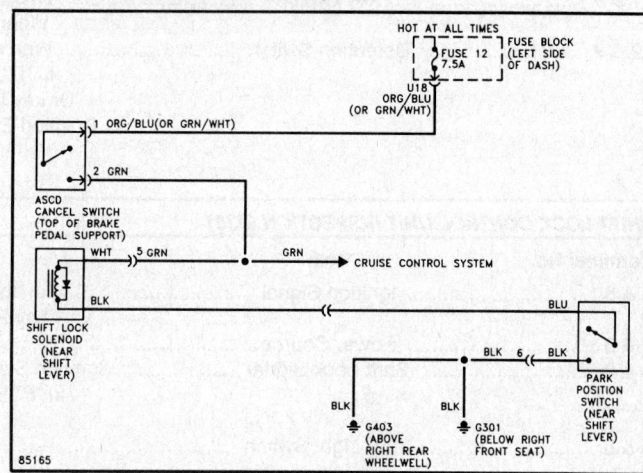

Fig. 5: Shift Lock System Circuit Diagram (1996 Pathfinder)

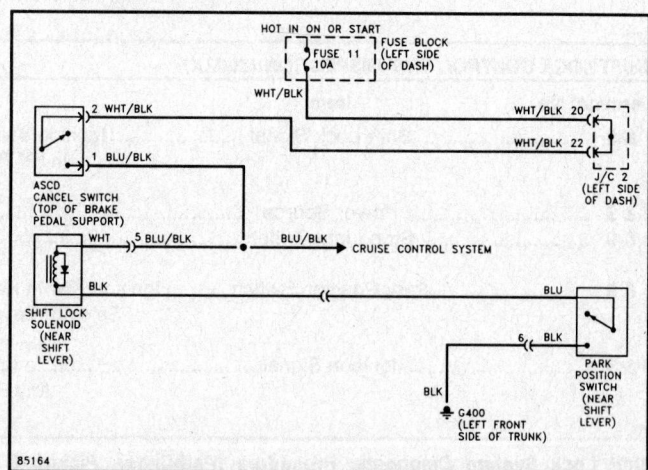

Fig. 6: Shift Lock System Circuit Diagram (1996 Pickup)

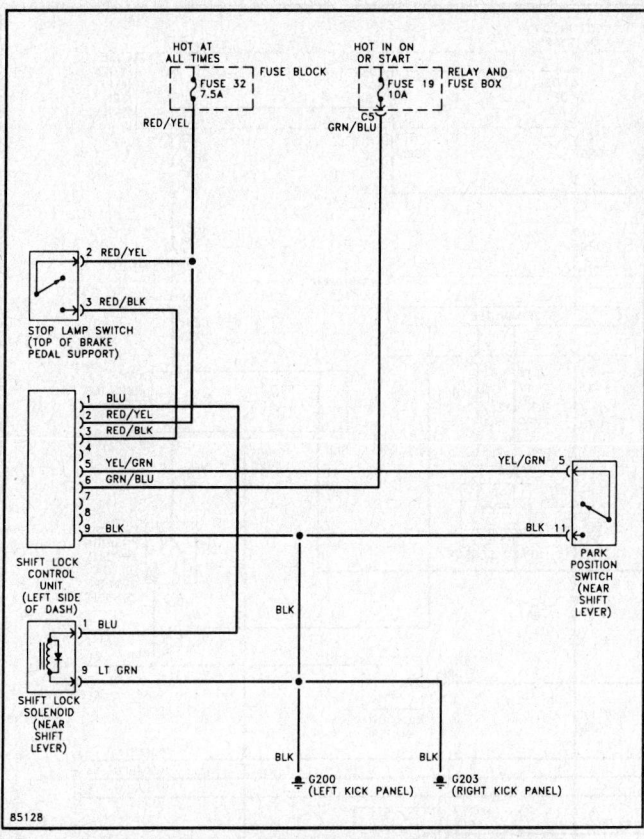

Fig. 7: Shift Lock System Circuit Diagram (1995-96 300ZX)

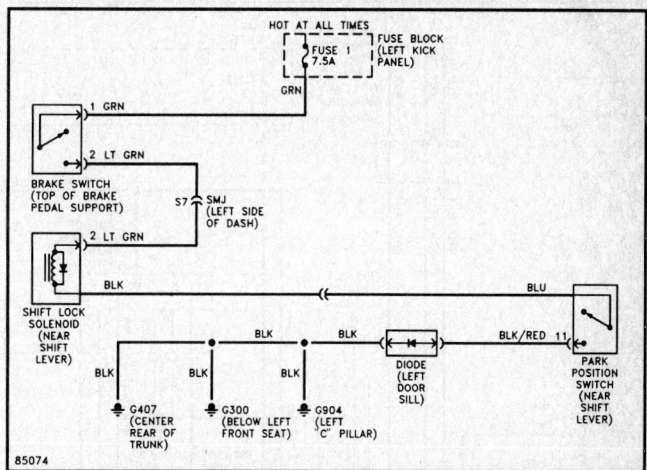

Fig. 9: Shift Lock System Circuit Diagram (1996 240SX)

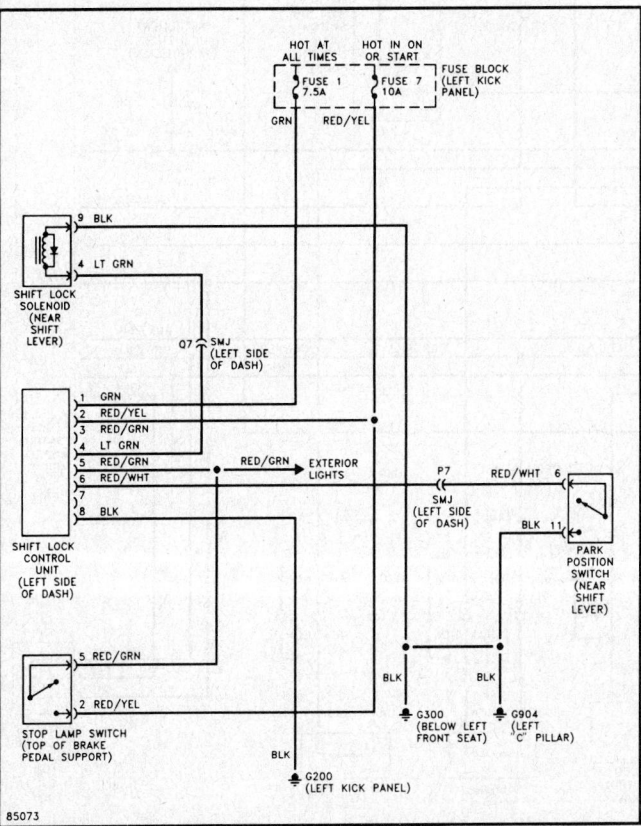

Fig. 8: Shift Lock System Circuit Diagram (1995 240SX)

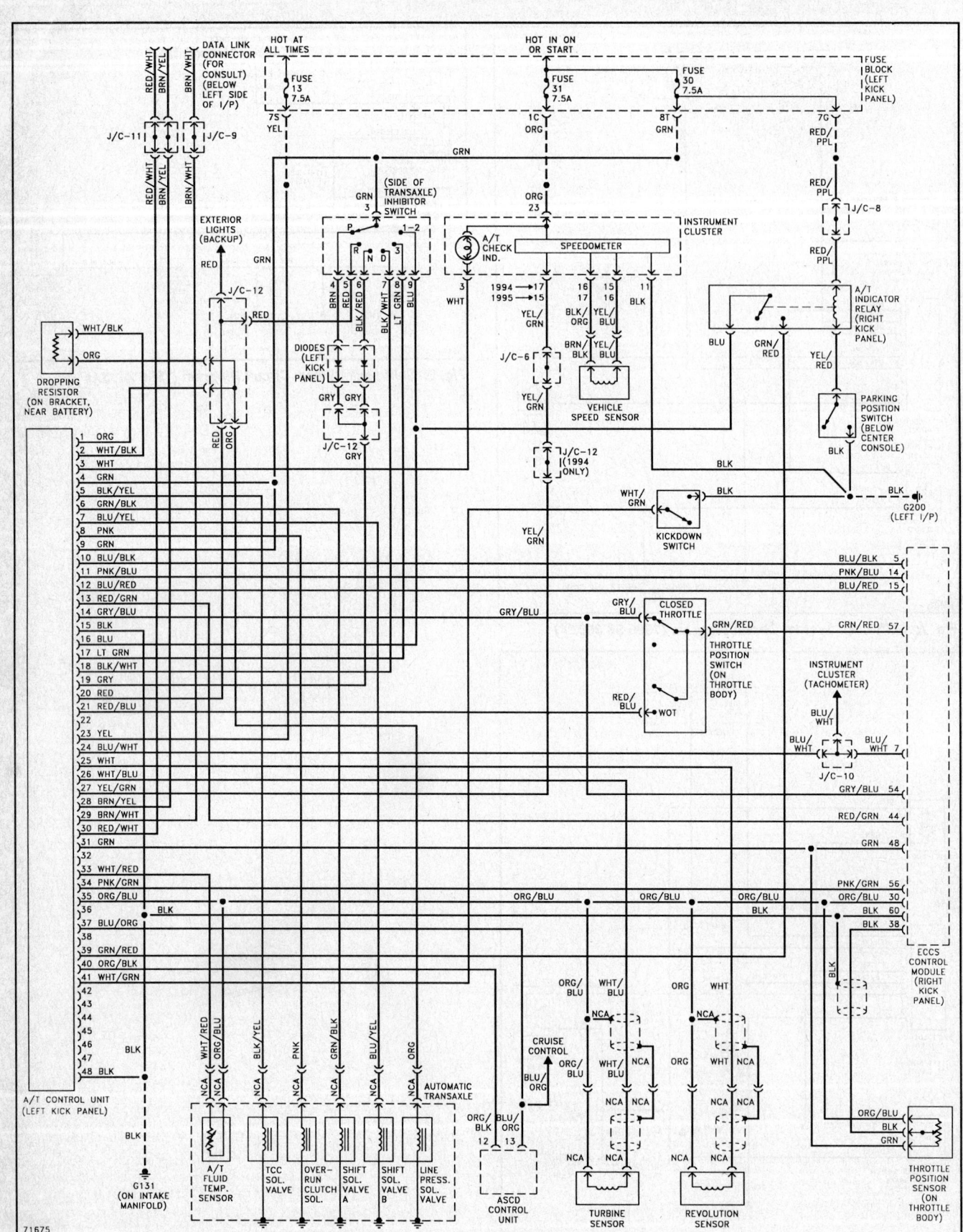

Fig. 10: 1995 Infiniti J30 Wiring Diagram (RE4R01A)

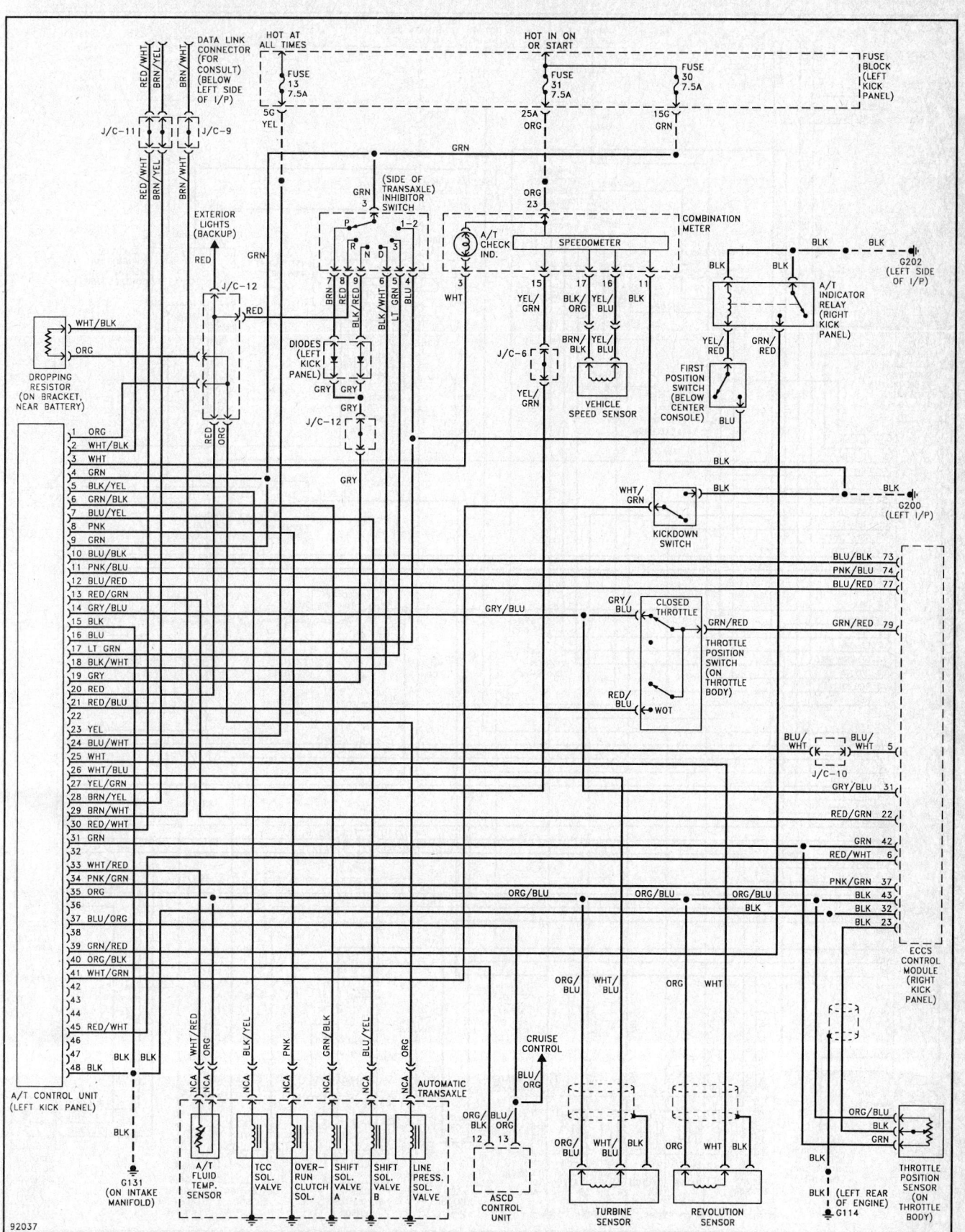

Fig. 11: 1996 Infiniti J30 Wiring Diagram (RE4R01A)

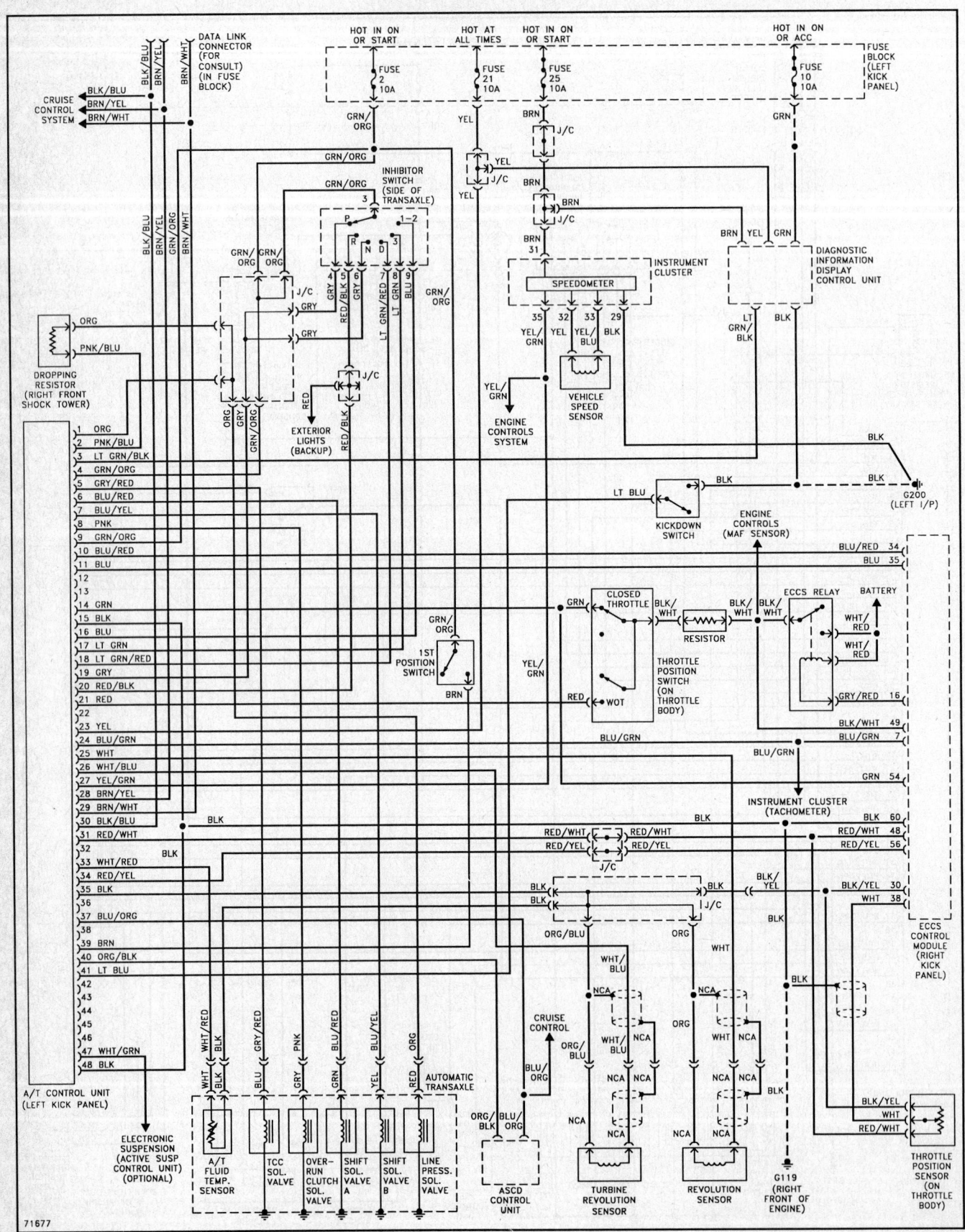

Fig. 12: 1995 Infiniti Q45 Wiring Diagram (RE4R03A)

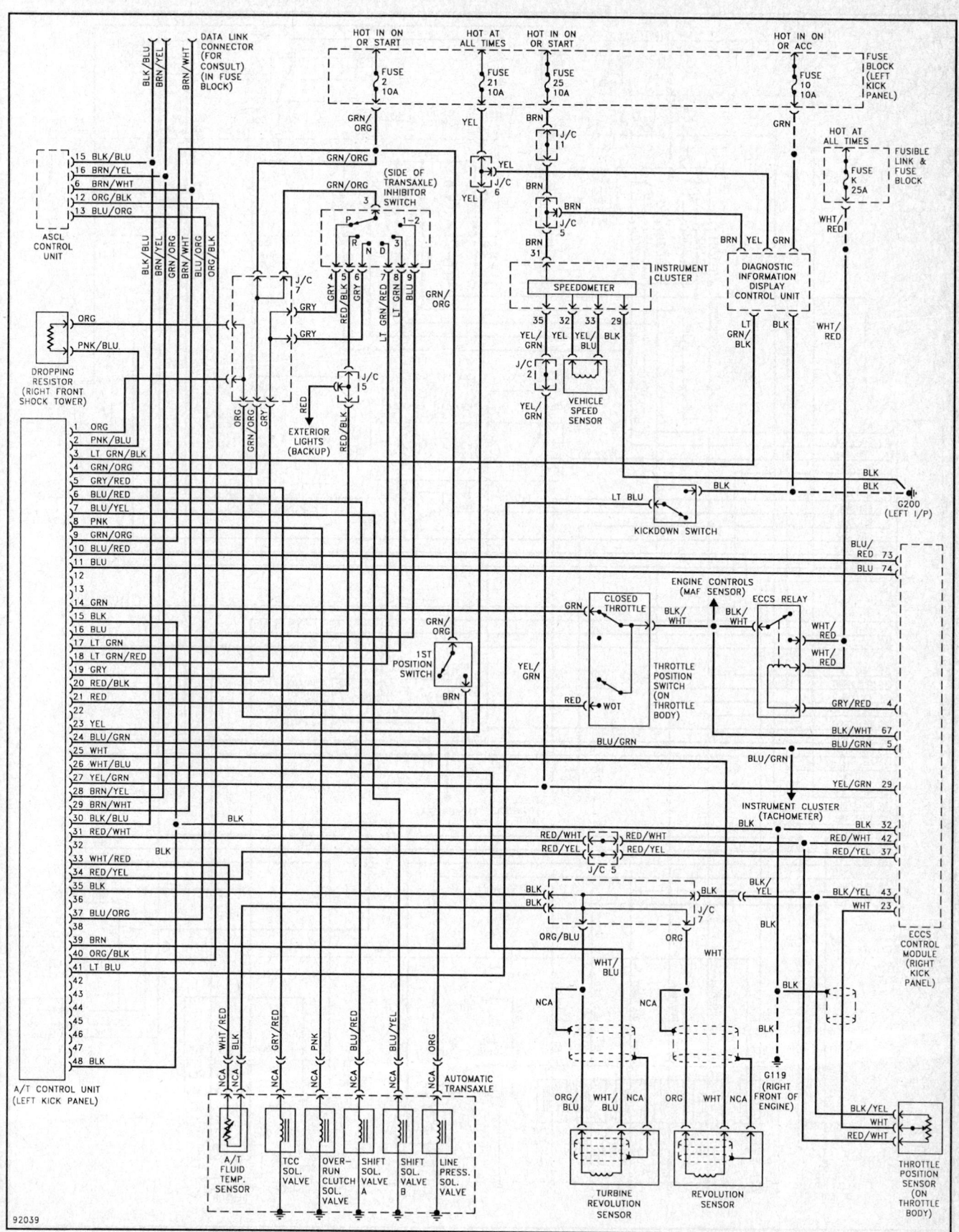

Fig. 13: 1996 Infiniti Q45 Wiring Diagram (RE4R03A)

92039

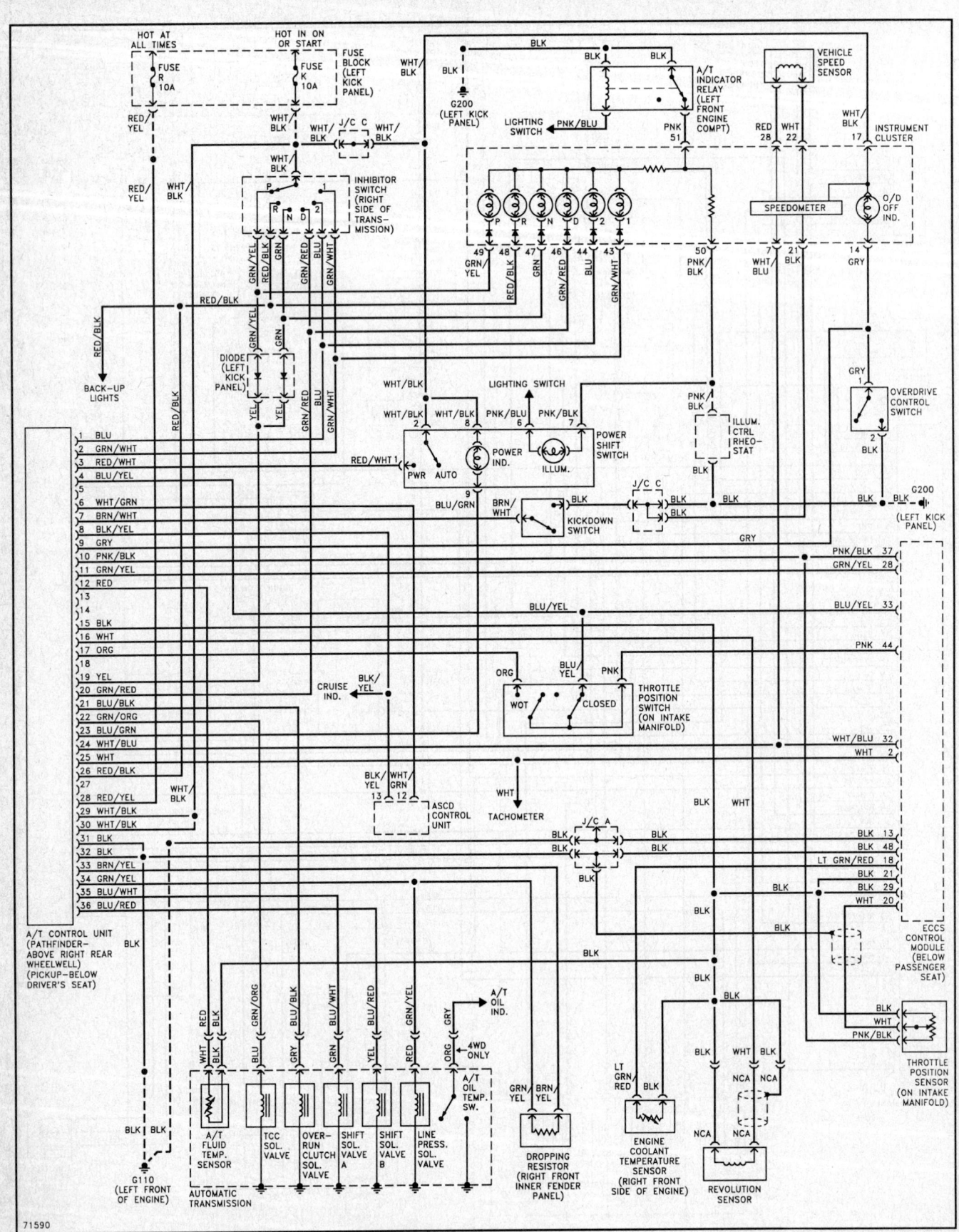

Fig. 14: 1995 Nissan Pathfinder & Pickup 3.0L Wiring Diagram (RE4R01A)

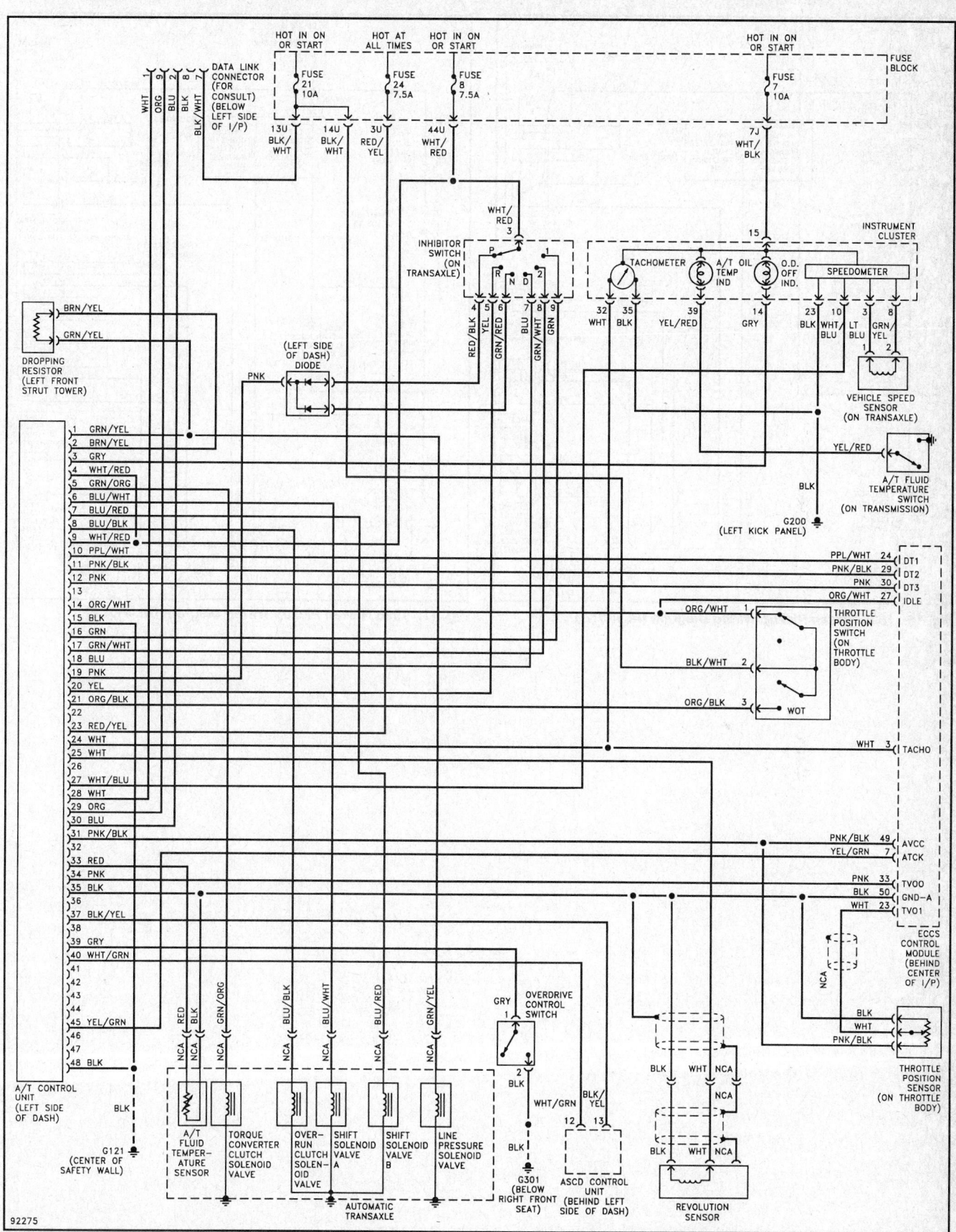

Fig. 15: 1996 Nissan Pathfinder Wiring Diagram (RE4R01A)

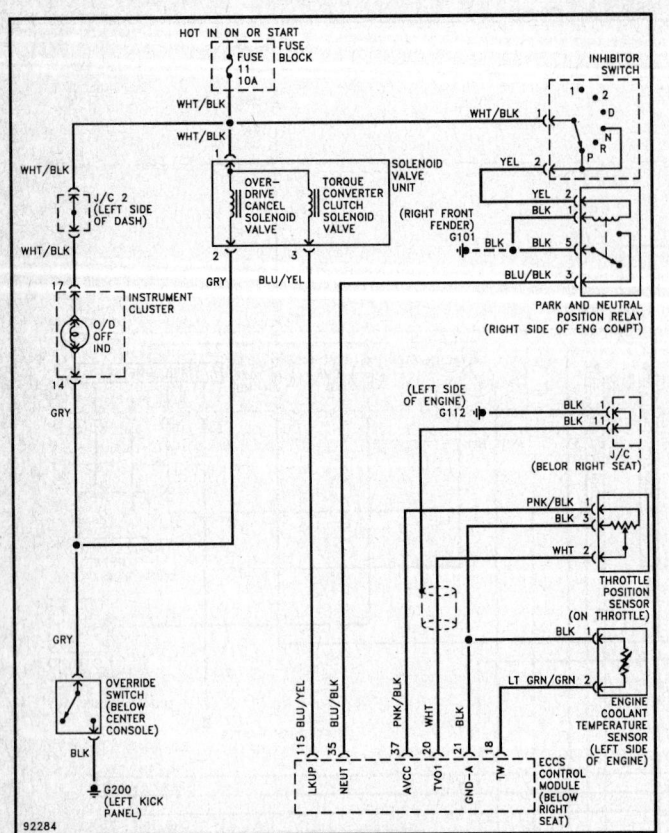

Fig. 16: 1995 Nissan Pickup Wiring Diagram (RL4R01A)

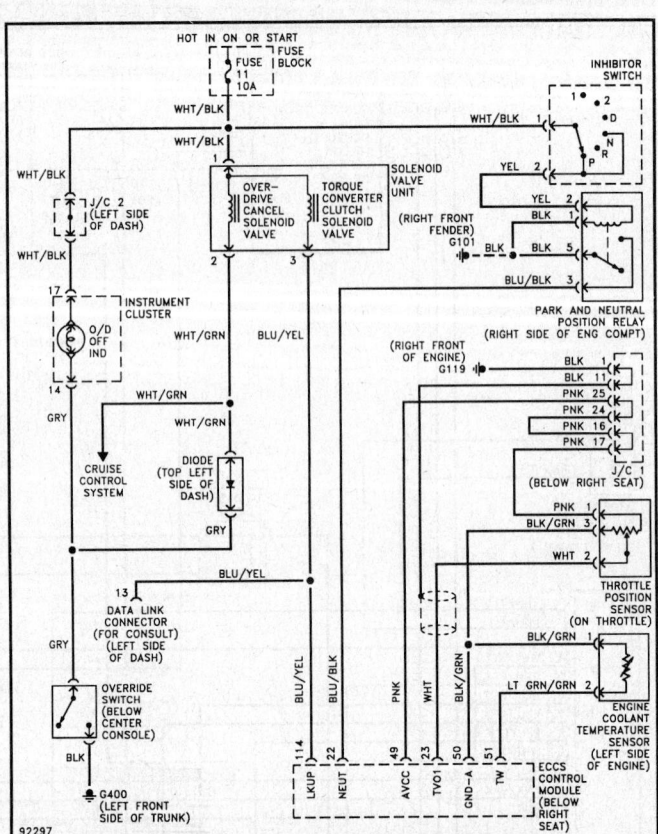

Fig. 17: 1996 Nissan Pickup Wiring Diagram (RL4R01A)

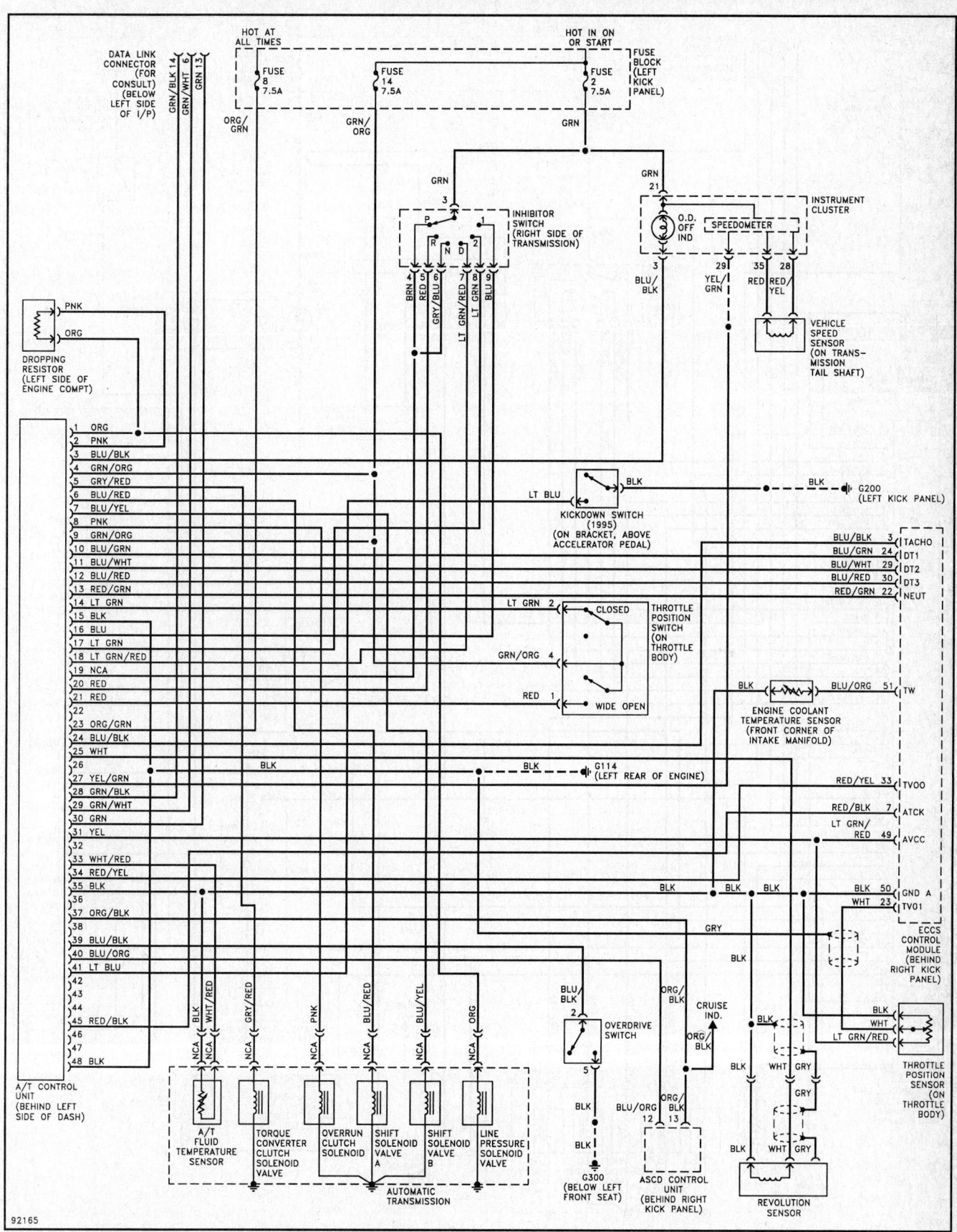

Fig. 18: 1995-96 Nissan 240SX Wiring Diagram (RE4R01A)

92165

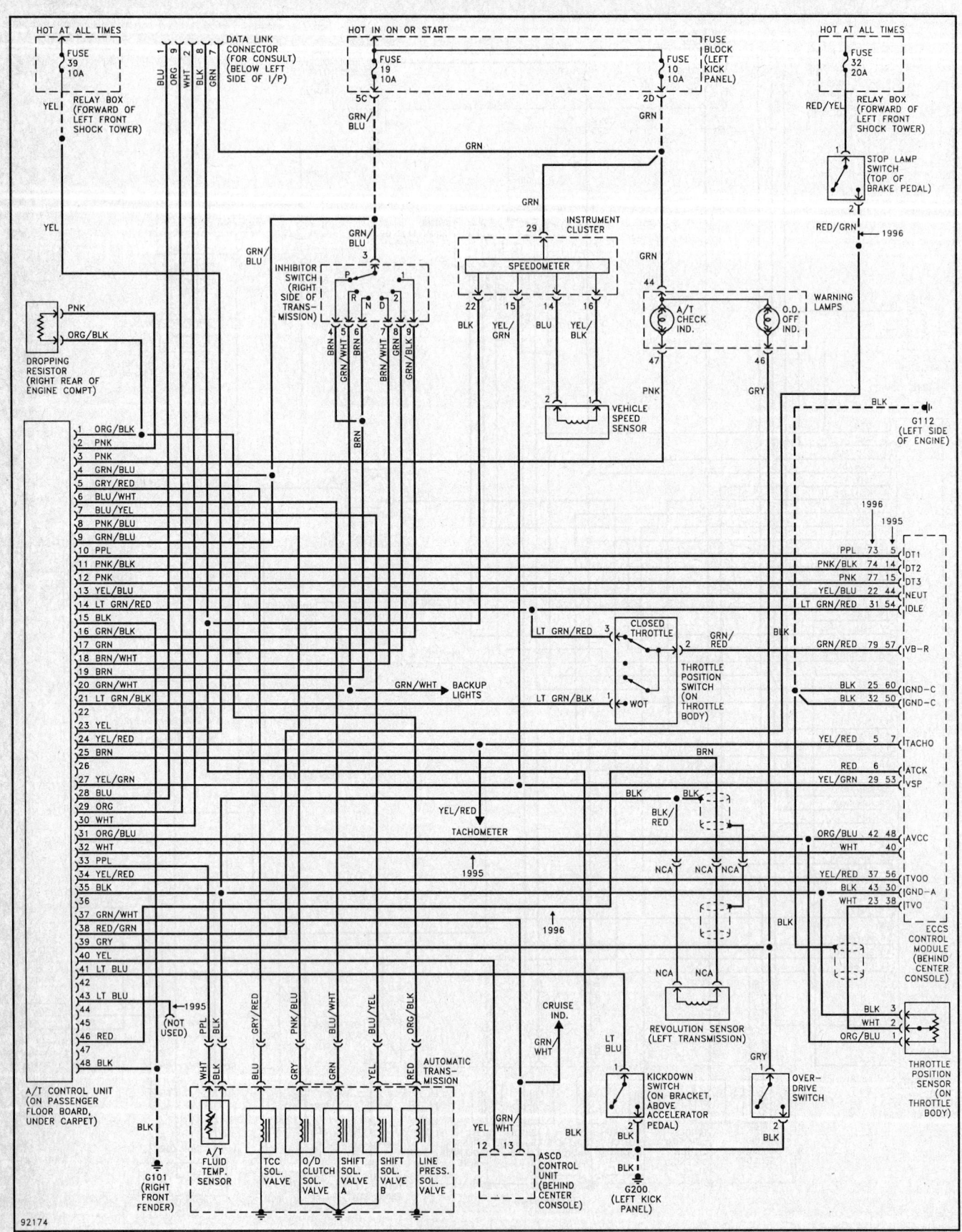

Fig. 19: 1995-96 300ZX Wiring Diagram (RE4R01A & RE4R03A)

Sentra, 200SX

APPLICATION & LABOR TIMES

APPLICATION & LABOR TIMES

Vehicle Application	Labor Times		Transaxle Model
	[1] R & I	[2] Overhaul	
Sentra & 200SX (1.6L)	5.0	9.0	[3] RL4F03A

[1] – Removal and installation of transmission from vehicle chassis.

[2] – Bench overhaul time for transmission and differential. DOES NOT include removal and installation.

[3] – With 1.6L engine.

IDENTIFICATION

Transaxle model is located on vehicle identification plate in engine compartment area, on firewall. Transaxle number is located on transaxle governor cap. See Fig. 1.

DESCRIPTION

Transaxle consists of 3 main components: automatic transaxle, torque converter and differential assembly. Automatic transaxle consists of forward clutch, high clutch, low-reverse brake, overrun clutch, reverse clutch and brake band servo. See Fig. 2.

LUBRICATION & ADJUSTMENTS

See appropriate AUTOMATIC TRANSMISSION SERVICING article in TRANSMISSION SERVICING section.

TROUBLE SHOOTING

NOTE: Always check fluid level and linkage. Fluid level should be checked using HOT range on dipstick with fluid temperatures of 122-176°F (50-80°C) after vehicle has been driven approximately 5 minutes after initial warm-up. Use caution not to overfill.

SYMPTOM DIAGNOSIS

Engine Will Not Start In "P" Or "N" – Inhibitor switch or control cable misadjusted, damaged ignition switch or starter.

Engine Starts In Position Other Than "P" Or "N" – Inhibitor switch or control cable misadjusted.

Excessive Shock From "N" To "D" – Incorrect fluid level, line pressure, engine idle RPM, control cable or throttle cable adjustment. Damaged N-D accumulator, oil pump, reverse clutch or control valve.

Excessive Shock During 1-2 Or 2-3 Upshift – Incorrect fluid level, line pressure, control cable or throttle cable adjustment. Damaged oil pump, servo release accumulator, brake band or control valve.

Excessive Shock During 3-4 Upshift – Incorrect fluid level, line pressure, control cable or throttle cable adjustment. Damaged oil pump, overrun clutch, brake band or control valve.

Excessive Shock During D-2 & D-1 Downshift – Incorrect fluid level, line pressure, control cable or throttle cable adjustment. Damaged high clutch, overrun clutch, brake band or control valve. See CLUTCH & BAND APPLICATION table.

Excessive Shock During 2-1 Downshift In "1" Position – Incorrect fluid level, line pressure, control cable or throttle cable adjustment. Damaged oil pump, low-reverse brake or control valve.

Excessive Shock When OD Switch Is Set From ON To OFF – Incorrect fluid level, line pressure, control cable or throttle cable adjustment. Damaged high clutch, overrun clutch, brake band or control valve.

Slips During 1-2 Upshift – Incorrect fluid level, line pressure, control cable or throttle cable adjustment. Damaged oil pump, brake band or control valve.

Slips During 2-3 Upshift – Incorrect fluid level, line pressure, control cable or throttle cable adjustment. Damaged oil pump, brake band, high clutch, servo release accumulator or control valve.

Slips During 3-4 Upshift – Incorrect fluid level, line pressure, control cable or throttle cable adjustment. Damaged oil pump, brake band, high clutch, or control valve.

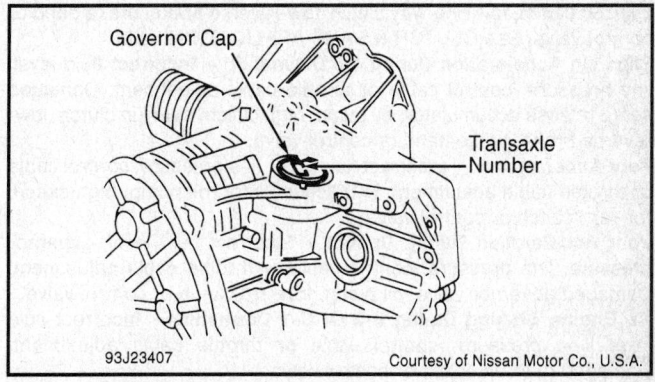

Fig. 1: Locating Automatic Transaxle Number

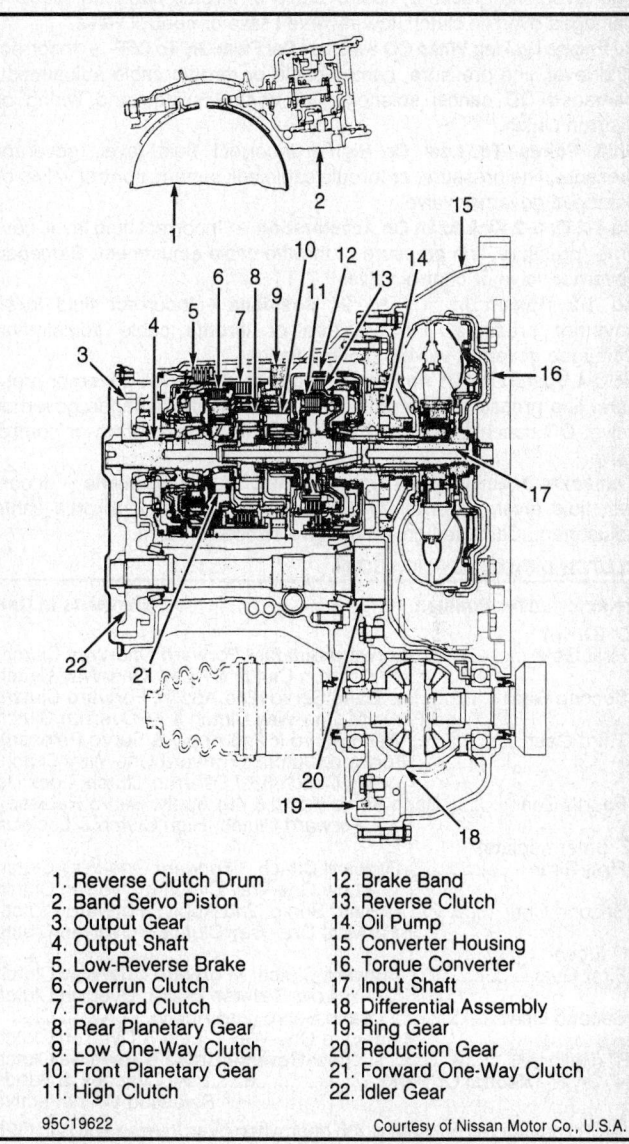

1. Reverse Clutch Drum	12. Brake Band
2. Band Servo Piston	13. Reverse Clutch
3. Output Gear	14. Oil Pump
4. Output Shaft	15. Converter Housing
5. Low-Reverse Brake	16. Torque Converter
6. Overrun Clutch	17. Input Shaft
7. Forward Clutch	18. Differential Assembly
8. Rear Planetary Gear	19. Ring Gear
9. Low One-Way Clutch	20. Reduction Gear
10. Front Planetary Gear	21. Forward One-Way Clutch
11. High Clutch	22. Idler Gear

Fig. 2: Identifying Transaxle Component Locations

Slips On Acceleration During 4-1 Or 3-1 Downshift – Incorrect fluid level, governor pressure, line pressure, control cable or throttle cable adjustment. Damaged governor valve, oil pump, high clutch, forward one-way clutch, brake band or control valve.

Slips On Acceleration During 4-2 Downshift – Incorrect fluid level, governor pressure, line pressure, control cable or throttle cable adjustment. Damaged governor valve, torque converter, oil pump, reverse clutch, high clutch, forward clutch, forward one-way clutch, overrun clutch, low one-way clutch, low-reverse brake, brake band or control valve. See CLUTCH & BAND APPLICATION table.

Slips On Acceleration During 4-3 Downshift – Incorrect fluid level, line pressure, control cable or throttle cable adjustment. Damaged servo release accumulator, oil pump, high clutch, overrun clutch, low-reverse brake, brake band or control valve.

Poor Acceleration – Incorrect fluid level, line pressure, control cable or throttle cable adjustment. N-D accumulator, oil pump, high clutch, forward clutch or control valve.

Poor Acceleration During Upshift – Incorrect fluid level, governor pressure, line pressure, control cable or throttle cable adjustment. Damaged governor valve, oil pump, forward clutch or control valve.

No Engine Braking During D-2 Or D-1 Downshift – Incorrect fluid level, line pressure, control cable or throttle cable adjustment. Damaged overrun clutch or control valve.

No Engine Braking During 2-1 Downshift In "1" Position – Incorrect fluid level, line pressure, control cable or throttle cable adjustment. Damaged overrun clutch, low-reverse brake or control valve.

No Engine Braking When OD Switch Is Set From ON To OFF – Incorrect fluid level, line pressure, control cable or throttle cable adjustment. Damaged OD cancel solenoid, OD control switch and wiring or overrun clutch.

Shift Points To Low Or High – Incorrect fluid level, governor pressure, line pressure, or throttle cable adjustment, control valve, or damaged governor valve.

No 4-2 Or 3-2 Kickdown On Acceleration – Incorrect fluid level, governor pressure, line pressure or throttle cable adjustment. Damaged governor valve or control valve.

No 1-2 Upshift In "D" & "2" Positions – Incorrect fluid level, governor pressure, line pressure or throttle cable adjustment. Damaged governor valve or control valve.

No 3-4 Upshift In "D" Position – Incorrect fluid level, governor pressure, line pressure or throttle cable adjustment. Damaged governor valve, OD cancel solenoid, OD control switch and wiring or control valve.

Transaxle Does Not Start From "1" In "D" & "2" Positions – Incorrect fluid level, governor pressure, line pressure or throttle cable adjustment. Damaged governor valve or control valve.

CLUTCH & BAND APPLICATION

Selector Lever Position	Elements In Use
"D" (Drive) [1]	
First Gear	Forward Clutch, [2] Forward One-Way Clutch, [3][4] Overrun Clutch & [2] Low One-Way Clutch
Second Gear	Band Servo (2nd Apply), Forward Clutch, [2] Forward One-Way Clutch & [3] Overrun Clutch
Third Gear	Band Servo ([5] 2nd Apply & Servo Release), Forward Clutch, [2] Forward One-Way Clutch, High Clutch & [3][4] Overrun Clutch, Lock Up
Fourth Gear	Band Servo ([6] 2nd & 4th Apply, Servo Release), Forward Clutch, High Clutch & Lock-up
"2" (Intermediate)	
First Gear	Forward Clutch, [2] Forward One-Way Clutch [2] Low One-Way Clutch & Overrun Clutch
Second Gear	Band Servo (2nd Apply), Forward Clutch, [2] Forward One-Way Clutch & Overrun Clutch
"1" (Low)	
First Gear	Forward Clutch, [2] Forward One-Way Clutch Low-Reverse Brake, Overrun Clutch
Second Gear	Band Servo (2nd Apply), Forward Clutch [2] Forward One-Way Clutch & Overrun Clutch
"R" (Reverse)	Low-Reverse Brake & Reverse Clutch
"N" Or "P" (Neutral Or Park)	All Clutches & Bands Released Or Ineffective

[1] – Transaxle will not shift to 4th gear when overdrive switch is in OFF position.
[2] – Operates during progressive acceleration.
[3] – Operates when overdrive switch is in OFF position.
[4] – Operates when throttle opening is less than 1/16.
[5] – Oil pressure is applied to both 2nd apply and 3rd release side of band servo piston. Brake band does not contract because oil pressure area on release side is greater than apply side.
[6] – Oil pressure is applied to 4th apply side in 3rd gear, and brake band contracts.

Shifts From 3rd To 1st (Skips 2nd) – Incorrect fluid level, governor pressure, line pressure or throttle cable adjustment. Damaged governor valve or control valve.

Shifts To "2" In "1" Position – Incorrect fluid level, governor pressure, line pressure or throttle cable adjustment. Damaged governor valve or control valve.

Lock-Up Point Is Extremely High Or Low – Incorrect fluid level, governor pressure, line pressure or throttle cable adjustment. Damaged governor valve or control valve.

Torque Converter Does Not Lock Up – Incorrect fluid level, governor pressure, line pressure or throttle cable adjustment. Damaged governor valve, torque converter clutch solenoid valve, torque converter or control valve.

Lock-Up Is Not Released On Deceleration – Incorrect fluid level, torque converter clutch solenoid valve, torque converter or control valve.

Vehicle Moves In "P" Position – Misadjusted control cable or damaged parking components.

ELECTRONIC TESTING

NOTE: For shift interlock system and transaxle electrical circuit and terminal identification, see WIRING DIAGRAMS. See Figs. 38 and 39.

SHIFT LOCK SYSTEM TESTING

Detention Switch – 1) Disconnect 8-pin shift lock control unit harness connector, located below shift lever housing. Check for continuity between shift lock harness connector, terminal No. 6 and terminal No. 1. *See Fig. 3.*
2) When selector lever is in Park and selector lever button is released, continuity should not exist. Continuity should exist for all other conditions. If continuity is not as specified, replace detention switch (located at base of shift lever).

Shift Lock Solenoid – Check operation by applying battery voltage to shift lock harness connector, terminals No. 7 and No. 8.

Shift Lock Control Module – 1) Check voltage at specified terminals of 8-pin shift lock control module connector, located to right of hood release handle. If voltage is not as specified, check appropriate component, connector or wiring harness and repair as necessary.
2) With ignition switch in ON position, check voltage between shift lock control module terminal No. 1 and terminal No. 7. Battery voltage should exist. Voltage should not exist under any other conditions. If voltage is not as specified, check 10-amp fuse in fuse block.
3) Check for voltage between shift lock control module terminal No. 6 and terminal No. 7. Battery voltage should exist under all conditions. If voltage is not as specified, check 15-amp fuse in fuse block.
4) With ignition switch in ON position, selector lever in Park, and brake pedal applied, check for voltage between shift lock control module terminal No. 4 and terminal No. 7. Battery voltage should exist. Voltage should not exist under any other conditions. If voltage is not as specified, check shift lock solenoid.
5) Check for voltage between shift lock control module terminal No. 8 and terminal No. 7. With brake pedal applied, battery voltage should exist. With brake pedal released, voltage should not exist. If voltage is not as specified, check stoplight switch.
6) Check for voltage between shift lock control module terminal No. 5 and terminal No. 7. When ignition key is inserted into key cylinder, selector lever is in Park and selector lever button is pushed, battery voltage should exist. When selector lever is set to any other position except Park, battery voltage should exist. Voltage should not exist under any other conditions. If voltage is not as specified, check detention switch.

OD SWITCH & OD CANCEL SOLENOID

OD OFF Indicator – 1) With KOEO, set OD switch to "OFF" position. OD OFF indicator light should come on. If indicator light does NOT come on, check indicator bulb, power supply from ignition switch and fuse. *See Fig. 3.* If indicator light functions properly, go to step 3).

2) If power supply is okay, check OD switch. Disconnect 8-pin connector of OD switch harness. Check continuity between terminals No. 4 and No. 5. With OD switch in "ON" position, continuity should not exist. Continuity should exist only in "OFF" position. If not as specified, replace OD switch.

3) If OD switch is okay, check resistance of OD cancel solenoid valve. Disconnect solenoid harness 3-pin connector. Check resistance at terminals No. 2 and No. 3. Resistance should be approximately 25 ohms. If resistance is not as specified, replace overdrive control solenoid valve.

4) If OD cancel solenoid is okay, check continuity in wiring harness between fuse and OD cancel solenoid valve and between OD cancel solenoid valve and OD switch. If equipped with Automatic Speed Control Device (ASCD) check condition of diode. *See Fig. 3.*

INHIBITOR SWITCH TESTING

Inhibitor Switch – 1) With KOEO, check voltage between ECM terminal No. 22 and ground while moving through each position. In "P" and "N" zero volts should be present. In all other positions, battery voltage should be present.

2) If voltage is not as specified, check continuity in "N", "P" and "R" positions. Continuity should exist 1.5 degrees of rotation in either direction. In "P" and "N" continuity should exist between terminals No. 1 and No. 2. In "R" position should show continuity between terminals No. 3 and No. 4.

3) If continuity does not exist equally in both directions, adjust inhibitor switch. To adjust, see appropriate AUTOMATIC TRANSMISSION SERVICING article in TRANSMISSION SERVICING section.

4) If continuity is not as specified, check continuity between ground, ECM, and back-up lamp to inhibitor switch. *See Fig. 3.*

SOLENOID TESTING

Torque Converter Clutch Solenoid Valve – 1) Torque converter lock-up is controlled by ECM. If an excessively low voltage from solenoid valve is sent to ECM, or if A/T torque converter slip is occurred in lock-up condition. ECM will set DTC P1550/0904. See appropriate SELF-DIAGNOSTICS article in ENGINE PERFORMANCE in appropriate MITCHELL® manual.

2) With ignition switch "OFF", disconnect ECM harness connector and TCC solenoid valve harness connector. Check resistance between

terminals No. 1 and No. 30. Resistance should be approximately zero ohms. Repair or replace if not as specified.

3) With ignition switch "ON", check voltage between terminal No. 3 and ground. Battery voltage should exist. If voltage is not as specified, check power supply, ignition switch, fuse and wiring. Check for continuity between fuse and TCC solenoid valve.

4) If voltage check is okay, check TCC solenoid valve resistance. Check resistance between TCC solenoid valve terminals No. 1 and No. 3. Resistance should be approximately 25 ohms. If not as specified, replace TCC solenoid valve.

5) If resistance was okay, remove TCC solenoid valve. See COMPONENT DISASSEMBLY & REASSEMBLY. To check solenoid operation, apply battery voltage to Terminals No. 1 and No. 3 of TCC solenoid valve harness. Replace or repair as needed.

6) If TCC solenoid valve operation is okay, check control valve. Disassemble control valve assembly. See COMPONENT DISASSEMBLY & REASSEMBLY. Repair or replace as needed.

7) Road test vehicle, ensure malfunction has been eliminated. Perform self-diagnostic test, ensure code does not return. *See Fig. 3.*

TESTING

ROAD TEST

Preliminary Checks – 1) Check fluid level using HOT range on dip stick with fluid temperatures of 122-176°F (50-80°C) after vehicle has been driven approximately 5 minutes after initial warm-up. COLD range on dipstick is for reference only.

2) Fluid level should be checked with vehicle on level surface and parking brake applied. Check fluid level while engine is idling and selector lever is in "P" position.

3) If fluid level is at low side of either range, add fluid. Check fluid condition. Check for fluid leakage. Examine fluid color, texture and odor. If fluid is Black and has a burnt odor, clutch friction plates are worn.

4) If fluid is milky Pink in color, fluid is water-contaminated. Water may be entering transaxle through filler tube or breather. If fluid is Light or Dark Brown in color and tacky, fluid level is incorrect or transaxle is overheating.

Check With Engine Idling – 1) Start engine and let idle. Release parking brake. Apply foot brake, move selector lever to "R" position. Vehicle should creep backwards after foot brake is released.

2) Move selector lever to "D", "2" and "1" positions. Vehicle should creep forward in all three positions. Move selector lever to "N" position. Vehicle should not creep forward or backward.

Road Test Procedure – 1) Place selector lever in "P" position, and start engine. Turn engine off and repeat procedure in all positions, including "N" position. Ensure engine starts in "P" and "N" positions only. In "P" position, transaxle parking mechanism should be locked and vehicle should not move. Release parking brake to ensure parking mechanism remains locked.

2) Start engine, move selector lever from "P" to "R" position, and note shift quality. Drive vehicle in reverse long enough to detect slippage or other abnormalities. Stop vehicle and move selector lever into "P" position.

3) Move selector lever from "R" and "D" positions to "N" position and note shift quality. With parking brake released and selector lever in "N" position, lightly depress accelerator to ensure vehicle does not move.

4) Move selector lever from "N" to "D" position, and note shift quality. Road test vehicle and note upshift/downshift speeds. Upshift/downshift speeds should be close to speeds shown in SHIFT SPEED SPECIFICATIONS table.

5) Shift speeds should be checked at half and full throttle positions. Note when shift shock occurs during shifting. Determine if lock-up occurs while driving vehicle in appropriate gear position and at correct speed. See LOCK-UP SPEED SPECIFICATIONS table. Ensure transaxle does not shift to overdrive with OD switch in OFF position.

6) When vehicle is being driven 37-43 MPH ("D" position) at half to light throttle position, fully depress accelerator pedal to ensure transaxle downshifts from 3rd to 2nd gear. When vehicle is being driven 16-22 MPH ("2" position) at half to light throttle position, fully depress accelerator pedal to ensure transaxle downshifts from 2nd to 1st gear.

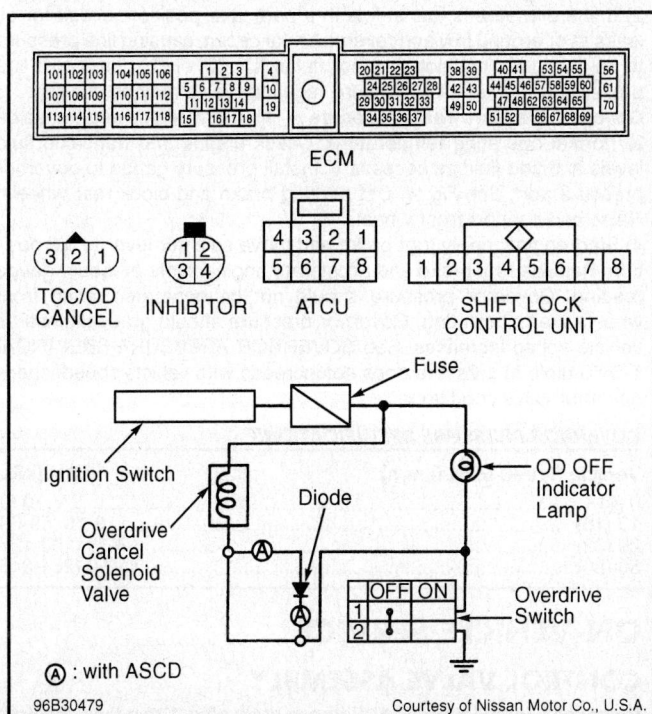

Fig. 3: Identifying Harness Connector Terminal Pins

96B30479   Courtesy of Nissan Motor Co., U.S.A.

7) Shift vehicle to "2" position and ensure vehicle starts in 1st gear. As vehicle speed is increased, ensure transaxle upshifts from 1st to 2nd gear. Further increase vehicle speed. Ensure transaxle does not upshift to 3rd gear.

8) While driving vehicle 16-22 MPH with throttle at half to light position ("2" position), fully depress accelerator pedal to ensure transaxle downshifts from 2nd to 1st gear. Decelerate vehicle and ensure 2-1 downshift. Shift to "D" position and drive vehicle at 19-25 MPH. Shift into "2" position. Ensure 3-2 downshift occurs.

9) Shift vehicle to "1" position. Transaxle should not upshift from 1st to 2nd as vehicle speed increases. Accelerate and decelerate vehicle to determine engine braking. Ensure engine compression acts as a brake. Drive vehicle in "2" position at 9-16 MPH. Ensure 2-1 downshift occurs when selector lever is moved to "1" position.

LOCK-UP SPEED SPECIFICATIONS [1]

Application	MPH
Lock-Up ON in 4th Gear	47-52
Lock-Up OFF in 4th Gear	42-47

[1] – With 1/4 throttle opening.

SHIFT SPEED SPECIFICATIONS

Application	Full Throttle MPH	Half Throttle MPH
1st-2nd	32-37	18-23
2nd-3rd	60-65	32-37
3rd-4th	N/A	63-68
4th-3rd	88-93	42-47
3rd-2nd	50-60	25-30
2nd-1st	24-29	5-10

STALL SPEED TEST

Stall Speed Test Procedure – 1) Check engine and transaxle fluid levels. Ensure engine and transaxle are at normal operating temperatures. Set parking brake and block wheels.

2) Install tachometer so it is visible to driver. Start engine, apply foot brake and move selector lever to "D" position. Gradually depress accelerator pedal to wide-open throttle position while applying foot brake. Note engine stall speed and release accelerator pedal immediately. Stall speed should be 2450-2750 RPM.

3) Place selector lever in "N" position and run engine at idle for one minute to allow transaxle to cool. Repeat stall speed test procedure in "2", "1" and "R" positions, allowing transaxle to cool between each test.

CAUTION: DO NOT hold wide-open throttle for more than 5 seconds during test.

Stall Speed Test Results
- **Stall Speed Low In All Positions** – Insufficient engine performance or faulty torque converter one-way clutch.
- **Stall Speed High In All Positions** – Low and reverse brake slipping, faulty low one-way clutch or hydraulic circuit for line pressure control.
- **Stall Speed High In "R" Position Only** – Reverse clutch slipping or low and reverse brake slipping.
- **Stall Speed High In "D", "2" & "R" Positions, Okay In "1" Position** – Defective reverse clutch, forward clutch, forward one-way clutch or low one-way clutch.
- **Stall Speed High In "D", "2" & "1" Positions, Okay In "R" Position** – Defective forward clutch, low one-way clutch or forward one-way clutch.
- **Stall Speed High In "D" & "2" Positions, Okay In "1" & "R" Positions** – Defective forward clutch, low one-way clutch and forward one way.

NOTE: Condition of high clutch and brake band cannot be confirmed by stall speed test.

HYDRAULIC PRESSURE TESTS

Line Pressure Test Procedure – 1) Warm engine and transaxle to normal operating temperature. Check engine and transaxle fluid levels and add fluid as necessary. Install pressure gauge to line pressure port. *See Fig. 4.*

2) Set parking brake and block wheels. Apply foot brake fully while line pressure test at stall speed is performed. Start engine and measure line pressure at idle and stall speed in "D", "2", "1" and "R" positions. When measuring line pressure at stall speed, follow stall speed test procedure. Note pressure readings and refer to LINE PRESSURE SPECIFICATIONS table.

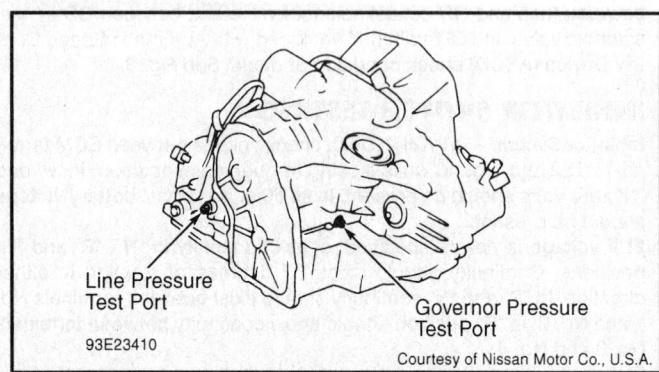

Line Pressure
Test Port

Governor Pressure
Test Port

93E23410

Courtesy of Nissan Motor Co., U.S.A.

Fig. 4: Identifying Hydraulic Pressure Test Ports

LINE PRESSURE SPECIFICATIONS

Application	psi (kPa)
At Idle	
In "D"	92 (637)
In "2" & "1"	166 (1,147)
In "R"	128 (883)
At Stall Speed	
In "D", "2" & "1"	185 (1275)
In "R"	256 (1765)

Line Pressure Test Results – 1) If line pressure is low at idle in all positions, possible causes are: oil pump wear; oil leakage at or around oil pump, control valve body, transmission case or governor; sticking pressure regulator or modifier valve.

2) If line pressure is low at idle in a particular position, check for oil leaks at or around low and reverse brake circuit, causing line pressure to be low in "R" position, but normal in "D", "2" or "1" position. If line pressure is high at idle, pressure regulator valve may be sticking.

Governor Pressure Test Procedure – 1) Warm engine and transaxle to normal operating temperature. Check engine and transaxle fluid levels and add fluid as necessary. Install pressure gauge to governor pressure port. *See Fig. 4.* Set parking brake and block rear wheels. Raise and support front wheels.

4) Start engine, apply foot brake and move selector lever to "D" position. Release foot brake and accelerate engine. Note pressure gauge reading. Governor pressure should not be generated when front wheels are not rotating. Governor pressure should gradually rise as vehicle speed increases. See GOVERNOR PRESSURE SPECIFICATIONS table. If pressure does not increase with vehicle speed, check governor valve condition.

GOVERNOR PRESSURE SPECIFICATIONS

Vehicle Speed MPH (km/h)	psi (kPa)
0 (0)	0 (0)
10 (16)	9-10 (59-69)
20 (32)	18-18 (108-127)
50 (80)	41-50 (284-343)

ON-VEHICLE SERVICE

CONTROL VALVE ASSEMBLY

Removal & Installation – 1) Remove drain plug. Drain fluid. Remove oil pan and gasket. Disconnect A/T solenoid harness connector.

Remove clip from A/T solenoid harness terminal body. Remove A/T solenoid harness by pushing terminal body into transmission case. Remove oil strainer. Remove control valve assembly by removing bolts. See CONTROL VALVE ASSEMBLY BOLT IDENTIFICATION table. *See Fig. 5.* Remove accumulators by applying compressed air (if necessary).

CONTROL VALVE ASSEMBLY BOLT IDENTIFICATION [1]

Letter ID	In. (mm)
A	.984 (25)
B	1.299 (33)
C	1.575 (40)
D	1.713 (43.5)

[1] – See Fig. 5 for bolt locations.

2) To install control valve assembly, set manual valve in Neutral position and align with manual plate. Install control valve assembly and tighten bolts to 61-78 INCH lbs. (7-9 N.m). Ensure selector lever can be moved to all positions. To complete installation, reverse removal procedure. Fill transaxle to appropriate fluid level.

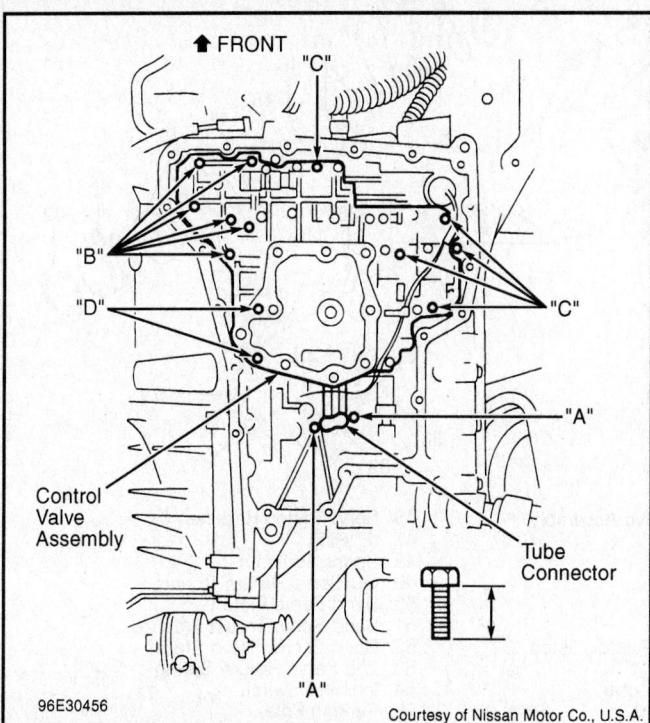

Fig. 5: Identifying Control Valve Assembly Bolt Locations

GOVERNOR VALVE ASSEMBLY

Removal & Installation – Remove air duct. Remove governor cap snap ring. Remove governor cap. Remove "O" ring from governor cap. Remove governor assembly from transaxle. To install, reverse removal procedure.

INHIBITOR SWITCH ADJUSTMENT

See appropriate AUTOMATIC TRANSMISSION SERVICING article in TRANSMISSION SERVICING section.

OIL COOLER FLUSHING PROCEDURE

Vehicles with tube type transaxle fluid cooler may be cleaned using cleaning solvent and compressed air. Cooler lines must also be flushed to remove any foreign material. Vehicles with fin type transaxle fluid cooler cannot be cleaned. Replace radiator (radiator incorporates transaxle cooler) and flush cooler lines to remove any foreign material.

REMOVAL & INSTALLATION

See appropriate AUTOMATIC TRANSMISSION REMOVAL article in TRANSMISSION SERVICING section.

TORQUE CONVERTER

1) Torque converter is a sealed unit and cannot be disassembled for service. Replace torque converter if damaged. Check converter one-way clutch using flat-blade screwdriver and suitable wire. *See Fig. 6.*
2) Hook wire into groove of bearing support unitized with one-way clutch outer race. While holding bearing support with wire, rotate one-way clutch spline using screwdriver. Ensure inner race rotates clockwise only. If inner race rotates in both directions, replace torque converter.

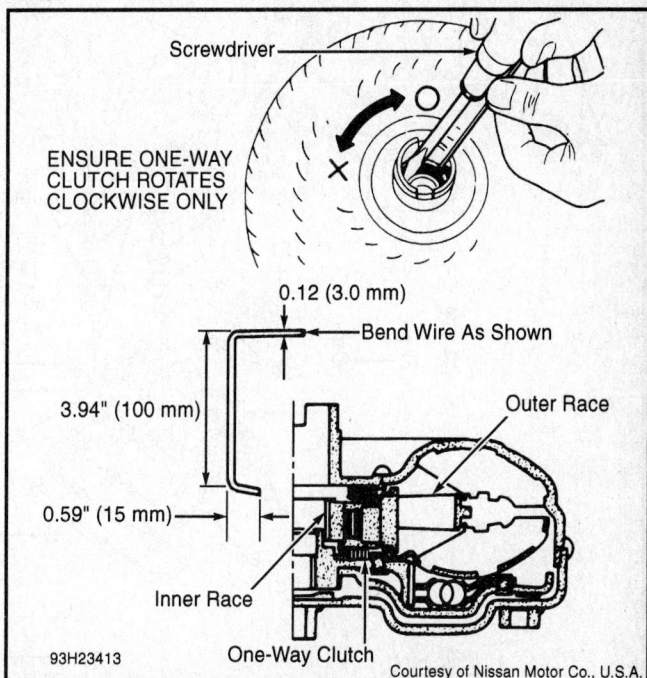

Fig. 6: Checking Torque Converter One-Way Clutch

TRANSAXLE DISASSEMBLY

1) Remove drain plug and drain fluid. Remove torque converter. Check torque converter one-way clutch. See TORQUE CONVERTER. Remove dipstick and dipstick tube. Remove oil cooler tube. Set manual lever to "P" position. Remove inhibitor switch. Remove oil pan and gasket. *See Fig. 7.* DO NOT reuse oil pan bolts.
2) Remove control valve assembly bolts. *See Fig. 5.* Remove clip from terminal body. Push terminal body into transaxle case and remove solenoid harness. Remove manual valve from control valve assembly. Remove return spring from servo release accumulator piston. Using compressed air, remove servo release accumulator piston. *See Fig. 8.*
3) Remove "O" rings from servo release accumulator piston. Using compressed air, remove N-D accumulator piston and return spring. *See Fig. 8.* Remove "O" rings from N-D accumulator piston. Check accumulator pistons and contact surface of transaxle case for damage. Check accumulator return springs free length and diameter. See ACCUMULATOR SPRING SPECIFICATIONS table.

ACCUMULATOR SPRING SPECIFICATIONS

Application	In. (mm)
N-D Accumulator Spring	
Free Length	1.713 (43.50)
Outer Diameter	1.102 (28.0)
Servo Release Accumulator Spring	
Free Length	2.220 (56.40)
Outer Diameter	.827 (21.00)

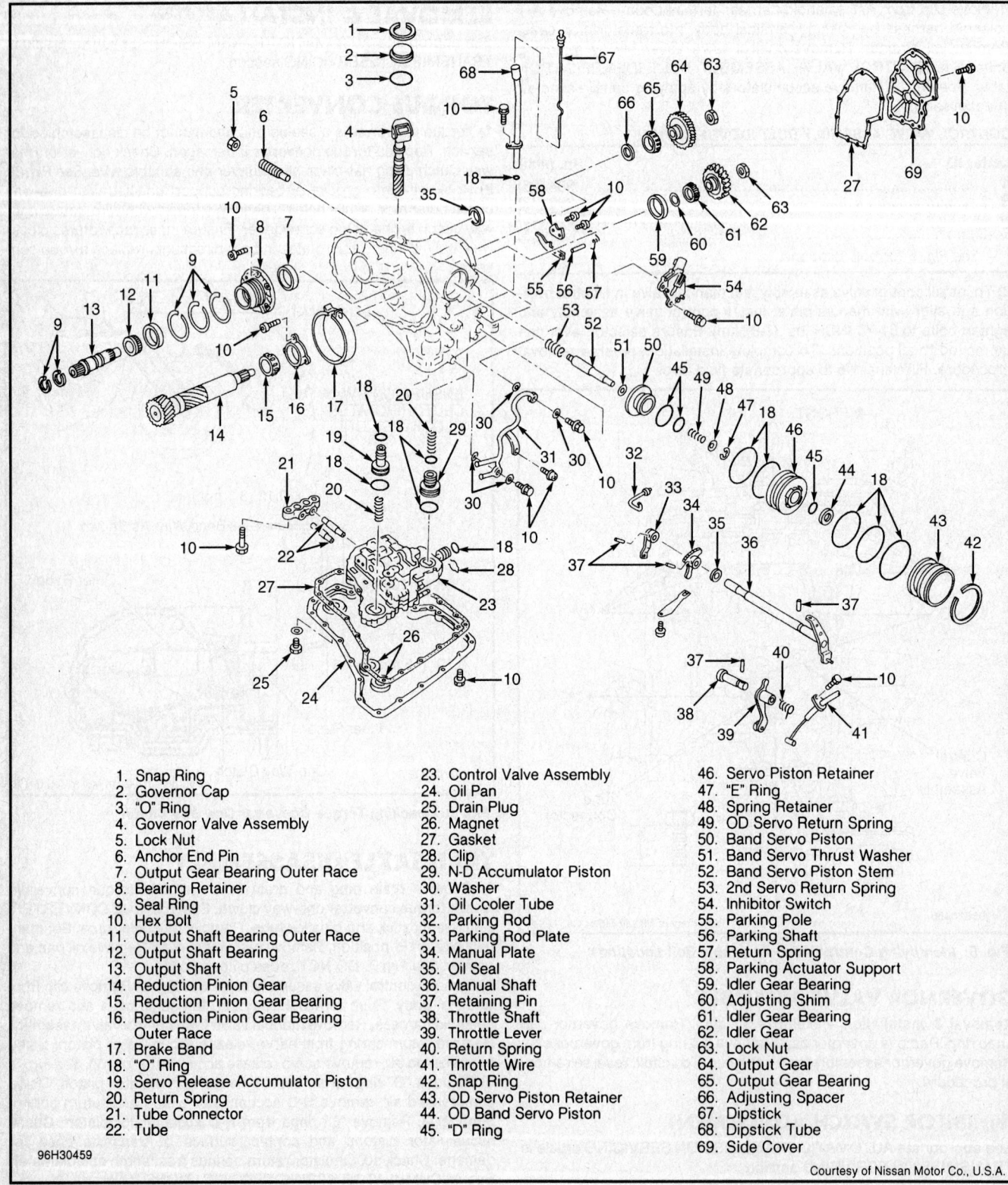

1. Snap Ring	23. Control Valve Assembly	46. Servo Piston Retainer
2. Governor Cap	24. Oil Pan	47. "E" Ring
3. "O" Ring	25. Drain Plug	48. Spring Retainer
4. Governor Valve Assembly	26. Magnet	49. OD Servo Return Spring
5. Lock Nut	27. Gasket	50. Band Servo Piston
6. Anchor End Pin	28. Clip	51. Band Servo Thrust Washer
7. Output Gear Bearing Outer Race	29. N-D Accumulator Piston	52. Band Servo Piston Stem
8. Bearing Retainer	30. Washer	53. 2nd Servo Return Spring
9. Seal Ring	31. Oil Cooler Tube	54. Inhibitor Switch
10. Hex Bolt	32. Parking Rod	55. Parking Pole
11. Output Shaft Bearing Outer Race	33. Parking Rod Plate	56. Parking Shaft
12. Output Shaft Bearing	34. Manual Plate	57. Return Spring
13. Output Shaft	35. Oil Seal	58. Parking Actuator Support
14. Reduction Pinion Gear	36. Manual Shaft	59. Idler Gear Bearing
15. Reduction Pinion Gear Bearing	37. Retaining Pin	60. Adjusting Shim
16. Reduction Pinion Gear Bearing Outer Race	38. Throttle Shaft	61. Idler Gear Bearing
17. Brake Band	39. Throttle Lever	62. Idler Gear
18. "O" Ring	40. Return Spring	63. Lock Nut
19. Servo Release Accumulator Piston	41. Throttle Wire	64. Output Gear
20. Return Spring	42. Snap Ring	65. Output Gear Bearing
21. Tube Connector	43. OD Servo Piston Retainer	66. Adjusting Spacer
22. Tube	44. OD Band Servo Piston	67. Dipstick
	45. "D" Ring	68. Dipstick Tube
		69. Side Cover

96H30459

Courtesy of Nissan Motor Co., U.S.A.

Fig. 7: Exploded View Of Transaxle Case Components

4) Remove lip seals from band servo oil port. Using snap ring pliers, remove governor valve oil filter. Check filter for damage or clogging. Remove throttle cable from throttle lever. Remove throttle cable mounting bolt and remove throttle cable from transaxle case. Remove converter housing bolts and remove converter housing by tapping housing with soft-faced hammer. Remove "O" ring from differential oil port.

5) Remove differential assembly from transaxle case. It may be necessary to tap differential assembly with soft-faced hammer to remove assembly from case. Using a hammer and screwdriver, remove oil seal from converter housing, being careful not to damage converter housing. Remove seal from transaxle case.

6) Remove oil tube from converter housing. Remove "O" ring from input shaft. *See Fig. 9.* Remove oil pump assembly bolts and remove

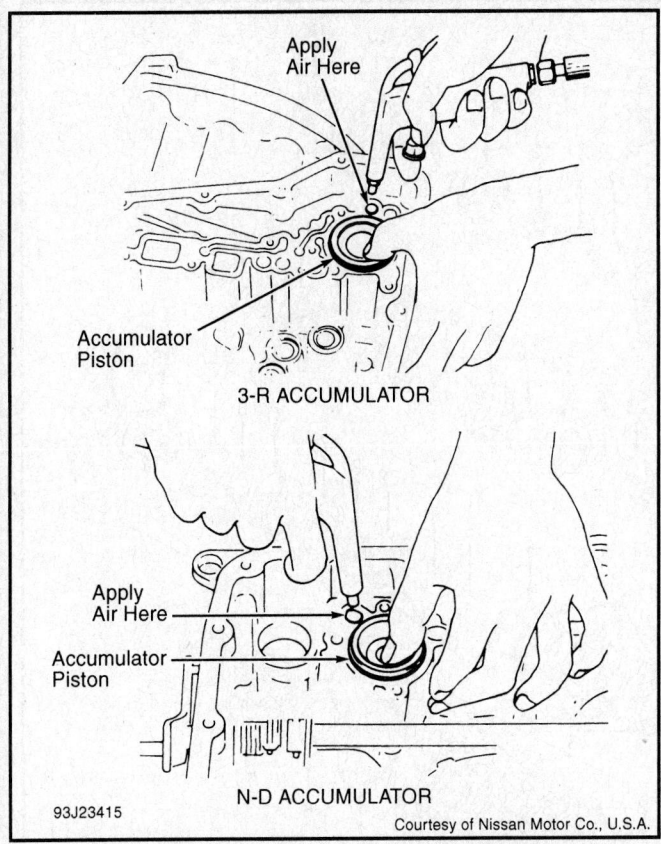

Apply
Air Here

Accumulator
Piston

3-R ACCUMULATOR

Apply
Air Here

Accumulator
Piston

N-D ACCUMULATOR

93J23415

Courtesy of Nissan Motor Co., U.S.A.

Fig. 8: Removing N-D & Servo Release Accumulator Pistons

oil pump assembly from transaxle case. Remove thrust washer and bearing race from oil pump assembly. Loosen anchor end pin lock nut, then back off anchor end pin.

7) Remove brake band from transaxle case. When removing brake band, insert wire clip into brake band ends for support. To prevent brake lining from cracking or peeling, DO NOT stretch brake band. Check brake band facing for damage, cracks, wear or burns. Remove high clutch (with input shaft assembly) and reverse clutch assemblies. Remove high clutch from reverse clutch. *See Fig. 10.*

8) Remove needle bearing from high clutch drum. Remove high clutch hub and needle bearing from transaxle case. Remove front sun gear and needle bearings from transaxle case. Check all components for damage or wear.

9) Remove snap ring and front planetary carrier assembly with low one-way clutch. Ensure low one-way clutch rotates counterclockwise only. Remove low one-way clutch from front planetary carrier by rotating one-way clutch counterclockwise. Remove needle bearing from planetary carrier. *See Fig. 10.* Check all components for damage or wear.

10) Remove rear planetary carrier assembly from transaxle case. Remove rear sun gear from rear planetary carrier. Remove needle bearings from rear planetary carrier. Check all components for damage or wear.

11) Using a feeler gauge, check clearance between pinion washer and planetary carrier on front and rear planetary carriers. Clearance between pinion washer and planetary carrier should be .006-.028" (.15-.70 mm). Replace appropriate planetary carrier if clearance exceeds .031" (.80 mm).

12) Remove rear internal gear from transaxle case. Remove needle bearing from rear internal gear and check bearing for damage or wear. Remove forward clutch assembly from transaxle case. Remove thrust washer and bearing race from transaxle case. Remove side cover bolts and side cover. *See Fig. 7.*

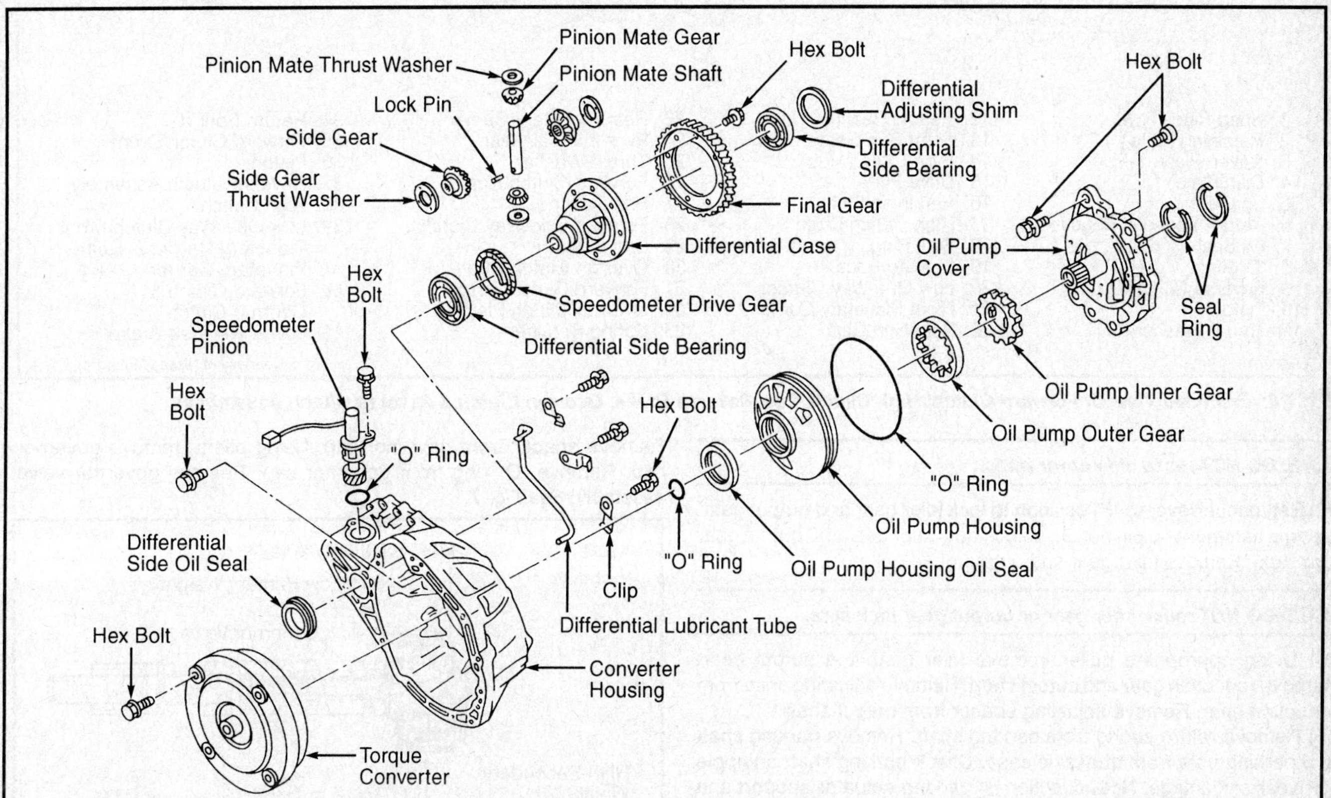

Pinion Mate Gear

Pinion Mate Thrust Washer

Pinion Mate Shaft

Hex Bolt

Hex Bolt

Differential Adjusting Shim

Lock Pin

Side Gear

Differential Side Bearing

Side Gear Thrust Washer

Final Gear

Differential Case

Oil Pump Cover

Seal Ring

Hex Bolt

Speedometer Pinion

Speedometer Drive Gear

Differential Side Bearing

Oil Pump Inner Gear

Oil Pump Outer Gear

Hex Bolt

Hex Bolt

"O" Ring

"O" Ring

Oil Pump Housing

Differential Side Oil Seal

"O" Ring

Oil Pump Housing Oil Seal

Hex Bolt

Clip

Differential Lubricant Tube

Converter Housing

Torque Converter

96A30460

Courtesy of Nissan Motor Co., U.S.A.

Fig. 9: Exploded View Of Torque Converter Housing & Differential Components

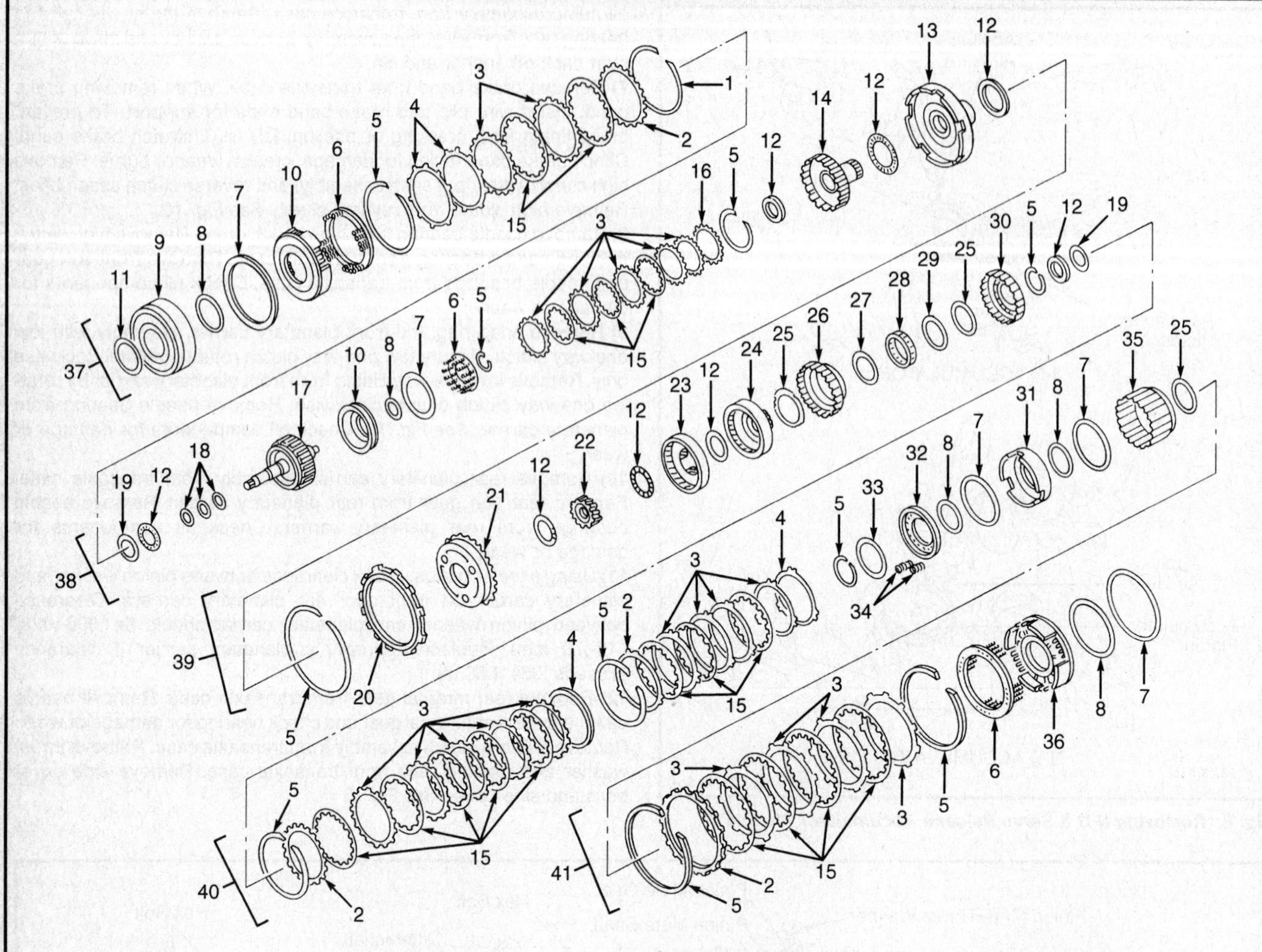

1. Snap Ring	12. Needle Bearing	23. Rear Planetary Carrier	34. Return Spring
2. Retaining Plate	13. Front Sun Gear	24. Rear Internal Gear	35. Forward Clutch Drum
3. Driven Plate	14. High Clutch Hub	25. Thrust Washer	36. Piston
4. Dish Plate	15. Drive Plate	26. Forward Clutch Hub	37. Reverse Clutch Assembly
5. Snap Ring	16. Retaining Plate	27. End Bearing	38. High Clutch
6. Return Spring & Retainer	17. High Clutch Drum	28. Forward One-Way Clutch	39. Low One-Way Clutch Front
7. Oil Seal	18. Seal Ring	29. End Bearing	Planetary Carrier & Rear
8. "D" Ring	19. Bearing Race	30. Overrun Clutch Hub	Planetary Carrier
9. Reverse Clutch Drum	20. Low One-Way Clutch	31. Forward Clutch Piston	40. Forward Clutch &
10. Piston	21. Front Planetary Carrier	32. Overrun Clutch Piston	Overrun Clutch
11. Thrust Washer	22. Rear Sun Gear	33. Spring Retainer	41. Low & Reverse Brake

96B30461

Courtesy of Nissan Motor Co., U.S.A.

Fig. 10: Exploded View Of Forward Clutch, High Clutch, Low-Reverse Brake, Overrun Clutch & Reverse Clutch Assemblies

---

NOTE: DO NOT reuse side cover bolts.

---

13) Set manual lever to "P" position to lock idler gear and output gear. Using a hammer and pin punch, unlock both idler gear and output gear lock nuts. Remove idler gear and output gear lock nuts.

NOTE: DO NOT reuse idler gear or output gear lock nuts.

---

14) Using appropriate puller, remove idler gear and output gear. Remove reduction gear and output shaft. Remove adjusting shim from reduction gear. Remove adjusting spacer from output shaft.

15) Remove return spring from parking shaft. Remove parking shaft and parking pole from transaxle case. Check parking shaft and pole for wear or damage. Note direction of parking actuator support and remove actuator support from transaxle case. Inspect actuator support for wear or damage. Remove governor assembly snap ring.

Remove spacer from governor cap. Using pliers, remove governor cap. Remove "O" ring from governor cap. Remove governor valve assembly. See Fig. 7.

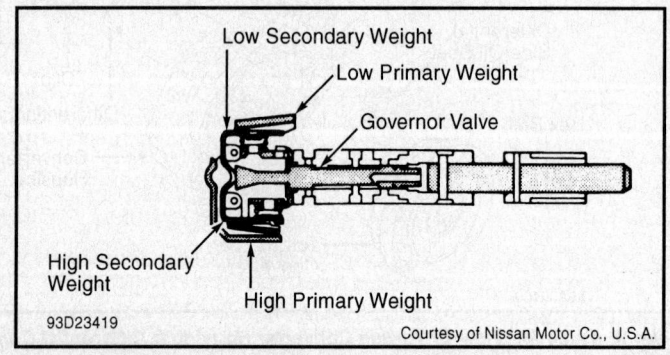

Courtesy of Nissan Motor Co., U.S.A.

Fig. 11: Identifying Governor Valve Components

16) With low primary weight closed, ensure governor valve lowers under its own weight. Check low and high secondary weight operation. Ensure governor valve move freely. *See Fig. 11.* Using a hammer and screwdriver, remove side oil seal from transaxle case. Remove manual shaft and throttle lever components. See MANUAL SHAFT & THROTTLE LEVER under COMPONENT DISASSEMBLY & REASSEMBLY.

COMPONENT DISASSEMBLY & REASSEMBLY

OIL PUMP

Disassembly – Remove seal rings. Remove oil pump cover bolts in numerical order and remove oil pump cover. *See Fig. 12.* Remove inner and outer gears from oil pump housing, noting direction of inner gear prior to removal. Remove "O" ring from oil pump housing. Using a screwdriver, pry out oil pump housing oil seal. *See Fig. 13.*

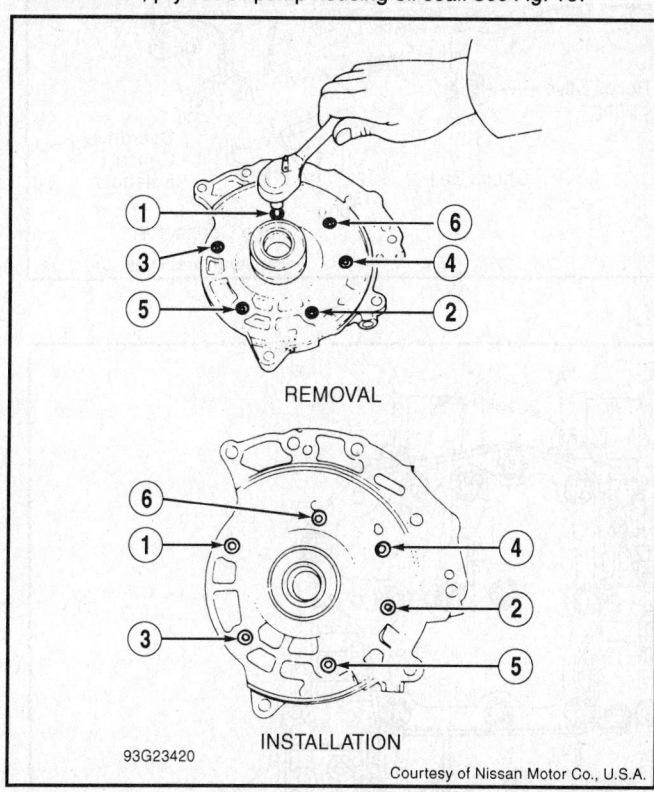

Fig. 12: *Removal & Installation Of Oil Pump Cover*

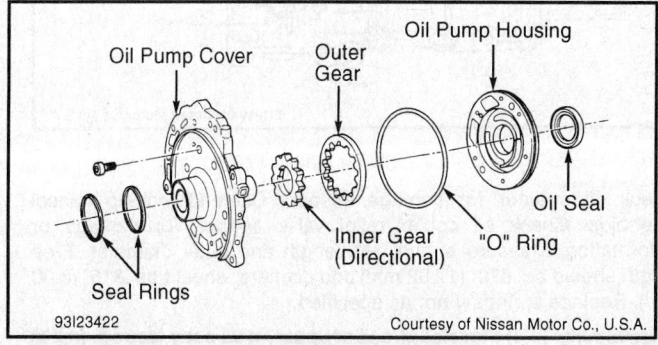

Fig. 13: *Exploded View Of Oil Pump Assembly*

Inspection – 1) Inspect oil pump housing, oil pump cover and inner and outer gear for wear or damage. Using a dial indicator, measure side clearance between end of oil pump housing and inner and outer gears in at least 4 places along their circumferences. Clearance should be .0008-.0016" (.020-.040 mm). *See Fig. 14.*

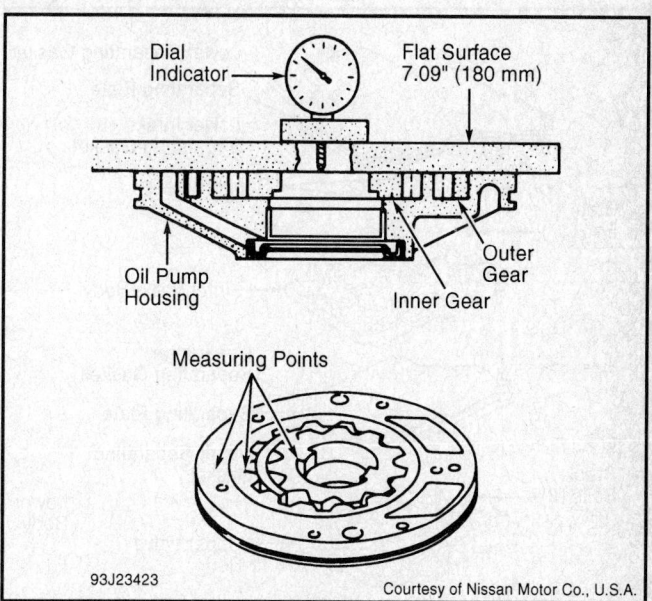

Fig. 14: *Measuring Oil Pump Side Clearance*

2) If clearance is less then specified, replace inner and outer gears as a set. Ensure clearance is as specified. Gears are available in thicknesses of .3925-.3929" (9.970-9.980 mm), .3929-.3933" (9.980-9.990 mm) and .3933-.3937" (9.990-10.000 mm). If clearance is greater than specified, replace oil pump assembly, except oil pump cover.
3) Using a feeler gauge, measure clearance between outer gear and oil pump housing. Clearance should be .003-.006" (.08-.15 mm). If clearance is not as specified, replace oil pump assembly, except oil pump cover. Install NEW seal rings onto oil pump cover. Measure clearance between seal ring and ring groove. Clearance should be .004-.010" (.10-.25 mm), with allowable limit of .010" (.25 mm). If clearance is not as specified, replace oil pump cover.

Reassembly – 1) Using appropriate adapter, install NEW oil seal on oil pump housing. Apply ATF to NEW "O" ring and install "O" ring on oil pump housing. Install inner and outer gears on oil pump housing. Ensure inner gear is installed in same direction as removed.
2) Wrap oil pump splines with masking tape to protect oil seal. Position oil pump cover on oil pump housing, then remove masking tape. Tighten bolts in numerical order to 62-97 INCH lbs. (7-11 N.m). *See Fig. 12.* Pack ring groove with petroleum jelly, then carefully install NEW seal rings. Connect seal ring hooks. DO NOT spread gap of seal ring excessively while installing as ring may become deformed.

CONTROL VALVE ASSEMBLY

Disassembly – 1) Remove tube connector and tube from control valve lower body. Disassemble upper, inter and lower valve bodies. *See Fig. 15.* Note bolt length, number of bolts and location. See VALVE BODY BOLT IDENTIFICATION table.

VALVE BODY BOLT IDENTIFICATION [1]

Bolt I.D. (Letter)	Length – In. (mm)	No. Of Bolts
A	.53 (13.5)	4
B	2.28 (58.0)	3
C	1.57 (40.0)	6
D	2.60 (66.0)	11
E	1.30 (33.0)	2
F	3.07 (78.0)	2

[1] – See Fig. 16 for bolt location.

2) Remove bolts "A", "D" and "F", and remove oil strainer from control valve assembly. Remove OD cancel solenoid and lock-up solenoid from control valve assembly. Remove "O" rings from OD cancel solenoid, lock-up solenoid and harness terminal body. Place upper valve body face down. Remove bolts "B", "C" and "F".

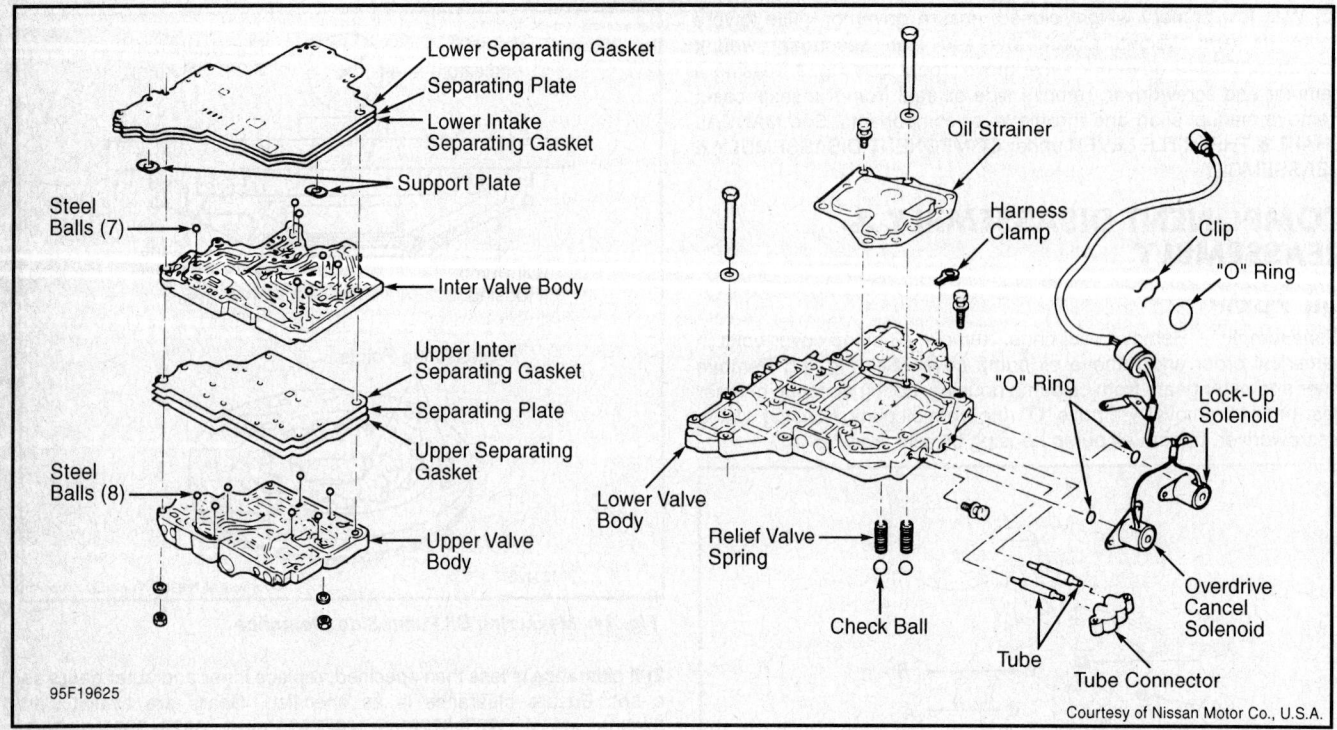

Fig. 15: Exploded View Of Control Valve Assembly

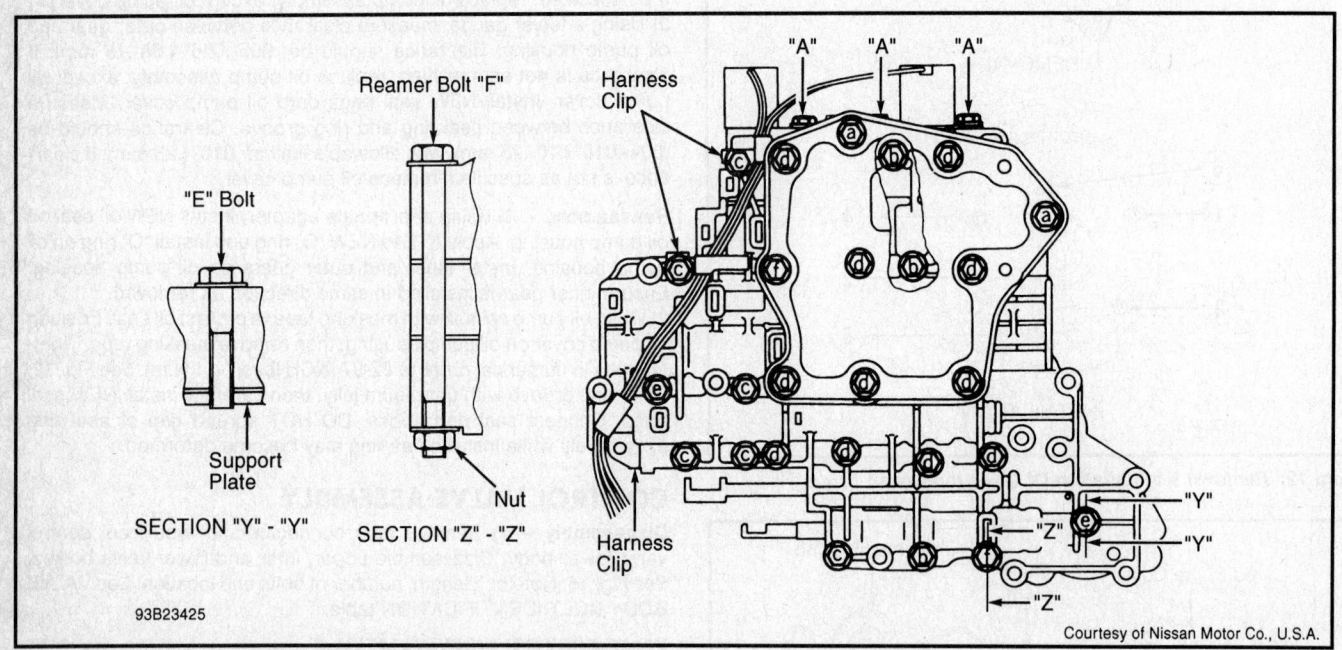

Fig. 16: Identifying Valve Body Bolt Locations

3) Remove inter valve body from lower valve body. Turn lower valve body over and remove accumulator support plate. Remove separating plate and separating gasket from lower valve body. *See Fig. 15.* Remove check balls and relief valve springs from lower valve body. DO NOT lose check balls or relief valve springs.

4) Remove inter valve body with separating plate and separating gasket from upper valve body. Ensure steel balls are properly positioned in upper and inter valve bodies, then remove balls from valve bodies. DO NOT lose steel balls.

Inspection – Ensure retainer plates are properly positioned in lower and upper valve bodies. *See Fig. 17.* DO NOT lose retainer plates.

Check oil strainer for damage. Inspect OD and lock-up cancel solenoids. Check oil cooler relief valve springs for damage or deformation. Measure spring free length and outer diameter. Free length should be .670" (17.02 mm) and diameter should be .315" (8.00 mm). Replace springs if not as specified.

Reassembly – 1) Place oil circuit of upper valve body face up. Install steel balls in proper positions. *See Fig. 18.* Install upper separating plate gasket, upper inter separating plate gasket and upper separating plate. Install reamer bolts "F" from bottom of upper valve body. Install separating gaskets and separating plates as a set on upper valve body, using reamer bolts as a guide.

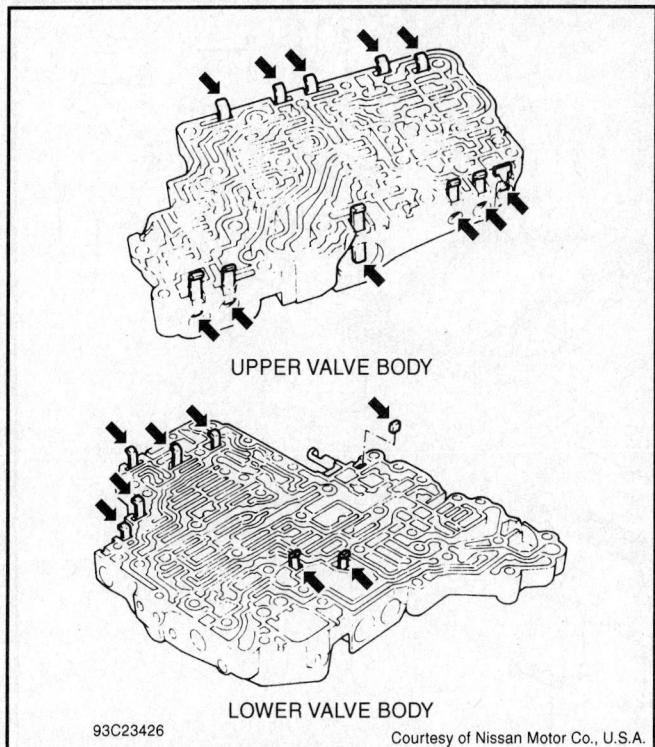

UPPER VALVE BODY

LOWER VALVE BODY

93C23426

Courtesy of Nissan Motor Co., U.S.A.

Fig. 17: Identifying Retainer Plate Locations

2) Place lower valve body side of inter valve body face up. Install steel balls in proper positions. Install inter valve body on upper valve body, using reamer bolts "F" as a guide. DO NOT lose steel balls. Install steel balls and relief valve springs in proper positions in lower valve body. Install lower separating gasket, inter separating gasket and lower separating plate. See Fig. 15.

3) Install support plate bolts "E" from bottom of lower valve body. Install separating gaskets and separating plate as a set on lower valve

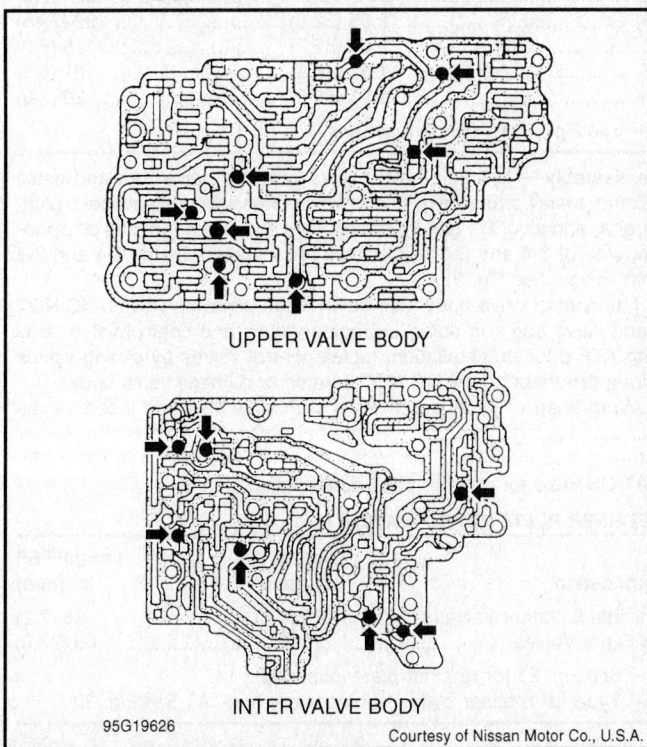

UPPER VALVE BODY

INTER VALVE BODY

95G19626

Courtesy of Nissan Motor Co., U.S.A.

Fig. 18: Identifying Steel Ball Locations

body using bolts "E" as a guide. Temporarily install support plates on lower valve body. Install lower valve body on inter valve body using reamer bolts "F" as a guide. See Fig. 16. Tighten bolts.

4) Install "O" rings to OD cancel solenoid, lock-up solenoid and harness connector. Apply ATF to "O" rings prior to installation. Install and snug bolts "B". Install OD cancel solenoid and lock-up solenoid to lower valve body. Install and snug bolts "A" and 'C'.

5) Remove both reamer bolts "F" previously installed as guides. Install one reamer bolt "F" from lower valve body side. Tighten bolts "A", "B", "C" and "F" to 62-80 INCH lbs. (7-9 N.m). Install oil strainer and other reamer bolt "F". Tighten bolts "A", "D" and "F" to 62-80 INCH lbs. (7-9 N.m). Install support plates and tighten bolts "E" to 30-39 INCH lbs. (3.4-4.4 N.m). Install tube connector and tubes to lower valve body. Install oil circuit side of tube connector face up.

CONTROL VALVE UPPER BODY

Disassembly – 1) Use a screwdriver to pry out retainer plates. Remove retainer plates while holding spring, plugs and sleeves. Remove plug slowly to prevent internal parts from jumping out.

2) Place mating surface of valve body face down and remove internal parts. If valve is hard to remove, lightly tap body with soft-faced hammer. DO NOT use a magnet to remove valves. DO NOT drop or damage valves or sleeves.

Inspection – Measure spring free length and outer diameter. See UPPER VALVE BODY SPRING IDENTIFICATION table. Check for deformation or damage. Replace valve springs if deformed or fatigued. Check sliding surfaces of valves, sleeves and plugs.

UPPER VALVE BODY SPRING IDENTIFICATION [1]

Spring No.	Length In. (mm)	Diameter In. (mm)
1	.98 (25.0)	.31 (7.92)
2	1.59 (40.5)	.35 (9.0)
3	2.01 (51.1)	.67 (17.0)
4	1.04 (26.3)	.28 (7.2)
5	.89 (22.6)	.29 (7.3)
6	.93 (23.5)	.29 (7.4)
7	1.16 (29.5)	.22 (5.5)
8	.85 (21.7)	.26 (6.7)
9	1.56 (39.5)	.19 (5.0)
10	1.56 (39.5)	.20 (5.1)

[1] – See Fig. 19 for spring locations.

Reassembly – 1) Lay control valve body face down when installing valves. DO NOT stand valve body on edge. Lubricate valves and control valve body with ATF prior to installation. Install control valves by sliding valves into appropriate bores. DO NOT scratch or damage valve body. Wrap shaft of small screwdriver with vinyl tape and insert valves into bores using screwdriver where necessary.

2) Install 1-2 accumulator valve, then align 1-2 accumulator retainer plate with 1-2 accumulator valve from opposite side of control valve body. Install return spring and 1-2 accumulator piston. See Fig. 20. While pushing plug or return spring, install retainer plates. See RETAINER PLATE IDENTIFICATION table for retainer plate dimensions.

RETAINER PLATE IDENTIFICATION [1]

Application	Length "A" In. (mm)	Length "B" In. (mm)
Lock-Up Control, Pressure Modifier & 4-2 Sequence Valves	.24 (6.0)	1.06 (27.0)
Torque Converter Relief Valve [2]	.51 (13.0)	.67 (17.0)
1-2 Accumulator Valve	.24 (6.0)	1.52 (38.5)
All Other Valves	.24 (6.0)	.85 (21.5)

[1] – See Fig. 17 for retainer plate locations.
[2] – Type "B" retainer plate. All others are type "A". See Fig. 20.

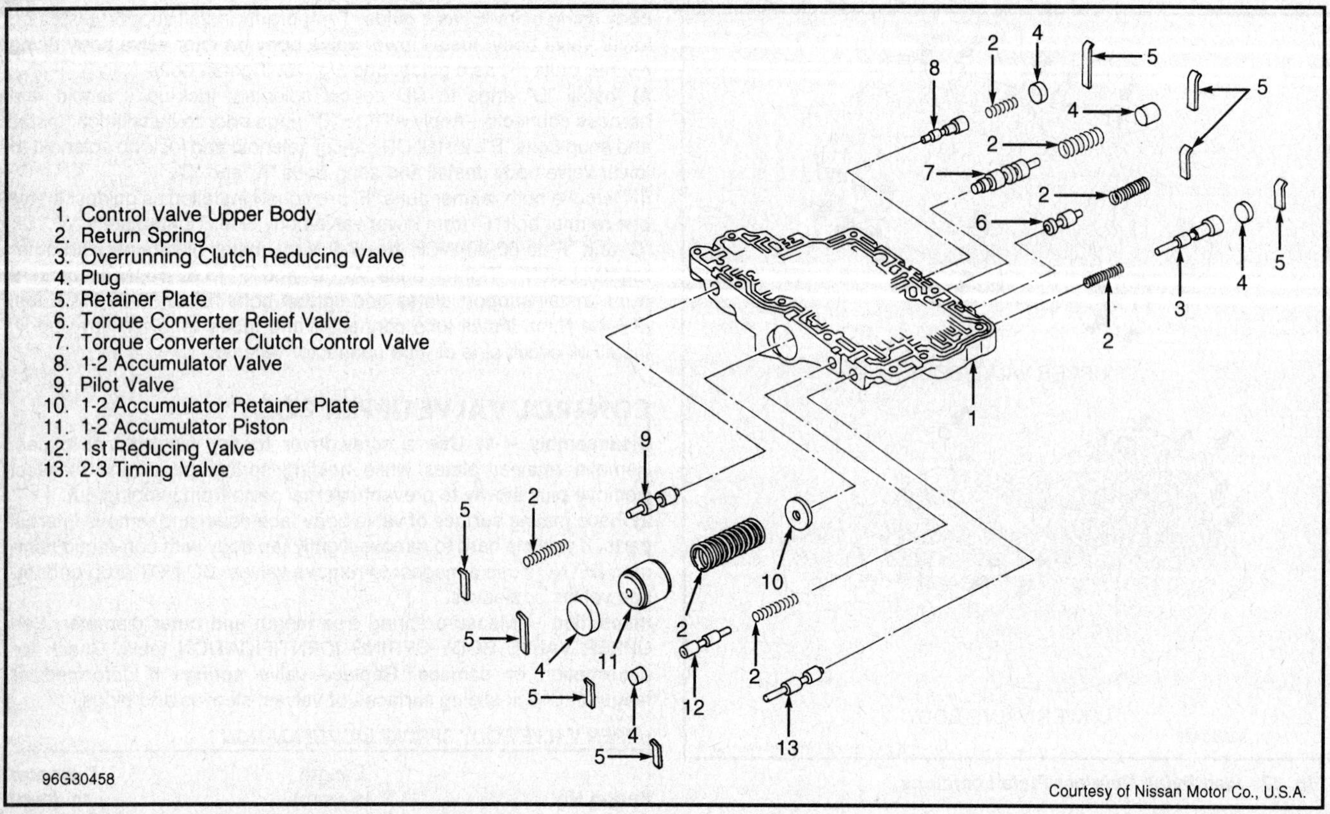

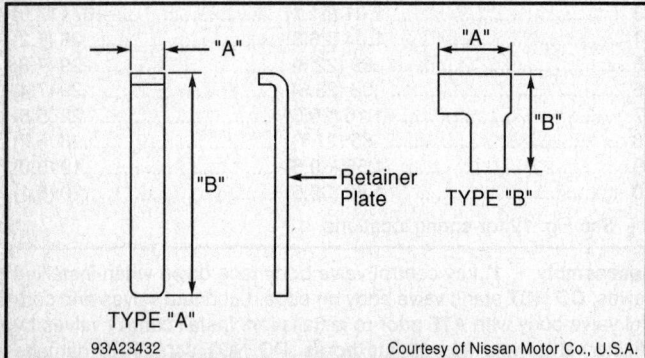

1. Control Valve Upper Body
2. Return Spring
3. Overrunning Clutch Reducing Valve
4. Plug
5. Retainer Plate
6. Torque Converter Relief Valve
7. Torque Converter Clutch Control Valve
8. 1-2 Accumulator Valve
9. Pilot Valve
10. 1-2 Accumulator Retainer Plate
11. 1-2 Accumulator Piston
12. 1st Reducing Valve
13. 2-3 Timing Valve

96G30458

Courtesy of Nissan Motor Co., U.S.A.

Fig. 19: Exploded View Of Control Valve Upper Body

93A23432   Courtesy of Nissan Motor Co., U.S.A.

Fig. 20: Measuring Retainer Plate Dimensions

CONTROL VALVE LOWER BODY

Disassembly – Use a screwdriver to pry out retainer plates. Remove retainer plates while holding spring, plugs and sleeves. Remove plug slowly to prevent internal parts from jumping out. Place mating surface of valve body face down and remove internal parts. If valve is hard to remove, lightly tap body with soft-faced hammer. DO NOT use a magnet to remove valves. DO NOT drop or damage valves or sleeves. Remove throttle valve "E" ring and throttle valve.

Inspection – Measure spring free length and outer diameter. See LOWER VALVE BODY SPRING IDENTIFICATION table. Also check for deformation or damage. Replace valve springs if deformed or fatigued. Check sliding surfaces of valves, sleeves and plugs.

LOWER VALVE BODY SPRING IDENTIFICATION [1]

Spring No.	Length In. (mm)	Diameter In. (mm)
1	1.30 (33.0)	.32 (8.1)
2	2.06 (52.24)	.59 (15.0)
3	2.05 (52.0)	.29 (7.45)
4	2.07 (52.7)	.28 (7.0)
5	1.81 (45.9)	.21 (5.3)
6	1.93 (48.9)	.28 (7.0)

[1] – See Fig. 21 for spring locations.

Reassembly – **1)** Insert throttle valve to control valve body and install "E" ring. Install pressure regulator valve after assembling sleeve plug, plug "A" and plug "B". Ensure spool plugs and retainer plates on opposite side of 3-4 and 2-3 shift valves are installed. Install 3-4 and 2-3 shift valves. See Fig. 21.

2) Lay control valve body face down when installing valves. DO NOT stand valve body on edge. Lubricate valves and control valve body with ATF prior to installation. Install control valves by sliding valves into appropriate bores. DO NOT scratch or damage valve body.

3) Wrap shaft of small screwdriver with vinyl tape and insert valves into bores using screwdriver where necessary. While pushing plug or return spring, install retainer plates. See RETAINER PLATE IDENTIFICATION table for retainer plate dimensions.

RETAINER PLATE IDENTIFICATION [1]

Application	Length "A" In. (mm)	Length "B" In. (mm)
Throttle & Detent Valves [2]	.24 (6.0)	.28 (7.2)
All Other Valves	.24 (6.0)	1.06 (27.0)

[1] – See Fig. 21 for retainer plate locations.
[2] – Type "B" retainer plate. All others are type "A". See Fig. 20.

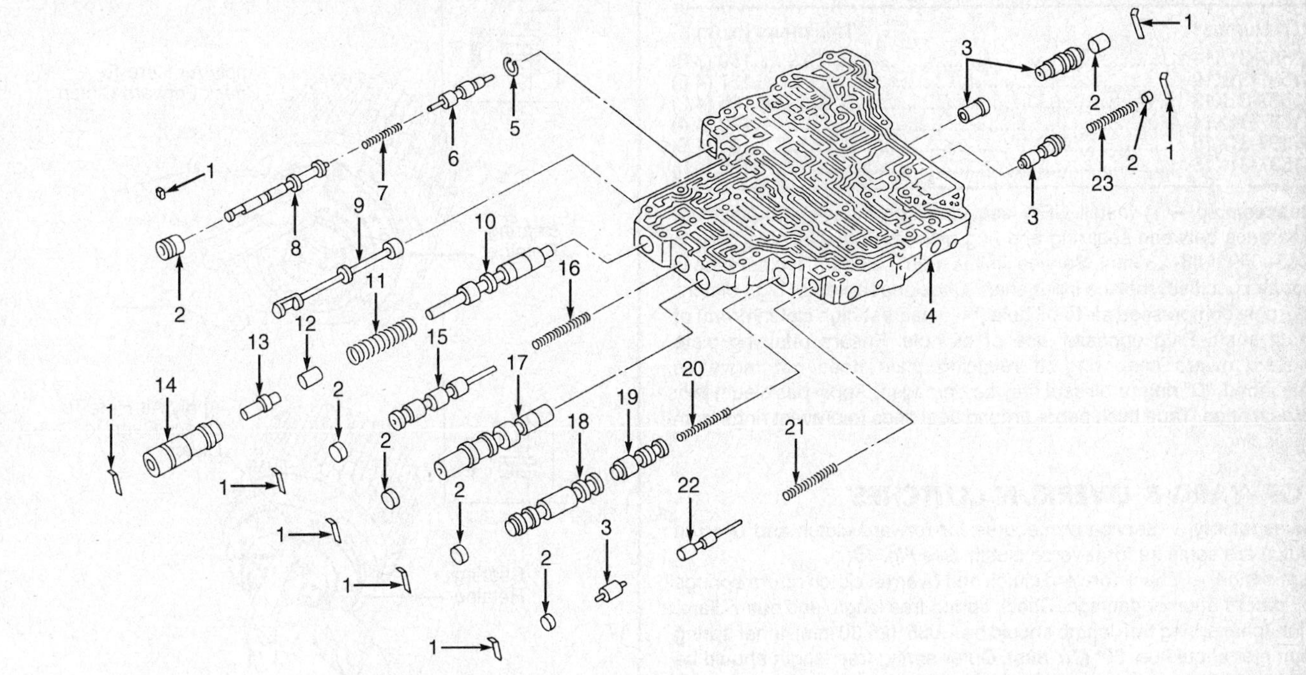

1. Retainer Plate
2. Plug
3. Spool Plug
4. Lower Body
5. "E" Ring
6. Throttle Valve
7. Return Spring No. 1
8. Detent Valve
9. Manual Valve
10. Pressure Regulator Valve
11. Return Spring No. 2
12. Plug "B"
13. Plug "A"
14. Sleeve Plug
15. 3-4 Shift Valve
16. Return Spring No. 3
17. 2-3 Shift Valve
18. 1-2 Shift Valve "B"
19. 1-2 Shift Valve "A"
20. Return Spring No. 5
21. Return Spring No. 6
22. Overrun Clutch Control Valve
23. Return Spring No. 4

96F30457

Courtesy of Nissan Motor Co., U.S.A.

Fig. 21: Exploded View Of Control Valve Lower Body

REVERSE CLUTCH

Disassembly – Remove snap ring from reverse clutch assembly. Remove drive plates, driven plates, retaining plate, and dish plates. *See Fig. 10.* Record number of plates for reassembly reference. Remove snap ring from clutch drum while compressing springs. Remove spring retainer and return springs. DO NOT remove return springs from spring retainer. Remove piston from clutch drum by turning piston clockwise. Remove "D" ring and oil seal from piston.

Inspection – Check dish plate and return springs for deformation, fatigue or damage. Always replace spring retainer and return springs as a set (if necessary). Inspect drive plate facing for burns, cracks or damage. Dish plate thickness should be .110" (2.80 mm). Drive plate thickness should be .079" (2.00 mm). Service limit is .071" (1.80 mm). If drive plate is not as specified, replace drive plate. Ensure check balls in reverse clutch piston are not seized.

Reassembly – **1)** Prior to installation, apply ATF to "D" ring, oil seal and inner surface of drum. Install "D" ring and oil seal on piston. Install piston assembly in drum while slowly turning clockwise. Install return springs and spring retainer on piston. Compress springs and install snap ring. Install dish plate, drive plates, driven plates, retaining plate and snap ring. DO NOT align projections of dish plates.

2) Measure clearance between retaining plate and snap ring. Specified clearance is .020-.031" (.50-.80 mm). Service limit is .047" (1.20 mm). Retaining plate is available in .008" (.20 mm) increments. See REVERSE CLUTCH RETAINING PLATE THICKNESS table.

REVERSE CLUTCH RETAINING PLATE THICKNESS

Part Number	Thickness In. (mm)
31537-31X00	.173 (4.4)
31537-31X01	.181 (4.6)
31537-31X02	.189 (4.8)
31537-31X03	.197 (5.0)
31537-31X04	.205 (5.2)

3) Check reverse clutch operation. Install seal ring onto drum support of oil pump cover. Install reverse clutch assembly. Apply compressed air to oil hole. *See Fig. 22.* Ensure retaining plates move toward snap ring. If retaining plate does not move as described, "D" ring or oil seal may be damaged.

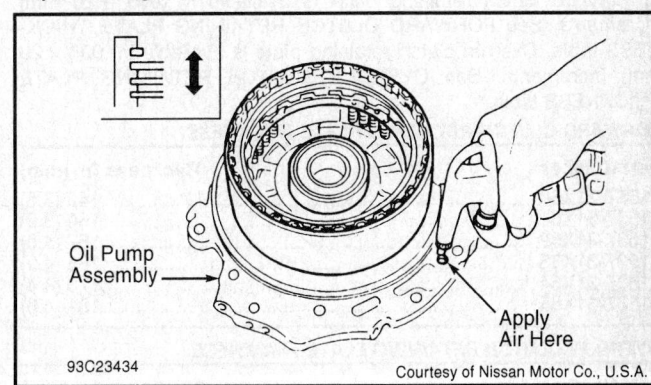

Oil Pump Assembly

Apply Air Here

93C23434

Courtesy of Nissan Motor Co., U.S.A.

Fig. 22: Checking Reverse Clutch Operation

HIGH CLUTCH

Disassembly & Inspection – **1)** Remove seal rings from input shaft. Service procedures for high clutch are same as for reverse clutch. Drive plate thickness should be .079" (2.00 mm). Service limit is .071" (1.80 mm).

2) Measure clearance between retaining plate and snap ring. Specified clearance is .055-.071" (1.40-1.80 mm). Service limit is .094" (2.40 mm). Retaining plate is available in .008" (.20 mm) increments. See HIGH CLUTCH RETAINING PLATE THICKNESS table. Ensure check balls in high clutch piston are not seized.

HIGH CLUTCH RETAINING PLATE THICKNESS

Part Number	Thickness In. (mm)
31537-31X11	.150 (3.8)
31537-31X12	.157 (4.0)
31537-31X13	.165 (4.2)
31537-31X14	.173 (4.4)
31537-31X15	.181 (4.6)
31537-31X16	.189 (4.8)

Reassembly – 1) Install NEW seal rings on input shaft. Measure clearance between seal ring and ring groove. Specified clearance is .003-.009" (.08-.23 mm). Service limit is .009" (.23 mm). If clearance is not as specified, replace input shaft. Check operation of high clutch.
2) Apply compressed air to oil hole (hole nearest high clutch drum) of input shaft. Plug opposite side of oil hole. Ensure retaining plate moves toward snap ring. If retaining plate does not move as described, "D" ring or oil seal may be damaged. Apply petroleum jelly to seal rings. Tape thick paper around seal rings to prevent rings from spreading.

FORWARD & OVERRUN CLUTCHES
Disassembly – Service procedures for forward clutch and overrun clutch are same as for reverse clutch. See Fig. 10.
Inspection – Check forward clutch and overrun clutch return springs for deformation or damage. Check spring free length and outer diameter. Inner spring free length should be 1.035" (26.30 mm). Inner spring diameter should be .30" (7.7 mm). Outer spring free length should be 1.047" (26.60 mm). Outer spring diameter should be .417" (10.60 mm). Inspect drive plate facing for burns, cracks or damage. Ensure check balls in forward clutch and overrun clutch pistons are not seized.
Reassembly – 1) Reassembly procedures for forward and overrun clutches are same as for reverse clutch. Dish plate thickness for forward clutch should be .098" (2.50 mm). Dish plate thickness for overrun clutch should be .085" (2.15 mm). Drive plate thickness for forward clutch should be .071" (.1.80 mm). Service limit is .063" (1.60 mm). Drive plate thickness for overrun clutch should be .063" (1.60 mm). Service limit is .055" (1.40 mm).
2) Measure clearance between retaining plate and snap ring. Specified clearance for forward clutch is .018-.034" (.45-.85 mm). Service limit is .073" (1.85 mm). Specified clearance for overrun clutch is .039-.055" (1.00-1.40 mm). Service limit is .079" (2.00 mm).
3) Forward clutch retaining plate is available in .008" (.20 mm) increments. See FORWARD CLUTCH RETAINING PLATE THICKNESS table. Overrun clutch retaining plate is available in .008" (.20 mm) increments. See OVERRUN CLUTCH RETAINING PLATE THICKNESS table.

FORWARD CLUTCH RETAINING PLATE THICKNESS

Part Number	Thickness In. (mm)
31537-31X60	.142 (3.6)
31537-31X61	.150 (3.8)
31537-31X62	.157 (4.0)
31537-31X63	.165 (4.2)
31537-31X64	.173 (4.4)
31537-31X65	.181 (4.6)

OVERRUN CLUTCH RETAINING PLATE THICKNESS

Part Number	Thickness In. (mm)
31567-31X71	.142 (3.6)
31567-31X72	.150 (3.8)
31567-31X73	.157 (4.0)
31567-31X74	.165 (4.2)
31567-31X75	.173 (4.4)

4) Check forward and overrun clutch operation. Install bearing retainer on forward clutch drum. Apply compressed air to appropriate oil hole of forward clutch drum. See Fig. 23. Ensure retaining plate moves toward snap ring. If retaining plate does not move as described, "D" ring or oil seal may be damaged.

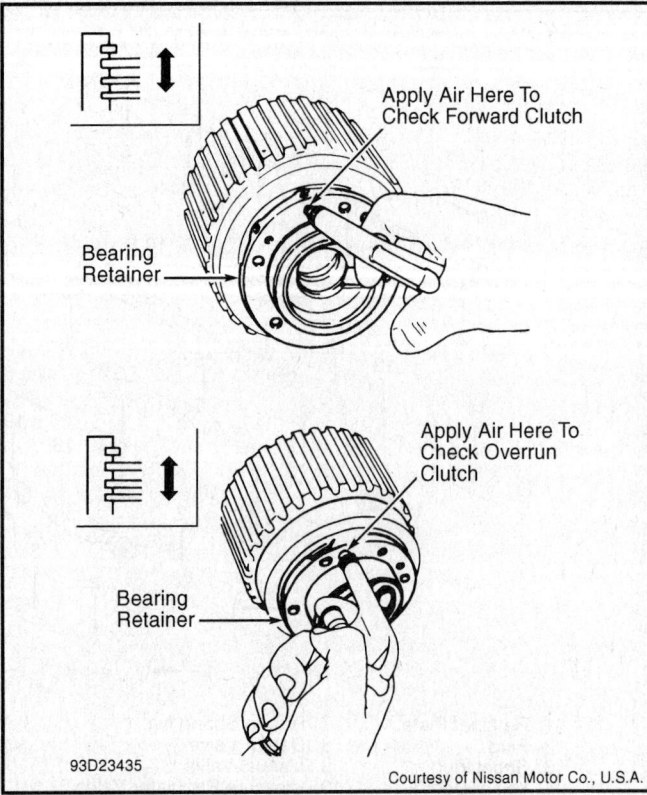

93D23435

Courtesy of Nissan Motor Co., U.S.A.

Fig. 23: Checking Forward & Overrun Clutch Operation

LOW- REVERSE BRAKE
Disassembly – Position transaxle case to obtain access to low-reverse brake snap ring. Remove snap ring. Remove drive plates, driven plates and retaining plate from transaxle case. See Fig. 10. Record number of plates for reassembly reference. Compress return springs and remove snap ring. Remove spring retainer and return springs from transaxle case. DO NOT remove return springs from spring retainer. Apply compressed air to oil hole in transaxle case and remove piston. See Fig. 24. Remove "D" ring and oil seal from piston.
Inspection – Check low-reverse brake snap ring, springs and retainer for deformation or damage. Always replace spring retainer and return springs as a set (if necessary). Check low and reverse drive plates for burns, cracks or damage.
Reassembly – 1) Reassembly procedures for low-reverse brake are same as for reverse clutch. Drive plate thickness should be .079" (2.00 mm). Service limit is .071" (1.8 mm). Specified clearance is .055-.071" (1.40 mm) service limit is .110" (2.80 mm). Retaining plate is available in increments of .008" (.20 mm). See LOW-REVERSE BRAKE RETAINING PLATE THICKNESS table.

LOW-REVERSE BRAKE RETAINING PLATE THICKNESS

Part Number	Thickness In. (mm)
31667-31X16	.142 (3.6)
31667-31X17	.150 (3.8)
31667-31X18	.157 (4.0)
31667-31X19	.165 (4.2)
31667-31X20	.173 (4.4)
31667-31X21	.181 (4.6)

2) Check low-reverse brake operation. Apply compressed air to oil hole in transaxle case. See Fig. 25. Ensure retaining plate moves toward snap ring. If retaining plate does not move, "D" ring or oil seal may be damaged.

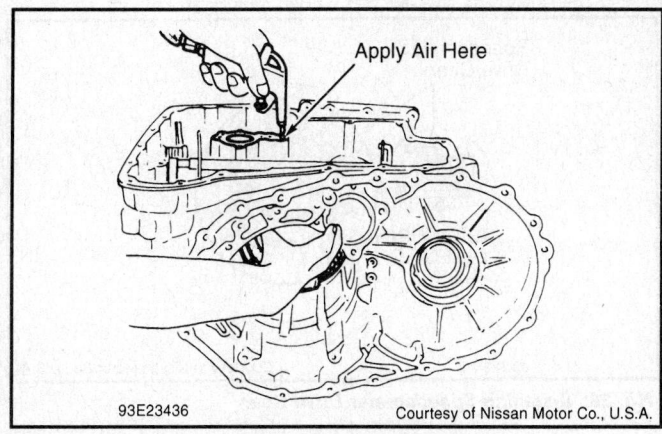

Fig. 24: *Removing Low-Reverse Brake Piston*

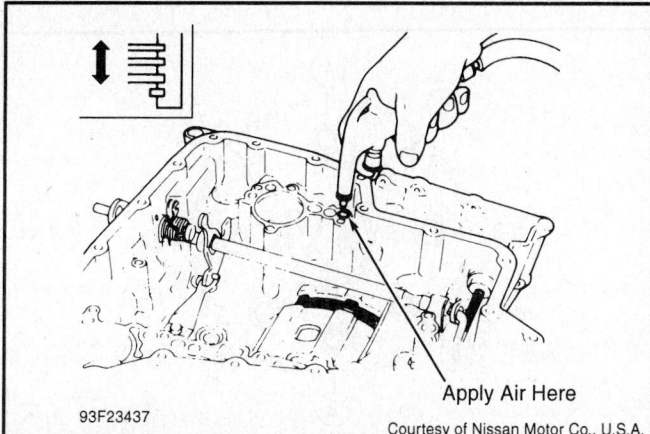

Fig. 25: *Checking Low & Reverse Operation*

REAR INTERNAL GEAR, FORWARD CLUTCH HUB & OVERRUN CLUTCH HUB

Disassembly – Remove snap ring from overrun clutch hub. Remove overrun clutch hub from forward clutch hub. *See Fig. 10.* Remove thrust washer from forward clutch hub. Remove forward clutch hub from rear internal gear. Remove end bearing from rear internal gear. Remove thrust washer from rear internal gear. Remove end bearing from forward one-way clutch. Remove one-way clutch from forward clutch hub.

Inspection – Check frictional surfaces for wear or damage. Check forward one-way clutch, end bearing and snap ring for wear or damage.

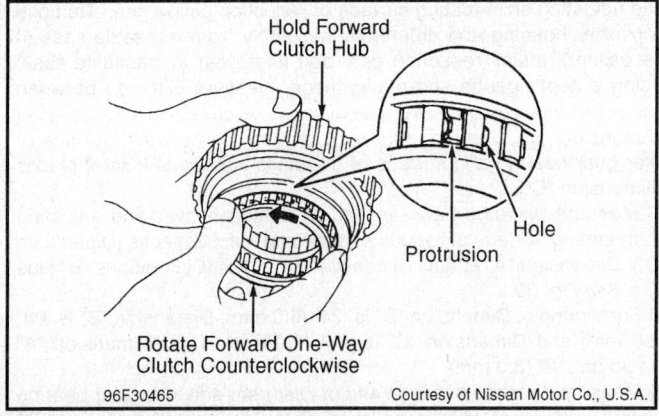

Fig. 26: *Checking Forward One-Way Clutch Rotation*

Reassembly – 1) Install forward one-way clutch on forward clutch hub with arrow facing forward. *See Fig. 26.* Apply petroleum jelly to end bearings and thrust washers. Install end bearing on forward one-way clutch.

2) Install thrust washer on rear internal gear. Align pawls of thrust washer with holes in rear internal gear. Install end bearing on rear internal gear. Install forward clutch hub on rear internal gear. Ensure forward clutch hub rotates counterclockwise only.

3) Install thrust washer on overrun clutch hub. Align pawls of thrust washer with holes in overrun clutch hub. Install overrun clutch hub on rear internal gear. Align projections of rear internal gear with holes in overrun clutch hub. Install snap ring to rear internal gear.

BAND SERVO PISTON ASSEMBLY

Disassembly – 1) Use appropriate puller to compress servo piston. Remove band servo piston snap ring. Apply compressed air to oil hole in transaxle case to remove OD servo piston retainer and band servo piston assembly. *See Fig. 27.*

2) Apply compressed air to oil hole in servo piston retainer to remove OD band servo piston from retainer. Secure OD band servo piston while applying compressed air. Remove "D" ring from OD band servo piston. Remove "O" rings from OD servo piston retainer. *See Fig. 7.*

3) Remove band servo piston assembly from servo piston retainer by pushing forward. Place piston stem end on wooden block. While pushing servo piston spring retainer down, remove "E" ring. Remove OD servo retainer spring, band servo thrust washer and band servo piston stem from band servo piston. Note direction of "O" rings and "D" rings. Remove "O" rings from servo piston retainer. Remove "D" rings from band servo piston.

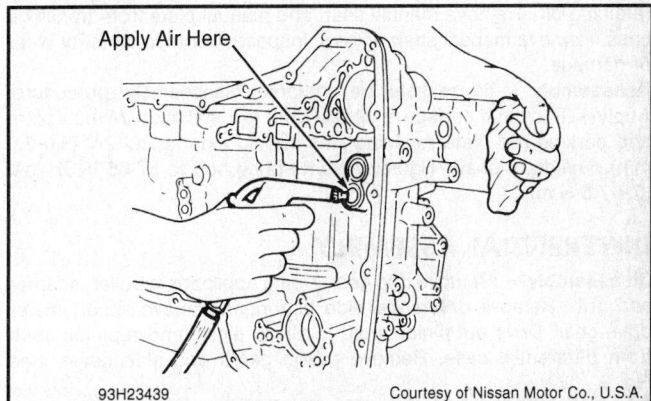

Fig. 27: *Removing OD Piston Retainer & Band Servo Piston*

Inspection – Check frictional surfaces for abnormal wear or damage. Check return springs for deformation or damage. Check spring free length and outer diameter. Free length of 2nd servo return spring should be 1.28" (32.5 mm), diameter should be 1.020" (25.90 mm). Free length of OD servo return spring should be 1.220" (31.00 mm), diameter should be .854" (21.70 mm). Replace spring(s) if not as specified.

Reassembly – 1) Apply ATF to all "D" rings and "O" rings prior to installation. Install "D" rings on servo piston retainer. Install band servo piston stem, band servo thrust washer, OD servo return spring and spring retainer on band servo piston. Place piston stem on wooden block. While pushing servo piston spring retainer down, install "E" ring.

2) Install "O" rings on servo piston retainer. Install band servo piston assembly into servo piston retainer by pushing inward. Install "D" ring on OD band servo piston. Install "O" rings on OD servo piston retainer.

3) Install OD band servo piston to OD servo piston retainer. Install band servo piston assembly and 2nd servo return spring in transaxle case. Install OD band servo piston assembly to transaxle case. Install band servo piston snap ring on transaxle case. *See Fig. 7.*

OUTPUT SHAFT & GEAR, IDLER GEAR, REDUCTION GEAR & BEARING RETAINER

Disassembly – 1) Remove seal rings from output shaft and bearing retainer. *See Fig. 7.* Using appropriate press and adapter, press off output shaft bearing. Using appropriate puller, remove output shaft bearing race from bearing retainer. Using appropriate puller and drift, remove output gear bearing.

2) Using appropriate puller and drift, remove idler gear bearing from idler gear. Using appropriate puller, remove idler gear bearing race from transaxle case. Using press and adapter, press reduction gear bearing from reduction gear. Remove 4 bolts and remove reduction gear bearing race from transaxle case. See Fig. 7.

Inspection – 1) Inspect output shaft for cracks, wear or damage. Check all gears for wear, chips and cracks. Ensure bearings roll freely and are free from noise, cracks, pitting or wear.

2) Install NEW seal rings to output shaft and bearing retainer. Measure clearance between seal ring and ring grooves of output shaft and bearing retainer. Specified clearance is .004-.010" (.10-.25 mm). Service limit is .010" (.25 mm). If clearance is not as specified, replace output shaft or bearing retainer as necessary.

Reassembly – To reassemble, reverse disassembly procedure. Tighten reduction gear bearing race bolts to 46-49 ft. lbs. (63-67 N.m). Apply petroleum jelly to NEW seal rings and install seal rings on output shaft and bearing retainer. Tape thick paper around seal rings to prevent rings from spreading.

MANUAL SHAFT & THROTTLE LEVER

Disassembly – 1) Remove detent spring from transaxle case. Pull out throttle shaft retaining pin, then remove throttle shaft from transaxle case. Drive out manual plate retaining pin. Drive and pull out parking rod plate retaining pin. Remove parking rod plate from manual shaft. See Fig. 7.

2) Remove parking rod from transaxle case. Pull out manual shaft retaining pin. Remove manual shaft and manual plate from transaxle case. Remove manual shaft oil seal. Inspect all components for wear or damage.

Reassembly – To reassemble, reverse disassembly procedure. Apply ATF to outer surface of oil seal prior to installation. Manual plate and parking rod plate retaining pins should extend .20-.24" (5.0-6.0 mm) outside of shaft. Tighten detent spring bolt to 57-66 INCH lbs. (6.4-7.5 N.m).

DIFFERENTIAL ASSEMBLY

Disassembly – Remove ring gear. Using appropriate puller, adapter and drift. Remove differential side bearings. Remove speedometer drive gear. Drive out pinion shaft retaining pin. Remove pinion shaft from differential case. Remove pinion gears and side gears. See Fig. 9.

Inspection – Check mating surfaces of differential case, side gears and pinion gears for wear, scoring or damage. Check washers for wear or damage. Ensure bearings roll freely and are free from cracks, pitting or wear.

Reassembly – 1) Install side gears and thrust washers in differential case. Install pinion gears and thrust washers in case by rotating gears. Apply ATF to all components. Position 2 feeler gauges of same thickness on opposite sides of differential case. Measure clearance between side gear thrust washers and differential case.

2) Specified clearance should be .004-.008" (0.10-0.20 mm). If clearance is not as specified, adjust clearance by changing thickness of side gear thrust washers. Washers are available in increments of .002" (.05 mm). See SIDE GEAR THRUST WASHER THICKNESS table.

SIDE GEAR THRUST WASHER THICKNESS

Part Number	Thickness In. (mm)
38424-D2111	.030-.032 (.75-.80)
38424-D2112	.032-.034 (.80-.85)
38424-D2113	.034-.035 (.85-.90)
38424-D2114	.035-.037 (.90-95.)
38424-D2114	.037-.039 (.95-1.00)

3) Install retaining pin. Ensure retaining pin is flush with case. Install speedometer drive gear in differential case. Align projections of speedometer drive gear with groove in differential case. See Fig. 28.

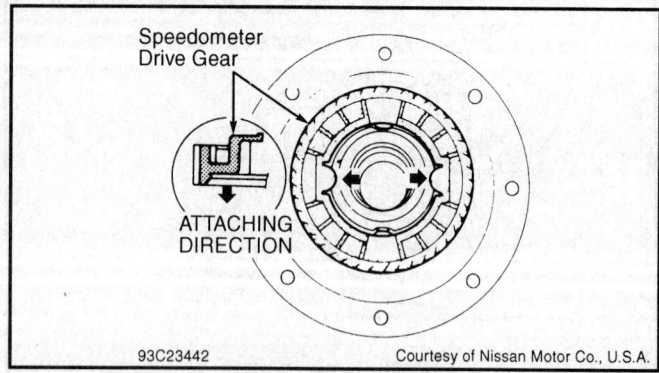

Fig. 28: Installing Speedometer Drive Gear

4) Press differential side bearings on differential case. Install ring gear and tighten bolts in numerical order. See Fig. 29. Tighten bolts to 54-65 ft. lbs. (74-88 N.m).

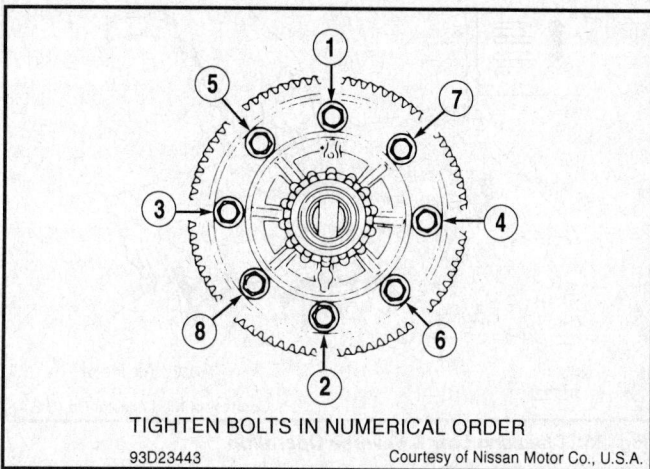

TIGHTEN BOLTS IN NUMERICAL ORDER

Fig. 29: Tightening Ring Gear Bolts

TRANSAXLE ADJUSTMENTS

NOTE: Transaxle adjustments are performed as part of transaxle assembly procedure. See TRANSAXLE REASSEMBLY.

REDUCTION GEAR BEARING PRELOAD

1) Preload is adjusted by adjusting shim thickness. To determine shim thickness, use the following equation:

$$A = D - (B + C)$$

"A" is the distance between surface of idler gear bearing inner race and adjusting shim mating surface of reduction pinion gear. Remove converter housing and differential assembly from transaxle case (if necessary). Install reduction gear and idler gear in transaxle case. Using a depth gauge and straightedge, measure distance between end of reduction gear and surface of transaxle case in at least 2 places (Dimension "B"). See Fig. 30. Measure distance between surface of idler gear bearing and surface of transaxle case in at least 2 places (Dimension "C").

2) Measure distance between end of reduction gear and adjusting shim mating surface of reduction gear in at least 2 places (Dimension "D"). Dimension "A" equals Dimension "D" minus (Dimensions "B" plus "C"). See Fig. 30.

3) For example, Dimension "D" is .24" (6.0 mm). Dimension "B" is .08" (2.0 mm) and Dimension "C" is .04" (1.0 mm). Total Dimension "A" would be .12" (3.0 mm).

4) Measure distance between end of idler gear and idler gear bearing mating surface of idler gear in at least 2 places (Dimension "E"). Reduction gear bearing preload should be .002" (.05 mm).

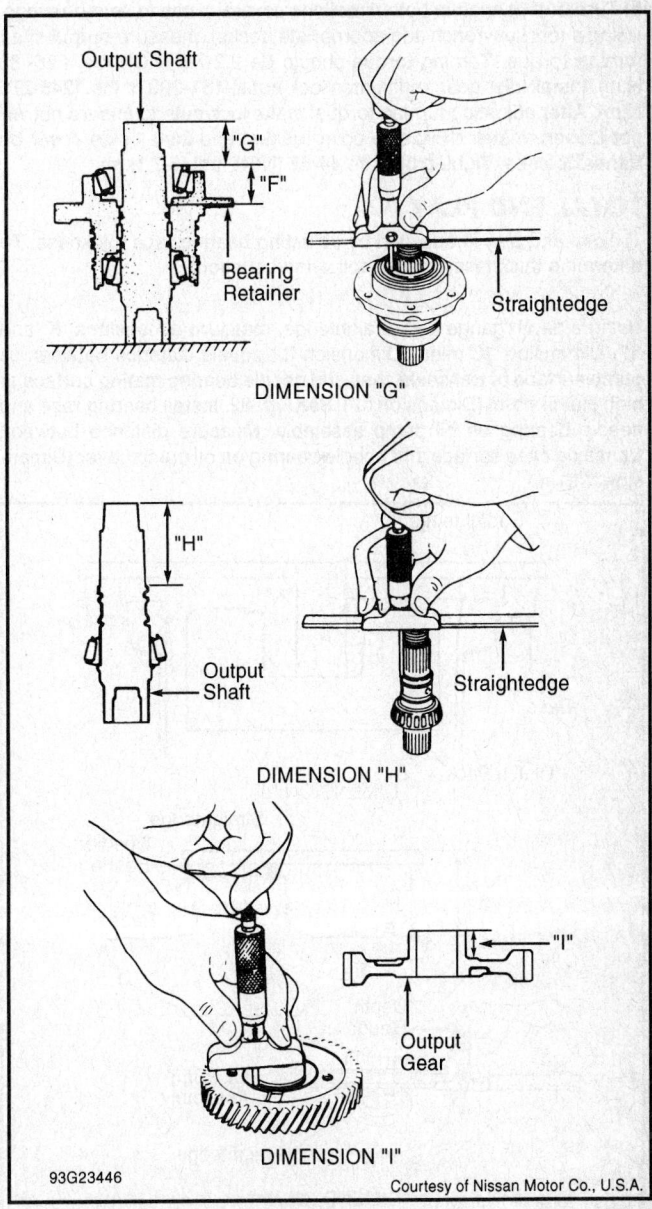

Shims are available in thicknesses of .069-.105" (1.74-2.66 mm), in increments of .002" (.04 mm). If dimension "T" is .070-.071" (1.77-1.81 mm), required shim thickness is .069" (1.74 mm). For each .002" (.04 mm) dimension increase, shim thickness will increase same amount.

6) Install selected adjusting shim. Press idler gear bearing on idler gear. Press idler gear on reduction gear. Ensure idler gear locks on parking pawl. Lock idler gear with parking pawl and tighten idler gear lock nut to 181-203 ft. lbs. (245-275 N.m).

7) Turn reduction gear in both directions several times to seat bearings. Using a torque wrench and appropriate socket, measure reduction gear turning torque. Turning torque should be .95-6.10 INCH lbs. (.11-.69 N.m). After adjusting turning torque, stake lock nut to ensure nut will not loosen.

OUTPUT SHAFT BEARING PRELOAD

1) Output shaft bearing preload is adjusted by adjusting thickness of output shaft adjusting spacer ("F"). Remove paper from output shaft. Install bearing retainer on output shaft. To determine dimension "F", output shaft bearing adjusting spacer thickness, use the following equation:

$$F = H - G$$

DIMENSION "G"

DIMENSION "H"

DIMENSION "I"

93G23446   Courtesy of Nissan Motor Co., U.S.A.

Fig. 31: Measuring Output Shaft Bearing Preload

DIMENSION "B"

DIMENSION "C"

DIMENSION "D"

DIMENSION "E"

EXAMPLE
Dimension "B" = .08" (2.0 mm)
PLUS +
Dimension "C" = .04" (1.0 mm)
EQUALS = .12" (3.0 mm)

Dimension "D" = .24" (6.0 mm)
MINUS -
Dimensions "B" + "C" .12" (3.0 mm)
EQUALS =
Dimension "A" .12" (3.0 mm)

Dimension "A" .12" (3.0 mm)
MINUS -
Dimension "E"
EQUALS =
Thickness Of Thrust Shim

95G19691   Courtesy of Nissan Motor Co., U.S.A.

Fig. 30: Measuring Reduction Gear Bearing Preload

5) Select proper thickness ("T") of reduction gear bearing adjusting shim by using the following equation:

$$T = A - E$$

Install output gear bearing in bearing retainer. Using a depth gauge and straightedge, measure distance between end of output shaft and surface of output gear bearing in at least 2 places (Dimension "G"). Measure distance between end of output shaft and adjusting spacer mating surface of output shaft (Dimension "H"). See Fig. 31.

2) Measure distance between end of output gear (adjusting spacer mating surface), and bearing surface (Dimension "I"). Dimension "F" minus Dimension "I" equals output shaft bearing preload. See Fig. 31. Output shaft bearing preload should be .001-.003" (0.03-0.08 mm). Select proper thickness of output shaft adjusting spacer.

3) Spacers are available in thicknesses of .247-.284" (6.26-7.22 mm), in increments of .002" (.04 mm). If total dimension is .247-.249" (6.29-6.33 mm), required shim thickness is 0.246" (6.26 mm). For each .002" (.04 mm) dimension increase, shim thickness will increase same amount.

4) Install bearing retainer on transaxle case. Tighten retainer bolts to 12-15 ft. lbs. (16-21 N.m). Install output shaft on bearing retainer. Install selected output shaft bearing adjusting spacer on output shaft. Press output gear bearing on output gear. Press output gear on output shaft. Tighten output gear lock nut to 181-203 ft. lbs. (245-275 N.m). Remove idler gear to measure output shaft preload.

5) Turn output shaft in both directions several times to seat bearings. Using a torque wrench and appropriate socket, measure output shaft turning torque. Turning torque should be 2.2-7.8 INCH lbs. (.25-.88 N.m). Install idler gear and tighten lock nut to 181-203 ft. lbs. (245-275 N.m). After adjusting turning torque, stake lock nuts to ensure nut will not loosen. Install NEW side cover gasket and install side cover on transaxle case. Tighten bolts to 44-62 INCH lbs. (5-7 N.m).

TOTAL END PLAY

1) Total end play is adjusted by adjusting bearing race thickness. To determine thickness, use the following equation:

$$J = K - L$$

Using a depth gauge and straightedge, measure dimensions "K" and "L". Dimension "K" minus Dimension "L" equals distance between oil pump surface of transaxle case and needle bearing mating surface of high clutch drum (Dimension "J"). See Fig. 32. Install bearing race and needle bearing on oil pump assembly. Measure distance between transaxle case surface and needle bearing on oil pump cover (Dimension "M").

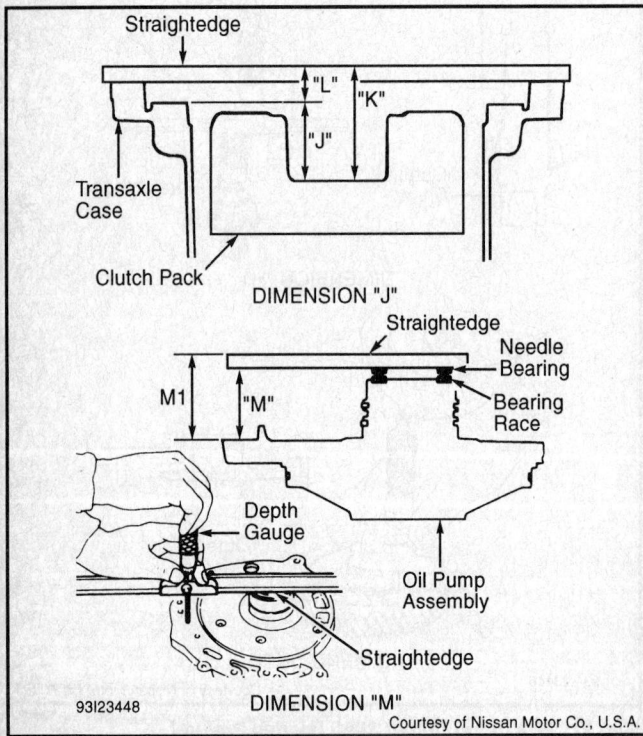

DIMENSION "J"

DIMENSION "M"

93I23448

Courtesy of Nissan Motor Co., U.S.A.

Fig. 32: Measuring Total End Play

2) Dimension "M1" minus straightedge thickness equals Distance "M". Dimension "J" minus Dimension "M" equals total end play. See Fig. 31. Total end play should be .010-.022" (.25-.55 mm). Bearing races are available in increments of .015" (.40 mm). See END PLAY BEARING RACE THICKNESS table. Select proper thickness of bearing race to ensure total end play is as specified.

END PLAY BEARING RACE THICKNESS

Part Number	Thickness In. (mm)
31435-31X01	.024 (.6)
31435-31X02	.031 (.8)
31435-31X03	.039 (1.0)
31435-31X04	.047 (1.2)
31435-31X05	.055 (1.4)
31435-31X06	.063 (1.6)
31435-31X07	.071 (1.8)
31435-31X08	.079 (2.0)

REVERSE CLUTCH END PLAY

1) Reverse clutch end play is adjusted by adjusting thrust washer thickness. To determine thrust washer thickness, use the following equation:

$$N = O - P$$

Place thrust washer on reverse clutch drum. Using a depth gauge and straightedge, measure distance between thrust washer and straightedge (Dimension "O"). Measure distance between oil pump mating surface on transaxle case and straightedge (Dimension "P"). See Fig. 33. Dimension "O" minus Dimension "P" equals distance between oil pump surface of transaxle case and thrust washer on reverse clutch drum (Dimension "N").

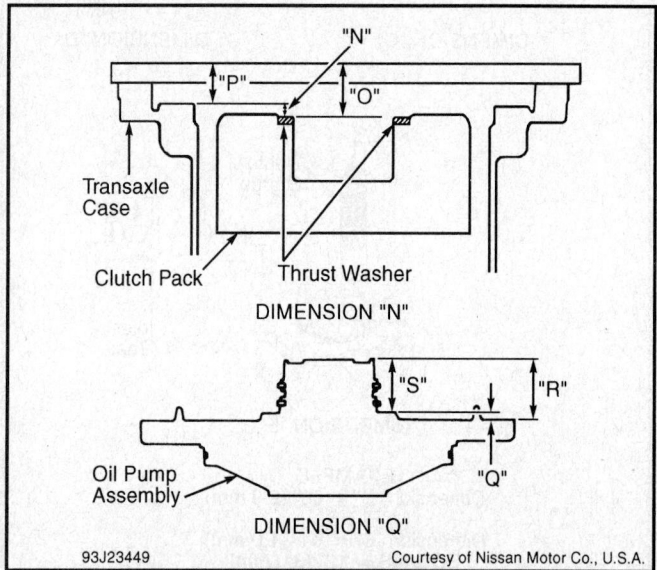

DIMENSION "N"

DIMENSION "Q"

93J23449

Courtesy of Nissan Motor Co., U.S.A.

Fig. 33: Measuring Reverse Clutch End Play

2) Measure distance between oil pump surface and straightedge (Dimension "R"). See Fig. 33. Measure distance between thrust washer mating surface and straightedge (Dimension "S") using the following equation:

$$Q = R - S$$

Dimension "R" minus Dimension "S" is distance between transaxle case surface and thrust washer mating surface (Dimension "Q").

3) Dimension "N" minus Dimension "Q" equals total reverse clutch end play. Reverse clutch end play should be .026-.039" (.65-1.00 mm). Thrust washers are available in increments of .006" (.15 mm). See REVERSE CLUTCH END PLAY THRUST WASHER THICKNESS table. Select proper thickness thrust washer to ensure reverse clutch end play is as specified.

REVERSE CLUTCH END PLAY THRUST WASHER THICKNESS

Part Number	Thickness In. (mm)
31508-31X00	.026 (.65)
31508-31X01	.031 (.80)
31508-31X02	.037 (.95)
31508-31X03	.043 (1.1)
31508-31X04	.049 (1.4)
31435-31X05	.055 (1.4)

DIFFERENTIAL ASSEMBLY END PLAY

1) Differential assembly end play is adjusted by adjusting differential side bearing shim thickness. To determine thickness of differential side bearing shim, use the following equation:

$$T - U + V$$

Using a depth gauge and straightedge, measure distance between side bearing surface of transaxle case and converter housing surface of transaxle case. Measure thickness of straightedge (Dimension "T2"). See Fig. 34.

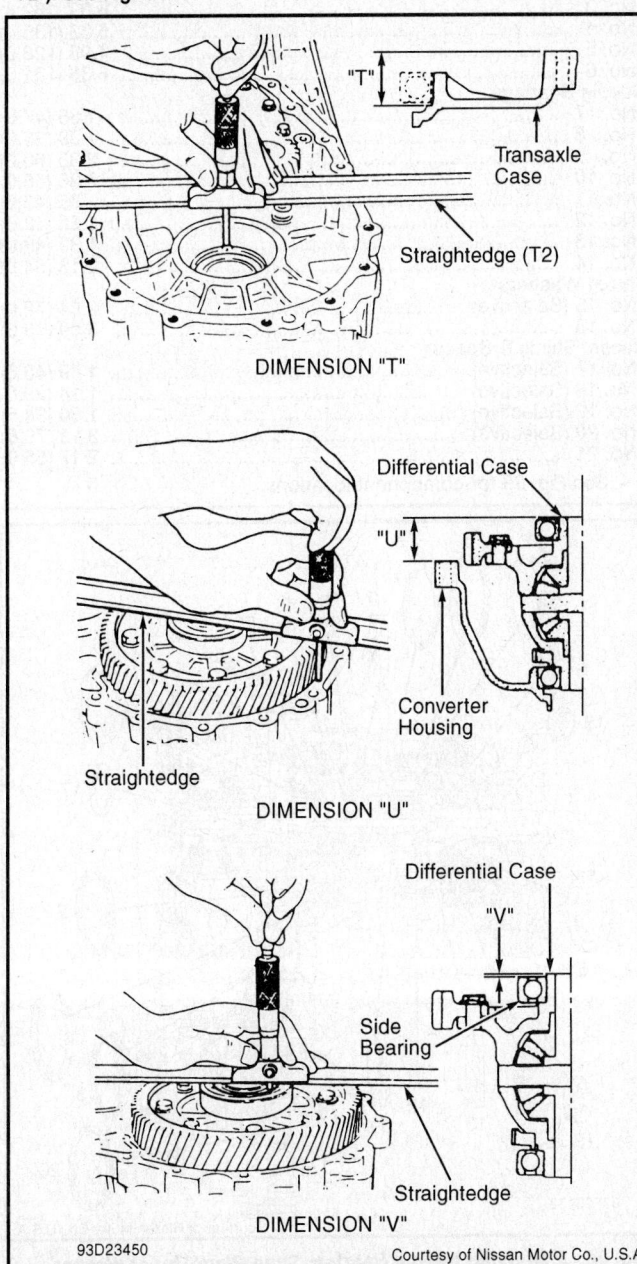

DIMENSION "T"

DIMENSION "U"

DIMENSION "V"

93D23450   Courtesy of Nissan Motor Co., U.S.A.

Fig. 34: Measuring Differential Assembly End Play

2) Depth gauge measurement minus thickness of straightedge equals total distance between side bearing surface of transaxle case and converter housing surface of transaxle case (Dimension "T"). Place differential assembly on converter housing. Measure distance between end of differential case and transaxle case surface of converter housing (Dimension "U"). See Fig. 34.

3) Measure distance between end of differential case and adjusting shim mating surface of differential side bearing (Dimension "V"). Dimension "T" minus Dimension "U" plus Dimension "V" equals differential assembly end play. Differential assembly end play should be 0-.006" (0-.15 mm).

4) Differential side bearing adjusting shims are available in increments of .015" (.40 mm). See DIFFERENTIAL SIDE BEARING ADJUSTING SHIM THICKNESS table. Select proper thickness differential side bearing adjustment shim to ensure differential end play is within specification.

DIFFERENTIAL SIDE BEARING ADJUSTING SHIM THICKNESS

Part Number	Thickness In. (mm)
38454-M8001	.019 (.48)
38454-M8003	.022 (.56)
38454-M8005	.025 (.64)
38454-M8007	.028 (.72)
38454-M8009	.032 (.80)
38454-M8011	.035 (.88)
38454-M8013	.038 (.96)
38454-M8015	.041 (1.04)

TRANSAXLE REASSEMBLY

NOTE: See NEEDLE BEARING, SNAP RING, THRUST WASHER & SHIM LOCATIONS table for component locations. Also see Fig. 36.

1) Install differential side oil seal in converter housing with .217-.256" (5.50-6.60 mm) of seal protruding from housing. Install differential side oil seal in transaxle case with 0.02" (0.5 mm) of seal recessed inside housing.

2) Install parking actuator support to transaxle case with beveled edge inward. Install parking pawl on transaxle case and secure with parking shaft. Install return spring. See Fig. 7. Perform Reduction Gear Bearing Preload and Output Shaft Bearing Preload adjustment procedures. See TRANSAXLE ADJUSTMENTS.

3) Remove paper from bearing retainer. Apply petroleum jelly to thrust washer, bearing race and needle bearing. Install thrust washer on bearing retainer. Ensure bearing retainer seal rings are not spread. Align teeth of low-reverse brake drive plates. Install forward clutch assembly. Install bearing race on bearing retainer. Install bearings on rear internal gear with smooth side down.

4) Hold forward clutch hub and turn overrun clutch hub. Ensure overrun clutch hub rotates counterclockwise and does not rotate clockwise. If overrun clutch hub does not operate as described, check installed direction of forward one-way clutch. Align forward clutch and overrun clutch drive plate teeth and install rear internal gear assembly. See Fig. 10.

5) Apply petroleum jelly to needle bearing and install needle bearing with smooth side down on rear planetary carrier. Install rear sun gear on rear planetary carrier with grooved side facing out. Install rear planetary carrier in transaxle case. Apply petroleum jelly to thrust needle bearing and install bearing on front planetary carrier with grooved side down.

6) Install low one-way clutch to front planetary carrier by rotating clutch counterclockwise. Ensure one-way clutch does not rotate in clockwise direction. Install front planetary carrier assembly in transaxle case. Install snap ring.

NOTE: Snap ring will not fit in groove of transaxle case if forward clutch and bearings are not installed correctly.

7) Apply petroleum jelly to thrust needle bearing and needle bearings. Install thrust needle bearing on front sun gear with flat side down.

Install front sun gear on front planetary carrier. Install needle bearing on front sun gear with smooth side down. Install high clutch hub on front sun gear. Install needle bearing on high clutch hub with smooth side up. *See Fig. 10.*

8) Remove paper from input shaft. Align teeth of high clutch drive plates and install input shaft assembly. Align teeth of reverse clutch drive plates. Apply petroleum jelly to needle bearing and install needle bearing on high clutch assembly with smooth side down.

9) Install reverse clutch assembly. Install anchor end pin, washer and lock nut on transaxle case. Place brake band on reverse clutch drum. Tighten anchor end pin enough that brake band is on reverse drum evenly.

10) Apply petroleum jelly on bearing race selected in TOTAL END PLAY adjustment procedure. See TRANSAXLE ADJUSTMENTS. Install bearing race on oil pump cover. Apply petroleum jelly on thrust washer selected in REVERSE CLUTCH END PLAY adjustment procedure. See TRANSAXLE ADJUSTMENTS. Install thrust washer on reverse clutch drum. Install oil pump assembly on transaxle case.

11) Tighten oil pump bolts to 13-15 ft. lbs. (18-21 N.m). Apply ATF to input shaft "O" ring and install "O" ring on input shaft. Adjust brake band. Tighten anchor end pin to 35-53 INCH lbs. (4-6 N.m). Back off anchor end pin 2 1/2 turns. While holding anchor end pin, tighten lock nut. Apply compressed air to oil holes in transaxle case to ensure correct brake band operation. *See Fig. 35.*

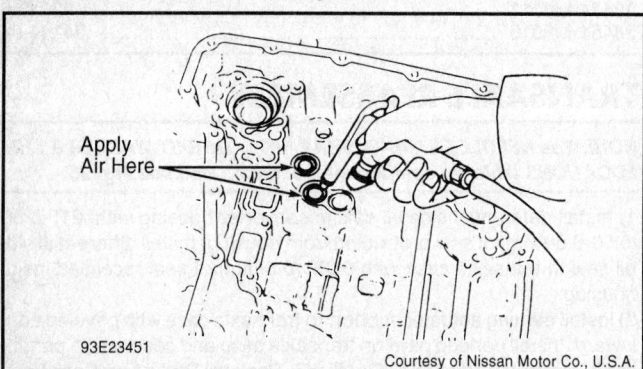

Apply Air Here

93E23451   Courtesy of Nissan Motor Co., U.S.A.

Fig. 35: Checking Brake Band Operation

12) Install differential side bearing adjusting shim selected in DIFFERENTIAL END PLAY adjustment procedure into transaxle case. See TRANSAXLE ADJUSTMENTS. Install differential assembly on transaxle case. Install oil tube on converter housing and tighten bolts to 44-62 INCH lbs. (5-7 N.m). Install "O" ring on differential oil port of transaxle case. Apply a bead of liquid gasket .060" (1.5 mm) in diameter on inside edge of converter housing mating surface. Install converter housing on transaxle case. Tighten bolts to 19-22 ft. lbs. (26-30 N.m).

13) Check contact surface of accumulator piston for damage. Apply ATF to "O" rings and install on accumulator piston. Install accumulator pistons and return springs in transaxle case. Apply petroleum jelly to lip seals for band servo oil holes and install in transaxle case. Install governor valve oil filter. Install throttle cable to transaxle case. Tighten throttle mounting bolt to 18-35 INCH lbs. (2-4 N.m). Install throttle cable to throttle lever.

14) Apply ATF to manual valve and insert valve into control valve assembly. Set manual shaft in Neutral position. Install control valve assembly on transaxle case while aligning manual valve with manual plate and detent valve with throttle lever.

15) Put solenoid harness into transaxle case and push terminal body onto transaxle case. Install clip to terminal body. Install and tighten control valve assembly bolts to 61-78 INCH lbs. (7-9 N.m). *See Fig. 5.* Attach magnet to oil pan. Install NEW oil pan gasket and install oil pan. Tighten NEW pan bolts in a crisscross pattern to 61-78 INCH lbs. (7-9 N.m). Install drain plug (if necessary) and tighten to 21-29 ft. lbs. (29-39 N.m).

NOTE: Always replace oil pan bolts. Bolts are self-sealing.

16) Install governor valve assembly into transaxle. Soak "O" ring in ATF and install on governor cap. Install governor cap on transaxle. Install spacer on governor cap. Install snap ring into transaxle case, aligning snap ring gap with notch on transaxle. Install inhibitor switch and adjust if necessary.

17) Apply ATF to NEW "O" ring and install on dipstick tube. Install dipstick tube and oil cooler tube to transaxle. Tighten dipstick tube bolt to 39-51 INCH lbs. (4.4-5.8 N.m). Tighten oil cooler tube bolts to 21-36 ft. lbs. (29-49 N.m).

18) Pour 1.1 qt. (1.0L) of ATF into torque converter and install torque converter. Measure distance "A" to ensure torque converter is installed correctly. *See Fig. 37.* Distance "A" should be 0.83" (21.1 mm).

NEEDLE BEARING, SNAP RING, THRUST WASHER & SHIM LOCATIONS [1]

Application & Number	Outer Diameter In. (mm)
Snap Rings	
No. 1	5.59 (142.0)
No. 2	4.45 (113.0)
No. 3	6.39 (162.4)
No. 4	5.33 (135.4)
No. 5	4.96 (126.0)
No. 6	6.36 (161.5)
Needle Bearings	
No. 7	1.85 (47.0)
No. 8	1.38 (35.0)
No. 9	2.36 (60.0)
No. 10	2.36 (60.0)
No. 11	1.85 (47.0)
No. 12	1.68 (42.6)
No. 13	1.89 (48.0)
No. 14	2.13 (54.0)
Thrust Washers	
No. 15 (Selective)	2.84 (72.0)
No. 16	3.09 (78.5)
Races, Shims & Spacer	
No. 17 (Selective)	1.89 (48.0)
No. 18 (Selective)	1.14 (29.0)
No. 19 (Selective)	1.36 (34.5)
No. 20 (Selective)	3.13 (79.5)
No. 21	2.17 (55.0)

[1] – See Fig. 36 for component locations.

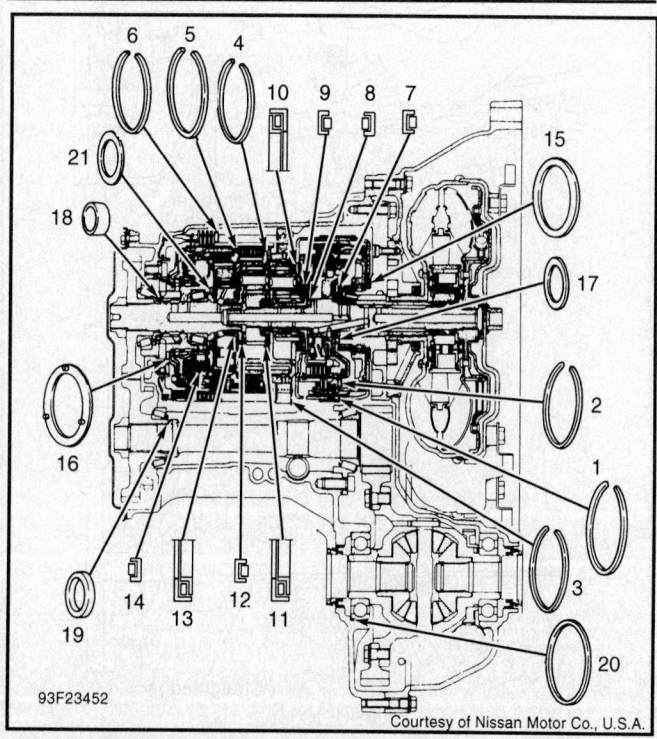

93F23452   Courtesy of Nissan Motor Co., U.S.A.

Fig. 36: Identifying Needle Bearing, Snap Ring, Thrust Washer & Selective Shim Locations (RL4F03A Shown)

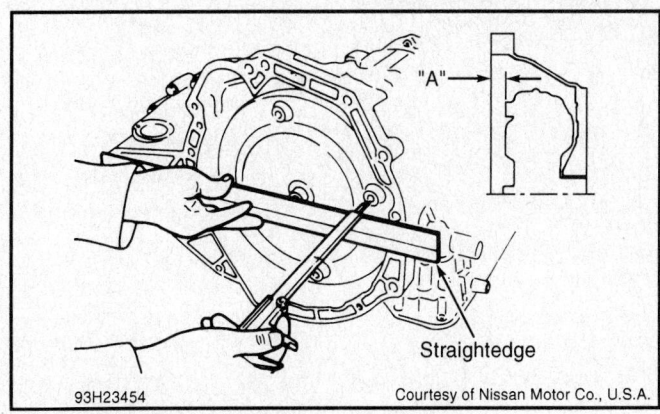

Fig. 37: Measuring Converter Installed Depth

TRANSAXLE SPECIFICATIONS

TRANSAXLE SPECIFICATIONS

Application	In. (mm)
Differential Assembly	
Side Gear-To-Differential Case	
Specified Clearance	.004-.008 (0.10-0.20)
Differential End Play	0-.006 (0-.15)
Forward & Overrun Clutches	
Dish Plate Thickness	
Forward Clutch	.098 (2.50)
Overrun Clutch	.085 (2.15)
Drive Plate Thickness (Forward Clutch)	.071 (1.80)
Allowable Limit	.063 (1.60)
Drive Plate Thickness (Overrun Clutch)	.063 (1.60)
Allowable Limit	.055 (1.40)
Retaining Plate-To-Snap Ring	
Specified Clearance (Forward Clutch)	.018-.033 (.45-.85)
Specified Clearance (Overrun Clutch)	.039-.055 (1.00-1.40)
Allowable Limit (Forward Clutch)	.073 (1.85)
Allowable Limit (Overrun Clutch)	.079 (2.00)
High Clutch	
Drive Plate Thickness	.079 (2.00)
Allowable Limit	.071 (1.80)
Retaining Plate-To-Snap Ring	
Specified Clearance	.055-.071 (1.40-1.80)
Allowable Limit	.094 (2.40)
Input Shaft Seal Ring-To-Ring Groove	
Specified Clearance	.003-.009 (.08-.23)
Allowable Limit	.009 (.23)
Low-Reverse Brake	
Drive Plate Thickness	.079 (2.00)
Allowable Limit	.071 (1.80)
Specified Clearance	.055-.071 (1.40-1.80)
Allowable Limit	.110 (2.80)
Oil Pump Seal Ring-To-Ring Groove	
Specified Clearance	.004-.010 (.10-.25)
Allowable Limit	.010 (.25)
Oil Pump Side Clearance	.0008-.0016 (.020-.040)
Output Shaft Bearing Preload	.001-.003 (.03-.08)
Output Shaft Seal Ring-To-Ring Groove	
Specified Clearance	.004-.010 (.10-.25)
Allowable Limit	.010 (.25)
Pinion Washer-To-Planetary Gear	
Specified Clearance	.006-.028 (.15-.70)
Allowable Limit	.031 (.80)
Reverse Clutch	
Drive Plate Thickness	.079 (2.00)
Allowable Limit	.071 (1.80)
Retaining Plate-To-Snap Ring	
Specified Clearance	.020-.031 (.50-.80)
Allowable Limit	.047 (1.20)
Reduction Gear Bearing Preload	.002 (.05)
Reverse Clutch End Play	.026-.039 (.65-1.00)
Total End Play	.010-.022 (.25-.55)

TORQUE SPECIFICATIONS

TORQUE SPECIFICATIONS

Application	Ft. Lbs. (N.m)
Anchor End Pin Lock Nut	23-27 (31-36)
Bearing Retainer	12-15 (16-21)
Converter Housing Bolt	19-22 (26-30)
Idler Gear Lock Nut	181-203 (245-275)
Oil Cooler Tube Bolt	21-36 (29-49)
Oil Pan Drain Plug	21-29 (29-39)
Oil Pump-To-Transaxle Case Bolt	13-15 (18-21)
Output Gear Lock Nut	181-203 (245-275)
Output Shaft Bearing Retainer Bolt	12-15 (16-21)
Parking Actuator Support Bolt	15-18 (20-24)
Reduction Gear Bearing	
Race Bolt	46-49 (63-67)
Ring Gear Bolt	54-65 (74-88)

	INCH Lbs. (N.m)
Control Valve Assembly Bolt	61-78 (7-9)
Control Valve Body Bolt	44-62 (5-7)
Detent Spring Bolt	57-66 (6.4-7.5)
Dipstick Tube	39-51 (4.4-5.8)
Inhibitor Switch Bolt	18-22 (2-2.5)
Oil Pan Bolt	61-78 (7-9)
Oil Pump Cover-To-Housing Bolt	62-97 (7-11)
Oil Tube	39-51 (4-6)
Side Cover Bolt	44-62 (5-7)
Speedometer Pinion Bolt	33-44 (3.7-5)
Throttle Cable Bolt	18-35 (2-4)

WIRING DIAGRAMS

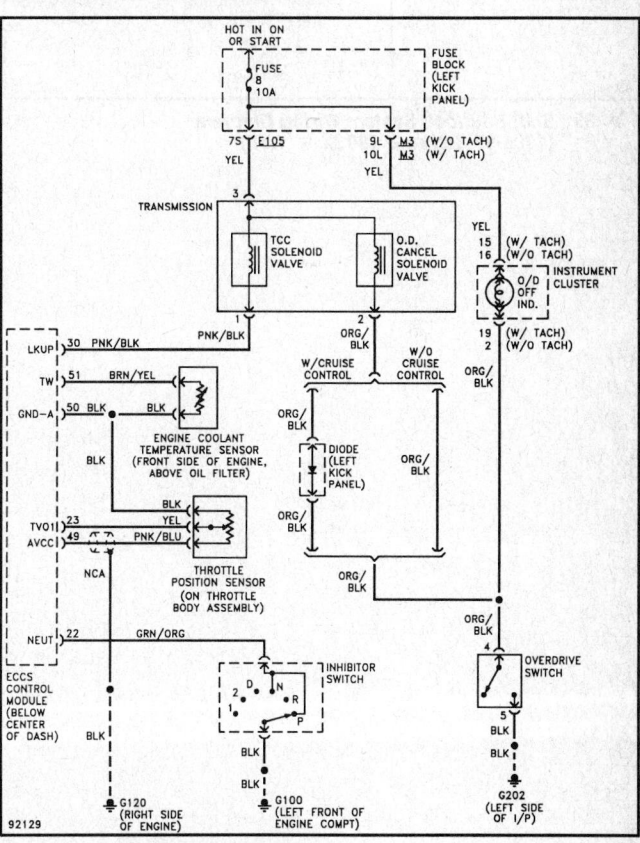

**Fig. 38: Transaxle Wiring Diagram
(1995-96 Sentra & 200SX — 1.6L)**

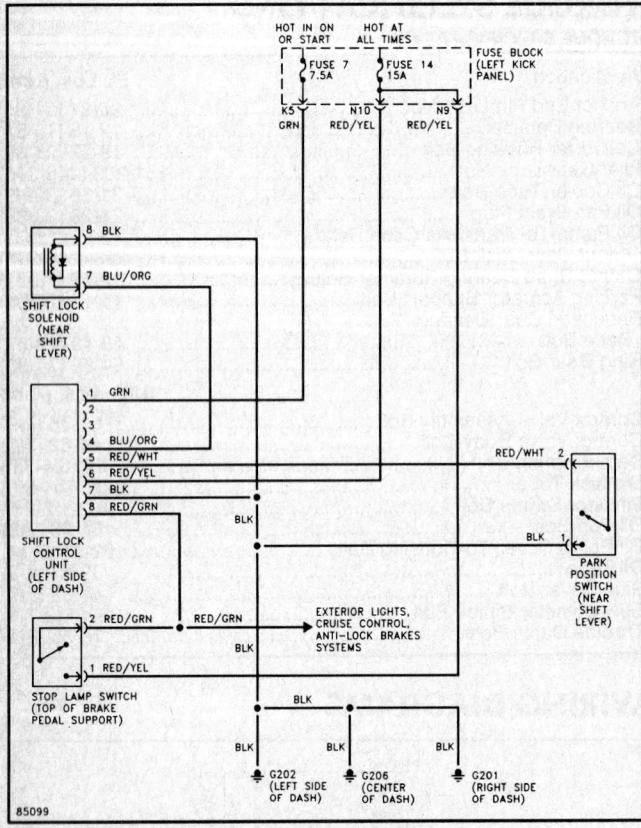

Fig. 39: Shift Interlock System Wiring Diagram
(1995-96 Sentra & 200SX – 1.6L)

911 Carrera 2 (2WD)

APPLICATION & LABOR TIMES

APPLICATION & LABOR TIMES

Vehicle Application	Labor Times		Series
	[1] R & I	[2] Overhaul	
911 Carrera 2 (2WD)	11.4	.... 15.5	A50/05

[1] – Removal and installation of transaxle from vehicle chassis.

[2] – Bench overhaul time for transaxle/differential. DOES NOT include removal and installation.

NOTE: The metric dimensions listed in this article are the preferred service measurement. Inch conversions are given to the 3rd or 4th decimal place for reference.

IDENTIFICATION

Vehicle identification label is located behind locking mechanism on underside of front hood. Label contains VIN, vehicle code, engine/transaxle code, paint/interior code and option codes.

NOTE: Manufacturer recommends transaxle repairs be made only to valve body, oil pump, sensors and final drive assembly. If repairs to multi-disc clutches, planetary gear sets and/or one-way clutch of transaxle is necessary, the entire transmission MUST be replaced.

DESCRIPTION & OPERATION

The Porsche Tiptronic automatic transaxle is a 4-speed electronically controlled unit that can be operated either as an automatic or manually shifted transaxle using a dual gate shift selector. The Robert Bosch electronic control unit monitors multiple inputs (every 30 or 100 milliseconds) to manage shift programs including lock-up torque converter in 2nd, 3rd and 4th gears.

Shift characteristics are affected by accelerator pedal position, throttle valve angle, vehicle speed, longitudinal and lateral vehicle acceleration and engine RPM. Forced upshift is interrupted during heavy cornering and heavy braking.

Transaxle consists of 6 multi-disc clutches, 2 planetary gear sets (one compound) and a one-way clutch (sprag type). *See Fig. 1.* Power is transferred from internal components through spur gears to longitudinal shaft (drive pinion). The drive pinion is connected to ring gear of open hypoid differential unit (final drive).

A/T fluid cooling is provided by auxiliary cooler mounted in conjunction with engine oil cooler in front of right front wheel and is ventilated by 2-speed electric fan.

LUBRICATION & ADJUSTMENTS

NOTE: See appropriate AUTOMATIC TRANSMISSION SERVICING article in TRANSMISSION SERVICING section.

TROUBLE SHOOTING

NOTE: Refer to Fig. 1 for component location.

Preliminary Checks – Automatic transaxle malfunction can be caused by either engine or transaxle problems. Isolate malfunction to engine or transaxle before proceeding with trouble shooting. Prior to trouble shooting check and adjust shift linkage, multifunctional switch and idle speed as needed. Ensure fluid level is correct. Check tires for correct inflation.

SYMPTOM DIAGNOSIS

Park Position Does Not Engage – Check shift cable adjustment between shift lever and transaxle. Defective parking lock mechanism.

Transaxle Does Not Remain In Park – Check shift cable adjustment between shift lever and transaxle.

Starter Will Not Operate In Park Or Neutral – Check multifunctional switch adjustment and operation.

No Reverse Gear – Check shift cable adjustment between shift lever and transaxle. Check if reverse lock does not release. Check for clogged oil strainer, worn clutch "B", "E" and/or brake "D".

Low Power In Reverse – Check for low pressure in clutch "B" or "E", and brake "D".

Slipping Or Shudder In Reverse – Check for worn clutch "B", "E" and/or brake "D".

Hard, Erratic P-R, N-R Engagement – Check for high idle speed. Clutch "B" faulty. Modulating pressure excessively high.

No Reverse & No Forward Gears – Main pressure valve or spring in valve body stuck or broken.

Vibration In Reverse Gear – Torque converter out of balance.

Vehicle Moves In Neutral – Check shift cable adjustment between shift lever and transaxle. Clutch "A" binding or 2nd seal ring or turbine shaft leaking.

No Power In Drive – Check shift cable adjustment between shift lever and transaxle. Check for clogged oil strainer, stuck main pressure valve, broken valve spring, faulty clutch "A" or faulty sprag.

Poor Power In Drive – Clutch "A" pressure too low.

Slipping Or Shudder When Starting Out – Damaged clutch "A".

Hard, Jerky N-D Engagement – Check for high idle speed and defective clutch "A".

Knocking Noise In Neutral – Torque converter out of balance.

No 1-2 Or 2-1 Shift – 1-2 shift valve stuck, pressure reducer valve No. 1 stuck or damaged brakes "C1" and "C2".

No 2-3 Or 3-2 Shift – 2-3 shift valve stuck or damaged clutch "B".

No 3-4 Or 4-3 Shift – 3-4 shift valve stuck or brake "F" damaged.

Vehicle Starts Off In 2nd – 1-2 shift valve stuck.

Vehicle Starts Off In 3rd – 1-2 and 2-3 shift valves stuck.

Vehicle Shifts From 1st To 3rd – 2-3 shift valve stuck.

No Engine Braking, 4-3 Shift – Faulty damper "E" and clutch "E".

No Manual 3-2 Shift – 2-3 shift valve stuck and damper "C1" faulty.

No Engine Braking In 2nd Gear – Check condition of brake "C1" and clutch "E".

No Manual 2-1 Shift – 1-2 shift valve stuck, damper "D" faulty and modulating valve binding.

No Engine Braking In 1st Gear – Check condition of brake "D" and clutch "E".

Harsh Converter Clutch Engagement – Faulty torque converter clutch.

No Converter Clutch Operation – Torque converter shift slide stuck or faulty torque converter clutch.

Torque Converter Clutch Always Engaged – Faulty valve body.

High Pitched Noise In All Shift Positions, Especially When Cold Or Oil Pump Intake Noise – Check fluid level. Leaking valve body or pump bushing is seized.

Noise In Reverse – Pump bushing is seized.

TESTING

PRELIMINARY CHECKS

Before testing transaxle, ensure fluid level is correct and shift linkage, multifunctional switch and idle speed are adjusted correctly.

AUTOMATIC TRANSMISSIONS
Porsche A50/05 Tiptronic (Cont.)

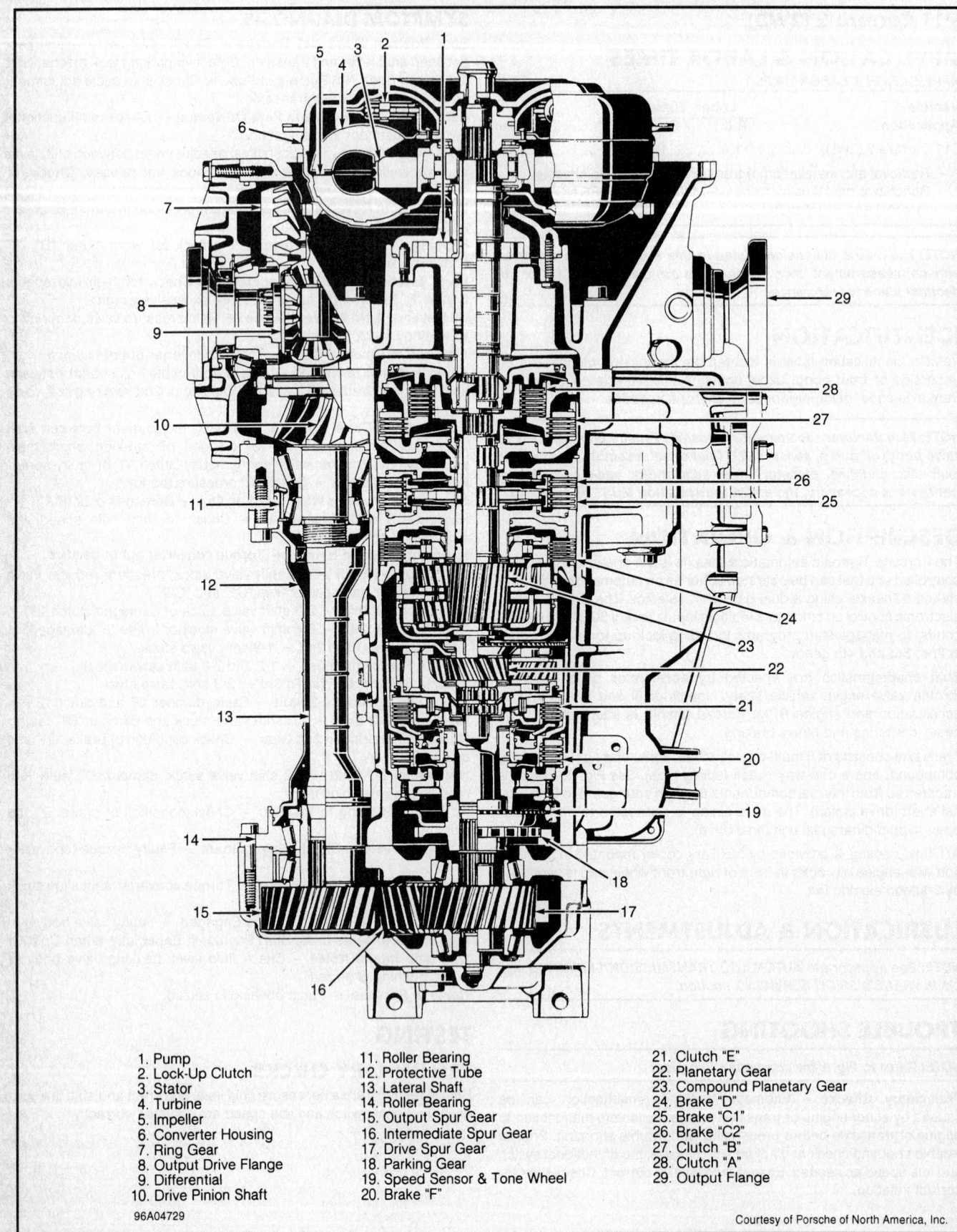

1. Pump
2. Lock-Up Clutch
3. Stator
4. Turbine
5. Impeller
6. Converter Housing
7. Ring Gear
8. Output Drive Flange
9. Differential
10. Drive Pinion Shaft
11. Roller Bearing
12. Protective Tube
13. Lateral Shaft
14. Roller Bearing
15. Output Spur Gear
16. Intermediate Spur Gear
17. Drive Spur Gear
18. Parking Gear
19. Speed Sensor & Tone Wheel
20. Brake "F"
21. Clutch "E"
22. Planetary Gear
23. Compound Planetary Gear
24. Brake "D"
25. Brake "C1"
26. Brake "C2"
27. Clutch "B"
28. Clutch "A"
29. Output Flange

96A04729

Courtesy of Porsche of North America, Inc.

Fig. 1: Cut-Away Of A50/05 Tiptronic Automatic Transaxle

Selector lever position	Gear	Clutches			Brakes				Freewheels		
		A	B	E	C'	C	D	F	1st gear	2nd gear	3rd gear
D	1.	X		X					X		X
D	2.	X		X	X	X				X	X
D	3.	X	X	X							X
D	4.	X	X			X		X			
3	1.	X		X					X		X
3	2.	X		X	X	X				X	X
3	3.	X	X	X		X					X
2	1.	X		X					X		X
2	2.	X		X	X	X				X	X
*1	1.	X		X			X		(X)		X
R	R		X	X			X				

* engine brake effective in overrun mode

96E04731

Courtesy of Porsche of North America, Inc.

Fig. 2: Clutch & Brake Application Table

ROAD TEST

During road test, transaxle must be checked for slipping of each friction element, engagement shock and proper upshift or downshift points. See Fig. 3. Once transaxle has shifted into each gear, determine if torque converter clutch has gone into lock-up. See Fig. 4.

STALL SPEED TEST

Stall speed testing procedures are not available from manufacturer. Stall speed specification is 1900-2700 RPM.

HYDRAULIC PRESSURE TESTS

Hydraulic pressure test procedures or specifications are not available from manufacturer.

REMOVAL & INSTALLATION

See appropriate AUTOMATIC TRANSMISSION REMOVAL article in TRANSMISSION SERVICING section.

TORQUE CONVERTER

Torque converter is sealed unit and must be serviced as complete assembly. Test procedures are not available from manufacturer. If contamination exists in transaxle, torque converter must be replaced.

TRANSMISSION DISASSEMBLY

NOTE: Detailed disassembly procedures are not available from manufacturer. Refer to illustrations for transaxle disassembly. See Figs. 5-12.

COMPONENT DISASSEMBLY & REASSEMBLY

NOTE: Detailed disassembly procedures are not available from manufacturer. Refer to illustrations for component disassembly. See Figs. 13-31.

Disassembly – When disassembling clutch assemblies, ensure number of discs and plates, component location and assembly order is recorded. Inspect all friction material for wear. Replace as needed. Use appropriate press to compress pistons for snap ring removal. Inspect discs, plates and flange. Clean all parts thoroughly in solvent except discs. Air dry parts with compressed air. Soak new discs in ATF before installation. Ensure all seals and "O" rings are installed in original position. Inspect clutch pack clearance after assembly. See TRANSMISSION SPECIFICATIONS.

AUTOMATIC TRANSMISSIONS
Porsche A50/05 Tiptronic (Cont.)

Upshift Points (mph)

Shift characteristic	1. → 2. A	1. → 2. B	1. → 2. C (Kick-down)	2. → 3. A	2. → 3. B	2. → 3. C (Kick-down)	3. → 4. A	3. → 4. B	3. → 4. C (Kick-down)
1	15	30	39	22	64	76	30	98	114
2	15	30	39	28	64	76	37	98	114
3	17	39	39	32	64	76	46	98	114
4	20	39	39	58	76	76	87	114	114
5	25	39	39	65	76	76	99	114	114

Downshift Points (mph)

Shift characteristic	4. → 3. A	4. → 3. B	4. → 3. C (Kick-down)	3. → 2. A	3. → 2. B	3. → 2. C (Kick-down)	2. → 1. A	2. → 1. B	2. → 1. C (Kick-down)
1	25	86	108	14	30	70	12	18	33
2	30	86	108	14	30	70	12	18	33
3	37	86	108	25	56	70	12	31	33
4	65	104	108	41	70	70	14	32	33
5	70	108	108	47	70	70	18	32	33

A = Rolling vehicle without pressure on the accelerator pedal
B = Full throttle position
C = Accelerator pedal pressed beyond full throttle position (kick-down)

Shift Characteristics are:
1 = Comfort/Economy
2 = Economy
3 = Normal
4 = Sport
5 = Intense/Sport

96C04730

Courtesy of Porsche of North America, Inc.

Fig. 3: Upshift & Downshift Speed Specifications

Gear Shift criteria	1	2	3	4	R
1 Comfort/Economy	Always open in all ranges	opens below 10 mph closes at 28 mph	opens below 22 mph closes at 28 mph	opens below 30 mph closes at 36 mph	Always open in all ranges
2 Economy		opens below 15 mph closes at 36 mph	opens below 22 mph closes at 28 mph	opens below 30 mph closes at 36 mph	
3 Normal		opens below 15 mph closes at 45 mph	opens below 22 mph closes at 25 mph	opens below 30 mph closes at 36 mph	
4 Sport		opens below 15 mph closes at 45 mph	opens below 22 mph closes at 25 mph	opens below 30 mph closes at 36 mph	
5 Intense/Sport		opens below 15 mph closes at 36 mph	opens below 22 mph closes at 50 mph	opens below 30 mph closes at 68 mph	

96G04732

Courtesy of Porsche of North America, Inc.

Fig. 4: Torque Converter Lock-Up Speed Specifications

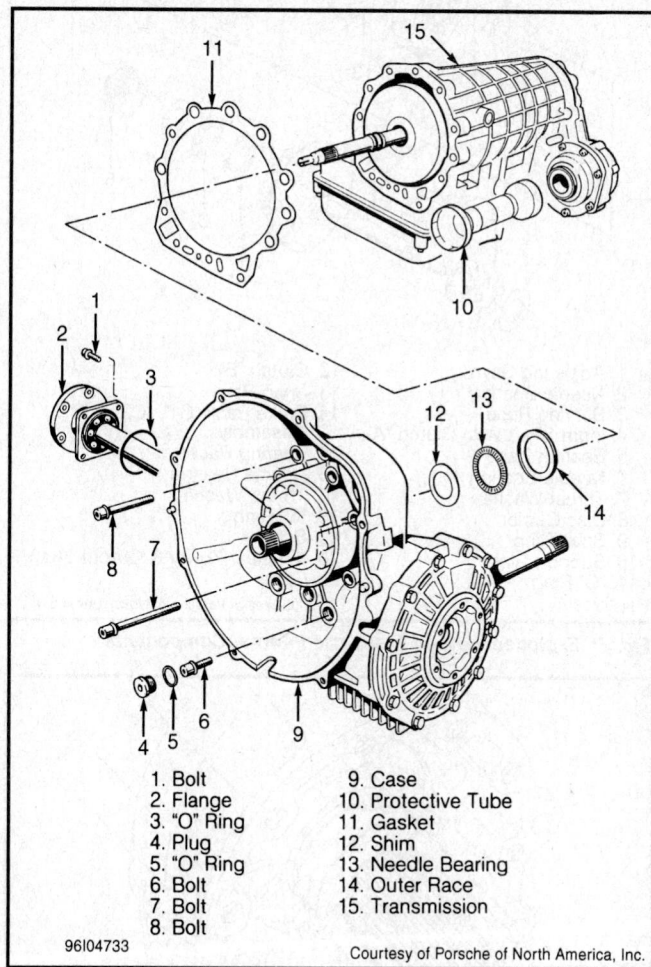

1. Bolt
2. Flange
3. "O" Ring
4. Plug
5. "O" Ring
6. Bolt
7. Bolt
8. Bolt
9. Case
10. Protective Tube
11. Gasket
12. Shim
13. Needle Bearing
14. Outer Race
15. Transmission

96I04733

Courtesy of Porsche of North America, Inc.

Fig. 5: Removing & Installing Final Drive Assembly

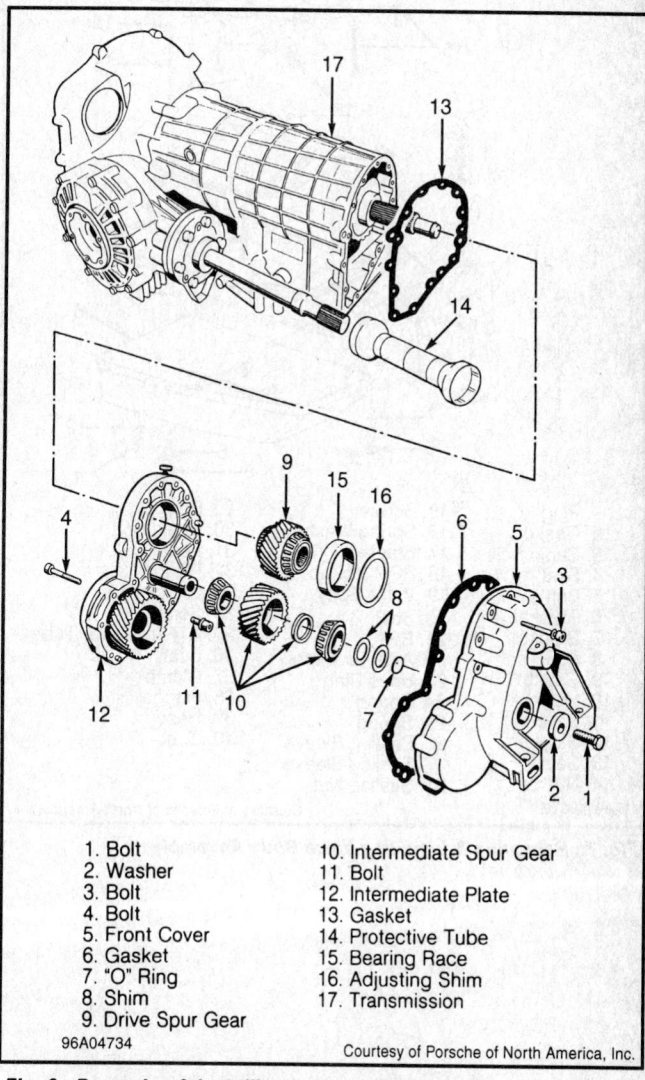

1. Bolt
2. Washer
3. Bolt
4. Bolt
5. Front Cover
6. Gasket
7. "O" Ring
8. Shim
9. Drive Spur Gear
10. Intermediate Spur Gear
11. Bolt
12. Intermediate Plate
13. Gasket
14. Protective Tube
15. Bearing Race
16. Adjusting Shim
17. Transmission

96A04734

Courtesy of Porsche of North America, Inc.

Fig. 6: Removing & Installing Intermediate Plate & Spur Gear Assembly

AUTOMATIC TRANSMISSIONS
Porsche A50/05 Tiptronic (Cont.)

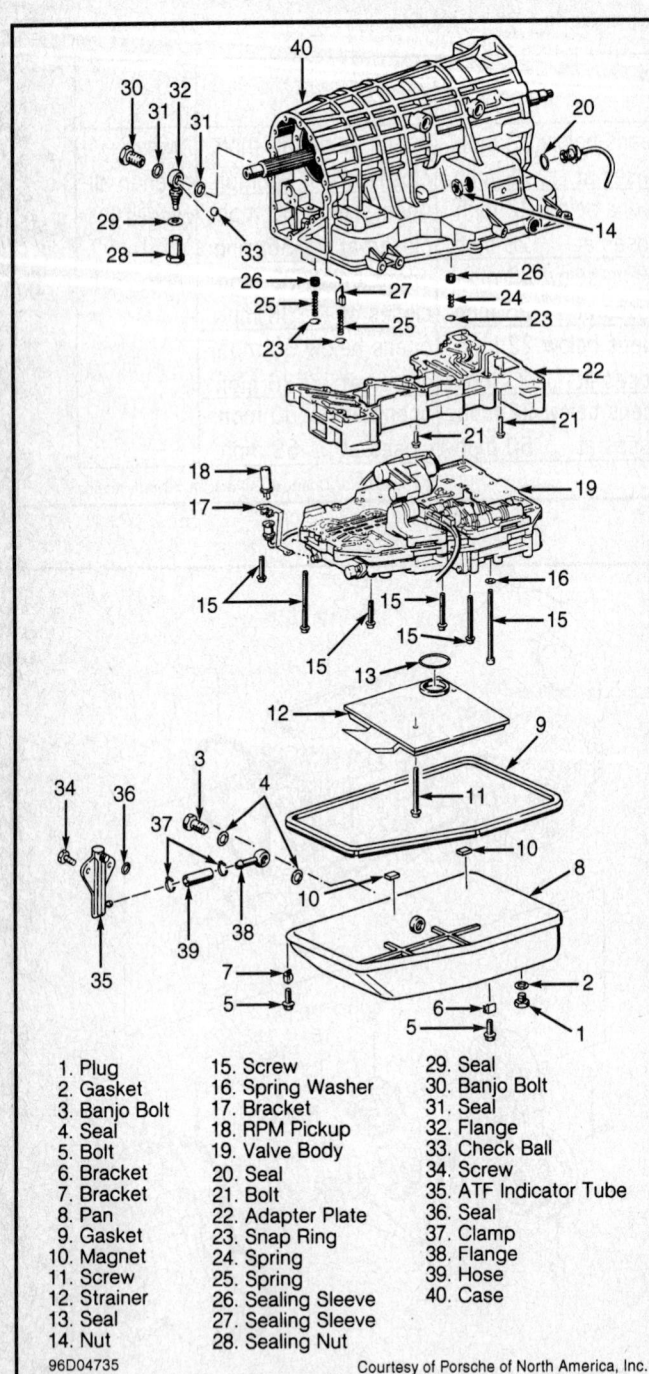

1. Plug
2. Gasket
3. Banjo Bolt
4. Seal
5. Bolt
6. Bracket
7. Bracket
8. Pan
9. Gasket
10. Magnet
11. Screw
12. Strainer
13. Seal
14. Nut
15. Screw
16. Spring Washer
17. Bracket
18. RPM Pickup
19. Valve Body
20. Seal
21. Bolt
22. Adapter Plate
23. Snap Ring
24. Spring
25. Spring
26. Sealing Sleeve
27. Sealing Sleeve
28. Sealing Nut
29. Seal
30. Banjo Bolt
31. Seal
32. Flange
33. Check Ball
34. Screw
35. ATF Indicator Tube
36. Seal
37. Clamp
38. Flange
39. Hose
40. Case

96D04735

Courtesy of Porsche of North America, Inc.

Fig. 7: Removing & Installing Valve Body Assembly

NOTE: See Figs. 9-12 before disassembling internal case components.

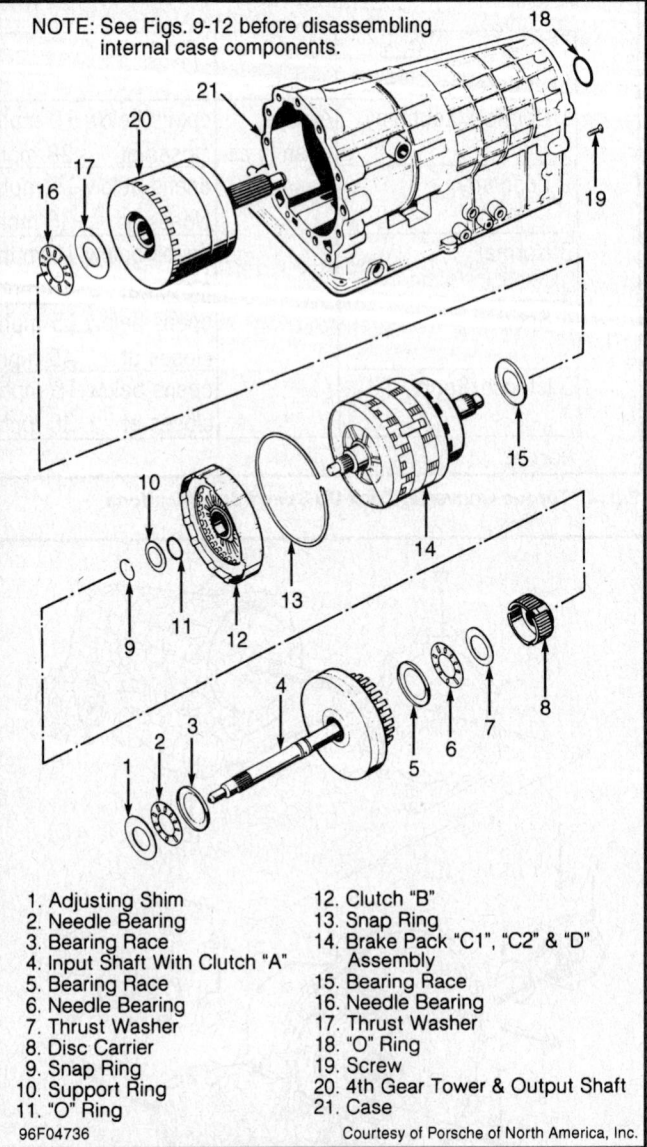

1. Adjusting Shim
2. Needle Bearing
3. Bearing Race
4. Input Shaft With Clutch "A"
5. Bearing Race
6. Needle Bearing
7. Thrust Washer
8. Disc Carrier
9. Snap Ring
10. Support Ring
11. "O" Ring
12. Clutch "B"
13. Snap Ring
14. Brake Pack "C1", "C2" & "D" Assembly
15. Bearing Race
16. Needle Bearing
17. Thrust Washer
18. "O" Ring
19. Screw
20. 4th Gear Tower & Output Shaft
21. Case

96F04736

Courtesy of Porsche of North America, Inc.

Fig. 8: Exploded View Of Transaxle Internal Components

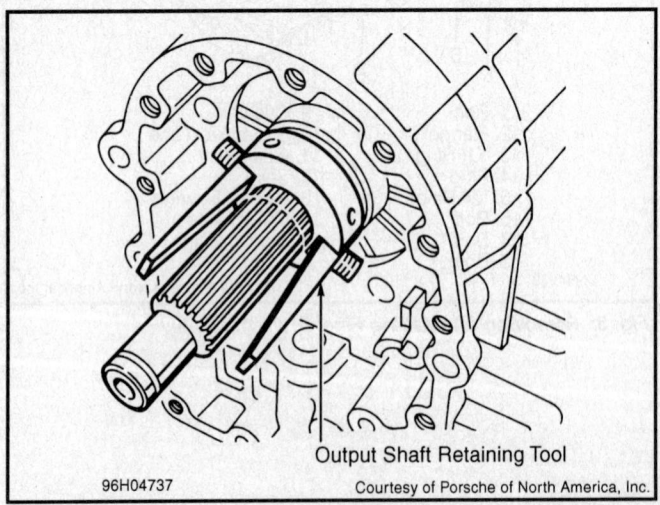

Output Shaft Retaining Tool

96H04737

Courtesy of Porsche of North America, Inc.

Fig. 9: Retaining Output Shaft To 4th Gear Tower Assembly During Disassembly

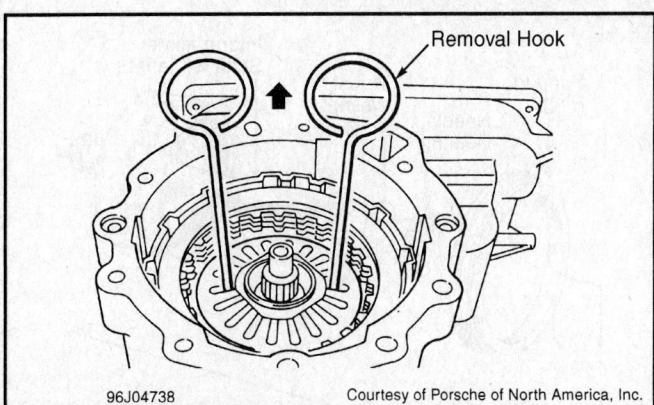

Fig. 10: Removing Clutch "B"

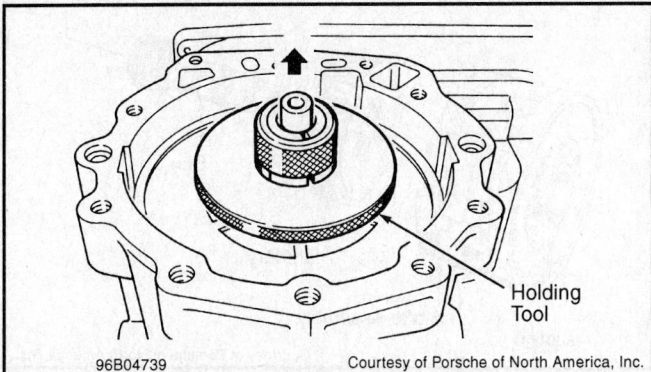

Fig. 11: Removing Brake Assembly ("C1", "C2" & "D") Using Holding Tool (9329/1)

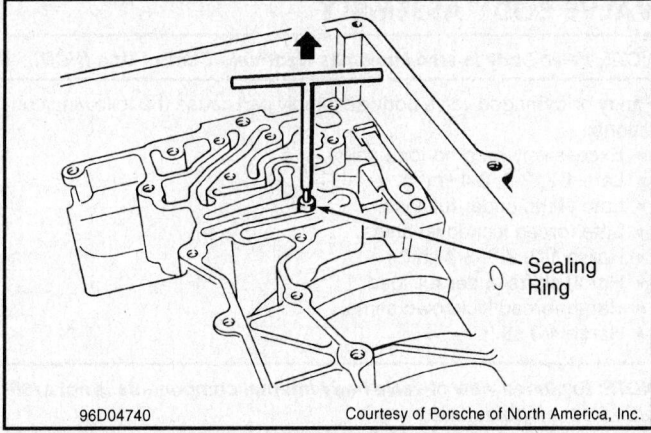

Fig. 12: Removing Sealing Rings From Case

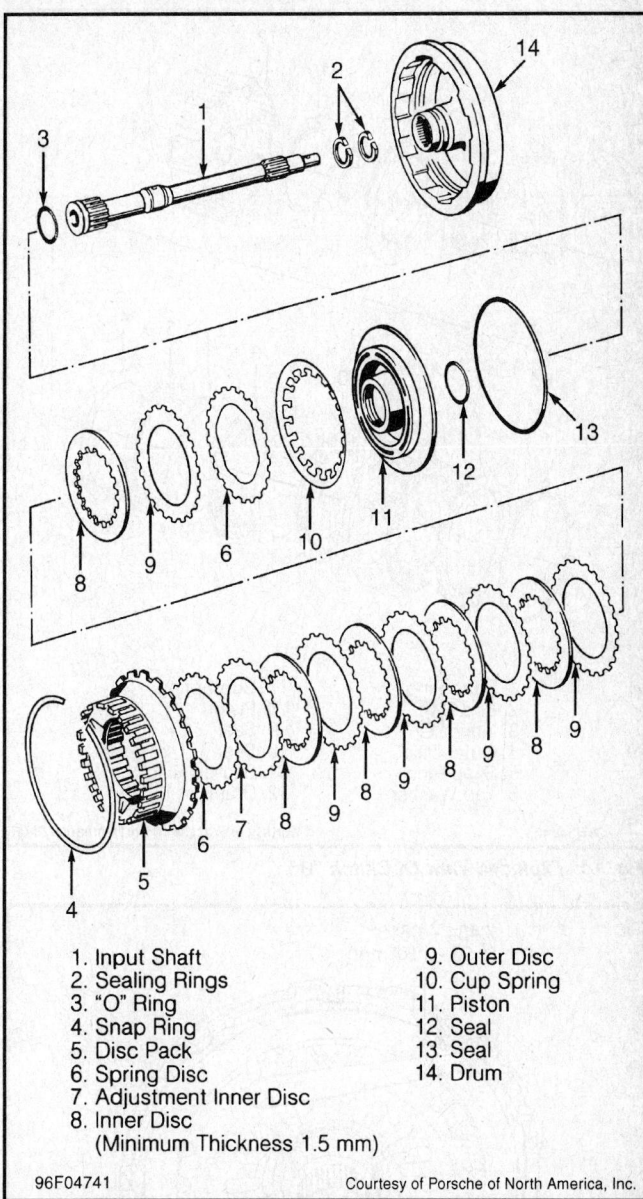

1. Input Shaft
2. Sealing Rings
3. "O" Ring
4. Snap Ring
5. Disc Pack
6. Spring Disc
7. Adjustment Inner Disc
8. Inner Disc
   (Minimum Thickness 1.5 mm)
9. Outer Disc
10. Cup Spring
11. Piston
12. Seal
13. Seal
14. Drum

Fig. 13: Exploded View Of Clutch "A"

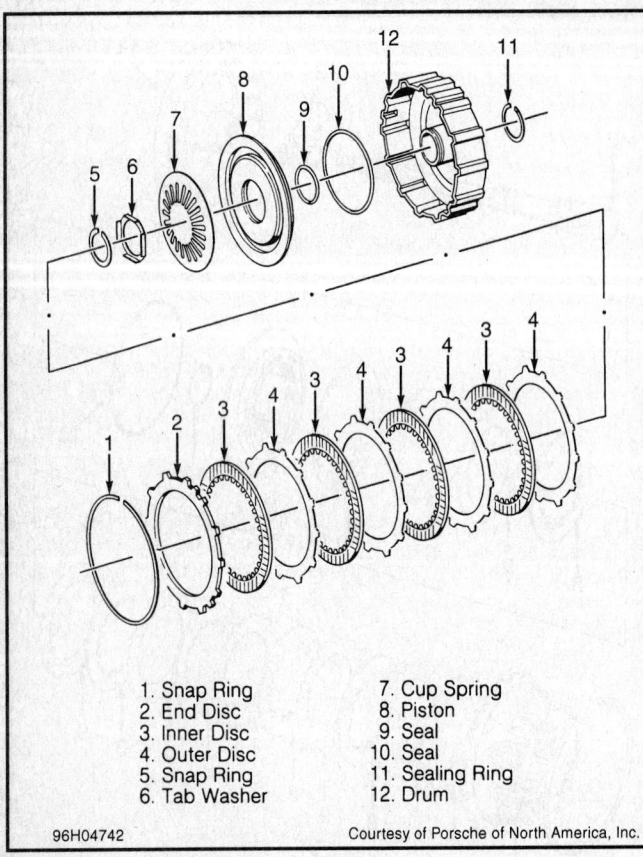

1. Snap Ring
2. End Disc
3. Inner Disc
4. Outer Disc
5. Snap Ring
6. Tab Washer
7. Cup Spring
8. Piston
9. Seal
10. Seal
11. Sealing Ring
12. Drum

96H04742   Courtesy of Porsche of North America, Inc.

Fig. 14: Exploded View Of Clutch "B"

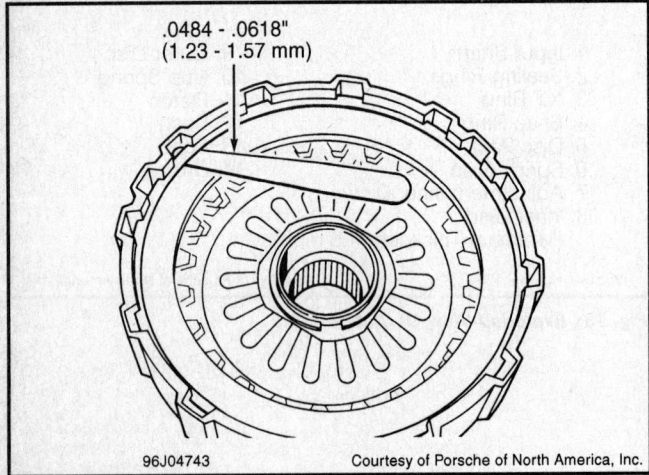

.0484 - .0618"
(1.23 - 1.57 mm)

96J04743   Courtesy of Porsche of North America, Inc.

Fig. 15: Measuring Clutch "B" Pack Clearance

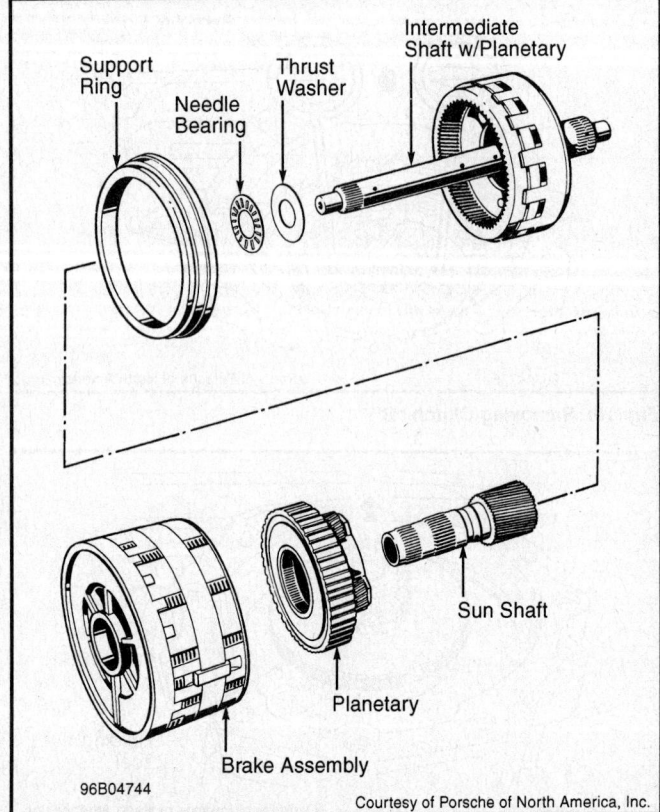

Support Ring
Needle Bearing
Thrust Washer
Intermediate Shaft w/Planetary
Sun Shaft
Planetary
Brake Assembly

96B04744   Courtesy of Porsche of North America, Inc.

**Fig. 16: Disassembling Brake Assembly From
Intermediate Shaft Assembly**

VALVE BODY ASSEMBLY

NOTE: Valve body is also known as Hydraulic Control Unit (HCU).

Faulty or damaged valve body assembly can cause the following conditions;
- Excessively hard no-load shifts.
- Late 1-2, 2-3, 3-4 shifts.
- Late shifts under full load.
- Late forced kickdown shifts.
- Harsh 1-2, 2-3, 3-4 shifts.
- Harsh shifts under full load.
- Harsh forced kickdown shifts.
- Harsh 4-3 shift.

NOTE: Exploded view of valve body internal components is not available from manufacturer.

If valve body is disassembled, ensure all components are installed in original location. Valves may be held in with pins, retainers and plugs. Lay all components in sequence during removal for reassembly reference. Clean all parts with solvent. Dry parts with compressed air. Ensure all valve body oil passages are clear. Inspect valves for scoring or roughness. Inspect valve springs for damage, squareness, rust and collapsed coils. Coat all components with ATF. Position any gaskets or separator plates in original position. Refer to illustrations for solenoid location. See Figs. 32 and 33.

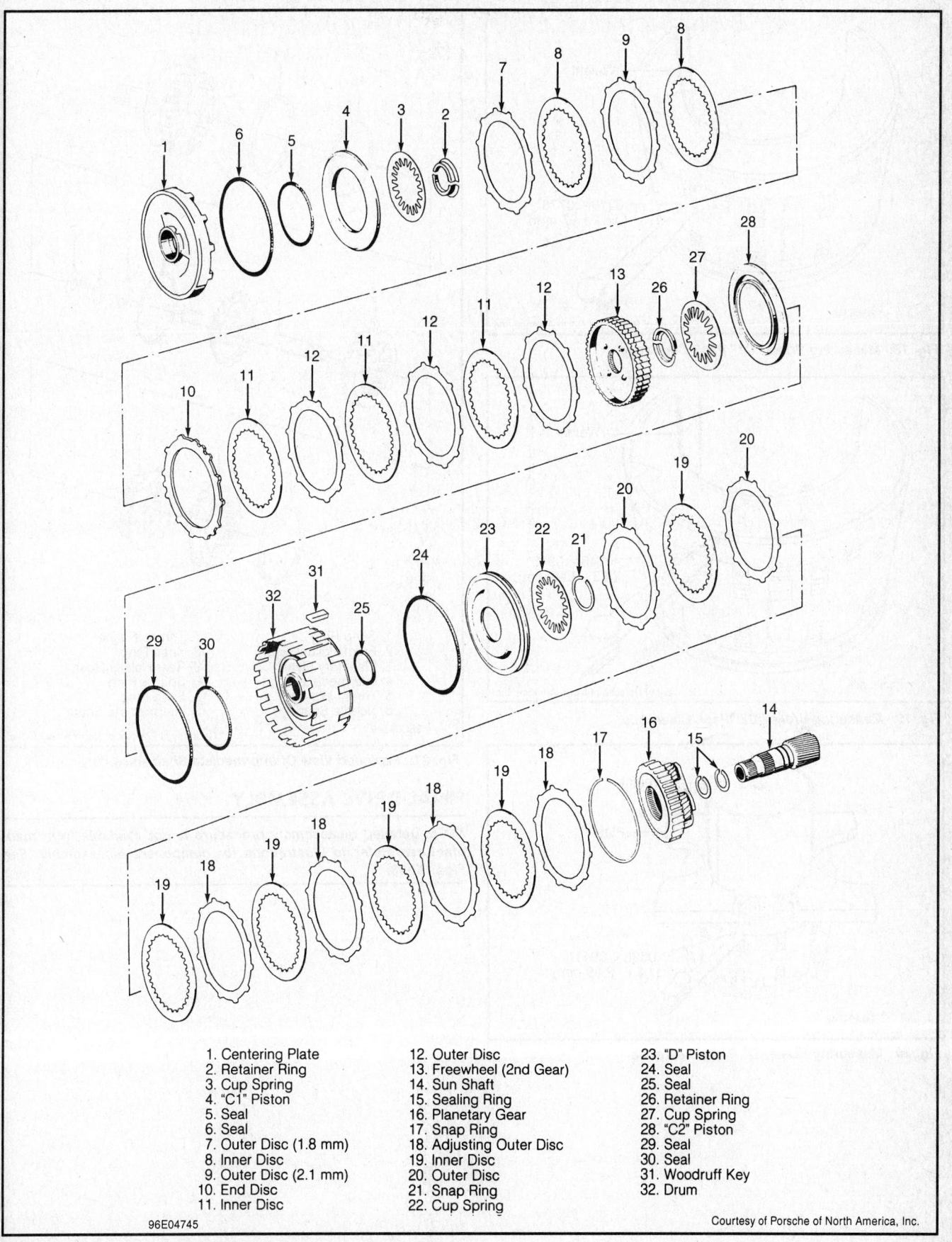

1. Centering Plate	12. Outer Disc	23. "D" Piston
2. Retainer Ring	13. Freewheel (2nd Gear)	24. Seal
3. Cup Spring	14. Sun Shaft	25. Seal
4. "C1" Piston	15. Sealing Ring	26. Retainer Ring
5. Seal	16. Planetary Gear	27. Cup Spring
6. Seal	17. Snap Ring	28. "C2" Piston
7. Outer Disc (1.8 mm)	18. Adjusting Outer Disc	29. Seal
8. Inner Disc	19. Inner Disc	30. Seal
9. Outer Disc (2.1 mm)	20. Outer Disc	31. Woodruff Key
10. End Disc	21. Snap Ring	32. Drum
11. Inner Disc	22. Cup Spring	

96E04745

Courtesy of Porsche of North America, Inc.

Fig. 17: Exploded View Of Brake Assemblies ("C1", "C2" & "D")

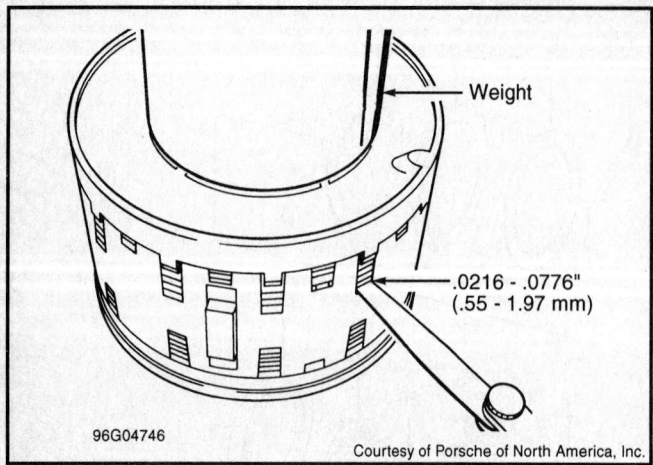

Fig. 18: Measuring Brake "C1" Pack Clearance

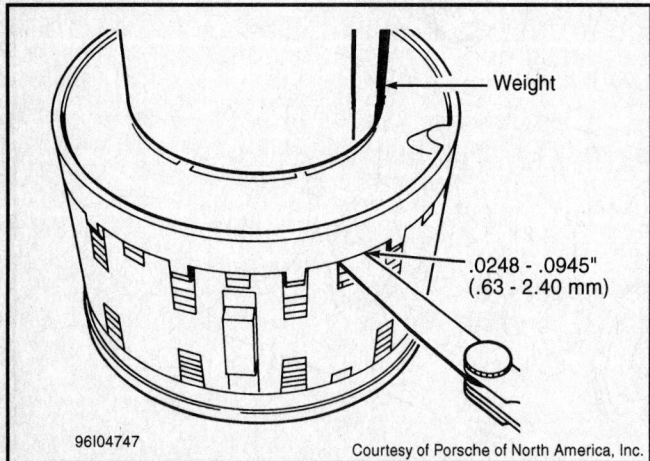

Fig. 19: Measuring Brake "C2" Pack Clearance

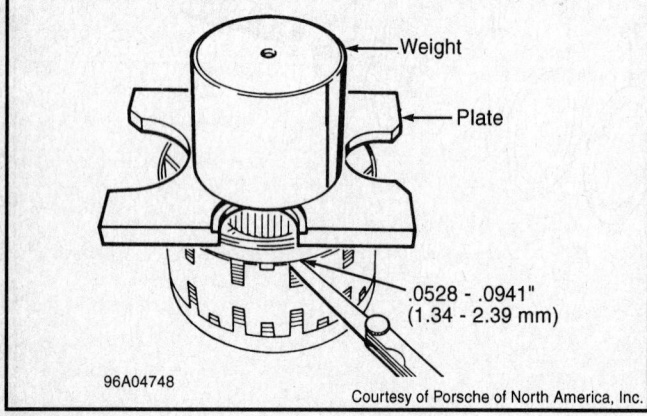

Fig. 20: Measuring Brake "D" Pack Clearance

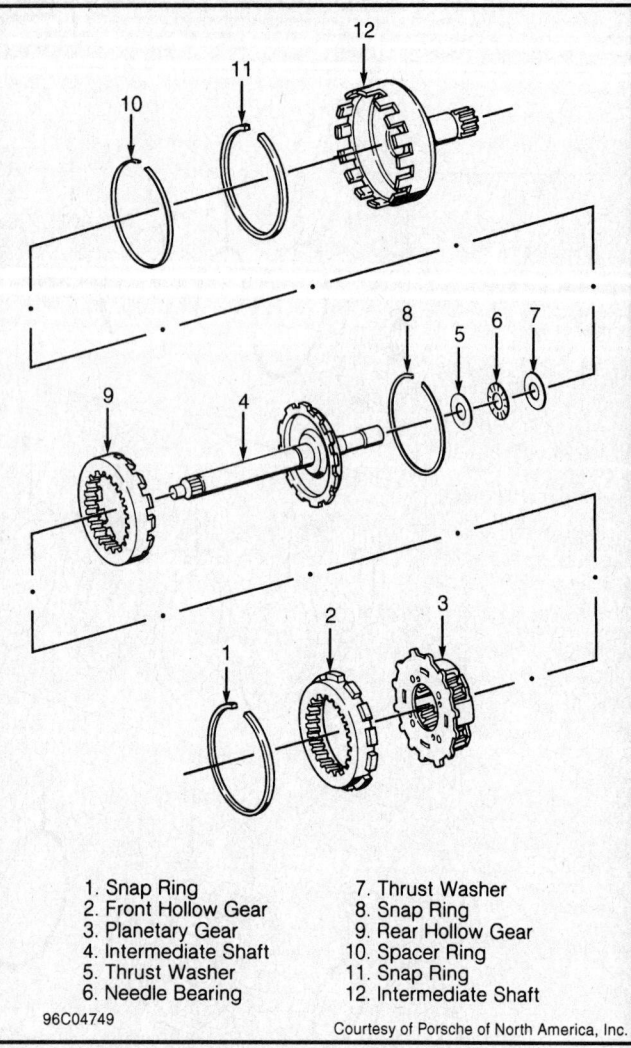

1. Snap Ring	7. Thrust Washer
2. Front Hollow Gear	8. Snap Ring
3. Planetary Gear	9. Rear Hollow Gear
4. Intermediate Shaft	10. Spacer Ring
5. Thrust Washer	11. Snap Ring
6. Needle Bearing	12. Intermediate Shaft

Fig. 21: Exploded View Of Intermediate Shaft Assembly

FINAL DRIVE ASSEMBLY

NOTE: Detailed disassembly procedure is not available from manufacturer. Refer to illustrations for component disassembly. See Figs. 33-38.

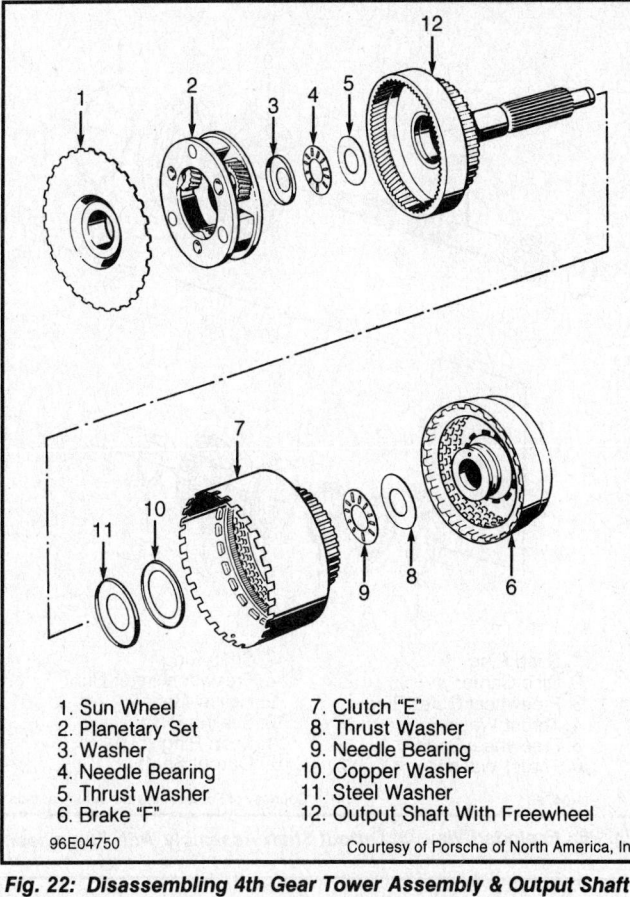

1. Sun Wheel
2. Planetary Set
3. Washer
4. Needle Bearing
5. Thrust Washer
6. Brake "F"
7. Clutch "E"
8. Thrust Washer
9. Needle Bearing
10. Copper Washer
11. Steel Washer
12. Output Shaft With Freewheel

96E04750

Courtesy of Porsche of North America, Inc.

Fig. 22: Disassembling 4th Gear Tower Assembly & Output Shaft

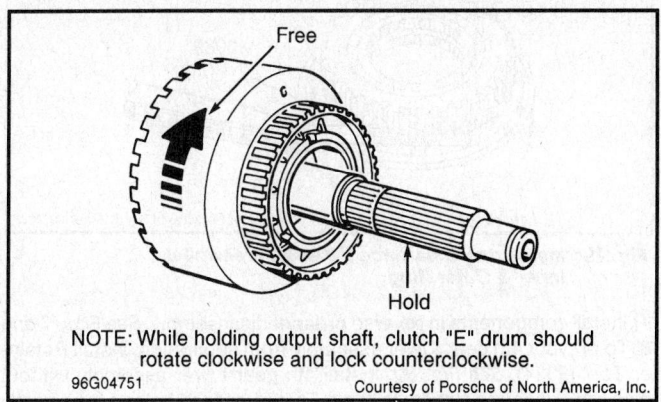

NOTE: While holding output shaft, clutch "E" drum should rotate clockwise and lock counterclockwise.

96G04751

Courtesy of Porsche of North America, Inc.

Fig. 23: Checking Output Shaft Freewheel Operation

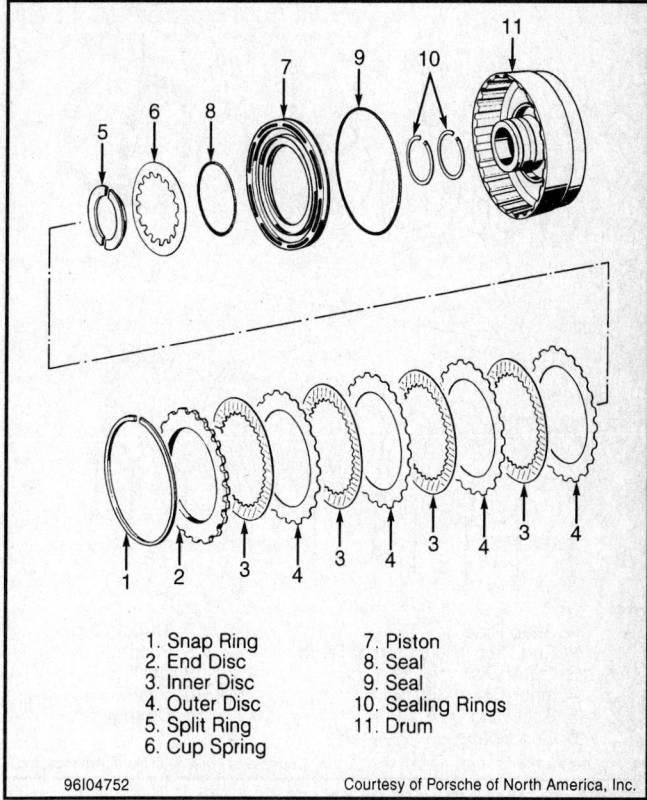

1. Snap Ring
2. End Disc
3. Inner Disc
4. Outer Disc
5. Split Ring
6. Cup Spring
7. Piston
8. Seal
9. Seal
10. Sealing Rings
11. Drum

96I04752

Courtesy of Porsche of North America, Inc.

Fig. 24: Exploded View Of Brake "F" Assembly

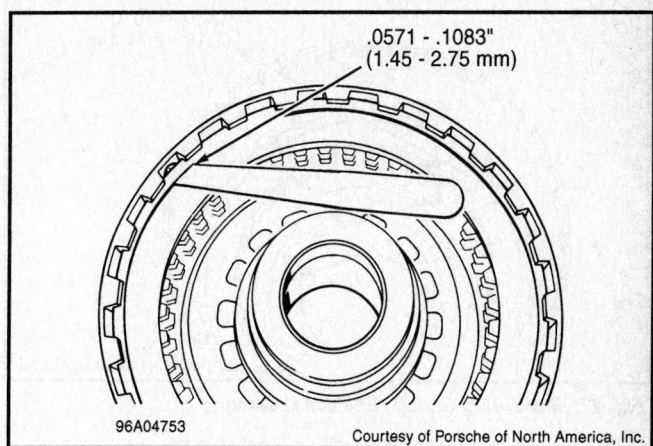

.0571 - .1083"
(1.45 - 2.75 mm)

96A04753

Courtesy of Porsche of North America, Inc.

Fig. 25: Measuring Brake "F" Pack Clearance

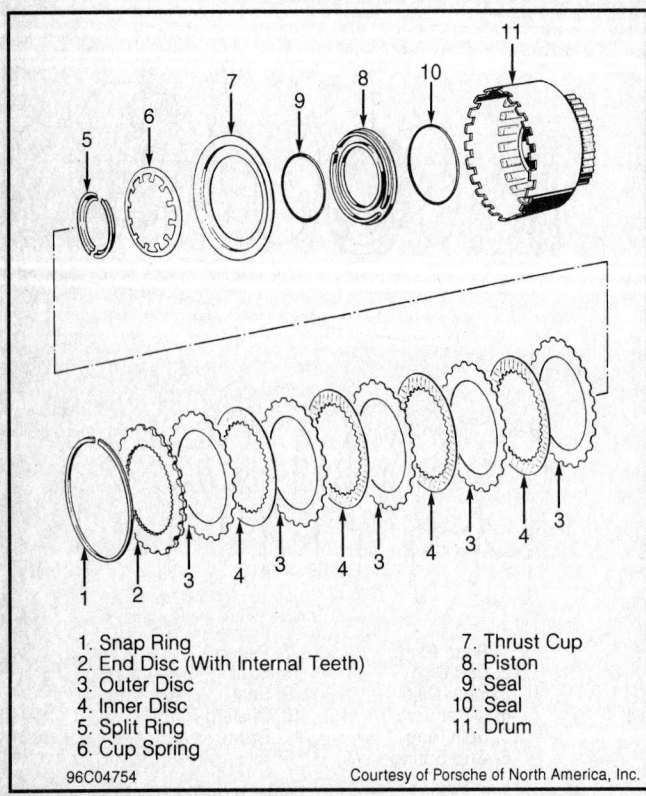

1. Snap Ring
2. End Disc (With Internal Teeth)
3. Outer Disc
4. Inner Disc
5. Split Ring
6. Cup Spring
7. Thrust Cup
8. Piston
9. Seal
10. Seal
11. Drum

96C04754   Courtesy of Porsche of North America, Inc.

Fig. 26: Exploded View Of Clutch "E" Assembly

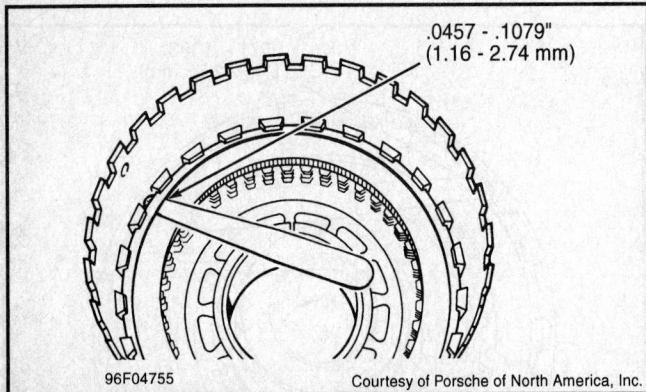

.0457 - .1079"
(1.16 - 2.74 mm)

96F04755   Courtesy of Porsche of North America, Inc.

Fig. 27: Measuring Clutch "E" Pack Clearance

TRANSAXLE REASSEMBLY

INTERNAL COMPONENTS & VALVE BODY

NOTE: Coat all oil seal rings, clutch discs, clutch plates, rotating parts, and sliding surfaces with ATF prior to reassembly. All gaskets and rubber "O" rings should be replaced. Ensure ends of snap rings are not aligned with cut-outs and are installed correctly in groove. If a worn bushing is to be replaced, replacement must be made with the subassembly containing that bushing. Check thrust bearings and races for wear or damage. Use petroleum jelly to hold parts in place. Replace parts as necessary. Soak clutch plates in ATF prior to installation.

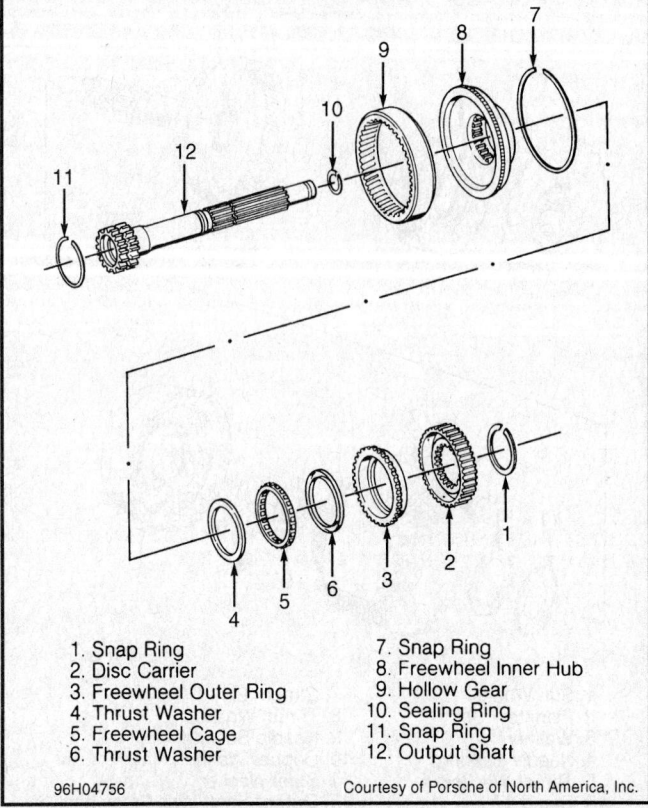

1. Snap Ring
2. Disc Carrier
3. Freewheel Outer Ring
4. Thrust Washer
5. Freewheel Cage
6. Thrust Washer
7. Snap Ring
8. Freewheel Inner Hub
9. Hollow Gear
10. Sealing Ring
11. Snap Ring
12. Output Shaft

96H04756   Courtesy of Porsche of North America, Inc.

Fig. 28: Exploded View Of Output Shaft Assembly With Freewheel

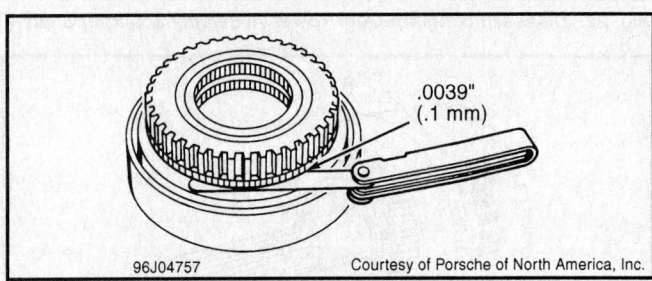

.0039"
(.1 mm)

96J04757   Courtesy of Porsche of North America, Inc.

Fig. 29: Measuring Clearance Between Freewheel Inner & Outer Ring

1) Install components in reverse order of disassembly. *See Figs. 7 and 8.* To prevent 4th gear tower assembly from separating, install Retainer Tool (9334). *See Fig. 39.* Install 4th gear tower assembly without planetary gear into transaxle case. Ensure oil feed holes are correctly aligned. *See Fig. 39.*

2) Install brake pack assembly. Ensure oil feed holes are correctly aligned. *See Fig. 40.* Ensure snap ring is installed in groove. Install clutch "B" assembly. Ensure "O" ring is installed in groove in intermediate shaft.

3) Install remaining components. Measure distance clutch "A" protrudes past transaxle case. *See Fig. 41.* If distance is greater than .3346" (8.5 mm), components are not assembled properly. Disassemble transaxle components and reassemble as necessary. Ensure oil pump gear alignment marks are aligned before installing pump. *See Fig. 42.* Install valve body assembly. Ensure correct length screws are installed in proper locations. *See Fig. 43.*

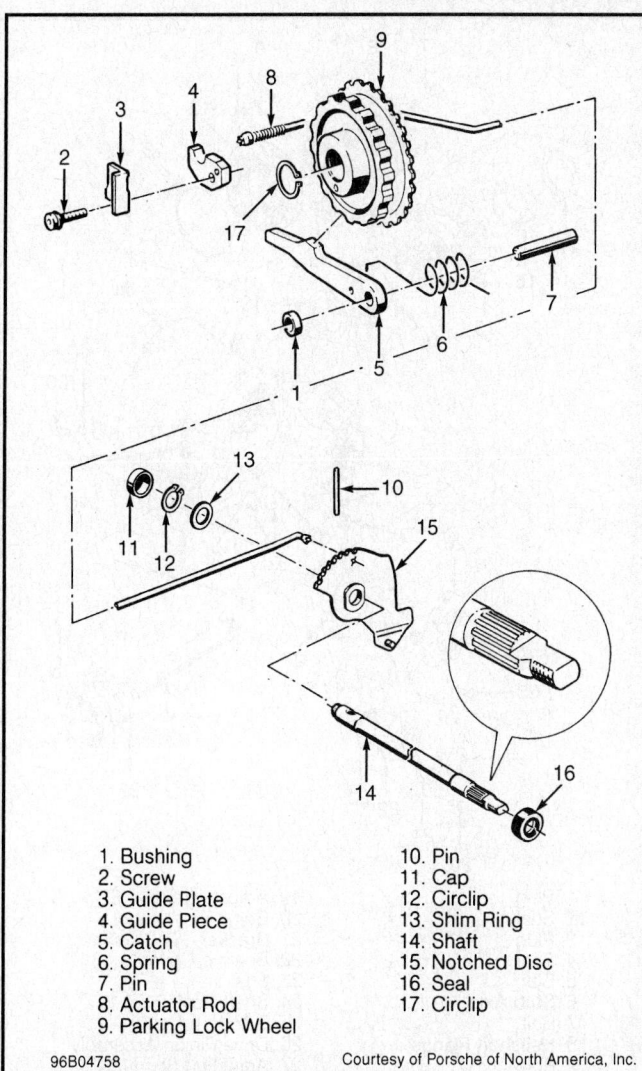

1. Bushing
2. Screw
3. Guide Plate
4. Guide Piece
5. Catch
6. Spring
7. Pin
8. Actuator Rod
9. Parking Lock Wheel
10. Pin
11. Cap
12. Circlip
13. Shim Ring
14. Shaft
15. Notched Disc
16. Seal
17. Circlip

96B04758   Courtesy of Porsche of North America, Inc.

Fig. 30: Exploded View Of Park Mechanism

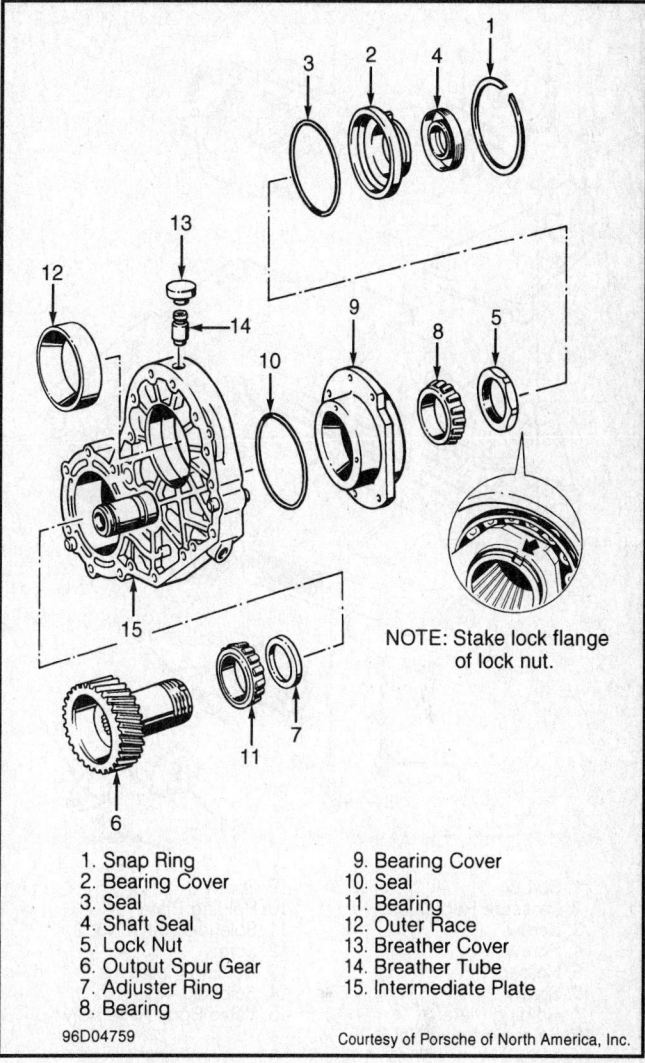

1. Snap Ring
2. Bearing Cover
3. Seal
4. Shaft Seal
5. Lock Nut
6. Output Spur Gear
7. Adjuster Ring
8. Bearing
9. Bearing Cover
10. Seal
11. Bearing
12. Outer Race
13. Breather Cover
14. Breather Tube
15. Intermediate Plate

NOTE: Stake lock flange of lock nut.

96D04759   Courtesy of Porsche of North America, Inc.

Fig. 31: Exploded View Of Intermediate Plate & Output Spur Gear Assembly

INTERMEDIATE PLATE & SPUR GEAR ASSEMBLY

CAUTION: The following procedure is for checking purposes only using original components. Individual parts are no longer available from manufacturer. See TECHNICAL SERVICE BULLETINS.

NOTE: Output spur gear turning torque specification is not available from manufacturer.

Intermediate Spur Gear – 1) Using vernier height gauge, measure and record distance between front cover mounting surface and intermediate spur gear bearing thrust surface (dimension "A"). *See Fig. 44.*
2) Measure and record distance from intermediate plate mounting surface and inner race surface of intermediate spur gear bearing inner race (dimension "B"). *See Fig. 45.*
3) Subtract dimension "B" from dimension "A". Add .0087" (.22 mm) (bearing preload and gasket thickness) to difference to determine thrust shim thickness. Always round shim thickness to nearest .05 mm.

Drive Spur Gear – 1) Remove outer bearing race and adjusting shim from front cover. *See Fig. 6.* Reinstall outer bearing race. Remove intermediate spur gear (if installed). Bolt front cover to intermediate plate without gasket. Use additional nuts and washers as needed to completely attach front cover to intermediate plate.
2) Mount dial indicator to intermediate plate. *See Fig. 46.* Set dial indicator to zero with a preload of 2 mm. Holding internal puller, move spur gear and read maximum deflection. Thrust washer thickness is equal to spur gear movement measurement plus .0079" (.20 mm) (bearing preload and gasket thickness). Always round shim thickness to nearest .05 mm.

Final Assembly – Install selected shims. Lubricate all components with ATF. Install intermediate plate to transaxle case. Complete reassembly of spur gears in reverse order of disassembly. Tighten bolts to specification. See TORQUE SPECIFICATIONS.

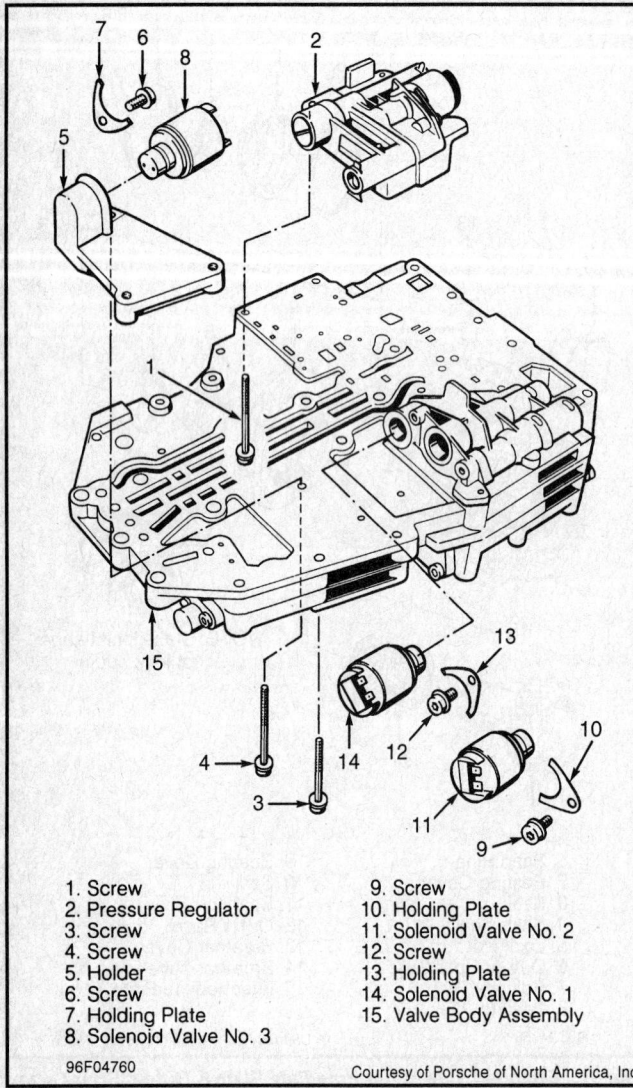

1. Screw	9. Screw
2. Pressure Regulator	10. Holding Plate
3. Screw	11. Solenoid Valve No. 2
4. Screw	12. Screw
5. Holder	13. Holding Plate
6. Screw	14. Solenoid Valve No. 1
7. Holding Plate	15. Valve Body Assembly
8. Solenoid Valve No. 3	

96F04760   Courtesy of Porsche of North America, Inc.

Fig. 32: *Exploded View Of Valve Body Solenoid Installation*

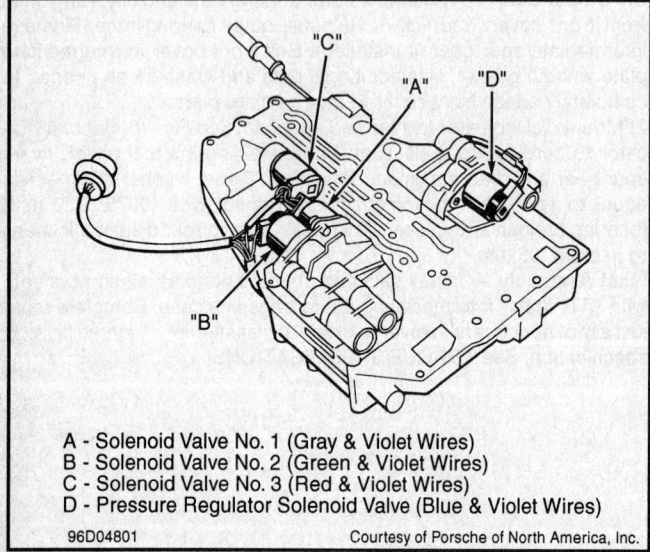

A - Solenoid Valve No. 1 (Gray & Violet Wires)
B - Solenoid Valve No. 2 (Green & Violet Wires)
C - Solenoid Valve No. 3 (Red & Violet Wires)
D - Pressure Regulator Solenoid Valve (Blue & Violet Wires)

96D04801   Courtesy of Porsche of North America, Inc.

Fig. 33: *Identifying Valve Body Solenoid Locations & Wire Colors*

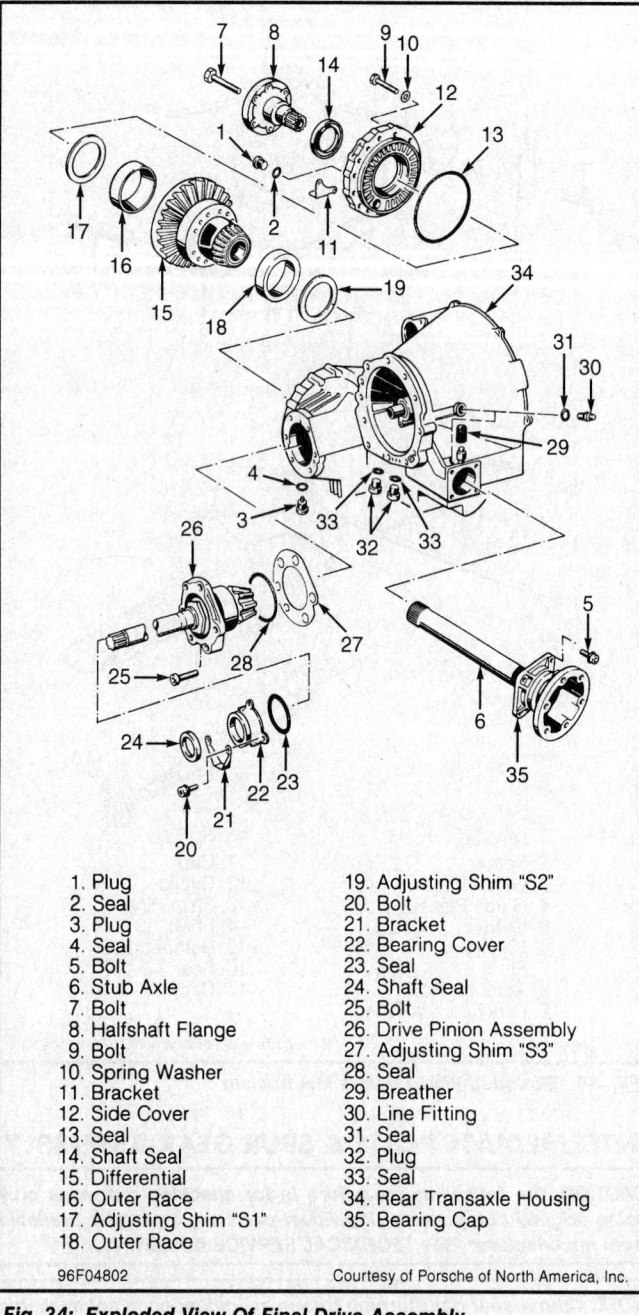

1. Plug	19. Adjusting Shim "S2"
2. Seal	20. Bolt
3. Plug	21. Bracket
4. Seal	22. Bearing Cover
5. Bolt	23. Seal
6. Stub Axle	24. Shaft Seal
7. Bolt	25. Bolt
8. Halfshaft Flange	26. Drive Pinion Assembly
9. Bolt	27. Adjusting Shim "S3"
10. Spring Washer	28. Seal
11. Bracket	29. Breather
12. Side Cover	30. Line Fitting
13. Seal	31. Seal
14. Shaft Seal	32. Plug
15. Differential	33. Seal
16. Outer Race	34. Rear Transaxle Housing
17. Adjusting Shim "S1"	35. Bearing Cap
18. Outer Race	

96F04802   Courtesy of Porsche of North America, Inc.

Fig. 34: *Exploded View Of Final Drive Assembly*

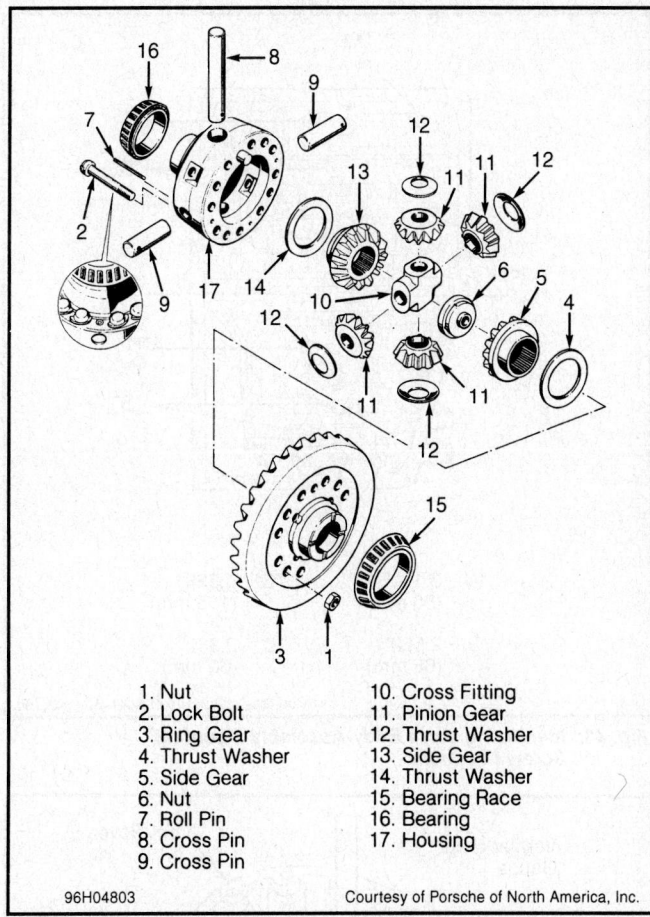

1. Nut
2. Lock Bolt
3. Ring Gear
4. Thrust Washer
5. Side Gear
6. Nut
7. Roll Pin
8. Cross Pin
9. Cross Pin
10. Cross Fitting
11. Pinion Gear
12. Thrust Washer
13. Side Gear
14. Thrust Washer
15. Bearing Race
16. Bearing
17. Housing

96H04803   Courtesy of Porsche of North America, Inc.

Fig. 35: Exploded View Of Differential Assembly

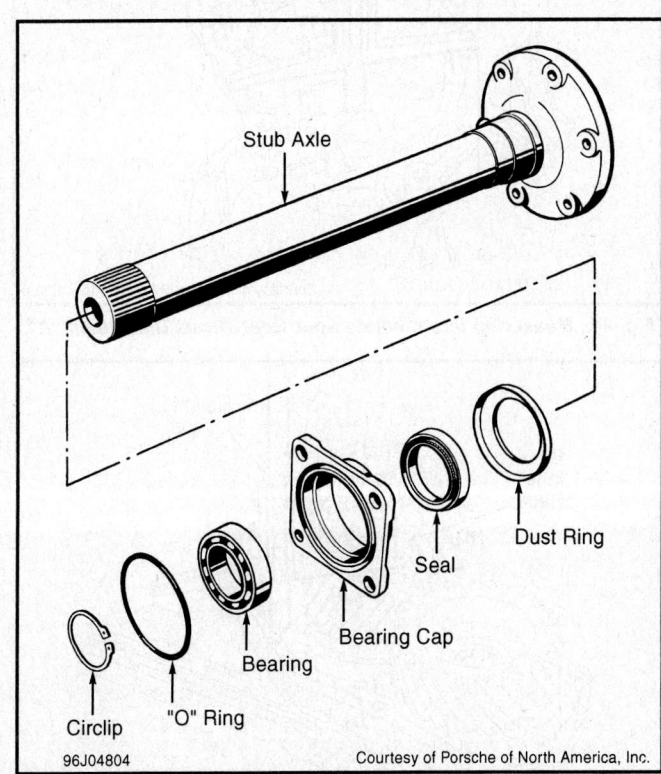

96J04804   Courtesy of Porsche of North America, Inc.

Fig. 36: Exploded View Of Joint Flange Assembly

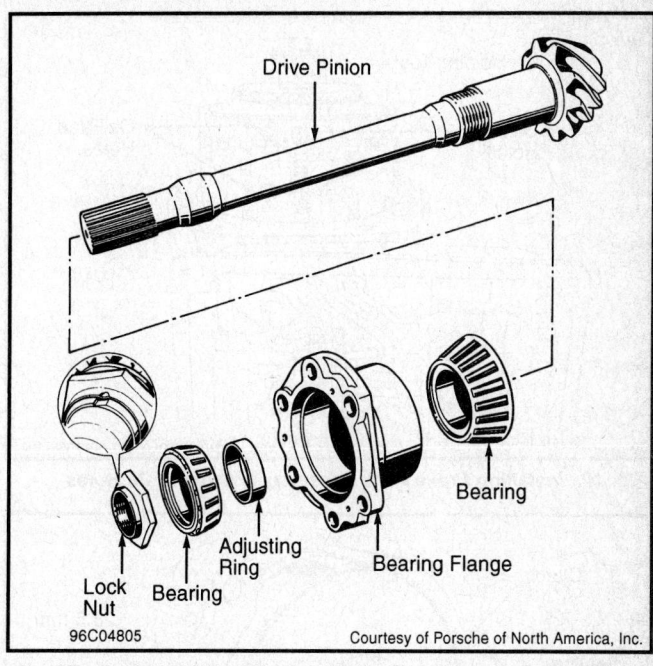

96C04805   Courtesy of Porsche of North America, Inc.

Fig. 37: Exploded View Of Drive Pinion Components Assembly

NOTE: Drive pinion turning torque and preload specification is not available from manufacturer.

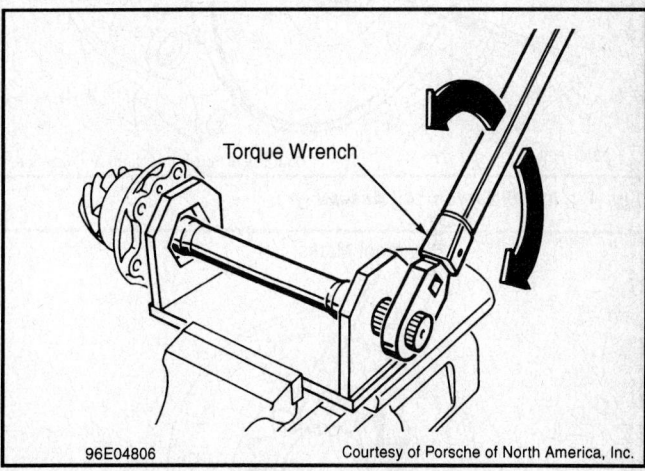

96E04806   Courtesy of Porsche of North America, Inc.

Fig. 38: Removing & Installing Drive Pinion Lock Nut

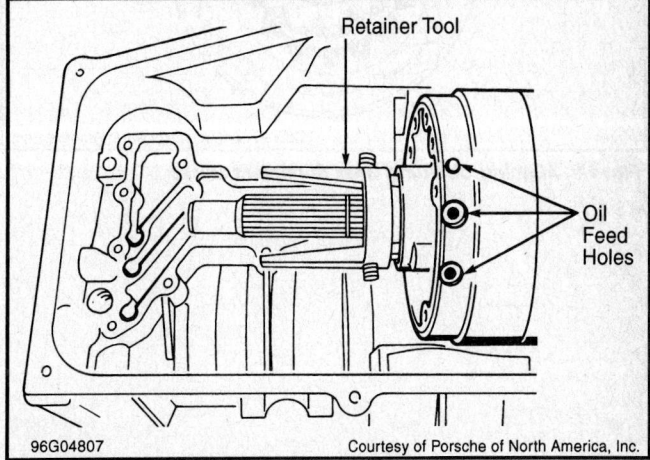

96G04807   Courtesy of Porsche of North America, Inc.

Fig. 39: Installing 4th Gear Tower Assembly

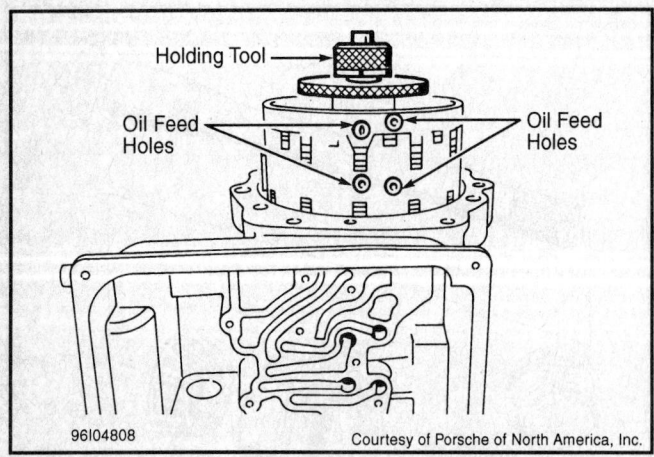

96I04808   Courtesy of Porsche of North America, Inc.

Fig. 40: Installing Brake Pack Assembly & Aligning Oil Holes

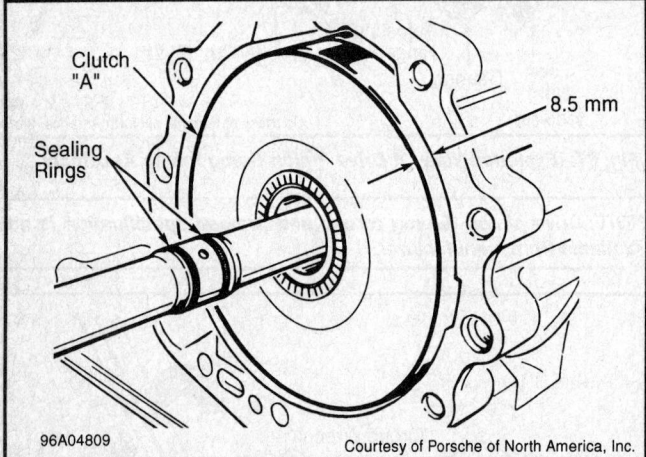

96A04809   Courtesy of Porsche of North America, Inc.

Fig. 41: Install Clutch "A" Assembly

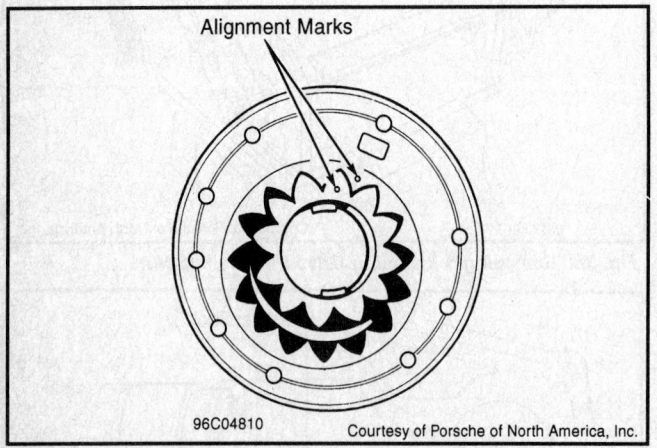

96C04810   Courtesy of Porsche of North America, Inc.

Fig. 42: Aligning Oil Pump Gear Alignment Marks

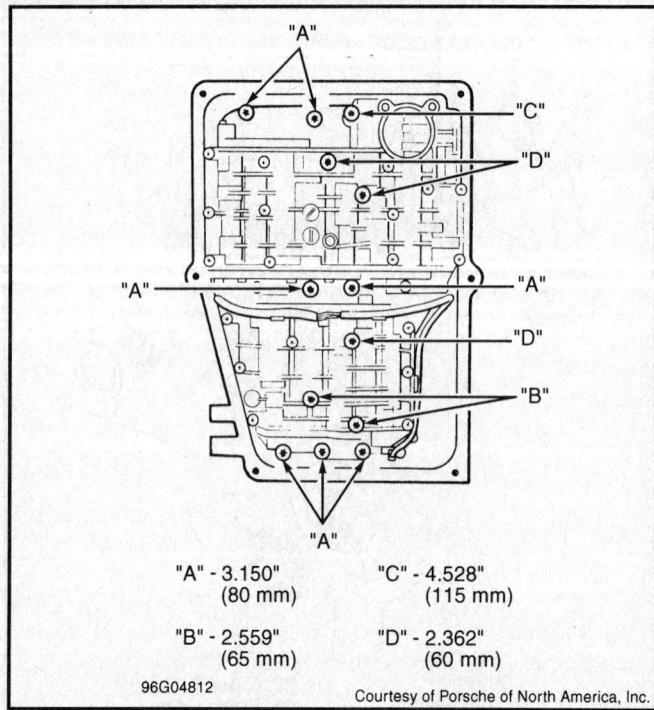

"A" - 3.150"   "C" - 4.528"
(80 mm)   (115 mm)

"B" - 2.559"   "D" - 2.362"
(65 mm)   (60 mm)

96G04812   Courtesy of Porsche of North America, Inc.

Fig. 43: Identifying Valve Body Assembly Mounting Screw Locations

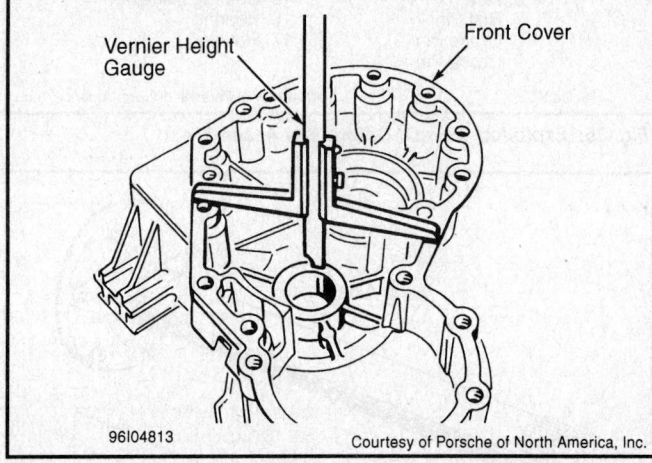

96I04813   Courtesy of Porsche of North America, Inc.

Fig. 44: Measuring Intermediate Spur Gear Thrust Dimension "A"

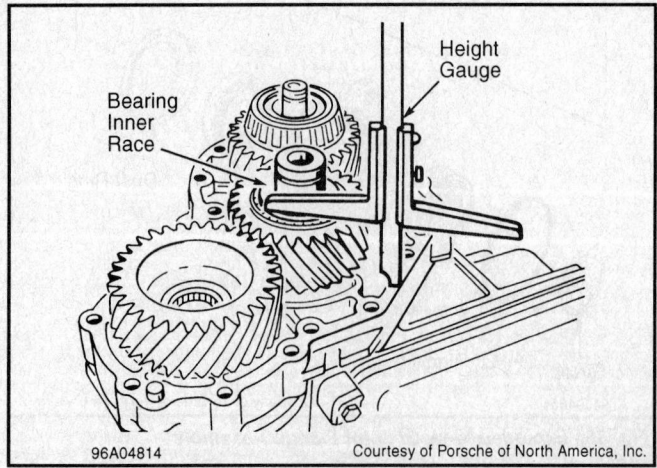

96A04814   Courtesy of Porsche of North America, Inc.

Fig. 45: Measuring Intermediate Spur Gear Thrust Dimension "B"

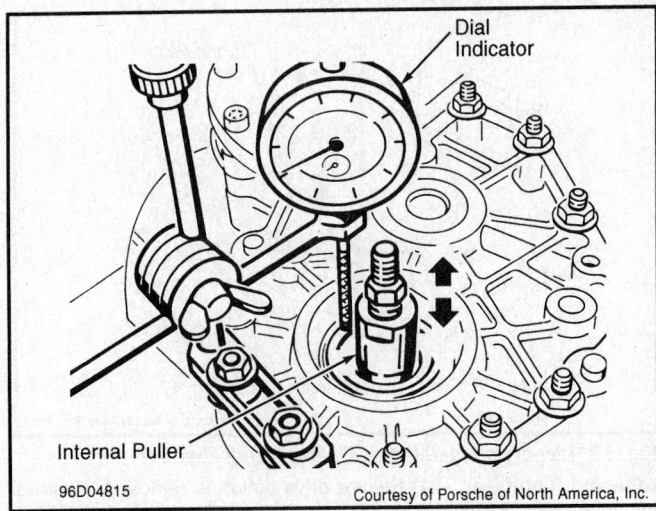

Fig. 46: Measuring Drive Spur Gear Thrust Clearance

FINAL DRIVE ASSEMBLY

Assemble final drive components in reverse order of disassembly. *See Figs. 34-37.* It is necessary to adjust drive pinion and/or ring gear if the following components have been replaced:

- Rear transaxle case.
- Transaxle side cover.
- Drive pinion bearings.
- Drive pinion and ring gear.
- Differential housing.
- Differential housing case bearings.

All adjustment procedures use specialized tools for measuring. For tool part number identification, *see Fig. 47.* Ensure all components are thoroughly cleaned. Any contamination will affect measurements. Following procedures will determine thickness of spacers "S1" and "S2", and adjusting shim "S3". *See Fig. 48.*

Drive Pinion & Ring Gear Identification – Drive pinion and ring gear are always replaced as matched set. Drive pinion is positioned axially to achieve smoothest operation. Deviation "r" from specified design dimension "Ro" is measured, added to design dimension "Ro" and engraved on ring gear as setting value "E". *See Fig. 49.*

NOTE: Setting dimension "E" is stamped on ring gear.

Adjusting Drive Pinion – **1)** Install drive pinion without shim "S3" to rear transaxle housing. *See Fig. 34.* Tighten drive pinion retainer bolts to 37 ft. lbs. (50 N.m).
2) Rotate adjustable stop ring along with spindle towards measuring plunger as far as possible. Set second setting ring to dimension "a" which is 1.181" (30 mm). *See Fig. 50.*
3) Assemble measuring mandrel and set with master gauge to setting dimension "E" (stamped on ring gear). Set dial indicator to zero with 1 mm preload. *See Fig. 51.*
4) Place gauge block plate on drive pinion head and insert measure mandrel with dial indicator toward transaxle side cover into rear transaxle case. Dial gage extension faces center of drive pinion. *See Fig. 52.*

NOTE: Do not use a hammer when installing side cover. Gauge block plate is magnetically held to drive pinion.

5) Install transaxle side cover without shaft seal and sealing ring. Tighten side cover bolts to specification in crisscross pattern. See TORQUE SPECIFICATIONS.
6) Using 24 mm socket, unscrew measuring mandrel until centering discs contact differential carrier bearing races. Do not tighten mandrel to point that mandrel cannot be rotated.

7) Carefully turn measuring mandrel back and forth so dial indicator extension (plunger) sweeps on either side of drive pinion vertical (center) line. Record dial indicator reading at maximum deflection (dial indicator needle reversing point).
8) Measured value is dial indicator movement from set dimension in clockwise direction. Measure value is shim thickness "S3" to be installed. Round dial indicator reading to nearest .05 mm.
9) Remove drive pinion and install selected shim. Recheck drive pinion dimension "E". A tolerance of 0 – .03 mm is allowed.

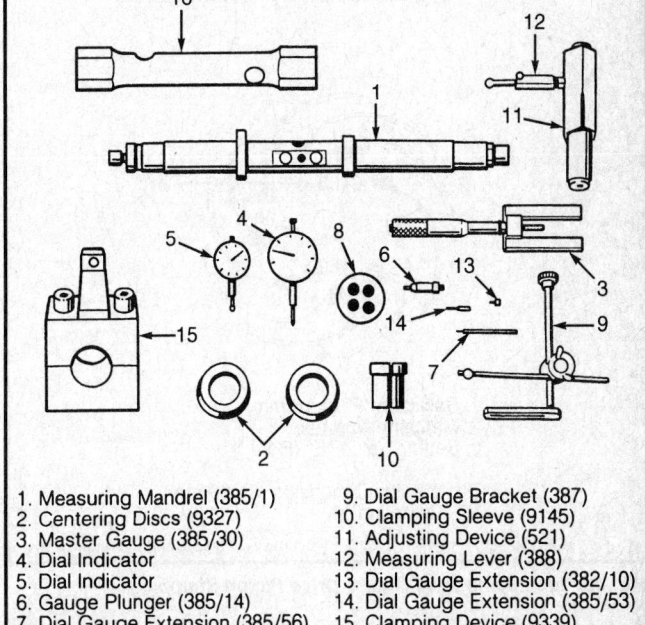

1. Measuring Mandrel (385/1)
2. Centering Discs (9327)
3. Master Gauge (385/30)
4. Dial Indicator
5. Dial Indicator
6. Gauge Plunger (385/14)
7. Dial Gauge Extension (385/56)
8. Gauge Block Plate (9281)
9. Dial Gauge Bracket (387)
10. Clamping Sleeve (9145)
11. Adjusting Device (521)
12. Measuring Lever (388)
13. Dial Gauge Extension (382/10)
14. Dial Gauge Extension (385/53)
15. Clamping Device (9339)
16. 24 mm Socket Wrench

Fig. 47: Identifying Final Drive Assembly Measuring Tool Set

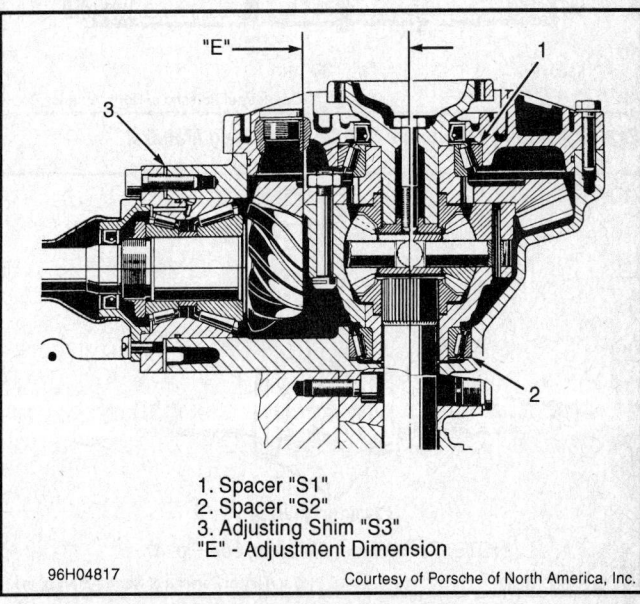

1. Spacer "S1"
2. Spacer "S2"
3. Adjusting Shim "S3"
"E" - Adjustment Dimension

Fig. 48: Cut-Away View Of Final Drive Assembly

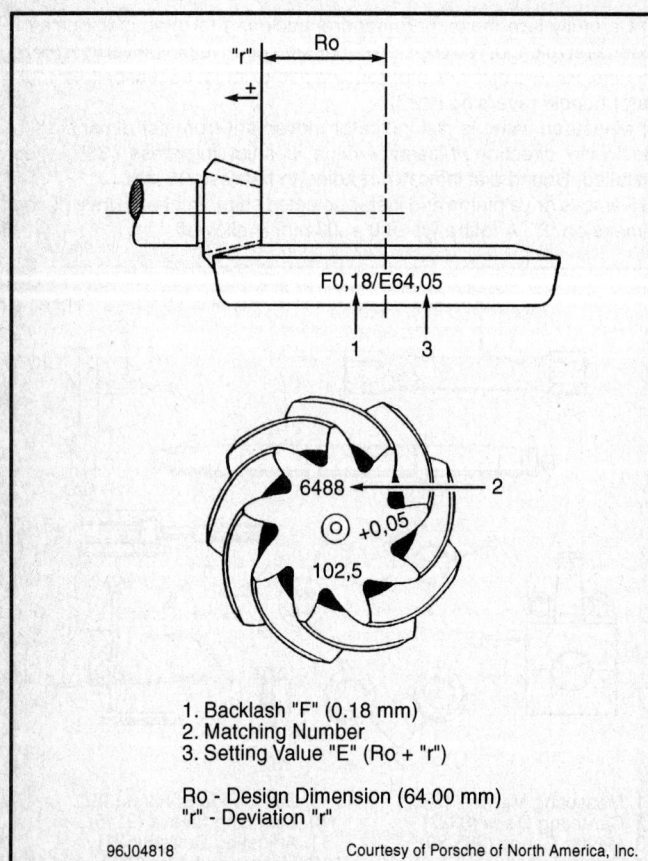

1. Backlash "F" (0.18 mm)
2. Matching Number
3. Setting Value "E" (Ro + "r")

Ro - Design Dimension (64.00 mm)
"r" - Deviation "r"

96J04818   Courtesy of Porsche of North America, Inc.

Fig. 49: Identifying Ring Gear & Drive Pinion Stamping

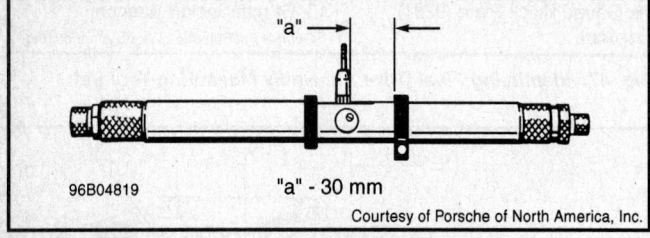

96B04819   "a" - 30 mm
                           Courtesy of Porsche of North America, Inc.

Fig. 50: Setting Dimension "a" On Measuring Mandrel

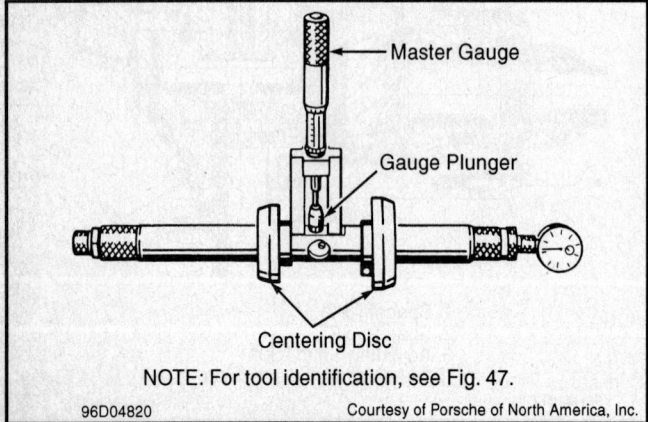

NOTE: For tool identification, see Fig. 47.
96D04820   Courtesy of Porsche of North America, Inc.

Fig. 51: Setting Measuring Mandrel For Dimension "E" Measurement

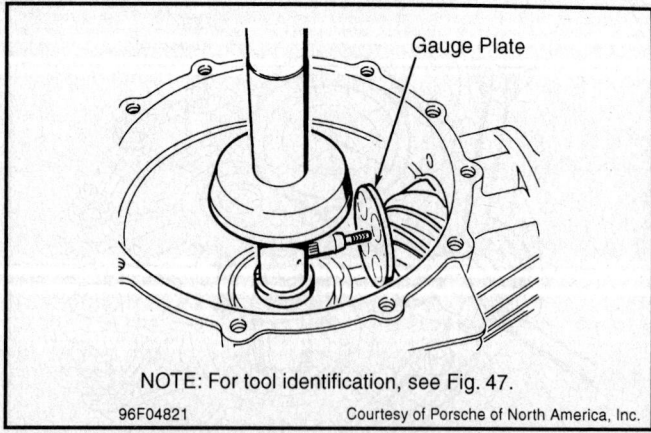

NOTE: For tool identification, see Fig. 47.
96F04821   Courtesy of Porsche of North America, Inc.

Fig. 52: Identifying Installation Of Measuring Mandrel

Adjusting Ring Gear – 1) Ensure drive pinion is removed. Remove adjusting shim "S1" from side cover. See Fig. 34. Install bearing race in side cover. Ensure adjusting shim "S2" is not removed. Install differential assembly in transaxle case. Install side cover without seals. Tighten bolts in crisscross pattern to 17 ft. lbs. (23 N.m).
2) Rotate differential to seat bearings. Place gauge block plate on differential collar. See Fig. 53. Mount dial indicator with 30 mm extension. Set dial indicator to zero with 2 mm preload.
3) Move differential up and down. Measure and record maximum dial indicator deflection. Do not turn differential during measuring process.
4) Disassemble side cover and remove differential assembly. Remove adjusting shim "S2". See Fig. 34. Measure thickness of adjusting shim "S2". Adjusting shim "S1" thickness is determined by adding measured deflection, adjusting shim "S2" thickness and .0094" (.24 mm) (bearing preload).
5) Total the thickness measurements of both shims and divide by 2. See following example:

Total Thickness Of Adjusting Shims

"S1" + "S2" = .1122" (2.85 mm)

Thickness Of Adjusting Shim "S1"

$$\frac{.1122" \ (2.85 \ mm)}{2} = \frac{.0561" \ (1.425 \ mm)}{-.0157" \ (.40 \ mm)}$$
$$= .0404" \ (1.025 \ mm)$$

Thickness Of Adjusting Shim "S2"

$$\frac{.1122" \ (2.85 \ mm)}{2} = \frac{.0561" \ (1.425 \ mm)}{+.0157" \ (.40 \ mm)}$$
$$= .0718" \ (1.825 \ mm)$$

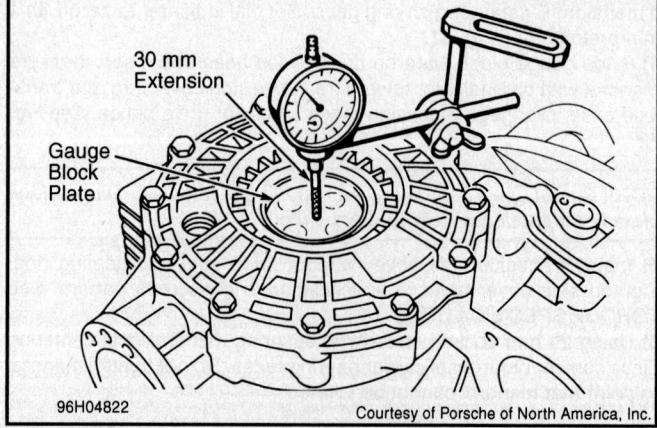

96H04822   Courtesy of Porsche of North America, Inc.

Fig. 53: Measuring Differential Axial Movement

6) Thickness of adjusting shim "S1" is total minus .0157" (.40 mm). Thickness of adjusting shim "S2" is total plus .0157" (.40 mm). Available adjusting shims range in thicknesses from 1.0 - 2.0 mm in increments of .05 mm. Shim thickness may be rounded up or down to next available shim as long as total thickness of both selected shims doesn't exceed original thickness measurement of both shims.

NOTE: Backlash specification is stamped on ring gear.

Adjusting Differential Backlash – 1) Install drive pinion with predetermined "S3" shim. Tighten pinion retainer bolts to specification. See TORQUE SPECIFICATIONS.

2) Install predetermined adjusting shims "S1" and "S2". See ADJUSTING RING GEAR. Install differential carrier bearing outer races. Install differential and side cover. Tighten side cover bolts to specification in crisscross pattern. See TORQUE SPECIFICATIONS. Ensure some backlash exists when tightening side cover bolts. Do not allow drive pinion to bind against ring gear.

3) Rotate differential. Assemble measuring lever and adjusting device. *See Fig. 54.* Adjust lever length to .3150" (80 mm) (dimension "a").

4) Mount clamp on drive pinion. *See Fig. 55.* Do not tighten clamp. Mount dial indicator at right angle to measuring lever. *See Fig. 54.* Tighten clamp on drive pinion.

5) Turn differential clockwise and hold. Zero dial indicator. Turn differential counterclockwise and hold. Record dial indicator reading. Loosen clamp on drive pinion. Turn differential 90 degrees. Repeat backlash measurement procedure.

6) Turn differential 90 degrees 2 more times while repeating backlash measurement procedure. Recorded readings should not deviate more than .05 mm. Backlash figure is stamped on ring gear.

7) Backlash is adjusted by changing shims "S1" and "S2". A shim thickness change of .05 mm will result in backlash change of about .1 mm. DO NOT change total thickness of both selected shims determined in ADJUSTING RING GEAR procedure.

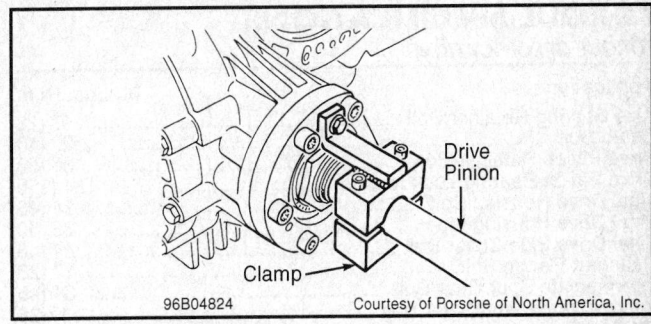

Fig. 55: **Clamping Drive Pinion**

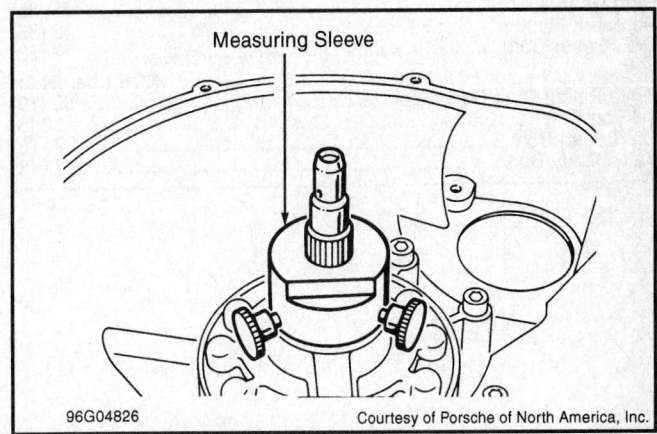

Fig. 56: **Installing Input Shaft Measuring Sleeve**

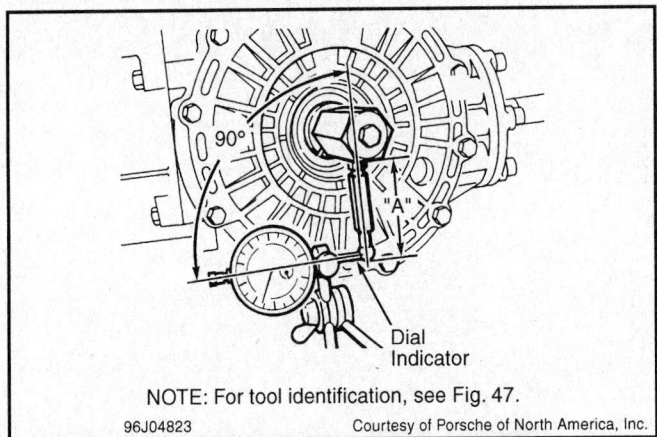

Fig. 54: **Measuring Drive Pinion-To-Ring Gear Backlash**

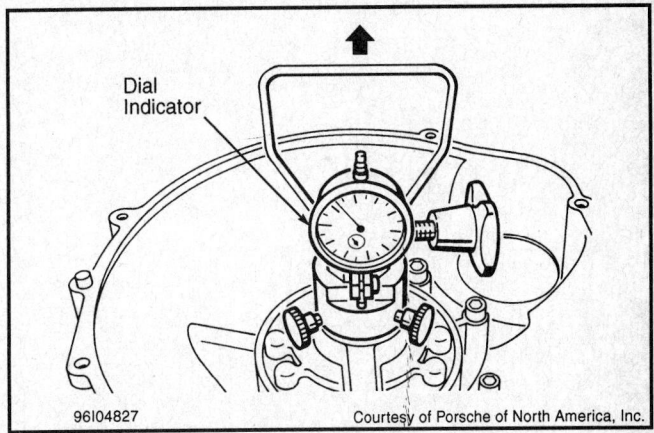

Fig. 57: **Measuring Input Shaft End Play**

NOTE: Alternative method can be used to determine input shaft end play.

FINAL ASSEMBLY

Adjusting Input Shaft End Play – 1) Install final drive assembly with gasket to transaxle case. Use centering pins to assist alignment of final drive assembly to transaxle case, if needed. Front section (intermediate plate/spur gear assembly) should already be installed.

2) Install Measuring Sleeve (9338). *See Fig. 56.* Mount dial indicator to input shaft and tighten clamp. *See Fig. 57.* Zero dial indicator. Pull up on handle and record maximum clearance. Install appropriate shim to achieve .0079 - .0157" (.2 - .4 mm) end play.

Torque Converter – Install torque converter in transaxle. Measure torque converter installed depth. *See Fig. 58.* Torque converter should protrude past case about .9842" (25 mm).

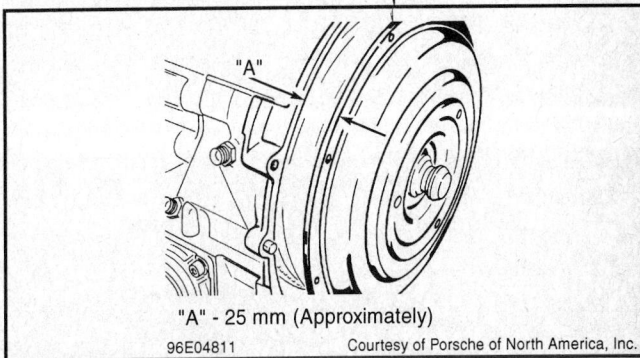

"A" - 25 mm (Approximately)

Fig. 58: **Measuring Torque Converter Installed Depth**

TORQUE SPECIFICATIONS
TORQUE SPECIFICATIONS

Application	Ft. Lbs. (N.m)
Axle Bearing Retainer Bolt	17 (23)
Banjo Bolt	29 (40)
Drive Pinion Retainer Bolt	36 (50)
Drive Pinion Bearing Lock Nut	184 (250)
Final Drive Housing Bolt	34 (46)
Final Drive Housing Plug	36 (50)
Final Drive Side Cover Bolt	34 (46)
Halfshaft Flange Bolt	17 (23)
Intermediate Spur Gear Bolt	34 (46)
Intermediate Plate Cover Bolt	17 (23)
Oil Pan Plug	29 (40)
Output Spur Gear Nut	184 (250)
Ring Gear Nut	63 (85)
Screw-In Flange	26 (35)
Side Cover Bolt	17 (23)

Application	INCH Lbs. (N.m)
Drive Pinion Dust Cover Bolt	89 (10)
Oil Pan Bolt	53 (6)
Oil Screen Bolt	71 (8)
Valve Body Bolt	71 (8)

TRANSMISSION SPECIFICATIONS
TRANSMISSION SPECIFICATIONS

Application	INCH (mm)
Brake & Clutch Pack Clearance	
Brake "C1"	.0217-.0776 (.55-1.97)
Brake "C2"	.0248-.0945 (.63-2.40)
Brake "D"	.0528-.0941 (1.34-2.39)
Brake "F"	.0571-.1082 (1.45-2.75)
Clutch "A"	N/A
Clutch "B"	.0484-.0618 (1.23-1.57)
Clutch "E"	.0457-.1079 (1.16-2.74)
End Play	
Input Shaft	.0079-.0158 (.2-.4)

TECHNICAL SERVICE BULLETINS

INTERMEDIATE PLATE/SPUR GEAR ASSEMBLY

Porsche of North America, Inc. TSB 9503 (4-4-95) – Should repairs to Tiptronic transaxle front cover, spur gears, bearings or intermediate plate become necessary, they must be replaced as a complete set. These parts are no longer available as separate items. 911 Carrera (993) 1995-on part number is 943 300 911 01.

Manufacturer recommends transaxle repairs be made only to valve body, oil pump, sensors and final drive assembly.

ROUGH 2-3 SHIFT &/OR ROUGH 2-1 SHIFT

Porsche of North America, Inc. TSB 9506 (11-28-95) – If customer experiences rough 2-3 shift and/or rough 2-1 shift, manufacturer recommends replacement of valve body assembly (943 325 001 02) and Transmission Control Module (TCM) (993 618 115 00).

Carrera 2 (1995)

APPLICATION

Vehicle	Transaxle Model
1995 Porsche Carrera 2	A50/05

NOTE: *Information for 1996 models is not available.*

DESCRIPTION

The A50/05 Tiptronic transaxle is a clutch and planetary type transaxle that can be operated in either automatic or manual mode by means of a dual-gate shift selector. Transaxle is controlled by an electronic Transmission Control Unit (TCU) that selects from 5 different shift programs (SK1-economical to SK5-sports) depending on information input from various components and sensors. *See Fig. 1.*

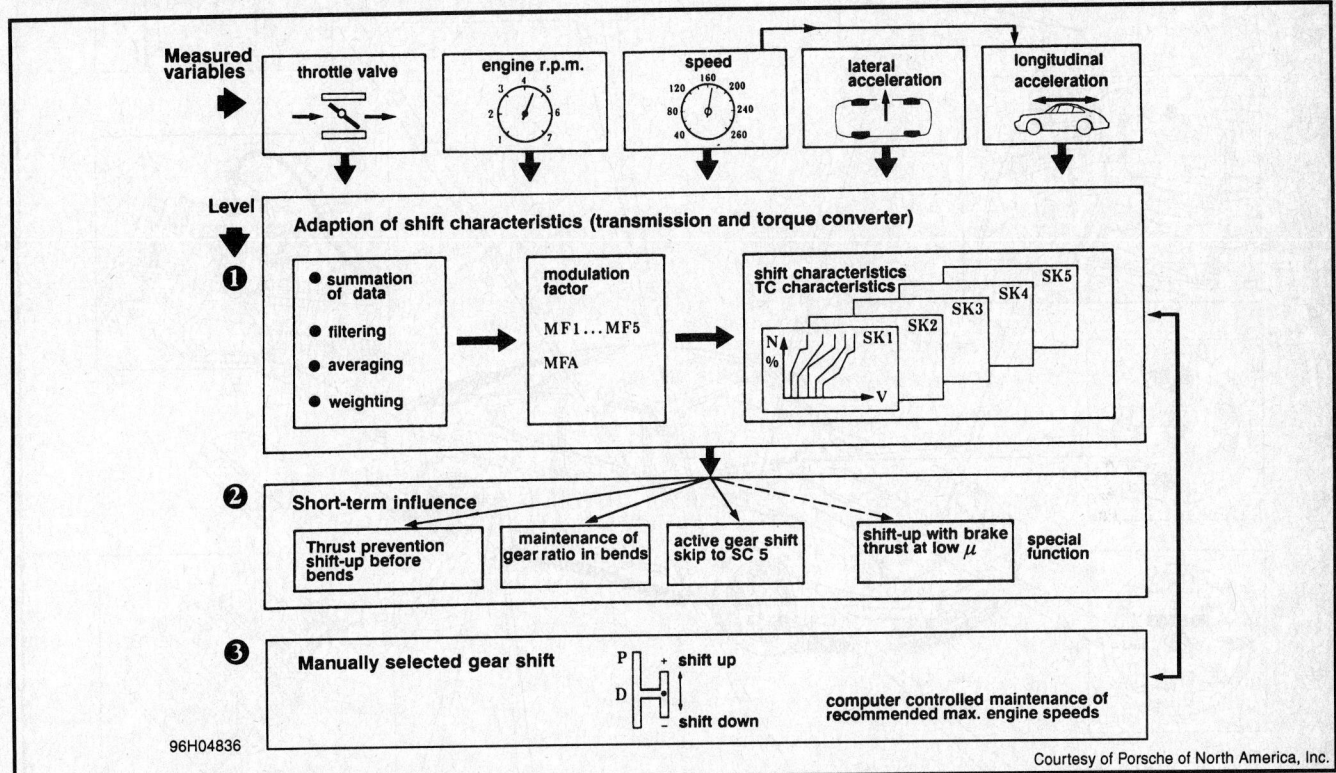

Fig. 1: Transaxle System Operational Overview

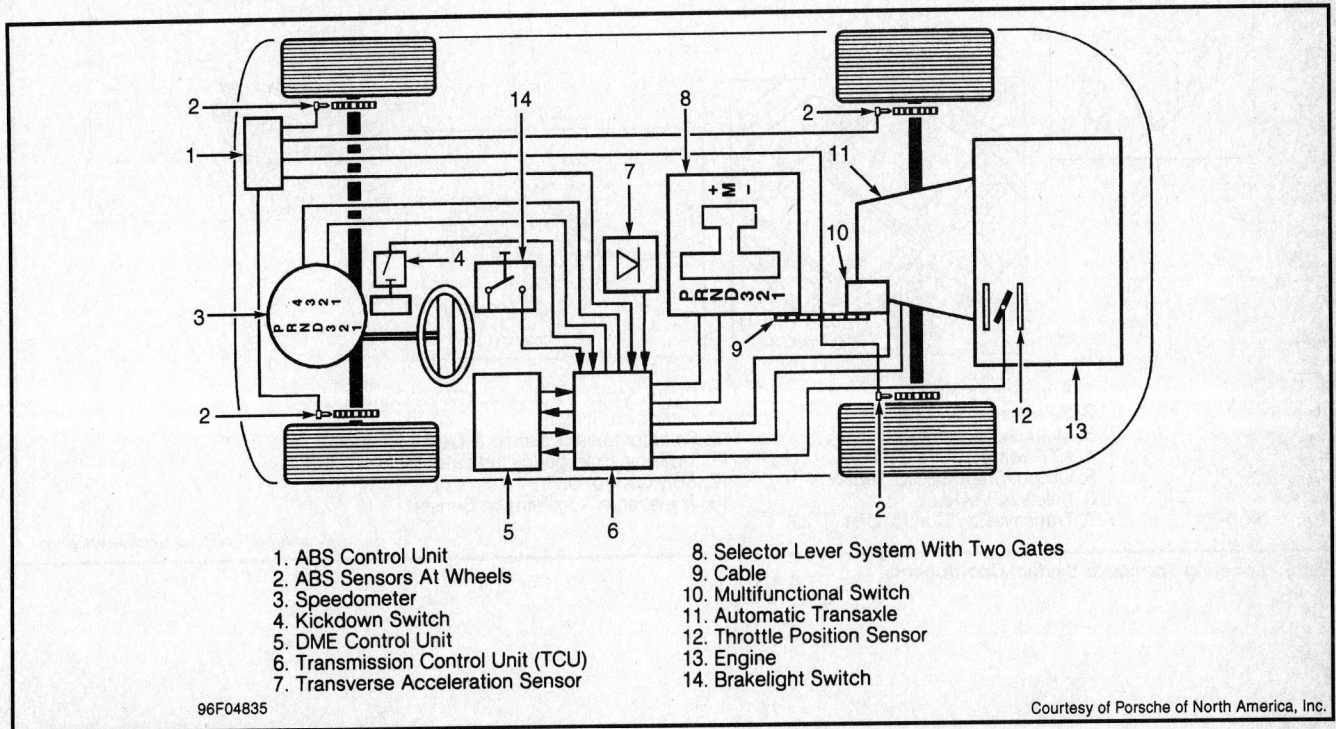

1. ABS Control Unit
2. ABS Sensors At Wheels
3. Speedometer
4. Kickdown Switch
5. DME Control Unit
6. Transmission Control Unit (TCU)
7. Transverse Acceleration Sensor
8. Selector Lever System With Two Gates
9. Cable
10. Multifunctional Switch
11. Automatic Transaxle
12. Throttle Position Sensor
13. Engine
14. Brakelight Switch

Courtesy of Porsche of North America, Inc.

Fig. 2: Identifying TCU Inputs & Outputs

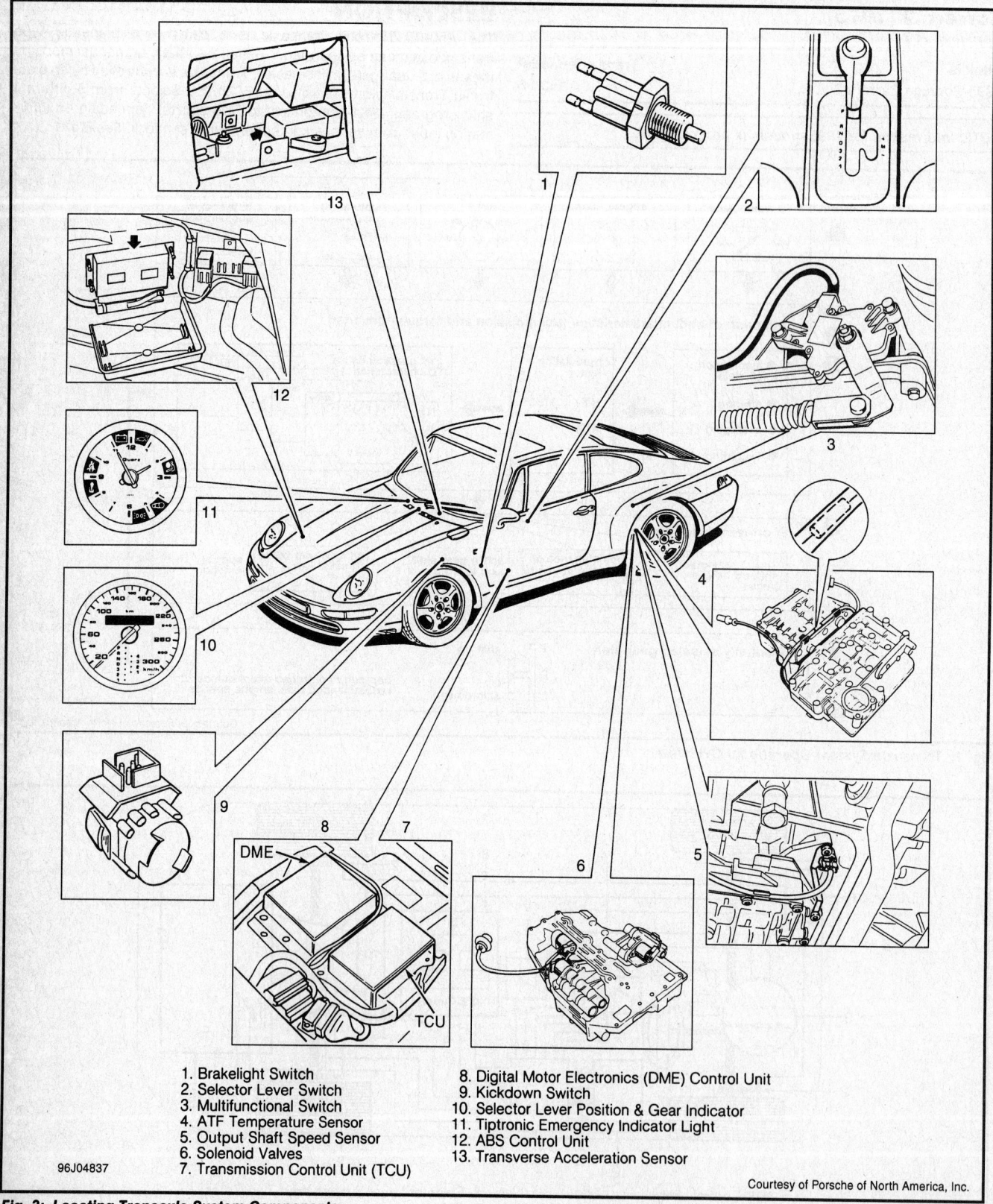

1. Brakelight Switch
2. Selector Lever Switch
3. Multifunctional Switch
4. ATF Temperature Sensor
5. Output Shaft Speed Sensor
6. Solenoid Valves
7. Transmission Control Unit (TCU)
8. Digital Motor Electronics (DME) Control Unit
9. Kickdown Switch
10. Selector Lever Position & Gear Indicator
11. Tiptronic Emergency Indicator Light
12. ABS Control Unit
13. Transverse Acceleration Sensor

96J04837

Courtesy of Porsche of North America, Inc.

Fig. 3: Locating Transaxle System Components

OPERATION

NOTE: For component location, see Fig. 3.

TRANSMISSION CONTROL UNIT (TCU)

The TCU is the information and command center for entire transaxle system. It compares various information inputs with stored driving and gearshift programs. *See Fig. 2.* The TCU then selects shift strategy that is best suited to driving mode and sends signals to transaxle solenoids.

TCU INPUT DEVICES

Brakelight Switch – Brakelight switch signal is sent to TCU to start downshifts.

Shift Selector Lever Switch – Shift selector lever switch includes manual, upshift, downshift and parking switches.

Multifunctional Switch – Switch is operated by selector lever. Selector lever position is transmitted to TCU. Switch also operates reverse lights and starter lock out (park and neutral position).

ATF Temperature Sensor – Sensor is built into transmission harness. Sensor controls modulating pressure of transmission in accordance with ATF temperature. If ATF temperature reaches excessive level, TCU selects shift program with minimum power loss and engages torque converter lock up to allow ATF to cool.

Output Shaft Speed Sensor – Inductive pickup transmits transaxle output shaft RPM to TCU for shift point calculation and slip monitoring.

Digital Motor Electronics (DME) Engine Management System – The DME control unit is located next to TCU. DME sends engine RPM, fuel consumption and throttle position signals to TCU. TCU responds by sending shift signal to DME control unit for ignition retard at moment of shifting.

ABS Control Unit – ABS inputs right front wheel speed to TCU.

Transverse Acceleration Sensor – Mounted below center console, sensor sends input signal to TCU if transverse (lateral) acceleration limits are exceeded during cornering. Will not downshift, even if accelerator is fully depressed.

TCU OUTPUT DEVICES

Shift Solenoid Valves – TCU controls operation of 3 transaxle solenoid valves. Solenoid valves control shifts and torque converter lock-up. A 4th frequency controlled valve regulates fluid pressure.

Kickdown Switch – Kickdown switch detects accelerator being depressed beyond full throttle position. Depending on engine RPM, transaxle immediately downshifts.

Tiptronic Emergency Indicator Light – Light located in clock is temporarily switched on (light check) and goes dim when engine is started. If light is illuminated while vehicle is operating, a system fault has been detected and emergency driving program is selected. Warning light also indicates that the electro-hydraulic reverse lock-out is inoperative. Vehicle can be shifted into reverse during forward movement, causing transaxle damage.

SELF-DIAGNOSTIC SYSTEM

NOTE: Before testing transmission, ensure fluid level is correct and shift cable is properly adjusted. Ensure engine starts with shift lever in Park and Neutral to ensure proper adjustment of multifunctional switch. Transaxle must first be tested by checking for stored codes. See RETRIEVING TROUBLE CODES.

Transmission Control Unit (TCU) can store fault codes. Detected faults are stored for at least 50 engine starts. If positive battery cable or TCU harness connector is disconnected, fault code memory will be cleared.

TIPTRONIC EMERGENCY INDICATOR LIGHT

Description – Vehicle is equipped with a light that indicates fault in Tiptronic control system. Indicator light is installed in clock. *See Fig. 4.* Light illuminates as a self-test when ignition switch is in ON position.

Emergency Driving Program – If an electrical or electronic fault occurs during operation with Tiptronic drive system, the TCU automatically switches itself off and switches over to emergency driving program. This switch-over occurs in event of the following:

*   Short circuit or electrical fault in a solenoid valve or pressure regulator for modulation pressure.
*   Missing injection signal from engine from DME control unit.
*   No supply voltage to TCU.
*   Open circuit in wiring harness between TCU and transaxle.

In emergency driving program, transaxle operates in 3rd gear only without torque converter lock-up. Reverse gear and parking gear can also be selected manually.

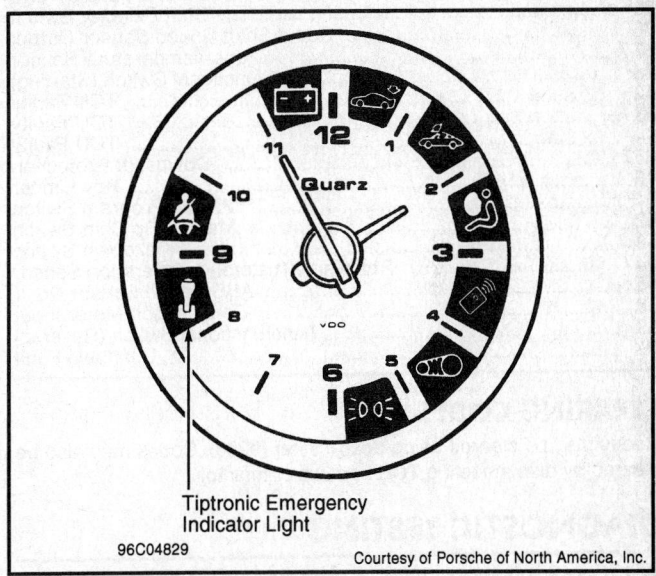

Tiptronic Emergency Indicator Light

96C04829

Courtesy of Porsche of North America, Inc.

Fig. 4: Locating Tiptronic Emergency Indicator Light

RETRIEVING TROUBLE CODES

NOTE: Before retrieving Diagnostic Trouble Codes (DTC), ensure sufficient battery voltage exists for proper self-diagnosis system operation.

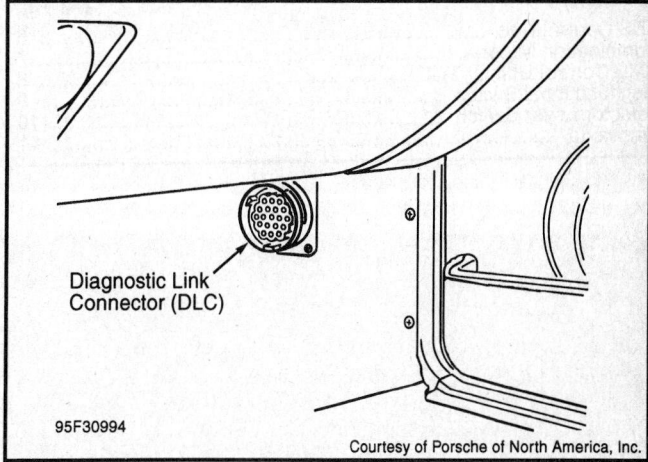

Diagnostic Link Connector (DLC)

95F30994

Courtesy of Porsche of North America, Inc.

Fig. 5: Locating Diagnostic Link Connector (DLC)

Using Diagnostic Connector – Ensure transaxle is in Park or Neutral and ignition is off. Connect Porsche System Tester (9288) to Diagnostic Link Connector (DLC). *See Fig. 5.* Turn tool on and follow instructions displayed. In addition to reading code memory, test can activate a number of components.

DTC IDENTIFICATION

DTC	Probable Cause
11	Supply Voltage (Terminal 15 Circuit)
13	Supply Voltage – Drive Links
14	Supply Voltage – 5 Volt Ref.
21	Engine RPM Signal
22	Load Signal
24	Ignition Timing Change
25	Throttle Position Sensor
31	Solenoid Valve No. 1
32	Solenoid Valve No. 2
33	TCC Solenoid Valve
34	Pressure Regulator Solenoid Valve
35	Shift Selector Switch
36	Ouput Shaft Speed Sensor Output
37	Trans Temperature Sensor
38	Multifunctional Switch (Starting)
42	TCU Faulty
43	TCU Faulty
44	TCU Faulty
45	Downshift Protection
46	Rev Limiter
51	Manual Program Switch
52	Manual Tip Shift Switch
53	Kickdown Switch
54	Transverse (Lateral) Acceleration Sensor
55	ABS Speed Sensor No. 1
56	Combination Meter Input
59	Multifunctional Switch (Reverse)
XX	Unknown Fault

CLEARING CODES

Codes may be cleared using Scan Tester (9288). Codes may also be cleared by disconnecting TCU harness connector.

DIAGNOSTIC TESTING

NOTE: For connector terminal identification, see CONNECTOR IDENTIFICATION. For circuit and wire color identification, see appropriate wiring diagram in WIRING DIAGRAMS. Manufacturer recommends use of Breakout Box for measuring voltage at TCU harness connector.

CONNECTOR IDENTIFICATION

CONNECTOR IDENTIFICATION

Component	See Fig.
ABS Control Unit	6
Combination Meter	7
DME Control Unit Or TCU	8
Multifunctional Switch	9
Selector Lever Switch	10
Transaxle	11

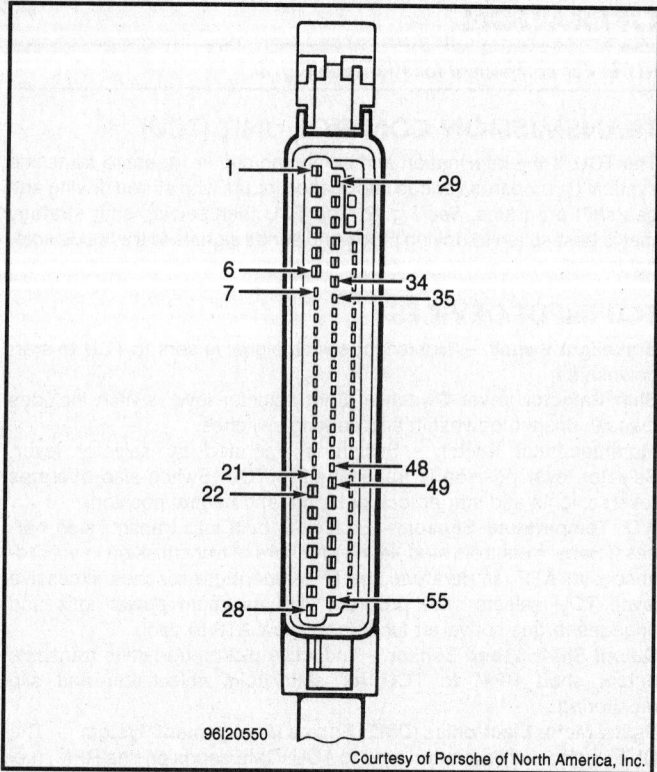

96I20550

Courtesy of Porsche of North America, Inc.

Fig. 6: Identifying ABS Control Unit Harness Connector Terminals

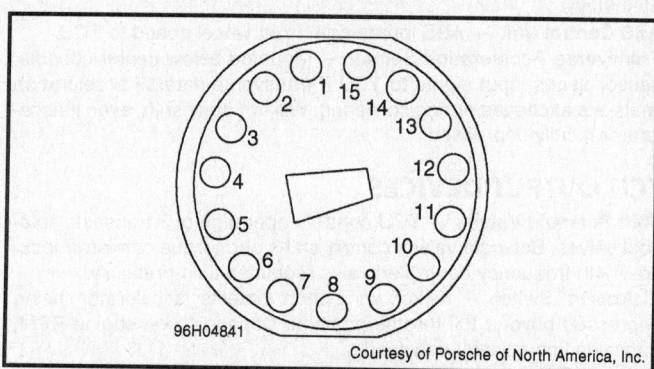

96H04841

Courtesy of Porsche of North America, Inc.

Fig. 7: Identifying Combination Meter Connector Terminals

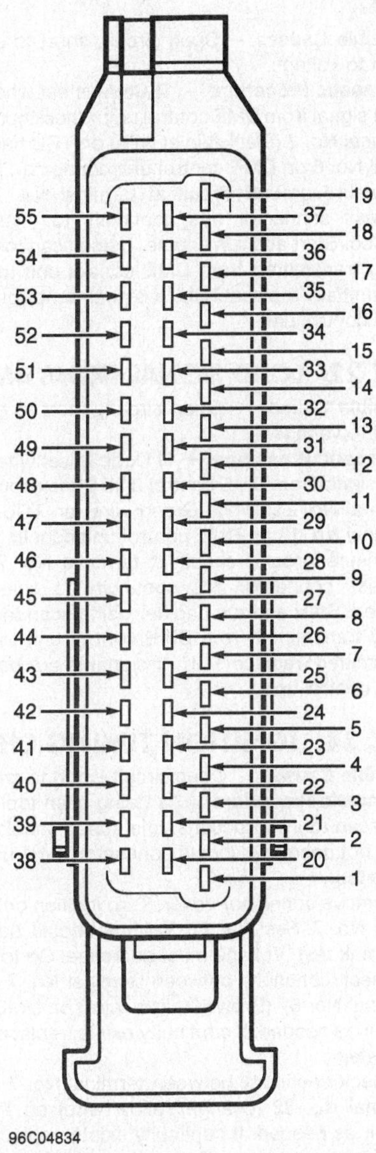

1. Terminal 15 E
2. Output RPM +
3. Engine RPM (TN)
4. Brakelight
5. Solenoid Valve No. 1
6. Modulating Pressure Solenoid Valve
7. Ground
8. 5 Volt Reference
9. Pin Coding "1"
10. Upshift
11. Throttle Signal
12. Front Wheel Speed
13. Manual Program Display
14. Position "Y" Switch
15. "L" Wire
16. 1st Gear Display
17. Not Used
18. Not Used
19. Positive Voltage For Solenoid Valves
20. Shield/Output RPM
21. Load Signal (TI)
22. Not Used
23. Warning Light
24. Solenoid Valve No. 2
25. Reverse Light Relay
26. Ground
27. Not Used
28. Pin Coding "2"
29. Downshift
30. Kickdown
31. 2nd Gear Display
32. Ignition Timing Signal
33. Position "Z" Switch
34. Not Used
35. Not Used
36. Not Used
37. Not Used
38. Output RPM
39. Terminal 30
40. Transverse Acceleration Sensor
41. Redundancy
42. Lock-Up Clutch Solenoid Valve
43. 3rd Gear Display
44. Ground
45. 5 Volt Output
46. ATF Temperature Sensor
47. Not Used
48. Manual Program Input Signal
49. Not Used
50. Position "X" Switch
51. "K" Wire
52. Not Used
53. Not Used
54. Not Used
55. 4th Gear Display

96C04834

Courtesy of Porsche of North America, Inc.

Fig. 8: Identifying DME Control Unit & TCU Harness Connector Terminals

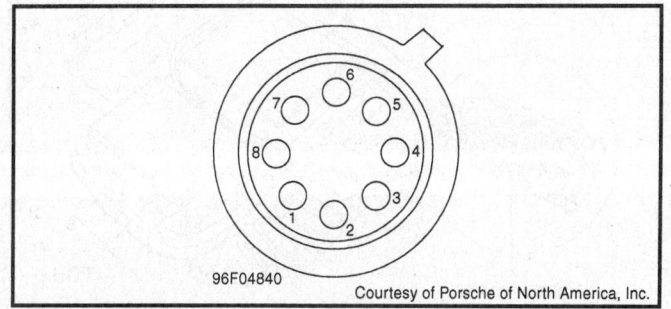

96F04840

Courtesy of Porsche of North America, Inc.

Fig. 9: Identifying Multifunctional Switch Terminals

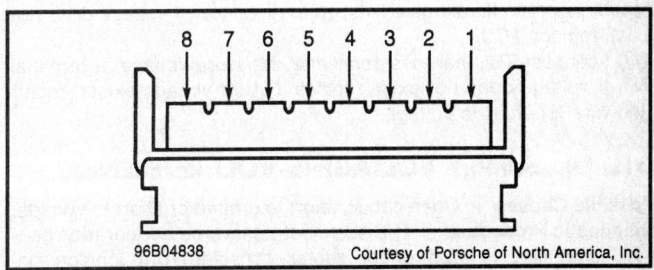

96B04838

Courtesy of Porsche of North America, Inc.

Fig. 10: Identifying Selector Lever Switch Connector Terminals

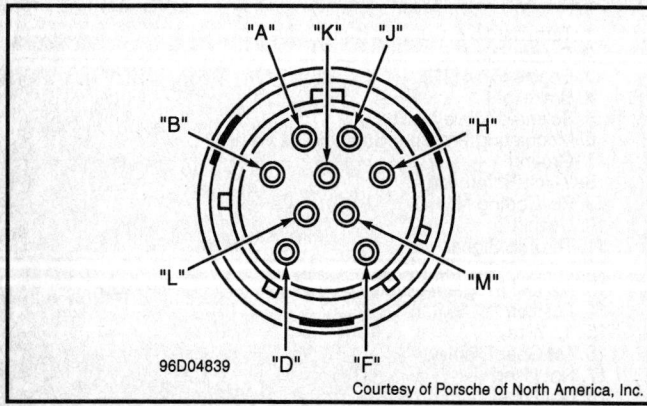

Fig. 11: *Identifying Transaxle Connector Terminals*

DTC 11: CONTROL UNIT VOLTAGE

Possible Causes – Open circuit, short to positive, short to ground, loose connection and/or voltage outside limits.

Diagnostic Procedure – 1) If tiptronic emergency indicator light does not illuminate when ignition is on, inspect fuse No. 27 (15-amp). Replace as needed. Measure voltage at fuse No. 27. If voltage does not exist, go to next step.

2) Inspect Orange/White wire between fuse No. 27 and relay No. 11. If circuit is okay, inspect operation of relay No. 11. Replace as needed.

3) Turn ignition off. Disconnect TCU harness connector. Turn ignition on. Measure voltage at terminal No. 1 (Red/White wire). If voltage is not present, repair Red/White wire between TCU harness connector and fuse No. 27. Go to next step.

4) If voltage measured is less than 11 volts or greater than 14.5 volts with engine running, inspect battery, alternator and/or regulator. See appropriate GENERATOR & REGULATORS article in STARTING & CHARGING SYSTEMS in appropriate MITCHELL® manual. Repair as needed.

DTC 13: SUPPLY VOLTAGE (SWITCHED VOLTAGE)

Possible Causes – Transaxle relay in TCU cannot energize or de-energize.

Diagnostic Procedure – 1) Ensure ignition is off. Disconnect transaxle harness connector. Turn ignition on. Measure voltage at terminal "M". If voltage is not present, go to next step. If voltage is present, go to step 3).

2) Turn ignition off. Disconnect TCU harness connector. Check continuity between terminal No. 19 (Red wire) on TCU harness connector and terminal "M" on transaxle harness connector. Repair as needed. If continuity exists, go to next step.

3) Turn ignition off. Measure voltage at terminal "M" on transaxle harness connector. If voltage exists, go to next step. If voltage does not exist, replace TCU.

4) Disconnect TCU harness connector. Measure voltage at terminal "M". If voltage does not exist, replace TCU. If voltage exists, repair Red wire for short to voltage.

DTC 14: SUPPLY VOLTAGE (5-VOLT REFERENCE)

Possible Causes – Open circuit, short to ground or short to voltage.
Diagnostic Procedure – 1) Disconnect transverse acceleration sensor connector, located under center console. Turn ignition on. Measure voltage at terminal No. 3 (Pink/White wire). If voltage is not present, check continuity of Pink/White wire between terminal No. 3 and terminal No. 45 on TCU harness connector. Repair as needed.

2) Inspect for short to ground between terminal No. 3 (Pink/White wire) on transverse acceleration sensor and terminal No. 7 (Brown wire) on TCU harness connector. Repair as needed. Go to next step.

3) Inspect for short to voltage between terminal No. 3 (Pink/White wire) on transverse acceleration sensor and terminal No. 1 (Red/White wire) on TCU harness connector. Repair as needed.

DTC 21: RPM SIGNAL FROM DME CONTROL UNIT

Possible Causes – Open circuit, short to ground, loose contact or short to voltage.
Diagnostic Procedure – 1) Code is set when TCU does not receive RPM signal from DME control unit. Check continuity of circuit between terminal No. 3 (Black/Violet wire) on TCU harness connector and terminal No. 6 on DME control unit connector. Repair as needed.

2) Ensure ground circuit at terminal No. 7 (Brown wire) on TCU harness connector has continuity to chassis ground. Repair as needed. Start and run engine. Using scan tool, check if RPM signal is being transmitted from DME control unit to TCU. If signal is being transmitted, replace TCU. If signal is not being transmitted, replace DME control unit.

DTC 22: LOAD SIGNAL FROM DME CONTROL UNIT

Possible Causes – Open circuit, short to ground, loose contact or short to voltage.
Diagnostic Procedure – 1) Code is set when TCU does not receive load signal from DME control unit. Check continuity of circuit between terminal No. 21 (White/Green wire) on TCU harness connector and terminal No. 17 on DME control unit connector. Repair as needed.

2) Ensure ground circuit at terminal No. 7 (Brown wire) on TCU harness connector has continuity to chassis ground. Repair as needed. Start and run engine. Using scan tool, check if load signal is being transmitted from DME control unit to TCU. If signal is being transmitted, replace TCU. If signal is not being transmitted, replace DME control unit.

DTC 24: IGNITION TIMING CHANGE

Possible Causes – Open circuit, short to ground or short to voltage.
Diagnostic Procedure – 1) Using scan tool, perform drive link test. See scan tool instructions. Idle speed should decrease. If idle speed does not decrease, locate connector X 4/1 under driver's seat. Go to next step.

2) Remove connector cover. Turn ignition on. Measure voltage at terminal No. 7. *See Fig. 12.* Voltage should be about 5 volts. Perform drive link test. Voltage must decrease. Go to next step.

3) Check continuity between terminal No. 7 on connector X 4/1 and terminal No. 51 (Brown/Yellow wire) on DME control unit connector. Repair as needed. If continuity exists, replace DME control unit. Go to next step.

4) Check continuity between terminal No. 7 on connector X 4/1 and terminal No. 32 (Orange/Yellow wire) on TCU harness connector. Repair as needed. If continuity exists, replace TCU. Check engine to chassis ground strap. Repair as needed.

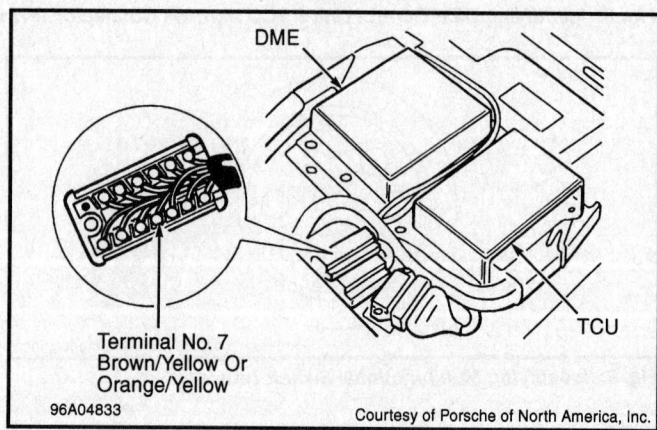

Fig. 12: *Identifying X 4/1 Connector Terminals*

DTC 25: THROTTLE POSITION (TP) SENSOR

Possible Causes – Open circuit, short to ground or short to voltage.
Diagnostic Procedure – 1) Determine if TP sensor trouble code is stored in DME control unit memory. See appropriate SELF-DIAGNOSTICS article in ENGINE PERFORMANCE in appropriate MITCHELL® manual. Repair as necessary. If code is not present, go to next step.
2) Check continuity between terminal No. 11 (White/Black wire) on TCU harness connector and terminal No. 52 on DME control unit connector. Repair as needed. If circuit is okay, go to next step.
3) Turn ignition on. Measure voltage at terminal No. 11 (White/Black wire) on TCU harness connector. Depress accelerator pedal to full throttle position. If voltage varies from one volt at idle to about 10 volts at wide open throttle, replace TCU. If voltage does not vary from one volt at idle to about 10 volts at wide open throttle, replace DME control unit.

DTC 31: SOLENOID VALVE NO. 1

Possible Causes – Open circuit, short to ground or short to positive.
Diagnostic Procedure – 1) Using scan tool, perform drive link test. Determine if clicking noise is audible from valve body. Turn ignition off. Disconnect TCU harness connector. Go to next step.
2) Measure resistance between terminals No. 5 (Gray wire) and No. 19 (Red wire) on TCU harness connector. If resistance is 31-37 ohms, go to next step. If resistance is not 31-37 ohms, go to step 4).
3) Check continuity between chassis ground and terminals No. 5 (Gray wire) and No. 19 (Red wire) on TCU harness connector. Repair as needed. If continuity does not exist, replace TCU.
4) Disconnect transaxle harness connector. Check continuity between terminal No. 5 (Gray wire) on TCU harness connector and terminal "H" on transaxle harness connector. Repair as needed. If continuity exists, go to next step.
5) Check continuity between terminal No. 19 (Red wire) on TCU harness connector and terminal "M" on transaxle harness connector. Repair as needed. If continuity exists, replace solenoid No. 1.

DTC 32: SOLENOID VALVE NO. 2

Possible Causes – Open circuit, short to ground or short to positive.
Diagnostic Procedure – 1) Using scan tool, perform drive link test. See scan tool instructions. Determine if clicking noise is audible from valve body. Turn ignition off. Disconnect TCU harness connector. Go to next step.
2) Measure resistance between terminals No. 24 (Green wire) and No. 19 (Red wire) on TCU harness connector. If resistance is 31-37 ohms, go to next step. If resistance is not 31-37 ohms, go to step 4).
3) Check continuity between chassis ground and terminals No. 24 (Green wire) and No. 19 (Red wire) on TCU harness connector. Repair as needed. If continuity does not exist, replace TCU.
4) Disconnect transaxle harness connector. Check continuity between terminal No. 24 (Green wire) on TCU harness connector and terminal "K" on transaxle harness connector. Repair as needed. If continuity exists, go to next step.
5) Check continuity between terminal No. 19 (Red wire) on TCU harness connector and terminal "M" on transaxle harness connector. Repair as needed. If continuity exists, replace solenoid No. 1.

DTC 33: TCC SOLENOID VALVE

Possible Causes – Open circuit, short to ground or short to positive.
Diagnostic Procedure – 1) Using scan tool, perform drive link test. Determine if clicking noise is audible from valve body. Turn ignition off. Disconnect TCU harness connector. Go to next step.
2) Measure resistance between terminals No. 42 (Red/White wire) and No. 19 (Red wire) on TCU harness connector. If resistance is 31-37 ohms, go to next step. If resistance is not 31-37 ohms, go to step 4).
3) Check continuity between chassis ground and terminals No. 42 (Red/White wire) and No. 19 (Red wire) on TCU harness connector. Repair as needed. If continuity does not exist, replace TCU.
4) Disconnect transaxle harness connector. Check continuity between terminal No. 42 (Red/White wire) on TCU harness connector and terminal "L" on transaxle harness connector. Repair as needed. If continuity exists, go to next step.
5) Check continuity between terminal No. 19 (Red wire) on TCU harness connector and terminal "M" on transaxle harness connector. Repair as needed. If continuity exists, replace solenoid No. 1.

DTC 34: PRESSURE REGULATOR SOLENOID VALVE

Possible Causes – Open circuit, short to ground or short to positive.
Diagnostic Procedure – 1) Turn ignition off. Disconnect TCU harness connector. Go to next step. Measure resistance between terminals No. 6 (Blue wire) and No. 19 (Red wire) on TCU harness connector. If resistance is 4-8 ohms, go to next step. If resistance is not 4-8 ohms, go to step 4).
2) Check continuity between chassis ground and terminals No. 6 (Blue wire) and No. 19 (Red wire) on TCU harness connector. Repair as needed. If continuity does not exist, replace TCU.
3) Disconnect transaxle harness connector. Check continuity between terminal No. 6 (Blue wire) on TCU harness connector and terminal "B" on transaxle harness connector. Repair as needed. If continuity exists, go to next step.
4) Check continuity between terminal No. 19 (Red wire) on TCU harness connector and terminal "M" on transaxle harness connector. Repair as needed. If continuity exists, replace solenoid No. 1.

DTC 35: SHIFT SELECTOR SWITCH

Possible Causes – Open circuit, short to ground or short to positive.
Diagnostic Procedure – 1) Using scan tool, select INPUT SIGNALS, then SELECTOR LEVER/MANUAL PROGRAM. Slowly move shift selector lever through all positions. Scan tool display change is slightly delayed. Compare scan tool display against lever position and indicator lights on speedometer. Go to next step.
2) Turn ignition off. Check continuity between ground and individual terminals No. 14 (Black/Yellow wire), 33 (Blue/Black wire), 41 (Gray/Brown wire) and 50 (Black/White wire). Move shift selector lever through all positions. Check for correct continuity in all positions. See Fig. 13. If continuity measurements are correct in all positions, replace TCU. If continuity measurement is not correct, go to next step.

Selector Position	Pin 14	Pin 33	Pin 41	Pin 50
P	X	X	0	0
R	0	X	0	0
N	0	X	X	X
D	0	0	X	X
3	0	0	0	X
2	X	0	0	X
1	X	0	X	X

X = No Continuity.
0 = Continuity.
96E04830

Fig. 13: Testing Shift Selector Switch At TCU Connector

Selector Position	Pin 4-1	Pin 4-2	Pin 4-3	Pin 5-6	Pin 7-8
P	X	X	0	0	0
R	0	X	0	X	0
N	0	X	X	0	X
D	0	0	X	X	X
3	0	0	0	X	X
2	X	0	0	X	X
1	X	0	X	X	X

X = No Continuity.
0 = Continuity.
96G04831

Fig. 14: Testing Shift Selector Switch

3) Ensure shift control cable is correctly adjusted. Disconnect shift selector switch connector. Check continuity of switch in all positions. *See Fig. 14.* Replace as needed. If continuity measurements are correct in all positions, inspect circuits between selector switch and TCU harness connector. Repair as necessary.

DTC 36: OUTPUT SHAFT SPEED SENSOR OUTPUT

NOTE: Sensor transmits transaxle speed to TCU. TCU compares transaxle speed to wheel speed.

Possible Causes – Open circuit, short to ground, short to positive or loose connector.

Diagnostic Procedure – **1)** Using scan tool, check if transaxle speed sensor is outputting signal. Turn ignition off. Disconnect TCU harness connector. Measure resistance between terminals No. 2 (White wire) and No. 38 (Brown wire) on TCU harness connector. Resistance should be approximately 350 ohms. Go to next step.

2) Check continuity between chassis ground and terminals No. 2 and 38. Repair as necessary. If continuity does not exist and sensor resistance is within specification, replace TCU. If resistance is not within specification, disconnect transaxle harness connector. Go to next step.

3) Check continuity exists between terminal No. 2 (White wire) on TCU harness connector and terminal "A" on transaxle harness connector. Repair as necessary. If continuity exists, go to next step.

4) Check continuity between terminal No. 38 (Brown wire) on TCU harness connector and terminal "F" on transaxle harness connector. Repair as necessary. If continuity exists, go to next step.

5) Check continuity between terminal No. 7 (Brown wire), and terminals No. 2 and 38 on TCU harness connector. If continuity exists, repair as needed. If continuity does not exist, go to next step.

6) Check continuity between terminal No. 20 (shielding), and terminals No. 2 and 38 on TCU harness connector. If continuity exists, repair as needed. If continuity does not exist, go to next step.

7) Measure voltage between terminal No. 1 (Red/White wire), and terminals No. 2 and 38 on TCU harness connector. If voltage is present, repair as needed. Check internal wiring harness.

DTC 37: ATF TEMPERATURE SENSOR

NOTE: If scan tool displays TEMPERATURE SENSOR SHORT TO POSITIVE or TRANSVERSE ACCELERATION SENSOR SHORT TO POSITIVE, check for short circuit between ATF temperature sensor and TCU. Repair as needed. Replace TCU.

Possible Causes – Open circuit, short to ground, short to voltage or faulty signal.

Diagnostic Procedure – **1)** Start and run engine. Using scan tool, read transmission temperature and record. Turn ignition off. Disconnect TCU harness connector. Measure resistance between terminals No. 44 (Pink/Brown wire) and 46 (Orange wire). Go to next step.

2) Resistance values vary with fluid temperature. Specifications are 1000 ohms at 68°F (20°C), 1150 ohms at 104°F (40°C) and 1300 ohms at 140°F (60°C). If measured values match scan tool display, replace TCU. If measured values do not match scan tool display, go to next step.

3) Check continuity of circuits between transmission temperature sensor and TCU. Repair as needed. If circuits are okay, replace internal harness that contains temperature sensor.

DTC 38: SHIFT SELECTOR SWITCH

NOTE: This code is set when engine can be started in other than Park or Neutral.

Possible Causes – Open circuit, short to ground or short to voltage.
Diagnostic Procedure – **1)** Check adjustment of shift selector cable to multifunctional switch. Adjust as needed. Check adjustment of multifunctional switch. Adjust as needed. Go to next step.

2) Disconnect shift selector switch connector. Check continuity of switch in all positions. *See Fig. 14.* Replace as needed. If continuity measurements are correct in all positions, inspect circuits between selector switch and TCU harness connector. Repair as necessary.

DTCs 42, 43, 44: TCU FAULTY
Repair Procedure – Replace TCU.

DTC 45, 46: DOWNSHIFT PROTECTION, REV LIMITER
Possible Causes – Faulty RPM signal from output source or engine. Incorrect output shaft to engine RPM ratio.
Diagnostic Procedure – Inspect transaxle shaft speed sensor. See DTC 36. Repair as needed. If sensor is okay, other possible cause is transaxle slipping internally. Repair as necessary.

DTC 51: MANUAL PROGRAM SWITCH
Possible Cause – Short to ground.
Diagnostic Procedure – **1)** Using scan tool, select INPUT SIGNALS. Check operation of manual program switch. Turn ignition off. Go to next step.

2) Disconnect TCU harness connector. Check continuity between chassis ground and terminal No. 26 (Brown wire) on TCU harness connector. Repair as needed. If continuity exists, go to next step.

3) Disconnect selector lever switch connector. Check continuity between terminal No. 48 (Green/Brown wire) on TCU harness connector and terminal No. 3 on selector lever connector. Repair as needed. If continuity exists, replace selector lever switch. If problem reoccurs, replace TCU.

DTC 52: MANUAL TIP SHIFT SWITCH
Possible Cause – Short to ground.
Diagnostic Procedure – **1)** Using scan tool, select INPUT SIGNALS. Check operation of manual program switch. Turn ignition off. Go to next step.

2) Disconnect TCU harness connector. Check continuity between chassis ground and terminal No. 26 (Brown wire) on TCU harness connector. Repair as needed. If continuity exists, go to next step.

3) Disconnect selector lever switch connector. For upshift circuit, check continuity between terminal No. 10 (Brown/Yellow wire) on TCU harness connector and terminal No. 2 on selector lever connector. Repair as needed. If continuity exists, go to next step.

4) For downshift circuit, check continuity between terminal No. 29 (Green/Yellow wire) on TCU harness connector and terminal No. 1 on selector lever connector. Repair as needed. If continuity exists, replace selector lever switch. If problem reoccurs, replace TCU.

DTC 53: KICKDOWN SWITCH
Possible Cause – Short to ground.
Diagnostic Procedure – **1)** Turn ignition on. Using scan tool, select INPUT SIGNALS. Check operation of kickdown switch. Determine if valve body solenoid can be heard operating. Turn ignition off. Go to next step.

2) Remove kickdown switch and check operation using ohmmeter. Replace as needed. If switch is okay, disconnect TCU harness connector. Check continuity between terminal No. 30 (Black/Yellow wire) on TCU harness connector and terminal No. 2 on kickdown switch harness connector. Repair as needed. If continuity exists, replace TCU.

DTC 54: TRANSVERSE ACCELERATION SENSOR
Possible Causes – Open circuit, short to ground or short to voltage.
Diagnostic Procedure – **1)** Using scan tool, select ACTUAL VALUES. Read transverse acceleration sensor value. On level ground sensor should output 0 g. Raise vehicle on one side and value should change.

2) Turn ignition off. Disconnect sensor connector. Turn ignition on. Measure voltage between terminal No. 1 (Pink/Brown wire) and terminal No. 3 (Pink/White wire) on sensor harness connector. If about 5 volts is present and scan tool displayed sensor changes when vehicle was raised in step 1), replace TCU. If 5 volts is not present, go to next step.

3) Check continuity of circuits between TCU harness connector and transverse acceleration sensor. See TRANSVERSE ACCELERATION SENSOR CIRCUIT IDENTIFICATION table. Repair circuit(s) as needed. If continuity exists in all circuits, go to next step.

TRANSVERSE ACCELERATION SENSOR CIRCUIT IDENTIFICATION

TCU Terminal No.	Sensor Terminal No.
44	1
40	2
45	3

4) Inspect for short between terminal No. 7 (Brown wire) on TCU harness connector and terminals No. 2 and 3 on transverse acceleration sensor harness connector. Repair as needed. If all circuits are okay, go to next step.

5) Inspect for short between terminal No. 1 (Red/White wire) on TCU harness connector and terminals No. 1, 2 and 3 on transverse acceleration sensor harness connector. Repair as needed.

DTC 55: ABS SPEED SENSOR NO. 1

Possible Causes – Open circuit, short to ground or short to voltage.
Diagnostic Procedure – 1) Determine if ABS system is functioning correctly. See appropriate ANTI-LOCK article in BRAKES in appropriate MITCHELL® manual. Repair as needed. Go to next step.

2) Raise right front wheel. Using scan tool, select INPUT SIGNALS. Rotate wheel and monitor scan tool for signal from wheel sensor. Go to next step.

3) Check continuity between terminal No. 12 (Violet/Green wire) on TCU harness connector and terminal No. 42 on ABS control unit harness connector. Repair as needed. If continuity exists, go to next step.

4) Inspect for short between terminals No. 7 (Brown wire) and 12 on TCU harness connector. Repair as needed. If circuit is okay, go to next step.

5) Inspect for short between terminals No. 1 (Red/White wire) and 12 on TCU harness connector. Repair as needed. If circuit is okay and wheel sensor output was displayed on scan tool in step 2), replace TCU.

DTC 56: COMBINATION METER INPUT

Possible Causes – Open circuit, short to ground or short to voltage.
Diagnostic Procedure – 1) Switch manual program on and off while observing indicator light on combination meter. Turn ignition off. Disconnect TCU harness connector. Connect jumper wire between

ground and terminal No. 13 on TCU harness connector. Turn ignition on. If scan tool displays EGS FAULTY, replace combination meter. If scan tool does not display EGS FAULTY, go to next step.

2) Turn ignition off. Check continuity between terminal No. 13 (Blue/Green wire) on TCU harness connector and terminal No. 9 on combination meter harness connector. Repair as needed. If continuity exists, replace combination meter.

DTC 59: MULTIFUNCTIONAL SWITCH (REVERSE CIRCUIT)

Possible Causes – Open circuit, short to ground or short to voltage.
Diagnostic Procedure – 1) Turn ignition off. Disconnect TCU harness connector. Check continuity between chassis ground and terminal No. 41 (Gray/Brown wire) on TCU connector. Continuity should exist in Park and Reverse. If continuity exists, go to step 3). If continuity does not exist, go to next step.

2) Disconnect selector lever switch. Check continuity between terminal No. 41 (Gray/Brown wire) on TCU connector and terminal No. 8 on selector lever switch connector. Repair as needed. If continuity exists, go to next step.

3) Ensure shift control cable is correctly adjusted. Disconnect shift selector switch connector. Check continuity of switch in all positions. See Fig. 14. Replace as needed. If continuity is correct in all positions, inspect circuits between selector switch and TCU harness connector. Repair as necessary.

DTC XX: UNKNOWN FAULT CODE

Diagnostic Procedure – Check all ground circuits and ground contact points. Repair as needed.

NO PERMANENT VOLTAGE SUPPLY TO TCU

Possible Causes – Open circuit, short to ground or loose contact.
Diagnostic Checks;
- If no codes are stored in memory, constant voltage (terminal 30) is not present at terminal No. 39.
- Inspect fuse No. 12 (15-amp). Replace as needed. Check for voltage to fuse connector. Ensure ground circuit has continuity to chassis ground.
- If fuse No. 12 is blown, disconnect TCU harness connector. Inspect terminal No. 39 (Red wire) for short to ground. Repair as needed.
- If previous checks have not found source of fault, replace TCU.

WIRING DIAGRAMS

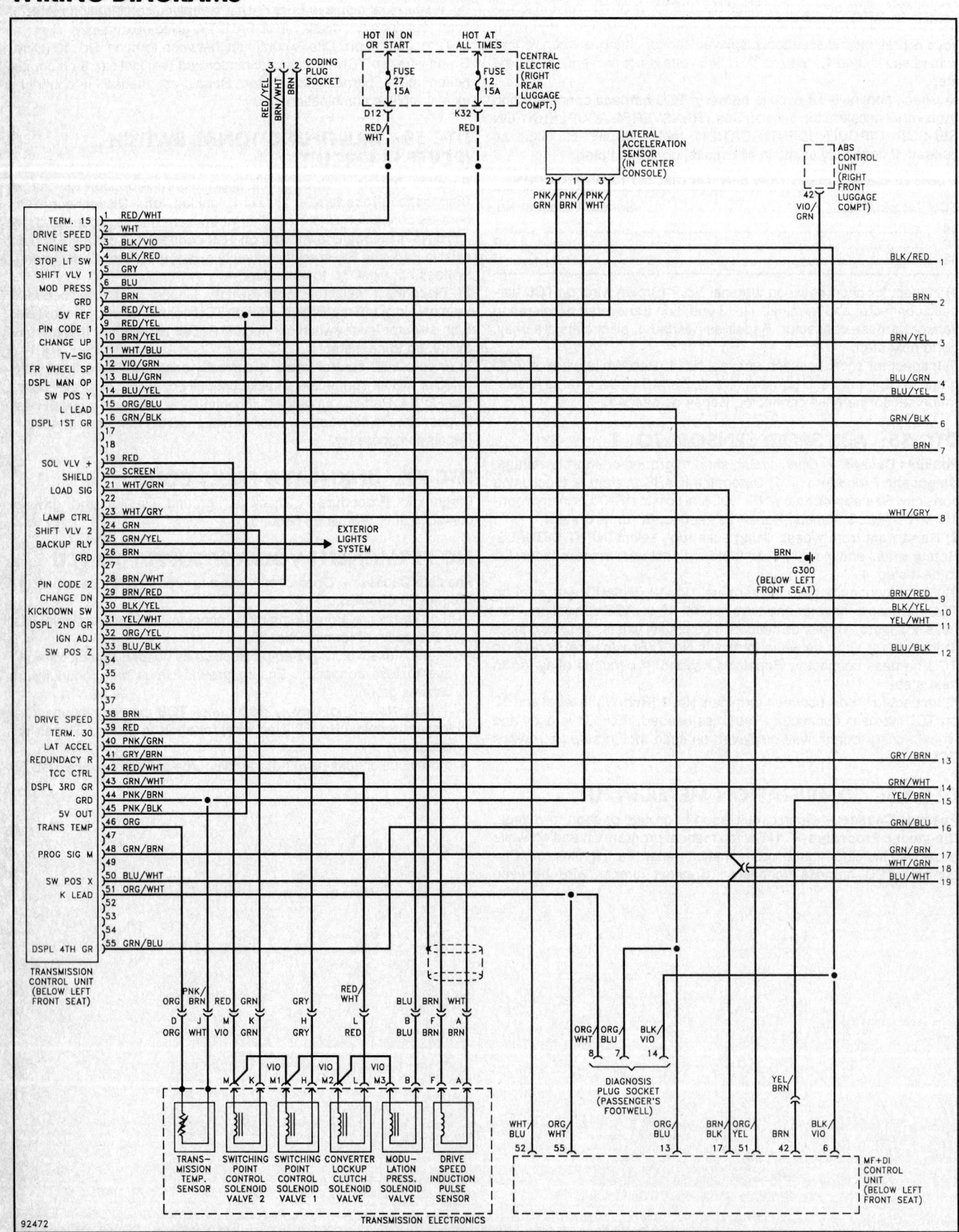

Fig. 15: Transaxle Wiring Diagram (1995 911 — Early Production, 1 Of 2)

92472

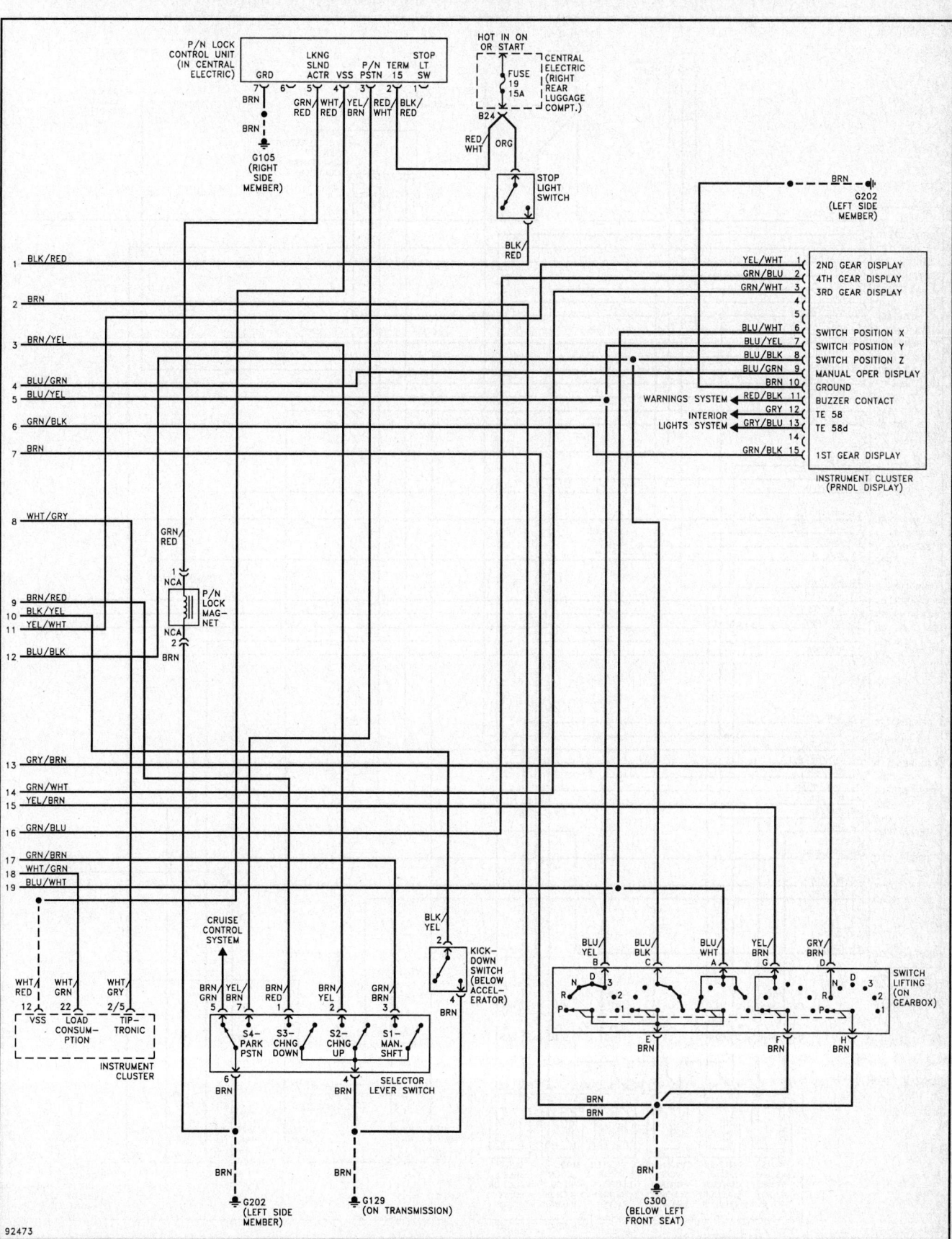

Fig. 16: Transaxle Wiring Diagram (1995 911 – Early Production, 2 Of 2)

92473

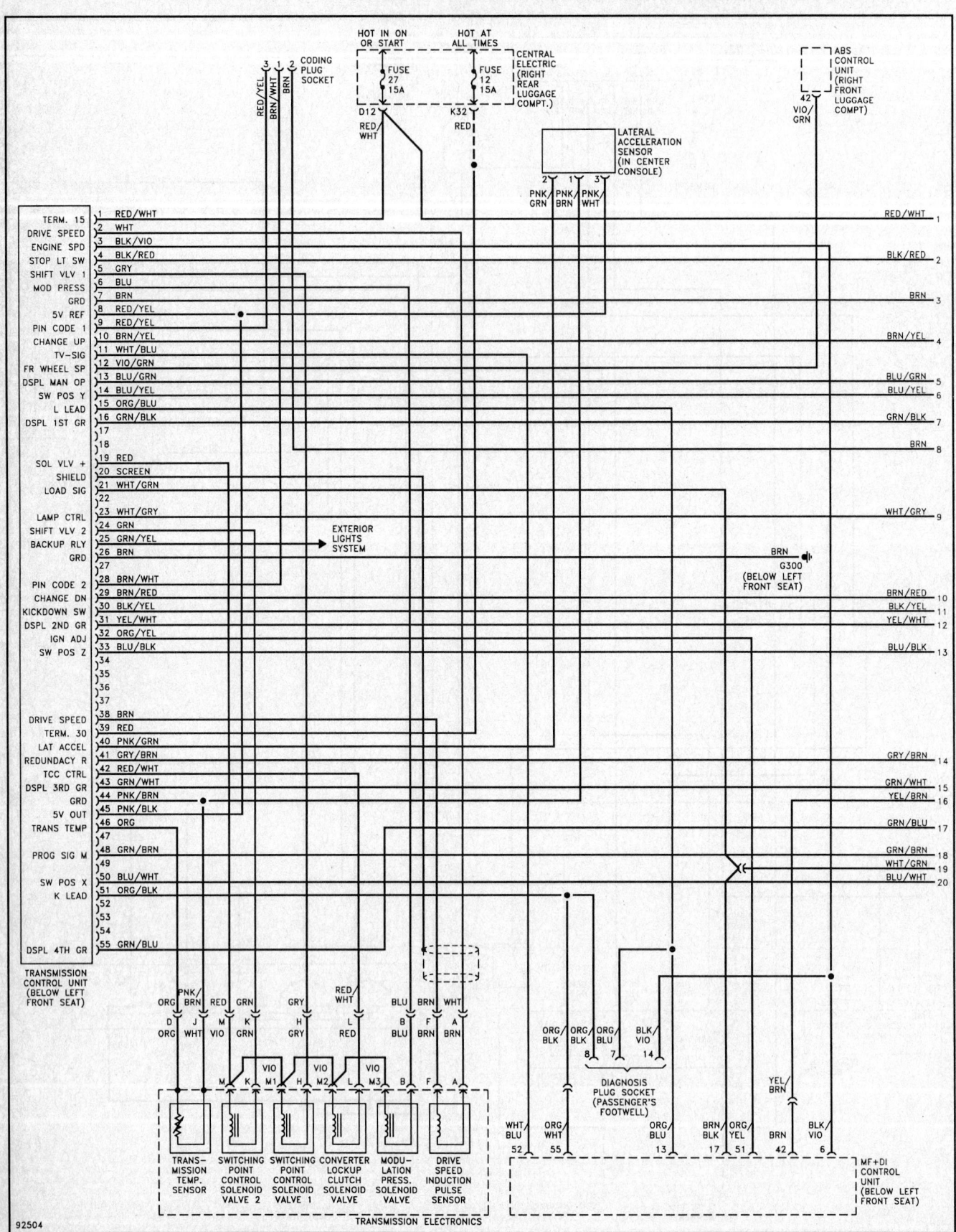

Fig. 17: Transaxle Wiring Diagram (1995 911 – Late Production, 1 Of 2)

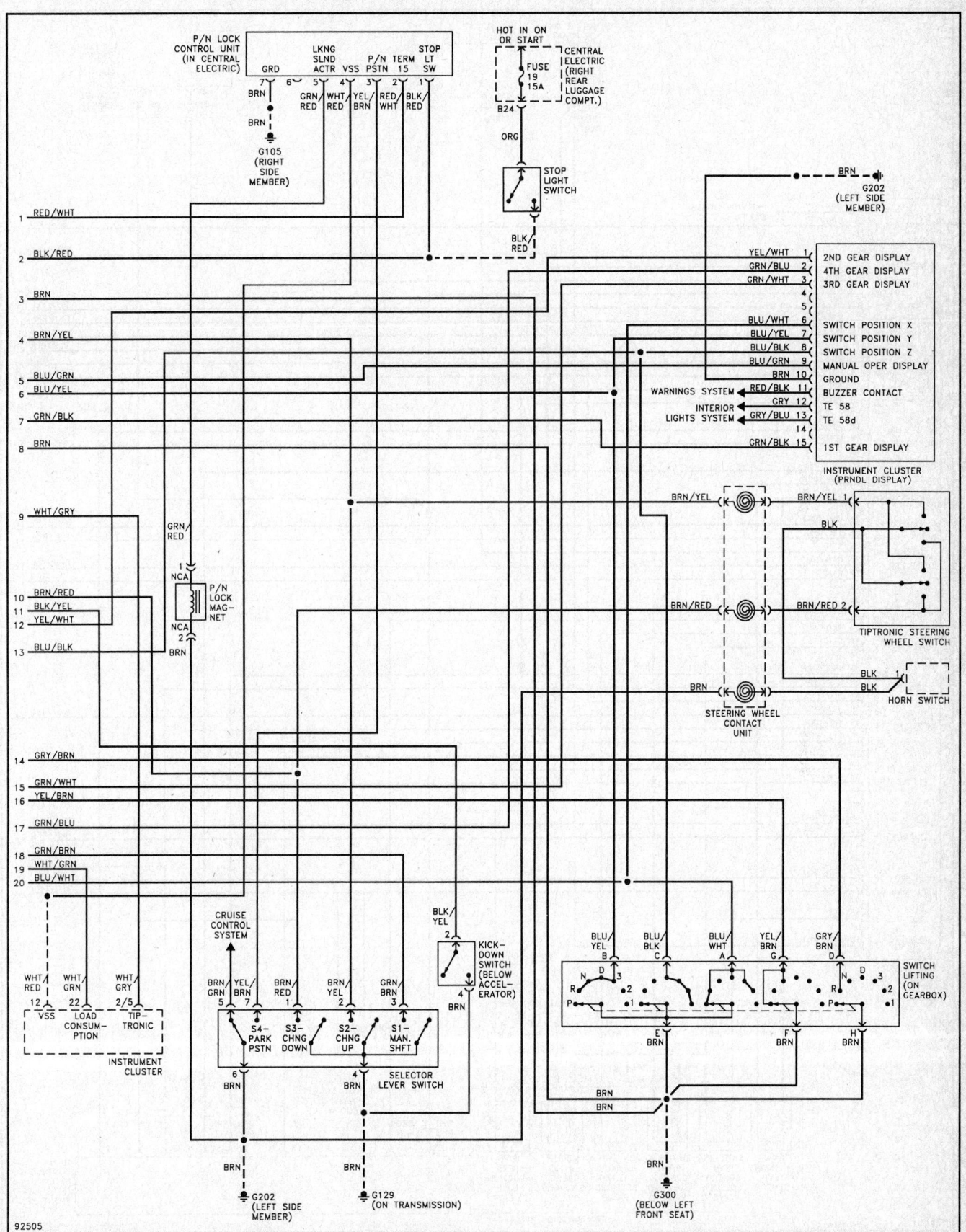

Fig. 18: Transaxle Wiring Diagram (1995 911 – Late Production, 2 Of 2)

92505

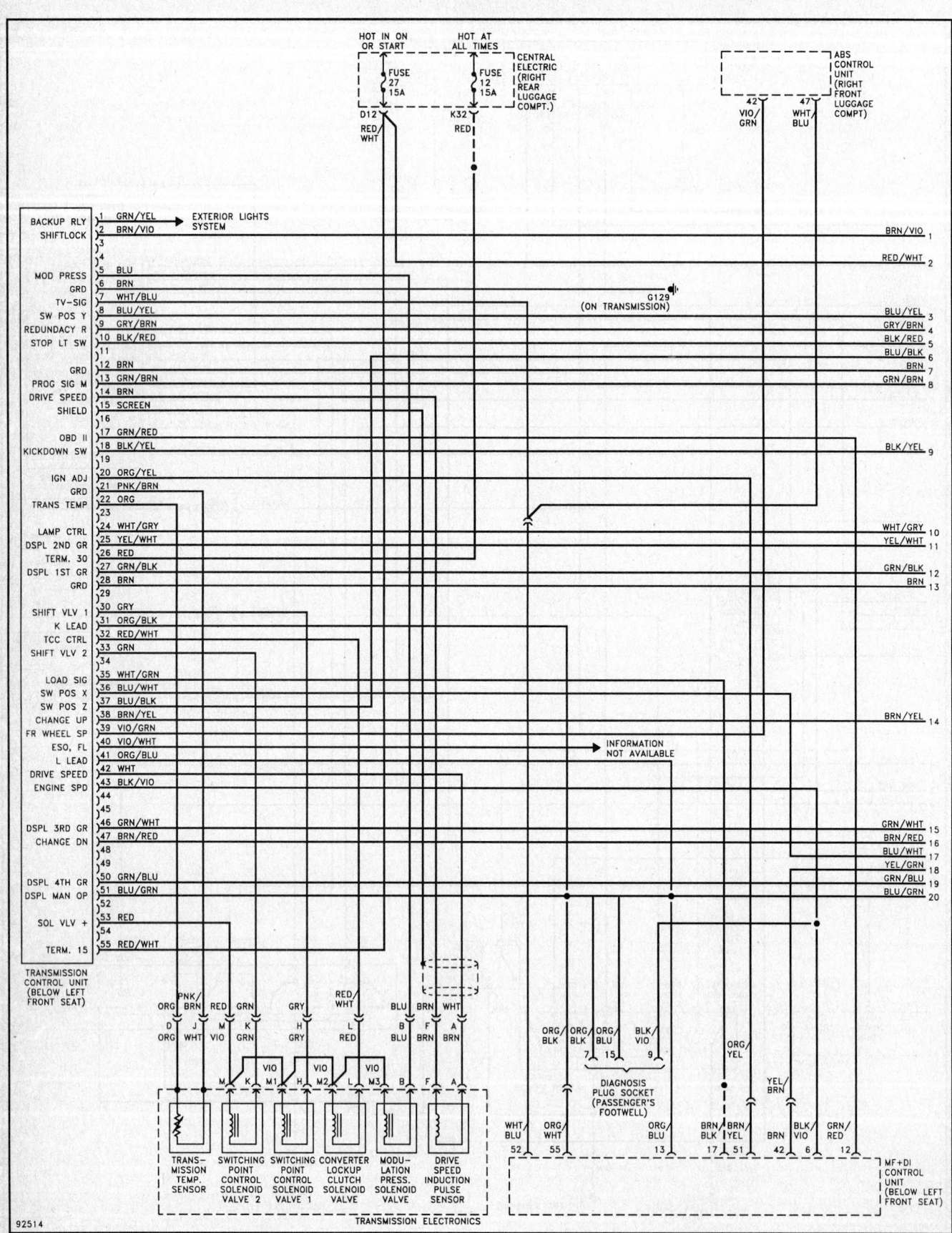

Fig. 19: Transaxle Wiring Diagram (1996 911, 1 Of 2)

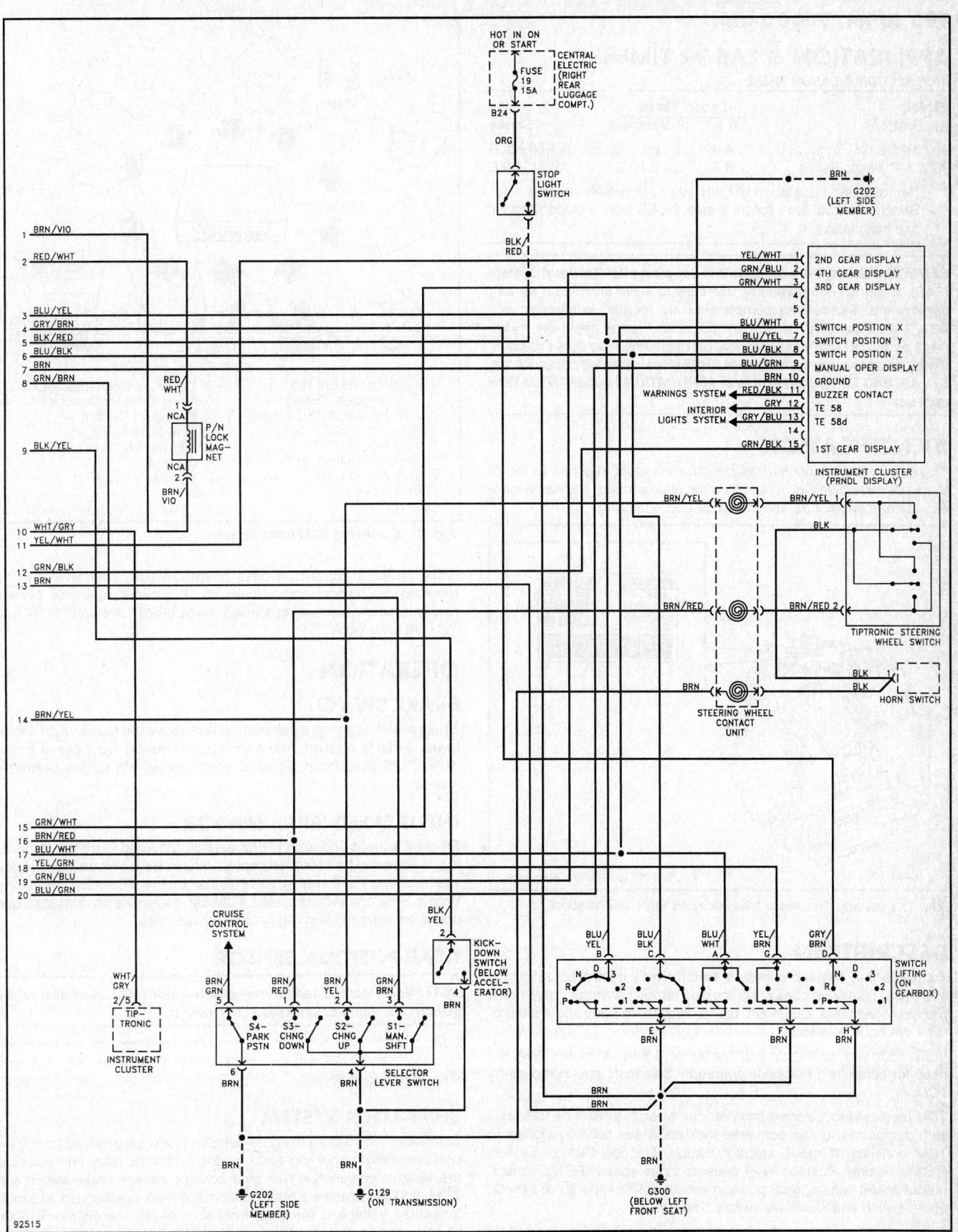

Fig. 20: Transaxle Wiring Diagram (1996 911, 2 Of 2)

92515

900 Series, 9000 Series

APPLICATION & LABOR TIMES

APPLICATION & LABOR TIMES

Vehicle Application	Labor Times		Series
	[1] R & I	[2] Overhaul	
900 Series	4.8	9.1	AW50-40LE
9000 4-Cylinder Series	8.2	9.1	AW50-40LE

[1] – Removal and installation of transaxle from vehicle chassis.
[2] – Bench overhaul time for transaxle. DOES NOT include removal and installation.

CAUTION: *Vehicle is equipped with a Supplemental Restraint System (SAS). When servicing vehicle, use care to avoid accidental air bag deployment. SRS-related components are located in steering column, center console, instrument panel and lower panel on instrument panel. DO NOT use electrical test equipment on these circuits. If may be necessary to deactivate SRS before servicing components. See AIR BAG SERVICING article in APPLICATIONS & IDENTIFICATION section.*

IDENTIFICATION

Transaxle can be identified by identification plate attached to top of transaxle case. *See Fig. 1.* Identification plate contains transaxle model, year of manufacture and transaxle part number.

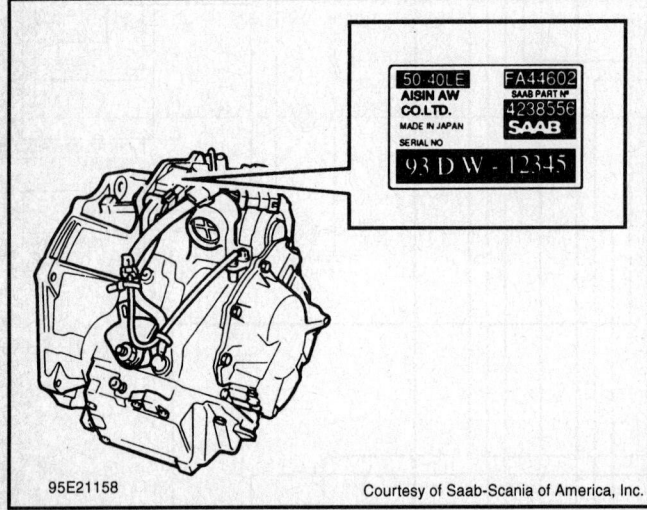

95E21158   Courtesy of Saab-Scania of America, Inc.

Fig. 1: Locating Transaxle Identification Plate Information

DESCRIPTION

Transaxle is a 4-speed overdrive electronically controlled automatic transaxle. Transaxle consists of lock-up torque converter, oil pump, 3 planetary gear sets, clutch and brake units, valve body and 4 electronic valve body solenoids.

Valve body with solenoids and Transaxle Control Module (TCM) are used for controlling transaxle operation. Solenoids are controlled by TCM.

TCM receives input signals from various areas to determine transaxle shift points and torque converter lock-up. Areas sending signals to TCM consists of mode selector switch, Traction Control System (TCS), Throttle Position (TP) sensor, input speed (RPM) sensor, output speed sensor, gear position sensor, ATF temperature sensor, brake switch and kickdown switch. *See Fig. 2.*

Transaxle is equipped with a mode selector switch. Switch is used for normal, sport and winter driving conditions. Transaxle is also equipped with a shift lock and starter interlock system. Shift lock system prevents shift lever from being moved from Park position unless

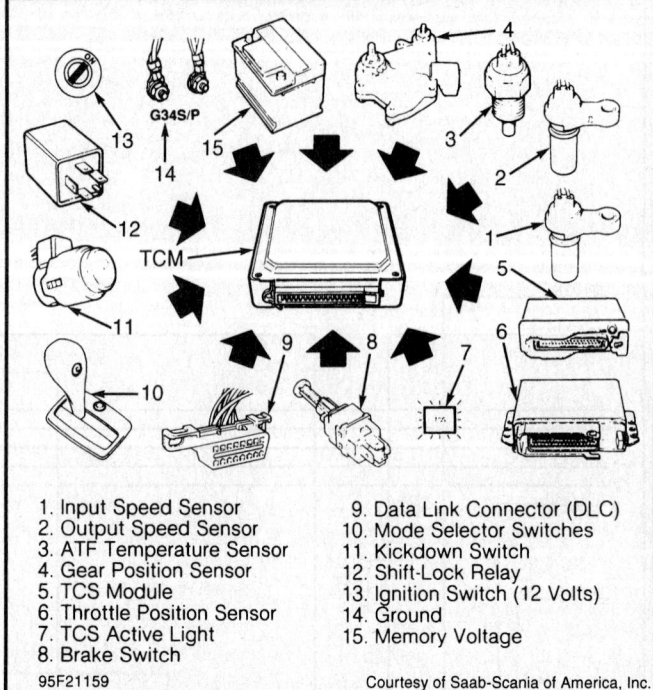

1. Input Speed Sensor	9. Data Link Connector (DLC)
2. Output Speed Sensor	10. Mode Selector Switches
3. ATF Temperature Sensor	11. Kickdown Switch
4. Gear Position Sensor	12. Shift-Lock Relay
5. TCS Module	13. Ignition Switch (12 Volts)
6. Throttle Position Sensor	14. Ground
7. TCS Active Light	15. Memory Voltage
8. Brake Switch	

95F21159   Courtesy of Saab-Scania of America, Inc.

Fig. 2: Identifying TCM Input Areas

brake pedal is applied. In case of malfunction, shift lever can be released by disconnecting fuse No. 9. Starter interlock system prevents power from being applied to starter circuit except in "P" and "N" shift lever positions.

OPERATION

BRAKE SWITCH

Brake switch is an input device mounted above the brake pedal. When brake pedal is applied, brake switch delivers an input signal to the TCM. TCM uses input signal to control (shut off) torque converter lock-up.

INPUT SPEED (RPM) SENSOR

Electromagnetic (inductive) RPM sensor, mounted in transaxle housing, is activated by a toothed impulse wheel. Sensor is an input device which delivers an engine RPM signal to the TCM. By comparing engine RPM and vehicle speed, TCM can determine amount of torque converter slippage and regulate fluid pressures.

GEAR POSITION SENSOR

NOTE: *Gear position sensor may also be referred to as neutral safety switch or Transmission Range (TR) switch.*

Gear position sensor is an input device mounted on the transaxle housing. Sensor delivers an input signal to TCM, indicating transaxle selector lever position.

SHIFT-LOCK SYSTEM

Shift-lock system prevents gear selector from being moved from Park position without applying brake pedal. Shift-lock relay and solenoid are wired in conjunction with gear position sensor, brake switch and TCM. If TCM receives a brake switch and Park position signal simultaneously, voltage is removed from solenoid by the shift-lock relay, allowing gear selector to be moved from Park position. If system fails, voltage can be disconnected to solenoid by removing fuse No. 9.

KICKDOWN SWITCH

Kickdown switch, located below accelerator pedal, sends input signal to TCM when accelerator pedal is fully depressed. TCM uses input signal for controlling transaxle shifting for maximum performance.

MODE SELECTOR SWITCHES

SPORT mode selector switch is located on shift lever. WINTER mode selector switch is located to right of shift selector lever. These switches effect transaxle shift points. Input signal from mode selector switches are sent to TCM. TCM uses input signals for controlling transaxle shifting and torque converter lock-up.

NORMAL mode, is for regular driving and provides early upshifts combined with lock-up as often as possible for top 3 gears. Transaxle line pressure is modulated to provide smooth gear engagement.

In SPORT mode, transaxle shift points are designed to provide the highest possible performance. When SPORT mode is selected, SPORT indicator light on dash is illuminated. Under normal acceleration, transaxle shifts occur the same as in NORMAL mode. During increased acceleration, TCM selects shift and lock-up points for best possible performance.

WINTER mode prevents wheel spin on slippery surfaces. Transaxle starts out in 3rd gear. When WINTER mode is selected, WINTER warning light on dash is illuminated. This mode may also be used when driver wants to control gear selection.

ATF TEMPERATURE SENSOR

ATF temperature sensor, located in transaxle housing, measures transaxle fluid temperature and delivers an input signal to TCM. TCM uses input signal for controlling transaxle shifting and torque converter lock-up.

TRANSAXLE CONTROL MODULE (TCM)

TCM is located behind glove box. See Fig. 3. TCM determines shift points and torque converter lock-up timing based on input signals received from various components. Components consist of mode selector switches, Throttle Position Sensor (TPS), input speed (RPM) sensor, output speed sensor, gear position sensor, TCS module, ATF temperature sensor, brake switch and kickdown switch. See Fig. 2.

TCM contains a self-diagnostic system which stores a Diagnostic Trouble Code (DTC). If a transaxle problem exists, DTC's can be retrieved to determine transaxle problem area.

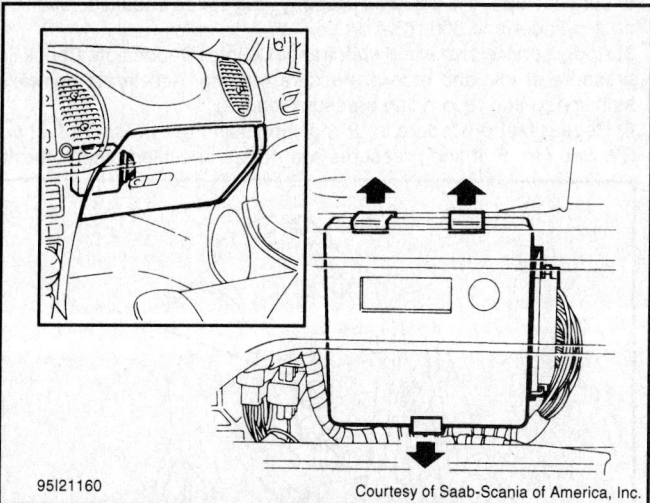

95I21160

Fig. 3: Locating TCM

Courtesy of Saab-Scania of America, Inc.

THROTTLE POSITION (TP) SENSOR

Throttle position sensor, mounted on throttle body, determines throttle position and delivers an input signal to Motronic ECM. Motronic ECM supplies signal to TCM. TCM uses input signal for controlling transaxle upshifts and regulate fluid pressures.

VALVE BODY SOLENOIDS

Valve body solenoids, mounted on the valve body, are output devices controlled by signals received from the TCM. The No. 1 and No. 2 solenoids are used to control transaxle shifting. The No. 1 solenoid controls 1-2 and 3-4 shifts, while No. 2 solenoid controls 2-3 shifts. Torque converter clutch solenoid is used to control torque converter lock-up. Pressure control solenoid is used to control transaxle line pressure. For solenoid locations, See Fig. 4. For valve body solenoid usage, see VALVE BODY SOLENOID APPLICATION table.

VALVE BODY SOLENOID APPLICATION

Shift Lever Position	No. 1 Solenoid	No. 2 Solenoid
"D"		
1st	OFF	ON
2nd	ON	ON
3rd	ON	OFF
4th	OFF	OFF
"3"		
1st	OFF	ON
2nd	ON	ON
3rd	ON	OFF
"2"		
1st	OFF	ON
2nd	ON	ON
"1"		
1st	OFF	ON
"R"		
4.35 MPH (7 km/h) Or Less	OFF	ON
More Than 4.35 MPH (7 km/h)	ON	ON
"N" Or "P"	OFF	ON

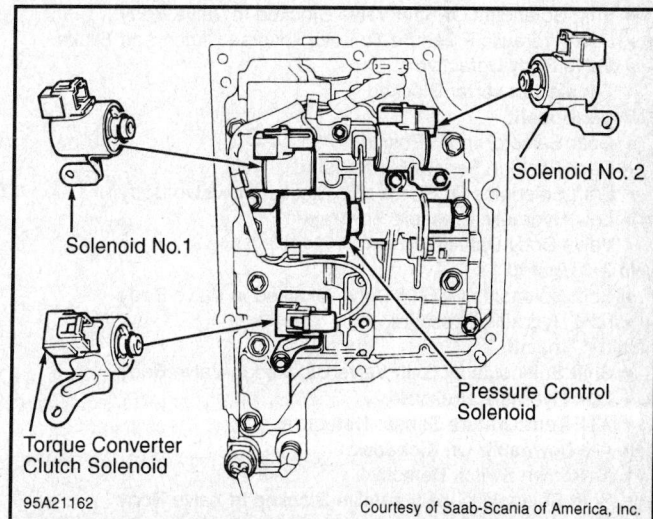

95A21162

Courtesy of Saab-Scania of America, Inc.

Fig. 4: Identifying Solenoid Valves

VEHICLE SPEED SENSORS (VSS)

Vehicle speed sensors, mounted in transaxle housing, are an input device consisting of speed sensor rotor and speed sensor. Input signal is delivered from speed sensor to TCM with each revolution of clutch drum or axle shaft. TCM uses speed sensor input signal for controlling transaxle operation.

LUBRICATION & ADJUSTMENTS

See appropriate AUTOMATIC TRANSMISSION SERVICING article in TRANSMISSION SERVICING section.

TROUBLE SHOOTING

NOTE: Before trouble shooting transmission, perform trouble shooting preliminary checks. Once trouble shooting preliminary procedure is performed, proceed to symptom diagnosis. See SYMPTOM DIAGNOSIS under TROUBLE SHOOTING.

Preliminary Checks – Perform in the following order:
- Read any fault codes before battery is disconnected, see SELF-DIAGNOSTIC SYSTEM.
- Ensure fluid level is correct.
- Inspect and adjust throttle cable, kickdown cable and gear position sensor (if necessary).
- Check idle speed RPM and adjust as necessary.
- Check stall speeds, see STALL SPEED TESTS.
- Check hydraulic pressure, see HYDRAULIC PRESSURE TEST.
- Test drive vehicle and document shift points, see ROAD TEST.

NOTE: Manufacturer recommends transaxle assembly replacement only. Manufacturer does not provide mechanical overhaul information.

SYMPTOM DIAGNOSIS

Vehicle Will Not Move In Forward Gears Or Jerks Or Slips
- ATF Fluid Level Low
- Transaxle Filter Clogged
- Oil Pump Blocked
- Low Hydraulic Pressure To Forward Clutch And Brake
- Defective One-Way Gear
- Valve Body Defective
- Torque Converter Blocked

Vehicle Will Not Move In Reverse
- ATF Fluid Level Low
- Transaxle Filter Clogged
- Oil Pump Blocked
- Shift Solenoids Or Shift Valve Blocked In Valve Body
- Low Hydraulic Pressure To Low/Reverse Clutch And Brake
- Valve Body Defective
- Torque Converter Blocked

No 1-2 Upshift
- Gear Selector In "1" Position
- Gear Position Sensor Misadjusted
- Shift Solenoids Or Shift Valve Blocked In Valve Body
- Low Hydraulic Pressure To Brake
- Valve Body Defective

No 2-3 Upshift
- Shift Solenoids Or Shift Valve Blocked In Valve Body
- Low Hydraulic Pressure

No 3-4 Upshift
- Shift Solenoids Or Shift Valve Blocked In Valve Body
- Low Hydraulic Pressure
- ATF Temperature Sensor Defective

No 4-3 Downshift On Kickdown
- Kickdown Switch Defective
- Shift Solenoids Or Shift Valve Blocked In Valve Body
- Low Hydraulic Pressure
- Defective One-Way Gear

No 3-2 Downshift On Kickdown
- Kickdown Switch Defective
- Shift Solenoids Or Shift Valve Blocked In Valve Body
- Low Hydraulic Pressure
- Defective One-Way Gear

No 2-1 Downshift On Kickdown
- Kickdown Switch Defective
- Shift Solenoids Or Shift Valve Blocked In Valve Body
- Defective One-Way Gear

NO Engine Braking
- Low Hydraulic Pressure
- Shift Solenoids Or Shift Valve Blocked In Valve Body

Rough Gear Shifting From "N" To "D"
- Valve Body Defective
- Low Hydraulic Pressure
- Defective One-Way Gear

Rough Gear Shifting From "N" To "R"
- Valve Body Defective
- Low Hydraulic Pressure

Rough Gear Shifting At All Gear Shifts
- Valve Body Defective
- Low Hydraulic Pressure

Torque Converter Clutch Does Not Engage
- Torque Converter Clutch Solenoid Defective
- Valve Body Defective
- Torque Converter Clutch Defective

TESTING

STALL SPEED TEST

1) Operate engine and transaxle at normal operating temperature. Connect tachometer to vehicle and ensure it is visible to driver. Apply parking brake and block all 4 wheels.

CAUTION: DO NOT maintain stall speed RPM for more than 5 seconds. Transaxle damage may occur.

2) Ensure A/C is off. Start engine, apply brakes and place transaxle in "D" position. Depress accelerator to full throttle and note maximum RPM obtained. Repeat test in "R" position. For stall speed specifications, see STALL SPEED SPECIFICATIONS table.

STALL SPEED SPECIFICATIONS

Engine Application	RPM
4-Cylinder	2150-2450
V6	2000-2300

HYDRAULIC PRESSURE TEST

1) Ensure transaxle is at normal operating temperature. Connect pressure gauge to line pressure test port C1. *See Fig. 5.*
2) Connect tachometer to vehicle and ensure it is visible to driver. Block all 4 wheels and fully apply parking brake. Start engine and ensure idle speed is adjusted properly. Idle speed should be 900 RPM on 4-cylinder and 800 RPM on V6.
3) Apply service brake and shift transaxle into "D" position. Check line pressure at idle and record pressure reading. Accelerate vehicle to stall speed and record line pressure reading.
4) Repeat test procedure in "R" position using line pressure test port C2. *See Fig. 5.* If line pressures are not as specified, check throttle

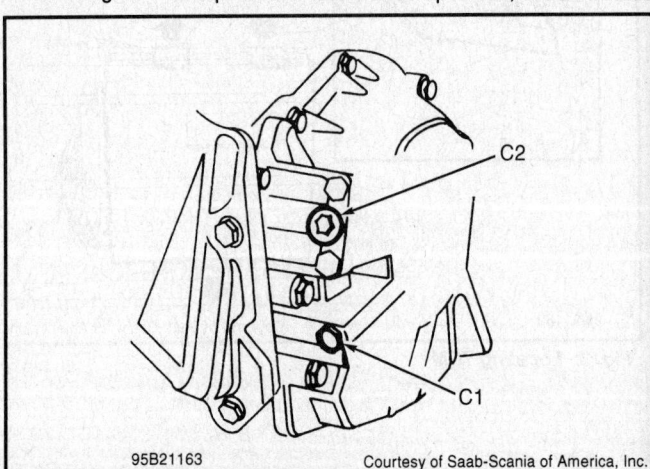

95B21163   Courtesy of Saab-Scania of America, Inc.

Fig. 5: Locating Line Pressure Test Ports

cable adjustment. Adjust throttle cable as necessary, and repeat test procedure and record pressure readings. Compare all readings to specification. See LINE PRESSURE SPECIFICATIONS table.

LINE PRESSURE SPECIFICATIONS

Engine Speed	"D" Position psi (bar)	"R" Position psi (bar)
Idle Speed	58 (4)	97 (6.7)
Stall Speed	174 (12)	261 (18)

5) If line pressures are not as specified, internal components in transaxle may be malfunctioning. Check self-diagnostic system for trouble codes. See SELF-DIAGNOSTIC SYSTEM. If no trouble codes are found, manufacturer recommends replacing transaxle as an assembly.

ROAD TEST

"D" Position – Engine and transaxle must be at normal operating temperature. Shift transaxle into "D" position. Set mode selector switch to SPORT position. Test drive vehicle and ensure all upshifts and downshifts occur at specified speeds. See SHIFT SPEED SPECIFICATIONS table.

SHIFT SPEED SPECIFICATIONS

Application	4 Cyl. Turbo MPH	4 Cyl. MPH	V6 MPH
Normal Mode			
Idle			
1st-2nd	9-14	12-16	9-14
2nd-3rd	16-25	16-28	16-25
3rd-4th	28-37	31-43	28-37
WOT [1]			
1st-2nd	28-34	30-36	28-34
2nd-3rd	56-62	61-67	56-62
3rd-4th	81-87	88-94	81-87
WOT [2]			
1st-2nd	31-37	36-42	33-39
2nd-3rd	62-68	69-75	65-71
3rd-4th	101-107	110-116	104-110
Sport Mode			
Idle			
1st-2nd	9-14	12-16	9-14
2nd-3rd	16-25	16-28	16-25
3rd-4th	28-37	31-43	28-37
WOT [3]			
1st-2nd	31-37	36-42	33-39
2nd-3rd	62-68	69-75	65-71
3rd-4th	101-107	110-116	104-110
Downshift Speed [4]			
4th-3rd	98-104	107-113	99-106
3rd-2nd	57-63	63-70	59-65
2nd-1st	26-32	30-36	28-34

[1] – Kickdown solenoid not engaged.
[2] – Kickdown solenoid engaged.
[3] – With or without kickdown solenoid engaged.
[4] – Normal or Sport mode downshift speeds.

ON-VEHICLE SERVICE

AXLE SHAFTS

See appropriate AXLE SHAFTS article in AXLE SHAFTS & TRANSFER CASES section.

THROTTLE & KICKDOWN CABLES

For throttle and kickdown cable adjustments, see appropriate AUTOMATIC TRANSMISSION SERVICING article in TRANSMISSION SERVICING section.

REMOVAL & INSTALLATION

TRANSAXLE

For transaxle removal and installation procedure, see appropriate AUTOMATIC TRANSMISSION REMOVAL article in TRANSMISSION SERVICING section.

VALVE BODY

Removal & Installation – **1)** On V6 models, remove engine cover. On all models, remove transaxle vent hose. Install engine support. Raise and support vehicle. Remove spoiler covers under vehicle. Remove negative battery cable at mount bracket and remove bracket.

2) Remove transaxle cooler lines and plug holes. Remove ATF temperature sensor cover. Remove valve body cover bolts. Using a rubber mallet, knock valve body cover to right.

3) Remove 9 bolts retaining valve body, noting length and location of bolts for installation reference. See Fig. 6. Remove manual valve from lifting eye and lift out valve body.

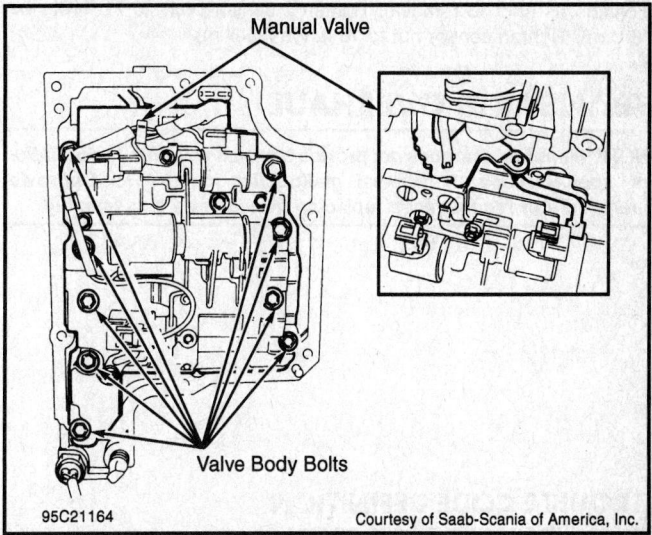

Fig. 6: Locating Valve Body Bolts & Manual Valve

95C21164   Courtesy of Saab-Scania of America, Inc.

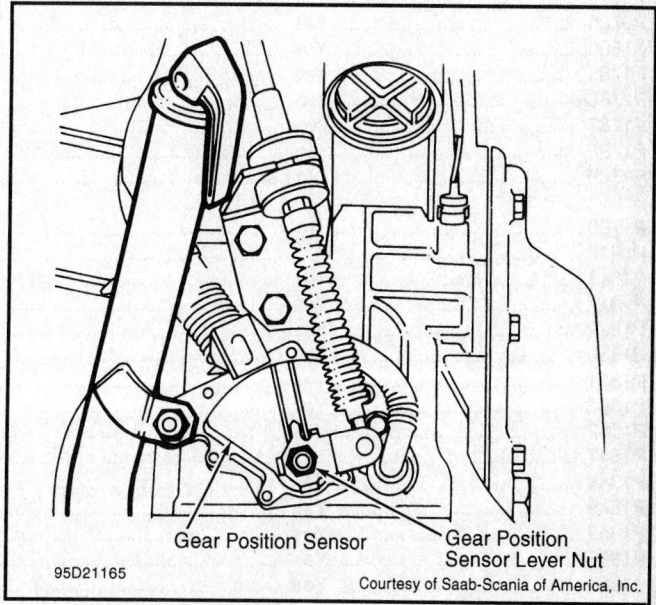

Fig. 7: Identifying Gear Position Sensor Components

95D21165   Courtesy of Saab-Scania of America, Inc.

4) To install, reverse removal procedure. Ensure bolts are installed in correct locations. Tighten bolts to 62 INCH lbs. (7 N.m). Install .12" (3 mm) thick bead of sealing compound on transaxle surface and install valve body cover. Tighten valve body cover bolts to 18 ft. lbs. (25 N.m).

GEAR POSITION SENSOR

NOTE: Gear position sensor may also be referred to as neutral safety switch or Transmission Range (TR) switch.

Removal & Installation – 1) Ensure transaxle is in "P" position and parking brake is applied. Remove battery, battery tray and air intake hose. Remove dipstick. Disconnect transaxle cable and bracket from lever at gear position sensor. Note position of notch on sensor for installation reference. *See Fig. 7.*
2) Remove lever nut from sensor. Remove 2 bolts securing sensor to transaxle. Remove sensor from control shaft. To install, reverse removal procedure. Ensure notch on sensor is located in exact position as prior to removal. Tighten 2 sensor bolts to 71 INCH lbs. (8 N.m). Tighten sensor nut to 18 ft. lbs (25 N.m).

TRANSAXLE OVERHAUL

NOTE: Manufacturer does not provide transaxle overhaul information or specifications. If internal malfunction occurs to transaxle, manufacturer recommends replacing transaxle as an assembly.

SELF-DIAGNOSTIC SYSTEM

DIAGNOSTIC PROCEDURE

When performing vehicle diagnosis ensure the following procedure is performed in order listed:
- Read any fault codes before battery is disconnected, see SELF-DIAGNOSTIC SYSTEM.
- Ensure transaxle fluid level is correct and fluid is neither contaminated or burnt.
- Inspect and adjust throttle cable, kickdown cable and gear position sensor (if necessary). See appropriate AUTOMATIC TRANSMISSION SERVICING article in TRANSMISSION SERVICING section.
- Check idle speed RPM and adjust as necessary.
- Check stall speeds, see STALL SPEED TESTS.
- Check hydraulic pressure, see HYDRAULIC PRESSURE TEST.
- Test drive vehicle and document shift points, see ROAD TEST.
- Repair diagnostic trouble codes in order displayed.

NOTE: Saab scan tool (ISAT) can be used in 6 different system test functions using manufacturer's instructions to activate system components and perform several tests on transaxle. See manufacturer's instructions.

SELF-DIAGNOSTICS

Signals from various sensors are monitored continuously by TCM. If signals are lost or become faulty, TCM will adapt electrical signals to transaxle components to protect transaxle. TCM adopts fixed replacement values (limp-home mode) to enable vehicle to be driven when certain failures occur. CHECK GEARBOX light will illuminate. Transaxle will not shift gears due to lack of electrical signal. Transaxle will operate in 4th gear in "D", and 3rd gear position. Transaxle will operate in 3rd gear in 2nd and 1st position. Manual shifting is possible into all other shift lever positions.

Faults are recorded in TCM memory in the form of Diagnostic Trouble Codes (DTC's). Codes can only be retrieved using Saab's ISAT tester. Follow manufacturer's instructions.

TROUBLE CODE DEFINITION
DIAGNOSTIC TROUBLE CODE DEFINITION

DTC	Check Gearbox Light On [1]	Fault/Repair
P0705	Yes	Gear Position Sensor Signal Incorrect
P1500	Yes	Low Battery Voltage
P1785	Yes	Incorrect TP Sensor Signal
P1786	No	Incorrect TCS Position Sensor Signal
P1787	No	Open Or Short To Ground In TCS Position Sensor Circuit
P1788	No	Erratic Throttle Position Sensor Signal
P1789	No	Open Or Short To Ground In ECM Idle Compensating Signal Circuit From Gear Position Sensor
P1790	No	Short To Ground In Kickdown Switch Circuit
P1812	No	Short To Ground In ATF Temperature Sensor Circuit
P1813	No	High ATF Temperature Or Short To Voltage In ATF Temperature Sensor Circuit
P1817	Yes	Input Speed Sensor Signal Missing
P1822	Yes	Output Speed Sensor Signal Missing
P1830	Yes	Gear Ratio Information Incorrect
P1831	Yes	Downshifting Fault
P1832	Yes	Incorrect Shift Length Slip/Jerk
P1842	Yes	Open Or Short In Torque Limiter Circuit
P1847	Yes	Open Or Short To Ground In Pressure Control Solenoid Circuit
P1848	Yes	Short To Voltage In Pressure Control Solenoid Circuit
P1849	Yes	Internal Short In Pressure Control Solenoid
P1852	Yes	Short To Ground In No. 1 Shift Solenoid Circuit
P1853	Yes	Short To Voltage In No. 1 Shift Solenoid Circuit
P1857	Yes	Short To Ground In No. 2 Shift Solenoid Circuit
P1858	Yes	Short To Voltage In No. 2 Shift Solenoid Circuit
P1862	No	Short To Ground In TCC Solenoid Circuit
P1863	No	Short To Voltage In TCC Solenoid Circuit

[1] – CHECK GEARBOX light is located in instrument panel. When a fault occurs, DTC is recorded and CHECK GEARBOX light comes on. If fault is intermittent, CHECK GEARBOX light will go out, but DTC will remain.

TCM VOLTAGE CHECKS

If Saab's ISAT tester is not available, TCM voltage checks can be made using a DVOM. TCM is located in passenger compartment behind glove box. See Fig. 3. Turn ignition on. Check voltage at each control module terminal. See Fig. 8. If voltage is not as specified at each terminal, repair or replace component(s) or wiring. See TCM VOLTAGE TESTS table. If no problem is found with any component or wiring, replace TCM. See following pin voltage chart.

TCM VOLTAGE TESTS

Terminal Number	Circuit Tested	[1] Test Conditions	Measure Between Terminals	Voltage Output
1	Solenoid No.1	Shifter In "D", Winter Mode On	1 – 35	12
		Winter Mode Off		0
3	Solenoid No. 2	Shifter In "D", Winter Mode On	3 – 35	0
		Winter Mode Off		12
4	TCS Signal	TCS Light On	4 – 17	12
		TCS Light Off		0
6	Check Gear Box Warning Light	Check Gear Box Light On	6 – 17	12
		Check Gear Box Light Off		0
7	Winter Mode Light	Winter Light On	7 – 17	12
		Winter Mode Off		0
8	Kickdown Switch	Accelerator Depressed	8 – 35	0
		Accelerator Not Depressed		12
9	Gear Position Sensor Pin "A"	Shift Lever In "P", "R", "3" & "2"	9 – 35	12
		Shift Lever In "N", "D" & "1"		0
10	Gear Position Sensor Pin "B"	Shift Lever In "R", "N", "D" & "3"	10 – 35	12
		Shift Lever In "P", "2" & "1"		0
11	Idling Compensation Drive Signal	Shift Lever Moved From "N"	11 – 35	12
12	Input Speed Sensor	Engine Idling	12 – 31	1.2-1.4
		Engine At 2500 RPM		2.2
13	Torque Limitation On Shifting	Engine Idling	13 – 31	[2]
15	TCS Throttle Position	Engine Idling	15 – 35	[2]
16	Pressure Control Solenoid	Ignition On	16 – 34	[2]
17	Battery Voltage 15 Amp Fuse	Ignition On	17 – B-	12
		Ignition Off		0
18	Battery Voltage 30 Amp Fuse	At All Times	18 – B-	12
19	Torque Converter Lockup Solenoid	Ignition On	19 – 35	[2]
20	Sport Mode Switch	Switch On	20 – 35	0
		Switch Off		12
21	Winter Mode Switch	Switch On	21 – 35	0
		Switch Off		12
22	Ground	At All Times	22 – B-	0
23	Data Link Connector	ISAT Scan Tool Connected	23 – 35	10
		ISAT Scan Tool Not Connected		0
24	Sport Mode Indicator Light	Sport Light On	17 – 24	12
		Sport Light Off		0
25	Throttle Position Sensor	Engine Idling	25 – 35	1.2
		Engine At 2500 RPM		2.0
		Starter Motor Cranking		.25-1.0
26	Brake Light Switch	Brake Applied	26 – 35	12
		Brake Not Applied		0
27	Gear Position Sensor Pin "D"	Shift Lever In "P", "N", "3" & "1"	27 – 35	12
		Shift Lever In "N", "D" & "2"		0
28	Gear Position Sensor Pin "C"	Shift Lever In "D", "3", "2" & "1"	28 – 35	12
		Shift Lever In "P", "R" & "N"		0
30	Output Shaft Speed Sensor	Engine Running, Wheel Speed @ 12.4 MPH (20 km/h)	30 – 31	1.1
31	Ground For Speed Sensors	Ignition On	31 – B-	0
33	ATF Temperature Sensor	Fluid Temp. @ 68°F (20°C)	33 – 35	2.3
		Fluid Temp. @ 122°F (50°C)		1.7
		Fluid Temp. @ 176°F (80°C)		1.0
34	Pressure Control Solenoid	Ignition On	34 – 35	[2]
35	Ground	Ignition On	35 – B-	0

[1] – Ignition should be On unless otherwise noted.

[2] – Circuit can only be tested with Saab ISAT tester. See manufacturers' instructions on operation.

AUTOMATIC TRANSMISSIONS
Saab AW50-40LE Electronic Controls (Cont.)

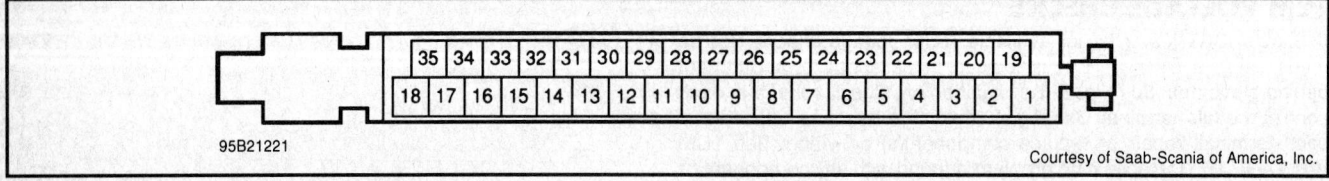

95B21221

Courtesy of Saab-Scania of America, Inc.

Fig. 8: Identifying TCM Connector Terminals

CIRCUIT & COMPONENT TESTING

BRAKE SWITCH

1) Ensure ignition is off. Remove underdash panel on left side to gain access to brake switch, located at top of brake pedal lever. Connect a voltmeter between brake switch terminal No. 2 (Yellow/Gray wire) and a good known ground. Battery voltage should be present. If battery voltage is not present, check for open circuit between terminal No. 2 and brake switch fuse (No. 17, 10 amp).
2) Disconnect brake switch connector. Connect an ohmmeter between brake switch terminals No. 1 (Violet wire) and No. 2 (Yellow/Gray wire). With brake pedal released, resistance should be infinite. With brake pedal depressed, resistance should be zero ohms. If resistance is not as specified, replace brake switch.

KICKDOWN SWITCH

Ensure ignition is off. Remove center console, left side panel to gain access to kickdown switch. Disconnect kickdown switch connector from switch. Using a DVOM, measure resistance between switch terminals when accelerator pedal is in WOT position. Resistance should be zero ohms. While slowly releasing accelerator pedal continue to measure resistance. Resistance should be infinite in all other pedal positions. If kickdown switch does not test as described, replace switch.

MODE SELECTOR SWITCHES

Sport Switch – Ensure ignition switch is off. Disconnect sport switch connector from switch. Using a DVOM, measure resistance between switch terminals when switch is in SPORT mode. Resistance should be infinite. When sport mode switch is switched off, zero ohms should exist. If resistance is not as specified, replace sport switch.

Winter Switch – Ensure ignition switch is off. Disconnect winter switch connector from switch. Using a DVOM, measure resistance between switch terminals when switch is in WINTER mode. Resistance should be infinite. When winter mode switch is switched off, zero ohms should exist. If resistance is not as specified, replace winter switch.

ATF TEMPERATURE SENSOR

Resistance Test – **1)** Ensure ignition switch is off. Using a DVOM, measure resistance between TCM terminals No. 33 and 35. If resistance is as specified in ATF TEMPERATURE SENSOR RESISTANCE & VOLTAGE table, sensor and wiring are okay.
2) If resistance is not as specified, test ground circuit from sensor to attachment below center console. If ATF temperature sensor ground circuit is okay, replace sensor.

Voltage Test – **1)** Ensure ignition switch is on and engine is off. Using a DVOM, measure voltage between Black/Blue wire of ATF temperature sensor and ground. If voltage is as specified in ATF TEMPERATURE SENSOR RESISTANCE & VOLTAGE table, sensor and wiring are okay.
2) If voltage is not as specified, test ground circuit from sensor to attachment below center console. If ATF temperature sensor ground circuit is okay, replace sensor.

ATF TEMPERATURE SENSOR RESISTANCE & VOLTAGE

Temperature °F (°C)	Resistance (Ohms)	Voltage (V)
-50 (-10)	5000	4.6
32 (0)	2000	4.1
68 (20)	900	3.4
104 (40)	400	2.4
176 (80)	125	1.1
212 (100)	75	0.7

SPEED SENSORS

1) Ensure ignition switch is off. Using a DVOM, measure resistance between sensor terminals. Resistance should be 300-600 ohms. If resistance is as specified, sensor and wiring are okay.
2) If resistance is not as specified, inspect wiring between sensor and TCM terminals No. 12 and No. 31 on input speed sensor or TCM terminals No. 30 and No. 31 for output speed sensor. If wiring is okay, replace speed sensor.

TORQUE LIMITING SIGNAL VOLTAGE

Torque limiting signal voltage can only be tested with Saab ISAT tester. If Saab ISAT tester is available, see manufacturers instructions.

VALVE BODY SOLENOIDS

1) Remove transaxle oil pan. Disconnect solenoid wire connector(s). For solenoid wire color identification, see SOLENOID WIRE COLOR IDENTIFICATION table. Using a DVOM, measure resistance between appropriate solenoid terminal and ground. Resistance should be approximately 13 ohms for No. 1, No. 2 and torque converter clutch solenoids. If resistance is not as specified, replace solenoid.
2) Using DVOM, measure resistance between pressure control solenoid terminals. Resistance should be about 4 ohms. If resistance is not as specified, replace solenoid.

SOLENOID WIRE COLOR IDENTIFICATION

Solenoid	Wire Color
No. 1	White
No. 2	Black
Pressure Control	Brown
Torque Converter Clutch	Yellow

WIRING DIAGRAMS

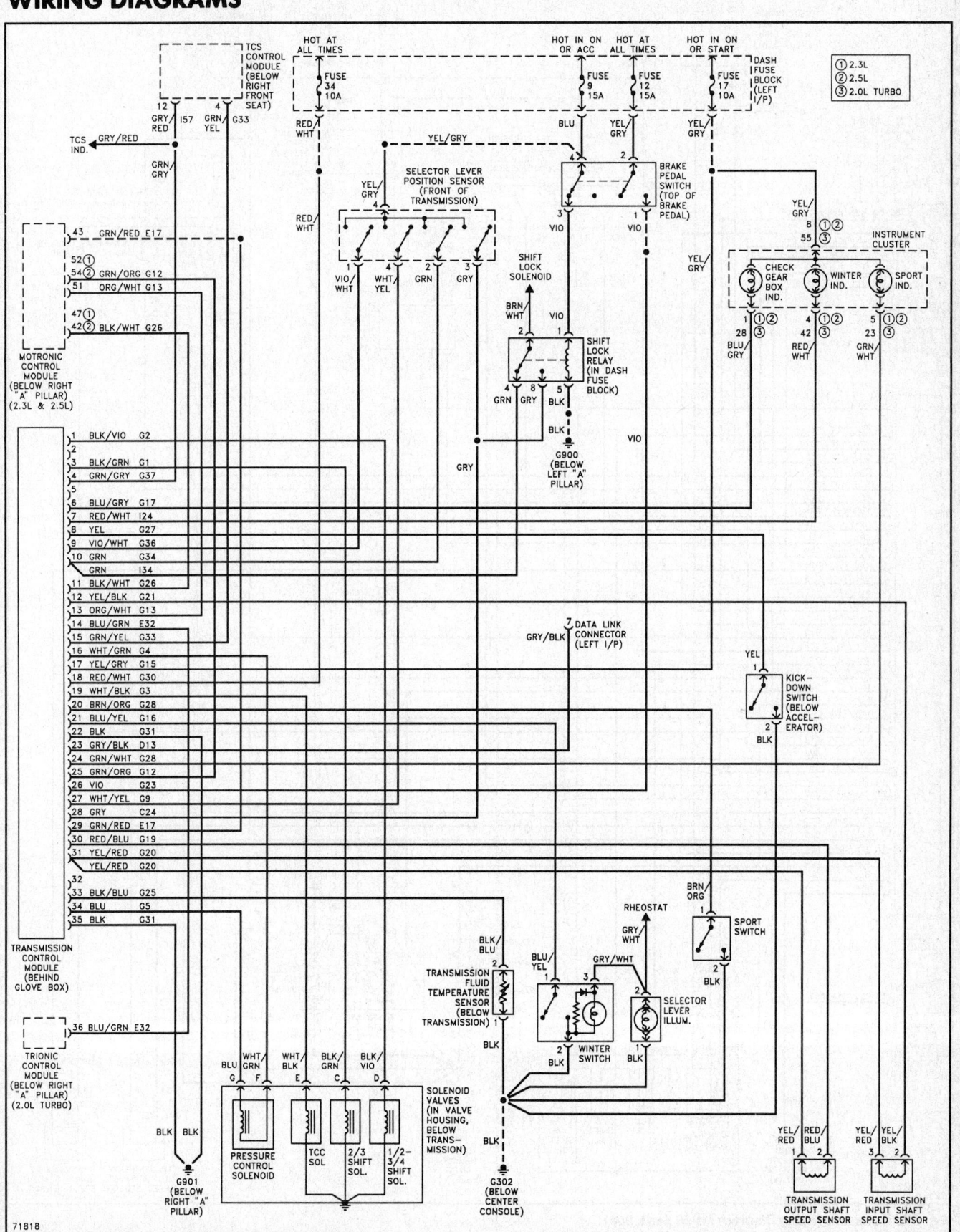

Fig. 9: Transaxle Wiring Diagram (1995 Saab 900)

AUTOMATIC TRANSMISSIONS
Saab AW50-40LE Electronic Controls (Cont.)

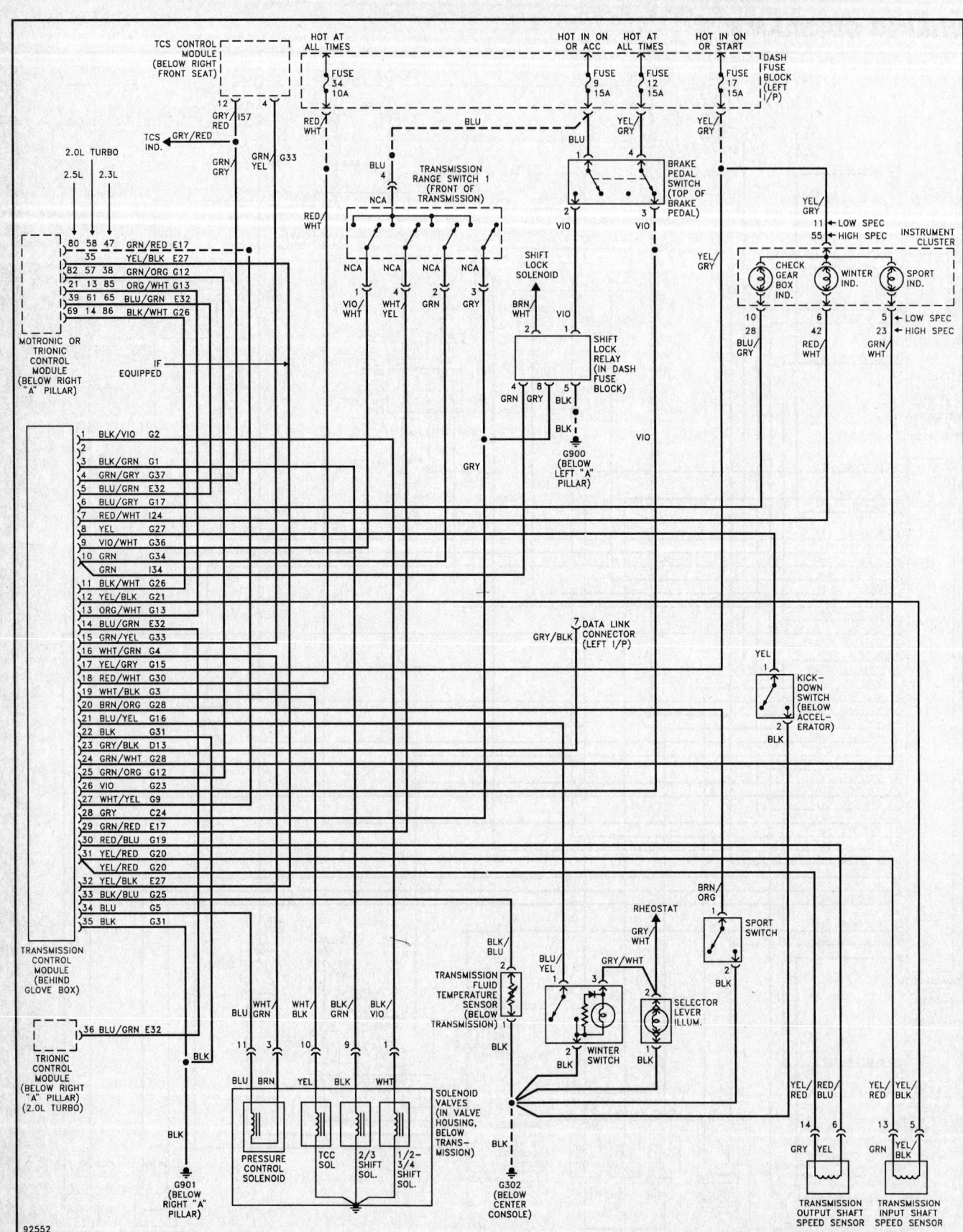

Fig. 10: Transaxle Wiring Diagram (1996 Saab 900)

9000 Series

APPLICATION & LABOR TIMES

APPLICATION & LABOR TIMES

Vehicle Application	Labor Times		Trans. Model
	[1] R & I	[2] Overhaul	
Saab 9000 V6 Series	8.2	9.1	ZF 4HP 18

[1] – Removal and installation of transmission from vehicle chassis.

[2] – Bench overhaul time for transmission and differential. DOES NOT include removal and installation.

IDENTIFICATION

Automatic Transaxle (A/T) can be identified by transaxle identification plate which is located on top of the torque converter cover. *See Fig. 1.*

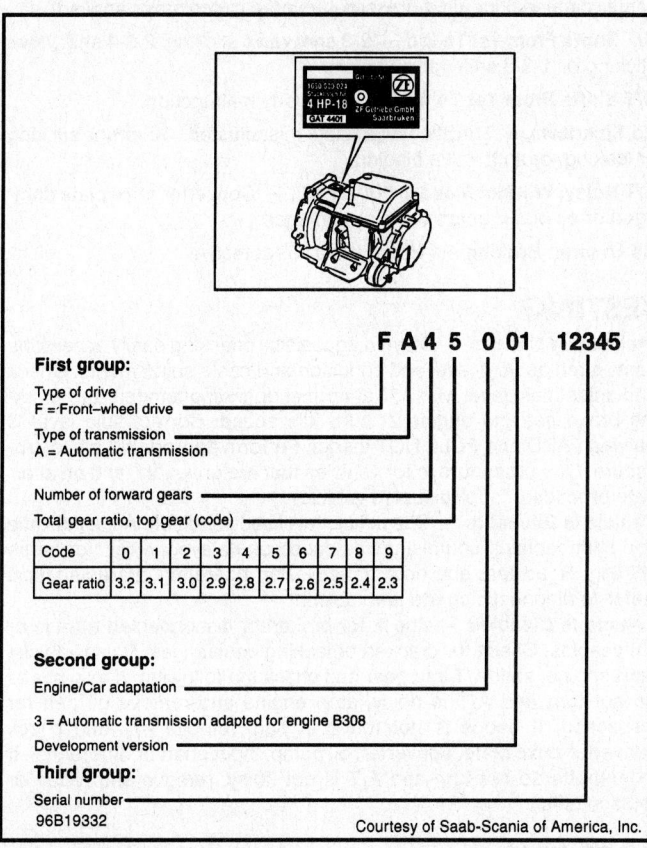

First group:

Type of drive
F = Front–wheel drive

Type of transmission
A = Automatic transmission

Number of forward gears

Total gear ratio, top gear (code)

Code	0	1	2	3	4	5	6	7	8	9
Gear ratio	3.2	3.1	3.0	2.9	2.8	2.7	2.6	2.5	2.4	2.3

Second group:

Engine/Car adaptation

3 = Automatic transmission adapted for engine B308

Development version

Third group:

Serial number

96B19332

Courtesy of Saab-Scania of America, Inc.

Fig. 1: Identifying Transaxle

DESCRIPTION

The ZF 4HP 18 Automatic Transaxle (A/T) has 4 speeds, providing an overdrive ratio of .74:1. A/T shifting is controlled by a governor valve, line pressure valve, throttle pressure regulator valve and a modulator valve. Valve operation is dependent on shift lever position, vehicle speed and throttle position. The A/T features a lock-up type torque converter and a planetary gear set, consisting of a total of 6 planetary pinions. Ignition TDC sensor is activated by a stamped steel trigger wheel attached to the torque converter drive plate. Two types of one-way clutches are used: roller and sprag. Roller type clutch operates in 1st gear, and a sprag type clutch in 2nd gear.

LUBRICATION & ADJUSTMENTS

NOTE: For lubrication information, see appropriate AUTOMATIC TRANSMISSION SERVICING article in TRANSMISSION SERVICING section.

BAND ADJUSTMENT

1) Remove battery. Remove battery tray. Remove dipstick and upper valve body cover. Remove valve body and adjusting screw lock nut. *See Fig. 2.*

2) Remove adjusting screw and dowel. Install new O-rings on dowel and reinstall. Install adjusting screw and tighten to 87.5 INCH lbs. (10 N.m). Mark adjusting screw and gearcase. Loosen adjusting screw 2 turns.

3) Install lock nut and tighten to 37 ft. lbs. (50 N.m) while ensuring adjusting screw does not rotate. To install, reverse removal procedure.

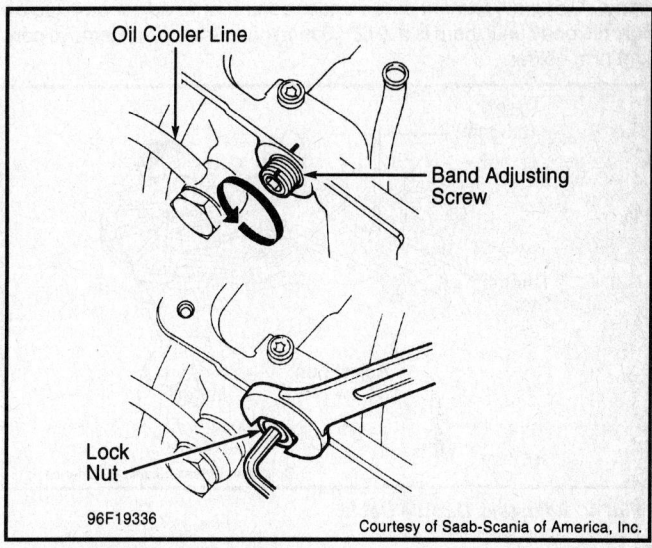

Fig. 2: Adjusting Brake Band

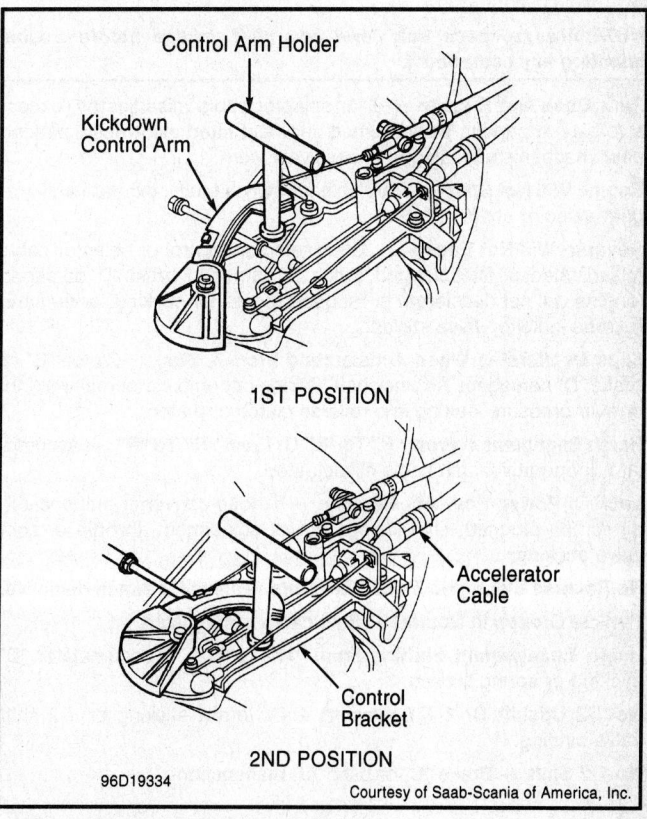

Fig. 3: Adjusting Kick-Down Threshold

THROTTLE CABLE

1) Move kick-down control arm to wide open throttle position. Install Kick-Down Control Arm Holder (87 92 459) into right side hole on control bracket. *See Fig. 3.* Release kick-down control arm and allow it to rest against holder. Ensure kick-down threshold is not crossed with conrol arm in this position.

2) Move kick-down control arm holder to left side hole on control bracket. Remove throttle cable from control arm. Loosen lock nuts and adjust control rod so there is a gap between control arm and holder. Tighten lock nuts and attach throttle cable.

3) Adjust throttle cable so there is a small amount of slack in throttle cable. Using adjustment screw under control arm, adjust stop lug on throttle body until there is a .012" (.3 mm) gap. *See Fig. 4.* Remove control arm holder.

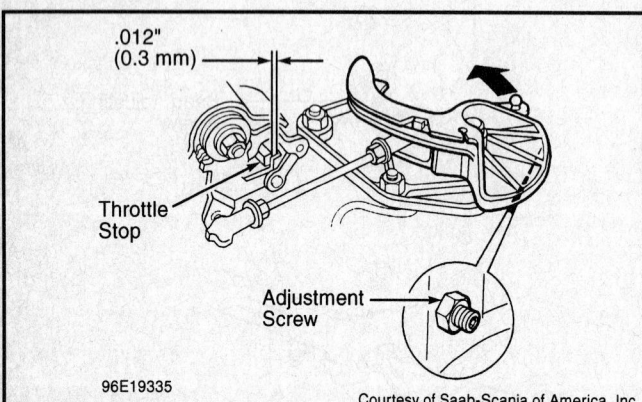

96E19335   Courtesy of Saab-Scania of America, Inc.

Fig. 4: Adjusting Throttle Cable

TROUBLE SHOOTING

NOTE: Always check fluid level and shift linkage before trouble shooting any component.

Park Does Not Engage – Gear selector cable misadjusted, excessive play at parking pawl washer, segment fitted incorrectly, parking pawl mechanism binding or excessively worn.

Engine Will Not Start – Start inhibitor switch faulty, excessive play at gear selector shaft.

Reverse Will Not Engage – Gear selector control or selector cable misadjusted, oil filter clogged, clutch "B" damaged, brake "D" damaged (engine will not decelerate in 1st gear), governor sticking, or first and reverse inhibitor valve sticking.

Slips Or Vibrates When Accelerating From A Stop – Clutch "B" or brake "D" damaged. Turbine shaft "O" ring or pump stator malfunction, or fluid pressure leaking into reverse clutch or piston.

Harsh Engagement From "P" To "R" Or From "N" To "R" – Accumulator inoperative, shift cable misadjusted.

Lack Of Power, Poor Acceleration – Torque converter malfunction, oil screen plugged, shift linkage out of adjustment, throttle or shift valve sticking.

No Reverse Lights; No Electrical Faults – Inhibitor switch defective.

Vehicle Creeps In Neutral – Shift cable misadjusted.

Harsh Engagement Shifting From "N" To "D" – Accumulator "D" sticking or spring broken.

No 1-2 Upshift Or 2-1 Downshift – Governor sticking or 1-2 shift valve binding.

No 1-2 Shift – Brake "C" or band "C" malfunction.

No 2-3 Upshift Or 3-2 Downshift – Governor sticking or 2-3 shift valve binding.

No 2-3 Shift – Clutch "E" damaged or oil supply for clutch "E" leaking.

No 3-4 Upshift Or 4-3 Downshift – Governor sticking or 3-4 shift valve sticking.

No 3-4 Shift – Brake band "C" inoperative or loose, 2-3-4 upshift valve sticking or position 3 valve sticks.

Shifting Points Incorrect – Throttle cable misadjusted, governor sticking, shift valves binding.

Vehicle Takes Off In 2nd Gear (No Downshift To 1st) – Governor piston binding, 1-2 shift valve sticking or band "C" not releasing (adjusted too tight).

Vehicle Takes Off In 3rd Gear (No Downshift To 1st Or 2nd) – Governor malfunction, 1-2 and 2-3 shift valves sticking or closing gap in center plate leaking fluid pressure (reverse clutch stays applied).

A/T Shifts From 1st To 3rd – 2-3 shift valve sticking, 2-3-4 shift valve sticking or 1-2-3 shift valve sticking.

A/T Shifts From 1st To 4th – Valve body malfunction.

No Kickdown – Throttle valve cable misadjusted. Governor sticking or leaking, or shift valve binding.

A/T Noisy; Will Not Move In "D" Or "R" – Converter drive plate damaged or oil pump gears worn or damaged.

No Overrun Braking – Brake band "C" defective.

TESTING

Preliminary Checks – Begin diagnosis by checking easily accessible items such as fluid level and condition and cable adjustments. Check and adjust fluid level with A/T at normal operating temperature, parking brake set and engine at curb idle speed. Correct fluid level is between ADD and FULL HOT marks. Perform appropriate basic procedure. One procedure is for vehicles that are driveable, and an alternate procedure is for disabled vehicles.

Vehicle Is Driveable – Check fluid level and condition. Adjust throttle and shift cables if complaint was based on delayed, erratic or harsh shifting. Road test and note transmission operating characteristics. Refer to diagnostic charts and tables.

Vehicle Is Disabled – Check for broken or disconnected throttle or shift cables. Check for cracked or leaking cooler lines. Raise vehicle, start engine, shift A/T into gear and check the following: If axle shafts do not turn and A/T is noisy, stop engine and remove oil pan for inspection. If debris is not found in pan, remove A/T and check converter drive plate, converter, oil pump, input shaft or differential. If axle shafts do not turn and A/T is not noisy, remove and repair or replace unit.

ROAD TEST

1) Operate A/T in all gear ranges while checking for slippage and shift variations. Note when shifts are harsh, spongy, delayed, early or if downshifts are sensitive.

2) Check closely for engine flare during shifts. Engine flare usually indicates clutch, band or overrunning clutch malfunctions.

Road Test Results – Use CLUTCH & BAND APPLICATION and SHIFT SPEED SPECIFICATIONS charts to provide a basis for analyzing road test results.

CLUTCH & BAND APPLICATION

Gear Position	Elements In Use
1st Gear	Clutch "A", Brake "D", 1st Gear One-Way Clutch
2nd Gear	Clutch "A", Brake "C", Band "C", 2nd Gear One-Way Clutch
3rd Gear	Clutch "A", Clutch "E"
4th Gear	Band "C", Clutch "E"
Reverse	Clutch "B", Brake "D"

SHIFT SPEED SPECIFICATIONS

Shift Point	MPH (km/h)
Minimum Throttle Application	
1st-2nd	13-17 (22-28)
2nd-3rd	26-32 (43-53)
3rd-4th	44-51 (72-83)
Maximum Throttle Application	
With Engine At 5100-5700 RPM	
1st-2nd	39-45 (63-73)
2nd-3rd	75-83 (122-136)
3rd-4th	101-117 (165-191)
Maximum Downshift Speed	
With Kick-Down Engaged	
4th-3rd	88-96 (142-154)
3rd-2nd	57-62 (92-102)
2nd-1st	28-34 (45-55)

LINE PRESSURE TEST

1) Perform line pressure test after A/T has reached operating temperature of 176°F (80°C). Ensure fluid level and condition have been checked and are acceptable.

2) Measure line pressure with gear selector in "N" and engine idling. Measure kickdown line pressure with throttle valve cable withdrawn fully and engine speed at 2000 RPM.

3) Connect oil pressure gauge to pressure port in A/T housing. *See Fig. 5.* Start engine, obtain pressure readings and refer to specifications. See appropriate LINE PRESSURE SPECIFICATIONS table.

LINE PRESSURE SPECIFICATIONS [1]

Gear Position	Idle RPM	Line Pressure At Idle (PSI)	[2] Line Pressure At Kickdown (PSI)
"R"	950	149.4-178.4	32.1-275.6
"N"	875	103.0-114.6	167.9-189.2
"D"	950	103.0-114.6	167.9-189.2
"1"	950	103.0-114.6	167.9-189.2

[1] – Specified system pressure applies when fluid temperature is 104-122°F (40-50°C).

[2] – Line pressure with throttle closed and kickdown cable fully retracted.

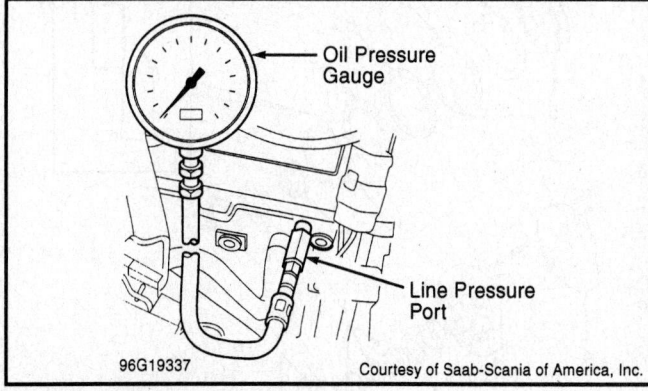

96G19337   Courtesy of Saab-Scania of America, Inc.

Fig. 5: Locating Pressure Test Ports

STALL SPEED TEST

1) Perform stall speed test with A/T at operating temperature. Check engine and A/T fluid to ensure proper levels and condition.

2) Stall speeds are measured with gear selector in "D" and "1" positions. Parking brake and service brake must be applied fully while performing stall test. Connect an engine tachometer visible to driver.

3) Start engine, apply parking brake and service brake fully, then shift gear selector to "D" position. Ensure no one is in front or behind vehicle and depress accelerator pedal to floor. Obtain engine RPM reading and release accelerator pedal immediately. Stall speed should be 1900-2400 RPM.

4) Allow ATF to cool, then repeat test with gear selector in "1" position. To prevent internal damage to A/T, DO NOT hold stall speed longer than 5 seconds. Stall speed should be 1900-2400 RPM.

ON-VEHICLE SERVICE

SPEEDOMETER DRIVE/SPEEDOMETER SENSOR

Removal & Installation – With a small hammer and pin punch, remove locking pin from A/T case. Pull speedometer cable from A/T case. If equipped with electronic sensor, remove retaining bracket and drive.

SERVO PISTON

Removal – **1)** Remove transmission fluid cooler. Compress piston and cover and remove cover snap ring.

2) Remove piston cover and band piston assembly. Remove and discard "O" rings from piston and cover. Clean piston and cover. Inspect for signs of wear or damage.

Installation – **1)** Install new "O" rings on band piston and piston cover. Install piston assembly and cover in case bore and ensure piston rod is seated in band.

2) Compress piston and cover and install cover snap ring. Remove tool and install transmission fluid cooler. Tighten cooler bolt to 37 ft. lbs. (50 N.m).

GEAR POSITION SWITCH REPLACEMENT

Removal – **1)** Disconnect neutral switch harness connector in engine compartment. Raise vehicle and remove splash shield.

2) Remove bolt attaching switch bracket to A/T case and remove switch from case.

Installation – **1)** While under vehicle, feed switch harness up into engine compartment. Install new "O" ring on neutral switch.

2) Insert neutral switch into A/T case, install switch bracket and tighten bolt to 89 INCH lbs. (10 N.m).

3) Install splash shield and lower vehicle. Connect neutral switch harness connector in engine compartment.

PARKING PAWL COMPONENTS

NOTE: Removal of parking pawl components is possible without transaxle removal. For disassembly procedures, see SELECTOR MECHANISM & PARKING PAWL under COMPONENT DISASSEMBLY & REASSEMBLY section.

REMOVAL & INSTALLATION

See appropriate AUTOMATIC TRANSMISSION REMOVAL article in AUTOMATIC TRANSMISSION SERVICING section.

AXLE SHAFTS

See appropriate AXLE SHAFTS article in AXLE SHAFTS & TRANSFER CASES section.

TORQUE CONVERTER

Torque converters used with ZF 4HP 18 transaxles are not serviceable. If damaged or contaminated in any way, converter must be replaced. The transaxle assembly must be removed to access torque converter.

TRANSAXLE DISASSEMBLY

1) Mount transmission on work bench and secure with oil pan facing upward. Remove torque converter. Remove bearing cover bolts and CV joint. Remove oil filter cover and oil dipstick. Remove valve body cover and valve body assembly. Remove 18 bolts and torque converter housing with input shaft housing attached. Lift out differential assembly.

2) Remove differential bearing race. Remove intermediate plate with oil pump and clutch "C". Remove angle washer and shims from turbine shaft. Loosen brake band "C" adjusting screw. Turn turbine shaft back and forth while removing clutch "A", clutch "B" and 2nd one-way clutch assembly.

3) Seperate clutch "A", clutch "B" and 2nd one-way clutch. Remove brake band and engine shaft with clutch "E". Remove intermediate shaft with 2 axial washers and axial needle bearing. Remove sun gear shaft with axial bearings, washer and angle washer. Remove drum with axial bearing, axial washer, angle washer and bearing holder. Lift out planetary spider assembly with axial bearing, washer and bearing holders.

4) Turn transmission over, remove spur gear cover and engage parking pawl. Loosen spur gear bolts, but DO NOT remove. Turn transmission over with oil pan side facing upward. Release parking pawl and remove spur gear bolts. Remove spur gear and output shaft.

5) Remove spider drum. Remove hexagon bolt, spur gear and adjusting washer. Remove countershaft. Remove inner race from spur gear (output shaft).

6) Remove tapered roller bearing inner shaft of spur gear (countershaft). Tapered roller bearing inner ring on countershaft can be pressed off. Turn transmission housing on end and remove bearing outer race with 2 jaw bearing puller. Remove sleeve and governor assembly.

7) Turn transmission with pan facing upward and remove slotted nut. Remove bearing ring with 1st one-way clutch assembly and retainer washer. Depress brake "C" servo cover. Remove retaining ring and piston "C" assembly. Remove adjusting bolt and pin.

8) Lift out brake "D" clutch discs and plate spring. Use compressed air to remove piston "D". Release snap ring and remove discs from clutch "B". Remove clutch "A" and "E" assembly and output shaft. Remove governor and differential assembly. Remove input shaft speedometer from converter housing. Remove selector mechanism and parking interlock from transmission housing. For further information on individual components, see COMPONENT DISASSEMBLY & REASSEMBLY.

COMPONENT DISASSEMBLY & REASSEMBLY

SERVO PISTON, BRAKE "C" & OIL PUMP

Disassembly – 1) Press down on servo piston cover and release snap ring with a screwdriver. Remove cover and servo piston "C" assembly. Disassemble piston by removing snap ring and separating plate springs. Remove piston "C" pin from housing by loosening adjusting pin. Remove band from housing. See Fig. 6.

2) Remove intermediate plate bolts and separate pump from intermediate plate. It may be necessary to tap plate with plastic hammer to remove pump. Rectangular plates and locating pin remain in intermediate plate. Disassemble pump by removing pump gears. Remove compression spring and valve with cap from intermediate plate. See Fig. 7.

3) Press brake "C" together with plate spring and remove snap ring. Remove all clutch discs. Press out piston "C" by screwing in 2 bolts from pump side.

Cleaning & Inspection – Clean all parts with solvent and dry with compressed air. Inspect all parts for excessive wear and damage. Replace parts as necessary. Replace all seals and "O" rings.

Reassembly – 1) Install new "O" ring on band anchor pin and insert into housing. Install adjusting bolt with wave washer partially into housing. If piston was disassembled from pin, install thicker washer against collar of pin. Install sleeve into servo cylinder housing using appropriate mandrel.

2) Lubricate and install new "O" ring on servo piston. Install springs over piston shaft and slide into housing. Install servo piston cover. Insert snap ring, remove mounting device and install screw plug. Install brake band. Fit flush with shoulder in transmission housing.

3) Install pump gears into pump housing. Ensure mark at top of pump housing and outer pump gear are visible. Install 2 straight pins into intermediate plate using a plastic hammer. Install assembled torque converter pressure relief valve into intermediate plate.

4) Insert compression spring into pump opening and install intermediate plate onto pump housing. Install intermediate plate and pump housing. Tighten 6 Torx bolts to 89 INCH lbs. (10 N.m). Spin pump shaft to ensure smooth rotation. Install rectangular rings onto hub.

5) Fit "O" ring on clutch piston "C", lubricate piston with petroleum jelly and press piston into intermediate plate. Insert complete set of clutch discs. Install end disc and secure with snap ring.

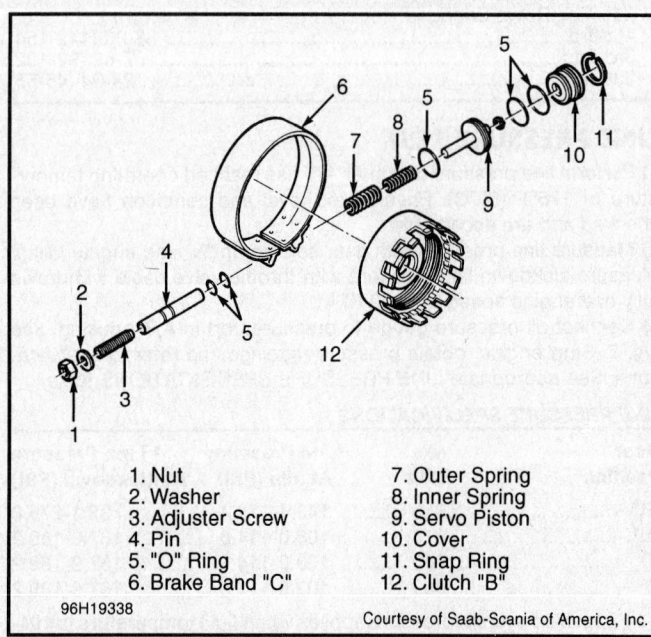

1. Nut	7. Outer Spring
2. Washer	8. Inner Spring
3. Adjuster Screw	9. Servo Piston
4. Pin	10. Cover
5. "O" Ring	11. Snap Ring
6. Brake Band "C"	12. Clutch "B"

96H19338

Courtesy of Saab-Scania of America, Inc.

Fig. 6: Exploded View Of Servo Piston & Band "C"

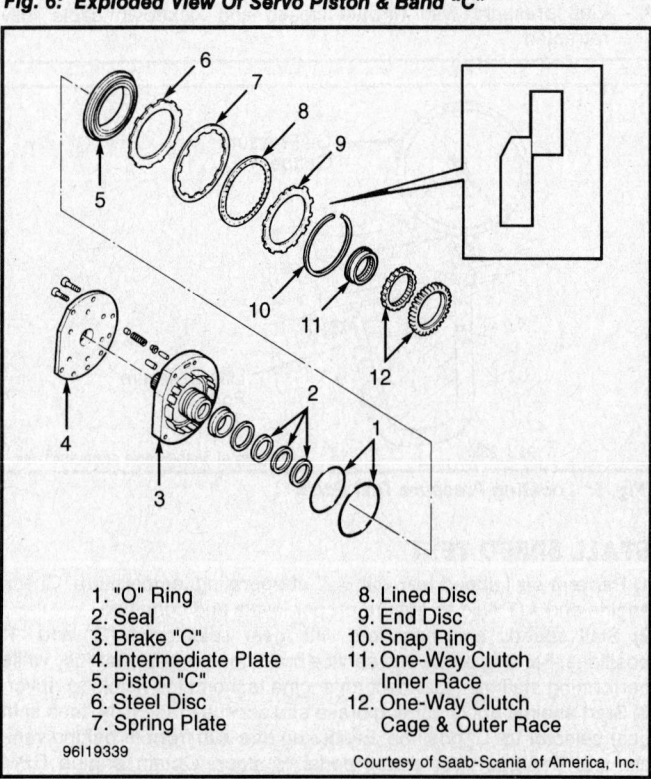

1. "O" Ring	8. Lined Disc
2. Seal	9. End Disc
3. Brake "C"	10. Snap Ring
4. Intermediate Plate	11. One-Way Clutch
5. Piston "C"	Inner Race
6. Steel Disc	12. One-Way Clutch
7. Spring Plate	Cage & Outer Race

96I19339

Courtesy of Saab-Scania of America, Inc.

Fig. 7: Exploded View Of Brake "C"
With Intermediate Plate & Oil Pump

6) Install measuring bar and dial indicator, position tip on end disc and zero gauge. Manually lift complete set of discs and record readings. Release clearance should be .05-.06" (1.3-1.6 mm). If clearance is not as specified, install different size snap ring to obtain specified clearance.

BRAKE "D"

Disassembly – Remove snap ring and remove complete set of brake "D" discs and plate spring. Use compressed air to remove piston "D" out of transmission housing oil passage. *See Fig. 8.*

Cleaning & Inspection – Clean all parts with solvent and dry with compressed air. Inspect for excessive wear and damage. Replace disc set as a unit.

Reassembly – **1)** Install new "O" rings into piston and insert piston into housing with raised face up. Insert plate spring with convex surface facing plate spring. Insert complete set of brake "D" discs. Begin with spring disc followed by outer disc and lined disc, end with end disc.

NOTE: Manufacturer does not provide snap ring thickness information.

---

2) Install .04 (1.0 mm) snap ring. Install measuring bar and dial indicator and zero dial. Manually lift complete set of discs and record clearance. Release clearance for 6 pairs of discs should be .09-.10" (2.0-2.5 mm). If readings differ from these readings, install correct size snap ring.

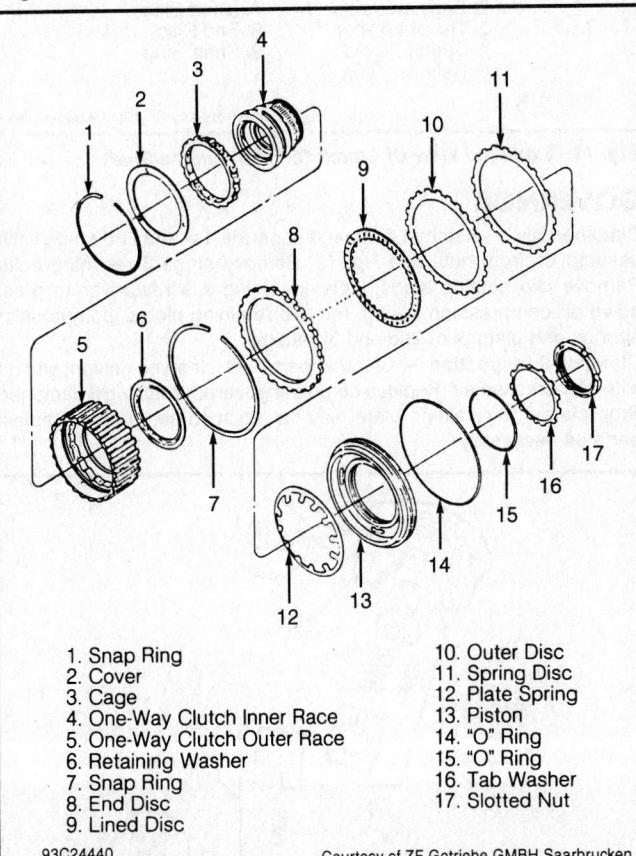

1. Snap Ring
2. Cover
3. Cage
4. One-Way Clutch Inner Race
5. One-Way Clutch Outer Race
6. Retaining Washer
7. Snap Ring
8. End Disc
9. Lined Disc
10. Outer Disc
11. Spring Disc
12. Plate Spring
13. Piston
14. "O" Ring
15. "O" Ring
16. Tab Washer
17. Slotted Nut

93C24440   Courtesy of ZF Getriebe GMBH Saarbrucken

Fig. 8: Exploded View Of Brake "D" With 1st One-Way Clutch

CLUTCH "B"

Disassembly – **1)** Remove snap ring from clutch and clutch discs. *See Fig. 9.* Using press and adapter, compress plate spring and release split retaining ring. Remove plate spring. Use compressed air to remove piston out of oil feed bore.

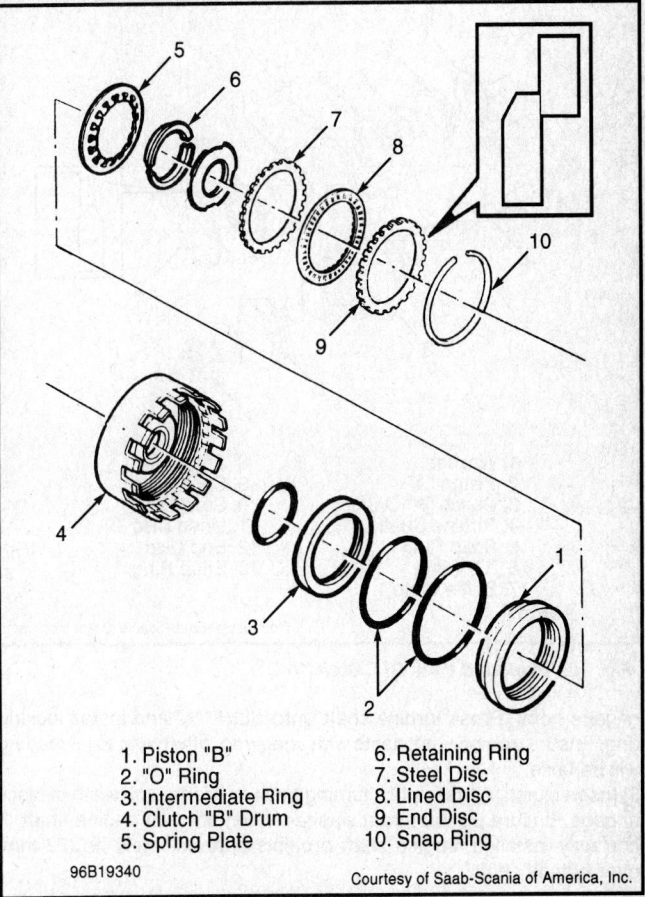

1. Piston "B"
2. "O" Ring
3. Intermediate Ring
4. Clutch "B" Drum
5. Spring Plate
6. Retaining Ring
7. Steel Disc
8. Lined Disc
9. End Disc
10. Snap Ring

96B19340   Courtesy of Saab-Scania of America, Inc.

Fig. 9: Exploded View Of Clutch "B"

2) Remove piston intermediate ring. Press out overrun clutch inner ring and separate 2 cover washers from outer ring.

Cleaning & Inspection – Clean all parts with solvent and dry with compressed air. Inspect all parts for excessive wear and damage. Replace parts as necessary.

Reassembly – **1)** Install new "O" ring on hub and lubricate with petroleum jelly. Install intermediate ring with chamfer facing inward. Install new "O" ring on piston, lubricate and install into clutch drum.

2) Using centering ring, insert plate spring. Using press and mounting device, depress plate spring, install thrust washer and secure with split retaining ring. Install clutch discs and secure with snap ring.

CLUTCH "A"

Disassembly – **1)** Use snap ring pliers to remove snap ring and turbine shaft from clutch "A". *See Fig. 10.* Remove snap ring from cylinder. Remove complete set of discs and spring disc.

2) Use press and adapter to press down baffle plate and release snap ring. Remove baffle plate and 2 plate springs. Place compressed air gun against one of 2 oil feed bores and, using care, remove piston with compressed air.

Cleaning & Inspection – Clean all parts with solvent and dry with compressed air. Inspect for excessive wear or damage. Replace parts (as necessary).

Reassembly – **1)** Install new "O" rings onto clutch piston and install piston into cylinder. *See Fig. 10.* Insert plate spring and plate spring with curved face pointing up. Fit "O" ring into baffle plate and apply petroleum jelly prior to seating baffle plate into clutch housing.

2) Install snap ring and insert clutch discs. Begin with spring disc, followed alternately by steel discs and lined discs. Install end disc and secure with snap ring. Install 2 rectangular rings onto turbine shaft and

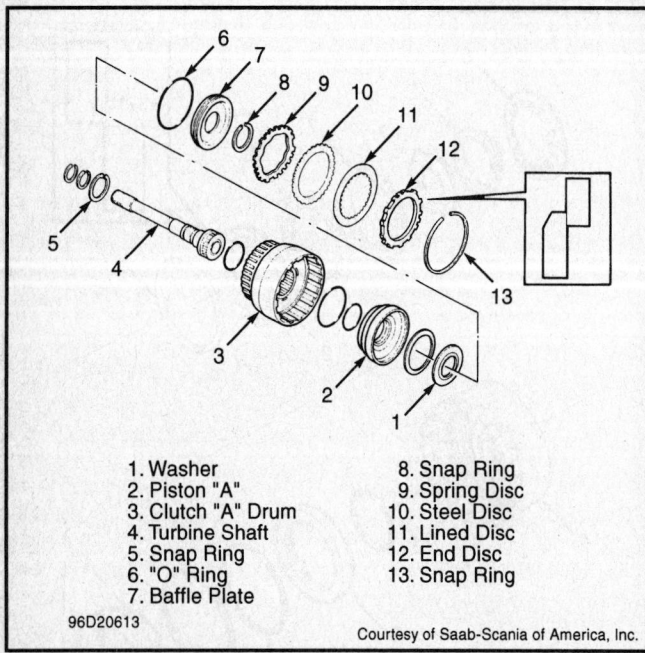

1. Washer
2. Piston "A"
3. Clutch "A" Drum
4. Turbine Shaft
5. Snap Ring
6. "O" Ring
7. Baffle Plate
8. Snap Ring
9. Spring Disc
10. Steel Disc
11. Lined Disc
12. End Disc
13. Snap Ring

96D20613

Courtesy of Saab-Scania of America, Inc.

Fig. 10: Exploded View Of Clutch "A"

engage hook. Press turbine shaft onto clutch "A" and install locking ring. Ensure turbine shaft seats with snap ring, otherwise axial reading will be false.

3) Insert clutch "A" assembly, turning back and forth until teeth of discs engage. Ensure plastic thrust washer is centered on engine shaft. If correctly installed, engine shaft projects approximately .9" (22 mm) over turbine shaft.

CLUTCH "E"

Disassembly – 1) Remove thrust washer off engine shaft. *See Fig. 11.* Remove snap ring and lift out complete set of discs. Press down plate spring "E" and remove split retaining ring.

2) Remove plate spring and use compressed air gun to force piston out. Rectangular rings remain on engine shaft. White plastic rings have chamfered ends.

Cleaning & Inspection – Clean all parts with cleaning solvent and dry with compressed air. Inspect all parts for excessive wear or damage. Replace parts as necessary.

Reassembly – 1) Install new "O" ring onto piston and apply a light coating of petroleum jelly. Press assembled piston onto cylinder of engine shaft. Using press and adapter, compress 2 plate springs. Secure with split retaining ring.

2) Insert clutch discs beginning with steel disc followed alternately by lined disc and steel disc. End disc is installed with recess faced outward. Secure disc sets with snap ring.

3) Install 2 rectangular rings onto engine shaft and engage hook. Coat rings with petroleum jelly. Install thrust washer. Install engine shaft while turning back and forth. If installed correctly, shoulder of clutch "E" is flush with edge of disc carrier on sun gear shaft.

OUTPUT SHAFT & 1ST ONE-WAY CLUTCH

Disassembly – Remove snap ring from housing and separate hollow gear from output shaft. Remove tapered roller bearing with inner race. Pull overrun clutch inner race from assembly. Remove snap ring from outer race and disassemble.

Cleaning & Inspection – Clean all parts in solvent and dry with compressed air. Inspect all parts for excessive wear and damage. Replace parts as necessary.

Reassembly – Install plate springs and install snap ring. Press in one-way clutch inner race in clutch housing. Press on tapered roller bearing with race. Install hollow shaft into overrun clutch housing and secure with snap ring.

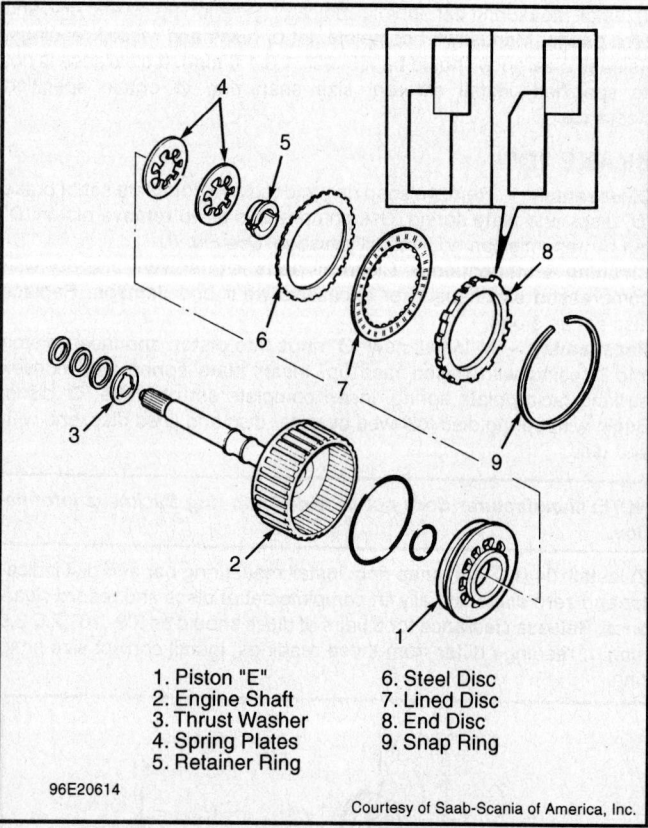

1. Piston "E"
2. Engine Shaft
3. Thrust Washer
4. Spring Plates
5. Retainer Ring
6. Steel Disc
7. Lined Disc
8. End Disc
9. Snap Ring

96E20614

Courtesy of Saab-Scania of America, Inc.

Fig. 11: Exploded View Of Clutch "E" With Engine Shaft

GOVERNOR

Disassembly – Remove bolts and separate 1st and 2nd stage valve assemblies from hub. *See Fig. 12.* Remove stage 3 retaining bolts. Remove clip holding stage 1 piston. Using a screwdriver to press down on compression spring, remove retaining plates, compression springs and pistons of 2nd and 3rd stage.

Cleaning & Inspection – Clean all parts with cleaning solvent and dry with compressed air. Replace complete governor housing if damaged. Stop plate and retaining plate may be replaced separately. Replace parts as necessary.

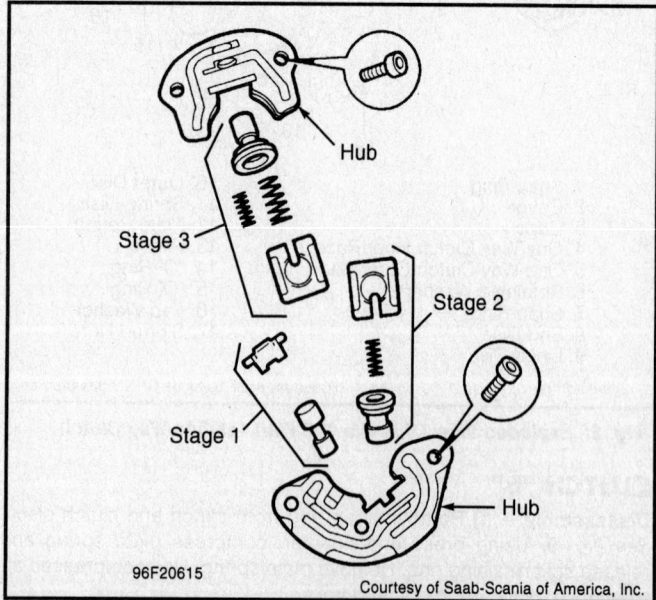

96F20615

Courtesy of Saab-Scania of America, Inc.

Fig. 12: Exploded View Of Governor Assembly

Reassembly – 1) Insert governor piston into valve housing and secure with a washer in 1st stage housing. To assemble 2nd and 3rd stages, insert governor pistons, install 2 compression springs into pistons and secure with retaining plates.

2) Install 1st, 2nd and 3rd stages of governor housing into governor flange with each stage covering one straight and one angled oil feed passage. Tighten Torx bolts to 89 INCH lbs. (10 N.m). Fit rectangular ring onto first governor flange and secure hook. Insert 2 rubber rings into middle and rear annular groove. DO NOT distort rubber ring excessively. Lubricate rubber rings with petroleum jelly when installing into transmission housing.

DIFFERENTIAL

Disassembly – Remove locking pin and differential shaft. *See Fig. 13.* Press 2 axle bevel gears and needle bearings out of differential cage. Install differential into soft jaw vise and remove ring gear from differential. Pull tapered roller bearing and race off differential and remove speedometer worm gear.

Cleaning & Inspection – Clean all parts with solvent and dry with compressed air. Inspect all parts for damage and excessive wear. Replace differential housing if damaged or worn.

Reassembly – 1) Insert 2 axle bevel gears into differential housing, ensuring both axle bores are aligned. Press tapered roller bearing and race onto housing. Turn differential over. Install tension pin into speedometer worm gear until seated. Install worm gear into differential with tension pin fitting into notch in housing.

2) Press on tapered roller bearing and race using press and adapter. Place differential housing into soft jawed vise. Install ring gear and tighten bolts to 57 ft. lbs. (77 N.m) in a crisscross pattern.

Remove dipstick tube and oil tubes. DO NOT damage sealing surface of housing or reuse oil tubes. Remove all screw plugs to clean housing. Leave locating pin in transmission housing.

Cleaning & Inspection – Clean all parts with cleaning solvent and dry with compressed air. Replace all seals and "O" rings. Inspect all parts for excessive wear and damage. Replace parts (as necessary).

Reassembly – 1) Install plugs into housing. Tighten plugs to 11 ft. lbs. (15 N.m). Screw 2 plastic plugs into housing oil cooler line connection hole. Install dowel into transmission housing using a plastic hammer.

2) With a heat gun, heat transmission housing to 158°F (70°C) and install countershaft tapered roller bearing outer ring. Install shaft seal into transmission housing. Assemble pawl and spring and press pin into housing, securing pin with Torx bolt. Tighten bolt to 89 INCH lbs. (10 N.m). Assemble locking cam and install into housing, tightening bolt to 23 ft. lbs. (32 N.m).

3) Install guide pin and locking spring. Press locking spring against spacer and secure with two bolts tightened to 89 INCH lbs. (10 N.m). Insert Detent Adjustment Tool (87 91 501) and install detent spring. *See Fig. 14.* Tighten detent spring bolt to 89 INCH lbs. (10 N.m). Install assembled selector mechanism into housing. Use following formula to determine thickness of washer used on selector assembly:

$$S = X - .004 \ (.10 \ mm)$$

S = Thickness of washer
X = Value to be measured
.004 (.10 mm) = Standard clearance

Insert correct size washer to meet standard clearance by removing stop plate and withdrawing selector shaft enough to install washer.

4) Assemble and install throttle cam and throttle cable into transmission housing and pretension throttle cam by rotating one revolution and inserting nipple of cable in cam.

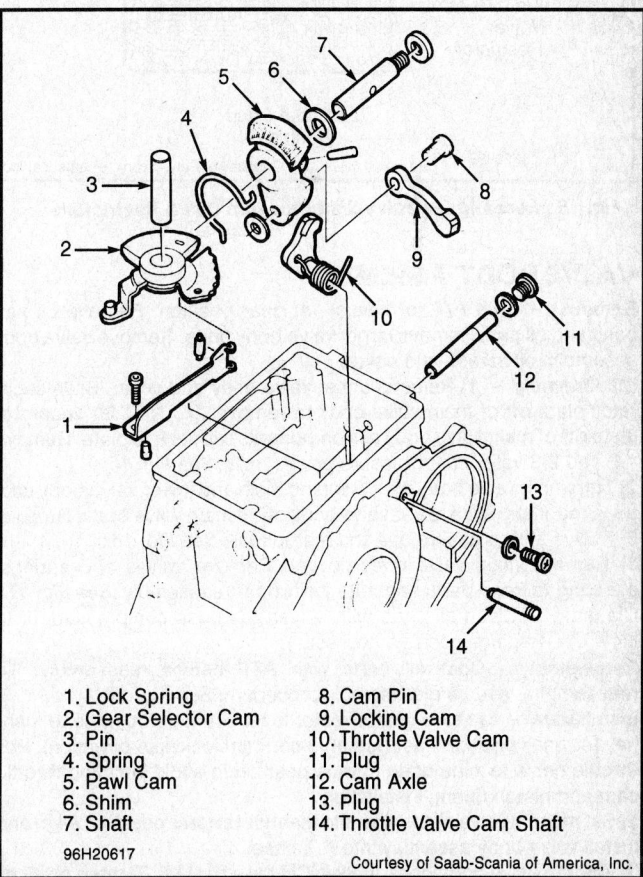

1. Needle Bearing	6. Tapered Roller Bearing
2. Washer	7. Speedometer Worm Gear
3. Bevel Gear	8. Differential Housing
4. Shaft	9. Ring Gear
5. Pin	

96G20616   Courtesy of Saab-Scania of America, Inc.

Fig. 13: Exploded View Of Differential Components

SELECTOR MECHANISM & PARKING PAWL

Disassembly – 1) Detach Throttle Valve (TV) cable from cam and pry out housing with 2 screwdrivers. Remove retaining bolt and remove accelerator cam axle together with leg spring and accelerator spring. Remove bolts and remove detent spring and pin. *See Fig. 14.*

2) Remove screw plug and support shaft. Use punch to move tension pin enough to remove selector shaft. Remove segment with locking cam and adjusting washer by pressing pawl down slightly.

3) Remove pin at annular groove and remove pawl with leg spring. Remove 2 bearings outer races. Remove shaft seal and selector shaft.

1. Lock Spring	8. Cam Pin
2. Gear Selector Cam	9. Locking Cam
3. Pin	10. Throttle Valve Cam
4. Spring	11. Plug
5. Pawl Cam	12. Cam Axle
6. Shim	13. Plug
7. Shaft	14. Throttle Valve Cam Shaft

96H20617   Courtesy of Saab-Scania of America, Inc.

Fig. 14: Exploded View Of Linkage Components

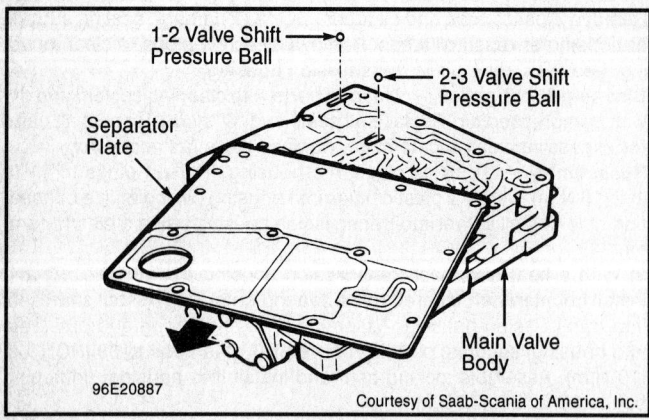

Fig. 15: Locating 1-2 & 2-3 Valve Shift Pressure Balls

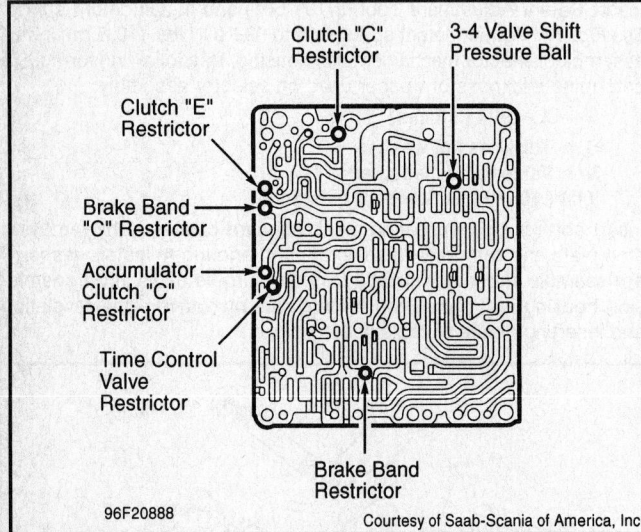

Fig. 16: Locating 3-4 Valve Shift Pressure Ball & Restrictors

VALVE BODY ASSEMBLY

Removal – Shift A/T to manual 1st gear position. Remove oil pan bolts and oil pan. Remove larger valve body bolts. Remove valve body assembly, oil screen and cover.

Disassembly – **1)** Remove upper valve body and cover. Slide separator plate off of main valve body to remove. DO NOT lift separator plate off of main valve body as components will stick to plate. Remove 1-2 and 2-3 valve shift pressure plastic balls. *See Fig. 15.*

2) Turn main valve body over, keeping main and lower valve body sections together. Slide lower valve body off of main valve body. Remove 3-4 valve shift pressure ball and restrictions. *See Fig. 16.*

3) Remove main valve body covers. Remove valves and springs, ensuring to keep parts separate for proper reassembly. *See Fig. 17.*

Cleaning – Clean all parts with solvent and use compressed air to blow dry. Replace parts as necessary.

Reassembly – Coat all parts with ATF before reassembly. To reassemble, reverse disassembly procedure. *See Fig. 17.*

Installation – **1)** Move gear selector lever counterclockwise to manual 1st gear position (last detent in counterclockwise direction). Pull throttle cable to wide open throttle position to avoid jamming throttle cam and piston during installation.

2) Set manual valve all the way into manual 1st gear position. Align and install valve body assembly into A/T case.

3) Tighten valve body bolts to 89 INCH lbs. (10 N.m). Tighten small oil screen bolts to 44 INCH lbs. (5 N.m) and large oil screen bolts to 71 INCH lbs. (8 N.m).

4) Install oil pan and tighten clamp nuts to 53 INCH lbs. (6 N.m). Install splash shield, and lower vehicle. Install ATF and adjust throttle cable.

TRANSAXLE REASSEMBLY

1) Install servo piston into transmission housing. With mounting device, press piston cover slightly and install snap ring to secure servo piston. Turn transmission over and install brake band "C" into housing. Fit lugs of brake band into 2 pins. Ensure brake band seats into transmission housing shoulder.

2) Assemble and install brake "D" clutch discs into transmission housing and secure with snap ring. Install measuring bar and dial indicator. Manually lift complete set of clutch discs and read clearance of discs. Clearance for 6 pairs of clutches should be .08-.10" (2.0-2.5 mm). Remove brake "D" disc set and insert 1st one-way clutch into transmission housing. Ensure inner ring of one-way clutch does not fall out. Turn transmission over while holding free-wheel in place.

3) Set tab washer with locking lug into transmission housing. Install slotted nut and tighten to 37 ft. lbs. (50 N.m). Bend lock tab into nut seat. Ensure free-wheel turns freely in clockwise direction. Reinstall brake "D" disc set and secure with correct washers. Install spider bowl into one-way clutch inner ring. Press tapered roller bearing inner ring onto output shaft. Insert output shaft into hollow gear and secure with snap ring. *See Fig. 18.*

4) Install output shaft/hollow gear assembly into transmission case. Install needle bearing assembly along with flat washer and angle washer in output shaft assembly. Install planetary carrier into hollow gear. Install sun gear into planetary carrier. Fit sun gear drum onto teeth of sun gear.

5) Install needle bearing assembly along with flat washer and angle washer into sun gear drum. Insert sun gear shaft into sun gear drum. Ensure when rotated, sun gear drum rotates in opposite direction from sun gear shaft. Install needle bearing assembly along with flat washer and angle washer over the end of the intermediate shaft. Insert intermediate shaft into sun gear shaft.

6) Fit rectangular rings and thrust washer on engine shaft. Install assembled clutch "E" and engine shaft assembly into case. Ensure shoulder of cylinder "E" is flush with edge of disc carrier on sun gear shaft.

7) Assemble clutch "A" and install 2 rectangular rings onto turbine shaft and engage hook. Press turbine shaft into clutch "A" cylinder and engage locking ring with snap ring pliers. Pull on turbine shaft until it seats with snap ring, otherwise axial clearance will be incorrect. Insert assembled clutch "A", rotating until teeth of discs engage. Plastic thrust washer must be centered on engine shaft. If correctly installed, engine shaft will project approximately .8" (22 mm) over turbine shaft.

8) Assemble clutch "B" and install into case by turning until discs fully engage. Clutch "B" must engage in recesses of drum for a gap of .04" (1.0 mm) to be still visible.

9) Assemble pump housing and torque converter pressure relief valve, and install on intermediate plate. Insert compression spring into opening in pump, place intermediate plate onto pump housing and align. Bolt intermediate plate to pump housing; tighten bolts to 89 INCH lbs. (10 N.m). Inspect torque converter relief valve to ensure it operates freely. Ensure pump operates freely. Install 3 rectangular rings onto hub of intermediate plate.

10) Assemble 2nd one-way clutch by inserting cage of one-way clutch into collar with collar facing down. If not installed properly, clamping direction will not be correct. Install cover rings on one-way clutch collar. Insert one-way clutch inner race by turning it clockwise. One-way clutch inner race must rotate freely in clockwise direction with collar pointing out.

11) Install .04" (1.0 mm) selective adjusting washer and angle washer onto shaft. DO NOT install 2nd one-way clutch during measurement process. Install assembled pump and intermediate plate. Rotate back and forth until fully engaged. Hold in place with 2 opposing bolts. Tighten bolts to 89 INCH lbs. (10 N.m). Install measuring tool onto turbine shaft and secure tightly.

12) Measuring tip of dial indicator must rest on impeller shaft. Pull on measuring tool to obtain reading. Axial clearance should be .004-.012" (.10-.30 mm). If clearance is not as specified, select correct washer. Remove intermediate plate assembly. Install angle washer and adjusting washer onto hub of intermediate plate.

13) Install 2nd one-way clutch into lined discs of brake "C" with inner teeth seated on washer. Ensure all lined discs mesh with one-way clutch inner race. Do this by rotating outer race; lined discs must also turn.

14) Tighten adjusting washer of brake band in order to secure cylinder "B" in place. Insert assembled pump, intermediate plate and 2nd gear one-way clutch into transmission. Rotate back and forth to seat unit.

When inserting unit, hold one-way clutch to avoid discs slipping out. When properly installed, plate springs seat into transmission housing when pressure is applied against pump housing.

15) Install 8 bolts into intermediate plate and tighten bolts to 89 INCH lbs. (10 N.m). Loosen brake band and check axial clearance. Assemble governor housing on governor hub. Tighten retaining bolts to 89

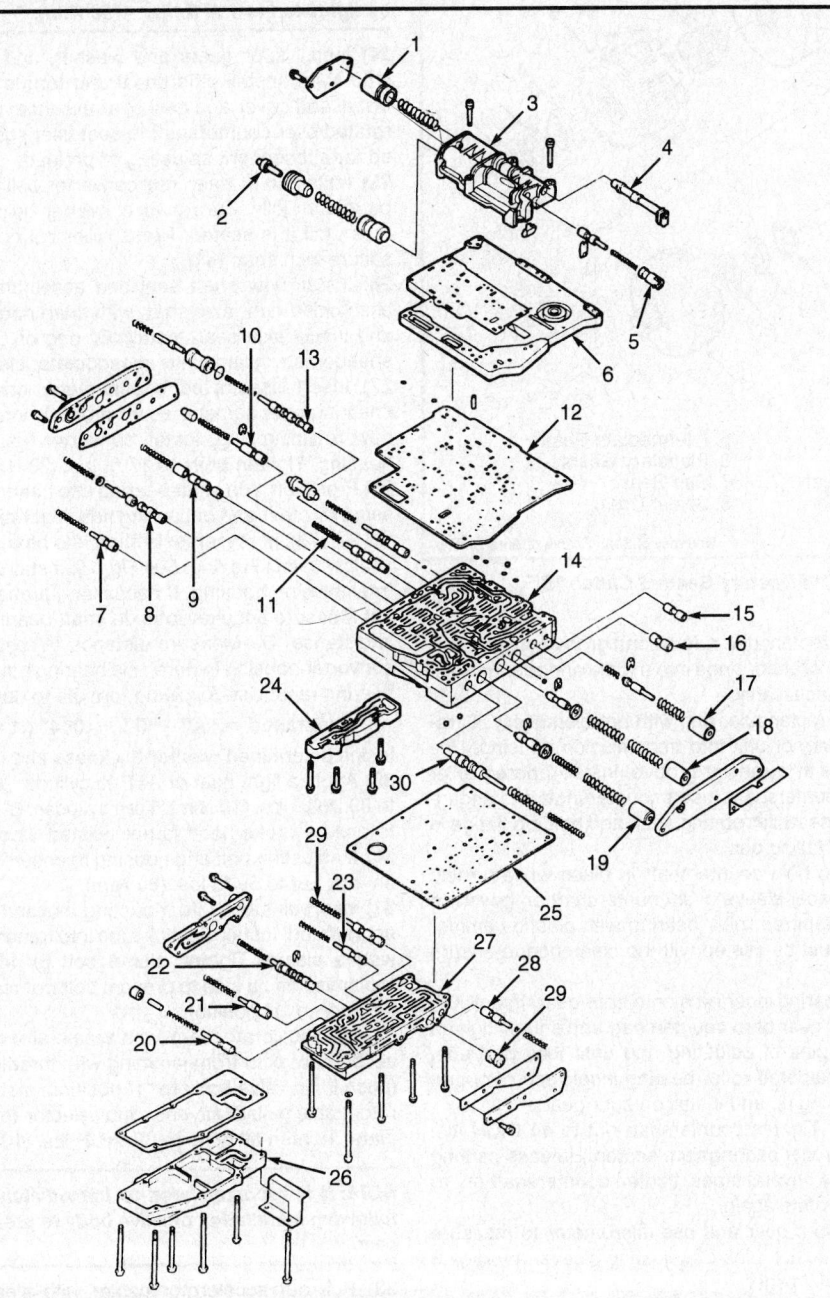

1. Clutch "D" Accumulator	11. 1st & "R" Gear Lock-Up Valve	21. 3rd Gear Lock-Up
2. Clutch "A" Accumulator	12. Separator Plate	22. Throttle Control Valve
3. Accumulator Housing	13. 1-2-3 Shift Sequencing Valve	23. 2nd Gear Lock-Up Valve
4. Selector Valve	14. Valve Body	24. Cover
5. Throttle Valve	15. 3-4 Shift Valve	25. Separator Plate
6. Lower Valve Body	16. 2-3 Shift Valve	26. Cover
7. 4-3 Traction Valve	17. Time Control Valve	27. Upper Valve Body
8. 3-4 Traction Valve	18. Clutch "C" Accumulator	28. 2-3-4 Shift Sequencing Valve
9. 4-3 Downshift Valve	19. Clutch "E" Accumulator	29. 1-2 Shift Valve
10. Modulator Valve	20. 4-3-2 Shift Sequencing Valve	30. Pressure Valve

96I20618

Courtesy of Saab-Scania of America, Inc.

Fig. 17: Identifying Valve Body Components

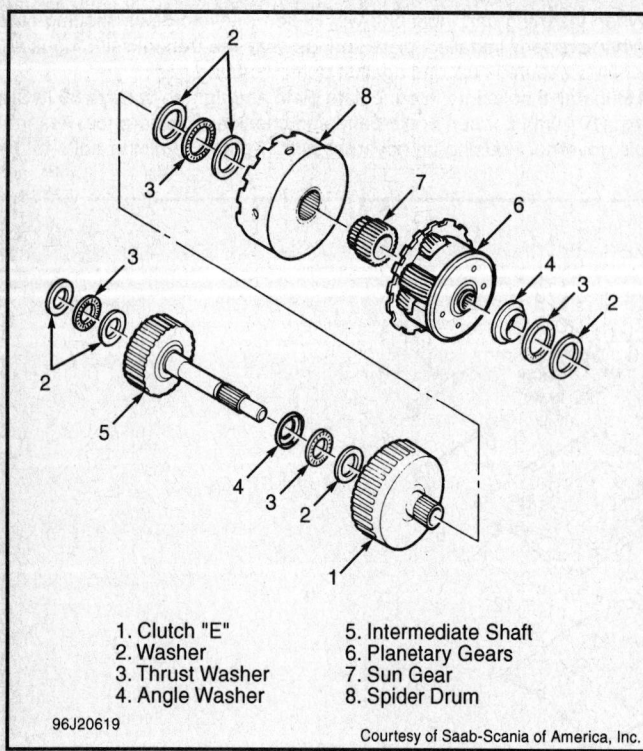

1. Clutch "E"
2. Washer
3. Thrust Washer
4. Angle Washer
5. Intermediate Shaft
6. Planetary Gears
7. Sun Gear
8. Spider Drum

96J20619

Courtesy of Saab-Scania of America, Inc.

Fig. 18: Exploded View Of Planetary Gears & Clutch "B"

INCH lbs. (10 N.m). Install rectangular ring on end groove of governor hub and snap hook. Insert 2 rubber rings into middle and rear groove. DO NOT stretch rings unnecessarily.

16) Coat rubber rings and rectangular ring with petroleum jelly. Carefully insert assembled governor unit into transmission housing. Use care installing rubber rings into annular groove. Install tapered roller bearing inner race onto countershaft. Insert countershaft into engaging gears of governor flange while rotating shaft and holding flange in position to prevent it from falling out.

17) Install retaining tool to hold countershaft in place while turning transmission over. Slip spacer sleeve over countershaft on governor unit. Install outer race of tapered roller bearing with plastic hammer until seated. Outer ring must be seated with no clearance to ensure correct adjustment.

18) Press tapered roller bearing inner race onto spur gear. Install .07" (1.9 mm) washer and spur gear onto countershaft and snugly tighten bolt. Drive the 3 tension pins of adjusting ring until they protrude. Install adjusting ring onto tapered roller bearing inner race of output shaft with tension pins facing up and install on spur gear.

19) Engage parking pawl. Tighten countershaft nut to 44 INCH lbs. (5 N.m) to ensure tapered roller bearings are seated. Release parking interlock, rotate spur gears several times, tighten countershaft nut to 44 INCH lbs. (5 N.m) and rotate again.

20) Loosen nut, remove spur gear and use micrometer to measure thickness of washer at 3 tension pins of adjusting sleeve. Average 3 readings and install correct washer.

21) Insert correct washer and spur gear onto countershaft. Tighten countershaft bolt to 110 ft. lbs. (150 N.m). Install Preloading Device (87 91 733) to transaxle case. Attach measuring tool with dial indicator.

22) Turn adjusting screw down for gauge pointer to move. While rotating spur gears several times, set gauge scale to zero. If pointer deflects to end of scale, record readings to determine average reading. Loosen pretensioning device on bottom of transmission. Tighten adjusting screw one turn.

23) Rotate spur gears several times until pointer of dial indicator has settled. Record readings and obtain an average. Use following formula to obtain correct washer thickness:

$$S = .07 - X + .03$$

S = Specific thickness of washer
.07 = Selected shim thickness when measured
X = Reading on dial indicator

NOTE: If it is necessary to install a washer of different thickness, it is recommended to repeat measurement steps. Countershaft bolt must be tightened to 110 ft. lbs. (150 N.m).

24) Install spur gears and washer, and tighten bolt to 110 ft. lbs. (150 N.m). Install differential and torque converter housing. Do not install end cover and gasket at this time; differential housing must be rotated over countershaft to seat bearings. This step must be repeated for subsequent adjusting of preload.

25) Install shaft seal into converter bellhousing and coat seal with petroleum jelly. Turn over converter bellhousing and install bearing race until it is seated. Press roller bearing onto right axle shaft and secure with snap ring.

26) Install new shaft seal and assembled right axle shaft. Secure assembled right axle shaft with snap ring. Slip new "O" ring on shaft and install axle seal. Install "O" ring on speedometer sleeve. Insert speedometer pinion into speedometer sleeve and install sleeve.

27) Insert assembled speedometer drive into converter housing ensuring speedometer seats properly into speedometer bore. Install new retaining ring. Install converter housing gasket and converter housing. Tighten bolts to 17 ft. lbs. (23 N.m).

28) Press left axle shaft bearing into bearing housing. Press axle shaft seal into other end of bearing housing. Using Differential Preload Tool (81 91 279), press left axle shaft into bearing housing and secure axle shaft with locking ring. *See Fig. 19.* Install differential bearing race into transmission housing. If necessary, preheat housing with heat gun.

29) Measure shoulder of axle shaft bearing housing and record, this is distance "B". Measure distance "A" between machined surface of converter housing (where axle bearing housing mates) and differential bearing race. Use following formula to determine washer thickness:

$$\text{Clearance} = \text{"A"} - \text{"B"} + .004\text{"} (.1 \text{ mm})$$

Install determined washer thickness and reassemble.

30) Apply a light coat of ATF to cylinder "B". Tighten brake band bolt to 89 INCH lbs. (10 N.m). Turn cylinder "B" during tightening operation to ensure brake band is not twisted. Loosen adjusting bolt 2 turns. Mark adjusting bolt and housing to ensure screw does not turn. Tighten lock nut to 59 ft. lbs. (80 N.m).

31) Insert oil tubes into mounting tool and install with plastic hammer until seated. Install dipstick tube into transmission housing and secure with a clamp. Tighten clamp bolt to 44 INCH lbs. (5 N.m). Turn transmission on side to prevent bolt from falling into housing. Set gear selector to "1" position.

32) Pull accelerator cam, with accelerator cable, far enough to prevent accelerator cam from jamming with throttle piston. Set selector valve (push in) in valve body to "1" position. Install valve body, with accelerator cable pulled out, ensuring selector valve is inserted in pin of stop plate. Tighten all bolts to 89 INCH lbs. (10 N.m).

NOTE: It is recommended to immediately adjust accelerator cable following installation of valve body to prevent cable from coming off cam.

33) Pull out accelerator cable, with sleeve extended, to point of kickdown (noticeable resistance). Clamp lead seal 1.51-1.55 (38.5-39.5 mm) from end of sleeve. Check operation of accelerator cable and selector mechanism.

34) Install new oil pan gasket and oil pan. Tighten bolts to 53 INCH lbs. (6 N.m). Install oil pan drain plug and tighten plug to 59 ft. lbs. (80 N.m). Install "O" ring and oil filter onto transmission housing.

35) Install filter cover, with magnet. Install bolt and tighten to 71 INCH lbs. (8 N.m). Install torque converter and secure with retaining clamp. Install new "O" ring on dipstick and install dipstick.

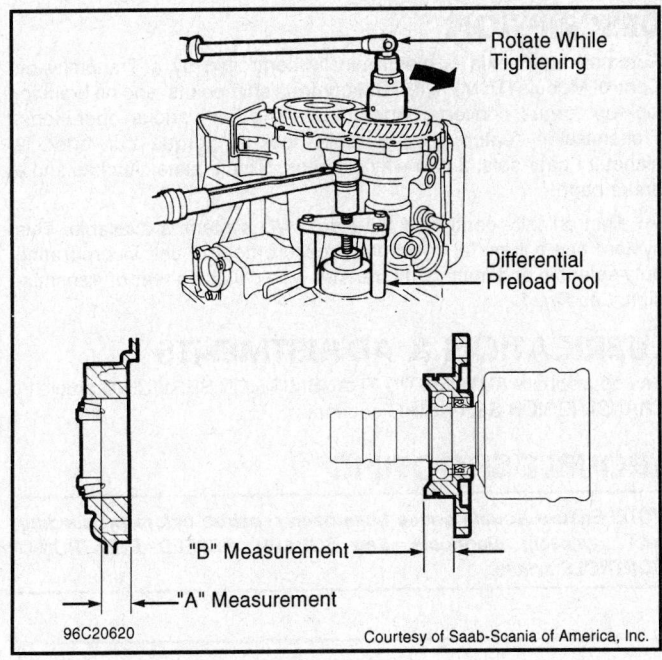

96C20620

Courtesy of Saab-Scania of America, Inc.

Fig. 19: Setting Differential Preload

TORQUE SPECIFICATIONS
TORQUE SPECIFICATIONS

Application	Ft. Lbs. (N.m)
Brake Band "C" Lock Nut	59 (80)
Converter Bell Housing Bolt	17 (23)
Countershaft Lock Nut	110 (150)
Differential Cover Bolts	17 (23)
Input Shaft Housing	17 (23)
Oil Pan Drain Plug	59 (80)
Output Shaft Center Bolt	18 (25)
Shift Cable Bracket-To-A/T Case Bolt	15 (21)
Shift Lever Nut (Non-Reusable)	13 (17)
Starter Bolts	31 (42)
Throttle Cable Jam Nuts	11 (15)
Transaxle Cooler Bolt	37 (50)

Application	INCH Lbs. (N.m)
Detent Spring Bolt	89 (10)
Dipstick Oil Tube Bolt	44 (5)
Governor Housing Bolts	89 (10)
Governor Support Retainer Bolt	89 (10)
Intermediate Pump Bolts	89 (10)
Neutral Start Switch Bracket Bolts	89 (10)
Oil Pan Bolts	53 (6)
Oil Pan Retaining Clamp Nuts	53 (6)
Oil Screen Cover	71 (8)
Speedometer Sensor Bolt	89 (10)
Spur Gear Cover	89 (10)
Throttle Cam Bolt	44 (5)
Valve Body Bolts	89 (10)

AUTOMATIC TRANSMISSIONS
Subaru 4-Speed

Impreza, Legend, SVX

APPLICATION & LABOR TIMES

APPLICATION & LABOR TIMES

Vehicle Application	Labor Times [1] R & I	[2] Overhaul	Transaxle Model
1995-96 Impreza	3.8	11.0	4-Speed
1995-96 Legacy	3.8	11.0	4-Speed
1995-96 SVX	3.8	11.0	4-Speed

[1] – Removal and installation of transmission from vehicle chassis. Add .5 hour for AWD models.

[2] – Bench overhaul time for transmission and differential. DOES NOT include removal and installation.

IDENTIFICATION

Transaxle is identified by the 11th character of VIN number. A "C" or "K" identifies FWD models, while "H" identifies AWD models. Transaxle serial number label is located on upper surface of case or converter housing.

DESCRIPTION

Automatic transaxle is electronically controlled by a Transmission Control Module (TCM). The TCM controls shift points, engine braking, lock-up torque converter operation and other various operations. Transmission features a hydraulic lock-up torque converter, 2 planetary gear sets, 2 one-way clutches, 5 multi-plate clutches and a brake band.

An electronically controlled full-time AWD system is available. This system has a transfer hydraulic pressure control unit incorporating duty solenoid and multi-plate transfer type clutch on rear of transmission. *See Fig. 1.*

LUBRICATION & ADJUSTMENTS

See appropriate AUTOMATIC TRANSMISSION SERVICING article in TRANSMISSION SERVICING section.

TROUBLE SHOOTING

NOTE: Ensure trouble codes have been repaired before proceeding with symptom diagnosis. See SUBARU 4-SPEED ELECTRONIC CONTROLS article.

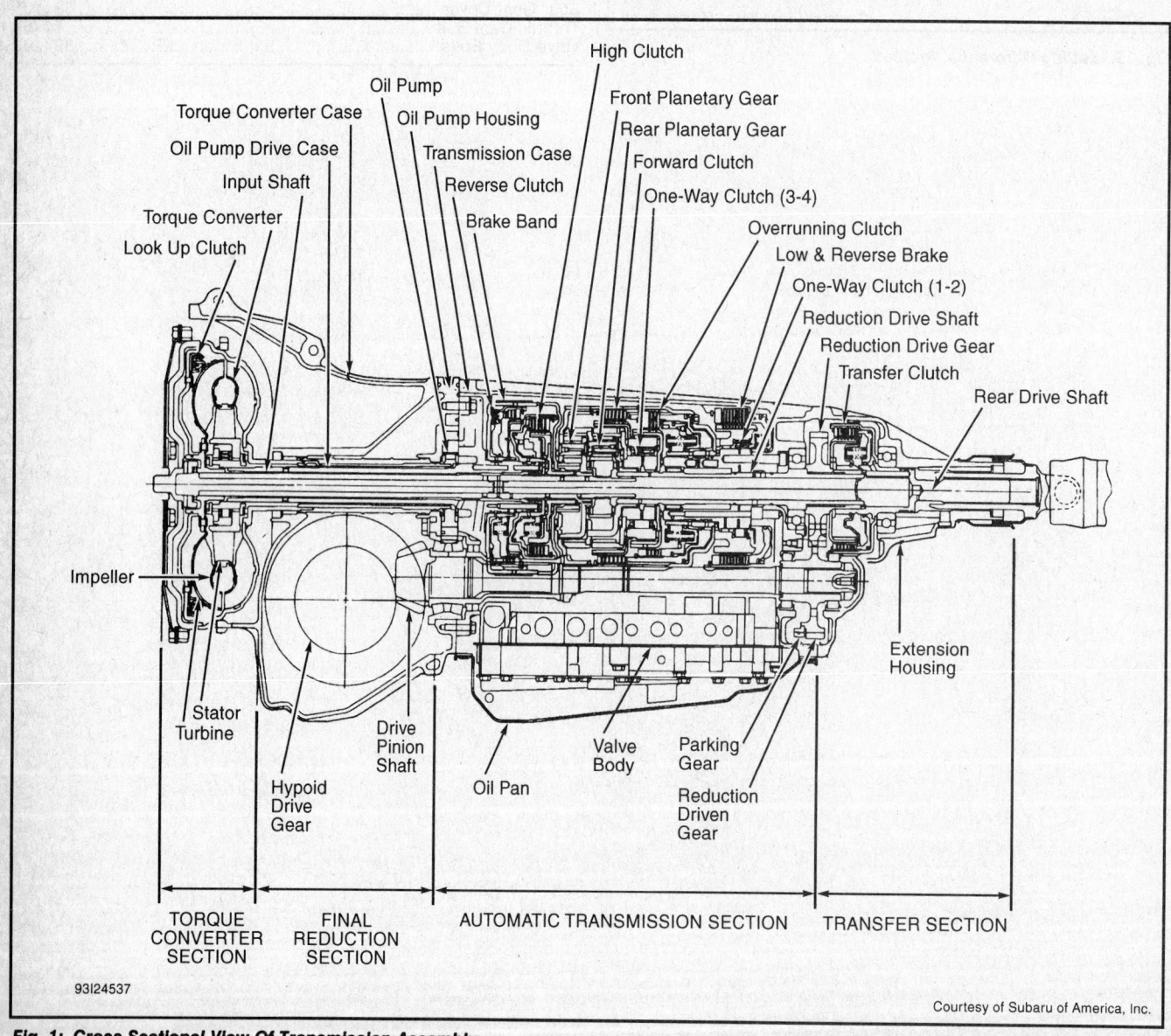

93124537

Courtesy of Subaru of America, Inc.

Fig. 1: Cross Sectional View Of Transmission Assembly

SYMPTOM DIAGNOSIS

Starter Does Not Rotate When Select Lever Is In "P" Or "N", Starter Rotates When Select Lever is "R", "D", "3" Or "2" – Check inhibitor switch, select cable, select lever and starter motor and cables.

Abnormal Noise When Select Lever Is In "P" Or "N" – Check filter, duty solenoid "C", oil pump, drive plate. Ensure ATF level is correct.

Hissing Noise During Standing Starts – Check filter and ensure ATF level is correct.

Noise Occurs While Driving In "D," Range – Check final gear, planetary gear and reduction gear. Ensure differential gear oil level is correct.

Noise Occurs While Driving In "D$_2$" Range – Check final gear, planetary gear and reduction gear. Ensure differential gear oil level is correct.

Noise Occurs While Driving In "D$_3$" Range – Check final gear and reduction gear. Ensure differential gear oil level is correct.

Noise Occurs While Driving In "D$_4$" Range – Check final gear, planetary gear and reduction gear. Ensure differential gear oil level is correct.

Engine Stalls While Shifting From One Range To Another – Check control valve, lock-up damper and engine performance.

Vehicle Moves When Select Lever Is In "N" – Check forward clutch.

Shock Occurs When Select Lever Is Moved From "N" To "D" – Check control module, N-D accumulator and control valve. Check for ATF deterioration.

Excessive Time Lag Occurs When Select Lever Is Moved From "N" To "D" – Check control valve and forward clutch.

Shock Occurs When Select Lever Is Moved From "N" To "R" – Check control module, 4A accumulator and control valve. Check for ATF deterioration.

Excessive Time Lag Occurs When Select Lever Is Moved From "N" To "R" – Check control valve, low and reverse clutch and reverse clutch.

Vehicle Does Not Start In Any Shift Range (Engine Revving Up) – Check filter, control valve, drive pinion, ring gear, axle shaft, differential gear, oil pump, input shaft, output shaft, planetary gear and drive plate. Ensure ATF level is correct.

Vehicle Does Not Start In Any Shift Range (Engine Stall) – Check parking brake mechanism.

Vehicle Does Not Start In "R" Range Only (Engine Revving Up) – Check select cable, select lever, control valve, low and reverse clutch and reverse clutch.

Vehicle Does Not Start In "R" Range Only (Engine Stall) – Check forward clutch, band brake and planetary gear.

Vehicle Does Not Start In "D" Or "3" Range (Engine Revving Up) – Check forward clutch (1-2).

Vehicle Does Not Start In "D", "3" Or "2" Range (Engine Flare Up) – Check forward clutch.

Vehicle Does Not Start In "D", "3" Or "2" Range (Engine Stall) – Check reverse clutch.

Vehicle Starts In "R" Range Only (Engine Revving Up) – Check control valve.

Acceleration During Standing Starts Is Poor (High Stall RPM) – Check control valve, forward clutch and reverse clutch. Ensure differential gear oil level is correct.

Acceleration During Standing Starts Is Poor (Low Stall RPM) – Check oil pump, torque converter one-way clutch and engine performance.

Acceleration Is Poor When Select Lever Is In "D", "3" Or "2" Range (Normal Stall RPM) – Check control module, control valve, high clutch, band brake and planetary gear.

Acceleration Is Poor When Select Lever Is In "R" (Normal Stall RPM) – Check control valve, overrunning clutch, high clutch, band brake and planetary gear.

No Shift Occurs From 1st To 2nd Gear – Check control module, vehicle speed sensor "1" and "2", throttle sensor, shift solenoid No. 1 and 2, throttle position sensor, control valve and band brake.

No Shift Occurs From 2nd To 3rd Gear – Check control module, control valve, high clutch and one-way clutch (3-4).

No Shift Occurs From 3rd To 4th Gear – Check control module, 3R accumulator, ATF temperature sensor, shift solenoid No. 3, control valve and band brake.

No Kickdown Shifts Occur – Check control module and throttle position sensor.

Engine Brake Is Not Effected When Select Lever Is In "3" Range – Check inhibitor switch, control module, throttle position sensor and control valve.

Engine Brake Is Not Effected When Select Lever Is In "3" Or "2" Range – Check overrunning clutch.

Engine Brake Is Not Effected When Select Lever Is In "1" Range – Check control valve and low and reverse clutch.

Shift Characteristics Are Erroneous – Check inhibitor switch, control module, vehicle speed sensor "1" and "2", and control valve.

No Lock-Up Occurs – Check control module, throttle position sensor, ATF temperature sensor, control valve, lock-up facing and engine speed signal.

Vehicle Cannot Be Set In "D" Range Power Mode – Check control module and throttle position sensor.

"D" Range Power Mode Cannot Be Released – Check control module, throttle position sensor and ATF temperature sensor.

Parking Gear Inoperative – Check select cable, select lever and park pawl mechanism.

Shift Lever Cannot Be Moved Or Is Hard To Move From "P" Range – Check select cable, select lever and parking brake mechanism.

Select Lever Is Hard To Move – Check select cable, select lever, detent spring and manual plate.

Select Lever Moves Too Easy (Little To No Resistance) – Check detent spring and manual plate.

ATF Spurts Out From Air Breather Hose &/Or Dipstick Tube – Ensure ATF level is correct.

Differential Oil Spurts Out – Ensure differential gear oil level is correct.

Differential Oil Level Changes Excessively – Check seal pipe and double oil seal between oil pump housing and transmission case.

Odor Is Produced From Oil Supply Pipe – Check transfer clutch, forward clutch, overrunning clutch, high clutch, band brake, low and reverse clutch, reverse clutch, lock-up facing and ATF deterioration.

Shock Occurs When Select Lever Is Moved From "1" To "2" Range – Check control unit, throttle position sensor, 2A accumulator, ATF temperature sensor, duty solenoid "A", control valve, band brake, ATF deterioration and engine performance.

Slippage Occurs When Select Lever Is Moved From "1" To "2" Range – Check control module, throttle position sensor, 2A accumulator, ATF temperature sensor, duty solenoid "A", control valve and band brake.

Shock Occurs When Select Lever Is Moved From "2" To "3" Range – Check control module, throttle position sensor, 3R accumulator, ATF temperature sensor, duty solenoid "A", control valve, high clutch, band brake, ATF deterioration and engine performance.

Slippage Occurs When Select Lever Is Moved From "2" To "3" Range – Check control module, throttle position sensor, 3R accumulator, ATF temperature sensor, duty solenoid "A", control valve, high clutch and band brake.

Shock Occurs When Select Lever Is Moved From "3" To "4" Range – Check control module, throttle position sensor, 4A accumulator, ATF temperature sensor, duty solenoid "A", control valve, overrunning clutch, band brake, ATF deterioration and engine performance.

Slippage Occurs When Select Lever Is Moved From "3" To "4" Range – Check control module, throttle position sensor, 4A accumulator, ATF temperature sensor, duty solenoid "A", control valve and band brake.

Shock Occurs When Select Lever Is Moved From "3" To "2" Range – Check control module, throttle position sensor, ATF temperature sensor, duty solenoid "A", control valve, overrunning clutch, band brake and ATF deterioration.

Shock Occurs When Select Lever Is Moved From "D" To "1" Range – Check control module, throttle position sensor, ATF temperature sensor, duty solenoid "A", control valve and ATF deterioration.

Shock Occurs When Select Lever Is Moved From "2" To "1" Range – Check control module, throttle position sensor, ATF temperature sensor, duty solenoid "A", control valve, low and reverse clutch and ATF deterioration.

Shock Occurs When Accelerator Pedal Is Released At Medium Speeds – Check control module, throttle position sensor, ATF temperature sensor, duty solenoid "A", control valve, lock-up damper and engine performance.

Vibration Occurs During Straight-Forward Operation – Check control module, duty solenoid "B", lock-up facing and lock-up damper.

Select Lever Slips Out Of Position During Acceleration Or While Driving On Rough Terrain – Check select cable, select lever, detent spring and manual plate.

Vibration Occurs During Turns (Tight Corner "Braking" Phenomenon) – Check control module, vehicle speed sensors "1" and "2", throttle sensor, ATF temperature sensor, transfer clutch, transfer valve, duty solenoid "C" and ATF deterioration.

Front Wheel Slippage Occurs During Standing Starts – Check control module, vehicle speed sensor "2", FWD switch, throttle sensor, ATF temperature sensor, control valve, transfer clutch, transfer valve, transfer pipe and duty solenoid "C".

Vehicle Is Not Set In FWD Mode – Check control module, FWD switch, transfer clutch, transfer valve and duty solenoid "C".

TIME LAG TEST

Testing Precautions – Perform test at normal fluid operating temperature. Allow one minute between tests to cool transaxle. Perform 3 measurements and take average value.

Testing Procedure – Fully apply parking brake and check idle speed (with A/C off). Idle speed should be 600-800 RPM. Move shift selector lever from "N" to "D" position. Using stopwatch, measure time lag from moving shifting lever until shock is felt. In same manner, measure time lag of "N" to "R" shift. See TIME LAG TEST SPECIFICATIONS table.

TIME LAG TEST SPECIFICATIONS

Selector Position	Time
"N" To "D"	Less Than 1.2 sec.
"N" To "R"	Less Than 1.5 sec.

Time Lag Test Results – If "N" to "D" time lag is longer than specified, line pressure is too low, forward clutch is worn and/or low one-way clutch is not operating properly. If "N" to "R" time lag is longer than specified, line pressure is too low, low and reverse brake is worn, reverse clutch is worn and/or low and reverse clutch is worn.

SHIFT SPEEDS

SHIFT SPEEDS MPH

Application & Shift Points	Throttle Fully-Closed	Throttle Fully-Open
"D" Range		
Normal		
1-2 Upshift	7-11	29-33
2-3 Upshift	17-21	56-60
3-4 Upshift	26-30	87-91
4-3 Downshift	23-27	81-85
3-2 Downshift	7-11	50-54
2-1 Downshift	4-8	23-27
Power [1]		
1-2 Upshift	7-11	33-37
2-3 Upshift	17-21	63-67
3-4 Upshift	29-33	110-115
4-3 Downshift	23-27	100-105
3-2 Downshift	10-14	65-75
2-1 Downshift	4-8	26-30

[1] – Changeover to power performed automatically corresponding to accelerator pedal depression.

ROAD TEST

FWD Mode – Road test should be conducted to properly diagnose condition of automatic transaxle. All shifts should be smooth, responsive and with no slippage or engine runaway. Slippage or engine runaway in any gear usually indicates clutch or band problems.

AWD Mode – With vehicle in AWD, turn vehicle in a circle while lightly depressing accelerator pedal. If tight-corner braking occurs check duty solenoid "C" for improper operation. If solenoid is operating correctly, check transfer clutch pressure. If oil pressure is normal, check transfer control valve for sticking and transfer clutch facing for wear.

STALL SPEED TEST

Testing Precautions – DO NOT hold throttle open longer than 5 seconds to obtain steady gauge reading. After each stall test, move shift selector lever to "N" position and allow engine to idle lower than 1200 RPM for one minute minimum to cool engine and transaxle. If engine speed exceeds limits shown in STALL SPEED TEST SPECIFICATIONS table, release accelerator immediately as clutch or band slippage is indicated.

Testing Procedures – With engine at normal operating temperature, tachometer installed and parking and service brakes applied, perform transaxle stall test in "D", "3", "2", and "R" ranges at full throttle and note maximum RPM obtained. Engine speed should be within limits in STALL SPEED TEST SPECIFICATIONS table.

STALL SPEED TEST SPECIFICATIONS [1]

Application	Stall RPM
Impreza	
1800 cc	2200-2600
2200 cc	2300-2700
Legacy	2300-2700
SVX	2350-2750

[1] – Test specifications are for vehicle at sea level. Specifications may vary slightly at higher elevations.

Stall Speed Test Results – **1)** If stall speed is below specification in "2" or "R" position, throttle is not fully opened, engine performance is unsatisfactory or one-way clutch is slipping.

2) If stall speed is high in "D" position, forward clutch slippage and/or one way clutch (1-2) malfunctioning.

3) If stall speed is high in "R" position, line pressure too low, reverse clutch slipping and/or low reverse brake slipping.

4) If stall speed is high in "2" position, line pressure too low, forward clutch slipping, brake band slipping and/or one way clutch (3-4) malfunctioning.

5) Verify low-reverse brake or reverse clutch slippage by road testing vehicle. If engine can be used as a brake with selector lever in "1" range, reverse clutch is slipping. If engine cannot be used as a brake, low-reverse brake is slipping.

PRESSURE TESTS

Line Pressure – **1)** Install oil pressure gauge in driver's compartment. Remove blind plug on floor board/firewall and pass hose of gauge into engine compartment. Remove test plug and install oil pressure gauge. See Figs. 2 and 3.

2) Raise and support vehicle on hoist. With ATF at normal operating temperature and correct level, perform line pressure test with throttle fully-closed. Pressures should be as shown in LINE PRESSURE TEST SPECIFICATIONS table.

3) Apply both foot and parking brakes. With ATF at normal operating temperature and correct level, perform line pressure test at Wide Open Throttle (WOT). Measure line pressure for 5 to 10 seconds. Before measuring again, idle engine for 2 to 5 minutes. Pressures should be as shown in LINE PRESSURE TEST SPECIFICATIONS table.

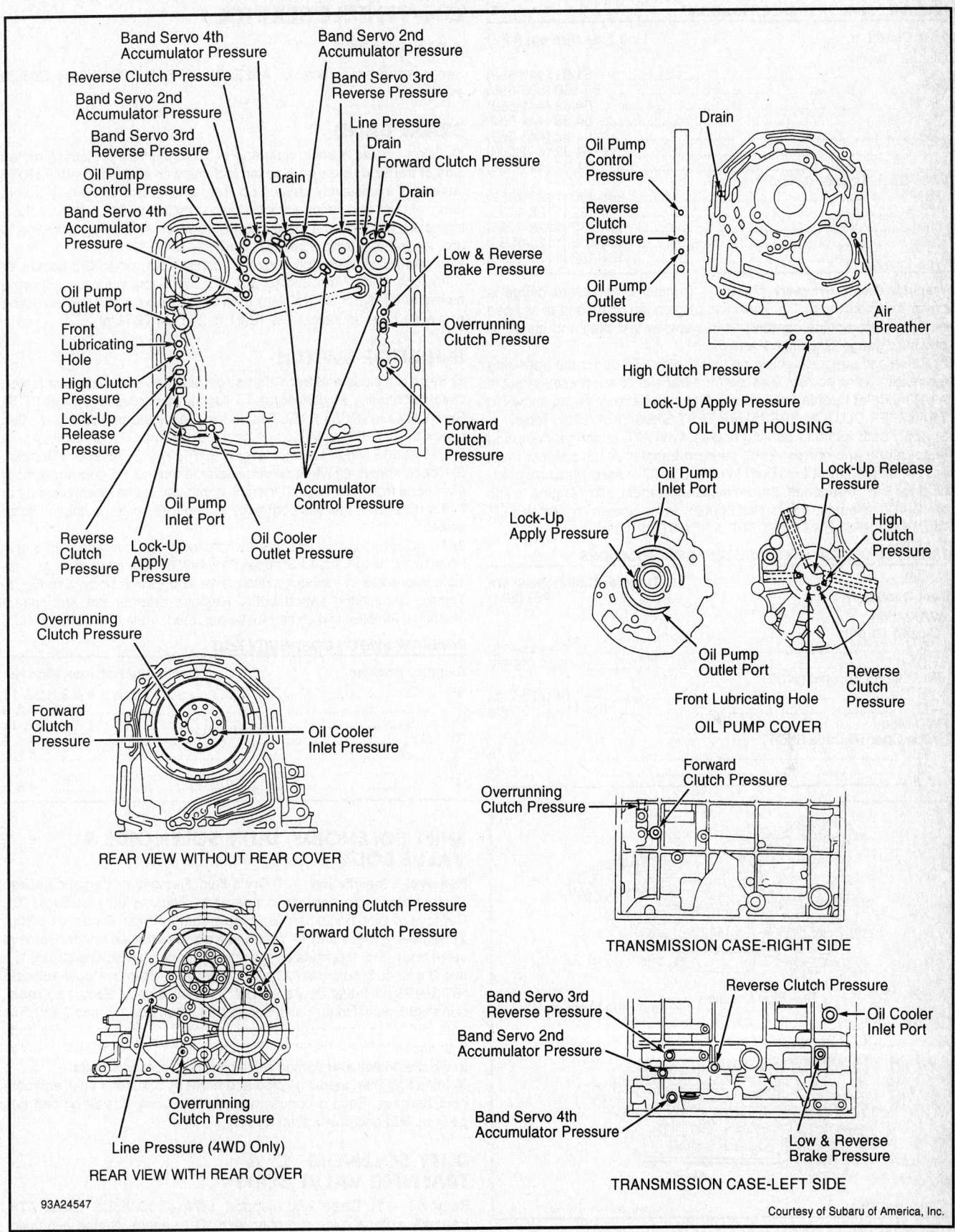

Fig. 2: Identifying Test Plug Locations

93A24547

Courtesy of Subaru of America, Inc.

LINE PRESSURE TEST SPECIFICATIONS

Test Condition	Line Pressure psi (kPa)
Closed Throttle	
"P"	64-82 (441-569)
"R"	85-100 (588-686)
"N"	64-82 (441-569)
"D"	64-82 (441-569)
"3"	64-82 (441-569)
"2"	64-82 (441-569)
"1"	64-82 (441-569)
Wide Open Throttle (WOT)	
"R"	206-230 (1422-1589)
"D"	164-182 (1128-1255)
"3"	164-182 (1128-1255)
"2"	164-182 (1128-1255)
"1"	164-182 (1128-1255)

Transfer Clutch Pressure (AWD) – 1) Install oil pressure gauge in driver's compartment. Remove blind plug on toe board and pass hose of gauge into engine compartment. Remove test plug and install oil pressure gauge. *See Figs. 2 and 3.*

2) Raise and support vehicle on hoist. With ATF at normal operating temperature and correct level, perform transfer clutch pressure test in AWD mode at throttle fully-closed. Pressures should be as shown in TRANSFER CLUTCH PRESSURE TEST SPECIFICATIONS table.

3) Apply both foot and parking brakes. With ATF at normal operating temperature and correct level, perform transfer clutch pressure test with wide open throttle in both FWD and AWD modes. Measure pressure for 5 to 10 seconds. Before measuring again, allow engine to idle for 2 to 5 minutes. Pressures should be as shown in TRANSFER CLUTCH PRESSURE TEST SPECIFICATIONS table.

TRANSFER CLUTCH PRESSURE TEST SPECIFICATIONS

Test Condition	Transfer Clutch Pressure PSI (kPa)
AWD Mode	
Closed Throttle	
"R"	7-11 (49-78)
"D"	7-11 (49-78)
Wide Open Throttle (WOT)	
"R"	104-114 (716-785)
"D"	104-114 (716-785)
FWD Mode	
Wide Open Throttle (WOT)	
"R"	0 (0)
"D"	0 (0)

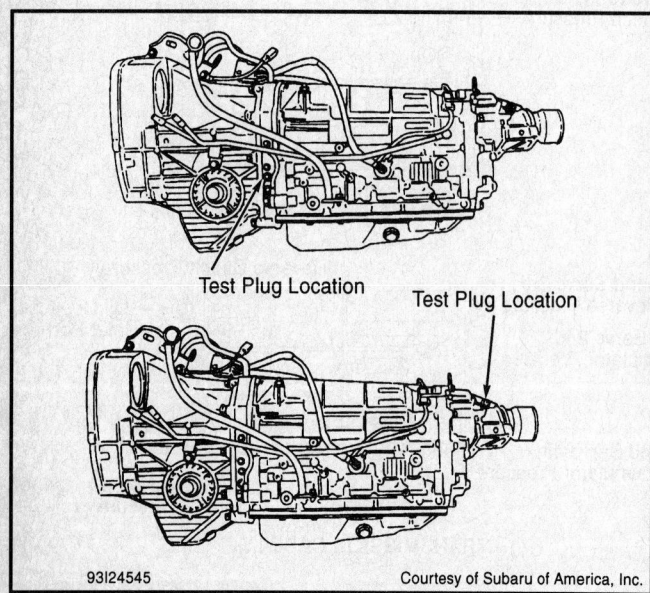

Test Plug Location

Test Plug Location

93I24545   Courtesy of Subaru of America, Inc.

Fig. 3: Identifying Oil Passage & Test Plug Locations

ON-VEHICLE SERVICE

AXLE SHAFTS

See appropriate article in AXLE SHAFTS & TRANSFER CASES section.

BRAKE BAND

1) Using socket wrench, hold end of 10 mm screw projecting on left side of transaxle case and loosen lock nut with wrench. If engine RPM increases excessively shifting up from 2nd to 3rd or there is a shift delay of over one second at kickdown from 3rd to 2nd, tighten adjusting screw 3/4 turn. If a braking is noted when shifting up from 2nd to 3rd, loosen adjusting screw 3/4 turn.

2) If, during acceleration a direct upshift from 1st to 3rd occurs or when upshifting from 2nd to 3rd, tire slip occurs, torque adjusting screw to 80 INCH lbs. (9 N.m) then back off 3 turns. Hold adjusting screw and torque lock nut to 18-21 ft. lbs. (24-28 N.m).

INHIBITOR SWITCH

1) Separate cable end from shift selector lever. Using a circuit tester, check continuity at connector T3 for all positions. See INHIBITOR SWITCH CONTINUITY TEST table for specificatons. *See Fig. 4.* Also check that continuity in ignition circuit does not exist at terminal pins No. 11 and 12. when selector lever is in "R", "D", "3", "2" and "1" ranges.

2) Check continuity when selector lever is moved 1.5 degrees in both directions from "N" range. If there is continuity in one direction and not in the other or if there is continuity at unequal points, adjust inhibitor switch.

3) To adjust, loosen 3 inhibitor switch securing bolts and shift select lever to "N" range. Insert Stopper Pin (499267300) as vertical as possible into holes in inhibitor switch lever and switch body. *See Fig. 5.* Tighten 3 inhibitor switch bolts. Remove stopper pin and repeat checks. If inhibitor switch cannot be adjusted, replace inhibitor switch.

INHIBITOR SWITCH CONTINUITY TEST

Selector Position	Continuity Between Pins No.
"P"	4 & 3, 12 & 11
"R"	4 & 2, 10 & 9
"N"	4 & 1, 12 & 11
"D"	4 & 8
"3"	4 & 7
"2"	4 & 6
"1"	4 & 5

SHIFT SOLENOIDS, DUTY SOLENOIDS & VALVE BODY

Removal & Installation – 1) Drain fluid. Remove oil pan and gasket. Disconnect wiring harness connectors. Remove duty solenoid "B". Remove oil pipe bolts, harness bracket and oil pipe. Remove oil filter.

2) Remove 6 Black and 11 Yellow valve body attaching bolts. Remove valve body and accumulator springs. Remove shift solenoids No. 1, 2 and 3 and duty solenoid "A" from valve body. Remove duty solenoid "B". *See Fig. 6.* Install duty solenoid "B" to valve body. Secure solenoid, hand tight, with 2 inner bolts. Install shift solenoids 1, 2 and 3 and duty solenoid "A" to valve body. Secure accumulator springs to valve body with assembly lube. Install valve body to transaxle with Black and Yellow bolts. Install and tighten remaining duty solenoid bolts.

3) Install oil filter. Install oil pipe and harness bracket. Install and connect harness. Secure connectors to valve body. Install oil pan and gasket. Add and check fluid level.

DUTY SOLENOID "C" & TRANSFER VALVE BODY

Removal – 1) Raise and support vehicle on hoist. Drain ATF. Remove exhaust pipe together with "O₂" sensor. Scribe alignment marks on drive shaft and rear differential flange. Remove drive shaft. Support transaxle using jack and raise slightly. Remove crossmember and vehicle speed sensor "1".

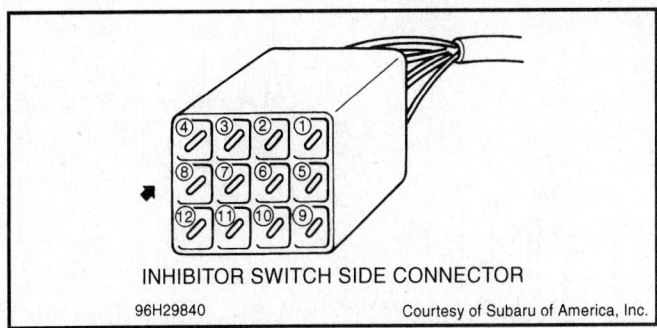

INHIBITOR SWITCH SIDE CONNECTOR

96H29840   Courtesy of Subaru of America, Inc.

Fig. 4: Identifying Inhibitor Switch Connector Terminals

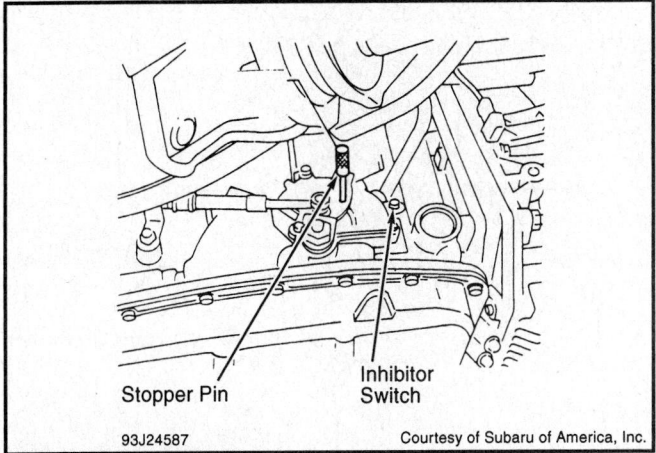

Stopper Pin   Inhibitor Switch

93J24587   Courtesy of Subaru of America, Inc.

Fig. 5: Installing Stopper Pin

2) Remove gear selector cable nut and move cable. Remove extension housing. Disconnect duty solenoid "C" connector. Remove oil pipe clamp and oil pipe. Remove duty solenoid "C" and transfer valve body. *See Fig. 6.*

Installation – 1) Install duty solenoid "C", transfer valve body and oil pipe with clamp. Connect duty solenoid "C" connectors and install extension housing to transaxle. Install gear selector cable and cable nut. Install vehicle speed sensor "1".

2) Install rear crossmember. Lower and remove jack. Install drive shaft by aligning scribe marks. Install exhaust pipe. Reconnect "O₂" sensor connector and multi-connector. Add fluid and check fluid level.

REMOVAL & INSTALLATION

For transaxle removal procedure, see appropriate AUTOMATIC TRANSMISSION REMOVAL article in TRANSMISSION SERVICING section.

TORQUE CONVERTER

Torque converter is a sealed unit and cannot be disassembled for service. Replace if found to be defective.

TRANSAXLE DISASSEMBLY

1) Pull out torque converter horizontally. DO NOT scratch bushing inside oil pump shaft. Remove oil pump shaft, input shaft and strut bar bracket. Disconnect air breather hoses and clips. Remove oil filler pipe. Remove "O" ring from flange face and attach to pipe. Remove oil cooler inlet and outlet pipes. Use caution not to lose balls and springs with retaining screws. Remove harness from bracket.

2) Remove converter case bolts and lightly tap off converter case from transmission case. Ensure not to damage oil seal and bushing inside converter case. On AWD models, remove vehicle speed sensor and extension housing bolts. Pull off extension housing slightly and disconnect duty solenoid "C" connector. On FWD models, remove transmission cover bolts and cover.

3) Remove reduction drive gear assembly from rear of transmission case. Set range selector lever to "P" position. Unstake and remove reduction driven gear lock nut. Drill 2 holes into Puller Set (899524100) plate. *See Fig. 8.* Remove reduction driven gear.

4) Remove park pawl, return spring and shaft. Loosen, but do not remove, roller bearing retainer bolts. Place 2 wooden blocks on workbench and stand transmission case with rear end facing down. Ensure rear mating surface of case is not scratched or damaged. Remove oil pan and gasket.

5) Remove oil cooler outlet pipe. DO NOT twist pipe. Disconnect harness connectors for shift solenoids, duty solenoids and ground cable. Remove oil filter. Ensure oil filter "O" ring is not damaged. Remove 11 Yellow bolts and 6 Black bolts and remove valve body. Remove 3 accumulator springs.

6) Loosen reverse clutch drum slightly by turning adjusting screw. Remove oil pump housing. Retain total end play adjusting thrust washer. Loosen and remove brake band screw and strut. Remove brake band and reverse clutch. Remove high clutch, high clutch hub, thrust bearing, front sun gear, thrust bearing, front planetary carrier, thrust bearing, rear planetary carrier, thrust bearing, rear sun gear and thrust bearing. *See Fig. 11.*

7) Remove rear internal gear, thrust bearing, one-way clutch outer race and thrust bearing. Remove overrunning clutch hub, thrust washer, and thrust bearing and forward clutch drum. Remove snap ring. Remove retaining plate, drive plates and dish plates as a unit.

8) Turn case upside-down. Remove one-way clutch inner race and spring retainer assembly. Remove low and reverse piston by applying compressed air. Remove servo piston inner snap ring. Hold servo piston with cloth and apply compressed air from the release pressure side.

CAUTION: DO NOT allow finger to be pinched between pipe and retainer.

9) Apply compressed air from operating pressure side and remove 4 accumulators. *See Fig. 9.* Remove range select lever and detent spring. Remove parking rod with manual lever. Drive out roll pin and remove manual shaft. Remove inhibitor switch and transmission harness.

10) Wrap left and right drive axle shafts with tape. Remove differential side retainers using Remover (499095500) and Installer (499247300). *See Fig. 9.* Hold differential case assembly by hand to avoid damaging retainer mounting hole of converter case and speedometer gears. Remove axle shaft circlip and pull out axle shaft.

11) Remove differential case assembly. Remove seal pipe if attached (DO NOT reuse). Use caution not to damage retainer mounting hole of torque converter clutch case and speedometer gears. Remove speedometer driven gear snap ring and speedometer driven gear. Remove vehicle speed sensor "2". Tap out speedometer shaft to outside of case. Remove oil seal. On AWD models, remove transfer clutch from extension by tapping end of rear drive shaft. DO NOT damage oil seal in extension housing. Remove transfer pipe and transfer valve body bolts. Remove duty solenoid "C" and transfer valve body. Remove inlet filter.

AUTOMATIC TRANSMISSIONS
Subaru 4-Speed (Cont.)

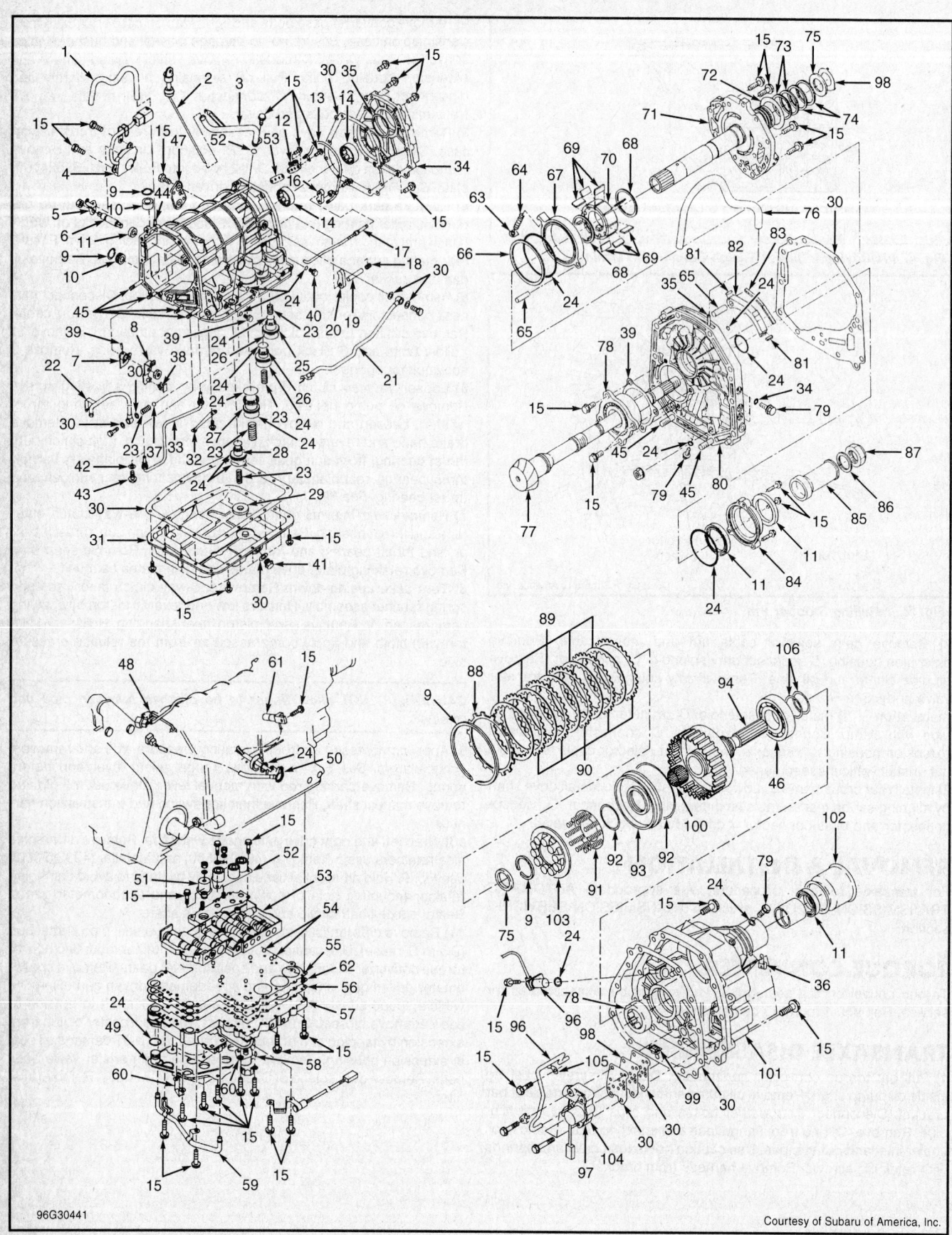

Fig. 6: Exploded View Of Transmission Assembly (1 Of 2)

96G30441

Courtesy of Subaru of America, Inc.

1. Air Breather Hose
2. Oil Level Gauge
3. Oil Filler Pipe
4. Inhibitor Switch
5. Range Selector Lever
6. Manual Shaft
7. Manual Plate
8. Manual Lever
9. Snap Ring
10. Plug
11. Oil Seal
12. Relief Pipe
13. Pipe
14. Roller Bearing
15. Hex Bolt
16. Parking Support
17. Parking Rod
18. Return Spring
19. Shaft
20. Parking Pawl
21. Inlet Pipe
22. Outlet Pipe
23. Spring
24. "O" Ring
25. Accumulator Piston (N-D)
26. Accumulator Piston (2-3)
27. Accumulator Piston (1-2)
28. Accumulator Piston (3-4)

29. Magnet
30. Gasket
31. Oil Pan
32. Detention Spring
33. Pipe (AWD Model)
34. Transmission Cover (FWD Model)
35. Shim
36. Clip
37. Ball
38. Stopper
39. Stopper Pin
40. Test Plug
41. Drain Plug
42. Gasket (FWD Model)
43. Plug (AWD Model)
44. Nipple
45. Stud Bolt
46. Ball Bearing
47. Plate Assembly
48. Stay
49. Oil Strainer
50. Transmission Harness
51. Duty Solenoid "A" (Line Pressure)
52. Solenoid
53. Upper Valve Body
54. Ball

55. Upper Separator Gasket
56. Lower Separator Gasket
57. Lower Valve Body
58. Duty Solenoid "B" (Lock-Up)
59. Pipe
60. Bracket
61. Vehicle Speed Sensor (FWD)
62. Separator Plate
63. Retainer
64. Return Spring
65. Pin
66. Friction Ring
67. Cam Ring
68. Vane Ring
69. Vane
70. Rotor
71. Oil Pump Cover
72. Thrust Washer
73. Right Seal Ring
74. Left Seal Ring
75. Thrust Needle Bearing
76. Air Breather Hose
77. Drive Pinion Shaft
78. Roller Bearing
79. Test Plug
80. Oil Pump Housing

81. Side Seal
82. Control Piston
83. Plane Seal
84. Oil Seal Retainer
85. Drive Pinion Collar
86. Lock Washer
87. Lock Nut
88. Pressure Plate
89. Drive Plate
90. Driven Plate
91. Spring Retainer
92. Lathe Cut Seal Ring
93. Transfer Clutch Piston
94. Rear Drive Shaft
95. Vehicle Speed Sensor "1" (AWD)
96. Transfer Clutch Pipe
97. Duty Solenoid "C" (Transfer Clutch)
98. Plate
99. Filter
100. Needle Roller Bearing
101. Extension Case
102. Dust Seal
103. Seal Transfer Piston
104. Transfer Valve Body
105. Stay
106. Seal Ring

96I30443

Courtesy of Subaru of America, Inc.

Fig. 7: Legend For Fig. 6 (2 Of 2)

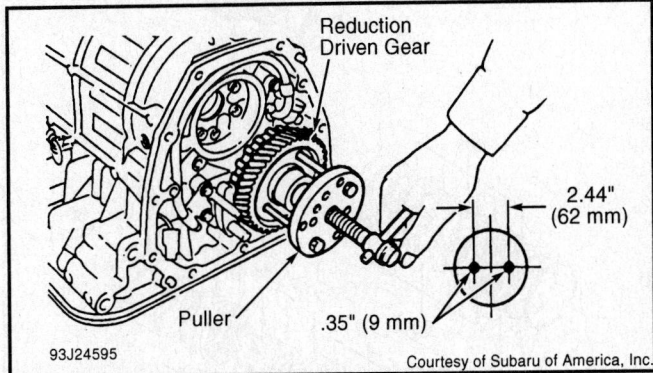

93J24595   Courtesy of Subaru of America, Inc.

Fig. 8: Removing Reduction Driven Gear

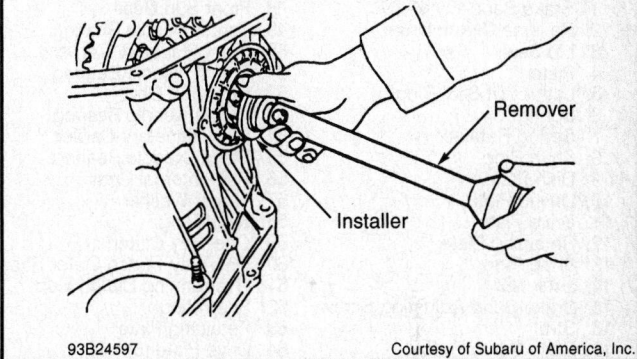

93B24597   Courtesy of Subaru of America, Inc.

Fig. 10: Removing Differential Side Retainer

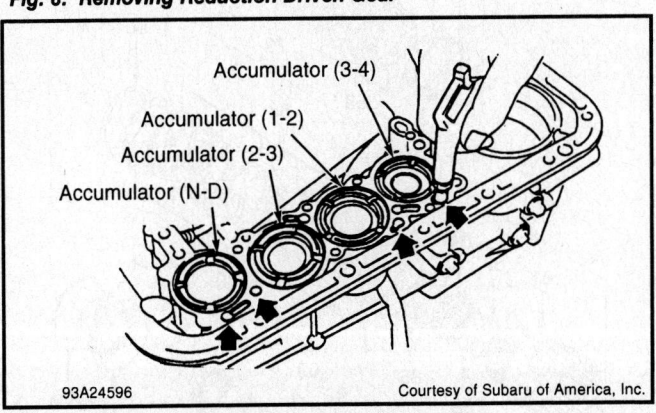

93A24596   Courtesy of Subaru of America, Inc.

Fig. 9: Removing Accumulator Piston Assemblies

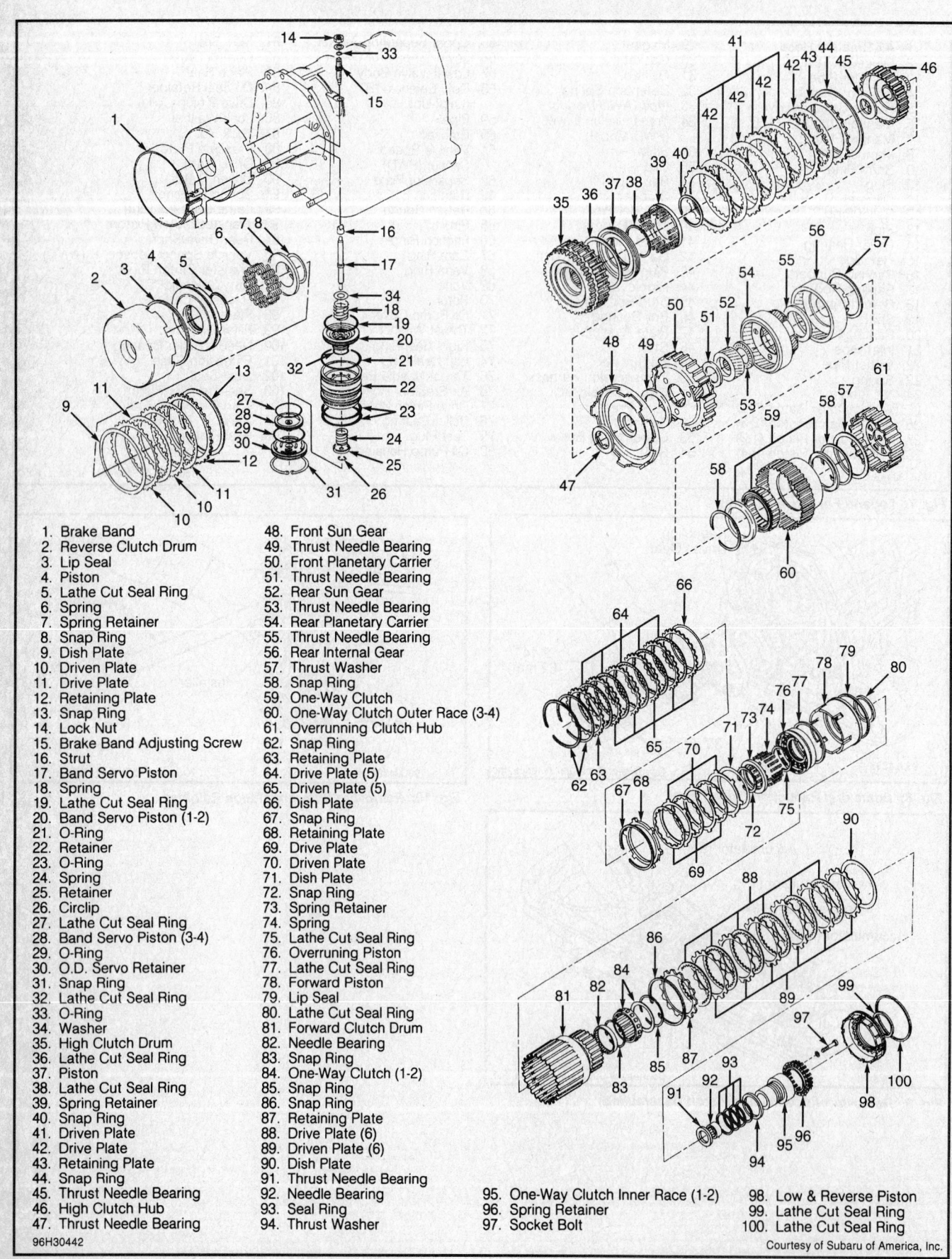

1. Brake Band
2. Reverse Clutch Drum
3. Lip Seal
4. Piston
5. Lathe Cut Seal Ring
6. Spring
7. Spring Retainer
8. Snap Ring
9. Dish Plate
10. Driven Plate
11. Drive Plate
12. Retaining Plate
13. Snap Ring
14. Lock Nut
15. Brake Band Adjusting Screw
16. Strut
17. Band Servo Piston
18. Spring
19. Lathe Cut Seal Ring
20. Band Servo Piston (1-2)
21. O-Ring
22. Retainer
23. O-Ring
24. Spring
25. Retainer
26. Circlip
27. Lathe Cut Seal Ring
28. Band Servo Piston (3-4)
29. O-Ring
30. O.D. Servo Retainer
31. Snap Ring
32. Lathe Cut Seal Ring
33. O-Ring
34. Washer
35. High Clutch Drum
36. Lathe Cut Seal Ring
37. Piston
38. Lathe Cut Seal Ring
39. Spring Retainer
40. Snap Ring
41. Driven Plate
42. Drive Plate
43. Retaining Plate
44. Snap Ring
45. Thrust Needle Bearing
46. High Clutch Hub
47. Thrust Needle Bearing
48. Front Sun Gear
49. Thrust Needle Bearing
50. Front Planetary Carrier
51. Thrust Needle Bearing
52. Rear Sun Gear
53. Thrust Needle Bearing
54. Rear Planetary Carrier
55. Thrust Needle Bearing
56. Rear Internal Gear
57. Thrust Washer
58. Snap Ring
59. One-Way Clutch
60. One-Way Clutch Outer Race (3-4)
61. Overrunning Clutch Hub
62. Snap Ring
63. Retaining Plate
64. Drive Plate (5)
65. Driven Plate (5)
66. Dish Plate
67. Snap Ring
68. Retaining Plate
69. Drive Plate
70. Driven Plate
71. Dish Plate
72. Snap Ring
73. Spring Retainer
74. Spring
75. Lathe Cut Seal Ring
76. Overruning Piston
77. Lathe Cut Seal Ring
78. Forward Piston
79. Lip Seal
80. Lathe Cut Seal Ring
81. Forward Clutch Drum
82. Needle Bearing
83. Snap Ring
84. One-Way Clutch (1-2)
85. Snap Ring
86. Snap Ring
87. Retaining Plate
88. Drive Plate (6)
89. Driven Plate (6)
90. Dish Plate
91. Thrust Needle Bearing
92. Needle Bearing
93. Seal Ring
94. Thrust Washer
95. One-Way Clutch Inner Race (1-2)
96. Spring Retainer
97. Socket Bolt
98. Low & Reverse Piston
99. Lathe Cut Seal Ring
100. Lathe Cut Seal Ring

96H30442

Courtesy of Subaru of America, Inc.

Fig. 11: Exploded View Of Clutch Assemblies & Components

COMPONENT DISASSEMBLY & REASSEMBLY

REDUCTION DRIVE GEAR

Disassembly – Remove seal rings and outer snap ring. Using press, remove reduction drive gear. Press off ball bearing.

Reassembly – Press on ball bearing and reduction drive gear. On AWD models, install snap ring in groove. On FWD models, press on ball bearing and install snap ring in groove. Install seal rings.

CONTROL VALVE BODY

Disassembly – **1)** Remove shift solenoids No. 1, 2 and 3 and duty solenoid "A" from upper valve body. *See Fig. 6.* Remove duty solenoid "B" and bracket from lower valve body.

2) Remove upper-lower valve body bolts and 2 locating bolts. Separate valve bodies. Remove 9 steel balls from upper valve body. Remove orifice and filter from lower valve body. *See Fig. 12.*

NOTE: *During minor overhaul, complete disassembly and cleaning of valve body is not necessary. If any contamination is present in transmission assembly, completely disassemble valve body and thoroughly clean all components. See Fig. 14. Ensure smooth operation of all valves.*

Reassembly – **1)** Reverse disassembly sequence. Ensure proper positioning of steel balls, orifice and filter. *See Fig. 12.* Tighten bolts and upper-lower valve body bolts to specification. See TORQUE SPECIFICATIONS table. See BOLT LOCATION & LENGTH table for correct installation location. *See Fig. 13.*

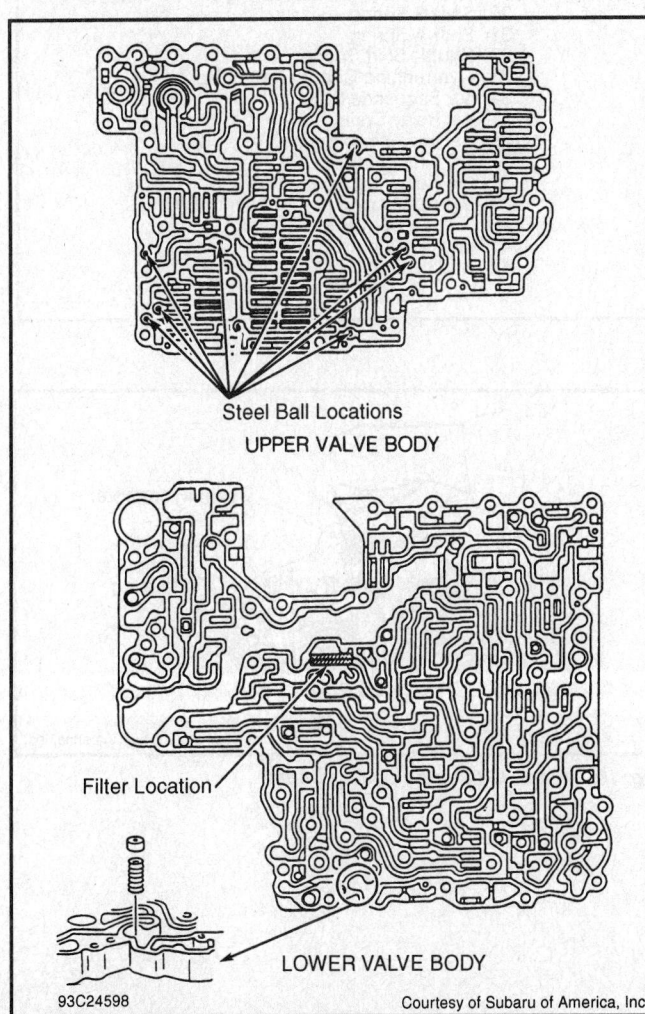

Steel Ball Locations
UPPER VALVE BODY

Filter Location

LOWER VALVE BODY

93C24598   Courtesy of Subaru of America, Inc.

Fig. 12: Identifying Valve Body Steel Ball & Filter Locations

2) Install shift solenoids and duty solenoid "A". Bolt length for shift solenoids is .63" (16 mm). Bolt length for duty solenoid "A" is 1.06" (27 mm).

BOLT LOCATION & LENGTH

Location [1]	Length In. (mm)
a	2.76 (70)
b	1.97 (50)
c	1.30 (33)
d	1.06 (27)
e	1.10 (28)

[1] – For bolt location, *see Fig. 13.*

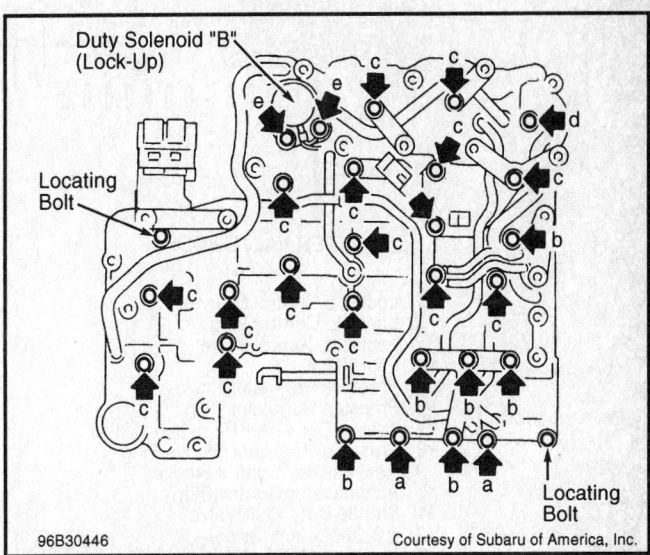

Duty Solenoid "B" (Lock-Up)

Locating Bolt

Locating Bolt

96B30446   Courtesy of Subaru of America, Inc.

Fig. 13: Valve Body Bolt Location

OIL PUMP ASSEMBLY

Disassembly – Remove oil seal retainer, "O" ring and oil seal air breather. Remove oil pump cover bolts and tap end of stator shaft to remove cover. Remove retainer and return spring, rotor, 2 vane rings and 9 vanes. Remove cam ring, control piston, "O" ring, friction ring, 2 side seals and plain seal. Remove seal rings. *See Fig. 6.*

Inspection – **1)** Using a micrometer, measure height of rotor, control piston and cam ring in at least 4 positions. Measure height at one location for each of 9 vanes. *See Fig. 15.* Remove control piston seals when measuring and remove friction ring from cam ring when measuring.

2) Using a depth gauge, measure depth of oil pump housing. *See Fig. 16.* Ensure clearances are within specified wear limits. See OIL PUMP COMPONENT SPECIFICATIONS table. If wear limit is exceeded, select components so standard clearance is obtained. Select vanes which are same height as rotor.

OIL PUMP COMPONENT SPECIFICATIONS

Component	Wear Limit In. (mm)	Standard Value In. (mm)
Rotor End Play, Control Piston-To Pump Housing & Vanes-To-Rotor	.0021 (.054)	.0012-.0017 (.030-.044)
Cam Ring-To-Housing	.0013 (.034)	.0004-.0009 (.010-.024)

Reassembly – **1)** Coat "O" ring and friction ring with lubricant, attach to cam ring and install into oil pump housing. Install vane ring, rotor, vanes and vane ring. Install return spring and retainer between housing and cam ring. Install control piston. Fit seal in piston groove, with Red seals facing top side.

2) Set rotor in center of housing bore. Apply ATF to components. Align 2 pivot pins with pivot holes of cover and install cover. Tighten bolts to 17-20 ft. lbs. (2.4-2.9 N.m). Install seal rings and oil seal retainer.

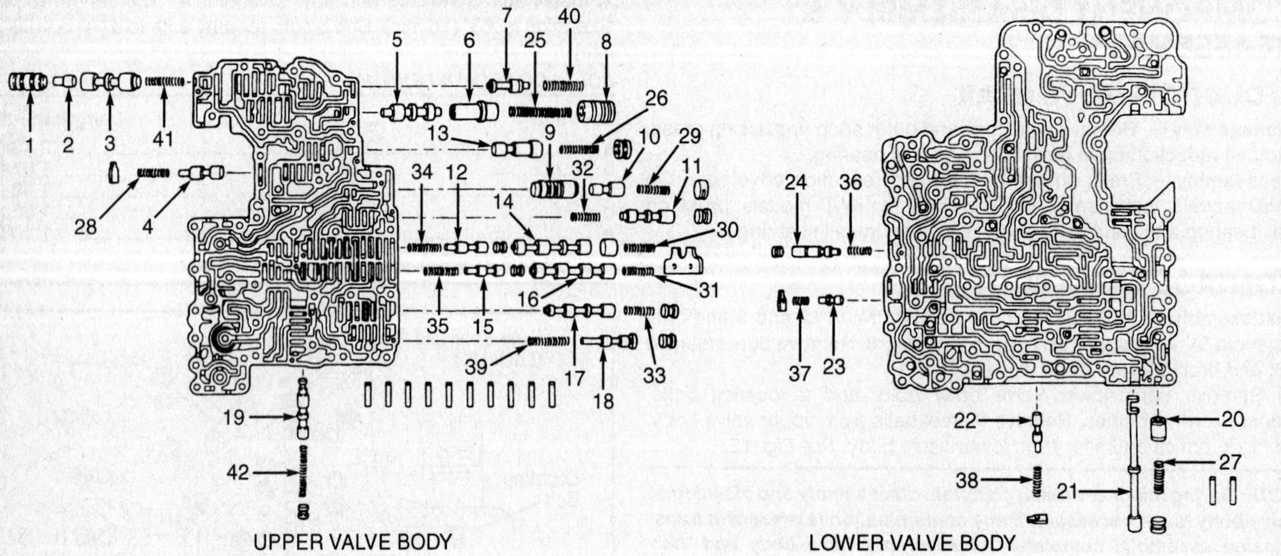

UPPER VALVE BODY

LOWER VALVE BODY

1. Lock-Up Control Sleeve
2. Lock-Up Control Plug
3. Lock-Up Control Valve
4. Pilot Valve
5. Pressure Regulator Valve
6. Pressure Regulator Plug
7. Torque Converter Regulation Valve
8. Pressure Regulator Sleeve Plug
9. Accumulator Control Sleeve
10. Accumulator Control Plug
11. Shuttle Duty Shift Valve
12. 4-2 Sequence Valve
13. Pressure Modifier Valve
14. Shift Valve B
15. 4-2 Relay Valve
16. Shift Valve A
17. Overrunning Clutch Control Valve
18. Overrunning Clutch Control Valve
19. Shuttle Shift Valve
20. Manual Valve
21. Forward Clutch Control Valve

22. 1st Reducing Valve
23. 3-2 Timing Valve
24. Servo Charger Valve
25. Pressure Regulator Spring
26. Pressure Modifier Spring
27. Modifier Accumulator Spring
28. Pilot Spring
29. Accumulator Control Spring
30. Shift B Spring
31. Shift A Spring
32. Shuttle Shift Spring
33. Overrunning Clutch Control Spring
34. 4-2 Sequence Spring
35. 4-2 Relay Spring
36. Servo Charger Spring
37. 3-2 Timing Spring
38. 1st Reducing Spring
39. Overrunning Clutch Reducing Spring
40. Torque Converter Regulator Spring
41. Lock-Up Control Spring
42. Shuttle Duty Shift Spring

96J30444

Courtesy of Subaru of America, Inc.

Fig. 14: Exploded View Of Valve Body Assembly

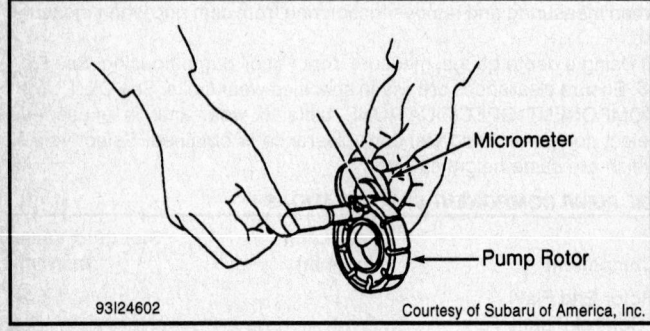

93124602   Courtesy of Subaru of America, Inc.

Fig. 15: Measuring Height Of Pump Rotor

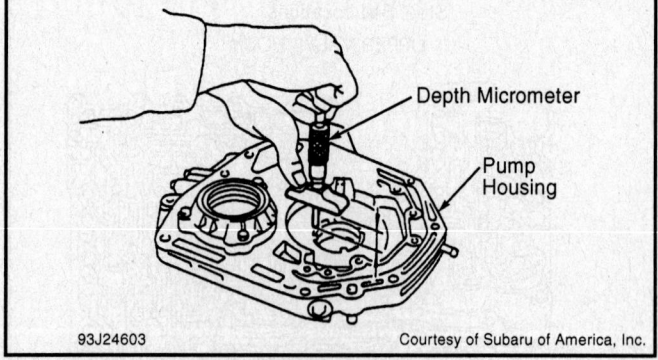

93J24603   Courtesy of Subaru of America, Inc.

Fig. 16: Measuring Pump Housing Depth

DRIVE PINION SHAFT

Disassembly – Unstake lock nut and remove, using Wrench (499787100) and Holder (498937100). *See Fig. 17.* Remove drive pinion collar. Remove "O" ring. Using press, remove rear roller bearing and outer race. Press off front roller bearing.

Reassembly – 1) Measure dimension "A" of drive pinion shaft. *See Fig. 19.* Press on roller bearings. DO NOT change positions of outer race and bearing cone. Install "O" ring and drive pinion collar. Install lock washer and lock nut. Using Wrench (499787100) and torque wrench, tighten to 80-87 ft. lbs. (108-118 N.m). *See Fig. 17.*

2) Using spring gauge, measure starting torque of bearing. *See Fig. 18.* Ensure starting torque of 3-18 INCH lbs. (0.3-2.0 N.m). If not in specified range, replace roller bearing and recheck. Stake lock nut in 2 places.

3) Measure dimension "B" of drive pinion shaft. *See Fig. 19.* Determine thickness of drive pinion shim(s) "t", using INCH dimensions in the the following equation:

$$\text{"t"} = .255\text{"} - (B - A)$$

The .255" may be +/- .002" (.253-.257"). Use 3 or fewer shims. See DRIVE PINION SHIMS table.

DRIVE PINION SHIMS

Part No.	Thickness – In. (mm)
31451AA050	.006 (.15)
31451AA060	.007 (.18)
31451AA070	.008 (.20)
31451AA080	.009 (.23)
31451AA090	.010 (.25)
31451AA100	.011 (.28)

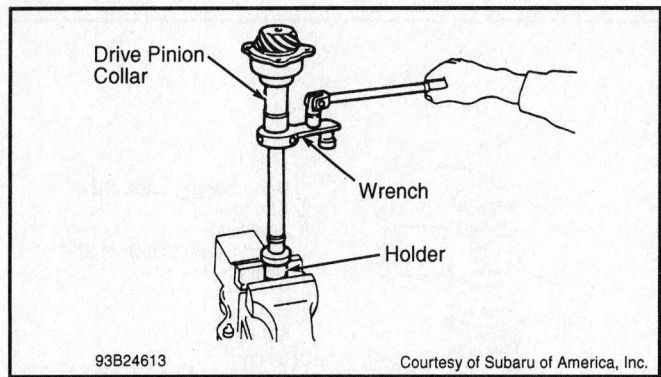

Fig. 17: Removing & Installing Lock Nut

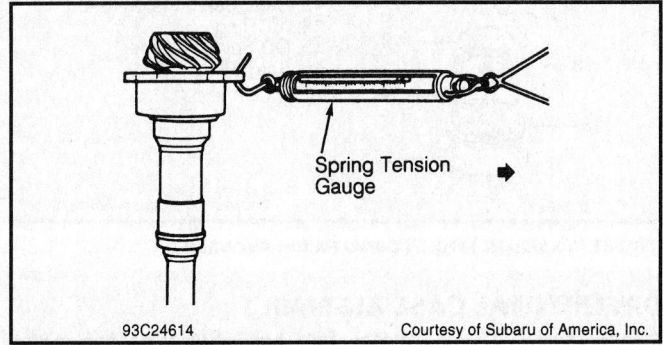

Fig. 18: Measuring Starting Torque

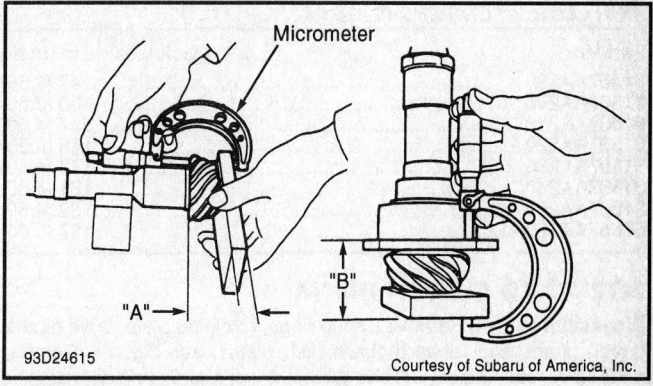

Fig. 19: Measuring Drive Pinion Shaft

REVERSE CLUTCH

Disassembly – Remove snap ring, retaining plate, drive plates, driven plates and dish plate. *See Fig. 11.* Using appropriate compressor, remove snap ring, spring retainer and springs. Apply compressed air and remove clutch piston.

Inspection – Check drive plate facing for wear and damage. Check snap ring for wear, return spring for breakage or settling, and spring retainer for deformation. Inspect lip seal and seal ring for damage and piston check ball operation.

Reassembly – 1) Using compressor, install clutch piston, return springs, spring retainer and snap ring. Install dish plate, driven plates, drive plates, retaining plate and snap ring. Ensure correct placement of dish plate. *See Fig. 11.*

2) Apply compressed air intermittently to oil hole and check reverse clutch for smooth operation. Using thickness gauge, measure clearance between retaining plate and snap ring. If clearance is not .020-.031" (.50-.80 mm) select retaining plate for proper clearance. See REVERSE CLUTCH RETAINING PLATE table.

REVERSE CLUTCH RETAINING PLATE

Part No.	Thickness – In. (mm)
31567AA350	.181 (4.60)
31567AA360	.189 (4.80)
31567AA370	.197 (5.00)
31567AA380	.205 (5.20)
31567AA390	.213 (5.40)
31567AA400	.220 (5.60)

HIGH CLUTCH

Disassembly – Remove snap ring, retaining plate, drive plates and driven plates. *See Fig. 11.* Using appropriate compressor, remove snap ring, spring retainer and springs. Apply compressed air and remove clutch piston.

Inspection – Check drive plate facing for wear and damage. Check snap ring for wear, return springs for breakage or settling and spring retainer for deformation. Inspect large and small seal ring for damage and piston check ball operation.

Reassembly – 1) Using compressor, install clutch piston, return springs, spring retainer and snap ring. Install thin driven plate, driven plates, drive plates, retaining plate and snap ring.

2) Apply compressed air intermittently to oil hole and check high clutch for smooth operation. Using thickness gauge, measure clearance between retaining plate and snap ring. Standard clearance is .071-.087" (1.80-2.20 mm), Maximum allowable limit is .102" (2.6 mm). If clearance is greater, select appropriate retaining plate for proper clearance. See HIGH CLUTCH RETAINING PLATE table.

HIGH CLUTCH RETAINING PLATE

Part No.	Thickness – In. (mm)
31567AA190	.142 (3.60)
31567AA200	.150 (3.80)
31567AA210	.157 (4.00)
31567AA220	.165 (4.20)
31567AA230	.173 (4.40)
31567AA240	.181 (4.60)
31567AA250	.189 (4.80)
31567AA260	.197 (5.00)

FORWARD CLUTCH DRUM

Disassembly – 1) Remove 2 snap rings, retaining plate, drive plates, driven plates and forward clutch dish plates. See Fig. 11. Remove snap ring, retaining plate, drive plates, driven plates and overrunning clutch dish plate. Compress spring retainer and remove snap ring.
2) Install one-way clutch inner race onto forward clutch drum and apply compressed air to remove overrunning piston and forward piston. Remove one-way clutch snap ring, needle bearing and one-way clutch.

Inspection – Check drive plate facing for wear or damage. Check snap ring for wear, return springs for breakage or setting and spring retainer for deformation. Inspect lip seal and lathe-cut ring for damage and piston and drum check ball operation.

Reassembly – 1) Align forward piston cut-out portion with spline of drum and install. Install overrunning piston. Install springs and spring retainer onto piston. Install snap ring.
2) Install overrunning clutch dish plate, driven plates, drive plates, retaining plate and snap ring. Ensure correct dish plate placement. Install forward clutch dish plates, driven plates, drive plates, retaining plate and snap rings. See Fig. 11. Install front planetary carrier snap ring.
3) Check forward clutch and overrunning clutch for operation. Set one-way clutch inner race and apply compressed air to check. Measure clearance between retaining plates and snap rings of forward clutch and overrunning clutch. See FORWARD & OVERRUNNING CLUTCH CLEARANCE table. If clearance is not within specifications, select appropriate retaining plate to obtain proper clearance. See FORWARD CLUTCH RETAINING PLATE table and OVERRUNNING CLUTCH RETAINING PLATE table.
4) Install one-way clutch needle bearing and snap ring. Install 1st-2nd one-way clutch, plate and snap ring. Set inner race and ensure forward clutch moves freely in clockwise direction and locks in counterclockwise direction. See Fig. 20.

FORWARD & OVERRUNNING CLUTCH CLEARANCE

Application	Standard Clearance – In. (mm)
Forward Clutch	.018-.034 (.45-.85)
Overrunning Clutch	.039-.055 (1.00-1.40)

FORWARD CLUTCH RETAINING PLATE

Part No.	Thickness – In. (mm)
31567AA270	.157 (4.00)
31567AA280	.165 (4.20)
31567AA290	.173 (4.40)
31567AA300	.181 (4.60)
31567AA310	.189 (4.80)
31567AA320	.197 (5.00)
31567AA330	.205 (5.20)

OVERRUNNING CLUTCH RETAINING PLATE

Part No.	Thickness – In. (mm)
31567AA120	.315 (8.00)
31567AA130	.323 (8.20)
31567AA140	.331 (8.40)
31567AA150	.339 (8.60)
31567AA160	.346 (8.80)
31567AA170	.354 (9.00)
31567AA180	.362 (9.20)

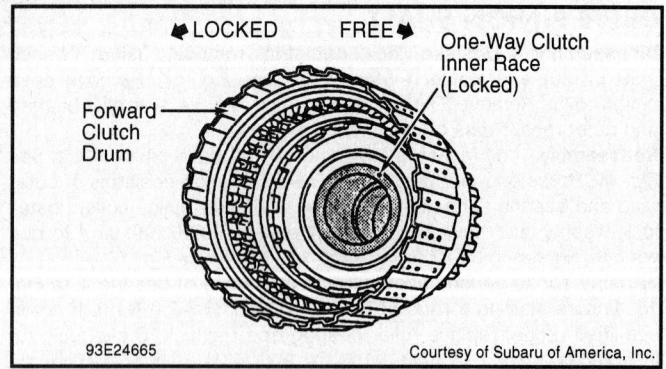

93E24665   Courtesy of Subaru of America, Inc.

Fig. 20: Checking Forward Clutch Operation

SERVO PISTON

Disassembly – Remove spring and 3rd-4th band servo piston. See Fig. 21. Compress retainer from above and remove snap ring, retainer, spring and stem. Remove 1st-2nd band servo piston.

Inspection – Check each component for cuts, damage and other faults. Inspect "O" rings and seal rings for damage. A variety of "O" rings and seal rings are used. DO NOT interchange them during disassembly and reassembly.

Reassembly – Install 1st-2nd band servo piston to retainer and insert stem. Install spring and retainer on piston. Compress spring and install snap ring. Install 3rd-4th band servo piston. Install spring securely to 1-2 band servo piston. DO NOT damage "O" rings and lathe-cut rings during reassembly. See Fig. 21.

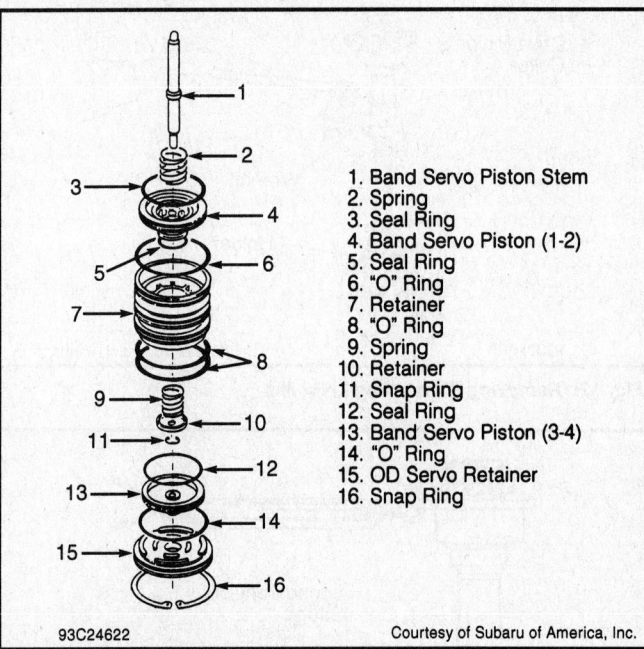

1. Band Servo Piston Stem
2. Spring
3. Seal Ring
4. Band Servo Piston (1-2)
5. Seal Ring
6. "O" Ring
7. Retainer
8. "O" Ring
9. Spring
10. Retainer
11. Snap Ring
12. Seal Ring
13. Band Servo Piston (3-4)
14. "O" Ring
15. OD Servo Retainer
16. Snap Ring

93C24622   Courtesy of Subaru of America, Inc.

Fig. 21: Exploded View Of Servo Piston Assembly

DIFFERENTIAL CASE ASSEMBLY

Disassembly – 1) Press off taper roller bearing using bearing splitter and press. DO NOT damage speedometer drive gear. Secure differential case in vise. Remove ring gear bolts and ring gear. Separate differential cases.
2) Drive out roll pin and remove pinion shaft from case. Remove differential side gear, thrust washer and pinion gears. See Fig. 22.
Reassembly – 1) Install pinion gears, thrust washer and side gear. Insert pinion shaft and drive in roll pin. Stake straight pin. Install thrust washer and side gear to left hand case. Assemble case halves. Install ring gear and tighten bolts to 42-49 ft. lbs. (57-67 N.m). See Fig. 20.

2) Measure pinion gear backlash by inserting dial indicator through access window of case. *See Fig. 23.* Backlash should be .005-.007" (.13-.18 mm). If backlash is not within specification, replace washers.

3) Position locking end of speedometer drive gear correctly and install onto differential case. Using press and Drift (398487700), install taper roller bearing.

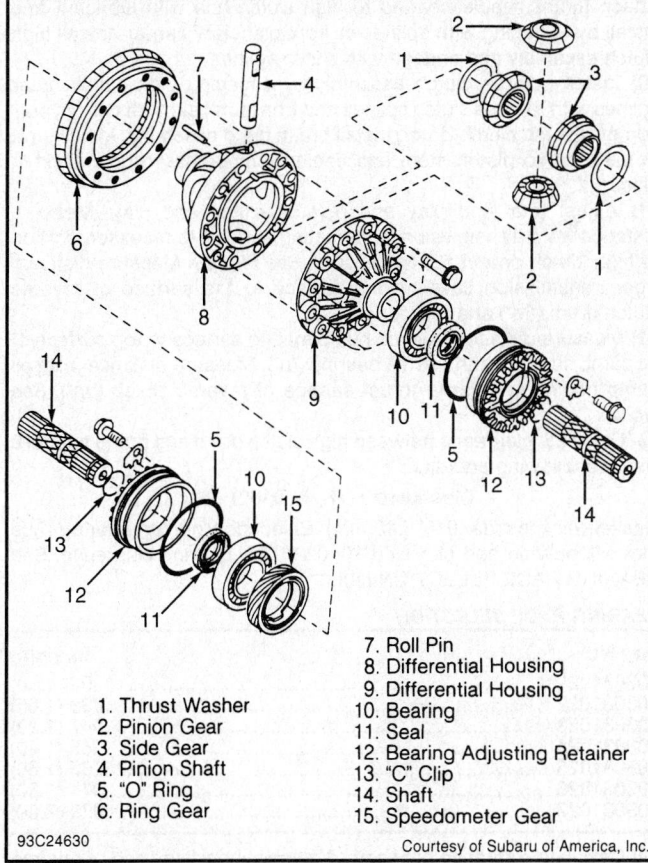

```
7. Roll Pin
8. Differential Housing
9. Differential Housing
10. Bearing
11. Seal
12. Bearing Adjusting Retainer
13. "C" Clip
14. Shaft
15. Speedometer Gear
```

```
1. Thrust Washer
2. Pinion Gear
3. Side Gear
4. Pinion Shaft
5. "O" Ring
6. Ring Gear
```

93C24630   Courtesy of Subaru of America, Inc.

Fig. 22: *Exploded View Of Differential Assembly*

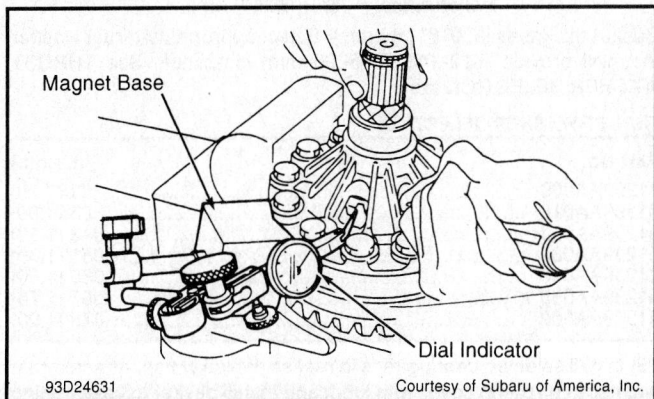

93D24631   Courtesy of Subaru of America, Inc.

Fig. 23: *Measuring Pinion Gear Backlash*

TRANSFER CLUTCH (AWD)

Disassembly – Remove seal ring. Support bearing in press and remove. Remove snap ring, pressure plate, drive plates and driven plates. Using appropriate compressor, remove snap ring, spring retainer and springs. Apply compressed air to rear drive shaft to remove piston. Remove seal ring from piston. *See Fig. 6.*

Inspection – Check drive plate facing for wear and damage. Inspect snap rings for wear, return springs for settling and breakage and spring retainer for deformation. Check seal ring and "O" ring for damage.

Reassembly – **1)** Install seal rings to transfer clutch piston. Install piston, springs and spring retainer. Using compressor, compress springs and install snap ring. Install driven plates, drive plates, pressure plate and snap ring. Apply compressed air to check clutch operation. *See Fig. 6.*

2) Measure between pressure plate and snap ring for clearance of .008-.024" (.20-.60 mm). If clearance is not within specified range, select proper pressure plate. See PRESSURE PLATES table.

PRESSURE PLATES

Part No.	Thickness – In. (mm)
31593AA151	.130 (3.30)
31593AA161	.146 (3.70)
31593AA171	.161 (4.10)
31593AA181	.177 (4.50)

3) Using press, install ball bearing. Coat seal ring with lubricant and install in seal ring groove of shaft. DO NOT expand seal ring excessively when installing.

TRANSFER VALVE BODY

Disassembly – Remove plate, spring and pilot valve. *See Fig. 24.* Remove straight pin, pry out plug and remove spring and transfer clutch valve.

Reassembly – To reassemble, reverse disassembly procedure. Ensure valves slide smoothly.

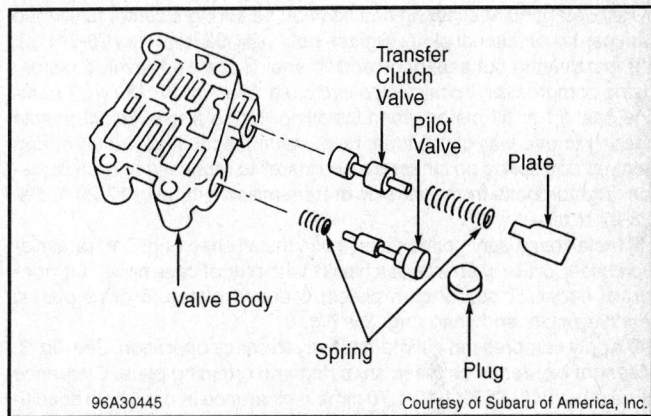

96A30445   Courtesy of Subaru of America, Inc.

Fig. 24: *Exploded View Of Transfer Valve Body*

TRANSAXLE REASSEMBLY

1) Install washer and snap ring to speedometer shaft and install oil seal. Using driver, install shaft into converter case. Install NEW vehicle speed sensor "2". Tighten to 39-65 INCH lbs. (4.4-7.4 N.m). Install speedometer driven gear to speedometer shaft, secure with snap ring.

2) Install oil seal to converter case. Install differential case. DO NOT damage speedometer drive and driven gears and differential side retainer contact surfaces. Install snap rings to axle shafts. Insert shafts into differential case and tap into place. Measure shaft end play. End play should be approximately .012-.020" (.30-.50 mm). If no play is felt or play is too large, replace axle shaft.

3) Wrap axle shafts splined portions with tape. Install oil seals and taper roller bearing outer races to differential side retainers. Install retainers to converter case. Using Handle (499787000), screw in retainers until light contact is felt. Screw in right side slightly deeper than left side.

4) Install drive pinion shaft with selected shim(s) to oil pump housing. Tighten bearing retainer bolts to 27-31 ft. lbs. (36-42 N.m). Clean oil pump housing and converter case mating surfaces. Install oil pump housing to converter case. Tighten bolts to 27-31 ft. lbs. (36-42 N.m).

5) Using Socket (498937100) and Wrench (499787100), rotate drive pinion several times. *See Fig. 25.* Tighten left side retainer until contact is felt when rotating shaft. Loosen right side retainer. Tighten left side retainer and loosen right side retainer until pinion shaft can no longer be turned. This is the "zero" state.

6) After zero state is established, loosen left side retainer 3 notches and secure with locking tab. Loosen right side retainer and retighten by hand until it stops. Repeat several times. Tighten right side retainer 1 3/4 notches further and secure with locking tab. This sets preload.

7) Using Socket (499787100), Magnet Base (498247001) and dial indicator, measure backlash. *See Fig. 26.* Backlash should be .005-.007" (.13-.18 mm). Turning retainers one notch changes backlash approximately .002" (.05 mm).

8) Remove pump housing and apply Red Lead to 3 or 4 tooth surfaces of ring gear. Install pump housing. Rotate drive pinion shaft forward and reverse several times. Remove oil pump housing and check tooth contact pattern. See GEAR TOOTH CONTACT PATTERNS article in APPLICATIONS & IDENTIFICATION section.

9) When tooth contact is correct, mark retainer positions and loosen. Install "O" rings and retighten to marked positions. Tighten lock tab bolts to 17-19 ft. lbs. (23-26 N.m). Install NEW seal pipe to converter case.

10) Install 2 oil seals to drive pinion shaft oil seal retainer with Installer (499247300). Install "O" ring to oil seal retainer with lubricant. Install seal to oil pump housing bore. Install oil seal retainer and tighten bolts to 53-71 INCH lbs. (6-8 N.m).

11) Apply lubricant to grooves on oil pump cover and install seal rings. Install rubber seal to converter case. Press bearing into transmission case. Install oil seal using plastic hammer. Install manual plate and shaft. Drive in roll pin and ensure smooth operation. Install manual lever, parking rod and nut. Tighten nut to 33-36 ft. lbs. (45-49 N.m). Install detent manual spring and position so spring's center is aligned with center of manual plate. Tighten bolt to 44-62 INCH lbs. (5-7 N.m).

12) Install lathe-cut seal rings and lip seal to low and reverse piston. Using compressor, install piston into case. *See Fig. 27.* DO NOT damage seal lip or tilt piston when installing. Using press, install needle bearing to one-way clutch inner race. Install 4 seal rings. Install spring retainer and spring on inner race and install to recessed portion of piston. Tighten bolts from rear side of transmission case to 17-20 ft. lbs. (23-27 N.m).

13) Install band servo piston assembly. Install snap ring. Set transmission case vertically on wooden blocks with rear of case down. On non-turbo models, install 2 dish plates, 6 driven plates, 6 drive plates, retaining plate and snap ring. *See Fig. 6.*

14) Apply compressed air intermittently to check operation. *See Fig. 3.* Measure clearance between snap ring and retaining plate. Clearance should be .043-.067" (1.10-1.70 mm). If clearance is not within specifications, install correct retaining plate. See LOW & REVERSE BRAKE RETAINING PLATE table.

LOW & REVERSE BRAKE RETAINING PLATE

Part No.	Thickness – In. (mm)
31667AA180	.256 (6.50)
31667AA190	.268 (6.80)
31667AA200	.280 (7.10)
31667AA210	.291 (7.40)
31667AA220	.303 (7.70)
31667AA230	.315 (8.00)
31667AA240	.323 (8.20)
31667AA250	.331 (8.40)

15) Install thrust needle bearing on one-way clutch inner race. Install forward clutch drum assembly. Rotate drum slowly, ensuring not to damage seal ring. Drum is installed correctly when its position is .098" (2.50 mm) below inner race surface.

16) Install thrust needle bearing and thrust washer to overrunning clutch hub. *See Fig. 6.* Install overrunning clutch hub into transmission case. Ensure splines are correctly engaged. Install one-way outer race assembly. Ensure splines are correctly engaged.

17) Install thrust needle bearing and thrust washer to rear internal gear. Install rear internal gear while rotating it. *See Fig. 5.* Engage thrust needle bearing with dog of overrunning clutch hub. Installation is complete when snap ring top surface of forward clutch drum is receded approximately .138" (3.50 mm) into rear internal gear.

18) Install thrust needle bearing to inside of rear planetary carrier with lubricant. Install carrier into transmission case while rotating. Install rear sun gear with oil hole facing up.

19) Attach thrust needle bearing to both sides of front planetary carrier with lubricant. Install front planetary carrier while aligning splines with forward clutch drum and while rotating pinion. Attach thrust needle bearing to front sun gear and install front sun gear while rotating. Attach thrust needle bearing to high clutch hub with lubricant and install by engaging with splines of front planetary carrier. Install high clutch assembly and engage with clutch splines.

20) Install reverse clutch assembly by engaging high clutch outer splines with reverse clutch splines and front sun gear with cut-out portion of reverse clutch drum. Install brake band assembly. Install strut to band servo piston stem and tighten temporarily to hold band in place.

21) Adjust total end play and reverse clutch end play. Measure distance from transmission case mating surface to recessed portion of high clutch drum ("H") and record. *See Fig. 28.* Measure distance from transmission case mating surface to top surface of reverse clutch drum ("M") and record.

22) Measure distance from oil pump mating surface to top surface of oil pump support with needle bearing ("h"). Measure distance from oil pump mating surface to thrust surface of reverse clutch ("m"). *See Fig. 28.*

23) Calculate clearance between high clutch drum and pump support. Use the following equation:

$$\text{Clearance} = (H + .016") - h.$$

Gasket thickness is .016" (.40 mm). Select appropriate bearing race that will provide end play of .010-.022" (.25-.55 mm) clearance. See BEARING RACE SELECTION table.

BEARING RACE SELECTION

Part No.	In. (mm)
803031021	.031 (.80)
803031022	.039 (1.00)
803031023	.047 (1.20)
803031024	.055 (1.40)
803031025	.063 (1.60)
803031026	.071 (1.80)
803031027	.079 (2.00)

24) Calculate clearance between oil pump support and end of reverse clutch drum. Use the following equation:

$$\text{Clearance} = (M + .016") - m.$$

Gasket thickness is .016" (.40 mm). Select appropriate thrust washer that will provide .022-.035" (.55-.90 mm) clearance. See THRUST WASHER SELECTION table.

THRUST WASHER SELECTION

Part No.	In. (mm)
31299AA000	.028 (.70)
31299AA010	.035 (.90)
31299AA020	.043 (1.10)
31299AA030	.051 (1.30)
31299AA040	.059 (1.50)
31299AA050	.067 (1.70)
31299AA060	.075 (1.90)

25) Install selected bearing race in recess of high clutch. Attach thrust washer to oil pump cover with lubricant. Install gasket to case mating surface. Align dowel pins and install oil pump housing to case. Ensure there is no clearance between mating surfaces. Clearance between mating surfaces indicates a damaged seal ring. Install oil pump housing nuts and tighten to 28-33 ft. lbs. (38-44 N.m).

26) Apply Liquid Gasket (Three-Bond 1215) to converter case mating surface. Ensure rubber seal and seal pipe are fitted in position. Install converter case to transmission case and tighten bolts to 28-33 ft. lbs. (38-44 N.m).

27) Install accumulators and springs to transmission case. Ensure proper spring installation positions. See ACCUMULATOR SPRING SPECIFICATIONS table.

ACCUMULATOR SPRING SPECIFICATIONS

Accumulator Spring	Outer Diameter In. (mm)	Free Length In. (mm)
1-2	1.122 (28.50)	1.752 (44.50)
2-3	.807 (20.50)	1.220 (31.00)
3-4	.681 (17.30)	1.720 (43.70)
N-D	.701 (17.80)	1.437 (36.50)

28) Install and route transmission harness. Set range select lever to No. 2 position. Install control valve body by engaging manual valve and manual lever and tightening bolts to 62-80 INCH lbs. (7-9 N.m). DO NOT pinch harness or damage gasket. Tighten control valve body bolts evenly in crisscross pattern.

29) Install oil filter to control valve body. Connect 4 electrical connectors. Install oil cooler outlet pipe. Install oil pan with magnet to transmission case. Tighten bolts evenly in crisscross pattern to 30-39 INCH lbs. (3.4-4.4 N.m).

30) On AWD models, press in NEW oil seal in extension housing. Install filter in extension housing. Install transfer clutch valve assembly and tighten bolts to 62-80 INCH lbs. (7-9 N.m). Install pipe and clamp and transfer clutch assembly to extension housing.

31) On FWD models, install vehicle speed sensor "1" to transmission case. On all models, install reduction driven gear, parking pawl and shaft. Set shift select lever to "P" and tighten drive pinion lock nut to 69-76 ft. lbs. (93-103 N.m). Stake lock nut securely.

32) On AWD models, determine extension housing end play. Measure distance from transmission case mating surface to reduction drive gear end surface ("h"). See Fig. 28. Measure distance from extension mating surface to rear drive shaft end face ("H"). On FWD models, measure distance from transmission case mating surface to bearing end face ("h"). Measure distance from cover case mating surface to bearing mounting surface ("H").

33) Calculate clearance between end of reduction drive gear and end of rear drive shaft (AWD). Use the following equation to calculate:

$$\text{Clearance} = (\text{H} + .016") - \text{h}.$$

Thickness of gasket is .016". Select appropriate thrust needle bearing to provide clearance of .002-.010" (.05-.25 mm). See THRUST BEARING SELECTION (AWD) table.

THRUST BEARING SELECTION (AWD)

Part No.	In. (mm)
806535020	.150 (3.80)
806535030	.157 (4.00)
806535040	.165 (4.20)
806535050	.173 (4.40)
806535060	.181 (4.60)
806535070	.189 (4.80)
806535090	.197 (5.00)

34) Calculate clearance between end of reduction drive gear and end of bearing (FWD). Use the following equation to calculate:

$$\text{Clearance} = (\text{H} + .016") - \text{h}.$$

Thickness of gasket is .016". Select appropriate combination of thrust shim(s) to provide clearance of .002-.010" (.05-.25 mm). Thrust washer is available in .006" (.15 mm) thickness. Part number is 31288AA000.

35) On AWD models, install selected thrust needle bearing to end surface of reduction drive gear with lubricant. Install parking return spring. Remove transfer clutch from extension housing. Install needle bearing on reduction drive shaft and install transfer clutch to transfer clutch hub. Ensure correct spline teeth engagement. Install gasket and extension housing halfway. Connect duty solenoid "C" connector. Complete gasket and extension housing installation. Tighten bolts to 17-20 ft. lbs. (23-27 N.m). Install vehicle speed sensor "1".

36) On FWD models, install selected aluminum washer(s) on cover case with lubricant. Set parking return spring. Install gasket and cover case to transmission case. Ensure proper alignment of bearing, parking shaft and reduction driven gear. Tighten bolts to 17-20 ft. lbs. (23-27 N.m).

37) On all models, install inhibitor switch to transmission case. Fit projecting portion of switch into recessed portion of case and tighten bolts temporarily. Insert range selector lever into shaft and tighten nut to 27-31 ft. lbs. (36-42 N.m). Set selector lever to "N" and adjust inhibitor switch so hole of range selector lever is aligned with inhibitor switch hole.

38) Attach transmission harness, inhibitor switch cord and vehicle sensor cord (AWD). Install oil cooler inlet and outlet pipe. Install oil charge pipe. Tighten brake band adjusting screw to 80 INCH lbs. (9 N.m) then back off 3 turns. Tighten lock nut to 18-21 ft. lbs. (25-28 N.m). Install strut bar bracket. Install air breather hoses to transmission case and oil pump housing.

39) Install input shaft while turning lightly. Install oil pump shaft to torque converter. Ensure clip fits securely in groove. Install torque converter assembly to converter case, ensuring not to damage bushing. Rotate shaft lightly by hand to engage splines securely.

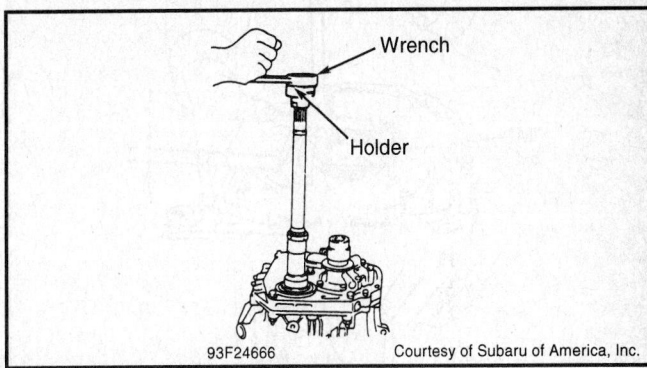

93F24666   Courtesy of Subaru of America, Inc.

Fig. 25: Setting Drive Pinion Preload

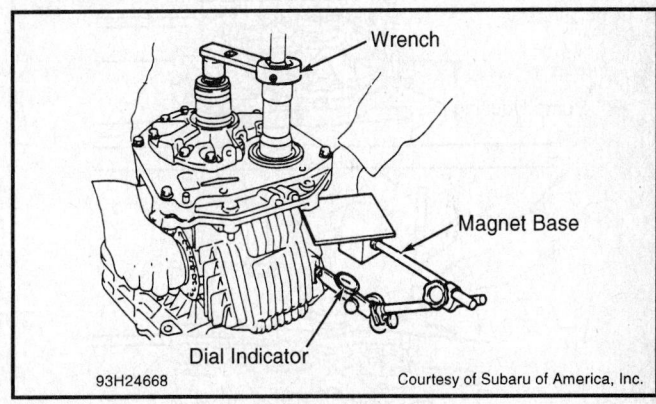

93H24668   Courtesy of Subaru of America, Inc.

Fig. 26: Measuring Differential Backlash

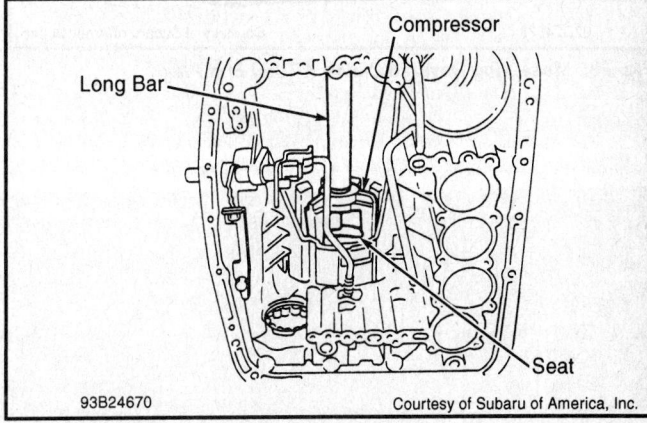

93B24670   Courtesy of Subaru of America, Inc.

Fig. 27: Installing Low & Reverse Piston

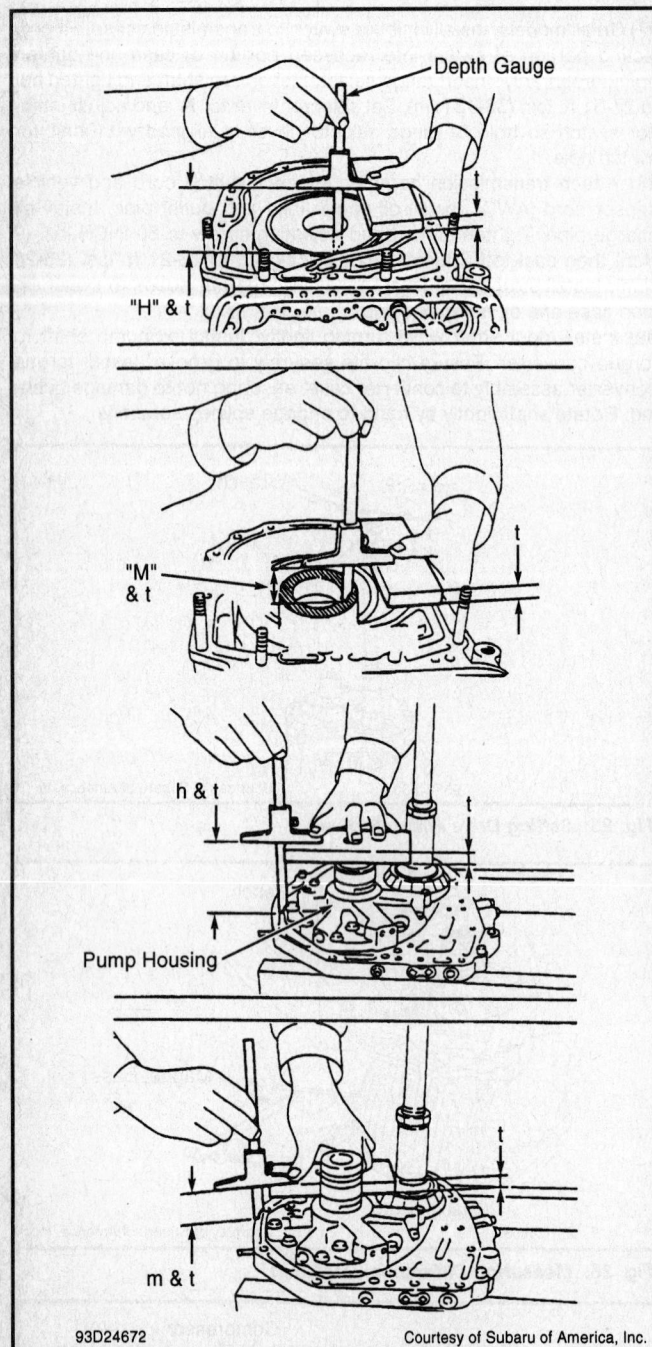

93D24672   Courtesy of Subaru of America, Inc.

Fig. 28: Measuring Reverse Clutch & Total End Play

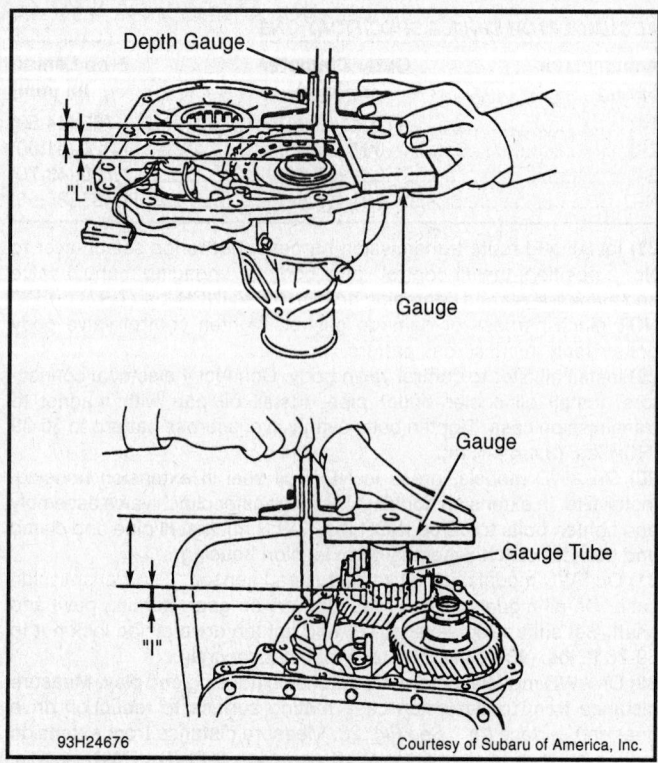

93H24676   Courtesy of Subaru of America, Inc.

Fig. 29: Measuring Transfer Clutch End Play

TORQUE SPECIFICATIONS

TORQUE SPECIFICATIONS

Application	Ft. Lbs. (N.m)
ATF Drain Plug	17-20 (23-27)
Brake Band Adjusting Screw Lock Nut	18-21 (24-28)
Converter Case Nut & Bolts	28-33 (38-44)
Cover Case Bolts (FWD)	28-33 (38-44)
Differential Drain Plug	30-35 (41-47)
Differential Oil Seal Retainer Lock Tab Bolts	17-19 (23-26)
Drive Pinion Lock Nut	79-87 (108-118)
Drive Pinion Shaft Bearing Bolts	27-31 (36-42)
Drive Pinion Shaft Lock Nut	65 (88)
Extension Bolts (AWD)	17-20 (23-27)
Manual Lever Nut	33-36 (44-49)
Oil Charge Pipe	28-33 (38-44)
Oil Cooler Inlet Pipe	17-20 (23-27)
Oil Cooler Outlet Pipe	23-28 (31-37)
Oil Pump Cover Bolts	17-20 (23-27)
Oil Pump Housing Bolts	28-33 (38-44)
Oil Pump Housing Nuts	28-33 (38-44)
Strut Bar Bracket Bolts	28-38 (38-52)
Range Selector Lever Shaft Nut	28-38 (38-52)
Rear Crossmember Bolts (On-Vehicle Service)	20-35 (27-47)
Ring Gear Bolts	42-49 (57-67)
Transaxle Pitch Stopper Bolts Body Side	35-49 (47-67)
Transaxle Pitch Stopper Bolt Engine Side	33-40 (44-54)

	INCH lbs. (N.m)
Control Valve Body Bolts	62-80 (7-9)
Control Valve Locating Bolts	62-80 (7-9)
Detent Manual Spring Bolt	44-62 (5-7)
Drive Pinion Shaft Oil Seal Retainer Bolts	53-71 (6-8)
Inhibitor Switch Bolts	26-35 (2.9-3.9)
Oil Cooler Outlet Pipe Bolts	62-80 (7-9)
Oil Pan Bolts	38-48 (4.4-5.4)
Oil Pipe Bolts	21-30 (2.4-3.4)
Oil Strainer Bolts	62-80 (7-9)
Vehicle Speed Sensor Bolt (FWD)	53-71 (6-8)
Vehicle Speed Sensor Bolt (AWD)	53-71 (6-8)
Vehicle Speed Sensor Bolt (AWD) (On-Vehicle Service)	71 (8)
Transfer Valve Body Bolts	62-80 (7-9)
Transfer Valve Body Bolts (On-Vehicle Service)	62-80 (7-9)

Impreza, Legacy, SVX

APPLICATION

APPLICATION

Vehicle	Transaxle
1995-96 Impreza	4-Speed
1995-96 Legacy	4-Speed
1995-96 SVX	4-Speed

CAUTION: Vehicle is equipped with a Supplemental Restraint System (SRS). When servicing vehicle, use care to avoid accidental air bag deployment. All SRS electrical connections and wiring harness are covered with Yellow insulation. SRS-related components are located in steering wheel, steering column, toe-board (center, left and right), instrument panel and lower panel on instrument panel, front seat floor and side seal, left lower front pillar, combination meter, and installment panel (passenger side, if equipped). DO NOT use electrical test equipment on these circuits. It may be necessary to deactivate SRS before servicing components. See AIR BAG SERVICING article in APPLICATIONS & IDENTIFICATION section.

DESCRIPTION

Automatic transaxle is electronically controlled by a Transmission Control Module (TCM). The TCM controls shift points, engine braking, lock-up torque converter operation and other various operations. The TCM receives information from various input devices and uses this information to operate duty and shift control solenoid valves. Depending on throttle position, the TCM controls shift points, lock-up torque converter operation and overdrive. An electronically controlled full-time AWD system is available. This system has a transfer hydraulic pressure control unit incorporating duty solenoid and multi-plate transfer type clutch on rear of transmission.

Vehicle also utilizes AT OIL TEMP light to indicate trouble codes. The TCM incorporates a self-diagnosis ability to detect electronic system or component malfunctions. On all models, transaxle is equipped with shift and key interlock systems. Shift interlock system prevents shift selector lever from being moved from Park unless brake pedal is depressed and accelerator is in idle position. In case of a malfunction, shift selector lever can be released by depressing button on front of shifter console. Key interlock system prevents ignition key from being removed from ignition lock assembly unless shift selector lever is in Park position.

OPERATION

NOTE: For component location, See Figs. 1 and 2.

TRANSAXLE CONTROL MODULE (TCM)

The TCM receives information from various input devices and uses this information to control shift and lock-up control solenoid valves. TCM contains a self-diagnostic system, which will store a trouble code if a failure or problem exists in electronic control system. trouble code can be retrieved to determine transaxle problem area. See RETRIEVING TROUBLE CODES.

SHIFT INTERLOCK SYSTEM

The shift lock system prevents shifting of selector lever from "P" to any other position unless brake pedal is depressed. Shifter can be moved with manual release button located in front of console in case of malfunction or lack of battery power. When shift position console switch is in Park, A/T shift lock control unit provides voltage to shift lock circuit in interlock control unit, provided brake pedal is depressed and accelerator is in idle position. Shift lock control unit then operates shift lock solenoid by controlling ground circuit. When shift lock solenoid is energized, shift selector lever is released and can be moved.

KEY INTERLOCK SYSTEM

Key interlock system prevents ignition key from being removed from ignition lock assembly on steering column unless shift selector lever is in Park. When ignition key is in ignition lock assembly, key interlock switch closes, providing voltage to key interlock solenoid and interlock control unit.

If shift selector lever is not in Park, interlock control unit energizes key interlock solenoid by completing ground circuit. When key interlock solenoid is energized, ignition key cannot be removed from ignition lock assembly. Key interlock switch and solenoid are located on ignition lock assembly.

TCM INPUT DEVICES

NOTE: For component location, See Figs. 1 and 2.

ABS Signal – When ABS system is operating, transfer clutch torque is controlled to eliminate influence of engine braking and reduce degree of coupling between front and rear wheels. This optimizes ABS control.

ATF Temperature Sensor – ATF sensor detects ATF temperature. This signal is used for inhibiting of torque converter lock-up and release of overdrive. Sensor is mounted to valve body.

Cruise Switch – The cruise switch, which is part of cruise control system, detects operation of cruise control and expands 4th gear operating range.

Engine Speed Sensor (Tach Signal) – Engine speed sensor detects engine speed. This signal is used for torque converter lock-up operation. This provides for smooth and controlled operation and prevents engine overrunning in 1st and 2nd range.

FWD Switch – FWD switch is used to change from AWD to FWD. Inserting of fuse into holder is necessary for testing purposes.

Inhibitor Switch – Inhibitor switch is used to determine shifting and line pressure for all shift ranges. Inhibitor switch also incorporates a neutral safety switch and back-up light switch. Switch is mounted to shift selector lever shaft. *See Fig. 1.*

Throttle Sensor – Throttle sensor detects throttle opening and speed of throttle being depressed. Sensor also determines shift point, line pressure and torque converter lock-up speed according to engine load.

Vehicle Speed Sensor "1" – Vehicle speed sensor "1" detects vehicle speed. This signal is used to control shifting, torque converter lock-up, line pressure and transfer clutch. Sensor is mounted to transmission. *See Fig. 1.*

Vehicle Speed Sensor "2" – In FWD mode, vehicle speed sensor "2" is used as a backup in case of failure of vehicle speed sensor "1". In AWD mode, sensor is used to control transfer clutch and as backup for sensor "1". Vehicle speed sensor "2" is built into combination meter.

TCM OUTPUT DEVICES

NOTE: For component location, See Figs. 1 and 2.

AT OIL TEMP Warning Light – Warning light illuminates when ATF exceeds a set temperature level.

Duty Solenoid "A" – Duty Solenoid "A" regulates line pressure according to driving conditions. Duty ratio of solenoid is controlled by TCM. Solenoid "A" is mounted to valve body. *See Fig. 1.*

Duty Solenoid "B" – Duty Solenoid "B" regulates hydraulic pressure of torque converter lock-up clutch and operates in 3 modes; open, smooth and lock-up. Duty ratio of solenoid is controlled by TCM. Solenoid "B" is mounted to valve body. *See Fig. 1.*

Duty Solenoid "C" – Duty Solenoid "C" regulates hydraulic pressure of transfer clutch and controls driving force to rear drive shaft. Duty ratio of solenoid is controlled by TCM. Solenoid is mounted to transfer control valve on side of extension case.

AT OIL TEMP light – Indicator light is used for oil temperature warning and self-diagnostics.

Shift Solenoids "1" & "2" – Shift Solenoids "1" and "2" controls shift stage by turning solenoid ON/OFF. When shifting, timing is controlled for each solenoid to reduce shock.

Shift Solenoid "3" – Shift Solenoid "3" controls shift timing and over-running clutch operation. Shift timing is controlled by controlling release speed of oil pressure to reduce shock while downshifting. Overrunning clutch is controlled so it will operate during coasting to apply engine brake.

SELF-DIAGNOSTIC SYSTEM

SYSTEM DIAGNOSIS

System Overview – Transmission control module (TCM) monitors transaxle operation. TCM contains a self-diagnostic system which stores trouble codes if failure or problem exists. If trouble code is stored, TCM will flash AT OIL TEMP indicator light after engine starts. Self-diagnostic system is capable of detecting any malfunction with speed sensors, throttle sensor, shift solenoids, duty solenoids, temperature sensor, ignition pulse and atmospheric pressure.

Fail Safe Function – A fail safe function is provided to maintain driveability even if trouble should occur in vehicle speed sensor, throttle sensor, inhibitor switch or or any of solenoids (duty and shift).

Vehicle Speed Sensor (VSS) – A dual speed sensing system is used. Speed signal is taken from transmission (output shaft revolution sensor) and also from a sensor built in speedometer. If one sensor system fails, vehicle can be controlled normally with other sensor system.

Throttle Sensor – If throttle sensor becomes faulty, throttle position input signal will be set to predetermined position.

Inhibitor Switch – If 2 signals are input due to inhibitor switch failure, vehicle can still be driven with limited shifting capability.

Shift Solenoids "1" & "2" – If a malfunction occurs in either solenoid, both solenoids are turned off. Vehicle can be driven only in 3rd gear. If both solenoids fail, mechanical hydraulic circuit is used.

Shift Solenoid "3" – If overrunning clutch solenoid fails, solenoid is turned off. Overrunning clutch will engage so engine brake will be applied when reducing vehicle speed.

Duty Solenoid "A" – If duty solenoid "A" fails, solenoid is turned off and line pressure is raised to maximum to enable vehicle operation.

Duty Solenoid "B" – If duty solenoid "B" fails, solenoid is turned off and torque converter lock-up is released.

Duty Solenoid "C" – If duty solenoid "C" fails, solenoid is turned off. This causes maximum oil pressure to be applied to transfer clutch so power is always transmitted to rear axle (direct coupling AWD).

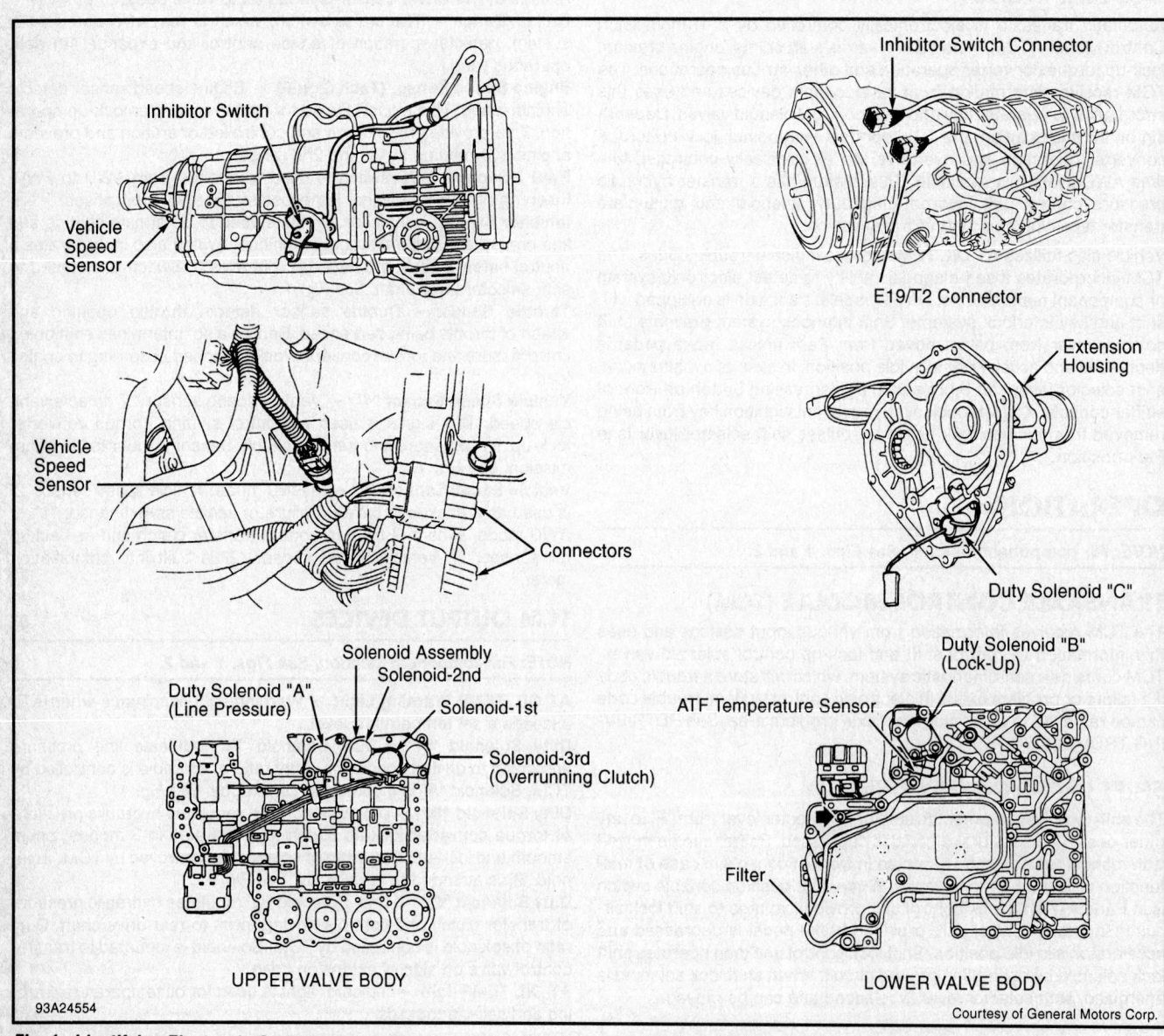

UPPER VALVE BODY

LOWER VALVE BODY

93A24554

Courtesy of General Motors Corp.

Fig. 1: Identifying Electronic Component Locations

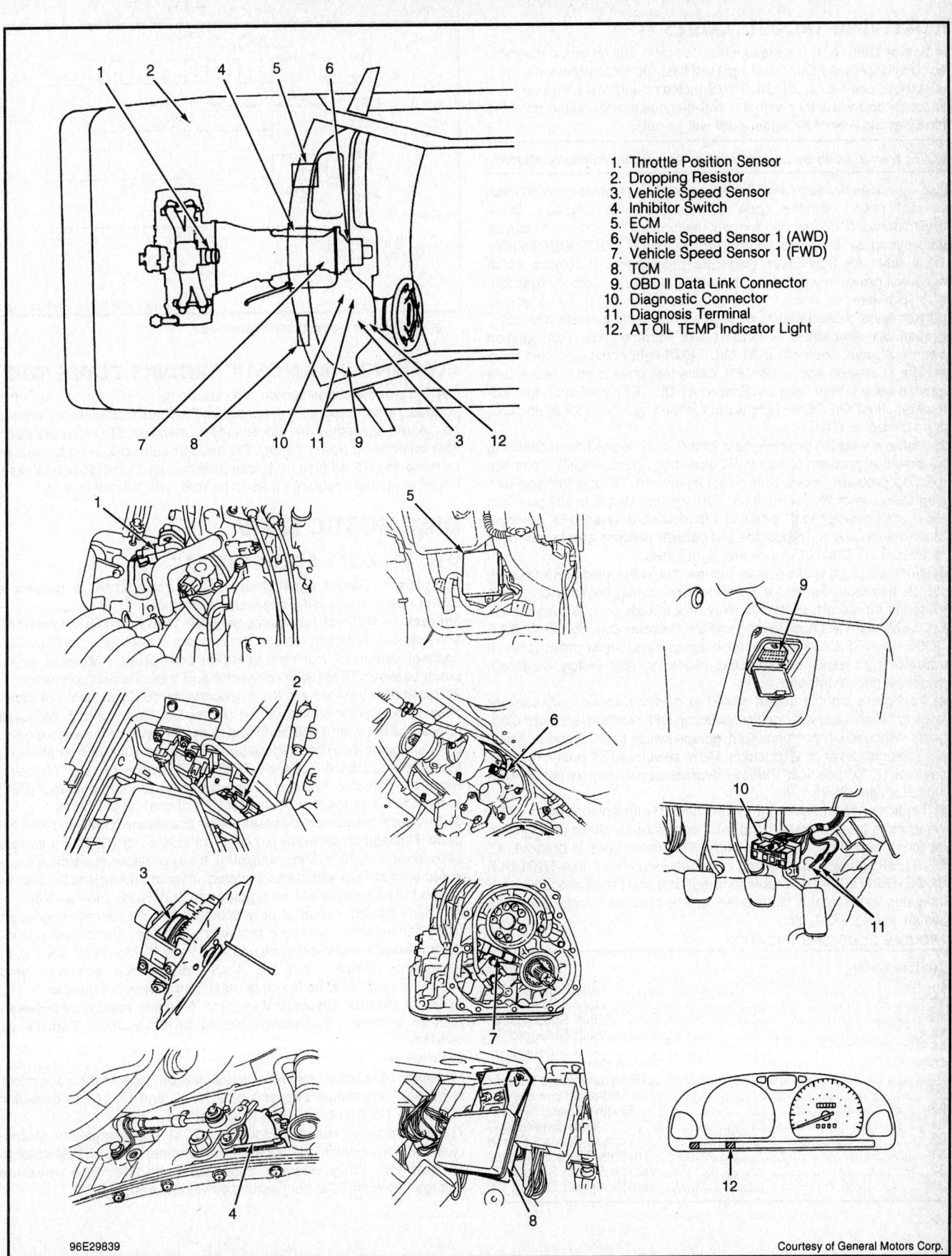

1. Throttle Position Sensor
2. Dropping Resistor
3. Vehicle Speed Sensor
4. Inhibitor Switch
5. ECM
6. Vehicle Speed Sensor 1 (AWD)
7. Vehicle Speed Sensor 1 (FWD)
8. TCM
9. OBD II Data Link Connector
10. Diagnostic Connector
11. Diagnosis Terminal
12. AT OIL TEMP Indicator Light

96E29839

Courtesy of General Motors Corp.

Fig. 2: Identifying Electronic Component Locations

RETRIEVING TROUBLE CODES

Indicator Light – **1)** If a malfunction occurs in any on board diagnostic components, AT OIL TEMP light will flash immediately when engine is started. *See Fig. 3.* AT OIL TEMP indicator light will come on for 2 seconds and will either signal a self-diagnosis malfunction (blinking for 8 seconds) or okay signal (light will go out).

NOTE: Warning can be noticed only when engine is initially started.

2) If light does not flash after initial 2 seconds, system is okay. In case of malfunction, trouble code is output as light flashes. Once preliminary procedure is performed, malfunctioning part or unit can be determined by a trouble code. See TROUBLE CODE IDENTIFICATION table for flow chart diagnosis procedures. Problems which occurred previously can also be identified through memory function. If a problem is occurring, it can be determined by checking performance characteristics of each sensor using a select monitor.

Preliminary Procedure – **1)** Start and warm engine. Turn ignition switch off, then back on. If AT OIL TEMP light comes on, test drive vehicle at speeds above 12 MPH. Once test drive is completed, turn ignition off and then back on. Ensure AT OIL TEMP indicator light illuminates. If AT OIL TEMP light is not functioning, check for faulty bulb, lamp circuit or TCM.

2) If lamp is working properly, turn ignition to OFF position. If checking for previous problem stored in ECU memory, go to step **6)**. To check existing problem, move shift selector lever to "D" position and turn diagnosis switch to ON position. Turn ignition switch to ON position. Move shift selector to "3" position. Move selector lever to "2" position. Move select lever to "1" position and partially depress accelerator pedal. Ensure AT OIL TEMP indicator light blinks.

3) If indicator light blinks 4 times per second (with ignition switch OFF), vehicle has faulty battery. If indicator continuously blinks until ignition switch is turned off, system is okay. If a trouble code is present, AT OIL TEMP light will flash in long and short sequences. See TROUBLE CODE IDENTIFICATION table for diagnosis and repair procedures. If indicator light remains illuminated, check inhibitor switch, diagnosis switch, wiring, TCM, etc.

4) To access trouble codes stored in memory, move shift selector lever to "1" position with ignition switch in OFF position, and turn diagnosis switch to ON position. Turn ignition switch to ON position. Move shift selector lever to "2" position. Move selector to "3" position. Move selector to "D" position. Partially depress accelerator pedal. Ensure indicator light blinks.

5) If indicator light blinks 4 times per second (with ignition switch OFF), vehicle has faulty battery. If indicator continuously blinks until ignition switch is turned off, system is okay. If a trouble code is present, AT OIL TEMP light will flash in long and short sequences. See TROUBLE CODE IDENTIFICATION table for diagnosis and repair procedures. If indicator light remains illuminated, check inhibitor switch, diagnosis switch, wiring, TCM, etc.

TROUBLE CODE IDENTIFICATION

Trouble Code	Component
11	Duty Solenoid "A"
12	Duty Solenoid "B"
13	Shift Solenoid "3"
14	Shift Solenoid "2"
15	Shift Solenoid "1"
16	Torque Control Cut Signal
21	ATF Temperature Sensor
22	Mass Airflow Sensor
23	Engine Speed Sensor
24	Duty Solenoid C
25	Torque Control Signal
31	Throttle Position Sensor
32	Vehicle Speed Sensor "1"
33	Vehicle Speed Sensor "2"

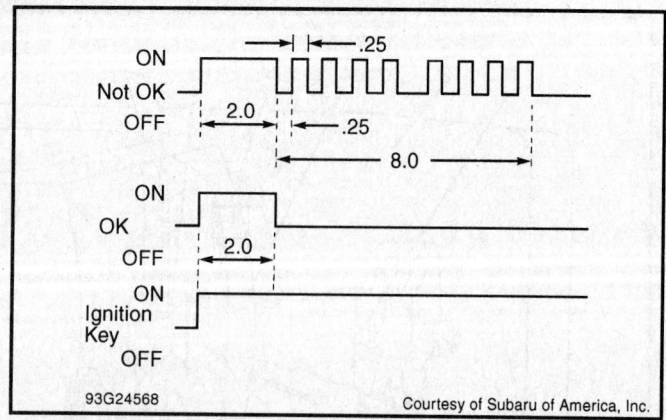

93G24568   Courtesy of Subaru of America, Inc.

Fig. 3: Trouble Code Blink Sequence

CLEARING DIAGNOSTIC TROUBLE CODES (DTC)

Current trouble codes shown are cleared by turning ignition off after conducting self-diagnosis procedures. Previous trouble codes cannot be cleared since they are stored in ECU memory. ECU memory operates on back-up power supply. Previous trouble codes can be cleared by removing No. 14 fuse from fuse panel located behind hood release. Clearing memory requires fuse to be removed for one minute.

DIAGNOSTIC TESTS

DTC 11: DUTY SOLENOID "A"

Symptom – Output signal circuit of duty solenoid "A" or resistor is open or shorted, causing excessive shift shock.

Impreza – **1)** Check harnesses between TCM and duty solenoid "A", and between TCM and resistor. Disconnect connector from TCM. Disconnect connector from transmission and resistor. Measure resistance between TCM (B52) connector and transmission connector.

2) Resistance between pin No. 8 of connector (B52) and No. 7 of transmission connector should be 0-1 ohms. *See Figs. 4 and 5.* Measure resistance between TCM (B52) and body. Resistance between pin No. 8 of connector (B52) and vehicle body should be 100k/ohms minimum. Measure resistance between TCM (B52) connector and dropping resistor connector. Resistance between pin No. 7 of connector (B52) and pin No. 1 of resistor connector (B1) should be 0-1 ohms.

3) Measure resistance between TCM connector (B52) and vehicle body. Resistance between pin No. 7 of connector (B52) and vehicle body should be 100k/ohms minimum. If any previous resistance measurements are not within specification, inspect and repair circuit(s) as needed. See appropriate wiring diagram in WIRING DIAGRAMS.

4) Check ground circuit of duty solenoid "A". Disconnect connector from transmission. Measure resistance between transmission connector receptacle (on transmission) and transmission case. *See Fig. 5.* Resistance between pin No. 4 of transmission connector and transmission should be 0-1 ohm maximum. Repair as needed.

5) Check resistor. Disconnect resistor. Measure resistance between resistor terminals. Resistance should be 9-15 ohms. Replace as needed.

6) Check duty solenoid "A". Disconnect connector from transmission. Measure resistance between transmission connector receptacle terminals. Resistance between pins No. 7 and No. 4 of connector should be 1.5-4.5 ohms. Replace as needed.

7) Measure signal voltage output from TCM. Warm engine and transmission. Turn ignition on. DO NOT start engine. Move shift selector to "N" position. While opening and closing throttle valve, measure voltage between TCM connector and vehicle body.

8) Voltage between pins No. 8 and 10 on (B52) connector with throttle fully closed should be 1.5-4.0 volts. *See Fig. 4.* With throttle fully open (WOT), voltage should not exceed one volt maximum. Voltage between pins No. 7 and No. 10 with throttle fully closed should be 5-14 volts. With throttle fully open voltage at pins No. 7 and No. 10 should be one volt maximum. If voltage is not within specification, replace TCM and retest.

NOTE: Connectors are identified for both models. Legacy model is listed first and SVX model second. Example; (B55/68)=(Legacy/ SVX). Pin locations and numbers that are not identical for Legacy/ SVX, may be identified as follows; Terminal No. 36/20.

Legacy & SVX – 1) Check Harnesses Between TCM and duty solenoid "A", and between TCM and resistor. Disconnect connector from TCM. Disconnect connector from transmission and resistor. Measure resistance between TCM (B55/68) connector and transmission connector.

2) Resistance between pin No. 8 of connector (B55/68) and pin No. 7 of transmission connector should be 0-1 ohms. *See Fig. 5.* Measure resistance between TCM (B55/68) and body. Resistance between pin No. 8 of connector (B55/68) and vehicle body should be 100k/ohms minimum. Measure resistance between TCM (B55/68) connector and dropping resistor connector. Resistance between pin No. 7 of connector (B55/68) and pin No. 1 of resistor connector should be 0-1 ohms.

3) Measure resistance between TCM connector (B55/68) and vehicle body. Resistance between pin No. 7 of connector (B55/68) and vehicle body should be 100 k/ohms minimum. If any previous resistance measurements are not within specification, inspect and repair circuit(s) as needed. See appropriate wiring diagram in WIRING DIAGRAMS.

4) Check ground circuit of duty solenoid "A". Disconnect connector from transmission. Measure resistance between transmission connector receptacle (on transmission) and transmission case. *See Fig. 5.* Resistance between pin No. 4 of transmission connector and transmission should be one ohm maximum. Repair as needed.

5) Check resistor. Disconnect resistor. Measure resistance between resistor terminals. Resistance should be 9-15 ohms. Replace as needed.

6) Check duty solenoid "A". Disconnect connector from transmission. Measure resistance between transmission connector receptacle terminals. Resistance between pins No. 7 and No. 4 of connector should be 1.5-4.5 ohms. Replace as needed.

7) Measure signal voltage output from TCM. Warm engine and transmission. Turn ignition on. DO NOT start engine. Move shift selector to "N" position. While opening and closing throttle valve, measure voltage between TCM connector (B55/68) and vehicle body.

8) Voltage between pins No. 8 and 10 on (B55/68) connector with throttle fully closed should be 1.5-4.0 volts. With throttle fully open (WOT), voltage should not exceed 1 volt. Measure voltage between pins No. 7 and 10 on (B55/68) connector. With throttle fully closed, voltage should be 5-14 volts. With throttle fully open (WOT), voltage should not exceed .05 volts. If voltage is not within specification,

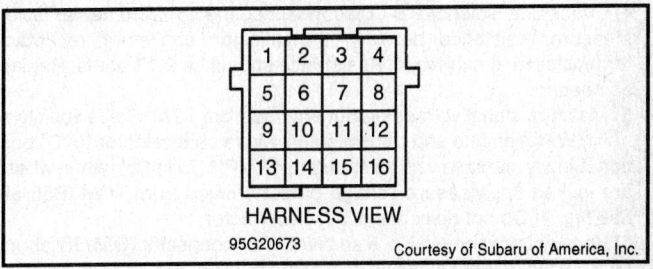

95G20673　　　　Courtesy of Subaru of America, Inc.

Fig. 5: Identifying Transmission Connector Pin Locations

replace TCM and retest. If voltage is not within specification, replace TCM and retest. Pin No. 10 is connected to vehicle ground through duty solenoid "A".

DTC 12: DUTY SOLENOID "B"

Symptom – Output signal circuit of duty solenoid "B" is open or shorted, causing no "lock-up" after engine warm-up.

Impreza – 1) Check harness between TCM and duty solenoid "B". Disconnect connector from TCM. Disconnect connector from transmission. Measure resistance between TCM (B52) connector and transmission connector. *See Figs. 4 and 5.*

2) Resistance between pin No. 7 of connector (B52) and pin No. 6 of transmission connector should be 0-1 ohms. Measure resistance between TCM (B52) connector and vehicle body. Resistance between pin No. 7 of connector (B52) and vehicle body should be 100 k/ohms minimum.

3) Check ground circuit of duty solenoid "B". Disconnect connector from transmission. Measure resistance between transmission connector receptacle and transmission case. *See Fig. 5.* Resistance between pin No. 4 of connector and case should be one ohm maximum. If any previously measured resistances are not within specification, repair circuit(s) as needed. See appropriate wiring diagram in WIRING DIAGRAMS.

4) Check duty solenoid "B". Disconnect connector from transmission. Measure resistance between transmission connector receptacle terminals No. 6 and No. 4. Resistance should be 10-17 ohms. Replace solenoid as needed.

5) Measure signal voltage output emitted from TCM. Raise vehicle on hoist. Warm engine and transmission. Move shift selector to "D" position. Slowly increase vehicle speed to 37 MPH (60 km/h), when wheels are locked up (converter lock-up). Measure voltage output emitted from TCM (B52). Do not disconnect TCM connector. *See Fig. 4.*

6) Voltage between pin No. 7 and No. 13 of connector (B52) should be 8.5 volts minimum. Move shift selector to "N" position. Voltage should be reduced to .5 volts, maximum. If voltage is not within specification, replace TCM and retest.

NOTE: Connectors are identified for both models. Legacy model is listed first and SVX model second. Example; (B55/68)=(Legacy/ SVX). Pin locations and numbers that are not identical for Legacy/ SVX, may be identified as follows; Terminal No. 36/20.

Legacy & SVX – 1) Check harness between TCM and duty solenoid "B". Disconnect connector from TCM. Disconnect connector from transmission. Measure resistance between TCM (B55/68) connector and transmission connector. *See Figs. 4 and 5.*

2) Resistance between pin No. 5 of connector (B55/68) and pin No. 6 of transmission connector should be 0-1 ohms. Measure resistance between TCM (B55/68) connector and vehicle body. Resistance between pin No. 5 of connector (B55/68) and vehicle body should be 100 k/ohms minimum.

3) Check ground line of duty solenoid "B". Disconnect connector from transmission. Measure resistance between transmission connector receptacle and transmission case. Resistance between pin No. 4 of connector and case should be one ohm maximum. If any previously measured resistances are not within specification, repair circuit(s) as needed. See appropriate wiring diagram in WIRING DIAGRAMS.

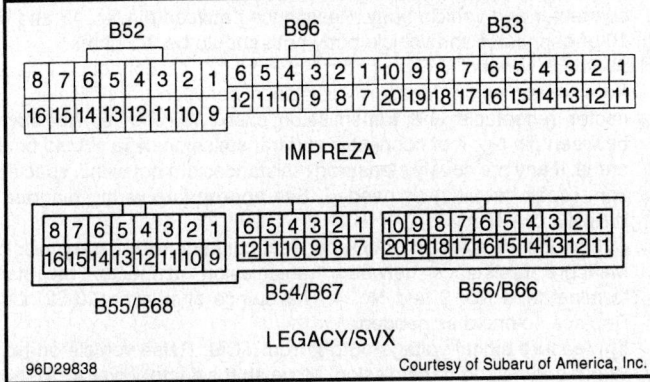

96D29838　　　　　　　Courtesy of Subaru of America, Inc.

**Fig. 4: Identifying TCM Connector Pin Locations
(Component View)**

4) Check duty solenoid "B". Disconnect connector from transmission. Measure resistance between transmission connector receptacle terminals No. 6 and No. 4. Resistance should be 9-17 ohms. Replace as needed.

5) Measure signal voltage output emitted from TCM. Raise vehicle on hoist. Warm engine and transmission. Move shift selector to "D" position. Slowly increase vehicle speed to 47 MPH (75 km/h), when wheels are locked up. Measure voltage output emitted from TCM (B55/68). *See Fig. 4.* Do not disconnect TCM connector.

6) Voltage between pin No. 5 and No. 10 of connector (B55/68) should be 8.5 volts or more when wheels are locked up. If voltage is not within specification, replace TCM and retest.

DTC 13: SHIFT SOLENOID "3"

Symptom – Output signal circuit of shift solenoid "3" is open or shorted, causing ineffective engine brake with shift lever in "3" position.

Impreza – **1)** Check harness between TCM and shift solenoid "3". Disconnect connector from TCM. Disconnect connector from transmission. Measure resistance between TCM (B52) connector and transmission connector. *See Figs. 4 and 5.*

2) Resistance between pin No. 8 of TCM connector and pin No. 1 of transmission connector should be 0-1 ohms. Resistance between pin No. 13 of TCM connector and pin No. 4 of transmission connector should be 0-1 ohms. Measure resistance between TCM connector and vehicle body. Resistance between pins No. 8 and 13 of connector and vehicle body should be 100 k/ohms minimum.

3) Check ground circuit of shift solenoid. Disconnect connector from transmission. Measure resistance between transmission connector receptacle and transmission case. Resistance between pin No. 4 of connector and transmission case should be 0-1 ohms. If previously measured resistances are not within specification, repair circuit(s) as needed. See appropriate wiring diagram in WIRING DIAGRAMS.

4) Check shift solenoid. Disconnect connector from transmission. Measure resistance between transmission connector receptacle terminals. *See Fig. 5.* Resistance between pin No. 1 and No. 4 of connector should be 20-30 ohms. Replace solenoid as needed.

5) Measure signal voltage output from TCM. Raise vehicle on hoist. Warm engine and transmission. Move shift selector lever to "D" position. Measure signal voltage output emitted from TCM connector while engine is idling. Do not disconnect connector. Measure voltage between pin No. 8 and No. 13 of connector B52. *See Fig. 4.* Voltage should be 10-14 volts. If voltage is not within specification, replace TCM and retest.

NOTE: Connectors are identified for both models. Legacy model is listed first and SVX model second. Example; (B55/68)=(Legacy/SVX). Pin locations and numbers that are not identical for Legacy/SVX, may be identified as follows; Terminal No. 36/20.

Legacy & SVX – **1)** Check harness between TCM and shift solenoid "3". Disconnect connector from TCM. Disconnect connector from transmission. Measure resistance between TCM (B55/68) connector and transmission connector. *See Figs. 4 and 5.*

2) Resistance between pin No. 15 of TCM connector and pin No. 1 of transmission connector should be 0-1 ohms. Resistance between pin No. 10 of TCM connector and pin No. 4 of transmission connector should be 0-1 ohms. Measure resistance between TCM connector and vehicle body. Resistance between pins No. 10 and 15 of connector and vehicle body should be 100 k/ohms minimum.

3) Check ground circuit of shift solenoid. Disconnect connector from transmission. Measure resistance between transmission connector receptacle and transmission case. Resistance between pin No. 4 of connector and transmission case should be 0-1 ohms. If any previously measured resistances are not within specification, repair circuit(s) as needed. See appropriate wiring diagram in WIRING DIAGRAMS.

4) Check shift solenoid. Disconnect connector from transmission. Measure resistance between transmission connector receptacle terminals. *See Fig. 5.* Resistance between pin No. 1 and No. 4 of connector should be 20-30 ohms. Replace solenoid as needed.

5) Measure signal voltage output from TCM. Raise vehicle on hoist. Warm engine and transmission. Move shift selector lever to "D" position. Measure signal voltage output emitted from TCM connector while engine is idling. Do not disconnect connector. Measure voltage between pin No. 15 and No. 10 of connector (B55/68). *See Fig. 4.* Voltage should be 10-14 volts. If voltage is not within specification, replace TCM and retest.

DTC 14: SHIFT SOLENOID "2"

Symptom – Output signal circuit of shift solenoid "2" is open or shorted, causing "No Shift" condition.

Impreza – **1)** Check harness between TCM and shift solenoid "2". Disconnect connector from TCM. Disconnect connector from transmission. Measure resistance between TCM (B52) connector and transmission connector. *See Figs. 4 and 5.*

2) Resistance between pin No. 9 of connector (B52) and pin No. 2 of transmission connector should be 0-1 ohms. Resistance between pin No. 13 of TCM connector and pin No. 4 of transmission connector should be 0-1 ohms. Measure resistance between TCM connector and vehicle body. Resistance between pin No. 9 and No. 13 of connector and vehicle body should be 0-1 ohms.

3) Check ground circuit of shift solenoid "2". Disconnect connector from transmission. Measure resistance between transmission connector receptacle and transmission case. *See Fig. 5.* Resistance between pin No. 4 of connector and transmission case should be 0-1 ohms. If any previously measured resistances are not within specification, repair circuit(s) as needed. See appropriate wiring diagram in WIRING DIAGRAMS.

4) Check shift solenoid "2". Disconnect connector from transmission. Measure resistance between transmission connector receptacle terminal pins No. 2 and No. 4. Resistance should be 20-30 ohms. Replace solenoid as needed.

5) Measure signal voltage output from TCM. Raise vehicle on hoist. Warm engine and transmission. Move shift selector lever to "D" position. Measure signal voltage output emitted from TCM (B52) when engine is idling. *See Fig. 4.* Do not disconnect connector.

6) Voltage between pin No. 13 and No. 9 of connector (B52) should be 10-14 volts. If voltage is not within specification, replace TCM and retest.

NOTE: Connectors are identified for both models. Legacy model is listed first and SVX model second. Example; (B55/68)=(Legacy/SVX). Pin locations and numbers that are not identical for Legacy/SVX, may be identified as follows; Terminal No. 36/20.

Legacy & SVX – **1)** Check harness between TCM and shift solenoid "2". Disconnect connector from TCM. Disconnect connector from transmission. Measure resistance between TCM (B55/68) connector and transmission connector. *See Figs. 4 and 5.*

2) Resistance between pin No. 13 of connector (B55/68) and pin No. 2 of transmission connector should be 0-1 ohms. Resistance between pin No. 10 of TCM connector and pin No. 4 of transmission connector should be 100 k/ohms minimum. Measure resistance between TCM connector and vehicle body. Resistance between pin No. 13 and No. 10 of connector and vehicle body both should be 0-1 ohms.

3) Check ground circuit of shift solenoid "2". Disconnect connector from transmission. Measure resistance between transmission connector receptacle and transmission case. *See Fig. 5.* Resistance between pin No. 4 of connector and transmission case should be 0-1 ohms. If any previously measured resistances are not within specification, repair circuit(s) as needed. See appropriate wiring diagram in WIRING DIAGRAMS.

4) Check shift solenoid "2". Disconnect connector from transmission. Measure resistance between transmission connector receptacle terminal pins No. 2 and No. 4. Resistance should be 20-32 ohms. Replace solenoid as needed.

5) Measure signal voltage output from TCM. Raise vehicle on hoist. Warm engine and transmission. Move shift selector lever to "D" position. Measure signal voltage output emitted from TCM (B55/68) when engine is idling. *See Fig. 4.* Do not disconnect connector.

6) Voltage between pin No. 13 and No. 10 of connector (B55/68) should be 10-14 volts. If voltage is not within specification, replace TCM and retest.

DTC 15: SHIFT SOLENOID "1"

Symptom – Output signal circuit of shift solenoid "1" is open or shorted causing a no shift condition.

Impreza – **1)** Check harness between TCM and shift solenoid "1". Disconnect connector from TCM. Disconnect connector from transmission. Measure resistance between TCM (B52) connector and transmission connector. *See Figs. 4 and 5.*

2) Resistance between pin No. 10 of (B52) connector and pin No. 3 of transmission connector should be 0-1 ohms. Resistance between pin No. 13 of (B52) connector and pin No. 4 of transmission connector should be 0-1 ohms. Measure resistance between TCM (B52) connector and vehicle body. Resistance between pins No. 10 and No. 13 and vehicle body should both be 100k/ohms minimum.

3) Check ground line of shift solenoid "1". Disconnect connector from transmission. Measure resistance between transmission connector receptacle and transmission case. Resistance between pin No. 4 of connector and transmission case should be 0-1 ohms. If any previously measured resistances are not within specification, repair circuit(s) as needed. See appropriate wiring diagram in WIRING DIAGRAMS.

4) Check shift solenoid "1". Disconnect connector from transmission. Measure resistance between transmission connector receptacle terminals. *See Fig. 5.* Resistance between pins No. 3 and No. 4 should be 20-30 ohms. Replace solenoid as needed.

5) Measure signal voltage output from TCM. Raise vehicle on hoist. Warm engine and transmission. Move shift selector to "D" position.

6) Measure signal voltage output emitted from TCM (B52) when engine is idling. *See Fig. 4.* Do not disconnect connector. Voltage between pin No. 10 and No. 13 of connector (B52) should be 10-14 volts. If voltage is not within specification, replace TCM.

NOTE: Connectors are identified for both models. Legacy model is listed first and SVX model second. Example; (B55/68)=(Legacy/SVX). Pin locations and numbers that are not identical for Legacy/SVX, may be identified as follows; Terminal No. 36/20.

Legacy & SVX – **1)** Check harness between TCM and shift solenoid "1". Disconnect connector from TCM. Disconnect connector from transmission. Measure resistance between TCM (B55/68) connector and transmission connector. *See Figs. 4 and 5.*

2) Resistance between pin No. 14 of (B55/68) connector and pin No. 3 of transmission connector should be 0-1 ohms. Resistance between pin No. 10 of (B55/68) connector and pin No. 4 of transmission connector should be 0-1 ohms. Measure resistance between TCM (B55/68) connector and vehicle body. Resistance between pins No. 14 and No. 10 and vehicle body should both be 100k/ohms minimum.

3) Check ground circuit of shift solenoid "1". Disconnect connector from transmission. Measure resistance between transmission connector receptacle and transmission case. Resistance between pin No. 4 of connector and transmission case should be 0-1 ohms. If any previously measured resistances are not within specification, repair circuit(s) as needed. See appropriate wiring diagram in WIRING DIAGRAMS.

4) Check shift solenoid "1". Disconnect connector from transmission. Measure resistance between transmission connector receptacle terminals. *See Fig. 5.* Resistance between pins No. 3 and No. 4 should be 20-30 ohms. Replace solenoid as needed.

5) Measure signal voltage output from TCM. Raise vehicle on hoist. Warm engine and transmission. Move shift selector to "D" position.

6) Measure signal voltage output emitted from TCM (B55/68) when engine is idling. *See Fig. 4.* Do not disconnect connector. Voltage between pins No. 14 and No. 10 of connector (B55/68) should be 10-14 volts. If voltage is not within specification, replace TCM and retest.

DTC 16: TORQUE CONTROL CUT SIGNAL

Symptom – Torque control signal is open or shorted from ECM.

Impreza – **1)** Check harness connector between TCM and ECM. With ignition OFF, disconnect connectors from ECM and TCM. Measure resistance between connector (B53) No. 16 and connector (E29) No. 36. Resistance should be 0-1 ohms. Measure resistance of harness connector (B53) No. 16 and body. Resistance should be 100k ohms minimum.

2) Check ground line of TCM. Measure resistance of harness connector (B53) terminal No. 1 and vehicle body. Resistance should be 0-1 ohms. If any previously measured resistances are not within specification, repair circuit(s) as needed. See appropriate wiring diagram in WIRING DIAGRAMS.

3) Measure signal voltage input of TCM. Turn igniton switch ON. Measure voltage between pins (B53) No. 16 and vehicle body. Voltage should be 6-9 volts. If voltage is not within specification replace TCM.

Legacy & SVX – **1)** Check resistance between TCM harness connector (B56/66) terminal No. 16 and ECM harness connector (B84/B59) terminal No. 36/20. Resistance should be 0-1 ohms. Measure resistance between TCM harness connector (B56/B66) terminal No. 16 and vehicle body. Resistance should be 100k ohms minimum.

2) Check TCM ground. Measure resistance of harness connector (B56/66) terminal No. 1 to vehicle body. Resistance should be 0-1 ohms. If any previously measured resistances are not within specification, repair circuit(s) as needed. See appropriate wiring diagram in WIRING DIAGRAMS.

3) Check voltage signal to TCM. With ignition switch on, measure voltage between TCM (B56/66) connector terminal No. 1 and body. Voltage should be 6-9 volts. If voltage is not within specifications, replace TCM and retest.

DTC 21: ATF TEMPERATURE SENSOR

Symptom – Input signal circuit of TCM to ATF temperature sensor is open or shorted causing harsh shift feel (excessive shift shock).

Impreza – **1)** Check harness between TCM and ATF temperature sensor. Disconnect connector from TCM. Disconnect connector from transmission. Measure resistance between TCM (B53) connector and transmission connector. *See Figs. 4 and 5.* Resistance between pin No. 19 of connector (B53) and pin No. 5 of transmission connector should be 0-1 ohms.

2) Measure resistance between TCM (B53) connector and transmission connector. Resistance between pin No. 4 of connector (B53) and pin No. 12 of transmission connector should be 0-1 ohms.

3) Measure resistance between TCM (B53) connector and vehicle body. Resistance between pin No. 19 of connector (B53) and vehicle body should be 100k/ohms minimum. If any previously measured resistances are not within specification, inspect and repair circuit(s) as needed. See appropriate wiring diagram in WIRING DIAGRAMS.

4) Check ATF temperature sensor. Disconnect connector from transmission. Measure resistance between transmission receptacle terminals. *See Fig. 5.* Resistance between pin No. 5 and No. 12 of connector receptacle should be 2.1-2.9 k/ohms with ATF temperature of 68°F (20°C).

5) Connect connector to transmission. Warm engine to increase ATF temperature. Stop engine and disconnect connector from transmission. Measure resistance between transmission connector receptacle terminals. Resistance between pin No. 5 and No. 12 should be 275-375 ohms with ATF temperature of 176°F (80°C). Replace sensor as needed.

6) Measure signal voltage input of TCM. Turn ignition on with engine not running. Measure signal voltage input of TCM. Do not disconnect TCM connector. Measure voltage between pins No. 19 and 4 of connector (B53). *See Fig. 4.* Voltage should be 2.9-4.0 volts with ATF temperature of 68°F (20°C).

7) Start and warm engine and transmission. Measure voltage. Voltage should be 1.0-1.4 volts with ATF temperature of 176°F (80°C). If voltage is not within specification, replace TCM and retest.

NOTE: Connectors are identified for both models. Legacy model is listed first and SVX model second. Example; (B55/68)=(Legacy/ SVX). Pin locations and numbers that are not identical for Legacy/ SVX, may be identified as follows; Terminal No. 36/20.

Legacy & SVX – 1) Check harness between TCM and ATF temperature sensor. Disconnect connector from TCM. Disconnect connector from transmission. Measure resistance between TCM (B54/67) connector and transmission connector. *See Figs. 4 and 5.* Resistance between pin No. 10 of connector (B54/67) and pin No. 5 of transmission connector should be 0-1 ohms.

2) Measure resistance between TCM (B56/66) connector and transmission connector. Resistance between pin No. 20 of connector (B56/66) and pin No. 12 of transmission connector should be 0-1 ohms.

3) Measure resistance between TCM (B54/67) connector and vehicle body. Resistance between pin No. 10 of connector (B54/67) and vehicle body should be 100k/ohms minimum. If any previously measured resistances are not within specification, inspect and repair circuit(s) as needed. See appropriate wiring diagram in WIRING DIAGRAMS.

4) Check ATF temperature sensor. Disconnect connector from transmission. Measure resistance between transmission receptacle terminals. *See Fig. 5.* Resistance between pin No. 5 and No. 12 of connector receptacle should be 2.1-2.9k/ohms for Legacy 2.3-2.7k/ohms for SVX with ATF temperature of 68°F (20°C).

5) Connect connector to transmission. Warm engine to increase ATF temperature. Stop engine and disconnect connector from transmission. Measure resistance between transmission connector receptacle terminals. Resistance between pin No. 5 and No. 12 should be 275-378 ohms for Legacy and 280-360 ohms for SVX with ATF temperature of 176°F (80°C). Replace sensor as needed.

6) Measure signal voltage input of TCM. Turn ignition on with engine not running. Measure signal voltage input of TCM. Do not disconnect TCM connector. Measure voltage between pin No. 10 of connector (B54/67) and pin No. 20 of connector (B56/66). *See Fig. 4.* Voltage should be 2.9-4.0 volts with ATF temperature of 68°F (20°C).

7) Start and warm engine and transmission. Measure voltage. Voltage should be 1.0-1.4 volt with ATF temperature of 176°F (80°C). If voltage is not within specification, replace TCM and retest.

DTC 22: MASS AIR FLOW SIGNAL

Symptom – Input signal circuit of TCM from ECM is open or shorted.
Impreza – 1) Check vehicle for engine related DTC'S. Using scan tool, check for mass air flow trouble code. Check harness connector between TCM and ECM. With ignition off, disconnect connectors from TCM and ECM. Measure resistance between TCM harness connector (B96) terminal No. 9 and ECM harness connector (E29) terminal No. 35. Resistance should be .0-1 ohms. Measure resistance of TCM harness connector (B96) terminal No. 9 and vehicle body. Resistance should be 100 k/ohms minimum. If any previously measured resistances are not within specification, inspect and repair circuit(s) as needed. See appropriate wiring diagram in WIRING DIAGRAMS.

2) Check input signal for TCM. Reconnect connectors to TCM and ECM. Start engine. After engine warm up, measure signal voltage between TCM connector (B96) terminal No. 9 and vehicle body. Voltage should be .5-1.2 volts. If voltage is not within specification, replace TCM and retest.

Legacy & SVX – 1) Check vehicle for engine related DTC'S. Using scan tool, check for mass air flow trouble code. Check harness connector between TCM and ECM. With ignition off, disconnect connectors from TCM and ECM. Measure resistance between TCM harness connector (B54/B67) terminal No. 9 and ECM connector (B84/ B59) terminal No. 35/16. Resistance should be 0-1 ohms.

2) Measure resistance between TCM harness connector (B54/67) terminal No. 9 and vehicle body. Resistance should be 100k/ohms minimum. If any previously measured resistances are not within specification, inspect and repair circuit(s) as needed. See appropriate wiring diagram in WIRING DIAGRAMS.

3) Check input signal for TCM. Check input signal for TCM. Reconnect connectors to TCM and ECM. Start engine. After engine warm up, measure signal voltage between TCM connector (B54/67) terminal No. 9 and vehicle body. Voltage should be .5-1.2 volts. If voltage is not within specification, replace TCM and retest.

DTC 23: ENGINE SPEED SIGNAL

Symptom – Engine speed input signal circuit is open or shorted causing a no lock-up condition after engine warm-up, and AT OIL TEMP indicator remains on when vehicle is not moving.
Impreza – 1) Check harness between TCM and ECU (MPFI). Disconnect connector from TCM. Disconnect connector from ECU. Measure resistance between TCM (B52) connector and ECU (B29) connector. *See Figs. 4 and 6.* Resistance between pin No. 4 of connector (B52) and pin No. 3 of connector (B29) should be 0-1 ohms.

2) Measure resistance between pin No. 4 of connector (B52) and vehicle body. Resistance should be 100 k/ohms minimum. If any measured resistances are not within specification, inspect and repair circuit(s) as needed. See appropriate wiring diagram in WIRING DIAGRAMS.

3) Measure signal voltage input of TCM. Turn ignition on with engine not running. Measure signal voltage input of TCM. Do not disconnect connector. *See Fig. 4.* Voltage between pin No. 4 of connector (B52) and vehicle body should be 10.5 volts minimum. If voltage is not within specification, replace TCM and retest.

NOTE: Connectors are identified for both models. Legacy model is listed first and SVX model second. Example; (B55/68)=(Legacy/ SVX). Pin locations and numbers that are not identical for Legacy/ SVX, may be identified as follows; Terminal No. 36/20.

Legacy & SVX – 1) Check harness between TCM and ECU (MPFI). Disconnect connector from TCM. Disconnect connector from ECU. Measure resistance between TCM (B54/67) connector and ECU (B56/ 61) connector. *See Figs. 4 and 6.* Resistance between pin No. 5 of connector (B54/67) and pin No. 16 of connector B56/61 should be 0-1 ohms.

2) Measure resistance between pin No. 5 of connector (B54/67) and vehicle body. Resistance should be 100 k/ohms minimum. If any measured resistances are not within specification, inspect and repair circuit(s) as needed. See appropriate wiring diagram in WIRING DIAGRAMS.

3) Measure signal voltage input of TCM. Turn ignition on with engine not running. Measure signal voltage input of TCM. Do not disconnect connector. *See Fig. 4.* Voltage between pin No. 5 of connector (B54/ 67) and vehicle body should be 10 volts minimum. If voltage is not within specification, replace TCM and retest.

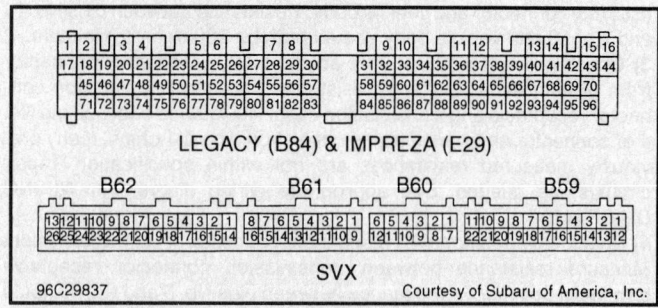

LEGACY (B84) & IMPREZA (E29)

B62   B61   B60   B59

SVX

96C29837   Courtesy of Subaru of America, Inc.

Fig. 6: Identifying ECU Connector Terminals

DTC 24: DUTY SOLENOID "C"

Symptom – Output signal circuit of duty solenoid "C" is open or shorted causing excessive engine braking in tight corners.
Impreza – 1) Check harness between TCM and duty solenoid "C". Disconnect connector from TCM. Disconnect connector from transmission. Measure resistance between TCM (B52) connector and transmission connector. *See Figs. 4 and 5.*

2) Resistance between pin No. 6 of connector (B52) and pin No. 11 of transmission connector should be 0-1 ohms. Resistance between pin No. 13 of connector (B52) and pin No. 4 of transmission connector should be 0-1 ohms.

3) Measure resistance between TCM (B52) connector and vehicle body. Resistance between pins No. 6 and No. 13 and vehicle body should be 100 k/ohms minimum for both circuits. If any measured resistances are not within specification, inspect and repair circuit(s) as needed. See appropriate wiring diagram in WIRING DIAGRAMS.

4) Check ground line of duty solenoid "C". Disconnect connector from transmission. Measure resistance between transmission connector receptacle and transmission case. See Fig. 5. Resistance between pin No. 4 of connector and transmission case should be one ohm maximum.

5) Check duty solenoid "C". Disconnect connector from transmission. Measure resistance between transmission connector receptacle terminals. Resistance between pins No. 11 and No. 4 should be 10-17 ohms. Replace solenoid as needed.

6) Check signal voltage output from TCM. Install spare fuse on FWD connector and set in FWD mode. Turn ignition on with engine not running. Move shift selector lever to "D" position. Measure voltage output from TCM (B52) with accelerator pedal released. See Fig. 4. Do not disconnect connector.

7) Voltage between pin No. 6 and No. 13 of (B52) connector should be 8-14 volts. Turn ignition switch off. Remove spare fuse from FWD switch. Turn ignition switch on with engine not running. Move shift selector lever to "D" position.

8) Measure voltage output emitted from TCM (B52) with accelerator pedal fully depressed (WOT). Voltage between pin No. 6 and No. 13 of connector (B52) should be .5 volts maximum. If voltage is not within specification, replace TCM and retest.

NOTE: Connectors are identified for both models. Legacy model is listed first and SVX model second. Example; (B55/68)=(Legacy/ SVX). Pin locations and numbers that are not identical for Legacy/ SVX, may be identified as follows; Terminal No. 36/20.

Legacy & SVX – 1) Check harness between TCM and duty solenoid "C". Disconnect connector from TCM. Disconnect connector from transmission. Measure resistance between TCM (B55/68) connector and transmission connector. See Figs. 4 and 5.

2) Resistance between pin No. 3 of connector (B55/68) and pin No. 11 of transmission connector should be 0-1 ohms. Resistance between pin No. 10 of connector (B55/68) and pin No. 4 of transmission connector should be 0-1 ohms.

3) Measure resistance between TCM (B55/68) connector and vehicle body. Resistance between pins No. 3 and No. 10 and vehicle body should be 100 k/ohms minimum for both circuits. If any measured resistances are not within specification, inspect and repair circuit(s) as needed. See appropriate wiring diagram in WIRING DIAGRAMS.

4) Check ground line of duty solenoid "C". Disconnect connector from transmission. Measure resistance between transmission connector receptacle and transmission case. See Fig. 5. Resistance between pin No. 4 of connector and transmission case should be one ohm maximum.

5) Check duty solenoid "C". Disconnect connector from transmission. Measure resistance between transmission connector receptacle terminals. Resistance between pins No. 11 and No. 4 should be 9-15 ohms. Replace solenoid as needed.

6) Check signal voltage output from TCM. Install spare fuse on FWD connector and set in FWD mode. Turn ignition on with engine not running. Move shift selector lever to "D". Measure voltage output from TCM (B55/68) with accelerator pedal released. See Fig. 4. Do not disconnect connector.

7) Voltage between pin No. 3 and No. 10 of (B55/68) connector should be 8-14 volts. Turn ignition switch off. Remove spare fuse from FWD switch. Turn ignition switch on with engine not running. Move shift selector lever to "D" position.

8) Measure voltage output emitted from TCM (B55/68) with accelerator pedal fully depressed (WOT). Voltage between pin No. 3 and No. 10 of connector (B55/68) should be .5 volts maximum. If voltage is not within specification, replace TCM and retest.

DTC 25: ENGINE TORQUE CONTROL SIGNAL

Symptom – Engine torque control output signal circuit is open or shorted causing harsh shift feel.

Impreza — 1) Check harness connector between TCM and ECM. Turn ignition switch OFF. Disconnect connectors from TCM and ECM. Measure resistance of TCM harness connector (B52) terminal No. 16 and ECM harness connector (E29) terminal No. 49. Resistance should be 0-1 ohms. Measure resistance of harness connector (B52) terminal No. 16 and vehicle body. Resistance should be 100 k/ohms minimum. If any measured resistances are not within specification, inspect and repair circuit(s) as needed. See appropriate wiring diagram in WIRING DIAGRAMS.

2) Check input signal for TCM. Reconnect connector to TCM and ECM. Turn ignition switch on. Measure voltage between TCM connector (B52) terminal No. 16 and vehicle body. Voltage should be 4-6 volts. If voltage is not within specification, replace TCM and retest

Legacy – 1) Check harness connector between TCM and ECM. Turn ignition switch OFF. Disconnect connectors from TCM and ECM. Measure resistance of TCM harness connector (B55) terminal No. 16 and ECM harness connector (B84) terminal No. 49. Resistance should be 0-1 ohms. Measure resistance of harness connector (B55) terminal No. 16 and vehicle body. Resistance should be 100 k/ohms minimum. If any measured resistances are not within specification, inspect and repair circuit(s) as needed. See appropriate wiring diagram in WIRING DIAGRAMS.

2) Check input signal for TCM. Reconnect connector to TCM and ECM. Turn ignition switch on. Measure voltage between TCM connector (B55) terminal No. 16 and vehicle body. Voltage should be 4-6 volts. If voltage is not within specification, replace TCM and retest

SVX – 1) Measure signal voltage output of ECU (MPFI). Turn ignition on with engine not running. Measure signal voltage output of ECU (MPFI). Do not disconnect connector.

2) Measure voltage between pin No. 20 of connector (B59) and vehicle body. See Fig. 6. Voltage should be 4-5 volts. If voltage is not within specification, replace ECU and retest.

3) Measure signal voltage input of TCM. Disconnect connector from TCM. Turn ignition on with engine not running. Measure signal voltage input of TCM. Measure voltage between pin No. 9 of connector (B68) and vehicle body. See Fig. 4.

4) Voltage should be 4-5 volts. If voltage is not within specification, inspect and repair circuit. See appropriate wiring diagram in WIRING DIAGRAMS. If circuit is okay, replace TCM and retest.

DTC 31: THROTTLE SENSOR

Symptom – Input signal circuit of throttle sensor is open or shorted causing shift points too high or too low, no engine braking in 3rd, erratic shifting and/or excessive engine braking in tight corners.

Impreza — 1) Check harness connector between TCM and Throttle Position Sensor. With ignition switch OFF, disconnect TCM connector (B96) and throttle position sensor (E10). Measure resistance at terminal (B96) terminal No. 8 and (E10) terminal No. 2. Resistance should be 0-1 ohms. Measure resistance at TCM connector (B53) No. 19 and TPS connector (E10) terminal No. 3. Resistance should be 0-1 ohms.

2) Check harness connector for short to ground. Check connector (B96) terminal No. 8 and vehicle body. Resistance should be 100 k/ohms minimum. Measure connector (B53) terminal No. 8 and vehicle body. Resistance should be 100 k/ohms minimum.

3) Measure resistance between throttle position sensor (E10) terminals. No. 1 to terminal No. 2 with throttle fully closed, resistance should be .3-.7 k/ohms. With throttle fully open, resistance should read 3-6 k/ohms. At terminal No. 1 and terminal No. 3 with throttle fully open, resistance should be 3.5-6.5 k/ohms. If resistance values are not within specifications, replace throttle position sensor.

4) Measure signal voltage input of TCM. With KOEO, measure signal voltage from throttle sensor at wide open throttle (WOT). Measure voltage between pin No. 8 (B96) and No. 7 (B96). Voltage should be 4.3-4.9 (throttle fully open). Voltage reading with throttle fully closed should be .3-.7 volts. If voltage is within specification, replace TCM and retest.

Legacy – 1) Check harness connector between TCM and throttle position sensor. With Ignition switch OFF, disconnect connectors from TCM and TPS. Measure resistance at TCM connector (B54) terminal No. 8 and TPS connector (E13). Resistance should be 0-1 ohms. Measure TPS connector (B56) terminal No. 19 and TPS connector (E13) terminal No. 3. Resistance should be 0-1 ohms.

2) Check for short to ground between TCM and vehicle body. At terminal (B54) No. 8 to vehicle body, Resistance should be 100 k/ohms minimum. At terminal (B56) No. 19 to vehicle body resistance should be 100 k/ohms minimum. If not within specification, repair or replace connectors or wiring.

3) Check Throttle Position Sensor (TPS). Measure resistance at TPS terminals (E13) No. 1 and No. 2. With throttle fully closed, resistance should be .3-.7 k/ohms. With throttle fully open, resistance should be 3-6 k/ohms. At terminal No. 1 and terminal No. 3 resistance should be 3.5-6.5 k/ohms. If results are not within specification, replace TPS and retest.

4) Check input signal to TCM. Connect connectors to TCM and TPS. With KOEO, measure voltage from TPS. At (B54) terminal No. 8 and No. 7 voltage should be .3-.7 volts with throttle fully closed. With throttle fully open, voltage should be 4.3-4.9 volts. If values are within specification, replace TCM and retest. *See Fig. 4.*

SVX – 1) Measure signal voltage input of TCM. With KOEO, Measure signal voltage input emitted from throttle sensor with accelerator pedal fully depressed (WOT). Measure voltage between pin No. 8 of TCM connector (B67) and vehicle body. Voltage should be .5 volt with throttle fully closed. With throttle fully open (WOT), voltage should be 4.5 volts.

2) Check harness/connector between TCM and throttle sensor. Disconnect connector from TCM. Disconnect connector from throttle sensor. Measure resistance between TCM (B67) and throttle sensor (E11) connector. Resistance between pin No. 8 of connector (B67) and pin No. 1 of connector (E11) should be 0-1 ohms. Resistance between pin No. 8 of connector (B67) and vehicle body should be 100 k/ohms minimum.

3) Check throttle sensor. Disconnect connector from throttle sensor. Measure resistance between throttle sensor terminals. Resistance between pins No. 1 and 2 should be 1 k/ohms with throttle fully closed. With wide open throttle, resistance should be 4.3 k/ohms.

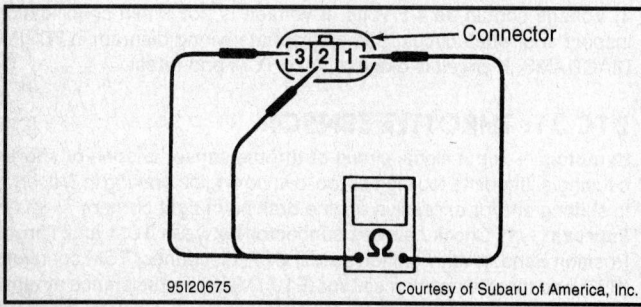

95120675   Courtesy of Subaru of America, Inc.

Fig. 7: Testing Throttle Sensor (Impreza)

DTC 32: VEHICLE SPEED SENSOR "1"

Symptom – Input signal circuit of TCM is open or shorted, causing no shifting or excessive transmission braking in tight corners.

Impreza – 1) Check harness/connector between TCM and vehicle speed sensor "1". Disconnect connector from TCM. Disconnect connector from transmission. Measure resistance between TCM connector and transmission connector. *See Figs. 4 and 5.* Resistance between pin No. 12 of connector (B96) and pin No. 16 of transmission connector (B9) should be 0-1 ohms. Resistance between pin No. 7 of connector (B96) and pin No. 9 of connector (B9) should be 0-1 ohms.

2) Check for short to ground. Measure resistance of pins No. 7 and No. 12 to vehicle body. Resistance should be 100 k/ohms minimum. If results are not within specifications, repair or replace harness connectors.

3) Check vehicle speed sensor "1". Measure resistance between transmission connector (T4) receptacles terminals No. 16 and terminal No. 9. Resistance should be 450-720 ohms. Measure resistance of harness connector between transmission connector and transmission case to check for short. Resistance between terminal pins No. 16 and No. 9 to transmission case should be 100 k/ohms minimum. *See Fig. 5.* If results are not within specification, replace speed sensor.

4) Measure signal voltage input of TCM. Raise vehicle on hoist. Ensure wheels are off floor. Start engine and set vehicle speed to 12 mph. Measure signal voltage input of TCM (B96). *See Fig. 4.* Measure voltage between pins No. 12 and 7 of connector (B96). Voltage should be one volt A/C minimum. If voltage is not within specification, replace TCM.

NOTE: Connectors are identified for both models. Legacy model is listed first and SVX model second. Example; (B33/68)=(Legacy/ SVX). Pin locations and numbers that are not Identical for Legacy/ SVX, may be Identified as follows; Terminal 36/20.

Legacy & SVX – 1) Check harness/connector between TCM and vehicle speed sensor "1". Disconnect connector from TCM. Disconnect connector from transmission. Measure resistance between TCM connector and transmission connector. *See Figs. 4 and 5.*

2) Resistance between pin No. 12 of connector (B54/67) and pin No. 16 of transmission connector (B11) should be 0-1 ohms. Resistance between pin No. 7 of connector (B54/67) and pin No. 9 of connector (B11) should be 0-1 ohms.

3) Measure resistance of harness connector between TCM and vehicle body to ensure there is no short to ground. Measure between terminal pins No. 1 and No. 12 to vehicle body. Resistance should be 100 k/ohms. If any resistances measured are not within specification, inspect and repair circuit as needed.

4) Check vehicle speed sensor "1". Disconnect connector from transmission. Measure resistance between connector receptacle terminals. *See Fig. 5.* Resistance between pins No. 16 and 9 of connector (T4) should be 450-720 ohms. If resistance is not within specification, replace vehicle speed sensor.

5) Measure signal voltage input of TCM. Raise vehicle on hoist. Start engine and set vehicle speed to 12 mph. Measure signal voltage input of TCM (B54/67). *See Fig. 4.* Measure voltage between pin No. 12 of connector (B54/67) and No. 7 of connector (B56/66). Voltage should be one volt A/C minimum. If voltage is not within specification, replace TCM and retest.

DTC 33: VEHICLE SPEED SENSOR "2"

Symptom – Input signal of vehicle speed sensor "2" is open or shorted, causing incorrect shift points. Poor driving performance.

Impreza – 1) Ensure speedometer indicates vehicle speed. Check harness connector between TCM and combination meter. With ignition OFF, remove combination meter. Disconnect connectors from TCM and combination meter. Measure resistance of harness connector (B53) terminal No. 11 and terminal pin No. 8 of connector (i18). Resistance should be 0-1 ohms.

2) Measure resistance of terminal pin No. 8 of connector (i18) and vehicle body. Resistance should be 100 k/ohms minimum. If not within specification, Check for short to ground.

3) Measure signal voltage input of TCM. Connect connector to combination meter and install. Raise and support vehicle. Ensure wheels are off floor. Start engine, drive wheels slowly. Measure voltage between TCM and body. From terminal pin No. 11, connector (B53) to vehicle body. Voltage should fluctuate from 0-1 volts to 4 volts minimum. If voltage is not within specification, replace TCM and retest. *See Fig. 4.*

Legacy – 1) Ensure speedometer indicates vehicle speed. Check harness connector between TCM and combination meter. With ignition OFF, remove combination meter. Disconnect connectors from TCM and combination meter. Measure resistance of harness connector (B56) terminal No. 11 and connector (i10) terminal No. 10. Resistance should be 0-1 ohms. If any resistances are not within specification, inspect and repair circuit as needed.

TCM PIN INPUT/OUTPUT RESISTANCE SPECIFICATIONS [1,2] (LEGACY & SVX)

Component	Terminal No.	Ohms Resistance
ATF Temp (68°F)	[4] 10	2.1-2.9k/2.3-2.7k
ATF Temp (176°F)	[4] 10	275-375/280-360
Duty Solenoid		
Solenoid "A"	[3] 8	2.0-4.5/1.5-4.5
Solenoid "B"	[3] 5	9-15
Solenoid "C"	[3] 3	9-15
Ground Circuits		
Speed Sensor Line "1"	[4] 7	0-1
Temperature Sensor Line "2"	[5] 20	0-1
System	[5] 1	0-1
Power System	[3] 10	0-1
Resistor (Drop)	[3] 7	9-15
Shift Solenoid		
Solenoid "1"	[3] 14	20-32
Solenoid "2"	[3] 13	20-32
Solenoid "3"	[3] 15	20-32
Speed Sensor		
Sensor "1"	[4] 12	450-720/450-650

[1] – For pin location, see Fig. 4.
[2] – Resistance to vehicle body.
[3] – Connector B33/68.
[4] – Connector B44/67.
[5] – Connector B46/66.

TCM PIN INPUT/OUTPUT RESISTANCE SPECIFICATIONS [1,2] (IMPREZA)

Component	Terminal No.	Ohms Resistance
ATF Temp (68°F)	[4] 19	2.1-2.9k
ATF Temp (176°F)	[4] 19	275-375
Duty Solenoid		
Solenoid "A"	[3] 11	2-4.5
Solenoid "B"	[3] 7	10-17
Solenoid "C"	[3] 6	10-17
Ground Circuits		
Sensor Line "1"	[4] 16	0-1
Sensor Line "2"	[4] 4	0-1
System	[3] 14	0-1
Power System	[3] 13	0-1
Resistor (Drop)	[3] 12	12-18
Shift Solenoid		
Solenoid "1"	[3] 10	20-30
Solenoid "2"	[3] 9	20-30
Solenoid "3"	[3] 8	20-30
Speed Sensor		
Sensor "1"	[4] 15	450-650

[1] – For pin location, see Fig. 4.
[2] – Resistance to vehicle body.
[3] – Connector B52.
[4] – Connector B53.

2) Measure resistance of harness connector (i10) terminal No. 10 and vehicle body. Resistance should be 100 k/ohms minimum. If not within specification, Check for short to ground.

3) Measure resistance of vehicle speed sensor "2". Install combination meter. Connect connector to TCM. Raise and support vehicle. Disconnect connector from vehicle speed sensor "2". Measure resistance between terminals of vehicle speed sensor "2". At (B17) terminal pins No. 1 and No. 2. Resistance should be 350-450 ohms. Resistance between terminal No. 1 and No. 2 to vehicle body should be 100 k/ohms minimum.

4) On models with TCS, Push TCS OFF switch to ON. Start engine and set vehicle speed to 12 MPH and measure output signal from vehicle speed sensor 2. Measure voltage between terminals (B17) No. 1 and No. 2. AC voltage should be 2 volts minimum. If any resistances are not within specification, replace vehicle speed sensor "2". Ensure no mechanical problem exists between vehicle speed sensor "2" and transmission.

5) Measure signal voltage input of TCM. Reconnect connector to vehicle speed sensor "2". With vehicle raised off the floor, push TCS OFF switch to ON. Start engine and drive wheels slowly. Measure voltage between connector (B56) terminal No. 11 and body. Voltage should fluctuate between 0-1 volts to 9 volts minimum. If voltage is not within specification, replace TCM and retest.

NOTE: Speed difference between front and rear wheels may light either ABS or ABS/TCS warning light. This indicates no malfunction. when AT control diagnosis is finished, clear ABS or ABS/TCS memory clearing procedure of self diagnosis system.

SVX – 1) Measure signal voltage input of TCM. Turn ignition on with engine not running. Move shift select lever to "N" position and slowly push vehicle. While vehicle is moving slowly, measure signal voltage input of TCM.

2) Measure voltage between pins No. 11 and 20 of connector (B66). See Fig. 4. Voltage should fluctuate between 0-1 and 5 volts. If voltage is not within specification, replace TCM and retest.

3) Check harness/connector between TCM and vehicle speed sensor "2". Disconnect connector from TCM. Disconnect connector from vehicle speed sensor "2".

4) Measure resistance between TCM (B66) connector and vehicle speed (B9) sensor "2" connector. Resistance between pin No. 11 of connector (B66) and pin No. 1 of connector (B9) should be 0-1 ohms. Resistance between pin No. 11 of connector (B66) and vehicle body should be 100 k/ohms minimum. Measure resistance between pin No. 2 of connector (B9) and vehicle body. Resistance should be 0-1 ohms. If any resistances measured are not within specification, inspect and repair circuits as needed.

5) Check voltage of power supply line. Turn ignition on with engine not running. Measure voltage between vehicle speed sensor "2" connector and vehicle body. Voltage between pin No. 3 of connector (B9) and vehicle body should be 10 volts minimum.

6) Check vehicle speed sensor "2". Remove vehicle speed sensor "2" from transmission, connect body harness connector (B9) to vehicle speed sensor "2" and turn ignition on with engine not running. Rotate vehicle speed sensor "2". Ensure voltage across pins No. 1 and 2 of connector (B9) changes from 0-1 to 5 volts 4 times per revolution. Replace sensor as needed.

TCM VOLTAGES

Access TCM. See Fig. 2. Turn ignition on. Using voltmeter, backprobe ECT ECU harness connector. Check voltage between selected terminal and vehicle ground. Voltage should be as specified. See TCM PIN INPUT/OUTPUT VOLTAGE SPECIFICATIONS tables.

NOTE: Connectors are identified for both models. Legacy model is listed first and SVX model second. Example; (B55/68)=(Legacy/SVX). Pin locations and numbers that are not identical for Legacy/SVX, may be identified as follows; Terminal 36/20.

ELECTRONIC SYSTEM TESTING
SHIFT & KEY INTERLOCK SYSTEM

NOTE: In the following procedures, connectors are identified for both models. Impreza/Legacy model is listed first and SVX model second. Example: (B55/68)=(Legacy/SVX). Pin locations and numbers are identical. For wire color and terminal identification, see appropriate wiring diagram in WIRING DIAGRAMS.

TCM PIN INPUT/OUTPUT VOLTAGE SPECIFICATIONS [1,2] (LEGACY & SVX)

Component	Terminal No.	Connector No.	Requirements	Voltage
ABS Signal	5	B56/66	ABS Switch On	0-1
ABS Signal	5	B56/66	ABS Switch Off	6.5-10
ATF Temp	10	B54/67	ATF 68°F	2.9-4.0
ATF Temp	10	B54/67	ATF 176°F	1.0-1.4
Battery Voltage	14	B56/66	Ignition Key Off	10-14
Brake Switch	7	B56/66	Pedal On	10.5-14
Brake Switch	7	B56/66	Pedal Off	0-1
Cruise Signal	3	B56/66	Cruise On	0-1
Cruise Signal	3	B56/66	Cruise Off	6-13
Duty Solenoid				
Solenoid "A"	8	B55/68	[5] Closed	1.5-4.0
Solenoid "A"	8	B55/68	[6] Open	0-1
Solenoid "B"	5	B55/68	[9] Lock	8.5-14
Solenoid "B"	5	B55/68	[10] No Lock	0-.5
Solenoid "C"	3	B55/68	[11] Fuse	8.5-14
Solenoid "C"	3	B55/68	[12] No Fuse	0-.5
Engine TCS [7]	16	B55/68	[3] "N"	4-6
FWD Switch	2	B46/66	No Fuse	8-9.1
FWD Switch	2	B46/66	Fuse	0-1
Ground Circuits				
Speed Sensor Line "1"	7	B54/68	N/A	0
Temperature Sensor Line "2"	20	B56/66	N/A	0
System	1	B56/66	N/A	0
Power System	10	B55/68	N/A	0
Ignition Voltage	1	B55/68	[2] KOEO	10-14
Ignition Voltage	6	B54/67	[2] KOEO	10-14
Inhibitor Switch				
"P" Range	9	B56/66	[3] "P"	0-1
"P" Range	9	B56/66	[4] "ALL"	9-13
"R" Range	10	B56/66	[3] "R"	0-1
"R" Range	10	B56/66	[4] All	6-13
"N" Range	8	B56/66	[3] "N"	0-1
"N" Range	8	B56/66	[4,13] All	9-13
"D" Range	1	B54/67	[3] "D"	0-1
"D" Range	1	B54/67	[4] All	6-123
"3" Range	2	B54/67	[3] "3"	0-1
"3" Range	2	B54/67	[4] All	6-10
"2" Range	3	B54/67	[3] "2"	0-1
"2" Range	3	B54/67	[4] All	6-10
"1" Range	4	B54/67	[3] "1"	0-1
"1" Range	4	B54/67	[4] All	6-10
Manual Switch	6	B56/66	Switch On	0-1
Manual Switch	6	B56/66	Switch Off	6-10
Resistor (Drop)	7	B55/68	[5] Closed	5-14
Resistor (Drop)	7	B55/68	[6] Open	0-.5
Shift Solenoid				
Solenoid "1"	14	B55/68	[3] 1st,4th	9-14
Solenoid "1"	14	B55/68	[3] 2nd,3rd	0-1
Solenoid "2"	13	B55/68	[3] 1st,2nd	9-14
Solenoid "2"	13	B55/68	[3] 3rd,4th	0-1
Solenoid "3"	15	B55/68	[3] "N"	0-1
Solenoid "3"	15	B55/68	[3] "D"	9-14
Speed Sensor				
Sensor "1"	12	B54/67	Stopped	0
Sensor "1"	12	B54/67	[8] 20 MPH	1-2 AC
Sensor "2"	11	B56/66	Push Car	0-1 to 9-14 Pulse
Throttle Sensor				
Legacy	8	B54/67	[5] Closed	.3-.7
Legacy	8	B54/67	[6] Open	4.3-4.9
SVX	8	B54/67	[5] Closed	.5
SVX	8	B54/67	[6] Open	4.5

[1] – For terminal identification, see Fig. 4.
[2] – Key On, Engine Off.
[3] – Shift lever selection (1 or 2 choices).
[4] – Select any gear selection other than previously used.
[5] – Throttle fully closed (engine at operating temperature, KOEO).
[6] – Throttle fully open (engine at operating temperature, KOEO).
[7] – Engine torque control signal.
[8] – 20 MPH minimum.
[9] – Torque converter lock-up engaged.
[10] – Torque converter Lock-up not engaged.
[11] – Fuse installed in FWD switch. See Fig. 5.
[12] – Fuse removed, wide open throttle, shift lever in 1st Gear.
[13] – Except in "P" range

AUTOMATIC TRANSMISSIONS
Subaru 4-Speed Electronic Controls (Cont.)

TCM PIN INPUT/OUTPUT VOLTAGE SPECIFICATIONS [1],[2] (IMPREZA)

Component	Terminal No.	Connector No.	Requirements	Voltage
ABS Signal	7	B53	ABS Switch On	0-1
ABS Signal	7	B53	ABS Switch Off	6.5-13
ATF Temp	19	B53	ATF 68°F	2.9-4.0
ATF Temp	19	B53	ATF 176°F	1.0-1.4
Battery Voltage	1	B52	Ignition Key Off	11-13
Brake Switch	8	B53	Pedal On	10-14
Brake Switch	8	B53	Pedal Off	0-1
Cruise Signal	6	B53	Cruise On	0-1
Cruise Signal	6	B53	Cruise Off	6-10
Duty Solenoid				
Solenoid "A"	11	B52	[5] Closed	1.5-4.0
Solenoid "A"	11	B52	[6] Open	0-1
Solenoid "B"	7	B52	[8] Lock	8-14
Solenoid "B"	7	B52	[9] No Lock	0-.5
Solenoid "C"	6	B52	[10] Fuse	8-14
Solenoid "C"	6	B52	[11] No Fuse	0-.5
FWD Switch	2	B52	No Fuse	10-14
FWD Switch	2	B52	Fuse	0-1
Ground Circuits				
Sensor Line "1"	16	B53	N/A	0
Sensor Line "2"	4	B53	N/A	0
System	14	B52	N/A	0
Power System	13	B52	N/A	0
Ignition Voltage	15	B52	[2] KOEO	11-13
Ignition Voltage	16	B52	[2] KOEO	11-13
Inhibitor Switch				
"P" Range	12	B53	"P" Or "N"	0-1
"P" Range	12	B53	[4] "ALL"	8-13
"R" Range	3	B52	[3] "R"	0-1
"R" Range	3	B52	[4] All	9.5-13
"N" Range	12	B53	[3] "N"	0-1
"N" Range	12	B53	[4] All	9.5-13
"D" Range	11	B53	[3] "D"	0-1
"D" Range	11	B53	[4] All	9.5-13
"3" Range	3	B53	[3] "3"	0-1
"3" Range	3	B53	[4] All	9.5-13
"2" Range	10	B53	[3] "2"	0-1
"2" Range	10	B53	[4] All	9.5-13
"1" Range	9	B53	[3] "1"	0-1
"1" Range	9	B53	[4] All	9.5-13
Resistor (Drop)	12	B52	[5] Closed	5-14
Resistor (Drop)	12	B52	[6] Open	0-.5
Shift Solenoid				
Solenoid "1"	10	B52	[3] 1st,4th	10-14
Solenoid "1"	10	B52	[3] 2nd,3rd	0-1
Solenoid "2"	9	B52	[3] 1st,2nd	10-14
Solenoid "2"	9	B52	[3] 3rd,4th	0-1
Solenoid "3"	8	B52	[3] "N"	0-1
Solenoid "3"	8	B52	[3] "D"	10-14
Speed Sensor				
Sensor "1"	15	B53	Stopped	0
Sensor "1"	15	B53	[7] 12 MPH	1-2 AC
Sensor "2"	5	B52	Push Car	0-1, 4+ Pulse
Throttle Sensor	20	B53	[5] Closed	.3-.7
Throttle Sensor	20	B53	[6] Open	3.9-4.3

[1] – For terminal identification, *see Fig. 4*.
[2] – Key On, Engine Off.
[3] – Shift lever selection (1 or 2 choices).
[4] – Select any gear selection other than previously used.
[5] – Throttle fully closed (engine at operating temperature, KOEO).
[6] – Throttle fully open (engine at operating temperature, KOEO).
[7] – 20 MPH minimum.
[8] – Torque converter lock-up engaged.
[9] – Torque converter lock-up not engaged.
[10] – Fuse installed in FWD switch. *See Fig. 5*.
[11] – Fuse removed, wide open throttle, shift lever in 1st Gear.

Preliminary Testing – Turn ignition switch to ON position. Ensure shift selector lever moves from "P" to any other position. If selector moves, see COMPONENT TESTING. If shift selector will not move, depress brake pedal and recheck. If selector still will not move, see SHIFT LOCK DOES NOT RELEASE.

If shift selector lever will move, shift to "N" position and turn ignition switch to OFF position. If ignition key can be removed from ignition switch, see KEY INTERLOCK DOES NOT OPERATE. If key cannot be removed, move shift selector lever to "P" position and attempt to remove key. If key can be removed, system is functioning properly. If key cannot be removed, see KEY INTERLOCK DOES NOT RELEASE.

Component Testing – 1) Check if brakelights remain on when brake pedal is released. If lights remain on, check and repair brakelight system as required. If lights go out when brake pedal is released, disconnect connector from shift lock control unit. Control unit is located behind right side of steering column lower panel.

2) If shift lock occurs when shift selector lever is moved to "P" position, replace shift lock control unit. If shift lock does not occur, disconnect connector from shift lock solenoid. Ensure shift lock function occurs when shift selector lever is moved to "P" position. If shift lock still occurs, there is a short in shift lock solenoid's RED/GRN harness. If shift lock does not occur, check shift selector lever assembly. *See Fig. 11, 12 or 13.*

CAUTION: When conducting operational checks of key lock solenoid, do not apply 12 volts to solenoid for more than one second, solenoid circuit damage may occur.

Shift Lock Does Not Release – 1) Ensure brakelight turns on when brake pedal is depressed. If brakelights fail to turn on, check and repair brakelight system as required. If brake lights turn on, ensure 10 volts minimum is present across pin No. 3 of control unit and vehicle ground. If voltage is not within specifications, check and repair harness or faulty connector between main fuse and control unit. *See Fig. 11, 12 or 13.*

2) If voltage is within specifications, check voltage across pin No. 4 of control unit and vehicle ground. Voltage should be 10 volts minimum when brake pedal is depressed. If voltage is not within specifications, check and repair harness or faulty connector contact between brake light switch and control unit.

3) Ensure voltage across pin No. 1 of control unit and vehicle ground is 10 volts minimum when ignition switch is turned on. If voltage is not within specifications, check fuse. If fuse is okay, check and repair harness or faulty connector contact between ignition switch and control unit. If voltage is within specifications, turn ignition switch to OFF position. Disconnect connector from shift lock control unit.

4) Check for continuity between pin No. 2 of connector (B57/R47) and vehicle ground. Place shift selector lever is in "P" position. If continuity does not exist, check inhibitor switch and/or repair harness. If continuity exists, measure resistance between pin No. 1 of connector (B57/R47) and vehicle ground.

5) If resistance is greater than 20 ohms, shift lock solenoid circuit is shorted. Check and repair harness or faulty connector contact between shift lock solenoid and connector (B57/R47). If resistance is less than 10 ohms, shift lock solenoid is shorted or poorly grounded. After repairs are completed, recheck solenoid operation. If malfunction is still present, replace shift lock control unit.

6) Ensure resistance between pin No. 10 of connector (B69/R47) and vehicle ground is less than 10 ohms. If resistance is not less than 10 ohms, control unit ground circuit is open or has poor connector contact. If resistance is less than 10 ohms, replace shift lock control unit.

NOTE: For shift and key interlock system wiring diagram, see appropriate wiring diagram in WIRING DIAGRAMS.

Key Interlock Does Not Operate – 1) Ensure shift lock operates properly. If not, recheck testing procedures previously listed. If shift lock is functioning properly, check if voltage across pin No. 3 of control unit and vehicle ground is 10 volts minimum. If voltage is not within specifications, check and repair harness of faulty connector contact between main fuse and control unit. If voltage is within specifications, check voltage across pin No. 8 of control unit and vehicle ground. *See Fig. 11, 12 or 13.*

2) Voltage should be 10 volts minimum when key is inserted into ignition switch. If voltage is not within specifications, check and replace faulty ignition switch. Check and replace harness or faulty connector contact between fuse block and control unit.

3) If voltage is within specifications, check voltage across pin No. 7 and vehicle ground. Voltage should be 10 volts minimum when ignition switch is set to ACC position. If voltage is not within specifications, check and repair harness or faulty connector contact between ignition switch and control unit.

4) If voltage is within specifications, disconnect harness connector from control unit. Check resistance between pins No. 9 and No. 11 of connector (B69/R47). If resistance is 8 ohms or greater, key lock solenoid circuit is open. Check and repair harness or faulty connector contact between key lock solenoid and control unit.

5) If resistance is less than 4 ohms, key lock solenoid is shorted. Check and repair harness or faulty connector contact between key lock solenoid and control unit. After repairs are completed, recheck solenoid operation. If malfunction is still present, replace shift lock control unit.

6) Check resistance between pin No. 11 of connector (B69/R47) and vehicle ground. If resistance is 1k/ohm minimum, replace shift lock control unit.

Key Interlock Does Not Release – 1) Ensure shift lock operates properly. If not, recheck testing procedures previously listed. If shift lock is functioning properly, check if voltage across pin No. 3 of control unit and vehicle ground is 10 volts minimum. If voltage is not within specifications, check and repair harness of faulty connector contact between main fuse and control unit. If voltage is within specifications, check voltage across pin No. 8 of control unit and vehicle ground. *See Fig. 11, 12 or 13.*

2) Voltage should be 10 volts minimum when key is inserted into ignition switch. If voltage is not within specifications, check and replace faulty ignition switch. Check and repair harness or faulty connector contact between fuse block and control unit.

3) If voltage is within specifications, check voltage across pin No. 7 and vehicle ground. Voltage should be 10 volts minimum when ignition switch is set to ACC position. If voltage is not within specifications, check and repair harness or faulty connector contact between ignition switch and control unit.

4) If voltage is within specifications, disconnect harness connector from control unit. Check resistance between pins No. 9 and No. 11 of connector (B69/R47). If resistance is 8 ohms or greater, key lock solenoid circuit is open. Check and repair harness or faulty connector contact between key lock solenoid and control unit.

5) If resistance is less than 4 ohms, key lock solenoid is shorted. Check and repair harness or faulty connector contact between key lock solenoid and control unit. Check resistance between pin No. 9 of connector (B69/R47) and vehicle ground. If resistance is 1k/ohm minimum, check and repair harness or faulty connector contact between key lock solenoid and control unit.

6) After repairs are completed, recheck solenoid operation. If malfunction is still present, replace shift lock control unit. If resistance between pin No. 9 of control unit and vehicle ground is less than 1k/ohm, replace shift lock control unit.

WIRING DIAGRAMS

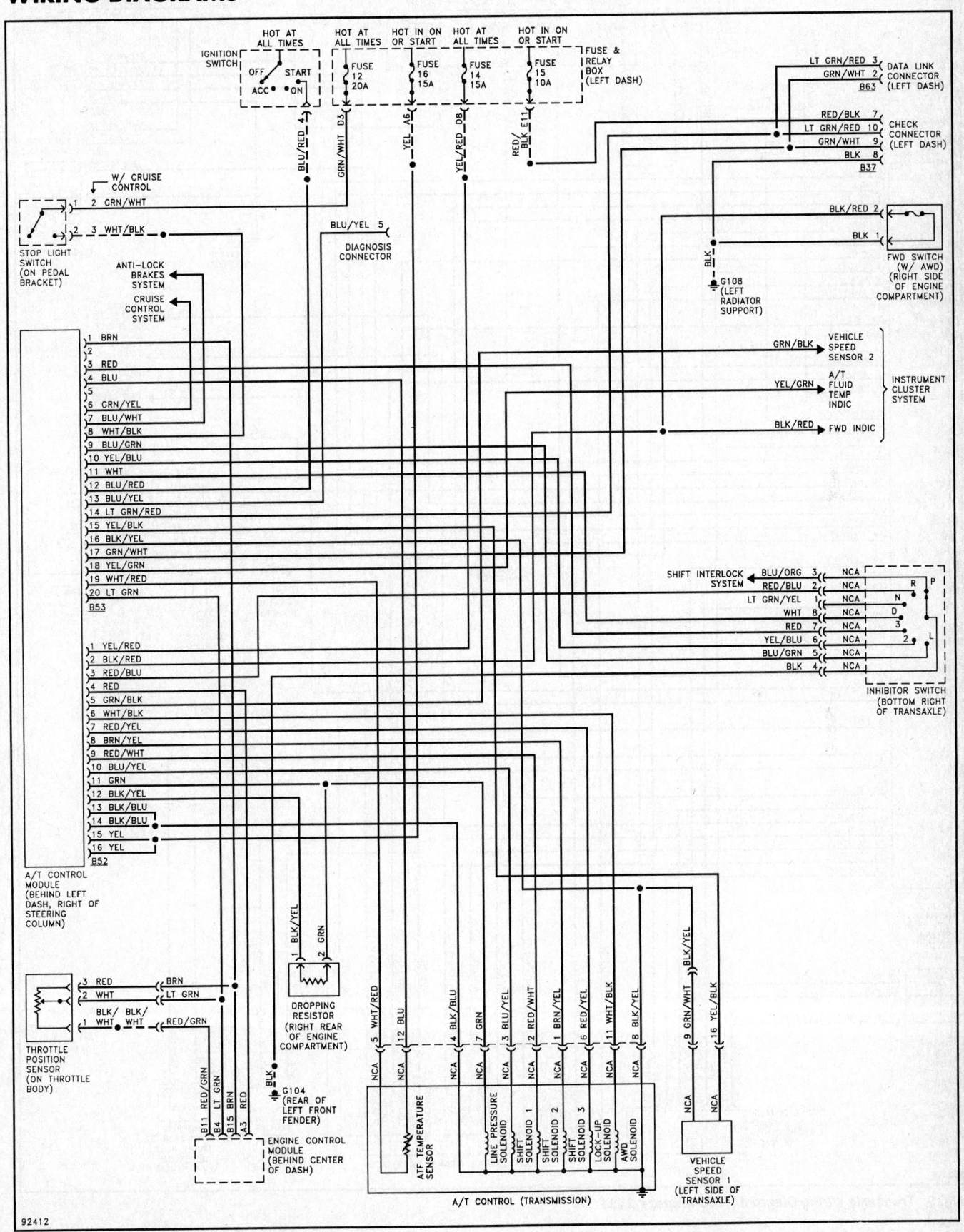

Fig. 8: Transaxle Wiring Diagram (1995 Impreza 1.8L)

AUTOMATIC TRANSMISSIONS
Subaru 4-Speed Electronic Controls (Cont.)

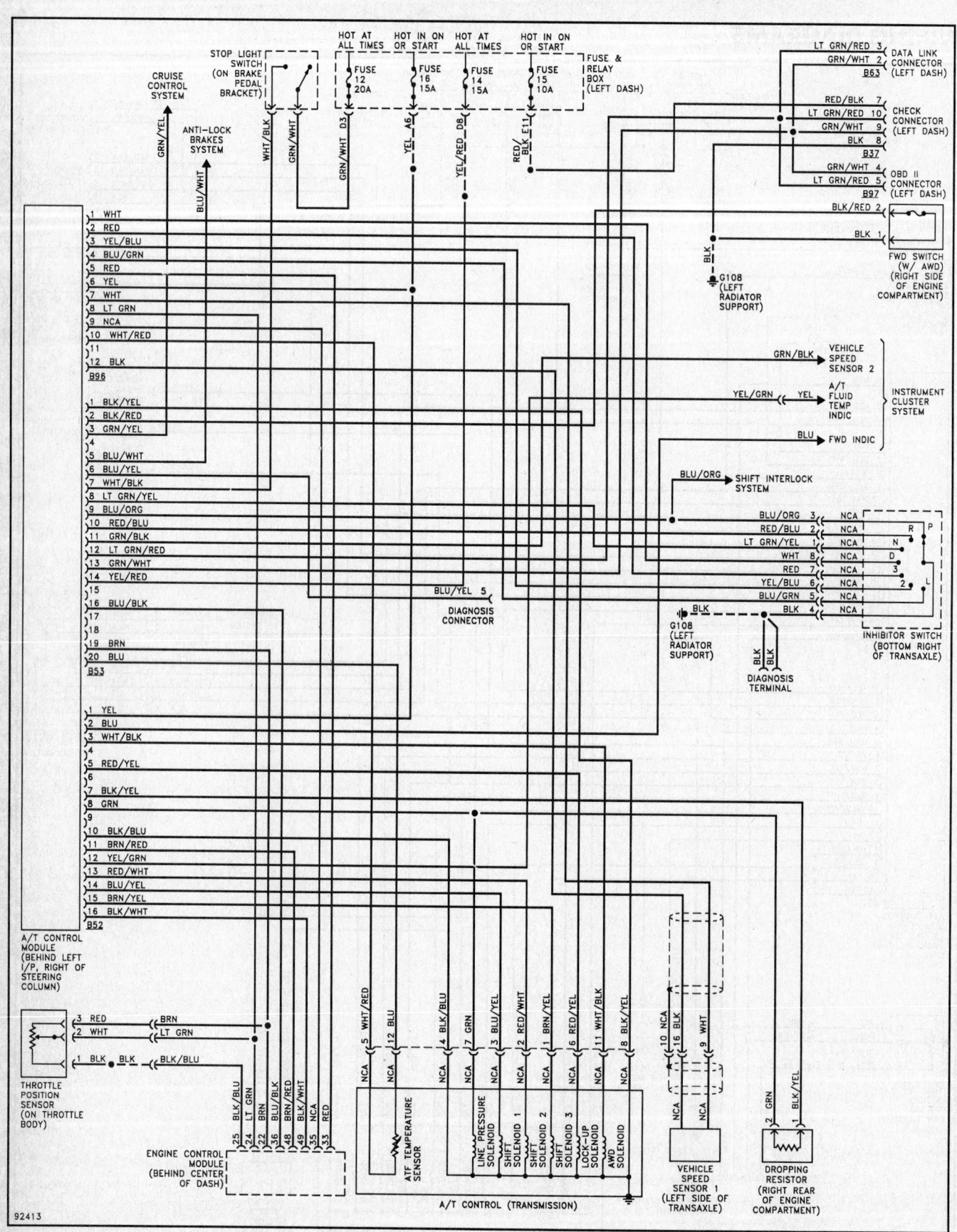

Fig. 9: Transaxle Wiring Diagram (1995 Impreza 2.2L)

92413

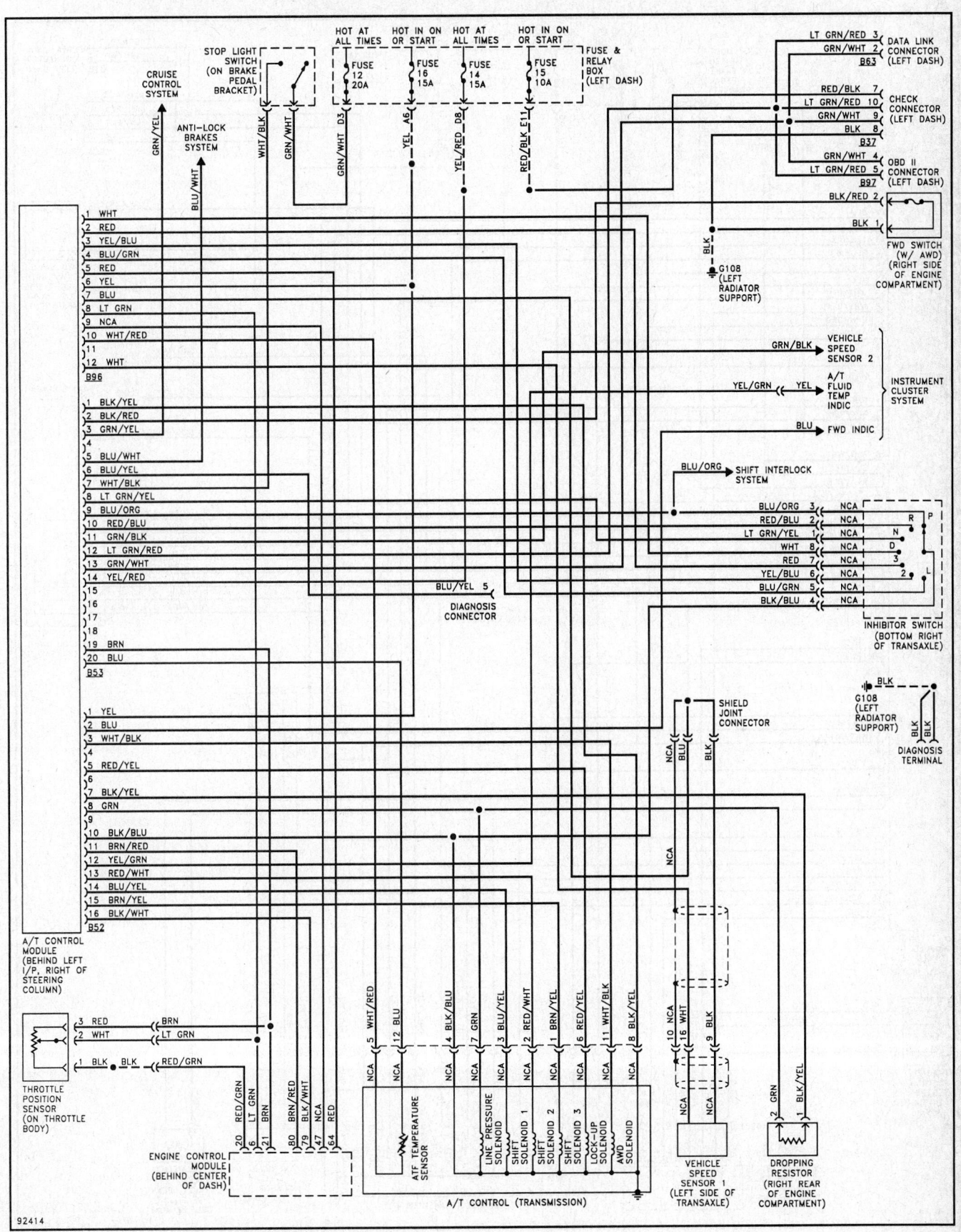

Fig. 10: Transaxle Wiring Diagram (1996 Impreza)

92414

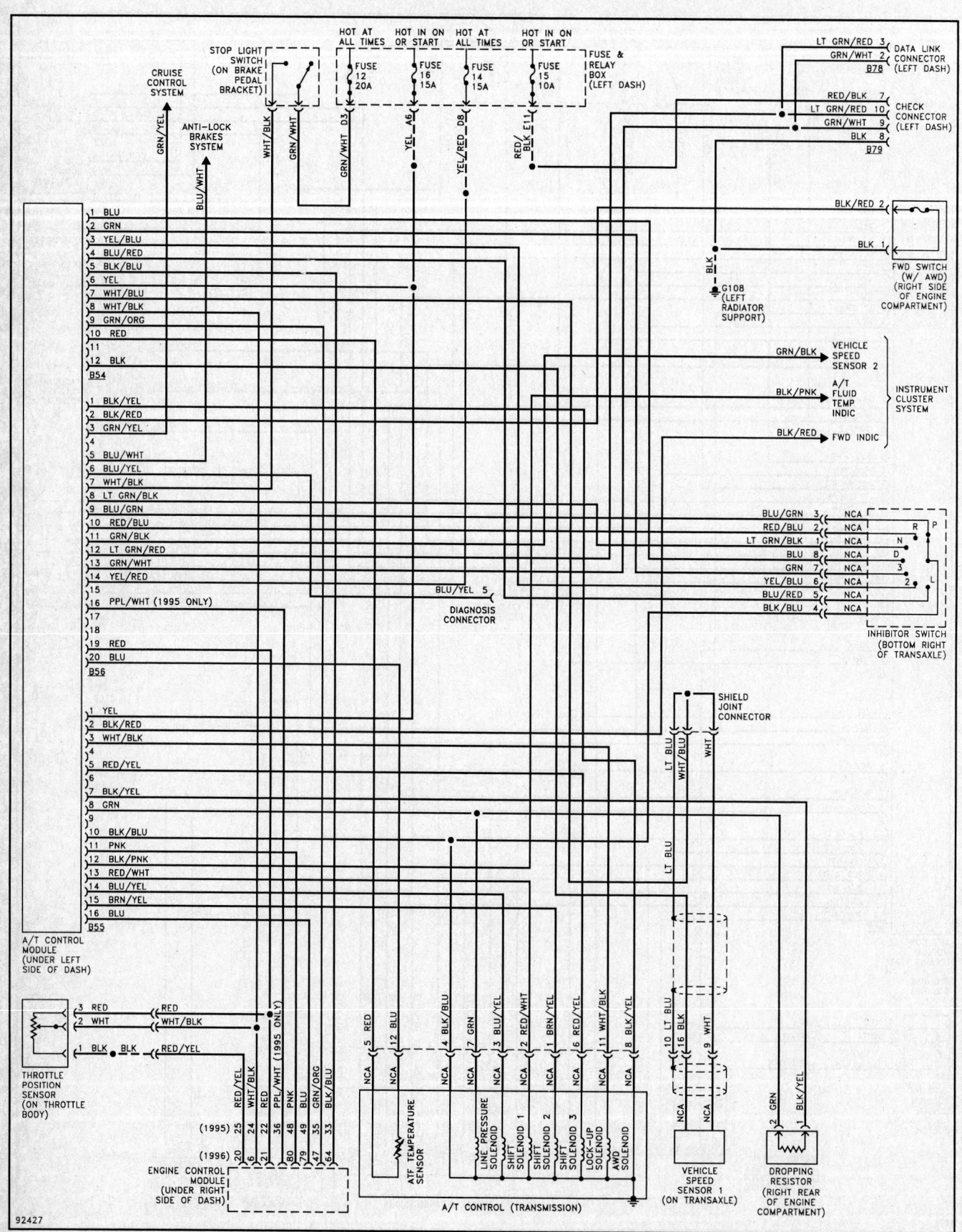

Fig. 11: Transaxle Wiring Diagram (1995-96 Legacy)

92427

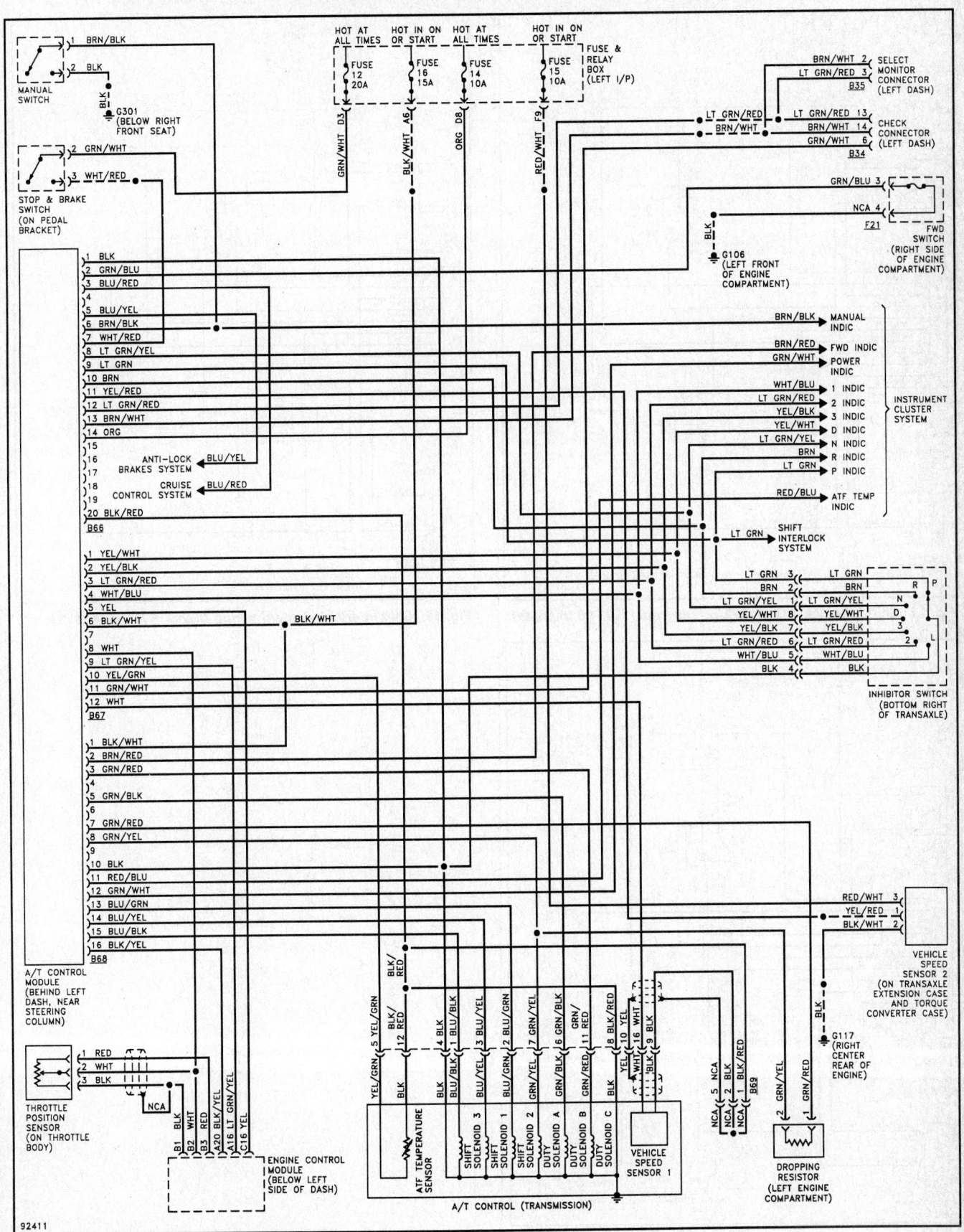

Fig. 12: Transaxle Wiring Diagram (1995-96 SVX)

92411

AUTOMATIC TRANSMISSIONS
Subaru 4-Speed Electronic Controls (Cont.)

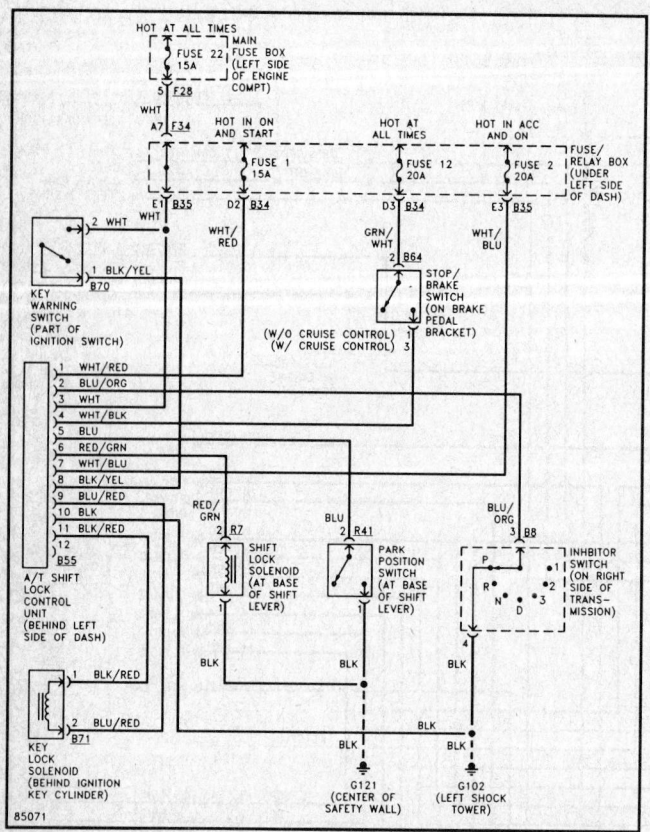

Fig. 13: Shift Interlock System Wiring Diagram (1995-96 Impreza)

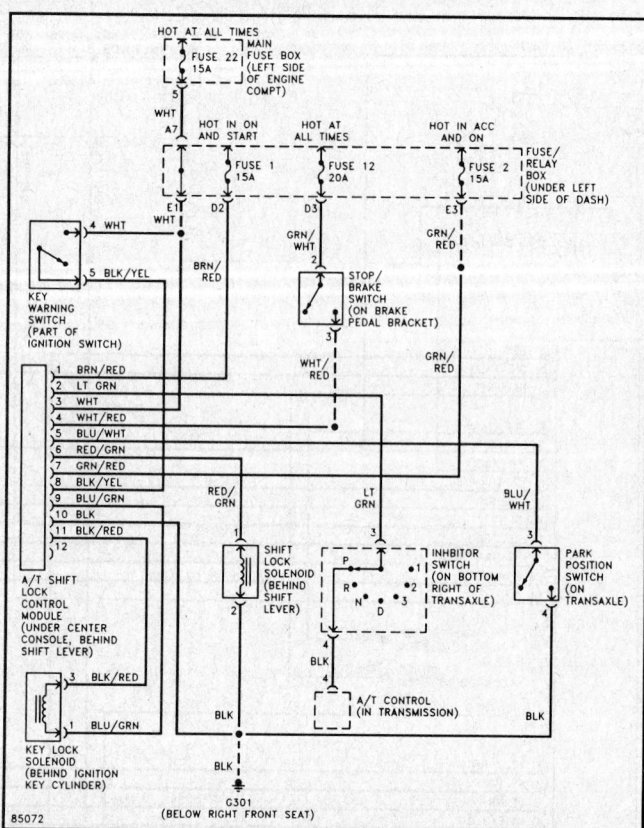

Fig. 15: Shift Interlock System Wiring Diagram (1995-96 SVX)

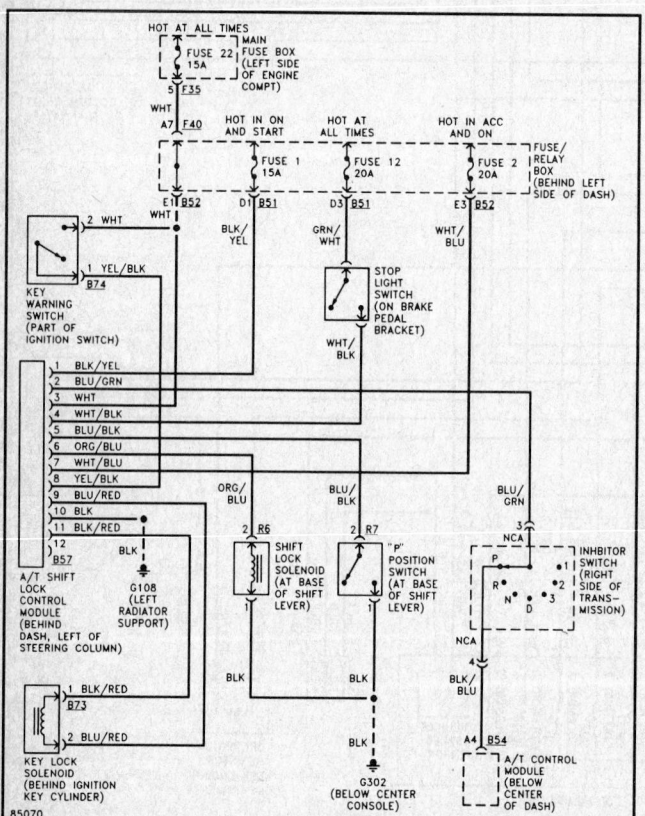

Fig. 14: Shift Interlock System Wiring Diagram (1995-96 Legacy)

AUTOMATIC TRANSMISSIONS
Suzuki ECC 3-Speed

Geo: Metro
Suzuki: Swift

APPLICATION & LABOR TIMES

APPLICATION & LABOR TIMES

Vehicle Application	Labor Times [1] R & I	[2] Overhaul	Trans. Model
Geo			
1995-96 Metro			
1.0L Engine	4.0	6.0	ECC
1.3L Engine			
W/Engine Removal [3]			
With A/C	8.2	6.0	ECC
Without A/C	7.2	6.0	ECC
W/O Engine Removed	4.0	6.0	ECC
Suzuki			
1995-96 Swift			
With A/C	8.2	6.0	ECC
Without A/C	7.2	6.0	ECC

[1] – Removal and installation of transaxle from vehicle chassis.
[2] – Bench overhaul time for transaxle and differential. DOES NOT include removal and installation.
[3] – Manufacturer gives procedures for transmission removal with and without engine removal. Some vehicles may require engine removal.

IDENTIFICATION

Vehicle Identification Number (VIN) is used for correct application of component parts and assemblies. VIN location is at top left of instrument panel. Transaxle identification tag is attached to side of transaxle case.

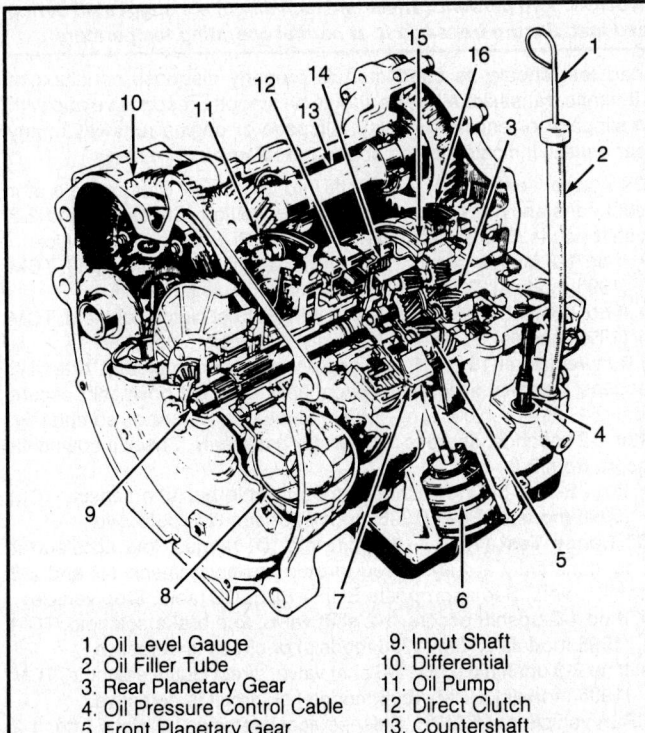

1. Oil Level Gauge
2. Oil Filler Tube
3. Rear Planetary Gear
4. Oil Pressure Control Cable
5. Front Planetary Gear
6. 2nd Brake Piston Cover
7. 2nd Brake Band
8. Torque Converter
9. Input Shaft
10. Differential
11. Oil Pump
12. Direct Clutch
13. Countershaft
14. Forward Clutch
15. One-Way Clutch
16. 1st-Reverse Brake

93C24358

Courtesy of Suzuki of America, Corp.

Fig. 1: Cross-Sectional View Of Automatic Transaxle

DESCRIPTION & OPERATION

NOTE: For electronic diagnosis information, see SUZUKI 3-SPEED ELECTRONIC CONTROLS article.

Model ECC is a 3-speed electronically controlled automatic transaxle with a hydraulic torque converter, countershaft and differential. The transaxle features 2 planetary gears, 2 disc clutches, one band brake, one disc brake and one one-way clutch. *See Fig. 1.*

Transaxle is equipped with shift and key interlock systems. Shift interlock system prevents shift selector lever from being moved from Park unless brake pedal is depressed and accelerator is in idle position. In case of a malfunction, shift selector lever can be released by depressing button on rear of shifter console. Key interlock system prevents ignition key from being removed from ignition lock assembly unless shift selector lever is in "P" position.

LUBRICATION & ADJUSTMENTS

See appropriate AUTOMATIC TRANSMISSION SERVICING article in TRANSMISSION SERVICING section.

TROUBLE SHOOTING

PRELIMINARY CHECK

Troubles occurring with electronically controlled transmissions can be caused by engine, electronic control or transmission. It is necessary to isolate these 3 areas before proceeding with trouble shooting.

SYMPTOM DIAGNOSIS

Harsh Engagement In Forward Gears – Check fluid level, T.V. cable adjustment, shift cable adjustment, valve body, accumulators and fluid pressure.
Slips In 1st Gear – Check fluid level, T.V. cable adjustment, shift cable adjustment, valve body, accumulators, forward clutch, one-way clutch and fluid pressure.
No Upshift From 1st Gear – Check T.V. cable adjustment, valve body, intermediate servo, 2nd brake band and fluid pressure.
Slipping Or Rough 1-2 Upshift – Check fluid level, T.V. cable adjustment, valve body, intermediate servo, 2nd brake band, torque converter, forward clutch and fluid pressure.
No 2-3 Shift Or 2-3 Shift Slipping – Check fluid level, T.V. cable, valve body, intermediate servo, 2nd brake band, torque converter, direct clutch and fluid pressure.
High Or Low Shift Points – Check fluid level, T.V. cable, valve body, torque converter, forward clutch, direct clutch and fluid pressure.
No Downshift At Part Throttle Or Delayed Downshift – Check T.V. cable adjustment, valve body, intermediate servo, 2nd brake band, 1st and reverse brake and one-way clutch.
No Engine Braking Or No 3-2-1 Manual Downshift – Check shift cable, valve body, intermediate servo, 2nd brake band, 1st and reverse brake and one-way clutch.
No Reverse Or Slips In Reverse – Check fluid level, shift cable adjustment, valve body, direct clutch and fluid pressure.
Vehicle Does Not Move In Any Gear – Check fluid level, shift cable, parking lock pawl, torque converter, valve body and fluid pressure.

CLUTCH & BAND APPLICATION

Selector Lever Position	Elements In Use
"D" (Drive)	
1st Gear	Forward Clutch & One-Way Clutch
2nd Gear	Forward Clutch & 2nd Brake
3rd Gear	Forward Clutch & Direct Clutch
"2" (Second)	
1st Gear	Forward Clutch & One-Way Clutch
2nd Gear	Forward Clutch & 2nd Brake
"L" (Low)	
1st Gear	Forward Clutch, 1st and Reverse Brake & One-Way Clutch
"R" (Reverse)	Direct Clutch & 1st and Reverse Brake
"N" (Neutral)	No Elements In Use
"P" (Park)	1st and Reverse Brake

TESTING

TIME LAG TEST

Testing Precautions – Perform test at normal fluid operating temperature. Allow one minute between tests to cool transaxle. Perform 3 measurements and take average value.

Testing Procedure – Fully apply parking brake and check idling speed (with A/C off). Idle speed should be 600-800 RPM. Move shift selector lever from "P" to "R" position. Using stopwatch, measure time lag from moving shifting lever until shock is felt. In same manner, measure time lag of "R" to "D" shift. See TIME LAG TEST SPECIFICATIONS table.

TIME LAG TEST SPECIFICATIONS

Selector Position	Time
"P" To "R"	About 1.4 sec.
"R" To "D"	About 1.0 sec.

Time Lag Test Results – If "P" to "R" time lag is longer than specified, line pressure is too low, direct clutch is worn and/or 1st and reverse brake is worn. If "R" to "D" time lag is longer than specified, line pressure is too low, forward clutch is worn and/or one-way clutch is faulty.

STALL SPEED TEST

CAUTION: DO NOT run engine continuously at stall speed for more than 5 seconds. Oil temperature may rise excessively high.

1) Object of test is to check overall performance of transaxle and engine by measuring stall speeds in "D" and "R" ranges. Perform test at normal operating temperature.
2) Connect engine tachometer. Apply parking brake. Block front and rear wheels. Start engine. Depress brake pedal.
3) Shift into "D" range. Fully depress accelerator pedal. Immediately note engine RPM. DO NOT perform test longer than 5 seconds. Stall speed should be 2200-2700 RPM for 1.0L engine, and 2000-2500 RPM for 1.3L engine. Perform same test in "R" range.
4) If stall speed is same for both ranges, but lower than specified RPM, engine output may be insufficient or torque converter is defective.
5) If stall speed in "D" range is higher than specifications, forward clutch may be slipping or one-way clutch is defective.
6) If stall speed in "R" range is higher than specifications, direct clutch is slipping or 1st and reverse brake is slipping.

LINE PRESSURE TEST

NOTE: Perform line pressure test when transmission fluid is at normal operating temperature. Ensure transaxle is not leaking. DO NOT run engine continuously at stall speed for more than 5 seconds.

1) With engine off, remove plug and connect oil pressure gauge to plug hole. *See Fig. 2.* Apply parking brake and block wheels. Start engine.
2) Apply brake and shift into "D" range. Depress accelerator. Note pressure readings at idle and stall speeds. Repeat test in "R" range. Compare pressure readings to those listed in LINE PRESSURE table.
3) Low pressure in both ranges indicates accelerator cable and/or T.V. cable may be out of adjustment, defective regulator valve, defective oil pump or defective valve body throttle valve.
4) High pressure in both ranges indicates accelerator cable and/or T.V. cable may be out of adjustment, defective regulator valve, or defective valve body throttle valve.
5) Low pressure in "D" range indicates "D" range oil circuit leaking pressure or defective forward clutch. Low pressure in "R" range indicates "R" range oil circuit leaking pressure, defective direct clutch, or defective 1st and reverse brake. Reinstall plug and tighten to 54-78 INCH lbs. (6.1-8.8 N.m).

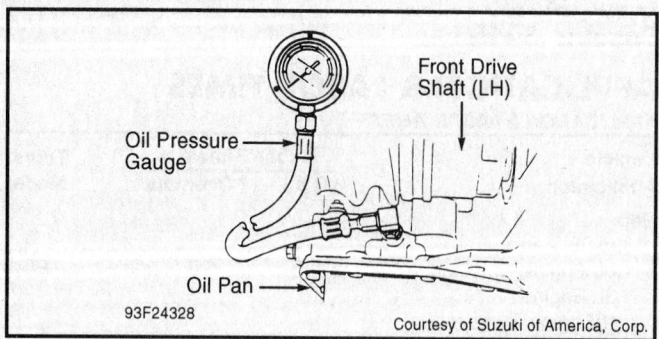

Fig. 2: Checking Line Pressure

LINE PRESSURE

Application	psi (kg/cm²)
1.0L Engine	
"D" Range	
Idle Speed (800-900 RPM)	29-57 (2-4)
Stall Speed (2200-2700 RPM)	57-85 (4-6)
"R" Range	
Idle Speed (800-900 RPM)	78-114 (5.5-8)
Stall Speed (2200-2700 RPM)	128-178 (9-12.5)
1.3L Engine	
"D" Range	
Idle Speed (800-900 RPM)	29-57 (2-4)
Stall Speed (2000-2500 RPM)	71-100 (5-7)
"R" Range	
Idle Speed (800-900 RPM)	78-114 (5.5-8)
Stall Speed (2000-2500 RPM)	149-199 (10.5-14)

ROAD TEST

CAUTION: Two persons (driver and technician) are suggested during road test. Ensure transaxle is at normal operating temperature.

Road test should be conducted to properly diagnose condition of automatic transaxle. All shifts should be smooth, responsive and with no slippage or engine runaway. Slippage or engine runaway in any gear usually indicates clutch or band problems.

"D" Range Test (1.0L) – 1) Shift into "D" range. Hold accelerator pedal constantly at fully closed throttle position. Check 1-2 and 2-3 upshift points. See appropriate SHIFT SPEEDS table. Stop vehicle.
- If no 1-2 upshift occurs, 1-2 shift valve, 2nd brake solenoid, TCM (1995 models), PCM (1996 models) or circuit is defective.
- If no 2-3 upshift occurs, 2-3 shift valve, direct clutch solenoid, TCM (1995 models), PCM (1996 models) or circuit is defective.

2) Run vehicle at 19 MPH. Release accelerator completely. After 1-2 seconds, depress accelerator pedal fully. Check if downshift occurs from 2-1. Run vehicle at 47 MPH. Release accelerator completely. After 1-2 seconds, depress accelerator pedal fully. Check if downshift occurs from 3-2.
- If no 2-1 or 3-2 downshift occurs, throttle position sensor, TCM (1995 models), PCM (1996 models) or circuit is defective.

"D" Range Test (1.3L) – 1) Shift into "D" range. Hold accelerator pedal constantly at fully closed throttle position. Check 1-2 and 2-3 upshift points. See appropriate SHIFT SPEEDS table. Stop vehicle.
- If no 1-2 upshift occurs, 1-2 shift valve, 2nd brake solenoid, TCM (1995 models), PCM (1996 models) or circuit is defective.
- If no 2-3 upshift occurs, 2-3 shift valve, direct clutch solenoid, TCM (1995 models), PCM (1996 models) or circuit is defective.

2) Run vehicle at 15 MPH. Release accelerator completely. After 1-2 seconds, depress accelerator pedal fully. Check if downshift occurs from 2-1. Run vehicle at 47 MPH. Release accelerator completely. After 1-2 seconds, depress accelerator pedal fully. Check if downshift occurs from 3-2.
- If no 2-1 or 3-2 downshift occurs, throttle position sensor, TCM (1995 models), PCM (1996 models) or circuit is defective.

SHIFT SPEEDS (METRO)

Application	MPH
"D" Range	
Fully Closed Throttle	
1-2	11
2-3	19
3-2	9
2-1	9
Wide Open Throttle	
1-2	37
2-3	70
3-2	60
2-1	25
"2" Range	
Fully Closed Throttle	
1-2	11
2-1	9
Wide Open Throttle	
1-2	37
2-1	25
"L" Range	
Fully Closed Throttle	
2-1	33
Wide Open Throttle	
2-1	33

SHIFT SPEEDS (SWIFT)

Application	MPH (1.0L)	MPH (1.3L)
"D" Range		
Fully Closed Throttle		
1-2	9	8
2-3	21	19
3-2	6	6
2-1	6	6
Wide Open Throttle		
1-2	32	34
2-3	60	62
3-2	51	51
2-1	23	22
"2" Range		
Fully Closed Throttle		
1-2	9	8
2-1	6	6
Wide Open Throttle		
1-2	32	34
2-1	23	22
"L" Range		
Fully Closed Throttle		
2-1	33	33
Wide Open Throttle		
2-1	33	33

ENGINE BRAKE TEST

1) While driving in "D" range, 3rd gear, shift down to "2" range and check engine braking effect. If there is no engine braking effect, 2nd brake is defective.
2) While driving in "D" range, 3rd gear, shift down to "L" range and check engine braking effect. If there is no engine braking effect, 1st and reverse brake is defective.

ON-VEHICLE SERVICE

THROTTLE VALVE (T.V.) CABLE

Removal – 1) Remove cable cover. Remove T.V. cable from accelerator cable. Drain transmission fluid. Remove oil pan.
2) Remove cable from throttle valve cam. Remove cable from transaxle case.

NOTE: Oil pressure control cable can be disconnected from throttle valve cam without removal of 2nd brake solenoid.

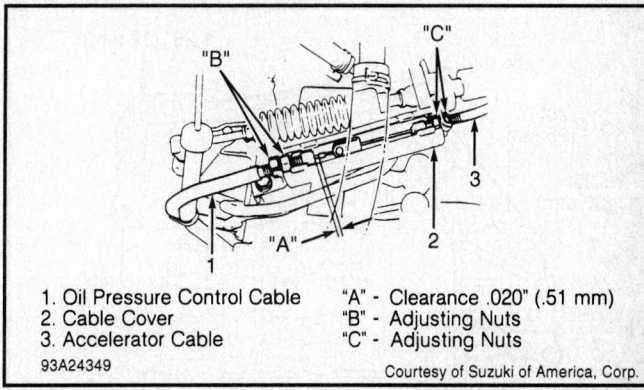

1. Oil Pressure Control Cable
2. Cable Cover
3. Accelerator Cable
"A" - Clearance .020" (.51 mm)
"B" - Adjusting Nuts
"C" - Adjusting Nuts
93A24349
Courtesy of Suzuki of America, Corp.

Fig. 3: Adjusting Throttle Valve (T.V.) Pressure Control Cable

Installation – 1) To install, reverse removal procedure. After connecting cable to accelerator cable, check and adjust cable play. *See Fig. 3.*
2) With cable cover removed, adjust clearance "A" to specification by turning adjusting nuts "B". Adjusting nuts "C" can be used for adjustment (if necessary). Tighten adjusting nuts and install cable cover.

TRANSMISSION RANGE (TR) SWITCH

Removal – Disconnect harness connector. Remove mounting bolt and remove TR switch from transaxle. DO NOT attempt to repair TR switch.
Installation – 1) Shift selector lever to "N" position. Using a flat-blade screwdriver, rotate TR switch joint full clockwise ("P" position). A "click" sound should be heard each time a gear position is selected. Next, rotate TR switch joint counterclockwise 3 clicks to obtain "N" position. *See Fig. 4.*
2) Install TR switch on manual shift shaft. Tighten TR switch mounting bolt to 10-17 ft. lbs. (14-23 N.m). Install harness connector. Check for proper installation. Apply parking brake and block vehicle wheels. Check for the following:

- With selector lever in "P", turn ignition switch to START position. Engine should start.
- With selector lever in "N", turn ignition switch to START position. Engine should start.
- With selector lever shifted from "N" to "L" and back to "N", turn ignition switch to START position. Engine should start.
- Shift selector lever from "N" to "P". Check starter for operation.
- Ensure starter and ignition switch operate in "P" and "N" position.
- Without starting engine, turn ignition switch to ON position and shift selector lever to "R". Ensure back-up lights illuminate.

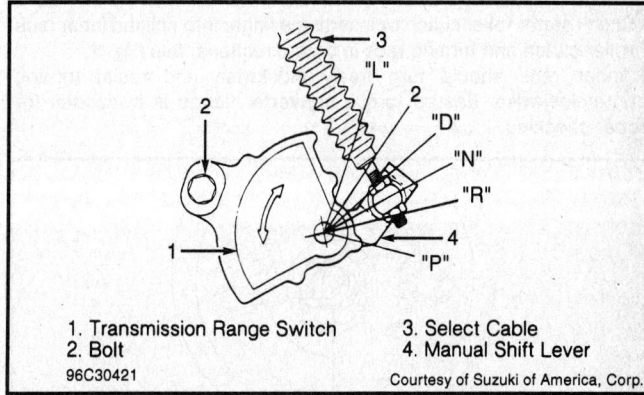

1. Transmission Range Switch
2. Bolt
3. Select Cable
4. Manual Shift Lever
96C30421
Courtesy of Suzuki of America, Corp.

Fig. 4: Adjusting Transmission Range (TR) Switch

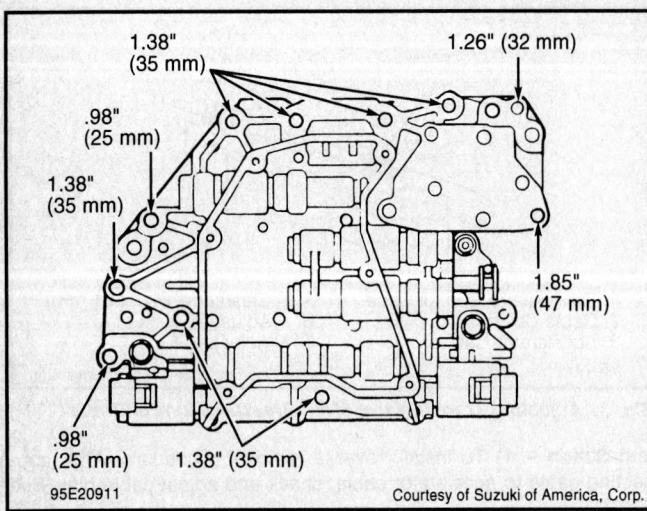

Fig. 5: Identifying Valve Body Bolts

VALVE BODY

Removal – **1)** Disconnect negative battery cable. Raise and support vehicle. Remove pan and drain fluid. Remove harness connectors from shift solenoids. Gently prying with screwdriver, remove fluid pipes.

2) Disconnect T.V. cable from cam. Remove screen (filter). Remove valve body retaining bolts and remove valve body. If necessary, forward clutch and 2nd brake accumulators may be removed.

Installation – To install, reverse removal procedure. Install bolts in correct location. See Fig. 5. Tighten bolts in a crisscross pattern to specified torque. See TORQUE SPECIFICATIONS. Fill transaxle with fluid (approximately 1.5 qts.).

REMOVAL & INSTALLATION

For transaxle removal procedure, see appropriate AUTOMATIC TRANSMISSION REMOVAL article in TRANSMISSION SERVICING section.

TORQUE CONVERTER

NOTE: The torque converter is a sealed unit and must be serviced as a complete unit. Torque converter and transaxle cooler must be thoroughly cleaned and flushed if transaxle is contaminated.

STATOR ROLLER CLUTCH TEST

1) Check stator roller clutch by inserting a finger into splined inner race of roller clutch and turning race in both directions. See Fig. 6.

2) Inner race should turn freely clockwise and resist turning counterclockwise. Ensure torque converter flange is horizontal for proper checking.

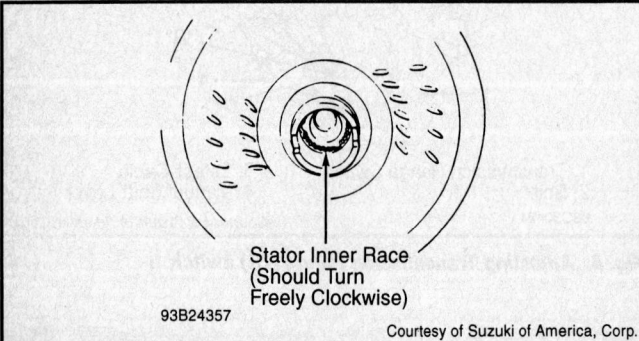

Fig. 6: Checking Stator Roller Clutch

TRANSMISSION DISASSEMBLY

NOTE: Thoroughly clean transaxle exterior prior to disassembly. Use special care in handling aluminum components. DO NOT turn transaxle over when removing oil pan. Turning transaxle will contaminate valve body with foreign matter from bottom of oil pan.

1) Remove torque converter. Remove engine mounting LH bracket. Remove oil level gauge and oil filler tube. Remove speedometer driven gear. Remove vehicle speed sensor. Remove park/neutral position switch. Drain transmission fluid. Remove oil pan and gasket.

2) Remove direct clutch and 2nd brake solenoid connectors. Using a screwdriver, carefully pry up 2 oil tubes from lower valve body. Remove cable from throttle valve cam. Remove oil strainer (filter). Remove 11 lower valve body bolts. Remove valve body assembly. Ensure manual valve does not drop when removing valve body.

3) Using 15 psi (1 kg/cm²) of compressed air in apply hole (beside accumulator piston bore), remove accumulator pistons into a shop towel. Remove pistons and springs. Remove 2nd brake band cover and gasket.

4) Check 2nd brake piston stroke. Scribe mark on piston rod. Apply compressed air into oil hole. Measure 2nd brake piston rod stroke. See Fig. 7. Piston stroke should be .060-.120" (1.5-3.0 mm). If piston stroke exceeds specification, inspect brake during disassembly.

5) Remove 2nd brake piston. Using valve spring compressor tool, push in piston cover. Remove snap ring. Remove 2nd brake piston cover and piston. See Fig. 8.

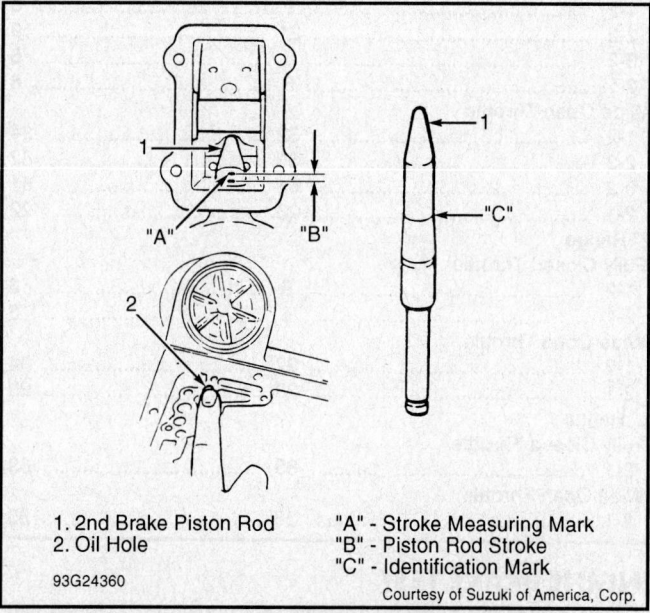

1. 2nd Brake Piston Rod	"A" - Stroke Measuring Mark
2. Oil Hole	"B" - Piston Rod Stroke
	"C" - Identification Mark

Fig. 7: Measuring 2nd Brake Piston Rod Stroke

6) Remove solenoid wire hold plate nut. Remove 2 wire harness clamps on transaxle. Remove solenoid wire. Remove 6 oil pump bolts. Using 2 slide hammers, remove oil pump. Ensure 2nd brake piston and piston rod have been removed prior to oil pump removal to prevent damage of 2nd brake band.

7) Remove transaxle case housing while tapping lightly with a plastic hammer. Remove 2nd brake band pin. Remove direct and forward clutch together while holding input shaft. DO NOT lose ring gear race and bearing, which may sometimes stick to input shaft.

8) Remove direct clutch from input shaft. Remove 2nd brake band. Remove front planetary ring gear and bearing. Remove front planetary gear. Remove planetary sun gear and front planetary gear bearing.

9) Carefully remove one-way clutch snap ring. Remove one-way clutch and rear planetary gear. Remove rear planetary ring gear, ring gear bearing and washers.

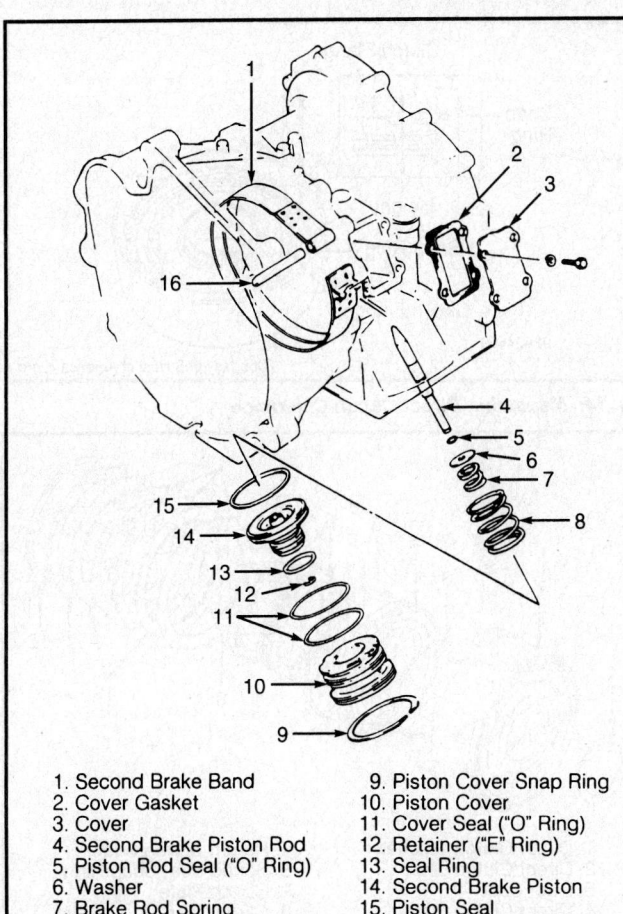

1. Second Brake Band
2. Cover Gasket
3. Cover
4. Second Brake Piston Rod
5. Piston Rod Seal ("O" Ring)
6. Washer
7. Brake Rod Spring
8. Piston Spring

9. Piston Cover Snap Ring
10. Piston Cover
11. Cover Seal ("O" Ring)
12. Retainer ("E" Ring)
13. Seal Ring
14. Second Brake Piston
15. Piston Seal
16. Pin

93B24498   Courtesy of Suzuki of America, Corp.

Fig. 8: Exploded View Of 2nd Brake Piston

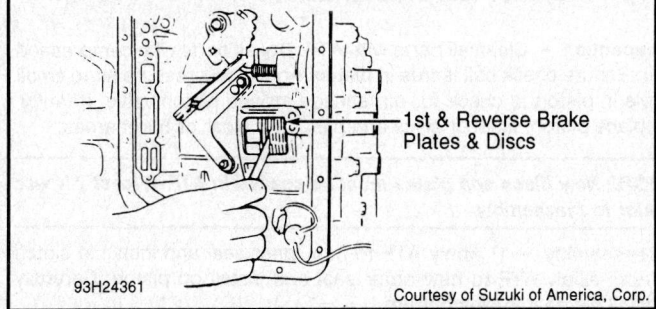

1st & Reverse Brake Plates & Discs

93H24361   Courtesy of Suzuki of America, Corp.

Fig. 9: Measuring 1st & Reverse Brake Clearance

10) Check 1st and reverse brake clearance. Measure clearance between snap ring and flange. Clearance should be .023-.075" (.58-1.91 mm). See Fig. 9. If clearance exceeds specification, inspect 1st and reverse brake discs and plates.

11) Remove 2 snap rings, 1st and reverse brake flange, discs, plates and damper. Remove differential gear. Remove 10 bolts and 2 nuts from rear cover. Remove rear cover by lightly tapping with a plastic hammer.

12) Unstake reduction driven gear lock nut. Shift manual shift lever to "P". This locks output shaft. Carefully loosen nut so as not to damage reduction gear or parking lock pawl. Remove reduction gear.

13) Drive out countershaft with a plastic hammer. Drive out output shaft by pushing outer race of internal output shaft bearing. To prevent damage, DO NOT hit output shaft or shaft end.

14) Remove parking lock pawl shaft and spring. Remove parking lock pawl and sleeve. Remove detent spring and manual shift shaft. Push down return spring and remove snap ring. Remove return spring. Apply compressed air into case passage to remove 1st and reverse brake piston. Passage is beside clutch, in middle of case. If piston does not pop out with compressed air, use needle-nose pliers to remove.

COMPONENT DISASSEMBLY & REASSEMBLY

NOTE: Clean all parts with cleaning solvent and air dry. DO NOT use wiping cloths or rags to clean or dry parts. Soak new clutch discs and brake band in ATF for 2 hours or more before assembly. Apply ATF to sliding, rolling and thrusting surfaces of all components. Replace all gaskets and "O" rings. Apply ATF to all "O" rings except oil pump cover seal. Replace oil seals that are removed. Apply grease to oil seal lips. Check each part for proper operation after installation.

OIL PUMP

Disassembly – Remove 2 oil pump cover seal rings. Remove oil pump cover seal. Remove 11 oil pump cover bolts. Remove cover. See Fig. 10.

Inspection – 1) Check pump body oil seal for wear, damage or cracks. Replace oil seal (if necessary). Apply grease to oil seal lip when installing.

2) Check driven gear-to-pump body clearance. Push driven gear against pump body. Measure clearance between driven gear and pump body. See Fig. 11. Replace driven gear if clearance is not within specification. See OIL PUMP CLEARANCE table.

OIL PUMP CLEARANCE

Application	Thickness – In. (mm)
Driven Gear-To-Pump Body Clearance	
Standard	.0028-.0059 (.071-.150)
Maximum	.012 (.305)
Gear-To-Crescent Clearance	
Standard	.0043-.0055 (.109-.140)
Maximum	.012 (.305)
Gear Side Clearance	
Standard	.0008-.0020 (.020-.051)
Maximum	.0039 (.100)

3) Measure tip clearance between both gears and crescent shaped part of pump body. See Fig. 12. Replace drive or driven gear if not within specification.

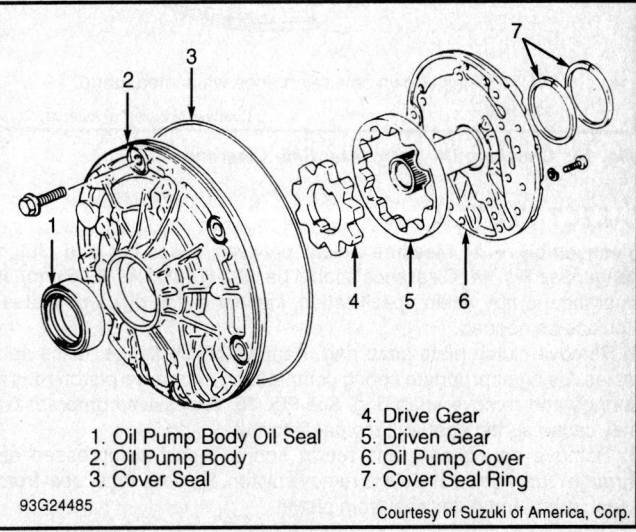

1. Oil Pump Body Oil Seal
2. Oil Pump Body
3. Cover Seal

4. Drive Gear
5. Driven Gear
6. Oil Pump Cover
7. Cover Seal Ring

93G24485   Courtesy of Suzuki of America, Corp.

Fig. 10: Exploded View Of Oil Pump

4) Using feeler gauge and straightedge, measure side clearance between drive and driven gears and pump body. *See Fig. 13.* Replace drive or driven gear if not within specification.

Reassembly – 1) Install pump body oil seal. Apply grease to oil seal lip. Coat driven and drive gears with ATF. Install gears to pump body. Install pump cover to pump body. Tighten 11 pump cover bolts to 72-102 INCH lbs. (8.1-11.5 N.m).

2) Apply ATF to oil pump bushings and 2 seal rings. Install 2 oil pump cover seal rings. Apply grease to oil pump cover seal ("O" ring) and install. Check drive gear for smooth rotation.

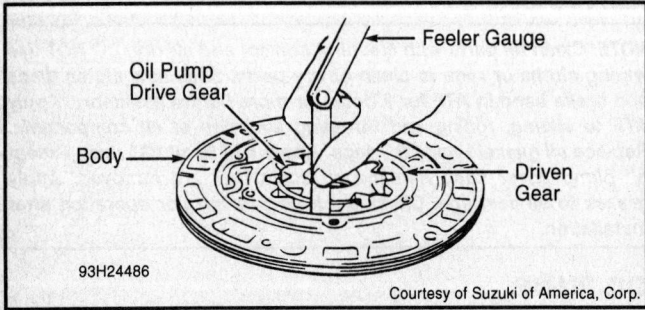

Fig. 11: Checking Oil Pump Driven Gear Clearance

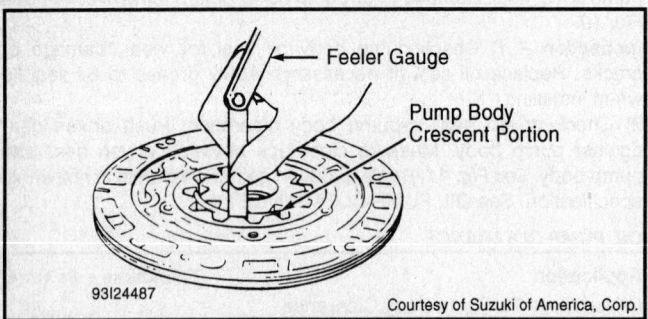

Fig. 12: Checking Oil Pump Tip Clearance

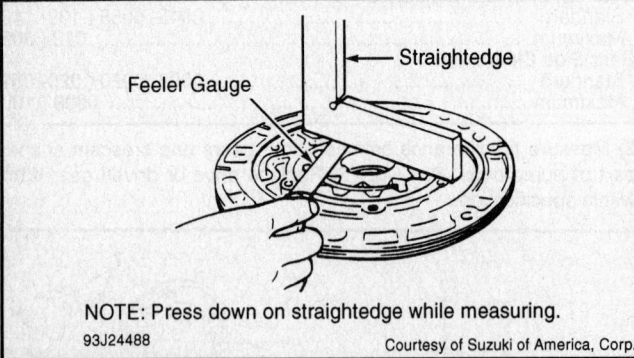

NOTE: Press down on straightedge while measuring.

Fig. 13: Checking Oil Pump Gear Side Clearance

DIRECT CLUTCH

Disassembly – 1) Measure height between snap ring and clutch flange. *See Fig. 14.* Clearance should be .098-.120" (2.49-3.05 mm). If clearance is not within specification, inspect clutch discs or plates. Replace as needed.

2) Remove clutch plate snap ring. Remove clutch flange, discs and plates. Using appropriate spring compressor, compress piston return springs and remove snap ring. *See Fig. 15.* Excessive compression may cause spring seat to become distorted.

3) Remove spring seat and return spring. Apply compressed air through clutch drum oil hole to remove piston. Remove inner seal from clutch drum and outer seal from piston.

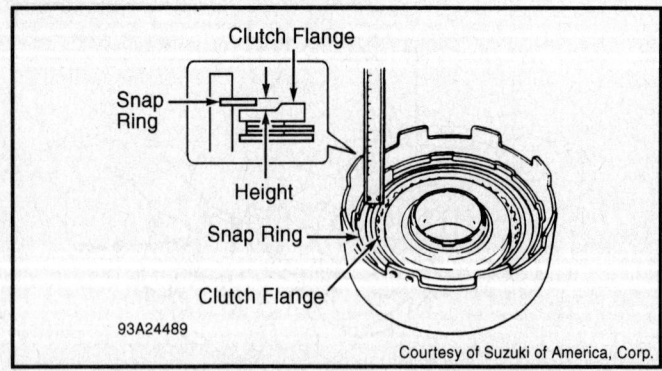

Fig. 14: Measuring Direct Clutch Clearance

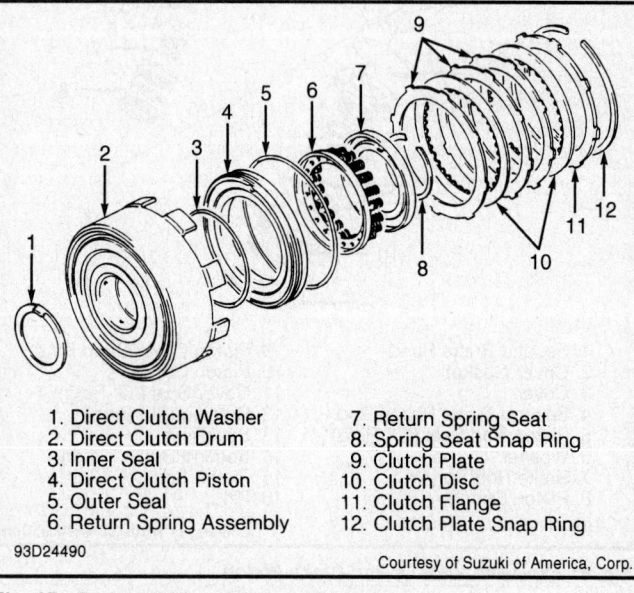

1. Direct Clutch Washer
2. Direct Clutch Drum
3. Inner Seal
4. Direct Clutch Piston
5. Outer Seal
6. Return Spring Assembly
7. Return Spring Seat
8. Spring Seat Snap Ring
9. Clutch Plate
10. Clutch Disc
11. Clutch Flange
12. Clutch Plate Snap Ring

Fig. 15: Exploded View Of Direct Clutch

Inspection – Clean all parts with ATF. Dry all parts with compressed air. Ensure check ball is free in piston. Apply low pressure air to small hole in piston to check for air leakage around piston valve. If faulty, replace piston. Inspect discs and plates for wear or burnt areas.

NOTE: New discs and plates must be soaked in ATF at least 2 hours prior to reassembly.

Reassembly – 1) Apply ATF to new inner seal and install in clutch drum. Apply ATF to new outer seal and install on piston. Carefully install piston into clutch drum.

2) Install clutch return spring and seat. Compress return springs using spring compressor and an arbor press. Install snap ring. Ensure snap ring is securely fitted in 4 projections of spring seat.

3) Install in order: plate, disc, plate, plate, disc and flange. Install clutch plate snap ring. Measure height between snap ring and clutch flange. *See Fig. 14.* Standard clearance should be .098-.120" (2.49-3.05 mm). If height is not within specification, replace flange. Flange is available in 2 thicknesses: .118" (3.00 mm) and .133" (3.38 mm). Check piston for proper movement by applying low compressed air through oil hole in clutch drum.

FORWARD CLUTCH

Disassembly – 1) Measure height between snap ring and clutch flange. *See Fig. 16.* Standard clearance should be .079-.106" (2.01-2.69 mm). If clearance is not within specification, inspect clutch discs or plates. replace as needed.

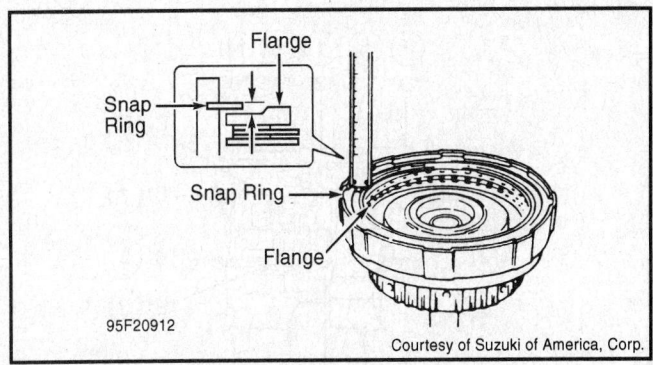

95F20912

Courtesy of Suzuki of America, Corp.

Fig. 16: Measuring Forward Clutch Clearance

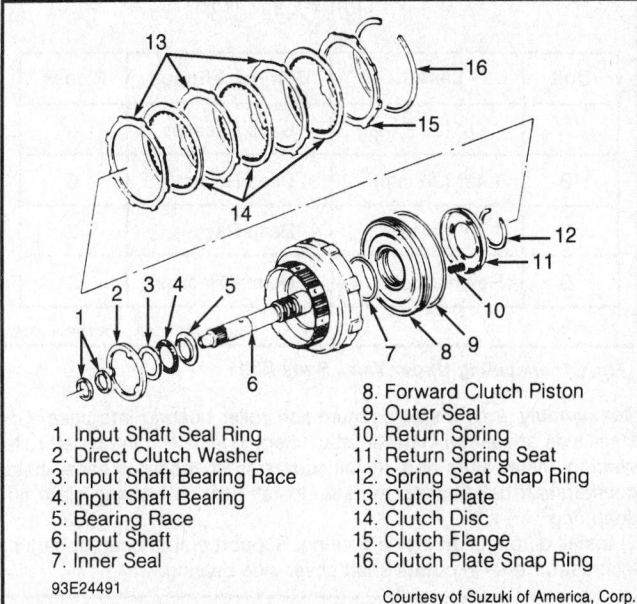

93E24491

1. Input Shaft Seal Ring
2. Direct Clutch Washer
3. Input Shaft Bearing Race
4. Input Shaft Bearing
5. Bearing Race
6. Input Shaft
7. Inner Seal

8. Forward Clutch Piston
9. Outer Seal
10. Return Spring
11. Return Spring Seat
12. Spring Seat Snap Ring
13. Clutch Plate
14. Clutch Disc
15. Clutch Flange
16. Clutch Plate Snap Ring

Courtesy of Suzuki of America, Corp.

Fig. 17: Exploded View Of Forward Clutch

2) Remove clutch plate snap ring. Remove clutch flange, discs and plates. *See Fig. 17.* Using appropriate spring compressor, compress piston return springs and remove snap ring. Excessive compression may cause spring seat to become distorted.

3) Remove spring seat and return spring. Apply compressed air through input shaft oil hole to remove piston. Remove inner and outer seals from piston.

Inspection – Clean all parts with ATF. Dry all parts with compressed air. Ensure check ball is free in piston. Apply low pressure air to small hole in piston to check for air leakage around piston valve. If faulty, replace piston. Inspect discs and plates for wear or burnt areas.

NOTE: New discs and plates must be soaked in ATF at least 2 hours prior to reassembly.

Reassembly – **1)** Apply ATF to new inner and outer seals. Install inner and outer seals to clutch piston. Carefully install piston into input shaft drum.

2) Install piston return springs and seat. Compress return springs using spring compressor and an arbor press. Install snap ring. Ensure snap ring is securely fitted in 4 projections of spring seat.

3) Install in order: plate, disc, plate, disc, plate, disc and flange. Install clutch plate snap ring. Measure height between snap ring and clutch flange. Clearance should be .079-.106" (2.01-2.69 mm). If height is not within specification, replace flange. Flange is available in 2 thicknesses: .118" (3.00 mm) and .133" (3.38 mm). Check piston for proper movement by applying low pressure compressed air through oil hole in input shaft.

VALVE BODY

Disassembly – **1)** Remove lower valve body cover bolts. Remove lower valve body cover and gasket. Remove direct clutch and 2nd brake solenoids from valve body. *See Fig. 18.*

2) Remove 16 bolts from upper valve body. Carefully remove upper valve body from lower valve body. DO NOT allow 4 steel check balls to drop out. Remove valve body gaskets. *See Fig. 19.*

3) All valve body components must be installed in original location. Lay all components out in sequence during removal for reassembly reference. Note diameter and check ball location. *See Fig. 20.*

Inspection – **1)** Clean all parts with ATF. Clean all fluid passages and holes. Using compressed air, ensure passages or holes are clear.

2) Inspect valves for scoring or roughness. Inspect valve springs for damage, squareness, rust and collapsed coils. Replace spring if necessary. Valve body springs must be arranged with corresponding valve.

Reassembly – **1)** Coat all components with ATF. To reassemble, reverse removal procedure. Note special procedures listed.

2) Install 4 steel check balls in upper valve body. *See Fig. 20.* Replace all gaskets with same type as old gaskets. When installing each valve to valve body, ensure parts are installed in correct direction.

3) When reassembling upper valve body, install same number of throttle valve rings as were removed.

4) Install lower valve body cover and gasket. Tighten lower valve body cover bolts to 36-48 INCH lbs. (4.1-5.4 N.m). Install throttle valve cam assembly. Tighten throttle valve cam bolt to 54-78 INCH lbs. (6.1-8.8 N.m).

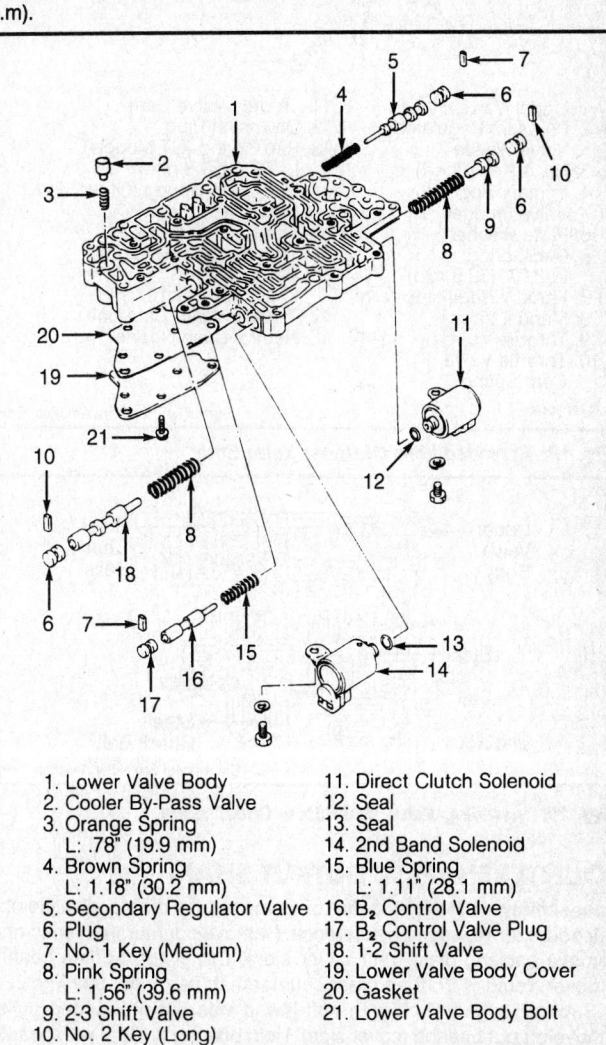

1. Lower Valve Body
2. Cooler By-Pass Valve
3. Orange Spring
   L: .78" (19.9 mm)
4. Brown Spring
   L: 1.18" (30.2 mm)
5. Secondary Regulator Valve
6. Plug
7. No. 1 Key (Medium)
8. Pink Spring
   L: 1.56" (39.6 mm)
9. 2-3 Shift Valve
10. No. 2 Key (Long)

11. Direct Clutch Solenoid
12. Seal
13. Seal
14. 2nd Band Solenoid
15. Blue Spring
    L: 1.11" (28.1 mm)
16. B₂ Control Valve
17. B₂ Control Valve Plug
18. 1-2 Shift Valve
19. Lower Valve Body Cover
20. Gasket
21. Lower Valve Body Bolt

93F24492

Courtesy of Suzuki of America, Corp.

Fig. 18: Exploded View Of Lower Valve Body

5) Install upper valve body to lower valve body. Install 2 reamer bolts finger tight. Install upper valve body bolts and tighten to 44-53 INCH lbs. (5-6 N.m). *See Fig. 21.*

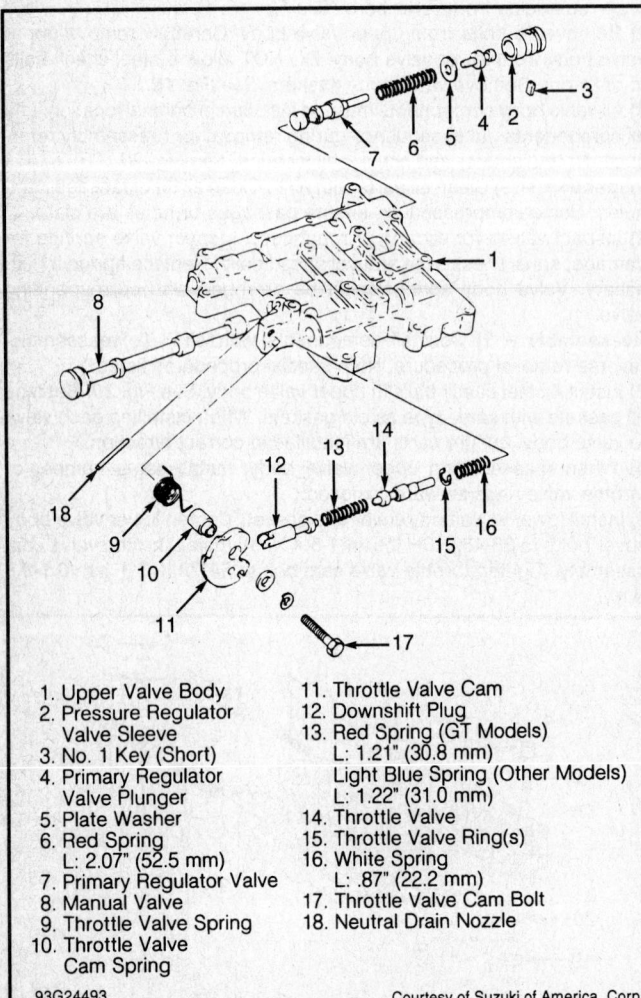

1. Upper Valve Body
2. Pressure Regulator Valve Sleeve
3. No. 1 Key (Short)
4. Primary Regulator Valve Plunger
5. Plate Washer
6. Red Spring L: 2.07" (52.5 mm)
7. Primary Regulator Valve
8. Manual Valve
9. Throttle Valve Spring
10. Throttle Valve Cam Spring
11. Throttle Valve Cam
12. Downshift Plug
13. Red Spring (GT Models) L: 1.21" (30.8 mm) Light Blue Spring (Other Models) L: 1.22" (31.0 mm)
14. Throttle Valve
15. Throttle Valve Ring(s)
16. White Spring L: .87" (22.2 mm)
17. Throttle Valve Cam Bolt
18. Neutral Drain Nozzle

93G24493   Courtesy of Suzuki of America, Corp.

Fig. 19: Exploded View Of Upper Valve Body

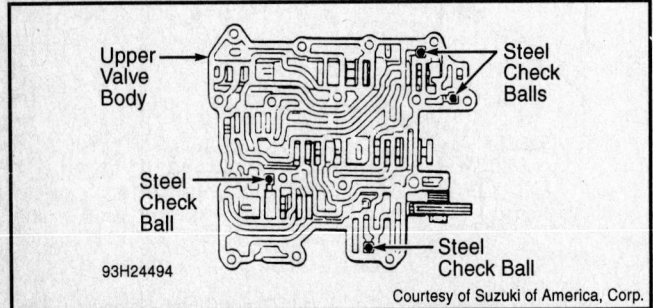

93H24494   Courtesy of Suzuki of America, Corp.

Fig. 20: Installing Valve Body Steel Check Balls

COUNTERSHAFT & OUTPUT SHAFT

Disassembly – 1) Note order of components during disassembly procedure for reassembly reference. Remove countershaft snap ring. Remove backing plate (rear cover side). Using appropriate bearing remover, remove front and rear countershaft bearings. *See Fig. 22.*
2) Support output shaft with soft-jawed vise. Using bearing puller, remove output bearing (cover side). Hold bearing (inside) with bearing puller, and remove output shaft with a press.

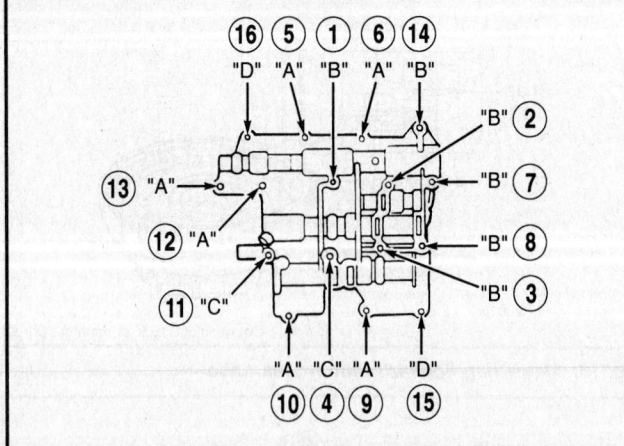

Bolt	Length	Bolt Head Shape	Pieces
A	1.16" (29.5 mm)	Deep Recess	6
B	1.49" (38 mm)	Deep Recess	6
C	1.73" (44 mm)	Deep Recess	2
D	Reamer Bolt	Normal Recess	2

96J04639   Courtesy of Suzuki of America, Corp.

Fig. 21: Installing Upper Valve Body Bolts

Reassembly – 1) Install countershaft roller bearing into case. Use small side of bearing installer attachment to install countershaft roller bearing. Install snap ring. Install countershaft spacer to case. Install countershaft ball bearing to case. Install bearing backing plate and snap ring.
2) Install output shaft inside bearing. Support output shaft at parking lock gear. Press in output shaft cover side bearing.

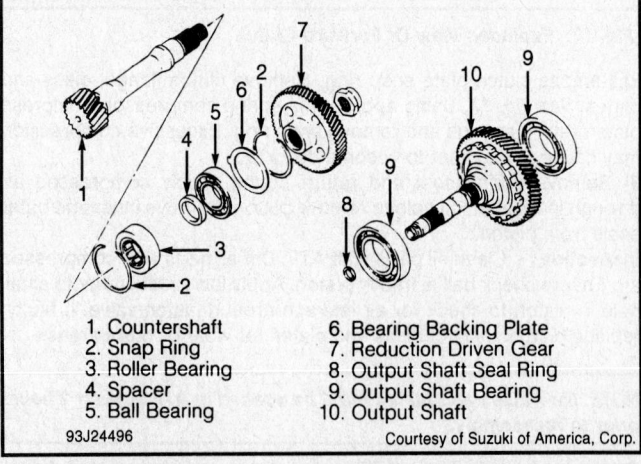

1. Countershaft
2. Snap Ring
3. Roller Bearing
4. Spacer
5. Ball Bearing
6. Bearing Backing Plate
7. Reduction Driven Gear
8. Output Shaft Seal Ring
9. Output Shaft Bearing
10. Output Shaft

93J24496   Courtesy of Suzuki of America, Corp.

Fig. 22: Exploded View Of Countershaft & Output Shaft (Typical)

DIFFERENTIAL

Disassembly – 1) Using appropriate bearing puller, remove differential left-side bearing. Support differential case with soft-jawed vise and remove 8 bolts. Remove final gear. Drive out differential right-side bearing.
2) Remove speedometer drive gear. Remove side pinion shaft spring pin. Remove side pinion shaft, 2 differential pinions, 2 side pinion washers, 2 differential gears and 2 side gear washers. *See Fig. 23.*

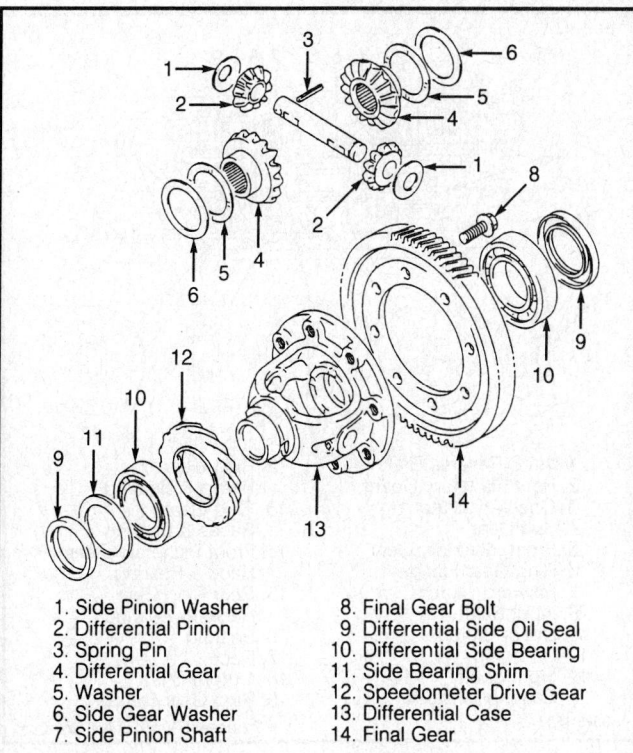

1. Side Pinion Washer
2. Differential Pinion
3. Spring Pin
4. Differential Gear
5. Washer
6. Side Gear Washer
7. Side Pinion Shaft
8. Final Gear Bolt
9. Differential Side Oil Seal
10. Differential Side Bearing
11. Side Bearing Shim
12. Speedometer Drive Gear
13. Differential Case
14. Final Gear

96B04640   Courtesy of Suzuki of America, Corp.

Fig. 23: Exploded View Of Differential Gear

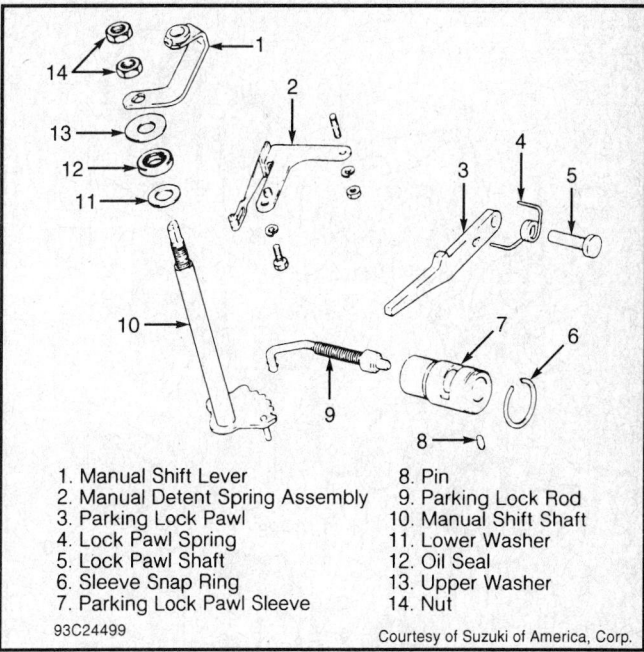

1. Manual Shift Lever
2. Manual Detent Spring Assembly
3. Parking Lock Pawl
4. Lock Pawl Spring
5. Lock Pawl Shaft
6. Sleeve Snap Ring
7. Parking Lock Pawl Sleeve
8. Pin
9. Parking Lock Rod
10. Manual Shift Shaft
11. Lower Washer
12. Oil Seal
13. Upper Washer
14. Nut

93C24499   Courtesy of Suzuki of America, Corp.

Fig. 24: Exploded View Of Manual Shift Shaft & Parking Lock Pawl

Inspection – Clean all parts with ATF. Use compressed air to dry all parts. Check bearings and gears for wear or damage.

Reassembly – **1)** Assemble differential case. Install side gear washers on differential gears. Install side pinion washers to differential pinions. Install side pinion shaft. Align lock pin holes with differential case.

2) Measure left-side differential gear thrust play by using 2 screwdrivers to move gear up and down. Read movement of dial indicator. Measure right-side differential gear thrust play by moving gear up and down by hand. Thrust play should be .002-.013" (.05-.33 mm). Select thrust washers that will ensure correct thrust play. On Geo models, thrust washer thickness is available in .022" (.56 mm), .028" (.71 mm), .031" (.79 mm) and .035" (.89 mm). On Suzuki models, thrust washer thickness is available from .035" (.89 mm) to .047" (1.19 mm) in .002" (.05 mm) increments. Install thrust washers and side gears in case. If possible, install same size thrust washers on both sides. Recheck thrust play.

3) Drive in spring pin from right side until flush with differential case surface. Press in differential left-side bearing.

4) Install speedometer drive gear. Support differential so left-side bearing is floating. Press in differential right-side bearing using bearing installer and copper hammer.

5) Hold differential with soft-jawed vise. Install final gear. Place offset side of final gear flange toward differential case. Tighten final gear bolts to 59-66 ft. lbs. (80-89 N.m). DO NOT substitute final gear bolts.

TRANSMISSION REASSEMBLY

NOTE: Coat all oil seal rings, clutch discs, clutch plates, rotating parts and sliding surfaces with ATF prior to reassembly. All gaskets and rubber "O" rings should be replaced. Ensure ends of snap rings are not aligned with cut-outs and are installed correctly in groove. If a worn bushing is to be replaced, replacement must be made with subassembly containing that bushing. Check thrust bearings and races for wear or damage. Use petroleum jelly to hold parts in place. Replace parts as necessary. Soak clutch plates in ATF for at least 2 hours prior to installation.

1) Place 2nd brake piston spring in transaxle case. Apply ATF to piston rod, seal and seal ring. Insert 2nd brake piston into case. Apply ATF to 2 cover seals. Install piston cover. Using valve spring compressor, push down piston cover and install snap ring. *See Fig. 8.*

2) Install lower washer and parking lock rod on manual shift shaft. *See Fig. 24.* Carefully install manual shift shaft into transmission case. Install manual detent spring. Tighten manual detent spring bolt and nut to 72-102 INCH lbs. (8.1-11.5 N.m). Install shift shaft upper washer and manual shift lever to manual shift shaft. Tighten shift shaft lower nut first, then tighten upper nut to 20-24 ft. lbs. (27-33 N.m). Check manual shift shaft for smooth rotation.

3) Install restrictor pin and snap ring to parking lock pawl sleeve. Install assembly into case. Shift manual shift lever to a position other than "P". Install parking lock pawl. Install lock pawl shaft and lock pawl spring. Ensure parking lock pawl moves smoothly when manual shift lever is activated.

4) Apply ATF to 1st and reverse brake piston inner and outer seals. Install new seals on piston. Carefully insert 1st and reverse piston with spring holes facing upward. Place return spring on piston. Push down on return spring and install snap ring. *See Fig. 25.*

5) Install countershaft. Ensure countershaft spacer is installed in correct position. DO NOT hammer shaft excessively hard.

6) Shift manual shift lever to position other than "P". Using bearing installer, install output shaft. Shift manual shift lever to "P" so output shaft is locked and cannot turn. Install reduction driven gear on countershaft. Tighten driven gear nut to 80-108 ft. lbs. (110-150 N.m). Stake driven gear nut in 2 places.

7) Install transaxle rear cover gasket. Install rear cover. Ensure output shaft bearing enters rear cover bearing hole smoothly. Install 10 bolts and 2 nuts. Tighten rear cover bolts to 12-17 ft. lbs. (16-23 N.m). Tighten rear cover nuts to 8-11 ft. lbs. (11-15 N.m). Ensure shafts rotate smoothly.

8) Push output shaft against rear cover side. Fit 4 projections of output shaft installer to 4 notches in case. To prevent damage to shaft, DO NOT hit output shaft directly.

9) Line up final gear and countershaft gear teeth. Carefully drive in differential by applying pressure to side bearing inner race using bearing installer.

10) Install 1st and reverse brake damper plate on return spring with convex side facing upward. Install in order: plate, disc, plate, disc, plate, disc, plate and disc. Install flange with flat area facing inward. Install snap ring. Measure 1st and reverse brake clutch clearance. Measure clearance between snap ring and flange. *See Fig. 9.*

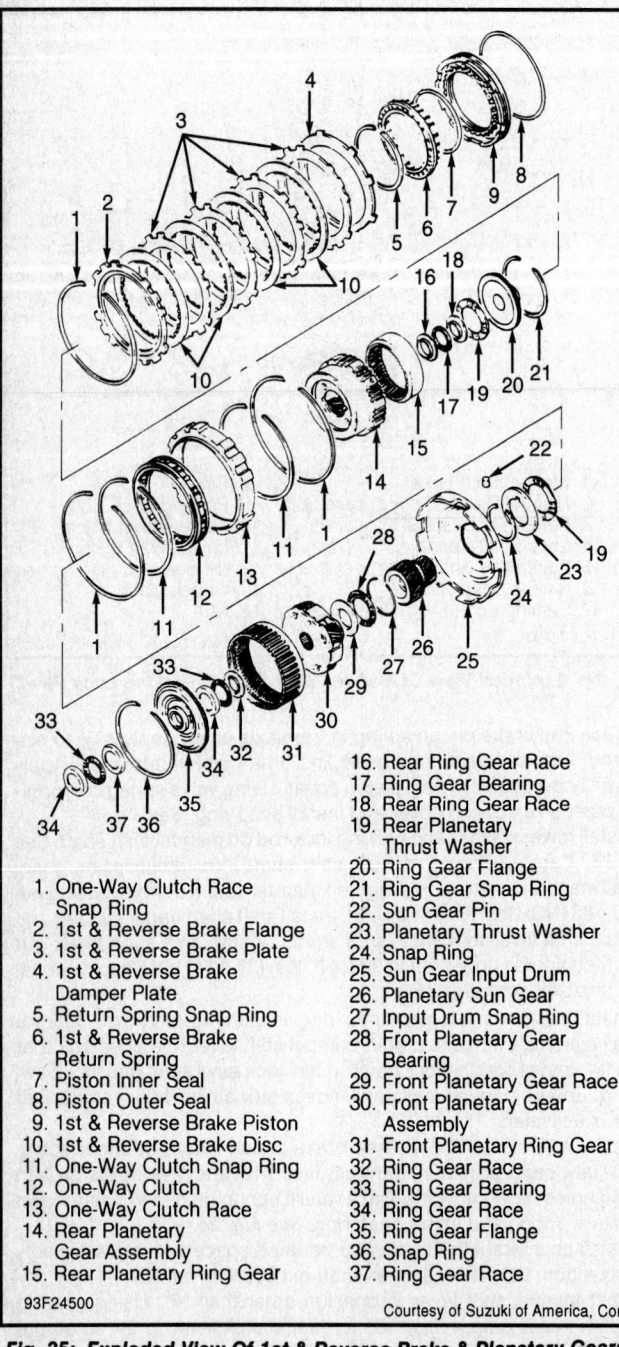

1. One-Way Clutch Race
   Snap Ring
2. 1st & Reverse Brake Flange
3. 1st & Reverse Brake Plate
4. 1st & Reverse Brake
   Damper Plate
5. Return Spring Snap Ring
6. 1st & Reverse Brake
   Return Spring
7. Piston Inner Seal
8. Piston Outer Seal
9. 1st & Reverse Brake Piston
10. 1st & Reverse Brake Disc
11. One-Way Clutch Snap Ring
12. One-Way Clutch
13. One-Way Clutch Race
14. Rear Planetary
    Gear Assembly
15. Rear Planetary Ring Gear

16. Rear Ring Gear Race
17. Ring Gear Bearing
18. Rear Ring Gear Race
19. Rear Planetary
    Thrust Washer
20. Ring Gear Flange
21. Ring Gear Snap Ring
22. Sun Gear Pin
23. Planetary Thrust Washer
24. Snap Ring
25. Sun Gear Input Drum
26. Planetary Sun Gear
27. Input Drum Snap Ring
28. Front Planetary Gear
    Bearing
29. Front Planetary Gear Race
30. Front Planetary Gear
    Assembly
31. Front Planetary Ring Gear
32. Ring Gear Race
33. Ring Gear Bearing
34. Ring Gear Race
35. Ring Gear Flange
36. Snap Ring
37. Ring Gear Race

93F24500

Courtesy of Suzuki of America, Corp.

Fig. 25: Exploded View Of 1st & Reverse Brake & Planetary Gears

Standard clearance should be .023-.075" (.58-1.91 mm). Check 1st and reverse brake piston operation by applying compressed air into oil hole. Confirm 1st and reverse brake piston moves smoothly.

11) Align ring gear and output shaft spline and insert rear planetary ring gear. *See Fig. 25.* Install rear planetary ring gear races and bearing. Ensure ring gear races are installed in proper positions and directions. *See Fig. 26.*

12) Temporarily assemble one-way clutch and rear planetary gear. Check one-way clutch operation. Clutch and gear should rotate freely in arrow direction "A" and lock in opposite direction. *See Fig. 27.* Remove one-way clutch.

13) Apply grease to rear planetary thrust washers. Install thrust washers on front and rear faces of rear planetary gear. Ensure washer lugs match slots in planetary gear.

14) Align 1st and reverse brake discs and install rear planetary gear. Check thrust washers and races for proper installation. Move rear planetary gear up and down lightly by hand. Listen for a click sound which indicates proper installation.

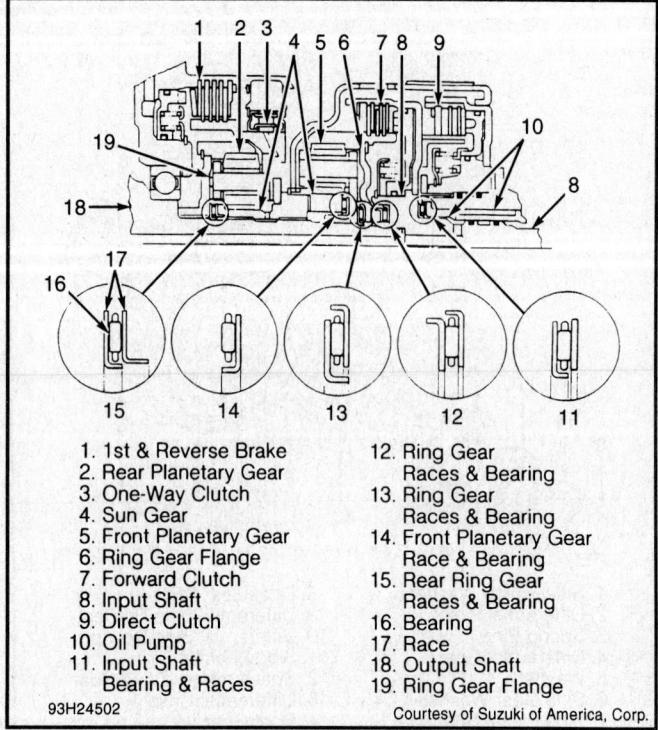

1. 1st & Reverse Brake
2. Rear Planetary Gear
3. One-Way Clutch
4. Sun Gear
5. Front Planetary Gear
6. Ring Gear Flange
7. Forward Clutch
8. Input Shaft
9. Direct Clutch
10. Oil Pump
11. Input Shaft
    Bearing & Races

12. Ring Gear
    Races & Bearing
13. Ring Gear
    Races & Bearing
14. Front Planetary Gear
    Race & Bearing
15. Rear Ring Gear
    Races & Bearing
16. Bearing
17. Race
18. Output Shaft
19. Ring Gear Flange

93H24502

Courtesy of Suzuki of America, Corp.

Fig. 26: Identifying Bearing & Race Locations

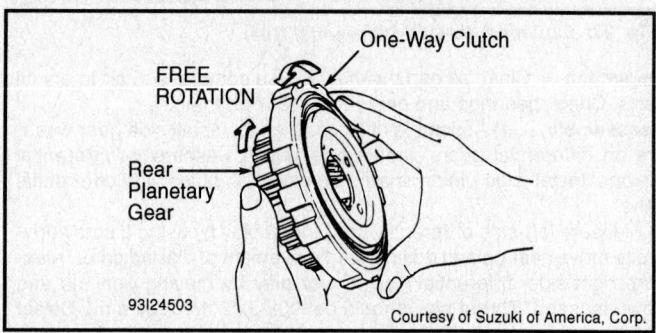

93I24503

Courtesy of Suzuki of America, Corp.

Fig. 27: Checking Free Rotation Of One-Way Clutch

15) Install one-way clutch race snap ring into groove of transaxle case. Place one-way clutch on rear planetary gear. While turning planetary gear clockwise, insert one-way clutch. Confirm planetary gear turns clockwise and locks counterclockwise.

16) Install one-way clutch race snap ring. Ensure snap ring end-gap is between lugs. Install sun gear pin and thrust washer on sun gear. Ensure pin is in thrust washer notch. Push in sun gear while engaging with rear planetary gear. DO NOT damage bushing inside sun gear. Check thrust washers for proper installation. Lightly move sun gear up and down. Listen for a click sound which indicates proper installation.

17) Install front planetary gear bearing and race to sun gear. *See Fig. 26.* Install front planetary gear while turning gear back and forth. Check bearing and race for proper installation. Move planetary gear up and down lightly with finger. If planetary gear makes a clicking sound, bearing and race are properly installed.

18) Install ring gear bearing and races on front planetary gear. *See Fig. 26.* Install front planetary ring gear. Check bearing and race for proper installation. Move ring gear up and down lightly with finger. If ring gear makes a clicking sound, bearing and race are properly installed.

19) Install 2nd brake band. DO NOT bend or damage. Check output shaft seal ring for wear or damage. Apply grease to direct clutch washer. Install direct clutch washer on direct clutch with washer grooves facing upward. Align washer protrusions to direct clutch drum groove.

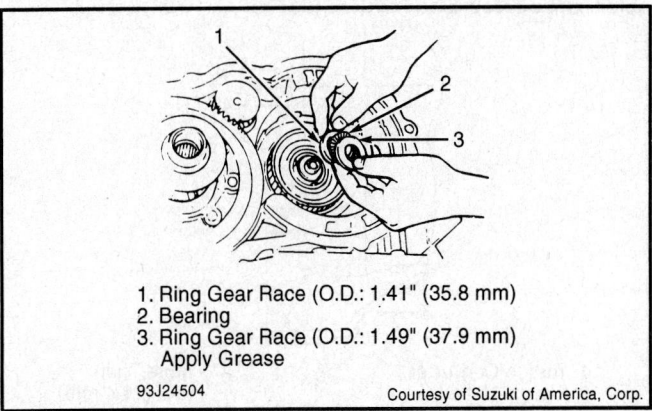

1. Ring Gear Race (O.D.: 1.41" (35.8 mm)
2. Bearing
3. Ring Gear Race (O.D.: 1.49" (37.9 mm)
   Apply Grease

93J24504   Courtesy of Suzuki of America, Corp.

Fig. 28: Installing Ring Gear Bearing

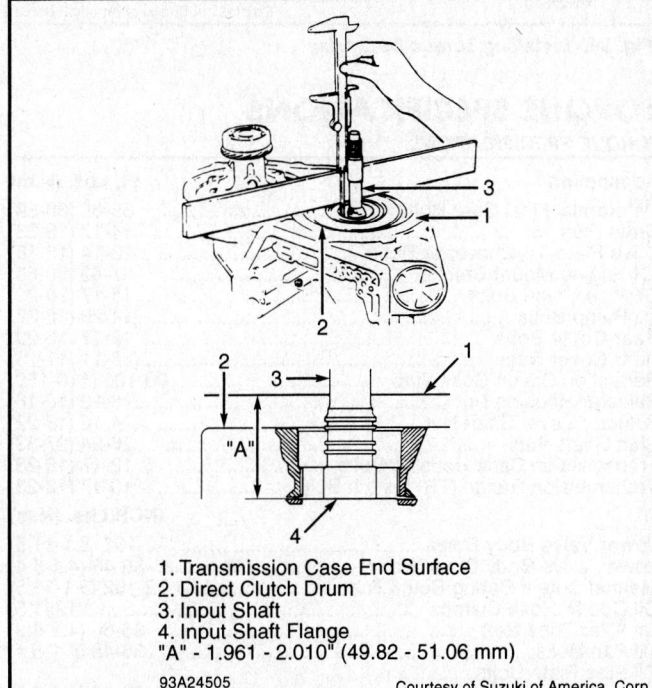

1. Transmission Case End Surface
2. Direct Clutch Drum
3. Input Shaft
4. Input Shaft Flange
"A" - 1.961 - 2.010" (49.82 - 51.06 mm)

93A24505   Courtesy of Suzuki of America, Corp.

Fig. 29: Measuring Distance Between Case End Surface & Input Shaft Flange

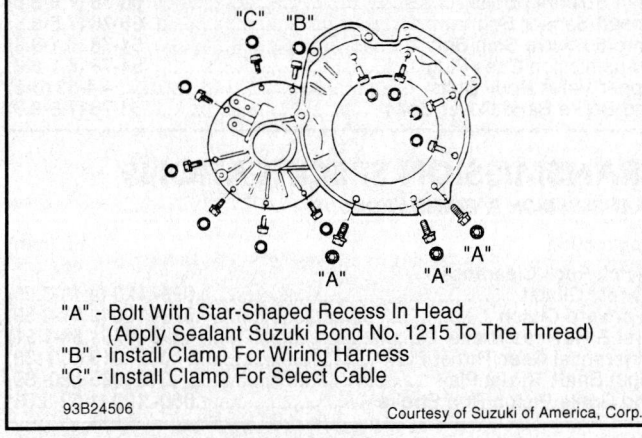

"A" - Bolt With Star-Shaped Recess In Head
  (Apply Sealant Suzuki Bond No. 1215 To The Thread)
"B" - Install Clamp For Wiring Harness
"C" - Install Clamp For Select Cable

93B24506   Courtesy of Suzuki of America, Corp.

Fig. 30: Installing Case Housing Bolts

20) Align direct clutch discs and install direct clutch on input shaft. Check direct clutch for proper installation. Move direct clutch up and down lightly by hand. Listen for a click sound which indicates proper installation. Install ring gear races and bearing. See Fig. 28.

21) While rotating input shaft and direct clutch, insert into case. Align forward clutch discs and install forward clutch. Check input shaft for proper installation. Move input shaft up and down lightly by hand. If input shaft makes a clicking sound, shaft is installed properly.

22) Place straightedge on transaxle case end surface and measure distance "A" by using vernier caliper. See Fig. 29. Distance "A" should be 1.961-2.010" (49.82-51.06 mm). To obtain distance "A", subtract width of straightedge from vernier reading. If distance "A" is within specification, component parts are installed properly. If distance "A" is not within specification, remove input shaft and direct clutch. Reinstall properly.

23) Align hole in 2nd brake band with case pin hole and insert 2nd brake band pin. Carefully install transaxle case housing and new case gasket. See Fig. 30. Install case housing bolts and tighten to 12-17 ft. lbs. (16-23 N.m). DO NOT apply thread locking compound to case housing bolts.

24) Measure input shaft seated position. See Fig. 31. Distance "A" should be 7.416-7.477" (188.37-189.92 mm).

25) Install input shaft bearing race and bearing on shaft. Install other input shaft bearing race on oil pump. Ensure seal rings installed in oil pump cover flange are in good condition and lubricated with ATF. Input shaft thrust play is adjusted with oil pump bearing race.

26) Install direct clutch washer flange into notch of oil pump body. Install new oil pump cover seal to oil pump. Align oil pump bolt hole with bolt hole and gently push oil pump into case. Ensure direct clutch washer does not fall. Ensure smooth rotation of input shaft. Gradually tighten 6 oil pump bolts to 14-20 ft. lbs. (18-27 N.m).

27) Measure input shaft thrust play. Input shaft thrust play should be .012-.035" (.30-.89 mm). If thrust play is incorrect remove oil pump and replace input shaft bearing race on oil pump side. Oil pump races are available in thicknesses of .031" (.79 mm) and .055" (1.40 mm). Ensure input shaft rotates smoothly.

28) Install wire harness to case. Check 2nd brake band for proper installation. Ensure 2nd brake piston rod end is aligned with center of recess in brake band. See Fig. 32. If rod end contacts outside of brake band recess, pull up 2nd brake band by inserting thin wire in brake band fitting to align band recess with rod end properly. Check 2nd brake piston stroke. See TRANSMISSION DISASSEMBLY step 4). See Fig. 7. Install 2nd brake band cover with new gasket. Tighten 2nd brake band cover bolts to 66-78 INCH lbs. (7.5-8.8 N.m).

29) Install oil pressure control cable in case. Install accumulator springs and pistons. Align manual valve with pin on manual shift lever. Ensure manual shift lever pin is between 2 flanges at end of manual shift valve. Lower valve body into position. Install 11 bolts in lower valve body. See Fig. 33. Tighten 3 reamer (positioning) bolts "C" and "D". Tighten all lower valve body bolts to 72-102 INCH lbs. (8.1-11.5 N.m).

30) Install oil pressure control cable on throttle valve cam. Using plastic hammer, tap in 2 oil tubes to valve body. DO NOT deform oil tubes. Install direct clutch and 2nd brake solenoid wires. Install oil strainer and solenoid wire clamp. Tighten oil strainer bolts to 44-53 INCH lbs. (5-6 N.m).

31) Install magnet in oil pan under oil strainer. Install oil pan bolts. Tighten 15 oil pan bolts to 36-48 INCH lbs. (4.1-5.4 N.m). Tighten oil pan drain plug to 14-17 ft. lbs. (19-23 N.m).

32) Install oil inlet and outlet pipes. Tighten union bolts to 15-17 ft. lbs. (20-23 N.m). Clamp pipes with oil pipe plate through rubber tubes. Tighten 8-mm plate bolts to 89-144 INCH lbs. (10.1-16.3 N.m). Tighten 6-mm plate bolt to 36-60 INCH lbs. (4.1-6.8 N.m).

33) Insert oil filler tube in case to flange. Tighten oil filler tube bolt to 36-60 INCH lbs. (4.1-6.8 N.m). Install engine mounting LH bracket. Tighten bolts to 37-43 ft. lbs. (50-60 N.m).

34) Carefully install torque converter to input shaft. Ensure distance "A" is within specification. See Fig. 34. Check torque converter for smooth rotation. Apply grease around cup at center of torque converter.

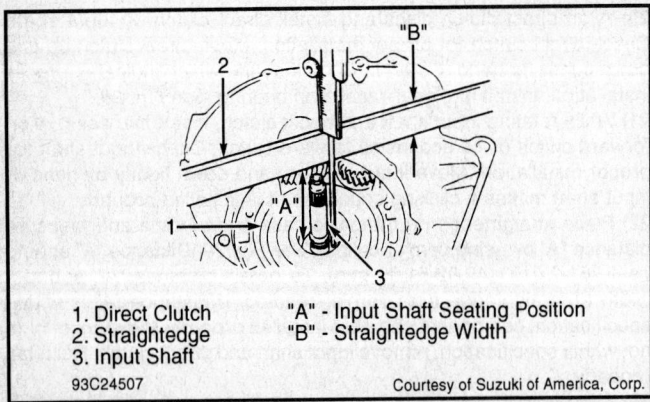

1. Direct Clutch   "A" - Input Shaft Seating Position
2. Straightedge   "B" - Straightedge Width
3. Input Shaft
93C24507   Courtesy of Suzuki of America, Corp.

Fig. 31: Measuring Input Shaft Seating Position

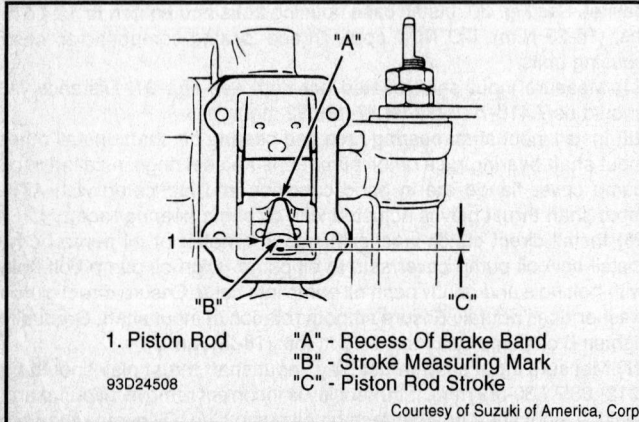

1. Piston Rod   "A" - Recess Of Brake Band
            "B" - Stroke Measuring Mark
93D24508   "C" - Piston Rod Stroke
          Courtesy of Suzuki of America, Corp.

Fig. 32: Checking 2nd Brake Band Alignment

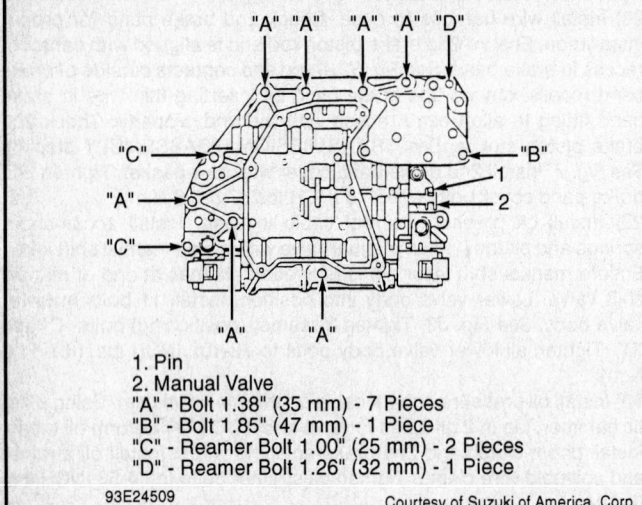

1. Pin
2. Manual Valve
"A" - Bolt 1.38" (35 mm) - 7 Pieces
"B" - Bolt 1.85" (47 mm) - 1 Piece
"C" - Reamer Bolt 1.00" (25 mm) - 2 Pieces
"D" - Reamer Bolt 1.26" (32 mm) - 1 Piece
93E24509   Courtesy of Suzuki of America, Corp.

Fig. 33: Installing Valve Body Bolts

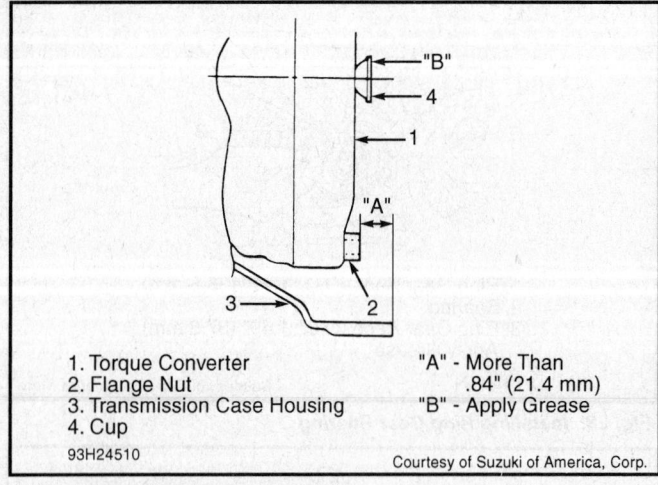

1. Torque Converter   "A" - More Than
2. Flange Nut   .84" (21.4 mm)
3. Transmission Case Housing   "B" - Apply Grease
4. Cup
93H24510   Courtesy of Suzuki of America, Corp.

Fig. 34: Installing Torque Converter

TORQUE SPECIFICATIONS
TORQUE SPECIFICATIONS

Application	Ft. Lbs. (N.m)
Differential Final Gear Bolts	59-66 (80-89)
Drain Plug	14-17 (19-23)
Drive Plate-To-Converter Bolts	13-14 (18-19)
LH Engine Mount Bracket	37-43 (50-60)
Oil Pipe Union Bolts	15-17 (20-23)
Oil Pump Bolts	14-20 (18-27)
Rear Cover Bolts	12-17 (16-23)
Rear Cover Nuts	8-11 (11-15)
Reduction Driven Gear Nuts	80-108 (110-150)
Selector Housing Nut	8-12 (10-16)
Selector Lever Shaft Nut	14-16 (18-22)
Shift Shaft Nuts	20-24 (27-33)
Transmission Case Housing Bolts	12-17 (16-23)
Transmission Range (TR) Switch Bolt	10-17 (13-23)

Application	INCH Lbs. (N.m)
Lower Valve Body Bolts	72-102 (8.1-11.5)
Lower Valve Body Cover Bolts	36-48 (4.1-5.4)
Manual Detent Spring Bolt & Nut	72-102 (8.1-11.5)
Oil Cooler Hose Clamps	12 (1.5)
Oil Filler Tube Bolt	36-60 (4.1-6.8)
Oil Pan Bolts	36-48 (4.1-5.4)
Oil Pipe Plate Bolts	
6-mm	36-60 (4.1-6.8)
8-mm	89-144 (10.1-16.3)
Oil Pump Cover Bolts	72-102 (8.1-11.5)
Oil Strainer Bolts	44-53 (5-6)
Shift Solenoid Bolts	66-78 (7.5-8.8)
Speed Sensor Bolt	66-78 (7.5-8.8)
Throttle Valve Cam Bolt	54-78 (6.1-8.8)
Transmission Case Plug	54-78 (6.1-8.8)
Upper Valve Body Bolts	44-53 (5-6)
2nd Brake Band Cover Bolts	66-78 (7.5-8.8)

TRANSMISSION SPECIFICATIONS
TRANSMISSION SPECIFICATIONS

Application	In. (mm)
Clutch Pack Clearance	
Direct Clutch	.098-.120 (2.49-3.05)
Forward Clutch	.079-.106 (2.01-2.69)
1st & Reverse Brake	.023-.075 (.58-1.91)
Differential Gear Thrust Play	.002-.013 (.05-.33)
Input Shaft Thrust Play	.012-.035 (.30-.89)
2nd Brake Piston Rod Stroke	.060-.120 (1.52-3.05)

Geo: Metro
Suzuki: Swift

APPLICATION

APPLICATION

Vehicle	Transmission Model
1995 Geo Metro	ECC
1995 Suzuki Swift	ECC

DESCRIPTION

Automatic transaxle is electronically controlled. Transaxle shifting is controlled by Transmission Control Module (TCM). TCM receives information from various input devices and uses this information to control shift solenoids. See Fig. 1.

Transaxle is equipped with a solenoid operated shift lock system, and a cable operated key lock system. Shift lock system prevents shift lever from being moved from "P" position unless brake pedal is depressed. Key lock system prevents ignition key from being moved from ACC to LOCK position unless shift lever is in "P" position.

NOTE: Direct clutch solenoid may also be known as shift solenoid "A", and 2nd brake solenoid may also be known as shift solenoid "B".

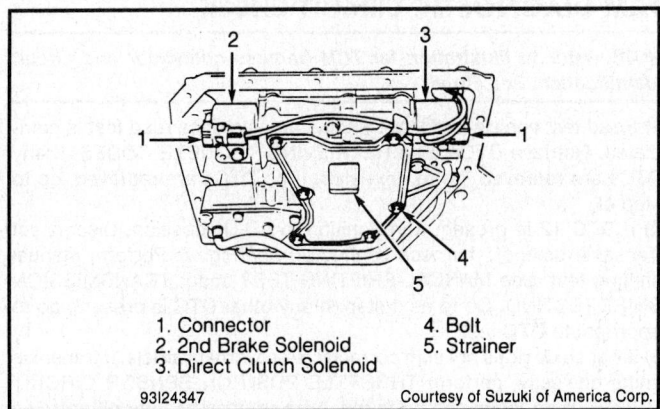

1. Connector   4. Bolt
2. 2nd Brake Solenoid   5. Strainer
3. Direct Clutch Solenoid

93124347   Courtesy of Suzuki of America Corp.

Fig. 1: Locating Transaxle Shift Solenoids

OPERATION

TRANSMISSION CONTROL MODULE (TCM)

The TCM receives information from various input devices and uses this information to control both solenoids on transaxle valve body for transaxle shifting.

The TCM contains a self-diagnostic system, which will store a Diagnostic Trouble Code (DTC) if a failure is detected in the electronic control system. DTCs can be retrieved to determine problem area. See SELF-DIAGNOSTIC SYSTEM.

INPUT DEVICES

Transmission Range (TR) Switch – TR switch may also be known as Park/Neutral Position (PNP) switch. TR switch delivers an input signal to TCM, indicating shift lever position. Switch is located on side of transaxle.

Throttle Position (TP) Sensor – TP sensor delivers closed throttle and variable throttle position input signals to TCM to assist in transaxle shifting. TP sensor is located on side of throttle body. See Fig. 2.

Vehicle Speed Sensor (VSS) – VSS is mounted on transaxle and transmits a vehicle speed signal to TCM. See Fig. 3.

OUTPUT DEVICES

Direct Clutch Solenoid (Shift Solenoid "A") – The TCM controls transaxle shifting by delivering an output signal to operate solenoid. Solenoid is located on transaxle valve body. See Fig. 1. Direct clutch solenoid controls delivery of line pressure to 2-3 shift valve.

2nd Brake Solenoid (Shift Solenoid "B") – The TCM controls transaxle shifting by delivering an output signal to operate solenoid. Solenoid is located on transaxle valve body. See Fig. 1. 2nd brake solenoid controls delivery of line pressure to 1-2 shift valve.

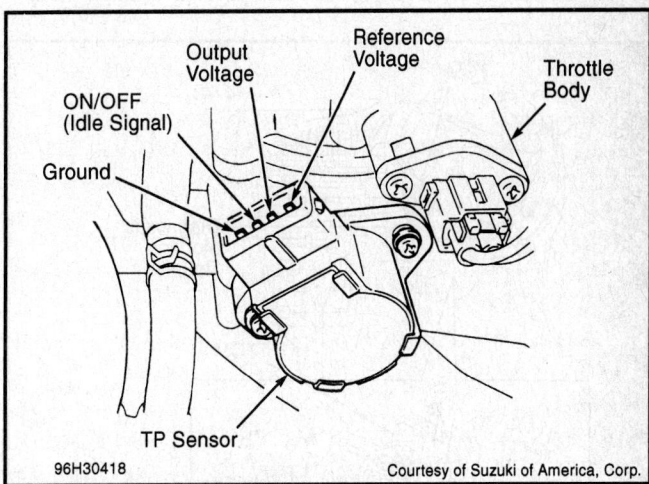

96H30418   Courtesy of Suzuki of America, Corp.

Fig. 2: Identifying Throttle Position (TP) Sensor Terminals

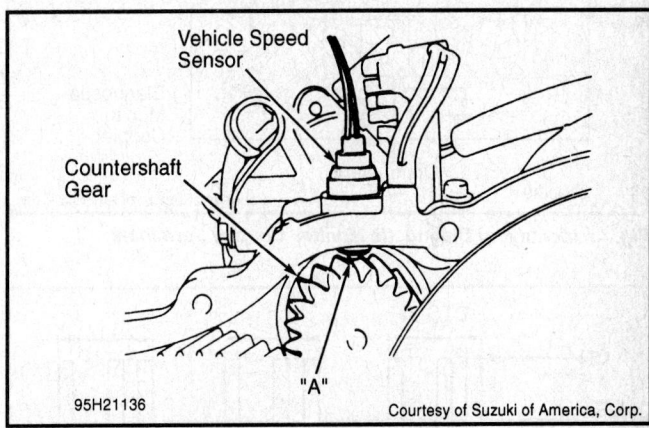

95H21136   Courtesy of Suzuki of America, Corp.

Fig. 3: Identifying Vehicle Speed Sensor (VSS)

SELF-DIAGNOSTIC SYSTEM

SYSTEM DIAGNOSIS

NOTE: Before testing transaxle, ensure fluid level is correct and throttle and shift cables are properly adjusted. Ensure engine starts with shift lever in Park and Neutral to ensure proper adjustment of transmission range switch. Transaxle must first be tested by checking for stored Diagnostic Trouble Codes (DTCs). See RETRIEVING TROUBLE CODES.

RETRIEVING TROUBLE CODES

CAUTION: Ensure engine remains running while retrieving DTCs. Any DTCs will be erased if ignition is turned off.

1) After test driving vehicle, apply parking brake and idle engine with gear selector in "P" position. Locate natural colored 6-pin diagnostic monitor coupler under instrument panel, to right of steering column. See Fig. 4.

3-1430

AUTOMATIC TRANSMISSIONS
1995 Suzuki ECC 3-Speed
Electronic Controls (Except OBD-II) (Cont.)

2) Using an analog ohmmeter, connect leads between chassis ground and terminal "A" of coupler. Using a jumper wire, jumper terminals "B" and "D" of coupler together. *See Fig. 4.*

3) To read DTCs, record sequence of ohmmeter indicator sweeps. All DTCs are 2-digit numbers. Each digit is separated by a 1.5 second pause. Additional DTCs are separated by a 2.5 second pause. *See Fig. 5.* Record all DTCs.

4) Once DTC is obtained, determine probable cause and symptom. See DTC IDENTIFICATION table. For trouble shooting of DTCs, see DIAGNOSTIC TESTING. Turn ignition off and remove jumper wire.

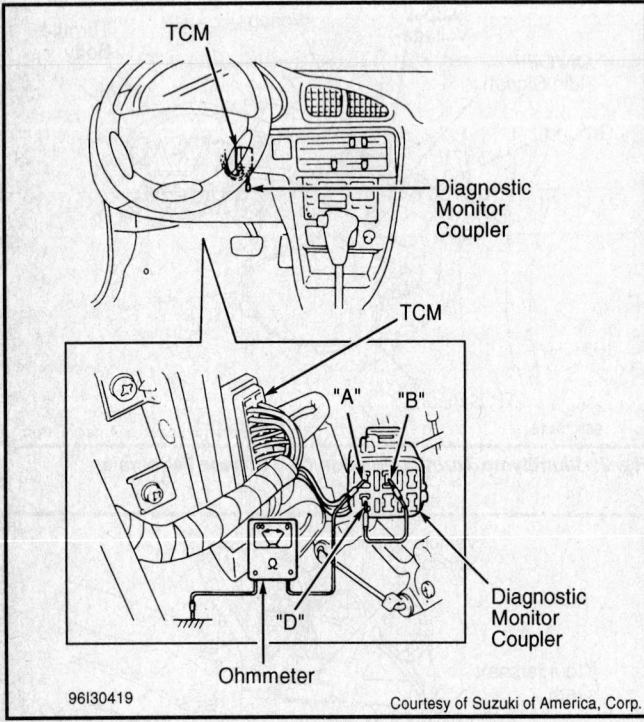

Fig. 4: Identifying Diagnostic Monitor Coupler Terminals

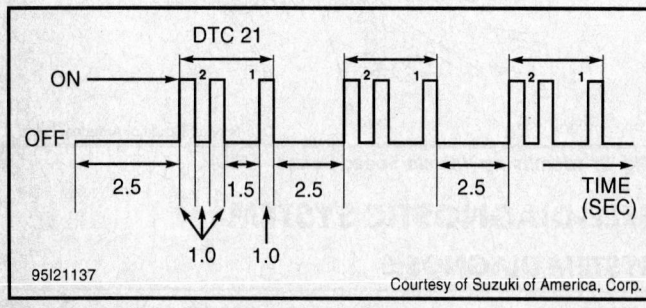

Fig. 5: *Identifying Trouble Code Displays*

DTC IDENTIFICATION

DTC	[1] Probable Cause
12	Normal
21	Open Direct Clutch Solenoid Circuit
22	Shorted Direct Clutch Solenoid Circuit
23	Open 2nd Brake Solenoid Circuit
24	Shorted 2nd Brake Solenoid Circuit
25	Shorted RD2L Signal
31	Open/Shorted Vehicle Speed Input Circuit
32	[2] Transmission Range (TR) Switch Circuit
33	Engine Speed Input Circuit

[1] – Check listed component for probable cause. Also check wiring and connections of specified component.
[2] – May also be known as Park/Neutral Position (PNP) switch.

CLEARING TROUBLE CODES

Once repairs have been performed, DTCs must be cleared from TCM memory. Turn ignition off to clear DTCs.

DIAGNOSTIC TESTING

When trouble shooting transaxle, first check for stored DTCs. Perform TCM DIAGNOSTIC CIRCUIT CHECK before diagnosing any DTCs. Repair as necessary. If no DTCs are present, perform manual shifting test to determine if problem is electrical or mechanical related. See MANUAL SHIFTING TEST under TRANSMISSION SHIFT TESTING.

TCM DIAGNOSTIC CIRCUIT CHECK

NOTE: Refer to illustration for TCM harness connector and circuit identification. See Fig. 6.

1) Road test vehicle and leave engine running once road test is completed. Retrieve DTCs. See RETRIEVING TROUBLE CODES. If any DTCs are retrieved, go to next step. If no DTCs are retrieved, go to step **4)**.

2) If DTC 12 is present, turn ignition to LOCK position. Disconnect transaxle solenoid harness connector. *See Fig. 7.* Perform manual shifting test. See MANUAL SHIFTING TEST under TRANSMISSION SHIFT TESTING. Go to next step. If any other DTC is present, go to appropriate DTC test.

3) If transaxle does not shift correctly, see overhaul article. If transaxle shifts correctly, perform THROTTLE POSITION SENSOR CIRCUIT CHECK. If no faults can be found, problem may be intermittent. See overhaul article.

4) If no DTCs are retrieved, or ohmmeter shows no reaction, go to step **6)**. If ohmmeter reacts, but needle does not sweep to indicate a DTC, go to next step.

5) Check Pink wire for a short to ground between monitor coupler and TCM. Repair as necessary. If wire is okay, replace TCM and retest system.

6) Check for poor harness connection at TCM. Check Pink wire and Pink/Black wire for an open between monitor coupler and TCM. Check for good ground connections at TCM and monitor coupler. See appropriate wiring diagram in WIRING DIAGRAMS. Repair as necessary. If circuits are okay, replace TCM and retest.

AUTOMATIC TRANSMISSIONS
1995 Suzuki ECC 3-Speed
Electronic Controls (Except OBD-II) (Cont.)

3-1431

4	3		2	1
10	9	8	7	6	5

CAVITY	WIRE COLOR	CIRCUIT	VOLTAGE KEY "ON"	VOLTAGE ENG. RUN
1	PNK/ BLK	DIAGNOSTIC ENABLE SIGNAL	B+	B+
2	RED	R POSITION SIGNAL	0* ①	0* ①
3	—	NOT USED	—	—
4	BRN	ENGINE SPEED INPUT	B+	6-11V ②
5	GRN	2 POSITION SIGNAL	0* ③	0* ③
6	GRN/ RED	D POSITION SIGNAL	0* ④	0* ④
7	GRN/ BLU	L POSITION SIGNAL	0* ⑤	0* ⑤
8	ORG/ BLK	P POSITION SIGNAL	0* ⑥	0* ⑥
9	ORG/ YEL	N POSITION SIGNAL	0* ⑦	0* ⑦
10	—	NOT USED	—	—

* LESS THAN 0.5 VOLTS
① B+ WITH PARK/NEUTRAL POSITION SWITCH IN "R"
② VARIES WITH ENGINE SPEED
③ B+ WITH PARK/NEUTRAL POSITION SWITCH IN "2"
④ B+ WITH PARK/NEUTRAL POSITION SWITCH IN "D"
⑤ B+ WITH PARK/NEUTRAL POSITION SWITCH IN "L"
⑥ B+ WITH PARK/NEUTRAL POSITION SWITCH IN "P"
⑦ B+ WITH PARK/NEUTRAL POSITION SWITCH IN "N"
⑧ VARIES WITH PARK/NEUTRAL POSITION SWITCH POSITION
⑨ B+ WITH PARK/NEUTRAL POSITION SWITCH IN "R","D","2" AND "L"
⑩ VARIES WITH THROTTLE POSITION
⑪ VARIES WITH VEHICLE FRONT WHEELS ROTATING
⑫ 0 V AT WIDE OPEN THROTTLE OR WITH HIGH ENGINE COOLANT TEMPERATURE

96D30422

6	5	4		3	2	1
14	13	12	11	10	9	8	7

CAVITY	WIRE COLOR	CIRCUIT	VOLTAGE KEY "ON"	VOLTAGE ENG. RUN
1	BLK	GROUND	0*	0*
2	BLK	GROUND	0*	0*
3	BLK/ WHT	IGNITION POWER INPUT	B+	B+
4	GRN OR ORG	DIRECT CLUTCH SOLENOID CONTROL	0* ⑧	0* ⑧
5	BRN/ WHT	RDL2 SIGNAL CONTROL	0* ⑨	0* ⑨
6	ORG/ GRN	2ND BRAKE SOLENOID CONTROL	0* ⑧	0* ⑧
7	BRN/ YEL	THROTTLE POSITION INPUT	⑩	⑩
8	BRN/ BLK	THROTTLE POSITION INPUT	⑩	⑩
9	BRN/ RED	THROTTLE POSITION INPUT	⑩	⑩
10	GRA	VEHICLE SPEED SENSOR SHIELD GROUND	0*	0*
11	LT GRN	VEHICLE SPEED INPUT	1-4V ⑪	1-4V ⑪
12	PPL	VEHICLE SPEED SENSOR GROUND	0*	0*
13	PNK	DIAGNOSTIC SIGNAL CONTROL	0*	0*
14	LT GRN/ RED	A/C CUTOUT CONTROL	B+ ⑫	B+ ⑫

Courtesy of Suzuki of America Corp.

Fig. 6: Identifying TCM Connector Terminals

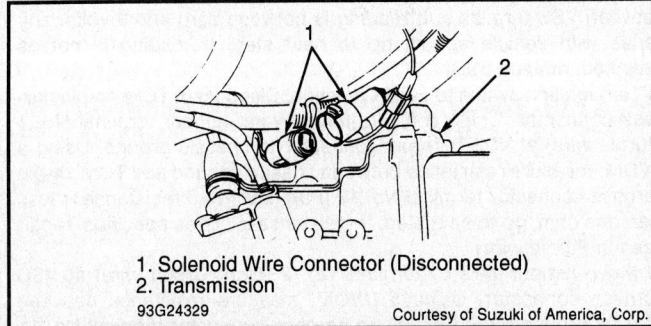

1. Solenoid Wire Connector (Disconnected)
2. Transmission

93G24329

Courtesy of Suzuki of America, Corp.

Fig. 7: Disconnecting Solenoid Harness Connector

DTC 21: OPEN DIRECT CLUTCH SOLENOID CIRCUIT

NOTE: Removal of transaxle oil pan may be necessary to complete the following diagnostic procedure.

1) Perform TCM DIAGNOSTIC CIRCUIT CHECK. Ensure ignition is on and shift selector is in "D" position. Disconnect solenoid harness connector. *See Fig. 7.* Using a DVOM, measure voltage between chassis ground and solenoid harness connector terminal No. 2 (Green wire on Geo, Orange wire on Suzuki). If battery voltage is present, go to step **3)**. If battery voltage is not present, go to next step.
2) Measure voltage (backprobe) between chassis ground and TCM 14-pin harness connector terminal No. 4 (Green wire on Geo, Orange wire on Suzuki). *See Fig. 6.* If battery voltage is present, repair open

3-1432

AUTOMATIC TRANSMISSIONS
1995 Suzuki ECC 3-Speed
Electronic Controls (Except OBD-II) (Cont.)

in Green wire (Geo), or Orange wire (Suzuki) between TCM and solenoid. If battery voltage is not present, check for poor TCM harness connection. Repair as necessary. If connection is okay, replace TCM and retest system.

3) Using a DVOM, measure resistance between chassis ground and solenoid harness connector terminal No. 2 (Red wire). If resistance is 10-15 ohms, check for poor connection at solenoid. Repair as necessary. If connection is okay, replace TCM and retest system. If resistance is not as specified, go to next step.

4) Move gear selector to "P" position. Turn ignition switch to LOCK position. Disconnect direct clutch solenoid harness connector. Using a DVOM, measure resistance of Red wire between solenoid and solenoid harness connector. If resistance is less than .5 ohms, replace solenoid. If resistance is not as specified, repair open in Red wire. Retest system.

DTC 22: SHORTED DIRECT CLUTCH SOLENOID CIRCUIT

NOTE: Removal of transaxle oil pan may be necessary to complete the following diagnostic procedure.

1) Perform TCM DIAGNOSTIC CIRCUIT CHECK. Ensure ignition is turned to LOCK position. Disconnect TCM 14-pin harness connector. See Fig. 6. Using a DVOM, measure resistance between chassis ground and TCM harness connector terminal No. 4 (Green wire on Geo, Orange wire on Suzuki). If resistance is 10-15 ohms, replace TCM and retest system. If resistance is not as specified, go to next step.

2) With DVOM still connected, disconnect solenoid harness connector. If DVOM displays infinite resistance, go to next step. If resistance is not as specified, repair Green wire (Geo), or Orange wire (Suzuki) for a short to ground. Retest system.

3) Disconnect direct clutch solenoid harness connector. Using a DVOM, measure resistance between chassis ground and solenoid harness connector terminal No. 2 (Red wire). If DVOM displays infinite resistance, replace solenoid. If resistance is not a specified, repair Red wire for a short to ground. Retest system.

DTC 23: OPEN 2ND BRAKE SOLENOID CIRCUIT

NOTE: Removal of transaxle oil pan may be necessary to complete the following diagnostic procedure.

1) Perform TCM DIAGNOSTIC CIRCUIT CHECK. Ensure ignition is on and gear selector is in "D" position. Disconnect solenoid harness connector. See Fig. 7. Using a DVOM, measure voltage between chassis ground and solenoid harness connector terminal No. 1 (Orange/Green wire). If battery voltage is present, go to step 3). If battery voltage is not present, go to next step.

2) Measure voltage (backprobe) between chassis ground and TCM 14-pin harness connector terminal No. 6 (Orange/Green wire). See Fig. 6. If battery voltage is present, repair open in Orange/Green wire between TCM and solenoid. If battery voltage is not present, check for poor TCM harness connection. Repair as necessary. If connection is okay, replace TCM and retest system.

3) Using a DVOM, measure resistance between chassis ground and solenoid connector terminal No. 1 (Yellow wire). If resistance is 10-15 ohms, check for poor connection at solenoid. Repair as necessary. If connection is okay, replace TCM and retest system. If resistance is not as specified, go to next step.

4) Move gear selector to "P" position. Turn ignition switch to LOCK position. Disconnect 2nd brake solenoid harness connector. Using a DVOM, measure resistance of Yellow wire between solenoid and solenoid harness connector. If resistance is less than .5 ohm, replace solenoid. If resistance is not as specified, repair open in Yellow wire. Retest system.

DTC 24: SHORTED 2ND BRAKE SOLENOID CIRCUIT

NOTE: Removal of transaxle oil pan may be necessary to complete the following diagnostic procedure.

1) Perform TCM DIAGNOSTIC CIRCUIT CHECK. Ensure ignition is turned to LOCK position. Disconnect TCU 14-pin harness connector. See Fig. 6. Using a DVOM, measure resistance between chassis ground and TCM harness connector terminal No. 6 (Orange/Green wire). If resistance is 10-15 ohms, replace TCM and retest system. If resistance is not as specified, go to next step.

2) With DVOM still connected, disconnect solenoid harness connector. If DVOM displays infinite resistance, go to next step. If resistance is not as specified, repair Orange/Green wire for a short to ground. Retest system.

3) Disconnect 2nd brake clutch solenoid harness connector. Using a DVOM, measure resistance between chassis ground and solenoid harness connector terminal No. 1 (Yellow wire). If DVOM displays infinite resistance, replace solenoid. If resistance is not a specified, repair Yellow wire for a short to ground. Retest system.

DTC 25: SHORTED RD2L SIGNAL

1) Perform TCM DIAGNOSTIC CIRCUIT CHECK. Ensure ignition is turned to LOCK position. Disconnect Powertrain Control Module (PCM) 16-pin harness connector, located near glove box. Turn ignition on. Move shift selector from "P" position to "D" position, then back to "P" position. Check if DTC 25 is still present. If DTC 25 is still present, go to next step. If DTC 25 is no longer present, replace PCM and retest system.

2) Turn ignition to LOCK position. Disconnect TCM 14-pin harness connector. Using a DVOM, measure resistance between chassis ground and TCM 14-pin harness connector terminal No. 5 (Brown/White wire). If DVOM displays infinite resistance, replace TCM and retest. If resistance is not as specified, repair Brown/White wire between PCM and TCM for a short to ground.

DTC 31: OPEN/SHORTED VEHICLE SPEED INPUT CIRCUIT

1) Preform TCM DIAGNOSTIC CIRCUIT CHECK. Raise and support front of vehicle. Start and operate vehicle in drive ("D") at idle. Using a DVOM, measure voltage (backprobe) between TCM 14-pin harness connector terminals No. 11 (Light/Green wire) and No. 12 (Purple wire). See Fig. 6. If reading varies between zero and 3 volts, and increases with wheel speed, go to next step. If reading is not as specified, go to step 3).

2) DTC may be set by an intermittent problem. Inspect harness connections. Check for corroded, damaged or backed-out terminal pins. Check VSS shielding and shield ground for breaks, cuts or opens. Repair as necessary. If no problem is found, problem cannot be duplicated at this time.

3) Disconnect VSS harness connector. Using DVOM, measure voltage between VSS terminals. If reading is between zero and 3 volts, and varies with vehicle speed, go to next step. If reading is not as specified, replace VSS.

4) Turn ignition switch to LOCK position. Disconnect TCM 14-pin harness connector. Using a fused jumper wire, jumper terminal No. 1 (Purple wire) at VSS harness connector to chassis ground. Using a DVOM, measure resistance between chassis ground and TCM 14-pin harness connector terminal No. 12 (Purple wire). If resistance is less than one ohm, go to next step. If resistance is not as specified, repair open in Purple wire.

5) Move jumper wire to terminal No. 2 (Light Green wire) at VSS harness connector. Using a DVOM, measure resistance between chassis ground and TCM 14-pin harness connector terminal No. 11 (Light Green wire). If resistance is less than one ohm, go to next step. If resistance is not as specified, repair open in Light Green wire.

AUTOMATIC TRANSMISSIONS
1995 Suzuki ECC 3-Speed
Electronic Controls (Except OBD-II) (Cont.)

3-1433

6) With DVOM still connected, remove jumper wire. If DVOM displays infinite resistance, check for poor connections at TCM. If connections are okay, replace TCM and retest system. If DVOM does not display infinite resistance, repair Light Green wire for a short to ground between TCM and VSS.

DTC 32: TRANSMISSION RANGE (TR) SWITCH CIRCUIT

NOTE: DTC is set if TCM does not receive any signal from TR switch, or receives 2 or more signals simultaneously. TR switch may also be known as Park/Neutral Position (PNP) switch.

1) Perform TCM DIAGNOSTIC CIRCUIT CHECK. Place gear selector in "P" position. Turn ignition on. Using a test light connected to ground, backprobe TCM 10-pin harness connector terminal No. 8 (Orange/Black wire). *See Fig. 6.* If test light comes on, go to next step. If test light does not come on, go to step **3)**.

2) Using test light connected to ground, backprobe TCM 10-pin harness connector terminals No. 2 (Red wire), No. 5 (Green wire), No. 6 (Green/Red wire), No. 7 (Green/Blue wire) and No. 9 (Orange/Yellow wire), one at a time. *See Fig. 6.* If test light does not come on at any terminal, go to step **5)**. If test light does come on for any terminal, go to step **6)**.

3) Using a test light connected to ground, backprobe TR switch harness connector terminal No. 9 (Orange/Black wire). *See Fig. 8.* If test light comes on, repair open in Orange/Black wire between TR switch and TCM. Retest system. If test light does not come on, go to next step.

4) Using a test light connected to ground, backprobe TR switch harness connector terminal No. 8 (Yellow wire). *See Fig. 8.* If test light comes on, replace TR switch. If test light does not come on, check TR switch harness connection. Repair as necessary. If connection is okay, repair open in Yellow wire between junction block and TR switch. Retest system.

5) Place gear selector in "R" position. Using a test light connected to ground, backprobe TCM 10-pin harness connector terminal No. 2 (Red wire). *See Fig. 6.* If test light comes on, go to step **7)**. If test light does not come on, go to step **8)**.

6) Disconnect TCM 10-pin harness connector and retest terminals as specified in step **2)**. If test light does not come on at any terminal, replace TR switch. If test light does come on for any terminal, repair short to power in appropriate circuit. Retest system.

7) Using a test light connected to ground, backprobe TCM 10-pin harness connector terminals No. 5 (Green wire), No. 6 (Green/Red wire), No. 7 (Green/Blue wire), No. 8 (Orange/Black wire) and No. 9 (Orange/Yellow wire), one at a time. *See Fig. 6.* If test light does not come on at any terminal, go to step **9)**. If test light does come on for any terminal, replace TR switch and retest system.

8) Using a test light connected to ground, backprobe TR switch harness connector terminal No. 1 (Red wire). *See Fig. 8.* If test light comes on, repair open in Red wire between TR switch and TCM. If test light does not come on, replace TR switch and retest system.

9) Place gear selector in "N" position. Using a test light connected to ground, backprobe TCM 10-pin harness connector terminal No. 9 (Orange/Yellow wire). *See Fig. 6.* If test light comes on, go to next step. If test light does not come on, go to step **11)**.

10) Using a test light connected to ground, backprobe TCM 10-pin harness connector terminals No. 2 (Red wire), No. 5 (Green wire), No. 6 (Green/Red wire), No. 7 (Green/Blue wire) and No. 8 (Orange/Black wire), one at a time. *See Fig. 6.* If test light does not come on at any terminal, go to step **12)**. If test light does come on at any terminal, replace TR switch and retest system.

11) Using a test light connected to ground, backprobe TR switch harness connector terminal No. 10 (Orange/Yellow wire). *See Fig. 8.* If test light comes on, repair open in Orange/Yellow wire between TR switch and TCM. If test light does not come on, replace TR switch and retest system.

12) Place gear selector in "D" position. Using a test light connected to ground, backprobe TCM 10-pin harness connector terminal No. 6

(Green/Red wire). *See Fig. 6.* If test light comes on, go to next step. If test light does not come on, go to step **14)**.

13) Using a test light connected to ground, backprobe TCM 10-pin harness connector terminals No. 2 (Red wire), No. 5 (Green wire), No. 7 (Green/Blue wire), No. 8 (Orange/Black wire) and No. 9 (Orange/Yellow wire), one at a time. *See Fig. 6.* If test light does not come on at any terminal, go to step **15)**. If test light does come on at any terminal, replace TR switch and retest system.

14) Using a test light connected to ground, backprobe TR switch harness connector terminal No. 2 (Green/Red wire). *See Fig. 8.* If test light comes on, repair open in Green/Red wire between TR switch and TCM. If test light does not come on, replace TR switch and retest system.

15) Place gear selector in "2" position. Using a test light connected to ground, backprobe TCM 10-pin harness connector terminal No. 5 (Green wire). *See Fig. 6.* If test light comes on, go to next step. If test light does not come on, go to step **17)**.

16) Using a test light connected to ground, backprobe TCM 10-pin harness connector terminals No. 2 (Red wire), No. 6 (Green/Red wire), No. 7 (Green/Blue wire), No. 8 (Orange/Black wire) and No. 9 (Orange/Yellow wire), one at a time. *See Fig. 6.* If test light does not come on at any terminal, go to step **18)**. If test light does come on at any terminal, replace TR switch and retest system.

17) Using a test light connected to ground, backprobe TR switch harness connector terminal No. 3 (Green wire). *See Fig. 8.* If test light comes on, repair open in Green wire between TR switch and TCM. If test light does not come on, replace TR switch and retest system.

18) Place gear selector in "L" position. Using a test light connected to ground, backprobe TCM 10-pin harness connector terminal No. 7 (Green/Blue wire). *See Fig. 6.* If test light comes on, go to next step. If test light does not come on, go to step **20)**.

19) Using a test light connected to ground, backprobe TCM 10-pin harness connector terminals No. 2 (Red wire), No. 5 (Green wire), No. 6 (Green/Red wire), No. 8 (Orange/Black wire) and No. 9 (Orange/Yellow wire), one at a time. *See Fig. 6.* If test light does not come on at any terminal, check for poor connection at TCM. Repair as necessary. If connection is okay, replace TCM. If test light does come on at any terminal, replace TR switch and retest system.

20) Using a test light connected to ground, backprobe TR switch harness connector terminal No. 4 (Green/Blue wire). *See Fig. 8.* If test light comes on, repair open in Green/Blue wire between TR switch and TCM. If test light does not come on, replace TR switch and retest system.

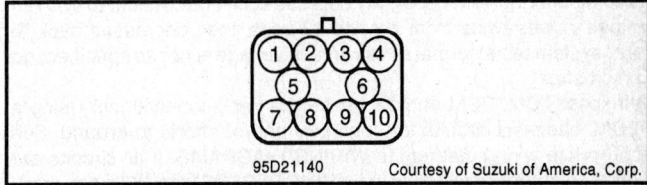

95D21140   Courtesy of Suzuki of America, Corp.

Fig. 8: Identifying TR Switch Harness Connector Terminals

DTC 33: ENGINE SPEED INPUT CIRCUIT

1) Perform TCM DIAGNOSTIC CIRCUIT CHECK. Ensure ignition is turned to LOCK position, and jumper wire is removed from diagnostic monitor coupler. Disconnect noise suppressor filter harness connector. *See Fig. 9.* Using a fused jumper wire, jumper noise suppressor filter harness connector terminals No. 3 (Brown wire) and No. 4 (Brown/White wire) together. Perform TCM DIAGNOSTIC CIRCUIT CHECK. If DTC 33 is still present, go to next step. If DTC 33 is not present, replace noise suppressor filter.

2) Turn ignition switch to LOCK position. Remove jumper wire from noise suppressor filter harness connector. Disconnect ignition coil harness connector. Using a DVOM, measure resistance between ignition coil harness connector terminal No. 2 (Brown/White wire), and noise suppressor filter harness connector terminal No. 4 (Brown/White wire). If resistance is less than .5 ohm, go to next step. If resistance is not as specified, repair open in Brown/White wire.

3-1434

AUTOMATIC TRANSMISSIONS
1995 Suzuki ECC 3-Speed
Electronic Controls (Except OBD-II) (Cont.)

3) Disconnect TCM 10-pin harness connector. Using a DVOM, measure resistance between noise suppressor filter harness connector terminal No. 3 (Brown wire), and TCM 10-pin harness connector terminal No. 4 (Brown wire). *See Fig. 6.* If resistance is less than .5 ohm, check for a poor connection at TCM. Repair as necessary. If connection is okay, replace TCM. If resistance is not as specified, repair open in Brown wire between noise suppressor filter and TCM.

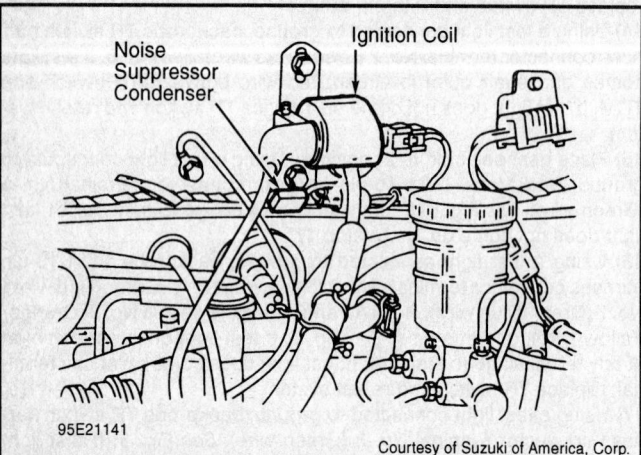

95E21141

Courtesy of Suzuki of America, Corp.

Fig. 9: Locating Noise Suppressor Filter

THROTTLE POSITION (TP) SENSOR CIRCUIT TEST

1) Ensure ignition is off. Disconnect TCM harness connectors. Turn ignition on. Using a DVOM, measure voltage between TCM 14-pin harness connector terminals No. 3 (Black/White wire) and No. 7 (Brown/Yellow wire). *See Fig. 6.* Go to next step.
2) While monitoring voltage, slowly depress accelerator pedal to Wide Open Throttle (WOT). If voltage increases from zero to 12 volts, go to next step. If voltage is not as specified, go to step **5)**.
3) Measure voltage between TCM 14-pin harness connector terminals No. 3 (Black/White wire), and No. 8 (Brown/Black wire) *See Fig. 6.* While monitoring voltage, slowly depress accelerator pedal to WOT. If voltage increases from zero to 12 volts, then decreases back to zero, go to next step. If voltage is not as specified, go to step **5)**.
4) Measure voltage between TCM 14-pin harness connector terminals No. 3 (Black/White wire), and No. 9 (Brown/Red wire). *See Fig. 6.* While monitoring voltage, slowly depress accelerator pedal to WOT. If voltage pulses twice from zero to 12 volts, then decreases back to zero, system tests normal at this time. If voltage is not as specified, go to next step.
5) Inspect TCM, PCM and TP sensor harness connections. Using a DVOM, check all circuits for continuity and/or shorts to ground. See appropriate wiring diagram in WIRING DIAGRAMS. If all circuits are okay, see appropriate article in ENGINE PERFORMANCE in appropriate MITCHELL® IMPORTED CARS, LIGHT TRUCKS & VANS SERVICE & REPAIR MANUAL for further TP sensor diagnostic procedures.

TRANSMISSION SHIFT TESTING

MANUAL SHIFTING TEST

1) Object of test is to check gears being used in "L", "2" or "D" range with electric gearshift control system disconnected. Test drive vehicle until engine is warm.
2) Disconnect solenoid harness connector. *See Fig. 7.* Shift transaxle into "L" range and accelerate to 19 MPH. Ensure 1st gear is operating properly. Shift to "2" range and accelerate to 37 MPH. Ensure 2nd gear is operating properly.
3) Shift to "D" range and accelerate to greater than 37 MPH. Ensure 3rd gear is operating properly. If transaxle shifts correctly, fault is electronic. If shifting is not correct or erratic, see appropriate overhaul article for further diagnosis. After test is complete, stop engine and reconnect solenoid harness connector.

COMPONENT TESTING

TRANSMISSION RANGE (TR) SWITCH

NOTE: TR switch may also be known as Park/Neutral Position (PNP) switch.

Ensure ignition is off. Disconnect TR switch harness connector. Check continuity of specified circuits. See TR SWITCH CONTINUITY table. Ensure there is no continuity to ground, or to any other terminals. See appropriate wiring diagram in WIRING DIAGRAMS. *See Fig. 8.* Replace TR switch if test results are not as specified.

TR SWITCH CONTINUITY

Selector Position	Terminals
"P" (Park)	8 & 9
"R" (Reverse)	1 & 8
"N" (Neutral)	8 & 10
"D" (Drive)	2 & 8
"2" (Second)	3 & 8
"1" (Low)	4 & 8

SHIFT SOLENOID TEST

1) When shift solenoids are removed from transaxle, verify valve function before reinstalling. Ensure ATF does not exhaust from solenoid-side oil passages when battery voltage is NOT applied. *See Fig. 10.*
2) Perform procedure in step 1) while applying battery voltage. Ensure ATF exhausts freely from solenoid-side oil passages. DO NOT reuse solenoid if oil flow is restricted.
3) Shift solenoid circuit resistance can be checked with an ohmmeter at connector. With ignition switch in OFF position, disconnect solenoid harness connector. Place ohmmeter probes on terminals and measure solenoid resistance. See appropriate wiring diagram in WIRING DIAGRAMS. See SHIFT SOLENOID RESISTANCE table.

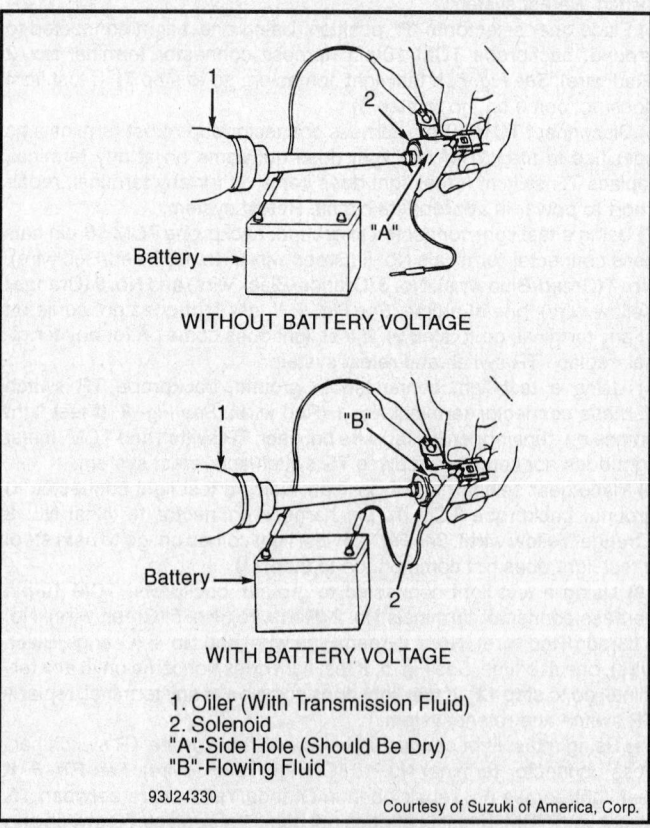

WITHOUT BATTERY VOLTAGE

WITH BATTERY VOLTAGE

1. Oiler (With Transmission Fluid)
2. Solenoid
"A"-Side Hole (Should Be Dry)
"B"-Flowing Fluid

93J24330

Courtesy of Suzuki of America, Corp.

Fig. 10: Checking Solenoid Valve Function

AUTOMATIC TRANSMISSIONS
1995 Suzuki ECC 3-Speed
Electronic Controls (Except OBD-II) (Cont.)

3-1435

SHIFT SOLENOID RESISTANCE

Solenoid	Ohms
Direct Clutch	10-15
2nd Brake	10-15

REMOVAL & INSTALLATION

SHIFT SOLENOIDS

Removal – Drain transmission fluid and remove oil pan. See appropriate AUTOMATIC TRANSMISSION SERVICING article. Remove couplers from direct clutch and 2nd brake solenoids. Remove shift solenoids. Remove solenoid wire harness and grommet from upper side.

Installation – **1)** Install grommet and solenoid wire harness to transaxle case. Install direct clutch and 2nd brake solenoids to lower valve body. Install new shift solenoid "O" ring. Tighten shift solenoid bolts to 35 INCH lbs. (4 N.m).

2) Install solenoid wires to each solenoid. Install oil pan and refill ATF. Install solenoid wire coupler. Warm up transaxle. Check for proper fluid level and ensure no leaks are present.

VEHICLE SPEED SENSOR (VSS)

Removal & Installation – **1)** Remove wiring harness clamp. Disconnect VSS harness connector. *See Fig. 3.* Remove speed sensor bolt.

2) Pull out speed sensor by gripping sensor body. To install, reverse removal procedure. Tighten speed sensor bolt to 62-80 INCH lbs. (7-9 N.m).

WIRING DIAGRAMS

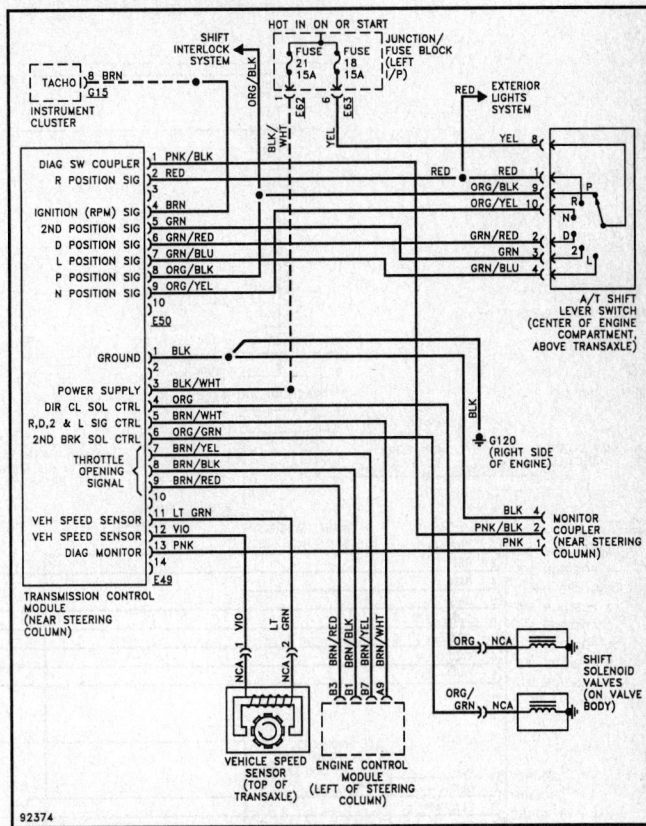

Fig. 11: 1995 Transaxle Wiring Diagram (Swift – 1.3L)

3-1436

AUTOMATIC TRANSMISSIONS
1995 Suzuki ECC 3-Speed
Electronic Controls (Except OBD-II) (Cont.)

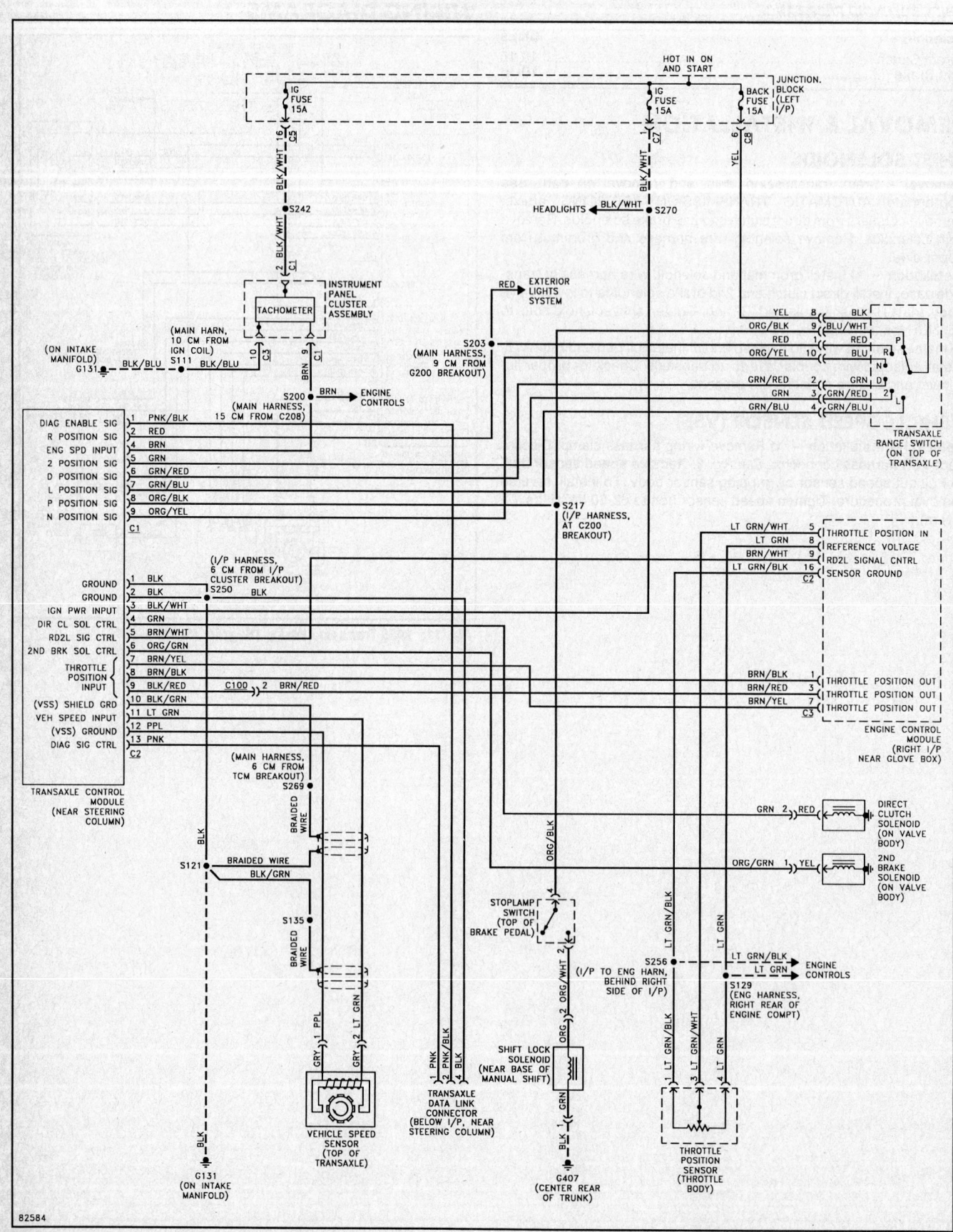

Fig. 12: 1995 Transaxle Wiring Diagram (Metro – 1.3L)

82584

Geo: Metro
Suzuki: Swift

APPLICATION

APPLICATION

Vehicle	Transmission Model
1996 Geo Metro	ECC
1996 Suzuki Swift	ECC

DESCRIPTION

Automatic transaxle is electronically controlled. Transaxle shifting is controlled by Powertrain Control Module (PCM). PCM receives information from various input devices and uses this information to control shift solenoids. *See Fig. 1.*

Transaxle is equipped with a solenoid operated shift lock system, and a cable operated key lock system. Shift lock system prevents shift lever from being moved from "P" position unless brake pedal is depressed. Key lock system prevents ignition key from being moved from ACC to LOCK position unless shift lever is in "P" position.

NOTE: Direct clutch solenoid may also be known as shift solenoid "A", and 2nd brake solenoid may also be known as shift solenoid "B".

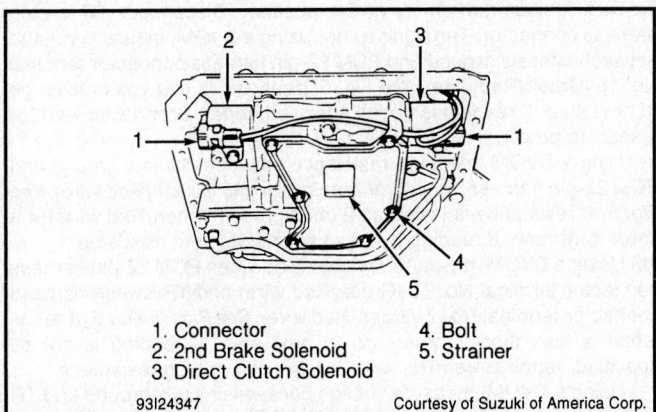

1. Connector
2. 2nd Brake Solenoid
3. Direct Clutch Solenoid
4. Bolt
5. Strainer

93124347   Courtesy of Suzuki of America Corp.

Fig. 1: Locating Transaxle Shift Solenoids

OPERATION

POWERTRAIN CONTROL MODULE (PCM)

The PCM receives information from various input devices and uses this information to control both solenoids on transaxle valve body for transaxle shifting.

The PCM contains a self-diagnostic system, which will store a Diagnostic Trouble Code (DTC) if a failure is detected in the electronic control system. DTCs can be retrieved to determine problem area. See SELF-DIAGNOSTIC SYSTEM.

INPUT DEVICES

Transmission Range (TR) Switch – TR switch may also be known as Park/Neutral Position (PNP) switch. TR switch delivers an input signal to PCM, indicating shift lever position. Switch is located on side of transaxle.

Throttle Position (TP) Sensor – TP sensor delivers closed throttle and variable throttle position input signals to PCM to assist in transaxle shifting. TP sensor is located on side of throttle body. *See Fig. 2.*

Vehicle Speed Sensor (VSS) – VSS is mounted on transaxle and transmits a vehicle speed signal to PCM. *See Fig. 3.*

OUTPUT DEVICES

Direct Clutch Solenoid (Shift Solenoid "A") – The PCM controls transaxle shifting by delivering an output signal to operate solenoid. Solenoid is located on transaxle valve body. *See Fig. 1.* Direct clutch solenoid controls delivery of line pressure to 2-3 shift valve.

2nd Brake Solenoid (Shift Solenoid "B") – The PCM controls transaxle shifting by delivering an output signal to operate solenoid. Solenoid is located on transaxle valve body. *See Fig. 1.* 2nd brake solenoid controls delivery of line pressure to 1-2 shift valve.

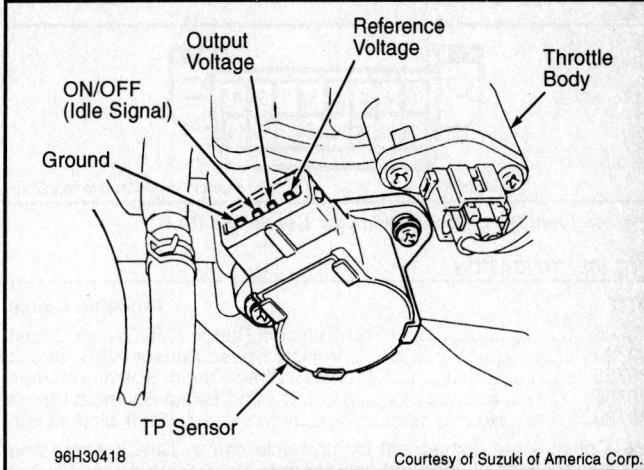

96H30418   Courtesy of Suzuki of America Corp.

Fig. 2: Identifying Throttle Position (TP) Sensor Terminals

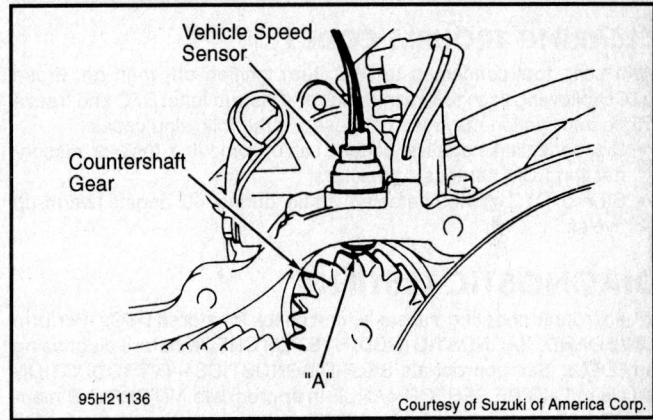

95H21136   Courtesy of Suzuki of America Corp.

Fig. 3: Identifying Vehicle Speed Sensor (VSS)

SELF-DIAGNOSTIC SYSTEM

NOTE: See appropriate ENGINE PERFORMANCE article in appropriate MITCHELL® manual for additional information on the self-diagnostic system. See WIRING DIAGRAMS to aid in component, wire color and terminal identification.

SYSTEM DIAGNOSIS

NOTE: Before testing transaxle, ensure fluid level is correct and throttle and shift cables are properly adjusted. Ensure engine starts with shift lever in Park and Neutral to ensure proper adjustment of transmission range switch. Transaxle must first be tested by checking for stored Diagnostic Trouble Codes (DTCs). See RETRIEVING TROUBLE CODES.

3-1438

AUTOMATIC TRANSMISSIONS
1996 Suzuki ECC 3-Speed
Electronic Controls (OBD-II) (Cont.)

RETRIEVING TROUBLE CODES

1) Ensure ignition is off. Using an OBD-II compatible scan tool, connect it to 16-pin Data Link Connector (DLC), located under instrument panel, to right of steering column. *See Fig. 4.*

2) Turn ignition on. Ensure Malfunction Indicator Light (MIL) on instrument cluster illuminates. Retrieve and record DTC and freeze frame data following scan tool manufacturer's instructions.

3) Once a DTC is obtained, determine probable cause and symptom. See DTC IDENTIFICATION table. For trouble shooting of DTCs, see DIAGNOSTIC TESTING.

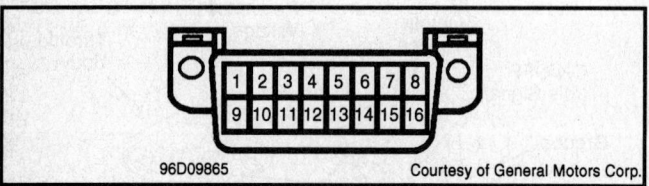

96D09865   Courtesy of General Motors Corp.

Fig. 4: Identifying OBD-II Data Link Connector (DLC)

DTC IDENTIFICATION

DTC	[1] Probable Cause
P0705	[2] Transmission Range (TR) Switch Circuit
P0720	Vehicle Speed Sensor (VSS) Circuit
P0753	Direct Clutch Solenoid Circuit
P0758	2nd Brake Solenoid Circuit
P0780	Shift Malfunction

[1] – Check listed component for probable cause. Check wiring and connections of specified component.
[2] – May also be known as Park/Neutral Position (PNP) switch.

CLEARING TROUBLE CODES

With scan tool connected to DLC, turn ignition off, then on. Erase DTCs following scan tool manufacturer's instructions. DTC and freeze frame information may also be erased in the following cases:

- Disconnecting negative battery cable, removing fuse or disconnecting PCM harness connectors.
- Stored DTC is not detected again during 40 engine warm-up cycles.

DIAGNOSTIC TESTING

When trouble shooting transaxle, first check for stored DTCs. Perform ON-BOARD DIAGNOSTIC (OBD) SYSTEM CHECK before diagnosing any DTCs. See appropriate SELF-DIAGNOSTICS – INTRODUCTION article in ENGINE PERFORMANCE in appropriate MITCHELL® manual. Repair as necessary. If no DTCs are present, perform manual shifting test to determine if problem is electrical or mechanical related. See MANUAL SHIFTING TEST under TRANSMISSION SHIFT TESTING.

DTC P0705: TRANSMISSION RANGE (TR) SWITCH CIRCUIT

NOTE: DTC is set if PCM does not receive any signal from TR switch, or receives 2 or more signals simultaneously. TR switch may also be known as Park/Neutral Position (PNP) switch.

1) Turn ignition switch to LOCK position. Disconnect PCM 22-pin harness connector, located under instrument panel, behind glove box. Turn ignition on. Using a DVOM, measure voltage between chassis ground and PCM 22-pin harness connector terminal No. 15 (Green/Red wire). *See Fig. 5.* Monitor voltage while moving gear selector through all gear ranges. If reading is 12 volts in "D" range, and less than one volt in any other gear range, go to next step. If reading is not as specified, go to step **8)**.

2) Using a DVOM, measure voltage between chassis ground and PCM 22-pin harness connector terminal No. 14 (Green/Blue wire). *See Fig.*

5. Monitor voltage while moving gear selector through all gear ranges. If reading is 12 volts in "L" range, and less than one volt in any other gear range, go to next step. If reading is not as specified, go to step **12)**.

3) Using a DVOM, measure voltage between chassis ground and PCM 22-pin harness connector terminal No. 4 (Orange/Yellow wire). *See Fig. 5.* Monitor voltage while moving gear selector through all gear ranges. If reading is 12 volts in "N" range, and less than one volt in any other gear range, go to next step. If reading is not as specified, go to step **16)**.

4) Using a DVOM, measure voltage between chassis ground and PCM 22-pin harness connector terminal No. 3 (Green wire). *See Fig. 5.* Monitor voltage while moving gear selector through all gear ranges. If reading is 12 volts in "2" range, and less than one volt in any other gear range, go to next step. If reading is not as specified, go to step **20)**.

5) Using a DVOM, measure voltage between chassis ground and PCM 22-pin harness connector terminal No. 16 (Red wire). *See Fig. 5.* Monitor voltage while moving gear selector through all gear ranges. If reading is 12 volts in "R" range, and less than one volt in any other gear range, go to next step. If reading is not as specified, go to step **24)**.

6) Inspect PCM 22-pin harness connector for poor connection. Repair as necessary and retest system. If connection is okay, go to next step.

7) Turn ignition switch to LOCK position. Reconnect PCM harness connector. Road test vehicle, then recheck for DTC P0705. If DTC resets, replace PCM. If DTC does not reset, malfunction can not be duplicated at this time.

8) Turn ignition switch to LOCK position. Disconnect TR switch harness connector. Turn ignition on. Using a DVOM, measure voltage between chassis ground and PCM 22-pin harness connector terminal No. 15 (Green/Red wire). *See Fig. 5.* If reading is one volt or less, go to next step. If reading is not as specified, repair Green/Red wire for a short to power.

9) Using a DVOM, measure resistance between chassis ground and PCM 22-pin harness connector terminal No. 15 (Green/Red wire). *See Fig. 5.* If resistance is less than 2 ohms, repair Green/Red wire for a short to ground. If reading is not as specified, go to next step.

10) Using a DVOM, measure resistance between PCM 22-pin harness connector terminal No. 15 (Green/Red wire) and TR switch harness connector terminal No. 2 (Green/Red wire). *See Figs. 5 and 6.* If resistance is less than 2 ohms, go to next step. If reading is not as specified, repair Green/Red wire for an open or high resistance.

11) Using a DVOM, measure voltage between chassis ground and TR switch harness connector terminal No. 8 (Yellow wire). *See Fig. 6.* If reading is 11-14 volts, check for proper TR switch adjustment. See ADJUSTMENTS in appropriate AUTOMATIC TRANSMISSION SERVICING article. If adjustment is okay, replace TR switch. If reading is not as specified, repair Yellow wire for an open or high resistance.

12) Turn ignition switch to LOCK position. Disconnect TR switch harness connector. Turn ignition on. Using a DVOM, measure voltage between chassis ground and PCM 22-pin harness connector terminal No. 14 (Green/Blue wire). *See Fig. 5.* If reading is one volt or less, go to next step. If reading is not as specified, repair Green/Blue wire for a short to power.

13) Using a DVOM, measure resistance between chassis ground and PCM 22-pin harness connector terminal No. 14 (Green/Blue wire). *See Fig. 5.* If resistance is less than 2 ohms, repair Green/Blue wire for a short to ground. If reading is not as specified, go to next step.

14) Using a DVOM, measure resistance between PCM 22-pin harness connector terminal No. 14 (Green/Blue wire) and TR switch harness connector terminal No. 4 (Green/Blue wire). *See Figs. 5 and 6.* If resistance is less than 2 ohms, go to next step. If reading is not as specified, repair Green/Blue wire for an open or high resistance.

15) Using a DVOM, measure voltage between chassis ground and TR switch harness connector terminal No. 8 (Yellow wire). *See Fig. 6.* If reading is 11-14 volts, check for proper TR switch adjustment. See ADJUSTMENTS in appropriate AUTOMATIC TRANSMISSION SERVICING article. If adjustment is okay, replace TR switch. If reading is not as specified, repair Yellow wire for an open or high resistance.

AUTOMATIC TRANSMISSIONS
1996 Suzuki ECC 3-Speed
Electronic Controls (OBD-II) (Cont.)

3-1439

16) Turn ignition switch to LOCK position. Disconnect TR switch harness connector. Turn ignition on. Using a DVOM, measure voltage between chassis ground and PCM 22-pin harness connector terminal No. 4 (Orange/Yellow wire). *See Fig. 5.* If reading is one volt or less, go to next step. If reading is not as specified, repair Orange/Yellow wire for a short to power.

17) Using a DVOM, measure resistance between chassis ground and PCM 22-pin harness connector terminal No. 4 (Orange/Yellow wire). *See Fig. 5.* If resistance is less than 2 ohms, repair Orange/Yellow wire for a short to ground. If reading is not as specified, go to next step.

18) Using a DVOM, measure resistance between PCM 22-pin harness connector terminal No. 4 (Orange/Yellow wire) and TR switch harness connector terminal No. 10 (Orange/Yellow wire). *See Figs. 5 and 6.* If resistance is less than 2 ohms, go to next step. If reading is not as specified, repair Orange/Yellow wire for an open or high resistance.

19) Using a DVOM, measure voltage between chassis ground and TR switch harness connector terminal No. 8 (Yellow wire). *See Fig. 6.* If reading is 11-14 volts, check for proper TR switch adjustment. See ADJUSTMENTS in appropriate AUTOMATIC TRANSMISSION SERVICING article. If adjustment is okay, replace TR switch. If reading is not as specified, repair Yellow wire for an open or high resistance.

20) Turn ignition switch to LOCK position. Disconnect TR switch harness connector. Turn ignition on. Using a DVOM, measure voltage between chassis ground and PCM 22-pin harness connector terminal No. 3 (Green wire). *See Fig. 5.* If reading is one volt or less, go to next step. If reading is not as specified, repair Green wire for a short to power.

21) Using a DVOM, measure resistance between chassis ground and PCM 22-pin harness connector terminal No. 3 (Green wire). *See Fig. 5.* If resistance is less than 2 ohms, repair Green wire for a short to ground. If reading is not as specified, go to next step.

22) Using a DVOM, measure resistance between PCM 22-pin harness connector terminal No. 3 (Green wire) and TR switch harness connector terminal No. 3 (Green wire). *See Figs. 5 and 6.* If resistance is less than 2 ohms, go to next step. If reading is not as specified, repair Green wire for an open or high resistance.

23) Using a DVOM, measure voltage between chassis ground and TR switch harness connector terminal No. 8 (Yellow wire). *See Fig. 6.* If reading is 11-14 volts, check for proper TR switch adjustment. See ADJUSTMENTS in appropriate AUTOMATIC TRANSMISSION SERVICING article. If adjustment is okay, replace TR switch. If reading is not as specified, repair Yellow wire for an open or high resistance.

24) Turn ignition switch to LOCK position. Disconnect TR switch harness connector. Turn ignition on. Using a DVOM, measure voltage between chassis ground and PCM 22-pin harness connector terminal No. 16 (Red wire). *See Fig. 5.* If reading is one volt or less, go to next step. If reading is not as specified, repair Red wire for a short to power.

25) Using a DVOM, measure resistance between chassis ground and PCM 22-pin harness connector terminal No. 16 (Red wire). *See Fig. 5.* If resistance is less than 2 ohms, repair Red wire for a short to ground. If reading is not as specified, go to next step.

26) Using a DVOM, measure resistance between PCM 22-pin harness connector terminal No. 16 (Red wire) and TR switch harness connector terminal No. 1 (Red wire). *See Figs. 5 and 6.* If resistance is less than 2 ohms, go to next step. If reading is not as specified, repair Red wire for an open or high resistance.

27) Using a DVOM, measure voltage between chassis ground and TR switch harness connector terminal No. 8 (Yellow wire). *See Fig. 6.* If reading is 11-14 volts, check for proper TR switch adjustment. See ADJUSTMENTS in appropriate AUTOMATIC TRANSMISSION SERVICING article. If adjustment is okay, replace TR switch. If reading is not as specified, repair Yellow wire for an open or high resistance.

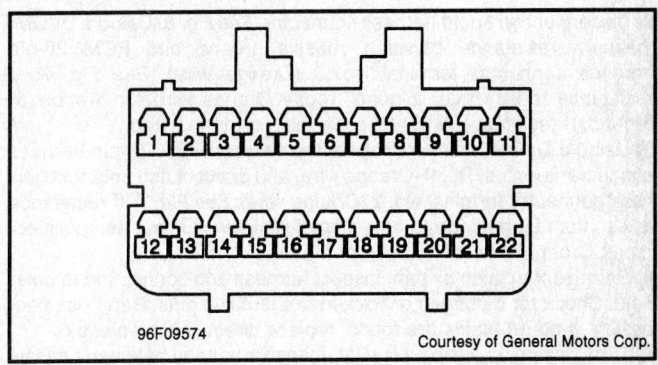

96F09574   Courtesy of General Motors Corp.

Fig. 5: Identifying PCM 22-Pin Harness Connector Terminals

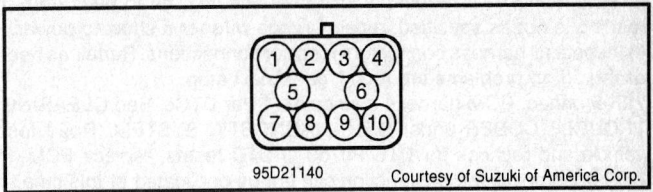

95D21140   Courtesy of Suzuki of America Corp.

Fig. 6: Identifying TR Switch Harness Connector Terminals

DTC P0720: VEHICLE SPEED SENSOR (VSS) CIRCUIT

1) Turn ignition switch to LOCK position. Disconnect PCM 22-pin harness connector. Using a DVOM, measure resistance between PCM 22-pin harness connector terminals No. 2 (Purple wire) and No. 13 (Light Green wire). *See Fig. 5.* If resistance is 100-300 ohms, go to step 6). If resistance is not as specified, go to next step.

2) Disconnect VSS harness connector at transaxle. Using a DVOM, measure resistance between VSS terminals (sensor side). If resistance is 100-300 ohms, go to next step. If resistance is not as specified, replace VSS.

3) Using a DVOM, measure resistance between PCM 22-pin harness connector terminal No. 13 (Light Green wire) and VSS harness connector terminal No. 1 (Light Green wire). *See Fig. 5.* If resistance is less than 2 ohms, go to next step. If resistance is not as specified, repair Light Green wire for an open or high resistance.

4) Using a DVOM, measure resistance between PCM 22-pin harness connector terminal No. 2 (Purple wire) and VSS harness connector terminal No. 2 (Purple wire). *See Fig. 5.* If resistance is less than 2 ohms, go to next step. If resistance is not as specified, repair Purple wire for an open or high resistance.

5) Reconnect all harness connectors. Clear DTCs. See CLEARING TROUBLE CODES under SELF-DIAGNOSTIC SYSTEM. Road test vehicle and recheck for DTC P0720. If DTC resets, replace PCM. If DTC does not reset, malfunction can not be duplicated at this time.

DTC P0753: DIRECT CLUTCH SOLENOID CIRCUIT

NOTE: Removal of transaxle oil pan may be necessary to complete the following diagnostic procedure.

1) Turn ignition switch to LOCK position. Disconnect PCM 26-pin harness connector. Using a DVOM, measure resistance between chassis ground and PCM 26-pin harness connector terminal No. 9 (Orange wire). *See Fig. 7.* If resistance is 8-20 ohms at room temperature, go to step 5). If resistance is not as specified, go to next step.

3-1440

AUTOMATIC TRANSMISSIONS
1996 Suzuki ECC 3-Speed
Electronic Controls (OBD-II) (Cont.)

2) Disconnect solenoid harness connector. *See Fig. 8.* Using a DVOM, measure resistance between chassis ground and PCM 26-pin harness connector terminal No. 9 (Orange wire). *See Fig. 7.* If resistance is less than 2 ohms, repair Orange wire for a short to ground. If resistance is not as specified, go to next step.

3) Using a DVOM, measure resistance between PCM 26-pin harness connector terminal No. 9 (Orange wire) and direct clutch solenoid harness connector terminal No. 2 (Orange wire). *See Fig. 7.* If resistance is less than 2 ohms, go to next step. If resistance is not as specified, repair Orange wire for an open or high resistance.

4) Remove transaxle oil pan. Inspect harness and connection to solenoid. Check for damaged or backed-out terminal pins. Repair as necessary. If no problems are found, replace direct clutch solenoid.

5) Turn ignition on. Using a DVOM, measure voltage between chassis ground and PCM 26-pin harness connector terminal No. 9 (Orange wire). *See Fig. 7.* If reading is less than one volt, go to next step. If reading is not as specified, repair Orange wire for a short to power.

6) Inspect all harness connectors for poor connections. Repair as necessary. If no problems are found, go to next step.

7) Reconnect PCM harness connector. Clear DTCs. See CLEARING TROUBLE CODES under SELF-DIAGNOSTIC SYSTEM. Road test vehicle and recheck for DTC P0753. If DTC resets, replace PCM. If DTC does not reset, malfunction can not be duplicated at this time.

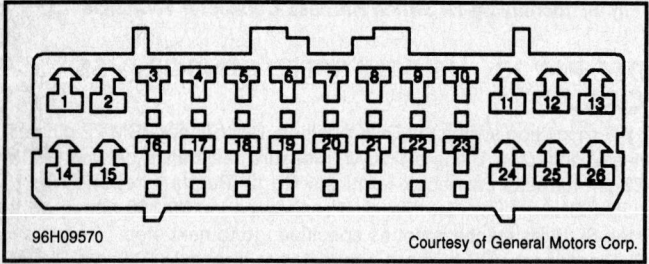

96H09570   Courtesy of General Motors Corp.

Fig. 7: Identifying PCM 26-Pin Harness Connector Terminals

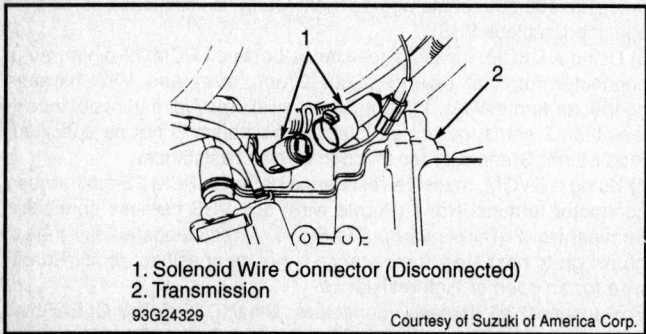

1. Solenoid Wire Connector (Disconnected)
2. Transmission

93G24329   Courtesy of Suzuki of America Corp.

Fig. 8: Disconnecting Solenoid Harness Connector

DTC P0758: 2ND BRAKE SOLENOID CIRCUIT

NOTE: Removal of transaxle oil pan may be necessary to complete the following diagnostic procedure.

1) Turn ignition switch to LOCK position. Disconnect PCM 26-pin harness connector. Using a DVOM, measure resistance between chassis ground and PCM 26-pin harness connector terminal No. 8 (Orange/Green wire). *See Fig. 7.* If resistance is 8-20 ohms at room temperature, go to step 5). If resistance is not as specified, go to next step.

2) Disconnect solenoid harness connector. *See Fig. 8.* Using a DVOM, measure resistance between chassis ground and PCM 26-pin harness connector terminal No. 8 (Orange/Green wire). *See Fig. 7.* If resistance is less than 2 ohms, repair Orange/Green wire for a short to ground. If resistance is not as specified, go to next step.

3) Using a DVOM, measure resistance between PCM 26-pin harness connector terminal No. 8 (Orange/Green wire) and direct clutch solenoid harness connector terminal No. 2 (Orange/Green wire). *See Fig. 7.* If resistance is less than 2 ohms, go to next step. If resistance is not as specified, repair Orange/Green wire for an open or high resistance.

4) Remove transaxle oil pan. Inspect harness and connection to solenoid. Check for damaged or backed-out terminal pins. Repair as necessary. If no problems are found, replace 2nd brake solenoid.

5) Turn ignition on. Using a DVOM, measure voltage between chassis ground and PCM 26-pin harness connector terminal No. 8 (Orange/Green wire). *See Fig. 7.* If reading is less than one volt, go to next step. If reading is not as specified, repair Orange/Green wire for short to power.

6) Inspect all harness connectors for poor connections. Repair as necessary. If no problems are found, go to next step.

7) Reconnect PCM harness connector. Clear DTCs. See CLEARING TROUBLE CODES under SELF-DIAGNOSTIC SYSTEM. Road test vehicle and recheck for DTC P0758. If DTC resets, replace PCM. If DTC does not reset, malfunction can not be duplicated at this time.

DTC P0780: SHIFT MALFUNCTION

NOTE: Removal of transaxle oil pan may be necessary to complete the following diagnostic procedure.

1) Turn ignition on. Check for any other DTCs that may be set. If any other DTCs are set in addition to DTC P0780, diagnose them first. If no other DTCs are set, go to next step.

2) Clear DTCs. See CLEARING TROUBLE CODES under SELF-DIAGNOSTIC SYSTEM. Start engine and allow it to reach normal operating temperature. Road test vehicle with gear selector in "D" position. Accelerate vehicle using steadily increasing throttle pressure. Note vehicle speeds and shift points. Stop vehicle. Recheck for DTC P0780. If DTC resets, go to next step. If DTC does not reset, malfunction can not be duplicated at this time.

3) Check Transmission Range (TR) switch and circuit. See DTC P0705: TRANSMISSION RANGE (TR) SWITCH CIRCUIT. Repair as necessary. If TR switch tests okay, go to next step.

4) Check Vehicle Speed Sensor (VSS) and circuit. See DTC P0720: VEHICLE SPEED SENSOR (VSS) CIRCUIT. Repair as necessary. If VSS tests okay, go to next step.

5) Check Throttle Position (TP) sensor and circuit. See DTC P0121 in appropriate SELF-DIAGNOSTICS article in ENGINE PERFORMANCE in appropriate MITCHELL® manual. Repair as necessary. If TP sensor tests okay, go to next step.

6) Remove transaxle oil pan. Remove shift solenoids and inspect. See SHIFT SOLENOID TEST under COMPONENT TESTING. Repair as necessary. If shift solenoids test okay, go to next step.

7) Clear DTCs. See CLEARING TROUBLE CODES under SELF-DIAGNOSTIC SYSTEM. Road test vehicle and recheck for DTC P0780. If DTC resets, replace PCM. If DTC does not reset, malfunction can not be duplicated at this time.

TRANSMISSION SHIFT TESTING
MANUAL SHIFTING TEST

1) Object of test is to check gears being used in "L", "2" or "D" range with electric gearshift control system disconnected. Test drive vehicle until engine is warm.

2) Disconnect solenoid harness connector. *See Fig. 8.* Place gear selector in "D" position. Slowly accelerate vehicle and verify transaxle shifts from 1st gear to 2nd gear, then from 2nd gear to 3rd gear.

3) Stop vehicle. Place gear selector in "2" position. Slowly accelerate vehicle and verify transaxle shifts from 1st gear to 2nd gear. Accelerate to 25 MPH and verify transaxle does not upshift from 2nd gear to 3rd gear.

AUTOMATIC TRANSMISSIONS
1996 Suzuki ECC 3-Speed
Electronic Controls (OBD-II) (Cont.)

3-1441

4) Stop vehicle. Place gear selector in "L" position. Slowly accelerate vehicle and verify transaxle does not upshift from 1st gear to 2nd gear.
5) Stop vehicle. Place gear selector in "R" position. Slowly accelerate and verify vehicle operates in reverse direction. If transaxle shifts correctly, fault is electronic. If shifting is not correct or erratic, see appropriate overhaul article for further diagnosis. After test is complete, stop engine and reconnect solenoid harness connector.

COMPONENT TESTING

TRANSMISSION RANGE (TR) SWITCH

NOTE: TR switch may also be known as Park/Neutral Position (PNP) switch.

Ensure ignition is off. Disconnect TR switch harness connector. Check continuity of specified circuits. See TR SWITCH CONTINUITY table. Ensure there is no continuity to ground, or to any other terminals. See appropriate wiring diagram in WIRING DIAGRAMS. *See Fig. 6.* Replace TR switch if test results are not as specified.

TR SWITCH CONTINUITY

Selector Position	Terminals
"P" (Park)	8 & 9
"R" (Reverse)	1 & 8
"N" (Neutral)	8 & 10
"D" (Drive)	2 & 8
"2" (Second)	3 & 8
"1" (Low)	4 & 8

SHIFT SOLENOID TEST

1) When shift solenoids are removed from transaxle, verify valve function before reinstalling. Ensure ATF does not exhaust from solenoid-side oil passages when battery voltage is NOT applied. *See Fig. 9.*
2) Perform procedure in step **1)** while applying battery voltage. Ensure ATF exhausts freely from solenoid-side oil passages. DO NOT reuse solenoid if oil flow is restricted.
3) Shift solenoid circuit resistance can be checked with an ohmmeter at connector. With ignition switch in OFF position, disconnect solenoid harness connector. Place ohmmeter probes on terminals and measure solenoid resistance. See appropriate wiring diagram in WIRING DIAGRAMS. See SHIFT SOLENOID RESISTANCE table.

SHIFT SOLENOID RESISTANCE

Solenoid	Ohms
Direct Clutch	10-15
2nd Brake	10-15

REMOVAL & INSTALLATION

SHIFT SOLENOIDS

Removal – Drain transmission fluid and remove oil pan. See appropriate AUTOMATIC TRANSMISSION SERVICING article. Remove couplers from direct clutch and 2nd brake solenoids. Remove shift solenoids. Remove solenoid wire harness and grommet from upper side.
Installation – **1)** Install grommet and solenoid wire harness to transaxle case. Install direct clutch and 2nd brake solenoids to lower valve body. Install new shift solenoid "O" ring. Tighten shift solenoid bolts to 35 INCH lbs. (4 N.m).
2) Install solenoid wires to each solenoid. Install oil pan and refill ATF. Install solenoid wire coupler. Warm up transaxle. Check for proper fluid level and ensure no leaks are present.

VEHICLE SPEED SENSOR (VSS)

Removal & Installation – **1)** Remove wiring harness clamp. Disconnect VSS harness connector. *See Fig. 3.* Remove speed sensor bolt.
2) Pull out speed sensor by gripping sensor body. To install, reverse removal procedure. Tighten speed sensor bolt to 62-80 INCH lbs. (7-9 N.m).

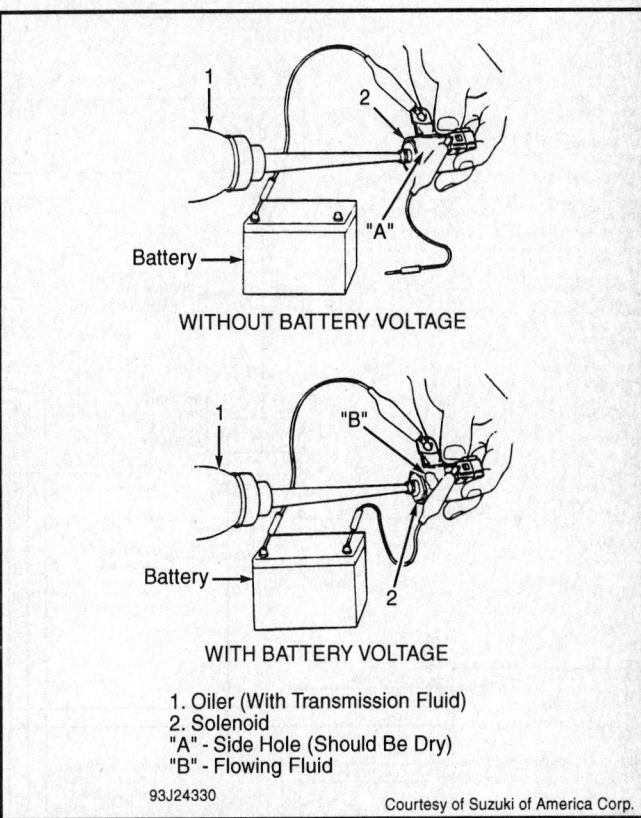

1. Oiler (With Transmission Fluid)
2. Solenoid
"A" - Side Hole (Should Be Dry)
"B" - Flowing Fluid

93J24330　　Courtesy of Suzuki of America Corp.

Fig. 9: Checking Solenoid Valve Function

WIRING DIAGRAMS

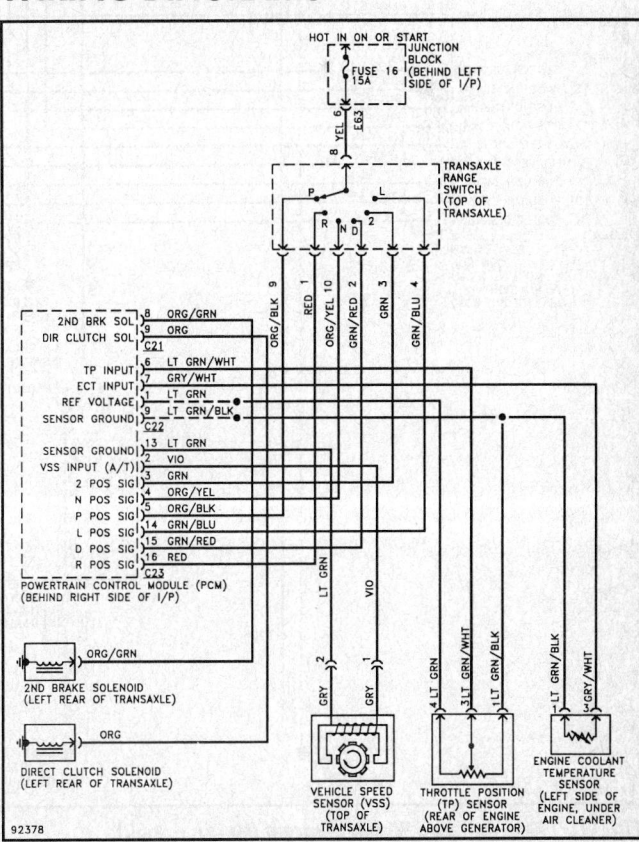

Fig. 10: 1996 Transaxle Wiring Diagram (Swift - 1.3L)

AUTOMATIC TRANSMISSIONS
1996 Suzuki ECC 3-Speed
Electronic Controls (OBD-II) (Cont.)

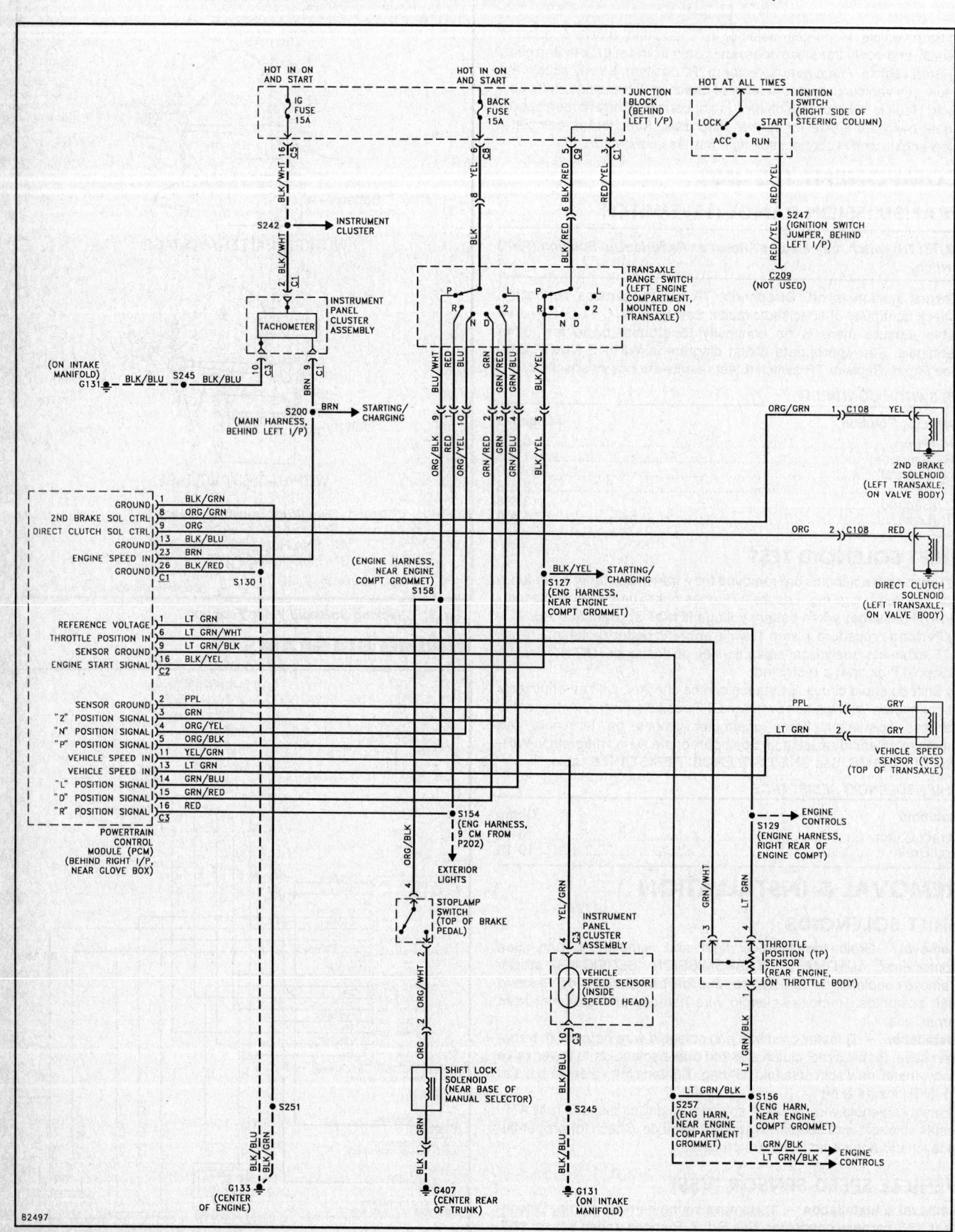

Fig. 11: 1996 Transaxle Wiring Diagram (Metro - 1.3L)

Esteem

APPLICATION & LABOR TIMES

APPLICATION & LABOR TIMES

Vehicle Application	Labor Times		Trans. Model
	[1] R & I	[2] Overhaul	
Suzuki			
1995-96 Esteem	4.5	6.0	[3] 4-Speed

[1] – Removal and installation of transaxle from vehicle chassis.

[2] – Bench overhaul time for transaxle. DOES NOT include removal and installation.

[3] – Transaxle model number is not available from manufacturer.

IDENTIFICATION

Vehicle Identification Number (VIN) is used for correct application of component parts and assemblies. VIN location is at top left of instrument panel. Transaxle is identified by transaxle identification number. Transaxle identification number is located on top of transaxle near engine mounting surface. *See Fig. 1.* This number contains transaxle production year, production month and serial number.

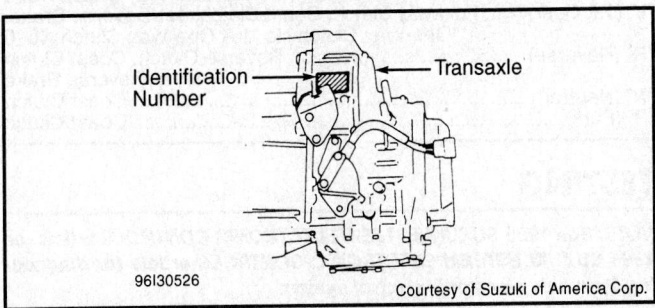

96I30526 Courtesy of Suzuki of America Corp.

Fig. 1: Locating Transaxle Identification Number

DESCRIPTION & OPERATION

Transaxle consists of a lock-up torque converter, oil pump, valve body assembly, 4 multi-disc clutch assemblies, 2 planetary gear sets, one multi-disc clutch style brake and 2 one-way clutches. *See Fig. 2.*

The Esteem 4-speed overdrive (OD) transaxle is electronically controlled. Transaxle shifting and torque converter lock-up are controlled by the Transmission Control Module (TCM), 2 shift solenoids and a Torque Converter Clutch (TCC) control solenoid valve. For electronic diagnosis, see appropriate ELECTRONIC CONTROLS article.

The TCM receives information from various input devices and uses this information to control TCC control solenoid valve, and shift solenoids No. 1 and 2 on transaxle valve body. Solenoids are responsible for transaxle shifting and TCC apply (lock-up). An O/D cut switch (mounted on gear selector lever) is used to select OD gear.

LUBRICATION & ADJUSTMENTS

See appropriate AUTOMATIC TRANSMISSION SERVICING article in TRANSMISSION SERVICING section.

TROUBLE SHOOTING

NOTE: Ensure engine is in good running condition before attempting transaxle diagnosis. A vehicle that runs improperly may exhibit poor transaxle performance or shift quality. All diagnosis should begin with a quick check of the self-diagnostic system to identify and eliminate any electrical problems that may be present. See appropriate ELECTRONIC CONTROLS article.

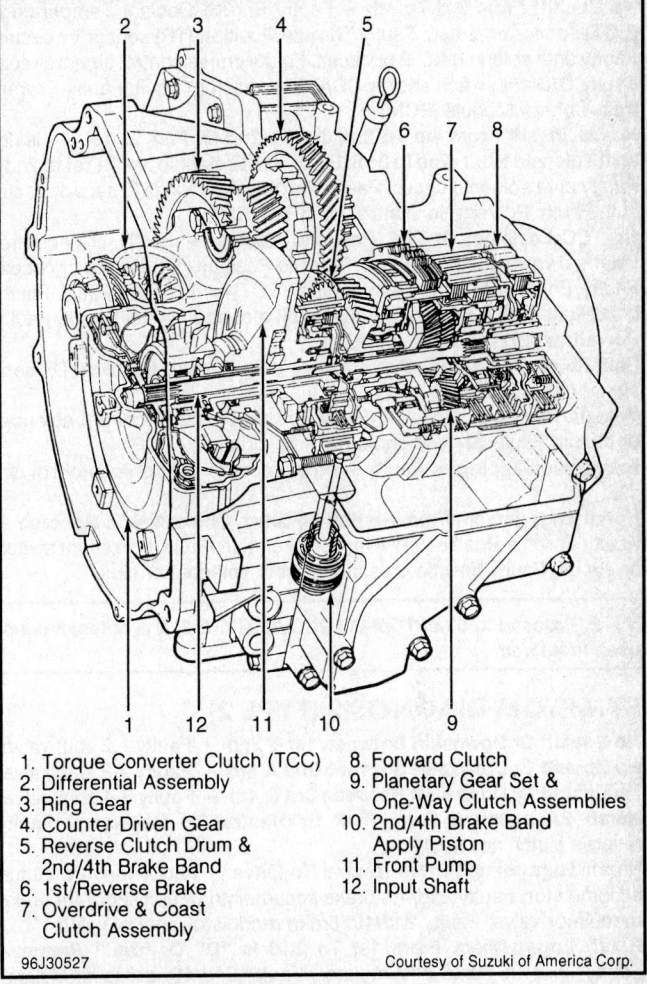

1. Torque Converter Clutch (TCC)
2. Differential Assembly
3. Ring Gear
4. Counter Driven Gear
5. Reverse Clutch Drum & 2nd/4th Brake Band
6. 1st/Reverse Brake
7. Overdrive & Coast Clutch Assembly
8. Forward Clutch
9. Planetary Gear Set & One-Way Clutch Assemblies
10. 2nd/4th Brake Band Apply Piston
11. Front Pump
12. Input Shaft

96J30527 Courtesy of Suzuki of America Corp.

Fig. 2: Cross-Sectional View Of Automatic Transaxle

PRELIMINARY CHECKS

1) Ensure engine is at normal operating temperature. Ensure ATF level is correct. Inspect and adjust shift linkage and Transmission Range (TR) switch (if necessary). Ensure electronic component harness connectors are properly connected. Check idle speed RPM and adjust if necessary.

2) After verifying proper operation of the transaxle electronic control system, perform a manual shifting test. See MANUAL SHIFT TEST under TRANSMISSION SHIFT TESTING in appropriate ELECTRONIC CONTROLS article. If transaxle passes test, proceed to SYMPTOM DIAGNOSIS (TYPE 1). If transaxle does not pass test, go to next step.

3) Perform stall test, time lag test, line pressure test, engine brake test and "P" range test. See appropriate test under TESTING. If all tests pass, proceed to SYMPTOM DIAGNOSIS (TYPE 2). If one or more tests do not pass, proceed to SYMPTOM DIAGNOSIS (TYPE 1), SYMPTOM DIAGNOSIS (TYPE 2), then SYMPTOM DIAGNOSIS (TYPE 3).

NOTE: To help identify problem area or component in transaxle, see TRANSMISSION COMPONENT APPLICATION CHART.

SYMPTOM DIAGNOSIS (TYPE 1)

No Upshift From 1st To 2nd Or 2nd To 3rd – Faulty Throttle Position (TP) sensor or circuit. Faulty shift solenoid No. 1 (2nd to 3rd). Faulty shift solenoid No. 2 (1st to 2nd). Faulty shift solenoid circuit. Faulty Powertrain Control Module (PCM).

No Upshift From 3rd To 4th – Faulty Engine Coolant Temperature (ECT) sensor or circuit. Faulty Throttle Position (TP) sensor or circuit. Faulty shift solenoid No. 2 or circuit. Faulty cruise control signal circuit. Faulty O/D cut switch and/or OD/OFF indicator circuit. Faulty Powertrain Control Module (PCM).

No Downshift From 4th To 3rd, 3rd To 2nd Or 2nd To 1st – Faulty shift solenoid No. 1 (2nd to 3rd). Faulty shift solenoid No. 2 (1st to 2nd). Faulty shift solenoid circuit. Faulty Throttle Position (TP) sensor or circuit. Faulty Powertrain Control Module (PCM).

No TCC Lock-Up, Or TCC Remains Applied – Faulty TCC control solenoid valve or circuit. Faulty Throttle Position (TP) sensor or circuit. Faulty Engine Coolant Temperature (ECT) sensor or circuit. Faulty brakelight switch or circuit. Faulty cruise control signal circuit. Faulty Powertrain Control Module (PCM).

Shift Points Too High Or Too Low – Faulty Throttle Position (TP) sensor or circuit.

Vehicle Does Not Move – Faulty throttle pressure control solenoid or circuit. Faulty shift solenoid No. 1 or circuit.

Excessive Slipping – Faulty throttle pressure control solenoid or circuit.

Harsh Engagement From Neutral To Drive, Or Neutral To Reverse – Faulty Throttle Position (TP) sensor or circuit. Faulty brakelight switch or circuit. Faulty throttle pressure control solenoid or circuit.

NOTE: Proceed to SYMPTOM DIAGNOSIS (TYPE 2) if problem has not been identified.

SYMPTOM DIAGNOSIS (TYPE 2)

No Upshift Or Downshift Between 1st & 2nd – Faulty 1-2 shift valve.
No Upshift Or Downshift Between 2nd & 3rd – Faulty 2-3 shift valve.
No Upshift Or Downshift Between 3rd & 4th – Faulty 3-4 shift valve.
Harsh Engagement From Park Or Neutral To Reverse – Faulty reverse clutch accumulator.
Harsh Engagement From Neutral To Drive – Faulty forward clutch accumulator. Faulty 2nd/4th brake accumulator. Faulty 2nd/4th brake modulator valve. Faulty 2nd/4th brake modulator control valve.
Harsh Engagement From 1st To 2nd In "D" Or "2nd" Range – Faulty 2nd/4th brake accumulator. Faulty 2nd/4th brake modulator valve. Faulty 2nd/4th brake modulator control valve.
Harsh Engagement From 2nd To 3rd In "D" Range – Faulty overdrive clutch accumulator. Faulty 2-3 timing valve.
Harsh Engagement From 3rd To 4th In "D" Range – Faulty 2nd/4th brake accumulator. Faulty 2nd/4th brake modulator valve. Faulty 2nd/4th brake modulator control valve.
Harsh Engagement In All Gear Ranges – Faulty throttle pressure control valve. Faulty primary regulator valve. Faulty accumulator control valve.
No TCC Lock-Up – Faulty TCC modulator valve. Faulty TCC control valve. Faulty TCC control solenoid. Faulty secondary regulator valve.
TCC Remains Applied – Faulty TCC control solenoid. Faulty TCC control valve.
Excessive Slipping (Low Line Pressure) – Faulty throttle pressure control valve. Faulty primary regulator valve.

NOTE: Proceed to SYMPTOM DIAGNOSIS (TYPE 3) if problem has not been identified.

SYMPTOM DIAGNOSIS (TYPE 3)

Vehicle Does Not Move In Any Forward Gear – Faulty forward clutch.
Vehicle Does Not Move In Reverse – Faulty reverse clutch. Faulty 1st/reverse brake.
Vehicle Does Not Move In 3rd Or 4th Gear – Faulty overdrive clutch.
Vehicle Does Not Move In 2nd Or 4th Gear – Faulty 2nd/4th brake.
Vehicle Does Not Move In 1st Gear ("D" Or "2" Range) – Faulty one-way clutch No. 1.
Vehicle Does Not Move In Any Forward Or Reverse Gear – Faulty parking lock pawl.

No TCC Lock-Up, TCC Remains Applied, Harsh Engagement During Lock-Up, Or Engine Stalls When Stopping Or Starting Vehicle Movement – Faulty TCC.
No Upshift From 1st To 2nd – Faulty 2nd/4th brake.
No Upshift From 2nd To 3rd – Faulty overdrive clutch.
No Upshift From 3rd To 4th – Faulty 2nd/4th brake.
No Engine Braking In 2nd Or 3rd – Faulty coast clutch.
No Engine Braking In 1st ("L" Range) – Faulty 1st/reverse brake.

TRANSMISSION COMPONENT APPLICATION CHART

Selector Lever Position	Elements In Use
"D" (Drive)	
First Gear	Forward Clutch, Coast Clutch, One-Way Clutch No. 1 & One-Way Clutch No. 0
Second Gear	Forward Clutch, Coast Clutch, 2nd/4th Brake & One-Way Clutch No. 0
Third Gear	Forward Clutch, Coast Clutch, OD Clutch & One-Way Clutch No. 0
Fourth Gear (OD)	Forward Clutch, OD Clutch & 2nd/4th Brake
"2" (Intermediate)	
First Gear	Forward Clutch, Coast Clutch, One-Way Clutch No. 1 & One-Way Clutch No. 0
Second Gear	Forward Clutch, Coast Clutch, 2nd/4th Brake & One-Way Clutch No. 0
"L" (1st Gear)	Forward Clutch, Coast Clutch, 1st/Reverse Brake, One-Way Clutch No. 1 & One-Way Clutch No. 0
"R" (Reverse)	Reverse Clutch, Coast Clutch & 1st/Reverse Brake
"N" (Neutral)	Coast Clutch
"P" (Park)	Coast Clutch

TESTING

NOTE: See 1995 SUZUKI ESTEEM ELECTRONIC CONTROLS article, or 1996 SUZUKI ESTEEM ELECTRONIC CONTROLS article for diagnosing transaxle electronic control system.

SHIFT POINT TEST

1) Engine and transmission must be at normal operating temperature. Road test vehicle with gear selector lever in "D" position. Ensure all upshifts and downshifts occur at specified shift points. See SHIFT POINT SPECIFICATIONS table.

2) Ensure lock-up occurs at appropriate speeds. See LOCK-UP SPEED SPECIFICATIONS table. Lightly depress accelerator pedal. If excessive increase in engine RPM is present, lock-up will not occur.

3) Check for shock and slippage at all upshifts. Check for abnormal noise and vibration. While driving in "D", "2" and "L" gear positions, ensure speeds at OD-3, 3-2 and 2-1 kickdown are within specification. Check for shock and slippage at kickdown.

SHIFT POINT SPECIFICATIONS

Application In "D" Position	Full Throttle MPH	Closed Throttle MPH
1st-2nd	35	9
2nd-3rd	67	15
3rd-OD	96	25
OD-3rd	87	12
3rd-2nd	59	6
2nd-1st	26	6

LOCK-UP SPEED SPECIFICATIONS

Application	MPH
Lock-Up ON	
3rd [1]	32
OD [2]	38
Lock-Up OFF	
3rd [1]	17
OD [2]	32

[1] – With gear selector lever in "D" position and throttle angle between 8 and 18 percent.
[2] – With gear selector lever in "D" position and throttle angle between zero and 18 percent.

STALL TEST

1) Ensure engine and transmission are at normal operating temperature. Check ATF level and add if necessary. Connect tachometer to vehicle and ensure it is visible to technician. Apply parking brake and block all 4 wheels.

CAUTION: DO NOT maintain stall speed RPM for more than 5 seconds. Ensure at least a 30 second pause is taken at idle between tests.

2) Start engine and depress brake pedal firmly. Place gear selector lever in "D" position. Depress accelerator pedal to full throttle and note maximum RPM obtained. Repeat test in "R" position. Stall speed should be 2280-2610 RPM.

Stall Speed Test Results:
- **Stall Speed Is Same In Both Positions, But Less Than Specified:** Engine output may be insufficient. Faulty torque converter.
- **Stall Speed High In "D" Position:** Low line pressure. Faulty one-way clutch No. 0 and/or coast clutch. Faulty forward clutch. Faulty one-way clutch No. 1.
- **Stall Speed High In "R" Position:** Low line pressure. Faulty reverse clutch. Faulty 1st/reverse brake.

TIME LAG TEST

1) Engine and transmission must be at normal operating temperature. Start engine and ensure idle speed RPM is within specification with A/C off. Apply service and parking brakes. Block all 4 wheels. Using a stop watch, measure amount of time until engagement shock is felt when gear selector lever is shifted from "N" to "D" position.

2) Allow one minute intervals between tests. Perform time measurements 2 more times and calculate average value. Time lag to "D" position should be less than .7 second. Repeat test procedure to test time lag when gear selector lever is shifted from "N" to "R" position. Time lag should be less than 1.2 seconds.

Time Lag Test Results:
- **"N" To "D" Position Time Lag Is Greater Than Specified:** Low line pressure. Faulty forward clutch.
- **"N" To "R" Position Time Lag Is Greater Than Specified:** Low line pressure. Faulty direct clutch. Faulty 1st/reverse brake.

LINE PRESSURE TEST

NOTE: Hydraulic pressure test should be performed with ATF temperature at normal operating temperature of 158-176°F (70-80°C).

1) Ensure ATF is at normal operating temperature. Check ATF level and add if necessary. Remove right-side engine undercover. Connect an appropriate pressure gauge to line pressure test port on transaxle. *See Fig. 3.*

2) Apply parking brake and block all 4 wheels. Connect tachometer to vehicle and ensure it is visible to technician. Start engine and ensure idle speed RPM is adjusted to specification.

CAUTION: DO NOT maintain stall speed RPM for more than 5 seconds. Ensure at least a one minute pause is taken at idle between tests.

3) Apply service brake and shift transmission to "D" position. Check line pressure at idle and record line pressure reading. Accelerate vehicle to stall speed and record line pressure reading. Repeat test procedure in "R" position. Compare all readings to specification. See LINE PRESSURE SPECIFICATIONS table.

LINE PRESSURE SPECIFICATIONS

Engine Speed	"D" Position psi (kg/cm²)	"R" Position psi (kg/cm²)
Idle Speed	53-58 (3.7-4.1)	79-86 (5.6-6.0)
Stall Speed	136-156 (9.6-11.0)	188-233 (13.2-16.4)

Line Pressure Test Results:
- **Line Pressure High In Both Positions:** Faulty pressure control solenoid valve. Faulty primary regulator valve.
- **Line Pressure Low In Both Positions:** Faulty pressure control solenoid valve. Faulty primary regulator valve. Faulty oil pump.
- **Line Pressure Low In "D" Position Only:** Fluid leak from "D" range pressure circuit.
- **Line Pressure Low In "R" Position Only:** Fluid leak from "R" range pressure circuit.

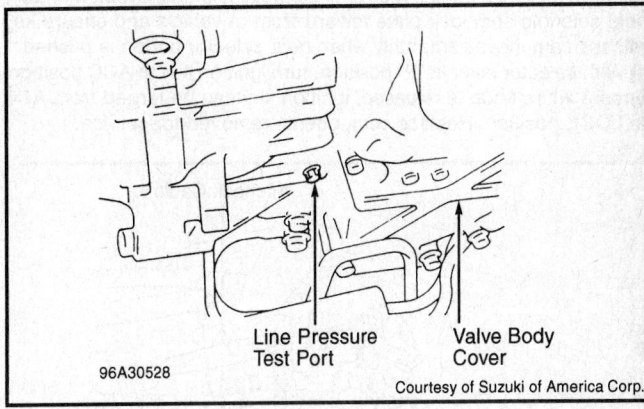

96A30528

Line Pressure Test Port   Valve Body Cover

Courtesy of Suzuki of America Corp.

Fig. 3: Locating Transaxle Line Pressure Test Port

ENGINE BRAKE TEST

Road test vehicle in 3rd gear while in "D" range. Shift gear selector lever into "2" range. Engine braking should be noticed. Repeat test in "L" range. Engine braking should also be noticed.

Engine Brake Test Results:
- **No Engine Braking In "2" Range:** Faulty 2nd/4th brake.
- **No Engine Braking In "L" Range:** Faulty 1st/reverse brake.

"P" RANGE TEST

1) Position vehicle on a slope, place gear selector lever in "P" position and apply parking brake. Turn engine off. Depress brake pedal and release parking brake.

2) Gradually release brake pedal and ensure vehicle remains stationary. Depress brake pedal and place gear selector lever in "N" position. Release brake pedal and ensure vehicle moves.

"P" Range Test Results:
- **Vehicle Moves In "P" Range:** Faulty parking lock pawl or spring.
- **Vehicle Remains Stationary In "N" Range:** Faulty parking lock pawl or spring.

ON-VEHICLE SERVICE

GEAR SELECTOR CABLE

Adjustment – 1) Place gear selector lever and transaxle control shaft in Neutral. Loosen cable lock nuts to provide cable slack and free movement. Push cable forward until it stops. Ensure gear selector lever is in Neutral.

2) Tighten rear cable lock nut until it contacts transaxle control shaft lever. Tighten front cable lock nut. Confirm the following: vehicle will not move with gear selector lever in Park. Vehicle will not drive in Neutral, but can be operated as indicated in all other positions.

SHIFT INTERLOCK SYSTEM

NOTE: Shift Interlock system will not allow gearshift to move from "P" position unless ignition is on. Ignition key removal is also prevented unless gearshift is in "P" position.

Interlock Cable (Adjustment) – 1) Disconnect negative battery cable and disable air bag system. See appropriate AIR BAG SERVICING article in APPLICATIONS & IDENTIFICATION section. Remove covers to access upper steering column. Ensure interlock cable clamp screw is tight and cable is attached to release shaft.

2) Loosen cable bracket nut at gear selector cable. Place gear selector lever in "P" position. Manually move solenoid lock plate towards front of vehicle and push gear selector lever lock knob. Insert Alignment Tool (09925-78210) into holes in gear selector key release cam and selector lever. See Fig. 4.

3) Ensure cable is connected to key release cam. Tighten cable bracket nut to 114 INCH lbs. (12.9 N.m). Remove alignment tool. Manually hold solenoid shift lock plate toward front of vehicle and ensure key release cam moves smoothly when gear selector button is pushed.

4) With selector lever in "P" position, turn ignition key to ACC position. Ensure when knob is released, ignition key can be turned from ACC to LOCK position. Replace components removed for service.

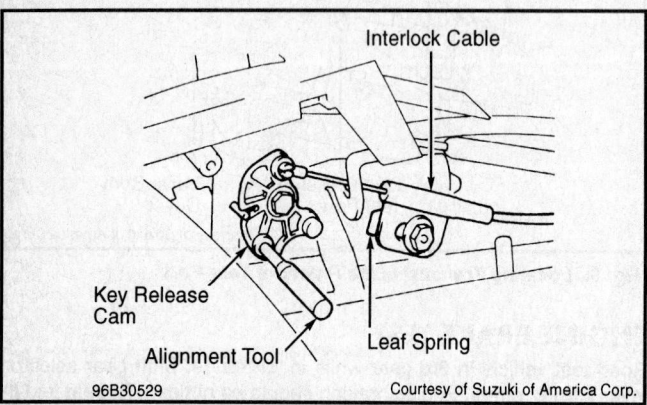

Fig. 4: Adjusting Interlock Cable

Shift Lock Solenoid (Inspection) – Remove parking brake cover and console box to access solenoid. Ensure detent pin is locked in Park position by lock plate. Ensure lock plate is pulled in when ignition switch is turned to ON position and brake pedal is depressed. This allows detent pin to be pushed down.

TRANSMISSION RANGE (TR) SWITCH

Adjustment – 1) Turn ignition switch to LOCK position. Place gear selector lever in "N" position. Disconnect TR switch harness connector. Using a DVOM, connect leads to TR switch terminals No. 7 and 9. See Fig. 5.

2) Turn TR switch gradually to find position where DVOM indicates continuity. Tighten TR switch at that position. Tighten bolts to 15 ft. lbs. (20 N.m).

3) Reconnect TR switch harness connector. Ensure engine starts with gear selector lever in "N" or "P" positions, but does not start in any other position. Ensure back-up lights illuminate with gear selector lever in "R" position.

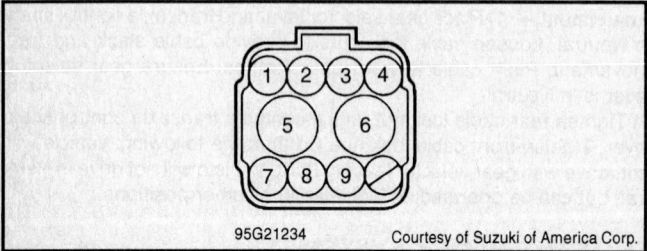

Fig. 5: Identifying Transmission Range (TR) Switch Terminals

VALVE BODY ASSEMBLY

CAUTION: DO NOT let manual valve fall off when removing valve body assembly.

Removal – 1) Disconnect transaxle solenoid harness connector. Drain ATF. Remove transaxle side cover and gasket. Discard 2 non-reusable bolts at position "A". See Fig. 6.

2) Release solenoid harness connector from clamp. Disconnect solenoid couplers. Remove 8 valve body assembly retaining bolts. Note bolt location and length. See Fig. 7. Remove valve body assembly.

Installation – 1) While holding valve body, connect manual valve to parking lock rod. Install valve body bolts and torque to 90 INCH lbs. (10.2 N.m). See Fig. 7. Reconnect solenoid couplers. Ensure couplers are connected as follows: shift solenoid No. 1 (White connector), shift solenoid No. 2 (Blue connector) and TCC control solenoid (Yellow connector).

2) Clean transaxle-to-side cover mating surfaces. Apply Sealant (99000-31160) to transaxle case and install side cover. Tighten bolts to 18 ft. lbs. (25 N.m). Ensure NEW bolts are used in position "A". See Fig. 6. Fill transaxle with ATF to proper level.

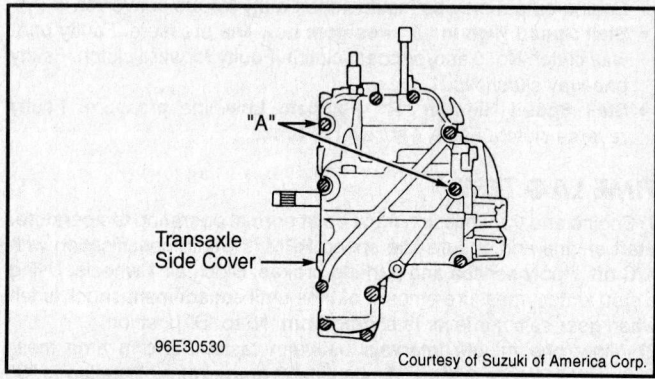

Fig. 6: Identifying NEW Side Cover Bolt Location

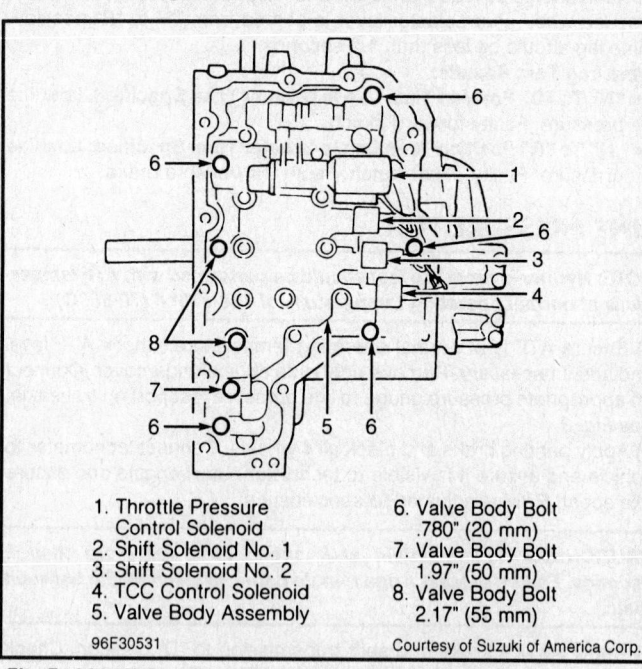

1. Throttle Pressure Control Solenoid
2. Shift Solenoid No. 1
3. Shift Solenoid No. 2
4. TCC Control Solenoid
5. Valve Body Assembly
6. Valve Body Bolt .780" (20 mm)
7. Valve Body Bolt 1.97" (50 mm)
8. Valve Body Bolt 2.17" (55 mm)

Fig. 7: Identifying Valve Body Bolt Length & Location

REMOVAL & INSTALLATION

For transmission removal and installation procedure, see appropriate AUTOMATIC TRANSMISSION REMOVAL article in TRANSMISSION SERVICING section.

TORQUE CONVERTER

NOTE: Torque converter is a sealed unit and must be serviced as a complete assembly. Torque converter and transmission oil cooler must be thoroughly cleaned and flushed if transmission fluid is contaminated. Manufacturer does not provide inspection procedures for torque converter.

TRANSMISSION DISASSEMBLY

CAUTION: Thoroughly clean transaxle exterior prior to disassembly. Use special care in handling aluminum components. DO NOT turn transaxle over when removing side cover. Turning transaxle may contaminate valve body with foreign matter from bottom of transaxle.

1) Remove torque converter. Using an INCH lb. torque wrench, measure starting torque of differential gear assembly. Specified starting torque is 12 INCH lbs. (1.4 N.m).

2) Remove oil cooler pipes and discard washers. Remove manual shift lever. Remove lock nut and lock washer. Discard lock washer. Remove lock washer and rubber plate. Remove 2 bolts, then Transmission Range (TR) switch.

3) Remove oil level dip stick, filler tube, forward clutch cylinder revolution sensor and each Vehicle Speed Sensor (VSS). One VSS is used for TCM input, the other is used for speedometer input.

4) Remove transaxle housing and discard 2 non-reusable bolts at position "A". *See Fig. 8.* Pull out differential gear assembly. Clean mating surfaces between transaxle case and housing. Remove 3 gaskets from transaxle case side. Remove oil pump body retaining bolts, then oil pump body.

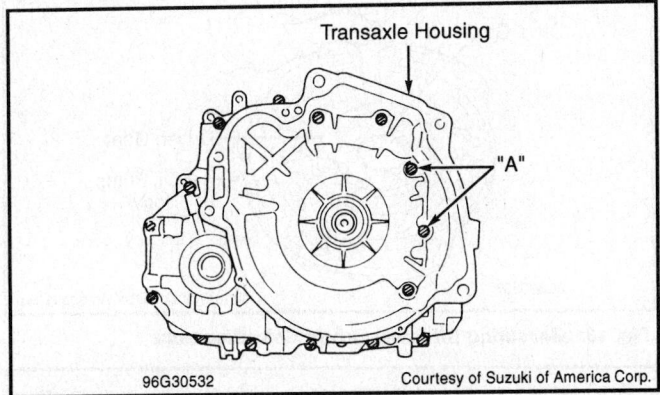

Fig. 8: Identifying NEW Transaxle Housing Bolt Location

5) Remove 2 bolts, oil reserve plate and oil strainer. Remove manual detent spring. Remove valve body assembly. See VALVE BODY ASSEMBLY under ON-VEHICLE SERVICE. Remove 2 gaskets ("O" rings). Using snap ring pliers, remove snap ring and pull out brake cover.

6) Using a dial indicator, measure 2nd/4th brake piston stroke as follows:
- Plug oil hole "A". *See Fig. 9.*
- Measure piston stroke while applying and releasing 57-113 psi (4-8 kg/cm²) of compressed air at oil hole "B".
- Specified piston stroke is .120-.130" (3.0-3.3 mm).

7) Pry off lock section of lock washer, loosen lock nut and remove piston rod with lock nut, lock washer and lock plate. NEVER reuse old lock washer. Remove lock plate from piston rod.

8) Pull out reverse clutch assembly. Remove 2nd/4th brake band assembly. Remove straight pin. Ensure length of straight pin is 1.770" (45 mm), and diameter is .310" (7.9 mm).

9) Using an appropriate press, push in piston cover and remove snap ring. Remove 2nd/4th brake piston cover, piston and spring. Remove 6 bolts from transaxle rear cover. Using a plastic hammer, tap 2 rib sections of rear cover. Remove 10 bolts and left-side engine mounting bracket. Discard 2 non-reusable bolts at position "A". *See Fig. 10.*

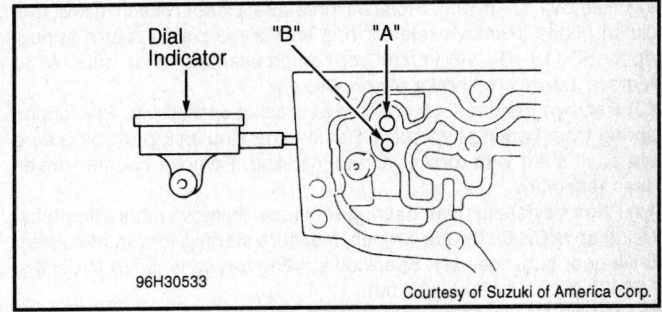

Fig. 9: Measuring 2nd/4th Brake Piston Stroke

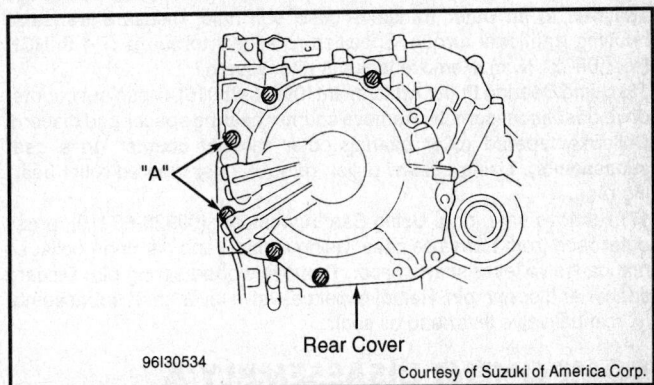

Fig. 10: Identifying NEW Rear Cover Bolt Location

10) Pull out transaxle rear cover with forward clutch subassembly installed. Remove 5 gaskets ("O" rings). Remove carrier for front/rear planetary ring gear and sun gear assembly with integral bearing installed. Pull out sun gear assembly.

11) Using a dial indicator, measure 1st/reverse brake piston stroke. Measure piston stroke while applying 57-113 psi (4-8 kg/cm²) of compressed air to oil hole "A". *See Fig. 11.* Specified piston stroke is .055-.087" (1.4-2.2 mm).

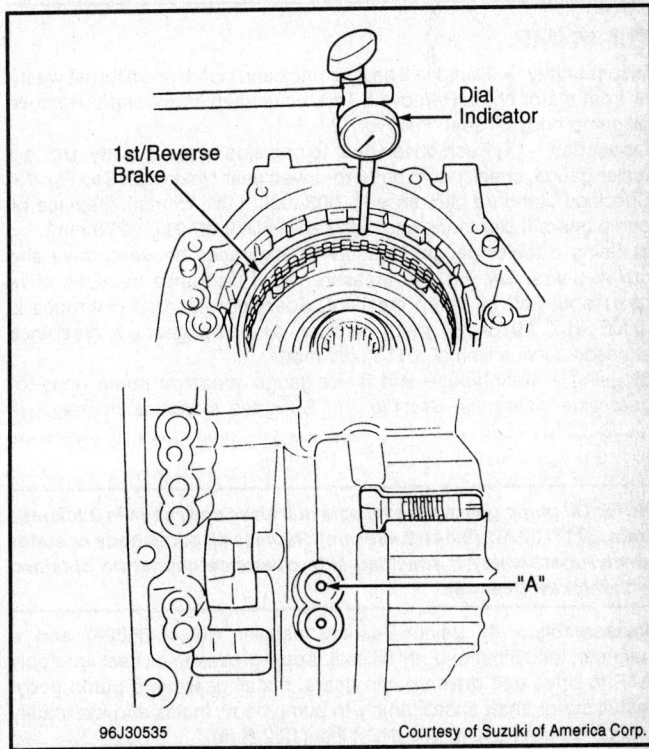

Fig. 11: Measuring 1st/Reverse Brake Piston Stroke

12) Remove snap ring. Remove pressure plates, clutch discs and clutch plates. Remove retainer ring and brake piston return spring. Apply 57-113 psi (4-8 kg/cm²) of compressed air to oil hole "A" to remove 1st/reverse brake piston. *See Fig. 11.*

13) Remove parking lock pawl, pawl bracket and spring. Pry torsion spring from parking lock pawl. Remove parking lock pawl by pulling out pawl shaft with torsion spring installed. Remove counter driven gear assembly.

14) Remove needle roller bearing with race. Remove lubrication tube. Using an INCH lb. torque wrench, measure starting torque of counter drive gear subassembly. Specified starting torque is .5-3.5 INCH lbs. (.05-.39 N.m). Unstake lock nut.

15) Clamp Counter Drive Gear Holder (09927-76040) in vise. Place transaxle housing onto holder. Using an appropriate push-pull gauge attached to an outer transaxle case bolt hole, measure transaxle housing rotational torque. Specified rotational torque is .7-1.9 INCH lbs. (.08-.21 N.m). Remove lock nut and discard.

16) Using Bearing Puller Attachment (09925-86010), press out counter drive gear subassembly. Remove counter bearing spacer and discard. Collapse tapered roller bearing outer race of counter drive gear subassembly. Using a 2-jaw puller, remove inner tapered roller bearing race.

17) Remove snap ring. Using Bearing Installer (09926-68310), press outer race from transaxle case. Using a chisel and hammer, collapse manual valve lever shaft spacer. Remove slotted spring pin. Discard spacer and spring pin. Remove manual valve lever shaft subassembly, manual valve lever and oil seal.

COMPONENT DISASSEMBLY & REASSEMBLY

NOTE: Clean all parts with cleaning solvent and air dry. DO NOT use wiping cloths or rags to clean or dry parts. Soak new clutch discs and brake band in ATF for 2 hours or more before assembly. Apply ATF to sliding, rolling and thrusting surfaces of all components. Replace all gaskets and "O" rings. Apply ATF to all "O" rings except oil pump cover seal. Replace oil seals that are removed. Apply grease to oil seal lips. Check each part for proper operation after installation.

OIL PUMP

Disassembly – Remove 2 sealing rings and clutch drum thrust washer from stator shaft. Remove 8 Torx bolts, then stator shaft. Remove oil pump body oil seal. *See Fig. 12.*

Inspection – **1)** Push driven gear to one side of pump body. Using a feeler gauge, check pump body-to-driven gear clearance. *See Fig. 13.* Specified standard clearance is .003-.006" (.08-.15 mm). Replace oil pump gears if clearance exceeds service limit of .011" (.280 mm).

2) Using a feeler gauge, measure tip clearance between drive and driven gears. *See Fig. 14.* Measure radial clearance between drive gear tooth and oil pump crescent. Specified standard clearance is .0005-.010" (.013-.254 mm). Replace oil pump gears if clearance exceeds service limit of .011" (.280 mm).

3) Using a straightedge and feeler gauge, measure pump body-to-gear side clearance. *See Fig. 15.* Specified standard clearance is .0008-.0019" (.020-.048 mm). Replace oil pump gears if clearance exceeds specification by .0039" (.100 mm).

NOTE: Oil pump gears are available in 5 sizes and range in thickness from .3717-.3736" (9.441-9.489 mm). Replace oil pump body or stator shaft subassembly if specified side clearance cannot be obtained with thickest gear set.

Reassembly – **1)** Using Bearing Installer (09944-66020) and a hammer, install pump body oil seal. Apply grease to oil seal lip. Apply ATF to drive and driven pump gears. Install gears into pump body. Install stator shaft subassembly to pump body. Install and alternately torque 8 Torx bolts to 108 INCH lbs. (12.2 N.m).

2) Install 2 NEW sealing rings to stator shaft. Apply ATF to clutch drum thrust washer and install. Using 2 screw drivers, turn drive gear and ensure rotation is smooth.

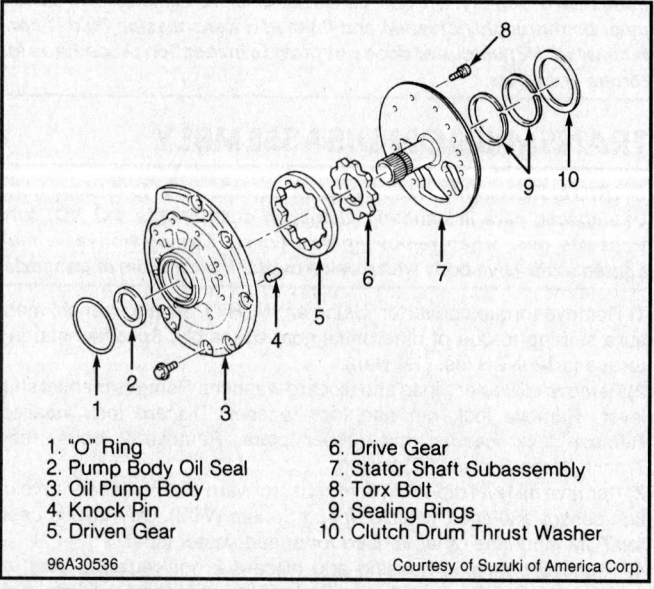

1. "O" Ring
2. Pump Body Oil Seal
3. Oil Pump Body
4. Knock Pin
5. Driven Gear
6. Drive Gear
7. Stator Shaft Subassembly
8. Torx Bolt
9. Sealing Rings
10. Clutch Drum Thrust Washer

96A30536   Courtesy of Suzuki of America Corp.

Fig. 12: Exploded View Of Oil Pump

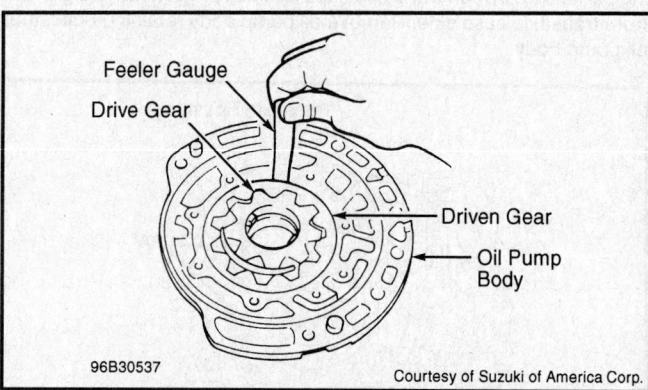

96B30537   Courtesy of Suzuki of America Corp.

Fig. 13: Measuring Oil Pump Driven Gear Clearance

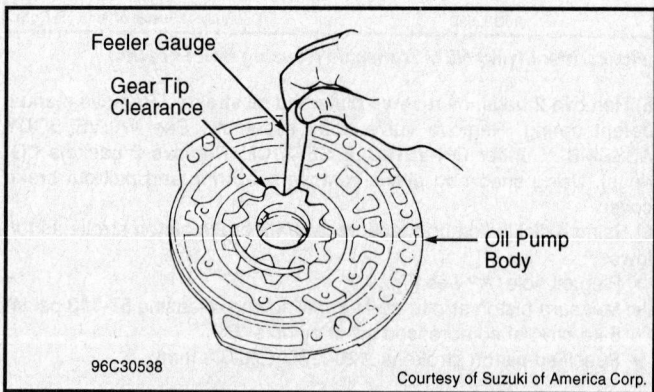

96C30538   Courtesy of Suzuki of America Corp.

Fig. 14: Measuring Oil Pump Gear Tip Clearance

FORWARD CLUTCH

Preliminary Check – Install forward clutch assembly into transaxle rear cover. Using a dial indicator, measure piston stroke while applying 57-113 psi (4-8 kg/cm²) of compressed air to oil hole "A". *See Fig. 16.* Specified piston stroke is .030-.057" (.76-1.45 mm).

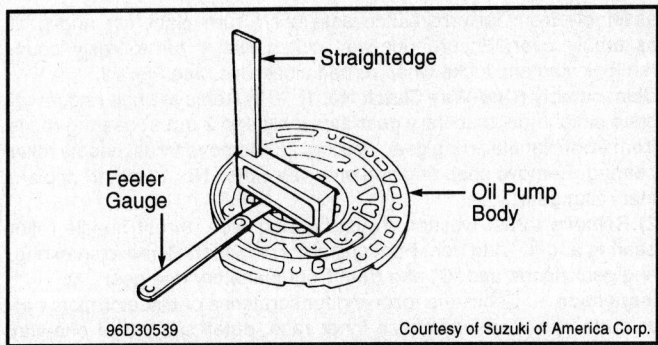

96D30539   Courtesy of Suzuki of America Corp.

Fig. 15: Measuring Oil Pump Gear Side Clearance

Disassembly – 1) Remove snap ring, flange, discs and plates. Remove clutch drum thrust washer. See Fig. 17. Using an appropriate press, compress forward clutch return spring. Remove snap ring and return spring subassembly.

2) Install forward clutch piston subassembly into transaxle rear cover. Apply 57-113 psi (4-8 kg/cm²) of compressed air into oil hole "A" to remove forward clutch piston. See Fig. 16. Remove clutch drum oil sealing rings from clutch drum and rear cover.

Inspection – 1) Check for worn, discolored (burnt) or cracked discs, plates and flanges. Replace if necessary. If printed numbers on clutch disc surfaces are defaced, replace them.

2) Using calipers, measure forward clutch return spring height. Perform measurement at several points. Replace return spring assembly if height is less than .866" (22 mm). Ensure check ball is free in piston and does not leak when compressed air is applied.

NOTE: Soak new clutch discs in ATF for 2 hours or more before assembly.

Reassembly – 1) Coat clutch drum oil sealing rings with ATF and position on clutch drum and rear cover. Coat "O" rings with ATF and position on clutch piston. Press clutch piston into clutch drum by hand.

2) Using an appropriate press, install piston return spring and secure with snap ring. Install plates, discs and flange in the following order: plate, disc, plate, disc and flange. Secure with snap ring, ensuring open end does not align with grooved section of clutch drum.

3) Coat race and clutch drum thrust washer with grease and install onto clutch drum. Measure forward clutch piston stroke as noted in PRELIMINARY CHECK.

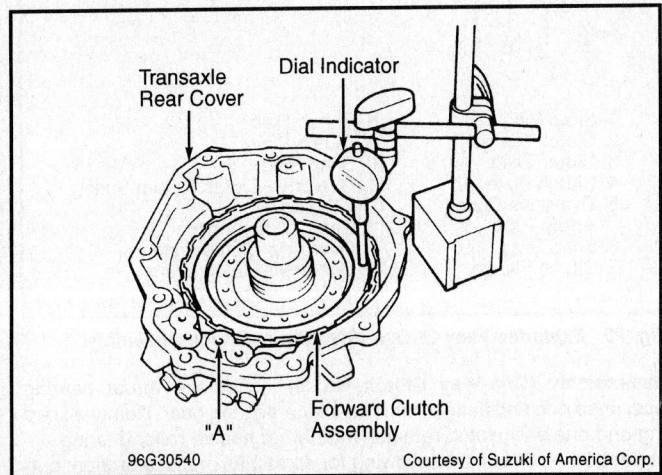

96G30540   Courtesy of Suzuki of America Corp.

Fig. 16: Measuring Forward Clutch Piston Stroke

OVERDRIVE/COAST CLUTCH

Preliminary Check – 1) Install forward clutch assembly and overdrive/coast clutch assembly into transaxle rear cover. Using a dial indicator, measure overdrive clutch piston stroke while applying 57-113 psi (4-8 kg/cm²) of compressed air to oil hole "A". See Fig. 18. Specified piston stroke is .030-.041" (.76-1.04 mm).

2) Using a dial indicator, measure coast clutch piston stroke while applying 57-113 psi (4-8 kg/cm²) of compressed air to oil hole "B". See Fig. 19. Specified piston stroke is .106-.119" (2.69-3.02 mm).

Disassembly – 1) Remove snap ring, flanges, discs and plate from overdrive clutch drum. See Fig. 20. Measure thickness of flange and record for reference of piston stroke confirmation.

2) Remove snap ring and overdrive clutch apply tube. Remove snap ring, flanges, discs and plate from coast clutch. Measure thickness of flange and record for reference of piston stroke confirmation.

3) Using an appropriate press, compress overdrive clutch return spring. Remove snap ring and return spring subassembly. Install forward clutch assembly, coast clutch piston and overdrive clutch piston into transaxle rear cover.

4) Apply 57-113 psi (4-8 kg/cm²) of compressed air into oil hole "B" to remove coast clutch piston. See Fig. 19. Remove "O" rings from coast clutch piston.

5) Apply 57-113 psi (4-8 kg/cm²) of compressed air into oil hole "A" to remove overdrive clutch piston. See Fig. 18. Remove "O" rings from overdrive clutch piston.

Inspection – 1) Check for worn, discolored (burnt) or cracked discs, plates and flanges. Replace if necessary. If printed numbers on clutch disc surfaces are defaced, replace them.

2) Using calipers, measure overdrive clutch return spring height. Perform measurement at several points. Replace return spring assembly if height is less than .740" (18.8 mm). Ensure check ball is free in piston and rattles when shaken.

NOTE: Soak new clutch discs in ATF for 2 hours or more before assembly.

Reassembly – 1) Apply ATF to "O" rings and position on pistons. Pushing by hand, set coast clutch piston to overdrive clutch piston. Press overdrive clutch and coast clutch pistons into overdrive clutch drum.

2) Using an appropriate press, install piston return spring and secure with snap ring. Select appropriate coast clutch flange to obtain correct piston stroke. Clutch flanges are available in 3 sizes and range in thickness from .142-.157" (3.61-3.99 mm).

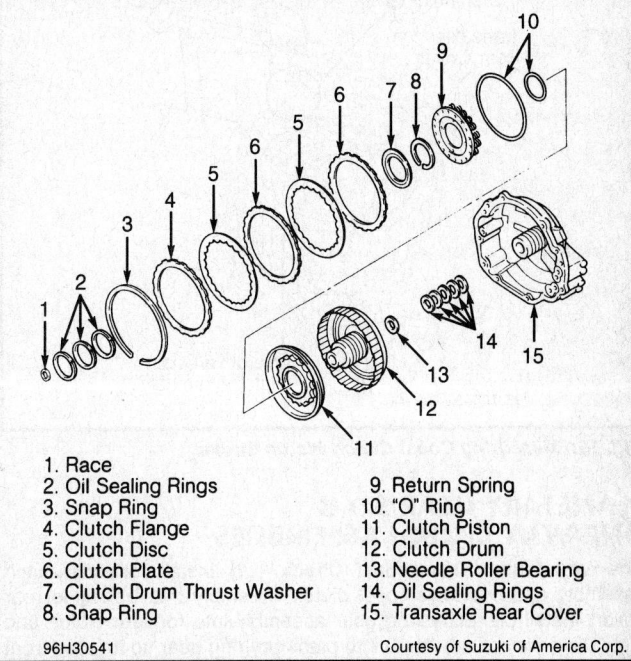

1. Race	9. Return Spring
2. Oil Sealing Rings	10. "O" Ring
3. Snap Ring	11. Clutch Piston
4. Clutch Flange	12. Clutch Drum
5. Clutch Disc	13. Needle Roller Bearing
6. Clutch Plate	14. Oil Sealing Rings
7. Clutch Drum Thrust Washer	15. Transaxle Rear Cover
8. Snap Ring	

96H30541   Courtesy of Suzuki of America Corp.

Fig. 17: Exploded View Of Forward Clutch Assembly

3) Install flanges, discs and plate in the following order: flange, disc, plate, disc and flange. Secure with snap ring, ensuring open end does not align with grooved section of clutch drum.

4) Install overdrive clutch apply tube. Select appropriate overdrive clutch flange to obtain correct piston stroke. Clutch flanges are available in 3 sizes and range in thickness from .142-.157" (3.61-3.99 mm).

5) Install flanges, discs and plate in the following order: flange, disc, plate, disc and flange. Secure with snap ring, ensuring open end does not align with grooved section of clutch drum.

6) Install forward clutch assembly and overdrive direct multiple "D" clutch assembly into transaxle rear cover. Measure overdrive and coast clutch piston strokes as noted in PRELIMINARY CHECK.

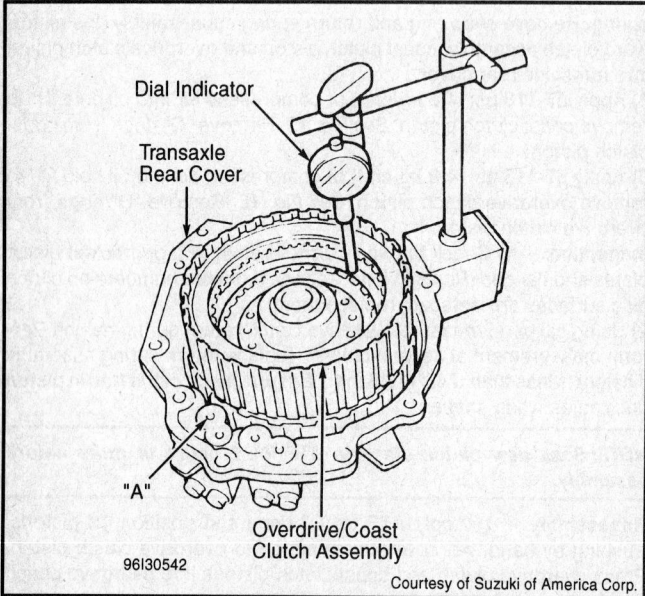

Fig. 18: *Measuring Overdrive Clutch Piston Stroke*

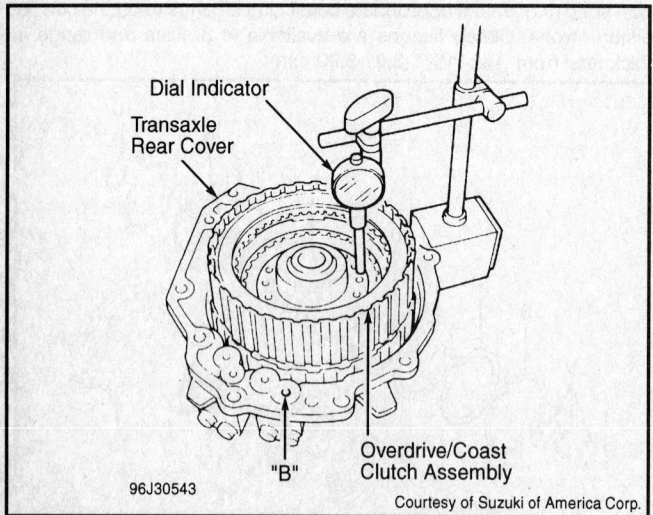

Fig. 19: *Measuring Coast Clutch Piston Stroke*

PLANETARY GEAR SET & ONE-WAY CLUTCH ASSEMBLIES

One-Way Clutch Operational Check – 1) Install forward clutch assembly and overdrive/coast clutch assembly into transaxle rear cover. Install planetary ring gear assembly into forward clutch and install one-way clutch No. 0 into planetary ring gear so it faces front side.

2) Ensure one-way clutch No. 0 turns freely clockwise and locks when turned counterclockwise. *See Fig. 21*. Remove planetary ring gear

assembly from forward clutch assembly. Turn planetary ring gear assembly over. Ensure one-way clutch No. 1 turns freely counterclockwise and locks when turned clockwise. *See Fig. 22*.

Disassembly (One-Way Clutch No. 1) – 1) Remove snap ring, overdrive clutch hub, planetary gear assembly and 2 thrust bearing races from front planetary ring gear. *See Fig. 23*. Remove thrust needle roller bearing. Remove snap ring and one-way clutch No. 1 from front planetary ring gear.

2) Remove thrust washer, thrust bearing race, thrust needle roller bearing and "O" ring from front planetary ring gear. Remove snap ring, ring gear flange and "O" ring from front planetary ring gear.

Inspection – Check the following for scratches or discoloration: outer surface of one-way clutch inner race, outer surface of one-way clutch roller and inner surface of front planetary ring gear subassembly. Replace as necessary.

Reassembly – 1) Apply ATF to "O" ring and install into front planetary ring gear. Install ring gear flange onto front planetary ring gear and secure with snap ring. Apply ATF to second "O" ring and install into front planetary ring gear.

2) Apply ATF and install thrust needle roller bearing, thrust bearing race and thrust washer into front planetary ring gear. Assemble one-way clutch No. 1 so section "A" (short side) faces front, and section "B" (thin side) faces rear. *See Fig. 24*.

3) Install one-way clutch No. 1 into front planetary ring gear and secure with snap ring. Install thrust needle bearing. Install planetary gear assembly and overdrive clutch hub into front planetary ring gear and secure with snap ring. Apply ATF to both thrust bearing races and install.

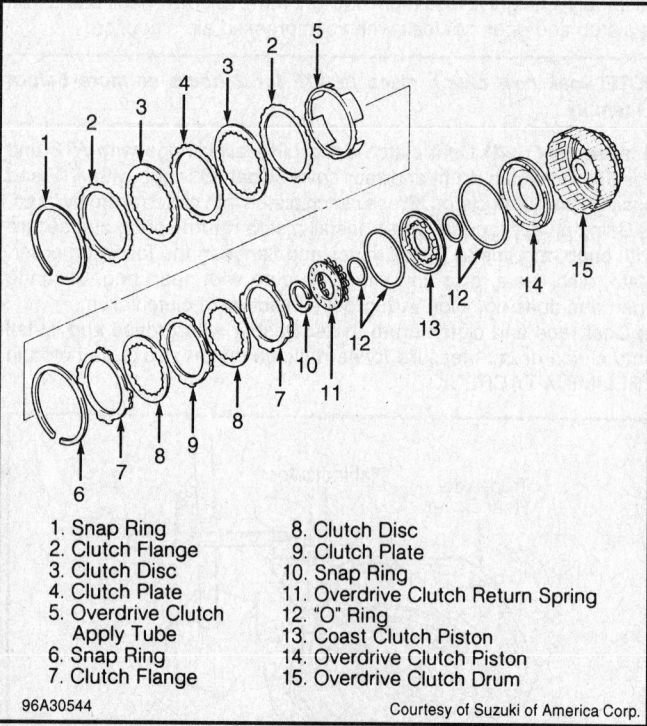

1. Snap Ring	8. Clutch Disc
2. Clutch Flange	9. Clutch Plate
3. Clutch Disc	10. Snap Ring
4. Clutch Plate	11. Overdrive Clutch Return Spring
5. Overdrive Clutch Apply Tube	12. "O" Ring
6. Snap Ring	13. Coast Clutch Piston
7. Clutch Flange	14. Overdrive Clutch Piston
	15. Overdrive Clutch Drum

Fig. 20: *Exploded View Of Overdrive/Coast Clutch Assembly*

Disassembly (One-Way Clutch No. 0) – Remove thrust bearing race, snap ring and flange from rear planetary ring gear. Remove snap ring and one-way clutch retainer with thrust needle roller bearing.

Inspection – Check the following for scratches or discoloration: outer surface of one-way clutch roller, inner surface of one-way clutch outer race and inner surface of rear planetary ring gear subassembly. Replace as necessary.

Reassembly – Assemble one-way clutch No. 0 so section "A" (thin side) faces front. *See Fig. 25*. To complete assembly, reverse disassembly procedure. Apply ATF to thrust bearing race and thrust needle roller bearing.

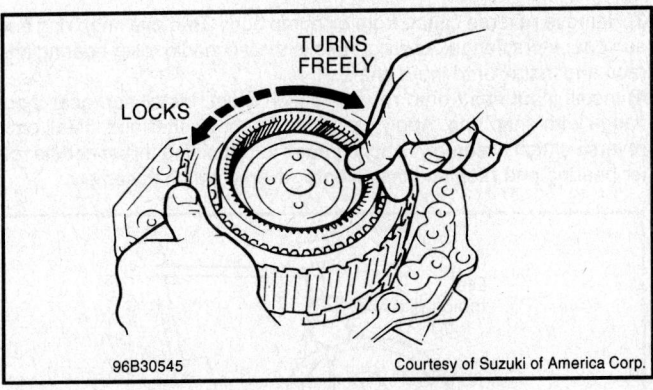

Fig. 21: Checking One-Way Clutch No. 0 Operation

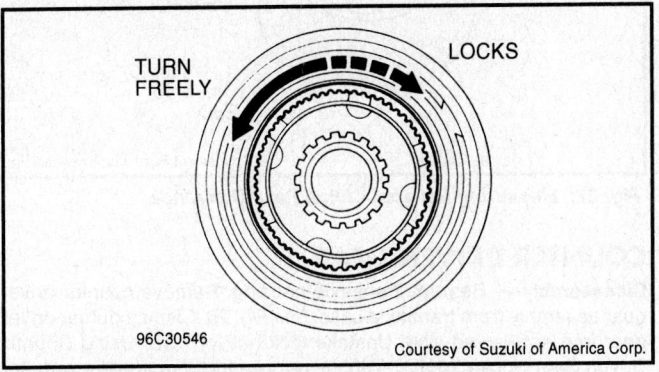

Fig. 22: Checking One-Way Clutch No. 1 Operation

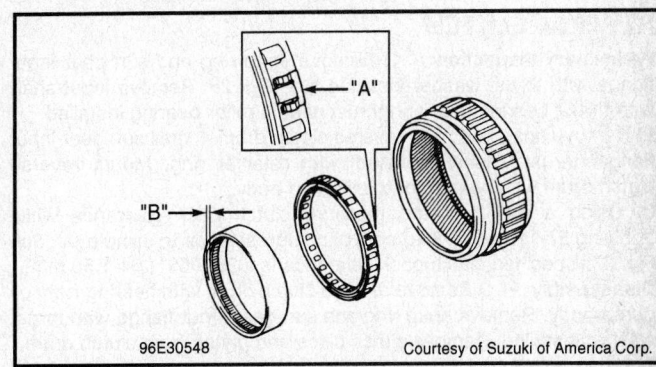

Fig. 24: Assembling One-Way Clutch No. 1

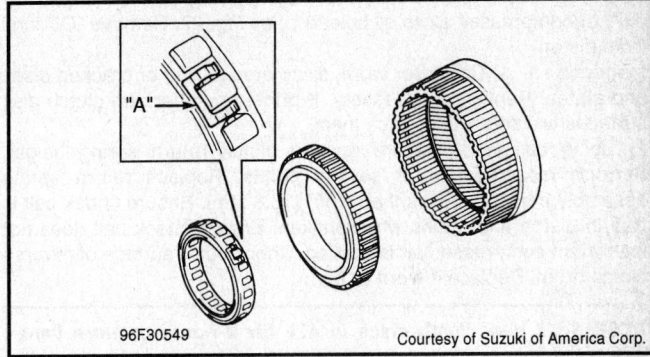

Fig. 25: Assembling One-Way Clutch No. 0

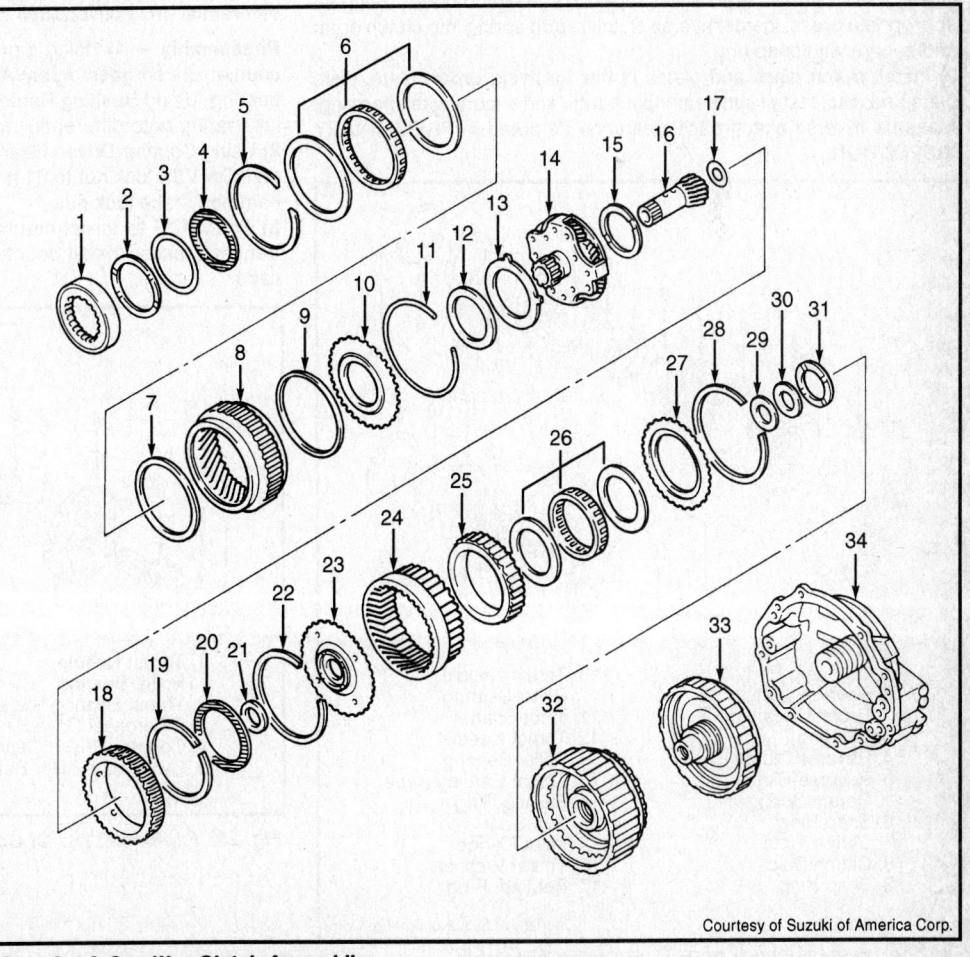

1. One-Way Clutch Inner Race
2. Thrust Washer
3. Thrust Bearing Race
4. Thrust Needle Roller Bearing
5. Snap Ring
6. One-Way Clutch
7. "O" Ring
8. Front Planetary Ring Gear Assembly
9. "O" Ring
10. Front Planetary Ring Gear Flange
11. Snap Ring
12. Thrust Needle Roller Bearing
13. Thrust Bearing Race
14. Planetary Gear Assembly
15. Thrust Bearing Race
16. Planetary Sun Gear Subassembly
17. Thrust Needle Roller Bearing
18. Overdrive Clutch Hub
19. Snap Ring
20. Thrust Needle Roller Bearing
21. Thrust Bearing Race
22. Snap Ring
23. Rear Planetary Ring Gear Flange
24. Rear Planetary Ring Gear Subassembly
25. One-Way Clutch Race
26. One-Way Clutch
27. One-Way Clutch Retainer
28. Snap Ring
29. Thrust Needle Roller Bearing
30. Thrust Bearing Race
31. Thrust Washer
32. Overdrive/Coast Clutch Assembly
33. Forward Clutch Assembly
34. Transaxle Rear Cover

Fig. 23: Exploded View Of Planetary Gear Set & One-Way Clutch Assemblies

REVERSE CLUTCH

Preliminary Inspection – 1) Remove snap ring and sun gear input flange with thrust washer installed. *See Fig. 26.* Remove input shaft with thrust bearing race and thrust needle roller bearing installed.

2) Remove snap ring from reverse clutch drum. Install sun gear input flange (thrust washer installed) with retainer ring. Mount reverse clutch drum with bearing onto oil pump body.

3) Using a dial indicator, measure clutch pack clearance while applying 57-113 psi (4-8 kg/cm²) of compressed air to oil hole "A". *See Fig. 27.* Specified clutch pack clearance is .025-.059" (.64-1.50 mm).

Disassembly – 1) Remove reverse clutch drum with bearing from oil pump body. Remove snap ring and sun gear input flange with thrust washer installed. Remove clutch discs and plates from clutch drum.

2) Using an appropriate press, remove snap ring and reverse clutch return spring. Position reverse clutch drum with bearing onto oil pump body. Remove reverse clutch piston by applying 57-113 psi (4-8 kg/cm²) of compressed air to oil hole "A". *See Fig. 27.* Remove "O" rings from piston.

Inspection – 1) Check for worn, discolored (burnt) or cracked discs and plates. Replace if necessary. If printed numbers on clutch disc surfaces are defaced, replace them.

2) Using calipers, measure reverse clutch return spring height. Perform measurement at several points. Replace return spring assembly if height is less than .740" (18.8 mm). Ensure check ball is free in piston and rattles when shaken. Ensure check ball does not leak when compressed air is applied. Check outer surface of reverse clutch drum. Replace if worn or burnt.

NOTE: Soak new clutch discs in ATF for 2 hours or more before assembly.

Reassembly – 1) Apply ATF to "O" rings and install onto reverse clutch piston. Press reverse clutch piston into clutch drum. Using an appropriate press, install reverse clutch return spring into clutch drum and secure with snap ring.

2) Install clutch discs and plates in the following order: plate, disc, plate and disc. Install sun gear input flange and secure with snap ring. Measure reverse clutch pack clearance as noted in PRELIMINARY INSPECTION.

3) Remove reverse clutch from oil pump body. Remove snap ring and sun gear input flange. Apply grease to thrust needle roller bearing and race and install onto input shaft.

4) Install input shaft onto reverse clutch drum. Install sun gear input flange with snap ring. Apply grease to thrust washer and install onto reverse clutch assembly. Apply grease to remaining thrust needle roller bearing and race and install onto reverse clutch assembly.

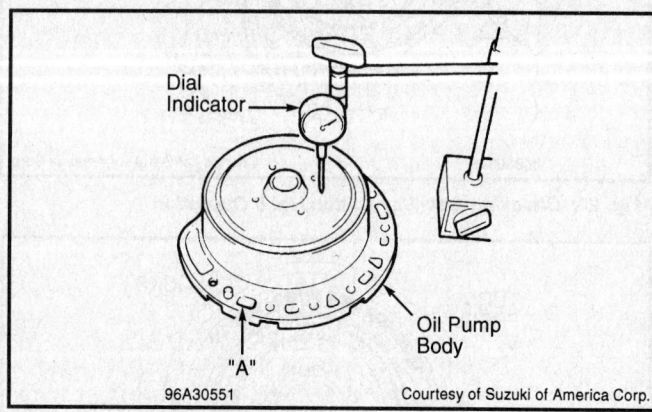

Fig. 27: Measuring Reverse Clutch Pack Clearance

COUNTER DRIVEN GEAR

Disassembly – Remove transaxle housing. Remove counter driven gear assembly from transaxle case. *See Fig. 28.* Clamp counter driven gear in a soft-jawed vice. Unstake lock nut for VSS. Using Counter Driven Gear Socket (09927-76050), remove lock nut and discard. *See Fig. 29.* Using a press, remove cylindrical roller bearing by pressing differential drive pinion. *See Fig. 30.*

Reassembly – 1) Using a press, press differential drive pinion onto counter driven gear. Apply ATF to inner surface of cylindrical roller bearing. Using Bushing Remover (09951-16060), press cylindrical roller bearing onto differential drive pinion.

2) Using Counter Driven Gear Socket (09927-76050), install and tighten NEW VSS lock nut to 91 ft. lbs. (123 N.m). Using a staking tool and hammer, stake lock nut.

3) Apply ATF to thrust needle roller bearings and races. Install into transaxle case. Install counter driven gear assembly into transaxle case.

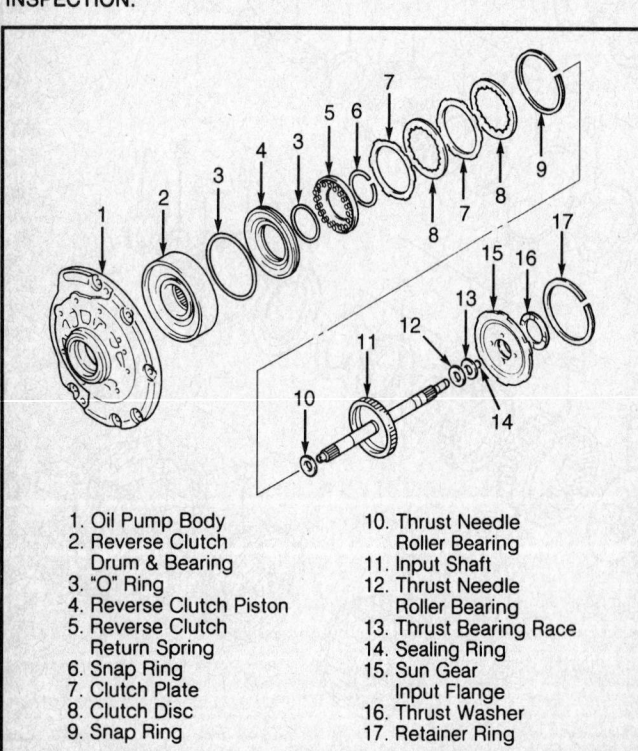

1. Oil Pump Body	10. Thrust Needle Roller Bearing
2. Reverse Clutch Drum & Bearing	11. Input Shaft
3. "O" Ring	12. Thrust Needle Roller Bearing
4. Reverse Clutch Piston	13. Thrust Bearing Race
5. Reverse Clutch Return Spring	14. Sealing Ring
6. Snap Ring	15. Sun Gear Input Flange
7. Clutch Plate	16. Thrust Washer
8. Clutch Disc	17. Retainer Ring
9. Snap Ring	

96J30550   Courtesy of Suzuki of America Corp.

Fig. 26: Exploded View Of Reverse Clutch Assembly

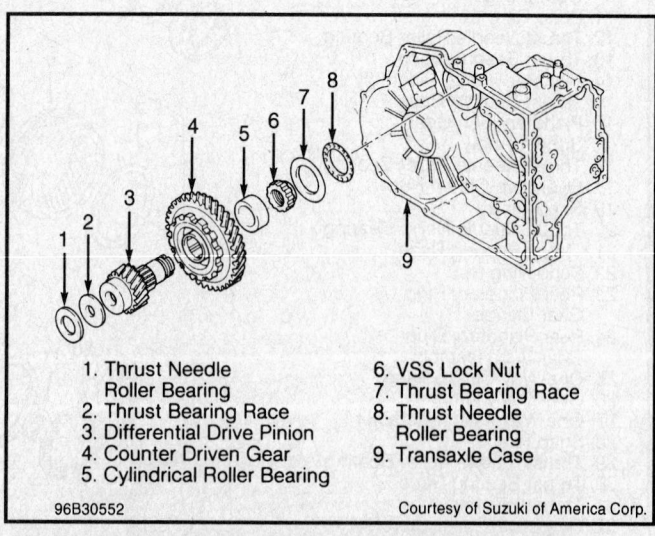

1. Thrust Needle Roller Bearing	6. VSS Lock Nut
2. Thrust Bearing Race	7. Thrust Bearing Race
3. Differential Drive Pinion	8. Thrust Needle Roller Bearing
4. Counter Driven Gear	9. Transaxle Case
5. Cylindrical Roller Bearing	

96B30552   Courtesy of Suzuki of America Corp.

Fig. 28: Exploded View Of Counter Driven Gear Assembly

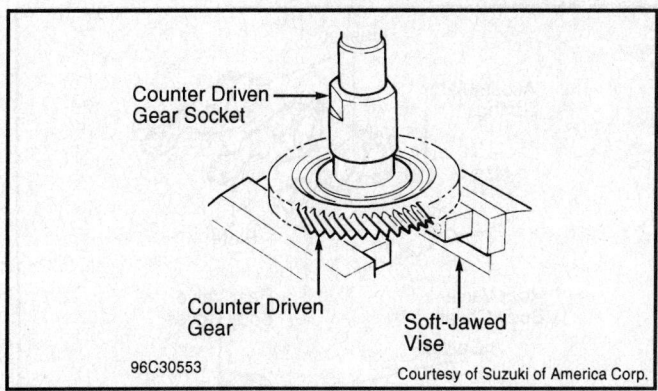

Fig. 29: Removing VSS Lock Nut

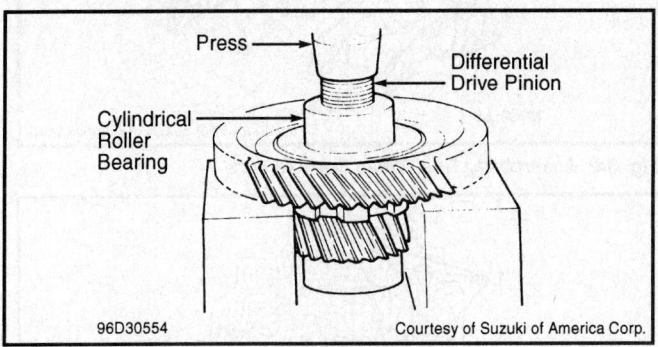

Fig. 30: Removing Cylindrical Roller Bearing

VALVE BODY

Disassembly – 1) Pull out manual valve. Remove control solenoids. Remove bolts from valve body (11 front side; 5 rear side). Remove rear valve body gaskets and separator plate together with rear valve body. **2)** Remove 6 check balls, solenoid oil strainer and check valves with springs. Remove check valve and spring from front valve body. Remove rear valve body cover and key. Remove components as shown. *See Fig. 31.*

3) Remove keys from front valve body and remove components as shown. *See Fig. 31.* Remove front valve body cover, gaskets and plate. Remove check valve, spring, 3 check balls and solenoid oil strainers. Remove keys and remaining components from front valve body.

Inspection – 1) Clean all parts with ATF. Clean all fluid passages and holes. Using compressed air, ensure passages or holes are clear. **2)** Inspect valves for scoring or roughness. Inspect valve springs for damage, squareness, rust and collapsed coils. Replace springs if necessary. Valve body springs must be arranged with corresponding valve. See VALVE BODY SPRING IDENTIFICATION table.

Reassembly – 1) Install valves and springs into torque converter side of front valve body. *See Fig. 31.* Ensure correct spring and valve are installed in appropriate bore. See VALVE BODY SPRING IDENTIFICATION table.

2) Install check balls, check valve, spring and solenoid oil strainers. *See Fig. 32.* Install gaskets, plate and front valve body cover. Tighten bolts to 60 INCH lbs. (6.8 N.m).

3) Install valves and springs into rear cover side of front valve body. *See Fig. 31.* Ensure correct spring and valve are installed in appropriate bore. See VALVE BODY SPRING IDENTIFICATION table.

1. Front Valve Body (Torque Converter Side)
2. 1-2 Shift Valve Spring
3. 2-3 Shift Valve Spring
4. 3-4 Shift Valve Spring
5. TCC Modulator Valve Spring
6. Front Valve Body (Rear Cover Side)
7. 2nd/4th Brake Modulator Valve Spring
8. Accumulator Control Valve Spring
9. Primary Regulator Valve Spring
10. Rear Valve Body (Torque Converter Side)
11. 2nd/4th Brake Accumulator Piston Spring
12. Reverse Clutch Accumulator Piston Spring (Outer)
13. Reverse Clutch Accumulator Piston Spring (Inner)
14. Solenoid Modulator Valve Spring
15. Low Coast Modulator Valve Spring
16. 2nd/4th Brake Modulator Control Valve Spring
17. Secondary Regulator Valve Spring
18. Rear Valve Body (Rear Cover Side)
19. TCC Control Valve Spring
20. Coast Clutch Modulator Valve Spring
21. 2-3 Timing Valve Spring
22. Overdrive Clutch Accumulator Piston Spring
23. Forward Clutch Accumulator Piston Spring (Outer)
24. Forward Clutch Accumulator Piston Spring (Inner)

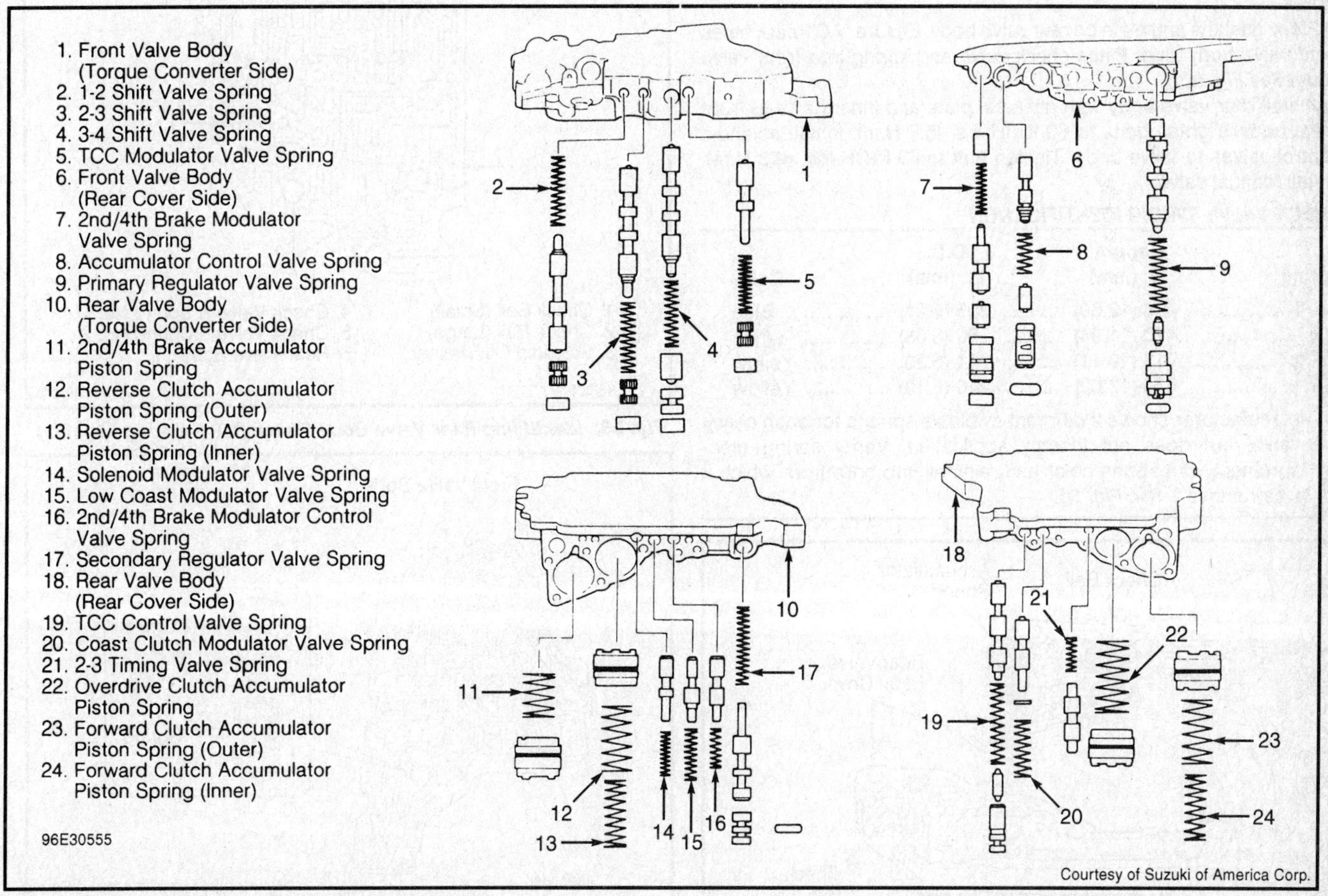

Fig. 31: Exploded View Of Valve Body Components

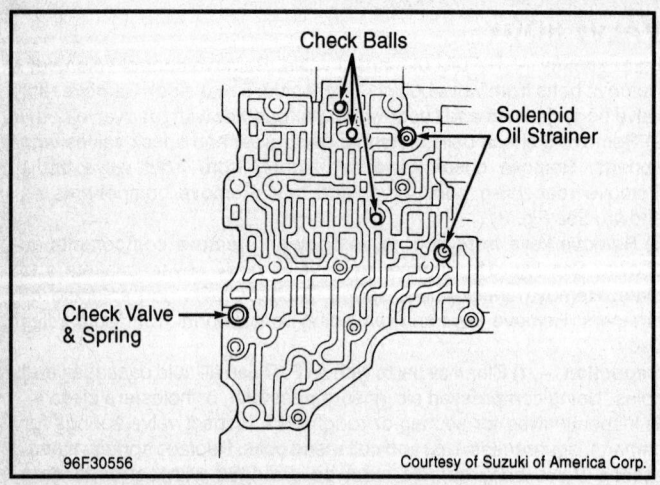

Fig. 32: Identifying Check Valve & Spring Location (Front Valve Body)

4) Install accumulator pistons, valves and springs into rear valve body. See Fig. 31. Ensure correct spring and valve are installed in appropriate bore. See VALVE BODY SPRING IDENTIFICATION table. DO NOT reuse accumulator "O" ring.

5) Install check balls and accumulator spring into rear valve body covers. See Fig. 33. Install gaskets, plates and rear valve body covers with check balls and accumulator spring. See Fig. 34. Tighten bolts to 96 INCH lbs. (10.8 N.m).

6) Install check balls, solenoid oil strainer, check valves and springs into rear valve body. Ensure correct spring is installed in appropriate bore. See Fig. 35. See CHECK VALVE SPRING IDENTIFICATION table.

7) Place gaskets and plate on rear valve body. Ensure "AO" mark faces front valve body side. Place check valve and spring into front valve body. See Fig. 36.

8) Install rear valve body with gaskets, plate and inner parts to front valve body. Tighten bolts to 60 INCH lbs. (6.8 N.m). Install solenoid control valves to valve body. Tighten bolt to 60 INCH lbs. (6.8 N.m). Install manual valve.

CHECK VALVE SPRING IDENTIFICATION [1]

Spring	Length In. (mm)	O.D. In. (mm)	Color
No. 1	.496 (12.60)	.205 (5.21)	Blue
Or	.470 (11.94)	.200 (5.08)	White
No. 2	.713 (18.11)	.244 (6.20)	Yellow
Or	.670 (17.02)	.240 (6.10)	Yellow

[1] – Manufacturer shows 2 different available springs for each check valve, but does not identify application. Verify spring measurement with spring color and reinstall into bore from which it was removed. See Fig. 35.

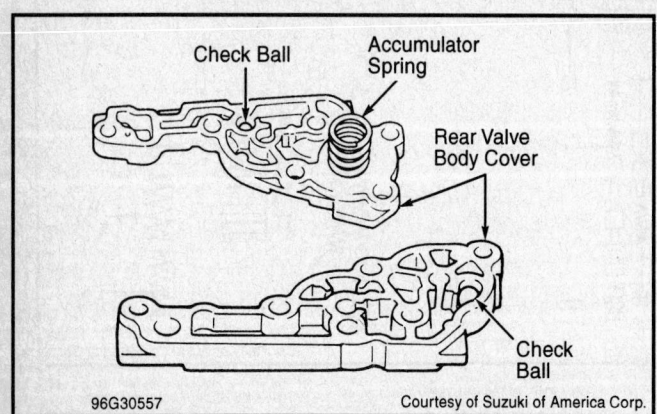

Fig. 33: Identifying Rear Cover Check Ball & Spring Location

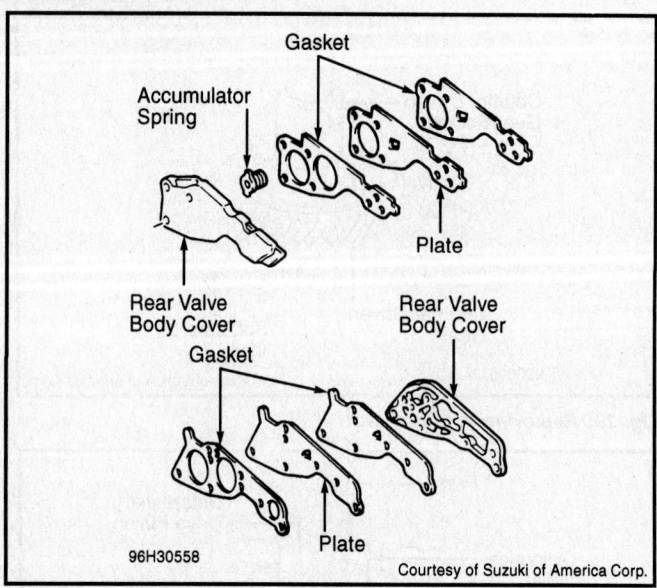

Fig. 34: Assembling Rear Valve Body Covers

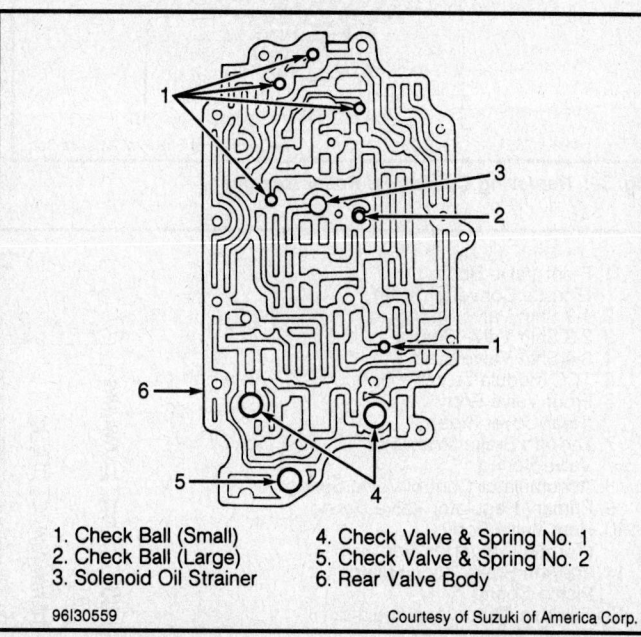

1. Check Ball (Small)
2. Check Ball (Large)
3. Solenoid Oil Strainer
4. Check Valve & Spring No. 1
5. Check Valve & Spring No. 2
6. Rear Valve Body

Fig. 35: Identifying Rear Valve Body Check Ball & Spring Location

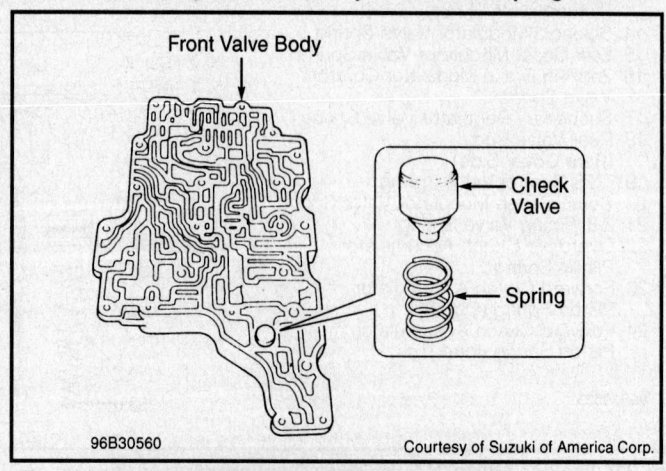

Fig. 36: Identifying Check Valve & Spring Location (Front Valve Body)

VALVE BODY SPRING IDENTIFICATION

Spring Application	Length In. (mm)	O.D. In. (mm)	Color
1-2 Shift Valve	1.340 (34.0)	.310 (7.9)	Blue
2-3 Shift Valve	1.340 (34.0)	.310 (7.9)	Blue
3-4 Shift Valve	1.340 (34.0)	.310 (7.9)	Blue
TCC Modulator Valve	1.100 (27.9)	.310 (7.9)	Green
2nd/4th Brake Modulator Valve	1.180 (30.0)	.330 (8.4)	Light Green
Accumulator Control Valve	.980 (24.9)	.450 (11.4)	Purple
Primary Regulator Valve	1.890 (48.0)	.520 (13.2)	White
2nd/4th Brake Accumulator Piston	1.110 (28.2)	.830 (21.1)	Blue
Reverse Clutch Accumulator Piston (Outer)	1.650 (41.9)	.830 (21.1)	Red
Reverse Clutch Accumulator Piston (Inner)	1.650 (41.9)	.610 (15.5)	Red
Solenoid Modulator Valve	1.120 (28.4)	.310 (7.9)	Purple
Low Coast Modulator Valve	1.290 (32.8)	.300 (7.6)	Red
2nd/4th Brake Modulator Control Valve	.940 (23.9)	.300 (7.6)	Pink
Secondary Regulator Valve	1.890 (48.0)	.370 (9.4)	None
TCC Control Valve	2.560 (65.0)	.380 (9.7)	None
Coast Clutch Modulator Valve	1.400 (35.6)	.300 (7.6)	Light Green
2-3 Timing Valve	.830 (21.1)	.430 (10.9)	White
Overdrive Clutch Accumulator Piston	1.780 (45.2)	.830 (21.8)	Light Green
Forward Clutch Accumulator Piston (Outer)	1.650 (41.9)	.830 (21.8)	Red
Forward Clutch Accumulator Piston (Inner)	1.650 (41.9)	.610 (15.5)	Red

DIFFERENTIAL

Inspection – Using a soft-jawed vice, hold differential assembly. Using a dial indicator, measure differential gear thrust play. *See Fig. 37.* Specified thrust play is .0024-.0087" (.061-.221 mm). Replace differential case if not within specification.

Disassembly – Release tabs on ring gear bolt lock plates. Remove ring gear bolts and lock plates. Remove ring gear. *See Fig. 38.* Remove differential side oil seal. Using appropriate bearing driver, remove tapper roller bearing outer race and washer from transaxle case.

Reassembly – To assemble, reverse disassembly procedure. Heat ring gear in oil bath to 212°F (100°C) to ease installation onto differential case. Tighten ring gear bolts to 72 ft. lbs. (98 N.m). Clamp bolts securely with lock plates.

Installation – 1) Using appropriate bearing driver, drive bearing outer race and washer into transaxle case. Install differential assembly into transaxle case. Tighten case bolts to 22 ft. lbs. (30 N.m).

2) Using an INCH lb. torque wrench and Preload Adapter (09928-06050), measure differential preload (starting torque). *See Fig. 39.* Specified preload is 12 INCH lbs. (1.4 N.m). If preload exceeds specification, select appropriate selective washer for both transaxle case and housing.

3) Selective washers are available from .083-.114" (2.10-2.90 mm) in .002" (.05 mm) increments. Preload changes about 3-4 INCH lbs. (.3-.5 N.m) with each washer thickness. Install differential side oil seal.

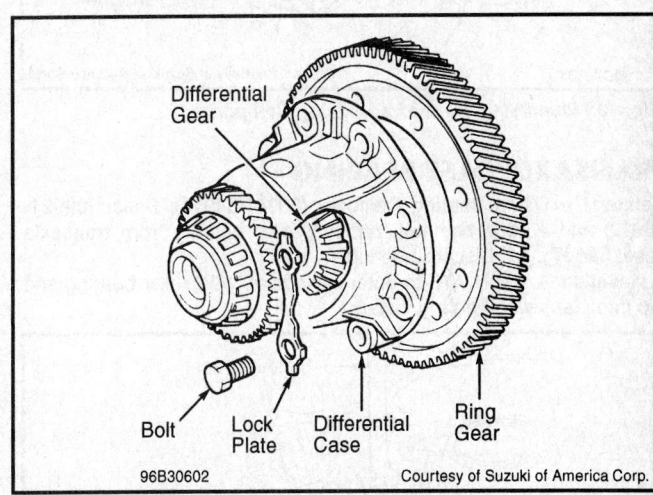

Fig. 38: Exploded View Of Differential Assembly

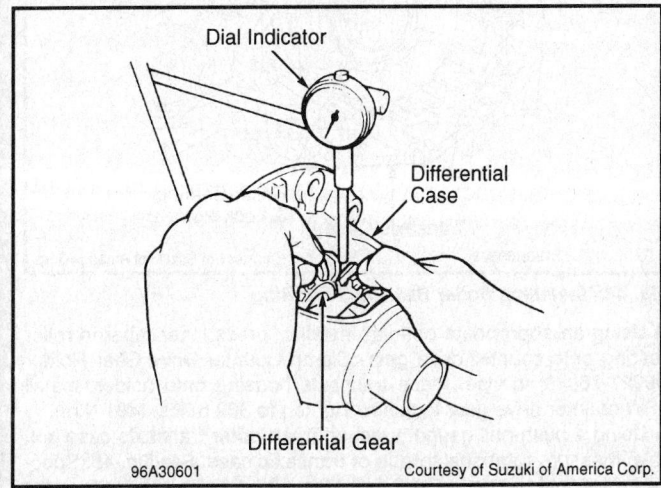

Fig. 37: Measuring Differential Gear Thrust Play

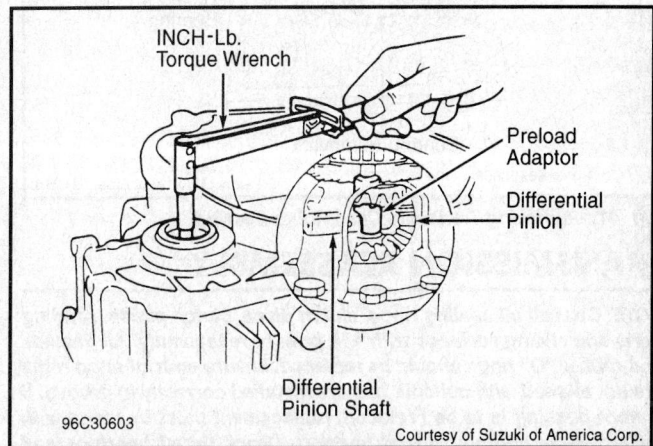

Fig. 39: Measuring Differential Preload (Starting Torque)

TRANSAXLE HOUSING COMPONENTS

Removal – Remove oil seal, oil reservoir plate, magnets, lubrication tube and roller bearing retainer. *See Fig. 40.* Using appropriate bearing puller, remove roller bearing. Discard oil seal and bearing.

2) Remove needle roller bearing with race from transaxle housing. Check oil pan for particles. Remove and clean magnets. Clean transaxle housing thoroughly.

Installation – **1)** Apply ATF to outer surface of roller bearing and tap into place with bearing installer. Install roller bearing retainer. Tighten retainer bolt to 120 INCH lbs. (13.6 N.m).

2) Install lubrication tube and clamp. Tighten clamp bolt to 48 INCH lbs. (5.4 N.m). Install oil reservoir plate with 3 magnets. Tighten bolts to 48 INCH lbs. (5.4 N.m).

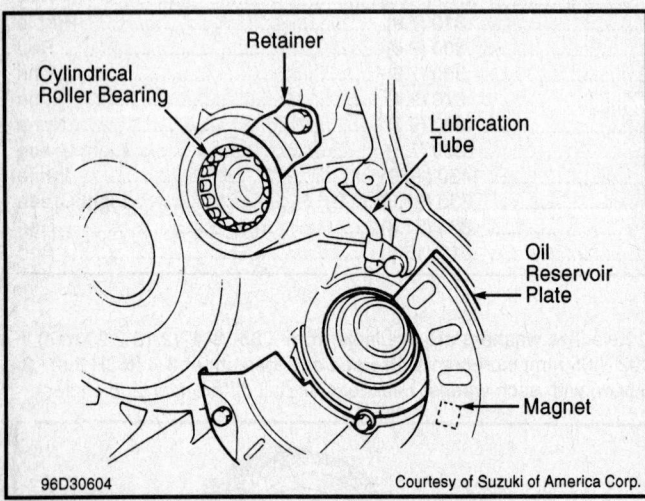

96D30604   Courtesy of Suzuki of America Corp.

Fig. 40: *Identifying Transaxle Housing Components*

TRANSAXLE CASE BEARING

Removal – Using Bearing Remover (09941-54911), Collar (09921-26010) and a slide hammer, remove roller bearing from transaxle case. *See Fig. 41.* Discard bearing.

Installation – Apply ATF to outer surface of NEW roller bearing and tap into place with bearing installer.

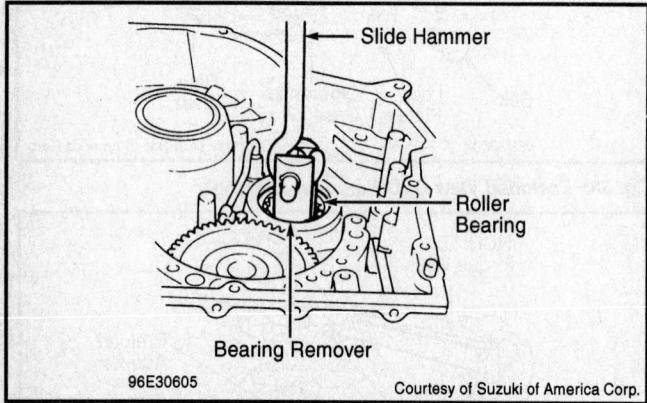

96E30605   Courtesy of Suzuki of America Corp.

Fig. 41: *Removing Transaxle Case Roller Bearing*

TRANSMISSION REASSEMBLY

NOTE: Coat all oil sealing rings, clutch discs, clutch plates, rotating parts and sliding surfaces with ATF prior to reassembly. All gaskets and rubber "O" rings should be replaced. Ensure ends of snap rings are not aligned with cut-outs and are installed correctly in groove. If a worn bushing is to be replaced, replacement must be made with subassembly containing that bushing. Check thrust bearings and races for wear or damage. Use petroleum jelly to hold parts in place. Replace parts as necessary. Soak clutch plates and brake band in ATF for 2 hours or more prior to installation.

1) Apply grease to lip portion of NEW manual valve lever shaft oil seal and install into transaxle case. Install manual valve lever and shaft into transaxle case with a NEW spacer and spring pin. *See Fig. 42.* Rotate spacer about 180 degrees, then stake small hole of spacer using a punch and hammer.

2) Using Bearing Installer (09926-68310), press outer bearing race into transaxle case. Secure with snap ring. *See Figs. 43 and 44.* Press outer tapered roller bearing onto counter drive gear. Apply ATF to bearing and install NEW spacer onto counter drive gear. Install assembly into transaxle case.

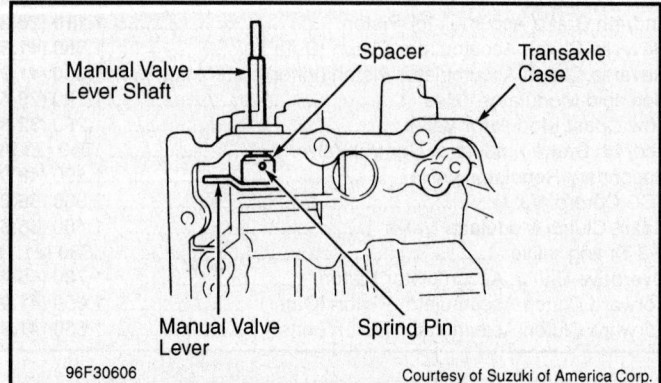

96F30606   Courtesy of Suzuki of America Corp.

Fig. 42: *Installing Manual Valve Linkage*

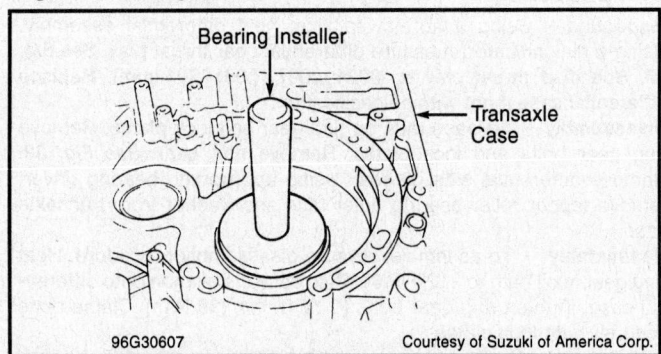

96G30607   Courtesy of Suzuki of America Corp.

Fig. 43: *Installing Transaxle Case Outer Bearing Race*

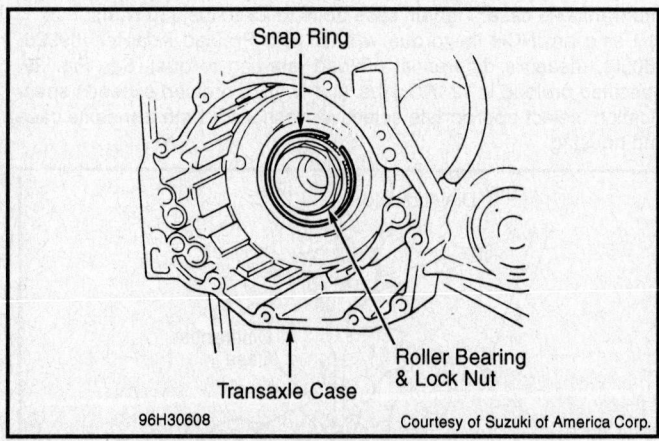

96H30608   Courtesy of Suzuki of America Corp.

Fig. 44: *Installing Roller Bearing Snap Ring*

3) Using an appropriate bearing installer, press inner tapered roller bearing onto counter drive gear. Clamp Counter Drive Gear Holder (09927-76040) in vise. Place transaxle housing onto holder. Install NEW counter drive gear lock nut. Tighten to 362 ft. lbs. (491 N.m).

4) Using a push-pull gauge attached to an outer transaxle case bolt hole, measure rotational torque of transaxle case. *See Fig. 45.* Specified rotational torque is .7-1.9 INCH lbs. (.08-.21 N.m). Using Counter Drive Gear Socket (09927-26010) and an INCH lb. torque wrench, measure starting torque of counter drive gear. *See Fig. 46.* Specified starting torque is .5-3.5 INCH lbs. (.05-.39 N.m).

5) Using a punch and a hammer, stake NEW lock nut. Install "O" rings coated with ATF onto 1st/reverse brake piston. Install piston into transaxle case. Install brake piston return spring, compress and secure with snap ring.

6) Install brake flanges, clutch discs and plates in the following order: flange, disc, plate, disc, plate, disc, plate, disc and flange. Install snap ring, ensuring open end does not align with grooved section of transaxle case. *See Fig. 47.*

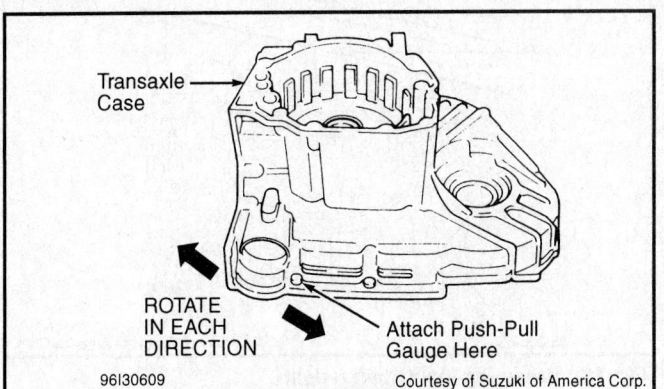

Fig. 45: *Measuring Transaxle Case Rotational Torque*

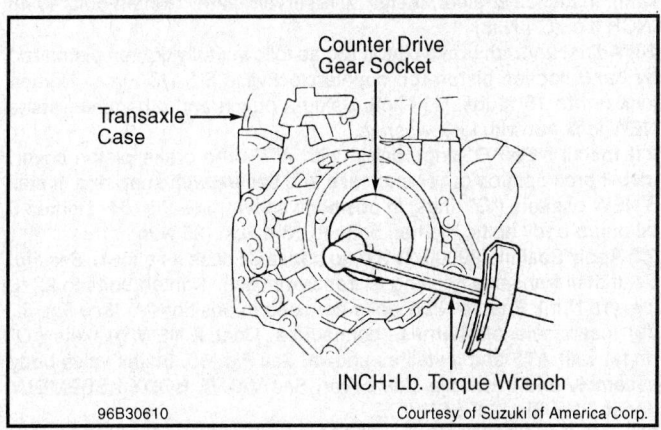

Fig. 46: *Measuring Counter Drive Gear Starting Torque*

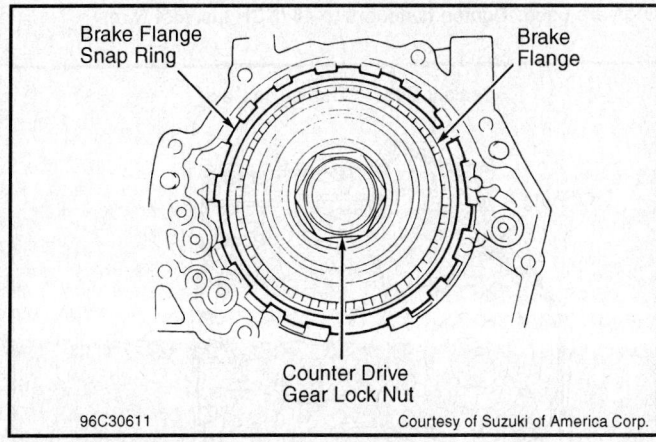

Fig. 47: *Installing Brake Flange Snap Ring*

7) Using a dial indicator, measure 1st/reverse brake piston stroke. Measure piston stroke while applying 57-113 psi (4-8 kg/cm²) of compressed air to oil hole "A". *See Fig. 11.* Specified piston stroke is .055-.087" (1.4-2-2 mm).

8) Place 2nd/4th brake spring into transaxle case. Install 2nd/4th brake piston with NEW "O" rings. Install piston cover, compress using appropriate press and secure with snap ring.

9) Temporarily install piston rod with lock plate, NEW lock washer and lock nut to transaxle case. Ensure tip of piston rod protrudes into inner side of transaxle case about .079-.118" (2.0-3.0 mm). *See Figs. 48 and 49.*

10) Apply ATF to outer surface of locating pins and install into transaxle case. *See Fig. 50.* Ensure correct pin is installed in its proper place. See LOCATING PIN IDENTIFICATION table.

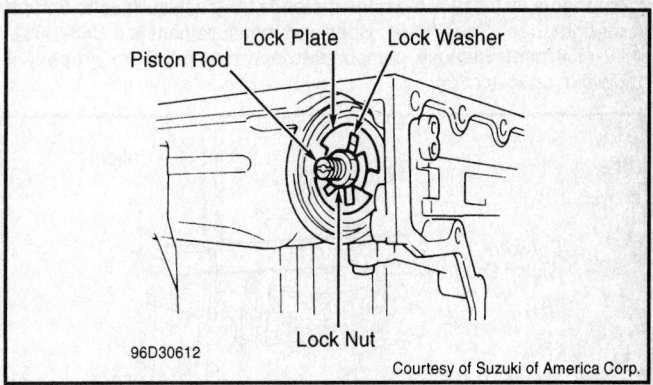

Fig. 48: *Installing Piston Rod & Lock Plate*

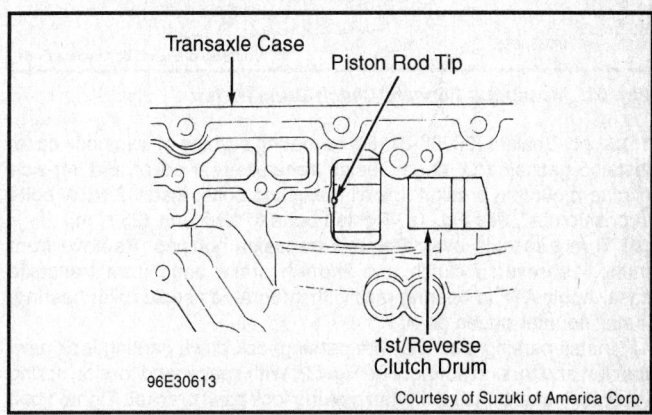

Fig. 49: *Piston Rod Protrusion*

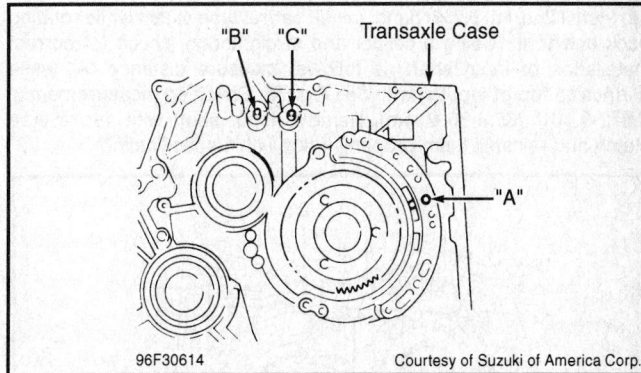

Fig. 50: *Transaxle Case Locating Pin Position*

LOCATING PIN IDENTIFICATION

Locating Pin	Length In. (mm)	O.D. In. (mm)
A	1.770 (45.0)	.310 (7.9)
B	1.330 (33.8)	.390 (9.9)
C	1.810 (46.0)	.470 (11.9)

11) Apply ATF to transaxle lubrication tube and install. Tighten to 48 INCH lbs. (5.4 N.m). Install 2nd/4th brake band. Install 1st/reverse clutch assembly. Temporarily install front pump. Temporarily tighten transaxle housing to case with 5-6 bolts. Stand transaxle on end (housing facing downward).

12) Install front and rear planetary carrier while rotating back and forth. Install sun gear with needle roller bearing. Coat bearing race with grease and install into planetary carrier.

13) Install overdrive/coast clutch while rotating back and forth. Ensure overdrive/coast clutch locks when turned counterclockwise, and turns freely clockwise. Install forward clutch while rotating.

14) Using a caliper and straightedge, check for correct installation of components as follows: measure distance "A" (case surface to bottom of straightedge). See Fig. 51. Specified measurement is 1.848-1.882" (46.9-47.8 mm). Remove components and reinstall them properly if not within specification.

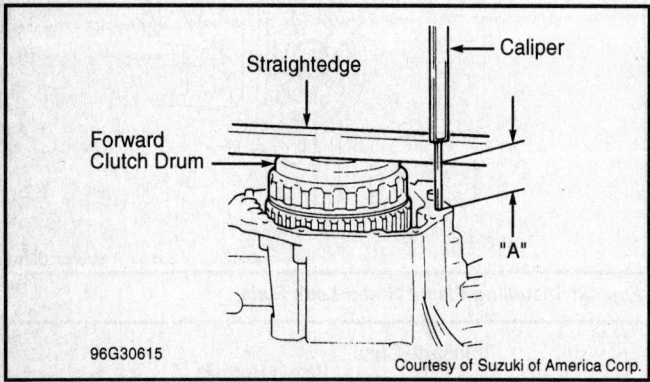

Fig. 51: Measuring Forward Clutch Drum Height

15) Apply Sealant (99000-31160) to mating surface of transaxle case. Install 5 gaskets ("O" rings). Install transaxle rear cover and left-side engine mounting bracket. Install 8 existing bolts. Install 2 NEW bolts in position "A". See Fig. 10. Tighten bolts to 18 ft. lbs. (25 N.m).

16) Turn transaxle over. Remove transaxle housing. Remove front pump, 1st/reverse clutch and 2nd/4th brake band from transaxle case. Apply ATF to bearing race with integrated needle roller bearing. Install counter driven gear.

17) Install parking lock rod with parking lock pawl, parking lock pawl bracket and torsion spring. See Fig. 52. With spacer and torsion spring in place, install bolt and tighten parking lock pawl bracket. Tighten bolt to 90 INCH lbs. (10.2 N.m). Insert parking lock rod to pawl bracket and connect parking lock rod with manual valve lever.

18) Install 2nd/4th brake band. Install 1st/reverse clutch while rotating back and forth. Using a caliper and straightedge, check for correct installation of input shaft as follows: measure distance "A" (case surface to top of input shaft). See Fig. 53. Specified measurement is 3.372-3.401" (85.6-86.4 mm). Remove input shaft with 1st/reverse clutch and reinstall them properly if not within specification.

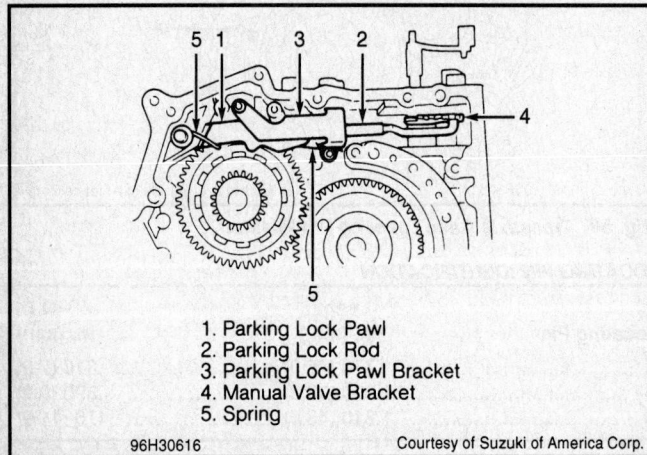

1. Parking Lock Pawl
2. Parking Lock Rod
3. Parking Lock Pawl Bracket
4. Manual Valve Bracket
5. Spring

Fig. 52: Installing Parking Lock Pawl Linkage

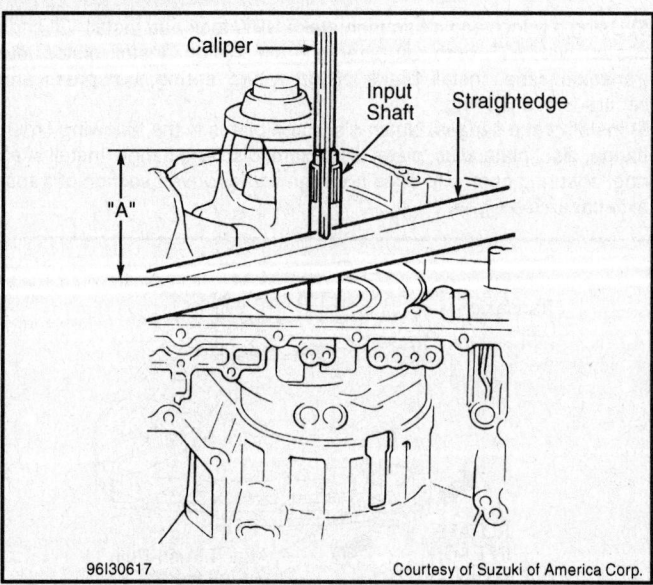

Fig. 53: Measuring Input Shaft Height

19) Install manual detent spring. Tighten bolts to 90 INCH lbs. (10.2 N.m). Install oil strainer. Install oil reservoir plate. Tighten bolts to 48 INCH lbs. (5.4 N.m).

20) Adjust 2nd/4th brake piston rod as follows: fully tighten piston rod by hand. loosen piston rod counterclockwise 3-3 1/3 turns. Tighten lock nut to 15 ft. lbs. (11 N.m). Using a punch and a hammer, stake NEW lock nut with lock washer.

21) Install NEW "O" ring coated with ATF onto brake piston cover. Install brake piston cover into case and secure with snap ring. Install 3 NEW gaskets ("O" rings) in positions shown. See Fig. 54. Tighten 6 oil pump body bolts. Tighten bolts to 18 ft. lbs. (25 N.m).

22) Apply Sealant (99000-31160) to transaxle case as shown. See Fig. 54. Install transaxle housing to transaxle case. Tighten bolts to 22 ft. lbs. (16 N.m). Ensure NEW bolts are used in position "A". See Fig. 8.

23) Insert solenoid harness connectors. Coat 2 NEW gaskets ("O" rings) with ATF and install as shown. See Fig. 55. Install valve body assembly and transaxle side cover. See VALVE BODY ASSEMBLY under ON-VEHICLE SERVICE.

24) Install solenoid coupler, VSS, forward clutch cylinder revolution sensor, oil filler tube and speedometer driven gear. Ensure NEW "O" rings are used. Tighten fasteners to 48 INCH lbs. (5.4 N.m).

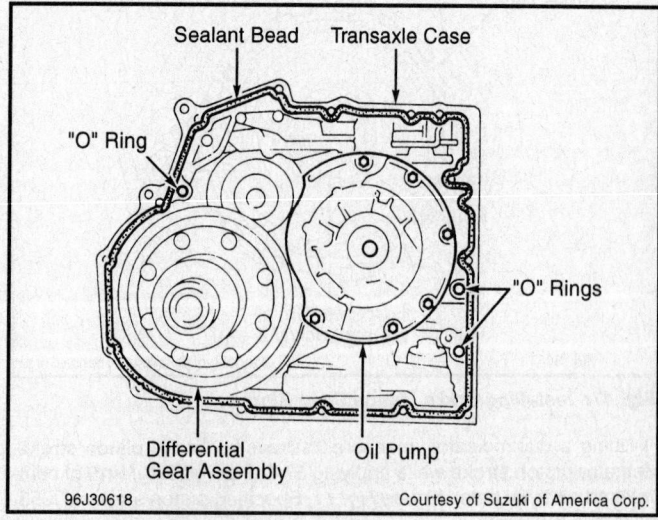

Fig. 54: "O" Ring & Sealant Placement

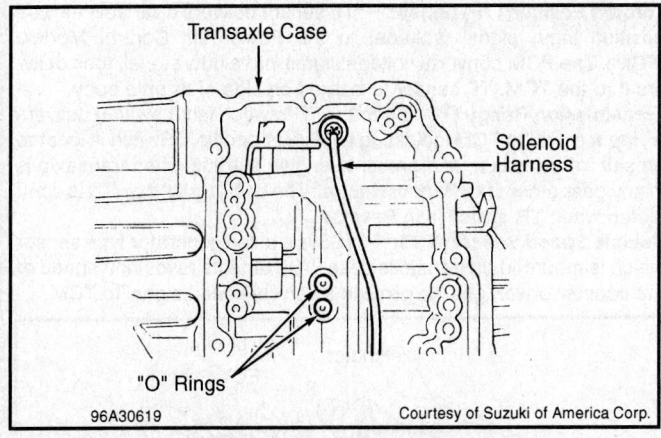

Fig. 55: Solenoid Harness & "O" Ring Placement

25) Install TR switch assembly. Place NEW rubber plate and lock washer on TR switch. Tighten lock nut to 60 INCH lbs. (6.8 N.m). Adjust TR switch. See TRANSMISSION RANGE (TR) SWITCH under ON-VEHICLE SERVICE. Tighten manual shift lever spring washer and nut to 60 INCH lbs. (6.8 N.m).

26) Install oil cooler pipes and tighten to 26 ft. lbs. (35 N.m). Using an INCH lb. torque wrench, measure starting torque of differential gear assembly. *See Fig. 39.* Specified starting torque is 12 INCH lbs. (1.4 N.m). Install torque converter onto input shaft.

27) Using a caliper and straightedge, measure torque converter set-back. *See Fig. 56.* Specified depth is .929-1.002" (23.6-25.4 mm). Check torque converter for smooth rotation.

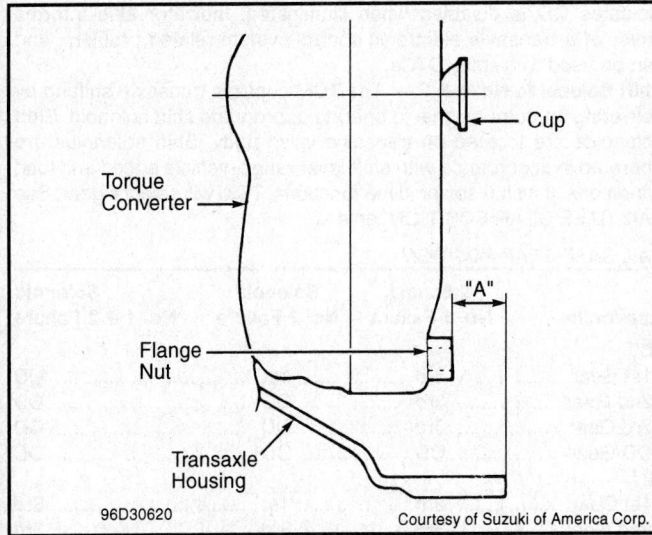

Fig. 56: Measuring Torque Converter Set-Back

TORQUE SPECIFICATIONS
TORQUE SPECIFICATIONS

Application	Ft. Lbs. (N.m)
Counter Drive Gear Lock Nut	362 (491)
Oil Cooler Pipes	26 (35)
Oil Pump-To-Transaxle Case Bolts	18 (25)
Ring Gear-To-Differential Housing Bolts	72 (98)
Transaxle Housing-To-Transaxle Case Bolts	22 (30)
Transaxle Rear Cover Bolts	18 (25)
Transaxle Side Cover Bolts	18 (25)
Transmission Range (TR) Switch Bolts	15 (20)
VSS Lock Nut-To-Counter Driven Gear	91 (123)
2nd/4th Brake Piston Rod Lock Nut	15 (11)

Application	INCH Lbs. (N.m)
Forward Clutch Revolution Sensor Bolt	48 (5.4)
Front Valve Body Cover Bolts	60 (6.8)
Front Valve Body-To-Rear Valve Body Bolts	60 (6.8)
Interlock Cable Bracket Nut	114 (12.9)
Manual Detent Spring Bolts	90 (10.2)
Manual Shift Lever Nut	60 (6.8)
Oil Filler Tube Bolt	48 (5.4)
Oil Reservoir Plate Bolts	48 (5.4)
Oil Strainer Bolts	48 (5.4)
Parking Lock Pawl Bracket Bolts	90 (10.2)
Rear Valve Body Cover Bolts	96 (10.8)
Solenoid Coupler Bolt	48 (5.4)
Solenoid-To-Valve Body Bolts	60 (6.8)
Speedometer Driven Gear Bolt	48 (5.4)
Stator Shaft-To-Pump Body Bolts	108 (12.2)
Transaxle Housing Bearing Retainer Bolt	120 (13.6)
Transaxle Housing Lubrication Tube Bolt	48 (5.4)
Transmission Range (TR) Switch Lock Nut	60 (6.8)
Valve Body-To-Transaxle Bolts	90 (10.2)
Vehicle Speed Sensor (VSS) Bolt	48 (5.4)

TRANSMISSION SPECIFICATIONS
TRANSMISSION SPECIFICATIONS

Application	In. (mm)
Differential Gear Thrust Play	.0024-.0087 (.061-.221)
Piston Stroke	
Coast Clutch	.106-.119 (2.69-3.02)
Forward Clutch	.030-.057 (.76-1.45)
Overdrive Clutch	.030-.041 (.76-1.04)
1st/Reverse Brake	.055-.087 (1.4-2.2)
2nd/4th Brake	.120-.130 (3.0-3.3)
Pump Gear Clearance	
Gear Tip	
Standard	.0005-.010 (.013-.254)
Service Limit	.011 (.280)
Pump Body-To-Driven Gear	
Standard	.003-.006 (.08-.15)
Service Limit	.0169 (.429)
Pump Body-To-Gear Side	
Standard	.0008-.0019 (.020-.048)
Service Limit	.0058 (.147)
Reverse Clutch Pack Clearance	.025-.059 (.64-1.50)
Torque Converter Set-Back Depth	.929-1.002 (23.6-25.4)

Application	INCH Lbs. (N.m)
Starting Torque (Bearing Preload)	
Counter Drive Gear Subassembly	.5-3.5 (.05-.39)
Differential Gear Assembly	12 (1.4)
Transaxle Case Rotational Torque	.7-1.9 (.08-.21)

AUTOMATIC TRANSMISSIONS
1995 Suzuki Esteem Electronic Controls

Esteem

APPLICATION

APPLICATION

Vehicle	Transaxle Model
1995 Esteem .... [1] 4-Speed

[1] – Transaxle model number is not available from manufacturer.

DESCRIPTION

Automatic transaxle is electronically controlled. Transaxle shifting and torque converter lock-up are controlled by Transmission Control Module (TCM).

The TCM receives information from various input devices and uses this information to control shift solenoids No. 1 and 2 on transaxle valve body for transaxle shifting, and Torque Converter Clutch (TCC) solenoid for torque converter lock-up.

An O/D cut switch is mounted on gear selector lever. When O/D cut switch is depressed to ON position, transaxle will shift into overdrive (OD) when gear selector lever is in "D" position, and O/D OFF indicator on instrument cluster will turn off. When O/D cut switch is released to OFF position, transaxle will shift into 3rd gear, and O/D OFF indicator will illuminate.

OPERATION

TCM

The TCM receives information from various input devices and uses this information to control shift solenoids No. 1 and 2 on transaxle valve body for transaxle shifting, and control TCC solenoid for torque converter lock-up.

The TCM contains a self-diagnostic system which will store a Diagnostic Trouble Code (DTC) if a malfunction is detected in the electronic control system. DTCs can be retrieved to determine problem area. See SELF-DIAGNOSTIC SYSTEM. TCM is located under instrument panel, to left of steering column.

TCM INPUT DEVICES

Brakelight Switch Signal – Brakelight switch delivers input signal to TCM, indicating vehicle braking which results in TCC disengagement if in operation. Brakelight switch is located on brake pedal support.

Cruise Control Electronic Control Unit (ECU) – Cruise control ECU delivers an input signal to control overdrive operation in accordance with vehicle speed when cruise control is operating. If vehicle speed drops 2 MPH less than the set speed during cruise control operation while in overdrive, overdrive is released to prevent reduction in vehicle speed. Once vehicle speed is greater than the set speed, overdrive is resumed. If coolant temperature is low, transaxle will not shift into overdrive. Cruise control ECU is located under center console.

Engine Coolant Temperature (ECT) Sensor – ECT sensor delivers an input signal to TCM, indicating engine coolant temperature. TCM uses this signal to prevent gear change to OD and TCC lock-up when coolant temperature is less than a predetermined value. ECT sensor is located on water outlet, next to distributor. See Fig. 1.

Forward Clutch Cylinder Revolution Sensor – This is a pulse generator type sensor (mounted on transaxle case) which detects revolution speed of forward clutch drum (input shaft). The TCM uses this signal to monitor revolution speed inputted into transaxle and compare it with that of the output revolution (vehicle speed) as determined by the Vehicle Speed Sensor (VSS).

O/D Cut Switch – The O/D cut switch (mounted on shift lever) provides an input signal to TCM to indicate when overdrive is selected by vehicle operator. When O/D cut switch is depressed to ON position with shift lever in "D" range, transaxle will upshift into OD, and OD/OFF indicator on instrument cluster will turn off. When O/D cut switch is released to OFF position, transaxle will downshift into 3rd gear, and OD/OFF indicator will illuminate.

Throttle Position (TP) Sensor – TP sensor delivers a variable throttle position input signal (voltage) to the Powertrain Control Module (PCM). The PCM converts voltage signal into a duty signal, then delivers it to the TCM. TP sensor is located on side of throttle body.

Transmission Range (TR) Switch – TR switch (shift switch) delivers an input signal to TCM indicating shift lever position. Switch is located on side of transaxle, and prevents engine starting when transaxle is in any gear other than Park or Neutral. The back-up light circuit is completed when TR switch is in Reverse.

Vehicle Speed Sensor (VSS) – VSS is a pulse generator type sensor which is mounted on transaxle case. VSS detects revolution speed of the counter driven gear to provide a vehicle speed signal to TCM.

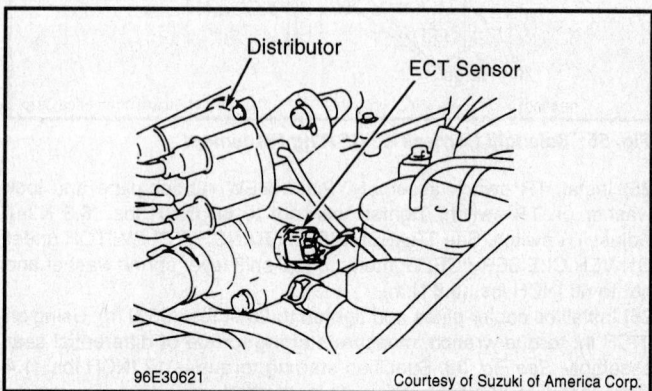

Fig. 1: Locating ECT Sensor

TCM OUTPUT DEVICES

OD/OFF Indicator – OD/OFF indicator, located in instrument cluster, indicates OD is disabled when illuminated. Indicator also informs driver of a transaxle electronic control system related problem, and can be used to display DTCs.

Shift Solenoids No. 1 & 2 – The TCM controls transaxle shifting by delivering an output signal to operate appropriate shift solenoid. Shift solenoids are located on transaxle valve body. Shift solenoids are operated in accordance with shift lever range, vehicle speed and load conditions. If a shift solenoid malfunctions, TCM will select a gear. See FAIL SAFE GEAR POSITION table.

FAIL SAFE GEAR POSITION

Application	Solenoid No. 1 Failure	Solenoid No. 2 Failure	Solenoid No. 1 & 2 Failure
"D"			
1st Gear	3rd	1st	OD
2nd Gear	3rd	OD	OD
3rd Gear	3rd	OD	OD
OD Gear	OD	OD	OD
"2"			
1st Gear	3rd	1st	3rd
2nd Gear	3rd	3rd	3rd
"L"			
1st Gear	1st	1st	1st

TCC Lock-Up Solenoid – The TCM controls torque converter lock-up by delivering an output signal to TCC lock-up solenoid. Lock-up solenoid is activated when shift lever is in "D" position, and vehicle is at a predetermined specified speed and temperature.

SELF-DIAGNOSTIC SYSTEM

SYSTEM DIAGNOSIS

NOTE: Before testing transaxle, ensure fluid level is correct and throttle and shift cables are properly adjusted. Ensure engine starts with gear selector lever in "P" and "N" positions to ensure proper adjustment of Transmission Range (TR) switch. The electronic control system must first be checked for stored DTCs. See RETRIEVING TROUBLE CODES.

The TCM monitors transaxle operation and contains a self-diagnostic system which stores a Diagnostic Trouble Code (DTC) if an electronic control system malfunction is detected. If a malfunction is detected and a DTC is set, the TCM will deliver a signal to flash OD/OFF indicator on instrument cluster to warn the driver.

The number of OD/OFF indicator flashes will equal first digit of DTC. After a one second pause, second digit of DTC is displayed. If more than one DTC is present, the next DTC will be displayed after a 3 second pause. Smallest number DTC will be displayed first. DTCs are repeated after each retrieval cycle. Once a DTC is retrieved, determine probable cause. See DTC IDENTIFICATION.

RETRIEVING TROUBLE CODES

NOTE: Before retrieving DTCs, ensure battery is fully charged for proper self-diagnostic system operation. DTCs must be cleared from TCM memory once repairs have been performed. See CLEARING TROUBLE CODES.

1) Ensure O/D cut switch is in OFF position. Turn ignition on. If OD/OFF indicator illuminates for about 4 seconds, go to next step. If OD/OFF indicator remains illuminated, go to step **3)**. If OD/OFF indicator does not illuminate, go to step **4)**.

2) Using a fused jumper wire, jumper ground terminal of diagnostic connector No. 1 to diagnosis switch terminal of diagnostic connector No. 2, located in engine compartment relay box. *See Fig. 2.* If OD/OFF indicator does not respond, go to step **6)**. If OD/OFF indicator flashes DTC 12 only, perform a visual inspection. See VISUAL INSPECTION under PRELIMINARY CHECK. If OD/OFF indicator flashes any DTC other than DTC 12, identify DTC and diagnose. See DTC IDENTIFICATION, then proceed to DIAGNOSTIC TESTING.

3) Check for faulty OD/OFF switch or a short to ground in OD/OFF indicator circuit (Light Green wire). Repair as necessary. If no problem is found, check TCM and its circuit. See TCM POWER & GROUND CIRCUIT under TCM CIRCUIT CHECK.

4) Turn ignition off. Disconnect TCM harness connector. Using a fused jumper wire, jumper TCM harness connector terminal A21 (Light Green wire) to ground. turn ignition on. If OD/OFF indicator illumi-

nates, go to next step. If OD/OFF indicator does not illuminate, check for an open in Light Green wire or faulty OD/OFF indicator bulb. Repair as necessary.

5) Check for poor TCM harness connection at terminal A21 (Light Green wire). Repair as necessary. If connection is okay, check TCM and its circuit. See TCM POWER & GROUND CIRCUIT under TCM CIRCUIT CHECK.

6) Check for poor TCM harness connection at terminal A18 (Green/Red wire). Check for an open in Green/Red wire between TCM and diagnostic connector No. 2, or defective jumper wire. Repair as necessary. If no problem is found, check TCM and its circuit. See PIN VOLTAGE CHART under TCM CIRCUIT CHECK.

DTC IDENTIFICATION

DTC IDENTIFICATION

DTC	[1] Probable Cause
12	System Operation Normal
21	Faulty Shift Solenoid No. 1 Or Circuit Open Or Shorted To Power
22	Faulty Shift Solenoid No. 1 Or Circuit Shorted To Ground
23	Faulty Shift Solenoid No. 2 Or Circuit Open Or Shorted To Power
24	Faulty Shift Solenoid No. 2 Or Circuit Shorted To Ground
25	Faulty TCC Solenoid Or Circuit Open Or Shorted To Power
26	Faulty TCC Solenoid Or Circuit Shorted To Ground
31	Faulty Vehicle Speed Sensor Or Circuit Open Or Shorted
32	Faulty TP Sensor Or Circuit (Signal Voltage Low)
33	Faulty TP Sensor Or Circuit (Signal Voltage High)
34	Faulty Transmission Range (TR) Switch Or Circuit
37	Faulty Forward Clutch Revolution Sensor Or Circuit
41	Faulty Throttle Pressure Control Solenoid Or Circuit Open Or Shorted To Ground
42	Faulty Throttle Pressure Control Solenoid Or Circuit Shorted
51	Engine Coolant Temperature (ECT) Sensor (Signal High/Low Temperature)

[1] – Check listed component for probable cause. Also check wiring and connections of specified component.

CLEARING TROUBLE CODES

Once repairs have been performed, trouble codes must be cleared from TCM memory. To clear, disconnect negative battery cable for at least 10 seconds.

PRELIMINARY CHECK

NOTE: As a preliminary step, perform a visual inspection of the following systems and components which directly relate to proper transaxle operation.

Visual Inspection – Check the following and repair as necessary:
- Engine Oil: check level and for evidence of leakage.
- Engine Coolant: check level and for evidence of leakage.
- ATF: check level, condition and for evidence of leakage.
- Battery: check water level and terminal corrosion.
- A/T Hoses: check for poor connections or deterioration.
- Harness Connectors: check for poor connections or worn insulation.
- Fuses: check for improper installation or for burning.
- Related Mechanical Parts: check for proper installation and condition.

If no problems are found during visual inspection, and only DTC 12 is retrieved even though a problem exists, perform a manual shifting test. See MANUAL SHIFTING TEST under TRANSMISSION SHIFT TESTING.

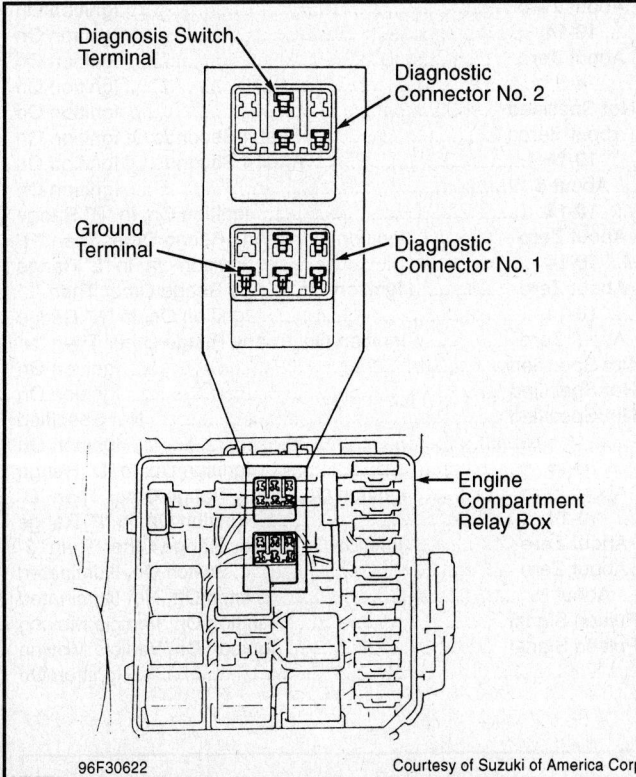

96F30622   Courtesy of Suzuki of America Corp.

Fig. 2: Identifying Diagnostic Connector Terminals

TCM CIRCUIT CHECK
TCM POWER & GROUND CIRCUIT

NOTE: Perform the following procedure if OD/OFF indicator does not illuminate with ignition switch in ON position, and transaxle does not shift to 1st gear at vehicle start with gear selector lever in "D" position.

1) Turn ignition on. Using a DVOM, measure voltage (backprobe) between ground and TCM harness connector terminal A15 (Black/White wire). If reading is 10-14 volts, go to next step. If reading is not as specified, repair open in Black/White wire between TCM and circuit fuses.

2) Turn ignition off. Disconnect PCM and TCM harness connectors. Using a DVOM, check for continuity between ground and TCM harness connector terminal A12 (Black/Red wire). If continuity is present, go to next step. If continuity is not present, repair open in Black/Red wire.

3) Check for poor TCM harness connections at terminal A15 (Black/White wire) or terminal A12 (Black/Red wire). Repair as necessary. If no problem is found, replace TCM with a known-good unit. Retest system.

PIN VOLTAGE CHART

Using a voltmeter, measure voltage (backprobe) specified terminals with harness connector connected to TCM. *See Fig. 3.* Ensure each check is made under conditions noted in chart.

NOTE: Values or conditions that are not specified in the following chart represent ground circuits, or signal circuits which may vary or toggle depending upon vehicle operation.

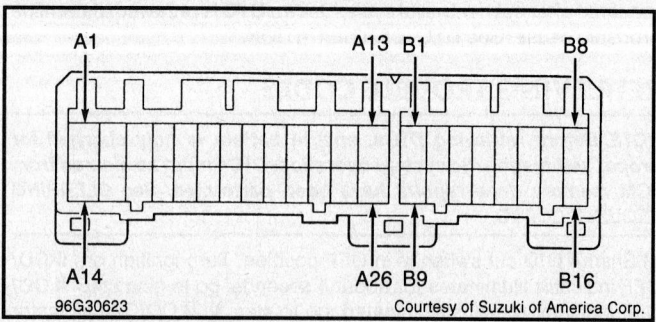

Fig. 3: Identifying TCM Harness Connector Terminals (Harness Side)

PIN VOLTAGE CHART

Terminal	Circuit	Normal Voltage	Condition
A1	Shift Solenoid No. 1	10-14	Ignition On
A2	Back-Up Power Source	10-14	Ignition On Or Off
A3	Throttle Pressure Control Solenoid	Varies	Vehicle Operation (Throttle Movement)
A4	Park/Neutral Position (PNP) Signal (PCM)	10-14	Ignition On, In "P" Or "N" Range
		About Zero	Ignition On, In "R", "D", "2" Or "L" Range
A5	Brake Light Switch	10-14	Brake Pedal Depressed
		About Zero	Brake Pedal Released
A11	TR Switch ("P" Range)	10-14	Ignition On, In "P" Range
		About Zero	Ignition On, In Any Range Other Than "P"
A12	Ground Supply	Zero	Detecated Ground
A13	Throttle Pressure Control Solenoid (Ground)	About Zero	Not Specified
A14	Shift Solenoid No. 2	About Zero	Ignition On
A15	Power Supply	10-14	Ignition On
A16	TCC Solenoid	About Zero	Ignition On
A17	Data Link Connector	4-5	Ignition On
A18	Diagnosis Switch Terminal	Not Specified	Ignition On
A21	OD/OFF Indicator	About Zero	First 4 Seconds Of Ignition On
		10-14	After 4 Seconds Of Ignition On
A22	Cruise Control Unit	About 5	Ignition On
A24	TR Switch ("R" Range)	10-14	Ignition On, In "R" Range
		About Zero	Ignition On, In Any Range Other Than "R"
B1	TR Switch ("L" Range)	10-14	Ignition On, In "L" Range
		About Zero	Ignition On, In Any Range Other Than "L"
B2	TR Switch ("N" Range)	10-14	Ignition On, In "N" Range
		About Zero	Ignition On, In Any Range Other Than "N"
B5	VSS (Ground)	Not Specified	Ignition On
B6	Forward Clutch Revolution Sensor (Ground)	Not Specified	Ignition On
B7	Shield Ground	Not Specified	Not Specified
B8	Throttle Opening Signal	[1]	Ignition On
B9	TR Switch ("D" Range)	10-14	Ignition On, In "D" Range
		About Zero	Ignition On, In Any Range Other Than "D"
B10	TR Switch ("2" Range)	10-14	Ignition On, In "2" Range
		About Zero	Ignition On, In Any Range Other Than "2"
B12	O/D Cut Switch	About Zero	Switch On, Illuminated
		About 5	Switch Off, Not Illuminated
B13	VSS	Pulsed Signal	Ignition On, Vehicle Moving
B14	Forward Clutch Revolution Sensor	Pulsed Signal	Ignition On, Vehicle Moving
B15	ECT Signal (PCM)	[2]	Ignition On

[1] – Varies with throttle position.
[2] – Varies with coolant temperature.

TRANSMISSION SHIFT TESTING
MANUAL SHIFTING TEST

NOTE: Perform manual shifting test if no DTCs are present. Manual shifting test determines if problem is an electrical or mechanical related problem.

1) Start and operate vehicle until normal operating temperature is achieved. Disconnect TCM harness connector. Road test vehicle and ensure transmission gear changes correspond with shift lever position. See GEAR APPLICATION table.
2) If a fault is present, problem is mechanically related. Perform STALL TEST, TIME LAG TEST, LINE PRESSURE TEST, ENGINE BRAKE TEST and "P" RANGE TEST. See TESTING in appropriate overhaul article. If all gears are correct, see PRELIMINARY CHECKS in appropriate overhaul article.
3) After testing is completed, reconnect TCM harness connector. Clear DTCs from TCM memory, as disconnecting electrical connector may set a DTC. See CLEARING TROUBLE CODES.

GEAR APPLICATION

Shift Lever Position	Gear
"D"	Overdrive
"2"	3rd Gear
"L"	1st Gear
"R"	Reverse
"P"	Park

DIAGNOSTIC TESTING

NOTE: When trouble shooting transaxle, ensure all proper steps are taken to eliminate the possibility of a mechanical malfunction. This can save diagnostic time and avoid unnecessary replacement of properly operating components. See SYSTEM DIAGNOSIS under SELF-DIAGNOSTIC SYSTEM. See wiring diagram in WIRING DIAGRAM to aid in component location, wire color and wire terminal identification.

DTC 21: SHIFT SOLENOID NO. 1

NOTE: DTC 21 will set if shift solenoid No. 1 or its circuit is open or shorted to power.

1) Turn ignition off. Disconnect TCM harness connectors. Using a DVOM, measure resistance between TCM harness connector terminal A1 (Green/White wire) and terminal A12 (Black/Red wire). If resistance is about 13 ohms, go to next step. If resistance is not as specified, test operation of shift solenoid No. 1. See SOLENOIDS under COMPONENT TESTING. Replace if necessary. If solenoid tests okay, repair Green/White wire for an open or short to power.
2) Turn ignition on. Using a DVOM, measure voltage between terminal A1 (Green/White wire) and terminal A12 (Black/Red wire). If reading is about zero volts, check for poor TCM harness connections. Repair as necessary. If connections are okay, substitute TCM with a known-good unit. If reading is not as specified, repair Green/White wire for a short to power.

DTC 22: SHIFT SOLENOID NO. 1

NOTE: DTC 22 will set if shift solenoid No. 1 or its circuit is shorted to ground.

1) Turn ignition off. Disconnect TCM harness connectors. Using a DVOM, measure resistance between TCM harness connector terminal A1 (Green/White wire) and terminal A12 (Black/Red wire). If resistance is about 13 ohms, check for an intermittent problem. See DIAGNOSTIC AIDS. If resistance is not as specified, go to next step.
2) Test operation of shift solenoid No. 1. See SOLENOIDS under COMPONENT TESTING. Replace if necessary. If solenoid tests okay, repair Green/White wire for a short to ground.

Diagnostic Aids – An intermittent condition may be caused by a poor connection, damaged wire insulation or a wire which is broken inside the insulation. Inspect TCM harness connectors for damaged, corroded or backed-out terminal pins. Repair as necessary and retest system.

DTC 23: SHIFT SOLENOID NO. 2

NOTE: DTC 23 will set if shift solenoid No. 2 or its circuit is open or shorted to power.

1) Turn ignition off. Disconnect TCM harness connectors. Using a DVOM, measure resistance between TCM harness connector terminal A14 (Green/Orange wire) and terminal A12 (Black/Red wire). If resistance is about 13 ohms, go to next step. If resistance is not as specified, test operation of shift solenoid No. 2. See SOLENOIDS under COMPONENT TESTING. Replace if necessary. If solenoid tests okay, repair Green/Orange wire for an open or short to power.
2) Turn ignition on. Using a DVOM, measure voltage between terminal A14 (Green/Orange wire) and terminal A12 (Black/Red wire). If reading is about zero volts, check for poor TCM harness connections. Repair as necessary. If connections are okay, substitute TCM with a known-good unit. If reading is not as specified, repair Green/Orange wire for a short to power.

DTC 24: SHIFT SOLENOID NO. 2

NOTE: DTC 24 will set if shift solenoid No. 2 or its circuit is shorted to ground.

1) Turn ignition off. Disconnect TCM harness connectors. Using a DVOM, measure resistance between TCM harness connector terminal A14 (Green/Orange wire) and terminal A12 (Black/Red wire). If resistance is about 13 ohms, check for an intermittent problem. See DIAGNOSTIC AIDS. If resistance is not as specified, go to next step.
2) Test operation of shift solenoid No. 2. See SOLENOIDS under COMPONENT TESTING. Replace if necessary. If solenoid tests okay, repair Green/Orange wire for a short to ground.

Diagnostic Aids – An intermittent condition may be caused by a poor connection, damaged wire insulation or a wire which is broken inside the insulation. Inspect TCM harness connectors for damaged, corroded or backed-out terminal pins. Repair as necessary and retest system.

DTC 25: TCC SOLENOID

NOTE: DTC 25 will set if TCC solenoid or its circuit is open or shorted to power.

1) Turn ignition off. Disconnect TCM harness connectors. Using a DVOM, measure resistance between TCM harness connector terminal A16 (Green/Yellow wire) and terminal A12 (Black/Red wire). If resistance is about 13 ohms, go to next step. If resistance is not as specified, test operation of TCC solenoid. See SOLENOIDS under COMPONENT TESTING. Replace if necessary. If solenoid tests okay, repair Green/Yellow wire for an open or short to power.
2) Turn ignition on. Using a DVOM, measure voltage between terminal A16 (Green/Yellow wire) and terminal A12 (Black/Red wire). If reading is about zero volts, check for poor TCM harness connections. Repair as necessary. If connections are okay, substitute TCM with a known-good unit. If reading is not as specified, repair Green/Yellow wire for a short to power.

DTC 26: TCC SOLENOID

NOTE: DTC 26 will set if TCC solenoid or its circuit is shorted to ground.

1) Turn ignition off. Disconnect TCM harness connectors. Using a DVOM, measure resistance between TCM harness connector terminal A16 (Green/Yellow wire) and terminal A12 (Black/Red wire). If

resistance is about 13 ohms, check for an intermittent problem. See DIAGNOSTIC AIDS. If resistance is not as specified, go to next step.

2) Test operation of TCC solenoid. See SOLENOIDS under COMPONENT TESTING. Replace if necessary. If solenoid tests okay, repair Green/Yellow wire for a short to ground.

Diagnostic Aids – An intermittent condition may be caused by a poor connection, damaged wire insulation or a wire which is broken inside the insulation. Inspect TCM harness connectors for damaged, corroded or backed-out terminal pins. Repair as necessary and retest system.

DTC 31: VEHICLE SPEED SENSOR (VSS)

NOTE: DTC 31 will set if no VSS signal is inputted while transaxle is in "D", "2" or "L" range, and forward clutch cylinder revolution sensor signal was inputted 5000 times.

1) Turn ignition off. Disconnect TCM harness connectors. Using a DVOM, measure resistance between TCM harness connector terminal B13 (Black wire) and terminal B5 (White wire). If resistance is 648-792 ohms, go to next step. If resistance is not as specified, go to step 3).

2) Test operation of Transmission Range (TR) switch. See TRANSMISSION RANGE (TR) SWITCH under COMPONENT TESTING. Adjust or replace if necessary. If TR switch tests okay, check for poor TCM harness connections. Repair as necessary. If connections are okay, substitute TCM with a known-good unit. Retest system.

3) Test operation of VSS. See VEHICLE SPEED SENSOR (VSS) under COMPONENT TESTING. Replace if necessary. If VSS switch tests okay, repair Black or White wire for an open or short.

DTC 32: THROTTLE OPENING SIGNAL

NOTE: DTC 32 will set if signal voltage is low (opening high).

1) Turn ignition on. Using a DVOM, measure voltage (backprobe) between ground and TCM harness connector terminal B8 (Orange wire). Reading should be 4.4-6.2 volts with throttle opening at 48 percent, and increase smoothly to 9.4-13.2 volts as throttle opening is increased to 95 percent. If reading is as specified, check for an intermittent problem or faulty TCM. See DIAGNOSTIC AIDS. If reading is not as specified, go to next step.

2) Check for PCM (engine control related) DTCs. See appropriate SELF-DIAGNOSTICS article in ENGINE PERFORMANCE in appropriate MITCHELL® manual. If only DTC 12 is present, go to next step. If any DTC other than DTC 12 is present, diagnose and repair referring to appropriate diagnostic procedure.

3) Turn ignition off. Disconnect TCM and PCM harness connectors. Using a DVOM, measure resistance between ground and TCM harness connector B8 (Orange wire). If DVOM displays infinity, go to next step. If DVOM displays continuity, repair Orange wire for a short to ground.

4) Reconnect TCM harness connector. Turn ignition on. Using a DVOM, measure voltage between ground and 16-pin PCM harness connector terminal B5 (Orange wire). If reading is 10-14 volts, check for an intermittent problem or faulty PCM. See DIAGNOSTIC AIDS. If reading is not as specified, substitute TCM with a known-good unit. Retest system.

Diagnostic Aids – An intermittent condition may be caused by a poor connection, damaged wire insulation or a wire which is broken inside the insulation. Inspect TCM harness connectors for damaged, corroded or backed-out terminal pins. Repair as necessary and retest system.

DTC 33: THROTTLE OPENING SIGNAL

NOTE: DTC 33 will set if signal voltage is high (opening low).

1) Turn ignition on. Using a DVOM, measure voltage (backprobe) between ground and TCM harness connector terminal B8 (Orange wire). Reading should be 4.4-6.2 volts with throttle opening at 48 per-

cent, and increase smoothly to 9.4-13.2 volts as throttle opening is increased to 95 percent. If reading is as specified, check for an intermittent problem or faulty TCM. See DIAGNOSTIC AIDS. If reading is not as specified, go to next step.

2) Check for PCM (engine control related) DTCs. See appropriate SELF-DIAGNOSTICS article in ENGINE PERFORMANCE in appropriate MITCHELL® manual. If only DTC 12 is present, go to next step. If any DTC other than DTC 12 is present, diagnose and repair referring to appropriate diagnostic procedure.

3) Turn ignition off. Disconnect PCM harness connectors. Turn ignition on. Using a DVOM, measure voltage between ground and 16-pin PCM harness connector terminal B5 (Orange wire). If reading is 10-14 volts, check for poor PCM harness connections. Repair as necessary. If connections are okay, substitute PCM with a known-good unit. If reading is not as specified, go to next step.

4) Check for poor connection or open in Orange wire between TCM and PCM. Repair as necessary. If no problems are found, substitute TCM with a known-good unit. Retest system.

Diagnostic Aids – An intermittent condition may be caused by a poor connection, damaged wire insulation or a wire which is broken inside the insulation. Inspect TCM harness connectors for damaged, corroded or backed-out terminal pins. Repair as necessary and retest system.

DTC 34: TRANSMISSION RANGE (TR) SWITCH

NOTE: DTC 34 will set if 2 or more TR switch signals are inputted at the same time.

1) Turn ignition on. Using a DVOM, measure voltage (backprobe) between TCM harness connector terminal A11 (White/Black wire) and terminal A12 (Black/Red wire). If reading is about 12 volts with gear selector lever in "P" position, and about zero volts with gear selector lever in any other position, go to next step. If reading is not as specified, go to step 7).

2) Measure voltage (backprobe) between TCM harness connector terminal A24 (Red/White wire) and terminal A12 (Black/Red wire). If reading is about 12 volts with gear selector lever in "R" position, and about zero volts with gear selector lever in any other position, go to next step. If reading is not as specified, go to step 7).

3) Measure voltage (backprobe) between TCM harness connector terminal B2 (White/Red wire) and terminal A12 (Black/Red wire). If reading is about 12 volts with gear selector lever in "N" position, and about zero volts with gear selector lever in any other position, go to next step. If reading is not as specified, go to step 7).

4) Measure voltage (backprobe) between TCM harness connector terminal B9 (Violet/Red wire) and terminal A12 (Black/Red wire). If reading is about 12 volts with gear selector lever in "D" position, and about zero volts with gear selector lever in any other position, go to next step. If reading is not as specified, go to step 7).

5) Measure voltage (backprobe) between TCM harness connector terminal B10 (Violet wire) and terminal A12 (Black/Red wire). If reading is about 12 volts with gear selector lever in "2" position, and about zero volts with gear selector lever in any other position, go to next step. If reading is not as specified, go to step 7).

6) Measure voltage (backprobe) between TCM harness connector terminal B1 (Red/Black wire) and terminal A12 (Black/Red wire). If reading is about 12 volts with gear selector lever in "L" position, and about zero volts with gear selector lever in any other position, check for an intermittent problem or faulty PCM. See DIAGNOSTIC AIDS. If reading is not as specified, go to next step.

7) Test TR switch operation. See TRANSMISSION RANGE (TR) SWITCH under COMPONENT TESTING. Adjust or replace if necessary. If TR switch tests okay, check wires in TR switch harness for shorting together. Repair as necessary. If no problems are found, substitute TCM with a known-good unit. Retest system.

DTC 37: FORWARD CLUTCH CYLINDER REVOLUTION SENSOR

NOTE: DTC 37 will set if no forward clutch cylinder revolution sensor signal is inputted while transaxle is in "D", "2" or "L" range, and VSS signal was inputted 2000 times.

1) Turn ignition off. Disconnect TCM harness connectors. Using a DVOM, measure resistance between TCM harness connector terminal B14 (Green wire) and terminal B6 (Red wire). If resistance is 387-475 ohms, go to next step. If resistance is not as specified, go to step 3).

2) Test TR switch operation. See TRANSMISSION RANGE (TR) SWITCH under COMPONENT TESTING. Adjust or replace if necessary. If TR switch tests okay, check for poor TCM harness connections. Repair as necessary. If connections are okay, substitute TCM with a known-good unit. Retest system.

3) Test forward clutch cylinder revolution sensor operation. See FORWARD CLUTCH CYLINDER REVOLUTION SENSOR under COMPONENT TESTING. Replace if necessary. If sensor tests okay, repair Green or Red wire for an open or short.

DTC 41: THROTTLE PRESSURE CONTROL SOLENOID

NOTE: DTC 41 will set if throttle pressure control solenoid or its circuit is open or shorted to ground.

1) Turn ignition off. Disconnect TCM harness connectors. Using a DVOM, measure resistance between TCM harness connector terminal A3 (Gray/Red wire) and terminal A13 (Gray/Black wire). If resistance is about 3.5 ohms, check for an intermittent problem or faulty TCM. See DIAGNOSTIC AIDS. If resistance is not as specified, go to next step.

2) Test throttle pressure control solenoid operation. See SOLENOIDS under COMPONENT TESTING. Replace if necessary. If solenoid tests okay, check Gray/Red wire or Gray/Black wire for an open or short to ground. Check for poor TCM or solenoid harness connections. Repair as necessary.

Diagnostic Aids – An intermittent condition may be caused by a poor connection, damaged wire insulation or a wire which is broken inside the insulation. Inspect TCM harness connectors for damaged, corroded or backed-out terminal pins. Repair as necessary and retest system.

DTC 42: THROTTLE PRESSURE CONTROL SOLENOID

NOTE: DTC 42 will set if throttle pressure control solenoid or its circuit is shorted.

1) Turn ignition off. Disconnect TCM harness connectors. Using a DVOM, measure resistance between TCM harness connector terminal A3 (Gray/Red wire) and terminal A13 (Gray/Black wire). If resistance is about 3.5 ohms, check for an intermittent problem or faulty TCM. See DIAGNOSTIC AIDS. If resistance is not as specified, go to next step.

2) Test throttle pressure control solenoid operation. See SOLENOIDS under COMPONENT TESTING. Replace if necessary. If solenoid tests okay, repair Gray/Red wire for a short to Gray/Black wire.

Diagnostic Aids – An intermittent condition may be caused by a poor connection, damaged wire insulation or a wire which is broken inside the insulation. Inspect TCM harness connectors for damaged, corroded or backed-out terminal pins. Repair as necessary and retest system.

DTC 51: ENGINE COOLANT TEMPERATURE SIGNAL

NOTE: DTC 51 will set if engine coolant temperature signal is high, or if a low temperature signal is inputted for 15 minutes while engine is running.

1) Allow engine to cool. Turn ignition on. Using a DVOM, measure voltage (backprobe) between ground and TCM harness connector terminal B15 (Gray/Black wire). If reading is 3.4-4.6 volts with engine coolant temperature at 32-122°F (0-50°C), go to next step. If reading is not as specified, go to step 3).

2) Start engine. Observe DVOM. If reading increases to 6.7-9.2 volts as engine coolant temperature increases to greater than 122°F (50°C), check for an intermittent problem or faulty TCM. See DIAGNOSTIC AIDS. If reading is okay, go to next step.

3) Check for PCM (engine control related) DTCs. See appropriate SELF-DIAGNOSTICS article in ENGINE PERFORMANCE in appropriate MITCHELL® manual. If only DTC 12 is present, go to next step. If any DTC other than DTC 12 is present, diagnose and repair referring to appropriate diagnostic procedure.

4) Turn ignition off. Disconnect PCM harness connectors. Turn ignition on. Using a DVOM, measure voltage between ground and 16-pin PCM harness connector terminal B13 (Gray/Black wire). If reading is about 12 volts, check for poor PCM harness connections. Repair as necessary. If connections are okay, substitute PCM with a known-good unit. If reading is not as specified, go to next step.

5) Check for poor connection or open in Gray/Black wire between TCM and PCM. Repair as necessary. If no problems are found, substitute TCM with a known-good unit. Retest system.

Diagnostic Aids – An intermittent condition may be caused by a poor connection, damaged wire insulation or a wire which is broken inside the insulation. Inspect TCM harness connectors for damaged, corroded or backed-out terminal pins. Repair as necessary and retest system.

COMPONENT TESTING

FORWARD CLUTCH CYLINDER REVOLUTION SENSOR

Ensure ignition is off. Disconnect forward clutch cylinder revolution sensor harness connector located on transaxle. *See Fig. 4.* Using a DVOM, measure resistance between forward clutch cylinder revolution sensor terminals. Resistance should be 387-473 ohms at 68°F (20°C). Replace forward clutch cylinder revolution sensor if resistance is not as specified.

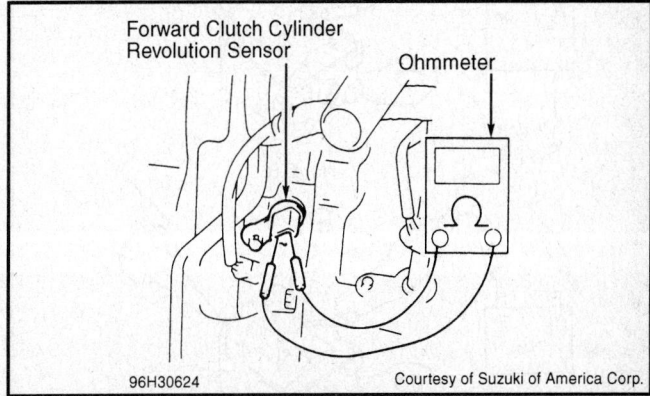

Fig. 4: *Testing Forward Clutch Cylinder Revolution Sensor*

O/D CUT SWITCH

Disconnect O/D cut switch harness connector. Using a DVOM, check for continuity between O/D cut switch terminals. Continuity should only be present with switch in ON position. Replace O/D cut switch if continuity is not as specified.

SOLENOIDS

Shift Solenoids – 1) Using a DVOM, measure resistance between solenoid body and terminal of solenoid. Resistance should be 11-15 ohms. Replace solenoid if resistance is not as specified.

2) Using an appropriate oiler (squirt can), apply ATF to oil feed hole of solenoid. *See Fig. 5.* ATF should not flow from solenoid. Using fused jumper wires, apply battery voltage to solenoid terminal, and ground to solenoid body. ATF should exhaust from solenoid. Replace solenoid if operation is not as specified.

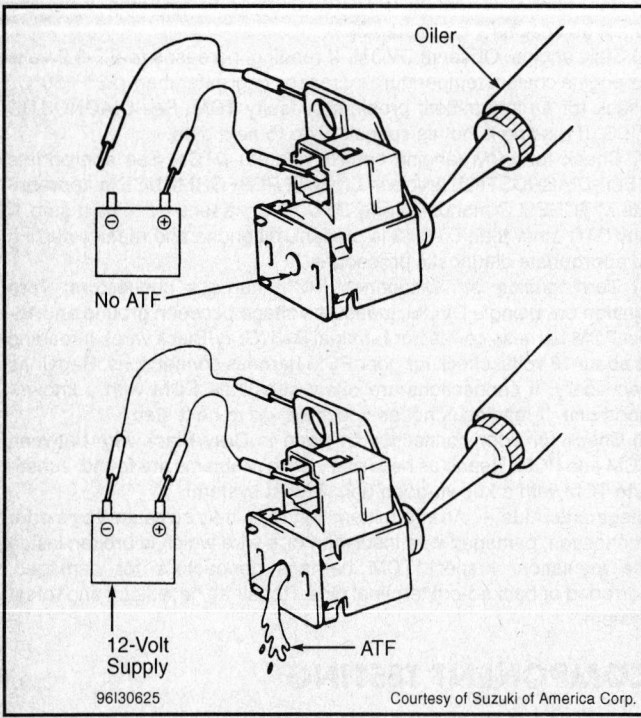

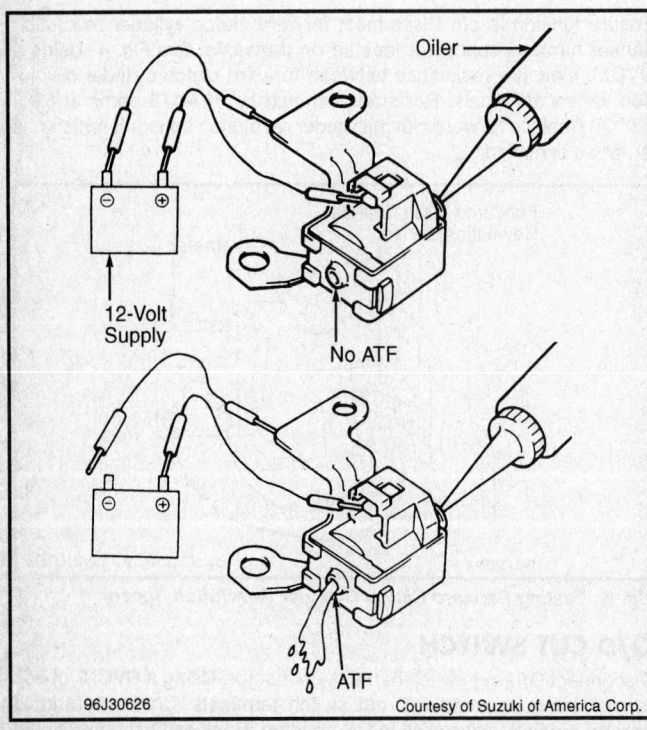

Fig. 5: Testing Shift Solenoids

Fig. 6: Testing TCC Solenoid

TCC Solenoid – Using an appropriate oiler (squirt can), apply ATF to oil feed hole of solenoid. *See Fig. 6.* ATF should exhaust from solenoid. Using fused jumper wires, apply battery voltage to solenoid terminal, and ground to solenoid body. ATF should not flow from solenoid. Replace solenoid if operation is not as specified.

Throttle Pressure Control Solenoid – Using a DVOM, measure resistance between solenoid terminals. *See Fig. 7.* Resistance should be 3.3-3.7 ohms. Replace solenoid if resistance is not as specified.

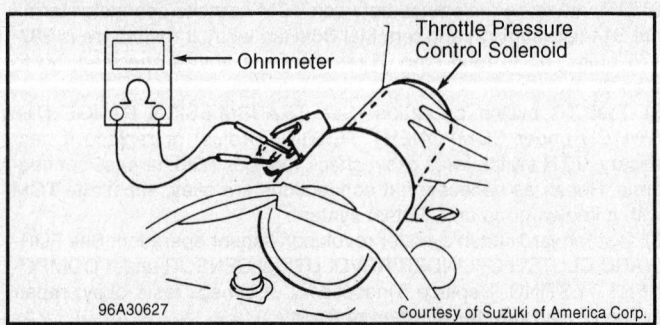

Fig. 7: Testing Throttle Pressure Control Solenoid

TRANSMISSION RANGE (TR) SWITCH

Turn ignition off. Disconnect TR switch harness connector located on side of transaxle. Using a DVOM, check for continuity between specified TR switch terminals in specified gear selector lever position. *See Fig. 8.* See TR SWITCH CONTINUITY table. Replace TR switch if continuity is not as specified.

TR SWITCH CONTINUITY

Lever Position	Continuity Between Terminals
"P"	5 & 6, 8 & 9
"R"	4 & 9
"N"	5 & 6, 7 & 9
"D"	3 & 9
"2"	2 & 9
"L"	1 & 9

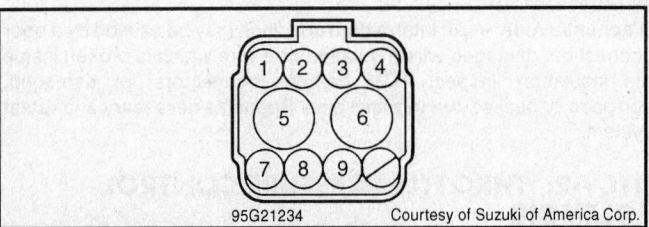

Fig. 8: Identifying TR Switch Terminals

VEHICLE SPEED SENSOR (VSS)

Ensure ignition is off. Disconnect VSS harness connector located on transaxle. *See Fig. 9.* Using a DVOM, measure resistance between VSS terminals. Resistance should be 648-792 ohms at 68°F (20°C). Replace VSS if resistance is not as specified.

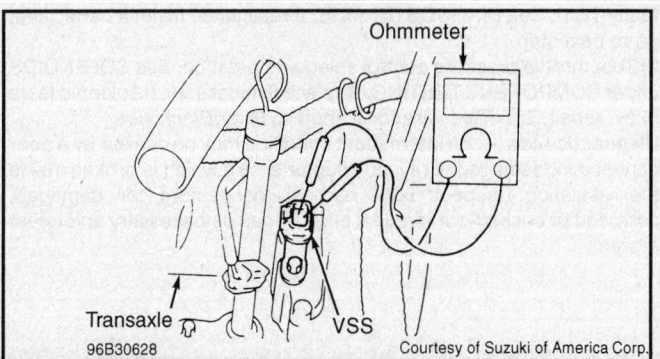

Fig. 9: Testing VSS

WIRING DIAGRAM

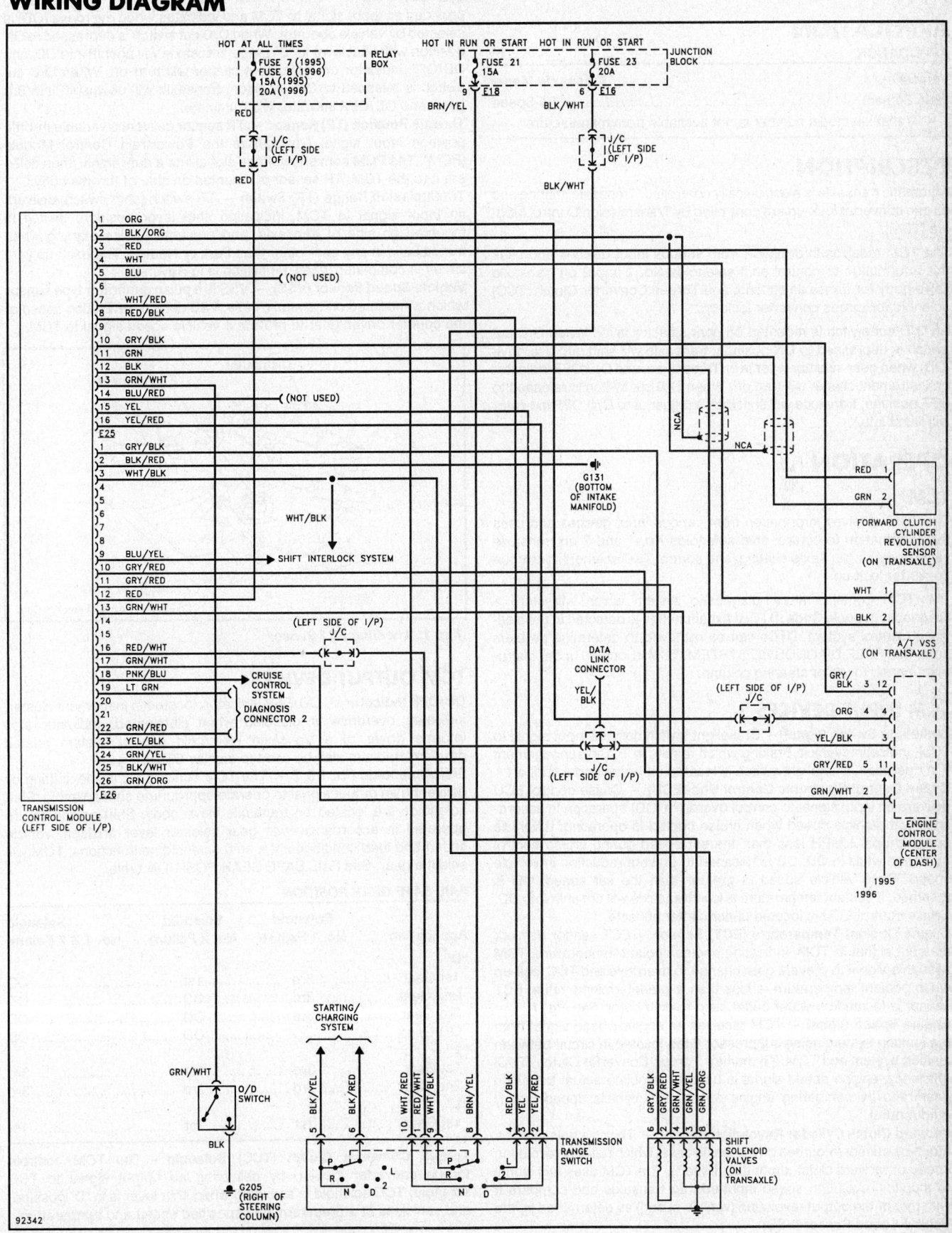

Fig. 10: Transaxle Wiring Diagram (1995 Suzuki Esteem)

AUTOMATIC TRANSMISSIONS
1996 Suzuki Esteem Electronic Controls

Esteem

APPLICATION

APPLICATION

Vehicle	Transaxle Model
1996 Esteem	[1] 4-Speed

[1] – Transaxle model number is not available from manufacturer.

DESCRIPTION

Automatic transaxle is electronically controlled. Transaxle shifting and torque converter lock-up are controlled by Transmission Control Module (TCM).

The TCM receives information from various input devices and uses this information to control shift solenoids No. 1 and 2 on transaxle valve body for transaxle shifting, and Torque Converter Clutch (TCC) solenoid for torque converter lock-up.

An O/D cut switch is mounted on gear selector lever. When O/D cut switch is depressed to ON position, transaxle will shift into overdrive (OD) when gear selector lever is in "D" position, and O/D OFF indicator on instrument cluster will turn off. When O/D cut switch is released to OFF position, transaxle will shift into 3rd gear, and O/D OFF indicator will illuminate.

OPERATION

TCM

The TCM receives information from various input devices and uses this information to control shift solenoids No. 1 and 2 on transaxle valve body for transaxle shifting, and control TCC solenoid for torque converter lock-up.

The TCM contains a self-diagnostic system which will store a Diagnostic Trouble Code (DTC) if a malfunction is detected in the electronic control system. DTCs can be retrieved to determine problem area. See SELF-DIAGNOSTIC SYSTEM. TCM is located under instrument panel, to left of steering column.

TCM INPUT DEVICES

Brakelight Switch Signal – Brakelight switch delivers input signal to TCM, indicating vehicle braking which results in TCC disengagement if in operation. Brakelight switch is located on brake pedal support.

Cruise Control Electronic Control Unit (ECU) – Cruise control ECU delivers an input signal to control overdrive (OD) operation in accordance with vehicle speed when cruise control is operating. If vehicle speed drops 2 MPH less than the set speed during cruise control operation while in OD, OD is released to prevent reduction in vehicle speed. Once vehicle speed is greater than the set speed, OD is resumed. If coolant temperature is low, transaxle will not shift into OD. Cruise control ECU is located under center console.

Engine Coolant Temperature (ECT) Sensor – ECT sensor delivers an input signal to TCM, indicating engine coolant temperature. TCM uses this signal to prevent gear change to overdrive and TCC lock-up when coolant temperature is less than a predetermined value. ECT sensor is located on water outlet, next to distributor. See Fig. 1.

Engine Speed Signal – TCM receives an engine speed signal from the ignition system noise suppressor filter, located in circuit between ignition system and TCM. To monitor Torque Converter Clutch (TCC) efficiency, engine speed signal is used to calculate actual transaxle gear ratio by comparing engine speed with vehicle speed (input/output ratio).

Forward Clutch Cylinder Revolution Sensor – This is a pulse generator type sensor (mounted on transaxle case) which detects revolution speed of forward clutch drum (input shaft). The TCM uses this signal to monitor revolution speed inputted into transaxle and compare it with that of the output revolution (vehicle speed) as determined by the Vehicle Speed Sensor (VSS).

O/D Cut Switch – The O/D cut switch (mounted on shift lever) provides an input signal to TCM and indicates when overdrive (OD) is selected by vehicle operator. When O/D cut switch is depressed to ON position with shift lever in "D" range, transaxle will upshift into OD, and OD/OFF indicator on instrument cluster will turn off. When O/D cut switch is released to OFF position, transaxle will downshift into 3rd gear, and OD/OFF indicator will illuminate.

Throttle Position (TP) Sensor – TP sensor delivers a variable throttle position input signal (voltage) to the Powertrain Control Module (PCM). The PCM converts voltage signal into a duty signal, then delivers it to the TCM. TP sensor is mounted on side of throttle body.

Transmission Range (TR) Switch – TR switch (shift switch) delivers an input signal to TCM, indicating shift lever position. Switch is mounted on side of transaxle, and prevents engine starting when transaxle is in any gear other than Park or Neutral. The back-up light circuit is completed when TR switch is in Reverse.

Vehicle Speed Sensor (VSS) – VSS is a pulse generator type sensor which is mounted on transaxle case. VSS detects revolution speed of the counter driven gear to provide a vehicle speed signal to TCM.

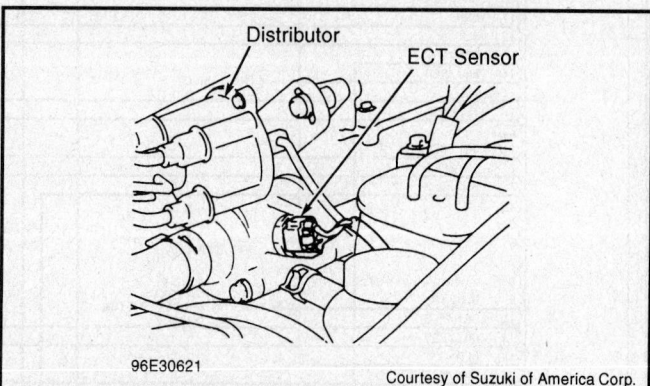

96E30621

Courtesy of Suzuki of America Corp.

Fig. 1: Locating ECT Sensor

TCM OUTPUT DEVICES

OD/OFF Indicator – OD/OFF indicator, located in instrument cluster, indicates overdrive is disabled when illuminated. Indicator also informs driver of a transaxle electronic control system related problem, and can also be used to display DTCs.

Shift Solenoids No. 1 & 2 – The TCM controls transaxle shifting by delivering an output signal to operate appropriate shift solenoid. Shift solenoids are located on transaxle valve body. Shift solenoids are operated in accordance with gear selector lever position, vehicle speed and load conditions. If a shift solenoid malfunctions, TCM will select a gear. See FAIL SAFE GEAR POSITION table.

FAIL SAFE GEAR POSITION

Application	Solenoid No. 1 Failure	Solenoid No. 2 Failure	Solenoid No. 1 & 2 Failure
"D"			
1st Gear	3rd	1st	OD
2nd Gear	3rd	OD	OD
3rd Gear	3rd	OD	OD
OD Gear	OD	OD	OD
"2"			
1st Gear	3rd	1st	3rd
2nd Gear	3rd	3rd	3rd
"L"			
1st Gear	1st	1st	1st

Torque Converter Clutch (TCC) Solenoid – The TCM controls torque converter lock-up by delivering an output signal to TCC solenoid. TCC solenoid is activated when shift lever is in "D" position, and vehicle is at a predetermined specified speed and temperature.

SELF-DIAGNOSTIC SYSTEM

SYSTEM DIAGNOSIS

NOTE: Before testing transaxle, ensure fluid level is correct and throttle and shift cables are properly adjusted. Ensure engine starts with gear selector lever in "P" and "N" positions to ensure proper adjustment of Transmission Range (TR) switch. The electronic control system must first be checked for stored DTCs. See RETRIEVING TROUBLE CODES.

The TCM continuously monitors transaxle operation and contains a self-diagnostic system which stores a Diagnostic Trouble Code (DTC) if an electronic control system malfunction is detected. If a malfunction is detected and a DTC is set, the TCM will deliver a signal to flash OD/OFF indicator on instrument cluster to indicate that a 2-digit "Flash Code" has been stored. In addition, TCM transmits DTC data to the Powertrain Control Module (PCM) which will be retained in memory as a 4-digit OBD-II DTC. As a result, PCM will illuminate the Malfunction Indicator Light (MIL).

When retrieving "Flash Codes", the number of OD/OFF indicator flashes will equal first digit of DTC. After a one second pause, second digit of DTC is displayed. If more than one DTC is present, the next DTC will be displayed after a 3 second pause. Smallest number DTC will be displayed first. DTCs are repeated after each retrieval cycle. Once a DTC is retrieved, determine probable cause. See DTC IDENTIFICATION.

DTCs may be retrieved using 3 methods. If OD/OFF indicator or MIL indicates a system malfunction, retrieve DTCs using desired method. See RETRIEVING TROUBLE CODES.

RETRIEVING TROUBLE CODES

NOTE: Before retrieving DTCs, ensure battery is fully charged for proper self-diagnostic system operation. DTCs must be cleared from TCM memory once repairs have been performed. See CLEARING TROUBLE CODES.

Scan Tool Method (PCM) – 1) Using an OBD-II compatible scan tool, interface PCM by connecting to OBD-II 16-pin Data Link Connector (DLC), located under instrument panel, accessible from driver's side. Retrieve DTCs following scan tool manufacturers instructions.
2) If a DTC is present, identify DTC and diagnose accordingly. See DTC IDENTIFICATION, then proceed to DIAGNOSTIC TESTING. After repairs are made, clear DTCs. See CLEARING TROUBLE CODES. Test drive vehicle and ensure OD/OFF indicator or MIL does not illuminate.
Scan Tool Method (TCM) – 1) Using SUZUKI scan tool with A/T cartridge, interface TCM by connecting to OBD-II 16-pin Data Link Connector (DLC), located under instrument panel, accessible from driver's side. Retrieve DTCs following scan tool manufacturers instructions.
2) If a DTC is present, identify DTC and diagnose accordingly. See DTC IDENTIFICATION, then proceed to DIAGNOSTIC TESTING. After repairs are made, clear DTCs. See CLEARING TROUBLE CODES. Test drive vehicle and ensure OD/OFF indicator or MIL does not illuminate.

NOTE: When using "Flash Code" (2-digit code) method to retrieve DTCs, convert trouble codes into 4-digit OBD-II DTCs for use in DIAGNOSTIC TESTING. See DTC IDENTIFICATION.

Flash Code Method – 1) Ensure O/D cut switch is in OFF (depressed) position. Turn ignition on. If OD/OFF indicator illuminates for about 2 seconds, go to next step. If OD/OFF indicator does not illuminate, go to OD/OFF INDICATOR DOES NOT ILLUMINATE. If OD/OFF indicator remains illuminated, go to OD/OFF INDICATOR REMAINS ILLUMINATED. If OD/OFF indicator flashes, go to OD/OFF INDICATOR FLASHES.

2) Using a fused jumper wire, jumper ground terminal of diagnostic connector No. 1 to diagnosis switch terminal of diagnostic connector No. 2, located in engine compartment relay box. *See Fig. 2.* If OD/OFF indicator flashes a DTC, record and identify DTC. See DTC IDENTIFICATION. If OD/OFF indicator does not respond, check for an open in diagnosis switch terminal circuit (Green/Red wire). Repair as necessary. If wire is okay, substitute TCM with a known-good unit. Retest system.

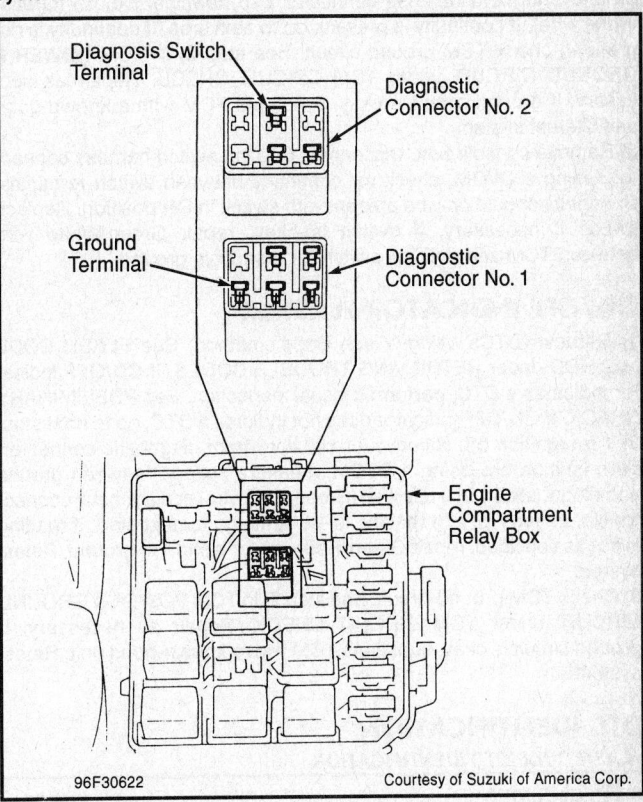

96F30622   Courtesy of Suzuki of America Corp.

Fig. 2: Identifying Diagnostic Connector Terminals

CLEARING TROUBLE CODES

Once repairs have been performed, DTCs must be cleared from both PCM and TCM memory. DTCs can be cleared using a scan tool following scan tool manufacturers instructions. If a scan tool is not available, turn ignition off and disconnect negative battery cable for at least one minute.

OD/OFF INDICATOR DOES NOT ILLUMINATE

1) Turn ignition on. If other indicator/warning lights in instrument cluster illuminate, go to next step. If no other indicators illuminate, check for: blown IG fuse (20-amp), blown main fuse (60-amp), open or poor connection in Black/White wire between IG fuse and instrument cluster, or faulty ignition switch.
2) Turn ignition off. Disconnect TCM harness connectors. Check TCM harness connector E26, terminal No. 19 (Light Green wire) for poor contact. Repair as necessary. If connection is okay, jumper Light Green wire to ground using a fused jumper wire (leave harness connector disconnected). Turn ignition on. If OD/OFF indicator illuminates, go to next step. If OD/OFF indicator does not illuminate, check for an open in Light Green wire, or for a faulty indicator bulb. Repair as necessary.
3) Check TCM ground circuit. See TCM POWER & GROUND CIRCUIT under TCM CIRCUIT CHECK. Repair as necessary. If no problems are found, substitute TCM with a known-good unit. Retest system.

OD/OFF INDICATOR REMAINS ILLUMINATED

1) Ensure O/D cut switch is in OFF position. Turn ignition off. Disconnect TCM harness connectors. Turn ignition on. If OD/OFF indicator illuminates steadily, repair Light Green wire between diagnostic connector and instrument cluster for a short to ground. If OD/OFF indicator does not illuminate steadily, go to next step.

2) Turn ignition off. Using a DVOM, check for continuity between ground and TCM harness connector E25, terminal No. 13 (Green/White wire). If continuity is present, go to next step. If continuity is not present, check TCM ground circuit. See step 2) in TCM POWER & GROUND CIRCUIT under TCM CIRCUIT CHECK. Repair as necessary. If ground circuit is okay, substitute TCM with a known-good unit. Retest system.

3) Remove console box. Disconnect O/D cut switch harness connector. Using a DVOM, check for continuity between switch terminals. Continuity should only be present with switch in ON position. Replace switch if necessary. If switch is okay, repair Green/White wire between TCM and O/D cut switch for a short to ground.

OD/OFF INDICATOR FLASHES

1) Retrieve DTCs using "Flash Code" method. See FLASH CODE METHOD under RETRIEVING TROUBLE CODES. If OD/OFF indicator indicates a DTC, perform a visual inspection. See PRELIMINARY CHECK. If OD/OFF indicator does not indicate a DTC, go to next step.

2) Turn ignition off. Remove jumper wire from diagnostic connector. Turn ignition on. Using a DVOM, measure voltage between ground and diagnostic switch terminal (Green/Red wire) at diagnostic connector No. 2. See Fig. 2. If reading is 4-6 volts, go to next step. If reading is not as specified, repair Green/Red wire for a short to ground. Retest system.

3) Check TCM ground circuit. See step 2) in TCM POWER & GROUND CIRCUIT under TCM CIRCUIT CHECK. Repair as necessary. If ground circuit is okay, substitute TCM with a known-good unit. Retest system.

DTC IDENTIFICATION

FLASH CODE/DTC IDENTIFICATION

Flash Code/DTC	Condition
12/ [1]	System Operation Normal
34/P0705	Transmission Range (TR) Switch Circuit
37/P0715	Forward Clutch Cylinder Revolution Sensor Circuit
31/P0720	VSS (Transaxle) Circuit
35/P0725	Engine Speed Input Circuit
41 & 42/P0745	Pressure Control Solenoid Malfunction
17/P0751	Shift Solenoid No. 1 Performance
21 & 22/P0753	Shift Solenoid No. 1 Circuit
28/P0756	Shift Solenoid No. 2 Performance
23 & 24/P0758	Shift Solenoid No. 2 Circuit
29/P0741 Or P0771	TCC Solenoid Performance
25 & 26/P0743 Or P0773	TCC Solenoid Circuit
32 & 33/P1700	TP Sensor Signal Input Malfunction
51/P1705	ECT Sensor Signal Input Malfunction

[1] – No 4-digit DTC set.

PRELIMINARY CHECK

NOTE: As a preliminary step, perform a visual inspection of the following systems and components which directly relate to proper transaxle operation.

Visual Inspection – Check the following and repair as necessary:
- Engine Oil: check level and for evidence of leakage.
- Engine Coolant: check level and for evidence of leakage.
- ATF: check level, condition and for evidence of leakage.
- Battery: check water level and terminal corrosion.
- A/T Hoses: check for poor connections or deterioration.
- Throttle Cable: excessive play or improper installation.
- Harness Connectors: check for poor connections or worn insulation.
- Fuses: check for improper installation or for burning.
- Related Mechanical Parts: check for proper installation and condition.

If no problems are found during visual inspection, and only DTC 12 is retrieved even though a problem exists, perform a manual shifting test. See MANUAL SHIFTING TEST under TRANSMISSION SHIFT TESTING.

TCM CIRCUIT CHECK

TCM POWER & GROUND CIRCUIT

1) Turn ignition off. Disconnect TCM harness connectors. Check for poor terminal contact. Repair as necessary. If connections are okay, turn ignition on. Using a DVOM, measure voltage between ground and TCM harness connector E26, terminal No. 25 (Black/White wire). If reading is 10-14 volts, go to next step. I reading is not as specified, repair open in Black/White wire.

2) Turn ignition off. Using A DVOM, check for continuity between ground and TCM harness connector E26, terminal No. 2 (Black/Red wire). If continuity is present, power and ground circuits are okay at this time. If continuity is not present, repair open in Black or Black/White wire between TCM and chassis ground. Retest system.

PIN VOLTAGE CHART

Using a DVOM, measure voltage (backprobe) at specified terminals with TCM harness connectors connected. See Fig. 3. Ensure each check is made under conditions noted in chart.

NOTE: Values or conditions that are not specified in the following chart represent ground circuits, or signal circuits which may vary or toggle depending upon vehicle operation.

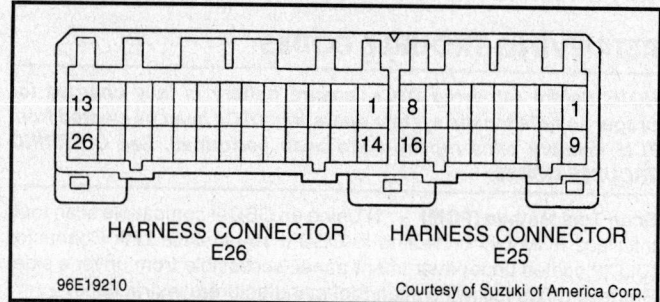

HARNESS CONNECTOR E26   HARNESS CONNECTOR E25

96E19210   Courtesy of Suzuki of America Corp.

Fig. 3: Identifying TCM Harness Connector Terminals (Harness Side)

TRANSMISSION SHIFT TESTING

MANUAL SHIFTING TEST

NOTE: Perform manual shifting test if no DTCs are present. Manual shifting test determines if problem is an electrical or mechanical related problem.

1) Start and operate vehicle until normal operating temperature is achieved. Disconnect TCM harness connectors. Road test vehicle in "L" range up to 13 MPH. Ensure 1st gear is being used. Manually upshift to "2" range and accelerate to 25 MPH. Ensure 3rd gear is being used.

2) Manually upshift to "D" range and ensure overdrive gear is used when vehicle is driven at speeds greater than 25 MPH. Stop vehicle and turn ignition off. Reconnect TCM harness connectors. Clear DTCs, as disconnecting harness connectors may set a DTC. See CLEARING TROUBLE CODES.

3) If a fault is present during manual operation, problem is mechanically related. Perform STALL TEST, TIME LAG TEST, LINE PRESSURE TEST, ENGINE BRAKE TEST and "P" RANGE TEST. See TESTING in appropriate overhaul article. If all gears are correct, see PRELIMINARY CHECKS in appropriate overhaul article.

PIN VOLTAGE CHART

Terminal	Circuit	Normal Voltage	Condition
E25			
1	Throttle Opening Signal	[1]	Ignition On
2	Shield Ground	Not Specified	Not Specified
3	Forward Clutch Revolution Sensor (−)	Not Specified	Not Specified
4	VSS (−)	Not Specified	Not Specified
5	Blank	N/A	N/A
6	Blank	N/A	N/A
7	TR Switch ("N" Range)	10-14	Ignition On, In "N" Range
		About Zero	Ignition On, In Any Range Other Than "N"
8	TR Switch ("L" Range)	10-14	Ignition On, In "L" Range
		About Zero	Ignition On, In Any Range Other Than "L"
9	Blank	N/A	N/A
10	ECT Signal (PCM)	[2]	Engine Running
11	Forward Clutch Revolution Sensor (+)	Not Specified	Not Specified
12	VSS (+)	Not Specified	Not Specified
13	O/D Cut Switch	About Zero	Switch On, Illuminated
		4-6	Switch Off, Not Illuminated
14	Blank	N/A	N/A
15	TR Switch ("2" Range)	10-14	Ignition On, In "2" Range
		About Zero	Ignition On, In Any Range Other Than "2"
16	TR Switch ("D" Range)	10-14	Ignition On, In "D" Range
		About Zero	Ignition On, In Any Range Other Than "D"
E26			
1	Throttle Pressure Control Solenoid (−)	Not Specified	Not Specified
2	Ground Supply	Not Specified	Not Specified
3	TR Switch ("P" Range)	10-14	Ignition On, In "P" Range
		About Zero	Ignition On, In Any Range Other Than "P"
4	Blank	N/A	N/A
5	Blank	N/A	N/A
6	Blank	N/A	N/A
7	Blank	N/A	N/A
8	Blank	N/A	N/A
9	Brake Light Switch	10-14	Brake Pedal Depressed
		About Zero	Brake Pedal Released
10	Park/Neutral Position (PNP) Signal (PCM)	10-14	Ignition On, In "P" Or "N" Range
		0-1	Ignition On, In "R", "D", "2" Or "L" Range
11	Throttle Pressure Control Solenoid (+)	Not Specified	Not Specified
12	Back-Up Power Source	10-14	Ignition On Or Off
13	Shift Solenoid No. 1	10-14	Ignition On, In "P" Range
14	Blank	N/A	N/A
15	Blank	N/A	N/A
16	TR Switch ("R" Range)	10-14	Ignition On, In "R" Range
		About Zero	Ignition On, In Any Range Other Than "R"
17	Serial Data Line (To PCM)	[3]	Ignition On
18	Cruise Control Unit	4-6	Ignition On
19	OD/OFF Indicator	0-1	First 2 Seconds Of Ignition On
		10-14	After 2 Seconds Of Ignition On
20	Blank	N/A	N/A
21	Ignition Signal	10-14	Ignition On
22	Diagnosis Switch Terminal	4-6	Ignition On
23	Data Link Connector	4-6	Ignition On
24	TCC Solenoid	About Zero	Ignition On
25	Power Supply	10-14	Ignition On
26	Shift Solenoid No. 2	About Zero	Ignition On, In "P" Range

[1] – Varies with throttle position.

[2] – Varies with coolant temperature.

[3] – Voltage varies between 0-1 and 4-6 volts.

AUTOMATIC TRANSMISSIONS
1996 Suzuki Esteem Electronic Controls (Cont.)

DIAGNOSTIC TESTING

NOTE: When diagnosing transaxle, ensure all proper steps are taken to eliminate the possibility of a mechanical malfunction. This can save diagnostic time and avoid unnecessary replacement of properly operating components. See SYSTEM DIAGNOSIS under SELF-DIAGNOSTIC SYSTEM. See wiring diagram in WIRING DIAGRAM to aid in component location, wire color and wire terminal identification. Refer to illustration for TCM harness connector and terminal identification. See Fig. 3.

DTC P0705: TRANSMISSION RANGE (TR) SWITCH

NOTE: DTC P0705 will set if no TR switch signal is inputted, or if multiple TR switch signals are inputted at the same time.

1) Turn ignition on. Using a DVOM, measure voltage (backprobe) between ground and TCM harness connector E26, terminal No. 3 (White/Black wire). If reading is about 12 volts with gear selector lever in "P" position, and about zero volts with gear selector lever in any other position, go to next step. If reading is not as specified, go to step 7).
2) Measure voltage (backprobe) between ground and TCM harness connector E26, terminal No. 16 (Red/White wire). If reading is about 12 volts with gear selector lever in "R" position, and about zero volts with gear selector lever in any other position, go to next step. If reading is not as specified, go to step 7).
3) Measure voltage (backprobe) between ground and TCM harness connector E25, terminal No. 7 (White/Red wire). If reading is about 12 volts with gear selector lever in "N" position, and about zero volts with gear selector lever in any other position, go to next step. If reading is not as specified, go to step 7).
4) Measure voltage (backprobe) between ground and TCM harness connector E25, terminal No. 16 (Yellow/Red wire). If reading is about 12 volts with gear selector lever in "D" position, and about zero volts with gear selector lever in any other position, go to next step. If reading is not as specified, go to step 7).
5) Measure voltage (backprobe) between ground and TCM harness connector E25, terminal No. 15 (Yellow wire). If reading is about 12 volts with gear selector lever in "2" position, and about zero volts with gear selector lever in any other position, go to next step. If reading is not as specified, go to step 7).
6) Measure voltage (backprobe) between ground and TCM harness connector E25, terminal No. 8 (Red/Black wire). If reading is about 12 volts with gear selector lever in "L" position, and about zero volts with gear selector lever in any other position, check for an intermittent problem. See DIAGNOSTIC AIDS. If reading is not as specified, go to next step.
7) Test TR switch operation. See TRANSMISSION RANGE (TR) SWITCH under COMPONENT TESTING. Adjust or replace if necessary. If TR switch is in good condition, check wires in TR switch harness for opens or shorts. Repair as necessary. If no problems are found, substitute TCM with a known-good unit. Retest system.
Diagnostic Aids – An intermittent condition may be caused by a poor connection, damaged wire insulation or a wire which is broken inside the insulation. Inspect TCM harness connectors for damaged, corroded or backed-out terminal pins. Repair as necessary and retest system.

DTC P0715: FORWARD CLUTCH CYLINDER REVOLUTION SENSOR

NOTE: DTC P0715 will set if no forward clutch cylinder revolution sensor signal is inputted while transaxle is in "D", "2" or "L" range, and VSS (transaxle) signal was inputted.

1) Turn ignition off. Disconnect forward clutch cylinder revolution sensor harness connector. Using a DVOM, measure resistance between sensor terminals. If resistance is 387-475 ohms at 68°F (20°C), go to next step. If resistance is not as specified, replace sensor.

2) Visually inspect sensor for damage, contamination or improper installation. Replace if necessary. If sensor is in good condition, check Red wire or Green wire between sensor and TCM for an open or short to ground. Repair as necessary, If wires are okay, check for an intermittent problem or faulty TCM. See DIAGNOSTIC AIDS.
Diagnostic Aids – An intermittent condition may be caused by a poor connection, damaged wire insulation or a wire which is broken inside the insulation. Inspect TCM harness connectors for damaged, corroded or backed-out terminal pins. Repair as necessary and retest system.

DTC P0720: VEHICLE SPEED SENSOR (VSS)

NOTE: DTC P0720 will set if no VSS (transaxle) signal is inputted while transaxle is in "D", "2" or "L" range, and forward clutch cylinder revolution sensor signal was inputted.

1) Turn ignition off. Disconnect VSS harness connector. Using a DVOM, measure resistance between VSS terminals. If resistance is 648-792 ohms at 68°F (20°C), go to next step. If resistance is not as specified, replace VSS.
2) Visually inspect VSS for damage, contamination or improper installation. Repair as necessary. If VSS is in good condition, check TR switch operation referring to step 1) of DTC P0705. Adjust or replace TR switch if necessary. If TR switch is in good condition, go to next step.
3) Check Black wire or White wire between VSS and TCM for an open or short to ground. Repair as necessary. If wires are okay, check for an intermittent problem or faulty TCM. See DIAGNOSTIC AIDS.
Diagnostic Aids – An intermittent condition may be caused by a poor connection, damaged wire insulation or a wire which is broken inside the insulation. Inspect TCM harness connectors for damaged, corroded or backed-out terminal pins. Repair as necessary and retest system.

DTC P0725: ENGINE SPEED INPUT CIRCUIT

NOTE: DTC P0725 will set if no engine speed signal is inputted with engine running, and normal ECT sensor signal values were inputted.

Turn ignition off. Disconnect TCM harness connectors. Turn ignition on. Using a DVOM, measure voltage between ground and TCM harness connector E26, terminal No. 21 (Brown wire). If reading is 10-14 volts, check for an intermittent problem or faulty TCM. See DIAGNOSTIC AIDS. If reading is not as specified, check for an open in Brown wire between TCM and noise suppressor filter, or a faulty noise suppressor filter. Repair as necessary. Retest system.
Diagnostic Aids – An intermittent condition may be caused by a poor connection, damaged wire insulation or a wire which is broken inside the insulation. Inspect TCM harness connectors for damaged, corroded or backed-out terminal pins. Repair as necessary and retest system.

DTC P0745: THROTTLE PRESSURE CONTROL SOLENOID

NOTE: DTC P0745 will set if throttle pressure control solenoid or its circuit is open or shorted.

1) Turn ignition off. Place gear selector lever in "P" position. Turn ignition on. Using a DVOM, measure voltage (backprobe) between TCM harness connector E26, terminals No. 1 (Gray/Black wire), and No. 2 (Black/Red wire). Observe DVOM as accelerator pedal is depressed. If voltage decreases as throttle opens, check for an intermittent problem or faulty TCM. See DIAGNOSTIC AIDS. If voltage did not decrease, go to next step.
2) Turn ignition off. Disconnect throttle pressure control solenoid harness connector at transaxle. Using a DVOM, measure resistance between solenoid terminals, then measure resistance between transaxle case and specified solenoid terminal. See Fig. 4. If resistance is 3.3-3.7 ohms at 68°F (20°C) between terminals, and infinity between

transaxle case and solenoid terminal, go to next step. If resistance is not as specified, solenoid or lead wire is faulty. Repair as necessary.
3) Check Gray/Red wire or Gray/Black wire between solenoid and TCM for an open or short to ground. Repair as necessary, If wires are okay, substitute TCM with a known-good unit. Retest system.
Diagnostic Aids – An intermittent condition may be caused by a poor connection, damaged wire insulation or a wire which is broken inside the insulation. Inspect TCM harness connectors for damaged, corroded or backed-out terminal pins. Repair as necessary and retest system.

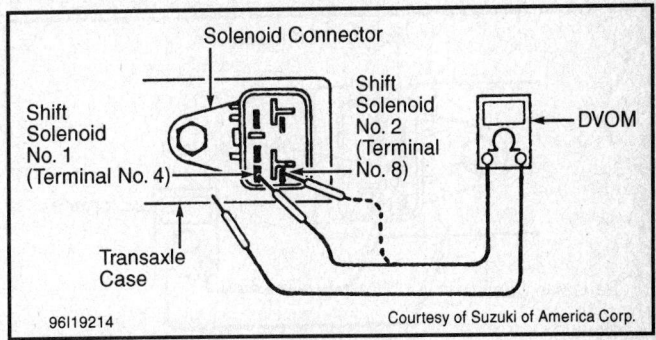

Fig. 5: Measuring Shift Solenoid Resistance

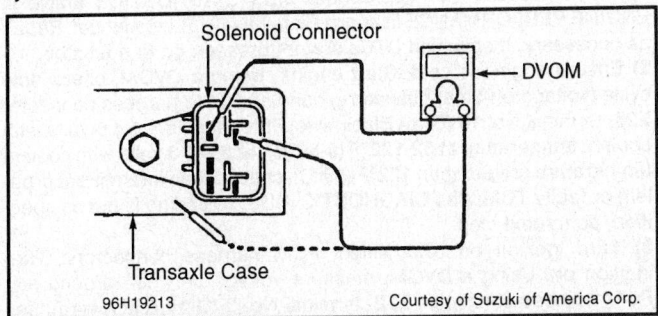

Fig. 4: Measuring Throttle Pressure Control Solenoid Resistance

DTC P0751 OR P0756: SHIFT SOLENOIDS NO. 1 OR 2 PERFORMANCE

NOTE: DTC P0751 or P0756 will set if detected transaxle gear ratio does not coincide with TCM command.

1) Perform manual shifting test. See MANUAL SHIFTING TEST under TRANSMISSION SHIFT TESTING. If test results are okay, go to next step. If test results are not okay, see PRELIMINARY CHECKS in appropriate overhaul article.
2) Check shift solenoid operation. See SOLENOIDS under COMPONENT TESTING. Repair as necessary. If shift solenoids are in good condition, go to next step.
3) Check valve body for clogged fluid passages or stuck valves. See ON-VEHICLE SERVICE and COMPONENT DISASSEMBLY & REASSEMBLY in appropriate overhaul article. Repair as necessary. If valve body is okay, substitute TCM with a known-good unit.

DTC P0753 OR P0758: SHIFT SOLENOIDS NO. 1 OR 2 CIRCUIT FAULT

NOTE: DTC P0753 or P0758 will set if a shift solenoid or its circuit is open or shorted.

1) Turn ignition off. Disconnect TCM harness connectors. Turn ignition on. Using a DVOM, measure voltage between ground and TCM harness connector E26, terminal No. 13 (Green/White wire), then No. 26 (Green/Orange wire). If reading is about zero volts at both terminals, go to next step. If reading is not as specified, repair Green/White wire or Green/Orange wire for a short to power.
2) Turn ignition off. Using a DVOM, measure resistance between ground and TCM harness connector E26, terminal No. 13 (Green/White wire), or No. 26 (Green/Orange wire). If resistance is 11-15 ohms at 68°F (20°C), at tested terminal, check for an intermittent problem or faulty TCM. See DIAGNOSTIC AIDS. If resistance is not as specified, go to next step.
3) Disconnect solenoid harness connector at transaxle. Using a DVOM, measure resistance between transaxle case and solenoid terminal No. 4, or No. 8. See Fig. 5. If resistance is 11-15 ohms at 68°F (20°C), at tested terminal, repair Green/White wire or Green/Orange wire for an open or short to ground. If resistance is not as specified, go to next step.
4) Check shift solenoid lead wires in transaxle for an open or short. Check solenoids for proper installation. Repair as necessary. If no problems are found, replace affected shift solenoid. Retest system.

Diagnostic Aids – An intermittent condition may be caused by a poor connection, damaged wire insulation or a wire which is broken inside the insulation. Inspect TCM harness connectors for damaged, corroded or backed-out terminal pins. Repair as necessary and retest system.

DTC P0741 OR P0771: TCC SOLENOID PERFORMANCE

NOTE: DTC P0741 or P0771 will set under the following conditions:
- *Difference in RPM between engine and transaxle input speed (forward clutch cylinder revolution sensor) is greater than specified value while TCC solenoid is commanded on.*
- *Difference in RPM between engine and transaxle input speed (forward clutch cylinder revolution sensor) is less than specified value while TCC solenoid is commanded off.*

1) Check TCC solenoid operation. See SOLENOIDS under COMPONENT TESTING. Replace if necessary. If TCC solenoid is in good condition, go to next step.
2) Check TCC control valve in valve body for smooth operation. Ensure fluid passages are unrestricted. See ON-VEHICLE SERVICE and COMPONENT DISASSEMBLY & REASSEMBLY in appropriate overhaul article. Repair as necessary. If no problems are found, replace torque converter.

DTC P0743 OR P0773: TCC SOLENOID CIRCUIT FAULT

NOTE: DTC P0743 or P0773 will set if voltage at TCM harness connector E26, terminal No. 24 (Green/Yellow wire) is high while TCC solenoid is commanded off, or low while commanded on.

1) Turn ignition off. Disconnect TCM harness connectors. Turn ignition on. Using a DVOM, measure voltage between ground and TCM harness connector E26, terminal No. 24 (Green/Yellow wire). If reading is about zero volts, go to next step. If reading is not as specified, repair Green/Yellow wire for a short to power.
2) Turn ignition off. Using a DVOM, measure resistance between ground and TCM harness connector E26, terminal No. 24 (Green/Yellow wire). If resistance is 11-15 ohms at 68°F (20°C), check for an intermittent problem or faulty TCM. See DIAGNOSTIC AIDS. If resistance is not as specified, go to next step.
3) Disconnect solenoid harness connector at transaxle. Using a DVOM, measure resistance between transaxle case and TCC solenoid harness connector terminal No. 3 (Green/Yellow wire). See Fig. 6. If resistance is 11-15 ohms at 68°F (20°C), repair Green/Yellow wire for an open or short to ground. If resistance is not as specified, go to next step.
4) Check TCC solenoid wires in transaxle for an open or short. Check TCC solenoid for proper installation. Repair as necessary. If no problems are found, replace TCC solenoid. Retest system.

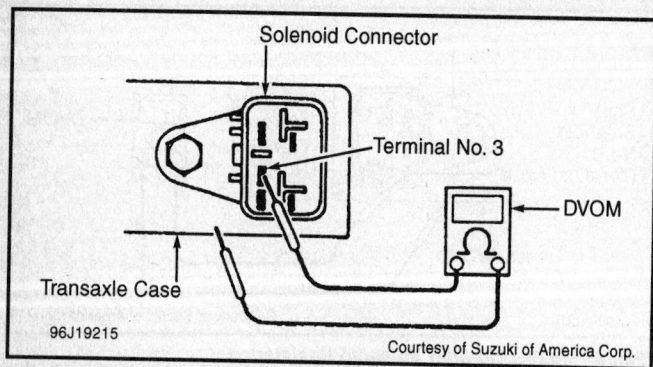

96J19215

Courtesy of Suzuki of America Corp.

Fig. 6: Measuring TCC Solenoid Resistance

Diagnostic Aids – An intermittent condition may be caused by a poor connection, damaged wire insulation or a wire which is broken inside the insulation. Inspect TCM harness connectors for damaged, corroded or backed-out terminal pins. Repair as necessary and retest system.

DTC P1700: THROTTLE POSITION (TP) SENSOR SIGNAL INPUT MALFUNCTION

NOTE: DTC P1700 will set if ON (zero volt) time of pulse signal from PCM to TCM is out of specified time.

1) Check for engine performance related DTCs. See SCAN TOOL METHOD under RETRIEVING TROUBLE CODES. If DTC P0122 or P0123 is present, see appropriate SELF-DIAGNOSTICS article in ENGINE PERFORMANCE in appropriate MITCHELL® manual. Repair as necessary. If specified DTCs are not present, go to next step.
2) Turn ignition on. Using a DVOM, check duty cycle (voltage on-time) between ground and TCM harness connector E25, terminal No. 1 (Orange wire). If reading is 8-13 volts at closed throttle, and 4-8 volts at Wide Open Throttle (WOT), check for an intermittent problem or faulty TCM. See DIAGNOSTIC AIDS. If reading is not as specified, go to next step.
3) Turn ignition off. Disconnect PCM harness connectors. Turn ignition on. Using a DVOM, measure voltage between ground and PCM harness connector E92, terminal No. 4 (Orange wire). *See Fig. 7.* If reading is 10-14 volts, check for an open in PCM power or ground circuits. See TCM POWER & GROUND CIRCUIT under TCM CIRCUIT CHECK. Repair as necessary. If no problems are found, substitute PCM with a known-good unit. If reading is not as specified, go to next step.
4) Check Orange wire for an open or short to ground. Check for short in cruise control module (if equipped). Repair as necessary. If no problems are found, substitute TCM with a known-good unit. Retest system.
Diagnostic Aids – An intermittent condition may be caused by a poor connection, damaged wire insulation or a wire which is broken inside the insulation. Inspect TCM harness connectors for damaged, corroded or backed-out terminal pins. Repair as necessary and retest system.

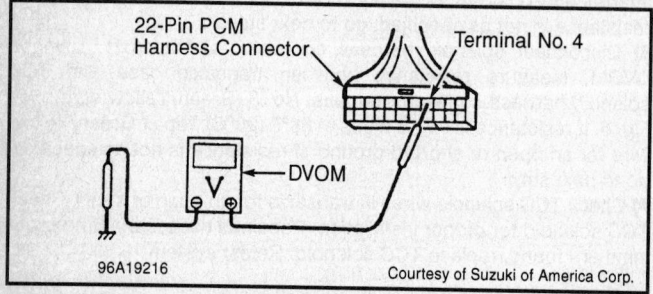

96A19216

Courtesy of Suzuki of America Corp.

Fig. 7: Measuring TP Sensor Signal Circuit Voltage

DTC P1705: ENGINE COOLANT TEMPERATURE (ECT) SENSOR SIGNAL INPUT MALFUNCTION

NOTE: DTC P1705 will set if voltage at TCM harness connector E25, terminal No. 10 (Gray/Black wire) is high (9-14 volts), or low (about zero volts) while engine is running.

1) Check for engine performance related DTCs. See SCAN TOOL METHOD under RETRIEVING TROUBLE CODES. If DTC P0117 or P0118 is present, see appropriate SELF-DIAGNOSTICS article in ENGINE PERFORMANCE in appropriate MITCHELL® manual. Repair as necessary. If specified DTCs are not present, go to next step.
2) Ensure engine is cold. Start engine. Using a DVOM, check duty cycle (voltage on-time) between ground and TCM harness connector E25, terminal No. 10 (Gray/Black wire). If reading is 3.4-4.6 volts with coolant temperature at 32-122°F (0-50°C), or 6.7-9.3 volts with coolant temperature greater than 122°F (50°C), check for an intermittent problem or faulty TCM. See DIAGNOSTIC AIDS. If reading is not as specified, go to next step.
3) Turn ignition off. Disconnect PCM harness connectors. Turn ignition on. Using a DVOM, measure voltage between ground and PCM harness connector E92, terminal No. 3 (Gray/Black wire). *See Fig. 8.* If reading is 9-14 volts, substitute PCM with a known-good unit. If reading is not as specified, go to next step.
4) Check Gray/Black wire for an open or short to ground. Repair as necessary. If wire is okay, substitute TCM with a known-good unit. Retest system.
Diagnostic Aids – An intermittent condition may be caused by a poor connection, damaged wire insulation or a wire which is broken inside the insulation. Inspect TCM harness connectors for damaged, corroded or backed-out terminal pins. Repair as necessary and retest system.

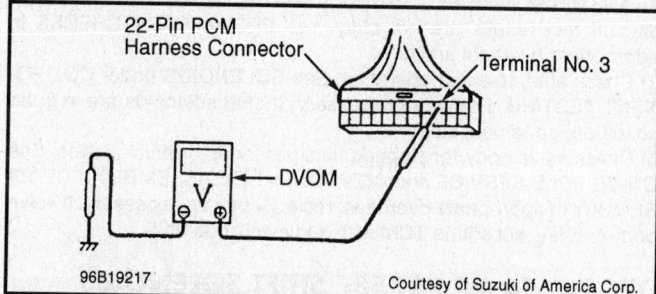

96B19217

Courtesy of Suzuki of America Corp.

Fig. 8: Measuring ECT Sensor Signal Circuit Voltage

COMPONENT TESTING

FORWARD CLUTCH CYLINDER REVOLUTION SENSOR

See DTC P0715: FORWARD CLUTCH CYLINDER REVOLUTION SENSOR under DIAGNOSTIC TESTING.

O/D CUT SWITCH

Turn ignition off. Remove console box. Disconnect O/D cut switch harness connector. Using a DVOM, check for continuity between O/D cut switch terminals. Continuity should only be present with switch in ON position. Replace O/D cut switch if continuity is not as specified.

SOLENOIDS

Shift Solenoids – 1) Using a DVOM, measure resistance between solenoid body and terminal of solenoid. Resistance should be 11-15 ohms at 68°F (20°C). Replace solenoid if resistance is not as specified.
2) Using an appropriate oiler (squirt can), apply ATF to oil feed hole of solenoid. *See Fig. 9.* ATF should not flow from solenoid. Using fused jumper wires, apply battery voltage to solenoid terminal, and ground to solenoid body. ATF should exhaust from solenoid. Replace solenoid if operation is not as specified.

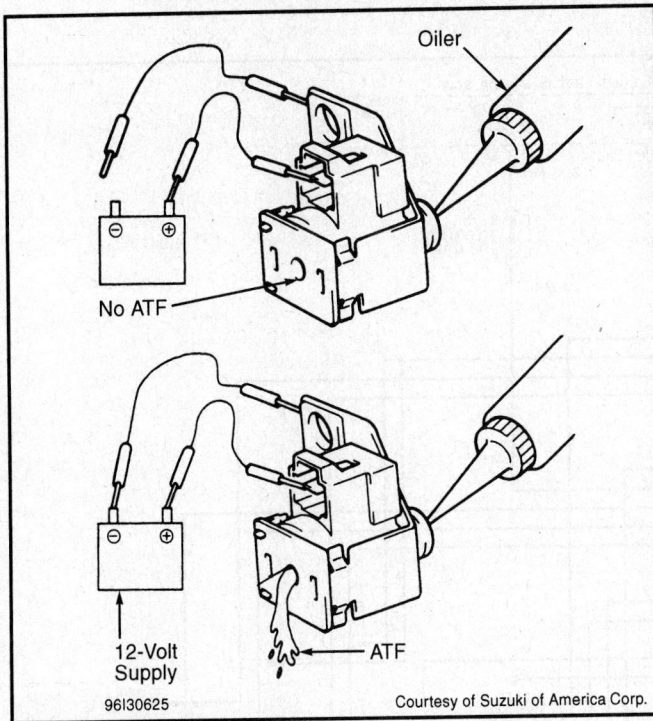

Fig. 9: Testing Shift Solenoids

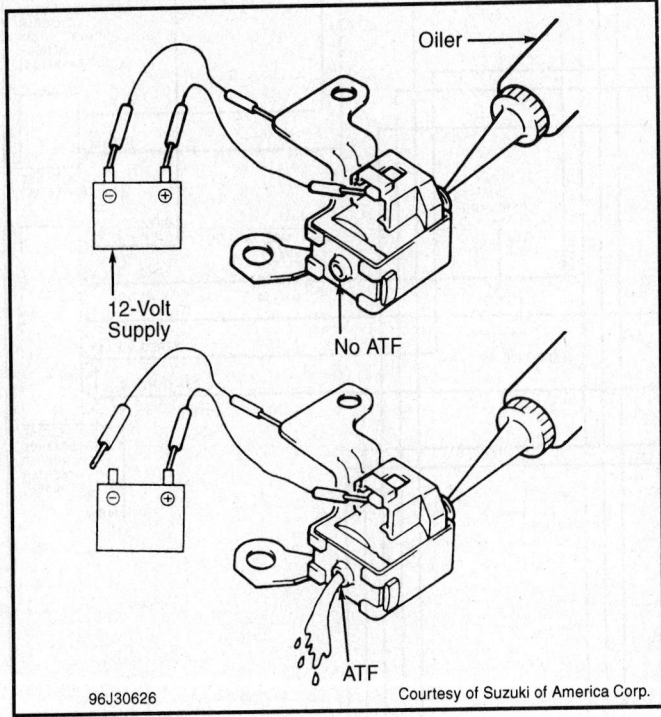

Fig. 10: Testing TCC Solenoid

TCC Solenoid – Using an appropriate oiler (squirt can), apply ATF to oil feed hole of solenoid. *See Fig. 10.* ATF should exhaust from solenoid. Using fused jumper wires, apply battery voltage to solenoid terminal, and ground to solenoid body. ATF should not flow from solenoid. Replace solenoid if operation is not as specified.

Throttle Pressure Control Solenoid – Using a DVOM, measure resistance between solenoid terminals. *See Fig. 11.* Resistance should be 3.3-3.7 ohms. Replace solenoid if resistance is not as specified.

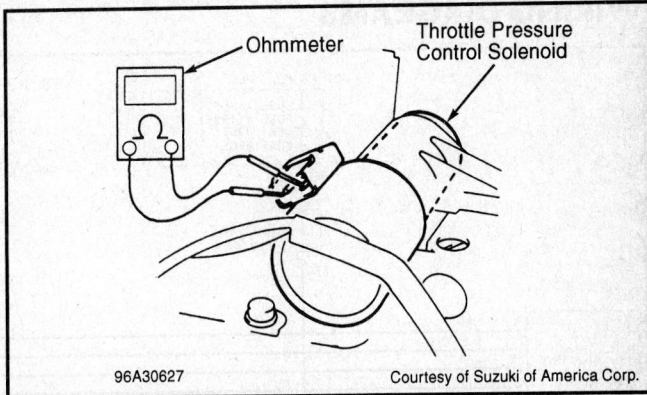

Fig. 11: Testing Throttle Pressure Control Solenoid

TRANSMISSION RANGE (TR) SWITCH

Turn ignition off. Disconnect TR switch harness connector located on side of transaxle. Using a DVOM, check for continuity between specified TR switch terminals in specified gear selector lever position. *See Fig. 12.* See TR SWITCH CONTINUITY table. Ensure continuity is not present between any terminal and transaxle case in any position. Replace TR switch if continuity is not as specified.

TR SWITCH CONTINUITY

Lever Position	Continuity Between Terminals
"P"	5 & 6, 8 & 9
"R"	1 & 8
"N"	5 & 6, 8 & 10
"D"	2 & 8
"2"	3 & 8
"L"	4 & 8

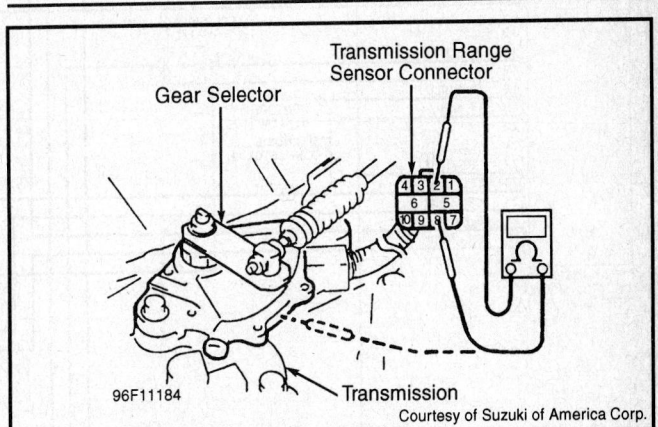

Fig. 12: Identifying TR Switch Terminals

VEHICLE SPEED SENSOR (VSS)

See steps **1)** and **2)** of DTC P0720: VEHICLE SPEED SENSOR (VSS) under DIAGNOSTIC TESTING.

AUTOMATIC TRANSMISSIONS
1996 Suzuki Esteem Electronic Controls (Cont.)

WIRING DIAGRAMS

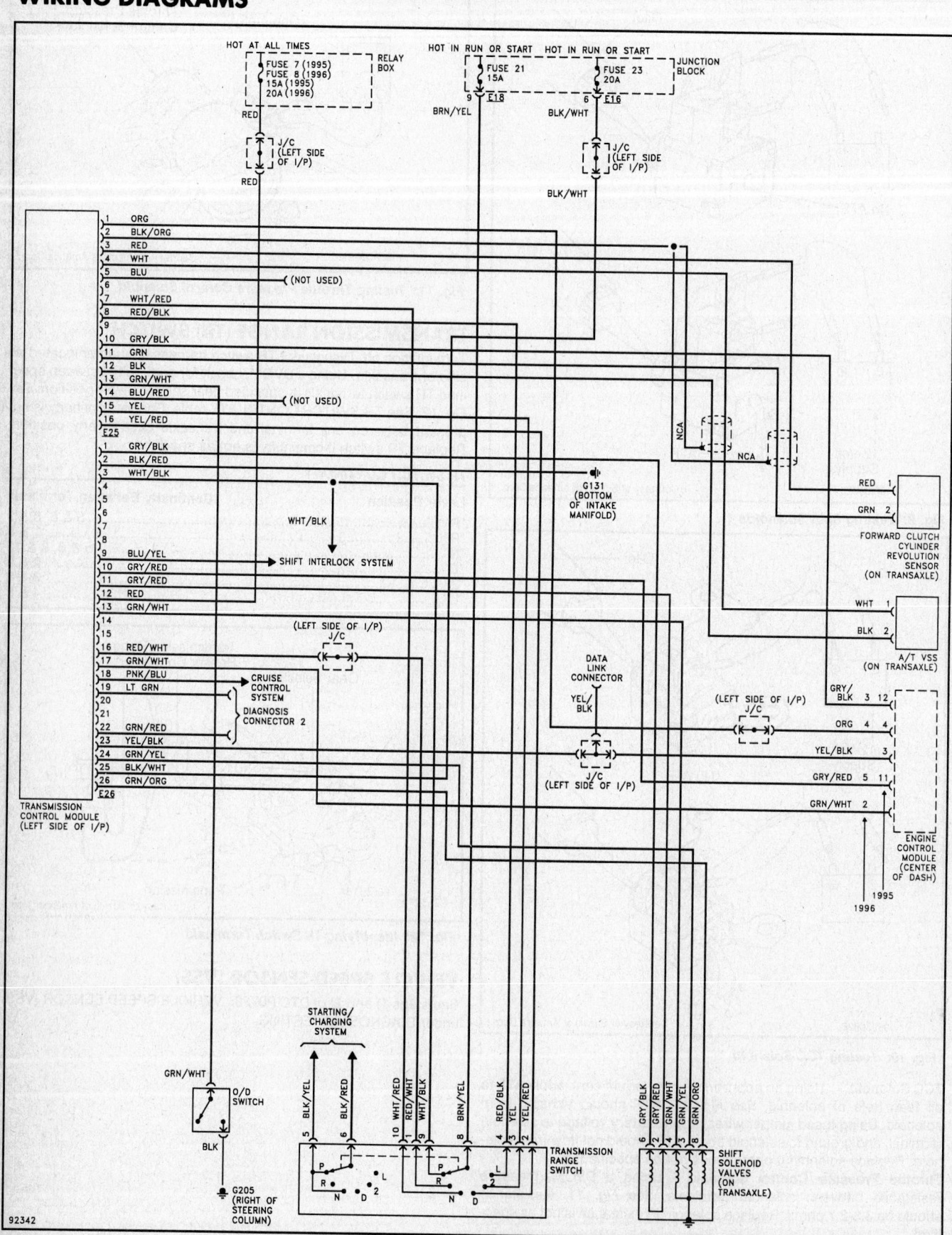

Fig. 13: Transaxle Wiring Diagram (1996 Suzuki Esteem)

Pickup, Previa, Tacoma

APPLICATION & LABOR TIMES

APPLICATION & LABOR TIMES

Vehicle Application	Labor Times [1] R & I	[2] Overhaul	Trans. Model
Pickup 2WD (2.4L) [3]	5.5	7.3	A-43D
Previa (Non-Supercharged) [3]			
2WD	4.1	6.6	A-46DE
AWD	4.6	6.7	A-46DF
Tacoma 2WD (2.4L)			
Manual Steering			
With A/C	10.2 [4]	7.3	A-43D
Without A/C	9.8 [4]	7.3	A-43D
Power Steering			
With A/C	10.8 [4]	7.3	A-43D
Without A/C	10.4 [4]	7.3	A-43D

[1] – Removal and installation of transmission from vehicle chassis.

[2] – Bench overhaul time for transmission. Does not include removal and installation.

[3] – 1995 only.

[4] – Requires engine removal.

CAUTION: Previa and Tacoma models are equipped with a Supplemental Restraint System (SRS). When servicing vehicle, use care to avoid accidental air bag deployment. All SRS electrical connections and wiring harness are covered by Yellow insulation. SRS-related components are located in steering column, center console, instrument panel and lower panel on instrument panel. DO NOT use electrical test equipment on these circuits. If necessary, deactivate SRS before servicing components. See AIR BAG SERVICING article in APPLICATIONS & IDENTIFICATION section.

IDENTIFICATION

Transmission is identified by Vehicle Identification Number (VIN). VIN locations are at front right side of frame, top left of instrument panel and driver's side door post. VIN is used to ensure correct application of component parts and assemblies.

DESCRIPTION

Transmission consists of a lock-up torque converter, oil pump, valve body assembly, front clutch, O/D direct clutch, rear clutch, 3 planetary gear sets, 4 clutch style brakes and 3 one-way clutches.

The A-46DE and A-46DF transmissions are electronically controlled. Transmission shifting and torque converter lock-up are controlled by 2 shift solenoids and a lock-up solenoid. Solenoids are controlled by an Electronic Controlled Transmission (ECT) Electronic Control Unit (ECU). Control unit is referred to as the ECT ECU. For electronic diagnosis, see TOYOTA A-46DE & A-46DF ELECTRONIC CONTROLS article.

The ECT ECU receives information from various input devices and uses this information to control No. 1 and No. 2 solenoids for transmission shifting and lock-up solenoid for torque converter lock-up.

An Overdrive (OD) switch is mounted on the shift lever. When OD switch is depressed to ON position, transmission will shift into 4th gear when shift lever is in "D" position, and OD OFF light on instrument panel will go off. When OD switch is released to OFF position, transmission will shift into 3rd gear, and OD OFF light on instrument panel will illuminate.

Transmission is equipped with a shift lock and key lock system. Shift lock system prevents shift lever from being moved from Park unless brake pedal is depressed. Key lock system prevents ignition key from being moved from ACC to LOCK position on ignition switch unless shift lever is in Park. For more information on shift lock and key lock system, see TOYOTA SHIFT LOCK SYSTEM article.

LUBRICATION & ADJUSTMENTS

See appropriate AUTOMATIC TRANSMISSION SERVICING article in TRANSMISSION SERVICING section.

TROUBLE SHOOTING

Preliminary Checks – Ensure fluid level is correct. Inspect and adjust throttle cable, shift linkage and park/neutral position switch (if necessary). Check idle speed RPM and adjust as necessary.

SYMPTOM DIAGNOSIS

Fluid Discolored Or Smells Burnt – Fluid contaminated, damaged torque converter or transmission assembly.

No Movement In Any Gear Position – Manual shift linkage or cable out of adjustment. Faulty valve body, primary regulator valve, parking lock pawl or torque converter. Damaged or broken converter drive plate or restricted oil filter.

Selector Lever Position Incorrect – Manual shift linkage or cable out of adjustment. Faulty manual valve and lever.

Harsh Engagement Into Any Forward Gear Position – Throttle cable out of adjustment. Faulty valve body, primary regulator valve, accumulator pistons or transmission assembly.

Delayed Upshifts Or Downshifts From OD-3 Or 3-2, Then Back To OD – Throttle cable or cam faulty or out of adjustment. Faulty governor, electronic controls, solenoid valve or valve body.

Slips On Upshift, Or Slips Or Shudders On Acceleration – Manual shift linkage, cable or throttle cable out of adjustment. Faulty valve body, solenoid valve or transmission assembly.

Drag Or Binding On Upshifts – Manual shift linkage or cable out of adjustment. Faulty valve body or transmission assembly. See CLUTCH & BRAKE APPLICATION CHART

Lock-Up Does Not Occur – Faulty electronic controls, valve body, solenoid valve or transmission assembly.

Harsh Downshift – Throttle cable or cam faulty or out of adjustment. Faulty accumulator pistons, valve body or transmission assembly.

No Downshift When Coasting – Faulty governor, valve body, electronic controls or solenoid valve.

Downshift Occurs Too Soon Or Too Late When Coasting – Throttle cable or cam faulty or out of adjustment. Faulty governor, valve body, electronic controls, solenoid valve or transmission assembly.

No OD-3, 3-2 Or 2-1 Kickdown – Throttle cable out of adjustment. Faulty governor, valve body, electronic controls or solenoid valve.

No Engine Braking In 2nd Or "L" Position – Faulty valve body, electronic controls, solenoid valve or transmission assembly.

Vehicle Does Not Hold In "P" Position – Manual shift linkage or cable out of adjustment. Faulty parking lock pawl cam and spring.

CLUTCH & BRAKE APPLICATION CHART

Selector Lever Position	Elements In Use
"D" (Drive)	
First Gear	Front Clutch, No. 2 One-Way Clutch, OD Direct Clutch & OD One-Way Clutch
Second Gear	Front Clutch, No. 1 One-Way Clutch, No. 2 Brake, OD Direct Clutch & OD One-Way Clutch
Third Gear	Front Clutch, No. 2 Brake, OD Direct Clutch, OD One-Way Clutch & Rear Clutch (Outer Piston)
OD (Fourth Gear)	Front Clutch, No. 2 Brake, OD Brake & Rear Clutch (Outer Piston)
"2" (Intermediate)	
First Gear	Front Clutch, No. 2 One-Way Clutch, OD Direct Clutch & OD One-Way Clutch
Second Gear	Front Clutch, No. 1 Brake, No. 2 Brake, No. 1 One-Way Clutch, OD Direct Clutch & OD One-Way Clutch
"L" (1st Gear)	Front Clutch, No. 3 Brake, No. 2 One-Way Clutch, OD Direct Clutch & OD One-Way Clutch
"R" (Reverse)	No. 3 Brake, OD Direct Clutch, OD One-Way Clutch & Rear Clutch
"N" (Neutral)	OD Direct Clutch & OD One-Way Clutch
"P" (Park)	No. 3 Brake, OD Direct Clutch & OD One-Way Clutch

3-1478

AUTOMATIC TRANSMISSIONS
Toyota A-43D, A-46DE & A-46DF (Cont.)

TESTING

NOTE: For electronic diagnosis and component testing of A-46DE and A-46DF transmissions, see appropriate TOYOTA ELECTRONIC CONTROLS article.

PRELIMINARY CHECKS

1) Before testing transmission, ensure fluid level is correct and selector lever, throttle cable and idle speed are adjusted correctly. Battery must be fully charged for accurate testing.

2) To aid in transmission fault diagnosis, determine if fault is hydraulic, electronic or a combination of both. Electronic control transmissions are capable of storing self-diagnostic codes. To determine if a fault is electrical, retrieve any stored diagnostic trouble codes. See TOYOTA A-46DE & A-46DF ELECTRONIC CONTROLS article for electronic diagnosis.

TIME LAG TEST

1) Engine and transmission must be at normal operating temperature. Start engine and ensure idle RPM is within specification with A/C off. Idle speed for Pickup and Previa is 750 RPM in Neutral. Idle speed for Tacoma is 700 RPM in Neutral. Apply service and parking brakes. Using stop watch, measure time until engagement shock is felt when selector lever is shifted from "N" to "D" position.

2) Allow one minute intervals between tests. Perform time measurements 2 more times and calculate average value. Time should be less than 1.2 seconds. Repeat test procedure to test time lag when selector lever is shifted from "N" to "R" position. Time lag should be less than 1.5 seconds.

Time Lag Test Results

- **"N" To "D" Position Time Lag Is Greater Than Specified:** Low line pressure, worn front clutch or OD one-way clutch not operating correctly.
- **"N" To "R" Position Time Lag Is Greater Than Specified:** Low line pressure, worn rear clutch, worn No. 3 brake or OD one-way clutch not operating correctly.

ROAD TEST

"D" Position Test – 1) Engine and transmission must be at normal operating temperature. Shift transmission into "D" position with OD switch in ON position. Depress accelerator pedal to full throttle. Ensure all upshifts and downshifts occur at specified points. Refer to appropriate SHIFT SPEED SPECIFICATIONS table.

2) Ensure lock-up occurs at appropriate speeds. See LOCK-UP SPEED SPECIFICATIONS table. Lightly depress accelerator pedal. If excessive increase in engine RPM exists, lock-up did not occur.

NOTE: A 3-OD upshift will not occur with a throttle valve opening greater than 86 percent or if coolant temperature is below 122°F (50°C). A OD-3 kickdown is always possible with throttle valve opening of 86 percent or greater. Lock-up does not occur at coolant temperatures below 158°F (70°C).

3) Check for shock and slippage at all upshifts. Drive vehicle in 3rd and OD. Check for abnormal noise and vibration. While driving in OD, "D", 3rd and 2nd gear, ensure speeds at 2-1, 3-2 and OD-3 kickdown are within specification. Check for shock and slippage at kickdown.

"D" Position Test Results

- **No 1-2 Upshift:** Defective governor or stuck 1-2 shift valve or No. 2 solenoid.
- **No 2-3 Upshift:** Stuck 2-3 shift valve or No. 1 solenoid.
- **No 3-OD Upshift With Throttle Opening Less Than 86 Percent:** Stuck 3-OD shift valve. If shift point is not within specification, check for misadjusted throttle cable or defective throttle valve, 1-2, 2-3 or 3-OD shift valve.
- **Lock-Up Does Not Occur:** Stuck shift solenoid or lock-up relay valve.

- **Excessive Shock & Slippage:** High line pressure, defective accumulator or check balls. Abnormal noise and vibration may be caused by unbalance in drive shaft, differential, tires or torque converter.

"2" Position Test – Shift transmission to "2" position. With accelerator pedal held at full throttle, check for proper 1-2 upshift at specified throttle positions. See appropriate SHIFT SPEED SPECIFICATIONS table. While driving vehicle in 2nd gear, release accelerator and check engine braking effect. If engine braking does not exist, No. 1 brake is defective.

"L" Position Test – While driving vehicle in "L" position, check for failure to upshift to 2nd gear. Check engine braking effect when accelerator is released. If engine braking does not exist, No. 3 brake is defective.

"R" Position Test – Shift vehicle to "R" position. Accelerate vehicle and check for transmission slippage.

"P" Position Test – Stop vehicle on incline of 5 degrees or steeper. Shift vehicle to "P" position and release parking brake. Ensure parking lock pawl prevents vehicle from moving.

PICKUP A-43D SHIFT SPEED SPECIFICATIONS [1]

Application	MPH
"D" Position	
1st-2nd	35-45
2nd-3rd	66-77
3rd-OD [2]	No Shift
OD-3rd	[3]
3rd-2nd	59-70
2nd-1st	22-30
"L" Position	
2nd-1st	29-39

[1] – At wide open throttle.
[2] – 3-OD upshift point with closed throttle is at 24-32 MPH.
[3] – OD-3 downshift is possible up to maximum speed.

PREVIA A-46DE & A-46DF SHIFT SPEED SPECIFICATIONS [1]

Application	MPH
"D" Position	
1st-2nd	35-38
2nd-3rd	62-68
3rd-OD	89-94
3rd-OD [2]	No Shift
OD-3rd	[3]
OD-3rd	85-91
3rd-2nd	58-64
2nd-1st	31-34
"2" Position	
1st-2nd	35-38
3rd-2nd	62-66
2nd-1st	31-34
"L" Position	
2nd-1st	31-34

[1] – At wide open throttle.
[2] – 3-OD upshift point with closed throttle is at 25-27 MPH.
[3] – OD-3 downshift point with closed throttle is at 16-19 MPH.

PREVIA A-46DE & A-46DF LOCK-UP SPEED SPECIFICATIONS [1]

Application	MPH
Lock-Up ON	
3rd [2] & OD	43-47
Lock-Up OFF	
3rd [2] & OD	40-43

[1] – With vehicle in "D" position and throttle valve opened 5 percent.
[2] – With OD switch in OFF position.

AUTOMATIC TRANSMISSIONS
Toyota A-43D, A-46DE & A-46DF (Cont.)

3-1479

TACOMA A-43D SHIFT SPEED SPECIFICATIONS [1]

Application	MPH
"D" Position	
1st-2nd	34-43
2nd-3rd	63-72
3rd-OD [2]	No Shift
OD-3rd	[3]
3rd-2nd	60-69
2nd-1st	27-35
"L" Position	
2nd-1st	29-40

[1] – At wide open throttle.
[2] – 3-OD upshift point with closed throttle is at 27-34 MPH.
[3] – OD-3 downshift is possible up to maximum speed.

STALL SPEED TEST

1) Ensure engine and transmission are at normal operating temperature. Connect tachometer to vehicle and ensure it is visible to driver. Apply parking brake and block front wheels.

CAUTION: DO NOT maintain stall speed RPM for more than 5 seconds.

2) Start engine, apply brakes and place transmission in "D" position. Depress accelerator to full throttle and note maximum RPM obtained. Repeat test in "R" position. Stall speed for Pickup should be 1750-2050 RPM. Stall speed for Previa should be 2450-2750 RPM. Stall speed for Tacoma should be 1700-2000 RPM.

Stall Speed Test Results
- **Stall Speed Is Same In Both Positions, But Less Than Specified:** Engine output may be insufficient or defective stator one-way clutch.

NOTE: If stall speed RPM is more than 600 RPM lower than specification, torque converter may be faulty.

- **Stall Speed High In "D" Position:** Low line pressure, slipping front clutch or defective No. 2 or OD one-way clutch.
- **Stall Speed High In "R" Position:** Low line pressure, rear clutch slipping, No. 3 brake slipping or defective OD one-way clutch.
- **Stall Speed High In Both Positions:** Low line pressure, improper fluid level or defective OD one-way clutch.

HYDRAULIC PRESSURE TESTS

NOTE: Hydraulic pressure tests should be performed with transmission fluid temperature at normal operating temperature of 122-176°F (50-80°C).

Line Pressure Test – 1) Ensure transmission fluid is at normal operating temperature. Connect appropriate pressure gauge to line pressure test port on transmission. *See Fig. 1.*
2) Connect tachometer to vehicle and ensure it is visible to driver. Block all 4 wheels and fully apply parking brake. Start engine and ensure idle speed is adjusted to specification.
3) Apply service brake and shift transmission to "D" position. Check line pressure at idle and record pressure reading. Accelerate vehicle to stall speed and record line pressure reading.
4) Repeat test procedure in "R" position. If line pressures are not as specified, check throttle cable adjustment. Adjust throttle cable (if necessary), and repeat test procedure and record pressure readings. Compare all readings to specification. See appropriate LINE PRESSURE SPECIFICATIONS table.

PICKUP & TACOMA LINE PRESSURE SPECIFICATIONS

Engine Speed	"D" Position psi (kg/cm²)	"R" Position psi (kg/cm²)
Idle Speed	64-73 (4.5-5.1)	97-108 (6.8-7.6)
Stall Speed	144-169 (10.1-11.9)	213-270 (15.0-19.0)

PREVIA LINE PRESSURE SPECIFICATIONS

Engine Speed	"D" Position psi (kg/cm²)	"R" Position psi (kg/cm²)
Idle Speed	53-58 (3.7-4.1)	73-81 (5.1-5.7)
Stall Speed	152-173 (10.6-12.2)	196-231 (13.8-16.3)

Line Pressure Test Results
- **Line Pressure High In Both Positions:** Defective regulator valve or throttle valve, or throttle cable out of adjustment.
- **Line Pressure Low In Both Positions:** Defective oil pump, regulator valve, throttle valve or OD direct clutch, or throttle cable out of adjustment.
- **Line Pressure Low In "D" Position Only:** Defective front clutch or fluid leak in "D" position circuit.
- **Line Pressure Low In "R" Position Only:** Defective rear clutch, No. 3 brake or internal fluid leak in reverse circuit.

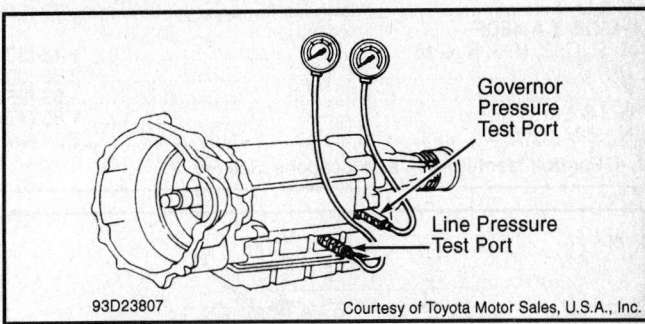

93D23807   Courtesy of Toyota Motor Sales, U.S.A., Inc.

Fig. 1: Identifying Transmission Hydraulic Pressure Test Ports

Governor Pressure Test (A-43D Only) – 1) Install pressure gauge to governor pressure port on transmission. *See Fig. 1.* Start engine and release parking brake. With transmission in "D" position, slowly depress accelerator and check governor pressure at specified speed. See GOVERNOR PRESSURE SPECIFICATIONS table.

CAUTION: Road test vehicle or use dynamometer to check governor pressures exceeding minimum vehicle speed specification.

2) If governor pressures are incorrect, possible causes are: incorrect line pressure, fluid leakage in governor pressure circuit or defective governor valve.

GOVERNOR PRESSURE SPECIFICATIONS (A-43D)

Vehicle & Speed (MPH)	Output Shaft RPM	Pressure psi (kg/cm²)
Pickup		
20	1000	13-21 (.9-1.5)
35	1800	23-31 (1.6-2.2)
69	3500	58-75 (4.1-5.3)
Tacoma		
20	1000	14-23 (1.0-1.6)
35	1800	28-37 (2.0-2.6)
69	3500	73-90 (5.1-6.3)

ON-VEHICLE SERVICE

VALVE BODY ASSEMBLY

Removal – Remove drain plug and drain ATF. Remove oil pan and gasket. Remove magnets from oil pan. Note location of oil tubes. Using screwdrivers, carefully pry at both ends of oil tubes and remove oil tubes. Disconnect solenoid wiring. Remove oil strainer (filter) and gasket. Remove valve body assembly retaining bolts. Note bolt location and length. See VALVE BODY ASSEMBLY BOLT SPECIFICATIONS table. *See Fig. 2.* Slightly lower valve body assembly. Disconnect throttle cable from valve assembly cam. Remove valve body assembly.

3-1480

AUTOMATIC TRANSMISSIONS
Toyota A-43D, A-46DE & A-46DF (Cont.)

Installation – **1)** To install, reverse removal procedure. Ensure manual shift lever in transmission case aligns with manual valve of valve body assembly. Connect throttle cable to cam.

2) Loosely install appropriate bolts in correct positions. *See Fig. 2.* Install valve body assembly and tighten bolts to 89 INCH lbs. (10 N.m). Install oil strainer and tighten bolts to 48 INCH lbs. (5.4 N.m). Ensure magnets are installed in oil pan. Install oil pan and tighten bolts to 48 INCH lbs. (5.4 N.m). Fill transmission with ATF to proper fluid level.

VALVE BODY ASSEMBLY BOLT SPECIFICATIONS [1]

Bolt Identification	In. (mm)
A-43D	
A, I & J	2.17 (55)
B	1.57 (40)
C, D & M	1.42 (36)
E & F	.98 (25)
G	1.85 (47)
H & N	1.18 (30)
K & L	.79 (20)
A-46DE & A-46DF	
A, B, C, E, H, J, K, & M	1.18 (30)
D	2.36 (60)
F	.98 (25)
G, I & L	1.85 (47)
N	N/A

[1] – For bolt identification and locations, *See Fig. 2.*

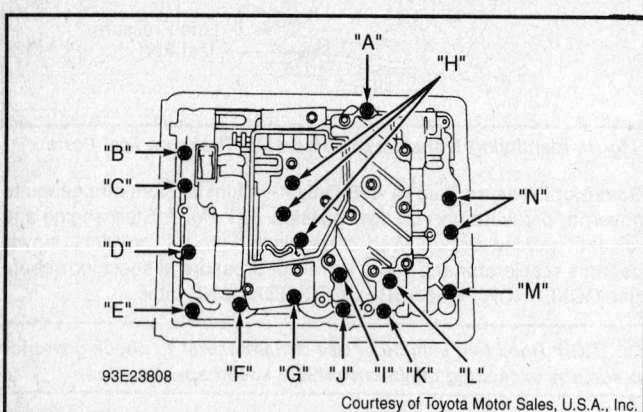

93E23808

Courtesy of Toyota Motor Sales, U.S.A., Inc.

Fig. 2: Identifying Control Valve Assembly Bolt Locations

EXTENSION HOUSING & GOVERNOR ASSEMBLY

Removal – **1)** Raise and support vehicle. Place reference marks on drive shaft and companion flange. Remove drive shaft, speedometer cable and speedometer driven gear. Remove speed sensors (if equipped). Support transmission with jack. Remove transmission-to-crossmember bolts and rear mount from extension housing.

2) Remove extension housing bolts and remove extension housing. Note bolt length and location. On 4WD vehicles, remove transfer case and adaptor. See appropriate article in AXLE SHAFTS & TRANSFER CASES section.

3) Remove snap ring, speedometer drive gear, lock ball and remaining snap ring from output shaft. Remove staked area on lock plate. Remove lock plate bolt. Using screwdriver, remove retaining clip from hole of output shaft. Remove governor assembly (if applicable).

Cleaning & Inspection – Clean components with solvent. Dry with compressed air. Inspect components for damage. Measure inside diameter of extension housing bushing. Replace extension housing if bushing inside diameter exceeds 1.4996" (38.090 mm).

Installation – **1)** To install, reverse removal procedure. Ensure output shaft bolt hole is aligned with governor assembly. Install lock plate and bolt and tighten bolt to 35 INCH lbs. (3.9 N.m). Stake lock plate. Install retaining clip so it engages with hole of output shaft. Install extension housing and NEW gasket. Clean all bolt threads.

2) Apply thread sealant to 4 upper extension housing bolts prior to installation. Install short bolts to bottom of extension housing. Tighten

bolts to 25 ft. lbs. (34 N.m). Install engine rear mount to extension housing. Tighten bolts to 18 ft. lbs. (25 N.m). Tighten rear mount bracket bolts to 115 INCH lbs. (13 N.m). Fill transmission to proper level with ATF.

PARKING LOCK PAWL

Removal & Installation – **1)** Remove valve body assembly. Remove parking lock pawl bolts and bracket. Disconnect parking lock rod from manual valve lever. Remove "E" ring from shaft. Pull out shaft and remove spring and parking lock pawl. *See Fig. 7.*

2) To install, reverse removal procedures. Prior to installing parking lock pawl bracket bolts, push lock rod forward. Finger tighten bolts and ensure parking lock pawl operates smoothly. Tighten bracket bolts to 65 INCH lbs. (7.4 N.m).

PARK/NEUTRAL POSITION (PNP) SWITCH

For PNP switch adjustment, see appropriate AUTOMATIC TRANSMISSION SERVICING article in TRANSMISSION SERVICING section.

SHIFT LINKAGE

For shift linkage adjustment, see appropriate AUTOMATIC TRANSMISSION SERVICING article in TRANSMISSION SERVICING section.

THROTTLE CABLE

For throttle cable adjustment, see appropriate AUTOMATIC TRANSMISSION SERVICING article in TRANSMISSION SERVICING section.

REMOVAL & INSTALLATION

For transmission removal and installation procedure, see appropriate AUTOMATIC TRANSMISSION REMOVAL article in TRANSMISSION SERVICING section.

TORQUE CONVERTER

NOTE: Torque converter is a sealed unit and must be serviced as complete assembly. Perform following tests to check converter condition. Torque converter and transmission cooler must be thoroughly cleaned and flushed if transmission fluid is contaminated.

ONE-WAY CLUTCH TEST

1) Install turner and stopper of One-Way Clutch Tester (09350-30020) in torque converter. *See Fig. 3.* Turner fits in inner race of one-way clutch. Stopper fits in notch of converter hub and outer race of one-way clutch.

2) Clutch should lock when rotated counterclockwise, and turn freely when rotated clockwise. If necessary, clean converter and retest clutch. Replace converter if clutch fails test.

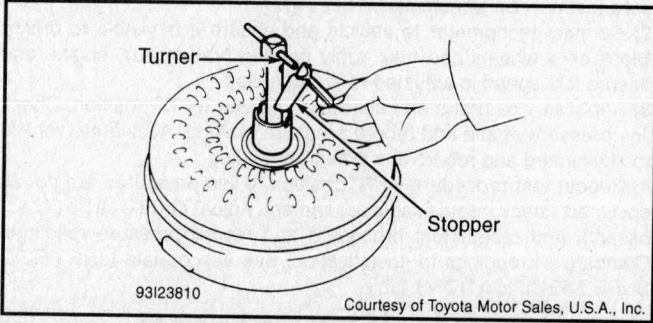

93I23810

Courtesy of Toyota Motor Sales, U.S.A., Inc.

Fig. 3: Checking Torque Converter One-Way Clutch

DRIVE PLATE RUNOUT TEST

Measure drive plate runout. *See Fig. 4.* If runout exceeds .008" (.20 mm), or if ring gear is damaged, replace drive plate. If installing a new

AUTOMATIC TRANSMISSIONS
Toyota A-43D, A-46DE & A-46DF (Cont.)

3-1481

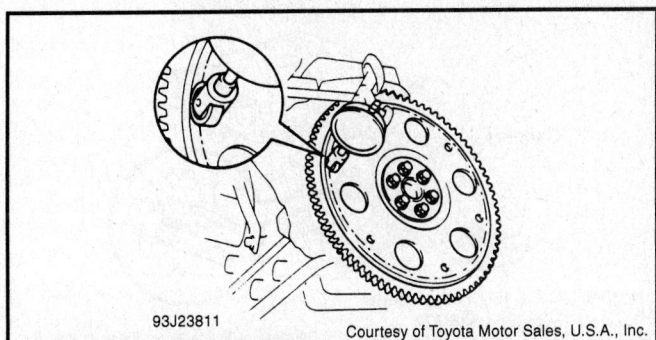

Fig. 4: Checking Drive Plate Runout

drive plate, note position of spacers. On Pickup, tighten bolts to 61 ft. lbs. (83 N.m). On Previa and Tacoma, tighten bolts to 55 ft. lbs. (74 N.m).

CONVERTER SLEEVE RUNOUT TEST

1) Temporarily mount torque converter to drive plate. Mount a dial indicator with needle resting on converter sleeve. *See Fig. 5.* Rotate converter. If runout exceeds .012" (.30 mm), ensure converter is properly mounted to drive plate and drive plate is not broken or bent.
2) If converter is properly mounted and runout exceeds specification, replace torque converter. Mark position of converter to ensure correct installation. Remove converter from drive plate.

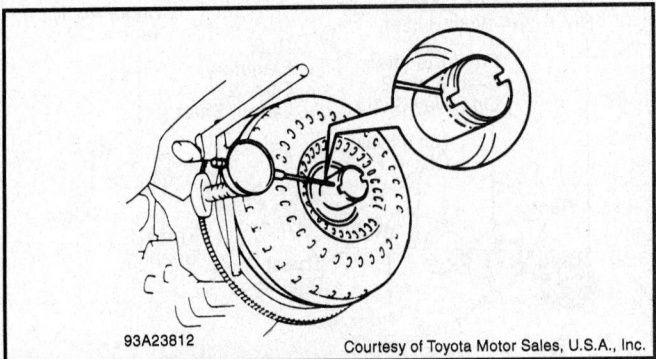

Fig. 5: Checking Converter Sleeve Runout

TRANSMISSION DISASSEMBLY

1) Remove wire harness clamp and throttle cable from converter housing. Remove control shaft lever. Remove overdrive solenoid, PNP switch, speedometer driven gear and speed sensors (if equipped). *See Fig. 6.* On AWD vehicles, remove transfer case. See appropriate article in AXLE SHAFTS & TRANSFER CASES section.

2) Remove oil pump bolts. Using appropriate 2-jaw puller, remove oil pump from transmission case. Remove bearing and race from rear of oil pump. Remove converter housing bolts. Note length and bolt location. While holding input shaft, remove converter housing. Remove "O" ring from OD case.
3) Remove extension housing and gasket. Note bolt length and location. Remove oil supply tube. Remove transfer adaptor (if equipped). On A-43D models, remove snap ring, speedometer drive gear, lock ball and remaining snap ring from output shaft. *See Fig. 6.*

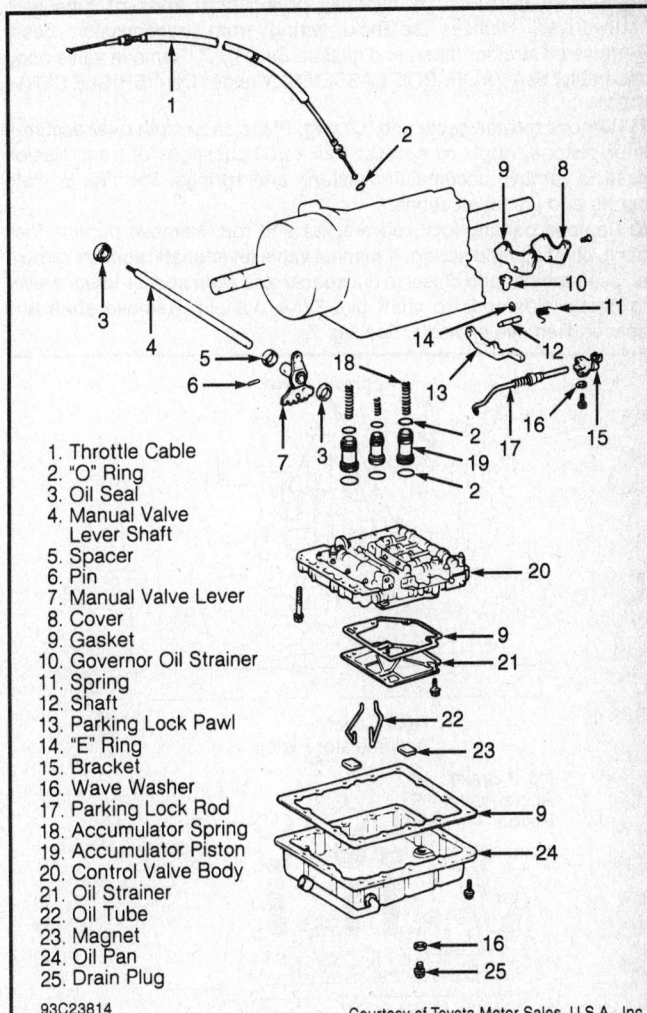

1. Throttle Cable
2. "O" Ring
3. Oil Seal
4. Manual Valve Lever Shaft
5. Spacer
6. Pin
7. Manual Valve Lever
8. Cover
9. Gasket
10. Governor Oil Strainer
11. Spring
12. Shaft
13. Parking Lock Pawl
14. "E" Ring
15. Bracket
16. Wave Washer
17. Parking Lock Rod
18. Accumulator Spring
19. Accumulator Piston
20. Control Valve Body
21. Oil Strainer
22. Oil Tube
23. Magnet
24. Oil Pan
25. Drain Plug

Fig. 7: Identifying Transmission Case Components

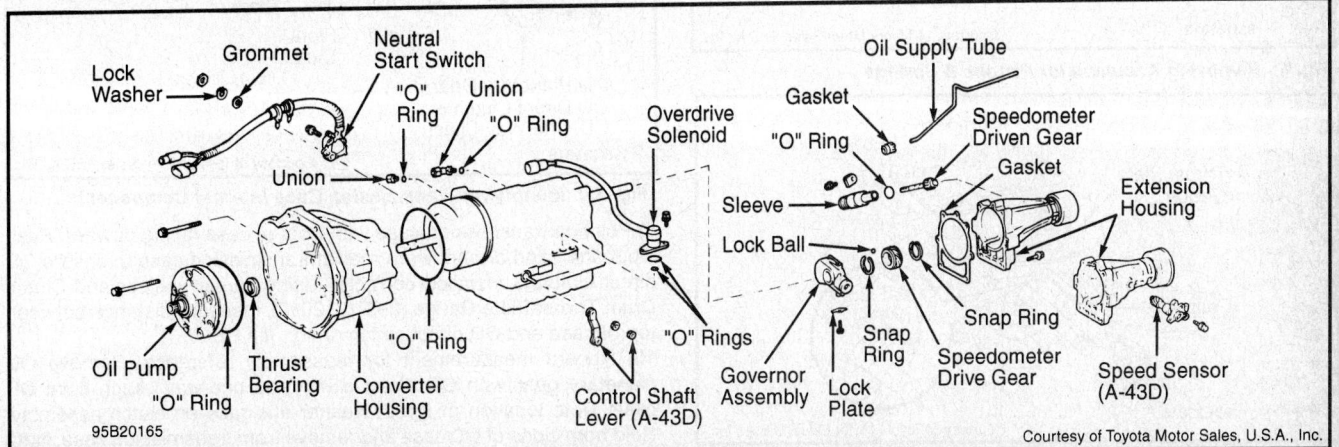

Fig. 6: Identifying Transmission & Extension Housing Components (A-43D Shown; A-46DE & A-46DF Are Similar)

3-1482

AUTOMATIC TRANSMISSIONS
Toyota A-43D, A-46DE & A-46DF (Cont.)

4) On all other models, remove snap ring from output shaft and remove speed sensor rotor and key. On A-43D models, remove staked area on lock plate. Remove governor assembly lock plate bolt. Using screwdriver, lift retaining clip from hole of output shaft. Remove governor assembly.

5) Remove cover, gasket and governor oil strainer from rear of transmission case. On all models, remove oil pan and gasket. Remove magnets from oil pan. Inspect magnets and pan for metal or brass particles.

6) Remove oil tubes by carefully prying both ends of tube with screwdriver. Remove solenoid wiring from transmission case. Remove oil strainer (filter) and gasket. See Fig. 7. Remove valve body assembly. See VALVE BODY ASSEMBLY under ON-VEHICLE SERVICE.

7) Remove throttle cable and "O" ring. Place shop cloth over accumulator pistons. Apply compressed air to oil passages of transmission case to remove accumulator pistons and springs. See Fig. 8. Note spring and piston locations.

8) Remove parking lock rod bracket and rod. Remove parking lock pawl, pivot pin and spring. If manual valve lever shaft requires removal, use hammer and chisel to cut spacer and slide spacer toward lever to obtain clearance to shaft pin. Drive out pin. Remove shaft and spacer. Remove oil seals. See Fig. 7.

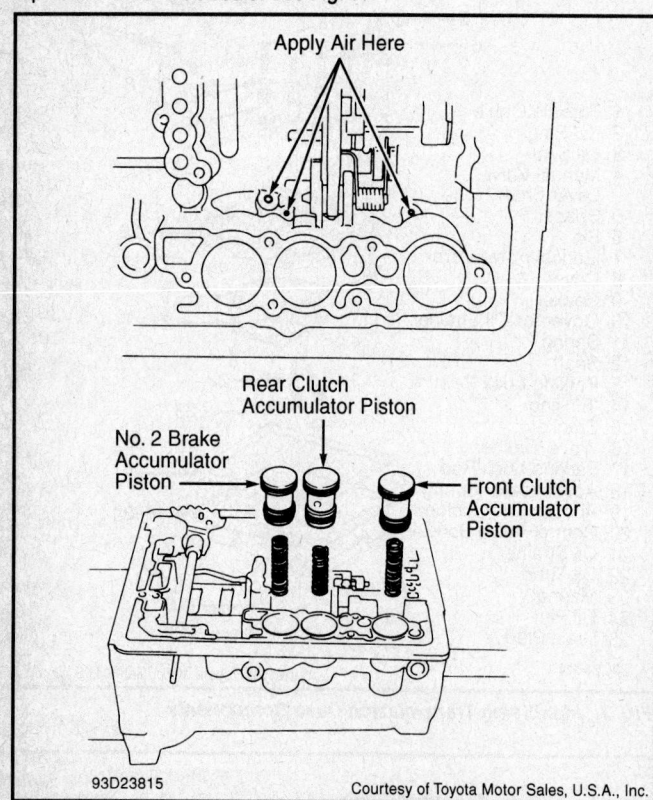

Fig. 8: Removing Accumulator Pistons & Springs

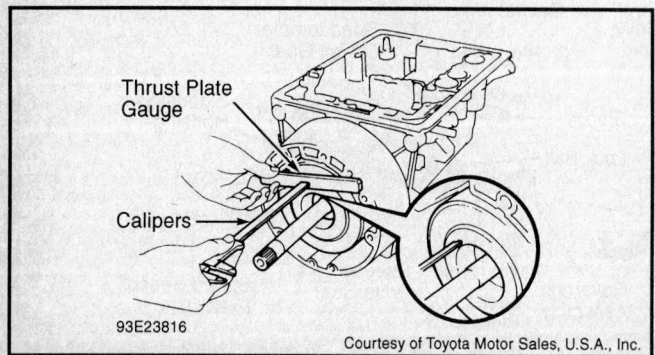

Fig. 9: Measuring OD Direct Clutch Drum Clearance

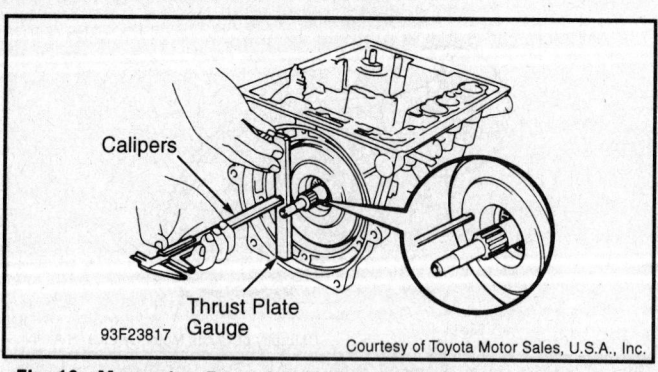

Fig. 10: Measuring Front Clutch Drum Clearance

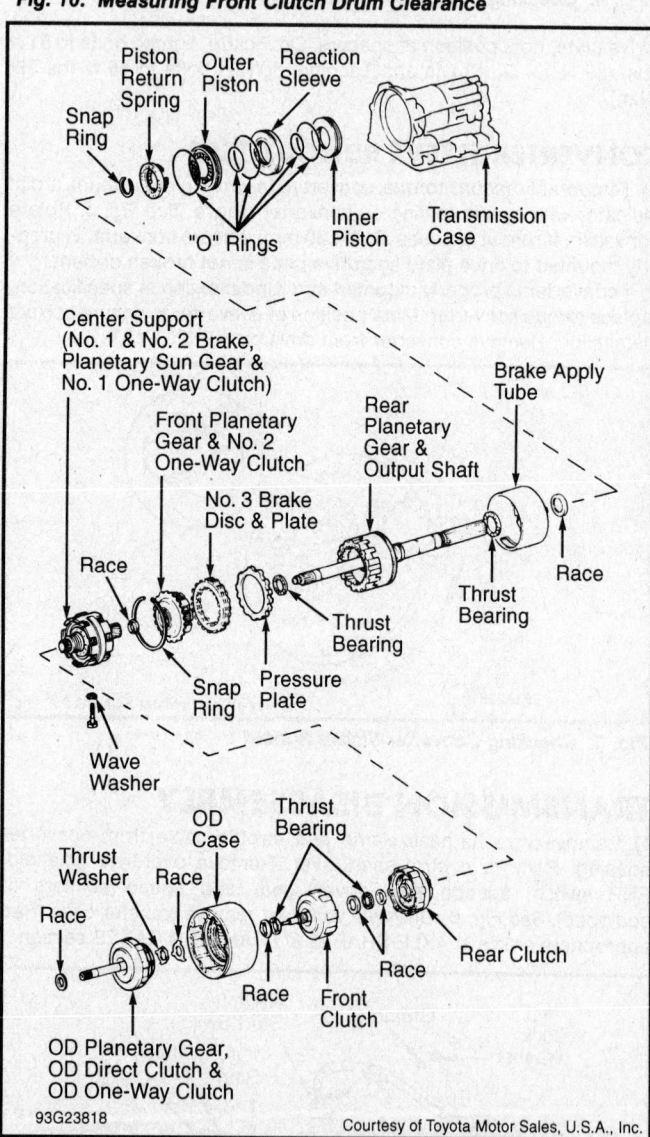

Fig. 11: Identifying Transmission Case Internal Components

9) Position transmission case with front of case facing upward. Push input shaft and drum toward rear of transmission case to ensure OD direct clutch is installed correctly. Using vernier caliper and Clutch Drum Thrust Plate Gauge (09370-12010), measure distance between top of case and OD direct clutch drum. See Fig. 9.

10) Record measurement for reassembly reference. Remove OD planetary gear with OD direct clutch and one-way clutch from OD case. Note location of thrust washer and race on clutch assembly. Hold both sides of OD case and remove from transmission case. Note location of bearing and race. See Fig. 11.

AUTOMATIC TRANSMISSIONS
Toyota A-43D, A-46DE & A-46DF (Cont.)

3-1483

11) Push input shaft and drum toward rear of transmission case. Ensure front clutch is installed correctly. Using vernier caliper and Clutch Drum Thrust Plate Gauge (09370-12010), measure distance between top of case and front clutch drum. *See Fig. 10.* Record measurement for reassembly reference.

12) Remove front clutch assembly from transmission case. Note location of bearings and race. Remove rear clutch assembly. Remove center support-to-case retaining bolts. Bolts are located at valve body side of case. *See Fig. 11.*

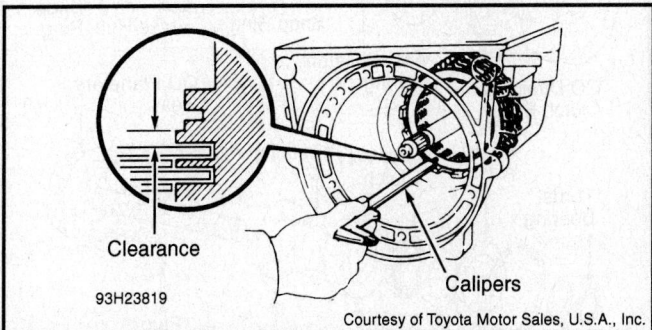

Clearance

93H23819

Calipers

Courtesy of Toyota Motor Sales, U.S.A., Inc.

Fig. 12: Measuring No. 3 Brake Pack Clearance

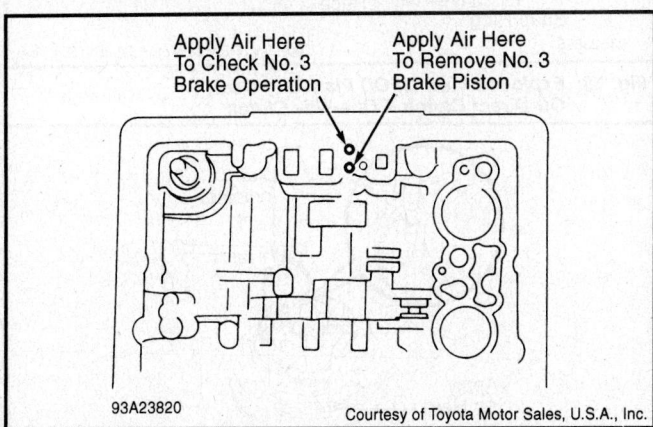

Apply Air Here To Check No. 3 Brake Operation

Apply Air Here To Remove No. 3 Brake Piston

93A23820

Courtesy of Toyota Motor Sales, U.S.A., Inc.

Fig. 13: Checking No. 3 Brake Operation & Removing Piston

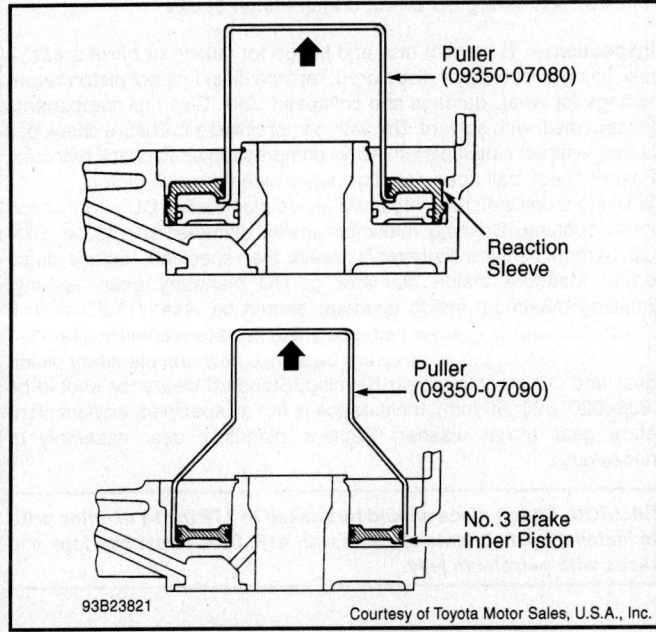

Puller (09350-07080)

Reaction Sleeve

Puller (09350-07090)

No. 3 Brake Inner Piston

93B23821

Courtesy of Toyota Motor Sales, U.S.A., Inc.

Fig. 14: Removing Reaction Sleeve & No. 3 Brake Piston

13) Remove center support and sun gear shaft assembly from transmission case. Note direction of bearing race on end of sun gear. Using 2 screwdrivers, remove front planetary gear snap ring. Remove snap ring. Insert 2 wires into planetary gear and remove gear. Using calipers, measure pack clearance of No. 3 brake between disc and transmission case. *See Fig. 12.* Pack clearance should be .024-.104" (.61-2.64 mm). If clearance is not as specified, inspect brake discs.

14) Remove No. 3 brake pack and pressure plate. Remove rear planetary gear, output shaft and 2 bearings. Remove brake apply tube. *See Fig. 11.* Remove race from transmission case. Ensure No. 3 brake pistons move smoothly when applying compressed air into transmission case. *See Fig. 13.*

15) Using appropriate spring compressor, compress No. 3 brake piston return spring. Remove snap ring. Remove piston return spring. Hold outer piston with hand, apply compressed air to case and remove outer piston.

16) Insert Puller (09350-07080) behind reaction sleeve and gradually lift sleeve out of transmission case. Insert Puller (09350-07090) behind inner piston and lift piston out of transmission case. *See Figs. 11 and 14.* Measure inside diameter of transmission case rear bushing. Replace transmission case if diameter exceeds 1.5035" (38.188 mm).

COMPONENT DISASSEMBLY & REASSEMBLY

OIL PUMP ASSEMBLY

Disassembly – Place oil pump assembly on torque converter. Remove seal rings from stator shaft. Remove stator shaft from oil pump housing. Place reference mark on drive and driven gears and remove from pump housing. If oil seal requires replacement, pry seal from housing with a screwdriver. *See Fig. 15.*

Inspection – **1)** Clean all components in solvent. Dry with compressed air. Inspect all components for damage or wear. Measure inside diameter of oil pump housing and stator shaft bushings. Measure driven gear-to-housing clearance and gear tip clearance. Using feeler gauge and straightedge, measure gear side clearance between pump housing face and top of gears. *See Fig. 16.*

2) Ensure all measurements are within specification. See OIL PUMP SPECIFICATIONS table. If bushing inside diameter exceeds specification, oil pump housing or stator shaft must be replaced. Replace necessary components to obtain correct clearances.

OIL PUMP SPECIFICATIONS

Application	Standard In. (mm)	Maximum In. (mm)
Gear Side Clearance	.0008-.0020 (.020-.050)	.004 (.10)
Gear Tip Clearance	.0043-.0055 (.109-.140)	.012 (.30)
Gear-To-Housing	.0028-.0059 (.071-.150)	.012 (.30)
Housing Bushing	N/A	1.5035 (38.190)
Stator Shaft Bushing		
A-43D Front & Rear	N/A	.8496 (21.58)
A-46DE & A-46DF		
Front	N/A	.8496 (21.58)
Rear	N/A	.9094 (23.10)

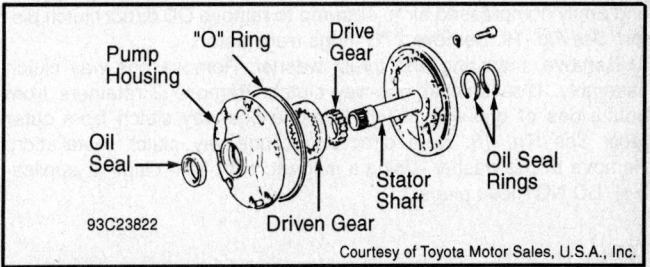

Pump Housing

"O" Ring

Drive Gear

Oil Seal

Stator Shaft

Driven Gear

Oil Seal Rings

93C23822

Courtesy of Toyota Motor Sales, U.S.A., Inc.

Fig. 15: Exploded View Of Oil Pump Assembly

AUTOMATIC TRANSMISSIONS
Toyota A-43D, A-46DE & A-46DF (Cont.)

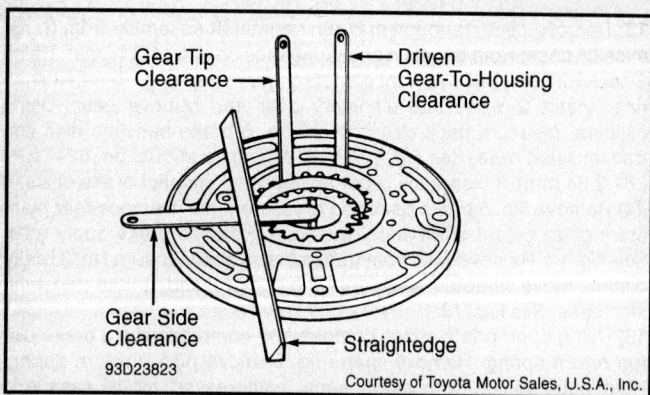

Fig. 16: Measuring Oil Pump Gear Clearances

Reassembly – 1) Place oil pump housing on torque converter. Coat all components with ATF. Align reference marks on driven and drive gears during installation. Align bolt holes and place stator shaft onto pump housing. Install but do not tighten attaching bolts. Install Oil Pump Aligning Tool (09363-20010) around outside of pump assembly to align pump housing and stator shaft. See Fig. 17.
2) Tighten oil pump bolts to 65 INCH lbs. (7.4 N.m). Remove aligning tool. Install oil seal rings. DO NOT spread ring ends more than necessary for installation. Ensure seal rings move smoothly after installation. Ensure pump drive gear rotates smoothly. Lubricate and install "O" ring on oil pump assembly.

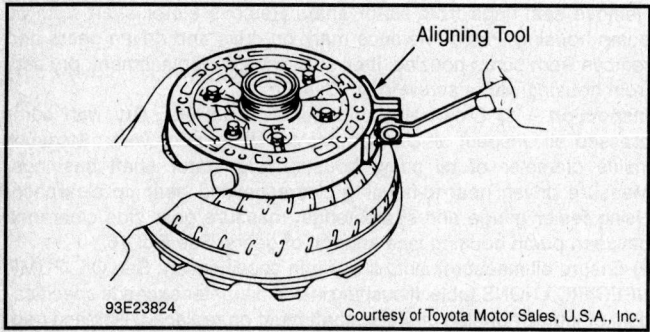

Fig. 17: Aligning Oil Pump Housing & Stator Shaft

OD PLANETARY GEAR, OD DIRECT CLUTCH & OD ONE-WAY CLUTCH

Disassembly – 1) Remove OD direct clutch drum from OD planetary gear. Remove thrust bearing and race (if equipped) from planetary gear. See Fig. 18. Place OD direct clutch assembly on oil pump assembly. Using a dial indicator, measure OD direct clutch piston stroke, while applying 57-114 psi (4-8 kg/cm²) to oil pump port. See Fig. 19.
2) Piston stroke should be .070-.102" (1.77-2.58 mm). If dial indicator reading is not within specified range, inspect discs for wear or damage. Remove OD direct clutch assembly from oil pump assembly. Remove OD brake hub snap ring and hub. Remove disc, snap ring, flange and cushion plate.
3) Using appropriate spring compressor, compress piston return spring and remove snap ring. Remove piston return spring. Install OD direct clutch drum on oil pump assembly. Hold OD direct clutch piston and apply compressed air to oil pump to remove OD direct clutch piston. See Fig. 19. Remove 2 "O" rings from piston.
4) Remove snap ring and thrust washer. Remove one-way clutch assembly. Disassemble one-way clutch. Remove 2 retainers from both sides of one-way clutch. Remove one-way clutch from outer race. See Fig. 18. Note direction of one-way clutch installation. Remove thrust washer. Using a magnet, remove 4 plugs (if applicable). DO NOT lose plugs.

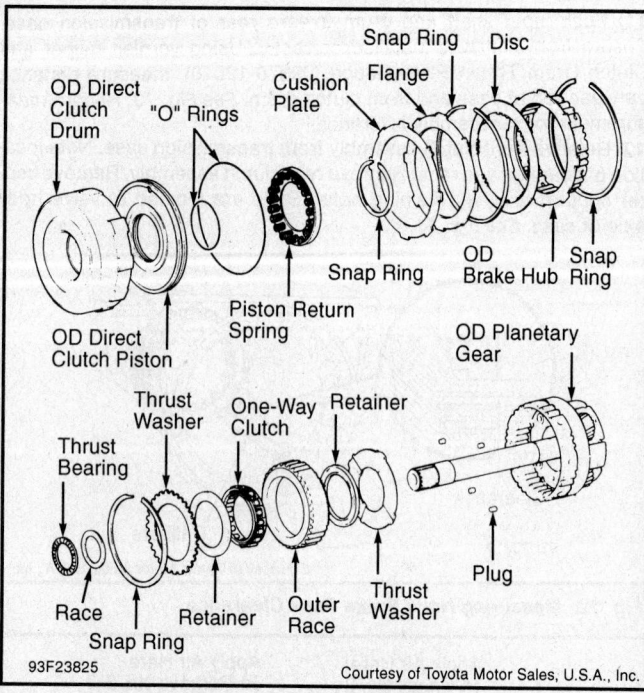

Fig. 18: Exploded View Of OD Planetary Gear, OD Direct Clutch & One-Way Clutch

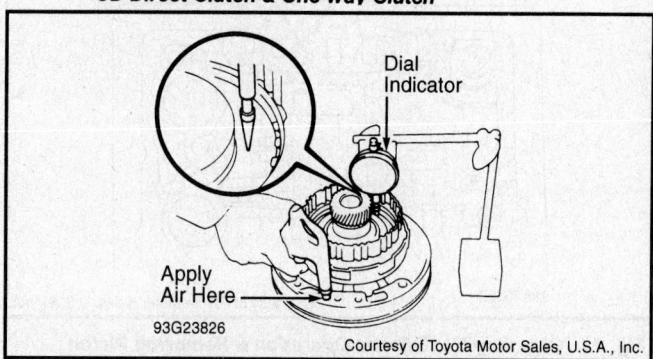

Fig. 19: Measuring OD Direct Clutch Piston Stroke

Inspection – 1) Inspect disc and flange for flaking or burnt areas. If disc lining is peeling or discolored, replace disc. Inspect piston return springs for wear, damage and collapsed coils. Clean all components (except disc) with solvent. Dry with compressed air. Ensure check ball is free in direct clutch piston. Apply compressed air to check ball area. Ensure check ball does not allow air to bleed through piston.
2) Using a dial indicator, measure inside diameter of OD direct clutch drum bushing. Bushing maximum inside diameter should be .911" (23.14 mm). If inside diameter is greater than specified, replace clutch drum. Measure inside diameter of OD planetary gear bushing. Bushing maximum inside diameter should be .444" (11.27 mm). If inside diameter is greater than specified, replace planetary gear.
3) Using a feeler gauge, measure clearance between planetary pinion gear and OD planetary gear housing. Standard clearance should be .008-.020" (.20-.50 mm). If clearance is not as specified, inspect planetary gear thrust washer. Replace planetary gear assembly (if necessary).

CAUTION: Clutch discs should be soaked in ATF for 15 minutes prior to installation. Lubricate all parts with ATF. Coat thrust bearings and races with petroleum jelly.

AUTOMATIC TRANSMISSIONS
Toyota A-43D, A-46DE & A-46DF (Cont.)

3-1485

Reassembly – 1) Install 4 plugs in planetary gear holes (if applicable). Install thrust washer to OD planetary gear with grooved side facing upward. Install one-way clutch in outer race with open end of retainers facing upward. Install retainer on both sides of one-way clutch. *See Fig. 20.* Install one-way clutch assembly. Install thrust washer and snap ring.

2) Coat NEW "O" rings with ATF and install on OD direct clutch piston. Carefully press direct clutch piston into clutch drum. Using spring compressor, compress piston return spring and install snap ring. Ensure end gap of snap ring is not aligned with spring seat claw.

3) Install cushion plate. Install flange with rounded edge facing upward. Install snap ring. Ensure end gap of snap ring is not aligned with cutout portion of clutch drum. Install disc, OD brake hub and snap ring. Ensure end gap of snap ring is not aligned with cutout portion of drum.

4) Recheck piston stroke of OD direct clutch. If piston stroke is less than specified, check for incorrect reassembly of components. Install race and thrust bearing on OD planetary gear. Install direct clutch assembly on OD planetary gear.

5) Rotate and push OD planetary gear to mesh splines of planetary gear with flukes of disc. Check one-way clutch operation. Hold OD direct clutch drum and rotate input shaft. Input shaft should rotate freely in clockwise direction and lock in counterclockwise direction. *See Fig. 21.*

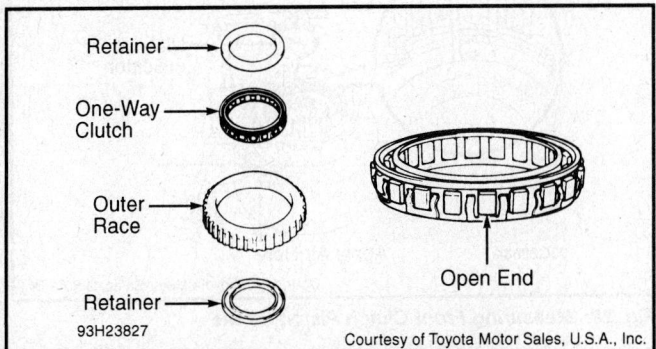

Fig. 20: Exploded View Of One-Way Clutch (Typical)

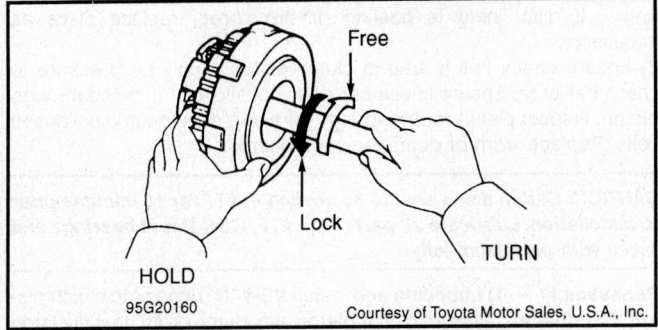

Fig. 21: Checking Operation Of One-Way Clutch

OVERDRIVE BRAKE

Disassembly – 1) Prior to disassembly, check OD brake piston stroke on A-43D transmissions. Install OD case on transmission case with cutout portion of OD case at 6 o'clock position. Ensure OD case oil hole is aligned with transmission case oil hole. *See Fig. 22.*

2) Using a dial indicator, measure brake piston stroke by applying compressed air to oil hole. *See Fig. 23.* Piston stroke should be .026-.087" (.65-2.21 mm). If piston stroke is not as specified, inspect discs. Remove OD case from transmission case. On A-46DE and A-46DF transmissions, using a feeler gauge, measure clearance between snap ring and flange. Standard clearance should be .014-.075" (.35-1.91 mm). On all transmissions, remove snap ring from OD case. Remove flange, discs, plates and cushion plate. Note location and number of components.

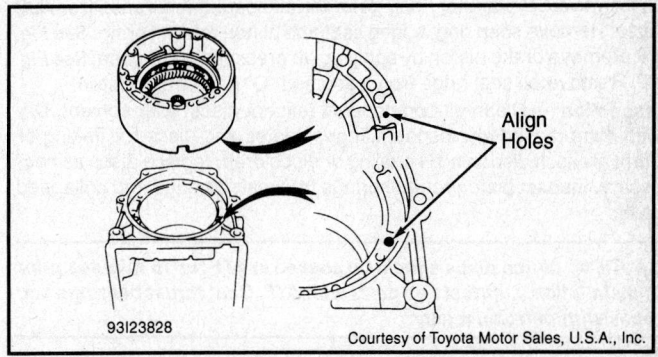

Fig. 22: Aligning OD Case & Transmission Case Oil Holes

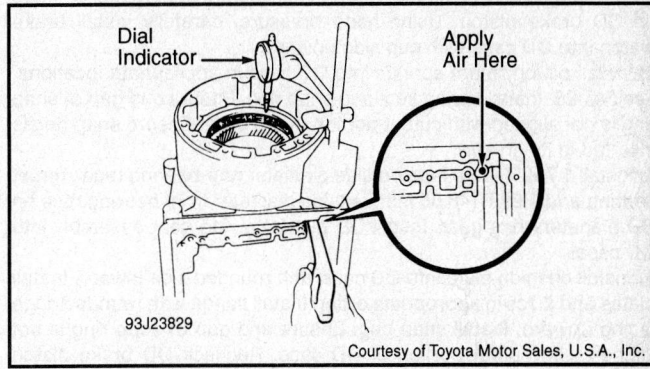

Fig. 23: Measuring OD Brake Piston Stroke (A-43D)

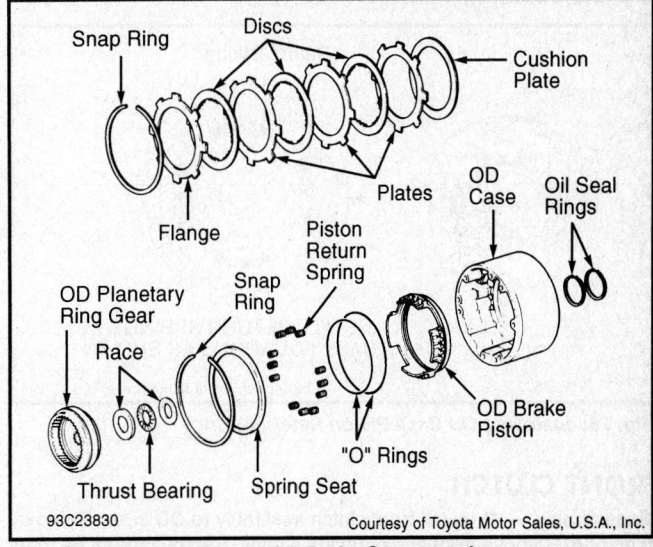

Fig. 24: Exploded View Of OD Brake Components

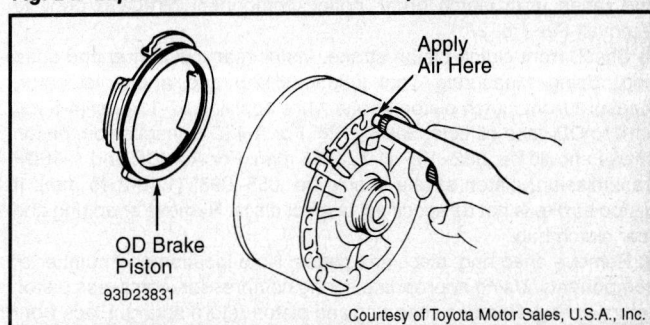

Fig. 25: Removing OD Brake Piston

3-1486

AUTOMATIC TRANSMISSIONS
Toyota A-43D, A-46DE & A-46DF (Cont.)

3) Remove OD planetary ring gear, thrust bearing and races from OD case. Remove snap ring, spring seat and piston return spring. *See Fig. 28.* Remove brake piston by applying air pressure to OD case. *See Fig. 29.* Remove oil seal rings from case and "O" rings from piston.

Inspection – Clean all components (except discs) with solvent. Dry with compressed air. Inspect flanges, plates and discs for flaking or burnt areas. If disc lining is peeling or discolored, replace discs as necessary. Inspect piston return springs for wear, damage and collapsed coils.

CAUTION: Clutch discs should be soaked in ATF for 15 minutes prior to installation. Lubricate all parts with ATF. Coat thrust bearings and races with petroleum jelly.

Reassembly – **1)** Lubricate and install oil seal rings on OD case. Ensure rings rotate smoothly after installation. Install NEW "O" rings on OD brake piston. Using hand pressure, carefully install brake piston into OD case with cup side upward.

2) Install piston return springs into OD case in appropriate locations. *See Fig. 26.* Install spring seat and snap ring. Ensure end gap of snap ring is not aligned with cutout portion of OD case. Ensure snap ring is inserted in its groove.

3) Install 1.752" (44.50 mm) outside diameter rear bearing race , thrust bearing and 1.909" (48.50 mm) outside diameter front bearing race on OD planetary ring gear. Install OD planetary ring gear assembly into OD case.

4) Install cushion plate into OD case with rounded side inward. Install plates and discs in appropriate order. Install flange with rounded edge facing upward. Install snap ring. Ensure end gap of snap ring is not aligned with cutout portion of OD case. Recheck OD brake piston stroke or clearance. If measurement is not as specified, check for incorrect reassembly of components.

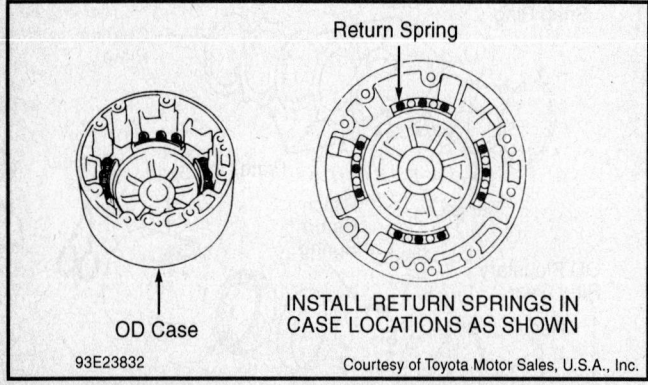

Fig. 26: Installing OD Case Piston Return Springs

FRONT CLUTCH

Disassembly – **1)** Install front clutch assembly to OD case. Remove snap ring. Remove front and rear clutch hubs. Remove thrust bearing and races from clutch drum, noting component direction prior to removal. *See Fig. 27.*

2) Check front clutch piston stroke. Install rear clutch hub and snap ring. Using Measuring Tool (09350-06120) and a dial indicator, measure front clutch piston stroke while applying 57-114 psi (4-8 kg/cm²) to OD case oil hole. *See Fig. 28.* For A-43D transmission, piston stroke should be .052-.105" (1.32-2.66 mm). For A-46DE and A-46DF transmission, piston stroke should be .055-.098" (1.40-2.48 mm). If piston stroke is not as specified, inspect discs. Remove snap ring and rear clutch hub.

3) Remove snap ring, discs and plates. Note location and number of components. Using appropriate spring compressor, compress piston return spring. Remove snap ring and piston return spring. Place front clutch drum on OD case. Carefully apply air pressure to case oil hole to remove piston. *See Fig. 28.* Remove "O" rings from clutch piston.

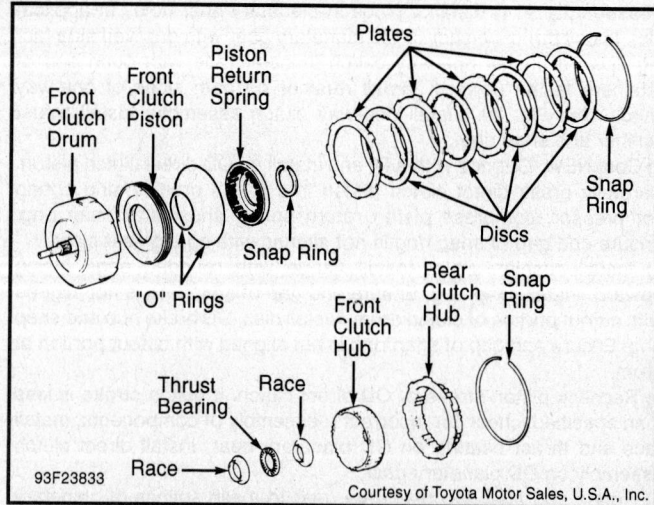

Fig. 27: Exploded View Of Front Clutch Components

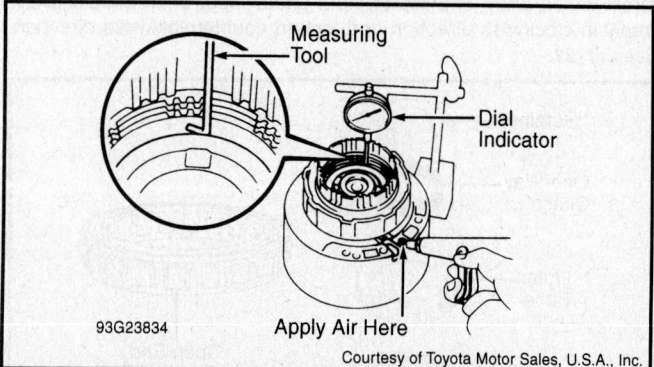

Fig. 28: Measuring Front Clutch Piston Stroke

Inspection – **1)** Clean all components (except discs) with solvent. Dry with compressed air. Inspect plates and discs for flaking or burnt areas. If disc lining is peeling or discolored, replace discs as necessary.

2) Ensure check ball is free in clutch piston. Apply air pressure to check ball area. Ensure check ball does not allow air to bleed through piston. Inspect piston return springs for wear, damage and collapsed coils. Replace worn or damaged components.

CAUTION: Clutch discs should be soaked in ATF for 15 minutes prior to installation. Lubricate all parts with ATF. Coat thrust bearings and races with petroleum jelly.

Reassembly – **1)** Lubricate and install NEW "O" rings onto clutch piston. Carefully install front clutch piston into clutch drum. Install piston return spring. Using spring compressor and appropriate press, compress return spring and install snap ring. Ensure end gap of snap ring is not aligned with claw area on spring seat.

2) Install plates, discs and snap ring in appropriate order. *See Fig. 27.* Ensure end gap of snap ring is not aligned with cutout portion of front clutch drum. Install rear clutch hub and snap ring. Recheck front clutch piston stroke.

3) If piston stroke is less than specified, check for incorrect reassembly of components. If piston stroke is greater than specified, select a new plate. Plates are available in thicknesses of .071" (1.80 mm) and .079" (2.00 mm). Remove snap ring and rear clutch hub. Install bearing races and thrust bearing into front clutch drum with flat surface of races facing away from clutch drum.

4) Rotate and push front clutch hub to mesh splines of front clutch hub with flukes of discs. Install front clutch hub into front clutch drum. Install rear clutch hub and snap ring. Ensure end gap of snap ring is not aligned with cutout portion of clutch drum.

AUTOMATIC TRANSMISSIONS
Toyota A-43D, A-46DE & A-46DF (Cont.)

3-1487

REAR CLUTCH

Disassembly – 1) Prior to disassembly, place rear clutch drum on center support. Using a dial indicator and compressed air, measure rear clutch piston stroke while applying 57-114 psi (4-8 kg/cm²) to OD case oil hole. *See Fig. 29.* Piston stroke should be .036-.078" (.91-1.99 mm) for A-43D transmission and .035-.069" (.90-1.75 mm) for A-46DE and A-46DF transmissions. If piston stroke is not as specified, inspect discs. Remove rear clutch from center support.

2) Remove snap ring, flange, discs and plates. Note location and number of components. Using appropriate spring compressor, compress piston return spring and remove snap ring. Remove piston return spring.

3) Place rear clutch drum on center support. Hold rear clutch piston with hand, and apply compressed air to center support to remove rear clutch piston. On A-46DE and A-46DF transmissions, apply compressed air to appropriate hole in center support to remove piston subassembly from rear clutch piston. *See Fig. 29.* Remove "O" rings from piston(s).

Inspection – 1) Clean all components (except discs) with solvent. Dry with compressed air. Inspect plates and discs for flaking or burnt areas. If disc lining is peeling or discolored, replace discs as necessary.

2) Ensure check ball is free in clutch piston. Apply air pressure to check ball area. Ensure check ball does not allow air to bleed through piston. Inspect piston return springs for wear, damage and collapsed coils. Replace worn or damaged components.

Reassembly – 1) Lubricate and install NEW "O" rings on clutch piston. On A-46DE and A-46DF transmissions, install piston subassembly into rear clutch piston. On A-43D transmission, carefully install rear clutch piston into clutch drum. On all models, using appropriate spring compressor and press, install piston return spring and snap ring. Ensure end gap of snap ring is not aligned with spring seat claw.

2) Install plates, discs and snap ring in appropriate order. *See Fig. 30.* Install flange with flat end facing down. Install snap ring. Ensure end gap of snap ring is not aligned with cutout portion of rear clutch drum. Recheck rear clutch piston stroke. If piston stroke is less than specified, check for incorrect reassembly of components.

CENTER SUPPORT ASSEMBLY

Disassembly – 1) Remove snap ring from end of sun gear shaft. Remove planetary sun gear with No. 1 one-way clutch from center support. Repeat procedure used in rear clutch disassembly to check No. 1 brake piston stroke. Piston stroke should be .031-.059" (.78-1.50 mm) for A-43D transmissions, and .032-.068" (.80-1.73 mm) for A-46DE and A-46DF transmissions. If piston stroke is not as specified, inspect discs. *See Fig. 31.*

2) Remove snap ring from front of center support. Remove flange, disc(s) and plate(s). *See Fig. 32.* Using appropriate spring compressor, compress piston return spring. Remove snap ring. Remove piston return spring.

3) Hold No. 1 brake piston and apply air pressure to center support oil hole to remove No. 1 brake piston. *See Fig. 31.* Remove "O" rings and oil seal rings. Turn center support over.

4) Check No. 2 brake piston stroke. Repeat test procedure used previously for checking piston stroke on No. 1 brake piston. *See Fig. 33.* Piston stroke should be .0398-.0886" (1.01-2.25 mm) for all transmissions. If piston stroke is not as specified, inspect discs. Remove rear snap ring, flange, discs and plates. Note location and number of components. *See Fig. 34.*

5) Using appropriate spring compressor and press, compress piston return spring. Remove snap ring. Remove piston return spring. Hold No. 2 brake piston and apply air pressure to center support oil hole to remove No. 2 brake piston. *See Fig. 33.* Remove "O" rings.

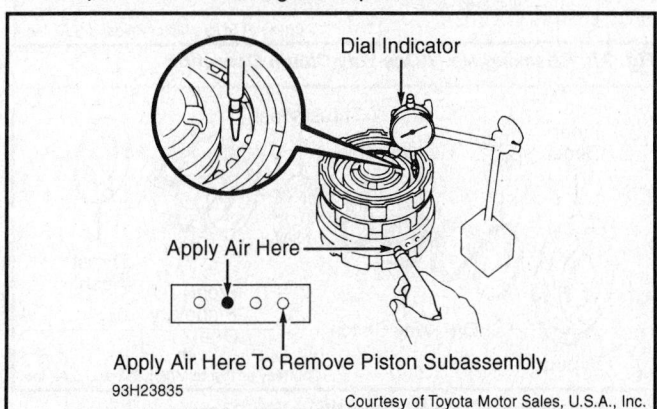

Dial Indicator

Apply Air Here

Apply Air Here To Remove Piston Subassembly

93H23835

Courtesy of Toyota Motor Sales, U.S.A., Inc.

Fig. 29: Measuring Rear Clutch Piston Stroke & Removing Piston Subassembly

CAUTION: Clutch discs should be soaked in ATF for 15 minutes prior to installation. Lubricate all parts with ATF.

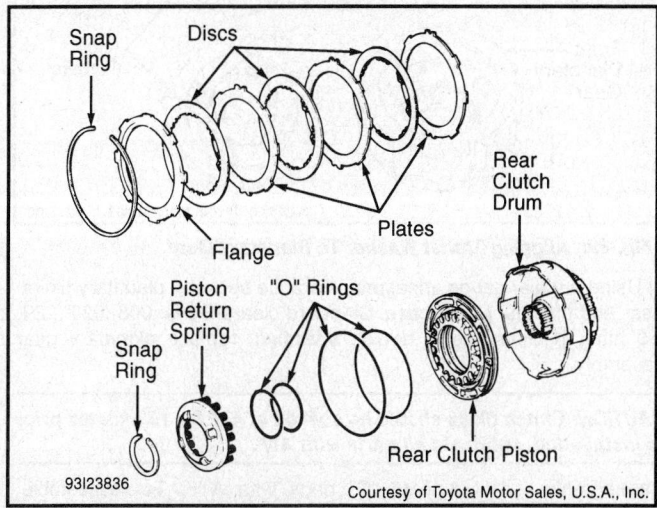

Snap Ring

Discs

Rear Clutch Drum

Flange

Plates

Piston Return Spring

"O" Rings

Snap Ring

Rear Clutch Piston

93I23836

Courtesy of Toyota Motor Sales, U.S.A., Inc.

Fig. 30: Exploded View Of Rear Clutch Components (A-43D Is Shown; A-46DE & A-46DF Are Similar)

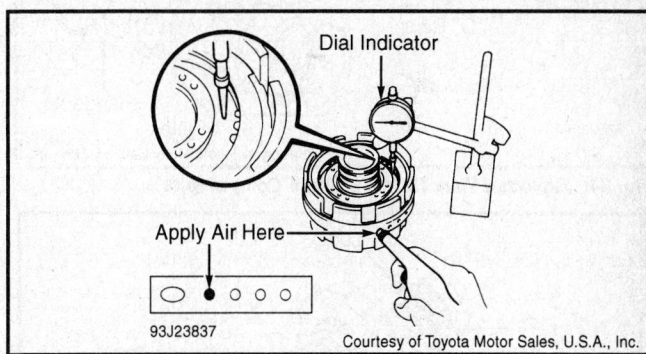

Dial Indicator

Apply Air Here

93J23837

Courtesy of Toyota Motor Sales, U.S.A., Inc.

Fig. 31: Measuring No. 1 Brake Piston Stroke

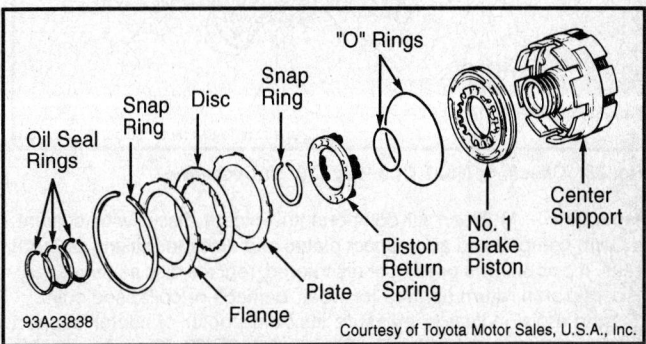

"O" Rings

Snap Ring

Disc

Snap Ring

Snap Ring

Oil Seal Rings

Piston Return Spring

Plate

Flange

No. 1 Brake Piston

Center Support

93A23838

Courtesy of Toyota Motor Sales, U.S.A., Inc.

Fig. 32: Exploded View Of No. 1 Brake Components

3-1488

AUTOMATIC TRANSMISSIONS
Toyota A-43D, A-46DE & A-46DF (Cont.)

6) Hold No. 1 one-way clutch and rotate planetary sun gear. Sun gear should rotate freely in counterclockwise direction and lock in clockwise direction. *See Fig. 35.* If component does not test as described, one-way clutch requires replacement. Loosen staked part of rear side retainer. Remove No. 1 one-way clutch and 2 retainers from outer race. *See Fig. 36.* Using a pin punch and hammer, remove front side retainer. Remove oil seal rings from sun gear.

7) Remove thrust washer from front planetary gear. Hold one-way clutch inner race and rotate planetary gear. Planetary gear should rotate freely in counterclockwise direction and lock in clockwise direction. *See Fig. 37.* Remove one-way clutch inner race. Remove snap ring, one-way clutch and 2 retainers. *See Fig. 38.*

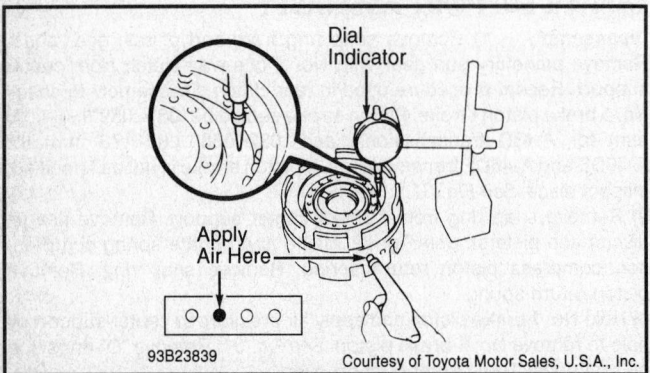

Fig. 33: Measuring No. 2 Brake Piston Stroke

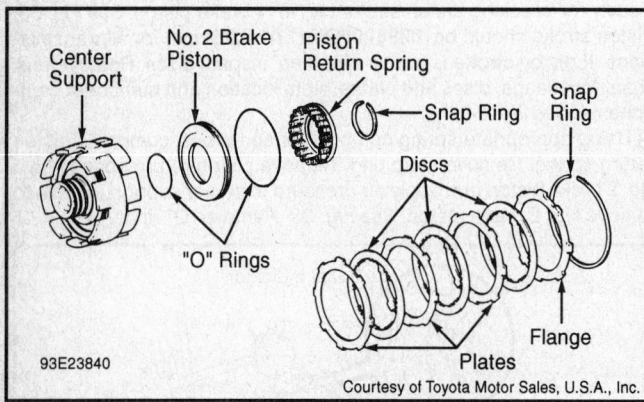

Fig. 34: Exploded View Of No. 2 Brake Components

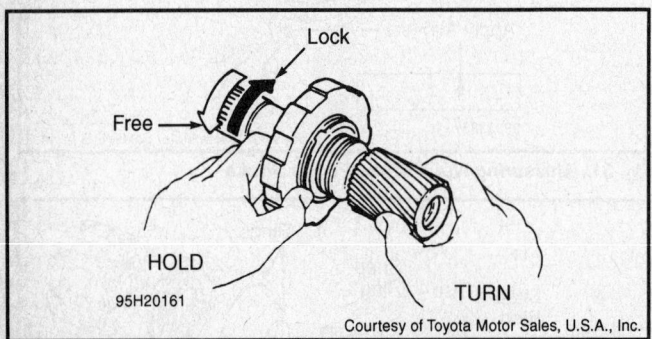

Fig. 35: Checking No. 1 One-Way Clutch Operation

Inspection – 1) Clean all components (except discs) with solvent. Dry with compressed air. Inspect plates and discs for flaking or burnt areas. If disc lining is peeling or discolored, replace disc as necessary. Inspect piston return springs for wear, damage or collapsed coils.

2) Using a dial indicator, measure inside diameter of center support bushing. Maximum inside diameter is 1.435" (36.46 mm). If inside diameter is greater than specified, replace center support. Measure inside diameter of planetary sun gear bushings. Maximum inside diameter is .8496" (21.58 mm). If inside diameter is greater than specified, replace planetary sun gear.

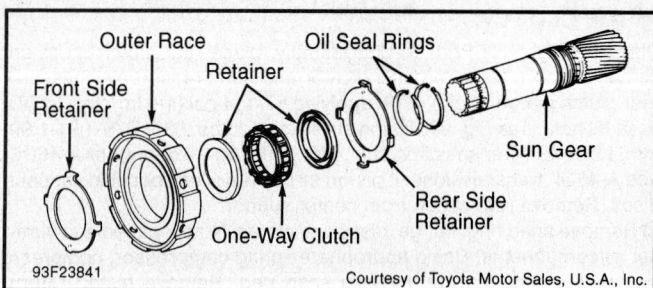

Fig. 36: Exploded View Of Planetary Sun Gear & No. 1 One-Way Clutch

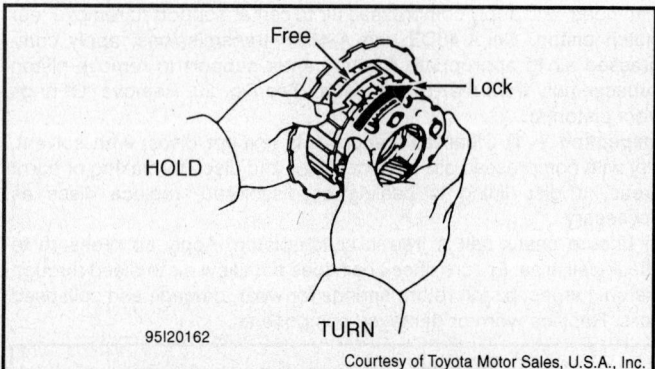

Fig. 37: Checking No. 2 One-Way Clutch Operation

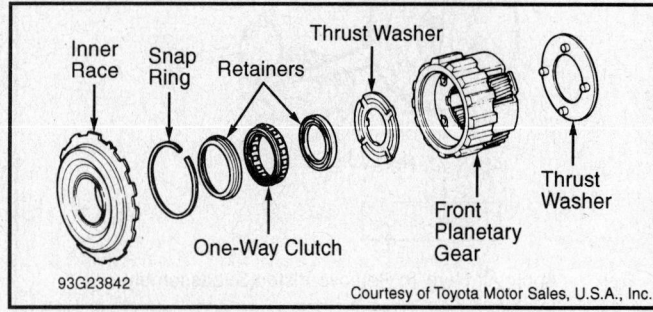

Fig. 38: Exploded View Of Front Planetary Gear & No. 2 One-Way Clutch

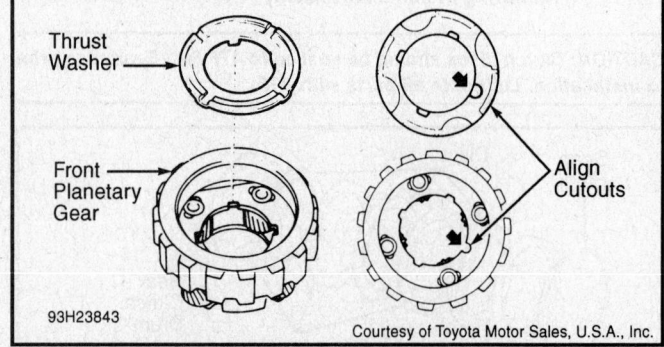

Fig. 39: Aligning Thrust Washer To Planetary Gear

3) Using a feeler gauge, measure clearance between planetary pinion gear and planetary gear case. Standard clearance is .008-.020" (.20-.50 mm). If clearance is not as specified, replace planetary gear assembly.

CAUTION: Clutch discs should be soaked in ATF for 15 minutes prior to installation. Lubricate all parts with ATF.

Reassembly – 1) Lubricate "O" rings with ATF. To reassemble, reverse disassembly procedure. Ensure end gap of snap ring does not align with claw area on spring seat of piston return spring. Install plates and discs in appropriate order. *See Figs. 32 and 34.*

2) Install No. 1 brake flange with rounded side facing down. Install No. 2 brake flange with flat side facing down. Install all snap rings. Ensure ends of snap rings do not align with cutout areas of center support.

3) Recheck No. 1 and No. 2 brake piston stroke. *See Figs. 31 and 33.* If piston stroke is not as specified, check for incorrect reassembly of components. Reassemble sun gear and No. 1 one-way clutch. *See Fig. 36.* While turning one-way clutch, install sun gear into center support. Install snap ring on end of sun gear. Ensure sun gear rotates in counterclockwise direction only.

4) Reassembly front planetary gear and No. 2 one-way clutch. *See Fig. 38.* Ensure lug shaped cutout on thrust washer for No. 2 one-way clutch is aligned with lug shaped cutout on front planetary gear. *See Fig. 39.* Ensure front planetary gear rotates in counterclockwise direction only.

REAR PLANETARY GEAR & OUTPUT SHAFT

Disassembly – 1) Remove thrust washer from front planetary ring gear. Compress snap ring and remove front planetary ring gear. Remove snap ring from ring gear. Remove rear planetary gear assembly from output shaft. Remove bearing and race.

2) Remove rear planetary carrier from rear planetary ring gear. Remove set ring. Remove rear planetary ring gear. Remove race from ring gear. Remove oil seal ring from intermediate shaft. Remove 3 oil seal rings from output shaft. *See Fig. 40.*

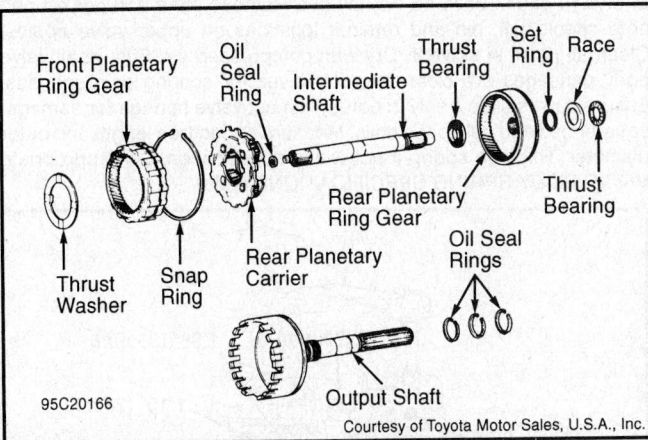

Fig. 40: Exploded View Of Rear Planetary Gear & Output Shaft

Inspection – 1) Clean all components with solvent. Dry with compressed air. Inspect all components for wear or damage. Using a dial indicator, measure inside diameter of output shaft bushing. Maximum inside diameter is .7117" (18.076 mm). If inside diameter is greater than specified, replace output shaft.

2) Using a feeler gauge, measure clearance between rear planetary carrier pinion gear and carrier case. Standard clearance should be .008-.020" (.20-.50 mm). If clearance is not as specified, inspect rear planetary carrier thrust washer. If necessary, replace rear planetary carrier assembly.

Reassembly – 1) Lubricate oil seal rings with ATF. Install oil seal rings on output shaft. Ensure rings rotate smoothly after installation. Lubricate and install NEW oil seal ring on output shaft. Ensure ring rotates smoothly. Apply petroleum jelly to race and install race on intermediate shaft with flat surface away from shaft.

2) Install rear planetary ring gear on intermediate shaft. Install set ring. Install rear planetary carrier to planetary ring gear. Apply petroleum jelly to bearing and race and install on rear planetary ring gear. Install rear planetary gear assembly to output shaft. Install front planetary ring gear. *See Fig. 40.*

3) Ensure snap ring is installed in groove of output shaft. Align snap ring end with wide cutout portion of output shaft. Apply petroleum jelly to thrust washer and install on rear planetary carrier. Ensure lug shapes match cutout portions on rear planetary carrier.

NO. 3 BRAKE PISTON

Disassembly – 1) Using appropriate spring compressor, compress piston return springs and remove snap ring. Remove spring retainer and return springs. Position transmission with front opening facing upward.

2) Place shop towels under case to prevent piston damage. Apply air pressure to case passages to remove No. 3 brake outer piston, reaction sleeve and No. 3 brake inner piston. *See Figs. 11 and 13.* It may be necessary to use long hooks to remove sleeve and inner piston. Using screwdriver, pry manual valve lever shaft seals from case if replacement is required.

Inspection – Clean all parts (except discs) in solvent. Dry with compressed air. Inspect pistons and sleeve for scoring, wear or damage. Check return springs for cracked or broken coils. If disc lining is peeled or discolored, replace discs as necessary. Replace damaged components as necessary.

Reassembly – Install manual valve lever shaft seals if removed. Lubricate and install all NEW "O" rings. Thin "O" ring goes on outside of reaction sleeve. Soak discs in ATF for 15 minutes prior to installation. To complete reassembly, reverse disassembly procedure. Check No. 3 brake operation. *See Fig. 13.*

VALVE BODY ASSEMBLY

CAUTION: All valve body components must be installed in original location. Lay all components in sequence during removal for reassembly reference.

NOTE: On A-43D valve body, throttle pressure is changed according to number of adjusting rings. When assembling valve body, install same number of adjusting rings as removed. Some valve bodies do not have adjusting rings.

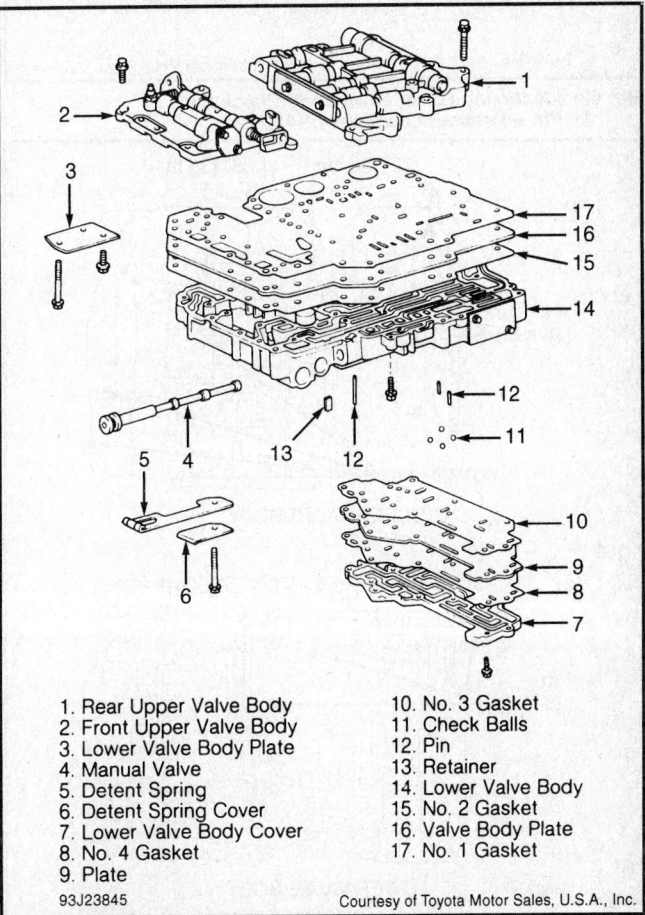

1. Rear Upper Valve Body	10. No. 3 Gasket
2. Front Upper Valve Body	11. Check Balls
3. Lower Valve Body Plate	12. Pin
4. Manual Valve	13. Retainer
5. Detent Spring	14. Lower Valve Body
6. Detent Spring Cover	15. No. 2 Gasket
7. Lower Valve Body Cover	16. Valve Body Plate
8. No. 4 Gasket	17. No. 1 Gasket
9. Plate	

93J23845   Courtesy of Toyota Motor Sales, U.S.A., Inc.

Fig. 41: Exploded View Of Valve Body Assembly
(A-43D Shown; A-46DE & A-46DF Are Similar)

3-1490

AUTOMATIC TRANSMISSIONS
Toyota A-43D, A-46DE & A-46DF (Cont.)

Disassembly (A-43D) – **1)** Remove detent spring, detent spring cover and manual valve from valve body assembly. Remove lower valve body cover, gaskets, plate, check balls, retainers and pins. Remove lower valve body plate. See Figs. 41 and 42.

2) Remove 3 lower valve body bolts. Turn over valve body assembly. Remove 5 front upper valve body bolts. Remove 5 rear upper valve body bolts. Note bolt length and location. See Fig. 43. Separate lower valve body and plate from upper valve bodies.

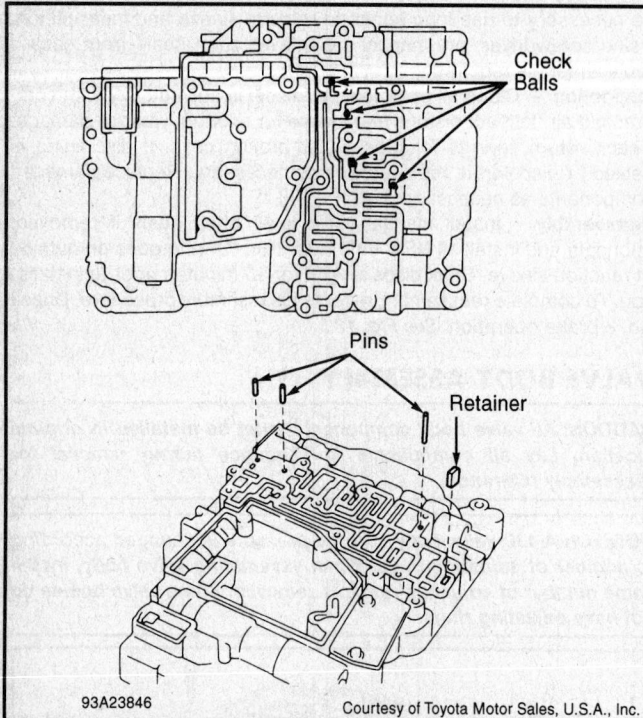

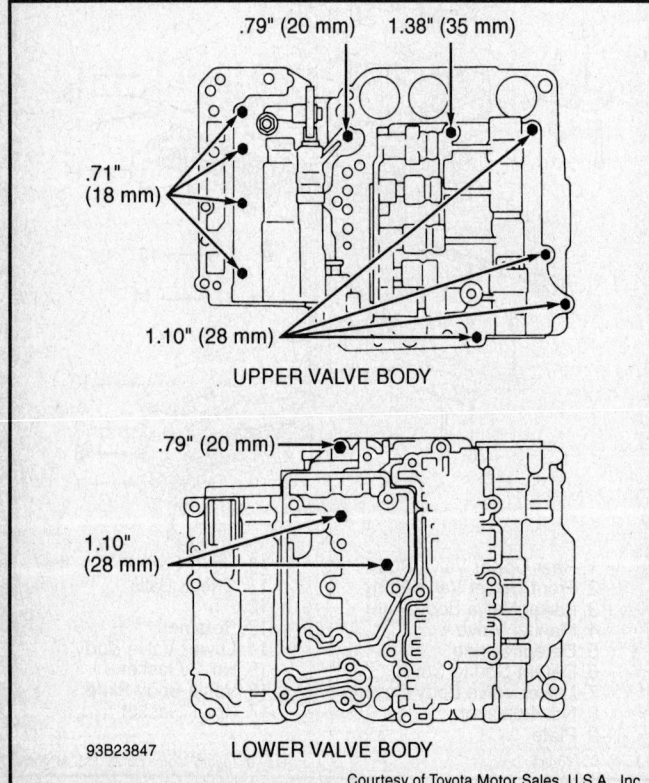

93A23846   Courtesy of Toyota Motor Sales, U.S.A., Inc.

Fig. 42: Identifying Lower Valve Body Check Ball, Pin & Retainer Locations (A-43D)

CAUTION: DO NOT allow plate to separate from lower valve body during removal or check balls and retainers may fall out.

Inspection – Remove plate and gaskets from lower valve body. Note location and diameter of check balls, springs and valves. Push inward on sleeves or plugs to remove all pins and retainers. Retainers may be removed using a magnet. Remove all check balls, springs and valves. Note location of pins, retainers and diameter of check balls. Clean all parts in solvent. Dry with compressed air. Ensure all valve body passages are clear. Inspect valves for scoring or roughness. Ensure valves slide freely in bores. Inspect valve springs for damage, squareness and collapsed coils. Measure spring free length and outer diameter. Replace spring if not within specification. See appropriate VALVE BODY SPRING SPECIFICATIONS table.

Disassembly (A-46DE & A-46DF) – Remove detent spring, detent spring cover and manual valve from valve body assembly. Remove 9 bolts from front and rear upper valve bodies. Note bolt length and location. Remove 7 bolts from lower valve body. See Fig. 44. Separate lower valve body and gasket from plate and upper valve bodies.

CAUTION: DO NOT allow plate to separate from upper valve bodies during removal or check balls, pins and retainers may fall out.

Inspection – Remove gasket from lower valve body. Note check ball, pin, spring and retainer location. Hold plate to upper valve bodies to ensure check balls do not fall out. Remove plate and gasket and note check ball, pin and retainer locations on upper valve bodies. Clean all parts in solvent. Dry with compressed air. Ensure all valve body passages are clear. Inspect valves for scoring or roughness. Ensure valves slide freely in bores. Inspect valve springs for damage, squareness and collapsed coils. Measure spring free length and outer diameter. Replace spring if not within specification. See appropriate VALVE BODY SPRING SPECIFICATIONS table.

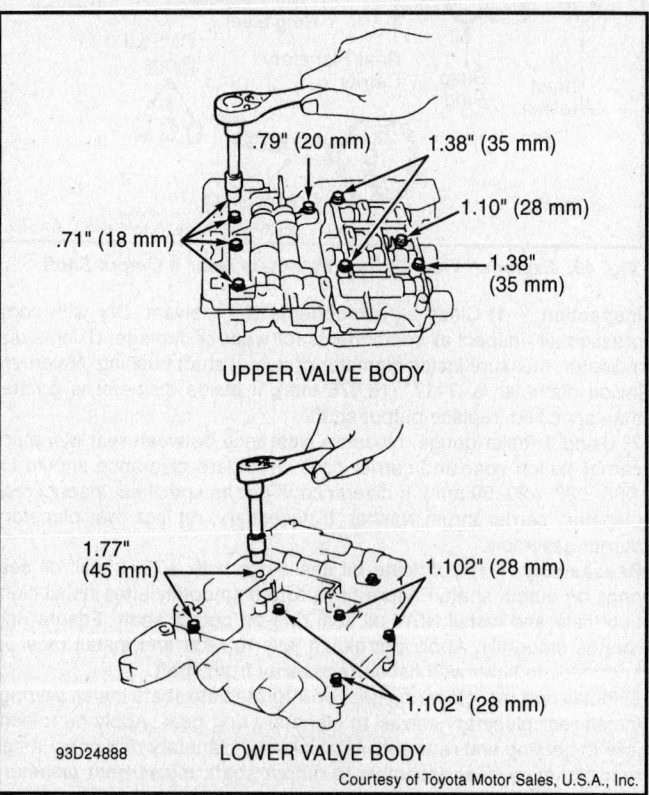

93D24888   Courtesy of Toyota Motor Sales, U.S.A., Inc.

Fig. 44: Identifying Valve Body Bolts (A-46DE & A-46DF)

Fig. 43: Identifying Valve Body Bolts (A-43D)

AUTOMATIC TRANSMISSIONS
Toyota A-43D, A-46DE & A-46DF (Cont.)

3-1491

LOWER VALVE BODY SPRING SPECIFICATIONS

Spring No.	Diameter In. (mm)	Free Length In. (mm)
A-43D [1]		
No. 1	.197 (5.00)	.787 (20.00)
No. 2	.543 (13.80)	.1.138 (28.90)
No. 3	.413 (10.50)	.539 (13.70)
No. 4	.299 (7.60)	1.362 (34.60)
No. 5	.417 (10.60)	1.327 (33.70)
No. 6	.516 (13.10)	1.264 (32.10)
No. 7	.669 (17.00)	2.173 (55.20)
A-46DE & A-46DF [2]		
No. 1	.670 (17.02)	1.980 (50.28)
No. 2	.362 (9.20)	.1.667 (42.35)
No. 3	.346 (8.80)	1.395 (35.43)
No. 4	.449 (11.40)	1.284 (32.60)
No. 5	.517 (13.14)	1.265 (32.14)
No. 6	.413 (10.50)	.539 (13.70)
No. 7	.196 (4.97)	.787 (20.00)
No. 8	.535 (13.60)	1.102 (28.00)

[1] – For spring locations, see Fig. 45.
[2] – For spring locations, see Figs. 46 and 48.

FRONT UPPER VALVE BODY SPRING SPECIFICATIONS

Spring No.	Diameter In. (mm)	Free Length In. (mm)
A-43D [1]		
No. 1	.425 (10.80)	1.567 (39.80)
No. 2	.339 (8.60)	.862 (21.90)
No. 3	.685 (17.40)	2.807 (71.30)
A-46DE & A-46DF [2]		
No. 1	.686 (17.43)	2.806 (71.27)
No. 2	.338 (8.58)	.864 (21.94)
No. 3	.429 (10.90)	1.557 (39.55)
No. 4	.270 (6.85)	.906 (23.00)

[1] – See Fig. 50 for spring locations.
[2] – See Fig. 51 for spring locations.

REAR UPPER VALVE BODY SPRING SPECIFICATIONS

Spring No.	Diameter In. (mm)	Free Length In. (mm)
A-43D [1]		
No. 1	.350 (8.90)	1.146 (29.10)
No. 2	.354 (9.00)	1.075 (27.30)
No. 3	.362 (9.20)	1.480 (37.60)
No. 4	.362 (9.20)	1.669 (42.40)
No. 5	.354 (9.00)	1.382 (35.10)
A-46DE & A-46DF [2]		
No. 1-3	.350 (8.90)	1.148 (29.15)
No. 4	.362 (9.20)	1.478 (37.55)

[1] – See Fig. 53 for spring locations.
[2] – See Fig. 54 for spring locations.

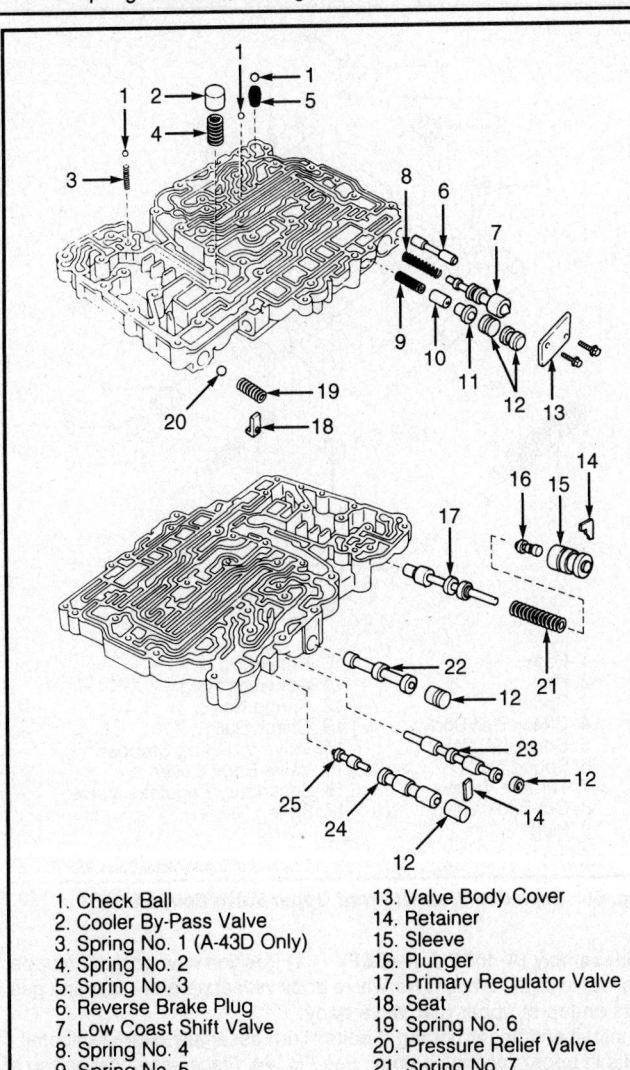

1. Check Ball
2. Cooler By-Pass Valve
3. Spring No. 1 (A-43D Only)
4. Spring No. 2
5. Spring No. 3
6. Reverse Brake Plug
7. Low Coast Shift Valve
8. Spring No. 4
9. Spring No. 5
10. 3-4 Coast Shift Valve
11. 3rd Coast Shift Valve
12. Plug
13. Valve Body Cover
14. Retainer
15. Sleeve
16. Plunger
17. Primary Regulator Valve
18. Seat
19. Spring No. 6
20. Pressure Relief Valve
21. Spring No. 7
22. D-2 Down Timing Valve
23. 3-4 Shift Valve
24. 1-2 Shift Lower Valve
25. 1-2 Shift Upper Valve

93C23848

Courtesy of Toyota Motor Sales, U.S.A., Inc.

Fig. 45: Exploded View Of Lower Valve Body (A-43D)

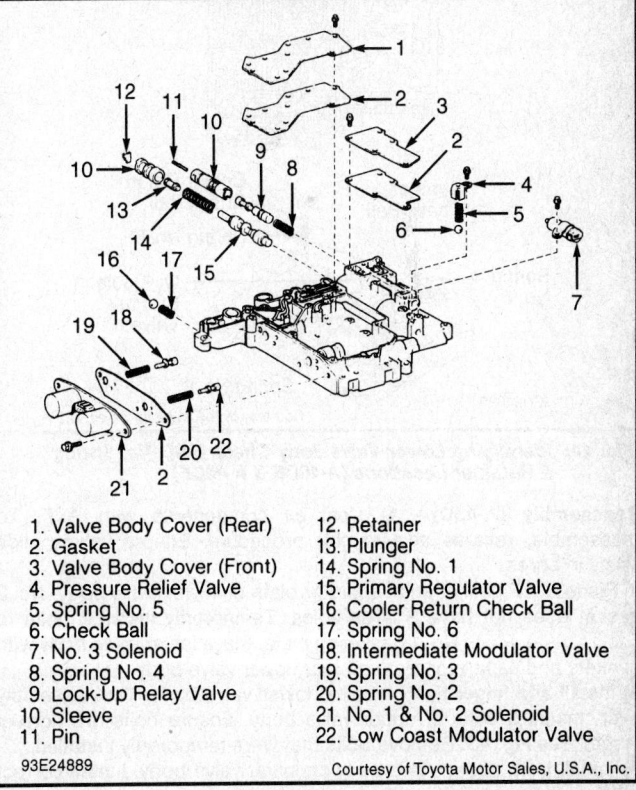

1. Valve Body Cover (Rear)
2. Gasket
3. Valve Body Cover (Front)
4. Pressure Relief Valve
5. Spring No. 5
6. Check Ball
7. No. 3 Solenoid
8. Spring No. 4
9. Lock-Up Relay Valve
10. Sleeve
11. Pin
12. Retainer
13. Plunger
14. Spring No. 1
15. Primary Regulator Valve
16. Cooler Return Check Ball
17. Spring No. 6
18. Intermediate Modulator Valve
19. Spring No. 3
20. Spring No. 2
21. No. 1 & No. 2 Solenoid
22. Low Coast Modulator Valve

93E24889

Courtesy of Toyota Motor Sales, U.S.A., Inc.

Fig. 46: Exploded View Of Lower Valve Body (A-46DE & A-46DF)

3-1492

AUTOMATIC TRANSMISSIONS
Toyota A-43D, A-46DE & A-46DF (Cont.)

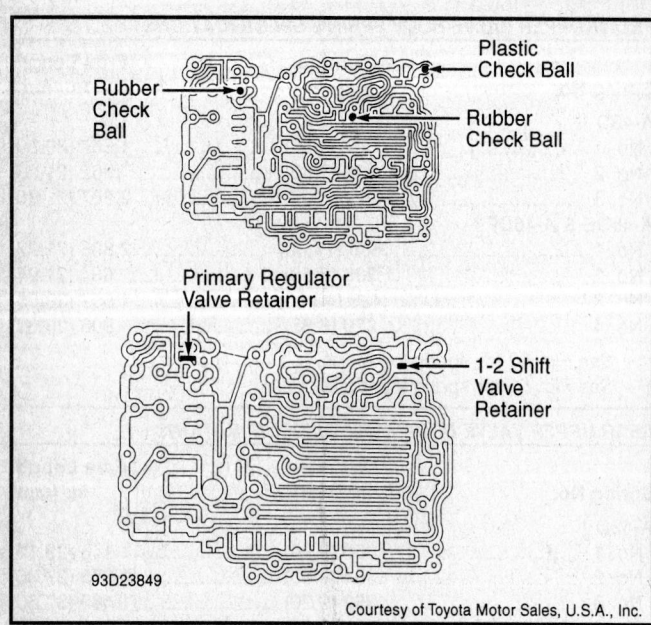

Fig. 47: Identifying Lower Valve Body Check Ball & Retainer Locations (A-43D)

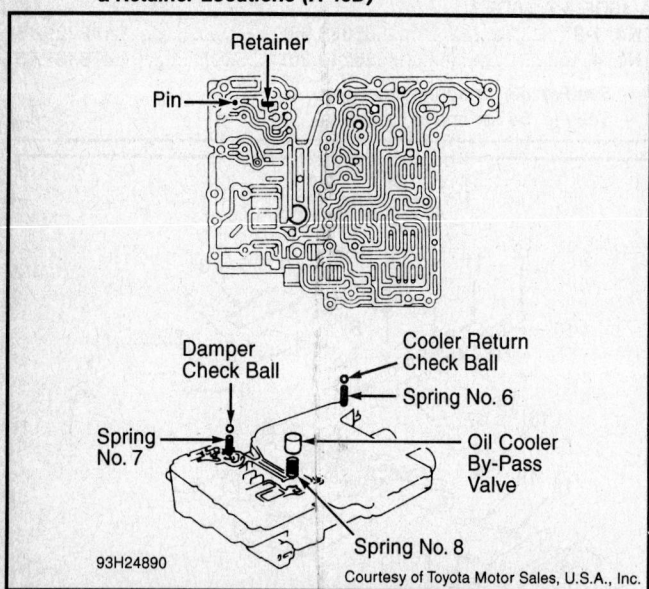

Fig. 48: Identifying Lower Valve Body Check Ball, Pin, Spring & Retainer Locations (A-46DE & A-46DF)

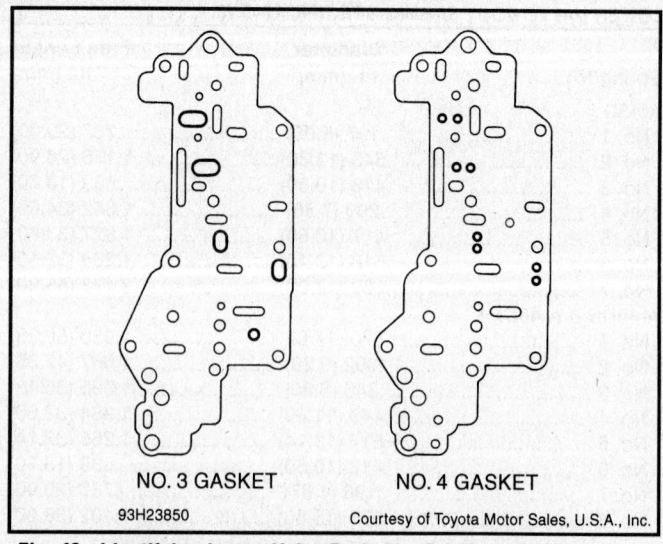

Fig. 49: Identifying Lower Valve Body No. 3 & No. 4 Gaskets (A-43D)

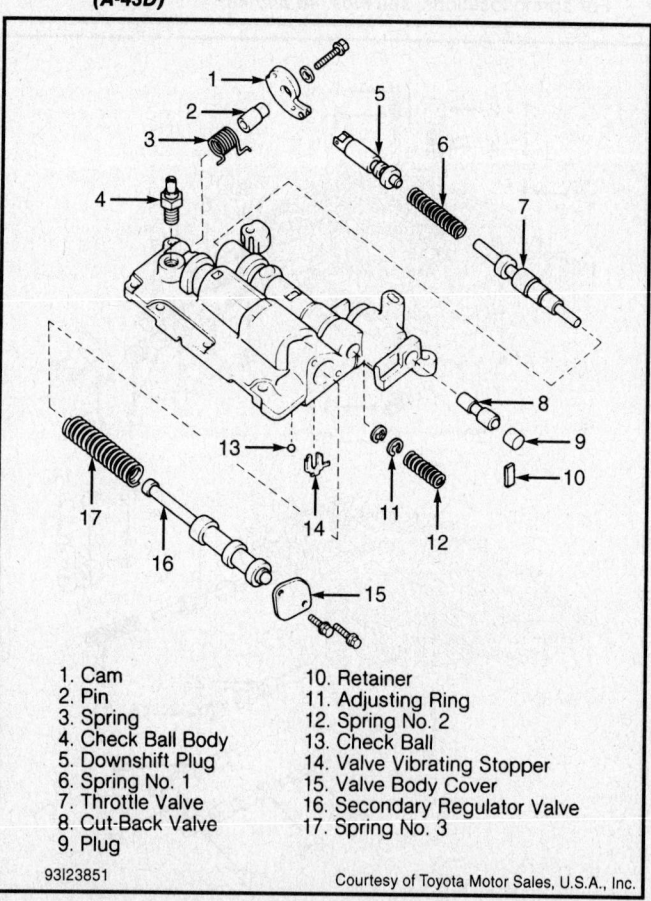

1. Cam
2. Pin
3. Spring
4. Check Ball Body
5. Downshift Plug
6. Spring No. 1
7. Throttle Valve
8. Cut-Back Valve
9. Plug
10. Retainer
11. Adjusting Ring
12. Spring No. 2
13. Check Ball
14. Valve Vibrating Stopper
15. Valve Body Cover
16. Secondary Regulator Valve
17. Spring No. 3

93I23851   Courtesy of Toyota Motor Sales, U.S.A., Inc.

Fig. 50: Exploded View Of Front Upper Valve Body (A-43D)

Reassembly (A-43D) – 1) Coat all components with ATF. To reassemble, reverse disassembly procedure. Ensure valves slide freely in bores.

2) Place No. 2 gasket and separator plate on lower valve body. No. 2 gasket does not have 3 large holes. Temporarily install 2 bolts to secure plate. Place No. 1 gasket on plate. Place lower valve body with gaskets and separator plate on rear upper valve body.

3) Install and finger tighten bolt in lower valve body. Turn assembly over. Install 5 bolts in upper valve body. Ensure bolts are correct length. See Fig. 43. Remove bolts that were temporarily installed.

4) Install front upper valve body on lower valve body. Install correct bolts and finger tighten. Turn assembly over and install remaining bolts. Tighten all bolts to specification. See TORQUE SPECIFICATIONS.

5) Install lower valve body plate. See Fig. 41. Install check balls in lower valve body. See Fig. 42. Install No. 3 gasket, separator plate, No. 4 gasket and lower valve body cover. For gasket identification, see Fig. 49. Install bolts and tighten to specification. Install manual valve and detent spring.

Reassembly (A-46DE & A-46DF) – 1) Position new gasket on upper rear valve body. Place lower valve body with separator plate and gaskets on top of upper rear valve body.

2) Install and finger tighten 3 bolts. Turn assembly over and install 4 bolts in upper rear valve body. See Fig. 44. Place assembly on top of upper front valve body. Install and finger tighten 3 bolts. Turn assembly over and install 5 bolts. Tighten bolts to specification. See TORQUE SPECIFICATIONS.

AUTOMATIC TRANSMISSIONS
Toyota A-43D, A-46DE & A-46DF (Cont.)

3-1493

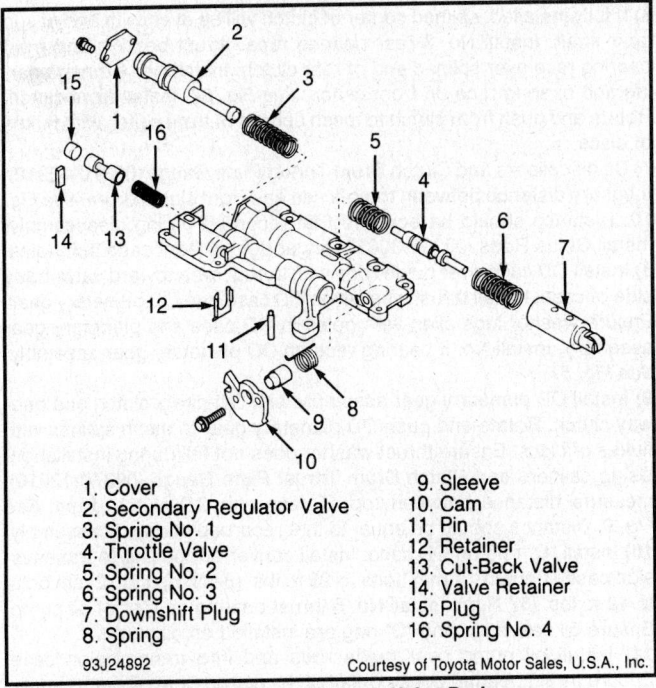

1. Cover	9. Sleeve
2. Secondary Regulator Valve	10. Cam
3. Spring No. 1	11. Pin
4. Throttle Valve	12. Retainer
5. Spring No. 2	13. Cut-Back Valve
6. Spring No. 3	14. Valve Retainer
7. Downshift Plug	15. Plug
8. Spring	16. Spring No. 4

93J24892   Courtesy of Toyota Motor Sales, U.S.A., Inc.

Fig. 51: Exploded View Of Front Upper Valve Body (A-46DE & A-46DF)

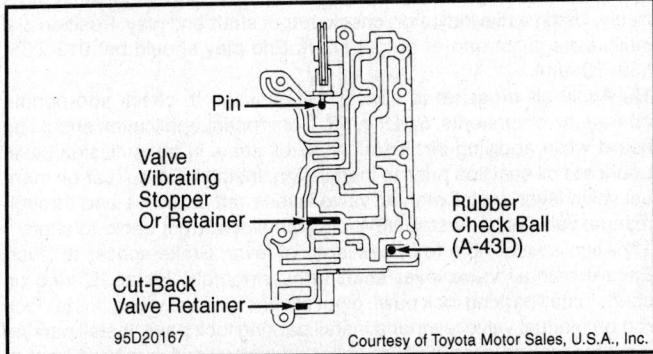

95D20167   Courtesy of Toyota Motor Sales, U.S.A., Inc.

Fig. 52: Identifying Front Upper Valve Body Check Ball, Pin, Stopper & Retainer Locations

GOVERNOR ASSEMBLY (A-43D ONLY)

Disassembly & Reassembly – Remove retaining clip (if necessary). Push downward on governor shaft. Remove "E" clip and remove governor components. See Fig. 56. Inspect all parts for wear and damage. Insert valve shaft into body. Ensure valve slides smoothly. Check oil passage for restrictions. To reassemble, reverse disassembly procedure. Ensure "E" clip is fully seated.

TRANSMISSION REASSEMBLY

NOTE: For bearing race and thrust bearing outer diameter specifications, see BEARING RACE & THRUST BEARING SPECIFICATIONS table. For bearing race and thrust bearing locations, see Fig. 57.

CAUTION: Lubricate all components with ATF. Clutch discs should be soaked in ATF for 15 minutes prior to installation. Coat thrust bearings and races with petroleum jelly. Ensure ends of snap rings are not aligned with cutout area of case.

1) Position transmission case with front facing upward. Assemble No. 3 brake inner piston, reaction sleeve and outer piston. Press assembled pistons into case with hand pressure. Using appropriate spring compressor, install piston return spring on outer piston. Install snap ring. Ensure No. 3 brake piston moves smoothly when compressed air is applied. See Fig. 13.

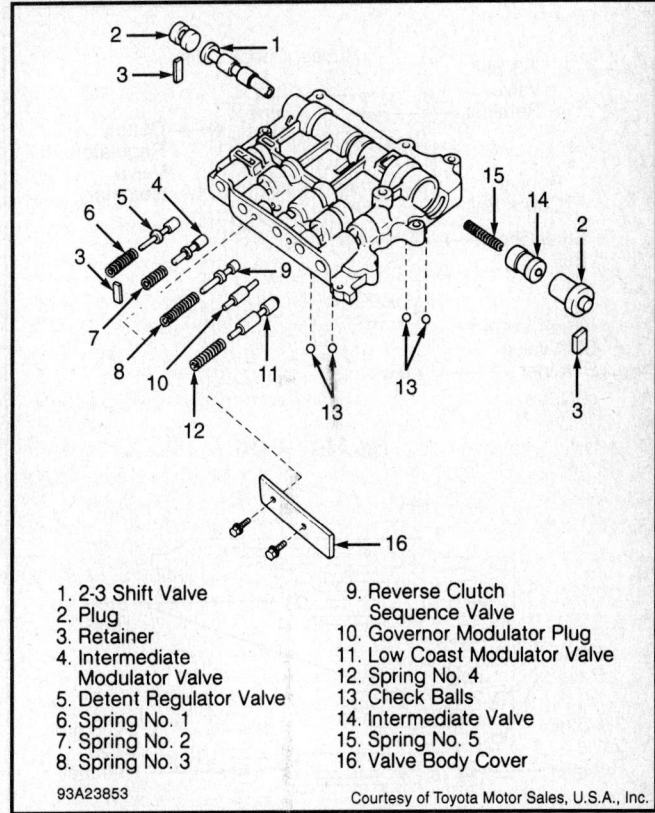

1. 2-3 Shift Valve	9. Reverse Clutch
2. Plug	Sequence Valve
3. Retainer	10. Governor Modulator Plug
4. Intermediate	11. Low Coast Modulator Valve
Modulator Valve	12. Spring No. 4
5. Detent Regulator Valve	13. Check Balls
6. Spring No. 1	14. Intermediate Valve
7. Spring No. 2	15. Spring No. 5
8. Spring No. 3	16. Valve Body Cover

93A23853   Courtesy of Toyota Motor Sales, U.S.A., Inc.

Fig. 53: Exploded View Of Rear Upper Valve Body (A-43D)

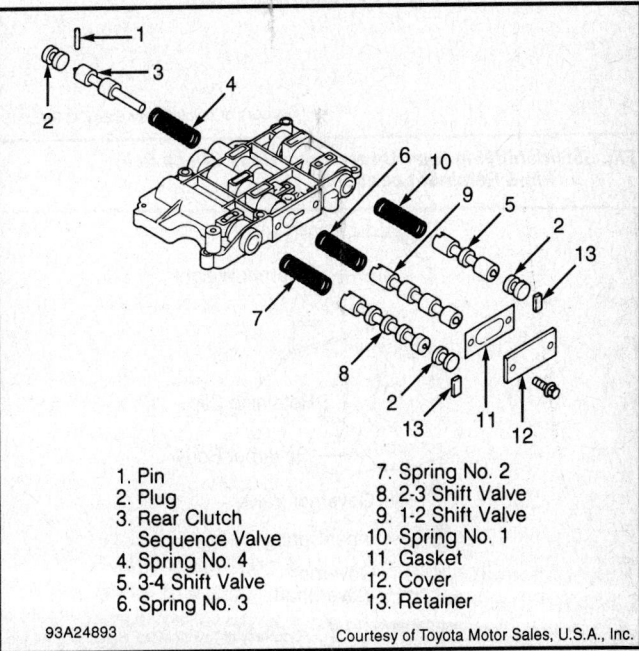

1. Pin	7. Spring No. 2
2. Plug	8. 2-3 Shift Valve
3. Rear Clutch	9. 1-2 Shift Valve
Sequence Valve	10. Spring No. 1
4. Spring No. 4	11. Gasket
5. 3-4 Shift Valve	12. Cover
6. Spring No. 3	13. Retainer

93A24893   Courtesy of Toyota Motor Sales, U.S.A., Inc.

Fig. 54: Exploded View Of Rear Upper Valve Body (A-46DE & A-46DF)

2) Install No. 1 bearing race. Install brake apply tube into transmission case, aligning locking tab with cutout in valve body side of transmission case. Ensure lips of tube end are completely inserted onto outer piston. Install output shaft No. 1 thrust bearing into case. Install rear planetary gear and output shaft into case. Install No. 2 thrust bearing. See Fig. 57.

3) Install pressure plate, with flat surface facing forward. Install 5 discs and 4 plates, starting with a disc and alternating each component. Measure No. 3 brake clutch pack clearance. See Fig. 12. Clearance should be .024-.104" (.61-2.64 mm).

3-1494

AUTOMATIC TRANSMISSIONS
Toyota A-43D, A-46DE & A-46DF (Cont.)

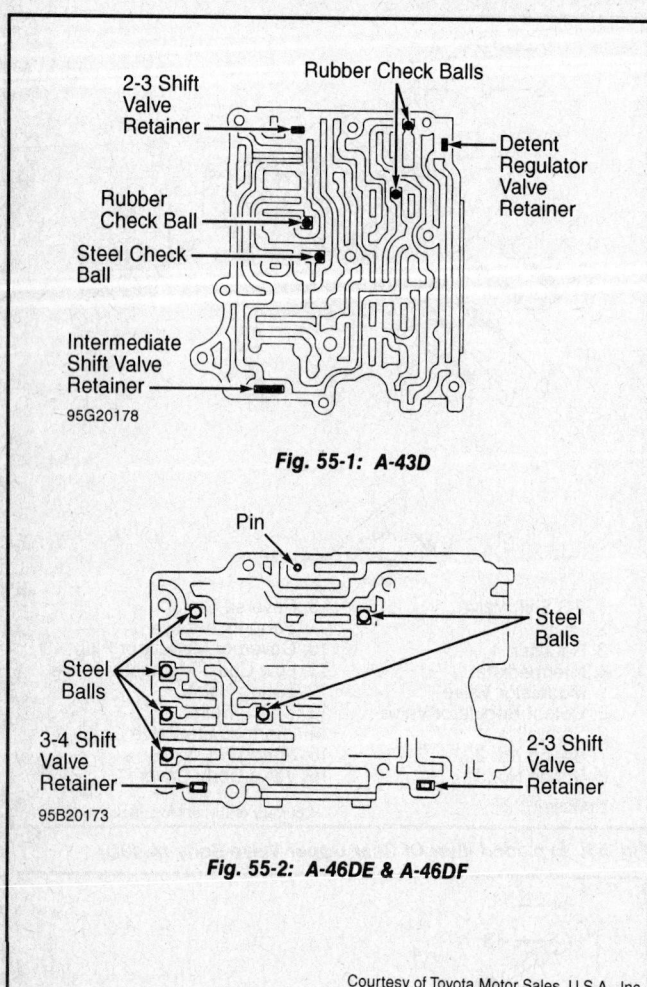

Fig. 55-1: A-43D

Fig. 55-2: A-46DE & A-46DF

Courtesy of Toyota Motor Sales, U.S.A., Inc.

Fig. 55: Identifying Rear Upper Valve Body Check Ball, Pin & Retainer Locations

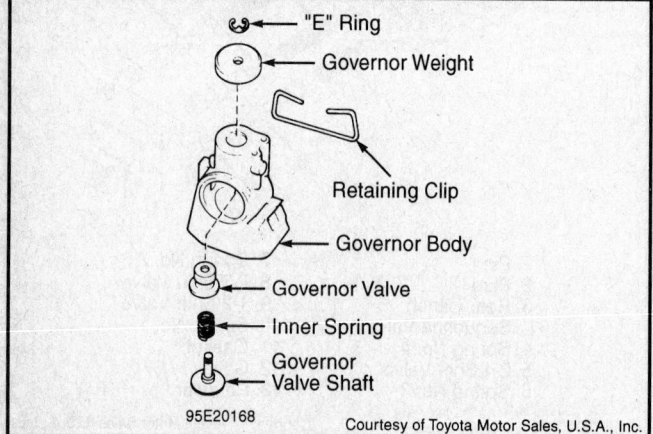

Courtesy of Toyota Motor Sales, U.S.A., Inc.

Fig. 56: Exploded View Of Governor Assembly

4) Remove one-way clutch inner race from planetary gear assembly. Install front planetary gear. Mesh splines of planetary gear with flukes of discs by rotating and pushing planetary gear. Position inner race with notched tooth toward valve body side of case. Push plate into place. Install snap ring. Ensure snap ring is fully seated.
5) Align oil and bolt holes of center support toward valve body side. Align center support bolt holes with case holes and install. Install bolts with wave washers. Tighten bolt on accumulator piston side first to 18 ft. lbs. (25 N.m). Install rear clutch assembly while rotating to align with center support.

6) If fully installed, splined center of clutch will be even with end of sun gear shaft. Install No. 3 rear bearing race, thrust bearing and front bearing race over splined end of rear clutch. Install No. 4 thrust bearing and bearing race on front clutch. *See Fig. 57*. Install front clutch. Rotate and push front clutch to mesh splines of front clutch with flukes of discs.
7) Using calipers and Clutch Drum Thrust Plate Gauge (09370-12010), measure distance between top of case and front clutch drum. *See Fig. 10*. Distance should be equal to that recorded during disassembly. Install Guide Rods (09362-30011) finger tight in front case bolt holes.
8) Install OD case over guide rods with cutout area toward valve body side of case. Install thrust washer on OD case and OD planetary gear. Ensure washer lugs align with holes in OD case and planetary gear assembly. Install No. 5 bearing race on OD planetary gear assembly. *See Fig. 57*.
9) Install OD planetary gear assembly with OD direct clutch and one-way clutch. Rotate and push OD planetary gear to mesh splines with flukes of discs. Ensure thrust washer does not fall during installation. Using calipers and Clutch Drum Thrust Plate Gauge (09370-12010), measure distance between top of case and OD clutch drum. *See Fig. 9*. Distance should be equal to that recorded during disassembly.
10) Install "O" ring on OD case. Install converter housing to transmission case. Tighten 10-mm bolts to 25 ft. lbs. (34 N.m) and 12 mm bolts to 42 ft. lbs. (57 N.m). Install No. 5 thrust bearing on rear of oil pump. Ensure oil seal rings and "O" ring are installed on oil pump.
11) Install oil pump over guide rods and into transmission case. Ensure thrust bearing does not fall off oil pump. Coat oil pump retaining bolts below bolt heads with thread sealer. Remove guide rods. Install bolts and tighten to 15 ft. lbs. (21 N.m). Ensure input shaft turns freely. Using a dial indicator, check output shaft end play. Position dial indicator against end of output shaft. End play should be .012-.035" (.30-.90 mm).
12) Apply air pressure to specific oil passage to check appropriate operating components. *See Fig. 58*. Component application should be heard while applying air. Install NEW oil seals in transmission case. Lubricate oil seal lips prior to installation. Install NEW spacer on manual valve lever. Install manual valve lever shaft into case and through manual valve lever. Install NEW pin with slot at right angle to shaft.
13) Align spacer hole to hollow area of lever. Stake spacer to lever. Ensure manual valve lever shaft turns smoothly. Install "E" ring on shaft. Install parking lock pawl, pivot pin and spring in case. Install lock rod on manual valve lever and install parking lock pawl. Install parking pawl bracket on case. Ensure collar on control rod is toward front of transmission. Tighten bracket bolts to 65 INCH lbs. (7.4 N.m).
14) Check operation of park lock pawl. Ensure output shaft is locked when manual valve lever is in "P" position. Determine proper accumulator piston locations. *See Fig. 8*. Ensure accumulator piston is proper diameter. See ACCUMULATOR PISTON DIAMETER table. Determine proper spring free length and outer diameter for accumulator piston application. See ACCUMULATOR SPRING SPECIFICATIONS table.

ACCUMULATOR PISTON DIAMETER

Application	In. (mm)
Front & Rear Clutch	1.252 (31.80)
No. 2 Brake	1.370 (34.80)

[1] – For accumulator piston locations, *See Fig. 8*.

ACCUMULATOR SPRING SPECIFICATIONS [1]

Application	Diameter In. (mm)	Free Length In. (mm)
Front Clutch		
A-43D	.689 (17.50)	2.547 (64.70)
A-46DE & A-46DF	.689 (17.50)	2.535 (64.40)
No. 2 Brake		
A-43D	.646 (16.40)	2.626 (66.70)
A-46DE & A-46DF	.606 (15.40)	1.260 (32.00)
Rear Clutch		
A-43D	.626 (15.90)	2.173 (55.20)
A-46DE & A-46DF	.626 (15.90)	2.260 (57.40)

[1] – For accumulator spring locations, *See Fig. 8*.

15) Install accumulator pistons and springs. Ensure accumulator pistons are pressed fully into bore. Install NEW "O" rings on throttle cable fitting. Install throttle cable. Align manual valve with pin on manual valve lever. Connect throttle cable to cam. Install valve body assembly and tighten bolts to 89 INCH lbs. (10 N.m). *See Fig. 2.*

16) Install gasket and oil strainer. Tighten bolts to 48 INCH lbs. (5.4 N.m). Using a plastic hammer, install oil tubes. Do not bend or damage oil tubes. Install magnets in oil pan. Ensure magnets do not interfere with oil tubes. Install NEW gasket to transmission case. Align cut part of gasket and transmission case. Install oil pan bolts and tighten to 39 INCH lbs. (4.4 N.m). On A-46DF, install transfer adapter and transfer case.

17) On A-43D models, install governor strainer and plate, if removed. Lift governor assembly retaining clip with screwdriver. Slide governor assembly onto output shaft. Install retaining clip into hole on output shaft. Install lock plate and bolt. Tighten bolt to 35 INCH lbs. (3.9 N.m). Stake lock plate in place.

18) Install snap ring, lock ball, speedometer drive gear and retaining snap rings. On all other models, install sensor rotor and snap ring. On all models, install oil supply tube and extension housing with NEW gasket. Clean all bolt threads. Apply thread sealer to top 4 extension housing bolts prior to installation. Install short bolts to bottom of extension housing. Tighten bolts to 25 ft. lbs. (34 N.m).

19) Install overdrive solenoid. Tighten bolts to 115 INCH lbs. (13 N.m). Lubricate and install NEW "O" rings on cooler unions. Install unions and tighten to 25 ft. lbs. (34 N.m). Lubricate and install "O" ring to sleeve. Insert speedometer driven gear into sleeve. Install sleeve to extension housing. Install lock plate and bolt. Using control shaft lever, turn manual valve lever shaft fully forward and return 2 notches.

20) Insert park/neutral position switch on manual valve lever shaft and temporarily tighten adjusting bolt. Install grommet and NEW lock washer. Install and tighten nut to 35 INCH lbs. (3.9 N.m). Align park/neutral position switch neutral basic line and switch groove. *See Fig. 59.* Tighten adjusting bolt to 40 INCH lbs. (4.5 N.m). Bend over at least 2 washer tabs.

21) Install control shaft lever with spring washer and nut. Tighten nut to 61 INCH lbs. (6.9 N.m). Install wire harness and throttle cable clamp. Install torque converter. Ensure torque converter is installed correctly. Using a straightedge and calipers, measure torque converter depth. For Pickup and Tacoma (1995), distance should be .787" (20.00 mm). For Previa and Tacoma (1996), distance should be 1.250" (31.75 mm). *See Fig. 60.*

BEARING RACE & THRUST BEARING SPECIFICATIONS [1]

Application & No.	Outer Diameter In. (mm)
Bearing Race	
No. 1	2.26 (57.5)
No. 3 (Rear)	1.75 (44.5)
No. 3 (Front)	1.91 (48.5)
No. 4	1.47 (37.3)
No. 5	1.54 (39.1)
Thrust Bearing	
No. 1 (A-43D)	1.74 (44.3)
No. 2	2.17 (55.2)
No. 3	1.83 (46.4)
No. 4	1.48 (37.5)
No. 5	1.70 (43.2)

[1] – See Fig. 57 for component locations.

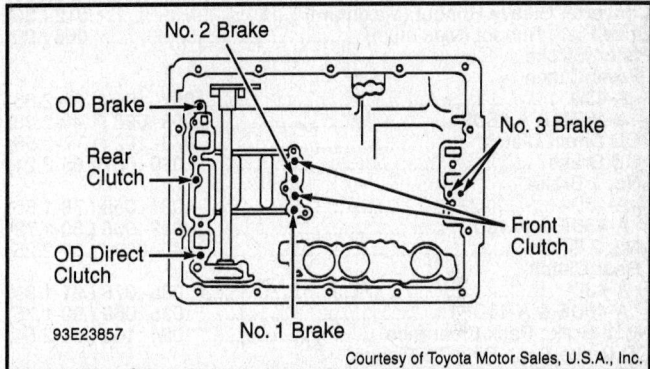

Fig. 58: *Checking Component Piston Operation*

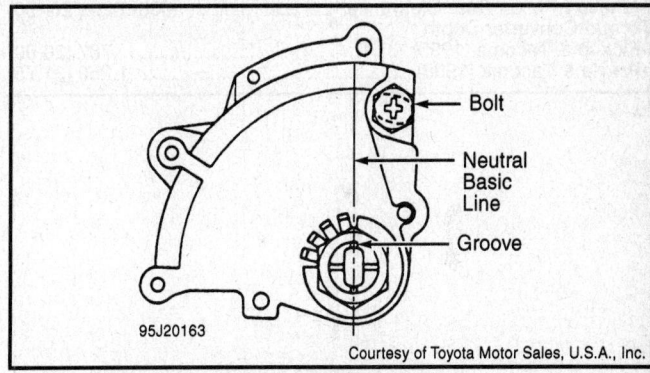

Fig. 59: *Aligning Park/Neutral Position Switch*

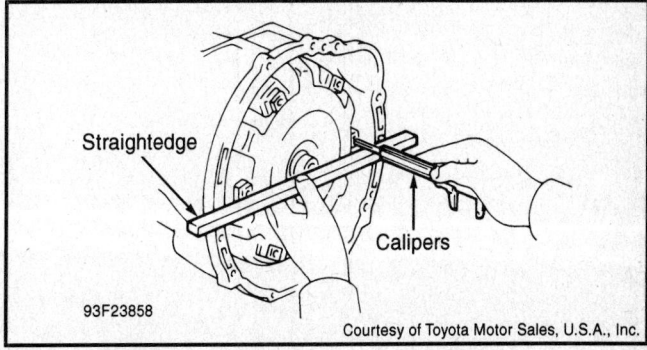

Fig. 60: *Measuring Torque Converter Installed Depth*

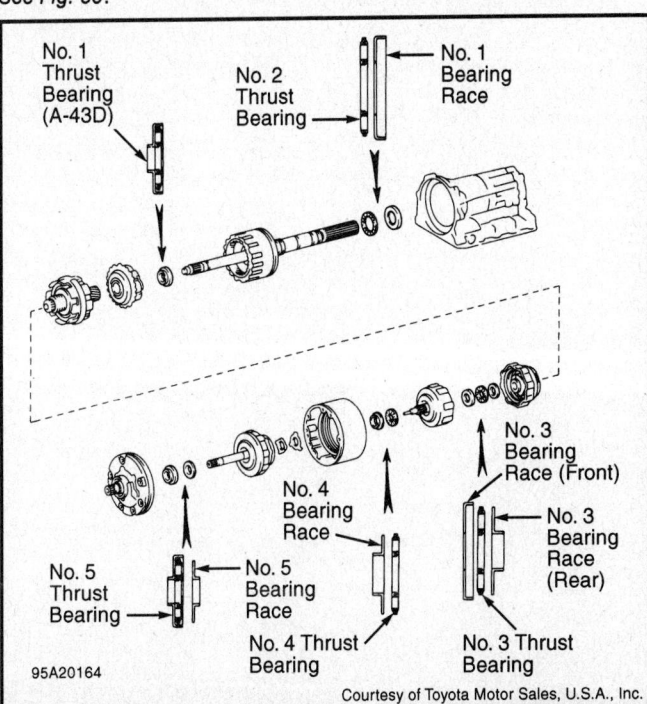

Fig. 57: *Identifying Bearing Race & Thrust Bearing Locations*

AUTOMATIC TRANSMISSIONS
Toyota A-43D, A-46DE & A-46DF (Cont.)

TRANSMISSION SPECIFICATIONS

TRANSMISSION SPECIFICATIONS

Application	In. (mm)
Bushing Diameter (Maximum)	
Center Support	1.435 (36.46)
Extension Housing	1.4996 (38.090)
OD Direct Clutch Drum	.911 (23.14)
OD Planetary Gear	.444 (11.27)
Oil Pump Body	1.5035 (38.190)
Oil Pump Stator Shaft	
A-43D Front & Rear	.8496 (21.58)
A-46DE & A-46DF	
Front	.8496 (21.58)
Rear	.9094 (23.10)
Output Shaft	.712 (18.08)
Planetary Sun Gear	.850 (21.58)
Transmission Case	1.5035 (38.190)
Converter Sleeve Runout (Maximum)	.012 (.30)
Drive Plate Runout (Maximum)	.008 (.20)
Piston Stroke	
Front Clutch	
A-43D	.052-.105 (1.32-2.66)
A-46DE & A-46DF	.055-.098 (1.40-2.48)
OD Direct Clutch	.070-.102 (1.77-2.58)
OD Brake	.026-.087 (.65-2.21)
No. 1 Brake	
A-43D	.031-.059 (.78-1.50)
A-46DE & A-46DF	.032-.068 (.80-1.73)
No. 2 Brake	.040-.089 (1.01-2.25)
Rear Clutch	
A-43D	.035-.078 (.91-1.99)
A-46DE & A-46DF	.035-.069 (.90-1.75)
No. 3 Brake Pack Clearance	.024-.104 (.61-2.64)
OD Brake Snap Ring-To-Flange	
Standard Clearance	.014-.075 (.35-1.91)
Output Shaft End Play	.012-.035 (.30-.90)
Planetary Pinion Gear Clearance	.008-.020 (.20-.50)
Torque Converter Depth	
Pickup & Tacoma (1995)	.787 (20.00)
Previa & Tacoma (1996)	1.250 (31.75)

TORQUE SPECIFICATIONS

TORQUE SPECIFICATIONS

Application	Ft. Lbs. (N.m)
Center Support-To-Case Bolt	18 (25)
Converter-To-Drive Plate Bolt	20 (27)
Cooler Union Nut	25 (34)
Drive Plate Bolt	
Pickup	61 (83)
Previa & Tacoma	55 (74)
Extension Housing-To-Case Bolt	25 (34)
Oil Pump-To-Case Bolt	15 (21)
Transfer Case Adapter Bolt (A-46DF)	25 (34)
Transfer Case-To-Adapter Bolt (A-46DF)	33 (45)
Transmission Case-To-Converter Housing Bolt	
10-mm	25 (34)
12-mm	42 (57)
Transmission Mounting Bolt	36 (49)

Application	INCH Lbs. (N.m)
Control Shaft Lever Bolt	61 (6.9)
Governor Lock Plate Bolt	35 (3.9)
Lock Pawl Bracket Bolt	65 (7.4)
Oil Pan Bolt	39 (4.4)
Oil Pump Housing Bolt	65 (7.4)
Oil Strainer Bolt	48 (5.4)
Overdrive Solenoid Bolt	115 (13)
Park/Neutral Position Switch	
Adjusting Bolt	48 (5.4)
Mounting Nut	35 (3.9)
Throttle Cam Bolt	65 (7.4)
Upper Valve Body-To-Lower	
Valve Body Bolt	48 (5.4)
Valve Assembly-To-Case Bolt	89 (10)

Pickup, Tacoma

APPLICATION

APPLICATION

Vehicle	Transmission Model
1995 Pickup (2.4L)	A-43D
1995-96 Tacoma (2.4L)	A-43D

CAUTION: Tacoma is equipped with a Supplemental Restraint System (SRS). When servicing vehicle, use care to avoid accidental air bag deployment. All SRS electrical connections and wiring harness are covered by Yellow insulation. SRS-related components are located in steering column, center console, instrument panel and lower panel on instrument panel. DO NOT use electrical test equipment on these circuits. If necessary, deactivate SRS before servicing components. See AIR BAG SERVICING article in APPLICATIONS & IDENTIFICATION section.

DESCRIPTION & OPERATION

A-43D transmission has an electronically controlled overdrive operation. Transmission overdrive shifting is controlled by electric solenoid. On Pickup, solenoid is turned on and off by overdrive relay. When engine reaches normal operating temperature, coolant temperature sensor sends signal to Electronic Controlled Transmission (ECT) Electronic Control Unit (ECU). ECT ECU sends signal to relay to activate overdrive solenoid. On Tacoma, solenoid is turned on and off by overdrive switch.

NOTE: On Pickup, Electronic Controlled Transmission (ECT) Electronic Control Unit (ECU) is used for controlling the engine fuel injection system and transmission (overdrive solenoid). Control unit is referred to as the ECT ECU. ECT ECU is located behind passenger's kick panel. On Tacoma, transmission is not equipped with ECT ECU input.

An Overdrive (OD) switch is mounted on shift lever. When OD switch is depressed to ON position, transmission will shift into 4th gear when shift lever is in "D" position, and OD OFF light on instrument panel will go off. When OD switch is released to OFF position, transmission will shift into 3rd gear, and OD OFF light on instrument panel will come on.

Transmission is equipped with a cable-operated (Pickup) or electronic (Tacoma) shift lock and key lock system. Shift lock system prevents shift lever from being moved from Park unless brake pedal is depressed. Key lock system prevents ignition key from being moved from ACC to LOCK position on ignition switch unless shift lever is in Park. For more information on shift lock and key lock system, see TOYOTA SHIFT LOCK SYSTEM article.

TROUBLE SHOOTING

NO OVERDRIVE ENGAGEMENT (PICKUP)

NOTE: For terminal locations, see WIRING DIAGRAMS. Manufacturer does not provide trouble shooting information for Tacoma.

1) Inspect main switch, relay and solenoid harness connectors. Clean and repair as needed. Inspect GAUGE and TURN fuses. Replace as needed.
2) Using DVOM, backprobe OD relay harness connector. Turn ignition switch on. Check for battery voltage between relay harness connector terminal No. 2 and ground. If voltage is not present, inspect and repair circuit between harness connector and TURN fuse.
3) If voltage is present, check voltage between relay harness connector terminal No. 1 and ground. With OD main switch in ON position, 10-12 volts should be present. With OD main switch in OFF position, zero volts should be present.

4) If voltage is within specification, check for internal transmission malfunction. See overhaul article for further testing information. Also check for faulty OD solenoid and/or solenoid circuit.
5) If voltage is not within specification, check voltage between relay harness connector terminal No. 3 and ground. With OD main switch in ON position, 10-12 volts should be present. With OD main switch in OFF position, zero volts should be present.
6) If voltage is not within specification, check for faulty OD main switch or switch circuit. If voltage is within specification, check for battery voltage between relay harness connector terminal No. 4 and ground.
7) If battery voltage is present, substitute known good relay and retest. If battery voltage is not present, turn ignition off. Disconnect ECT ECU harness connector. ECT ECU is located behind passenger's kick panel.
8) Turn ignition on. Check for battery voltage between OD relay harness connector terminal No. 4 and ground. If battery voltage is present, substitute known good ECT ECU and retest. If condition still exists, check for faulty coolant temperature sensor.
9) If battery voltage is not present, check for faulty OD relay. If relay is okay, inspect circuit between ECT ECU and OD relay. Repair as needed. See WIRING DIAGRAMS.

COMPONENT TESTS

Engine Coolant Temperature (ECT) Sensor (Pickup) – Disconnect electrical connector from ECT. ECT is located on front of engine next to injector time switch. Using ohmmeter, check resistance between terminals of coolant temperature sensor. Resistance should be as specified. *See Fig. 1.* Replace sensor if resistance is not within specification.

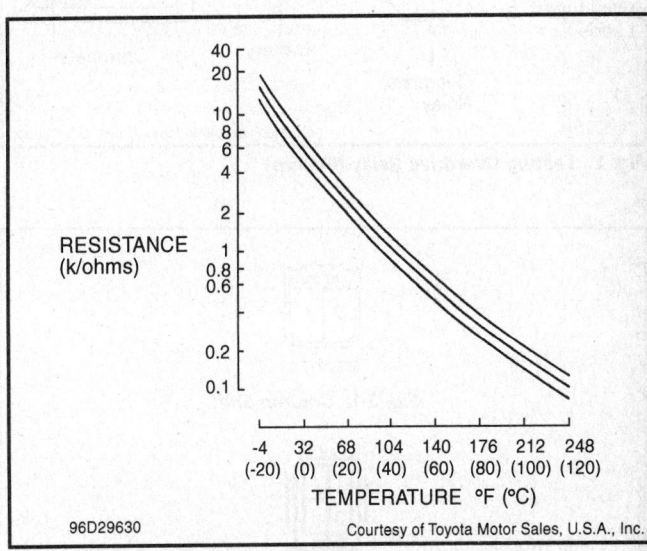

96D29630   Courtesy of Toyota Motor Sales, U.S.A., Inc.

Fig. 1: Checking Engine Coolant Temperature (ECT) Sensor

Overdrive Relay (Pickup) – 1) Remove overdrive relay from pedal bracket. Using an ohmmeter, ensure continuity exists between terminals No. 1 and 2 of overdrive relay. *See Fig. 2.* Replace relay if continuity does not exist.
2) Apply battery voltage across terminals No. 2 and 3. Using an ohmmeter, ensure continuity does not exist between terminals No. 1 and 2. Apply battery voltage across terminals No. 2 and 4. *See Fig. 2.* Ensure continuity does not exist at terminals No. 1 and 2. Replace relay if continuity exists. Reinstall overdrive relay to pedal bracket.

Overdrive Solenoid – 1) Using an ohmmeter, measure resistance between solenoid terminal and solenoid body (Pickup), or between solenoid terminals (Tacoma). Resistance should be 11-15 ohms. If resistance is not as described, replace overdrive solenoid. Apply battery voltage to solenoid. Check for solenoid operating sound.
2) To check operation of solenoid seals, remove solenoid from transmission. Apply low pressure compressed air to solenoid. Air should pass through solenoid when battery voltage is connected to component connector. Air should not pass through solenoid when voltage is disconnected.

Overdrive Off Indicator – Turn ignition switch to ON position. Depress OD switch to ON position. Ensure OD OFF indicator light is not activated. Depress OD switch to OFF position. OD OFF indicator light should activate. If OD OFF indicator light does not activate, replace indicator light.

Overdrive Main Switch – 1) On Pickup, remove steering column cover or console box. Locate overdrive main switch connector. *See Fig. 3* for terminal identification. With OD switch in OFF position, continuity should exist between terminals No. 1 and 2 on column shifter models, and between terminals No. 1 and 3 on floor shifter models. Replace switch if continuity is not as indicated.

2) On Tacoma, remove lower finish panel. Locate overdrive main switch connector. *See Fig. 4* for terminal identification. With OD switch in OFF position, continuity should not exist between terminals No. 1 and 3. Replace switch if continuity is not as indicated.

Park/Neutral Position (PNP) Switch – Disconnect harness connector at park/neutral position switch. Switch is located on side of transmission. Using ohmmeter, check for continuity between specified terminals in accordance with shift lever position. *See Figs. 5 and 6.* Replace PNP switch if defective.

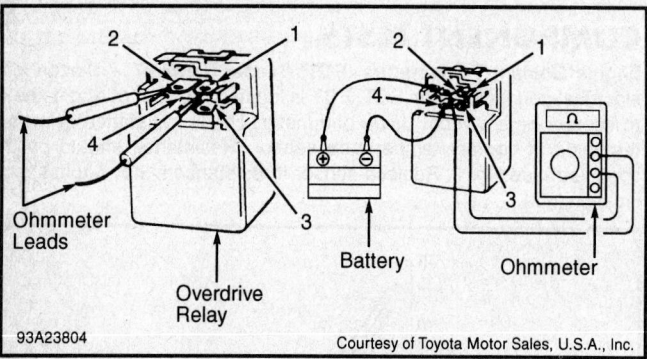

Fig. 2: Testing Overdrive Relay (Pickup)

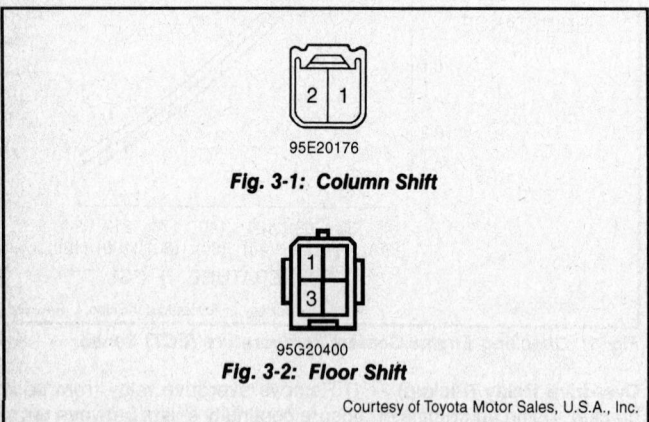

Fig. 3-1: Column Shift

Fig. 3-2: Floor Shift

Courtesy of Toyota Motor Sales, U.S.A., Inc.

Fig. 3: Identifying Overdrive Main Switch Terminals (Pickup)

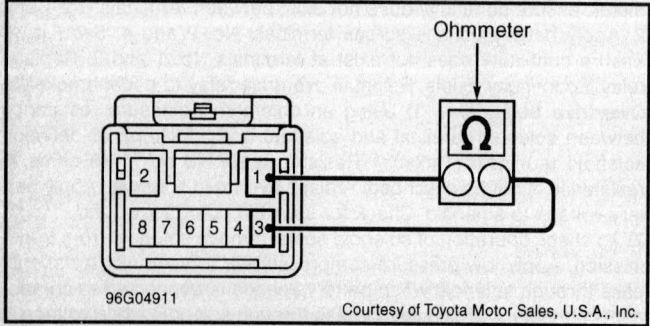

Fig. 4: Identifying Overdrive Main Switch Terminals (Tacoma)

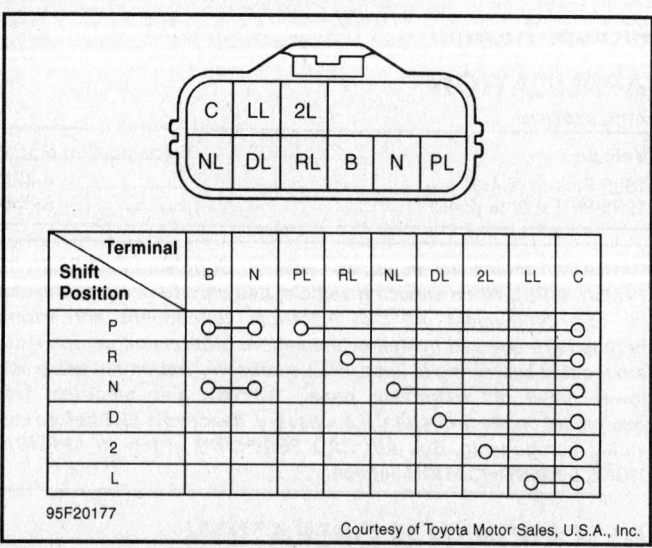

Terminal Shift Position	B	N	PL	RL	NL	DL	2L	LL	C
P	○	○	○						○
R				○					○
N	○	○			○				○
D						○			
2							○		
L								○	○

95F20177

Courtesy of Toyota Motor Sales, U.S.A., Inc.

Fig. 5: Testing Park/Neutral Position Switch (Pickup)

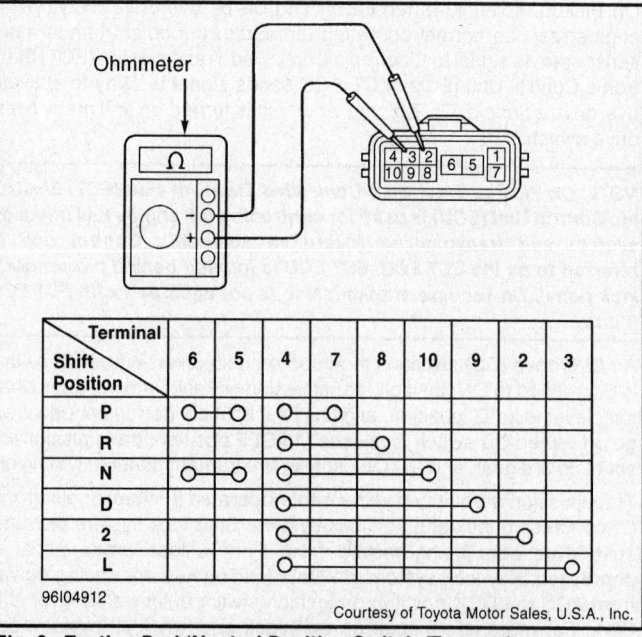

Terminal Shift Position	6	5	4	7	8	10	9	2	3
P	○	○	○	○					
R			○		○				
N	○	○	○			○			
D			○				○		
2			○					○	
L			○						○

96I04912

Courtesy of Toyota Motor Sales, U.S.A., Inc.

Fig. 6: Testing Park/Neutral Position Switch (Tacoma)

WIRING DIAGRAMS

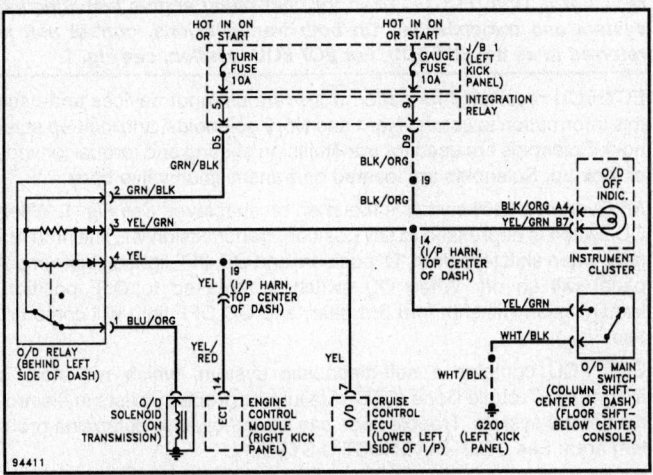

Fig. 7: Overdrive Control System Wiring Diagram (1995 Pickup – 2.4L)

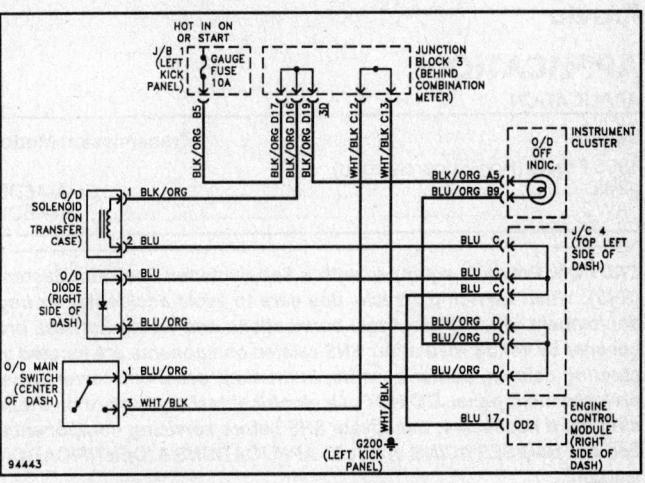

Fig. 8: Overdrive Control System Wiring Diagram (1995-96 Tacoma – 2.4L)

AUTOMATIC TRANSMISSIONS
Toyota A-46DE & A-46DF Electronic Controls

Previa

APPLICATION

APPLICATION

Vehicle	Transmission Model
1995 Previa (Non-Supercharged)	
2WD	A-46DE
AWD	A-46DF

CAUTION: Previa is equipped with a Supplemental Restraint System (SRS). When servicing vehicle, use care to avoid accidental air bag deployment. All SRS electrical connections and wiring harness are covered by Yellow insulation. SRS-related components are located in steering column, center console, instrument panel and lower panel on instrument panel. DO NOT use electrical test equipment on these circuits. If necessary, deactivate SRS before servicing components. See AIR BAG SERVICING article in APPLICATIONS & IDENTIFICATION section.

DESCRIPTION & OPERATION

A-46DE and A-46DF automatic transmissions are electronically controlled. Transmission shifting and torque converter lock-up are controlled by Engine and Electronic Controlled Transmission (ECT) Electronic Control Unit (ECU). A-46DF transmission is equipped with a full time transfer case.

NOTE: Engine and Electronic Controlled Transmission (ECT) Electronic Control Unit (ECU) is used for controlling engine fuel injection system and transmission. On both transmissions, control unit is referred to as the ECT ECU. For ECT ECU location, see Fig. 1.

ECT ECU receives information from various input devices and uses this information to control No. 1 and No. 2 solenoids, and lock-up solenoid. Solenoids are used for transmission shifting and torque converter lock-up. Solenoids are located on transmission valve body.

An Overdrive (OD) switch is mounted on shift lever. *See Fig. 1.* When OD switch is depressed to ON position, transmission will shift into 4th gear when shift lever is in "D" position, and OD OFF light on instrument panel will go off. When OD switch is released to OFF position, transmission will shift into 3rd gear, and OD OFF light will come on. *See Fig. 1.*

ECT ECU contains a self-diagnostic system, which will store a Diagnostic Trouble Code (DTC) if failure or problem exists in electronic control system. Trouble code can be retrieved to determine problem area. See SELF-DIAGNOSTIC SYSTEM.

Transmission is equipped with a cable-operated shift lock and key lock system. Shift lock system prevents shift lever from being moved from Park unless brake pedal is depressed. Key lock system prevents ignition key from being moved from ACC to LOCK position on ignition switch unless shift lever is in Park.

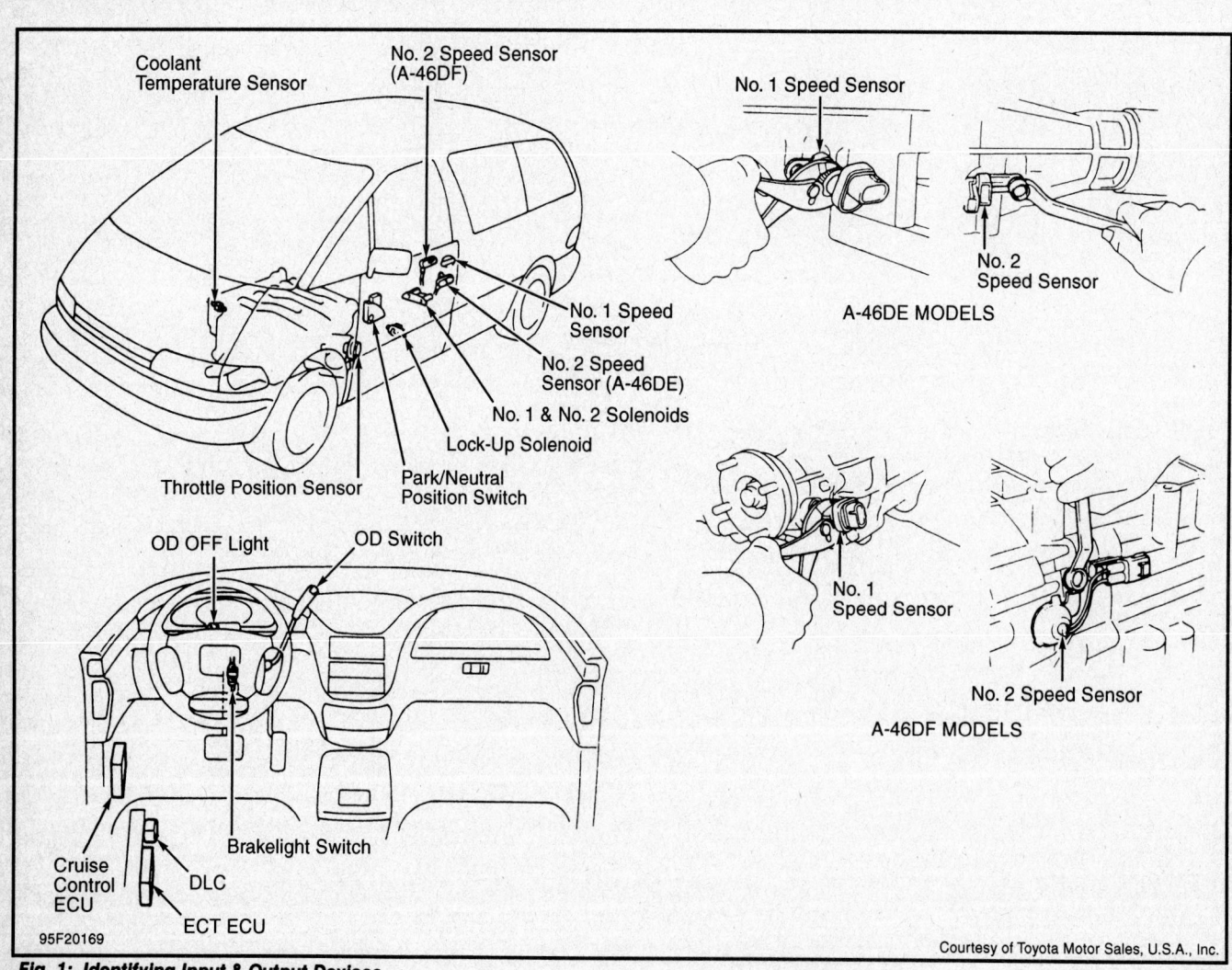

95F20169

Courtesy of Toyota Motor Sales, U.S.A., Inc.

Fig. 1: Identifying Input & Output Devices

AUTOMATIC TRANSMISSIONS
Toyota A-46DE & A-46DF Electronic Controls (Cont.)

3-1501

ECT ECU INPUT DEVICES

Distributor (Tach Signal) – Distributor delivers an input signal to ECT ECU indicating engine RPM and crankshaft position signal.

Park/Neutral Position (PNP) Switch Signal – PNP switch (also referred to as neutral start switch) delivers an input signal to ECT ECU indicating shift lever position. Switch is located on side of transmission. *See Fig. 1.*

Throttle Position (TP) Sensor – TP sensor delivers closed throttle and variable throttle position input signals to ECT ECU. TP sensor is located on side of throttle body. *See Fig. 1.*

Vehicle Speed Sensor (VSS) – Vehicle speed signal is delivered to ECT ECU by No. 1 and No. 2 speed sensors. *See Fig. 1.*

Brakelight Switch Signal – Brakelight switch delivers input signal to ECT ECU, indicating vehicle braking. Brakelight switch is located on brake pedal support. *See Fig. 1.*

OD Switch – OD switch provides an input signal to ECT ECU to indicate when overdrive is selected by operator. When OD switch is depressed to ON position, transmission will shift into 4th gear when shift lever is in "D" position, and OD OFF light on instrument panel will go off. OD switch is released to OFF position, transmission will shift into 3rd gear, and OD OFF light will come on. OD switch is mounted on shift lever. *See Fig. 1.*

Engine Coolant Temperature (ECT) Sensor – Coolant temperature sensor delivers input signal to ECT ECU, indicating engine coolant temperature. Coolant temperature sensor is located at top of water outlet pipe on front of engine. *See Fig. 1.*

Cruise Control Electronic Control Unit (ECU) – Cruise control ECU delivers an input signal to control overdrive operation in accordance with vehicle speed when cruise control is operating. When in overdrive with cruise control on, if vehicle speed drops 2 MPH less than set speed, overdrive is released to prevent reduction in vehicle speed. Once vehicle speed is more than set speed, overdrive is resumed. If coolant temperature is low, transmission will not shift into overdrive. Cruise control ECU is located near driver-side kick panel. *See Fig. 1.*

ECT ECU OUTPUT DEVICES

No. 1 & No. 2 Solenoids – ECT ECU controls transmission shifting by delivering an output signal to operate proper solenoid. Solenoids are located on transmission valve body. *See Fig. 1.* No. 1 solenoid has a Brown/White wire and No. 2 solenoid has a Brown/Yellow wire. Solenoids are operated in accordance with shift lever range. *See Fig. 2.* If a solenoid malfunctions, ECT ECU may select a preselected gear. *See Fig. 2.*

NOTE: ECT ECU provides a fail-safe system which will place transmission in preselected gear depending on solenoid failure. In other gears, fail-safe system will not be activated and transmission will be placed in a specified gear. See Fig. 2.

Lock-Up Solenoid – ECT ECU controls torque converter lock-up by delivering an output signal to lock-up solenoid. Lock-up solenoid is activated when shift lever is in "D" position and vehicle is at specified speed. Lock-up solenoid has a Green/Yellow wire.

SELF-DIAGNOSTIC SYSTEM

SYSTEM DIAGNOSIS

NOTE: Before testing transmission, ensure fluid level is correct and throttle and shift cables are properly adjusted. Ensure engine starts with shift lever in Park and Neutral to ensure proper adjustment of park/neutral position switch. Transmission must first be tested by checking for stored codes. See RETRIEVING TROUBLE CODES.

ECT ECU monitors transmission operation and contains a self-diagnostic system which stores a trouble code if an electronic control system failure or problem exists. If a problem exists in No. 1 solenoid, No. 2 solenoid or speed sensors and trouble code is set, ECT ECU delivers a signal to blink OD OFF light on instrument panel to warn driver.

NOTE: OD OFF light on instrument panel will not blink to warn driver if a problem exists or trouble code is stored for the following components:
- *Lock-Up Solenoid*
- *Brakelight Switch*
- *Throttle Position (TP) Sensor*

RETRIEVING TROUBLE CODES

NOTE: Before retrieving trouble codes, ensure battery voltage exists for proper self-diagnosis system operation. Perform diagnostic circuit check before retrieving trouble codes to ensure operation of OD OFF light. See DIAGNOSTIC CIRCUIT CHECK.

Diagnostic Circuit Check – 1) Turn ignition on. Release OD switch to OFF position. Ensure OD OFF light on instrument panel comes on. *See Fig. 1.* If OD OFF light does not come on, check OD switch and wiring circuit.

Range	NORMAL			NO. 1 SOLENOID MALFUNCTIONING			NO. 2 SOLENOID MALFUNCTIONING			BOTH SOLENOIDS MALFUNCTIONING		
	Solenoid Valve		Gear Position	Solenoid Valve		Gear Position	Solenoid Valve		Gear Position	Solenoid Valve		Gear Position
	No. 1	No. 2		No. 1	No. 2		No. 1	No. 2		No. 1	No. 2	
D range	ON	OFF	1st	X	ON (OFF)	3rd (O/D)	ON	X	1st	X	X	O/D
	ON	ON	2nd	X	ON	3rd	OFF (ON)	X	O/D (1st)	X	X	O/D
	OFF	ON	3rd	X	ON	3rd	OFF	X	O/D	X	X	O/D
	OFF	OFF	O/D	X	OFF	O/D	OFF	X	O/D	X	X	O/D
2 range	ON	OFF	1st	X	ON (OFF)	3rd (O/D)	ON	X	1st	X	X	3rd
	ON	ON	2nd	X	ON	3rd	OFF (ON)	X	3rd (1st)	X	X	3rd
	OFF	ON	3rd	X	ON	3rd	OFF	X	3rd	X	X	3rd
L range	ON	OFF	1st	X	OFF	1st	ON	X	1st	X	X	1st
	ON	ON	2nd	X	ON	2nd	ON	X	1st	X	X	1st

93E25019   ( ): No fail-safe function   X: Malfunctions   Courtesy of Toyota Motor Sales, U.S.A., Inc.

Fig. 2: Checking No. 1 & No. 2 Solenoid Operation

3-1502

AUTOMATIC TRANSMISSIONS
Toyota A-46DE & A-46DF Electronic Controls (Cont.)

2) Depress OD switch to the ON position. Ensure OD OFF light on instrument panel goes off. If OD OFF light remains on, check OD switch and wiring circuit. If OD OFF light is blinking, check for stored trouble codes. See ECT ECU TROUBLE CODES.

ECT ECU Trouble Codes – **1)** Turn ignition on. DO NOT start engine. Depress OD switch to ON position.

NOTE: Trouble codes can only be retrieved with OD switch in the ON position. If OD switch is in OFF position, OD OFF light will be on continuously and will not blink trouble code.

---

2) Install jumper wire between terminals T_E, and E_1 of data link connector. *See Fig. 3.* Data link connector is located on floor next to parking brake handle. *See Fig. 1.*

3) Note number of flashes from OD OFF light on instrument panel. If normal system operation exists, OD OFF light will blink 2 times per second. *See Fig. 4.*

4) If system is operating correctly and no trouble code exists, turn ignition off and remove jumper wire. Perform MANUAL SHIFT TEST to determine if problem is an electrical or mechanical transmission problem. Check system by symptom. See appropriate symptom under SYMPTOM TROUBLE SHOOTING.

5) If trouble code exists, OD OFF light will flash once every second. Number of flashes will equal first digit of trouble code. After a pause of 1.5 seconds, second digit will be displayed. *See Fig. 4.*

6) If more than one trouble code exists, next trouble code will be displayed after pause of 2.5 seconds. Smallest number trouble code will be first. Trouble codes will be repeated.

7) Once trouble code is obtained, determine probable cause and symptom. See DIAGNOSTIC TROUBLE CODE (DTC) IDENTIFICATION table. For trouble shooting of trouble codes, see DIAGNOSTIC TESTS. Turn ignition off and remove jumper wire.

NOTE: Once repairs have been performed, trouble codes must be cleared from ECT ECU memory. See CLEARING TROUBLE CODES under SELF-DIAGNOSTIC SYSTEM.

DIAGNOSTIC TROUBLE CODE (DTC) IDENTIFICATION

DTC	[1] Probable Cause
42	[2] No. 1 Speed Sensor
61	[2] No. 2 Speed Sensor
62	No. 1 Solenoid
63	No. 2 Solenoid
64	Lock-Up Solenoid

[1] – Check listed component for probable cause. Check wiring and connections of specified component.

[2] – If both No. 1 and No. 2 speed sensors fail simultaneously, trouble code will not exist and transmission will not upshift from 1st gear with shift lever in "D" position.

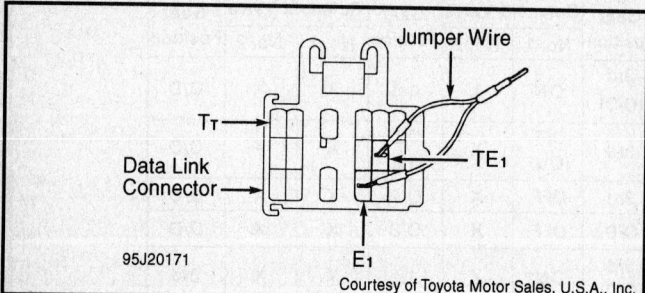

Fig. 3: Identifying Check Connector Terminals

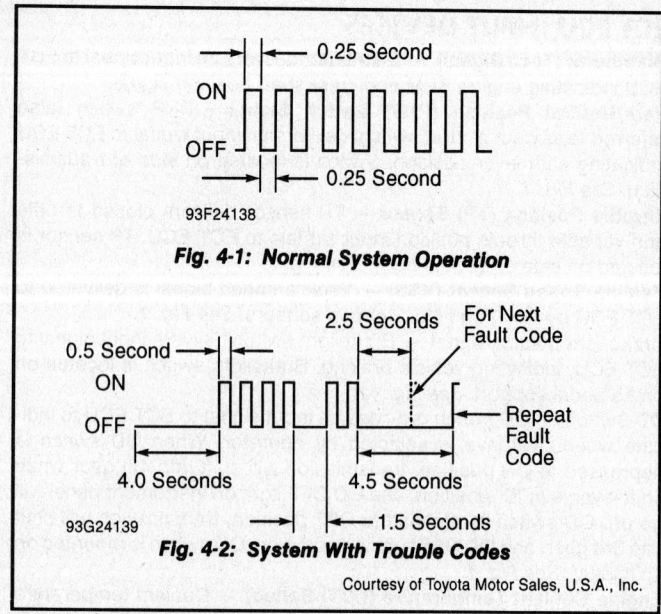

Fig. 4-1: Normal System Operation

Fig. 4-2: System With Trouble Codes

Courtesy of Toyota Motor Sales, U.S.A., Inc.

Fig. 4: Identifying Trouble Code Displays

CLEARING TROUBLE CODES

Once repairs have been performed, trouble codes must be cleared from ECT ECU memory. Remove EFI 15-amp fuse for 10 seconds to clear memory in ECT ECU. EFI fuse is in fuse/relay box, located at center of instrument panel. *See Fig. 5.* Fuse may need to be removed for more than 10 seconds in cold ambient temperatures. Reinstall fuse.

NOTE: Trouble codes may also be cleared by disconnecting negative battery cable. However, memory for electronic components will also be canceled.

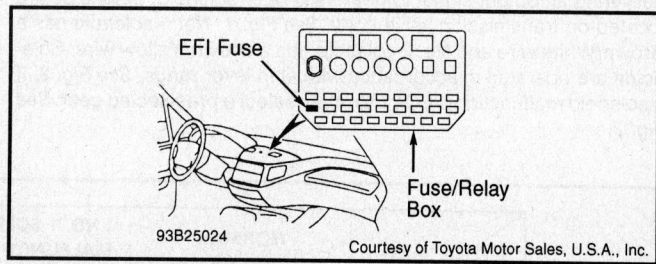

Courtesy of Toyota Motor Sales, U.S.A., Inc.

Fig. 5: Identifying Fuse/Relay Box Location

DIAGNOSTIC TESTS

When trouble shooting transmission, first check for stored trouble codes and repair as necessary. If no trouble codes exist, perform manual shift test to determine if problem area is in electrical circuits or a mechanical transmission problem. See MANUAL SHIFT TEST.

DTC 42: NO. 1 VEHICLE SPEED SENSOR (VSS)

1) Obtain access to ECT ECU. *See Fig. 1.* Using ohmmeter, backprobe ECT ECU harness connector. Check for continuity between terminal SP_1 of ECT ECU connector and body ground. *See Fig. 7.*

2) If continuity exists, replace ECT ECU. If continuity does not exist, check No. 1 vehicle speed sensor. See NO. 1 VEHICLE SPEED SENSOR under COMPONENT TESTS.

3) Replace No. 1 vehicle speed sensor if defective. If No. 1 vehicle speed sensor is okay, check wiring between ECT ECU and combination meter in instrument panel.

AUTOMATIC TRANSMISSIONS
Toyota A-46DE & A-46DF Electronic Controls (Cont.)

3-1503

DTC 61: NO. 2 VEHICLE SPEED SENSOR (VSS)

1) Obtain access to ECT ECU. *See Fig. 1.* Using ohmmeter, backprobe ECT ECU harness connector. Check for continuity between terminal SP$_2$ of ECT ECU connector and body ground. *See Fig. 7.*

2) If continuity exists, replace ECT ECU. If continuity does not exist, check No. 2 vehicle speed sensor. See NO. 2 VEHICLE SPEED SENSOR under COMPONENT TESTS.

3) Replace No. 2 vehicle speed sensor if defective. If No. 2 vehicle speed sensor is okay, check wiring between ECT ECU and No. 2 vehicle speed sensor, located on transmission. *See Fig. 1.*

DTC 62: NO. 1 SOLENOID CIRCUIT

1) Access ECT ECU. *See Fig. 1.* Using ohmmeter, backprobe ECT ECU harness connector. Check resistance between ECT ECU terminal S$_1$ and body ground with connector removed from ECT ECU. *See Fig. 7.*

2) Resistance should be 11-15 ohms. If resistance is okay, replace ECT ECU. If resistance is not within specification, remove oil pan. Disconnect electrical connector at No. 1 solenoid, located on transmission valve body. *See Fig. 1.* No. 1 solenoid contains a Brown/White wire.

3) Check resistance between electrical terminal on No. 1 solenoid and body ground. Replace No. 1 solenoid if resistance is not 11-15 ohms. If resistance is 11-15 ohms, check wiring between No. 1 solenoid and ECT ECU.

DTC 63: NO. 2 SOLENOID CIRCUIT

1) Obtain access to ECT ECU. *See Fig. 1.* Using ohmmeter, backprobe ECT ECU harness connector. Check resistance between terminal S$_2$ and body ground with connector removed from ECT ECU. *See Fig. 7.*

2) Resistance should be 11-15 ohms. If resistance is okay, replace ECT ECU. If resistance is not within specification, remove oil pan. Disconnect electrical connector at No. 2 solenoid, located on transmission valve body. *See Fig. 1.* No. 2 solenoid contains a Brown/Yellow wire.

3) Check resistance between electrical terminal on No. 2 solenoid and body ground. Replace No. 2 solenoid if resistance is not 11-15 ohms. If resistance is 11-15 ohms, check wiring between No. 2 solenoid and ECT ECU.

DTC 64: LOCK-UP SOLENOID CIRCUIT

1) Obtain access to ECT ECU. *See Fig. 1.* Using ohmmeter, backprobe ECT ECU harness connector. Check resistance between terminal S$_L$ and body ground with connector removed from ECT ECU. *See Fig. 7.*

2) Resistance should be 11-15 ohms. If resistance is okay, replace ECT ECU. If resistance is not within specification, remove oil pan. Disconnect electrical connector at lock-up solenoid, located on transmission valve body. *See Fig. 1.* Lock-up solenoid contains a Green/Yellow wire.

3) Check resistance between electrical terminal on lock-up solenoid and body ground. Replace lock-up solenoid if resistance is not 11-15 ohms. If resistance is 11-15 ohms, check wiring between lock-up solenoid and ECT ECU.

MANUAL SHIFT TEST

NOTE: Perform manual shift test if no trouble codes exist. Manual shift test determines if problem area is in electrical circuits or a mechanical transmission problem.

1) With ignition off, disconnect electrical connector for solenoids from rear of transmission. *See Fig. 6.*

2) Road test vehicle and ensure transmission gear changes corresponds with shift lever position. See GEAR APPLICATION table.

3) If abnormality exists, a mechanical transmission problem exists. If all gears are correct, perform trouble shooting in accordance with symptom. See SYMPTOM TROUBLE SHOOTING. Turn ignition off.

4) Reconnect electrical connector. Clear trouble codes from ECT ECU memory, as disconnecting electrical connector may set a trouble code. See CLEARING TROUBLE CODES under SELF-DIAGNOSTIC SYSTEM.

GEAR APPLICATION

Shift Lever Position	Gear
"D"	Overdrive
"2"	3rd
"L"	1st
"R"	Reverse
"P"	Park

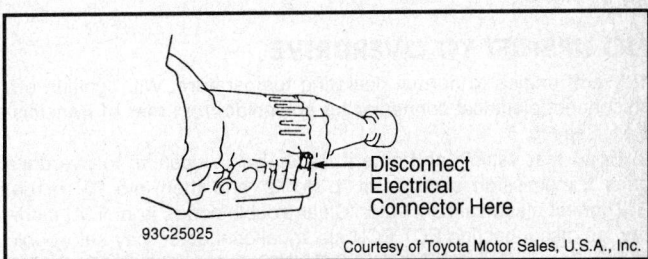

93C25025   Disconnect Electrical Connector Here

Courtesy of Toyota Motor Sales, U.S.A., Inc.

Fig. 6: Identifying Solenoid Electrical Connector

SYMPTOM TROUBLE SHOOTING

NOTE: If problem area is not listed under symptom trouble shooting, check throttle position sensor signal, brake switch signal, gear selector signal and ECT ECU voltages. See CIRCUIT TESTS.

TRANSMISSION WILL NOT SHIFT

1) Warm engine to normal operating temperature. Connect voltmeter between terminals T$_T$ and E$_1$ of data link connector. *See Fig. 3.* Data link connector is located next to parking brake handle on driver's side.

2) Turn ignition on. Note that voltage changes with throttle opening. If voltage changes with throttle opening, proceed to step **6)**. If voltage does not change with throttle opening, proceed to next step.

3) Obtain access to ECT ECU. Connect voltmeter between terminals STP and E$_1$ on ECT ECU with connector installed on ECT ECU. *See Fig. 7.*

4) No voltage should exist with brake pedal released. About 9-14 volts should exist with brake pedal depressed. If voltage is not correct, check for defective brakelight switch or wiring circuit.

5) If voltage is correct, check for short or open circuit in wire to terminal T$_T$ of data link connector. Check for defective throttle position sensor or wiring.

6) Perform MANUAL SHIFT TEST. If transmission does not perform correctly, repair transmission. If transmission operates correctly, road test vehicle and ensure voltage at terminal T$_T$ increases from zero to 7 volts.

7) If no voltage exists, proceed to step **9)**. If voltage increases from zero to 7 volts, transmission or solenoid is faulty. If voltage increases from zero to 5 volts, perform NO UPSHIFT TO OVERDRIVE under SYMPTOM TROUBLE SHOOTING.

8) If voltage increases from zero to 3 volts, check for 12 volts between terminals No. 2 and E$_1$ on ECT ECU with connector installed on ECT ECU and shift lever in "D" position. *See Fig. 7.* If 12 volts exist, check for defective neutral start switch or wiring circuit. If 12 volts does not exist, replace ECT ECU.

9) Check for 12 volts between terminals "L" and E$_1$ on ECT ECU with connector installed on ECT ECU and shift lever in "D" position. If 12 volts exist, check for defective neutral start switch or wiring circuit. If 12 volts does not exist, replace ECT ECU.

SHIFT POINTS TOO HIGH OR LOW

1) Warm engine to normal operating temperature. Connect voltmeter between terminals T$_T$ and E$_1$ of data link connector. *See Fig. 3.* Data link connector is located next to parking brake handle on driver's side.

3-1504

AUTOMATIC TRANSMISSIONS
Toyota A-46DE & A-46DF Electronic Controls (Cont.)

2) Turn ignition on. Note that voltage changes with throttle opening. If voltage changes with throttle opening, ECT ECU or transmission is defective. If voltage does not change with throttle opening, proceed to next step.

3) Obtain access to ECT ECU. See Fig. 1. Connect voltmeter between terminals STP and E, on ECT ECU with connector installed on ECT ECU. See Fig. 7.

4) No voltage should exist with brake pedal released. About 9-14 volts should exist with brake pedal depressed. If voltage is not correct, check for defective brakelight switch or wiring circuit.

5) If voltage is correct, check for short or open circuit in wire to T$_T$ terminal of data link connector. Check for defective throttle position sensor or wiring.

NO UPSHIFT TO OVERDRIVE

1) Warm engine to normal operating temperature. With ignition off, disconnect electrical connector for solenoids from rear of transmission. See Fig. 6.

2) Road test vehicle and note if transmission upshifts to overdrive once transmission shifts from "L" to "2" and then into "D" range. Reconnect electrical connector. Clear trouble codes from ECU memory, as disconnecting ECT ECU electrical connector may set trouble codes. See CLEARING TROUBLE CODES under SELF-DIAGNOSTIC SYSTEM. If no overdrive upshift exists, transmission is defective. If overdrive upshift exists, proceed to next step.

3) Connect voltmeter between terminals T$_T$ and E, of data link connector. See Fig. 3. Data link connector is located next to parking brake handle on driver's side.

4) Road test vehicle and ensure voltage at terminal T$_T$ increases from zero to 7 volts. If no voltage exists, check for 9-14 volts between terminals "L" and E, on ECT ECU with connector installed on ECT ECU and shift lever in "D" position with ignition on. See Fig. 7. If 9-14 volts exist, check for defective neutral start switch or wiring circuit. If 9-14 volts does not exist, replace ECT ECU.

5) If voltage increases from zero to 3 volts, check for 9-14 volts between terminals "2" and E, on ECT ECU with connector installed on ECT ECU and shift lever in "D" position with ignition on. If 9-14 volts exist, check for defective neutral start switch or wiring circuit. If 9-14 volts does not exist, replace ECT ECU.

6) If voltage increases from zero to 7 volts, transmission or solenoid is faulty. If voltage increases from zero to 5 volts, connect voltmeter between terminals OD$_2$ and E, on ECT ECU with connector installed on ECT ECU.

7) Turn ignition on. Check voltage with OD switch in released (OFF position) and depressed (ON position). No voltage should exist with switch released and 9-14 volts should exist with switch depressed.

8) If voltage is correct, proceed to next step. If voltage is not correct, check for defective OD switch or wiring circuit.

9) Check voltage between terminals OD$_1$ and E, on ECT ECU with connector installed on ECT ECU and ignition on. Voltage should be about 5 volts. If voltage is correct, replace ECT ECU. If voltage is not correct, proceed to next step.

10) Disconnect electrical connector from cruise control Electronic Control Unit (ECU). See Fig. 1. Check voltage between terminals OD$_1$ and E, on ECT ECU with connector installed on ECT ECU and ignition on. If voltage is now about 5 volts, replace cruise control ECU. If voltage is not about 5 volts, check for defective cruise control ECU wiring. If wiring is okay, replace ECT ECU.

NO LOCK-UP

1) Warm engine to normal operating temperature. Connect voltmeter between terminals T$_T$ and E, of data link connector. See Fig. 3. Data link connector is located next to parking brake handle on driver's side.

2) Road test vehicle and ensure voltage at terminal T$_T$ is 3-7 volts in lock-up range. If voltage is correct, lock-up solenoid, torque converter or transmission is defective.

3) If voltage is not correct, obtain access to ECT ECU. Connect voltmeter between terminals STP and E, on ECT ECU with connector installed on ECT ECU. See Fig. 7.

4) No voltage should exist with brake pedal released. About 9-14 volts should exist with brake pedal depressed. If voltage is not correct, check for defective brakelight switch or wiring circuit. If voltage is correct, check for defective throttle position sensor or wiring.

CIRCUIT TESTS

THROTTLE POSITION SENSOR SIGNAL

1) Connect voltmeter between terminals T$_T$ and E, of data link connector. See Fig. 3. Data link connector is next to parking brake handle on driver's side.

2) Turn ignition on. DO NOT start engine. Note that voltage gradually increases as accelerator is depressed. Voltage should gradually increase to about 8 volts with throttle fully open.

3) If voltage does not change with throttle opening, check throttle position sensor. See THROTTLE POSITION SENSOR under COMPONENT TESTS. If throttle position sensor is okay, check wiring circuit for throttle position sensor.

BRAKE SWITCH SIGNAL

1) Connect voltmeter between terminals T$_T$ and E, of data link connector. See Fig. 3. Data link connector is located next to parking brake handle on driver's side.

2) Depress accelerator pedal until 8 volts exists. Depress brake pedal and note that voltage decreases to zero voltage. Release brake pedal and note that voltage increases to 8 volts.

3) If voltage is not correct, check brakelight switch. See BRAKELIGHT SWITCH under COMPONENT TESTS. If brakelight switch is okay, check wiring circuit for brakelight switch.

GEAR SELECTOR SIGNAL

1) Warm engine to normal operating temperature. Depress OD switch to the ON position. Connect voltmeter between terminals T$_T$ and E, of data link connector. Data link connector is located next to parking brake handle on driver's side. See Fig. 3.

2) Road test vehicle with shift lever in "D" position and vehicle speed greater than 6 MPH. Voltage should increase as specified. See GEAR SIGNAL VOLTAGE table.

NOTE: Lock-up clutch will come on infrequently during normal 2nd and 3rd gear operation. To get lock-up clutch to operate, depress accelerator pedal to more than 1/2 of pedal travel. With accelerator pedal at less than 1/2 of pedal travel, voltage may increase to 2, 4, 6 and then 7 volts.

3) If voltages are correct, the electronic control system is operating correctly. If voltages are not correct, system must be checked.

GEAR SIGNAL VOLTAGE

Gear Position	Volts
1st	0
2nd	2
2nd With Lock-Up	3
3rd	4
3rd With Lock-Up	5
Overdrive	6
Overdrive With Lock-Up	7

ECT ECU VOLTAGE CHECK

Access ECT ECU. See Fig. 1. Turn ignition on. Using DVOM, backprobe ECT ECU harness connector. Check voltage between designated terminals on ECT ECU between connector and ground terminal (E,). Voltage should be as specified. See Fig. 7.

AUTOMATIC TRANSMISSIONS
Toyota A-46DE & A-46DF Electronic Controls (Cont.)

3-1505

			SL
E1			S1 S2

	THW	VC
TE1	IDL VTA	E2

SP1 SP2 T T		BATT
OD1 OD2 STP	N 2 L	+B

	Terminal ID.	Function/Description	Voltage Value (DC Volts Unless Otherwise Specified)
Brown/White	S_1	No. 1 Solenoid	9-14 Volts With KOEO [1]
Brown/Yellow	S_2	No. 2 Solenoid	0-1.5 Volts With KOEO [1]
Green/Yellow	S_L	Lock-Up Solenoid	0-1.5 Volts With KOEO [1]
Green/White	STP	Brakelight Switch Signal	7.5-14 Volts With Pedal Depressed
Blue	THW	Coolant Temperature Sensor Signal	.1-1.0 Volts @ 176°F (80°C)
Blue/Yellow	IDL	Closed Throttle Sensor Signal	0-3 Volts With Throttle Closed, KOEO [1]
Yellow/Red	VTA	Throttle Position Sensor Output Signal	3-5 Volts With Throttle Fully Open
Violet/Yellow	OD_1	OD Output To Cruise Control ECU	5 Volts With KOEO [1]
Blue/White	OD_2	Overdrive Switch Signal	9-14 Volts With Switch On
Violet/White	SP_1	No. 1 Vehicle Speed Sensor Signal	0-1.5 Volts With Cruise Control Off (Car Parked)
Brown/White	SP_2	No. 2 Vehicle Speed Sensor Signal	1.5-4.5 Volts (Pulse Signal) With Vehicle Moving
Black/Red	2	Park/Neutral Position Switch "2" Signal	7.5-14 Volts In "2", KOEO [1]
Black/Blue	L	Park/Neutral Position Switch "L" Signal	7.5-14 Volts In "L", KOEO [1]
Black/Yellow	N	Park/Neutral Position Switch "N" Signal	7.5-14 Volts With KOEO [1]
Black/Orange	+B	EFI Main Relay Power Supply	9-14 Volts With KOEO [1]
White/Red	BATT	Power Supply Voltage	9-14 Volts (Constant)

96A04913   [1] – Key On, Engine Off.   Courtesy of Toyota Motor Sales, U.S.A., Inc.

Fig. 7: ECT ECU Pin Voltage Table (ECT ECU Connector Shown)

COMPONENT TESTS

SOLENOIDS

1) Obtain access to ECT ECU. *See Fig. 1.* Ensure ignition is off. Disconnect electrical connector from ECT ECU that contains S_L, S_1 and S_2 terminals. *See Fig. 7.*

2) Using ohmmeter, measure resistance between S_L, S_1 or S_2 terminal on wiring harness side of ECT ECU connector and body ground. Replace solenoid if resistance is not 11-15 ohms.

3) To check solenoid operation, apply battery voltage to S_L, S_1 or S_2 terminal of ECT ECU connector. Ensure operating sound can be heard when battery voltage is connected. Replace solenoid if operating sound cannot be heard.

4) To check solenoid seals, connect battery voltage to solenoid. Apply 71 psi (5 kg/cm²) to solenoid with battery voltage connected. *See Fig. 8.*

5) On No. 1 and No. 2 solenoids, with battery voltage applied, air should pass through solenoid. Disconnect battery and ensure air does not pass through solenoid. Replace solenoid if defective.

6) On lock-up solenoid, with battery voltage applied, air should not pass through solenoid. Disconnect battery and ensure air passes through solenoid. Replace solenoid if defective.

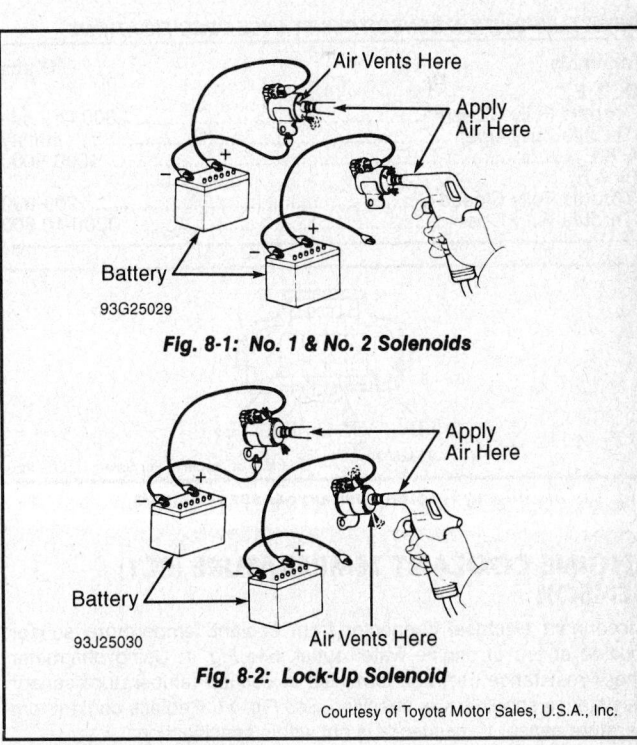

Air Vents Here

Apply Air Here

Battery

93G25029

Fig. 8-1: No. 1 & No. 2 Solenoids

Apply Air Here

Battery

93J25030

Air Vents Here

Fig. 8-2: Lock-Up Solenoid

Courtesy of Toyota Motor Sales, U.S.A., Inc.

Fig. 8: Checking Solenoids

3-1506

AUTOMATIC TRANSMISSIONS
Toyota A-46DE & A-46DF Electronic Controls (Cont.)

PARK/NEUTRAL POSITION (PNP) SWITCH

Disconnect electrical connector at PNP switch (also referred to as neutral start switch). Switch is located on side of transmission. Using ohmmeter, check for continuity between specified terminals in accordance with shift lever position. See Fig. 9. Replace neutral start switch if continuity is not as specified. Install electrical connector.

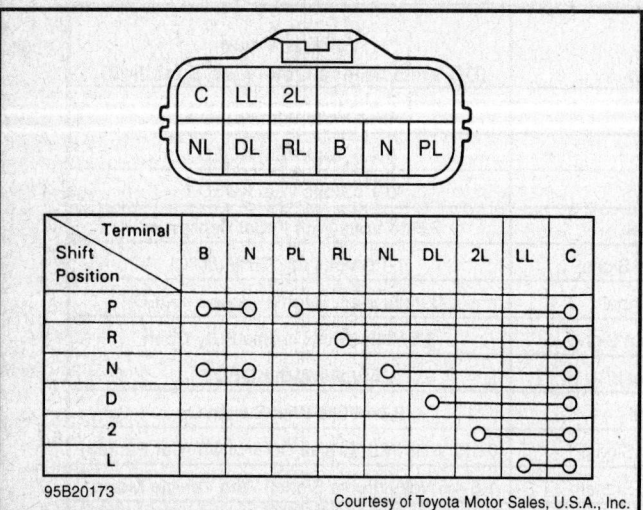

Fig. 9: Testing Park/Neutral Position (PNP) Switch

THROTTLE POSITION (TP) SENSOR

1) Disconnect electrical connector at throttle position sensor, located on side of throttle body. Note throttle position sensor terminal identification. See Fig. 10.

2) Using ohmmeter, check resistance between specified terminals in relation to throttle position. See THROTTLE POSITION SENSOR RESISTANCE SPECIFICATIONS table. Replace throttle position sensor if resistance is not as specified.

THROTTLE POSITION SENSOR RESISTANCE SPECIFICATIONS

Terminals	Ohms
IDL & E_2	
Throttle Fully Closed	2300 Or Less
Throttle Fully Open	Infinity
V_C & E_2	4000-9000
V_{TA} & E_2	
Throttle Fully Closed	200-800
Throttle Fully Open	3300-10,000

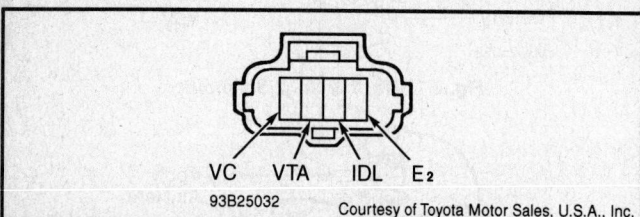

Fig. 10: Identifying Throttle Position Sensor Terminals

ENGINE COOLANT TEMPERATURE (ECT) SENSOR

Disconnect electrical connector from coolant temperature sensor, located at top of engine water outlet. See Fig. 1. Using ohmmeter, check resistance between terminals of coolant temperature sensor. Resistance should be as specified. See Fig. 11. Replace coolant temperature sensor if resistance is not within specification.

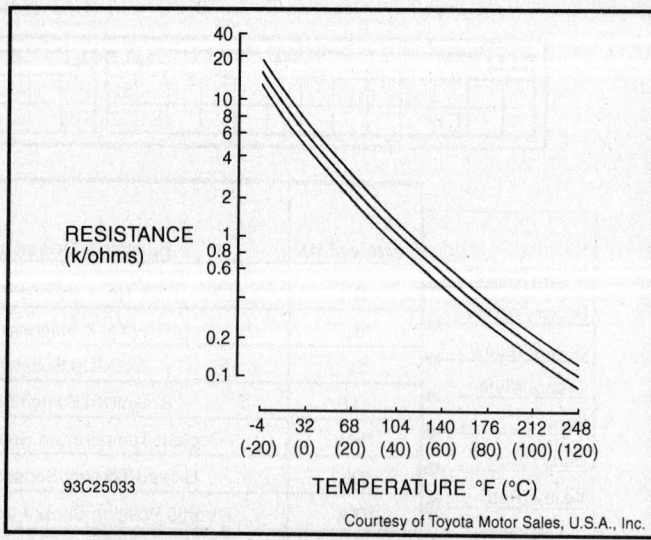

Fig. 11: Checking Engine Coolant Temperature Sensor

NO. 1 VEHICLE SPEED SENSOR

1) Remove No. 1 vehicle speed sensor from transmission. See Fig. 1. Connect voltmeter positive lead to speed sensor terminal No. 3, and negative lead to speed sensor terminal No. 2. Connect battery positive terminal to speed sensor terminal No. 1, and negative terminal to speed sensor terminal No. 2. See Fig. 12.

2) Rotate shaft of No. 1 vehicle speed sensor. Ensure that voltage changes from zero to 11 volts or more, 4 times per each shaft revolution. Replace No. 1 vehicle speed sensor if voltage does not change correctly.

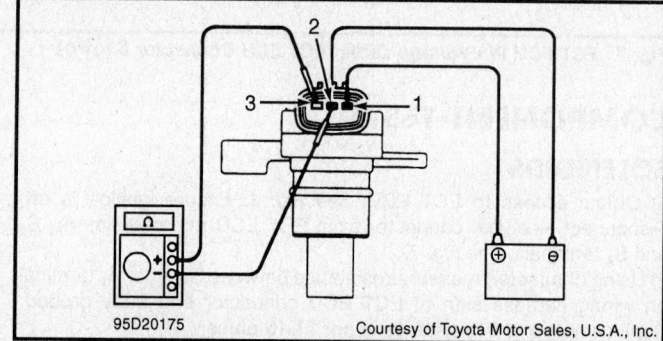

Fig. 12: Checking No. 1 Vehicle Speed Sensor

NO. 2 VEHICLE SPEED SENSOR

1) Disconnect electrical connector from No. 2 vehicle speed sensor, located on transmission. See Fig. 1. Raise and support vehicle so one rear wheel can rotate. Connect ohmmeter between terminals of No. 2 vehicle speed sensor.

2) Rotate rear wheel. Note that ohmmeter needle fluctuates from continuity to no continuity. Replace speed sensor or check for worn components in transmission if reading does not fluctuate.

OVERDRIVE (OD) SWITCH

Disconnect electrical connector from OD switch. Using ohmmeter, ensure continuity exists between both electrical terminals of OD switch with switch released (OFF position). Ensure no continuity exists between both terminals with switch depressed (ON position). Replace switch if defective.

AUTOMATIC TRANSMISSIONS
Toyota A-46DE & A-46DF Electronic Controls (Cont.)

3-1507

BRAKELIGHT SWITCH

1) Disconnect electrical connector from brakelight switch, located near brake pedal. Note brakelight switch terminal identification. *See Fig. 13.*

2) Using ohmmeter, ensure continuity exists between terminals No. 2 and 4 with brake pedal released. Replace brakelight switch if continuity does not exist.

3) Using ohmmeter, ensure continuity exists between terminals No. 1 and 3 with brake pedal depressed. If continuity does not exist, ensure brake pedal is properly adjusted so brakelight switch has proper travel for switch operation. If proper brakelight switch travel exists, replace brakelight switch.

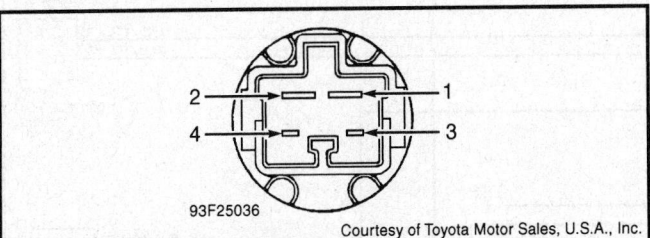

93F25036

Courtesy of Toyota Motor Sales, U.S.A., Inc.

Fig. 13: Identifying Brakelight Switch Terminals

REMOVAL & INSTALLATION

BRAKELIGHT SWITCH

Removal & Installation – 1) Disconnect electrical connector. Remove lock nut, and unscrew brakelight switch. To install, screw brakelight switch inward until brakelight plunger contacts brake pedal.

2) Ensure distance between threaded end of brakelight switch and brake pedal is .02-.09" (.5-2.4 mm). Install and tighten lock nut on brakelight switch. Install electrical connector. Ensure brakelights and cruise control operate properly.

ENGINE COOLANT TEMPERATURE (ECT) SENSOR

Removal & Installation – Coolant temperature sensor is located at top of engine water outlet. *See Fig. 1.* Drain cooling system. Remove coolant temperature sensor. To install, reverse removal procedure. Fill cooling system and check for leaks.

NO. 1 & NO. 2 SOLENOIDS

Removal & Installation – Solenoids are located on transmission valve body. *See Fig. 1.* Remove bolt, solenoid and "O" ring from valve body. To install, reverse removal procedure using NEW "O" ring.

NOTE: *The No. 1 and 2 solenoids must be replaced as an assembly.*

LOCK-UP SOLENOID

Removal & Installation – Solenoid is located on transmission valve body. *See Fig. 1.* Remove bolt and solenoid from transmission valve body. To install, reverse removal procedure.

PARK/NEUTRAL POSITION (PNP) SWITCH

Removal – PNP switch is located on side of transmission. Remove manual lever from control shaft on transmission. Bend up tabs on lock washer. Remove lock nut, lock washer and seal from control shaft. Remove retaining bolt and park/neutral position switch (also referred to as neutral start switch). *See Fig. 14.*

Installation – 1) Install switch on control shaft. Loosely install switch retaining bolt. Install seal and lock washer. Install lock nut and tighten to specification. See TORQUE SPECIFICATIONS.

2) Switch must be adjusted. Ensure parking brake is applied. Temporarily install manual lever on control shaft. Place shift lever in Neutral. Remove manual lever. Rotate park/neutral position switch and align reference mark on switch with groove. *See Fig. 14.*

3) Hold switch in this position. Tighten retaining bolt to specification. Bend tabs on lock washer over against lock nut. To install remaining components, reverse removal procedure.

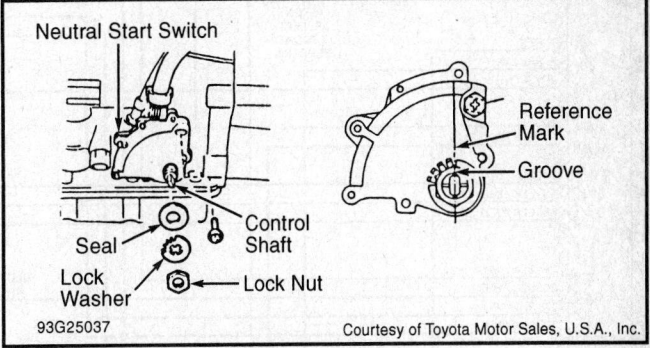

93G25037

Courtesy of Toyota Motor Sales, U.S.A., Inc.

Fig. 14: Removing & Installing PNP Switch

THROTTLE POSITION (TP) SENSOR

Removal – Ensure ignition is off. Disconnect electrical connector from throttle position sensor. Throttle position sensor is located on throttle body. Remove screws and throttle position sensor.

Installation – 1) Ensure throttle valve is closed. Install throttle position sensor on throttle body with screws loosely installed. Throttle position sensor must be adjusted. Connect ohmmeter leads to IDL and E_2 terminals of throttle position sensor. *See Fig. 10.*

2) Insert .029" (.73 mm) feeler gauge between throttle stop screw and stop lever. Gradually rotate throttle position sensor until ohmmeter deflects and tighten retaining screws. Remove feeler gauge.

NO. 1 VEHICLE SPEED SENSOR

Removal & Installation – Disconnect electrical connector. Remove No. 1 vehicle speed sensor from transmission. *See Fig. 1.* To install, reverse removal procedure.

NO. 2 VEHICLE SPEED SENSOR

Removal & Installation – Disconnect electrical connector from No. 2 vehicle speed sensor. Remove bolt and No. 2 vehicle speed sensor from transmission. *See Fig. 1.* To install, reverse removal procedure.

TORQUE SPECIFICATIONS
TORQUE SPECIFICATIONS

Application	INCH Lbs. (N.m)
PNP Switch	
Bolt	48 (5.4)
Lock Nut	35 (4.0)

AUTOMATIC TRANSMISSIONS
Toyota A-46DE & A-46DF Electronic Controls (Cont.)

WIRING DIAGRAMS

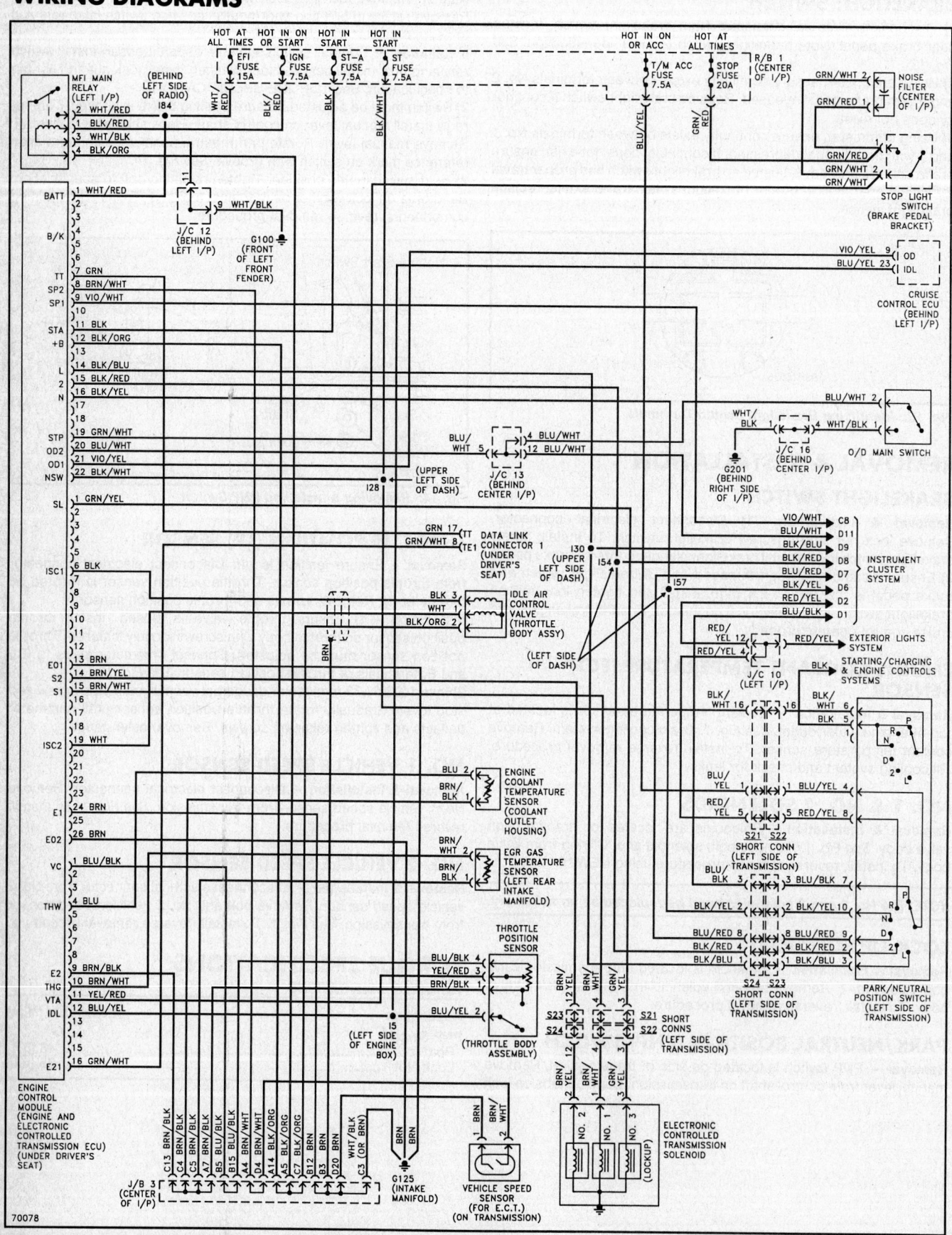

Fig. 15: Transmission Wiring Diagram (1995 Previa Non-Supercharged)

Geo: Prizm
Toyota: Corolla, Tercel

APPLICATION & LABOR TIMES

APPLICATION & LABOR TIMES

Vehicle Application	Labor Times R & I [1]	Overhaul [2]	Trans. Model
Geo			
Prizm	5.5	10.5	A-131L
Toyota			
Corolla	5.5	10.5	A-131L
Tercel	5.2	10.5	A-132L

[1] – Removal and installation of transmission from vehicle chassis.

[2] – Bench overhaul time for transmission and differential. Does not include removal and installation.

NOTE: Geo models and other imported vehicles sold by domestic manufacturers are normally covered in MITCHELL® TRANSMISSION SERVICE & REPAIR for DOMESTIC CARS, LIGHT TRUCKS & VANS. The Geo Prizm is covered in this article due to limited use of this model transmission in domestic vehicles.

CAUTION: All models are equipped with a Supplemental Restraint System (SRS). When servicing vehicle, use care to avoid accidental air bag deployment. All SRS electrical connections and wiring harness are covered by Yellow insulation. SRS-related components are located in steering column, center console, instrument panel and lower panel on instrument panel. DO NOT use electrical test equipment on these circuits. If necessary, deactivate SRS before servicing components. See AIR BAG SERVICING article in APPLICATIONS & IDENTIFICATION section.

IDENTIFICATION

This transmission may be manufactured by either Aisin Warner or Toyota. On Geo Prizm, transaxle identification number is located above left drive axle. 1995 transaxle is manufactured by Toyota. 1996 transaxle is manufactured by Aisin Warner. On Corolla, transaxle identification number is located on converter housing (Aisin Warner), or on top of transaxle case, near carrier cover (Toyota). On Tercel, transaxle identification number is located on top of transaxle case near carrier cover (Toyota).

DESCRIPTION

Transaxles have 3 forward speeds and reverse. Transaxle assembly consists of torque converter, oil pump, control valve assembly, differential, input shaft, intermediate shaft, 2 planetary gear sets, 2 clutch style brakes, forward clutch, direct clutch and 2 one-way clutches.

LUBRICATION & ADJUSTMENTS

See appropriate AUTOMATIC TRANSMISSION SERVICING article in TRANSMISSION SERVICING section.

TROUBLE SHOOTING

Preliminary Checks – Automatic transaxle malfunction can be caused by either engine or transaxle. Isolate malfunction to engine or transaxle before proceeding with trouble shooting. Prior to trouble shooting, check and adjust throttle cable, shift linkage, park/neutral position switch and idle speed RPM as necessary. Ensure fluid level is correct. Check tires for correct inflation.

SYMPTOM DIAGNOSIS

Fluid Discolored Or Smells Burnt – Contaminated fluid, faulty torque converter or transaxle assembly.

No Movement In Any Gear Position – Shift cable out of adjustment, faulty valve body assembly, primary regulator valve, parking lock pawl, torque converter or front/rear planetary gear. Broken converter drive plate or blocked oil pump intake screen.

No Forward Gears – Faulty governor valve, forward clutch, No. 2 one-way clutch, 1st and reverse brake, 2nd coast brake, No. 1 one-way clutch or direct clutch.

No Reverse – Faulty 2nd coast brake, front or rear planetary gear, 1-2 shift valve, 2-3 shift valve, direct clutch or 1st and reverse brake.

Selector Lever Position Incorrect – Shift cable out of adjustment, faulty manual valve and/or lever.

Harsh Engagement Into Any Forward Gear Position – Throttle cable out of adjustment, faulty valve body assembly, primary regulator valve or accumulators. See CLUTCH & BRAKE APPLICATION table.

Delayed Upshifts, Or Downshifts From 3-2 Then Shifts Back To 3rd – Throttle cable out of adjustment, faulty valve body assembly or governor assembly.

Slips On Upshift, Or Slips Or Shudders On Acceleration – Shift cable or throttle cable out of adjustment, faulty valve body assembly or clutch assemblies. See CLUTCH & BRAKE APPLICATION table.

Drag, Binding Or Tie-Up On Upshifts – Shift cable out of adjustment, faulty valve body assembly or transaxle assembly.

No Lock-Up – Lock-up relay valve, lock-up signal valve or torque converter.

No Kickdown – Faulty 1-2 or 2-3 shift valve.

Poor Acceleration – Faulty torque converter.

Harsh Downshift – Throttle cable out of adjustment, throttle modulator valve or primary regulator valve.

Downshift Occurs Too Soon Or Too Late While Coasting – Throttle cable out of adjustment, faulty valve body assembly, transaxle assembly or governor assembly.

No Engine Braking In "2" Or "L" Position – 1st and reverse brake or 2nd coast brake.

Vehicle Does Not Hold In "P" Position – Shift cable out of adjustment, faulty parking lock pawl cam and spring.

CLUTCH & BRAKE APPLICATION

Selector Lever Position	Elements In Use
"D" (Drive)	
1st Gear	Forward Clutch & No. 2 One-Way Clutch
2nd Gear	Forward Clutch, No. 1 One-Way Clutch & 2nd Brake
3rd Gear	Forward Clutch, Direct Clutch & 2nd Brake
"2" (Second)	
1st Gear	Forward Clutch & No. 2 One-Way Clutch
2nd Gear	Forward Clutch, No. 1 One-Way Clutch, 2nd Brake & 2nd Coast Brake Band
"L" (Low)	
1st Gear	Forward Clutch, No. 2 One-Way Clutch & 1st & Reverse Brake
2nd Gear [1]	Forward Clutch, No. 1 One-Way Clutch, 2nd Brake & 2nd Coast Brake Band
"R" (Reverse)	Direct Clutch & 1st & Reverse Brake
"N" Or "P" (Neutral Or Park)	All Clutches & Brakes Released Or Ineffective

[1] – Downshift in "L" position, second gear only. No upshift.

TESTING

PRELIMINARY CHECKS

Before testing transaxle, ensure fluid level is correct and selector lever, throttle cable and idle speed are adjusted correctly.

TIME LAG TEST

NOTE: Perform test with fluid at normal operating temperature of 122-176°F (50-80°C). Wait one minute between tests. Record 3 measurements and use average value.

1) If selector lever is actuated with engine idling, a time lag will be noted before shock can be felt. Apply parking brake and block front and rear wheels. Start engine and check idle speed. See IDLE SPEED SPECIFICATIONS table.

IDLE SPEED SPECIFICATIONS [1]

Application	RPM
Geo	
Prizm	650-750
Toyota	
Corolla	650-750
Tercel	700-800

[1] – Idle speed is computer controlled and is not adjustable.

2) Move selector lever from "N" to "D" position. Measure time required for shock to be felt. Time lag must be less than 1.2 seconds. Repeat procedure, shifting from "N" to "R" position. Time lag must be less than 1.5 seconds.

Time Lag Test Results

- **Excessive Time Lag From "N" To "D" Position:** – Low line pressure or defective forward clutch.
- **Excessive Time Lag From "N" To "R" Position** – Low line pressure, defective direct clutch or 1st and reverse brake.

ROAD TEST

NOTE: Perform test with fluid at normal operating temperature of 122-176°F (50-80°C).

"D" Position Test – 1) Shift vehicle into "D" position. While driving vehicle, hold accelerator constantly at full throttle position. Check 1-2 and 2-3 upshift points. Refer to appropriate SHIFT SPEED SPECIFICATIONS table.

- If 1-2 upshift does not occur, 1-2 shift valve is stuck or governor valve is defective.
- If 2-3 upshift does not occur, 2-3 shift valve is stuck.
- If all shift points are incorrect, throttle cable is out of adjustment or throttle valve, 1-2 or 2-3 shift valves are defective.

2) Repeat procedure and check shock and slip during 1-2 and 2-3 upshifts. Excessive shock can be caused by excessive line pressure, defective accumulator or defective check ball.

3) While driving vehicle in "D" position, check for abnormal noise or vibration. Abnormal noise or vibration may be due to an unbalanced axle shaft, differential, tires or torque converter.

4) While driving vehicle in 3rd gear, confirm correct kickdown speed limits for 3-2 and 2-1 shift points. Check for abnormal shock or slip at kickdown. If kickdown speed limit is incorrect, throttle cable is out of adjustment or throttle valve, 1-2 or 2-3 shift valves are defective.

5) Drive vehicle in "D" position at 37 MPH. Release accelerator pedal and shift into "L" position. Confirm correct downshift speed limits for 2-1 shift point.

Lock-Up Mechanism – Drive vehicle in "D" position with lock-up on and hold vehicle at specified speed. See appropriate LOCK-UP SPEED SPECIFICATIONS table. Lightly depress accelerator pedal. Ensure engine RPM does not change abruptly. Large increase in engine RPM indicates lock-up function is faulty.

"2" Position Test – While driving vehicle in "2" position, release accelerator pedal and check engine braking effect. If no engine braking occurs, 2nd coast brake is defective. Check for abnormal noise during acceleration and deceleration. Check for shock during upshift and downshift.

"L" Position Test – While driving vehicle in "L" position, ensure upshift to 2nd gear does not occur. Release accelerator pedal. If engine braking does not occur, 1st and reverse brake are defective.

"R" Position Test – Shift vehicle to "R" position. Accelerate vehicle from a stop to full throttle. Ensure slipping does not occur.

"P" Position Test – Stop vehicle on slight incline. Shift vehicle to "P" position. Release parking brake. Ensure parking lock pawl holds vehicle.

COROLLA SHIFT SPEED SPECIFICATIONS (3.526 GEAR RATIO)

Application	MPH
"D" Position [1]	
1995	
1-2	33-44
2-3	64-73
3-2	60-71
2-1	24-30
1996	
1-2	31-42
2-3	60-72
3-2	56-70
2-1	22-30
"L" Position [2]	
1995	
2-1	25-33
1996	
2-1	26-34

[1] – Wide open throttle.
[2] – Fully closed throttle.

COROLLA SHIFT SPEED SPECIFICATIONS (3.722 GEAR RATIO)

Application	MPH
"D" Position [1]	
1995	
1-2	31-42
2-3	60-72
3-2	57-70
2-1	22-29
1996	
1-2	29-40
2-3	58-68
3-2	53-65
2-1	21-29
"L" Position [2]	
1995	
2-1	24-31
1996	
2-1	25-32

[1] – Wide open throttle.
[2] – Fully closed throttle.

COROLLA LOCK-UP SPEED SPECIFICATIONS (3.526 GEAR RATIO) [1]

Application	MPH
"D" Position [2]	
1995	
Lock-Up ON	44-51
Lock-Up OFF	42-48
1996	
Lock-Up ON	42-48
Lock-Up OFF	39-46

[1] – Fully closed throttle.
[2] – There is no lock-up in "L" or "2" position.

COROLLA LOCK-UP SPEED SPECIFICATIONS (3.722 GEAR RATIO) [1]

Application	MPH
"D" position [2]	
1995	
Lock-Up ON	42-48
Lock-Up OFF	39-46
1996	
Lock-Up ON	40-46
Lock-Up OFF	37-43

[1] – Fully closed throttle.
[2] – There is no lock-up in "L" or "2" position.

PRIZM SHIFT SPEED SPECIFICATIONS

Application	MPH
"D" Position [1]	
1995	
1-2	33-44
2-3	64-73
3-2	60-71
2-1	24-30
1996	
1-2	31-40
2-3	60-70
3-2	56-67
2-1	22-29
"L" Position [2]	
1995	
2-1	25-33
1996	
2-1	26-32

[1] – Wide open throttle.
[2] – Fully closed throttle.

NOTE: Prizm lock-up speed specifications are not provided by manufacturer.

TERCEL SHIFT SPEED SPECIFICATIONS

Application	MPH
"D" Position [1]	
1-2	29-39
2-3	57-66
3-2	53-65
2-1	22-29
"L" Position [2]	
2-1	24-30

[1] – Wide open throttle.
[2] – Fully closed throttle.

TERCEL LOCK-UP SPEED SPECIFICATIONS [1]

Application	MPH
"D" Position [2]	
Lock-Up ON	39-45
Lock-Up OFF	37-42

[1] – Fully closed throttle.
[2] – There is no lock-up in "L" or "2" position.

STALL SPEED TEST

1) Operate engine and transaxle at normal operating temperature. Connect tachometer to vehicle and ensure it is visible to driver. Apply parking brake and block front and rear wheels.

CAUTION: DO NOT maintain stall speed RPM for more than 5 seconds.

2) Start engine, apply brakes and place transaxle in "D" position. Depress accelerator to full throttle and note maximum RPM obtained. Repeat test in "R" position. For stall speeds, see STALL SPEED SPECIFICATIONS table.

STALL SPEED SPECIFICATIONS

Application	RPM
Corolla & Prizm	
1995	2250-2550
1996	2150-2450
Tercel	2100-2500

Stall Speed Test Results

- **Stall Speed Is Same In Both Positions, But Less Than Specified** – Insufficient engine output or defective stator one-way clutch.

NOTE: If stall speed RPM is more than 600 RPM less than specification, torque converter may be faulty.

- **Stall Speed High In "D" Position** – Low line pressure, forward clutch slipping or defective No. 2 one-way clutch.
- **Stall Speed High In "R" Position** – Low line pressure or direct clutch or 1st and reverse brake slipping.
- **Stall Speed High In Both Positions** – Low line pressure or improper fluid level.

HYDRAULIC PRESSURE TESTS

CAUTION: Perform tests with fluid at normal operating temperature of 122-176°F (50-80°C).

Line Pressure Test – 1) Remove appropriate transaxle case plug and connect pressure gauge. See Fig. 1. Block all wheels. Apply parking brake. Start engine and shift into "D" position. Ensure idle speed RPM is set to specification.

2) Apply service brakes and depress accelerator. Note pressure readings at idle and stall speeds. Repeat test in "R" position. Compare pressure readings to those listed in LINE PRESSURE SPECIFICATIONS table.

3) If pressure is lower than specified, check throttle cable adjustment. Adjust as necessary. See appropriate AUTOMATIC TRANSMISSION SERVICING article in TRANSMISSION SERVICING section for adjustment procedure. Repeat pressure test procedure if throttle cable adjustment was necessary.

Line Pressure Test Results

- **Line Pressure High In Both Positions** – Throttle cable out of adjustment, defective throttle valve or regulator valve.
- **Line Pressure Low In Both Positions** – Throttle cable out of adjustment, defective oil pump, throttle valve or regulator valve.
- **Line Pressure Low In "D" Position Only** – "D" position circuit leaking pressure or defective forward clutch.
- **Line Pressure Low In "R" Position Only** – "R" position circuit leaking pressure, defective 1st and reverse brake or direct clutch.

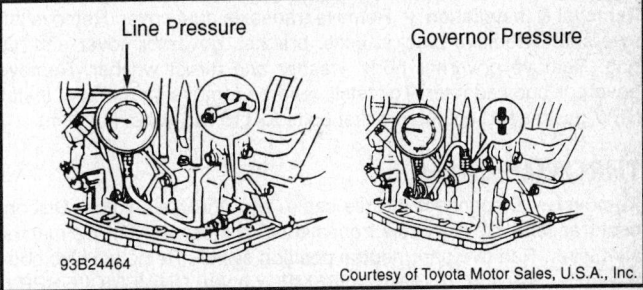

93B24464   Courtesy of Toyota Motor Sales, U.S.A., Inc.

Fig. 1: Checking Governor & Line Pressure

LINE PRESSURE SPECIFICATIONS

Application	psi (kg/cm²)
"D" Position	
Idle Speed	53-61 (3.7-4.3)
Stall Speed	131-152 (9.2-10.7)
"R" Position	
Idle Speed	
Corolla	80-102 (5.6-7.2)
All Others	77-102 (5.4-7.2)
Stall Speed	205-239 (14.4-16.8)

Governor Pressure Test – 1) Apply parking brake. Raise and support front of vehicle with safety stands. Remove appropriate transaxle case plug and connect pressure gauge. See Fig. 1.

CAUTION: Road test vehicle or use chassis dynamometer to check governor pressures exceeding minimum vehicle speed specification.

2) Start engine and shift to "D" position. Note governor pressure at specified speeds and engine RPM. See GOVERNOR PRESSURE SPECIFICATIONS table. Incorrect governor pressure may be caused by incorrect line pressure, leakage at governor pressure circuit or defective governor valve.

GOVERNOR PRESSURE SPECIFICATIONS

Speed (MPH)	psi (kg/cm²)
Corolla	
Gear Ratio – 3.526	
1995	
19	6-17 (.4-1.2)
37	26-37 (1.8-2.6)
56	41-53 (2.9-3.7)
1996	
19	6-17 (.4-1.2)
37	24-36 (1.7-2.5)
56	44-55 (3.0-3.8)
Gear Ratio – 3.722	
1995	
19	13-24 (.9-1.7)
37	26-37 (1.8-2.6)
56	48-60 (3.3-4.1)
1996	
19	7-18 (.5-1.3)
37	26-37 (1.8-2.6)
56	48-60 (3.3-4.1)
Prizm	
19	5-17.1 (.34-1.2)
37	22.8-34.1 (1.6-2.4)
56	41.2-52.6 (2.8-3.6)
Tercel	
19	9-20 (.6-1.4)
37	27-38 (1.9-2.7)
56	51-63 (3.5-4.3)

ON-VEHICLE SERVICE

DRIVE AXLE SHAFTS

See appropriate AXLE SHAFTS article in AXLE SHAFTS & TRANSFER CASES section.

GOVERNOR ASSEMBLY

Removal & Installation – Remove transaxle dust cover. Remove left axle shaft. Remove bracket bolts, bracket, governor cover and "O" ring. Remove governor body, washer and thrust washer. Remove governor body adapter. To install, reverse removal procedure. Install NEW gasket and tighten bracket bolts to 115 INCH lbs. (13 N.m).

THROTTLE CABLE

Removal – Disconnect throttle cable from throttle linkage. Disconnect transaxle control cable from manual shift lever. Remove manual shift lever. Remove park/neutral position switch. Remove valve body assembly. See VALVE BODY ASSEMBLY under ON-VEHICLE SERVICE. Remove throttle cable bolt and retaining plate. Pull throttle cable from transaxle case.

Installation – 1) Install throttle cable in transaxle case. Ensure cable is fully seated. Install retaining bolt and plate. Install valve body assembly. On NEW throttle cables, stopper must be staked on inner cable. Bend cable in approximately a 7.87" (200 mm) radius.
2) Pull inner cable lightly, until a slight resistance is felt, and hold in place. Stake stopper on inner cable, leaving a .031-.059" (.78-1.49 mm) gap between cable housing and stopper. See Fig. 2.

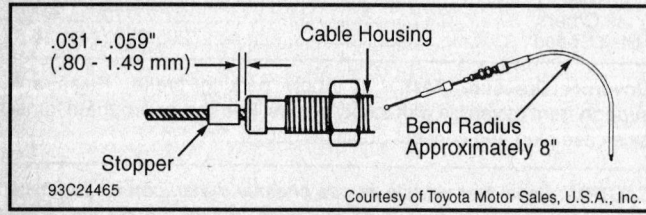

Fig. 2: Locating Throttle Cable Stopper

3) Adjust throttle cable and park/neutral position switch (if necessary). See appropriate AUTOMATIC TRANSMISSION SERVICING article in TRANSMISSION SERVICING section. Install manual shift lever. Install transaxle control cable. Test drive vehicle.

VALVE BODY ASSEMBLY

CAUTION: Note valve body assembly bolts length and location. Proper length bolts must be installed in correct locations to prevent transaxle case damage.

Removal – 1) Raise and support vehicle. Clean exterior of transaxle oil pan. Drain transaxle fluid. Remove oil pan and gasket. Remove strainer and oil tube bracket. Note location of oil tubes. Using large screwdriver, remove oil tubes.
2) Remove detent spring. Remove manual valve and manual valve body. See Fig. 3. Note bolt length and location. Remove valve body assembly bolts. See Fig. 4. Remove throttle cable. Remove valve body assembly. Remove governor oil strainer. Remove governor apply gasket.

Installation – 1) Install governor apply gasket. Install governor oil strainer. Hold valve body cam downward. Install throttle cable in slot. Install valve body assembly. Ensure kickdown switch wire is not under valve body assembly. Install valve body assembly bolts finger tight. Ensure bolts are installed correctly. See Fig. 4. Tighten bolts to 89 INCH lbs. (10 N.m).
2) Align manual valve with pin on manual shift lever. Install manual valve body. Install manual valve body bolts and tighten to 89 INCH lbs. (10 N.m). Install detent spring and tighten bolts to 89 INCH lbs. (10 N.m). Ensure manual valve lever contacts center of roller on detent spring. Using a plastic hammer, tap oil tubes into place. Install oil tube bracket. Tighten bolts to 89 INCH lbs. (10 N.m).
3) Install oil strainer. Tighten bolts to 89 INCH lbs. (10 N.m). Install magnets in oil pan. Ensure magnets do not interfere with oil tubes. Install oil pan and gasket. Tighten bolts to 43 INCH lbs. (4.9 N.m). Fill transaxle with fluid.

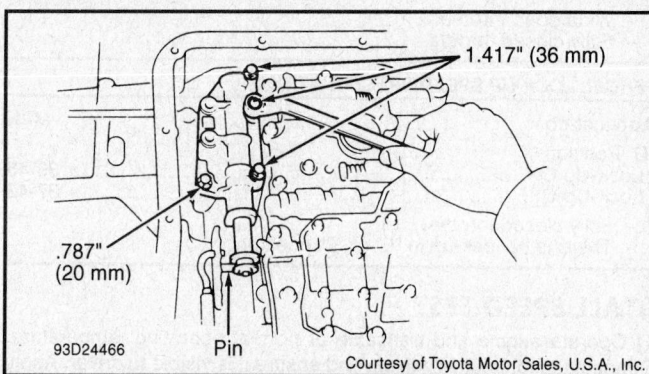

Fig. 3: Identifying Manual Valve Body Bolts

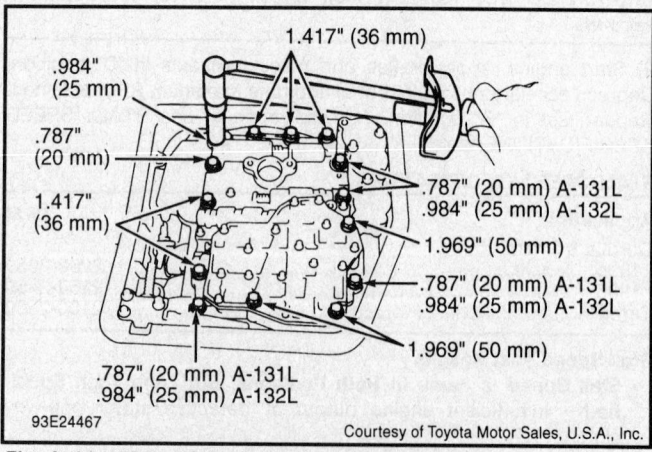

Fig. 4: Identifying Valve Body Assembly Bolts

REMOVAL & INSTALLATION

For transaxle removal and installation procedure, see appropriate AUTOMATIC TRANSMISSION REMOVAL article in TRANSMISSION SERVICING section.

TORQUE CONVERTER

NOTE: Torque converter is sealed unit and must be serviced as complete assembly. Perform following tests to check converter condition. Torque converter and oil cooler lines must be thoroughly cleaned and flushed if transaxle fluid is contaminated.

ONE-WAY CLUTCH TEST

1) Install turner and stopper of One-Way Clutch Tester (09350-32014) in torque converter. *See Fig. 5.* Turner fits in inner race of one-way clutch. Stopper fits in notch of converter hub and outer race of one-way clutch.
2) Clutch should lock when rotated counterclockwise, and turn freely when rotated clockwise. If necessary, clean converter and retest clutch. Replace converter if clutch does not test as described.

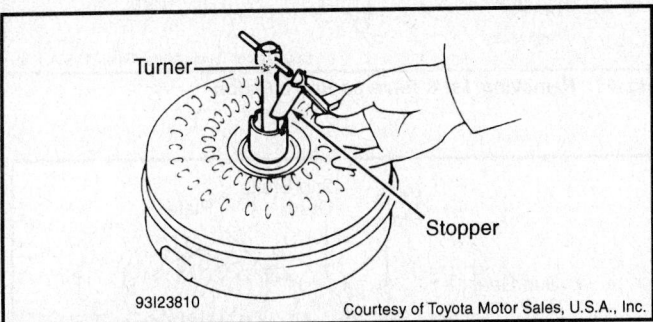

93I23810   Courtesy of Toyota Motor Sales, U.S.A., Inc.

Fig. 5: Checking Torque Converter One-Way Clutch

DRIVE PLATE RUNOUT TEST

Measure drive plate runout. *See Fig. 6.* If runout exceeds .008" (.20 mm), or if ring gear is damaged, replace drive plate. If installing a NEW drive plate, note position of spacers. Tighten bolts to specification. See TORQUE SPECIFICATIONS.

CONVERTER SLEEVE RUNOUT TEST

1) Temporarily mount torque converter to drive plate. Mount a dial indicator with needle resting on converter sleeve. *See Fig. 7.* Rotate converter. If runout exceeds .012" (.30 mm), ensure converter is properly mounted to drive plate.
2) If converter is properly mounted and runout exceeds specification, replace torque converter. Mark position of converter on drive plate to ensure correct installation. Remove converter from drive plate.

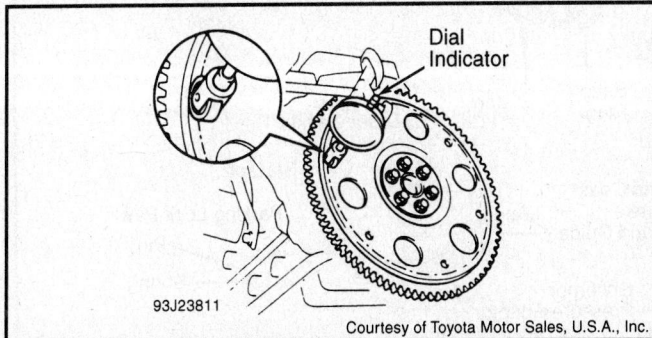

93J23811   Courtesy of Toyota Motor Sales, U.S.A., Inc.

Fig. 6: Checking Drive Plate Runout

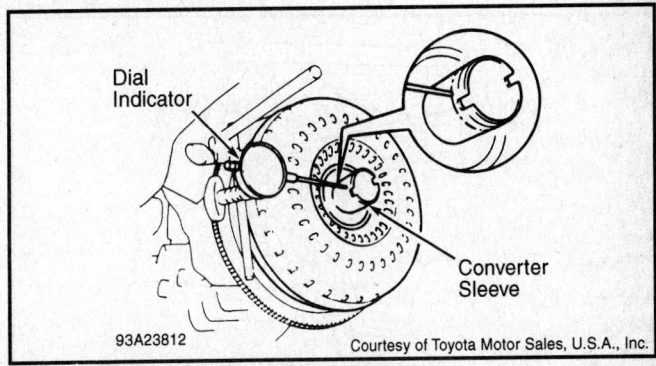

93A23812   Courtesy of Toyota Motor Sales, U.S.A., Inc.

Fig. 7: Checking Converter Sleeve Runout

TRANSAXLE DISASSEMBLY

1) Remove oil cooler pipes and unions, manual shift lever and park/neutral position switch. Remove filler tube and dipstick. Remove throttle cable retaining plate. Remove governor cover bracket. Remove governor cover and "O" ring. Remove thrust washer. Remove governor assembly, plate washer and governor body adapter.
2) Remove oil pan and gasket. Remove 3 magnets from oil pan. Remove oil tube bracket and oil strainer. Remove valve body assembly. See VALVE BODY ASSEMBLY under ON-VEHICLE SERVICE. Remove throttle cable from transaxle case. Remove governor apply gasket and governor oil strainer. *See Fig. 8.*
3) Loosen accumulator cover bolts evenly until spring tension is released. Remove cover and gasket. Remove forward clutch and direct clutch accumulator pistons and springs. Apply 14 psi (1 kg/cm²) of compressed air to oil passage to force 2nd brake piston and springs from bore. *See Fig. 9.* Remove snap ring. Remove 2nd coast brake piston cover. Remove 2nd coast brake piston and outer return spring.

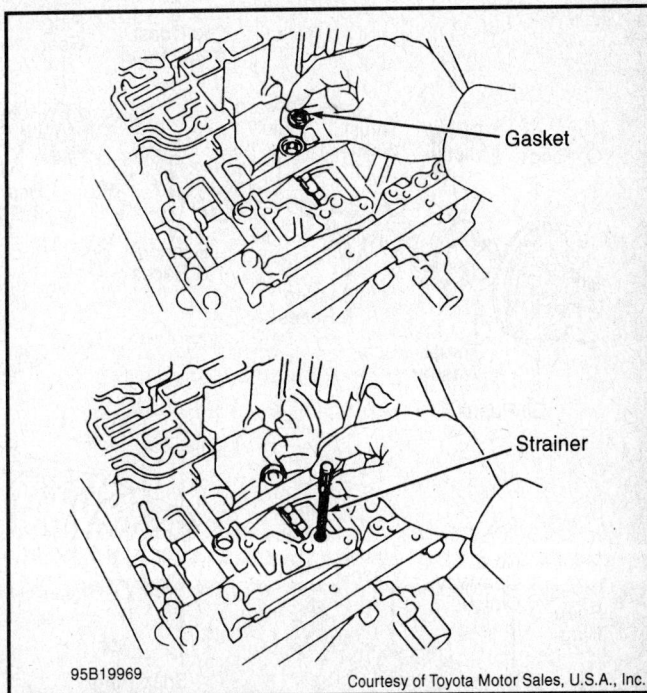

95B19969   Courtesy of Toyota Motor Sales, U.S.A., Inc.

Fig. 8: Removing 2nd Brake Apply Gasket & Governor Oil Strainer

AUTOMATIC TRANSMISSIONS
Toyota A-131L & A-132L (Cont.)

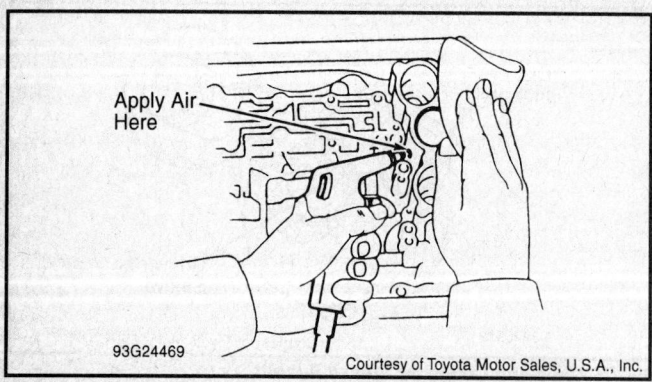

Fig. 9: Removing 2nd Brake Accumulator Piston & Springs

93G24469

Courtesy of Toyota Motor Sales, U.S.A., Inc.

4) Remove oil pump bolts. Using appropriate puller, pull oil pump free from case. Hold input shaft, grasp pump stator shaft and remove oil pump and direct clutch from transaxle case. Firmly push 2nd coast brake band into transaxle case. Ensure brake band does not catch on direct clutch drum. Remove direct clutch and thrust washer from rear of oil pump.

5) Remove forward clutch. Remove race and thrust bearings from forward clutch. Using small screwdriver, push 2nd coast brake band pin inward and remove from oil pump mounting bolt hole. Remove 2nd coast brake band. Remove front planetary ring gear. See Fig. 10. Remove bearing and race from ring gear.

6) Remove front planetary gear. Remove bearings and races from planetary gear. Remove sun gear, sun gear input drum, 2nd brake hub and No. 1 one-way clutch. Remove 2nd coast brake band guide. Remove 2nd brake drum snap ring. Remove 2nd brake drum. Remove 2nd brake piston return spring.

7) Remove plates, discs and flange. Note number and location of components. Remove 2nd brake drum gasket. Remove No. 2 one-way clutch snap ring. Remove No. 2 one-way clutch and rear planetary gear. Remove thrust washers from both sides of planetary gear. Remove rear planetary ring gear, races and thrust bearings. Using compressed air, confirm 1st and reverse brake piston moves smoothly. See Fig. 11.

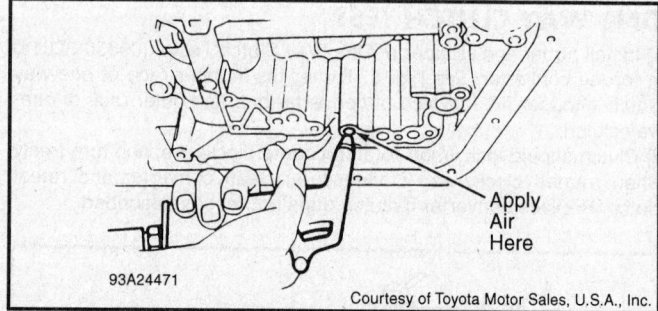

93A24471

Courtesy of Toyota Motor Sales, U.S.A., Inc.

Fig. 11: Removing 1st & Reverse Brake Piston

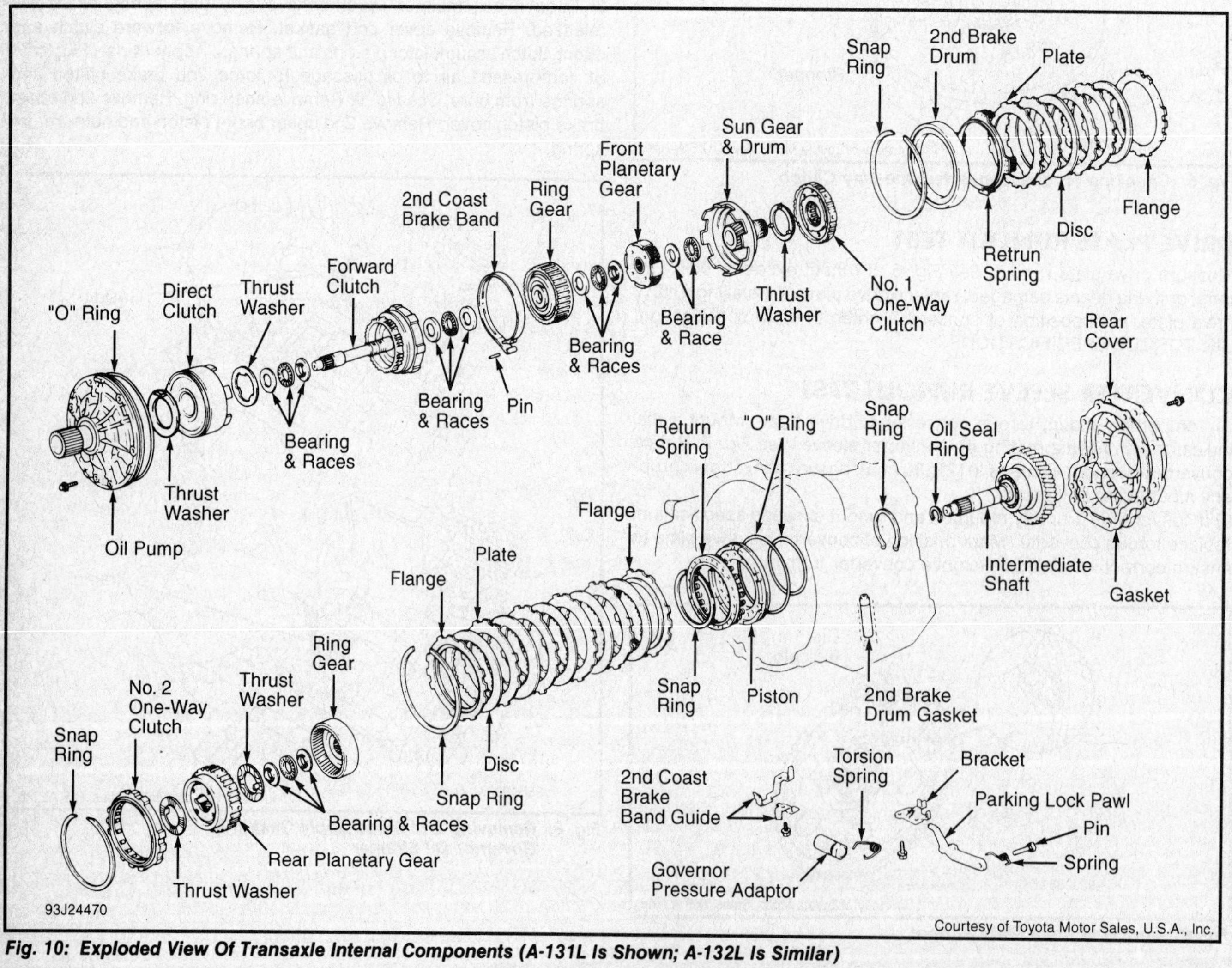

Fig. 10: Exploded View Of Transaxle Internal Components (A-131L Is Shown; A-132L Is Similar)

93J24470

Courtesy of Toyota Motor Sales, U.S.A., Inc.

8) Remove flange snap ring. Remove flange, plates and discs. Note number and location of components. Remove transaxle rear cover bolts. Tap rear cover using a plastic hammer. Remove cover. Remove intermediate shaft. Remove snap ring. Using appropriate spring compressor, remove piston return spring from transaxle case. Apply compressed air into oil passage. Remove 1st and reverse brake piston. See Figs. 11 and 12.

9) Remove parking lock pawl bracket. Remove parking lock rod. Remove pin, spring and parking lock pawl. Remove manual valve shaft spring, collar and pin. Remove manual valve lever from transaxle case. Remove manual shaft oil seal. Remove governor pressure adapter from transaxle case. See Fig. 10.

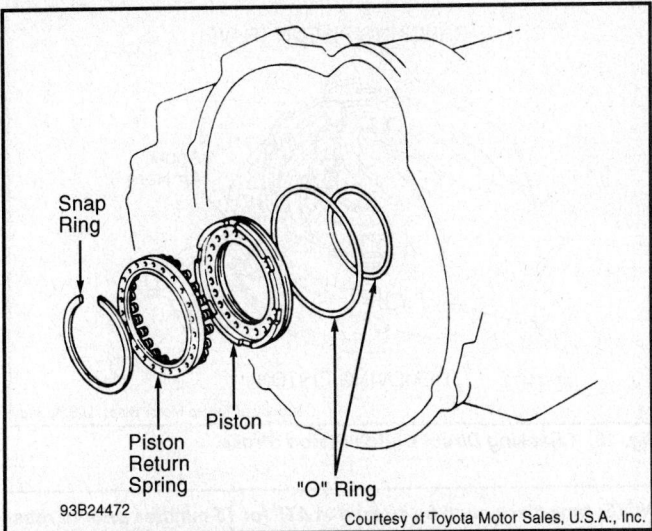

Fig. 12: Exploded View Of 1st & Reverse Brake Piston

COMPONENT DISASSEMBLY & REASSEMBLY

OIL PUMP ASSEMBLY

Disassembly – 1) Remove race from stator shaft. Remove "O" ring and oil seal rings from pump body and stator shaft. Remove clutch drum thrust washer from stator shaft.

2) Mark stator shaft and pump body for reassembly reference. Remove stator shaft bolts. Separate stator shaft and pump body. Mark gear location for reassembly reference. Remove pump gears. Using screwdriver, remove oil seal. See Fig. 13.

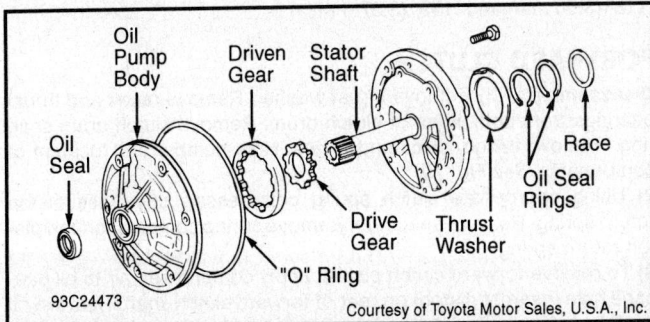

Fig. 13: Exploded View Of Oil Pump Assembly

Inspection – 1) Note position of oil pump gears. Clean all parts with solvent. Use compressed air to ensure oil passages are clear. Check driven gear-to-body clearance. Push driven gear against one side of pump. Using a feeler gauge, measure clearance between driven gear and pump body. See Fig. 14. Replace pump body if clearance is not within specification. See OIL PUMP CLEARANCE SPECIFICATIONS table.

2) Using a feeler gauge, measure tip clearance between both gears and crescent-shaped part of pump body. See Fig. 15. Replace pump body if clearance is not within specification. See OIL PUMP CLEARANCE SPECIFICATIONS table.

3) Using a feeler gauge and straightedge, measure side clearance of both gears. See Fig. 16. Replace pump body if clearance is not within specification. See OIL PUMP CLEARANCE SPECIFICATIONS table. Drive and driven gears are available in 3 different thicknesses. See DRIVE & DRIVEN GEAR THICKNESS SPECIFICATIONS table.

OIL PUMP CLEARANCE SPECIFICATIONS

Application	In. (mm)
Driven Gear-To-Pump Body	
Standard	.0028-.0059 (.071-.149)
Maximum	.012 (.30)
Gear-To-Crescent Tip Clearance	
Standard	.0043-.0055 (.109-.139)
Maximum	.012 (.30)
Gear Side Clearance	
Standard	.0008-.0020 (.020-.050)
Maximum	.004 (.10)

DRIVE & DRIVEN GEAR THICKNESS SPECIFICATIONS

I.D. Mark	In. (mm)
A	.3717-.3723 (9.440-9.456)
B	.3723-.3730 (9.456-9.474)
C	.3730-.3736 (9.474-9.490)

4) Using a dial indicator, measure inside diameter of oil pump body bushing. Maximum inside diameter is 1.503" (38.18 mm). If inside diameter exceeds specification, replace oil pump body.

5) Using a dial indicator, measure inside diameter of stator shaft bushings. Maximum front side bushing inside diameter is .849" (21.57 mm). Maximum rear side bushing inside diameter is 1.066" (27.07 mm). If inside diameter exceeds specification, replace stator shaft.

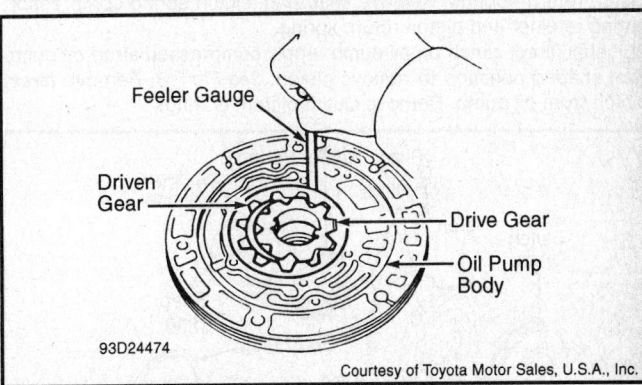

Fig. 14: Checking Oil Pump Driven Gear Clearance

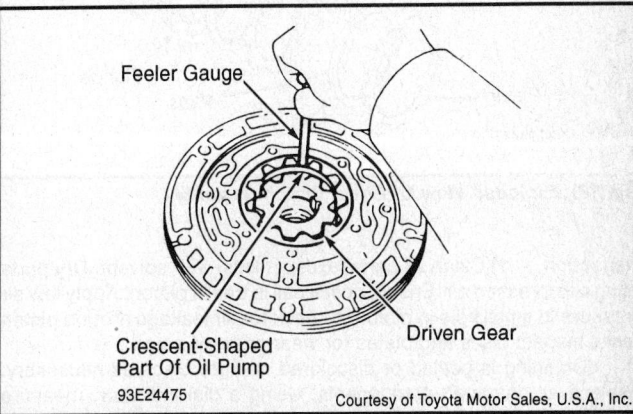

Fig. 15: Checking Oil Pump Gear Tip Clearance

Reassembly – 1) Install NEW oil seal. Seal must be even with edge of pump body. Coat all components with ATF. Install pump gears, aligning reference marks. Install stator shaft on pump body. Align bolt holes and tighten bolts to 89 INCH lbs. (10 N.m). Coat thrust washer with petroleum jelly.

2) Install thrust washer on pump body. Align washer tab with hollow of pump body. Install oil seal rings. Ensure rings rotate smoothly after installation. DO NOT spread oil seal ring ends more than necessary for installation . Using screwdrivers, check drive gear for smooth rotation. Install "O" ring. Install race on stator shaft. *See Fig. 13.*

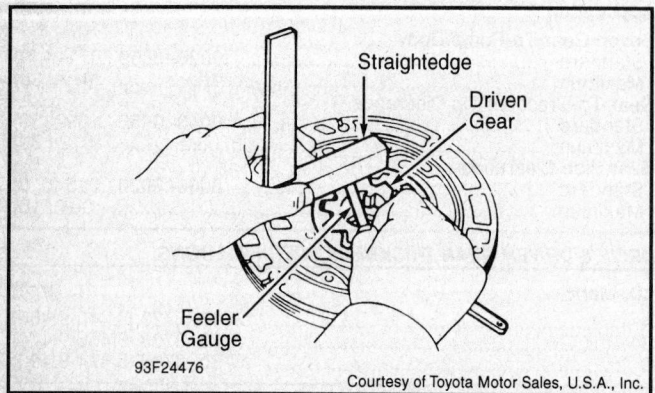

Fig. 16: Checking Oil Pump Gear Side Clearance

DIRECT CLUTCH

Disassembly – 1) Remove snap ring from clutch drum. Remove flange, discs and plates. Note number and location of components. *See Fig. 17.* Using appropriate clutch spring compressor, compress piston return springs. Remove snap ring, clutch spring compressor, spring retainer and piston return spring.

2) Install direct clutch on oil pump. Apply compressed air to oil pump oval shaped passage to remove piston. *See Fig. 18.* Remove direct clutch from oil pump. Remove clutch piston "O" rings.

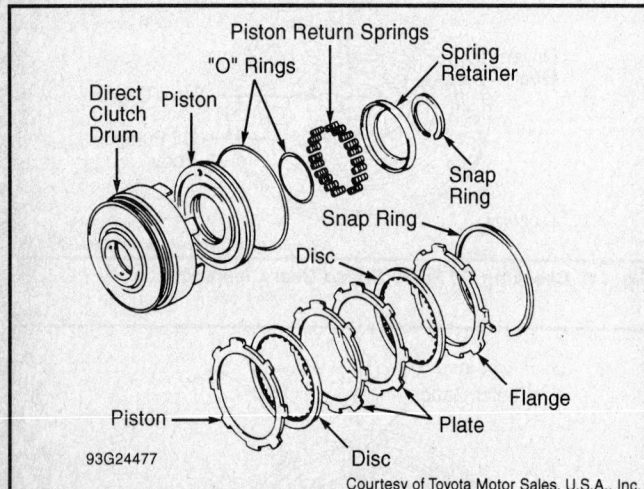

Fig. 17: Exploded View Of Direct Clutch Assembly

Inspection – 1) Clean all parts (except discs) with solvent. Dry parts using compressed air. Ensure check ball is free in piston. Apply low air pressure to small hole in piston to check for air leakage around piston valve. Inspect discs and plates for wear or burnt areas.

2) If disc lining is peeled or discolored, replace discs as necessary. Replace all damaged components. Using a dial indicator, measure inside diameter of direct clutch bushing. Maximum inside diameter is 1.853" (47.07 mm). If inside diameter exceeds specification, replace direct clutch.

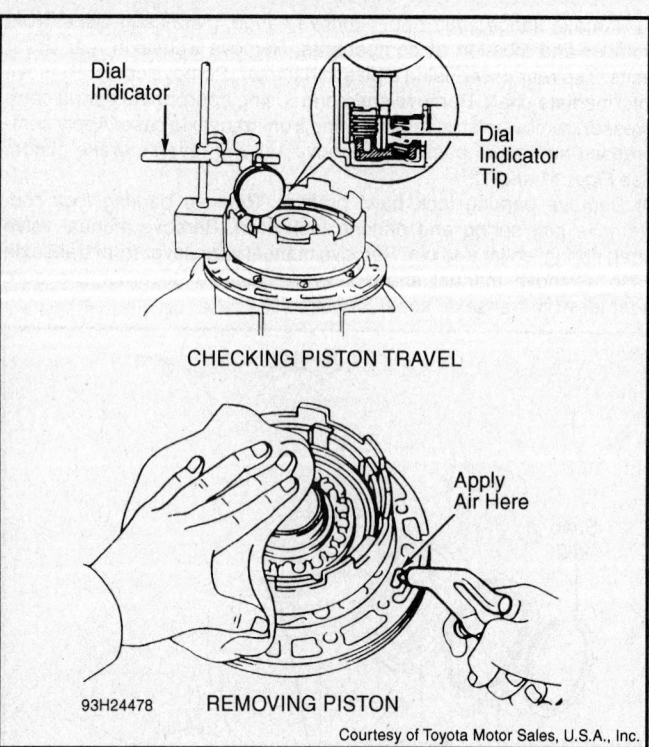

CHECKING PISTON TRAVEL

REMOVING PISTON

Fig. 18: Checking Direct Clutch Piston Stroke

NOTE: New discs must be soaked in ATF for 15 minutes prior to reassembly.

Reassembly – 1) Install NEW "O" rings on piston and coat with ATF. Using hand pressure, press direct clutch piston into clutch drum with cup side up. Install piston return spring and retainer. Compress piston return spring and install snap ring.

2) Ensure snap ring gap does not align with spring retainer claw. Install plates, discs, and flange. Install flange with flat side facing downward. Install snap ring. Ensure snap ring gap does not align with drum cutout.

3) Install direct clutch on oil pump. Use dial indicator to check direct clutch piston stroke. Apply air pressure to oil pump passage and note reading. *See Fig. 18.* Clutch piston stroke should be .054-.067" (1.37-1.70 mm). If piston stroke is not as specified, select appropriate flange to obtain correct piston stroke. Flange is available in thicknesses of .118" (3.00 mm) and .133" (3.37 mm).

FORWARD CLUTCH

Disassembly – 1) Remove thrust washer. Remove races and thrust bearings from both sides of clutch drum. Remove clutch drum snap ring. Remove flange, discs and plates. Note number and location of components. *See Fig. 19.*

2) Using appropriate clutch spring compressor, compress piston return spring. Remove snap ring. Remove spring compressor and piston return spring.

3) To remove forward clutch piston, apply compressed air to oil passage hole (nearest piston) on rear of forward clutch shaft. Remove oil seal rings (if necessary).

Inspection – Clean all parts (except discs) with solvent. Dry parts using compressed air. Ensure check ball is free in piston. Apply low air pressure to small hole in piston to check for air leakage around piston valve. Inspect discs and plates for wear or burnt areas. If disc lining is peeled or discolored, replace discs as necessary. Replace all damaged components.

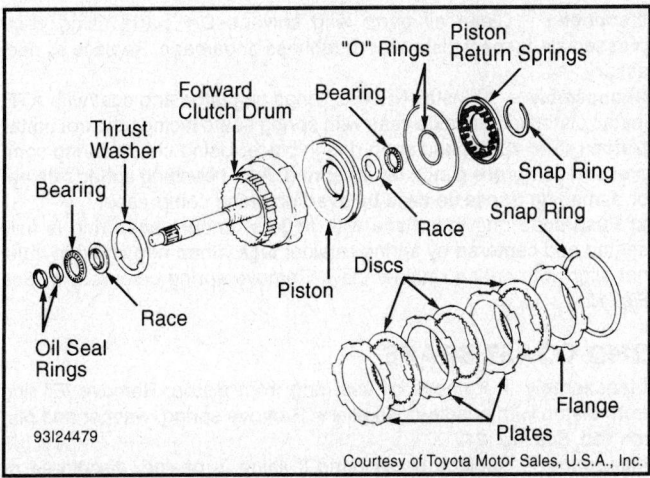

Fig. 19: Exploded View Of Forward Clutch Assembly

NOTE: New discs must be soaked in ATF 15 for minutes prior to reassembly.

Reassembly – 1) Install NEW seal rings (if necessary). Use care not to over expand seal rings. Install NEW "O" rings on piston and coat with ATF. Using hand pressure, install piston in clutch drum with cup side upward.

2) Install piston return spring. Compress piston return spring using clutch spring compressor. Install snap ring. Ensure snap ring gap does not align with spring retainer claw.

3) Install plates and discs in appropriate order. See Fig. 19. Install flange with flat side facing downward. Install snap ring. Ensure snap ring gap does not align with drum cutout.

4) Measure piston stroke by applying compressed air to oil passage hole (nearest piston) on rear of forward clutch shaft and note reading. Clutch piston stroke should be .044-.058" (1.11-1.47 mm).

5) If piston stroke is not as specified, select appropriate flange to obtain correct piston stroke. Flange is available in thicknesses of .118" (3.00 mm) and .133" (3.37 mm). Coat thrust washer, races and bearing with petroleum jelly and install.

FRONT PLANETARY GEAR

Disassembly – 1) Check No. 1 one-way clutch operation. Hold sun gear and rotate hub. Hub should rotate freely in clockwise direction and lock when rotated in counterclockwise direction. See Fig. 20. Turn hub clockwise and remove 2nd brake hub and one-way clutch from sun gear.

2) Remove thrust washer and snap ring. Remove sun gear from input drum. Remove shaft snap ring from sun gear. Remove one-way clutch retainer if clutch requires replacement. Remove one-way clutch from hub.

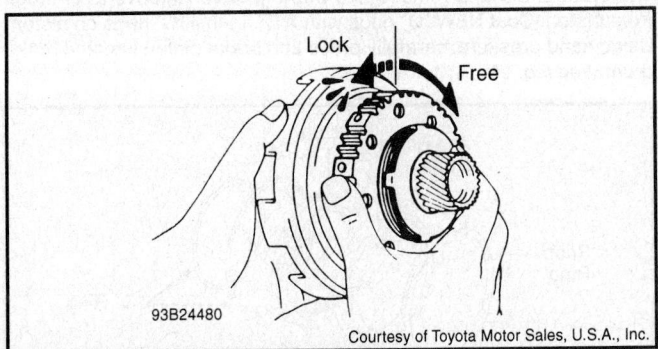

Fig. 20: Checking No. 1 One-Way Clutch

Inspection – 1) Clean all parts with solvent. Dry parts using compressed air. Check thrust bearings, races and one-way clutch for wear or damage. Replace if necessary.

2) Using a dial indicator, measure inside diameter of sun gear bushing. Standard inside diameter should be .867-.868" (22.03-22.05 mm). Maximum inside diameter is .870" (22.10 mm). If inside diameter exceeds specification, replace sun gear.

3) Using a feeler gauge, measure clearance between planetary pinion gear and planetary gear case. Standard clearance should be .008-.020" (.20-.50 mm). Maximum clearance is .020" (.50 mm). If clearance exceeds specification, replace planetary gear.

4) Using a dial indicator, measure inside diameter of ring gear flange bushing. Standard inside diameter should be .749-.750" (19.03-19.05 mm). If inside diameter exceeds specification, replace flange.

Reassembly – Install shaft snap ring to sun gear. Install sun gear to drum. Install snap ring to drum. Install thrust washer to sun gear input drum. See Fig. 21. Rotate hub clockwise. Install one-way clutch and 2nd brake hub. Hold sun gear and rotate hub. Hub should rotate freely in clockwise direction and lock when rotated in counterclockwise direction.

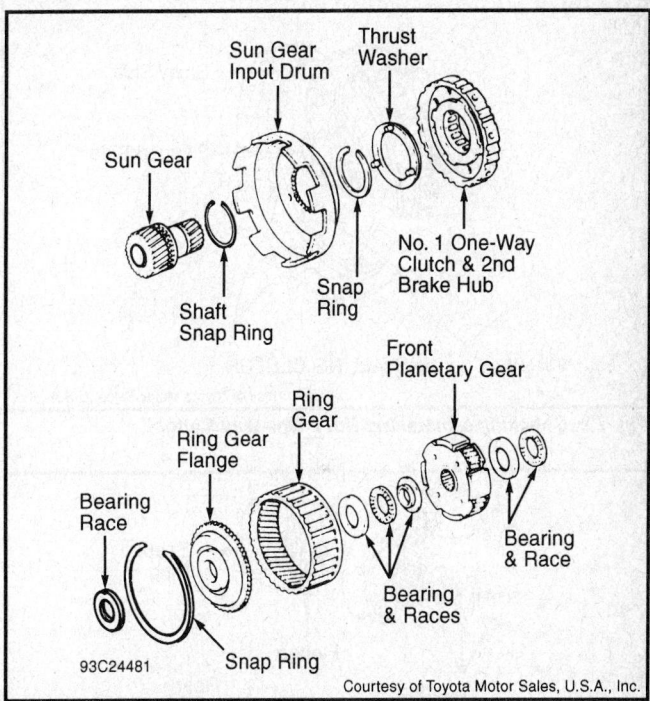

Fig. 21: Exploded View Of Front Planetary Gear Assembly

REAR PLANETARY GEAR

Disassembly – 1) Check No. 2 one-way clutch operation. Hold outer race and rotate hub. Hub should rotate freely in counterclockwise direction and lock when rotated in clockwise direction. See Fig. 22.

2) Remove thrust washers from both sides of rear planetary gear. Separate No. 2 one-way clutch and planetary gear. Remove snap rings and retainers from No. 2 one-way clutch. Note position of No. 2 one-way clutch. Remove one-way clutch from outer race.

Inspection – 1) Clean all parts with solvent. Dry parts using compressed air. Check thrust washers and one-way clutch for wear or damage. Replace if necessary.

2) Using a feeler gauge, measure clearance between planetary pinion gear and planetary gear case. Standard clearance should be .008-.020" (.20-.50 mm). Maximum clearance is .020" (.50 mm). If clearance exceeds specification, replace planetary gear.

Reassembly – 1) Coat all parts with ATF. Install one-way clutch into outer race. Flanged side of one-way clutch should face toward shiny side of outer race. See Fig. 22. Install retainers and snap rings.

2) Install planetary gear into one-way clutch. Planetary gear inner race should face toward back side of outer race. Check operation of one-way clutch. Coat thrust washers with petroleum jelly. Install thrust washers on both sides of planetary gear. Ensure thrust washer tab is aligned with hollow area in gear. See Fig. 23.

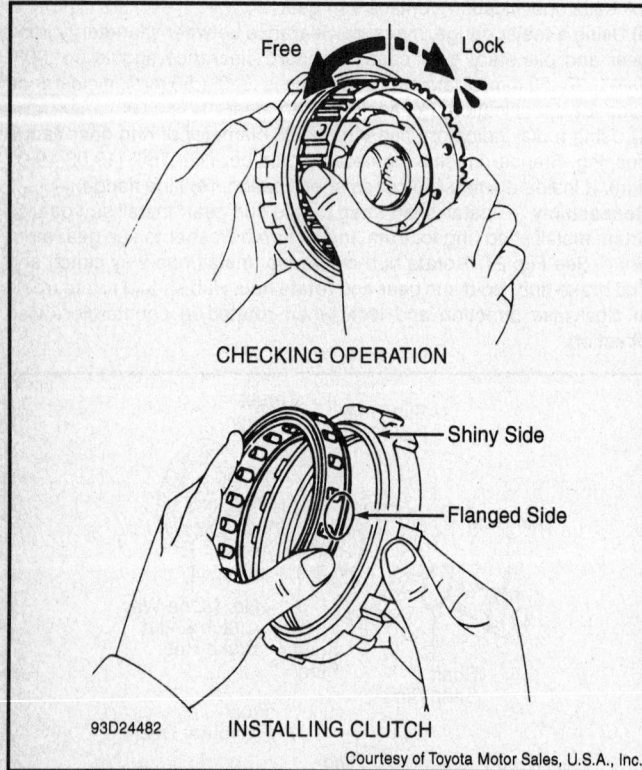

Fig. 22: Checking & Installing No. 2 One-Way Clutch

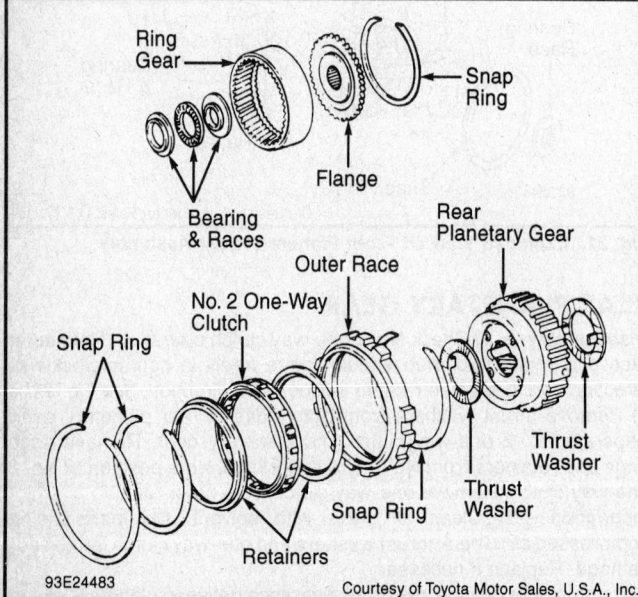

Fig. 23: Exploded View Of Rear Planetary Gear Assembly

1ST & REVERSE BRAKE PISTON

Disassembly – Using appropriate spring compressor, compress springs by tightening bolt gradually. Remove snap ring and compressor. Remove piston return spring. Apply compressed air to oil passage in transaxle case to remove piston. See Fig. 11. Remove piston "O" rings.

Inspection – Clean all parts with solvent. Dry parts using compressed air. Inspect piston for roughness or damage. Replace as necessary.

Reassembly – **1)** Install NEW "O" rings on piston and coat with ATF. Install piston in transaxle case with spring seats facing upward. Install piston return spring and snap ring in place. Using clutch spring compressor, compress piston return spring. Avoid bending spring retainer or damaging transaxle case by overtightening compressor.

2) Push snap ring into place with fingers. Ensure snap ring is fully seated and centered by spring retainer lugs. Snap ring end gap must not align with spring retainer claw. Remove spring compressor. See Fig. 12.

2ND COAST BRAKE

Disassembly – Remove oil seal ring from piston. Remove "E" ring from piston with needle-nose pliers. Remove spring, washer and piston rod. See Fig. 24.

Inspection – Replace brake band if lining is peeled, discolored or printed numbers are defaced. Before assembling NEW band, soak in ATF for 15 minutes. If band is serviceable but piston rod stroke is not within specification, select a NEW piston rod. Piston stroke should be .059-.118" (1.50-3.00 mm). Piston rods are available in lengths of 2.811" (71.40 mm) and 2.870" (72.90 mm).

Reassembly – Install washer and spring to piston rod. Install "E" ring while pushing piston. Apply ATF to oil seal ring. Install oil seal ring to piston. DO NOT spread oil seal ring ends more than necessary for installation. See Fig. 24.

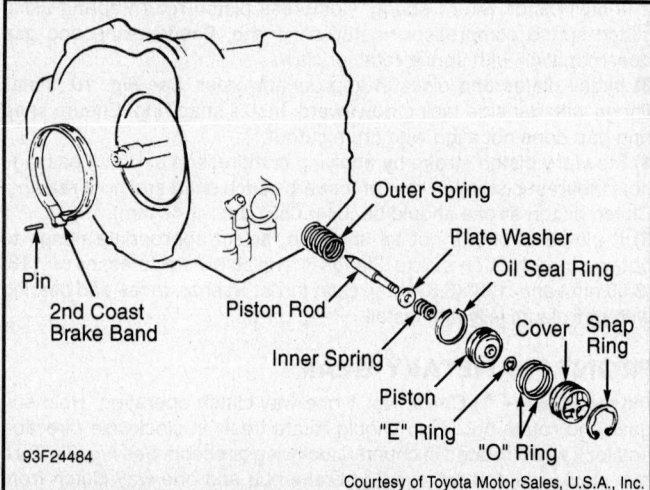

Fig. 24: Exploded View Of 2nd Coast Brake

2ND BRAKE PISTON

Disassembly & Reassembly – Apply compressed air to oil hole on 2nd brake drum and remove 2nd brake piston. Remove 2 "O" rings from piston. Coat NEW "O" rings with ATF. Install "O" rings on piston. Using hand pressure, carefully press 2nd brake piston into 2nd brake drum. See Fig. 25.

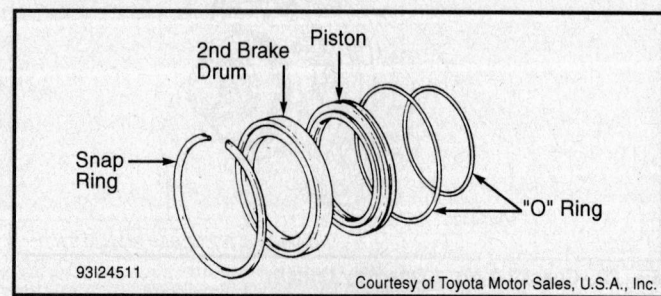

Fig. 25: Exploded View Of 2nd Brake Piston

INTERMEDIATE SHAFT

Disassembly & Reassembly – Using appropriate bearing splitter and puller or press, remove intermediate shaft bearings from shaft. Install intermediate shaft bearings. Ensure gear flange end to intermediate shaft end measurement is 4.560" (115.82 mm). See Fig. 26.

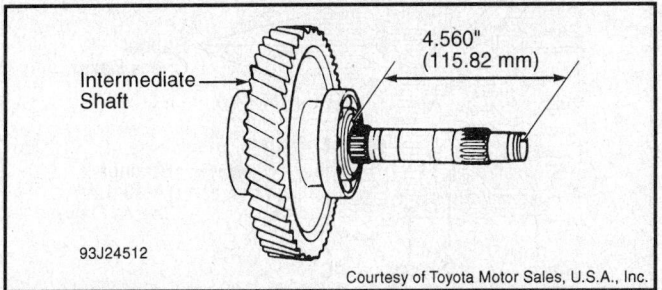

Fig. 26: Checking Intermediate Shaft Gear Flange

VALVE BODY ASSEMBLY

NOTE: All valve body assembly components must be installed in original location. Lay all components in sequence during removal for reassembly reference. Throttle pressure is changed according to number of adjusting rings. See Fig. 27. When assembling valve body, install same number of adjusting rings as were removed. Some valve bodies do not have adjusting rings.

Disassembly – Remove 9 bolts and upper valve body cover. Remove strainer, 2 gaskets and plate. Remove sleeve stopper. Remove 3 bolts and upper valve body. Remove 14 bolts, lower valve body cover and gasket. Remove 3 lower valve body bolts. Hold plate against lower valve body and carefully remove lower valve body. DO NOT lose check balls. Note location of check balls, retainers and pins in valve body. Remove plate and gasket. See Fig. 27.

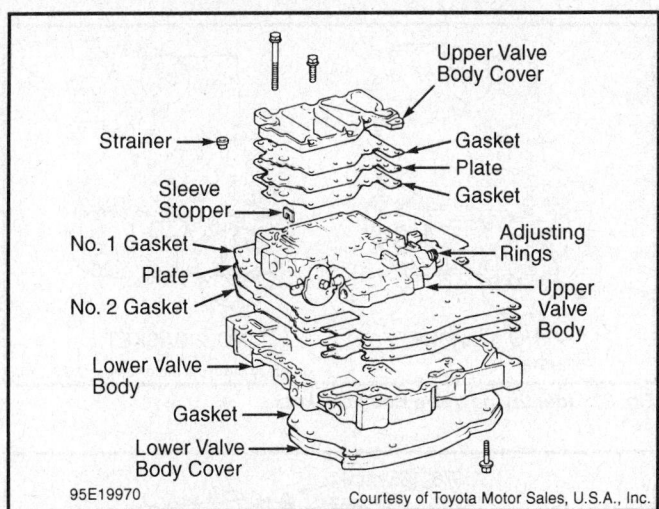

Fig. 27: Exploded View Of Valve Body Assembly

UPPER VALVE BODY SPRING SPECIFICATIONS

Spring No. [1]	Diameter In. (mm)	Free Length In. (mm)
1	.374 (9.50)	.854 (21.70)
2 (Geo)	.409 (10.40)	1.307 (33.20)
2 (Toyota)	.417 (10.60)	1.106 (28.10)
3	.311 (7.90)	.921 (23.40)
4	.343 (8.70)	1.173 (29.80)
5	.362 (9.20)	1.209 (30.70)
6	.335 (8.50)	.823 (20.90)
7	.402 (10.20)	1.047 (26.60)

[1] – For spring locations, See Fig. 28.

Inspection – 1) Clean all parts with solvent. Dry parts with compressed air. Ensure all valve body oil passages are clear. Inspect valves for scoring or roughness. Inspect valve springs for damage, squareness, rust and collapsed coils. Measure spring free length and outer diameter.

2) Replace spring if not within specification. See appropriate VALVE BODY SPRING SPECIFICATIONS table. Ensure valve body springs correspond with appropriate valve. Ensure retainers are installed in appropriate locations.

LOWER VALVE BODY SPRING SPECIFICATIONS

Spring No. [1]	Diameter In. (mm)	Free Length In. (mm)
1	.429 (10.90)	1.717 (43.60)
2	.252 (6.40)	1.071 (27.20)
3	.327 (8.30)	1.091 (27.70)
4	.315 (8.00)	1.236 (31.40)
5 (Aisin Warner)	.311 (7.90)	1.146 (29.10)
5 (Toyota)	.311 (7.90)	1.169 (29.70)
6	.732 (18.60)	2.626 (66.70)
7	.433 (11.00)	.783 (19.90)
8	.252 (6.40)	.441 (11.20)

[1] – For spring locations, See Fig. 30.

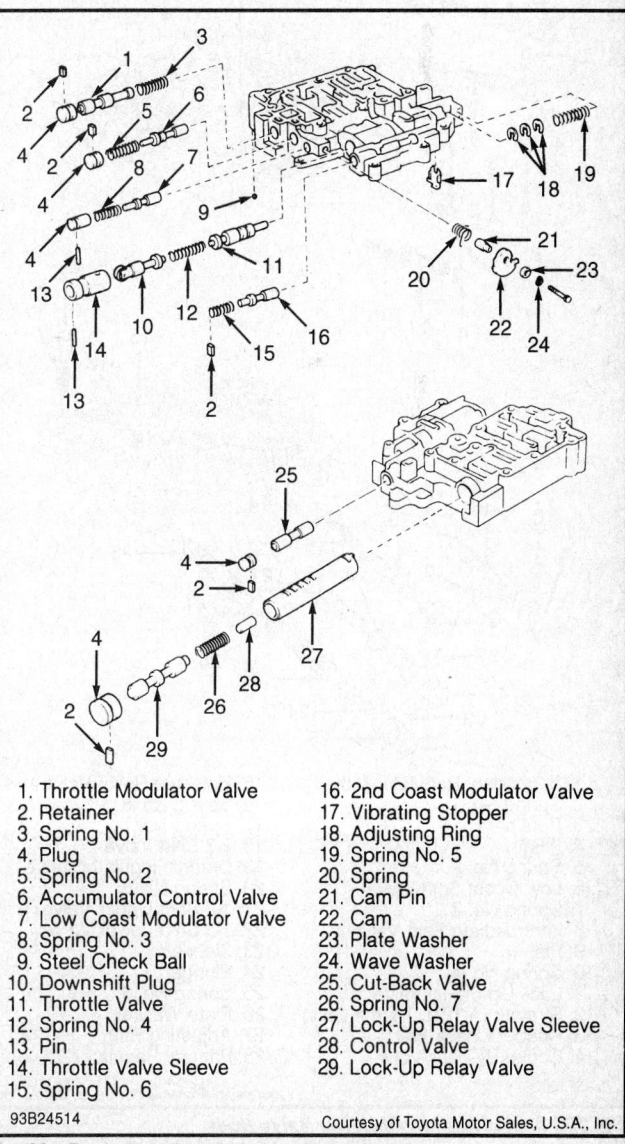

1. Throttle Modulator Valve
2. Retainer
3. Spring No. 1
4. Plug
5. Spring No. 2
6. Accumulator Control Valve
7. Low Coast Modulator Valve
8. Spring No. 3
9. Steel Check Ball
10. Downshift Plug
11. Throttle Valve
12. Spring No. 4
13. Pin
14. Throttle Valve Sleeve
15. Spring No. 6
16. 2nd Coast Modulator Valve
17. Vibrating Stopper
18. Adjusting Ring
19. Spring No. 5
20. Spring
21. Cam Pin
22. Cam
23. Plate Washer
24. Wave Washer
25. Cut-Back Valve
26. Spring No. 7
27. Lock-Up Relay Valve Sleeve
28. Control Valve
29. Lock-Up Relay Valve

93B24514   Courtesy of Toyota Motor Sales, U.S.A., Inc.

Fig. 28: Exploded View Of Upper Valve Body

AUTOMATIC TRANSMISSIONS
Toyota A-131L & A-132L (Cont.)

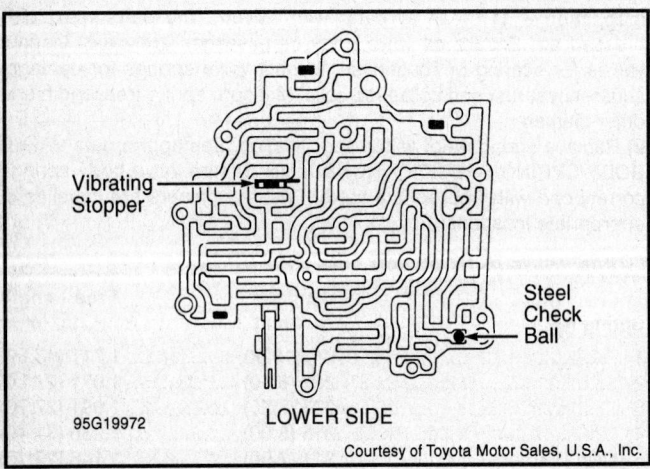

Vibrating Stopper

Steel Check Ball

LOWER SIDE

95G19972

Courtesy of Toyota Motor Sales, U.S.A., Inc.

Fig. 29: Identifying Upper Valve Body Check Ball, Pin & Retainer Locations

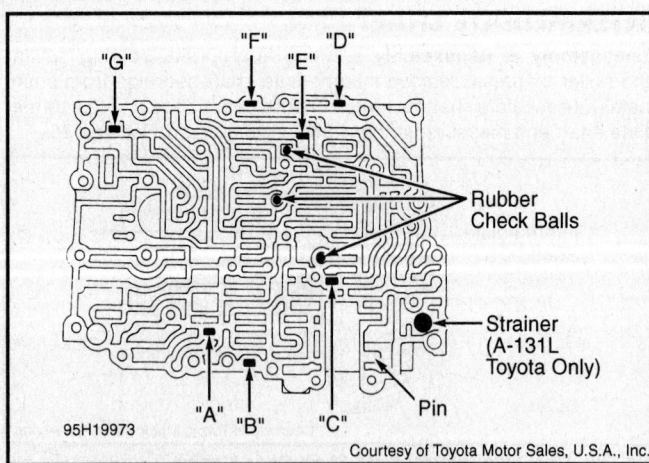

"G" "F" "E" "D"

Rubber Check Balls

Strainer (A-131L Toyota Only)

"A" "B" "C" Pin

95H19973

Courtesy of Toyota Motor Sales, U.S.A., Inc.

Fig. 31: Identifying Lower Valve Body Check Ball, Pin & Retainer Locations

NOTE: Valves may be held in with pins or retainers and plugs. Remove components and note locations. Arrange parts in order for reassembly reference.

Reassembly – 1) Coat all components with ATF. To reassemble, reverse disassembly procedure. Ensure check balls, pins and strainer on upper side of lower valve body are installed correctly. See Fig. 31. Ensure check ball, pins, retainers and vibrating stopper on lower side of upper valve body are installed correctly. See Fig. 29.

2) Position NEW No. 2 gasket, plate and NEW No. 1 gasket on lower valve body. Ensure gaskets are installed in correct locations. See Fig. 32. Place lower valve body with plate and gaskets on upper valve body. DO NOT let components separate. Align each bolt hole in valve bodies with gaskets and plate.

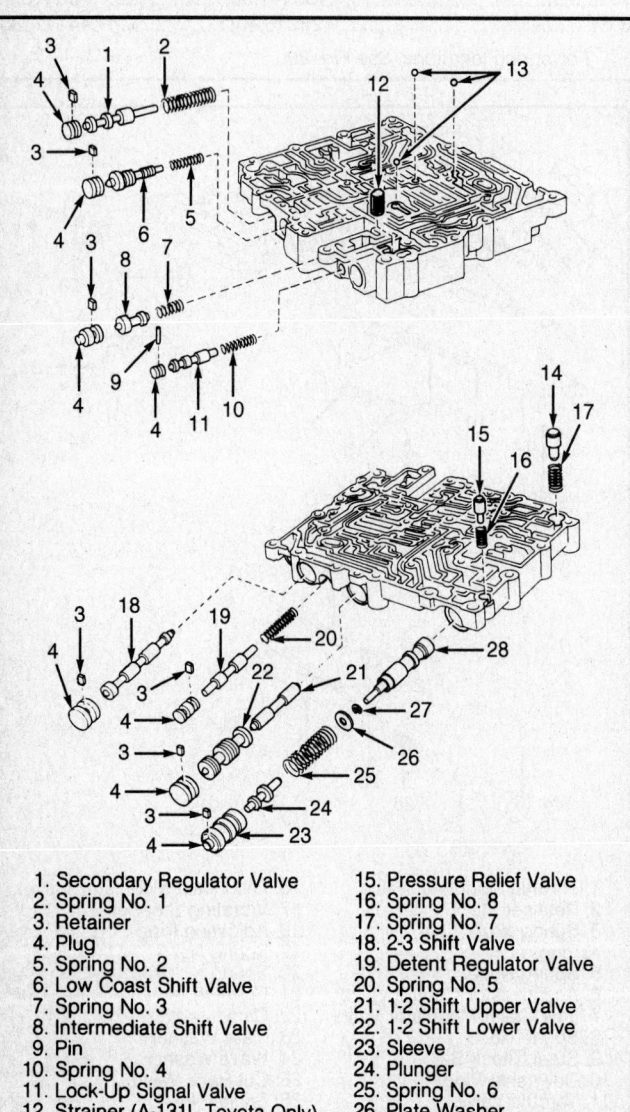

1. Secondary Regulator Valve
2. Spring No. 1
3. Retainer
4. Plug
5. Spring No. 2
6. Low Coast Shift Valve
7. Spring No. 3
8. Intermediate Shift Valve
9. Pin
10. Spring No. 4
11. Lock-Up Signal Valve
12. Strainer (A-131L Toyota Only)
13. Rubber Check Ball
14. Cooler By-Pass Valve
15. Pressure Relief Valve
16. Spring No. 8
17. Spring No. 7
18. 2-3 Shift Valve
19. Detent Regulator Valve
20. Spring No. 5
21. 1-2 Shift Upper Valve
22. 1-2 Shift Lower Valve
23. Sleeve
24. Plunger
25. Spring No. 6
26. Plate Washer
27. Adjusting Ring
28. Primary Regulator Valve

95F19971

Courtesy of Toyota Motor Sales, U.S.A., Inc.

Fig. 30: Exploded View Of Lower Valve Body

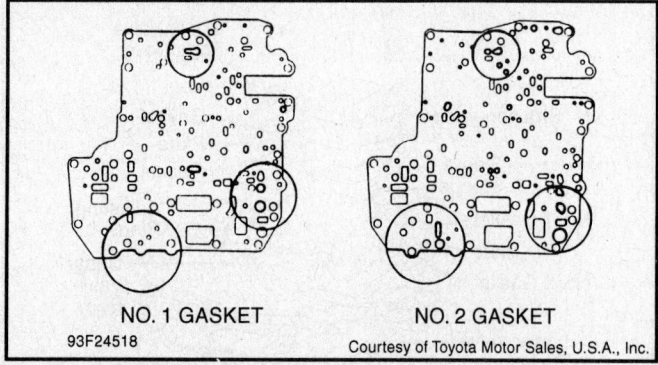

NO. 1 GASKET   NO. 2 GASKET

93F24518

Courtesy of Toyota Motor Sales, U.S.A., Inc.

Fig. 32: Identifying Valve Body Gaskets

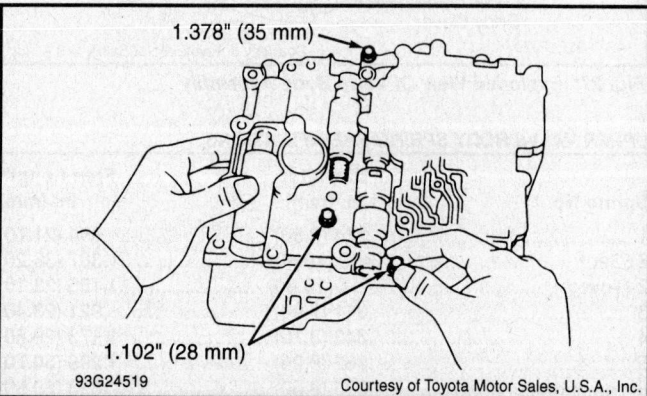

1.378" (35 mm)

1.102" (28 mm)

93G24519

Courtesy of Toyota Motor Sales, U.S.A., Inc.

Fig. 33: Installing Lower Valve Body-To-Upper Valve Body Bolts

3) Install and finger tighten bolts in lower valve body to secure upper valve body. *See Fig. 33.* Install lower valve body cover over NEW gasket. Install and finger tighten 14 cover bolts. *See Fig. 34.* Install and finger tighten 1.102" (28 mm) bolts (3) in upper valve body.

4) Ensure retainers are installed correctly on upper side of upper valve body. Install sleeve stopper. Position NEW gasket, plate and gasket. Install strainer onto plate. Position upper valve body cover and install and finger tighten 9 bolts. *See Fig. 34.* Check alignment of gaskets and plates. Tighten upper and lower valve body bolts to 48 INCH lbs. (5.4 N.m).

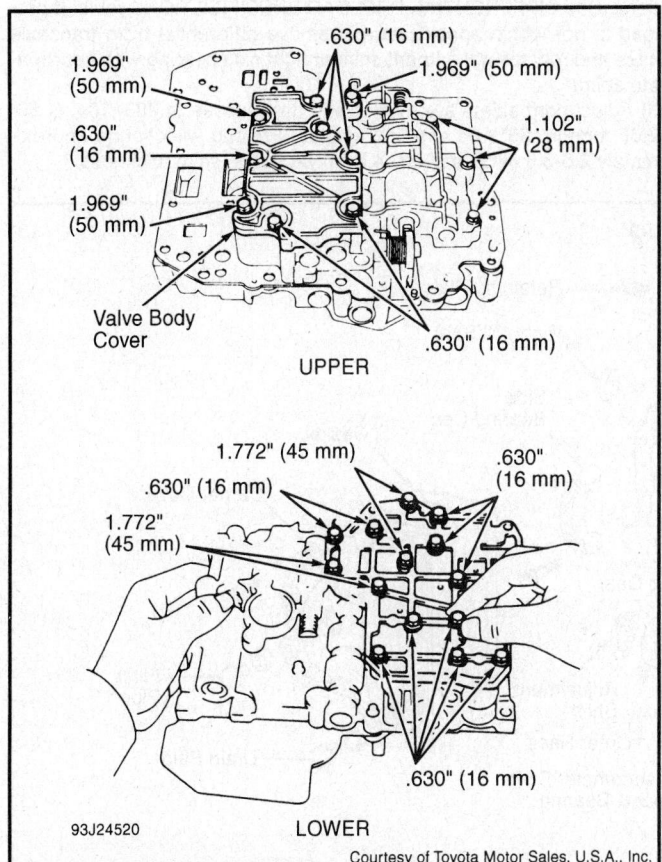

Fig. 34: Identifying Upper & Lower Valve Body Cover Bolt Locations

DIFFERENTIAL ASSEMBLY

Disassembly – 1) Remove carrier cover. Attach an INCH lb. torque wrench to end of pinion shaft. *See Fig. 35.* Measure total preload required to rotate pinion. Note and record reading. Position dial indicator assembly on transaxle case. Position dial indicator tip against side gear. *See Fig. 36.* Measure side gear backlash while holding one pinion toward case. Backlash should be .002-.008" (.05-.20 mm). Note and record reading.

2) Remove left side bearing retainer bolts. Remove bearing retainer. Remove "O" ring from retainer. Remove right side bearing cap. Remove differential, outer race and adjustment shim from transaxle case.

3) Attach an INCH lb. torque wrench to end of pinion shaft. Measure drive pinion preload. Note and record reading. Starting preload should be 4-7 INCH lbs. (.5-.8 N.m) for a used bearing. Total preload reading minus drive pinion preload should equal 1-2 INCH lbs. (.1-.2 N.m). If not within specification, side bearing preload requires adjustment.

4) Remove bearings from differential case using appropriate puller. Remove speedometer drive gear. Mark ring gear and case for reassembly reference. Spread ring gear bolt locking plates. Remove ring gear bolts and locking plates. Using brass hammer, tap ring gear from differential case.

5) Using a dial indicator, check side gear backlash. Hold one pinion against case. Measure side gear backlash. Backlash must be .002-.008" (.05-.20 mm). If backlash is not within specification, side gear thrust washers must be replaced.

6) Drive out pinion shaft lock pin from ring gear side. Remove pinion shaft, pinion gears, side gears and thrust washers. Remove left oil seals from transaxle case or bearing retainer. Using a long screwdriver, remove right oil seal from transaxle case. Remove left outer bearing race and shim from retainer.

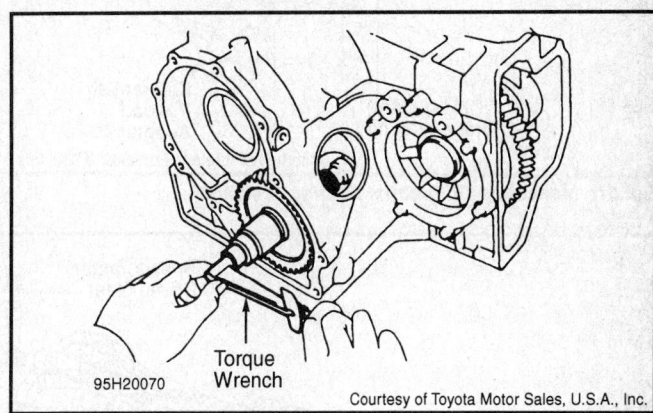

Fig. 35: Measuring Total Preload

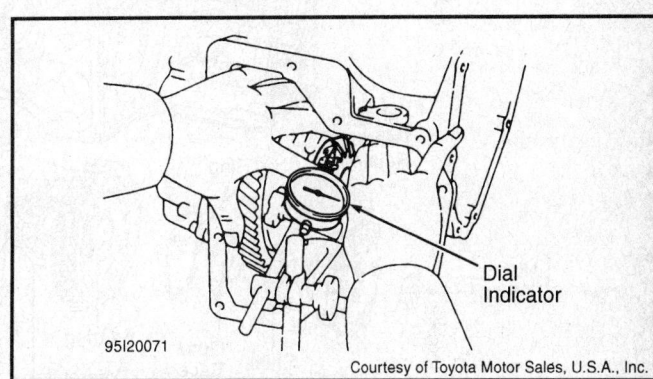

Fig. 36: Measuring Differential Side Gear Backlash

Cleaning & Inspection – Clean all parts with solvent. Dry with compressed air. Check bearings and gears for wear or damage. Replace if necessary.

Reassembly – 1) Install original shim onto retainer. Install outer race. Lubricate oil seal lip. Install oil seals until oil seal surface is flush with surface of transaxle case or bearing retainer.

2) Select thrust washers that will ensure correct side gear backlash. Thrust washers are available in thicknesses of .037-.047" (.95-1.20 mm) in .20" (.05 mm) increments. Install thrust washers and side gears in differential case. If possible, install same size thrust washers on both sides. Install pinion gears and pinion shaft. Check side gear backlash to ensure proper thrust washers are used.

3) Once backlash is correct, using hammer and punch, drive lock pin through differential case and into pinion shaft. Stake differential case to retain lock pin. Install speedometer drive gear onto differential case. Install side bearings onto differential case.

4) Clean ring gear contact surface of differential case. Heat ring gear to 212°F (100°C) in an oil bath. DO NOT heat ring gear above 230°F (110 °C). Clean contact surface of ring gear using cleaning solvent. Align ring gear with differential case. Install ring gear on differential case.

5) Install NEW locking plates and bolts. Tighten bolts evenly and in several steps to 72 ft. lbs. (97 N.m) for A-131L transaxle and 91 ft. lbs. (124 N.m) for A-132L transaxle. Stake lock plates. Stake one tab flush with flat surface of bolt. Stake 2nd tab against corner of bolt.

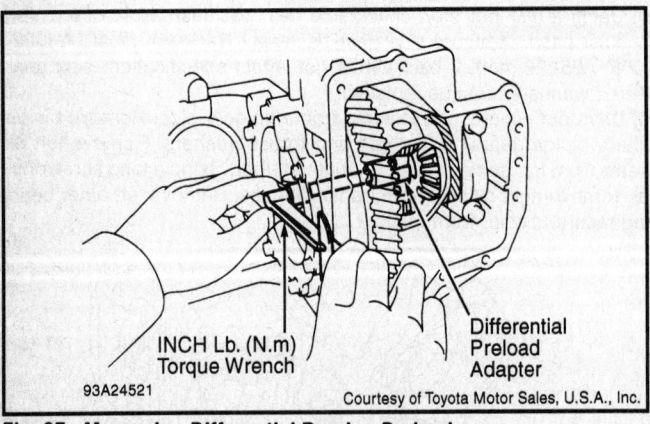

INCH Lb. (N.m) Torque Wrench

Differential Preload Adapter

93A24521

Courtesy of Toyota Motor Sales, U.S.A., Inc.

Fig. 37: Measuring Differential Bearing Preload

6) Install outer race and original adjusting shim on right side bearing. Remove differential drive pinion. See DIFFERENTIAL DRIVE PINION ASSEMBLY. Install differential in transaxle case. Install left bearing outer race, shim and retainer without "O" ring. Snug bolts evenly and gradually while turning ring gear. Tighten bolts to 14 ft. lbs. (19 N.m). Install right side bearing cap. Snug bolts evenly and gradually while turning ring gear. Tighten bolts to 36 ft. lbs. (49 N.m).

7) Using Differential Preload Adapter (09564-32011) and an INCH lb. torque wrench, measure differential bearing preload with differential drive pinion removed. See Fig. 37. Preload must be within specifications. See DIFFERENTIAL PRELOAD SPECIFICATIONS table. If preload is not within specifications, remove differential from transaxle case and replace adjustment shim at right side bearing with appropriate shim.

8) Adjustment shims are available in thicknesses of 063-.104" (1.60-2.65 mm) in .20" (.05 mm) increments. Preload will change approximately 2.6-3.5 INCH lbs. (.3-.4 N.m) with each shim thickness.

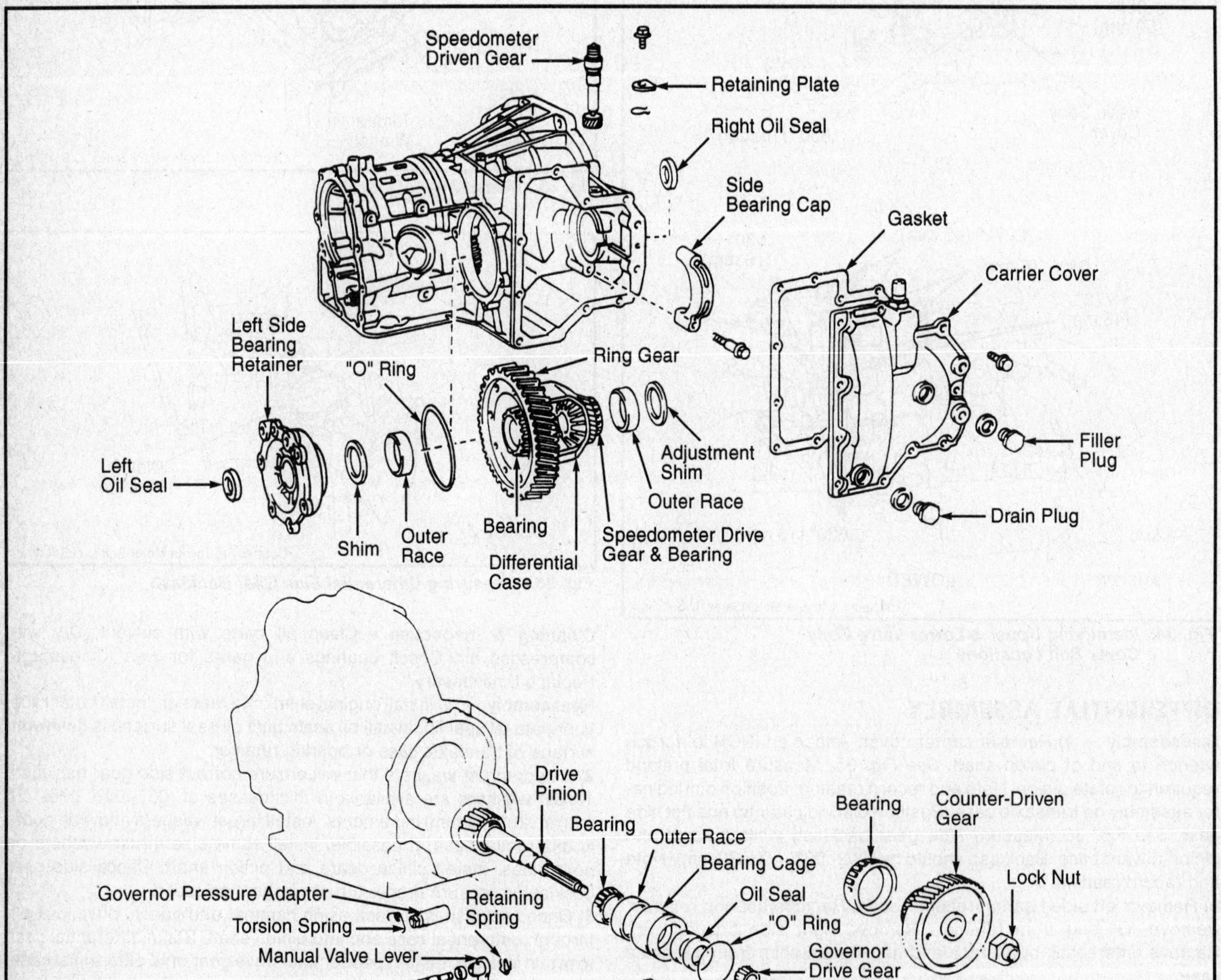

Speedometer Driven Gear

Retaining Plate

Right Oil Seal

Side Bearing Cap

Gasket

Carrier Cover

Left Side Bearing Retainer

"O" Ring

Ring Gear

Filler Plug

Left Oil Seal

Adjustment Shim

Outer Race

Drain Plug

Shim

Outer Race

Bearing

Differential Case

Speedometer Drive Gear & Bearing

Drive Pinion

Bearing

Outer Race

Bearing Cage

Oil Seal

"O" Ring

Governor Drive Gear

Bearing

Counter-Driven Gear

Lock Nut

Governor Pressure Adapter

Torsion Spring

Manual Valve Lever

Retaining Spring

Oil Slinger

Outer Race

Oil Seal

Pin

Collar

Spacer

Manual Valve Lever Shaft

Parking Lock Rod

Spring

Pin

Snap Ring

Parking Lock Pawl Bracket

Parking Lock Pawl

93B24522

Courtesy of Toyota Motor Sales, U.S.A., Inc.

Fig. 38: Exploded View Of A-131L & A-132L Transaxle Differential Assembly

DIFFERENTIAL PRELOAD SPECIFICATIONS

Application	INCH Lbs. (N.m)
New Bearings	9-14 (1.0-1.6)
Used Bearings	4-7 (.5-.8)

9) If preload is within specification, remove left bearing retainer. DO NOT lose selected adjustment shim. Install "O" ring on left bearing retainer. Remove right side bearing cap bolts and coat threads with sealant. Tighten bolts evenly and gradually to 36 ft. lbs. (49 N.m), while turning ring gear.

10) With drive pinion installed in case, measure total preload using procedure used during disassembly. Starting preload should be drive pinion preload of 4-7 INCH lbs. (.5-.8 N.m) plus 3-4 INCH lbs. (.3-.4 N.m) for NEW bearings or 1-2 INCH lbs. (.1-.2 N.m) for used bearings.

11) If total preload is not within specification, disassemble differential and readjust. If total preload is correct, stake counter-driven gear lock nut. Install drive pinion cap. Coat carrier cover bolt threads with sealant. Install carrier cover and gasket. Install bolts and tighten to 18 ft. lbs. (25 N.m). To complete reassembly, reverse disassembly procedure. Tighten all bolts to specification. See Fig. 38.

DIFFERENTIAL DRIVE PINION ASSEMBLY

Disassembly – 1) Using an INCH lb. torque wrench, measure drive pinion preload with differential assembly removed. Starting preload should be 4-7 INCH lbs. (.5-.8 N.m) for used bearings. Remove drive pinion bolt and cap. Using chisel, loosen staked area of counter-driven gear lock nut. Secure gear from turning. Remove lock nut. Using appropriate puller, remove counter-driven gear and bearing.

2) Remove bearing race from transaxle case. Remove oil slinger, bearing spacer and governor drive gear. Remove snap ring from transaxle case. Using brass drift and hammer, drive pinion and bearing cage from bore. Press governor drive gear from drive pinion shaft. Remove bearing cage from drive pinion. Remove "O" ring from bearing cage. See Fig. 38.

3) Press bearing from counter-driven gear. Using bearing remover, remove pinion shaft bearing. Using hammer and brass drift, drive out drive bearing outer race from cage. Note position of oil seal lips. Remove seals from cage.

Cleaning & Inspection – Clean all parts with solvent. Dry parts with compressed air. Check bearings and gears for wear or damage. Replace if necessary.

Reassembly – 1) Lubricate lips of oil seals. Install inner seal with lip facing downward. Oil seal must be installed to proper depth of .315" (8.00 mm) for A-131L transaxle, and .374" (9.50 mm) for A-132L transaxle.

2) Using seal installer, install outer seal with lip facing upward. Position oil seal flush with cage surface. Install outer bearing race in bearing cage.

3) Install drive pinion shaft bearing. Using remover/installer, install bearing on counter-driven gear. Install "O" ring on bearing cage. Install cage on drive pinion shaft. Use care not to damage oil seals. Install governor drive gear. Install shaft assembly into transaxle case.

4) Tap bearing cage into transaxle case. Ensure cage is past snap ring groove. Install snap ring. Insert brass bar into hole and tap drive pinion shaft against snap ring. Ensure snap ring is fully seated. Install oil slinger with lip facing outward. Install outer race in transaxle case with narrow end facing out. Install NEW bearing spacer, small end first.

5) Drive counter-driven gear onto shaft until lock nut can be installed. DO NOT tap on transaxle case. Lubricate lock nut threads and install lock nut on shaft. Install holder on gear. Tighten counter-driven gear lock nut to 127 ft. lbs. (172 N.m). Rotate counter-driven gear both directions several times.

6) Using an INCH lb. torque wrench, measure drive pinion preload. Starting preload should be 9-14 INCH lbs. (1.0-1.6 N.m) for NEW bearings and 4-7 INCH lbs. (.5-.8 N.m) for used bearings. Replace bearing spacer if preload exceeds specifications. Recheck preload procedure (if necessary).

7) If preload is less than specification, tighten lock nut in additional increments of 9.5 ft. lbs. (13 N.m) . Tighten lock nut until specified preload is obtained. If maximum torque of 213 ft. lbs. (289 N.m) is exceeded while tightening nut, replace bearing spacer and repeat procedure. DO NOT back off nut to reduce preload.

TRANSAXLE REASSEMBLY

NOTE: Coat all oil seal rings, clutch discs, clutch plates, rotating parts and sliding surfaces with ATF prior to reassembly. Soak clutch discs in ATF for 15 minutes prior to installation. For bearing race and thrust bearing installation direction and locations, See Fig. 41. For bearing race and thrust bearing outer diameter specifications, see BEARING RACE & THRUST BEARING SPECIFICATIONS table.

1) Install governor pressure adapter into case. Align adapter and transaxle case hole and install torsion spring. Ensure adapter does not slide and spring does not fall out when pulled. Install manual valve lever shaft oil seal to transaxle case. Install NEW collar on manual valve lever. See Fig. 38.

2) Install manual valve lever shaft to transaxle case through manual valve lever. Using a pin punch, drive in roll pin until flush with manual valve lever surface. Align collar hole with notch in lever and stake in position using a hammer and punch. Install retaining spring. Ensure lever moves smoothly.

3) Install parking lock pawl in transaxle case. Hook spring end on pawl and transaxle case. Install pin into hole of transaxle case, through spring and pawl. Install parking lock rod.

4) Install parking lock pawl bracket. Tighten to 65 INCH lbs. (7.4 N.m). Check operation of parking lock pawl to ensure counter-driven gear is locked when manual valve lever is in "P" position. Install 1st and reverse brake piston (if necessary). See 1ST & REVERSE BRAKE PISTON under COMPONENT DISASSEMBLY & REASSEMBLY. Install intermediate shaft. Install transaxle rear cover and gasket. Tighten bolts to 18 ft. lbs. (25 N.m).

5) Ensure intermediate shaft turns smoothly. Using a dial indicator, check intermediate shaft end play. End play should be .019-.059" (.49-1.51 mm). If end play is not as specified, check installation of intermediate shaft. Install 1st and reverse inner flange with flat end facing upward. Install discs and plates starting with disc, alternating with plate and ending with disc.

NOTE: The 1st and reverse clutch may include a manufacturer modification. On some transaxles, an additional clutch plate has been added, and clutch disc thickness has been reduced. Clutch disc thickness has been reduced from .067" (1.7 mm) to .059"(1.50 mm). Piston thickness has been increased from .49" (12.4 mm) to .60" (15.3 mm) on A-131L transaxle, or from .64" (16.3 mm) to .75" (19.0 mm) on A-132L transaxle.

6) Install outer flange with flat side toward piston. Install snap ring. Ensure end gap of snap ring is not aligned with cutout of transaxle case. Apply compressed air to oil passage to ensure piston moves. See Fig. 11. Coat bearings and races "E" with petroleum jelly and install on ring gear. See Fig. 41. Install ring gear in transaxle case.

7) Align flukes of discs in 1st and reverse brake. Coat thrust washer with petroleum jelly. Align tab of thrust washer with hollow of planetary carrier. Align planetary carrier splines with flukes of discs. Install rear planetary gear. Install No. 2 one-way clutch in transaxle case with shiny side upward. Install one-way clutch on inner race while turning planetary gear clockwise.

8) Coat thrust washer with petroleum jelly and install on planetary gear. Check No. 2 one-way clutch operation by turning planetary gear. Gear should rotate freely in clockwise direction and lock in counterclockwise direction. Install snap ring. Ensure snap ring end is not aligned with cutout of transaxle case.

9) Install 2nd coast brake band guide with tip contacting transaxle case. Install 2nd brake flange with flat side facing upward. Install discs and plates in the following order: for A-131L transaxle install disc, plate, disc, plate, disc, plate. For A-132L transaxle install disc, plate, plate, disc, plate, plate.

10) Install piston return spring assembly with springs over protrusions in transaxle case. Align groove of 2nd brake drum with guide. Install drum in transaxle case. Install snap ring. Using 2 hammers, compress piston return springs with handles. Install snap ring into groove. Ensure end gap of ring is not aligned with cutout in transaxle case.

11) Install 2nd brake drum gasket until gasket makes contact with 2nd brake drum. See Fig. 8. Apply compressed air to center oil passage (next to manual valve lever shaft) and ensure piston movement. Align flukes of 2nd brake discs. Install hub on 2nd brake discs. Check distance between surfaces of 2nd brake hub and rear planetary gear. Distance should be approximately .20" (5.0 mm).

12) Install sun gear and input drum on No. 1 one-way clutch while turning sun gear clockwise. Ensure thrust washer is on sun gear input drum. Coat bearings and races "D" and "C" with petroleum jelly and install on ring gear and front planetary gear. See Fig. 41. Install planetary gear on ring gear. Install front planetary gear assembly on sun gear.

13) If planetary gear is correctly installed, ring gear flange bushing will be flush with or below intermediate shaft shoulder. Coat race with petroleum jelly and install on ring gear flange. Install intermediate shaft oil seal ring.

14) Install 2nd coast brake band in transaxle case. Install pin through oil pump mounting bolt hole. Coat bearings and races "A" and "B" with petroleum jelly and install on both sides of forward clutch drum. See Fig. 41. Coat clutch drum thrust washer with petroleum jelly and install with oil groove facing upward on direct clutch drum. Align flukes of direct clutch discs.

15) Mesh hub with direct clutch flukes while turning clutch drum or forward clutch. If disc flukes are meshed with hub correctly, end of direct clutch drum bushing will be flush with surface of forward clutch. Place direct clutch and forward clutch into transaxle case. Rotate forward clutch to mesh front planetary ring gear and discs. Assembly is fully seated when distance is about .118" (3.00 mm) between direct clutch drum and sun gear input drum (shell).

16) Coat race "A" with petroleum jelly and install on stator shaft. See Fig. 41. Install "O" ring on oil pump. Install oil pump into transaxle case. Hold input shaft and lightly press oil pump body to slide oil seal rings on stator shaft through direct clutch drum. Install and tighten bolts to 16 ft. lbs. (22 N.m).

NOTE: DO NOT apply excessive pressure on oil pump. If excessive pressure is used, seal rings will stick to direct clutch drum.

---

17) Measure input shaft end play. End play should be .012-.035" (.30-.90 mm). If end play is not as specified, replace oil pump race. Oil pump races are available in thicknesses of .031" (.80 mm) and .055" (1.40 mm). Ensure input shaft rotates smoothly. Install "O" rings on brake piston cover. Install outer spring, 2nd coast brake piston and cover into bore. Install snap ring. Ensure front end of piston rod contacts center of 2nd brake band depression.

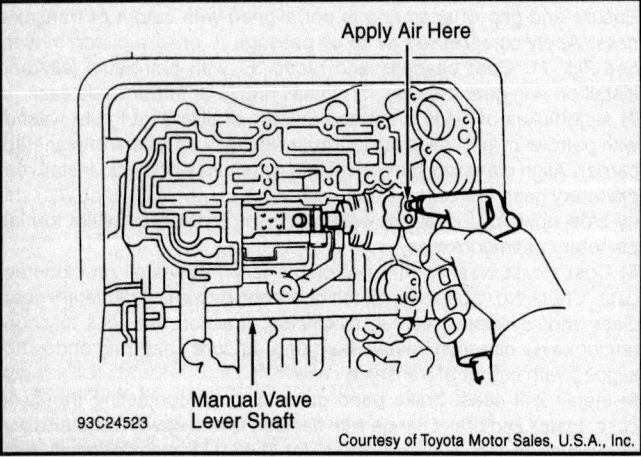

Apply Air Here

Manual Valve Lever Shaft

93C24523   Courtesy of Toyota Motor Sales, U.S.A., Inc.

Fig. 39: Checking 2nd Coast Brake Band

18) Measure 2nd coast brake piston stroke by applying compressed air to oil passage in transaxle case. See Fig. 39. Piston stroke should be .059-.118" (1.50-3.00 mm). If piston stroke is not within specification, replace piston rod. Piston rods are available in lengths of 2.811" (71.40 mm) and 2.870" (72.90 mm). Recheck piston travel after changing piston rod. It travel still exceeds specification, replace 2nd coast brake band.

19) Apply compressed air to oil passage and check piston rod movement. See Fig. 39. Coat accumulator piston "O" rings with ATF. Install "O" rings on accumulator pistons. Check accumulator spring free length. See appropriate ACCUMULATOR SPRING SPECIFICATIONS table. Replace as necessary. Install pistons and springs in appropriate locations. See Fig. 40. Install accumulator cover and gasket. Tighten bolts to 89 INCH lbs. (10 N.m).

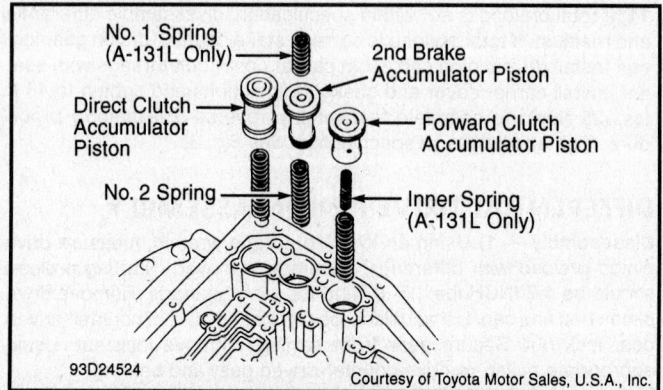

No. 1 Spring (A-131L Only)
2nd Brake Accumulator Piston
Direct Clutch Accumulator Piston
Forward Clutch Accumulator Piston
No. 2 Spring
Inner Spring (A-131L Only)

93D24524   Courtesy of Toyota Motor Sales, U.S.A., Inc.

Fig. 40: Identifying Accumulator Piston & Spring Locations

ACCUMULATOR SPRING SPECIFICATIONS (AISIN WARNER A-131L)

Application	Color	Length – In. (mm)
Geo		
Forward Clutch		
Inner	Red	1.890 (48.00)
Outer	Yellow/Green	3.193 (81.10)
Direct Clutch	Blue	2.935 (74.54)
2nd Brake		
No. 1	Yellow	1.385 (35.18)
No. 2	Yellow	2.231 (56.68)
Toyota		
Forward Clutch		
Inner	Brown	1.523 (38.68)
Outer	Yellow/Green	2.074 (52.68)
Direct Clutch	Blue/Red	2.935 (74.54)
2nd Brake		
No. 1	Yellow	1.385 (35.18)
No. 2	Yellow	2.231 (56.68)

ACCUMULATOR SPRING SPECIFICATIONS (TOYOTA A-131L)

Application	Color	Length – In. (mm)
Geo		
Forward Clutch		
Inner	Red	1.890 (48.00)
Outer	Yellow	3.193 (81.10)
Direct Clutch	Yellow	2.842 (72.18)
2nd Brake	Purple	2.625 (66.68)
Toyota		
Forward Clutch		
Inner	Brown	1.523 (38.68)
Outer	Yellow/Green	2.074 (52.68)
Direct Clutch	Yellow/Red	3.101 (78.76)
2nd Brake	Green/Red	2.482 (63.05)

ACCUMULATOR SPRING SPECIFICATIONS (A-132L)

Application	Color	Length – In. (mm)
Forward Clutch	Red/White	2.067 (52.50)
Direct Clutch	None	2.618 (66.50)
2nd Brake	Orange	2.625 (66.68)

20) Install 2nd brake apply gasket and governor oil strainer. Install throttle cable into transaxle case. Use care not to damage "O" ring. Ensure cable is fully seated in transaxle case. Install control valve assembly. Ensure proper length bolt is used in proper location. See VALVE BODY ASSEMBLY under ON-VEHICLE SERVICE. Tighten bolts to 89 INCH lbs. (10 N.m).

21) Align manual valve with pin on manual shift lever. Install manual valve body. Tighten bolts to 89 INCH lbs. (10 N.m). Install detent spring on manual valve body. Tighten bolts to 89 INCH lbs. (10 N.m). Ensure manual valve lever is touching center of detent spring tip roller.

22) Install oil tubes. DO NOT bend or damage tubes. Install oil tube bracket. Tighten bolts to 89 INCH lbs. (10 N.m). Install oil strainer (filter). Tighten bolts to 89 INCH lbs. (10 N.m). Install magnets into oil pan. Ensure magnets do not interfere with oil tubes. Install oil pan with NEW gasket. Tighten bolts to 43 INCH lbs. (4.9 N.m).

23) Install governor body adapter, governor body with plate washer and thrust washer onto governor body. Install cover and "O" ring. Install cover bracket with 2 bolts. Tighten bolts to 115 INCH lbs. (13 N.m). Install throttle cable retaining plate. Install filler tube and dipstick. Install seal and park/neutral position switch. Tighten and secure with lock plate. Tighten nut to 61 INCH lbs. (6.9 N.m).

24) Adjust park/neutral position switch and tighten adjusting bolts to 48 INCH lbs. (5.4 N.m). Install manual shift lever. Tighten nut to 115 INCH lbs. (13 N.m). Install oil cooler pipes and unions. Tighten unions to 20 ft. lbs. (27 N.m).

25) Install torque converter on transaxle. Using a straightedge and calipers, measure torque converter installed depth. Distance should be .898" (22.80 mm) for Corolla, .906" (23.00 mm) for Prizm and .512" (13.00 mm) for Tercel. See Fig. 42.

BEARING RACE & THRUST BEARING SPECIFICATIONS

Application (Letter I.D.) [1]	Outer Diameter In. (mm)
Front Bearing Race	
A	1.693 (43.00)
B & C	1.492 (37.90)
D	1.772 (45.00)
E	1.469 (37.30)
Thrust Bearing	
A	1.654 (42.00)
B & C	1.421 (36.10)
D	1.772 (45.00)
E	1.480 (37.60)
Rear Bearing Race	
A	1.654 (42.00)
B	1.406 (35.70)
C	1.378 (35.00)
D	N/A
E	1.480 (37.60)

[1] – For bearing race and thrust bearing locations, See Fig. 41.

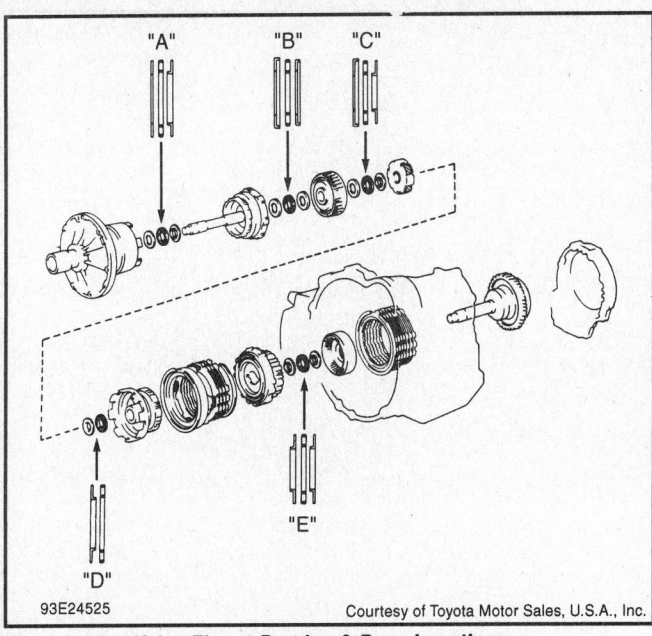

"A"   "B"   "C"

"E"

"D"

93E24525   Courtesy of Toyota Motor Sales, U.S.A., Inc.

Fig. 41: Identifying Thrust Bearing & Race Locations

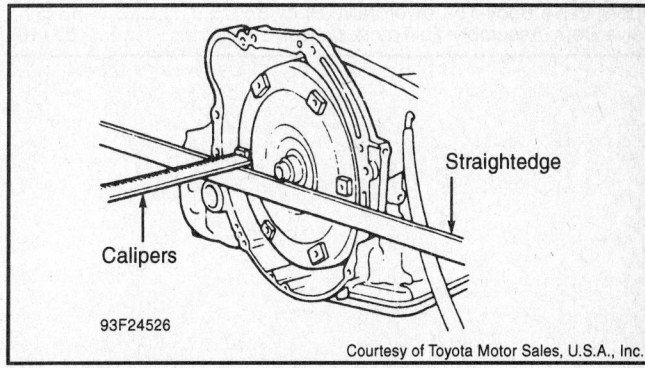

Straightedge

Calipers

93F24526   Courtesy of Toyota Motor Sales, U.S.A., Inc.

Fig. 42: Measuring Torque Converter Depth

AUTOMATIC TRANSMISSIONS
Toyota A-131L & A-132L (Cont.)

TORQUE SPECIFICATIONS
TORQUE SPECIFICATIONS

Application	Ft. Lbs. (N.m)
Bearing Retainer Bolt	14 (19)
Converter-To-Drive Plate Bolt	
A-131L	20 (27)
A-132L	13 (18)
Counter-Driven Lock Nut	
Standard	127 (172)
Maximum	213 (289)
Drive Plate Mounting Bolt	
Corolla	
1995	65 (88)
1996	47 (64)
Prizm	47 (64)
Tercel	65 (88)
Oil Cooler Union Nut	20 (27)
Oil Pan Drain Plug	36 (49)
Oil Pump Mounting Bolt	16 (22)
Ring Gear Bolt	
A-131L	72 (97)
A-132L	91 (124)
Side Bearing Cap Bolt	36 (49)
Transaxle-To-Engine Bolt	
10 mm	34 (46)
12 mm	47 (64)
Transaxle Rear Cover Bolt	18 (25)

Application	INCH Lbs. (N.m)
Accumulator Cover Bolt	89 (10)
Manual Shift Lever Nut	115 (13)
Manual Valve Body Bolt	89 (10)
Oil Pan Bolt	43 (4.9)
Oil Pump Stator Shaft Bolt	89 (10)
Oil Strainer Bolt	89 (10)
Park/Neutral Position Switch	
Adjusting Bolt	48 (5.4)
Retaining Nut	61 (6.9)
Parking Lock Pawl Bracket Bolt	65 (7.4)
Upper Valve Body-To-Lower Valve Body Bolt	48 (5.4)
Valve Body Assembly-To-Transaxle Bolt	89 (10)

TRANSAXLE SPECIFICATIONS
TRANSAXLE SPECIFICATIONS

Application	In. (mm)
Bushing Inside Diameter (Maximum)	
Direct Clutch	1.853 (47.07)
Oil Pump Body	1.503 (38.18)
Ring Gear Flange	.749-.750 (19.03-19.05)
Stator Shaft	
Front	.849 (21.57)
Rear	1.066 (27.07)
Sun Gear	
Standard	.867-.868 (22.03-22.05)
Maximum	.870 (22.10)
Input Shaft End Play	.012-.035 (.30-.90)
Intermediate Shaft End Play	.019-.059 (.49-1.51)
Piston Stroke	
Direct Clutch	.054-.067 (1.37-1.70)
Forward Clutch	.044-.058 (1.11-1.47)
2nd Coast Brake	.059-.118 (1.5-3.0)
Planetary Pinion Gear Clearance	.008-.020 (.20-.50)
Side Gear Backlash	.002-.008 (.05-.20)
Torque Converter Depth	
Corolla	.898 (22.80)
Prizm	.906 (23.00)
Tercel	.512 (13.00)

Camry, Celica

APPLICATION & LABOR TIMES

APPLICATION & LABOR TIMES

Vehicle Application	Labor Times R & I [1]	Overhaul [2]	Trans. Model
Camry DX, LE & XLE	6.3	11.5	A-140E
Celica GT	6.0	11.5	A-140E

[1] – Removal and installation of transmission from vehicle chassis.
[2] – Bench overhaul time for transmission and differential. DOES NOT include removal and installation.

CAUTION: All models are equipped with a Supplemental Restraint System (SRS). When servicing vehicle, use care to avoid accidental air bag deployment. All SRS electrical connections and wiring harness are covered by Yellow insulation. SRS-related components are located in steering column, center console, instrument panel and lower panel on instrument panel. DO NOT use electrical test equipment on these circuits. If necessary, deactivate SRS before servicing components. See AIR BAG SERVICING article in APPLICATIONS & IDENTIFICATION section.

IDENTIFICATION

Vehicle Identification Number (VIN) is used for correct identification of component parts and assemblies. VIN locations are at top left corner of instrument panel, on driver's door post and stamped on front cowl of engine compartment.

DESCRIPTION

The A-140E automatic transaxle is a 4-speed Electronic Controlled Transaxle (ECT) which controls shift and lock-up timing. This transaxle features a lock-up type torque converter, forward clutch, direct clutch, overdrive (OD) direct clutch, 3 one-way clutches, planetary gear unit, 2 clutch style brakes, hydraulic control system and electronic control system.

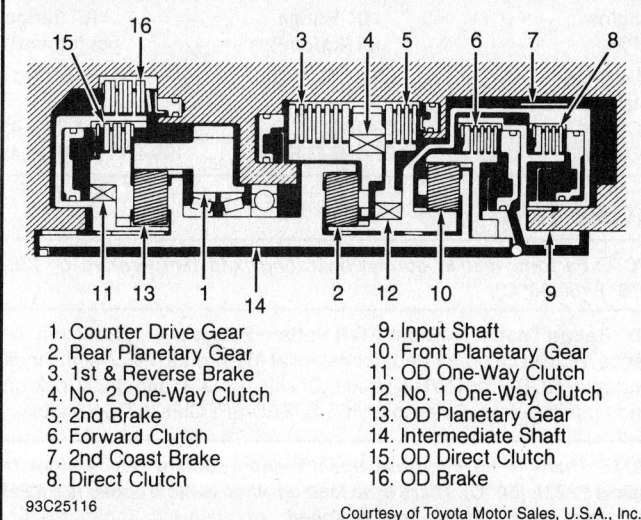

1. Counter Drive Gear
2. Rear Planetary Gear
3. 1st & Reverse Brake
4. No. 2 One-Way Clutch
5. 2nd Brake
6. Forward Clutch
7. 2nd Coast Brake
8. Direct Clutch
9. Input Shaft
10. Front Planetary Gear
11. OD One-Way Clutch
12. No. 1 One-Way Clutch
13. OD Planetary Gear
14. Intermediate Shaft
15. OD Direct Clutch
16. OD Brake

93C25116

Courtesy of Toyota Motor Sales, U.S.A., Inc.

Fig. 1: Identifying Transaxle Component Locations

LUBRICATION & ADJUSTMENTS

See appropriate AUTOMATIC TRANSMISSION SERVICING article in TRANSMISSION SERVICING section.

TROUBLE SHOOTING

SYMPTOM DIAGNOSIS

NOTE: Items listed after symptom are recommended to be checked in order listed.

Vehicle Does Not Move In Any Forward Or Reverse Gear – Check manual valve, primary regulator valve, parking lock pawl, OD one-way clutch, OD direct clutch, OD brake, front planetary gear, rear planetary gear and OD planetary gear.

Vehicle Does Not Move In Any Forward Gear – Check forward clutch, No. 2 one-way clutch, 1st and reverse brake, 2nd coast brake, 2nd brake and direct clutch.

Vehicle Does Not Move In Reverse ("R") Gear – Check 1-2 shift valve, 2-3 shift valve, 2nd coast brake, front planetary gear, rear planetary gear, direct clutch, OD direct clutch and 1st and reverse brake.

No 1-2 &/Or 2-3 Upshift – Check Throttle Position (TP) sensor circuit, No. 1 and No. 2 shift solenoid circuit, Vehicle Speed Sensor (VSS) circuit, Electronic Control Module (ECM), 1-2 shift valve, 2-3 shift valve, 2nd brake, direct clutch and No. 1 one-way clutch.

No 3-OD Upshift – Check OD switch and OD OFF indicator switch circuit, OD cancel signal circuit, No. 1 and No. 2 shift solenoid circuit, VSS circuit, Engine Coolant Temperature (ECT) circuit, ECM, 3-4 shift valve and OD brake.

No OD-3 Downshift – Check No. 1 and No. 2 shift solenoid valve, VSS circuit, OD cancel signal circuit, ECM and 3-4 shift valve.

No 3-2 &/Or 2-1 Downshift – Check No. 1 and No. 2 shift solenoid valve, VSS circuit, TP sensor circuit, ECM, 2-3 shift valve, 1-2 shift valve and 2nd coast brake.

No Torque Converter Lock-Up – Check shift solenoid valve SL circuit, TP sensor circuit, VSS circuit, OD cancel circuit, brakelight circuit, ECT circuit, ECM, lock-up relay valve and torque converter clutch.

Torque Converter Lock-Up Will Not Release – Check shift solenoid valve SL circuit, TP sensor circuit, IDL switch circuit, brakelight circuit, ECT circuit, ECM, lock-up relay valve and torque converter clutch.

Shift Speeds, Too High Or Too Low – Check TP sensor circuit, VSS circuit, shift solenoid valve SL circuit, OD cancel signal circuit, pattern select switch circuit and ECM.

CLUTCH & BRAKE APPLICATION

Selector Position	Elements In Use
"P" (Park)	OD Direct Clutch
"R" (Reverse)	OD Direct Clutch, Direct Clutch & 1st & Reverse Brake
"N" (Neutral)	OD Direct Clutch
"D" (Drive)	
1st Gear	OD Direct Clutch, Forward Clutch, OD One-Way Clutch & No. 2 One-Way Clutch
2nd Gear	OD Direct Clutch, Forward Clutch, 2nd Brake, OD One-Way Clutch & No. 1 One-Way Clutch
3rd Gear	OD Direct Clutch, Forward Clutch, Direct Clutch, 2nd Brake & OD One-Way Clutch
Overdrive	Forward Clutch, Direct Clutch, OD Brake & 2nd Brake
"2" (Second)	
1st Gear	OD Direct Clutch, Forward Clutch, OD One-Way Clutch & No. 2 One-Way Clutch
2nd Gear	OD Direct Clutch, Forward Clutch, 2nd Coast Brake, 2nd Brake, OD One-Way Clutch & No. 1 One-Way Clutch
3rd Gear [1]	OD Direct Clutch, Forward Clutch, Direct Clutch, 2nd Brake & OD One-Way Clutch
"L" (Low)	
1st Gear	OD Direct Clutch, Forward Clutch, 1st & Reverse Brake, OD One-Way Clutch & No. 2 One-Way Clutch
2nd Gear [1]	OD Direct Clutch, Forward Clutch, 2nd Coast Brake, 2nd Brake, OD One-Way Clutch & No. 1 One-Way Clutch

[1] – Gear available only during downshift. No upshift occurs.

Harsh Engagement, Neutral To Reverse – Check direct clutch accumulator, direct clutch, throttle valve and 1st and reverse brake.

Harsh Engagement, Neutral To Drive – Check forward clutch accumulator, throttle valve and forward clutch.

No Engine Braking In Low – Check low modulator valve and 1st and reverse brake.

No Engine Braking In 2nd – Check 2nd modulator valve and 2nd coast brake.

TESTING

PRELIMINARY CHECK

Ensure a thorough explanation of when and how transaxle malfunction occurs is received from customer. Check fluid level and condition. Retrieve trouble codes. See TOYOTA A-140E ELECTRONIC CONTROLS article. Proceed as necessary. If no codes are present, proceed with symptom diagnosis. See TROUBLE SHOOTING. Check throttle cable adjustment. See LUBRICATION & ADJUSTMENTS. Perform STALL SPEED, TIME LAG and HYDRAULIC TESTS as needed. After repairs are completed, perform ROAD TEST to confirm repairs.

STALL SPEED TEST

CAUTION: Perform test at normal operating fluid temperature, 122-176°F (50-80°C). DO NOT continue test longer than 5 seconds.

1) Testing is done to check overall performance of transaxle and engine by measuring maximum engine speeds in "D" and "R" ranges.

2) Block front and rear wheels. Connect engine tachometer. Apply parking and service brakes. Start engine. Shift transaxle into "D" range. Fully depress accelerator pedal. Release throttle after 5 seconds.

3) Record highest engine RPM. Compare reading obtained to specification. Stall speed should be 2300-2600. Repeat test in "R" range.

4) If engine speed is same for both ranges, but lower than specified RPM, engine output may be insufficient or stator one-way clutch is not operating properly.

NOTE: If stall speed RPM is more than 600 RPM less than specification, torque converter may be faulty.

5) If stall speed in "D" range is higher than specifications, forward clutch may be slipping, No. 2 one-way clutch and overdrive one-way clutch may not operating be properly, or line pressure too low.

6) If stall speed in "R" range is higher than specifications, direct clutch is slipping, 1st and reverse brake is slipping, line pressure is too low or overdrive direct clutch is slipping.

7) If stall speed in "R" and "D" ranges is higher than specifications, line pressure is too low, incorrect fluid level or overdrive one-way clutch not operating properly.

TIME LAG TEST

CAUTION: Perform this test at normal operating fluid temperature 122-176°F (50-80°C). Allow one minute between tests. Record 3 measurements and average results.

1) If shift lever is actuated with engine idling, a time lag will be noted before shock can be felt. This test is used for checking condition of overdrive direct clutch, forward clutch, direct clutch and 1st and reverse brake.

2) Apply parking brake. Start engine. Ensure idle speed is 750 RPM. Shift transaxle from "N" into "D" range. Use a stop watch to measure elapsed time between shifting lever until shock is felt.

3) Standard time lag is less than 1.2 seconds. Repeat test to measure time lag for "N" to "R". Standard lag is less than 1.5 seconds. If "N" to "D" time lag is longer than specification, line pressure is too low, forward clutch may be worn, overdrive one-way clutch not operating properly.

4) If "N" to "R" time lag is longer than specified, direct clutch may be worn, 1st and reverse brake may be worn, line pressure is too low or overdrive direct clutch worn.

HYDRAULIC TEST

CAUTION: Perform test at normal operating fluid temperature of 122-176°F (50-80°C).

1) Ensure transaxle fluid is at operating temperature. Raise and support vehicle. Remove transaxle case test plug. Install hydraulic pressure gauge. *See Fig. 2.*

2) Fully apply parking brake. Start engine. Shift into "D" range. Read and record pressure at idle. Fully apply brakes. Depress accelerator pedal to floor. DO NOT apply full throttle for more than 5 seconds.

3) Measure highest line pressure. Refer to LINE PRESSURE SPECIFICATIONS table. Repeat test in "R" range. If pressures exceed specifications in all ranges, regulator valve or throttle valve is defective or throttle cable out of adjustment.

4) If pressures in all ranges are lower than specifications, oil pump, regulator valve, throttle valve or overdrive direct clutch is defective or throttle cable is out of adjustment.

5) If pressure is lower than specifications in "D" range only, forward clutch is defective or "D" range circuit has a fluid leak. If pressure is lower than specifications in "R" range only, direct clutch is defective, 1st and reverse brake is defective or "R" range circuit has a fluid leak.

Pressure Gauge

Measuring Line Pressure

96B04895

Courtesy of Toyota Motor Sales, U.S.A., Inc.

Fig. 2: Locating Line Pressure Test Connection

LINE PRESSURE SPECIFICATIONS

Engine RPM	"D" Range psi (kg/cm²)	"R" Range psi (kg/cm²)
Idle Speed	53-61 (3.7-4.3)	90-115 (6.3-8.1)
Stall Speed		
Camry	109-130 (7.7-9.2)	199-233 (14.0-16.4)
Celica	107-125 (7.5-8.8)	199-233 (14.0-16.4)

ROAD TEST

NOTE: Perform test at normal operating fluid temperature of 122-176°F (50-80°C).

"D" Range Test In NORM & PWR Pattern Ranges – 1) Shift into "D" range. Hold accelerator pedal constant at full throttle. Place shift mode button in NORM or PWR position. Check 1-2, 2-3, and 3-OD lock-up and upshift points. Refer to SHIFT SPEED SPECIFICATIONS table.

NOTE: There is no overdrive upshift when coolant temperature is below 122°F (50°C). There is no lock-up when vehicle speed is 6 MPH less than the set cruise control speed.

- If no 1-2 upshift occurs, check 1-2 shift valve or solenoid.
- If no 2-3 upshift occurs, check 2-3 shift valve or solenoid.
- If no 3-OD upshift occurs, check 3-OD shift valve.
- If all shift points are incorrect, check throttle valve, 1-2 shift valve, 2-3 shift valve and 3-OD shift valve.
- If all lock-up points are incorrect, check lock-up relay valve or solenoid.

2) Use procedure outlined in step 1) to check for shock and slip between 1-2, 2-3, and 3-OD upshifts. If shock is harsh, line pressure may be too high. Also check accumulator or check ball.

3) Run vehicle in "D" range lock-up or overdrive gear. Check for abnormal noise and vibration.

NOTE: Check for cause of abnormal noise and vibration must be made with extreme care as problem could be due to an unbalanced drive shaft, differential, tire, torque converter, etc.

---

4) While running in "D" range, confirm correct kickdown vehicle speed limits for 2-1, 3-2, OD-3 shift points. Check for abnormal shock and slip at kickdown.

5) Check lock-up function. Drive vehicle in OD gear of "D" range with lock-up on. Hold vehicle speed steady at 47 MPH. Lightly depress accelerator pedal. Ensure engine RPM does not change abruptly. Large increase in engine RPM indicates lock-up function is faulty.

"2" Range Test – 1) Shift to "2" range. Drive with accelerator pedal held constantly at full throttle. Ensure 1-2 upshift points take place and are operating properly.

NOTE: In "2" range there will be no lock-up to 2nd gear.

---

2) While driving in "2" range, release accelerator pedal and check engine breaking effect. If there is no engine braking effect, 2nd coast brake is defective. Check for abnormal noise and shock at acceleration and deceleration.

A-140E SHIFT SPEED SPECIFICATIONS [1] (Camry)

Application	MPH
"D" Range	
NORM	
1st-2nd	36-40
2nd-3rd	68-75
3rd-OD	91-98
3rd-OD [2]	24-28
OD-3rd [2]	11-15
OD-3rd	86-93
3rd-2nd	61-67
2nd-1st	26-30
PWR	
1st-2nd	36-40
2nd-3rd	68-75
3rd-OD	91-98
3rd-OD [2]	24-28
OD-3rd [2]	11-15
OD-3rd	86-93
3rd-2nd	63-69
2nd-1st	32-36
"2" Range	
NORM or PWR	
1st-2nd	36-40
3rd-2nd	55-62
2nd-1st	26-30
"L" Range	
NORM or PWR	
2nd-1st	31-35

[1] – Wide open throttle.
[2] – Fully closed throttle.

A-140E SHIFT SPEED SPECIFICATIONS [1] (Celica)

Application	MPH
"D" Range	
1st-2nd	33-37
2nd-3rd	62-68
3rd-OD	89-95
3rd-OD [2]	33-37
OD-3rd [2]	12-14
OD-3rd	83-89
3rd-2nd	56-61
2nd-1st	26-29
"2" Range	
1st-2nd	33-37
2nd-1st	26-29
"L" Range	
2nd-1st	28-31

[1] – Wide open throttle.
[2] – Fully closed throttle.

"L" Range Test – While running in "L" range, ensure there is no upshift to 2nd gear. While running in "L" range, release accelerator pedal. If there is no engine braking effect, 1st and reverse brake are defective. Check for abnormal noise during acceleration and deceleration.

"R" Range Test – Shift into "R" range. Accelerate in reverse from a stop at full throttle. Ensure slipping does not occur.

"P" Range Test – Stop vehicle on slight grade. Shift transaxle into "P". Release parking brake. Ensure parking pawl holds vehicle.

LOCK-UP SPEEDS [1] (Camry)

Application	MPH
"D" Range [2]	
NORM	
Lock-Up ON in 3rd [3]	53-57
Lock-Up OFF in 3rd [3]	49-53
Lock-Up ON in OD	42-46
Lock-Up OFF in OD	40-44
PWR	
Lock-Up ON in 3rd [3]	53-57
Lock-Up OFF in 3rd [3]	49-53
Lock-Up ON in OD	45-50
Lock-Up OFF in OD	43-48

[1] – Throttle valve opening 5 percent.
[2] – There is no lock-up in "L" or "2" range.
[3] – With OD switch off.

LOCK-UP SPEEDS [1] (Celica)

Application	MPH
"D" Range [2]	
Lock-Up ON in 3rd [3]	41-44
Lock-Up OFF in 3rd [3]	38-41
Lock-Up ON in OD	48-51
Lock-Up OFF in OD	44-47

[1] – Throttle valve opening 5 percent.
[2] – There is no lock-up in "L" or "2" range.
[3] – With OD switch off.

ON-VEHICLE SERVICE

DRIVE AXLE SHAFTS

See appropriate AXLE SHAFTS article in AXLE SHAFTS & TRANSFER CASES section.

VEHICLE SPEED SENSOR

Removal & Installation – Disconnect speed sensor connector. Remove bolt and speed sensor. Remove clip and speedometer driven gear from speed sensor. Remove speed sensor and "O" ring. To install, reverse removal procedure. Coat NEW "O" ring with ATF. Tighten bolt to 12 ft. lbs. (16 N.m).

THROTTLE VALVE (TV) CABLE

Removal – Disconnect throttle cable from throttle valve linkage. Disconnect housing from bracket. Disconnect transaxle control cable from manual shift lever. Remove manual shift lever. Remove park/neutral position switch at transaxle. Remove valve body. See VALVE BODY ASSEMBLY. Remove cable housing retainer bolt. Pull throttle cable out of transaxle.

Installation – 1) Push cable into transaxle housing and install retainer bolt. Install valve body. See VALVE BODY ASSEMBLY. If new cable is being installed, it is necessary to install NEW cable stopper.

2) Bend cable so there is a radius of about 7.87" (200 mm). *See Fig. 3.* Lightly pull cable until a slight resistance is felt. Hold cable in place. Stake stopper within .031-.059" (.8-1.5 mm) of cable housing. *See Fig. 4.*

3) To complete installation, reverse removal procedure. Ensure throttle cable is correctly adjusted. See appropriate AUTOMATIC TRANSMISSION SERVICING article in TRANSMISSION SERVICING section. Also check park/neutral position switch and transaxle control cable adjustment (Cont.

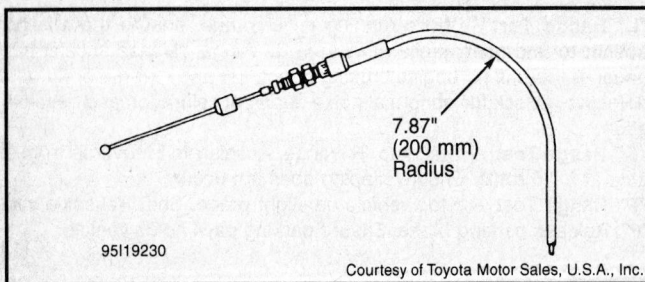

Fig. 3: Identifying Throttle Cable Bend

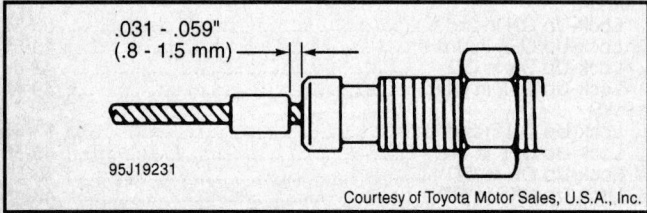

Fig. 4: Installing Throttle Cable Stopper

VALVE BODY ASSEMBLY

Removal – **1)** Clean exterior of transaxle. Remove oil pan plug. Drain transaxle fluid. Remove oil pan and gasket. Remove 2 bolts and apply tube bracket. Note bolt length and location during disassembly of valve body for reassembly reference. Remove 3 bolts and oil strainer. **2)** Disconnect solenoid harness connectors. Remove oil tubes. Remove manual detent spring. Remove manual valve and valve body. Remove 12 bolts. Disconnect throttle cable from cam. Remove valve body. Remove 2nd brake apply gasket.

Installation – **1)** Install 2nd brake apply gasket. While holding cam down, slip cable end into slot. DO NOT entangle cable with kickdown switch or solenoid wire. Install valve body. Hand tighten valve body bolts first, then tighten bolts in crisscross pattern to 89 INCH lbs. (10 N.m). *See Fig. 5.* Connect solenoid harness connectors.

2) Align manual valve with pin on manual shift lever. Place lower valve body into position. Initially install 4 bolts hand tight. Tighten bolts in crisscross pattern to 89 INCH lbs. (10 N.m). *See Fig. 6.*

3) Install detent spring. Tighten bolts to 89 INCH lbs. (10 N.m). Ensure manual valve lever is in contact with center of roller at end of detent spring. Tap oil tubes into position. DO NOT bend or damage tubes during installation. Install apply tube bracket. Tighten bolts to 89 INCH lbs. (10 N.m).

4) Install oil strainer. Tighten bolts to 89 INCH lbs. (10 N.m). *See Fig. 7.* Install magnets in oil pan. Ensure magnet does not interfere with oil tubes. Install oil pan. Tighten bolts to 43 INCH lbs. (4.9 N.m). Install drain plug with new washer gasket. Tighten plug to 36 ft. lbs. (49 N.m). Fill transaxle with oil. See LUBRICATION & ADJUSTMENTS.

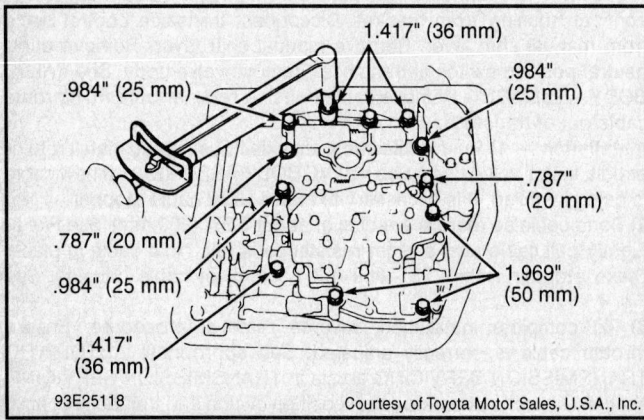

Fig. 5: Identifying Valve Body Bolt Length & Location

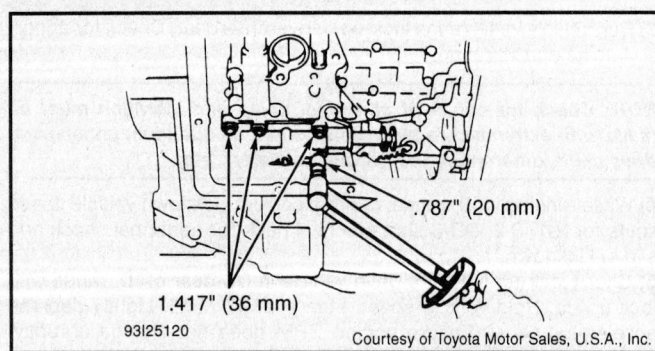

Fig. 6: Identifying Manual Valve Body Bolt Length & Location

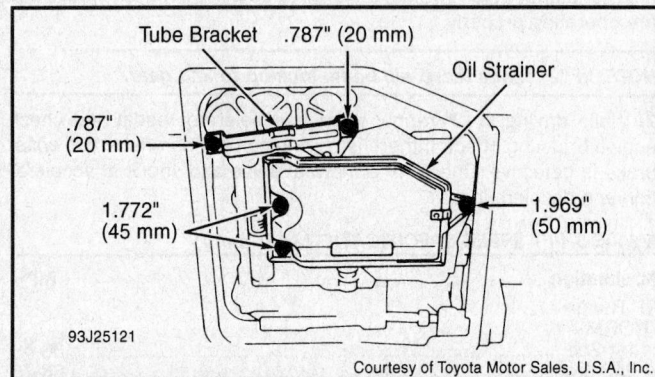

**Fig. 7: Identifying Tube Bracket & Oil Strainer
Bolt Length & Location**

REMOVAL & INSTALLATION

For transaxle removal procedure, see appropriate AUTOMATIC TRANSMISSION REMOVAL article in TRANSMISSION SERVICING section.

TORQUE CONVERTER

NOTE: Torque converter is a sealed unit and must be serviced as complete assembly. Perform following tests to check converter condition. Torque converter and oil cooler lines must be thoroughly cleaned and flushed if transaxle fluid is contaminated.

ONE-WAY CLUTCH TEST

1) Insert a turning tool into inner race of one-way clutch. Install Tester (09351-32010) so that it fits in notch of converter hub and other race of one-way clutch.

2) With converter in normal operating position, clutch should lock-up when turned counterclockwise and should rotate freely and smoothly when turned clockwise. *See Fig. 8.* If one-way clutch fails test in either direction, clean converter. Retest clutch. If clutch fails test, replace converter.

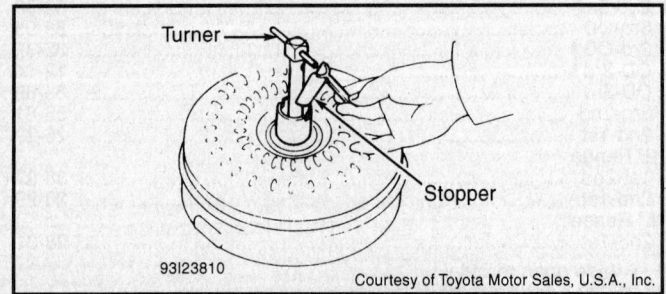

Fig. 8: Testing Torque Converter One-Way Clutch

CONVERTER SLEEVE RUNOUT TEST

1) Temporarily mount torque converter to drive plate. Mount a dial indicator with needle resting on converter sleeve. *See Fig. 9.* Rotate converter. If runout exceeds .012" (.30 mm), ensure converter is properly mounted to drive plate.

2) If converter is properly mounted and runout exceeds specifications, replace torque converter. Mark position of converter to ensure correct installation. Remove converter from drive plate.

DRIVE PLATE (FLYWHEEL) RUNOUT TEST

Measure drive plate runout. *See Fig. 10.* If runout exceeds .008" (.20 mm), or if ring gear is damaged, replace drive plate. If installing a NEW drive plate, note position of spacers. Tighten bolts to 61 ft. lbs. (83 N.m).

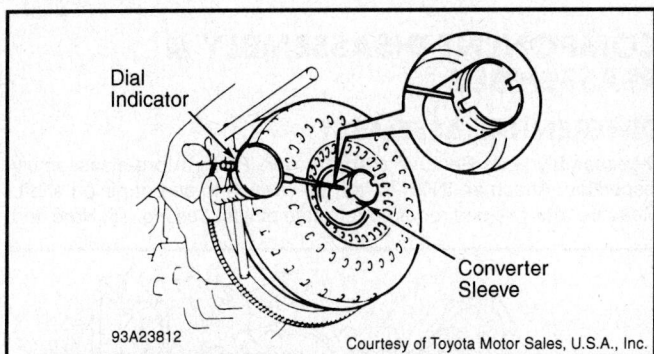

Fig. 9: *Measuring Torque Converter Sleeve Runout*

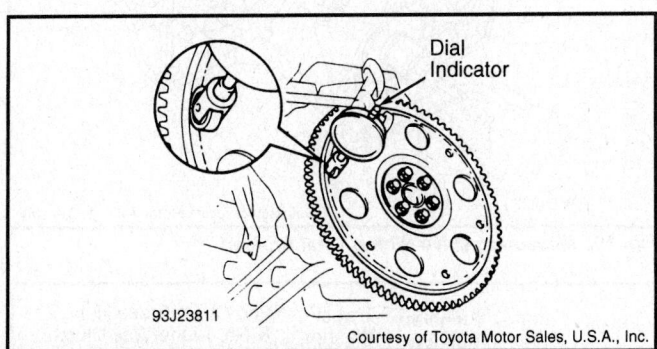

Fig. 10: *Checking Drive Plate Runout*

TRANSAXLE DISASSEMBLY

1) Remove oil cooling tubes. Remove union and elbow. Remove manual shift lever and park/neutral position switch. Remove 2 solenoid attaching bolts and solenoid. Remove oil filler tube. Unbolt throttle cable retaining plate. Remove solenoid wire retaining bolt.

2) Remove cover bracket, cover and "O" ring. Remove 15 oil pan bolts and remove oil pan. DO NOT turn transaxle over. This will contaminate valve body with foreign material.

3) Place transaxle on wooden blocks to prevent damage to pipe bracket. Examine particles found in oil pan. If particles are magnetic (steel), bearing, gear and clutch plate wear are indicated. If particles are brass, bushing wear is indicated.

4) Turn transaxle over. Remove tube bracket, oil strainer and solenoid connectors. Using screwdriver, carefully remove 4 oil tubes. Remove manual detent spring, manual valve and valve body.

5) Remove valve body bolts. Disconnect throttle cable from throttle valve cam. Remove valve body. Remove throttle cable. Remove solenoid wiring from case. Remove 2nd brake apply gasket.

6) Loosen 5 bolts one turn at a time until spring tension is released. Remove cover and gasket. Remove piston and spring for forward clutch and direct clutch. Using 15 psi (1 kg/cm²) of air pressure in apply hole, pop out 2nd brake piston into a shop cloth. Remove piston and spring. *See Fig. 11.*

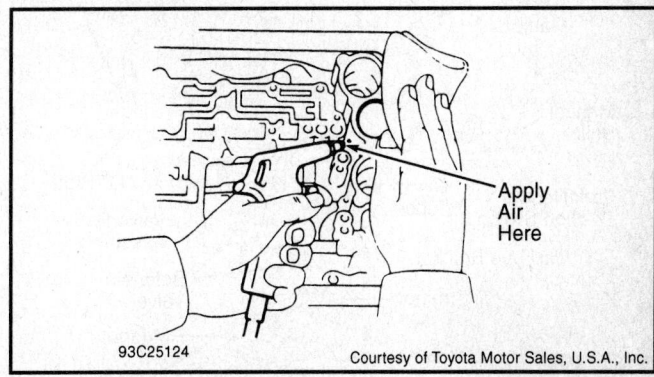

Fig. 11: *Removing 2nd Brake Accumulator Piston & Spring*

7) Remove 2nd coast brake piston snap ring and cover. Remove piston and outer return spring. Remove 7 oil pump-to-case bolts. Using appropriate puller, remove oil pump.

8) Direct clutch assembly should be attached to oil pump. Remove direct clutch from oil pump. DO NOT lose race located behind oil pump. Remove clutch drum thrust washer.

9) Remove forward clutch with thrust bearing and race. Remove 2nd coast brake band. Push pin with a small screwdriver to remove pin from bolt hole of oil pump mounting. Remove brake band.

10) Remove front planetary ring gear. Remove race and bearing from ring gear. Remove planetary gear. Remove bearing from planetary gear. Remove sun gear, sun gear input drum, 2nd brake hub and No. 1 one-way clutch. Stand transaxle case up and remove 2nd coast brake band guide.

11) Remove snap ring holding 2nd brake drum to case. Remove 2nd brake drum. If brake drum is difficult to remove, lightly tap drum with a wooden block. Remove 2nd brake drum gasket from bottom of case. Remove 2nd brake piston return spring.

12) Remove clutch plates, discs and flange. Remove snap ring holding No. 2 one-way clutch outer race to case. Remove No. 2 one-way clutch and rear planetary gear. Retain planetary carrier thrust washers, located on both sides.

13) Remove rear planetary ring gear, bearing and race. Remove snap ring holding 1st and reverse brake flange to case. Remove flanges, plates and discs. Turn transaxle around. Remove 11 bolts attaching overdrive unit to transaxle case. Remove overdrive unit. Tap on outside of overdrive case with a plastic hammer. Remove overdrive planetary gear and countergear.

14) Remove overdrive brake drum from transaxle case. Remove case gasket. Remove overdrive clutch apply gasket and overdrive brake apply gasket. Using Spring Compressor (09351-32040), compress 1st and reverse piston return springs.

15) Remove snap ring. Remove return spring from case. Remove 1st and reverse brake piston with compressed air. *See Fig. 14.* Remove "O" rings from piston.

16) Remove parking lock pawl bracket and lock rod. Remove pin, spring and parking lock pawl. Remove manual valve shaft. Remove retaining spring. Using a hammer and chisel, pry and turn collar. Using a hammer and punch, drive out pin. Slide shaft out and remove manual valve lever from case. Remove manual shaft oil seal with a screwdriver.

NOTE: *For differential and drive pinion assembly removal and installation procedures, see COMPONENT DISASSEMBLY & REASSEMBLY.*

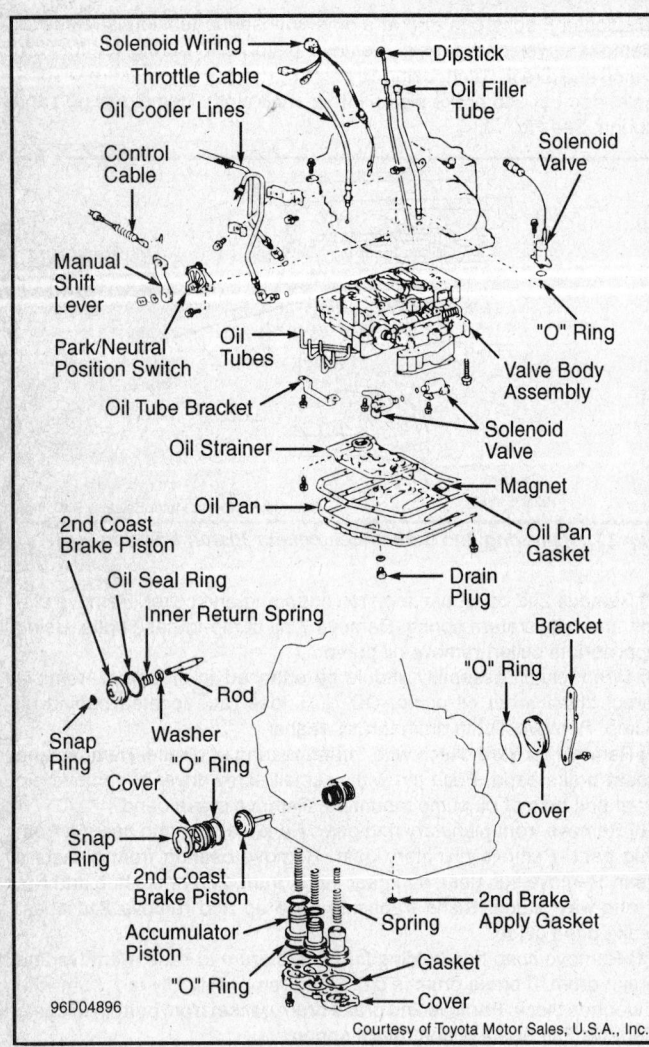

Fig. 12: Locating Transaxle External Components

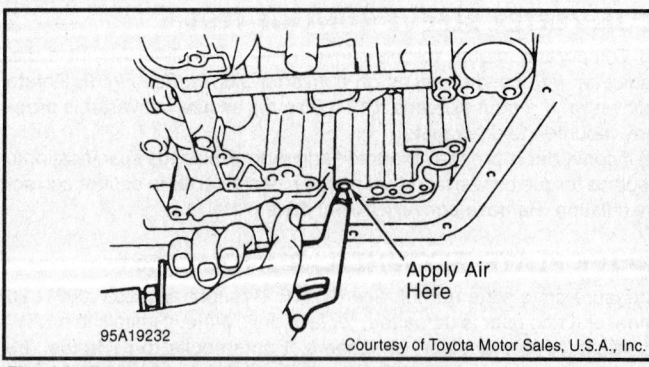

95A19232   Courtesy of Toyota Motor Sales, U.S.A., Inc.

Fig. 14: Removing 1st & Reverse Brake Piston

COMPONENT DISASSEMBLY & REASSEMBLY

DIFFERENTIAL ASSEMBLY

Disassembly – 1) Remove carrier cover. Perform pre-disassembly inspection. Attach an INCH-lb. torque wrench to end of pinion shaft. Measure total preload required to rotate pinion. *See Fig. 15.* Note and

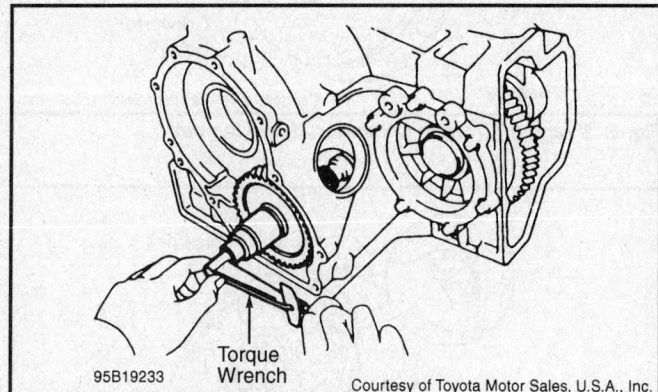

95B19233   Courtesy of Toyota Motor Sales, U.S.A., Inc.

Fig. 15: Measuring Drive Pinion Total Preload

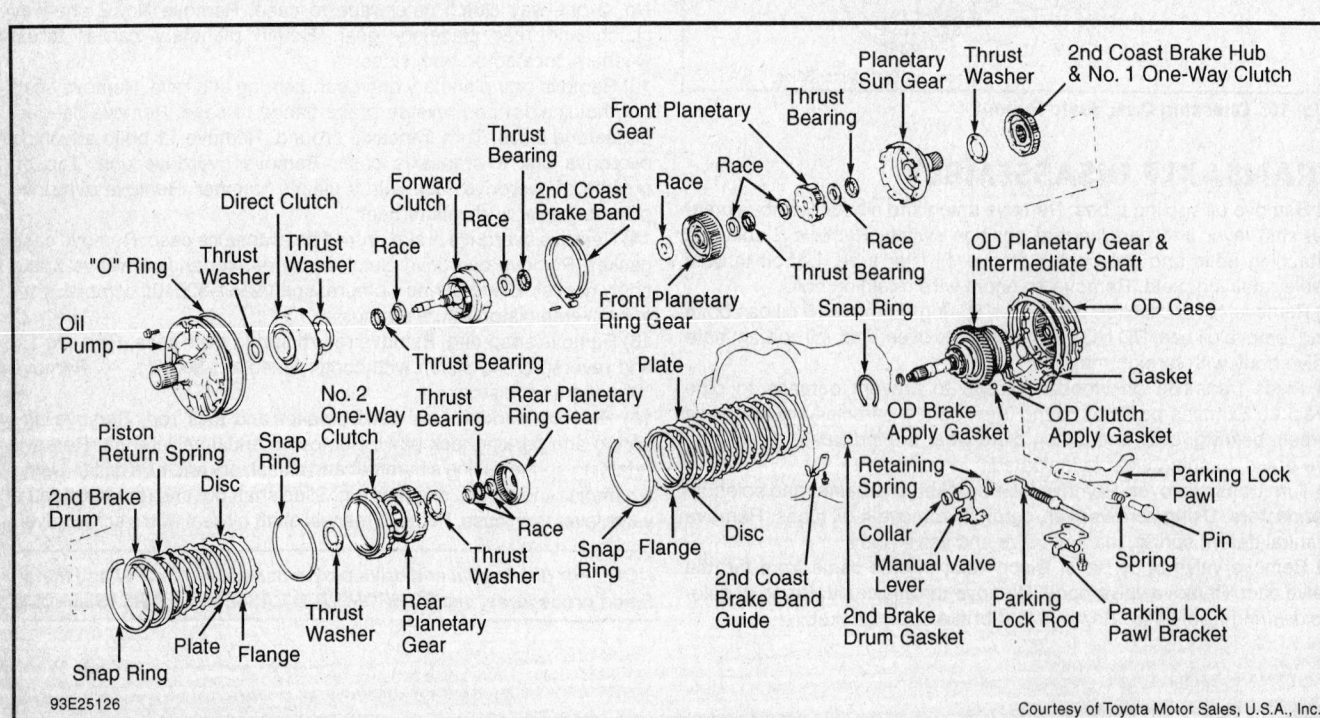

Fig. 13: Exploded View Of Transaxle Internal Components

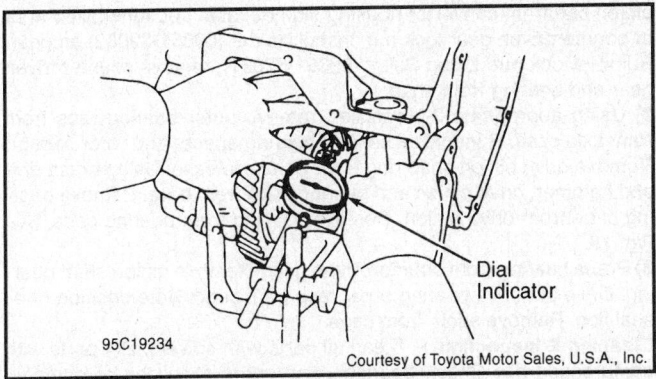

95C19234

Courtesy of Toyota Motor Sales, U.S.A., Inc.

Fig. 16: Measuring Differential Side Gear Backlash

record reading. Position dial indicator assembly on transaxle case. Position dial indicator tip against side gear. *See Fig. 16.* Measure side gear backlash while holding one pinion toward case. Backlash should be .002-.008" (.05-.20 mm). Note and record reading.

2) Remove left side bearing retainer bolts. Remove bearing retainer. Remove "O" ring from retainer. Remove right side bearing cap. Remove differential, outer race and adjustment shim from transaxle case.

3) Attach an INCH-lb. torque wrench to end of pinion shaft. Measure drive pinion preload. Note and record reading. Starting preload should be 4-7 INCH lbs. (.5-.8 N.m) for a used bearing, 9-14 INCH lbs. (1-1.6 N.m) for new bearing. Total preload reading minus drive pinion preload should equal 1-2 INCH lbs. (.1-.2 N.m). If measurement is not within specification, side bearing preload requires adjustment or bearing replacement. See DRIVE PINION ASSEMBLY.

4) Remove side bearings from differential case using appropriate puller. Remove speedometer drive gear. Mark ring gear and case for reassembly reference. Spread ring gear bolt locking plates. Remove ring gear bolts and locking plates. Using brass hammer, tap ring gear from differential case.

5) Mount differential case in vise. Using a dial indicator, check side gear backlash. Hold one pinion against case. Measure side gear backlash. Backlash must be .002-.008" (.05-.20 mm). If backlash is not within specification, side gear thrust washers must be replaced.

6) Drive out pinion shaft lock pin from ring gear side. Remove pinion shaft, pinion gears, side gears and thrust washers. *See Fig. 17.* Remove left oil seal from bearing retainer. Using a press, remove bearing outer race and shim from bearing retainer. Using a long screwdriver, remove right oil seal from transaxle case.

Cleaning & Inspection – Clean all parts with solvent. Dry with compressed air. Check bearings and gears for wear or damage. Replace if necessary.

Reassembly – 1) Using appropriate seal installer and handle, install right oil seal until oil seal surface is flush with surface of transaxle case. Install original shim onto retainer. Using appropriate race installer and press, install outer race. Install left oil seal to a depth of .106" (2.7 mm). Lubricate oil seal lip.

2) Select thrust washers that will ensure correct side gear backlash. Thrust washers are available in thicknesses of .037-.047" (.95-1.20 mm) in .20" (5.0 mm) increments. Install thrust washers and side gears in differential case. *See Fig. 14.* If possible, install same size thrust washers on both sides. Install pinion gears and pinion shaft. Check side gear backlash to ensure proper thrust washers are used.

3) Drive lock pin through differential case and into pinion shaft. Stake differential case to retain lock pin. Install speedometer drive gear onto differential case. Using Adapters (09351-32090 and 09351-32120) and press, install side bearings onto differential case.

4) Clean ring gear contact surface of differential case. Clean contact surface of ring gear using cleaning solvent. Heat ring gear to 212°F (100°C) in an oil bath. DO NOT heat ring gear above 230°F (110 °C). Align ring gear with differential case. Install ring gear on differential case.

5) Install NEW locking plates and bolts. Tighten bolts in crisscross pattern to 72 ft. lbs. (97 N.m). Stake locking plates. Stake one tab flush with flat surface of bolt. Stake 2nd tab against corner of bolt.

6) Install outer race and original adjusting shim on right side bearing. Remove drive pinion. See DRIVE PINION ASSEMBLY. Install differential in transaxle case. Install left bearing outer race, shim and retainer without "O" ring. Tighten bolts evenly to 14 ft. lbs. (19 N.m). Install right side bearing cap. Snug bolts evenly in crisscross pattern while turning ring gear. Tighten bolts to 53 ft. lbs. (72 N.m).

7) Using Differential Preload Adapter (09564-32011) and an INCH-lb. torque wrench, measure differential bearing preload with drive pinion removed. *See Fig. 18.* See DIFFERENTIAL PRELOAD SPECIFICATIONS table. If preload is not within specifications, remove differential from transaxle case and replace adjustment shim at right side bearing with appropriate shim.

8) Adjustment shims are available in thicknesses from .075-.110" (1.90-2.80 mm) in .20" (5.0 mm) increments. Preload will increase approximately 2.6-3.5 INCH lbs. (.3-.4 N.m) with each .20" (5.0 mm) shim thickness increase.

DIFFERENTIAL PRELOAD SPECIFICATIONS

Application	INCH Lbs. (N.m)
New Bearings	9-14 (1.0-1.6)
Used Bearings	4-7 (.5-.8)

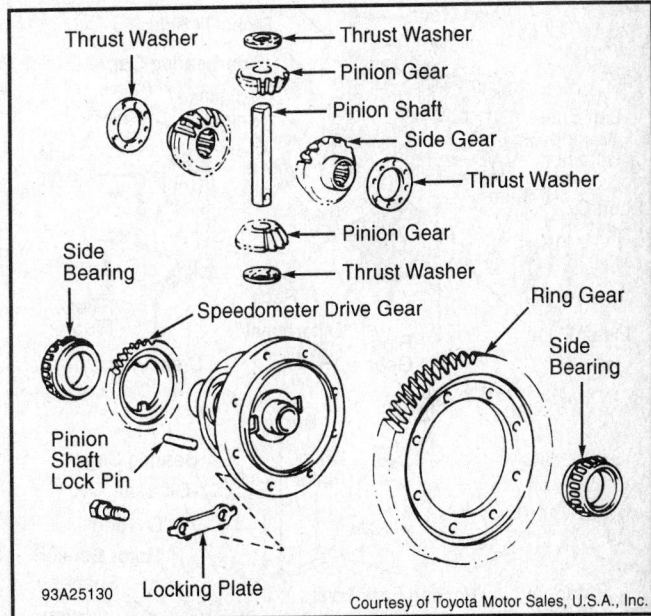

93A25130

Courtesy of Toyota Motor Sales, U.S.A., Inc.

Fig. 17: Exploded View Of Differential Unit

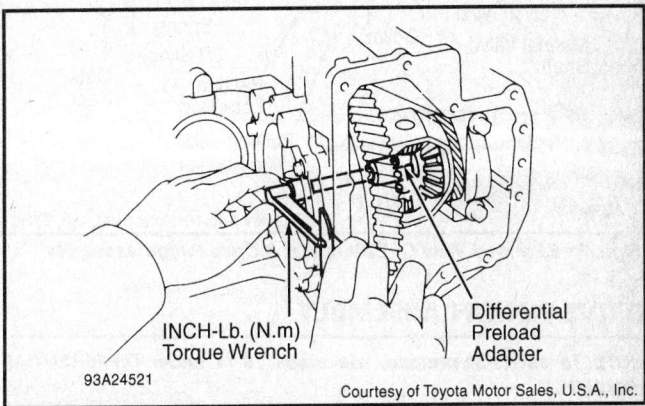

93A24521

Courtesy of Toyota Motor Sales, U.S.A., Inc.

Fig. 18: Measuring Differential Bearing Preload

NOTE: Proceed with steps 9-11 once drive pinion has been removed, inspected and reassembled. See DRIVE PINION ASSEMBLY. It is necessary to measure bearing preload of each individual component without the other component installed in transaxle case.

9) If preload is within specification, remove left bearing retainer. DO NOT misplace selected adjustment shim. Install "O" ring on left bearing retainer. Remove right side bearing cap bolts and coat threads with sealant. Tighten bolts evenly and gradually in crisscross pattern to 53 ft. lbs. (73 N.m), while turning ring gear. Recheck preload.

10) With drive pinion installed in case, measure total preload using procedure in step 1) under DISASSEMBLY. Starting preload should be the drive pinion preload of 4-7 INCH lbs. (.5-.8 N.m), plus 3-4 INCH lbs. (.3-.4 N.m) for new bearings or 1-2 INCH lbs. (.1-.2 N.m) for used bearings.

11) If total preload is not within specification, disassemble differential and readjust. If total preload is correct, stake counterdriven gear lock nut. Install drive pinion cap. Coat carrier cover bolt threads with sealant. Install carrier cover and gasket. Install bolts and tighten in crisscross pattern to 18 ft. lbs. (25 N.m). To complete reassembly, reverse disassembly procedure. Tighten all bolts to specification. See Fig. 19.

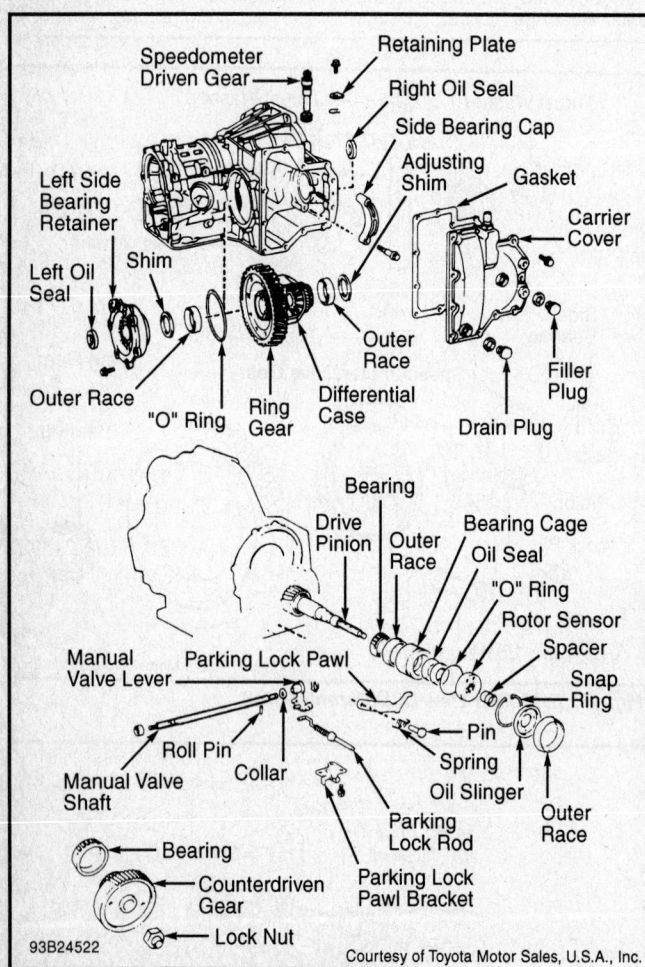

93B24522   Courtesy of Toyota Motor Sales, U.S.A., Inc.

Fig. 19: Exploded View Of Differential & Drive Pinion Assembly

DRIVE PINION ASSEMBLY

NOTE: To set total preload, see steps 10-11 under DIFFERENTIAL ASSEMBLY.

Disassembly – 1) Using an INCH-lb. torque wrench, measure drive pinion preload with differential assembly removed. Starting preload should be 4-7 INCH lbs. (.5-.8 N.m) for used bearings. Remove drive

pinion cap from converter housing side of case. Loosen staked area of counterdriven gear lock nut. Install Holder (09351-32032) on gear. Remove lock nut. Using Puller (09351-32061), remove counterdriven gear and bearing from shaft.

2) Using appropriate 2-jaw puller, remove outer bearing race from transaxle case. Remove oil slinger, bearing spacer and rotor sensor. Remove drive pinion snap ring from transaxle case. Using brass drift and hammer, drive pinion and bearing cage from bore. Remove bearing cage from drive pinion. Remove "O" ring from bearing cage. See Fig. 19.

3) Press bearing from counterdriven gear. Remove pinion shaft bearing. Drive out drive bearing outer race from cage. Note position of oil seal lips. Remove seals from cage.

Cleaning & Inspection – Clean all parts with solvent. Dry parts with compressed air. Check bearings and gears for wear or damage. Replace if necessary.

Reassembly – 1) Lubricate lips of oil seals. Install inner seal with lip facing downward. Oil seal must be installed to proper depth of .374" (9.50 mm).

2) Install outer seal with lip facing upward. Position oil seal flush with cage surface. Install outer bearing race in bearing cage.

3) Install drive pinion shaft bearing. Install bearing on counterdriven gear. Install "O" ring on bearing cage. Install cage on drive pinion shaft. Use care not to damage oil seals. Install rotor sensor. Install shaft assembly into transaxle case.

4) Tap bearing cage into transaxle case. Ensure cage is past snap ring groove. Install snap ring. Insert brass bar into hole and tap drive pinion shaft against snap ring. Ensure snap ring is fully seated. Install oil slinger with lip facing outward. Install outer race in transaxle case with narrow end facing out. Install NEW bearing spacer, small end first.

5) Drive counterdriven gear onto shaft until lock nut can be installed. DO NOT tap on transaxle case. Lubricate lock nut threads and install lock nut on shaft. Install holder on gear. Tighten counterdriven gear lock nut to 127 ft. lbs. (172 N.m). Rotate counterdriven gear both directions several times.

6) Using an INCH-lb. torque wrench, measure drive pinion preload. Starting preload should be 9-14 INCH lbs. (1.0-1.6 N.m) for new bearings and 4-7 INCH lbs. (.5-.8 N.m) for used bearings. Replace bearing spacer (crush sleeve) if preload exceeds specifications. Recheck preload procedure (if necessary).

7) If preload is less than specification, tighten lock nut in additional increments of 9.5 ft. lbs. (13 N.m). Tighten lock nut until specified preload is obtained. If maximum torque of 213 ft. lbs. (289 N.m) is exceeded while tightening nut, replace bearing spacer and repeat procedure. DO NOT back off (loosen) nut to reduce preload.

OIL PUMP ASSEMBLY

Disassembly – Remove race from stator shaft (if equipped). Remove "O" ring from pump body. Remove 2 oil seal rings from back of stator shaft (pump support). Remove thrust washer from stator shaft. Remove 11 bolts attaching oil pump body and stator shaft. See Fig. 20.

Inspection – 1) Check body clearance of driven gear. Push gear to one side of body. Using a feeler gauge, measure clearance. See Fig. 21. Body clearance should be .003-.006" (.07-.15 mm). Maximum body clearance is .012" (.30 mm). If body clearance exceeds specification, replace pump body.

2) Check tip clearance of both gears. Measure between gear teeth and crescent-shaped part of pump body. Tip clearance is .004-.006" (.11-.15 mm). Maximum tip clearance is .012" (.30 mm). If tip clearance exceeds specification, replace pump body.

3) Check side clearance of both gears. Use a steel straightedge and feeler gauge to measure side clearance of both gears. Clearance is .0008-.0020" (.020-.050 mm). Maximum side clearance is .004" (.10 mm). Drive and driven gears are available in 3 different thicknesses. See DRIVE & DRIVEN GEAR THICKNESS SPECIFICATIONS table. If thickest gear does not bring side clearance within specification, replace pump body.

DRIVE & DRIVEN GEAR THICKNESS SPECIFICATIONS

I.D. Mark	Thickness In. (mm)
A	.3717-.3723 (9.440-9.456)
B	.3723-.3730 (9.456-9.474)
C	.3730-.3736 (9.474-9.490)

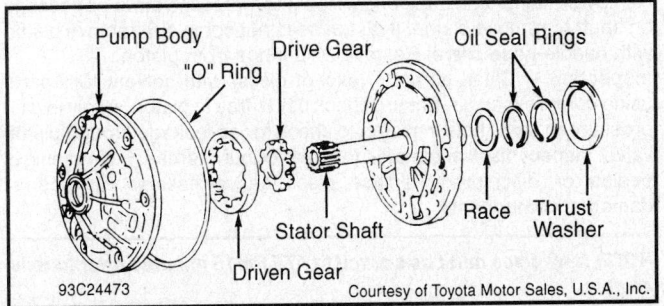

93C24473 Courtesy of Toyota Motor Sales, U.S.A., Inc.

Fig. 20: Exploded View Of Oil Pump Assembly

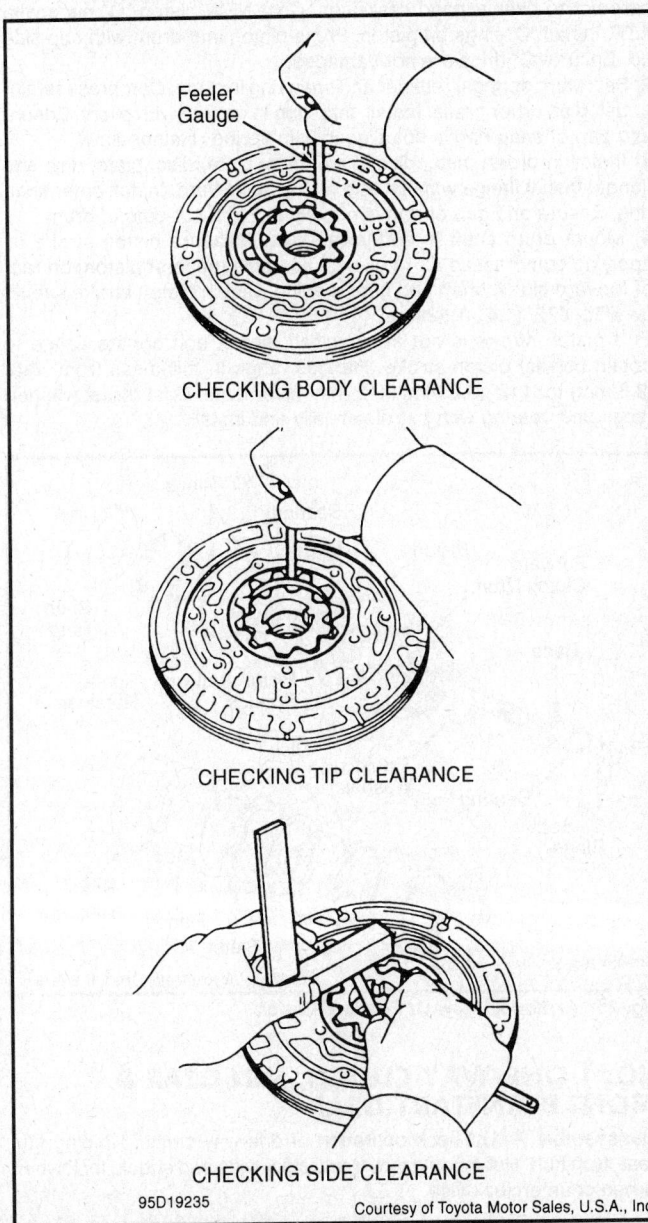

95D19235 Courtesy of Toyota Motor Sales, U.S.A., Inc.

Fig. 21: Measuring Oil Pump Clearances

4) Using a dial indicator, measure inside diameter of oil pump body bushing. Maximum inside diameter is 1.503" (38.18 mm). If inside diameter exceeds specification, replace oil pump body.

5) Using a dial indicator, measure inside diameter of stator shaft bushings. Maximum front side bushing inside diameter is .849" (21.57 mm). Maximum rear side bushing inside diameter is 1.066" (27.07 mm). If inside diameter exceeds specification, replace stator shaft.

6) Inspect front oil seal for cracks, damage or wear. Replace oil seal (if necessary). Remove oil seal with screwdriver. Install a NEW oil seal. Seal is properly installed when it is flush with outer edge of pump body.

Reassembly – **1)** Install front oil seal. Install driven gear and drive gear. Ensure top of gears are facing upward. Install stator shaft on pump body. Align bolt holes. Install 11 stator shaft-to-oil pump body bolts. Tighten bolts in crisscross pattern to 89 INCH lbs. (10 N.m).

2) Coat thrust bearing with petroleum jelly. Align tab of washer with hollow of pump body. Install thrust washer. Install 2 oil seal rings on oil pump. DO NOT spread ring ends too much. Turn drive gear with screwdrivers to ensure a smooth rotation. DO NOT damage oil seal lip. Install race on stator shaft (if equipped).

DIRECT CLUTCH

Disassembly – **1)** Prior to disassembly, measure piston stroke of direct clutch. Measure direct clutch piston stroke by applying compressed air. See Fig. 22. Piston stroke should be .044-.057" (1.11-1.44 mm). If piston stroke exceeds specification, inspect each component.

2) Remove snap ring from clutch drum. Remove flange, discs and plates. Note number and location of components. Compress piston return springs and remove snap ring. See Fig. 23.

3) Remove piston return spring. See Fig. 24. Slide direct clutch on oil pump. Remove piston by applying low pressure compressed air. If piston does not completely come out, remove with needle-nose pliers. Remove direct clutch from oil pump. Remove 2 "O" rings from clutch piston.

Inspection – **1)** Clean all parts (except discs) with solvent. Dry parts using compressed air. Ensure check ball is free in piston. Apply low air pressure to small hole in piston to check for air leakage around piston valve. Inspect discs and plates for wear or burnt areas.

2) If disc lining is peeled or discolored, replace discs as necessary. Replace all damaged components. Using a dial indicator, measure inside diameter of direct clutch bushing. Maximum inside diameter is 1.853" (47.07 mm). If inside diameter exceeds specification, replace direct clutch.

NOTE: New discs must be soaked in ATF at least 15 minutes prior to reassembly.

Reassembly – **1)** Install NEW "O" rings on piston. Coat rings with ATF. Press piston in drum with cup side up. Ensure "O" rings are not damaged. Install piston return springs. Set retainer and snap ring in position.

2) Using arbor press, compress return springs. See Fig. 23. Using snap ring pliers, install snap ring in groove. Ensure end gap of spring is not aligned with spring retainer claw.

3) Install in order: plate, disc, plate, disc, plate, disc and flange. See Fig. 24. Install flange with flat end facing inward. Install outer snap ring. Ensure end gap of snap ring is not aligned with cut-outs of drum.

4) If disc, plate or flange have been replaced, check piston stroke. Using a dial indicator, measure piston stroke by applying and releasing 57-114 psi (4-8 kg/cm²) compressed air. See Fig. 22.

5) Piston stroke should be .044-.057" (1.11-1.44 mm). If piston stroke is less than specification, disassemble and reassemble direct clutch parts.

6) Measure piston stroke again. If measurement is still not to specification, replace flange. Flange is available in 2 thicknesses, .102" (2.60 mm) or .118" (3.00 mm).

7) Check operation of direct clutch. Install direct clutch on oil pump. Apply compressed air into passage of oil pump body. See Fig. 22. Ensure movement of piston. If piston does not move, disassemble and inspect unit.

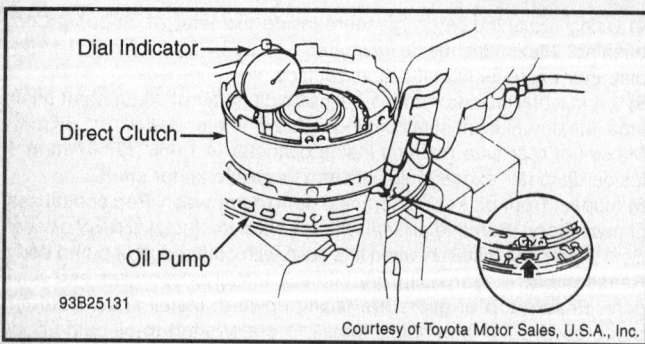

Fig. 22: Checking Direct Clutch Piston Stroke

Courtesy of Toyota Motor Sales, U.S.A., Inc.

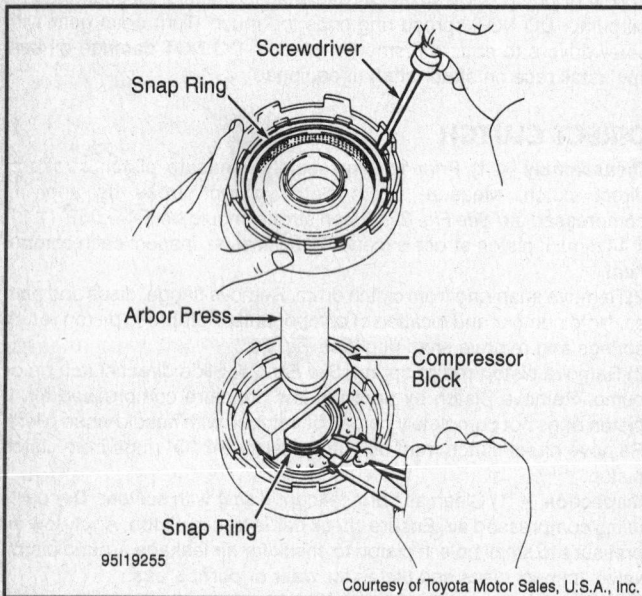

Fig. 23: Removing & Installing Direct Clutch

Courtesy of Toyota Motor Sales, U.S.A., Inc.

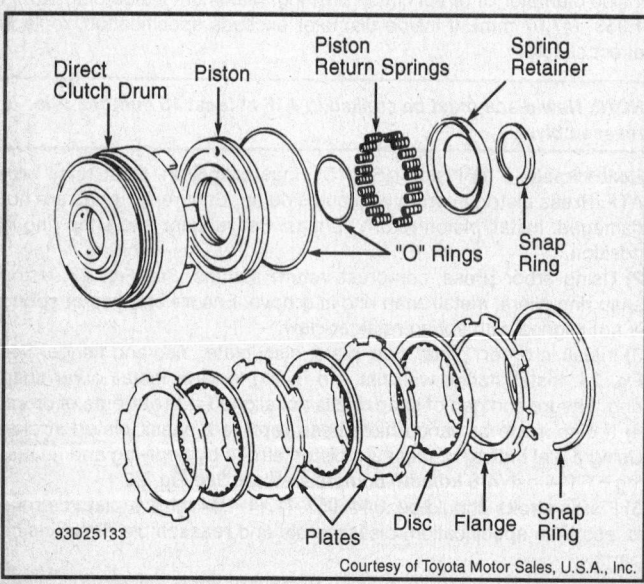

Fig. 24: Exploded View Of Direct Clutch

Courtesy of Toyota Motor Sales, U.S.A., Inc.

FORWARD CLUTCH

Disassembly – 1) Remove thrust bearings and races from both sides of clutch. Remove snap ring from clutch drum. Remove flange, discs and plates. Note number and location of components. See Fig. 25.

2) Using an arbor press, compress return springs. Remove snap ring. Remove retainer and 18 springs. Apply compressed air to oil passage on shaft to remove piston. If piston does not come out, remove piston with needle-nose pliers. Remove 2 "O" rings from piston.

Inspection – Clean all parts (except discs) with solvent. Dry parts using compressed air. Ensure check ball is free in piston. Apply low air pressure to small hole in piston to check for air leakage around piston valve. Inspect discs and plates for wear or burnt areas. If disc lining is peeled or discolored, replace discs as necessary. Replace all damaged components.

NOTE: New discs must be soaked in ATF for 15 minutes prior to reassembly.

Reassembly – 1) Install NEW seal rings on shaft (if necessary). Use care not to over expand seal rings. Coat NEW piston "O" rings with ATF. Install "O" rings on piston. Press piston into drum with cup side up. Ensure "O" rings are not damaged.

2) Set return springs, retainer and snap ring in drum. Compress retainer using an arbor press. Install snap ring in groove with pliers. Ensure end gap of snap ring is not aligned with spring retainer claw.

3) Install in order: plate, disc, plate, disc, plate, disc, plate, disc and flange. Install flange with flat end facing downward. Install outer snap ring. Ensure end gap of ring is not aligned with cut-outs of drum.

4) Mount drum shaft in soft-jawed vise. Measure piston stroke by applying compressed air to oil passage hole (nearest piston) on rear of forward clutch shaft and note reading. Clutch piston stroke should be .056-.072" (1.41-1.82 mm).

5) If piston stroke is not as specified, select appropriate flange to obtain correct piston stroke. Flanges range in thickness from .110" (2.8 mm) to .142" (3.6 mm) in .2 mm increments. Coat thrust washer, races and bearing with petroleum jelly and install.

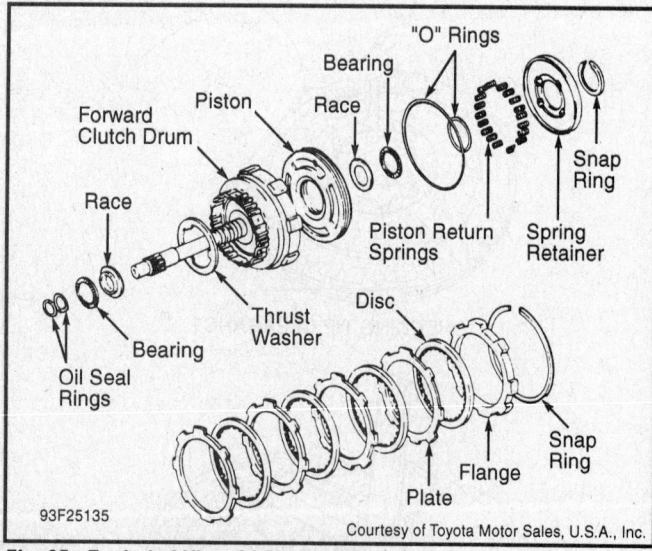

Fig. 25: Exploded View Of Forward Clutch

Courtesy of Toyota Motor Sales, U.S.A., Inc.

NO. 1 ONE-WAY CLUTCH, SUN GEAR & FRONT PLANETARY GEAR

Disassembly – 1) Check operation of one-way clutch. Holding sun gear, turn hub. Hub should turn freely clockwise and should lock when turned counterclockwise.

2) Turning hub clockwise, remove one-way clutch from sun gear. Remove thrust washer from sun gear input drum. Remove snap ring. Remove sun gear from input drum. *See Fig. 26.* Remove shaft snap ring from sun gear.

Inspection – Inspect ring gear flange bushing. Measure inside diameter of flange bushing. Standard inside diameter is .749-.750" (19.035-19.05 mm). If inside diameter exceeds specification, replace flange. Measure planetary pinion gear thrust clearance with a feeler gauge. Standard clearance should be .008-.020" (.20-.50 mm).

Reassembly – Install shaft snap ring on sun gear. Install sun gear input drum on sun gear. Install shaft snap ring. Install thrust washer on sun gear input drum. *See Fig. 26.* While turning hub clockwise, slide one-way clutch on sun gear. Recheck operation of No. 1 one-way clutch. Ensure hub turns clockwise while holding outer hub.

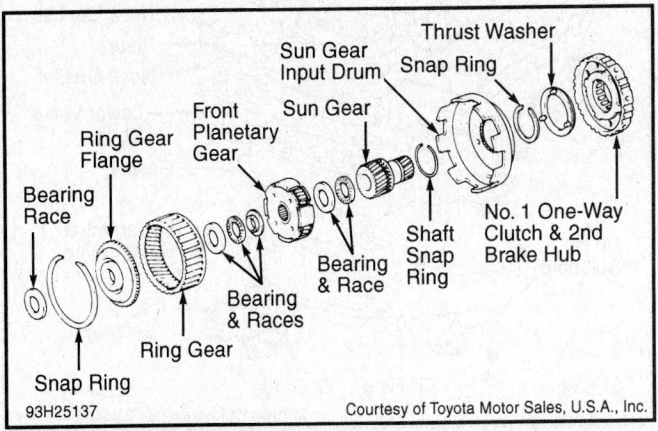

Fig. 26: Exploded View Of No. 1 One-Way Clutch, Sun Gear & Front Planetary Gear

NO. 2 ONE-WAY CLUTCH & REAR PLANETARY GEAR

Disassembly – **1)** Check operation of one-way clutch. Hold outer race and turn hub. Hub should turn freely counterclockwise and should lock when turned clockwise.

2) Separate No. 2 one-way clutch and rear planetary gear. Remove thrust washers from each side of planetary gear. Remove both side snap rings and 2 side retainers. Remove one-way clutch from outer race. *See Fig. 27.*

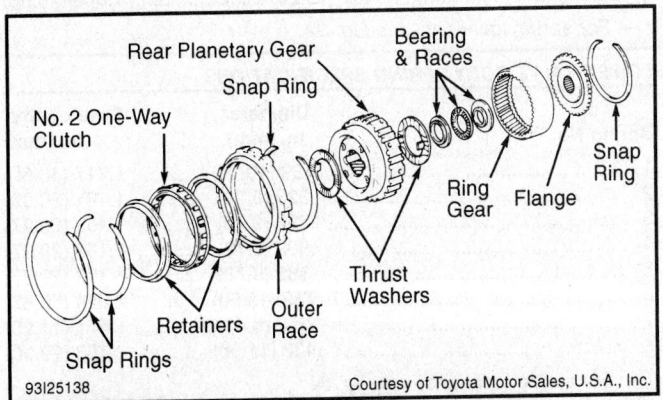

Fig. 27: Exploded View Of No. 2 One-Way Clutch & Rear Planetary Gear

Inspection – Measure planetary pinion gear thrust clearance with a feeler gauge. Standard clearance should be .0079-.0197" (.200-.500 mm).

Reassembly – **1)** Install one-way clutch in outer race. Face flanged side of one-way clutch inward from shiny side of outer race. Install 2 side retainers and 2 snap rings.

2) Install rear planetary gear into one-way clutch facing inner race of planetary gear inward from Black side of outer race. Check operation of one-way clutch. Coat thrust washers with petroleum jelly. Install thrust washer on each side of carrier. Align tab of washers with hollow of rear planetary gear.

1ST & REVERSE BRAKE PISTON

Disassembly – Using appropriate spring compressor, gradually and evenly tighten tool bolt to compress springs. Using snap ring pliers, remove snap ring. Remove piston return spring assembly. Apply compressed air into oil passage of case to remove piston. *See Fig. 14.* Hold air gun away from hole. Ensure piston does not tilt during removal. Remove "O" rings from piston.

Reassembly – **1)** Install NEW "O" rings on piston. Coat rings with ATF. Install piston in bore of case facing spring seats upward. Place base of spring compressor under case. Install piston return springs and retainer. Set snap ring in place.

2) Compress piston return springs slowly and evenly to allow installation of snap ring. DO NOT overtighten bolt as it will cause spring retainer to bend.

3) Push snap ring in place with fingers. Ensure snap ring is fully seated and centered on 3 lugs of spring retainer. Ensure end gap of ring is not aligned with spring retainer claw. Remove compressor tool. *See Fig. 28.*

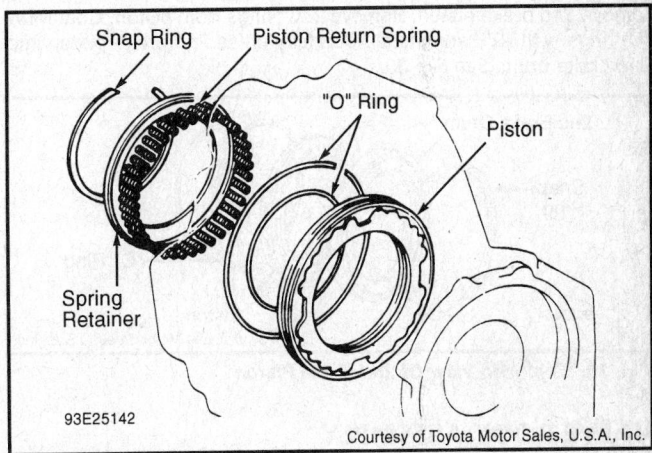

Fig. 28: Exploded View Of 1st & Reverse Brake Piston

2ND COAST BRAKE

Disassembly – Remove oil seal ring from piston. Remove "E" ring while pushing piston with needle nose pliers. Remove spring, washer and piston rod.

Inspection – **1)** Replace brake band if lining is peeled off or discolored or printed numbers are defaced. Before assembling NEW band, soak in ATF for at least 2 hours.

2) If brake band is serviceable but piston rod stroke is not within specification, select a NEW piston rod. Piston stroke should be .059-.118" (1.50-3.00 mm). There are 2 lengths of piston rods, 2.811" (71.40 mm) and 2.870" (72.90 mm).

Reassembly – Install washer and spring to piston rod. Install "E" ring. Install oil seal ring. DO NOT spread oil seal ring ends more than necessary for installation. *See Fig. 29.*

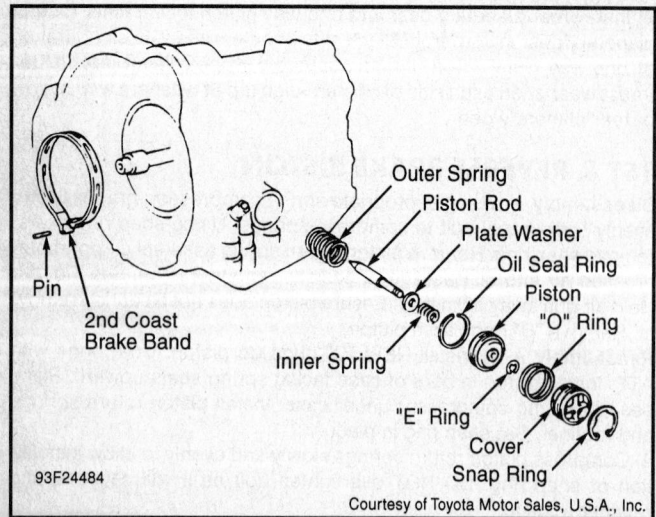

Fig. 29: Exploded View Of 2nd Coast Brake

2ND BRAKE PISTON

Disassembly & Reassembly – Apply compressed air to oil hole and remove 2nd brake piston. Remove 2 "O" rings from piston. Coat NEW "O" rings with ATF and install. Carefully press 2nd brake piston into 2nd brake drum. *See Fig. 30.*

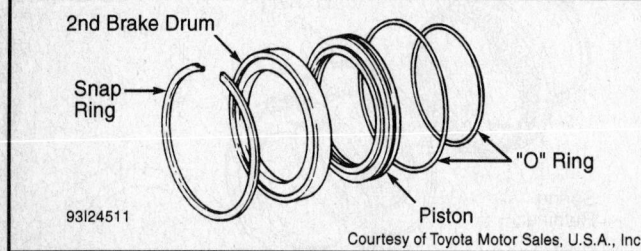

Fig. 30: Exploded View Of 2nd Brake Piston

VALVE BODY ASSEMBLY

NOTE: All valve body components must be installed in original location. Lay all components in sequence during removal for reassembly reference. Throttle pressure is changed according to number of adjusting rings. When assembling valve body, install same number of adjusting rings as were removed. Some valve bodies do not have adjusting rings.

Disassembly – 1) Remove 9 bolts and upper valve body cover. Remove strainer, 2 gaskets and plate. Remove sleeve stopper. Remove 3 bolts and upper valve body. Remove 10 bolts, lower valve body cover and gasket. Remove 3 lower valve body bolts.
2) Hold plate against lower valve body and carefully remove lower valve body. DO NOT lose check balls. Note location of check balls, retainers and pins in valve body. Remove plate and gasket. *See Fig. 31.*
Inspection – 1) Clean all parts with solvent. Dry parts with compressed air. Ensure all valve body oil passages are clear. Inspect valves for scoring or roughness. Inspect valve springs for damage, squareness, rust and collapsed coils. Measure spring free length and outer diameter.
2) Replace spring if not within specification. See appropriate VALVE BODY SPRING SPECIFICATIONS table. Ensure valve body springs correspond with appropriate valve. Ensure retainers are installed in appropriate locations. See appropriate VALVE BODY RETAINER SPECIFICATIONS table.

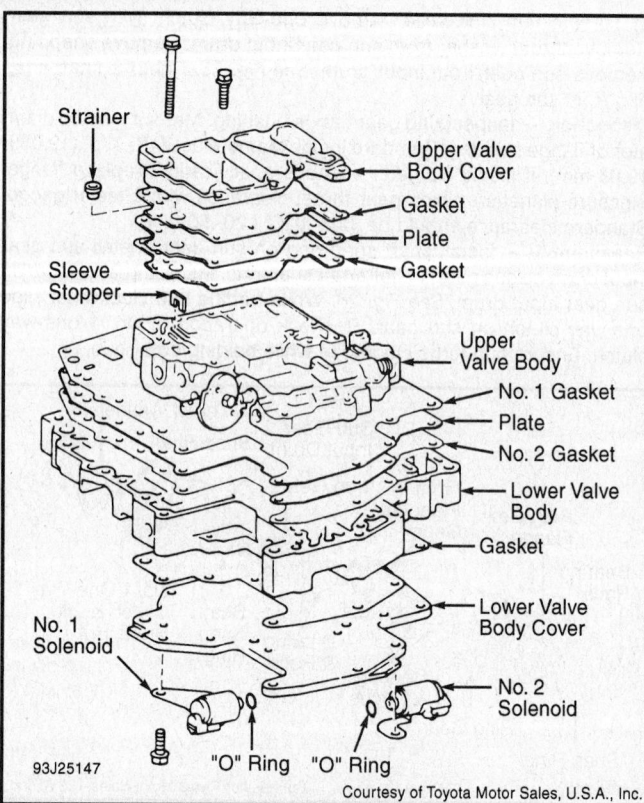

Fig. 31: Exploded View Of Valve Body Assembly

UPPER VALVE BODY SPRING SPECIFICATIONS

Spring No. [1]	Diameter In. (mm)	Free Length In. (mm)
1	.374 (9.50)	.854 (21.70)
2	.417 (10.60)	1.105 (28.06)
3	.311 (7.90)	.850 (21.60)
4	.344 (8.73)	1.173 (29.80)
5	.362 (9.20)	1.209 (30.70)
6	.335 (8.50)	.824 (20.93)
7	.236 (6.00)	.858 (21.80)
8	.402 (10.20)	1.046 (26.56)

[1] – For spring locations, see Fig. 32.

LOWER VALVE BODY SPRING SPECIFICATIONS

Spring No. [1]	Diameter In. (mm)	Free Length In. (mm)
1	.429 (10.90)	1.717 (43.60)
2	.323 (8.20)	1.181 (30.00)
3	.382 (9.70)	1.152 (29.27)
4	.382 (9.70)	1.152 (29.27)
5	.382 (9.70)	1.152 (29.27)
6	.732 (18.60)	2.624 (66.65)
7	.252 (6.40)	.441 (11.20)
8	.433 (11.00)	.783 (19.90)

[1] – For spring locations, see Fig. 34.

UPPER VALVE BODY RETAINER SPECIFICATIONS [1]

Application (Letter I.D.) [2]	Height In. (mm)
Accumulator Control Valve ("B")	.453 (11.50)
Lock-Up Relay Valve ("D") & 2nd Coast Modulator Valve ("C")	.591 (15.00)
Throttle Modulator ("A") & Cut-Back Valve ("C")	.362 (9.20)

[1] – Width is .197" (5.00 mm) for all retainers. Thickness is .126" (3.20 mm) for all retainers.
[2] – For retainer locations, see Fig. 33.

LOWER VALVE BODY RETAINER SPECIFICATIONS

Application (Letter I.D.) [1]	Height In. (mm)
Lock-Up Signal Valve ("F")	[2] .591 (15.00)
Primary Regulator ("A") & 1-2 Shift Valves ("C")	[2] .362 (9.20)
Secondary Regulator ("E")	[3] .512 (13.00)
2-3 Shift ("B") & 3-4 Shift Valves ("D")	[3] .315 (8.00)

[1] – For retainer locations, see Fig. 33.
[2] – Retainer width is .197" (5.00 mm).
[3] – Retainer width is .236 (6.00).

NOTE: Valves may be held in with pins or retainers and plugs. Remove components and note locations. Arrange parts in order for reassembly reference.

Reassembly – 1) Coat all components with ATF. To reassemble, reverse disassembly procedure. Ensure check balls, pins and strainer on upper side of lower valve body are installed correctly. See Fig. 35. Ensure check ball, pins, retainers and vibrating stopper on lower side of upper valve body are installed correctly. See Fig. 33.
2) Position NEW No. 2 gasket, plate and NEW No. 1 gasket on lower valve body. Ensure gaskets are installed in correct locations. See Fig. 37. Place lower valve body with plate and gaskets on upper valve body. DO NOT let components separate. Align each bolt hole in valve bodies with gaskets and plate.
3) Install and finger-tighten bolts in lower valve body to secure upper valve body. Use proper length bolt. See Fig. 36. Install lower valve body cover over new gasket. Install and finger-tighten 10 cover bolts. Install and finger-tighten 3 upper valve body 1.102" (28.00 mm) bolts.

4) Ensure retainers are installed correctly on upper side of upper valve body. See Fig. 33. Install sleeve stopper. Position NEW gasket, plate and strainer. Install strainer onto plate. Position and install upper valve body cover, and finger-tighten 9 bolts. See Fig. 36. Place and install NEW "O" rings on solenoids. Check alignment of gaskets and plates. Tighten upper and lower valve body bolts to 48 INCH lbs. (5.4 N.m).

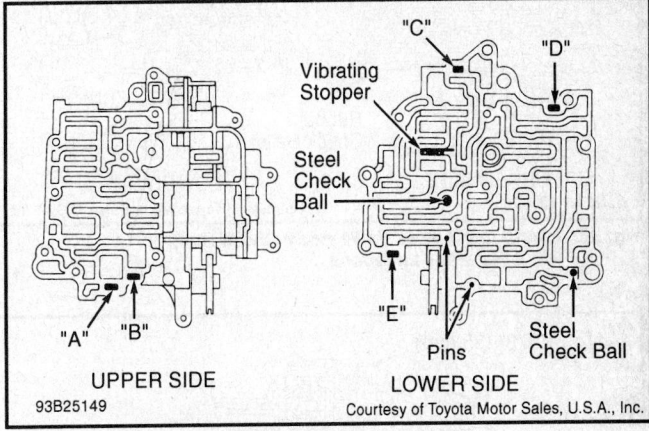

93B25149   Courtesy of Toyota Motor Sales, U.S.A., Inc.

Fig. 33: Identifying Upper Valve Body Check Ball, Pin & Retainer Locations

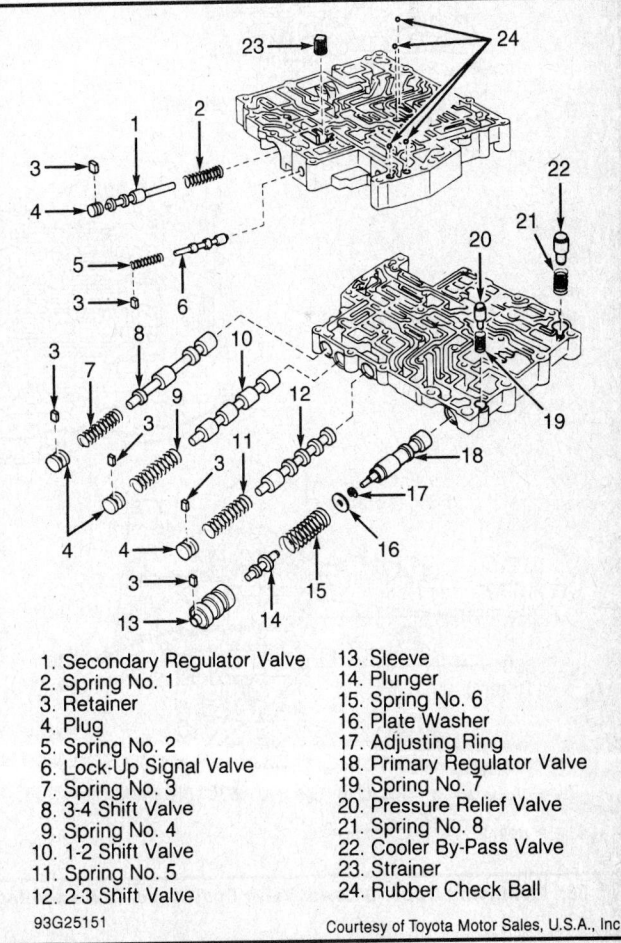

1. Secondary Regulator Valve	13. Sleeve
2. Spring No. 1	14. Plunger
3. Retainer	15. Spring No. 6
4. Plug	16. Plate Washer
5. Spring No. 2	17. Adjusting Ring
6. Lock-Up Signal Valve	18. Primary Regulator Valve
7. Spring No. 3	19. Spring No. 7
8. 3-4 Shift Valve	20. Pressure Relief Valve
9. Spring No. 4	21. Spring No. 8
10. 1-2 Shift Valve	22. Cooler By-Pass Valve
11. Spring No. 5	23. Strainer
12. 2-3 Shift Valve	24. Rubber Check Ball

93G25151   Courtesy of Toyota Motor Sales, U.S.A., Inc.

Fig. 34: Exploded View Of Lower Valve Body

1. Throttle Modulator Valve	16. 2nd Coast Modulator Valve
2. Retainer	17. Vibrating Stopper
3. Spring No. 1	18. Adjusting Ring
4. Plug	19. Spring No. 5
5. Spring No. 2	20. Spring
6. Accumulator Control Valve	21. Cam Pin
7. Low Coast Modulator Valve	22. Cam
8. Spring No. 3	23. Plate Washer
9. Steel Check Ball	24. Wave Washer
10. Downshift Plug	25. Cut-Back Valve
11. Throttle Valve	26. Spring No. 7
12. Spring No. 4	27. Lock-Up Relay Valve
13. Pin	28. Spring No. 8
14. Throttle Valve Sleeve	29. Control Valve
15. Spring No. 6	30. Lock-Up Relay Valve Sleeve

95D19276   Courtesy of Toyota Motor Sales, U.S.A., Inc.

Fig. 32: Exploded View Of Upper Valve Body

AUTOMATIC TRANSMISSIONS
Toyota A-140E (Cont.)

"A"
"B"
"C"
"D"
Rubber Check Balls
"E"
Strainer
Rubber Check Balls
UPPER SIDE
"F"
LOWER SIDE
93I25153
Courtesy of Toyota Motor Sales, U.S.A., Inc.

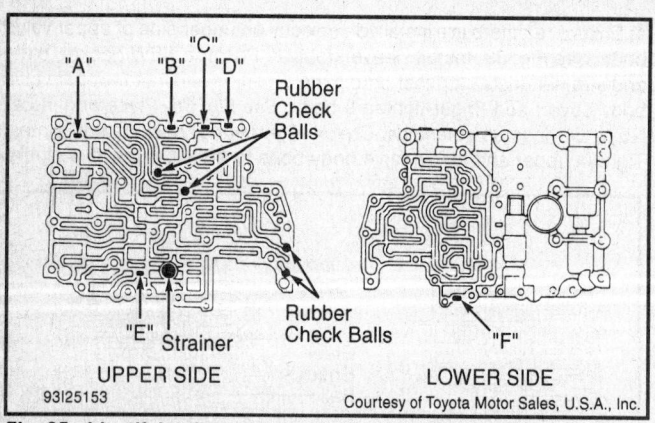

Fig. 35: Identifying Lower Valve Body Check Ball, Pin & Retainer Locations

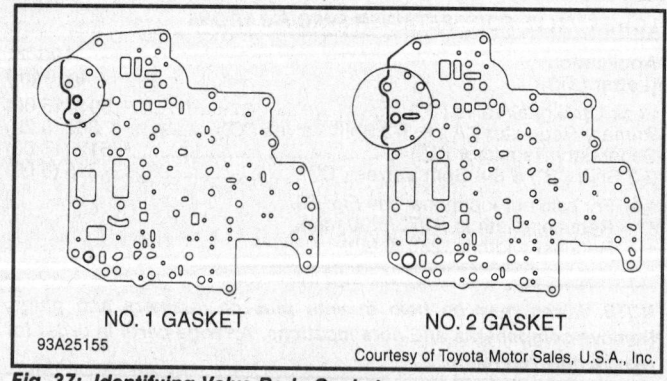

NO. 1 GASKET
NO. 2 GASKET
93A25155
Courtesy of Toyota Motor Sales, U.S.A., Inc.

Fig. 37: Identifying Valve Body Gaskets

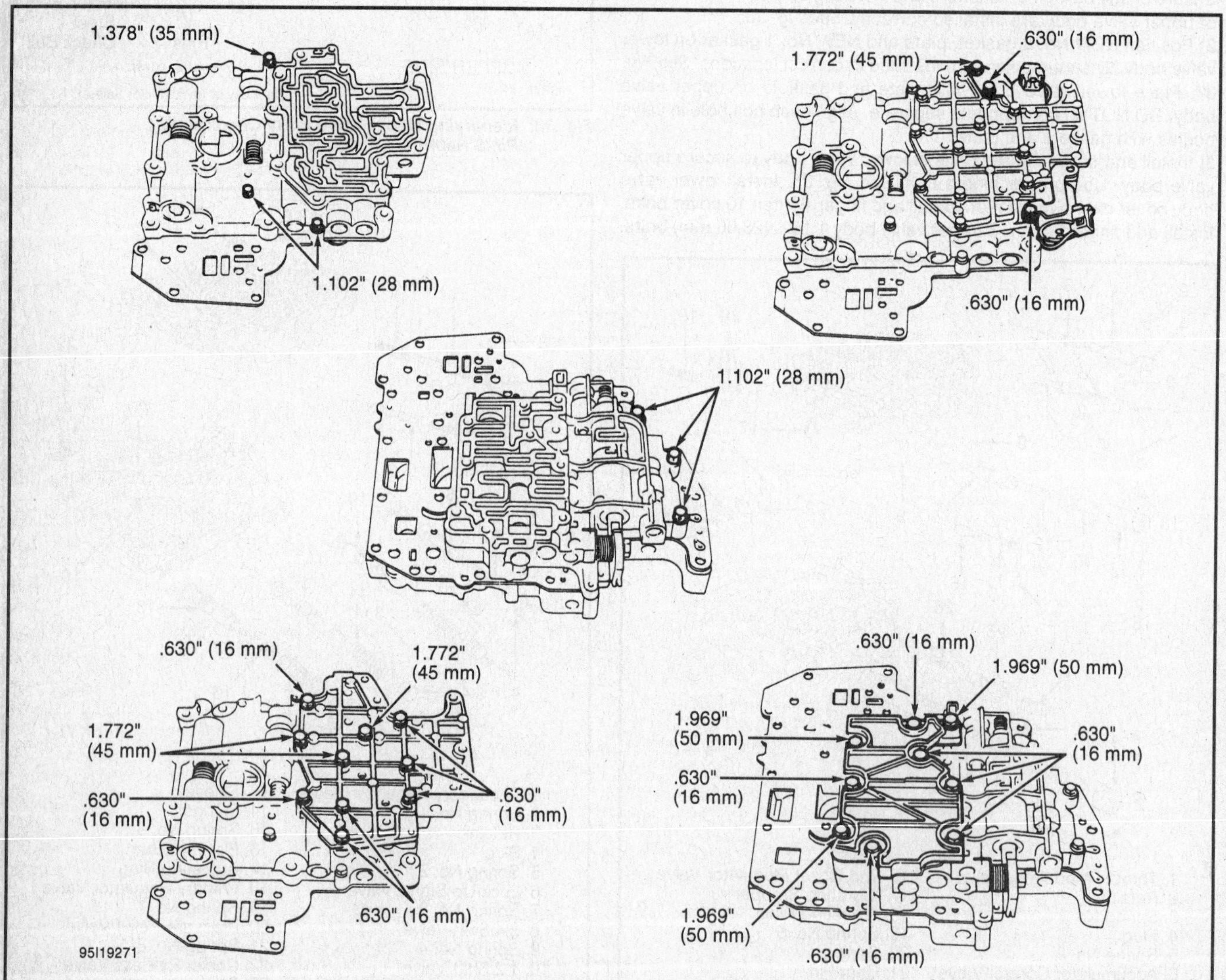

1.378" (35 mm)
1.102" (28 mm)
.630" (16 mm)
1.772" (45 mm)
.630" (16 mm)
1.102" (28 mm)
.630" (16 mm)
1.772" (45 mm)
1.772" (45 mm)
.630" (16 mm)
.630" (16 mm)
.630" (16 mm)
.630" (16 mm)
1.969" (50 mm)
1.969" (50 mm)
.630" (16 mm)
.630" (16 mm)
.630" (16 mm)
1.969" (50 mm)
.630" (16 mm)
95I19271
Courtesy of Toyota Motor Sales, U.S.A., Inc.

Fig. 36: Identifying Upper & Lower Valve Body Cover Bolt Locations

OVERDRIVE BRAKE

Disassembly – 1) Remove overdrive brake drum. Push in return spring and using a screwdriver, remove snap ring. Remove cushion plate. Remove plates, discs and flange. Note number and location of components. *See Fig. 41.*

2) Remove piston from drum by applying compressed air to oil hole. *See Fig. 38.* Ensure piston does not tilt. Remove "O" ring from piston.

Inspection – Inspect disc, plate and flange. If disc lining is peeled or discolored, replace discs as necessary. If discs are replaced, allow discs to soak at least 15 minutes in ATF.

Reassembly – 1) Install "O" rings on piston. Coat "O" rings with ATF. Install piston in drum. Ensure "O" ring is not damaged. Install flange facing flat end upward.

2) Install following parts in order: disc, .150" (3.8 mm) plate, .098" (2.5 mm) plate, disc, plate. Install cushion plate with rounded end upward. Install piston return spring assembly. Install snap ring in case. Ensure end gap of snap ring is not aligned with cutouts. While turning overdrive gear clockwise, install overdrive gear to case. If overdrive gear is properly installed to case, height will be .94" (24.0 mm). *See Fig. 39.*

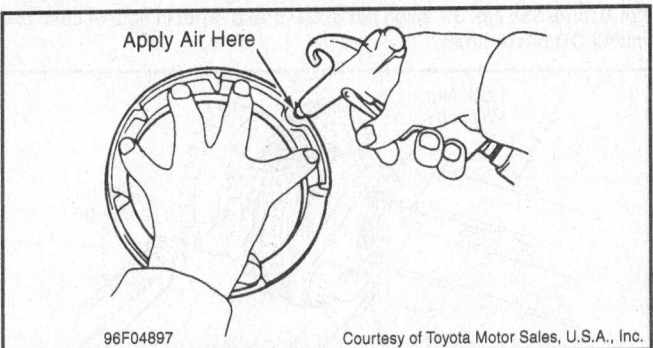

Fig. 38: *Removing OD Brake Piston From Case*

Apply Air Here

96F04897   Courtesy of Toyota Motor Sales, U.S.A., Inc.

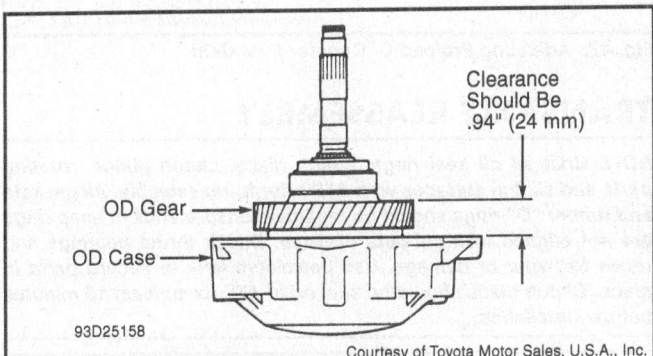

Clearance Should Be .94" (24 mm)

OD Gear

OD Case

93D25158   Courtesy of Toyota Motor Sales, U.S.A., Inc.

Fig. 39: *Checking Installed Height Between OD Gear & Case*

OVERDRIVE DIRECT CLUTCH

Disassembly – 1) Remove OD direct clutch from case. Remove bearing and race from clutch drum and case. Using a screwdriver, remove snap ring. Remove flanges, discs and plates. Note number and location of components.

2) Using appropriate spring compressor, compress piston return spring. Remove snap ring and piston return spring. Install clutch drum on case.

3) Apply compressed air to pressure apply hole. Remove OD direct clutch piston from case. *See Fig. 40.* If piston does not completely come out, use needle-nose pliers to remove piston. Remove "O" rings from piston.

Inspection – 1) Inspect piston check ball for free movement by shaking piston. Ensure valve does not leak by applying low pressure com-

pressed air. If disc lining is peeled or discolored, replace discs as necessary. If discs are replaced, allow discs to soak at least 15 minutes in ATF.

2) Measure inside diameter of both OD direct clutch drum bushings. Maximum inside diameter is .870" (22.09 mm). If inside diameter exceeds specification, replace OD direct clutch drum.

Reassembly – 1) Coat NEW "O" rings with ATF. Install "O" rings on piston. Press piston in drum with cup side up. DO NOT damage "O" rings. Install return spring. Set retainer and snap ring in place.

2) Compress spring retainer. Install snap ring with a screwdriver. Ensure end gap of ring is aligned with groove of clutch drum.

3) Install following parts in order: flange, disc, plate, disc and flange. Using a screwdriver, install snap ring. Ensure snap ring end gap is aligned with groove of clutch drum.

4) Coat race with petroleum jelly and install race to case. Coat assembled bearing and race with petroleum jelly and install with race side facing downward to clutch drum.

5) Install OD direct clutch to case. Measure OD direct clutch piston stroke by applying compressed air into case passage. Piston stroke should be .048-.075" (1.21-1.91 mm). *See Fig. 40.* If piston does not move, disassemble and inspect.

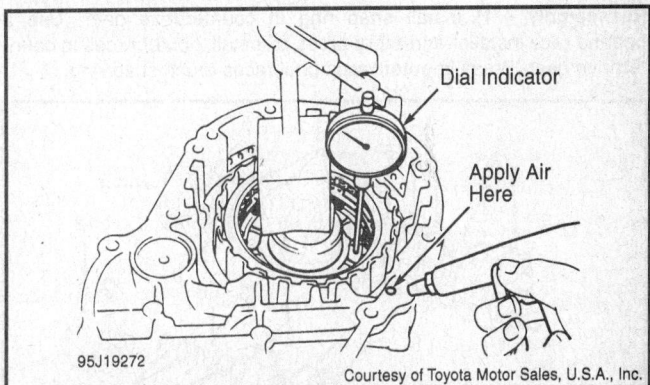

Dial Indicator

Apply Air Here

95J19272   Courtesy of Toyota Motor Sales, U.S.A., Inc.

Fig. 40: *Removing OD Direct Clutch Piston & Measuring Piston Stroke*

OVERDRIVE ONE-WAY CLUTCH

Disassembly – 1) Install OD direct clutch in OD planetary gear while turning OD gear clockwise. Hold OD direct clutch and turn intermediate shaft. Shaft should turn freely clockwise and lock counterclockwise. If not, proceed to next step.

2) Remove snap ring and retaining plate. Remove one-way clutch and outer race as an assembly. Remove No. 3 overdrive planetary thrust washer. *See Fig. 41.*

3) Remove one-way clutch from outer race, noting direction of one-way clutch. Using magnet, carefully remove 4 plugs from planetary gear.

Reassembly – 1) Install 4 plugs into planetary gear. Install No. 3 thrust washer with groove facing overdrive case. Install one-way clutch into outer race.

2) Install retainers on both sides of one-way clutch. Place overdrive one-way clutch assembly into hub. Ensure one-way clutch is installed in correct direction and is the correct part. Install retaining plate and snap ring.

3) Hold OD direct clutch and turn intermediate shaft. Shaft should turn freely clockwise and lock counterclockwise. Remove OD direct clutch from planetary gear.

OVERDRIVE CASE

Disassembly – Remove OD direct clutch accumulator piston snap ring. Remove retaining plate and 2 springs. Remove accumulator piston. Remove oil seal rings from case. Push one end of ring into groove and unhook both ends of ring by hand. Spread rings and remove.

Reassembly – Spread rings and install in groove. Push one end of ring in groove and hook both ends by hand. Coat NEW "O" ring with ATF and install on OD direct clutch accumulator piston. Install accumulator piston, spring, retainer plate and snap ring.

COUNTERDRIVE GEAR & BEARING

Disassembly – **1)** Pry back tabs of lock washer with chisel. Hold shaft in soft-jawed vise. Loosen adjusting nut. Remove nut and washer. Use a bearing puller and arbor press to remove intermediate shaft bearing.

2) Use a press to remove counterdrive gear and front bearing together. Remove rear bearing using bearing puller and arbor press. To remove OD planetary ring gear from counterdrive gear, pull up ring gear. Compress snap ring with needle-nose pliers. Remove snap ring from groove.

3) Remove ring gear from counterdrive gear. Use a brass drift and hammer to drive outer races from counterdrive gear. Using a screwdriver, remove snap ring from counterdrive gear.

Inspection – Using a feeler gauge, measure overdrive planetary pinion gear thrust clearance. Standard clearance is .008-.020" (.20-.50 mm).

Reassembly – **1)** Install snap ring in counterdrive gear. Use a bearing race installer and arbor press to install 2 outer races in counterdrive gear. Press in outer races until races touch snap ring.

2) While pushing down on ring gear, squeeze snap ring end with needle-nose pliers. Install OD planetary ring gear in counterdrive gear. When snap ring is fully seated, end is free.

3) Use a plate and arbor press to install rear bearing on shaft. Press in bearing until side surface of inner race touches shaft. Install counterdrive gear on shaft. Mesh ring gear with planetary pinions. Place front bearing on shaft. Hold ring gear to prevent shaft from falling.

4) Press in bearing until axial play between bearings is .020" (.50 mm). Press bearing onto intermediate shaft until bearing touches front bearing of counterdrive gear.

5) Place NEW locking washer and adjusting nut on intermediate shaft. Adjust preload of counterdrive gear. Hold shaft in a soft-jawed vise. Using a spring gauge and wrench on adjusting nut, tighten adjusting nut.

6) Rotate counterdrive gear right and left several times before measuring preload. Torque adjusting nut until preload is 2.0-3.4 INCH lbs. (9-15 N). *See Fig. 42.* Bend lock washer tab until even with adjusting nut groove.

7) Install snap ring. Ensure snap ring end gap is not aligned with cutouts. Turn OD gear clockwise and install OD gear in case. If OD gear is properly installed, clearance between OD gear and case will be .94" (24.0 mm). *See Fig. 39.* Align pin of OD brake drum in hole of case and install OD brake drum.

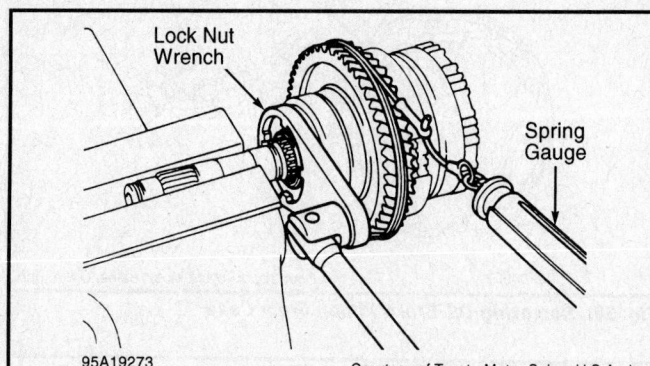

95A19273   Courtesy of Toyota Motor Sales, U.S.A., Inc.

Fig. 42: Adjusting Preload Of Counterdrive Gear

TRANSAXLE REASSEMBLY

NOTE: Coat all oil seal rings, clutch discs, clutch plates, rotating parts and sliding surfaces with ATF prior to reassembly. All gaskets and rubber "O" rings should be replaced. Ensure ends of snap rings are not aligned with cut-outs of drum. Check thrust bearings and races for wear or damage. Use petroleum jelly to secure parts in place. Clutch discs should be soaked in ATF for at least 15 minutes before installation.

NOTE: For thrust bearing and race locations, see Fig. 53.

1) Install drive pinion. Refer to DRIVE PINION ASSEMBLY under COMPONENT DISASSEMBLY & REASSEMBLY. Install differential assembly. Refer to DIFFERENTIAL REASSEMBLY under COMPONENT DISASSEMBLY & REASSEMBLY.

2) Install manual valve shaft. Install NEW shaft oil seal to case. Assemble a NEW collar to manual valve lever. Install manual valve lever shaft to case through lever. Drive in roll pin until flush with lever surface. Align collar hole with notch in lever and stake in position using a hammer and punch. Install retaining spring. Ensure lever moves smoothly.

3) Install parking pawl. Hook spring ends to case and pawl. Install pin in hole of case through spring and pawl. Install parking lock rod. Install parking lock pawl bracket. Tighten bolts to 65 INCH lbs. (7.4 N.m). Check operation of parking pawl. Ensure counterdriven gear is locked when manual lever is in "P" range.

4) Coat 1st and reverse brake piston "O" rings with ATF and install on piston. Install 1st and reverse brake piston to case with spring seat upward. Place piston return spring and snap ring on piston. Compress return spring until snap ring can be installed.

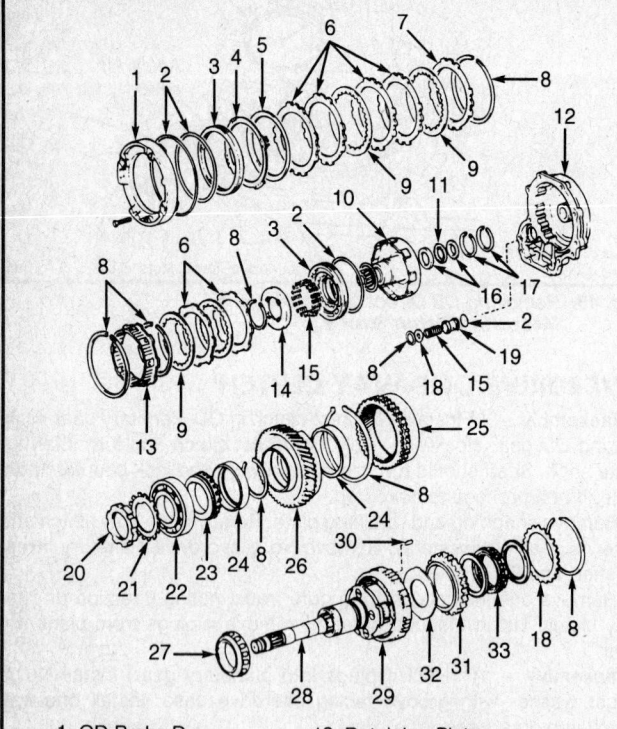

1. OD Brake Drum	18. Retaining Plate
2. "O" Ring	19. OD Clutch
3. Piston	Accumulator Piston
4. Piston Return Spring	20. Adjusting Nut
5. Cushion Plate	21. Lock Washer
6. Plate	22. Intermediate Shaft Bearing
7. Flange	23. Front Bearing
8. Snap Ring	24. Outer Race
9. Disc	25. Ring Gear
10. OD Clutch Drum	26. Counter Drive Gear
11. Thrust Bearing	27. Rear Bearing
12. OD Case	28. Intermediate Shaft
13. OD Brake Hub	29. OD Planetary Gear
14. Spring Retainer	30. Plug
15. Spring	31. One-Way Clutch Outer Race
16. Races	32. No. 3 Thrust Washer
17. Oil Seal Rings	33. OD One-Way Clutch

93J25162   Courtesy of Toyota Motor Sales, U.S.A., Inc.

Fig. 41: Exploded View Of Overdrive Assembly

5) Coat OD apply gaskets with petroleum jelly to hold in place. Install gaskets on transaxle case. Install both overdrive brake and governor apply gaskets over appropriate case opening.

6) Align each bolt hole in NEW gasket and case. Install overdrive unit and case to transaxle case. Tighten bolts to 18 ft. lbs. (25 N.m). Check intermediate shaft end play. Ensure shaft has thrust play in axial (in and out) direction. Thrust clearance should be .019-.059" (.49-1.51 mm). Ensure shaft turns smoothly.

7) Install 1st and reverse brake in case. Install brake inner flange facing flat end toward oil pump side. Install following parts in order: disc, plate, disc, plate, disc, plate, disc, plate, disc, plate and disc. Install outer flange flat side facing toward piston side.

8) Install snap ring. Ensure snap ring end gap is not aligned with cutouts. Check operation of 1st and reverse brake. Apply compressed air at oil passage of transaxle case to confirm piston movement. *See Fig. 43.*

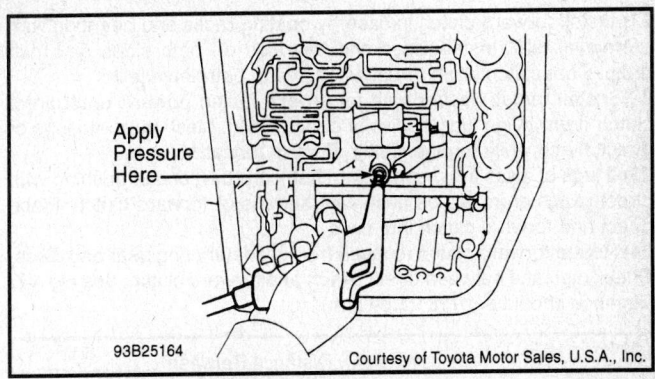

Apply Pressure Here

93B25164   Courtesy of Toyota Motor Sales, U.S.A., Inc.

Fig. 44: Checking Operation Of 2nd Brake

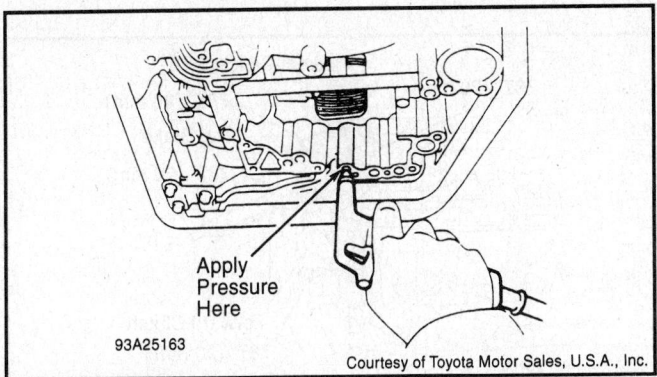

Apply Pressure Here

93A25163   Courtesy of Toyota Motor Sales, U.S.A., Inc.

Fig. 43: Checking Operation Of 1st & Reverse Brake

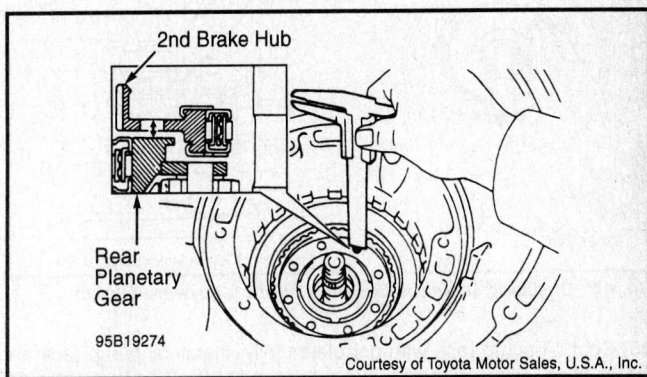

2nd Brake Hub

Rear Planetary Gear

95B19274   Courtesy of Toyota Motor Sales, U.S.A., Inc.

Fig. 45: Checking Distance Between 2nd Brake Hub & Rear Planetary Gear

9) Coat rear planetary gear thrust washers with petroleum jelly. Install washers on gear. Ensure that different lug shapes match openings on gear. *See Fig. 13.* Coat races and bearing with petroleum jelly. Install planetary gear on ring gear. Install ring gear into case.

10) Install rear planetary gear in case by aligning lugs of discs in 1st and reverse brake. Align spline of carrier with lugs of discs. Install planetary gear in 1st and reverse brake discs.

11) Install No. 2 one-way clutch in case with shiny side upward. Install one-way clutch on inner race while turning planetary gear clockwise with snap ring pliers. Check operation of No. 2 one-way clutch by turning planetary carrier. Carrier should turn freely clockwise and lock counterclockwise. Install snap ring. Ensure end gap is not aligned with cutouts.

12) Install 2nd coast brake band guide and 2nd brake drum guide. Install band guide so tip touches case. Install 2nd brake in case. Install brake flange facing flat end toward oil pump.

13) Install following parts in order: flange, disc, plate, disc, plate, disc, plate. Install piston return spring assembly with each spring end installed in protrusion of case.

14) Install 2nd brake drum in case. Align groove of drum with bolt. Place drum in case. Place snap ring in case so end gap is installed in groove. While compressing piston return springs over drum with 2 hammer handles, install snap ring in groove. Ensure snap ring end gap is not aligned with cutouts. Install NEW 2nd brake drum gasket.

15) Check operation of 2nd brake by applying compressed air into case oil passage. Ensure piston moves freely. *See Fig. 44.* Install NEW drum gasket until contact is made with 2nd brake drum.

16) Install No. 1 one-way clutch and 2nd brake hub by aligning flukes of discs in 2nd brake. Align spline of hub with flukes of discs. Install hub into 2nd brake discs. Check distance between surfaces of 2nd brake hub and rear planetary gear. *See Fig. 45.* Distance should be approximately .20" (5.0 mm).

17) Install sun gear and sun gear input drum by turning sun gear clockwise and installing in one-way clutch. Ensure sun gear is placed in center of intermediate shaft to protect bushing from damage.

18) To install front planetary gear on ring gear, coat races and bearings with petroleum jelly. Install races and bearings onto ring gear. Install planetary gear on ring gear.

NOTE: *For thrust bearing and race locations, see Fig. 53.*

---

19) Install front planetary gear assembly on sun gear. If planetary gear and other parts are installed correctly in case, end of bushing with ring gear flange will be flush with or below shoulder of intermediate shaft.

20) Coat race with petroleum jelly. Install race onto tip of ring gear flange. Install intermediate shaft oil seal ring. Install 2nd coast brake band in case. Install pin through oil pump mounting bolt hole. *See Fig. 46.*

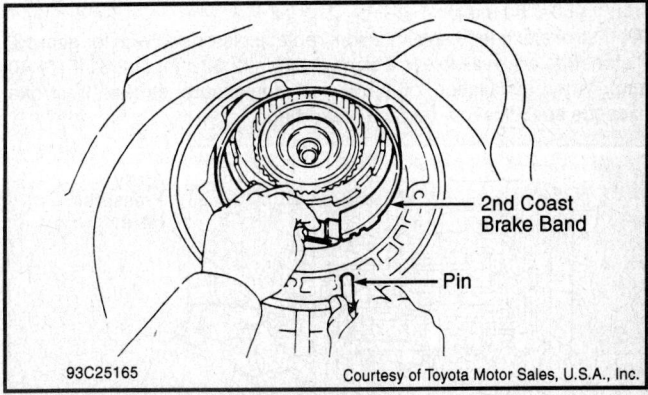

2nd Coast Brake Band

Pin

93C25165   Courtesy of Toyota Motor Sales, U.S.A., Inc.

Fig. 46: Installing 2nd Coast Brake Band

21) Install forward clutch in case by coating races and bearings with petroleum jelly. Install races and bearings on both sides of clutch drum. Coat clutch drum thrust washer with petroleum jelly.

22) Install thrust washer with oil groove facing upward onto direct clutch drum. Align lugs of disc in direct clutch. Mesh hub with lugs of direct clutch while turning clutch drum or forward clutch.

23) If lugs of discs are meshed with hub correctly, end of bushing with direct clutch drum will be flush with surface of forward clutch. Place direct and forward clutch into case.

24) Rotate forward clutch to mesh front planetary ring gear and discs. Check distance between direct clutch and forward clutch. *See Fig. 47.* Distance should be .118" (3.00 mm).

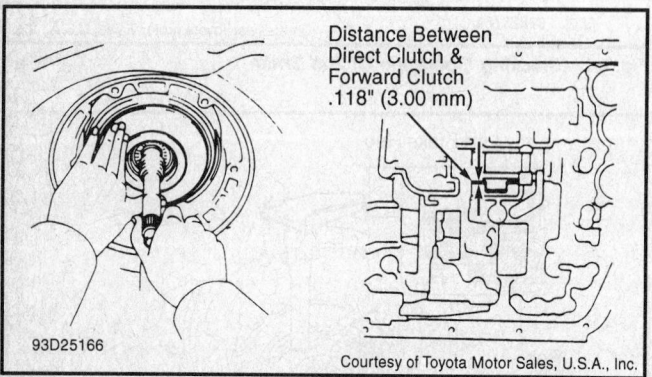

Fig. 47: **Checking Distance Between Direct & Forward Clutch**

25) Coat oil pump race with petroleum jelly. Install oil pump race on stator shaft. Place oil pump through input shaft. Align bolt holes of pump body at transaxle case. Hold input shaft. Lightly press oil pump body to slide oil seal rings on stator shaft through direct clutch drum.

26) DO NOT push on oil pump hard or oil seal ring will stick to direct clutch drum. Install and tighten oil pump mounting bolts to 16 ft. lbs. (22 N.m). Measure end play of input shaft in axial direction.

27) End play should be .012-.035" (.30-.90 mm). If end play is not within specification, select alternate bearing race. There are 2 different thicknesses of races for end of stator shaft, .031" (.80 mm) and .055". (1.40 mm). If end play is still not within specification, recheck all sub-component assemblies. Check input shaft rotation. Ensure shaft turns smoothly.

28) Install drive pinion cap. Install 2nd coast brake piston. Install outer spring with piston. Place cover in bore. Install snap ring while pressing in on cover. Ensure front end of piston rod contacts center of 2nd brake band depression.

29) Check 2nd coast brake piston stroke. Apply a small amount of paint to piston rod at point were piston rod contacts case. Measure 2nd coast piston stroke by applying and releasing 57-114 psi (4-8 kg/cm²) of compressed air. *See Fig. 48.* Piston stroke should be .059-.118" (1.50-3.00 mm).

30) If stroke exceeds specification, replace piston rod with longer rod. Piston rods are available in 2 sizes, 2.870" (72.90 mm) or 2.811" (71.40 mm). After installation of NEW rod, remeasure stroke. If stroke exceeds specification, replace brake band.

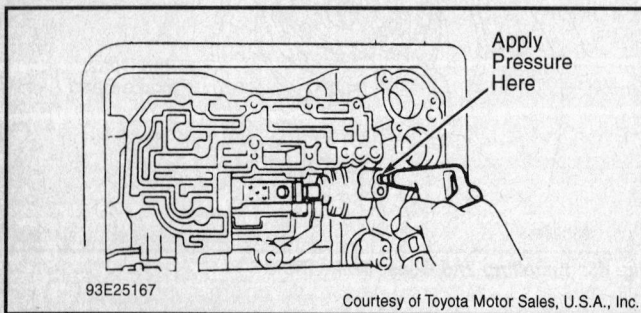

Fig. 48: **Checking Operation Of 2nd Coast Brake**

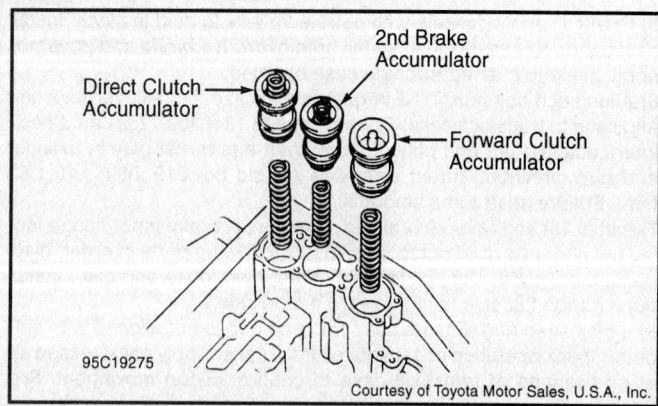

Fig. 49: **Identifying Accumulator Locations**

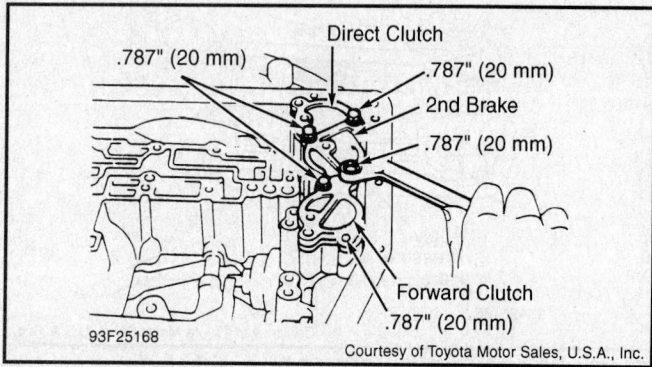

Fig. 50: **Identifying Length & Location Of Accumulator Bolts**

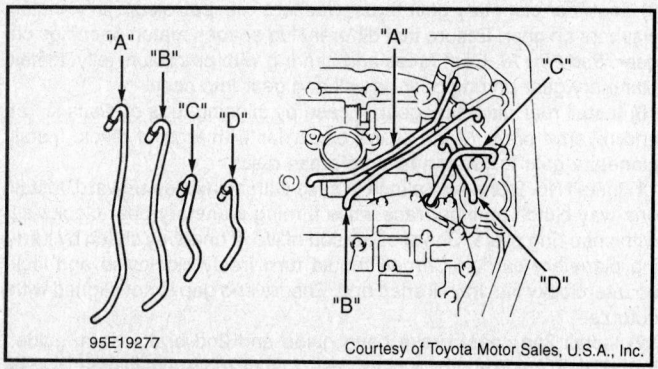

Fig. 51: **Identifying Oil Tubes**

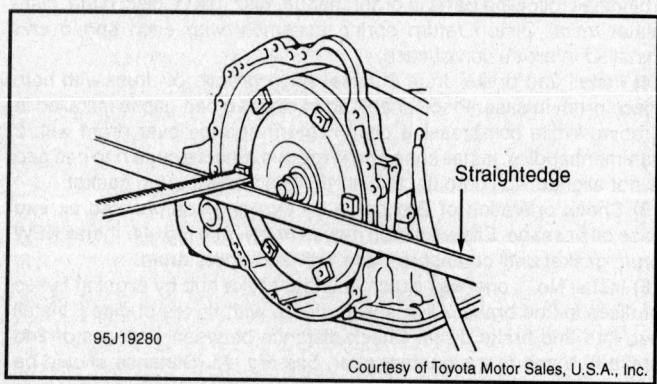

Fig. 52: **Measuring Torque Converter Depth**

31) Install accumulator pistons and springs in bore. *See Fig. 49.* Verify correct spring installation. See SPRING FREE LENGTH SPECIFICATIONS table. Install cover with gasket. Tighten 5 bolts gradually to 89 INCH lbs. (10 N.m). Ensure proper length bolts are used. *See Fig. 50.*

SPRING FREE LENGTH SPECIFICATIONS

Application	Free Length In. (mm)	Color
Forward Clutch	2.269 (57.64)	Red & Purple
Direct Clutch	2.764 (70.21)	Purple
2nd Brake	2.732 (69.39)	Green & White

32) Install throttle cable and solenoid wiring through case. DO NOT roll case over cable. Cable fitting will be damaged. Ensure "O" ring is not damaged. Ensure all components are fully seated. Place valve body on transaxle. While holding cam down with hand, slip cable end in slot. Lower valve body in position. DO NOT entangle throttle cable, solenoid or kickdown wiring.

33) Install valve body bolts. Ensure proper length and location of bolts. *See Fig. 5.* Finger tighten all bolts. Tighten bolts in crisscross pattern to 89 INCH lbs. (10 N.m). Connect solenoid wire connectors.

34) Place manual valve and body on transaxle. Align manual lever with pin of manual shaft lever. Lower valve body into position. Finger tighten bolts. Evenly tighten bolts to 89 INCH lbs. (10 N.m).

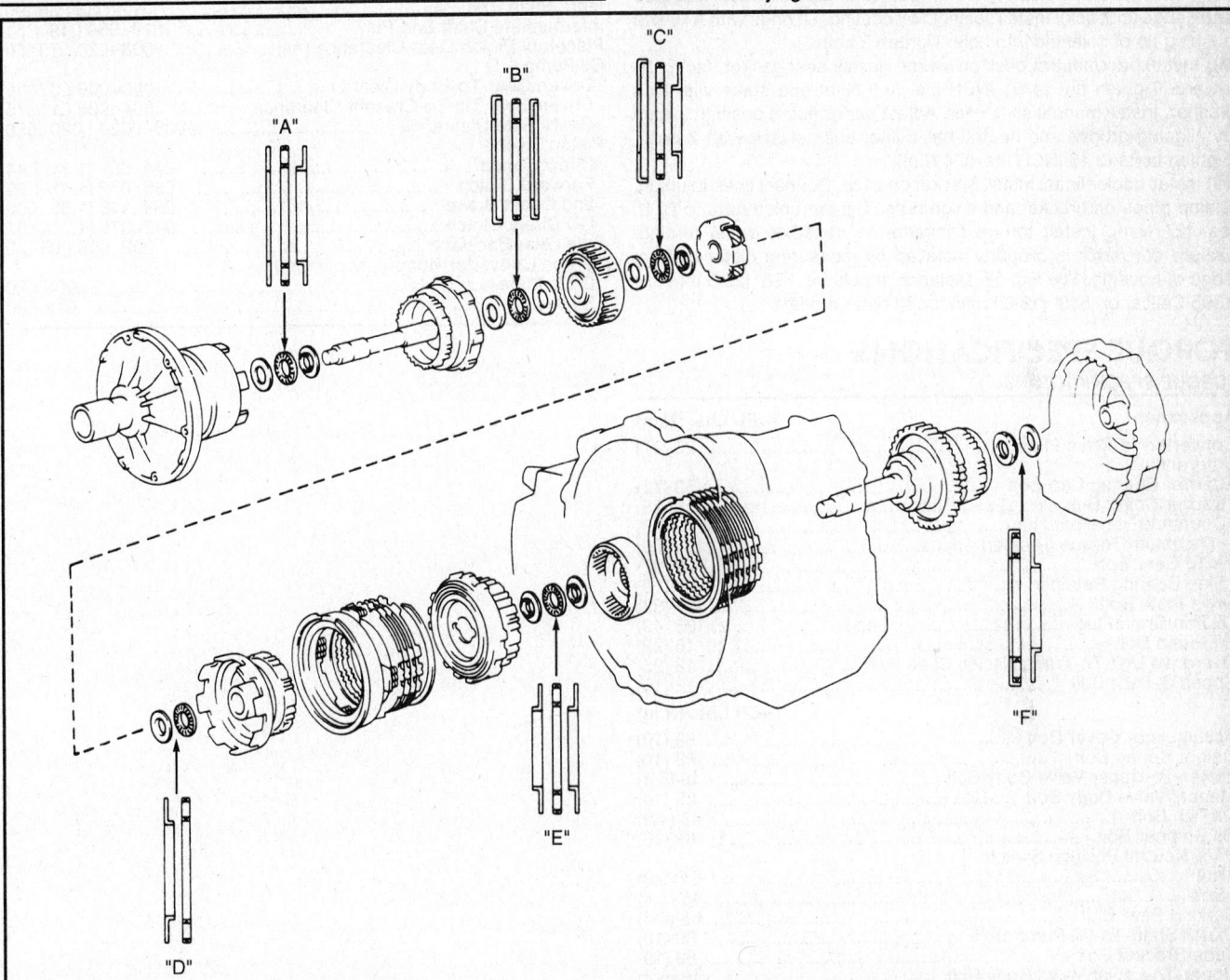

THRUST BEARING & RACE SPECIFICATIONS

Application	Outer Diameter In. (mm)	Inner Diameter In. (mm)
"A"		
Front Race	1.693 (43)	1.201 (30.5)
Rear Race	1.654 (42)	1.067 (27.1)
Bearing	1.654 (42)	1.138 (28.9)
"B"		
Front Race	1.492 (37.9)	.866 (22)
Rear Race	1.406 (35.7)	.906 (23)
Bearing	1.421 (36.1)	.874 (22.2)
"C"		
Front Race	1.492 (37.9)	.866 (22)
Rear Race	1.378 (35)	.748 (19)
Bearing	1.421 (36.1)	.874 (22.2)

THRUST BEARING & RACE SPECIFICATIONS (Cont.)

Application	Outer Diameter In. (mm)	Inner Diameter In. (mm)
"D"		
Front Race	1.772 (45)	1.102 (28)
Bearing	1.772 (45)	1.181 (30)
"E"		
Front Race	1.469 (37.3)	949 (24.1)
Rear Race	1.480 (37.6)	.874 (22.2)
Bearing	1.480 (37.6)	.945 (24.0)
"F"		
Rear Race	1.693 (43)	.965 (24.5)
Bearing	1.823 (46.3)	1.031 (26.2)

95A19281

Courtesy of Toyota Motor Sales, U.S.A., Inc.

Fig. 53: Identifying Thrust Bearing & Race Locations

35) Install detent spring. Ensure proper length and location of each bolt. Finger tighten bolts. Tighten to 89 INCH lbs. (10 N.m). Check for correct operation of manual valve lever. Ensure lever is touching center of detent spring tip roller.

36) Install oil tubes using plastic hammer. *See Fig. 51*. DO NOT bend or damage tubes. Install tube bracket. Tighten bolts to 89 INCH lbs. (10 N.m). Install oil strainer. Tighten bolts to 89 INCH lbs. (10 N.m). Install 3 magnets in oil pan.

37) Ensure magnets do not interfere with oil tubes. Install oil pan with NEW gasket. Tighten pan bolts to 43 INCH lbs. (4.9 N.m). Install cover and bracket with 2 bolts.

38) Install throttle and solenoid wiring retainer plates. Install filler tube and gauge (dipstick). Install solenoid by coating "O" rings with ATF and pushing tip of solenoid into hole. Tighten 2 bolts.

39) Install park/neutral position switch. Install seal gasket, facing lip inward. Tighten nut to 61 INCH lbs. (6.9 N.m) and stake with lock washer. Install manual shift lever. Adjust park/neutral position switch by aligning groove and neutral basic line. Lock switch with 2 bolts. Tighten bolts to 48 INCH lbs. (5.4 N.m).

40) Install cooler lines. Install bracket on case. Connect lines to union. Clamp pipes on bracket and union nuts. Tighten union nuts to 20 ft. lbs. (27 N.m). Install torque converter in transaxle while turning. Ensure converter is properly installed by measuring distance from edge of housing. *See Fig. 52*. Distance should be .898" (22.8 mm) for 1995 Celica, or .510" (13.00 mm) for all other models.

TORQUE SPECIFICATIONS
TORQUE SPECIFICATIONS

Application	Ft. Lbs. (N.m)
Converter-To-Drive Plate Bolt	20 (27)
Differential	
Carrier Bearing Cap Bolt	53 (72)
Carrier Cover Bolt	18 (25)
Counterdriven Gear Nut	127 (172)
Maximum Torque (Preload Adj.)	213 (289)
Ring Gear Bolt	72 (97)
Side Bearing Retainer	14 (19)
Drive Plate Bolt	61 (83)
Oil Pan Drain Plug	36 (49)
Oil Pump Bolt	16 (22)
Overdrive Unit-To-Transmission Case Bolt	18 (25)
Speed Sensor Bolt	12 (16)

Application	INCH Lbs. (N.m)
Accumulator Cover Bolt	89 (10)
Detent Spring Bolt	89 (10)
Lower-To-Upper Valve Body Bolt	48 (5.4)
Manual Valve Body Bolt	89 (10)
Oil Pan Bolt	43 (4.9)
Oil Strainer Bolt	89 (10)
Park/Neutral Position Switch	
Nut	61 (6.9)
Bolt	48 (5.4)
Parking Pawl Bolt	65 (7.4)
Stator Shaft-To-Oil Pump Bolt	89 (10)
Tube Bracket Bolt	89 (10)
Upper-To-Lower Valve Body Bolt	48 (5.4)
Valve Body Bolt	89 (10)

TRANSAXLE SPECIFICATIONS
TRANSAXLE SPECIFICATIONS

Application	In. (mm)
Bushing Inside Diameter (Maximum)	
Direct Clutch	1.853 (47.07)
Oil Pump Body	1.503 (38.18)
Oil Pump Stator	
Front Bushing	.849 (21.57)
Rear Bushing	1.066 (27.07)
OD Direct Clutch	.870 (22.09)
Planetary Ring Gear Flange	.749-.750 (19.03-19.05)
Stator Shaft	.849 (21.57)
Input Shaft End Play	.012-.035 (.30-.90)
Intermediate Shaft End Play	.019-.059 (.49-1.51)
Planetary Pinion Gear Clearance (All)	.008-.020 (.20-.50)
Oil Pump	
Driven Gear-To-Body Clearance	.003-.006 (.07-.15)
Driven Gear Tip-To-Cresent Clearance	.004-.006 (.11-.15)
Gears Side Clearance	.0008-.0020 (.020-.050)
Piston Stroke	
Direct Clutch	.044-.057 (1.11-1.44)
Forward Clutch	.056-.072 (1.41-1.82)
2nd Coast Brake	.059-.118 (1.50-3.00)
OD Direct Clutch	.048-.075 (1.21-1.91)
Side Gear Backlash	.002-.008 (.05-.20)
Torque Converter Runout (Maximum)	
Drive Plate	.008 (.20)
Sleeve	.012 (.30)

Camry, Celica

APPLICATION

APPLICATION

Vehicle	Transaxle Model
Camry DX, LE & XLE	A-140E
Celica GT	A-140E

CAUTION: All models are equipped with a Supplemental Restraint System (SRS). When servicing vehicle, use care to avoid accidental air bag deployment. All SRS electrical connections and wiring harness are covered by Yellow insulation. SRS-related components are located in steering column, center console, instrument panel and lower panel on instrument panel. DO NOT use electrical test equipment on these circuits. If necessary, deactivate SRS before servicing components. See AIR BAG SERVICING article in APPLICATIONS & IDENTIFICATION section.

DESCRIPTION

The A-140E automatic transaxle is electronically controlled. Transaxle shifting and torque converter lock-up are controlled by an Electronic Controlled Transmission (ECT) Electronic Control Unit (ECU). Control unit is referred to as the ECT ECU. ECT ECU is combined with engine ECU into one unit.

ECT ECU receives information from various input devices and uses this information to control No. 1 and No. 2 solenoids for transaxle shifting and lock-up solenoid (also called SL solenoid) for torque converter lock-up.

On Camry, a pattern select switch is located on center console. *See Figs. 1 and 2.* Pattern select switch contains a POWER (depressed) and a NORMAL (released) operating position. When pattern select switch is depressed, transaxle upshifts and downshifts will occur at a higher vehicle speed than with switch released. An indicator light will indicate pattern select switch position.

An Overdrive (OD) switch is mounted on the shift lever. *See Figs. 1-4.* When OD switch is depressed to ON position, transaxle will shift into 4th gear when shift lever is in "D" position, and OD OFF light on instrument panel will go off. When OD switch is released to OFF position, transaxle will shift into 3rd gear, and OD OFF light will illuminate.

Transaxle is equipped with a shift lock and key lock system. Shift lock system prevents shift lever from being moved from Park unless brake pedal is depressed. In case of a malfunction, shift lever can be released by depressing shift lock override button, located near shift lever. Key lock system prevents ignition key from being moved from ACC to LOCK position on ignition switch unless shift lever is in Park. For more information on shift lock and key lock system, see TOYOTA SHIFT LOCK SYSTEM article.

OPERATION

ECT ECU

ECT ECU receives information from various input devices and uses this information to control No. 1, No. 2 and lock-up solenoids (also called SL solenoid). ECT ECU contains a self-diagnostic system, which will store a Diagnostic Trouble Code (DTC) if failure or problem exists in the electronic control system.

DTC can be retrieved to determine transaxle problem area. See SELF-DIAGNOSTIC SYSTEM. ECT ECU is located near glove box on Camry models and behind center console on Celica models. *See Figs. 1-4.*

ECT ECU INPUT DEVICES

Pattern Select Switch (Camry) – Pattern select switch delivers an input signal to ECT ECU to indicate transaxle shift points selected by vehicle operator. Pattern select switch is located near shift lever. *See Figs. 1 and 2.*

Park/Neutral Position Switch – Park/Neutral position switch delivers an input signal to ECT ECU to indicate shift lever position. Park/Neutral position switch is located on side of transaxle. *See Figs. 1-4.*

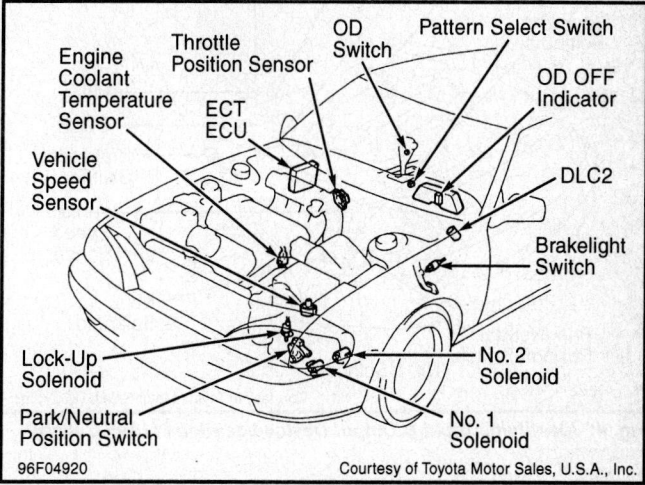

Fig. 1: Identifying Input & Output Device Locations (1995 Camry)

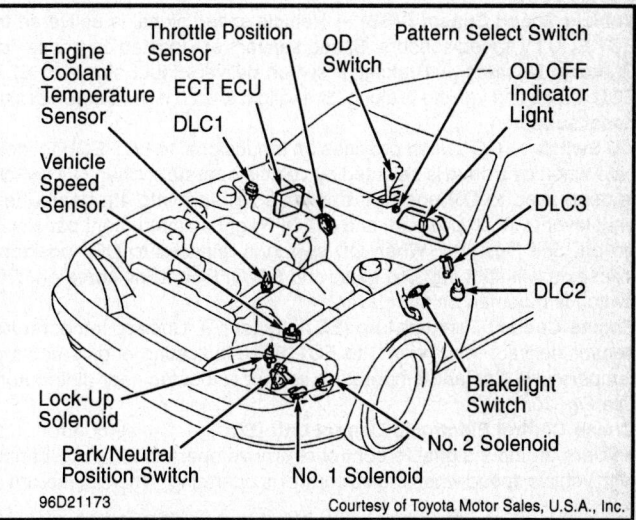

Fig. 2: Identifying Input & Output Device Locations (1996 Camry)

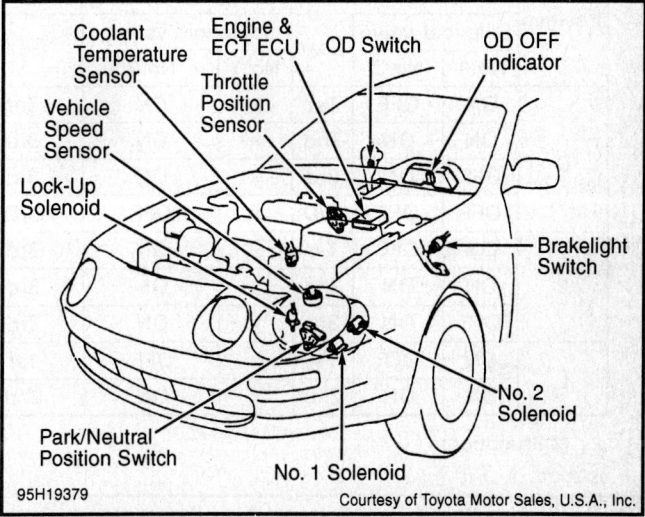

Fig. 3: Identifying Input & Output Device Locations (1995 Celica)

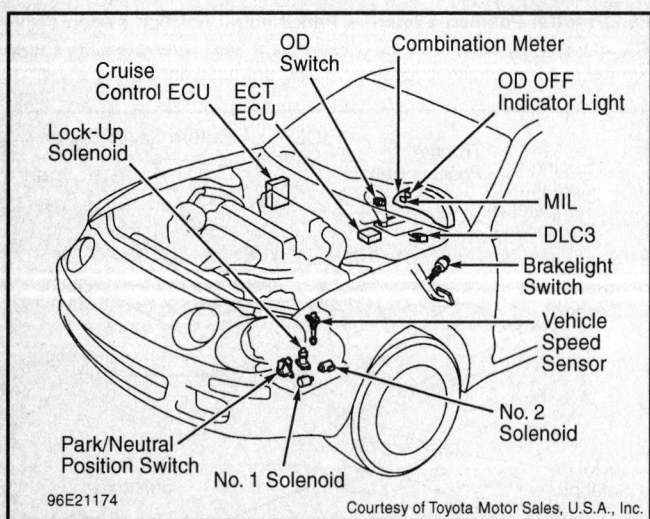

96E21174   Courtesy of Toyota Motor Sales, U.S.A., Inc.

Fig. 4: Identifying Input & Output Device Locations (1996 Celica)

Throttle Position (TP) Sensor – TP sensor delivers an input signal to ECT ECU indicating throttle position. TP sensor is located on side of throttle body.

Vehicle Speed Sensor (VSS) – Vehicle speed signal is delivered to ECT ECU by speed sensors. Speed sensors are located on transaxle.

Brakelight Switch – Brakelight switch delivers input signal to ECT ECU, indicating vehicle braking. Brakelight switch is located on brake pedal support.

OD Switch – OD switch provides an input signal to ECT ECU to indicate when overdrive is selected by vehicle operator. When OD switch is depressed to ON position, transaxle will shift into 4th gear when shift lever is in "D" position, and OD OFF light on instrument panel will go off. See Figs. 1-4. When OD switch is released to OFF position, transaxle will shift into 3rd gear, and OD OFF light will come on. OD switch is mounted on shift lever.

Engine Coolant Temperature (ECT) Sensor – Coolant temperature sensor delivers input signal to ECT ECU, indicating engine coolant temperature. Coolant temperature sensor is located near distributor. See Fig. 20.

Cruise Control Electronic Control Unit (ECU) – Cruise control ECU delivers an input signal to control overdrive operation in accordance with vehicle speed when cruise control is operating. When in overdrive

with cruise control on, if vehicle speed drops 3 MPH less than set speed, overdrive is released to prevent reduction in vehicle speed. Once vehicle speed is more than set speed, overdrive is resumed. Cruise control ECU is located behind instrument panel on passenger side of vehicle.

ECT ECU OUTPUT DEVICES

No. 1 & No. 2 Solenoids – ECT ECU controls transaxle shifting by delivering an output signal to operate proper solenoid. Solenoids are located on transaxle valve body. See Figs. 1-4. Solenoids are operated in accordance with shift lever range. See Fig. 5. If a solenoid malfunctions, ECT ECU places transaxle in a designated gear. See Fig. 5.

NOTE: In some gears, ECT ECU provides a fail-safe system which places transaxle in a designated gear depending on which solenoid fails. In some gears, fail-safe system will not be activated and transaxle will be placed in specified gear. See Fig. 5.

Lock-Up Solenoid – ECT ECU controls torque converter lock-up by delivering an output signal to lock-up solenoid. Lock-up solenoid (also called SL solenoid) is activated when shift lever is in "D" position and vehicle is at specified speed. Lock-up solenoid is located on transaxle valve body.

SELF-DIAGNOSTIC SYSTEM

SYSTEM DIAGNOSIS

NOTE: Before testing transaxle, ensure fluid level is correct and throttle and shift cables are properly adjusted. Ensure engine starts with shift lever in Park and Neutral to ensure proper adjustment of park/neutral position switch. Transaxle must first be tested by checking for stored trouble codes. See RETRIEVING TROUBLE CODES.

ECT ECU monitors transaxle operation and contains a self-diagnostic system which stores trouble codes if transaxle electronic control system failure or problem exists. If a problem exists in No. 1 or No. 2 solenoids or speed sensors and trouble code is set, ECT ECU blinks OD OFF light on instrument panel to warn driver.

OD OFF light will not blink to warn driver if a problem exists or trouble code is stored for lock-up solenoid, or problem exists with brakelight switch or throttle position sensor signal.

Position	NORMAL			NO.1 SOLENOID MALFUNCTIONING			NO.2 SOLENOID MALFUNCTIONING			BOTH SOLENOIDS MALFUNCTIONING
	Solenoid valve		Gear	Solenoid valve		Gear	Solenoid valve		Gear	Gear when shift selector is manually operated
	No.1	No.2		No.1	No.2		No.1	No.2		
D	ON	OFF	1st	×	ON	3rd	ON	×	1st	O/D
	ON	ON	2nd	×	ON	3rd	OFF	×	O/D	O/D
	OFF	ON	3rd	×	ON	3rd	OFF	×	O/D	O/D
	OFF	OFF	O/D	×	OFF	O/D	OFF	×	O/D	O/D
2	ON	OFF	1st	×	ON	3rd	ON	×	1st	3rd
	ON	ON	2nd	×	ON	3rd	OFF	×	3rd	3rd
	OFF	ON	3rd	×	ON	3rd	OFF	×	3rd	3rd
L	ON	OFF	1st	×	OFF	1st	ON	×	1st	1st
	ON	ON	2nd	×	ON	2nd	ON	×	1st	1st

×: Malfunctions

96F21175   Courtesy of Toyota Motor Sales, U.S.A., Inc.

Fig. 5: Checking No. 1 & No. 2 Solenoid Operation

RETRIEVING TROUBLE CODES

NOTE: On 1995 models, trouble codes are a 2 digit code. See DIAGNOSTIC TROUBLE CODE (DTC) IDENTIFICATION (1995) table. Before retrieving trouble codes, ensure proper battery voltage exists for proper self-diagnosis system operation. Perform diagnostic circuit check before retrieving trouble codes to ensure proper operation of OD OFF light. See DIAGNOSTIC CIRCUIT CHECK.

NOTE: On 1996 models, trouble codes are a 4 digit code (OBD-II). See DIAGNOSTIC TROUBLE CODE (DTC) IDENTIFICATION (1996) table. Trouble codes can only be retrieved using scan tool connected to 16-pin Data Link Connector (DLC3). See Fig. 6. For DLC3 location, see Figs. 2 and 4. When trouble code is present, Malfunction Indicator Light (MIL), located on instrument panel will light. To retrieve trouble codes using scan tool, follow scan tool manufacturer's operating instructions.

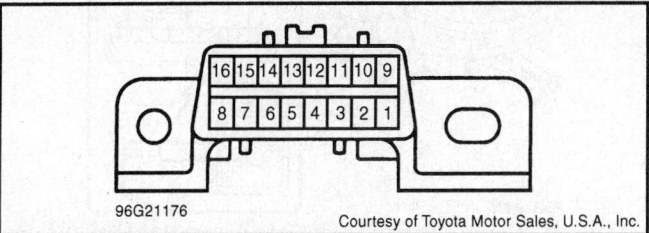

96G21176

Courtesy of Toyota Motor Sales, U.S.A., Inc.

Fig. 6: Identifying Data Link Connector (DLC3) Terminals (1996)

Diagnostic Circuit Check (1995) – 1) Turn ignition on. Release OD switch on shift lever to OFF position. Ensure OD OFF light on instrument panel turns on. If OD OFF light does not illuminate, check OD switch and wiring circuit.

2) Depress OD switch to ON position. Ensure OD OFF light goes off. If OD OFF light remains on, check OD switch and wiring circuit. If OD OFF light is blinking, check for stored trouble codes. See ECT ECU CODES.

ECT ECU Codes (1995) – 1) Turn ignition on. DO NOT start engine. Depress OD switch on shift lever to ON position.

NOTE: Codes can only be retrieved with OD switch on. If OD switch is off, OD OFF light will be on continuously and will not blink the code.

2) Install jumper wire between terminals TE₁ and E₁ of DLC1 or DLC2 connector. *See Figs. 7-9.*

3) Note number of flashes from OD OFF light on instrument panel. If normal system operation exists, OD OFF light will flash 2 times per second. *See Fig. 10.*

4) If system is operating correctly and no code exists, turn ignition off and remove jumper wire. Perform MANUAL SHIFT TEST to determine if problem is an electrical or mechanical transaxle problem.

5) If code exists, OD OFF light will blink once every .5 second. Number of blinks equals first digit of code. After a pause of 1.5 seconds, second digit will be displayed. *See Fig. 10.*

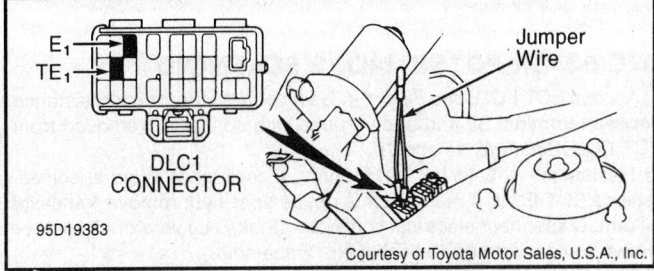

95D19383

Courtesy of Toyota Motor Sales, U.S.A., Inc.

Fig. 7: Identifying DLC1 Location (Camry – 1995)

6) If more than one code exists, next code will be displayed after pause of 2.5 seconds. *See Fig. 10.* Smallest number code will display first and system will progress to largest code. Codes will be repeated.

7) Once code is obtained, determine probable cause and symptom. See DIAGNOSTIC TROUBLE CODE (DTC) IDENTIFICATION (1995) table. For diagnosis and repair of trouble codes, see DIAGNOSTIC TESTS. Turn ignition off and remove jumper wire.

NOTE: Once repairs have been performed, codes must be cleared from ECT ECU memory. See CLEARING TROUBLE CODES under SELF-DIAGNOSTIC SYSTEM.

DIAGNOSTIC TROUBLE CODE (DTC) IDENTIFICATION (1995)

DTC	[1] Probable Cause
42	Vehicle Speed Sensor
62	No. 1 Solenoid
63	No. 2 Solenoid
64	[2] Lock-Up Solenoid

[1] – Check listed component for probable cause. Check wiring and connections of specified component.
[2] – Also called SL solenoid.

DIAGNOSTIC TROUBLE CODE (DTC) IDENTIFICATION (1996)

DTC	[1] Probable Cause
P0500	Vehicle Speed Sensor
P0750	[2] No. 1 Solenoid
P0753	No. 1 Solenoid Circuit Malfunction
P0755	[2] No. 2 Solenoid
P0758	No. 2 Solenoid Circuit Malfunction
P0770	[2][3] Lock-Up Solenoid
P0773	[3] Lock-Up Solenoid Circuit Malfunction
P1780	Park/Neutral Position Switch Malfunction

[1] – Check listed component for probable cause. Check wiring and connections of specified component.
[2] – To diagnose this DTC, see SOLENOIDS under COMPONENT TESTS.
[3] – Also called SL solenoid.

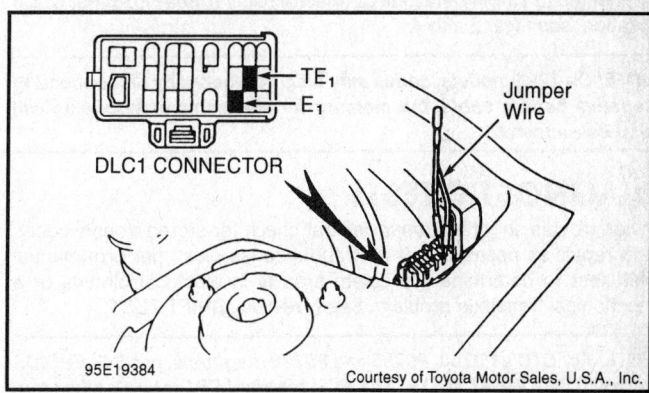

95E19384

Courtesy of Toyota Motor Sales, U.S.A., Inc.

Fig. 8: Identifying DLC1 Location (Celica – 1995)

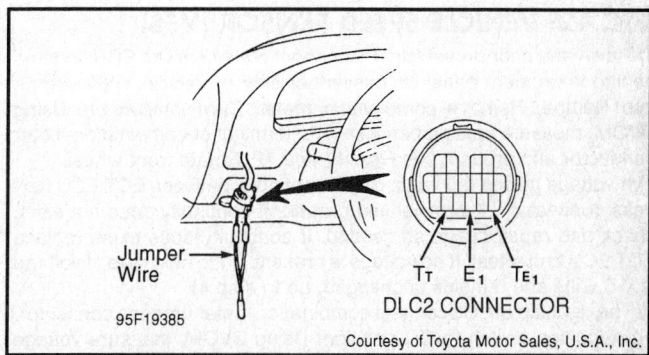

95F19385

Courtesy of Toyota Motor Sales, U.S.A., Inc.

Fig. 9: Identifying DLC2 Location (Camry – 1995)

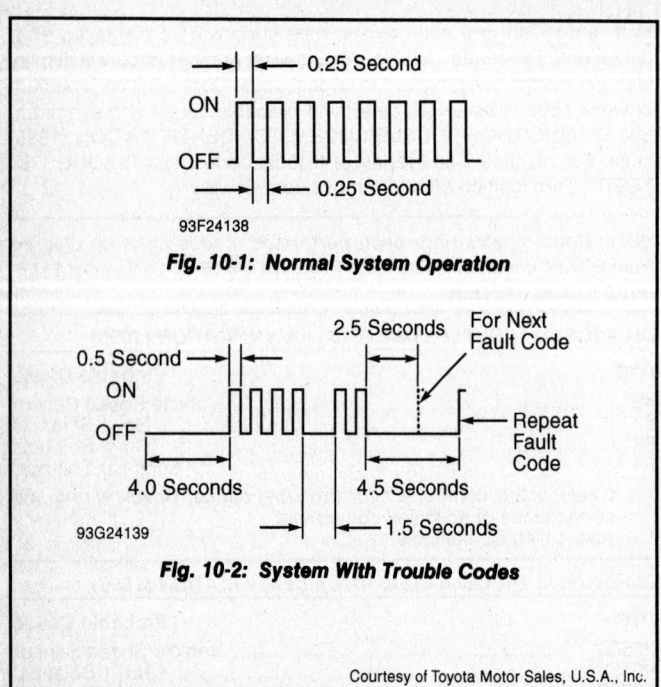

Fig. 10-1: *Normal System Operation*

Fig. 10-2: *System With Trouble Codes*

Courtesy of Toyota Motor Sales, U.S.A., Inc.

Fig. 10: Identifying Code Displays (1995)

CLEARING TROUBLE CODES

1995 Models – Once repairs have been performed, codes must be cleared from ECT ECU memory. Remove EFI fuse (15-amp) from engine compartment fuse box, near battery, for 10 seconds or more to clear memory in ECT ECU.

1996 Models – Trouble codes can only be cleared using scan tool connected to 16-pin Data Link Connector (DLC3). *See Fig. 6.* For DLC3 location, *see Figs. 2 and 4.*

NOTE: On 1995 models, codes may also be cleared by disconnecting negative battery cable, but memory for electronic components will also be canceled.

DIAGNOSTIC TESTS

When trouble shooting transaxle, first check for stored trouble codes and repair as necessary. If no trouble codes exist, perform manual shift test to determine if problem area is in electrical circuits or a mechanical transaxle problem. See MANUAL SHIFT TEST.

NOTE: For DTC's P0750, P0755 and P0770 diagnosis, see SOLENOIDS under COMPONENT TESTS. ECT ECU terminal SP1 may also be identified as terminal SPD in wiring diagrams.

DTC 42: VEHICLE SPEED SENSOR (VSS)

1) Raise and support vehicle. Disconnect cruise control ECU, located behind instrument panel on passenger side of vehicle. Shift vehicle into Neutral. Remove combination meter. Turn ignition on. Using DVOM, measure voltage between SP1 terminal of combination meter connector and ground. *See Figs. 11 and 12.* Rotate front wheel.

2) If voltage pulses 0-5 volts, check continuity between ECT ECU harness connector E1 terminal and ground. If continuity does not exist, check and repair circuit as needed. If continuity does exist, replace ECT ECU and retest. If no voltage is present, go to next step. If voltage is 4-6 volts and remains unchanged, go to step **4)**.

3) Turn ignition off. Disconnect combination meter harness connector. Turn ignition switch to ON position. Using DVOM, measure voltage between ECT ECU harness connector terminals SP1 and E1. *See Figs.*

15 and 16. If voltage is 4-6 volts, check and repair wiring harness or connector between combination meter and ECT ECU. If voltage is not 4-6 volts, replace ECT ECU and retest.

4) Check continuity of 2 circuits between combination meter and VSS. See appropriate wiring diagram in WIRING DIAGRAMS. If continuity does not exist, check and repair circuit(s) as needed. If continuity exists, inspect VSS. See VEHICLE SPEED SENSOR under COMPONENT TESTS. Replace as needed. If VSS is okay, go to next step.

5) Disconnect VSS harness connector. Turn ignition on. Measure voltage between VSS harness connector terminal No. 1 (Red/Blue wire) and ground. If battery voltage is not present, inspect and repair circuit as needed. If battery voltage is present, replace combination meter and retest.

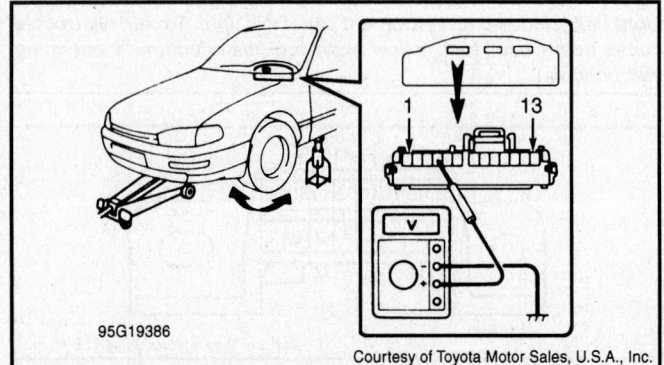

Courtesy of Toyota Motor Sales, U.S.A., Inc.

Fig. 11: Identifying Combination Meter Harness Connector (Camry)

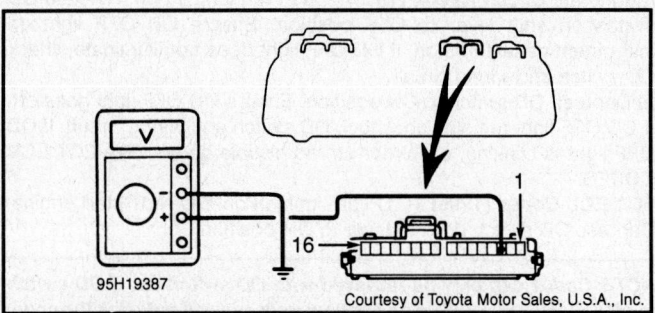

Courtesy of Toyota Motor Sales, U.S.A., Inc.

Fig. 12: Identifying Combination Meter Harness Connector (Celica)

DTC 62 OR P0753: NO. 1 SOLENOID

1) Access ECT ECU. *See Figs. 1-4.* Using ohmmeter, check resistance between terminal S1 and body ground with connector removed from ECT ECU. *See Figs. 15 and 16.*

2) Resistance should be 11-15 ohms. If resistance is as specified, replace ECT ECU. If resistance is not as specified, remove transaxle oil pan. Disconnect electrical connector (Violet wire) at No. 1 solenoid.

3) Check resistance between electrical terminal on No. 1 solenoid and body ground. Replace No. 1 solenoid if resistance is not 11-15 ohms. If resistance is 11-15 ohms, check and repair wiring between No. 1 solenoid and ECT ECU.

DTC 63 OR P0758: NO. 2 SOLENOID

1) Access ECT ECU. *See Figs. 1-4.* Using ohmmeter, check resistance between terminal S2 and body ground with connector removed from ECT ECU. *See Figs. 15 and 16.*

2) Resistance should be 11-15 ohms. If resistance is as specified, replace ECT ECU. If resistance is not as specified, remove transaxle oil pan. Disconnect electrical connector (Pink/Blue wire on Camry, or Brown/Yellow wire on Celica) at No. 2 solenoid.

3) Check resistance between electrical terminal on No. 2 solenoid and body ground. Replace No. 2 solenoid if resistance is not 11-15 ohms. If resistance is 11-15 ohms, check and repair wiring between No. 2 solenoid and ECT ECU.

DTC 64 OR P0773: LOCK-UP SOLENOID

1) Access ECT ECU. *See Figs. 1-4.* Using ohmmeter, check resistance between terminal SL and body ground with connector removed from ECT ECU. *See Figs. 15 and 16.*

2) Resistance should be 11-15 ohms. If resistance is as specified, replace ECT ECU. If resistance is not as specified, remove transaxle oil pan. Disconnect electrical connector (Blue/Yellow wire on Camry or Yellow/Black wire on Celica) at lock-up solenoid.

3) Check resistance between electrical terminal on lock-up solenoid and body ground. Replace lock-up solenoid if resistance is not 11-15 ohms. If resistance is 11-15 ohms, check and repair wiring between lock-up solenoid and ECT ECU.

DTC P0500: VEHICLE SPEED SENSOR (VSS)

1) Raise and support vehicle. Disconnect cruise control ECU, located behind instrument panel on passenger side of vehicle. Shift vehicle into Neutral. Remove combination meter. Turn ignition on. Using DVOM, backprobe between SP1 terminal of ECT ECU harness connector and ground. *See Figs. 15 and 16.* Rotate front wheel.

2) If voltage pulses between 4.5-5.5 volts, check continuity between ECT ECU harness connector E1 terminal and ground. If continuity does not exist, check and repair circuit as needed. If continuity does exist, replace ECT ECU and retest. If voltage is not as specified, check and repair wiring harness or connector between combination meter and ECT ECU. For VSS testing, see VEHICLE SPEED SENSOR under COMPONENT TESTS.

DTC P1780: PARK/NEUTRAL POSITION SWITCH

1) Access ECT ECU. *See Figs. 2 and 4.* Turn ignition switch to ON position. Using DVOM, measure voltage at terminals NSW, "2" and "L" of ECT ECU harness connector between terminal and body ground with gear selector in each shift position. *See Figs. 15 and 16.*

2) Ensure 9-14 volts is present at NSW terminal at ECT ECU harness connector in all shift positions. Ensure 9-14 volts is present at "2" and "L" terminals at ECT ECU harness connector with gear selector in "2" and "L" position. If voltage is not as specified, check park/neutral position switch. See PARK/NEUTRAL POSITION SWITCH under COMPONENT TESTS.

MANUAL SHIFT TEST

NOTE: Perform manual shift test if no trouble codes exist. Manual shift test determines if problem is in electrical circuits or is a mechanical transaxle problem.

1) Ensure ignition is off. Disconnect electrical connectors from solenoids on transaxle. Electrical connectors are located near park/neutral position switch on transaxle.

2) Road test vehicle and ensure transaxle gear changes corresponds with shift lever position. See GEAR APPLICATION table. If abnormality exists, a mechanical transaxle problem may exist. Turn ignition off.

3) Reconnect all electrical connectors. Clear trouble codes from ECT ECU memory, as disconnecting electrical connectors will set a trouble code. See CLEARING TROUBLE CODES under SELF-DIAGNOSTIC SYSTEM.

GEAR APPLICATION

Shift Lever Position	Gear
"D"	Overdrive
"2"	3rd
"L"	1st
"R"	Reverse
"P"	Park

TORQUE CONVERTER

LOCK-UP TEST

NOTE: Refer to appropriate SHIFT SPEED SPECIFICATION table in TOYOTA A-140E overhaul article for lock-up shift speed.

Road test vehicle. Increase vehicle speed until lock-up should occur. To confirm lock-up operation, very lightly depress brake pedal with left foot and release while maintaining constant speed. Monitor vehicle tachometer. Transaxle should downshift into 3rd gear and then upshift into lock-up once brake pedal is released.

CIRCUIT TESTS

THROTTLE POSITION (TP) SENSOR SIGNAL

1) Connect voltmeter between terminals T_T and E_1 of DLC connector. *See Figs. 7-9.* Turn ignition on. Note that voltage gradually increases as accelerator is depressed. Voltage should gradually increase to about 8 volts with throttle fully open.

2) If voltage does not increase as throttle is opened, check throttle position sensor. See THROTTLE POSITION (TP) SENSOR under COMPONENT TESTS. If throttle position sensor is okay, check circuit(s) between TP sensor and ECT ECU. See appropriate wiring diagram in WIRING DIAGRAMS.

BRAKELIGHT SIGNAL

1) Connect voltmeter between terminals T_T and E_1 of DLC connector. *See Figs. 7-9.* Depress accelerator pedal until 8 volts exists. Hold brake pedal and note that voltage decreases to zero voltage. Release brake pedal and note that voltage increases to 8 volts.

2) If voltage is not as specified, check brakelight switch. See BRAKELIGHT SWITCH under COMPONENT TESTS. If brakelight switch is okay, check circuit between brakelight switch and ECT ECU.

GEAR SELECTOR SIGNAL

1) Warm engine to normal operating temperature. Place pattern select switch in NORMAL position (if equipped). Depress OD switch, mounted on shift lever, to ON position.

2) Connect voltmeter between terminals T_T and E_1 of DLC2 connector on Camry or DLC1 connector on Celica. *See Figs. 8 and 9.*

3) On all models, road test vehicle with shift lever in "D" position and vehicle speed greater than 6 MPH. Voltage should increase as specified in accordance with transaxle gear position. See GEAR SIGNAL VOLTAGE table.

4) If voltages are as specified, electronic control system is operating correctly. If voltages are not as specified, further diagnosis must be performed. Inspect throttle position sensor, brakelight switch, park/neutral position switch and/or T_T circuit.

GEAR SIGNAL VOLTAGE

Gear Position	Voltage
1st	Less Than .5
2nd	1.5-2.6
2nd With Lock-Up	2.5-3.6
3rd	3.5-4.6
3rd With Lock-Up	4.5-5.6
Overdrive	5.5-6.6
Overdrive With Lock-Up	6.5-7.6

OVERDRIVE CANCEL SIGNAL

1) Access ECT ECU. *See Figs. 1-4.* Turn ignition on. Measure voltage (backprobe) between terminal OD1 of ECT ECU harness connector and ground. If 9-14 volts is present, substitute known good ECT ECU and retest. If voltage is not as specified, go to next step.

2) Turn ignition off. Disconnect cruise control ECU harness connector. *See Figs. 13 and 14.* Turn ignition on. Measure voltage between terminal OD and ground. *See Figs. 13 and 14.* If 9-14 volts is present, replace cruise control ECU and retest. If 9-14 volts is not present, check and repair circuit between cruise control ECU and ECT ECU.

AUTOMATIC TRANSMISSIONS
Toyota A-140E Electronic Controls (Cont.)

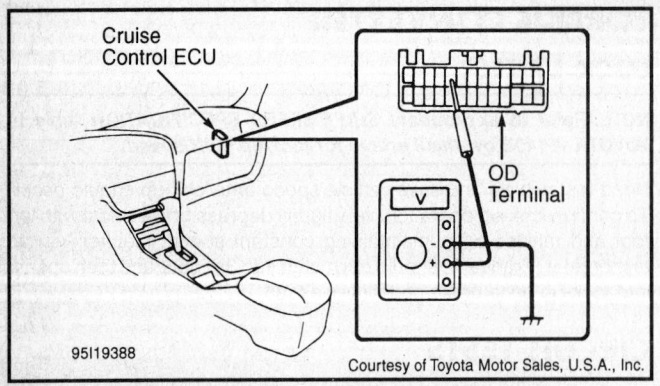

Fig. 13: Identifying Cruise Control ECU Terminals (Camry)

95I19388
Courtesy of Toyota Motor Sales, U.S.A., Inc.

95J19389
Courtesy of Toyota Motor Sales, U.S.A., Inc.

Fig. 14: Identifying Cruise Control ECU Terminals (Celica)

ECT ECU VOLTAGES

Access ECT ECU. See Figs. 1-4. Turn ignition on. Using voltmeter, backprobe ECT ECU harness connector. Check voltage between selected terminal and terminal E_1 or E_2. Voltage should be as specified. See Figs. 15 and 16.

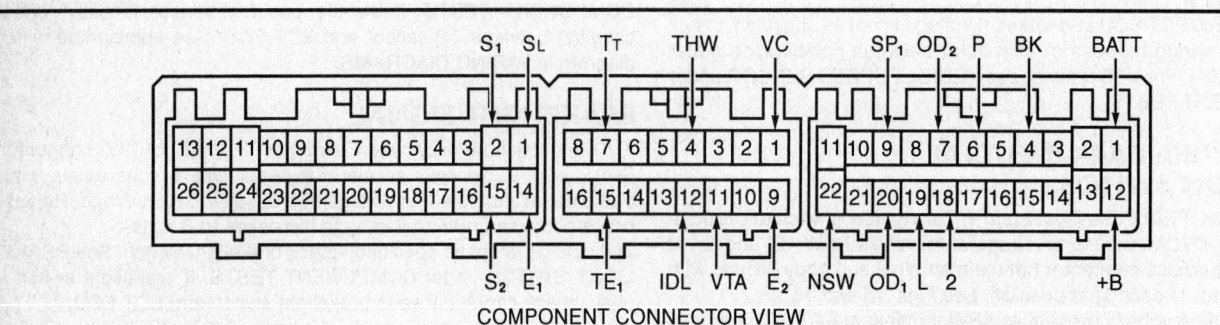

COMPONENT CONNECTOR VIEW

	Terminal ID.	Function/Description	Voltage Value (DC Volts Unless Otherwise Specified)
Violet	S_1	No. 1 Solenoid	9-14 Volts With KOEO [1]
Pink/Blue	S_2	No. 2 Solenoid	1 Volt Or Less With KOEO [1]
Blue/Yellow	S_L	Lock-Up Solenoid	1 Volt Or Less With KOEO [1]
Blue/Red	P	Pattern Select Switch Signal	9-14 Volts In PWR Position
Green/White	B/K	Brakelight Switch Signal	9-14 Volts With Pedal Depressed
Green	THW	Coolant Temperature Sensor Signal	.1-1.0 Volts @ 176°F (80°C)
Blue	IDL	Closed Throttle Sensor Signal	1 Volt Or Less With Throttle Closed
Black	VTA	Throttle Position Sensor Output Signal	3.0-5.5 Volts With Throttle Fully Open
Yellow/Black	OD_1	OD Output To Cruise Control ECU	9-14 Volts With KOEO [1]
Green/Orange	OD_2	Overdrive Switch Signal	9-14 Volts With Switch On
Violet/Yellow	SP_1	Vehicle Speed Sensor Signal	1 Volt Or Less With ECU Unplugged [2] (Car Parked)
Black/White	NSW	Ignition Switch (ST1) Signal	9-14 Volts In "P" Or "N", KOEO [1]
Orange	2	Park/Neutral Position Switch "2" Signal	9-14 Volts In "2", KOEO [1]
Yellow/Blue	L	Park/Neutral Position Switch "L" Signal	9-14 Volts In "L", KOEO [1]
Black/Orange	+B	EFI Main Relay Power Supply	9-14 Volts With KOEO [1]
White/Green	BATT	Power Supply Voltage	9-14 Volts (Constant)
Brown	E_1	Ground	Not Applicable
Brown	E_2	Ground	Not Applicable

[1] – Key On, Engine Off.
[2] – Disconnect cruise control ECU harness connector.

96H21177
Courtesy of Toyota Motor Sales, U.S.A., Inc.

Fig. 15: ECT ECU Pin Voltage Table (1995-96 Camry)

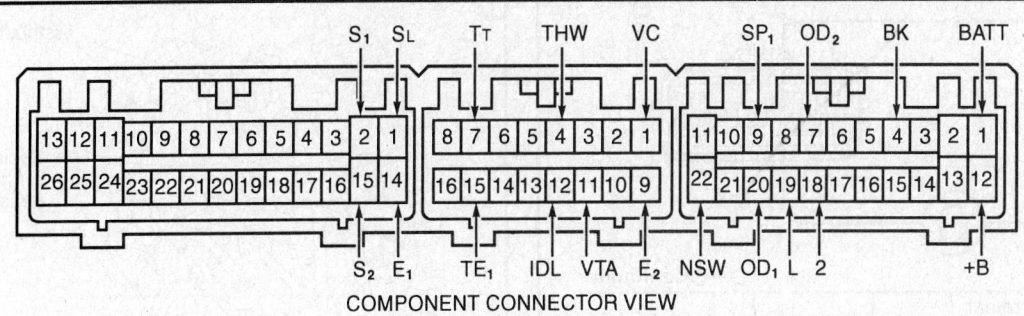

COMPONENT CONNECTOR VIEW

	Terminal ID.	Function/Description	Voltage Value (DC Volts Unless Otherwise Specified)
Violet	S_1	No. 1 Solenoid	9-14 Volts With KOEO [1]
Brown/Yellow	S_2	No. 2 Solenoid	1 Volt Or Less With KOEO [1]
Yellow/Black	S_L	Lock-Up Solenoid	1 Volt Or Less With KOEO [1]
Green/White	B/K	Brakelight Switch Signal	9-14 Volts With Pedal Depressed
Green	THW	Coolant Temperature Sensor Signal	.1-1.0 Volts @ 176°F (80°C)
Blue/White	IDL	Closed Throttle Sensor Signal	1 Volt Or Less With Throttle Closed
Black/White	VTA	Throttle Position Sensor Output Signal	3.0-5.5 Volts With Throttle Fully Open
Pink	OD_1	OD Output To Cruise Control ECU	9-14 Volts With KOEO [1]
Gray/Blue	OD_2	Overdrive Switch Signal	9-14 Volts With Switch On
Orange	SP_1	Vehicle Speed Sensor Signal	1 Volt Or Less With ECU Unplugged [2] (Car Parked)
Black/Yellow	NSW	Ignition Switch (ST1) Signal	9-14 Volts In "P" Or "N", KOEO [1]
Violet/Green	2	Park/Neutral Position Switch "2" Signal	9-14 Volts In "2", KOEO [1]
Violet/Red	L	Park/Neutral Position Switch "L" Signal	9-14 Volts In "L", KOEO [1]
Black/Yellow	+B	EFI Main Relay Power Supply	9-14 Volts With KOEO [1]
Pink	BATT	Power Supply Voltage	9-14 Volts (Constant)
Brown	E_1	Ground	Not Applicable
Brown	E_2	Ground	Not Applicable

[1] – Key On, Engine Off.
[2] – Disconnect cruise control ECU harness connector.

96I21178

Courtesy of Toyota Motor Sales, U.S.A., Inc.

Fig. 16: ECT ECU Pin Voltage Table (1995-96 Celica)

COMPONENT TESTS

SOLENOIDS

NOTE: The following information can also be used to diagnose DTC's P0750, P0755 and P0770.

1) Access ECT ECU. See Figs. 1-4. Ensure ignition is off. Disconnect ECT ECU harness connector. Using ohmmeter, measure resistance between S_L, S_1 and S_2 terminal and ground for appropriate solenoid. *See Figs. 15 and 16.*
2) Replace solenoid if resistance is not 11-15 ohms. To check solenoid operation, apply battery voltage to S_L, S_1 or S_2 terminal of ECT ECU harness connector for appropriate solenoid. Ensure operating sound can be heard when battery voltage is connected. Replace solenoid if operating sound cannot be heard.
3) To check solenoid seals, remove suspect solenoid. Connect battery voltage to solenoid. Apply 71 psi (5 kg/cm²) to solenoid with battery voltage connected. *See Fig. 17.*
4) With battery voltage applied, air should pass through No. 1 and 2 solenoids. Disconnect voltage to solenoid. Ensure air does not pass through solenoid. Replace solenoid if defective.

5) With battery voltage applied, air should not pass through lock-up solenoid. Disconnect voltage to solenoid. Ensure air passes through solenoid. Replace solenoid if defective.

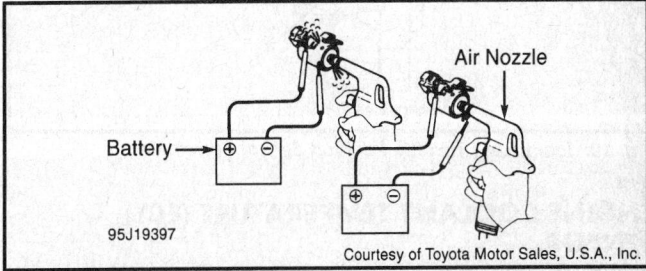

95J19397

Courtesy of Toyota Motor Sales, U.S.A., Inc.

Fig. 17: Checking Solenoids

PARK/NEUTRAL POSITION (PNP) SWITCH

Disconnect harness connector at park/neutral position switch. Switch is located on side of transaxle. Using ohmmeter, check for continuity between specified terminals in accordance with shift lever position. *See Figs. 18.* Replace PNP switch if continuity is not as specified.

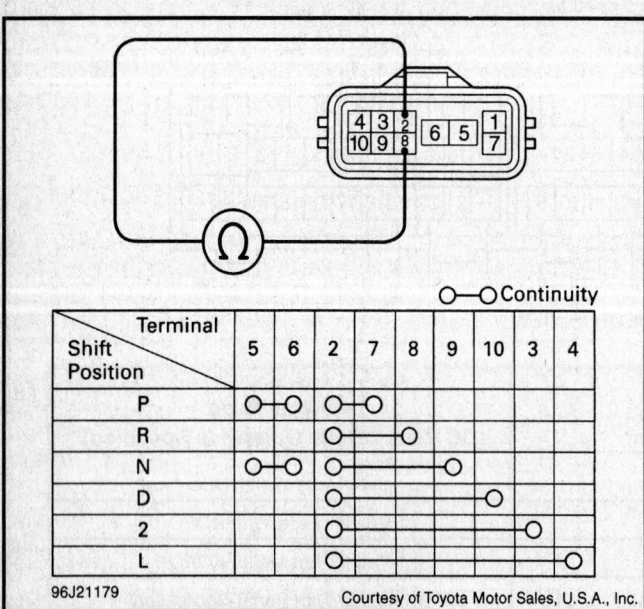

Terminal Shift Position	5	6	2	7	8	9	10	3	4
P	O—O		O—O						
R			O	O					
N	O—O		O			O			
D			O						
2			O				O		
L			O						O

O—O Continuity

96J21179   Courtesy of Toyota Motor Sales, U.S.A., Inc.

Fig. 18: Testing Park/Neutral Position Switch

THROTTLE POSITION (TP) SENSOR

Disconnect harness connector at throttle position sensor, located on side of throttle body. Using ohmmeter, check resistance between specified terminals in relation to throttle position. See Fig. 19. See THROTTLE POSITION SENSOR RESISTANCE SPECIFICATIONS table. Replace throttle position sensor if resistance is not as specified.

THROTTLE POSITION SENSOR RESISTANCE SPECIFICATIONS

Terminals	Ohms
IDL & E_2	
Throttle Fully Closed	2300 Or Less
Throttle Fully Open	Infinity
V_C & E_2	2500-5900
V_{TA} & E_2	
Throttle Fully Closed	200-5700
Throttle Fully Open	2000-10,200

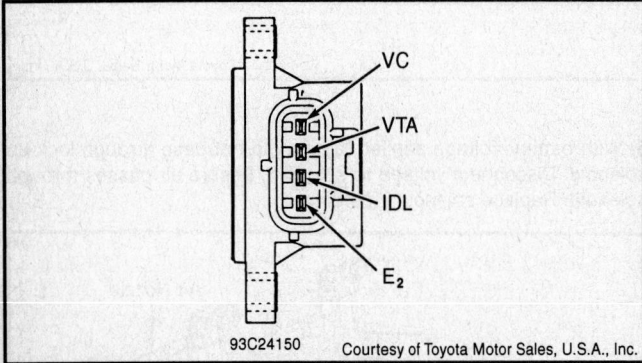

93C24150   Courtesy of Toyota Motor Sales, U.S.A., Inc.

Fig. 19: Identifying Throttle Position Sensor Terminals

ENGINE COOLANT TEMPERATURE (ECT) SENSOR

Disconnect electrical connector from ECT. ECT is located in coolant passage on rear of engine. See Fig. 20. Using ohmmeter, check resistance between terminals of coolant temperature sensor. Resistance should be as specified in accordance with coolant temperature. See Fig. 21. Replace sensor if resistance is not within specification.

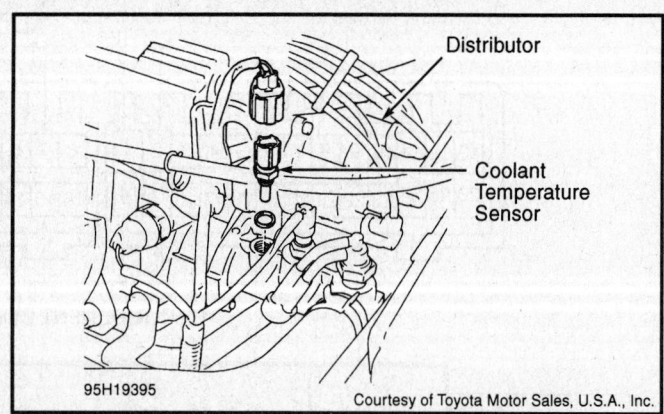

95H19395   Courtesy of Toyota Motor Sales, U.S.A., Inc.

Fig. 20: Locating Engine Coolant Temperature (ECT) Sensor

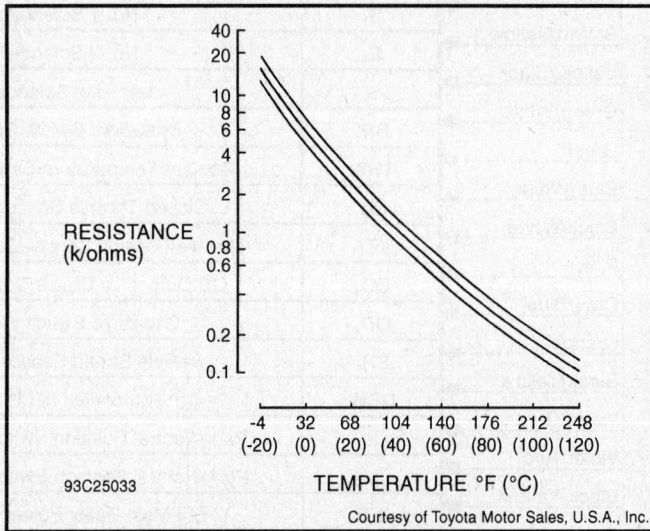

93C25033   Courtesy of Toyota Motor Sales, U.S.A., Inc.

Fig. 21: Checking Engine Coolant Temperature Sensor

VEHICLE SPEED SENSOR (VSS)

1) Disconnect electrical connector from VSS, located on top of transaxle. See Figs. 1-4. Connect positive battery lead to terminal No. 1 and negative lead to terminal No. 2. Connect positive lead of voltmeter to terminal No. 3 and negative lead to terminal No. 2. See Fig. 22.
2) Rotate speedometer cable shaft on speed sensor. Ensure voltage changes from zero to 11 volts. Voltage should change 4 times per each revolution of speedometer cable shaft. Replace speed sensor if voltage does not change as specified.

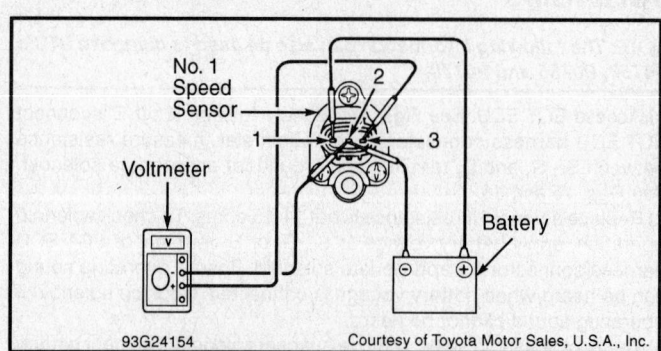

93G24154   Courtesy of Toyota Motor Sales, U.S.A., Inc.

Fig. 22: Checking Vehicle Speed Sensor

PATTERN SELECT SWITCH (CAMRY)

Disconnect electrical connector from pattern select switch. *See Fig. 23.* Using ohmmeter, ensure continuity exists between terminals No. 3 and 6 with switch in PWR position. No continuity should exist in NORM position.

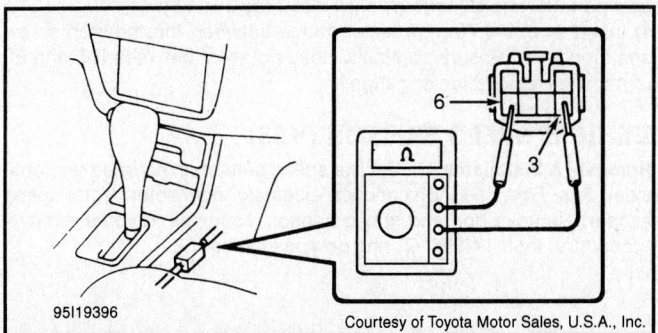

95I19396   Courtesy of Toyota Motor Sales, U.S.A., Inc.

Fig. 23: Identifying Pattern Select Switch Terminals (Camry)

OVERDRIVE (OD) SWITCH

Disconnect electrical connector from OD switch, located on shift lever. Using ohmmeter, ensure continuity exists between terminals No. 1 and 3 on Camry, or terminals No. 2 and 4 on Celica, with switch released (OFF position). *See Fig. 24.* Ensure no continuity exists with switch depressed (ON position). Replace switch if defective.

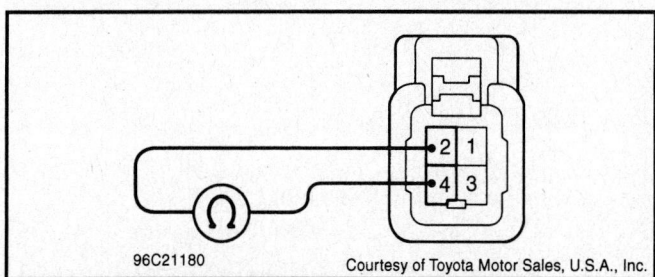

96C21180   Courtesy of Toyota Motor Sales, U.S.A., Inc.

Fig. 24: Identifying Overdrive (OD) Switch Terminals

BRAKELIGHT SWITCH

Disconnect electrical connector from brakelight switch, located near brake pedal. Using ohmmeter, ensure continuity exists between switch terminals No. 1 and 2 with brake pedal depressed. *See Fig. 25.* Continuity should exist between terminals No. 3 and 4 with pedal released. Replace switch if continuity is not as specified.

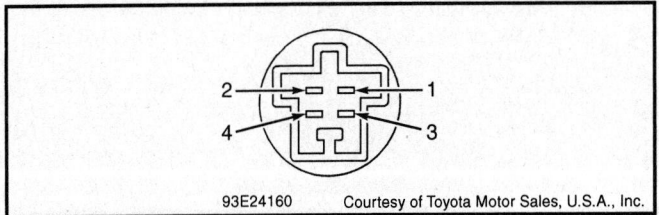

93E24160   Courtesy of Toyota Motor Sales, U.S.A., Inc.

Fig. 25: Identifying Brakelight Switch Terminals

REMOVAL & INSTALLATION

BRAKELIGHT SWITCH

Removal & Installation – 1) Disconnect electrical connector. Remove lock nut, and unscrew brakelight switch. To install, screw brakelight switch inward until brakelight plunger contacts brake pedal.

2) Unscrew brakelight switch one revolution. Ensure distance between threaded end of brakelight switch and brake pedal is .02-.09" (.5-2.4 mm). Install and tighten lock nut on brakelight switch. Install electrical connector. Ensure brakelights and cruise control operate properly.

ENGINE COOLANT TEMPERATURE (ECT) SENSOR

Removal & Installation – Coolant temperature sensor is located in coolant passage near distributor. *See Fig. 20.* Drain cooling system. Remove coolant temperature sensor. To install, reverse removal procedure. Fill cooling system.

NO. 1 & NO. 2 SOLENOIDS

Removal & Installation – Solenoids are located on transaxle valve body. Remove oil pan. Remove bolt, solenoid and "O" ring from valve body. To install, reverse removal procedure using NEW "O" ring.

LOCK-UP SOLENOID

Removal & Installation – Solenoid is located on transaxle valve body. Remove oil pan. Remove bolt, solenoid and "O" ring from transaxle. body. To install, reverse removal procedure using NEW "O" ring.

PARK/NEUTRAL POSITION (PNP) SWITCH

Removal – 1) Park/neutral position switch is located on side of transaxle. Remove lock nut, washer and manual lever from control shaft. *See Fig. 26.*

2) Bend up tabs on lock washer. Remove lock nut, lock washer and seal from control shaft. Remove retaining bolts and park/neutral position switch.

Installation – 1) Install switch on control shaft. Loosely install park/neutral position switch retaining bolts. Install seal and lock washer. Install lock nut and tighten to 62 INCH lbs. (7 N.m). Bend tabs on lock washer over against lock nut.

2) Ensure parking brake is applied. Temporarily install manual lever on control shaft. Place shift lever in Neutral. Remove manual lever. Rotate switch and align reference mark on switch with groove. *See Fig. 26.* Hold switch in this position. Tighten retaining bolts to 48 INCH lbs. (5 N.m). To install remaining components, reverse removal procedure.

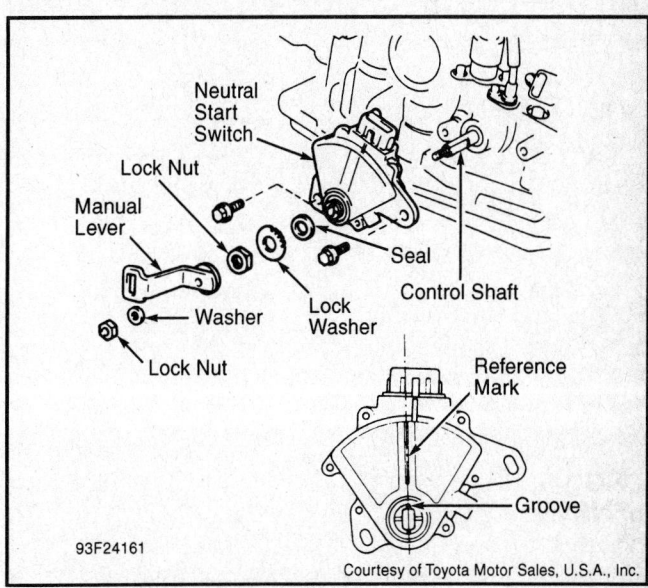

93F24161   Courtesy of Toyota Motor Sales, U.S.A., Inc.

Fig. 26: Removing & Installing PNP Switch

OVERDRIVE (OD) SWITCH

Overdrive (OD) switch is mounted on shift lever. *See Figs. 1-4.* Replacement information not available from manufacturer.

PATTERN SELECT SWITCH (CAMRY)

Pattern select switch is located on center console. *See Figs. 1 and 2.* Replacement information not available from manufacturer.

THROTTLE POSITION (TP) SENSOR

Removal – Ensure ignition is off. Disconnect electrical connector from TP sensor. TP sensor is located on throttle body. Remove screws and TP sensor.

Installation – 1) Install TP sensor on throttle body with screws loosely installed. Connect ohmmeter leads to IDL and E2 terminals of TP sensor. *See Fig. 19.*

2) Apply vacuum to throttle opener on throttle body. Insert a .024" (.60 mm) feeler gauge between throttle stop screw and stop lever. Gradually rotate TP sensor until ohmmeter indicates a reading and tighten retaining screws.

3) Remove feeler gauge. Insert a .020" (.50 mm) feeler gauge between throttle stop screw and stop lever. Ensure continuity now exists between IDL and E2 terminals. Remove feeler gauge.

4) Insert a .028" (.70 mm) feeler gauge between throttle stop screw and stop lever. Ensure continuity does not exist between IDL and E2 terminals. Remove feeler gauge.

VEHICLE SPEED SENSOR (VSS)

Removal & Installation – Vehicle speed sensor is mounted on transaxle. *See Figs. 1-4.* Disconnect electrical connector from speed sensor. Remove bolt and speed sensor. To install, reverse removal procedure. Install NEW "O" ring on speed sensor.

WIRING DIAGRAMS

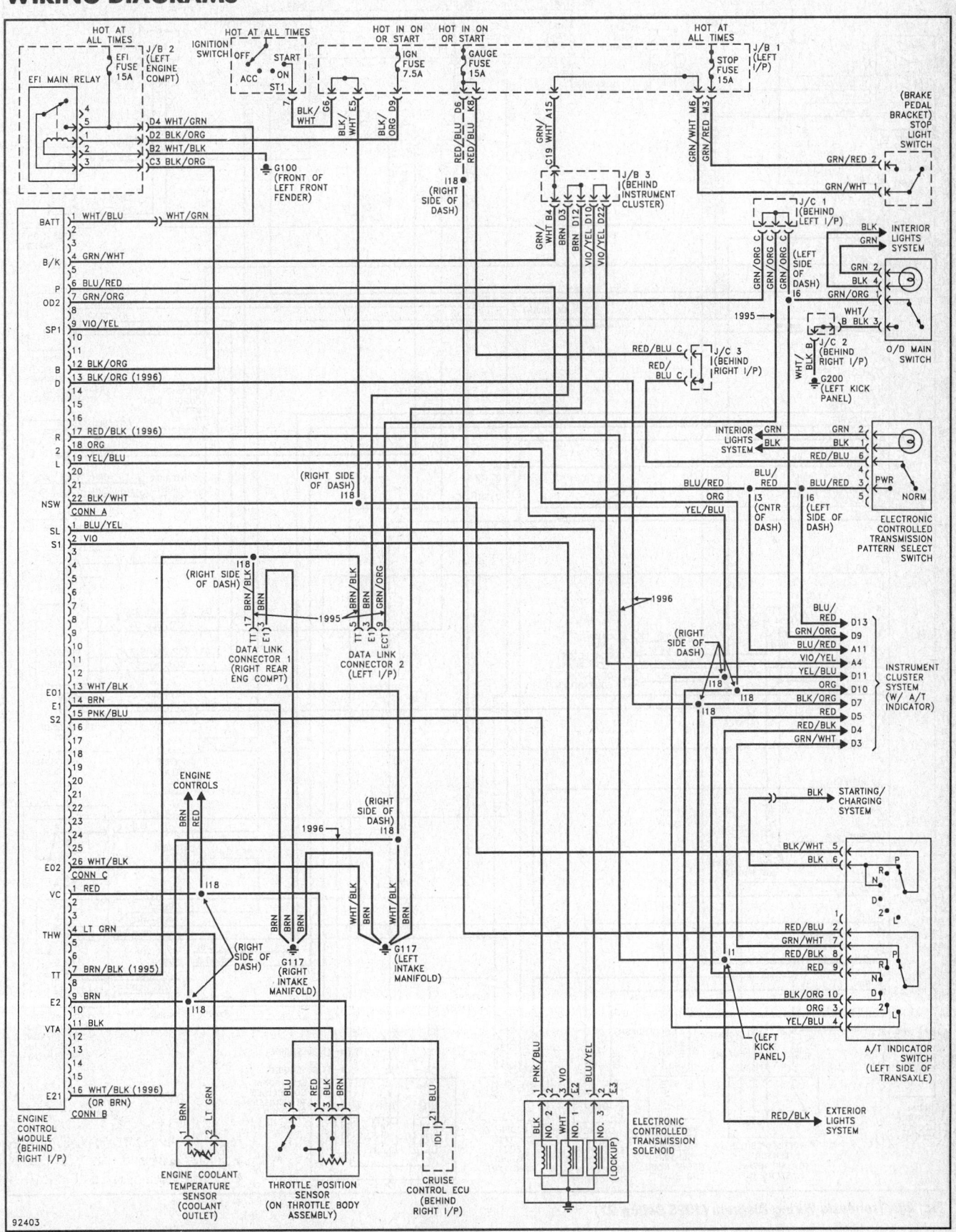

Fig. 27: Transaxle Wiring Diagram (1995-96 Camry - 4-Cylinder)

92403

AUTOMATIC TRANSMISSIONS
Toyota A-140E Electronic Controls (Cont.)

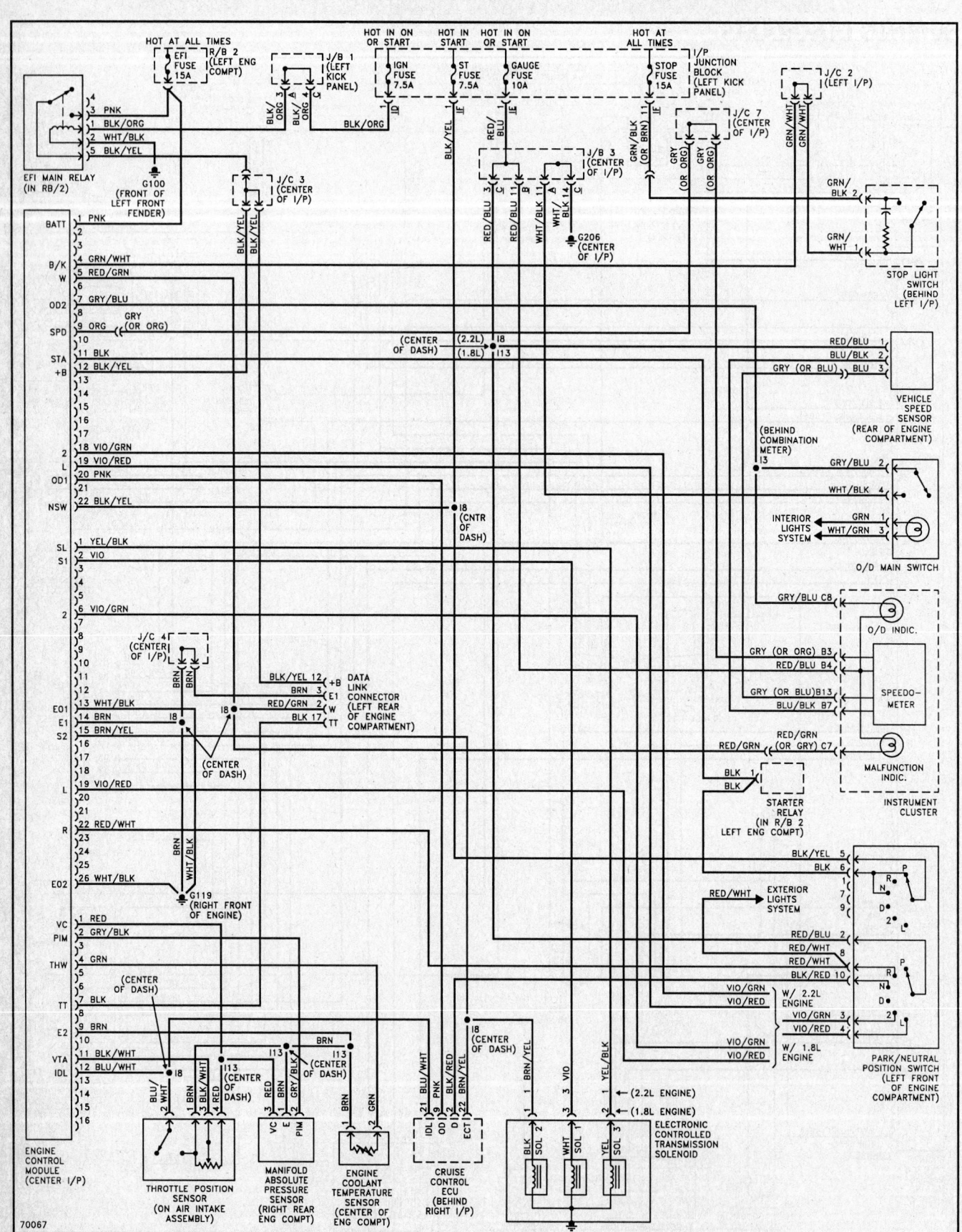

Fig. 28: *Transaxle Wiring Diagram (1995 Celica GT)*

70067

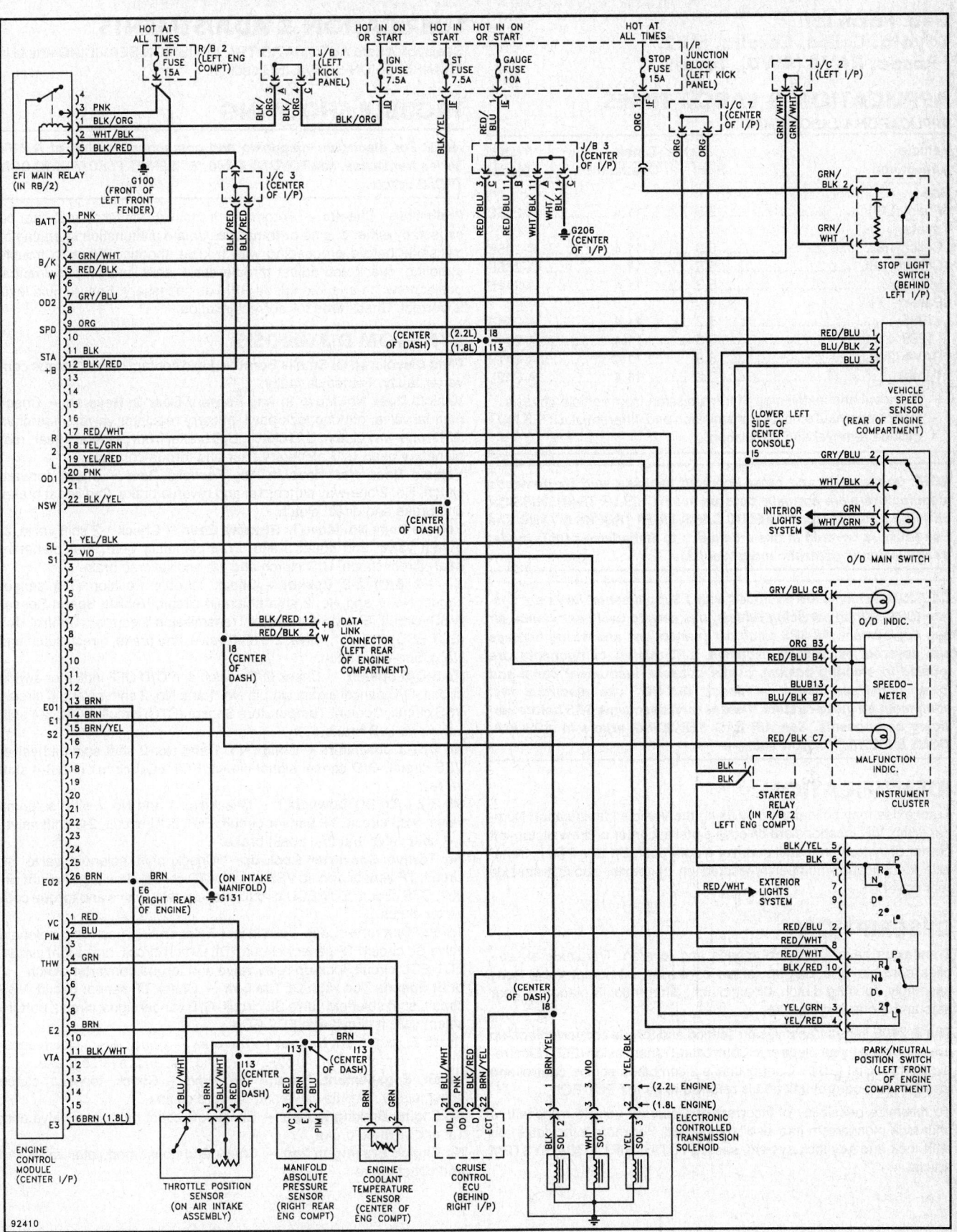

Fig. 29: Transaxle Wiring Diagram (1996 Celica GT)

92410

AUTOMATIC TRANSMISSIONS
Toyota A-240 "E" & "L" Series

Geo: Prizm LSi
Toyota: Celica, Corolla, MR2,
　Paseo, RAV4 (4WD), Tercel

APPLICATION & LABOR TIMES

APPLICATION & LABOR TIMES

Vehicle Application	Labor Times R & I [1]	Overhaul [2]	Trans. Model
Geo			
Prizm (LSi)	5.5	11.4	A-245E
Toyota			
Celica 1.8L	6.0	11.4	A-246E
Corolla 1.8L	5.5	11.4	A-245E
MR2	5.8	11.4	A-241E
Paseo			
1995	5.2	11.4	A-244E
1996	5.5	11.4	A-244E
RAV4 (2WD)	8.5	11.4	A-241E
Tercel	5.2	11.4	A-242L

[1] – Removal and installation of transmission from vehicle chassis.
[2] – Bench overhaul time for transmission and differential. DOES NOT include removal and installation.

NOTE: Geo models and other imported vehicles sold by domestic manufacturers are normally covered in MITCHELL® TRANSMISSION SERVICE & REPAIR for DOMESTIC CARS, LIGHT TRUCKS & VANS. The Geo Prizm is covered in this article due to limited use of this model transmission in domestic model vehicles.

CAUTION: Vehicles are equipped with a Supplemental Restraint System (SRS). When servicing vehicle, use care to avoid accidental air bag deployment. All SRS electrical connections and wiring harness are covered by Yellow insulation. SRS-related components are located in steering column, center console, instrument panel and lower panel on instrument panel. DO NOT use electrical test equipment on these circuits. If necessary, deactivate SRS before servicing components. See AIR BAG SERVICING article in APPLICATIONS & IDENTIFICATION section.

IDENTIFICATION

Transaxles may be identified by using the Vehicle Identification Number (VIN). VIN locations are on cowl panel at center of firewall, top left corner of instrument panel or driver's door post. On Geo Prizm, transaxle identification number is located on transaxle, above transaxle rear cover.

DESCRIPTION

Transaxles have 4 forward speeds and reverse. Transaxle assemblies consists of a lock-up torque converter, oil pump, valve body assembly, forward clutch, direct clutch, differential, 3 planetary gear sets and 3 one-way clutches.

The A-240E series transmission shifting and torque converter lock-up are controlled by an Electronic Controlled Transmission (ECT) Electronic Control Unit (ECU). Control unit is a combined engine control and transmission control unit and is referred to as the ECT ECU.

To minimize possibility of incorrect operation of vehicle transaxle, a shift lock mechanism has also been added. For more information on shift lock and key lock system, see TOYOTA SHIFT LOCK SYSTEM article.

LUBRICATION & ADJUSTMENTS

See appropriate AUTOMATIC TRANSMISSION SERVICING article in TRANSMISSION SERVICING section.

TROUBLE SHOOTING

NOTE: For electronic diagnosis and component testing of A-240E series transaxles, see TOYOTA A-240 "E" SERIES ELECTRONIC CONTROLS article.

Preliminary Checks – Automatic transaxle malfunctions can be caused by either engine or transaxle. Isolate malfunction to engine or transaxle before proceeding with trouble shooting. Prior to trouble shooting, check and adjust throttle cable, shift linkage, park/neutral position switch and idle speed RPM as necessary. Ensure fluid level is correct. Check tires for correct inflation.

SYMPTOM DIAGNOSIS

Fluid Discolored Or Smells Burnt – Fluid contaminated. Torque converter faulty. Transaxle faulty.

Vehicle Does Not Move In Any Forward Gear Or Reverse – Check manual valve, parking lock pawl, primary regulator valve, underdrive (U/D) one-way clutch, U/D clutch, U/D brake, front planetary gear, rear planetary gear, U/D planetary gear and torque converter.

Vehicle Does Not Move In Any Forward Gear – Check forward clutch, No. 2 one-way clutch, 1st and reverse brake, 2nd coast brake, 2nd brake and direct clutch.

Vehicle Does Not Move In Reverse Gear – Check 1-2 shift valve, 2-3 shift valve, 2nd coast brake, front planetary gear, rear planetary gear, direct clutch, U/D clutch and 1st and reverse brake.

No 1-2 &/Or 2-3 Upshift – Check Throttle Position (TP) sensor circuit, No. 1 and No. 2 shift solenoid circuit, Vehicle Speed Sensor (VSS) circuit, Electronic Control Transmission Electronic Control Unit (ECT ECU), 1-2 shift valve, 2-3 shift valve, 2nd brake, direct clutch and No. 1 one-way clutch.

No 3-O/D Upshift – Check O/D switch and O/D OFF indicator switch circuit, O/D cancel signal circuit, No. 1 and No. 2 shift solenoid circuit, VSS circuit, Coolant Temperature Sensor (CTS) circuit, ECM, 3-4 shift valve and U/D brake.

No O/D-3 Downshift – Check No. 1 and No. 2 shift solenoid valve, VSS circuit, O/D cancel signal circuit, ECT ECU circuit and 3-4 shift valve.

No 3-2 &/Or 2-1 Downshift – Check No. 1 and No. 2 shift solenoid valve, VSS circuit, TP sensor circuit, ECT ECU circuit, 2-3 shift valve, 1-2 shift valve and 2nd coast brake.

No Torque Converter Lock-Up – Check shift solenoid valve SL circuit, TP sensor circuit, VSS circuit, O/D cancel circuit, brakelight circuit, CTS circuit, ECT ECU circuit, lock-up relay valve and torque converter clutch.

Torque Converter Lock-Up Will Not Release – Check shift solenoid valve SL circuit, TP sensor circuit, IDL switch circuit, brakelight circuit, ECT ECU circuit, lock-up relay valve and torque converter clutch.

Shift Speeds Too High Or Too Low – Check TP sensor circuit, VSS circuit, shift solenoid valve SL circuit, O/D cancel signal circuit, pattern select switch circuit and ECT ECU.

Harsh Engagement Neutral To Reverse – Check direct clutch accumulator, direct clutch, throttle valve and, 1st and reverse brake.

Harsh Engagement Neutral To Drive – Check forward clutch accumulator, throttle valve and forward clutch.

No Engine Braking In Low – Check low coast modulator valve and, 1st and reverse brake.

No Engine Braking In 2nd – Check 2nd coast modulator valve and 2nd coast brake.

CLUTCH & BRAKE APPLICATION

Selector Lever Position	Elements In Use
"D" (Drive)	
1st Gear	Forward Clutch, No. 2 One-Way Clutch, Underdrive One-Way Clutch & Underdrive Brake
Second Gear	Forward Clutch, No. 1 One-Way Clutch 2nd Brake, Underdrive Brake & Underdrive One-Way Clutch
3rd Gear	Direct Clutch, Forward Clutch, 2nd Brake, Underdrive Brake & Underdrive One-Way Clutch
Overdrive	Direct Clutch, Forward Clutch, 2nd Brake & Underdrive Clutch
"2" (Second)	
1st Gear	Forward Clutch, No. 2 One-Way Clutch Underdrive One-Way Clutch & Underdrive Brake
2nd Gear	Forward Clutch, 2nd Brake, No. 1 One-Way Clutch, Underdrive Brake Underdrive One-Way Clutch & 2nd Coast Brake
3rd Gear [1]	Direct Clutch, Forward Clutch 2nd Brake, Underdrive Brake & Underdrive One-Way Clutch
"L" (Low)	
First Gear	Forward Clutch, Underdrive Brake, No. 2 One-Way Clutch, Underdrive One-Way Clutch & 1st & Reverse Brake
Second Gear [2]	Forward Clutch, 2nd Coast Brake 2nd Brake, No. 1 One-Way Clutch, Underdrive One-Way Clutch & Underdrive Brake
"R" (Reverse)	Direct Clutch, Underdrive Brake & 1st & Reverse Brake
"N" (Neutral)	Underdrive Brake
"P" (Park)	Underdrive Brake

[1] – Downshift only in 3rd gear for "2" position.
[2] – Downshift only in 2nd gear for "L" position. Upshift does not occur.

TESTING

NOTE: For electronic diagnosis and component testing of A-240E series transaxles, see TOYOTA A-240 "E" SERIES ELECTRONIC CONTROLS article.

PRELIMINARY CHECKS

1) Before testing transaxle, ensure fluid level is correct and selector lever, throttle cable and idle speed are adjusted correctly. Battery must be fully charged for accurate testing.

2) To aid in transaxle fault diagnosis, determine if fault is hydraulic, electronic or a combination of both. Electronic control transaxles are capable of storing self-diagnostic codes. To determine if a fault is electrical, retrieve any stored diagnostic trouble codes. See TOYOTA A-240 "E" SERIES ELECTRONIC CONTROLS article for electronic diagnosis.

TIME LAG TEST

CAUTION: Perform test with fluid at normal operating temperature of 122-176°F (50-80°C). Allow a one minute interval between tests. Record 3 measurements and use average value.

1) If selector lever is actuated with engine idling, a time lag will be noted before shock can be felt. This test is used for checking condition of underdrive clutch, forward clutch, direct clutch and 1st and reverse brake. Apply parking brake and start engine. Ensure idle speed is set to specification. See IDLE SPEED SPECIFICATIONS table.

IDLE SPEED SPECIFICATIONS [1]

Vehicle Application	Transaxle Model	RPM
Geo		
Prizm	A-245E	700
Toyota		
Celica 1.8L	A-246E	700
Corolla 1.8L	A-245E	700
MR2	A-241E	750
Paseo		
1995	A-244E	800
1996	A-244E	750
RAV4	A-241E	700
Tercel	A-242L	750

[1] – Idle speed is computer controlled and is not adjustable.

2) Move selector lever from "N" to "D" position. Measure time required for shock to be felt. Time lag must be less than 1.2 seconds. Repeat procedure shifting from "N" to "R" position. Time lag must be less than 1.5 seconds. See TIME LAG TEST RESULTS.

Time Lag Test Results
- **Excessive Time Lag From "N" To "D" Position:** Low line pressure, defective forward clutch or No. 2 and underdrive one-way clutch.
- **Excessive Time Lag From "N" To "R" Position:** Low line pressure, defective direct clutch, 1st and reverse brake or underdrive brake worn.

ROAD TEST

NOTE: Ensure transmission is at normal operating temperature. There is no OD upshift or torque converter lock-up when fluid temperature is less than 140°F (60°C).

"D" Range Test – **1)** Shift into "D" range. Hold accelerator pedal constant at full throttle. Check 1-2, 2-3, and 3-OD lock-up and upshift points. Refer to appropriate SHIFT SPEED SPECIFICATIONS table.

NOTE: There is no lock-up when vehicle speed is 6 MPH less than the set cruise control speed. Ensure cruise control is off during road test.

- If no 1-2 upshift occurs, check 1-2 shift valve or governor valve.
- If no 2-3 upshift occurs, check 2-3 shift valve.
- If no 3-OD upshift occurs, check 3-OD shift valve or solenoid.
- If all shift points are incorrect, check throttle valve, 1-2 shift valve, 2-3 shift valve and 3-OD shift valve.
- If all lock-up points are incorrect, check lock-up relay valve or solenoid.

2) Use procedure outlined in step **1)** to check for shock and slip between 1-2, 2-3, and 3-OD upshifts. If shock is harsh, line pressure may be too high. Check accumulator or check ball.

3) Run vehicle in "D" range lock-up or overdrive gear. Check for abnormal noise and vibration.

NOTE: Check for cause of abnormal noise and vibration must be made with extreme care as problem could be due to an unbalanced drive shaft, differential, tire, torque converter, etc.

4) While running in "D" range, confirm correct kickdown vehicle speed limits for 2-1, 3-2, OD-3 shift points. Check for abnormal shock and slip at kickdown.

5) Check lock-up function. Drive vehicle in OD gear of "D" range with lock-up on. Hold vehicle speed steady between 37-43 MPH. Lightly depress accelerator pedal. Ensure engine RPM does not change abruptly. Large increase in engine RPM indicates lock-up function is faulty.

"2" Range Test – **1)** Shift to "2" range. Drive with accelerator pedal held constantly at full throttle. Ensure 1-2 upshift points take place and are operating properly. See appropriate SHIFT SPEED SPECIFICATIONS table.

NOTE: *In "2" range there will be no lock-up to 2nd gear.*

---

2) While driving in "2" range, 2nd gear, release accelerator pedal and check engine braking effect. If there is no engine braking effect, 2nd coast brake is faulty. Check for abnormal noise and shock at acceleration and deceleration.

"L" Range Test – While running in "L" range, ensure there is no upshift to 2nd gear. While running in "L" range, release accelerator pedal. If there is no engine braking effect, 1st and reverse brake is faulty. Check for abnormal noise at acceleration and deceleration.

"R" Range Test – Shift into "R" range. Accelerate vehicle from a stop at full throttle. Ensure slipping does not occur.

"P" Range Test – Stop vehicle on 5 degree or more gradient. Shift transaxle into "P". Release parking brake. Ensure parking pawl holds vehicle.

NOTE: *For A-245E (PRIZM LSi) shift speed specifications, See Fig. 1.*

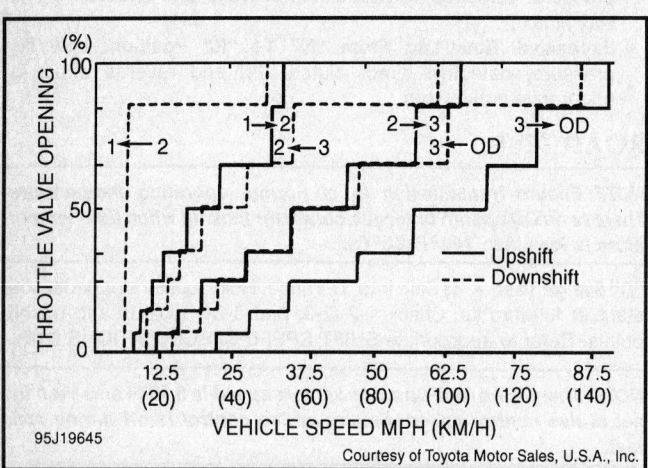

Fig. 1: Prizm LSi (A-245E) Shift Speed Diagram

A-246E (CELICA 1.8L) SHIFT SPEED SPECIFICATIONS [1] (1995)

Application	MPH
"D" Position	
1st-2nd	33-38
2nd-3rd	61-67
3rd-OD	89-98
3rd-OD [2]	22-27
OD-3rd [2]	17-23
OD-3rd	86-94
3rd-2nd	58-63
2nd-1st	25-29
"2" Position	
1st-2nd	33-38
2nd-1st	25-29
"L" Position	
2nd-1st	29-32

[1] – Wide open throttle.
[2] – Fully closed throttle.

A-246E (CELICA 1.8L) SHIFT SPEED SPECIFICATIONS [1] (1996)

Application	MPH
"D" Position	
1st-2nd	30-35
2nd-3rd	57-62
3rd-OD	81-89
3rd-OD [2]	22-27
OD-3rd [2]	17-23
OD-3rd	77-85
3rd-2nd	53-58
2nd-1st	25-29
"2" Position	
1st-2nd	33-38
2nd-1st	25-29
"L" Position	
2nd-1st	29-32

[1] – Wide open throttle.
[2] – Fully closed throttle.

A-246E (CELICA 1.8L) LOCK-UP SPEED SPECIFICATIONS [1]

Application	MPH
"D" Position [2]	
3rd Gear	
Lock-Up ON	42-47
Lock-Up OFF	37-42
OD Gear	
Lock-Up ON	49-54
Lock-Up OFF	43-48

[1] – With throttle valve open 5 percent.
[2] – There is no lock-up in "2" or "L" position.

A-245E (COROLLA 1.8L) SHIFT SPEED SPECIFICATIONS [1]

Application	MPH
"D" Position	
1st-2nd	32-37
2nd-3rd	59-63
3rd-OD	86-94
3rd-OD [2]	22-25
OD-3rd [2]	11-14
OD-3rd	83-89
3rd-2nd	55-59
2nd-1st	26-29
"2" Position	
3rd-2nd	55-60
2nd-1st	26-29
"L" Position	
2nd-1st	26-29

[1] – Wide open throttle.
[2] – Fully closed throttle.

A-245E (COROLLA 1.8L) LOCK-UP SPEED SPECIFICATIONS [1]

Application	MPH
"D" Position [2]	
3rd Gear	
Lock-Up ON	40-45
Lock-Up OFF	36-40
OD	
Lock-Up ON	40-45
Lock-Up OFF	36-40

[1] – With throttle valve open 5 percent.
[2] – There is no lock-up in "2" or "L" position.

A-241E (MR2) SHIFT SPEED SPECIFICATIONS [1]

Application	MPH
"D" Position	
1st-2nd	33-37
2nd-3rd	61-68
3rd-OD	81-89
3rd-OD [2]	27-31
OD-3rd [2]	11-14
OD-3rd	78-85
3rd-2nd	58-65
2nd-1st	27-31
"2" Position	
1st-2nd	33-37
2nd-1st	26-30
"L" Position	
2nd-1st	29-33

[1] – Wide open throttle.
[2] – Fully closed throttle.

A-241E (MR2) LOCK-UP SPEED SPECIFICATIONS [1]

Application	MPH
"D" Position [2]	
3rd Gear	
Lock-Up ON	39-43
Lock-Up OFF	35-40
OD	
Lock-Up ON	40-44
Lock-Up OFF	37-40

[1] – With throttle valve opened 5 percent.
[2] – There is no lock-up in "2" or "L" position.

A-244E (PASEO) SHIFT SPEED SPECIFICATIONS [1] (1995)

Application	MPH
California	
"D" Position	
1st-2nd	27-31
2nd-3rd	52-56
3rd-OD	123-127
3rd-OD [2]	24-27
OD-3rd [2]	10-13
OD-3rd	119-123
3rd-2nd	47-51
2nd-1st	23-26
2" Position	
1st-2nd	27-31
2nd-1st	23-26
"L" Position	
2nd-1st	25-29
Except California	
"D" Position	
1st-2nd	33-37
2nd-3rd	61-67
3rd-OD	123-127
3rd-OD [2]	24-27
OD-3rd [2]	10-13
OD-3rd	119-123
3rd-2nd	57-63
2nd-1st	27-30
2" Position	
1st-2nd	33-37
2nd-1st	27-30
"L" Position	
2nd-1st	30-34

[1] – Wide open throttle.
[2] – Fully closed throttle.

A-244E (PASEO) LOCK-UP SPEED SPECIFICATIONS [1] (1995)

Application	MPH
"D" Position [2]	
Lock-Up ON	42-45
Lock-Up OFF	38-42

[1] – With throttle valve opened 5 percent.
[2] – There is no lock-up in "2" or "L" position.

A-244E (PASEO) SHIFT SPEED SPECIFICATIONS [1] (1996)

Application	MPH
"D" Position	
1st-2nd	27-32
2nd-3rd	52-56
3rd-OD	85-92
3rd-OD [2]	24-27
OD-3rd [2]	10-13
OD-3rd	81-88
3rd-2nd	47-51
2nd-1st	23-26
"2" Position	
1st-2nd	27-32
2nd-1st	23-26
OD-3rd [2]	52-56
"L" Position	
3rd-2nd	52-56
2nd-1st	25-29

[1] – Wide open throttle.
[2] – Fully closed throttle.

A-244E (PASEO) LOCK-UP SPEED SPECIFICATIONS [1] (1996)

Application	MPH
"D" Position [2]	
3rd Gear	
Lock-Up ON	40-43
Lock-Up OFF	36-39
OD	
Lock-Up ON	42-45
Lock-Up OFF	38-41

[1] – With throttle valve opened 5 percent.
[2] – There is no lock-up in "2" or "L" position.

A-241E (RAV4 2WD) SHIFT SPEED SPECIFICATIONS [1]

Application	MPH
"D" Position	
1st-2nd	37-42
2nd-3rd	69-73
3rd-OD	103-110
3rd-OD [2]	22-25
OD-3rd [2]	10-13
OD-3rd	91-98
3rd-2nd	65-69
2nd-1st	25-29
"2" Position	
1st-2nd	37-42
4th-3rd	69-73
3rd-2nd	55-58
2nd-1st	25-28
"L" Position	
3rd-2nd	67-71
2nd-1st	36-40

[1] – Wide open throttle.
[2] – Fully closed throttle.

A-241E (RAV4 2WD) LOCK-UP SPEED SPECIFICATIONS [1]

Application	MPH
"D" Position [2]	
3rd Gear	
Lock-Up ON	61-65
Lock-Up OFF	53-57
OD	
Lock-Up ON	46-50
Lock-Up OFF	43-47

[1] – With throttle valve opened 5 percent.
[2] – There is no lock-up in "2" or "L" position.

A-242L (TERCEL) SHIFT SPEED SPECIFICATIONS [1]

Application	MPH
"D" Position	
1st-2nd	28-38
2nd-3rd	55-66
3rd-OD [2]	12-21
3rd-2nd	52-63
2nd-1st	19-27
"L" Position	
2nd-1st	27-35

[1] – Wide open throttle.
[2] – Fully closed throttle.

A-242L (TERCEL) LOCK-UP SPEED SPECIFICATIONS [1]

Application	MPH
"D" Position [2]	
Lock-Up ON In OD	40-47
Lock-Up OFF In OD	38-45

[1] – With throttle valve opened 5 percent.
[2] – There is no lock-up in "2" or "L" position.

STALL SPEED TEST

1) Operate engine and transaxle at normal operating temperature. Connect tachometer to vehicle and ensure it is visible to driver. Apply parking brake and block front and rear wheels.

CAUTION: DO NOT maintain stall speed RPM for more than 5 seconds. Allow vehicle to idle in Neutral or Park for at least 2 minutes before performing next test.

2) Start engine, apply service brakes and shift vehicle into "D" position. Depress accelerator to full throttle and note maximum RPM obtained. Repeat test in "R" position. For stall speeds, see STALL SPEED SPECIFICATIONS table. See STALL SPEED TEST RESULTS.

STALL SPEED SPECIFICATIONS

Vehicle Application	Transaxle Model	RPM
Geo		
Prizm	A-245E	2300-2600
Toyota		
Celica 1.8L		
1995	A-246E	2500-2800
1996	A-246E	2400-2700
Corolla 1.8L	A-245E	2300-2600
MR2	A-241E	2500-2800
Paseo		
1995		
Calif.	A-244E	2100-2500
Except Calif.	A-244E	2300-2700
1996	A-244E	2300-2700
RAV4 2WD	A-241E	2170-2570
Tercel	A-242L	2100-2500

Stall Speed Test Results
- **Stall Speed Is Same In Both Positions, But Less Than Specified:** Insufficient engine output or defective stator one-way clutch.

NOTE: If stall speed RPM is more than 600 RPM below specified value, torque converter may be faulty.

- **Stall Speed High In "D" Position:** Low line pressure, forward clutch slipping or defective No. 2 one-way clutch or underdrive one-way clutch.
- **Stall Speed High In "R" Position:** Low line pressure, direct clutch, 1st and reverse brake or underdrive brake slipping.
- **Stall Speed High In Both Positions:** Low line pressure, improper fluid level or underdrive brake slipping.

HYDRAULIC PRESSURE TESTS

CAUTION: Perform test at normal operating fluid temperature of 122-176°F (50-80°C)

Line Pressure Test – 1) Remove appropriate transaxle plug and connect pressure gauge. *See Fig. 2.* Block all wheels. Apply parking brake. Start engine and shift into "D" position.

2) Apply service brakes. Note pressure readings at idle. Depress accelerator and note pressure readings at stall speed. Repeat test in "R" position. Compare pressure readings to those listed in appropriate LINE PRESSURE SPECIFICATIONS table. See LINE PRESSURE TEST RESULTS.

3) If pressure is lower than specified, check throttle cable adjustment. Adjust as necessary. See appropriate AUTOMATIC TRANSMISSION SERVICING article in TRANSMISSION SERVICING section. Repeat pressure test procedure if throttle cable adjustment was necessary.

Line Pressure Test Results
- **Line Pressure High In Both Positions:** Throttle cable out of adjustment, defective throttle valve or regulator valve.
- **Line Pressure Low In Both Positions:** Throttle cable out of adjustment, defective oil pump, throttle valve, regulator valve, underdrive brake or underdrive one-way clutch.
- **Line Pressure Low In "D" Position Only:** "D" position circuit leaking pressure, defective forward clutch or underdrive one-way clutch.
- **Line Pressure Low In "R" Position Only:** "R" position circuit leaking pressure, defective direct clutch, 1st and reverse brake or underdrive one-way clutch.

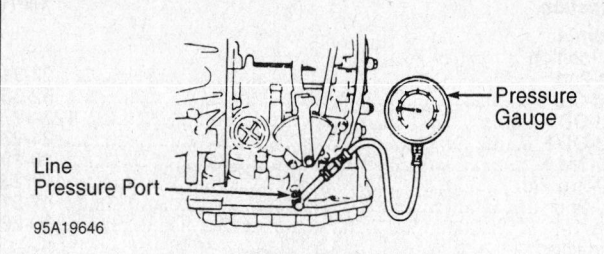

Fig. 2-1: A-242L, A-241E & A-244E

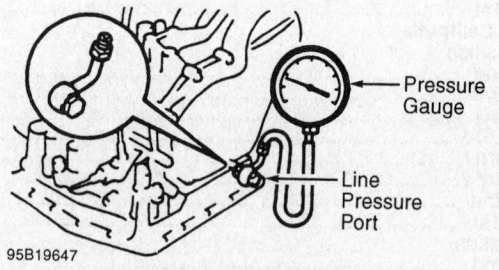

Fig. 2-2: A-245E & A-246E

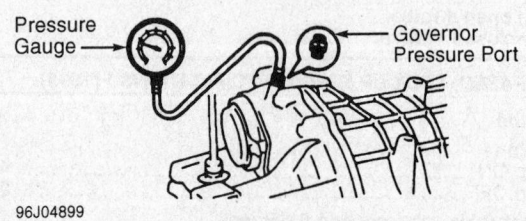

Fig. 2-3: A-242L

Courtesy of Toyota Motor Sales, U.S.A., Inc.

Fig. 2: Checking Governor & Line Pressure

A-245E (PRIZM) LINE PRESSURE SPECIFICATIONS

Application	psi (kg/cm²)
"D" Position	
Idle Speed	54-64 (3.8-4.5)
Stall Speed	139-162 (9.8-11.4)
"R" Position	
Idle Speed	85-102 (6.0-7.2)
Stall Speed	198-244 (13.9-17.2)

A-246E (CELICA) LINE PRESSURE SPECIFICATIONS

Application	psi (kg/cm²)
"D" Position	
Idle Speed	54-64 (3.8-4.5)
Stall Speed	142-165 (10.0-11.6)
"R" Position	
Idle Speed	87-104 (6.1-7.3)
Stall Speed	202-249 (14.2-17.5)

A-245E (COROLLA) LINE PRESSURE SPECIFICATIONS

Application	psi (kg/cm²)
"D" Position	
Idle Speed	54-64 (3.8-4.5)
Stall Speed	142-165 (10.0-11.6)
"R" Position	
Idle Speed	87-104 (6.1-7.3)
Stall Speed	202-249 (14.2-17.5)

A-241E (MR2) & A-244E (PASEO) LINE PRESSURE SPECIFICATIONS

Application	psi (kg/cm²)
"D" Position	
Idle Speed	54-61 (3.8-4.3)
Stall Speed	104-125 (7.3-8.8)
"R" Position	
Idle Speed	92-115 (6.5-8.1)
Stall Speed	193-229 (13.6-16.1)

A-241E (RAV4 2WD) LINE PRESSURE SPECIFICATIONS

Application	psi (kg/cm²)
"D" Position	
Idle Speed	51-61 (3.6-4.3)
Stall Speed	119-141 (8.4-9.9)
"R" Position	
Idle Speed	87-117 (6.1-8.2)
Stall Speed	222-257 (15.6-18.1)

A-242L (TERCEL) LINE PRESSURE SPECIFICATIONS

Application	psi (kg/cm²)
"D" Position	
Idle Speed	54-61 (3.8-4.3)
Stall Speed	131-152 (9.2-10.7)
"R" Position	
Idle Speed	80-102 (5.6-7.2)
Stall Speed	238-276 (16.7-19.4)

Governor Pressure Test (A-242L) – 1) Transaxle must be at normal operating temperature of 122-176°F (50-80°C). Block rear wheels. DO NOT apply parking brake. Raise and support front of vehicle with safety stands.

2) Remove appropriate transaxle plug and connect pressure gauge. See Fig. 2. Start engine and shift vehicle into "D" position. Note governor pressure at specified vehicle speeds. See GOVERNOR PRESSURE SPECIFICATIONS table.

CAUTION: *Road test vehicle or use chassis dynamometer to check governor pressures exceeding minimum vehicle speed specification.*

3) Incorrect governor pressure may be caused by incorrect line pressure, leakage at governor pressure circuit or defective governor valve.

GOVERNOR PRESSURE SPECIFICATIONS (A-242L)

Speed (MPH)	psi (kg/cm²)
19	9-20 (.6-1.4)
37	28-40 (2.0-2.8)
56	53-64 (3.7-4.5)

ON-VEHICLE SERVICE

DRIVE AXLE SHAFTS

See appropriate AXLE SHAFTS article in AXLE SHAFTS & TRANSFER CASES section.

GOVERNOR ASSEMBLY (A-242L)

Removal & Installation – Disconnect speedometer cable. Remove governor cover bolts. Using a screwdriver, remove governor cover. Remove "O" ring from cover. Remove governor body with thrust washer. Remove governor body adapter. Remove governor oil strainer. To install, reverse removal procedure. Install NEW gasket and tighten bolts to 115 INCH lbs. (13 N.m).

SPEED SENSOR & ROTOR (A-240 "E" SERIES)

Removal & Installation – Remove retaining plate and pull out speed sensor. Remove "O" ring from speed sensor. Remove 2 bolts and sensor cover bracket. Using a screwdriver, remove sensor cover. DO NOT damage cover. Remove sensor rotor. To install, reverse removal procedure. Tighten bolts to 48 INCH lbs. (5.4 N.m).

THROTTLE CABLE

Removal – Disconnect throttle cable from throttle linkage. Disconnect transaxle control cable from manual shift lever. Remove manual shift lever. Remove park/neutral position switch. Remove valve body assembly. See VALVE BODY ASSEMBLY under ON-VEHICLE SERVICE. Remove throttle cable retaining bolt. Pull throttle cable from transaxle.

Installation – 1) Install throttle cable in transaxle case. Ensure cable is fully seated. Install retaining bolt. Install valve body assembly. On NEW throttle cables, stopper must be staked on inner cable. Bend cable in approximately 7.87" (200 mm) radius.

2) Pull inner cable lightly, until a slight resistance is felt, and hold in place. Stake stopper on inner cable, leaving a .031-.059" (.80-1.49 mm) gap between cable housing and stopper. See Fig. 3.

3) Adjust throttle cable and park/neutral position switch (if necessary). See appropriate AUTOMATIC TRANSMISSION SERVICING article in TRANSMISSION SERVICING section. Install manual shift lever. Install transaxle control cable. Test drive vehicle.

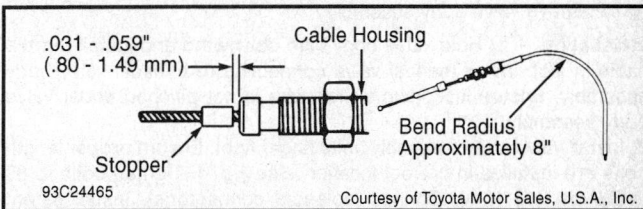

Fig. 3: Locating Throttle Cable Stopper

VALVE BODY ASSEMBLY

CAUTION: *Note valve body assembly bolts length and location. Proper length bolts must be installed in correct location to prevent case damage.*

Removal – 1) Clean exterior of transaxle oil pan. Remove drain plug and drain transaxle. Remove oil pan and gasket. Remove oil strainer (filter) and apply tube bracket. Note location of oil tubes. Using large screwdriver, carefully remove oil tubes.

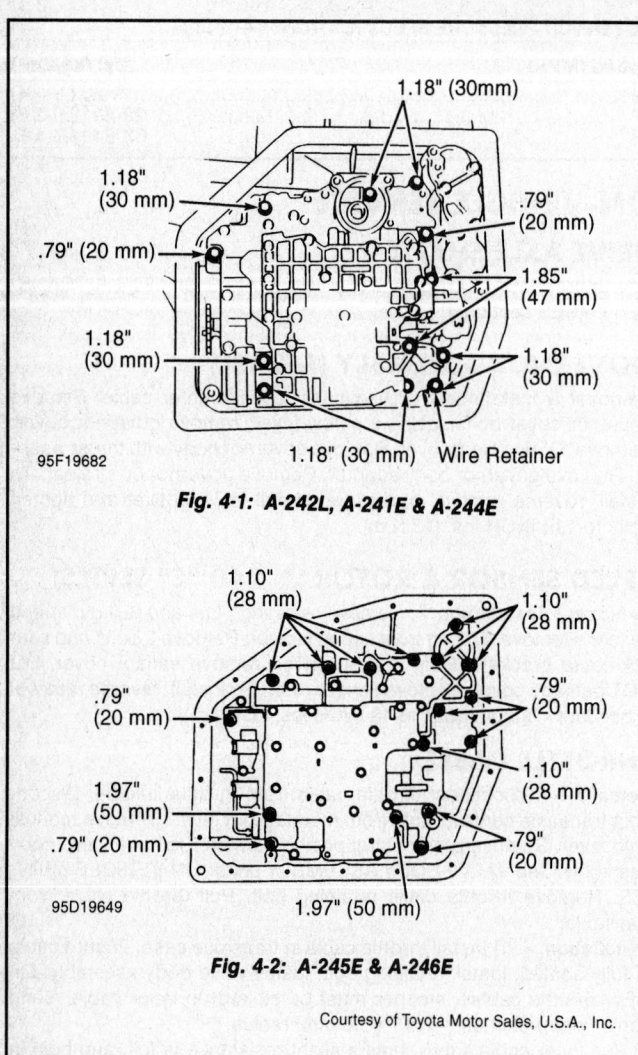

Fig. 4-1: A-242L, A-241E & A-244E

Fig. 4-2: A-245E & A-246E

Courtesy of Toyota Motor Sales, U.S.A., Inc.

Fig. 4: Identifying Valve Body Assembly Bolts

2) Remove manual detent spring. Disconnect solenoid connector(s). Remove valve body assembly bolts. Note bolt length and location. See Fig. 4. Remove throttle cable. Disconnect manual valve connecting rod. Remove valve body assembly.

Installation – 1) Hold valve body cam downward and install throttle cable in slot. Install manual valve connecting rod. Install valve body assembly. Ensure kickdown switch wire is not pinched under valve body assembly.

2) Install valve body assembly bolts finger tight. Ensure proper length bolts are installed in correct location. See Fig. 4. Tighten bolts to 89 INCH lbs. (10 N.m). Connect solenoid connector(s). Install detent spring and tighten bolt to 89 INCH lbs. (10 N.m). Ensure manual valve lever contacts center of roller on detent spring. Using a plastic hammer, tap oil tubes into place.

3) Install oil tube clamp and bolt and tighten bolt to 89 INCH lbs. (10 N.m). Install oil strainer. Install magnet in oil pan. Ensure magnet does not interfere with oil tubes. Install oil pan and gasket. Tighten oil pan bolts to 43 INCH lbs. (4.9 N.m). Install drain plug and tighten to 13 ft. lbs. (17 N.m). Fill transaxle with fluid and check for leaks.

REMOVAL & INSTALLATION

For transaxle removal and installation procedure, see appropriate AUTOMATIC TRANSMISSION REMOVAL article in TRANSMISSION SERVICING section.

TORQUE CONVERTER

NOTE: Torque converter is a sealed unit and must be serviced as complete assembly. Perform following tests to check converter condition. Torque converter and oil cooler lines must be thoroughly cleaned and flushed if transaxle fluid is contaminated.

ONE-WAY CLUTCH TEST

1) Install turner and stopper of One-Way Clutch Tester (09350-32014) in torque converter. See Fig. 5. Turner fits in inner race of one-way clutch. Stopper fits in notch of converter hub and outer race of one-way clutch.

2) Clutch should lock when rotated counterclockwise, and turn freely when rotated clockwise. If necessary, clean converter and retest clutch. Replace converter if clutch does not test as described.

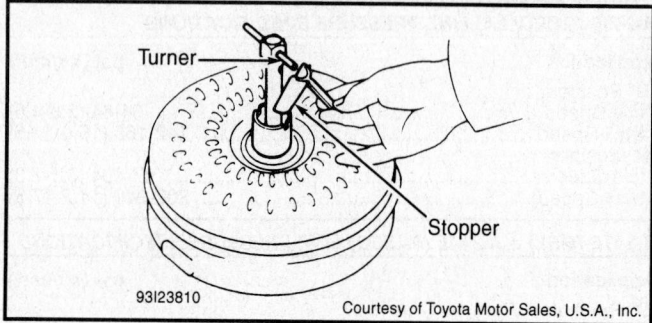

Courtesy of Toyota Motor Sales, U.S.A., Inc.

Fig. 5: Checking Torque Converter One-Way Clutch

DRIVE PLATE RUNOUT TEST

Measure drive plate runout. See Fig. 6. If runout exceeds .008" (.20 mm), or if ring gear is damaged, replace drive plate. If installing a new drive plate, note position of spacers. On Corolla, Celica and Prizm, tighten bolts to 47 ft. lbs. (64 N.m). On Tercel, tighten bolts to 65 ft. lbs. (88 N.m). On all other models, tighten bolts to 61 ft. lbs. (83 N.m).

CONVERTER SLEEVE RUNOUT TEST

1) Temporarily mount torque converter to drive plate. Mount a dial indicator with needle resting on converter sleeve. See Fig. 7. Rotate converter. If runout exceeds .012" (.30 mm), ensure converter is properly mounted to drive plate.

2) If converter is properly mounted and runout exceeds specification, replace torque converter. Mark position of converter on drive plate to ensure correct installation. Remove converter from drive plate.

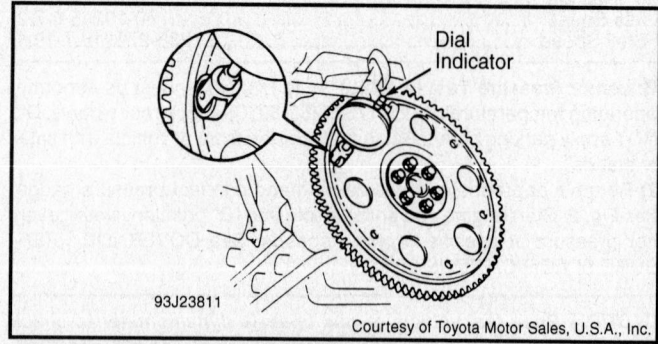

Courtesy of Toyota Motor Sales, U.S.A., Inc.

Fig. 6: Checking Drive Plate Runout

TRANSAXLE DISASSEMBLY

DISASSEMBLY (A-242L, A-241E & A-244E)

1) Remove oil cooler pipes, manual shift lever and park/neutral position switch. Remove filler tube and dipstick. Remove throttle cable retaining plate. Remove solenoid harness connector retainer plate.

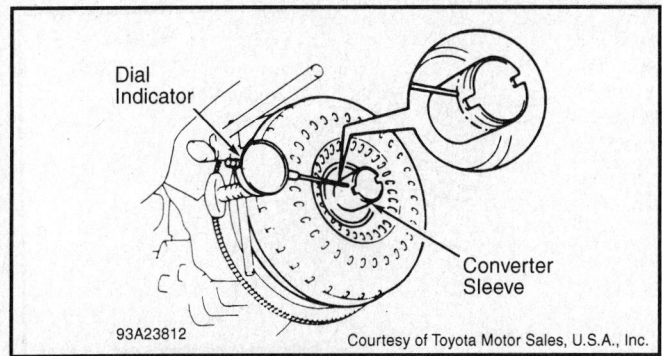

93A23812

Courtesy of Toyota Motor Sales, U.S.A., Inc.

Fig. 7: Checking Converter Sleeve Runout

2) On A-242L transaxle, remove governor cover. Remove "O" ring from cover. Remove governor assembly with thrust washer. Remove governor body adapter. Remove oil strainer. See Fig. 8.

3) On A-241E and A-244E transaxles, remove retainer plate and pull out vehicle speed sensor. Remove "O" ring from speed sensor. Remove 2 bolts and sensor cover bracket. Using a screwdriver, remove sensor cover. DO NOT damage cover. Remove sensor rotor. Remove sensor adapter. See Fig. 8.

4) On all models, remove oil pan and gasket. Remove magnet(s) from oil pan. Remove oil strainer (filter) and tube bracket. Carefully remove all oil tubes. Remove manual detent spring. Disconnect solenoid harness connectors. Remove valve body assembly. See VALVE BODY ASSEMBLY under ON-VEHICLE SERVICE. Remove throttle cable and solenoid sub-harness from transaxle case. Remove 2nd brake apply gasket. Remove 2nd brake drum seal. See Fig. 9.

5) Apply 14 psi (1 kg/cm²) of compressed air to oil passage to remove underdrive clutch accumulator piston and spring. See Fig. 10. Loosen accumulator cover bolts evenly until spring tension is released. Remove cover and gasket. Remove forward clutch accumulator piston and springs.

6) Apply 14 psi (1 kg/cm²) of compressed air to oil passage to remove direct clutch accumulator piston and spring. See Fig. 11. Apply 14 psi (1 kg/cm²) of compressed air to oil passage to remove 2nd brake accumulator piston and spring. See Fig. 12.

7) Apply mark to 2nd coast brake servo apply piston rod where it meets case. Apply air (57-114 psi (4-8 kg/cm²) and measure piston rod travel (stroke). See Fig. 13. Piston rod travel should be .059-.118" (1.5-3.0 mm). If rod travel is not within specification, further inspect band during disassembly.

8) Using snap ring expander, remove 2nd coast brake piston snap ring. Apply 14 psi (1 kg/cm²) of compressed air to oil passage to remove 2nd coast brake cover. Remove 2nd coast brake piston and spring. See Fig. 14.

9) Remove oil pump retaining bolts. Using appropriate puller, pull oil pump free from transaxle case. Remove oil pump. Remove race from oil pump. Remove direct clutch and forward clutch from transaxle case. Remove direct clutch from forward clutch. Remove thrust washer, bearings and races from both sides of forward clutch. See Fig. 15.

10) Using small screwdriver, push 2nd coast brake band pin inward and remove pin from oil pump mounting bolt hole. Remove 2nd coast brake band. Remove front planetary ring gear. Remove race and bearing from ring gear. See Fig. 15.

11) Remove front planetary gear. Remove bearings and races from both sides of planetary gear. Remove sun gear, sun gear input drum, thrust washer, 2nd brake hub and No. 1 one-way clutch. Using compressed air, confirm 2nd brake piston operates smoothly. See Fig. 16. Remove 2nd coast brake band guide.

12) Remove 2nd brake drum retaining snap ring. Remove 2nd brake drum. Remove thrust washer and 2nd brake piston return spring. Remove plates, discs and flange. Note number and location of components. Remove No. 2 one-way clutch retaining snap ring. Remove No. 2 one-way clutch and rear planetary gear. See Fig. 15.

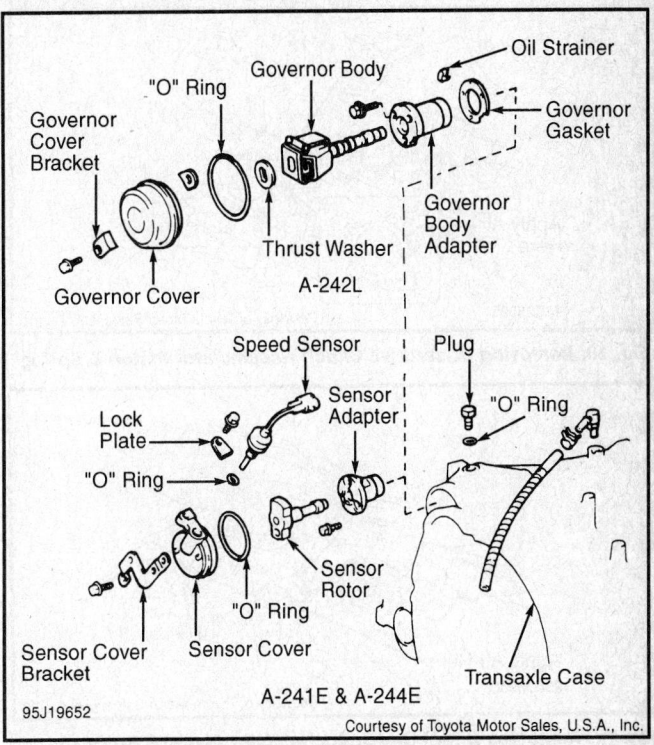

95J19652

Courtesy of Toyota Motor Sales, U.S.A., Inc.

Fig. 8: Exploded View Of Governor/Speed Sensor Assemblies

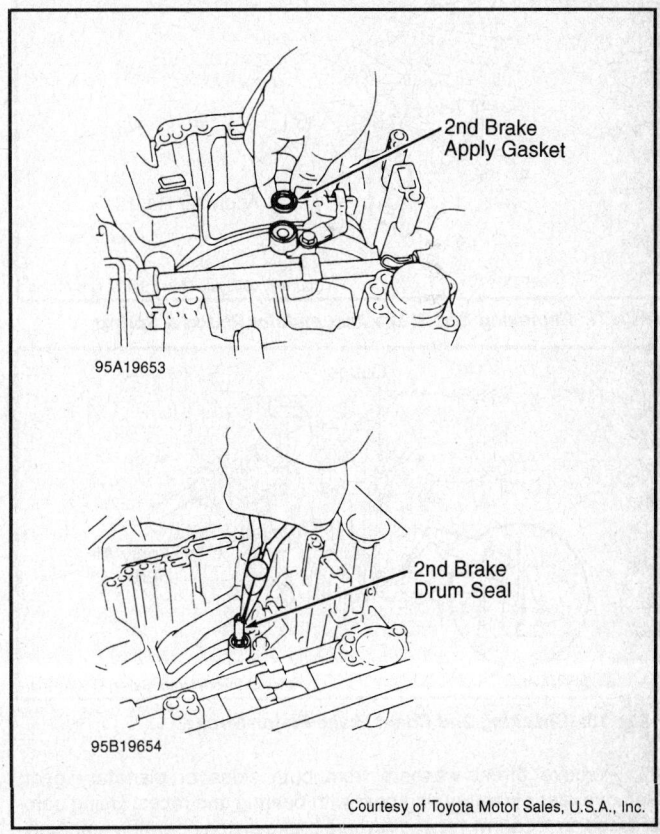

95A19653

95B19654

Courtesy of Toyota Motor Sales, U.S.A., Inc.

Fig. 9: Removing 2nd Brake Apply Gasket & Drum Seal

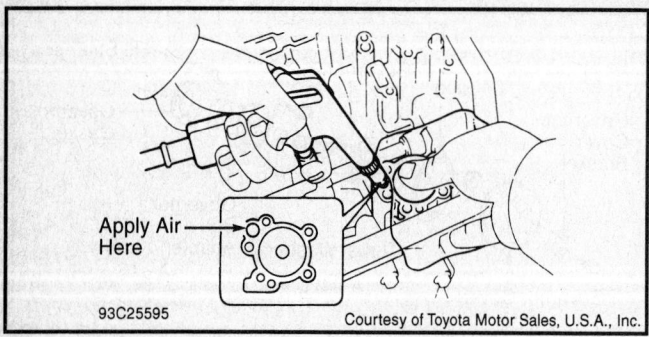

93C25595   Courtesy of Toyota Motor Sales, U.S.A., Inc.

Fig. 10: Removing Underdrive Clutch Accumulator Piston & Spring

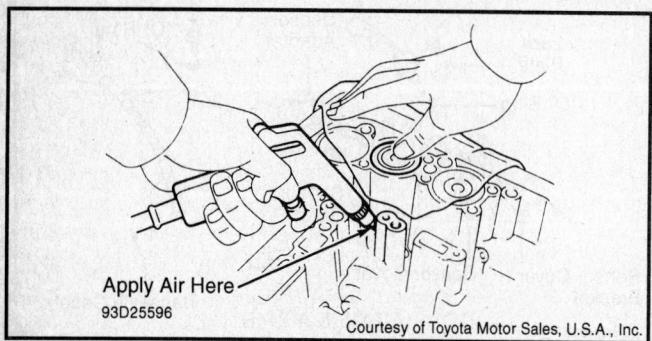

93D25596   Courtesy of Toyota Motor Sales, U.S.A., Inc.

Fig. 11: Removing Direct Clutch Accumulator Piston & Spring

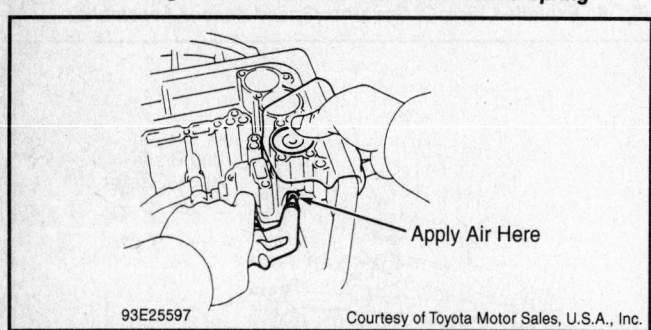

93E25597   Courtesy of Toyota Motor Sales, U.S.A., Inc.

Fig. 12: Removing 2nd Brake Accumulator Piston & Spring

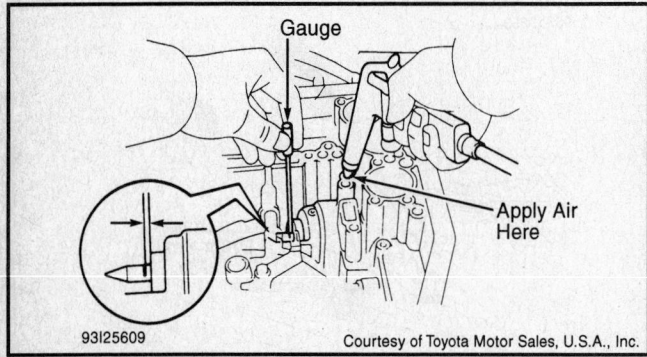

93I25609   Courtesy of Toyota Motor Sales, U.S.A., Inc.

Fig. 13: Checking 2nd Coast Brake Piston Stroke

13) Remove thrust washers from both sides of planetary gear. Remove rear planetary ring gear with bearing and races. Using compressed air, confirm 1st and reverse brake piston operates smoothly. *See Fig. 17.* Remove flange retaining snap ring. Remove flange, plates and discs. Note number and location of components. Remove rear transaxle cover bolts. Tap rear cover using a plastic hammer. Remove cover. Remove intermediate shaft.

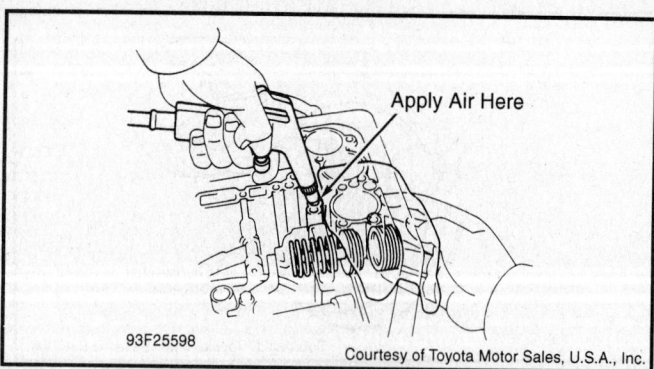

93F25598   Courtesy of Toyota Motor Sales, U.S.A., Inc.

Fig. 14: Removing 2nd Coast Brake Cover

14) Remove snap ring. Remove transaxle housing-to-case bolts. Remove transaxle housing. Remove differential assembly, governor driven gear and thrust washer. Remove apply gaskets from transaxle case. *See Fig. 18.* Using chisel, release staked area of countershaft lock nuts. Secure countershaft driven gear with appropriate holder and remove front and rear countershaft lock nuts.

15) Using appropriate puller, remove counterdriven gear. Remove thrust needle bearing. Remove countershaft assembly. Remove thrust bearing and race from countershaft. Remove underdrive clutch drum and anti-rattle clip. Note location and position of anti-rattle clip. Using compressed air, confirm underdrive brake piston operates smoothly. *See Fig. 19.* Remove oil seal rings. Using appropriate press and adapter, carefully remove underdrive brake snap ring.

16) Remove flange, plates and discs. Note number and location of components. Remove brake return spring. Using compressed air, remove underdrive brake piston. *See Fig. 19.* Using appropriate compressor, gradually compress spring assembly and remove snap ring. *See Fig. 20.*

17) Remove return spring assembly. Apply compressed air to oil passage in transaxle case and remove 1st and reverse brake piston. *See Fig. 17.* If piston does not pop out, remove using needle-nose pliers. Remove parking lock pawl stopper plate, torsion spring and spring guide. Remove pawl shaft clamp, shaft and lock pawl. *See Fig. 18.*

NOTE: *If manual shift linkage is damaged or needs to be disassembled, see MANUAL SHIFT LINKAGE under COMPONENT DISASSEMBLY & REASSEMBLY.*

18) Remove parking lock sleeve and cam guide bracket. Remove oil gallery cover and gasket. Remove underdrive brake accumulator piston and spring. *See Fig. 18.*

A-245E & A-246E

1) Remove oil cooler pipes, breather hose, manual shift lever and park/neutral position switch. Remove filler tube and dipstick. Remove throttle cable retaining bolt. Remove solenoid harness connector retaining bolt.

2) Remove oil pan and gasket. Remove magnet(s) from oil pan. Remove oil strainer (filter). Remove manual detent spring. Disconnect solenoid connectors. Remove valve body assembly. See VALVE BODY ASSEMBLY under ON-VEHICLE SERVICE. Remove throttle cable and solenoid sub-harness from transaxle case. Remove check ball body and ball, next to 2nd brake accumulator. Remove 2nd brake apply gasket. Remove 2nd brake drum seal. *See Fig. 9.*

3) Apply 14 psi (1 kg/cm²) of compressed air to oil passage to remove underdrive clutch accumulator piston and spring. *See Fig. 21.* Remove forward clutch accumulator piston and springs. Apply 14 psi (1 kg/cm²) of compressed air to oil passage to remove direct clutch accumulator piston and spring. *See Fig. 11.*

4) Apply 14 psi (1 kg/cm²) of compressed air to oil passage to remove 2nd brake accumulator piston and spring. *See Fig. 12.*

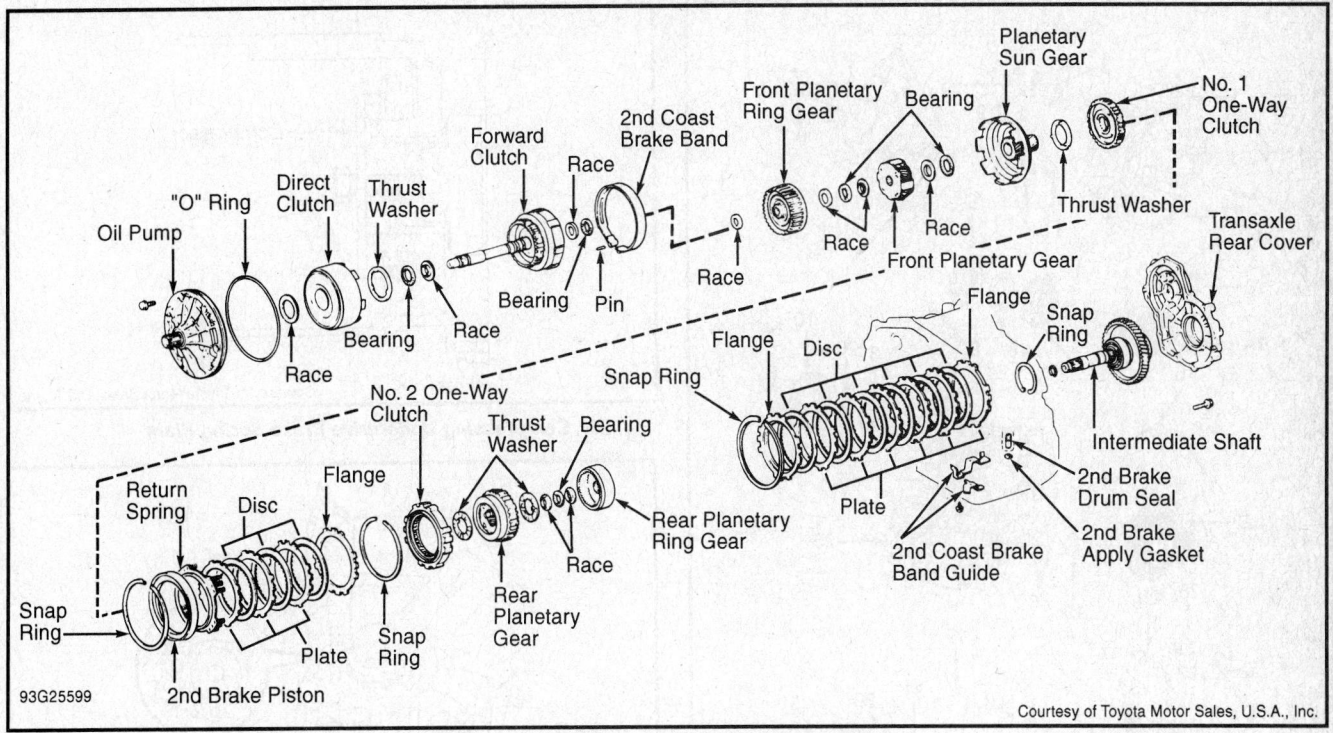

Fig. 15: Exploded View Of Transaxle Case Internal Components (A-242L, A-241E & A-244E)

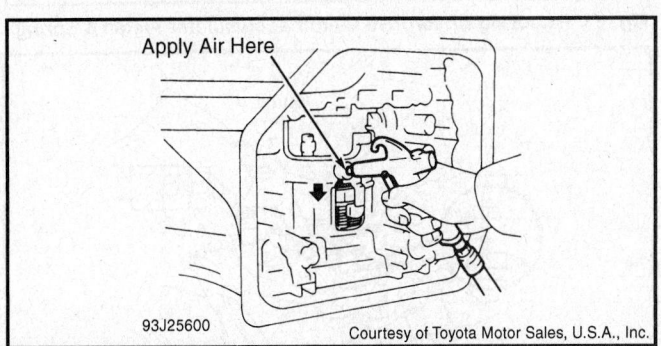

Fig. 16: Checking & Removing 2nd Brake Piston

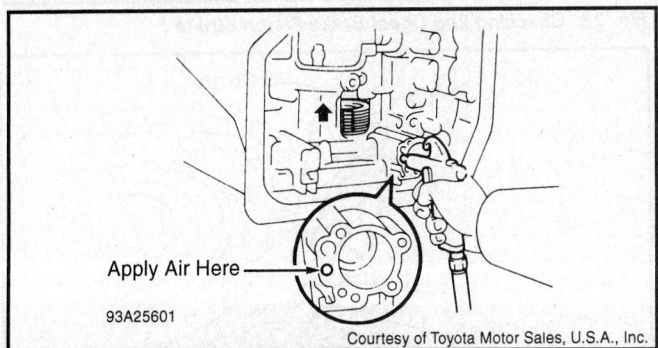

Fig. 17: Checking & Removing 1st & Reverse Piston

NOTE: If manual shift linkage is damaged or needs to be disassembled, see MANUAL SHIFT LINKAGE under COMPONENT DISASSEMBLY AND REASSEMBLY.

5) Remove 2nd brake band guide. Remove transaxle assembly bolts. Remove converter housing. Remove differential assembly. Remove apply gasket. Unbolt and remove oil pump assembly.

6) Apply mark to 2nd coast brake servo apply piston rod where it meets case. Apply air 57-114 psi (4-8 kg/cm²) and measure piston rod travel (stroke). See Fig. 22. Piston rod travel should be .059-.118" (1.5-3.0 mm). If rod travel is not within specification, further inspect band during disassembly.

7) Remove 2nd coast brake piston snap ring. Apply 14 psi (1 kg/cm²) of compressed air to oil passage to remove 2nd coast brake cover. Remove 2nd coast brake piston and spring. See Fig. 23.

8) Remove direct clutch with forward clutch from transaxle case. Remove direct clutch from forward clutch. Remove thrust washer, bearings and races from forward clutch. See Fig. 24.

9) Pull 2nd coast brake band pin and remove. Remove 2nd coast brake band. Remove front planetary ring gear. Remove race and bearing from ring gear. See Fig. 24.

10) Remove front planetary gear. Remove bearings and races from both sides of planetary gear. Remove sun gear, sun gear input drum, thrust washer, 2nd brake hub and No. 1 one-way clutch. Using compressed air, confirm 2nd brake piston operates smoothly. See Fig. 16. Remove 2nd coast brake band guide.

11) Remove 2nd brake drum retaining snap ring. Remove 2nd brake drum. Remove thrust washer and 2nd brake piston return spring. Remove plates, discs and flange. Note number and location of components. Remove No. 2 one-way clutch retaining snap ring. Remove No. 2 one-way clutch and rear planetary gear. See Fig. 24.

12) Remove thrust washers from both sides of planetary gear. Remove rear planetary ring gear with bearing and races. Using feeler gauge, measure 1st and reverse pack clearance. See Fig. 25. Clearance should be .095-.125" (2.42-3.18 mm).

13) Remove flange retaining snap ring. Remove flange, plates and discs. Note number and location of components. Remove rear transaxle cover bolts. Tap rear cover using a plastic hammer. Remove cover. Using chisel, release staked area of intermediate shaft lock nut.

14) Secure counterdriven gear with appropriate holder. Remove intermediate gear lock nut. Remove intermediate shaft. Press out counterdrive gear. Using chisel, release staked area of countershaft lock nuts. Remove both lock nuts.

15) Using appropriate puller, remove counterdriven gear with thrust bearing. Remove countershaft assembly. Remove thrust bearing and

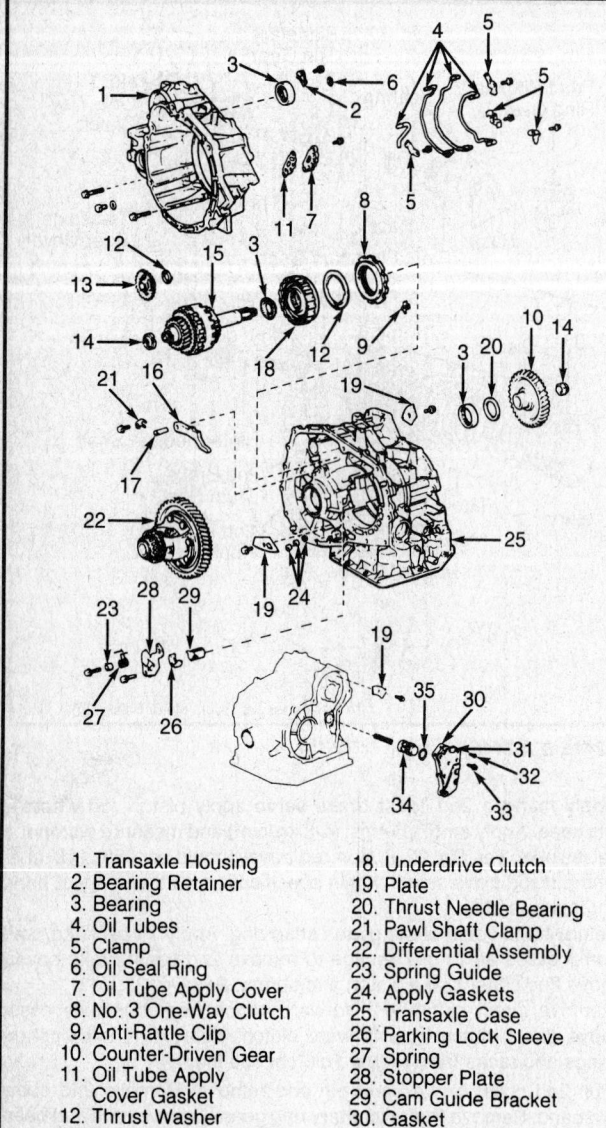

1. Transaxle Housing
2. Bearing Retainer
3. Bearing
4. Oil Tubes
5. Clamp
6. Oil Seal Ring
7. Oil Tube Apply Cover
8. No. 3 One-Way Clutch
9. Anti-Rattle Clip
10. Counter-Driven Gear
11. Oil Tube Apply Cover Gasket
12. Thrust Washer
13. Governor Driven Gear
14. Lock Nut
15. Underdrive Planetary Gear With Countershaft
16. Parking Lock Pawl
17. Pawl Shaft
18. Underdrive Clutch
19. Plate
20. Thrust Needle Bearing
21. Pawl Shaft Clamp
22. Differential Assembly
23. Spring Guide
24. Apply Gaskets
25. Transaxle Case
26. Parking Lock Sleeve
27. Spring
28. Stopper Plate
29. Cam Guide Bracket
30. Gasket
31. Oil Gallery Cover
32. Screw
33. Bolt
34. Underdrive Brake Accumulator Piston
35. "O" Ring

93B25602

Courtesy of Ford Motor Co.

Fig. 18: Exploded View Of Transaxle Housing & Case Components

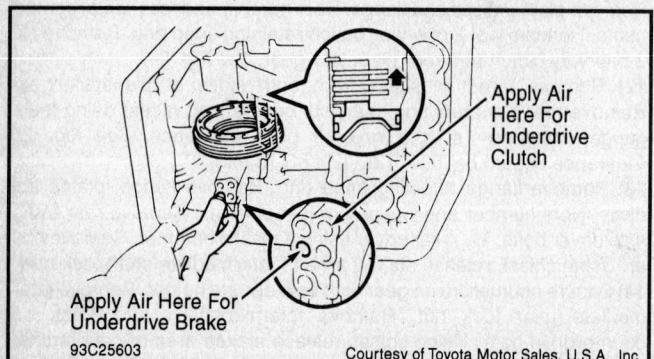

Apply Air Here For Underdrive Clutch

Apply Air Here For Underdrive Brake

93C25603

Courtesy of Toyota Motor Sales, U.S.A., Inc.

Fig. 19: Checking Underdrive Brake & Clutch Piston Operation

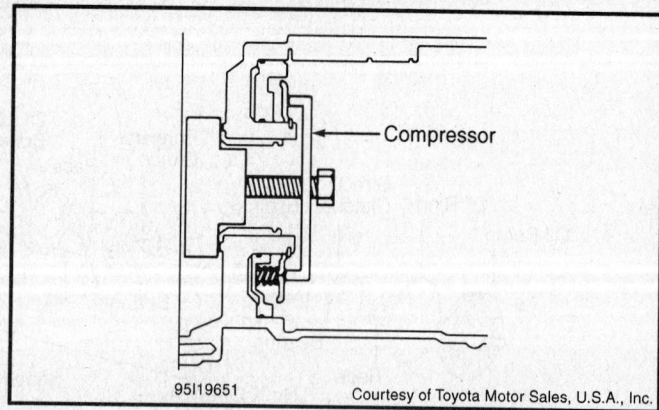

Compressor

95I19651

Courtesy of Toyota Motor Sales, U.S.A., Inc.

Fig. 20: Compressing Underdrive Brake Spring Plate

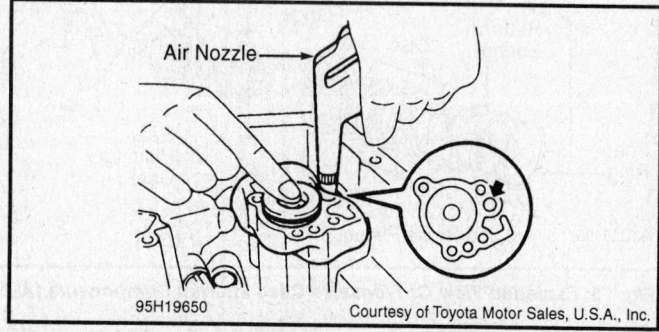

Air Nozzle

95H19650

Courtesy of Toyota Motor Sales, U.S.A., Inc.

Fig. 21: Removing Underdrive Clutch Accumulator Piston & Spring

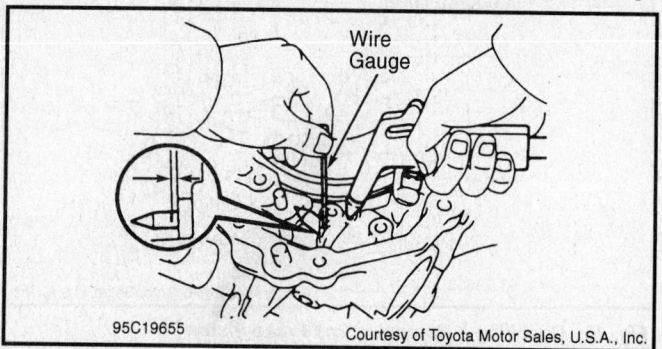

Wire Gauge

95C19655

Courtesy of Toyota Motor Sales, U.S.A., Inc.

Fig. 22: Checking 2nd Coast Brake Piston Stroke

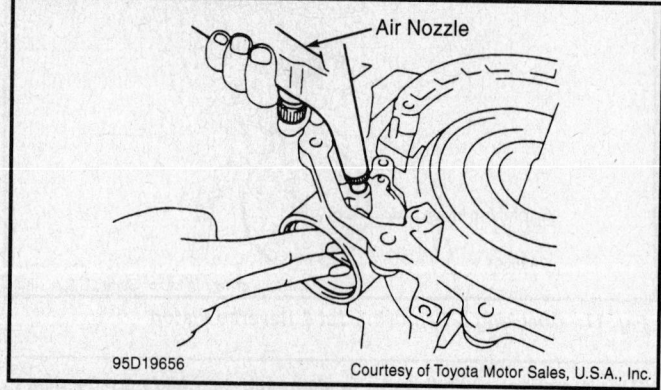

Air Nozzle

95D19656

Courtesy of Toyota Motor Sales, U.S.A., Inc.

Fig. 23: Removing 2nd Coast Brake Cover

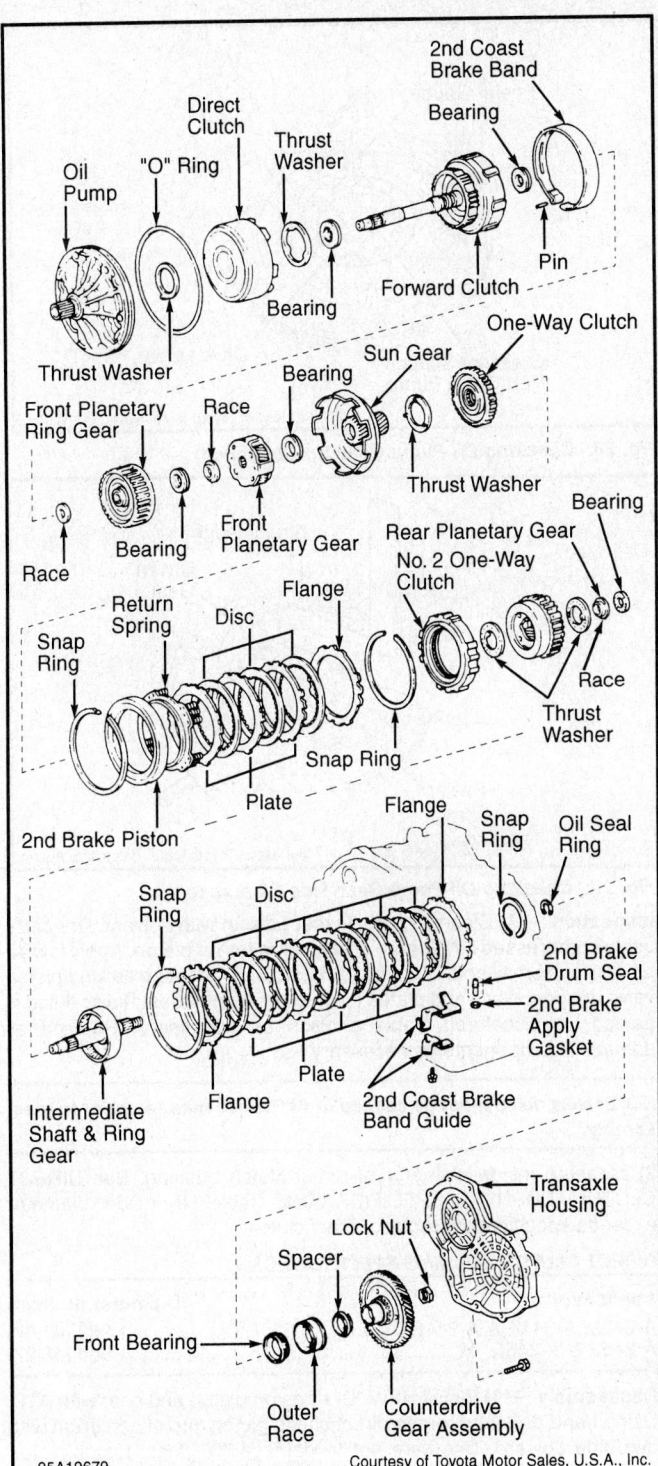

Fig. 24: Exploded View Of Transaxle Case Internal Components (A-245E & A-246)

95A19679 — Courtesy of Toyota Motor Sales, U.S.A., Inc.

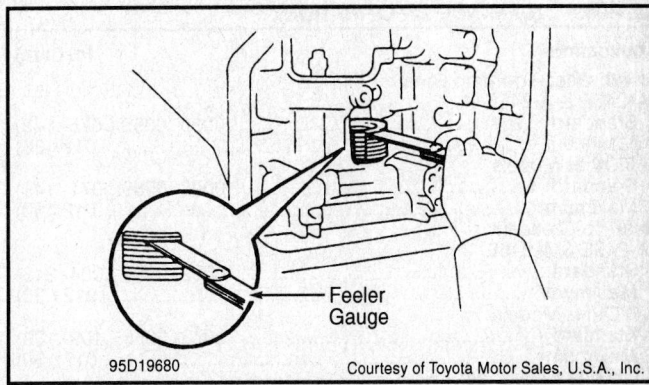

95D19680 — Courtesy of Toyota Motor Sales, U.S.A., Inc.

Fig. 25: Check 1st & Reverse Brake Clutch Pack Clearance

17) Remove return spring assembly. Apply compressed air to oil passage in transaxle case and remove 1st and reverse brake piston. *See Fig. 17.* If piston does not pop out, remove using needle-nose pliers.

18) Remove parking lock pawl stopper plate, torsion spring and spring guide. Remove pawl shaft clamp, shaft and lock pawl. *See Fig. 18.* Remove underdrive brake accumulator piston cover and gasket. Remove accumulator piston and spring.

COMPONENT DISASSEMBLY & REASSEMBLY

OIL PUMP

Disassembly – 1) Remove race from stator shaft (if equipped). Remove "O" ring and oil seal rings from oil pump body and stator shaft. Remove clutch drum thrust washer from stator shaft.

2) Mark stator shaft and oil pump body for reassembly reference. Remove stator shaft bolts. Separate stator shaft and oil pump body. Mark gear location for reassembly reference. Remove pump gears. Using screwdriver, remove front seal. *See Fig. 26.*

Inspection – 1) Note position of oil pump gears. Clean all parts with solvent. Dry parts using compressed air. Ensure oil passages are clear. Check driven gear-to-body clearance. Push driven gear against one side of oil pump. Measure clearance between driven gear and oil pump body. *See Fig. 27.* Replace oil pump body if clearance is not within specification. See OIL PUMP CLEARANCE SPECIFICATIONS table.

2) Measure tip clearance between driven gear and crescent-shaped part of oil pump body. *See Fig. 28.* Replace oil pump body if clearance is not within specification. See OIL PUMP CLEARANCE SPECIFICATIONS table.

3) Using feeler gauge and straightedge, measure side clearance of both gears. *See Fig. 29.* Replace oil pump body if clearance is not within specification. See OIL PUMP CLEARANCE SPECIFICATIONS table. Gears are available in 3 different thicknesses. See DRIVE & DRIVEN GEAR THICKNESS SPECIFICATIONS table.

DRIVE & DRIVEN GEAR THICKNESS SPECIFICATIONS

Identifying Mark	Thickness In. (mm)
A-242L	
A	.371-.372 (9.44-9.46)
B	.372-.373 (9.46-9.47)
C	.373-.374 (9.47-9.49)
All Other Models	
None	N/A

4) Using a dial indicator, measure inside diameter of oil pump body bushing. Maximum inside diameter should be 1.503" (38.18 mm). If inside diameter exceeds specification, replace oil pump body.

5) Measure inside diameter of stator shaft bushings. Maximum front side bushing inside diameter should be .849" (21.57 mm). Maximum rear side bushing inside diameter should be 1.066" (27.07 mm). If inside diameter exceeds specification, replace stator shaft.

race from countershaft. Remove underdrive clutch drum and anti-rattle clip. Using compressed air, confirm underdrive brake piston operates smoothly. *See Fig. 19.* Remove oil seal rings. Using appropriate press and adapter, carefully remove underdrive brake snap ring.

16) Remove flange, plates and discs. Note number and location of components. Remove brake return spring. Using compressed air, remove underdrive brake piston. *See Fig. 19.* Using appropriate compressor, gradually compress spring assembly and remove snap ring. *See Fig. 20.*

OIL PUMP CLEARANCE SPECIFICATIONS

Application	In. (mm)
Driven Gear-To-Pump Body	
A-245E & A-246E	
Standard	.0030-.0059 (.075-.149)
Maximum	.012 (.30)
All Other Models	
Standard	.0028-.0059 (.071-.149)
Maximum	.012 (.30)
Gear-To-Crescent	
A-245E & A-246E	
Standard	.0002-.0098 (.004-.248)
Maximum	.012 (.30)
All Other Models	
Standard	.0043-.0055 (.109-.139)
Maximum	.012 (.30)
Gear Side Clearance	
Standard	.0008-.0020 (.020-.050)
Maximum	.004 (.10)

Reassembly – 1) Install NEW oil seal. Seal must be even with edge of oil pump body. Coat all components with ATF. Install pump gears aligning reference marks. Install stator shaft on pump body. Align bolt holes and tighten bolts to 89 INCH lbs. (10 N.m).
2) Coat thrust washer with petroleum jelly. Install thrust washer on oil pump body. Align washer tab with oil pump body. Install oil seal rings. Use care not to over expand rings. Using screwdrivers, check drive gear for smooth rotation. Install "O" ring. Install race on stator shaft (if equipped). *See Fig. 26.*

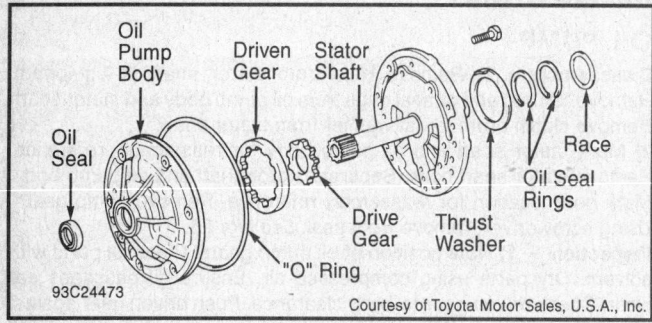

93C24473   Courtesy of Toyota Motor Sales, U.S.A., Inc.

Fig 26: Exploded View Of Oil Pump Assembly

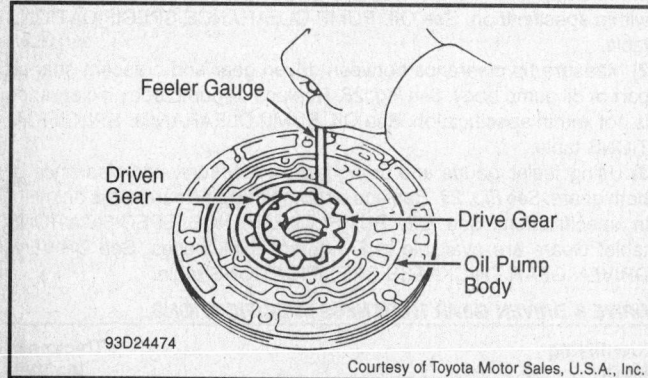

93D24474   Courtesy of Toyota Motor Sales, U.S.A., Inc.

Fig. 27: Checking Oil Pump Driven Gear Clearance

DIRECT CLUTCH

Disassembly – 1) Remove snap ring from direct clutch drum. Remove flange, discs and plates. Note number and location of components. *See Fig. 30.* Using appropriate spring compressor, compress spring retainer and springs. Remove snap ring, clutch spring compressor, spring retainer and piston return springs.
2) Install direct clutch on oil pump. Apply compressed air to oil pump oval shaped oil passage to remove piston. *See Fig. 31.* Remove direct clutch from oil pump. Remove clutch piston "O" rings.

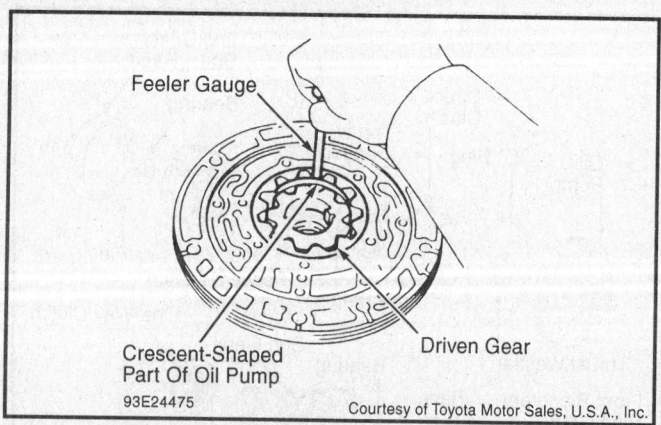

93E24475   Courtesy of Toyota Motor Sales, U.S.A., Inc.

Fig. 28: Checking Oil Pump Gear Tip Clearance

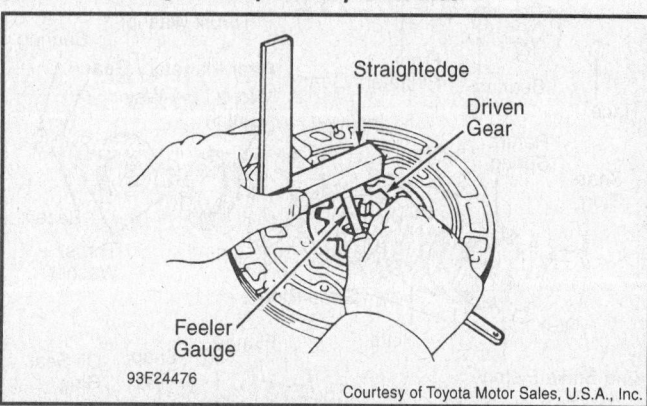

93F24476   Courtesy of Toyota Motor Sales, U.S.A., Inc.

Fig. 29: Checking Oil Pump Gear Side Clearance

Inspection – 1) Clean all parts (except discs) with solvent. Dry parts using compressed air. Ensure check ball is free in piston. Apply low air pressure to small hole in piston to check for air leakage around piston valve. Inspect discs and plates for wear or burnt areas. If disc lining is peeled or discolored, replace discs as necessary. Replace all damaged components as necessary.

NOTE: New discs must be soaked in ATF for 15 minutes prior to reassembly.

2) Measure inside diameter of direct clutch bushing. See DIRECT CLUTCH BUSHING SPECIFICATIONS table. If inside diameter exceeds specification, replace direct clutch.

DIRECT CLUTCH BUSHING SPECIFICATIONS

Application	Diameter In. (mm)
A-242L, A-241E & A-244E	1.853 (47.07)
A-245E & A-246E	1.900 (48.27)

Reassembly – 1) Install NEW "O" rings on piston and coat with ATF. Using hand pressure, press direct clutch piston into clutch drum with cup side upward. Use care not to damage "O" rings. Install piston return springs, retainer and snap ring. Compress return springs and retainer using clutch spring compressor.
2) Ensure snap ring gap does not align with spring retainer claw. Install plates and discs in reverse order of removal. Install flange with flat side facing downward. Install snap ring. Ensure snap ring gap does not align with drum cutout.
3) Install direct clutch on oil pump. Using a dial indicator, measure direct clutch piston stroke. Apply compressed air to oil pump passage and note dial indicator reading. *See Fig. 31.* See DIRECT CLUTCH PISTON STROKE SPECIFICATIONS table for stroke specification. If piston stroke is not as specified, select appropriate flange to obtain correct piston stroke. See DIRECT CLUTCH FLANGE SIZES table for flange thicknesses.

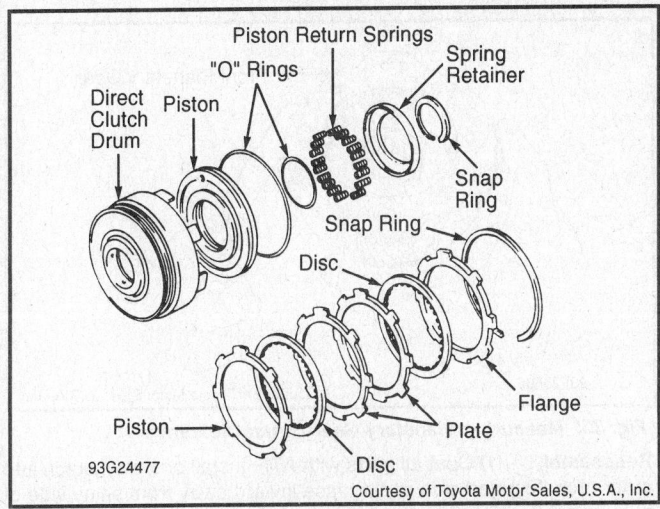

Fig. 30: Exploded View Of Direct Clutch Assembly (Typical)

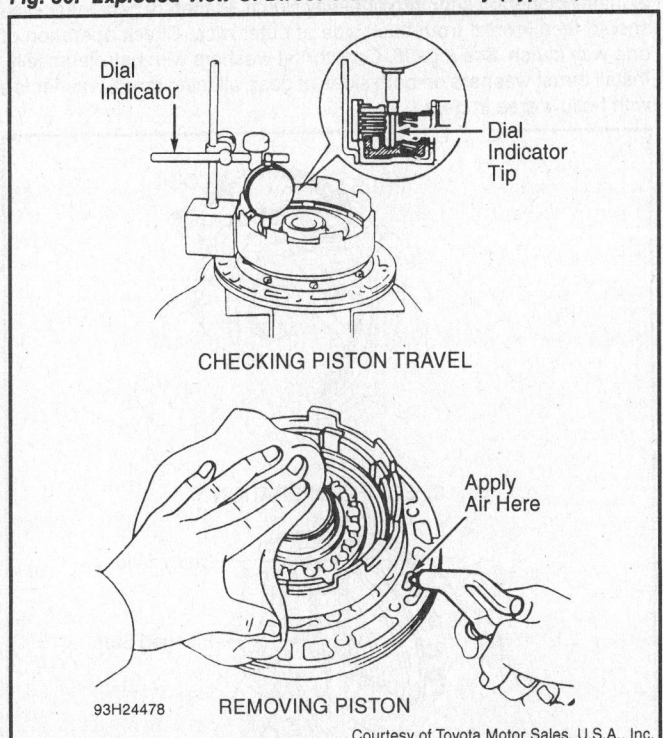

Fig. 31: Checking & Removing Direct Clutch Piston

DIRECT CLUTCH PISTON STROKE SPECIFICATIONS

Application	In. (mm)
A-241E	.044-.058 (1.11-1.47)
A-242L & A-244E	.064-.078 (1.63-1.97)
A-245E & A-246E	.044-.060 (1.11-1.52)

DIRECT CLUTCH FLANGE SIZES

Application	In. (mm)
A-241E	.102 (2.60), .118 (3.00)
A-242L & A-244E	.102 (2.60), .110 (2.80), .118 (3.00)
A-245E & A-246E	.102 (2.60), .110 (2.80), .118 (3.00), .126 (3.20)

FORWARD CLUTCH

Disassembly – 1) Remove thrust washer. Remove thrust bearings and races from both sides of clutch. Remove clutch drum snap ring.

Remove flange, discs and plates. Note number and location of components. See Fig. 32. Using appropriate spring compressor, compress spring retainer and return springs.

2) Remove snap ring. Remove spring compressor, spring retainer and return springs. To remove piston from clutch drum, apply compressed air to oil passage (hole nearest piston) on rear of forward clutch shaft. Remove "O" rings from piston. If necessary, remove oil seal rings.

Inspection – Clean all parts (except discs) with solvent. Dry parts using compressed air. Ensure check ball is free in piston. Apply low air pressure to small hole in piston to check for air leakage around piston valve. Inspect discs and plates for wear or burnt areas. If disc lining is peeled or discolored, replace discs as necessary. Replace all damaged components as necessary.

NOTE: New discs must be soaked in ATF for 15 minutes prior to reassembly.

Reassembly – 1) Install NEW oil seal rings (if necessary). DO NOT over expand seal rings. Install NEW "O" rings on piston and coat with ATF. Using hand pressure, install piston in clutch drum with cup side upward. Use care not to damage "O" rings. Install piston return springs, retainer and snap ring. Compress return springs and retainer using clutch spring compressor. Install snap ring so ring gap does not align with spring retainer claw.

2) Install plate and disc in reverse order of removal. Install flange with flat side facing inward. Install snap ring. Ensure end gap of snap ring is not aligned with drum cutout. Position dial indicator on piston flange. Measure piston stroke by applying compressed air to oil passage (hole nearest piston) on rear of forward clutch shaft and note dial indicator reading.

3) Piston stroke for A-244E transaxle should be .044-.058" (1.11-1.47 mm). Piston stroke for all other transaxles should be .056-.071" (1.42-1.81 mm). If piston stroke is not as specified, select appropriate flange to obtain correct piston stroke.

4) Flanges are available in thicknesses of .110" (2.80 mm) to .126" (3.20 mm) in .008" (.20 mm) increments. Also available are .132" (3.37 mm) and .141" (3.60 mm) flanges. Coat thrust washer, races and bearings with petroleum jelly and install components. See Fig. 32.

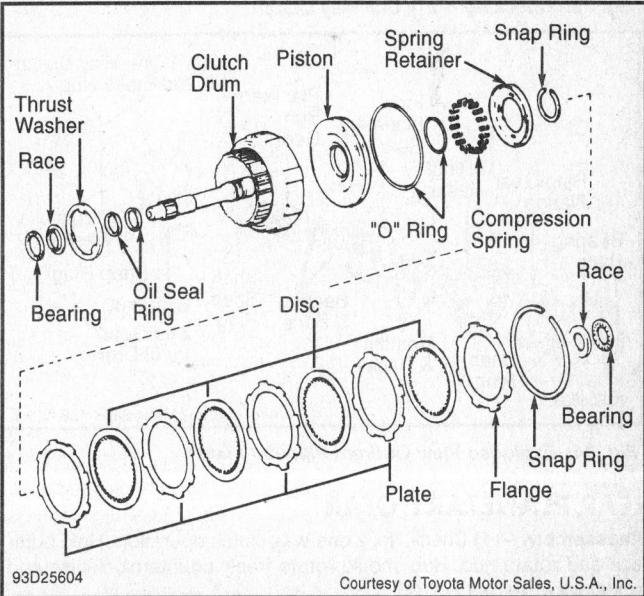

Fig. 32: Exploded View Of Forward Clutch

FRONT PLANETARY GEAR

Disassembly – 1) Check No. 1 one-way clutch operation. Hold sun gear (shell) and turn hub. Hub should rotate freely clockwise and lock when turned counterclockwise. See Fig. 33. Remove 2nd brake hub and No. 1 one-way clutch from sun gear.

2) Remove thrust washer from sun gear input drum. Remove snap ring. Remove sun gear from input drum. Remove shaft snap ring from sun gear. Remove one-way clutch retainer if clutch requires replacement. Remove one-way clutch from hub. *See Fig. 34.*

Inspection – 1) Clean all parts with solvent. Dry parts using compressed air. Check thrust bearings, races and one-way clutch for wear or damage. Replace if necessary.

2) Measure inside diameter of sun gear flange bushing. Standard inside diameter should be .867-.868" (22.03-22.05 mm). Maximum inside diameter is .870" (22.10 mm). If inside diameter exceeds specification, replace flange.

3) Measure planetary pinion gear thrust clearance. Standard clearance should be .008-.020" (.20-.50 mm). Maximum clearance is .020" (.50 mm). If clearance exceeds specification, replace planetary gear. *See Fig. 35.*

4) Measure inside diameter of ring gear flange bushing. Standard inside diameter should be .749-.750" (19.03-19.05 mm). If inside diameter exceeds specification, replace flange.

Reassembly – Install shaft snap ring to sun gear. Install sun gear to drum. Install snap ring to drum. Install thrust washer to sun gear input drum. *See Fig. 34.* Rotate hub clockwise. Install one-way clutch and 2nd brake hub. Check one-way clutch operation. Hold sun gear and rotate hub. Hub should rotate freely clockwise and lock counterclockwise.

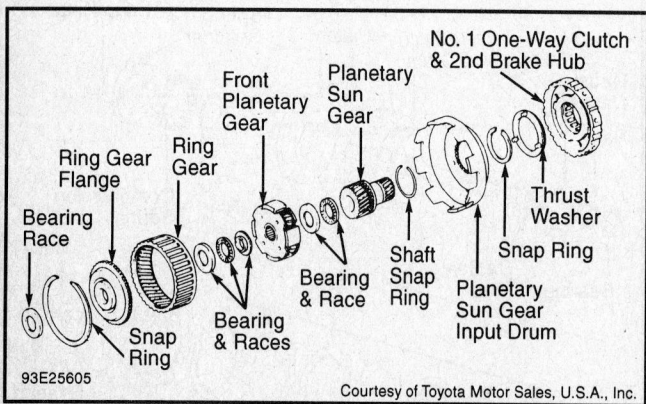

Fig. 33: Checking No. 1 One-Way Clutch

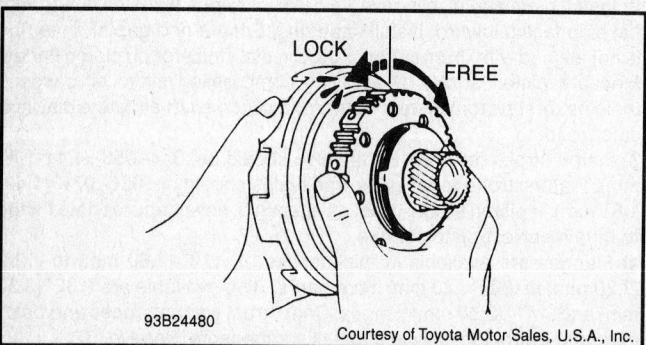

Fig. 34: Exploded View Of Front Planetary Gear

REAR PLANETARY GEAR

Disassembly – 1) Check No. 2 one-way clutch operation. Hold outer race and rotate hub. Hub should rotate freely counterclockwise and lock clockwise. *See Fig. 36.*

2) Remove thrust washers from both sides of planetary gear. Separate No. 2 one-way clutch and planetary gear. Remove snap rings and side retainers from No. 2 one-way clutch. Note position of No. 2 one-way clutch and remove from outer race. *See Fig. 37.*

Inspection – Clean all parts with solvent. Dry parts using compressed air. Check thrust washers and one-way clutch for wear or damage. Replace damaged parts as necessary.

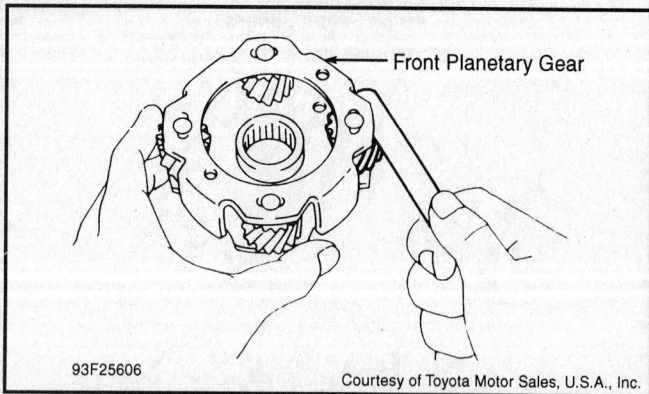

Fig. 35: Measuring Planetary Gear Thrust Clearance

Reassembly – 1) Coat all parts with ATF. Install one-way clutch into outer race. Flanged side should face inward away from shiny side of outer race. *See Fig. 36.* Install side retainers and snap rings.

2) Install planetary gear into one-way clutch. Planetary gear inner race should face inward from back side of outer race. Check operation of one-way clutch. *See Fig. 36.* Coat thrust washers with petroleum jelly. Install thrust washers on both sides of gear, aligning thrust washer tab with hollow area in gear.

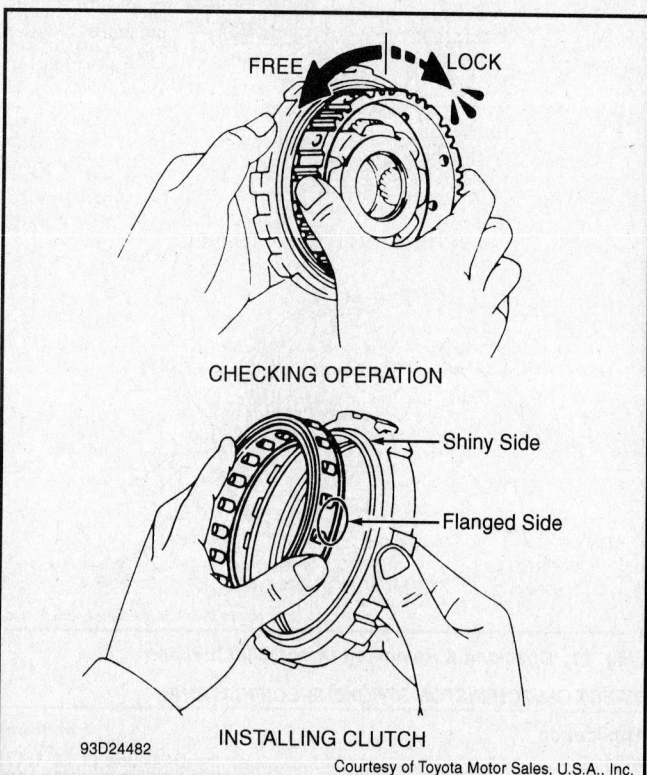

Fig. 36: Installing & Checking No. 2 One-Way Clutch

1ST & REVERSE BRAKE PISTON

Disassembly – 1) Using appropriate compressor, compress piston return springs. *See Fig. 38.* Remove spring retainer snap ring and compressor.

2) Remove piston return spring assembly. Apply compressed air to oil passage in transaxle case to remove piston. *See Fig. 17.* Remove piston "O" rings.

Inspection – Clean all parts with solvent. Dry parts using compressed air. Inspect piston for roughness or damage. Replace as necessary.

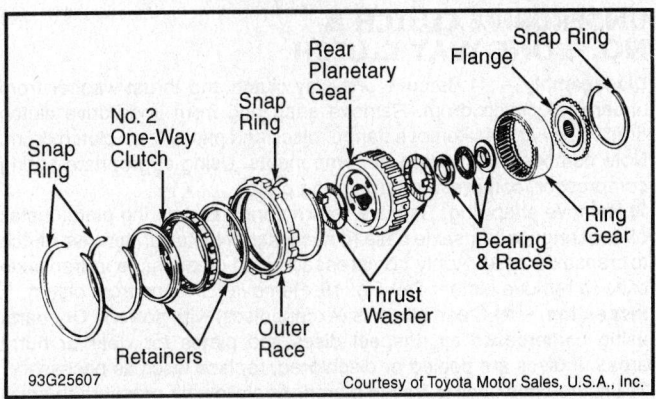

Fig. 37: Exploded View Of Rear Planetary Gear

Reassembly – 1) Install NEW "O" rings on piston and coat with ATF. Install piston in transaxle case with spring seats facing upward. Install piston return spring assembly and snap ring in place. See Fig. 38.
2) Using clutch spring compressor, compress piston return springs. Avoid bending spring retainer or damaging transaxle case by overtightening compressor. Push snap ring into place with fingers.
3) Ensure snap ring is fully seated and centered by spring retainer lugs. Ensure snap ring end gap is not aligned with cutouts. Remove spring compressor.

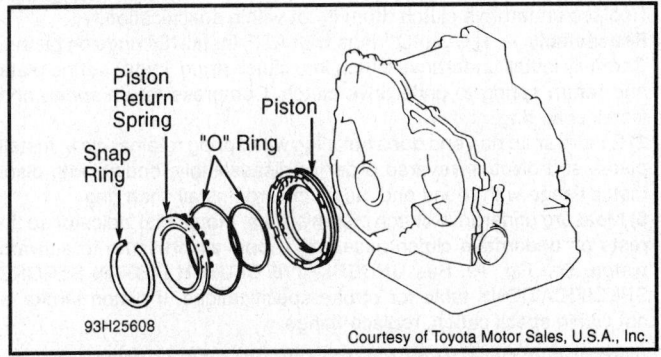

Fig. 38 Exploded View Of 1st & Reverse Brake Piston

2ND COAST BRAKE

Disassembly – 1) Prior to disassembly, check brake piston stroke. Apply paint to piston rod at point rod meets transaxle case. Apply compressed air to oil passage and measure piston stroke using appropriate wire gauge set. Piston stroke should be .059-.118" (1.50-3.00 mm). See Fig. 13 and 22.
2) If piston stroke exceeds specification, check brake band. If brake band is serviceable but piston rod stroke is not within specification, select NEW piston rod. Piston rod is available in lengths of 2.811" (71.40 mm) and 2.870" (72.90 mm).
3) Remove oil seal ring from piston. Remove "E" ring while pushing piston with needle-nose pliers. Remove spring, washer and piston rod. See Fig. 39.
Inspection – Replace brake band if lining is peeled or discolored or printed numbers are defaced. Before assembling NEW band, soak in ATF for 15 minutes.
Reassembly – Install washer and spring to piston rod. Install "E" ring. Install oil seal ring. DO NOT expand oil seal ring ends more than necessary for installation. See Fig. 39.

2ND BRAKE PISTON

Disassembly & Reassembly – Apply compressed air to oil passage and remove 2nd brake piston. See Fig. 16. Remove "O" rings from piston. Coat NEW "O" rings with ATF and install. Carefully press 2nd brake piston into 2nd brake drum. See Fig. 40.

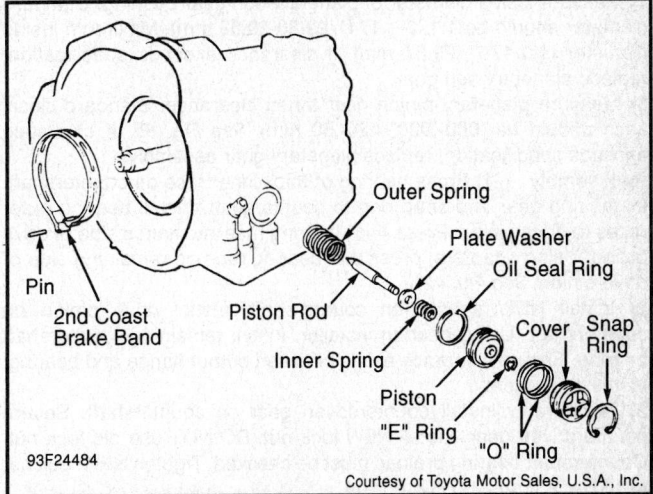

Fig. 39: Exploded View Of 2nd Coast Brake

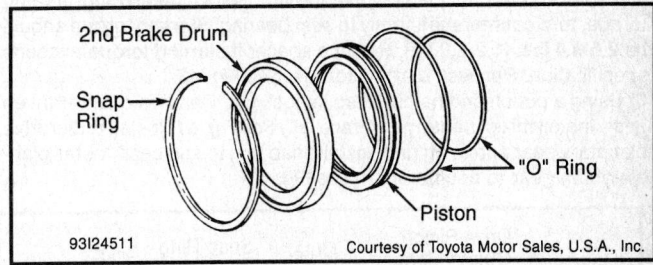

Fig. 40: Exploded View Of 2nd Brake Piston

INTERMEDIATE SHAFT

Disassembly & Reassembly (A-242L, A-241E & A-244E Only) – Using appropriate puller, press intermediate shaft bearings from shaft. Install intermediate shaft bearings using proper adapter and press. Ensure gear flange end to intermediate shaft end measurement is 4.560" (115.82 mm). See Fig. 41.

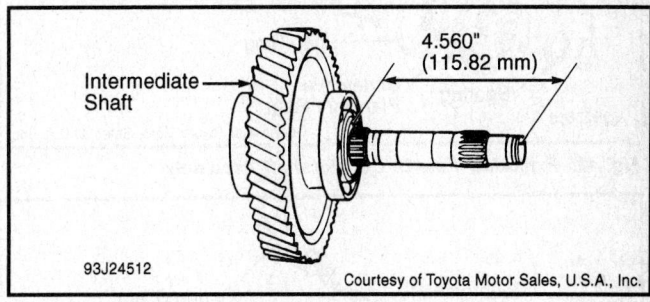

Fig. 41: Checking Intermediate Shaft Gear Flange

COUNTERSHAFT ASSEMBLY

Disassembly – 1) Remove planetary sun gear from countershaft. Remove snap ring from sun gear and countershaft assembly. Remove underdrive planetary gear, thrust bearing and race. See Fig. 42.
2) Remove drive pinion with output flange, outer bearing, race and spacer. Note thickness and size of bearing race. Remove ring gear retaining snap ring. Remove ring gear from countershaft.
3) Remove remaining bearing from countershaft. Remove outer bearing race from drive pinion using a brass punch and hammer. Note size of bearing and bearing race.
Inspection – 1) Clean all parts with solvent. Dry parts using compressed air. Inspect bearings, races, thrust bearing and race, drive pinion and gears for wear or damage. Replace components as necessary.

2) Measure inside diameter of planetary sun gear bushing. Standard diameter should be 1.173-1.174" (29.80-29.83 mm). Maximum inside diameter is 1.176" (29.87 mm). If clearance exceeds specification, replace planetary sun gear.

3) Measure planetary pinion gear thrust clearance. Standard clearance should be .008-.020" (.20-.50 mm). See Fig. 35. If clearance exceeds specification, replace planetary gear assembly.

Reassembly – 1) Press bearing of thick inner race on countershaft. Install ring gear and snap ring to countershaft. Install bearing outer races to drive pinion. Press thick bearing race into flange side of drive pinion. Using adapters, press thin bearing race on remaining side of drive pinion. See Fig. 42.

2) Install NEW spacer on countershaft. Install drive pinion on countershaft. Using bearing installer, install remaining countershaft bearing. Ensure clearance exists between output flange and bearing. Install inner race.

3) Temporarily install counterdriven gear on countershaft. Secure counterdriven gear. Install NEW lock nut. DO NOT use old lock nut. Countershaft bearing preload must be checked. Tighten NEW lock nut to 131-159 ft. lbs. (177-216 N.m).

4) Using Countershaft Adapter (09351-32170) and a spring scale, measure starting torque of countershaft. Before measuring starting torque, turn countershaft firmly to seat bearing. Starting torque should be 2.6-4.4 lbs. (1.2-2.0 kg). Replace spacer if starting torque exceeds specification. Recheck starting torque. See Fig. 43.

5) Using a punch and hammer, stake lock nut. Remove counterdriven gear. Install thrust bearing and race "H". See Fig. 81. Install underdrive planetary gear and snap ring. Install snap ring to sun gear. Install planetary sun gear to countershaft. See Fig. 42.

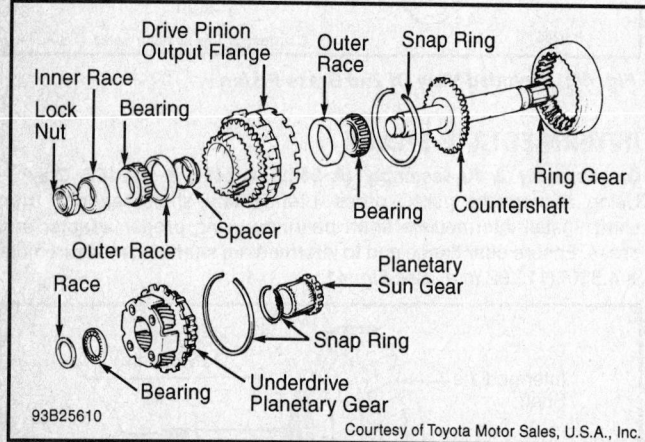

Fig. 42: Exploded View Of Countershaft Assembly

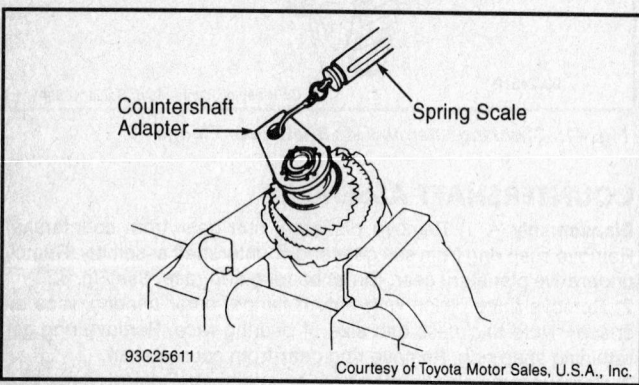

Fig. 43: Measuring Countershaft Torque

UNDERDRIVE CLUTCH & NO. 3 ONE-WAY CLUTCH

Disassembly – 1) Remove one-way clutch and thrust washer from underdrive clutch drum. Remove snap ring from underdrive clutch drum. See Fig. 44. Remove flange, discs and plates from clutch drum. Note number and location of components. Using appropriate spring compressor, compress return spring plate.

2) Remove snap ring. Remove return spring and spring plate. Install oil seal rings to transaxle case (if necessary). Install underdrive clutch to transaxle case. Apply compressed air to oil passage in transaxle case to remove piston. See Fig. 19. Remove "O" rings from piston.

Inspection – 1) Clean all parts (except discs) with solvent. Dry parts using compressed air. Inspect discs and plates for wear or burnt areas. If discs are peeled or discolored, replace discs as necessary.

2) Ensure check ball is free in piston. Apply low air pressure to small hole in piston to check for air leakage around piston valve. Replace all damaged components.

NOTE: New discs must be soaked in ATF for 15 minutes prior to installation.

3) Measure inside diameter of underdrive clutch drum bushing. Standard diameter for front side of bushing should be 1.831-1.832" (46.50-46.53 mm). Standard diameter for rear side of bushing should be 2.165-2.167" (55.00-55.03 mm). Maximum inside diameter should be 1.833" (46.57 mm) for front side and 2.169" (55.08 mm) for rear side. Replace underdrive clutch drum if not within specification.

Reassembly – 1) Coat "O" rings with ATF. Install "O" rings on piston. Carefully install underdrive clutch into clutch drum. Install spring plate and return spring to underdrive clutch. Compress return spring and install snap ring.

2) Ensure snap ring end does not align with spring retainer claw. Install plates and discs in reverse order of disassembly, ending with disc. Install flange with round end facing inward. Install snap ring.

3) Measure underdrive clutch piston stroke. Mount dial indicator so tip rests on underdrive clutch assembly. Apply air pressure to activate piston. See Fig. 19. See UNDERDRIVE CLUTCH PISTON STROKE SPECIFICATIONS table for stroke specifications. If piston stroke is not within specification, replace flange.

UNDERDRIVE CLUTCH PISTON STROKE SPECIFICATIONS

Application	In. (mm)
A-242L & A-244E	.059-.073 (1.50-1.86)
A-241E	.048-.061 (1.21-1.55)
A-245E & A-246E	.059-.075 (1.50-1.90)

4) For A-241E and A-242L transaxle, flange is available in thicknesses of .091" (2.30 mm), .098" (2.50 mm) and .106" (2.70 mm). For A-244E transaxle, flange is available in thicknesses of .080" (2.04 mm) and .094" (2.40 mm). For all other transaxles, flange is available in thicknesses of .080" (2.04 mm), .087" (2.20 mm), .094" (2.40 mm) and .098" (2.50 mm). Install appropriate flange to obtain correct clearance.

5) Install thrust washer on underdrive clutch drum. Install underdrive one-way clutch on underdrive clutch drum. Retainer claw must be facing upward. Check operation of one-way clutch. Hold clutch drum and rotate one-way clutch. One-way clutch should turn freely counterclockwise and lock clockwise. See Fig. 44.

UNDERDRIVE BRAKE & ACCUMULATOR

Disassembly – 1) Compress return spring and remove snap ring. Remove plates, discs and flange. Note number and location of components. Remove return spring. Remove oil seal rings (if necessary).

2) Apply compressed air to oil passage in transaxle case to remove underdrive piston from transaxle case. See Fig. 19. Remove "O" rings from piston. Remove oil gallery cover and gasket. Remove accumulator piston and spring from transaxle case. Remove "O" ring from piston. See Fig. 45.

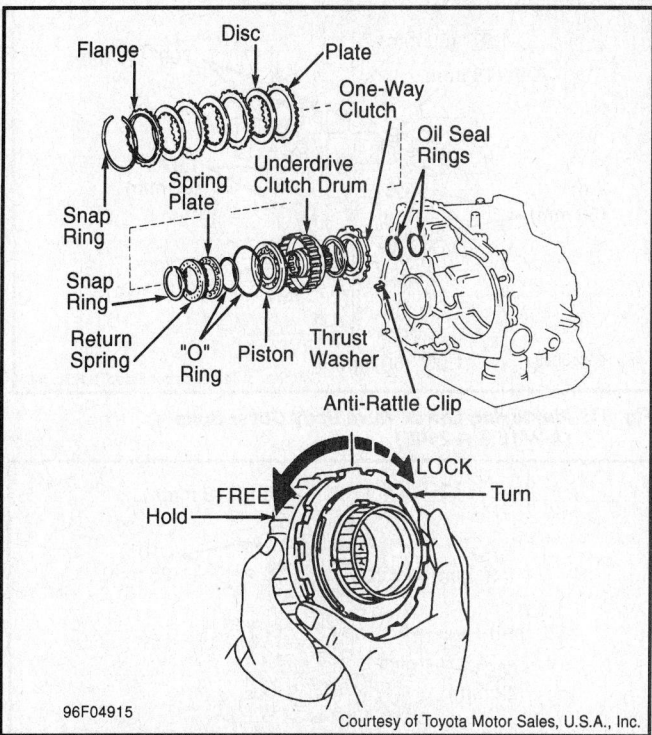

Fig. 44: Exploded View Of Underdrive Clutch & Checking No. 3 One-Way Clutch Operation

Inspection – 1) Clean all parts (except discs) with solvent. Dry parts using compressed air. Inspect discs and plates for wear or burnt areas. If discs are peeled or discolored, replace discs as necessary. **2)** Inspect underdrive brake piston. Ensure check ball is free by shaking piston. Ensure valve does not leak by applying low pressure compressed air to small hole in piston.

NOTE: New discs must be soaked in ATF for 15 minutes prior to reassembly.

Reassembly – 1) Coat NEW "O" ring with ATF and install on accumulator piston. Install accumulator piston and spring. Install oil gallery gasket and cover. Tighten bolts to 89 INCH lbs. (10 N.m). Apply thread sealant to screws for oil gallery cover. Install screws and tighten to 65 INCH lbs. (7.4 N.m).
2) Install underdrive brake piston "O" rings. Coat "O" rings with ATF. Install piston in transaxle case with cupped side upward. Use care not to damage "O" rings. Install brake piston return spring. Install plates and discs. Install flange with flat end facing inward.
3) Using spring compressor, compress return spring. Install snap ring. Ensure snap ring end gap is not aligned with cutout. Using compressed air, ensure underdrive brake piston operates smoothly. See Fig. 19.

VALVE BODY ASSEMBLY

NOTE: All valve body assembly components must be installed in original location. Arrange components in sequence during removal for reassembly reference. Throttle pressure is changed according to number of adjusting rings. When assembling valve body, install same number of adjusting rings as were removed. Some valve bodies do not have adjusting rings.

CAUTION: Note which step at end of plunger sleeve contacts valve body prior to removal. Line pressure is affected by plunger location. See Fig. 46.

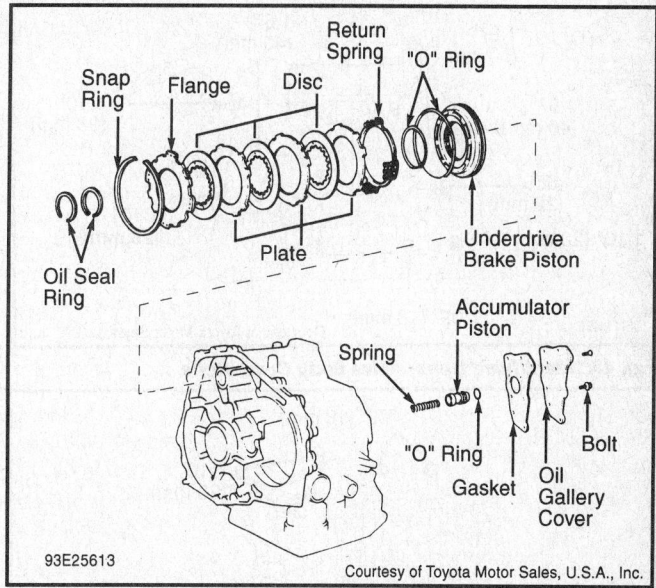

Fig. 45: Exploded View Of Underdrive Brake & Accumulator

Disassembly (A-242L) – Remove solenoid. Remove 17 bolts and lower valve body cover. See Fig. 47. Remove strainer, gaskets and plate. Remove 8 bolts from upper valve body. See Fig. 48. Remove 5 bolts from lower valve body. See Fig. 49. Hold plate against lower valve body and carefully remove lower valve body. DO NOT lose check balls. Note location of check balls, retainers, pins and plugs in valve body. Remove plate and gasket. See Fig. 50.

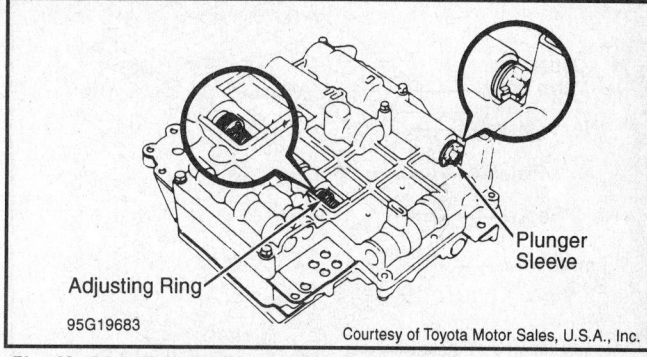

Fig. 46: Identifying Adjusting Ring & Plunger Sleeve Locations

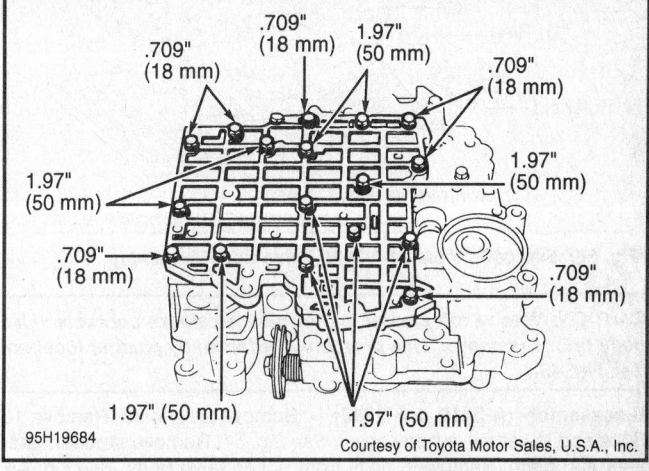

Fig. 47: Identifying Lower Valve Body Cover Bolts (A-242L)

AUTOMATIC TRANSMISSIONS
Toyota A-240 "E" & "L" Series (Cont.)

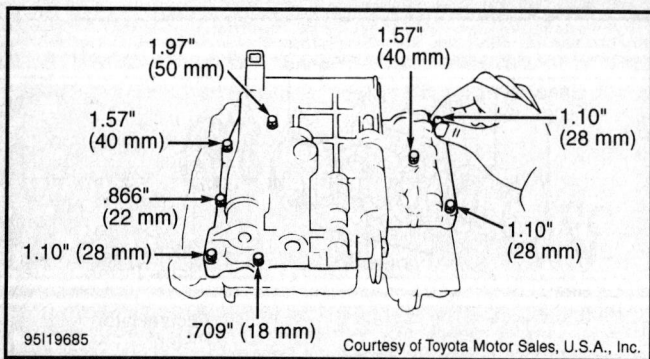

95I19685   Courtesy of Toyota Motor Sales, U.S.A., Inc.

Fig. 48: Identifying Upper Valve Body Cover Bolts

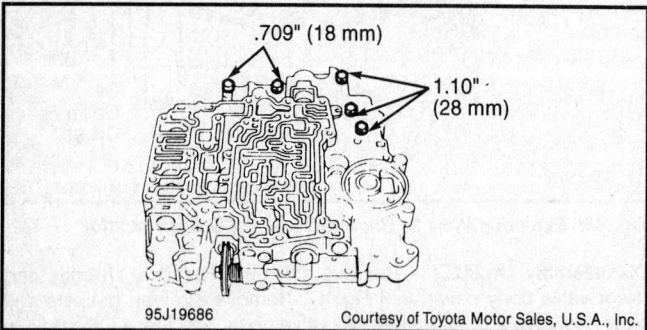

95J19686   Courtesy of Toyota Motor Sales, U.S.A., Inc.

Fig. 49: Identifying Lower Valve Body Bolts

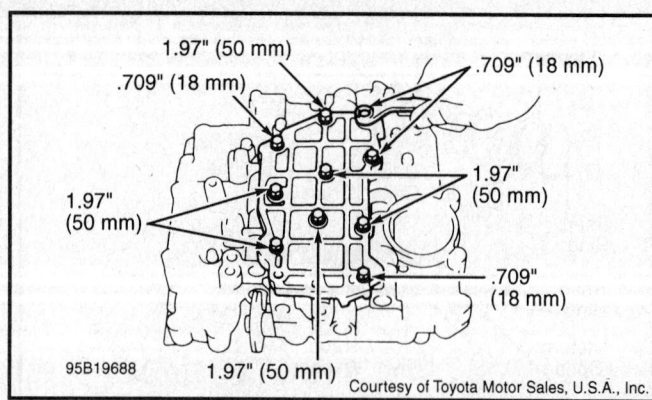

95B19688   Courtesy of Toyota Motor Sales, U.S.A., Inc.

Fig. 51: Identifying Lower Valve Body Cover Bolts (A-241E & A-244E)

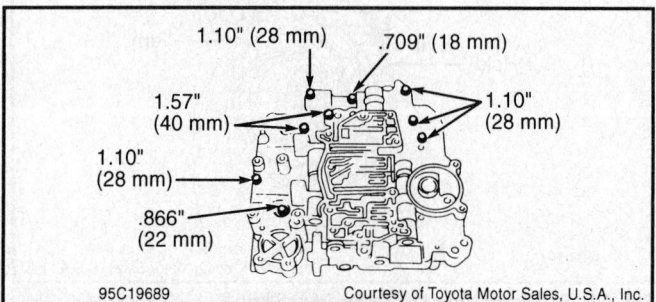

95C19689   Courtesy of Toyota Motor Sales, U.S.A., Inc.

Fig. 52: Identifying Lower Valve Body Bolts

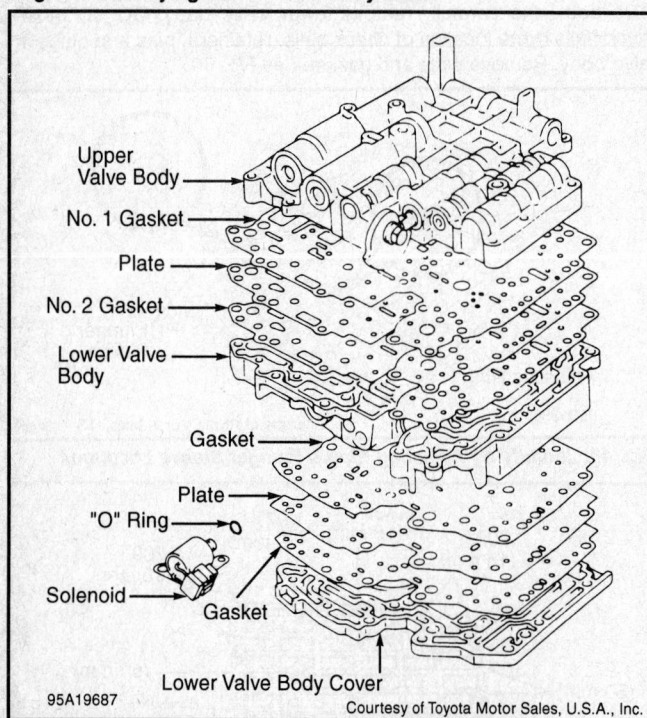

95A19687   Courtesy of Toyota Motor Sales, U.S.A., Inc.

Fig. 50: Exploded View Of A-242L Valve Body Assembly

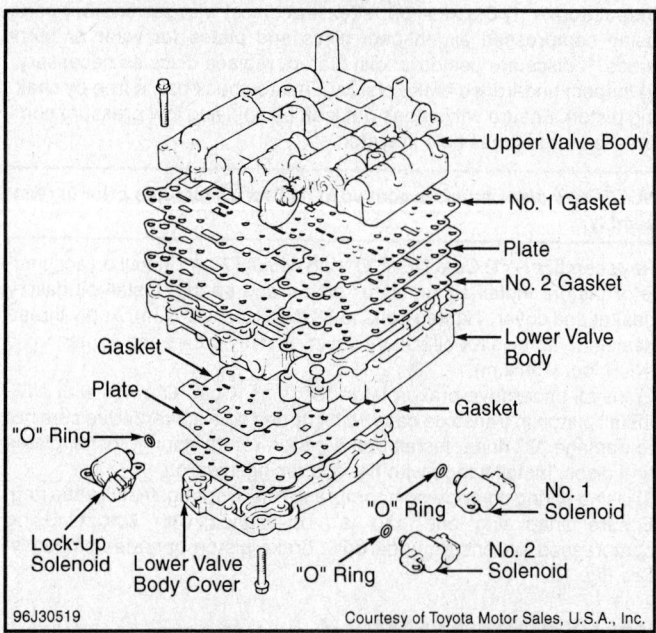

96J30519   Courtesy of Toyota Motor Sales, U.S.A., Inc.

Fig. 53: Exploded View Of A-241E & A-244E Valve Body Assembly

CAUTION: Note which step at end of plunger sleeve contacts valve body prior to removal. Line pressure is affected by plunger location. See Fig. 46.

Disassembly (A-241E & A-244E) – Remove solenoids. Remove 10 bolts and lower valve body cover. *See Fig. 51*. Remove strainer, gaskets and plate. Remove 8 bolts from upper valve body. *See Fig. 48*. Remove 9 bolts from lower valve body. *See Fig. 52*. Hold plate against lower valve body and carefully remove lower valve body. DO NOT lose check balls. Note location of check balls, retainers, pins and plugs in valve body. Remove plate and gasket. *See Fig. 53*.

CAUTION: Note position of throttle valve adjusting screw before disassembly. Also note which step at end of plunger sleeve contacts valve body prior to removal. Line pressure is affected by plunger location. See Fig. 54.

Disassembly (A-245E & A-246E) – Remove throttle cam. Remove solenoids. Remove pressure relief valve. Remove 21 bolts from lower valve body. *See Fig. 55*. Hold plate against lower valve body and carefully remove lower valve body. DO NOT lose check balls. Note location of check balls, retainers, pins and plugs in valve body. Remove plate and gasket. *See Fig. 56*.

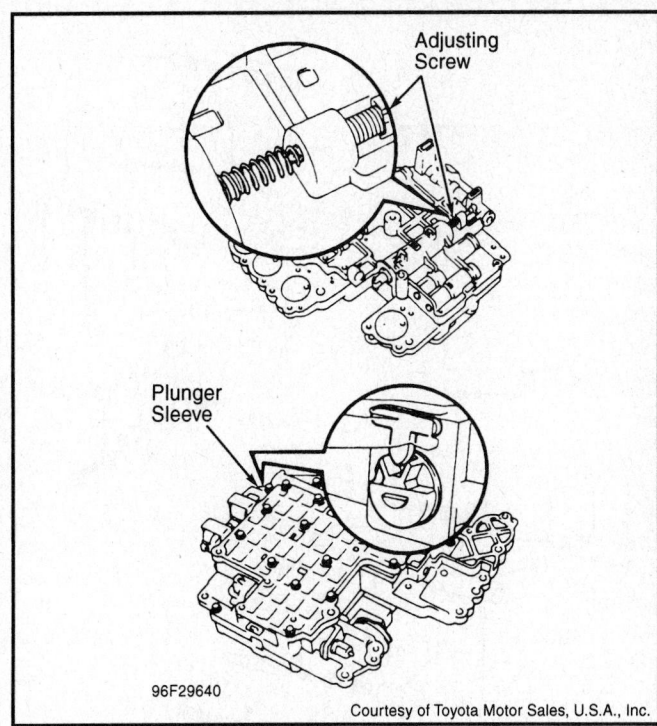

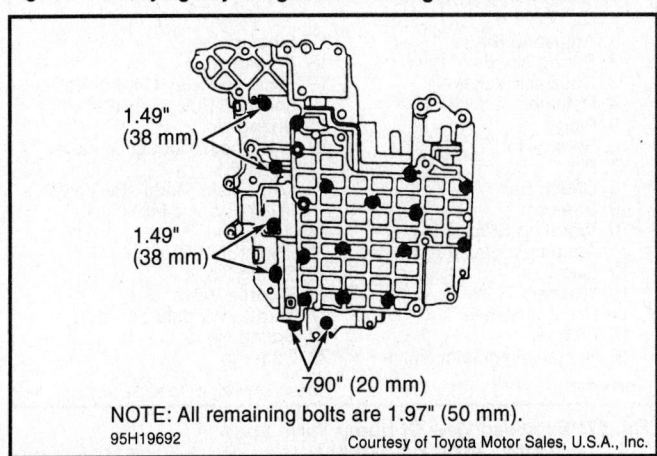

Fig. 54: Identifying Adjusting Screw & Plunger Sleeve Locations

Fig. 55: Identifying Lower Valve Body Bolts (A-245E & A-246E)

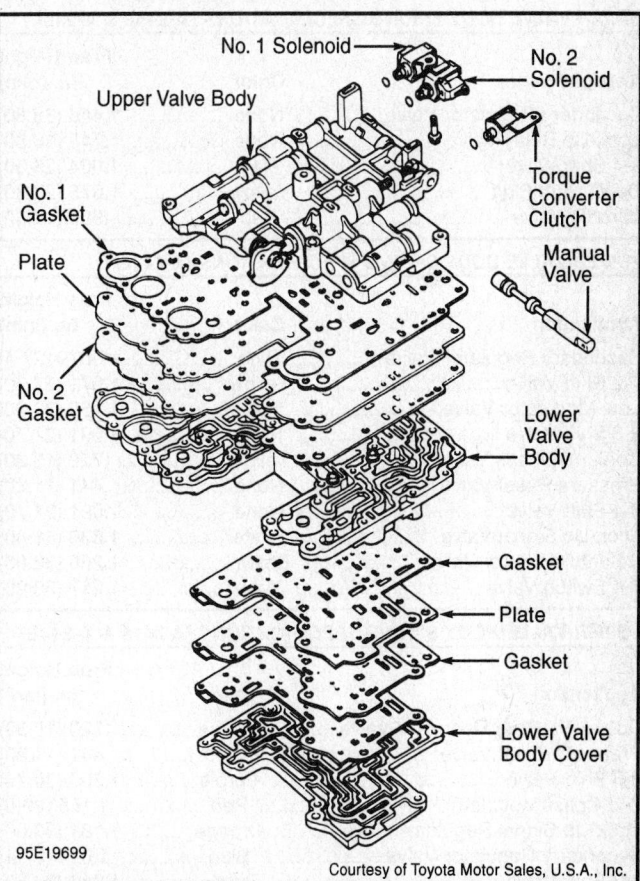

Fig. 56: Exploded View Of Valve Body Assembly (A-245E & A-246E)

UPPER VALVE BODY SPRING SPECIFICATIONS (A-242L)

Application	Color	Free Height In. (mm)
Primary Regulator Valve	Purple	2.626 (66.70)
Lock-Up Relay Valve	None	.740 (18.80)
2nd Coast Modulator Valve	Red	1.165 (29.60)
Throttle Valve	Blue	1.181 (30.00)
Down Shift Plug	Lt. Green	1.150 (29.20)
Throttle Modulator Valve	Green	1.177 (29.90)
Accumulator Control Valve	None	1.370 (34.80)

UPPER VALVE BODY SPRING SPECIFICATIONS (A-241E & A-244E)

Application	Color	Free Height In. (mm)
Primary Regulator Valve	None	2.626 (66.70)
Lock-Up Relay Valve	None	.740 (18.80)
Low Coast Modulator Valve	Yellow	1.083 (27.50)
Down Shift Plug	Red [1]	.957 (24.30)
Throttle Valve	Lt. Green	1.150 (29.20)
Throttle Modulator Valve	Green	1.177 (29.90)
Accumulator Control Valve	Orange [2]	[3] 1.307 (33.20)

[1] – A-244E spring color is Blue.
[2] – Spring for A-244E has no color.
[3] – Spring length is 1.370" (34.80 mm) for A-244E.

Inspection (All Models) – 1) Clean all parts with solvent. Dry parts with compressed air. When disassembling upper or lower valve body, maintain parts in order for reassembly reference. Ensure each valve is kept with corresponding spring. For upper valve body exploded views, *see Figs. 57 and 58*. For lower valve body exploded views, *See Figs. 58-60*.
2) Ensure all valve body oil passages are clear. Inspect valves for scoring or roughness. Inspect valve springs for damage, squareness, rust and collapsed coils. Measure spring free height and outer diameter.
3) Replace spring if not within specification. See appropriate VALVE BODY SPRING SPECIFICATIONS table. Ensure valve body springs correspond with appropriate valve. Ensure check balls are installed in appropriate locations. *See Fig. 61.* Ensure pins, retainers, strainers and vibrating stopper is installed in appropriate locations.

UPPER VALVE BODY SPRING SPECIFICATIONS (A-245E & A-246E)

Application	Color	Free Height In. (mm)
Secondary Regulator Valve	None	1.449 (36.80)
Lock-Up Relay Valve	None	.740 (18.80)
3-4 Shift Valve	Red	1.004 (25.50)
Down Shift Plug	Yellow	1.075 (27.30)
Throttle Valve	Red	.689 (17.50)

LOWER VALVE BODY SPRING SPECIFICATIONS (A-242L)

Application	Color	Free Height In. (mm)
Secondary Regulator Valve	Blue	1.079 (27.4)
1-2 Shift Valve	Yellow	1.071 (27.20)
Low Modulator Valve	None	1.150 (29.20)
2-3 Shift Valve	None	1.091 (27.70)
Cooler By-Pass Valve	Yellow	.720 (18.30)
Pressure Relief Valve	None	.441 (11.20)
3-4 Shift Valve	None	1.091 (27.70)
Lock-Up Signal Valve	White	1.630 (41.40)
Detent Regulator Valve	Brown	1.260 (32.00)
3-4 Switch Valve	None	1.217 (30.90)

LOWER VALVE BODY SPRING SPECIFICATIONS (A-241E & A-244E)

Application	Color	Free Height In. (mm)
Cooler By-Pass Regulator Valve	Yellow	.720 (18.30)
Pressure Relief Valve	None	.441 (11.20)
2-3 Shift Valve	Purple	1.209 (30.70)
2nd Coast Modulator Valve	Red	1.165 (29.6)
Lock-Up Signal Regulator Valve	Orange	1.181 (30.00)
Secondary Regulator Valve	Blue	1.079 (27.4)
1-2 Shift Valve	Purple	1.213 (30.80)
3-4 Shift Valve	Purple	1.213 (30.80)

LOWER VALVE BODY SPRING SPECIFICATIONS (A-245E & A-246E)

Application	Color	Free Height In. (mm)
Cooler By-Pass Valve	None	.965 (24.50)
Pressure Relief Valve	Red	.709 (18.00)
2-3 Shift Valve	Red	1.004 (25.50)
2nd Coast Modulator Valve	White	1.268 (32.20)
Cut-Back Valve	None	.740 (18.80)
Primary Regulator Valve	Red	1.638 (41.60)
1-2 Shift Valve	Red	1.004 (25.50)
Reverse Control Valve	None	1.008 (25.60)
Accumulator Control Valve	Pink	1.154 (29.30)
Low Coast Modulator Valve	Blue	1.122 (28.50)

Reassembly (A-242L) – **1)** Coat all components with ATF. Position NEW No. 2 gasket, plate and NEW No. 1 gasket on lower valve body. Ensure gaskets are installed in correct locations. *See Fig. 62.*

2) Place lower valve body with plate and gaskets on upper valve body. DO NOT let components separate. Align each bolt hole in valve bodies with gaskets and plate.

3) Install and finger tighten bolts in lower valve body to secure upper valve body. *See Fig. 49.* Install lower valve body cover over NEW gasket. Install and finger tighten cover bolts. *See Fig. 47.* Install and finger tighten bolts in upper valve body. *See Fig. 48.*

4) Tighten upper and lower valve body bolts to 58 INCH lbs. (6.5 N.m). Install NEW "O" ring on solenoid. Lubricate "O" ring with ATF and install solenoid. Tighten bolts for single solenoid to 58 INCH lbs. (6.5 N.m).

Reassembly (A-241E & A-244E) – **1)** Coat all components with ATF. To reassemble, reverse disassembly procedure. Position NEW No. 2 gasket, plate and NEW No. 1 gasket on lower valve body. Ensure gaskets are installed in correct locations. *See Fig. 63.*

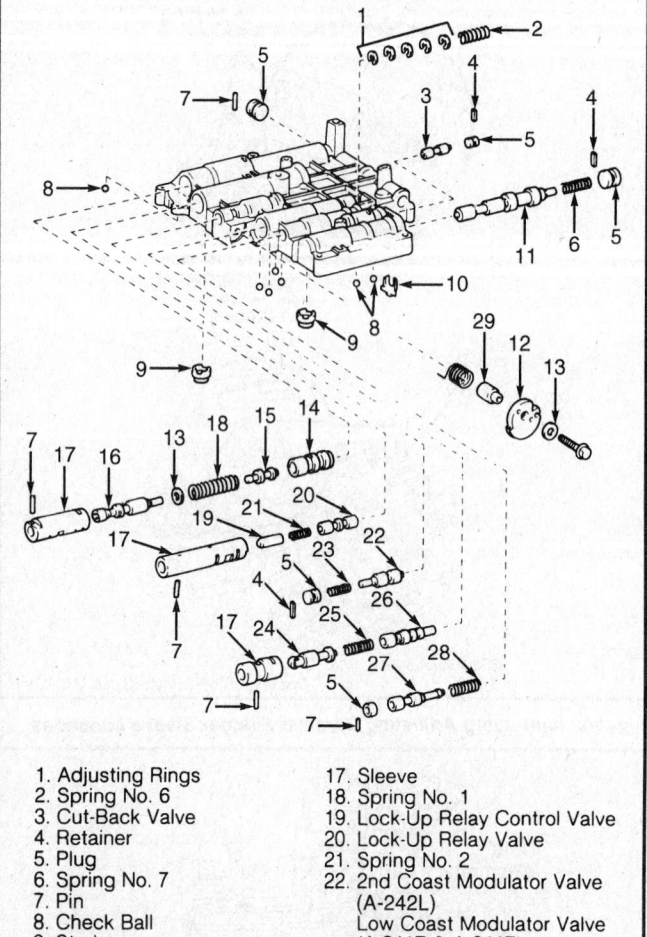

1. Adjusting Rings
2. Spring No. 6
3. Cut-Back Valve
4. Retainer
5. Plug
6. Spring No. 7
7. Pin
8. Check Ball
9. Strainer
10. Vibrating Stopper
11. Accumulator Control Valve
12. Cam
13. Washer
14. Plunger Sleeve
15. Plunger
16. Primary Regulator Valve
17. Sleeve
18. Spring No. 1
19. Lock-Up Relay Control Valve
20. Lock-Up Relay Valve
21. Spring No. 2
22. 2nd Coast Modulator Valve (A-242L) Low Coast Modulator Valve (A-241E & A-244E)
23. Spring No. 3
24. Down Shift Plug
25. Spring No. 4
26. Throttle Valve
27. Throttle Modulator Valve
28. Spring No. 5
29. Cam Pin

95I19693   Courtesy of Toyota Motor Sales, U.S.A., Inc.

Fig. 57: Exploded View Of Upper Valve Body (A-242L, A-241E & A-244E)

2) Place lower valve body with plate and gaskets on upper valve body. DO NOT let components separate. Align each bolt hole in valve bodies with gaskets and plate.

3) Install and finger tighten bolts in lower valve body to secure upper valve body. *See Fig. 52.* Install lower valve body cover over NEW gasket. Install and finger tighten cover bolts. *See Fig. 51.* Install and finger tighten bolts in upper valve body. *See Fig. 48.*

4) Ensure retainers are installed correctly. Position NEW gasket, plate and gasket. Tighten upper and lower valve body bolts to 58 INCH lbs. (6.5 N.m). Install NEW "O" rings on solenoids. Lubricate "O" rings with ATF and install solenoids. Tighten bolts for single solenoid to 58 INCH lbs. (6.5 N.m). Tighten bolts for 2 solenoids mounted together to 89 INCH lbs. (10 N.m).

Reassembly (A-245E & A-246E) – **1)** Coat all components with ATF. To reassemble, reverse disassembly procedure. Position NEW No. 2 gasket, plate and NEW No. 1 gasket on lower valve body. Ensure gaskets are installed in correct locations. *See Fig. 64.*

2) Place lower valve body with plate and gaskets on upper valve body. DO NOT let components separate. Align each bolt hole in valve bodies with gaskets and plate. Turn assembly over and install lower valve body cover.

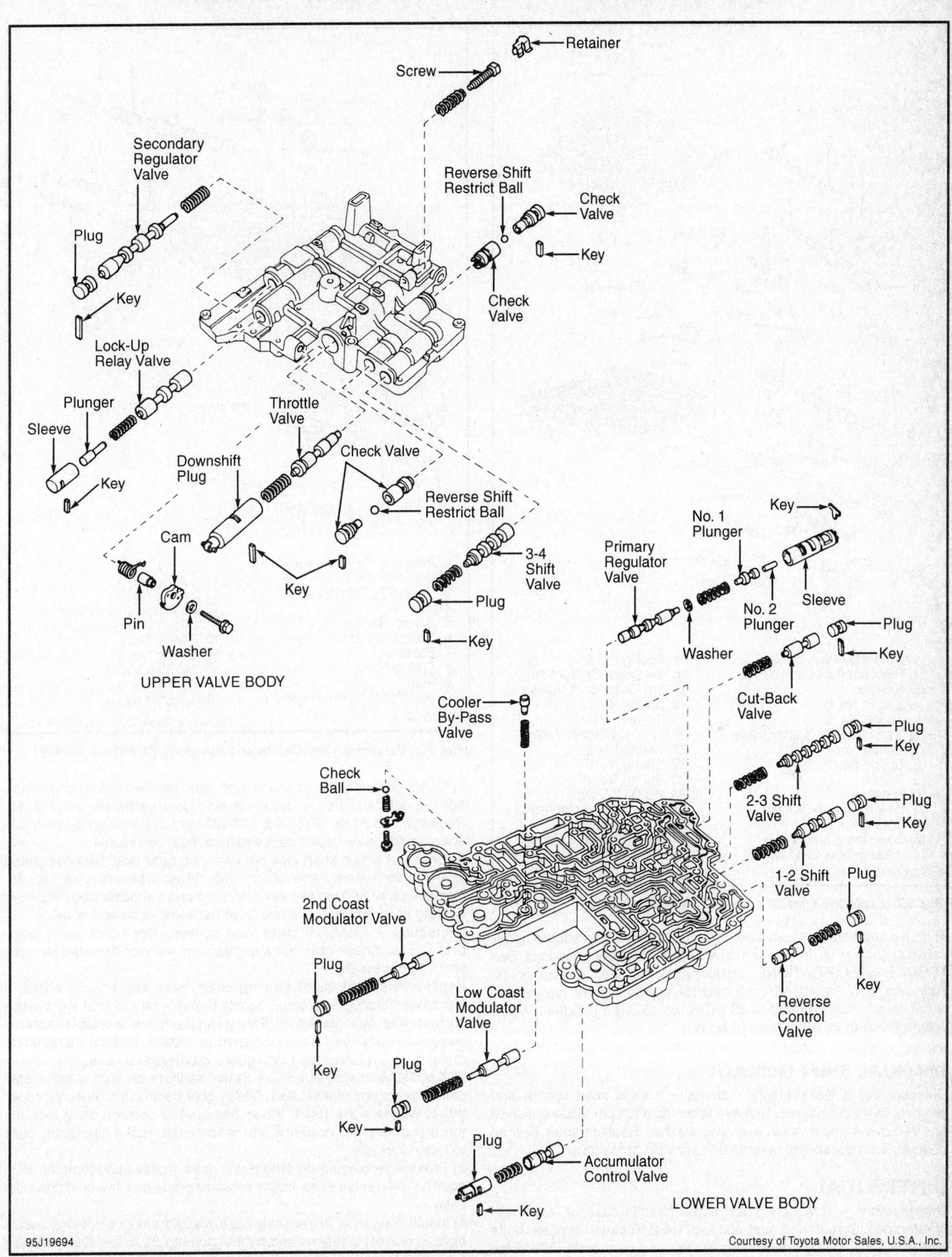

Courtesy of Toyota Motor Sales, U.S.A., Inc.

Fig. 58: Exploded View Of Upper & Lower Valve Bodies (A-245E & A-246E)

AUTOMATIC TRANSMISSIONS
Toyota A-240 "E" & "L" Series (Cont.)

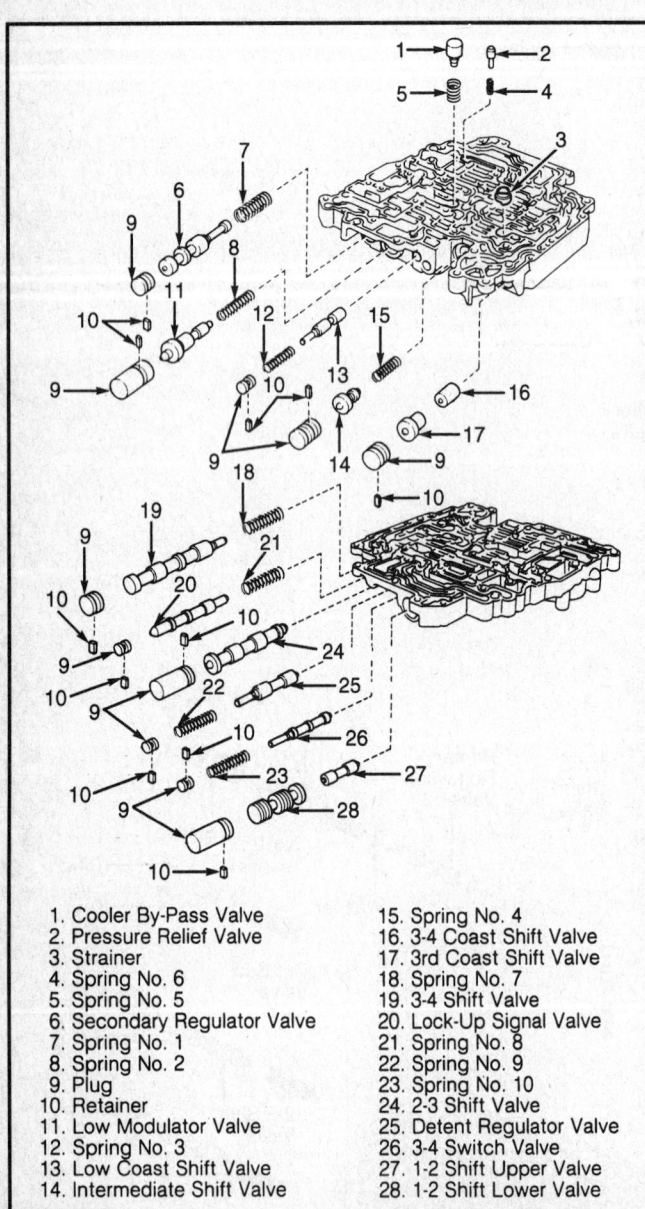

1. Cooler By-Pass Valve
2. Pressure Relief Valve
3. Strainer
4. Spring No. 6
5. Spring No. 5
6. Secondary Regulator Valve
7. Spring No. 1
8. Spring No. 2
9. Plug
10. Retainer
11. Low Modulator Valve
12. Spring No. 3
13. Low Coast Shift Valve
14. Intermediate Shift Valve

15. Spring No. 4
16. 3-4 Coast Shift Valve
17. 3rd Coast Shift Valve
18. Spring No. 7
19. 3-4 Shift Valve
20. Lock-Up Signal Valve
21. Spring No. 8
22. Spring No. 9
23. Spring No. 10
24. 2-3 Shift Valve
25. Detent Regulator Valve
26. 3-4 Switch Valve
27. 1-2 Shift Upper Valve
28. 1-2 Shift Lower Valve

93D25620   Courtesy of Toyota Motor Sales, U.S.A., Inc.

Fig. 59: Exploded View Of Lower Valve Body (A-242L)

3) Install and finger tighten bolts in lower valve body to secure upper valve body. See Fig. 55. Tighten valve body bolts to specifications. See TORQUE SPECIFICATIONS. Install NEW "O" rings on solenoids. Lubricate "O" rings with ATF and install solenoids. Tighten torque converter clutch solenoid bolt to 58 INCH lbs. (6.5 N.m). Tighten No. 2 solenoid bolt to 89 INCH lbs. (10 N.m).

MANUAL SHIFT LINKAGE

Disassembly & Reassembly – Unstake manual shaft spacer and remove. Drive out roll pin. Remove retaining hitch pin. Slide out shaft and remove manual valve lever and washer. Replace shaft seal as needed. To reassemble, reverse disassembly procedure.

DIFFERENTIAL

Disassembly – 1) Mark ring gear and differential case for reassembly reference. Spread ring gear bolt lock tabs. Remove ring gear bolts and lock tabs. Using brass hammer, tap ring gear from differential case. Remove bearings from differential case using appropriate bearing splitter and puller. Remove speedometer drive gear.

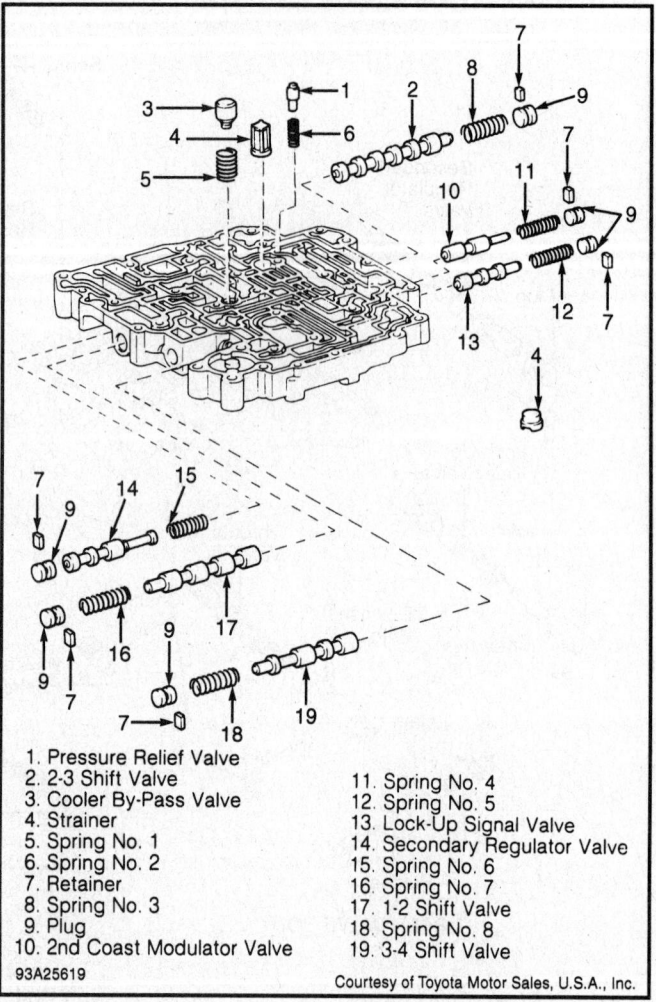

1. Pressure Relief Valve
2. 2-3 Shift Valve
3. Cooler By-Pass Valve
4. Strainer
5. Spring No. 1
6. Spring No. 2
7. Retainer
8. Spring No. 3
9. Plug
10. 2nd Coast Modulator Valve

11. Spring No. 4
12. Spring No. 5
13. Lock-Up Signal Valve
14. Secondary Regulator Valve
15. Spring No. 6
16. Spring No. 7
17. 1-2 Shift Valve
18. Spring No. 8
19. 3-4 Shift Valve

93A25619   Courtesy of Toyota Motor Sales, U.S.A., Inc.

Fig. 60: Exploded View Of Lower Valve Body (A-241E & A-244E)

2) Use a dial indicator to check side gear backlash. Hold one pinion against differential case. Measure side gear backlash. See Fig. 65. Backlash should be .002-.008" (.05-.20 mm). If backlash is not within specification, side gear thrust washers must be replaced.

3) Drive out pinion shaft lock pin from ring gear side. Remove pinion shaft, pinion gears, side gears, and thrust washers. See Fig. 66. Remove oil seals from transaxle housing and transaxle case. Remove bearing outer races and shims from transaxle case and housing.

Inspection – Clean all parts with solvent. Dry parts using compressed air. Check bearings and gears for wear or damage. Replace parts as necessary.

Reassembly – 1) Install bearing outer races and original shims in transaxle housing and case. Select thrust washers that will ensure correct side gear backlash. Thrust washers are available in thicknesses of .037-.047" (.95-1.20 mm) in .002" (.05 mm) increments. Install thrust washers and side gears in differential case.

2) If possible, install same size thrust washers on both sides. Install pinion gears and pinion shaft. Check gear backlash to ensure proper thrust washers are used. When backlash is correct, drive lock pin through differential case and into pinion shaft. Stake differential case to retain lock pin.

3) Press side bearing on differential case. Install speedometer drive gear on differential case. Install remaining side bearing on differential case.

4) Install differential in transaxle case. Install transaxle housing. Install bolts in correct locations and tighten bolts to 21 ft. lbs. (29 N.m). See Fig. 67. Measure differential bearing preload, using Differential Preload Adapter (09564-32011) and an INCH-lb. torque wrench. See Fig. 68.

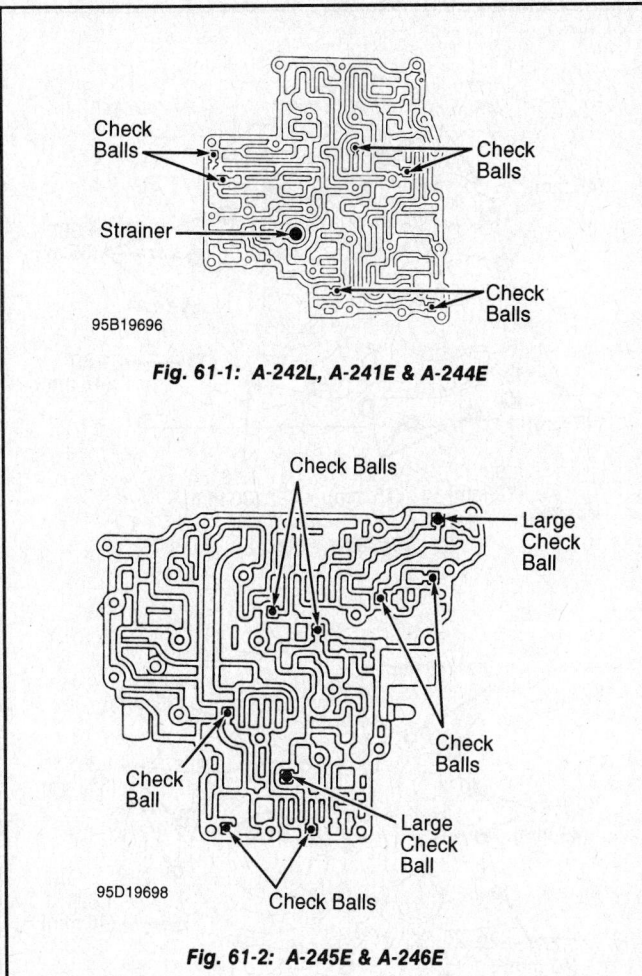

Fig. 61-1: A-242L, A-241E & A-244E

Fig. 61-1: A-242L, A-241E & A-244E

Fig. 61-2: A-245E & A-246E

Courtesy of Toyota Motor Sales, U.S.A., Inc.

Fig. 61: Identifying Upper Valve Body Check Ball Locations

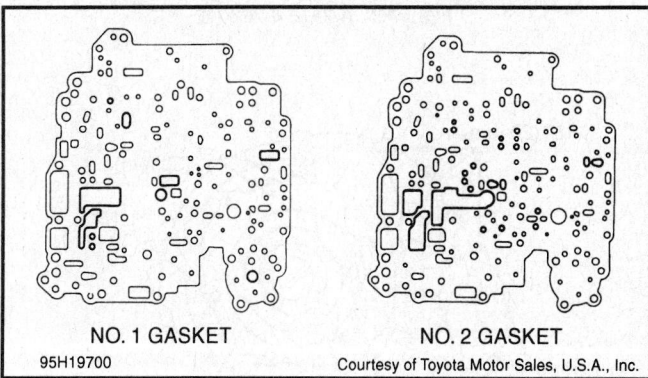

NO. 1 GASKET   NO. 2 GASKET

Courtesy of Toyota Motor Sales, U.S.A., Inc.

Fig. 62: Identifying Valve Body Gaskets (A-242L)

5) Preload must be within specification. See DIFFERENTIAL PRE-LOAD SPECIFICATIONS table. If preload is incorrect, remove differential from transaxle case and replace adjusting shim under bearing. Adjusting shims are available in thicknesses of .079" (2.00 mm) to .114" (2.90 mm) in .002" (.05 mm) increments. Preload will change approximately 2.6-3.5 INCH lbs. (.3-.4 N.m) with each shim thickness.

6) When correct preload is obtained, remove differential from transaxle case. Install ring gear on differential case. Clean ring gear and mounting surface. Heat ring gear to 212°F (100°C) in an oil bath.

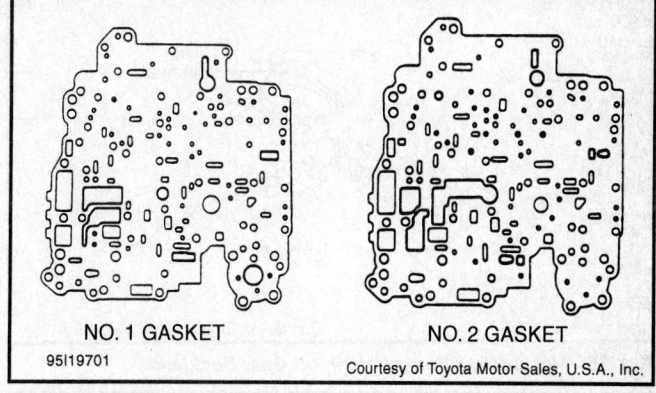

NO. 1 GASKET   NO. 2 GASKET

Courtesy of Toyota Motor Sales, U.S.A., Inc.

Fig. 63: Identifying Valve Body Gaskets (A-241E & A-244E)

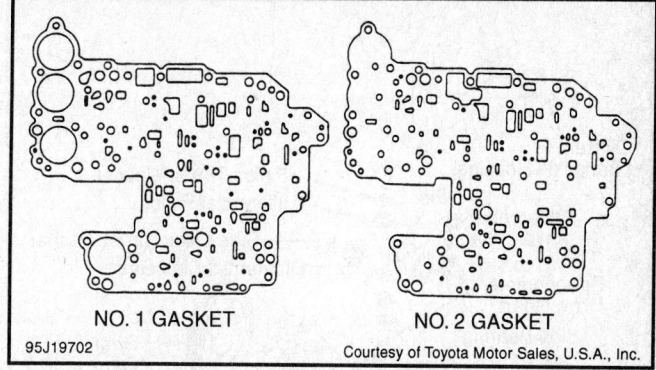

NO. 1 GASKET   NO. 2 GASKET

Courtesy of Toyota Motor Sales, U.S.A., Inc.

Fig. 64: Identifying Valve Body Gaskets (A-245E & A-246E)

DO NOT heat ring gear at temperatures greater than 230°F (110°C). Align ring gear on differential case and install NEW bolts. Tighten bolts evenly in crisscross pattern to 72 ft. lbs. (97 N.m).

7) Stake locking tabs. Stake one tab flush with flat surface of nut. Stake 2nd tab against corner of nut on tightening side. Coat lip of oil seals with multipurpose grease.

DIFFERENTIAL PRELOAD SPECIFICATIONS

Application	INCH Lbs. (N.m)
New Bearings	7.1-12.4 (.8-1.4)
Used Bearings	3.5-6.2 (.4-.7)

TRANSAXLE REASSEMBLY

A-242L, A-241E & A-244E

NOTE: Coat all oil seal rings, discs, plates, rotating parts and sliding surfaces with ATF prior to reassembly. Use petroleum jelly to hold bearings and races in place. Discs should be soaked in ATF for 15 minutes prior to installation.

NOTE: For bearing race and thrust bearing specifications and location, see Fig. 81.

1) Install oil tube apply cover and gasket. Install oil tubes. Install oil tube clamps. Install underdrive brake accumulator piston and spring. See Fig. 18.

2) Install oil gallery cover and gasket. Tighten bolts to 89 INCH lbs. (10 N.m). Apply thread sealant to screws for oil gallery cover. Install screws and tighten.

3) Install cam guide bracket. Install parking lock rod in guide bracket. Install parking lock sleeve with raised portion up. Install stopper plate on raised portion of lock sleeve. Install guide sleeve and spring. Install parking lock pawl, pawl shaft and shaft clamp. See Fig. 18.

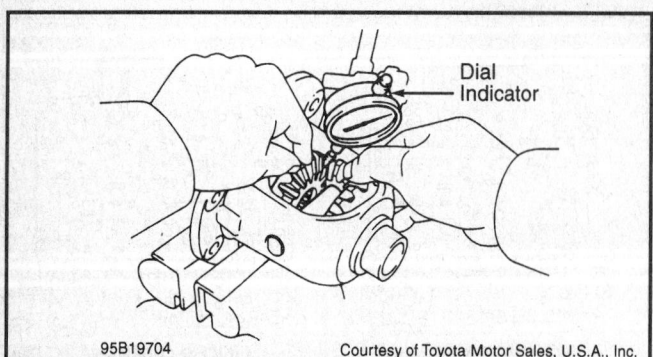

Fig. 65: **Measuring Differential Pinion Gear Backlash**

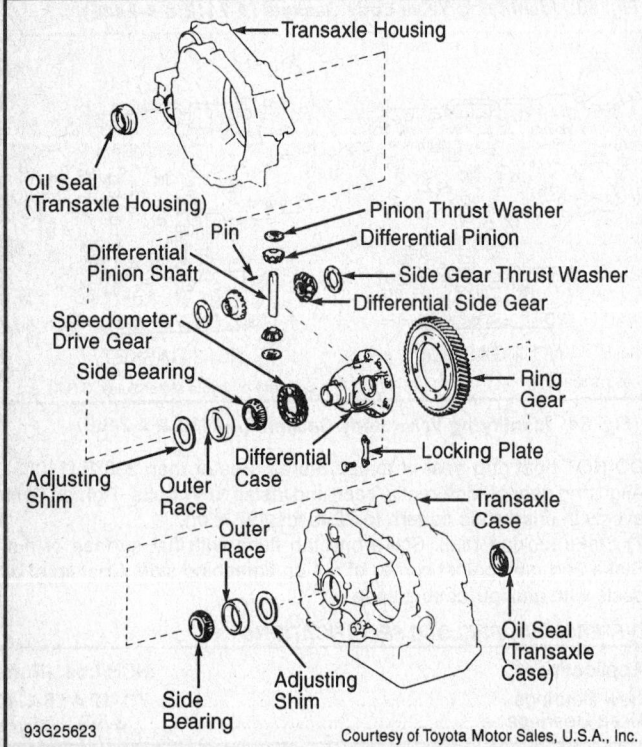

Fig 66: **Exploded View Of Differential Assembly**

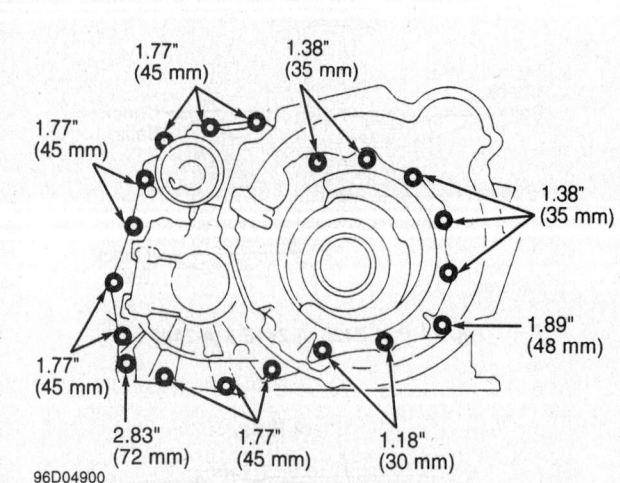

Fig. 67-1: **A-242L**

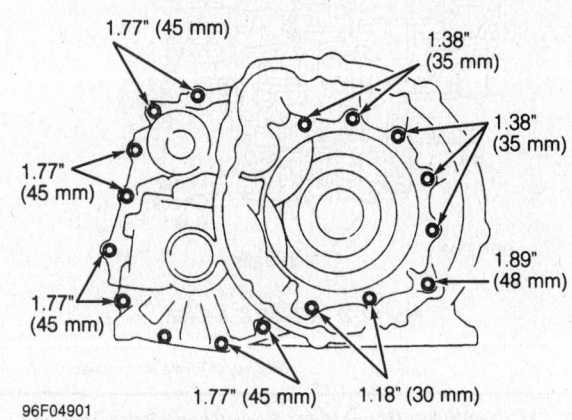

Fig. 67-2: **A-241E & A-244E**

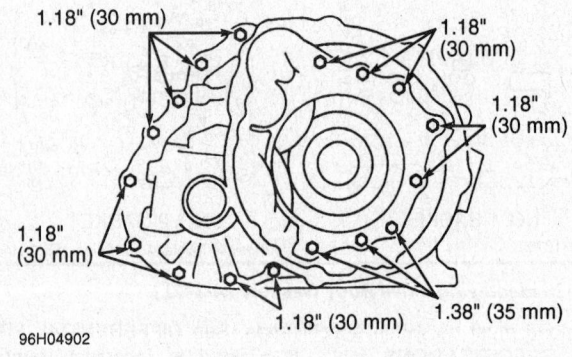

Fig. 67-3: **A-245E & A-246E**

Fig. 67: **Installing Transaxle Housing Bolts**

4) Install NEW "O" rings on 1st and reverse brake piston. Lubricate "O" rings with ATF. Using appropriate compressor, press 1st and reverse brake piston into transaxle case.

5) Install piston return spring and snap ring. Avoid bending spring retainer by overtightening bolt. See Fig. 20. Ensure snap ring is fully seated and centered by 3 lugs on spring retainer. Ensure end gap of snap ring is not aligned with spring retainer claw.

6) Install underdrive brake piston "O" rings. Coat "O" rings with ATF. Install piston in transaxle case with cup side upward. Use care not to damage "O" rings. Install brake piston return spring. Install plates and discs. Start with plate and alternate with disc ending with disc. Install flange with flat end down.

7) Using appropriate compressor, compress return spring. Install snap ring. Ensure snap ring end gap is not aligned with cutout. Using compressed air, confirm underdrive brake piston moves smoothly. See Fig. 19. Install oil seal rings to transaxle case.

8) Install underdrive one-way clutch assembly. Install anti-rattle clip. Align clutch disc tabs and install underdrive clutch assembly. Check operation of underdrive one-way clutch. Clutch should turn freely counterclockwise and lock clockwise. See Fig. 69.

9) Measure clutch assembly height from sleeve to inner race. Height should be .681-.717" (17.29-18.21 mm). See Fig. 70. Check underdrive

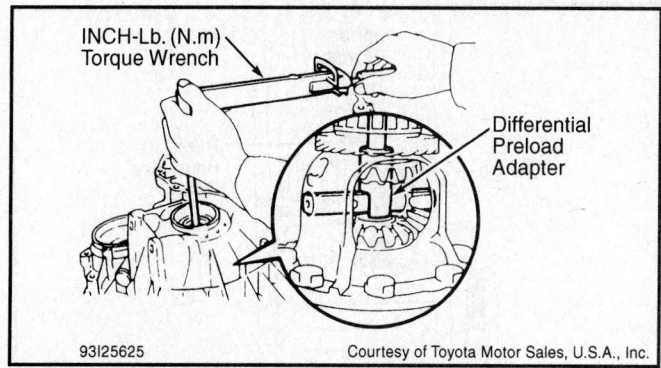

Fig. 68: Measuring Differential Bearing Preload

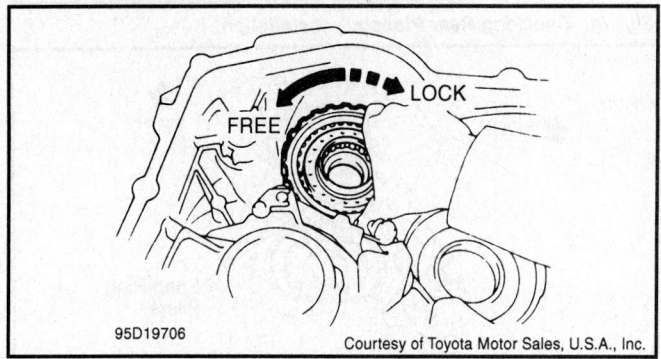

Fig. 69: Checking Underdrive Clutch Operation

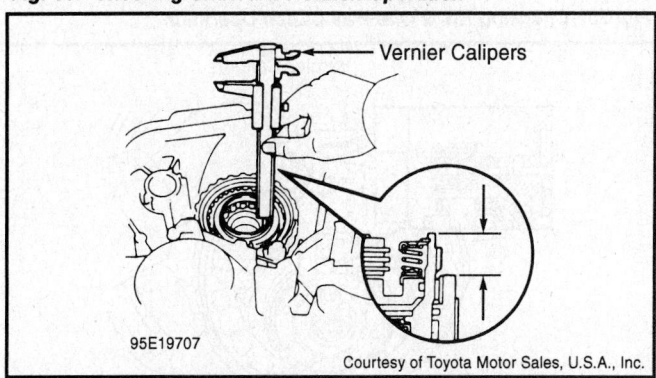

Fig. 70: Measuring Underdrive Clutch Assembly Height

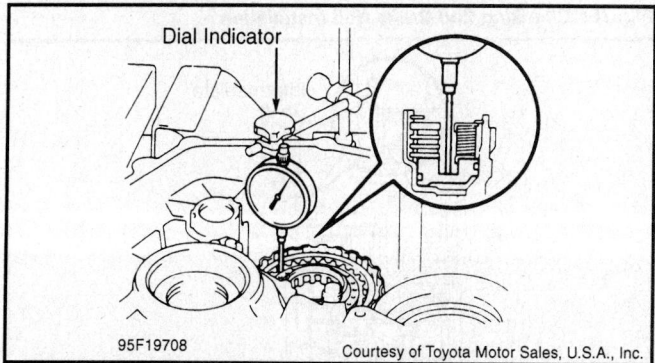

Fig. 71: Measuring Underdrive Clutch Piston Stroke

clutch piston stroke. Position dial indicator stem on underdrive clutch assembly. *See Fig. 71.* Apply compressed air to oil passage in transaxle case. *See Fig. 19.*

10) For A-241E and A-242L transaxles, piston stroke should be .048-.061" (1.21-1.55 mm). For A-244E transaxles, piston stroke should be .059-.073" (1.50-1.86 mm). If piston stroke is not within specification, install correct flange.

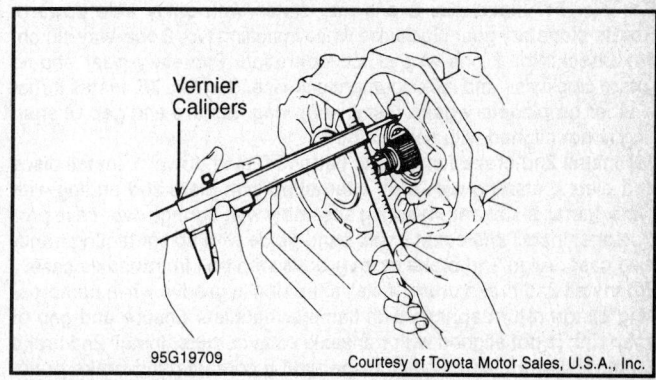

Fig. 72: Measuring Height Of Countershaft

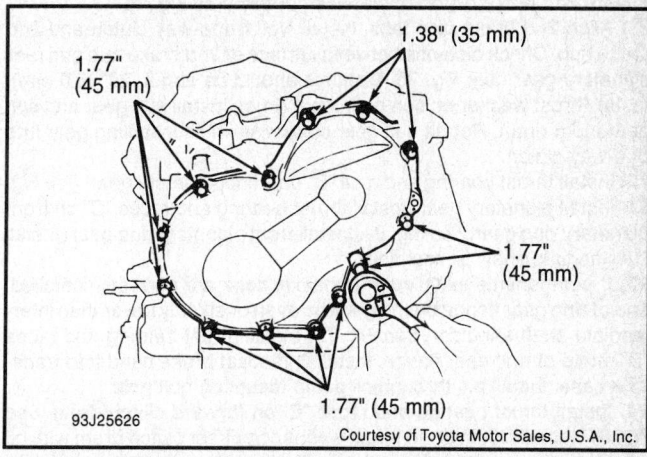

Fig. 73: Identifying Transaxle Rear Cover Bolts

11) Flanges are available in thicknesses of .080" (2.04 mm) and .094" (2.40 mm) for A-244E. Flanges for A-241E and A-242L transaxle are available in thicknesses of .091" (2.30 mm), .098" (2.50 mm) and .106" (2.70 mm) . Install thrust bearing "G". *See Fig. 81.* Install sun gear in transaxle case.

12) Align clutch disc tabs in underdrive clutch. Install countershaft assembly. Check countershaft height. Measure distance from tip of countershaft to bolt seat of clutch support. *See Fig. 72.* Countershaft height should be 1.311-1.398" (33.30-35.50 mm).

13) Install thrust bearing "F". *See Fig. 81.* Press in counterdriven gear. Install NEW lock nut. Using holder and adapter, tighten lock nut to 116 ft. lbs. (157 N.m). Using a dial indicator, measure countershaft end play. End play should be .009-.035" (.23-.89 mm). Stake lock nut. Install snap ring in transaxle case.

14) Install intermediate shaft. Apply gasket sealer to rear cover sealing areas. Install transaxle rear cover and bolts. Ensure bolts are installed in correct locations. *See Fig. 73.* Tighten bolts to 21 ft. lbs. (29 N.m). Install apply gaskets in transaxle case. Install thrust washer and governor driven gear. *See Fig. 18.* Ensure intermediate shaft rotates smoothly.

15) Install 1st and reverse brake components in transaxle case. Install inner flange with flat end facing upward. Install discs and plates. Start with disc, alternate with plate, ending with disc. Install outer flange with flat area facing inward. Install snap ring in groove. Ensure end gap does not align with transaxle case cutout.

16) Check 1st and reverse brake operation. Apply light air pressure to oil passage. *See Fig. 17.* Ensure piston moves smoothly. Install thrust bearing and races "A" in rear planetary ring gear. *See Fig. 81.* Align disc tabs. Install rear planetary ring gear in transaxle case. Install thrust washer on rear planetary gear. Ensure tabs align with grooves of gear.

17) Align spline of planetary gear with tabs of 1st and reverse brake discs. Install rear planetary gear into 1st and reverse brake. Ensure inner surface of rear planetary gear is below upper surface of flange.

See Fig. 74. Install No. 2 one-way clutch with shiny side upward. Rotate planetary gear clockwise while installing No. 2 one-way clutch.

18) Check No. 2 one-way clutch operation. Planetary gear should rotate clockwise and lock counterclockwise. *See Fig. 75.* Install thrust washer on planetary gear. Install snap ring. Ensure end gap of snap ring is not aligned with case cutouts.

19) Install 2nd brake flange with flat end facing upward. Install discs and plates, starting with disc, alternating with plate and ending with plate. Install piston return spring assembly with springs over case protrusions. Install 2nd coast brake band guide with tip contacting transaxle case. Align 2nd brake drum groove with bolt in transaxle case.

20) Install 2nd brake drum. Install snap ring in groove while compressing piston return springs with hammer handles. Ensure end gap of snap ring is not aligned with transaxle case cutouts. Install 2nd brake drum gasket in center oil passage until it contacts 2nd brake drum. Apply compressed air into 2nd brake oil passage in transaxle case. Ensure 2nd brake piston operates smoothly. *See Fig. 16.*

21) Align 2nd brake disc tabs. Install No. 1 one-way clutch and 2nd brake hub. Check distance between surface of 2nd brake hub and rear planetary gear. *See Fig. 76.* Distance should be about .20" (5.0 mm). Install thrust washer on sun gear input drum. Install sun gear and sun gear input drum. Rotate sun gear clockwise while installing gear into one-way clutch.

22) Install thrust bearing and race "B" on front planetary gear. *See Fig. 81.* Install planetary gear. Install thrust bearing and races "C" on front planetary ring gear. *See Fig. 81.* Install front planetary ring gear. Install intermediate shaft oil seal ring.

23) If components installed in transaxle case are correctly installed, end of ring gear flange bushing will be even or slightly lower than intermediate shaft shoulder. *See Fig. 77.* Install thrust bearing and races "D" on tip of ring gear flange. Install 2nd coast brake band into transaxle case. Install pin through oil pump mounting bolt hole.

24) Install thrust bearing and races "E" on forward clutch drum. *See Fig. 81.* Install clutch drum thrust washer on direct clutch drum with oil groove facing upward. Align clutch disc tabs. Install direct clutch into forward clutch. If tabs are aligned with hub correctly, end of direct clutch drum bushing will be flush with surfaces of forward clutch.

25) Rotate forward clutch to mesh with front planetary gear and discs. Install direct clutch and forward clutch into transaxle case. Check installation of direct/forward clutch assembly. Measure distance between direct clutch and sun gear drum (shell). *See Fig. 78.* Distance should be .118" (3.0 mm).

26) Install differential. Apply gasket sealer (Loctite 518 or equivalent) to transaxle housing. Install transaxle housing. Install mounting bolts in original locations. *See Fig. 67.* Tighten bolts to 21 ft. lbs. (29 N.m). Check differential side bearing preload. See DIFFERENTIAL under COMPONENT DISASSEMBLY & REASSEMBLY.

27) Install race on stator shaft. Install "O" ring on oil pump. Install oil pump. Hold input shaft and lightly press oil pump body to slide oil seal rings on stator shaft through direct clutch drum. Install and tighten bolts to 18 ft. lbs. (25 N.m).

NOTE: DO NOT apply excessive pressure on oil pump. Seal rings will stick to direct clutch drum if excessive pressure is used.

---

28) Ensure input shaft rotates smoothly. Using a dial indicator, measure input shaft end play. End play should be .012-.035" (.30-.90 mm). Replace oil pump race if end play is incorrect. Oil pump races are available in thicknesses of .031" (.80 mm) and .055" (1.40 mm).

29) Install spring, 2nd coast brake piston and cover into bore. Install snap ring. Ensure front end of piston rod contacts center of 2nd brake band depression.

30) Measure 2nd coast brake piston stroke by applying compressed air to oil passage in transaxle case. *See Fig. 13.* Piston stroke should be .059-.118" (1.50-3.00 mm). Replace band if stroke is not within specification.

31) Recheck piston stroke after band replacement. Coat accumulator piston "O" rings with ATF. Install "O" rings on accumulator pistons. Measure spring free length and replace as necessary.

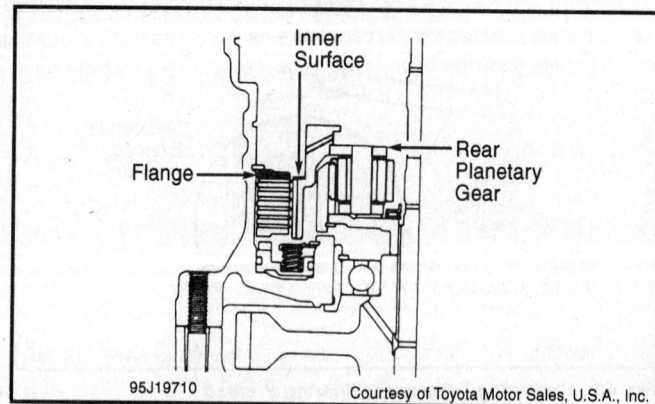

Fig. 74: Checking Rear Planetary Installation

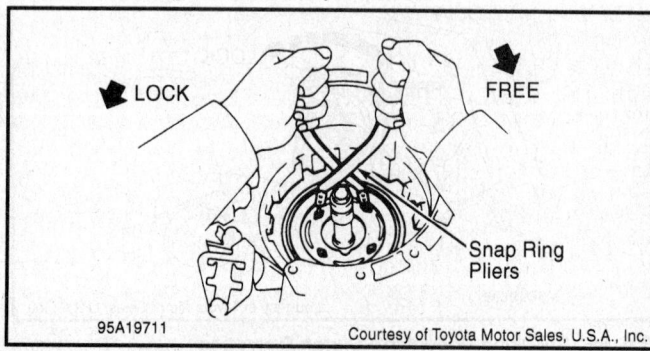

Fig. 75: Checking No. 2 One-Way Clutch Operation

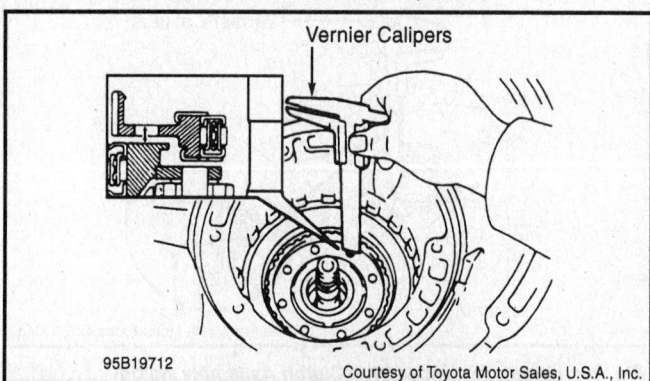

Fig. 76: Checking 2nd Brake Hub Installation

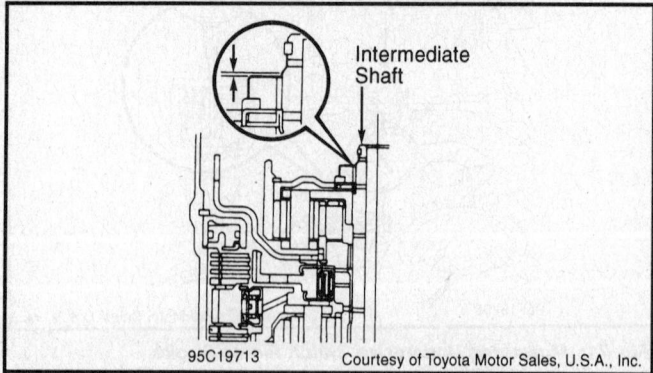

Fig. 77: Checking Front Planetary Ring Gear Installation

32) See ACCUMULATOR SPRING SPECIFICATIONS table. Install pistons and springs in transaxle case. *See Fig. 79.* Install accumulator cover and NEW gasket. Tighten bolts to 89 INCH lbs. (10 N.m).

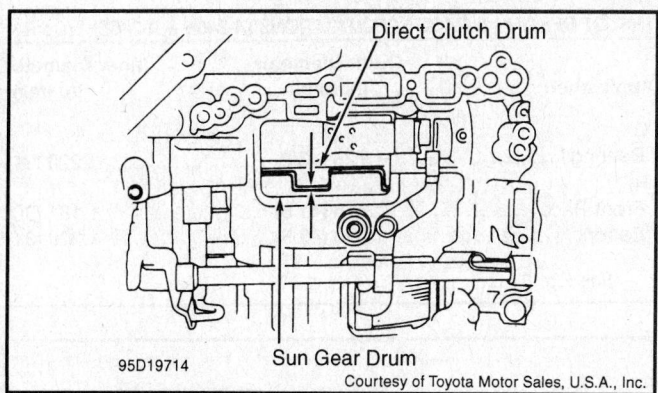

Fig. 78: *Checking Direct/Forward Clutch Drum Assembly Installation*

ACCUMULATOR SPRING SPECIFICATIONS [1]

Application	Color	Free Length In. (mm)
A-242L		
Direct Clutch	Orange	2.500 (63.50)
Forward Clutch		
Inner Spring	Brown	1.287 (32.68)
Outer Spring	None	2.009 (51.04)
Underdrive Clutch	Yellow	2.231 (56.68)
2nd Brake	White	1.197 (30.40)
A-241E		
Direct Clutch		
No. 1 Spring	Pink	2.446 (62.12)
No. 2 Spring	Pink	2.462 (62.54)
Forward Clutch		
Inner Spring	Pink	1.614 (41.00)
Outer Spring	Pink	2.917 (74.10)
Underdrive Clutch	Purple	2.397 (60.88)
2nd Brake		
No. 1 Spring	Green	.610 (15.50)
No. 2 Spring	Green	2.539 (64.50)
A-244E		
Direct Clutch	Red/White	2.446 (62.12)
Forward Clutch		
Inner Spring	None	1.457 (37.00)
Outer Spring	None	3.063 (77.80)
Underdrive Clutch	Yellow	2.231 (56.68)
2nd Brake	Blue	2.314 (58.77)

[1] – For accumulator spring locations, *see Fig. 79.*

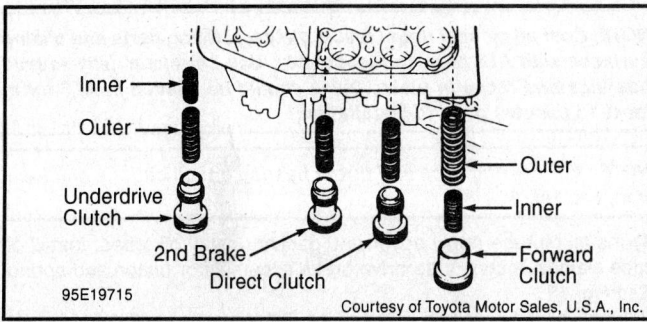

Fig. 79: *Identifying Accumulator Pistons & Springs*

33) Install 2nd brake apply gasket. Install throttle cable. Use care not to damage "O" ring. Ensure cable is fully seated in transaxle case. Install solenoid wire(s) in transaxle case. Install VALVE BODY assembly. See VALVE BODY ASSEMBLY under ON-VEHICLE SERVICE. Ensure proper length bolt is installed in proper location. Connect solenoid wiring.

34) Install manual detent spring and cover. Install bolt and tighten bolt to 89 INCH lbs. (10 N.m). Ensure manual valve lever is in contact with center of roller at tip of detent spring. Install oil tubes. Install oil tube clamp and bracket. Tighten bolts to 89 INCH lbs. (10 N.m). Install oil strainer (filter) with NEW gasket.

35) Install magnet(s) in oil pan. Install NEW oil pan gasket and install oil pan. Tighten oil pan bolts to 43 INCH lbs. (4.9 N.m). Install speed sensor and sensor rotor (if equipped). Install NEW "O" ring on sensor cover and install cover. Install sensor bracket and tighten bolts to 48 INCH lbs. (5.4 N.m).

36) On A-242L transaxles, install governor oil strainer. Install NEW gasket to governor body adapter. Install governor body adapter, governor body and thrust washer. Install NEW "O" ring on cover. Install cover and cover brackets. Tighten bracket bolts to 115 INCH lbs. (13 N.m). Install throttle cable and solenoid lock plates.

37) On all transaxles, install oil cooler pipe unions (if necessary). Install park/neutral position switch to manual valve shaft. Install packing, nut, stopper and nut. Tighten nut to 61 INCH lbs. (6.9 N.m). Adjust park/neutral position switch (if necessary) and tighten adjusting bolts to 48 INCH lbs. (5.4 N.m). See appropriate AUTOMATIC TRANSMISSION SERVICING article in TRANSMISSION SERVICING section. Stake nut to stopper. Install manual shift lever and tighten nut. Install filler tube and dipstick. Install oil cooler pipes.

38) Install torque converter on transaxle. Using a straightedge and calipers, measure torque converter installed depth. For torque converter depth specifications, see TORQUE CONVERTER DEPTH SPECIFICATIONS table. See Fig. 80.

TORQUE CONVERTER DEPTH SPECIFICATIONS

Application	In. (mm)
MR2	.502 (12.75)
Paseo	.528 (13.40)
RAV4	.502 (12.75)
Tercel	.512 (13.00)

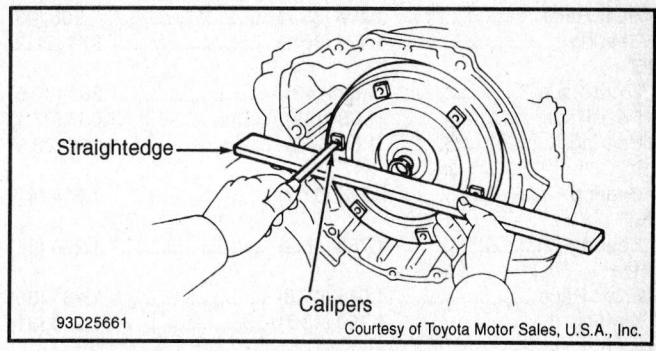

Fig. 80: *Measuring Torque Converter Depth*

THRUST BEARING & RACE SPECIFICATIONS (A-242L) [1]

Application	Outer Diameter In. (mm)	Inner Diameter In. (mm)
"A"		
Front Race	1.469 (37.3)	.949 (24.1)
Rear Race	1.480 (37.6)	.874 (22.2)
Bearing	1.480 (37.6)	.945 (24)
"B"		
Front Race	1.772 (45)	1.102 (28)
Bearing	1.772 (45)	1.181 (30)
"C"		
Front Race	1.492 (37.9)	.866 (22)
Rear Race	1.378 (35)	.748 (19)
Bearing	1.421 (36.1)	.874 (22.2)
"D"		
Front Race	1.492 (37.9)	.866 (22)
Bearing	1.421 (36.1)	1.181 (30)

[1] – See Fig. 81.

THRUST BEARING & RACE SPECIFICATIONS (A-242L) [1] (Cont.)

Application	Outer Diameter In. (mm)	Inner Diameter In. (mm)
"E"		
Front Race	1.693 (43)	1.201 (30.5)
Rear Race	1.654 (42)	1.067 (27.1)
Bearing	1.654 (42)	1.138 (28.9)
"F"		
Bearing	2.272 (57.7)	1.614 (41)
"G"		
Bearing	1.780 (45.2)	1.220 (31)
"H"		
Front Race	1.646 (41.8)	1.181 (30)
Bearing	1.720 (43.7)	1.220 (31)

[1] – See Fig. 81.

THRUST BEARING & RACE SPECIFICATIONS (A-241E & A-244E) [1]

Application	Outer Diameter In. (mm)	Inner Diameter In. (mm)
"A"		
Front Race	1.469 (37.3)	.949 (24.1)
Rear Race	1.480 (37.6)	.874 (22.2)
Bearing	1.480 (37.6)	.945 (24)
"B"		
Front Race	1.772 (45)	1.102 (28)
Bearing	1.772 (45)	1.181 (30)
"C"		
Front Race	1.492 (37.9)	.866 (22)
Rear Race	1.378 (35)	.748 (19)
Bearing	1.421 (36.1)	.874 (22.2)
"D"		
Front Race	1.492 (37.9)	.866 (22)
Rear Race	1.406 (35.7)	.906 (23)
Bearing	1.421 (36.1)	.874 (22.2)
"E"		
Front Race	1.693 (43)	1.201 (30.5)
Rear Race	1.654 (42)	1.067 (27.1)
Bearing	1.654 (42)	1.138 (28.9)
"F"		
Bearing	2.272 (57.7)	1.614 (41)
"G"		
Bearing	1.780 (45.2)	1.220 (31)
"H"		
Front Race	1.646 (41.8)	1.181 (30)
Bearing	1.720 (43.7)	1.220 (31)

[1] – See Fig. 81.

THRUST BEARING & RACE SPECIFICATIONS (A-245E & A-246E) [1]

Application	Outer Diameter In. (mm)	Inner Diameter In. (mm)
"A"		
Front Race	1.480 (37.6)	.949 (24.1)
Bearing	1.480 (37.6)	.870 (22.1)
"B"		
Bearing	1.772 (45)	1.106 (28.1)
"C"		
Rear Race	1.378 (35)	.748 (19)
Bearing	1.496 (38)	.866 (22)
"D"		
Rear Race	1.555 (39.5)	1.024 (26)
Bearing	1.654 (42)	1.016 (25.8)
"E"		
Bearing	1.811 (46)	1.209 (30.7)
"F"		
Bearing	2.283 (58)	1.614 (41)

[1] – See Fig. 81.

THRUST BEARING & RACE SPECIFICATIONS (A-245E & A-246E) [1] (Cont.)

Application	Outer Diameter In. (mm)	Inner Diameter In. (mm)
"G"		
Bearing	1.728 (43.9)	1.220 (31)
"H"		
Front Race	1.646 (41.8)	1.181 (30)
Bearing	1.728 (43.9)	1.220 (31)

[1] – See Fig. 81.

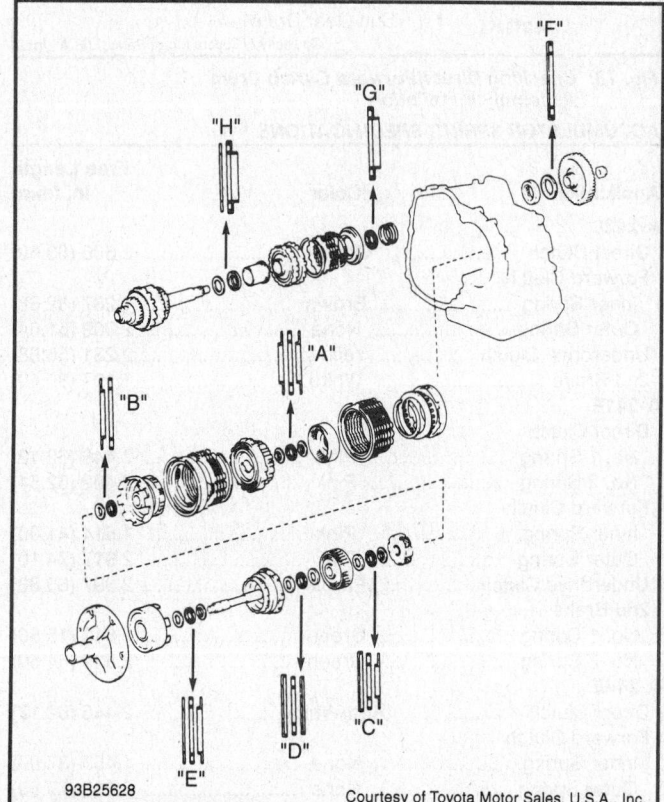

93B25628   Courtesy of Toyota Motor Sales, U.S.A., Inc.

Fig. 81: Identifying Bearing Race & Thrust Bearing Locations

A-245E & A-246E

NOTE: Coat all oil seal rings, discs, plates, rotating parts and sliding surfaces with ATF prior to reassembly. Use petroleum jelly to hold bearings and races in place. Discs should be soaked in ATF for at least 15 minutes prior to installation.

NOTE: For bearing race and thrust bearing specifications and location, see Fig. 81.

1) Install oil tube apply cover and gasket. Install oil tubes. Install oil tube clamps. Install underdrive brake accumulator piston and spring. See Fig. 18.
2) Install oil gallery cover and gasket. Tighten bolts to 89 INCH lbs. (10 N.m). Apply thread sealant to screws for oil gallery cover. Install screws and tighten.
3) Install cam guide bracket. Install parking lock rod in guide bracket. Install parking lock sleeve with raised portion up. Install stopper plate on raised portion of lock sleeve. Install guide sleeve and spring. Install parking lock pawl, pawl shaft and shaft clamp. See Fig. 18.
4) Install NEW "O" rings on 1st and reverse brake piston. Lubricate "O" rings with ATF. Using appropriate compressor, press 1st and reverse brake piston into transaxle case.

5) Install piston return spring and snap ring. Avoid bending spring retainer by overtightening bolt. *See Fig. 20.* Ensure snap ring is fully seated and centered by 3 lugs on spring retainer. Ensure end gap of snap ring is not aligned with spring retainer claw.

6) Install underdrive brake piston "O" rings. Coat "O" rings with ATF. Install piston in transaxle case with cup side upward. Use care not to damage "O" rings. Install brake piston return spring. Install plates and discs. Start with plate and alternate with disc ending with disc. Install flange with flat end down.

7) Using appropriate compressor, compress return spring. Install snap ring. Ensure snap ring end gap is not aligned with cutout. Using compressed air, confirm underdrive brake piston moves smoothly. *See Fig. 19.* Install oil seal rings to transaxle case.

8) Place counterdrive on press platform with NEW spacer installed. Place case on gear. Press bearing onto counterdrive shaft until seated. Install intermediate shaft. Install lock nut. Secure counterdrive gear from turning and tighten lock nut to 131 ft. lbs. (177 N.m).

9) Using INCH lb. torque wrench, measure starting torque of intermediate shaft at counterdrive gear lock nut. Starting torque for new bearings is 2.7-6.2 INCH lbs. (.3-.7 N.m). Starting torque for used bearings is 1.8-3.5 INCH lbs. (.2-.4 N.m).

10) If starting torque is less than specification, replace spacer and recheck. Loosen lock nut if starting torque is greater than specification. Stake lock nut in place.

11) Install underdrive one-way clutch assembly. Install anti-rattle clip. Align clutch disc tabs and install underdrive clutch assembly. Check operation of underdrive one-way clutch. Clutch should turn freely counterclockwise and lock clockwise. *See Fig. 69.*

12) Measure clutch assembly height from sleeve to inner race. Height should be .681-.717" (17.29-18.21 mm). *See Fig. 82.* Check underdrive clutch piston stroke. Position dial indicator stem on underdrive clutch assembly. *See Fig. 71.* Apply compressed air to oil passage in transaxle case. *See Fig. 19.*

13) Piston stroke should be .059-.075" (1.50-1.90 mm). If piston stroke is not within specification, install correct flange. Flanges are available in thicknesses of .080" (2.04 mm), .087" (2.20 mm), .094" (2.40 mm) and .098" (2.50 mm). Install thrust bearing "G". *See Fig. 81.* Install sun gear in transaxle case.

14) Align clutch disc tabs in underdrive clutch. Install countershaft assembly. Check countershaft height. Measure distance from tip of countershaft to bolt seat of clutch support. *See Fig. 72.* Countershaft height should be 1.193-1.280" (30.30-32.50 mm).

15) Install thrust bearing "F". *See Fig. 81.* Press in counterdriven gear. Install NEW lock nut. Using holder and adapter, tighten lock nut to 133 ft. lbs. (180 N.m). Using a dial indicator, measure countershaft end play. End play should be .009-.035" (.23-.89 mm). Stake lock nut.

16) Apply gasket sealer to rear cover sealing areas. Install transaxle rear cover and bolts. Ensure bolts are installed in correct locations. *See Fig. 83.* Tighten bolts to 89 INCH lbs. (10 N.m). Ensure intermediate shaft turns smoothly.

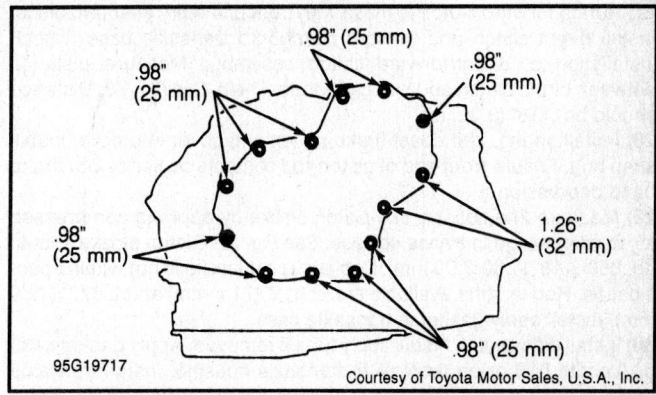

95G19717

Courtesy of Toyota Motor Sales, U.S.A., Inc.

Fig. 83: Identifying Transaxle Rear Cover Bolts

17) Install 1st and reverse brake components in transaxle case. Install discs and plates. Start with plate, alternate with disc, ending with disc. Install outer flange with flat area facing inward. Install snap ring in groove. Ensure end gap does not align with transaxle case cutout.

18) Check 1st and reverse brake clutch pack clearance. *See Fig. 25.* Clearance should be .047-.093" (1.19-2.35 mm). Install thrust bearing and races "A" in rear planetary ring gear. *See Fig. 81.* Align disc tabs. Install thrust washer on rear planetary gear. Ensure tabs align with grooves of gear.

19) Align spline of planetary gear with tabs of 1st and reverse brake discs. Install rear planetary gear into 1st and reverse brake. Ensure inner surface of rear planetary gear is below upper surface of flange. *See Fig. 74.* Install No. 2 one-way clutch with shiny side upward. Rotate planetary gear clockwise while installing No. 2 one-way clutch.

20) Check No. 2 one-way clutch operation. Planetary gear should rotate clockwise and lock counterclockwise. *See Fig. 75.* Install thrust washer on planetary gear. Install snap ring. Ensure end gap of snap ring is not aligned with case cutouts.

21) Install 2nd brake flange with flat end facing upward. Install discs and plates, starting with disc, alternating with plate and ending with plate. Install piston return spring assembly with springs over case protrusions. Install 2nd coast brake band guide with tip contacting transaxle case. Align 2nd brake drum groove with bolt in transaxle case.

22) Install 2nd brake drum. Install snap ring in groove while compressing piston return springs with hammer handles. Ensure end gap of snap ring is not aligned with transaxle case cutouts. Install 2nd brake drum gasket in center oil passage until it contacts 2nd brake drum. Apply compressed air into 2nd brake oil passage in transaxle case. Ensure 2nd brake piston operates smoothly. *See Fig. 16.*

23) Align 2nd brake disc tabs. Install No. 1 one-way clutch and 2nd brake hub. Check distance between surface of 2nd brake hub and rear planetary gear. *See Fig. 76.* Distance should be approximately .20" (5.0 mm). Install thrust washer on sun gear input drum. Install sun gear and sun gear input drum. Rotate sun gear clockwise while installing gear into one-way clutch.

24) Install thrust bearing and race "B" on front planetary gear. *See Fig. 81.* Install planetary gear. Install thrust bearing and race "C" on front planetary ring gear. *See Fig. 81.* Install front planetary ring gear. Install intermediate shaft oil seal ring.

25) If components installed in transaxle case are correctly installed, end of ring gear flange bushing will be even or slightly lower than intermediate shaft shoulder. *See Fig. 77.* Install thrust bearing and races "D" on tip of ring gear flange. Install 2nd coast brake band into transaxle case. Install pin.

26) Install thrust bearing and race "E" on forward clutch drum. *See Fig. 81.* Install clutch drum thrust washer on direct clutch drum with oil groove facing upward. Align clutch disc tabs. Install direct clutch into forward clutch. If tabs are aligned with hub correctly, end of direct clutch drum bushing will be flush with surfaces of forward clutch.

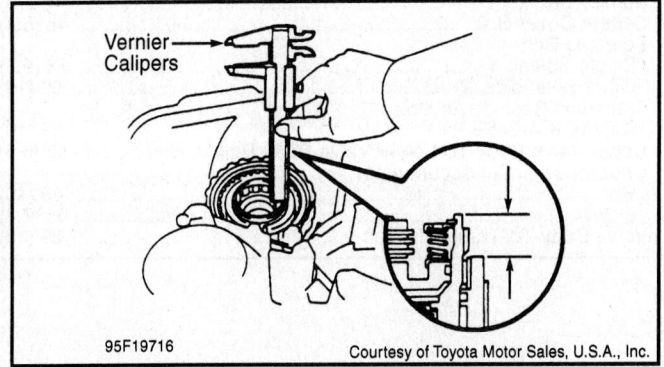

Vernier Calipers

95F19716

Courtesy of Toyota Motor Sales, U.S.A., Inc.

Fig. 82: Measuring Underdrive Clutch Assembly Height

27) Rotate forward clutch to mesh with front planetary gear and discs. Install direct clutch and forward clutch into transaxle case. Check installation of direct/forward clutch assembly. Measure distance between direct clutch and sun gear drum (shell). *See Fig. 78.* Distance should be .118" (3.0 mm).

28) Install spring, 2nd coast brake piston and cover into bore. Install snap ring. Ensure front end of piston rod contacts center of 2nd brake band depression.

29) Measure 2nd coast brake piston stroke by applying compressed air to oil passage in transaxle case. *See Fig. 22.* Piston stroke should be .059-.118" (1.50-3.00 mm). Replace rod if stroke is not within specification. Rod lengths available are, 2.811" (71.4 mm) and 2.870" (72.9 mm). Install apply gasket in transaxle case.

30) Install differential. Install apply tube if removed. Apply gasket sealer (Loctite 518 or equivalent) to transaxle housing. Install transaxle housing. Install mounting bolts in original locations. *See Fig. 67.* Tighten bolts to 21 ft. lbs. (29 N.m). Check differential side bearing preload. See DIFFERENTIAL under COMPONENT DISASSEMBLY & REASSEMBLY.

31) Install race on stator shaft. Install "O" ring on oil pump. Install oil pump. Hold input shaft and lightly press oil pump body to slide oil seal rings on stator shaft through direct clutch drum. Install and tighten bolts to 18 ft. lbs. (25 N.m).

NOTE: DO NOT apply excessive pressure on oil pump. Seal rings will stick to direct clutch drum if excessive pressure is used.

32) Ensure input shaft rotates smoothly. Using a dial indicator, measure input shaft end play. End play should be .012-.035" (.30-.90 mm). Replace oil pump race if end play is incorrect. Oil pump races are available in thicknesses of .031" (.80 mm) and .055" (1.40 mm).

33) Coat accumulator piston "O" rings with ATF. Install "O" rings on accumulator pistons. Measure spring free length and replace as necessary. See ACCUMULATOR SPRING SPECIFICATIONS table. Install pistons and springs in transaxle case. *See Fig. 79.*

ACCUMULATOR SPRING SPECIFICATIONS [1]

Application	Color	Free Length In. (mm)
A-245E & A-246E		
Direct Clutch	Blue	2.768 (70.30)
Forward Clutch		
Inner Spring	Red	1.437 (36.50)
Outer Spring	Red	2.480 (63.00)
Underdrive Clutch		
Inner Spring	Yellow	1.969 (50.00)
Outer Spring	White	[2] 2.815 (71.50)
2nd Brake	Brown	2.547 (64.70)

[1] – For accumulator spring locations, *see Fig. 79.*
[2] – Spring length on A-246E is 2.692" (68.40 mm).

---

34) Install 2nd brake apply gasket. Install check ball body and spring in passage next to 2nd brake accumulator. Install throttle cable. Use care not to damage "O" ring. Ensure cable is fully seated in transaxle case. Install solenoid wire(s) in transaxle case. Install VALVE BODY assembly. See VALVE BODY ASSEMBLY under ON-VEHICLE SERVICE. Ensure proper length bolt is installed in proper location. Connect solenoid wiring.

35) Install manual detent spring and cover. Install bolt and tighten bolt to 89 INCH lbs. (10 N.m). Ensure manual valve lever is in contact with center of roller at tip of detent spring. Install oil tubes. Install oil tube clamp and bracket. Tighten bolts to 89 INCH lbs. (10 N.m). Install oil strainer (filter) with NEW gasket.

36) Install magnet(s) in oil pan. Install NEW oil pan gasket and install oil pan. Tighten oil pan bolts to 46 INCH lbs. (5.2 N.m). Install throttle cable and solenoid lock plates.

37) Install oil cooler pipe unions (if necessary). Install park/neutral position switch to manual valve shaft. Install packing, nut, stopper and nut. Tighten nut to 106 INCH lbs. (12 N.m). Adjust park/neutral position switch (if necessary) and tighten adjusting bolts to 48 INCH lbs. (5.4 N.m). See appropriate AUTOMATIC TRANSMISSION SERVICING article in TRANSMISSION SERVICING section. Stake nut to stopper. Install manual shift lever and tighten nut. Install filler tube and dipstick. Install oil cooler pipes.

38) Install torque converter on transaxle. Using a straightedge and calipers, measure torque converter installed depth. For torque converter depth specifications, see TORQUE CONVERTER DEPTH SPECIFICATIONS table. *See Fig. 80.*

TORQUE CONVERTER DEPTH SPECIFICATIONS

Application	In. (mm)
Celica 1.8L	.898 (22.80)
Corolla 1.8L	.898 (22.80)
Prizm	.906 (23.00)

TORQUE SPECIFICATIONS

TORQUE SPECIFICATIONS

Application	Ft. Lbs. (N.m)
Converter-To-Drive Plate Bolt	
Paseo	18 (25)
All Other Models	20 (27)
Countershaft Lock Nut	131-159 (177-216)
Drain Plug	13 (17)
Drive Plate Bolt	
Celica, Corolla & Prizm	47 (64)
Tercel	65 (88)
All Other Models	61 (83)
Oil Cooler Union Nut	25 (34)
Oil Pump Bolt	18 (25)
Ring Gear Bolt	72 (97)
Transaxle Housing Bolt	21 (29)
Transaxle Rear Cover Bolt	
A-242L, A-241E & A-244E	21 (29)

	INCH lb. (N.m)
Accumulator Cover Bolt	89 (10)
Brake Band Guide Bolt	48 (5.4)
Governor Cover Bolt	115 (13)
Oil Gallery Cover Bolt	89 (10)
Oil Pan Bolt	43 (4.9)
Oil Pump Stator Shaft Bolt	89 (10)
Oil Strainer Bolt	89 (10)
Oil Tube Clamp Bolt	89 (10)
Park/Neutral Position Switch	
A-242L, A-241E & A-244E	
Adjusting Bolt	48 (5.4)
Retaining Nut	61 (6.9)
A-245E & A-246E	
Adjusting Bolt	106 (12)
Retaining Nut	46 (5.2)
Parking Lock Pawl Bracket Bolt	65 (7.4)
Sensor Bracket Bolt	115 (13)
Sensor Cover Bolt	48 (5.4)
Solenoid Bolt	
Single Solenoid	58 (6.5)
Other Solenoids (2)	89 (10)
Transaxle Rear Cover Bolt	
A-245E & A-245E	89 (10)
Upper Valve Body-To-Lower Valve Body Bolt	58 (6.5)
Underdrive Brake Accumulator	
Bolt	89 (10)
Screw	65 (7.4)
Valve Body-To-Transaxle Bolt	89 (10)

TRANSMISSION SPECIFICATIONS

TRANSMISSION SPECIFICATIONS

Application	In. (mm)
A-242L, A-241E & A-244E	
Assembly Height	
Underdrive Clutch	.681-.717 (17.29-18.21)
Bushing Inside Diameter	
Direct Clutch	1.853 (47.07)
Oil Pump Body	1.503 (38.18)
Planetary Sun Gear	
Standard	1.173-1.174 (29.80-29.83)
Maximum	1.176 (29.87)
Ring Gear Flange	.749-.750 (19.03-19.05)
Stator Shaft	
Front	.849 (21.57)
Rear	1.066 (27.07)
Sun Gear Flange	.867-.868 (22.03-22.05)
Underdrive Clutch (Front)	
Standard	1.831-1.832 (46.50-46.53)
Maximum	1.833 (45.57)
Underdrive Clutch (Rear)	
Standard	2.165-2.167 (55.00-55.03)
Maximum	2.169 (55.08)
Countershaft End Play	.009-.035 (.23-.89)
Countershaft Height	1.311-1.398 (33.30-35.50)
1st & Reverse Clutch Pack Clearance	.080-.109 (2.04-2.76)
Input Shaft End Play	.012-.035 (.30-.90)
Piston Stroke	
Direct Clutch	
A-241E	.044-.058 (1.11-1.47)
A-242L & A-244E	.064-.078 (1.63-1.97)
Forward Clutch	
A-244E	.044-.058 (1.11-1.47)
All Other Transaxles	.056-.071 (1.42-1.81)
Underdrive Clutch	
A-242L & A-244E	.059-.073 (1.50-1.86)
A-241E	.048-.061 (1.21-1.55)
2nd Coast Brake	.059-.118 (1.50-3.00)
Planetary Pinion Gear	
Thrust Clearance	.008-.020 (.20-.50)
Side Gear Backlash	.002-.008 (.05-.20)
A-245E & A-246E	
Assembly Height	
Underdrive Clutch	.681-.717 (17.29-18.21)
Bushing Inside Diameter	
Direct Clutch	1.900 (48.27)
Oil Pump Body	1.503 (38.18)
Planetary Sun Gear	
Standard	1.173-1.174 (29.80-29.83)
Maximum	1.176 (29.87)
Ring Gear Flange	.749-.750 (19.03-19.05)
Stator Shaft	
Front	.849 (21.57)
Rear	1.066 (27.07)
Sun Gear Flange	.867-.868 (22.03-22.05)
Underdrive Clutch (Front)	
Standard	1.831-1.832 (46.50-46.53)
Maximum	1.833 (45.57)
Underdrive Clutch (Rear)	
Standard	2.165-2.167 (55.00-55.03)
Maximum	2.169 (55.08)
Countershaft End Play	.009-.035 (.23-.89)
Countershaft Height	1.193-1.280 (30.30-32.50)
1st & Reverse Clutch Pack Clearance	.095-.125 (2.42-3.18)
Input Shaft End Play	.012-.035 (.30-.90)
Piston Stroke	
Direct Clutch	.044-.060 (1.12-1.52)
Forward Clutch	.056-.071 (1.41-1.81)
Underdrive Clutch	.059-.075 (1.50-1.90)
2nd Coast Brake	.059-.118 (1.50-3.00)
Planetary Pinion Gear	
Thrust Clearance	.008-.020 (.20-.50)
Side Gear Backlash	.002-.008 (.05-.20)

AUTOMATIC TRANSMISSIONS
Toyota A-240 "E" Series Electronic Controls

Geo: Prizm
Toyota: Celica, Corolla, MR2, Paseo, RAV4

APPLICATION

APPLICATION

Vehicle	Transaxle Model
Geo	
Prizm (LSi)	A-245E
Toyota	
Celica 1.8L	A-246E
Corolla 1.8L	A-245E
MR2 (1995)	A-241E
Paseo	A-244E
RAV4 (1996)	A-241E

CAUTION: All models are equipped with a Supplemental Restraint System (SRS). When servicing vehicle, use care to avoid accidental air bag deployment. All SRS electrical connections and wiring harness are covered by Yellow insulation. SRS-related components are located in steering column, center console, instrument panel and lower panel on instrument panel. DO NOT use electrical test equipment on these circuits. If necessary, deactivate SRS before servicing components. See AIR BAG SERVICING article in APPLICATIONS & IDENTIFICATION section.

NOTE: Geo models and other imported vehicles sold by domestic manufacturers are normally covered in MITCHELL® TRANSMISSION SERVICE & REPAIR for DOMESTIC CARS, LIGHT TRUCKS & VANS. Geo Prizm is covered in this article due to limited use of this transaxle model in domestic vehicles.

DESCRIPTION

The A-240 "E" series automatic transaxle is electronically controlled. Transaxle shifting and torque converter lock-up are controlled by an Electronic Controlled Transmission (ECT) Electronic Control Unit (ECU). Control unit is referred to as the ECT ECU. ECT ECU is combined with engine ECU into one unit.

ECT ECU receives information from various input devices and uses this information to control No. 1 and No. 2 solenoids for transaxle shifting and lock-up solenoid (also called SL solenoid) for torque converter lock-up.

On 1995 Celica, 1995 Corolla and 1996 RAV4, a pattern select switch is located on center console. Pattern select switch contains a POWER (depressed) and a NORMAL (released) operating position. When pattern select switch is depressed, transaxle upshifts and downshifts will occur at a higher vehicle speed than with switch released. An indicator light will indicate pattern select switch position.

NOTE: Celica and Corolla pattern select switch test information is not available.

An Overdrive (OD) switch is mounted on shift lever. *See Figs. 1-8.* When OD switch is depressed to ON position, transaxle will shift into 4th gear when shift lever is in "D" position, and OD OFF light on instrument panel will go off. When OD switch is released to OFF position, transaxle will shift into 3rd gear, and OD OFF light will illuminate.

Transaxle is equipped with a shift lock and key lock system. Shift lock system prevents shift lever from being moved from Park unless brake pedal is depressed. In case of a malfunction, shift lever can be released by depressing shift lock override button, located near shift lever. Key lock system prevents ignition key from being moved from ACC to LOCK position on ignition switch unless shift lever is in Park. For more information on shift lock and key lock system, see TOYOTA SHIFT LOCK SYSTEM article.

OPERATION

ECT ECU

ECT ECU receives information from various input devices and uses this information to control No. 1, No. 2 and lock-up solenoids (also called SL solenoid). ECT ECU contains a self-diagnostic system, which will store a Diagnostic Trouble Code (DTC) if failure or problem exists in electronic control system.

DTC can be retrieved to determine transaxle problem area. See SELF-DIAGNOSTIC SYSTEM. On all models except MR2, ECT ECU is located near front of center console. *See Figs. 1-4 and 6-8.* On MR2 models, ECT ECU is located near left rear corner of engine compartment. *See Fig. 5.*

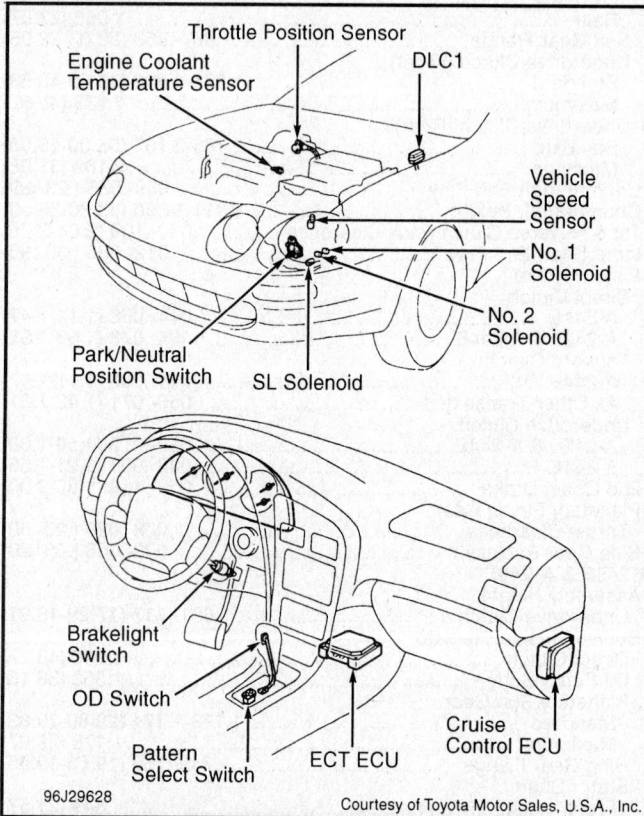

Fig. 1: Identifying Input & Output Devices (1995 Celica)

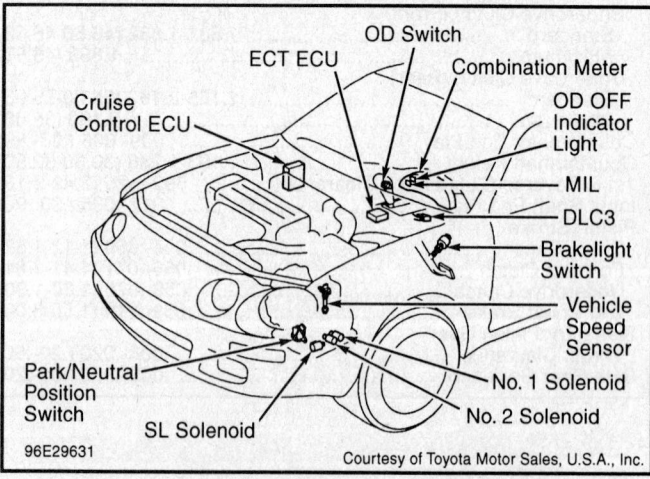

Fig. 2: Identifying Input & Output Devices (1996 Celica)

AUTOMATIC TRANSMISSIONS
Toyota A-240 "E" Series Electronic Controls (Cont.)

3-1593

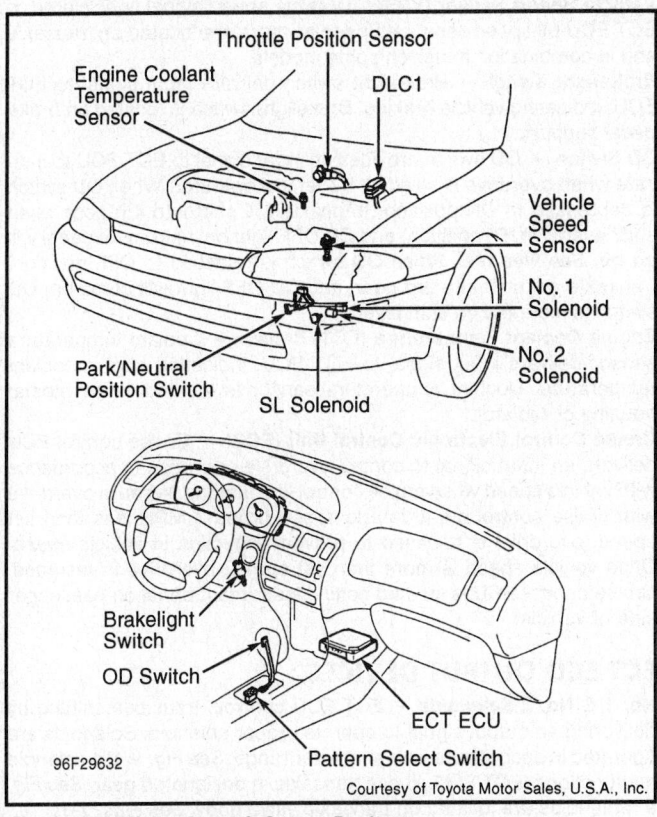

Fig. 3: Identifying Input & Output Devices
(1995 Corolla Is Shown; 1995-96 Prizm Is Similar)

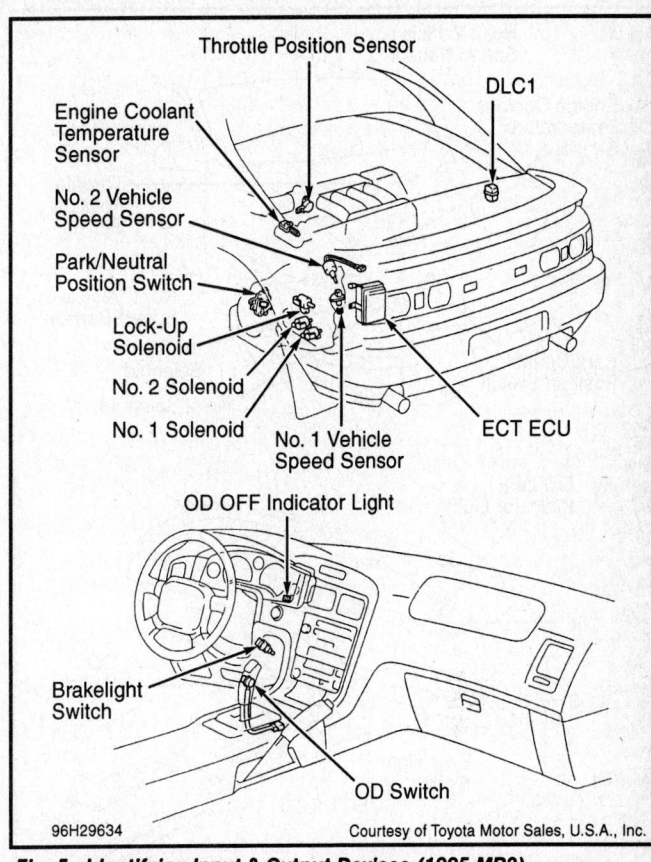

Fig. 5: Identifying Input & Output Devices (1995 MR2)

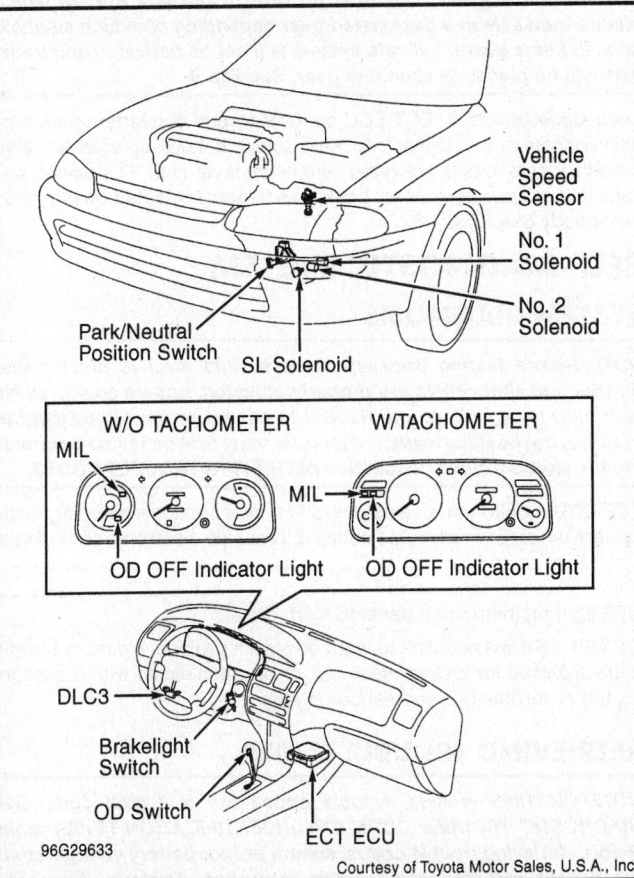

Fig. 4: Identifying Input & Output Devices (1996 Corolla)

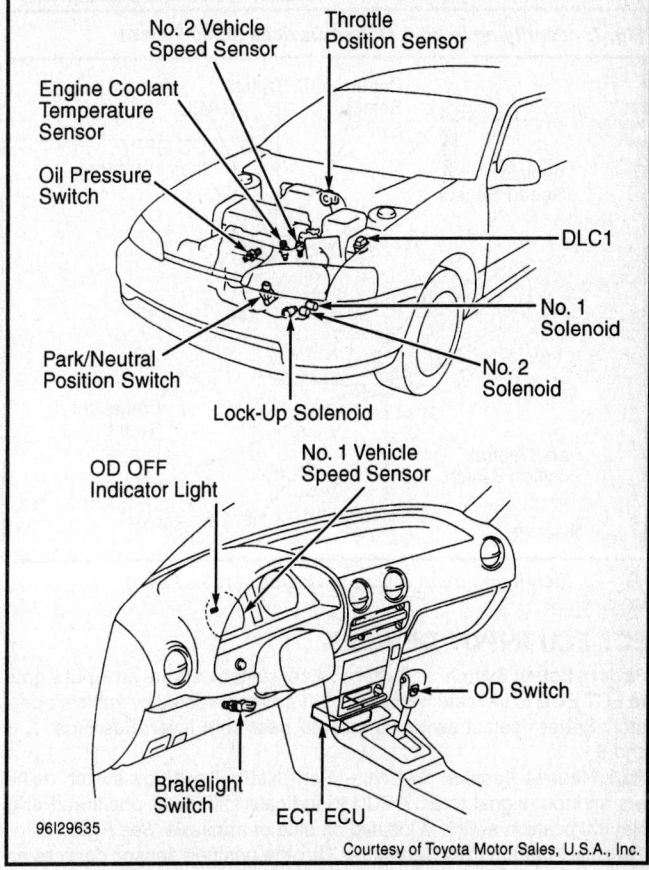

Fig. 6: Identifying Input & Output Devices (1995 Paseo)

3-1594

AUTOMATIC TRANSMISSIONS
Toyota A-240 "E" Series Electronic Controls (Cont.)

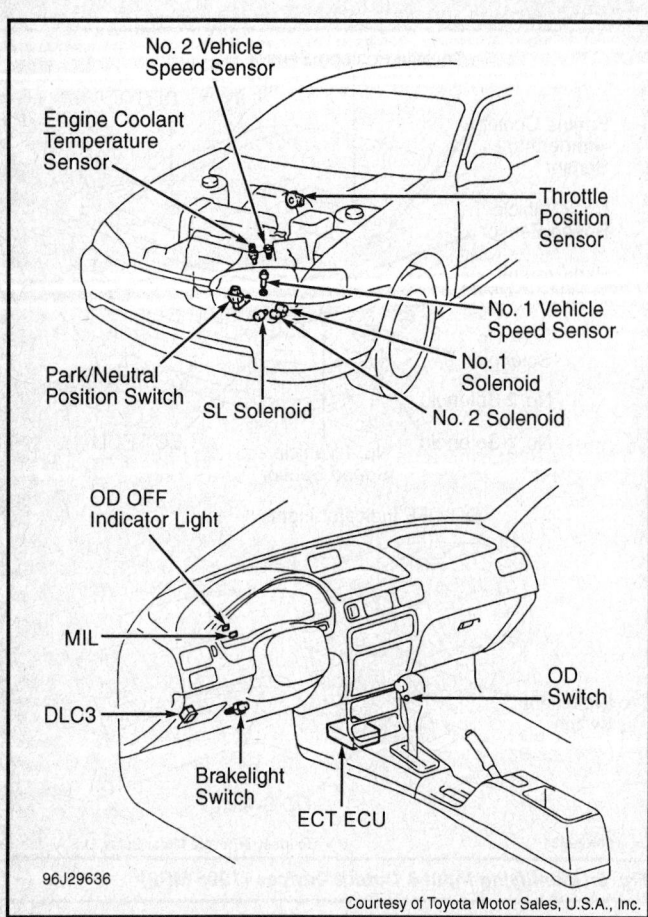

Fig. 7: Identifying Input & Output Devices (1996 Paseo)

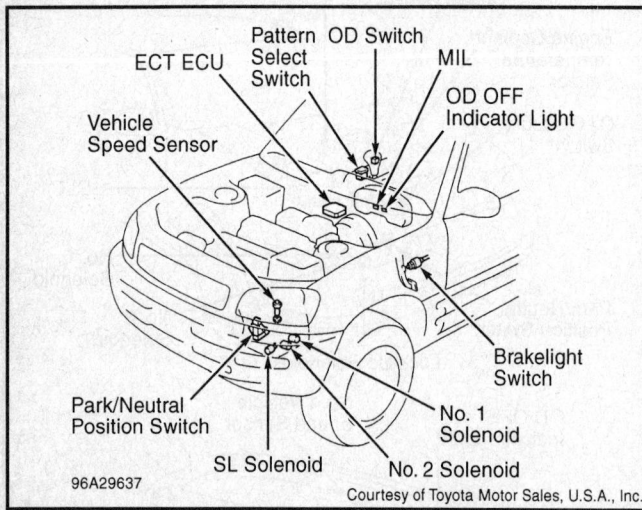

Fig. 8: Identifying Input & Output Devices (1996 RAV4)

ECT ECU INPUT DEVICES

Pattern Select Switch – Pattern select switch delivers an input signal to ECT ECU to indicate transaxle shift points selected by vehicle operator. Pattern select switch is located near shift lever. See Figs. 1, 3 and 8.

Park/Neutral Position Switch – Park/Neutral position switch delivers an input signal to ECT ECU to indicate shift lever position. Park/Neutral position switch is located on side of transaxle. See Figs. 1-8.

Throttle Position (TP) Sensor – Throttle position sensor delivers an input signal to ECT ECU indicating throttle position. Throttle position sensor is located on side of throttle body.

Vehicle Speed Sensor (VSS) – Vehicle speed signal is delivered to ECT ECU by speed sensors. Speed sensors are located on transaxle and in combination meter on some models.

Brakelight Switch – Brakelight switch delivers input signal to ECT ECU, indicating vehicle braking. Brakelight switch is located on brake pedal support.

OD Switch – OD switch provides an input signal to ECT ECU to indicate when overdrive is selected by vehicle operator. When OD switch is depressed to ON position, transaxle will shift into 4th gear when shift lever is in "D" position, and OD OFF light on instrument panel will go off. See Figs. 1-8. When OD switch is released to OFF position, transaxle will shift into 3rd gear, and OD OFF light will come on. OD switch is mounted on shift lever.

Engine Coolant Temperature (ECT) Sensor – Coolant temperature sensor delivers input signal to ECT ECU, indicating engine coolant temperature. Coolant temperature sensor is located in thermostat housing or radiator.

Cruise Control Electronic Control Unit (ECU) – Cruise control ECU delivers an input signal to control overdrive operation in accordance with vehicle speed when cruise control is operating. When in overdrive with cruise control on, if vehicle speed drops 3 MPH less than set speed, overdrive is released to prevent reduction in vehicle speed. Once vehicle speed is more than set speed, overdrive is resumed. Cruise control ECU is located behind instrument panel on passenger side of vehicle.

ECT ECU OUTPUT DEVICES

No. 1 & No. 2 Solenoids – ECT ECU controls transaxle shifting by delivering an output signal to operate proper solenoid. Solenoids are operated in accordance with shift lever range. See Fig. 9. If a solenoid malfunctions, ECT ECU places transaxle in designated gear. See Fig. 9. Solenoids are located on transaxle valve body. See Figs. 1-8.

NOTE: In some gears, ECT ECU provides a fail-safe system which places transaxle in a designated gear depending on which solenoid fails. In some gears, fail-safe system will not be activated and transaxle will be placed in specified gear. See Fig. 9.

Lock-Up Solenoid – ECT ECU controls torque converter lock-up by delivering an output signal to lock-up solenoid. Lock-up solenoid (also called SL solenoid) is activated when shift lever is in "D" position and vehicle is at specified speed. Lock-up solenoid is located on transaxle valve body See Figs. 1-8.

SELF-DIAGNOSTIC SYSTEM

SYSTEM DIAGNOSIS

NOTE: Before testing transaxle, ensure fluid level is correct and throttle and shift cables are properly adjusted. Ensure engine starts with shift lever in Park and Neutral to ensure proper adjustment of park/neutral position switch. Transaxle must first be tested by checking for stored trouble codes. See RETRIEVING TROUBLE CODES.

ECT ECU monitors transaxle operation and contains a self-diagnostic system which stores trouble codes if transaxle electronic control system failure or problem exists. If a problem exists in No. 1 or No. 2 solenoids or speed sensors and trouble code is set, ECT ECU blinks OD OFF light on instrument panel to warn driver.

OD OFF light will not blink to warn driver if a problem exists or trouble code is stored for lock-up solenoid, or problem exists with brakelight switch or throttle position sensor signal.

RETRIEVING TROUBLE CODES

NOTE: ON 1995 models, trouble codes are a 2 digit code. See DIAGNOSTIC TROUBLE CODE (DTC) IDENTIFICATION (1995) table. Before retrieving trouble codes, ensure proper battery voltage exists for proper self-diagnosis system operation. Perform diagnostic circuit check before retrieving trouble codes to ensure proper operation of OD OFF light. See DIAGNOSTIC CIRCUIT CHECK.

AUTOMATIC TRANSMISSIONS
Toyota A-240 "E" Series Electronic Controls (Cont.)

3-1595

Position	NORMAL			NO.1 SOLENOID MALFUNCTIONING			NO.2 SOLENOID MALFUNCTIONING			BOTH SOLENOIDS MALFUNCTIONING
	Solenoid valve		Gear	Solenoid valve		Gear	Solenoid valve		Gear	Gear when shift selector is manually operated
	No. 1	No. 2		No. 1	No. 2		No. 1	No. 2		
D	ON	OFF	1st	×	ON	3rd	ON	×	1st	O/D
	ON	ON	2nd	×	ON	3rd	OFF	×	O/D	O/D
	OFF	ON	3rd	×	ON	3rd	OFF	×	O/D	O/D
	OFF	OFF	O/D	×	OFF	O/D	OFF	×	O/D	O/D
2	ON	OFF	1st	×	ON	3rd	ON	×	1st	3rd
	ON	ON	2nd	×	ON	3rd	OFF	×	3rd	3rd
	OFF	ON	3rd	×	ON	3rd	OFF	×	3rd	3rd
L	ON	OFF	1st	×	OFF	1st	ON	×	1st	1st
	ON	ON	2nd	×	ON	2nd	ON	×	1st	1st

×: Malfunctions

96F21175   Courtesy of Toyota Motor Sales, U.S.A., Inc.

Fig. 9: Checking No. 1 & No. 2 Solenoid Operation

NOTE: On 1996 models, trouble codes are a 4 digit code (OBD-II). See DIAGNOSTIC TROUBLE CODE (DTC) IDENTIFICATION (1996) table. Trouble codes can only be retrieved using scan tool connected to 16-pin Data Link Connector (DLC3). See Fig. 10. For DLC3 location, see Figs. 2, 4 and 7. On RAV4, DLC3 is located behind instrument panel, above pedal assembly. When trouble code is present, Malfunction Indicator Light (MIL) located on instrument panel will light. To retrieve trouble codes using scan tool, follow scan tool manufacturer's operating instructions.

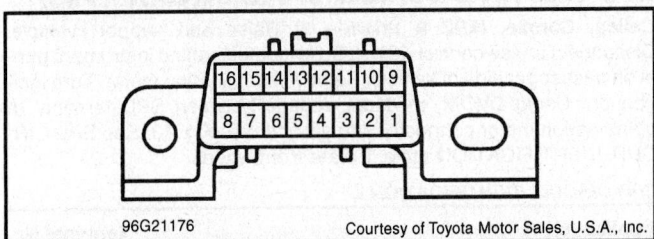

96G21176   Courtesy of Toyota Motor Sales, U.S.A., Inc.

Fig. 10: Identifying Data Link Connector (DLC3) Terminals (1996)

Diagnostic Circuit Check (1995) – 1) Turn ignition on. Release OD switch on shift lever to OFF position. Ensure OD OFF light on instrument panel turns on. If OD OFF light does not illuminate, check OD switch and wiring circuit.
2) Depress OD switch to ON position. Ensure OD OFF light on instrument panel goes off. If OD OFF light remains on, check OD switch and wiring circuit. If OD OFF light is blinking, check for stored codes. See ECT ECU CODES.
ECT ECU Codes (1995) – 1) Turn ignition on. DO NOT start engine. Depress OD switch on shift lever to ON position.

NOTE: Codes can only be retrieved with OD switch on. If OD switch is off, OD OFF light will be on continuously and will not blink the code.

2) Install jumper wire between terminals TE₁ and E₁ of DLC1 connector. See Fig. 11.
3) Note number of flashes from OD OFF light on instrument panel. If normal system operation exists, OD OFF light will flash 2 times per second. See Fig. 12.
4) If system is operating correctly and no code exists, turn ignition off and remove jumper wire. Perform MANUAL SHIFT TEST to determine if problem is electrical or mechanical transaxle problem. Check system by symptom. See appropriate symptom under SYMPTOM TROUBLE SHOOTING.

5) If code exists, OD OFF light will blink once every .5 second. Number of blinks equals first digit of code. After a pause of 1.5 seconds, second digit will be displayed. See Fig. 12.
6) If more than one code exists, next code will be displayed after pause of 2.5 seconds. See Fig. 12. Smallest number code will display first and system will progress to largest code. Codes will be repeated.
7) Once code is obtained, determine probable cause and symptom. See DIAGNOSTIC TROUBLE CODE (DTC) IDENTIFICATION (1995) table. For diagnosis and repair of trouble codes, see DIAGNOSTIC TESTS. Turn ignition off and remove jumper wire.

NOTE: Once repairs have been performed, codes must be cleared from ECT ECU memory. See CLEARING TROUBLE CODES under SELF-DIAGNOSTIC SYSTEM.

DIAGNOSTIC TROUBLE CODE (DTC) IDENTIFICATION (1995)

DTC	[1] Probable Cause
42	[2] No. 1 Speed Sensor
61	[2][3] No. 2 Speed Sensor
62	No. 1 Solenoid
63	No. 2 Solenoid
64	[4] Lock-Up Solenoid

[1] – Check listed component for probable cause. Check wiring and connections of specified component.
[2] – If both No. 1 and No. 2 speed sensors fail simultaneously, DTC will not exist, but transaxle will not upshift from 1st gear with shift lever in "D" position.
[3] – MR2 and Paseo.
[4] – Also called SL solenoid.

DIAGNOSTIC TROUBLE CODE (DTC) IDENTIFICATION (1996)

DTC	[1] Probable Cause
P0500	[2] Vehicle Speed Sensor
P0750	[3] No. 1 Solenoid
P0753	No. 1 Solenoid Circuit Malfunction
P0755	[3] No. 2 Solenoid
P0758	No. 2 Solenoid Circuit Malfunction
P0770	[3][4] Lock-Up Solenoid
P0773	[4] Lock-Up Solenoid Circuit Malfunction
P1700	[5] No. 2 Vehicle Speed Sensor
P1780	Park/Neutral Position Switch Malfunction

[1] – Check listed component for probable cause. Check wiring and connections of specified component.
[2] – Except Prizm.
[3] – To diagnose this DTC, see SOLENOIDS under COMPONENT TESTS.
[4] – Also called SL solenoid.
[5] – Paseo only.

3-1596

AUTOMATIC TRANSMISSIONS
Toyota A-240 "E" Series Electronic Controls (Cont.)

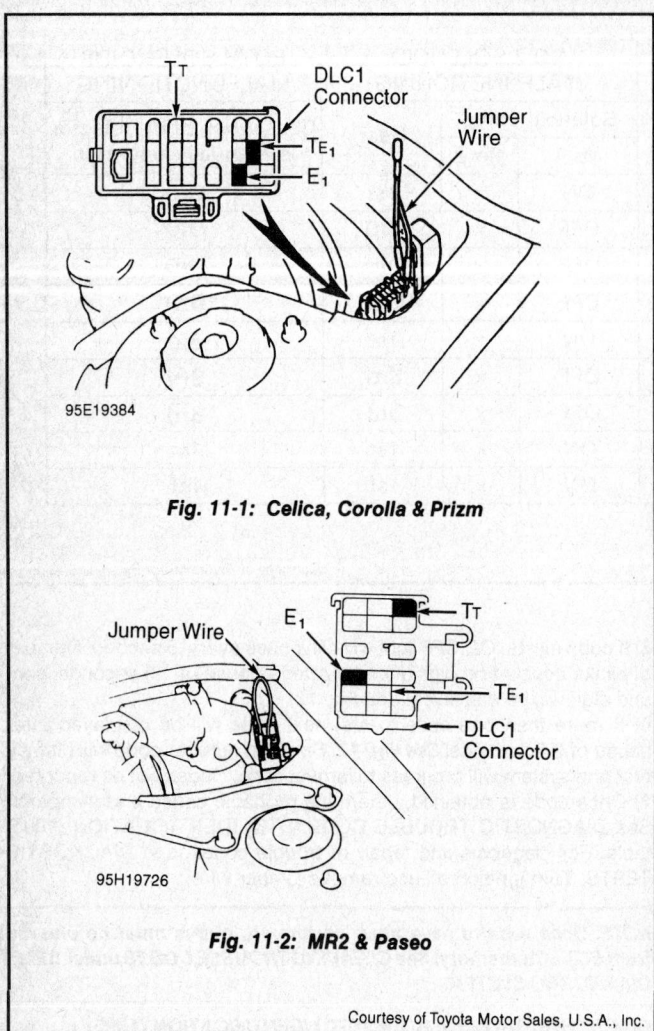

Fig. 11-1: Celica, Corolla & Prizm

Fig. 11-2: MR2 & Paseo

Courtesy of Toyota Motor Sales, U.S.A., Inc.

Fig. 11: Identifying DLC1 Terminals & Location

CLEARING TROUBLE CODES

1995 Models – Once repairs have been performed, codes must be cleared from ECT ECU memory. Remove EFI fuse (15-amp) from engine compartment fuse box, near battery, for 10 seconds or more to clear memory in ECT ECU. On all models except MR2, engine compartment fuse box is located near battery in engine compartment. On MR2, engine compartment fuse box is located on driver's side of engine compartment. Fuse may need to be removed for more than 10 seconds in cold ambient temperatures. Reinstall fuse.

1996 Models – Trouble codes can only be cleared using scan tool connected to 16-pin Data Link Connector (DLC3). See Fig. 10. For DLC3 location, see Figs. 2, 4 and 7. On RAV4, DLC3 is located behind instrument panel, above pedal assembly.

NOTE: On 1995 models, codes may also be cleared by disconnecting negative battery cable, but memory for electronic components will also be canceled.

DIAGNOSTIC TESTS

When trouble shooting transaxle, first check for stored trouble codes and repair as necessary. If no trouble codes exist, perform manual shift test to determine if problem area is in electrical circuits or a mechanical transaxle problem. See MANUAL SHIFT TEST.

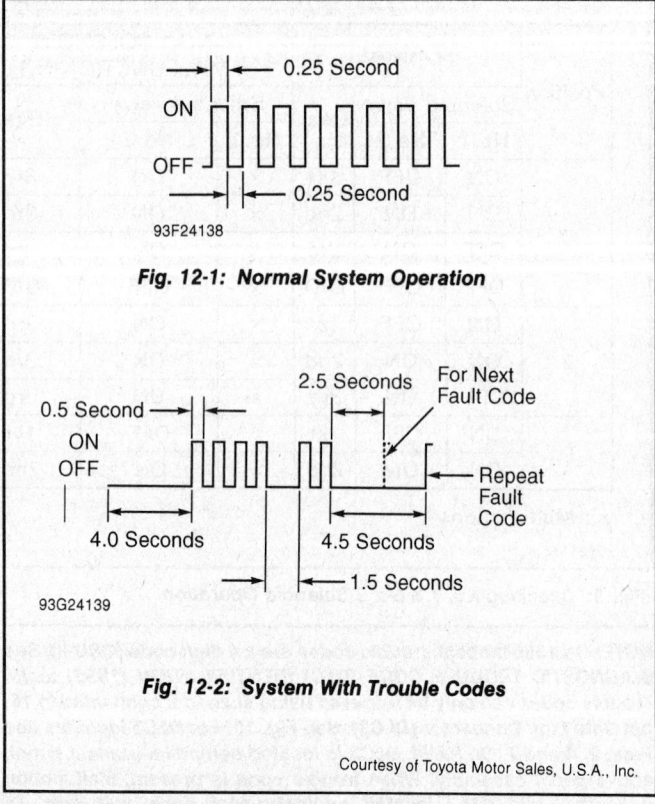

Fig. 12-1: Normal System Operation

Fig. 12-2: System With Trouble Codes

Courtesy of Toyota Motor Sales, U.S.A., Inc.

Fig. 12: Identifying Trouble Code Displays

DTC 42: NO. 1 VEHICLE SPEED SENSOR (VSS)

Celica, Corolla, MR2 & Prizm – 1) Raise and support vehicle. Disconnect cruise control ECU. ECU is located behind instrument panel on passenger side of vehicle. Remove combination meter. Turn ignition on. Using DVOM, measure voltage between SPD terminal of combination meter connector and ground. *See Fig. 13.* See SPD CIRCUIT IDENTIFICATION table. Rotate front wheel.

SPD CIRCUIT IDENTIFICATION

Application	Terminal No.
Corolla	9
Celica	3
MR2	10
Prizm	12

2) If voltage pulses 0-5 volts, check continuity between ECT ECU harness connector E_1 terminal and ground. If continuity does not exist, inspect and repair circuit as needed. If continuity does exist, replace ECT ECU and retest. If no voltage is present, go to next step. If voltage is 4-6 volts and remains unchanged, go to step 5).

3) Turn ignition off. Disconnect ECT ECU harness connector. *See Figs. 1, 3 and 5.* Using ohmmeter, check continuity between combination meter harness connector SPD terminal and ECT ECU SPD terminal. *See Fig. 15.* If continuity exists, go to next step. If continuity does not exist, inspect and repair circuit as needed.

4) Check continuity of 2 circuits between combination meter and VSS. See appropriate wiring diagram in WIRING DIAGRAMS. If continuity does not exist, inspect and repair circuit(s) as needed. If continuity exists, inspect VSS. See VEHICLE SPEED SENSOR under COMPONENT TESTS. Replace as needed.

5) Disconnect VSS harness connector. Turn ignition on. Measure voltage between VSS harness connector terminal No. 1 and ground. See WIRING DIAGRAMS. If battery voltage is not present, inspect and repair circuit as needed. If battery voltage is present, replace combination meter and retest.

AUTOMATIC TRANSMISSIONS
Toyota A-240 "E" Series Electronic Controls (Cont.)

3-1597

6) Turn ignition off. Disconnect ECT ECU harness connector. See Fig. 1, 3 and 5. Using ohmmeter, check continuity between combination meter harness connector SPD terminal and ECT ECU SPD terminal. See Fig. 15. If continuity exists, replace combination meter and retest. If continuity does not exist, inspect and repair circuit as needed.

Paseo – 1) Determine if speedometer is operating properly. Inspect and repair speedometer drive gear, cable and combination meter as needed.

2) Turn ignition off. Access ECT ECU harness connector. See Fig. 6. Raise and support front wheels of vehicle. Backprobing ECT ECU harness connector with DVOM, check voltage between SPD terminal and vehicle ground while turning front wheel.

3) If voltage pulses as wheel is turned, replace ECT ECU and retest. If pulse is not present, turn ignition off. Remove combination meter. Connect ohmmeter to test terminals and rotate combination meter shaft. See Fig. 14. If ohmmeter pulses, inspect and repair circuits between combination meter and ECT ECU. See appropriate wiring diagram in WIRING DIAGRAMS. If ohmmeter does not pulse, replace combination meter and retest.

DTC 61: NO. 2 VEHICLE SPEED SENSOR (VSS)

MR2 & Paseo – 1) Access ECT ECU. See Figs. 5 and 6. Using ohmmeter, check for continuity between terminal SP_2 of ECT ECU connector and body ground. See Fig. 15.

2) If continuity exists, replace ECT ECU. If continuity does not exist, check No. 2 speed sensor. See NO. 2 SPEED SENSOR under COMPONENT TESTS.

3) Replace No. 2 speed sensor if defective. If No. 2 speed sensor is okay, check wiring between ECT ECU and No. 2 speed sensor. See appropriate wiring diagram in WIRING DIAGRAMS.

DTC 62 OR DTC P0753: NO. 1 SOLENOID

1) Access ECT ECU. See Figs. 1-8. Using ohmmeter, check resistance between terminal S_1 and body ground with connector removed from ECT ECU. See Fig. 15.

2) Resistance should be 11-15 ohms. If resistance is okay, replace ECT ECU. If resistance is not within specification, remove transaxle oil pan. Disconnect electrical connector at No. 1 solenoid. See WIRING DIAGRAMS.

3) Check resistance between electrical terminal on No. 1 solenoid and body ground. Replace No. 1 solenoid if resistance is not 11-15 ohms. If resistance is 11-15 ohms, inspect and repair wiring between No. 1 solenoid and ECT ECU.

DTC 63 OR DTC P0758: NO. 2 SOLENOID

1) Access ECT ECU. See Figs. 1-8. Using ohmmeter, check resistance between terminal S_2 and body ground with connector removed from ECT ECU. See Fig. 15.

2) Resistance should be 11-15 ohms. If resistance is okay, replace ECT ECU. If resistance is not within specification, remove transaxle oil pan. Disconnect electrical connector at No. 2 solenoid. See WIRING DIAGRAMS.

3) Check resistance between electrical terminal on No. 2 solenoid and body ground. Replace No. 2 solenoid if resistance is not 11-15 ohms. If resistance is 11-15 ohms, inspect and repair wiring between No. 2 solenoid and ECT ECU.

DTC 64 OR DTC P0773: LOCK-UP/SL SOLENOID

1) Access ECT ECU. See Figs. 1-8. Using ohmmeter, check resistance between terminal S_L and body ground with connector removed from ECT ECU. See Fig. 15.

2) Resistance should be 11-15 ohms. If resistance is okay, replace ECT ECU. If resistance is not within specification, disconnect electrical connector at lock-up solenoid. See WIRING DIAGRAMS.

3) Check resistance between electrical terminal on lock-up solenoid and body ground. Replace lock-up solenoid if resistance is not 11-15 ohms. If resistance is 11-15 ohms, inspect and repair wiring between lock-up solenoid and ECT ECU.

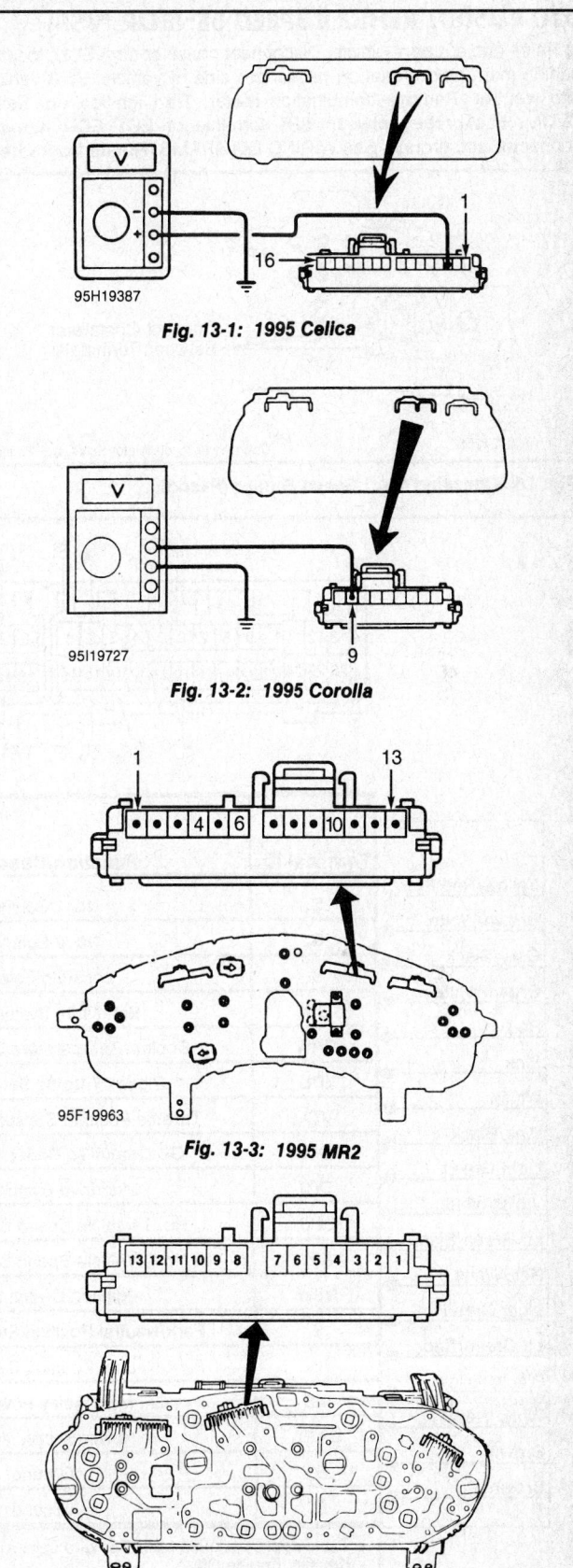

Fig. 13-1: 1995 Celica

Fig. 13-2: 1995 Corolla

Fig. 13-3: 1995 MR2

Fig. 13-4: 1995 Prizm

Courtesy of Toyota Motor Sales, U.S.A., Inc.

Fig. 13: Identifying Combination Meter Harness Connector

3-1598

AUTOMATIC TRANSMISSIONS
Toyota A-240 "E" Series Electronic Controls (Cont.)

DTC P0500: VEHICLE SPEED SENSOR (VSS)

1) Raise and support vehicle. Disconnect cruise control ECU, located behind instrument panel on passenger side of vehicle. Shift vehicle into Neutral. Remove combination meter. Turn ignition on. Using DVOM, backprobe between SP1 terminal of ECT ECU harness connector and ground. See WIRING DIAGRAMS. Rotate front wheel.

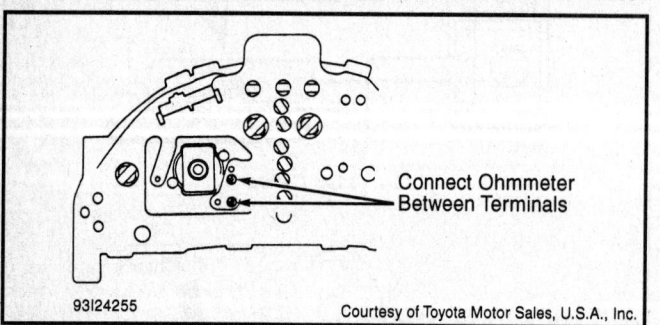

Connect Ohmmeter Between Terminals

93124255   Courtesy of Toyota Motor Sales, U.S.A., Inc.

Fig. 14: Checking No. 1 Speed Sensor (Paseo)

2) If voltage pulses between 4.5-5.5 volts, check continuity between ECT ECU harness connector E1 terminal and ground. If continuity does not exist, check and repair circuit as needed. If continuity does exist, replace ECT ECU and retest. If voltage is not as specified, check and repair wiring harness or connector between combination meter and ECT ECU. For VSS testing, see VEHICLE SPEED SENSOR under COMPONENT TESTS.

DTC P1700: NO. 2 VEHICLE SPEED SENSOR FAULT (PASEO)

1) Ensure ignition is off. Access ECT ECU. *See Fig.* 7. Raise and support vehicle. Shift transaxle into Neutral. Rotate front wheel. Back-probing ECT ECU harness connector with ohmmeter, measure resistance between terminal SP_2 and ground terminal E_1. See WIRING DIAGRAMS. Resistance should pulse between zero ohms and infinite ohms. If resistance is within specification, replace ECT ECU. If resistance is not within specification, go to next step.

2) Remove No. 2 speed sensor from extension housing of transaxle. Measure resistance between sensor terminals. Resistance should pulse between zero ohms and infinite ohms when a magnet is put

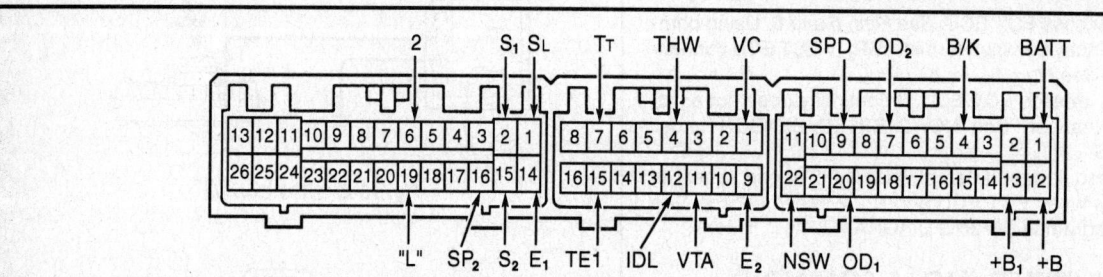

	Terminal ID.	Function/Description	Voltage Value (DC Volts Unless Otherwise Specified)
Yellow/Red [1]	S_1	No. 1 Solenoid	9-14 Volts With KOEO [2]
Brown/White	S_2	No. 2 Solenoid	1.5 Volt Or Less With KOEO [2]
Gray/Black	S_L	Lock-Up Solenoid	1.5 Volt Or Less With KOEO [2]
Green/White	B/K	Brakelight Switch Signal	9-14 Volts With Pedal Depressed
Red	THW	Coolant Temperature Sensor Signal	.2-1.0 Volts @ 176°F (80°C)
Pink	IDL	Closed Throttle Sensor Signal	0-3 Volts With Throttle Closed, KOEO [2]
White	VTA	Throttle Position Sensor Output Signal	3.2-4.9 Volts With Throttle Fully Open
Pink/Black	OD_1	OD Output To Cruise Control ECU	9-14 Volts With KOEO [2]
Light Green	OD_2	Overdrive Switch Signal	9-14 Volts With Switch On
Violet/White	SPD	No. 1 Vehicle Speed Sensor Signal	1 Volt Or Less With ECU Unplugged [3] (Car Parked)
Lt. Green/Black	SP_2	No. 2 Vehicle Speed Sensor Signal	One Pulse Per Each Output Shaft Revolution
Red/White	NSW	Ignition Switch Signal	9-14 Volts In "P" Or "N", KOEO [2]
Light Green	2	Park/Neutral Position Switch "2" Signal	9-14 Volts In "2", KOEO [2]
Lt. Green/Red	L	Park/Neutral Position Switch "L" Signal	9-14 Volts In "L", KOEO [2]
Black/Yellow	+B	EFI Main Relay Power Supply	9-14 Volts With KOEO [2]
White/Red	BATT	Power Supply Voltage	9-14 Volts (Constant)
Brown	E_1	Ground	Not Applicable
Brown	E_2	Ground	Not Applicable

[1] – Table applies to 1995 MR2. For wire color identification for all other models, see appropriate wiring diagram.
[2] – Key On, Engine Off.
[3] – Disconnect cruise control ECU harness connector, located behind instrument panel on passenger side of vehicle.

96B29638

Courtesy of Toyota Motor Sales, U.S.A., Inc.

Fig. 15: Identifying ECT ECU Harness Connector (MR2 Is Shown; Other Models Are Similar)

AUTOMATIC TRANSMISSIONS
Toyota A-240 "E" Series Electronic Controls (Cont.)

3-1599

close to tip of speed sensor. If resistance is not as specified, replace sensor. If resistance is as specified, check and repair circuits between sensor and ECT ECU.

DTC P1780: PARK/NEUTRAL POSITION SWITCH

1) Access ECT ECU. *See Figs. 2, 4, 7 and 8.* Turn ignition switch to ON position. Using DVOM, measure voltage at terminals NSW, "2" and "L" of ECT ECU harness connector between terminal and body ground with gear selector in each shift position. *See Fig. 15.*

2) Ensure 9-14 volts is present at NSW terminal at ECT ECU harness connector in all shift positions. Ensure 9-14 volts is present at terminals "2" and "L" at ECT ECU harness connector with gear selector in "2" and "L" position. If voltage is not as specified, check park/neutral position switch. See PARK/NEUTRAL POSITION (PNP) SWITCH under COMPONENT TESTS.

MANUAL SHIFT TEST

NOTE: Perform manual shift test if no trouble codes exist. Manual shift test determines if problem area is in electrical circuits or a mechanical transaxle problem.

1) With ignition off, disconnect electrical connector from solenoids on transaxle. Electrical connector is located near park/neutral position switch on transaxle.

2) Road test vehicle and ensure transaxle gear changes corresponds with shift lever position. See GEAR APPLICATION table. If abnormality exists, a mechanical transaxle problem exists.

3) If all gears are correct, perform trouble shooting in accordance with symptom. See SYMPTOM TROUBLE SHOOTING. Turn ignition off.

4) Reconnect electrical connector. Clear trouble codes from ECT ECU memory. See CLEARING TROUBLE CODES under SELF-DIAGNOSTIC SYSTEM.

GEAR APPLICATION

Shift Lever Position	Transaxle Gear
"D"	Overdrive
"2"	3rd
"L"	1st
"R"	Reverse
"P"	Park

TORQUE CONVERTER

LOCK-UP TEST

NOTE: Refer to appropriate SHIFT SPEED SPECIFICATION table in TOYOTA A-240 "E" & "L" SERIES overhaul article for lock-up shift speed.

Road test vehicle. Increase vehicle speed until lock-up should occur. To confirm lock-up operation, very lightly depress brake pedal with left foot and release while maintaining constant speed. Monitor vehicle tachometer. Torque converter should release and then return to lock-up once brake pedal is released.

SYMPTOM TROUBLE SHOOTING

NOTE: Symptom trouble shooting is for 1995 models only. Manufacturer does not provide trouble shooting information for 1996 models.

NOTE: If problem area is not listed under symptom trouble shooting, check throttle position sensor signal, brakelight signal, gear selector signal and ECT ECU voltages. See CIRCUIT TESTS.

TRANSAXLE WILL NOT SHIFT

1) Warm engine to normal operating temperature. Connect voltmeter between terminals T_T and E_1 of DLC1. *See Fig. 11.* Turn ignition on. Note that voltage changes as throttle pedal is depressed.

2) If voltage changes with throttle opening, go to step **6)**. If voltage does not change with throttle opening, go to next step. Access ECT ECU. *See Figs. 1, 3, 5 and 6.*

3) Connect voltmeter between terminals B/K and E_1 on ECT ECU connector. *See Fig. 15.* No voltage should exist with brake pedal released. About 10-14 volts should exist with brake pedal depressed.

4) If voltage is not as specified, check for defective brakelight switch. If brakelight switch is okay, inspect and repair circuit between brakelight switch and ECT ECU. See appropriate wiring diagram in WIRING DIAGRAMS.

5) If voltage is as specified, check for defective ECT ECU power source or ground connections. Check for short or open circuit in wire to T_T terminal of DLC1. Check for defective throttle position sensor or wiring. See THROTTLE POSITION (TP) SENSOR under COMPONENT TESTS.

6) Perform MANUAL SHIFT TEST. If transaxle does not perform correctly, disassemble and inspect transaxle. If transaxle operates correctly, road test vehicle and ensure voltage at terminal T_T increases from zero to 7 volts. See GEAR SELECTOR SIGNAL under CIRCUIT TESTS.

7) If no voltage exists, proceed to step **9)**. If voltage increases from zero to 7 volts, transaxle or solenoids are faulty. If voltage increases from zero to 4 volts, perform NO UPSHIFT TO OVERDRIVE under SYMPTOM TROUBLE SHOOTING.

8) If voltage increases from zero to 2 volts, check for 10-14 volts between terminals 2 and E_1 on ECT ECU with connector connected and shift lever in "D" position. *See Fig. 15.* If 10-14 volts exist, check for defective park/neutral position switch. If switch is okay, inspect and repair circuit(s) between switch and ECT ECU. See appropriate wiring diagram in WIRING DIAGRAMS. If 10-14 volts does not exist, replace ECT ECU.

9) Check for 10-14 volts between terminals "L" and E_1 on ECT ECU with connector connected and shift lever in "D" position. *See Fig. 15.* If 10-14 volts exist, check for defective park/neutral position switch. If switch is okay, inspect and repair circuit(s) between switch and ECT ECU. See appropriate wiring diagram in WIRING DIAGRAMS. If 10-14 volts does not exist, replace ECT ECU.

SHIFT POINTS TOO HIGH OR LOW

1) Warm engine to normal operating temperature. Connect voltmeter between terminals T_T and E_1 of DLC1. *See Fig. 11.*

2) Turn ignition on. Depress and release throttle pedal. Note if voltage changes with throttle opening. If voltage changes with throttle opening, check for faulty ECT ECU or internal transaxle malfunction. If voltage does not change with throttle opening, go to next step.

3) Access ECT ECU. *See Figs. 1, 3, 5 and 6.* Connect voltmeter between terminals B/K and E_1 on ECT ECU with connector connected. *See Fig. 15.* No voltage should exist with brake pedal released. About 10-14 volts should exist with brake pedal depressed. If voltage is not as specified, check for defective brakelight switch or wiring circuit.

4) If voltage is as specified, check for defective ECT ECU power source or ground connections. See appropriate wiring diagram in WIRING DIAGRAMS. Check for short or open circuit in wire to T_T terminal of DLC1. Check for defective throttle position sensor or wiring.

NO UPSHIFT TO OVERDRIVE

1) Warm engine to normal operating temperature. With ignition off, disconnect solenoid harness connector from transaxle. Electrical connectors are located near park/neutral position switch on transaxle.

2) Road test vehicle and note if transaxle upshifts to overdrive. Reconnect harness connector. Clear trouble codes from ECT ECU memory, as disconnecting electrical connectors may set DTC's. See CLEARING TROUBLE CODES under SELF-DIAGNOSTIC SYSTEM. If no overdrive upshift exists, disassemble and inspect transaxle. If overdrive upshift exists, go to next step.

3) Connect voltmeter between terminals T_T and E_1 of DLC1. *See Fig. 11.* Road test vehicle and ensure voltage at terminal T_T increases from zero to 7 volts. See GEAR SELECTOR SIGNAL under CIRCUIT TESTS.

3-1600

AUTOMATIC TRANSMISSIONS
Toyota A-240 "E"Series Electronic Controls (Cont.)

4) If no voltage exists, check for 10-14 volts between terminals L and E_1 on ECT ECU with connector connected, shift lever in "D" position and ignition on. See Fig. 15. If 10-14 volts exist, check for defective park/neutral position switch. See PARK/NEUTRAL POSITION (PNP) SWITCH under COMPONENT TESTS.

5) If switch is okay, inspect and repair circuit(s) between switch and ECT ECU. See appropriate wiring diagram in WIRING DIAGRAMS. If 10-14 volts does not exist, replace ECT ECU.

6) If voltage increases from zero to 2 volts, check for 10-14 volts between terminals 2 and E_1 on ECT ECU with connector connected, shift lever in "D" position and ignition on.

7) If 10-14 volts exist, check for defective park/neutral position switch. If switch is okay, inspect and repair circuit(s) between switch and ECT ECU. See appropriate wiring diagram in WIRING DIAGRAMS. If 10-14 volts does not exist, replace ECT ECU.

8) If voltage increases from zero to 7 volts between terminals L and E_1, solenoids may be faulty. See SOLENOIDS under COMPONENT TESTS. If solenoids are okay, disassemble and inspect transaxle. If voltage increases from zero to 4 volts between terminals L and E_1, connect voltmeter between terminals OD_2 and E_1 on ECT ECU with connector connected. See Fig. 15.

9) Turn ignition on. Check voltage with OD switch on shift lever released (OFF position) and depressed (ON position). No voltage should exist with switch released and 10-14 volts should exist with switch depressed.

10) If voltage is as specified, go to next step. If voltage is not as specified, check for defective OD switch or wiring circuit.

11) Check voltage between terminals OD_1 and E_1 on ECT ECU with connector connected and ignition on. Voltage should be about 5 volts. If voltage is as specified, replace ECT ECU. If voltage is not as specified, go to next step.

12) Disconnect electrical connector from cruise control ECU. ECU is located behind instrument panel on passenger side of vehicle. Check voltage between terminals OD_1 and E_1 on ECT ECU with connector connected and ignition on. If voltage is about 5 volts, replace cruise control ECU. If voltage is not about 5 volts, inspect and repair circuit(s) between cruise control ECU and ECT ECU. See appropriate wiring diagram in WIRING DIAGRAMS. If wiring is okay, replace ECT ECU.

NO LOCK-UP

1) Warm engine to normal operating temperature. Connect voltmeter between terminals T_T and E_1 of DLC1. See Fig. 11.

2) Road test vehicle and ensure voltage at terminal T_T is 7 volts in lock-up range. See GEAR SELECTOR SIGNAL under CIRCUIT TESTS. If voltage is as specified, lock-up solenoid, torque converter or transaxle is defective.

3) If voltage is not as specified, access ECT ECU. See Figs. 1, 3, 5 and 6. Connect voltmeter between terminals B/K and E_1 on ECT ECU with connector connected. See Fig. 15.

4) No voltage should exist with brake pedal released. About 10-14 volts should exist with brake pedal depressed. If voltage is not as specified, check for defective brakelight switch or wiring circuit.

5) If voltage is as specified, check for defective ECT ECU power source or ground connections. See appropriate wiring diagram in WIRING DIAGRAMS. Check for short or open circuit in wire to T_T terminal of DLC1. Check for defective throttle position sensor or wiring. See THROTTLE POSITION (TP) SENSOR under COMPONENT TESTS.

CIRCUIT TESTS

NOTE: All voltage checks are made with ignition switch in ON position unless otherwise stated.

THROTTLE POSITION (TP) SENSOR SIGNAL

1) Locate DLC1 in engine compartment. See Fig. 1, 3, 5 and 6. Connect voltmeter between terminals T_T and E_1 of DLC1. See Fig. 11.

2) Turn ignition on. Note that voltage gradually increases as accelerator is depressed. Voltage should gradually increase to about 8 volts with throttle fully open.

3) If voltage does not increase as throttle is opened, check throttle position sensor. See THROTTLE POSITION (TP) SENSOR under COMPONENT TESTS. If throttle position sensor is okay, check circuits between TP sensor and ECT ECU. See appropriate wiring diagram in WIRING DIAGRAMS.

BRAKELIGHT SIGNAL

1) Locate DLC1 in engine compartment. See Figs. 1, 3, 5 and 6. Connect voltmeter between terminals T_T and E_1 of DLC1. See Fig. 11.

2) Depress accelerator pedal until 6-8 volts exists. Hold brake pedal and note that voltage decreases to zero voltage. Release brake pedal and note that voltage increases to 6-8 volts.

3) If voltage is not as specified, check brakelight switch. See BRAKELIGHT SWITCH under COMPONENT TESTS. If brakelight switch is okay, check circuits between brakelight switch and ECT ECU. See appropriate wiring diagram in WIRING DIAGRAMS.

GEAR SELECTOR SIGNAL

1) Warm engine to normal operating temperature. Place pattern select switch in NORMAL position (if equipped). Pattern select switch is located near shift lever.

2) Depress OD switch, mounted on shift lever, to ON position. Locate DLC1 in engine compartment. See Figs. 1, 3, 5 and 6. Connect voltmeter between terminals T_T and E_1 of DLC1. See Fig. 11.

3) Road test vehicle with shift lever in "D" position and vehicle speed greater than 6 MPH. Voltage should increase as specified in accordance with transaxle gear position. See GEAR SIGNAL VOLTAGE table.

4) If voltages are as specified, electronic control system is operating correctly. If voltages are not as specified, further diagnosis must be performed. Inspect throttle position sensor, brakelight switch, park/neutral position switch and/or T_T circuit.

GEAR SIGNAL VOLTAGE [1]

Gear Position	Voltage (Approximate)
Celica & Corolla	
1st	Less Than .5
2nd	1.5-2.6
2nd With Lock-Up	2.5-3.6
3rd	3.5-4.6
3rd With Lock-Up	4.5-5.6
Overdrive	5.5-6.6
Overdrive With Lock-Up	6.5-7.6
MR2 & Paseo	
1st	0
2nd	2
3rd	4
Overdrive	6
Overdrive With Lock-Up	7

[1] – Information for Prizm is not available from manufacturer.

OVERDRIVE CANCEL SIGNAL

1) Access ECT ECU. See Figs. 1, 3, 5 and 6. Turn ignition on. Measure voltage (backprobe) between terminal OD_1 of ECT ECU harness connector and ground. If 10-14 volts is present, substitute known good ECT ECU and retest. If voltage is not as specified, go to next step.

2) Turn ignition off. Disconnect cruise control ECU harness connector. ECU is located behind instrument panel on passenger side of vehicle. Turn ignition on. Measure voltage between terminal OD and ground. See Fig. 16. If 10-14 volts is present, replace cruise control ECU and retest. If voltage is not as specified, inspect and repair circuit between cruise control ECU and ECT ECU.

ECT ECU VOLTAGES

Access ECT ECU. See Figs. 1-8. Turn ignition on. Using voltmeter, backprobe ECT ECU harness connector. Check voltage between selected terminal and E_1 or E_2 terminal. Voltage should be as specified. See Fig. 15.

AUTOMATIC TRANSMISSIONS
Toyota A-240 "E" Series Electronic Controls (Cont.)

3-1601

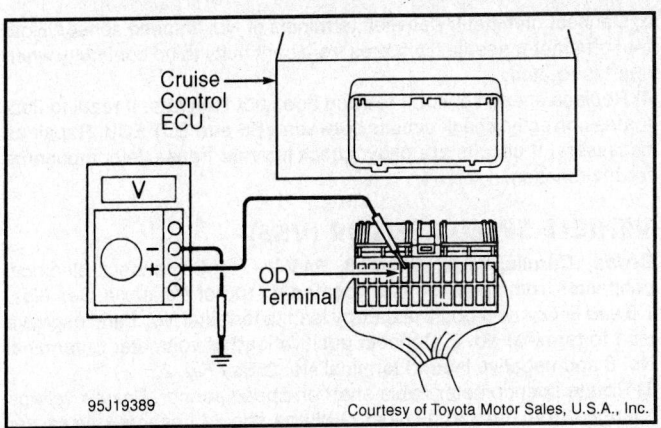

95J19389   Courtesy of Toyota Motor Sales, U.S.A., Inc.

Fig. 16: Identifying Cruise Control ECU Terminals

COMPONENT TESTS

NOTE: Not all components are used on all vehicles. Components identified for specific models are used only on those models.

SOLENOIDS

1) Access ECT ECU. See Figs. 1-8. Ensure ignition is off. Disconnect ECT ECU harness connector. Using ohmmeter, measure resistance between S_L, S_1 and S_2 terminal and ground for appropriate solenoid. See Fig. 15.

2) Replace solenoid if resistance is not 11-15 ohms. To check solenoid operation, apply battery voltage to S_L, S_1 or S_2 terminal of ECT ECU connector for appropriate solenoid. Ensure operating sound can be heard when battery voltage is connected. Replace solenoid if operating sound cannot be heard.

3) To check solenoid seals, remove suspect solenoid. Connect battery voltage to solenoid. Apply 71 psi (5 kg/cm²) of compressed air to solenoid with battery voltage connected. See Fig. 17.

4) With battery voltage applied, air should pass through No. 1 and 2 solenoids. Disconnect voltage to solenoid. Ensure air does not pass through solenoid. Replace solenoid if defective.

5) With battery voltage applied, air should not pass through lock-up solenoid. Disconnect voltage to solenoid. Ensure air passes through solenoid. Replace solenoid if defective.

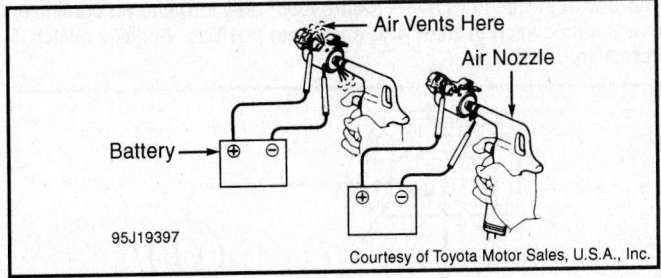

95J19397   Courtesy of Toyota Motor Sales, U.S.A., Inc.

Fig. 17: Checking Solenoids

PARK/NEUTRAL POSITION (PNP) SWITCH

Disconnect harness connector at park/neutral position switch. Switch is located on side of transaxle. Using ohmmeter, check for continuity between specified terminals in accordance with shift lever position. See Figs. 18, 19 and 20. Replace PNP switch if defective.

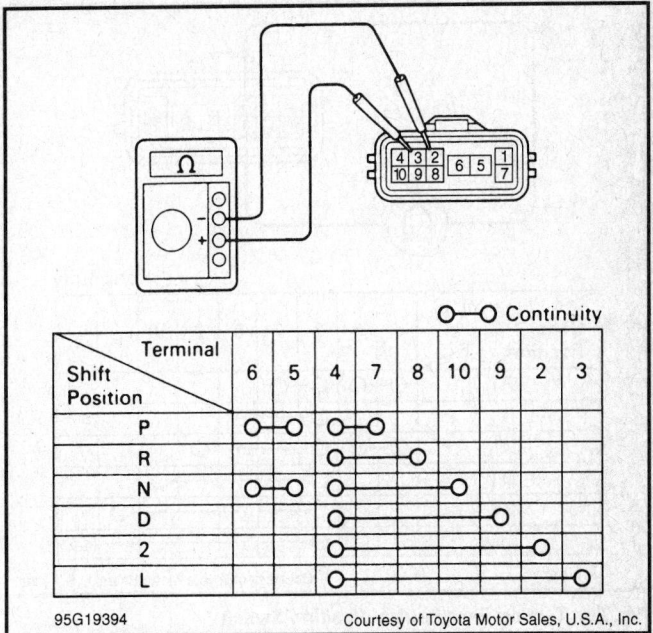

O—O Continuity

Terminal / Shift Position	6	5	4	7	8	10	9	2	3
P	O	O	O	O					
R			O		O				
N	O	O	O			O			
D			O				O		
2			O					O	
L			O						O

95G19394   Courtesy of Toyota Motor Sales, U.S.A., Inc.

Fig. 18: Testing Park/Neutral Position Switch (1995 Celica Is Shown; 1995-96 Prizm Is Similar)

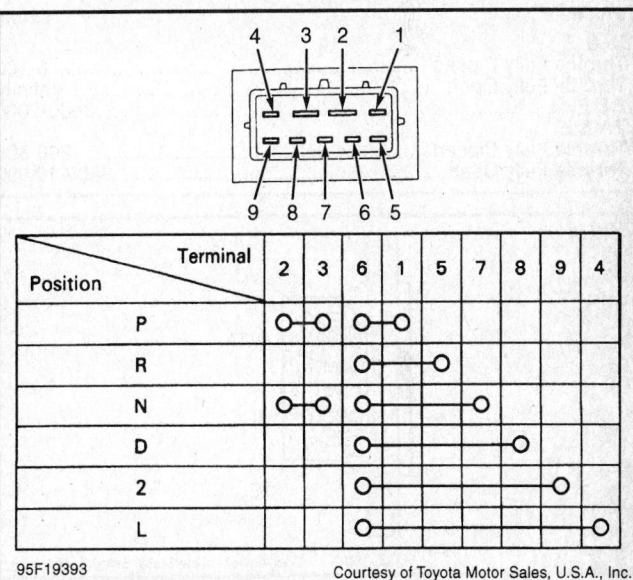

Terminal / Position	2	3	6	1	5	7	8	9	4
P	O	O	O	O					
R			O		O				
N	O	O	O			O			
D			O				O		
2			O					O	
L			O						O

95F19393   Courtesy of Toyota Motor Sales, U.S.A., Inc.

Fig. 19: Testing Park/Neutral Position Switch (1995 MR2 & 1995 Paseo)

THROTTLE POSITION (TP) SENSOR

Disconnect electrical connector at TP sensor, located on side of throttle body. Note TP sensor terminal identification. See Fig. 21. Using ohmmeter, check resistance between specified terminals in relation to throttle position. See THROTTLE POSITION (TP) SENSOR RESISTANCE SPECIFICATIONS table. Replace TP sensor if resistance is not as specified.

3-1602

AUTOMATIC TRANSMISSIONS
Toyota A-240 "E" Series Electronic Controls (Cont.)

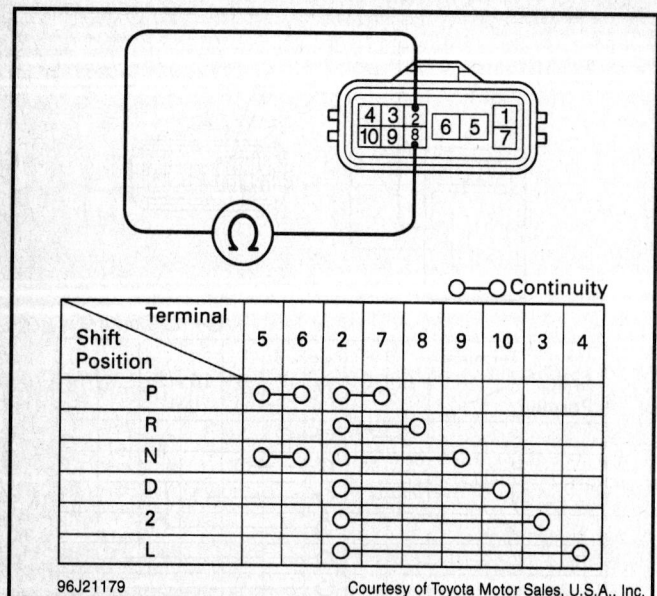

Fig. 20: Testing Park/Neutral Position Switch (All Other Models)

Shift Position \ Terminal	5	6	2	7	8	9	10	3	4
P	O—O		O—O						
R			O		O				
N	O—O		O			O			
D			O				O		
2			O					O	
L			O						O

O—O Continuity

96J21179   Courtesy of Toyota Motor Sales, U.S.A., Inc.

THROTTLE POSITION (TP) SENSOR RESISTANCE SPECIFICATIONS

Terminals	Ohms
IDL & E_2	
Throttle Fully Closed	0-100
Throttle Fully Open	Infinity
Vc & E_2	3000-7000
VTA & E_2	
Throttle Fully Closed	200-800
Throttle Fully Open	3200-10,000

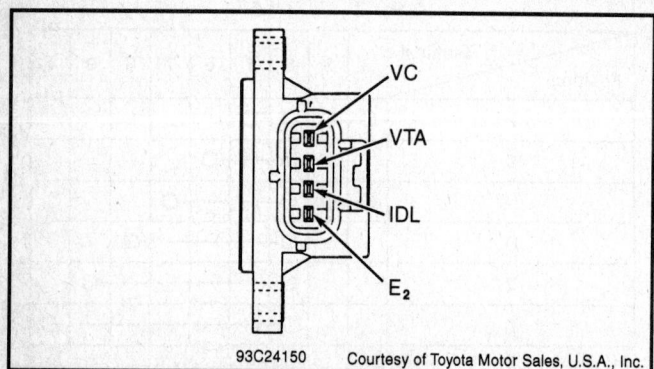

93C24150   Courtesy of Toyota Motor Sales, U.S.A., Inc.

Fig. 21: Identifying Throttle Position (TP) Sensor Terminals

NO. 1 VEHICLE SPEED SENSOR

NOTE: For MR2 No. 1 speed sensor test information, see VEHICLE SPEED SENSOR.

Paseo – Remove instrument panel. Connect ohmmeter between terminals on rear of instrument panel. See Fig. 14. Rotate speedometer cable shaft on instrument panel. Note that ohmmeter needle fluctuates from continuity to no continuity. If reading does not fluctuate correctly, replace speedometer or speed sensor as necessary.

NO. 2 VEHICLE SPEED SENSOR

MR2 & Paseo – 1) Disconnect electrical connector from No. 2 speed sensor, located on transaxle. Raise and support vehicle so wheels can rotate. Connect ohmmeter between terminals of No. 2 speed sensor.
2) Rotate appropriate wheel. Note that ohmmeter needle fluctuates from continuity to no continuity. If reading does not fluctuate correctly, remove No. 2 speed sensor from transaxle.

3) Connect ohmmeter between terminals of No. 2 speed sensor. Note that ohmmeter needle fluctuates from continuity to no continuity when shaft is rotated.
4) Replace speed sensor if reading does not fluctuate. If reading fluctuates correctly, check circuits between VSS and ECT ECU. Repair as necessary. If circuits are okay, check internal transaxle components for malfunction.

VEHICLE SPEED SENSOR (VSS)

Celica, Corolla, MR2, Prizm & RAV4 – 1) Disconnect electrical connector from speed sensor, located on top of transaxle. See Figs. 1-5 and 8. Connect positive battery lead to terminal No. 1 and negative lead to terminal No. 2. Connect positive lead of voltmeter to terminal No. 3 and negative lead to terminal No. 2. See Fig. 22.
2) Rotate speedometer cable shaft on speed sensor. Ensure voltage changes from zero to 11 volts. Voltage should change 4 times per each revolution of speedometer cable shaft. Replace speed sensor if voltage dose not change as specified.

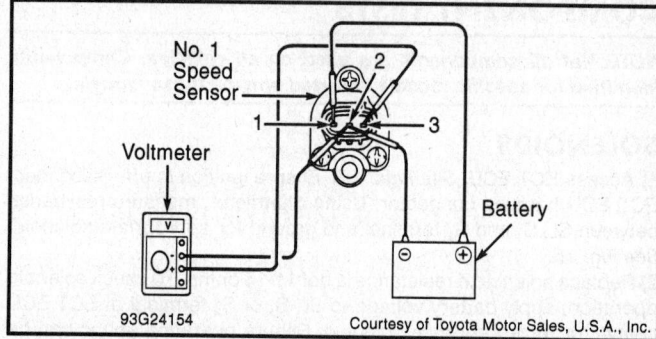

93G24154   Courtesy of Toyota Motor Sales, U.S.A., Inc.

Fig. 22: Checking Vehicle Speed Sensor

PATTERN SELECT SWITCH

NOTE: Information for Celica and Corolla is not available from manufacturer.

1996 RAV4 – 1) Disconnect electrical connector from pattern select switch, located near shift lever. See Fig. 8. Note terminal identification on pattern select switch. See Fig. 23.
2) Using ohmmeter, ensure continuity exists between terminals No. 1 and 3 with switch in POWER (depressed) position, and no continuity exists with switch in NORMAL (released) position. Replace switch if defective.

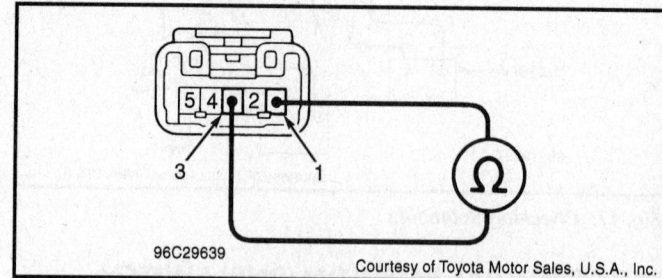

96C29639   Courtesy of Toyota Motor Sales, U.S.A., Inc.

Fig. 23: Identifying Pattern Select Switch Terminals (RAV4)

OVERDRIVE (OD) SWITCH

Disconnect electrical connector from OD switch, located on shift lever. Note terminal identification on OD switch. See Fig. 24. Using ohmmeter, ensure continuity exists between terminals No. 1 and 3 with switch released (OFF position). Ensure no continuity exists between terminals No. 1 and 3 with switch depressed (ON position). Replace switch if defective.

AUTOMATIC TRANSMISSIONS
Toyota A-240 "E" Series Electronic Controls (Cont.)

3-1603

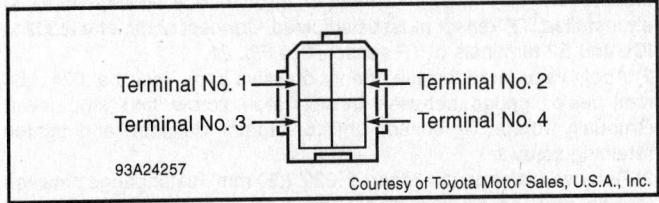

Fig. 24: Identifying Overdrive (OD) Switch Terminals

BRAKELIGHT SWITCH

1) Disconnect electrical connector from brakelight switch, located near brake pedal. Note brakelight switch terminal identification. *See Fig. 25.*
2) Using ohmmeter, ensure no continuity exists between terminals No. 1 and 3 with brake pedal released. Replace brakelight switch if continuity exists.
3) Using ohmmeter, ensure continuity exists between terminals No. 1 and 3 with brake pedal depressed. If continuity does not exist, ensure brake pedal is properly adjusted so brakelight switch has proper travel for switch operation. If proper brakelight switch travel exists, replace brakelight switch.

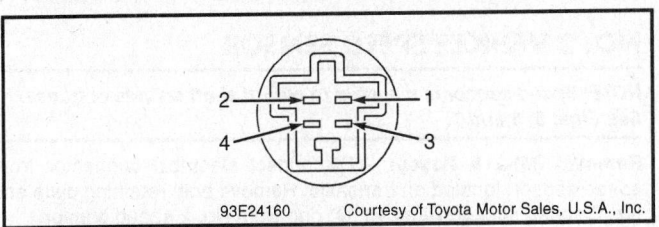

Fig. 25: Identifying Brakelight Switch Terminals

ENGINE COOLANT TEMPERATURE (ECT) SENSOR

Disconnect electrical connector from ECT. ECT is located in radiator on MR2, or in thermostat housing on all other models. Using ohmmeter, check resistance between terminals of coolant temperature sensor. Resistance should be as specified in accordance with coolant temperature. *See Fig. 26.* Replace sensor if resistance is not within specification.

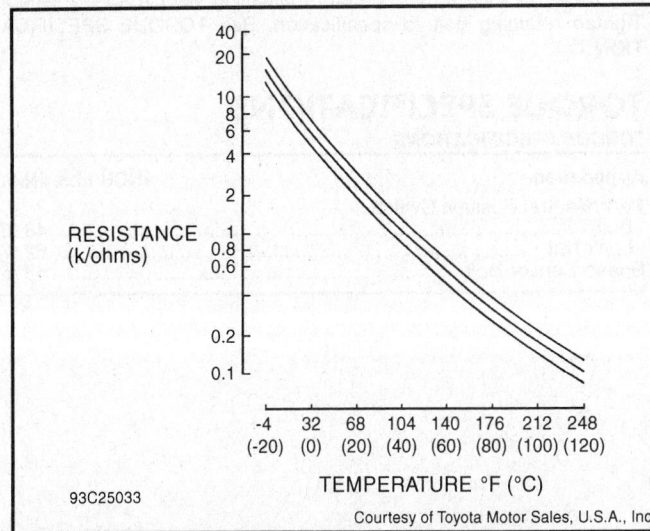

Fig. 26: Checking Engine Coolant Temperature Sensor

REMOVAL & INSTALLATION

BRAKELIGHT SWITCH

Removal & Installation – 1) Disconnect electrical connector. Remove lock nut, and unscrew brakelight switch. To install, screw brakelight switch inward until brakelight plunger contacts brake pedal. **2)** Install and tighten lock nut on brakelight switch. Install electrical connector. Ensure brakelights and cruise control (if equipped) operate properly.

ENGINE COOLANT TEMPERATURE (ECT) SENSOR

Removal (MR2) – Coolant temperature sensor is located in radiator. Drain cooling system. Remove coolant temperature sensor.
Installation – 1) To install, reverse removal procedure. Proper cooling system bleeding procedure must be followed.
2) Remove spare tire, front luggage compartment trim and upper radiator support seal. Connect air bleed hoses to heater and radiator air bleed plugs. Attach and support opposite end of hoses to hood or hood support. *See Fig. 27.* Ensure hoses are not pinched.
3) Place heater control lever on instrument panel to warmest position. Open heater and radiator air bleed plugs at least 3 turns.
4) Slowly add coolant through coolant filler. Air will bleed from hoses on heater and radiator air bleed plugs. Ensure coolant in air bleed hoses and coolant filler are at same level.
5) If coolant level in air bleed hoses is lower than lever in coolant filler, air still exists in cooling system. Check for pinched or restriction in air bleed hoses. If necessary, repeat step **4).** When proper coolant level is obtained in air bleed hoses, close air bleed plugs. Remove air bleed hoses.
Removal & Installation (Except MR2) – Coolant temperature sensor is located in thermostat housing. Drain cooling system and remove sensor. To install, reverse removal procedure. Fill cooling system and check for leaks.

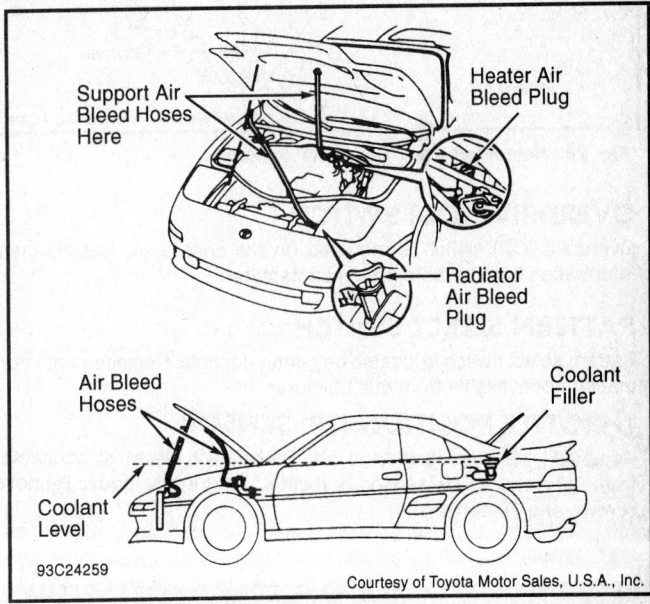

Fig. 27: Installing Air Bleed Hoses (MR2)

SOLENOIDS

Removal & Installation – Solenoids are located on transaxle valve body. Remove transaxle oil pan. Remove bolt, solenoid and "O" ring from valve body. To install, reverse removal procedure using NEW "O" ring.

3-1604

AUTOMATIC TRANSMISSIONS
Toyota A-240 "E" Series Electronic Controls (Cont.)

PARK/NEUTRAL POSITION (PNP) SWITCH

Removal – Park/neutral position switch is located on side of transaxle. Remove lock nut, washer and manual lever from control shaft. *See Fig. 28.* Bend up tabs on lock washer. Remove lock nut, lock washer and seal from control shaft. Remove retaining bolts and park/neutral position switch.

Installation – 1) Install switch on control shaft. Loosely install park/neutral position switch retaining bolts. Install seal and lock washer. Install lock nut and tighten to specification. See TORQUE SPECIFICATIONS. Bend tabs on lock washer over against lock nut.

2) Ensure parking brake is applied. Temporarily install manual lever on control shaft. Place shift lever in Neutral. Remove manual lever. Rotate switch and align reference mark on PNP switch with groove. *See Fig. 28.*

3) Hold park/neutral position switch in this position. Tighten retaining bolts to specification. To install remaining components, reverse removal procedure.

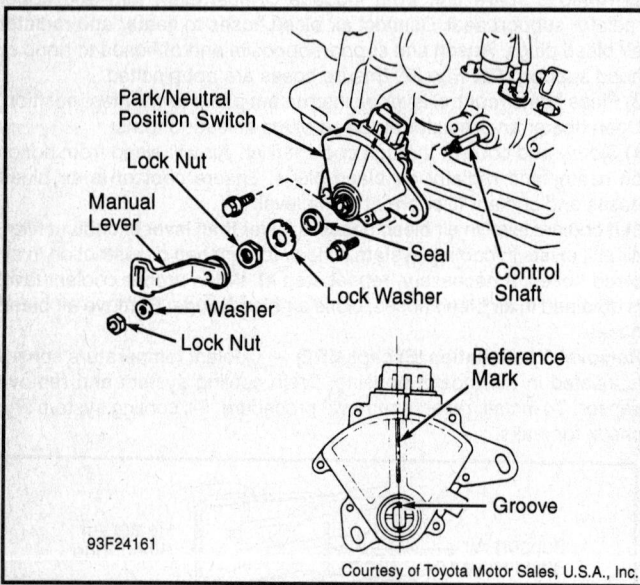

Park/Neutral
Position Switch

Lock Nut

Manual
Lever

Seal

Control
Shaft

Washer — Lock Washer

Lock Nut

Reference
Mark

Groove

93F24161

Courtesy of Toyota Motor Sales, U.S.A., Inc.

Fig. 28: Removing & Installing PNP Switch

OVERDRIVE (OD) SWITCH

Overdrive (OD) switch is mounted on the shift lever. Replacement information not available from manufacturer.

PATTERN SELECT SWITCH

Pattern select switch is located on center console. Replacement information not available from manufacturer.

THROTTLE POSITION (TP) SENSOR

Removal – Ensure ignition is off. Disconnect electrical connector from TP sensor. TP sensor is located on throttle body. Remove screws and TP sensor.

Installation – 1) Install TP sensor on throttle body with screws loosely installed. TP sensor must be adjusted. Connect ohmmeter leads to IDL and E2 terminals of TP sensor. *See Fig. 21.*

2) Apply vacuum to throttle opener on valve body. Insert a .024" (.60 mm) feeler gauge between throttle stop screw and stop lever. Gradually rotate TP sensor until ohmmeter deflects, and tighten retaining screws.

3) Remove feeler gauge. Insert a .020" (.50 mm) feeler gauge between throttle stop screw and stop lever. Ensure continuity now exists between IDL and E2 terminals. Remove feeler gauge.

4) Insert a .028" (.70 mm) feeler gauge between throttle stop screw and stop lever. Ensure no continuity now exists between IDL and E2 terminals. Remove feeler gauge.

NO. 1 VEHICLE SPEED SENSOR

NOTE: For No. 1 speed sensor removal and installation on MR2, see VEHICLE SPEED SENSOR (VSS).

Removal & Installation (1995 Paseo) – No. 1 speed sensor is mounted on rear of instrument panel at combination meter. *See Fig 6.* Remove combination meter from instrument panel. Disconnect speedometer cable from combination meter. Remove No. 1 speed sensor. To install, reverse removal procedure.

NO. 2 VEHICLE SPEED SENSOR

NOTE: Speed sensor is mounted to output shaft on side of transaxle. See Figs. 5, 6 and 7.

Removal (MR2 & Paseo) – Disconnect electrical connector from speed sensor, located on transaxle. Remove bolt, retaining plate and No. 2 speed sensor. Remove "O" ring from No. 2 speed sensor.

Installation – To install, reverse removal procedure using NEW "O" ring. Coat "O" ring with ATF before installing No. 2 speed sensor. Tighten retaining bolt to specification. See TORQUE SPECIFICATIONS.

VEHICLE SPEED SENSOR (VSS)

Removal (Celica, Corolla, MR2, Prizm & RAV4) – Disconnect electrical connector from speed sensor, located on transaxle. Remove bolt, retaining plate and vehicle speed sensor. Remove "O" ring from speed sensor.

Installation – To install, reverse removal procedure using NEW "O" ring. Coat "O" ring with ATF before installing vehicle speed sensor. Tighten retaining bolt to specification. See TORQUE SPECIFICATIONS.

TORQUE SPECIFICATIONS
TORQUE SPECIFICATIONS

Application	INCH Lbs. (N.m)
Park/Neutral Position Switch	
Bolt	48 (5)
Lock Nut	62 (7)
Speed Sensor Bolt	48 (5)

AUTOMATIC TRANSMISSIONS
Toyota A-240 "E" Series Electronic Controls (Cont.)

3-1605

WIRING DIAGRAMS

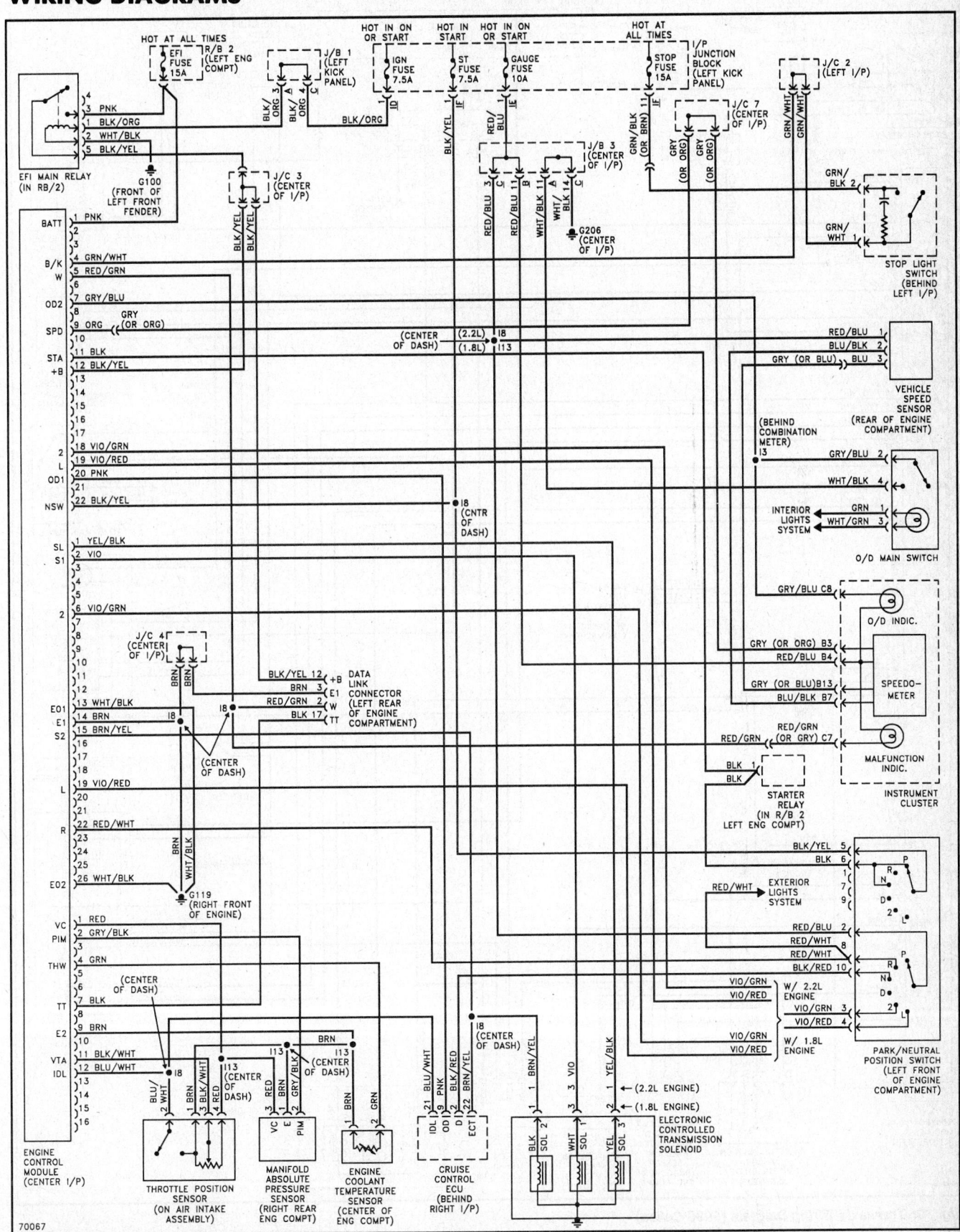

Fig. 29: Transaxle Wiring Diagram (1995 Celica)

3-1606

AUTOMATIC TRANSMISSIONS
Toyota A-240 "E" Series Electronic Controls (Cont.)

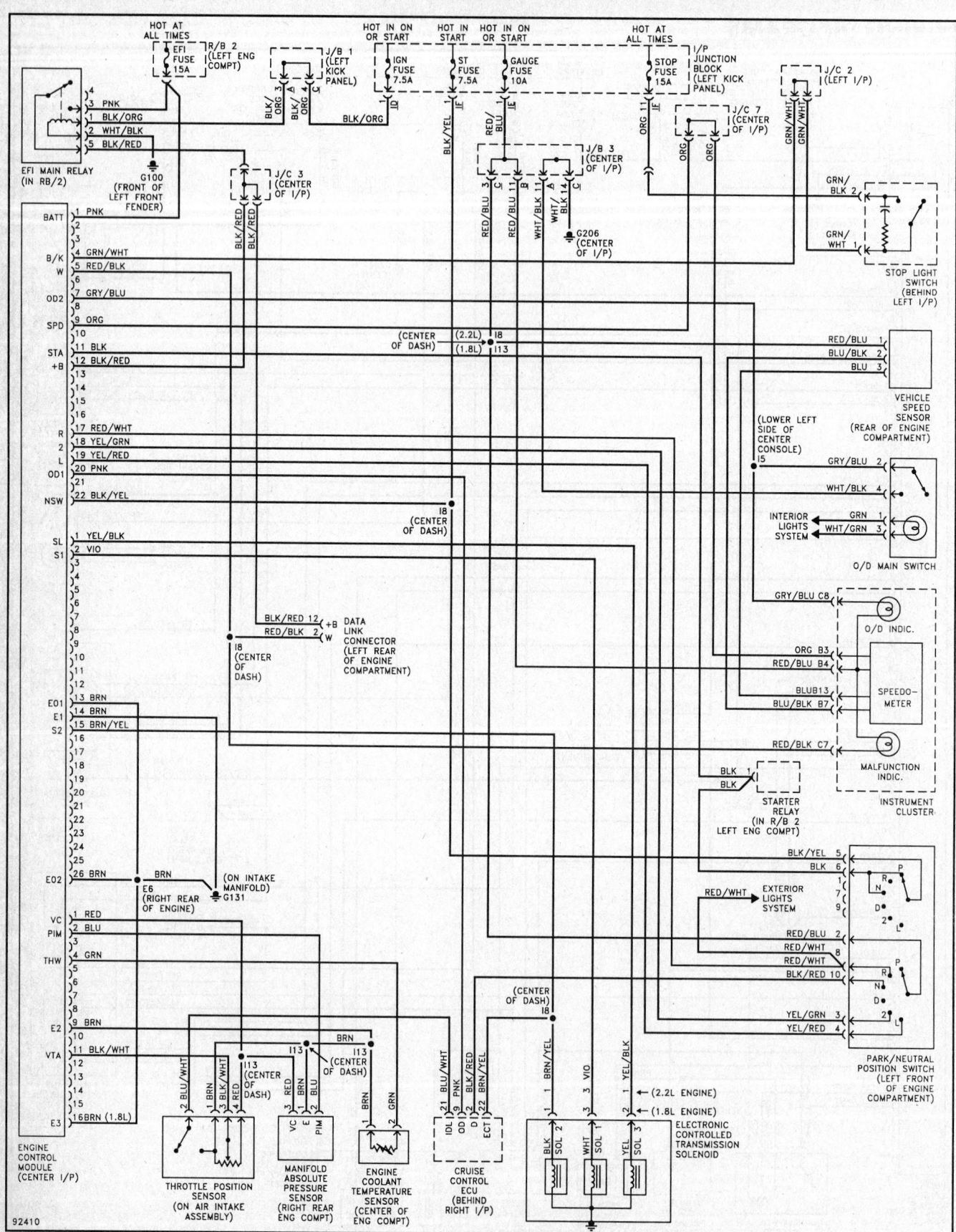

Fig. 30: Transaxle Wiring Diagram (1996 Celica)

92410

AUTOMATIC TRANSMISSIONS
Toyota A-240 "E" Series Electronic Controls (Cont.)

3-1607

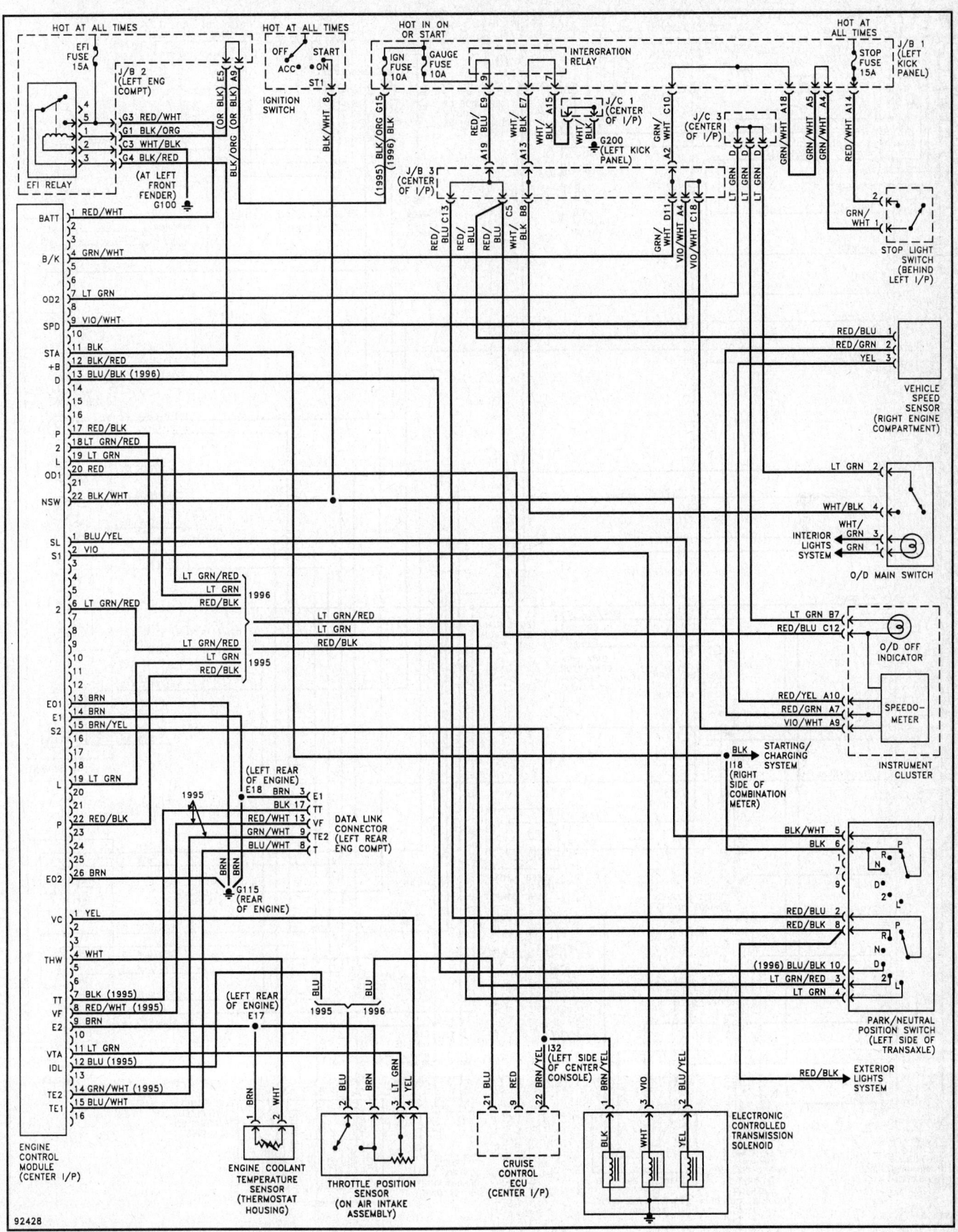

Fig. 31: Transaxle Wiring Diagram (1995-96 Corolla)

92428

3-1608

AUTOMATIC TRANSMISSIONS
Toyota A-240 "E"Series Electronic Controls (Cont.)

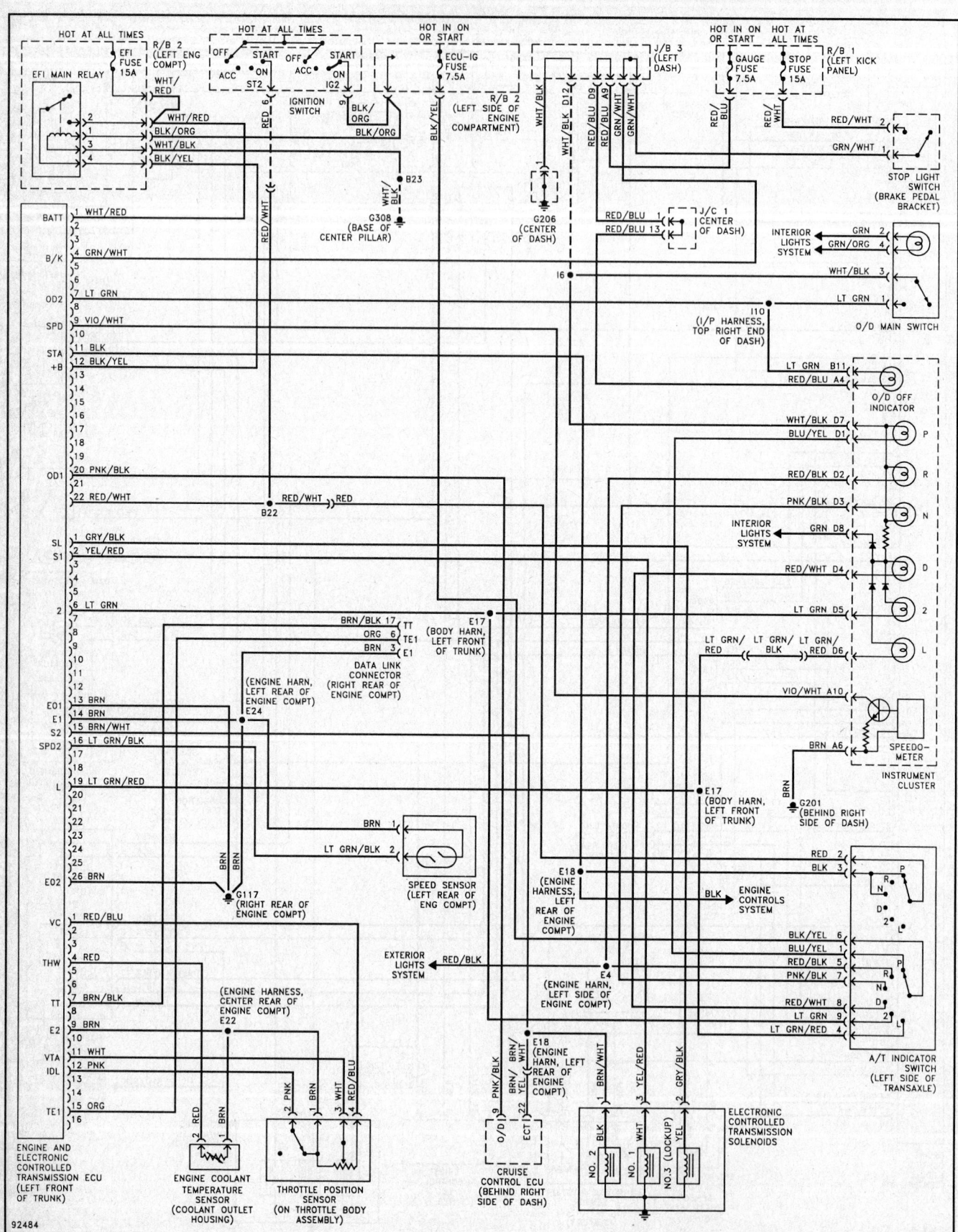

Fig. 32: *Transaxle Wiring Diagram (1995 MR2)*

AUTOMATIC TRANSMISSIONS
Toyota A-240 "E" Series Electronic Controls (Cont.)

3-1609

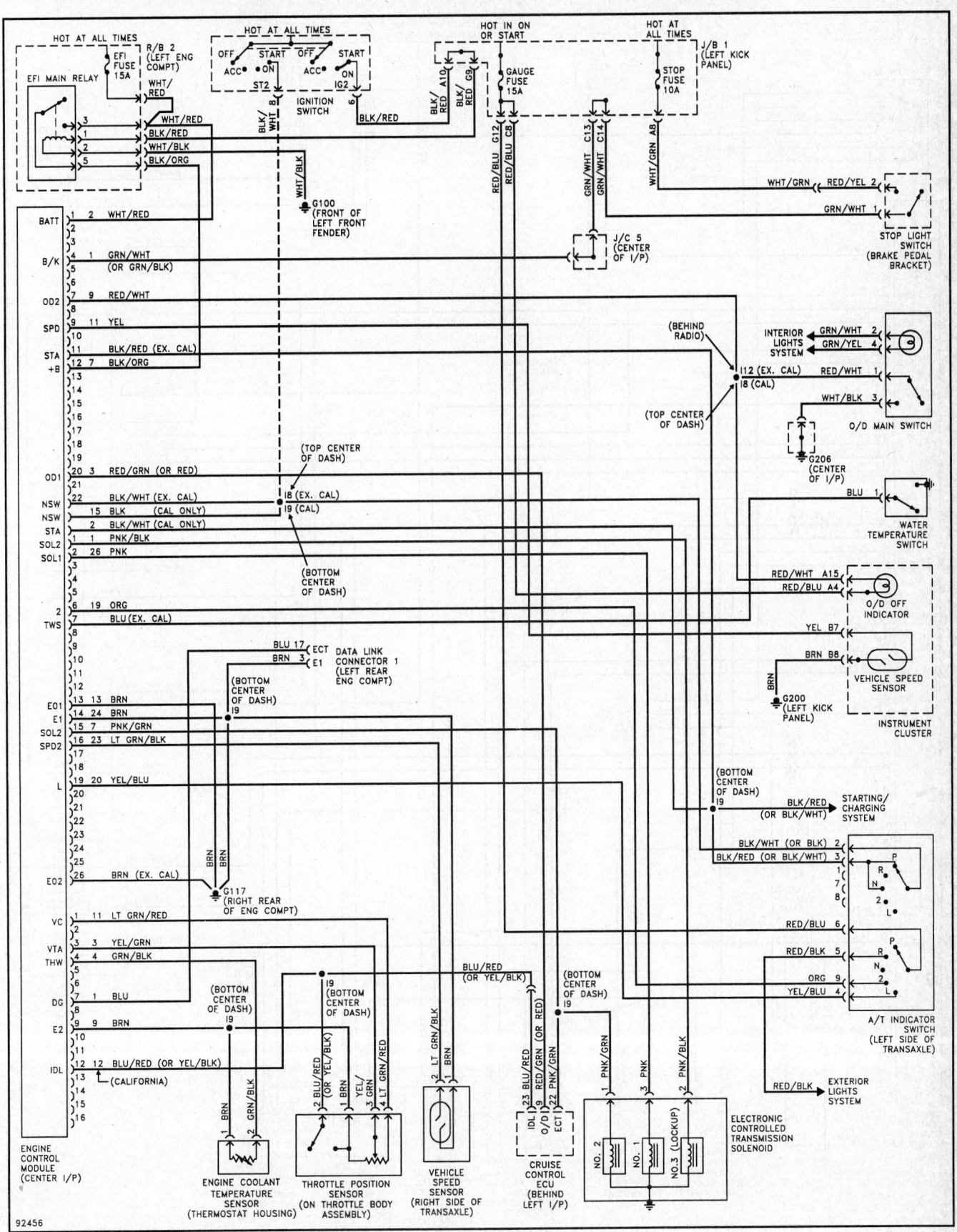

Fig. 33: Transaxle Wiring Diagram (1995 Paseo)

92456

3-1610

AUTOMATIC TRANSMISSIONS
Toyota A-240 "E" Series Electronic Controls (Cont.)

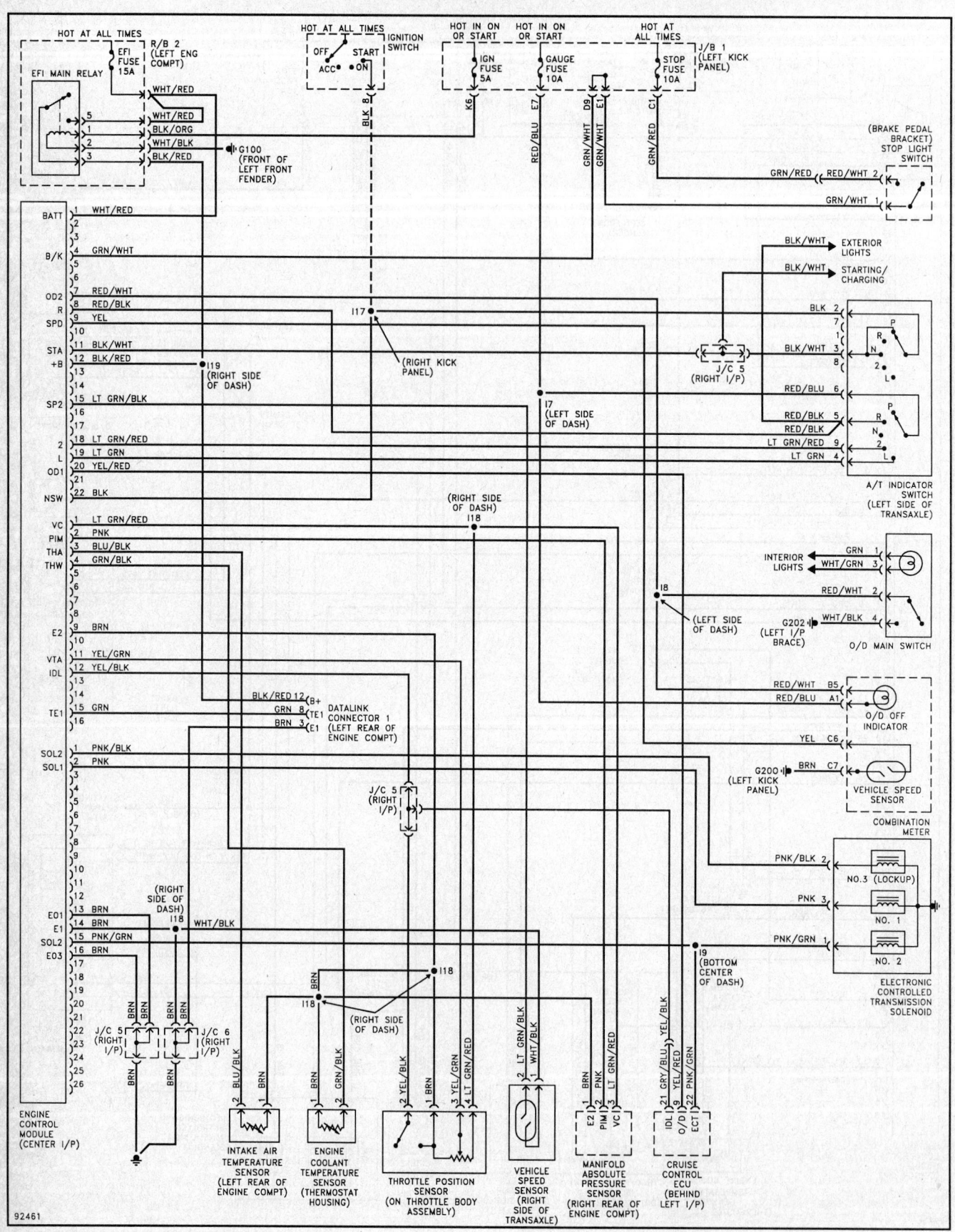

Fig. 34: Transaxle Wiring Diagram (1996 Paseo)

AUTOMATIC TRANSMISSIONS
Toyota A-240 "E" Series Electronic Controls (Cont.)

3-1611

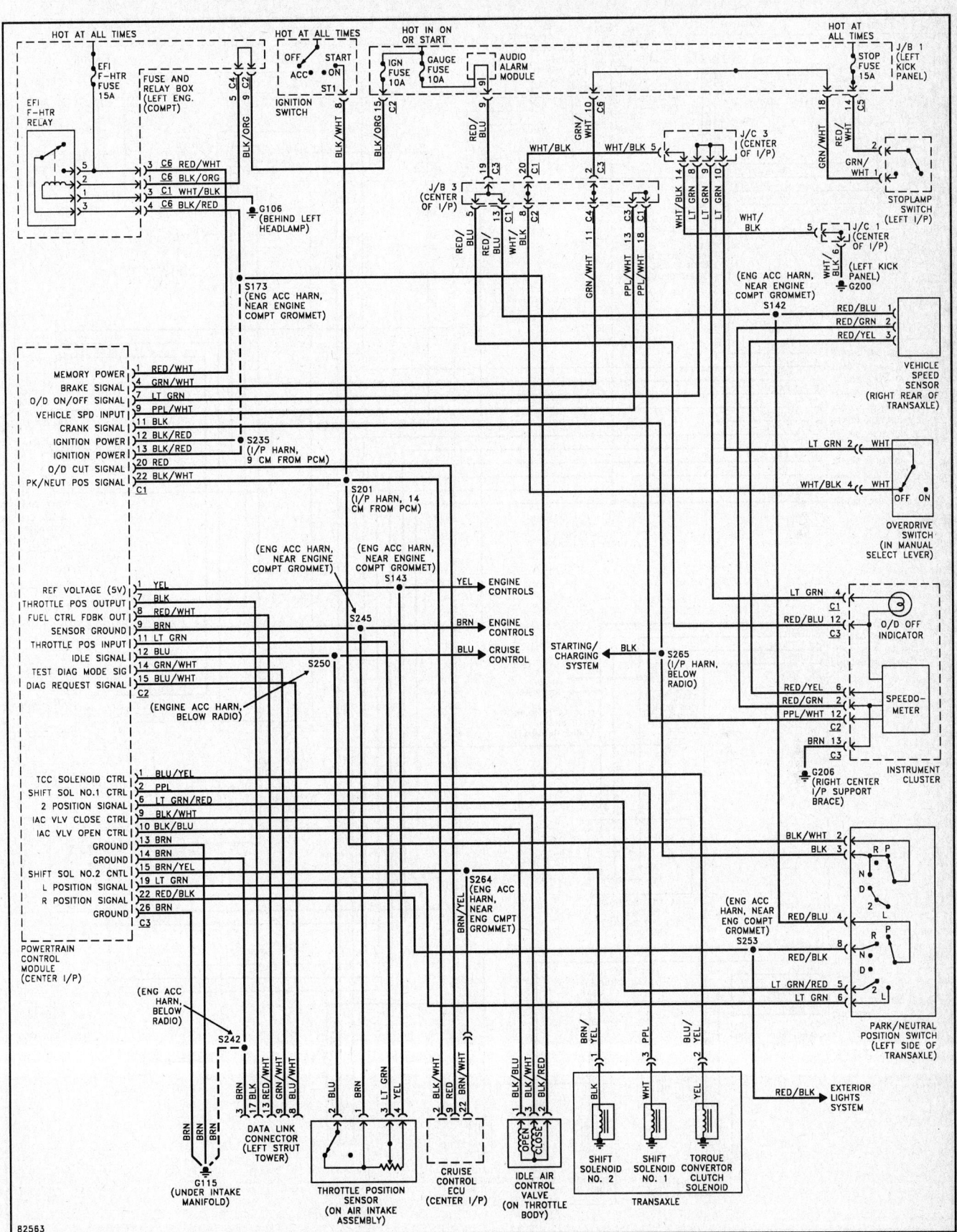

Fig. 35: Transaxle Wiring Diagram (1995 Prizm LSI)

82563

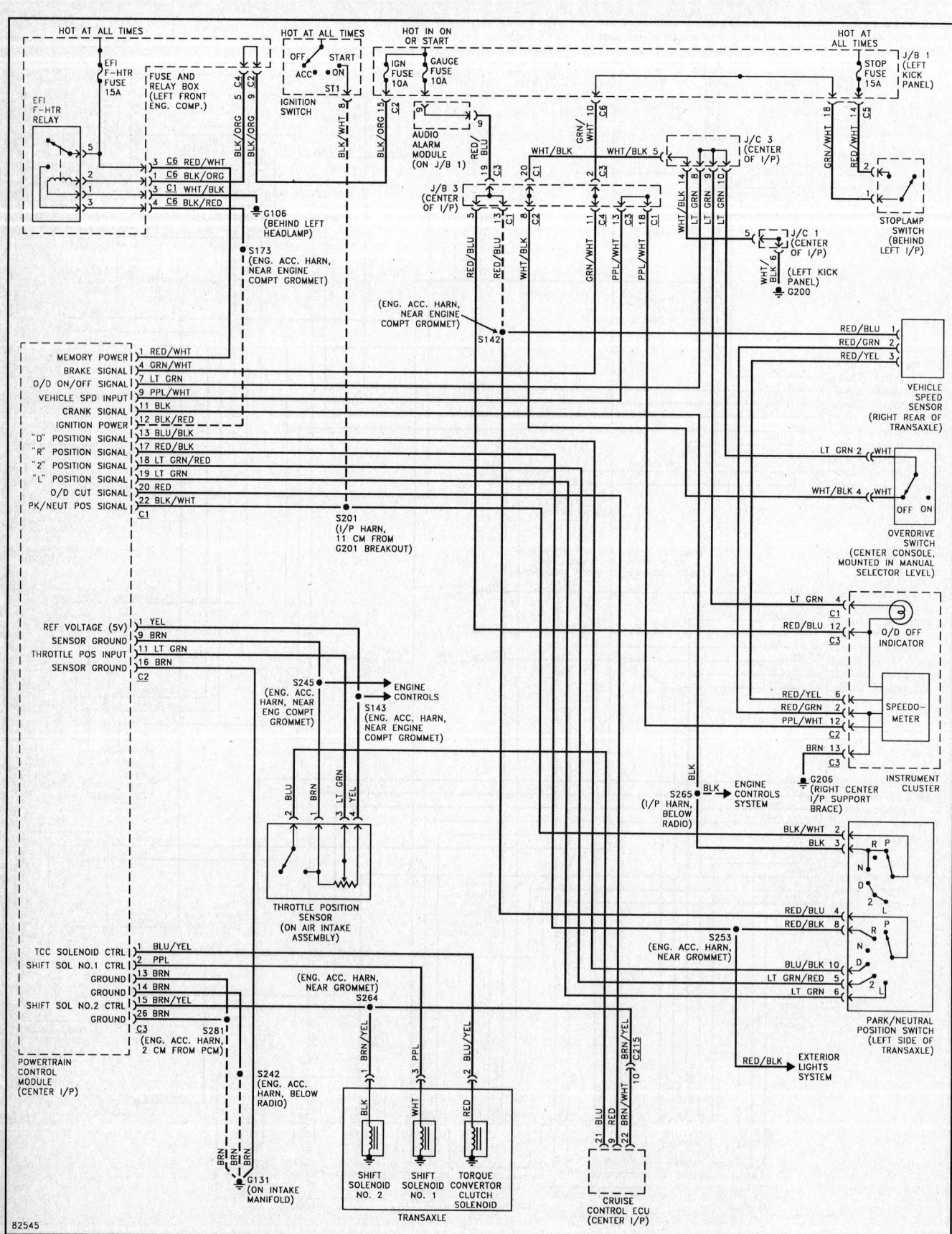

Fig. 36: Transaxle Wiring Diagram (1996 Prizm LSI)

AUTOMATIC TRANSMISSIONS
Toyota A-240 "E" Series Electronic Controls (Cont.)

3-1613

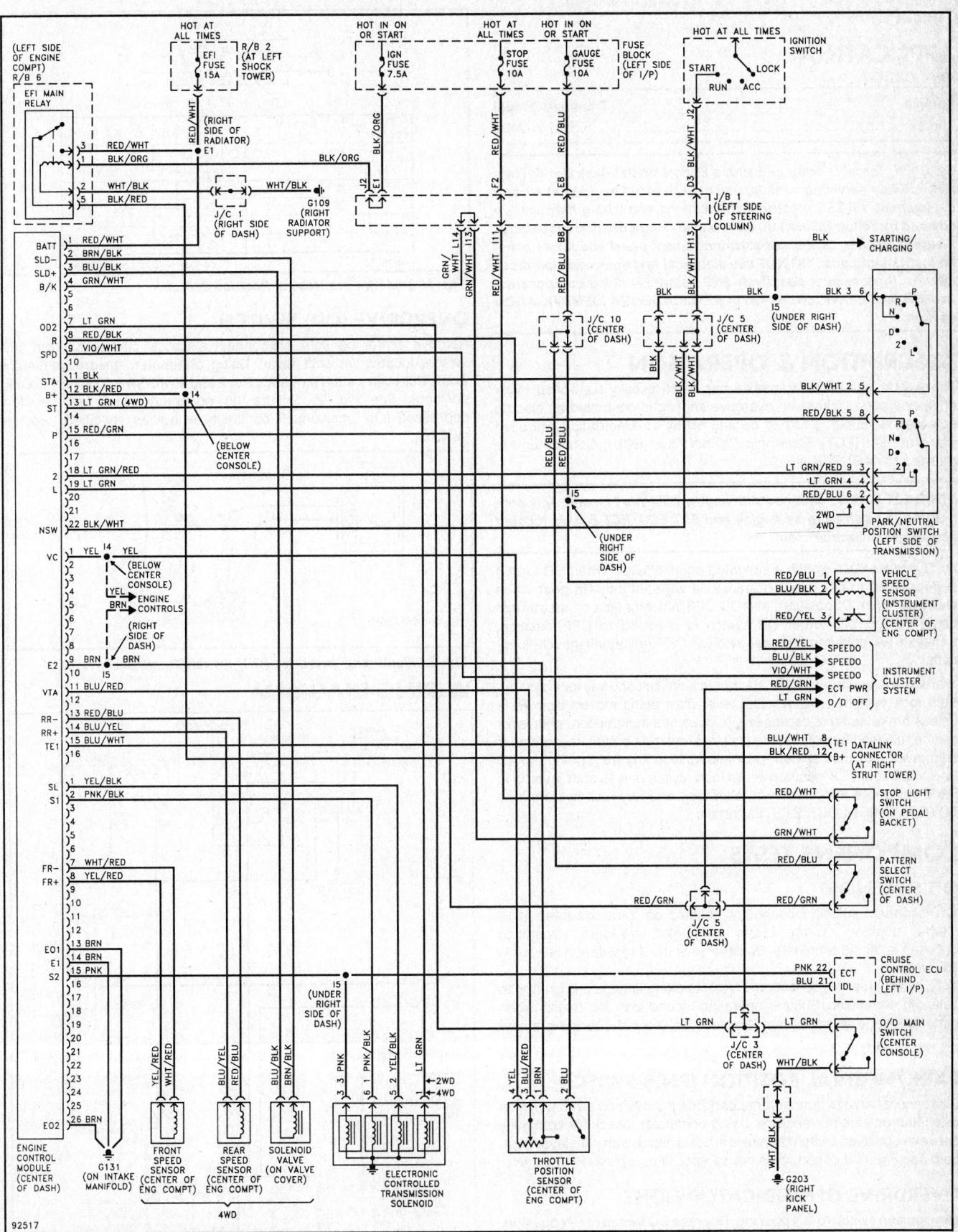

Fig. 37: Transaxle Wiring Diagram (1996 RAV4)

AUTOMATIC TRANSMISSIONS
Toyota A-242L Electronic Controls

Tercel

APPLICATION

APPLICATION

Vehicle	Transaxle Model
Tercel	A-242L

CAUTION: Tercel is equipped with a Supplemental Restraint System (SRS). When servicing vehicle, use care to avoid accidental air bag deployment. All SRS electrical connections and wiring harness are covered by Yellow insulation. SRS-related components are located in steering column, center console, instrument panel and lower panel on instrument panel. DO NOT use electrical test equipment on these circuits. If necessary, deactivate SRS before servicing components. See AIR BAG SERVICING article in APPLICATIONS & IDENTIFICATION section.

DESCRIPTION & OPERATION

The A-242L automatic transaxle has electronically controlled overdrive operation. Transaxle overdrive shifting is controlled by electric solenoid. Solenoid is turned on and off by an Electronic Controlled Transmission (ECT) Electronic Control Unit (ECU). Control unit is referred to as ECT ECU.

NOTE: ECT ECU is combined with engine ECU into one unit. This control unit is referred to as engine and ECT ECU. ECT ECU is located behind glove compartment.

An Overdrive (OD) switch is mounted on shift lever. When OD switch is depressed to ON position, transaxle will shift into 4th gear when shift lever is in "D" position, and OD OFF indicator light on instrument panel will go off. When OD switch is released to OFF position, transaxle will shift into 3rd gear, and OD OFF indicator light will illuminate.

Transaxle is equipped with a electronic shift lock and key lock system. Shift lock system prevents shift lever from being moved from Park unless brake pedal is depressed. In case of a malfunction, shift lever can be released by depressing shift lock override button, located near shift lever. Key lock system prevents ignition key from being moved from ACC to LOCK position on ignition switch unless shift lever is in Park. For more information on shift lock and key lock system, see TOYOTA SHIFT LOCK SYSTEM article.

COMPONENT TESTS

OD SOLENOID

1) Disconnect solenoid connector, located on transaxle near park/neutral position switch. Using ohmmeter, measure resistance between solenoid terminals. Replace solenoid if resistance is not 11-15 ohms.
2) To check solenoid operation, connect battery voltage and ground to solenoid terminals. Ensure operating sound can be heard when battery voltage is connected. Replace solenoid if operating sound cannot be heard.

PARK/NEUTRAL POSITION (PNP) SWITCH

Disconnect harness connector at park/neutral position switch. Switch is located on side of transaxle. Using ohmmeter, check for continuity between specified switch terminals in accordance with shift lever position. *See Fig. 1.* If continuity is not as specified, replace PNP switch.

OVERDRIVE OFF INDICATOR LIGHT

Turn ignition switch to ON position. Depress OD switch to ON position. Ensure OD OFF indicator light is not activated. Depress OD switch to OFF position. OD OFF indicator light should activate. If OD OFF indicator light does not activate, replace indicator light.

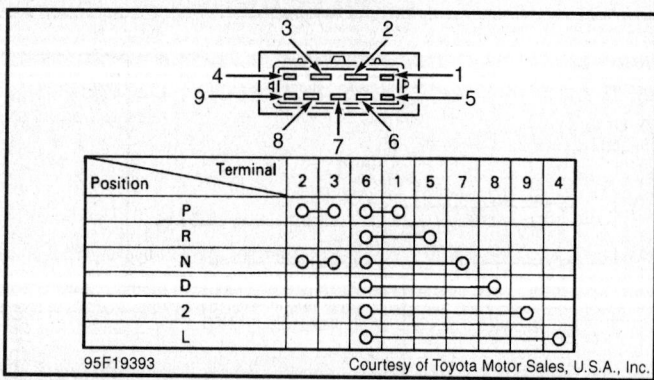

Position \ Terminal	2	3	6	1	5	7	8	9	4
P	O—O		O—O	O—O					
R			O			O			
N	O—O		O—O				O		
D			O					O	
2			O						
L			O						O

95F19393 Courtesy of Toyota Motor Sales, U.S.A., Inc.

Fig. 1: Testing Park/Neutral Position Switch

OVERDRIVE (OD) SWITCH

Remove center console. Disconnect electrical connector from OD switch, located on shift lever. Using ohmmeter, ensure continuity exists between switch terminals No. 2 and 4 with switch released (OFF position). *See Fig. 2.* Ensure no continuity exists with switch depressed (ON position). If continuity is not as specified, replace switch.

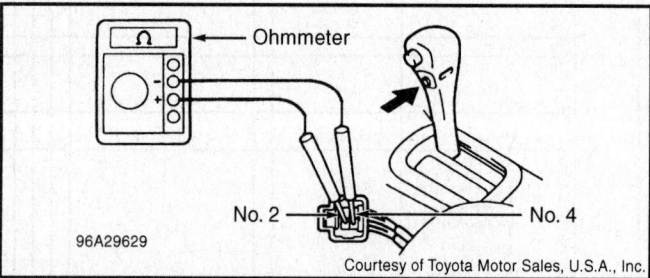

96A29629 Courtesy of Toyota Motor Sales, U.S.A., Inc.

Fig. 2: Identifying Overdrive (OD) Switch Terminals

WIRING DIAGRAM

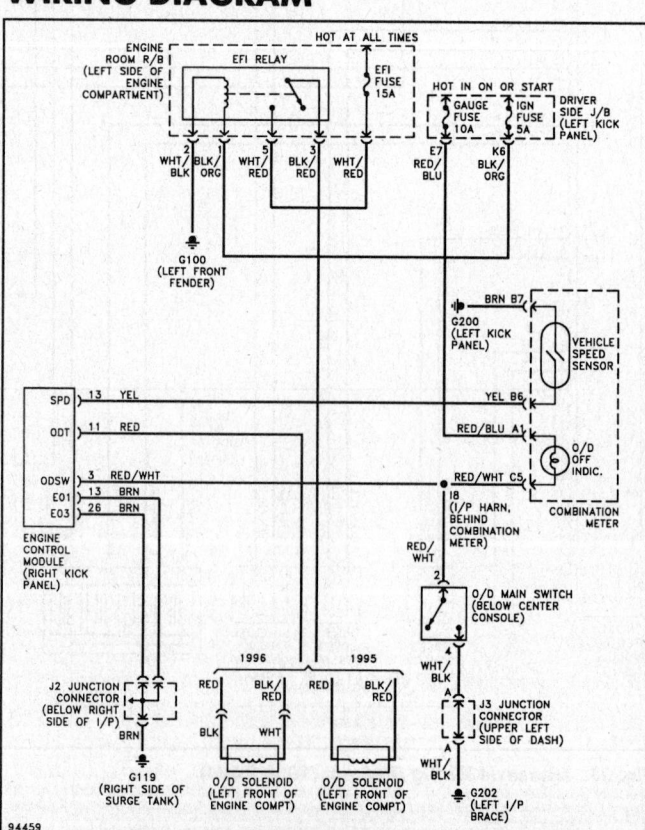

Fig. 3: Overdrive Control System Wiring Diagram (A-242L)

Lexus: GS300, LS400, LX450, SC300, SC400
Toyota: Land Cruiser, Pickup, Previa, Supra, Tacoma, T100, 4Runner

APPLICATION & LABOR TIMES

APPLICATION & LABOR TIMES

Vehicle Application	Labor Times		Trans. Model
	[1] R & I	[2] Overhaul	
Lexus			
GS300			
1995	5.0	12.8	A-340E
1996	5.0	12.8	A-350E
LS400	5.0	12.8	A-340E
LX450	6.3	11.9	A-343F
SC300	5.0	12.8	A-340E
SC400	5.0	12.8	A-340E
Toyota			
Land Cruiser	6.3	11.9	A-343F
Pickup			
2WD V6	5.5	12.8	A-340E
4WD 4-Cyl.	6.0	12.8	A-340F
4WD V6	9.2	12.8	A-340H
Previa (Supercharged)			
2WD	4.1	12.8	A-340E
AWD	4.6	12.8	A-340F
Supra			
Turbo	4.7	12.8	A-340E
Non-Turbo	4.7	12.8	A-340E
Tacoma			
2WD V6			
Manual Steering			
With A/C	12.2 [3]	12.8	A-340E
Without A/C	11.8 [3]	12.8	A-340E
Power Steering			
With A/C	12.8 [3]	12.8	A-340E
Without A/C	12.4 [3]	12.8	A-340E
4WD 4-Cyl. (2.7L)	6.0	12.8	A-340F
4WD V6	6.0	12.8	A-340F
T-100			
2WD 4-Cyl. (2.7L)			
With A/C	11.6 [3]	12.8	A-340E
Without A/C	11.2 [3]	12.8	A-340E
2WD V6			
With A/C	11.6 [3]	12.8	A-340E
Without A/C	11.2 [3]	12.8	A-340E
4WD V6	9.2	12.8	A-340F
4Runner			
1995			
2WD V6	5.5	12.8	A-340E
4WD 4-Cyl. (2.4L)	6.0	12.8	A-340F
4WD V6	9.2	12.8	A-340H
1996			
2WD 4-Cyl. (2.7L)	4.6	12.8	A-340E
2WD V6	4.6	12.8	A-340E
4WD 4-Cyl. (2.7L)	5.2	12.8	A-340F
4WD V6	5.2	12.8	A-340F

[1] – Removal and installation of transmission from vehicle chassis.
[2] – Bench overhaul time for transmission, DOES NOT include removal and installation.
[3] – Requires engine removal.

CAUTION: Most models are equipped with a Supplemental Restraint System (SRS). When servicing vehicle, use care to avoid accidental air bag deployment. All SRS electrical connections and wiring harness are covered by Yellow insulation. SRS-related components are located in steering column, center console, instrument panel and lower panel on instrument panel. DO NOT use electrical test equipment on these circuits. If necessary, deactivate SRS before servicing components. See AIR BAG SERVICING article in APPLICATIONS & IDENTIFICATION section.

IDENTIFICATION

Vehicle Identification Number (VIN) is located on front right side frame, top left of instrument panel, driver-side door post and front cowl of engine compartment. Fifth digit denotes transmission type.

DESCRIPTION

All A-340 series automatic transmissions are 4-speed Electronic Controlled Transmissions (ECT). A-350E transmission is a 5-speed Electronic Controlled Transmission (ECT). A new gear ratio has been added between 1st and 2nd gear. This gear is used by activating overdrive while vehicle is in 1st gear. A-350E valve body and planetary gear unit are different than A-340 series transmissions. All other internal components are the same for both A-340 series and A-350E transmissions.

On all models, solenoids that control shifts are located in valve body. Transmission consists of lock-up type torque converter, overdrive planetary gear unit, planetary gear unit, hydraulic control system and electronic control system. See Fig. 1.

Solenoids are controlled by an Electronic Controlled Transmission (ECT) Electronic Control Unit (ECU). Control unit is referred to as the ECT ECU. For electronic diagnosis, see appropriate ELECTRONIC CONTROLS article. The ECT ECU receives information from various input devices and uses this information to control solenoids for transmission shifting and lock-up solenoid for torque converter lock-up.

An Overdrive (OD) switch is mounted on the shift lever. When OD switch is depressed to ON position, transmission will shift into 4th gear when shift lever is in "D" position, and OD OFF light on instrument panel will go off. When OD switch is released to OFF position, transmission will shift into 3rd gear, and OD OFF light on instrument panel will illuminate.

A pattern select switch is located near shift lever on center console. Pattern select switch contains a POWER (PWR) and a NORMAL operating position. When pattern select switch is depressed (PWR position), transmission upshifts and downshifts will occur at a higher vehicle speed than with switch released. An indicator light on instrument panel indicates pattern select switch is in PWR (on) position.

A-340F and A-343F transmission has a mechanically controlled 2-speed 4WD transfer case. A-340H transmission has a electronically controlled 4WD transfer case. The transfer case consists of planetary gears, hydraulic clutches and hydraulic brake. The transfer case is mounted to rear of transmission case.

Transmission is equipped with a shift lock and key lock system. Shift lock system prevents shift lever from being moved from Park unless brake pedal is depressed. Key lock system prevents ignition key from being moved from ACC to LOCK position on ignition switch unless shift lever is in Park. For more information on shift lock and key lock system, see TOYOTA SHIFT LOCK SYSTEM article.

AUTOMATIC TRANSMISSIONS
Toyota A-340 & A-350 Series (Cont.)

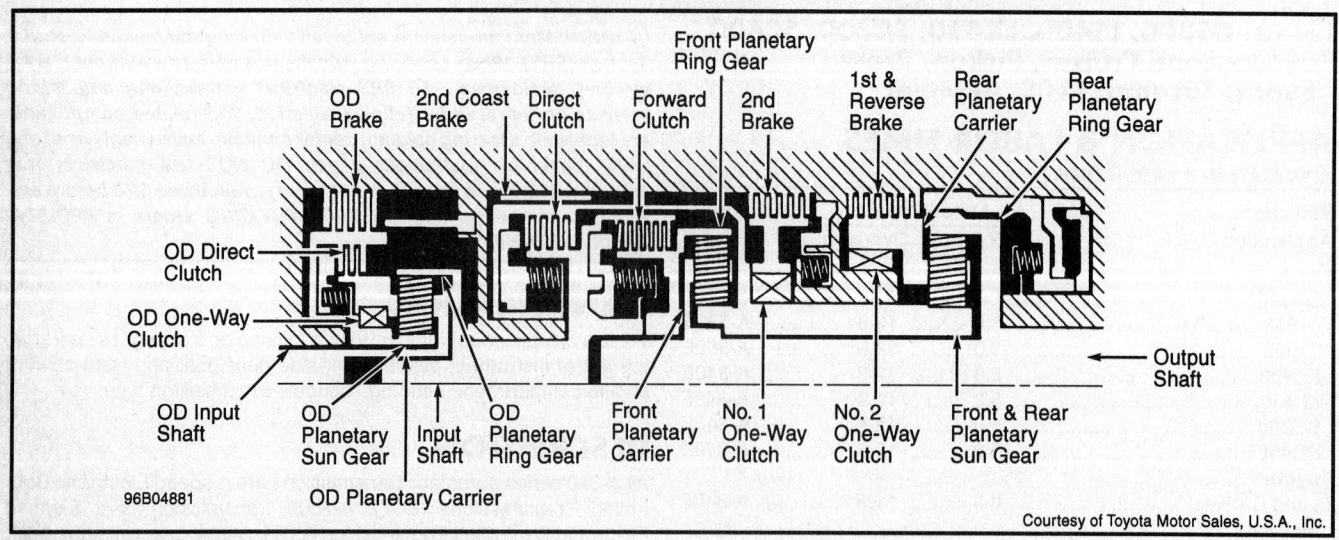

96B04881

Courtesy of Toyota Motor Sales, U.S.A., Inc.

Fig. 1: Identifying Transmission Component Locations

LUBRICATION & ADJUSTMENTS

See appropriate AUTOMATIC TRANSMISSION SERVICING article in TRANSMISSION SERVICING section.

TROUBLE SHOOTING

NOTE: See appropriate ELECTRONIC CONTROLS article for trouble shooting solenoids, sensors and computer control unit. Ensure transmission fluid level is correct before diagnosing transmission.

Preliminary Checks – Ensure fluid level is correct. Inspect and adjust throttle cable, shift linkage and park/neutral position switch (if necessary). Check idle speed RPM and adjust as necessary.

SYMPTOM DIAGNOSIS

Fluid Discolored Or Smells Burnt – Fluid contaminated. Torque converter or transmission faulty.

No Movement In Any Gear – Shift linkage out of adjustment. Faulty valve body or primary regulator. Park lock pawl faulty. Faulty torque converter. Converter drive plate damaged or broken. Oil pump intake screen blocked. ECT computer faulty. Control shaft lever out of adjustment. Faulty OD one-way clutch, OD brake, OD direct clutch or OD planetary gear.

Selector Lever Position Incorrect – Shift linkage out of adjustment. Faulty manual valve and lever.

Harsh Engagement Into Any Drive Range – Throttle cable out of adjustment. Faulty valve body, primary regulator or accumulator pistons. Faulty OD brake, OD direct clutch, OD planetary gear unit or torque converter. Faulty 1st and reverse brake, direct clutch or forward clutch.

Delayed 1-2, 2-3 Or 3-OD Upshifts, Or Downshifts From OD-3 Or 3-2, Then Changes Back To OD Or 3rd – Faulty valve body, ECT computer or solenoid valve.

Slips On Any Upshift Or Slips Or Shudders On Acceleration – Shift linkage or throttle cable out of adjustment. Faulty valve body or solenoid valve.

Drag Or Binding On Upshifts – Shift linkage out of adjustment or faulty valve body.

No Lock-Up In 2nd, 3rd Or OD – Faulty valve body, solenoid valve or electronic control unit.

Harsh Downshift – Throttle cable out of adjustment or faulty. Accumulator pistons or valve body faulty.

No Downshift When Coasting – Faulty valve body, electronic control or solenoid valve.

Downshifts Too Soon Or Too Late When Coasting – Throttle cable out of adjustment or faulty. Faulty valve body, electronic control or solenoid valve.

No OD-4, OD-3, 3-2 Or 2-1 Kickdown – Faulty valve body, electronic control or solenoid valve faulty.

No Engine Braking In "2" Or "L" Range – Faulty valve body, electronic control or solenoid valve.

Vehicle Does Not Move In "R" Range – Faulty 2nd coast brake, front and rear planetary gear unit or direct clutch. Faulty 1st and reverse brake. Faulty OD direct clutch.

Vehicle Does Not Move In "D", "2" Or "L" Range – Faulty forward clutch. Faulty No. 2 one-way clutch. Faulty 2nd brake. Faulty 1st and reverse brake. Faulty 2nd coast brake, direct clutch or 2nd brake.

No Upshift 1-2, 2-3, 3-OD, 3-4, 4-OD – Faulty 2nd brake or No. 1 one-way clutch. Faulty direct clutch. Faulty OD brake.

No Downshift 2-1 – Faulty 2nd coast brake. Faulty 2nd brake.

No Lock-Up Or No Lock-Up Off – Faulty torque converter or solenoid.

Slip Or Shudder In "D" Range, "R" Range, 1st, 2nd, 3rd, 4th Or OD – Faulty torque converter, OD one-way clutch or OD direct clutch. Faulty 1st and reverse brake or direct clutch. Faulty forward clutch or No. 2 one-way clutch. Faulty 2nd brake, 2nd coast brake or No. 1 one-way clutch. Faulty OD brake.

No Engine Braking 1st-3rd – Faulty OD direct brake, faulty 1st and reverse clutch. Faulty 2nd coast brake.

Poor Acceleration – Faulty torque converter, OD direct clutch, OD planetary gear unit or OD brake. Faulty 2nd coast brake, direct clutch, 2nd brake or 1st and reverse brake. Faulty forward clutch.

Engine Stalls When Starting Off Or Stopping – Faulty torque converter.

Vehicle Does Not Hold In "P" Range – Shift linkage faulty or out of adjustment. Defective park lock pawl assembly.

No Transfer Case Gear Changes On 4WD Models – Transfer linkage out of adjustment. Faulty electronic control, valve body or transfer case.

CLUTCH & BAND APPLICATION CHART (EXCEPT A-350E)

Selector Lever Position	Elements In Use
"D" (Drive)	
1st Gear	Forward Clutch, No. 2 One-Way Clutch, OD One-Way Clutch & OD Direct Clutch
2nd Gear	Forward Clutch, No. 1 One-Way Clutch, 2nd Brake, OD Direct Clutch & OD One-Way Clutch
3rd Gear	Forward Clutch, 2nd Brake, Direct Clutch, OD Direct Clutch & OD One-Way Clutch
OD (4th Gear)	Forward Clutch, 2nd Brake, OD Brake & Direct Clutch
"2" (Intermediate)	
1st Gear	Forward Clutch, No. 2 One-Way Clutch OD Direct Clutch & OD One-Way Clutch
2nd Gear	Forward Clutch, 2nd Coast Brake, 2nd Brake, No. 1 One-Way Clutch, OD Direct Clutch & OD One-Way Clutch
3rd Gear [1]	Forward Clutch, OD Direct Clutch, Direct Clutch 2nd Brake & OD One-Way Clutch
"L" (Low)	
1st Gear	Forward Clutch, OD One-Way Clutch, No. 2 One-Way Clutch, OD Direct Clutch & 1st & Reverse Brake
2nd Gear [2]	Forward Clutch, 2nd Coast Brake, 2nd Brake, No. 1 One-Way Clutch, OD Direct Clutch & OD One-Way Clutch
"R" (Reverse)	OD Direct Clutch, Direct Clutch, OD One-Way Clutch & 1st & Reverse Brake
"N" (Neutral)	OD Direct Clutch
"P" (Park)	OD Direct Clutch

[1] – Downshift only in "2" range and 3rd gear. No upshift.
[2] – Downshift only in "L" range and 2nd gear. No upshift.

CLUTCH & BAND APPLICATION CHART (A-350E)

Selector Lever Position	Elements In Use
"D" (Drive)	
1st Gear	Forward Clutch, No. 2 One-Way Clutch, OD One-Way Clutch & OD Direct Clutch
2nd Gear	Forward Clutch, OD Brake & No. 2 One-Way Clutch
3rd Gear	Forward Clutch, 2nd Brake, No. 1 One-Way Clutch, OD Direct Clutch & OD One-Way Clutch
4th Gear	Forward Clutch, 2nd Brake, Direct Clutch, OD Direct Clutch & OD One-Way Clutch
OD	Forward Clutch, 2nd Brake, OD Brake & Direct Clutch
"2" (Intermediate)	
1st Gear	Forward Clutch, No. 2 One-Way Clutch OD Direct Clutch & OD One-Way Clutch
3rd Gear	Forward Clutch, 2nd Coast Brake, 2nd Brake, No. 1 One-Way Clutch, OD Direct Clutch & OD One-Way Clutch
4th Gear [1]	Forward Clutch, OD Direct Clutch, Direct Clutch 2nd Brake & OD One-Way Clutch
"L" (Low)	
1st Gear	Forward Clutch, OD One-Way Clutch, No. 2 One-Way Clutch, OD Direct Clutch & 1st & Reverse Brake
3rd Gear [2]	Forward Clutch, 2nd Coast Brake, 2nd Brake, No. 1 One-Way Clutch, OD Direct Clutch & OD One-Way Clutch
"R" (Reverse)	OD Direct Clutch, Direct Clutch, OD One-Way Clutch & 1st & Reverse Brake
"N" (Neutral)	OD Direct Clutch
"P" (Park)	OD Direct Clutch

[1] – Downshift only in "S" range and 4th gear. No upshift.
[2] – Downshift only in "L" range and 3rd gear. No upshift.

TESTING

ELECTRICAL TESTING

Electrical tests should be performed prior to hydraulic testing to ensure problem is not in electrical circuit. See appropriate ELECTRONIC CONTROLS article.

PRELIMINARY CHECKS

Before testing transmission and transfer case, perform following procedures:
- Ensure fluid level is correct.
- Inspect and adjust throttle cable.
- Ensure battery is fully charged for accurate testing.
- Adjust shift linkage.
- Adjust park/neutral position switch.
- Inspect and adjust transfer shift linkage on A-340H.
- Inspect idle speed RPM.

TIME LAG TEST

Test Procedure – 1) Engine and transmission must be at normal operating temperature. Start engine and ensure idle RPM is within specification. See IDLE SPEED SPECIFICATIONS table. On Pickup, 4Runner and T100 models, place transfer gear shift selector in "H2".
2) On all models, apply service and parking brakes. Using stop watch, measure time until engagement shock is felt when lever is shifted from "N" to "D". Allow one minute interval between tests. Perform time measurements 2 more times and calculate average value. Time should be less than 1.2 seconds.
3) Use same procedure to test time lag when gear selector is moved from "N" to "R". Time lag should be less than 1.5 seconds.

Test Results – 1) If "N" to "D" time lag exceeds specification, check for low main line pressure, worn forward clutch or overdrive one-way clutch not operating correctly.
2) If "N" to "R" time lag exceeds specification, check for low main line pressure, worn direct clutch, worn 1st and reverse brake or overdrive one-way clutch not operating correctly.

IDLE SPEED SPECIFICATIONS [1] [2]

Vehicle Application	Transmission Application	RPM
Lexus		
GS300		
1995	A-340E	700
1996	A-350E	700
LS400	A-340E	650
LX450	A-343F	650
SC300	A-340E	650
SC400	A-340E	650
Toyota		
Land Cruiser	A-343F	650
Pickup		
2WD V6	A-340E	850
4WD 4-Cyl.	A-340F	800
4WD V6	A-340H	850
Previa		
2WD	A-340E	750
AWD	A-340F	750
Supra		
Non-Turbo	A-340E	700
Turbo	A-340E	650
Tacoma & T100		
4-Cyl.	A-340E	700
V6	A-340E & A-340F	700
4Runner		
1995		
2WD V6	A-340E	800
4WD 4-Cyl.	A-340F	750
4WD V6	A-340H	800
1996		
4-Cyl	A-340E & A-340F	700
V6	A-340E & A-340F	700

[1] – Plus or minus 50 RPM.
[2] – Check idle speed in Neutral range with A/C off.

ROAD TEST

CAUTION: Perform test at normal operating fluid temperature of 122-176°F (50-80°C).

Test Procedure – Before road testing, note following information:
- No overdrive upshift or lock-up will occur when engine coolant is below 140°F (60°C) on Supra and Lexus models. On Previa models, no overdrive upshift or lock-up will occur when engine coolant is below 122°F (50°C).
- No 3rd upshift or lock-up will occur when engine coolant temperature is below 95°F (35°C) and speed is below 25 MPH on Supra or Lexus models.
- No overdrive upshift or lock-up will occur when engine coolant temperature is below 133°F (55°C) on Land Cruiser or below 158°F (70°C) on Pickup, Tacoma, T100 and 4Runner models.
- No overdrive upshift or lock-up will occur if a 6 MPH difference between set cruise control speed and actual speed exists on Pickup and 4Runner models.
- All shift points vary due to transfer case gear position on Pickup, Tacoma, T100 and 4Runner models.
- Overdrive gear and lock-up are cancelled when transfer case is engaged in L4 on Pickup, Tacoma, T100 and 4Runner models.

"D" Range Test in NORM Or PWR Pattern Ranges – **1)** Shift into "D" range. Hold accelerator pedal constant at full throttle position. Check 1-2, 2-3 and 3-OD (1-2, 2-3, 3-4 and 4-OD on A-350E) upshift points. Refer to appropriate SHIFT SPEED SPECIFICATIONS table.
- If no 1st-2nd gear upshift occurs, 1-2 shift valve or No. 2 solenoid is stuck.
- If no 2nd-3rd gear upshift occurs, 2-3 shift valve or No. 1 solenoid is stuck.
- If no 3-OD gear upshift occurs, 3-4 shift valve is stuck.
- If all shift points are incorrect, throttle, 1-2 shift, 2-3 shift and 3-OD shift valves are defective.
- If all lock-up points are incorrect, lock-up control valve, lock-up signal valve or lock-up solenoid is stuck.

2) Use procedure outlined in step **1)** to check shock and slip between 1-2 gear, 2-3 gear and 3-OD gear upshifts (1-2, 2-3, 3-4 and 4-OD on A-350E). Excessive shock can be caused by excessive line pressure, defective accumulator or defective check ball.
3) Run in OD or lock-up in "D" range. Check for abnormal noise and vibration. Noise and vibration may be caused by unbalanced drive shaft, differential, torque converter or other drive train components.
4) While running in "D" range, 2nd, 3rd and OD gears, check correct kickdown speed for 2-1, 3-2 and OD-3 gears (2-1, 3-2, 4-3 and OD-4 on A-350E). Check for abnormal shock and slip at kickdown.
5) Check lock-up mechanism. Drive in OD gear of "D" range, at steady speed (lock-up ON) of 36-43 MPH for Lexus (except LX450), 47 MPH for Pickup, Previa, 4Runner, Tacoma, T100 and Supra models, and 59 MPH for Land Cruiser and LX450 models. Lightly depress accelerator pedal. Ensure engine RPM does not change abruptly. Large increase in engine RPM indicates there is no lock-up.

"2" Range Test – **1)** Shift to "2" range. Drive with accelerator pedal held constant at full throttle. Push in one pattern selection button. Ensure 1-2 upshift (1-3 upshift on A-350E) points at each accelerator opening take place and are operating properly.

NOTE: There is no OD upshift (4th upshift on A-350E) and lock-up in "2" range. To prevent overrun, transmission upshifts into 3rd gear at 68-71 MPH for Supra, 62 MPH for Pickup and 4Runner.

---

2) While driving in "2" range, ("3" range on A-350E) 2nd gear, release accelerator pedal and check engine braking. If there is no engine braking, second coast brake is defective. Check for abnormal noise and shock at acceleration and deceleration.
"L" Range Test – **1)** While running in "L" range, ensure there is no upshift to 2nd gear.
2) While running in "L" range, release accelerator pedal. If there is no engine braking effect, 1st and reverse brake is defective. Note abnormal noise at acceleration and deceleration.

"R" Range Test – Shift into "R" range. Accelerate vehicle from a stop at full throttle. Ensure slipping does not occur.
"P" Range Test – Stop vehicle on 5 degree or more gradient. Shift transmission into "P". Release parking brake. Ensure parking pawl holds vehicle.
Transfer Test – **1)** On A-340H model, ensure vehicle shifts from 2WD to 4WD when transfer gear lever is shifted from H2 to H4. Transfer case assembly is defective if unit does NOT shift from 2WD to 4WD.
2) Shift transfer gear lever from H4 to L4. Gear changes should occur within specification. If transfer did not change from H4 to L4 gears within specification, No. 4 solenoid, ECT computer or transfer is defective.

LANDCRUISER & LEXUS (LX450) A-343F (1995-96) SHIFT SPEED SPECIFICATIONS [1]

Application	MPH
"D" Range	
1st-2nd	35-39
2nd-3rd	64-71
3rd-OD	94-101
OD-3rd	90-97
3rd-2nd	59-63
2nd-1st	26-29
"2" Range [2]	
3rd-2nd	72-79
"L" Range	
2nd-1st	38-39

[1] – Wide open throttle.
[2] – No 1-2 upshift or 2-1 downshift with 2nd start switch on.

LANDCRUISER & LEXUS (LX450) A-343F (1995-96) LOCK-UP SPEED SPECIFICATIONS [1]

Application	MPH
"D" Range [2]	
NORM Or PWR	
Lock-Up ON	48-52
Lock-Up OFF	42-46

[1] – Throttle valve opened 5 percent.
[2] – No lock-up in "L" or "2" range.

LEXUS (GS300) A-340E (1995) SHIFT SPEED SPECIFICATIONS

Application	MPH
"D" Range	
NORM Or PWR	
1st-2nd [1]	34-39
2nd-3rd [1]	68-73
3rd-OD [1]	106-113
3rd-OD [2]	22-25
OD-3rd [2]	13-16
OD-3rd [1]	102-109
3rd-2nd [1]	63-68
2nd-1st [1]	27-31
"2" Range	
NORM Or PWR	
1st-2nd [1]	34-39
3rd-2nd [1]	63-68
2nd-1st [1]	27-31
3rd-2nd [2]	63-68
"L" Range	
2nd-1st [2]	35-38

[1] – Wide open throttle.
[2] – Fully closed throttle.

LEXUS (GS300) A-340E (1995) LOCK-UP SPEED SPECIFICATIONS [1]

Application	MPH
"D" Range [2]	
NORM Or PWR	
Lock-Up ON In 3rd [3]	39-42
Lock-Up OFF In 3rd [3]	35-38
Lock-Up ON In OD	35-39
Lock-Up OFF In OD	35-38

[1] – Throttle valve opened 5 percent.
[2] – No lock-up in "L" or "2" range.
[3] – With OD switch off.

LEXUS (GS300) A-350E (1996) SHIFT SPEED SPECIFICATIONS

Application	MPH
"D" Range	
NORM Or PWR	
1st-2nd [1]	35-40
2nd-3rd [1]	50-56
3rd-4th [1]	65-73
4th-OD [1]	101-110
4th-OD [2]	21-24
OD-4th [1]	98-104
OD-4th [2]	12-16
4th-3rd [1]	60-66
3rd-2nd [1]	36-39
2nd-1st [1]	26-29
"2" Range	
NORM Or PWR	
1st-3rd [1]	35-40
4th-3rd [1]	60-66
3rd-1st [1]	26-29
4th-3rd [2]	60-66
"L" Range	
3rd-1st [1]	34-37
3rd-1st [2]	34-37

[1] – Wide open throttle.
[2] – Fully closed throttle.

LEXUS (GS300) A-350E (1996) LOCK-UP SPEED SPECIFICATIONS [1]

Application	MPH
"D" Range [2]	
NORM Or PWR	
Lock-Up ON In 4th [3]	34-37
Lock-Up OFF In 4th [3]	34-37
Lock-Up ON In OD	34-37
Lock-Up OFF In OD	34-37

[1] – Throttle valve opened 5 percent.
[2] – No lock-up in "L", "2" or "3" range.
[3] – With OD switch off.

LEXUS (LS400) A-340E (1995-96) SHIFT SPEED SPECIFICATIONS

Application	MPH
"D" Range	
NORM Or PWR	
1st-2nd [1]	42-52
2nd-3rd [1]	78-84
3rd-OD [1]	123-130
3rd-OD [2]	19-23
OD-3rd [2]	16-19
OD-3rd [1]	119-126
3rd-2nd [1]	71-76
2nd-1st [1]	34-38
"2" Range	
NORM Or PWR	
1st-2nd [1]	42-52
3rd-2nd [1]	74-78
2nd-1st [1]	34-38
"L" Range	
NORM Or PWR	
2nd-1st [1]	36-40

[1] – Wide open throttle.
[2] – Fully closed throttle.

LEXUS (LS400) A-340E (1995-96) LOCK-UP SPEED SPECIFICATIONS [1]

Application	MPH
"D" Range [2]	
NORM Or PWR	
Lock-Up ON In 3rd [3]	57-62
Lock-Up OFF In 3rd [3]	53-57
Lock-Up ON In OD	36-40
Lock-Up OFF In OD	34-38

[1] – Throttle valve opened 5 percent.
[2] – No lock-up in "2" or "L" range.
[3] – With OD switch off.

LEXUS (SC300) A-340E (1995-96) SHIFT SPEED SPECIFICATIONS

Application	MPH
"D" Range)	
NORM Or PWR	
1st-2nd [1]	32-36
2nd-3rd [1]	65-69
3rd-OD [1]	101-108
3rd-OD [2]	24-27
OD-3rd [2]	16-19
OD-3rd [1]	98-104
3rd-2nd [1]	61-65
2nd-1st [1]	26-29
"2" Range	
NORM Or PWR	
1st-2nd [1]	32-36
3rd-2nd [1]	61-65
2nd-1st [1]	26-29
3rd-2nd [2]	61-65
"L" Range	
NORM Or PWR	
2nd-1st [1]	30-36
2nd-1st [2]	30-36

[1] – Wide open throttle.
[2] – Fully closed throttle.

LEXUS (SC300) A-340E (1995-96) LOCK-UP SPEED SPECIFICATIONS [1]

Application	MPH
"D" Range [2]	
NORM	
Lock-Up ON In 3rd [3]	35-38
Lock-Up OFF In 3rd [3]	37-40
Lock-Up ON In OD	35-37
Lock-Up OFF In OD	34-37
PWR	
Lock-Up ON In 3rd [3]	34-37
Lock-Up OFF In 3rd [3]	35-38
Lock-Up ON In OD	37-40
Lock-Up OFF In OD	35-38

[1] – Throttle valve opened 5 percent.
[2] – No lock-up in "L" or "2" range.
[3] – With OD switch off.

LEXUS (SC400) A-340E (1995) SHIFT SPEED SPECIFICATIONS

Application	MPH
"D" Range	
NORM Or PWR	
1st-2nd [1]	42-44
2nd-3rd [1]	73-77
3rd-OD (NORM) [1]	106-110
3rd-OD (PWR) [1]	111-116
3rd-OD [2]	20-22
OD-3rd [2]	14-16
OD-3rd [1]	102-106
3rd-2nd [1]	65-69
2nd-1st [1]	33-35
"2" Range	
NORM Or PWR	
1st-2nd [1]	42-44
3rd-2nd [1]	66-70
2nd-1st [1]	33-35
3rd-2nd [2]	66-70
NORM Or PWR	
2nd-1st [1]	35-39
2nd-1st [2]	35-39

[1] – Wide open throttle.
[2] – Fully closed throttle.

LEXUS (SC400) A-340E (1995) LOCK-UP SPEED SPECIFICATIONS [1]

Application	MPH
"D" Range [2]	
NORM OR PWR	
Lock-Up ON In 3rd [3]	52-55
Lock-Up OFF In 3rd [3]	48-51
Lock-Up ON In OD	35-37
Lock-Up OFF In OD	33-35

[1] – Throttle valve opened 5 percent.
[2] – No lock-up in "L" or "2" range.
[3] – With OD switch off.

LEXUS (SC400) A-340E (1996) SHIFT SPEED SPECIFICATIONS

Application	MPH
"D" Range	
NORM Or PWR	
1st-2nd [1]	36-45
2nd-3rd [1]	71-76
3rd-OD (NORM) [1]	107-114
3rd-OD (PWR) [1]	103-110
3rd-OD [2]	17-21
OD-3rd [2]	12-16
OD-3rd [1]	103-110
3rd-2nd [1]	64-68
2nd-1st [1]	30-33
"2" Range	
NORM Or PWR	
1st-2nd [1]	33-35
3rd-2nd [1]	66-70
2nd-1st [1]	30-33
3rd-2nd [2]	66-70
NORM Or PWR	
2nd-1st [1]	33-35
2nd-1st [2]	33-35

[1] – Wide open throttle.
[2] – Fully closed throttle.

LEXUS (SC400) A-340E (1996) LOCK-UP SPEED SPECIFICATIONS [1]

Application	MPH
"D" Range [2]	
NORM OR PWR	
Lock-Up ON In 3rd [3]	52-54
Lock-Up OFF In 3rd [3]	48-50
Lock-Up ON In OD	34-35
Lock-Up OFF In OD	32-33

[1] – Throttle valve opened 5 percent.
[2] – No lock-up in "L" or "2" range.
[3] – With OD switch off.

PICKUP 2WD [1] A-340E (1995) SHIFT SPEED SPECIFICATIONS (3.417 GEAR RATIO)

Application	MPH
"D" Range	
NORM	
1st-2nd [2]	38-41
2nd-3rd [2]	67-73
3rd-OD [2]	89-94
3rd-OD [3]	27-30
OD-3rd [3]	16-19
OD-3rd [2]	85-90
3rd-2nd [2]	62-65
2nd-1st [2]	27-30
PWR	
1st-2nd [2]	38-41
2nd-3rd [2]	74-79
3rd-OD [2]	91-97
3rd-OD [3]	29-32
OD-3rd [3]	16-19
OD-3rd [2]	87-93
3rd-2nd [2]	68-74
2nd-1st [2]	27-30
"2" Range	
NORM Or PWR	
1st-2nd [2]	33-35
2nd-3rd [2]	78-84
3rd-2nd [2]	74-80
2nd-1st [2]	29-32
"L" Range	
3rd-2nd [2]	63-68
2nd-1st [2]	35-39

[1] – Tire size P205/75R14 and P215/65R15.
[2] – Wide open throttle.
[3] – Fully closed throttle.

PICKUP 2WD [1] A-340E (1995) LOCK-UP SPEED SPECIFICATIONS (3.417 GEAR RATIO) [2]

Application	MPH
"D" Range [3]	
NORM	
Lock-Up ON In 3rd [4]	49-52
Lock-Up OFF In 3rd [4]	44-47
Lock-Up ON In OD	49-52
Lock-Up OFF In OD	42-45
PWR	
Lock-Up ON In 3rd [4]	38-41
Lock-Up OFF In 3rd [4]	42-45
Lock-Up ON In OD	49-52
Lock-Up OFF In OD	42-47

[1] – Tire size P205/75R14 or P215/65R15.
[2] – Throttle valve opened 5 percent.
[3] – No lock-up in "L" or "2" range.
[4] – With OD switch off.

PICKUP 2WD [1] A-340E (1995) SHIFT SPEED SPECIFICATIONS (3.90 GEAR RATIO)

Application	MPH
"D" Range	
NORM	
1st-2nd [2]	32-35
2nd-3rd [2]	45-62
3rd-OD [2]	84-88
3rd-OD [3]	23-25
OD-3rd [3]	14-16
OD-3rd [2]	81-85
3rd-2nd [2]	53-56
2nd-1st [2]	27-29
PWR	
1st-2nd [2]	32-35
2nd-3rd [2]	63-68
3rd-OD [2]	92-96
3rd-OD [3]	25-27
OD-3rd [3]	14-16
OD-3rd [2]	88-92
3rd-2nd [2]	59-63
2nd-1st [2]	27-29
"2" Range	
NORM Or PWR	
1st-2nd [2]	28-30
2nd-3rd [2]	67-71
3rd-2nd [2]	63-68
2nd-1st [2]	25-27
"L" Range	
3rd-2nd [2]	54-48
2nd-1st [2]	30-33

[1] – Tire size 185R14.
[2] – Wide open throttle.
[3] – Fully closed throttle.

PICKUP 2WD [1] A-340E (1995) LOCK-UP SPEED SPECIFICATIONS (3.90 GEAR RATIO) [2]

Application	MPH
"D" Range [3]	
NORM	
Lock-Up ON In 3rd [4]	42-44
Lock-Up OFF In 3rd [4]	38-40
Lock-Up ON In OD	42-44
Lock-Up OFF In OD	36-39
PWR	
Lock-Up ON In 3rd [4]	36-39
Lock-Up OFF In 3rd [4]	32-35
Lock-Up ON In OD	42-44
Lock-Up OFF In OD	38-40

[1] – Tire size 185R14.
[2] – Throttle valve opened 5 percent.
[3] – No lock-up in "L" or "2" range.
[4] – With OD switch off.

PICKUP 2WD (CAB & CHASSIS) [1] A-340E (1995)
SHIFT SPEED SPECIFICATIONS (4.10 GEAR RATIO)

Application	MPH
"D" Range	
NORM	
1st-2nd [2]	27-29
2nd-3rd [2]	52-57
3rd-OD [2]	80-84
3rd-OD [3]	45-48
OD-3rd [3]	13-16
OD-3rd [2]	76-81
3rd-2nd [2]	48-50
2nd-1st [2]	24-26
PWR	
1st-2nd [2]	32-34
2nd-3rd [2]	60-64
3rd-OD [2]	82-86
3rd-OD [3]	45-48
OD-3rd [3]	13-16
OD-3rd [2]	78-82
3rd-2nd [2]	56-60
2nd-1st [2]	28-30
"2" Range	
NORM Or PWR	
1st-2nd [2]	27-29
2nd-3rd [2]	64-68
3rd-2nd [2]	60-65
2nd-1st [2]	24-26
"L" Range	
3rd-2nd [2]	52-55
2nd-1st [2]	29-32

[1] – Tire size 185R14 (single or dual rear tires).
[2] – Wide open throttle.
[3] – Fully closed throttle.

PICKUP 2WD (CAB & CHASSIS) [1] A-340E (1995)
LOCK-UP SPEED SPECIFICATIONS [2] (4.10 GEAR RATIO)

Application	MPH
"D" Range [3]	
NORM	
Lock-Up ON In 3rd [4]	45-48
Lock-Up OFF In 3rd [4]	38-40
Lock-Up ON In OD	45-48
Lock-Up OFF In OD	42-44
PWR	
Lock-Up ON In 3rd [4]	45-48
Lock-Up OFF In 3rd [4]	42-44
Lock-Up ON In OD	45-48
Lock-Up OFF In OD	42-44

[1] – Tire size 185R14 (single or dual rear tires).
[2] – Throttle valve opened 5 percent.
[3] – No lock-up in "L" or "2" range.
[4] – With OD switch off.

PICKUP 2WD (CAB & CHASSIS) [1] A-340E (1995)
SHIFT SPEED SPECIFICATIONS (4.30 GEAR RATIO)

Application	MPH
"D" Range	
NORM	
1st-2nd [2]	25-28
2nd-3rd [2]	50-54
3rd-OD [2]	76-80
3rd-OD [3]	43-45
OD-3rd [3]	12-15
OD-3rd [2]	73-77
3rd-2nd [2]	45-48
2nd-1st [2]	23-25
PWR	
1st-2nd [2]	30-33
2nd-3rd [2]	57-62
3rd-OD [2]	78-82
3rd-OD [3]	43-45
OD-3rd [3]	12-15
OD-3rd [2]	75-78
3rd-2nd [2]	53-57
2nd-1st [2]	26-29
"2" Range	

[1] – Tire size 185R14 (dual rear tires).
[2] – Wide open throttle.
[3] – Fully closed throttle.

PICKUP 2WD (CAB & CHASSIS) [1] A-340E (1995)
SHIFT SPEED SPECIFICATIONS (4.30 GEAR RATIO) (Cont.)

Application	MPH
NORM Or PWR	
1st-2nd [2]	25-28
2nd-3rd [2]	61-65
3rd-2nd [2]	58-62
2nd-1st [2]	23-25
"L" Range	
3rd-2nd [2]	49-53
2nd-1st [2]	28-30

[1] – Tire size 185R14 (dual rear tires).
[2] – Wide open throttle.
[3] – Fully closed throttle.

PICKUP 2WD (CAB & CHASSIS) [1] A-340E (1995)
LOCK-UP SPEED SPECIFICATIONS (4.30 GEAR RATIO) [2]

Application	MPH
"D" Range [3]	
NORM	
Lock-Up ON In 3rd [4]	49-52
Lock-Up OFF In 3rd [4]	44-47
Lock-Up ON In OD	43-45
Lock-Up OFF In OD	40-42
PWR	
Lock-Up ON In 3rd [4]	38-41
Lock-Up OFF In 3rd [4]	42-45
Lock-Up ON In OD	43-45
Lock-Up OFF In OD	40-42

[1] – Tire size 185R14 (dual tires).
[2] – Throttle valve opened 5 percent.
[3] – No lock-up in "L" or "2" range.
[4] – With OD switch off.

PICKUP & 4RUNNER 4WD A-340F (1995)
SHIFT SPEED SPECIFICATIONS

Application	MPH
"D" Range	
NORM	
1st-2nd [1]	27-30
2nd-3rd [1]	58-61
3rd-OD [1]	83-87
3rd-OD [2]	22-24
OD-3rd [2]	13-16
OD-3rd [1]	79-84
3rd-2nd [1]	54-58
2nd-1st [1]	25-27
PWR	
1st-2nd [1]	29-32
2nd-3rd [1]	58-61
3rd-OD [1]	92-96
3rd-OD [2]	31-33
OD-3rd [2]	13-16
OD-3rd [1]	89-92
3rd-2nd [1]	54-58
2nd-1st [1]	25-28
"2" Range	
NORM Or PWR	
1st-2nd [1]	27-29
2nd-3rd [1]	64-68
3rd-2nd [1]	60-64
2nd-1st [1]	24-26
"L" Range	
NORM Or PWR	
3rd-2nd [1]	51-55
2nd-1st [1]	29-32

[1] – Wide open throttle.
[2] – Fully closed throttle.

PICKUP & 4RUNNER 4WD A-340F (1995)
LOCK-UP SPEED SPECIFICATIONS [1]

Application	MPH
"D" Range [2]	
NORM	
Lock-Up ON In 3rd [3]	25-28
Lock-Up OFF In 3rd [3]	24-26
Lock-Up ON In OD	37-39
Lock-Up OFF In OD	34-37
PWR	
Lock-Up ON In 3rd [3]	34-37
Lock-Up OFF In 3rd [3]	31-33
Lock-Up ON In OD	47-49
Lock-Up OFF In OD	43-45

[1] – Throttle valve opened 5 percent.
[2] – No lock-up in "L" or "2" range.
[3] – With OD switch off.

PICKUP & 4RUNNER 4WD A-340H (1995)
SHIFT SPEED SPECIFICATIONS

Application	MPH
"D" Range	
NORM	
1st-2nd [1]	31-33
2nd-3rd [1]	56-60
3rd-OD [1]	81-86
3rd-OD [2]	22-24
OD-3rd [2]	13-16
OD-3rd [1]	78-82
3rd-2nd [1]	52-57
2nd-1st [1]	25-27
PWR	
1st-2nd [2]	31-33
2nd-3rd [2]	56-60
3rd-OD [2]	81-86
3rd-OD [3]	24-26
OD-3rd [3]	13-16
OD-3rd [2]	78-82
3rd-2nd [2]	52-57
2nd-1st [2]	25-27
"2" Range	
NORM Or PWR	
1st-2nd [2]	27-29
2nd-3rd [2]	64-68
3rd-2nd [2]	60-64
2nd-1st [2]	24-26
"L" Range	
NORM Or PWR	
3rd-2nd [2]	51-55
2nd-1st [2]	29-32

[1] – Transfer shift position "H2" or "H4".
[2] – Wide open throttle.
[3] – Fully closed throttle.

PICKUP & 4RUNNER 4WD A-340H (1995)
LOCK-UP SPEED SPECIFICATIONS [1]

Application	MPH
"D" Range [2], [3]	
NORM	
Lock-Up ON In 3rd [4]	32-35
Lock-Up OFF In 3rd [4]	31-33
Lock-Up ON In OD	40-42
Lock-Up OFF In OD	34-37
PWR	
Lock-Up ON In 3rd [4]	32-35
Lock-Up OFF In 3rd [4]	31-33
Lock-Up ON In OD	40-42
Lock-Up OFF In OD	36-39

[1] – Throttle valve opened 5 percent.
[2] – No lock-up in "L" or "2" range.
[3] – Transfer shift position "H2" or "H4".
[4] – With OD switch off.

PREVIA A-340E & A-340F (1995-96) SHIFT SPEED SPECIFICATIONS [1]

Application	MPH
"D" Range	
1st-2nd	34-37
2nd-3rd	62-68
3rd-OD	101-108
OD-3rd	97-104
3rd-2nd	57-63
2nd-1st	27-30
"2" Range	
3rd-2nd	39-54
"L" Range	
2nd-1st	32-36

[1] – Wide open throttle.

PREVIA A-340E & A-340F (1995-96)
LOCK-UP SPEED SPECIFICATIONS [1]

Application	MPH
"D" Range [2]	
Lock-Up ON In 3rd [3]	42-46
Lock-Up OFF In 3rd [3]	39-42
Lock-Up ON In OD	45-49
Lock-Up OFF In OD	44-48

[1] – Throttle valve opened 5 percent.
[2] – No lock-up in "L" or "2" range.
[3] – With OD switch off.

4RUNNER 2WD A-340E (1995) SHIFT SPEED SPECIFICATIONS

Application	MPH
"D" Range	
NORM	
1st-2nd [1]	36-39
2nd-3rd [1]	64-69
3rd-OD [1]	89-94
3rd-OD [2]	25-29
OD-3rd [2]	16-18
OD-3rd [1]	85-90
3rd-2nd [1]	59-62
2nd-1st [1]	28-30
PWR	
1st-2nd [1]	36-39
2nd-3rd [1]	70-75
3rd-OD [1]	91-96
3rd-OD [2]	28-30
OD-3rd [2]	16-18
OD-3rd [1]	87-93
3rd-2nd [1]	65-70
2nd-1st [1]	28-30
"2" Range	
NORM Or PWR	
1st-2nd [1]	31-34
2nd-3rd [1]	75-79
3rd-2nd [1]	70-75
2nd-1st [1]	28-30
"L" Range	
3rd-2nd [1]	60-65
2nd-1st [1]	34-37

[1] – Wide open throttle.
[2] – Fully closed throttle.

4RUNNER 2WD A-340E (1995) LOCK-UP SPEED SPECIFICATIONS [1]

Application	MPH
"D" Range [2]	
NORM	
Lock-Up ON In 3rd [3]	47-49
Lock-Up OFF In 3rd [3]	42-45
Lock-Up ON In OD	47-49
Lock-Up OFF In OD	40-43
PWR	
Lock-Up ON In 3rd [3]	40-43
Lock-Up OFF In 3rd [3]	36-39
Lock-Up ON In OD	47-49
Lock-Up OFF In OD	42-45

[1] – Throttle valve opened 5 percent.
[2] – No lock-up in "L" or "2" range.
[3] – With OD switch off.

4RUNNER 2.7L 2WD A-340E (1996) SHIFT SPEED SPECIFICATIONS

Application	MPH
"D" Range	
NORM Or PWR	
1st-2nd [1]	36-40
2nd-3rd [1]	66-72
3rd-OD [1]	88-94
3rd-OD [2]	21-24
OD-3rd [2]	16-19
OD-3rd [1]	84-90
3rd-2nd [1]	61-67
2nd-1st [1]	29-32
"2" Range	
NORM Or PWR	
1st-2nd [1]	36-40
3rd-2nd [1]	70-75
2nd-1st [1]	29-32
"L" Range	
NORM Or PWR	
2nd-1st [1]	34-37

[1] – Wide open throttle.
[2] – Fully closed throttle.

4RUNNER 2.7L 2WD A-340E (1996) LOCK-UP SPEED SPECIFICATIONS [1]

Application	MPH
"D" Range [2]	
NORM	
Lock-Up ON In OD	48-52
Lock-Up OFF In OD	43-47
PWR	
Lock-Up ON In OD	52-55
Lock-Up OFF In OD	43-47

[1] – Throttle valve opened 5 percent.
[2] – No lock-up in "L" or "2" range.

4RUNNER 3.4L 2WD A-340E (1996) SHIFT SPEED SPECIFICATIONS

Application	MPH
"D" Range	
NORM Or PWR	
1st-2nd [1]	37-40
2nd-3rd [1]	70-75
3rd-OD [1]	94-99
3rd-OD [2]	27-30
OD-3rd [2]	14-17
OD-3rd [1]	89-94
3rd-2nd [1]	64-69
2nd-1st [1]	29-32
"2" Range	
NORM Or PWR	
1st-2nd [1]	37-40
3rd-2nd [1]	74-79
2nd-1st [1]	29-32
"L" Range	
NORM Or PWR	
2nd-1st [1]	36-39

[1] – Wide open throttle.
[2] – Fully closed throttle.

4RUNNER 3.4L 2WD A-340E (1996) LOCK-UP SPEED SPECIFICATIONS [1]

Application	MPH
"D" Range [2]	
NORM Or PWR	
Lock-Up ON in OD	47-50
Lock-Up OFF in OD	42-45

[1] – Throttle valve opened 5 percent.
[2] – No lock-up in "L" or "2" range.

4RUNNER 2.7L 4WD A-340F (1996) SHIFT SPEED SPECIFICATIONS

Application	MPH
"D" Range	
NORM Or PWR	
1st-2nd [1]	34-38
2nd-3rd [1]	63-69
3rd-OD [1]	83-90
3rd-OD [2]	20-23
OD-3rd [2]	15-18
OD-3rd [1]	79-86
3rd-2nd [1]	58-64
2nd-1st [1]	27-30
"2" Range	
NORM Or PWR	
1st-2nd [1]	34-38
3rd-2nd [1]	65-72
2nd-1st [1]	27-30
"L" Range	
NORM Or PWR	
2nd-1st [1]	32-35

[1] – Wide open throttle.
[2] – Fully closed throttle.

4RUNNER 2.7L 4WD A-340F (1996) LOCK-UP SPEED SPECIFICATIONS [1]

Application	MPH
"D" Range [2]	
NORM Or PWR	
Lock-Up ON in OD	48-52
Lock-Up OFF in OD	44-48

[1] – Throttle valve opened 5 percent.
[2] – No lock-up in "L" or "2" range.

4RUNNER 3.4L 4WD A-340F (1996) SHIFT SPEED SPECIFICATIONS

Application	MPH
"D" Range	
NORM Or PWR	
1st-2nd [1]	35-39
2nd-3rd [1]	66-73
3rd-OD [1]	89-97
3rd-OD [2]	25-29
OD-3rd [2]	14-17
OD-3rd [1]	85-93
3rd-2nd [1]	61-68
2nd-1st [1]	28-32
"2" Range	
NORM Or PWR	
1st-2nd [1]	35-39
3rd-2nd [1]	71-78
2nd-1st [1]	28-32
"L" Range	
NORM Or PWR	
2nd-1st [1]	34-38

[1] – Wide open throttle.
[2] – Fully closed throttle.

4RUNNER 3.4L 4WD A-340F (1996) LOCK-UP SPEED SPECIFICATIONS [1]

Application	MPH
"D" Range [2]	
NORM Or PWR	
Lock-Up ON in OD	45-48
Lock-Up OFF in OD	40-44

[1] – Throttle valve opened 5 percent.
[2] – No lock-up in "L" or "2" range.

SUPRA (NON-TURBO) A-340E (1995-96) SHIFT SPEED SPECIFICATIONS

Application	MPH
"D" Range	
NORM	
1st-2nd [1]	33-39
2nd-3rd [1]	65-70
3rd-OD [1]	101-109
3rd-OD [2]	21-24
OD-3rd [2]	12-16
OD-3rd [1]	98-105
3rd-2nd [1]	61-65
2nd-1st [1]	26-30
MANUAL	
2nd-3rd [1]	65-70
3rd-OD [1]	101-109
3rd-OD [2]	101-109
OD-3rd [2]	12-16
OD-3rd [1]	98-109
3rd-2nd [1]	61-65
"2" Range	
NORM	
1st-2nd [1]	33-39
3rd-2nd [3]	75-82
2nd-1st [1]	26-30
"2" Range	
MANUAL	
3rd-2nd [3]	75-82
"L" Range	
2nd-1st [3]	30-33

[1] – Wide open throttle.
[2] – Fully closed throttle.
[3] – Wide open or fully closed throttle.

SUPRA (NON-TURBO) A-340E (1995-96) LOCK-UP SPEED SPECIFICATIONS [1]

Application	MPH
"D" Range [2]	
NORM	
Lock-Up ON In 3rd [3]	35-39
Lock-Up OFF In 3rd [3]	35-39
Lock-Up ON In OD	35-39
Lock-Up OFF In OD	35-39
MANUAL	
Lock-Up ON In 3rd [3]	61-65
Lock-Up OFF In 3rd [3]	57-62
Lock-Up ON In OD	101-109
Lock-Up OFF In OD	35-39

[1] – Throttle valve opened 5 percent.
[2] – No lock-up in "L" or "2" range.
[3] – With OD switch off.

SUPRA (TURBO) A-340E (1995-96) SHIFT SPEED SPECIFICATIONS

Application	MPH
"D" Range	
NORM	
1st-2nd [1]	39-45
2nd-3rd [1]	75-80
3rd-OD [1]	116-125
3rd-OD [2]	18-25
OD-3rd [2]	14-17
OD-3rd [1]	112-121
3rd-2nd [1]	68-73
2nd-1st [1]	25-29
MANUAL	
2nd-3rd [1]	76-81
3rd-OD [1]	121-129
3rd-OD [2]	112-121
OD-3rd [2]	14-17
OD-3rd [1]	116-125
3rd-2nd [1]	68-73
"2" Range	
NORM Or MANUAL	
1st-2nd [1]	39-45
3rd-2nd [3]	84-91
2nd-1st [1]	25-29
"L" Range	
2nd-1st [3]	37-41

[1] – Wide open throttle.
[2] – Fully closed throttle.
[3] – Wide open or fully closed throttle.

SUPRA (TURBO) A-340E (1995-96) LOCK-UP SPEED SPECIFICATIONS [1]

Application	MPH
"D" Range	
NORM	
Lock-Up ON In 3rd [2]	37-41
Lock-Up OFF In 3rd [2]	31-35
Lock-Up ON In OD	33-37
Lock-Up OFF In OD	31-35
PWR	
Lock-Up ON In 2nd Or 3rd [2]	37-41
Lock-Up OFF In 2nd Or 3rd [2]	35-39
Lock-Up ON In OD	112-121
Lock-Up OFF In OD	43-47

[1] – Throttle valve opened 5 percent.
[2] – With OD switch off.

TACOMA 2.7L (WITH P255/75R15 TIRES) A-340E (1995-96) SHIFT SPEED SPECIFICATIONS

Application	MPH
"D" Range	
NORM Or PWR	
1st-2nd [1]	33-36
2nd-3rd [1]	60-65
3rd-OD [1]	84-89
3rd-OD [2]	21-23
OD-3rd [2]	15-18
OD-3rd [1]	80-86
3rd-2nd [1]	55-59
2nd-1st [1]	26-29
"2" Range	
NORM Or PWR	
1st-2nd [1]	33-36
3rd-2nd [1]	66-72
2nd-1st [1]	26-29
"L" Range	
NORM Or PWR	
3rd-2nd [1]	57-62
2nd-1st [1]	32-35

[1] – Wide open throttle.
[2] – Fully closed throttle.

TACOMA 2.7L (WITH P255/75R15 TIRES) A-340E (1995-96) LOCK-UP SPEED SPECIFICATIONS [1]

Application	MPH
"D" Range [2]	
NORM Or PWR	
Lock-Up ON In OD	48-52
Lock-Up OFF In OD	45-48

[1] – Throttle valve opened 5 percent.
[2] – No lock-up in "L" or "2" range.

TACOMA 2.7L (WITH 31X10.5R15 TIRES) A-340E (1995-96) SHIFT SPEED SPECIFICATIONS

Application	MPH
"D" Range	
NORM Or PWR	
1st-2nd [1]	32-35
2nd-3rd [1]	58-63
3rd-OD [1]	82-87
3rd-OD [2]	20-22
OD-3rd [2]	15-17
OD-3rd [1]	78-83
3rd-2nd [1]	54-57
2nd-1st [1]	25-28
"2" Range	
NORM Or PWR	
1st-2nd [1]	32-35
3rd-2nd [1]	65-70
2nd-1st [1]	25-28
"L" Range	
NORM Or PWR	
3rd-2nd [1]	55-60
2nd-1st [1]	31-34

[1] – Wide open throttle.
[2] – Fully closed throttle.

TACOMA 2.7L (WITH 31X10.5R15 TIRES) A-340E (1995-96) LOCK-UP SPEED SPECIFICATIONS [1]

Application	MPH
"D" Range [2]	
NORM Or PWR	
Lock-Up ON In OD	47-50
Lock-Up OFF In OD	44-47

[1] – Throttle valve opened 5 percent.
[2] – No lock-up in "L" or "2" range.

TACOMA 3.4L A-340E (1995-96) SHIFT SPEED SPECIFICATIONS

Application	MPH
"D" Range	
NORM Or PWR	
1st-2nd [1]	40-43
2nd-3rd [1]	75-81
3rd-OD [1]	101-107
3rd-OD [2]	29-32
OD-3rd [2]	16-19
OD-3rd [1]	96-102
3rd-2nd [1]	69-75
2nd-1st [1]	32-35
"2" Range	
NORM Or PWR	
1st-2nd [1]	40-43
3rd-2nd [1]	80-85
2nd-1st [1]	32-35
"L" Range	
NORM Or PWR	
3rd-2nd [1]	68-73
2nd-1st [1]	38-42

[1] – Wide open throttle.
[2] – Fully closed throttle.

TACOMA 3.4L A-340E (1995-96) LOCK-UP SPEED SPECIFICATIONS [1]

Application	MPH
"D" Range [2]	
NORM Or PWR	
Lock-Up ON In OD	50-53
Lock-Up OFF In OD	45-49

[1] – Throttle valve opened 5 percent.
[2] – No lock-up in "L" or "2" range.

TACOMA 3.4L (WITH P225/75R15 TIRES) A-340F (1995-96) SHIFT SPEED SPECIFICATIONS

Application	MPH
"D" Range	
NORM Or PWR	
1st-2nd [1]	35-38
2nd-3rd [1]	65-71
3rd-OD [1]	88-94
3rd-OD [2]	25-29
OD-3rd [2]	14-16
OD-3rd [1]	84-90
3rd-2nd [1]	60-66
2nd-1st [1]	27-30
"2" Range	
NORM Or PWR	
1st-2nd [1]	35-38
3rd-2nd [1]	70-75
2nd-1st [1]	27-30
"L" Range	
NORM Or PWR	
3rd-2nd [1]	59-65
2nd-1st [1]	34-37

[1] – Wide open throttle.
[2] – Fully closed throttle.

TACOMA 3.4L (WITH P225/75R15 TIRES) A-340F (1995-96) LOCK-UP SPEED SPECIFICATIONS [1]

Application	MPH
"D" Range [2]	
NORM Or PWR	
Lock-Up ON In OD	44-47
Lock-Up OFF In OD	40-43

[1] – Throttle valve opened 5 percent.
[2] – No lock-up in "L" or "2" range.

TACOMA 3.4L (WITH 31X10.5R15 TIRES) A-340F (1995-96) SHIFT SPEED SPECIFICATIONS

Application	MPH
"D" Range	
NORM Or PWR	
1st-2nd [1]	36-39
2nd-3rd [1]	68-73
3rd-OD [1]	91-97
3rd-OD [2]	26-29
OD-3rd [2]	14-18
OD-3rd [1]	87-93
3rd-2nd [1]	62-68
2nd-1st [1]	29-31
"2" Range	
NORM Or PWR	
1st-2nd [1]	36-39
3rd-2nd [1]	72-78
2nd-1st [1]	29-31
"L" Range	
NORM Or PWR	
3rd-2nd [1]	62-68
2nd-1st [1]	35-38

[1] – Wide open throttle.
[2] – Fully closed throttle.

TACOMA 3.4L (WITH 31X10.5R15 TIRES) A-340F (1995-96) LOCK-UP SPEED SPECIFICATIONS [1]

Application	MPH
"D" Range [2]	
NORM Or PWR	
Lock-Up ON In OD	45-48
Lock-Up OFF In OD	41-44

[1] – Throttle valve opened 5 percent.
[2] – No lock-up in "L" or "2" range.

T100 2.7L 2WD A-340E (1995-96) SHIFT SPEED SPECIFICATIONS

Application	MPH
"D" Range	
1st-2nd [1]	34-37
2nd-3rd [1]	62-67
3rd-OD [1]	79-85
3rd-OD [2]	21-24
OD-3rd [2]	16-19
OD-3rd [1]	75-81
3rd-2nd [1]	57-61
2nd-1st [1]	27-30
"2" Range	
1st-2nd [1]	34-37
3rd-2nd [1]	68-75
2nd-1st [1]	27-30
"L" Range	
2nd-1st [1]	33-36

[1] – Wide open throttle.
[2] – Fully closed throttle.

T100 2.7L 2WD A-340E (1995-96) LOCK-UP SPEED SPECIFICATIONS [1]

Application	MPH
"D" Range [2]	
Lock-Up ON In OD	52-55
Lock-Up OFF In OD	44-47

[1] – Throttle valve opened 5 percent.
[2] – No lock-up in "L" or "2" range.

T100 3.4L 2WD A-340E (1995-96)
SHIFT SPEED SPECIFICATIONS

Application	MPH
"D" Range	
1st-2nd [1]	35-39
2nd-3rd [1]	67-73
3rd-OD [1]	91-96
3rd-OD [2]	27-30
OD-3rd [2]	14-17
OD-3rd [1]	86-92
3rd-2nd [1]	62-67
2nd-1st [1]	29-32
"2" Range	
1st-2nd [1]	35-39
3rd-2nd [1]	71-77
2nd-1st [1]	29-32
"L" Range	
2nd-1st [1]	32-36

[1] – Wide open throttle.
[2] – Fully closed throttle.

T100 3.4L 2WD A-340E (1995-96) LOCK-UP SPEED SPECIFICATIONS [1]

Application	MPH
"D" Range [2]	
Lock-Up ON In OD	49-52
Lock-Up OFF In OD	45-48

[1] – Throttle valve opened 5 percent.
[2] – No lock-up in "L" or "2" range.

T100 3.4L 4WD A-340F (1995-96) SHIFT SPEED SPECIFICATIONS

Application	MPH
"D" Range	
1st-2nd [1]	34-37
2nd-3rd [1]	64-69
3rd-OD [1]	86-91
3rd-OD [2]	26-29
OD-3rd [2]	13-16
OD-3rd [1]	83-88
3rd-2nd [1]	59-64
2nd-1st [1]	27-30
"2" Range	
1st-2nd [1]	34-37
3rd-2nd [1]	68-73
2nd-1st [1]	27-30
"L" Range	
2nd-1st [1]	33-36

[1] – Wide open throttle.
[2] – Fully closed throttle.

T100 3.4L 4WD A-340F (1995-96) LOCK-UP SPEED SPECIFICATIONS [1]

Application	MPH
"D" Range [2]	
Lock-Up ON In OD	47-50
Lock-Up OFF In OD	42-45

[1] – Throttle valve opened 5 percent.
[2] – No lock-up in "L" or "2" range.

STALL SPEED TEST

Test Procedure – 1) Operate engine and transmission at normal operating temperature. Install tachometer. Apply parking brake and block front wheels.

CAUTION: DO NOT maintain stall RPM for more than 5 seconds. Allow engine to idle for one minute between tests to allow fluid to cool.

2) On Pickup, Tacoma, 4Runner and T100 4WD models, place transfer case in "H2" position. On all models, start engine, apply brake pedal and place transmission in "D". Accelerate engine to full throttle and note maximum RPM obtained. Repeat test in "R". Compare reading obtained to specification. See STALL SPEED SPECIFICATIONS table.

Stall Test Results – 1) If stall speed is the same for both ranges but lower than specification, engine output may be insufficient or stator one-way clutch may not be operating properly.

NOTE: If stall RPM is more than 600 RPM below specifications, torque converter may be faulty.

2) Stall speed exceeding specification in "D" range may be caused by a slipping forward clutch, defective No. 2 or overdrive one-way clutch, low main line pressure or transfer case direct clutch slipping.
3) Stall speeds exceeding specification in "R" range may be caused by a low main line pressure, direct clutch slipping, 1st and reverse brake slipping, overdrive one-way clutch defective or transfer case direct clutch slipping.
4) Stall speeds exceeding specification in both ranges may be caused by a low main line pressure, improper fluid level, overdrive one-way clutch defective or transfer case direct clutch slipping.

STALL SPEED SPECIFICATIONS

Vehicle Application	Transmission Application	Stall RPM
Lexus		
GS300		
1995	A-340E	2300-2600
1996	A-350E	2300-2600
LS400	A-340E	2050-2350
LX450	A-343F	1800-2100
SC300	A-340E	2050-2350
SC400	A-340E	2050-2350
Toyota		
Land Cruiser	A-343F	1800-2100
Pickup		
C & C [1]	A-340E	2050-2350
Except C & C	A-340E	2300-2600
4WD 4-Cyl	A-340F	2050-2350
4WD V6	A-340H	2700-3000
Previa		
2WD	A-340E	1900-2200
AWD	A-340F	1900-2200
Supra		
Non-Turbo	A-340E	2300-2600
Turbo	A-340E	2450-2750
Tacoma & T100		
4-Cyl.	A-340E	1800-2100
V6	A-340E & A-340F	2000-2300
4Runner		
1995		
2WD V6	A-340E	2300-2600
4WD 4-Cyl.	A-340F	2050-2350
4WD V6	A-340H	2700-3000
1996		
4-Cyl	A-340E & A-340F	1850-2150
V6	A-340E & A-340F	2100-2400

[1] – Cab & Chassis.

HYDRAULIC PRESSURE TEST

NOTE: Hydraulic pressure test should be performed with transmission fluid temperature of 122-176°F (50-80°C).

Main Line Pressure – 1) Ensure transmission fluid is at normal operating temperature. Remove plug from right side of transmission case and install appropriate pressure gauge.
2) Apply parking and service brakes. Start engine. Ensure idle speed is within manufacturer's specifications. Place transmission in "D" range.
3) Check main line pressure at engine idle. See A-340 & A-350 SERIES LINE PRESSURE SPECIFICATIONS table. Repeat procedure in "R" range. Compare all readings to specification. See A-340 & A-350 SERIES LINE PRESSURE SPECIFICATIONS table.

4) Check main line pressure at full throttle (stall speed). Read highest pressure when engine reaches stall speed. See A-340 & A-350 SERIES LINE PRESSURE SPECIFICATIONS table. Repeat procedure in "R" range. Compare all readings to specification. See A-340 & A-350 SERIES LINE PRESSURE SPECIFICATIONS table.

Main Line Pressure Test Results – 1) If line pressure in all ranges exceeds specification, check for defective regulator valve, defective throttle valve, defective SLT solenoid valve (A-350E) or throttle cable out of adjustment.

2) If line pressure is below specification in all ranges, check for defective oil pump, defective regulator valve, defective SLT solenoid valve (A-350E), defective throttle valve, throttle cable out of adjustment, defective OD direct clutch or transfer case direct clutch, front drive clutch or low speed brake defective.

3) If line pressure is below specification in "D" range only, check for defective forward clutch, fluid leak in "D" range circuit, or defective OD clutch.

4) If line pressure is low in "R" range only, check for defective direct clutch, fluid leak in "R" range or defective 1st and reverse brake.

A-340 & A-350 SERIES LINE PRESSURE SPECIFICATIONS

Application & Engine RPM	"D" Range psi (kg/cm²)	"R" Range psi (kg/cm²)
Lexus		
GS300		
1995		
Idle Speed	55-64 (3.9-4.5)	89-104 (6.3-7.3)
Stall Speed	183-203	250-299
	(12.9-14.3)	(17.6-21.0)
1996		
Idle Speed	54-63 (3.8-4.4)	88-102 (6.2-7.2)
Stall Speed	175-195	240-289
	(12.3-13.7)	(16.9-20.3)
LS400		
1995		
Idle Speed	55-63 (3.9-4.4)	84-95 (5.9-6.7)
Stall Speed	181-198	238-270
	(12.7-13.9)	(16.7-19.0)
1996		
Idle Speed	61-70 (4.3-4.9)	94-105 (6.6-7.4)
Stall Speed	189-209	245-293
	(13.3-14.7)	(17.2-20.6)
LX450		
Idle Speed	61-70 (4.3-4.9)	74-88 (5.2-6.2)
Stall Speed	186-222	229-280
	(13.1-15.6)	(16.1-19.7)
SC300 & SC400 (1995)		
Idle Speed	55-64 (3.9-4.5)	92-104 (6.5-7.3)
Stall Speed	183-203	250-299
	(12.9-14.3)	(17.6-21.0)
SC400 (1996)		
Idle Speed	61-70 (4.3-4.9)	91-105 (6.4-7.4)
Stall Speed	189-209	245-293
	(13.3-14.7)	(17.2-20.6)
Toyota		
Land Cruiser		
1995		
Idle Speed	61-70 (4.3-4.9)	74-88 (5.2-6.2)
Stall Speed	135-171	188-238
	(9.5-12.0)	(13.2-16.7)
1996		
Idle Speed	61-70 (4.3-4.9)	74-88 (5.2-6.2)
Stall Speed	186-222	229-280
	(13.1-15.6)	(16.1-19.7)

A-340 & A-350 SERIES LINE PRESSURE SPECIFICATIONS (Cont.)

Application & Engine RPM	"D" Range psi (kg/cm²)	"R" Range psi (kg/cm²)
Toyota		
Pickup		
A-340E		
Idle Speed	53-61 (3.7-4.3)	71-85 (5.0-6.0)
Stall Speed	135-171	188-238
	(9.5-12.0)	(13.2-16.7)
A-340F		
Idle Speed	61-70 (4.3-4.9)	74-88 (5.2-6.2)
Stall Speed	162-198	199-249
	(11.4-13.9)	(14.0-17.5)
A-340H		
Idle Speed	61-70 (4.3-4.9)	75-90 (5.2-6.3)
Stall Speed	162-198	199-249
	(11.4-13.9)	(14.0-17.5)
Previa (A-340E & A-340F)		
Idle Speed	53-61 (3.7-4.3)	88-101 (6.2-7.1)
Stall Speed	131-166	208-282
	(9.2-11.7)	(14.6-19.8)
Supra		
Non-Turbo		
Idle Speed	53-61 (3.7-4.3)	73-87 (5.1-6.1)
Stall Speed	131-166	179-230
	(9.2-11.7)	(12.6-16.2)
Turbo		
Idle Speed	68-77 (4.8-5.4)	100-114 (7.0-8.0)
Stall Speed	193-213	246-294
	(13.6-15.0)	(17.3-20.7)
Tacoma & T100		
4-Cyl. (A-340E)		
Idle Speed	53-61 (3.7-4.3)	71-85 (5.0-6.0)
Stall Speed	135-171	188-238
	(9.5-12.0)	(13.2-16.7)
V6 (A-340E & A-340F)		
Idle Speed	53-61 (3.7-4.3)	88-101 (6.2-7.1)
Stall Speed	131-166	208-282
	(9.2-11.7)	(14.6-19.8)
4Runner		
1995		
A-340E & A-340F		
Idle Speed	53-61 (3.7-4.3)	71-85 (5.0-6.0)
Stall Speed	135-171	188-238
	(9.5-12.0)	(13.2-16.7)
A-340H		
Idle Speed	61-70 (4.3-4.9)	75-90 (5.2-6.3)
Stall Speed	162-198	199-249
	(11.4-13.9)	(14.0-17.5)
1996		
4-Cyl. (A-340E & A-340F)		
Idle Speed	53-61 (3.7-4.3)	88-102 (6.2-7.2)
Stall Speed	135-171	228-277
	(9.5-12.0)	(16.0-19.5)
V6 (A-340E & A-340F)		
Idle Speed	53-61 (3.7-4.3)	88-101 (6.2-7.1)
Stall Speed	131-166	208-282
	(9.2-11.7)	(14.6-19.8)

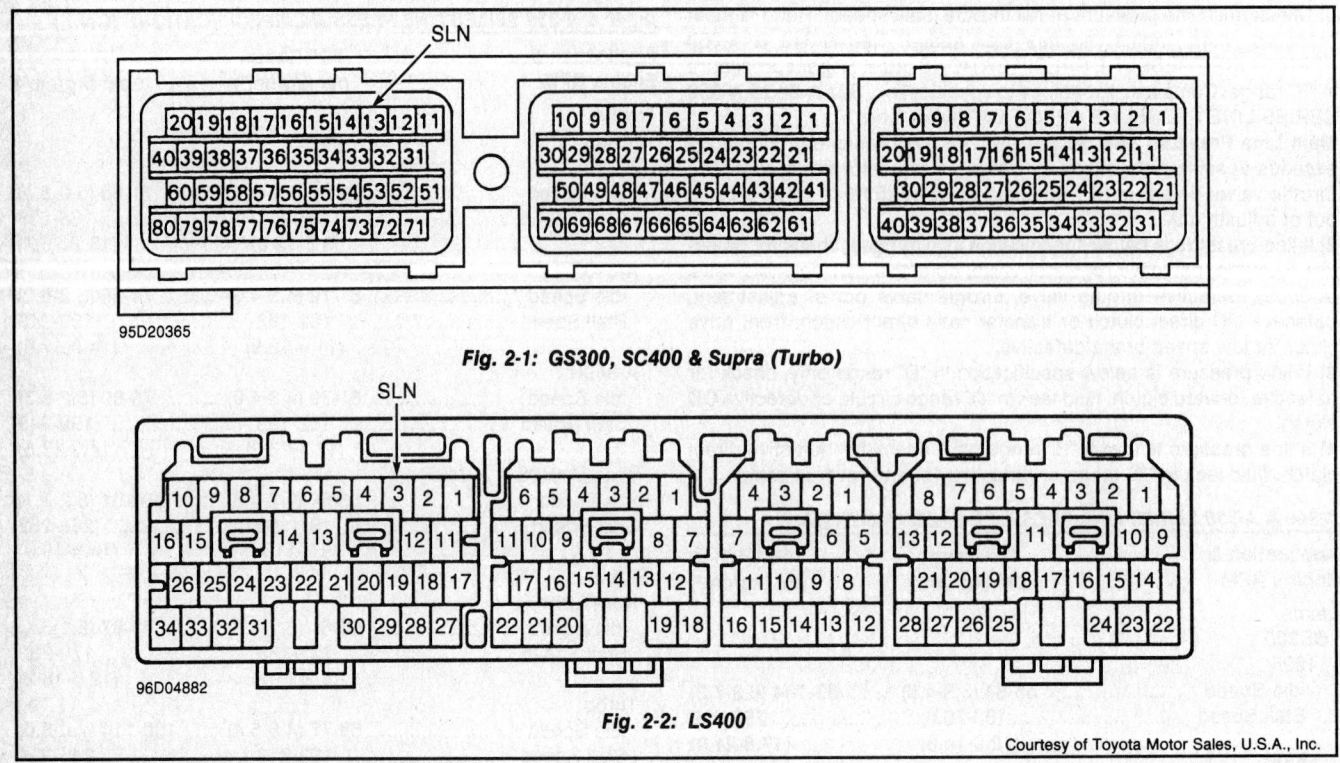

SLN

Fig. 2-1: GS300, SC400 & Supra (Turbo)

95D20365

SLN

Fig. 2-2: LS400

96D04882

Courtesy of Toyota Motor Sales, U.S.A., Inc.

Fig. 2: Identifying ECT ECU "SLN" Terminal

ACCUMULATOR BACKPRESSURE TEST (LEXUS: GS300, LS400 & SC400, TOYOTA: SUPRA TURBO)

NOTE: Perform test at normal operating fluid temperature 122-176°F (50-80°C). Ensure oil pressure gauge hose does not come in contact with exhaust pipe.

Line Pressure Test – 1) Move right side heat insulator aside (if applicable). Remove plug from transmission case and install appropriate pressure gauge.
2) Remove passenger side No. 2 undercover to gain access to ECT ECU. Backprobe ECT ECU harness connector. Connect a jumper lead with an 8 watt in-line bulb to terminal SLN of harness connector. *See Fig. 2.* DO NOT ground jumper at this time.
3) Apply parking brake. Block wheels. Start engine. Ensure idle speed is within manufacturer's specification. Place transmission in "D" range.
4) Measure accumulator backpressure. See ACCUMULATOR BACK-PRESSURE SPECIFICATIONS table. Repeat procedure with jumper lead connected to ground. Compare all readings to specification.

ACCUMULATOR BACKPRESSURE SPECIFICATIONS

Application	Backpressure psi (kg/cm2)
"D" Range (Idle)	
GS300, SC400 & Supra (Turbo)	
Not Grounded [1]	26-37 (1.8-2.6)
Grounded [1]	0 (0)
LS400	
Not Grounded [1]	0-36 (0-2.5)
Grounded [1]	0 (0)
[1] – Condition of ECT ECU terminal SLN.	

Line Pressure Test Results – If accumulator backpressure is not as specified when terminal SLN is not grounded, check for throttle cable out of adjustment (if applicable), throttle valve defective, solenoid modulator valve defective, SLN solenoid valve defective, SLT solenoid valve defective (A-350E) or accumulator control valve defective. If accumulator backpressure does not become zero when terminal SLN is grounded, check for defective SLN solenoid valve.

ON-VEHICLE SERVICE

DRIVE AXLE SHAFTS

See appropriate article in AXLE SHAFTS & TRANSFER CASES section.

TRANSMISSION VALVE BODY

Removal – 1) Drain fluid. Remove oil pan, filler tube, gasket, oil filter and magnets from oil pan. Disconnect connectors from each solenoid. Remove solenoid wiring and stopper plate.
2) Note location of oil tubes. Using screwdrivers, pry at both ends of oil tubes and remove oil tubes. Remove transmission fluid temperature sensor (if applicable). Remove valve body bolts. Note location and bolt length. *See Fig. 3.*
3) Lower valve body slightly and remove accumulator piston springs. Note location of springs. Disconnect throttle cable from valve body cam. Remove valve body. Use care not to lose check ball and spring located above valve body (if equipped).

NOTE: During valve body removal, note location of accumulator piston springs, oil tubes, bolt length and location, check ball and spring (if equipped). Component locations should be marked for reassembly reference.

Installation – 1) To install, reverse removal procedure. Ensure check ball and spring are installed above valve body (if equipped). Ensure manual shift lever in transmission case aligns with manual valve of valve body.
2) Install accumulator piston springs and spacers in original location. See TRANSMISSION REASSEMBLY. Proper length bolts must be installed in designated areas. *See Fig. 3.* Use NEW "O" ring on solenoid, oil filter and gasket if necessary. Ensure oil tubes do not contact oil pan. Install magnets in oil pan. Install pan with NEW gasket. Fill fluid to proper level.

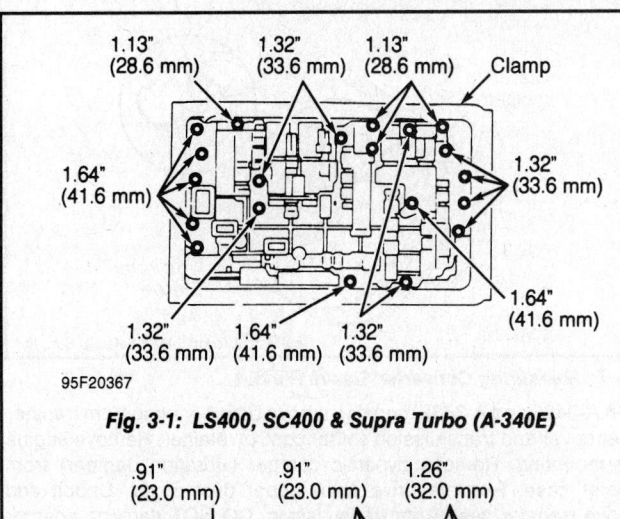

95F20367

Fig. 3-1: LS400, SC400 & Supra Turbo (A-340E)

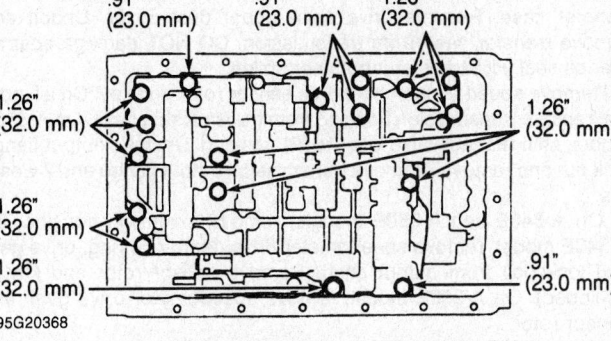

95G20368

Fig. 3-2: All Other A-340 Series Models

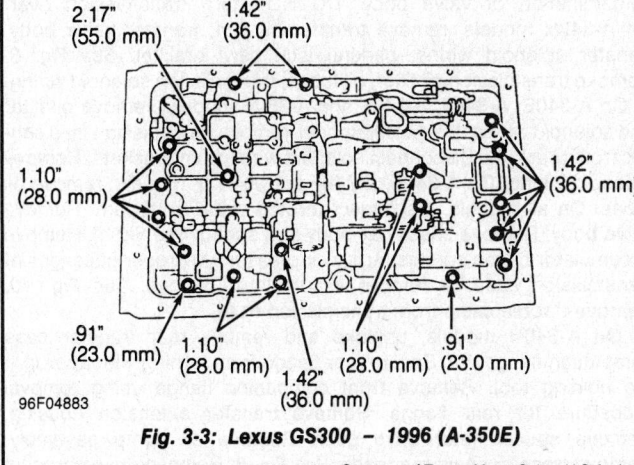

96F04883

Fig. 3-3: Lexus GS300 – 1996 (A-350E)

Courtesy of Toyota Motor Sales, U.S.A., Inc.

Fig. 3: Identifying Valve Body Mounting Bolts

TRANSFER CASE VALVE BODY (A-340H)

Removal & Installation – 1) Drain fluid. Support transmission with jack. Remove rear support crossmember from body and transfer case bracket. Remove transfer case bracket from transfer case.

2) Remove oil pan. Remove magnets from oil pan. Disconnect No. 4 solenoid connector and transfer pressure switch. Remove valve body. Remove solenoid wiring stopper plate. Remove solenoid wiring from transfer case. Note bolt location and length.

3) To install, reverse removal procedures. Ensure manual shift lever in case aligns with manual valve of valve body. Proper length bolts must be installed. Install oil pan with NEW gasket. Fill to proper fluid level.

PARKING LOCK PAWL

Removal & Installation – 1) Remove valve body on A-340E, A-340F and A-343F models or transfer case valve body on A-340H model. On all models, remove parking lock pawl bracket. Disconnect parking lock rod from manual valve lever on A-340E and A-340F. Remove transfer manual valve lever and shaft on A-340H model.

2) On all models, note location of shaft spring. Remove shaft spring from shaft. Remove shaft and parking lock pawl. Remove "E" ring from shaft. To install, reverse removal procedure.

EXTENSION HOUSING & SENSOR ROTOR (A-340E)

Removal – 1) Raise and support vehicle. Place reference marks on drive shaft and companion flange. Remove drive shaft and center bearing assembly.

2) Remove front exhaust pipe and converter. Disconnect speedometer cable. Remove speedometer driven gear and speed sensor from extension housing.

3) Using jack, support transmission. Remove ground cable and rear support member from extension housing. Remove extension housing bolts. Note bolt length and location. Remove extension housing.

4) If sensor rotor is to be replaced, remove snap ring, speedometer drive gear and lock ball from output shaft. Use care not to lose lock ball when removing drive gear. Remove sensor rotor.

Cleaning & Inspection – Clean components with solvent. Dry with compressed air. Inspect components for damage. Measure inside diameter of extension housing bushing bore. Replace extension housing if inside diameter exceeds 1.578" (40.09 mm).

Installation – Install sensor rotor on output shaft, ensuring key is installed in groove. Install extension housing using a NEW housing gasket. Apply sealant to extension housing bolt threads prior to installation. Shorter mounting bolts go on bottom of extension housing. To complete installation, reverse removal procedure.

THROTTLE CABLE

Removal – Disconnect throttle cable from cam. Remove transmission valve body. See TRANSMISSION VALVE BODY. Pull out throttle cable.

Installation – 1) Install throttle cable in transmission case. Ensure cable is fully seated. Install valve body. Connect throttle cable to cam. New cables do not have cable stopper installed. To make adjustment possible, stake stopper as described.

2) Pull inner cable lightly until a slight resistance is felt. Stake stopper .031-.059" (.80-1.50 mm) from end of outer cable. See Fig. 4. Connect throttle cable on throttle linkage. Adjust throttle cable. See appropriate article in TRANSMISSION SERVICING section. Test drive vehicle.

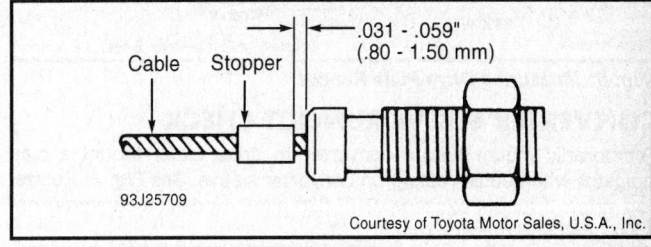

93J25709

Courtesy of Toyota Motor Sales, U.S.A., Inc.

Fig. 4: Staking Throttle Cable Stopper

REMOVAL & INSTALLATION

For transmission removal procedure, see appropriate AUTOMATIC TRANSMISSION REMOVAL article in TRANSMISSION SERVICING section.

TORQUE CONVERTER

NOTE: Torque converter is a sealed unit and is serviced as complete assembly. Perform following tests to check for defective converter. Torque converter and transmission cooler must be thoroughly cleaned and flushed if transmission is contaminated.

ONE-WAY CLUTCH CHECK

1) Install turner and stopper of One-Way Clutch Tester (09350-30020) in torque converter. *See Fig. 5.* Turner fits in inner race of one-way clutch. Stopper fits in notch of converter hub and outer race of one-way clutch.

2) Clutch should lock when turned counterclockwise, but should turn freely when rotated clockwise. Torque required to turn clutch clockwise should be less than 22 INCH lbs. (2.5 N.m). If necessary, clean converter and retest clutch. Replace converter if clutch still fails test.

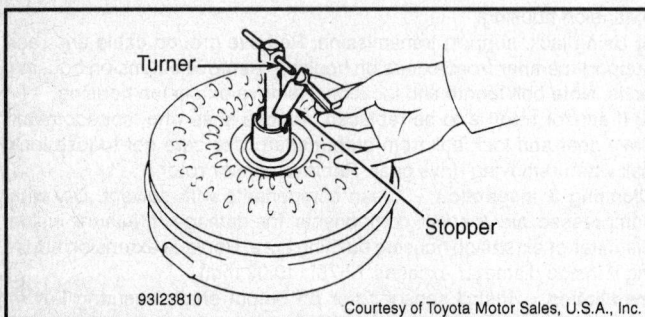

93I23810   Courtesy of Toyota Motor Sales, U.S.A., Inc.

Fig. 5: Checking Condition Of One-Way Clutch

DRIVE PLATE (FLYWHEEL) RUNOUT CHECK

Using dial indicator, measure drive plate runout. *See Fig. 6.* If runout exceeds .008" (.20 mm), or if ring gear is damaged, replace drive plate. If installing a new drive plate, note position of spacers.

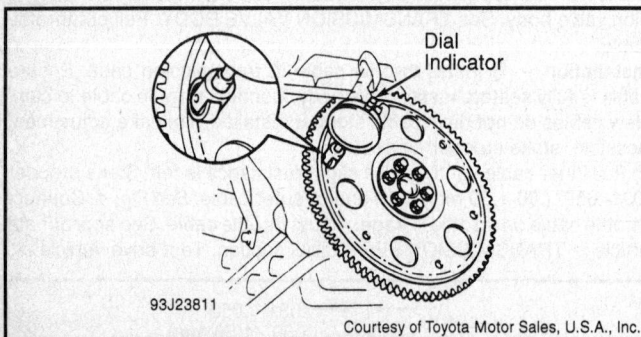

93J23811   Courtesy of Toyota Motor Sales, U.S.A., Inc.

Fig. 6: Measuring Drive Plate Runout

CONVERTER SLEEVE RUNOUT CHECK

Temporarily mount torque converter to drive plate. Mount a dial indicator with needle resting on converter sleeve. *See Fig. 7.* Rotate converter. If runout exceeds .012" (.30 mm), reposition converter on drive plate and recheck runout.

TRANSMISSION DISASSEMBLY

1) Remove wire harness and throttle cable clamp. Remove transmission shaft lever and park/neutral position switch. Remove cooler line side unions. On A-340E, A-340F, A-340H and A-350E models, remove speedometer driven gear or No. 1 and No. 2 speed sensors (if equipped) from extension housing. On A-350E model, remove OD direct clutch speed sensor from left forward side of transmission case.

2) On A-343F model, remove transmission fluid temperature sensor from right side of transmission case. On A-340F and A-340H models, remove transmission and transfer fluid temperature sensors. Remove transfer oil cooler tubes and transfer cooler line side unions. Remove transfer control shaft lever. Remove transfer position switch.

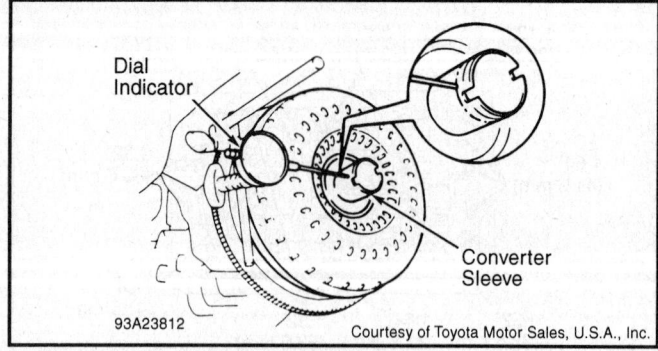

93A23812   Courtesy of Toyota Motor Sales, U.S.A., Inc.

Fig. 7: Measuring Converter Sleeve Runout

3) On A-340F and A-343F models, remove breather hose from transfer upper cover and transmission shifter control retainer. Remove engine rear mounting. Remove dynamic damper (vibration damper) from transfer case. Remove drive shaft upper dust cover. Unbolt and remove transfer case from transmission. DO NOT damage adapter rear oil seal with transfer input gear spline.

4) Remove speed sensor snap ring, sensor rotor and key. On all models, remove transmission housing from transmission case. On A-350E model, shift manual valve lever to "P" position. Unstake output flange lock nut and remove. Remove transmission output flange and 2 washers.

5) On A-340E and A-350E models, remove extension housing. On A-340E model, remove speedometer drive gear snap ring, drive gear and lock ball from output shaft. Remove sensor rotor and key (if equipped). On A-350E model, remove speedometer drive gear with sensor rotor.

6) On A-340F and A-343F models, remove transfer case from transmission. On all models, remove transmission oil pan. To prevent contamination of valve body, DO NOT turn transmission over. On A-340H models, remove transfer oil pan, transfer valve body, transfer solenoid wiring, parking lock pawl bracket. *See Fig. 8.* Remove transmission oil filter, oil tubes, transmission solenoid wiring.

7) On A-340E, A-340F, A-343F and A-350E models, remove oil filter and solenoid wiring. On A-350E model, remove transmission fluid sensor from brackets. Disconnect solenoid wires from brackets. Remove solenoid wiring. On A-340E, A-340F and A-343F models, remove oil tubes. On all models, disconnect throttle cable from cam. Remove valve body. Remove check ball body and spring. *See Fig. 9.* Remove accumulator piston springs. Apply air pressure to proper passages of transmission case to remove accumulator pistons. *See Fig. 10.* Remove throttle cable from transmission case.

8) On A-340H models, unstake and remove rear transfer case companion flange nut. Secure rear flange from turning with appropriate holding tool. Remove front companion flange using removal procedure for rear flange. Remove transfer extension housing. Remove speedometer drive gear. Remove oil pump assembly. Remove transfer chain rear case. *See Fig. 8.* Remove drive sprocket snap ring. Remove drive chain with drive sprocket and driven shaft. Remove transfer chain oil receiver. Remove transfer chain front case with front output shaft. Remove front output shaft from transfer chain front case.

9) Remove transfer front drive clutch snap ring and remove clutch. Remove output shaft snap ring. Check pack clearance of transfer low speed brake. Using feeler gauge, measure clearance between snap ring and flange. *See Fig. 11.* Clearance should be .036-.083" (.91-2.10 mm). If clearance is not within specifications, inspect discs. Remove transfer center support and transfer low speed brake. Remove front flange, thrust bearing race and thrust bearing. Remove sun gear. Remove bearing and race from transfer direct clutch. Remove transfer direct clutch snap ring and direct clutch. Remove front support. Remove bearing and race from front support. Unbolt and remove transfer case. Remove speed sensor and key.

NOTE: For additional information on A-340H transfer case, see appropriate transfer case article in AXLE SHAFTS & TRANSFER CASES section.

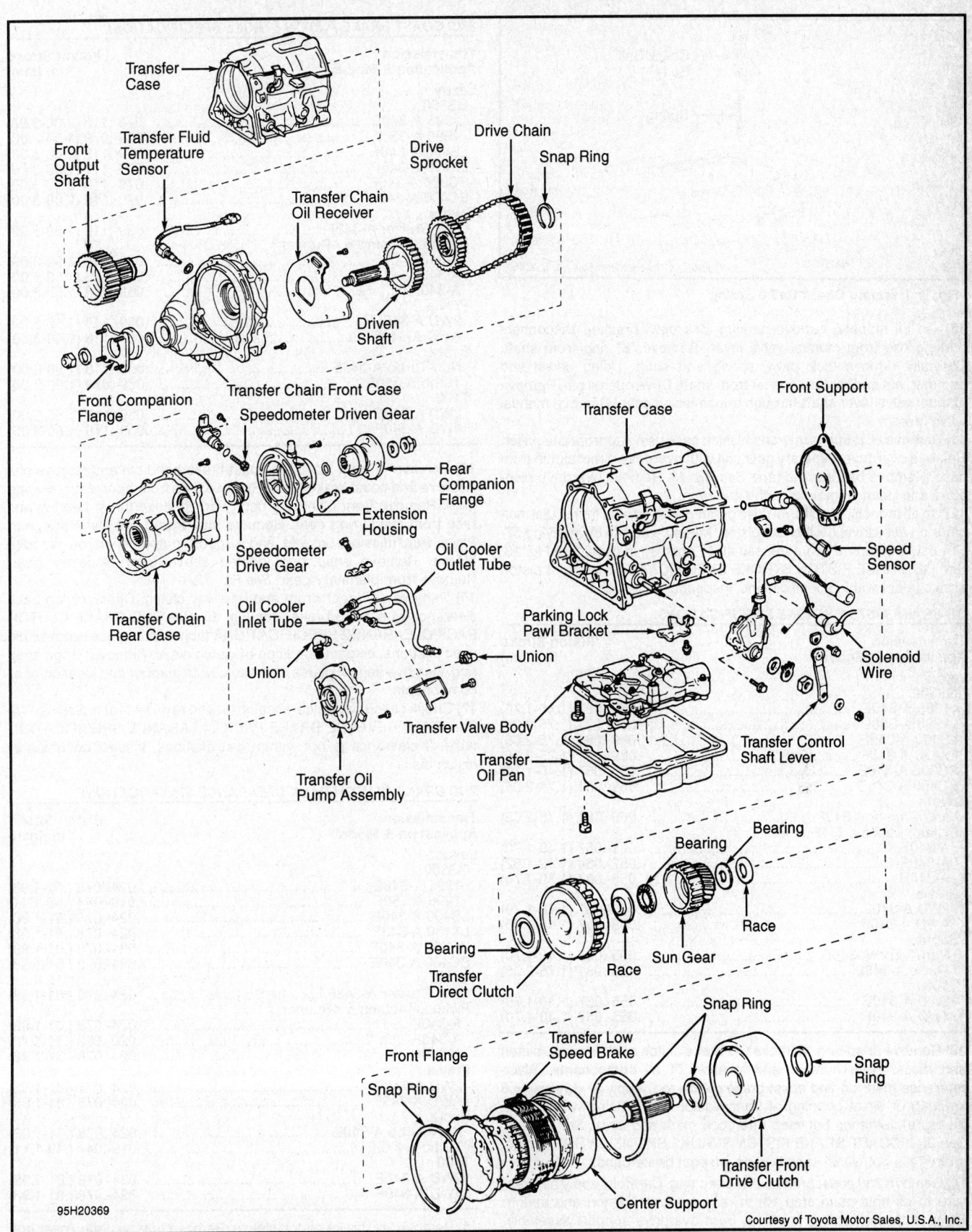

95H20369

Courtesy of Toyota Motor Sales, U.S.A., Inc.

Fig. 8: Exploded View Of A-340H Transfer Case

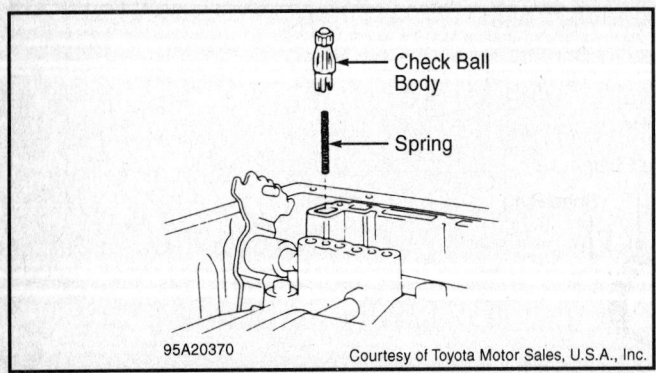

95A20370   Courtesy of Toyota Motor Sales, U.S.A., Inc.

Fig. 9: Locating Check Ball & Spring

10) On all models, remove parking lock pawl bracket. Disconnect parking rod from manual valve lever. Remove "E" ring from shaft. Carefully remove lock pawl, spring and shaft. Using chisel and hammer, cut and remove spacer from shaft. Drive out roll pin. Remove manual valve lever shaft through transmission case. Remove manual valve lever.

11) Remove oil pump from transmission case using appropriate puller. Remove overdrive planetary gear unit with overdrive direct clutch from case. Remove bearing and race. *See Fig. 12.* Remove overdrive planetary ring gear. Remove bearing and race.

12) On all models, check overdrive brake piston stroke. Install dial indicator on overdrive, (OD) brake piston. Measure stroke by applying 57-114 psi (4-8 kg/cm2) compressed air to opening in case. *See Fig. 13.* See OD BRAKE PISTON STROKE SPECIFICATIONS table. If piston stroke is not within specifications, inspect clutch discs.

OD BRAKE PISTON STROKE SPECIFICATIONS

Transmission Application & Model	Piston Stroke In. (mm)
Lexus	
GS300	
1995 A-340E	.055-.067 (1.40-1.70)
1996 A-350E	.069-.081 (1.75-2.05)
LS400 A-340E	.069-.081 (1.75-2.05)
LX450 A-343F	.069-.081 (1.75-2.05)
SC300 A-340E	.055-.067 (1.40-1.70)
SC400 A-340E	.069-.081 (1.75-2.05)
Toyota	
Land Cruiser A-343F	.069-.081 (1.75-2.05)
Pickup, Tacoma & 4Runner	
A-340E	.055-.067 (1.40-1.70)
A-340F	.052-.064 (1.32-1.62)
A-340H	.055-.067 (1.40-1.70)
Previa	
2WD A-340E	.055-.067 (1.40-1.70)
AWD A-340F	.055-.067 (1.40-1.70)
Supra	
Non-Turbo A-340E	.055-.067 (1.40-1.70)
Turbo A-340E	.069-.081 (1.75-2.05)
T100	
2WD A-340E	.055-.067 (1.40-1.70)
4WD A-340F	.055-.067 (1.40-1.70)

13) Remove snap ring. Remove OD brake clutch pack flanges, plates and discs. Note number and location of all components. Place reference mark on 2nd coast brake piston rod. Apply 57-114 psi (4.8 kg/cm2) of air at opening of transmission case. Using wire gauge, measure clearance between reference mark and case. *See Fig. 14.* See 2ND COAST BRAKE PISTON STROKE SPECIFICATIONS table. If stroke is not within specification, inspect brake band.

14) Remove 2nd coast brake cover snap ring. Carefully apply air pressure to oil hole as in step **13)** to remove cover, piston and spring. Remove thrust bearing and race from overdrive support assembly. Remove overdrive support-to-case bolts. Remove snap ring. Using appropriate puller, remove overdrive support assembly. Remove race from rear of support assembly. Remove direct clutch with forward clutch from case. Remove bearings and race from clutch assembly.

2ND COAST BRAKE PISTON STROKE SPECIFICATIONS

Transmission Application & Model	Piston Stroke In. (mm)
Lexus	
GS300	
1995 A-340E	.079-.118 (2.00-3.00)
1996 A-350E	.039-.079 (1.00-2.00)
LS400 A-340E	.079-.118 (2.00-3.00)
LX450 A-343F	.059-.118 (1.50-3.00)
SC300 A-340E	.079-.118 (2.00-3.00)
SC400 A-340E	.079-.118 (2.00-3.00)
Toyota	
Land Cruiser A-343F	.059-.118 (1.50-3.00)
Pickup, Tacoma & 4Runner	
A-340E	.059-.118 (1.50-3.00)
A-340F	.059-.118 (1.50-3.00)
A-340H	.059-.118 (1.50-3.00)
Previa	
2WD A-340E	.059-.118 (1.50-3.00)
AWD A-340F	.059-.118 (1.50-3.00)
Supra	
Non-Turbo A-340E	.059-.118 (1.50-3.00)
Turbo A-340E	.039-.079 (1.00-2.00)
T100	
2WD A-340E	.059-.118 (1.50-3.00)
4WD A-340F	.059-.118 (1.50-3.00)

15) Remove "E" ring from 2nd coast brake band pin and remove pin. Remove 2nd coast brake band. Remove race from front planetary ring gear. Remove front planetary ring gear. Remove thrust bearing and race from inside ring gear. Remove race from front planetary gear. Place transmission on end and support output shaft on wooden blocks. Remove snap ring located above front planetary gear. Remove front planetary gear. *See Fig. 12.*

16) Remove sun gear drum and one-way clutch. Check clutch pack clearance of second brake. *See Fig. 15.* See 2ND BRAKE CLUTCH PACK CLEARANCE SPECIFICATIONS table. If clearance is not within specifications, inspect condition of clutch discs. Remove flange snap ring. Remove flange, plates and discs. Note number and location of all components.

17) Check clutch pack clearance of 1st and reverse brake. *See Fig. 15.* See 1ST & REVERSE BRAKE PACK CLEARANCE SPECIFICATION table. If clearance is not within specifications, inspect condition of clutch discs.

2ND BRAKE CLUTCH PACK CLEARANCE SPECIFICATIONS

Transmission Application & Model	Piston Stroke In. (mm)
Lexus	
GS300	
1995 A-340E	.024-.078 (.61-1.98)
1996 A-350E	.019-.044 (.49-1.11)
LS400 A-340E	.024-.078 (.61-1.98)
LX450 A-343F	.024-.078 (.61-1.98)
SC300 A-340E	.024-.078 (.61-1.98)
SC400 A-340E	.024-.078 (.61-1.98)
Toyota	
Land Cruiser A-343F	.024-.078 (.61-1.98)
Pickup, Tacoma & 4Runner	
A-340E	.024-.078 (.61-1.98)
A-340F	.020-.069 (.50-1.76)
A-340H	.024-.078 (.61-1.98)
Previa	
2WD A-340E	.024-.078 (.61-1.98)
AWD A-340F	.024-.078 (.61-1.98)
Supra	
Non-Turbo A-340E	.024-.078 (.61-1.98)
Turbo A-340E	.019-.044 (.49-1.11)
T100	
2WD A-340E	.024-.078 (.61-1.98)
4WD A-340F	.024-.078 (.61-1.98)

18) Remove 2nd brake piston sleeve. Remove rear planetary gear unit snap ring. Remove rear planetary gear, 2nd brake drum, 1st and reverse brake pack and output shaft as an assembly. Remove thrust bearing and race from case. Remove 2nd brake drum assembly. *See Fig. 12.*

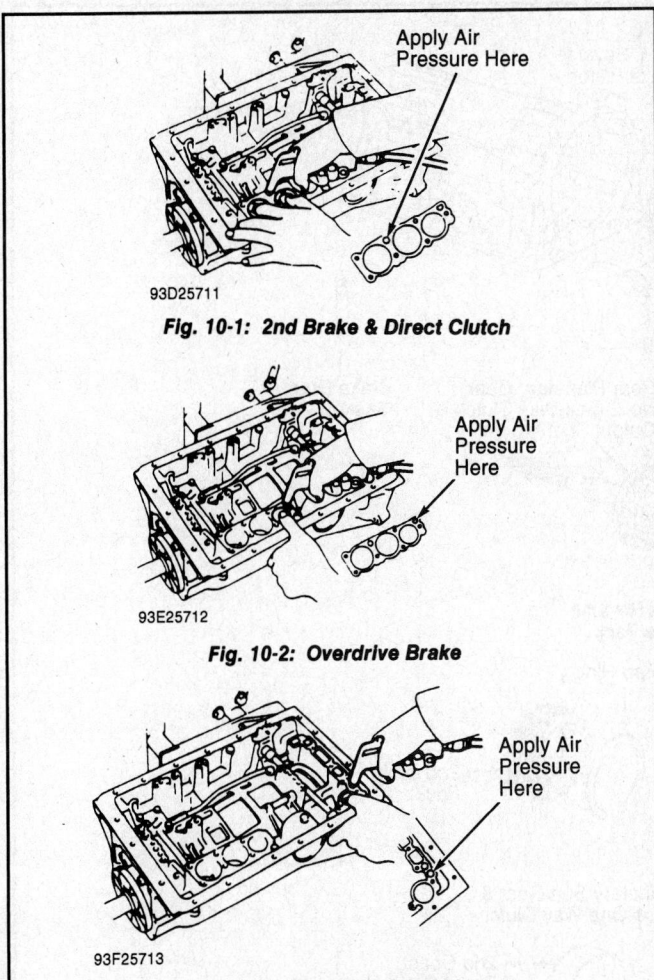

93D25711

Fig. 10-1: 2nd Brake & Direct Clutch

Apply Air Pressure Here

93E25712

Fig. 10-2: Overdrive Brake

Apply Air Pressure Here

93F25713

Fig. 10-3: Overdrive Direct Clutch

Courtesy of Toyota Motor Sales, U.S.A., Inc.

Fig. 10: Removing Accumulator Pistons & Springs

1ST & REVERSE BRAKE PACK CLEARANCE SPECIFICATION

Application	Clearance – In. (mm)
Lexus	
GS300	
1995 A-340E	.024-.044 (.61-1.12)
1996 A-350E	.024-.035 (.61-.90)
LS400 A-340E	.028-.039 (.70-1.00)
LX450 A-343F	.028-.048 (.70-1.22)
SC300 A-340E	.024-.044 (.61-1.12)
SC400 A-340E	.028-.039 (.71-1.00)
Toyota	
Land Cruiser A-343F	.028-.048 (.70-1.22)
Pickup, Tacoma & 4Runner	
A-340E	.024-.044 (.61-1.12)
A-340F	.020-.040 (.50-1.02)
A-340H	.024-.052 (.61-1.32)
Previa	
2WD A-340E	.024-.044 (.61-1.12)
AWD A-340F	.024-.044 (.61-1.12)
Supra	
Non-Turbo A-340E	.024-.044 (.61-1.12)
Turbo A-340E	.028-.039 (.70-1.00)
T100	
2WD A-340E	.024-.044 (.61-1.12)
4WD A-340F	.024-.044 (.61-1.12)

19) Remove 1st and reverse brake cushion plate, flange, plates and discs. Note number and location of all components. Remove leaf spring from case. Remove brake drum gasket from case.

20) Ensure 1st and reverse brake pistons move smoothly when applying compressed air into case. See Fig. 16. Disassemble 1st and reverse brake piston. Install appropriate compressor on spring retainer and compress return spring. See Fig. 17. Remove snap ring. Remove piston return spring. Using compressed air, remove 1st and reverse brake piston No. 2. See Fig. 16.

21) Insert Sleeve Remover (09350-07080) behind reaction sleeve. Remove reaction sleeve from case. See Fig. 18. Insert Piston Remover (09350-07090) behind No. 1 brake piston. Remove No. 1 brake piston from case. On A-340E and A-340H models, remove manual valve lever spacer from shaft. Remove pin. Pull shaft out through case and remove lever. Remove 2 oil seals.

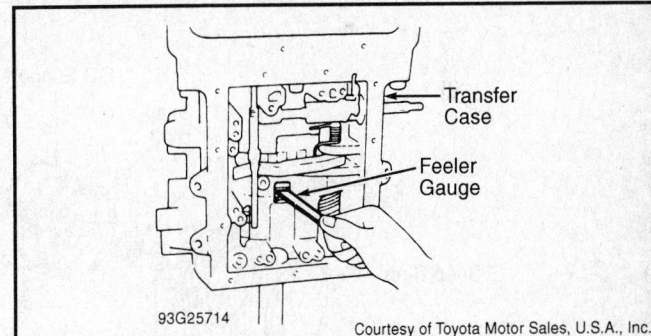

Transfer Case

Feeler Gauge

93G25714

Courtesy of Toyota Motor Sales, U.S.A., Inc.

Fig. 11: Measuring Transfer Low Speed Brake Clearance

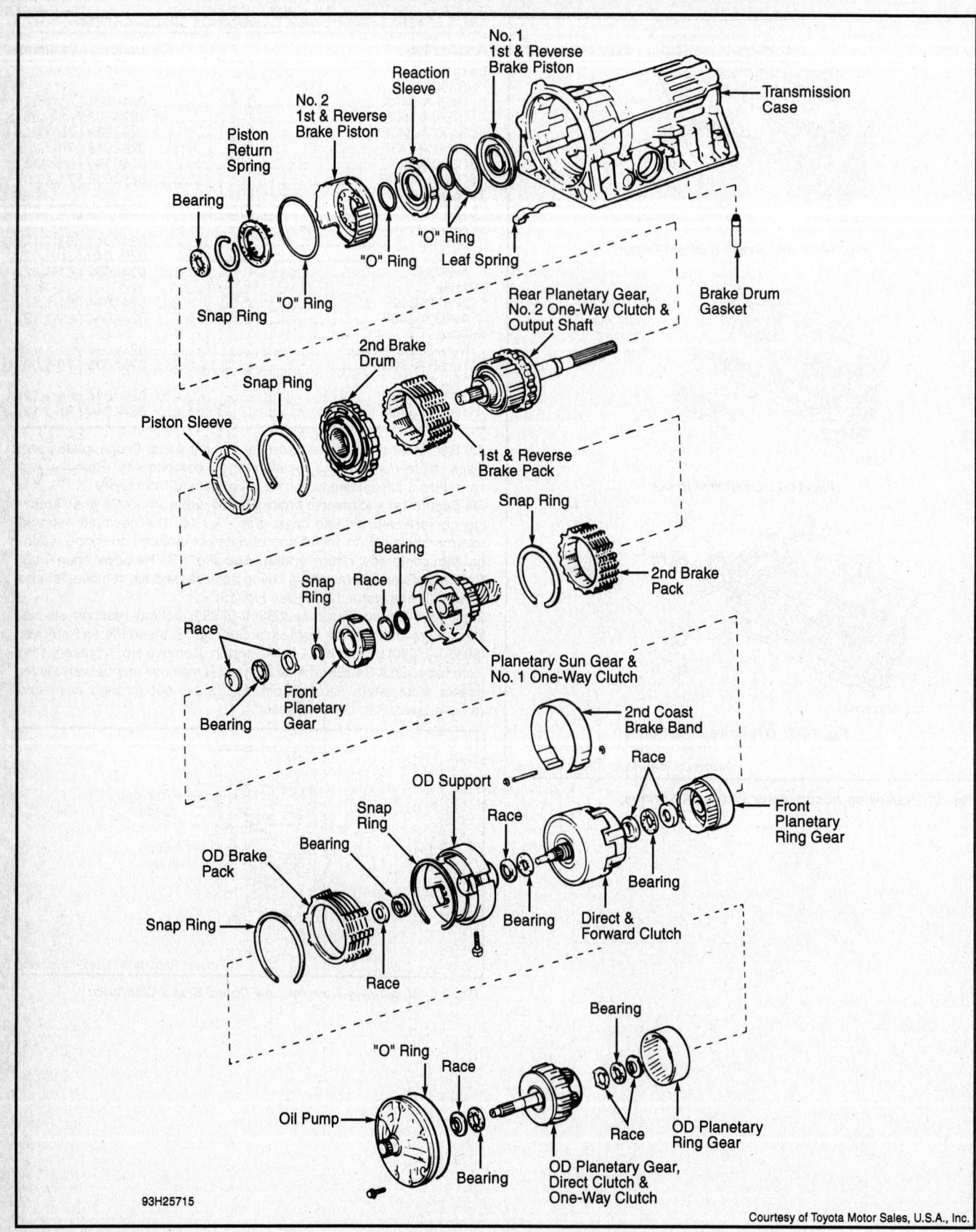

93H25715

Courtesy of Toyota Motor Sales, U.S.A., Inc.

Fig. 12: Exploded View Of A-340E, A-340F, A-343F & A-340H Internal Components (A-350E Is Similar)

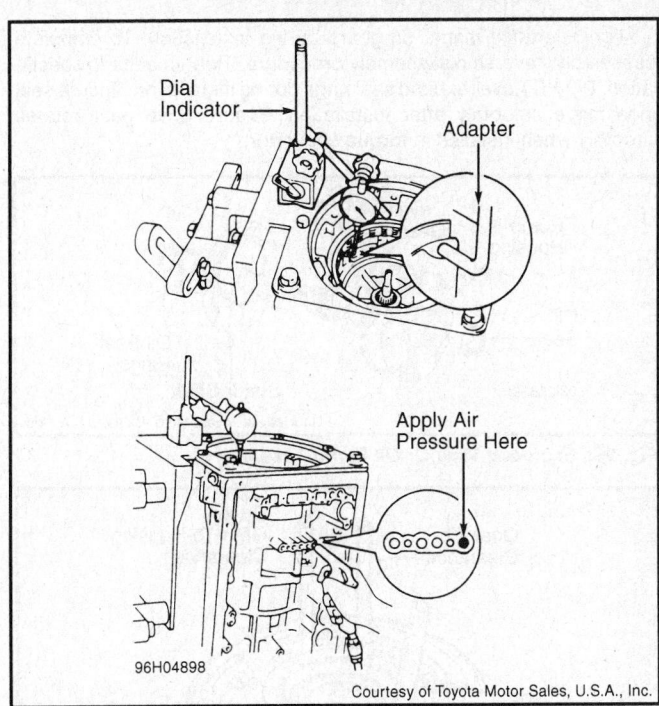

Fig. 13: Measuring Overdrive Brake Piston Stroke

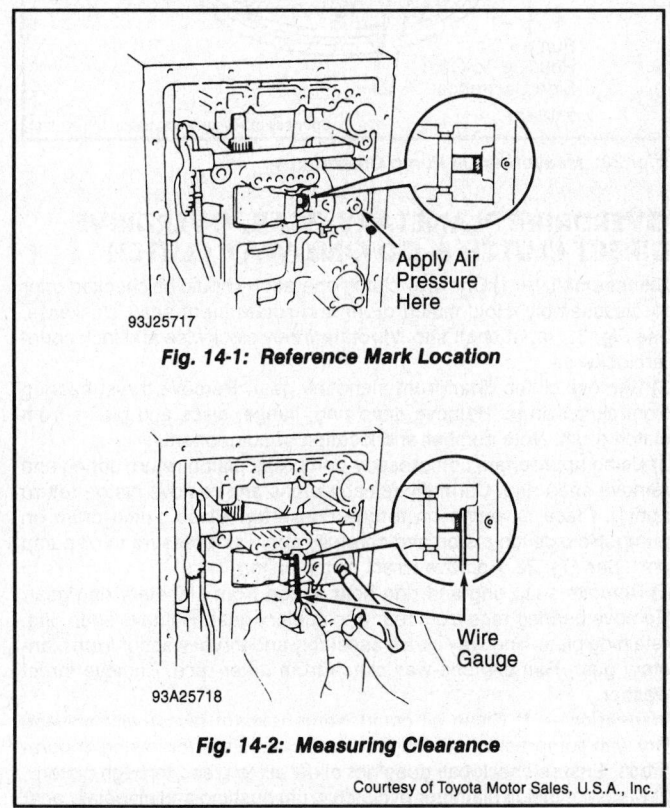

Fig. 14-1: Reference Mark Location

Fig. 14-2: Measuring Clearance

Fig. 14: Measuring 2nd Coast Brake Piston Stroke

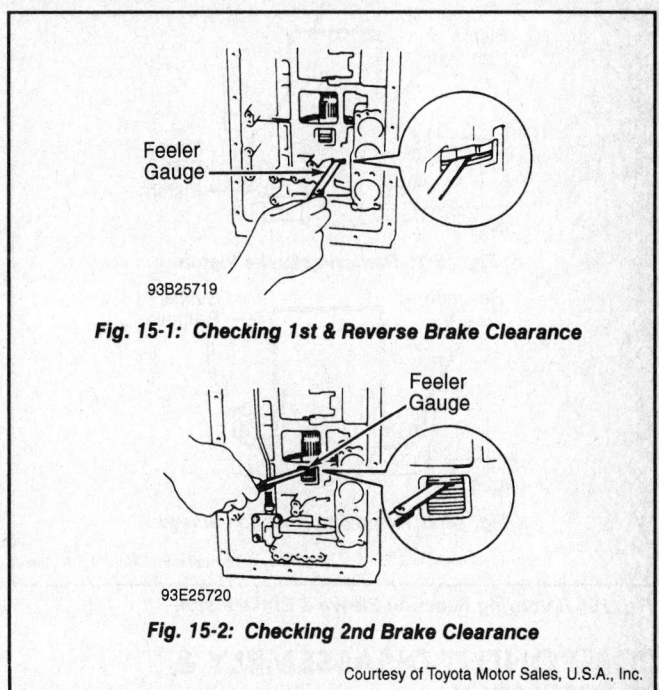

Fig. 15-1: Checking 1st & Reverse Brake Clearance

Fig. 15-2: Checking 2nd Brake Clearance

Fig. 15: Measuring Brake Clearance

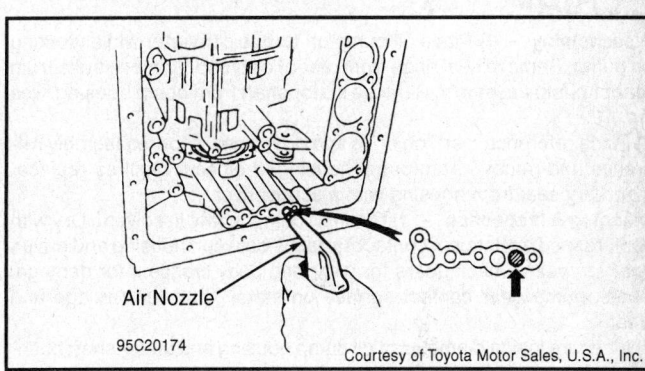

Fig. 16: Checking 1st & Reverse Brake Piston Travel

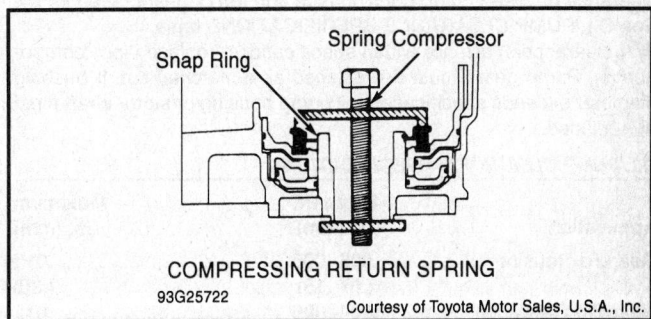

COMPRESSING RETURN SPRING

Fig. 17: Compressing 1st & Reverse Brake Return Spring

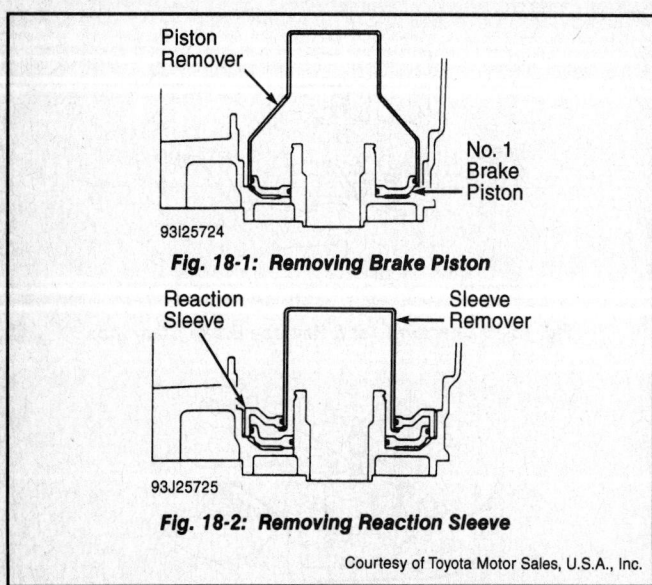

Fig. 18-1: Removing Brake Piston

Fig. 18-2: Removing Reaction Sleeve

Courtesy of Toyota Motor Sales, U.S.A., Inc.

Fig. 18: Removing Reaction Sleeve & Brake Piston

COMPONENT DISASSEMBLY & REASSEMBLY

OIL PUMP

Disassembly – 1) Place oil pump on torque converter while working on pump. Remove seal rings from rear of oil pump. Remove bolts from rear of pump assembly. Remove stator shaft from pump housing. See Fig. 19.

2) Place reference mark on drive and driven gears for reassembly reference and remove from pump housing. If oil seal requires replacement, pry seal from housing with a screwdriver.

Cleaning & Inspection – 1) Clean all components in solvent. Dry with compressed air. Inspect contact surfaces between housing and driven gear for wear. Check gears for wear and body crescent for damage. Check pump gear contact surface on stator shaft for damage and wear.

2) Measure inside diameter of oil pump housing and stator shaft bushings. Measure driven gear-to-housing clearance and gear tip clearance. Using feeler gauge and straightedge, measure gear side clearance between pump housing face and top of gears. See Fig. 20. See OIL PUMP CLEARANCE SPECIFICATIONS table.

3) If clearance(s) are not within specifications, replace worn component(s). Pump gears must be replaced as a matched set. If bushing diameter exceeds specification, oil pump housing or stator shaft must be replaced.

OIL PUMP CLEARANCE SPECIFICATIONS

Application	Standard In. (mm)	Maximum In. (mm)
Gear-To-Housing	.003-.006 (.07-.15)	.012 (.30)
Gear Tip Clearance	.004-.006 (.11-.14)	.012 (.30)
Gear Side Clearance	.0008-.0020 (.020-.050)	.004 (.10)
Housing Bushing		1.504 (38.19)
Stator Shaft Bushing Front		.850 (21.58)
Rear		1.066 (27.08)

Reassembly – 1) Install oil seal until seal is even with outer edge of pump housing. Place stator shaft in torque converter while working on pump. Coat all components with ATF. See Fig. 19.

2) Align reference marks on gears during installation. To complete reassembly, reverse disassembly procedure. Tighten bolts to specification. DO NOT over expand seal rings during installation. Ensure seal rings move smoothly after installation. Ensure drive gear rotates smoothly when installed in torque converter.

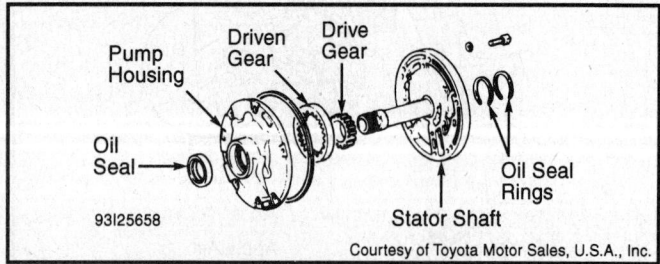

Courtesy of Toyota Motor Sales, U.S.A., Inc.

Fig. 19: Exploded View Of Oil Pump Assembly

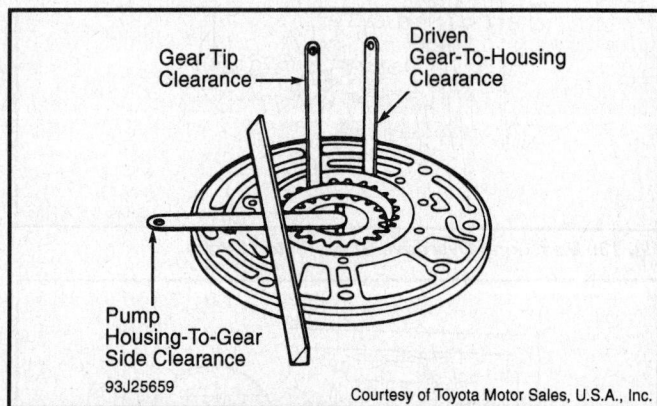

Courtesy of Toyota Motor Sales, U.S.A., Inc.

Fig. 20: Measuring Oil Pump Clearances

OVERDRIVE PLANETARY GEAR, OVERDRIVE DIRECT CLUTCH & OD ONE-WAY CLUTCH

Disassembly – 1) One-way clutch operation should be checked prior to disassembly. Hold clutch drum and rotate input shaft clockwise. See Fig. 21. Input shaft should rotate freely clockwise and lock counterclockwise.

2) Remove clutch drum from planetary gear. Remove thrust bearing from clutch drum. Remove snap ring, flange, discs and plates from clutch drum. Note number and location of components.

3) Using appropriate compressor, compress piston return spring and remove snap ring. Carefully release press and remove piston return spring. Place oil pump on torque converter. Place clutch drum on pump. Hold clutch piston and carefully apply air pressure to oil pump port. See Fig. 22. Remove direct clutch piston.

4) Remove snap ring and ring gear flange from planetary ring gear. Remove bearing race from rear of planetary gear. Remove snap ring, retaining plate, one-way clutch assembly and thrust washer from planetary gear. Remove one-way clutch from outer race. Remove thrust washer.

Inspection – 1) Clean all components (except discs) with solvent. Dry with compressed air. Inspect plates and discs for flaking or burnt areas. Ensure check ball does not allow air to bleed through piston.

2) Measure inside diameter of clutch drum bushing and planetary gear bushing. Maximum diameter for overdrive direct clutch drum bushing is 1.067" (27.11 mm). Maximum diameter for overdrive planetary gear bushing is .444" (11.27 mm). Replace components if damaged or not within specifications.

3) Measure planetary pinion gear thrust clearance. Standard clearance should be .008-.024" (.20-.61 mm). Maximum clearance is .039" (1.00 mm). If clearance is not within specifications, replace planetary gear assembly. Check OD direct clutch return spring free length. Include spring seat in measurement. Standard free length is .622" (15.80 mm).

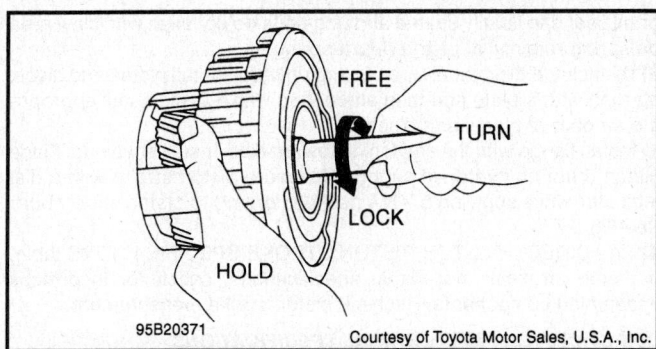

Fig. 21: Checking OD One-Way Clutch Operation

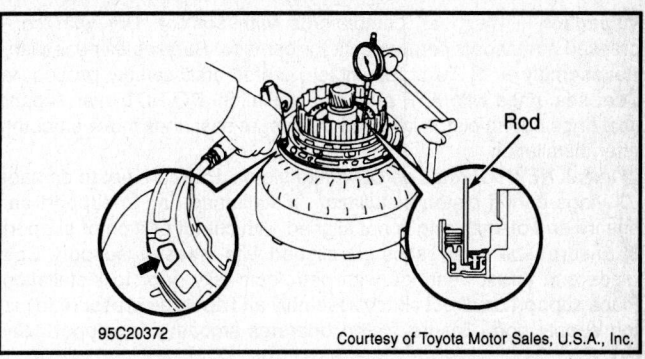

Fig. 22: Removing Clutch Piston & Measuring Stroke

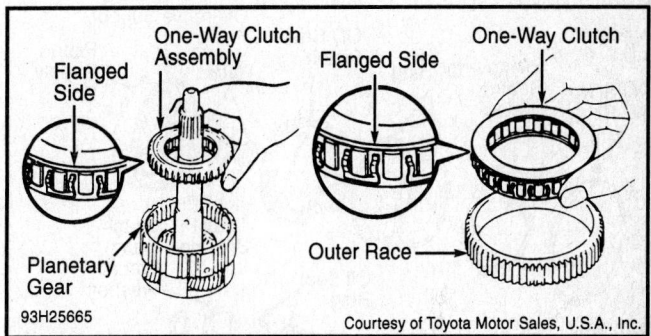

Fig. 23: Installing Overdrive One-Way Clutch

CAUTION: Clutch discs should be soaked in ATF for 15 minutes prior to installation. Coat all parts with ATF prior to installation. Coat thrust bearings and races with petroleum jelly prior to installation.

Reassembly – 1) Position planetary gear with input shaft pointing upward. Install thrust washer in planetary gear with grooved side facing upward. Install one-way clutch into outer race with flanged side facing upward. See Fig. 23.

2) Install one-way clutch assembly on planetary gear. Install retaining plate and snap ring. Install race on back of planetary gear. Race tabs must be engaged in planetary gear. See Fig. 24.

3) Install ring gear flange and snap ring . Install thrust bearing and race in planetary ring gear. Race tabs must be engaged in ring gear. Coat "O" rings with ATF and install on clutch piston. Carefully install clutch piston in clutch drum. Install piston return spring. Using appropriate compressor, compress return spring and install snap ring. Ensure ring is fully seated.

CAUTION: Ensure ends of snap ring do not align with claw area on spring retainer of piston return spring.

4) With clutch drum open area facing upward, install plates and discs, starting with plate. Install flange with flat end facing toward disc. Install snap ring. Place oil pump on torque converter. Place clutch drum on the oil pump. Measure piston stroke while applying 57-114 psi (4-8 kg/cm²) to oil pump port. See Fig. 22. See OVERDRIVE DIRECT CLUTCH PISTON STROKE SPECIFICATIONS table. If piston stroke is not within specifications, check for incorrectly assembled components. Recheck piston stroke.

OVERDRIVE DIRECT CLUTCH PISTON STROKE SPECIFICATIONS

Application	In. (mm)
Lexus	
GS300 (1995) & SC300	.073-.085 (1.85-2.15)
GS300 (1996), LS400, LX450 & SC400	.057-.067 (1.45-1.70)
Toyota	
A-340E (Supra Non-Turbo)	.057-.067 (1.45-1.70)
A-340E (Supra Turbo)	.057-.067 (1.45-1.70)
A-340E (All Others)	.073-.085 (1.85-2.15)
A-340F (T100)	.073-.085 (1.85-2.15)
A-340F (All Others)	.070-.082 (1.77-2.07)
A-340H	.073-.085 (1.85-2.15)
A-343F	.073-.085 (1.85-2.15)

5) If piston stroke exceeds specification, install different thickness flange. Flanges are available in thicknesses of .122" (3.09 mm) to .142" (3.60 mm) in .004" (.10 mm) increments.

6) Remove clutch assembly from oil pump. Install thrust bearing and race in clutch drum with race toward clutch drum. Align tabs of clutch discs. See Fig. 24. Install direct clutch drum on planetary gear. Hold clutch drum and rotate input shaft clockwise. Input shaft should rotate freely clockwise and lock counterclockwise.

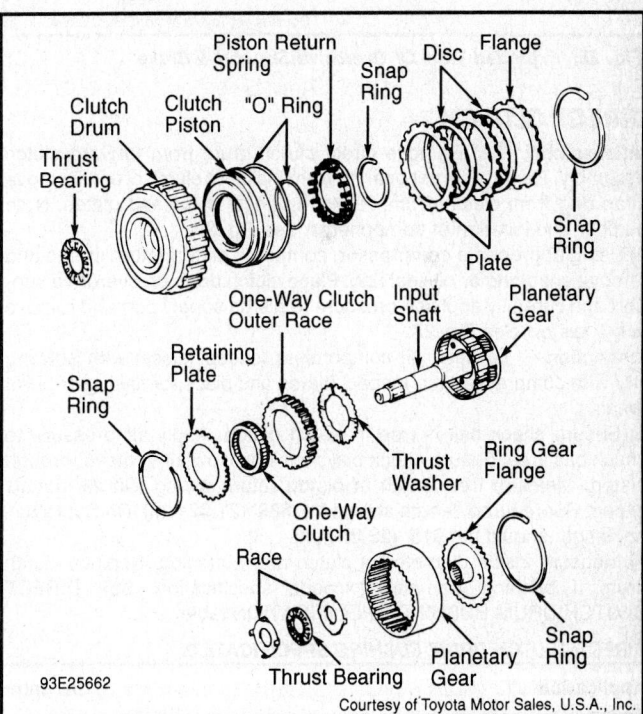

Fig. 24: Exploded View Of Overdrive Clutch Assembly

OVERDRIVE BRAKE

Disassembly – Remove all thrust washers from overdrive support. Using appropriate compressor, compress piston return spring and remove snap ring. Place support on direct clutch assembly. Hold brake piston in a level position. Carefully apply air pressure to piston supply port and remove piston. Remove oil seal rings from rear of support. See Fig. 25.

Inspection – Clean all components with solvent. Dry with compressed air. Inspect components for damage. Replace as necessary.

Reassembly – **1)** To reassemble, reverse disassembly procedure. Coat seal rings with ATF prior to installation. DO NOT over expand seal rings during piston installation. Ensure seal rings move smoothly after installation.

2) Install NEW "O" rings on OD brake piston. Use care not to damage "O" rings during piston installation. Install snap ring in support and ensure end of snap ring is not aligned with cutout portion of support.

3) Ensure tabs on all races are aligned with areas on support. Coat races and thrust bearings with petroleum jelly prior to installation. Place support on direct clutch assembly and apply air pressure to piston supply port. Ensure piston operates smoothly in support. See Fig. 25.

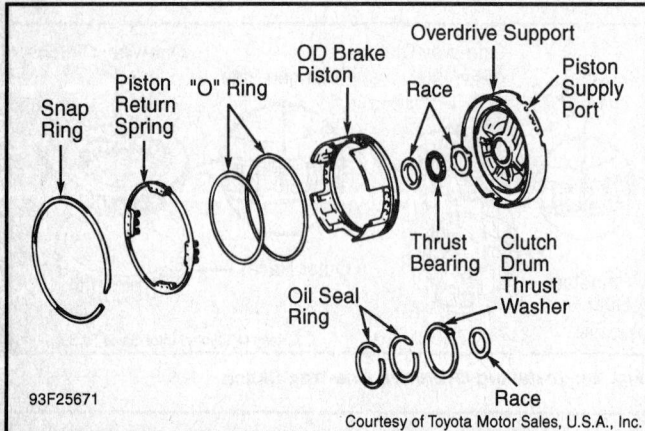

Fig. 25: Exploded View Of Overdrive Support & Brake

DIRECT CLUTCH

Disassembly – **1)** Remove direct clutch drum from forward clutch assembly. Remove thrust bearing from inside of clutch drum. Remove snap ring from clutch drum. Remove flange, discs and plates. Note number and location of components. See Fig. 26.

2) Using appropriate compressor, compress piston return spring and remove snap ring or oil seal ring. Place clutch drum on overdrive support and carefully apply air pressure to piston supply port and remove clutch piston. See Fig. 27.

Inspection – **1)** Clean all components (except discs) with solvent. Dry with compressed air. Inspect plates and discs for flaking or burnt areas.

2) Ensure check ball is free in clutch piston. Apply air pressure to check ball area. Ensure check ball does not allow air to bleed through piston. Measure free length of piston return spring. On all models except Supra turbo, length should be .839" (21.32 mm). On Supra turbo, length should be .915" (23.25 mm).

3) Measure inside diameter of clutch drum bushing. Replace clutch drum if bushing diameter exceeds specification. See DIRECT CLUTCH DRUM BUSHING SPECIFICATION table.

DIRECT CLUTCH DRUM BUSHING SPECIFICATION

Application	In. (mm)
Lexus	
GS300 (1995), LX450 & SC300	2.126 (53.99)
GS300 (1996), LS400 & SC400	2.124 (53.97)
Toyota	
Supra	2.124 (53.97)
All Other Models	2.126 (53.99)

CAUTION: Clutch discs should be soaked in ATF for 15 minutes prior to installation. Thrust washers and races should be coated with petroleum jelly prior to installation.

Reassembly – **1)** Coat "O" rings with ATF. To complete reassembly, reverse disassembly procedure. Ensure piston return spring snap ring

or oil seal ring is fully seated and ring ends do not align with claw area on spring retainer of piston return spring.

2) With clutch drum open area facing upward, install plates and discs, starting with a plate and then alternating with a disc. Install appropriate amount of plates and discs.

3) Install flange with flat end facing toward disc. Install snap ring. Place clutch drum on overdrive support. Measure piston stroke with a dial indicator while applying 57-114 psi (4-8 kg/cm²) to piston supply port. See Fig. 27.

4) See DIRECT CLUTCH PISTON STROKE SPECIFICATIONS table. If piston stroke is not within specifications, check for incorrectly assembled components. Recheck piston stroke measurement.

DIRECT CLUTCH PISTON STROKE SPECIFICATIONS

Application	In. (mm)
Lexus	
GS300 (1995), LX450 & SC300	.054-.063 (1.37-1.60)
GS300 (1996), LS400 & SC400	.015-.028 (.40-.70)
Toyota	
A-340E (Supra Turbo)	.020-.032 (.50-.80)
A-340E (All Others)	.054-.063 (1.37-1.60)
A-340F (T100)	.054-.063 (1.37-1.60)
A-340F (All Others)	.041-.052 (1.03-1.33)
A-340H	.054-.063 (1.37-1.60)
A-343F	.054-.063 (1.37-1.60)

5) If piston stroke is not within specifications, install different thickness flange. Flanges for Toyota A-340E, A-340F, A-343F and A-340H are available in thicknesses of .106" (2.70 mm) to .146" (3.70 mm) in .004" (.10 mm) increments. Flanges for Lexus A-340E are available in thicknesses of .118" (2.99 mm) to .146" (3.70 mm) in .004" (.10 mm) increments. Flanges for Lexus A-350E are available in thicknesses of .106" (2.70 mm) to .146" (3.70 mm) in .004" (.10 mm) increments.

6) Install thrust bearing in clutch drum. Align tabs of clutch discs. Install direct clutch assembly on forward clutch assembly. Measure distance from end of direct clutch to shaft end of forward clutch. Distance should be 2.803" (71.2 mm). See Fig. 27. If distance is not within specifications, components may be incorrectly assembled.

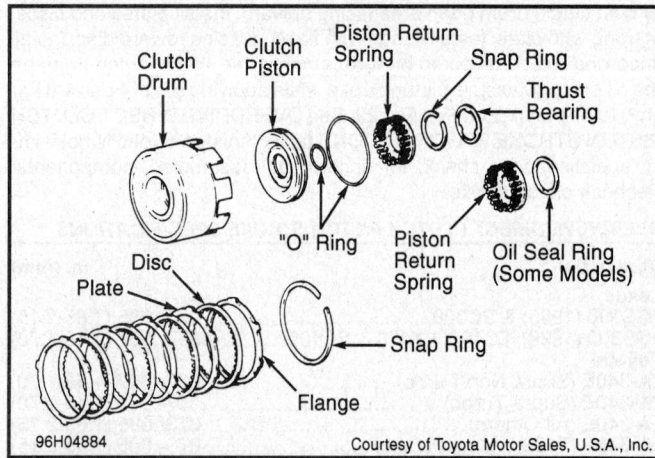

Fig. 26: Exploded View Of Direct Clutch Assembly

FORWARD CLUTCH

Disassembly – **1)** Separate front clutch assembly from direct clutch. Place overdrive support on wooden blocks and install front clutch in overdrive support. Remove snap ring from clutch drum. Remove flange, discs, plates and cushion plate. See Fig. 28. Note number and location of components.

2) Using appropriate compressor, compress piston return spring and remove snap ring. Place clutch drum on overdrive support. Carefully apply air pressure to piston supply port and remove clutch piston. Remove "O" rings from clutch piston and clutch hub. Remove oil seal rings.

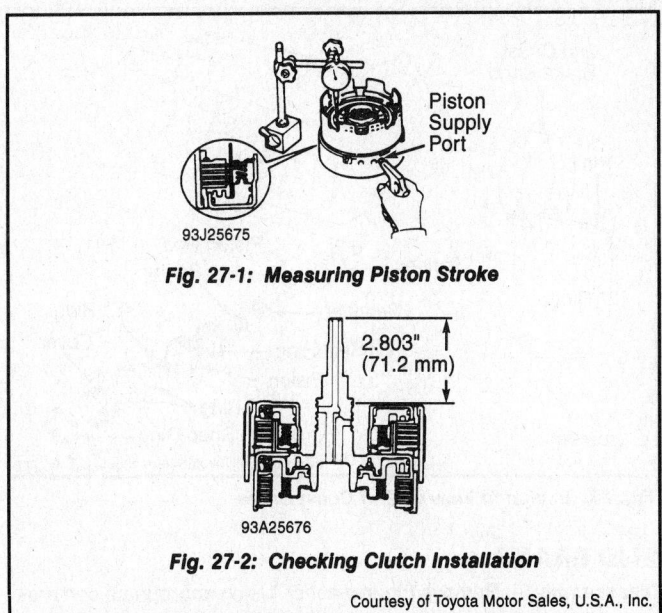

Fig. 27-1: Measuring Piston Stroke

Fig. 27-2: Checking Clutch Installation

Courtesy of Toyota Motor Sales, U.S.A., Inc.

Fig. 27: Checking Direct Clutch Piston Stroke & Installation

Inspection – Clean all components (except discs) with solvent. Dry with compressed air. Inspect plates and discs for flaking or burnt areas. Ensure check ball is free in clutch piston. Apply air pressure to check ball area. Ensure check ball does not allow air to bleed through piston. Measure inside diameter of clutch drum bushing. Replace clutch drum if bushing diameter exceeds .948" (24.089 mm).

CAUTION: Clutch disc should be soaked in ATF for 15 minutes prior to installation.

Reassembly – 1) Coat "O" rings with ATF. To complete reassembly, reverse disassembly procedure. Ensure piston return spring snap ring is fully seated and ends do not align with claw area on spring retainer of piston return spring.

2) Install cushion plate with rounded end toward inside of clutch drum. Install plates and discs, starting with a plate. Install appropriate amount of plates and discs. See Fig. 28.

3) Install flange with rounded edge toward disc. Install snap ring. Ensure end gap of snap ring is not aligned with forward clutch drum cut out portion. Place clutch drum on overdrive support. Measure piston stroke while applying 57-114 psi (4-8 kg/cm²) to piston supply port. See Fig. 29. See FORWARD CLUTCH PISTON STROKE SPECIFICATIONS table.

4) If clearance is not within specifications, install different thickness flange. Flanges are available in thicknesses of .118" (3.0 mm) to .173" (4.4 mm) in .008" (.20 mm) increments. Install thrust bearing and race. Align tabs of the clutch discs.

FORWARD CLUTCH PISTON STROKE SPECIFICATIONS

Application	In. (mm)
Lexus	
GS300 & SC300	.024-.035 (.61-.90)
LX450	.024-.039 (.61-.100)
LS400 & SC400	.028-.039 (.70-1.00)
Toyota	
A-340E (Supra Turbo)	.028-.039 (.70-1.00)
A-340E (All Others)	.020-.035 (.50-.90)
A-340F (T100)	.020-.035 (.50-.90)
A-340F (All Others)	.016-.031 (.40-.80)
A-340H	.020-.035 (.50-.90)
A-343F	.024-.039 (.61-.100)

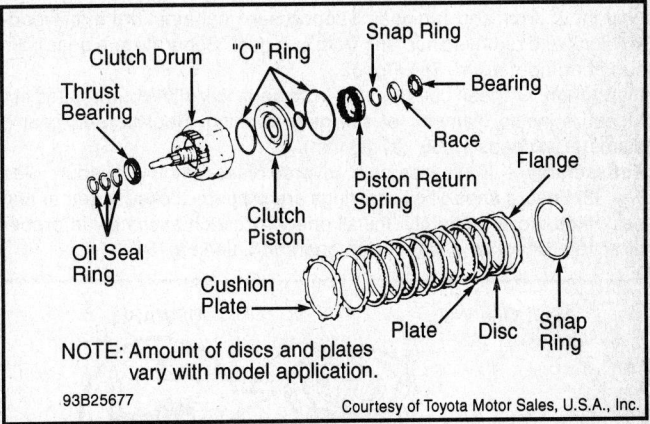

NOTE: Amount of discs and plates vary with model application.

Courtesy of Toyota Motor Sales, U.S.A., Inc.

Fig. 28: Exploded View Of Forward Clutch

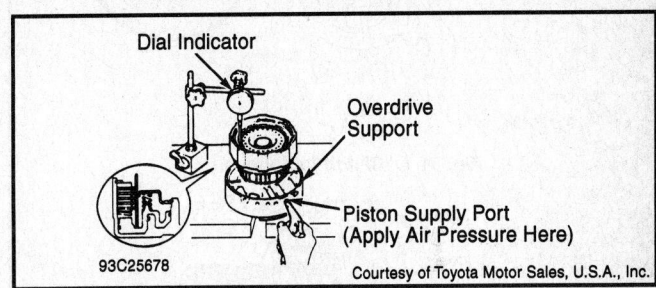

Courtesy of Toyota Motor Sales, U.S.A., Inc.

Fig. 29: Checking Front Clutch Piston Stroke

FRONT PLANETARY GEAR

Disassembly & Inspection – Remove thrust bearings and races from planetary gear and front planetary ring gear. Note direction of race installation. Measure front planetary ring gear bushing inside diameter. Replace planetary ring gear if bushing diameter exceeds .948" (24.08 mm) on all models except A-350E. On A-350E model, replace planetary ring gear if bushing diameter exceeds 1.578" (40.09 mm). Measure planetary pinion gear thrust clearance. Clearance should be .008-.024" (.20-.61 mm). Maximum clearance is .039" (1.00 mm). If clearance is not within specifications, replace planetary gear assembly.

Reassembly – Coat thrust bearings and races with petroleum jelly. Install thrust bearings and races, ensuring tabs on race align with planetary gear. Install races in planetary ring gear and planetary gear with the flat side against the gear surface. See Fig. 30.

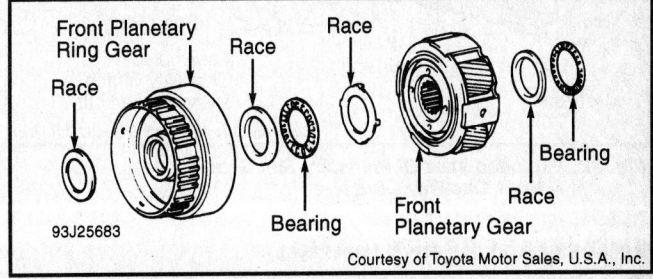

Courtesy of Toyota Motor Sales, U.S.A., Inc.

Fig. 30: Exploded View Of Front Planetary Gear

PLANETARY SUN GEAR & NO. 1 ONE-WAY CLUTCH

Disassembly – Hold sun gear input drum and check rotation of one-way clutch. Clutch should turn freely clockwise and lock counterclockwise. See Fig. 31. Remove one-way clutch assembly. Note direction of clutch installation. Remove thrust washer and oil seal rings from sun gear input drum and sun gear. Support sun gear input drum on wooden block and remove snap ring from sun gear. Separate sun gear from sun gear input drum. *See Fig. 32.*

Inspection – Clean components in solvent. Dry with compressed air. Measure inside diameter of sun gear bushing. Replace sun gear if diameter exceeds 1.066" (27.08 mm).

Reassembly – To reassemble, reverse disassembly procedure. *See Fig. 32.* Ensure ends of oil seal rings are properly locked together and seal rings move smoothly. Install one-way clutch assembly in proper direction. Check one-way clutch operation. *See Fig. 31.*

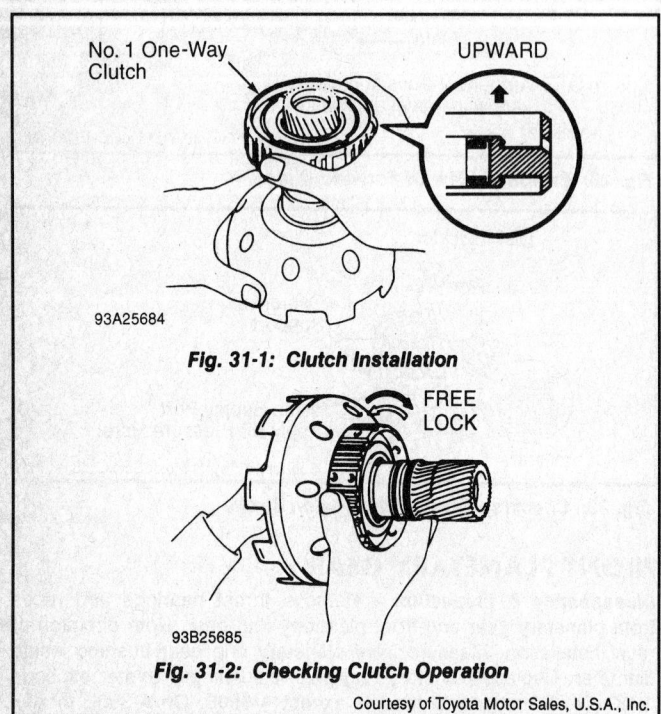

Fig. 31-1: Clutch Installation

Fig. 31-2: Checking Clutch Operation

Courtesy of Toyota Motor Sales, U.S.A., Inc.

Fig. 31: Installing & Checking No. 1 One-Way Clutch

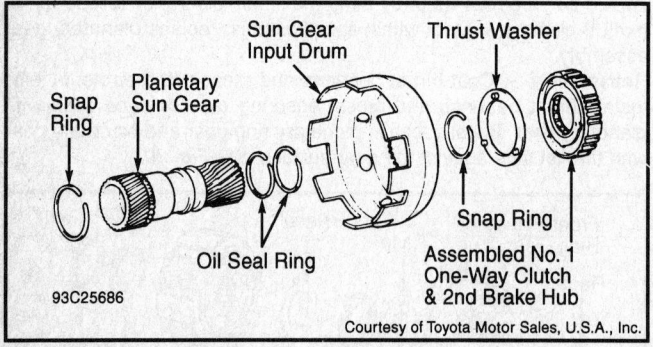

93C25686   Courtesy of Toyota Motor Sales, U.S.A., Inc.

Fig. 32: Exploded View Of Planetary Sun Gear & No. 1 One-Way Clutch

2ND COAST BRAKE (BAND)

Disassembly – Compress spring and remove "E" ring from piston rod. Remove 2nd coast brake piston, spring and retainer from piston rod. Remove oil seal ring.

Inspection – 1) Replace brake band if lining is peeled off or discolored or printed numbers are defaced. Before assembling NEW band, soak band in ATF for at least 15 minutes.

2) If brake band is serviceable but piston rod stroke is not within specification, select replacement rod. Rods are available in lengths of 2.78" (70.7 mm), 2.81" (71.4 mm), 2.84" (72.2 mm), 2.87" (72.9 mm) and 2.09" (73.1 mm).

Reassembly – Install oil seal ring on piston. Install retainer, spring and piston to piston rod. Install "E" ring. *See Fig. 33.*

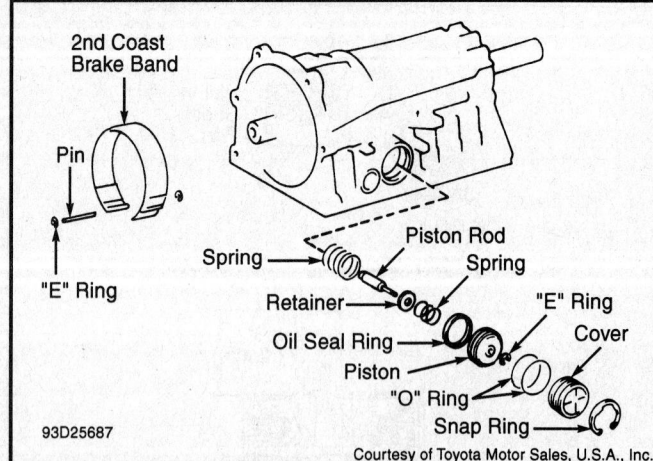

93D25687   Courtesy of Toyota Motor Sales, U.S.A., Inc.

Fig. 33: Exploded View Of 2nd Coast Brake

2ND BRAKE

Disassembly – Remove thrust washer. Using appropriate compressor, compress piston return spring with an arbor press. Remove snap ring. Remove spring retainer and piston return spring. Hold 2nd brake piston and apply compressed air to 2nd brake drum to remove piston.

Inspection – Check all parts for wear and damage. Soak NEW discs in ATF for 15 minutes before installation.

Reassembly – Coat NEW "O" rings with ATF and install. Carefully press 2nd brake piston into 2nd brake drum. Install piston return spring and spring retainer. *See Fig. 34.* Compress return spring and install snap ring. Apply compressed air to 2nd brake drum. Ensure 2nd brake piston moves smoothly. Install thrust washer. Ensure cutout portions of thrust washer match teeth of spring retainer.

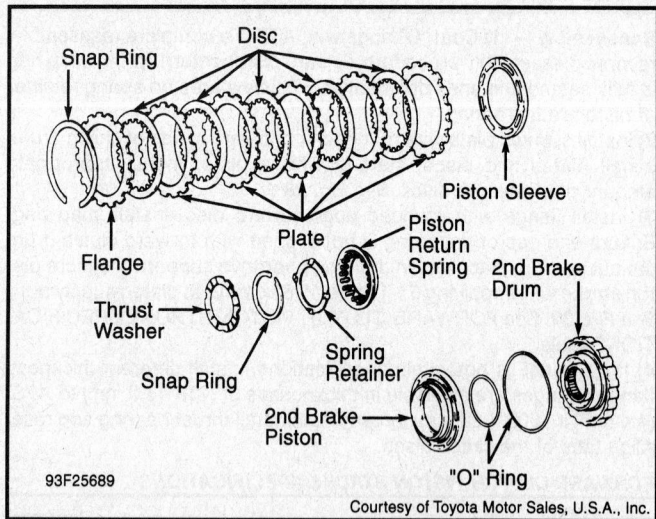

93F25689   Courtesy of Toyota Motor Sales, U.S.A., Inc.

Fig. 34: Exploded View Of 2nd Brake Assembly

REAR PLANETARY GEAR, NO. 2 ONE- WAY CLUTCH & OUTPUT SHAFT

Disassembly – 1) Remove output shaft from rear planetary gear. Remove oil seal from output shaft. Remove rear planetary gear from rear ring gear. Hold planetary gear and check operation of No. 2 one-way clutch. Clutch should turn freely counterclockwise and lock clockwise. *See Fig. 35.* Remove No. 2 one-way clutch inner race from rear planetary gear.

2) Remove snap ring and No. 2 one-way clutch using retainers from planetary gear. Note direction of one-way clutch in planetary gear. Remove No. 1 and 2 thrust washers from planetary gear. Remove bearings and races from ring gear. Remove snap ring and ring gear flange from ring gear. *See Fig. 36.*

Inspection – Clean all components with solvent. Dry with compressed air. Inspect all components for damage. Replace if necessary. Measure planetary pinion gear thrust clearance. Standard clearance should be .008-.024" (.20-.61 mm). Maximum clearance is .039" (1.00 mm). If clearance is not within specifications, replace planetary gear assembly.

Reassembly – **1)** To reassemble, reverse disassembly procedure. Coat all thrust bearings and races with petroleum jelly. When installing thrust bearings and races in ring gear, flat side of race must be placed against ring gear.

2) Ensure No. 1 and 2 thrust washer tangs align with cutout area of planetary gear. Install No. 2 one-way clutch with the open ends facing upward. *See Fig. 35.*

3) Rotate one-way clutch inner race counterclockwise during installation into rear planetary gear. Ensure No. 2 one-way clutch turns freely counterclockwise and locks clockwise. *See Fig. 35.*

4) Install rear planetary gear on rear planetary ring gear. Install oil seal ring. DO NOT spread oil seal ring too much. After installing oil seal ring, ensure seal ring rotates smoothly. Install output shaft into rear planetary gear assembly. *See Fig. 36.*

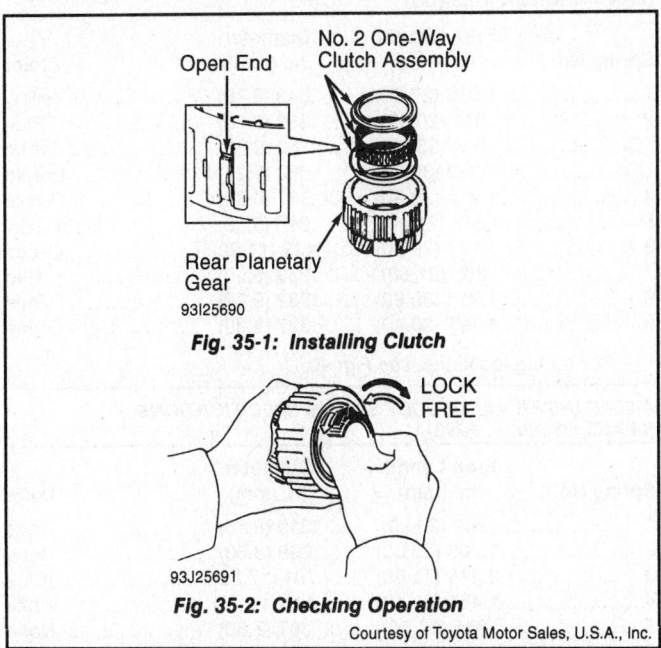

Fig. 35-1: Installing Clutch

Fig. 35-2: Checking Operation

Courtesy of Toyota Motor Sales, U.S.A., Inc.

Fig. 35: Installing No. 2 One-Way Clutch & Checking Operation

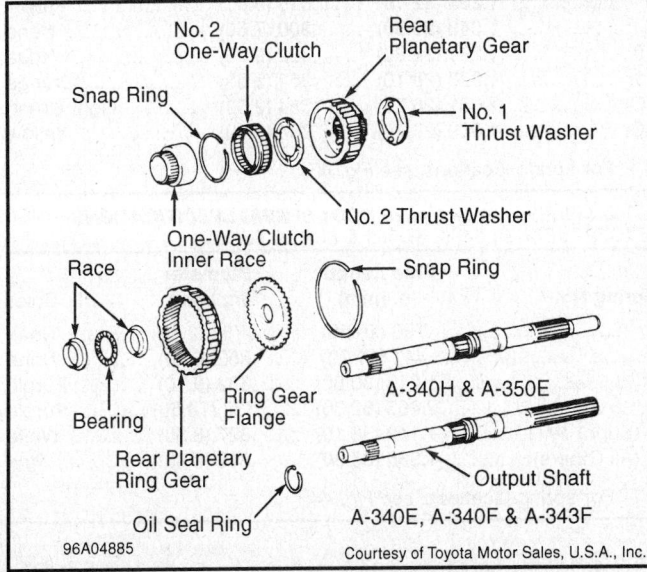

Fig. 36: Exploded View Of Output Shaft Assembly

Courtesy of Toyota Motor Sales, U.S.A., Inc.

VALVE BODY ASSEMBLY

CAUTION: All valve body components must be installed in original location. Lay all components in sequence during removal for reassembly reference. Note diameter and check ball location. Throttle pressure is changed according to number of adjusting rings. When assembling valve body, install same number of adjusting rings as removed. Some valve bodies do not have adjusting rings.

Disassembly – Remove detent spring and manual valve from valve body assembly. Remove solenoids and lock plate (if applicable), oil strainer and pressure relief valve. Remove lower valve body-to upper valve body bolts. Note bolt length and location. Separate upper valve body and valve body plate from lower valve body. *See Figs. 37-39.*

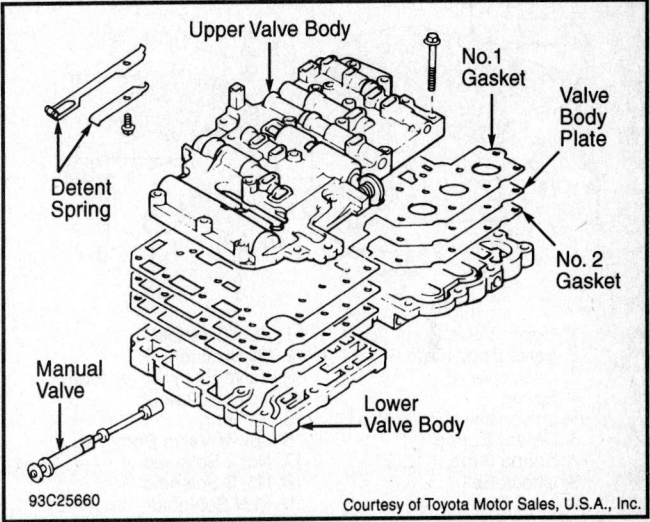

Courtesy of Toyota Motor Sales, U.S.A., Inc.

Fig. 37: Exploded View Of A-340 Series Control Valve Assembly (Except Lexus LS400, SC400 & Supra Turbo)

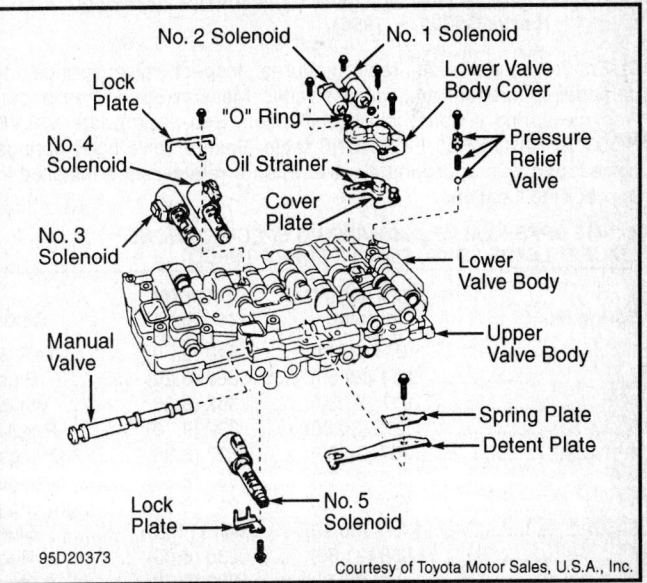

Courtesy of Toyota Motor Sales, U.S.A., Inc.

Fig. 38: Exploded View Of A-340 Series Control Valve Assembly (Lexus LS400, SC400 & Supra Turbo)

CAUTION: DO NOT allow valve body plate to separate from upper valve body during removal or check balls and strainer may fall out.

Inspection – **1)** Clean all parts in solvent. Dry with compressed air. Ensure all valve body passages are clear. Ensure strainers are not damaged or clogged. Inspect valves for scoring or roughness.

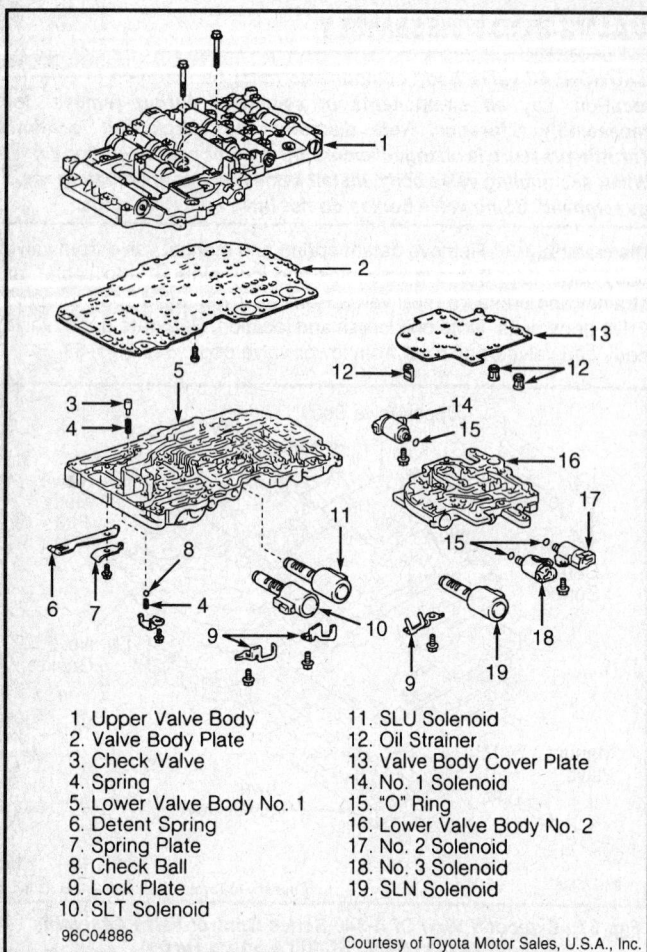

1. Upper Valve Body
2. Valve Body Plate
3. Check Valve
4. Spring
5. Lower Valve Body No. 1
6. Detent Spring
7. Spring Plate
8. Check Ball
9. Lock Plate
10. SLT Solenoid
11. SLU Solenoid
12. Oil Strainer
13. Valve Body Cover Plate
14. No. 1 Solenoid
15. "O" Ring
16. Lower Valve Body No. 2
17. No. 2 Solenoid
18. No. 3 Solenoid
19. SLN Solenoid

96C04886   Courtesy of Toyota Motor Sales, U.S.A., Inc.

**Fig. 39: Exploded View Of A-350E Control Valve Assembly
(Lexus GS300 – 1996)**

2) Ensure valves slide freely in bores. Inspect valve springs for damage, squareness and collapsed coils. Measure spring free length. Replace spring if not within specification. See appropriate VALVE BODY SPRING SPECIFICATIONS table. Ensure valve body springs correspond with appropriate valve. Ensure retainers are installed in appropriate locations.

A-340E UPPER VALVE BODY SPRING SPECIFICATIONS (EXCEPT LEXUS LS400, SC400 & SUPRA TURBO)

Spring No. [1]	Free Length In. (mm)	Diameter In. (mm)	Color
1	1.075 (27.30)	.343 (8.70)	Yellow
2	.811 (20.60)	.362 (9.20)	Blue
Or	.917 (23.30)	.362 (9.20)	White
3	1.213 (30.80)	.382 (9.70)	Purple
4 [2]	.967 (24.60)	.327 (8.30)	[3] Orange
4 [4]	.996 (25.30)	.339 (8.60)	Orange
5	.843 (21.40)	.217 (5.50)	Light Gray
6	1.217 (30.90)	.441 (11.20)	Blue
7	.858 (21.80)	.236 (6.00)	Red
8	1.213 (30.80)	.382 (9.70)	[5] Blue
9 [2]	1.039 (26.40)	.327 (8.30)	Yellow
9 [4]	1.197 (30.40)	.327 (8.30)	[6] Yellow

[1] – For spring locations, see Fig. 40.
[2] – GS300, Previa, SC300 and Supra Non-Turbo.
[3] – Blue on GS300 and SC300.
[4] – All Other Models.
[5] – Purple on GS300 and SC300.
[6] – Light Green on Pickup and 4Runner with A-340H.

A-340E UPPER VALVE BODY SPRING SPECIFICATIONS (LEXUS LS400, SC400 & SUPRA TURBO)

Spring No. [1]	Free Length In. (mm)	Diameter In. (mm)	Color
1	.922 (23.42)	.231 (5.86)	Red
2 (Lexus Models)	1.448 (36.78)	.363 (9.22)	None
2 (Supra Turbo)	1.291 (32.79)	.370 (9.40)	Blue
3	1.462 (37.13)	.439 (11.14)	White
4	.847 (21.50)	.306 (7.76)	None
5 [2]	1.072 (27.25)	.343 (8.73)	Yellow
6 [2]	.689 (17.50)	.283 (7.20)	Red
7	2.962 (75.26)	.519 (15.02)	Pink
8	1.211 (30.77)	.382 (9.70)	Purple
9	1.211 (30.77)	.382 (9.70)	Purple
10	1.007 (25.58)	.340 (8.64)	None

[1] – For spring locations, see Figs. 41 and 42.
[2] – Lexus models only.

A-343F UPPER VALVE BODY SPRING SPECIFICATIONS (LAND CRUISER & LEXUS)

Spring No. [1]	Free Length In. (mm)	Diameter In. (mm)	Color
1	1.075 (27.30)	.343 (8.70)	Yellow
2	.811 (20.60)	.362 (9.20)	Blue
Or	.917 (23.30)	.362 (9.20)	White
3	1.213 (30.80)	.382 (9.70)	Purple
4	1.217 (30.90)	.327 (8.30)	Purple
5	.843 (21.40)	.217 (5.50)	Light Gray
6	1.177 (29.90)	.433 (11.00)	Green
7	.858 (21.80)	.236 (6.00)	Red
8	1.213 (30.80)	.382 (9.70)	Blue
9	1.197 (30.40)	.327 (8.30)	Light Green

[1] – For spring locations, see Fig. 40.

A-350E UPPER VALVE BODY SPRING SPECIFICATIONS (LEXUS GS300 – 1996)

Spring No. [1]	Free Length In. (mm)	Diameter In. (mm)	Color
1	.941 (23.90)	.319 (8.10)	None
2	1.008 (25.60)	.339 (8.60)	None
3	2.815 (71.50)	.701 (17.80)	Blue
4	1.461 (37.10)	.437 (11.10)	White
5	.846 (21.50)	.307 (7.80)	None
6	1.358 (34.50)	.362 (9.20)	Red
7	.921 (23.40)	.232 (5.90)	Red
8	1.264 (32.10)	.315 (8.00)	Yellow
9	1.043 (26.50)	.300 (7.60)	None
10	1.295 (32.90)	.382 (9.70)	None
11	1.028 (26.10)	.354 (9.00)	Orange
Or	1.051 (26.70)	.354 (9.00)	Light Green
Or	1.079 (27.40)	.354 (9.00)	Yellow

[1] – For spring locations, see Fig. 43.

A-340 SERIES LOWER VALVE BODY SPRING SPECIFICATIONS (EXCEPT LEXUS LS400, SC400 & SUPRA TURBO)

Spring No. [1]	Free Length In. (mm)	Diameter In. (mm)	Color
1	.796 (20.20)	.476 (12.10)	None
2	.441 (11.20)	.252 (6.40)	None
3	1.213 (30.80)	.382 (9.70)	Purple
4	2.453 (62.30)	.732 (18.60)	Purple
5 (Supra N/T)	1.142 (36.10)	.327 (8.30)	White
5 (All Others)	1.335 (33.90)	.346 (8.80)	Pink

[1] – For spring locations, see Fig. 44.

A-340 SERIES LOWER VALVE BODY SPRING SPECIFICATIONS (SUPRA TURBO)

Spring No. [1]	Free Length In. (mm)	Diameter In. (mm)	Color
1	1.796 (45.62)	.645 (16.88)	Blue
2	.729 (18.52)	.209 (5.30)	White
3	.740 (18.80)	.300 (7.48)	None
4	.740 (18.80)	.300 (7.48)	None
5	1.265 (32.13)	.315 (8.00)	Yellow
6	.799 (20.30)	.240 (6.10)	None
7	1.227 (31.17)	.348 (8.85)	White
8	1.211 (30.77)	.382 (9.70)	Purple
9	.859 (21.83)	.315 (8.00)	Green
10	1.027 (26.09)	.322 (8.19)	Blue
Or	1.047 (26.60)	.322 (8.19)	Light Blue
Or	1.067 (27.11)	.322 (8.19)	White

[1] – For spring locations, *see Fig. 45.*

A-340 SERIES LOWER VALVE BODY SPRING SPECIFICATIONS (LEXUS LS400 & SC400)

Spring No. [1]	Free Length In. (mm)	Diameter In. (mm)	Color
1	1.639 (41.62)	.645 (16.88)	Red
2	.729 (18.52)	.209 (5.30)	White
3	.740 (18.80)	.300 (7.48)	None
4	.740 (18.80)	.300 (7.48)	None
5	1.2078 (30.63)	.315 (8.00)	None
6	.799 (20.30)	.240 (6.10)	None
7	1.358 (34.50)	.348 (8.85)	None
8	1.211 (30.77)	.382 (9.70)	Purple
9	.859 (21.83)	.315 (8.00)	Green
10	1.028 (26.11)	.317 (8.04)	Orange
Or	1.052 (26.71)	.317 (8.04)	Light Green
Or	1.079 (27.41)	.317 (8.04)	Yellow

[1] – For spring locations, *see Fig. 45.*

A-350E LOWER VALVE BODY SPRING SPECIFICATIONS (LEXUS GS300 – 1996)

Spring No. [1]	Free Length In. (mm)	Diameter In. (mm)	Color
1	1.004 (25.50)	.382 (9.70)	Red
2	1.004 (25.50)	.382 (9.70)	Red
3	1.638 (41.60)	.665 (16.90)	Red
4	.890 (22.60)	.319 (8.10)	None
5	.740 (18.80)	.295 (7.50)	None
6	1.358 (34.50)	.350 (8.90)	None
7	.799 (20.30)	.240 (6.10)	None
8	1.004 (25.50)	.382 (9.70)	Red
9	.839 (21.30)	.323 (8.20)	Yellow
10	.858 (21.80)	.315 (8.00)	Green
11	1.043 (26.50)	.299 (7.60)	None

[1] – For spring locations, *see Fig. 46.*

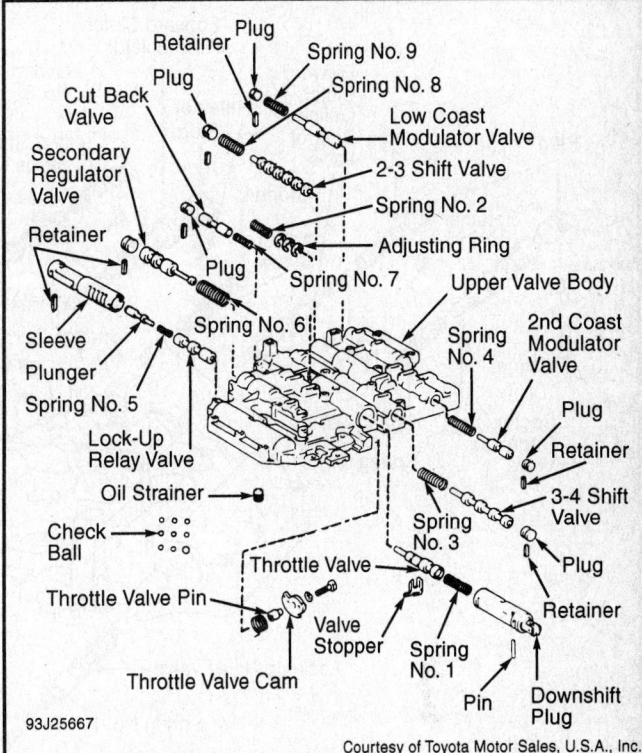

93J25667

Courtesy of Toyota Motor Sales, U.S.A., Inc.

Fig. 40: Exploded View Of A-340 Series Upper Valve Body (Except Lexus LS400, SC400 & Supra Turbo)

NOTE: *Valves may be held in with pins or retainers and plugs. Remove components and note locations. Arrange parts in order for reassembly reference.*

Reassembly – 1) Coat all components with ATF. To reassemble, reverse disassembly procedure. Ensure check balls in upper and lower valve body are installed correctly. *See Figs. 47-51.*

2) Position NEW No. 1 gasket, plate and NEW No. 2 gasket on upper valve body. Place lower valve body on upper valve body with plate and gaskets. DO NOT let components separate. Align each bolt hole in valve bodies with gaskets and plate.

3) Install and finger tighten bolts in upper valve body. Ensure proper bolt length is used. *See Figs. 52-54.* Tighten bolts to 56 INCH lbs. (6.4 N.m). Install oil strainer, pressure relief and solenoids (as applicable). Install manual valve and detent spring. Tighten bolts to 89 INCH lbs. (10 N.m). Ensure manual valve moves freely.

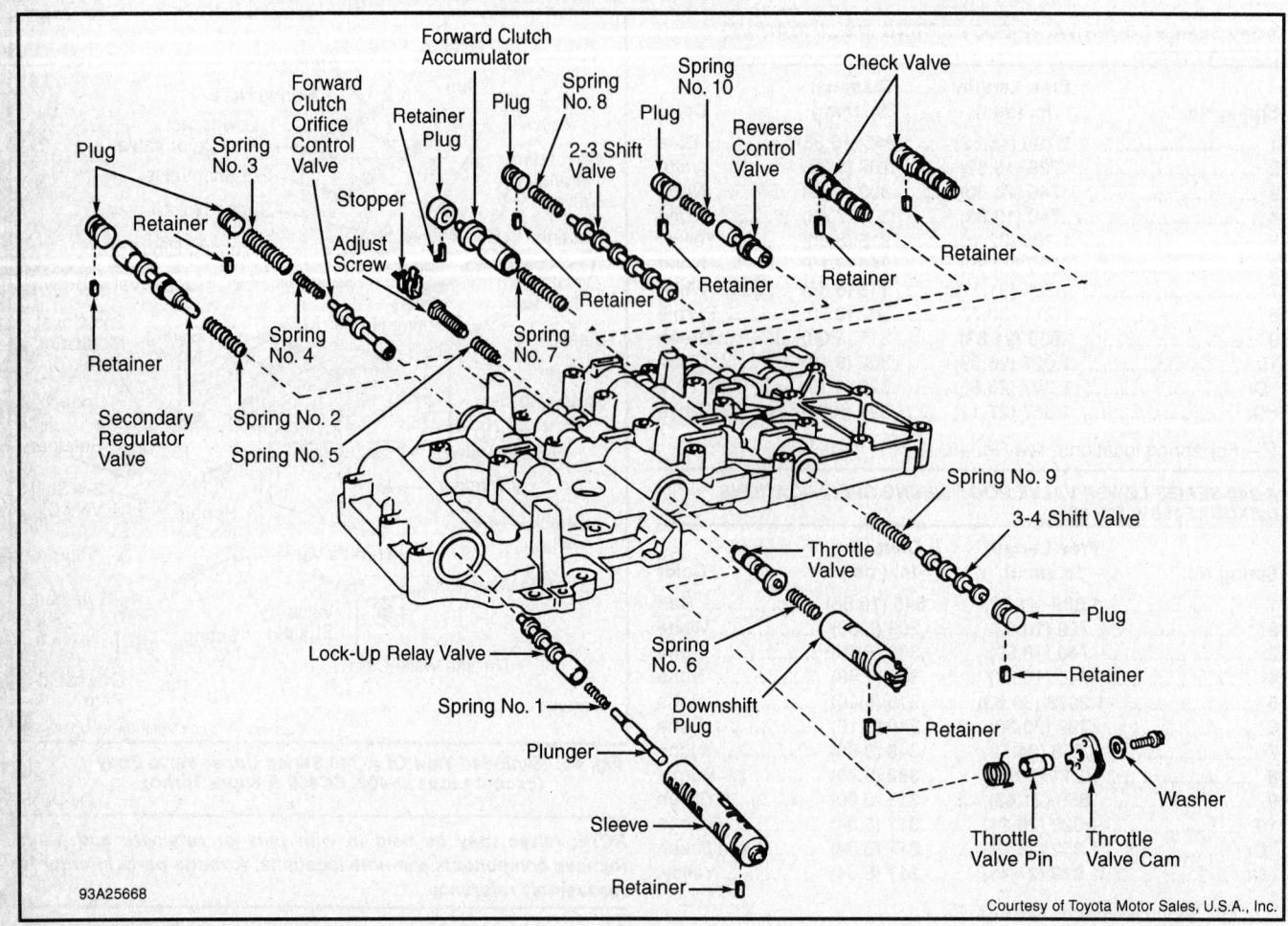

93A25668

Courtesy of Toyota Motor Sales, U.S.A., Inc.

Fig. 41: Exploded View Of A-340E Upper Valve Body (Lexus LS400 & SC400)

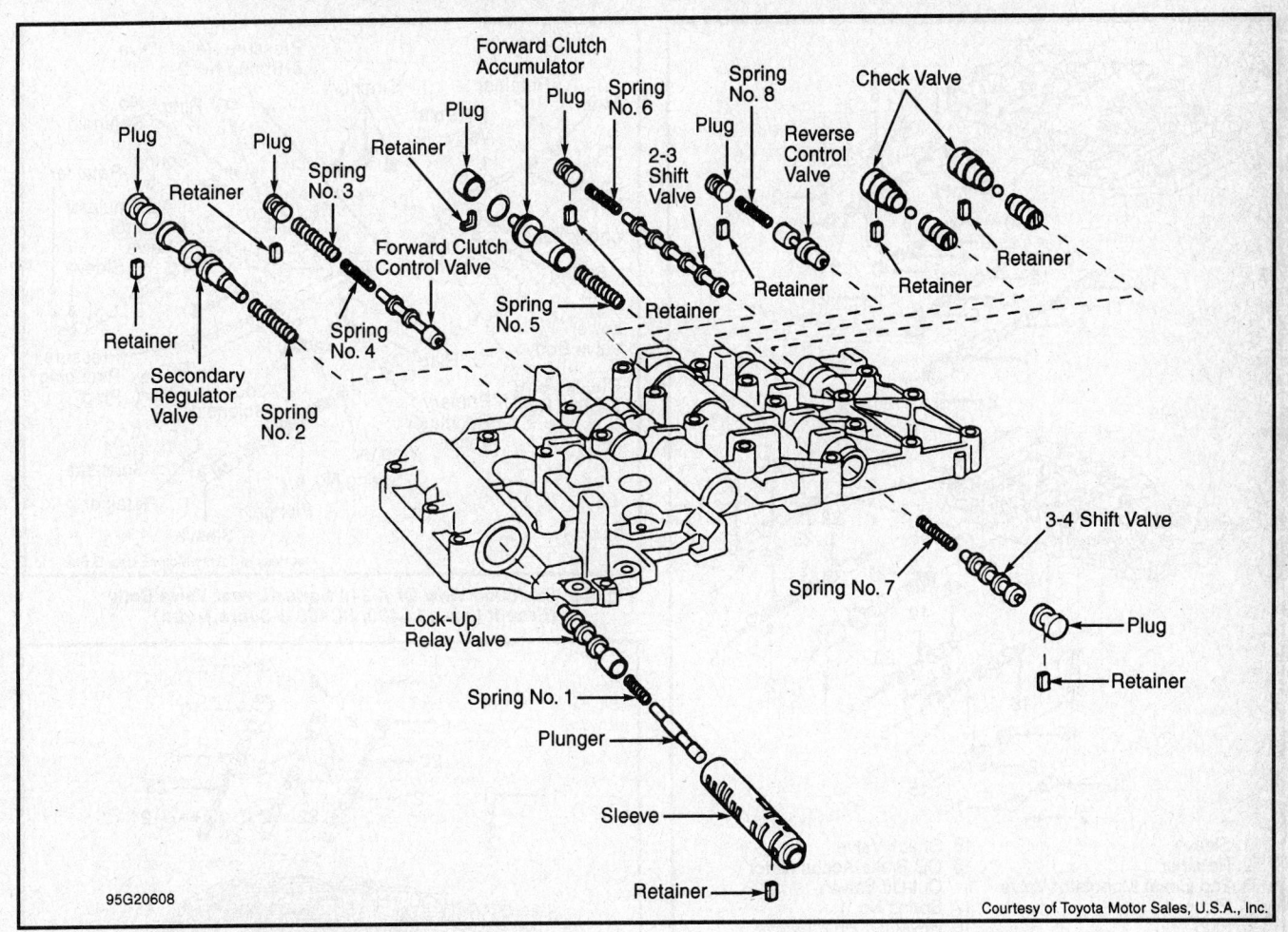

95G20608

Courtesy of Toyota Motor Sales, U.S.A., Inc.

Fig. 42: Exploded View Of A-340E Upper Valve Body (Supra Turbo)

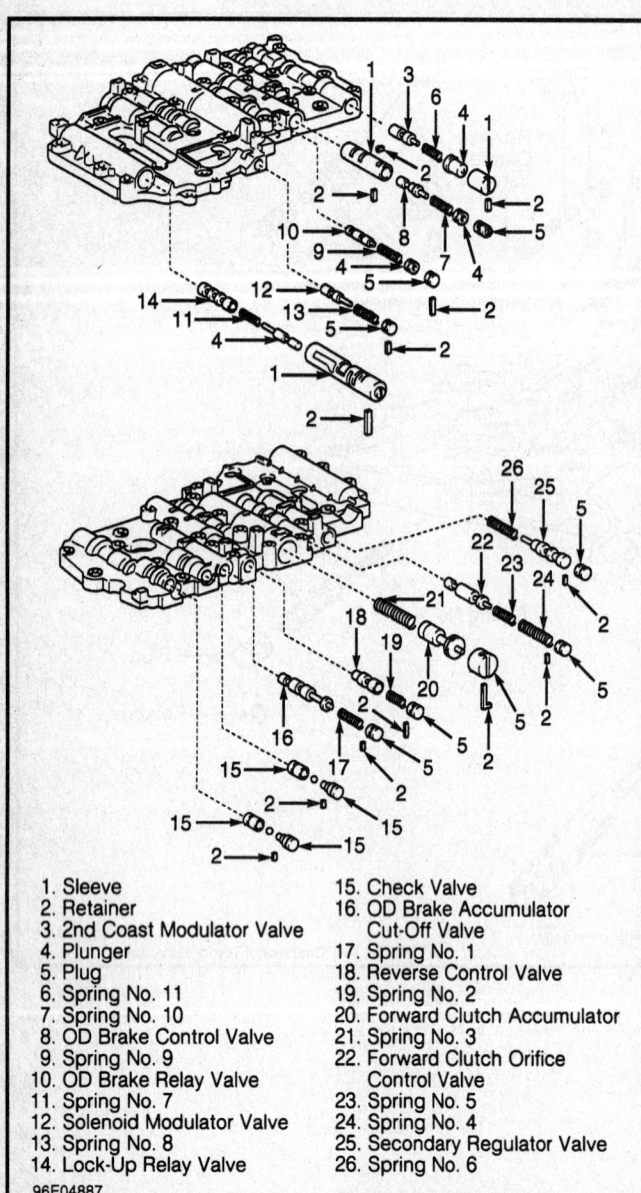

1. Sleeve
2. Retainer
3. 2nd Coast Modulator Valve
4. Plunger
5. Plug
6. Spring No. 11
7. Spring No. 10
8. OD Brake Control Valve
9. Spring No. 9
10. OD Brake Relay Valve
11. Spring No. 7
12. Solenoid Modulator Valve
13. Spring No. 8
14. Lock-Up Relay Valve
15. Check Valve
16. OD Brake Accumulator Cut-Off Valve
17. Spring No. 1
18. Reverse Control Valve
19. Spring No. 2
20. Forward Clutch Accumulator
21. Spring No. 3
22. Forward Clutch Orifice Control Valve
23. Spring No. 5
24. Spring No. 4
25. Secondary Regulator Valve
26. Spring No. 6

96E04887

Courtesy of Toyota Motor Sales, U.S.A., Inc.

Fig. 43: *Exploded View Of A-350E Upper Valve Body (Lexus GS300 – 1996)*

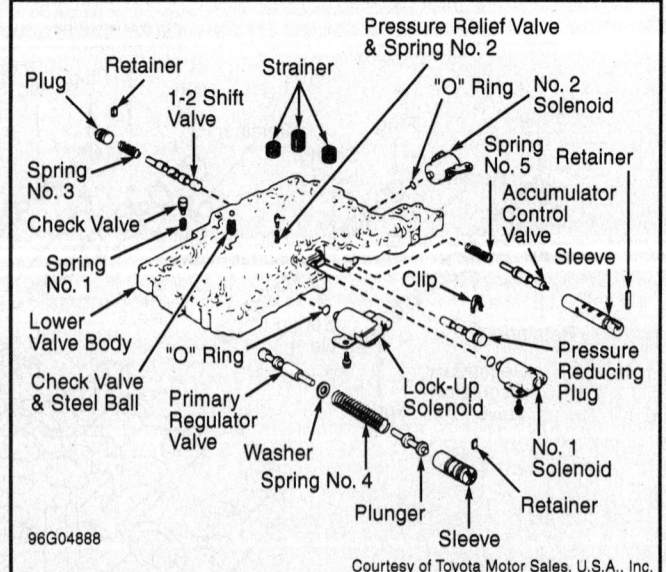

96G04888

Courtesy of Toyota Motor Sales, U.S.A., Inc.

Fig. 44: *Exploded View Of A-340 Series Lower Valve Body (Except Lexus LS400, SC400 & Supra Turbo)*

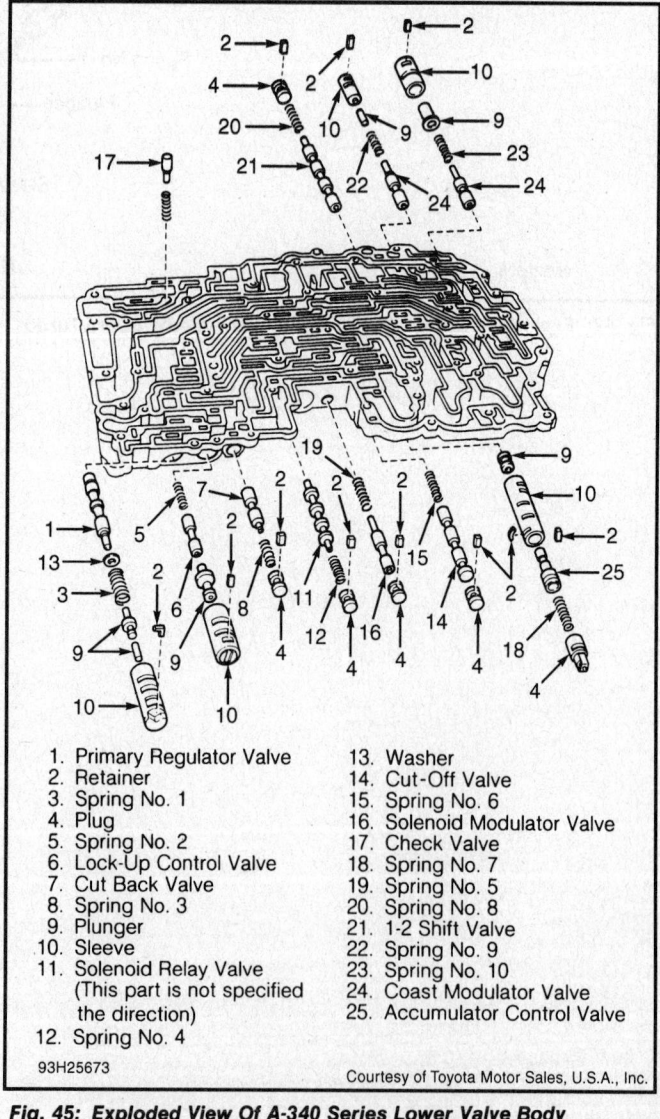

1. Primary Regulator Valve
2. Retainer
3. Spring No. 1
4. Plug
5. Spring No. 2
6. Lock-Up Control Valve
7. Cut Back Valve
8. Spring No. 3
9. Plunger
10. Sleeve
11. Solenoid Relay Valve (This part is not specified the direction)
12. Spring No. 4
13. Washer
14. Cut-Off Valve
15. Spring No. 6
16. Solenoid Modulator Valve
17. Check Valve
18. Spring No. 7
19. Spring No. 5
20. Spring No. 8
21. 1-2 Shift Valve
22. Spring No. 9
23. Spring No. 10
24. Coast Modulator Valve
25. Accumulator Control Valve

93H25673

Courtesy of Toyota Motor Sales, U.S.A., Inc.

Fig. 45: *Exploded View Of A-340 Series Lower Valve Body (Lexus LS400, SC400 & Supra Turbo)*

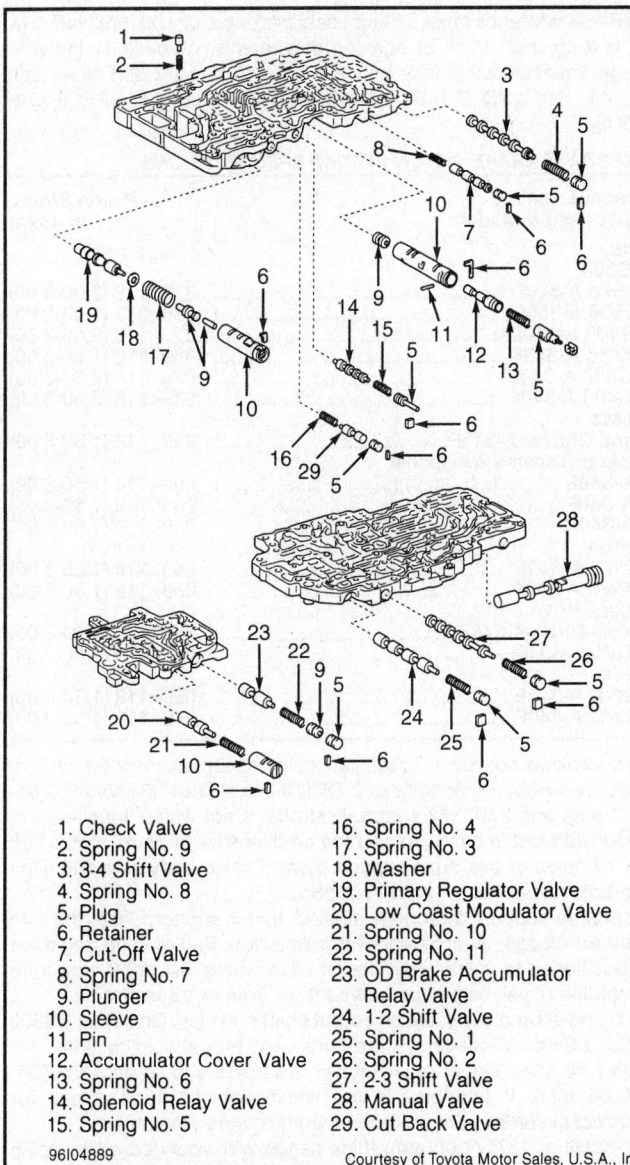

1. Check Valve	16. Spring No. 4
2. Spring No. 9	17. Spring No. 3
3. 3-4 Shift Valve	18. Washer
4. Spring No. 8	19. Primary Regulator Valve
5. Plug	20. Low Coast Modulator Valve
6. Retainer	21. Spring No. 10
7. Cut-Off Valve	22. Spring No. 11
8. Spring No. 7	23. OD Brake Accumulator
9. Plunger	Relay Valve
10. Sleeve	24. 1-2 Shift Valve
11. Pin	25. Spring No. 1
12. Accumulator Cover Valve	26. Spring No. 2
13. Spring No. 6	27. 2-3 Shift Valve
14. Solenoid Relay Valve	28. Manual Valve
15. Spring No. 5	29. Cut Back Valve

96I04889   Courtesy of Toyota Motor Sales, U.S.A., Inc.

Fig. 46: Exploded View Of A-350E Lower Valve Body (Lexus GS300 – 1996)

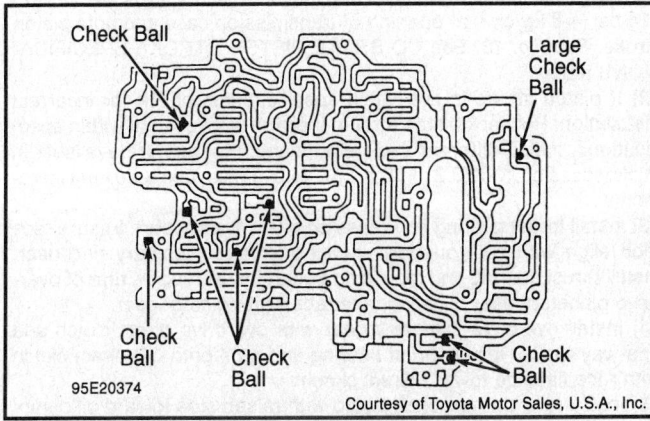

95E20374   Courtesy of Toyota Motor Sales, U.S.A., Inc.

Fig. 47: Identifying Upper Valve Body Check Ball Locations (GS300 – 1995 & SC300 A-340E Models & Pickup & 4Runner A-340H Models)

TRANSMISSION REASSEMBLY

NOTE: Coat all oil seal rings, clutch discs, clutch plates, rotating parts, and sliding surfaces with ATF prior to reassembly. All gaskets and rubber "O" rings should be replaced. Ensure ends of snap rings are not aligned with cutouts and are installed correctly in groove. If a worn bushing is to be replaced, replacement must be made with subassembly containing that bushing. Check thrust bearings and races for wear or damage. Use petroleum jelly to hold parts in place. Replace parts as necessary. Clutch discs should be soaked in ATF for 15 minutes before installation.

1) Before transmission reassembly, inspect case bushing and extension housing bushing (if equipped). Maximum transmission case bushing inside diameter is 1.504" (38.19 mm). Maximum extension housing bushing inside diameter is 1.578" (40.09 mm). If bushings are not within specifications, manufacturer recommends replacing transmission case and/or extension housing.

NOTE: For thrust bearing and race identification and installation positions, see Figs. 60 and 61.

2) Install 1st and reverse brake No. 1 piston to reaction sleeve. Install No. 1 piston with reaction sleeve on No. 2 piston. Align No. 2 piston teeth into proper grooves. Carefully press No. 1 and No. 2 brake pistons into case. Position piston return spring on No. 2 piston. Using Spring Compressor (09350-07050), compress return spring. *See Fig. 17.*

3) Install snap ring. Ensure snap ring end-gap is not aligned with spring retainer claw. Ensure 1st and reverse brake pistons move smoothly by applying compressed air to case. *See Fig. 16.*

4) Install leaf spring (if equipped). Install rear planetary gear unit with 1st and reverse brake pack and output shaft. Install flange with rounded edge toward planetary ring gear. On A340H, install plate and cushion plate. Cushion plate must be installed with rounded end toward brake drum end of output shaft. On all other models, install flange. Install plates and discs, starting with disc. Install correct number of plates and discs.

5) Install 2nd brake drum assembly. Install thrust bearing in case. Align teeth of 2nd brake drum, flange, discs and plates. Align splines of transmission case, assembled rear planetary gear, 2nd brake drum, 1st and reverse brake pack and output shaft into case.

6) Support output shaft on wooden blocks. Install snap ring in case with chamfered edge toward front of transmission. Ensure ends of snap ring are not aligned with cutout area of case. Measure 1st and reverse brake clearance between 2nd brake drum and plate. *See Fig. 15.* See 1ST & REVERSE BRAKE PACK CLEARANCE SPECIFICATIONS table.

1ST & REVERSE BRAKE PACK CLEARANCE SPECIFICATION

Application	Clearance – In. (mm)
Lexus	
GS300	
1995 A-340E	.024-.044 (.61-1.12)
1996 A-350E	.024-.035 (.61-.90)
LS400 A-340E	.028-.039 (.70-1.00)
LX450 A-343F	.028-.048 (.70-1.22)
SC300 A-340E	.024-.044 (.61-1.12)
SC400 A-340E	.028-.039 (.70-1.00)
Toyota	
Land Cruiser A-343F	.028-.048 (.70-1.22)
Pickup, Tacoma & 4Runner	
A-340E	.024-.044 (.61-1.12)
A-340F	.020-.040 (.50-1.02)
A-340H	.024-.052 (.61-1.32)
Previa	
2WD A-340E	.024-.044 (.61-1.12)
AWD A-340F	.024-.044 (.61-1.12)
Supra	
Non-Turbo A-340E	.024-.044 (.61-1.12)
Turbo A-340E	.028-.039 (.70-1.00)
T100	
2WD A-340E	.024-.044 (.61-1.12)
4WD A-340F	.024-.044 (.61-1.12)

7) If clearance is not within specification, select a different thickness flange. Flanges are available in thicknesses of .157" (4.0 mm) to .213" (5.4 mm) in .008" (.20 mm) increments.

8) Install 2nd brake piston sleeve. Install NEW brake drum gasket in case. Install No. 1 one-way clutch assembly. On Lexus GS300, LS400, SC400 and Supra Turbo, install No. 1 thrust washer on second brake. On all models, install No. 1 one-way clutch. On all models except A-340F, install .071" (1.8 mm) flange plate with rounded edge side of plate facing disc. Install plates and discs starting with disc. Install end flange with rounded edge facing disc. Install snap ring.

9) On A-340F, install .098" (2.5 mm) flange plate with rounded edge side of plate facing disc. Install plates and discs. Install end flange with rounded edge facing disc. Install snap ring.

10) Measure 2nd brake clearance between snap ring and flange. *See Fig. 15.* See 2ND BRAKE CLUTCH PACK CLEARANCE SPECIFICATIONS. If clearance is not within specifications, check for incorrect assembly.

2ND BRAKE CLUTCH PACK CLEARANCE SPECIFICATIONS

Transmission Application & Model	Piston Stroke In. (mm)
Lexus	
GS300	
1995 A-340E	.024-.078 (.61-1.98)
1996 A-350E	.019-.044 (.49-1.11)
LS400 A-340E	.024-.078 (.61-1.98)
LX450 A-343F	.024-.078 (.61-1.98)
SC300 A-340E	.024-.078 (.61-1.98)
SC400 A-340E	.024-.078 (.61-1.98)
Toyota	
Land Cruiser A-343F	.024-.078 (.61-1.98)
Pickup, Tacoma & 4Runner	
A-340E	.024-.078 (.61-1.98)
A-340F	.020-.069 (.50-1.76)
A-340H	.024-.078 (.61-1.98)
Previa	
2WD A-340E	.024-.078 (.61-1.98)
AWD A-340F	.024-.078 (.61-1.98)
Supra	
Non-Turbo A-340E	.024-.078 (.61-1.98)
Turbo A-340E	.019-.044 (.49-1.11)
T100	
2WD A-340E	.024-.078 (.61-1.98)
4WD A-340F	.024-.078 (.61-1.98)

11) Install planetary sun gear. Turn planetary sun gear clockwise into No. 1 one-way clutch. Ensure all thrust washers are correctly installed. Install front planetary gear bearing and race. Install front planetary gear into sun gear. Install snap ring. Remove wooden block from under output shaft. Install race on front of planetary gear so race tabs align with planetary gear holes.

12) Install 2nd coast brake band and pin. Pin must be installed so "E" ring is toward front of transmission. Install "E" ring. Coat thrust bearing and race with petroleum jelly and install on forward clutch. Raised portion of race must be toward front.

NOTE: For thrust bearing and race identification and installation positions, see Figs. 60 and 61.

---

13) Install race on front planetary ring gear. Smooth flat surface must be toward front. Align disc tabs of forward clutch. Install front planetary gear in forward clutch. Ensure gear is aligned with all clutch discs.

14) Install bearing race and thrust bearing on ring gear. Raised portion of race must be toward rear. Install forward and direct clutch assembly and front planetary ring gear in transmission case. Measure distance between sun gear input drum and direct clutch drum. *See Fig. 49.* Clearance for Lexus GS300, LS400, SC400 and Supra Turbo should be .386-.465" (9.80-11.80 mm). Clearance for all other models should be .209-.287" (5.30-7.30 mm). If clearance is not within specifications, check for incorrect installation.

15) Install thrust bearing and race on forward clutch assembly with flat side toward the clutch assembly. Install NEW "O" ring on 2nd coast brake cover. Install spring, 2nd coast brake piston assembly and cover to case. Install snap ring.

16) Place reference mark on 2nd coast brake piston rod. Apply 57-114 psi (4.8 kg/cm2) of air at opening of transmission case. Using wire gauge, measure clearance between reference mark and case. *See Fig. 14.* See 2ND COAST BRAKE PISTON STROKE SPECIFICATIONS.

2ND COAST BRAKE PISTON STROKE SPECIFICATIONS

Transmission Application & Model	Piston Stroke In. (mm)
Lexus	
GS300	
1995 A-340E	.079-.118 (2.00-3.00)
1996 A-350E	.039-.079 (1.00-2.00)
LS400 A-340E	.079-.118 (2.00-3.00)
LX450 A-343F	.059-.118 (1.50-3.00)
SC300 A-340E	.079-.118 (2.00-3.00)
SC400 A-340E	.079-.118 (2.00-3.00)
Toyota	
Land Cruiser A-343F	.059-.118 (1.50-3.00)
Pickup, Tacoma & 4Runner	
A-340E	.059-.118 (1.50-3.00)
A-340F	.059-.118 (1.50-3.00)
A-340H	.059-.118 (1.50-3.00)
Previa	
2WD A-340E	.059-.118 (1.50-3.00)
AWD A-340F	.059-.118 (1.50-3.00)
Supra	
Non-Turbo A-340E	.059-.118 (1.50-3.00)
Turbo A-340E	.039-.079 (1.00-2.00)
T100	
2WD A-340E	.059-.118 (1.50-3.00)
4WD A-340F	.059-.118 (1.50-3.00)

17) If stroke is not within specification, install replacement piston rod. Rods are available in lengths of 2.78" (70.7 mm), 2.81" (71.4 mm), 2.84" (72.2 mm) and 2.87" (72.9 mm). If stroke is not within specification, install NEW brake band. Install race on overdrive support. Install bolt and oil holes of overdrive support toward valve body side and align with bolt holes of case. Install support.

18) Ensure support is properly aligned. Install support snap ring with chamfered edge toward front of transmission. End of snap ring must be positioned to valve body side of case within .94" (23.9 mm) from center line of valve body as viewed from front of transmission.

19) Using dial indicator, check output shaft end play. On Lexus GS300 (1996), LS400, SC400 and Supra Turbo, end play should be .064-.114" (1.63-2.89 mm). On all other modes, end play should be .011-.034" (.27-.86 mm). If end play is not within specifications, check for incorrect assembly. Ensure output shaft rotates smoothly.

20) Install a .157" (4.00 mm) thick flange with rounded edge facing disc. Install correct amount of discs and plates, beginning with plate. Install end flange (stepped ring) with flat side toward disc. Install snap ring. Ensure ends of snap ring are not located at cutout areas of case.

21) Install dial indicator on case and measure piston stroke. Apply 57-114 psi (4-8 kg/cm²) at opening of transmission case and note piston stroke. *See Fig. 13.* See OD BRAKE PISTON STROKE SPECIFICATIONS table.

22) If piston stroke is not within specifications, check for incorrect installation. Recheck piston stroke. If piston stroke is not within specifications, install different thickness flange. Flanges are available in thicknesses of .130" (3.3 mm) to .157" (4.0 mm) in .008" (.20 mm) increments.

23) Install thrust bearing and races on overdrive support. Ensure race tabs align with hole support. Install overdrive planetary ring gear. Install thrust bearing and race in ring gear. Install race on rear of overdrive planetary gear, aligning race tabs with holes of gear.

24) Install overdrive planetary gear with overdrive direct clutch and one-way clutch. Install thrust bearing and race onto OD direct clutch with race flat side toward direct clutch.

25) Install race on rear of oil pump with raised side toward oil pump. Install NEW "O" ring on outer diameter of oil pump. Ensure oil seal rings are installed on rear of oil pump. Align holes of oil pump and transmission case. Install oil pump while holding input shaft and lightly pressing on oil pump.

OD BRAKE PISTON STROKE SPECIFICATIONS

Transmission Application & Model	Piston Stroke In. (mm)
Lexus	
GS300	
1995 A-340E	.055-.067 (1.40-1.70)
1996 A-350E	.069-.081 (1.75-2.05)
LS400 A-340E	.069-.081 (1.75-2.05)
LX450 A-343F	.069-.081 (1.75-2.05)
SC300 A-340E	.055-.067 (1.40-1.70)
SC400 A-340E	.069-.081 (1.75-2.05)
Toyota	
Land Cruiser A-343F	.069-.081 (1.75-2.05)
Pickup, Tacoma & 4Runner	
A-340E	.055-.067 (1.40-1.70)
A-340F	.052-.064 (1.32-1.62)
A-340H	.055-.067 (1.40-1.70)
Previa	
2WD A-340E	.055-.067 (1.40-1.70)
AWD A-340F	.055-.067 (1.40-1.70)
Supra	
Non-Turbo A-340E	.055-.067 (1.40-1.70)
Turbo A-340E	.069-.081 (1.75-2.05)
T100	
2WD A-340E	.055-.067 (1.40-1.70)
4WD A-340F	.055-.067 (1.40-1.70)

CAUTION: DO NOT apply excessive pressure on oil pump during installation or oil seal rings will stick to direct clutch drum.

26) Install oil pump bolts and tighten to specification. See TORQUE SPECIFICATIONS. Ensure input shaft rotates smoothly. Install throttle cable. Apply air pressure to specified oil passage to check operating components. *See Fig. 57.* When air checking OD direct clutch, overdrive accumulator piston hole must be plugged.

27) Assemble NEW spacer-to-manual valve lever. Install manual lever shaft to case through manual valve lever. Install pin to shaft. Align spacer hole with lever hole and stake spacer to lever. Ensure manual valve lever shaft turns smoothly.

28) Install "E" ring, parking lock pawl, shaft and spring. Connect parking lock rod to manual valve lever. Position parking lock pawl, shaft and spring. Connect parking lock rod to manual valve lever. Position parking lock pawl bracket on case and install.

29) Install accumulator pistons with NEW "O" rings and springs. *See Fig. 58.* Accumulator pistons and springs must be correct diameter and height. Accumulator pistons are stamped with identification codes. Determine correct spring free length. See appropriate ACCUMULATOR SPRING SPECIFICATIONS table.

30) Install check ball body and spring. *See Fig. 9.* Install valve body. See VALVE BODY under ON-VEHICLE SERVICE. Install sensor rotor and key on output shaft with snap ring. Install speedometer drive gear and lock ball and snap ring on output shaft. Install extension housing and NEW gasket. Shorter mounting bolts go to bottom of extension housing.

31) On A-340F and A-343F models, install transfer case assembly. Install transfer and drive shaft upper dust cover to transmission. Install engine rear mounting. Install dynamic damper. Install breather hose. Hose depth is .51" (13 mm).

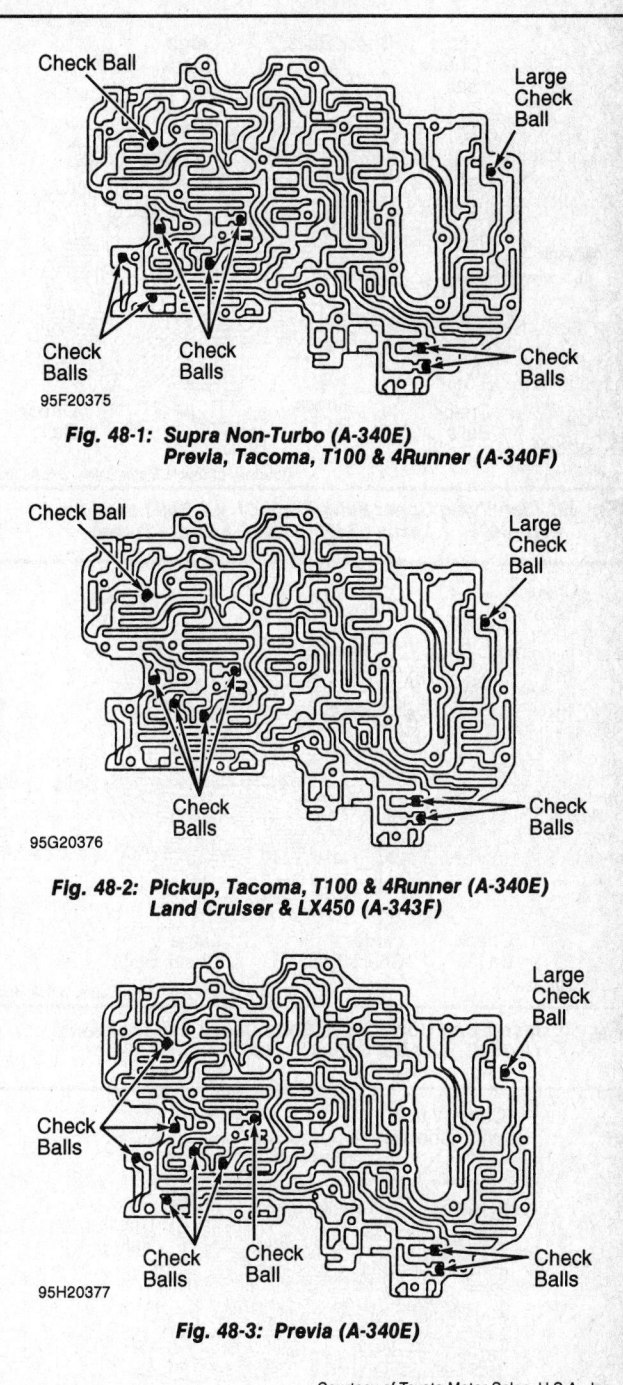

Fig. 48-1: Supra Non-Turbo (A-340E)
Previa, Tacoma, T100 & 4Runner (A-340F)

Fig. 48-2: Pickup, Tacoma, T100 & 4Runner (A-340E)
Land Cruiser & LX450 (A-343F)

Fig. 48-3: Previa (A-340E)

Courtesy of Toyota Motor Sales, U.S.A., Inc.

Fig. 48: Identifying Upper Valve Body Check Ball Locations

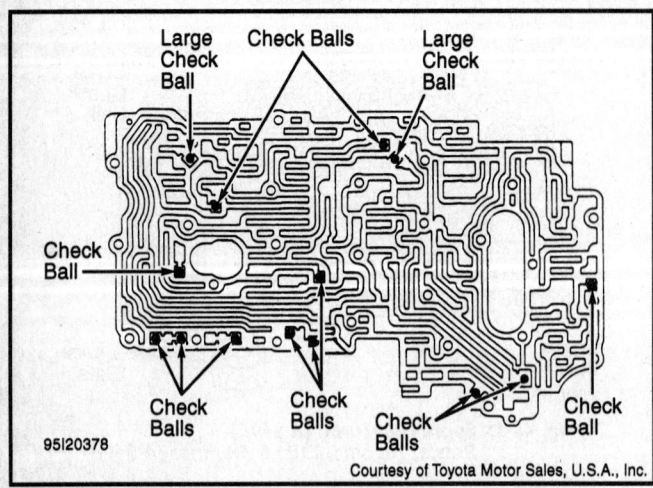

Fig. 49: Identifying Upper Valve Body Check Ball Locations (A-340E – Lexus LS400, SC400 & Supra Turbo)

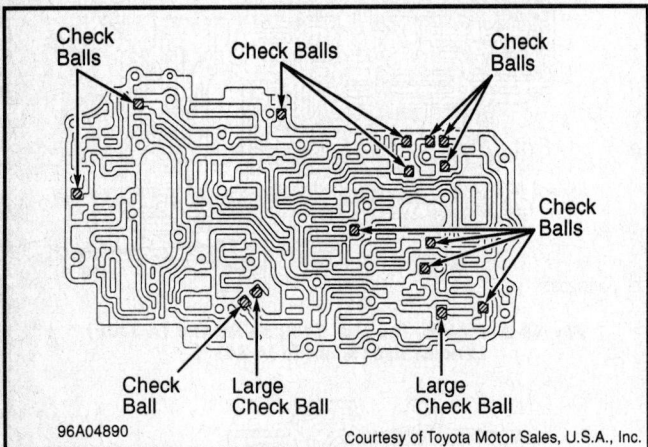

Fig. 50: Identifying Upper Valve Body Check Ball Locations (A-350E – Lexus GS300 – 1996)

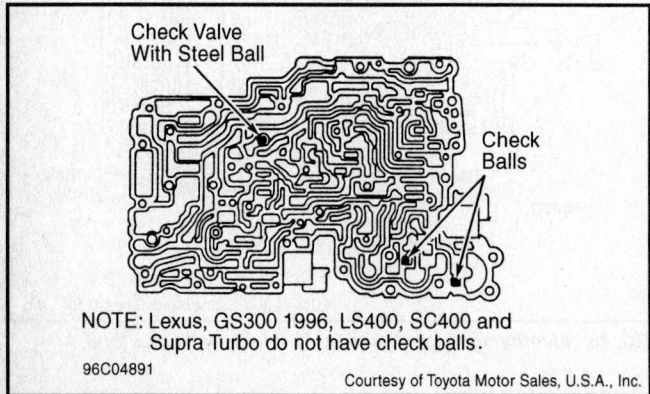

NOTE: Lexus, GS300 1996, LS400, SC400 and Supra Turbo do not have check balls.

Fig. 51: Identifying Lower Valve Body Check Ball Locations (A-340 Series Models)

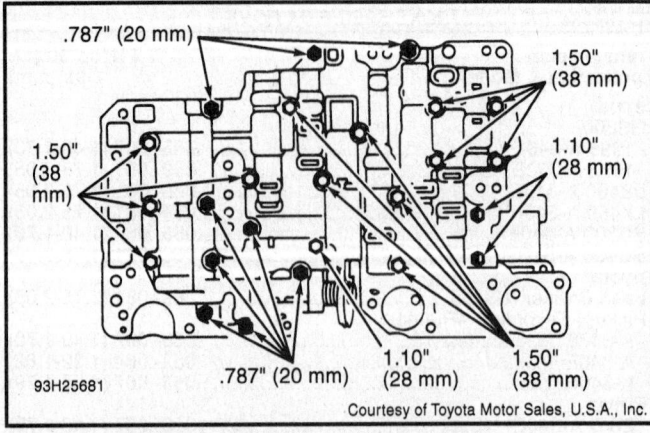

Fig. 52: Identifying A-340 Series Valve Body Bolts (All Except Lexus LS400, SC400 & Supra Turbo)

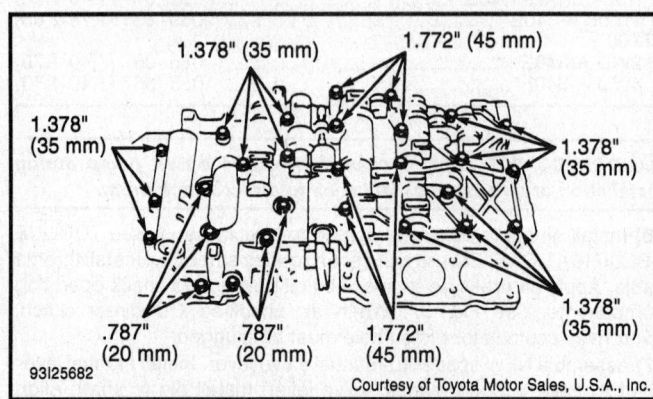

Fig. 53: Identifying A-340 Series Valve Body Bolts (Lexus LS400, SC400 & Supra Turbo)

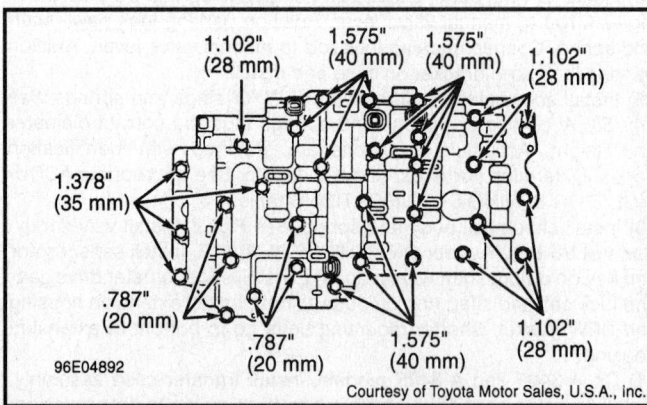

Fig. 54: Identifying A-350E Upper Valve Body Bolts (Lexus GS300 – 1996)

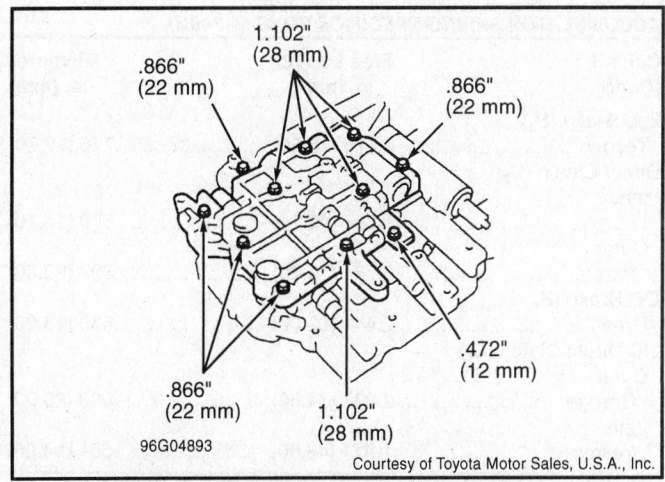

Fig. 55: Identifying A-350E Lower Valve Body Bolts (Lexus GS300 – 1996)

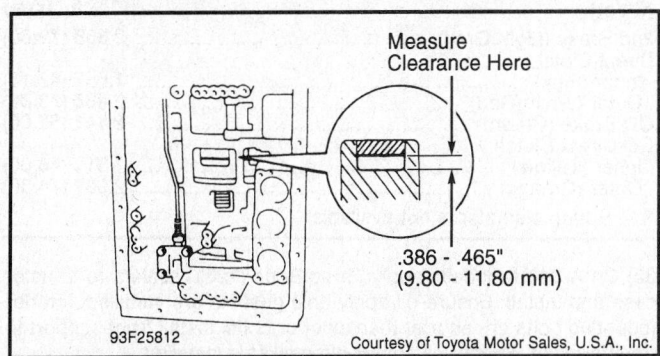

Fig. 56: Measuring Input Drum & Direct Clutch Drum Clearance

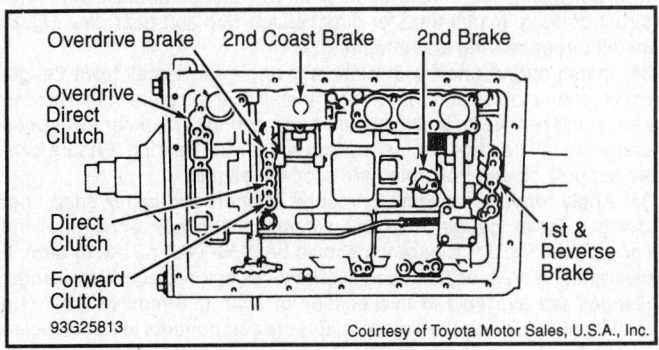

Fig. 57: Air Testing Transmission Components

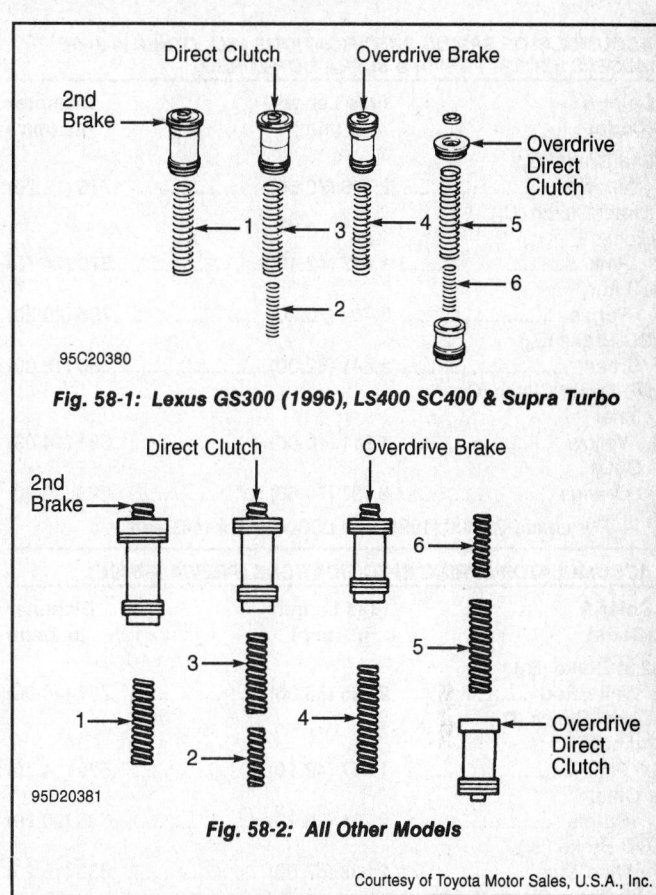

Fig. 58-1: Lexus GS300 (1996), LS400 SC400 & Supra Turbo

Fig. 58-2: All Other Models

Courtesy of Toyota Motor Sales, U.S.A., Inc.

Fig. 58: Identifying Accumulator Piston Assemblies

**ACCUMULATOR SPRING SPECIFICATIONS
(LEXUS GS300 1996, LS400, SC400 & SUPRA TURBO)**

Color & (Code)	Free Length In. (mm)	Diameter In. (mm)
2nd Brake (B_2)		
White/Red	2.963 (75.25)	.786 (19.97)
Direct Clutch (C_2)		
Inner		
White/Blue	1.575 (40.00)	.556 (14.11)
Outer		
Light Blue	3.0516 (77.51)	.791 (20.09)
OD Brake (B_0)		
White/Blue	2.637 (66.97)	.639 (16.24)
OD Direct Clutch (C_0)		
Inner		
White	1.513 (38.42)	.552 (14.03)
Outer		
White/Orange	2.573 (65.35)	.810 (20.59)

ACCUMULATOR SPRING SPECIFICATIONS (ALL OTHER A-340E MODELS EXCEPT PREVIA & SUPRA NON-TURBO)

Color & (Code)	Free Length In. (mm)	Diameter In. (mm)
2nd Brake (B_2)		
Yellow [1]	2.776 (70.50)	.776 (19.70)
Direct Clutch (C_2)		
Inner		
Pink	1.657 (42.10)	.579 (14.70)
Outer		
Purple	2.764 (70.20)	.795 (20.20)
OD Brake (B_0)		
Green	2.441 (62.00)	.630 (16.00)
OD Direct Clutch (C_0)		
Inner		
Yellow	1.811 (46.00)	.551 (14.00)
Outer		
Orange	2.937 (74.60)	.823 (20.90)

[1] – For Lexus GS300 (1995) and LS300, color is Green.

ACCUMULATOR SPRING SPECIFICATIONS (PREVIA A-340E)

Color & (Code)	Free Length In. (mm)	Diameter In. (mm)
2nd Brake (B_2)		
White/Red	2.965 (75.30)	.787 (20.00)
Direct Clutch (C_2)		
Inner		
Pink	1.657 (42.10)	.579 (14.70)
Outer		
Purple	2.764 (70.20)	.795 (20.20)
OD Brake (B_0)		
White/Blue	2.638 (67.00)	.638 (16.20)
OD Direct Clutch (C_0)		
Outer		
Orange	2.937 (74.60)	.823 (20.90)
Inner		
Yellow	1.811 (46.00)	.551 (14.00)

ACCUMULATOR SPRING SPECIFICATIONS (SUPRA NON-TURBO A-340E)

Color & (Code)	Free Length In. (mm)	Diameter In. (mm)
2nd Brake (B_2)		
Red	2.890 (73.40)	.783 (19.90)
Direct Clutch (C_2)		
Inner		
Pink	1.657 (42.10)	.579 (14.70)
Outer		
Purple	2.764 (70.20)	.795 (20.20)
OD Brake (B_0)		
White/Blue	2.638 (67.00)	.638 (16.20)
OD Direct Clutch (C_0)		
Outer		
Orange	2.937 (74.60)	.823 (20.90)
Inner		
Yellow	1.811 (46.00)	.551 (14.00)

ACCUMULATOR SPRING SPECIFICATIONS (A-340F)

Color & (Code)	Free Length In. (mm)	Diameter In. (mm)
2nd Brake (B_2)		
Yellow	2.776 (70.50)	.776 (19.70)
Direct Clutch (C_2)		
Blue	2.697 (68.50)	.795 (20.20)
OD Brake (B_0)		
Light Green	2.744 (69.70)	.657 (16.70)
OD Direct Clutch (C_0)		
White	2.638 (67.00)	.701 (17.80)

ACCUMULATOR SPRING SPECIFICATIONS (A-340H)

Color & (Code)	Free Length In. (mm)	Diameter In. (mm)
2nd Brake (B_2)		
Yellow	2.776 (70.50)	.776 (19.70)
Direct Clutch (C_2)		
Inner		
Purple	1.657 (42.10)	.579 (14.70)
Outer		
Purple	2.764 (70.20)	.795 (20.20)
OD Brake (B_0)		
Green	2.441 (62.00)	.630 (16.00)
OD Direct Clutch (C_0)		
Outer		
Orange	2.937 (74.60)	.823 (20.90)
Inner		
Yellow	1.811 (46.00)	.551 (14.00)

ACCUMULATOR SPRING SPECIFICATIONS [1] (A-343F)

Spring (Color)	Free Length In. (mm)
2nd Brake (Light Gray)	2.858 (72.60)
Direct Clutch	
Inner (Pink)	1.657 (42.10)
Outer (White/Red)	2.886 (73.30)
OD Brake (Green)	2.441 (62.00)
OD Direct Clutch	
Inner (Yellow)	1.811 (46.00)
Outer (Orange)	2.937 (74.60)

[1] – Spring diameter is not available.

32) On A-340H models, apply Three Bond (1281) sealant to transfer case and install. Ensure oil apply hole gaskets are installed. Interior mounting bolts are shorter than exterior bolts. Install front support to transfer case. Ensure oil apply hole gasket is installed.

33) Install thrust washer with inner and outer races on front of support with petroleum jelly. Install sun gear to transfer direct clutch with thrust bearing. Install transfer direct clutch with sun gear. See Fig. 8. Install thrust bearing and snap ring.

34) Install output shaft with planetary ring gear. Install front flange, clutch plates, discs and rear flange. Install cushion plate with rounded end facing rearward. Install piston return spring of transfer low speed brake. Install transfer center support with thrust bearing. Ensure center support oil and bolt holes are properly aligned.

35) Apply forward pressure on center support and install snap ring. Using a feeler gauge, measure clearance between snap ring and flange. See Fig. 11. Clearance should be .039-.083" (.91-2.10 mm). If clearance is not within specifications, select replacement flange. Flanges are available in thicknesses of .150" (3.8 mm) to .181" (4.6 mm) in .008" (.20 mm) increments. Ensure components are assembled correctly.

36) Install snap ring on output shaft. Install front drive clutch and snap ring. Install front output shaft and transfer front drive clutch. Mesh splines of front output shaft with discs. Apply sealant to transfer chain front cover and install. Install transfer chain front case to transfer case.

37) Install oil receiver. Install drive chain with drive and driven sprocket as single assembly. Install snap ring on output shaft. Apply sealant to transfer chain rear case and install. All bolts are equal length except 2 end bolts. Apply sealant to oil pump and install. Install speedometer drive gear. Apply sealant to extension housing and install. Install longer bolts with bracket.

38) Secure companion flange and install nut. Air-check piston operation. See Fig. 59. Install oil tubes. Install parking lock pawl bracket. Install transfer solenoid wiring. Install transfer valve body. Align manual valve groove to lever pin. Connect No. 4 solenoid and transfer pressure switch connectors. Install transfer oil pan. Install magnets in oil pan and install.

39) On A-350E models, install transmission output flange. Shift manual valve lever to "P" position. Tighten and stake nut. On all models, install transmission housing. On A-340E models, install speed sensor and speedometer driven gear. Install front and rear cooler line unions. On A-350E models, install direct clutch speed sensor. Install No. 1 and No. 2 speed sensors (if applicable).

40) Install speed sensor and fluid temperature sensor (if applicable). On A-340H models, install speed sensors. Install transfer position switch. Shift control lever into "H4" position. Align basic line and switch groove. Bend at least 2 lock washer tabs. Install transfer control shaft lever. Install speedometer driven gear.

41) Install transfer cooler line side unions. Install transfer oil cooler tubes. Install transmission and transfer fluid temperature sensors. On all models, install park/neutral position switch. Tighten nut to 61 INCH lbs. (6.9 N.m). Align neutral basic line and switch groove. Bend at least 2 lock washer tabs.

42) Install control shaft lever. If throttle cable is new, stake stopper on inner cable. Install wire harness and throttle cable clamp. Install torque converter. Using straightedge and depth gauge, measure distance from front of converter to front mounting surface of transmission housing. See TORQUE CONVERTER DISTANCE SPECIFICATIONS table to determine if converter is fully installed.

TORQUE CONVERTER DISTANCE SPECIFICATIONS

Application	Distance In. (mm)
Lexus	
GS300	
1995 A-340E	.004 (.10)
1996 A-350E	.004 (.10)
LS400 A-340F	.673 (17.10)
LX450 A-343F	.618 (15.70)
SC300 A-340E	1.039 (26.40)
SC400 A-340E	.673 (17.10)
Toyota	
Land Cruiser A-343F	.618 (15.70)
Pickup & 4Runner (1995)	
A-340E	.787 (20.00)
A-340F	.787 (20.00)
A-340H	.709 (18.00)
Previa	
2WD A-340E	1.250 (31.75)
AWD A-340F	1.250 (31.75)
Supra	
Non-Turbo A-340E	.004 (.10)
Turbo A-340E	.004 (.10)
Tacoma & 4Runner (1996)	
4-Cyl. A-340E & A-340F	1.250 (31.75)
V6 A-340E & A-340F	.707 (17.95)
T100	
A-340E	
4-Cyl.	1.250 (31.75)
V6	.707 (17.95)
A-340F	.707 (17.95)

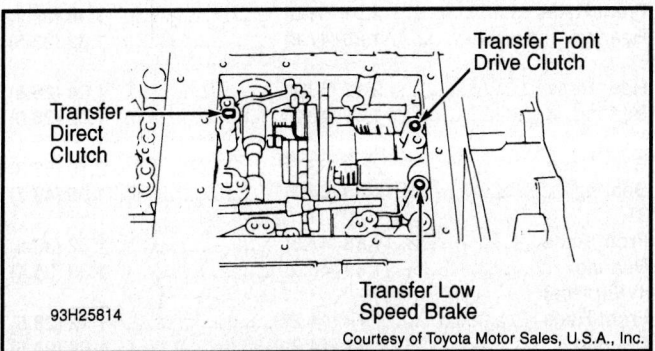

Transfer Front Drive Clutch

Transfer Direct Clutch

Transfer Low Speed Brake

93H25814

Courtesy of Toyota Motor Sales, U.S.A., Inc.

Fig. 59: Air Testing Transfer Components

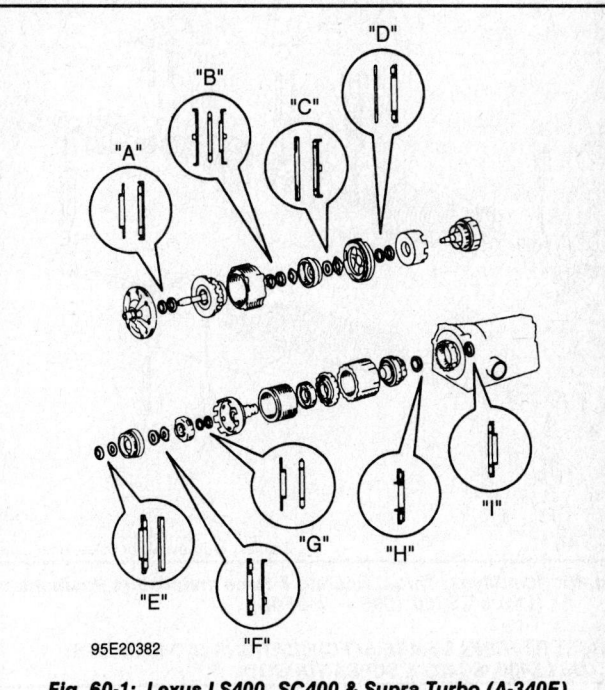

95E20382

Fig. 60-1: Lexus LS400, SC400 & Supra Turbo (A-340E) Land Cruiser & Lexus LX450 (A-343F)

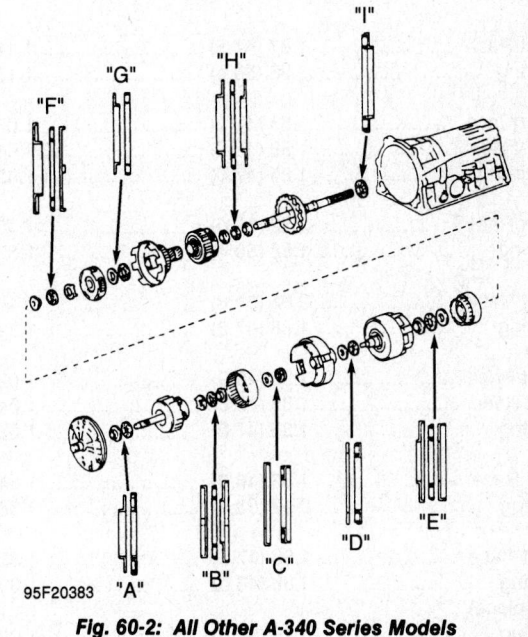

95F20383

Fig. 60-2: All Other A-340 Series Models

Courtesy of Toyota Motor Sales, U.S.A., Inc.

Fig. 60: Identifying Thrust Bearing & Race Installation Positions (A-340 Series Models)

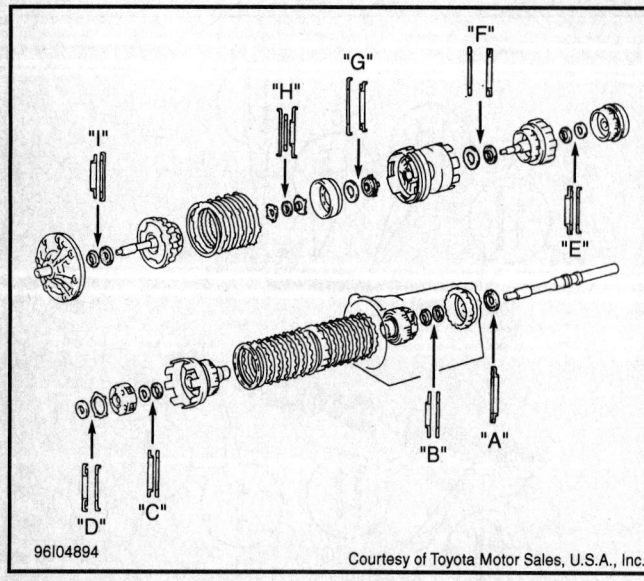

96I04894

Courtesy of Toyota Motor Sales, U.S.A., Inc.

Fig. 61: Identifying Thrust Bearing & Race Installation Positions (Lexus GS300 1996 – A-350E)

**THRUST BEARING & RACE SPECIFICATIONS (A-340 SERIES)
(LEXUS LS400, SC400 & SUPRA TURBO)**

Application	Outer Diameter In. (mm)	Inner Diameter In. (mm)
"A"		
Front Race	1.87 (47.5)	1.11 (28.1)
Bearing	1.98 (50.4)	1.13 (28.8)
"B"		
Front Race	1.65 (42.0)	1.07 (27.2)
Rear Race	1.89 (48.0)	.94 (24.0)
Bearing	1.85 (47.0)	1.02 (26.0)
"C"		
Front Race	2.32 (59.0)	1.46 (37.0)
Bearing	1.98 (50.4)	1.32 (33.5)
"D"		
Front Race	2.01 (51.0)	1.46 (37.0)
Bearing	1.88 (47.8)	1.32 (33.5)
"E"		
Front Race	1.93 (48.9)	1.02 (26.0)
Rear Race	1.85 (47.0)	1.04 (26.5)
Bearing	1.85 (47.0)	1.02 (26.0)
"F"		
Rear Race	1.89 (48.0)	1.34 (34.0)
Bearing	2.12 (53.8)	1.38 (35.0)
"G"		
Front Race	1.88 (47.8)	1.32 (33.5)
Bearing	1.89 (48.0)	1.39 (35.4)
"H" (1-piece)		
Bearing	2.15 (54.5)	1.09 (27.7)
"H" (3-piece)		
Front Race	1.76 (44.8)	1.13 (28.8)
Rear Race	1.76 (44.8)	1.09 (28.7)
Bearing	1.76 (44.8)	1.19 (30.1)
"I"		
Bearing	2.27 (57.7)	1.54 (39.0)

**THRUST BEARING & RACE SPECIFICATIONS
A-340 SERIES – ALL OTHER MODELS (EXCEPT A-343F)**

Application	Outer Diameter In. (mm)	Inner Diameter In. (mm)
"A"		
Front Race	1.86 (47.3)	1.11 (28.1)
Bearing	1.98 (50.2)	1.14 (28.9)
"B"		
Front Race	1.65 (41.8)	1.07 (27.3)
Rear Race	1.88 (47.8)	.953 (24.2)
Bearing	1.84 (46.8)	1.02 (26.0)
"C"		
Front Race	2.31 (58.8)	1.46 (37.2)
Bearing	2.01 (51.1)	1.33 (33.7)
"D"		
Front Race	2.00 (50.9)	1.45 (36.8)
Bearing	1.87 (47.6)	1.33 (33.7)
"E"		
Front Race	1.93 (48.9)	1.02 (26.0)
Rear Race	1.85 (47.0)	1.06 (26.8)
Bearing	1.84 (46.7)	1.02 (26.0)
"F"		
Front Race	2.11 (53.6)	1.20 (30.6)
Rear Race	1.88 (47.8)	1.35 (34.3)
Bearing	1.88 (47.8)	1.28 (32.6)
"G"		
Front Race	1.87 (47.6)	1.33 (33.7)
Bearing	1.88 (47.8)	1.40 (35.5)
"H"		
Front Race	1.76 (44.8)	1.13 (28.8)
Rear Race	1.76 (44.8)	1.13 (28.8)
Bearing	1.76 (44.8)	1.19 (30.1)
"I"		
Bearing	2.27 (57.7)	1.54 (39.2)

**THRUST BEARING & RACE SPECIFICATIONS
(LAND CRUISER & LEXUS LX450 – A-343F)**

Application	Outer Diameter In. (mm)	Inner Diameter In. (mm)
"A"		
Front Race	1.87 (47.5)	1.11 (28.1)
Bearing	1.98 (50.4)	1.13 (28.8)
"B"		
Front Race	1.65 (42.0)	1.07 (27.2)
Rear Race	1.89 (48.0)	.94 (24.0)
Bearing	1.85 (47.0)	1.02 (26.0)
"C"		
Front Race	2.32 (59.0)	1.46 (37.0)
Bearing	1.98 (50.4)	1.32 (33.5)
"D"		
Front Race	2.01 (51.0)	1.46 (37.0)
Bearing	1.88 (47.8)	1.32 (33.5)
"E"		
Rear Race	2.11 (53.7)	1.04 (26.5)
Bearing	1.69 (43.0)	1.02 (26.0)
"F"		
Rear Race	2.50 (63.6)	2.10 (53.3)
Bearing	2.55 (64.7)	1.96 (49.7)
"G"		
Front Race	1.88 (47.8)	1.32 (33.5)
Bearing	1.89 (48.0)	1.39 (35.4)
"H" (2-piece)		
Front Race	1.74 (44.2)	1.12 (28.5)
Bearing	1.74 (44.2)	1.08 (27.5)
"I"		
Bearing	2.27 (57.7)	1.54 (39.2)

THRUST BEARING & RACE SPECIFICATIONS
(LEXUS GS300 – 1996 – A-350E)

Application	Outer Diameter In. (mm)	Inner Diameter In. (mm)
"A"		
Bearing	2.27 (57.5)	1.54 (39.0)
"B"		
Front Race	1.74 (44.2)	1.12 (28.5)
Bearing	1.74 (44.2)	1.09 (27.6)
"C"		
Front Race	1.88 (47.8)	1.32 (33.6)
Bearing	1.89 (48.0)	1.40 (35.5)
"D"		
Rear Race	2.50 (63.6)	2.10 (53.3)
Bearing	2.55 (64.7)	1.96 (49.7)
"E"		
Rear Race	2.11 (53.7)	1.04 (26.5)
Bearing	1.93 (48.9)	1.02 (26.0)
"F"		
Front Race	2.00 (50.7)	1.44 (36.5)
Bearing	1.88 (47.8)	1.32 (33.6)
"G"		
Front Race	2.32 (59.0)	1.46 (37.0)
Bearing	1.98 (50.4)	1.32 (33.6)
"H" (3-piece)		
Front Race	1.65 (42.0)	1.07 (27.2)
Rear Race	1.89 (48.0)	1.02 (26.0)
Bearing	1.89 (48.0)	.945 (24.0)
"I"		
Front Race	1.84 (46.7)	1.13 (28.8)
Bearing	1.98 (50.4)	1.13 (28.8)

TORQUE SPECIFICATIONS
TORQUE SPECIFICATIONS

Application	Ft. Lbs. (N.m)
Chain Case Bolt (A-340H)	25 (34)
Companion Flange Nut (A-340H)	91 (123)
Cooler Union	21 (29)
Dynamic Damper	27 (37)
Extension Housing Bolt	
A-340H & A-350E	25 (34)
All Other Models	27 (37)
Fluid Temperature Sensor Bolt (A-340H)	11 (15)
Front Support Bolt (A340H)	25 (34)
No. 1 Speed Sensor Bolt	12 (16)
Oil Cooler Pipe Union Nut	25 (34)
Oil Pump-To-Case Bolt	16 (22)
Overdrive-To-Case Bolt	18 (25)
Rear Mounting-To-Extension Housing Bolt	18 (25)
Shift Lever Nut	12 (16)
Speedometer Driven Gear Bolt	12 (16)
Support Crossmember-To-Body Bolt	18 (25)
Torque Converter-To-Drive Plate Bolt	30 (41)
Transfer Case-To-Transmission Bolt (A-340H)	25 (34)
Transfer Oil Cooler Tube Union Nut (A-340H)	25 (34)
Transfer Oil Pump-To-Rear Chain Case Bolt (A-340H)	12 (16)
Transmission Housing Bolt	
10 mm	25 (34)
12 mm	42 (57)
14 mm	25 (34)
17 mm	42 (57)
Transmission Output Flange Bolt (A-350E)	91 (123)

Application	INCH Lbs. (N.m)
Detent Spring Bolt	89 (10)
Park/Neutral Position Switch	
Adjusting Bolt	115 (13)
Retaining Nut	61 (6.9)
No. 2 Speed Sensor Bolt	48 (5.4)
Oil Pan Bolt	65 (7.3)
Oil Pump-To-Stator Shaft Bolt	89 (10)
Oil Strainer Bolt	89 (10)
Overdrive Direct Clutch Speed Sensor Bolt (A-350E)	48 (5.4)

TORQUE SPECIFICATIONS (Cont.)

Application	INCH Lbs. (N.m)
Parking Lock Pawl Bracket Bolt	65 (7.3)
Solenoid-To-Valve Body Bolt	89 (10)
Throttle Cable-To-Transmission Case Bolt	48 (5.4)
Transfer Detent Spring-To-Valve Body Bolt (A-340H)	61 (6.9)
Transfer Lock Pawl Bracket Bolt (A-340H)	61 (6.9)
Transfer Oil Pump Body Bolt (A-340H)	89 (10)
Transfer Oil Strainer Bolt (A-340H)	61 (6.9)
Transfer Position Switch	
Adjusting Bolt	115 (13)
Mounting Nut	35 (3.9)
Transfer Pressure Switch-To-Valve Body (A-340H)	61 (6.9)
Transfer Valve Body-To-Case Bolt (A-340H)	89 (10)
Upper Valve Body-To-Lower Valve Body Bolt	57 (6.4)
Valve Body-To-Case Bolt	89 (10)

TRANSMISSION SPECIFICATIONS
TRANSMISSION SPECIFICATIONS

Application	In. (mm)
Bushing Diameter (Maximum)	
Direct Clutch Drum	
Lexus GS300 (1995), LX450 & SC300	2.126 (53.99)
Lexus GS300 (1996), LS400 & SC400	2.124 (53.97)
Toyota	
Supra	2.124 (53.97)
All Others	2.126 (53.99)
Extension Housing	1.578 (40.09)
Forward Clutch Drum	.948 (24.08)
OD Direct Clutch Drum	1.067 (27.11)
OD Planetary Gear	.444 (11.27)
Planetary Ring Gear	
A-340 Series	.948 (24.08)
A-350E	1.578 (40.09)
Sun Gear	1.066 (27.08)
Transmission Case	1.504 (38.19)
Clutch Pack Clearance	
Transfer Low Speed Brake	.036-.083 (.91-2.10)
1st & Reverse Brake	
Lexus	
GS300	
1995 A-340E	.024-.078 (.61-1.98)
1996 A-350E	.024-.035 (.61-.90)
LS400 A-340E	.024-.078 (.61-1.98)
LX450 A-343F	.028-.048 (.70-1.22)
SC300 A-340E	.024-.044 (.61-1.12)
SC400 A-340E	.028-.039 (.70-1.00)
Land Cruiser A-343F	.028-.048 (.70-1.22)
Pickup, Tacoma & 4Runner	
A-340E	.024-.044 (.61-1.12)
A-340F	.020-.040 (.50-1.02)
A-340H	.024-.052 (.61-1.32)
Previa	
2WD A-340E	.024-.044 (.61-1.12)
AWD A-340F	.024-.044 (.61-1.12)
Supra	
Non-Turbo A-340E	.024-.044 (.61-1.12)
Turbo A-340E	.028-.039 (.70-1.00)
T100	
2WD A-340E	.024-.044 (.61-1.12)
4WD A-340F	.024-.044 (.61-1.12)
2nd Brake Clutch	
Lexus	
GS300	
1995 A-340E	.024-.078 (.61-1.98)
1996 A-350E	.019-.044 (.49-1.11)
LS400 A-340E	.024-.078 (.61-1.98)
LX450 A-343F	.024-.078 (.61-1.98)
SC300 A-340E	.024-.078 (.61-1.98)
SC400 A-340E	.024-.078 (.61-1.98)
Land Cruiser A-343F	.024-.078 (.61-1.98)
Pickup, Tacoma & 4Runner	
A-340E	.024-.078 (.61-1.98)
A-340F	.020-.069 (.50-1.76)
A-340H	.024-.078 (.61-1.98)
Previa	
2WD A-340E	.024-.078 (.61-1.98)
AWD A-340F	.024-.078 (.61-1.98)

TRANSMISSION SPECIFICATIONS (Cont.)

Application	In. (mm)
Supra	
Non-Turbo A-340E	.024-.078 (.61-1.98)
Turbo A-340E	.019-.044 (.49-1.11)
T100	
2WD A-340E	.024-.078 (.61-1.98)
4WD A-340F	.024-.078 (.61-1.98)
Output Shaft End Play	
GS300 (1996), LS400, SC400	
& Supra Turbo	.064-.114 (1.63-2.89)
All Other Models	.011-.034 (.27-.86)
Piston Stroke	
Direct Clutch	
Lexus	
GS300 (1995), LX450 & SC300	.054-.063 (1.37-1.60)
GS300 (1996), LS400 & SC400	.015-.028 (.40-.70)
Toyota	
A-340E (Supra Turbo)	.020-.032 (.50-.80)
A-340E (All Others)	.054-.063 (1.37-1.60)
A-340F (T100)	.054-.063 (1.37-1.60)
A-340F (All Others)	.041-.052 (1.03-1.33)
A-340H	.054-.063 (1.37-1.60)
A-343F	.054-.063 (1.37-1.60)
Forward Clutch	
Lexus	
GS300 & SC300	.024-.035 (.61-.90)
LX450	.024-.039 (.61-1.00)
LS400 & SC400	.028-.039 (.70-1.00)
Toyota	
A-340E (Supra Turbo)	.028-.039 (.70-1.00)
A-340E (All Others)	.020-.035 (.50-.90)
A-340F (T100)	.020-.035 (.50-.90)
A-340F (All Others)	.016-.031 (.40-.80)
A-340H	.020-.035 (.50-.90)
A-343F	.024-.039 (.61-1.00)
OD Brake	
Lexus	
GS300	
1995 A-340E	.055-.067 (1.40-1.70)
1996 A-350E	.069-.081 (1.75-2.05)
LS400 A-340E	.069-.081 (1.75-2.05)
LX450 A-343F	.069-.081 (1.75-2.05)
SC300 A-340E	.055-.067 (1.40-1.70)
SC400 A-340E	.069-.081 (1.75-2.05)
Land Cruiser A-343F	.069-.081 (1.75-2.05)
Pickup, Tacoma & 4Runner	
A-340E	.055-.067 (1.40-1.70)
A-340F	.052-.064 (1.32-1.62)
A-340H	.055-.067 (1.40-1.70)
Previa	
2WD A-340E	.055-.067 (1.40-1.70)
AWD A-340F	.055-.067 (1.40-1.70)
Supra	
Non-Turbo A-340E	.055-.067 (1.40-1.70)
Turbo A-340E	.069-.081 (1.75-2.05)
T100	
2WD A-340E	.055-.067 (1.40-1.70)
4WD A-340F	.055-.067 (1.40-1.70)

TRANSMISSION SPECIFICATIONS (Cont.)

Application	In. (mm)
Piston Stroke (Cont.)	
OD Direct Clutch	
Lexus	
GS300 (1995) & SC300	.073-.085 (1.85-2.15)
GS300 (1996), LS400, LX450 & SC400	.057-.067 (1.45-1.70)
Toyota	
A-340E (Supra Non-Turbo)	.057-.067 (1.45-1.70)
A-340E (Supra)	.057-.067 (1.45-1.70)
A-340E (All Others)	.073-.085 (1.85-2.15)
A-340F (T100)	.073-.085 (1.85-2.15)
A-340F (All Others)	.070-.082 (1.77-2.07)
A-340H	.073-.085 (1.85-2.15)
A-343F	.073-.085 (1.85-2.15)
2nd Coast Brake	
Lexus	
GS300	
1995 A-340E	.079-.118 (2.00-3.00)
1996 A-350E	.039-.079 (1.00-2.00)
LS400 A-340E	.079-.118 (2.00-3.00)
LX450 A-343F	.059-.118 (1.50-3.00)
SC300 A-340E	.079-.118 (2.00-3.00)
SC400 A-340E	.079-.118 (2.00-3.00)
Land Cruiser A-343F	.059-.118 (1.50-3.00)
Pickup, Tacoma & 4Runner	
A-340E	.059-.118 (1.50-3.00)
A-340F	.059-.118 (1.50-3.00)
A-340H	.059-.118 (1.50-3.00)
Previa	
2WD A-340E	.059-.118 (1.50-3.00)
AWD A-340F	.059-.118 (1.50-3.00)
Supra	
Non-Turbo A-340E	.059-.118 (1.50-3.00)
Turbo A-340E	.039-.079 (1.00-2.00)
T100	
2WD A-340E	.059-.118 (1.50-3.00)
4WD A-340F	.059-.118 (1.50-3.00)
Planetary Pinion Gear Clearance	.008-.024 (.20-.61)

Toyota A-340 Series – Electronic Controls (Except OBD-II)

Lexus: GS300, SC300, SC400
Toyota: Pickup, Supra Turbo, 4Runner

APPLICATION

APPLICATION

Vehicle	Transmission Model
1995 Lexus	
GS300	A-340E
SC300	A-340E
SC400	A-340E
1995 Toyota	
Pickup	
2WD V6	A-340E
4WD 4-Cyl.	A-340F
4WD V6	A-340H
Supra	
Turbo	A-340E
4Runner	
2WD V6	A-340E
4WD 4-Cyl.	A-340F
4WD V6	A-340H

CAUTION: Lexus models and Toyota Supra are equipped with Supplemental Restraint System (SRS). When servicing vehicle, use care to avoid accidental air bag deployment. All SRS electrical connections and wiring harnesses are covered with Yellow insulation. SRS-related components are located in steering column, center console, instrument panel and lower panel on instrument panel. DO NOT use electrical test equipment on these circuits. If necessary, deactivate SRS before servicing components. See AIR BAG SERVICING article in APPLICATIONS & IDENTIFICATION section.

DESCRIPTION

Automatic transmission for all models is electronically controlled. The A-340E is an electronically controlled transmission without a transfer case. The A-340F is an electronically controlled transmission with a mechanically controlled transfer case. The A-340H is an electronically controlled transmission with an electronically controlled transfer case.

On all models, transmission shifting and torque converter lock-up are controlled by an Electronic Controlled Transmission (ECT) Electronic Control Unit (ECU). Control unit is referred to as the ECT ECU. ECT ECU is combined with engine ECU into one unit.

ECT ECU receives information from various input devices and uses this information to control shift solenoids for transmission shifting and lock-up solenoid (also called No. 3 or SL solenoid) for torque converter lock-up. Solenoids are mounted on transmission valve body. *See Figs. 1-4.*

On A-340H transmission, transfer case valve body is equipped with an additional solenoid (No. 4 solenoid) to assist in smooth shifting. On Lexus models, transmission valve body is equipped with a additional solenoid (No. 4 solenoid) that affects shift feel by controlling accumulator pressure. Supra Turbo is also equipped with this solenoid and an additional variably controlled orifice solenoid (No. 5 solenoid) for line pressure control. Supra Turbo does not have a throttle valve and/or throttle valve cable.

An Overdrive (OD) switch is mounted on shift lever. *See Figs. 1-4.* When OD switch is depressed to ON position, transmission will shift into 4th gear when shift lever is in "D" position, and OD OFF light on instrument panel will go off. When OD switch is released to OFF position, transmission will shift into 3rd gear, and OD OFF light will illuminate.

A pattern select switch is located on instrument panel (Pickup with column shift) or near shift lever (all other models). *See Figs. 1-4.* Pattern select switch has a POWER (depressed) and a NORMAL (released) operating position. When pattern select switch is depressed, transmission upshifts and downshifts will occur at a higher vehicle speed than with switch released. An indicator light on instrument panel indicates when pattern select switch is in POWER position.

Transmission is equipped with shift and key lock system. Shift lock system prevents shift lever from being moved from Park unless brake pedal is depressed. In case of malfunction, shift lever can be released by pressing shift lock override button, located near shift lever. Key lock system prevents ignition key from being moved from ACC to LOCK position unless shift lever is in Park. For more information on shift lock and key lock system, see TOYOTA SHIFT LOCK SYSTEM article.

OPERATION

ECT ECU

ECT ECU receives information from various input devices and uses this information to control solenoids on transmission or transfer case valve body for transmission shifting, shift feel, line pressure and torque converter lock-up.

ECT ECU contains a self-diagnostic system, which will store a Diagnostic Trouble Code (DTC) if failure or problem exists in electronic control system. DTC can be retrieved to determine transmission problem area. See SELF-DIAGNOSTIC SYSTEM. Note location of ECT ECU. *See Figs. 1-4.*

ECT ECU INPUT DEVICES

Brakelight Switch Signal – Brakelight switch delivers input signal to ECT ECU, indicating vehicle braking. Brakelight switch is located on brake pedal support. *See Figs. 1-4.*

Engine Coolant Temperature (ECT) Sensor Signal – Coolant temperature sensor delivers input signal to ECT ECU, indicating engine coolant temperature. Coolant temperature sensor is located in coolant passage on engine. *See Figs. 1-4.*

Cruise Control Electronic Control Unit (ECU) – Cruise control ECU delivers an input signal to control overdrive in accordance with vehicle speed when cruise control is operating. When in overdrive with cruise control on, if vehicle speed drops 3 MPH less than set speed, overdrive is released to prevent reduction in vehicle speed. Once vehicle speed is more than set speed, overdrive is resumed. If coolant temperature is low, transmission will not shift into overdrive.

On GS300, ECU is located under console, in front of shift lever. On SC300 and SC400, ECU is located behind instrument panel, to left of steering column. On Pickup and 4Runner, ECU is located at left kick panel. On Supra Turbo, ECU is located behind instrument panel cluster. *See Figs. 2-4.*

Distributor – Distributor delivers an input signal to ECT ECU indicating engine RPM and crankshaft position.

Kickdown Switch Signal (Supra Turbo) – Kickdown switch sends a signal to ECT ECU when accelerator is fully pressed. *See Fig. 4.* ECT ECU uses this input signal to control downshifts.

OD Direct Clutch Speed Sensor (Lexus Models & Supra Turbo) – OD direct clutch speed sensor sends input shaft speed signal to ECT ECU. OD direct clutch speed sensor is located on transmission, near park/neutral position switch. *See Figs. 1, 2 and 4.*

OD Switch Signal – OD switch provides an input signal to ECT ECU to indicate when overdrive is selected by vehicle operator. When OD switch is depressed to ON position, transmission will shift into 4th gear when shift lever is in "D" position, and OD OFF light on instrument panel will go off. When OD switch is released to OFF position, transmission will shift into 3rd gear, and OD OFF light will illuminate. OD switch is mounted on shift lever. *See Figs 1-4.*

Park/Neutral Position (PNP) Switch Signal – PNP switch delivers an input signal to ECT ECU indicating shift lever position. Switch is located on left side of transmission. *See Figs. 1-4.*

Throttle Position (TP) Sensor Signal – TP sensor delivers a closed throttle and variable throttle position input signals to ECT ECU. TP sensor is located on side of throttle body. *See Figs. 1-4.*

Vehicle Speed Sensor (VSS) Signal – Vehicle speed signal is delivered to ECT ECU by No. 1 and No. 2 speed sensors. No. 1 vehicle speed sensor is located in combination meter, or at left side of transmission housing. No. 2 vehicle speed sensor is located at left side of transmission housing. *See Figs. 1-4.*

3-1658

AUTOMATIC TRANSMISSIONS
Toyota A-340 Series - Electronic Controls (Except OBD-II) (Cont.)

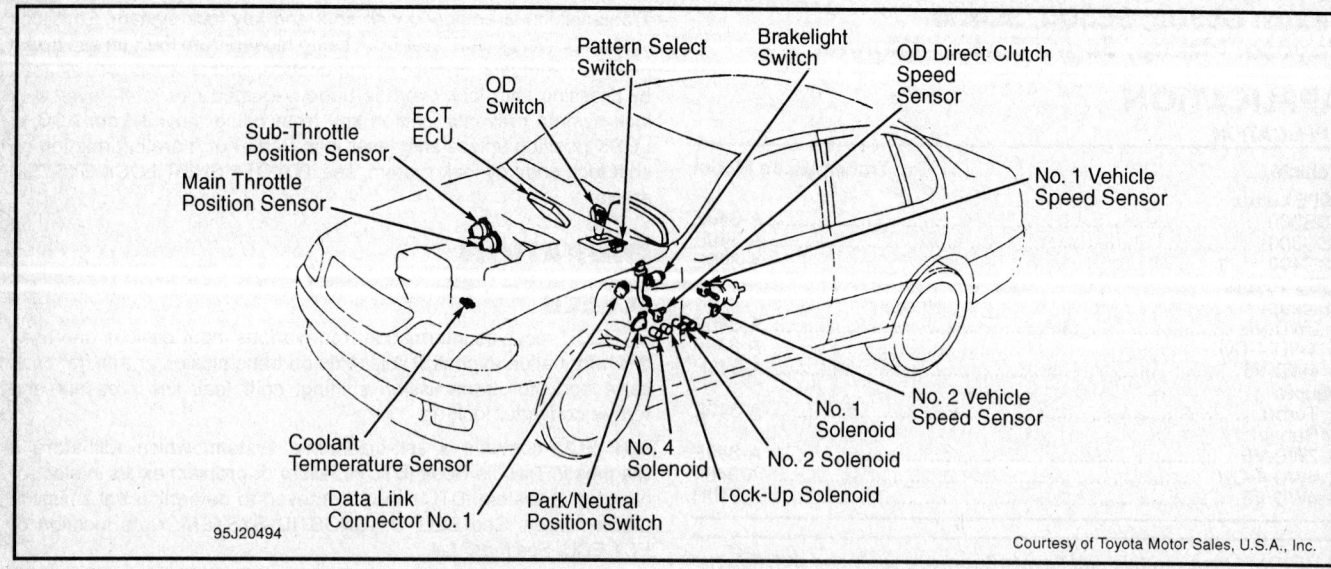

Fig. 1: Identifying Input & Output Devices (1995 Lexus GS300)

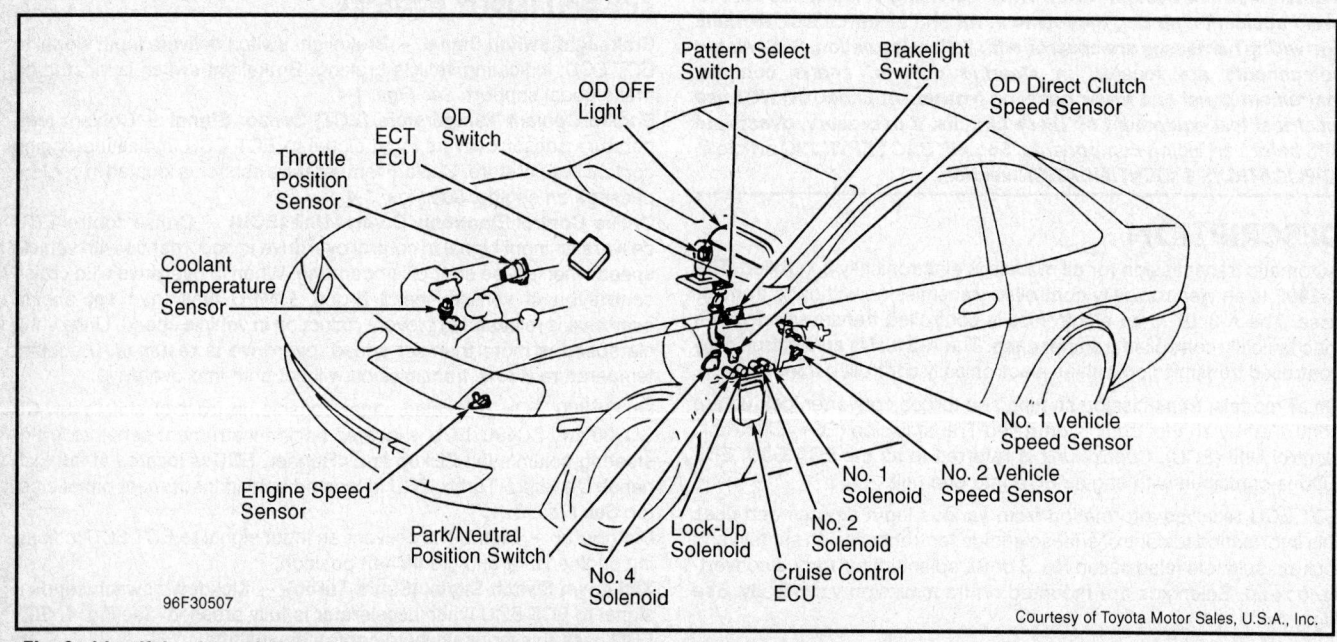

Fig. 2: Identifying Input & Output Devices (1995 Lexus SC400 Shown, SC300 Is Similar)

ATF Temperature Sensor (Pickup, Supra Turbo & 4Runner) – Sensor delivers an input signal to ECT ECU to indicate fluid temperature. Sensor converts fluid temperature into a resistance value. Sensor is located on left side of transmission. See Figs. 3 and 4.

Transfer Case Fluid Temperature Sensor (A-340H Transmission) – Sensor delivers an input signal to ECT ECU to indicate transfer case fluid temperature. Sensor converts fluid temperature into a resistance value. Sensor is located on transfer case rear extension housing. See Fig. 3.

Transfer Case Position Switch (A-340H Transmission) – Switch delivers an input signal to ECT ECU to indicate transfer case shift position. Sensor is located on transfer case rear extension housing. See Fig. 3.

ECT ECU OUTPUT DEVICES

No. 1 & No. 2 Solenoids – ECT ECU controls transmission shifting by delivering an output signal to operate proper solenoid. Solenoids are located on transmission valve body. See Figs. 1-4. Solenoids are operated in accordance with shift lever range. If a solenoid malfunctions, ECT ECU may select a preselected gear. See Fig. 5.

NOTE: ECT ECU provides a fail-safe system which will place transmission in preselected gear depending on solenoid failure. In other gears, fail-safe system will not be activated and transmission will be placed in a specified gear. See Fig. 5.

No. 3 Solenoid (Lock-Up Solenoid) – ECT ECU controls torque converter lock-up by delivering an output signal to lock-up solenoid. Lock-up solenoid is activated when shift lever is in "D" position and vehicle is at specified speed.

No. 4 Solenoid (Accumulator Back Pressure Modulation – Lexus Models & Supra Turbo) – ECT ECU receives information from various input devices and uses this information to control No. 4 solenoid for smooth clutch and brake engagement during shifting. No. 4 solenoid is located on transmission valve body.

No. 4 Solenoid (Transfer Case Shift Solenoid – A-340H Transmission) – ECT ECU receives information from various input devices and uses this information to control No. 4 solenoid for smooth engagement during shifting. No. 4 solenoid is located on transfer case valve body.

AUTOMATIC TRANSMISSIONS
Toyota A-340 Series - Electronic Controls (Except OBD-II) (Cont.)

3-1659

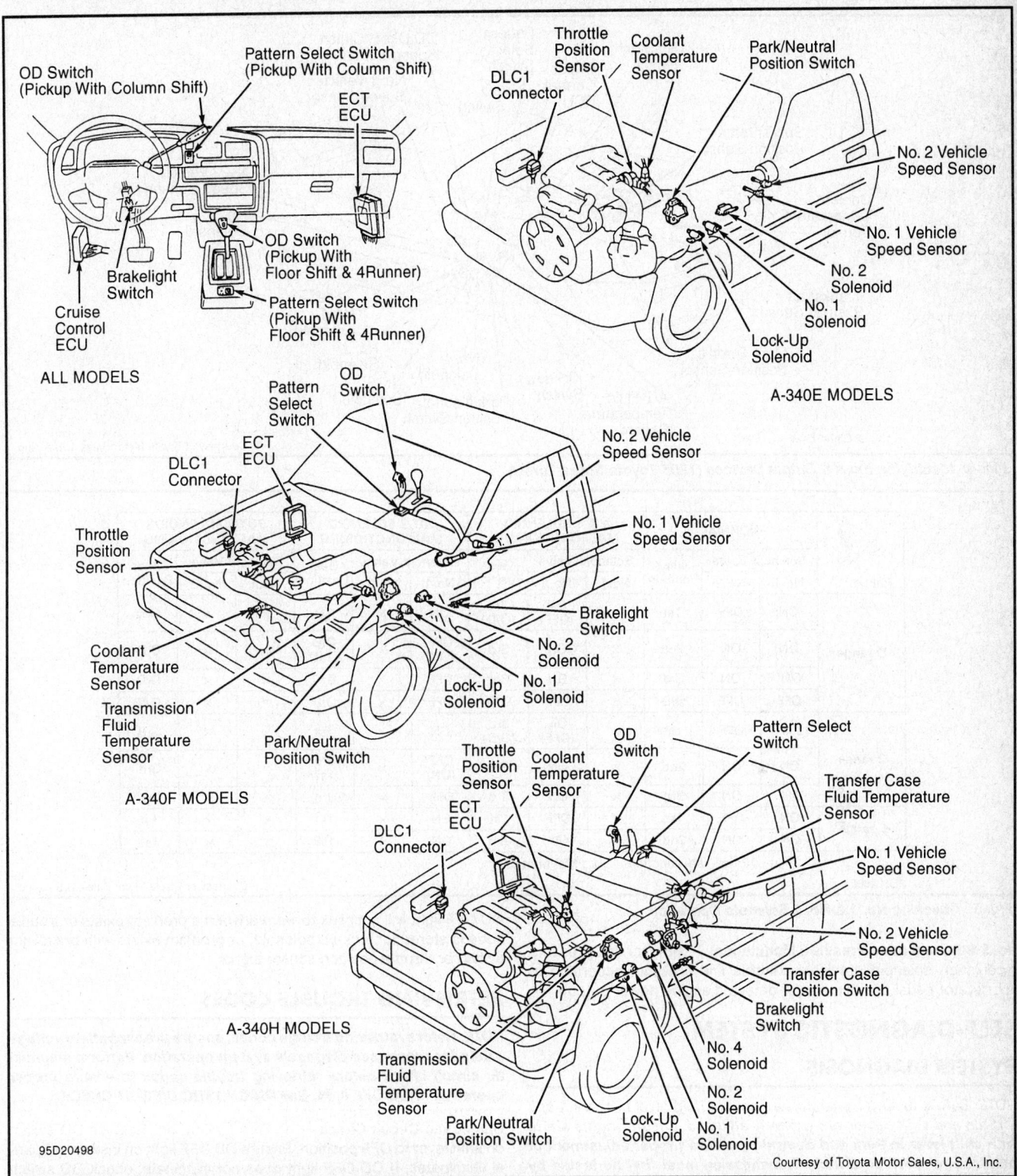

Fig. 3: Identifying Input & Output Devices (1995 Toyota Pickup & 4Runner)

95D20498

Courtesy of Toyota Motor Sales, U.S.A., Inc.

3-1660

AUTOMATIC TRANSMISSIONS
Toyota A-340 Series - Electronic Controls (Except OBD-II) (Cont.)

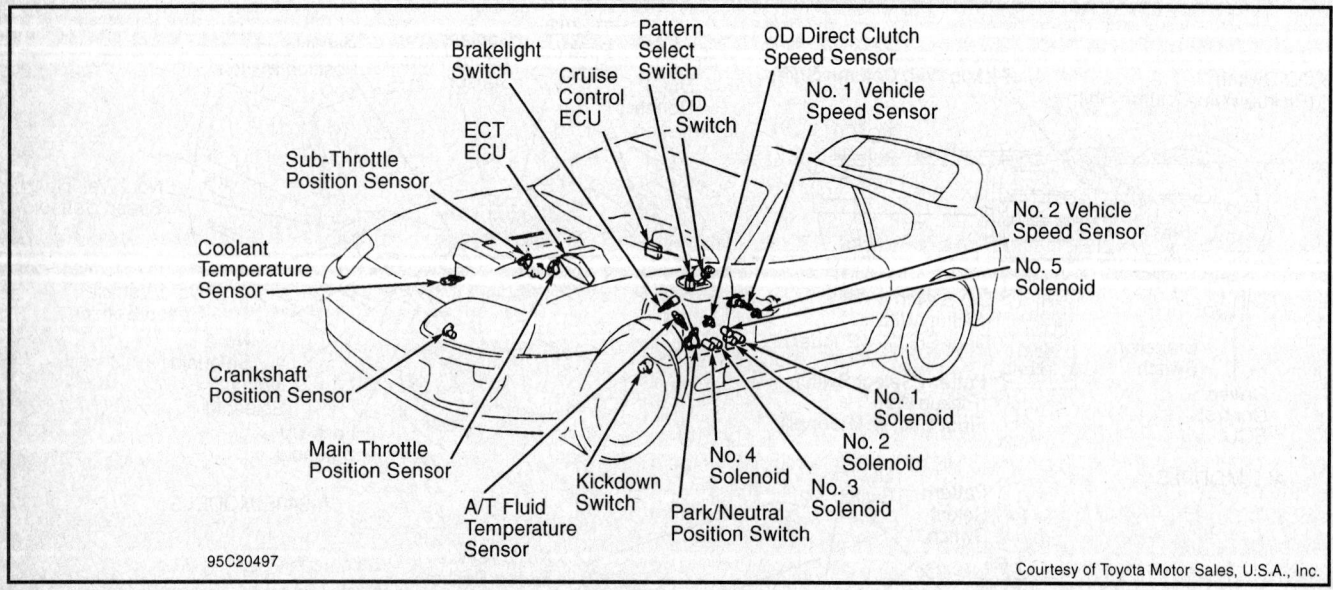

Courtesy of Toyota Motor Sales, U.S.A., Inc.

Fig. 4: Identifying Input & Output Devices (1995 Toyota Supra Turbo)

Range	NORMAL Solenoid Valve No.1	NORMAL Solenoid Valve No.2	NORMAL Gear Position	NO.1 SOLENOID MALFUNCTIONING Solenoid Valve No.1	NO.1 SOLENOID MALFUNCTIONING Solenoid Valve No.2	NO.1 SOLENOID MALFUNCTIONING Gear Position	NO.2 SOLENOID MALFUNCTIONING Solenoid Valve No.1	NO.2 SOLENOID MALFUNCTIONING Solenoid Valve No.2	NO.2 SOLENOID MALFUNCTIONING Gear Position	BOTH SOLENOIDS MALFUNCTIONING Solenoid Valve No.1	BOTH SOLENOIDS MALFUNCTIONING Solenoid Valve No.2	BOTH SOLENOIDS MALFUNCTIONING Gear Position
D range	ON	OFF	1st	×	ON (OFF)	3rd (O/D)	ON	×	1st	×	×	O/D
	ON	ON	2nd	×	ON	3rd	OFF (ON)	×	O/D (1st)	×	×	O/D
	OFF	ON	3rd	×	ON	3rd	OFF	×	O/D	×	×	O/D
	OFF	OFF	O/D	×	OFF	O/D	OFF	×	O/D	×	×	O/D
2 range	ON	OFF	1st	×	ON (OFF)	3rd (O/D)	ON	×	1st	×	×	3rd
	ON	ON	2nd	×	ON	3rd	OFF (ON)	×	3rd (1st)	×	×	3rd
	OFF	ON	3rd	×	ON	3rd	OFF	×	3rd	×	×	3rd
L range	ON	OFF	1st	×	OFF	1st	ON	×	1st	×	×	1st
	ON	ON	2nd	×	ON	2nd	ON	×	1st	×	×	1st

( ): No fail-safe function   × : Malfunctions

95C24689

Courtesy of Toyota Motor Sales, U.S.A., Inc.

Fig. 5: Checking No. 1 & No. 2 Solenoid Operation

No. 5 Solenoid (Line Pressure Modulation) – No. 5 or line pressure modulation solenoid precisely controls line pressure according to accelerator pedal position and/or detected engine power output.

SELF-DIAGNOSTIC SYSTEM

SYSTEM DIAGNOSIS

NOTE: Before testing transmission, ensure fluid level is correct and throttle and shift cables are properly adjusted. Ensure engine starts with shift lever in Park and Neutral to ensure proper adjustment of park/neutral position switch. Transmission must first be tested by checking for stored trouble codes. See RETRIEVING TROUBLE CODES.

ECT ECU monitors transmission operation and contains a self-diagnostic system which stores Diagnostic Trouble Codes (DTC's) if transmission electronic control system failure or problem exists. If a problem exists in any of the solenoids or speed sensors and trouble code is set, ECT ECU delivers a signal to blink OD OFF light on instrument panel to warn driver. Trouble codes may be set if a failure exists and can be retrieved for transmission diagnosis.

OD OFF light will not blink to warn driver if a problem exists or trouble code is stored for lock-up solenoid, or problem exists with brakelight switch or throttle position sensor signal.

RETRIEVING TROUBLE CODES

NOTE: Before retrieving trouble codes, ensure proper battery voltage exists for proper self-diagnosis system operation. Perform diagnostic circuit check before retrieving trouble codes to ensure proper operation of OD OFF light. See DIAGNOSTIC CIRCUIT CHECK.

Diagnostic Circuit Check – 1) Turn ignition on. Release OD switch on shift lever to OFF position. Ensure OD OFF light on instrument panel illuminates. If OD OFF light does not illuminate, check OD switch and wiring circuit.

2) Depress OD switch to ON position. Ensure OD OFF light goes off. If OD OFF light remains on, check OD switch and wiring circuit. If OD OFF light is blinking, check for stored trouble codes. See ECT ECU CODES.

ECT ECU Codes – 1) Turn ignition on. DO NOT start engine. Depress OD switch on shift lever to ON position.

NOTE: Trouble codes can only be retrieved with OD switch on. If OD switch is off, OD OFF light will be on continuously and will not blink the code.

2) Install jumper wire between terminals T_E, and E_1 of DLC1 or DLC2. *See Fig. 6.* On Lexus models, DLC1 is located in engine compartment, near left strut tower. On Pickup and 4Runner, DLC1 is located on right inner fender panel, near fuse/relay box. On Supra Turbo, DLC1 is located at right rear of engine compartment on firewall. On all models, DLC2 is located under instrument panel, left of steering column.

3) Note number of flashes from OD OFF light on instrument panel. If normal system operation exists, OD OFF light will blink 2 times per second. *See Fig. 7.*

NOTE: A stuck solenoid will not set a trouble code. Trouble codes are only set for circuit malfunctions, not mechanical failures.

4) If system is operating correctly and no code exists, turn ignition off and remove jumper wire. Perform MANUAL SHIFT TEST to determine if problem is an electrical or mechanical transmission problem. Check system by symptom. See appropriate symptom under SYMPTOM TROUBLE SHOOTING.

5) If trouble code exists, OD OFF light will blink once every second. Number of blinks equals first digit of trouble code. After a pause of 1.5 seconds, second digit will be displayed. *See Fig. 7.*

6) If more than one trouble code exists, next trouble code will be displayed after pause of 2.5 seconds. Smallest number trouble code will be first and system will progress to largest code. Trouble codes will be repeated.

7) Once trouble code is obtained, determine probable cause and symptom. See DIAGNOSTIC TROUBLE CODE (DTC) IDENTIFICATION table. For diagnosis and repair of trouble codes, see DIAGNOSTIC TESTS. Turn ignition off and remove jumper wire.

NOTE: Once repairs have been performed, trouble codes must be cleared from ECT ECU memory. See CLEARING TROUBLE CODES under SELF-DIAGNOSTIC SYSTEM.

DIAGNOSTIC TROUBLE CODE (DTC) IDENTIFICATION

DTC	[1] Probable Cause
38	[2] A/T Fluid Temperature Sensor
42	[3] No. 1 Vehicle Speed Sensor
46	[4] No. 4 Solenoid
61	[3] No. 2 Vehicle Speed Sensor
62	No. 1 Solenoid
63	No. 2 Solenoid
64	Lock-Up Solenoid
65	[5] No. 4 Solenoid
67	[4] OD Direct Clutch Speed Sensor
77	[2] No. 5 Solenoid
89	[2][6] TRAC ECU Circuit

[1] – Check listed component for probable cause. Check wiring and connections of specified component.
[2] – Supra Turbo.
[3] – If both No. 1 and No. 2 vehicle speed sensors fail simultaneously, trouble code will not exist and transmission will not upshift from 1st gear with shift lever in "D" position.
[4] – GS300, SC400 and Supra Turbo.
[5] – A-340H transmission.
[6] – Traction control system equipped.

CLEARING TROUBLE CODES

Once repairs have been performed, trouble codes must be cleared from ECT ECU memory. Remove EFI 15-amp fuse for 10 seconds to clear memory in ECT ECU. EFI fuse is in fuse/relay box, located in engine compartment. Fuse may need to be removed for more than 10 seconds in cold ambient temperatures. Reinstall fuse.

NOTE: Trouble codes may also be cleared by disconnecting negative battery cable but memory for electronic components will also be canceled.

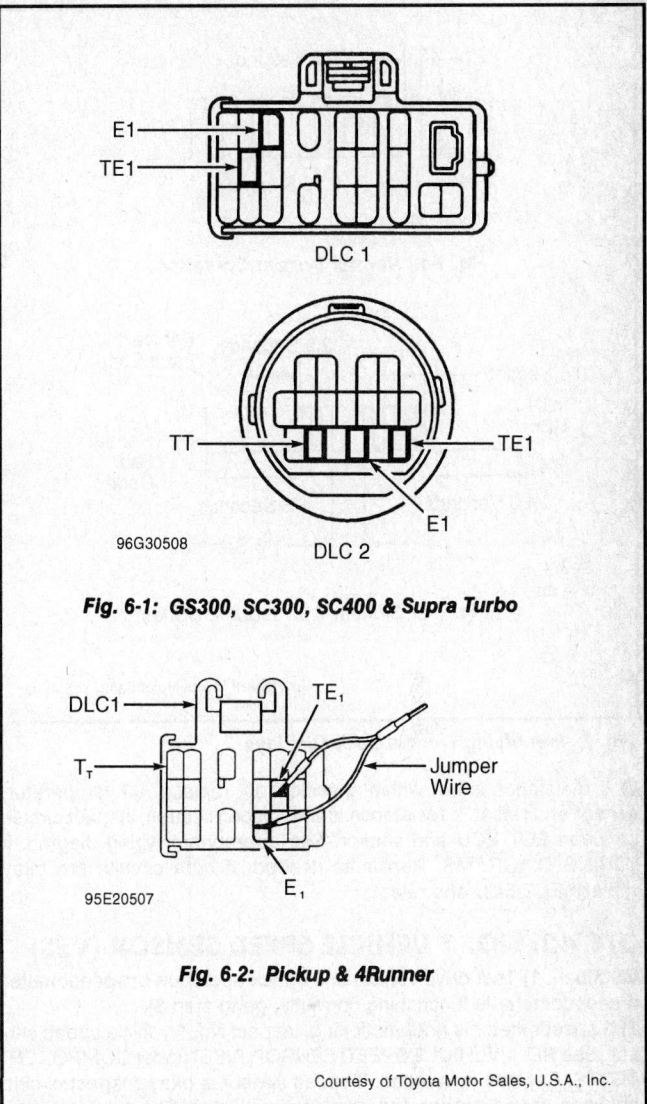

DLC 1

DLC 2

96G30508

Fig. 6-1: GS300, SC300, SC400 & Supra Turbo

DLC1 — TE₁ — Jumper Wire

95E20507

Fig. 6-2: Pickup & 4Runner

Courtesy of Toyota Motor Sales, U.S.A., Inc.

Fig. 6: Identifying Data Link Connector Terminals

DIAGNOSTIC TESTS

When trouble shooting transmission, first check for stored trouble codes and repair as necessary. If no trouble codes exist, perform manual shift test to determine if problem area is in transmission electrical circuits or a mechanical problem. See MANUAL SHIFT TEST.

NOTE: On Lexus models and Supra Turbo, manufacturer recommends using Check Harness (09990-0100) connected to ECT ECU when performing circuit tests at ECT ECU harness connector. Harness connects between ECT ECU terminals and ECT ECU harness connector. Check harness test terminals are same as ECT ECU harness connector terminals. For ECT ECU locations, see Figs. 1, 2 and 4.

DTC 38: A/T FLUID TEMPERATURE SENSOR (SUPRA TURBO)

1) Remove sensor from transmission housing. Using ohmmeter, check resistance between terminals of sensor. Resistance should be 12.08 k/ohms at 68°F (20°C) and 780 ohms at 230°F (110°C).

AUTOMATIC TRANSMISSIONS
Toyota A-340 Series - Electronic Controls (Except OBD-II) (Cont.)

3-1662

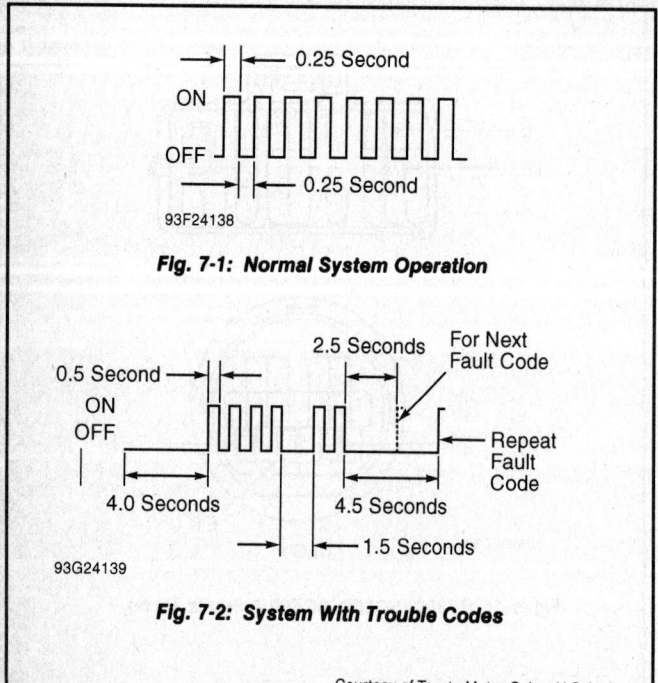

Fig. 7-1: Normal System Operation

Fig. 7-2: System With Trouble Codes

Courtesy of Toyota Motor Sales, U.S.A., Inc.

Fig. 7: Identifying Trouble Code Displays

2) If resistance is not within specification, replace A/T temperature sensor and retest. If resistance is within specification, inspect circuits between ECT ECU and sensor. See appropriate wiring diagram in WIRING DIAGRAMS. Repair as needed. If both circuits are okay, replace ECT ECU and retest.

DTC 42: NO. 1 VEHICLE SPEED SENSOR (VSS)

GS300 – 1) Test drive vehicle and check operation of speedometer. If speedometer is functioning correctly, go to step 3).

2) If speedometer is not functioning, inspect No. 1 vehicle speed sensor. See NO. 1 VEHICLE SPEED SENSOR (VSS) under COMPONENT TESTS. Replace as needed. If speed sensor is okay, inspect circuits between speed sensor and combination meter. Check combination meter circuits as necessary.

3) Access ECT ECU. See Fig. 1. Disconnect harness connector and install check harness between ECT ECU and harness connector. Raise and support rear of vehicle. Turn ignition on. Using DVOM, measure voltage between check harness terminal SP_1 and ground. See Fig. 8. Turn rear wheel.

4) If voltage pulses between 4-6 volts, replace ECT ECU and retest. If voltage does not pulse within specification, inspect and repair circuit between combination meter and ECT ECU. See appropriate wiring diagram in WIRING DIAGRAMS.

Pickup & 4Runner – 1) Access ECT ECU. See Fig. 3. Using ohmmeter, backprobe ECT ECU harness connector. Check for continuity between terminal SP_1 of ECT ECU connector and body ground. See Fig. 9.

2) If continuity exists, replace ECT ECU. If continuity does not exist, check No. 1 vehicle speed sensor. See NO. 1 VEHICLE SPEED SENSOR (VSS) under COMPONENT TESTS.

3) Replace No. 1 vehicle speed sensor if defective. If No. 1 vehicle speed sensor is okay, check wiring between ECT ECU and combination meter. Repair as needed. See appropriate wiring diagram in WIRING DIAGRAMS.

SC300 – 1) Remove combination meter. Raise and support rear of vehicle. Turn ignition on. Using DVOM, backprobe combination meter harness connector C14. Measure voltage between terminal SP_1 and ground while turning rear wheels. See Fig. 10.

2) If voltage is zero, go to step 4). If voltage is 5 volts (constant), inspect No. 1 vehicle speed sensor. See NO. 1 VEHICLE SPEED SENSOR (VSS) under COMPONENT TESTS. Replace as needed.

3) If speed sensor is okay, inspect circuit between speed sensor and combination meter. Repair as needed. If voltage measured is 0-5 volt pulse, replace ECT ECU and retest.

4) Turn ignition off. Disconnect combination meter harness connector. Disconnect cruise control ECU harness connector. See Fig. 2. Disconnect harness connector and install check harness between ECT ECU and harness connector. Turn ignition on.

5) Using DVOM, measure voltage between check harness terminal SP, and ground. See Fig. 8. If 5 volts is present, inspect and repair circuit between combination meter and ECT ECU. If 5 volts is not present, replace ECT ECU and retest.

SC400 – 1) Test drive vehicle and check operation of speedometer. If speedometer is functioning correctly, go to step 3).

2) If speedometer is not functioning, inspect No. 1 vehicle speed sensor. See NO. 1 VEHICLE SPEED SENSOR (VSS) under COMPONENT TESTS. Replace as needed. If speed sensor is okay, inspect circuits between speed sensor and combination meter. Also check combination meter circuits as necessary.

3) Access ECT ECU. See Fig. 2. Disconnect harness connector and install check harness between ECT ECU and harness connector. Raise and support rear of vehicle. Turn ignition on. Using DVOM, measure voltage between check harness terminal SPD and ground. See Fig. 8. Turn rear wheel.

4) If voltage pulses between 10-14 volts, replace ECT ECU and retest. If voltage does not pulse within specification, inspect and repair circuit between combination meter and ECT ECU. See appropriate wiring diagram in WIRING DIAGRAMS.

Supra Turbo – 1) Access ECT ECU. See Fig. 4. Disconnect harness connector and install check harness between ECT ECU and harness connector. Disconnect cruise control ECU. Disconnect power steering ECU, located at right kick panel. Raise and support rear of vehicle. Turn ignition on. Using DVOM, measure voltage between check harness terminal SP_1 and ground. See Fig. 8. Turn rear wheel.

2) Voltage should pulse between zero volts to 4-6 volts. If voltage is within specification, replace ECT ECU and retest. If voltage is not within specification, inspect odometer/trip meter.

NOTE: Odometer/trip meter is also known as Right Telltale Light Assembly.

---

3) Remove odometer/trip meter. Ensure harness connector is connected. Turn ignition on. Using DVOM, backprobe meter harness connector. Check continuity and voltage between specified terminals. See Fig. 11.

4) If meter is okay, inspect and repair circuit between odometer/trip meter and ECT ECU. See appropriate ACCESSORIES & EQUIPMENT section of appropriate MITCHELL® publication for IMPORTED CARS, LIGHT TRUCKS & VANS. Replace meter if continuity or voltage is not within specification.

5) Inspect No. 1 vehicle speed sensor. See NO. 1 VEHICLE SPEED SENSOR (VSS) under COMPONENT TESTS. Replace as needed. If speed sensor is okay, inspect circuit between speed sensor and odometer/trip meter.

DTC 46: NO. 4 SOLENOID CIRCUIT (GS300, SC400 & SUPRA TURBO)

1) Ensure ignition is off. Raise and support vehicle. Remove transmission oil pan. Disconnect No. 4 solenoid connector (Blue and Red wires). Using a DVOM, check resistance between No. 4 solenoid terminals. Resistance should be 5.1-5.5 ohms. If resistance is 5.1-5.5 ohms, go to next step. If resistance is not 5.1-5.5 ohms, replace No. 4 solenoid. Clear trouble code. See CLEARING TROUBLE CODES. Retest vehicle.

2) Connect a jumper wire with an 8-10 watt bulb in series between battery positive terminal and No. 4 solenoid terminal No. 1 (Red wire). Connect another jumper wire between battery negative terminal and No. 4 solenoid terminal No. 2. See Fig. 12.

AUTOMATIC TRANSMISSIONS
Toyota A-340 Series - Electronic Controls (Except OBD-II) (Cont.)

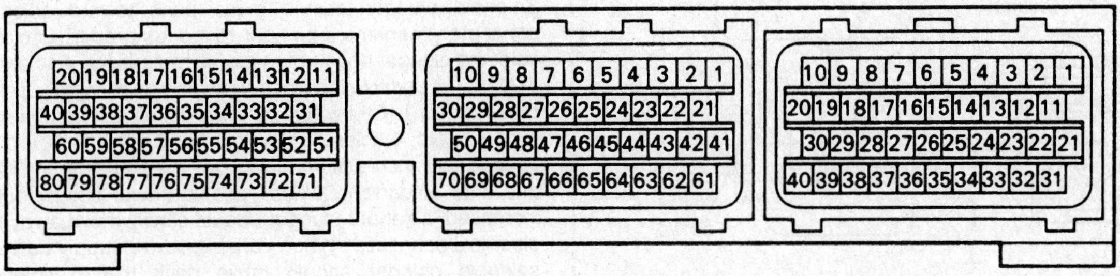

3-1663

"A" "B"

ECT ECU TERMINAL IDENTIFICATION

Circuit	Connector	Terminal No.
S_1 (SOL1)	A	10
S_2 (SOL2)	A	9
SLU	A	14
SLN	A	13
NSW	A	76
VTA1	A	43
IDL1	A	64
SP$_1$ Or SPD	B	2
SP$_2$-	A	3
SP$_2$+	A	23
KD	B	3
R	B	7
2	B	9
L	B	10

ECT ECU TERMINAL IDENTIFICATION (Cont.)

Circuit	Connector	Terminal No.
OD$_1$	B	12
OD$_2$	B	28
PWR	B	18
NCO-	A	1
NCO+	A	21
TRC+	B	14
TRC-	A	13
SLT+	A	31
SLT-	A	12
EFI+	B	27
EFI-	B	26
+B	B	31
Batt	B	33
E$_1$	A	69

NOTE: All circuits are not used on all models. See appropriate wiring diagrams under WIRING DIAGRAMS for circuit identification.

95D20514

Courtesy of Toyota Motor Sales, U.S.A., Inc.

Fig. 8: Identifying ECT ECU Terminals (GS300, SC300, SC400 & Supra Turbo)

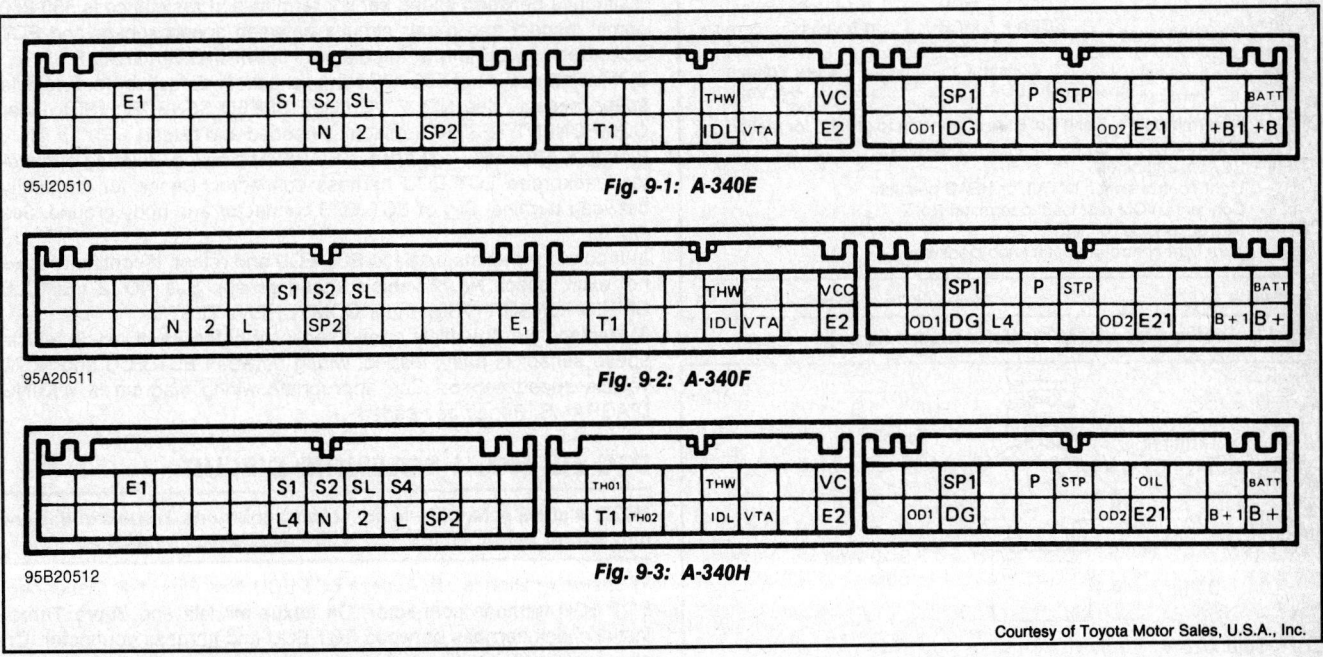

95J20510 **Fig. 9-1: A-340E**

95A20511 **Fig. 9-2: A-340F**

95B20512 **Fig. 9-3: A-340H**

Courtesy of Toyota Motor Sales, U.S.A., Inc.

Fig. 9: Identifying ECT ECU Terminals (Pickup & 4Runner)

3-1664

AUTOMATIC TRANSMISSIONS
Toyota A-340 Series - Electronic Controls (Except OBD-II) (Cont.)

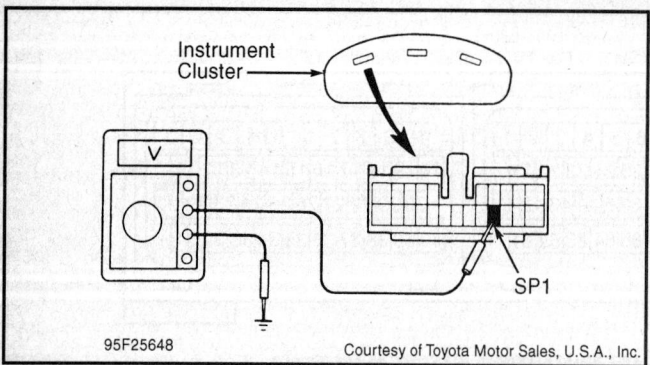

95F25648

Courtesy of Toyota Motor Sales, U.S.A., Inc.

Fig. 10: Measuring No. 1 Vehicle Speed Sensor Voltage (SC300)

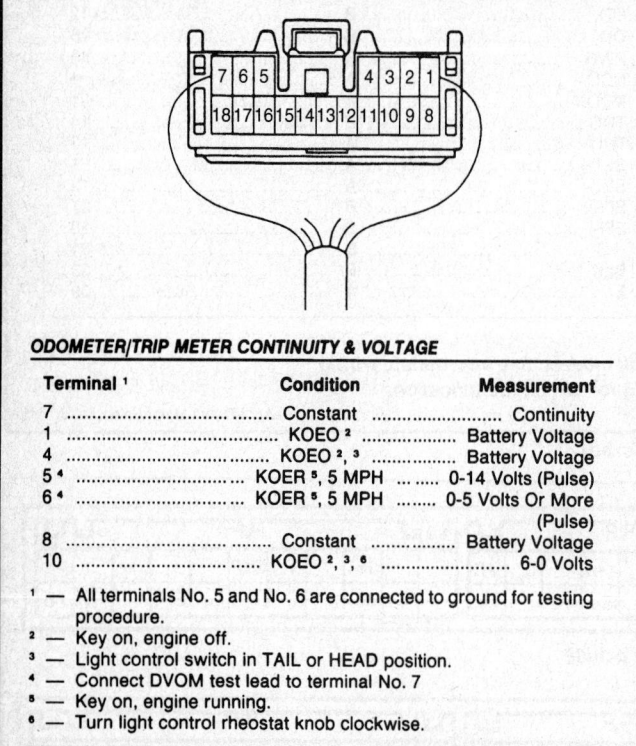

ODOMETER/TRIP METER CONTINUITY & VOLTAGE

Terminal [1]	Condition	Measurement
7	Constant	Continuity
1	KOEO [2]	Battery Voltage
4	KOEO [2], [3]	Battery Voltage
5 [4]	KOER [5], 5 MPH	0-14 Volts (Pulse)
6 [4]	KOER [5], 5 MPH	0-5 Volts Or More (Pulse)
8	Constant	Battery Voltage
10	KOEO [2], [3], [6]	6-0 Volts

[1] — All terminals No. 5 and No. 6 are connected to ground for testing procedure.
[2] — Key on, engine off.
[3] — Light control switch in TAIL or HEAD position.
[4] — Connect DVOM test lead to terminal No. 7
[5] — Key on, engine running.
[6] — Turn light control rheostat knob clockwise.

95I20899

Courtesy of Toyota Motor Sales, U.S.A., Inc.

Fig. 11: Testing Odometer/Trip Meter (Supra Turbo)

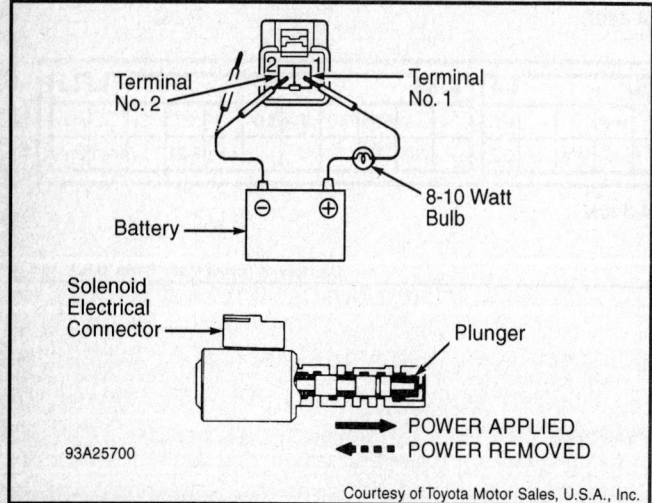

93A25700

Courtesy of Toyota Motor Sales, U.S.A., Inc.

Fig. 12: Testing No. 3, No. 4 & No. 5 Solenoid

3) Solenoid plunger should move away from solenoid electrical connector. Remove jumper wire from solenoid terminal No. 2. Solenoid plunger should move back toward solenoid electrical connector. If solenoid plunger responds properly, go to next step. If solenoid plunger does not respond, replace No. 4 solenoid and retest.

4) Connect positive lead of a variable power supply to No. 4 solenoid terminal No. 1 (Red wire). Connect negative lead of a variable power supply to No. 4 solenoid terminal No. 2.

5) Gradually increase variable power supply output. DO NOT exceed one amp of current. When variable power supply output is slowly increased, solenoid plunger should slowly move away from solenoid electrical connector. When variable power supply output is removed, solenoid plunger should move back toward solenoid electrical connector. If solenoid plunger responds properly, go to next step. If solenoid plunger does not respond properly, replace No. 4 solenoid.

6) Check for defective power supply circuit to No. 4 solenoid. If power supply circuit is okay, check for defective ground circuit between ECT ECU and No. 4 solenoid. See appropriate wiring diagram in WIRING DIAGRAMS. Repair as necessary. If circuits are okay, replace ECT ECU and retest.

DTC 61: NO. 2 VEHICLE SPEED SENSOR (VSS)

NOTE: When No. 2 vehicle speed sensor circuit fails, ECT ECU uses input signal from No. 1 vehicle speed sensor as a back-up signal.

GS300, SC300, SC400 & Supra Turbo – 1) Ensure ignition off. Access ECT ECU. *See Figs. 1, 2 and 4.* Disconnect harness connector and install check harness between ECT ECU and harness connector. Using ohmmeter, measure resistance between terminal SP2+ and SP2– at check harness. *See Fig. 8.* Resistance should be 560-680 ohms. If resistance is 560-680 ohms, replace ECT ECU and retest.

2) If resistance is not 560-680 ohms, remove No. 2 vehicle speed sensor from transmission. *See Figs. 1, 2 and 4.* Using ohmmeter, check resistance between speed sensor terminals. If resistance is 560-860 ohms, inspect and repair circuits between speed sensor and ECT ECU. *See appropriate wiring diagram in WIRING DIAGRAMS.*

3) If resistance is not 560-680 ohms, check for defective No. 2 vehicle speed sensor. See NO. 2 VEHICLE SPEED SENSOR (VSS) under COMPONENT TESTS. Replace as needed and retest.

Pickup & 4Runner – 1) Access ECT ECU. *See Fig. 3.* Using ohmmeter, backprobe ECT ECU harness connector. Check for continuity between terminal SP2 of ECT ECU connector and body ground. *See Fig. 9.*

2) If continuity exists, replace ECT ECU and retest. If continuity does not exist, check No. 2 vehicle speed sensor. See NO. 2 VEHICLE SPEED SENSOR (VSS) under COMPONENT TESTS.

3) Replace No. 2 vehicle speed sensor if defective. If No. 2 vehicle speed sensor is okay, inspect wiring between ECT ECU and No. 2 vehicle speed sensor. See appropriate wiring diagram in WIRING DIAGRAMS. Repair as needed.

DTC 62: NO. 1 SOLENOID CIRCUIT

NOTE: A stuck solenoid will not set a trouble code. Trouble codes are only set for circuit malfunctions, not mechanical failures.

1) Ensure ignition is off. Access ECT ECU. *See Figs. 1-4.* Disconnect ECT ECU harness connector. On Lexus models and Supra Turbo, install check harness between ECT ECU and harness connector. On all models, using ohmmeter, check resistance between ECT ECU terminal S1 and body ground at ECT ECU harness connector or at check harness. *See Figs. 8 and 9.*

2) Resistance should be 10-16 ohms. If resistance is okay, replace ECT ECU. If resistance is not within specification, remove transmission oil pan. Disconnect electrical connector at No. 1 solenoid (Blue/Red wire on 4-cylinder models, White wire on all other models).

3) Check resistance between electrical terminal on No. 1 solenoid and body ground. Replace No. 1 solenoid if resistance is not 10-16 ohms. If resistance is 10-16 ohms, check wiring between No. 1 solenoid and ECT ECU. See appropriate wiring diagram in WIRING DIAGRAMS.

AUTOMATIC TRANSMISSIONS
Toyota A-340 Series - Electronic Controls (Except OBD-II) (Cont.)

3-1665

4) If wiring is okay, check performance of solenoid. See SOLENOIDS under COMPONENT TESTS. Replace as needed. If solenoid is functioning okay, replace ECT ECU and retest.

DTC 63: NO. 2 SOLENOID CIRCUIT

NOTE: A stuck solenoid will not set a trouble code. Trouble codes are only set for circuit malfunctions, not mechanical failures.

1) Ensure ignition is off. Access ECT ECU. *See Figs. 1-4.* Disconnect ECT ECU harness connector. On Lexus models and Supra Turbo, install check harness between ECT ECU and harness connector. On all models, using ohmmeter, check resistance between ECT ECU terminal S_2 and body ground at ECT ECU harness connector or at check harness. *See Figs. 8 and 9.*

2) Resistance should be 10-16 ohms. If resistance is okay, replace ECT ECU. If resistance is not within specification, remove transmission oil pan. Disconnect electrical connector at No. 2 solenoid (Red/White wire on 4-cylinder models, Black wire on all other models).

3) Check resistance between electrical terminal on No. 2 solenoid and body ground. Replace No. 2 solenoid if resistance is not 10-16 ohms. If resistance is 10-16 ohms, check wiring between No. 2 solenoid and ECT ECU. See appropriate wiring diagram in WIRING DIAGRAMS.

4) If wiring is okay, check performance of solenoid. See SOLENOIDS under COMPONENT TESTS. Replace as needed. If solenoid is functioning okay, replace ECT ECU and retest.

DTC 64: NO. 3 LOCK-UP SOLENOID CIRCUIT

NOTE: A stuck solenoid will not set a trouble code. Trouble codes are only set for circuit malfunctions, not mechanical failures.

GS300, SC400 & Supra Turbo – 1) Ensure ignition is off. Raise and support vehicle. Remove transmission oil pan. Disconnect No. 3 solenoid connector (Brown and Yellow wires). Using a DVOM, check resistance between No. 3 solenoid terminals. Resistance should be 3.5-3.9 ohms. If resistance is 3.5-3.9 ohms, go to next step. If resistance is not 3.5-3.9 ohms, replace No. 3 solenoid. Clear trouble code. See CLEARING TROUBLE CODES. Retest vehicle.

2) Connect a jumper wire with an 8-10 watt bulb in series between battery positive terminal and No. 3 solenoid terminal No. 1 (Yellow wire). Connect another jumper wire between battery negative terminal and No. 3 solenoid terminal No. 2. *See Fig. 12.*

3) Solenoid plunger should move away from solenoid electrical connector. Remove jumper wire from solenoid terminal No. 2. Solenoid plunger should move back toward solenoid electrical connector. If solenoid plunger responds properly, go to next step. If solenoid plunger does not respond, replace No. 3 solenoid and retest.

4) Connect positive lead of a variable power supply to No. 3 solenoid terminal No. 1 (Yellow wire). Connect negative lead of a variable power supply to No. 3 solenoid terminal No. 2.

5) Gradually increase variable power supply output. DO NOT exceed one amp of current. When variable power supply output is slowly increased, solenoid plunger should slowly move away from solenoid electrical connector. When variable power supply output is removed, solenoid plunger should move back toward solenoid electrical connector. If solenoid plunger responds properly, go to next step. If solenoid plunger does not respond properly, replace No. 3 solenoid.

6) Check for defective power supply circuit to No. 3 solenoid. If power supply circuit is okay, check for defective ground circuit between ECT ECU and No. 3 solenoid. See appropriate wiring diagram in WIRING DIAGRAMS. Repair as necessary. If circuits are okay, replace ECT ECU and retest.

NOTE: On Pickup and 4Runner, No. 3 solenoid is also referred to as SL solenoid. See Fig. 9.

Pickup, SC300 & 4Runner – 1) Access ECT ECU. *See Figs. 2 and 3.* Disconnect ECT ECU harness connector. On SC300, install check harness between ECT ECU and harness connector. On all models, using ohmmeter, check resistance between terminal S_3 and body ground at ECT ECU harness connector or at check harness. *See Figs. 8 and 9.*

2) Resistance should be 10-16 ohms. If resistance is okay, replace ECT ECU. If resistance is not within specification, disconnect electrical connector at lock-up solenoid, located on transmission valve body. *See Figs. 2 and 3.*

3) Check resistance between electrical terminal on lock-up solenoid and body ground. Replace lock-up solenoid if resistance is not 10-16 ohms. If resistance is 10-16 ohms, check wiring between lock-up solenoid and ECT ECU. See appropriate wiring diagram in WIRING DIAGRAMS.

4) If wiring is okay, check performance of solenoid. See SOLENOIDS under COMPONENT TESTS. Replace as needed. If solenoid is functioning okay, replace ECT ECU and retest.

DTC 65: NO. 4 SOLENOID CIRCUIT (PICKUP & 4RUNNER WITH A-340H)

NOTE: A stuck solenoid will not set a trouble code. Trouble codes are only set for circuit malfunctions, not mechanical failures.

1) Access ECT ECU. *See Fig. 3.* Using ohmmeter, backprobe ECT ECU harness connector. Check resistance between terminal S_4 and body ground with connector removed from ECT ECU. *See Fig. 9.*

2) Resistance should be 11-15 ohms. If resistance is okay, replace ECT ECU. If resistance is not within specification, disconnect electrical connector at No. 4 solenoid, located on transmission valve body. *See Fig. 3.*

3) Check resistance between electrical terminal on No. 4 solenoid and body ground. Replace solenoid if resistance is not 11-15 ohms. If resistance is 11-15 ohms, check wiring between No. 4 solenoid and ECT ECU. See appropriate wiring diagram in WIRING DIAGRAMS.

4) If wiring is okay, check performance of solenoid. See SOLENOIDS under COMPONENT TESTS. Replace as needed. If solenoid is functioning okay, replace ECT ECU and retest.

DTC 67: OD DIRECT CLUTCH SPEED SENSOR (GS300, SC400 & SUPRA TURBO)

1) Ensure ignition is off. Access ECT ECU. *See Figs. 1, 2 and 4.* Disconnect ECT ECU harness connector and install check harness between ECT ECU and harness connector. Using ohmmeter, measure resistance between check harness terminals NCO+ and NCO−. *See Fig. 8.* Resistance should be 560-680 ohms. If resistance is 560-680 ohms, replace ECT ECU and retest.

2) If resistance is not 560-680 ohms, remove OD direct clutch speed sensor from transmission. *See Figs. 1, 2 and 4.* Measure resistance between speed sensor terminals. Resistance should be 560-680 ohms. If resistance is not 560-860 ohms, replace sensor and retest.

3) If resistance is 560-680 ohms, inspect both circuits between ECT ECU and OD direct clutch speed sensor. See appropriate wiring diagram in WIRING DIAGRAMS. Repair as necessary. If continuity exists in both circuits, check performance of OD direct clutch speed sensor. See OD DIRECT CLUTCH SPEED SENSOR under COMPONENT TESTS.

DTC 77: NO. 5 SOLENOID CIRCUIT (SUPRA TURBO)

NOTE: A stuck solenoid will not set a trouble code. Trouble codes are only set for circuit malfunctions, not mechanical failures.

1) Ensure ignition is off. Raise and support vehicle. Remove transmission oil pan. Disconnect No. 5 solenoid connector (Green and Orange wires). Using ohmmeter, check resistance between No. 5 solenoid terminals. Resistance should be 3.6-4.0 ohms. If resistance is 3.6-4.0 ohms, go to next step. If resistance is not 3.6-4.0 ohms, replace No. 5 solenoid. Clear trouble code. See CLEARING TROUBLE CODES. Retest vehicle.

2) Connect a jumper wire with an 8-10 watt bulb in series between battery positive terminal and No. 5 solenoid terminal No. 1 (Orange wire). Connect another jumper wire between battery negative terminal and No. 5 solenoid terminal No. 2. *See Fig. 12.*

3-1666

AUTOMATIC TRANSMISSIONS
Toyota A-340 Series - Electronic Controls (Except OBD-II) (Cont.)

3) Solenoid plunger should move away from solenoid electrical connector. Remove jumper wire from solenoid terminal No. 2. Solenoid plunger should move back toward solenoid electrical connector. If solenoid plunger responds properly, go to next step. If solenoid plunger does not respond, replace No. 5 solenoid and retest.

4) Connect positive lead of a variable power supply to No. 5 solenoid terminal No. 1 (Orange wire). Connect negative lead of a variable power supply to No. 5 solenoid terminal No. 2.

5) Gradually increase variable power supply output. DO NOT exceed one amp of current. When variable power supply output is slowly increased, solenoid plunger should slowly move away from solenoid electrical connector. When variable power supply output is removed, solenoid plunger should move back toward solenoid electrical connector. If solenoid plunger responds properly, go to next step. If solenoid plunger does not respond properly, replace No. 5 solenoid.

6) Check for defective power supply circuit to No. 5 solenoid. If power supply circuit is okay, check for defective ground circuit between ECT ECU and No. 5 solenoid. See appropriate wiring diagram in WIRING DIAGRAMS. Repair as necessary. If circuits are okay, replace ECT ECU and retest.

DTC 89: TRAC ECU CIRCUIT (SUPRA TURBO)

Ensure ignition is off. Disconnect harness connectors from ECT ECU and TRAC ECU. Both ECU's are located behind glove box. TRAC ECU is located next to ECT ECU. Check continuity between circuits that connect both ECU's. See Figs. 8 and 13. Repair as needed. If all circuits are okay, substitute TRAC ECU with known good unit and retest. If more diagnostic information is required for Toyota TRAC system, see appropriate article under BRAKES section of appropriate MITCHELL® publication for IMPORTED CARS, LIGHT TRUCKS & VANS.

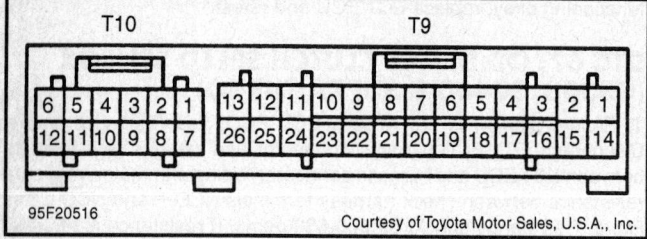

95F20516   Courtesy of Toyota Motor Sales, U.S.A., Inc.

Fig. 13: Identifying TRAC ECU Terminals (Supra Turbo)

MANUAL SHIFT TEST

NOTE: Perform manual shift test if no trouble codes exist. Manual shift test determines if problem area is in electrical circuits or a mechanical transmission problem.

1) With ignition off, disconnect electrical connector for solenoids from rear of transmission. Road test vehicle and ensure transmission gear changes corresponds with shift lever position. See GEAR APPLICATION table.

2) If abnormality exists, a mechanical transmission problem exists. If all gears are correct, perform trouble shooting in accordance with symptom. See SYMPTOM TROUBLE SHOOTING. Turn ignition off.

3) Reconnect electrical connector. Clear trouble codes from ECT ECU memory, as disconnecting electrical connector may set a trouble code. See CLEARING TROUBLE CODES under SELF-DIAGNOSTIC SYSTEM.

GEAR APPLICATION

Shift Lever Position	Gear
"D"	Overdrive
"2"	3rd
"L"	1st
"R"	Reverse
"P"	Park

SYMPTOM TROUBLE SHOOTING

NOTE: Following symptom trouble shooting applies to Pickup and 4Runner. Manufacturer does not supply trouble shooting information for other models.

NOTE: If problem area is not listed under symptom trouble shooting, check throttle position sensor signal, brakelight signal, gear selector signal and ECT ECU voltages. See CIRCUIT TESTS.

TRANSMISSION WILL NOT SHIFT

1) Warm engine to normal operating temperature. Connect voltmeter between terminals T_T and E_1 of data link connector. See Fig. 6.

2) Turn ignition on. Note that voltage changes with throttle opening. If voltage changes with throttle opening, proceed to step 6). If voltage does not change with throttle opening, proceed to next step.

3) Access ECT ECU. See Fig. 3. Connect voltmeter between terminals STP and E_1 on ECT ECU with connector installed on ECT ECU. See Fig. 9.

4) No voltage should exist with brake pedal released. About 10-14 volts should exist with brake pedal depressed. If voltage is not correct, check for defective brakelight switch or wiring circuit.

5) If voltage is correct, check for short or open circuit in wire to T_T terminal of data link connector. Check for defective throttle position sensor or wiring.

6) Perform MANUAL SHIFT TEST. If transmission does not perform correctly, repair transmission. If transmission operates correctly, road test vehicle and ensure voltage at terminal T_T increases from zero to 7 volts.

7) If no voltage exists, proceed to step 9). If voltage increases from zero to 7 volts, transmission or solenoid is faulty. If voltage increases from zero to 5 volts, perform NO UPSHIFT TO OVERDRIVE under SYMPTOM TROUBLE SHOOTING.

8) If voltage increases from zero to 3 volts, check for 12 volts between terminals 2 and E_1 on ECT ECU with connector installed on ECT ECU and shift lever in "D" position. See Fig. 9. If 12 volts exist, check for defective park/neutral position switch or wiring circuit. If 12 volts does not exist, replace ECT ECU.

9) Check for 12 volts between terminals "L" and E_1 on ECT ECU with connector installed on ECT ECU and shift lever in "D" position. If 12 volts exist, check for defective park/neutral position switch or wiring circuit. If 12 volts do not exist, replace ECT ECU.

SHIFT POINTS TOO HIGH OR LOW

1) Warm engine to normal operating temperature. Connect voltmeter between terminals T_T and E_1 of data link connector. See Fig. 6.

2) Turn ignition on. Note that voltage changes with throttle opening. If voltage changes with throttle opening, ECT ECU or transmission is defective. If voltage does not change with throttle opening, proceed to next step.

3) Access ECT ECU. See Fig. 3. Connect voltmeter between terminals STP and E_1 on ECT ECU with connector installed on ECT ECU. See Fig. 9.

4) No voltage should exist with brake pedal released. About 10-14 volts should exist with brake pedal depressed. If voltage is not correct, check for defective brakelight switch or wiring circuit.

5) If voltage is correct, check for short or open circuit in wire to T_T terminal of data link connector. Check for defective throttle position sensor or wiring.

NO UPSHIFT TO OVERDRIVE

1) Warm engine to normal operating temperature. With ignition off, disconnect electrical connector for solenoid from rear of transmission.

2) Road test vehicle and note if transmission upshifts to Overdrive once transmission shifts from "L" to "2" and then into "D" range. Reconnect electrical connector. Clear trouble codes from ECU memory, as disconnecting ECT ECU electrical connector may set trouble

codes. See CLEARING TROUBLE CODES under SELF-DIAGNOSTIC SYSTEM. If no overdrive upshift exists, transmission is defective. If overdrive upshift exists, proceed to step next step.

3) Connect voltmeter between terminals T_T and E_1 of data link connector. See Fig. 6.

4) Road test vehicle and ensure voltage at terminal T_T increases from zero to 7 volts. If no voltage exists, check for 12 volts between terminals "L" and E_1 on ECT ECU with connector installed on ECT ECU and shift lever in "D" position with ignition on. See Fig. 9. If 12 volts exist, check for defective park/neutral position switch or wiring circuit. If 12 volts do not exist, replace ECT ECU.

5) If voltage increases from zero to 3 volts, check for 12 volts between terminals "2" and E_1 on ECT ECU with connector installed on ECT ECU and shift lever in "D" position with ignition on. If 12 volts exist, check for defective park/neutral position switch or wiring circuit. If 12 volts do not exist, replace ECT ECU.

6) If voltage increases from zero to 7 volts, transmission or solenoid is faulty. If voltage increases from zero to 5 volts, connect voltmeter between terminals OD_2 and E_1 on ECT ECU with connector installed on ECT ECU.

7) Turn ignition on. Check voltage with OD switch released (OFF position) and depressed (ON position). No voltage should exist with switch released and 10-14 volts with switch depressed.

8) If voltage is correct, proceed to next step. If voltage is not correct, check for defective OD switch or wiring circuit.

9) Check voltage between terminals OD_1 and E_1 on ECT ECU with connector installed on ECT ECU and ignition on. Voltage should be about 5 volts. If voltage is correct, replace ECT ECU. If voltage is not correct, proceed to next step.

10) Disconnect electrical connector from cruise control Electronic Control Unit (ECU). See Fig. 3. Check voltage between terminals OD_1 and E_1 on ECT ECU with connector installed on ECT ECU and ignition on. If voltage is now about 5 volts, replace cruise control ECU. If voltage is not about 5 volts, check for defective cruise control ECU wiring. If wiring is okay, replace ECT ECU.

NO LOCK-UP

1) Warm engine to normal operating temperature. Connect voltmeter between terminals T_T and E_1 of data link connector. See Fig. 6.

2) Road test vehicle and ensure voltage at terminal T_T is 3-7 volts in lock-up range. If voltage is correct, lock-up solenoid, torque converter or transmission is defective.

3) If voltage is not correct, obtain access to ECT ECU. Connect voltmeter between terminals STP and E_1 on ECT ECU with connector installed on ECT ECU. See Fig. 9.

4) No voltage should exist with brake pedal released. About 10-14 volts should exist with brake pedal depressed. If voltage is not correct, check for defective brakelight switch or wiring circuit. If voltage is correct, check for defective throttle position sensor or wiring.

TRANSFER CASE DOES NOT SHIFT FROM H4 TO L4 (A-340H TRANSMISSION)

1) Check transfer position switch operation. See COMPONENT TESTS. Replace switch as necessary. If switch is okay, connect voltmeter between terminals T_T and E_1 of data link connector. See Fig. 6.

2) Turn ignition on. Note that voltage changes with throttle opening. If voltage does not change with throttle opening, check for defective throttle position sensor or wiring. If voltage does change with throttle opening, proceed to next step.

3) With engine idling, check voltage between terminals S_4 and E_1 at ECT ECU with harness connector installed on ECT ECU while shifting transfer shift lever from H4 to L4 position. See Fig. 9. If voltage is 12 volts, check for defective No. 4 solenoid or transfer case. If voltage is not 12 volts, replace ECT ECU.

CIRCUIT TESTS

THROTTLE POSITION (TP) SENSOR SIGNAL

1) Connect voltmeter between terminals T_T and E_1 of data link connector. See Fig. 6. Turn ignition on. Note that voltage gradually increases as accelerator is depressed. Voltage should gradually increase to about 8 volts with throttle fully open.

2) If voltage does not increase as throttle is opened, check throttle position sensor. See THROTTLE POSITION (TP) SENSOR under COMPONENT TESTS. If throttle position sensor is okay, check circuit(s) between TP sensor and ECT ECU. See appropriate wiring diagram in WIRING DIAGRAMS.

SUB-THROTTLE POSITION SENSOR SIGNAL

For diagnosis and testing information, see appropriate MITCHELL® ENGINE PERFORMANCE publication for IMPORTED CARS, LIGHT TRUCKS & VANS.

BRAKELIGHT SWITCH SIGNAL

1) Connect voltmeter between terminals T_T and E_1 of data link connector. See Fig. 6. Turn ignition on. Depress accelerator pedal until 8 volts exists. Depress brake pedal and note that voltage decreases to zero volts. Release brake pedal and note that voltage increases to 8 volts.

2) If voltage is not correct, check brakelight switch. See BRAKELIGHT SWITCH under COMPONENT TESTS. If brakelight switch is okay, check wiring circuit for brakelight switch. See appropriate wiring diagram in WIRING DIAGRAMS.

GEAR SELECTOR SIGNAL

1) Warm engine to normal operating temperature. Place pattern select switch in NORMAL position. Depress OD switch, mounted on shift lever, to ON position.

2) Connect voltmeter between terminals T_T and E_1 of data link connector. See Fig. 6.

3) Road test vehicle with shift lever in "D" position and vehicle speed greater than 6 MPH. Voltage should increase as specified in accordance with transmission gear position. See GEAR SIGNAL VOLTAGE table.

NOTE: Lock-up clutch will come on infrequently during normal 2nd and 3rd gear operation. To get lock-up clutch to operate, depress accelerator pedal to more than 1/2 of pedal travel. With accelerator pedal at less than 1/2 of pedal travel, voltage may change in sequence of 2, 4, 6 and then 7 volts.

---

4) If voltages are correct, the electronic control system is operating correctly. If voltages are not correct, system must be checked.

GEAR SIGNAL VOLTAGE

Gear Position	[1] Volts
1st	0
2nd	2
2nd With Lock-Up	3
3rd	4
3rd With Lock-Up	5
Overdrive	6
Overdrive With Lock-Up	7

[1] – Voltages are approximate. Voltage measured may vary from specification plus or minus .5 volt.

OVERDRIVE CANCEL SIGNAL

1) Access ECT ECU. See Figs. 1-4. Turn ignition on. Using DVOM, backprobe ECT ECU harness connector. Measure voltage between terminal OD_1 of ECT ECU harness connector and ground. See Figs. 8 and 9. If 4-6 volts is present, substitute known good ECT ECU and retest. If 4-6 volts is not present, go to next step.

3-1668

AUTOMATIC TRANSMISSIONS
Toyota A-340 Series - Electronic Controls (Except OBD-II) (Cont.)

2) Turn ignition off. Disconnect cruise control ECU harness connector. *See Figs. 1-4.* Turn ignition on. Measure voltage between terminal OD and ground. *See Fig. 14.* If 4-6 volts is present, replace cruise control ECU and retest. If 4-6 volts is not present, inspect and repair circuit between cruise control ECU and ECT ECU.

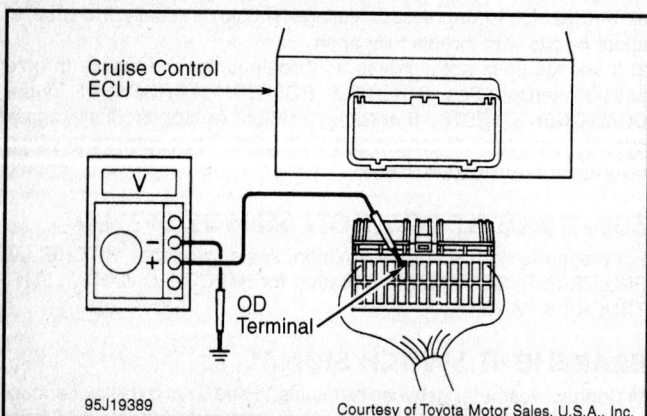

Cruise Control ECU

OD Terminal

95J19389

Courtesy of Toyota Motor Sales, U.S.A., Inc.

Fig. 14: Identifying Cruise Control ECU Terminals

ECT ECU VOLTAGES

Access ECT ECU. *See Figs. 1-4.* On Lexus models and Supra Turbo, disconnect ECT ECU harness connector and install check harness between ECT ECU and harness connector. On all models, turn ignition on. Using DVOM, backprobe ECT ECU harness connector or check harness. Check voltage between designated terminals on ECT ECU and ground terminal (E_1). Voltage should be as specified. *See Figs. 15-20.*

COMPONENT TESTS

NOTE: On Pickup and 4Runner, No. 3 solenoid (S3) may also be referred to as SL solenoid.

SOLENOIDS

1) Access ECT ECU. *See Figs. 1-4.* Ensure ignition is off. Disconnect electrical connector from ECT ECU.
2) Using ohmmeter, measure resistance between S1, S2, S3 or S4 terminal and body ground. *See Figs. 8 and 9.* Replace solenoid if resistance is not 11-16 ohms.
3) To check solenoid operation, apply battery voltage to appropriate terminal of ECT ECU harness connector and ground. Ensure operating sound can be heard when battery voltage is connected. Replace solenoid if operating sound cannot be heard.
4) To check solenoid seals, connect battery voltage to appropriate solenoid. Apply 71 psi (5 kg/cm²) to solenoid with battery voltage connected. *See Fig. 21.*
5) On S1, S2 or S4 solenoids, with battery voltage applied, air should pass through solenoid. Disconnect battery and ensure air does not pass through solenoid. Replace solenoid if defective.
6) On lock-up solenoid (S3 or SL), with battery voltage applied, air should not pass through solenoid. Disconnect battery and ensure air passes through solenoid. Replace solenoid if defective.

PARK/NEUTRAL POSITION (PNP) SWITCH

Disconnect electrical connector at PNP switch. Switch is located on side of transmission. Using ohmmeter, check for continuity between specified terminals in accordance with shift lever position. *See Figs. 22 and 23.* Replace PNP switch if defective.

	Terminal ID.	Function/Description	Voltage Value (DC Volts Unless Otherwise Specified)
Blue/Yellow	S_1	No. 1 Solenoid	9-14 Volts With KOEO [1]
Red/Blue	S_2	No. 2 Solenoid	.5 Volt Or Less With KOEO [1]
Blue	SLU	No. 3 (Lock-Up) Solenoid	9-14 Volts With KOEO [1]
Gray	SLN	No. 4 Solenoid	9-14 Volts With KOEO [1]
Black/White	NSW	Park/Neutral Position Switch	0-1 Volt In Park Or Neutral, KOEO [1]
Yellow/Red	VTA1	Throttle Position Sensor Output Signal	3.0-5.5 Volts With Throttle Fully Open
Pink/Black	IDL1	Closed Throttle Sensor Signal	0-1 Volt With Throttle Closed, KOEO [1]
Violet/White	SP_1	No. 1 Vehicle Speed Sensor	0-8 Volts (Pulse), Car Moving, KOEO [1]
Red/Black	R	Park/Neutral Position Switch "R" Signal	9-14 Volts With KOEO [1]
Green/Orange	2	Park/Neutral Position Switch "2" Signal	9-14 Volts In "2", KOEO [3]
Green/Black	L	Park/Neutral Position Switch "L" Signal	9-14 Volts In "L", KOEO [1]
Violet	OD_1	Input From Cruise Control ECU	4-6 Volts With KOEO [1]
Black/Red	OD_2	Overdrive Switch Signal	9-14 Volts With Switch On
Blue/White	P	Pattern Select Switch Signal	9-14 Volts In PWR Position
Black/Red	+B	EFI Main Relay Power Supply	9-14 Volts With KOEO [1]
White/Blue	BATT	Power Supply Voltage	9-14 Volts (Constant)
Brown	E_1	Ground	Not Applicable

96H30509   [1] – Key On, Engine Off.

Fig. 15: ECT ECU Pin Voltage Table (1995 Lexus GS300)

AUTOMATIC TRANSMISSIONS
Toyota A-340 Series - Electronic Controls (Except OBD-II) (Cont.)

3-1669

	Terminal ID.	Function/Description	Voltage Value (DC Volts Unless Otherwise Specified)
Lt. Green	S₁	No. 1 Solenoid	10-14 Volts With KOEO [1]
White/Red	S₂	No. 2 Solenoid	.5 Volt Or Less With KOEO [1]
Black/White	NSW	Park/Neutral Position Switch	0-1 Volt In Park Or Neutral, KOEO [1]
Yellow	VTA1	Throttle Position Sensor Output Signal	3.0-5.5 Volts With Throttle Fully Open
Red	IDL1	Closed Throttle Sensor Signal	0-1 Volt With Throttle Closed, KOEO [1]
Pink	SP1	No. 1 Vehicle Speed Sensor	0-8 Volts (Pulse), Car Moving, KOEO [1]
Green	2	Park/Neutral Position Switch "2" Signal	10-14 Volts In "2", KOEO [1]
White	L	Park/Neutral Position Switch "L" Signal	10-14 Volts In "L", KOEO [1]
Brown/Yellow	OD₁	Input From Cruise Control ECU	4-6 Volts With KOEO [1]
Gray/Red	OD₂	Overdrive Switch Signal	10-14 Volts With Switch On
Green/Orange	P	Pattern Select Switch Signal	10-14 Volts In PWR Position
Black/Red	+B	EFI Main Relay Power Supply	10-14 Volts With KOEO [1]
Black/Yellow	BATT	Power Supply Voltage	10-14 Volts (Constant)
Brown	E₁	Ground	Not Applicable

96A30510   [1] – Key On, Engine Off.

Fig. 16: ECT ECU Pin Voltage Table (1995 Lexus SC300)

	Terminal ID.	Function/Description	Voltage Value (DC Volts Unless Otherwise Specified)
Lt. Green	SOL1	No. 1 Solenoid	10-14 Volts With KOEO [1]
White/Red	SOL2	No. 2 Solenoid	.5 Volt Or Less With KOEO [1]
Blue	SLU	No. 3 (Lock-Up) Solenoid	10-14 Volts With KOEO [1]
Red/Black	SLN	No. 4 Solenoid	10-14 Volts With KOEO [1]
Black/White	NSW	Park/Neutral Position Switch	0-1 Volt In Park Or Neutral, KOEO [1]
Yellow	VTA1	Throttle Position Sensor Output Signal	3.0-5.5 Volts With Throttle Fully Open
Red	IDL1	Closed Throttle Sensor Signal	0-1 Volt With Throttle Closed, KOEO [1]
Pink	SPD	No. 1 Vehicle Speed Sensor	0-8 Volts (Pulse), Car Moving, KOEO [1]
Red/Black	R	Park/Neutral Position Switch "R" Signal	10-14 Volts With KOEO [1]
Green	2	Park/Neutral Position Switch "2" Signal	10-14 Volts In "2", KOEO [3]
White	L	Park/Neutral Position Switch "L" Signal	10-14 Volts In "L", KOEO [1]
Brown/Yellow	OD₁	Input From Cruise Control ECU	4-6 Volts With KOEO [1]
Gray/Red	OD₂	Overdrive Switch Signal	10-14 Volts With Switch On
Green/Orange	P	Pattern Select Switch Signal	10-14 Volts In PWR Position
Black/Red	+B	EFI Main Relay Power Supply	10-14 Volts With KOEO [1]
Black/Yellow	BATT	Power Supply Voltage	10-14 Volts (Constant)
Brown	E₁	Ground	Not Applicable

96B30511   [1] – Key On, Engine Off.

Fig. 17: ECT ECU Pin Voltage Table (1995 Lexus SC400)

AUTOMATIC TRANSMISSIONS
Toyota A-340 Series - Electronic Controls (Except OBD-II) (Cont.)

	Terminal ID.	Function/Description	Voltage Value (DC Volts Unless Otherwise Specified)
Blue/Red	S_1	No. 1 Solenoid	10-14 Volts With KOEO [1]
Red/White	S_2	No. 2 Solenoid	1 Volt Or Less With KOEO [1]
Red/Green	S_3 (SL)	Lock-Up Solenoid	1 Volt Or Less With KOEO [1]
Red/Blue	PWR	Pattern Select Switch Signal	10-14 Volts In PWR Position
Green/White	STP	Brakelight Switch Signal	10-14 Volts With Pedal Depressed
Green/Blue	THW	Coolant Temperature Sensor Signal	.1-1.0 Volts @ 176°F (80°C)
Yellow/Blue	IDL	Closed Throttle Sensor Signal	1 Volt Or Less With Throttle Closed
Yellow	VTA	Throttle Position Sensor Output Signal	3-5 Volts With Throttle Fully Open
Green/Yellow	VC	Throttle Position Sensor Input Signal	4-6 Volts With KOEO [1]
Yellow/Red	OD_1	OD Output To Cruise Control ECU	5 Volts With KOEO [1]
Yellow/Green	OD_2	Overdrive Switch Signal	10-14 Volts With Switch On
Green/Blue	SPD (SP_1)	Vehicle Speed Sensor Signal	0 Or 5 Volts [2] (Car Parked)
Blue	SP_2	Vehicle Speed Sensor Signal	0 Or 5 Volts With Car Parked
Violet/Red	N	Park/Neutral Position Switch "N" Signal	10-14 Volts In "N", KOEO [1]
Pink/Green	2	Park/Neutral Position Switch "2" Signal	10-14 Volts In "2", KOEO [1]
Violet/White	L	Park/Neutral Position Switch "L" Signal	10-14 Volts In "L", KOEO [1]
White/Red	+B	EFI Main Relay Power Supply	10-14 Volts With KOEO [1]
Black/Green	BATT	Power Supply Voltage	10-14 Volts (Constant)
Brown	E_1	Ground	Not Applicable
Brown/Black	E_2	Ground	Not Applicable

[1] – Key On, Engine Off.
[2] – Cruise control main switch off.

96C30512

Fig. 18: ECT ECU Pin Voltage Table (1995 Toyota Pickup & 4Runner – 4-Cylinder)

KICKDOWN SWITCH

Disconnect electrical connector at kickdown switch. See Fig. 4. Using ohmmeter, check for continuity between switch terminals. Continuity should exist when switch is in ON position. Continuity should not exist when switch is in OFF position. Replace switch if defective.

THROTTLE POSITION (TP) SENSOR

1) Disconnect electrical connector at throttle position sensor, located on side of throttle body. Note throttle position sensor terminal identification. See Fig. 24.
2) Using ohmmeter, check resistance between specified terminals in relation to throttle position. See THROTTLE POSITION SENSOR RESISTANCE SPECIFICATIONS table. Replace throttle position sensor if resistance is not as specified.

THROTTLE POSITION SENSOR RESISTANCE SPECIFICATIONS

Terminals	Ohms
IDL & E_2	
Throttle Fully Closed	2300 Or Less
Throttle Fully Open	Infinity
Vc & E_2	3900-9000
VTA & E_2	
Throttle Fully Closed	500-6100
Throttle Fully Open	3100-12,100

SUB-THROTTLE POSITION SENSOR

For diagnosis and testing, see appropriate MITCHELL® ENGINE PERFORMANCE publication for IMPORTED CARS, LIGHT TRUCKS & VANS.

ENGINE COOLANT TEMPERATURE (ECT) SENSOR

Disconnect electrical connector from coolant temperature sensor. Using ohmmeter, check resistance between terminals of coolant temperature sensor. Resistance should as specified in accordance with coolant temperature. See Fig. 25. Replace coolant temperature if resistance is not within specification.

NO. 1 VEHICLE SPEED SENSOR (VSS)

1) Disconnect electrical connector from VSS, located on side of transmission. See Figs. 1-4. Connect positive battery lead to terminal No. 1 and negative lead to terminal No. 2. Connect positive lead of voltmeter to terminal No. 3 and negative lead to terminal No. 2. See Fig. 26.
2) Rotate speedometer cable shaft on speed sensor. Ensure voltage changes from zero to 11 volts. Voltage should change 4 times per each revolution of speedometer cable shaft. Replace speed sensor if voltage does not change as specified.

AUTOMATIC TRANSMISSIONS
Toyota A-340 Series - Electronic Controls (Except OBD-II) (Cont.)

3-1671

	Terminal ID.	Function/Description	Voltage Value (DC Volts Unless Otherwise Specified)
White	S_1	No. 1 Solenoid	9-14 Volts With KOEO [1]
Black	S_2	No. 2 Solenoid	1 Volt Or Less With KOEO [1]
Yellow/Black	S_3 (SL)	Lock-Up Solenoid	1 Volt Or Less With KOEO [1]
Green/Red	S_4	Transfer Case Solenoid	1 Volt Or Less With KOEO [1]
Green/Orange	PWR	Pattern Select Switch Signal	9-14 Volts In PWR Position
Green/White	STP	Brakelight Switch Signal	9-14 Volts With Pedal Depressed
Green/Blue	THW	Coolant Temperature Sensor Signal	.1-1.0 Volts @ 176°F (80°C)
Yellow/White	IDL	Closed Throttle Sensor Signal	1 Volt Or Less With Throttle Closed
Yellow	VTA	Throttle Position Sensor Output Signal	3-5 Volts With Throttle Fully Open
Green/Black	VC	Throttle Position Sensor Input Signal	4-6 Volts With KOEO [1]
Yellow/Red	OD_1	OD Output To Cruise Control ECU	5 Volts With KOEO [1]
Yellow/Green	OD_2	Overdrive Switch Signal	9-14 Volts With Switch On
Green/Blue	SPD (SP$_1$)	Vehicle Speed Sensor Signal	0 Or 5 Volts [2] (Car Parked)
Brown/Red	SP_2	Vehicle Speed Sensor Signal	0 Or 5 Volts With Car Parked
Violet/Red	N	Park/Neutral Position Switch "N" Signal	9-14 Volts In "N", KOEO [1]
Pink/Green	2	Park/Neutral Position Switch "2" Signal	9-14 Volts In "2", KOEO [1]
Violet/White	L	Park/Neutral Position Switch "L" Signal	9-14 Volts In "L", KOEO [1]
Yellow/Red	L4	Transfer Shift Position Switch Signal	9-14 Volts In "L", KOEO [1]
Green/Black	THO1	Transmission Fluid Temperature Sensor	4-5 Volts @ 68°F (20°C)
Lt. Green	THO2	Transfer Fluid Temperature Sensor	4-5 Volts @ 68°F (20°C)
Blue/White	OIL	Indicator Light Signal	9-14 Volts With KOEO [1]
White/Red	+B	EFI Main Relay Power Supply	9-14 Volts With KOEO [1]
Black/Green	BATT	Power Supply Voltage	9-14 Volts (Constant)
Brown	E_1	Ground	Not Applicable
Brown/Black	E_2	Ground	Not Applicable

[1] – Key On, Engine Off.
[2] – Cruise control main switch off.

96D30513

Fig. 19: ECT ECU Pin Voltage Table (1995 Toyota Pickup & 4Runner – V-6)

NO. 2 VEHICLE SPEED SENSOR (VSS)

GS300, SC300, SC400 & Supra Turbo – Remove No. 2 vehicle speed sensor. See Figs. 1, 2 and 4. Connect voltmeter between terminals of sensor. Place a magnet near speed sensor tip. Quickly move magnet away from speed sensor tip. Move magnet quickly several times while observing voltmeter. Voltmeter should intermittently indicate a voltage less than one volt when magnet is brought close to sensor and then moved away. See Fig. 27. If voltage is not as specified, replace speed sensor.

Pickup & 4Runner – Disconnect electrical connector from No. 2 vehicle speed sensor, located on transmission. See Fig. 3. Raise and support vehicle so one rear wheel can rotate. Connect ohmmeter between terminals of No. 2 vehicle speed sensor. Rotate rear wheel. Ohmmeter needle should fluctuate from continuity to no continuity. Replace sensor as needed.

ATF & TRANSFER CASE FLUID TEMPERATURE SENSOR (PICKUP & 4RUNNER)

1) Raise and support vehicle. Disconnect appropriate temperature sensor connector. Remove temperature sensor from transmission. See Fig. 3. Connect ohmmeter leads between sensor terminals.

2) Submerge sensor in container of water. Heat water while measuring sensor resistance. At 68°F (20°C), sensor resistance should be 5000-20,000 ohms. At 248°F (120°C), sensor resistance should be 540-690 ohms. At 302°F (150°C), sensor resistance should be 300-340 ohms. If resistance is not as specified, replace sensor. If resistance is as specified, inspect and repair wiring circuits between sensor and ECT ECU. If circuits are okay, replace ECT ECU.

3-1672

AUTOMATIC TRANSMISSIONS
Toyota A-340 Series - Electronic Controls (Except OBD-II) (Cont.)

	Terminal ID.	Function/Description	Voltage Value (DC Volts Unless Otherwise Specified)
White/Red	S_1	No. 1 Solenoid	10-14 Volts With KOEO [1]
Red/Blue	S_2	No. 2 Solenoid	.5 Volt Or Less With KOEO [1]
Lt. Green/Black	SLU	No. 3 (Lock-Up) Solenoid	10-14 Volts With KOEO [1]
Yellow/Green	SLN	No. 4 Solenoid	10-14 Volts With KOEO [1]
Black/White	NSW	Park/Neutral Position Switch	0-1 Volt In Park Or Neutral, KOEO [1]
Yellow	VTA1	Throttle Position Sensor Output Signal	3.0-5.5 Volts With Throttle Fully Open
Red	IDL1	Closed Throttle Sensor Signal	0-1 Volt With Throttle Closed, KOEO [1]
Pink	SP_1	No. 1 Vehicle Speed Sensor	0-8 Volts (Pulse), Car Moving, KOEO [1]
Yellow	KD	Kickdown Switch	10-14 Volts With Switch Off, KOEO [1]
Red/Black	R	Park/Neutral Position Switch "R" Signal	10-14 Volts With KOEO [1]
Lt. Green/Red	2	Park/Neutral Position Switch "2" Signal	10-14 Volts In "2", KOEO [1]
Green/Black	L	Park/Neutral Position Switch "L" Signal	10-14 Volts In "L", KOEO [1]
Brown/Black	OD_1	Input From Cruise Control ECU	4-6 Volts With KOEO [1]
Violet/Green	OD_2	Overdrive Switch Signal	10-14 Volts With Switch On
Green/Yellow	M	Pattern Select Switch Signal	10-14 Volts In PWR Position
Orange	TRC+	TRAC ECU Signal	10-14 Volts With KOEO [1]
White/Red	TRC-	TRAC ECU Signal	10-14 Volts With KOEO [1]
[2]	SLT-, SLT+	No. 5 Solenoid	10-14 Volts With KOEO [1]
Black	EFI+	TRAC ECU Signal	10-14 Volts With KOEO [1]
White	EFI-	TRAC ECU Signal	10-14 Volts With KOEO [1]
Black/Red	+B	EFI Main Relay Power Supply	10-14 Volts With KOEO [1]
Black/Yellow	BATT	Power Supply Voltage	10-14 Volts (Constant)
Brown	E_1	Ground	Not Applicable

[1] – Key On, Engine Off.
[2] – Wire color for terminal SLT– is Lt. Green/Red. Wire color for terminal SLT+ is White/Green.

96E30514

Fig. 20: ECT ECU Pin Voltage Table (1995 Toyota Supra Turbo)

OD DIRECT CLUTCH SPEED SENSOR

1) Remove sensor from transmission. Connect ohmmeter between OD direct clutch speed sensor terminals. Place a magnet near speed sensor tip. See Fig. 27. Quickly move magnet away from speed sensor tip. Move magnet quickly several times while observing ohmmeter.
2) DVOM should intermittently indicate a voltage less than one volt. If DVOM intermittently indicates a voltage less than one volt, OD direct clutch speed sensor is okay. If DVOM does not intermittently indicate a voltage less than one volt, replace OD direct clutch speed sensor.

BRAKELIGHT SWITCH

1) Disconnect electrical connector from brakelight switch, located near brake pedal. Using ohmmeter, ensure continuity exists between switch terminals No. 1 and 2 with brake pedal depressed. See Fig. 28.
2) Continuity should exist between terminals No. 3 and 4 with brake pedal released. If continuity does not exist, ensure brake pedal is properly adjusted so brakelight switch has proper travel for switch operation. If proper brakelight switch travel exists, replace brakelight switch.

PATTERN SELECT SWITCH

Disconnect electrical connector from pattern select switch. See Figs. 1-4. Using ohmmeter, ensure continuity exists between specified terminals with switch in PWR position. See PATTERN SELECT SWITCH TERMINAL IDENTIFICATION table. No continuity should exist in NORM position. See Fig. 29.

PATTERN SELECT SWITCH TERMINAL IDENTIFICATION

Application	Terminal No.
Lexus	
GS300	1 & 2
SC300 & SC400	3 & 4
Toyota	
Pickup & 4Runner	
Column Shift	2 & 3
Floor Shift	4 & 6
Supra Turbo	3 & 4

AUTOMATIC TRANSMISSIONS
Toyota A-340 Series – Electronic Controls (Except OBD-II) (Cont.)

3-1673

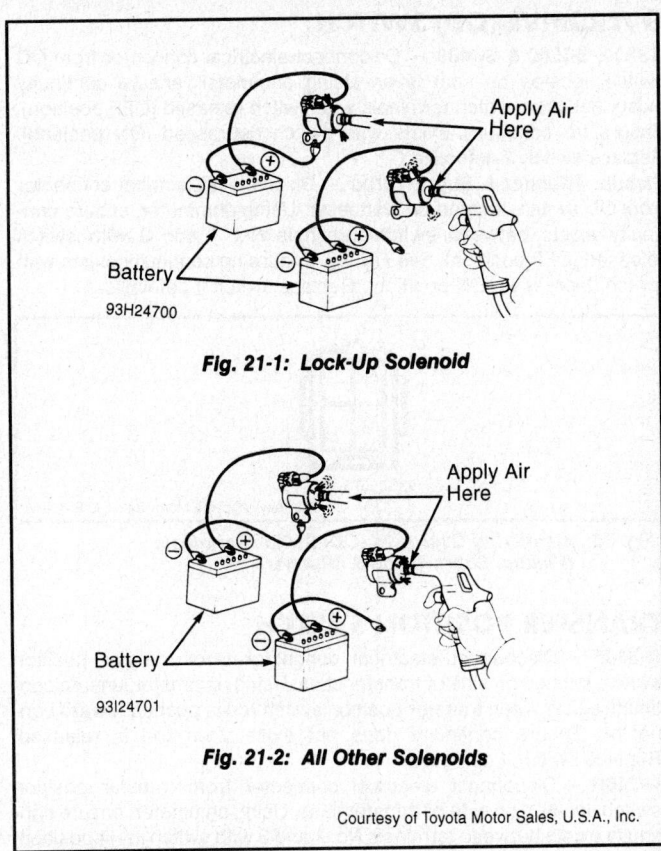

Fig. 21-1: Lock-Up Solenoid

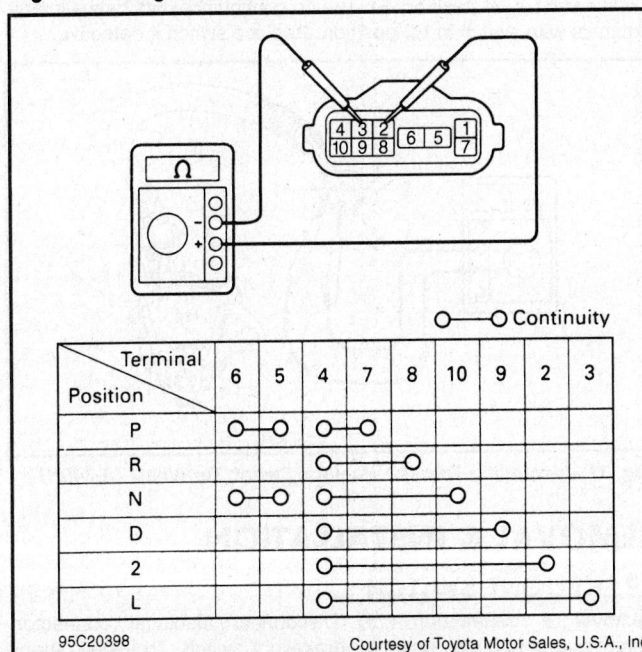

Fig. 21-2: All Other Solenoids

Courtesy of Toyota Motor Sales, U.S.A., Inc.

Fig. 21: Testing Solenoids

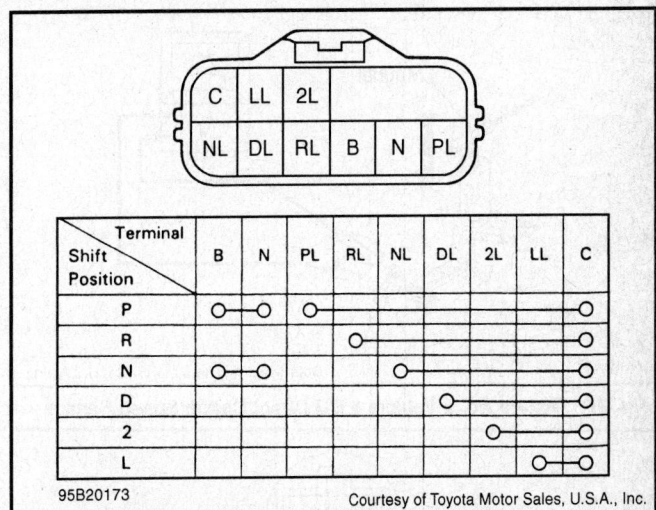

Terminal Shift Position	B	N	PL	RL	NL	DL	2L	LL	C
P	O—O		O						O
R				O					O
N	O—O				O				O
D						O			O
2							O		O
L								O—O	O

95B20173

Courtesy of Toyota Motor Sales, U.S.A., Inc.

Fig. 23: Testing Park/Neutral Position (PNP) Switch (Pickup & 4Runner)

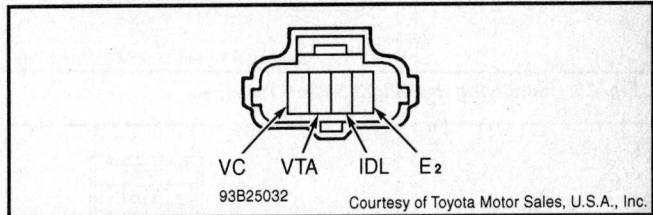

VC   VTA   IDL   E₂

93B25032

Courtesy of Toyota Motor Sales, U.S.A., Inc.

Fig. 24: Identifying Throttle Position Sensor Terminals

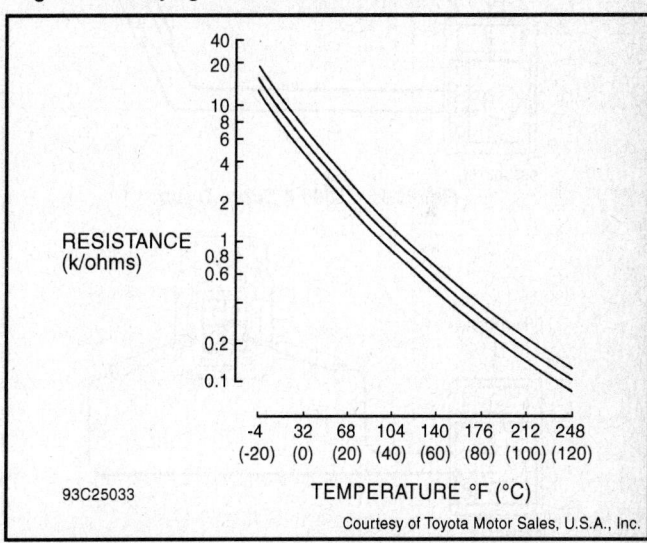

93C25033

Courtesy of Toyota Motor Sales, U.S.A., Inc.

Fig. 25: Checking Engine Coolant Temperature (ECT) Sensor

O—O Continuity

Terminal Position	6	5	4	7	8	10	9	2	3
P	O—O		O—O						
R			O	O					
N	O—O		O		O				
D			O			O			
2			O				O		
L			O						O

95C20398

Courtesy of Toyota Motor Sales, U.S.A., Inc.

Fig. 22: Testing Park/Neutral Position (PNP) Switch (GS300, SC300, SC400 & Supra Turbo)

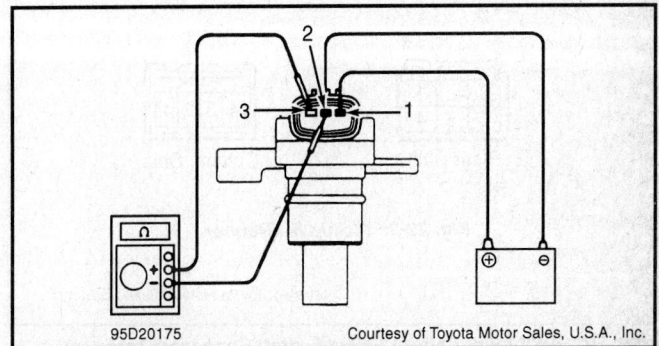

95D20175

Courtesy of Toyota Motor Sales, U.S.A., Inc.

Fig. 26: Checking No. 1 Vehicle Speed Sensor

3-1674

AUTOMATIC TRANSMISSIONS
Toyota A-340 Series - Electronic Controls (Except OBD-II) (Cont.)

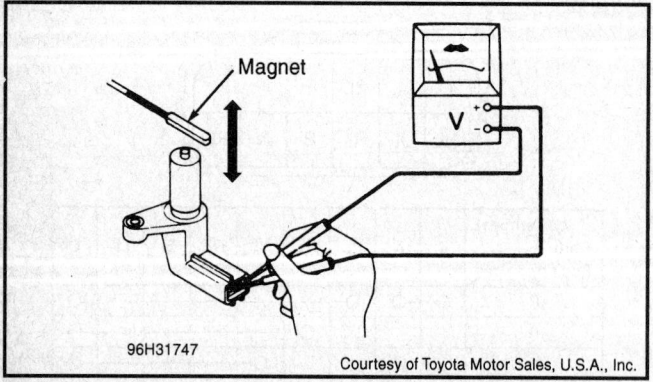

96H31747

Courtesy of Toyota Motor Sales, U.S.A., Inc.

Fig. 27: Testing No. 2 Vehicle & OD Direct Clutch Speed Sensor

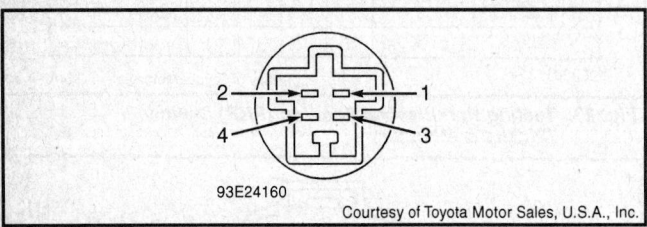

93E24160

Courtesy of Toyota Motor Sales, U.S.A., Inc.

Fig. 28: Identifying Brakelight Switch Terminals

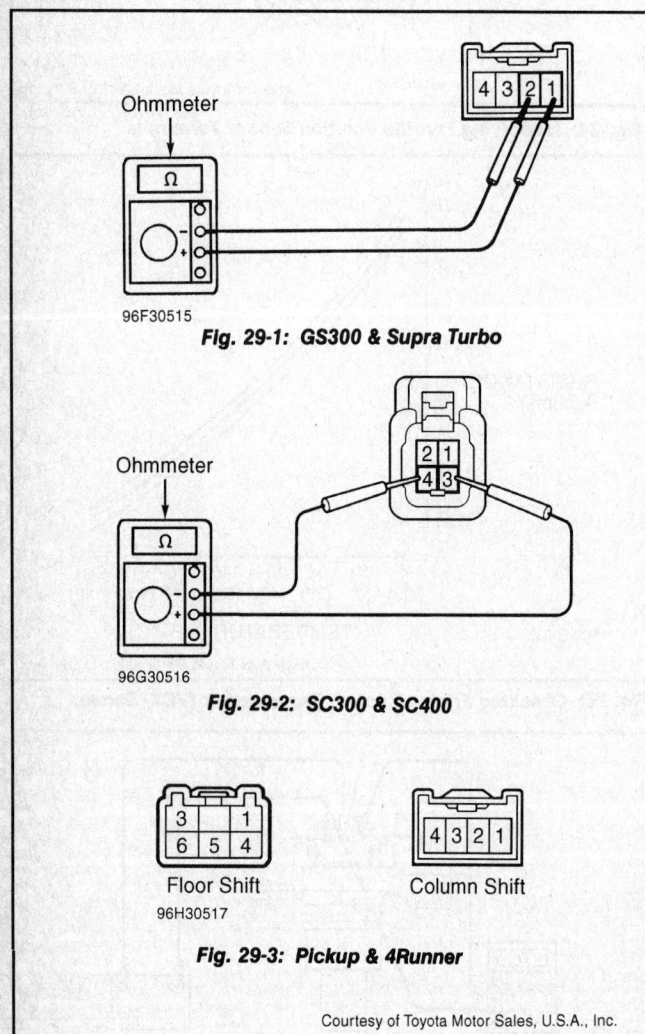

96F30515

Fig. 29-1: GS300 & Supra Turbo

96G30516

Fig. 29-2: SC300 & SC400

Floor Shift   Column Shift
96H30517

Fig. 29-3: Pickup & 4Runner

Courtesy of Toyota Motor Sales, U.S.A., Inc.

Fig. 29: Identifying Pattern Select Switch Connector Terminals

OVERDRIVE (OD) SWITCH

GS300, SC300 & SC400 – Disconnect electrical connector from OD switch, located on shift lever. Using ohmmeter, ensure continuity exists between switch terminals with switch released (OFF position). Ensure no continuity exists with switch depressed (ON position). Replace switch if defective.

Pickup, 4Runner & Supra Turbo – Disconnect electrical connector from OD switch, located on shift lever. Using ohmmeter, ensure continuity exists between switch terminals No. 1 and 3 with switch released (OFF position). See Fig. 30. Ensure no continuity exists with switch depressed (ON position). Replace switch if defective.

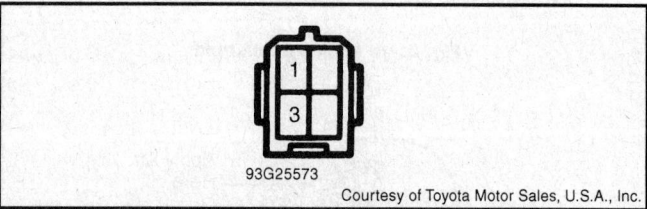

93G25573

Courtesy of Toyota Motor Sales, U.S.A., Inc.

Fig. 30: Identifying Overdrive (OD) Switch Terminals (Pickup, Supra Turbo & 4Runner)

TRANSFER POSITION SWITCH

A-340F – Disconnect electrical connector from transfer position switch, located on side of transfer case. Using ohmmeter, ensure continuity exists when transfer position switch rod is pushed toward connector. Ensure continuity does not exist when rod is released. Replace switch if defective.

A-340H – Disconnect electrical connector from transfer position switch, located on side of transfer case. Using ohmmeter, ensure continuity exists between terminals No. 1 and 3 with switch in H4 position. See Fig. 31. Ensure continuity exists between terminals No. 1, 2 and 3 with switch in L4 position. Ensure no continuity exists between any terminals with switch in H2 position. Replace switch if defective.

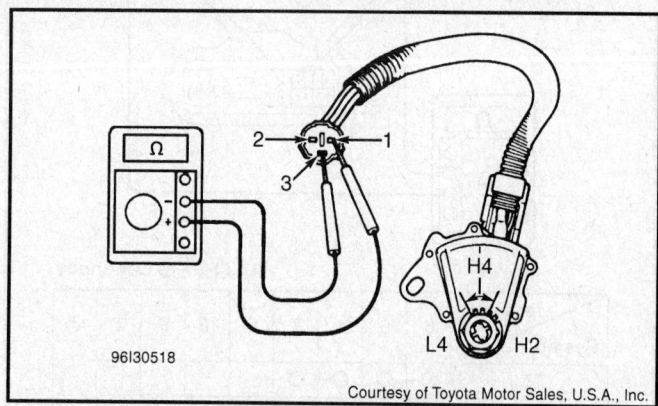

96I30518

Courtesy of Toyota Motor Sales, U.S.A., Inc.

Fig. 31: Identifying Transfer Position Switch Terminals (A-340H)

REMOVAL & INSTALLATION
BRAKELIGHT SWITCH

Removal & Installation – 1) Disconnect electrical connector. Remove lock nut, and unscrew brakelight switch. To install, screw brakelight switch inward until brakelight plunger contacts brake pedal. **2)** Ensure distance between threaded end of brakelight switch and brake pedal is .02-.09" (.5-2.4 mm). Install and tighten lock nut on brakelight switch. Install electrical connector. Ensure brakelights and cruise control operate properly.

SOLENOIDS

Removal & Installation – Solenoids are located on transmission valve body. See Figs. 1-4. Remove bolt, solenoid and "O" ring from valve body. To install, reverse removal procedure using NEW "O" ring.

PARK/NEUTRAL POSITION (PNP) SWITCH

Removal – **1)** PNP switch is located on side of transmission. Remove manual lever from control shaft on transmission.
2) Bend up tabs on lock washer. Remove lock nut, lock washer and seal from control shaft. Remove retaining bolt and switch.
Installation – **1)** Install switch on control shaft. Loosely install switch retaining bolt. Install seal and lock washer. Install lock nut and tighten to specification. See TORQUE SPECIFICATIONS.
2) Switch must be adjusted. Ensure parking brake is applied. Temporarily install manual lever on control shaft. Place shift lever in Neutral. Remove manual lever. Rotate switch and align neutral basic line on switch with groove. See Fig. 32.
3) Hold switch in this position. Tighten retaining bolt to specification. Bend tabs on lock washer over against lock nut. To install remaining components, reverse removal procedure.

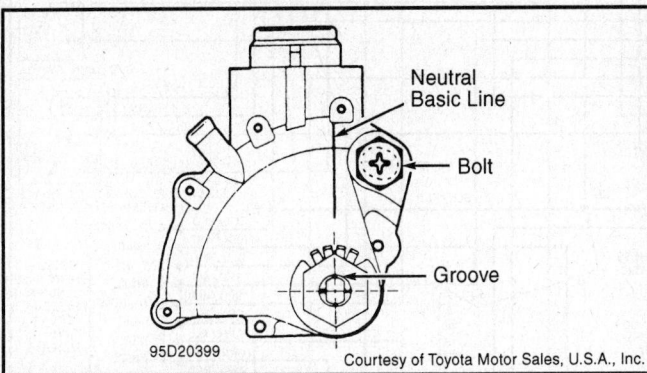

95D20399   Courtesy of Toyota Motor Sales, U.S.A., Inc.

Fig. 32: Aligning PNP Switch

THROTTLE POSITION (TP) SENSOR

Removal – Ensure ignition is off. Disconnect electrical connector from throttle position sensor. Throttle position sensor is located on throttle body. Remove screws and throttle position sensor.

Installation – **1)** Ensure throttle valve is closed. Install throttle position sensor on throttle body with screws loosely installed. Throttle position sensor must be adjusted. Connect ohmmeter leads to IDL and E_2 terminals of throttle position sensor. See Fig. 24.
2) Insert .020" (.50 mm) feeler gauge between throttle stop screw and stop lever. Gradually rotate throttle position sensor until ohmmeter deflects and tighten retaining screws. Remove feeler gauge.

NO. 1 & NO. 2 VEHICLE SPEED SENSOR (VSS)

Removal & Installation – Disconnect electrical connector. Remove appropriate vehicle speed sensor from transmission. See Figs. 1-4. To install, reverse removal procedure.

OD DIRECT CLUTCH SPEED SENSOR

Removal & Installation – Disconnect electrical connector from sensor. Remove bolt and sensor. See Figs. 1, 2 and 4. To install, reverse removal procedure.

TORQUE SPECIFICATIONS
TORQUE SPECIFICATIONS

Application	Ft. Lbs (N.m)
No. 1 Vehicle Speed Sensor	
GS300, SC300, SC400 & Supra Turbo	12 (16)
Pickup & 4Runner	[1]
No. 2 Vehicle Speed Sensor	
Pickup & 4Runner	12 (16)

	INCH Lbs. (N.m)
No. 2 Vehicle Speed Sensor	
GS300, SC300, SC400 & Supra Turbo	48 (5.4)
OD Direct Clutch Speed Sensor	48 (5.4)
PNP Switch	
Bolt	9 (13)
Lock Nut	61 (6.9)

[1] – Information is not available from manufacturer.

3-1676

AUTOMATIC TRANSMISSIONS
Toyota A-340 Series - Electronic Controls (Except OBD-II) (Cont.)

WIRING DIAGRAMS

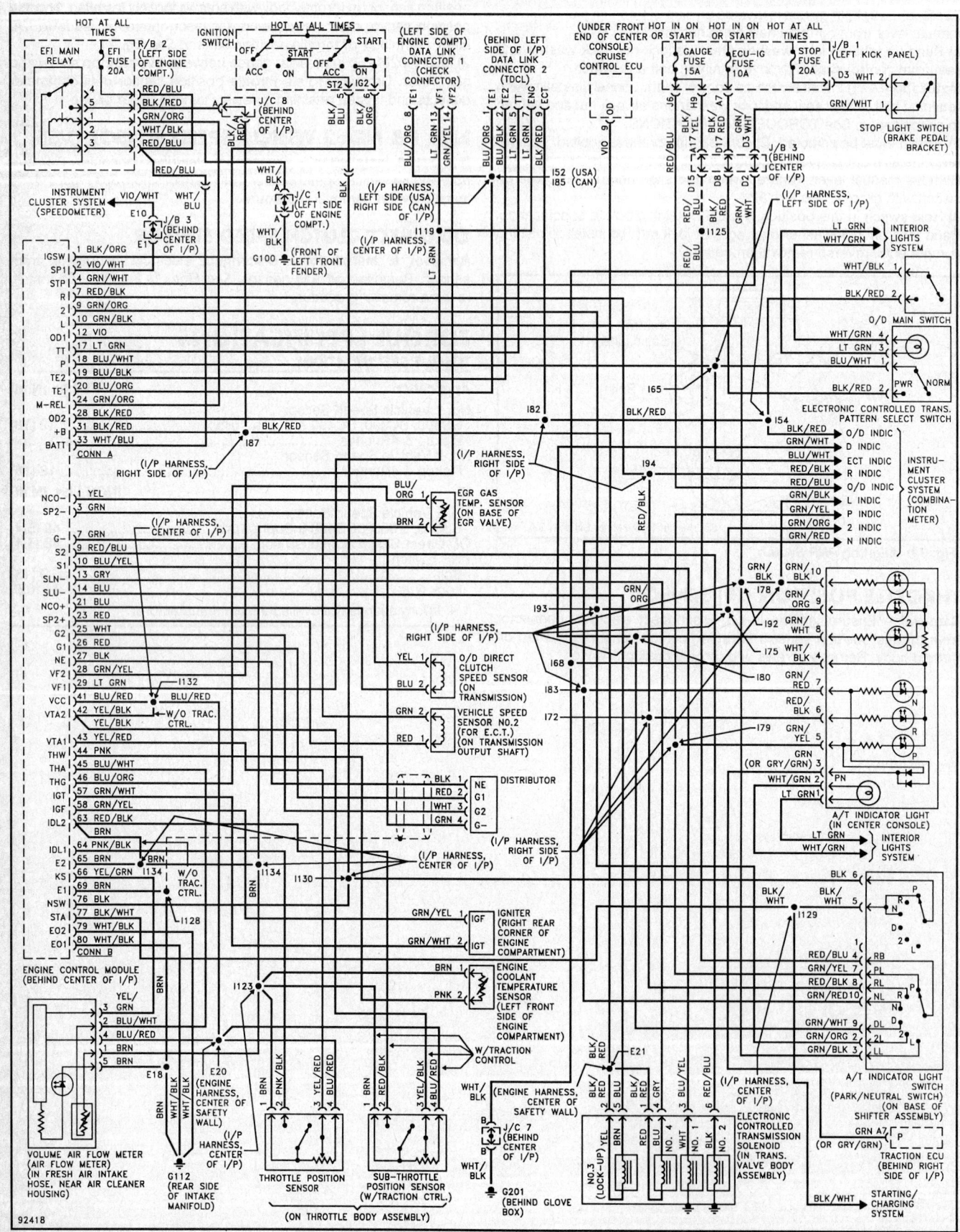

Fig. 33: Transmission Wiring Diagram (1995 Lexus GS300)

AUTOMATIC TRANSMISSIONS
Toyota A-340 Series - Electronic Controls (Except OBD-II) (Cont.)

3-1677

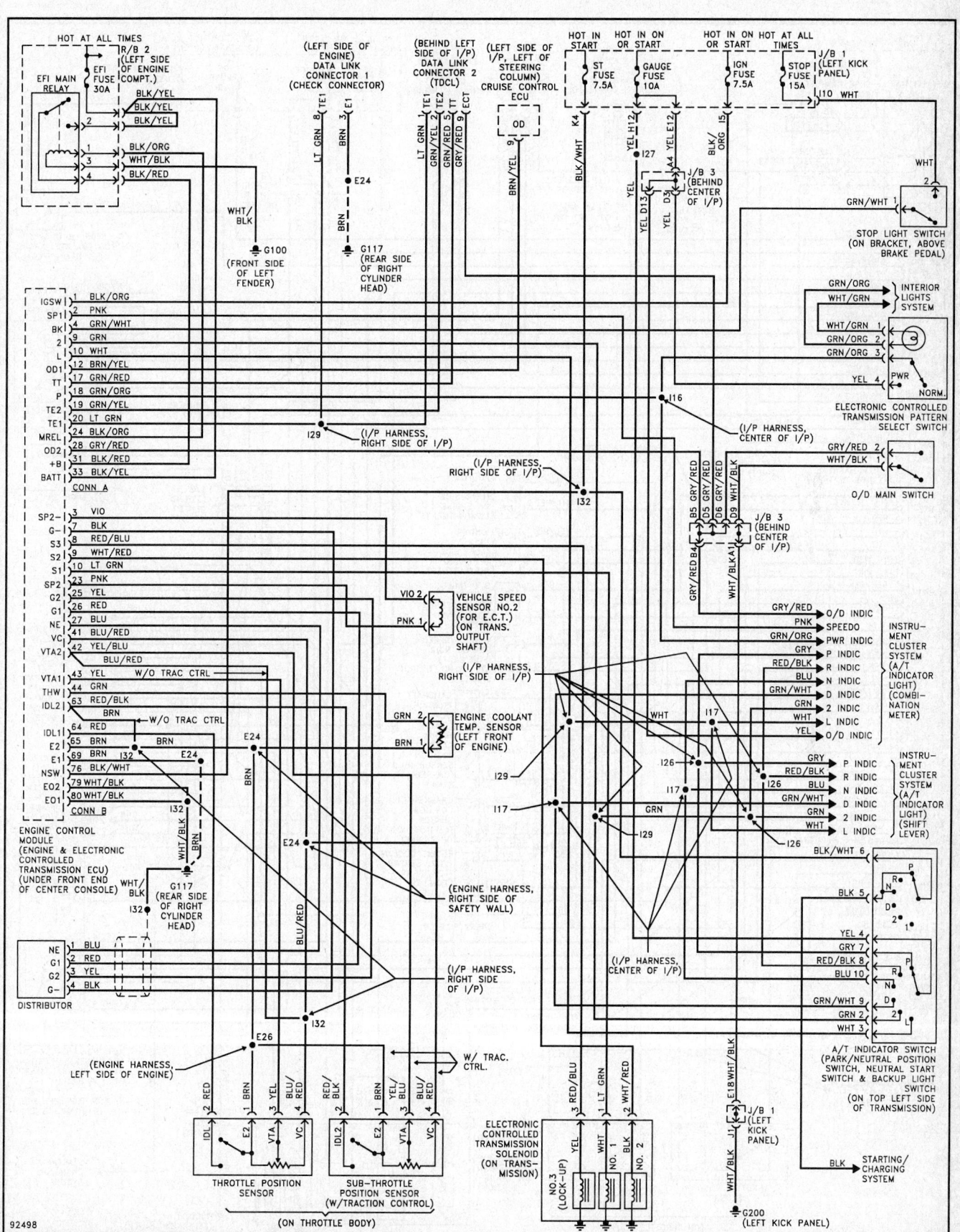

Fig. 34: Transmission Wiring Diagram (1995 Lexus SC300)

92498

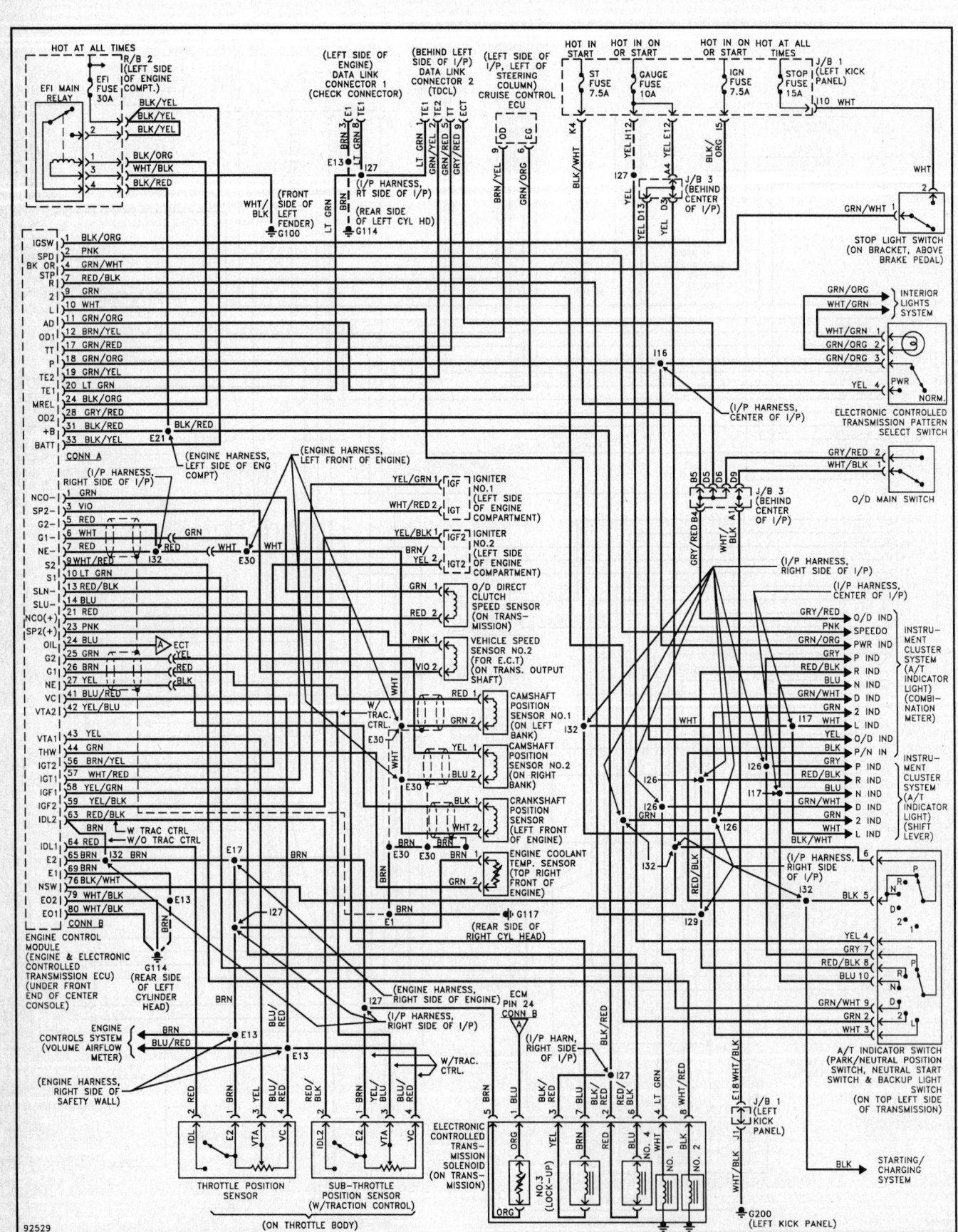

Fig. 35: Transmission Wiring Diagram (1995 Lexus SC400)

AUTOMATIC TRANSMISSIONS
Toyota A-340 Series - Electronic Controls (Except OBD-II) (Cont.)

3-1679

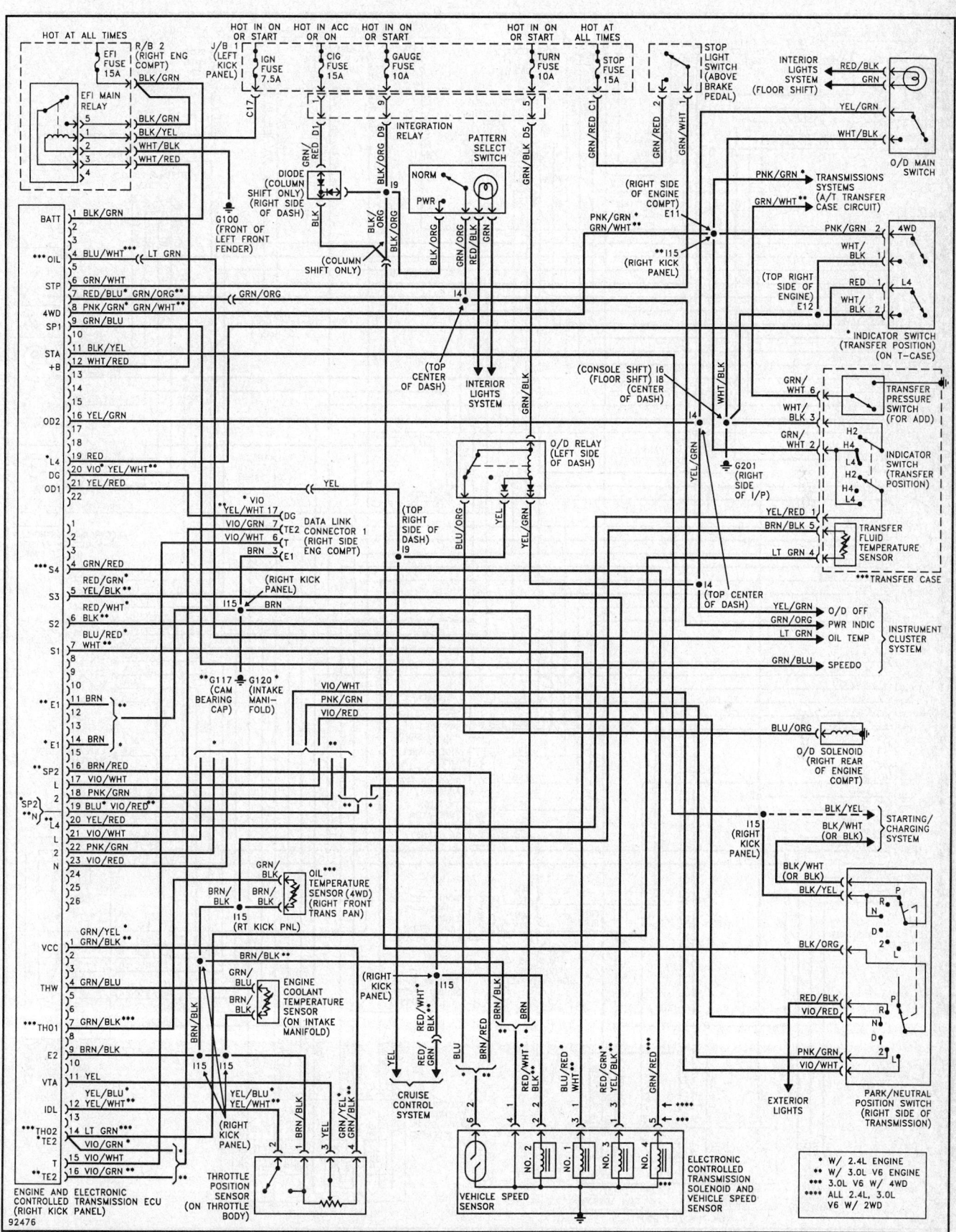

Fig. 36: *Transmission Wiring Diagram (1995 Toyota Pickup)*

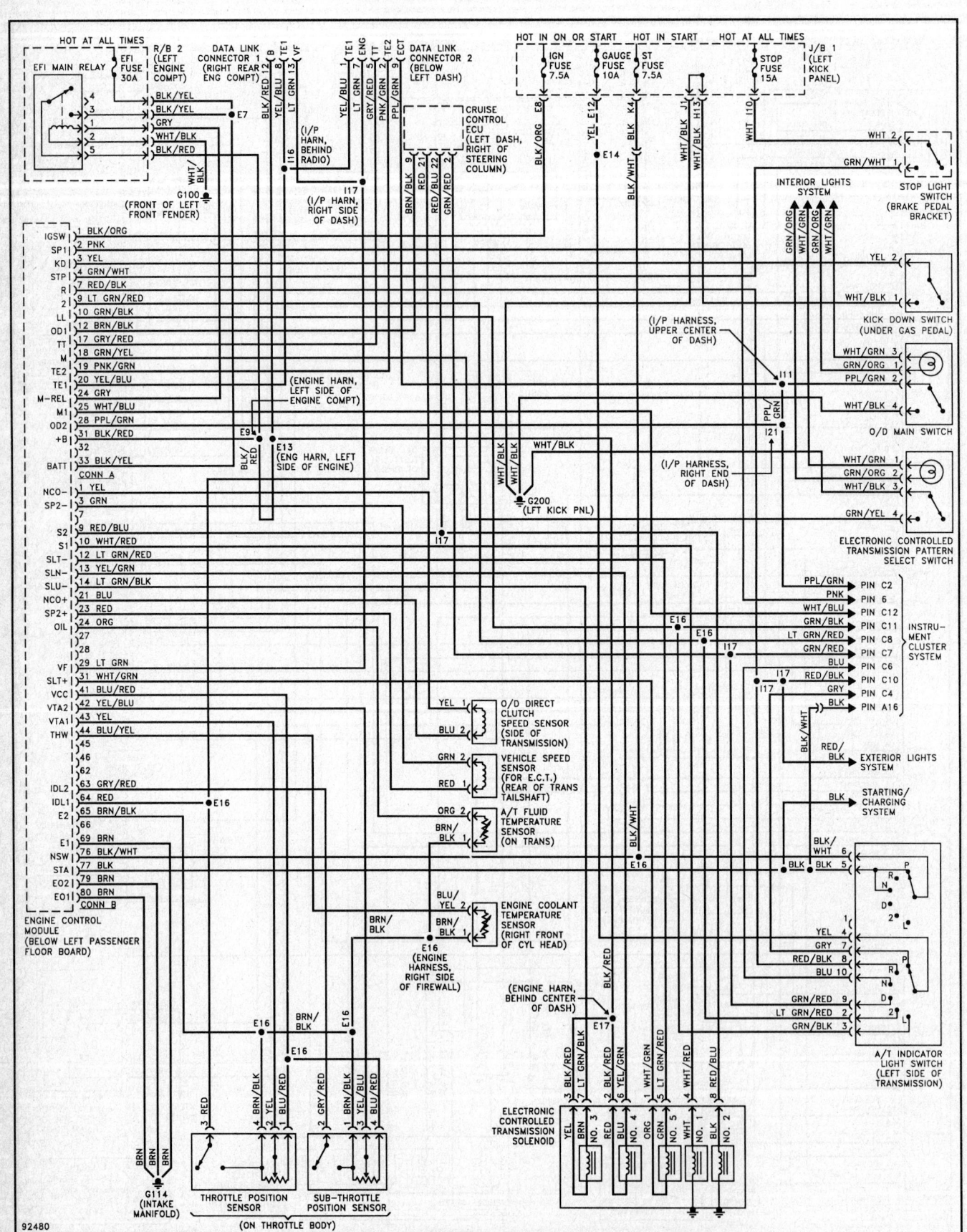

Fig. 37: Transmission Wiring Diagram (1995 Toyota Supra Turbo)

AUTOMATIC TRANSMISSIONS
Toyota A-340 Series - Electronic Controls (Except OBD-II) (Cont.)

3-1681

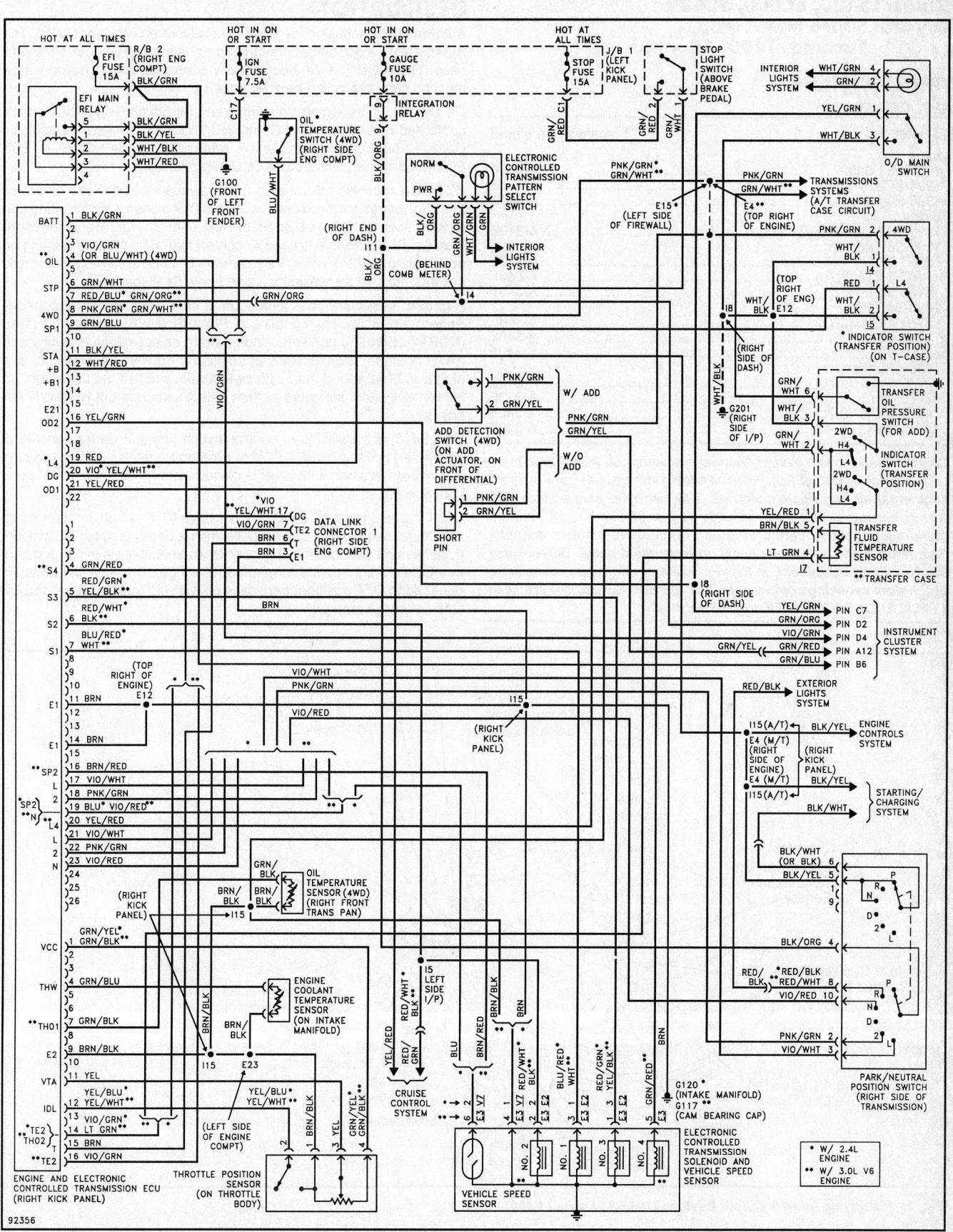

Fig. 38: Transmission Wiring Diagram (1995 Toyota 4Runner)

AUTOMATIC TRANSMISSIONS
Toyota A-340 Series – Electronic Controls (With OBD-II)

Lexus: LS400, SC300, SC400
Toyota: Supra Non-Turbo,
Tacoma, T100, 4Runner

APPLICATION

APPLICATION

Vehicle	Transmission Model
Lexus	
1995-96 LS400	A-340E
1996 SC300	A-340E
1996 SC400	A-340E
Toyota	
1995-96 Supra Non-Turbo	A-340E
1995-96 Tacoma	
2WD V6	A-340E
4WD 4-Cyl. (2.7L)	A-340F
4WD V6	A-340F
1995-96 T100	
2WD 4-Cyl. (2.7L)	A-340E
2WD V6	A-340E
4WD V6	A-340F
1996 4Runner	
2WD 4-Cyl. (2.7L)	A-340E
2WD V6	A-340E
4WD 4-Cyl. (2.7L)	A-340F
4WD V6	A-340F

CAUTION: All models except 4Runner are equipped with Supplemental Restraint System (SRS). When servicing vehicle, use care to avoid accidental air bag deployment. All SRS electrical connections and wiring harnesses are covered with Yellow insulation. SRS-related components are located in steering column, center console, instrument panel and lower panel on instrument panel. DO NOT use electrical test equipment on these circuits. If necessary, deactivate SRS before servicing components. See AIR BAG SERVICING article in APPLICATIONS & IDENTIFICATIONS section.

DESCRIPTION

Automatic transmission for all models is electronically controlled. The A-340E is an electronically controlled transmission without a transfer case. The A-340F is an electronically controlled transmission with a mechanically controlled transfer case.

On all models, transmission shifting and torque converter lock-up are controlled by an Electronic Controlled Transmission (ECT) Electronic Control Unit (ECU). Control unit is referred to as the ECT ECU. ECT ECU is combined with engine ECU into one unit.

ECT ECU receives information from various input devices and uses this information to control shift solenoids for transmission shifting and lock-up solenoid (also called SL or SLU solenoid) for torque converter lock-up. SLN solenoid is used to control hydraulic pressure acting on accumulator control valve. Valve assists in smooth shifting. Solenoids are mounted on transmission valve body. *See Figs. 1-7.*

A pattern select switch is located near shift lever on center console. Pattern select switch contains a POWER (PWR) and a NORMAL (NORM) operating position. When pattern select switch is depressed (PWR position), transmission upshifts and downshifts will occur at a higher vehicle speed than with switch released. An indicator light on instrument panel indicates pattern select switch is depressed (PWR position).

On LS400, a transmission control switch (located under console at shift lever) is used by ECT ECU to prohibit transmission from shifting into overdrive when shift lever is moved from "D" position to "3" position. *See Fig. 1.*

On all models except LS400, an Overdrive (OD) switch is mounted on shift lever. *See Figs. 2-7.* When OD switch is depressed to ON position, transmission will shift into 4th gear when shift lever is in "D" position, and OD OFF light on instrument panel will go off. When OD switch is released to OFF position, transmission will shift into 3rd gear, and OD OFF light will come on.

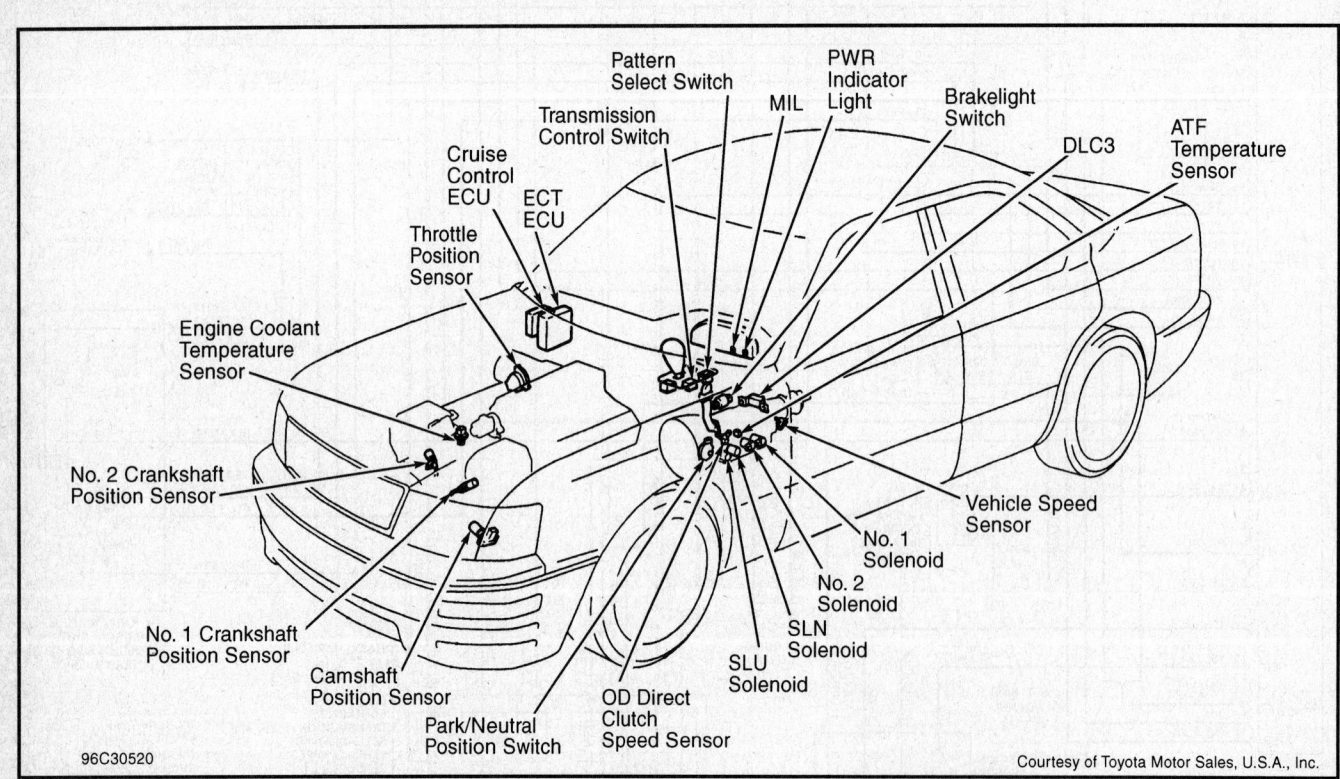

96C30520

Courtesy of Toyota Motor Sales, U.S.A., Inc.

Fig. 1: Identifying Input & Output Devices (1995-96 Lexus LS400)

AUTOMATIC TRANSMISSIONS
Toyota A-340 Series – Electronic Controls (With OBD-II) (Cont.)

3-1683

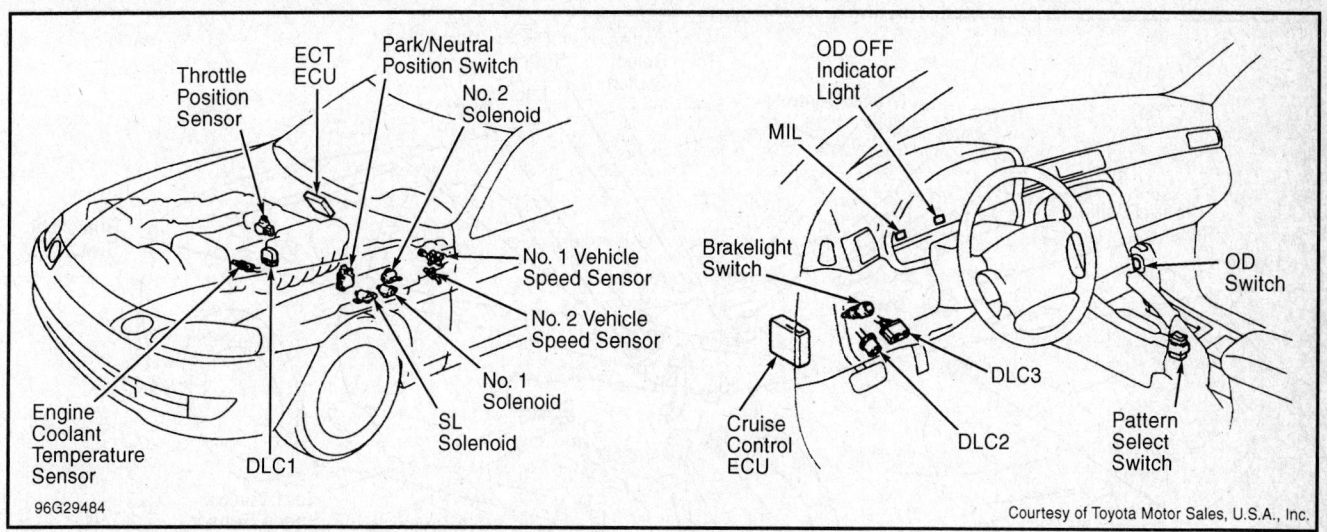

Fig. 2: Identifying Input & Output Devices (1996 Lexus SC300)

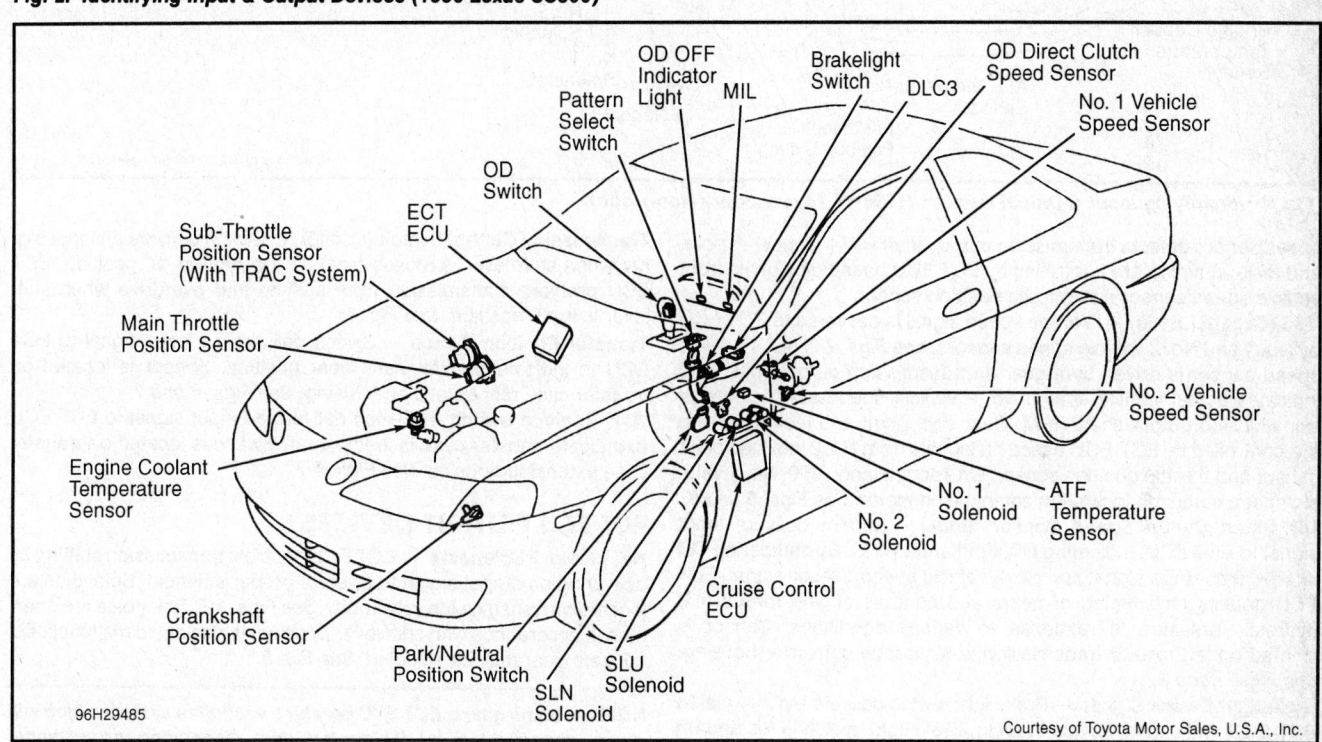

Fig. 3: Identifying Input & Output Devices (1996 Lexus SC400)

Transmission is equipped with a shift lock and key lock system. Shift lock system prevents shift lever from being moved from Park unless brake pedal is depressed. In case of a malfunction, shift lever can be released by depressing shift lock override button, located near shift lever. Key lock system prevents ignition key from being moved from ACC to LOCK position on ignition switch unless shift lever is in Park. For more information on shift lock and key lock system, see TOYOTA SHIFT LOCK SYSTEM article.

OPERATION

ECT ECU

ECT ECU receives information from various input devices and uses this information to control No. 1 and No. 2 solenoids on transmission valve body for transmission shifting and lock-up solenoid (also called SL or SLU solenoid) for torque converter lock-up. ECT ECU contains a self-diagnostic system, which will store a Diagnostic Trouble Code

(DTC) if a failure or problem exists in electronic control system. Trouble code can be retrieved to determine problem area. See SELF-DIAGNOSTIC SYSTEM. Note location of ECT ECU. *See Figs. 1-7.*

ECT ECU INPUT DEVICES

Pattern Select Switch Signal – Pattern select switch delivers an input signal to ECT ECU to indicate transmission shift points selected by vehicle operator. Pattern select switch is located near shift lever on center console. *See Figs. 1-5 and 7.* T100 is not equipped with a pattern select switch.

Park/Neutral Position (PNP) Switch Signal – PNP switch delivers an input signal to ECT ECU indicating shift lever position. Switch is located on side of transmission. *See Figs. 1-7.*

Throttle Position (TP) Sensor Signal – TP sensor delivers an input signal to ECT ECU indicating throttle position. TP sensor is located on side of throttle body. *See Figs. 1-7.*

Vehicle Speed Sensor (VSS) Signal (LS400) – Vehicle speed signal is delivered to ECT ECU by vehicle speed sensor. *See Fig. 1.* Vehicle

3-1684

AUTOMATIC TRANSMISSIONS
Toyota A-340 Series – Electronic Controls (With OBD-II) (Cont.)

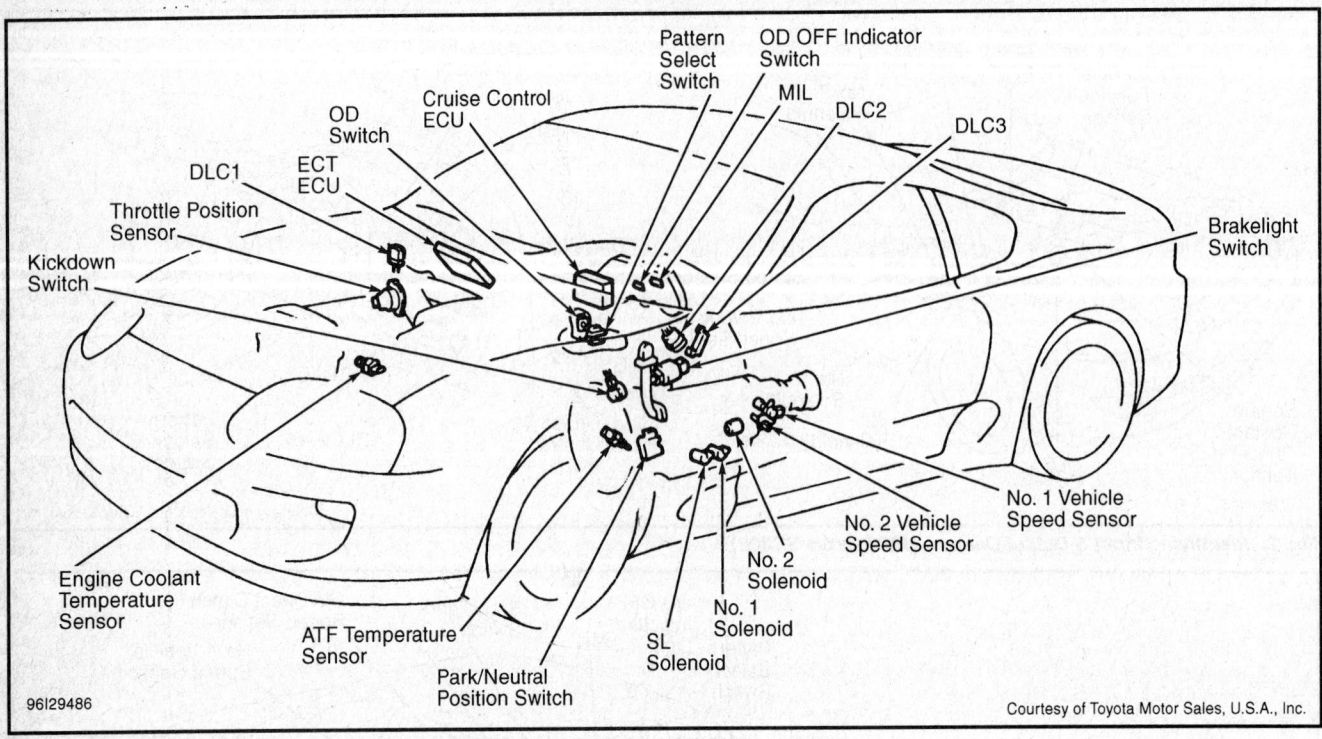

96l29486

Courtesy of Toyota Motor Sales, U.S.A., Inc.

Fig. 4: Identifying Input & Output Devices (1995-96 Toyota Supra Non-Turbo)

speed sensor detects transmission output shaft RPM. Gear shift point and lock-up timing are controlled by ECT ECU based on signals from vehicle speed sensor and throttle position sensor.

VSS (Except LS400) – Vehicle speed signal is delivered to ECT ECU by No. 1 and No. 2 vehicle speed sensors. *See Figs. 2-7.* No. 1 vehicle speed sensor is driven by a gear on transmission output shaft, and indicates actual vehicle speed. No. 2 vehicle speed sensor detects transmission output shaft RPM. Gear shift point and lock-up timing are controlled by ECT ECU based on signals from No. 2 vehicle speed sensor and throttle position sensor. On Tacoma and T100, No. 1 vehicle speed sensor is located in combination meter. *See Figs. 5 and 6.*

OD Direct Clutch Speed Sensor Signal – Sensor delivers input signal to ECT ECU, indicating OD input shaft RPM. By comparing OD direct clutch drum signal and No. 2 vehicle speed sensor signal, ECT ECU detects shift timing of gears and controls engine torque and hydraulic pressure in response to various conditions. Sensor is located on left side of transmission, near torque converter housing. *See Figs. 1 and 3.*

Brakelight Switch Signal – Brakelight switch delivers input signal to ECT ECU, indicating vehicle braking. Brakelight switch is located on brake pedal support.

OD Switch Signal – OD switch provides an input signal to ECT ECU to indicate when overdrive is selected by vehicle operator. OD switch is mounted on shift lever. *See Figs. 2-7.*

Engine Coolant Temperature (ECT) Sensor Signal – Coolant temperature sensor delivers input signal to ECT ECU, indicating engine coolant temperature. For engine coolant temperature sensor location, *see Figs. 1-7.*

ATF Temperature Sensor – Sensor delivers an input signal to ECT ECU to indicate fluid temperature. Sensor converts fluid temperature into a resistance value. Sensor is located on side of transmission. *See Figs. 1-7.*

Cruise Control Electronic Control Unit (ECU) – Cruise control ECU delivers an input signal to control overdrive operation in accordance with vehicle speed when cruise control is operating. *See Figs. 1-7.*

Transmission Control Switch (LS400) – Switch delivers an input signal when shift lever is moved from "D" position to "3" position. ECT ECU prohibits transmission from shifting into overdrive when shift lever is in "3" position. *See Fig. 1.*

Transfer Position Switch – Switch delivers an input signal to ECT ECU to indicate transfer case gear position. Sensor is located on transfer case rear extension housing. *See Figs. 6 and 7.*

"L4" Position Switch – Switch delivers an input signal to ECT ECU to indicate transfer case is in low gear. Switch is located on transfer case extension housing. *See Figs. 5-7.*

ECT ECU OUTPUT DEVICES

No. 1 & No. 2 Solenoids – ECT ECU controls transmission shifting by delivering an output signal to operate proper solenoid. Solenoids are located on transmission valve body. *See Figs. 1-7.* Solenoids are operated in accordance with shift lever position. If a solenoid malfunctions, fail-safe gear may be selected. *See Fig. 8.*

NOTE: In some gears, ECT ECU provides a fail-safe system which will place transmission in designated gear depending on solenoid failure.

Lock-Up Solenoid – ECT ECU controls torque converter lock-up by delivering an output signal to lock-up solenoid. Lock-up solenoid (also called SL or SLU solenoid) is activated when shift lever is in "D" position and vehicle is at specified speed. Lock-up solenoid is located on transmission valve body. *See Figs. 1-7.*

SLN Solenoid – SLN solenoid controls hydraulic pressure acting on accumulator control valve when transmission shifts and assists in smooth shifting. ECT ECU determines optimum control pressure according to signals from TP sensor, vehicle speed sensor and direct clutch drum speed sensor, and controls volume of current flow to SLN solenoid. Amount of current flow to SLN solenoid is controlled by duty cycle ratio of ECT ECU output signal, causing a momentary change in hydraulic pressure acting on clutches during shifting. When duty cycle ratio is high, pressure is low. SLN solenoid is located on transmission valve body. *See Figs. 1 and 3.*

AUTOMATIC TRANSMISSIONS
Toyota A-340 Series – Electronic Controls (With OBD-II) (Cont.)

3-1685

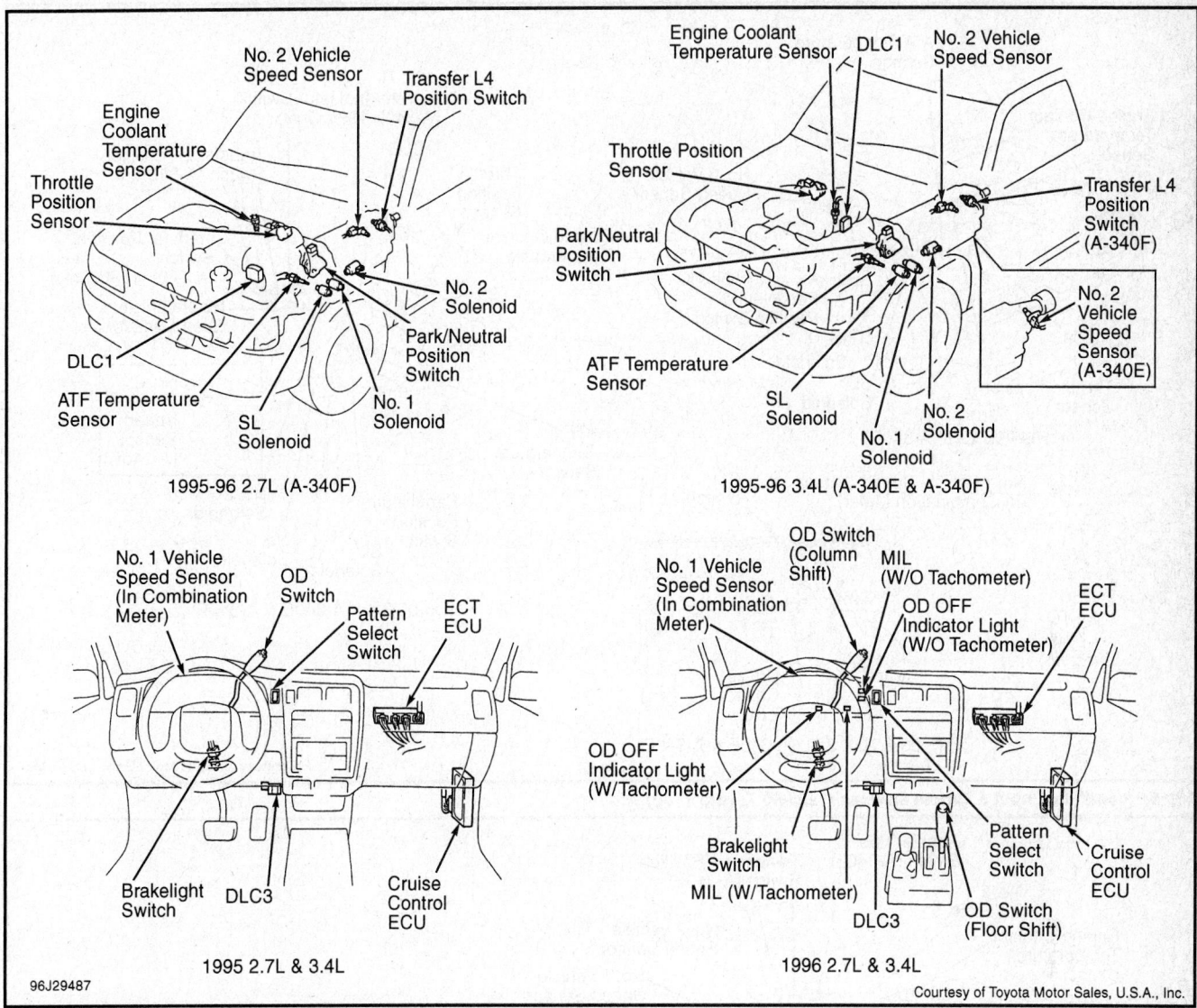

Fig. 5: Identifying Input & Output Devices (1995-96 Toyota Tacoma)

SELF-DIAGNOSTIC SYSTEM

SYSTEM DIAGNOSIS

NOTE: Before testing transmission, ensure fluid level is correct and throttle and shift cables are properly adjusted. Ensure engine starts with shift lever in "P" (Park) and "N" (Neutral) to ensure proper adjustment of park/neutral position switch. Transmission must first be tested by checking for stored trouble codes. See RETRIEVING TROUBLE CODES.

ECT ECU monitors engine and transmission operation and contains a self-diagnostic system which stores Diagnostic Trouble Codes (DTC). A Malfunction Indicator Light (MIL), also called CHECK ENGINE light, located on instrument panel, will illuminate if a system or component fails and sets a DTC.

MIL illuminates with ignition switch in ON position, engine off (KOEO). Once engine is started, MIL should go out. If MIL remains illuminated, ECT ECU has detected a malfunction or abnormality in system. If MIL does not illuminate, inspect circuit and light. See WIRING DIAGRAMS.

If malfunction does not reoccur in 3 trips, MIL goes off, but Diagnostic Trouble Code (DTC) remains recorded in ECT ECU memory. Trouble codes may only be retrieved using an appropriate scan tool or Lexus/Toyota scan tool connected to 16-pin Data Link Connector (DLC3), located at lower left corner of instrument panel or below parking brake handle. *See Figs. 9 and 10.* Scan tool also provides freeze-frame data and can be used to clear trouble codes.

ECT ECU records engine operating condition (fuel system, calculated load, coolant temperature, fuel trim (mixture), engine speed, vehicle speed, etc.) with 1st malfunction ONLY. Information is ONLY for 1st recorded failure, even if more than one code has been recorded. Freeze-frame data is only updated when all trouble codes have been cleared, or a misfire or fuel-trim malfunction has occurred.

RETRIEVING TROUBLE CODES

NOTE: Before retrieving trouble codes, ensure sufficient battery voltage exists for proper self-diagnosis system operation. Ensure proper operation of MIL light.

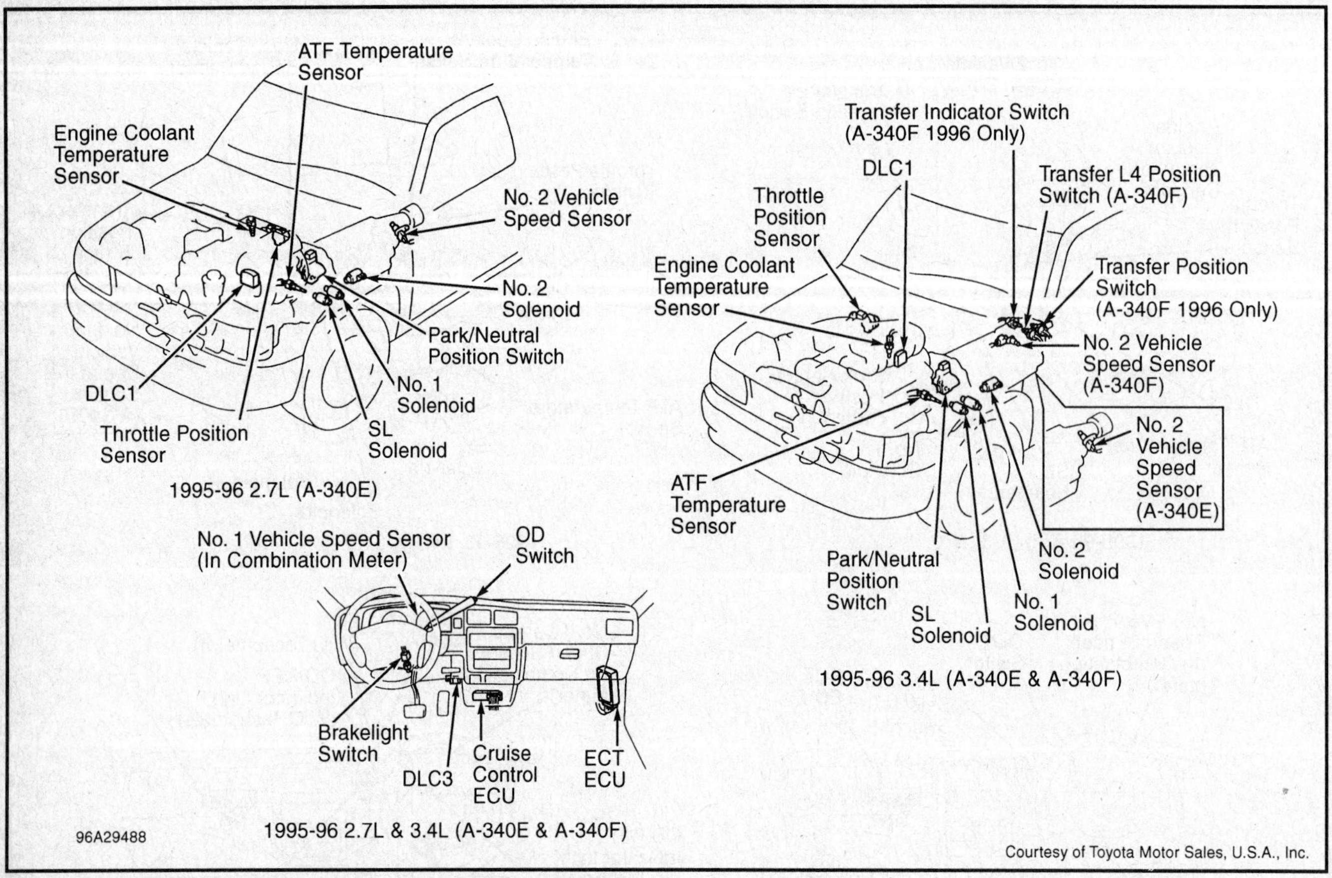

Fig. 6: Identifying Input & Output Devices (1995-96 Toyota T100)

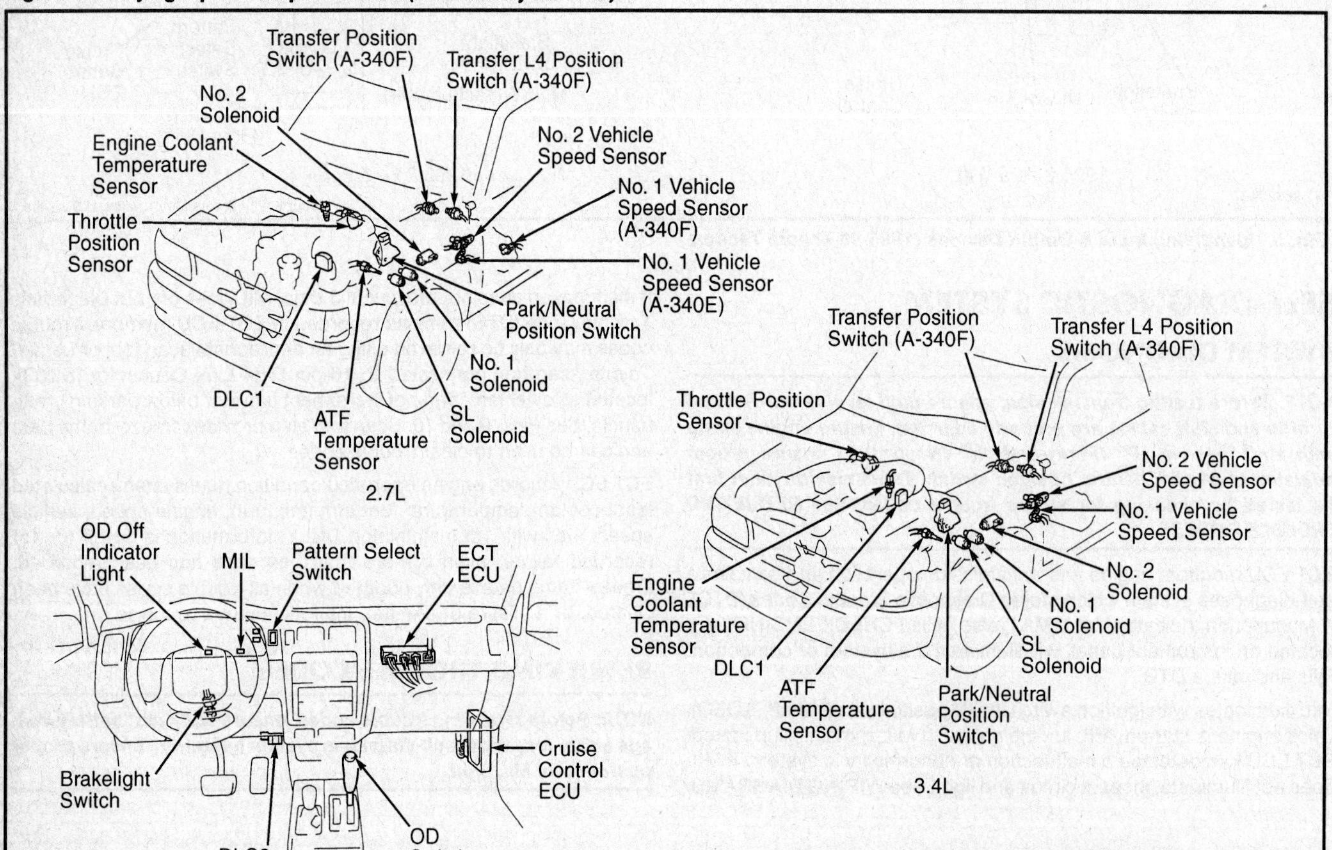

Fig. 7: Identifying Input & Output Devices (1996 Toyota 4Runner)

AUTOMATIC TRANSMISSIONS
Toyota A-340 Series – Electronic Controls (With OBD-II) (Cont.)

3-1687

Position	NORMAL			NO.1 SOLENOID MALFUNCTIONING			NO.2 SOLENOID MALFUNCTIONING			BOTH SOLENOIDS MALFUNCTIONING
	Solenoid valve		Gear	Solenoid valve		Gear	Solenoid valve		Gear	Gear when shift selector is manually operated
	No.1	No.2		No.1	No.2		No.1	No.2		
D	ON	OFF	1st	×	ON	3rd	ON	×	1st	O/D
	ON	ON	2nd	×	ON	3rd	OFF	×	O/D	O/D
	OFF	ON	3rd	×	ON	3rd	OFF	×	O/D	O/D
	OFF	OFF	O/D	×	OFF	O/D	OFF	×	O/D	O/D
2	ON	OFF	1st	×	ON	3rd	ON	×	1st	3rd
	ON	ON	2nd	×	ON	3rd	OFF	×	3rd	3rd
	OFF	ON	3rd	×	ON	3rd	OFF	×	3rd	3rd
L	ON	OFF	1st	×	OFF	1st	ON	×	1st	1st
	ON	ON	2nd	×	ON	2nd	ON	×	1st	1st

×: Malfunctions
96F21175

8-1: All Except 1995 Tacoma & T100

Position	NORMAL			NO.1 SOLENOID MALFUNCTIONING			NO.2 SOLENOID MALFUNCTIONING			BOTH SOLENOIDS MALFUNCTIONING
	Solenoid valve		Gear	Solenoid valve		Gear	Solenoid valve		Gear	Gear when shift selector is manually operated
	No.1	No.2		No.1	No.2		No.1	No.2		
D	ON	OFF	1st	x	ON	3rd	ON	x	1st	O/D
	ON	ON	2nd	x	ON	3rd	OFF	x	O/D	O/D
	OFF	ON	3rd	x	ON	3rd	OFF	x	O/D	O/D
	OFF	OFF	O/D	x	OFF	O/D	OFF	x	O/D	O/D
2	ON	OFF	1st	x	ON	3rd	ON	x	1st	O/D
	ON	ON	2nd	x	ON	3rd	OFF	x	O/D	O/D
	OFF	ON	3rd	x	ON	3rd	OFF	x	O/D	O/D
L	ON	OFF	1st	x	OFF	1st	ON	x	1st	1st
	ON	ON	2nd	x	ON	2nd	ON	x	1st	1st

x: Malfunctions
95C20364

8-2: 1995 Tacoma & T100

Courtesy of Toyota Motor Sales, U.S.A., Inc.

Fig. 8: Checking No. 1 & No. 2 Solenoid Operation

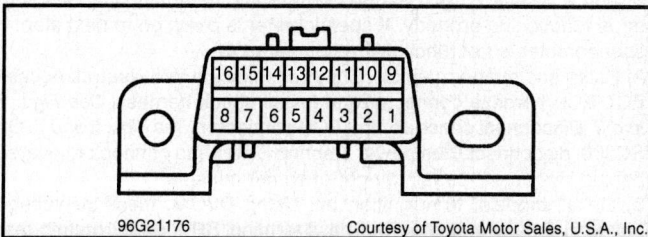

96G21176　　　　Courtesy of Toyota Motor Sales, U.S.A., Inc.

Fig. 9: Identifying Data Link Connector (DLC3) Terminals

NOTE: MIL will illuminate for all trouble codes except DTC P1765.

NOTE: For additional engine performance or other system related trouble codes present that are not listed in DIAGNOSTIC TROUBLE CODE (DTC) IDENTIFICATION table, see appropriate MITCHELL® ENGINE PERFORMANCE publication for IMPORTED CARS, LIGHT TRUCKS & VANS.

ECT ECU Codes – 1) Connect scan tool to Data Link Connector (DLC3). DLC3 is located at lower left corner of instrument panel or below parking brake handle. See Fig. 10.
2) Turn ignition on. Turn on scan tool. Retrieve any trouble codes stored in memory following scan tool instructions. See DIAGNOSTIC TROUBLE CODE (DTC) IDENTIFICATION table.
3) Trouble codes recorded may not have illuminated MIL. When certain malfunctions or trouble codes initially occur, they will be temporarily stored in ECT ECU memory, but MIL will not illuminate.
4) Second time malfunction or trouble code is detected, MIL will illuminate, provided ignition is turned off and then back on after malfunction or trouble code was first detected. This process is referred to as 2 trip detection logic and only applies to specific trouble codes.
5) Record freeze-frame data. If using Lexus/Toyota scan tool, ensure tool is in NORMAL mode. CHECK MODE will erase all codes.

3-1688

AUTOMATIC TRANSMISSIONS
Toyota A-340 Series – Electronic Controls (With OBD-II) (Cont.)

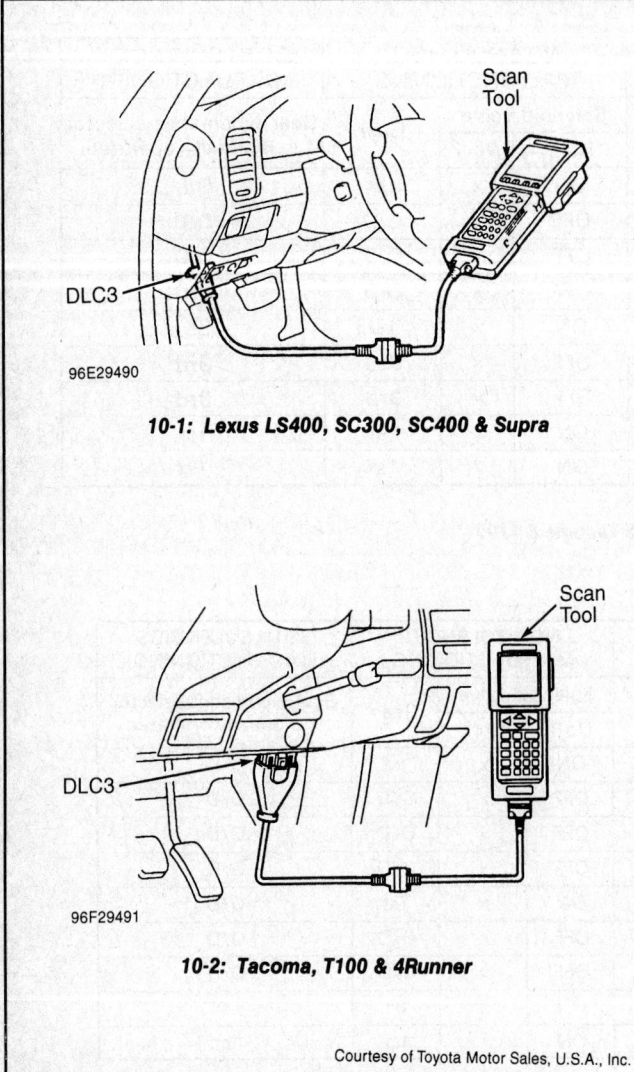

10-1: Lexus LS400, SC300, SC400 & Supra

10-2: Tacoma, T100 & 4Runner

Courtesy of Toyota Motor Sales, U.S.A., Inc.

Fig. 10: Connecting Scan Tool To Data Link Connector (DLC3)

DIAGNOSTIC TROUBLE CODE (DTC) IDENTIFICATION

DTC	[1] Probable Cause
P0500 (1996)	No. 1 Vehicle Speed Sensor
P0710	ATF Temperature Sensor
P0715	[3] OD Direct Clutch Speed Sensor
P0720 (1995)	No. 1 Vehicle Speed Sensor
P0750	No. 1 Solenoid
P0753	No. 1 Solenoid Circuit
P0755	No. 2 Solenoid
P0758	No. 2 Solenoid Circuit
P0770	[2] Lock-Up Solenoid
P0773	Lock-Up Solenoid Circuit
P1700	No. 2 Vehicle Speed Sensor Circuit
P1765	[3] SLN Solenoid Circuit
P1780	Park/Neutral Position Switch

[1] – Check listed component for probable cause. Check wiring and connections of specified component.
[2] – Also called SL or SLU solenoid.
[3] – LS400 and SC400.

CLEARING TROUBLE CODES

Once repairs have been performed, trouble codes must be cleared from ECT ECU memory. DTCs may be cleared by following methods:
- Scan tool (follow manufacturers instructions).
- Remove EFI fuse (15-amp) from engine compartment relay box on left fender panel, for 10 seconds or more to clear memory in ECT ECU.
- Disconnect negative battery cable (memory for electronic components will be also be canceled).

DIAGNOSTIC TESTS

When trouble shooting transmission, first check for stored trouble codes and repair as necessary. If no trouble codes exist, perform manual shift test to determine if problem area is in electrical circuits or a mechanical transmission problem. See MANUAL SHIFT TEST.

NOTE: On Lexus SC300, SC400 and Supra, manufacturer recommends using Check Harness (09990-0100) connected to ECT ECU when performing circuit tests at ECT ECU harness connector. Harness connects between ECT ECU terminals and ECT ECU harness connector. See Fig. 12. Check harness test terminals are same as ECT ECU harness connector terminals. For ECT ECU locations, see Figs. 2-4.

DTC P0500: NO. 1 VEHICLE SPEED SENSOR (VSS) FAULT (1996)

Circuit Description – No. 1 Vehicle Speed Sensor (VSS), driven by transmission output shaft, outputs a pulse signal to combination meter. Combination meter converts signal to a more precise waveform for ECT ECU. DTC is set when ECT ECU does not detect any signal while vehicle is in motion. Possible causes are:
- Open or short in vehicle speed sensor circuit.
- No. 1 VSS failure.
- Combination meter malfunction.
- ECT ECU malfunction.

Diagnosis & Repair Procedure – LS400 – 1) Test drive vehicle and determine if speedometer is functioning properly. If speedometer is okay, go to next step. If speedometer is not functioning, go to NO. 1 VEHICLE SPEED SENSOR under COMPONENT TESTS.
2) Gain access to ECT ECU. *See Fig. 1.* Disconnect appropriate ECT ECU connector. Using DVOM, measure resistance between ECT ECU terminals SP2+ and SP2-. *See Fig. 11.* If resistance is 560-680 ohms, replace ECT ECU and retest. If resistance is not 560-680 ohms, test speed sensor. See NO. 1 VEHICLE SPEED SENSOR under COMPONENT TESTS. Replace as necessary. If sensor is okay, check and repair circuits between ECT ECU and speed sensor. See WIRING DIAGRAMS.
SC300 & SC400 – 1) Test drive vehicle and determine if speedometer is functioning properly. If speedometer is okay, go to next step. If speedometer is not functioning, go to step **4)**.
2) Raise and support vehicle. Shift transmission into Neutral. Access ECT ECU harness connector and install check harness. *See Figs. 2 and 3.* Disconnect cruise control ECU connector. *See Figs. 2 and 3.* On SC300, disconnect Blue power steering ECU 6-pin connector, located behind instrument panel, to right of center console.
3) On all models, turn ignition on. Using DVOM, measure voltage between ground and check harness terminal SPD, while rotating rear wheel. *See Fig. 12.* If voltage is not 4.5-5.5 volts, check and repair open circuit between combination meter and ECT ECU. See WIRING DIAGRAMS. If voltage is as specified, replace ECT ECU and retest.
4) Check odometer operation. If odometer does not operate, go to step **6)**. If odometer operates, check trip meter operation. If trip meter operates while driving, replace speedometer. If trip meter does not operate, remove combination meter. Disconnect combination meter 23-pin connector. Connect jumper wires from harness connector terminals A1, A13, A15 and A23 to combination meter terminals A1, A13, A15 and A23. *See Fig. 13.*

AUTOMATIC TRANSMISSIONS
Toyota A-340 Series – Electronic Controls (With OBD-II) (Cont.)

3-1689

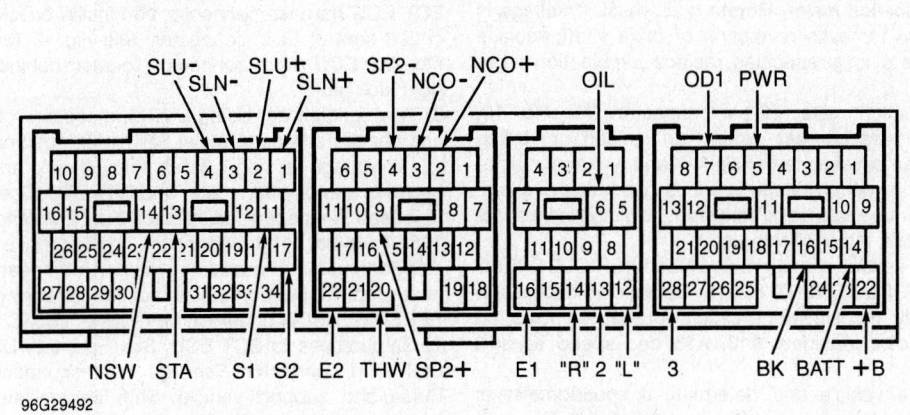

11-1: * LS400, Tacoma (3.4L), T100 (3.4L) & 4Runner (3.4L)

96G29492

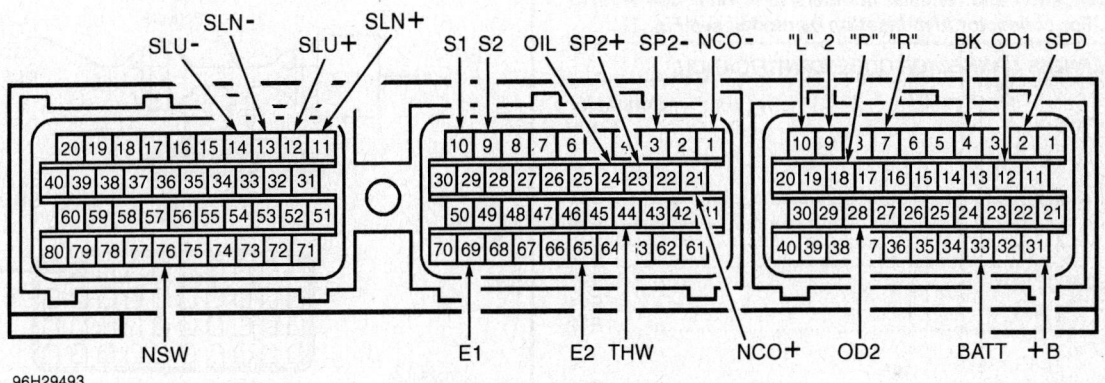

11-2: SC300, * SC400 & Supra Non-Turbo

96H29493

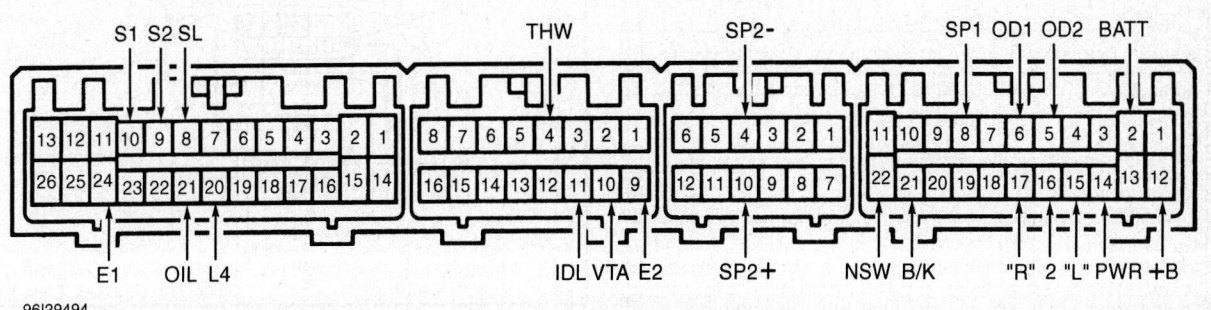

11-3: * Tacoma (2.7L), T100 (2.7L) & 4Runner (2.7L)

96I29494

Courtesy of Toyota Motor Sales, U.S.A., Inc.

Fig. 11: Identifying ECT ECU Connector Terminals

NOTE: *Terminal identification applies to LS400, SC400 eend Tacoma (2.7L). For terminal identification for all other models, see WIRING DIAGRAMS.

3-1690

AUTOMATIC TRANSMISSIONS
Toyota A-340 Series – Electronic Controls (With OBD-II) (Cont.)

5) Turn ignition on. Using DVOM, measure voltage between terminals A13 and A15 at combination meter. Rotate rear wheel. If voltage is zero to battery voltage for each revolution of drive shaft, replace speedometer. If voltage is not as specified, replace combination meter circuit plate.

6) Disconnect combination meter 23-pin connector. *See Fig. 13.* Inspect connector on wire harness side. Turn ignition on. Using DVOM, measure voltage between terminals A13 and A15 at combination meter. Rotate rear wheel. If voltage is not zero to battery voltage for each revolution of drive shaft, go to next step. If voltage is as specified, replace combination meter circuit plate.

7) Inspect No. 1 speed sensor operation. See NO. 1 VEHICLE SPEED SENSOR (VSS) under COMPONENT TESTS. Replace as necessary. If speed sensor is okay, inspect wiring circuit between combination meter harness connector terminals A13, A15 and speed sensor. Repair as necessary.

Supra – 1) Test drive vehicle and determine if speedometer is functioning properly. If speedometer is okay, go to next step. If speedometer is not functioning, see NO. 1 VEHICLE SPEED SENSOR (VSS) under COMPONENT TESTS.

NOTE: ECT ECU harness connectors have different connector identification codes. For ECT ECU connector identification code reference, see ECT ECU HARNESS CONNECTOR CODE IDENTIFICATION table. Circuit identification and terminal numbers may vary. See WIRING DIAGRAMS. For connector identification by model, see Fig. 11.

ECT ECU HARNESS CONNECTOR CODE IDENTIFICATION

Model & Number Of Pins	Connector Code
Lexus	
LS400	
28	E11
16	E12
22	E13
34	E14
SC300 & SC400	
40	E11
80	E12
Toyota	
Supra	
40	E10
80	E9
Tacoma	
2.7L	
22	E5
12	E6
16	E7
26	E8
3.4L	
28	E5
16	E6
22	E7
34	E8
T100	
2.7L	
22	E4
12	E5
16	E6
26	E7
3.4L	
28	E4
16	E5
22	E6
34	E7
4Runner	
2.7L	
22	E9
12	E8
16	E7
26	E6
3.4L	
28	E13
16	E12
22	E11
34	E10

2) Raise and support vehicle. Shift transmission into Neutral. Access ECT ECU harness connector and install check harness. Disconnect cruise control ECU connector. *See Fig. 4.* Disconnect Blue power steering ECU 6-pin connector, located behind instrument panel, at right kick panel.

3) Turn ignition on. Using DVOM, measure voltage between ground and check harness terminal SP1, while rotating rear wheel. *See Fig. 12.* If voltage is not 4.5-5.5 volts, check and repair open circuit between combination meter and ECT ECU. See WIRING DIAGRAMS. If voltage is as specified, replace ECT ECU and retest.

1996 Tacoma, T100 & 4Runner – 1) Test drive vehicle and determine if speedometer is functioning properly. If speedometer is okay, go to next step. If speedometer is not functioning, go to NO. 1 VEHICLE SPEED SENSOR (VSS) under COMPONENT TESTS.

2) Gain access to ECT ECU. *See Figs. 5-7.* Disconnect appropriate ECT ECU connector. *See Fig. 11.* Disconnect cruise control ECU. Raise and support vehicle. Shift transmission into Neutral. Turn ignition on. Using DVOM, measure voltage between ECT ECU terminal SP1 and ground while rotating rear wheel. *See Fig. 11.* If voltage is not 4.5-5.5 volts and generated intermittently, check and repair open circuit between combination meter and ECT ECU. See WIRING DIAGRAMS. If voltage is 4.5-5.5 volts and generated intermittently, replace ECT ECU and retest.

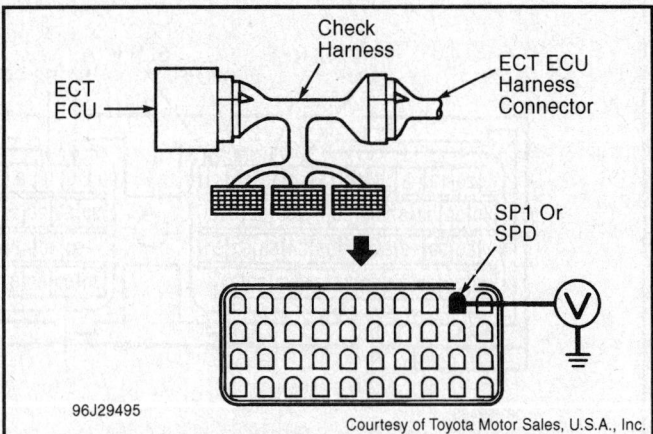

Fig. 12: Checking VSS Voltage At Check Harness Terminals (SC300, SC400 & Supra)

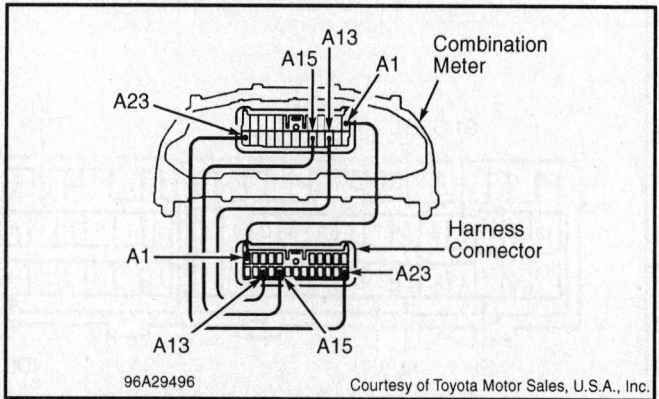

Fig. 13: Identifying Combination Meter 23-Pin Connector Terminals (SC300 & SC400)

DTC P0710: ATF TEMPERATURE SENSOR

Circuit Description – ATF temperature sensor converts fluid temperature into a resistance value which is input to ECT ECU. DTC is set when temperature sensor resistance is less than 79 ohms, or after

AUTOMATIC TRANSMISSIONS
Toyota A-340 Series – Electronic Controls (With OBD-II) (Cont.)

3-1691

engine has been operating for 15 minutes or more, temperature sensor resistance is more than 156 k/ohms. Either condition must be set for .5 second or more. Possible causes are:
- Open or short in ATF temperature sensor circuit.
- ATF temperature sensor malfunction.
- ECT ECU malfunction.

Diagnosis & Repair Procedure – 1) Raise and support vehicle. Disconnect ATF temperature sensor connector. *See Figs. 1-7.* On all models except LS400, SC300 and SC400, connect ohmmeter leads between sensor terminals. On LS400, SC300 and SC400, connect ohmmeter leads to terminals No. 1 and 5. *See Fig. 14.*
2) On all models, submerge sensor in container of water. Heat water while measuring sensor resistance. See ATF TEMPERATURE SENSOR RESISTANCE table. If resistance is not as specified, replace sensor. If resistance is as specified, inspect and repair wiring harness circuits between sensor and ECT ECU. If circuits are okay, replace ECT ECU.

ATF TEMPERATURE SENSOR RESISTANCE

Application & Temperature	Ohms
LS400, SC300 & SC400	
@ 50°F (10°C)	6500
@ 230°F (110°C)	300
Supra	
@ 68°F (20°C)	12,080
@ 230°F (110°C)	780
Tacoma, T100 (1995) & 4Runner	
@ 68°F (20°C)	4,290
@ 230°F (110°C)	690
T100 (1996)	
@ 68°F (20°C)	13,000
@ 230°F (110°C)	800

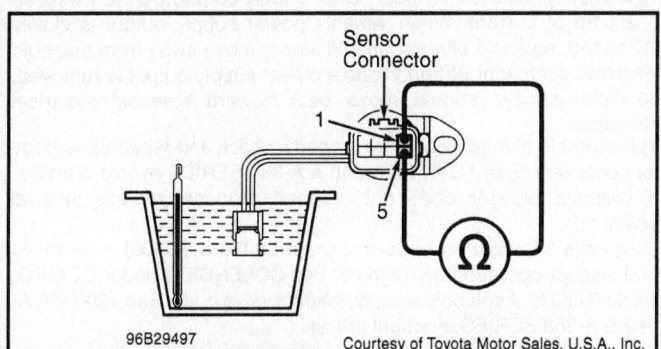

Fig. 14: Identifying ATF Temperature Sensor Connector Terminals (LS400, SC300 & SC400)

DTC P0715: OD DIRECT CLUTCH SPEED SENSOR (LS400 & SC400)

Circuit Description – OD direct clutch speed sensor, located at left front side of transmission near torque converter housing, detects OD input shaft RPM from rotation of OD direct clutch drum. By comparing OD direct clutch speed signal and vehicle speed sensor signal, ECT ECU detects shift timing of gears and controls engine torque and hydraulic pressure in response to various conditions. This assists in smooth shifting. DTC is set when gear change cannot be performed, gear position is 1st, 2nd or 3rd, output shaft RPM is 1000 RPM or more, input shaft RPM is 300 RPM or less, speed sensor operation is normal, and No. 1, No. 2 and SLU solenoid operation is normal. All conditions must be set for 5 seconds or more. Possible causes are:
- Open or short in OD direct clutch speed sensor circuit.
- OD direct clutch speed sensor malfunction.
- ECT ECU malfunction.

Diagnosis & Repair Procedure – 1) Ensure ignition is off. Access ECT ECU. *See Figs. 1 and 3.* Disconnect ECT ECU harness connector and install check harness to ECT ECU harness connector. *See Fig. 12.*

DO NOT connect check harness to ECT ECU. Using ohmmeter, measure resistance between terminal NCO+ and terminal NCO- at check harness. *See Fig. 11.* Resistance should be 560-680 ohms. If resistance is within specification, replace ECT ECU. If resistance is not within specification, go to next step.
2) Remove OD direct clutch speed sensor from transmission. Measure resistance between sensor terminals. Resistance should be 560-680 ohms. If resistance is not as specified, replace sensor. If resistance is as specified, check and repair circuits between sensor and ECT ECU.
3) Check voltage between sensor terminals when a magnet is put close to tip of speed sensor. *See Fig. 15.* If a low intermittent voltage is generated, sensor is okay. If no voltage is generated, replace speed sensor.

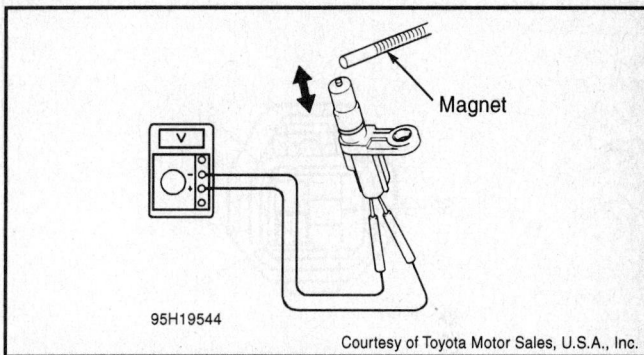

Fig. 15: Testing Speed Sensors

DTC P0720: NO. 1 VEHICLE SPEED SENSOR FAULT (1995 TACOMA & T100)

Circuit Description – No. 1 Vehicle Speed Sensor (VSS), (also called output speed sensor), is mounted in combination meter. Sensor contains a magnet which is rotated by speedometer cable. Reed switch in speed sensor is turned on and off 4 times for every revolution of speedometer. Signal is transmitted to ECT ECU. ECT ECU determines vehicle speed based on frequency of pulse signals. DTC is set when ECT ECU detects one or more of the following 500 times continuous: When no No. 1 vehicle speed sensor signal is received after 16 pulses of No. 2 vehicle speed sensor. Vehicle speed is 5.6 MPH or more for at least 4 seconds, and transmission and transfer case are in any shift lever position except Park and Neutral. Possible causes are:
- Open or short in vehicle speed sensor circuit.
- No. 1 VSS failure.
- Combination meter malfunction.
- ECT ECU malfunction.

Diagnosis & Repair Procedure – 1) Test drive vehicle and determine if speedometer is functioning properly. If speedometer is okay, go to next step. If speedometer is not functioning, go to NO. 1 VEHICLE SPEED SENSOR under COMPONENT TESTS.
2) Disconnect cruise control ECU. Raise and support vehicle. Shift transmission into Neutral. Turn ignition on. Using DVOM, measure voltage between ECT ECU terminal SP1 and ground while rotating rear wheel. *See Fig. 11.* If voltage is not 4-6 volts and generated intermittently, check and repair open circuit between combination meter and ECT ECU. See WIRING DIAGRAMS. If voltage is 4-6 volts and generated intermittently, replace ECT ECU and retest.

DTC P0750 & P0755: NO. 1 & NO. 2 SOLENOID FAULT

Circuit Description – ECT ECU uses signal from No. 1 vehicle speed sensor to determine actual gear position. ECT ECU compares actual gear with shift schedule in memory to detect mechanical trouble of solenoids and/or valve body. DTC is set if during normal driving, gear required by ECT ECU does not match actual gear after 2 trips have been completed. Possible causes are:
- No. 1 and/or No. 2 solenoid is stuck open or closed.
- Valve body is clogged or valve(s) is stuck.

3-1692

AUTOMATIC TRANSMISSIONS
Toyota A-340 Series – Electronic Controls (With OBD-II) (Cont.)

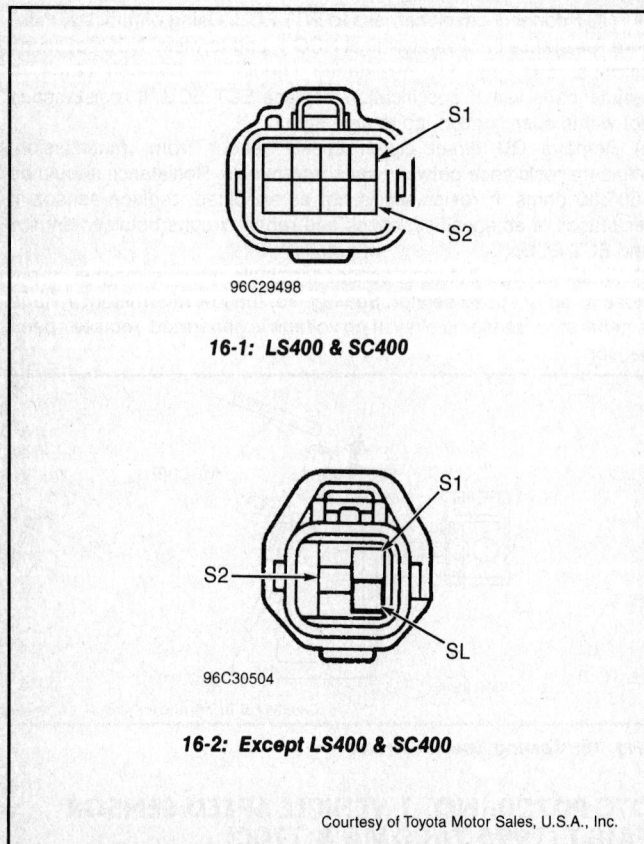

96C29498

16-1: LS400 & SC400

96C30504

16-2: Except LS400 & SC400

Courtesy of Toyota Motor Sales, U.S.A., Inc.

Fig. 16: Identifying Transmission Solenoid Harness Connector Terminals

Diagnosis & Repair Procedure – Remove and inspect operation of solenoids. See appropriate solenoid test under COMPONENT TESTS. If solenoids are okay, inspect valve body. See TOYOTA A-340 & A-350 SERIES overhaul article.

DTC P0753 & P0758: NO. 1 & NO. 2 SOLENOID CIRCUIT

Circuit Description – Shifting is performed in combination with ON and OFF position of shift solenoids controlled by ECT ECU. If an open or short circuit occurs in any shift solenoid, ECT ECU reverts to fail-safe mode. See Fig. 8. ECT ECU turns lock-up (also called SL or SLU) solenoid off at same time. DTCs are output when a open or short circuit occurs. Possible causes are:

- No. 1 and/or No. 2 solenoid circuit.
- No. 1 and/or No. 2 solenoid malfunction.
- ECT ECU malfunction.

Diagnosis & Repair Procedure – 1) Ensure ignition is off. Access ECT ECU. See Figs. 1-7. On Lexus LS400, SC400 and Toyota Supra, disconnect ECT ECU harness connector and install check harness on wiring harness connector. See Fig. 12. DO NOT connect check harness to ECT ECU. On all other models, disconnect appropriate ECT ECU connector. See Fig. 11. On all models, using ohmmeter, measure resistance between ground and terminal S1 and/or S2 at check harness or ECT ECU connector. If resistance is 11-15 ohms, replace ECT ECU and retest. If resistance is not within specification, go to next step.

2) Disconnect solenoid harness connectors (next to PNP switch) at transmission. Check continuity between terminal S1 and/or S2 of transmission harness connectors and corresponding terminal of check harness or ECT ECU. See Figs. 11 and 16.

3) If continuity exists for all circuits, go to next step. If continuity does not exist for any circuit, inspect and repair circuit(s) as needed.

4) Measure resistance between transmission connector terminal S1 and/or S2 and ground. See Fig. 16. If resistance is 11-15 ohms, replace solenoid. If resistance is not as specified, replace transmission sub-harness as needed.

DTC P0770: LOCK-UP (SL/SLU) SOLENOID

Circuit Description – ECT ECU uses signals from throttle position sensor, airflow meter and crankshaft position sensor to monitor engagement of Torque Converter Clutch (TCC). ECT ECU compares engagement condition of TCC with lock-up schedule in memory to detect mechanical trouble of lock-up solenoid, valve body and torque converter. DTC is set when TCC lock-up does not occur during appropriate speed, or lock-up does not release at appropriate speed. Possible causes are:

- Lock-up solenoid is stuck open or closed.
- Valve body clogged or valve stuck.
- TCC malfunction.

Diagnosis & Repair Procedure (LS400 & SC400) – 1) Connect a jumper wire with an 8-10 watt bulb in series between battery positive terminal and lock-up solenoid terminal No. 1 (Brown wire). Connect another jumper wire between battery negative terminal and lock-up solenoid terminal No. 2. See Fig. 17.

2) Solenoid plunger should move away from solenoid electrical connector. Remove jumper wire from solenoid terminal No. 2. Solenoid plunger should move back toward solenoid electrical connector. If solenoid plunger responds properly, go to next step. If solenoid plunger does not respond, replace lock-up solenoid and retest.

3) Connect positive lead of a variable power supply to lock-up solenoid terminal No. 1 (Brown wire). Connect negative lead of a variable power supply to lock-up solenoid terminal No. 2.

4) Gradually increase variable power supply output. DO NOT exceed one amp of current. When variable power supply output is slowly increased, solenoid plunger should slowly move away from solenoid electrical connector. When variable power supply output is removed, solenoid plunger should move back toward solenoid electrical connector.

5) If solenoid plunger responds properly, check and repair valve body as necessary. See TOYOTA A-340 & A-350 SERIES overhaul article. If solenoid plunger does not respond properly, replace lock-up solenoid.

Diagnosis & Repair Procedure (Except LS400 & SC400) – Remove and inspect operation of solenoid. See SOLENOIDS under COMPONENT TESTS. If solenoid is okay, inspect valve body. See TOYOTA A-340 & A-350 SERIES overhaul article.

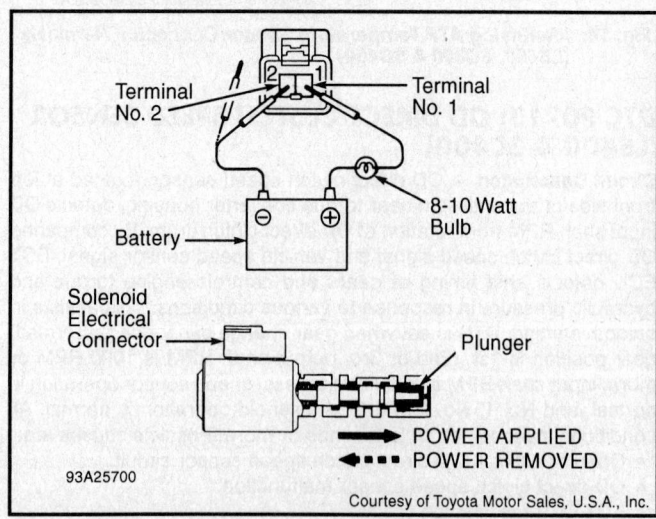

93A25700

Courtesy of Toyota Motor Sales, U.S.A., Inc.

Fig. 17: Testing Lock-Up & SLN Solenoid (LS400 & SC400)

DTC P0773: LOCK-UP (SL/SLU) SOLENOID CIRCUIT

Circuit Description (LS400 & SC400) – Lock-up solenoid is turned on and off by signals from ECT ECU. Amount of current flow to solenoid is controlled by duty cycle ratio of ECT ECU output signal. The higher the duty cycle ratio, the higher the lock-up hydraulic pressure becomes during lock-up operation. DTC is output when ECT ECU outputs a duty signal to lock-up solenoid of at least 95 percent for 3.3 milliseconds. Possible causes are:
- Lock-up solenoid open or short circuit.
- Lock-up solenoid malfunction.
- ECT ECU malfunction.

Diagnosis & Repair Procedure – 1) Raise and support vehicle. Remove transmission oil pan. Disconnect solenoid connector (Brown and Yellow wires). Using ohmmeter, measure resistance between solenoid connector terminals.

2) If resistance is 7.5-8.5 ohms, check and repair transmission sub-harness as needed. If sub-harness is okay, replace ECT ECU. If resistance is not 7.5-8.5 ohms, remove and inspect operation of solenoid. See appropriate solenoid test under COMPONENT TESTS. If solenoid is okay, inspect valve body. See TOYOTA A-340 & A-350 SERIES overhaul article.

Circuit Description (Except LS400 & SC400) – Lock-up solenoid is turned on and off by signals from ECT ECU to control hydraulic pressure affecting lock-up relay valve. Lock-up relay valve controls operation of Torque Converter Clutch (TCC). If ECT ECU detects a malfunction, fail-safe function is enabled. See Fig. 8. DTC is output when an open or short circuit occurs. Possible causes are:
- Lock-up solenoid open or short circuit.
- Lock-up solenoid malfunction.
- ECT ECU malfunction.

Diagnosis & Repair Procedure – 1) Ensure ignition is off. Access ECT ECU. See Figs. 2 and 4-7. Disconnect appropriate ECT ECU harness connector. On Lexus SC300 and Supra, install check harness to ECT ECU harness connector. On all models, backprobing ECT ECU harness connector with ohmmeter, measure resistance between terminal SL and ground. See Fig. 11. If resistance is 11-15 ohms, replace ECT ECU and retest. If resistance is not within specification, go to next step.

2) Disconnect solenoid harness connector at transmission. Check continuity between terminal SL of transmission harness connector and corresponding terminal of ECT ECU harness connector. See Figs. 11 and 16.

3) If continuity does not exist, check and repair circuit as needed. If continuity exists, measure resistance between transmission connector terminals SL and ground. See Fig. 16. If resistance is 11-15 ohms, replace solenoid. If resistance is not as specified, replace transmission sub-harness as needed.

DTC P1700: NO. 2 VEHICLE SPEED SENSOR (VSS) CIRCUIT

Circuit Description (Except T100 With 3.4L) – No. 2 vehicle speed sensor detects transmission output shaft RPM and sends signals to ECT ECU. An AC voltage is generated in No. 2 vehicle speed sensor coil as rotor mounted on output shaft rotates. This voltage is sent to ECT ECU. Gear shift point and lock-up timing are controlled by ECT ECU based on signals from No. 2 vehicle speed sensor and throttle position sensor. If No. 2 vehicle speed sensor malfunctions, ECT ECU uses input signals from No. 1 vehicle speed sensor as a back-up signal. DTC is output when no signal is detected from No. 2 vehicle speed sensor while No. 1 vehicle speed sensor sends 4 pulses to ECT ECU. Vehicle speed is more than 5.6 MPH for at least 4 seconds. Possible causes are:
- Sensor open or short circuit.
- Sensor malfunction.
- ECT ECU malfunction.

Diagnosis & Repair Procedure – 1) Ensure ignition is off. Access ECT ECU. See Figs. 1-7. Disconnect ECT ECU harness connector. On Lexus SC300, SC400 and Supra, install check harness on wiring harness connector. See Fig. 12. DO NOT connect check harness to ECT ECU. On all models, using ohmmeter, measure resistance between terminals SP2+ and SP2- at check harness. See Fig. 11. Resistance should be 560-680 ohms. If resistance is as specified, replace ECT ECU and retest. If resistance is not within specification, go to next step.

2) Remove No. 2 vehicle speed sensor from transmission. Measure resistance between sensor terminals. Resistance should be 560-680 ohms. If resistance is not as specified, replace sensor. If resistance is as specified, check and repair circuits between sensor and ECT ECU.

3) Check voltage between sensor terminals when a magnet is put close to tip of speed sensor. See Fig. 15. If a low intermittent voltage is generated, sensor is okay. If no voltage is generated, replace speed sensor.

Circuit Description (T100 With 3.4L) – A rotor with a built-in magnet is mounted on output shaft. Each time output shaft completes one revolution, permanent magnet activates reed switch. Reed switch is built into No. 2 vehicle speed sensor. Signal is generated and is sent to ECT ECU. ECT ECU controls shift points and lock-up operation. Sensor outputs one pulse for every revolution of output shaft. If No. 2 vehicle speed sensor malfunctions, ECT ECU uses input signal from No. 1 vehicle speed sensor as a back-up signal. DTC is output when no signal is detected from No. 2 vehicle speed sensor while No. 1 vehicle speed sensor sends 4 pulses to ECT ECU. Vehicle speed is more than 5.6 MPH for at least 4 seconds. Possible causes are:
- Sensor open or short circuit.
- Sensor malfunction.
- ECT ECU malfunction.

Diagnosis & Repair Procedure – 1) Ensure ignition is off. Access ECT ECU. See Fig. 6. Raise and support vehicle. Shift transmission into Neutral. Rotate rear wheel. Backprobing ECT ECU harness connector with ohmmeter, measure resistance between terminal No. SP2+ and ground (E1). See Fig. 11. Resistance should pulse between zero ohms and infinite ohms. If resistance is within specification, replace ECT ECU. If resistance is not within specification, go to next step.

2) Remove No. 2 speed sensor from transmission extension housing. Measure resistance between sensor terminals. Resistance should pulse between zero ohms and infinite ohms when a magnet is put close to tip of speed sensor. See Fig. 15. If resistance is not as specified, replace sensor. If resistance is as specified, check and repair circuits between sensor and ECT ECU.

DTC P1765: SLN SOLENOID CIRCUIT (ACCUMULATOR BACK PRESSURE MODULATION)

Circuit Description – SLN solenoid controls hydraulic pressure acting on accumulator control valve. ECT ECU determines optimum operating pressure according to signals from throttle position sensor, vehicle speed sensor and direct clutch speed sensor. Amount of current flow to solenoid is controlled by duty cycle ratio of ECT ECU output signal, causing a momentary change to hydraulic pressure acting on clutches during shifting. When duty cycle ratio is high, hydraulic pressure acting on clutches is low. DTC is output when ECT ECU outputs a duty signal to lock-up solenoid of at least 5 percent for 3.3 milliseconds. Possible causes are:
- SLN solenoid open or short circuit.
- SLN solenoid malfunction.
- ECT ECU malfunction.

Diagnosis & Repair Procedure – 1) Ensure ignition is off. Raise and support vehicle. Remove transmission oil pan. Disconnect SLN solenoid connector (Red and Blue wires). Using an ohmmeter, measure resistance between solenoid connector terminals. Ensure resistance is 7.5-8.5 ohms. If resistance is not as specified, check solenoid operation.

3-1694

AUTOMATIC TRANSMISSIONS
Toyota A-340 Series – Electronic Controls (With OBD-II) (Cont.)

2) Connect a jumper wire with an 8-10 watt bulb in series between battery positive terminal and SLN solenoid terminal No. 1 (Blue wire). Connect another jumper wire between battery negative terminal and SLN solenoid terminal No. 2. *See Fig. 17.*

3) Solenoid plunger should move away from solenoid electrical connector. Remove jumper wire from solenoid terminal No. 2. Solenoid plunger should move back toward solenoid electrical connector. If solenoid plunger responds properly, go to next step. If solenoid plunger does not respond, replace SLN solenoid and retest.

4) Connect positive lead of a variable power supply to SLN solenoid terminal No. 1 (Blue wire). Connect negative lead of a variable power supply to SLN solenoid terminal No. 2.

5) Gradually increase variable power supply output. DO NOT exceed one amp of current. When variable power supply output is slowly increased, solenoid plunger should slowly move away from solenoid electrical connector. When variable power supply output is removed, solenoid plunger should move back toward solenoid electrical connector.

6) If solenoid plunger responds properly, inspect and repair circuit(s) between SLN solenoid and ECT ECU. If circuits are okay, replace ECT ECU and retest. If solenoid plunger does not respond properly, replace lock-up solenoid.

DTC P1780: PARK/NEUTRAL POSITION (PNP) SWITCH

Circuit Description – PNP switch verifies shift lever position and sends signals to ECT ECU. If no signal is received from PNP switch, ECT ECU defaults to Drive ("D") position. DTC is output when ECT ECU detects 2 or more circuits are on. Vehicle speed has to be 25-44 MPH for 30 seconds or more with engine speed at 1500-2500 RPM. Possible causes are:

- Short in PNP switch circuit.
- PNP switch malfunction.
- ECT ECU malfunction.

Diagnosis & Repair Procedure – **1)** Turn ignition off. Access ECT ECU. *See Figs. 1-7* Disconnect ECT ECU harness connector. On Lexus SC300, SC400 and Supra, install check harness between ECT ECU and wiring harness. *See Fig. 12.* On all models, turn ignition on. Using DVOM, measure voltage at terminals NSW, "R", "2" and "L" of ECT ECU wiring harness or check harness between terminal and body ground with gear selector in each shift position. *See Fig. 11.*

2) On Lexus SC300, Toyota Supra and 1996 T100, ensure 7.5-14 volts is present at NSW terminal at ECT ECU harness connector or check harness in all shift positions. Ensure 7.5-14 volts is present at terminals "R", "2" and "L" at ECT ECU harness connector or check harness with gear selector in "R", "2" and "L" position.

3) On all other models, ensure 9-14 volts is present at NSW terminal at ECT ECU harness connector or check harness in all shift positions. Ensure 9-14 volts is present at terminals "R", "2" and "L" at ECT ECU harness connector or check harness with gear selector in "R", "2" and "L" position.

4) On all models, if voltage is not as specified, check park/neutral position switch. See PARK/NEUTRAL POSITION (PNP) SWITCH under COMPONENT TESTS. If switch is okay, check and repair circuit(s) between PNP switch and ECT ECU. See WIRING DIAGRAMS.

MANUAL SHIFT TEST

NOTE: Perform manual shift test if no trouble codes exist. Manual shift test determines if problem area is in electrical circuits or a mechanical transmission problem.

1) With ignition off, disconnect electrical connector for solenoids from transmission. Road test vehicle and ensure transmission gear changes correspond with shift lever position. See GEAR APPLICATION table.

2) If abnormality exists, a mechanical transmission problem exists. Turn ignition off. Reconnect electrical connector. Clear trouble codes from ECT ECU memory, as disconnecting electrical connector may set a trouble code. See CLEARING TROUBLE CODES under SELF-DIAGNOSTIC SYSTEM.

GEAR APPLICATION

Shift Lever Position	Gear
"D"	Overdrive
"2"	3rd
"L"	1st
"R"	Reverse
"P"	Park

CIRCUIT TESTS

BRAKELIGHT SIGNAL

1) Inspect operation of brakelights. Repair as needed. If switch is suspect, see BRAKELIGHT SWITCH under COMPONENT TESTS. If circuit is suspect, diagnose and repair as necessary. See WIRING DIAGRAMS.

2) Connect scan tool to DLC3. *See Figs. 1-7.* Turn ignition on. Read STP signal while depressing and releasing brake pedal. Ensure signal cycles when pressing brake pedal. If signal cycles, replace ECT ECU. If signal does not cycle, inspect and repair circuit between brakelight switch and ECT ECU. If circuit is okay, replace ECT ECU.

OVERDRIVE CANCEL SIGNAL

1) Access ECT ECU. *See Figs. 1-7.* On Lexus SC300, SC400 and Supra, connect check harness to ECT ECU. On all models, turn ignition on. Measure voltage between terminal OD1 of ECT ECU harness connector or check harness and ground. *See Fig. 11.* If voltage is 4-6 volts, substitute known good ECT ECU and retest. If voltage is not 4-6 volts, go to next step.

2) Turn ignition off. Disconnect cruise control ECU harness connector. *See Figs. 1-7.* Turn ignition on. Measure voltage between terminal OD and ground. *See Fig. 18.* If 4-6 volts is present, replace cruise control ECU and retest. If 4-6 volts is not present, inspect and repair circuit between cruise control ECU and ECT ECU.

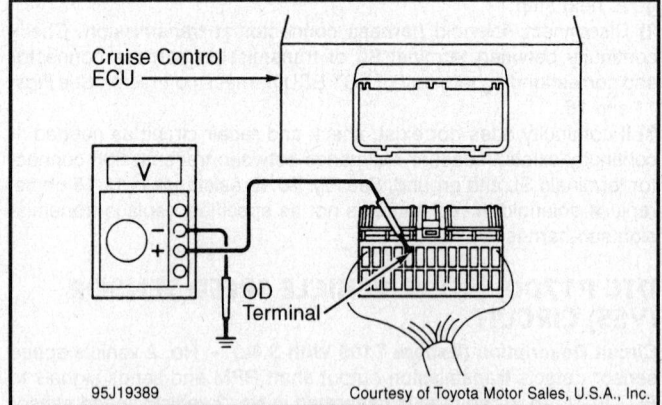

95J19389   Courtesy of Toyota Motor Sales, U.S.A., Inc.

Fig. 18: Identifying Cruise Control ECU Terminals

ECT ECU VOLTAGES

Access ECT ECU. *See Figs. 1-7.* On Lexus SC300, SC400 and Supra, connect check harness to ECT ECU. On all models, turn ignition on. Using voltmeter, measure voltage at ECT ECU or check harness. Check voltage between selected terminal and terminal E_1 (ground). Voltage should be as specified in pin voltage tables. *See Figs. 19-25.*

	Terminal ID.	Function/Description	Voltage Value (DC Volts Unless Otherwise Specified)
Red	S_1	No. 1 Solenoid	10-14 Volts With KOEO [1]
White	S_2	No. 2 Solenoid	1 Volt Or Less With KOEO [1]
[2]	SLU+, SLU-	Lock-Up Solenoid	3 Volts Or Less With KOEO [1]
[3]	SLN+, SLN-	No. 4 Solenoid	3 Volts Or Less With KOEO [1]
[4]	NSW	Ignition Switch Signal	0-1 Volt In Park Or Neutral, KOEO [1]
[5]	SP2+, SP2-	Vehicle Speed Sensor Signal	1 Volt Or Less, Or 4-5 Volts [6]
[7]	NCO+, NCO-	OD Direct Clutch Speed Sensor Signal	1 Volt Or Less, Or 4-5 Volts [6]
Yellow	VTA1	Throttle Position Sensor Output Signal	3.0-5.5 Volts With Throttle Fully Open
Green	IDL1	Closed Throttle Sensor Signal	0-1 Volt With Throttle Closed, KOEO [1]
Green/Red	BK	Brakelight Switch Signal	10-14 Volts With Brake Pedal Depressed
Red/Black	R	Park/Neutral Position Switch "R" Signal	10-14 Volts With KOEO [1]
Blue/Yellow	3	Park/Neutral Position Switch "3" Signal	10-14 Volts In "3", KOEO [1]
Green	2	Park/Neutral Position Switch "2" Signal	10-14 Volts In "2", KOEO [1]
Green/Black	L	Park/Neutral Position Switch "L" Signal	10-14 Volts In "L", KOEO [1]
Violet/Red	OD₁	Input From Cruise Control ECU	10-14 Volts With KOEO [1]
Blue/White	PWR	Pattern Select Switch Signal	10-14 Volts In PWR Position
Yellow	OIL	A/T Fluid Temperature Sensor	1.5 Volts Or Less @ 230°F (110°C)
[8]	+B	EFI Main Relay Power Supply	10-14 Volts With KOEO [1]
Black/Yellow	BATT	Power Supply Voltage	10-14 Volts (Constant)
Brown	E₁	Ground	Not Applicable

[1] – Key On, Engine Off.
[2] – Wire color for SLU+ for 1995 is Black/White. Wire color for SLU+ for 1996 is Blue/Yellow. Wire color for SLU- is Black.
[3] – Wire color for SLN+ is Yellow. Wire color for SLN- for 1995 is Gray. Wire color for SLN- for 1996 is Black.
[4] – Wire color for 1995 is Black/White. Wire color for 1996 is Blue/Yellow.
[5] – Wire color for SP2+ is Green. Wire color for SP2- is Red.
[6] – With engine running.
[7] – Wire color for NCO+ is Yellow. Wire color for NCO- is Blue.
[8] – Wire color for 1995 is Black/Blue. Wire color for 1996 is White.

96D29499

Fig. 19: ECT ECU Pin Voltage Table – LS400 (Component Connector View)

	Terminal ID.	Function/Description	Voltage Value (DC Volts Unless Otherwise Specified)
Light Green →	S₁	No. 1 Solenoid	9-14 Volts With KOEO [1]
White/Red →	S₂	No. 2 Solenoid	1.5 Volts Or Less With KOEO [1]
Red/Blue →	SL	Lock-Up Solenoid	1.5 Volts Or Less With KOEO [1]
Pink →	SPD	No. 1 Vehicle Speed Sensor Signal	1.5 Volts Or Less, Or 4-6 Volts [1][2]
Black/White →	NSW	Park/Neutral Position Switch	3 Volts Or Less In Park Or Neutral, KOEO [1]
Yellow →	VTA1	Throttle Position Sensor Output Signal	3.2-4.9 Volts With Throttle Fully Open
Red → [3]	IDL1	Closed Throttle Sensor Signal	1.5 Volts Or Less With Throttle Closed, KOEO [1]
→	SP2+, SP2-	No. 2 Vehicle Speed Sensor Signal	1.5 Volts Or Less, Or 4-6 Volts [4]
Green/White →	STP	Brakelight Switch Signal	7.5-14 Volts With Pedal Depressed
Green →	THW	Engine Coolant Temperature Sensor Signal	1.5 Volts Or Less @ 176°F (80°C)
Green →	2	Park/Neutral Position Switch "2" Signal	7.5-14 Volts In "2", KOEO [3]
White →	L	Park/Neutral Position Switch "L" Signal	7.5-14 Volts In "L", KOEO [1]
Brown/Yellow →	OD₁	Input From Cruise Control ECU	9-14 Volts With KOEO [1]
Gray/Red →	OD₂	Overdrive Switch Signal	9-14 Volts With Switch On
Green/Orange →	PWR	Pattern Select Switch Signal	7.5-14 Volts In PWR Position
Black/Red →	+B	EFI Main Relay Power Supply	9-14 Volts With KOEO [1]
Black/Yellow →	BATT	Power Supply Voltage	9-14 Volts (Constant)
Brown →	E₁	Ground	Not Applicable

[1] – Key On, Engine Off.
[2] – Disconnect cruise control ECU.
[3] – Wire color for SP2+ is Pink. Wire color for SP2- is Violet.
[4] – With engine running.

96G29500

Fig. 20: ECT ECU Pin Voltage Table – SC300 (Component Connector View)

AUTOMATIC TRANSMISSIONS
Toyota A-340 Series – Electronic Controls (With OBD-II) (Cont.)

3-1697

Wire Color	Terminal ID.	Function/Description	Voltage Value (DC Volts Unless Otherwise Specified)
Light Green	S_1	No. 1 Solenoid	10-14 Volts With KOEO [1]
White/Red	S_2	No. 2 Solenoid	10-14 Volts With KOEO [1]
Black/White	NSW	Park/Neutral Position Switch	0-1 Volt In Park Or Neutral, KOEO [1]
Yellow	VTA	Throttle Position Sensor Output Signal	3.0-5.5 Volts With Throttle Fully Open
Red	IDL1	Closed Throttle Sensor Signal	0-1 Volt With Throttle Closed, KOEO [1]
Pink	SPD	No. 1 Vehicle Speed Sensor	0-8 Volts (Pulse), Car Moving, KOEO [1]
Green/White	BK	Brakelight Switch Signal	1 Volt Or Less With Pedal Depressed
Blue	OIL	A/T Fluid Temperature Sensor Signal	1 Volt Or Less @ 230°F (110°C)
[2]	SP2+, SP2-	No. 2 Vehicle Speed Sensor	1.5 Volts Or Less, Or 4-5 Volts [3]
[4]	SLN+, SLN-	No. 4 Solenoid	10-14 Volts With KOEO [1]
[5]	SLU+, SLU-	Lock-Up Solenoid	10-14 Volts With KOEO [1]
[6]	NCO+, NCO-	OD Direct Clutch Speed Sensor	1 Volt Or Less, Or 4-5 Volts [3]
Green	2	Park/Neutral Position Switch "2" Signal	10-14 Volts In "2", KOEO [1]
Red/Black	R	Park/Neutral Position Switch "R" Signal	10-14 Volts In "R", KOEO [1]
White	L	Park/Neutral Position Switch "L" Signal	10-14 Volts In "L", KOEO [1]
Brown/Yellow	OD_1	Input From Cruise Control ECU	4-6 Volts With KOEO [1]
Gray/Red	OD_2	Overdrive Switch Signal	10-14 Volts With Switch On
Green/Orange	PWR	Pattern Select Switch Signal	7.5-14 Volts In PWR Position
Black/Red	+B	EFI Main Relay Power Supply	10-14 Volts With KOEO [1]
Black/Yellow	BATT	Power Supply Voltage	10-14 Volts (Constant)
Brown	E_1	Ground	Not Applicable

[1] – Key On, Engine Off.
[2] – Wire color for SP2+ is Pink. Wire color for SP2- is Violet.
[3] – With engine running.
[4] – Wire color for SLN+ is Black/Red. Wire color for SLN- is Red/Black.
[5] – Wire color for SLU+ is Black/White. Wire color for SLU- is Blue.
[6] – Wire color for NCO+ is Red. Wire color for NCO- is Green.

96H29501

Fig. 21: ECT ECU Pin Voltage Table – SC400 (Component Connector View)

Wire Color	Terminal ID.	Function/Description	Voltage Value (DC Volts Unless Otherwise Specified)
White/Red	S_1	No. 1 Solenoid	9-14 Volts With KOEO [1]
Red/Blue	S_2	No. 2 Solenoid	1.5 Volt Or Less With KOEO [1]
Black/Red [2]	S_3	Lock-Up Solenoid	1.5 Volt Or Less With KOEO [1]
	SP2+, SP2-	No. 2 Vehicle Speed Sensor	1.5 Volts Or Less, Or 4-6 Volts [3]
Green/White	STP	Brakelight Switch Signal	7.5-14 Volts With Pedal Depressed
Blue/Yellow	THW	Engine Coolant Temperature Sensor Signal	1.5 Volts Or Less @ 176°F (80°C)
Black/White	NSW	Park/Neutral Position Switch	0-3 Volt In Park Or Neutral, KOEO [1]
Yellow	VTA1	Throttle Position Sensor Output Signal	3.2-4.9 Volts With Throttle Fully Open
Red	IDL1	Closed Throttle Sensor Signal	1.5 Volts Or Less With Throttle Closed, KOEO [1]
Pink	SP_1	No. 1 Vehicle Speed Sensor	1.5 Volts Or Less, Or 4-6 Volts [1][3][4]
Yellow	KD	Kickdown Switch Signal	9-14 Volts With Switch Off, KOEO [1]
Lt. Green/Red	2	Park/Neutral Position Switch "2" Signal	7.5-14 Volts In "2", KOEO [1]
Green/Black	L	Park/Neutral Position Switch "L" Signal	7.5-14 Volts In "L", KOEO [1]
Brown/Black	OD_1	Input From Cruise Control ECU	9-14 Volts With KOEO [1]
Violet/Green	OD_2	Overdrive Switch Signal	9-14 Volts With Switch On
Green/Yellow	M	Pattern Select Switch Signal	9-14 Volts In PWR Position
Orange	OIL	A/T Fluid Temperature Sensor	1.5 Volts Or Less @ 230°F (110°C)
Black/Red	+B	EFI Main Relay Power Supply	9-14 Volts With KOEO [1]
Black/Yellow	BATT	Power Supply Voltage	9-14 Volts (Constant)
Brown	E_1	Ground	Not Applicable

[1] – Key On, Engine Off.
[2] – Wire color for SP2+ is Red. Wire color for SP2- is Green.
[3] – With engine running.
[4] – Disconnect cruise control ECU.

96I29502

Fig. 22: ECT ECU Pin Voltage Table – Supra Non-Turbo (Component Connector View)

AUTOMATIC TRANSMISSIONS
Toyota A-340 Series – Electronic Controls (With OBD-II) (Cont.)

3-1699

	Terminal ID.	Function/Description	Voltage Value (DC Volts Unless Otherwise Specified)
Violet/Yellow	S_1	No. 1 Solenoid	9-14 Volts With KOEO [1]
Light Green	S_2	No. 2 Solenoid	1.5 Volts Or Less With KOEO [1]
Red/Green	SL	Lock-Up Solenoid	1.5 Volts Or Less With KOEO [1]
Green/Orange	PWR	Pattern Select Switch Signal	9-14 Volts In PWR Position
Green/White	B/K	Brakelight Switch Signal	7.5-14 Volts With Pedal Depressed
Green/Red	THW	Engine Coolant Temperature Sensor Signal	1.5 Volts Or Less @ 176°F (80°C)
Yellow/Blue	IDL	Closed Throttle Sensor Signal	1.5 Volts Or Less With Throttle Closed
Black	NSW	Ignition Switch Signal	9-14 Volts In Park Or Neutral, KOEO [1]
Yellow [2]	VTA	Throttle Position Sensor Output Signal	3.2-4.9 Volts With Throttle Fully Open
Green	L4	Transfer Position Switch Signal	9-14 Volts In H2 Or H4 [1]
Green/Orange	SP₁ (SPD)	Vehicle Speed Sensor Signal	1.5 Volts Or Less, Or 4-6 Volts [1][3]
Blue	OD₁	OD Output To Cruise Control ECU	9-14 Volts With KOEO [1]
Blue/Orange	OD₂	Overdrive Switch Signal	9-14 Volts With Switch On
[4]	SP2+, SP2-	Vehicle Speed Sensor Signal	1.5 Volts Or Less, Or 4-6 Volts [1][5]
Red/Black	R [6]	Park/Neutral Position Switch "R" Signal	9-14 Volts In "R", KOEO [1]
Pink	2	Park/Neutral Position Switch "2" Signal	9-14 Volts In "2", KOEO [1]
Violet/White	L	Park/Neutral Position Switch "L" Signal	9-14 Volts In "L", KOEO [1]
Yellow/Red	OIL	A/T Fluid Temperature Sensor	1.5 Volts Or Less @ 239°F (115°C)
White/Red	+B	EFI Main Relay Power Supply	9-14 Volts With KOEO [1]
Black/Yellow	BATT	Power Supply Voltage	9-14 Volts (Constant)
Brown	E_1	Ground	Not Applicable
Brown/Black	E_2	Ground	Not Applicable

[1] – Key On, Engine Off.
[2] – Wire color is Green/Orange on models with 3.4L.
[3] – Disconnect cruise control ECU.
[4] – Wire color for SP2+ is Yellow/Red. Wire color for SP2- is White/Red.
[5] – Engine is running.
[6] – 1996 models only.

96J29503

Fig. 23: ECT ECU Pin Voltage Table – Tacoma (Component Connector View)

3-1700

AUTOMATIC TRANSMISSIONS
Toyota A-340 Series – Electronic Controls (With OBD-II) (Cont.)

	Terminal ID.	Function/Description	Voltage Value (DC Volts Unless Otherwise Specified)
White	S_1	No. 1 Solenoid	9-14 Volts With KOEO [1]
Black/White	S_2	No. 2 Solenoid	1.5 Volts Or Less With KOEO [1]
Yellow/Black	SL	Lock-Up Solenoid	1.5 Volts Or Less With KOEO [1]
Green/White	B/K	Brakelight Switch Signal	7.5-14 Volts With Pedal Depressed
Green/Yellow	THW	Engine Coolant Temperature Sensor Signal	1.5 Volts Or Less @ 176°F (80°C)
Yellow/Blue	IDL	Closed Throttle Sensor Signal	1.5 Volts Or Less With Throttle Closed
Yellow/Black	VTA	Throttle Position Sensor Output Signal	3.2-4.9 Volts With Throttle Fully Open
Black/Yellow [2]	NSW	Ignition Switch Signal	3 Volts Or Less In Park Or Neutral, KOEO [1]
Red/Green	4WD	Transfer Position Switch Signal	9-14 Volts In H2 With KOEO [1]
Yellow/Red	OD_1	OD Output To Cruise Control ECU	9-14 Volts With KOEO [1]
Yellow/Green	OD_2	Overdrive Switch Signal	9-14 Volts With Switch On
Green	SPD (SP_1)	Vehicle Speed Sensor Signal	1.5 Volts Or Less, Or 4-6 Volts [1] [3]
[4]	SP2+, SP2-	Vehicle Speed Sensor Signal	1.5 Volts Or Less, Or 4-6 Volts [1]
Red/Black	R	Park/Neutral Position Switch "R" Signal	7.5-14 Volts In "R", KOEO [1]
Pink/Green	2	Park/Neutral Position Switch "2" Signal	7.5-14 Volts In "2", KOEO [1]
Violet/White	L	Park/Neutral Position Switch "L" Signal	7.5-14 Volts In "L", KOEO [1]
Red	L4	Transfer Position Switch Signal	7.5-14 Volts In L4, KOEO [1]
Yellow	TFN	Transfer Position Switch Signal	3 Volts Or Less In "N" Position, KOEO [1]
Green/Black	OIL	A/T Fluid Temperature Sensor Signal	1.5 Volts Or Less @ 230°F (110°C)
White/Red	+B	EFI Main Relay Power Supply	9-14 Volts With KOEO [1]
Black/Green	BATT	Power Supply Voltage	9-14 Volts (Constant)
Brown	E_1	Ground	Not Applicable

[1] – Key On, Engine Off.
[2] – Wire color is Black/Orange on models with 3.4L.
[3] – Disconnect cruise control ECU.
[4] – Wire color for SP2+ is Brown/Red. Wire color for SP2- is Black/Red.

96A29504

Fig. 24: ECT ECU Pin Voltage Table – T100 (Component Connector View)

AUTOMATIC TRANSMISSIONS
Toyota A-340 Series – Electronic Controls (With OBD-II) (Cont.)

3-1701

	Terminal ID.	Function/Description	Voltage Value (DC Volts Unless Otherwise Specified)
Lt. Green/Red	S_1	No. 1 Solenoid	9-14 Volts With KOEO [1]
Light Green	S_2	No. 2 Solenoid	1.5 Volts Or Less With KOEO [1]
Green/Red	SL	Lock-Up Solenoid	1.5 Volts Or Less With KOEO [1]
[2]	SP2+, SP2-	No. 2 Vehicle Speed Sensor	1.5 Volts Or Less, Or 4-6 Volts [1] [3]
[4]	VTA	Throttle Position Sensor Output Signal	3.2-4.9 Volts With Throttle Fully Open
Yellow/Blue	IDL	Closed Throttle Sensor Signal	9-14 Volts With Throttle Closed, KOEO [1]
Green/Orange	SP_1	No. 1 Vehicle Speed Sensor	1.5 Volts Or Less, Or 4-6 Volts [1]
Green/Red	THW	Engine Coolant Temperature Sensor Signal	9-14 Volts Or Less @ 176°F (80°C)
Blue/Red	L4	Transfer Position Switch	9-14 Volts In H2.Or H4, KOEO [1]
Black	NSW	Ignition Switch Signal	9-14 Volts In Park Or Neutral, KOEO [1]
Green/White	BK	Brakelight Switch Signal	9-14 Volts With Pedal Depressed
Violet/Red	2	Park/Neutral Position Switch "2" Signal	9-14 Volts In "2", KOEO [1]
Light Green	L	Park/Neutral Position Switch "L" Signal	9-14 Volts In "L", KOEO [1]
Red/Yellow	R	Park/Neutral Position Switch "R" Signal	9-14 Volts In "R", KOEO [1]
Brown/Yellow	OD_1	Input From Cruise Control ECU	9-14 Volts With KOEO [1]
Blue/Orange	OD_2	Overdrive Switch Signal	9-14 Volts With Switch On
Green/Red	PWR	Pattern Select Switch Signal	9-14 Volts In PWR Position
Violet/Yellow	OIL	A/T Fluid Temperature Sensor	1.5 Volts Or Less @ 239°F (115°C)
White/Blue	+B	EFI Main Relay Power Supply	9-14 Volts With KOEO [1]
Black/White	BATT	Power Supply Voltage	9-14 Volts (Constant)
Brown	E_1	Ground	Not Applicable

[1] – Key On, Engine Off.
[2] – Wire color for SP2+ is Yellow/Red. Wire color for SP2- is White/Red.
[3] – With engine running.
[4] – Wire color for 2.7L is Yellow. Wire color for 3.4L is Black/Yellow.

96B29505

Fig. 25: ECT ECU Pin Voltage Table – 4Runner (Component Connector View)

3-1702

AUTOMATIC TRANSMISSIONS
Toyota A-340 Series – Electronic Controls (With OBD-II) (Cont.)

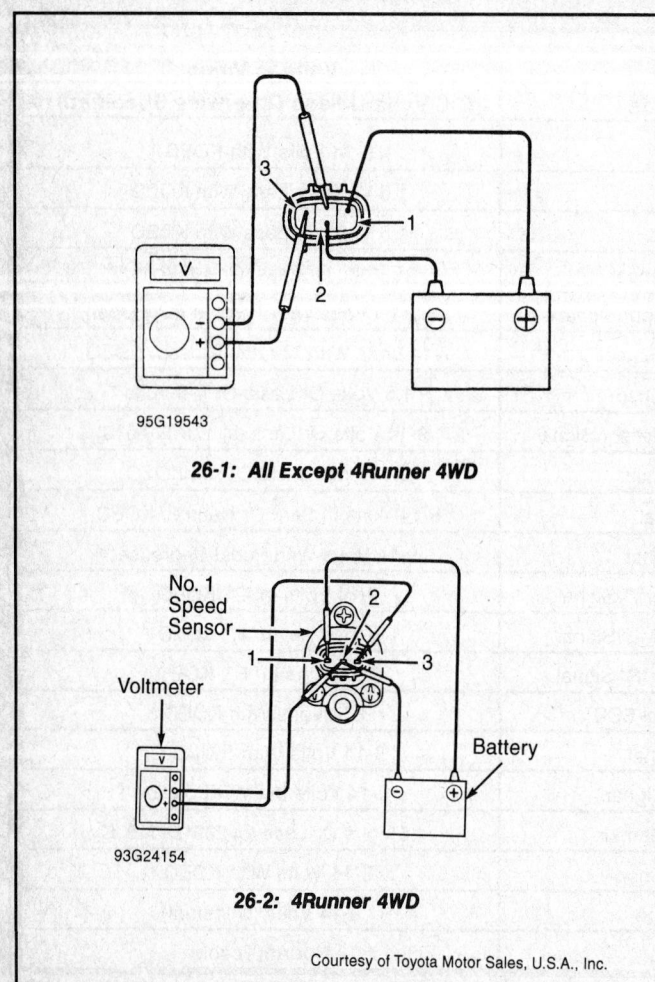

95G19543

26-1: All Except 4Runner 4WD

93G24154

26-2: 4Runner 4WD

Courtesy of Toyota Motor Sales, U.S.A., Inc.

Fig. 26: Checking No. 1 Vehicle Speed Sensor (Except Tacoma & T100)

COMPONENT TESTS

NO. 1 VEHICLE SPEED SENSOR (VSS)

NOTE: LS400 is equipped with only one speed sensor.

LS400 – 1) Remove speed sensor from transmission. *See Fig. 1.* Using DVOM, measure resistance between sensor terminals. Resistance should be 560-680 ohms. If resistance is not as specified, replace sensor. If resistance is as specified, check and repair circuits between sensor and ECT ECU.

2) Check voltage between sensor terminals when a magnet is put close to tip of speed sensor. *See Fig. 15.* If a low intermittent voltage is generated, sensor is okay. If no voltage is generated, replace speed sensor.

Except Tacoma & T100 – 1) Disconnect electrical connector from No. 1 vehicle speed sensor. *See Figs. 2, 3, 4 and 7.* Connect positive battery lead to terminal No. 1 and negative lead to terminal No. 2. Connect positive lead of voltmeter to terminal No. 3 and negative lead to terminal No. 2. *See Fig. 26.*

2) Raise and support one vehicle rear wheel. Rotate wheel and monitor voltmeter. Ensure voltage changes from zero to 11 volts. Voltage should change 4 times per each revolution of speedometer cable shaft. Replace speed sensor if voltage does not change as specified.

Tacoma & T100 – Ensure continuity exists between terminals "A" and "B" 4 times per revolution of speedometer shaft. *See Fig. 27.* If continuity is as specified, replace speedometer.

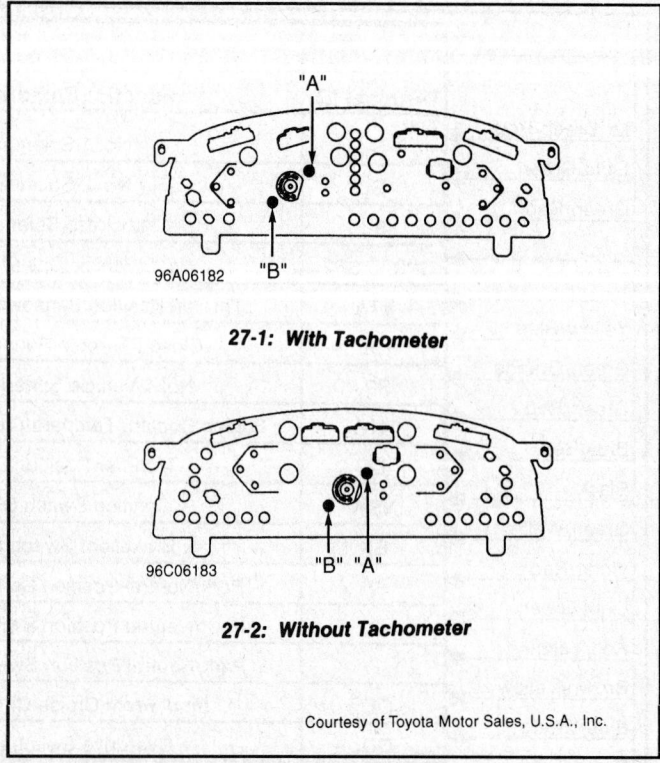

96A06182

27-1: With Tachometer

96C06183

27-2: Without Tachometer

Courtesy of Toyota Motor Sales, U.S.A., Inc.

Fig. 27: Checking No. 1 Vehicle Speed Sensor (Tacoma & T100)

NO. 1 & NO. 2 SOLENOIDS

1) To check solenoid seals, remove suspect solenoid. Connect battery voltage to solenoid. Apply 71 psi (5 kg/cm²) to solenoid with battery voltage connected. *See Fig. 28.*

2) With battery voltage applied, air should pass through solenoid. Disconnect voltage to solenoid. Ensure air does not pass through solenoid. Replace solenoid if defective.

LOCK-UP SOLENOID

1) To check solenoid seals, remove suspect solenoid. Connect battery voltage to solenoid. Apply 71 psi (5 kg/cm²) to solenoid with battery voltage connected. *See Fig. 28.*

2) With battery voltage applied, air should not pass through solenoid. Disconnect voltage to solenoid. Ensure air does pass through solenoid. Replace solenoid if defective.

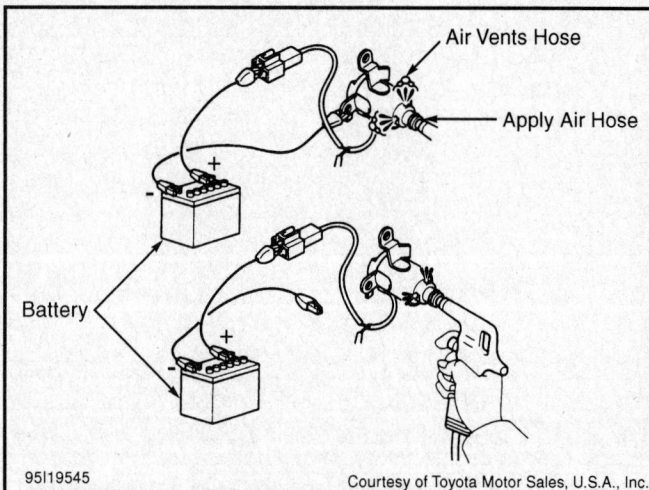

95I19545

Courtesy of Toyota Motor Sales, U.S.A., Inc.

Fig. 28: Checking Solenoids

AUTOMATIC TRANSMISSIONS
Toyota A-340 Series – Electronic Controls (With OBD-II) (Cont.)

3-1703

SLN SOLENOID

Raise and support vehicle. Remove transmission oil pan. Remove appropriate solenoid. To check solenoid operation, connect positive battery voltage to solenoid terminal No. 1. Ensure a 8-10 watt bulb is placed in-line of positive lead. *See Fig. 17.* Connect negative lead to terminal No. 2 and monitor valve's movement. Replace as needed.

PARK/NEUTRAL POSITION (PNP) SWITCH

Disconnect harness connector at park/neutral position switch. Switch is located on side of transmission. Using ohmmeter, check for continuity between specified terminals in accordance with shift lever position. *See Fig. 29.* Replace PNP switch if defective.

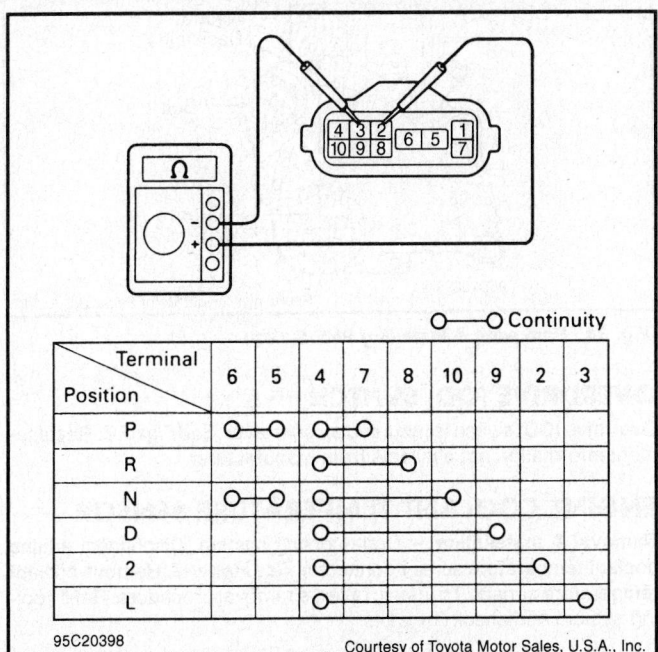

Terminal / Position	6	5	4	7	8	10	9	2	3
P	O—O		O—O						
R			O	O					
N	O—O		O			O			
D			O				O		
2			O					O	
L			O						O

O—O Continuity

95C20398   Courtesy of Toyota Motor Sales, U.S.A., Inc.

Fig. 29: Testing Park/Neutral Position (PNP) Switch

PATTERN SELECT SWITCH

NOTE: T100 is not equipped with a pattern select switch.

Disconnect electrical connector from pattern select switch. Using ohmmeter, ensure continuity exists between terminals No. 3 and 4 with switch in PWR position on Lexus LS400, SC300, SC400 and Supra. Ensure continuity exists between terminals No. 2 and 3 with switch in PWR position on Tacoma and 4Runner. *See Fig. 30.* No continuity should exist in NORM position. Replace switch as necessary.

OVERDRIVE (OD) SWITCH

Except Tacoma & 4Runner – Disconnect electrical connector from OD switch, located on shift lever. Using ohmmeter, ensure continuity exists between switch terminals with switch released (OFF position). Ensure no continuity exists with switch depressed (ON position). Replace switch if defective.

Tacoma & 4Runner – Disconnect electrical connector from OD switch, located on shift lever. Using ohmmeter, ensure continuity exists between switch terminals No. 1 and 3 on Tacoma with column shift, or terminals No. 5 and 10 on Tacoma with floor shift and 4Runner, with switch released (OFF position). Ensure no continuity exists with switch depressed (ON position). *See Fig. 31.* Replace switch if defective.

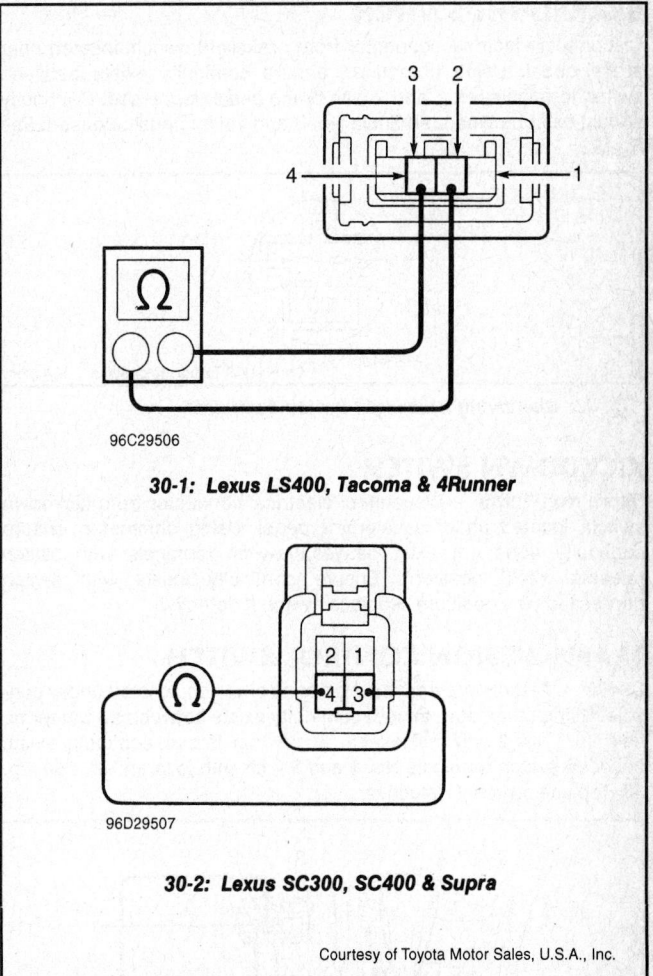

30-1: Lexus LS400, Tacoma & 4Runner

30-2: Lexus SC300, SC400 & Supra

Courtesy of Toyota Motor Sales, U.S.A., Inc.

Fig. 30: Identifying Pattern Select Switch Terminals

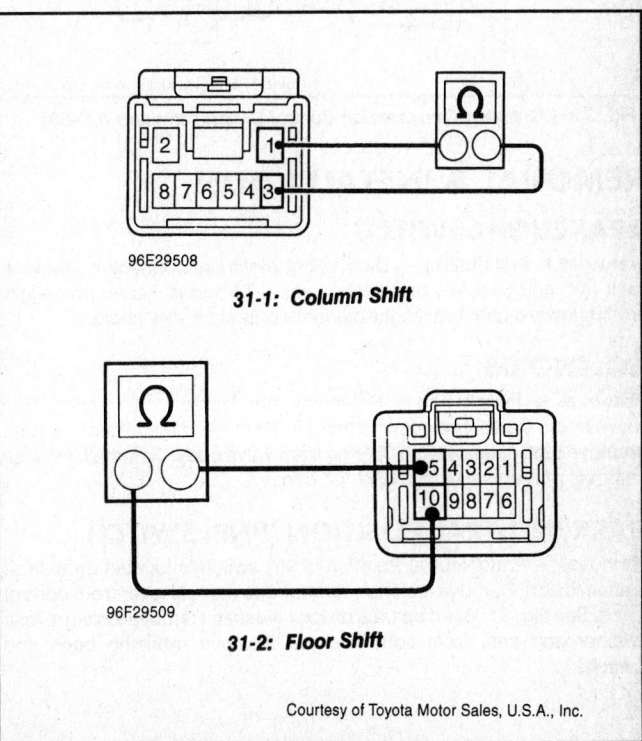

31-1: Column Shift

31-2: Floor Shift

Courtesy of Toyota Motor Sales, U.S.A., Inc.

Fig. 31: Checking OD Switch (Tacoma & 4Runner)

3-1704

AUTOMATIC TRANSMISSIONS
Toyota A-340 Series – Electronic Controls (With OBD-II) (Cont.)

BRAKELIGHT SWITCH

Disconnect electrical connector from brakelight switch, located near brake pedal. Using ohmmeter, ensure continuity exists between switch terminals No. 1 and 2 with brake pedal depressed. Continuity should exist between terminals No. 3 and 4 with pedal released. *See Fig. 32.*

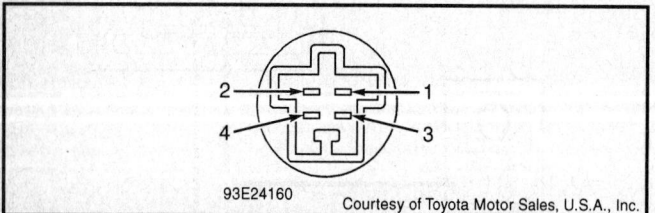

Fig. 32: Identifying Brakelight Switch Terminals

KICKDOWN SWITCH

Supra Non-Turbo – Disconnect electrical connector from kickdown switch, located under accelerator pedal. Using ohmmeter, ensure continuity does not exist between switch terminals with switch released (OFF position). Ensure continuity exists with switch depressed (ON position). Replace switch if defective.

TRANSMISSION CONTROL SWITCH

LS400 – Disconnect transmission control switch, located under console. Using ohmmeter, ensure continuity exists between switch terminals No. 1 and 2 with shift lever in "3" position. Ensure continuity exists between switch terminals No. 2 and 3 with shift lever in "D". *See.Fig. 33* Replace switch if defective.

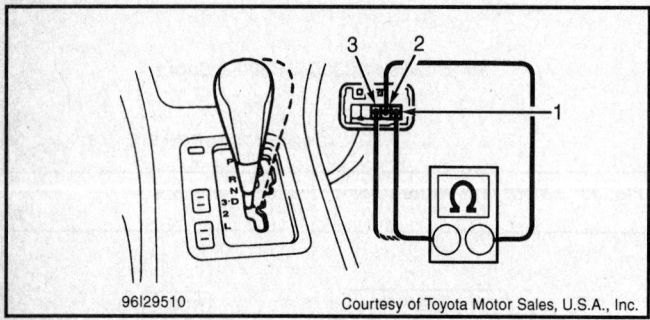

Fig. 33: Identifying Transmission Control Switch Terminals (LS400)

REMOVAL & INSTALLATION

BRAKELIGHT SWITCH

Removal & Installation – Disconnect electrical connector. Remove lock nut, and unscrew brakelight switch. To install, screw brakelight switch inward until brakelight plunger contacts brake pedal.

SOLENOIDS

Removal & Installation – Solenoids are located on transmission valve body. Raise and support vehicle. Remove transmission oil pan. Remove bolt, solenoid and "O" ring from valve body. To install, reverse removal procedure using NEW "O" ring.

PARK/NEUTRAL POSITION (PNP) SWITCH

Removal – Park/Neutral Position (PNP) switch is located on side of transmission. Remove lock nut, washer and manual lever from control shaft. *See Fig. 34.* Bend up tabs on lock washer. Remove lock nut, lock washer and seal from control shaft. Remove retaining bolts and switch.

Installation – 1) Install switch on control shaft. Loosely install switch retaining bolts. Install seal and lock washer. Install lock nut and tighten to specification. See TORQUE SPECIFICATIONS. Bend tabs on lock washer over against lock nut.

2) Ensure parking brake is applied. Temporarily install manual lever on control shaft. Place shift lever in Neutral. Remove manual lever. Rotate park/neutral position switch and align neutral basic line on PNP switch with groove. *See Fig. 34.*

3) Hold PNP switch in this position. Tighten retaining bolts to specification. To install remaining components, reverse removal procedure.

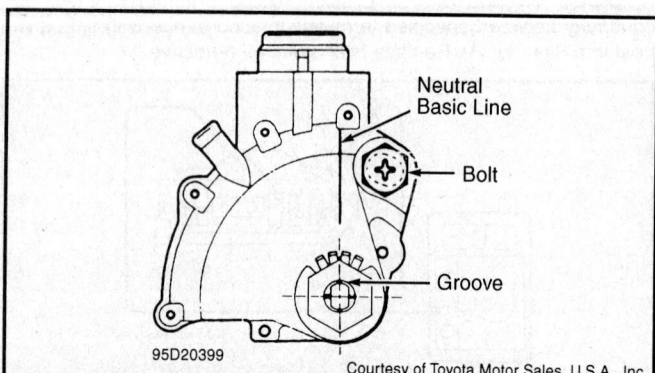

Fig. 34: Removing & Installing PNP Switch

OVERDRIVE (OD) SWITCH

Overdrive (OD) switch is mounted on shift lever. *See Figs 2-7.* Replacement information not available from manufacturer.

ENGINE COOLANT TEMPERATURE SENSOR

Removal & Installation – Drain cooling system. Disconnect engine coolant temperature sensor connector. *See Figs. 1-7.* Remove coolant temperature sensor. To install, reverse removal procedure. Refill cooling system and check for leaks.

NO. 1 & NO. 2 VEHICLE SPEED SENSOR (VSS)

NOTE: No. 1 vehicle speed sensor on Tacoma and T100 is located in combination meter. For removal and installation procedures, see appropriate MITCHELL® ELECTRICAL supplement for IMPORTED CARS, LIGHT TRUCKS & VANS.

Removal & Installation (All Except Tacoma & T100) – Disconnect electrical connector. Remove appropriate vehicle speed sensor from transmission. *See Figs. 1-4 and 7.* To install, reverse removal procedure.

OD DIRECT CLUTCH SPEED SENSOR

Removal & Installation – Disconnect electrical connector from sensor. Remove bolt and sensor. *See Figs. 1 and 3.* To install, reverse removal procedure.

TORQUE SPECIFICATIONS
TORQUE SPECIFICATIONS

Application	Ft. Lbs. (N.m)
ATF Temperature Sensor	11 (15)
No. 1 Vehicle Speed Sensor	12 (16)

	INCH Lbs. (N.m)
PNP Switch	
Bolt	115 (13)
Nut	
Lexus SC300, Supra, T100 & 4Runner	35 (3.9)
All Other Models	61 (6.9)
Solenoid Bolt	89 (10)
Speed Sensor Bolt	
LS400	48 (5.4)
No. 2 & OD Direct Clutch	48 (5.4)

AUTOMATIC TRANSMISSIONS
Toyota A-340 Series – Electronic Controls (With OBD-II) (Cont.)

3-1705

WIRING DIAGRAMS

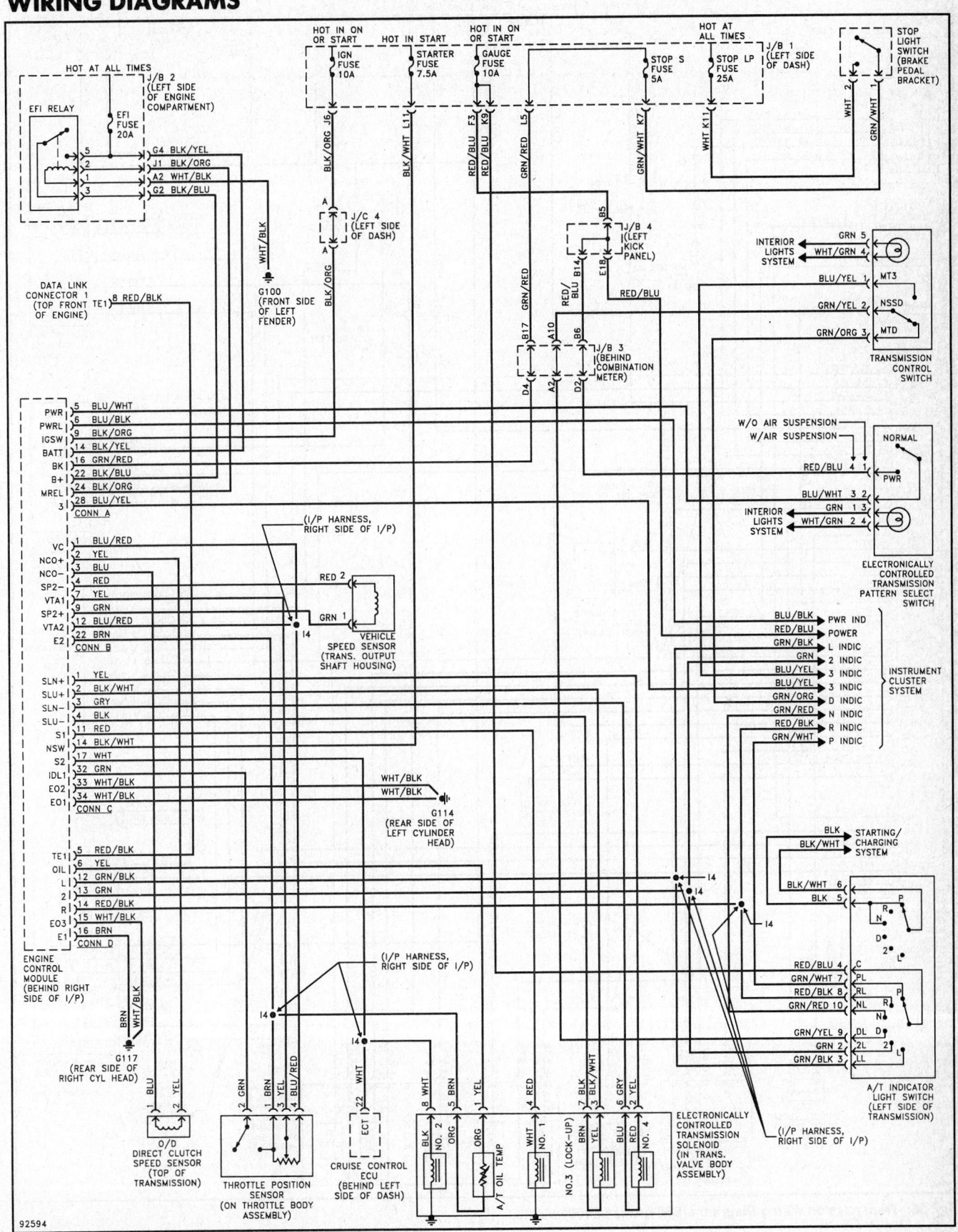

Fig. 35: Transmission Wiring Diagram (1995 Lexus LS400)

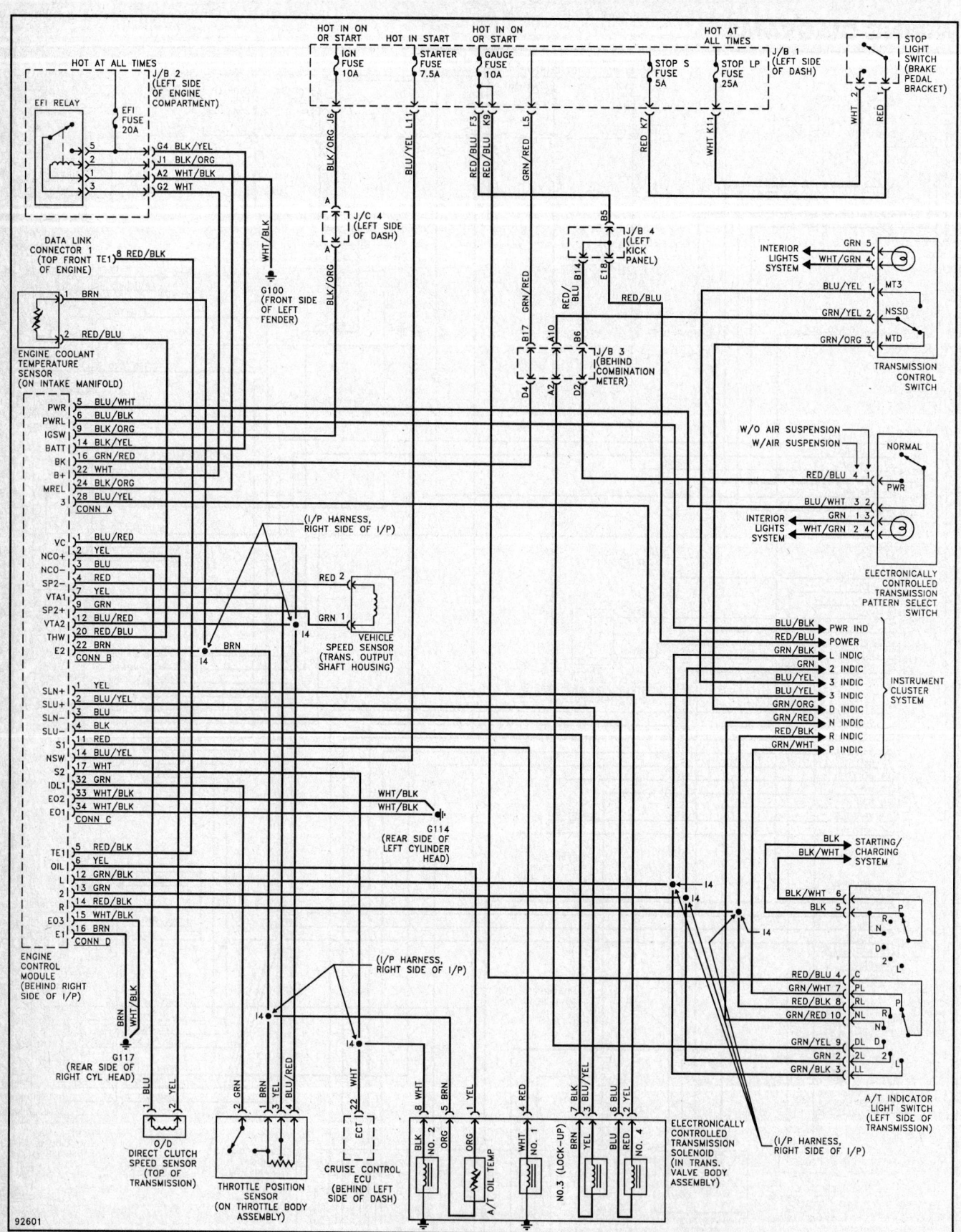

Fig. 36: *Transmission Wiring Diagram (1996 Lexus LS400)*

AUTOMATIC TRANSMISSIONS
Toyota A-340 Series – Electronic Controls (With OBD-II) (Cont.)

3-1707

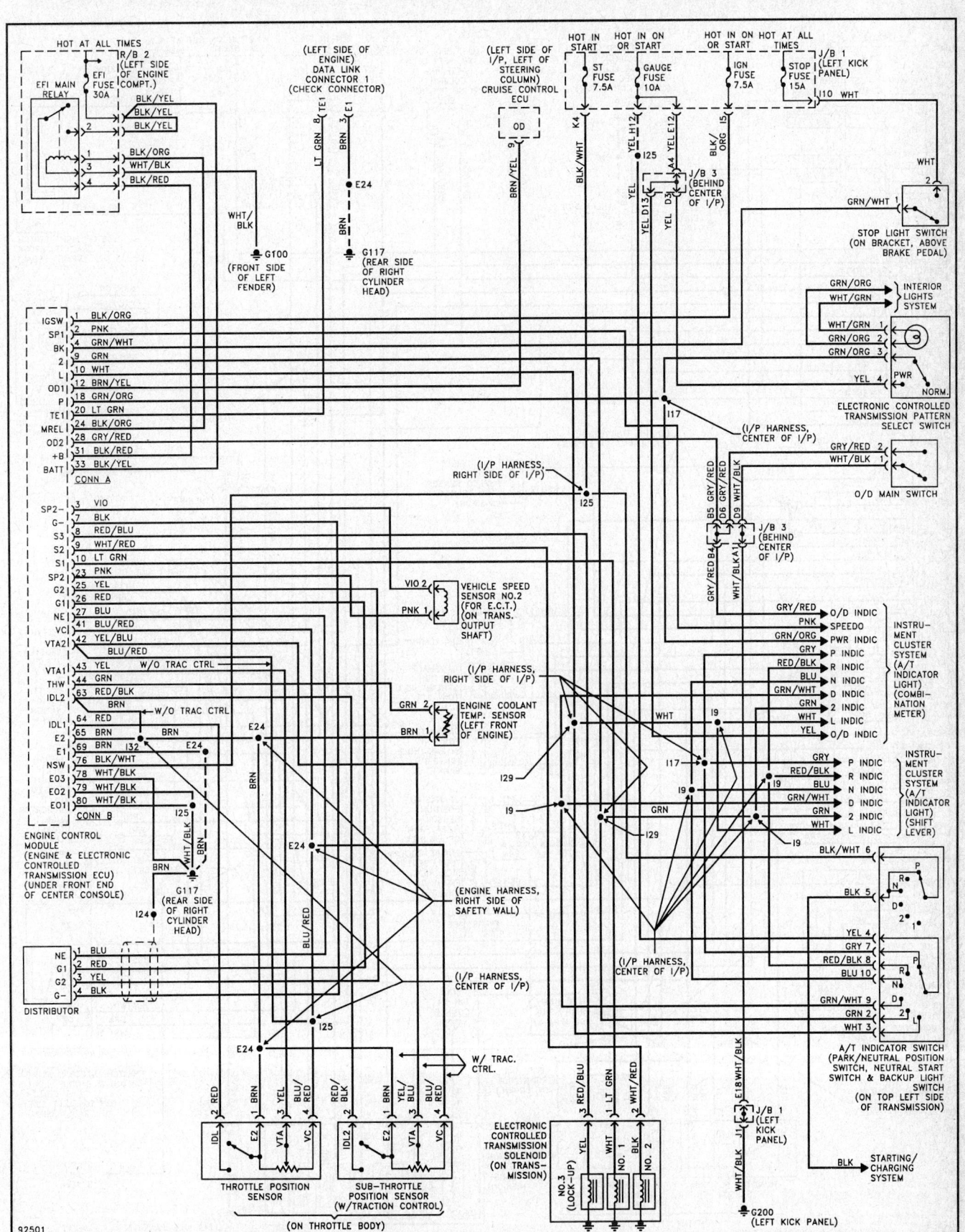

Fig. 37: Transmission Wiring Diagram (1996 Lexus SC300)

AUTOMATIC TRANSMISSIONS
Toyota A-340 Series – Electronic Controls (With OBD-II) (Cont.)

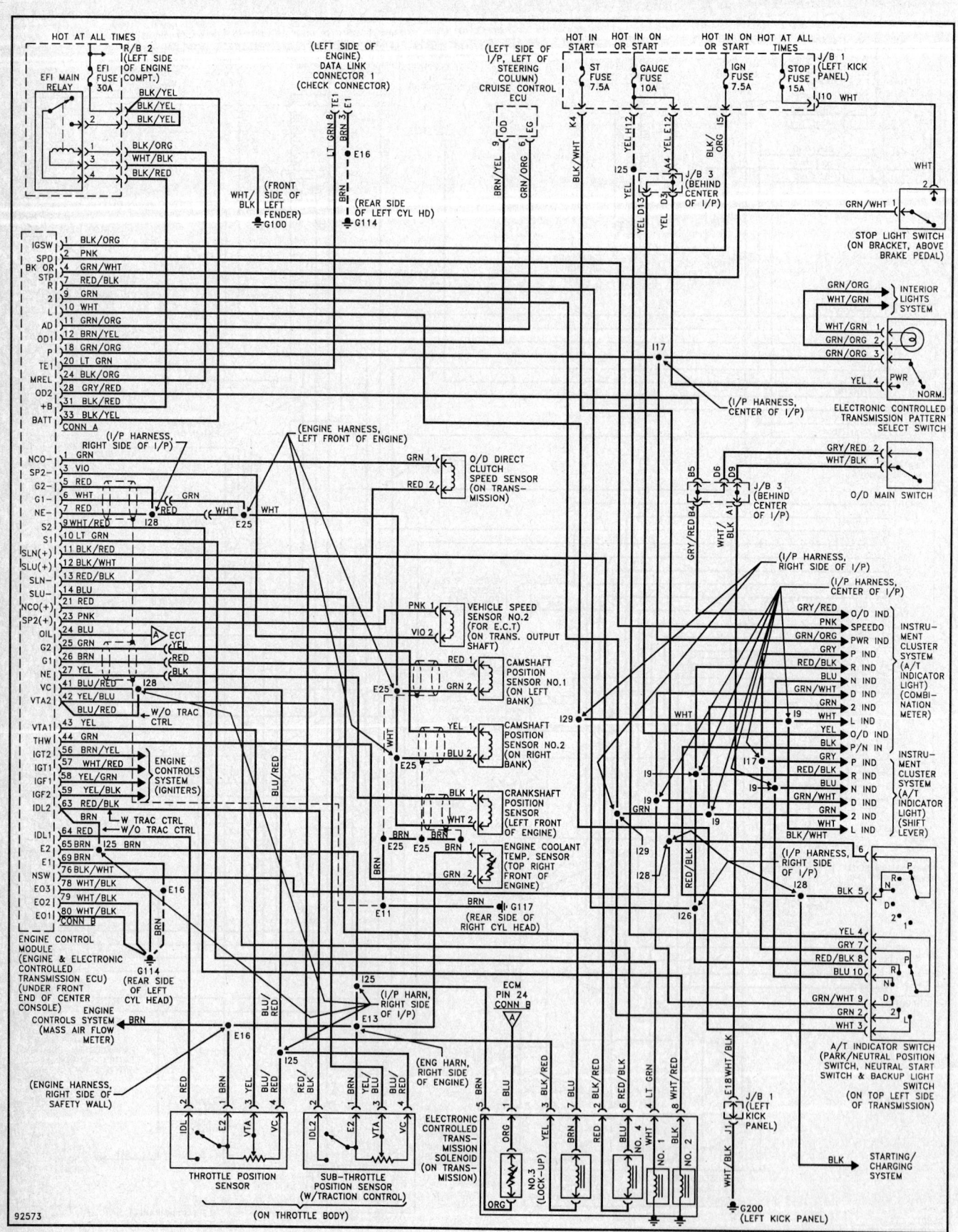

Fig. 38: Transmission Wiring Diagram (1996 Lexus SC400)

AUTOMATIC TRANSMISSIONS
Toyota A-340 Series – Electronic Controls (With OBD-II) (Cont.)

3-1709

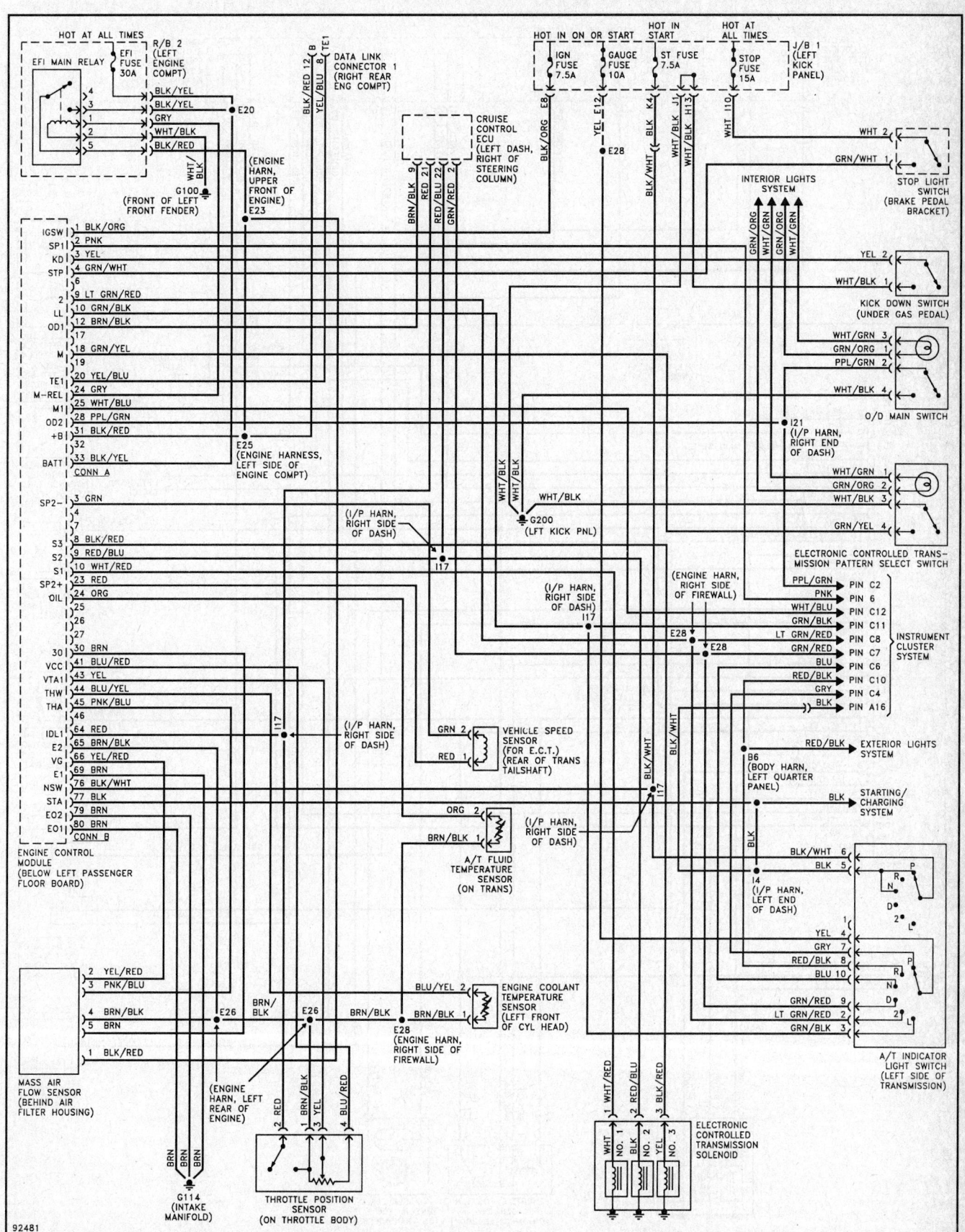

Fig. 39: Transmission Wiring Diagram (1995-96 Toyota Supra Non-Turbo)

AUTOMATIC TRANSMISSIONS
Toyota A-340 Series – Electronic Controls (With OBD-II) (Cont.)

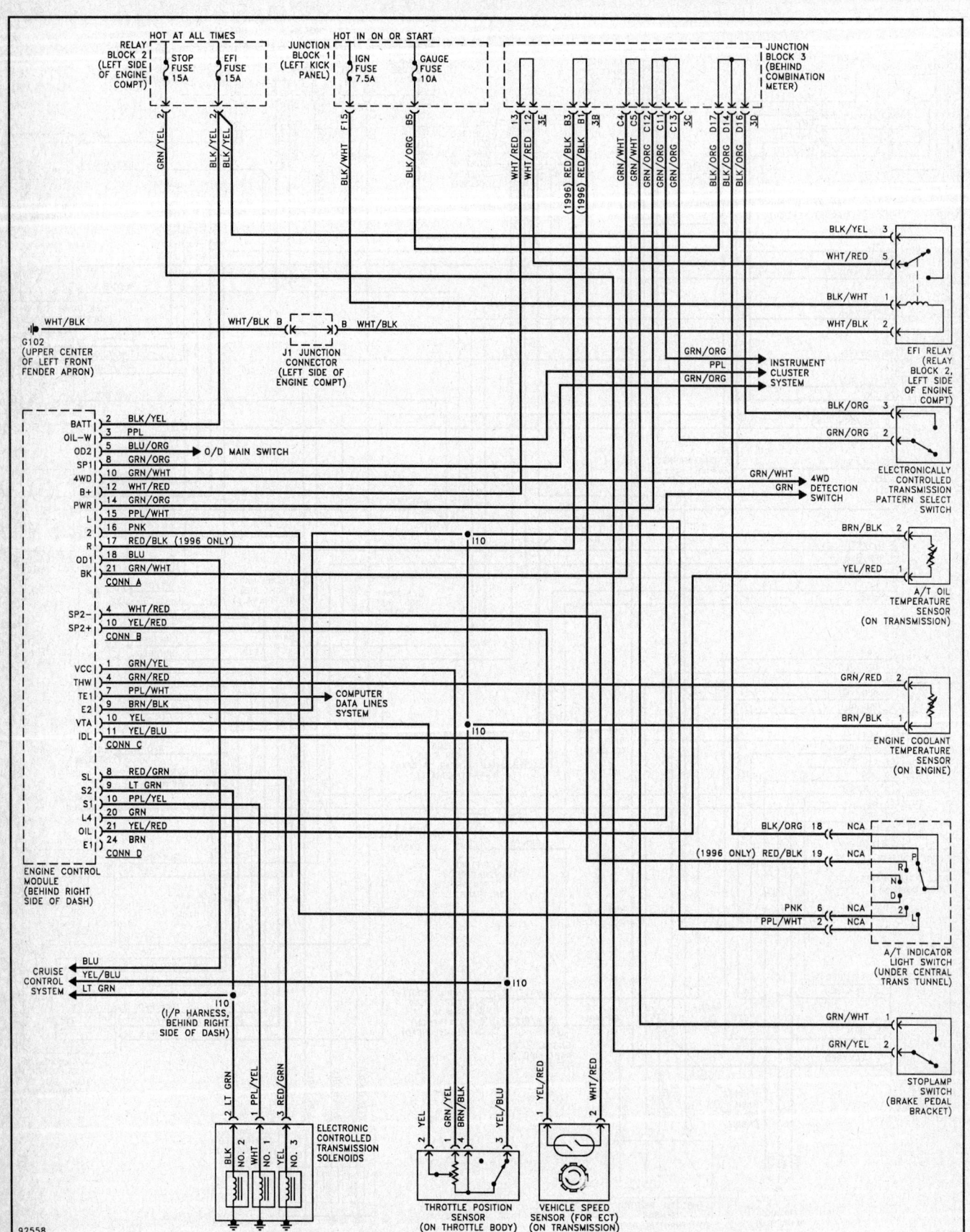

Fig. 40: Transmission Wiring Diagram (1995-96 Toyota Tacoma With 2.7L)

92558

AUTOMATIC TRANSMISSIONS
Toyota A-340 Series – Electronic Controls (With OBD-II) (Cont.)

3-1711

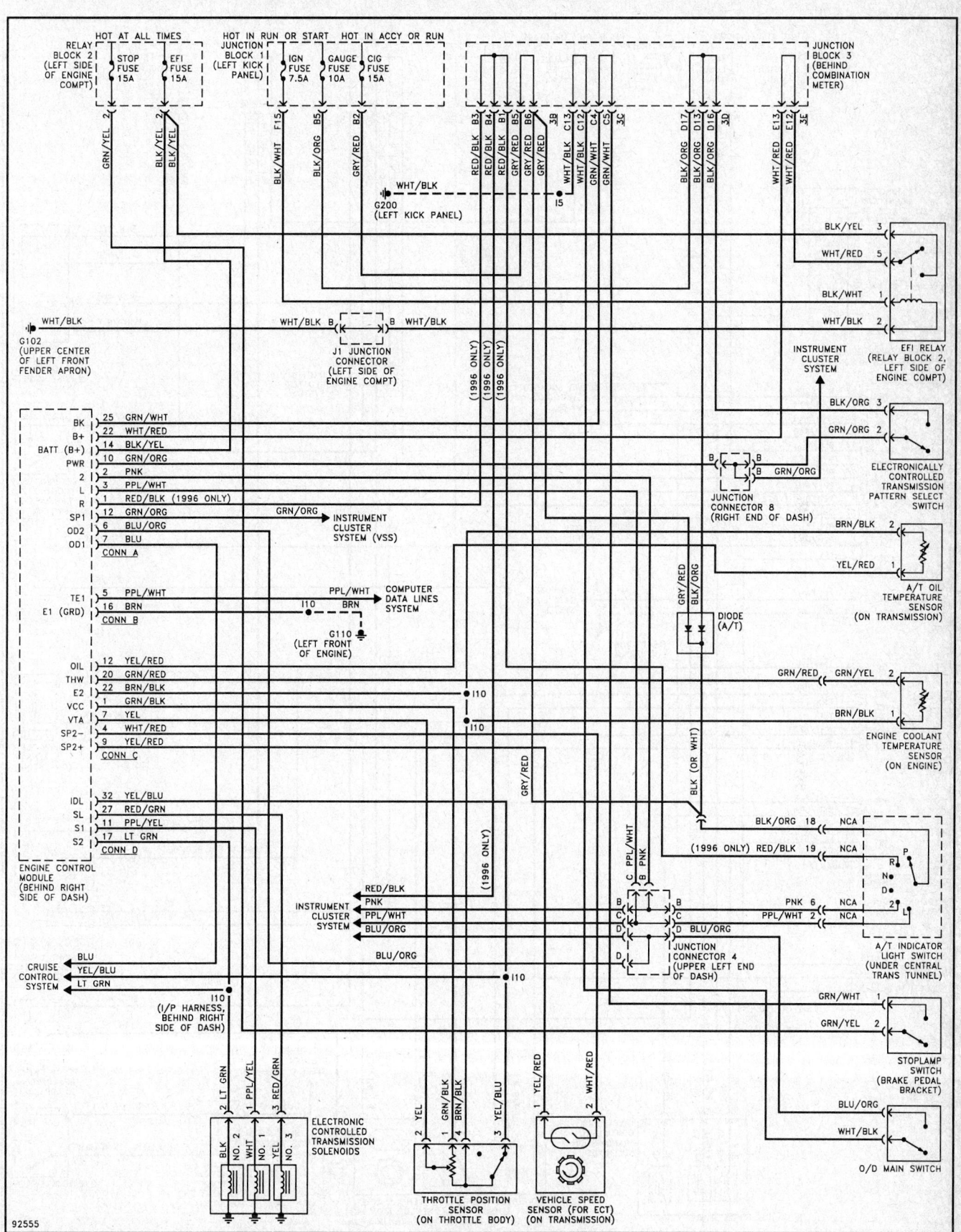

Fig. 41: Transmission Wiring Diagram (1995-96 Toyota Tacoma With 3.4L – 2WD)

92555

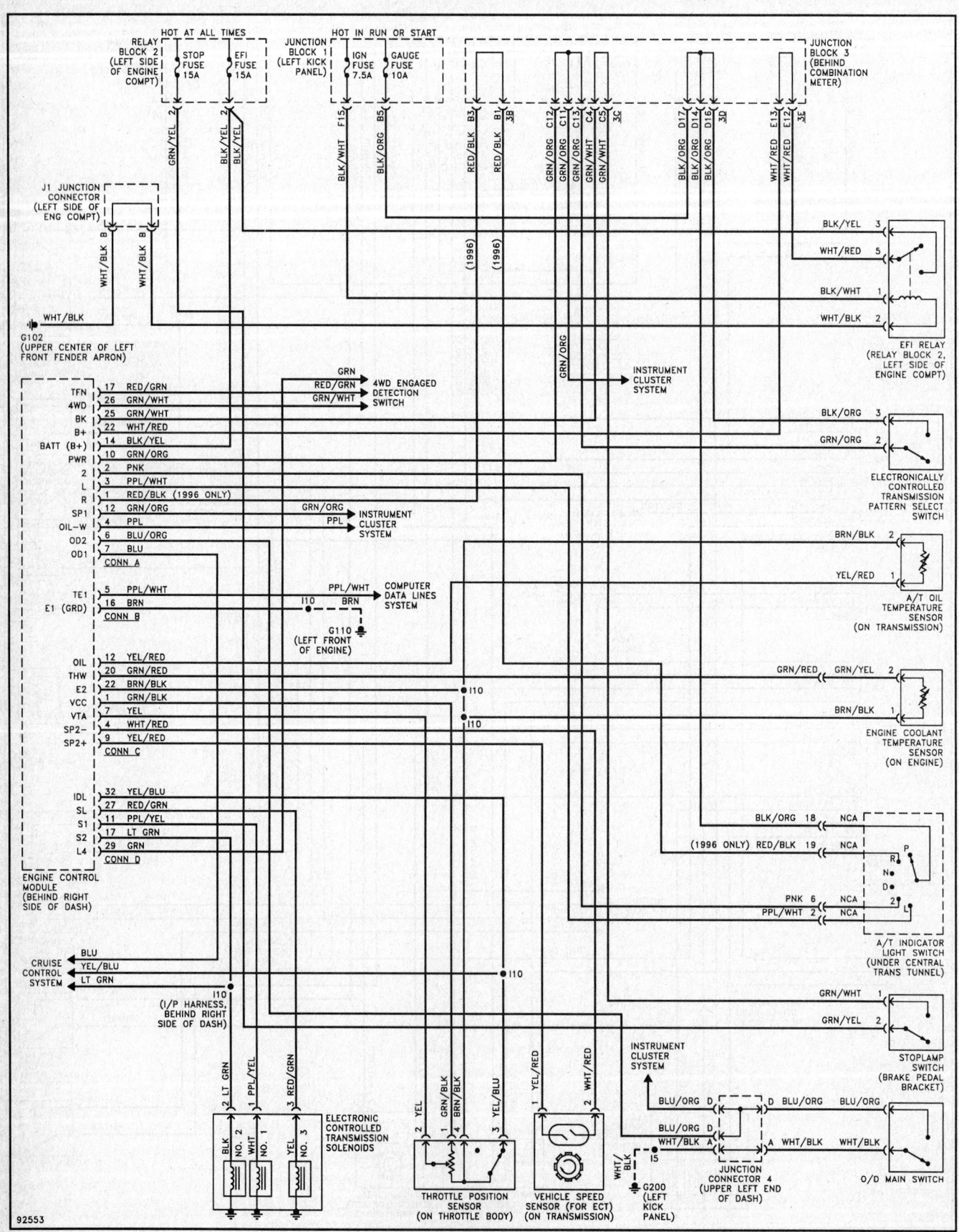

Fig. 42: Transmission Wiring Diagram (1995-96 Toyota Tacoma With 3.4L – 4WD)

92553

AUTOMATIC TRANSMISSIONS
Toyota A-340 Series – Electronic Controls (With OBD-II) (Cont.)

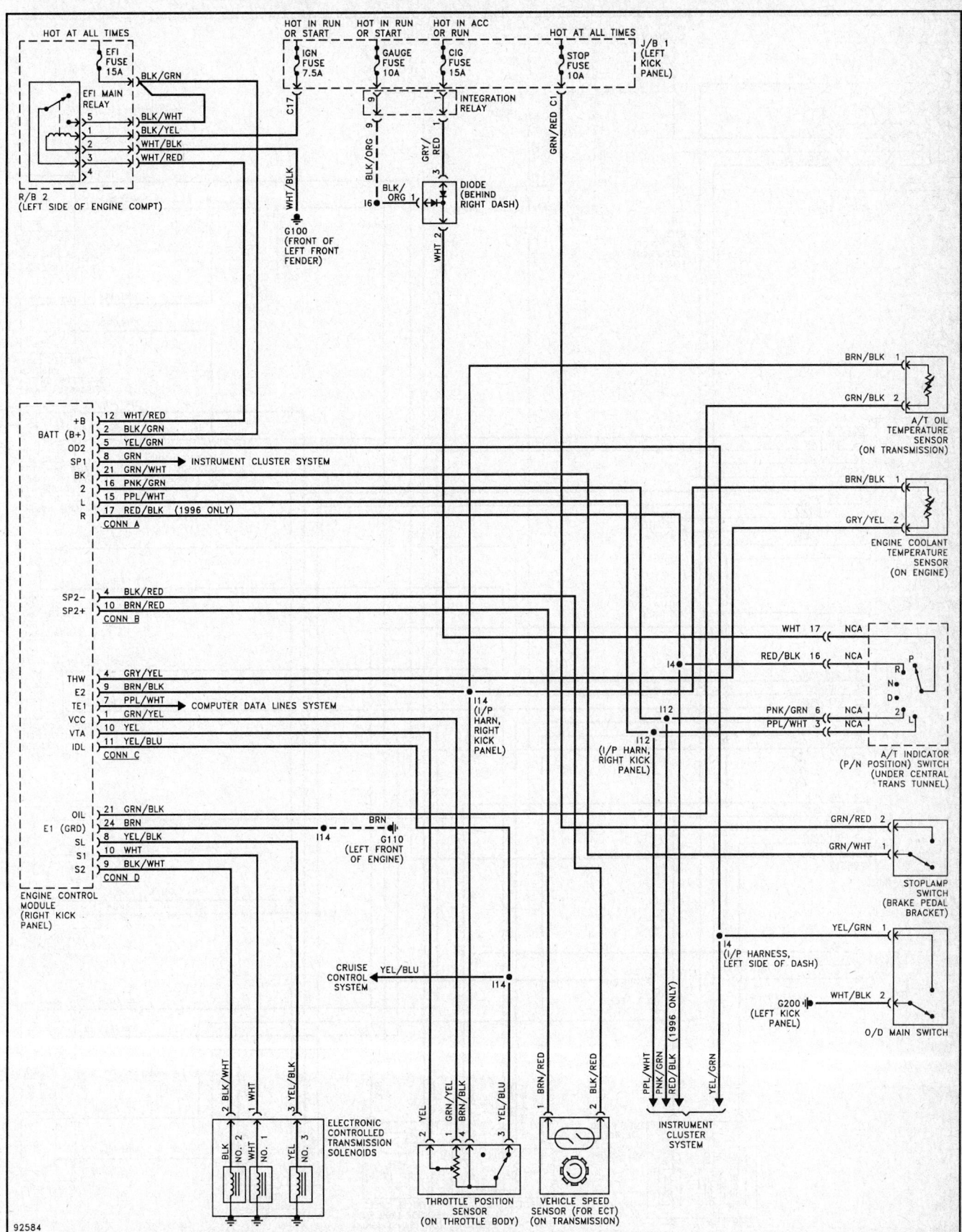

Fig. 43: Transmission Wiring Diagram (1995-96 Toyota T100 With 2.7L)

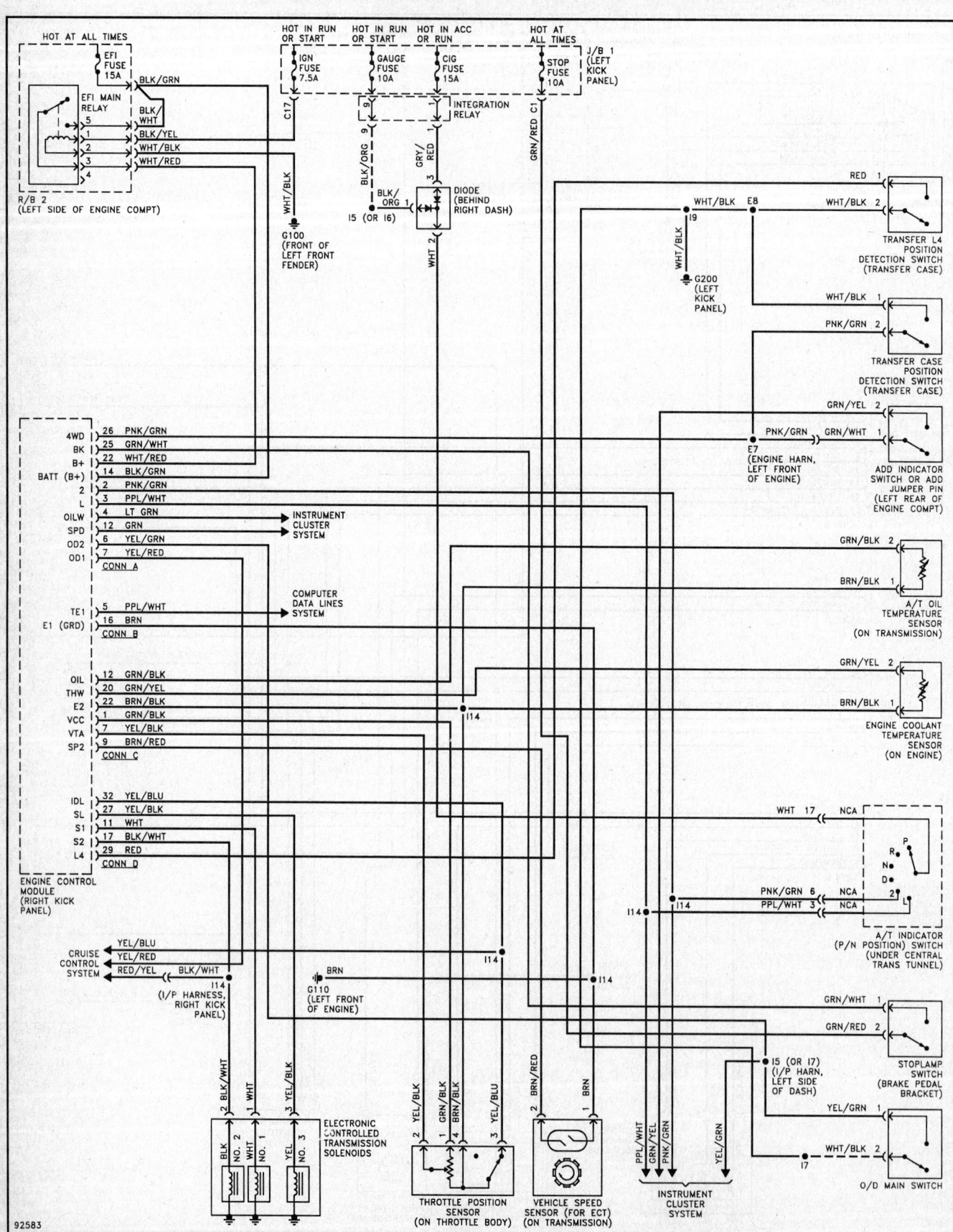

Fig. 44: Transmission Wiring Diagram (1995 Toyota T100 With 3.4L)

AUTOMATIC TRANSMISSIONS
Toyota A-340 Series – Electronic Controls (With OBD-II) (Cont.)

3-1715

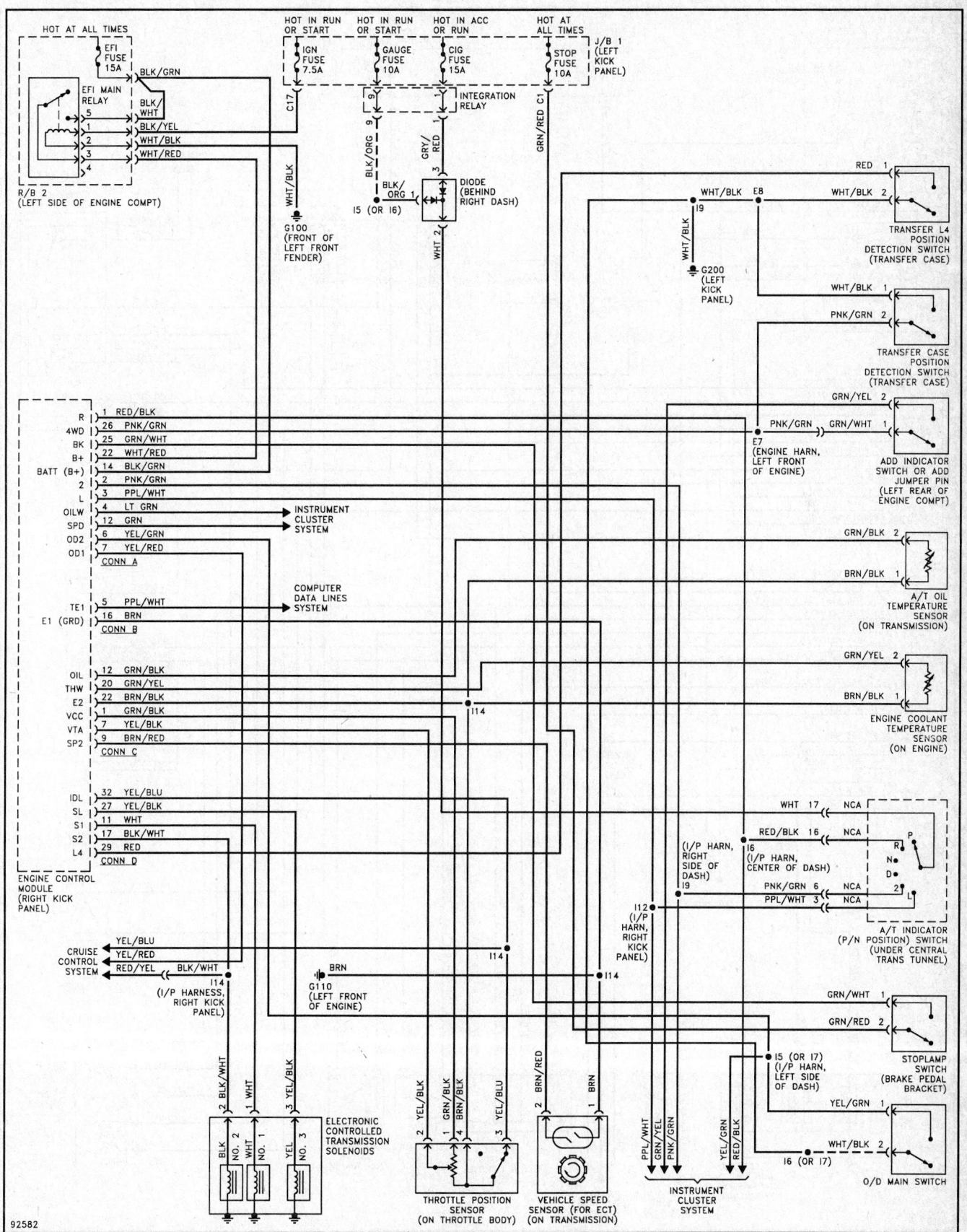

Fig. 45: Transmission Wiring Diagram (1996 Toyota T100 With 3.4L)

92582

AUTOMATIC TRANSMISSIONS
Toyota A-340 Series – Electronic Controls (With OBD-II) (Cont.)

3-1716

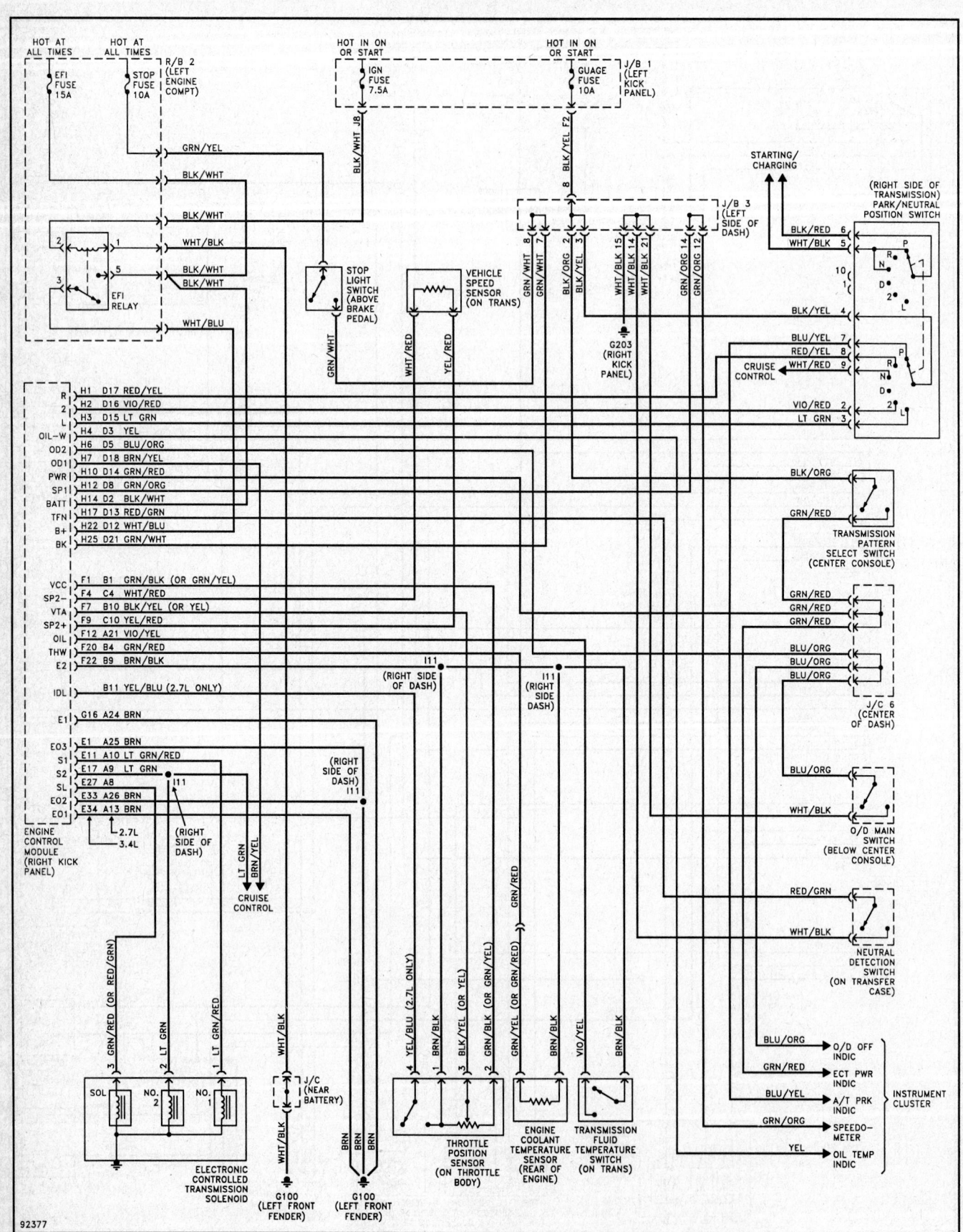

Fig. 46: Transmission Wiring Diagram (1996 Toyota 4Runner)

Previa

APPLICATION

APPLICATION

Vehicle	Transmission Model
Supercharged	
2WD	A-340E
AWD	A-340F

CAUTION: *Previa is equipped with a Supplemental Restraint System (SRS). When servicing vehicle, use care to avoid accidental air bag deployment. All SRS electrical connections and wiring harness are covered with Yellow insulation. SRS-related components are located in steering column, center console, instrument panel and lower panel of instrument panel. DO NOT use electrical test equipment on these circuits. It may be necessary to deactivate SRS before servicing components. See AIR BAG SERVICING article in APPLICATIONS & IDENTIFICATION section.*

DESCRIPTION & OPERATION

The A-340E and A-340F automatic transmissions are electronically controlled. Transmission shifting and torque converter lock-up are controlled by an Electronic Controlled Transmission (ECT) Electronic Control Unit (ECU). *See Fig. 1.* Control unit is a combined engine control and transmission control unit and is referred to as the ECT ECU.

ECT ECU receives information from various input devices and uses this information to control No. 1 and No. 2 shift solenoids on transmission valve body for transmission shifting and lock-up solenoid (also called SL solenoid) for torque converter lock-up.

ECT ECU contains a self-diagnostic system, which will store a Diagnostic Trouble Code (DTC) if a failure or problem exists in electronic control system. Trouble code can be retrieved to determine problem area. See SELF-DIAGNOSTIC SYSTEM.

An Overdrive (OD) switch is mounted on end of shift lever. *See Fig. 1.* When OD switch is depressed to ON position, transmission will shift into 4th gear when shift lever is in "D" position, and OD OFF light on

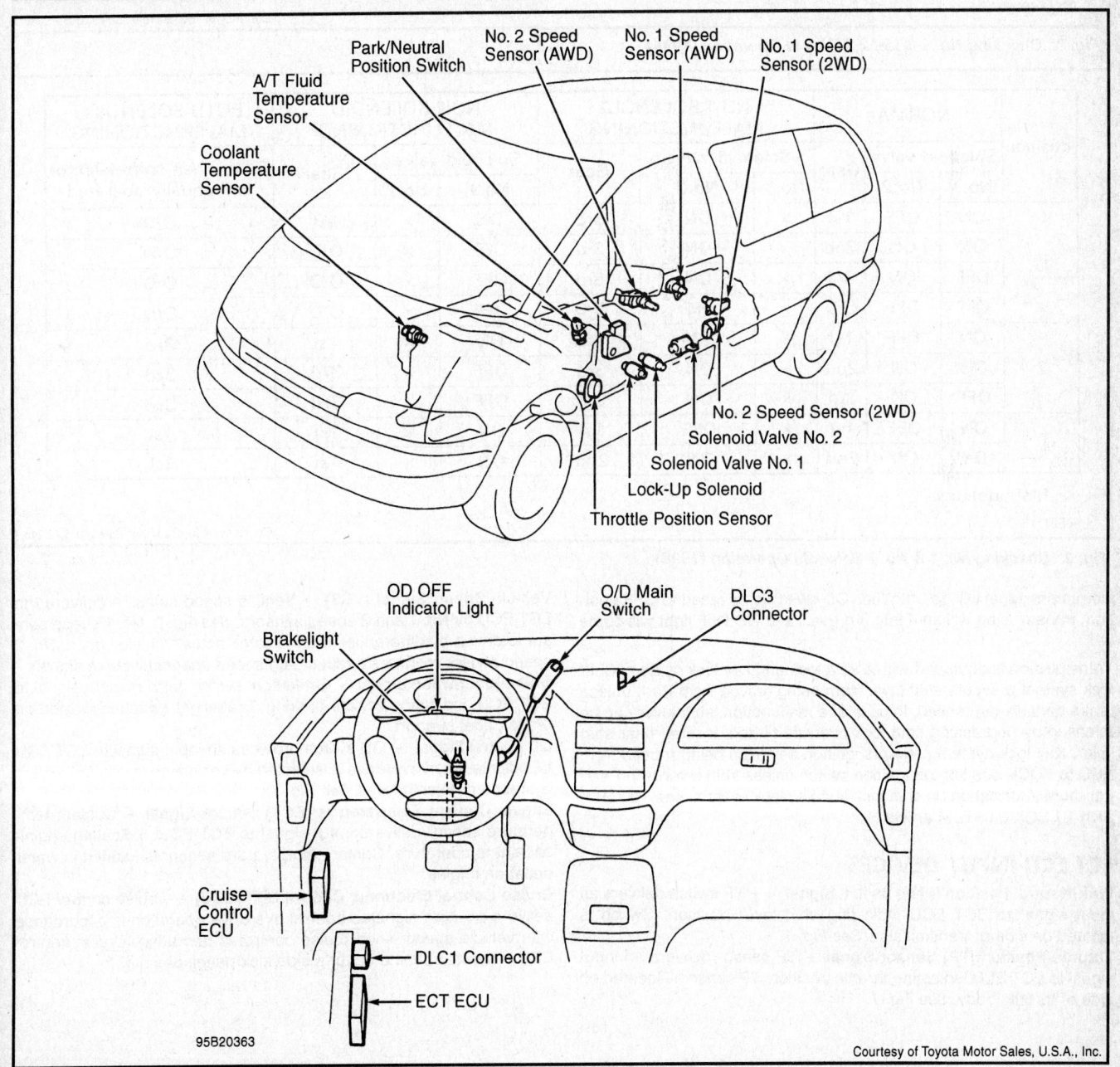

Courtesy of Toyota Motor Sales, U.S.A., Inc.

95B20363

Fig. 1: Identifying Input & Output Device Locations

Position	NORMAL			NO.1 SOLENOID MALFUNCTIONING			NO.2 SOLENOID MALFUNCTIONING			BOTH SOLENOIDS MALFUNCTIONING
	Solenoid valve		Gear	Solenoid valve		Gear	Solenoid valve		Gear	Gear when shift selector is manually operated
	No.1	No.2		No.1	No.2		No.1	No.2		
D	ON	OFF	1st	x	ON	3rd	ON	x	1st	O/D
	ON	ON	2nd	x	ON	3rd	OFF	x	O/D	O/D
	OFF	ON	3rd	x	ON	3rd	OFF	x	O/D	O/D
	OFF	OFF	O/D	x	OFF	O/D	OFF	x	O/D	O/D
2	ON	OFF	1st	x	ON	3rd	ON	x	1st	O/D
	ON	ON	2nd	x	ON	3rd	OFF	x	O/D	O/D
	OFF	ON	3rd	x	ON	3rd	OFF	x	O/D	O/D
L	ON	OFF	1st	x	OFF	1st	ON	x	1st	1st
	ON	ON	2nd	x	ON	2nd	ON	x	1st	1st

x: Malfunctions

95C20364

Courtesy of Toyota Motor Sales, U.S.A., Inc.

Fig. 2: Checking No. 1 & No. 2 Solenoid Operation (1995)

Position	NORMAL			NO.1 SOLENOID MALFUNCTIONING			NO.2 SOLENOID MALFUNCTIONING			BOTH SOLENOIDS MALFUNCTIONING
	Solenoid valve		Gear	Solenoid valve		Gear	Solenoid valve		Gear	Gear when shift selector is manually operated
	No.1	No.2		No.1	No.2		No.1	No.2		
D	ON	OFF	1st	×	ON	3rd	ON	×	1st	O/D
	ON	ON	2nd	×	ON	3rd	OFF	×	O/D	O/D
	OFF	ON	3rd	×	ON	3rd	OFF	×	O/D	O/D
	OFF	OFF	O/D	×	OFF	O/D	OFF	×	O/D	O/D
2	ON	OFF	1st	×	ON	3rd	ON	×	1st	3rd
	ON	ON	2nd	×	ON	3rd	OFF	×	3rd	3rd
	OFF	ON	3rd	×	ON	3rd	OFF	×	3rd	3rd
L	ON	OFF	1st	×	OFF	1st	ON	×	1st	1st
	ON	ON	2nd	×	ON	2nd	ON	×	1st	1st

×: Malfunctions

96F21175

Courtesy of Toyota Motor Sales, U.S.A., Inc.

Fig. 3: Checking No. 1 & No. 2 Solenoid Operation (1996)

instrument panel will go off. When OD switch is released to OFF position, transmission will shift into 3rd gear, and OD OFF light will come on.

Transmission is equipped with a shift lock and key lock system. Shift lock system prevents shift lever from being moved from Park unless brake pedal is depressed. In case of a malfunction, shift lever can be released by depressing shift lock override button, located near shift lever. Key lock system prevents ignition key from being moved from ACC to LOCK position on ignition switch unless shift lever is in Park. For more information on shift lock and key lock system, see TOYOTA SHIFT LOCK SYSTEM article.

ECT ECU INPUT DEVICES

Park/Neutral Position (PNP) Switch Signal – PNP switch delivers an input signal to ECT ECU indicating shift lever position. Switch is located on side of transmission. *See Fig. 1.*

Throttle Position (TP) Sensor Signal – TP sensor delivers an input signal to ECT ECU indicating throttle position. TP sensor is located on side of throttle body. *See Fig. 1.*

Vehicle Speed Signal (VSS) – Vehicle speed signal is delivered to ECT ECU by No. 1 and 2 speed sensors. *See Fig. 1.* No. 1 speed sensor is driven by differential and indicates actual vehicle speed. No. 2 speed sensor monitors direct clutch speed (magnetic pulse signal).

Brakelight Switch Signal – Brakelight switch delivers input signal to ECT ECU, indicating vehicle braking. Brakelight switch is located on brake pedal support.

OD Switch Signal – OD switch provides an input signal to ECT ECU to indicate when overdrive is selected by vehicle operator. OD switch is mounted on shift lever. *See Fig. 1.*

Engine Coolant Temperature (ECT) Sensor Signal – Coolant temperature sensor delivers input signal to ECT ECU, indicating engine coolant temperature. Coolant temperature sensor is located in water outlet on engine.

Cruise Control Electronic Control Unit (ECU) – Cruise control ECU delivers an input signal to control overdrive operation in accordance with vehicle speed when cruise control is operating. Cruise control ECU is located behind driver's side kick panel. *See Fig. 1.*

AUTOMATIC TRANSMISSIONS
Toyota Previa A-340E & A-340F — Electronic Controls (Cont.)

3-1719

ECT ECU OUTPUT DEVICES

No. 1 & No. 2 Solenoids – ECT ECU controls transmission shifting by delivering an output signal to operate proper solenoid. Solenoids are located on transmission valve body. *See Fig. 1.* Solenoids are operated in accordance with shift lever position. *See Figs. 2 and 3.* If a solenoid malfunctions, fail-safe gear may be selected.

NOTE: In some gears, ECT ECU provides a fail-safe system which will place transmission in designated gear depending on solenoid failure.

Lock-Up Solenoid – ECT ECU controls torque converter lock-up by delivering an output signal to lock-up solenoid. Lock-up solenoid (also called SL solenoid) is activated when shift lever is in "D" position and vehicle is at specified speed. Lock-up solenoid is located on transmission valve body. *See Fig. 1.*

SELF-DIAGNOSTIC SYSTEM

SYSTEM DIAGNOSIS

NOTE: Before testing transmission, ensure fluid level is correct and throttle and shift cables are properly adjusted. Ensure engine starts with shift lever in "P" (Park) and "N" (Neutral) to ensure proper adjustment of park/neutral position switch. Transmission must first be tested by checking for stored trouble codes. See RETRIEVING TROUBLE CODES.

ECT ECU monitors engine and transmission operation and contains a self-diagnostic system which stores diagnostic trouble code(s). A Malfunction Indicator Light (MIL), located on instrument panel, will illuminate if a system or component fails and sets a DTC.

MIL illuminates with ignition switch in ON position, engine off (KOEO). Once engine is started, MIL should go out. If MIL remains illuminated, ECT ECU has detected a malfunction or abnormality in system. If MIL does not illuminate, inspect circuit and light. See WIRING DIAGRAM.

If malfunction does not reoccur in 3 trips, MIL goes off, but Diagnostic Trouble Codes (DTC) remain recorded in ECT ECU memory. Trouble codes may only be retrieved using an appropriate scan tool or Toyota scan tool connected to standardized 16-pin Data Link Connector (DLC3) located in center dash area. *See Figs. 1 and 4.* Scan tool also provides freeze-frame data and can be used to clear trouble codes.

ECT ECU records engine operating condition (fuel system, calculated load, coolant temperature, fuel trim (mixture), engine speed, vehicle speed, etc.) with 1st malfunction ONLY. Information is ONLY for 1st recorded failure, even if more than one code has been recorded. Freeze-frame data is only updated when all trouble codes have been cleared, or a misfire or fuel-trim malfunction has occurred.

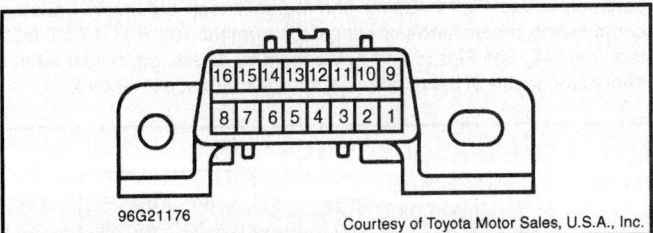

Fig. 4: Identifying Data Link Connector (DLC3) Terminals

96G21176   Courtesy of Toyota Motor Sales, U.S.A., Inc.

RETRIEVING TROUBLE CODES

NOTE: Before retrieving trouble codes, ensure sufficient battery voltage exists for proper self-diagnosis system operation. Ensure proper operation of MIL.

NOTE: For additional engine performance or other system related trouble codes present that are not listed in DIAGNOSTIC TROUBLE CODE (DTC) IDENTIFICATION table, see appropriate MITCHELL® ENGINE PERFORMANCE publication for IMPORTED CARS, LIGHT TRUCKS & VANS.

ECT ECU Codes – 1) Connect scan tool to Data Link Connector (DLC3). *See Fig. 5.* DLC3 is located in fuse box at left side of instrument panel.

2) Turn ignition on. Turn on scan tool. Retrieve any trouble codes stored in memory following scan tool instructions. See DIAGNOSTIC TROUBLE CODE (DTC) IDENTIFICATION table.

3) Trouble codes recorded may not have illuminated MIL. When certain malfunctions or trouble codes initially occur, they will be temporarily stored in ECT ECU memory, but MIL will not illuminate.

4) Second time malfunction or trouble code is detected, MIL will illuminate, provided ignition is turned off and then back on after malfunction or trouble code was first detected. This process is referred to as 2 trip detection logic and only applies to specific trouble codes.

5) Record freeze-frame data. If using Toyota scan tool, ensure tool is in NORMAL mode. CHECK MODE will erase all codes.

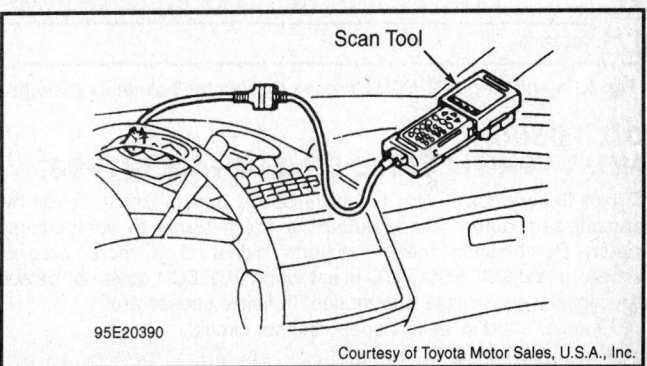

Scan Tool

95E20390   Courtesy of Toyota Motor Sales, U.S.A., Inc.

Fig. 5: Connecting Scan Tool To Data Link Connector (DLC3)

DIAGNOSTIC TROUBLE CODE (DTC) IDENTIFICATION

DTC	[1] Probable Cause
P0500 (1996)	No. 1 Speed Sensor
P0710 (1996)	Trans. Fluid Temp. Sensor
P0720 (1995)	No. 1 Speed Sensor
P0750	No. 1 Solenoid
P0753	No. 1 Solenoid Circuit
P0755	No. 2 Solenoid
P0758	No. 2 Solenoid Circuit
P0770	[2] Lock-Up Solenoid
P0773	[2] Lock-Up Solenoid Circuit
P1700	No. 2 Speed Sensor
P1780	Park/Neutral Position Switch

[1] – Check listed component for probable cause. Check wiring and connections of specified component.
[2] – Also called SL solenoid.

CLEARING TROUBLE CODES

Once repairs have been performed, trouble codes must be cleared from ECT ECU memory. DTCs may be cleared by following methods:

- Scan tool (follow manufacturers instructions).
- Remove EFI fuse (15-amp) from instrument panel fuse box for 10 seconds or more to clear memory in ECT ECU.
- Disconnect negative battery cable (memory for electronic components will also be canceled).

DIAGNOSTIC TESTS

When trouble shooting transmission, first check for stored trouble codes and repair as necessary. If no trouble codes exist, perform manual shift test to determine if problem area is in electrical circuits or a mechanical transmission problem. See MANUAL SHIFT TEST.

3-1720

AUTOMATIC TRANSMISSIONS
Toyota Previa A-340E & A-340F – Electronic Controls (Cont.)

Circuit	Terminal No.	Connector No.
+B	12	E9
BATT	2	E9
STP	14	E9
E$_1$	24	E8
IDL	11	E6
L	10	E9
NSW	22	E9
OD$_1$	18	E9
OD$_2$	9	E9
THO	9	E7
R	20	E9

ECT ECU TERMINAL/CIRCUIT IDENTIFICATION

Circuit	Terminal No.	Connector No.
S$_L$	8	E8
S$_1$	10	E8
S$_2$	9	E8
SP$_1$	8	E9
SP$_2$	16	E6
THW	4	E6
TE$_1$	7	E6
VTA	10	E6
2	21	E9
OIL.W	19	E9

ECT ECU TERMINAL/CIRCUIT IDENTIFICATION (Cont.)

96G29625

Courtesy of Toyota Motor Sales, U.S.A., Inc.

Fig. 6: Identifying ECT ECU Harness Connector Terminals (Component Connector View)

DTC P0500:
NO. 1 VEHICLE SPEED SENSOR FAULT (1996)

Circuit Description – No. 1 Vehicle Speed Sensor (VSS), driven by transmission output shaft, outputs a pulse signal to combination meter. Combination meter converts signal to a more precise waveform for ECT ECU. DTC is set when ECT ECU does not detect any signal while vehicle is in motion. Possible causes are:
- Open or short in vehicle speed sensor circuit.
- No. 1 VSS failure.
- Combination meter malfunction.
- ECT ECU malfunction.

Diagnosis & Repair Procedure – **1)** Test drive vehicle and determine if speedometer is functioning properly. If speedometer is okay, go to next step. If speedometer is not functioning, go to step **3)**.
2) Access ECT ECU harness connector. Disconnect ECT ECU connector E9. *See Figs. 1 and 6.* Using ohmmeter, check continuity between terminal SP$_1$ and ground. *See Fig. 6.* If continuity exists, check and repair circuit for short to ground. If continuity does not exist, raise and support vehicle.
3) Shift transmission into Neutral. Turn ignition on. Using DVOM, measure voltage between terminal SP$_1$ and ground while rotating rear wheel. If voltage is not 4.5-5.5 volts, check and repair open circuit between combination meter and ECT ECU. See WIRING DIAGRAM. If voltage is as specified, replace ECT ECU and retest.

DTC P0710: ATF TEMPERATURE SENSOR (1996)

Circuit Description – ATF temperature sensor converts fluid temperature into a resistance value which is input into ECT ECU. Control which changes shift point according to signal from ATF temperature sensor has been adopted in order to prevent ATF temperature from becoming excessive. Possible causes are:
- Open or short in ATF temperature sensor circuit.
- ATF temperature sensor.
- ECT ECU malfunction.

Diagnosis & Repair Procedure – 1) Remove ATF temperature sensor from transmission. Measure resistance between sensor terminals at 68°F (20°C). Resistance should be about 12,200 ohms. Measure resistance between sensor terminals at 230°F (110°C). Resistance should be about 770 ohms.
2) If resistance is as specified, check and repair circuit as needed. If circuit is okay, replace ECT ECU and retest. If resistance is not as specified, replace ATF temperature sensor.

DTC P0720:
NO. 1 VEHICLE SPEED SENSOR FAULT (1995)

Circuit Description – No. 1 Vehicle Speed Sensor (VSS), driven by transmission output shaft, outputs a pulse signal to combination meter. Combination meter converts signal to a more precise waveform for ECT ECU. DTC is set when ECT ECU does not detect any signal while vehicle is in motion. Possible causes are:
- Open or short in vehicle speed sensor circuit.
- No. 1 VSS failure.
- Combination meter malfunction.
- ECT ECU malfunction.

Diagnosis & Repair Procedure – 1) Disconnect combination meter and cruise control ECU harness connectors. Turn ignition on. Using a DVOM, measure voltage between terminal SP$_1$ and ground. If 4-6 volts is present, go to next step. If 4-6 volts is not present, go to step **4)**.
2) Raise and support vehicle. Shift transmission into Neutral. Reconnect combination meter harness connector. Remove combination meter. Turn ignition on. Using DVOM, measure voltage between terminal No. 8 of combination meter connector and ground. *See Fig. 7.* Rotate rear wheel.
3) If voltage is 4-6 volts and remains unchanged, go to step **6)**. If voltage is not as specified, turn ignition off. Disconnect ECT ECU harness connector. *See Fig. 1.* Using ohmmeter, check continuity between combination meter harness connector terminal No. 8 and ECT ECU terminal SP$_1$. *See Figs. 6 and 7.* If continuity exists, go to next step. If continuity does not exist, check and repair circuit as needed.

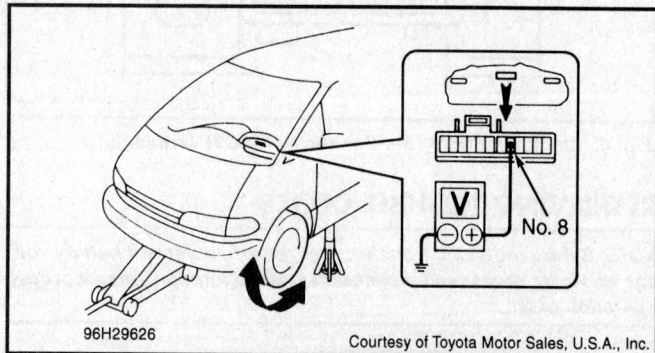

96H29626

Courtesy of Toyota Motor Sales, U.S.A., Inc.

Fig. 7: Identifying Combination Meter Harness Connector

AUTOMATIC TRANSMISSIONS
Toyota Previa A-340E & A-340F — Electronic Controls (Cont.)

3-1721

4) Access ECT ECU harness connector. Disconnect ECT ECU connector E9. *See Figs. 1 and 6.* Using ohmmeter, check continuity between terminal SP$_1$ and ground. *See Fig. 6.*
5) If continuity exists, replace ECT ECU and retest. If continuity does not exist, check and repair circuit for short to ground between ECT ECU, cruise control ECU and combination meter. Repair as necessary.
6) Check continuity of 2 circuits between combination meter and VSS. See WIRING DIAGRAM. If continuity does not exist, check and repair circuit(s) as needed. If continuity exists, check VSS. See NO.1 VEHICLE SPEED SENSOR under COMPONENT TESTS. Replace as needed.

DTC P0750 & P0755: NO. 1 & NO. 2 SOLENOID FAULT

Circuit Description – ECT ECU uses signal from vehicle speed sensor to determine actual gear position. ECT ECU compares actual gear with shift schedule in memory to detect mechanical trouble of shift solenoid and/or valve body. DTC is set if during normal driving gear required by ECT ECU does not match actual gear after 2 trips have been completed. Possible causes are:
- No. 1 and/or No. 2 solenoid is stuck open or closed.
- Valve body is clogged or valve(s) is stuck.

Diagnosis & Repair Procedure – Remove and inspect operation of solenoids. See SOLENOIDS under COMPONENT TESTS. If solenoids are okay, inspect valve body. See TOYOTA A-340 & A-350 SERIES overhaul article.

DTC P0753 & P0758: NO. 1 & NO. 2 SOLENOID CIRCUIT

Circuit Description – Shifting is performed in combination with ON and OFF position of shift solenoids controlled by ECT ECU. If an open or short circuit occurs in either shift solenoid, ECT ECU reverts to fail-safe mode. *See Figs. 2 and 3.* DTC(s) are output when a open or short circuit occurs. Possible causes are:
- No. 1 and/or No. 2 solenoid circuit.
- No. 1 and/or No. 2 solenoid.
- ECT ECU malfunction.

Diagnosis & Repair Procedure – **1)** Ensure ignition is off. Access ECT ECU. *See Fig. 1.* Backprobing ECT ECU harness connector with ohmmeter, measure resistance between terminal S$_1$ and/or S$_2$ and ground. *See Fig. 6.* If resistance is 10-16 ohms, replace ECT ECU and retest. If resistance is not within specification, go to next step.
2) Disconnect solenoid harness connector at transmission. Check continuity between terminal S$_1$ of transmission harness connector and corresponding terminal of ECT ECU harness connector. *See Figs. 6 and 8.*
3) Check continuity between terminal S$_2$ of transmission harness connector and corresponding terminal of ECT ECU harness connector. If continuity exists for both circuits, go to next step. If continuity does not exist for either circuit, check and repair circuit(s) as needed.
4) Measure resistance between transmission solenoid harness connector terminals S$_1$ and/or S$_2$, and ground. *See Fig. 8.* If resistance is 10-16 ohms, replace solenoid. If resistance is not as specified, replace transmission sub-harness as needed.

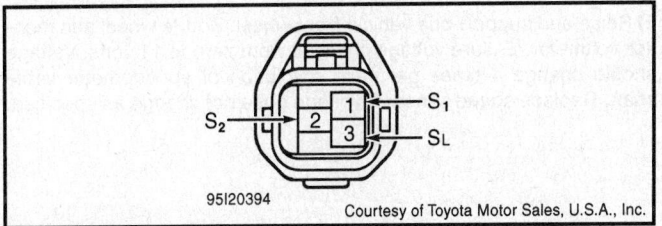

S$_2$ ▭ | 2 | 1 | ▯ — S$_1$
| 3 | — S$_L$

95l20394

Courtesy of Toyota Motor Sales, U.S.A., Inc.

Fig. 8: Identifying Transmission Solenoid Harness Connector Terminals

DTC P0770: LOCK-UP/SL SOLENOID

Circuit Description – ECT ECU uses signals from throttle position sensor, air flow meter and crankshaft position sensor to monitor engagement of Torque Converter Clutch (TCC). ECT ECU compares engagement condition of TCC with lock-up schedule in memory to detect mechanical trouble of solenoid, valve body and torque converter. DTC is set when TCC lock-up does not occur at appropriate speed (50 MPH), or lock-up does not release at appropriate speed. Possible causes are:
- Lock-up solenoid is stuck open or closed.
- Valve body clogged or valve stuck.
- TCC malfunction.

Diagnosis & Repair Procedure – Remove and inspect operation of solenoid. See SOLENOIDS under COMPONENT TESTS. If solenoid is okay, inspect valve body. See TOYOTA A-340 & A-350 SERIES overhaul article.

DTC P0773: LOCK-UP/SL SOLENOID CIRCUIT

Circuit Description – Lock-up solenoid is turned on and off by signals from ECT ECU to control hydraulic pressure affecting lock-up relay valve. Lock-up relay valve controls operation of Torque Converter Clutch (TCC). If ECT ECU detects a malfunction, fail-safe function is enabled. *See Figs. 2 and 3.* DTC is output when a open or short circuit occurs. Possible causes are:
- Lock-up solenoid open or short circuit.
- Lock-up solenoid malfunction.
- ECT ECU malfunction.

Diagnosis & Repair Procedure – **1)** Ensure ignition is off. Access ECT ECU. *See Fig. 1.* Disconnect appropriate ECT ECU harness connector. Backprobing ECT ECU harness connector with ohmmeter, measure resistance between terminal S$_L$ and ground. If resistance is 8-100 k/ohms, replace ECT ECU and retest. If resistance is not within specification, go to next step.
2) Disconnect solenoid harness connector at transmission. Check continuity between terminal S$_L$ of transmission harness connector and corresponding terminal of ECT ECU harness connector. *See Figs. 6 and 8.*
3) If continuity does not exist, check and repair circuit as needed. If continuity exists, measure resistance between transmission connector terminals S$_L$, and ground. *See Fig. 8.* If resistance is 10-16 ohms, replace solenoid. If resistance is not as specified, replace transmission sub-harness as needed.

DTC P1700: NO. 2 VEHICLE SPEED SENSOR FAULT

Circuit Description – Sensor detects rotation speed of transmission output shaft. ECT ECU controls shift points by comparing throttle position sensor signal and vehicle speed. DTC is output when no signal is detected after 4 pulses of No. 1 speed sensor. Possible causes are:
- Sensor open or short circuit.
- Sensor malfunction.
- ECT ECU malfunction.

Diagnosis & Repair Procedure – **1)** Ensure ignition is off. Access ECT ECU. *See Fig. 1.* Raise and support vehicle. Shift transmission into Neutral. Rotate rear wheel. Backprobing ECT ECU harness connector with ohmmeter, measure resistance between terminal SP$_2$ and ground terminal E$_1$. Resistance should pulse between zero ohms and infinite ohms. If resistance is within specification, replace ECT ECU. If resistance is not within specification, go to next step.
2) Remove No. 2 speed sensor from extension housing of transmission. Measure resistance between sensor terminals. Resistance should pulse between zero ohms and infinite ohms when a magnet is put close to tip of speed sensor. *See Fig. 9.* If resistance is not as specified, replace sensor. If resistance is as specified, check and repair circuits between sensor and ECT ECU.

3-1722

AUTOMATIC TRANSMISSIONS
Toyota Previa A-340E & A-340F — Electronic Controls (Cont.)

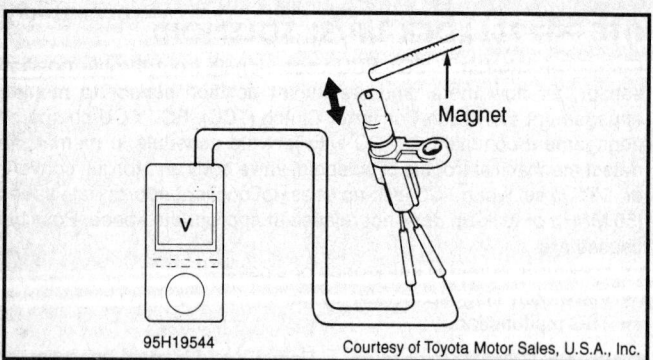

95H19544   Courtesy of Toyota Motor Sales, U.S.A., Inc.

Fig. 9: Testing No. 2 Speed Sensor

DTC P1780: PARK/NEUTRAL POSITION (PNP) SWITCH

Circuit Description – PNP switch verifies shift lever position and sends signals to ECT ECU. If no signal is received from PNP switch, ECT ECU defaults to drive ("D") position. DTC is output when ECT ECU detects 2 or more circuits are on. Also vehicle speed has to be above 44 MPH for more than 30 seconds with engine RPM at 1200-2500. Possible causes are:

- Short in PNP switch circuit.
- PNP switch malfunction.
- ECT ECU malfunction.

Diagnosis & Repair Procedure – **1)** Turn ignition on. Access ECT ECU. Using DVOM, measure voltage at terminals NSW, "R", "2" and "L" of ECT ECU harness connector between terminal and body ground with gear selector in each shift position. *See Fig. 6.*

2) Ensure 7.5-14 volts is present at NSW terminal at ECT ECU harness connector in all shift positions. Ensure 7.5-14 volts is present at "R", "2" and "L" terminals at ECT ECU harness connector with gear selector in "R", "2" and "L" position. If voltage is not as specified, check park/neutral position switch. See PARK/NEUTRAL POSITION (PNP) SWITCH under COMPONENT TESTS. If switch is okay, check and repair circuit(s) between PNP switch and ECT ECU. See WIRING DIAGRAM.

MANUAL SHIFT TEST

NOTE: Perform manual shift test if no trouble codes exist. Manual shift test determines if problem area is in electrical circuits or a mechanical transmission problem.

1) With ignition off, disconnect electrical connector for solenoids from rear of transmission. Road test vehicle and ensure transmission gear changes corresponds with shift lever position. See GEAR APPLICATION table.

2) If abnormality exists, a mechanical transmission problem exists. Turn ignition off. Reconnect electrical connector. Clear trouble codes from ECT ECU memory, as disconnecting electrical connector may set a trouble code. See CLEARING TROUBLE CODES under SELF-DIAGNOSTIC SYSTEM.

GEAR APPLICATION

Shift Lever Position	Gear
"D"	Overdrive
"2"	3rd
"L"	1st
"R"	Reverse
"P"	Park

CIRCUIT TESTS

BRAKELIGHT SIGNAL

1) Inspect operation of brakelights. Repair as needed. If switch is suspect, see BRAKELIGHT SWITCH under COMPONENT TESTS. If circuit is suspect, diagnose and repair as necessary. See WIRING DIAGRAM.

2) Connect scan tool to DLC3. *See Figs. 1 and 4.* Turn ignition on. Read STP signal while depressing and releasing brake pedal. Ensure signal cycles when pressing brake pedal. If signal cycles, replace ECT ECU. If signal does not cycle, check and repair circuit between brakelight switch and ECT ECU. If circuit is okay, replace ECT ECU.

OVERDRIVE CANCEL SIGNAL

1) Access ECT ECU. *See Fig. 1.* Turn ignition on. Backprobe ECT ECU harness connector with DVOM. Measure voltage between terminal OD, of ECT ECU harness connector and ground. *See Fig. 6.* If voltage is 4-6 volts, substitute known good ECT ECU and retest. If voltage is not 4-6 volts, go to next step.

2) Turn ignition off. Disconnect cruise control ECU harness connector. *See Fig. 1.* Turn ignition on. Measure voltage between terminal OD and ground. *See Fig. 10.* If 4-6 volts is present, replace cruise control ECU and retest. If 4-6 volts is not present, inspect and repair circuit between cruise control ECU and ECT ECU.

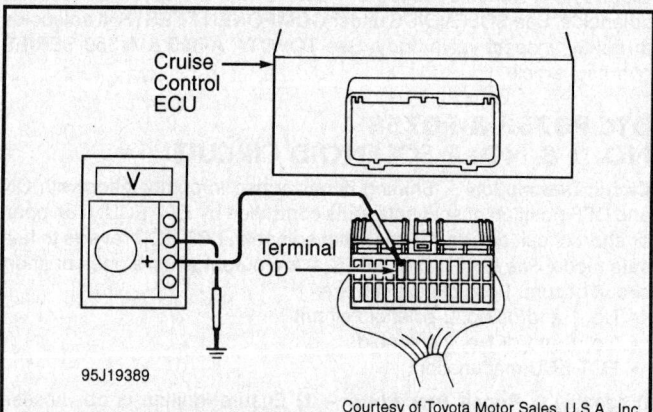

95J19389   Courtesy of Toyota Motor Sales, U.S.A., Inc.

Fig. 10: Identifying Cruise Control ECU Terminals

ECT ECU VOLTAGES

Access ECT ECU. *See Fig. 1.* Turn ignition on. Using voltmeter, backprobe ECT ECU harness connector. Check voltage between selected terminal and E, terminal. Voltage should be as specified. *See Fig. 11.*

COMPONENT TESTS

NO. 1 VEHICLE SPEED SENSOR (VSS)

1) Disconnect electrical connector from No. 1 VSS, located on extension housing of transmission. *See Fig. 1.* Connect positive battery lead to terminal No. 1 and negative lead to terminal No. 2. Connect positive lead of voltmeter to terminal No. 3 and negative lead to terminal No. 2. *See Fig. 12.*

2) Raise and support one vehicle front wheel. Rotate wheel and monitor voltmeter. Ensure voltage changes from zero to 11 volts. Voltage should change 4 times per each revolution of speedometer cable shaft. Replace speed sensor if voltage dose not change as specified.

AUTOMATIC TRANSMISSIONS
Toyota Previa A-340E & A-340F — Electronic Controls (Cont.)

3-1723

	Terminal ID.	Function/Description	Voltage Value (DC Volts Unless Otherwise Specified)
Brown/White	S_1	No. 1 Solenoid	9-14 Volts With KOEO [1]
Brown/Yellow	S_2	No. 2 Solenoid	1.5 Volt Or Less With KOEO [1]
Green/Yellow	S_L	Lock-Up Solenoid	1.5 Volt Or Less With KOEO [1]
Green/White	STP	Brakelight Switch Signal	9-14 Volts With Pedal Depressed
Blue	THW	Coolant Temperature Sensor Signal	1.5 Volts Or Less @ 176°F (80°C)
Blue/Yellow	IDL	Closed Throttle Sensor Signal	1.5 Volts Or Less With Throttle Closed, KOEO [1]
Yellow/Red	VTA	Throttle Position Sensor Output Signal	3.2-4.9 Volts With Throttle Fully Open
Violet/Yellow	OD_1	OD Output To Cruise Control ECU	9-14 Volts With KOEO [1]
Blue/White	OD_2	Overdrive Switch Signal	9-14 Volts With Switch On
Violet/White	SP_1	No. 1 Vehicle Speed Sensor Signal	1.5 Volt Or Less With ECU Unplugged [2] (Car Parked)
Black/White	NSW	Ignition Switch (ST1) Signal	9-14 Volts In "P" Or "N", KOEO [1]
Black/Red	2	Park/Neutral Position Switch "2" Signal	9-14 Volts In "2", KOEO [1]
Black/Blue	L	Park/Neutral Position Switch "L" Signal	9-14 Volts In "L", KOEO [1]
Black/Orange	+B	EFI Main Relay Power Supply	9-14 Volts With KOEO [1]
White/Red	BATT	Power Supply Voltage	9-14 Volts (Constant)
Brown/White	SP_2	No. 2 Vehicle Speed Sensor	1.5 Volt Or Less With KOEO [1]
Black/Blue	THO	ATF Temperature Sensor	1.5 Volt Or Less With KOEO [1]
Black	OIL.W	ATF Temperature Sensor (Light On)	3.0 Volts Or Less With KOEO [1]
Brown	E_1	Ground	Not Applicable

[1] – Key On, Engine Off.
[2] – Disconnect cruise control ECU. See Fig. 1.

96129627

Courtesy of Toyota Motor Sales, U.S.A., Inc.

Fig. 11: ECT ECU Pin Voltage Table

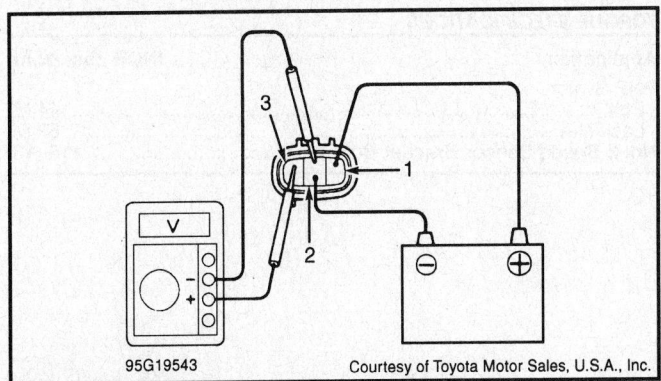

95G19543   Courtesy of Toyota Motor Sales, U.S.A., Inc.

Fig. 12: Checking No. 1 Vehicle Speed Sensor (VSS)

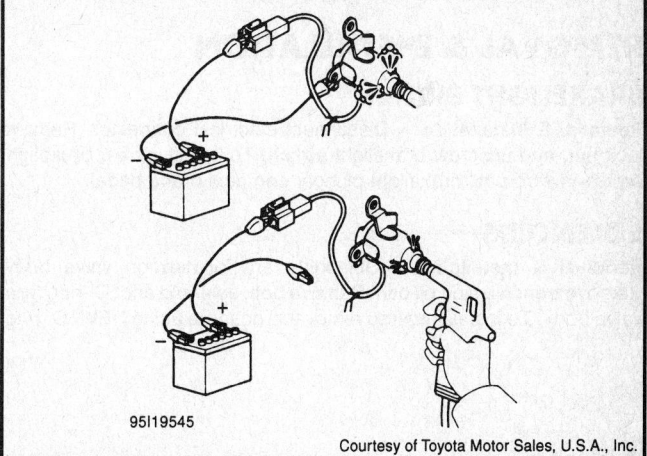

95I19545   Courtesy of Toyota Motor Sales, U.S.A., Inc.

Fig. 13: Checking Solenoids

SOLENOIDS

1) To check solenoid seals, remove suspect solenoid. Connect battery voltage to solenoid. Apply 71 psi (5 kg/cm²) to solenoid with battery voltage connected. See Fig. 13.
2) With battery voltage applied, air should pass through solenoid. Disconnect voltage to solenoid. Ensure air does not pass through solenoid. Replace solenoid if defective.

PARK/NEUTRAL POSITION (PNP) SWITCH

Disconnect harness connector at park/neutral position switch. Switch is located on side of transmission. Using ohmmeter, check for continuity between specified terminals in accordance with shift lever position. See Fig. 14. Replace PNP switch if defective.

OVERDRIVE (OD) SWITCH

Disconnect electrical connector from OD switch, located on shift lever. Using ohmmeter, ensure continuity exists between terminals with switch released (OFF position). Ensure no continuity exists with switch depressed (ON position). Replace switch if defective.

BRAKELIGHT SWITCH

Disconnect electrical connector from brakelight switch, located near brake pedal. Using ohmmeter, ensure continuity exists between switch terminals No. 1 and 2 with brake pedal depressed. Continuity should exist between terminals No. 3 and 4 with pedal released. See Fig. 15.

3-1724

AUTOMATIC TRANSMISSIONS
Toyota Previa A-340E & A-340F – Electronic Controls (Cont.)

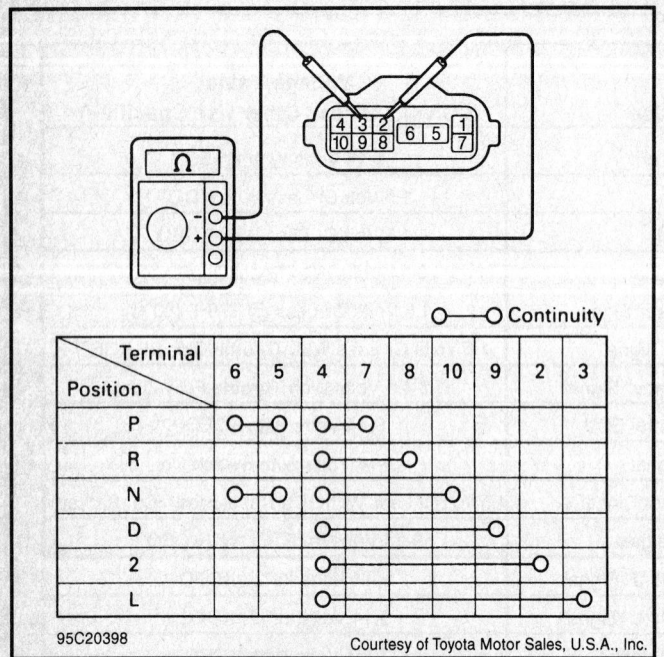

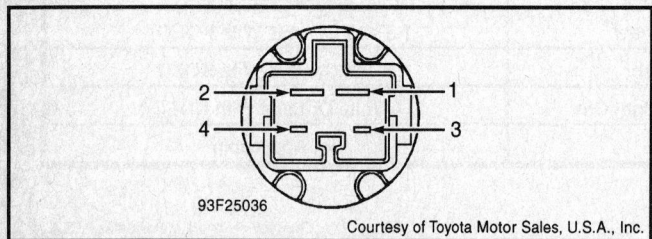

Terminal / Position	6	5	4	7	8	10	9	2	3
P	O—O		O—O						
R			O	O					
N	O—O		O			O			
D			O				O		
2			O					O	
L			O						O

O—O Continuity

95C20398   Courtesy of Toyota Motor Sales, U.S.A., Inc.

Fig. 14: Testing Park/Neutral Position (PNP) Switch

93F25036   Courtesy of Toyota Motor Sales, U.S.A., Inc.

Fig. 15: Identifying Brakelight Switch Terminals

REMOVAL & INSTALLATION

BRAKELIGHT SWITCH

Removal & Installation – Disconnect electrical connector. Remove lock nut, and unscrew brakelight switch. To install, screw brakelight switch inward until brakelight plunger contacts brake pedal.

SOLENOIDS

Removal & Installation – Solenoids are located on valve body. Remove transmission oil pan. Remove bolt, solenoid and "O" ring from valve body. To install, reverse removal procedure using NEW "O" ring.

PARK/NEUTRAL POSITION (PNP) SWITCH

Removal – Park/Neutral Position (PNP) switch is located on side of transmission. Remove lock nut, washer and manual lever from control shaft. Bend up tabs on lock washer. Remove lock nut, lock washer and seal from control shaft. Remove retaining bolts and switch.

Installation – **1)** Install switch on control shaft. Loosely install switch retaining bolts. Install seal and lock washer. Install lock nut and tighten to specification. See TORQUE SPECIFICATIONS. Bend tabs on lock washer over against lock nut.

2) Ensure parking brake is applied. Temporarily install manual lever on control shaft. Place shift lever in Neutral. Remove manual lever. Rotate park/neutral position switch and align neutral basic line on PNP switch with groove. See Fig. 16. Hold PNP switch in this position. Tighten retaining bolts to specification. To install remaining components, reverse removal procedure.

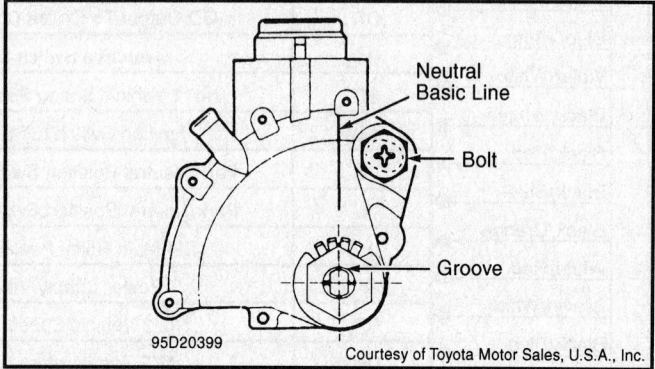

95D20399   Courtesy of Toyota Motor Sales, U.S.A., Inc.

Fig. 16: Installing PNP Switch

OVERDRIVE (OD) SWITCH

Overdrive (OD) switch is mounted on the shift lever. See Fig. 1. Replacement information not available from manufacturer.

TORQUE SPECIFICATIONS
TORQUE SPECIFICATIONS

Application	INCH Lbs. (N.m)
PNP Switch	
Bolt	44 (5)
Lock Nut	62 (7)
No. 2 Speed Sensor Bracket Bolt	115 (13)

AUTOMATIC TRANSMISSIONS
Toyota Previa A-340E & A-340F — Electronic Controls (Cont.)

3-1725

WIRING DIAGRAMS

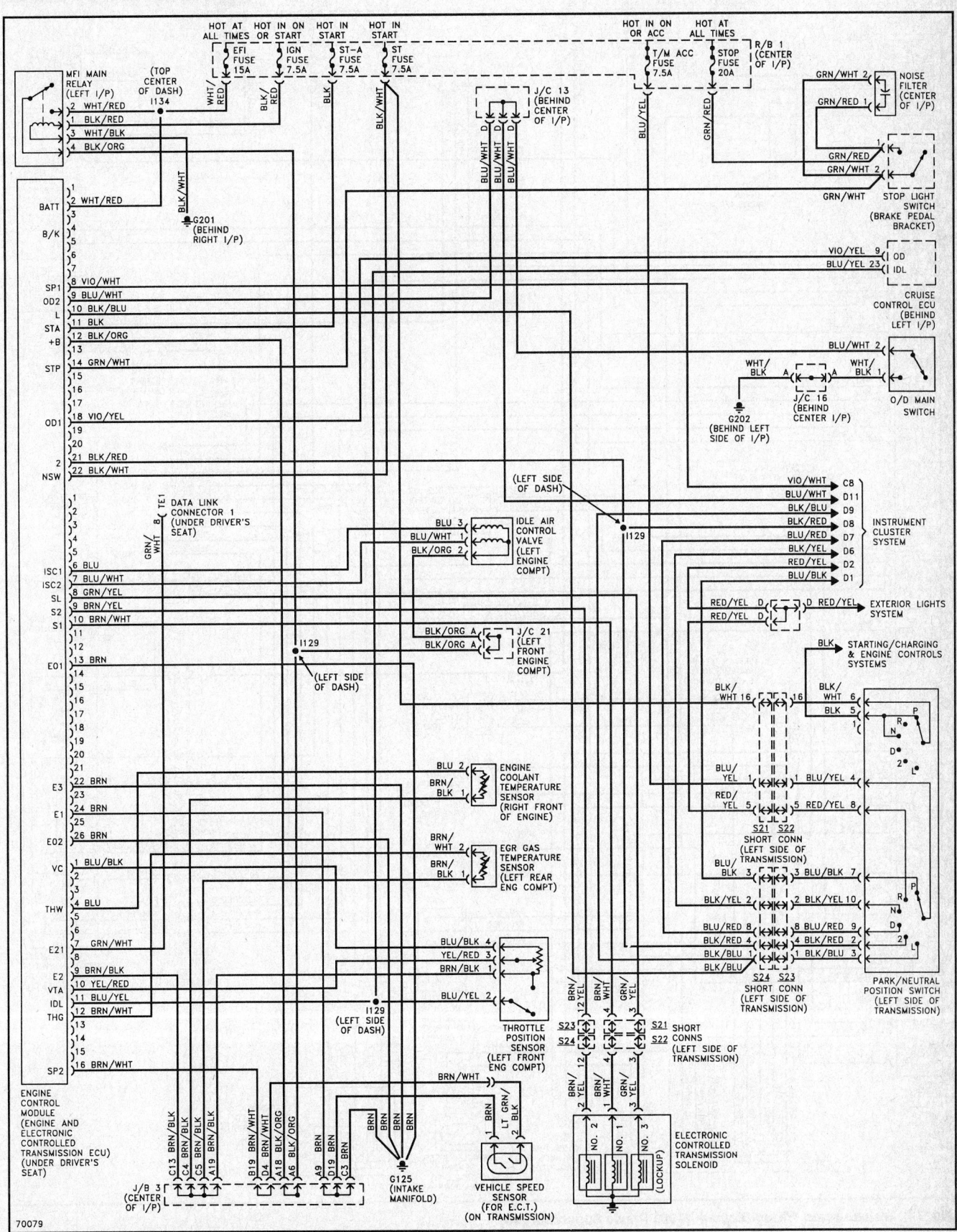

Fig. 17: Transmission Wiring Diagram (1995 Previa Supercharged)

70079

3-1726

AUTOMATIC TRANSMISSIONS
Toyota Previa A-340E & A-340F – Electronic Controls (Cont.)

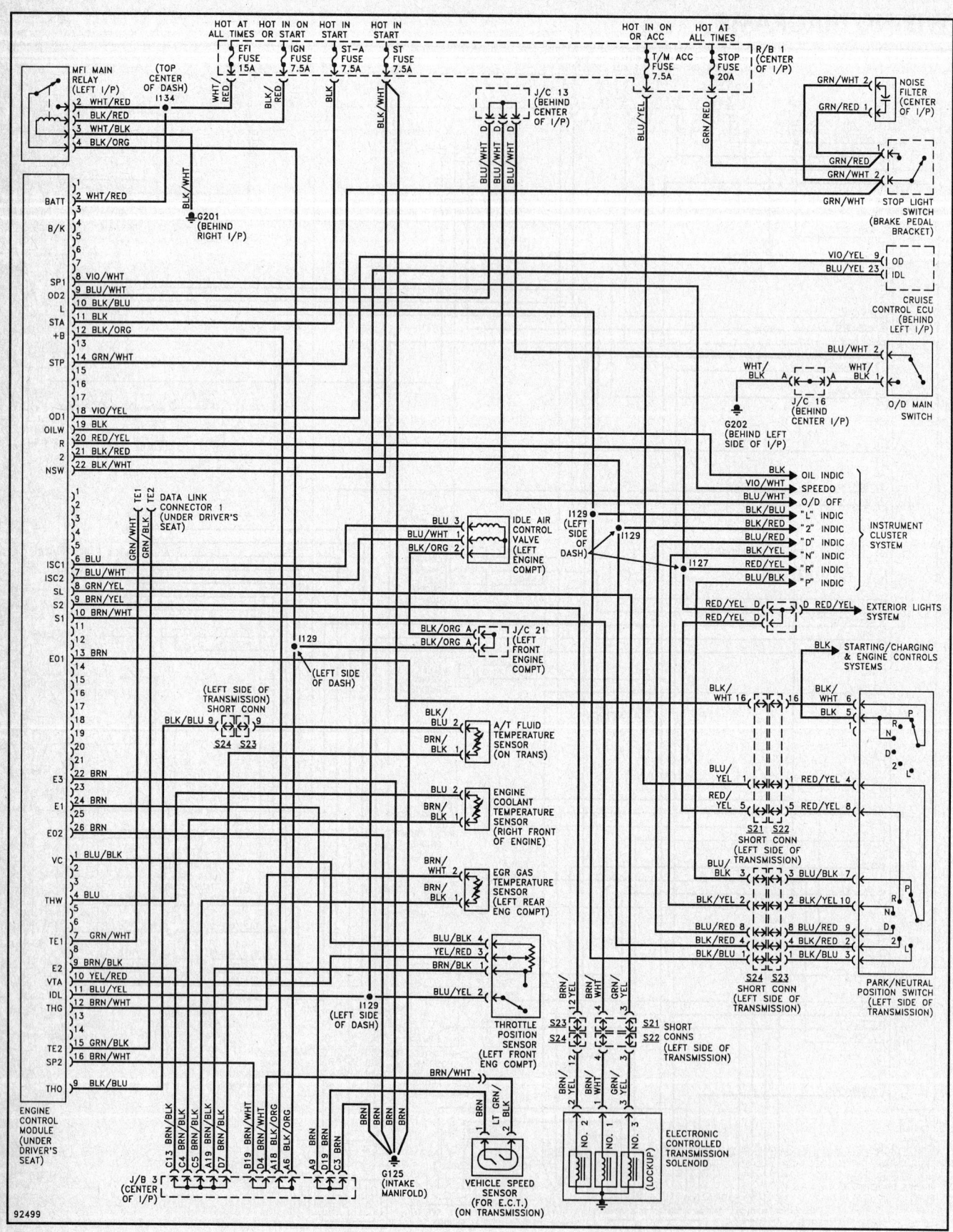

Fig. 18: *Transmission Wiring Diagram (1996 Previa Supercharged)*

92499

Lexus: LX450
Toyota: Land Cruiser

APPLICATION

APPLICATION

Vehicle	Transmission Model
Land Cruiser	A-343F
LX450 (1996)	A-343F

CAUTION: Vehicles are equipped with a Supplemental Restraint System (SRS). When servicing vehicles, use care to avoid accidental air bag deployment. All SRS electrical connections and wiring harness are covered with Yellow insulation. SRS-related components are located in steering column, center console, instrument panel and lower panel of instrument panel. DO NOT use electrical test equipment on these circuits. It may be necessary to deactivate SRS before servicing components. See AIR BAG SERVICING article in APPLICATIONS & IDENTIFICATION section.

DESCRIPTION

The A-343F automatic transmission is electronically controlled. Transmission shifting and torque converter lock-up are controlled by an Electronic Controlled Transmission (ECT) Electronic Control Unit (ECU). Control unit is a combined engine control and transmission control unit and is referred to as the ECT ECU. *See Figs. 1 and 2.*

ECT ECU receives information from various input devices and uses this information to control No. 1 and No. 2 solenoids on transmission valve body for transmission shifting and lock-up solenoid (also called SL solenoid) for torque converter lock-up.

A pattern select switch is located near shift lever on center console. Pattern select switch contains a POWER (PWR) and a NORMAL operating position. When pattern select switch is depressed (PWR position), transmission upshifts and downshifts will occur at a higher vehicle speed than with switch released. An indicator light on instrument panel indicates pattern select switch is in PWR (on) position.

Pattern select switch also includes a 2nd start switch. When switch is activated, transmission will start out in 2nd gear. If gear selector is in "D" position, transmission will shift up through 3rd gear to OD. If transmission is in 2nd gear, transmission is held in 2nd gear.

An Overdrive (OD) switch is mounted on shift lever. *See Figs. 1 and 2.* When OD switch is depressed to ON position, transmission will shift into 4th gear when shift lever is in "D" position, and OD OFF light on instrument panel will go off. When OD switch is released to OFF position, transmission will shift into 3rd gear, and OD OFF light will come on.

Transmission is equipped with a shift lock and key lock system. Shift lock system prevents shift lever from being moved from Park unless brake pedal is depressed. In case of a malfunction, shift lever can be released by depressing shift lock override button, located near shift lever. Key lock system prevents ignition key from being moved from ACC to LOCK position on ignition switch unless shift lever is in Park. For more information on shift lock and key lock system, see TOYOTA SHIFT LOCK SYSTEM article.

OPERATION

ECT ECU

ECT ECU receives information from various input devices and uses this information to control No. 1 and No. 2 solenoids on transmission valve body for transmission shifting and lock-up solenoid for torque converter lock-up. ECT ECU contains a self-diagnostic system, which will store a Diagnostic Trouble Code (DTC) if a failure or problem exists in the electronic control system. Trouble code can be retrieved to determine problem area. See SELF-DIAGNOSTIC SYSTEM. Note location of ECT ECU. *See Figs. 1 and 2.*

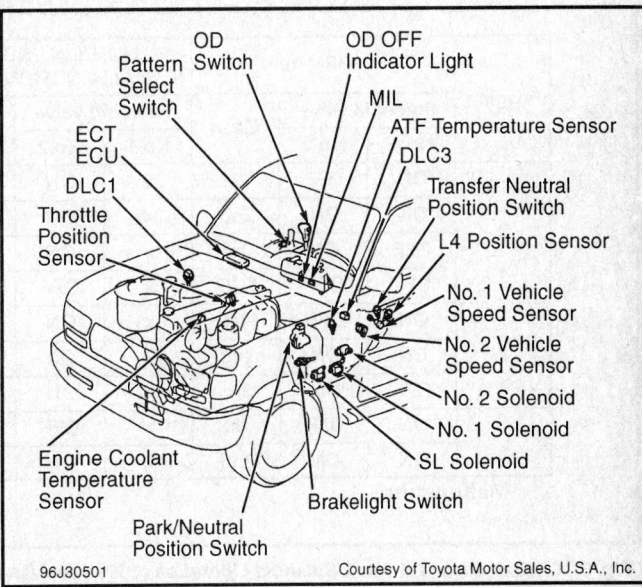

Fig. 1: Identifying Input & Output Devices (Land Cruiser)

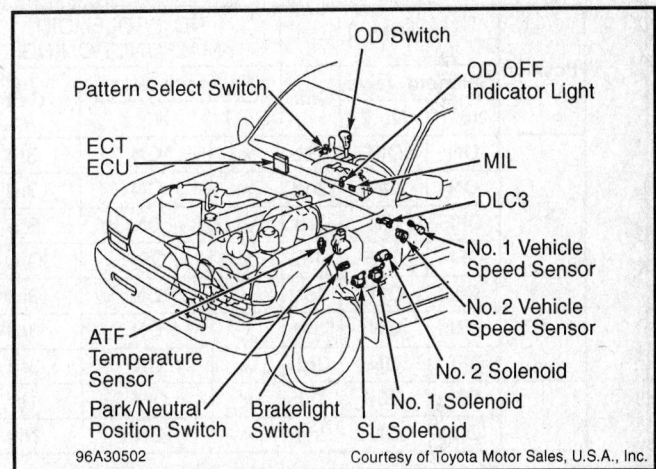

Fig. 2: Identifying Input & Output Devices (LX450)

ECT ECU INPUT DEVICES

Pattern Select Switch Signal – Pattern select switch delivers an input signal to ECT ECU to indicate transmission shift points selected by vehicle operator. Pattern select switch is located near shift lever on center console. *See Figs. 1 and 2.*

Park/Neutral Position (PNP) Switch Signal – PNP switch delivers an input signal to ECT ECU indicating shift lever position. Switch is located on side of transmission. *See Figs. 1 and 2.*

Throttle Position (TP) Sensor Signal – TP sensor delivers an input signal to ECT ECU indicating throttle position. TP sensor is located on side of throttle body. *See Figs. 1 and 2.*

Vehicle Speed Sensor Signal (VSS) – Vehicle speed signal is delivered to ECT ECU by No. 1 and No. 2 vehicle speed sensors. *See Figs. 1 and 2.* No. 1 vehicle speed sensor is driven by gear on transmission output shaft, and indicates actual vehicle speed. No. 2 vehicle speed sensor detects transmission output shaft RPM. Gear shift point and lock-up timing are controlled by ECT ECU based on signals from No. 2 vehicle speed sensor and throttle position sensor.

Brakelight Switch Signal – Brakelight switch delivers input signal to ECT ECU, indicating vehicle braking. Brakelight switch is located on brake pedal support.

OD Switch Signal – OD switch provides an input signal to ECT ECU to indicate when overdrive is selected by vehicle operator. OD switch is mounted on shift lever. *See Figs. 1 and 2.*

Position	NORMAL			NO.1 SOLENOID MALFUNCTIONING			NO.2 SOLENOID MALFUNCTIONING			BOTH SOLENOIDS MALFUNCTIONING
	Solenoid valve		Gear	Solenoid valve		Gear	Solenoid valve		Gear	Gear when shift selector is manually operated
	No.1	No.2		No.1	No.2		No.1	No.2		
D	ON	OFF	1st	x	ON	3rd	ON	x	1st	O/D
	ON	ON	2nd	x	ON	3rd	OFF	x	O/D	O/D
	OFF	ON	3rd	x	ON	3rd	OFF	x	O/D	O/D
	OFF	OFF	O/D	x	OFF	O/D	OFF	x	O/D	O/D
2	ON	OFF	1st	x	ON	3rd	ON	x	1st	O/D
	ON	ON	2nd	x	ON	3rd	OFF	x	O/D	O/D
	OFF	ON	3rd	x	ON	3rd	OFF	x	O/D	O/D
L	ON	OFF	1st	x	OFF	1st	ON	x	1st	1st
	ON	ON	2nd	x	ON	2nd	ON	x	1st	1st

x: Malfunctions

95C20364

Courtesy of Toyota Motor Sales, U.S.A., Inc.

Fig. 3: Checking No. 1 & No. 2 Solenoid Operation (1995 Land Cruiser)

Position	NORMAL			NO.1 SOLENOID MALFUNCTIONING			NO.2 SOLENOID MALFUNCTIONING			BOTH SOLENOIDS MALFUNCTIONING
	Solenoid valve		Gear	Solenoid valve		Gear	Solenoid valve		Gear	Gear when shift selector is manually operated
	No.1	No.2		No.1	No.2		No.1	No.2		
D	ON	OFF	1st	×	ON	3rd	ON	×	1st	O/D
	ON	ON	2nd	×	ON	3rd	OFF	×	O/D	O/D
	OFF	ON	3rd	×	ON	3rd	OFF	×	O/D	O/D
	OFF	OFF	O/D	×	OFF	O/D	OFF	×	O/D	O/D
2	ON	OFF	1st	×	ON	3rd	ON	×	1st	3rd
	ON	ON	2nd	×	ON	3rd	OFF	×	3rd	3rd
	OFF	ON	3rd	×	ON	3rd	OFF	×	3rd	3rd
L	ON	OFF	1st	×	OFF	1st	ON	×	1st	1st
	ON	ON	2nd	×	ON	2nd	ON	×	1st	1st

×: Malfunctions

96F21175

Courtesy of Toyota Motor Sales, U.S.A., Inc.

Fig. 4: Checking No. 1 & No. 2 Solenoid Operation (1996 Land Cruiser & LX450)

Engine Coolant Temperature (ECT) Sensor Signal – Coolant temperature sensor delivers input signal to ECT ECU, indicating engine coolant temperature. Coolant temperature sensor is located in coolant passage on left side of cylinder head, above oil filter (connector with Brown/Black and Red/White wires). See Fig. 1.

ATF Temperature Sensor – Sensor delivers an input signal to ECT ECU to indicate fluid temperature. Sensor converts fluid temperature into a resistance value. Sensor is located on transmission valve body. See Fig. 1.

2nd Start Switch – When switch is activated, input signal is delivered to ECT ECU. ECT ECU controls solenoids to ensure transmission will start out in 2nd gear. The 2nd start switch is included in pattern select switch.

Transfer Neutral Position Switch – Switch delivers an input signal to ECT ECU to indicate transfer case is in Neutral. Sensor is located on transfer case rear extension housing. See Fig. 1.

L4 Position Sensor – Sensor delivers an input signal to ECT ECU to indicate transfer case is in low gear. Sensor is located on transfer case extension housing. See Fig. 1.

Cruise Control Electronic Control Unit (ECU) – Cruise control ECU delivers an input signal to control overdrive operation in accordance with vehicle speed when cruise control is operating. Cruise control ECU is located at left side of combination meter, behind instrument panel on Land Cruiser, or behind instrument panel fuse box on LX450.

ECT ECU OUTPUT DEVICES

No. 1 & No. 2 Solenoids – ECT ECU controls transmission shifting by delivering an output signal to operate proper solenoid. Solenoids are located on transmission valve body. See Figs. 1 and 2. Solenoids are operated in accordance with shift lever position. If a solenoid malfunctions, fail-safe gear may be selected. See Figs. 3 and 4.

NOTE: *In some gears, ECT ECU provides a fail-safe system which will place transmission in designated gear depending on solenoid failure.*

Lock-Up Solenoid – ECT ECU controls torque converter lock-up by delivering an output signal to lock-up solenoid. Lock-up solenoid (also called SL solenoid) is activated when shift lever is in "D" position and vehicle is at specified speed. Lock-up solenoid is located on transmission valve body. See Figs. 1 and 2.

SELF-DIAGNOSTIC SYSTEM

SYSTEM DIAGNOSIS

NOTE: Before testing transmission, ensure fluid level is correct and throttle and shift cables are properly adjusted. Ensure engine starts with shift lever in "P" (Park) and "N" (Neutral) to ensure proper adjustment of park/neutral position switch. Transmission must first be tested by checking for stored trouble codes. See RETRIEVING TROUBLE CODES.

ECT ECU monitors engine and transmission operation and contains a self-diagnostic system which stores diagnostic trouble code(s). A Malfunction Indicator Light (MIL), located on instrument panel, will illuminate if a system or component fails and sets a DTC. *See Figs. 1 and 2.*

MIL illuminates with ignition switch in ON position, engine off (KOEO). Once engine is started, MIL should go out. If MIL remains illuminated, ECT ECU has detected a malfunction or abnormality in system. If MIL does not illuminate, inspect circuit and light. See WIRING DIAGRAMS.

If malfunction does not reoccur in 3 trips, MIL goes off, but Diagnostic Trouble Code (DTC) remains recorded in ECT ECU memory. Trouble codes may only be retrieved using an appropriate scan tool or Lexus/Toyota scan tool connected to 16-pin Data Link Connector (DLC3), located at lower left corner of instrument panel. *See Figs. 5 and 6.* Scan tool also provides freeze-frame data and can be used to clear trouble codes.

ECT ECU records engine operating condition (fuel system, calculated load, coolant temperature, fuel trim (mixture), engine speed, vehicle speed, etc.) with 1st malfunction ONLY. Information is ONLY for 1st recorded failure, even if more than one code has been recorded. Freeze-frame data is only updated when all trouble codes have been cleared, or a misfire or fuel-trim malfunction has occurred.

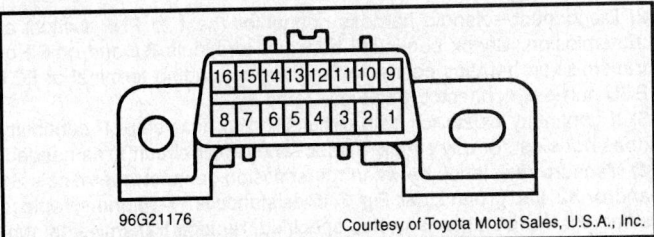

Fig. 5: Identifying Data Link Connector (DLC3) Terminals

RETRIEVING TROUBLE CODES

NOTE: Before retrieving trouble codes, ensure sufficient battery voltage exists for proper self-diagnosis system operation. Ensure proper operation of MIL light.

NOTE: MIL will illuminate for all trouble codes.

NOTE: For additional engine performance or other system related trouble codes present that are not listed in DIAGNOSTIC TROUBLE CODE (DTC) IDENTIFICATION table, see appropriate MITCHELL® ENGINE PERFORMANCE publication for IMPORTED CARS, LIGHT TRUCKS & VANS.

ECT ECU Codes – 1) Connect scan tool to Data Link Connector (DLC3). DLC3 is located at lower left corner of instrument panel. *See Fig. 6.*
2) Turn ignition on. Turn on scan tool. Retrieve any trouble codes stored in memory following scan tool instructions. See DIAGNOSTIC TROUBLE CODE (DTC) IDENTIFICATION table.
3) Trouble codes recorded may not have illuminated MIL. When certain malfunctions or trouble codes initially occur, they will be temporarily stored in ECT ECU memory, but MIL will not illuminate.
4) Second time malfunction or trouble code is detected, MIL will illuminate, provided ignition is turned off and then back on after malfunction

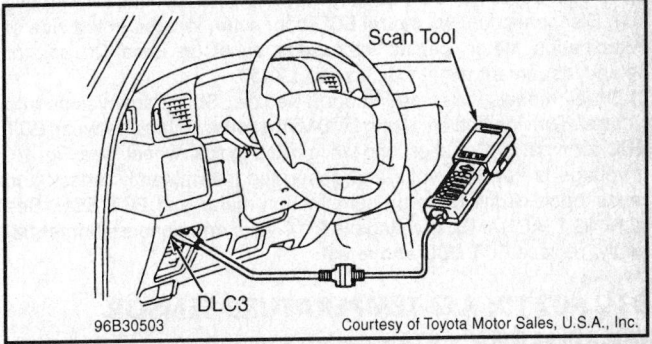

Fig. 6: Connecting Scan Tool To Data Link Connector (DLC3)

or trouble code was first detected. This process is referred to as 2 trip detection logic and only applies to specific trouble codes.
5) Record freeze-frame data. If using Lexus/Toyota scan tool, ensure tool is in NORMAL mode. CHECK MODE will erase all codes.

DIAGNOSTIC TROUBLE CODE (DTC) IDENTIFICATION

DTC	[1] Probable Cause
P0500 (1996)	No. 1 Vehicle Speed Sensor
P0710	ATF Temperature Sensor
P0720 (1995 Land Cruiser)	No. 1 Vehicle Speed Sensor
P0750	No. 1 Solenoid
P0753	No. 1 Solenoid Circuit
P0755	No. 2 Solenoid
P0758	No. 2 Solenoid Circuit
P0770	[2] Lock-Up Solenoid
P0773	Lock-Up Solenoid Circuit
P1700	No. 2 Vehicle Speed Sensor Circuit
P1780	Park/Neutral Position Switch

[1] – Check listed component for probable cause. Check wiring and connections of specified component.
[2] – Also called SL solenoid.

CLEARING TROUBLE CODES

Once repairs have been performed, trouble codes must be cleared from ECT ECU memory. DTC's may be cleared by following methods:
* Scan tool (follow manufacturers instructions).
* Remove EFI fuse (15-amp) from engine compartment relay box on left fender panel, for 10 seconds or more to clear memory in ECT ECU.
* Disconnect negative battery cable (memory for electronic components will be also be canceled).

DIAGNOSTIC TESTS

When trouble shooting transmission, first check for stored trouble codes and repair as necessary. If no trouble codes exist, perform manual shift test to determine if problem area is in electrical circuits or a mechanical transmission problem. See MANUAL SHIFT TEST.

DTC P0500:
NO. 1 VEHICLE SPEED SENSOR (VSS) FAULT

Circuit Description – No. 1 Vehicle Speed Sensor (VSS), driven by transmission output shaft, outputs a pulse signal to combination meter. Combination meter converts signal to a more precise waveform for ECT ECU. DTC is set when ECT ECU does not detect any signal while vehicle is in motion. Possible causes are:
* Open or short in vehicle speed sensor circuit.
* No. 1 VSS failure.
* Combination meter malfunction.
* ECT ECU malfunction.

Diagnosis & Repair Procedure – 1) Test drive vehicle and determine if speedometer is functioning properly. If speedometer is okay, go to next step. If speedometer is not functioning, go to NO. 1 VEHICLE SPEED SENSOR (VSS) under COMPONENT TESTS.

2) To gain access to ECT ECU, remove speaker panel next to glove box. Disconnect cruise control ECU connector, located at left side of combination meter, behind instrument panel on Land Cruiser, or behind instrument panel fuse box on LX450.

3) On all models, raise and support vehicle. Shift transmission into Neutral. Turn ignition on. Using DVOM, measure voltage between ECT ECU terminal SPD and ground while rotating rear wheel. *See Fig. 10.* If voltage is not 9-14 volts and generated intermittently, check and repair open circuit between combination meter and ECT ECU. See WIRING DIAGRAMS. If voltage is 9-14 volts and generated intermittently, replace ECT ECU and retest.

DTC P0710: ATF TEMPERATURE SENSOR

Circuit Description – ATF temperature sensor converts fluid temperature into a resistance value which in input to ECT ECU. DTC is set when temperature sensor resistance is less than 79 ohms, or after engine has been operating for 15 minutes or more, temperature sensor resistance is more than 156 k/ohms. Either condition must be set for .5 second or more. Possible causes are:
- Open or short in ATF temperature sensor circuit.
- ATF temperature sensor malfunction.
- ECT ECU malfunction.

Diagnosis & Repair Procedure – **1)** Raise and support vehicle. Remove transmission oil pan. Disconnect ATF temperature sensor connector (Red/White and Brown/Black wires). Remove sensor from valve body. Connect ohmmeter leads between sensor terminals.

2) Submerge sensor in container of water. Heat water while measuring sensor resistance. At 68°F (20°C), sensor resistance should be about 12.2 k/ohms. At 230°F (110°C), sensor resistance should be about 770 ohms. If resistance is not as specified, replace sensor. Tighten sensor to 11 ft. lbs. (15 N.m). If resistance is as specified, inspect and repair wiring harness circuits between sensor and ECT ECU. If circuits are okay, replace ECT ECU and retest.

DTC P0720: NO. 1 VEHICLE SPEED SENSOR (VSS) FAULT (1995 LAND CRUISER)

Circuit Description – No. 1 Vehicle Speed Sensor (VSS), driven by transmission output shaft, outputs a pulse signal to combination meter. Combination meter converts signal to a more precise waveform for ECT ECU. DTC is set when ECT ECU detects one or more of the following 500 times or more continuously.

When transfer case is not in L4 position and No. 1 vehicle speed sensor signal is not received by ECT ECU after 16 pulses of No. 2 vehicle speed sensor. When transfer case is in L4 position and No. 1 vehicle speed sensor signal is not received by ECT ECU after 40 pulses of No. 2 vehicle speed sensor. Vehicle speed is 5.6 MPH or more for at least 4 seconds, and transmission and transfer case are in any shift lever position except Park and Neutral. Possible causes are:
- Open or short in vehicle speed sensor circuit.
- No. 1 VSS failure.
- Combination meter malfunction.
- ECT ECU malfunction.

Diagnosis & Repair Procedure – **1)** Test drive vehicle and determine if speedometer is functioning properly. If speedometer is okay, go to next step. If speedometer is not functioning, go to NO. 1 VEHICLE SPEED SENSOR (VSS) under COMPONENT TESTS.

2) To gain access to ECT ECU, remove speaker panel next to glove box. Disconnect cruise control ECU connector, located at left side of combination meter, behind instrument panel.

3) Raise and support vehicle. Shift transmission into Neutral. Turn ignition on. Using DVOM, measure voltage between ECT ECU terminal SPD and ground while rotating rear wheel. *See Fig. 10.* If voltage is not 4-6 volts and generated intermittently, check and repair open circuit between combination meter and ECT ECU. See WIRING DIAGRAMS. If voltage is 4-6 volts and generated intermittently, replace ECT ECU and retest.

DTC P0750 & P0755: NO. 1 & NO. 2 SOLENOID FAULT

Circuit Description – ECT ECU uses signal from No. 1 vehicle speed sensor to determine actual gear position. ECT ECU compares actual gear with shift schedule in memory to detect mechanical trouble of solenoids and/or valve body. DTC is set if during normal driving gear required by ECT ECU does not match actual gear after 2 trips have been completed. Possible causes are:
- No. 1 and/or No. 2 solenoid is stuck open or closed.
- Valve body is clogged or valve(s) is stuck.

Diagnosis & Repair Procedure – Remove and inspect operation of solenoids. See appropriate solenoid test under COMPONENT TESTS. If solenoids are okay, inspect valve body. See TOYOTA A-340 SERIES & A-350 SERIES overhaul article.

DTC P0753 & P0758: NO. 1 & NO. 2 SOLENOID CIRCUIT

Circuit Description – Shifting is performed in combination with ON and OFF position of shift solenoids controlled by ECT ECU. If an open or short circuit occurs in either shift solenoid, ECT ECU reverts to fail-safe mode. *See Figs. 3 and 4.* ECT ECU turns off SL solenoid at same time. DTC's are output when a open or short circuit occurs. Possible causes are:
- No. 1 and/or No. 2 solenoid circuit.
- No. 1 and/or No. 2 solenoid malfunction.
- ECT ECU malfunction.

Diagnosis & Repair Procedure – **1)** Ensure ignition is off. To gain access to ECT ECU, remove speaker panel next to glove box. Disconnect appropriate ECT ECU harness connector. Using ohmmeter, measure resistance between ECT ECU harness connector terminal S1 and/or S2 and ground. *See Fig. 10.* If resistance is 11-15 ohms, replace ECT ECU and retest. If resistance is not within specification, go to next step.

2) Disconnect solenoid harness connector (next to PNP switch) at transmission. Check continuity between terminals S1 and/or S2 of transmission harness connector and corresponding terminal of ECT ECU harness connector. *See Figs. 7 and 10.*

3) If continuity exists for both circuits, go to next step. If continuity does not exist for any circuit, inspect and repair circuit(s) as needed.

4) Measure resistance between transmission connector terminals S1 and/or S2, and ground. *See Fig. 7.* If resistance is 11-15 ohms, replace solenoid. If resistance is not as specified, replace transmission sub-harness as needed.

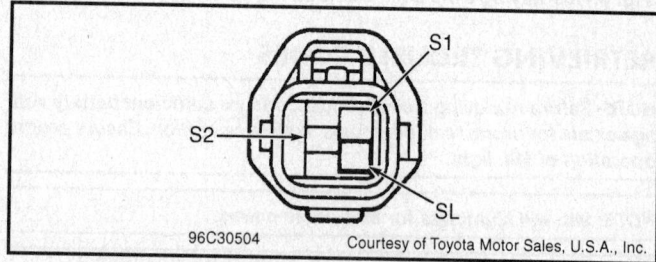

96C30504   Courtesy of Toyota Motor Sales, U.S.A., Inc.

Fig. 7: Identifying Transmission Solenoid Harness Connector Terminals

DTC P0770: LOCK-UP/SL SOLENOID

Circuit Description – ECT ECU uses signals from throttle position sensor, air flow meter and crankshaft position sensor to monitor engagement of Torque Converter Clutch (TCC). ECT ECU compares engagement condition of TCC with lock-up schedule in memory to detect mechanical trouble of solenoid, valve body and torque converter. DTC is set when TCC lock-up does not occur at appropriate speed (50 MPH), or lock-up does not release at appropriate speed. Possible causes are:

- Lock-up solenoid is stuck open or closed.
- Valve body clogged or valve stuck.
- TCC malfunction.

Diagnosis & Repair Procedure – Remove and inspect operation of solenoid. See appropriate solenoid test under COMPONENT TESTS. If solenoid is okay, inspect valve body. See TOYOTA A-340 & A-350 SERIES overhaul article.

DTC P0773: LOCK-UP/SL SOLENOID CIRCUIT

Circuit Description – Lock-up solenoid is turned on and off by signals from ECT ECU to control hydraulic pressure affecting lock-up relay valve. Lock-up relay valve controls operation of Torque Converter Clutch (TCC). If ECT ECU detects a malfunction, fail-safe function is enabled. See Figs. 3 and 4. DTC is output when a open or short circuit occurs. Possible causes are:

- Lock-up solenoid open or short circuit.
- Lock-up solenoid malfunction.
- ECT ECU malfunction.

Diagnosis & Repair Procedure – **1)** Ensure ignition is off. To gain access to ECT ECU, remove speaker panel next to glove box. Disconnect appropriate ECT ECU harness connector. See Fig. 10. Backprobing ECT ECU harness connector with ohmmeter, measure resistance between terminal SL and ground. If resistance is 11-15 ohms, replace ECT ECU and retest. If resistance is not within specification, go to next step.
2) Disconnect solenoid harness connector at transmission. Check continuity between terminal SL of transmission harness connector and corresponding terminal of ECT ECU harness connector. See Figs. 7 and 10.
3) If continuity does not exist, check and repair circuit as needed. If continuity exists, measure resistance between transmission connector terminal SL, and ground. See Fig. 7. If resistance is 11-15 ohms, replace solenoid. If resistance is not as specified, replace transmission sub-harness as needed.

DTC P1700: NO. 2 VEHICLE SPEED SENSOR (VSS) CIRCUIT

Circuit Description – No. 2 vehicle speed sensor detects transmission output shaft RPM and sends signals to ECT ECU. An AC voltage is generated in No. 2 vehicle speed sensor coil as rotor mounted on output shaft rotates. This voltage is sent to ECT ECU. Gear shift point and lock-up timing are controlled by ECT ECU based on signals from No. 2 vehicle speed sensor and throttle position sensor. If No. 2 vehicle speed sensor malfunctions, ECT ECU uses input signals from No. 1 vehicle speed sensor as a back-up signal. DTC is output when no signal is detected from No. 2 vehicle speed sensor while No. 1 vehicle speed sensor sends 4 pulses to ECT ECU. Vehicle speed is more than 5.6 MPH for at least 4 seconds. Possible causes are:

- Sensor open or short circuit.
- Sensor malfunction.
- ECT ECU malfunction.

Diagnosis & Repair Procedure – **1)** Ensure ignition is off. To gain access to ECT ECU, remove speaker panel next to glove box. Disconnect appropriate ECT ECU harness connector. Using ohmmeter, measure resistance between terminals SP2+ and SP2- at ECT ECU harness connector. See Fig. 10. Resistance should be 560-680 ohms. If resistance is as specified, replace ECT ECU and retest. If resistance is not within specification, go to next step.
2) Remove No. 2 vehicle speed sensor from transmission. Measure resistance between sensor terminals. Resistance should be 560-680 ohms. If resistance is not as specified, replace sensor. If resistance is as specified, check and repair circuits between sensor and ECT ECU.
3) Check voltage between sensor terminals when a magnet is put close to tip of speed sensor. See Fig. 8. If a low intermittent voltage is generated, sensor is okay. If no voltage is generated, replace speed sensor.

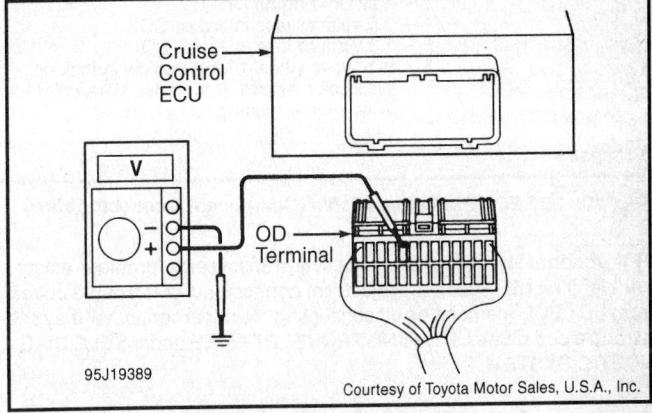

95H19544   Courtesy of Toyota Motor Sales, U.S.A., Inc.

Fig. 8: Testing No. 2 Vehicle Speed Sensor

DTC P1780: PARK/NEUTRAL POSITION (PNP) SWITCH

Circuit Description – PNP switch verifies shift lever position and sends signals to ECT ECU. If no signal is received from PNP switch, ECT ECU defaults to drive ("D") position. DTC is output when ECT ECU detects 2 or more circuits are on. Also vehicle speed has to be above 44 MPH for more than 30 seconds with engine speed at 1500-2500 RPM. Possible causes are:

- Short in PNP switch circuit.
- PNP switch malfunction.
- ECT ECU malfunction.

Diagnosis & Repair Procedure – **1)** To gain access to ECT ECU, remove speaker panel next to glove box. Turn ignition on. Using DVOM, measure voltage at terminals NSW, "R", "2" and "L" of ECT ECU harness connector between terminal and body ground with gear selector in each shift position. See Fig. 10.
2) Ensure 7.5-14 volts is present at NSW terminal at ECT ECU harness connector in all shift positions. Ensure 7.5-14 volts is present at terminals "R", "2" and "L" at ECT ECU harness connector with gear selector in "R", "2" and "L" position. If voltage is not as specified, check park/neutral position switch. See PARK/NEUTRAL POSITION (PNP) SWITCH under COMPONENT TESTS. If switch is okay, check and repair circuit(s) between PNP switch and ECT ECU. See WIRING DIAGRAMS.

MANUAL SHIFT TEST

NOTE: Perform manual shift test if no trouble codes exist. Manual shift test determines if problem area is in electrical circuits or a mechanical transmission problem.

1) With ignition off, disconnect electrical connector for solenoids from transmission. Road test vehicle and ensure transmission gear changes correspond with shift lever position. See GEAR APPLICATION table.

Cruise Control ECU

OD Terminal

95J19389   Courtesy of Toyota Motor Sales, U.S.A., Inc.

Fig. 9: Identifying Cruise Control ECU Terminals

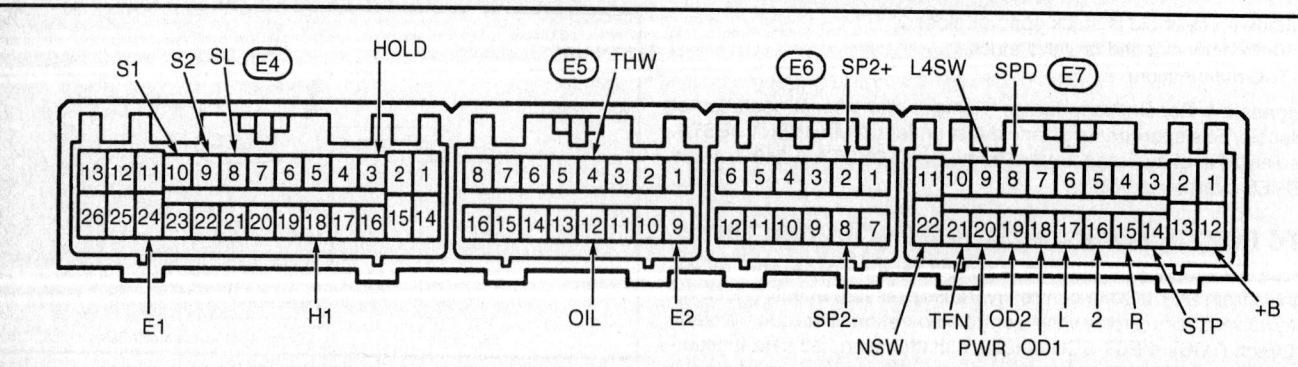

	Terminal ID.	Function/Description	Voltage Value (DC Volts Unless Otherwise Specified)
Red	S1	No. 1 Solenoid	9-14 Volts With KOEO [1][2]
Red/Yellow	S2	No. 2 Solenoid	9-14 Volts With KOEO [1][3]
Red/Blue	SL	Lock-Up Solenoid	Less Than 1.5 Volts With KOEO [1][4]
[5]	SP2+, SP2-	No. 2 Vehicle Speed Sensor	1.5 Volts Or Less, Or 4-6 Volts [6]
Green/White	STP	Brakelight Switch Signal	7.5-14 Volts With Pedal Depressed
Red/White	THW	Engine Coolant Temperature Sensor Signal	1.5 Volts Or Less @ 176°F (80°C)
Blue/White	SPD	No. 1 Vehicle Speed Sensor Signal	1.5 Volts Or Less, Or 4-6 Volts [1][7]
Red/White	OIL	ATF Temperature Sensor	1.5 Volts Or Less @ 230°F (110°C)
Green/Orange	OD1	OD Output To Cruise Control ECU	9-14 Volts With KOEO [1]
Pink/Blue	OD2	Overdrive Switch Signal	9-14 Volts With Switch On
Black/White	NSW	Ignition Switch Signal	9-14 Volts In "P" Or "N", KOEO [1]
Orange	2	Park/Neutral Position Switch "2" Signal	7.5-14 Volts In "2", KOEO [1]
Green/White	L	Park/Neutral Position Switch "L" Signal	7.5-14 Volts In "L", KOEO [1]
Red/Black	R	Park/Neutral Position Switch "R" Signal	7.5-14 Volts With KOEO [1]
Pink/Blue	PWR	Pattern Select Switch Signal	7.5-14 Volts In PWR Position
Yellow	+B	EFI Main Relay Power Supply	9-14 Volts With KOEO [1]
Yellow/Blue	TFN	Transfer Case "N" Position Signal	3 Volts Or Less With KOEO [1]
Black/Blue	L4SW	Transfer Case "L4" Position Signal	7.5-14 Volts With KOEO [1]
Orange	HOLD	2nd Start Switch Signal	9-14 Volts With Switch On
Brown/Black	E1	Ground	Not Applicable
Brown/Black	E2	Ground	Not Applicable

[1] – Key On, Engine Off.
[2] – 1.5 volts or less in 3rd or OD.
[3] – 1.5 volts or less in 1st or OD.
[4] – 9-14 volts while driving vehicle in lock-up.
[5] – Wire color for SP2+ is Violet. Wire color for SP2- is Violet/Green.
[6] – With engine running.
[7] – Disconnect cruise control ECU.

96D30505

Courtesy of Toyota Motor Sales, U.S.A., Inc.

Fig. 10: ECT ECU Pin Voltage Table (Component Connector View)

2) If abnormality exists, a mechanical transmission problem exists. Turn ignition off. Reconnect electrical connector. Clear trouble codes from ECT ECU memory, as disconnecting electrical connector may set a trouble code. See CLEARING TROUBLE CODES under SELF-DIAGNOSTIC SYSTEM.

GEAR APPLICATION

Shift Lever Position	Gear
"D"	Overdrive
"2"	3rd
"L"	1st
"R"	Reverse
"P"	Park

CIRCUIT TESTS

BRAKELIGHT SIGNAL

1) Inspect operation of brakelights. Repair as needed. If switch is suspect, see BRAKELIGHT SWITCH under COMPONENT TESTS. If circuit is suspect, diagnose and repair as necessary. See WIRING DIAGRAMS.

2) Connect scan tool to DLC3. See Fig. 6. Turn ignition on. Read STP signal while depressing and releasing brake pedal. Ensure signal cycles when pressing brake pedal. If signal cycles, replace ECT ECU. If signal does not cycle, inspect and repair circuit between brakelight switch and ECT ECU. If circuit is okay, replace ECT ECU.

OVERDRIVE CANCEL SIGNAL

1) To gain access to ECT ECU, remove speaker panel next to glove box. Turn ignition on. Measure voltage between ground and ECT ECU harness connector terminal OD1. See Fig. 10. If voltage is 9-14 volts, substitute known good ECT ECU and retest. If voltage is not 9-14 volts, go to next step.

2) Turn ignition off. Disconnect cruise control ECU connector, located at left side of combination meter, behind instrument panel on Land Cruiser, or behind instrument panel fuse box on LX450. Turn ignition on. Measure voltage between cruise control ECU connector terminal OD and ground. See Fig. 9. If 9-14 volts is present, replace cruise control ECU and retest. If 9-14 volts is not present, inspect and repair circuit between cruise control ECU and ECT ECU.

ECT ECU VOLTAGES

To gain access to ECT ECU, remove speaker panel next to glove box. Turn ignition on. Using voltmeter, measure voltage at ECT ECU harness connector. Check voltage between selected terminal and E_1 terminal. Voltage should be as specified. See Fig. 10.

COMPONENT TESTS

NO. 1 VEHICLE SPEED SENSOR (VSS)

1) Disconnect electrical connector from No. 1 VSS, located at left rear side of transmission. See Figs. 1 and 2. Connect positive battery lead to terminal No. 1 and negative lead to terminal No. 2. Connect positive lead of voltmeter to terminal No. 3 and negative lead to terminal No. 2. See Fig. 11.

2) Raise and support one vehicle rear wheel. Rotate wheel and monitor voltmeter. Ensure voltage changes from zero to 11 volts. Voltage should change 4 times per each revolution of speedometer cable shaft. Replace speed sensor if voltage does not change as specified.

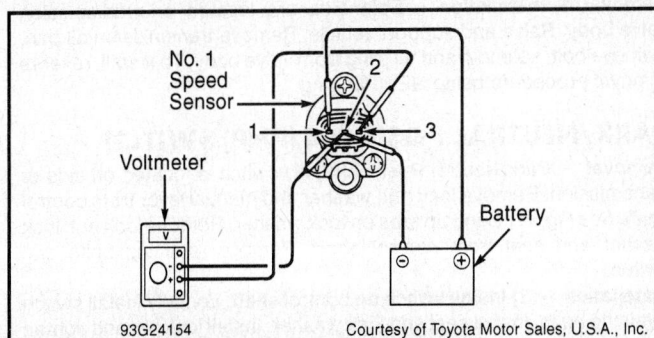

Fig. 11: Checking No. 1 Vehicle Speed Sensor

NO. 1 & NO. 2 SOLENOIDS

1) To check solenoid seals, remove suspect solenoid. Connect battery voltage to solenoid. Apply 71 psi (5 kg/cm²) to solenoid with battery voltage connected. See Fig. 12.

2) With battery voltage applied, air should pass through solenoid. Disconnect voltage to solenoid. Ensure air does not pass through solenoid. Replace solenoid if defective.

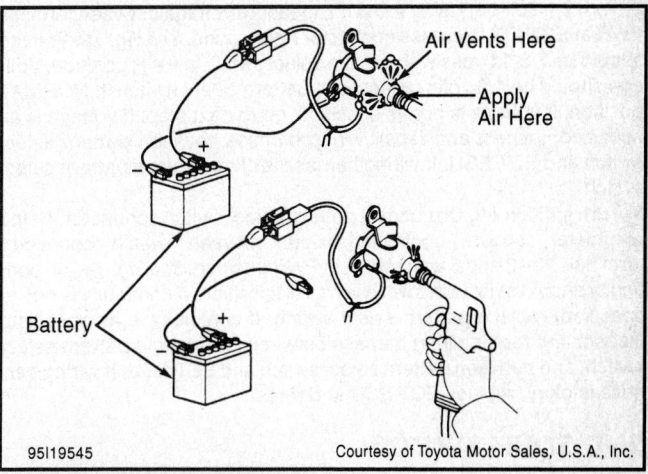

Fig. 12: Checking Solenoids

LOCK-UP/SL SOLENOID

1) To check solenoid seals, remove suspect solenoid. Connect battery voltage to solenoid. Apply 71 psi (5 kg/cm²) to solenoid with battery voltage connected. See Fig. 12.

2) With battery voltage applied, air should not pass through solenoid. Disconnect voltage to solenoid. Ensure air does pass through solenoid. Replace solenoid if defective.

PARK/NEUTRAL POSITION (PNP) SWITCH

Disconnect harness connector at park/neutral position switch. Switch is located on left side of transmission. Using ohmmeter, check for continuity between specified terminals in accordance with shift lever position. See Fig. 13. Replace PNP switch if defective.

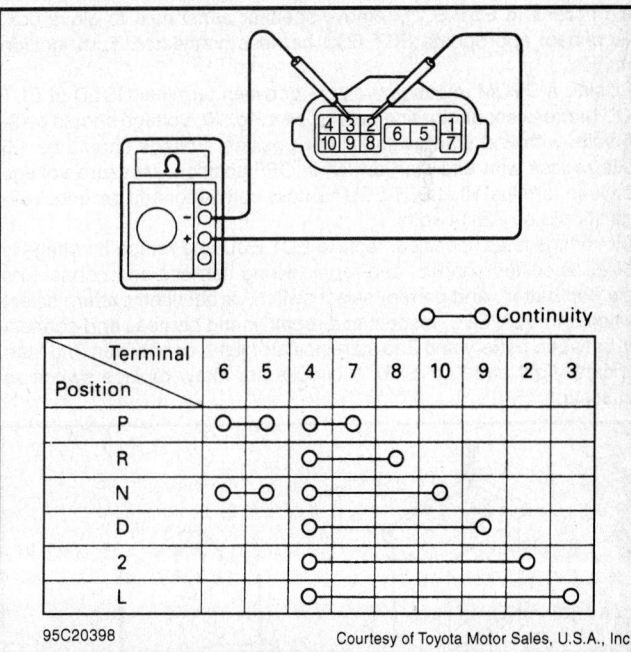

Fig. 13: Testing Park/Neutral Position (PNP) Switch

PATTERN SELECT SWITCH

1) Check pattern select switch light operation. Turn ignition on. Ensure pattern select switch (PWR) indicator light is on when switch is pushed to ON position. Ensure PWR indicator light is off when switch is pushed to OFF position. If indicator light operates as described, go to next step. If indicator light does not operate as described, inspect and repair wiring harness as necessary. If wiring harness is okay, replace indicator bulb.

2) Turn ignition on. Using a DVOM, measure voltage between terminal PWR at ECT ECU harness connector and ground. *See Fig. 10.* Voltage should be 7.5-14 volts with pattern select switch in PWR position. Voltage should be 1.5 volts or less with pattern select switch in NORMAL position. If voltage is not as specified, go to next step. If voltage is as specified, inspect and repair wiring harness between pattern select switch and ECT ECU. If wiring harness is okay, replace pattern select switch.

3) Turn ignition off. Disconnect pattern select switch connector. Using ohmmeter, ensure continuity exists between switch connector terminals No. 3 and 6 with switch in PWR position. *See Fig. 14.* No continuity should exist with switch in NORM position. If continuity is not as specified, replace pattern select switch. If continuity is as specified, inspect and repair wiring harness between battery and pattern select switch, and between pattern select switch and ECT ECU. If wiring harness is okay, replace ECT ECU and retest.

2ND START SWITCH

NOTE: Pattern select switch includes 2nd start switch. When 2nd start switch is activated, transmission will start out in 2nd gear. If gear selector is in "D" position, transmission will shift up through 3rd gear to OD. If transmission is in 2nd gear, transmission is held in 2nd gear.

1) Check 2nd start switch operation. Turn ignition on. Ensure 2nd STRT indicator light is on when switch is pushed to ON position. Ensure 2nd STRT indicator light is off when switch is pushed to OFF position. If indicator light operates as described, go to next step. If indicator light does not operate as described, inspect and repair wiring harness as necessary. If wiring harness is okay, replace indicator bulb.

2) Disconnect pattern select switch connector. Using ohmmeter, ensure continuity exists between terminals No. 2 and 5 with switch in ON position. *See Fig. 14.* No continuity should exist in OFF position. To gain access to ECT ECU, remove speaker panel next to glove box. Disconnect appropriate ECT ECU harness connector. Turn ignition on.

3) Using a DVOM, measure voltage between terminal HOLD at ECT ECU harness connector and ground. *See Fig. 10.* Voltage should be 9-14 volts with 2nd start switch in ON position. Voltage should be 1.5 volts or less with 2nd start switch in OFF position. Measure voltage between terminal HI at ECT ECU harness connector and ground. Voltage should be 7.5-14 volts.

4) If voltage is as specified, replace ECT ECU and retest. If voltage is not as specified, inspect and repair wiring harness and connectors between battery and pattern select switch, or between pattern select switch and ECT ECU. Inspect and repair wiring harness and connector between battery and 2nd start indicator light, or between 2nd start indicator light and ECT ECU. If circuits are okay, replace switch as necessary.

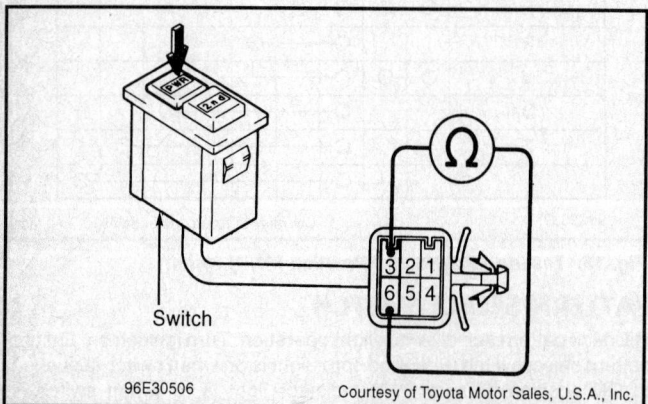

Fig. 14: Identifying Pattern Select Switch & 2nd Start Switch Terminals

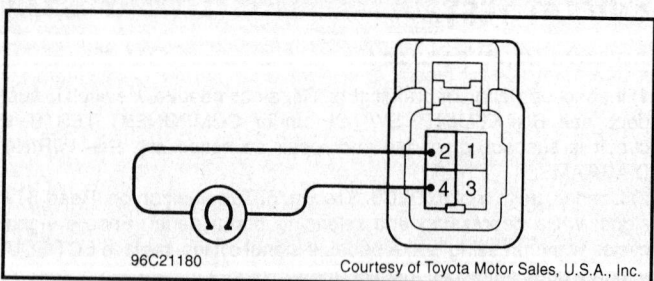

Fig. 15: Identifying Overdrive (OD) Switch Terminals

OVERDRIVE (OD) SWITCH

Disconnect electrical connector from OD switch, located on shift lever. Using ohmmeter, ensure continuity exists between switch terminals No. 2 and 4 with switch released (OFF position). *See Fig. 15.* Ensure no continuity exists with switch depressed (ON position). Replace switch if defective.

BRAKELIGHT SWITCH

Disconnect electrical connector from brakelight switch, located near brake pedal. Using ohmmeter, ensure continuity exists between switch terminals No. 1 and 2 with brake pedal depressed. Continuity should exist between terminals No. 3 and 4 with pedal released. *See Fig. 16.*

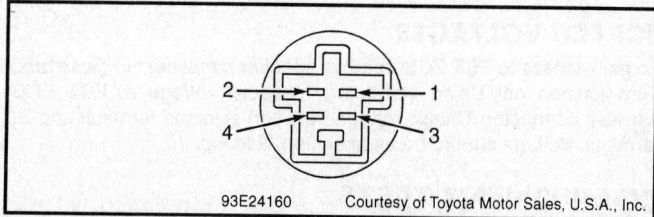

Fig. 16: Identifying Brakelight Switch Terminals

REMOVAL & INSTALLATION
BRAKELIGHT SWITCH

Removal & Installation – Disconnect electrical connector. Remove lock nut, and unscrew brakelight switch. To install, screw brakelight switch inward until brakelight plunger contacts brake pedal.

SOLENOIDS

Removal & Installation – Solenoids are located on transmission valve body. Raise and support vehicle. Remove transmission oil pan. Remove bolt, solenoid and "O" ring from valve body. To install, reverse removal procedure using NEW "O" ring.

PARK/NEUTRAL POSITION (PNP) SWITCH

Removal – Park/Neutral Position (PNP) switch is located on side of transmission. Remove lock nut, washer and manual lever from control shaft. *See Fig. 17.* Bend up tabs on lock washer. Remove lock nut, lock washer and seal from control shaft. Remove retaining bolts and switch.

Installation – **1)** Install switch on control shaft. Loosely install switch retaining bolts. Install seal and lock washer. Install lock nut and tighten to specification. See TORQUE SPECIFICATIONS. Bend tabs on lock washer over against lock nut.

2) Ensure parking brake is applied. Temporarily install manual lever on control shaft. Place shift lever in Neutral. Remove manual lever. Rotate park/neutral position switch and align neutral basic line on PNP switch with groove. *See Fig. 17.*

3) Hold PNP switch in this position. Tighten retaining bolts to specification. To install remaining components, reverse removal procedure.

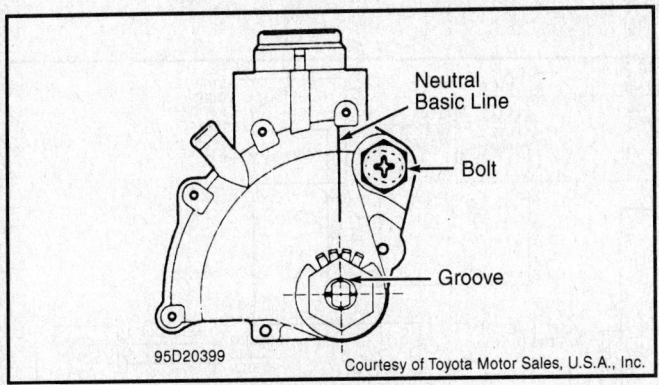

95D20399 — Courtesy of Toyota Motor Sales, U.S.A., Inc.

Fig. 17: Removing & Installing PNP Switch

OVERDRIVE (OD) SWITCH

Overdrive (OD) switch is mounted on shift lever. *See Figs. 1 and 2.* Replacement information not available from manufacturer.

ENGINE COOLANT TEMPERATURE SENSOR

Removal & Installation – Drain cooling system. Disconnect engine coolant temperature sensor connector (connector with Brown/Black and Red/White wires). Sensor is located in coolant passage on left side of cylinder head, above oil filter. Remove coolant temperature sensor. To install, reverse removal procedure. Refill cooling system and check for leaks.

TORQUE SPECIFICATIONS
TORQUE SPECIFICATIONS

Application	INCH Lbs. (N.m)
PNP Switch	
Bolt	115 (13)
Nut	35 (3.9)
Solenoid Bolt	89 (10)
Speed Sensor Bolt	48 (5.4)

WIRING DIAGRAMS

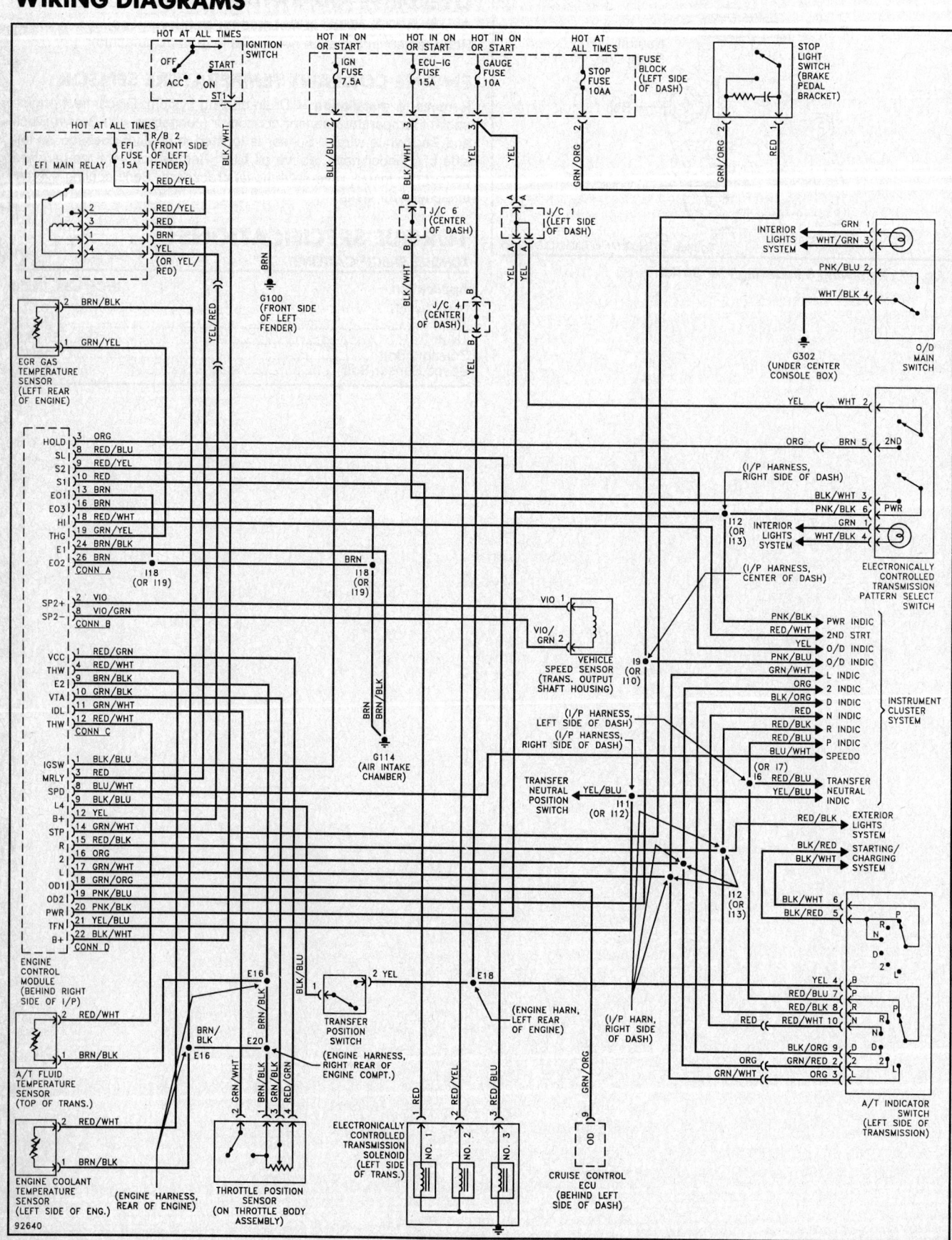

Fig. 18: Transmission Wiring Diagram (1995-96 Land Cruiser & 1996 LX450)

Lexus: ES300
Toyota: Avalon, Camry, RAV4

APPLICATION & LABOR TIMES

APPLICATION & LABOR TIMES

Vehicle Application	Labor Times [1] R & I	[2] Overhaul	Trans. Model
Avalon	6.3	11.5	A-541E
Camry (V6) LE, SE & XLE	6.3	11.5	A-541E
Lexus ES300	6.3	11.5	A-541E
RAV4 4WD			
With A/C	12.8 [3]	11.5	A-540H
Without A/C	12.5 [3]	11.5	A-540H

[1] – Removal and installation of transmission from vehicle chassis.
[2] – Bench overhaul time for transmission and differential. DOES NOT include removal and installation.
[3] – Requires engine removal.

NOTE: RAV4 is equipped with a transfer case. For transfer case overhaul procedures, see TOYOTA RAV4 – WITH A-540H A/T in TRANSFER CASES.

CAUTION: All models are equipped with a Supplemental Restraint System (SRS). When servicing vehicle, use care to avoid accidental air bag deployment. All SRS electrical connections and wiring harness are covered by Yellow insulation. SRS-related components are located in steering column, center console, instrument panel and lower panel on instrument panel. DO NOT use electrical test equipment on these circuits. If necessary, deactivate SRS before servicing components. See AIR BAG SERVICING article in APPLICATIONS & IDENTIFICATION section.

IDENTIFICATION

Vehicle Identification Number (VIN) is used for correct application of component parts and assemblies. VIN is stamped on cowl panel, manufacturer's plate, vehicle identification number plate and certification regulation plate.

DESCRIPTION

The A-540H 4WD transaxle has a center differential and electronic transfer case attached. Transaxle internal components are the same or similar to the A-541E transaxle. Transaxle has 4 shift solenoids in the valve body to control engagement speed and throttle pressure for shift feel. Torque is distributed to front and rear wheels at all times to maximize traction of 4WD vehicle.

The A-541E transaxle features a torque converter with lock-up clutch, 4-speed planetary gear unit, differential, hydraulic control system and electronic control system. Transaxle also has 4 shift solenoids in the valve body to control engagement speed and throttle pressure for shift feel. A shift lock mechanism is used to minimize possibility of incorrect operation of transaxle.

LUBRICATION & ADJUSTMENTS

See appropriate AUTOMATIC TRANSMISSION SERVICING article in TRANSMISSION SERVICING section.

TROUBLE SHOOTING

NOTE: For electronic diagnosis and component testing of A-540H and A-541E transaxles, see appropriate TOYOTA ELECTRONIC CONTROLS article. For diagnosis and testing of shift lock system, See TOYOTA SHIFT LOCK SYSTEM article.

CLUTCH & BRAKE APPLICATION

Selector Lever Position	Elements In Use
"D" (Drive)	
1st Gear	Forward Clutch, OD Direct Clutch, OD One-Way Clutch & No. 2 One-Way Clutch
2nd Gear	Forward Clutch, OD Direct Clutch, OD One-Way Clutch, No. 1 One-Way Clutch & 2nd Brake
3rd Gear	Forward Clutch, Direct Clutch, OD Direct Clutch, OD One-Way Clutch & 2nd Brake
Overdrive	Direct Clutch, Forward Clutch, OD Brake & 2nd Brake
"2" (Second)	
1st Gear	Forward Clutch, OD One-Way Clutch, OD Direct Clutch & No. 2 One-Way Clutch
2nd Gear	Forward Clutch, OD Direct Clutch, OD One-Way Clutch, 2nd Brake, 2nd Coast Brake & No. 1 One-Way Clutch
3rd Gear [1]	Forward Clutch, Direct Clutch OD Direct Clutch, OD One-Way Clutch & 2nd Brake
"L" (Low)	
1st Gear	Forward Clutch, OD Direct Clutch, OD One-Way Clutch, & 1st & Reverse Brake & No. 2 One-Way Clutch
2nd Gear [2]	Forward Clutch, OD Direct Clutch, OD One-Way Clutch, No. 1 One-Way Clutch, 2nd Brake & 2nd Coast Brake
"R" (Reverse)	Direct Clutch, OD Direct Clutch & 1st & Reverse Brake
"N" (Neutral)	OD Direct Clutch
"P" (Park)	OD Direct Clutch

[1] – Downshift only in 3rd gear for "2" position.
[2] – Downshift only in 2nd gear for "L" position. Upshift does not occur.

SYMPTOM DIAGNOSIS

Fluid Discolored Or Smells Burnt – Fluid contaminated. Torque converter faulty. Transaxle faulty.

Vehicle Does Not Move In Any Forward Gear Or Reverse – Check manual valve, parking lock pawl, primary regulator valve, overdrive (OD) one-way clutch, OD direct clutch, OD brake, front planetary gear, rear planetary gear and OD planetary gear.

Vehicle Does Not Move In Any Forward Gear – Check forward clutch, No. 2 one-way clutch, 1st and reverse brake, 2nd coast brake, 2nd brake and direct clutch.

Vehicle Does Not Move In Reverse ("R") – Check 1-2 shift valve, 2-3 shift valve, 2nd coast brake, front planetary gear, rear planetary gear, direct clutch, OD direct clutch and 1st and reverse brake.

No 1-2 &/Or 2-3 Upshift – Check Throttle Position (TP) sensor circuit, No. 1 and No. 2 shift solenoid circuit, Vehicle Speed Sensor (VSS) circuit, Electronic Control Transmission Electronic Control Module (ECT ECM), 1-2 shift valve, 2-3 shift valve, 2nd brake, direct clutch and No. 1 one-way clutch.

No 3-O/D Upshift – Check OD switch and OD OFF indicator switch circuit, OD cancel signal circuit, No. 1 and No. 2 shift solenoid circuit, VSS, Engine Coolant Temperature (ECT) circuit, ECM, 3-4 shift valve and OD brake.

No O/D-3 Downshift – Check No. 1 and No. 2 shift solenoid valve, VSS circuit, OD cancel signal circuit, ECM and 3-4 shift valve.

No 3-2 &/Or 2-1 Downshift – Check No. 1 and No. 2 shift solenoid valve, VSS circuit, TP sensor circuit, ECM, 2-3 shift valve, 1-2 shift valve and 2nd coast brake.

No Torque Converter Lock-Up – Check shift solenoid valve SL circuit, TP sensor circuit, VSS circuit, OD cancel circuit, brakelight circuit, ECT circuit, ECM, lock-up relay valve and torque converter clutch.

Torque Converter Lock-Up Will Not Release – Check shift solenoid valve SL circuit, TP sensor circuit, brakelight circuit, ECT ECM circuit, lock-up relay valve and torque converter clutch.

Shift Speeds Too High Or Too Low – Check TP sensor circuit, VSS circuit, shift solenoid valve SL circuit, OD cancel signal circuit, pattern select switch circuit and ECM.

Harsh Engagement Neutral To Reverse – Check direct clutch accumulator, direct clutch, throttle valve and 1st and reverse brake.

Harsh Engagement Neutral To Drive – Check forward clutch accumulator, throttle valve and forward clutch.

No Engine Braking In Low – Check low coast modulator valve and 1st and reverse brake.

No Engine Braking In 2nd – Check 2nd coast modulator valve and 2nd coast brake.

TESTING

PRELIMINARY CHECK

Ensure a thorough explanation of when and how transmission malfunction occurs is received from customer. Check fluid level and condition. Retrieve Diagnostic Trouble Codes (DTC's). See appropriate TOYOTA ELECTRONIC CONTROLS article. Proceed as necessary. If no codes are present, proceed with symptom diagnosis. See TROUBLE SHOOTING. Check throttle cable adjustment. See LUBRICATION & ADJUSTMENTS. Perform STALL SPEED, TIME LAG and HYDRAULIC TESTS as needed. After repairs are completed, perform ROAD TEST to confirm repairs.

TIME LAG TEST

CAUTION: Perform this test at normal operating fluid temperature of 122-176°F (50-80°C). Allow a one minute interval between tests. Record 3 measurements and average results.

1) If shift lever is actuated with engine idling, a time lag will be noted before shock can be felt. This test is used for checking condition of OD direct clutch, forward clutch, direct clutch, and 1st and reverse brake.

2) Apply parking brake. Start engine. On RAV4, ensure idle speed is 700-800 RPM. On all other models, ensure idle speed is 650-750 RPM. Shift transaxle from "N" into "D" range. Use a stop watch to measure elapsed time between shifting of lever until shock is felt. Standard time lag is less than 1.2 seconds.

3) Repeat procedure outlined in step **2)** to measure time lag for "N" to "R". Standard lag time is less than 1.5 seconds.

4) If "N" to "D" time lag is longer than specification, line pressure is too low, forward clutch may be worn, or OD one-way clutch is not operating properly.

5) If "N" to "R" time lag is longer than specified, direct clutch may be worn, 1st and reverse brake may be worn, line pressure is too low or OD one-way clutch is not operating properly.

ROAD TEST

NOTE: Perform test at normal operating fluid temperature of 122-176°F (50-80°C).

"D" Range Test In NORM & PWR Pattern Ranges – **1)** Shift into "D" range. Hold accelerator pedal constant at full throttle. Place shift mode button in NORM or PWR position. Check 1-2, 2-3, and 3-OD lock-up and upshift points. Refer to appropriate SHIFT SPEED SPECIFICATIONS table.

NOTE: There is no overdrive upshift when coolant temperature is below 122°F (50°C). There is no lock-up when vehicle speed is 6 MPH less than the set cruise control speed.

- If no 1-2 upshift occurs, check 1-2 shift valve or solenoid.
- If no 2-3 upshift occurs, check 2-3 shift valve or solenoid.
- If no 3-OD upshift occurs, check 3-OD shift valve.
- If all shift points are incorrect, check throttle valve, 1-2 shift valve, 2-3 shift valve and 3-OD shift valve.
- If all lock-up points are incorrect, check lock-up relay valve or shift solenoid valve SL.

2) Use procedure outlined in step **1)** to check for shock and slip between 1-2, 2-3, and 3-OD upshifts. If shock is harsh, line pressure may be too high. Also check accumulator or check ball.

3) Run vehicle in "D" range lock-up or overdrive gear. Check for abnormal noise and vibration.

NOTE: Check for cause of abnormal noise and vibration must be made with extreme care as problem could be due to an unbalanced drive shaft, differential, tire, torque converter, etc.

4) While running in "D" range, confirm correct kickdown vehicle speed limits for 2-1, 3-2, OD-3 shift points. Check for abnormal shock and slip at kickdown.

5) Check lock-up function. Drive vehicle in OD gear of "D" range with lock-up on. Hold vehicle speed steady at 47 MPH. Lightly depress accelerator pedal. Ensure engine RPM does not change abruptly. Large increase in engine RPM indicates lock-up function is faulty.

"2" Range Test – **1)** Shift into "2" range and fully depress accelerator pedal to full throttle. Ensure 1-2 upshift takes place and shift point conforms to specifications. See appropriate SHIFT SPEED SPECIFICATIONS table.

2) While driving in "2" range, 2nd gear, release accelerator pedal and check engine braking effect. If there is no engine braking effect, 2nd coast brake is faulty. Check for abnormal noise and shock at acceleration and deceleration.

"L" Range Test – While running in "L" range, ensure there is no upshift to 2nd gear. While running in "L" range, release accelerator pedal. If there is no engine braking effect, 1st and reverse brake is faulty. Check for abnormal noise at acceleration and deceleration.

"R" Range Test – Shift into "R" range. Accelerate vehicle from a stop at full throttle. Ensure slipping does not occur.

"P" Range Test – Stop vehicle on 5 degree or more gradient. Shift transaxle into "P" range. Release parking brake. Ensure parking pawl holds vehicle.

AVALON A-541E SHIFT SPEED SPECIFICATIONS [1]

Application	MPH
"D" Range [2]	
NORM Or PWR	
1st-2nd	41-44
2nd-3rd	76-81
3rd-OD	117-123
3rd-OD [2]	24-27
OD-3rd [2]	12-15
OD-3rd	113-118
3rd-2nd	70-75
2nd-1st	34-37
"2" Range	
NORM Or PWR	
1st-2nd	41-44
3rd-2nd	83-88
2nd-1st	34-37
"L" Range	
NORM Or PWR	
3rd-2nd	72-77
2nd-1st	37-39

[1] – Wide open throttle.
[2] – Fully closed throttle.

AVALON A-541E LOCK-UP SPEEDS [1]

Application	MPH
"D" Range [2]	
NORM Or PWR	
Lock-Up ON In 3rd [3]	40-43
Lock-Up OFF In 3rd [3]	36-39
Lock-Up ON In OD	40-43
Lock-Up OFF In OD	36-39

[1] – Throttle valve opening 5 percent.
[2] – There is no lock-up in "L" or "2" ranges.
[3] – With OD switch off.

CAMRY (V6) A-541E SHIFT SPEED SPECIFICATIONS [1]
(1995 & 1996 SE MODELS)

Application	MPH
"D" Range	
1st-2nd	37-41
2nd-3rd	70-75
3rd-OD	108-113
3rd-OD [2]	22-24
OD-3rd [2]	12-15
OD-3rd	104-109
3rd-2nd	65-70
2nd-1st	31-34
"2" Range	
1st-2nd	37-41
3rd-2nd	76-81
2nd-1st	31-34
"L" Range	
3rd-2nd	66-71
2nd-1st	34-37

[1] – Wide open throttle.
[2] – Fully closed throttle.

CAMRY (V6) A-541E SHIFT SPEED SPECIFICATIONS [1]
(1996 EXCEPT SE MODELS)

Application	MPH
"D" Range	
1st-2nd	41-44
2nd-3rd	76-82
3rd-OD	118-124
3rd-OD [2]	24-27
OD-3rd [2]	14-17
OD-3rd	114-119
3rd-2nd	71-76
2nd-1st	34-37
"2" Range	
1st-2nd	41-44
3rd-2nd	83-88
2nd-1st	34-37
"L" Range	
3rd-2nd	73-78
2nd-1st	37-40

[1] – Wide open throttle.
[2] – Fully closed throttle.

CAMRY (V6) A-541E LOCK-UP SPEEDS [1]

Application	MPH
"D" Range [2]	
1995 & 1996 Except SE Models	
Lock-Up ON In 3rd [3]	37-40
Lock-Up OFF In 3rd [3]	33-35
Lock-Up ON In OD	37-40
Lock-Up OFF In OD	33-35
1996 SE Models	
Lock-Up ON In 3rd [3]	40-44
Lock-Up OFF In 3rd [3]	36-39
Lock-Up ON In OD	40-44
Lock-Up OFF In OD	36-39

[1] – Throttle valve opening 5 percent.
[2] – There is no lock-up in "L" or "2" ranges.
[3] – With OD switch off.

LEXUS ES300 A-541E LOCK-UP SPEEDS [1]

Application	MPH
"D" Range [2]	
Lock-Up ON In 3rd [3]	37-40
Lock-Up OFF In 3rd [3]	33-35
Lock-Up ON In OD	37-40
Lock-Up OFF In OD	33-35

[1] – Throttle valve opening 5 percent.
[2] – There is no lock-up in "L" or "2" ranges.
[3] – With OD switch off.

LEXUS ES300 A-541E SHIFT SPEED SPECIFICATIONS [1]

Application	MPH
"D" Range [2]	
1st-2nd	37-41
2nd-3rd	70-75
3rd-OD	108-113
3rd-OD [2]	22-24
OD-3rd [2]	12-15
OD-3rd	104-109
3rd-2nd	65-70
2nd-1st	31-34
"2" Range	
1st-2nd	37-41
3rd-2nd	76-81
2nd-1st	31-34
"L" Range	
3rd-2nd	66-71
2nd-1st	34-37

[1] – Wide open throttle.
[2] – Fully closed throttle.

RAV4 A-540H SHIFT SPEED SPECIFICATIONS [1]

Application	MPH
"D" Range [2]	
NORM Or PWR	
1st-2nd	35-39
2nd-3rd	64-70
3rd-OD	101-108
3rd-OD [2]	19-22
OD-3rd [2]	10-12
OD-3rd	90-96
3rd-2nd	58-64
2nd-1st	27-30
"2" Range	
NORM Or PWR	
1st-2nd	35-39
2nd-1st	27-30
"L" Range	
NORM Or PWR	
3rd-2nd	62-68
2nd-1st	27-30

[1] – Wide open throttle.
[2] – Fully closed throttle.

RAV4 A-540H LOCK-UP SPEEDS [1]

Application	MPH
"D" Range [2]	
NORM	
Lock-Up ON In 3rd [3]	39-43
Lock-Up OFF In 3rd [3]	35-38
Lock-Up ON In OD	37-40
Lock-Up OFF In OD	30-33
PWR	
Lock-Up ON In 3rd [3]	48-51
Lock-Up OFF In 3rd [3]	37-40
Lock-Up ON In OD	41-44
Lock-Up OFF In OD	34-37

[1] – Throttle valve opening 5 percent.
[2] – There is no lock-up in "L" or "2" ranges.
[3] – With OD switch off.

STALL SPEED TEST

CAUTION: Perform test at normal operating fluid temperature of 122-176°F (50-80°C). DO NOT maintain stall speed RPM for more than 5 seconds. Allow vehicle to idle in Neutral or Park for at least 5 minutes before performing next test.

1) Object of test is to check overall performance of transaxle and engine by measuring maximum engine speeds in "D" and "R" ranges.
2) Block front and rear wheels. Connect tachometer to vehicle and ensure it is visible to driver. Apply parking and service brakes. Start engine. Position transmission in "D" range. Fully depress accelerator pedal. Immediately note highest engine RPM. DO NOT perform test longer than 5 seconds. Repeat test in "R" range. See STALL SPEED SPECIFICATIONS table.

STALL SPEED SPECIFICATIONS

Applications	RPM
A-540H	2250-2550
A-541E	2450-2750

3) If stall speed is same for both ranges, but lower than specified RPM, engine output may be insufficient or stator one-way clutch is not operating properly.

NOTE: If stall speed RPM is more than 600 RPM below specified value, torque converter may be faulty.

4) If stall speed in "D" range is higher than specifications, forward clutch may be slipping, No. 2 one-way clutch and OD one-way clutch are not operating properly, or line pressure is too low.

5) If stall speed in "R" range is higher than specifications, direct clutch is slipping, 1st and reverse brake is slipping, line pressure is too low or OD direct clutch is not operating properly.

6) If stall speed in "R" and "D" ranges is higher than specifications, line pressure is too low, fluid level is incorrect or OD one-way clutch is not operating properly.

HYDRAULIC PRESSURE TEST

CAUTION: Hydraulic pressure test should be performed with transmission fluid temperature of 122-176°F (50-80°C).

Line Pressure Test – 1) Ensure transmission fluid is at operating temperature. Block wheels. Support vehicle on safety stands. Remove transaxle case test plug and install pressure gauge. *See Fig. 1.*

2) Fully apply parking brake. Start engine. Apply brakes. Shift into "D" range. On A-540H transaxle, apply battery voltage between ground and terminal No. 1 of shift solenoid valve ST connector. *See Fig. 2.* On both transaxles, measure line pressure at idle. Accelerate to full throttle. Measure line pressure at stall speed. See LINE PRESSURE SPECIFICATIONS table.

3) On all models, repeat test in "R" range. DO NOT ground shift solenoid valve ST in "R" range.

4) If pressures exceed specifications in all ranges, regulator valve or throttle valve is faulty or throttle cable is out of adjustment.

5) If pressures in all ranges are lower than specifications, oil pump, regulator valve, throttle valve or OD direct clutch is faulty or throttle cable is out of adjustment.

6) If pressure is lower than specifications in "D" range only, forward clutch is faulty or "D" range circuit has a fluid leak.

7) If pressure is lower than specifications in "R" range only, direct clutch is faulty, 1st and reverse brake is faulty or "R" range circuit has a fluid leak.

LINE PRESSURE SPECIFICATIONS

Selector Position	Pressure psi (kg/cm²)
A-540H [1]	
"D" Position	
Idle Speed	
With Solenoid Valve ST On	76-102 (5.4-7.2)
With Solenoid Valve ST Off	53-61 (3.7-4.3)
Stall Speed	
With Solenoid Valve ST On	192-225 (13.5-15.8)
With Solenoid Valve ST Off	106-125 (7.5-8.8)
"R" Position	
Idle Speed	76-102 (5.4-7.2)
Stall Speed	192-225 (13.5-15.8)
A-541E	
"D" Position	
Idle Speed	58-66 (4.1-4.7)
Stall Speed	165-179 (11.6-12.6)
"R" Position	
Idle Speed	117-128 (8.2-9.0)
Stall Speed	249-269 (17.5-18.9)

[1] – See Fig. 2 for shift solenoid valve ST activation location.

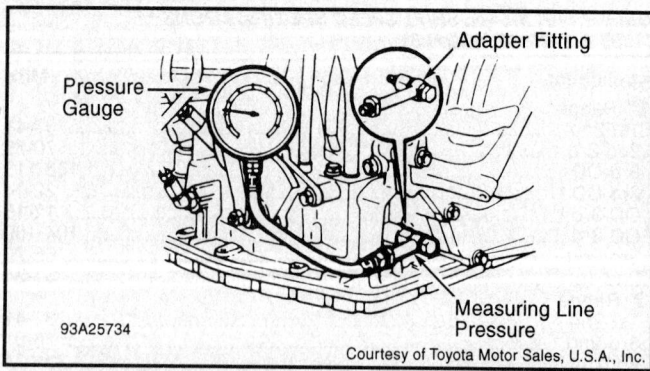

93A25734

Courtesy of Toyota Motor Sales, U.S.A., Inc.

Fig. 1: Checking Hydraulic Pressure

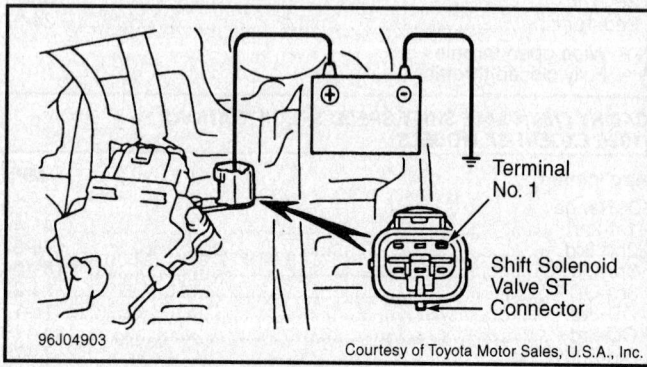

96J04903

Courtesy of Toyota Motor Sales, U.S.A., Inc.

Fig. 2: Activating Shift Solenoid Valve ST

ON-VEHICLE SERVICE
PARK/NEUTRAL POSITION (PNP) SWITCH

Removal & Installation – 1) Remove manual shift lever. Pry back locking tab on manual shaft washer. Remove nut and washer. Remove park/neutral position (PNP) switch.

2) Install PNP switch to manual valve shaft. Install NEW locking plate. Tighten nut and stake with locking plate. Adjust switch by aligning groove and neutral basic line. Tighten bolts to 48 INCH lbs. (5.4 N.m). Install manual shift lever.

THROTTLE CABLE

See appropriate AUTOMATIC TRANSMISSION SERVICING article in TRANSMISSION SERVICING section.

VALVE BODY ASSEMBLY

CAUTION: Note bolt length and location during disassembly. Proper length bolts must be installed to prevent case damage.

Removal – 1) Clean exterior of transaxle. Remove oil pan plug. Drain transaxle. Remove oil pan and gasket. Discard gasket. Remove oil strainer. Note location of magnets in oil pan. Remove magnets. Examine particles in pan. Steel (magnetic) particles indicate bearing, gear, or plate wear. Brass (non-magnetic) particles indicate bushing wear.

2) Remove tube bracket. Note location of oil tubes, and remove oil tubes. Disconnect solenoid wiring harness connector(s). Remove manual detent spring. Remove manual valve. Disconnect throttle cable from cam. Remove valve body assembly. Remove 2nd brake apply gasket.

Installation – 1) Install NEW 2nd brake apply gasket. While holding cam down, slip cable end into slot. DO NOT tangle solenoid wire. Install valve body assembly. Hand tighten valve body assembly bolts. *See Fig. 3.* Tighten bolts to specification. See TORQUE SPECIFICATIONS. Connect solenoid wiring connector(s).

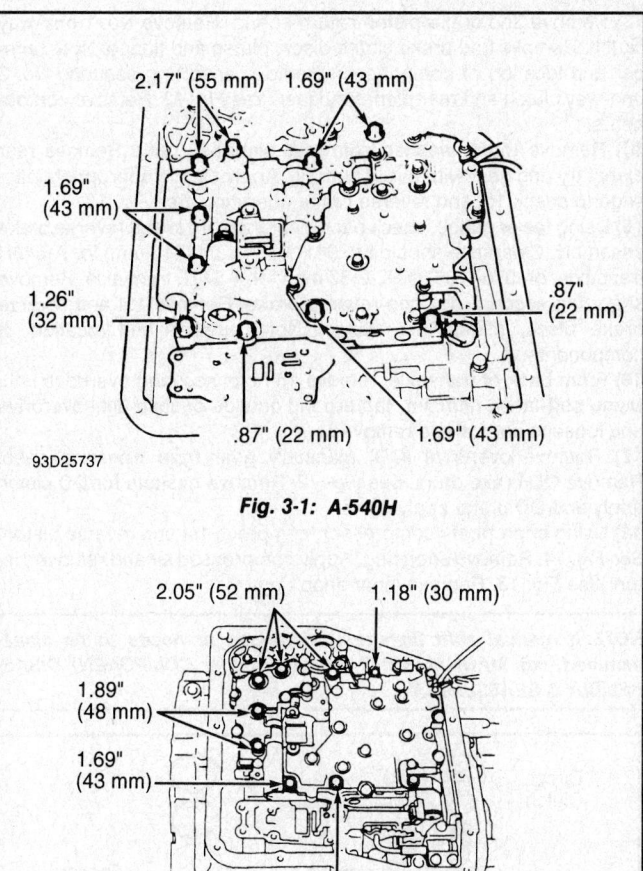

Fig. 3-1: A-540H

Fig. 3-2: A-541E

Courtesy of Toyota Motor Sales, U.S.A., Inc.

Fig. 3: Locating Valve Body Assembly Bolts

2) Align manual valve with pin on manual shaft lever. Lower manual valve body into position. Install 5 bolts finger tight. See Fig. 4. Install detent spring. Ensure manual valve lever is in contact with center of roller at tip of detent spring. Install 2 bolts finger tight. Tap oil tubes into position. DO NOT bend or damage tubes during installation. Install oil tube bracket.

3) Install oil strainer. Install magnets in oil pan. Ensure magnets do not interfere with oil tubes. Install oil pan and new gasket. Install drain plug with NEW washer gasket. Fill transaxle with ATF.

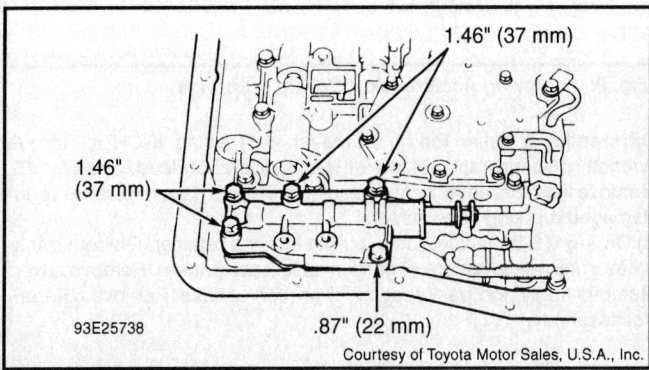

Courtesy of Toyota Motor Sales, U.S.A., Inc.

Fig. 4: Locating Manual Valve Body Bolts

REMOVAL & INSTALLATION

For transaxle removal procedure, see appropriate AUTOMATIC TRANSMISSION REMOVAL article in TRANSMISSION SERVICING section.

TORQUE CONVERTER

NOTE: Torque converter is a sealed unit and must be serviced as complete assembly. Perform following tests to check converter condition. Torque converter and oil cooler lines must be thoroughly cleaned and flushed if transaxle fluid is contaminated.

ONE-WAY CLUTCH TEST

1) Insert a turning tool into inner race of one-way clutch. Install Tester (09350-32014) so that it fits in notch of converter hub and other race of one-way clutch.

2) With torque converter in normal operating position, clutch should lock-up when turned counterclockwise and should rotate freely and smoothly when turned clockwise. See Fig. 5. If one-way clutch fails test in either direction, clean converter. Retest clutch. If clutch fails test, replace converter.

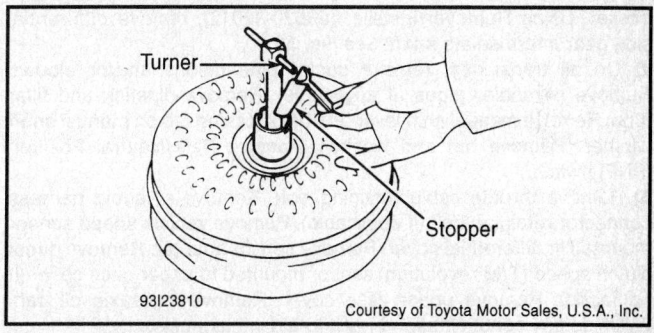

Courtesy of Toyota Motor Sales, U.S.A., Inc.

Fig. 5: Testing Torque Converter One-Way Clutch

CONVERTER SLEEVE RUNOUT TEST

1) Temporarily mount torque converter to drive plate. Mount a dial indicator with needle resting on converter sleeve. See Fig. 6. Rotate converter. If runout exceeds .012" (.30 mm), ensure converter is properly mounted to drive plate.

2) If converter is properly mounted and runout exceeds specifications, replace torque converter. Mark position of converter to ensure correct installation. Remove converter from drive plate.

DRIVE PLATE (FLYWHEEL) RUNOUT TEST

Measure drive plate runout. See Fig. 7. If runout exceeds .008" (.20 mm), or if ring gear is damaged, replace drive plate. If installing a NEW drive plate, note position of spacers. Tighten bolts to 61 ft. lbs. (83 N.m).

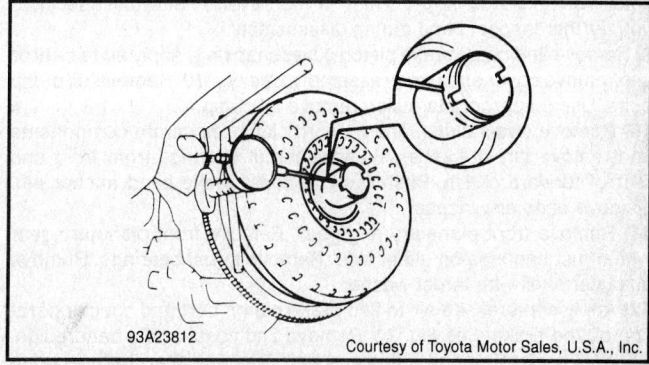

Courtesy of Toyota Motor Sales, U.S.A., Inc.

Fig. 6: Measuring Torque Converter Sleeve Runout

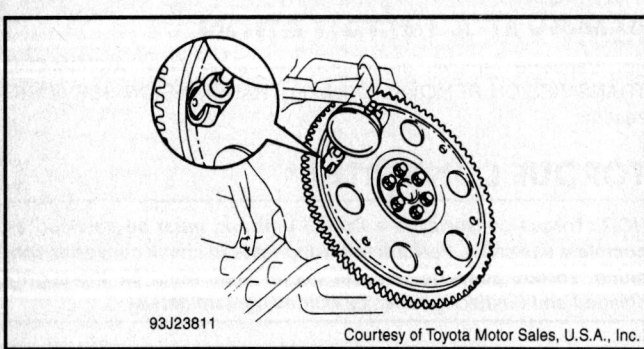

93J23811   Courtesy of Toyota Motor Sales, U.S.A., Inc.

Fig. 7: Checking Drive Plate Runout

TRANSAXLE DISASSEMBLY

NOTE: RAV4 is equipped with a transfer case. For transfer case overhaul procedures, see TOYOTA RAV4 in TRANSFER CASES.

1) On A-540H, remove bolts and nuts on transfer case assembly. Remove transfer case assembly from transaxle. Remove apply gasket. Using Remover/Installer (09520-32012), remove differential side gear intermediate shaft. *See Fig. 53.*

2) On all transaxles, remove cooler pipe unions and/or elbows Remove oil cooler pipes (if applicable). Remove dipstick and filler tube. Remove manual shift lever. Pry back locking tab on manual shaft washer. Remove nut and washer. Remove Park/Neutral Position (PNP) switch.

3) Remove throttle cable retaining bolt. Remove solenoid harness connector retaining bolt (if applicable). Remove vehicle speed sensor mounted in differential cover. Remove sensor adapter. Remove direct clutch speed (T/M revolution) sensor mounted to upper case cover (if equipped). Remove upper case cover. Remove transaxle oil pan. Examine any contamination in pan to aid in diagnosis.

4) Remove oil stainer (filter) and oil pipe hold-down bracket. Remove manual valve body including detent spring. Gently remove all oil pipes by prying up on end of pipe with screwdriver.

5) Disconnect solenoid harness connectors. Remove connector clamp and apply pipe retainer. Remove 1st and reverse apply pipe. Remove valve body bolts. Remove wiring harness clamp. Disconnect throttle cable from cam and remove valve body.

6) Remove throttle cable and solenoid wiring harness. Remove 2nd brake apply gasket. Loosen accumulator cover bolts in crisscross pattern. Remove cover and gasket. Remove forward clutch accumulator. *See Fig. 8.*

7) Remove remaining accumulators by applying 14 psi (1kg/cm²) of air pressure to apply hole. *See Fig. 9.* Cover accumulator bores with a rag when applying air.

8) Mark 2nd coast brake servo apply piston rod where it meets case. Apply 57-114 psi (4-8 kg/cm²) of air pressure to apply hole and measure piston rod travel (stroke). *See Fig. 10.* Piston rod travel should be .079-.138" (2.0-3.5 mm). If rod travel is not within specification, further inspect band during disassembly.

9) Remove 2nd coast brake piston cover snap ring. Apply air to oil hole and remove cover and piston assembly. *See Fig. 10.* Remove oil pump bolts. Using appropriate puller, remove oil pump.

10) Remove direct clutch and forward clutch. Separate components and remove thrust washer. Remove thrust bearings from front and rear of forward clutch. Push out 2nd coast brake band anchor pin. Remove band and inspect.

11) Remove front planetary ring gear. Remove front planetary gear with thrust bearings on either side. Remove thrust bearings. Remove sun gear shell with thrust washer.

12) Apply compressed air to 2nd brake piston port and check operation of 2nd brake. *See Fig. 11.* Remove 2nd coast brake band guide. DO NOT separate band guide and bolt. Remove snap ring securing 2nd brake drum. Remove drum.

13) Remove 2nd brake piston return spring. Remove No. 1 one-way clutch. Remove 2nd brake clutch discs, plates and flange. Note number and location of components. Remove snap ring securing No. 2 one-way clutch and rear planetary gear. *See Fig. 12.* Remove components.

14) Remove thrust washer from rear planetary gear. Remove rear planetary ring gear with thrust bearing. Apply air into appropriate passage to check 1st and reverse brake operation. *See Fig. 13.*

15) Using feeler gauge, check pack clearance of 1st and reverse brake assembly. Clearance should be .041-.085" (1.04-2.16 mm) for A-540H transaxle, or .076-.106" (1.92-2.68 mm) for A-541E transaxle. Remove snap ring securing 1st and reverse brake. Remove 1st and reverse brake discs, plates and flange. Note number and location of components.

16) From back of transaxle, remove 13 bolts securing overdrive unit. Using soft-faced hammer, tap around outside of case until overdrive unit loosens and can be removed.

17) Remove overdrive (OD) planetary gear from transaxle case. Remove OD brake drum. *See Fig. 12.* Remove gaskets for OD clutch apply and OD brake apply ports.

18) Using appropriate compressor, compress 1st and reverse piston. *See Fig. 14.* Remove snap ring. Apply compressed air and remove piston. *See Fig. 13.* Remove inner snap ring.

NOTE: If manual shift linkage is damaged or needs to be disassembled, see MANUAL SHIFT LINKAGE under COMPONENT DISASSEMBLY & REASSEMBLY.

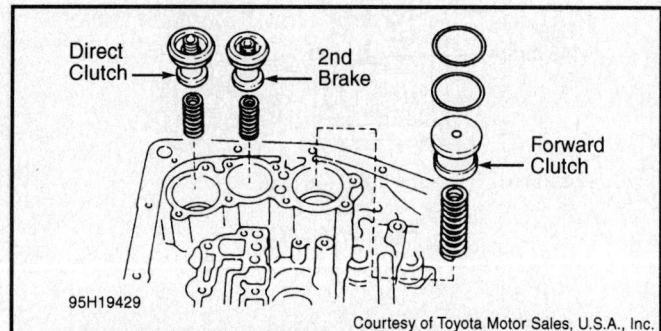

95H19429   Courtesy of Toyota Motor Sales, U.S.A., Inc.

Fig. 8: Exploded View Of Accumulator Piston Assemblies

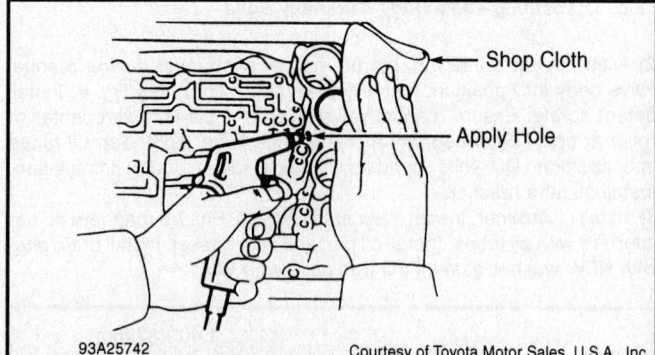

93A25742   Courtesy of Toyota Motor Sales, U.S.A., Inc.

Fig. 9: Removing Accumulator Pistons & Springs

Differential & Drive Pinion Removal – 1) Using INCH lb. torque wrench, measure and record differential total preload. *See Fig. 15.* Remove left differential bearing retainer. Ensure case or retainer is not damaged if prying is necessary.

2) On A-541E transaxle, remove right bearing retainer. On both transaxles, remove carrier cover bolts in crisscross pattern. Remove cover. Remove apply port gasket at lower portion of case. Remove differential assembly.

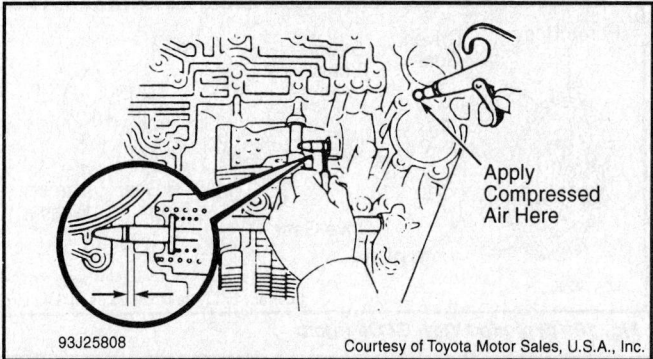

Fig. 10: Checking Operation & Removing 2nd Coast Brake

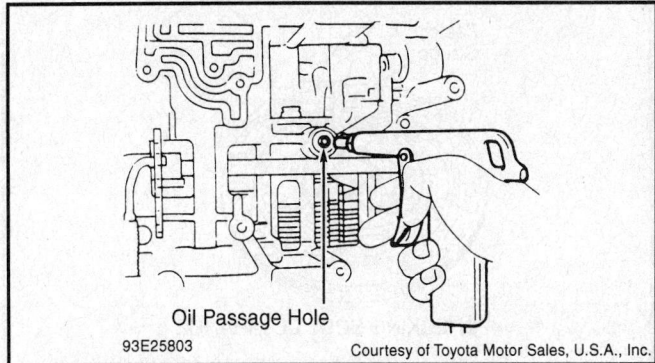

Fig. 11: Checking Operation & Removing 2nd Brake

3) From converter side of case, remove drive pinion cap. Using INCH lb. torque wrench, measure drive pinion preload. *See Fig. 15.* Starting preload should be 4.3-6.9 INCH lbs. (.5-.8 N.m). Subtract the drive pinion preload from total preload.

4) If difference is not 1.1-1.7 INCH lbs. (about .1 N.m), differential side bearing preload may not have been within specification. Carefully inspect condition of all bearings and replace as needed. See COMPONENT DISASSEMBLY & REASSEMBLY.

5) Bend back locking washer securing nut on drive pinion shaft. Secure driven gear and remove nut. Using appropriate puller, remove driven gear and bearing. Using appropriate 2-jaw puller, remove outer race, spacer and oil slinger. Remove snap ring.

6) Turn transaxle case, converter side facing up. Install appropriate bar into hole in drive pinion. Press out drive pinion shaft. Remove bearing cage from drive pinion. Press off bearing if replacement is needed.

COMPONENT DISASSEMBLY & REASSEMBLY

MANUAL SHIFT LINKAGE

Disassembly & Reassembly – 1) Remove parking lock pawl bracket. Using hammer and chisel, cut collar on manual valve shaft. Remove retaining spring. Drive out roll pin on shaft.

2) Slide out shaft from case and remove manual valve lever and parking lock rod. Remove shaft oil seal. Remove pin, spring and parking lock pawl.

3) To assemble, reverse disassembly procedure. Use NEW collar. Lubricate seal before installing manual valve lever shaft. Check operation of parking lock pawl.

OIL PUMP

Disassembly – Remove "O" ring and 2 oil seal rings from pump body and stator shaft. Remove clutch drum thrust washer from stator shaft. Remove bolts attaching oil pump body and stator shaft. Identify top and bottom and keep parts in order. Separate stator shaft and pump body. Mark gear locations for reassembly reference. *See Fig. 16.* Remove front seal.

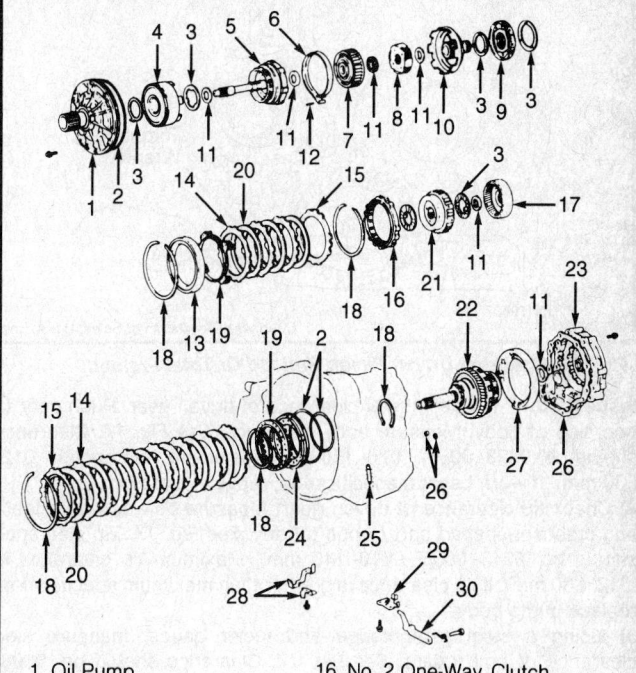

1. Oil Pump	16. No. 2 One-Way Clutch
2. "O" Ring	17. Rear Planetary Ring Gear
3. Thrust Washer	18. Snap Ring
4. Direct Clutch	19. Spring
5. Forward Clutch	20. Disc
6. 2nd Coast Brake Band	21. Rear Planetary Gear
7. Front Planetary Ring Gear	22. Overdrive Planetary Gear
8. Front Planetary Gear	23. Overdrive Case
9. No. 1 One-Way Clutch	24. 1st & Reverse Brake Piston
10. Drum & Sun Gear	25. 2nd Brake Drum Gasket
11. Bearing	26. Gasket
12. Pin	27. Overdrive Brake Drum
13. Second Brake Drum	28. 2nd Coast Brake Band Guide
14. Plate	29. Bracket
15. Flange	30. Parking Lock Pawl

Fig. 12: Exploded View Of Transaxle Internal Components

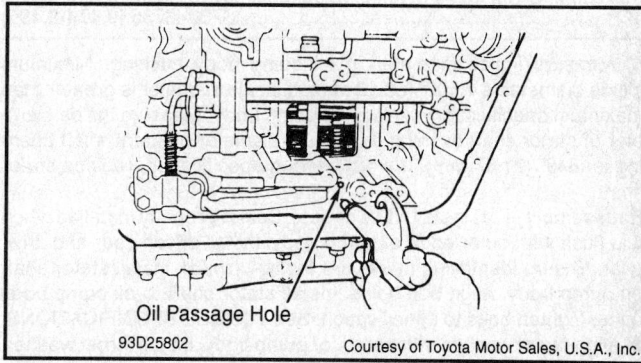

Fig. 13: Checking Operation & Removing 1st & Reverse Brake

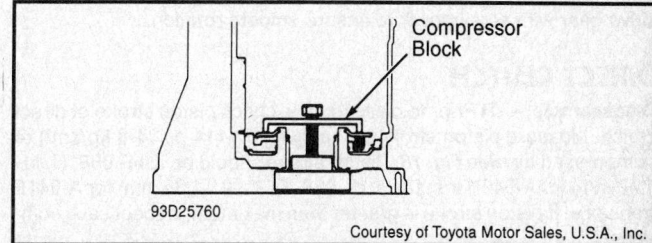

Fig. 14: Compressing 1st & Reverse Brake Piston Springs

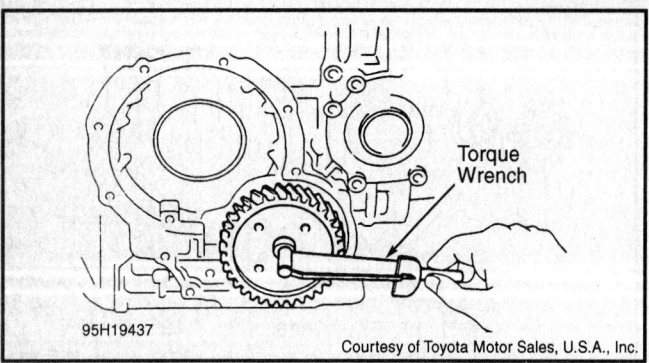

95H19437

Courtesy of Toyota Motor Sales, U.S.A., Inc.

Fig. 15: Checking Driven Pinion Preload Or Total Preload

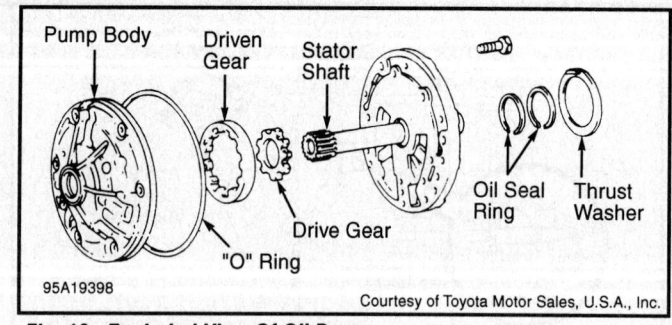

95A19398

Courtesy of Toyota Motor Sales, U.S.A., Inc.

Fig. 16: Exploded View Of Oil Pump

Inspection – 1) Check body clearance of driven gear. Push gear to one side of body. Measure body clearance. See Fig. 17. Clearance should be .0028-.0059" (.070-.150 mm). Maximum clearance is .012" (.30 mm). If worn beyond specification, replace pump body.

2) Check tip clearance of driven gear. Measure between gear teeth and crescent-shaped part of pump body. See Fig. 17. Tip clearance should be .0043-.0055" (.110-.140 mm). Maximum tip clearance is .012" (.30 mm). If tip clearance is greater than maximum specification, replace pump body.

3) Using a steel straightedge and feeler gauge, measure side clearance of both gears. See Fig. 17. Clearance should be .0008-.0020" (.020-.050 mm). Maximum side clearance is .004" (.10 mm). If worn beyond specification, replace pump body. Drive and driven gears are available in different thicknesses. See OIL PUMP DRIVE & DRIVEN GEAR SPECIFICATIONS table.

OIL PUMP DRIVE & DRIVEN GEAR SPECIFICATIONS

ID Mark	Thickness In. (mm)
A-540H	
F	.4209-.4212 (10.690-10.699)
G	.4213-.4216 (10.700-10.709)
H	.4217-.4220 (10.710-10.720)
J	.4221-.4224 (10.721-10.730)
K	.4225-.4228 (10.731-10.740)
A-541E	
A	.3717-.3723 (9.440-9.456)
B	.3723-.3730 (9.456-9.474)
C	.3730-.3736 (9.474-9.490)

4) Measure inside diameter of oil pump body bushing. Maximum inside diameter is 1.503" (38.18 mm). If inside diameter is greater than maximum specification, replace oil pump body. Measure inside diameter of stator shaft bushing. Maximum diameter of stator shaft bushing is .849" (21.57 mm). If worn beyond specification, replace stator shaft.

Reassembly – 1) Install NEW oil seal. Seal is properly installed when it is flush with outer edge of pump body. Install driven gear and drive gear. Ensure identifying marks are facing upward. Install stator shaft on pump body. Align bolt holes. Install stator shaft-to-oil pump body bolts. Tighten bolts to specification. See TORQUE SPECIFICATIONS.

2) Align tab of washer with hollow of pump body. Install thrust washer. Install 2 oil seal rings on oil pump. DO NOT spread ring ends more than required for installation. Ensure oil seal rings move freely. Turn drive gear with screwdriver to ensure smooth rotation.

DIRECT CLUTCH

Disassembly – 1) Prior to disassembly, check piston stroke of direct clutch. Measure piston stroke by applying 57-114 psi (4-8 kg/cm²) of compressed air. See Fig. 18. Piston stroke should be .044-.058" (1.11-1.47 mm) for A-540H transaxle, or .036-.053" (.91-1.35 mm) for A-541E transaxle. If piston stroke is greater than maximum, inspect each component.

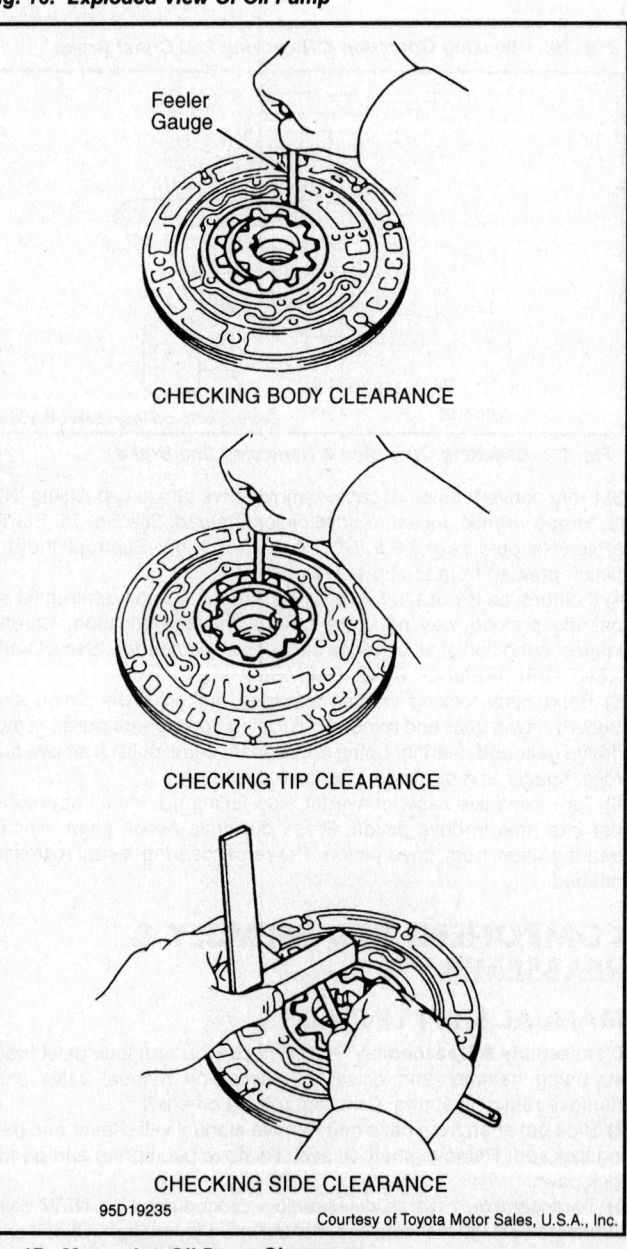

CHECKING BODY CLEARANCE

CHECKING TIP CLEARANCE

CHECKING SIDE CLEARANCE

95D19235

Courtesy of Toyota Motor Sales, U.S.A., Inc.

Fig. 17: Measuring Oil Pump Clearances

2) Remove snap ring from clutch drum. Remove flange, discs and plates. Note number and location of components. See Fig. 19. Compress piston return springs and remove snap ring. Remove spring retainer. Slide direct clutch onto oil pump. Remove piston by applying low pressure compressed air. See Fig. 18. Remove direct clutch from oil pump. Remove "O" ring from clutch piston.

Inspection – Shake piston to ensure direct clutch piston check ball is free. Ensure valve does not leak by applying low pressure compressed air. Inspect discs, plates and flange. Measure inside diameter of direct clutch bushing. Maximum inside diameter is 1.853" (47.07 mm) for A-540H transaxle, or 1.900" (48.27 mm) for A-541E transaxle. If inside diameter is excessive, replace direct clutch.

Reassembly – 1) Install NEW "O" rings on piston. Coat rings with ATF. Press piston in drum with cup side up. Ensure "O" ring is not damaged. Install piston return springs. Install retainer and snap ring.

2) Install plates, discs and flange. Install flange with flat side facing inward. Install outer snap ring. Ensure end gap of snap ring is not aligned with cut-outs in direct clutch drum.

3) Install direct clutch on oil pump. Check piston stroke. Using a dial indicator, measure piston stroke by applying and releasing 57-114 psi (4-8 kg/cm²) of compressed air. *See Fig. 18.*

4) Piston stroke should be .044-.058" (1.11-1.47 mm) for A-540H transaxle, or .036-.053" (.91-1.35 mm) for A-541E transaxle. If piston stroke is less than specification, replace flange. Flange is available in thicknesses of .102" (2.60 mm), .110" (2.80 mm) and .118" (3.00 mm) for A-540H transaxle, or .106" (2.70 mm) and .118" (3.00 mm) for A-541E transaxle.

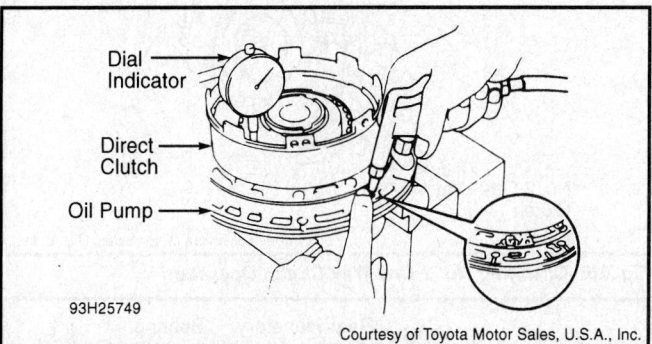

93H25749
Courtesy of Toyota Motor Sales, U.S.A., Inc.

Fig. 18: Checking Direct Clutch Piston Stroke

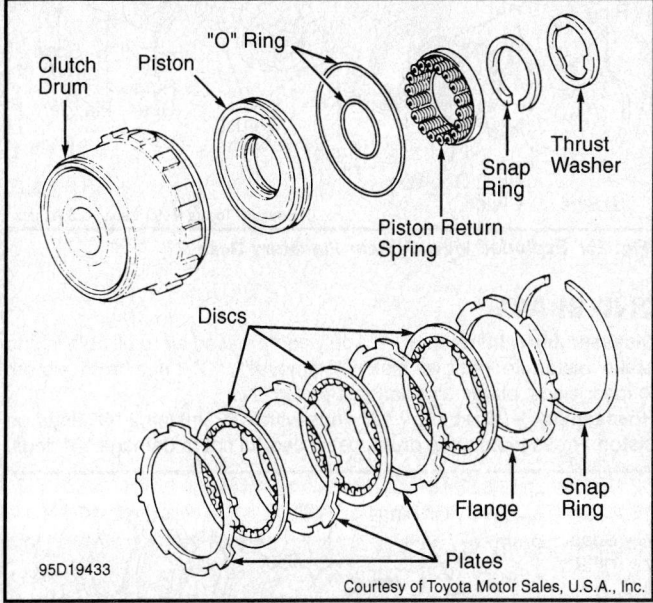

95D19433
Courtesy of Toyota Motor Sales, U.S.A., Inc.

Fig. 19: Exploded View Of Direct Clutch

FORWARD CLUTCH

Disassembly – 1) Prior to disassembly, check piston stroke of forward clutch. Using a dial indicator, measure piston stroke by applying and releasing 54-114 psi (4-8 kg/cm²) of compressed air. *See Fig. 20.* Piston stroke should be .056-.072" (1.41-1.82 mm) for A-540H transaxle, or 071-.087" (1.79-2.21 mm) for A-541E transaxle. If piston stroke is greater than maximum, inspect each component.

2) Remove snap ring from clutch drum. *See Fig. 21.* Remove flange, discs and plates. Note number and location of components. Using appropriate compressor, compress springs and remove snap ring. Remove return spring assembly. Remove retainer and springs. Apply compressed air to oil passage to remove piston. If piston does not come out, remove piston with needle-nose pliers. Remove oil seal rings.

Inspection – Inspect clutch piston. Shake piston to ensure check ball is free. Ensure valve does not leak by applying low pressure compressed air. Replace oil seal rings. DO NOT spread ring ends more than required for installation. Inspect discs, plates and flanges.

Reassembly – 1) Coat NEW "O" rings with ATF. Install "O" rings on piston. Press piston into drum with cup side up. Ensure "O" ring is not damaged.

2) Install return springs, retainer and snap ring in drum. Compress retainer using compressor. Using pliers, install snap ring in groove. Ensure end gap of snap ring is not aligned with spring retainer claw.

3) Install plates, discs and flange. Install flange with flat end facing inward. Install outer snap ring. Ensure end gap of ring is not aligned with cut-outs in clutch drum.

4) Check piston stroke. Piston stroke should be .056-.072" (1.41-1.82 mm) for A-540H transaxle, or 071-.087" (1.79-2.21 mm) for A-541E transaxle. If piston stroke is less than specification, replace flange. Flange is available in thicknesses of .110" (2.80 mm), .118" (3.00 mm), .126" (3.20 mm), .134" (3.40 mm) and .142" (3.60 mm) for A-540H transaxle, or .091" (2.30 mm) and 1.06" (2.70 mm) for A-541E transaxle.

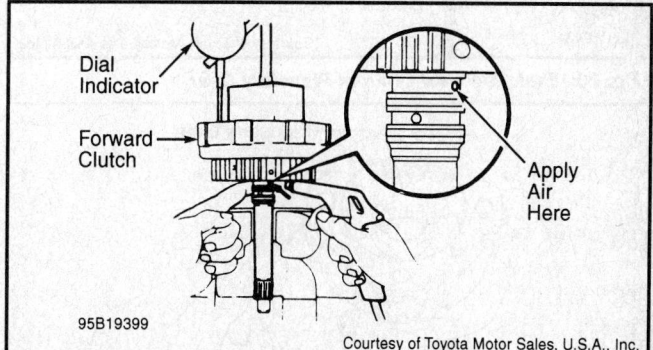

95B19399
Courtesy of Toyota Motor Sales, U.S.A., Inc.

Fig. 20: Checking Forward Clutch Piston Stroke

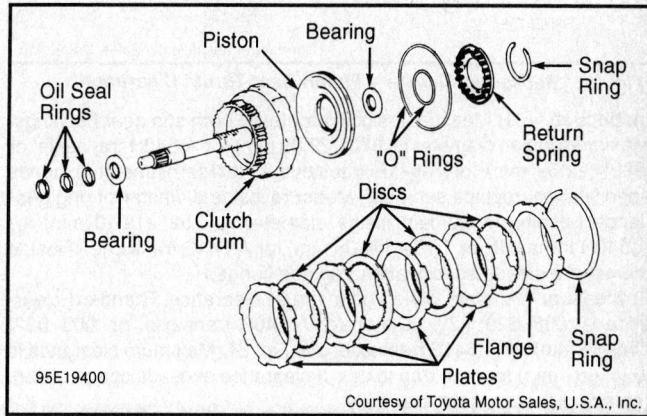

95E19400
Courtesy of Toyota Motor Sales, U.S.A., Inc.

Fig. 21: Exploded View Of Forward Clutch

FRONT PLANETARY GEAR

Disassembly – 1) Check operation of No. 1 one-way clutch. Holding sun gear input drum (shell), turn hub. Hub should turn freely clockwise and should lock when turned counterclockwise. *See Fig. 22.*

2) While turning hub clockwise, remove No. 1 one-way clutch from sun gear. Remove thrust washer from sun gear input drum. Remove snap ring. Remove sun gear from drum. *See Fig. 23.*

3) Using a screwdriver, remove ring gear snap ring. Remove ring gear flange from ring gear. Remove front planetary gear from sun gear.

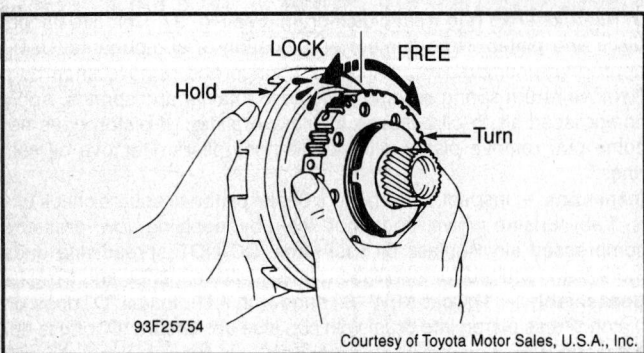

Fig. 22: Checking No. 1 One-Way Clutch Operation

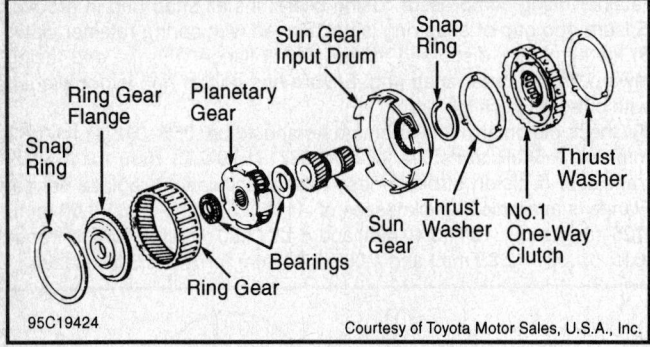

Fig. 23: Exploded View Of Front Planetary Gear

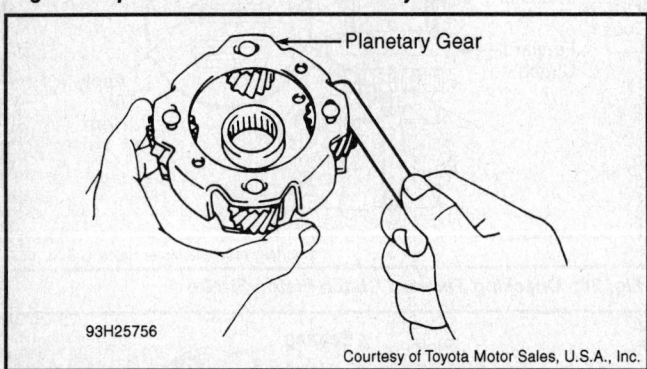

Fig. 24: Measuring Planetary Pinion Gear Thrust Clearance

Inspection – 1) Measure inside diameter of both sun gear bushings. Maximum inside diameter is .870" (22.09 mm) for A-540H transaxle, or .889" (22.59 mm) for A-541E transaxle. If inside diameter exceeds specification, replace sun gear. Measure inside diameter of ring gear flange bushing. Maximum inside diameter is .752" (19.10 mm) for A-540H transaxle, or 1.184" (30.08 mm) for A-541E transaxle. If inside diameter exceeds specification, replace flange.

2) Measure planetary pinion gear thrust clearance. Standard clearance is .008-.020" (.20-.50 mm) for A-540H transaxle, or .006-.022" (.16-.56 mm) for A-541E transaxle. See Fig. 24. Maximum clearance is .024" (.61 mm) for both transaxles. If clearance exceeds specification, replace planetary gear assembly.

Reassembly – Position flange into ring gear. Using a screwdriver, install snap ring. See Fig. 23. Install shaft snap ring on sun gear. Install sun gear input drum on sun gear. Install shaft snap ring. Install thrust washer on sun gear input drum. While turning hub clockwise, slide one-way clutch on sun gear. Recheck operation of one-way clutch.

REAR PLANETARY GEAR

Disassembly – 1) Check operation of No. 2 one-way clutch. Hold outer race and turn rear planetary gear. Gear should turn freely counterclockwise and should lock when turned clockwise. See Fig. 25. Separate No. 2 one-way clutch and rear planetary gear.

2) Remove thrust washer(s) from rear side of planetary gear. Remove snap rings and retainers from both sides. Remove No. 2 one-way clutch from outer race. See Fig. 26.

Inspection – Measure rear planetary pinion gear thrust clearance. Standard clearance is .008-.020" (.20-.50 mm) for A-540H transaxle, or .006-.022" (.16-.56 mm) for A-541E transaxle. Maximum clearance is .024" (.61 mm) for both transaxles. Replace planetary gear assembly if clearance is excessive.

Reassembly – 1) Install No. 2 one-way clutch into outer race. Face No. 2 one-way clutch flanged side toward outer race shiny side. Install retainers and snap rings to both sides of No. 2 one-way clutch.

2) Install planetary gear into No. 2 one-way clutch facing inner race of planetary gear inward toward Black side of outer race. Check operation of No. 2 one-way clutch. Coat thrust washers with petroleum jelly. Install thrust washer on both sides of carrier. Align tab of washers with hollow of carrier.

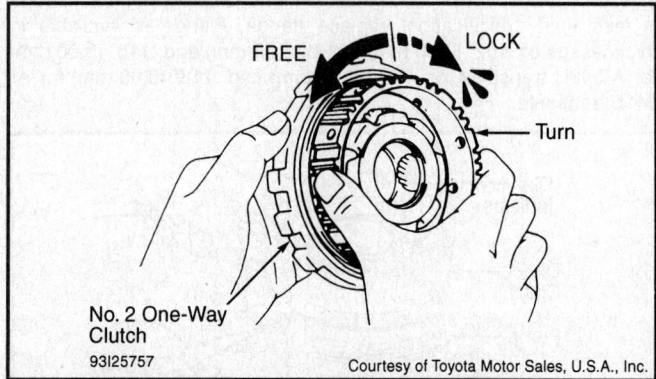

Fig. 25: Checking No. 2 One-Way Clutch Operation

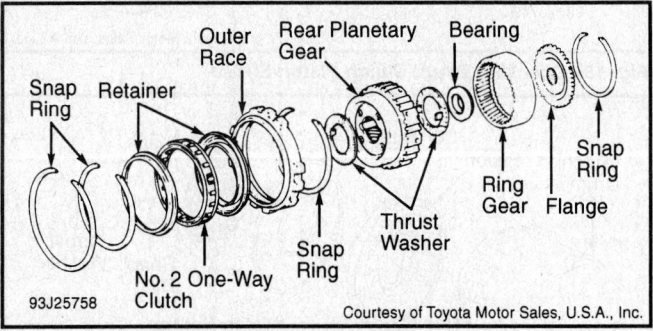

Fig. 26: Exploded View Of Rear Planetary Gear

2ND BRAKE

Disassembly & Inspection – Apply compressed air to oil hole in 2nd brake piston to remove piston. Remove 2 "O" rings from piston. Inspect discs, plates and flange. See Fig. 27.

Reassembly – Coat NEW "O" rings with ATF. Install 2 "O" rings on piston. Press piston into drum, being careful not to damage "O" rings.

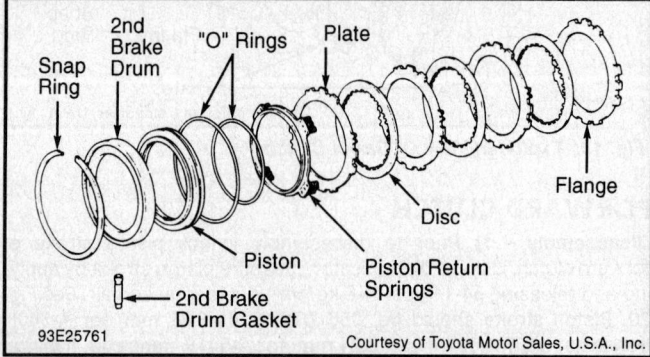

Fig. 27: Exploded View Of 2nd Brake

2ND COAST BRAKE

Disassembly – Remove oil seal ring from piston. Remove piston rod "E" ring while pushing piston with needle-nose pliers. Remove inner spring, plate washer and piston rod. *See Fig. 28.*

Inspection – Inspect brake band lining condition. If brake band is serviceable but piston stroke is not within standard value, select a new piston rod. Piston stroke should be .079-.138" (2.00-3.50 mm). Piston rod is available in lengths of 3.748" (95.20 mm) and 3.791" (96.30 mm).

Reassembly – Install plate washer and inner spring to piston rod. Install "E" ring while pushing piston. Apply ATF to oil seal ring. Install oil seal ring to piston. DO NOT spread ring ends more than necessary for installation.

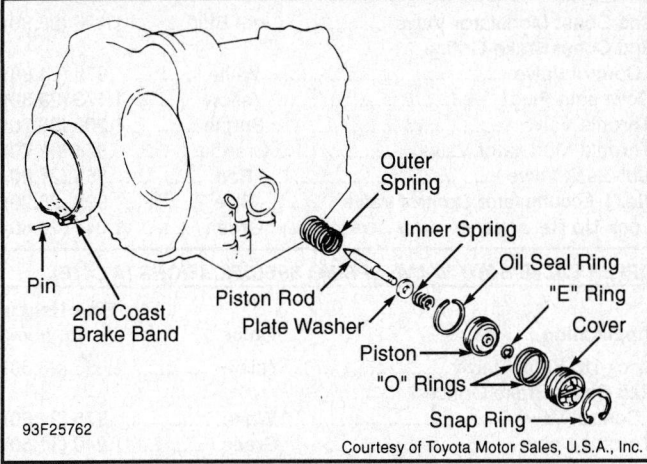

93F25762

Courtesy of Toyota Motor Sales, U.S.A., Inc.

Fig. 28: Exploded View Of 2nd Coast Brake

VALVE BODY ASSEMBLY

CAUTION: When disassembling valve body assembly, DO NOT damage or deform plate that overhangs valve body. Throttle pressure is changed according to number of rings behind throttle valve. Some valve bodies DO NOT have adjusting rings. Note which step at end of plunger sleeves is in contact with valve body before disassembly. Line pressure is affected by plunger location.

The following headings are used to identify valve bodies and component procedures:

- *Disassembly (A-540H)*
- *Disassembly (A-541E)*
- *Disassembly & Reassembly (Upper Valve Body – A-540H & A-541E)*
- *Disassembly & Reassembly (Lower Valve Body – A-540H & A-541E)*
- *Reassembly (Valve Body Assembly – A-540H)*
- *Reassembly (Valve Body Assembly – A-541E)*

Disassembly (A-540H) – **1)** Remove No. 1 and No. 2 solenoids. *See Fig. 29.* DO NOT use a screwdriver to pry up solenoid(s). Remove "O" ring(s) from solenoid(s). Remove shift solenoid valve SL. Remove shift solenoid valve ST with check valve sleeve. Remove shift solenoid valve ST from check valve sleeve.

2) Remove key, 2 check valves and check ball from check valve sleeve. Remove OD brake accumulator assembly. Applying compressed air to accumulator cylinder hole, remove piston and spring. Remove 2 "O" rings from piston.

3) Remove bolts from upper valve body and cover. Note bolt length and location for reassembly reference. Remove upper valve body cover, oil strainer, gaskets and plate. Remove lock-up relay valve sleeve stopper. Turn assembly over.

4) Remove bolts from lower valve body and cover. Carefully remove lower valve body cover gaskets and plate. Note location of check balls, retainers, keys and pins in valve body.

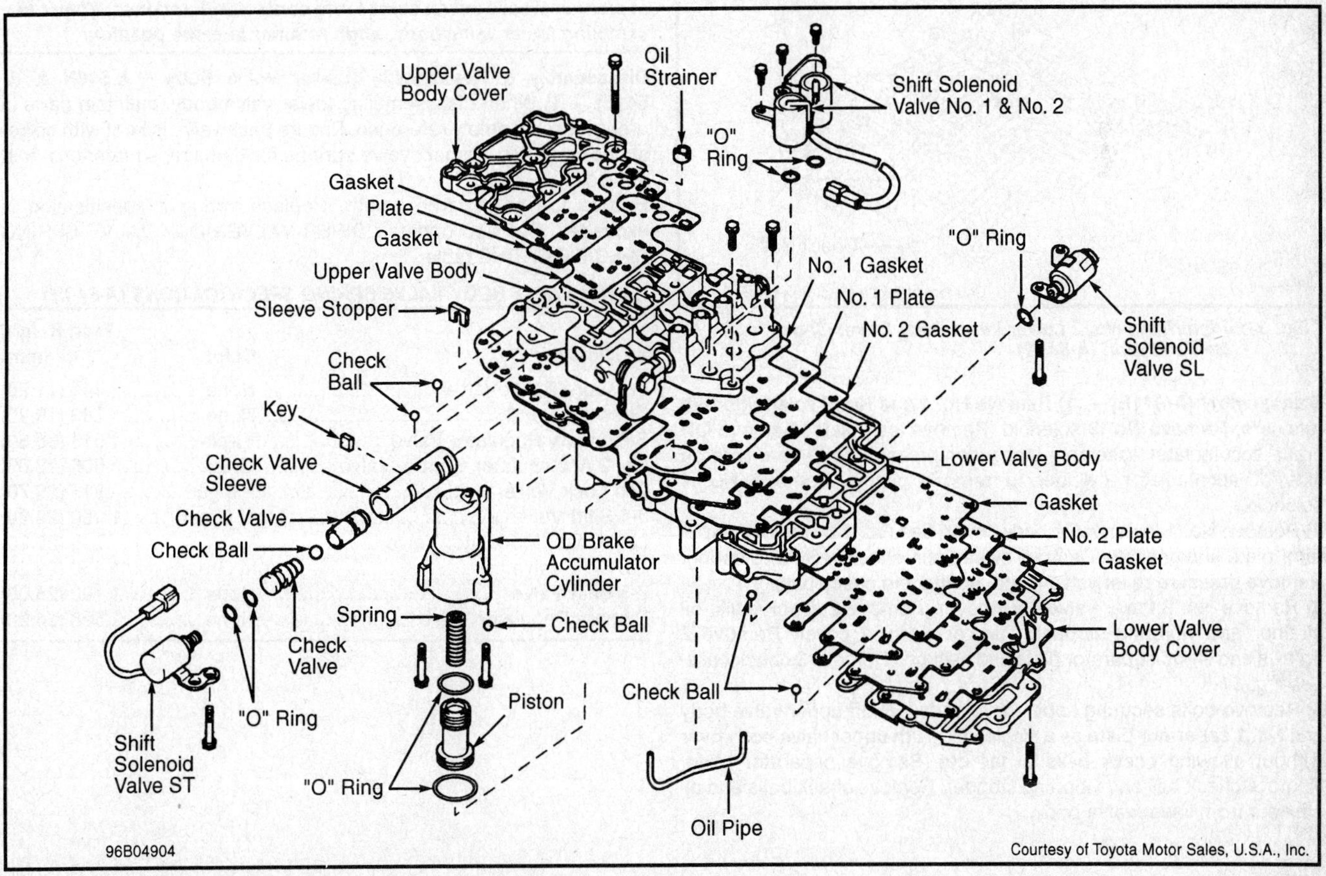

96B04904

Courtesy of Toyota Motor Sales, U.S.A., Inc.

Fig. 29: Exploded View Of Valve Body Assembly (A-540H)

5) Remove 2 check balls from lower valve body. Remove 1 bolt from lower valve body. Remove 3 bolts from upper valve body. Hold No. 1 plate to upper valve body. Lift off upper valve body and plate as a unit. DO NOT lose steel balls, retainers and pins in valve body.

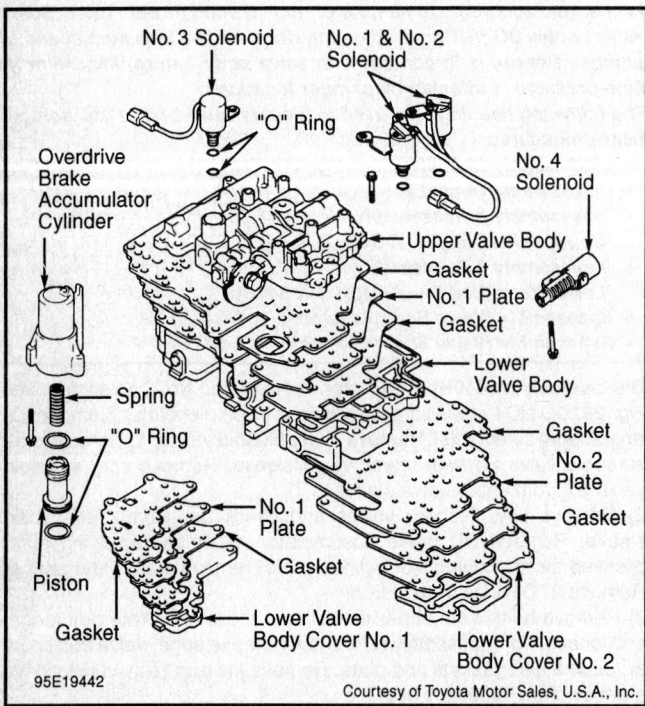

Fig. 30: Exploded View Of Valve Body Assembly (A-541E)

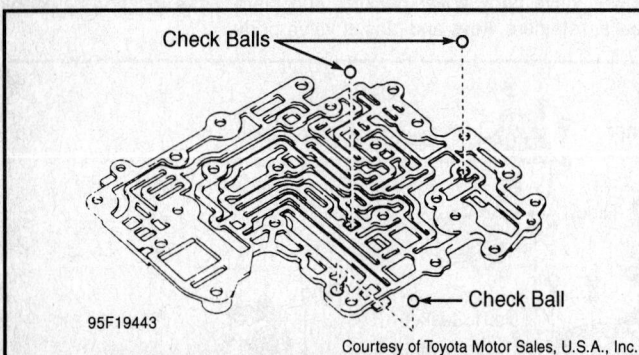

Fig. 31: Identifying No. 2 Lower Valve Body Cover Check Ball Location (A-541E)

Disassembly (A-541E) – 1) Remove No. 1 and No. 2 solenoids with retainers. Remove No. 3 solenoid. Remove lock plate. Remove OD brake accumulator assembly. Apply compressed air to vent hole on side of accumulator cylinder to remove piston. Remove No. 4 solenoid.

2) Remove No. 1 lower valve body cover. *See Fig. 30.* Remove separator plate and gaskets. Remove oil strainer, check valve and spring. Remove pressure relief valve (plate, spring and check ball).

3) Remove No. 2 lower valve body cover. Remove 2 check balls, oil strainer and vibrating stopper. Turn over No. 2 cover. Remove 2 screws and lift off separator plate and gaskets. Remove 3 check balls. *See Fig. 31.*

4) Remove bolts securing upper valve body. Lift off upper valve body and No. 1 separator plate as a single unit. Turn upper valve body over without allowing check balls to fall out. Remove separator plate. Remove check ball and vibrating stopper. Remove check balls and oil strainers from lower valve body.

Disassembly & Reassembly (Upper Valve Body – A-540H & A-541E) – 1) When disassembling upper valve body, maintain parts in order for reassembly reference. Ensure each valve is kept with corresponding spring. Inspect valve springs for damage, squareness, rust and collapsed coils.

2) Measure spring free height. Replace spring if specification is exceeded. See appropriate UPPER VALVE BODY VALVE SPRING SPECIFICATIONS table. Clean all components with solvent and lubricate with ATF. For parts identification, *see Figs. 32 and 33.*

UPPER VALVE BODY VALVE SPRING SPECIFICATIONS (A-540H)

Application	Color	Free Height In. (mm)
2nd Coast Modulator Valve	Light Blue	1.126 (28.60)
2nd Coast Brake Orifice Control Valve	White	.976 (24.80)
Downshift Plug	Yellow	1.173 (29.80)
Throttle Valve	Purple	1.209 (30.70)
Throttle Modulator Valve	Orange	.854 (21.70)
Cut-Back Valve	Red	.858 (21.80)
No. 1 Accumulator Control Valve	Blue	.992 (25.20)
Lock-Up Relay Valve	Green	1.047 (26.60)

UPPER VALVE BODY VALVE SPRING SPECIFICATIONS (A-541E)

Application	Color	Free Height In. (mm)
Lock-Up Relay Valve	Yellow	1.055 (26.80)
2nd Coast Brake Orifice Control Valve	White	.976 (24.80)
Throttle Valve	Green	1.240 (31.50)
Downshift Plug	None	.591 (15.00)
Low Coast Modulator Valve	Purple	.795 (20.20)

NOTE: On A-540H transaxle, line pressure changes according to part of plunger sleeve which comes into contact with retainer. When reassembling lower valve body, align retainer in same position.

Disassembly & Reassembly (Lower Valve Body – A-540H & A-541E) – 1) When disassembling lower valve body, maintain parts in order for reassembly reference. Ensure each valve is kept with corresponding spring. Inspect valve springs for damage, squareness, rust and collapsed coils.

2) Measure spring free height. Replace spring if specification is exceeded. See appropriate LOWER VALVE BODY VALVE SPRING SPECIFICATIONS table.

LOWER VALVE BODY VALVE SPRING SPECIFICATIONS (A-540H)

Application	Color	Free Height In. (mm)
Pressure Relief Valve	None	.441 (11.20)
Check Valve	None	.783 (19.90)
Secondary Regulator Valve	Purple	1.516 (38.50)
No. 2 Accumulator Control Valve	Gray	.906 (23.00)
2nd Lock Valve	Orange	.815 (20.70)
3-4 Shift Valve	Light Green	1.150 (29.20)
Low Coast Modulator Valve	Purple	.795 (20.20)
1-2 Shift Valve	Light Green	1.150 (29.20)
2-3 Shift Valve	None	1.102 (28.00)
Primary Regulator Valve	None	2.528 (64.20)

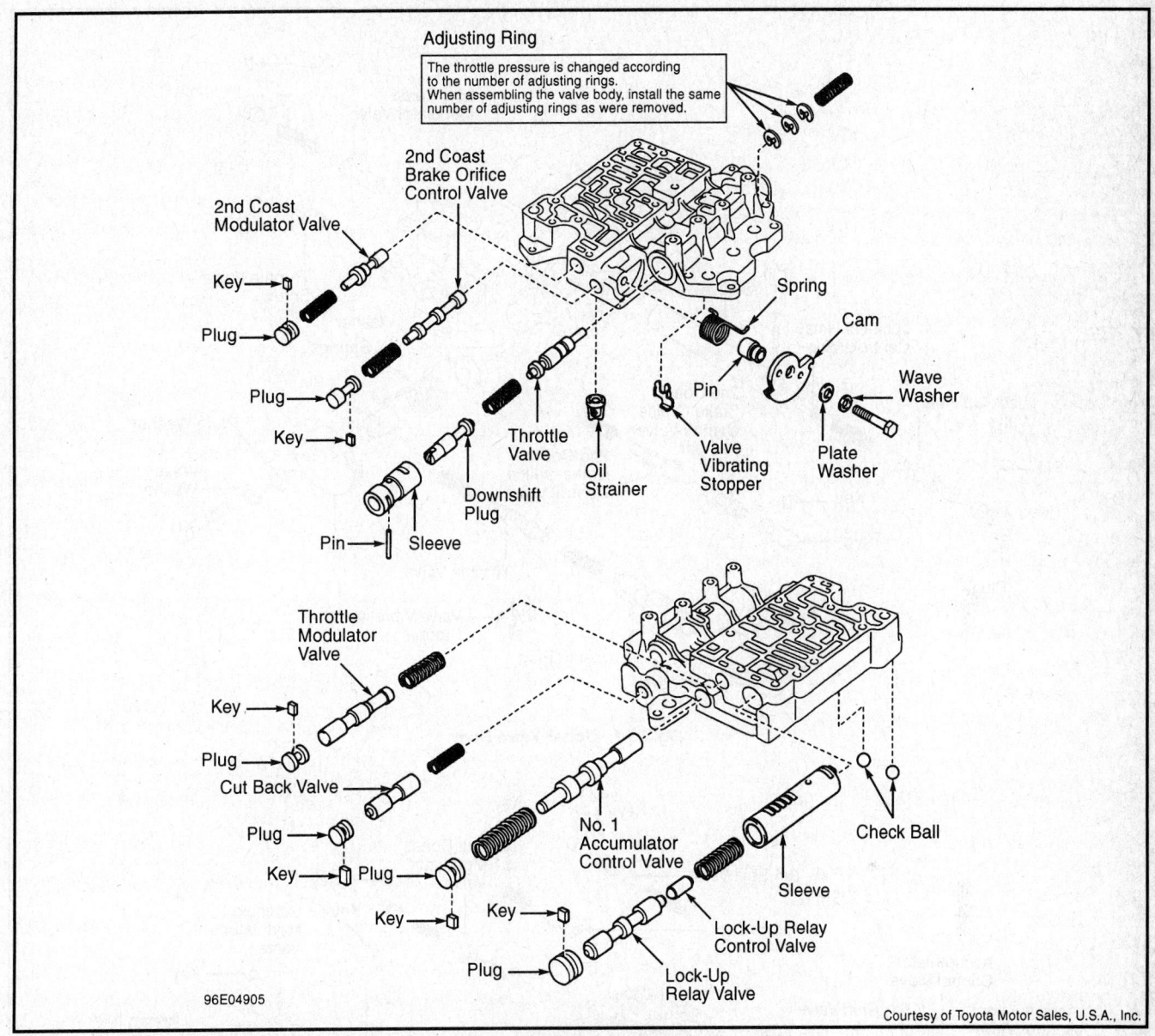

Adjusting Ring

The throttle pressure is changed according to the number of adjusting rings. When assembling the valve body, install the same number of adjusting rings as were removed.

96E04905

Courtesy of Toyota Motor Sales, U.S.A., Inc.

Fig. 32: Exploded View Of A-540H Upper Valve Body (Viewed From Both Ends)

LOWER VALVE BODY VALVE SPRING SPECIFICATIONS (A-541E)

Application	Color	Free Height In. (mm)
Accumulator Control Valve	Red	.988 (25.10)
2-3 Shift Valve	None	1.102 (28.00)
1-2 Shift Valve	Light Green	1.150 (29.20)
Reverse Control Valve	White/Purple	1.50 (38.1)
Cut-Back Valve	None	.858 (21.80)
Primary Regulator Valve	None	1.441 (36.60)
3-4 Shift Valve	None	1.102 (28.0)
2nd Lock Valve	None	.815 (20.70)
2nd Coast Modulator Valve	White	1.268 (32.20)
Solenoid Modulator Valve	Purple/Pink	1.189 (30.20)
Secondary Regulator Valve	None	1.846 (46.90)

Reassembly (Valve Body Assembly – A-540H) – 1) Position NEW No. 1 gasket, No. 1 separator plate and NEW No. 2 gasket on upper valve body. For gasket identification, *see Fig. 35.* Ensure check balls are correctly installed. *See Fig. 36.* Place upper valve body with No. 1 plate and gaskets on lower valve body.

2) Hold upper valve body, No. 1 plate and gaskets so they do not separate. Align each bolt hole in valve bodies with gaskets and plate. Note length and location of bolts. Install and finger tighten 3 bolts in upper valve body to secure lower valve body. *See Fig. 37.*

3) Install lock-up relay valve sleeve stopper. Install upper valve body cover gaskets, plate and throttle modulator oil strainer. Install upper valve body cover, and finger tighten 11 bolts in valve body cover. *See Fig. 37.* Install and finger tighten bolts in lower valve body.

4) Install check balls into lower valve body. Install NEW lower valve body cover gaskets and No. 2 plate. Install NEW lower valve body cover and finger tighten 12 bolts in valve body cover. Tighten bolts to specification. See TORQUE SPECIFICATIONS.

5) Coat NEW "O" rings with ATF. Install "O" rings on piston. Insert spring and piston into cylinder. Place check ball on No. 1 gasket. Install accumulator. Install and tighten 2 bolts. Install shift solenoids valves SL and ST. Install No. 1 and No. 2 shift solenoids.

Reassembly (Valve Body Assembly – A-541E) – 1) Install check ball and vibrating stopper to upper valve body. *See Fig. 38.* Install oil strainers and check ball to lower valve body. Position No. 1 gasket against upper valve body. *See Fig. 39.* Place separator plate and No. 2 gasket on No. 1 gasket.

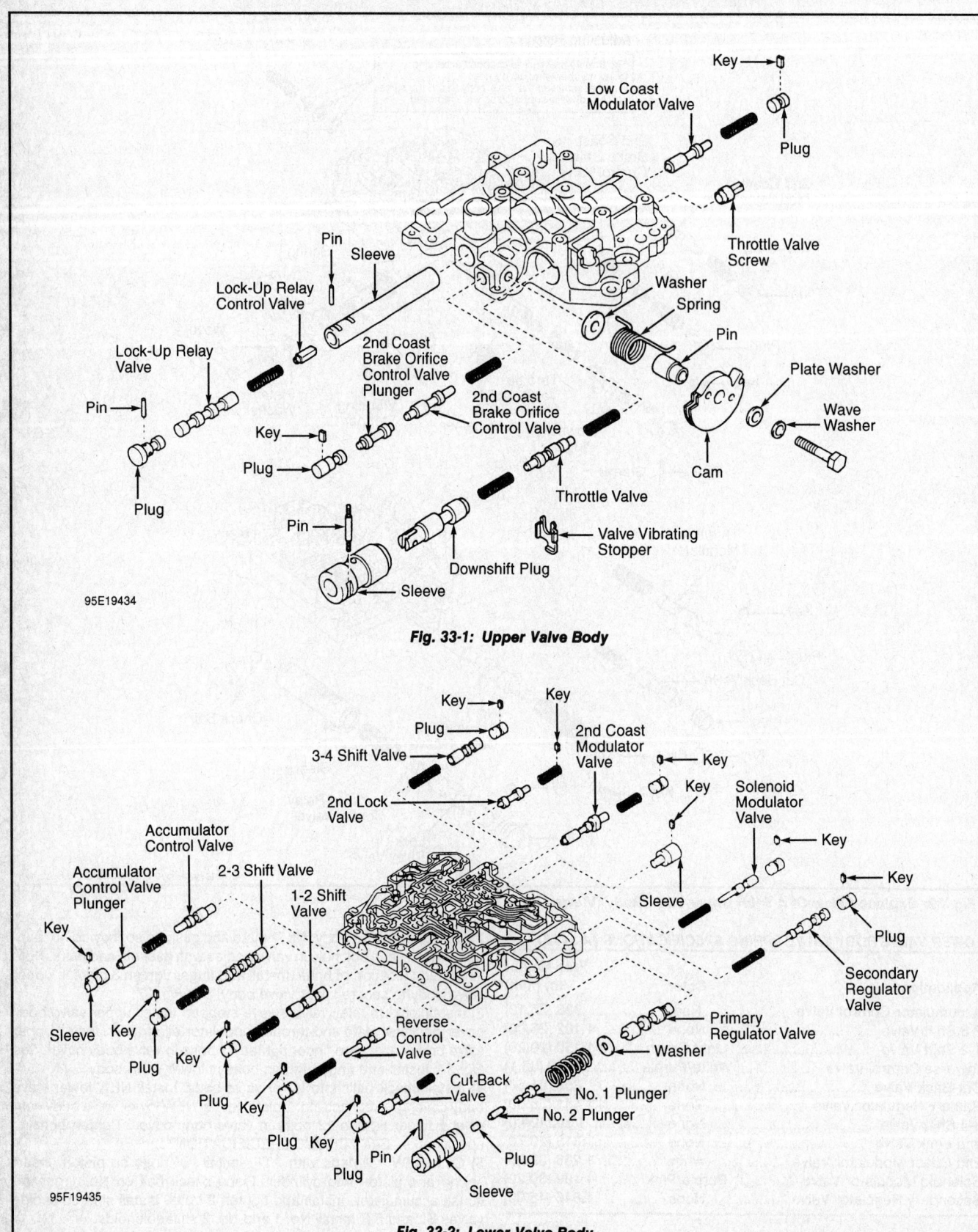

95E19434

Fig. 33-1: Upper Valve Body

95F19435

Fig. 33-2: Lower Valve Body

Courtesy of Toyota Motor Sales, U.S.A., Inc.

Fig. 33: Exploded View Of A-541E Upper & Lower Valve Bodies

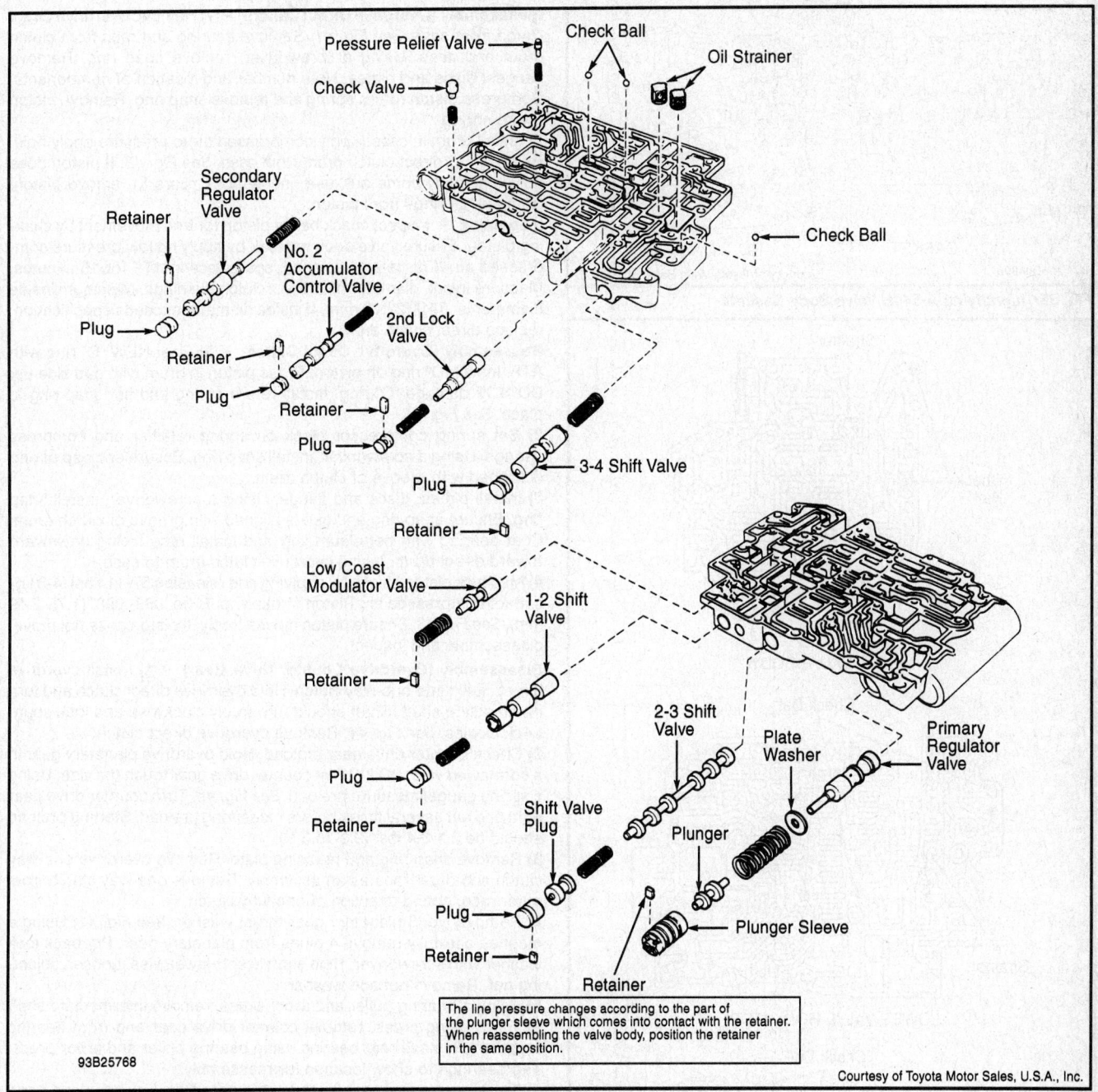

Pressure Relief Valve
Check Ball
Oil Strainer
Check Valve
Check Ball
Secondary Regulator Valve
Retainer
No. 2 Accumulator Control Valve
Plug
Retainer
2nd Lock Valve
Plug
Retainer
Plug
3-4 Shift Valve
Plug
Retainer
Low Coast Modulator Valve
1-2 Shift Valve
Retainer
2-3 Shift Valve
Plate Washer
Primary Regulator Valve
Plug
Plunger
Retainer
Shift Valve Plug
Plunger Sleeve
Plug
Retainer

The line pressure changes according to the part of the plunger sleeve which comes into contact with the retainer. When reassembling the valve body, position the retainer in the same position.

93B25768

Courtesy of Toyota Motor Sales, U.S.A., Inc.

Fig. 34: Exploded View Of A-540H Lower Valve Body (Viewed From Both Ends)

2) Hold gasket and plate assembly against upper valve body. Turn assembly over and install on lower valve body assembly. Align bolt holes and install bolts. *See Fig. 40.*

3) Install check balls in No. 2 lower valve body. Place gaskets and separator plate on valve body. Secure in place with screws. Install oil strainer, check ball and vibrating stopper in lower valve body. Install No. 2 lower valve body. Align bolt holes and install bolts. *See Fig. 40.*

4) Install oil strainer and check valve in lower valve body. Install No. 1 lower valve body cover with gaskets and separator plate. Install bolts. Tighten bolts to specification. See TORQUE SPECIFICATIONS.

5) Install pressure relief valve. Tighten 3 upper valve body bolts. Install OD brake accumulator assembly. Install lock plate. Install all solenoids.

OVERDRIVE UNIT

Disassembly (Overdrive Brake) – 1) While pushing return spring, remove snap ring with a screwdriver. Remove piston return spring. Remove plates, discs and flange. Note number and location of components. *See Fig. 41.*

2) Remove piston from drum by applying compressed air to oil hole. *See Fig. 42.* Ensure piston does not tilt. Remove "O" rings from piston. Inspect disc, plate and flange. If discs are replaced, soak discs in ATF for 15 minutes.

Reassembly (Overdrive Brake) – 1) Install "O" rings on piston. Coat "O" rings with ATF. Install piston in drum. Ensure "O" ring is not damaged. Install flange facing flat end upward.

2) Install discs, plates. Install cushion plate with rounded end upward. Install piston return spring assembly. Install snap ring into case. Ensure end gap of snap ring is not aligned with cutouts.

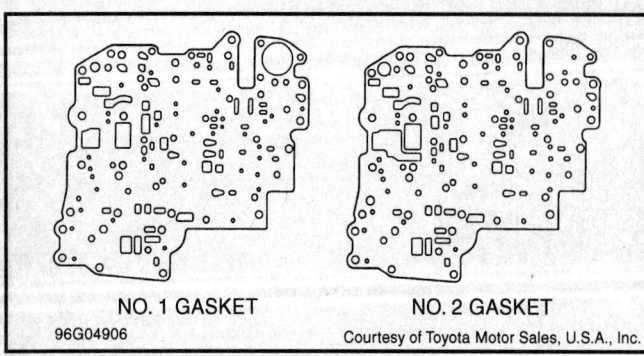

NO. 1 GASKET   NO. 2 GASKET

96G04906   Courtesy of Toyota Motor Sales, U.S.A., Inc.

Fig. 35: Identifying A-540H Valve Body Gaskets

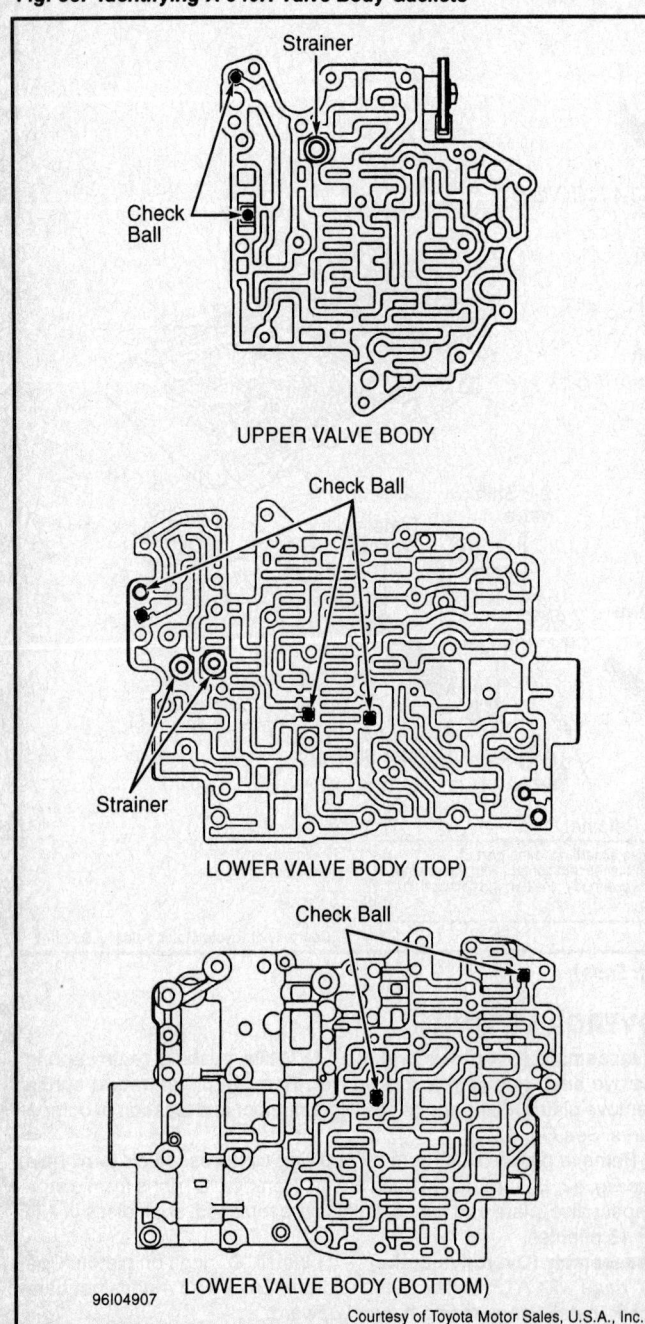

96I04907   Courtesy of Toyota Motor Sales, U.S.A., Inc.

Fig. 36: Locating A-540H Valve Body Check Balls

Disassembly (Overdrive Direct Clutch) – **1)** Remove overdrive direct clutch from case. See Fig. 41. Remove bearing and race from clutch drum and case. Using a screwdriver, remove snap ring. Remove flanges, discs and plates. Note number and location of components. Compress piston return spring and remove snap ring. Remove piston return spring.

2) Install drum in case. Apply compressed air to pressure apply hole. Remove OD direct clutch drum from case. See Fig. 43. If piston does not completely come out, use needle-nose pliers to remove piston. Remove "O" rings from piston.

Inspection – Inspect check ball of piston for free movement by shaking piston. Ensure valve does not leak by applying low pressure compressed air. If discs are replaced, soak discs in ATF for 15 minutes. Measure inside diameter of 2 direct clutch bushings. Maximum inside diameter is .871" (22.13 mm). If inside diameter exceeds specification, replace direct clutch drum.

Reassembly (Overdrive Direct Clutch) – **1)** Coat NEW "O" ring with ATF. Install "O" ring on piston. Press piston in drum with cup side up. DO NOT damage "O" ring. Install return spring and set snap ring in place. See Fig. 41.

2) Set spring compressor block on spring retainer and compress springs. Using a screwdriver, install snap ring. Ensure end gap of ring is aligned with groove of clutch drum.

3) Install plates, discs and flange. Using a screwdriver, install snap ring. Ensure snap ring end gap is aligned with groove of clutch drum. Coat bearing with petroleum jelly and install race facing downward toward direct drum. Install overdrive clutch drum to case.

4) Measure piston stroke by applying and releasing 57-114 psi (4-8 kg/cm²) of compressed air. Piston stroke should be .069-.098" (1.75-2.49 mm). See Fig. 43. Ensure piston moves freely. If piston does not move, disassemble and inspect.

Disassembly (Overdrive Counter Drive Gear) – **1)** Install overdrive direct clutch into one-way clutch. Hold overdrive direct clutch and turn intermediate shaft. Shaft should turn freely clockwise and lock counterclockwise. See Fig. 44. Remove overdrive direct clutch.

2) Check counter drive gear preload. Hold overdrive planetary gear in a soft-jawed vise. DO NOT let counter drive gear touch the vise. Using a spring gauge, measure preload. See Fig. 45. Turn counter drive gear right and left several times before measuring preload. Starting preload should be 2.1-3.4 lbs. (9.2-15.3 N).

3) Remove snap ring and retaining plate. Remove overdrive one-way clutch and outer race as an assembly. Remove one-way clutch from outer race, noting direction of one-way clutch.

4) Remove No. 3 planetary gear thrust washer. See Fig. 41. Using a magnet, carefully remove 4 plugs from planetary gear. Pry back lock washer with screwdriver. Hold shaft in soft-jawed vise. Loosen adjusting nut. Remove nut and washer.

5) Using a bearing puller and arbor press, remove intermediate shaft bearing. Using press, remove counter drive gear and front bearing together. Remove rear bearing using bearing puller and arbor press. Tag bearings to show location for reassembly.

6) To remove overdrive planetary ring gear from counter drive gear, pull up ring gear while compressing snap ring with needle-nose pliers. Remove snap ring from groove.

7) Remove ring gear from counter drive gear. Using a brass drift bar and hammer, drive outer races from counter drive gear. Remove snap ring from counter drive gear. Tag races to show location for reassembly.

Inspection – Measure planetary pinion gear thrust clearance. Standard clearance is .006-.022" (.16-.56 mm). Maximum clearance is .024" (.61 mm). If clearance is excessive, replace planetary gear assembly.

Reassembly (Overdrive Counter Drive Gear) – **1)** Install snap ring in counter drive gear. Install 2 outer races to both sides of counter drive gear. Press in outer races until races touch snap ring.

2) Install snap ring to ring gear. While pushing down on ring gear, squeeze snap ring end with needle-nose pliers. Install overdrive planetary ring gear into counter drive gear.

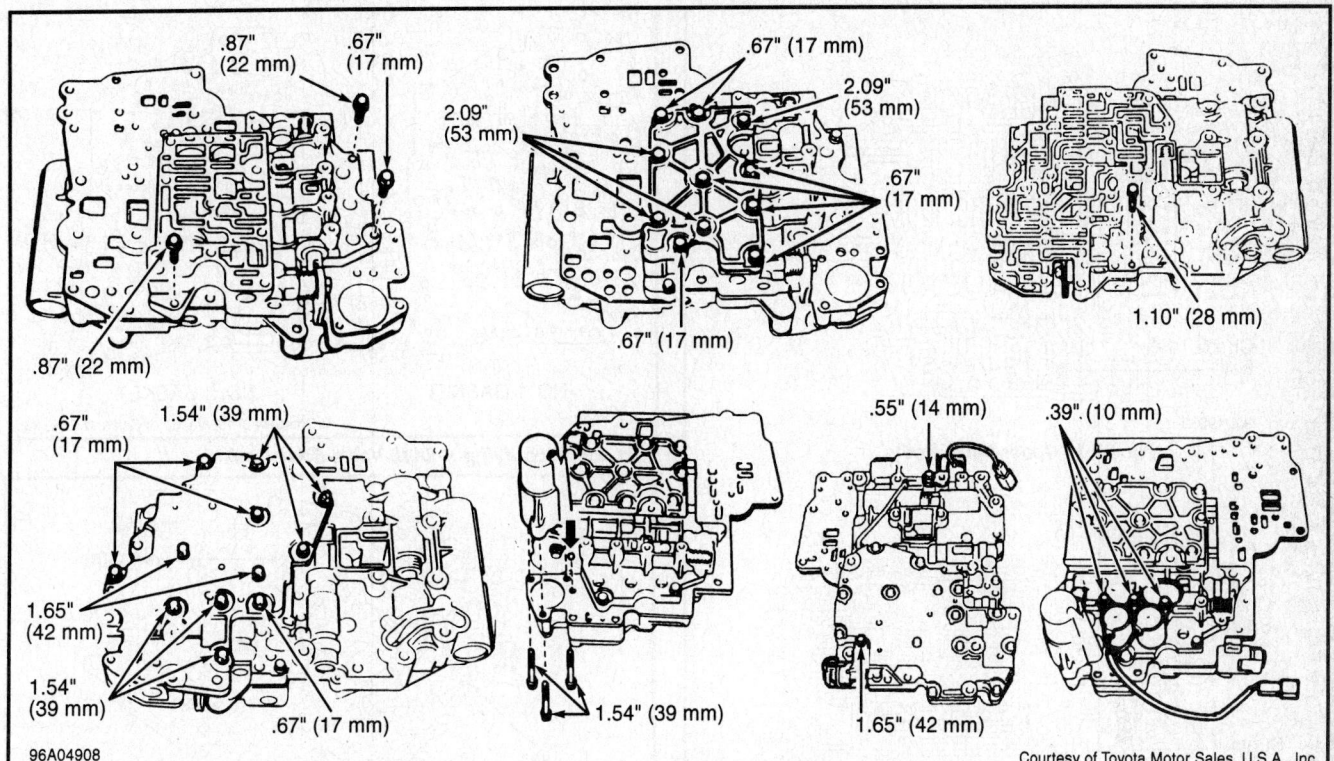

96A04908   Courtesy of Toyota Motor Sales, U.S.A., Inc.

Fig. 37: Locating A-540H Valve Body Bolts

3) Install rear bearing on shaft. Press in bearing until side surface of inner race touches planetary carrier. Install counter drive gear on shaft. Mesh ring gear with planetary pinions. Place front bearing on shaft. Hold ring gear to prevent shaft from falling.

4) Press in bearing until there is slight play between bearings. Install intermediate shaft bearing. Press bearing until bearing slightly touches front bearing of counter drive gear.

5) Place NEW locking washer and adjusting nut on intermediate shaft. Adjust preload of counter drive gear. Holding shaft in a soft-jawed vise and using a tension gauge and lock nut wrench on adjusting nut, tighten adjusting nut. See Fig. 45.

6) Rotate counter drive gear right and left several times before measuring preload. Tighten adjusting nut until preload is 2.1-3.4 lbs. (9.2-15.3 N). Bend locking washer tab until even with adjusting nut groove.

7) Install 4 plugs into pinion shaft. Install No. 3 thrust washer with groove facing overdrive case. Install one-way clutch into outer race. Install retainers on both sides of one-way clutch. Install one-way clutch into overdrive planetary gear. Ensure one-way clutch is installed in correct direction. Install retaining plate and snap ring.

8) Hold overdrive clutch and turn intermediate shaft. Shaft should turn freely clockwise and lock counterclockwise. See Fig. 44. Remove overdrive clutch from one-way clutch.

9) While turning overdrive planetary gear clockwise, install gear on overdrive direct clutch. If overdrive planetary gear is properly installed, clearance between counter drive gear and overdrive case will be .94" (24.0 mm). See Fig. 46.

Disassembly (Overdrive Case) – Remove snap ring. Remove retaining plate and 2 springs. Remove OD direct clutch accumulator piston from overdrive case. Remove "O" ring from piston. Spread 2 oil seal rings apart and remove rings.

Reassembly (Overdrive Case) – Spread rings and install in grooves. After installing oil seal rings, check for smooth movement. Coat "O" ring with ATF. Install NEW "O" ring on accumulator piston. Install accumulator piston, springs, retaining plate and snap ring.

DIFFERENTIAL ASSEMBLY (A-540H)

Disassembly – **1)** Remove right case bearing outer race. See Fig. 47. Use a dial indicator to measure differential end play. End play should be .0071-.0323" (.180-.820 mm). See Fig. 48. Remove ring gear mounting case sleeve. Remove 4 oil seal rings from ring gear mounting right case. Remove snap ring and speedometer drive gear.

2) Place match marks on ring gear mounting left case and right case. Remove bolts and left case. Place match marks on ring gear and left case. Place left case on A/T Tool Set (09350-32014). Using a plastic hammer, remove ring gear from left case.

3) Remove No. 2 thrust washer. Remove front differential left case from ring gear mounting right case. Using a Torx wrench, remove screws from left case. Separate left and right cases. DO NOT scratch contact surface of needle bearing.

4) Remove the following parts from front differential cases: 2 differential side gears and 2 side thrust washers, differential spider, 4 differential pinions and 4 pinion washers.

5) Remove No. 1 thrust washer. Check operation of clutch pistons. Plug one hole in right case with your hand. Apply compressed air into other hole and confirm pistons move. See Fig. 49.

6) Remove hydraulic multi-plate clutch discs and plates. Remove snap ring. Remove flange, discs and plates. Note number and location of components. Using Spring Compressor (09350-32014), compress return spring. Remove snap ring. Apply compressed air to right case hole. Remove No. 1 piston. Remove "O" ring from No. 1 piston. Using small screwdriver, remove reaction sleeve and No. 2 piston. Remove 3 "O" rings from reaction sleeve and No. 2 piston.

7) Using Bearing Remover and Attachment (09950-00020, 09950-00030), remove ring gear mounting left case bearing. Using A/T Tool Set (09350-32014) and arbor press, install ring gear mounting left case bearing.

8) Using a chisel and hammer, cut out ring gear mounting right case bearing cage. DO NOT damage right case. Using A/T Tool Set (09350-32014) and arbor press, remove bearing inner race. Using Bearing Replacer (09316-60010) and arbor press, install NEW ring gear mounting right case bearing.

AUTOMATIC TRANSMISSIONS
Toyota A-540H & A-541E (Cont.)

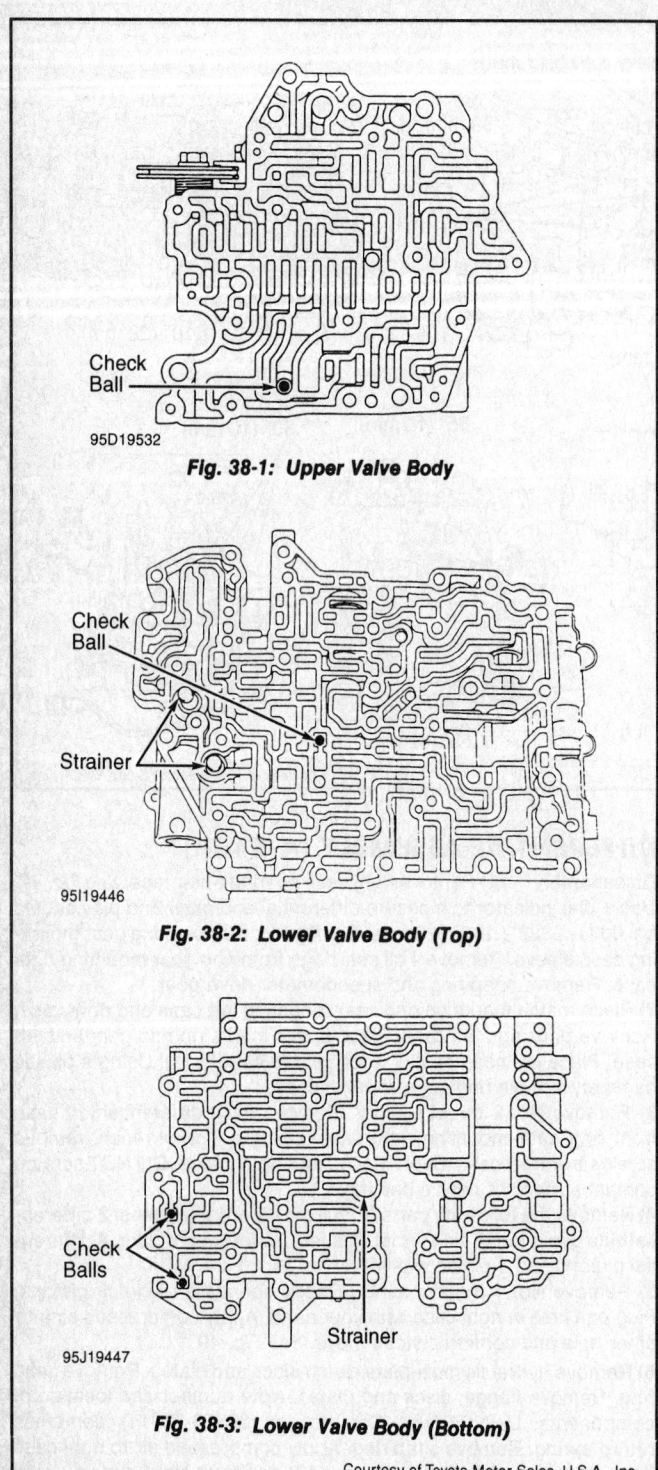

Fig. 38-1: Upper Valve Body

Fig. 38-2: Lower Valve Body (Top)

Fig. 38-3: Lower Valve Body (Bottom)

Courtesy of Toyota Motor Sales, U.S.A., Inc.

Fig. 38: Locating A-541E Valve Body Check Balls

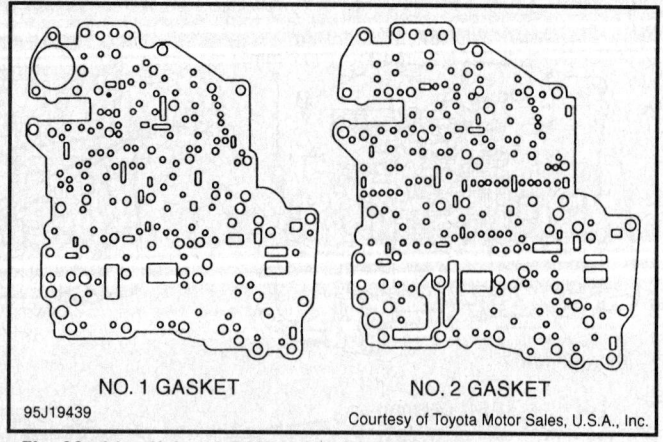

NO. 1 GASKET   NO. 2 GASKET

Courtesy of Toyota Motor Sales, U.S.A., Inc.

Fig. 39: Identifying A-541E Valve Body Gaskets

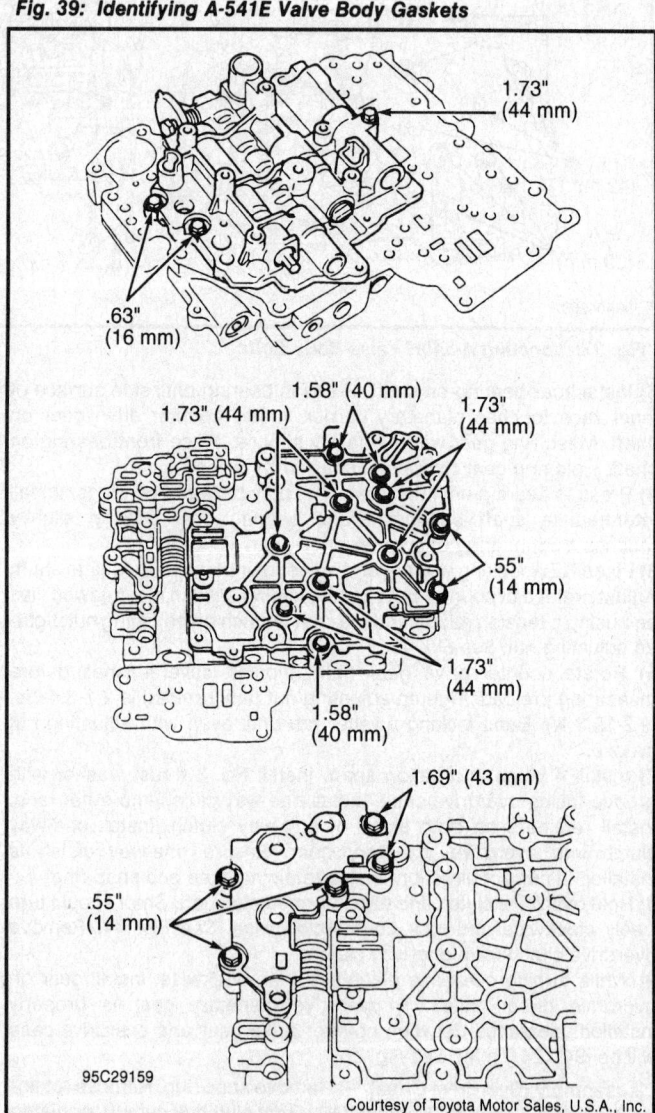

Courtesy of Toyota Motor Sales, U.S.A., Inc.

Fig. 40: Locating A-541E Valve Body Bolts

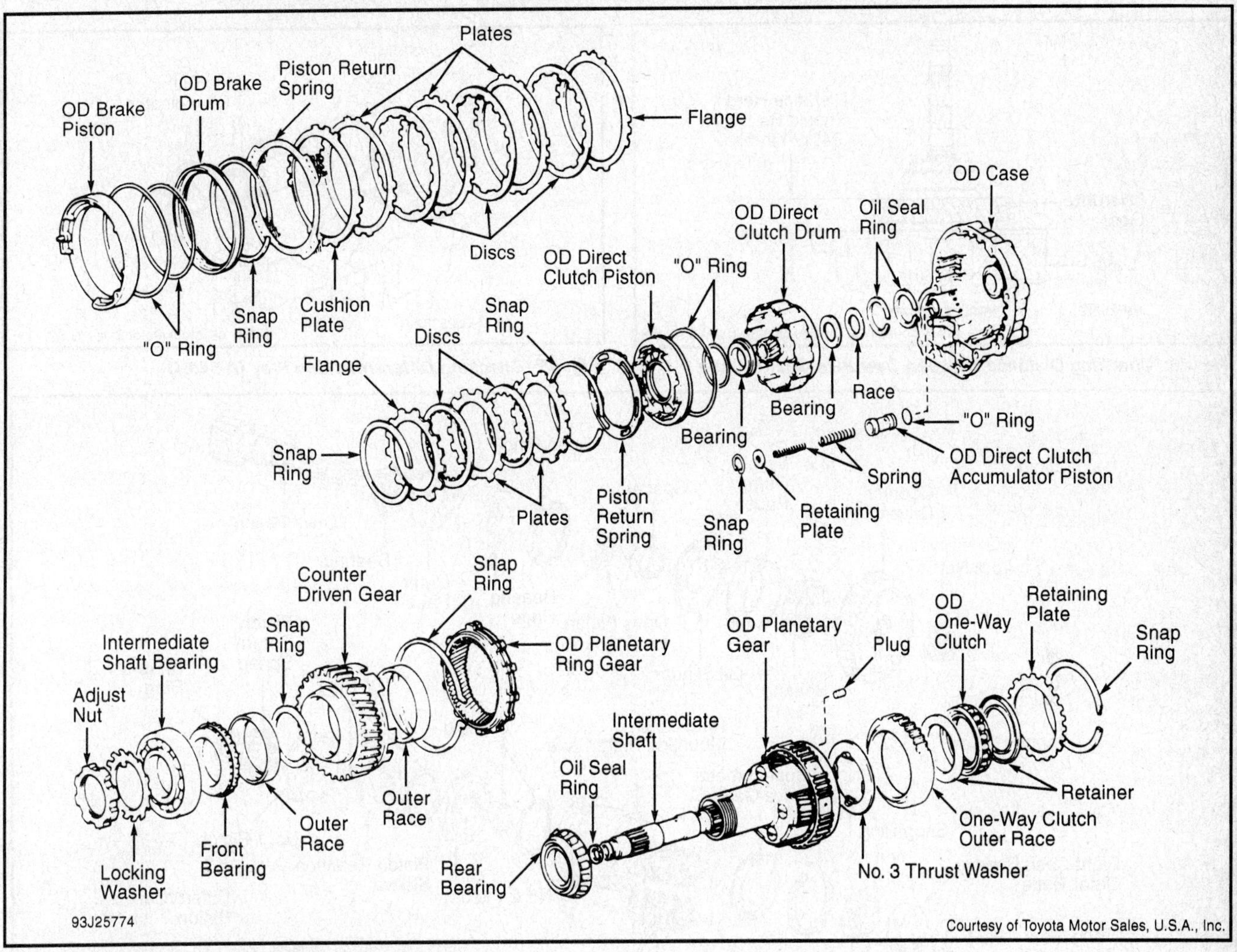

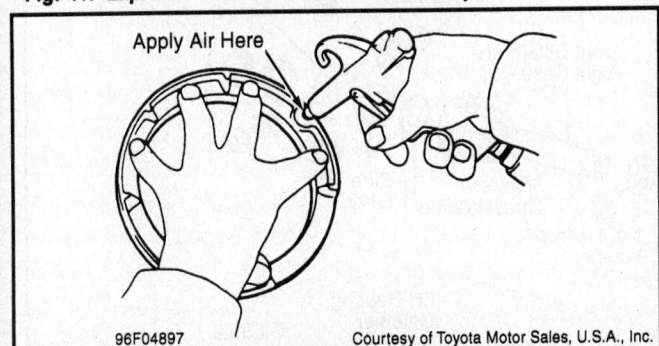

Fig. 41: Exploded View Of Overdrive Assembly

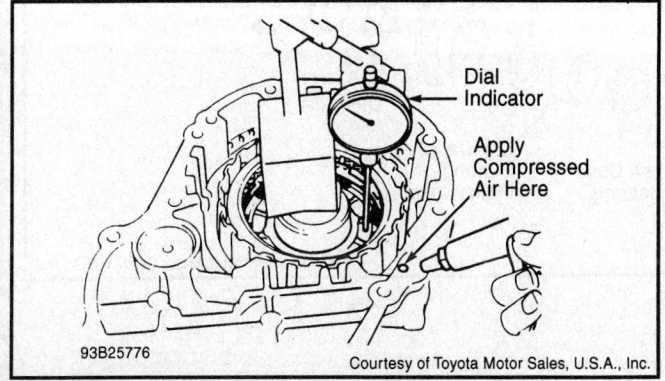

Fig. 42: Removing Overdrive Brake Piston

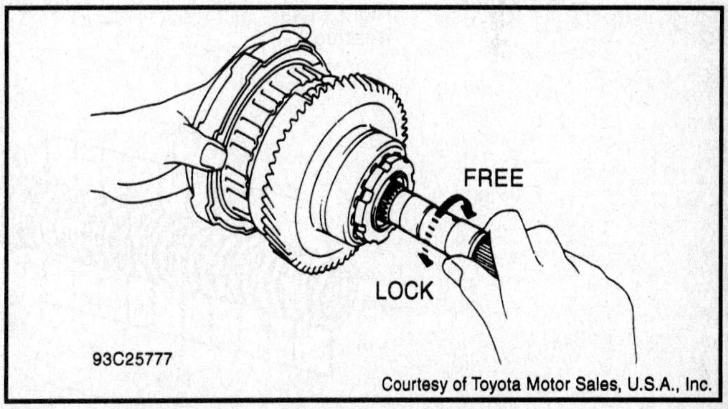

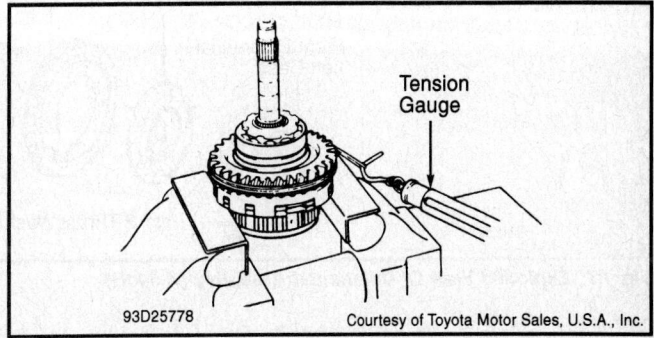

Fig. 44: Checking OD One-Way Clutch Operation

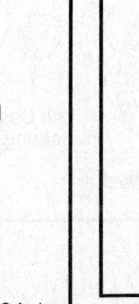

Fig. 43: Checking OD Direct Clutch Piston Stroke

Fig. 45: Checking Counter Drive Gear Preload

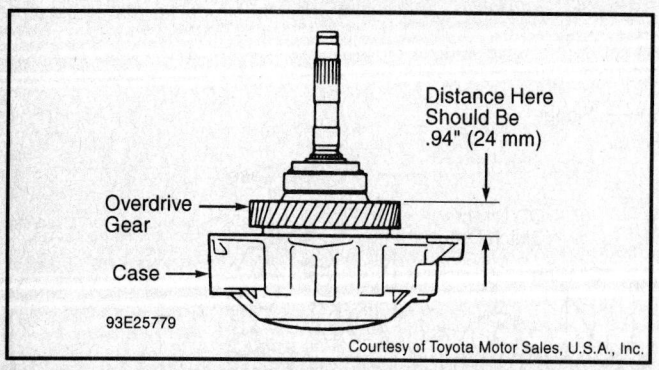

Distance Here Should Be .94" (24 mm)

Overdrive Gear

Case

93E25779

Courtesy of Toyota Motor Sales, U.S.A., Inc.

Fig. 46: Checking Distance Between Overdrive Gear & Case

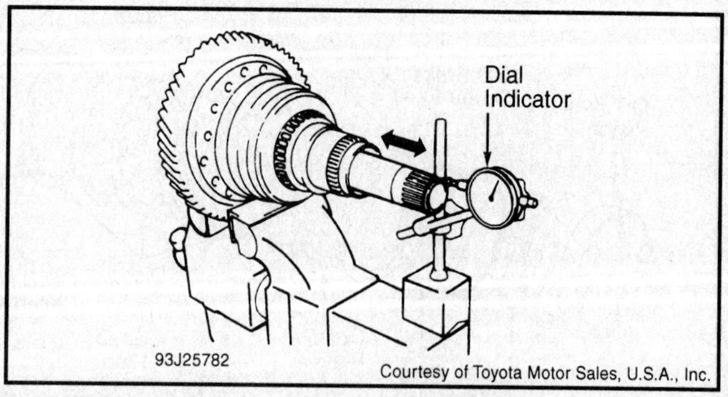

Dial Indicator

93J25782

Courtesy of Toyota Motor Sales, U.S.A., Inc.

Fig. 48: Checking Differential End Play (A-540H)

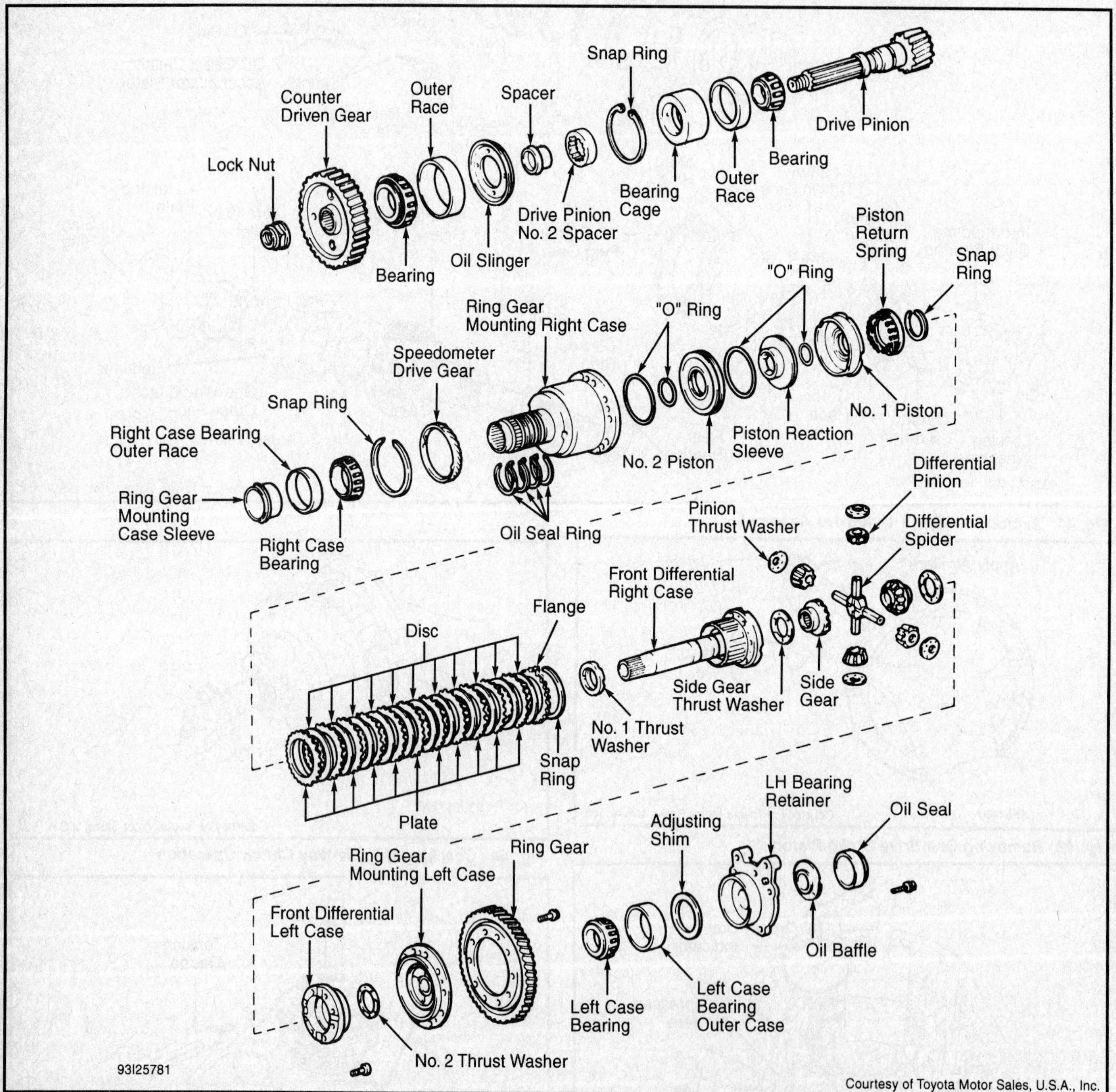

Lock Nut

Counter Driven Gear

Outer Race

Spacer

Snap Ring

Drive Pinion

Bearing

Drive Pinion No. 2 Spacer

Bearing Cage

Outer Race

Bearing

Oil Slinger

Ring Gear Mounting Right Case

Speedometer Drive Gear

"O" Ring

"O" Ring

Piston Return Spring

Snap Ring

Snap Ring

Right Case Bearing Outer Race

Ring Gear Mounting Case Sleeve

Right Case Bearing

Oil Seal Ring

No. 2 Piston

Piston Reaction Sleeve

No. 1 Piston

Differential Pinion

Differential Spider

Pinion Thrust Washer

Disc

Flange

Front Differential Right Case

Side Gear Thrust Washer

Side Gear

No. 1 Thrust Washer

Snap Ring

Plate

LH Bearing Retainer

Oil Seal

Ring Gear Mounting Left Case

Ring Gear

Adjusting Shim

Oil Baffle

Front Differential Left Case

Left Case Bearing

Left Case Bearing Outer Case

No. 2 Thrust Washer

93I25781

Courtesy of Toyota Motor Sales, U.S.A., Inc.

Fig. 47: Exploded View Of Differential Assembly (A-540H)

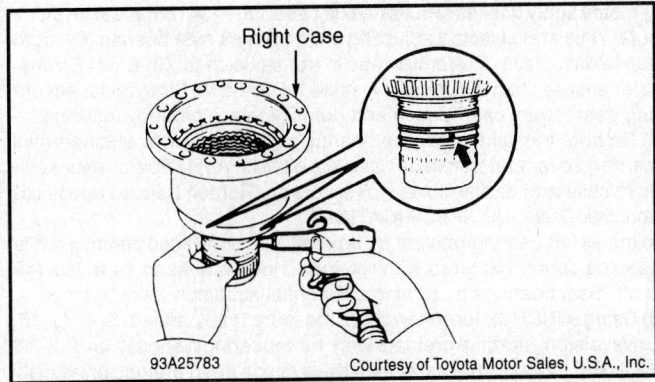

Fig. 49: Checking Operation Of Differential Clutch Pistons (A-540H)

9) Use hammer and screwdriver to remove oil seal from ring gear mounting left case. Remove oil baffle from left bearing retainer. Use hammer and brass bar to drive out outer race and adjusting shim from left bearing retainer. Place adjusting shim into left bearing retainer. Use either original shim or shim with thickness of .0945" (2.400 mm). Use A/T Tool Set (09350-32014) and arbor press to install outer race and shim. Install oil baffle and oil seal after adjusting differential side bearing preload. See TRANSAXLE REASSEMBLY.

Reassembly – 1) Coat 4 "O" rings with ATF. Install "O" rings on reaction sleeve and pistons. Install No. 1 piston, No. 2 piston and reaction sleeve to ring gear mounting right case.

2) Place return spring on piston. Install A/T Tool Set (09350-32014) on piston return spring retainer. Compress spring with arbor press. Install snap ring.

3) Install plates and discs, starting with plate, alternating with disc and ending with disc. Install flange with flat end facing downward. Install snap ring. Check operation of clutch pistons. Plug one hole with your hand. Apply compressed air into other hole. Ensure pistons move. Install No. 1 thrust washer.

4) Install following parts into front differential left case: side gear thrust washer, side gear, 4 differential pinion gears, 4 pinion gear thrust washers and differential spider. Use a dial indicator to measure backlash of one pinion gear while holding side gear toward case. See Fig. 50. Backlash should be .0020-.0079" (.050-.200 mm).

5) If backlash exceeds specification, install thrust washers of different thickness. DO NOT overtighten vise. See SIDE GEAR THRUST WASHER SPECIFICATIONS table. Perform same procedure described in step **4)** for front differential right case. See Fig. 50.

SIDE GEAR THRUST WASHER SPECIFICATIONS

ID Mark	Thickness In. (mm)
A	.0394 (1.000)
B	.0413 (1.050)
C	.0433 (1.100)
D	.0453 (1.150)
E	.0472 (1.200)
F	.0492 (1.250)
G	.0512 (1.300)

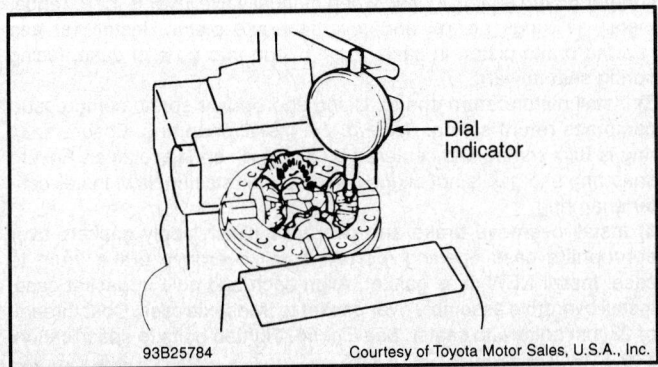

Fig. 50: Measuring Front Differential Side Gear Backlash

6) Install front differential left case to right case. Align match marks on left and right cases. Tighten Torx screws to 24 ft. lbs. (33 N.m). Install front differential case to ring gear right case. Align flukes of discs in hydraulic multi-plate clutch. Install No. 2 washer.

7) Clean ring gear left case contact surface. Heat ring gear to about 212°F (100°C) in an oil bath. DO NOT heat ring gear above 230°F (110°C). Clean contact surface of ring gear with cleaning solvent. Quickly install ring gear on differential case. Align match marks on ring gear left case and ring gear. Install ring gear and left case on right case. Install 12 bolts. Align match marks on ring gear left and right cases. Tighten bolts to 91 ft. lbs. (124 N.m).

8) Ensure front differential turns smoothly. Place speedometer drive gear on ring gear case. Install snap ring. Install oil seal rings to ring gear right case. Install ring gear case sleeve. Install right case bearing outer race.

DIFFERENTIAL ASSEMBLY (A-541E)

Disassembly – 1) Using appropriate puller, remove differential case side bearings. Remove speedometer drive gear. Place reference marks on differential case and ring gear. Remove ring gear bolts. Using soft-face hammer, remove ring gear.

2) Mount differential in vise. Using dial indicator, measure pinion gear backlash. See Fig. 51. Backlash should be .0020-.0079" (.050-.200 mm). From ring gear side of case, drive out pinion shaft roll pin. Remove pinion shaft. Remove pinion gears, side gears and all thrust washers. See Fig. 52. Examine all components for wear and replace as needed.

Reassembly – 1) Match side gears and pinion gears with corresponding thrust washers. Install gears in differential case. Install pinion shaft. Check pinion gear backlash.

2) If backlash is not within specification, replace side gear thrust washers with matched set. Washers are available in 3 thicknesses; .063" (1.60 mm), .067" (1.70 mm) and .071" (1.80 mm). Recheck backlash after washers have been replaced.

3) Drive in pinion shaft roll pin. Ensure ring gear mounting surface is clean and free of burrs or scratches. Heat ring gear in oil bath to 212°F (100°C). DO NOT exceed temperature. Install ring gear, aligning reference marks made during disassembly. Tighten bolts to specification. See TORQUE SPECIFICATIONS. Install speedometer drive gear. Press side bearing onto differential case. Lubricate all moving parts with ATF.

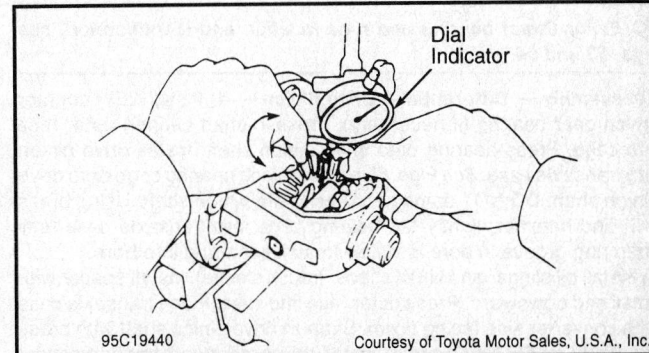

Fig. 51: Measuring Differential Pinion Bearing Backlash (A-541E)

TRANSAXLE REASSEMBLY

NOTE: Coat all oil seal rings, clutch discs, clutch plates, rotating parts, and sliding surfaces with ATF prior to reassembly. All gaskets and rubber "O" rings should be replaced. Ensure ends of snap rings are not aligned with cut-outs and are installed correctly in groove. If a worn bushing is to be replaced, replacement must be made with the subassembly containing that bushing. Check thrust bearings and races for wear or damage. Use petroleum jelly to hold parts in place. Replace parts as necessary. Soak clutch plates in ATF for 15 minutes prior to installation.

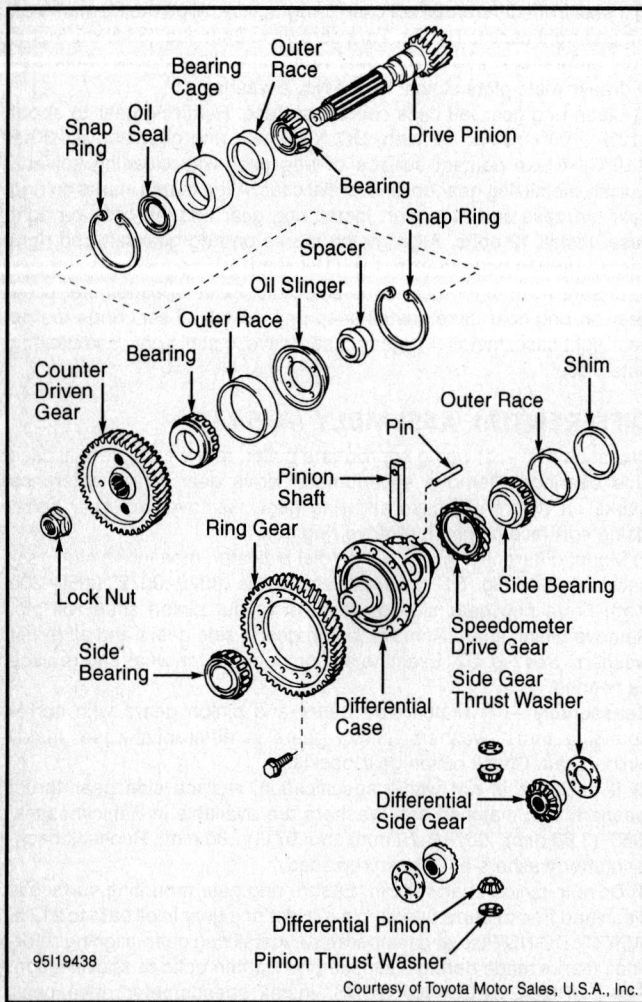

95I19438

Courtesy of Toyota Motor Sales, U.S.A., Inc.

Fig. 52: Exploded View Of Differential Assembly (A-541E)

NOTE: *For thrust bearing and race location and identification, see Figs. 63 and 64.*

Reassembly – Differential & Drive Pinion – 1) Install NEW counter driven gear bearing (if necessary). Press in shaft bearing outer race into cage. Press bearing onto drive pinion shaft. Install drive pinion into transaxle case. *See Figs. 53 and 54.* Place bearing cage onto drive pinion shaft. DO NOT damage oil seals with pinion shaft. Using brass drift and hammer, lightly tap bearing cage into transaxle case until snap ring groove in bore is visible. Install snap ring into bore.
2) Install oil slinger and NEW spacer (crush sleeve). Install spacer with small end downward. Press outer race into case. Place transaxle case with converter side facing down. Support drive pinion shaft with brass bar. *See Fig. 55.* Using press, install driven gear until bearing almost touches counter gear.
3) Install NEW lock nut. Secure gear from turning. Tighten nut to 207 ft. lbs. (280 N.m). Rotate gear both directions while tightening nut. Using a INCH lb. torque wrench, measure starting preload of drive pinion.
4) Starting preload with new bearing should be 8.7-13.9 INCH lbs. (1.0-1.6 N.m). With used bearing, preload should be 4.3-6.9 INCH lbs. (.5-.8 N.m). If preload exceeds specification, replace bearing spacer (crush sleeve). DO NOT loosen nut to adjust starting preload.
5) If starting preload is less than specification, retighten shaft nut 115 INCH lbs. (13 N.m) at a time until specified preload is reached. Maximum shaft nut torque is 260 ft. lbs. (353 N.m). If maximum torque is exceeded while tightening shaft nut, replace bearing spacer. Repeat preload procedure. DO NOT loosen nut to reduce preload. Stake lock nut.

6) Install apply gasket(s) in transaxle case. On A-541E transaxle, place outer race and selected adjusting shim on right side bearing. On both transaxles, place differential case in transaxle case. On A-541E transaxle, ensure shim is properly installed. On A-540H transaxle, ensure ring gear mount case sleeve and outer race are properly installed.
7) On both transaxles, ensure bearing contact surfaces of differential (carrier) cover and transaxle case are oil free. Apply appropriate sealer to case and carrier cover. Install cover. Tighten bolts to specification. See TORQUE SPECIFICATIONS.
8) Install left bearing retainer by tapping with soft-faced hammer while keeping carrier centered with retainer. Tighten bolts to 14 ft. lbs. (19 N.m). Seat bearings by turning differential assembly several times.
9) Using a INCH lb. torque wrench, measure total preload. *See Fig. 15.* Drive pinion starting preload with new bearings should be 2.2-3.8 INCH lbs. (.2-.4 N.m) greater than drive pinion shaft preload previously measured in step 4).
10) If used bearings are used, preload should be 1.2-1.9 INCH lbs. (.1-.2 N.m) greater than drive pinion shaft preload previously measured. If preload exceeds specifications, replace adjusting shim in left bearing retainer. Remove left bearing retainer. Remove bearing race from retainer. Select shim from DIFFERENTIAL SIDE BEARING ADJUSTING SHIM SELECTION table.

DIFFERENTIAL SIDE BEARING ADJUSTING SHIM SELECTION

ID Mark	Thickness In. (mm)
0	.0787 (2.000)
1	.0807 (2.050)
2	.0827 (2.100)
3	.0846 (2.150)
4	.0866 (2.200)
5	.0886 (2.250)
6	.0906 (2.300)
7	.0925 (2.350)
8	.0945 (2.400)
9	.0965 (2.450)
A	.0984 (2.500)
B	.1004 (2.550)
C	.1024 (2.600)
D	.1043 (2.650)
E	.1063 (2.700)
F	.1083 (2.750)
G	.1102 (2.800)
H	.1122 (2.850)

11) Install selected shim in retainer. Install bearing race. Install left bearing retainer by tapping with soft-faced hammer while keeping carrier centered with retainer. Tighten bolts to specification. See TORQUE SPECIFICATIONS. Recheck total starting preload.
12) If starting preload is within specification, remove left bearing retainer. Apply appropriate sealant to retainer mounting surface. Apply thread sealer to bolts. Install retainer.
13) Place oil baffle on left bearing retainer. Press in oil seal until flush with surface of retainer. Apply sealant to right retainer. Coat bolt threads with sealer. Tighten bolts to specification. See TORQUE SPECIFICATIONS. Install drive pinion cap to converter side of transaxle case .

Reassembly – 1) Check operation of parking lock pawl. Ensure counter driven gear is locked when manual valve lever is in "P" range. Install "O" rings on 1st and reverse brake piston. Install 1st and reverse brake piston in case. Push piston into bore of case, facing spring seat upward.
2) Install piston return spring. Using appropriate spring compressor, compress return spring. *See Fig. 14.* Install snap ring. Ensure snap ring is fully seated and centered by 3 lugs on spring retainer. Ensure snap ring end gap is not aligned with spring retainer claw. Install center snap ring.
3) Install overdrive brake and overdrive clutch apply gaskets over appropriate case opening (ports). Install overdrive brake drum to case. Install NEW case gasket. Align each bolt hole in gasket case. Install overdrive assembly over gasket to transaxle case. Coat threads of 23 mm bolts with sealer. *See Fig. 56.* Tighten bolts to specification. See TORQUE SPECIFICATIONS.

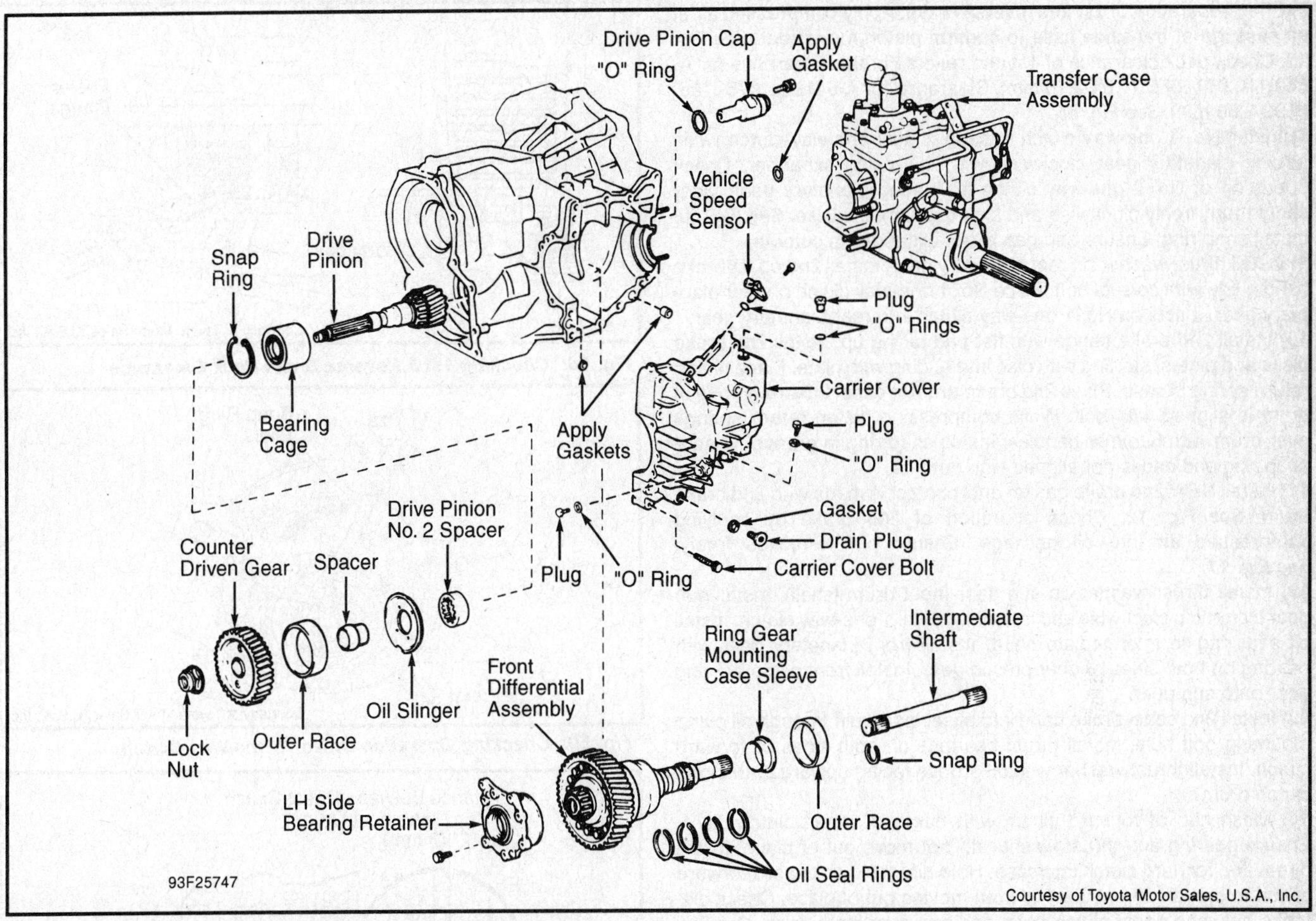

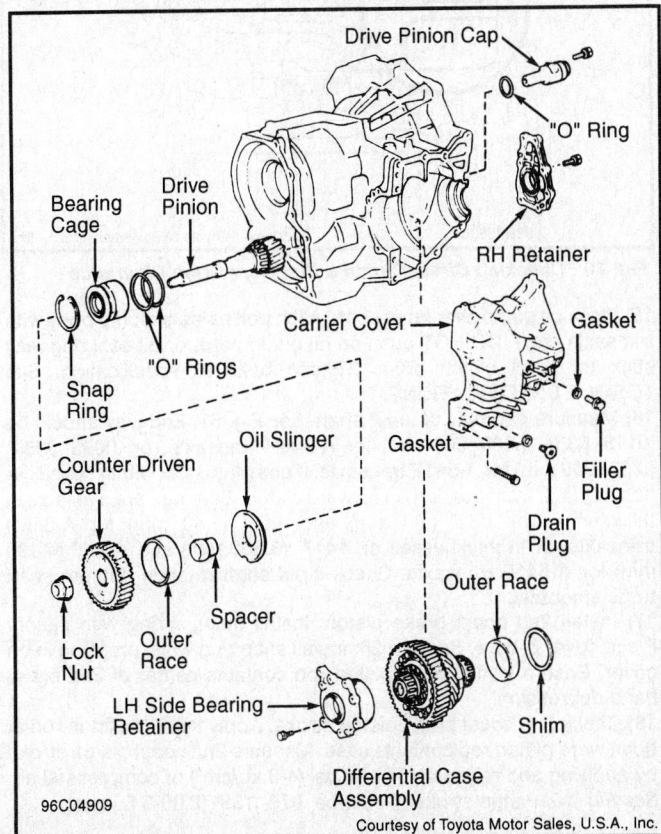

Fig. 53: **Exploded View Of Final Drive Components (A-540H)**

Fig. 54: **Exploded View Of Final Drive Components (A-541E)**

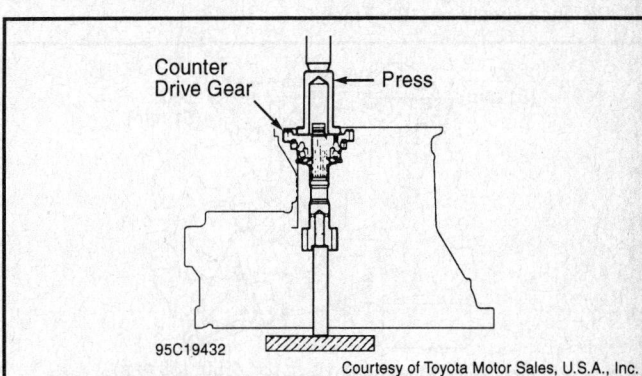

Fig. 55: **Installing Driven Pinion**

4) Check intermediate shaft end play (axial). *See Fig. 57.* End play should be .019-.059" (.47-1.50 mm). Ensure shaft turns smoothly. If end play is not within specification, check installation of intermediate shaft.

NOTE: *For thrust bearing and race location and identification, see Figs. 63 and 64.*

5) Install rear planetary ring gear. Place bearing on ring gear. Coat thrust washer with petroleum jelly and install on rear planetary gear. Install rear planetary gear. *See Fig. 26.*

6) Install 1st and reverse brake discs, plates and flange. *See Fig. 12.* Start with plate, alternating with disc, and ending with disc. Install outer flange with flat side facing toward piston side. Install snap ring. Ensure snap ring end-gap is not aligned with cutouts.

7) Check operation of 1st and reverse brake. Apply compressed air at oil passage of transaxle case to confirm piston movement. *See Fig. 13.* Check pack clearance of 1st and reverse brake. Clearance for A-540H is .041-.085" (1.04-2.16 mm). Clearance for A-541E is .076-.106" (1.92-2.86 mm). *See Fig. 58.*

8) Install No. 2 one-way clutch in case. Install one-way clutch while turning planetary gear clockwise with snap ring expander. Check operation of No. 2 one-way clutch by turning planetary gear. Gear should turn freely clockwise and lock counterclockwise. *See Fig. 59.* Install snap ring. Ensure end gap is not aligned with cutouts.

9) Install thrust washer on rear planetary gear. Install 2nd coast brake band guide with correct bolt. Place No. 1 one-way clutch on rear planetary gear. Install on No. 1 one-way clutch into rear planetary gear.

10) Install 2nd brake flange with flat end facing up. Install 2nd brake discs and plates, starting with disc and ending with plate. Place piston return spring in case. Place 2nd brake drum in case. Ensure groove of drum is aligned with bolt. While compressing piston return springs over drum with hammer handles, install snap ring in groove. Ensure snap ring end gap is not aligned with cutouts.

11) Install NEW 2nd brake gasket until contact is made with 2nd brake drum. *See Fig. 12.* Check operation of 2nd brake by applying compressed air into oil passage. Ensure piston moves freely. *See Fig. 11.*

12) Install thrust washer on sun gear input drum (shell). Install sun gear by turning clockwise and installing in No. 1 one-way clutch. Install oil seal ring to intermediate shaft. Install front planetary gear with bearing on both sides of gear on sun gear. Install front planetary ring gear onto sun gear.

13) Install 2nd coast brake band into case. Install pin through oil pump mounting bolt hole. Install thrust bearings on both sides of forward clutch. Install thrust washer with oil groove facing upward onto direct clutch drum.

14) Mesh hub of forward clutch with flukes of direct clutch discs. Ensure bearing and thrust washer do not move out of place. Install direct and forward clutch into case. Hold direct clutch toward forward clutch to prevent thrust washer from moving out of place. Check distance between direct clutch drum and sun gear input drum. *See Fig. 60.* Distance should be .12" (3 mm).

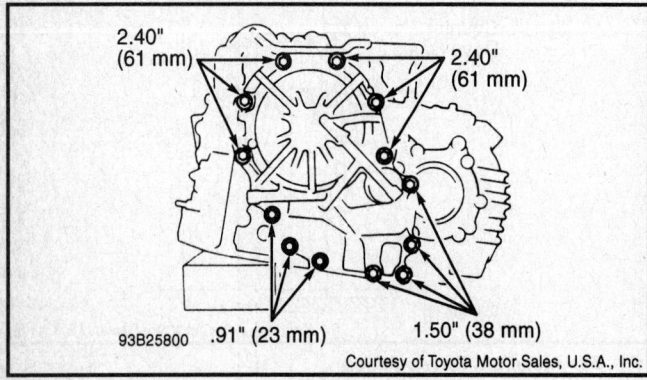

Fig. 56: **Locating Overdrive Assembly Bolts**

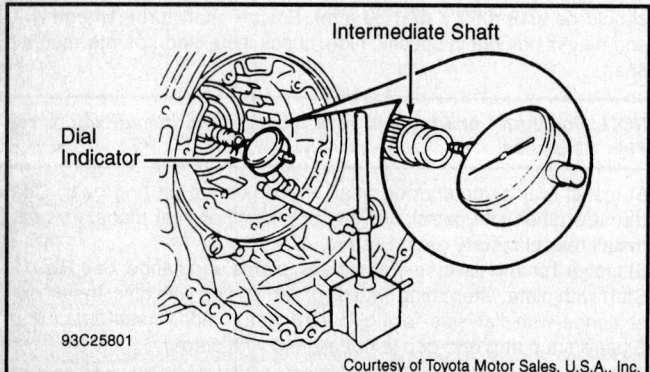

Fig. 57: **Checking Intermediate Shaft End Play**

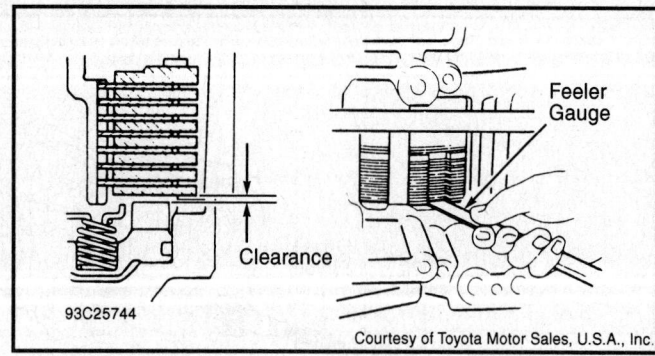

Fig. 58: *Checking 1st & Reverse Brake Pack Clearance*

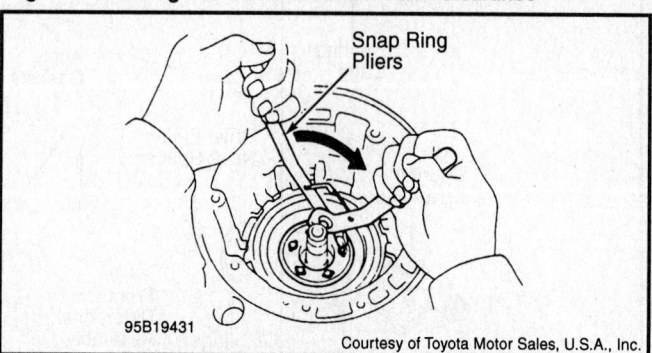

Fig. 59: *Checking Operation Of No. 2 One-Way Clutch*

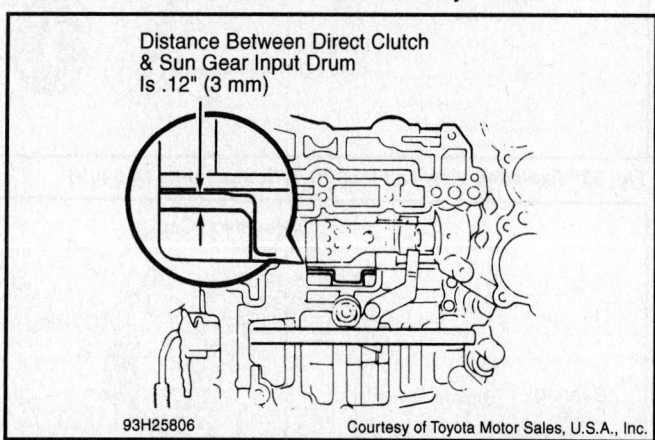

Fig. 60: *Checking Direct Clutch & Sun Gear Drum Clearance*

15) Place oil pump over input shaft. Align bolt holes of pump body with transaxle case. DO NOT push on oil pump hard, or oil seal ring may stick to direct clutch drum. Tighten bolts to specification. See TORQUE SPECIFICATIONS.

16) Measure end play of input shaft. *See Fig. 61.* End play should be .0118-.0354" (.300-.900 mm) for A-540H transaxle, or .0098-.0354" (.250-.900 mm) for A-541E transaxle. If end play is not within specification, replace front bearing on forward clutch. Bearings are available in thicknesses of .031" (.08 mm) and .055" (1.40 mm) for A-540H transaxle, or in thicknesses of .1417" (3.600 mm) and .1650" (4.190 mm) for A-541E transaxle. Check input shaft rotation. Ensure shaft turns smoothly.

17) Install 2nd coast brake piston. Install outer spring with piston. Place cover in bore. *See Fig. 28.* Install snap ring while pressing in on cover. Ensure front end of piston rod contacts center of 2nd brake band depression.

18) Check 2nd coast brake piston stroke. Apply mark to piston rod at point were piston rod contacts case. Measure 2nd coast piston stroke by applying and releasing 57-114 psi (4-8 kg/cm²) of compressed air. *See Fig. 10.* Piston stroke should be .079-.138" (2.00-3.50 mm).

19) If stroke exceeds specification, replace piston rod with longer rod. Piston rods are available in 2 sizes: 3.748" (95.20 mm) or 3.791" (96.30 mm). After installation of NEW rod, re-measure stroke. If stroke exceeds specification, replace brake band.

20) Install accumulator pistons and springs in bores. See Fig. 8. See ACCUMULATOR SPRING SPECIFICATIONS table. Install accumulator cover with NEW gasket. Tighten bolts in crisscross pattern to specification.

ACCUMULATOR SPRING SPECIFICATIONS

Application	Color	Free Length In. (mm)
A-540H		
Direct Clutch	Red	2.008 (51.00)
2nd Brake	Blue/White	2.701 (68.60)
Forward Clutch	Pink	2.433 (61.80)
A-541E		
Direct Clutch	Yellow/Purple	2.039 (51.08)
2nd Brake		
Inner	None	3.472 (88.20)
Outer	None	2.768 (70.30)
Forward Clutch	None	2.898 (73.60)

21) Install 2nd brake apply gasket. Install throttle cable and solenoid wire. Place valve body on transaxle. While holding cam down with hand, slip cable end in slot. Lower valve body into position. DO NOT entangle throttle valve cable. Install valve body bolts. Ensure proper length and location of bolts. See Fig. 3. Finger tighten all bolts. Tighten bolts in crisscross pattern to specification. See TORQUE SPECIFICATIONS.

22) Install 1st and reverse brake apply tube. Install connector clamp and tube retainer. Connect solenoid connectors. Using a plastic hammer, install oil tubes. DO NOT bend or damage tubes. Place manual valve body on transmission. Align manual lever with pin of manual shaft lever. Lower manual valve body into position. Ensure proper length and location of bolts. See Fig. 4. Finger tighten bolts. Evenly tighten bolts in crisscross pattern.

23) Install detent spring. Ensure proper length and location of each bolt. Finger tighten bolts. Check for correct operation of manual valve lever. Ensure lever is touching center of detent spring tip roller.

24) Install tube bracket and oil strainer. Install magnets in oil pan. Ensure magnets do not interfere with oil tubes. Install oil pan with NEW gasket. Install vehicle speed sensor with "O" ring (as applicable). Install speed sensor connector. Install throttle cable retaining plate. Install solenoid wire.

25) Install transaxle case upper cover. Install direct clutch speed (T/M revolution) sensor (if equipped). Install park/neutral position switch to manual valve shaft. Install NEW locking plate. Tighten nut and stake with locking plate. Adjust switch by aligning groove and neutral basic line. Tighten bolts. Install manual shift lever.

26) On A-540H transaxle, install NEW snap ring to shaft groove and install differential side gear intermediate shaft. See Fig. 53. Keeping intermediate shaft on pinion shaft of differential, measure shaft protrusion length from transaxle case surface to end of shaft. Protrusion length should be 10.059" (255.50 mm).

27) Install NEW apply gasket on differential carrier cover. Install transfer case assembly to transaxle. Apply seal packing Three Bond (1281) or Loctite (518) to contacting surface of transaxle case. Coat threads of bolts with Three Bond (1324) sealer. Install and tighten nuts and bolts to 51 ft. lbs. (69 N.m). Install breather hose to driven pinion bearing cage and transaxle upper cover.

28) On both transaxles, install cooler line union and elbow. Install elbow at right angles to bottom of case. Install torque converter. Ensure converter is full of ATF before installation. Check installed position by measuring installed depth from edge of case. See Fig. 62. Distance should be .539" (13.7 mm).

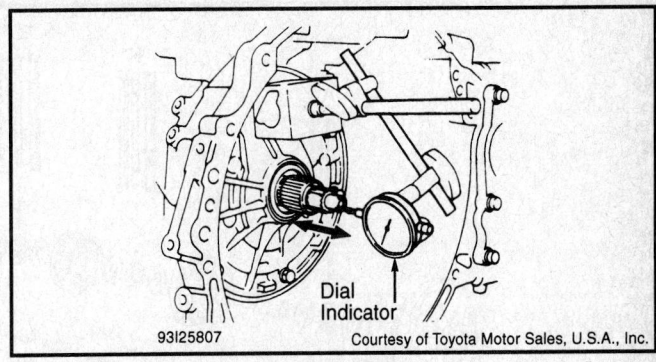

Fig. 61: *Measuring Input Shaft End Play*

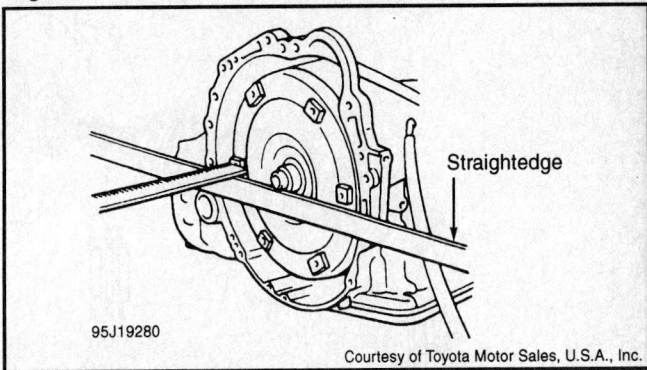

Fig. 62: *Measuring Torque Converter Installed Depth*

TRANSAXLE SPECIFICATIONS
TRANSAXLE SPECIFICATIONS

Application	In. (mm)
Bushing Inside Diameter (Maximum)	
Direct Clutch	
A-540H	1.853 (47.07)
A-541E	1.900 (48.27)
Oil Pump Body	1.503 (38.18)
OD Direct Clutch	.871 (22.13)
Planetary Ring Gear Flange	1.184 (30.08)
Sun Gear	
A-540H	.870 (22.09)
A-541E	.889 (22.59)
Stator Shaft	.849 (21.57)
Clutch Pack Clearances	
1st & Reverse Brake	
A-540H	.041-.085 (1.04-2.16)
A-541E	.076-.106 (1.92-2.68)
End Play	
Differential	.0071-.323 (.180-.820)
Input Shaft	
A-540H	.0118-.0354" (.300-.900 mm)
A-541E	.0098-.0354" (.250-.900 mm)
Intermediate Shaft	.019-.059 (.47-1.50)
Intermediate Shaft Protrusion Length	10.059 (255.50)
Oil Pump (Standard Measurements)	
Body Clearance Of Driven Gear	.0028-.0059 (.070-.150)
Tip Clearance Of Driven Gear	.0043-.0055 (.110-.140)
Gear Side Clearance	.0008-.0020 (.020-.050)
Piston Stroke	
Direct Clutch	
A-540H	.044-.058 (1.11-1.47)
A-541E	.036-.053 (.91-1.35)
Forward Clutch	
A-540H	.056-.072 (1.41-1.82)
A-541E	.071-.087 (1.79-2.21)
2nd Coast Brake	.079-.138 (2.00-3.50)
OD Direct Clutch	.069-.098 (1.75-2.49)
Planetary Pinion Gear Thrust Clearance	
A-540H	.008-.020 (.20-.50)
A-541E	.006-.022 (.16-.56)
Pinion Gear Backlash	.0020-.0080 (.050-.200)
Torque Converter Runout (Maximum)	
Drive Plate	.008 (.20)
Sleeve	.012 (.30)

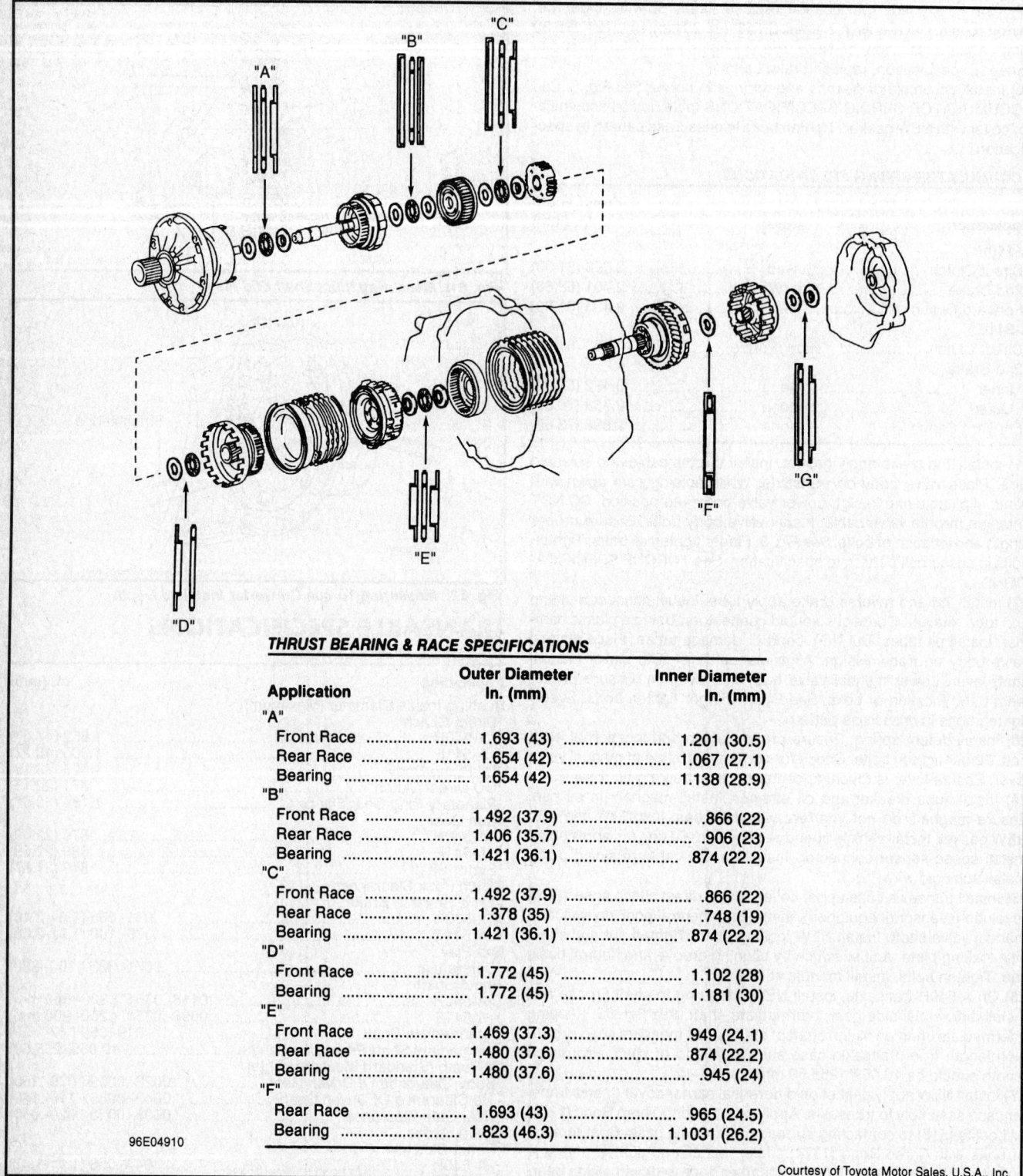

THRUST BEARING & RACE SPECIFICATIONS

Application	Outer Diameter In. (mm)	Inner Diameter In. (mm)
"A"		
Front Race	1.693 (43)	1.201 (30.5)
Rear Race	1.654 (42)	1.067 (27.1)
Bearing	1.654 (42)	1.138 (28.9)
"B"		
Front Race	1.492 (37.9)	.866 (22)
Rear Race	1.406 (35.7)	.906 (23)
Bearing	1.421 (36.1)	.874 (22.2)
"C"		
Front Race	1.492 (37.9)	.866 (22)
Rear Race	1.378 (35)	.748 (19)
Bearing	1.421 (36.1)	.874 (22.2)
"D"		
Front Race	1.772 (45)	1.102 (28)
Bearing	1.772 (45)	1.181 (30)
"E"		
Front Race	1.469 (37.3)	.949 (24.1)
Rear Race	1.480 (37.6)	.874 (22.2)
Bearing	1.480 (37.6)	.945 (24)
"F"		
Rear Race	1.693 (43)	.965 (24.5)
Bearing	1.823 (46.3)	1.1031 (26.2)

96E04910

Courtesy of Toyota Motor Sales, U.S.A., Inc.

Fig. 63: Identifying Thrust Bearing & Race Locations (A-540H)

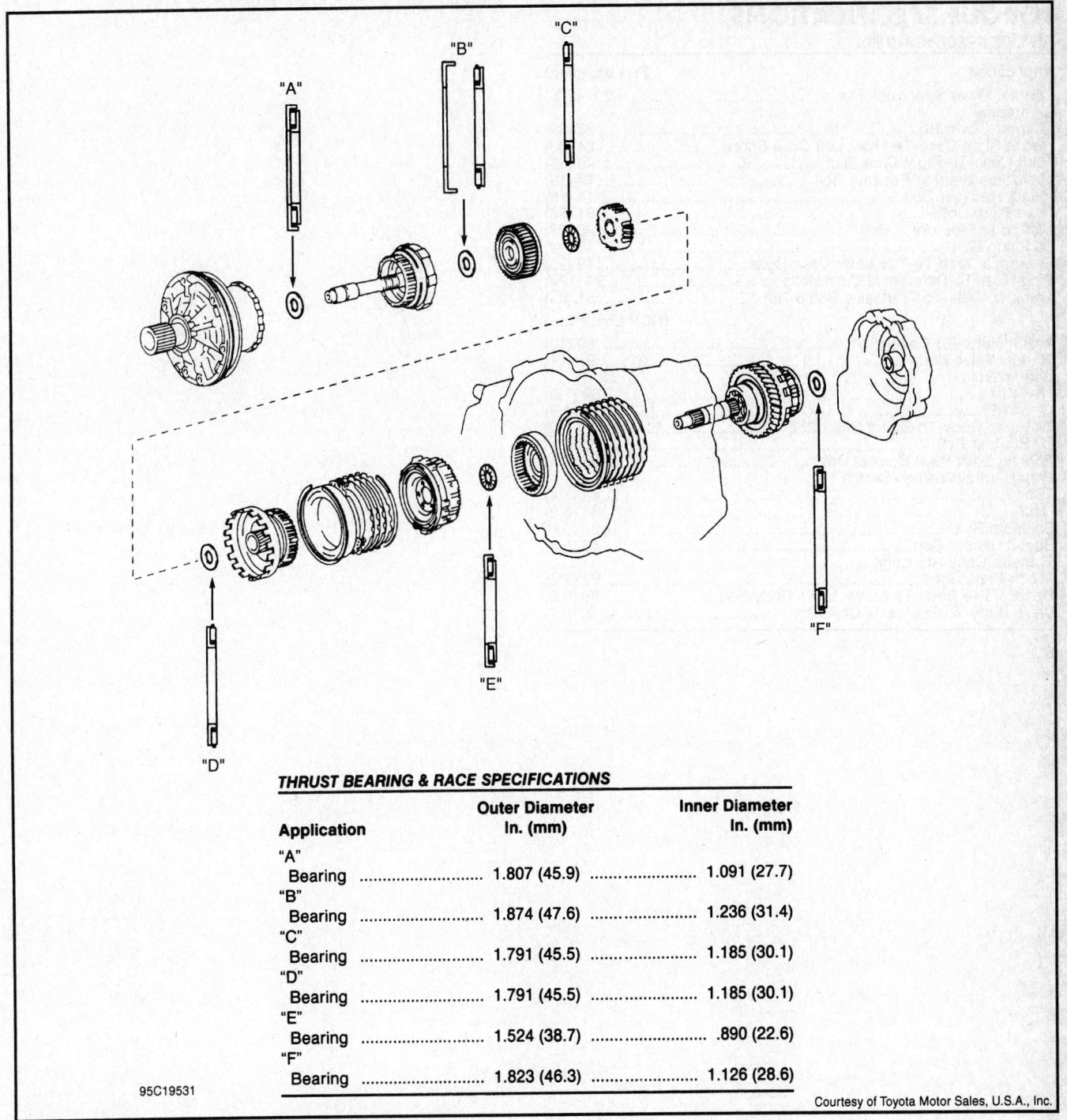

THRUST BEARING & RACE SPECIFICATIONS

Application	Outer Diameter In. (mm)	Inner Diameter In. (mm)
"A"		
Bearing	1.807 (45.9)	1.091 (27.7)
"B"		
Bearing	1.874 (47.6)	1.236 (31.4)
"C"		
Bearing	1.791 (45.5)	1.185 (30.1)
"D"		
Bearing	1.791 (45.5)	1.185 (30.1)
"E"		
Bearing	1.524 (38.7)	.890 (22.6)
"F"		
Bearing	1.823 (46.3)	1.126 (28.6)

95C19531

Courtesy of Toyota Motor Sales, U.S.A., Inc.

Fig. 64: Identifying Thrust Bearing & Race Locations (A-541E)

TECHNICAL SERVICE BULLETINS

IMPROVED SHIFT QUALITY (A-541E)

Toyota Motor Sales, U.S.A., Inc. TSB TC95-007 (8-11-95) – 1) Customer may complain of harsh upshift on Camry SE with 3.90 ratio differential. Upshift quality can be improved by adjusting accumulator backpressure control.
2) Ensure condition exists and throttle cable is adjusted properly. Drain transaxle fluid. Remove oil pan and gasket. Set accumulator backpressure to lowest position. Using a screwdriver, depress accumulator backpressure plug down slightly inward. Plug is located on corner side of valve body, below axle shaft.
3) Turn plug clockwise to full right position. Plug will be set to most protruded position. Install oil pan and refill transaxle. Test drive vehicle for 30 minutes with pattern select switch at NORMAL position.

NOTE: ECU must relearn logic. Ensure vehicle is driven for full 30 minutes.

TORQUE SPECIFICATIONS

TORQUE SPECIFICATIONS

Application	Ft. Lbs. (N.m)
Counter Drive Gear Lock Nut	207 (280)
Differential	
Carrier Cover Bolt	29 (39)
Front Right Case-To-Front Left Case Screw	24 (33)
Left Case-To-Right Case Bolt	46 (63)
Left Side Bearing Retainer Bolt	14 (19)
Right Retainer Bolt	14 (19)
Drive Plate Bolt	61 (83)
Oil Cooler Pipe Union Bolt	20 (27)
Oil Pump Bolt	16 (22)
Overdrive Case-To-Transaxle Case Bolts	18 (25)
Ring Gear-To-Differential Case Bolts	91 (124)
Transfer Case-To-Transaxle Bolt & Nut	51 (69)

	INCH Lbs. (N.m)
Accumulator-To-Cover Bolt	89 (10)
Manual Valve Bolt	97 (11)
Oil Pan Bolt	
A-540H	69 (7.8)
A-541E	43 (4.9)
Oil Pump Body-To-Stator Shaft Bolt	89 (10)
Oil Strainer Bolt	97 (11)
Parking Lock Pawl Bracket Bolt	65 (7.4)
Park Neutral Position Switch	
Bolt	48 (5.4)
Nut	61 (6.9)
Solenoid Bolt	58 (6.6)
Speed Sensor Bolt	48 (5.4)
Transfer Case Adjusting	
Lock-Plate Bolt	63 (7.2)
Upper Valve Body-To-Lower Valve Body Bolt	58 (6.6)
Valve Body-To-Transaxle Case Bolt	97 (11)

RAV4

APPLICATION

APPLICATION

Vehicle	Transaxle Model
RAV4 (4WD)	A-540H

CAUTION: RAV4 is equipped with a Supplemental Restraint System (SRS). When servicing vehicle, use care to avoid accidental air bag deployment. All SRS electrical connections and wiring harness are covered with Yellow insulation. SRS-related components are located in steering column, center console, instrument panel and lower panel of instrument panel. DO NOT use electrical test equipment on these circuits. It may be necessary to deactivate SRS before servicing components. See AIR BAG SERVICING article in APPLICATIONS & IDENTIFICATION section.

DESCRIPTION

The A-540H automatic transaxle is electronically controlled. Transaxle shifting and torque converter lock-up are controlled by an Electronic Controlled Transmission (ECT) Electronic Control Unit (ECU). Control unit is a combined engine control and transaxle control unit and is referred to as the ECT ECU. See Fig. 1.

ECT ECU receives information from various input devices and uses this information to control No. 1 and No. 2 solenoids on transaxle valve body for transaxle shifting and lock-up solenoid (also called SL solenoid) for torque converter lock-up. SLD solenoid is used to control hydraulic pressure acting on center differential clutch and maintains limited slip differential operation. ST solenoid is used to control transaxle line pressure.

A pattern select switch is located near shift lever on center console. Pattern select switch contains a POWER (PWR) and a NORMAL (NORM) operating position. When pattern select switch is depressed (PWR position), transaxle upshifts and downshifts will occur at a higher vehicle speed than with switch released. An indicator light on instrument panel indicates pattern select switch is depressed (PWR position).

An Overdrive (OD) switch is mounted on shift lever. See Fig. 1. When OD switch is depressed to ON position, transaxle will shift into 4th gear when shift lever is in "D" position, and OD OFF light on instrument panel will go off. When OD switch is released to OFF position, transaxle will shift into 3rd gear, and OD OFF light will come on.

Transaxle is equipped with a shift lock and key lock system. Shift lock system prevents shift lever from being moved from Park unless brake pedal is depressed. In case of a malfunction, shift lever can be released by depressing shift lock override button, located near shift lever. Key lock system prevents ignition key from being moved from ACC to LOCK position on ignition switch unless shift lever is in Park. For more information on shift lock and key lock system, see TOYOTA SHIFT LOCK SYSTEM article.

OPERATION

ECT ECU

ECT ECU receives information from various input devices and uses this information to control No. 1 and 2 solenoids on transaxle valve body for transaxle shifting and lock-up solenoid (also called SL solenoid) for torque converter lock-up. ECT ECU contains a self-diagnostic system, which will store a Diagnostic Trouble Code (DTC) if a failure or problem exists in electronic control system. Trouble code can be retrieved to determine problem area. See SELF-DIAGNOSTIC SYSTEM. Note location of ECT ECU. See Fig. 1.

ECT ECU INPUT DEVICES

Pattern Select Switch Signal – Pattern select switch delivers an input signal to ECT ECU to indicate transaxle shift points selected by vehicle operator. Pattern select switch is located near shift lever on center console. See Fig. 1.

Park/Neutral Position (PNP) Switch Signal – PNP switch delivers an input signal to ECT ECU indicating shift lever position. Switch is located on side of transaxle. See Fig. 1.

Throttle Position (TP) Sensor Signal – TP sensor delivers an input signal to ECT ECU indicating throttle position. TP sensor is located on side of throttle body.

Vehicle Speed Sensor Signal (VSS) – Vehicle speed signal is delivered to ECT ECU by No. 1 vehicle speed sensor, and front and rear speed sensors. See Fig. 1. No. 1 speed sensor is driven by transaxle output shaft by a driven gear, and indicates actual vehicle speed. Front speed sensor detects vehicle speed based on ring gear RPM. Rear speed sensor detects rear wheel speed based on transfer drive gear RPM.

Brakelight Switch Signal – Brakelight switch delivers input signal to ECT ECU, indicating vehicle braking. Brakelight switch is located on brake pedal support.

OD Switch Signal – OD switch provides an input signal to ECT ECU to indicate when overdrive is selected by vehicle operator. OD switch is mounted on shift lever. See Fig. 1.

Engine Coolant Temperature (ECT) Sensor Signal – Coolant temperature sensor delivers input signal to ECT ECU, indicating engine coolant temperature. Coolant temperature sensor is located in coolant passage on engine. See Fig. 17.

Cruise Control Electronic Control Unit (ECU) – Cruise control ECU delivers an input signal to control overdrive operation in accordance with vehicle speed when cruise control is operating. Cruise control ECU is located behind instrument panel, near passenger's side kick panel.

ECT ECU OUTPUT DEVICES

No. 1 & No. 2 Solenoids – ECT ECU controls transaxle shifting by delivering an output signal to operate proper solenoid. Solenoids are located on transaxle valve body. See Fig. 1. Solenoids are operated in accordance with shift lever position. If a solenoid malfunctions, fail-safe gear may be selected. See Fig. 2.

NOTE: In some gears, ECT ECU provides a fail-safe system which will place transaxle in designated gear depending on solenoid failure.

Lock-Up Solenoid – ECT ECU controls torque converter lock-up by delivering an output signal to lock-up solenoid. Lock-up solenoid (also called SL solenoid) is activated when shift lever is in "D" position and vehicle is at specified speed. Lock-up solenoid is located on transaxle valve body. See Fig. 1.

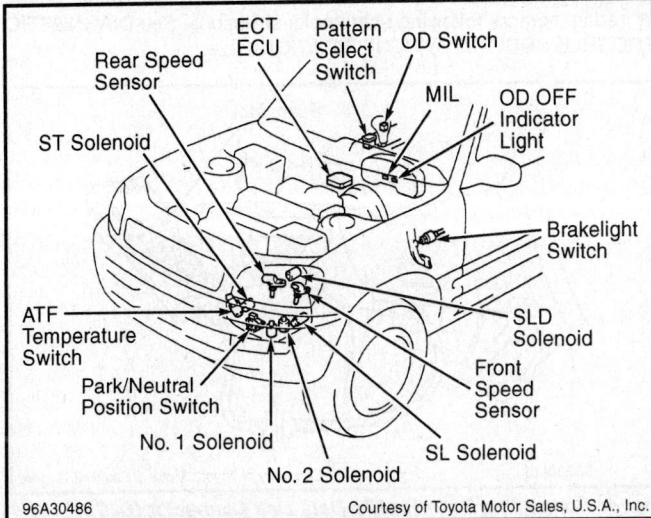

Rear Speed Sensor · ECT ECU · Pattern Select Switch · OD Switch · MIL · OD OFF Indicator Light · ST Solenoid · Brakelight Switch · ATF Temperature Switch · SLD Solenoid · Park/Neutral Position Switch · Front Speed Sensor · No. 1 Solenoid · SL Solenoid · No. 2 Solenoid

96A30486   Courtesy of Toyota Motor Sales, U.S.A., Inc.

Fig. 1: Identifying Input & Output Devices

Position	NORMAL			NO.1 SOLENOID MALFUNCTIONING			NO.2 SOLENOID MALFUNCTIONING			BOTH SOLENOIDS MALFUNCTIONING
	Solenoid valve		Gear	Solenoid valve		Gear	Solenoid valve		Gear	Gear when shift selector is manually operated
	No.1	No.2		No.1	No.2		No.1	No.2		
D	ON	OFF	1st	×	ON	3rd	ON	×	1st	O/D
	ON	ON	2nd	×	ON	3rd	OFF	×	O/D	O/D
	OFF	ON	3rd	×	ON	3rd	OFF	×	O/D	O/D
	OFF	OFF	O/D	×	OFF	O/D	OFF	×	O/D	O/D
2	ON	OFF	1st	×	ON	3rd	ON	×	1st	O/D
	ON	ON	2nd	×	ON	3rd	OFF	×	O/D	O/D
	OFF	ON	3rd	×	ON	3rd	OFF	×	O/D	O/D
L	ON	OFF	1st	×	OFF	1st	ON	×	1st	1st
	ON	ON	2nd	×	ON	2nd	ON	×	1st	1st

x: Malfunctions

95I19537

Courtesy of Toyota Motor Sales, U.S.A., Inc.

Fig. 2: Checking No. 1 & No. 2 Solenoid Operation

ST Solenoid – When difference in speed between front and rear wheels is extreme, and condition takes place during low speed operation in "D", "2" or "L" position, ST solenoid is turned on by ECT ECU to adjust transaxle line pressure. ST solenoid is located on transaxle valve body. *See Fig. 1.*

SLD Solenoid – SLD solenoid controls hydraulic pressure applied to center differential clutch and maintains limited slip differential level. ECT ECU determines optimum control pressure according to signals from TP sensor, front and rear speed sensors, and volume of current flow to SLD solenoid. Amount of current flow to SLD solenoid is controlled by duty ratio of ECT ECU output signal. The higher the duty ratio becomes, the higher center differential control pressure becomes during center differential operation. SLD solenoid is located on transaxle valve body. *See Fig. 1.*

SELF-DIAGNOSTIC SYSTEM

SYSTEM DIAGNOSIS

NOTE: Before testing transaxle, ensure fluid level is correct and throttle and shift cables are properly adjusted. Ensure engine starts with shift lever in "P" (Park) and "N" (Neutral) to ensure proper adjustment of park/neutral position switch. Transaxle must first be tested by checking for stored trouble codes. See RETRIEVING TROUBLE CODES.

ECT ECU monitors engine and transaxle operation and contains a self-diagnostic system which stores diagnostic trouble code(s). A Malfunction Indicator Light (MIL), located on instrument panel, will illuminate if a system or component fails and sets a DTC. *See Fig. 1.*

MIL illuminates with ignition switch in ON position, engine off (KOEO). Once engine is started, MIL should go out. If MIL remains illuminated, ECT ECU has detected a malfunction or abnormality in system. If MIL does not illuminate, inspect circuit and light. See WIRING DIAGRAM.

If malfunction does not reoccur in 3 trips, MIL goes off, but Diagnostic Trouble Code (DTC) remains recorded in ECT ECU memory. Trouble codes may only be retrieved using an appropriate scan tool or Toyota scan tool connected to 16-pin Data Link Connector (DLC3), located under instrument panel, above pedal assembly. *See Figs. 3 and 4.* Scan tool also provides freeze-frame data and can be used to clear trouble codes.

ECT ECU records engine operating condition (fuel system, calculated load, coolant temperature, fuel trim (mixture), engine speed, vehicle speed, etc.) with 1st malfunction ONLY. Information is ONLY for 1st recorded failure, even if more than one code has been recorded. Freeze-frame data is only updated when all trouble codes have been cleared, or a misfire or fuel-trim malfunction has occurred.

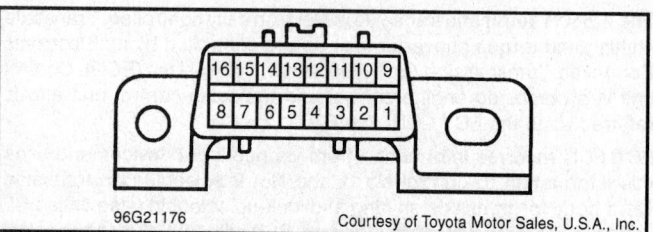

96G21176

Courtesy of Toyota Motor Sales, U.S.A., Inc.

Fig. 3: Identifying Data Link Connector (DLC3) Terminals

RETRIEVING TROUBLE CODES

NOTE: Before retrieving trouble codes, ensure sufficient battery voltage exists for proper self-diagnosis system operation. Ensure proper operation of MIL light. MIL will illuminate and OD OFF indicator will flash for all trouble codes.

NOTE: For additional engine performance or other system related trouble codes present that are not listed in DIAGNOSTIC TROUBLE CODE (DTC) IDENTIFICATION table, see appropriate MITCHELL® ENGINE PERFORMANCE publication for IMPORTED CARS, LIGHT TRUCKS & VANS.

ECT ECU Codes – **1)** Connect scan tool to Data Link Connector (DLC3). DLC3 is located under instrument panel, above pedal assembly. *See Fig. 4.*
2) Turn ignition on. Turn on scan tool. Retrieve any trouble codes stored in memory following scan tool instructions. See DIAGNOSTIC TROUBLE CODE (DTC) IDENTIFICATION table.

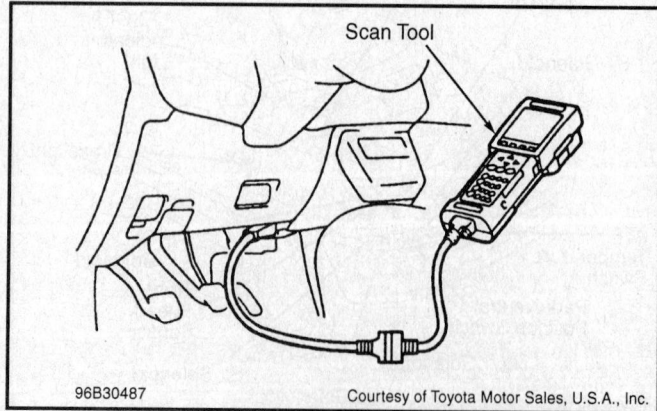

Scan Tool

96B30487

Courtesy of Toyota Motor Sales, U.S.A., Inc.

Fig. 4: Connecting Scan Tool To Data Link Connector (DLC3)

3) Trouble codes recorded may not have illuminated MIL. When certain malfunctions or trouble codes initially occur, they will be temporarily stored in ECT ECU memory, but MIL will not illuminate.

4) Second time malfunction or trouble code is detected, MIL will illuminate, provided ignition is turned off and then back on after malfunction or trouble code was first detected. This process is referred to as 2 trip detection logic and only applies to specific trouble codes.

5) Record freeze-frame data. If using Toyota scan tool, ensure tool is in NORMAL mode. CHECK MODE will erase all codes.

DIAGNOSTIC TROUBLE CODE (DTC) IDENTIFICATION

DTC	¹ Probable Cause
P0500	No. 1 Vehicle Speed Sensor
P0750	No. 1 Solenoid
P0753	No. 1 Solenoid Circuit
P0755	No. 2 Solenoid
P0758	No. 2 Solenoid Circuit
P0770	² Lock-Up Solenoid
P0773	Lock-Up Solenoid Circuit
P1700	Front Speed Sensor Circuit
P1715	Rear Speed Sensor Circuit
P1760	ST Solenoid Circuit
P1770	SLD Solenoid Circuit
P1780	Park/Neutral Position Switch

¹ – Check listed component for probable cause. Check wiring and connections of specified component.

² – Also called SL solenoid.

CLEARING TROUBLE CODES

Once repairs have been performed, trouble codes must be cleared from ECT ECU memory. DTCs may be cleared by following methods:

- Scan tool (follow manufacturers instructions).
- Remove EFI fuse (15-amp) from engine compartment fuse box, near battery, for 10 seconds or more to clear memory in ECT ECU.
- Disconnect negative battery cable (memory for electronic components will be also be canceled).

DIAGNOSTIC TESTS

When trouble shooting transaxle, first check for stored trouble codes and repair as necessary. If no trouble codes exist, perform manual shift test to determine if problem area is in electrical circuits or a mechanical transaxle problem. See MANUAL SHIFT TEST.

DTC P0500:
NO. 1 VEHICLE SPEED SENSOR (VSS) FAULT

Circuit Description – No. 1 Vehicle Speed Sensor (VSS), driven by transaxle output shaft, outputs a pulse signal to combination meter. Combination meter converts signal to a more precise waveform for ECT ECU. DTC is set when ECT ECU does not detect any signal while vehicle is in motion. Possible causes are:

- Open or short in vehicle speed sensor circuit.
- No. 1 VSS failure.
- Combination meter malfunction.
- ECT ECU malfunction.

Diagnosis & Repair Procedure – **1)** Test drive vehicle and determine if speedometer is functioning properly. If speedometer is okay, go to next step. If speedometer is not functioning, go to step **3)**.

2) Access ECT ECU harness connector. Disconnect ECT ECU harness connector. See Figs. 1 and 8. Using ohmmeter, check continuity between terminal SPD and ground. See Fig. 8. If continuity exists, check and repair circuit for short to ground. If continuity does not exist, raise and support vehicle.

3) Shift transaxle into Neutral. Turn ignition on. Using DVOM, measure voltage between terminal SPD and ground while rotating front wheel. If voltage is not 4.5-5.5 volts, check and repair open circuit between combination meter and ECT ECU. See WIRING DIAGRAM. If voltage is as specified, replace ECT ECU and retest.

DTC P0750 & P0755:
NO.1 & NO. 2 SOLENOID FAULT

Circuit Description – ECT ECU uses signal from No. 1 vehicle speed sensor to determine actual gear position. ECT ECU compares actual gear with shift schedule in memory to detect mechanical trouble of solenoids and/or valve body. DTC is set if during normal driving gear required by ECT ECU does not match actual gear after 2 trips have been completed. Possible causes are:

- No. 1 and/or No. 2 solenoid is stuck open or closed.
- Valve body is clogged or valve(s) is stuck.

Diagnosis & Repair Procedure – Remove and inspect operation of solenoids. See SOLENOIDS under COMPONENT TESTS. If solenoids are okay, inspect valve body. See TOYOTA A-540H & A-541E overhaul article.

DTC P0753 & P0758:
NO. 1 & NO. 2 SOLENOID CIRCUIT

Circuit Description – Shifting is performed in combination with ON and OFF position of shift solenoids controlled by ECT ECU. If an open or short circuit occurs in either shift solenoid, ECT ECU reverts to fail-safe mode. See Fig. 2. DTCs are output when a open or short circuit occurs. Possible causes are:

- No. 1 and/or No. 2 solenoid circuit.
- No. 1 and/or No. 2 solenoid.
- ECT ECU malfunction.

Diagnosis & Repair Procedure – **1)** Ensure ignition is off. Access ECT ECU. See Fig. 1. Backprobing ECT ECU harness connector with ohmmeter, measure resistance between terminal S1 and/or S2 and ground. See Fig. 8. If resistance is 11-15 ohms, replace ECT ECU and retest. If resistance is not within specification, go to next step.

2) Disconnect solenoid harness connector (next to PNP switch) at transaxle. Check continuity between terminal S1 of transaxle harness connector and corresponding terminal of ECT ECU harness connector. See Figs. 5 and 8.

3) Check continuity between terminal S2 of transaxle harness connector and corresponding terminal of ECT ECU harness connector. If continuity exists for both circuits, go to next step. If continuity does not exist for either circuit, inspect and repair circuit(s) as needed.

4) Measure resistance between transaxle connector terminals S1 and/or S2, and ground. See Fig. 5. If resistance is 11-15 ohms, replace solenoid. If resistance is not as specified, replace transaxle sub-harness as needed.

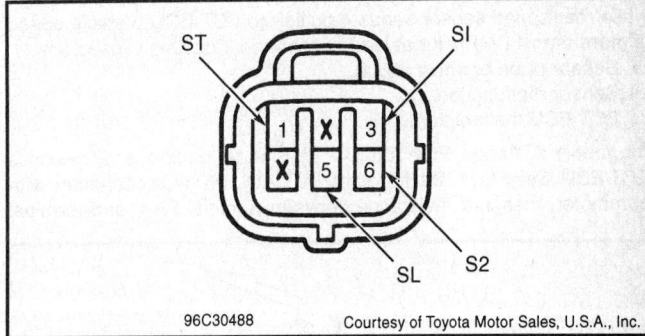

Fig. 5: Identifying Transaxle Solenoid Harness Connector Terminals

DTC P0770: LOCK-UP/SL SOLENOID

Circuit Description – ECT ECU uses signals from throttle position sensor and airflow meter to monitor engagement of Torque Converter Clutch (TCC). ECT ECU compares engagement condition of TCC with lock-up schedule in memory to detect mechanical trouble of solenoid, valve body and torque converter. DTC is set when TCC lock-up does not occur at appropriate speed, or lock-up does not release at appropriate speed. Possible causes are:

- Lock-up solenoid is stuck open or closed.
- Valve body clogged or valve stuck.
- TCC malfunction.

Diagnosis & Repair Procedure – Remove and inspect operation of solenoid. See SOLENOIDS under COMPONENT TESTS. If solenoid is okay, inspect valve body. See TOYOTA A-540H & A-541E overhaul article.

DTC P0773: LOCK-UP/SL SOLENOID CIRCUIT

Circuit Description – Lock-up solenoid is turned on and off by signals from ECT ECU to control hydraulic pressure affecting lock-up relay valve. Lock-up relay valve controls operation of Torque Converter Clutch (TCC). If ECT ECU detects a malfunction, fail-safe function is enabled. DTC is output when a open or short circuit occurs. Possible causes are:

- Lock-up solenoid open or short circuit.
- Lock-up solenoid malfunction.
- ECT ECU malfunction.

Diagnosis & Repair Procedure – **1)** Ensure ignition is off. Access ECT ECU. See Fig. 1. Backprobing ECT ECU harness connector with ohmmeter, measure resistance between terminal SL and ground. If resistance is 8-100 k/ohms, replace ECT ECU and retest. If resistance is not within specification, go to next step.

2) Disconnect solenoid harness connector (next to PNP switch) at transaxle. Check continuity between terminal SL of transaxle harness connector and corresponding terminal of ECT ECU harness connector. See Figs. 5 and 8.

3) If continuity does not exist, inspect and repair circuit as needed. If continuity exists, measure resistance between transaxle connector terminal SL and ground. See Fig. 5. If resistance is 11-15 ohms, replace solenoid. If resistance is not as specified, replace transaxle sub-harness as needed.

DTC P1700: FRONT SPEED SENSOR CIRCUIT

Circuit Description – Front speed sensor detects vehicle speed based on ring gear RPM and sends signals to ECT ECU. An AC voltage is generated in front speed sensor coil as ring gear rotates. This voltage is sent to ECT ECU. Center differential clutch is controlled by ECT ECU based on signals from front and rear speed sensor signals. DTC is output when no signal is detected from front speed sensor while rear speed sensor sends 4 pulses to ECT ECU. Vehicle speed is more than 11 MPH for at least 4 seconds. Possible causes are:

- Sensor open or short circuit.
- Sensor malfunction.
- ECT ECU malfunction.

Diagnosis & Repair Procedure – **1)** Ensure ignition is off. Access ECT ECU. See Fig. 1. Backprobing ECT ECU harness connector with ohmmeter, measure resistance between terminal FR+ and terminal

FR-. See Fig. 8. Resistance should be 560-680 ohms. If resistance is within specification, replace ECT ECU. If resistance is not within specification, go to next step.

2) Remove front speed sensor from transaxle. Measure resistance between sensor terminals. Resistance should be 560-680 ohms. If resistance is not as specified, replace sensor. If resistance is as specified, check and repair circuits between sensor and ECT ECU.

3) Check voltage between sensor terminals when a magnet is put close to tip of speed sensor. See Fig. 6. If a low intermittent voltage is generated, sensor is okay. If no voltage is generated, replace speed sensor.

DTC P1715: REAR SPEED SENSOR CIRCUIT

Circuit Description – Rear speed sensor detects rear wheel speed based on revolution of transfer drive gear and sends signals to ECT ECU. An AC voltage is generated in rear speed sensor coil as ring gear rotates. This voltage is sent to ECT ECU. Center differential clutch is controlled by ECT ECU based on signals from front and rear speed sensor signals. DTC is output when no signal is detected from rear speed sensor at ECT ECU. Vehicle speed is more than 19 MPH. Possible causes are:

- Sensor open or short circuit.
- Sensor malfunction.
- ECT ECU malfunction.

Diagnosis & Repair Procedure – **1)** Ensure ignition is off. Access ECT ECU. See Fig. 1. Backprobing ECT ECU harness connector with ohmmeter, measure resistance between terminal RR+ and terminal RR-. See Fig. 8. Resistance should be 560-680 ohms. If resistance is within specification, replace ECT ECU. If resistance is not within specification, go to next step.

2) Remove rear speed sensor from transaxle. Measure resistance between sensor terminals. Resistance should be 560-680 ohms. If resistance is not as specified, replace sensor. If resistance is as specified, check and repair circuits between sensor and ECT ECU.

3) Check voltage between sensor terminals when a magnet is put close to tip of speed sensor. See Fig. 6. If a low intermittent voltage is generated, sensor is okay. If no voltage is generated, replace speed sensor.

DTC P1760: ST SOLENOID CIRCUIT (LINE PRESSURE CONTROL)

Circuit Description – ST solenoid controls hydraulic pressure. When difference in speed between front and rear wheels is extreme, and occurs during extreme low speed operation in "D", "2" and "L" positions, ST solenoid is turned on by signal from ECT ECU. DTC is output when open or short circuit is occurs. Possible causes are:

- ST solenoid open or short circuit.
- ST solenoid malfunction.
- ECT ECU malfunction.

Diagnosis & Repair Procedure – **1)** Ensure ignition is off. Access ECT ECU. See Fig. 1. Backprobing ECT ECU harness connector with ohmmeter, measure resistance between terminal ST and ground. See Fig. 8. Resistance should be 11-15 ohms. If resistance is within specification, replace ECT ECU. If resistance is not within specification, go to next step.

2) Disconnect solenoid harness connector (next to PNP switch) at transaxle. Check continuity between terminal ST of transaxle harness connector and corresponding terminal of ECT ECU harness connector. See Figs. 5 and 8.

3) If continuity does not exist, inspect and repair circuit as needed. If continuity exists, measure resistance between transaxle connector terminal ST and ground. See Fig. 5. If resistance is 11-15 ohms, replace solenoid. If resistance is not as specified, replace transaxle sub-harness as needed.

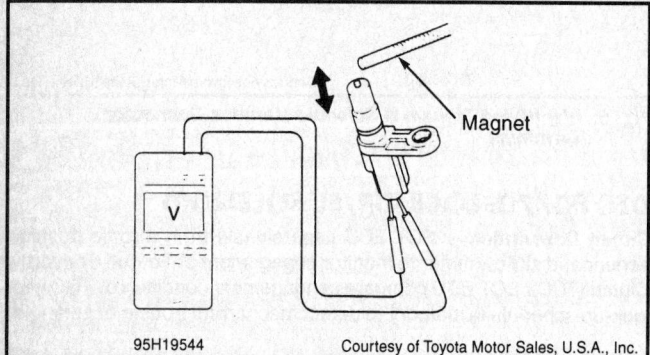

95H19544   Courtesy of Toyota Motor Sales, U.S.A., Inc.

Fig. 6: Testing Front & Rear Speed Sensors

Magnet

V

DTC P1770: SLD SOLENOID CIRCUIT (DIFFERENTIAL LOCK SOLENOID)

Circuit Description – SLD solenoid controls hydraulic pressure applied to center differential clutch and maintains limited slip differential level. ECT ECU determines optimum operating pressure according to signals from throttle position sensor, and front and rear speed sensors, and control volume of current flow to SLD solenoid. DTC is output when SLD solenoid output signal is on for 3.3 milliseconds or more with duty ratio of at least 5 percent. Possible causes are:

- SLD solenoid open or short circuit.
- SLD solenoid malfunction.
- ECT ECU malfunction.

Diagnosis & Repair Procedure – Ensure ignition is off. Raise and support vehicle. Remove transaxle oil pan. Disconnect SLD solenoid connector. Using an ohmmeter, measure resistance between solenoid connector terminals. Ensure resistance is 5.1-5.5 ohms. If resistance is not as specified, inspect and repair circuit(s) between SLD solenoid and ECT ECU. See WIRING DIAGRAM. Also conduct performance check of solenoid. See SLD SOLENOID under COMPONENT TESTS. Replace as needed. If solenoid is okay, replace ECT ECU and retest.

DTC P1780: PARK/NEUTRAL POSITION (PNP) SWITCH

Circuit Description – PNP switch verifies shift lever position and sends signals to ECT ECU. If no signal is received from PNP switch, ECT ECU defaults to drive ("D") position. DTC is output when ECT ECU detects 2 or more circuits are on. Vehicle speed has to be above 50 MPH for more than 30 seconds with engine RPM at 1500-3000. Possible causes are:

- Short in PNP switch circuit.
- PNP switch malfunction.
- ECT ECU malfunction.

Diagnosis & Repair Procedure – 1) Turn ignition on. Access ECT ECU. Using DVOM, measure voltage at terminals NSW, "R", "2" and "L" of ECT ECU harness connector between terminal and body ground with gear selector in each shift position. See Fig. 8.

2) Ensure 10-14 volts is present at NSW terminal at ECT ECU harness connector in all shift positions. Ensure 10-14 volts is present at "R", "2" and "L" terminals at ECT ECU harness connector with gear selector in "R", "2" and "L" position. If voltage is not as specified, check park/neutral position switch. See PARK/NEUTRAL POSITION (PNP) SWITCH under COMPONENT TESTS. If switch is okay, check and repair circuit(s) between PNP switch and ECT ECU. See WIRING DIAGRAM.

MANUAL SHIFT TEST

NOTE: Perform manual shift test if no trouble codes exist. Manual shift test determines if problem area is in electrical circuits or a mechanical transaxle problem.

1) With ignition off, disconnect electrical connector for solenoids from transaxle. Road test vehicle and ensure transaxle gear changes correspond with shift lever position. See GEAR APPLICATION table.

2) If abnormality exists, a mechanical transaxle problem exists. Turn ignition off. Reconnect electrical connector. Clear trouble codes from ECT ECU memory, as disconnecting electrical connector may set a trouble code. See CLEARING TROUBLE CODES under SELF-DIAGNOSTIC SYSTEM.

GEAR APPLICATION

Shift Lever Position	Gear
"D"	Overdrive
"2"	3rd
"L"	1st
"R"	Reverse
"P"	Park

CIRCUIT TESTS

BRAKELIGHT SIGNAL

1) Inspect operation of brakelights. Repair as needed. If switch is suspect, see BRAKELIGHT SWITCH under COMPONENT TESTS. If circuit is suspect, diagnose and repair as necessary. See WIRING DIAGRAM.

2) Connect scan tool to DLC3. See Fig. 4. Turn ignition on. Read STP signal while depressing and releasing brake pedal. Ensure signal cycles when pressing brake pedal. If signal cycles, replace ECT ECU. If signal does not cycle, inspect and repair circuit between brakelight switch and ECT ECU. If circuit is okay, replace ECT ECU.

OVERDRIVE CANCEL SIGNAL

1) Access ECT ECU. See Fig. 1. Turn ignition on. Backprobe ECT ECU harness connector with DVOM. Measure voltage between terminal OD1 of ECT ECU harness connector and ground. See Fig. 8. If voltage is 4-6 volts, substitute known good ECT ECU and retest. If voltage is not 4-6 volts, go to next step.

2) Turn ignition off. Disconnect cruise control ECU harness connector, located behind instrument panel, near passenger's side kick panel. Turn ignition on. Measure voltage between terminal OD and ground. See Fig. 7. If 4-6 volts is present, replace cruise control ECU and retest. If 4-6 volts is not present, inspect and repair circuit between cruise control ECU and ECT ECU.

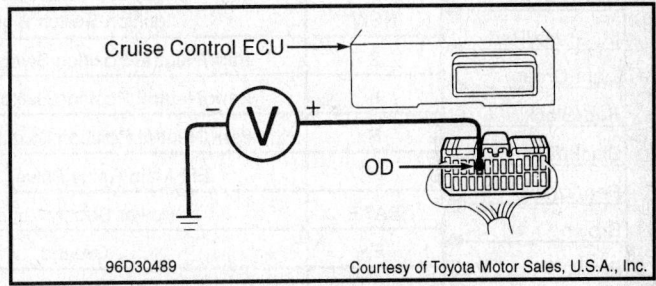

96D30489   Courtesy of Toyota Motor Sales, U.S.A., Inc.

Fig. 7: Identifying Cruise Control ECU Terminals

ECT ECU VOLTAGES

Access ECT ECU. See Fig. 1. Turn ignition on. Using voltmeter, backprobe ECT ECU harness connector. Check voltage between selected terminal and E_1 terminal. Voltage should be as specified. See Fig. 8.

AUTOMATIC TRANSMISSIONS
Toyota A-540H Electronic Controls (Cont.)

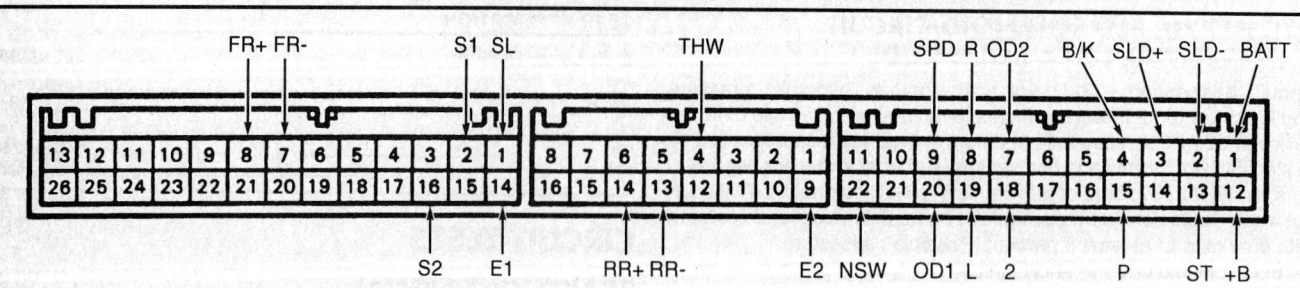

	Terminal ID.	Function/Description	Voltage Value (DC Volts Unless Otherwise Specified)
Pink/Black	S1	No. 1 Solenoid	10-14 Volts With KOEO [1]
Pink	S2	No. 2 Solenoid	1 Volt Or Less With KOEO [1]
Yellow/Black	SL	Lock-Up Solenoid	1 Volt Or Less With KOEO [1]
Light Green	ST	ST Solenoid	Less Than 1 Volt With KOEO [1]
Red/Green	P	Pattern Select Switch Signal	7.5-14 Volts In PWR Position
Green/White	B/K	Brakelight Switch Signal	7.5-14 Volts With Pedal Depressed
White	THW	Coolant Temperature Sensor Signal	.2-1.0 Volts @ 176°F (80°C)
Violet/White	SPD	Vehicle Speed Sensor Signal	1 Volt Or Less With ECU Unplugged [2] (Car Parked)
[3]	FR+, FR-	Front Speed Sensor Signal	1 Volt Or Less With KOEO [1] (Car Parked)
[4]	RR+, RR-	Rear Speed Sensor Signal	1 Volt Or Less With KOEO [1] (Car Parked)
[5]	SLD+, SLD-	SLD Solenoid	Pulse Generation With KOEO [1]
Yellow/Black	OD1	OD Output To Cruise Control ECU	4-6 Volts With KOEO [1]
Light Green	OD2	Overdrive Switch Signal	10-14 Volts With Switch On
Black/White	NSW	Ignition Switch Signal	10-14 Volts In "P" Or "N", KOEO [1]
Lt. Green/Red	2	Park/Neutral Position Switch "2" Signal	10-14 Volts In "2", KOEO [1]
Light Green	L	Park/Neutral Position Switch "L" Signal	10-14 Volts In "L", KOEO [1]
Red/Black	R	Park/Neutral Position Switch "R" Signal	10-14 Volts With KOEO [1]
Black/Red	+B	EFI Main Relay Power Supply	10-14 Volts With KOEO [1]
Red/White	BATT	Power Supply Voltage	10-14 Volts (Constant)
Brown	E₁	Ground	Not Applicable
Brown	E₂	Ground	Not Applicable

[1] – Key On, Engine Off.
[2] – Disconnect cruise control ECU.
[3] – Wire color for FR+ is Yellow/Red. Wire color for FR- is White/Red.
[4] – Wire color for RR+ is Blue/Yellow. Wire color for RR- is Red/Blue.
[5] – Wire color for SLD+ is Blue/Black. Wire color for SLD- is Brown/Black.

96G30490

Courtesy of Toyota Motor Sales, U.S.A., Inc.

Fig. 8: ECT ECU Pin Voltage Table (Component Connector View)

COMPONENT TESTS

NO. 1 VEHICLE SPEED SENSOR (VSS)

1) Disconnect electrical connector from No. 1 VSS, located on top of transaxle. *See Fig. 1.* Connect positive battery lead to terminal No. 1 and negative lead to terminal No. 2. Connect positive lead of voltmeter to terminal No. 3 and negative lead to terminal No. 2. *See Fig. 9.*
2) Raise and support one vehicle front wheel. Rotate wheel and monitor voltmeter. Ensure voltage changes from zero to 11 volts. Voltage should change 4 times per each revolution of speedometer cable shaft. Replace speed sensor if voltage does not change as specified.

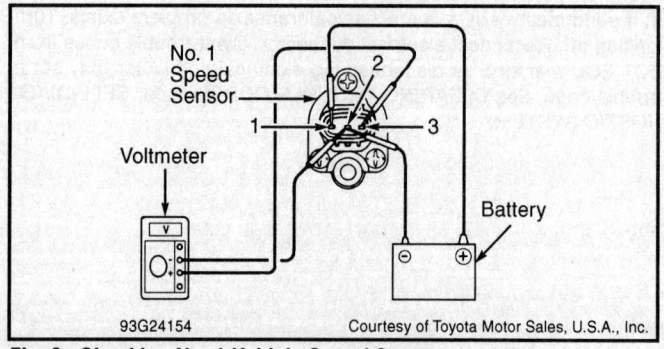

93G24154

Courtesy of Toyota Motor Sales, U.S.A., Inc.

Fig. 9: Checking No. 1 Vehicle Speed Sensor

SOLENOIDS

1) To check solenoid seals, remove suspect solenoid. Connect battery voltage to solenoid. Apply 71 psi (5 kg/cm²) to solenoid with battery voltage connected. *See Fig. 10.*

2) With battery voltage applied, air should pass through solenoid. Disconnect voltage to solenoid. Ensure air does not pass through solenoid. Replace solenoid if defective.

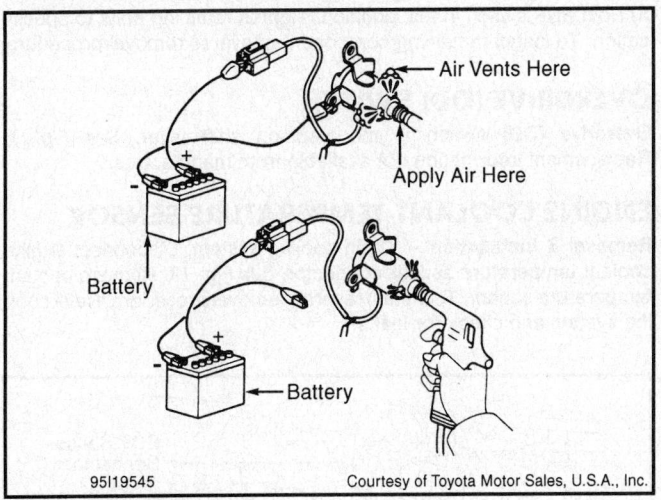

95I19545 Courtesy of Toyota Motor Sales, U.S.A., Inc.

Fig. 10: Checking Solenoids

SLD SOLENOID

Raise and support vehicle. Remove transaxle oil pan. Remove SLD solenoid. To check solenoid operation, connect positive battery voltage to solenoid terminal No. 1. Ensure a 8-10 watt bulb is placed in-line of positive lead. *See Fig. 11.* Connect negative lead to terminal No. 2 and monitor valve's movement. Replace as needed.

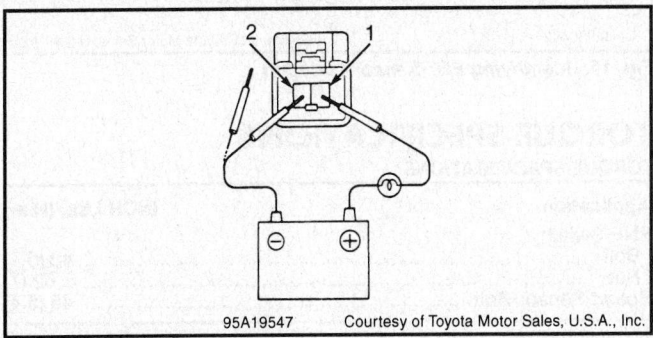

95A19547 Courtesy of Toyota Motor Sales, U.S.A., Inc.

Fig. 11: Testing SLD Solenoid

PARK/NEUTRAL POSITION (PNP) SWITCH

Disconnect harness connector at park/neutral position switch. Switch is located on side of transaxle. Using ohmmeter, check for continuity between specified terminals in accordance with shift lever position. *See Fig. 12.* Replace PNP switch if defective.

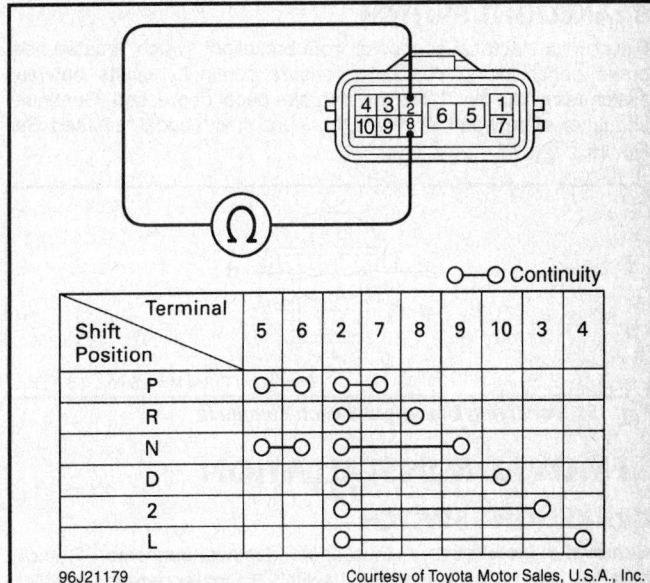

Terminal Shift Position	5	6	2	7	8	9	10	3	4
P	O—O		O—O						
R			O		O				
N	O—O		O			O			
D			O				O		
2			O					O	
L			O						O

O—O Continuity

96J21179 Courtesy of Toyota Motor Sales, U.S.A., Inc.

Fig. 12: Testing Park/Neutral Position (PNP) Switch

PATTERN SELECT SWITCH

Disconnect electrical connector from pattern select switch. *See Fig. 13.* Using ohmmeter, ensure continuity exists between terminals No. 1 and 3 with switch in PWR position. No continuity should exist in NORM position. Replace switch as necessary.

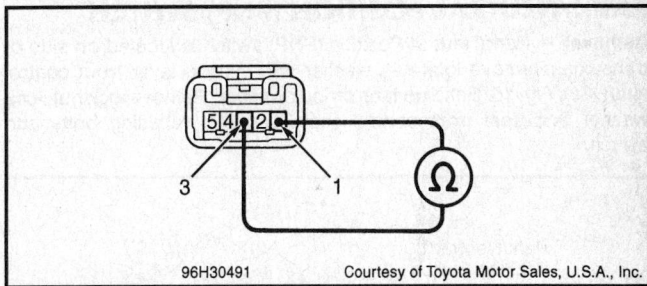

96H30491 Courtesy of Toyota Motor Sales, U.S.A., Inc.

Fig. 13: Identifying Pattern Select Switch Terminals

OVERDRIVE (OD) SWITCH

Disconnect electrical connector from OD switch, located on shift lever. Using ohmmeter, ensure continuity exists between terminals No. 2 and 4 with switch released (OFF position). *See Fig. 14.* Ensure no continuity exists with switch depressed (ON position). Replace switch if defective.

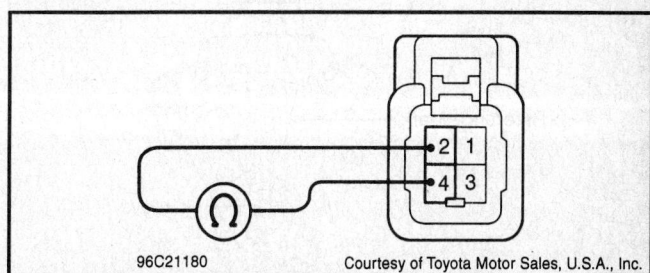

96C21180 Courtesy of Toyota Motor Sales, U.S.A., Inc.

Fig. 14: Identifying Overdrive (OD) Switch Terminals

BRAKELIGHT SWITCH

Disconnect electrical connector from brakelight switch, located near brake pedal. Using ohmmeter, ensure continuity exists between switch terminals No. 1 and 2 with brake pedal depressed. Continuity should exist between terminals No. 3 and 4 with pedal released. *See Fig. 15.*

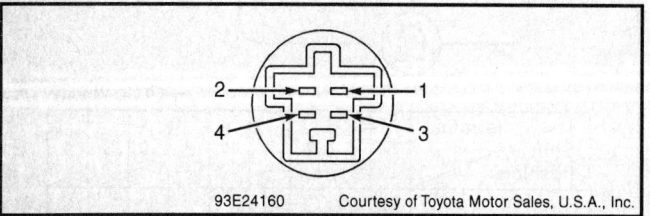

93E24160   Courtesy of Toyota Motor Sales, U.S.A., Inc.

Fig. 15: Identifying Brakelight Switch Terminals

REMOVAL & INSTALLATION

BRAKELIGHT SWITCH

Removal & Installation – Disconnect electrical connector. Remove lock nut, and unscrew brakelight switch. To install, screw brakelight switch inward until brakelight plunger contacts brake pedal.

SOLENOIDS

Removal & Installation – Solenoids are located on transaxle valve body. Raise and support vehicle. Remove transaxle oil pan. Remove bolt, solenoid and "O" ring from valve body. To install, reverse removal procedure using NEW "O" ring.

PARK/NEUTRAL POSITION (PNP) SWITCH

Removal – Park/Neutral Position (PNP) switch is located on side of transaxle. Remove lock nut, washer and manual lever from control shaft. *See Fig. 16.* Bend up tabs on lock washer. Remove lock nut, lock washer and seal from control shaft. Remove retaining bolts and switch.

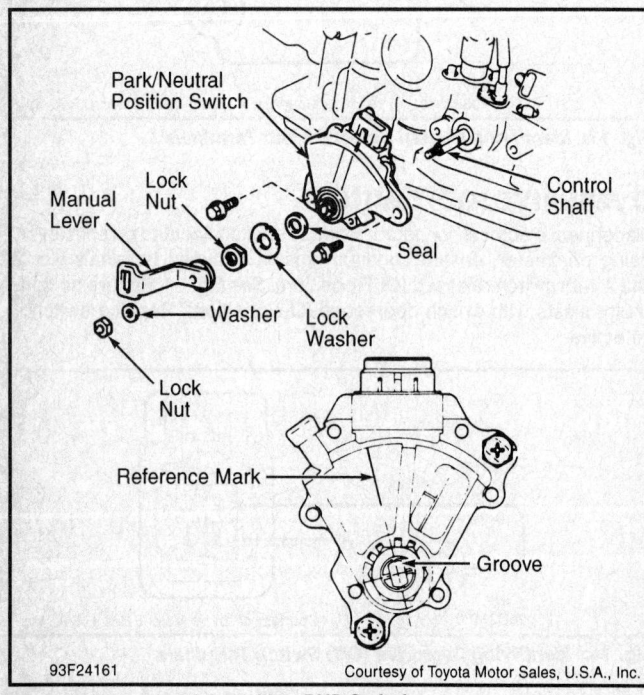

93F24161   Courtesy of Toyota Motor Sales, U.S.A., Inc.

Fig. 16: Removing & Installing PNP Switch

Installation – **1)** Install switch on control shaft. Loosely install switch retaining bolts. Install seal and lock washer. Install lock nut and tighten to specification. See TORQUE SPECIFICATIONS. Bend tabs on lock washer over against lock nut.

2) Ensure parking brake is applied. Temporarily install manual lever on control shaft. Place shift lever in Neutral. Remove manual lever. Rotate park/neutral position switch and align reference mark on PNP switch with groove. *See Fig. 16.*

3) Hold PNP switch in this position. Tighten retaining bolts to specification. To install remaining components, reverse removal procedure.

OVERDRIVE (OD) SWITCH

Overdrive (OD) switch is mounted on shift lever. *See Fig. 1.* Replacement information not available from manufacturer.

ENGINE COOLANT TEMPERATURE SENSOR

Removal & Installation – Drain cooling system. Disconnect engine coolant temperature sensor connector. *See Fig. 17.* Remove coolant temperature sensor. To install, reverse removal procedure. Refill cooling system and check for leaks.

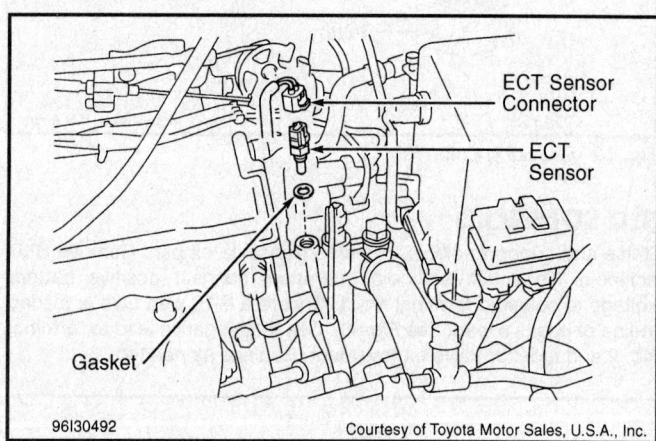

96I30492   Courtesy of Toyota Motor Sales, U.S.A., Inc.

Fig. 17: Identifying ECT Sensor Location

TORQUE SPECIFICATIONS
TORQUE SPECIFICATIONS

Application	INCH Lbs. (N.m)
PNP Switch	
Bolt	48 (5.4)
Nut	62 (7)
Speed Sensor Bolt	48 (5.4)

WIRING DIAGRAMS

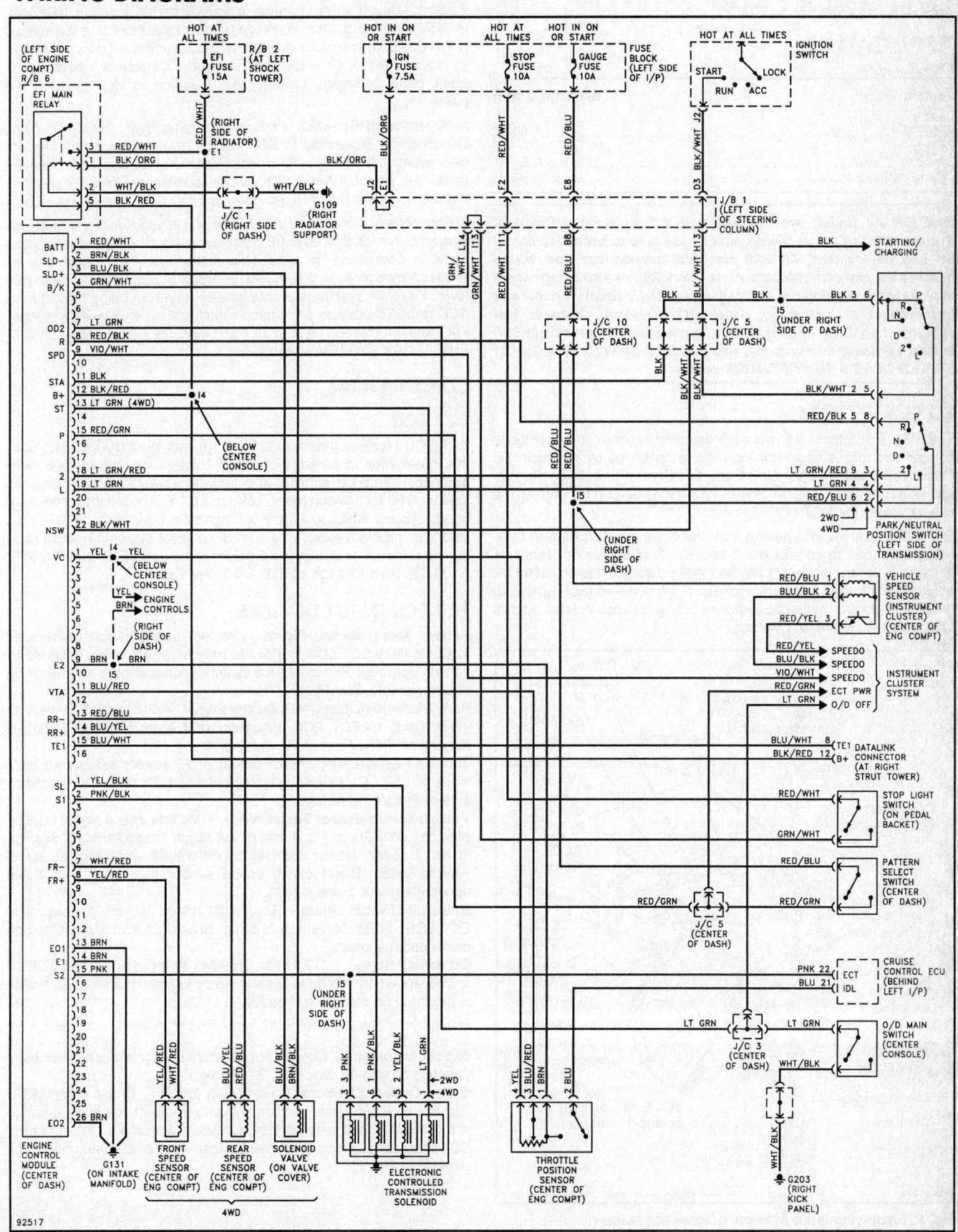

Fig. 18: Transaxle Wiring Diagram (1996 RAV4)

92517

AUTOMATIC TRANSMISSIONS
Toyota A-541E Electronic Controls

Lexus: ES300
Toyota: Avalon, Camry

APPLICATION

APPLICATION

Vehicle	Transaxle Model
Lexus	
ES300	A-541E
Toyota	
Avalon	A-541E
Camry V6	A-541E

CAUTION: All models are equipped with a Supplemental Restraint System (SRS). When servicing vehicle, use care to avoid accidental air bag deployment. All SRS electrical connections and wiring harness are covered with Yellow Insulation. SRS-related components are located in steering column, center console, instrument panel and lower panel of instrument panel. DO NOT use electrical test equipment on these circuits. It may be necessary to deactivate SRS before servicing components. See AIR BAG SERVICING article in APPLICATIONS & IDENTIFICATION section.

DESCRIPTION

The A-541E automatic transaxle is electronically controlled. Transaxle shifting and torque converter lock-up are controlled by an Electronic Controlled Transmission (ECT) Electronic Control Unit (ECU). Control unit is a combined engine control and transaxle control unit and is referred to as the ECT ECU. *See Fig. 1.*

ECT ECU receives information from various input devices and uses this information to control No. 1 and No. 2 solenoids on transaxle valve body for transaxle shifting and lock-up solenoid (also called SL solenoid) for torque converter lock-up. A 4th solenoid (SLN solenoid) is used to control hydraulic pressure acting on accumulator control valve to assist in smooth shifting.

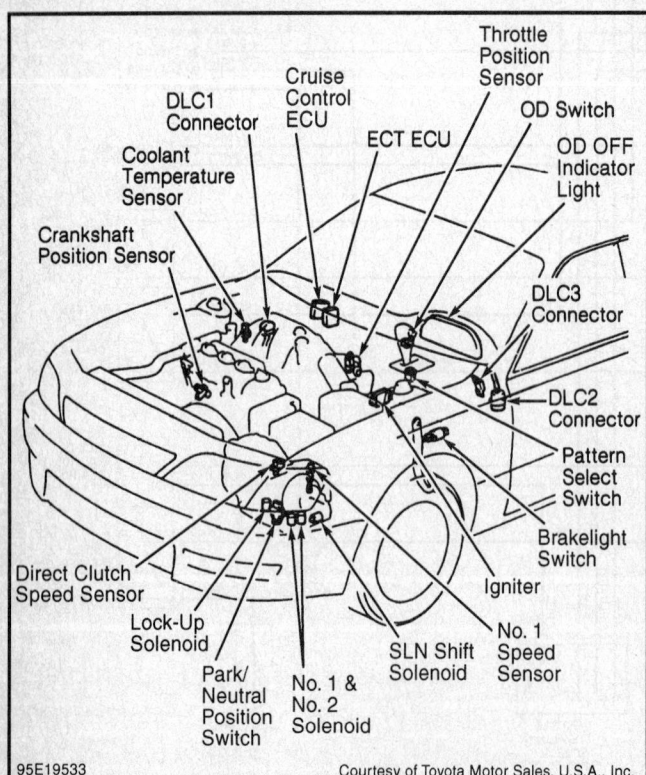

DLC1 Connector
Coolant Temperature Sensor
Crankshaft Position Sensor
Cruise Control ECU
ECT ECU
Throttle Position Sensor
OD Switch
OD OFF Indicator Light
DLC3 Connector
DLC2 Connector
Pattern Select Switch
Brakelight Switch
Igniter
No. 1 Speed Sensor
SLN Shift Solenoid
No. 1 & No. 2 Solenoid
Park/ Neutral Position Switch
Lock-Up Solenoid
Direct Clutch Speed Sensor

95E19533   Courtesy of Toyota Motor Sales, U.S.A., Inc.

Fig. 1: Identifying Input & Output Devices (All Models)

A pattern select switch is located near shift lever on center console. Pattern select switch contains a POWER (PWR) and a NORMAL (NORM) operating position. When pattern select switch is depressed (PWR position), transaxle upshifts and downshifts will occur at a higher vehicle speed than with switch released. An indicator light on instrument panel indicates pattern select switch is depressed (PWR position).

An Overdrive (OD) switch is mounted on shift lever. *See Fig. 1.* When OD switch is depressed to ON position, transaxle will shift into 4th gear when shift lever is in "D" position, and OD OFF light on instrument panel will go off. When OD switch is released to OFF position, transmission will shift into 3rd gear, and OD OFF light will come on.

Transaxle is equipped with a shift lock and key lock system. Shift lock system prevents shift lever from being moved from Park unless brake pedal is depressed. In case of a malfunction, shift lever can be released by depressing shift lock override button, located near shift lever. Key lock system prevents ignition key from being moved from ACC to LOCK position on ignition switch unless shift lever is in Park. For more information on shift lock and key lock system, see TOYOTA SHIFT LOCK SYSTEM article.

OPERATION

ECT ECU

ECT ECU receives information from various input devices and uses this information to control No. 1 and 2 solenoids on transaxle valve body for transaxle shifting and lock-up solenoid (also called SL solenoid) for torque converter lock-up. ECT ECU contains a self-diagnostic system, which will store a Diagnostic Trouble Code (DTC) if a failure or problem exists in electronic control system. Trouble code can be retrieved to determine problem area. See SELF-DIAGNOSTIC SYSTEM. Note location of ECT ECU. *See Fig. 1.*

ECT ECU INPUT DEVICES

Pattern Select Switch Signal – Pattern select switch delivers an input signal to ECT ECU to indicate transaxle shift points selected by vehicle operator. Pattern select switch is located near shift lever on center console. *See Fig. 1.*

Park/Neutral Position (PNP) Switch Signal – PNP switch delivers an input signal to ECT ECU indicating shift lever position. Switch is located on side of transaxle. *See Fig. 1.*

Throttle Position (TP) Sensor Signal – TP sensor delivers an input signal to ECT ECU indicating throttle position. TP sensor is located on side of throttle body. *See Fig. 1.*

Vehicle Speed Sensor Signal (VSS) – Vehicle speed signal is delivered to ECT ECU by No. 1 and direct clutch speed sensors. *See Fig. 1.* No. 1 speed sensor is driven by differential and indicates actual vehicle speed. Direct clutch speed sensor monitors direct clutch speed (magnetic pulse signal).

Brakelight Switch Signal – Brakelight switch delivers input signal to ECT ECU, indicating vehicle braking. Brakelight switch is located on brake pedal support.

OD Switch Signal – OD switch provides an input signal to ECT ECU to indicate when overdrive is selected by vehicle operator. OD switch is mounted on shift lever. *See Fig. 1.*

Engine Coolant Temperature (ECT) Sensor Signal – Coolant temperature sensor delivers input signal to ECT ECU, indicating engine coolant temperature. Coolant temperature sensor is located in coolant passage on engine. *See Figs. 23 and 24.*

Cruise Control Electronic Control Unit (ECU) – Cruise control ECU delivers an input signal to control overdrive operation in accordance with vehicle speed when cruise control is operating. Cruise control ECU is located behind instrument panel, near passenger's side kick panel. *See Fig. 1.*

Position	NORMAL			NO.1 SOLENOID MALFUNCTIONING			NO.2 SOLENOID MALFUNCTIONING			BOTH SOLENOIDS MALFUNCTIONING
	Solenoid valve		Gear	Solenoid valve		Gear	Solenoid valve		Gear	Gear when shift selector is manually operated
	No.1	No.2		No.1	No.2		No.1	No.2		
D	ON	OFF	1st	×	ON	3rd	ON	×	1st	O/D
	ON	ON	2nd	×	ON	3rd	OFF	×	O/D	O/D
	OFF	ON	3rd	×	ON	3rd	OFF	×	O/D	O/D
	OFF	OFF	O/D	×	OFF	O/D	OFF	×	O/D	O/D
2	ON	OFF	1st	×	ON	3rd	ON	×	1st	O/D
	ON	ON	2nd	×	ON	3rd	OFF	×	O/D	O/D
	OFF	ON	3rd	×	ON	3rd	OFF	×	O/D	O/D
L	ON	OFF	1st	×	OFF	1st	ON	×	1st	1st
	ON	ON	2nd	×	ON	2nd	ON	×	1st	1st

x: Malfunctions

95I19537

Courtesy of Toyota Motor Sales, U.S.A., Inc.

Fig. 2: Checking No. 1 & No. 2 Solenoid Operation

ECT ECU OUTPUT DEVICES

No. 1 & No. 2 Solenoids – ECT ECU controls transaxle shifting by delivering an output signal to operate proper solenoid. Solenoids are located on transaxle valve body. See Fig. 1. Solenoids are operated in accordance with shift lever position. If a solenoid malfunctions, fail-safe gear may be selected. See Fig. 2.

NOTE: In some gears, ECT ECU provides a fail-safe system which will place transaxle in designated gear depending on solenoid failure.

Lock-Up Solenoid – ECT ECU controls torque converter lock-up by delivering an output signal to lock-up solenoid. Lock-up solenoid (also called SL solenoid) is activated when shift lever is in "D" position and vehicle is at specified speed. Lock-up solenoid is located on transaxle valve body. See Fig. 1.

SELF-DIAGNOSTIC SYSTEM

SYSTEM DIAGNOSIS

NOTE: Before testing transaxle, ensure fluid level is correct and throttle and shift cables are properly adjusted. Ensure engine starts with shift lever in "P" (Park) and "N" (Neutral) to ensure proper adjustment of park/neutral position switch. Transaxle must first be tested by checking for stored trouble codes. See RETRIEVING TROUBLE CODES.

ECT ECU monitors engine and transaxle operation and contains a self-diagnostic system which stores diagnostic trouble code(s). A Malfunction Indicator Light (MIL), located on instrument panel, will illuminate if a system or component fails and sets a DTC.

MIL illuminates with ignition switch in ON position, engine off (KOEO). Once engine is started, MIL should go out. If MIL remains illuminated, ECT ECU has detected a malfunction or abnormality in system. If MIL does not illuminate, inspect circuit and light. See appropriate wiring diagram in WIRING DIAGRAMS.

If malfunction does not reoccur in 3 trips, MIL goes off, but Diagnostic Trouble Code (DTC) remains recorded in ECT ECU memory. Trouble codes may only be retrieved using an appropriate scan tool or Toyota/Lexus scan tool connected to 16-pin Data Link Connector (DLC3), located in fuse box. See Figs. 3 and 4. Scan tool also provides freeze-frame data and can be used to clear trouble codes.

ECT ECU records engine operating condition (fuel system, calculated load, coolant temperature, fuel trim (mixture), engine speed, vehicle speed, etc.) with 1st malfunction ONLY. Information is ONLY for 1st recorded failure, even if more than one code has been recorded. Freeze-frame data is only updated when all trouble codes have been cleared, or a misfire or fuel-trim malfunction has occurred.

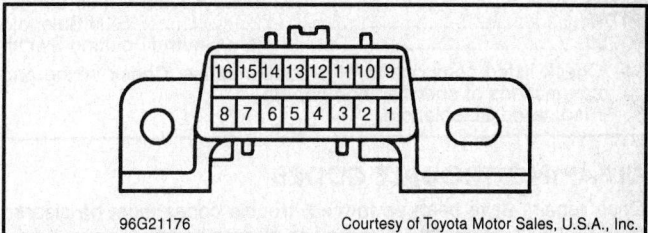

96G21176   Courtesy of Toyota Motor Sales, U.S.A., Inc.

Fig. 3: Identifying Data Link Connector (DLC3) Terminals

RETRIEVING TROUBLE CODES

NOTE: Before retrieving trouble codes, ensure sufficient battery voltage exists for proper self-diagnosis system operation. Ensure proper operation of MIL light.

NOTE: MIL will illuminate and OD OFF indicator will flash for all trouble codes except DTC P1765 (SLN solenoid).

NOTE: For additional engine performance or other system related trouble codes present that are not listed in DIAGNOSTIC TROUBLE CODE (DTC) IDENTIFICATION table, see appropriate MITCHELL® ENGINE PERFORMANCE publication for IMPORTED CARS, LIGHT TRUCKS & VANS.

ECT ECU Codes – 1) Connect scan tool to Data Link Connector (DLC3). DLC3 is located in fuse box at lower left of instrument panel. See Fig. 4.
2) Turn ignition on. Turn on scan tool. Retrieve any trouble codes stored in memory following scan tool instructions. See DIAGNOSTIC TROUBLE CODE (DTC) IDENTIFICATION table.

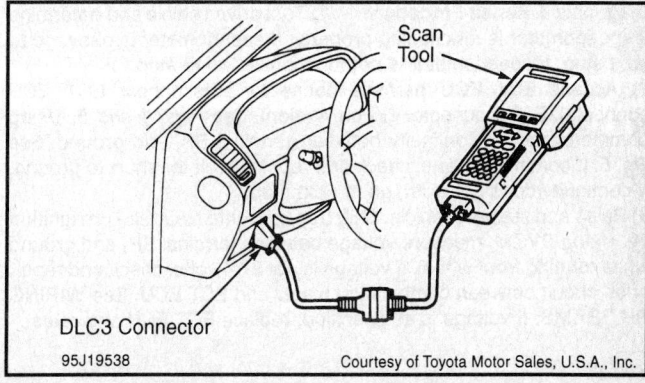

95J19538   Courtesy of Toyota Motor Sales, U.S.A., Inc.

Fig. 4: Connecting Scan Tool To Data Link Connector (DLC3)

3) Trouble codes recorded may not have illuminated MIL. When certain malfunctions or trouble codes initially occur, they will be temporarily stored in ECT ECU memory, but MIL will not illuminate.
4) Second time malfunction or trouble code is detected, MIL will illuminate, provided ignition is turned off and then back on after malfunction or trouble code was first detected. This process is referred to as 2 trip detection logic and only applies to specific trouble codes.
5) Record freeze-frame data. If using Toyota/Lexus scan tool, ensure tool is in NORMAL mode. CHECK MODE will erase all codes.

DIAGNOSTIC TROUBLE CODE (DTC) IDENTIFICATION

DTC	[1] Probable Cause
P0500 (1996)	No. 1 Speed Sensor
P0720 (1995)	Output Speed Sensor Circuit
P0750	No. 1 Solenoid
P0753	No. 1 Solenoid Circuit
P0755	No. 2 Solenoid
P0758	No. 2 Solenoid Circuit
P0770	[2] Lock-Up Solenoid
P0773	Lock-Up Solenoid Circuit
P1705	Direct Clutch Speed Sensor
P1765	SLN Solenoid
P1780	Park/Neutral Position Switch

[1] – Check listed component for probable cause. Check wiring and connections of specified component.
[2] – Also called SL solenoid.

CLEARING TROUBLE CODES

Once repairs have been performed, trouble codes must be cleared from ECT ECU memory. DTCs may be cleared by following methods:
- Scan tool (follow manufacturers instructions).
- Remove EFI fuse (15-amp) from engine compartment fuse box, near battery, for 10 seconds or more to clear memory in ECT ECU.
- Disconnect negative battery cable (memory for electronic components will be also be canceled).

DIAGNOSTIC TESTS

When trouble shooting transaxle, first check for stored trouble codes and repair as necessary. If no trouble codes exist, perform manual shift test to determine if problem area is in electrical circuits or a mechanical transaxle problem. See MANUAL SHIFT TEST.

DTC P0500:
NO. 1 VEHICLE SPEED SENSOR FAULT (1996)

Circuit Description – No. 1 Vehicle Speed Sensor (VSS), driven by transaxle output shaft, outputs a pulse signal to combination meter. Combination meter converts signal to a more precise waveform for ECT ECU. DTC is set when ECT ECU does not detect any signal while vehicle is in motion. Possible causes are:
- Open or short in vehicle speed sensor circuit.
- No. 1 VSS failure.
- Combination meter malfunction.
- ECT ECU malfunction.

Diagnosis & Repair Procedure – **1)** Test drive vehicle and determine if speedometer is functioning properly. If speedometer is okay, go to next step. If speedometer is not functioning, go to step **3)**.
2) Access ECT ECU harness connector. Disconnect ECT ECU connector E10 (connector E5 on Avalon). *See Figs. 1 and 5.* Using ohmmeter, check continuity between terminal SP_1 and ground. *See Fig. 5.* If continuity exists, check and repair circuit for short to ground. If continuity does not exist, go to next step.
3) Raise and support vehicle. Shift transaxle into Neutral. Turn ignition on. Using DVOM, measure voltage between terminal SP_1 and ground while rotating front wheel. If voltage is not 9-14 volts, check and repair open circuit between combination meter and ECT ECU. See WIRING DIAGRAMS. If voltage is as specified, replace ECT ECU and retest.

DTC P0720:
OUTPUT SPEED SENSOR CIRCUIT FAULT (1995)

NOTE: DTC P0720 is output when DTC P0500 (No. 1 Vehicle Speed Sensor) is detected.

Circuit Description – Vehicle Speed Sensor (VSS), driven by the differential, outputs a pulse signal to combination meter. Combination meter converts signal to a more precise waveform for ECT ECU. DTC is set when DTC P0500 (No. 1 Vehicle Speed Sensor) is detected. Possible causes are:
- Open or short in vehicle speed sensor circuit.
- No. 1 VSS failure.
- Combination meter malfunction.
- ECT ECU malfunction.

Diagnosis & Repair Procedure – **1)** Test drive vehicle and determine is speedometer is functioning properly. If speedometer is okay, go to next step. If speedometer is not functioning, go to step **5)**.
2) Access ECT ECU harness connector. Disconnect ECT ECU connector E10 (connector E5 on Avalon). *See Figs. 1 and 5.* Using ohmmeter, check continuity between terminal SP_1 and ground. *See Fig. 5.*
3) If continuity exists, inspect and repair circuit for short to ground. If continuity does not exist, turn ignition on. Measure voltage between terminals SP_1 and E_1 at ECT ECU harness connector.
4) If 4-6 volts is not present, inspect and repair open circuit between combination meter and ECT ECU. See appropriate wiring diagram in WIRING DIAGRAMS. If 4-6 volts is present, replace ECT ECU and retest.
5) Raise and support vehicle. Disconnect cruise control ECU. *See Fig. 1.* Remove combination meter. Turn ignition on. Using DVOM, measure voltage between SP_1 terminal of combination meter connector and ground. *See Figs. 6-8.* Rotate front wheel.
6) If voltage pulses 0-5 volts, check continuity between ECT ECU harness connector E_1 terminal and ground. If continuity does not exist, inspect and repair circuit as needed. If continuity does exist, replace ECT ECU and retest. If no voltage is present, go to next step. If voltage is 4-6 volts and remains unchanged, go to step **8)**.
7) Turn ignition off. Disconnect ECT ECU harness connector. *See Fig. 1.* Using ohmmeter, check continuity between combination meter harness connector terminal SP_1 and ECT ECU terminal SP_1. *See Fig. 5.* If continuity exists, go to next step. If continuity does not exist, inspect and repair circuit as needed.
8) Check continuity of 2 circuits between combination meter and VSS. See appropriate wiring diagram in WIRING DIAGRAMS. If continuity does not exist, inspect and repair circuit(s) as needed. If continuity exists, inspect VSS. See NO.1 VEHICLE SPEED SENSOR under COMPONENT TESTS. Replace as needed.
9) Disconnect VSS harness connector. Turn ignition on. Measure voltage between VSS harness connector terminal No. 1 and ground. If battery voltage is not present, inspect and repair circuit as needed. If battery voltage is present, replace combination meter and retest.
10) Turn ignition off. Disconnect ECT ECU harness connector. *See Fig. 1.* Using ohmmeter, check continuity between combination meter harness connector SP_1 terminal and ECT ECU SP_1 terminal. *See Figs. 5-8.* If continuity exists, replace combination meter and retest. If continuity does not exist, inspect and repair circuit as needed.

NOTE: Avalon ECT ECU harness connectors have different connector identification code. Circuit Identification and terminal numbers are the same as Camry and ES300. For ECT ECU connector identification code cross reference, see ECT ECU HARNESS CONNECTOR REFERENCE table.

ECT ECU HARNESS CONNECTOR REFERENCE

Connector No. (Avalon)	Connector No. (Camry & ES300)
E8	E7
E7	E8
E6	E9
E5	E10

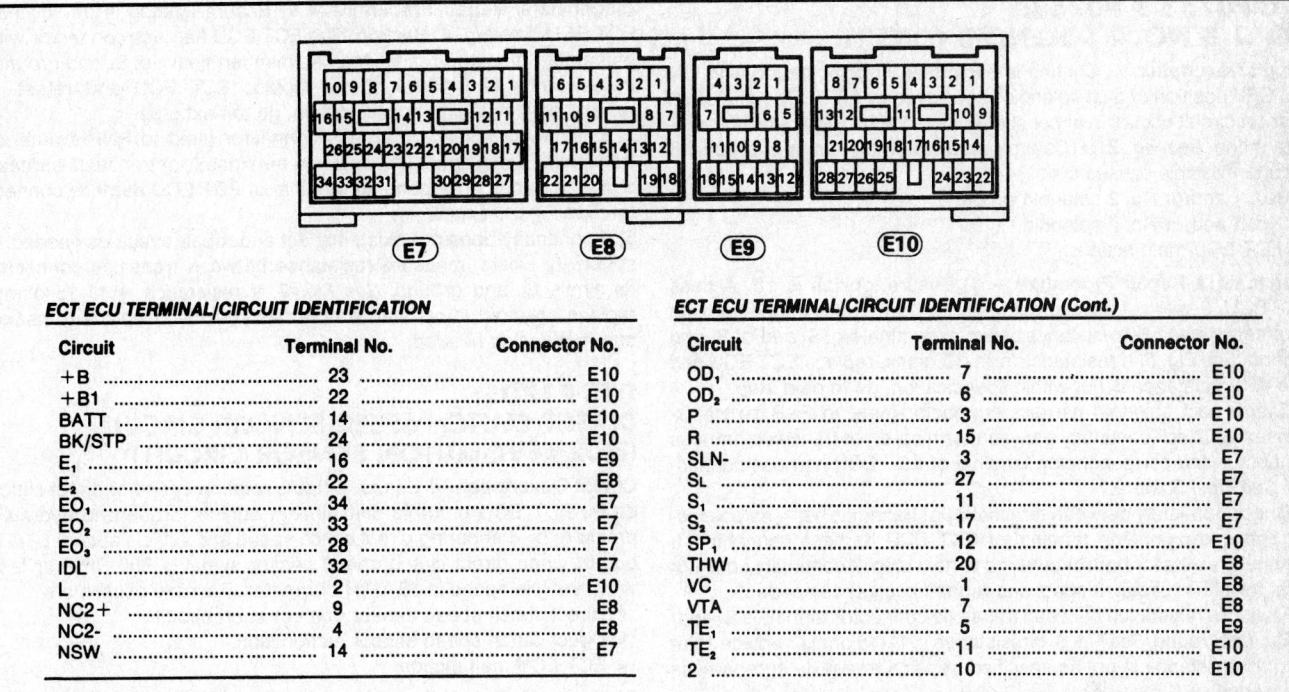

ECT ECU TERMINAL/CIRCUIT IDENTIFICATION

Circuit	Terminal No.	Connector No.
+B	23	E10
+B1	22	E10
BATT	14	E10
BK/STP	24	E10
E_1	16	E9
E_2	22	E8
EO_1	34	E7
EO_2	33	E7
EO_3	28	E7
IDL	32	E7
L	2	E10
NC2+	9	E8
NC2-	4	E8
NSW	14	E7

ECT ECU TERMINAL/CIRCUIT IDENTIFICATION (Cont.)

Circuit	Terminal No.	Connector No.
OD_1	7	E10
OD_2	6	E10
P	3	E10
R	15	E10
SLN-	3	E7
S_L	27	E7
S_1	11	E7
S_2	17	E7
SP_1	12	E10
THW	20	E8
VC	1	E8
VTA	7	E8
TE_1	5	E9
TE_2	11	E10
2	10	E10

95A19539

Courtesy of Toyota Motor Sales, U.S.A., Inc.

Fig. 5: Identifying ECT ECU Harness Connectors (Component Connector View)

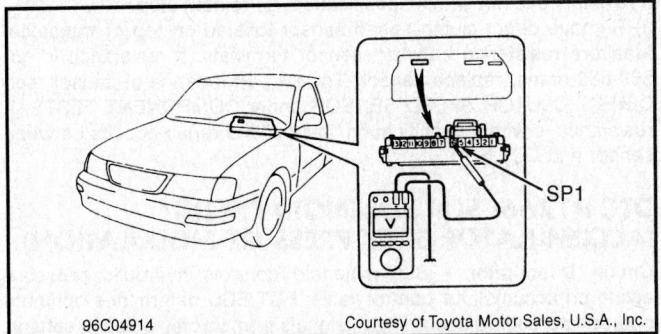

96C04914 Courtesy of Toyota Motor Sales, U.S.A., Inc.

Fig. 6: Identifying Combination Meter Harness Connector (Avalon)

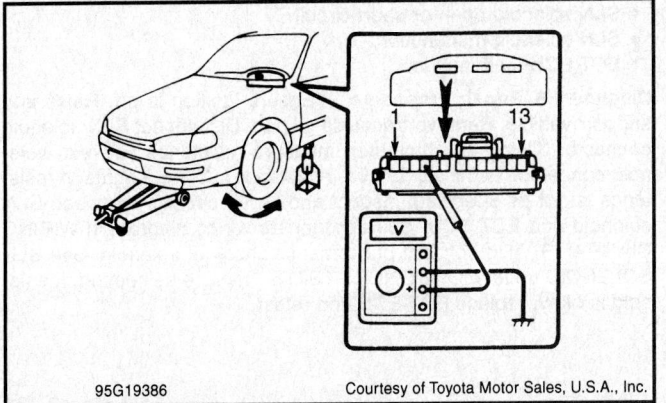

95G19386 Courtesy of Toyota Motor Sales, U.S.A., Inc.

Fig. 7: Identifying Combination Meter Harness Connector (Camry)

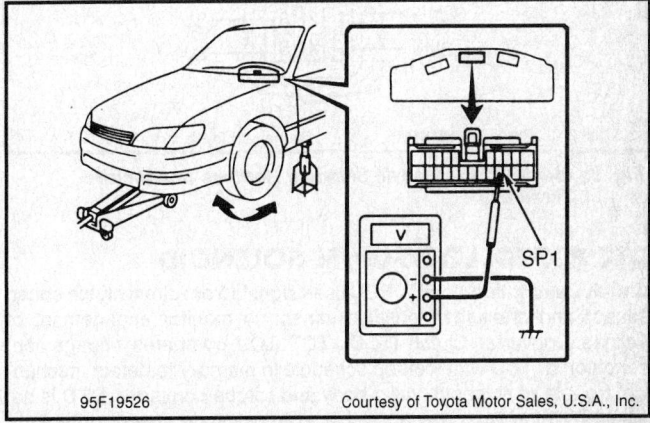

95F19526 Courtesy of Toyota Motor Sales, U.S.A., Inc.

Fig. 8: Identifying Combination Meter Harness Connector (ES300)

DTC P0750 & P0755: NO.1 & NO. 2 SOLENOID FAULT

Circuit Description – ECT ECU uses signal from direct clutch speed sensor and vehicle speed sensor to determine actual gear position. ECT ECU compares actual gear with shift schedule in memory to detect mechanical trouble of solenoids and/or valve body. DTC is set if during normal driving gear required by ECT ECU does not match actual gear after 2 trips have been completed. Possible causes are:

- No. 1 and/or No. 2 solenoid is stuck open or closed.
- Valve body is clogged or valve(s) is stuck.

Diagnosis & Repair Procedure – Remove and inspect operation of solenoids. See SOLENOIDS under COMPONENT TESTS. If solenoids are okay, inspect valve body. See TOYOTA A-540H & A-541E overhaul article.

DTC P0753 & P0758:
NO. 1 & NO. 2 SOLENOID CIRCUIT

Circuit Description – Shifting is performed in combination with ON and OFF position of shift solenoids controlled by ECT ECU. If an open or short circuit occurs in either shift solenoid, ECT ECU reverts to fail-safe mode. *See Fig. 2*. DTCs are output when a open or short circuit occurs. Possible causes are:
- No. 1 and/or No. 2 solenoid circuit.
- No. 1 and/or No. 2 solenoid.
- ECT ECU malfunction.

Diagnosis & Repair Procedure – 1) Ensure ignition is off. Access ECT ECU. *See Fig. 1*. Backprobing ECT ECU harness connector with ohmmeter, measure resistance between terminal No. S_1 and/or S_2 and ground. *See Fig. 5*. If resistance is 11-15 ohms, replace ECT ECU and retest. If resistance is not within specification, go to next step.
2) Disconnect solenoid harness connector (next to PNP switch) at transaxle. Check continuity between terminal S_1 of transaxle harness connector and corresponding terminal of ECT ECU harness connector. *See Figs. 5 and 9*.
3) Check continuity between terminal S_2 of transaxle harness connector and corresponding terminal of ECT ECU harness connector. If continuity exists for both circuits, go to next step. If continuity does not exist for either circuit, inspect and repair circuit(s) as needed.
4) Measure resistance between transaxle connector terminals S_1 and/or S_2, and ground. *See Fig. 9*. If resistance is 11-15 ohms, replace solenoid. If resistance is not as specified, replace transaxle sub-harness as needed.

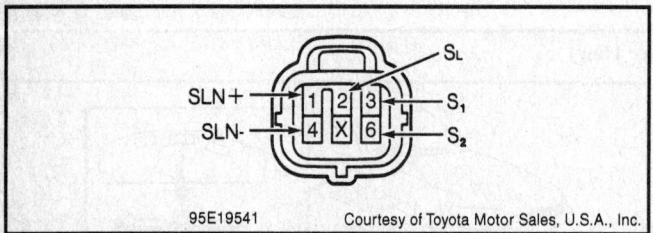

95E19541   Courtesy of Toyota Motor Sales, U.S.A., Inc.

Fig. 9: Identifying Transaxle Solenoid Harness Connector Terminals

DTC P0770: LOCK-UP/SL SOLENOID

Circuit Description – ECT ECU uses signals from direct clutch speed sensor and crankshaft position sensor to monitor engagement of Torque Converter Clutch (TCC). ECT ECU compares engagement condition of TCC with lock-up schedule in memory to detect mechanical trouble of solenoid, valve body and torque converter. DTC is set when TCC lock-up does not occur at appropriate speed, or lock-up does not release at appropriate speed. Possible causes are:
- Lock-up solenoid is stuck open or closed.
- Valve body clogged or valve stuck.
- TCC malfunction.

Diagnosis & Repair Procedure – Remove and inspect operation of solenoid. See SOLENOIDS under COMPONENT TESTS. If solenoid is okay, inspect valve body. See TOYOTA A-540H & A-541E overhaul article.

DTC P0773: LOCK-UP/SL SOLENOID CIRCUIT

Circuit Description – Lock-up solenoid is turned on and off by signals from ECT ECU to control hydraulic pressure affecting lock-up relay valve. Lock-up relay valve controls operation of Torque Converter Clutch (TCC). If ECT ECU detects a malfunction, fail-safe function is enabled. DTC is output when a open or short circuit occurs. Possible causes are:
- Lock-up solenoid open or short circuit.
- Lock-up solenoid malfunction.
- ECT ECU malfunction.

Diagnosis & Repair Procedure – 1) Ensure ignition is off. Access ECT ECU. *See Fig. 1*. Backprobing ECT ECU harness connector with ohmmeter, measure resistance between terminal No. S_L and ground. If resistance is 8-100 k/ohms, replace ECT ECU and retest. If resistance is not within specification, go to next step.
2) Disconnect solenoid harness connector (next to PNP switch) at transaxle. Check continuity between terminal S_L of transaxle harness connector and corresponding terminal of ECT ECU harness connector. *See Figs. 5 and 9*.
3) If continuity does not exist, inspect and repair circuit as needed. If continuity exists, measure resistance between transaxle connector terminals S_L and ground. *See Fig. 9*. If resistance is 11-15 ohms, replace solenoid. If resistance is not as specified, replace transaxle sub-harness as needed.

DTC P1705:
DIRECT CLUTCH SPEED SENSOR CIRCUIT
(NC2 REVOLUTION SENSOR CIRCUIT)

Circuit Description – Sensor detects rotation speed of direct clutch drum. ECT ECU controls shift timing, engine torque and hydraulic pressure by comparing direct clutch speed and vehicle speed. DTC is output when direct clutch speed sensor signal is 300 RPM or less when vehicle speed is 20 MPH or greater. Possible causes are:
- Direct clutch speed sensor open or short circuit.
- Direct clutch speed sensor malfunction.
- ECT ECU malfunction.

Diagnosis & Repair Procedure – 1) Ensure ignition is off. Access ECT ECU. *See Fig. 1*. Backprobing ECT ECU harness connector with ohmmeter, measure resistance between terminal NC2+ and NC2-. *See Fig. 5*. If resistance is 560-680 ohms, replace ECT ECU and retest. If resistance is not within specification, go to next step.
2) Remove direct clutch speed sensor located on top of transaxle. Measure resistance between sensor terminals. If resistance is not 560-680 ohms, replace sensor. To test performance of sensor, see DIRECT CLUTCH SPEED SENSOR under COMPONENT TESTS. If resistance is within specification, inspect and repair circuits between sensor and ECT ECU.

DTC P1765: SLN SOLENOID CIRCUIT
(ACCUMULATOR BACK PRESSURE MODULATION)

Circuit Description – SLN solenoid controls hydraulic pressure acting on accumulator control valve. ECT ECU determines optimum operating pressure according to signals from throttle position sensor, vehicle speed sensor and direct clutch speed sensor. DTC is output when current flow is .2 amps or less. Possible causes are:
- SLN solenoid open or short circuit.
- SLN solenoid malfunction.
- ECT ECU malfunction.

Diagnosis & Repair Procedure – Ensure ignition is off. Raise and support vehicle. Remove transaxle oil pan. Disconnect SLN solenoid connector. Using an ohmmeter, measure resistance between solenoid connector terminals. Ensure resistance is 5.1-5.5 ohms. If resistance is not as specified, inspect and repair circuit(s) between SLN solenoid and ECT ECU. See appropriate wiring diagram in WIRING DIAGRAMS. Also conduct performance check of solenoid. See SLN SOLENOID under COMPONENT TESTS. Replace as needed. If solenoid is okay, replace ECT ECU and retest.

DTC P1780: PARK/NEUTRAL POSITION (PNP) SWITCH

Circuit Description – PNP switch verifies shift lever position and sends signals to ECT ECU. If no signal is received from PNP switch, ECT ECU defaults to drive ("D") position. DTC is output when ECT ECU detects 2 or more circuits are on. Vehicle speed has to be above 44 MPH for more than 30 seconds with engine RPM at 1500-2500. Possible causes are:

- Short in PNP switch circuit.
- PNP switch malfunction.
- ECT ECU malfunction.

Diagnosis & Repair Procedure – **1)** Turn ignition on. Access ECT ECU. Using DVOM, measure voltage at terminals NSW, R, 2 and L of ECT ECU harness connector between terminal and body ground with gear selector in each shift position. *See Fig. 5.*

2) Ensure 10-14 volts is present at NSW terminal at ECT ECU harness connector in all shift positions. Ensure 10-14 volts is present at R, 2 and L terminals at ECT ECU harness connector with gear selector in R, 2 and L position. If voltage is not as specified, check park/neutral position switch. See PARK/NEUTRAL POSITION (PNP) SWITCH under COMPONENT TESTS. If switch is okay, check and repair circuit(s) between PNP switch and ECT ECU. See WIRING DIAGRAMS.

MANUAL SHIFT TEST

NOTE: Perform manual shift test if no trouble codes exist. Manual shift test determines if problem area is in electrical circuits or a mechanical transaxle problem.

1) With ignition off, disconnect electrical connector for solenoids from rear of transaxle. Road test vehicle and ensure transaxle gear changes correspond with shift lever position. See GEAR APPLICATION table.

2) If abnormality exists, a mechanical transaxle problem exists. Turn ignition off. Reconnect electrical connector. Clear trouble codes from ECT ECU memory, as disconnecting electrical connector may set a trouble code. See CLEARING TROUBLE CODES under SELF-DIAGNOSTIC SYSTEM.

GEAR APPLICATION

Shift Lever Position	Gear
"D"	Overdrive
"2"	3rd
"L"	1st
"R"	Reverse
"P"	Park

CIRCUIT TESTS

BRAKELIGHT SIGNAL

1) Inspect operation of brakelights. Repair as needed. If switch is suspect, see BRAKELIGHT SWITCH under COMPONENT TESTS. If circuit is suspect, diagnose and repair as necessary. See WIRING DIAGRAMS.

2) Connect scan tool to DLC3. *See Fig. 4.* Turn ignition on. Read STP signal while depressing and releasing brake pedal. Ensure signal cycles when pressing brake pedal. If signal cycles, replace ECT ECU. If signal does not cycle, inspect and repair circuit between brakelight switch and ECT ECU. If circuit is okay, replace ECT ECU.

OVERDRIVE CANCEL SIGNAL

1) Access ECT ECU. *See Fig. 1.* Turn ignition on. Backprobe ECT ECU harness connector with DVOM. Measure voltage between terminal OD_1 of ECT ECU harness connector and ground. *See Fig. 5.* If voltage is 4-6 volts, substitute known good ECU and retest. If voltage is not 4-6 volts, go to next step.

2) Turn ignition off. Disconnect cruise control ECU harness connector. *See Fig. 1.* Turn ignition on. Measure voltage between terminal OD and ground. *See Fig. 10.* If 4-6 volts is present, replace cruise control ECU and retest. If 4-6 volts is not present, inspect and repair circuit between cruise control ECU and ECT ECU.

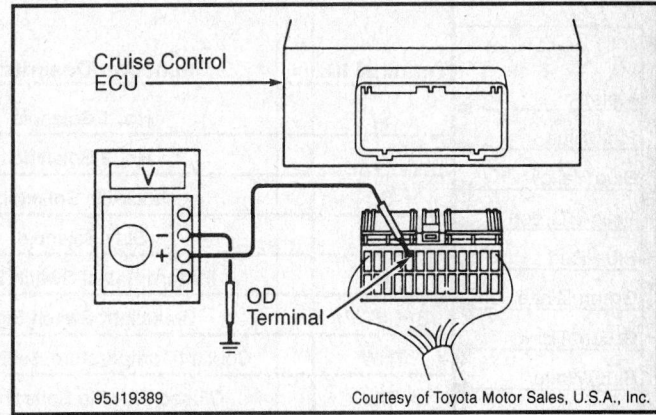

95J19389   Courtesy of Toyota Motor Sales, U.S.A., Inc.

Fig. 10: Identifying Cruise Control ECU Terminals

ECT ECU VOLTAGES

Access ECT ECU. *See Fig. 1.* Turn ignition on. Using voltmeter, backprobe ECT ECU harness connector. Check voltage between selected terminal and E_1 terminal. Voltage should be as specified. *See Fig. 11.*

COMPONENT TESTS

NO. 1 VEHICLE SPEED SENSOR (VSS)

1) Disconnect electrical connector from No. 1 VSS, located on top of transaxle. *See Fig. 1.* Connect positive battery lead to terminal No. 1 and negative lead to terminal No. 2. Connect positive lead of voltmeter to terminal No. 3 and negative lead to terminal No. 2. *See Fig. 12.*

2) Raise and support one vehicle front wheel. Rotate wheel and monitor voltmeter. Ensure voltage changes from zero to 11 volts. Voltage should change 4 times per each revolution of speedometer cable shaft. Replace speed sensor if voltage does not change as specified.

SLN SOLENOID

Raise and support vehicle. Remove transaxle oil pan. Remove SLN solenoid. To check solenoid operation, connect positive battery voltage to solenoid terminal No. 1. Ensure a 8-10 watt bulb is placed in-line of positive lead. *See Fig. 15.* Connect negative lead to terminal No. 2 and monitor valve's movement. Replace as needed.

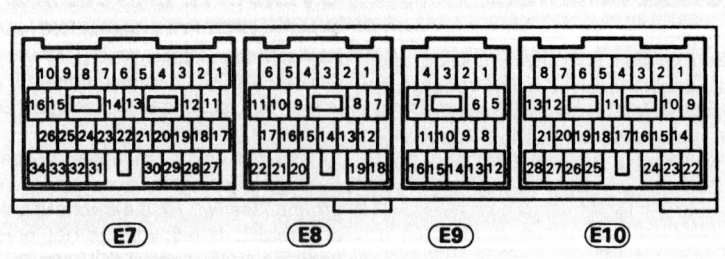

Wire Color	Terminal ID.	Function/Description	Voltage Value (DC Volts Unless Otherwise Specified)
Violet	S₁	No. 1 Solenoid	10-14 Volts With KOEO ¹
Pink/Blue	S₂	No. 2 Solenoid	1 Volt Or Less With KOEO ¹
Blue/Yellow	Sʟ	Lock-Up Solenoid	1 Volt Or Less With KOEO ¹
Yellow/Green	SLN-	SLN Solenoid	10-14 Volts With KOEO ¹
Blue/Red	P	Pattern Select Switch Signal	10-14 Volts In PWR Position
Green/White	B/K (STP)	Brakelight Switch Signal	10-14 Volts With Pedal Depressed
Green/Black	THW	Coolant Temperature Sensor Signal	.2-1.0 Volts @ 176°F (80°C)
Blue/White	IDL	Closed Throttle Sensor Signal	0-3 Volts With Throttle Closed, KOEO ¹
Black/Yellow	VTA	Throttle Position Sensor Output Signal	3.2-4.9 Volts With Throttle Fully Open
Yellow/Black	OD₁	OD Output To Cruise Control ECU	10-14 Volts With KOEO ¹
Green/Orange	OD₂	Overdrive Switch Signal	10-14 Volts With Switch On
Violet/Yellow	SP₁	Vehicle Speed Sensor Signal	1 Volt Or Less With ECU Unplugged ² (Car Parked)
³ Black/White	NC2+, NC2-	Direct Clutch Speed Sensor Signal	1-5 Volts (Pulse Signal) With Engine Running
Orange	NSW	Ignition Switch Signal	10-14 Volts In "P" Or "N", KOEO ¹
Yellow/Blue	2	Park/Neutral Position Switch "2" Signal	10-14 Volts In "2", KOEO ¹
Red/Black	L	Park/Neutral Position Switch "L" Signal	10-14 Volts In "L", KOEO ¹
Black/Orange	R	Park/Neutral Position Switch "R" Signal	10-14 Volts With KOEO ¹
White/Blue ⁴	+B	EFI Main Relay Power Supply	10-14 Volts With KOEO ¹
Brown	BATT	Power Supply Voltage	10-14 Volts (Constant)
Brown	E₁	Ground	Not Applicable
	E₂	Ground	Not Applicable

¹ – Key On, Engine Off.
² – Disconnect cruise control ECU. *See Fig. 1.*
³ – Wire color for NC2- is White/Blue. Wire color for NC2+ is Yellow/Blue.
⁴ – Wire color is Black/Yellow for Avalon.

96F30481

Courtesy of Toyota Motor Sales, U.S.A., Inc.

Fig. 11: ECT ECU Pin Voltage Table

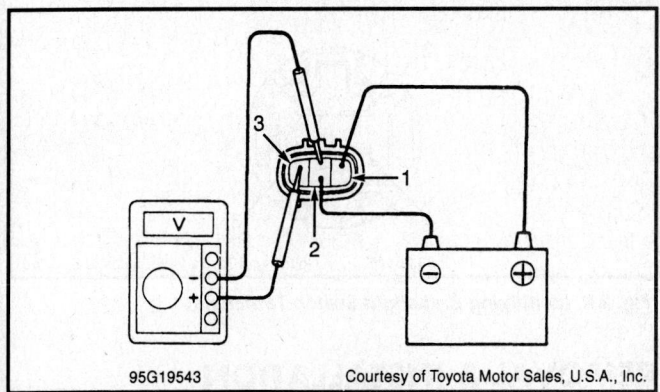

Fig. 12: Checking No. 1 Vehicle Speed Sensor

DIRECT CLUTCH SPEED SENSOR

Connect voltmeter between sensor terminals. Ensure voltage is generated intermittently when a magnet is brought close to sensor and then moved away. *See Fig. 13.* Voltage generated is very low.

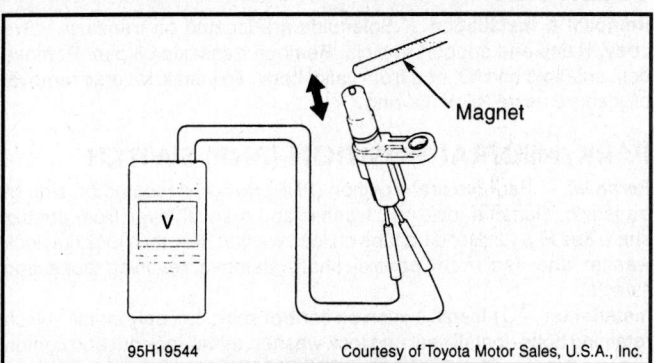

Fig. 13: Testing Direct Clutch Speed Sensor

SOLENOIDS

1) To check solenoid seals, remove suspect solenoid. Connect battery voltage to solenoid. Apply 71 psi (5 kg/cm²) to solenoid with battery voltage connected. *See Fig. 14.*

2) With battery voltage applied, air should pass through solenoid. Disconnect voltage to solenoid. Ensure air does not pass through solenoid. Replace solenoid if defective.

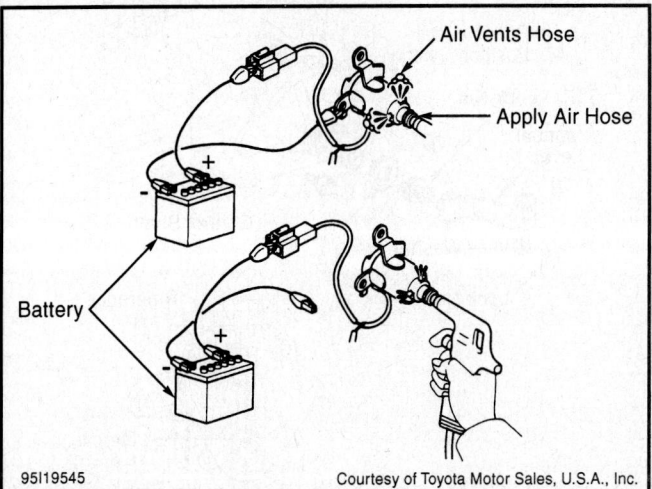

Fig. 14: Checking Solenoids

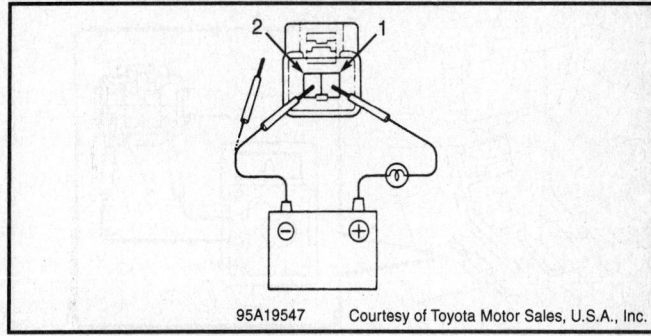

Fig. 15: Testing SLN Solenoid

PARK/NEUTRAL POSITION (PNP) SWITCH

Disconnect harness connector at park/neutral position switch. Switch is located on side of transaxle. Using ohmmeter, check for continuity between specified terminals in accordance with shift lever position. *See Fig. 16.* Replace PNP switch if defective.

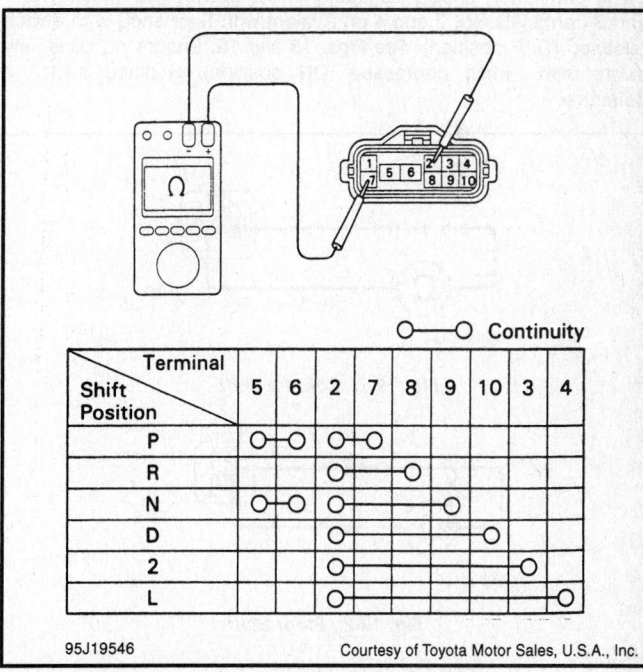

○——○ Continuity

Terminal Shift Position	5	6	2	7	8	9	10	3	4
P	○—○		○—○						
R			○			○			
N	○—○		○				○		
D			○					○	
2			○						○
L			○						○

Fig. 16: Testing Park/Neutral Position (PNP) Switch

PATTERN SELECT SWITCH

Disconnect electrical connector from pattern select switch. *See Figs. 17 and 18.* Using ohmmeter, ensure continuity exists between terminals No. 3 and 6 (terminals No. 12 and 13 on Avalon) with switch in PWR position. No continuity should exist in NORM position. Replace switch as necessary.

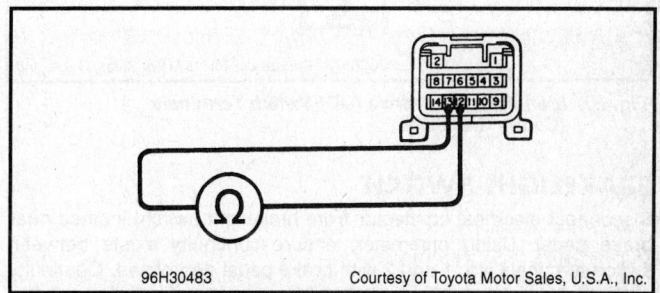

Fig. 17: Identifying Pattern Select Switch Terminals (Avalon)

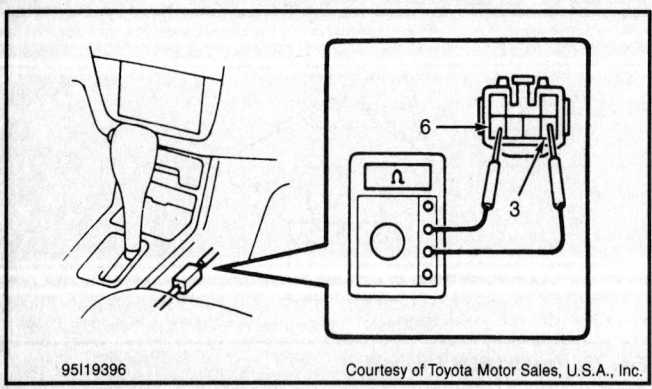

95I19396   Courtesy of Toyota Motor Sales, U.S.A., Inc.

Fig. 18: Identifying Pattern Select Switch Terminals (Camry & ES300)

OVERDRIVE (OD) SWITCH

Disconnect electrical connector from OD switch, located on shift lever. Using ohmmeter, ensure continuity exists between terminals No. 1 and 3 (terminals No. 2 and 4 on Avalon with floor shift) with switch released (OFF position). See Figs. 18 and 19. Ensure no continuity exists with switch depressed (ON position). Replace switch if defective.

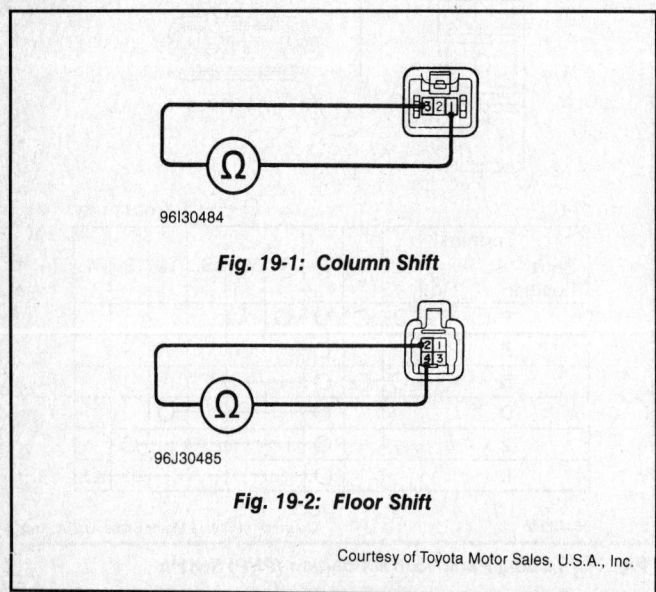

96I30484

Fig. 19-1: Column Shift

96J30485

Fig. 19-2: Floor Shift

Courtesy of Toyota Motor Sales, U.S.A., Inc.

Fig. 19: Identifying Overdrive (OD) Switch Terminals (Avalon)

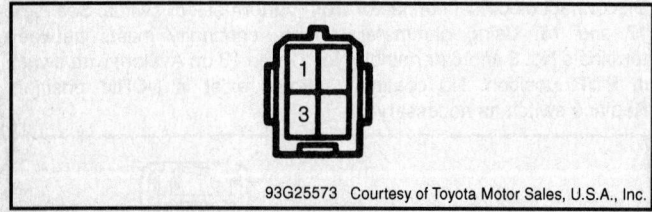

93G25573   Courtesy of Toyota Motor Sales, U.S.A., Inc.

Fig. 20: Identifying Overdrive (OD) Switch Terminals (Camry & ES300)

BRAKELIGHT SWITCH

Disconnect electrical connector from brakelight switch, located near brake pedal. Using ohmmeter, ensure continuity exists between switch terminals No. 1 and 2 with brake pedal depressed. Continuity should exist between terminals No. 3 and 4 with pedal released. See Fig. 21.

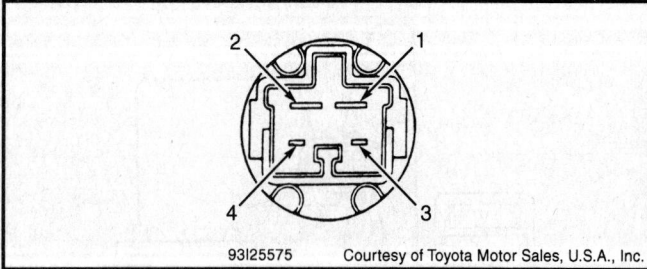

93I25575   Courtesy of Toyota Motor Sales, U.S.A., Inc.

Fig. 21: Identifying Brakelight Switch Terminals

REMOVAL & INSTALLATION

BRAKELIGHT SWITCH

Removal & Installation – Disconnect electrical connector. Remove lock nut, and unscrew brakelight switch. To install, screw brakelight switch inward until brakelight plunger contacts brake pedal.

SOLENOIDS

Removal & Installation – Solenoids are located on transaxle valve body. Raise and support vehicle. Remove transaxle oil pan. Remove bolt, solenoid and "O" ring from valve body. To install, reverse removal procedure using NEW "O" ring.

PARK/NEUTRAL POSITION (PNP) SWITCH

Removal – Park/Neutral Position (PNP) switch is located on side of transaxle. Remove lock nut, washer and manual lever from control shaft. See Fig. 22. Bend up tabs on lock washer. Remove lock nut, lock washer and seal from control shaft. Remove retaining bolts and switch.

Installation – 1) Install switch on control shaft. Loosely install switch retaining bolts. Install seal and lock washer. Install lock nut and tighten to specification. See TORQUE SPECIFICATIONS. Bend tabs on lock washer over against lock nut.

2) Ensure parking brake is applied. Temporarily install manual lever on control shaft. Place shift lever in Neutral. Remove manual lever. Rotate park/neutral position switch and align reference mark on PNP switch with groove. See Fig. 22.

3) Hold PNP switch in this position. Tighten retaining bolts to specification. To install remaining components, reverse removal procedure.

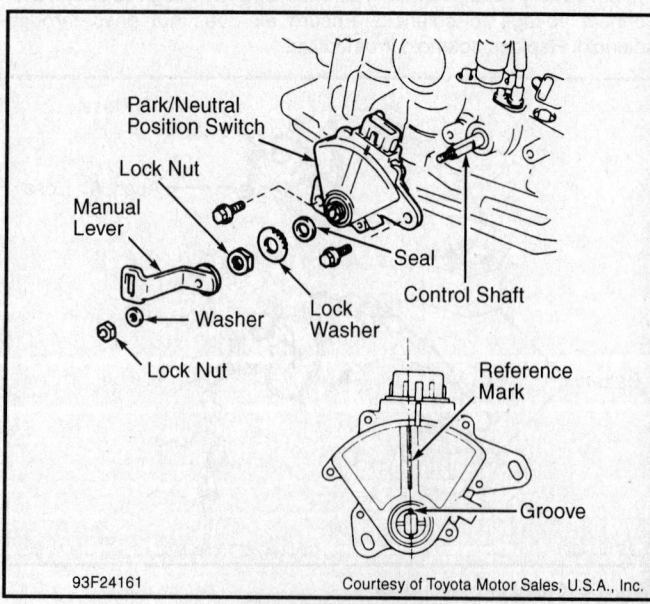

93F24161   Courtesy of Toyota Motor Sales, U.S.A., Inc.

Fig. 22: Removing & Installing PNP Switch

OVERDRIVE (OD) SWITCH

Overdrive (OD) switch is mounted on shift lever. *See Fig. 1.* Replacement information not available from manufacturer.

ENGINE COOLANT TEMPERATURE SENSOR

Removal & Installation – Drain cooling system. Disconnect engine coolant temperature sensor connector. *See Figs. 23 and 24.* Remove coolant temperature sensor. To install, reverse removal procedure. Refill cooling system and check for leaks.

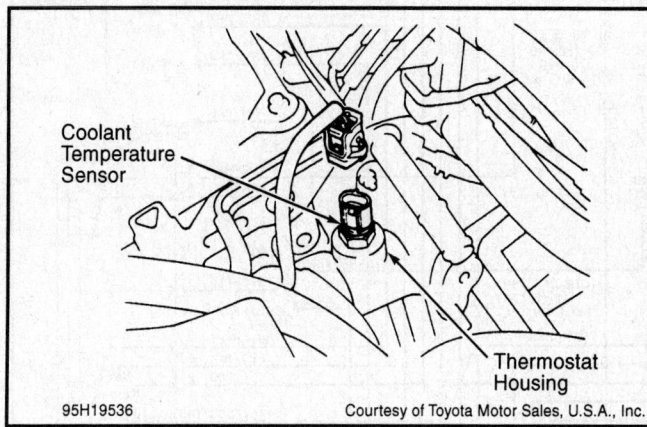

Fig. 23: Identifying ECT Sensor Location (Avalon & ES300)

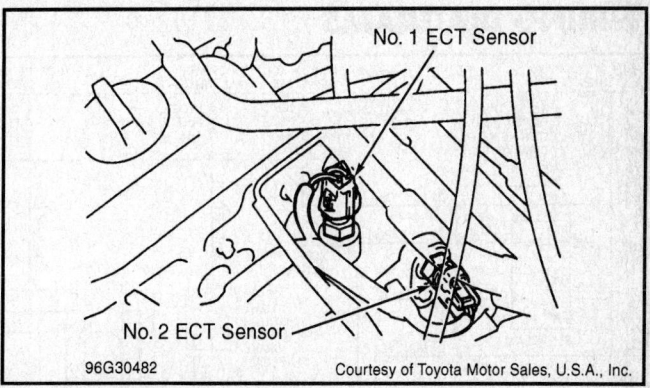

Fig. 24: Identifying ECT Sensor Location (Camry)

TORQUE SPECIFICATIONS

TORQUE SPECIFICATIONS

Application	INCH Lbs. (N.m)
Direct Clutch Speed Sensor Bolt	48 (5.4)
PNP Switch	
Bolt	44 (5)
Nut	62 (7)
No. 1 Speed Sensor Bracket Bolt	115 (13)

AUTOMATIC TRANSMISSIONS
Toyota A-541E Electronic Controls (Cont.)

WIRING DIAGRAMS

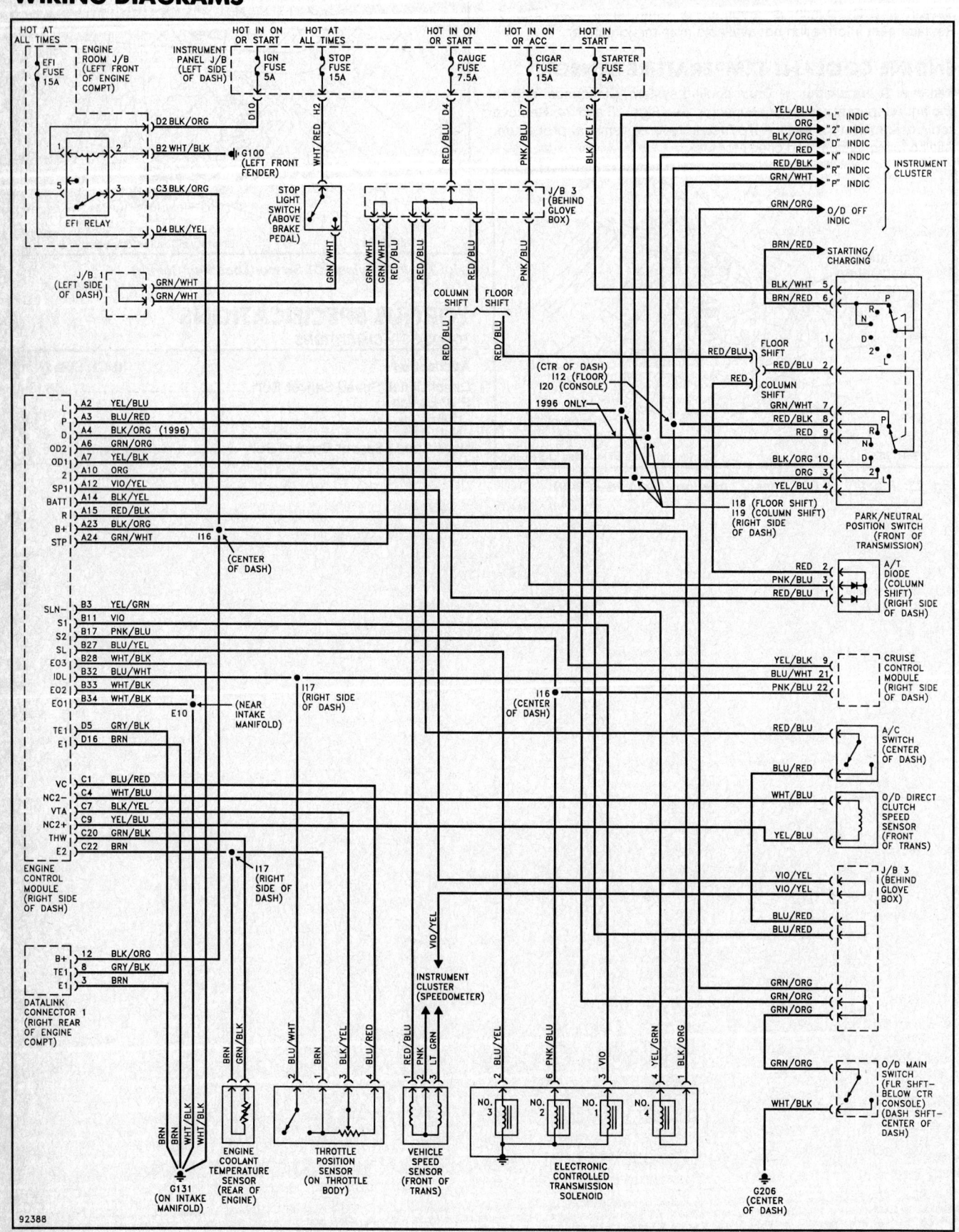

Fig. 25: Transaxle Wiring Diagram (1995-96 Avalon)

92388

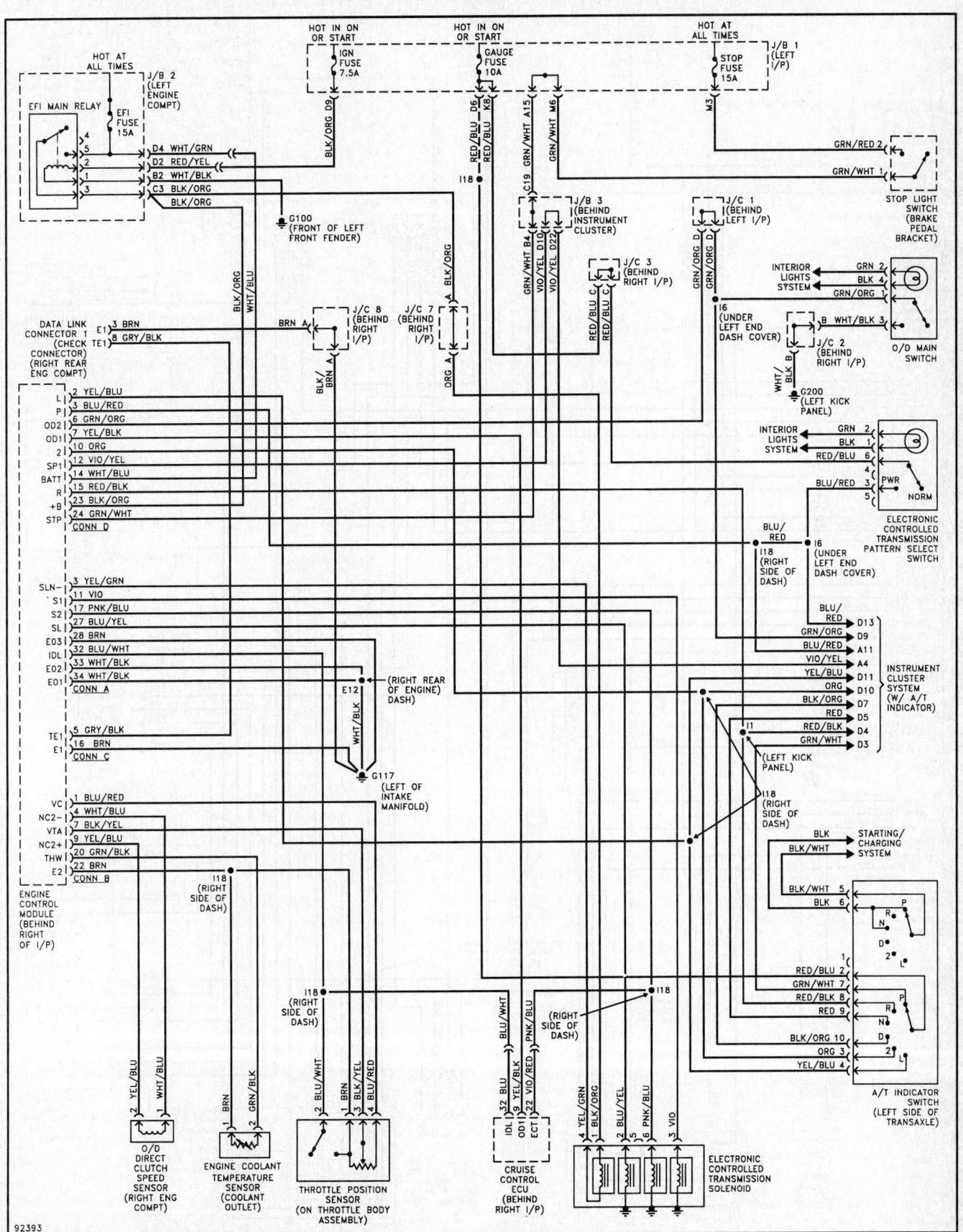

Fig. 26: Transaxle Wiring Diagram (1995-96 Camry V6)

92393

AUTOMATIC TRANSMISSIONS
Toyota A-541E Electronic Controls (Cont.)

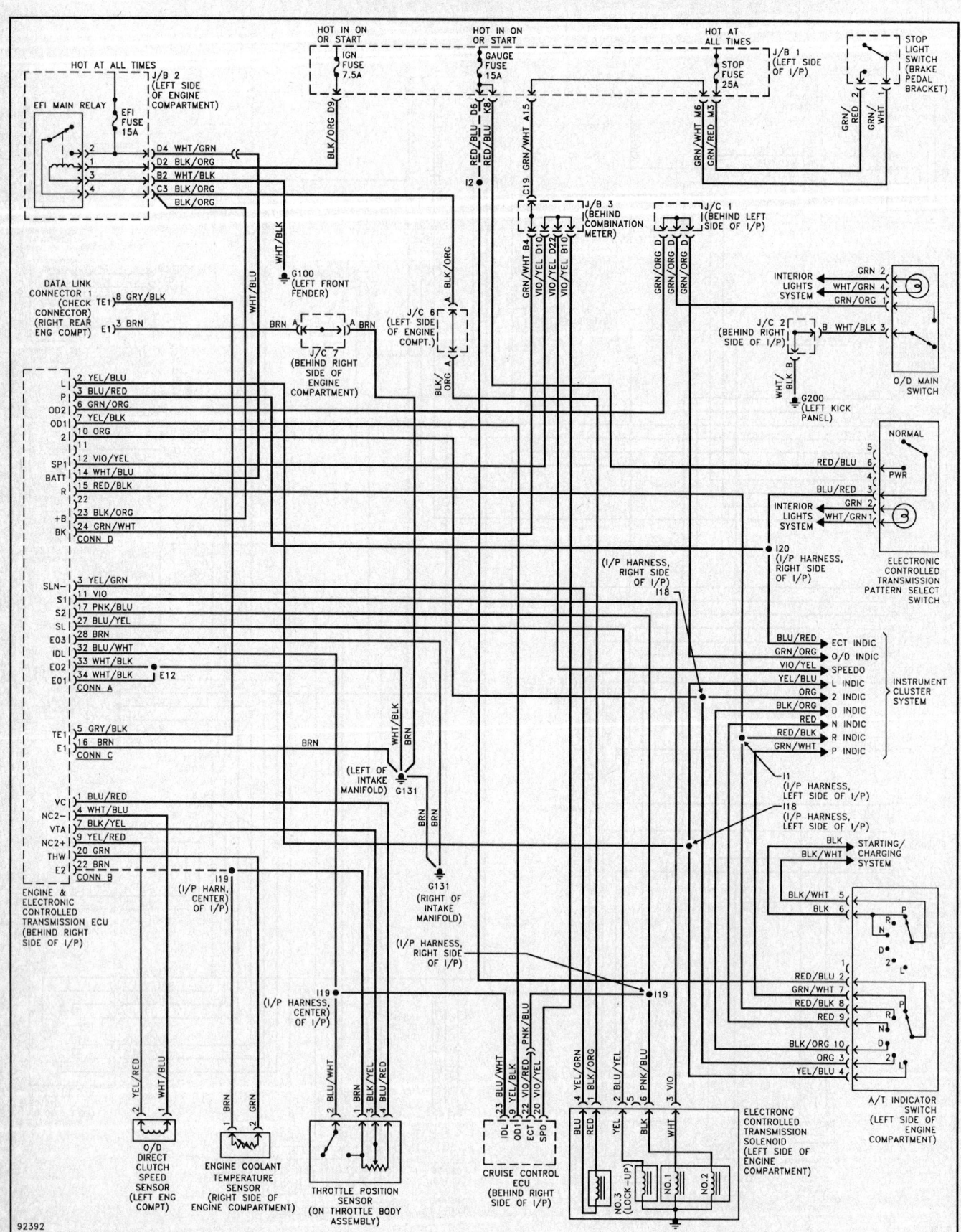

Fig. 27: Transaxle Wiring Diagram (1995-96 ES300)

Lexus: ES300, GS300, LS400, LX450, SC300, SC400
Toyota: Avalon, Camry, Celica, Corolla, Land Cruiser, MR2, Paseo, Previa, Pickup, RAV4, Supra, Tacoma, Tercel, T100, 4Runner

DESCRIPTION

Transmission is equipped with a electronically controlled shift lock and key lock system. *See Fig. 1.* Shift lock system prevents shift lever from being moved from Park unless brake pedal is depressed. In case of a malfunction, shift lever can be released by depressing shift lock override button, located near shift lever. Key lock system prevents ignition key from being moved from ACC to LOCK position on ignition switch unless shift lever is in Park.

System consists of brakelight switch, key interlock solenoid, shift lock control switch, shift lock Electronic Control Unit (ECU), shift lock solenoid and shift lock override button. *See Fig. 1.*

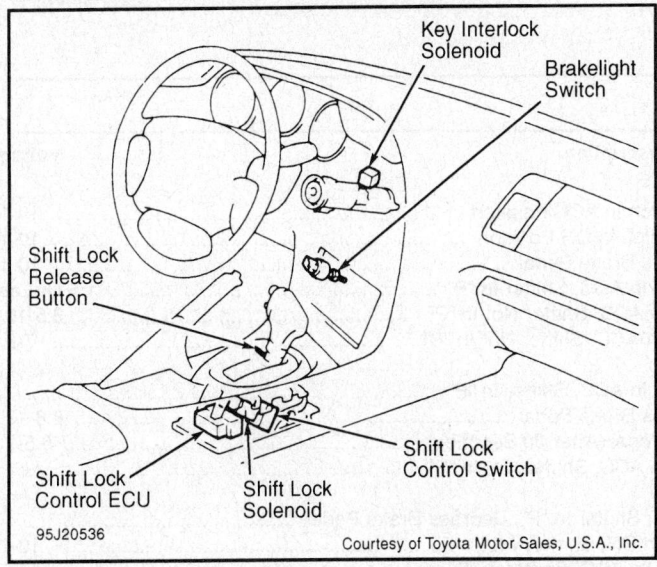

Fig. 1: Shift & Key Lock System Component Locations (Typical)

NOTE: Previa and T100 are equipped with cable operated shift lock system. See CABLE OPERATED SHIFT LOCK SYSTEM CHECK and ADJUSTMENTS.

OPERATION

SHIFT LOCK SYSTEM

With ignition on, when brake pedal is depressed, an input signal is sent from brakelight switch to ECU. With shift lever in Park, an input signal from shift control switch is input to ECU, indicating shift lever is in Park. ECU then operates shift lock solenoid, so shift lever can be moved from Park.

KEY LOCK SYSTEM

With ignition in ON or ACC position and shift lever in Park, shift lock control switch opens and voltage from ECU to key interlock solenoid is turned off. When key interlock solenoid is turned off, ignition key can be turned from ACC to LOCK position on ignition switch.

NOTE: If ignition is left in ACC or ON position with shift lever in any gear range except Park for about one hour, ECU then operates to release lock mechanism.

COMPONENT TESTS

ELECTRONIC CONTROL UNIT (ECU)

Access ECU. *See Fig. 1.* ECU is under center console, in front or back of shifter. Turn ignition on. Backprobing ECU harness connector with DVOM, check voltage between designated terminals. Voltage should be as specified. See appropriate SHIFT LOCK SYSTEM PIN VOLTAGES table. For circuit identification, see appropriate wiring diagram in WIRING DIAGRAMS.

NOTE: Ground (GND) terminal is also referred to as "E" terminal.

SHIFT LOCK SYSTEM PIN VOLTAGES (AVALON, CAMRY & MR2)

Application & Terminals	Description	Voltage
ECU		
ACC – GND	Ignition Switch In ACC Position	10-14
IG – GND	Ignition Switch In ON Position	10-14
STP – GND	Depress Brake Pedal	10-14
KLS – GND	Ignition Switch In ACC, Shifter In "P"	0
	Ignition Switch In ACC, Shifter Not In "P"	7.5-11.5
	[1] Ignition Switch In ACC, Shifter Not In "P"	6-9
Shift Lock Solenoid		
SLS+ – GND	Ignition Switch In ACC, Shifter In "P"	0
	Depress Brake Pedal	8-13.5
	Ignition Switch In ACC, Shifter Not In "P"	0
Shift Lock Control Switch		
P_1 – P	Ignition Switch In ON Position, Shifter In "P", Depress Brake Pedal	0
	Ignition Switch In ON, Shifter Not In "P"	9-13.5
P_2 – P	Ignition Switch In ACC, Shifter In "P"	9-13.5

[1] – Voltage measurement after one second.

SHIFT LOCK SYSTEM PIN VOLTAGES (CELICA, COROLLA, ES300, GS300, LAND CRUISER, LX450, PASEO, TACOMA & TERCEL)

Application & Terminals	Description	Voltage
ECU		
ACC – GND	Ignition Switch In ACC Position	10-14
IG – GND	Ignition Switch In ON Position	10-14
STP – GND	Depress Brake Pedal	10-14
KLS – GND	Ignition Switch In ACC, Shifter In "P"	0
	Ignition Switch In ACC, Shifter Not In "P"	[2] 10-14
	[1] Ignition Switch In ACC, Shifter Not In "P"	6-9
Shift Lock Solenoid		
SLS+ – SLS–	Ignition Switch In ACC, Shifter In "P"	0
	Depress Brake Pedal	8-13.5
	Depress Brake Pedal (After 20 Seconds)	5.5-9.5
	Ignition Switch In ACC, Shifter Not In "P"	0
Shift Lock Control Switch		
P₁ – P	Ignition Switch In ON Position, Shifter In "P", Depress Brake Pedal	0
	Ignition Switch In ON, Shifter Not In "P"	9-13.5
P₂ – P	Ignition Switch In ACC, Shifter In "P"	9-13.5
	Ignition Switch In ACC, Shifter Not In "P"	0

[1] – Voltage measurement after one second.
[2] – Voltage is 7.5-11 volts on 1996 ES300.

SHIFT LOCK SYSTEM PIN VOLTAGES (LS400)

Application & Terminals	Description	Voltage
ECU		
ACC – GND	Ignition Switch In ACC Position	10-14
IG – GND	Ignition Switch In ON Position	10-14
STP – GND	Depress Brake Pedal	10-14
KLS – GND	Ignition Switch In ACC, Shifter In "P"	1.5 Or Less
	Ignition Switch In ACC, Shifter Not In "P"	8.5-10.5
	[1] Ignition Switch In ACC, Shifter Not In "P"	7-8.5
Shift Lock Solenoid		
SLS+ – SLS–	Ignition Switch In ACC, Shifter In "P"	0
	Depress Brake Pedal	8.8-12.5
	Depress Brake Pedal (After 20 Seconds)	6.5-9.2
	Ignition Switch In ACC, Shifter Not In "P"	0
Shift Lock Control Switch		
P₁ – P	Ignition Switch In ON Position, Shifter In "P", Depress Brake Pedal	0
	Ignition Switch In ON, Shifter Not In "P"	10-14
P₂ – P	Ignition Switch In ACC, Shifter In "P"	10-14
	Ignition Switch In ACC, Shifter Not In "P"	0

[1] – Voltage measurement after one second.

SHIFT LOCK SYSTEM PIN VOLTAGES (PICKUP & 1995 4RUNNER)

Application & Terminals	Description	Voltage
ECU		
ACC – GND	Ignition Switch In ACC Position	10-14
IG – GND	Ignition Switch In ON Position	10-14
STP – GND	Depress Brake Pedal	10-14
KLS – GND	Ignition Switch In ACC, Shifter In "P"	0
	Ignition Switch In ACC, Shifter Not In "P"	10-14
	[1] Ignition Switch In ACC, Shifter Not In "P"	6-9
Shift Lock Solenoid		
SLS+ – SLS–	Ignition Switch In ACC, Shifter In "P"	0
	Depress Brake Pedal	10-14
	Ignition Switch In ACC, Shifter Not In "P"	0
Shift Lock Control Switch		
P₁ – P	Ignition Switch In ON Position, Shifter In "P", Depress Brake Pedal	0
	Ignition Switch In ON, Shifter Not In "P"	10-14
P₂ – P	Ignition Switch In ACC, Shifter In "P"	10-14
	Ignition Switch In ACC, Shifter Not In "P"	0

[1] – Voltage measurement after one second.

SHIFT LOCK SYSTEM PIN VOLTAGES (RAV4)

Application & Terminals	Description	Voltage
ECU		
ACC – GND	Ignition Switch In ACC Position	10-14
IG – GND	Ignition Switch In ON Position	10-14
STP – GND	Depress Brake Pedal	10-14
KLS – GND	Ignition Switch In ACC, Shifter In "P"	0
	Ignition Switch In ACC, Shifter Not In "P"	7.5-11
	[1] Ignition Switch In ACC, Shifter Not In "P"	5.5-10
Shift Lock Solenoid		
SLS+ – GND	Ignition Switch In ACC, Shifter In "P"	0
	Depress Brake Pedal	8-14
	Ignition Switch In ACC, Shifter Not In "P"	0
Shift Lock Control Switch		
P$_1$ – P	Ignition Switch In ON Position, Shifter In "P", Depress Brake Pedal	0
	Ignition Switch In ON, Shifter Not In "P"	10-14
P$_2$ – P	Ignition Switch In ACC, Shifter In "P"	10-14

[1] – Voltage measurement after one second.

SHIFT LOCK SYSTEM PIN VOLTAGES (SC300, SC400, SUPRA & 1996 4RUNNER)

Application & Terminals	Description	Voltage
ECU		
ACC – GND	Ignition Switch In ACC Position	10-14
IG – GND	Ignition Switch In ON Position	10-14
STP – GND	Depress Brake Pedal	10-14
KLS – GND	Ignition Switch In ACC, Shifter In "P"	0
	Ignition Switch In ACC, Shifter Not In "P"	7.5-11
	[1] Ignition Switch In ACC, Shifter Not In "P"	6-9.5
Shift Lock Solenoid		
SLS+ – SLS–	Ignition Switch In ACC, Shifter In "P"	0
	Depress Brake Pedal	8-13.5
	Depress Brake Pedal (After 20 Seconds)	6-8.5
	Ignition Switch In ACC, Shifter Not In "P"	0
Shift Lock Control Switch		
P$_1$ – P	Ignition Switch In ON Position, Shifter In "P", Depress Brake Pedal	0
	Ignition Switch In ON, Shifter Not In "P"	9-13.5
P$_2$ – P	Ignition Switch In ACC, Shifter In "P"	9-13.5
	Ignition Switch In ACC, Shifter Not In "P"	0

[1] – Voltage measurement after one second.

NOTE: Ground (GND) terminal is also referred to as "E" terminal.

SHIFT LOCK SOLENOID

1) Disconnect electrical connector from shift lock solenoid. Using ohmmeter, measure resistance between shift lock solenoid terminals. See WIRING DIAGRAMS.

2) Replace shift lock solenoid if resistance is not within specification. See SHIFT LOCK SOLENOID RESISTANCE SPECIFICATIONS table. Apply battery voltage between shift lock solenoid terminals. Replace shift lock solenoid if operating sound cannot be heard.

SHIFT LOCK SOLENOID RESISTANCE SPECIFICATIONS

Application	Ohms
Avalon, Camry, Paseo, Tacoma (A-43D) & Tercel	30-35
Celica, Corolla, 1995 ES300, GS300	
MR2 & 1996 4Runner	21-27
Land Cruiser, LS400, LX450,	
SC300, SC400, Supra & Tacoma (A-340E/F)	20-28
1996 ES300, Pickup & 1995 4Runner	29-36
RAV4	26-33

KEY INTERLOCK SOLENOID

1) Disconnect electrical connector from key interlock solenoid. Using ohmmeter, measure resistance between key interlock solenoid terminals. See WIRING DIAGRAMS.

2) Replace key interlock solenoid if resistance is not 12-17 ohms. Apply battery voltage between of key interlock solenoid terminals. Replace key interlock solenoid if operating sound cannot be heard.

SHIFT LOCK CONTROL SWITCH

Disconnect electrical connector from shift lock control switch. Using ohmmeter, check continuity between specified terminals in relation to shift lever. See WIRING DIAGRAMS. See SHIFT LOCK CONTROL SWITCH CONTINUITY table. Replace switch if continuity is not as specified.

NOTE: Continuity must be checked in accordance with position of release button on shift lever and shift lever position.

SHIFT LOCK CONTROL SWITCH CONTINUITY

Shift Lever Position & Condition	Terminals
Any Other Gear Except Park	P & P$_2$
Park & Release Button Not Pushed	P & P$_1$
Park & Release Button Is Pushed	P & P$_1$ Or P & P$_2$

CABLE OPERATED SHIFT LOCK SYSTEM CHECK

Previa – Ensure shift lock cable does not interfere with wiring harness. Ensure ignition switch turns to LOCK position when shift lever is in "P" position. Ensure brake pedal returns fully. Ensure shift lock is released when brake pedal is depressed with ignition switch at ACC, ON or START position.

T100 – Ensure parking lock cable is lubricated and does not scrape or knock during component operation. Place shift lever in "P" position and ensure lever is locked when parking lock cable is pushed .28" (7 mm). Ensure shift lever is released when parking lock cable is free. Ensure free play at tip of shift lever is .24" (6 mm).

ADJUSTMENTS

SHIFT LOCK PIN

Previa – Adjust pin length by loosening and tightening nut. Pin length should be .012" (.3 mm) above or .028" (.7 mm) below shift lever assembly surface. With pin within length specifications, tighten nut to 18 ft. lbs. (25 N.m). *See Fig. 2.*

PARKING LOCK CABLE

Previa – Place shift lever in "P" position. Turn ignition switch to LOCK position. Loosen 2 nuts and ensure slide pin strikes cushion rubber. Tighten 2 nuts to 48 INCH lbs. (5.4 N.m). *See Fig. 3.*

SHIFT LOCK PLATE CLEARANCE

T100 – Turn ignition switch key to ACC position. Set control shaft to "D" position. Measure clearance between stopper and shift lock plate. Clearance should be .039" (1.0 mm) plus or minus .031" (.8 mm). *See Fig. 4.* When control shaft is set to "D" position, ensure ignition key does not turn to LOCK position.

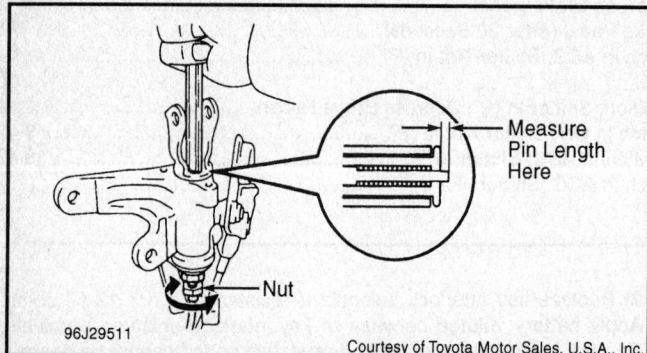

Fig. 2: Measuring Shift Lock Pin Length (Previa)

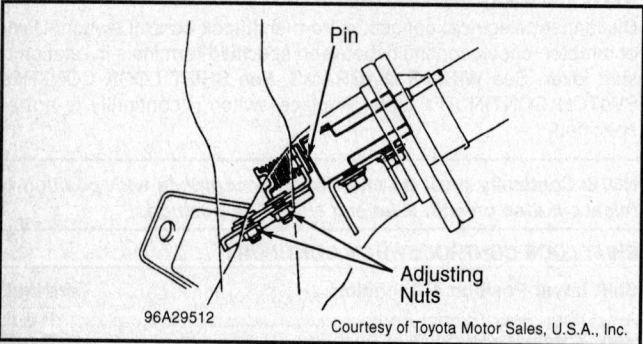

Fig. 3: Adjusting Parking Lock Cable (Previa)

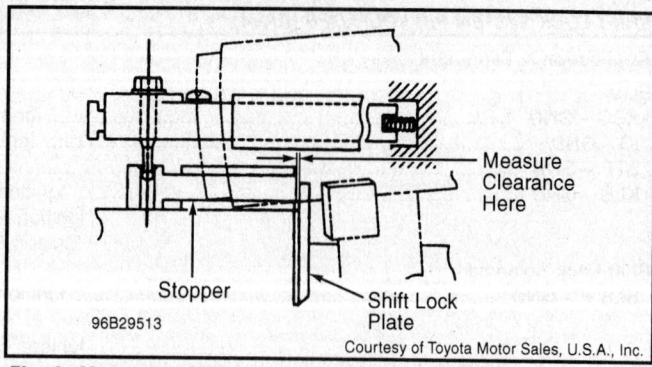

Courtesy of Toyota Motor Sales, U.S.A., Inc.

Fig. 4: Measuring Shift Lock Plate Clearance (T100)

WIRING DIAGRAMS

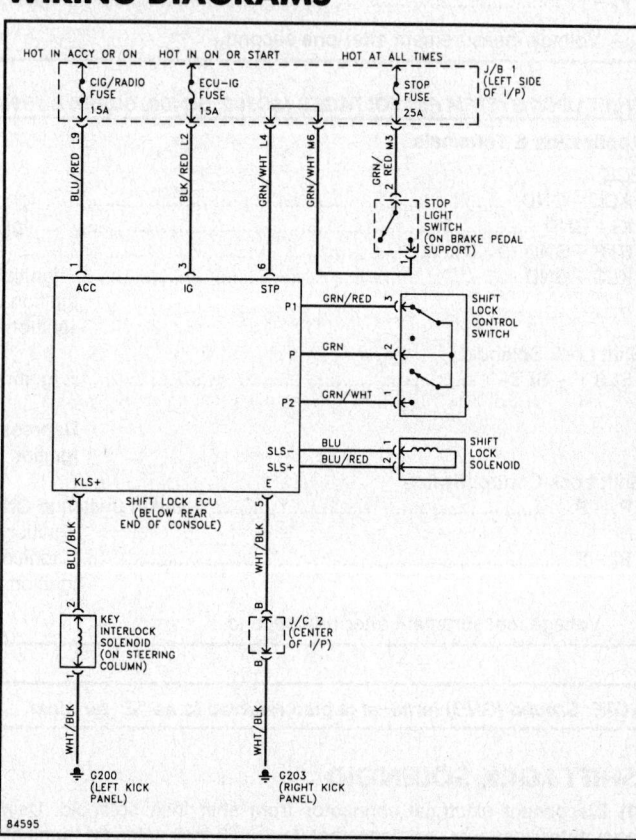

Fig. 5: Shift Interlock System Wiring Diagram (1995-96 ES300)

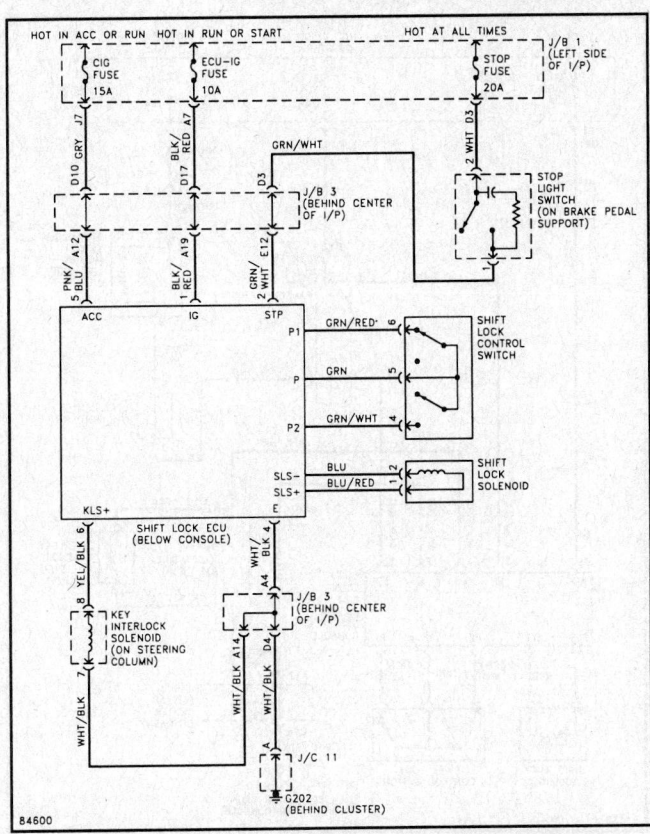

Fig. 6: Shift Interlock System Wiring Diagram (1995-96 GS300)

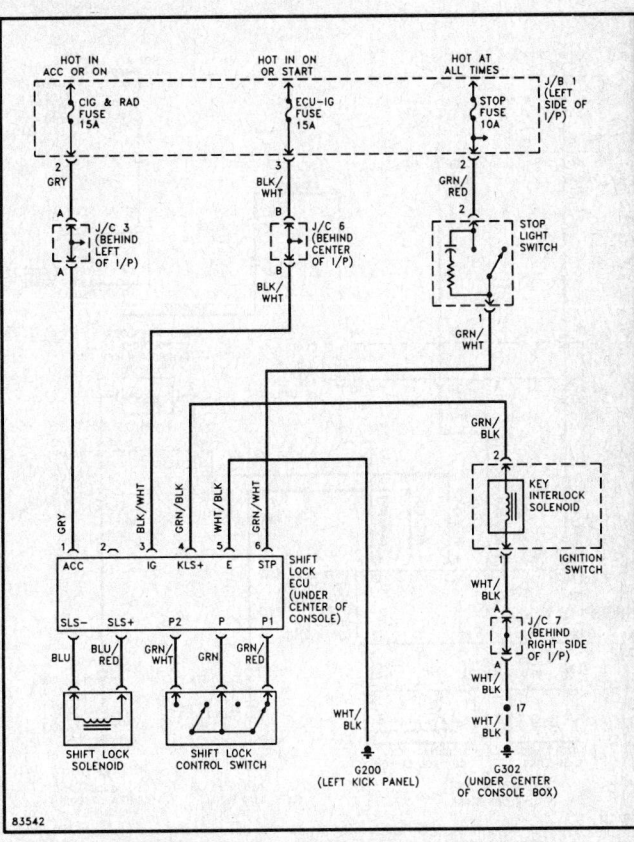

Fig. 8: Shift Interlock System Wiring Diagram (1996 LX450)

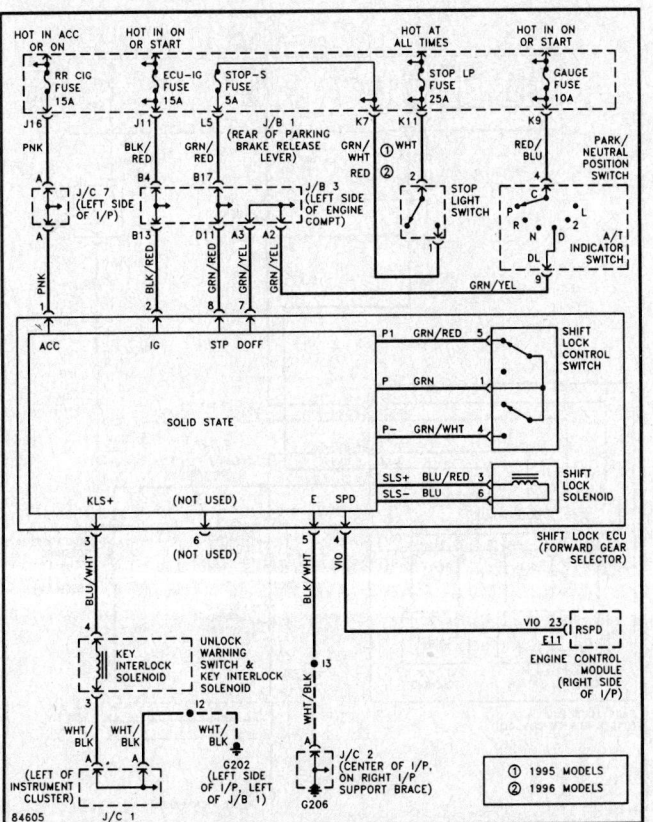

Fig. 7: Shift Interlock System Wiring Diagram (1995-96 LS400)

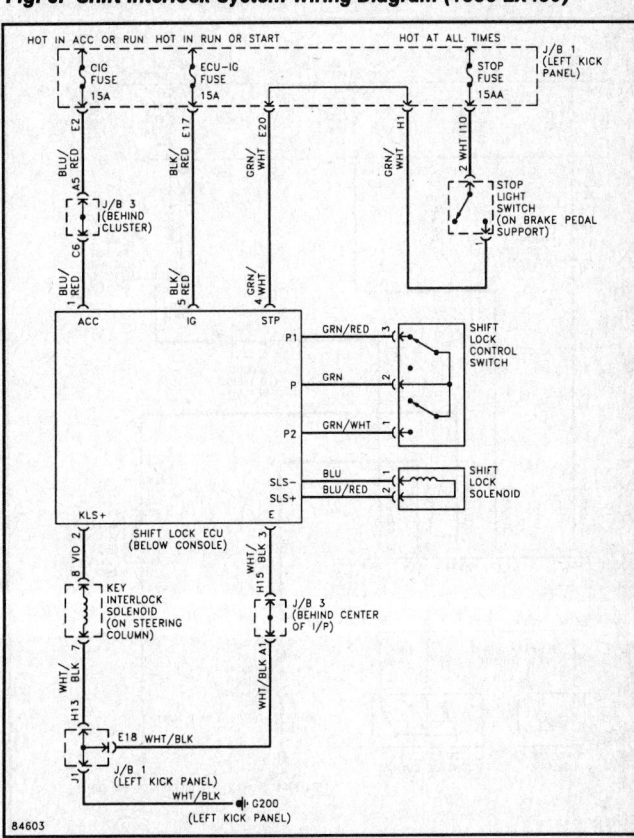

Fig. 9: Shift Interlock System Wiring Diagram (1995-96 SC300 & SC400)

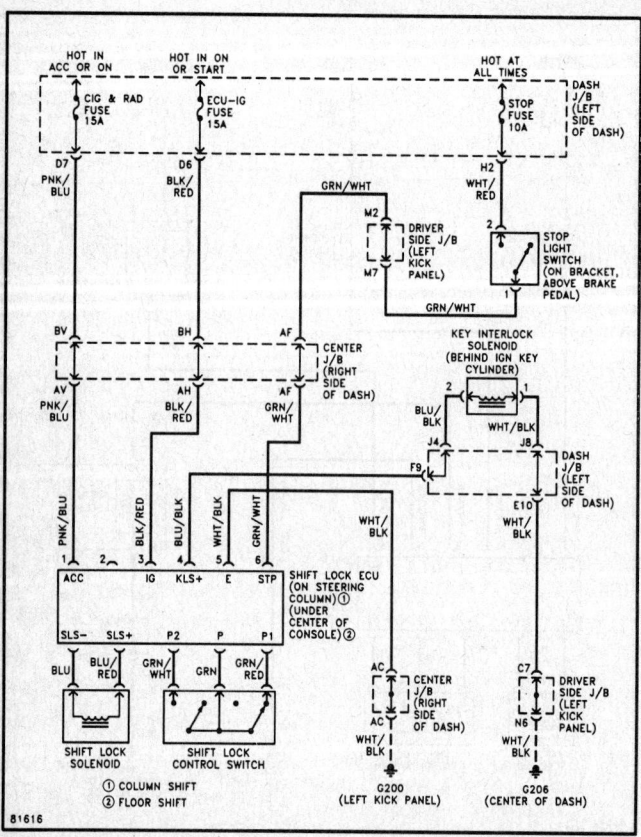

Fig. 10: Shift Interlock System Wiring Diagram (1995-96 Avalon)

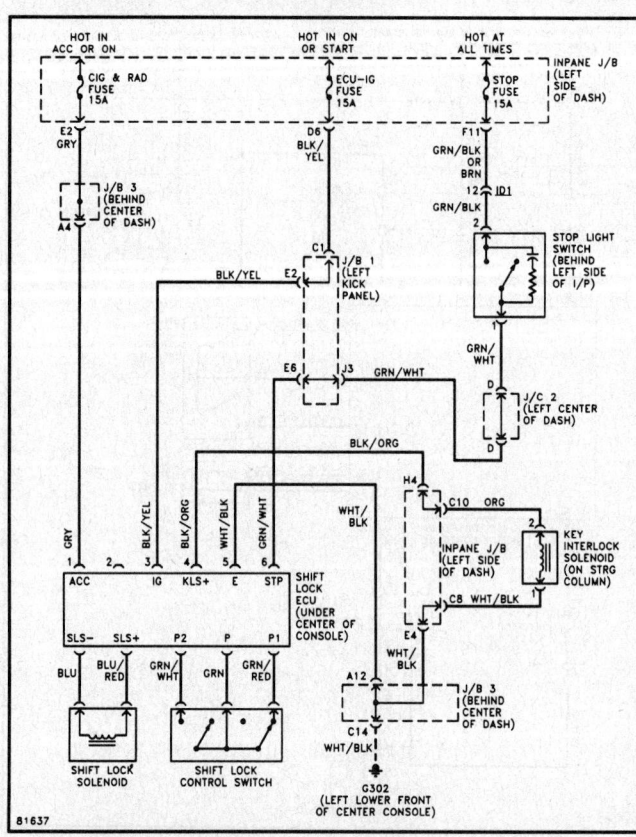

Fig. 12: Shift Interlock System Wiring Diagram (1995-96 Celica)

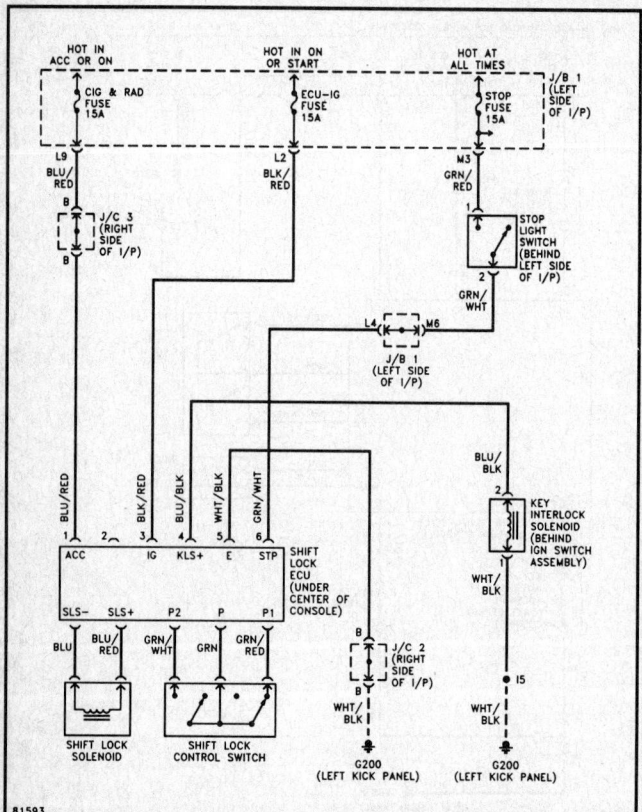

Fig. 11: Shift Interlock System Wiring Diagram (1995-96 Camry)

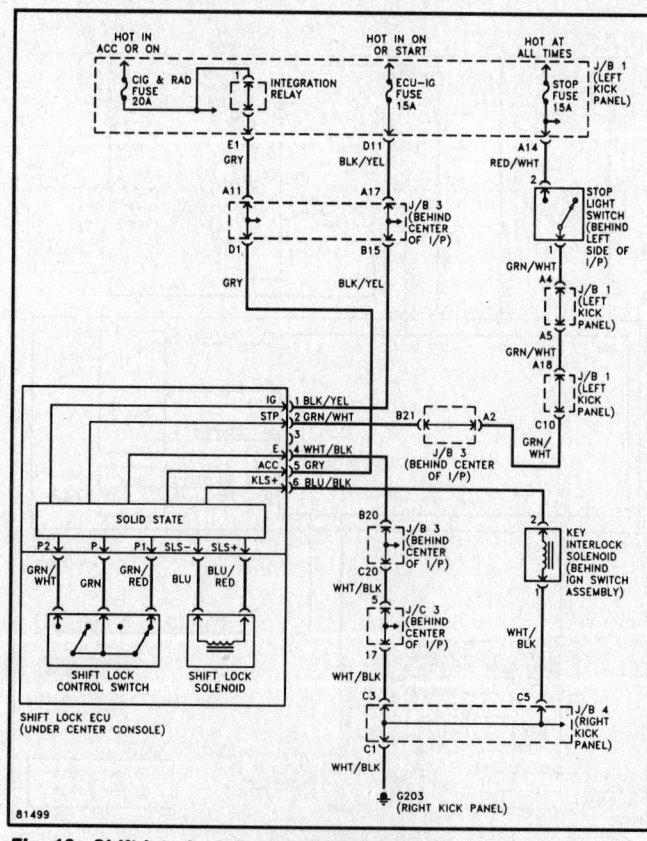

Fig. 13: Shift Interlock System Wiring Diagram (1995-96 Corolla)

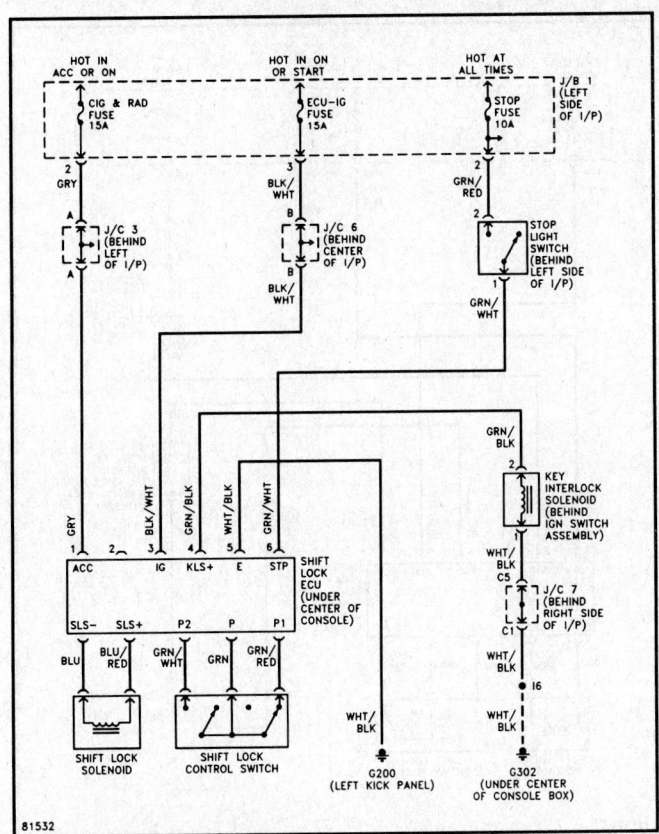

Fig. 14: *Shift Interlock System Wiring Diagram (1995-96 Land Cruiser)*

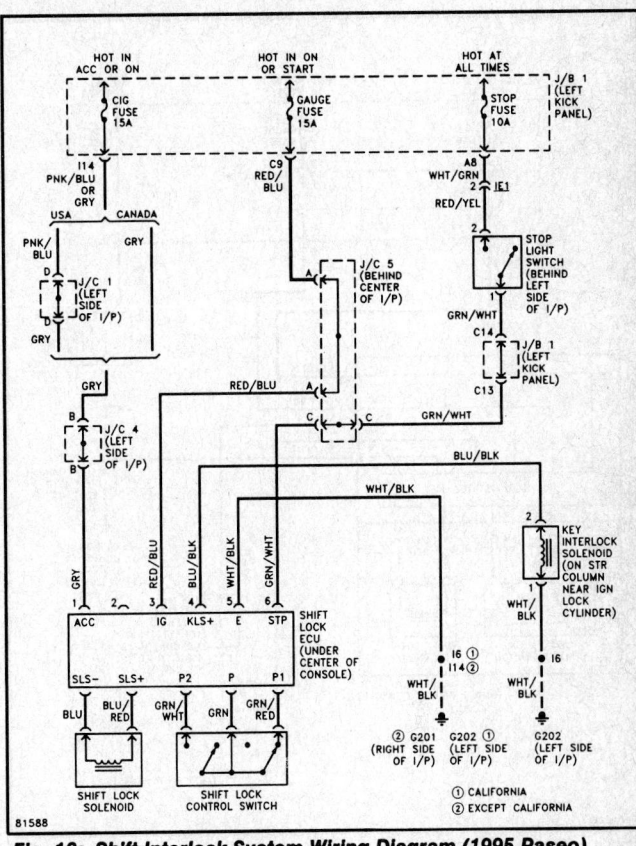

Fig. 16: *Shift Interlock System Wiring Diagram (1995 Paseo)*

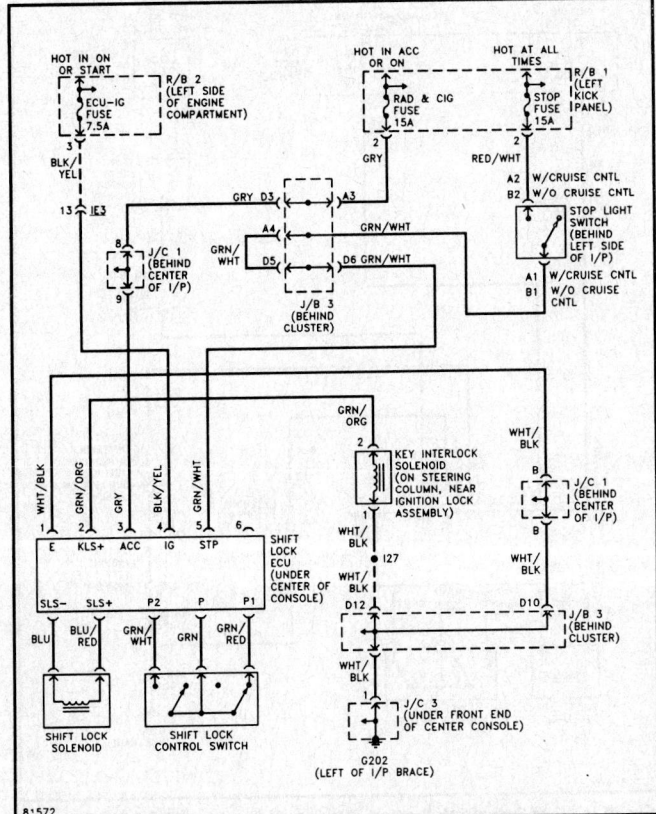

Fig. 15: *Shift Interlock System Wiring Diagram (1995 MR2)*

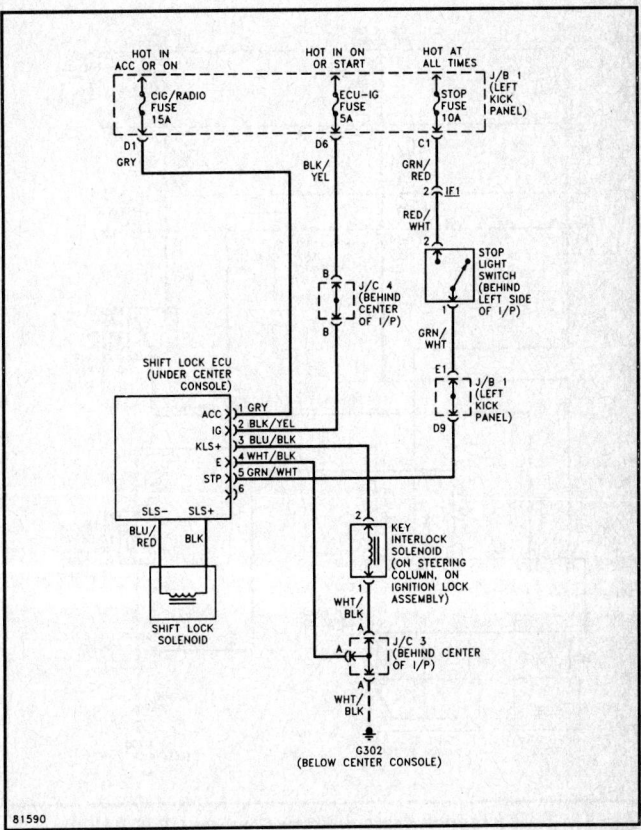

Fig. 17: *Shift Interlock System Wiring Diagram (1996 Paseo)*

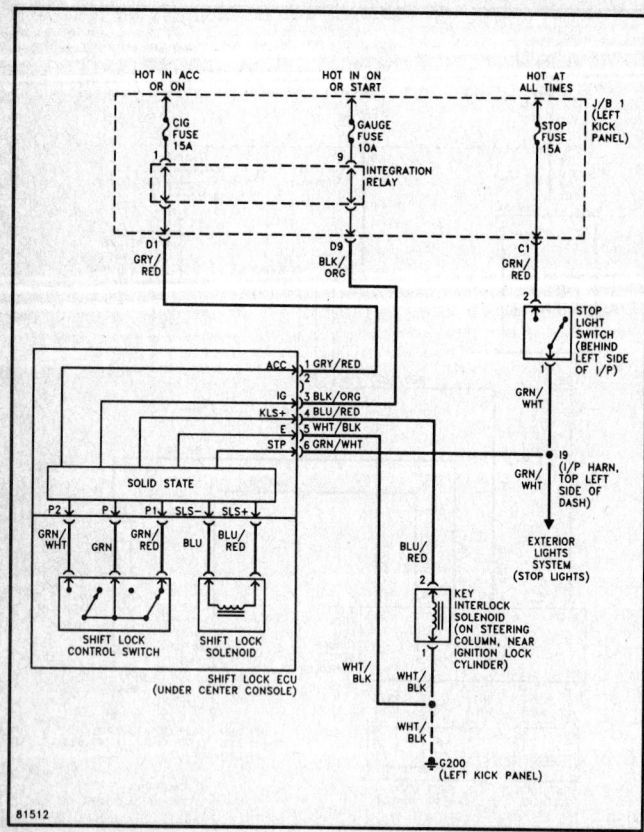

Fig. 18: Shift Interlock System Wiring Diagram (1995 Pickup)

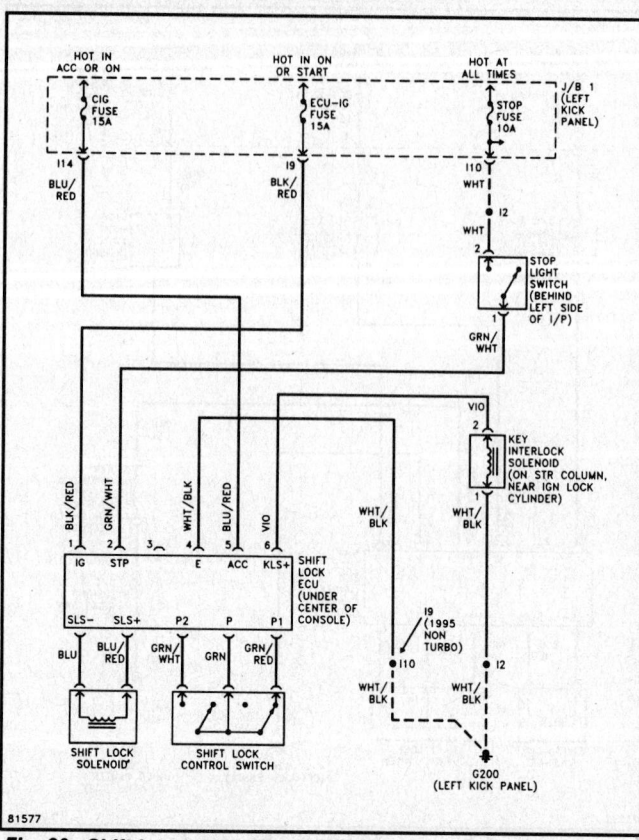

Fig. 20: Shift Interlock System Wiring Diagram (1995-96 Supra)

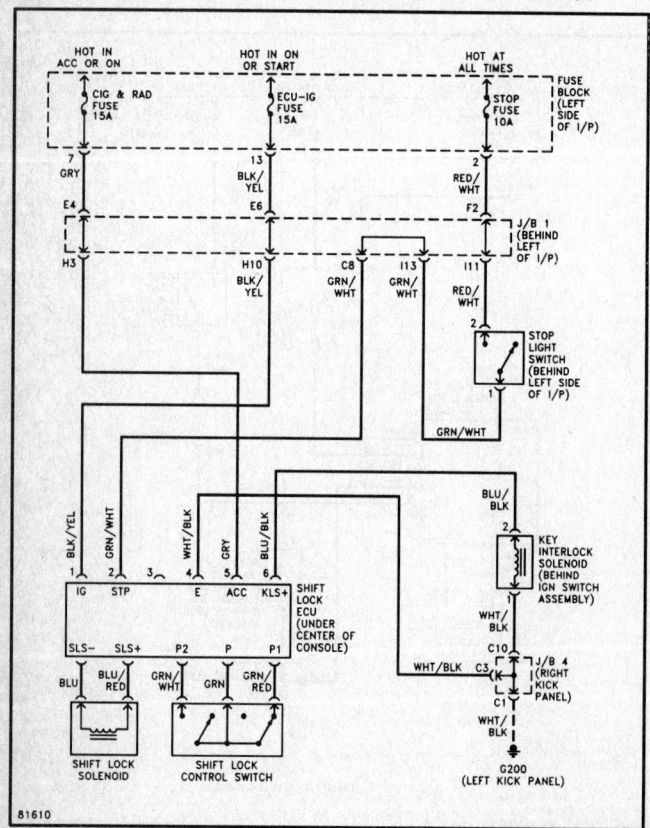

Fig. 19: Shift Interlock System Wiring Diagram (1996 RAV4)

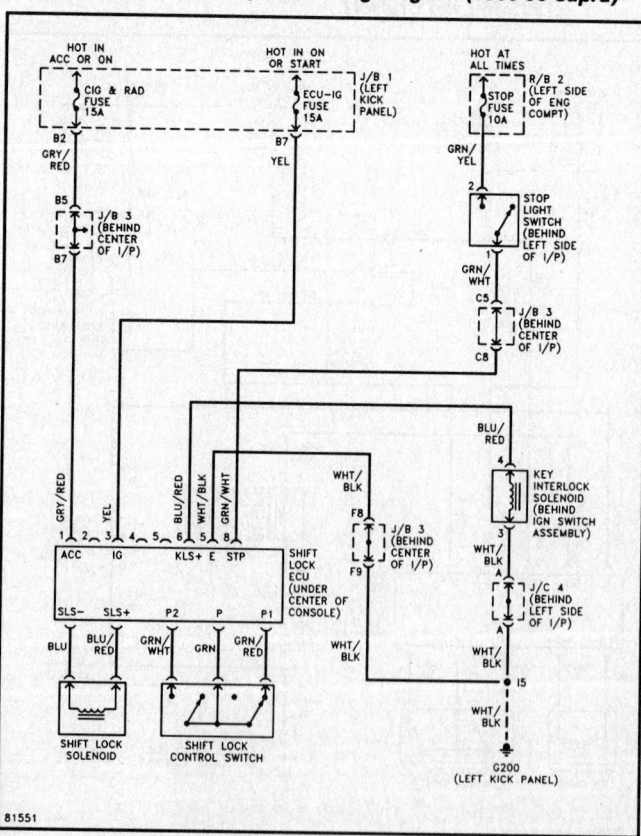

Fig. 21: Shift Interlock System Wiring Diagram (1995-96 Tacoma)

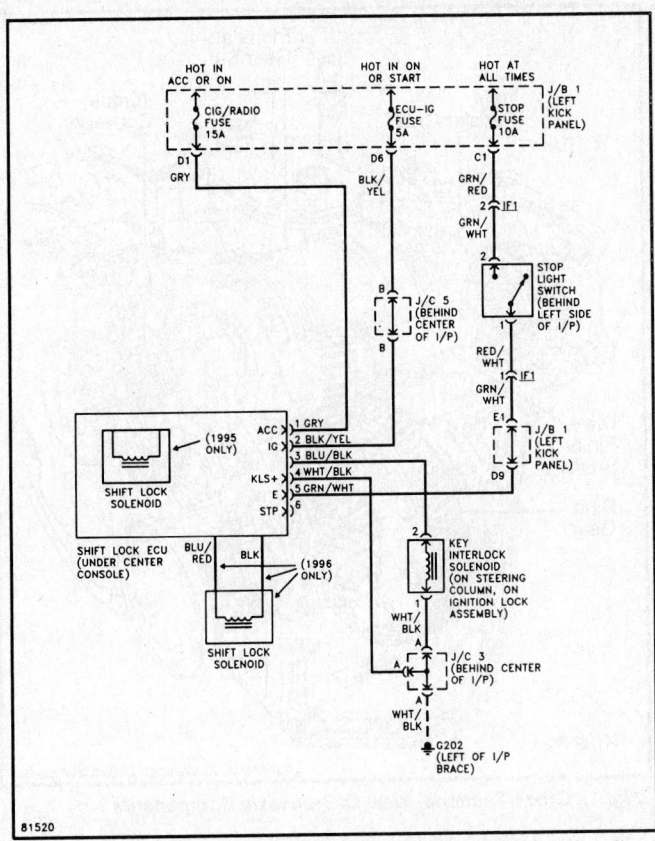

Fig. 22: Shift Interlock System Wiring Diagram (1995-96 Tercel)

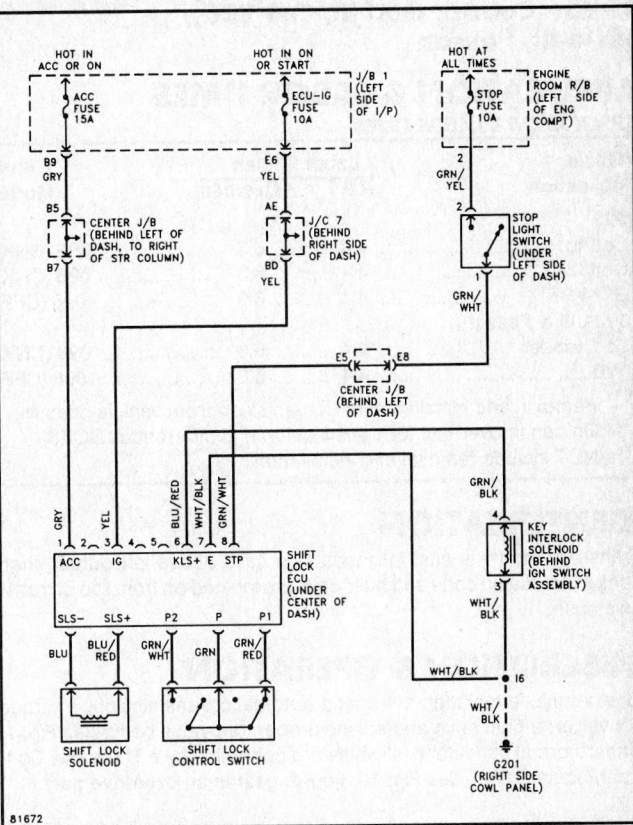

Fig. 24: Shift Interlock System Wiring Diagram (1996 4Runner)

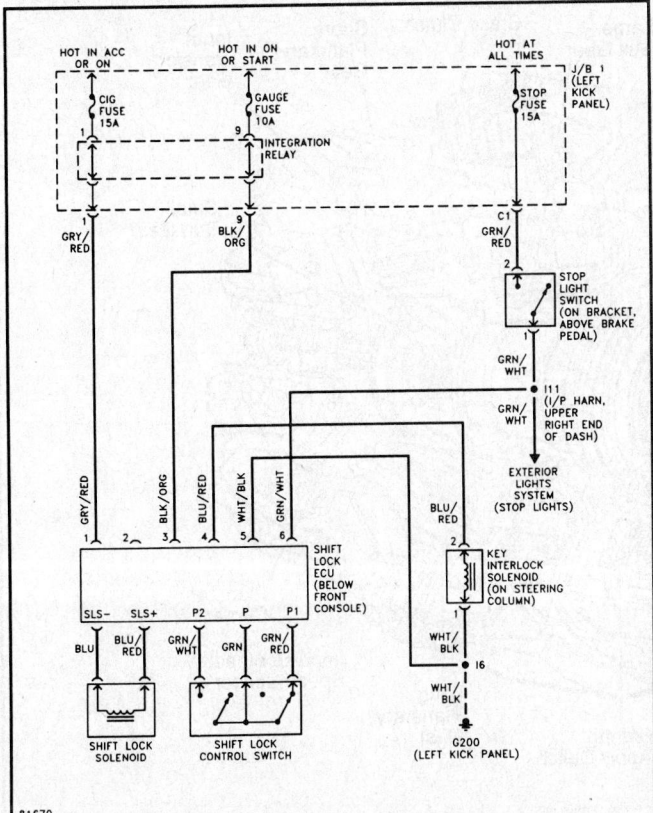

Fig. 23: Shift Interlock System Wiring Diagram (1995 4Runner)

AUTOMATIC TRANSMISSIONS
Volkswagen Model 096

1995: Cabrio, Golf III, GTI VR6, Jetta III, Passat

APPLICATION & LABOR TIMES

APPLICATION & LABOR TIMES

Vehicle Application	Labor Times [1] R & I	Labor Times [2] Overhaul	Trans. Model
1995			
Cabrio	4.4	6.3	096 (CNK)
Golf III	4.4	6.3	096 (CNK)
GTI VR6	4.4	6.3	096 (CFF)
Jetta III & Passat			
4-Cylinder	4.4	6.3	096 (CNK)
V6	4.4	6.3	096 (CFF)

[1] – Removal and installation of transmission from vehicle chassis.
[2] – On bench overhaul for transmission and differential. DOES NOT include removal and installation.

IDENTIFICATION

Transaxle model is cast into transaxle case above left output shaft flange. Transaxle code and build date are located on front top of transaxle case.

DESCRIPTION & OPERATION

This transaxle includes a 4-speed automatic transmission, a torque converter, a final drive and solenoid-operated valve body. See Fig. 1. Under normal conditions, all shifts are controlled by a Transaxle Control Module (TCM). See Fig. 10. Fourth gear is an overdrive gear.

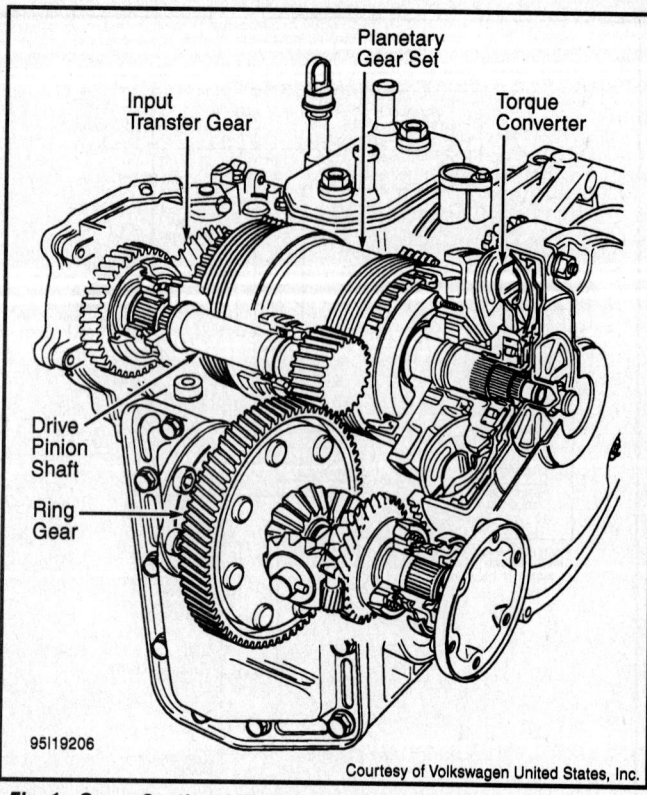

95I19206

Courtesy of Volkswagen United States, Inc.

Fig. 1: Cross-Sectional View Of Transaxle Components

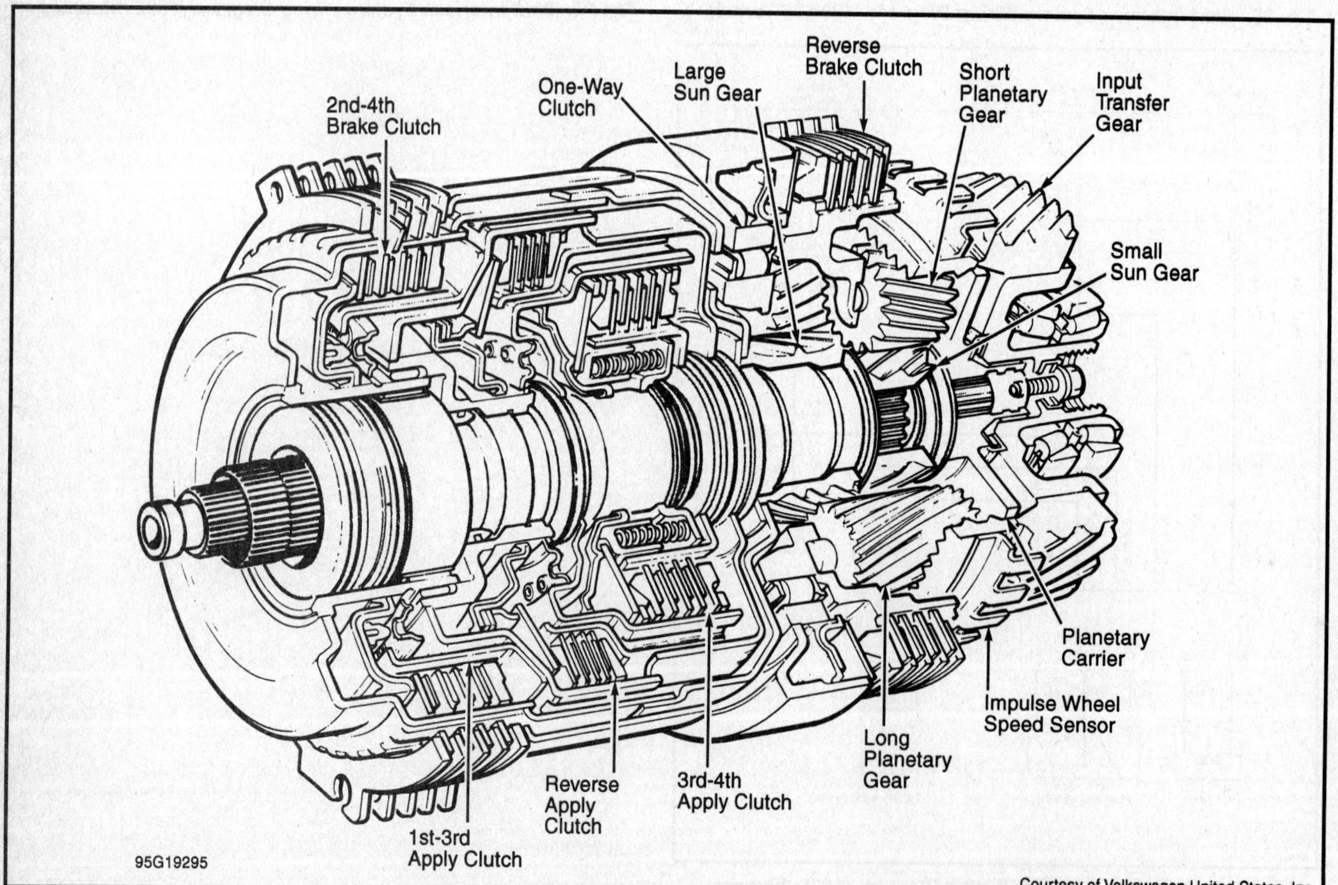

95G19295

Courtesy of Volkswagen United States, Inc.

Fig. 2: View Of Transmission Clutches, Shafts & Planetary Assemblies

The transmission elements consist of a planetary gear set, one-way roller clutch, 3 apply clutches and 2 brake clutches. See Fig. 2. Power from the transmission is connected to the drive pinion through transfer gears. A ring gear and differential assembly are connected to flanges which spin the drive axles.

The electronic control consists of a TCM (located under rear seat), control solenoids, various sensors and switches. The control solenoids direct oil pressure inside the valve body. Solenoid valves No. 1-4 control the apply and brake clutches. Solenoid valves No. 5 and 7 control shift smoothness.

Control solenoid valve No. 6 is a frequency valve and controls the main hydraulic pressure. The TCM controls the main hydraulic pressure by varying the duty cycle.

The TCM monitors input and output signals. If electrical problems occur, TCM will record faults in TCM memory and may go into fail-safe mode. If TCM enters fail-safe mode, the transaxle will operate manually in reverse, 1st or 3rd gear. In fail-safe mode, 3rd gear operates with gear selector in 2nd, 3rd or "D". The TCM memory can only be read using Scan Tool (VAG 1551) and Adapter (VAG 1551/3).

The TCM also controls shift lock system. This system locks the gear selector in Park or Neutral unless the brake pedal is pushed down. The TCM uses a shift lock control relay to release a gear-selector mounted solenoid.

LUBRICATION & ADJUSTMENTS

NOTE: See appropriate AUTOMATIC TRANSMISSION SERVICING article in TRANSMISSION SERVICING section.

TROUBLE SHOOTING

SYMPTOM DIAGNOSIS

Leak At Torque Converter – Check drive plate clearance, torque converter bushing, oil seal or oil pump assembly. Repair as necessary.

Transaxle Fluid In Coolant – Faulty transaxle oil cooler. Replace transaxle oil cooler and friction plates in transaxle. Clean transaxle.

Transaxle & Differential Oils Mixed – Replace "O" ring and drive pinion seal on inner bearing support.

Gear Selector Hard To Move – Check gear selector between shifter and transaxle. Repair as necessary. Check parking lock assembly inside transaxle. Repair as necessary.

No Drive In 1st Gear – Check for faulty 1st-3rd apply clutch or reverse brake clutch.

No Drive In "D", "2" Or "3" – Check for faulty 1st-3rd apply clutch or one-way clutch.

No 2nd Gear In "D", "2" Or "3" – Check for faulty 2nd-4th brake clutch.

No 3rd Gear In "D" Or "3" – Check for faulty reverse apply clutch.

No 4th Gear In "D" – Check for faulty 2nd-4th brake clutch.

No Reverse – Check for faulty reverse apply clutch or reverse brake clutch.

No Drive In All Forward Gear Positions – Check for faulty 1st-3rd apply clutch, reverse brake clutch or one-way clutch.

Missing Shifts Up Or Down – Check valve body for sticking valve(s) or faulty shift solenoid(s).

Erratic Or Harsh Shifts – Short in wiring to shift solenoid(s) or faulty shift solenoid(s). Check for proper throttle angle adjustment. See TECHNICAL SERVICE BULLETINS.

Harsh Shift In One Gear Only – Determine elements involved. Air check elements. Check for faulty shift solenoid or shift valve.

Stuck In Emergency Running Mode – Check for incorrect TCM installed, faulty wiring, bad solenoid electrical strip (inside oil pan) or stuck valve.

Park Lock Will Not Engage – Check for misadjusted selector lever cable. Check for faulty locking mechanism.

Bucking Or Poor Idling – Check throttle housing and air ducts for leaks. Check for possible air entering oil pump pickup.

Excess Engine RPM Drop When Shifting Into 1st Gear – Faulty Engine Control Module (ECM).

Engine Starts In Gear Or No Start In Park/Neutral – Check for faulty Park/Neutral safety switch.

Shift-Lock Not Holding Selector In Park/Neutral – Check for faulty shift lock solenoid, shift lock mechanism or bad TCM.

MECHANICAL, HYDRAULIC & ELECTRICAL COMPONENTS

1) If gear selector is stuck in Park or Neutral, go to SHIFT LOCK SYSTEM under TROUBLE SHOOTING. If gear positions are missing, shift quality is poor or no shifts are possible, ensure all electrical connections are okay and fluid level is correct.

2) If problems are still present, disconnect electrical connector at transaxle. Test drive vehicle. Check if transaxle will operate manually in reverse and 1st gear. Move gear selector to 2nd, 3rd or "D" position. Transaxle should operate in 3rd gear (2nd, 3rd or "D").

3) If transaxle operates as described, problem may be electrical. See ELECTRONIC SELF-DIAGNOSTICS. If transaxle does not operate as described, problem may be mechanical or hydraulic. See ROAD TEST.

NOTE: If transaxle does not operate in manual 1st gear, check 1st-3rd apply clutch and reverse brake clutch for damage or wear. If transaxle does not operate in manual reverse gear, check reverse apply clutch and reverse brake clutch for damage or wear.

ROAD TEST

WARNING: DO NOT exceed safe or legal speed limits during road test.

1) Road test vehicle with transaxle in "D" range. With vehicle at a speed above kickdown speed, press throttle pedal down and note kickdown shift speeds. Compare kickdown shift speeds to kickdown shift speed specifications. See KICKDOWN SHIFT SPEED SPECIFICATIONS table.

KICKDOWN SHIFT SPEED SPECIFICATIONS

Application	Kickdown (MPH)
4-Cylinder	
1-2	32-35
2-3	62-66
3-4	89-95
4-3	91-87
3-2	61-57
2-1	29-25
V6	
1-2	38-42
2-3	76-80
3-4	109-113
4-3	111-107
3-2	74-70
2-1	31-27

2) Connect scan tool and appropriate adapter to diagnostic connector. Select function 08 "READ MEASURING VALUE BLOCK". Test solenoid valves and upshift speeds following scan tool manufacturers instructions.

3) If transaxle does not shift within specified MPH range, and scan tool values are within specification, determine affected elements. See APPLY & BRAKE CLUTCH APPLICATION.

4) If all apply and brake clutch elements are affected, check oil pump, oil filter, cooler lines, solenoid valve No. 6 and condition of torque converter and/or engine. Repair as necessary.

5) If one or more apply and brake clutch elements are affected, remove valve body. Locate appropriate fluid circuit in transaxle case and valve body. See Figs. 3-10. Check for leaks and blockage. Repair as necessary.

6) If hydraulic circuits are okay or problems with apply and brake clutch elements are mechanical, repair transaxle.

NOTE: *If transaxle does not operate in manual 1st gear, check 1st-3rd apply clutch and reverse brake clutch for damage or wear. If transaxle does not operate in manual reverse gear, check reverse apply clutch and reverse brake clutch for damage or wear.*

APPLY & BRAKE CLUTCH APPLICATION

APPLY & BRAKE CLUTCH APPLICATION

Gear Selector Position	Elements In Use
"D" (Drive)	
1st Gear	1st-3rd Apply & One-Way Clutch Holding
2nd Gear	1st-3rd Apply & 2nd-4th Brake
3rd Gear [1]	1st-3rd & Reverse Apply Clutches
4th Gear	3rd-4th Apply & 2nd-4th Brake
3rd (Drive)	
1st Gear	1st-3rd Apply & One-Way Clutch Holding
2nd Gear	1st-3rd Apply & 2nd-4th Brake
3rd Gear	1st-3rd & Reverse Apply Clutches
2nd (Drive)	
1st Gear	1st-3rd Apply & One-Way Clutch Holding
2nd Gear	1st-3rd Apply & 2nd-4th Brake
1st (Manual)	
1st Gear	1st-3rd Apply & Reverse Brake
Reverse	Reverse Apply & Reverse Brake
Park & Neutral	All Apply & Brake Clutches Released Or Ineffective

[1] – 1st-3rd and reverse apply clutches are engaged. However, main power path is the 3rd-4th apply clutch.

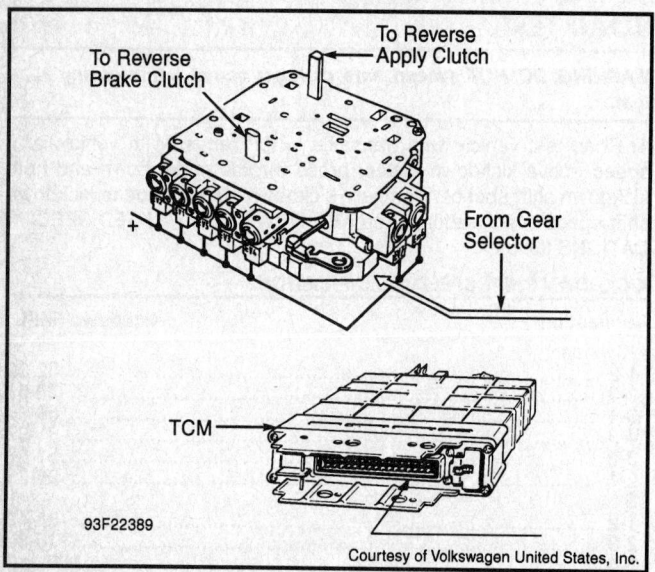

Fig. 3: *Reverse Gear Oil Circuits*

SHIFT LOCK SYSTEM

Operation – All models are equipped with an electronic shift lock system. TCM controls shift lock system. *See Fig. 10.* This system locks gear selector in Park or Neutral position unless brake pedal is pushed down. TCM uses shift lock control relay to release a solenoid mounted on gear selector assembly.

NOTE: *Shift lock relay will not lock gear selector when vehicle speed is greater than 3 MPH.*

A mechanical control cable prevents ignition key from being removed unless gear selector is in Park. With ignition key removed, gear selector locks in Park.

NOTE: *If battery is disconnected or discharged, gear selector can be moved out of Park by turning ignition key to START position.*

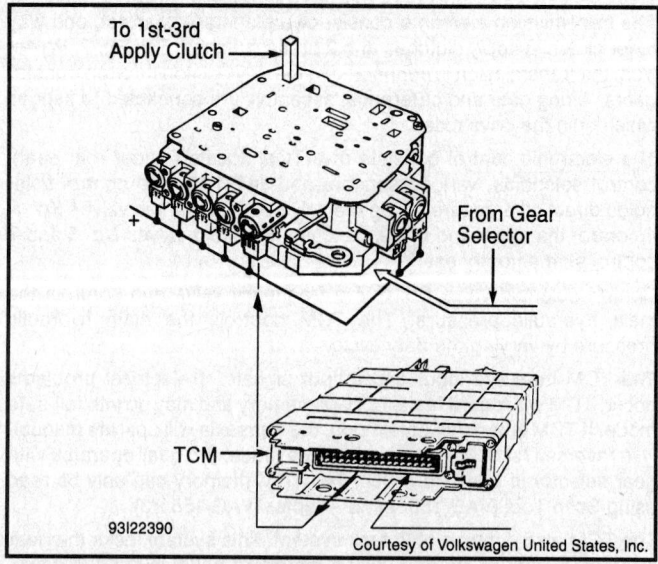

Fig. 4: *1st (In "D") Gear Oil Circuits*

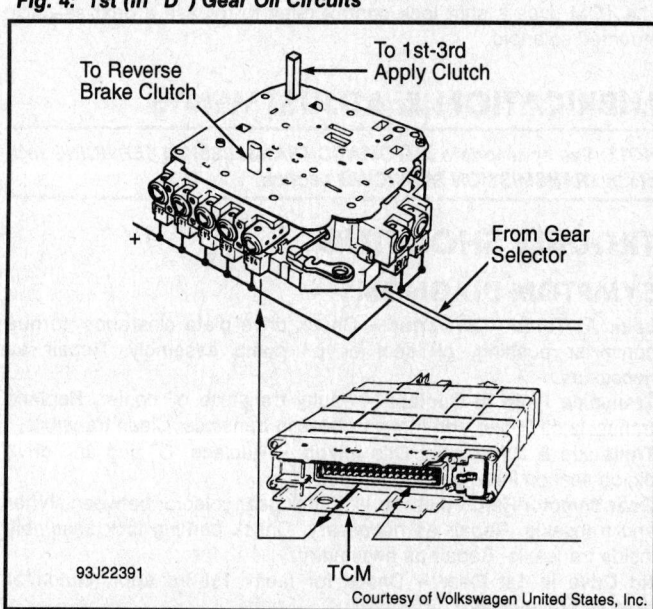

Fig. 5: *1st (In Manual 1st) Gear Oil Circuits*

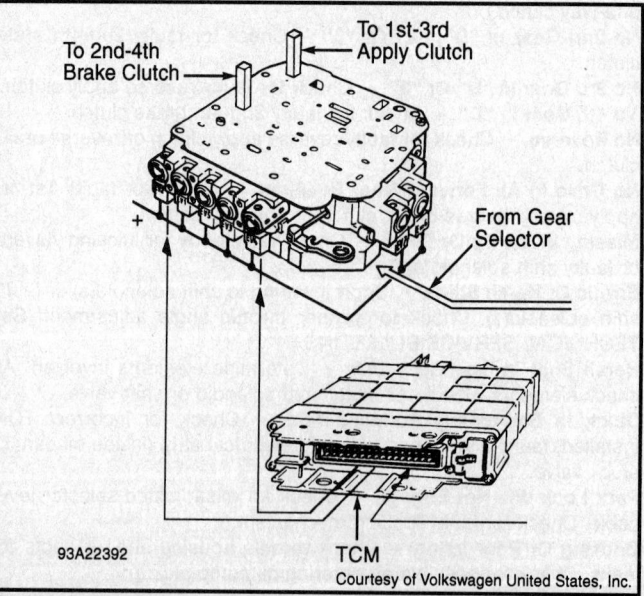

Fig. 6: *2nd Gear Oil Circuits*

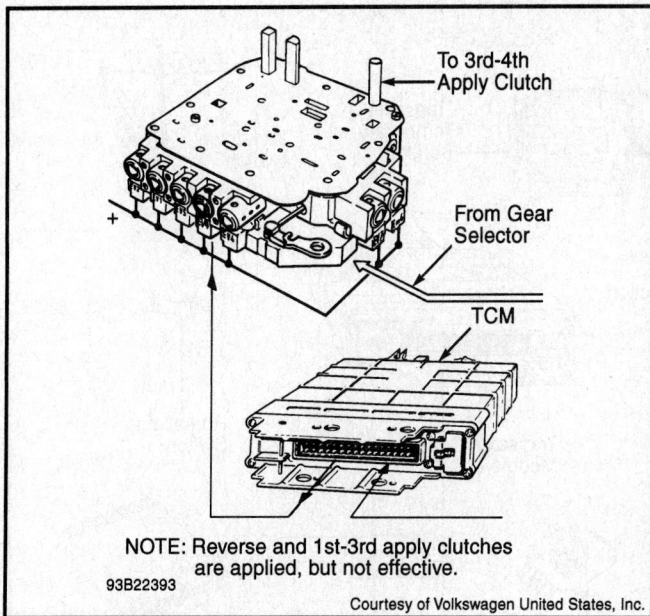

NOTE: Reverse and 1st-3rd apply clutches
are applied, but not effective.

93B22393

Courtesy of Volkswagen United States, Inc.

Fig. 7: 3rd (In "D") Gear Oil Circuits

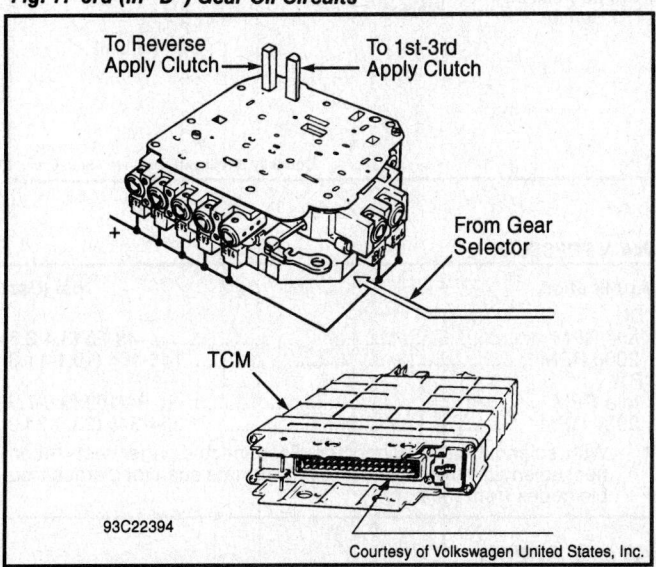

93C22394

Courtesy of Volkswagen United States, Inc.

Fig. 8: 3rd (In Manual) Gear Oil Circuits

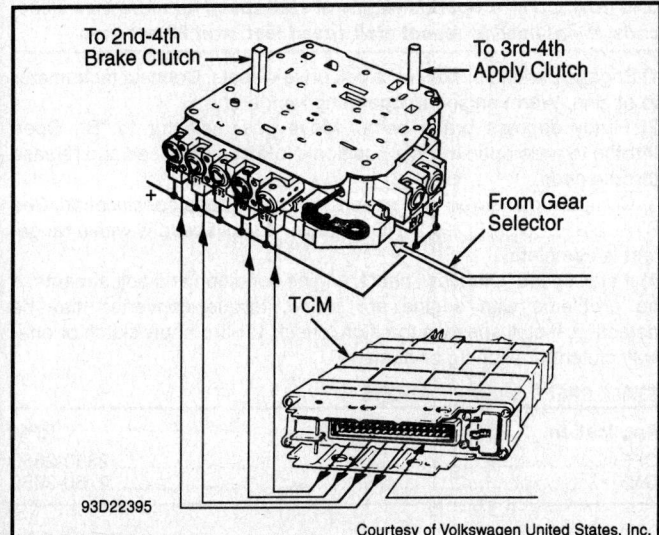

93D22395

Courtesy of Volkswagen United States, Inc.

Fig. 9: 4th Gear Oil Circuits

Functional Check – 1) With ignition key removed, ensure gear selector cannot be moved from Park. Insert key in ignition switch.
2) Turn ignition on. Ensure gear selector can only be moved with brake pedal pressed down. Move gear selector to Neutral position.
3) Without pressing brake pedal, ensure gear selector cannot move out of Neutral. Press brake pedal down. Ensure it is now possible to move gear selector.
4) If shift lock system does not operate as described, adjust gear selector, solenoid and control cable. If shift lock system does not operate after adjustments are made, check shift lock electrical system with Scan Tool (VAG 1551).
5) See testing information under ELECTRONIC SELF-DIAGNOSTICS. *See Figs. 17-24.* If any problems are found, service harness or components. If no problems are found, TCM may be defective. If shift lock system still does not operate correctly, check for worn or damaged parts and replace as necessary. *See Figs. 10 and 11.*

NOTE: *Perform the following adjustments in order given.*

Control Cable Adjustment – Loosen lock screw at gear selector lever on transaxle. Move gear selector in center console to Park position. Ensure front wheels are locked. Tighten cable housing to gear selector lever lock screw.

Shift Lock Solenoid Adjustment – Place gear selector in Neutral or Park. Loosen shift lock solenoid mounting screws. Insert a .019" (.30 mm) feeler gauge between shift lock solenoid push rod and shift lever. *See Fig. 12.* If necessary, move shift lock solenoid and tighten screws.

Shift Lock Cable Adjustment – 1) Move gear selector to "1" position. Remove steering column covers. Turn ignition key to Start position and release. Check clearance between shift lock cable lever and ignition switch locking pin.
2) Clearance should be .028" (.70 mm). If clearance is not correct, loosen lock nut on shift lock cable sheath. Position shift lock cable lever to obtain correct clearance. Tighten lock nut. *See Fig. 13.* Tighten gear selector housing screws and install steering column covers.

Removal & Installation (Control Cable) – Remove cover from center console. Remove circlip from control cable end. Remove exhaust covers. On V6 engines, remove catalytic converter. On all engines, loosen lock nut and remove control cable from shift lever on transaxle. To install, reverse removal procedure. Adjust control cable. See CONTROL CABLE ADJUSTMENT.

Removal & Installation (Shift Lock Cable) – 1) Remove shift lever handle. Remove center console cover. Disconnect negative battery cable and wait 30 seconds.
2) Using Torx wrench, remove air bag retaining screws from rear side of steering wheel. Lift off air bag unit from steering wheel, and tilt air bag unit downward. Disconnect wiring connector from air bag unit. Remove steering wheel. Remove dash panel.
3) Place gear selector in rear position. Loosen screw holding cable sheath to gear selector support. Remove cable from lever. *See Fig. 14.*
4) Remove cover from ignition switch. Remove spring clip holding cable housing to ignition assembly. Lift and tilt shift lock cable housing upward. Pull up shift lock cable until shift lock cable unhooks from ignition switch. *See Fig. 15.*
5) Remove shift-lock cable from under dash near A/C-heater housing and remove from vehicle. To install, position shift lock cable through under-dash panels. *See Fig. 16.* To complete installation, reverse removal procedure. Adjust shift lock control cable. See SHIFT LOCK CABLE ADJUSTMENT.

ELECTRONIC SELF-DIAGNOSTICS

RETRIEVING TROUBLE CODES

1) Electronic control consists of a TCM (located under rear seat), control solenoids, and various sensors and switches. TCM monitors input and output signals. *See Fig. 10.*
2) If TCM detects problems in transaxle-related circuits or devices, TCM may record a trouble code in memory. To retrieve obtain trouble codes, use Scan Tool (VAG 1551) and Adapter (VAG 1551/3). All trouble code and related testing information is contained in scan tool.

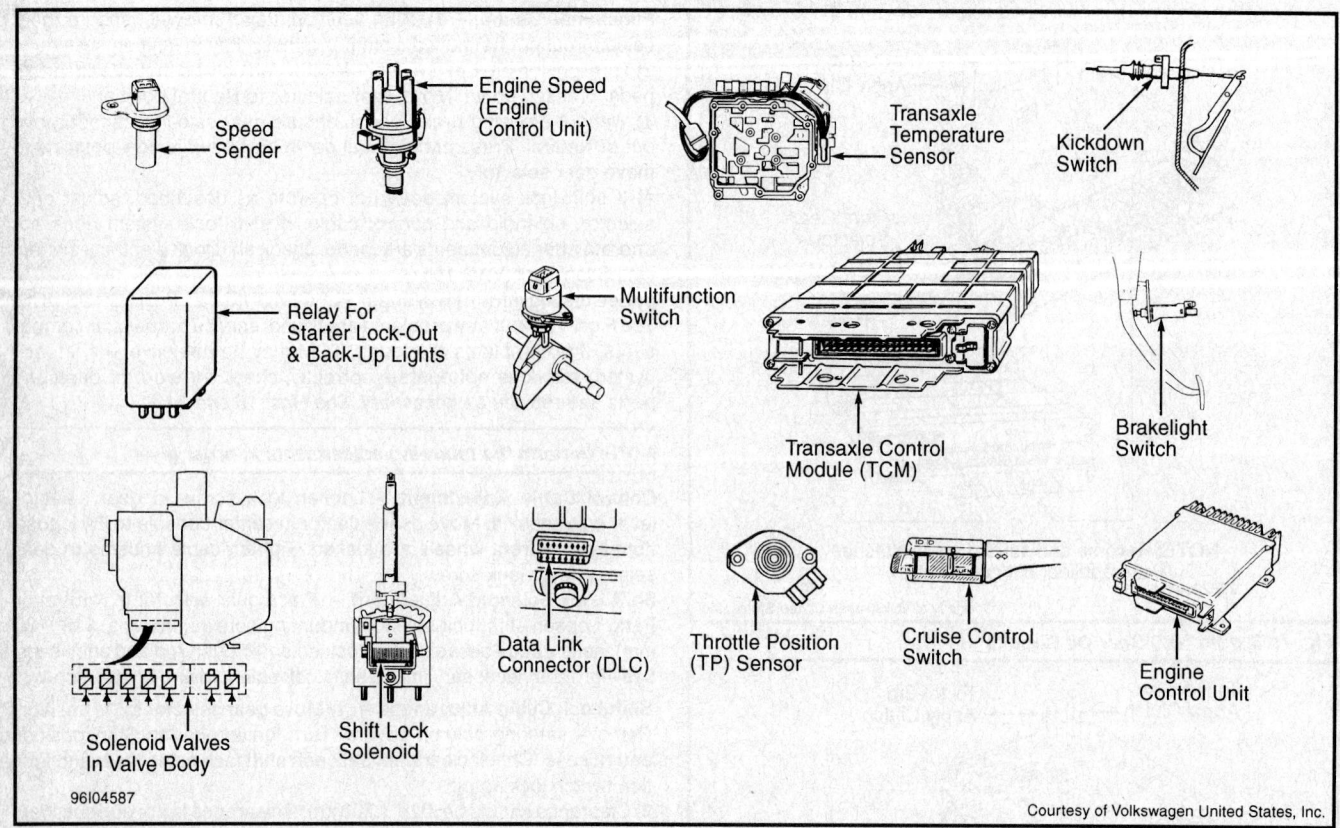

96I04587

Courtesy of Volkswagen United States, Inc.

Fig. 10: Identifying TCM & Shift Lock Electrical Components

TESTING

ELECTRICAL

NOTE: Manufacturer does not provide electrical component tests or specifications. All testing information is contained in Scan Tool (VAG 1551).

1) To isolate TCM circuit problems without a scan tool, circuit resistance and voltage can be checked using appropriate test box and adapter. For 38-pin TCM connectors, use Test Box (VAG 1598) and Adapter (VAG 1598/9). For 68-pin TCM connectors, use Test Box (VAG 1598/18).
2) When checking circuit voltage, leave battery connected with test box connected to TCM and TCM vehicle harness. When checking circuit resistance, disconnect negative battery cable and connect test box to TCM vehicle harness. Leave TCM disconnected.
3) Measure voltage and resistance between specified sockets on test box. *See Figs. 17-24.* If a problem is found, service harness or components. If no problem is found, TCM may be defective.

HYDRAULIC PRESSURE

Check operation of apply and brake clutches by air checking fluid passages of valve body and transaxle case. *See Figs. 3-9.* Install Pressure Gauge (VAG 1702) to transaxle pressure tap located near dipstick tube. Check main hydraulic pressure under normal driving conditions. See MAIN PRESSURE table. If main hydraulic pressures are not correct, check for incorrect idle speed, problem with pump or sticking valves in valve body. Repair as necessary.

MAIN PRESSURE

Application	psi (Bar)
"D"	
Idle RPM	49-55 (3.4-3.8)
2000 RPM [1]	146-164 (10.1-11.3)
"R"	
Idle RPM	94-109 (6.5-7.5)
2000 RPM [1]	334-348 (23.0-24.0)

[1] – With solenoid valve connector disconnected. After test, reconnect solenoid valves and using appropriate scan tool, erase trouble codes from memory.

STALL SPEED

CAUTION: DO NOT operate engine at stall speed for more than 5 seconds. If you need to repeat stall speed test, wait 20 seconds.

1) Engage parking brake and block drive wheels. Connect tachometer to engine. Warm engine to operating temperature.
2) Firmly depress brake pedal. Move gear selector to "D". Open throttle to wide open throttle position. Note engine speed and release throttle pedal.
3) Compare measured stall speed with stall speed specification. See STALL SPEED SPECIFICATIONS table. If stall speed is within range, test is complete.
4) If stall speed is too low, check engine condition and adjustments. If no problems with engine are found, torque converter may be defective. If stall speed is too high, check 1st-3rd apply clutch or one-way clutch for slipping or damage.

STALL SPEED SPECIFICATIONS

Application	RPM
CFF	2350-2650
CNK	2750-3050

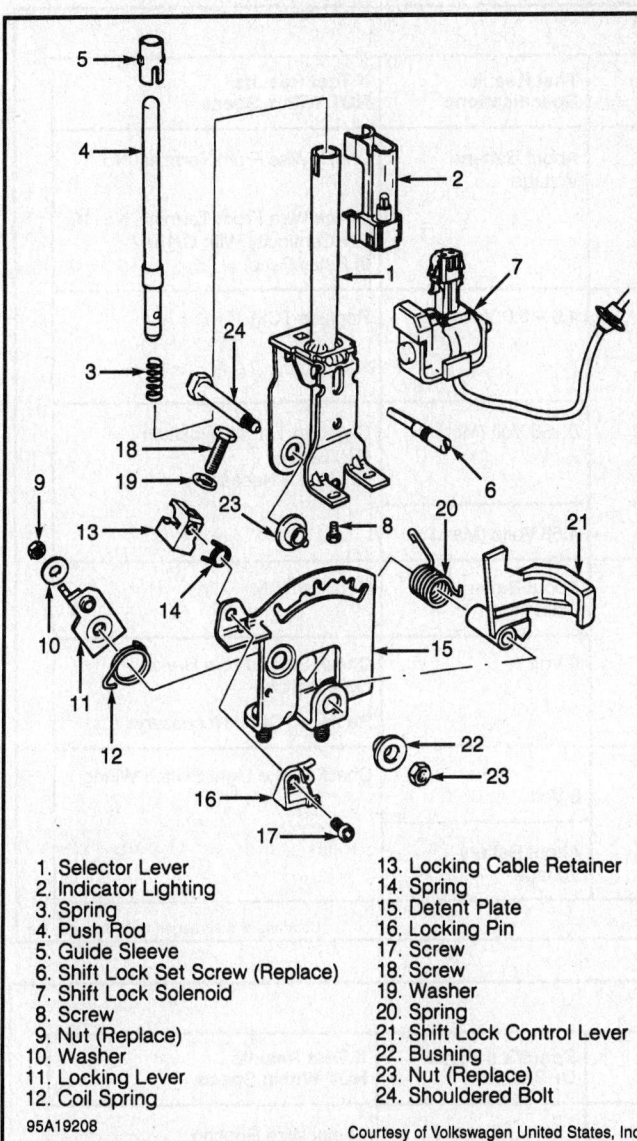

1. Selector Lever
2. Indicator Lighting
3. Spring
4. Push Rod
5. Guide Sleeve
6. Shift Lock Set Screw (Replace)
7. Shift Lock Solenoid
8. Screw
9. Nut (Replace)
10. Washer
11. Locking Lever
12. Coil Spring
13. Locking Cable Retainer
14. Spring
15. Detent Plate
16. Locking Pin
17. Screw
18. Screw
19. Washer
20. Spring
21. Shift Lock Control Lever
22. Bushing
23. Nut (Replace)
24. Shouldered Bolt

95A19208

Courtesy of Volkswagen United States, Inc.

Fig. 11: Exploded View Of Shift Lock & Gear Selector Assembly

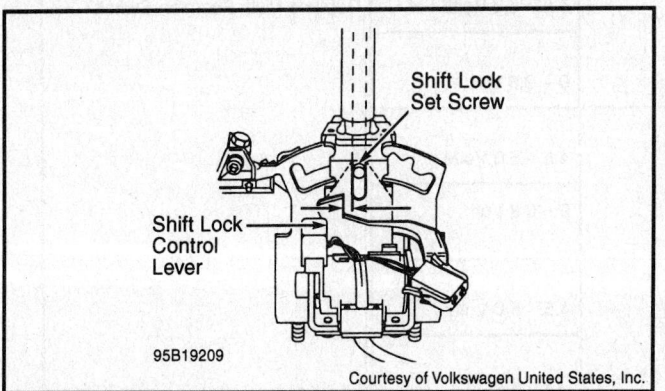

95B19209

Courtesy of Volkswagen United States, Inc.

Fig. 12: Adjusting Shift Lock Solenoid

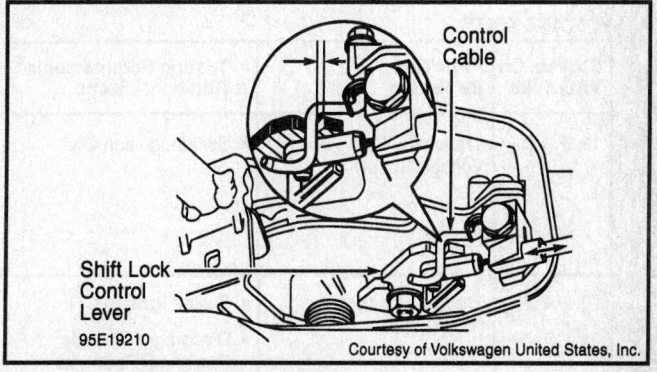

95E19210

Courtesy of Volkswagen United States, Inc.

Fig. 13: Adjusting Shift Lock Cable

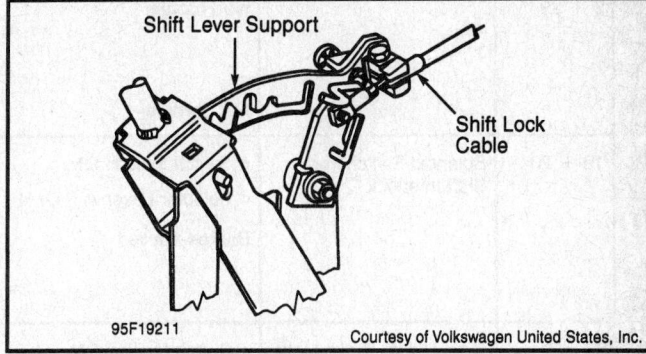

95F19211

Courtesy of Volkswagen United States, Inc.

Fig. 14: Removing Shift Lock Cable From Shift Lever Support

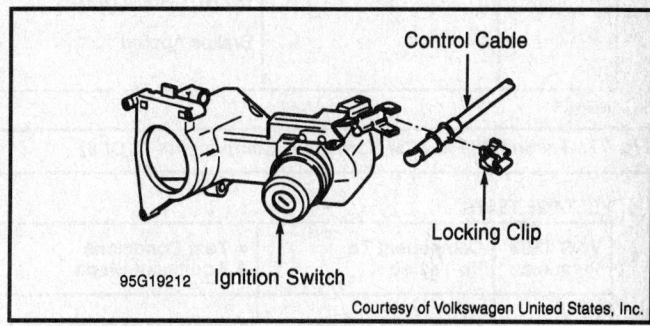

95G19212

Courtesy of Volkswagen United States, Inc.

Fig. 15: Removing Shift Lock Cable From Ignition Switch

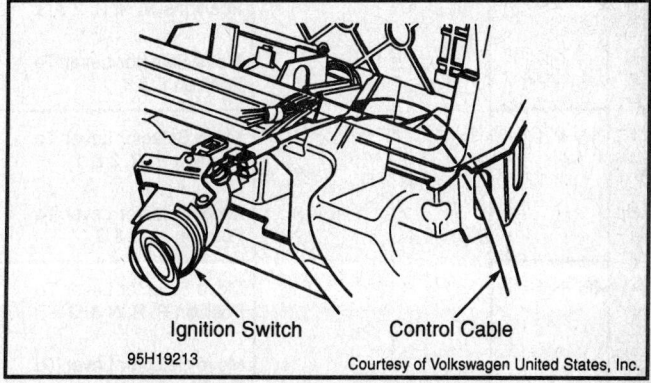

95H19213

Courtesy of Volkswagen United States, Inc.

Fig. 16: Routing Shift Lock Cable To Ignition Switch

VOLTAGE TESTS

Sockets On VAG 1598	Area To Be Tested	• Testing Requirements & Additional Steps	Test Result Specifications	If Test Results NOT Within Specs
19 + 1	Transaxle TCM Voltage Supply	• Switch Ignition ON	About Battery Voltage	Check Wire From Terminal No. 1 Check Wire From Terminal No. 19 For Continuity With C/15A In Relay Panel
10 + 29	Throttle Position (TP) Sensor	• Switch Ignition ON • Disconnect Throttle Position (TP) Sensor	4.6 – 5.0 Volts	Replace TCM
9 + 29		No Throttle	0.156 Volt (Min.)	Calibrate Throttle Position (TP) Sensor Replace If Necessary
		Full Throttle	4.68 Volts (Max.)	
19 + 20	Solenoid Switch For Shift Interlock	• Switch Ignition ON • Selector Lever In P Or N	.About Battery Voltage	Replace TCM
		Brakes Applied	0 Volt	Check Signal From Brake Light Switch Replace TCM If Necessary
26 + 1	Signal From Brake Light Switch	• Switch Ignition ON DO NOT Apply Brakes	0 Volt	Check Brake Light Switch Wiring
		Brakes Applied	About Battery Voltage	

96G04591

Courtesy of Volkswagen United States, Inc.

Fig. 17: Testing 38-Pin TCM Harness & Components (1 Of 8)

VOLTAGE TESTS

VAG 1598 Terminals	Component To Be Tested	• Test Conditions & Additional Steps	Specified Value Or Results	If Test Results NOT Within Specs
34 + 1	Multi-Function Switch	• Switch Ignition ON Move Selector Lever To Positions R, N, D, 2 & 3	4.5 – 5.0 Volts	Check Wire Routing Replace Multi-Function Switch
		Move Selector Lever To Position P & 1	0 – 0.8 Volt	
15 + 1		Move Selector Lever To Position P, R, 2 & 1	4.5 – 5.0 Volts	
		Move Selector Lever To Position N, D & 3	0 – 0.8 Volt	
35 + 1		Move Selector Lever To Position P, R, N & D	4.5 – 5.0 Volts	
		Move Selector Lever To Position 3, 2 & 1	0 – 0.8 Volt	
16 + 1		Move Selector Lever To Position R, R & N	About Battery Voltage	
		Move Selector Lever To Position D, 3, 2 & 1	0 – 0.8 Volt	

96I04592

Courtesy of Volkswagen United States, Inc.

Fig. 18: Testing 38-Pin TCM Harness & Components (2 Of 8)

RESISTANCE TESTS

Sockets On VAG 1598	Area To Be Tested	• Testing Requirements & Additional Steps	Test Result Specifications	If Test Results NOT Within Specs
22 + 18	Solenoid Valve No. 1	• Switch Ignition OFF	55 – 65 Ohms	Check Harness
22 + 1		TCM Disconnected	Open	Replace Valve Body
23 + 18	Solenoid Valve No. 2	• Switch Ignition OFF	55 – 65 Ohms	Check Harness
23 + 1		TCM Disconnected	Open	Replace Valve Body
3 + 18	Solenoid Valve No. 3	• Switch Ignition OFF	55 – 65 Ohms	Check Harness Routing
3 + 1		TCM Disconnected	Open	Replace Valve Body
2 + 18	Solenoid Valve No. 4	• Switch Ignition OFF	55 – 65 Ohms	Check Harness Routing
2 + 1		TCM Disconnected	Open	Replace Valve Body
24 + 18	Solenoid Valve No. 5	• Switch Ignition OFF	55 – 65 Ohms	Check Harness Routing
24 + 1		TCM Disconnected	Open	Replace Valve Body
25 + 18	Solenoid Valve No. 6	• Switch Ignition OFF	4.5 – 6.5 Ohms	Check Harness Routing
25 + 1		TCM Disconnected	Open	Replace Valve Body
21 + 18	Solenoid Valve No. 7	• Switch Ignition OFF	55 – 65 Ohms	Check Harness Routing
21 + 1		TCM Disconnected	Open	Replace Valve Body

96A04593

Courtesy of Volkswagen United States, Inc.

Fig. 19: Testing 38-Pin TCM Harness & Components (3 Of 8)

ON-VEHICLE SERVICE

DRIVE AXLE SHAFTS

See appropriate AXLE SHAFTS article in AXLE SHAFTS & TRANSFER CASES section.

OIL COOLER FLUSHING

1) Remove external oil filter. Remove oil lines and allow fluid to drain. Using pressurized solvent, flush remaining fluid and debris from oil lines and cooler. Repeat flushing if necessary.
2) Use pressurized shop air to remove solvent from oil lines and oil cooler. Install a new external oil filter.

TRANSAXLE COMPONENTS

Following components may be serviced with transaxle in vehicle. For removal and installation procedures, see TRANSAXLE DISASSEMBLY.
• Drive Flanges
• External Oil Filter
• Gear Selector Lever
• Multifunction Switch, Speedometer Drive Shaft & Speed Sensor
• Oil Pan & Valve Body Assembly
• Planetary Gear Cover

REMOVAL & INSTALLATION

See appropriate AUTOMATIC TRANSMISSION REMOVAL article in TRANSMISSION SERVICING section.

TORQUE CONVERTER

1) Remove torque converter. Check torque converter for any wear or damage, and replace if necessary. If torque converter is being reused, drain old fluid.
2) Slightly tilt torque converter on bench. Place a .53-gallon (2.0L) plastic bottle below torque converter.
3) Create a small round hole in bottle cap. Ensure outside diameter of a small hose fits tightly in bottle cap. Insert hose into bottle cap, and install cap and hose on bottle.
4) Squeeze bottle and place other end of hose into torque converter. Release bottle and allow fluid to drain in bottle. Loosen bottle cap, and allow remaining fluid to siphon into bottle.

TRANSAXLE DISASSEMBLY

TRANSMISSION ASSEMBLY

1) Remove torque converter. Remove oil pan and valve body assembly. Remove sealing plug from transaxle case. See Figs. 25 and 27.
2) Measure and record turbine shaft end play. See Fig. 26. Remove oil pump bolts. Using two M8 bolts, remove oil pump from front of transaxle. See Fig. 29.
3) Remove turbine shaft complete with 2nd-4th brake clutch, support tube, 1st-3rd and reverse apply clutch assemblies. Remove impeller shaft and 3rd-4th apply clutch assembly. See Figs. 28 and 30.
4) Remove planetary cover from transaxle case. Engage parking gear. Using a screwdriver, lock small sun gear drive shell to large sun gear drive shell. See Fig. 31. Remove bolt from end of small planetary drive shaft, and remove shaft.
5) Remove small sun gear drive shell, large sun gear drive shell, circlips and one-way clutch. Remove planetary carrier and bearing assembly. Remove reverse brake clutch assembly. See Figs. 28, 32 and 33. DO NOT remove input gear assembly, unless bearing or gear damage is present. See Fig. 33.

RESISTANCE TESTS

VAG 1598 Terminals	Component To Be Tested	• Test Conditions & Additional Steps	Specified Value Or Results	If Test Results NOT Within Specs
19 + 20	Solenoid Switch for Shift Interlock	• Switch Ignition OFF • TCM Disconnected	14 – 25 Ohms	Check Harness Routing Replace Shift Interlock Solenoid Assembly
1 + 17	Kickdown Switch	• Switch Ignition OFF • TCM Disconnected DO NOT Press Accelerator Pedal Depress Accelerator Fully	 Open Less Than 1.5 Ohms	Check Harness Routing Adjust Or Replace Accelerator Cable
32 + 33	Vehicle Speed Sensor	• Switch Ignition OFF • TCM Disconnected • Set Ohmmeter To 2 k/ohm Scale	800 – 900 Ohms	Check Harness Routing Replace Vehicle Speed Sensor
36 + 1	Program Switch	• Switch Ignition OFF • TCM Disconnected • Set Ohmmeter To 200-Ohm Scale Program Switch Not Activated Program Switch Activated	 Open Less Than 1.5 Ohms	Check Harness Routing Replace Program Switch
30 + 18	ATF Temperature Sensor	• Switch Ignition OFF • TCM Disconnected • Set Ohmmeter To 200 k/ohm Scale ATF Temperature 68°F (20°C) ATF Temperature 140°F (60°C) ATF Temperature 248°F (120°C)	 About 24,700 Ohms About 48,800 Ohms About 7400 Ohms	Check Harness Routing Replace Valve Body

96C04594

Courtesy of Volkswagen United States, Inc.

Fig. 20: Testing 38-Pin TCM Harness & Components (4 Of 8)

RESISTANCE TESTS

VAG 1598/18 Terminals	Component To Be Tested	• Test Conditions & Additional Steps	Specified Value Or Results	If Test Results NOT Within Specs
20 + 65	Vehicle Speed Sensor	• Switch Ignition OFF • TCM Disconnected • Set Ohmmeter To 2 k-Ohm Scale	800 – 900 Ohms	Check Harness Routing Replace Vehicle Speed Sensor
6 + 67	ATF Temperature Sensor	• Switch Ignition OFF • TCM Disconnected • Set Ohmmeter To 200 k-Ohm Scale ATF Temperature 68°F (20°C) Set Ohmmeter to 200 k-Ohm scale ATF Temperature 140°F (60°C) ATF Temperature 248°F (120°C)	 24,700 Ohms About 48,800 Ohms About 7400 Ohms	Check Harness Routing Replace Valve Body

96F04595

Courtesy of Volkswagen United States, Inc.

Fig. 21: Testing 68-Pin TCM Harness & Components (5 Of 8)

RESISTANCE TESTS

VAG 1598/18 Terminals	Component To Be Tested	• Test Conditions & Additional Steps	Specified Value Or Results	If Test Results NOT Within Specs
63 + 1	Multi-Function Switch	• Switch Ignition OFF		Check Wire Routing
		Move Selector Lever To Positions R, N, D, 2 & 3	Open	Replace Multi-Function Switch
		Move Selector Lever To Position P & 1	.8 – 1.0 Ohms	
40 + 1		Move Selector Lever To Position P, R, 2 & 1	Open	
		Move Selector Lever To Position N, D & 3	.8 – 1.0 Ohms	
62 + 1		• Switch Ignition ON		
		Move Selector Lever To Position P, R, N & D	Open	
		Move Selector Lever To Position 3, 2 & 1	.8 – 1.0 Ohms	
18 + 1		• Switch Ignition ON		
		Move Selector Lever To Position P, R & N	About Battery Voltage	
		Move Selector Lever To Position D, 3, 2 & 1	0 Volt	
55 + 67	Solenoid Valve No. 1	• Switch Ignition OFF	55 – 65 Ohms	Check Harness
55 + 1		Control Unit Removed	Open	Replace Valve Body
54 + 67	Solenoid Valve No. 2	• Switch Ignition OFF	55 – 65 Ohms	Check Harness
54 + 1		Control Unit Removed	Open	Replace Valve Body

96H04596

Courtesy of Volkswagen United States, Inc.

Fig. 22: Testing 68-Pin TCM Harness & Components (6 Of 8)

FINAL DRIVE & TRANSFER GEARS

1) Drain gear oil. Attach INCH-lb. torque wrench to a 1 5/8" (41 mm) socket wrench. See Fig. 58. Measure and record total roller bearing turning torque of drive pinion gear. This measurement is required for reassembly reference if roller bearings are reused.
2) Engage parking pawl. Using a 7/8" (22 mm) Allen wrench socket, remove fastener nut. See Fig. 35. Remove dished washer, bearing and shim.
3) Install fastener nut. Using Pressing Adapter (VW771), thread tool until 1/8" clearance is present between bearing race and fastener nut.
4) Pull input gear out until it bottoms in pressing adapter. Remove pressing adapter. Remove input transfer gear assembly from transaxle case.
5) Remove speedometer drive shaft. See Fig. 34. On left axle flange, remove bolt and remove axle flange. On right axle flange, remove circlip. Using puller, remove right axle flange.
6) Remove differential ring gear cover. If bearings are being reused, mark differential adjuster ring (torque converter side) bearing carrier to transaxle case. Using Bearing Adjuster Ring Socket (3155), remove both differential bearing carriers. See Fig. 36. Remove differential assembly from transaxle case. See Fig. 34.

NOTE: Differential bearing carrier on left (torque converter) side is tightened to 111 ft. lbs. (150 N.m).

7) Remove drive pinion and input transfer gear cover (if not already removed). See Fig. 33. Using INCH-lb. torque wrench, measure turning force of drive pinion and transfer gear bearings. Record measurement for reassembly.
8) Engage parking pawl. Remove nut from pinion. See Fig. 37. Using puller, remove output gear. See Fig. 38. Remove selector shaft and parking pawl assembly. See Fig. 48. Remove outer bearing support. Remove parking gear from pinion. Remove pinion and bearing from transaxle. Using pin socket, remove inner bearing support with drive pinion seal.

COMPONENT DISASSEMBLY & REASSEMBLY

FINAL DRIVE

1) Disassemble differential. See Fig. 39. If ring gear or differential housing is damaged, replace differential housing. To reassemble differential, reverse disassembly.

RESISTANCE TESTS

Sockets On VAG 1598/18	Area To Be Tested	• Testing Requirements & Additional Steps	Test Result Specifications	If Test Results NOT Within Specs
9 + 67	Solenoid Valve No. 3	• Switch Ignition OFF	55 – 65 Ohms	Check Harness Routing
9 + 1		TCM Disconnected	Open	Replace Valve Body
47 + 67	Solenoid Valve No. 4	• Switch Ignition OFF	55 – 65 Ohms	Check Harness Routing
47 + 1		TCM Disconnected	Ohms	Replace Valve Body
56 + 67	Solenoid Valve No. 5	• Switch Ignition OFF	55 – 65 Ohms	Check Harness Routing
56 + 1		TCM Disconnected	Open	Replace Valve Body
58 + 22	Solenoid Valve No. 6	• Switch Ignition OFF	4.5 – 6.5 Ohms	Check Harness Routing
58 + 1/22 + 1		TCM Disconnected	Open	Replace Valve Body
10 + 67	Solenoid Valve No. 7	• Switch Ignition OFF	55 – 65 Ohms	Check Harness Routing
10 + 1		TCM Disconnected	Open	Replace Valve Body
23 + 29	Solenoid Switch for Shift Interlock	• Switch Ignition OFF, TCM Disconnected	14 – 25 Ohms	Check Harness Routing, Replace Shiftlock Solenoid Assembly
1 + 16	Kickdown Switch	• Switch Ignition OFF, • TCM Disconnected, DO NOT Press Accelerator Pedal	Open	Check Harness Routing, Adjust Or Replace Accelerator Cable
		Depress Accelerator Fully	Less Than 1.5 Ohms	

96J04597

Courtesy of Volkswagen United States, Inc.

Fig. 23: Testing 68-Pin TCM Harness & Components (7 Of 8)

NOTE: If differential bearings are replaced, check differential side bearing preload and ring gear position. See FINAL DRIVE & TRANSFER GEARS under TRANSAXLE REASSEMBLY.

2) Using puller, remove roller bearing from differential housing. Remove speedometer drive gear and bushing.
3) Check all bearing races in adjuster rings and replace if necessary. Using hydraulic press, replace bearing race(s). Replace each roller bearing and race as a set.

OIL PUMP & 2ND-4TH BRAKE CLUTCH PISTON

Disassemble oil pump and 2nd-4th brake clutch piston. Check for worn or damaged parts and replace as necessary. Replace all seals and reassemble. See Fig. 40.

NOTE: Specifications are not available from manufacturer.

ONE-WAY CLUTCH

1) Disassemble one-way clutch. Check for worn or damaged parts and replace as necessary. Compress each spring and install into cage. See Fig. 41.
2) Hold cage assembly with large lugs up. Install cage assembly into outer ring. See Figs. 42-44. Rotate cage clockwise until lugs touch stop. Install piston into outer ring.

PLANETARY CARRIER

NOTE: Disassembly and reassembly procedures are not available from manufacturer.

Inspection & Adjustment – 1) Inspect planetary carrier, pinion gears, sun gears and related parts for wear or damage. Replace parts as necessary.
2) Assemble sun gear drive shells, planetary carrier, small sun gear, pinion drive transfer gear and all related bearings and washers onto small planetary drive shaft. See Fig. 45.
3) Place assembly into transaxle case. Install adjustment shim, washer and bolt to pinion drive transfer gear end of small planetary drive shaft. Using a screwdriver, lock small sun gear drive shell to large sun gear drive shell. See Fig. 31. Tighten bolt to 22 ft. lbs. (30 N.m).
4) Place Dial Indicator Support (VW 382/7) on top of assembly. See Fig. 46. Measure end play of small sun gear drive shaft.
5) If end play is not .009-.014 (.23-.37 mm), replace adjustment shim. Adjustment shims range in thickness from .040" (1.00 mm) to .114" (2.90 mm) in .004" (.10 mm) increments.

RESISTANCE & VOLTAGE TESTS

Sockets On VAG 1598/18	Area To Be Tested	• Testing Requirements & Additional Steps	Test Result Specifications	If Test Results NOT Within Specs
23 + 1	Transaxle TCM Voltage Supply	• Switch Ignition ON	About Battery Voltage	Check Wire From Terminal No. 1 Check Wire From Terminal No. 23 For Continuity With C/15A In Relay Panel
5 + 28	Throttle Position (TP) Sensor	• Switch Ignition OFF No Throttle Full Throttle	 700-1800 Ohms 2100-3900 Ohms	Check Wiring Calibrate Throttle Position (TP) Sensor
5 + 50	Throttle Position (TP) Sensor	• Switch Ignition OFF No Throttle Full Throttle	 2100-3900 Ohms 700-1800 Ohms	Check Wiring Calibrate Throttle Position (TP) Sensor
29 + 15	Solenoid Switch For Shift Interlock	• Switch Ignition ON • Selector Lever In P Or N Brakes Applied	About Battery Voltage About 0.2 Volt	Check Wiring Replace Shiftlock Solenoid
15 + 1	Signal From Brake Light Switch	• Switch Ignition ON DO NOT Apply Brakes Brakes Applied	0 Volt About Battery Voltage	Check Wiring Replace Brake Light Switch

96B04598

Courtesy of Volkswagen United States, Inc.

Fig. 24: Testing 68-Pin TCM Harness & Components (8 Of 8)

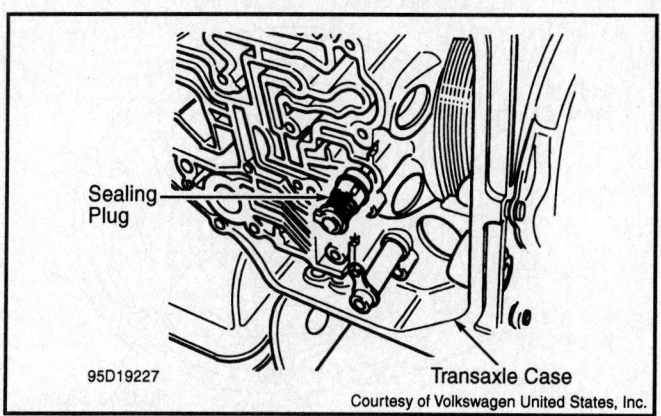

Sealing Plug

Transaxle Case

95D19227

Courtesy of Volkswagen United States, Inc.

Fig. 25: Locating Sealing Plug

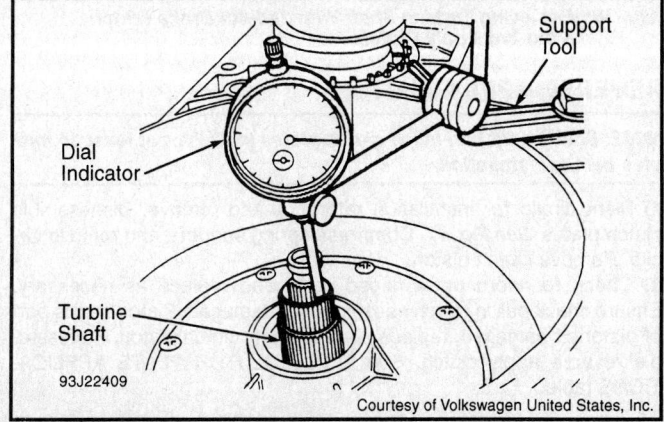

Support Tool

Dial Indicator

Turbine Shaft

93J22409

Courtesy of Volkswagen United States, Inc.

Fig. 26: Checking Turbine Shaft End Play

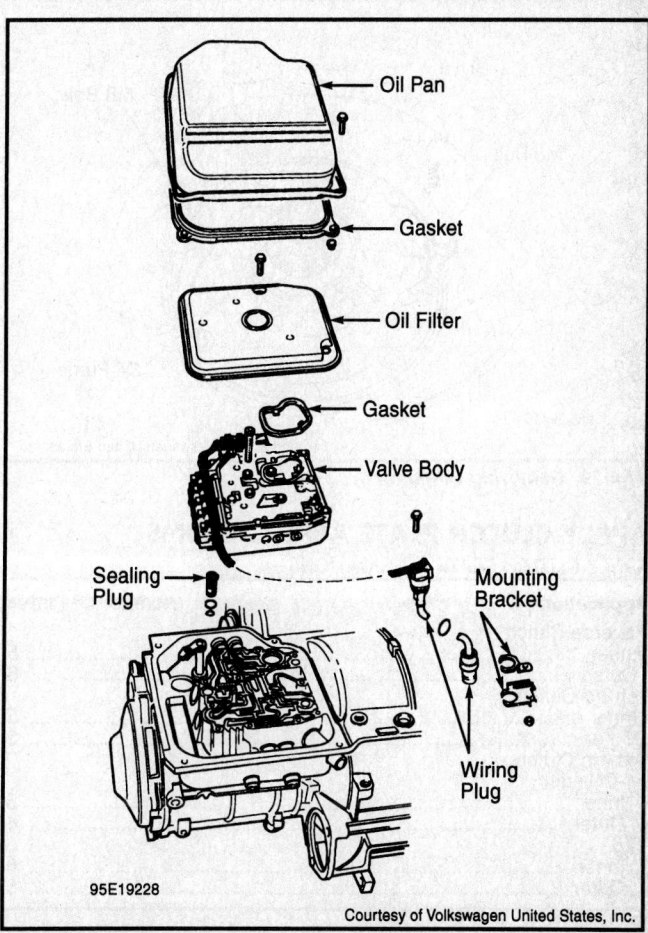

Oil Pan

Gasket

Oil Filter

Gasket

Valve Body

Sealing Plug

Mounting Bracket

Wiring Plug

95E19228

Courtesy of Volkswagen United States, Inc.

Fig. 27: Exploded View Of Oil Pan & Valve Body

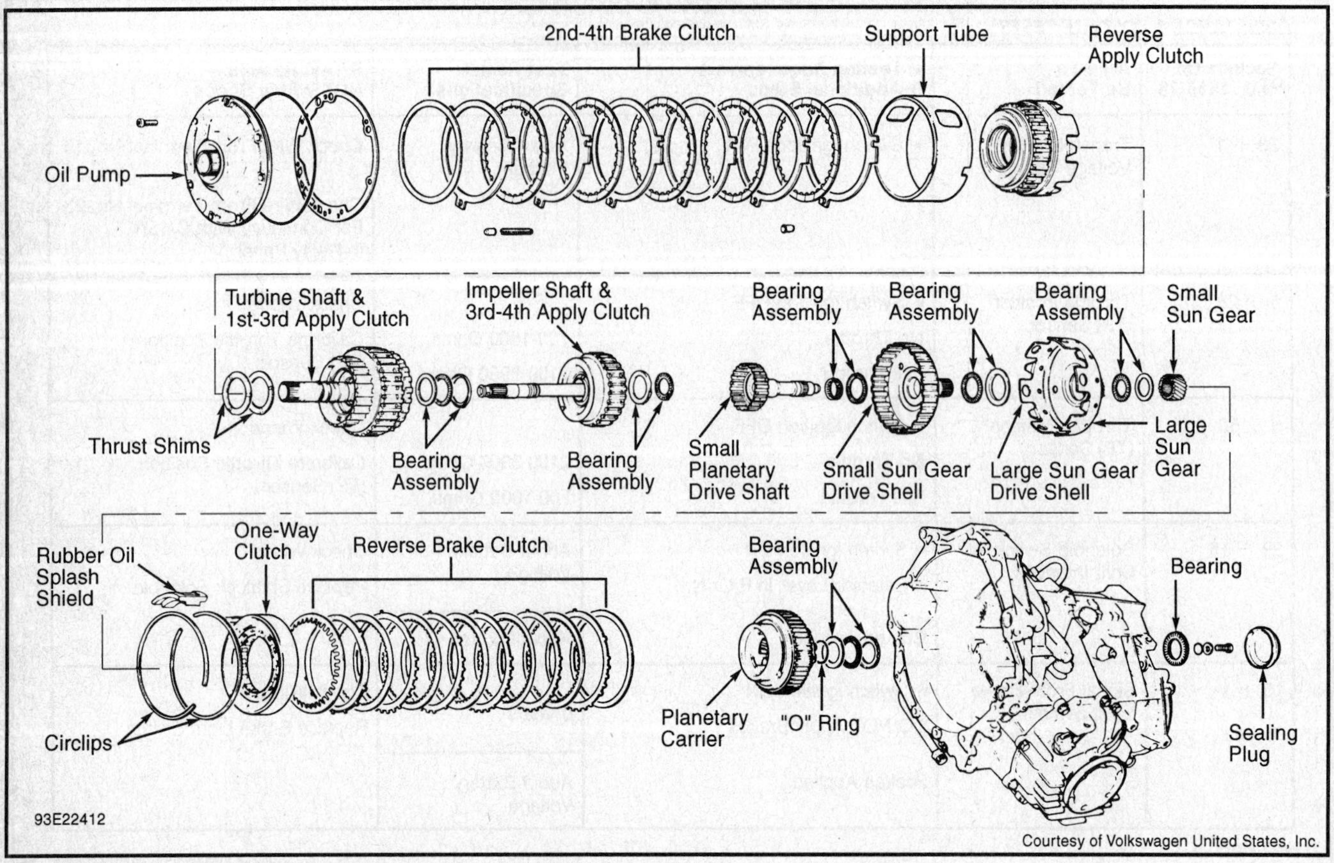

AUTOMATIC TRANSMISSIONS
Volkswagen Model 096 (Cont.)

Fig. 28: Exploded View Of Transmission Components (097 Is Shown As Example; 096 Is Similar)

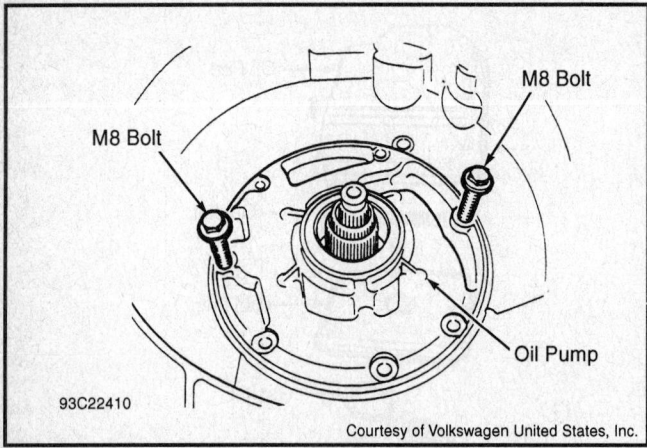

Fig. 29: Removing Oil Pump

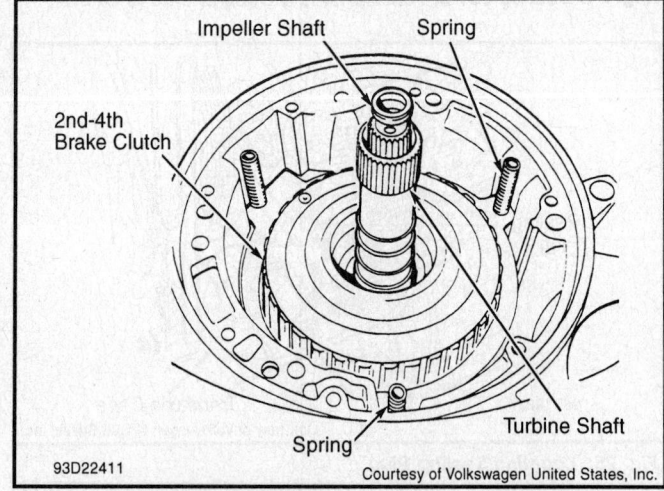

Fig. 30: Removing Turbine Shaft With 2nd-4th Brake Clutch & 1st-3rd Apply Clutch

APPLY CLUTCH PLATE APPLICATIONS

APPLY CLUTCH PLATE APPLICATIONS

Application	Number Of Plates
Reverse Clutch	
Inner	5
Outer	5
1st-3rd Clutch	
Inner	5
Outer	5
3rd-4th Clutch	
4-Cylinder	
Inner	5
Outer	4
V6	
Inner	6
Outer	5

REVERSE APPLY CLUTCH

NOTE: Soak all friction-faced clutch plates in ATF for at least 15 minutes before installation.

1) Mark circlip for installation reference and remove. Disassemble clutch plates. *See Fig. 47.* Compress spring support, and remove circlip. Remove clutch piston.

2) Check for worn or damaged parts and replace as necessary. Ensure check ball in clutch housing is not damaged. Piston seal is part of piston. If damaged, replace reverse apply clutch piston. Reassemble reverse apply clutch. See APPLY CLUTCH PLATE APPLICATIONS table.

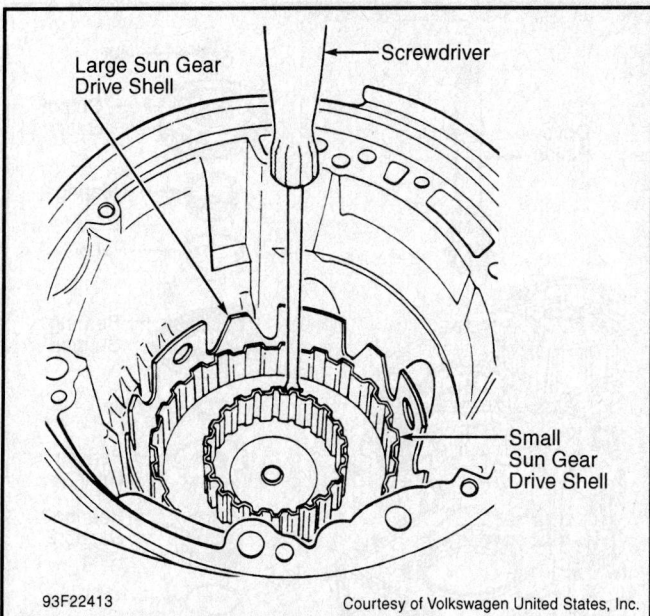

Fig. 31: Locking Small Sun Gear Drive Shell

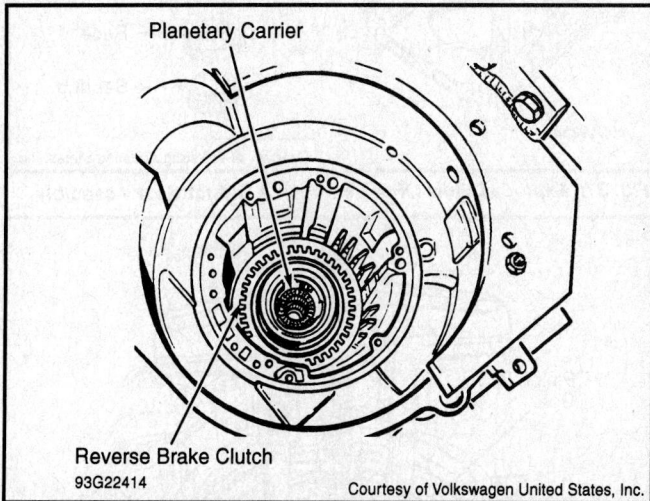

Fig. 32: Removing Planetary Carrier & Reverse Brake Clutch

NOTE: Assembled clutch clearance specification is not available from manufacturer. Ensure thrust plate is installed with shouldered side facing circlip.

REVERSE & 2ND-4TH BRAKE CLUTCHES

Reverse and 2nd-4th brake clutches are disassembled and reassembled during transaxle disassembly and reassembly. See TRANSAXLE DISASSEMBLY and TRANSAXLE REASSEMBLY.

TRANSAXLE CASE

1) Remove multifunction switch, all seals, manual valve assembly, parking pawl and sensors. If necessary, remove parking pawl pin, detent spring screws and selector rod for manual valve from case. See Fig. 48. Inspect bushings and bearing races, and replace if necessary.
2) Install new "O" ring to gear change shaft. Install gear change shaft. Install parking pawl pin (if removed). Using a center punch, peen parking pawl pin. Install operating rod for manual valve, detent spring screws, multifunction switch and new seals.

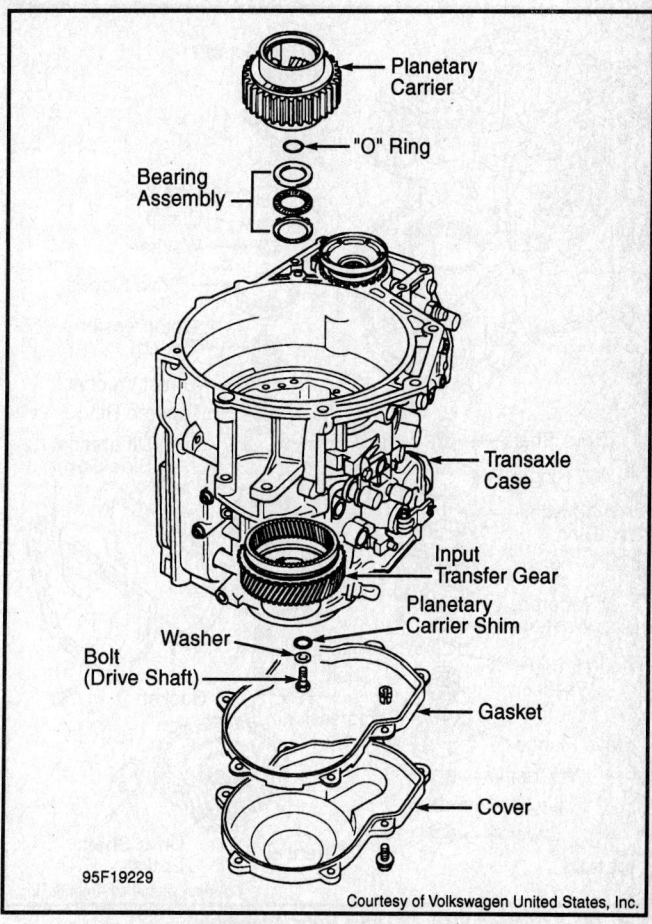

Fig. 33: Locating Planetary & Input Gear Assembly

TRANSFER GEARS

Using puller and adapter, remove tapered bearing from output gear. See Fig. 49. Using hydraulic press, install bearing to drive pinion transfer gear. Set transfer and drive pinion gears aside.

VALVE BODY

NOTE: Disassembly and reassembly procedures are not available from manufacturer.

1ST & 3RD APPLY CLUTCH

1) Remove support ring. Mark circlip for installation reference, and remove circlip. Disassemble clutch plates. See Fig. 50. Remove diaphragm spring circlip. Compress spring support, and remove circlip. See Fig. 51. Remove spring plates and clutch piston.
2) Remove piston rings from piston. Piston seal is part of piston. If damaged, replace 1st-3rd apply clutch piston. Remove seal rings from turbine shaft. Check for worn or damaged parts and replace as necessary. Ensure check ball in clutch housing is not damaged.
3) Install new seal rings to clutch piston, and install piston in clutch housing. Install plate springs. Compress spring support and install circlip. See Fig. 51.
4) Install bottom thrust plate with smooth side facing clutch plate. Install one inner splined and one outer splined clutch plate into clutch housing. See Fig. 50.
5) Place inner plate carrier on bench. Install remaining clutch plates to inner plate carrier. See APPLY CLUTCH PLATE APPLICATIONS. Insert top thrust plate with smooth side facing clutch plate. Install support ring with step tabs up after installing thrust plate, friction plates and steel plates. See Fig. 52.
6) Install inner plate carrier into clutch housing. Install circlip in clutch housing. See Fig. 53.

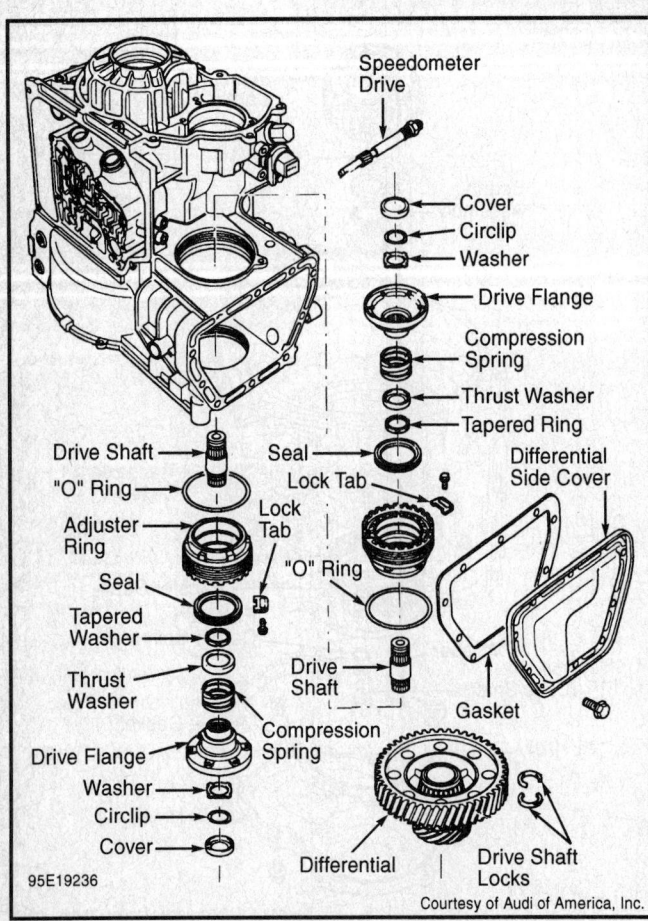

Fig. 34: Exploded View Of Drive Gear Assembly

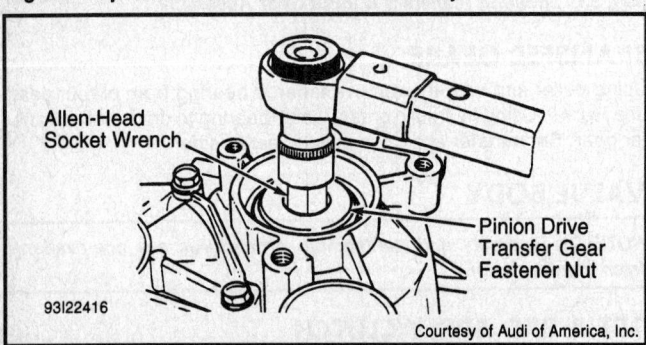

Fig. 35: Removing Input Transfer Gear Fastener Nut (097 Is Shown As Example; 096 Is Similar)

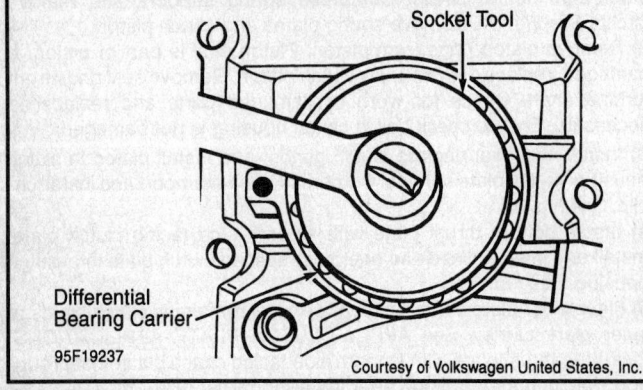

Fig. 36: Removing Bearing Adjuster Ring Bearing Carrier

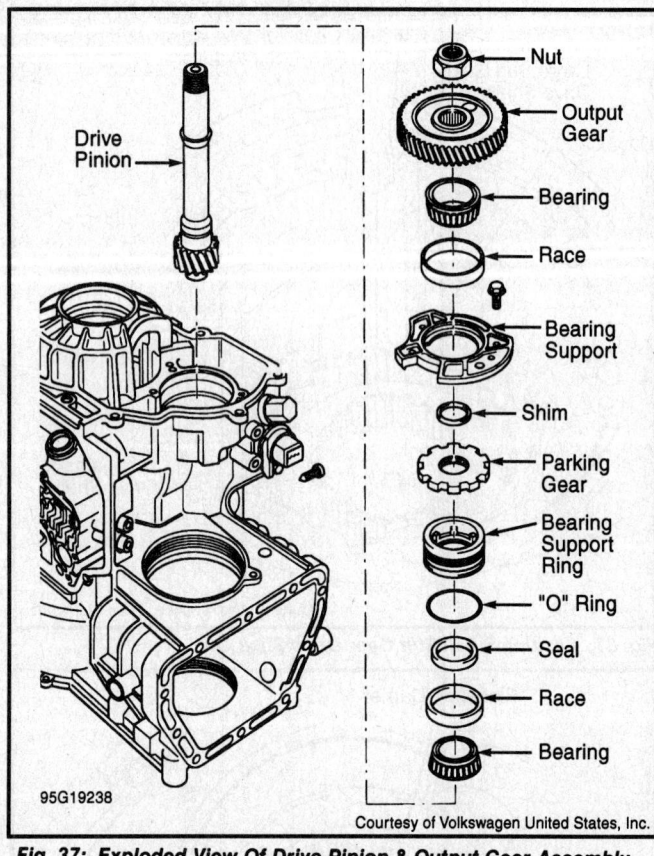

Courtesy of Volkswagen United States, Inc.

Fig. 37: Exploded View Of Drive Pinion & Output Gear Assembly

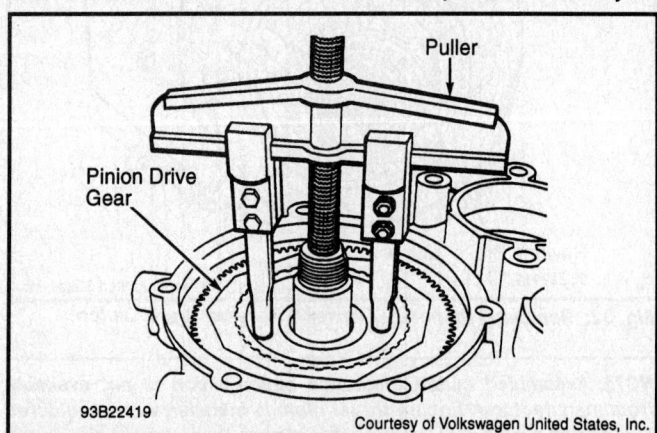

Courtesy of Volkswagen United States, Inc.

Fig. 38: Removing Pinion Drive Gear

3RD-4TH APPLY CLUTCH

NOTE: Soak all friction-faced clutch plates in ATF for at least 15 minutes before installation.

1) Mark circlip for installation reference and remove. Disassemble clutch plates. See Fig. 54. Compress spring support ring, and remove circlip. Remove spring support ring and spring. Remove clutch piston.
2) Remove front impeller seal rings. DO NOT remove inner impeller seal rings unless damaged. Check for worn or damaged parts and replace as necessary.
3) Piston seal is part of piston. If damaged, replace 3rd-4th apply clutch piston. Reassemble 3rd-4th apply clutch. See APPLY CLUTCH PLATE APPLICATIONS table.

NOTE: Assembled clutch clearance specification is not available from manufacturer. Ensure top thrust plate is installed with shouldered side facing circlip.

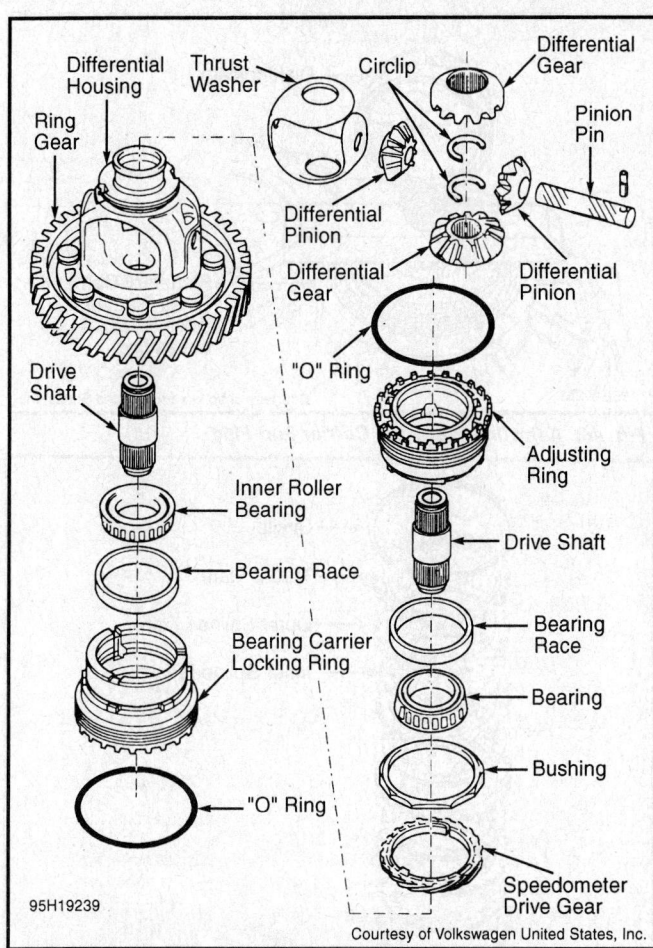

Fig. 39: Exploded View Of Differential

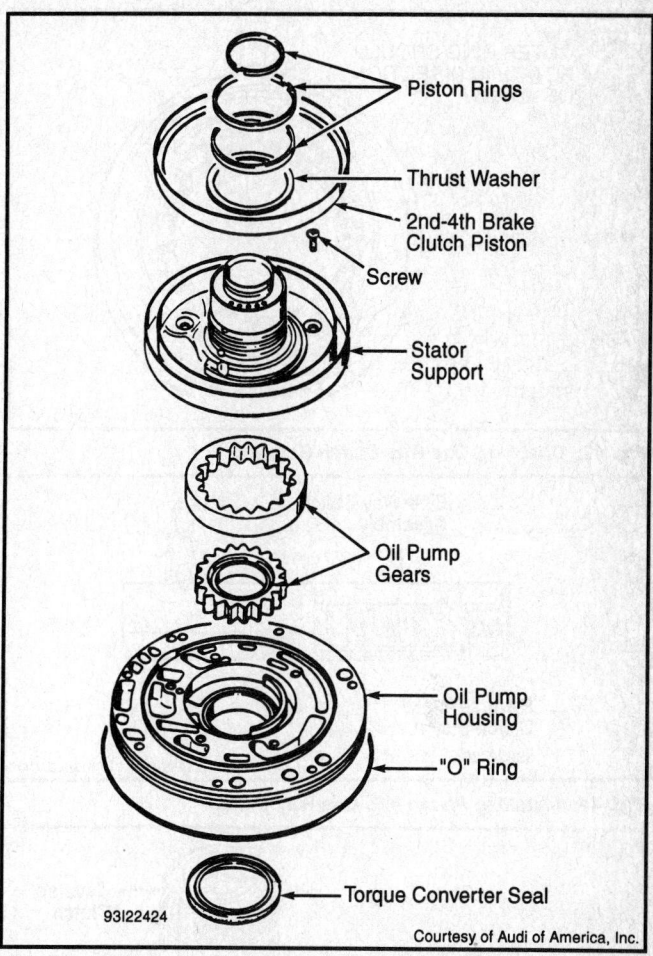

Fig. 40: Exploded View Of Oil Pump & 2nd-4th Brake Clutch Piston

TRANSAXLE REASSEMBLY

FINAL DRIVE & TRANSFER GEARS

NOTE: Reassembly procedures include bearing and shim adjustments. Perform all steps in the order given. If no parts were replaced, skip adjustment steps and reassemble final drive and transfer gear assembly using new seals. Ensure turning torque of complete assembly is within specifications. See INPUT TRANSFER GEAR ADJUSTMENT & REASSEMBLY procedure. If turning torque is not within specifications, check all adjustments.

Drive Pinion Roller Bearing Adjustment – 1) Install drive pinion assembly with smaller bearing and inner bearing support (with pinion seal and "O" ring). Install parking gear (rounded side facing drive pinion gear), park lock lug and large pinion bearing race support. Go to next step.

NOTE: Install drive pinion seal with lip opening facing closest roller bearing.

2) If reusing drive pinion and large pinion bearing, DO NOT remove existing shims from drive pinion shaft. *See Fig. 56.* Go to step **4)**. If replacing drive pinion and/or pinion bearings, install large pinion roller bearing to drive pinion. Go to next step.

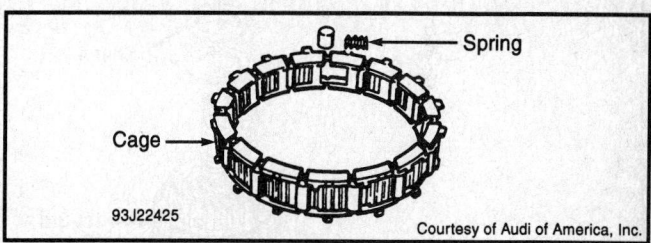

Fig. 41: Installing Springs Into Cage

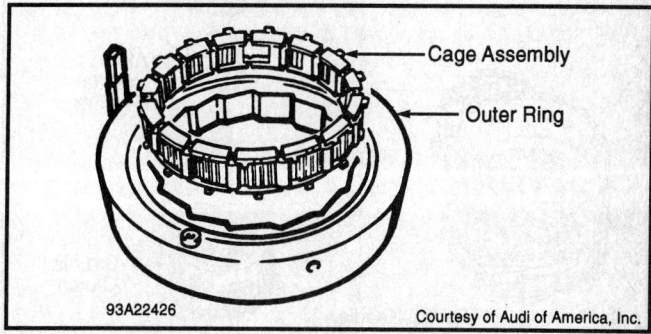

Fig. 42: Installing Cage Assembly Into Outer Ring

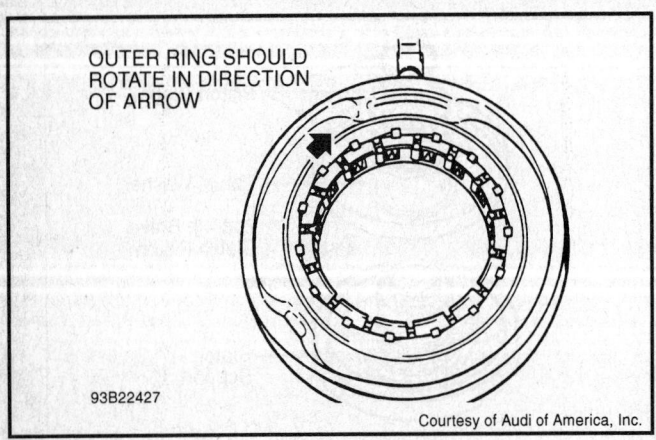

OUTER RING SHOULD
ROTATE IN DIRECTION
OF ARROW

93B22427

Courtesy of Audi of America, Inc.

Fig. 43: Checking One-Way Clutch Rotation

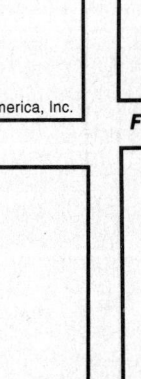

One-Way Clutch
Assembly

Reverse Brake
Clutch Piston

93C22428

Courtesy of Audi of America, Inc.

Fig. 44: Installing Piston Into One-Way Clutch

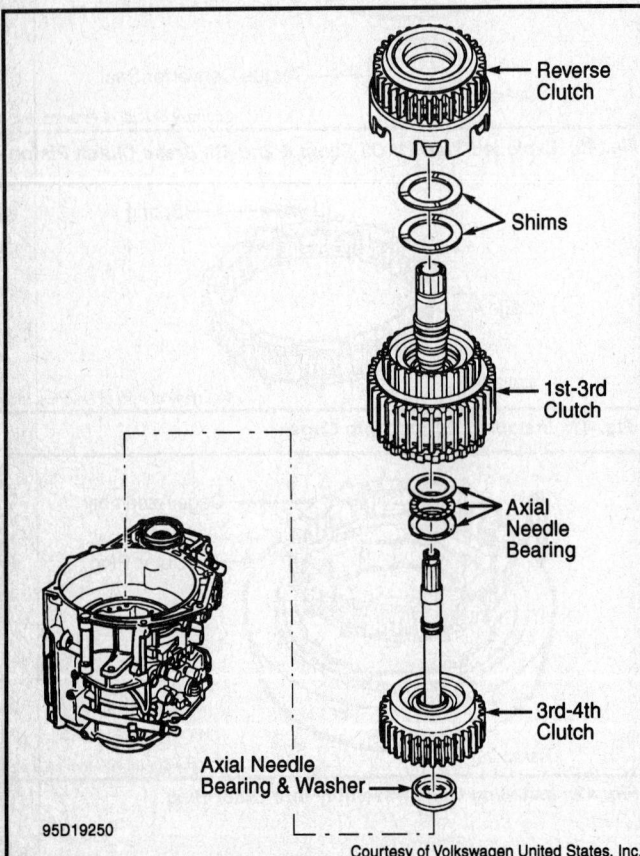

Reverse
Clutch

Shims

1st-3rd
Clutch

Axial
Needle
Bearing

3rd-4th
Clutch

Axial Needle
Bearing & Washer

95D19250

Courtesy of Volkswagen United States, Inc.

Fig. 45: Locating Planetary Carrier Elements

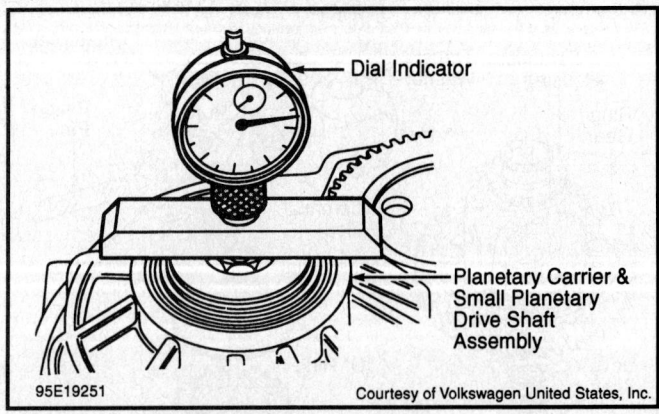

Dial Indicator

Planetary Carrier &
Small Planetary
Drive Shaft
Assembly

95E19251

Courtesy of Volkswagen United States, Inc.

Fig. 46: Adjusting Planetary Carrier End Play

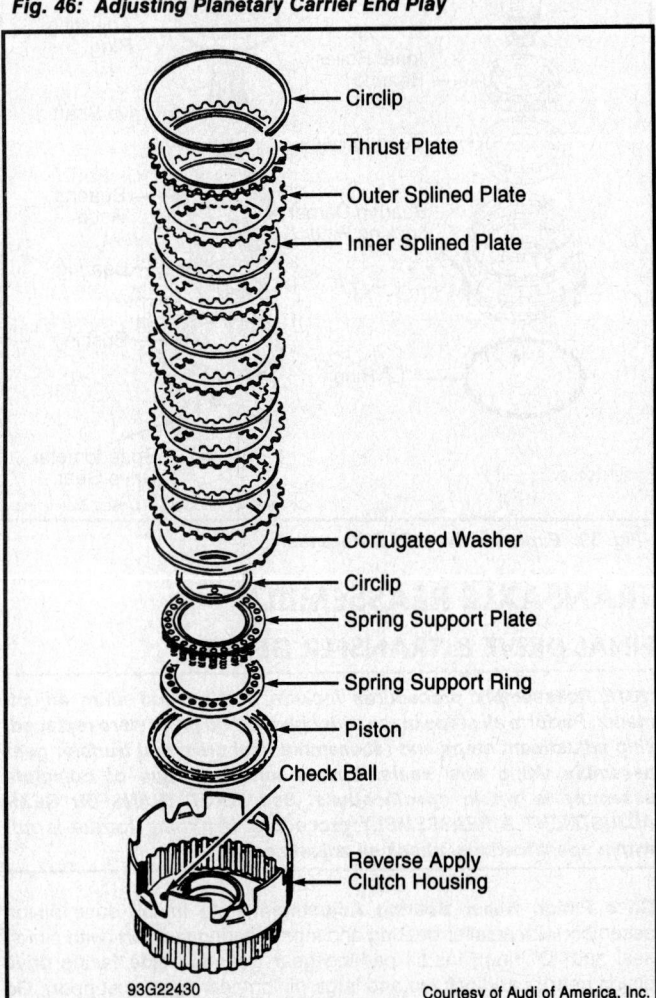

Circlip

Thrust Plate

Outer Splined Plate

Inner Splined Plate

Corrugated Washer

Circlip

Spring Support Plate

Spring Support Ring

Piston

Check Ball

Reverse Apply
Clutch Housing

93G22430

Courtesy of Audi of America, Inc.

Fig. 47: Exploded View Of Reverse Apply Clutch

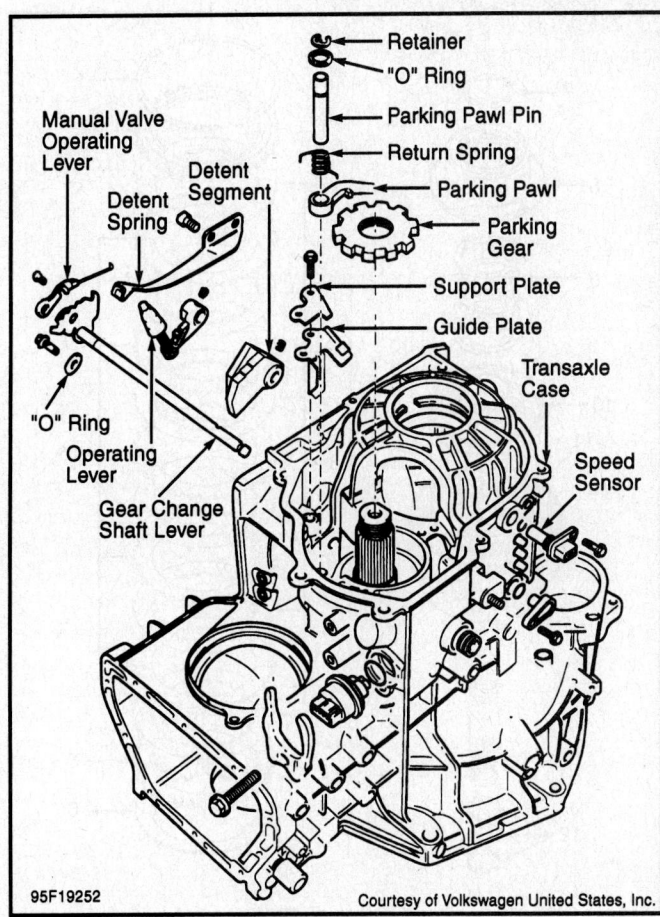

Fig. 48: Exploded View Of Transaxle Case Components

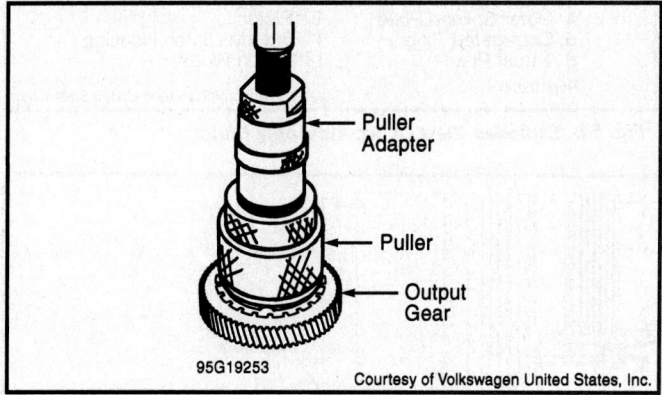

Fig. 49: Removing Output Gear Roller Bearing

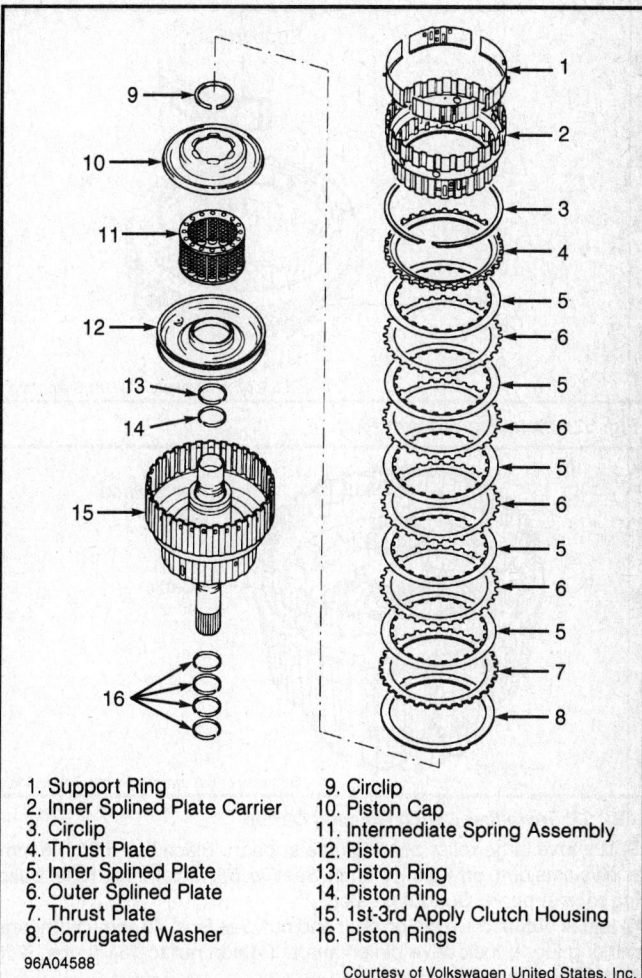

1. Support Ring
2. Inner Splined Plate Carrier
3. Circlip
4. Thrust Plate
5. Inner Splined Plate
6. Outer Splined Plate
7. Thrust Plate
8. Corrugated Washer
9. Circlip
10. Piston Cap
11. Intermediate Spring Assembly
12. Piston
13. Piston Ring
14. Piston Ring
15. 1st-3rd Apply Clutch Housing
16. Piston Rings

Courtesy of Volkswagen United States, Inc.

Fig. 50: Exploded View Of 1st-3rd Apply Clutch

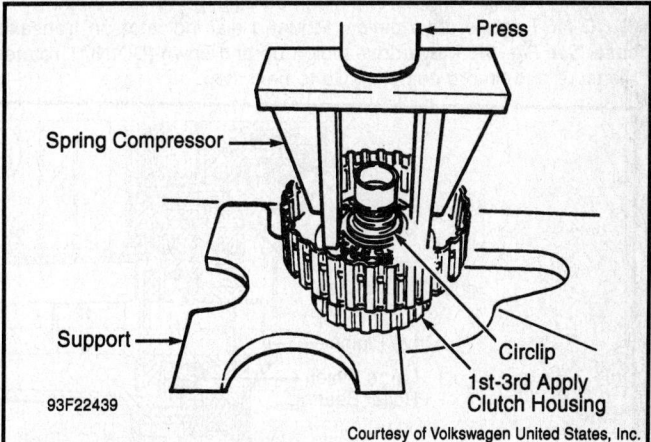

Fig. 51: Removing & Installing Spring Circlip

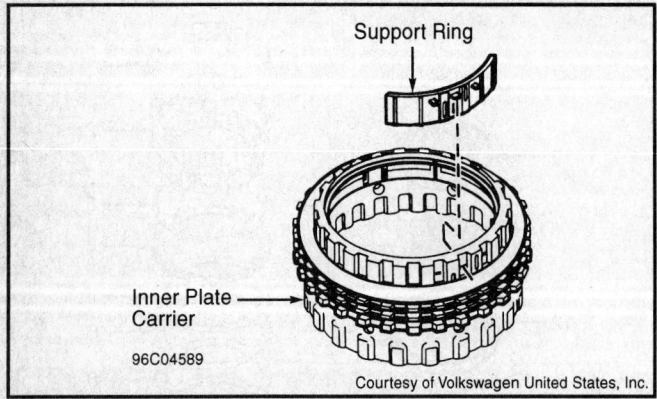

Fig. 52: Installing Support Ring

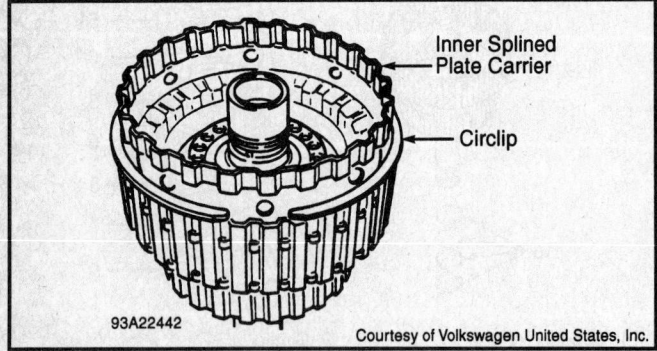

Fig. 53: Installing Clutch Housing Circlip

3) Remove large roller bearing race support. Place two .06" (1.5 mm) thick shims onto drive pinion shaft. *See Fig. 56.* Install large roller bearing race support. Go to next step.

4) Install output drive pinion gear and nut. *See Figs. 48 and 55.* Engage parking lug to lock drive pinion shaft. Tighten nut to 184 ft. lbs. (250 N.m). Go to next step.

5) If reusing drive pinion and large pinion bearing, go to step **9)**. If replacing drive pinion and/or pinion bearings, go to next step.

6) DO NOT rotate drive pinion. Mount a dial indicator on transaxle case. *See Fig. 57.* Move drive pinion up and down (DO NOT rotate). Measure and record end play. Go to next step.

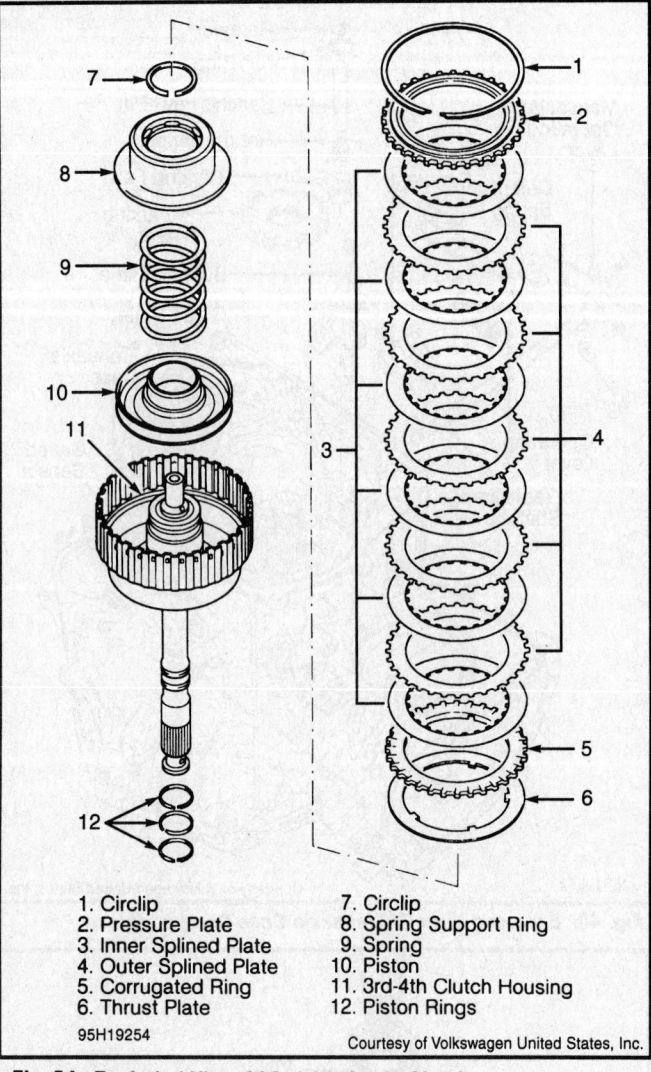

1. Circlip	7. Circlip
2. Pressure Plate	8. Spring Support Ring
3. Inner Splined Plate	9. Spring
4. Outer Splined Plate	10. Piston
5. Corrugated Ring	11. 3rd-4th Clutch Housing
6. Thrust Plate	12. Piston Rings

95H19254

Fig. 54: Exploded View Of 3rd-4th Apply Clutch

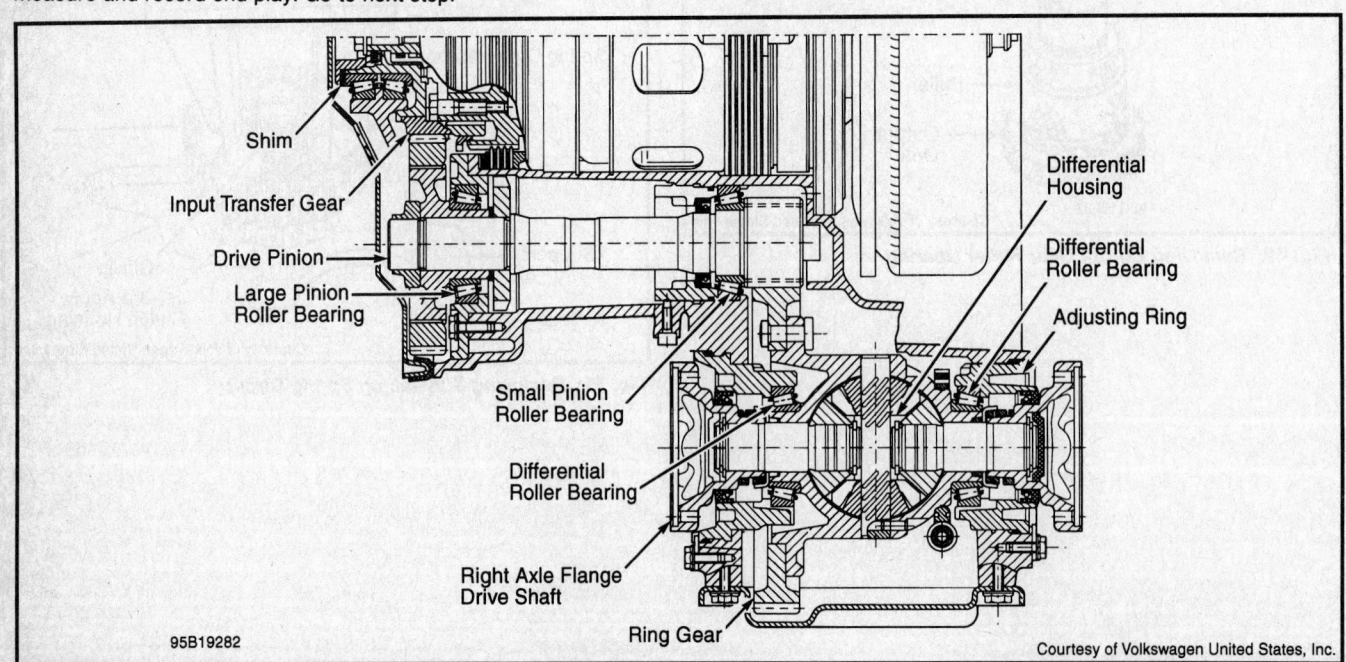

95B19282

Fig. 55: Locating Final Drive Roller Bearings, Races & Adjustment Shims

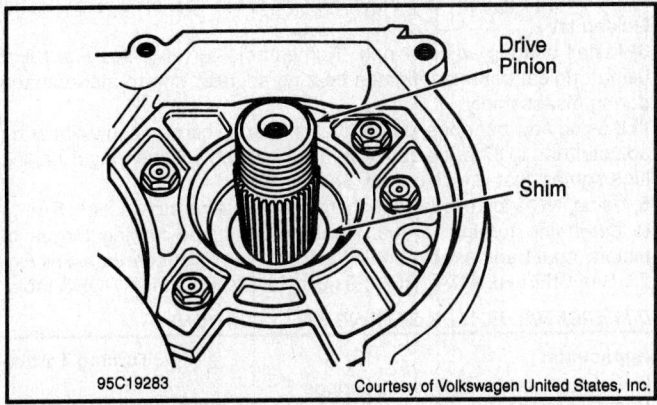

95C19283   Courtesy of Volkswagen United States, Inc.

Fig. 56: Installing Drive Pinion Shim

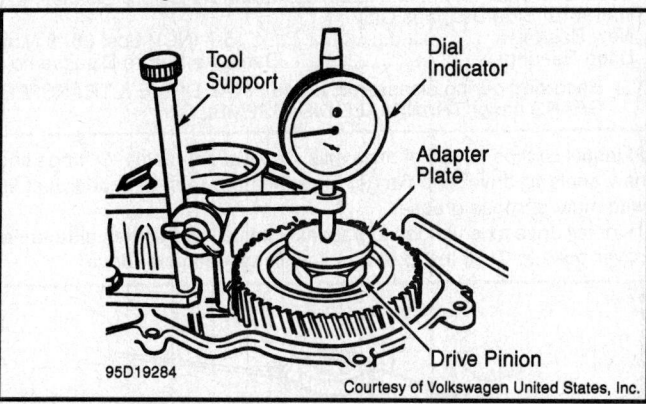

95D19284   Courtesy of Volkswagen United States, Inc.

Fig. 57: Checking Drive Pinion Roller Bearing End Play

7) Drive pinion requires .008" (.220 mm) preload. To determine correct shim thickness, perform the following procedure. Dimensions are given as an EXAMPLE ONLY:

- Subtract end play reading .037" (0.93 mm) recorded in step 6) from .118" (3.00 mm) shim pack added in step 3). This will result in zero end play.
- Next, subtract .008" (.220 mm) to achieve required preload.
- Total shim thickness required to achieve correct preload would be .073" (1.85 mm).
- Shims are available in thickness ranging from .040-.106" (1.00-2.70 mm), in .001" (.025 mm) increments.

8) Remove nut, drive pinion gear and bearing. Install shim calculated in step 7). Apply gear oil to bearings. Install drive pinion gear and nut. Tighten nut to 184 ft. lbs. (250 N.m) to seat bearings.

9) Using INCH-lb. torque wrench, rotate torque wrench at least 8 turns to determine turning torque. Measure turning torque of drive pinion

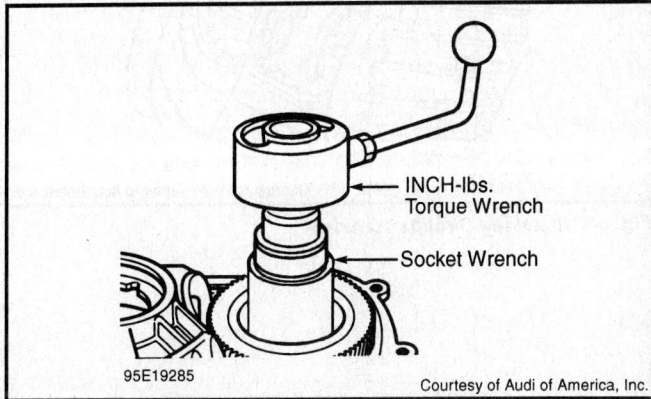

95E19285   Courtesy of Audi of America, Inc.

Fig. 58: Checking Pinion Roller Bearing Preload

roller bearings. See Fig. 58. See DRIVE PINION ROLLER BEARING SPECIFICATIONS table. After turning torque is correct, bend locking plate on nut.

DRIVE PINION ROLLER BEARING SPECIFICATIONS

Application	Turning Torque
New Bearings	7-11 INCH Lbs. (.73-1.20 N.m)
Used Bearings	[1] Same As Before Disassembly

[1] – Recorded during disassembly. See FINAL DRIVE & TRANSFER GEARS under TRANSAXLE DISASSEMBLY.

Input Transfer Gear Adjustment & Reassembly – 1) Ensure inner race for roller bearing is installed in transaxle case.

2) Install input transfer gear with roller bearing and axial needle bearing (flat side facing input gear) into transaxle case. See Figs. 1, 55 and 60. Align lugs on outer roller bearing to fit between lugs on inner roller bearing. See Fig. 59.

3) Install outer roller bearing (without dished washer or shim) on input transfer gear. See Figs. 55 and 60. Engage parking gear. Using an Allen-head socket, tighten fastener nut to 74 ft. lbs. (100 N.m). See Fig. 61.

4) Remove fastener nut. Using a dial indicator, measure distance between input transfer gear and inner race of roller bearing. See Fig. 62. Measure thickness of dished washer.

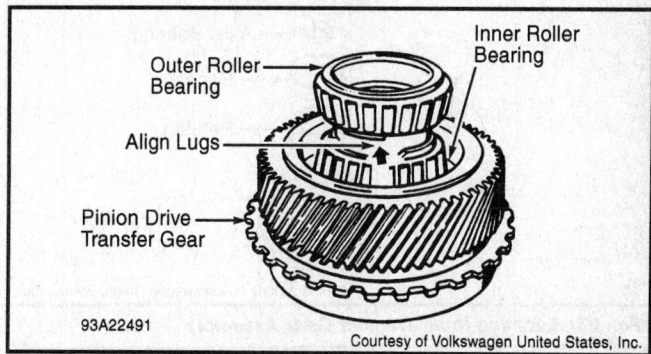

93A22491   Courtesy of Volkswagen United States, Inc.

Fig. 59: Aligning Lugs On Input Transfer Gear Roller Bearings

5) Add dished washer thickness to distance measured in step 3). Subtract .007" (.180 mm) to obtain shim thickness for desired roller bearing preload. Shims are available in thickness ranging from .040-.106" (1.00-2.70 mm), in .001" (.025 mm) increments.

6) Install selected shim. Install dished washer with curved side facing fastener nut. Apply ATF to bearings. Install and tighten fastener nut to 184 ft. lbs. (250 N.m) to seat bearings.

7) Using INCH-lb. torque wrench, rotate torque wrench at least 8 turns to determine turning torque. Measure combined turning torque of pinion and input transfer gear roller bearings. See Fig. 58. See INPUT TRANSFER GEAR ROLLER BEARING SPECIFICATIONS table.

INPUT TRANSFER GEAR ROLLER BEARING SPECIFICATIONS

Application	Turning Torque
New Bearings	
Without Drive Pinion Bearings	18 INCH Lbs. (2.0 N.m)
With Drive Pinion Bearings	[1] 27 INCH Lbs. (3.0 N.m)
Used Bearings	[2] Same As Before Disassembly

[1] – Based on a drive pinion torque of 9 INCH Lbs. (1.0 N.m).
[2] – Recorded during disassembly. See FINAL DRIVE & TRANSFER GEARS under TRANSAXLE DISASSEMBLY.

8) Remove fastener nut. If necessary, select a shim and recheck roller bearing preload. If roller bearing preload is okay, apply Locking Compound (AMV 100 01) to shaft side of roller bearing.

9) Align lugs with notches of opposite roller bearing. See Fig. 59. Install axial needle bearing with flat side facing drive shaft. Engage parking gear lug. Install fastener nut and tighten to 184 ft. lbs. (250 N.m).

Final Drive Assembly – 1) Oil bearings and place differential assembly inside transaxle. Install seals, "O" rings and new bearing races (if required) to bearing carrier and bearing adjuster ring.

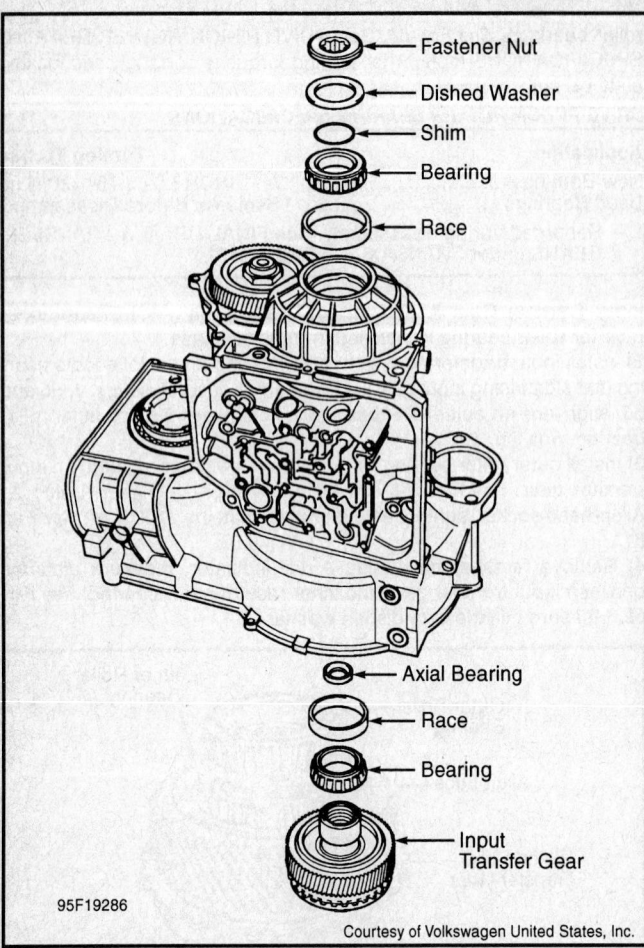

Fig. 60: Locating Input Transfer Gear Assembly

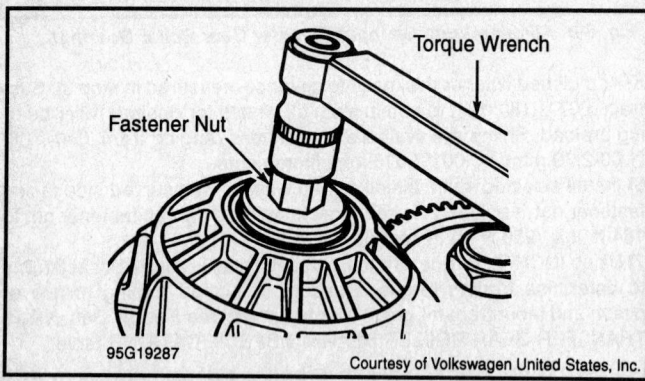

Fig. 61: Tightening Fastener Nut On Input Transfer Gear Roller Bearings

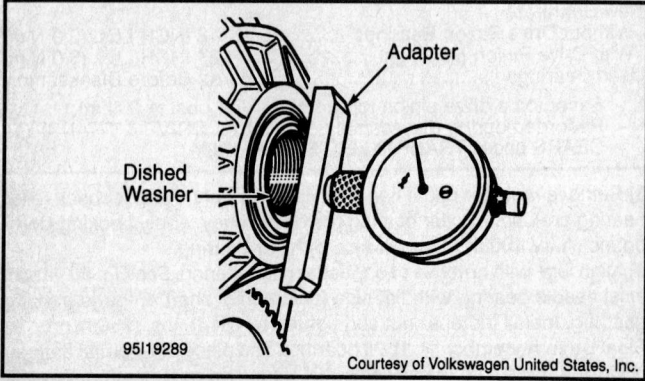

Fig. 62: Checking Distance Between Input Transfer Gear & Inner Race Of Roller Bearings

2) Install and tighten bearing carrier to 111 ft. lbs. (150 N.m). Install locking tab.

3) Install bearing adjuster ring. Tighten adjuster ring. *See Fig. 63.* If using original bearings, tighten bearing adjuster ring to marks made during disassembly.

4) If using new bearings, differential or bearing carrier, tighten bearing adjuster ring to 37 ft. lbs. (50 N.m). Turn bearing adjuster ring 5 locking lugs tighter. Install locking tab. *See Fig. 63.*

5) Using INCH-lb. torque wrench, rotate torque wrench at least 8 turns to determine turning torque. Measure combined turning torque of pinion, input transfer gear and differential side roller bearings. *See Fig. 58.* See DIFFERENTIAL ROLLER BEARING SPECIFICATIONS table.

DIFFERENTIAL ROLLER BEARING SPECIFICATIONS

Application	Turning Torque
Including Transfer & Pinion Bearings	
New Bearings	33 INCH Lbs. (3.7 N.m)
Used Bearings	Same As Before Disassembly
Differential Side Bearings Only	
New Bearings	5-7 INCH Lbs. (.6-.8 N.m)
Used Bearings	Same As Before Disassembly

¹ – Recorded during disassembly. See FINAL DRIVE & TRANSFER GEARS under TRANSAXLE DISASSEMBLY.

6) Install circlips to end of each axle. *See Fig. 64.* Install "O" rings and new seals to drive axle flange. Fill space between seal and dust lip with multi-purpose grease.

7) Install drive axle flanges to transaxle. Install and tighten differential cover bolts to 21 ft. lbs. (28 N.m). Install speedometer drive.

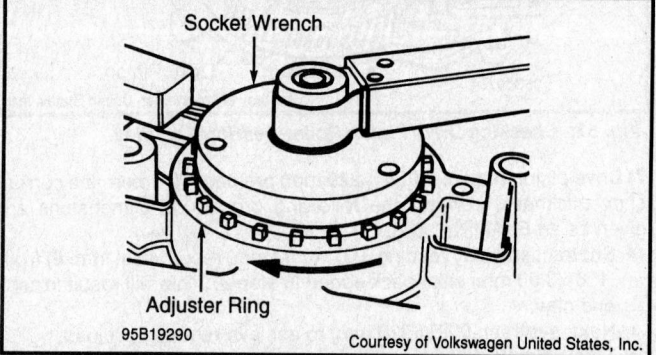

Fig. 63: Preloading Differential Side Bearings

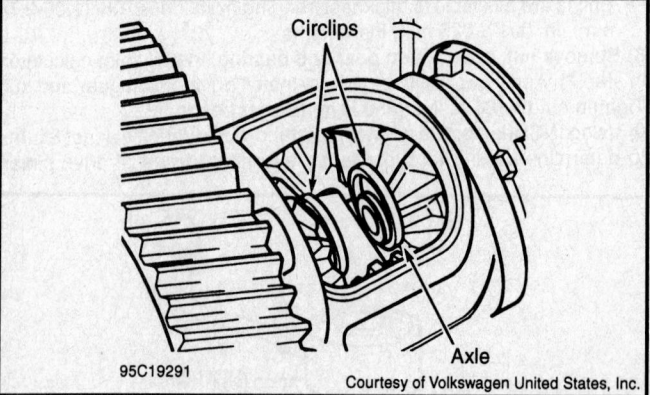

Fig. 64: Installing Circlips To Axles

TRANSMISSION

NOTE: Soak all friction-faced clutch plates in ATF for at least 15 minutes before installation. Apply assembly lubrication to all bushings, washers, shims and bearings before installation. See Fig. 28.

1) Input transfer gear, drive pinion and differential assemblies should be adjusted and installed at this time. Install axial needle bearing to input transfer gear. *See Fig. 65.* Install "O" ring and planetary carrier. Install washer and axial needle bearing into planetary carrier. *See Figs. 33 and 66.* Install end plate shim for reverse brake clutch plates. *See Fig. 67.*

2) Install reverse brake clutch plates. *See Fig. 68.* See BRAKE CLUTCH PLATE APPLICATIONS table. Using Assembly Ring (VW 3267), install one-way clutch and secure using circlip. *See Figs. 69 and 70.*

3) Using a feeler gauge, check installed reverse brake clutch clearance. *See Fig. 71.* Clearance should be .047-.071" (1.2-1.8 mm). If clearance is not as specified, replace end plate shim. End plate shims are available in thicknesses ranging from .040" (1.0 mm) to .070" (1.9 mm) in .004" (.10 mm) increments.

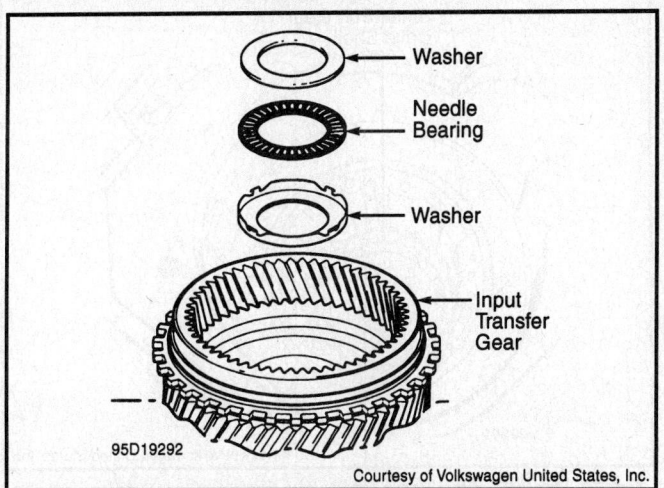

Fig. 65: *Installing Axial Needle Bearing To Input Transfer Gear*

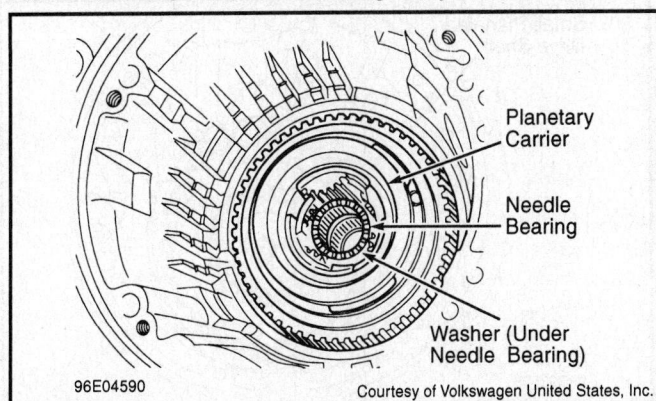

Fig. 66: *Installing Planetary Carrier & Axial Needle Bearing*

BRAKE CLUTCH PLATE APPLICATIONS

Application	Number Of Plates
Reverse Clutch	
Inner	5
Outer	5
2nd-4th Clutch	
Inner	6
Outer	7

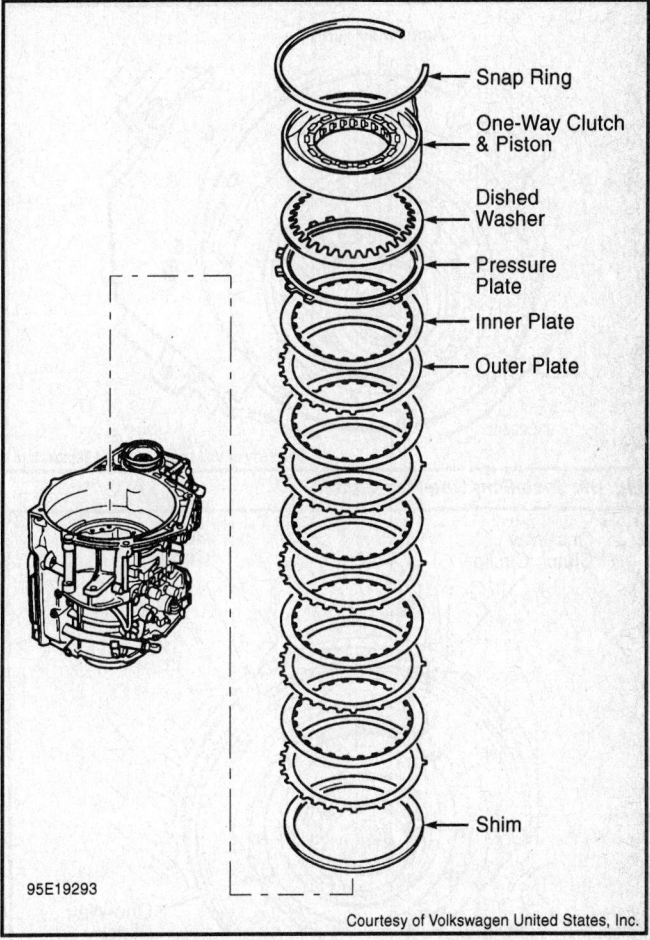

Fig. 67: *Exploded View Reverse Brake Clutch Assembly*

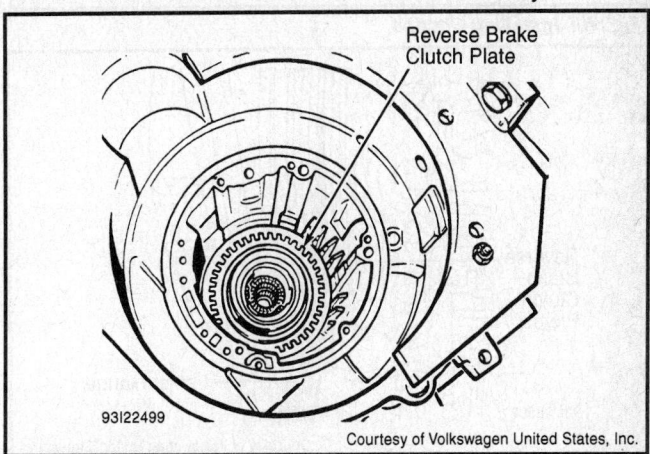

Fig. 68: *Installing Reverse Brake Clutch Plates*

4) Install upper circlip for support tube. *See Fig. 70.* Install washer and needle bearing into large sun gear drive shell. *See Fig. 28.* Install large sun gear drive shell. *See Fig. 72.*

5) Install small sun gear drive shell. Install small planetary drive shaft with needle bearings. *See Figs. 28, 73 and 74.* Using a screwdriver, lock small sun gear drive shell to large sun gear drive shell. *See Fig. 75.* Install adjustment shim, washer and bolt on end of small planetary drive shaft. Tighten bolt to 22 ft. lbs. (30 N.m).

6) Ensure end play is .009-.014" (.23-.37 mm). If end play is not as specified, recheck assembly or adjustment. See PLANETARY CARRIER under COMPONENT DISASSEMBLY & REASSEMBLY.

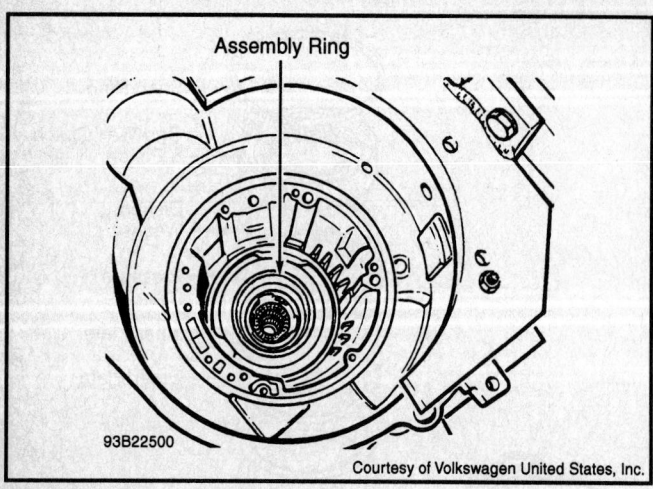

Fig. 69: Installing One-Way Clutch

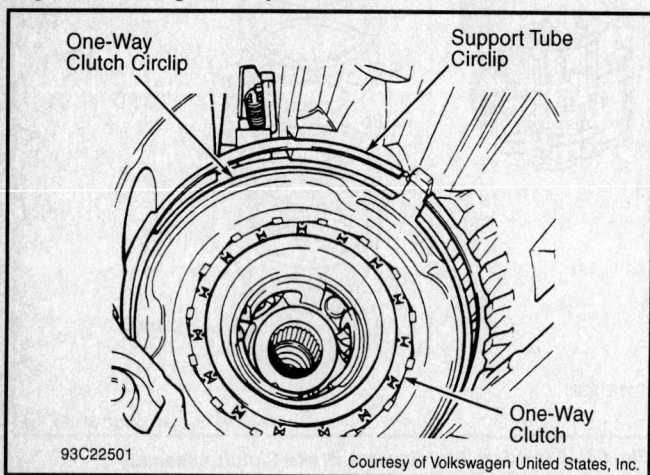

Fig. 70: Installing Circlips

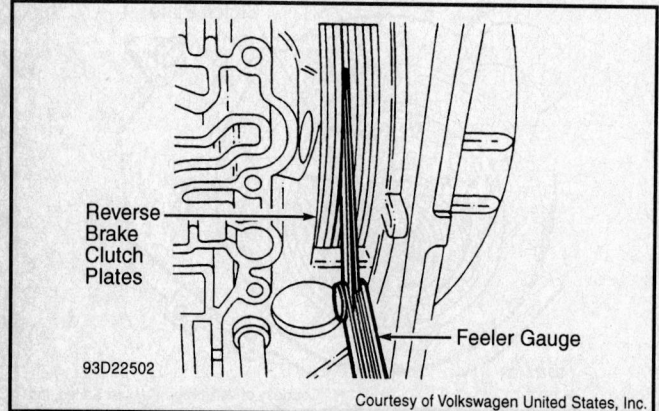

Fig. 71: Checking Reverse Brake Clutch Clearance

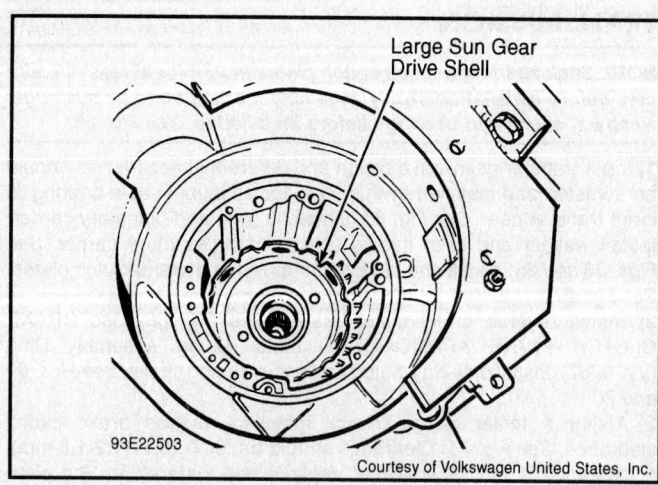

Fig. 72: Installing Large Sun Gear Drive Shell

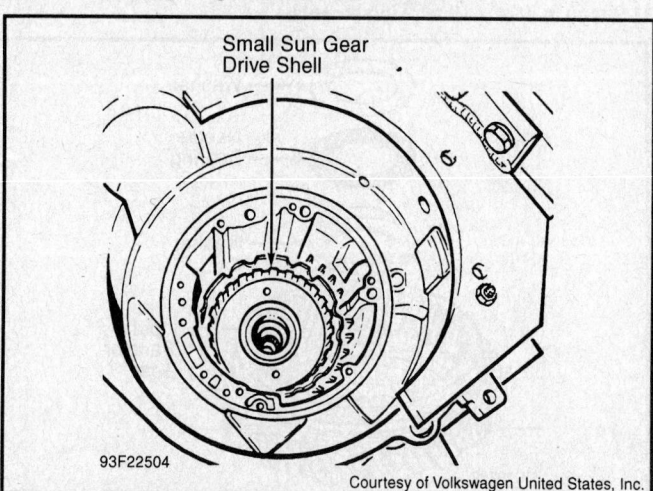

Fig. 73: Installing Small Sun Gear Drive Shell

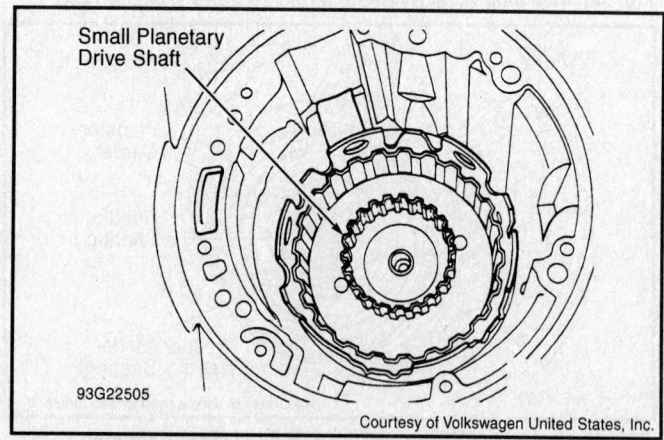

Fig. 74: Installing Small Planetary Drive Shaft

7) Install bearing, washer, and impeller shaft and 3rd-4th apply clutch. See Fig. 76. Install bearing, washer and 1st-3rd apply clutch with turbine shaft assembly. See Fig. 77. Install thrust shims on 1st-3rd apply clutch housing. Install reverse apply clutch and support tube. See Fig. 78.

NOTE: Turbine shaft end play was measured before disassembly. If end play is okay, use original thrust shims. If end play is not okay or new parts are installed, calculate end play and install required thrust shims.

8) For checking purposes, install oil pump gasket and oil pump. See Fig. 28. Position dial indicator and Support (VW 387) on transaxle case. See Fig. 79.

9) Press dial indicator on turbine shaft, and apply .040" (1.0 mm) preload. Move turbine shaft up and down. Turbine shaft end play should be .019-.047" (.50-1.20 mm).

10) If end play is okay, go to next step. If end play is not okay, install required thrust shims. Thrust shims are available in thicknesses ranging from .04" (1.0 mm) to .07" (1.8 mm) in .008" (.20 mm) increments. Recheck turbine shaft end play.

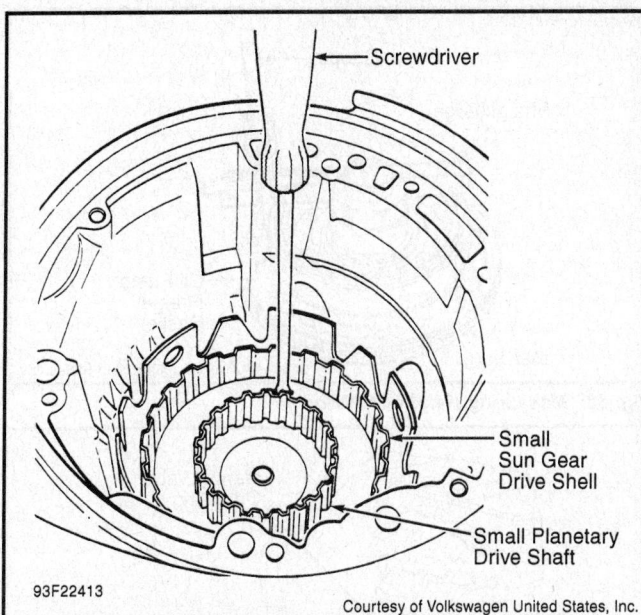

Fig. 75: Holding Small Sun Gear Drive Shell

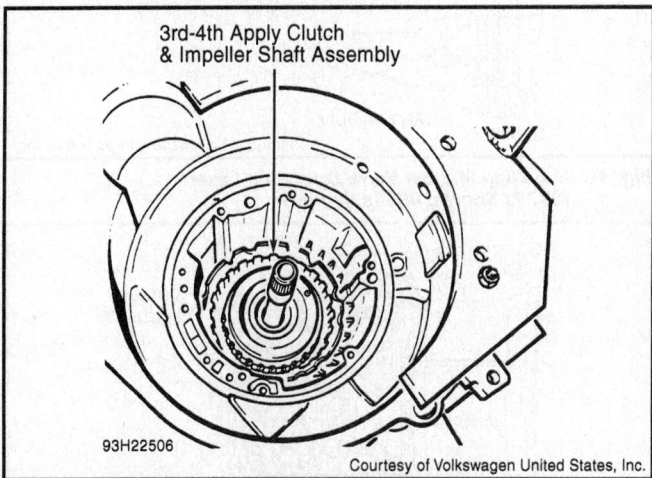

Fig. 76: Installing 3rd-4th Apply Clutch & Impeller Shaft

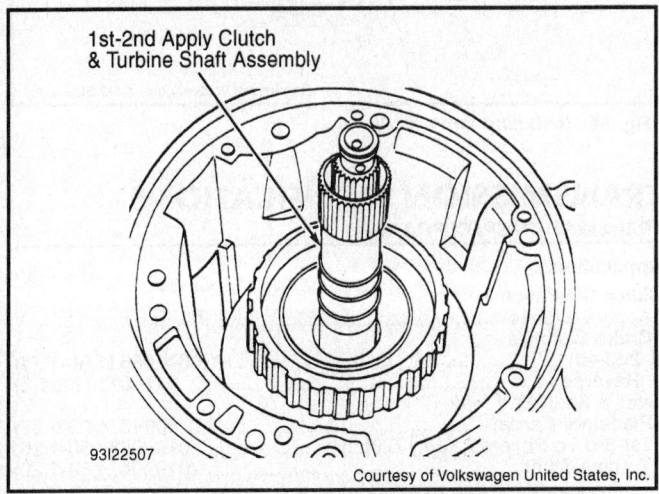

Fig. 77: Installing 1st-3rd Apply Clutch & Turbine Shaft

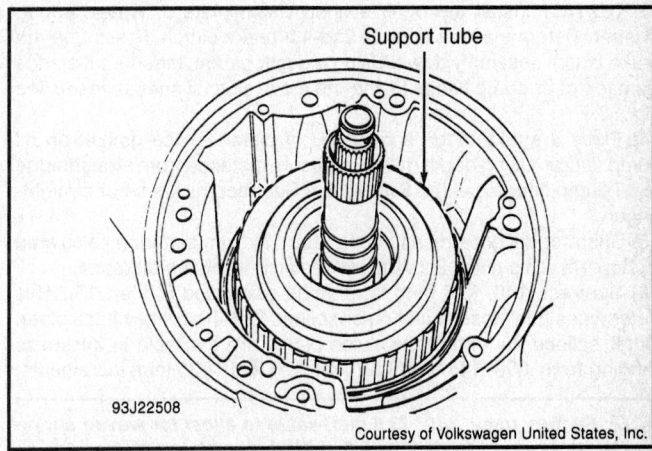

Fig. 78: Installing Support Tube

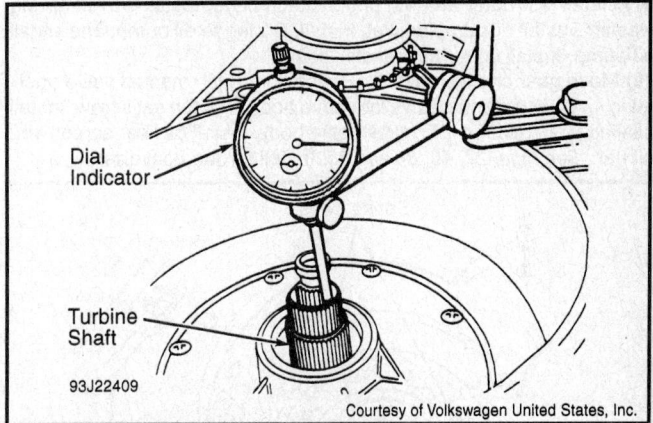

Fig. 79: Checking Turbine Shaft End Play

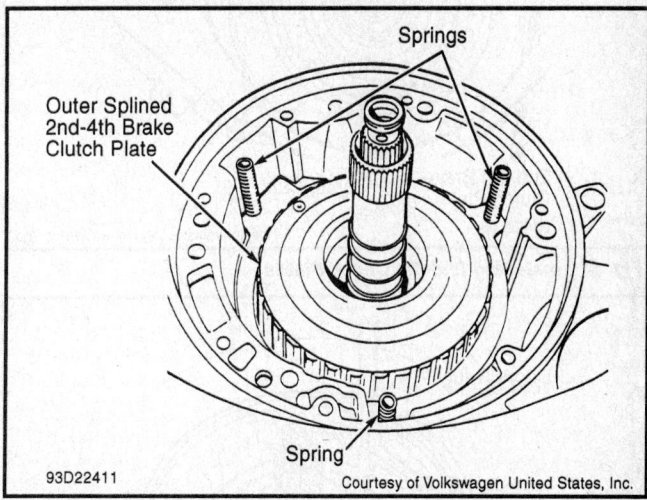

Fig. 80: Installing 2nd-4th Brake Clutch Plate & Springs

11) Remove oil pump and oil pump gasket. Install support tube and .118" (3.0 mm) thick outer splined plate for reverse apply clutch. Ensure groove on support tube engages wedge of one-way clutch. See Figs. 28 and 78.

12) Install friction plates and outer splined plates for reverse apply clutch into transaxle case. See Fig. 80. Install 3 caps and springs. Install 2nd-4th brake clutch plates. See Fig. 81. See BRAKE CLUTCH PLATE APPLICATIONS table. Install 3 spring caps to springs.

13) DO NOT install top outer splined clutch plate or waved spring washer. Determine clearance of 2nd-4th brake clutch. Press 2nd-4th brake clutch assembly down. Using a depth gauge, measure distance from top of oil pump flange to 2nd-4th brake clutch (inner splined). *See Fig. 82.*

14) Place a straightedge across top of piston. Place gasket on oil pump flange. Using depth gauge, measure distance from straightedge to oil pump flange gasket. *See Fig. 83.* Subtract thickness of straightedge.

15) Subtract distance measured in step **13)** from distance calculated in step **14)**. This gives 2nd-4th brake clutch-to-piston distance.

16) Subtract .140" (3.6 mm) from value calculated in step **15)**. This determines thickness of last outer splined 2nd-4th brake clutch plate. Outer splined 2nd-4th brake clutch plates are available in thickness ranging from .080-.148" (2.00-3.75 mm), in .010" (.25 mm) increments.

NOTE: Factory uses .140" (3.6 mm) value to allow for waved spring washer thickness installed with 2nd-4th brake clutch plates.

---

17) Install last outer 2nd-4th brake clutch plate. Install waved spring washer. Install oil pump gasket. Install "O" ring to oil pump, and install oil pump. Install cover for transfer gears.

18) Move gear change shaft to "P" position. Push manual valve operating lever with manual valve into valve body. Tighten set screw. Install sealing plug. *See Fig. 25.* Install valve body. Install oil filter screen and oil pan. *See Figs. 27, 48, 84 and 85.* Install torque converter.

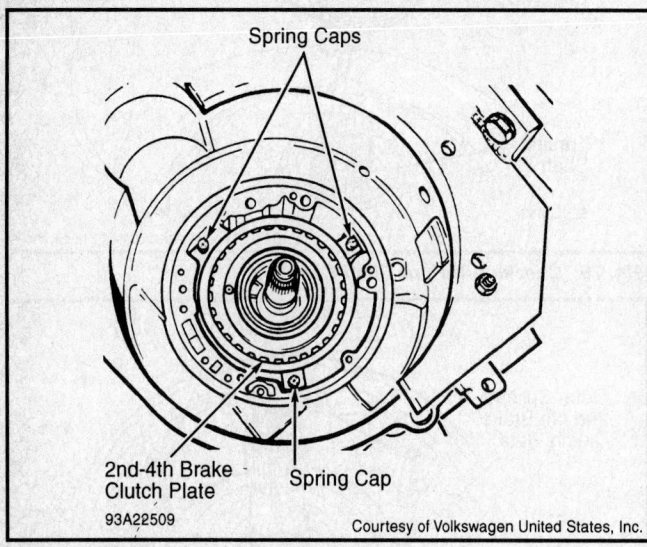

Fig. 81: **Installing 2nd-4th Clutch Plates**

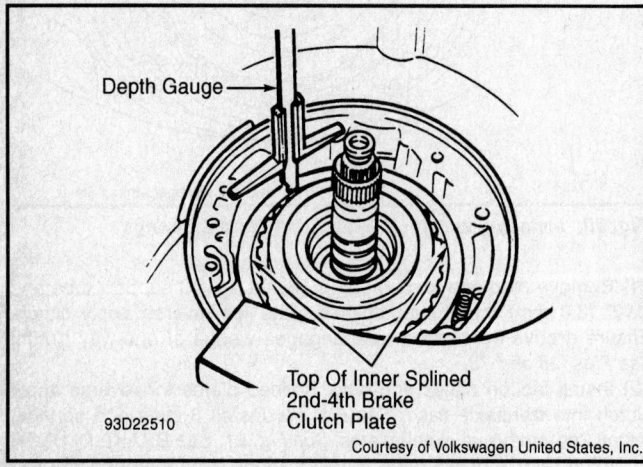

Fig. 82: **Measuring Oil Pump Flange-To-Clutch Plate**

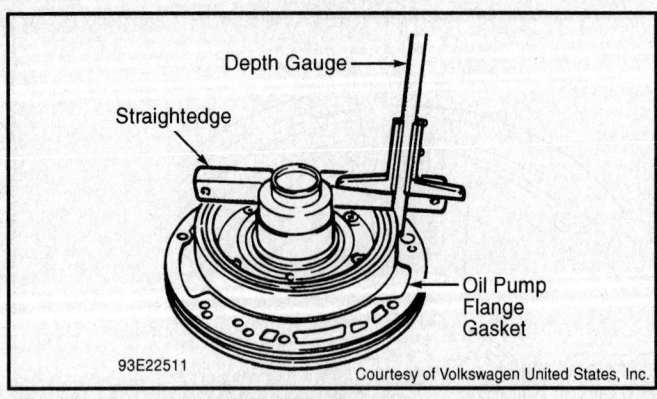

Fig. 83: **Measuring Height Of Piston**

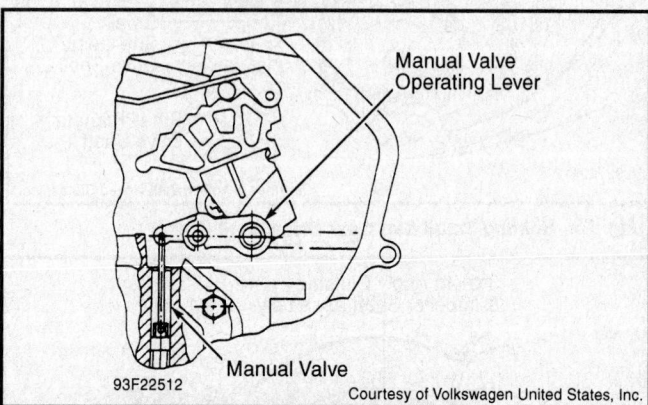

Fig. 84: **Installing Manual Valve Operating Lever (097 Is Shown; 096 Is Similar)**

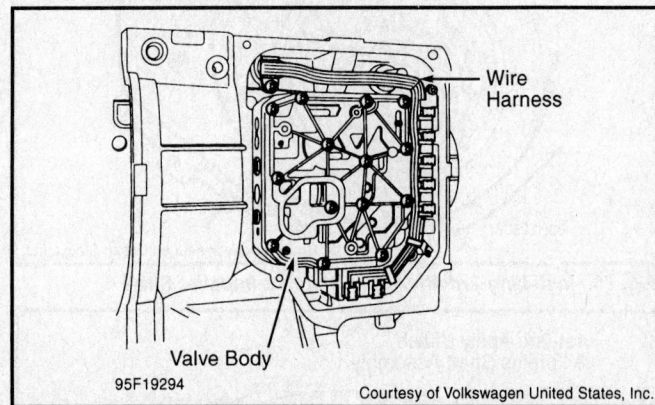

Fig. 85: **Installing Valve Body**

TRANSMISSION SPECIFICATIONS
TRANSMISSION SPECIFICATIONS

Application	In. (mm)
Clutch Clearance	
Apply Clutches	[1]
Brake Clutches	
2nd-4th	[2] .060-.068 (1.50-1.74)
Reverse	.047-.071 (1.2-1.8)
Gear & Shaft End Play	
Planetary Carrier	.009-.014 (.23-.37)
1st-3rd To Reverse Apply Clutch	.019-.047 (.50-1.20)
Turbine Shaft	.019-.047 (.50-1.20)

[1] – Assembled clutch clearance is not available.
[2] – See TRANSMISSION under TRANSAXLE REASSEMBLY.

TECHNICAL SERVICE BULLETINS

SHIFTING ERRATIC, HARSH OR DELAYED

1993-On Cabrio, Golf, GTI, Jetta & Passat (Group 01, TSB No. 97-01, 1-8-97) – Transaxle may shift erratic, harsh or hold shifts too long (delayed upshifts) with no trouble codes stored in memory. This condition is normally caused by improper throttle angle setting. If shifting quality is a concern, perform THROTTLE ANGLE SETTING.

NOTE: On a newly installed TCM, basic settings must be set prior to performing the following procedure. Basic settings can be set with Scan Tool (VAG 1551) using Function "04", Display "OOO".

Throttle Angle Setting – 1) Connect scan tool. Turn ignition on. Press "1" to select RAPID DATA TRANSFER. Enter address word 02 "TRANSMISSION ELECTRONICS" and advance until "SELECT FUNCTION XX" appears in scan tool display.

2) Press buttons "0", then "8" to select function 08 "READ MEASURING VALUE BLOCK". Press "Q" button to confirm input. Press "Q" button once more, then enter group No. 001. Press "Q" button to confirm input.

3) Print screen. While observing scan tool display, slowly press accelerator pedal until display reads 25 percent. DO NOT release pedal. Print screen.

4) While observing scan tool display, slowly press accelerator pedal until display reads 50 percent. DO NOT release pedal. Print screen.

5) While observing scan tool display, slowly press accelerator pedal until display reads 75 percent. DO NOT release pedal. Print screen.

6) While observing scan tool display, slowly press accelerator pedal until display reads 99 percent. DO NOT release pedal (resistance of kickdown switch should be felt). Print screen.

7) Continue pressing accelerator pedal to its stop while observing fourth digit on right-side 8 digit display. Fourth digit must change from 0 to 1, indicating kickdown. Hold for 5 seconds to set throttle angle.

8) Release accelerator pedal, then press right arrow button on scan tool. Select function 06 "END OUTPUT". Repeat procedure from beginning.

9) Compare voltage readings and throttle angle percentages on printout from first test with that of second test. If readings do not match, throttle angle was set incorrectly.

10) If readings do match, road test vehicle and activate kickdown switch several times to ensure proper operation.

TORQUE SPECIFICATIONS

TORQUE SPECIFICATIONS

Application	Ft. Lbs. (N.m)
Differential Bearing Carrier	111 (150)
Differential Housing Cover Bolts	21 (28)
Drive Axle Flange Bolts	33 (45)
Drive Pinion Bearing & "O" Ring Support	148 (200)
Drive Pinion Nut	184 (250)
Input Transfer Gear Nut	184 (250)
Oil Cooler Banjo Bolts	26 (35)
Small Planetary Drive Shaft Bolt	22 (30)
Starter-To-Transaxle Bolts	44 (60)
Subframe-To-Transaxle Support Nut	44 (60)
Torque Converter Nuts	44 (60)
Transaxle-To-Engine Bolts	
10-mm Diameter	44 (60)
12-mm Diameter	59 (80)
Transaxle-To-Transaxle Support Bolts	44 (60)
	INCH Lbs. (N.m)
Detent Spring Screws	84 (10)
Differential Bearing Carrier/Adjuster	
Locking Tab Bolt	108 (12)
Oil Filter Bolts	71 (8)
Oil Pan Bolts	108 (12)
Oil Pump-To-Transaxle Bolts	
Step 1	71 (8)
Step 2	Additional 90 Degrees
Transfer Gear Cover Bolts	71 (8)
Valve Body Bolts	44 (5)
Valve Body Conductor Strip Bolt	89 (10)

AUTOMATIC TRANSMISSIONS
Volkswagen Model 096 (Cont.)

WIRING DIAGRAMS

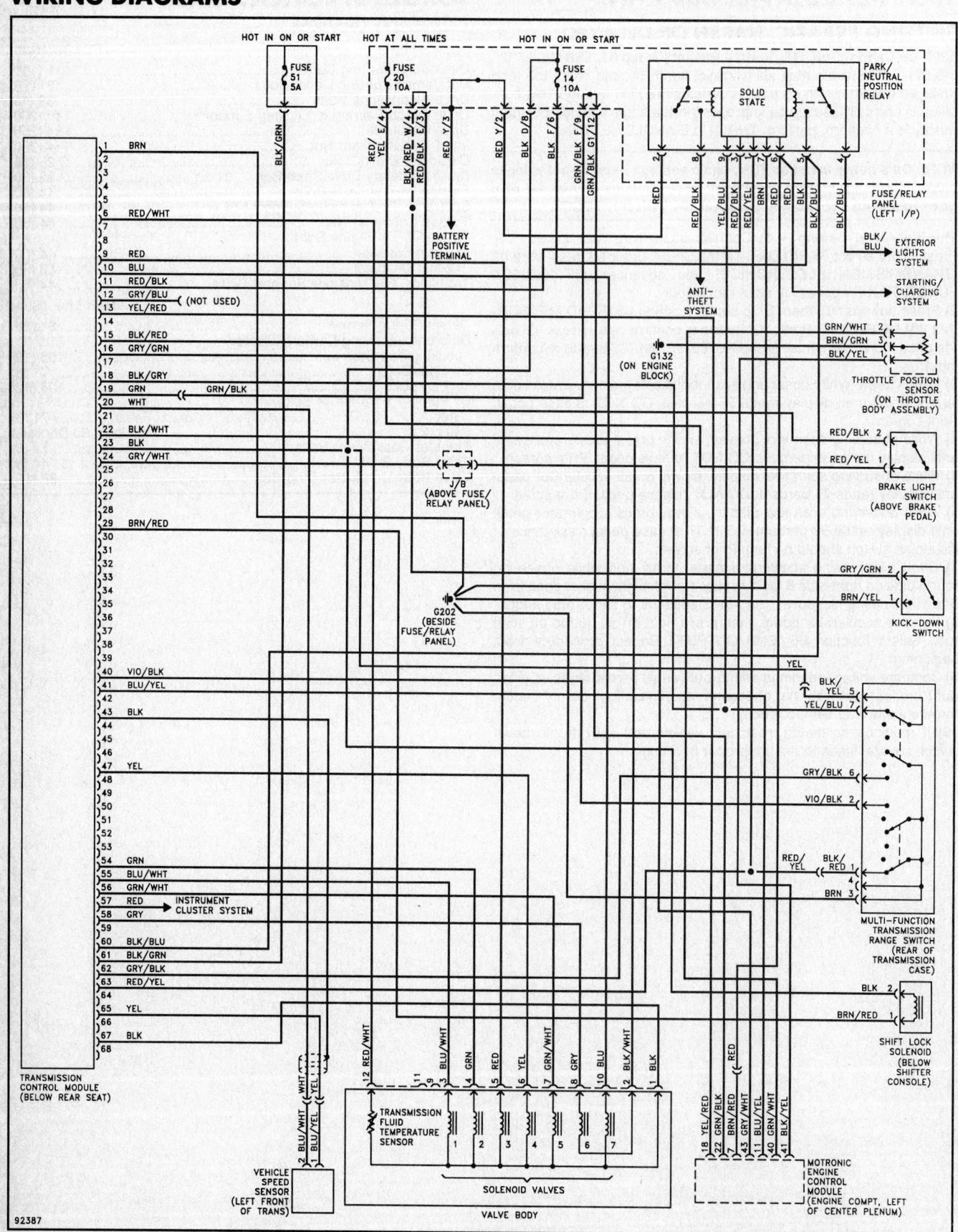

Fig. 86: 1995 Transaxle Wiring Diagram (Cabrio, Golf & Jetta 2.0L – Early Production)

92387

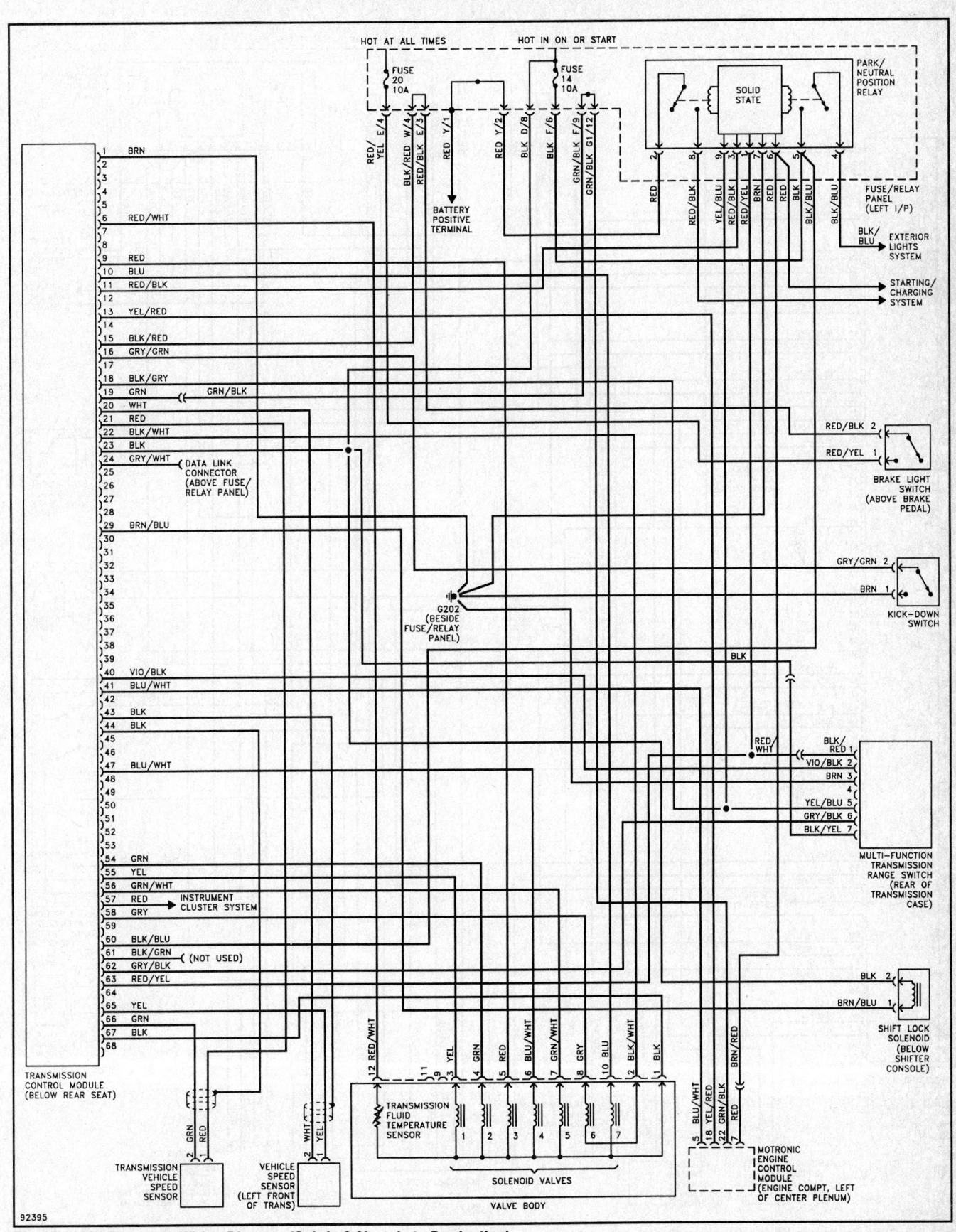

Fig. 87: 1995 Transaxle Wiring Diagram (Cabrio 2.0L — Late Production)

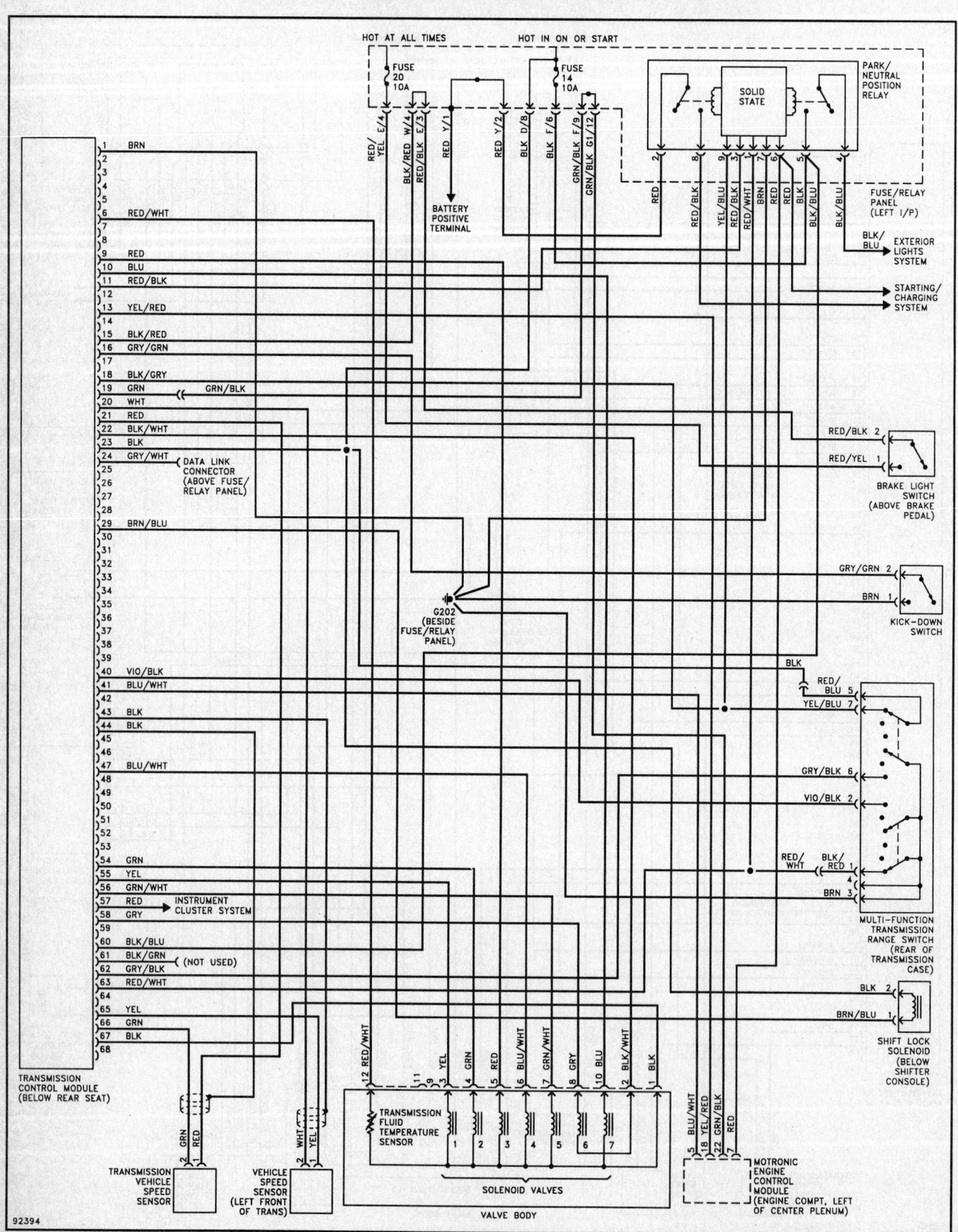

Fig. 88: 1995 Transaxle Wiring Diagram (Golf & Jetta 2.0L – Late Production)

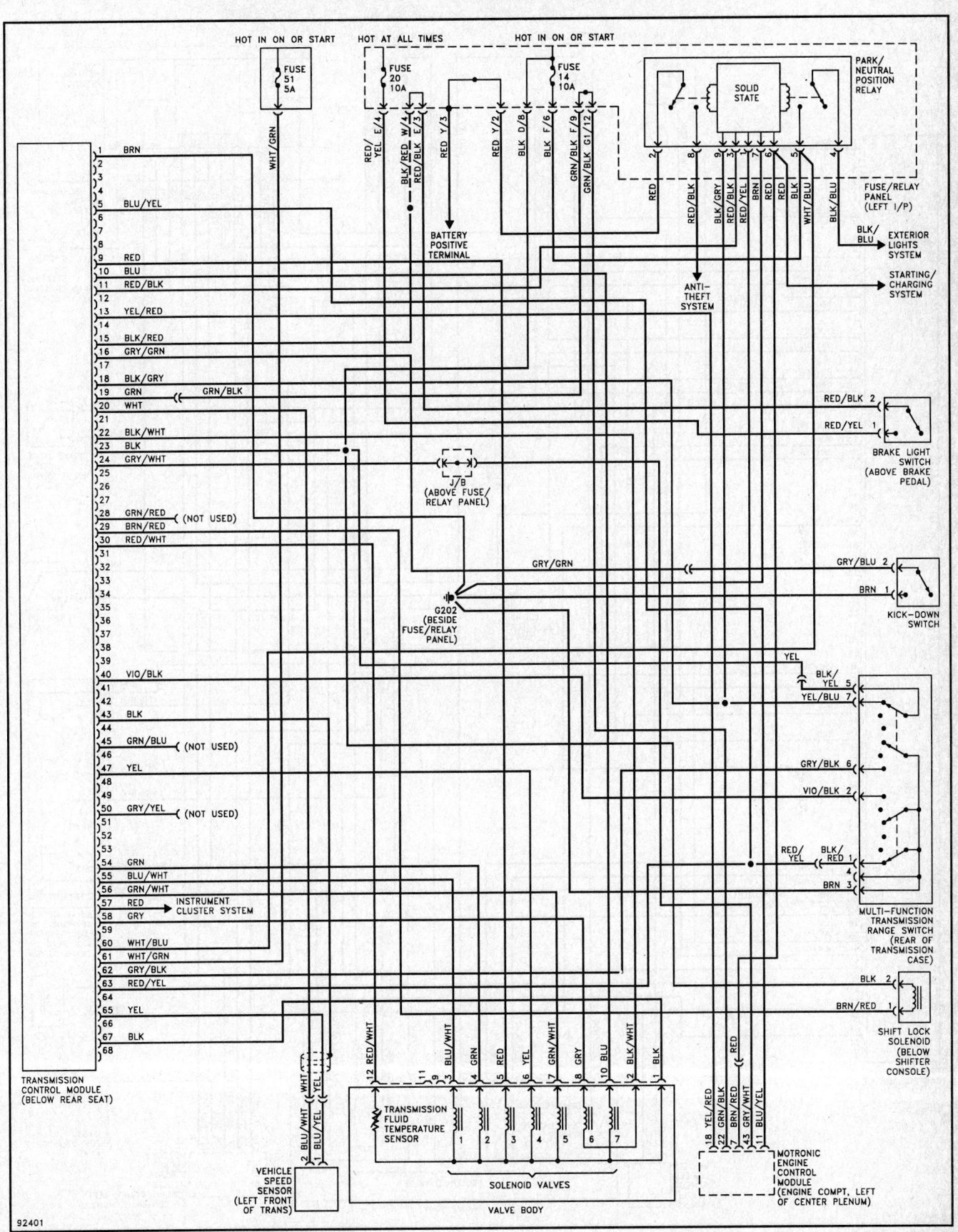

Fig. 89: 1995 Transaxle Wiring Diagram (Jetta 2.8L)

92401

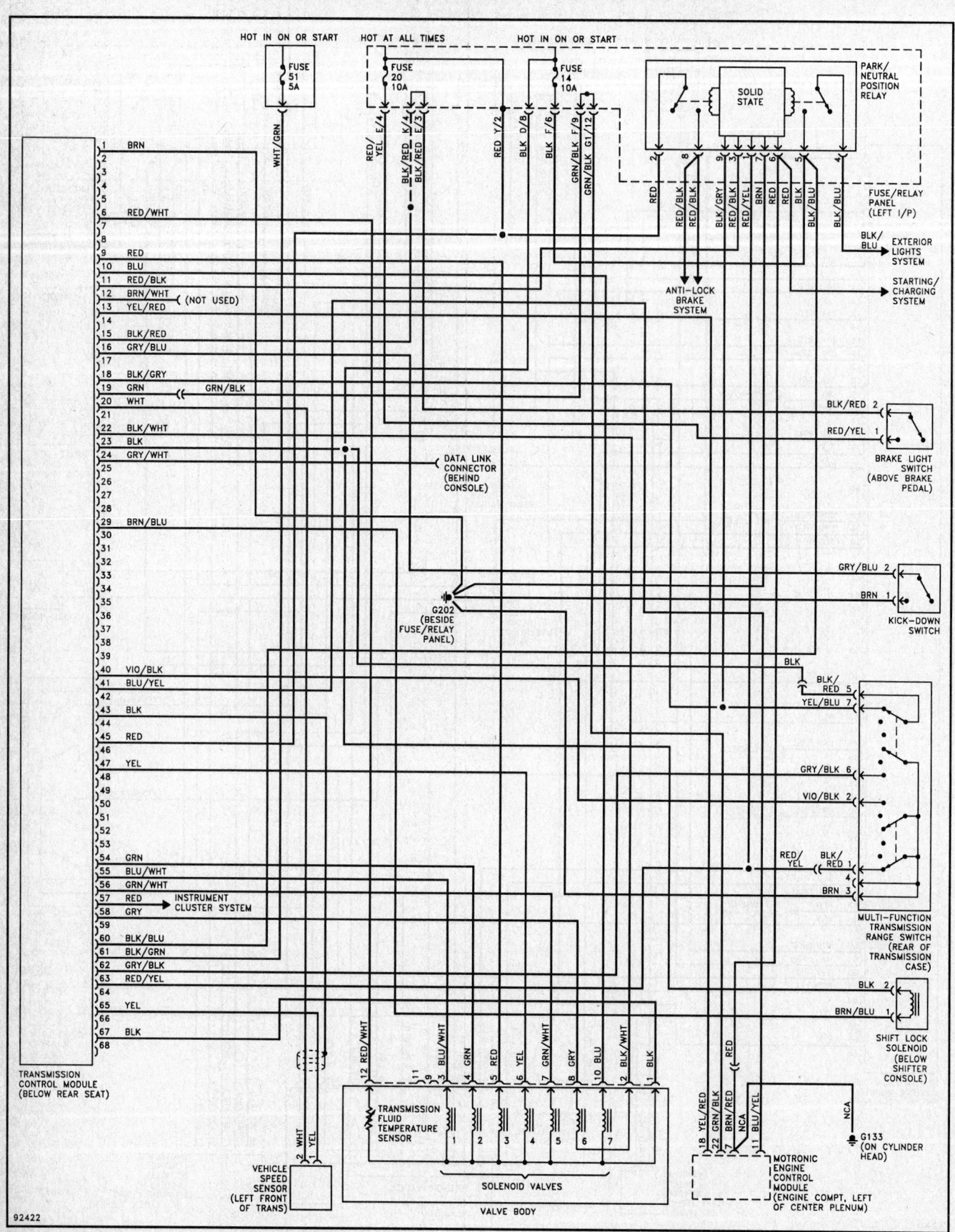

Fig. 90: 1995 Transaxle Wiring Diagram (Passat)

Cabrio, Golf, Golf III, GTI
Jetta, Jetta III, Passat

APPLICATION & LABOR TIMES

APPLICATION & LABOR TIMES

Vehicle Application	Labor Times		Trans. Model
	¹ R & I	² Overhaul	
1995-96			
Cabrio	4.4	6.3	01M (CLK)
Golf, GTI & Jetta			
4-Cylinder			
Gas	4.4	6.3	01M (CLK)
Turbo Diesel	4.4	6.3	01M (CKZ)
V6	4.4	6.3	01M (CLB)
Passat			
4-Cylinder			
Gas	4.9	6.3	01M (CLK)
Turbo Diesel	4.9	6.3	01M (CKZ)
V6	4.9	6.3	01M (CLB)

¹ – Removal and installation of transmission from vehicle chassis.
² – On bench overhaul for transmission and differential. DOES NOT include removal and installation.

IDENTIFICATION

Volkswagen Audi Group (VAG) transaxle type is cast into top of transaxle case, next to ATF cooler. Transaxle code and build date are located on top of transaxle case, next to starter.

DESCRIPTION & OPERATION

Transaxle includes a 4-speed automatic transmission, lock-up torque converter, final drive and solenoid-operated valve body. *See Fig. 1.* Under normal conditions, all shifts are controlled by a Transaxle Control Module (TCM). *See Fig. 2.* Fourth gear is an overdrive gear.

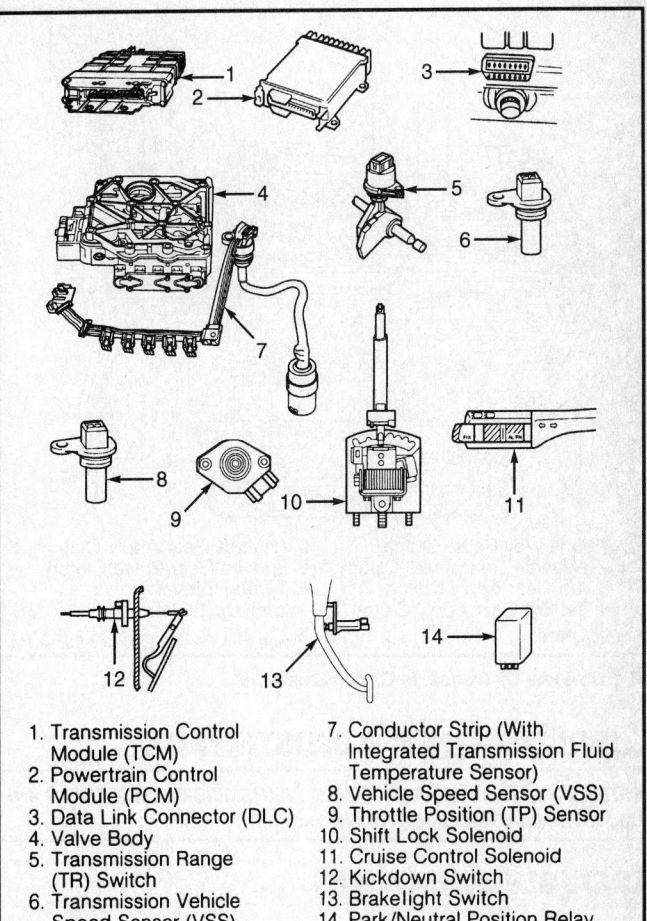

1. Transmission Control Module (TCM)
2. Powertrain Control Module (PCM)
3. Data Link Connector (DLC)
4. Valve Body
5. Transmission Range (TR) Switch
6. Transmission Vehicle Speed Sensor (VSS)
7. Conductor Strip (With Integrated Transmission Fluid Temperature Sensor)
8. Vehicle Speed Sensor (VSS)
9. Throttle Position (TP) Sensor
10. Shift Lock Solenoid
11. Cruise Control Solenoid
12. Kickdown Switch
13. Brakelight Switch
14. Park/Neutral Position Relay

96C04631   Courtesy of Volkswagen United States, Inc.

Fig. 2: Identifying TCM & Shift Lock Electrical Components

The transmission elements consist of a planetary gear set, one-way roller clutch, 3 apply clutches, 2 brake clutches and a torque converter lock-up clutch. *See Figs. 1 and 3.*

All 4 forward gears are hydraulically activated. When the lock-up clutch is engaged, the forward gears become mechanically driven by eliminating torque converter slip. The lock-up clutch is engaged depending on engine load and vehicle speed.

Power from the transmission is connected to the drive pinion through transfer gears. A ring gear and differential assembly are connected to flanges which spin the drive axles.

The electronic control consists of a TCM (located under rear seat), control solenoids, various sensors and switches. The control solenoids direct oil pressure inside the valve body. Solenoid valves No. 1-4 control the apply and brake clutches. Solenoid valves No. 5 and 7 control shift smoothness. Solenoid valve No. 6 is a frequency valve and controls the main hydraulic pressure. The TCM controls the main hydraulic pressure by varying the duty cycle.

The TCM monitors input and output signals. If electrical problems occur, TCM will record faults in TCM memory and may go into fail-safe mode (also known as emergency running mode). If TCM enters fail-safe mode, the transaxle will operate manually in reverse, 1st or 3rd gear. In fail-safe mode, 3rd gear operates with gear selector in 2nd, 3rd or "D". If engine is started with TCM in fail-safe mode, TCM activates 3rd gear hydraulically. The TCM memory can only be read using Scan Tool (VAG 1551) and Adapter (VAG 1551/3).

The TCM also controls shift lock system. This system locks the gear selector in Park or Neutral position unless the brake pedal is pressed. The TCM uses a shift lock control relay to release a gear-selector mounted solenoid. *See Fig. 2.*

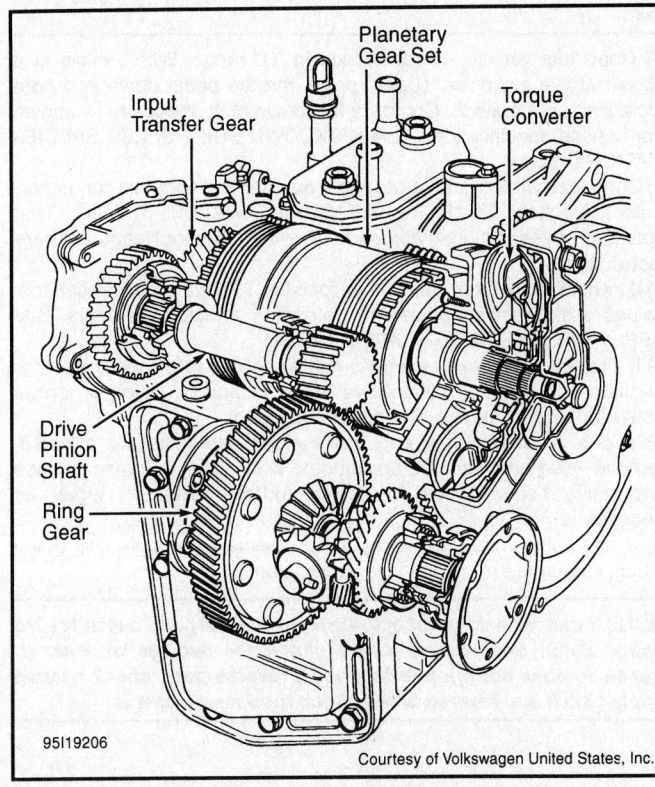

95I19206   Courtesy of Volkswagen United States, Inc.

Fig. 1: Cross-Sectional View Of Transaxle Components

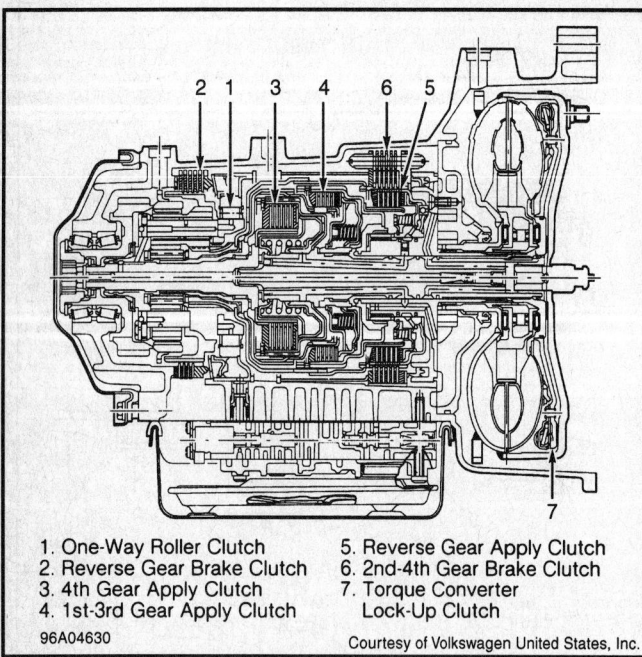

1. One-Way Roller Clutch
2. Reverse Gear Brake Clutch
3. 4th Gear Apply Clutch
4. 1st-3rd Gear Apply Clutch
5. Reverse Gear Apply Clutch
6. 2nd-4th Gear Brake Clutch
7. Torque Converter Lock-Up Clutch

96A04630   Courtesy of Volkswagen United States, Inc.

Fig. 3: View Of Transaxle Clutch Elements

LUBRICATION & ADJUSTMENTS

NOTE: See appropriate AUTOMATIC TRANSMISSION SERVICING article in TRANSMISSION SERVICING section.

TROUBLE SHOOTING

SYMPTOM DIAGNOSIS

Leak At Torque Converter – Check drive plate clearance, torque converter bushing, oil seal or oil pump assembly. Repair as necessary.

Transaxle Fluid In Coolant – Faulty transaxle oil cooler. Replace transaxle oil cooler and friction plates in transaxle. Clean transaxle.

Transaxle & Differential Oils Mixed – Replace "O" ring and drive pinion seal on inner bearing support.

Gear Selector Hard To Move – Check gear selector between shifter and transaxle. Repair as necessary. Check parking lock assembly inside transaxle. Repair as necessary.

No Drive In 1st Gear – Check for faulty 1st-3rd apply clutch or reverse brake clutch.

No Drive In "D", "2" Or "3" – Check for faulty 1st-3rd apply clutch or one-way clutch.

No 2nd Gear In "D", "2" Or "3" – Check for faulty 2nd-4th brake clutch.

No 3rd Gear In "D" Or "3" – Check for faulty reverse apply clutch.

No 4th Gear In "D" – Check for faulty 2nd-4th brake clutch.

No Reverse – Check for faulty reverse apply clutch or reverse brake clutch.

No Drive In All Forward Gear Positions – Check for faulty 1st-3rd apply clutch, reverse brake clutch or one-way clutch.

Missing Shifts Up Or Down – Check valve body for sticking valve(s) or faulty shift solenoid(s).

Erratic Or Harsh Shifts – Short in wiring to shift solenoid(s) or faulty shift solenoid(s). Check for proper throttle angle adjustment. See TECHNICAL SERVICE BULLETINS.

Harsh Shift In One Gear Only – Determine elements involved. Air check elements. Check for faulty shift solenoid or shift valve.

Stuck In Emergency Running Mode – Check for incorrect TCM installed, faulty wiring, bad solenoid electrical strip (inside oil pan) or stuck valve.

Park Lock Will Not Engage – Check for misadjusted selector lever cable. Check for faulty locking mechanism.

Bucking Or Poor Idling – Check throttle housing and air ducts for leaks. Check for possible air entering oil pump pickup.

Excess Engine RPM Drop When Shifting Into 1st Gear – Faulty Powertrain Control Module (PCM).

Engine Starts In Gear Or No Start In Park/Neutral – Check for faulty Park/Neutral safety switch.

Shift Lock Not Holding Selector In Park/Neutral – Check for faulty shift lock solenoid, shift lock mechanism or bad TCM.

MECHANICAL, HYDRAULIC & ELECTRICAL COMPONENTS

1) If gear selector is stuck in Park or Neutral position, go to SHIFT LOCK SYSTEM under TROUBLE SHOOTING. If gear positions are missing, shift quality is poor or no shifts are possible, ensure all electrical connections are okay and fluid level is correct.

2) If problems are still present, disconnect electrical connector at transaxle. Test drive vehicle. Check if transaxle will operate manually in reverse and 1st gear. Move gear selector to 2nd, 3rd or "D" position. Transaxle should operate in 3rd gear (2nd, 3rd or "D").

3) If transaxle operates as described, problem may be electrical. See ELECTRONIC SELF-DIAGNOSTICS. If transaxle does not operate as described, problem may be mechanical or hydraulic. See ROAD TEST.

NOTE: If transaxle does not operate in manual 1st gear, check 1st-3rd apply clutch and reverse brake clutch for damage or wear. If transaxle does not operate in manual reverse gear, check reverse apply clutch and reverse brake clutch for damage or wear.

ROAD TEST

WARNING: DO NOT exceed safe or legal speed limits during road test.

1) Road test vehicle with transaxle in "D" range. With vehicle at a speed above kickdown speed, press throttle pedal down and note kickdown shift speeds. Compare kickdown shift speeds to kickdown shift speed specifications. See KICKDOWN SHIFT SPEED SPECIFICATIONS table.

2) Connect scan tool and appropriate adapter to diagnostic connector. Select function 08 "READ MEASURING VALUE BLOCK". Test solenoid valves and upshift speeds following scan tool manufacturers instructions.

3) If transaxle does not shift within specified MPH range, and scan tool values are within specification, determine affected elements. See APPLY & BRAKE CLUTCH APPLICATION.

4) If all apply and brake clutch elements are affected, check oil pump, oil filter, cooler lines, solenoid valve No. 6, and condition of torque converter and/or engine. Repair as necessary.

5) If one or more apply and brake clutch elements are affected, remove valve body. Locate appropriate fluid circuit in transaxle case and valve body. Check for leaks and/or blockage. Repair as necessary.

6) If hydraulic circuits are okay, or problems with apply and brake clutch elements are mechanical, repair transaxle.

NOTE: If transaxle does not operate in manual 1st gear, check 1st-3rd apply clutch and reverse brake clutch for damage or wear. If transaxle does not operate in manual reverse gear, check reverse apply clutch and reverse brake clutch for damage or wear.

NOTE: In the following table, letter suffix following gear application refers to Hydraulic ("H") or Mechanical ("M") gear operation. Hydraulic or manual gear operation depends on operating mode of torque converter lock-up clutch.

KICKDOWN SHIFT SPEED SPECIFICATIONS

Application	Kickdown (MPH)
4-Cylinder (CLK)	
1H-1M	30-34
1M-2H	30-34
2H-2M	61-65
2M-3H	61-65
3H-3M	85-89
3M-4H	85-89
4H-4M	85-89
4M-4H	86-83
4H-3M	86-83
3M-3H	61-57
3H-2M	61-57
2M-2H	61-57
2H-1M	26-22
1M-1H	26-22
Turbo Diesel (CKZ)	[1]
V6 (CLB)	
1H-1M	37-41
1M-2H	37-41
2H-2M	76-80
2M-3H	76-80
3H-3M	111-115
3M-4H	111-115
4H-4M	111-115
4M-4H	112-108
4H-3M	112-108
3M-3H	75-71
3H-2M	75-71
2M-2H	75-71
2H-1M	32-28
1M-1H	32-28

[1] – Information not available from manufacturer.

APPLY & BRAKE CLUTCH APPLICATION

APPLY & BRAKE CLUTCH APPLICATION [1]

Gear Application	Elements In Use
1st Gear	1st-3rd Apply & One-Way Clutch Holding
2nd Gear	1st-3rd Apply & 2nd-4th Brake
3rd Gear	1st-3rd & 4th Apply Clutches
4th Gear	4th Apply & 2nd-4th Brake
Reverse	Reverse Apply & Reverse Brake
Park & Neutral	All Apply & Brake Clutches Released Or Ineffective

[1] – All forward gear elements shown are in "hydraulic-state". Forward gear elements switch to a "mechanical-state" with the addition of torque converter lock-up clutch apply.

SHIFT LOCK SYSTEM

Operation – All models are equipped with an electronic shift lock system. TCM controls shift lock system. *See Fig. 2.* This system locks gear selector in Park or Neutral position unless brake pedal is pressed. TCM uses shift lock control relay to release a solenoid mounted on gear selector assembly.

NOTE: Shift lock relay will not lock gear selector when vehicle speed is greater than 3 MPH.

A mechanical control cable prevents ignition key from being removed unless gear selector is in Park position. With ignition key removed, gear selector locks in Park position.

NOTE: If battery is disconnected or discharged, gear selector can be moved out of Park position by turning ignition key to START position.

Functional Check – 1) With ignition key removed, ensure gear selector cannot be moved from "P" position. Insert key in ignition switch.

2) Turn ignition on. Ensure gear selector can only be moved with brake pedal pressed. Move gear selector to "N" position.
3) Without pressing brake pedal, ensure gear selector cannot move out of "N" position. Press brake pedal down. Ensure it is now possible to move gear selector.
4) If shift lock system does not operate as described, adjust gear selector, solenoid and control cable. If shift lock system does not operate after adjustments are made, check shift lock electrical system with Scan Tool (VAG 1551).
5) See testing information under ELECTRONIC SELF-DIAGNOSTICS. *See Figs. 10-13.* If any problems are found, service harness or components. If no problems are found, TCM may be defective. If shift lock system still does not operate correctly, check for worn or damaged parts and replace as necessary. *See Figs. 2 and 4.*

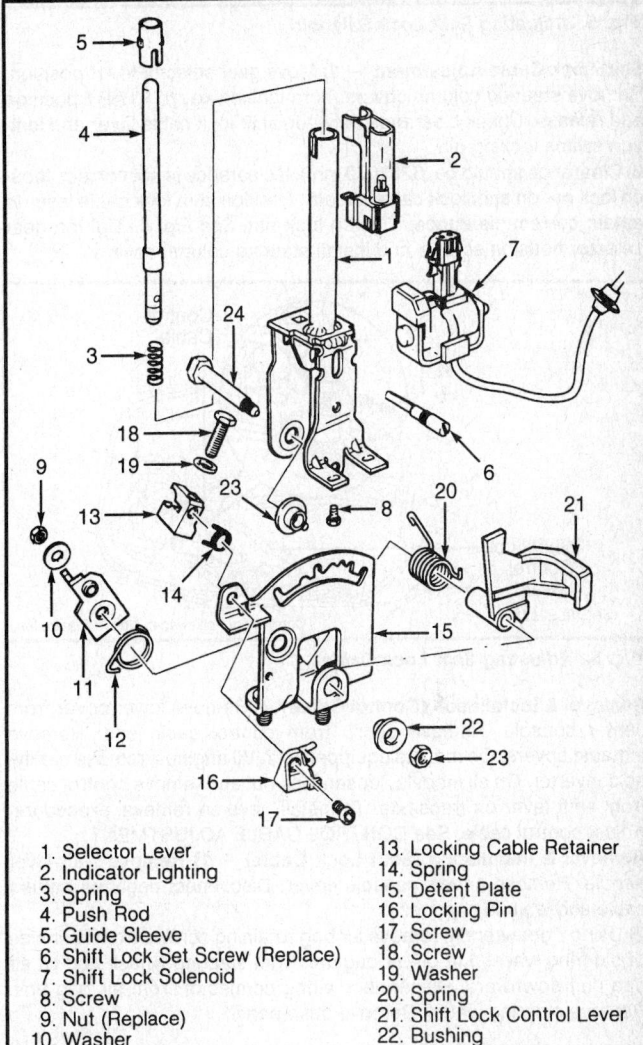

1. Selector Lever
2. Indicator Lighting
3. Spring
4. Push Rod
5. Guide Sleeve
6. Shift Lock Set Screw (Replace)
7. Shift Lock Solenoid
8. Screw
9. Nut (Replace)
10. Washer
11. Locking Lever
12. Coil Spring
13. Locking Cable Retainer
14. Spring
15. Detent Plate
16. Locking Pin
17. Screw
18. Screw
19. Washer
20. Spring
21. Shift Lock Control Lever
22. Bushing
23. Nut (Replace)
24. Shouldered Bolt

95A19208   Courtesy of Volkswagen United States, Inc.

Fig. 4: Exploded View Of Shift Lock & Gear Selector Assembly

NOTE: Perform the following adjustments in order given.

Control Cable Adjustment – Loosen lock screw at gear selector lever on transaxle. Move gear selector in center console to Park position. Ensure front wheels are locked. Tighten cable housing to gear selector lever lock screw.

Shift Lock Solenoid Adjustment – Place gear selector in "N" or "P" position. Loosen shift lock solenoid mounting screws. Insert a .019" (.30 mm) feeler gauge between shift lock solenoid push rod and shift lever. *See Fig. 5.* If necessary, move shift lock solenoid and tighten screws.

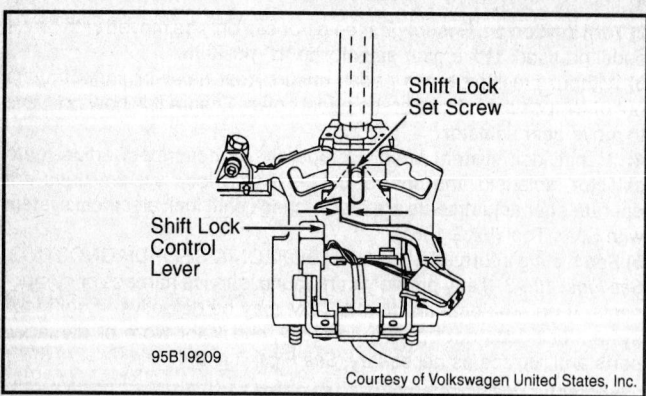

95B19209

Courtesy of Volkswagen United States, Inc.

Fig. 5: Adjusting Shift Lock Solenoid

Shift Lock Cable Adjustment – **1)** Move gear selector to "1" position. Remove steering column covers. Turn ignition key to START position and release. Check clearance between shift lock cable lever and ignition switch locking pin.

2) Clearance should be .028" (.70 mm). If clearance is not correct, loosen lock nut on shift lock cable sheath. Position shift lock cable lever to obtain correct clearance. Tighten lock nut. See Fig. 6. Tighten gear selector housing screws and install steering column covers.

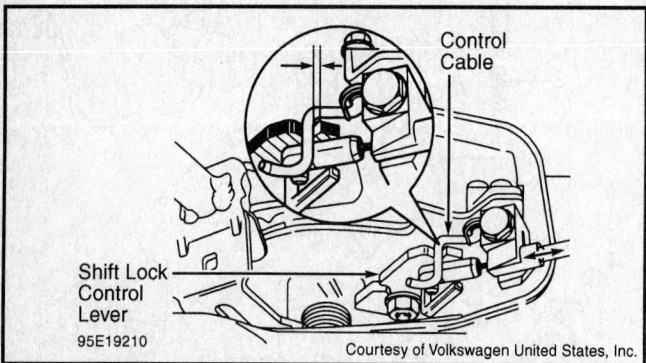

95E19210

Courtesy of Volkswagen United States, Inc.

Fig. 6: Adjusting Shift Lock Cable

Removal & Installation (Control Cable) – Remove lower cover from center console. Remove circlip from control cable end. Remove exhaust covers. On models equipped with V6 engines, remove catalytic converter. On all models, loosen lock nut and remove control cable from shift lever on transaxle. To install, reverse removal procedure. Adjust control cable. See CONTROL CABLE ADJUSTMENT.

Removal & Installation (Shift Lock Cable) – **1)** Remove shift lever handle. Remove center console cover. Disconnect negative battery cable and wait 30 seconds.

2) Using Torx wrench, remove air bag retaining screws from rear side of steering wheel. Lift off air bag unit from steering wheel, and tilt air bag unit downward. Disconnect wiring connector from air bag unit. Remove steering wheel. Remove dash panel.

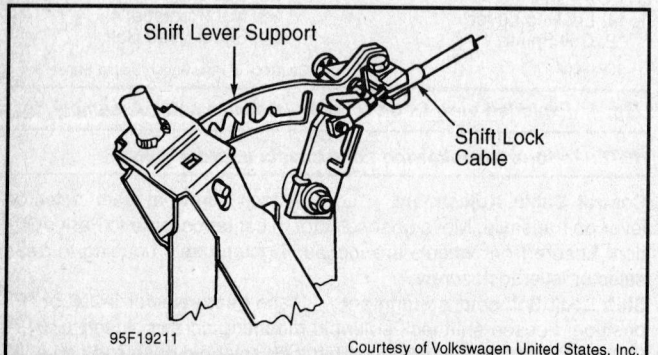

95F19211

Courtesy of Volkswagen United States, Inc.

Fig. 7: Removing Shift Lock Cable From Shift Lever Support

3) Place gear selector in rear position. Loosen screw holding cable sheath to gear selector support. Remove cable from lever. See Fig. 7.

4) Remove cover from ignition switch. Remove spring clip holding cable housing to ignition assembly. Lift and tilt shift lock cable housing upward. Pull up shift lock cable until shift lock cable unhooks from ignition switch. See Fig. 8.

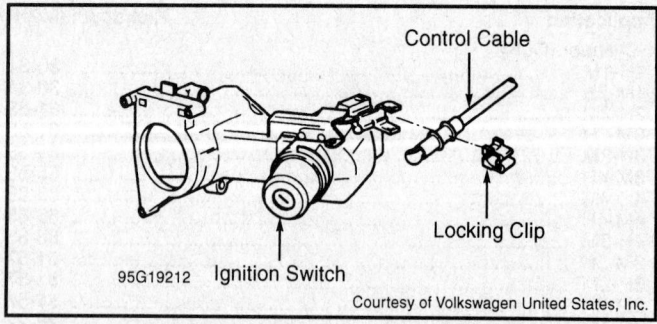

95G19212

Courtesy of Volkswagen United States, Inc.

Fig. 8: Removing Shift Lock Cable From Ignition Switch

5) Remove shift lock cable from under dash near A/C-heater housing and remove from vehicle. To install, position shift lock cable through under-dash panels. See Fig. 9. To complete installation, reverse removal procedure. Adjust shift lock control cable. See SHIFT LOCK CABLE ADJUSTMENT.

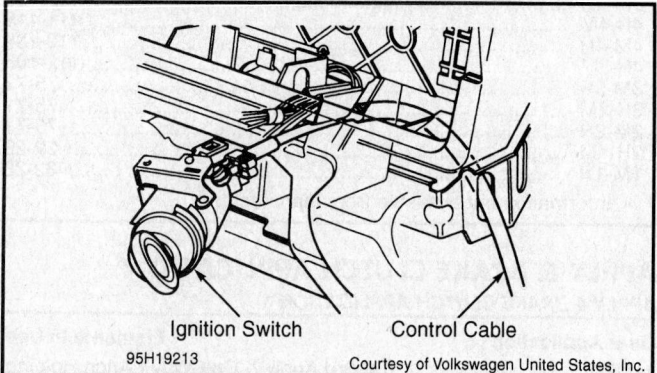

95H19213

Courtesy of Volkswagen United States, Inc.

Fig. 9: Routing Shift Lock Cable To Ignition Switch

ELECTRONIC SELF-DIAGNOSTICS
RETRIEVING TROUBLE CODES

1) Electronic control consists of a TCM (located under rear seat), control solenoids, and various sensors and switches. TCM monitors input and output signals. See Fig. 2.

2) If TCM detects problems in transaxle-related circuits or devices, TCM may record a trouble code in memory. To retrieve obtain trouble codes, use Scan Tool (VAG 1551) and Adapter (VAG 1551/3). All trouble code and related testing information is contained in scan tool.

TESTING
ELECTRICAL

NOTE: Manufacturer does not provide electrical component tests or specifications. All testing information is contained in Scan Tool (VAG 1551).

1) To isolate TCM circuit problems without a scan tool, circuit resistance and voltage can be checked by using Test Box (VAG 1598/18).

2) When checking circuit voltage, leave battery connected with test box connected to TCM and TCM vehicle harness. When checking circuit resistance, disconnect negative battery cable and connect test box to TCM vehicle harness. Leave TCM disconnected.

3) Measure voltage and resistance between specified sockets on test box. *See Figs. 10-13.* If a problem is found, service harness or components as necessary. If no problem is found, TCM may be defective.

HYDRAULIC PRESSURE

Check operation of apply and brake clutches by air checking fluid passages of valve body and transaxle case. Install Pressure Gauge (VAG 1702) to transaxle pressure tap located near dipstick tube. Check main hydraulic pressure under normal driving conditions. See MAIN PRESSURE table. If main hydraulic pressures are not correct, check for incorrect idle speed, problem with pump or sticking valves in valve body. Repair as necessary.

MAIN PRESSURE

Application	psi (Bar)
"D"	
Idle RPM	49-55 (3.4-3.8)
2000 RPM [1]	146-164 (10.1-11.3)
"R"	
Idle RPM	94-109 (6.5-7.5)
2000 RPM [1]	334-348 (23.0-24.0)

[1] – With solenoid valve connector disconnected. After test, reconnect solenoid valves and using appropriate scan tool, erase trouble codes from memory.

STALL SPEED

CAUTION: DO NOT operate engine at stall speed for more than 5 seconds. If you need to repeat stall speed test, wait 20 seconds.

1) Engage parking brake and block drive wheels. Connect tachometer to engine. Warm engine to normal operating temperature.
2) Firmly press brake pedal. Move gear selector to "D" position. Open throttle to wide open throttle position. Note engine speed and release throttle pedal.
3) Compare measured stall speed with stall speed specification. See STALL SPEED SPECIFICATIONS table. If stall speed is within range, test is complete.
4) If stall speed is up to 200 RPM too low, check engine condition and adjustments. If stall speed is greater than 200 RPM too low, torque converter is faulty. If stall speed is too high, check 1st-3rd apply clutch or one-way clutch for slipping or damage.

STALL SPEED SPECIFICATIONS

Application	RPM
CLK	2600-2900
CLB & CKZ	2250-2550

RESISTANCE & VOLTAGE TESTS

Sockets On VAG 1598/18	Area To Be Tested	• Testing Requirements & Additional Steps	Test Result Specifications	If Test Results NOT Within Specs
23 + 1	Transaxle TCM Voltage Supply	• Switch Ignition ON	About Battery Voltage	Check Wire From Terminal No. 1 Check Wire From Terminal No. 23 For Continuity With C/15A In Relay Panel
5 + 28	Throttle Position (TP) Sensor	• Switch Ignition OFF No Throttle Full Throttle	 700-1800 Ohms 2100-3900 Ohms	Check Wiring Calibrate Throttle Position (TP) Sensor
5 + 50	Throttle Position (TP) Sensor	• Switch Ignition OFF No Throttle Full Throttle	 2100-3900 Ohms 700-1800 Ohms	Check Wiring Calibrate Throttle Position (TP) Sensor
29 + 15	Solenoid Switch For Shift Interlock	• Switch Ignition ON • Selector Lever In P Or N Brakes Applied	About Battery Voltage About 0.2 Volt	Check Wiring Replace Shiftlock Solenoid
15 + 1	Signal From Brake Light Switch	• Switch Ignition ON DO NOT Apply Brakes Brakes Applied	0 Volt About Battery Voltage	Check Wiring Replace Brake Light Switch

96B04598

Courtesy of Volkswagen United States, Inc.

Fig. 10: Testing TCM Harness & Components (1 Of 4)

AUTOMATIC TRANSMISSIONS
Volkswagen Type 01M (Cont.)

RESISTANCE TESTS

VAG 1598/18 Terminals	Component To Be Tested	• Test Conditions & Additional Steps	Specified Value Or Results	If Test Results NOT Within Specs
63 + 1	Multifunction Switch	• Switch Ignition OFF		Check Wire Routing
		Move Selector Lever To Positions R, N, D, 2 & 3	Open	Replace Multifunction Switch
		Move Selector Lever To Position P & 1	.8 – 1.0 Ohms	
40 + 1		Move Selector Lever To Position P, R, 2 & 1	Open	
		Move Selector Lever To Position N, D & 3	.8 – 1.0 Ohms	
62 + 1		• Switch Ignition OFF		
		Move Selector Lever To Position P, R, N & D	Open	
		Move Selector Lever To Position 3, 2 & 1	.8 – 1.0 Ohms	
18 + 1		• Switch Ignition ON		
		Move Selector Lever To Position P, R & N	About Battery Voltage	
		Move Selector Lever To Position D, 3, 2 & 1	0 Volt	
55 + 67	Solenoid Valve No. 1	• Switch Ignition OFF	55 – 65 Ohms	Check Harness
55 + 1		Control Unit Removed	Open	Replace Valve Body
54 + 67	Solenoid Valve No. 2	• Switch Ignition OFF	55 – 65 Ohms	Check Harness
54 + 1		Control Unit Removed	Open	Replace Valve Body

96E04627

Courtesy of Volkswagen United States, Inc.

Fig. 11: Testing TCM Harness & Components (2 Of 4)

RESISTANCE TESTS

Sockets On VAG 1598/18	Area To Be Tested	• Testing Requirements & Additional Steps	Test Result Specifications	If Test Results NOT Within Specs
9 + 67	Solenoid Valve No. 3	• Switch Ignition OFF	55 – 65 Ohms	Check Harness Routing
9 + 1		TCM Disconnected	Open	Replace Valve Body
47 + 67	Solenoid Valve No. 4	• Switch Ignition OFF	4.5 – 6.5 Ohms	Check Harness Routing
47 + 1		TCM Disconnected	Ohms	Replace Valve Body
56 + 67	Solenoid Valve No. 5	• Switch Ignition OFF	55 – 65 Ohms	Check Harness Routing
56 + 1		TCM Disconnected	Open	Replace Valve Body
58 + 22	Solenoid Valve No. 6	• Switch Ignition OFF	4.5 – 6.5 Ohms	Check Harness Routing
58 + 1/22 + 1		TCM Disconnected	Open	Replace Valve Body
10 + 67	Solenoid Valve No. 7	• Switch Ignition OFF	55 – 65 Ohms	Check Harness Routing
10 + 1		TCM Disconnected	Open	Replace Valve Body
23 + 29	Solenoid Switch for Shift Interlock	• Switch Ignition OFF TCM Disconnected	14 – 25 Ohms	Check Harness Routing Replace Shiftlock Solenoid Assembly
1 + 16	Kickdown Switch	• Switch Ignition OFF • TCM Disconnected		Check Harness Routing Adjust Or Replace Accelerator Cable
		DO NOT Press Accelerator Pedal	Open	
		Depress Accelerator Fully	Less Than 1.5 Ohms	

96G04628

Courtesy of Volkswagen United States, Inc.

Fig. 12: Testing TCM Harness & Components (3 Of 4)

RESISTANCE TESTS

VAG 1598/18 Terminals	Component To Be Tested	• Test Conditions & Additional Steps	Specified Value Or Results	If Test Results NOT Within Specs
20 + 65	Vehicle Speed Sensor	• Switch Ignition OFF • TCM Disconnected • Set Ohmmeter To 2 k/ohm Scale	800 – 900 Ohms	Check Harness Routing Replace Vehicle Speed Sensor
6 + 67	ATF Temperature Sensor	• Switch Ignition OFF • TCM Disconnected • Set Ohmmeter To 200 k/ohm Scale ATF Temperature 68°F (20°C)	24,700 Ohms	Check Harness Routing Replace Valve Body
		• Set Ohmmeter to 200 k/ohm scale ATF Temperature 140°F (60°C)	About 48,800 Ohms	
		ATF Temperature 248°F (120°C)	About 7400 Ohms	
21 + 66	Transmission Vehicle Speed Sensor	• Switch Ignition OFF • TCM Disconnected • Set Ohmmeter To 2 k/ohm Scale	800 – 900 Ohms	Check Harness Routing Replace Vehicle Speed Sensor

96I04629

Courtesy of Volkswagen United States, Inc.

Fig. 13: Testing TCM Harness & Components (4 Of 4)

ON-VEHICLE SERVICE

DRIVE AXLE SHAFTS

See appropriate AXLE SHAFTS article in AXLE SHAFTS & TRANSFER CASES section.

OIL COOLER FLUSHING

1) Remove external oil filter. Remove oil lines and allow fluid to drain. Using pressurized solvent, flush remaining fluid and debris from oil lines and cooler. Repeat flushing if necessary.
2) Use pressurized shop air to remove solvent from oil lines and oil cooler. Install a new external oil filter.

TRANSAXLE COMPONENTS

Following components may be serviced with transaxle in vehicle. For removal and installation procedures, see TRANSAXLE DISASSEMBLY.

- Drive Flanges
- External Oil Filter
- Gear Selector Lever
- Multifunction Switch, Speedometer Drive Shaft & Speed Sensor
- Oil Pan & Valve Body Assembly
- Planetary Gear Cover

REMOVAL & INSTALLATION

See appropriate AUTOMATIC TRANSMISSION REMOVAL article in TRANSMISSION SERVICING section.

TORQUE CONVERTER

1) Remove torque converter. Check torque converter for any wear or damage, and replace if necessary. If torque converter is being reused, drain old fluid.
2) Extract ATF from torque converter using Torque Converter Service Station (VAG 1358 A) and Probe (VAG 1358 A/1).

TRANSAXLE DISASSEMBLY

TRANSAXLE UNIT

1) Remove torque converter. Remove oil pan and valve body assembly. Remove sealing plug from transaxle case. See Fig. 14.
2) Measure and record turbine shaft end play. See Fig. 15. Remove oil pump bolts. Using two M8 bolts, remove oil pump from front of transaxle. See Fig. 16.
3) Remove all clutches with support tube, 2nd-4th gear clutch plates, springs and spring caps together. See Figs. 17 and 18.
4) Lock drive shell in place by inserting a screwdriver through hole of large sun gear into side of transaxle case. See Fig. 19. Loosen and remove small planetary drive shaft bolt, washer and shim. See Fig. 20. Remove small planetary drive shaft.
5) Remove large drive shaft and sun gear. Remove Vehicle Speed Sensor (VSS) from transaxle case. Remove supporting tube and one-way clutch circlips. Remove one-way clutch assembly.
6) Remove planetary carrier with dished spring. Remove reverse brake clutch assembly. See Figs. 17, 20 and 21. DO NOT remove input gear assembly, unless bearing or gear damage is present.

FINAL DRIVE & TRANSFER GEARS

1) Drain gear oil. Attach INCH-lb. torque wrench to a 1 5/8" (41 mm) socket wrench. See Fig. 22. Measure and record total roller bearing turning torque of drive pinion gear. This measurement is required for reassembly reference if roller bearings are reused.
2) Engage parking pawl. Using a 7/8" (22 mm) Allen wrench socket, remove fastener nut. See Fig. 22. Remove dished washer, shim and bearing.
3) Install fastener nut. Using Pressing Adapter (VW771), thread tool until 1/8" clearance is present between bearing race and fastener nut.

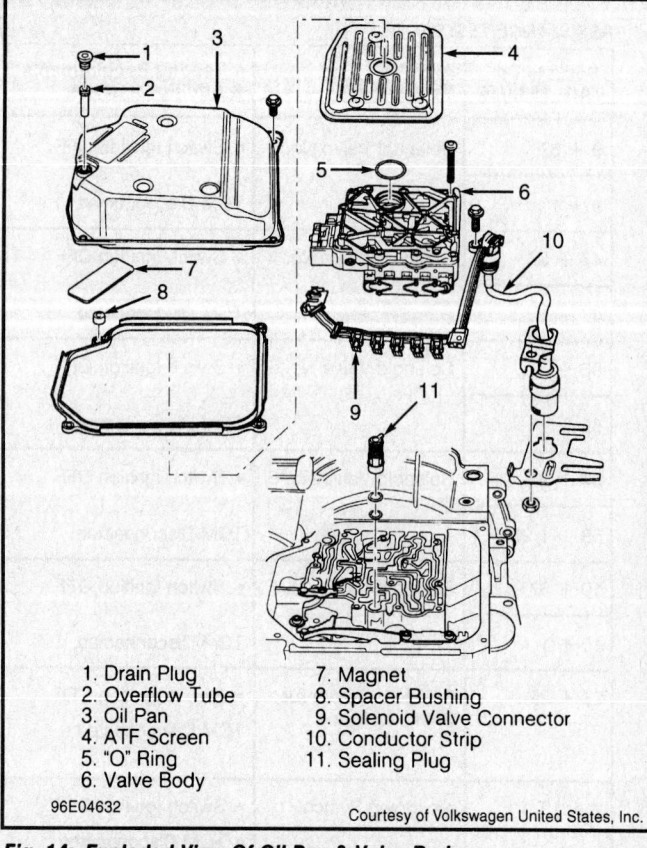

1. Drain Plug	7. Magnet
2. Overflow Tube	8. Spacer Bushing
3. Oil Pan	9. Solenoid Valve Connector
4. ATF Screen	10. Conductor Strip
5. "O" Ring	11. Sealing Plug
6. Valve Body	

96E04632
Courtesy of Volkswagen United States, Inc.

Fig. 14: Exploded View Of Oil Pan & Valve Body

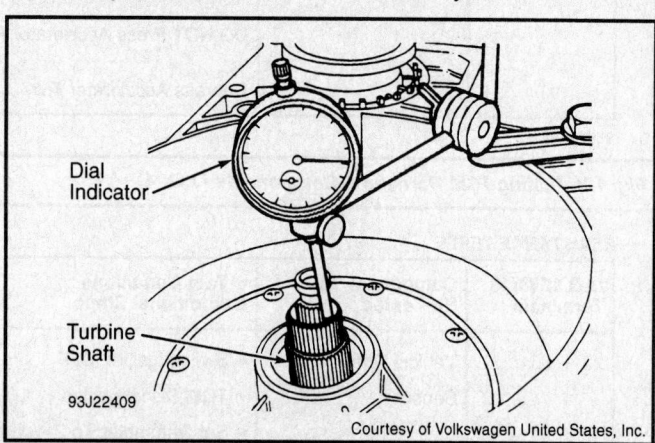

93J22409
Courtesy of Volkswagen United States, Inc.

Fig. 15: Checking Turbine Shaft End Play

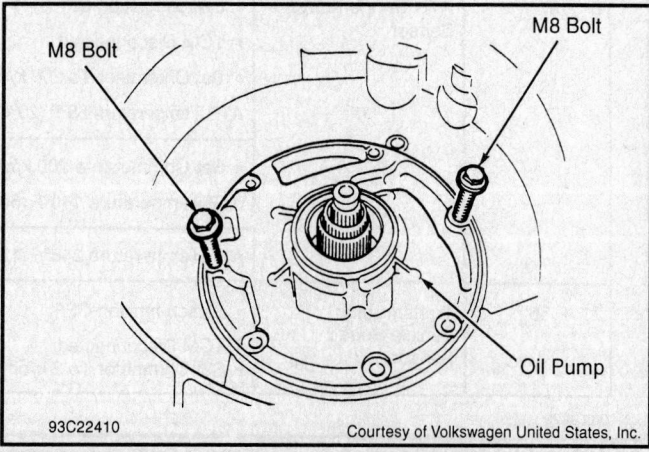

93C22410
Courtesy of Volkswagen United States, Inc.

Fig. 16: Removing Oil Pump

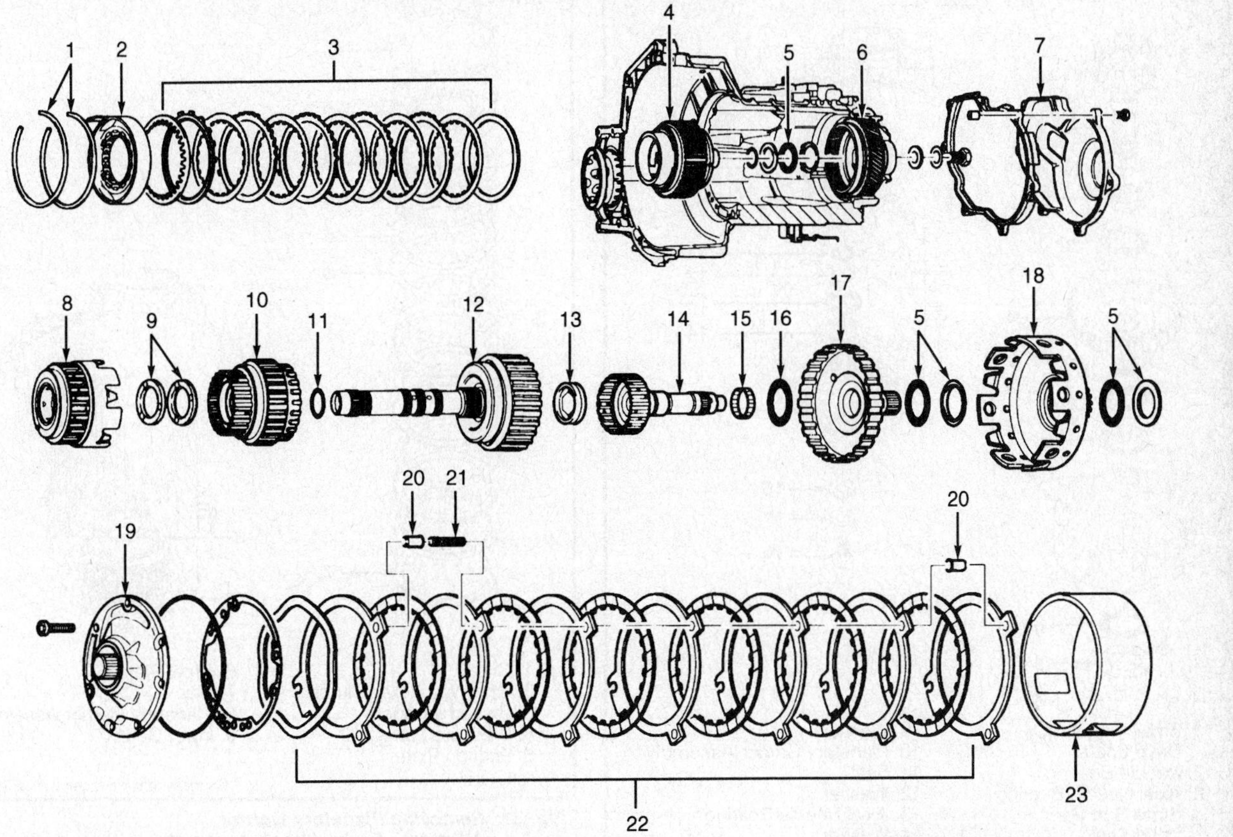

1. Circlips
2. One-Way Roller Clutch
3. Reverse Brake Clutch Assembly
4. Planetary Carrier Assembly
5. Bearing Assembly
6. Input Gear
7. Cover
8. Reverse Apply Clutch Assembly
9. Shims
10. 1st-3rd Apply Clutch Assembly
11. Seal
12. Turbine Shaft & 4th Apply Clutch Assembly
13. Axial Needle Bearing With Washer
14. Small Planetary Drive Shaft
15. Needle Bearing
16. Axial Needle Bearing
17. Small Sun Gear Drive Shell
18. Large Sun Gear Drive Shell
19. Oil Pump
20. Spring Cap
21. Spring
22. 2nd-4th Brake Clutch Assembly
23. Support Tube

96G04633

Courtesy of Volkswagen United States, Inc.

Fig. 17: Exploded View Of Transaxle Components

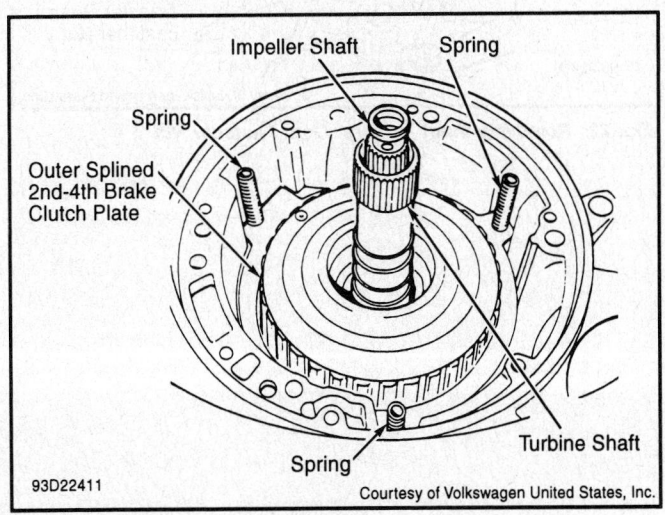

93D22411

Courtesy of Volkswagen United States, Inc.

**Fig. 18: Removing Turbine Shaft With 2nd-4th Brake Clutch
& 1st-3rd Apply Clutch**

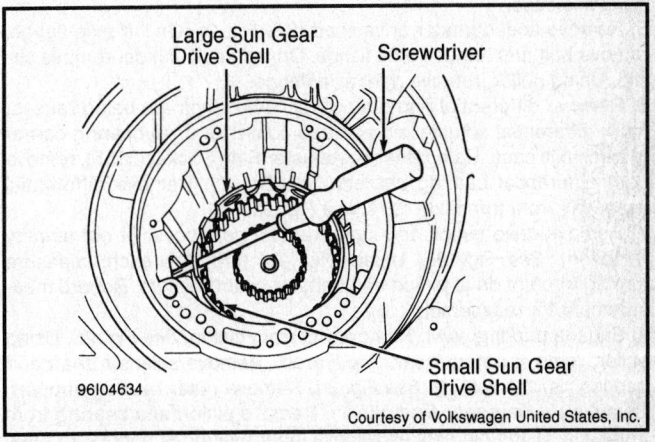

96I04634

Courtesy of Volkswagen United States, Inc.

Fig. 19: Locking Small Sun Gear Drive Shell

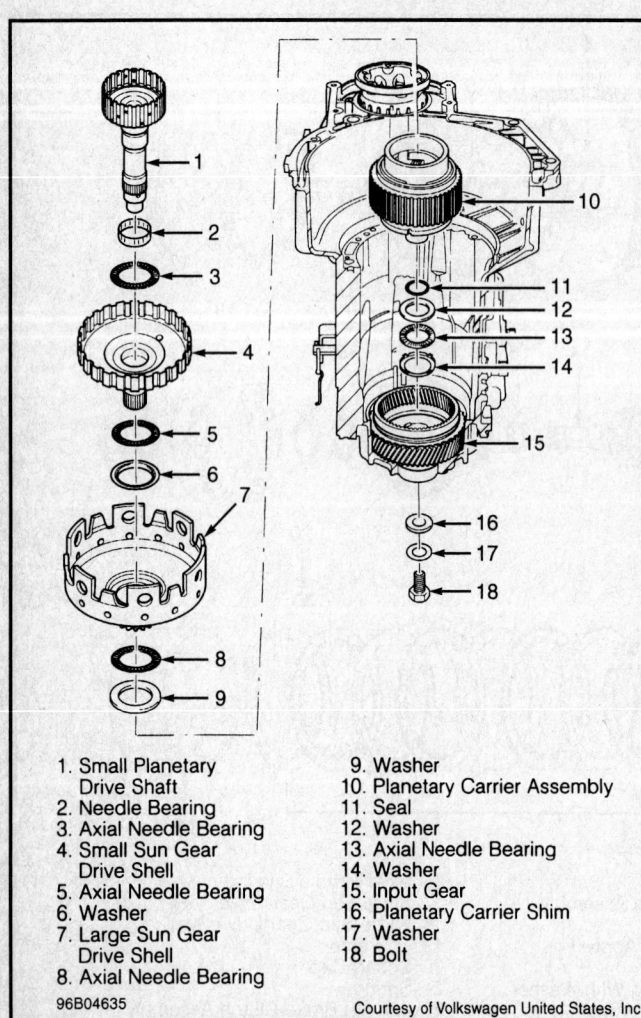

1. Small Planetary Drive Shaft
2. Needle Bearing
3. Axial Needle Bearing
4. Small Sun Gear Drive Shell
5. Axial Needle Bearing
6. Washer
7. Large Sun Gear Drive Shell
8. Axial Needle Bearing
9. Washer
10. Planetary Carrier Assembly
11. Seal
12. Washer
13. Axial Needle Bearing
14. Washer
15. Input Gear
16. Planetary Carrier Shim
17. Washer
18. Bolt

96B04635   Courtesy of Volkswagen United States, Inc.

Fig. 20: *Removing Small Planetary Drive Shaft*

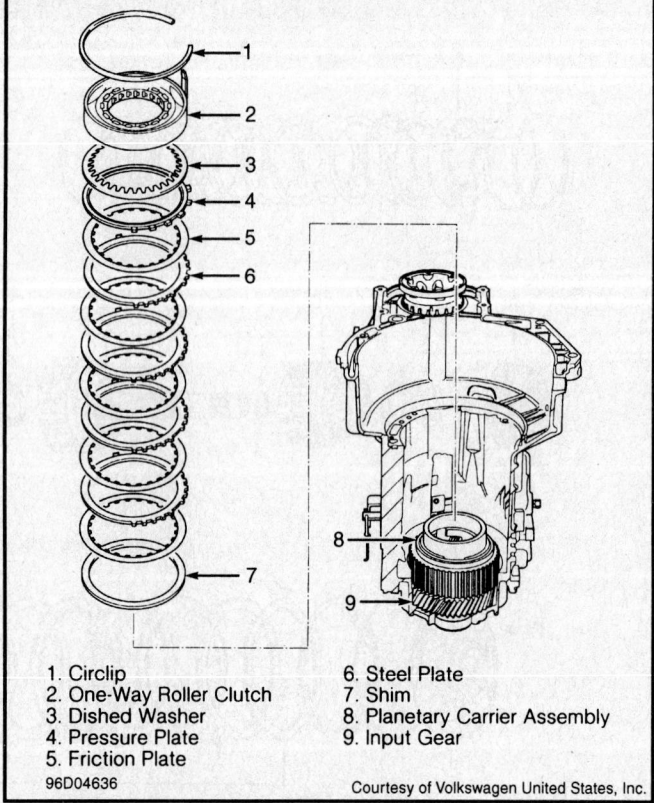

1. Circlip
2. One-Way Roller Clutch
3. Dished Washer
4. Pressure Plate
5. Friction Plate
6. Steel Plate
7. Shim
8. Planetary Carrier Assembly
9. Input Gear

96D04636   Courtesy of Volkswagen United States, Inc.

Fig. 21: *Removing Planetary Carrier & Reverse Brake Clutch Assembly*

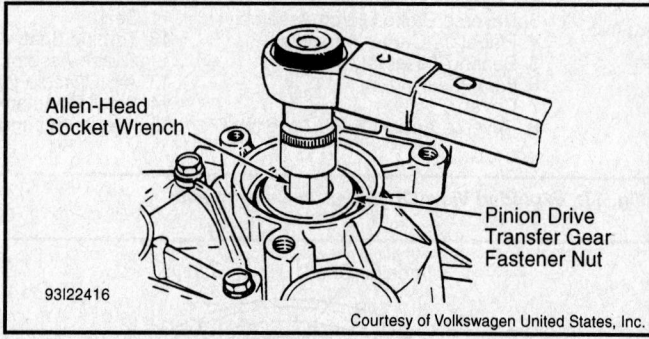

Allen-Head Socket Wrench

Pinion Drive Transfer Gear Fastener Nut

93I22416   Courtesy of Volkswagen United States, Inc.

Fig. 22: *Removing Input Transfer Gear Fastener Nut*

4) Pull input gear out until it bottoms in pressing adapter. Remove pressing adapter. Remove input transfer gear assembly from transaxle case.

5) Remove speedometer drive shaft. *See Fig. 23.* On left axle flange, remove bolt and remove axle flange. On right axle flange, remove circlip. Using puller, remove right axle flange.

6) Remove differential ring gear cover. If bearings are being reused, mark differential adjuster ring (torque converter side) bearing carrier to transaxle case. Using Bearing Adjuster Ring Socket (3155), remove both differential bearing carriers. *See Fig. 24.* Remove differential assembly from transaxle case. *See Fig. 23.*

7) Remove drive pinion and input transfer gear cover (if not already removed). *See Fig. 25.* Using INCH-lb. torque wrench, measure turning force of drive pinion and transfer gear bearings. Record measurement for reassembly.

8) Engage parking pawl. Remove nut from pinion. *See Fig. 26.* Using puller, remove output gear. *See Fig. 27.* Remove selector shaft and parking pawl assembly. *See Fig. 36.* Remove outer bearing support. Remove parking gear from pinion. Remove pinion and bearing from transaxle. Using pin socket, remove inner bearing support with drive pinion seal.

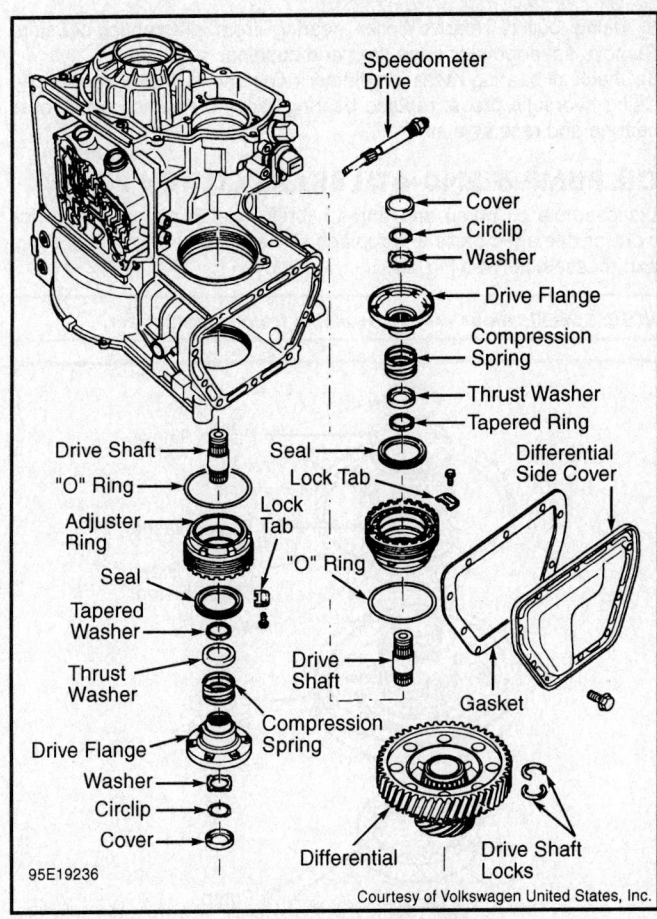

Speedometer Drive

Cover
Circlip
Washer
Drive Flange
Compression Spring
Thrust Washer
Tapered Ring

Drive Shaft
"O" Ring
Adjuster Ring
Seal
Tapered Washer
Thrust Washer
Drive Flange
Washer
Circlip
Cover

Seal
Lock Tab
Lock Tab
"O" Ring
Drive Shaft

Differential Side Cover
"O" Ring
Gasket

Differential
Drive Shaft Locks

95E19236

Courtesy of Volkswagen United States, Inc.

Fig. 23: Exploded View Of Drive Gear Assembly

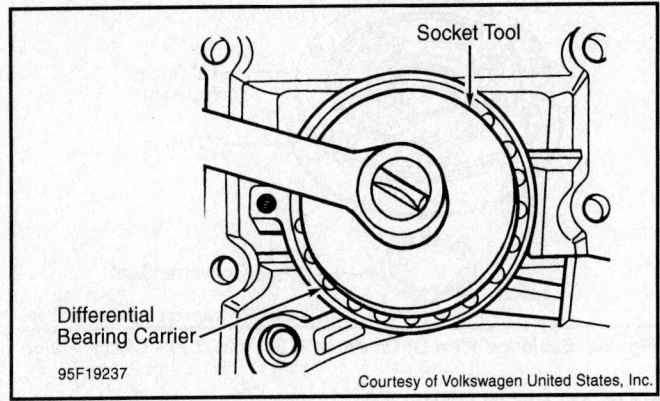

Socket Tool

Differential Bearing Carrier

95F19237

Courtesy of Volkswagen United States, Inc.

Fig. 24: Removing Bearing Adjuster Ring Bearing Carrier

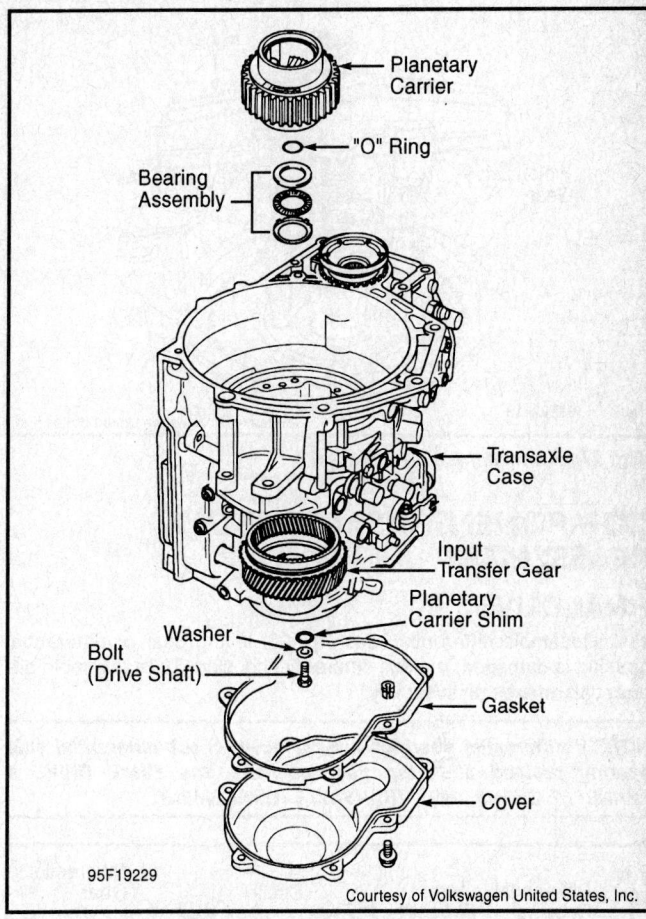

Planetary Carrier
"O" Ring
Bearing Assembly

Transaxle Case

Input Transfer Gear
Planetary Carrier Shim

Bolt (Drive Shaft)
Washer

Gasket

Cover

95F19229

Courtesy of Volkswagen United States, Inc.

Fig. 25: Locating Planetary & Input Gear Assembly

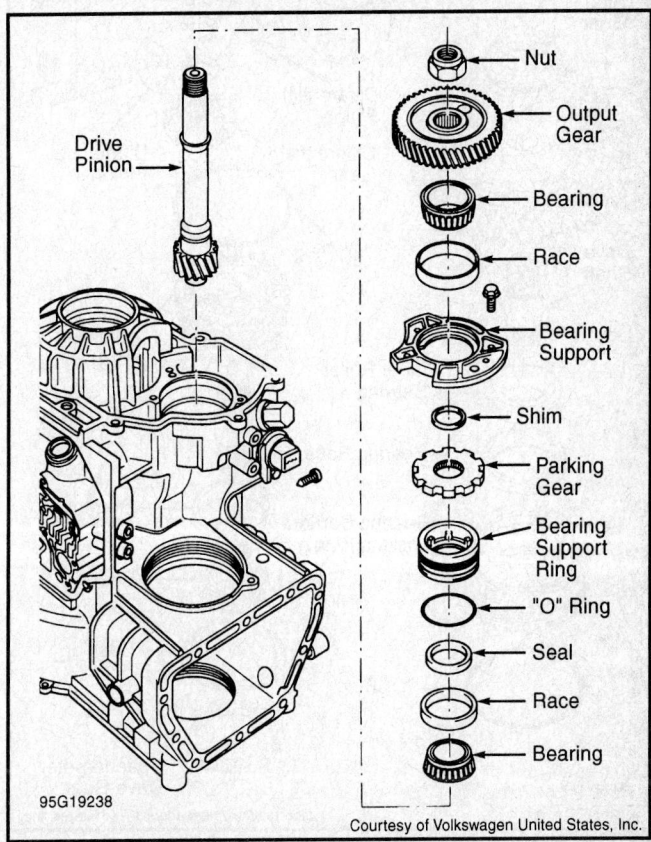

Drive Pinion

Nut
Output Gear
Bearing
Race
Bearing Support
Shim
Parking Gear
Bearing Support Ring
"O" Ring
Seal
Race
Bearing

95G19238

Courtesy of Volkswagen United States, Inc.

Fig. 26: Exploded View Of Drive Pinion & Output Gear Assembly

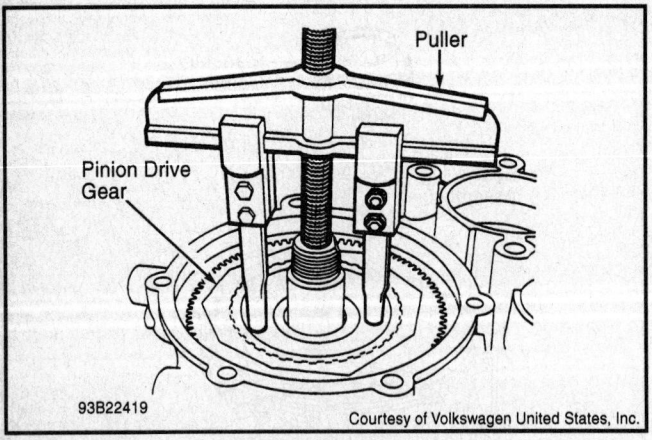

93B22419

Courtesy of Volkswagen United States, Inc.

Fig. 27: Removing Pinion Drive Gear

COMPONENT DISASSEMBLY & REASSEMBLY

FINAL DRIVE

1) Disassemble differential. See Fig. 28. If ring gear or differential housing is damaged, replace differential housing. To reassemble differential, reverse disassembly.

NOTE: If differential bearings are replaced, check differential side bearing preload and ring gear position. See FINAL DRIVE & TRANSFER GEARS under TRANSAXLE REASSEMBLY.

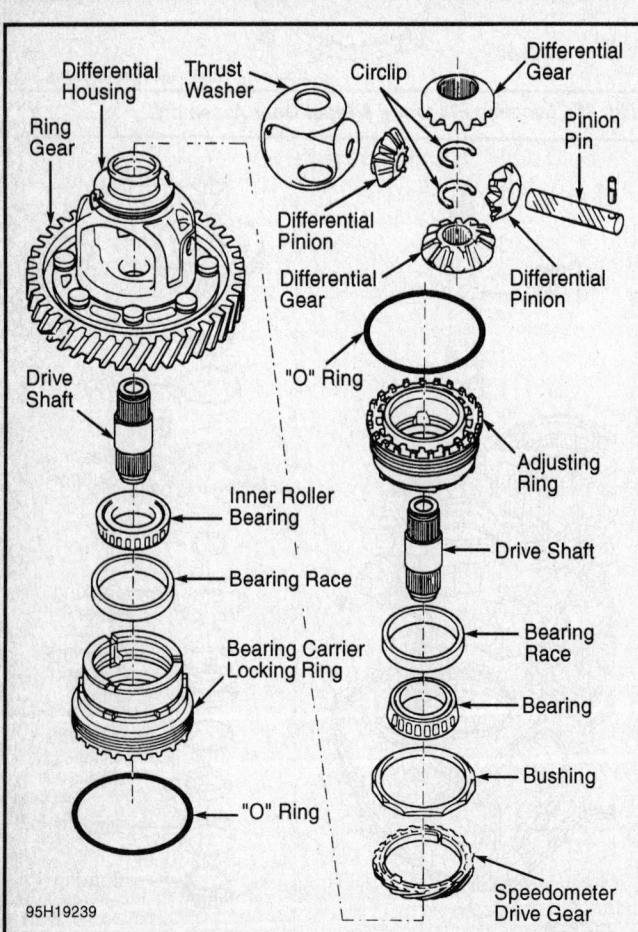

95H19239

Courtesy of Volkswagen United States, Inc.

Fig. 28: Exploded View Of Differential

2) Using puller, remove roller bearing from differential housing. Remove speedometer drive gear and bushing.

3) Check all bearing races in adjuster rings and replace if necessary. Using hydraulic press, replace bearing race(s). Replace each roller bearing and race as a set.

OIL PUMP & 2ND-4TH BRAKE CLUTCH PISTON

Disassemble oil pump and 2nd-4th brake clutch piston. Check for worn or damaged parts and replace as necessary. Replace all seals and reassemble. See Fig. 29.

NOTE: Specifications are not available from manufacturer.

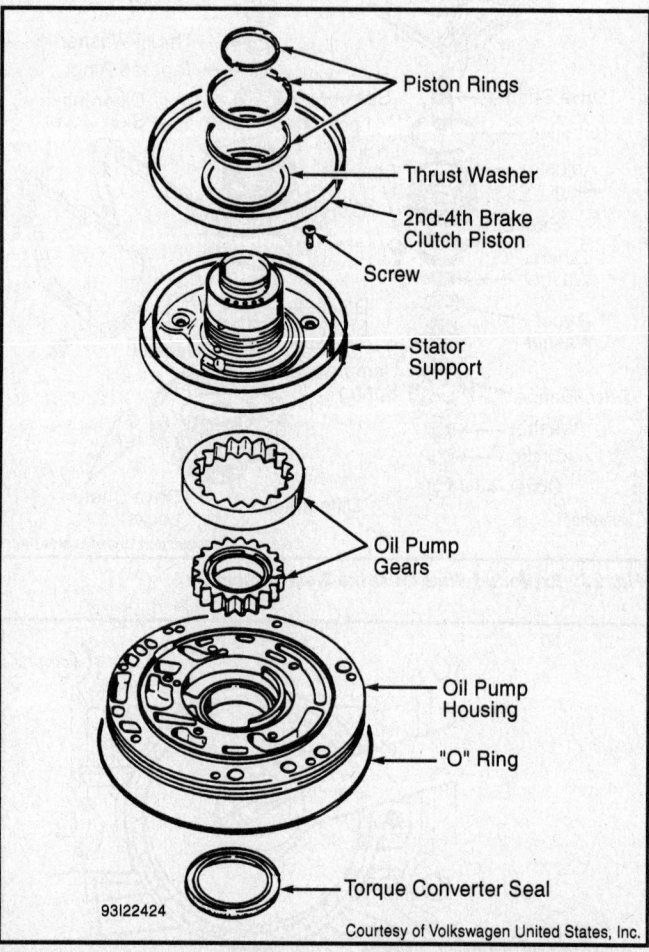

93I22424

Courtesy of Volkswagen United States, Inc.

Fig. 29: Exploded View Of Oil Pump & 2nd-4th Brake Clutch Piston

ONE-WAY CLUTCH

1) Disassemble one-way clutch. Check for worn or damaged parts and replace as necessary. Compress each spring and install into cage. See Fig. 30.

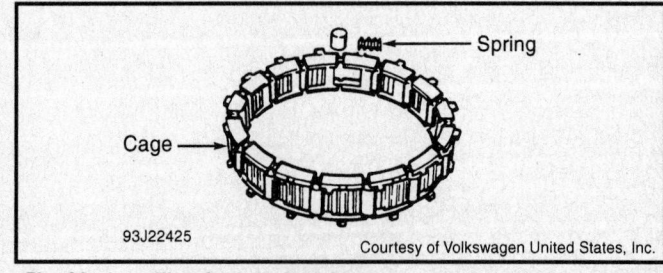

93J22425

Courtesy of Volkswagen United States, Inc.

Fig. 30: Installing Springs Into Cage

2) Hold cage assembly with large lugs up. Install cage assembly into outer ring. *See Figs. 31-33.* Rotate cage clockwise until lugs touch stop. Install piston into outer ring.

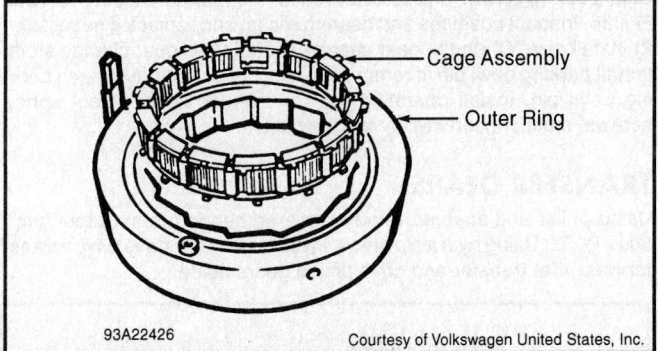

93A22426   Courtesy of Volkswagen United States, Inc.

Fig. 31: Installing Cage Assembly Into Outer Ring

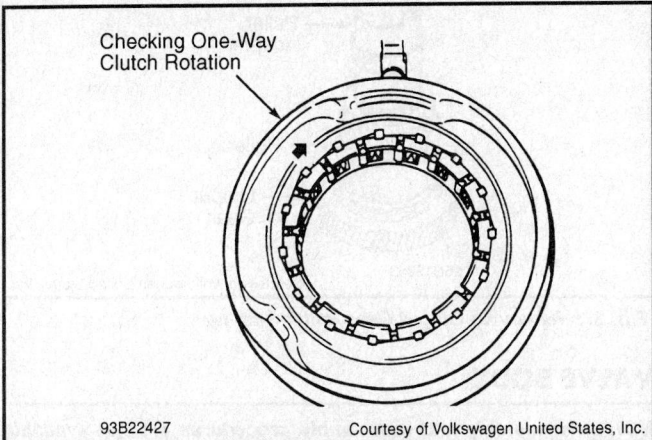

93B22427   Courtesy of Volkswagen United States, Inc.

Fig. 32: Checking One-Way Clutch Rotation

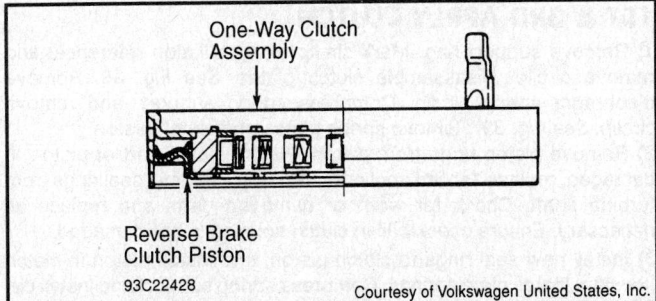

93C22428   Courtesy of Volkswagen United States, Inc.

Fig. 33: Installing Piston Into One-Way Clutch

PLANETARY CARRIER

NOTE: Disassembly and reassembly procedures are not available from manufacturer.

Inspection & Adjustment – 1) Inspect planetary carrier, pinion gears, sun gears and related parts for wear or damage. Replace parts as necessary.

2) Assemble sun gear drive shells, planetary carrier, small sun gear, pinion drive transfer gear and all related bearings and washers onto small planetary drive shaft. *See Figs. 17 and 20.*

3) Place assembly into transaxle case. Install adjustment shim, washer and bolt to pinion drive transfer gear end of small planetary drive shaft. Using a screwdriver, lock large sun gear drive shell to transaxle case. *See Fig. 19.* Tighten bolt to 22 ft. lbs. (30 N.m).

4) Place Dial Indicator Support (VW 382/7) on top of assembly. *See Fig. 34.* Measure end play of small sun gear drive shaft.

5) If end play is not .009-.014 (.23-.37 mm), replace adjustment shim. Adjustment shims range in thickness from .040" (1.00 mm) to .114" (2.90 mm) in .004" (.10 mm) increments.

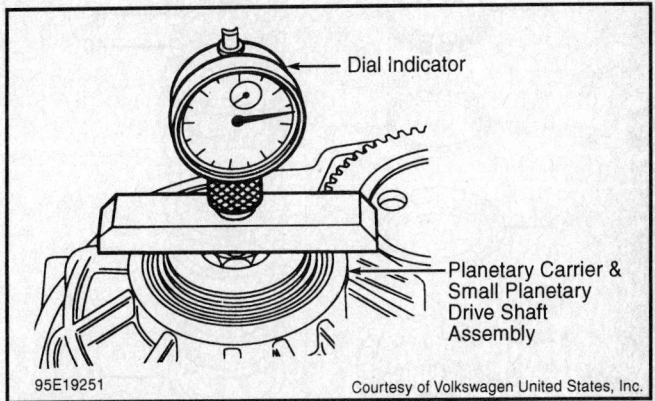

95E19251   Courtesy of Volkswagen United States, Inc.

Fig. 34: Adjusting Planetary Carrier End Play

APPLY CLUTCH PLATE APPLICATIONS

APPLY CLUTCH PLATE APPLICATIONS

Application	Number Of Plates
Reverse Clutch	
Inner	5
Outer	5
1st-3rd Clutch	
Inner	5
Outer	
CLB & CLK	5
CKZ	4
4th Clutch	
Inner	
CLB & CKZ	6
CLK	5
Outer	
CLB & CKZ	5
CLK	4

REVERSE APPLY CLUTCH

NOTE: Soak all friction-faced clutch plates in ATF for at least 15 minutes before installation.

1) Mark circlip for installation reference and remove. Disassemble clutch plates. *See Fig. 35.* Compress spring support, and remove circlip. Remove clutch piston.

2) Check for worn or damaged parts and replace as necessary. Ensure check ball in clutch housing is not damaged. Piston seal is part of piston. If damaged, replace reverse apply clutch piston. Reassemble reverse apply clutch. See APPLY CLUTCH PLATE APPLICATIONS table.

NOTE: Assembled clutch clearance specification is not available from manufacturer. Ensure thrust plate is installed with shouldered side facing circlip.

REVERSE & 2ND-4TH BRAKE CLUTCHES

Reverse and 2nd-4th brake clutches are disassembled and reassembled during transaxle disassembly and reassembly. See TRANSAXLE DISASSEMBLY and TRANSAXLE REASSEMBLY.

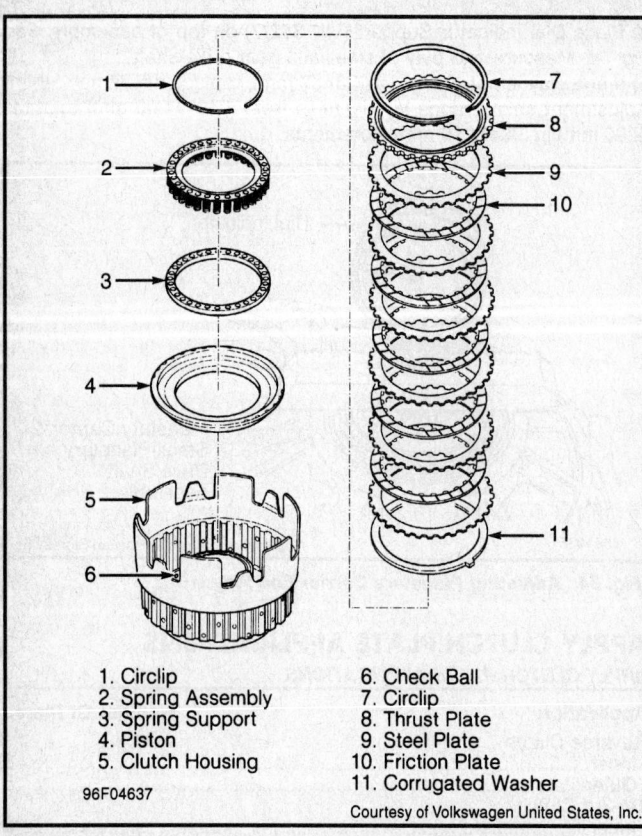

1. Circlip
2. Spring Assembly
3. Spring Support
4. Piston
5. Clutch Housing
6. Check Ball
7. Circlip
8. Thrust Plate
9. Steel Plate
10. Friction Plate
11. Corrugated Washer

96F04637

Courtesy of Volkswagen United States, Inc.

Fig. 35: Exploded View Of Reverse Apply Clutch Assembly

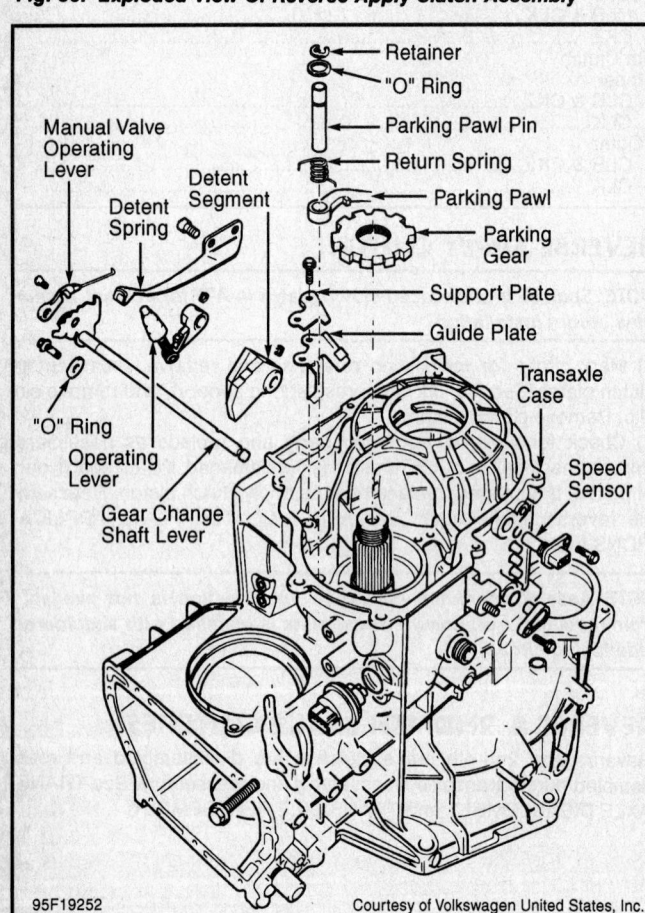

95F19252

Courtesy of Volkswagen United States, Inc.

Fig. 36: Exploded View Of Transaxle Case Components

TRANSAXLE CASE

1) Remove multifunction switch, all seals, manual valve assembly, parking pawl and sensors. If necessary, remove parking pawl pin, detent spring screws and selector rod for manual valve from case. See Fig. 36. Inspect bushings and bearing races, and replace if necessary.
2) Install new "O" ring to gear change shaft. Install gear change shaft. Install parking pawl pin (if removed). Using a center punch, peen parking pawl pin. Install operating rod for manual valve, detent spring screws, multifunction switch and new seals.

TRANSFER GEARS

Using puller and adapter, remove tapered bearing from output gear. See Fig. 37. Using hydraulic press, install bearing to drive pinion transfer gear. Set transfer and drive pinion gears aside.

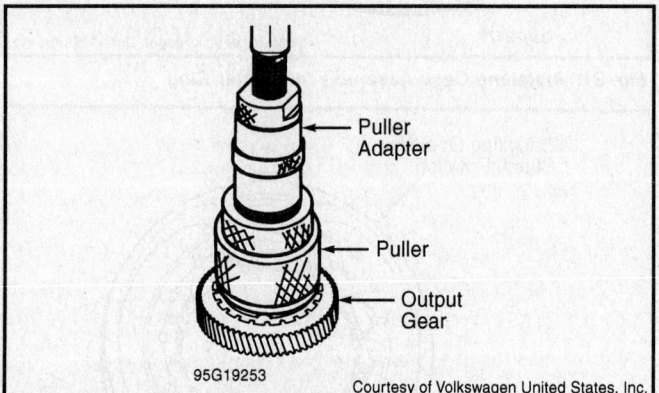

95G19253

Courtesy of Volkswagen United States, Inc.

Fig. 37: Removing Output Gear Roller Bearing

VALVE BODY

NOTE: Disassembly and reassembly procedures are not available from manufacturer.

1ST & 3RD APPLY CLUTCH

1) Remove support ring. Mark circlip for installation reference, and remove circlip. Disassemble clutch plates. See Fig. 38. Remove diaphragm spring circlip. Compress spring support, and remove circlip. See Fig. 39. Remove spring plates and clutch piston.
2) Remove piston rings from piston. Piston seal is part of piston. If damaged, replace 1st-3rd apply clutch piston. Remove seal rings from turbine shaft. Check for worn or damaged parts and replace as necessary. Ensure check ball in clutch housing is not damaged.
3) Install new seal rings to clutch piston, and install piston in clutch housing. Install plate springs. Compress spring support and install circlip. See Fig. 39.
4) Install bottom thrust plate with smooth side facing clutch plate. Install one inner splined and one outer splined clutch plate into clutch housing. See Fig. 38.
5) Place inner plate carrier on bench. Install remaining clutch plates to inner plate carrier. See APPLY CLUTCH PLATE APPLICATIONS. Insert top thrust plate with smooth side facing clutch plate. Install support ring with step tabs up after installing thrust plate, friction plates and steel plates. See Fig. 40.
6) Install inner plate carrier into clutch housing. Install circlip in clutch housing. See Fig. 41.

4TH APPLY CLUTCH

NOTE: Soak all friction-faced clutch plates in ATF for at least 15 minutes before installation.

1) Mark circlip for installation reference and remove. Disassemble clutch plates. See Fig. 42. Compress spring support ring, and remove circlip. Remove spring support ring and spring. Remove clutch piston.

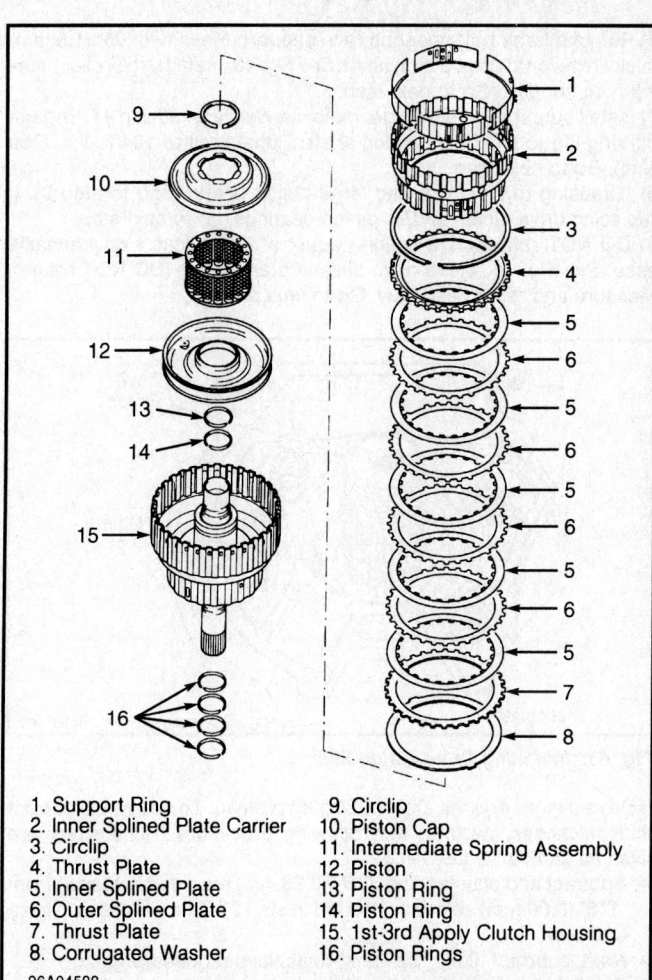

1. Support Ring
2. Inner Splined Plate Carrier
3. Circlip
4. Thrust Plate
5. Inner Splined Plate
6. Outer Splined Plate
7. Thrust Plate
8. Corrugated Washer
9. Circlip
10. Piston Cap
11. Intermediate Spring Assembly
12. Piston
13. Piston Ring
14. Piston Ring
15. 1st-3rd Apply Clutch Housing
16. Piston Rings

96A04588

Courtesy of Volkswagen United States, Inc.

Fig. 38: *Exploded View Of 1st-3rd Apply Clutch*

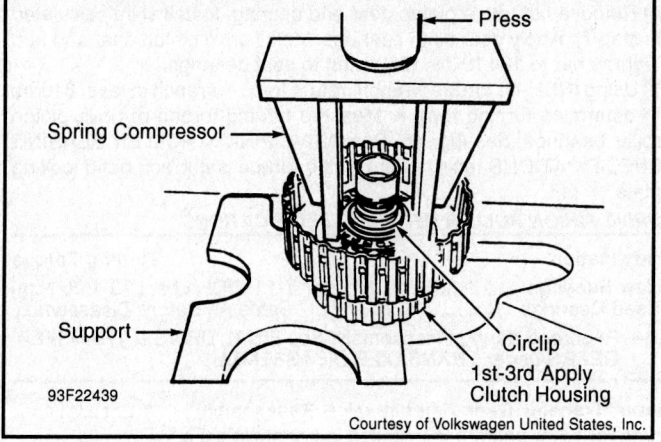

93F22439

Courtesy of Volkswagen United States, Inc.

Fig. 39: *Removing & Installing Spring Circlip*

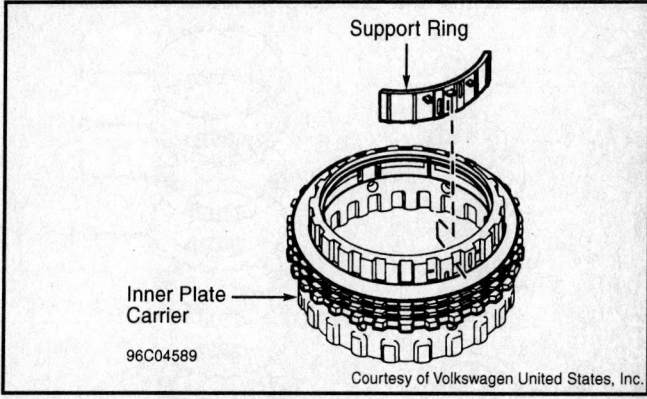

96C04589

Courtesy of Volkswagen United States, Inc.

Fig. 40: *Installing Support Ring*

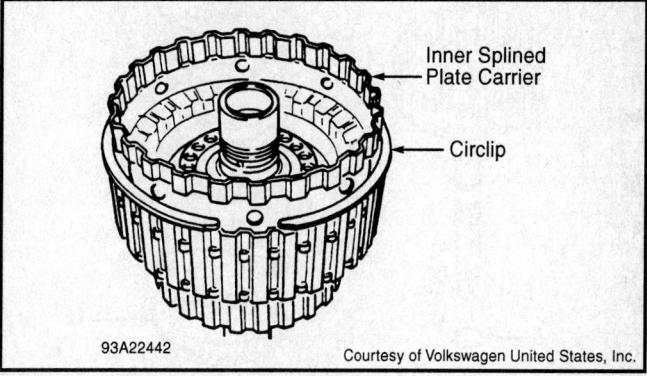

93A22442

Courtesy of Volkswagen United States, Inc.

Fig. 41: *Installing Clutch Housing Circlip*

2) Remove front impeller seal rings. DO NOT remove inner impeller seal rings unless damaged. Check for worn or damaged parts and replace as necessary.

3) Piston seal is part of piston. If damaged, replace 3rd-4th apply clutch piston. Reassemble 3rd-4th apply clutch. See APPLY CLUTCH PLATE APPLICATIONS table.

NOTE: Assembled clutch clearance specification is not available from manufacturer. Ensure top thrust plate is installed with shouldered side facing circlip.

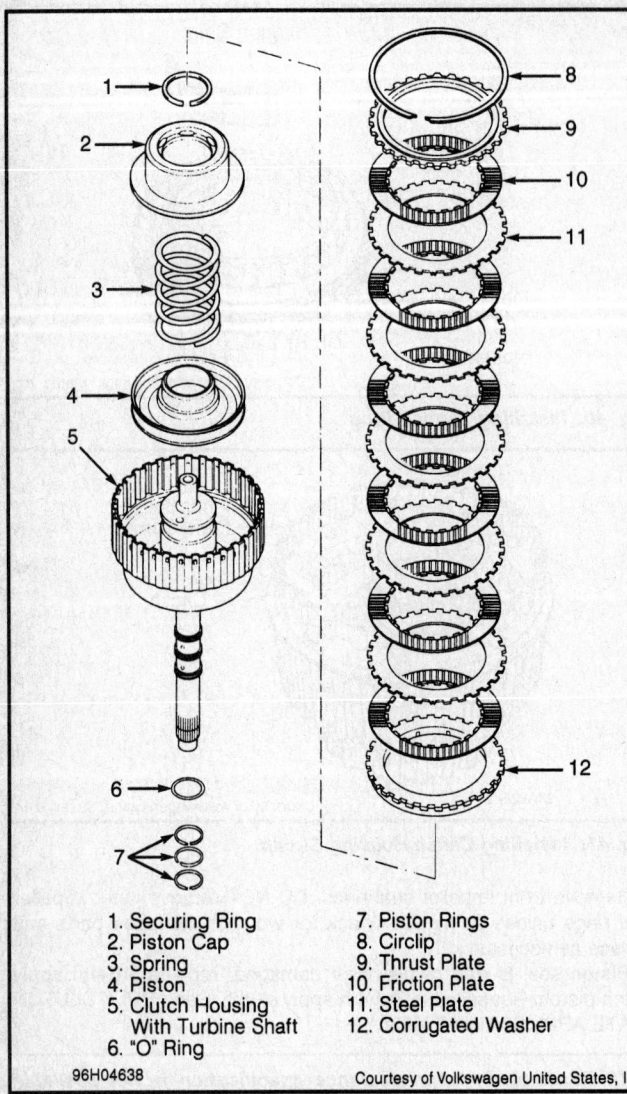

1. Securing Ring
2. Piston Cap
3. Spring
4. Piston
5. Clutch Housing
   With Turbine Shaft
6. "O" Ring
7. Piston Rings
8. Circlip
9. Thrust Plate
10. Friction Plate
11. Steel Plate
12. Corrugated Washer

96H04638   Courtesy of Volkswagen United States, Inc.

Fig. 42: Exploded View Of 4th Apply Clutch

TRANSAXLE REASSEMBLY

FINAL DRIVE & TRANSFER GEARS

NOTE: Reassembly procedures include bearing and shim adjustments. Perform all steps in the order given. If no parts were replaced, skip adjustment steps and reassemble final drive and transfer gear assembly using new seals. Ensure turning torque of complete assembly is within specifications. See INPUT TRANSFER GEAR ADJUSTMENT & REASSEMBLY procedure. If turning torque is not within specifications, check all adjustments.

Drive Pinion Roller Bearing Adjustment – 1) Install drive pinion assembly with smaller bearing and inner bearing support (with pinion seal and "O" ring). Install parking gear (rounded side facing drive pinion gear), park lock lug and large pinion bearing race support. Go to next step.

NOTE: Install drive pinion seal with lip opening facing closest roller bearing.

2) If reusing drive pinion and large pinion bearing, DO NOT remove existing shims from drive pinion shaft. *See Fig. 43*. Go to step 4). If replacing drive pinion and/or pinion bearings, install large pinion roller bearing to drive pinion. Go to next step.

3) Remove large roller bearing race support. Place two .06" (1.5 mm) thick shims onto drive pinion shaft. *See Fig. 43*. Install large roller bearing race support. Go to next step.

4) Install output drive pinion gear and nut. *See Figs. 36 and 44*. Engage parking lug to lock drive pinion shaft. Tighten nut to 184 ft. lbs. (250 N.m). Go to next step.

5) If reusing drive pinion and large pinion bearing, go to step 9). If replacing drive pinion and/or pinion bearings, go to next step.

6) DO NOT rotate drive pinion. Mount a dial indicator on transaxle case. *See Fig. 45*. Move drive pinion up and down (DO NOT rotate). Measure and record end play. Go to next step.

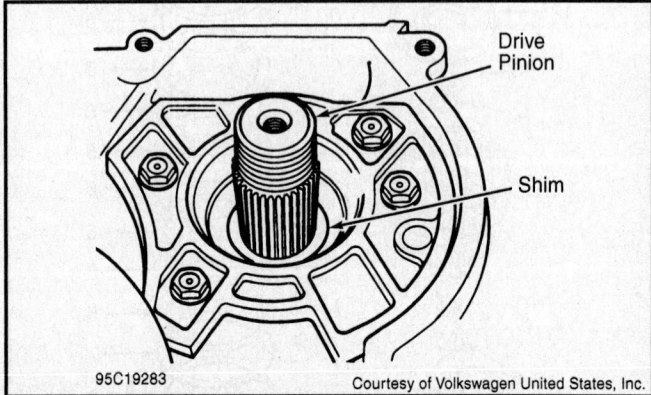

95C19283   Courtesy of Volkswagen United States, Inc.

Fig. 43: Installing Drive Pinion Shim

7) Drive pinion requires .008" (.220 mm) preload. To determine correct shim thickness, perform the following procedure. Dimensions are given as an EXAMPLE ONLY:
- Subtract end play reading .037" (0.93 mm) recorded in step 6) from .118" (3.00 mm) shim pack added in step 3). This will result in zero end play.
- Next, subtract .008" (.220 mm) to achieve required preload.
- Total shim thickness required to achieve correct preload would be .073" (1.85 mm).
- Shims are available in thickness ranging from .040-.106" (1.00-2.70 mm), in .001" (.025 mm) increments.

8) Remove nut, drive pinion gear and bearing. Install shim calculated in step 7). Apply gear oil to bearings. Install drive pinion gear and nut. Tighten nut to 184 ft. lbs. (250 N.m) to seat bearings.

9) Using INCH-lb. torque wrench, rotate torque wrench at least 8 turns to determine turning torque. Measure turning torque of drive pinion roller bearings. *See Fig. 46*. See DRIVE PINION ROLLER BEARING SPECIFICATIONS table. After turning torque is correct, bend locking plate on nut.

DRIVE PINION ROLLER BEARING SPECIFICATIONS

Application	Turning Torque
New Bearings	7-11 INCH Lbs. (.73-1.20 N.m)
Used Bearings	[1] Same As Before Disassembly

[1] – Recorded during disassembly. See FINAL DRIVE & TRANSFER GEARS under TRANSAXLE DISASSEMBLY.

Input Transfer Gear Adjustment & Reassembly – 1) Ensure inner race for roller bearing is installed in transaxle case.

2) Install input transfer gear with roller bearing and axial needle bearing (flat side facing input gear) into transaxle case. *See Figs. 1, 44 and 47*. Align lugs on outer roller bearing to fit between lugs on inner roller bearing. *See Fig. 48*.

3) Install outer roller bearing (without dished washer or shim) on input transfer gear. *See Figs. 44 and 47*. Engage parking gear. Using an Allen-head socket, tighten fastener nut to 74 ft. lbs. (100 N.m). *See Fig. 49*.

4) Remove fastener nut. Using a dial indicator, measure distance between input transfer gear and inner race of roller bearing. *See Fig. 50*. Measure thickness of dished washer.

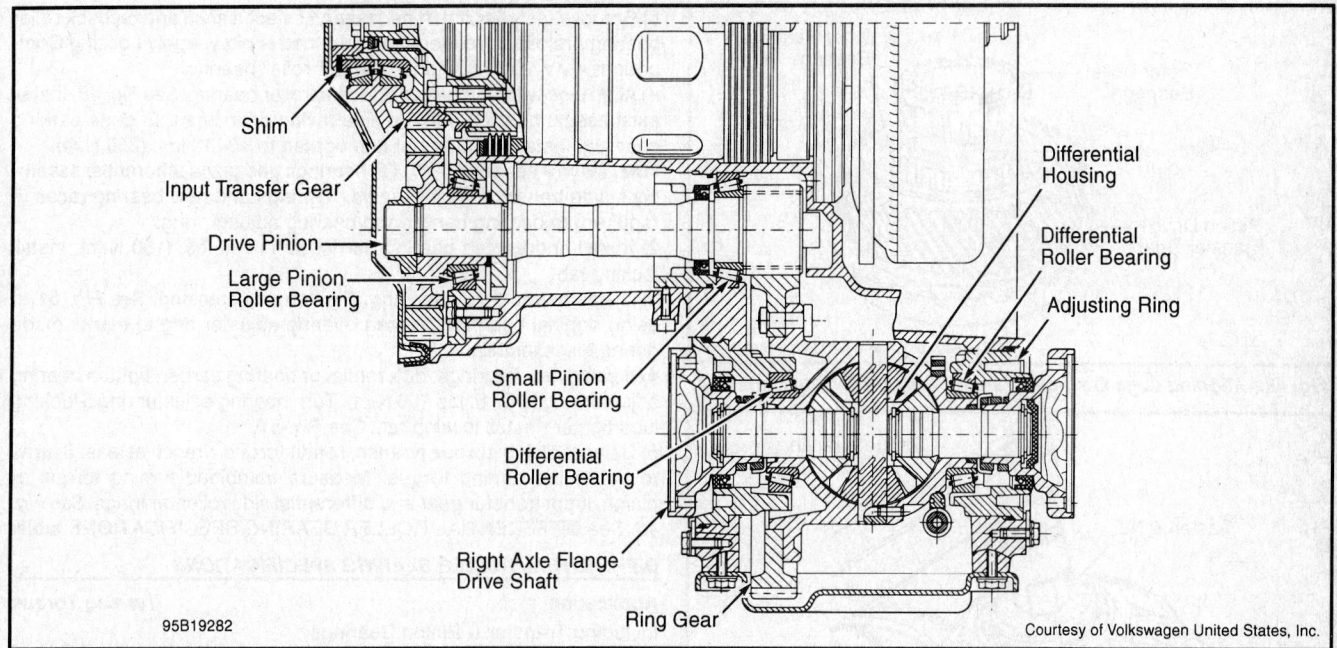

Shim

Input Transfer Gear

Drive Pinion

Large Pinion Roller Bearing

Differential Housing

Differential Roller Bearing

Adjusting Ring

Small Pinion Roller Bearing

Differential Roller Bearing

Right Axle Flange Drive Shaft

Ring Gear

95B19282

Courtesy of Volkswagen United States, Inc.

Fig. 44: Locating Final Drive Roller Bearings, Races & Adjustment Shims

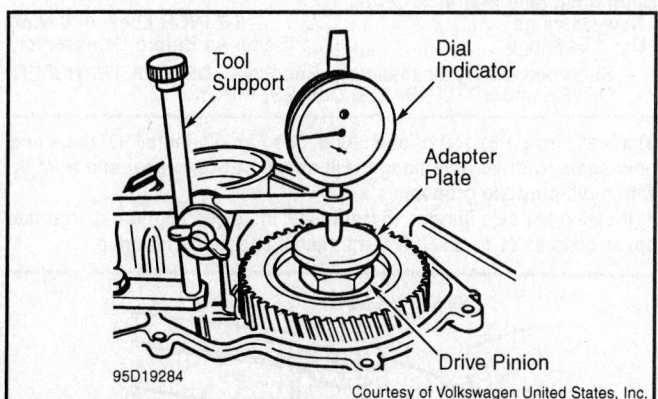

Tool Support

Dial Indicator

Adapter Plate

Drive Pinion

95D19284

Courtesy of Volkswagen United States, Inc.

Fig. 45: Checking Drive Pinion Roller Bearing End Play

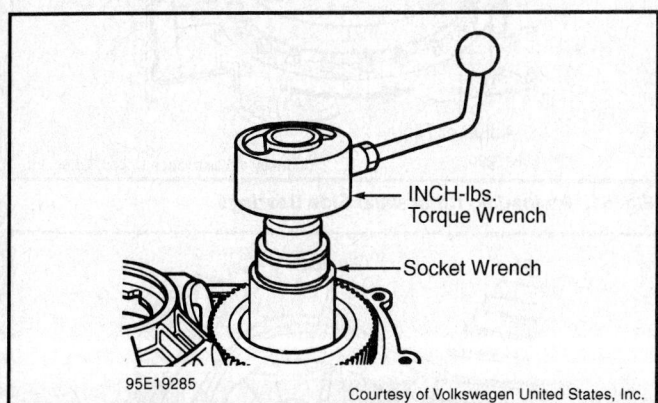

INCH-lbs. Torque Wrench

Socket Wrench

95E19285

Courtesy of Volkswagen United States, Inc.

Fig. 46: Checking Pinion Roller Bearing Preload

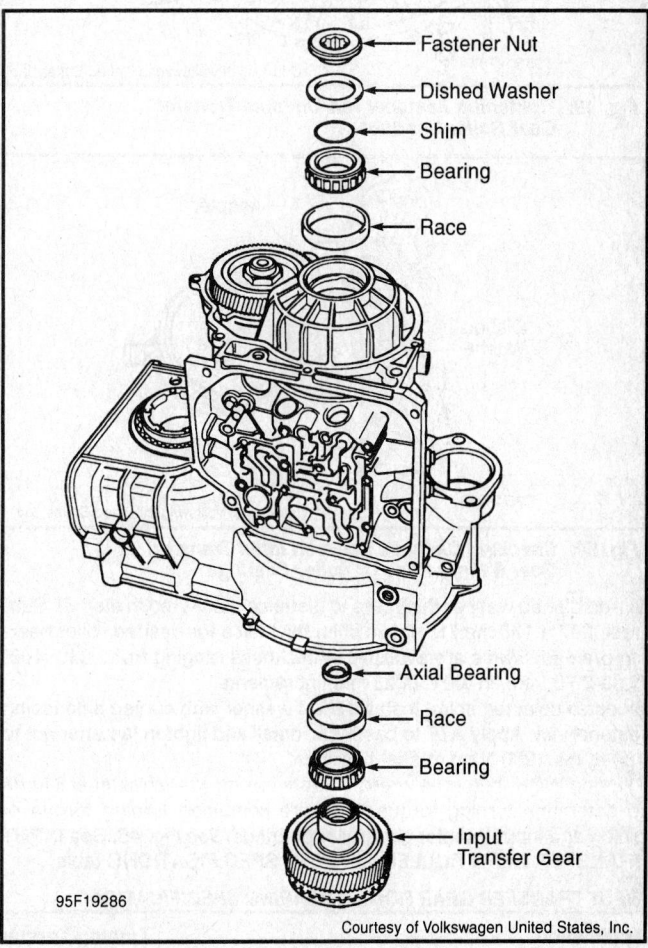

Fastener Nut

Dished Washer

Shim

Bearing

Race

Axial Bearing

Race

Bearing

Input Transfer Gear

95F19286

Courtesy of Volkswagen United States, Inc.

Fig. 47: Locating Input Transfer Gear Assembly

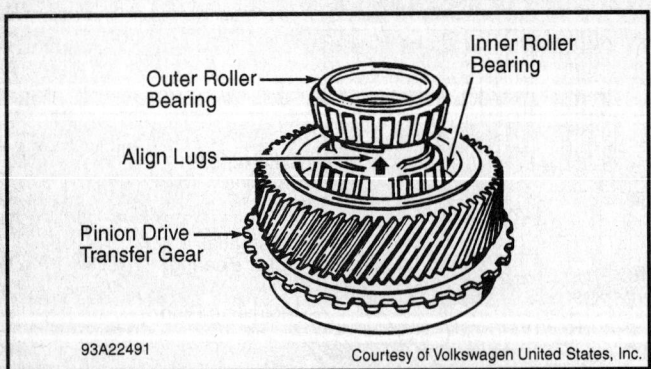

Fig. 48: Aligning Lugs On Input Transfer Gear Roller Bearings

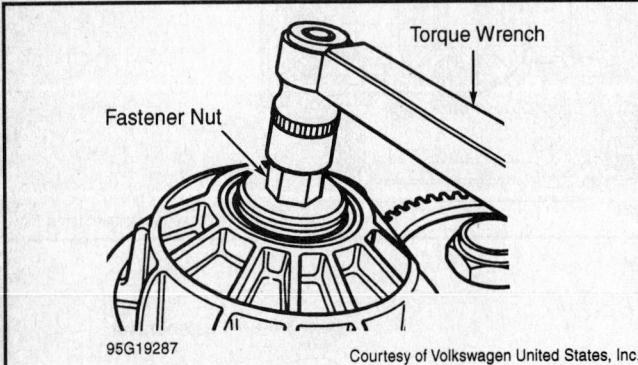

Fig. 49: Tightening Fastener Nut On Input Transfer Gear Roller Bearings

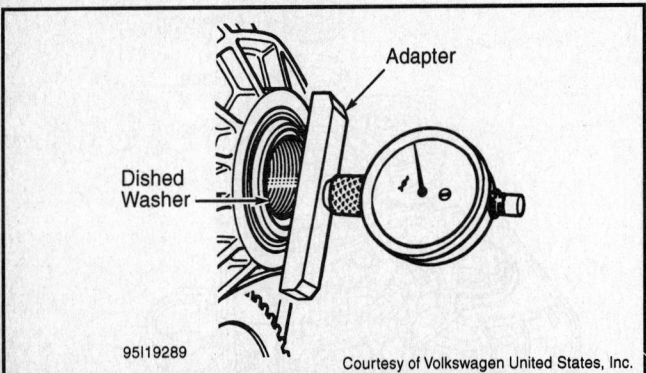

Fig. 50: Checking Distance Between Input Transfer Gear & Inner Race Of Roller Bearings

5) Add dished washer thickness to distance measured in step **3)**. Subtract .007" (.180 mm) to obtain shim thickness for desired roller bearing preload. Shims are available in thickness ranging from .040-.106" (1.00-2.70 mm), in .001" (.025 mm) increments.

6) Install selected shim. Install dished washer with curved side facing fastener nut. Apply ATF to bearings. Install and tighten fastener nut to 184 ft. lbs. (250 N.m) to seat bearings.

7) Using INCH-lb. torque wrench, rotate torque wrench at least 8 turns to determine turning torque. Measure combined turning torque of pinion and input transfer gear roller bearings. See Fig. 46. See INPUT TRANSFER GEAR ROLLER BEARING SPECIFICATIONS table.

INPUT TRANSFER GEAR ROLLER BEARING SPECIFICATIONS

Application	Turning Torque
New Bearings	
Without Drive Pinion Bearings	18 INCH Lbs. (2.0 N.m)
With Drive Pinion Bearings	[1] 27 INCH Lbs. (3.0 N.m)
Used Bearings	[2] Same As Before Disassembly

[1] – Based on a drive pinion torque of 9 INCH Lbs. (1.0 N.m).
[2] – Recorded during disassembly. See FINAL DRIVE & TRANSFER GEARS under TRANSAXLE DISASSEMBLY.

8) Remove fastener nut. If necessary, select a shim and recheck roller bearing preload. If roller bearing preload is okay, apply Locking Compound (AMV 100 01) to shaft side of roller bearing.

9) Align lugs with notches of opposite roller bearing. See Fig. 48. Install axial needle bearing with flat side facing drive shaft. Engage parking gear lug. Install fastener nut and tighten to 184 ft. lbs. (250 N.m).

Final Drive Assembly – **1)** Oil bearings and place differential assembly inside transaxle. Install seals, "O" rings and new bearing races (if required) to bearing carrier and bearing adjuster ring.

2) Install and tighten bearing carrier to 111 ft. lbs. (150 N.m). Install locking tab.

3) Install bearing adjuster ring. Tighten adjuster ring. See Fig. 51. If using original bearings, tighten bearing adjuster ring to marks made during disassembly.

4) If using new bearings, differential or bearing carrier, tighten bearing adjuster ring to 37 ft. lbs. (50 N.m). Turn bearing adjuster ring 5 locking lugs tighter. Install locking tab. See Fig. 51.

5) Using INCH-lb. torque wrench, rotate torque wrench at least 8 turns to determine turning torque. Measure combined turning torque of pinion, input transfer gear and differential side roller bearings. See Fig. 46. See DIFFERENTIAL ROLLER BEARING SPECIFICATIONS table.

DIFFERENTIAL ROLLER BEARING SPECIFICATIONS

Application	Turning Torque
Including Transfer & Pinion Bearings	
New Bearings	33 INCH Lbs. (3.7 N.m)
Used Bearings	Same As Before Disassembly
Differential Side Bearings Only	
New Bearings	5-7 INCH Lbs. (.6-.8 N.m)
Used Bearings	Same As Before Disassembly

[1] – Recorded during disassembly. See FINAL DRIVE & TRANSFER GEARS under TRANSAXLE DISASSEMBLY.

6) Install circlips to end of each axle. See Fig. 52. Install "O" rings and new seals to drive axle flange. Fill space between seal and dust lip with multi-purpose grease.

7) Install drive axle flanges to transaxle. Install and tighten differential cover bolts to 21 ft. lbs. (28 N.m). Install speedometer drive.

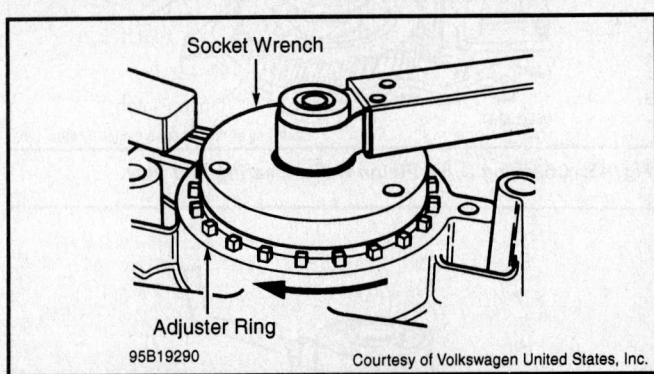

Fig. 51: Preloading Differential Side Bearings

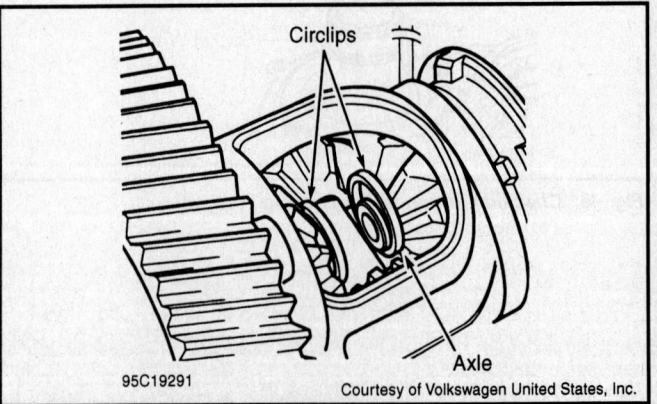

Fig. 52: Installing Circlips To Axles

TRANSMISSION

NOTE: Soak all friction-faced clutch plates in ATF for at least 15 minutes before installation. Apply assembly lubrication to all bushings, washers, shims and bearings before installation. See Fig. 17.

1) Input transfer gear, drive pinion and differential assemblies should be adjusted and installed at this time. Install axial needle bearing to input transfer gear. *See Fig. 53.* Install "O" ring and planetary carrier. Install washer and axial needle bearing into planetary carrier. *See Figs. 25 and 54.* Install end plate shim for reverse brake clutch plates. *See Fig. 55.*

2) Install reverse brake clutch plates. *See Fig. 56.* See BRAKE CLUTCH PLATE APPLICATIONS table. Using Assembly Ring (VW 3267), install one-way clutch and secure using circlip. *See Figs. 57 and 58.*

3) Using a feeler gauge, check installed reverse brake clutch clearance. *See Fig. 59.* Clearance should be .047-.071" (1.2-1.8 mm). If clearance is not as specified, replace end plate shim. End plate shims are available in thicknesses ranging from .040" (1.0 mm) to .070" (1.9 mm) in .004" (.10 mm) increments.

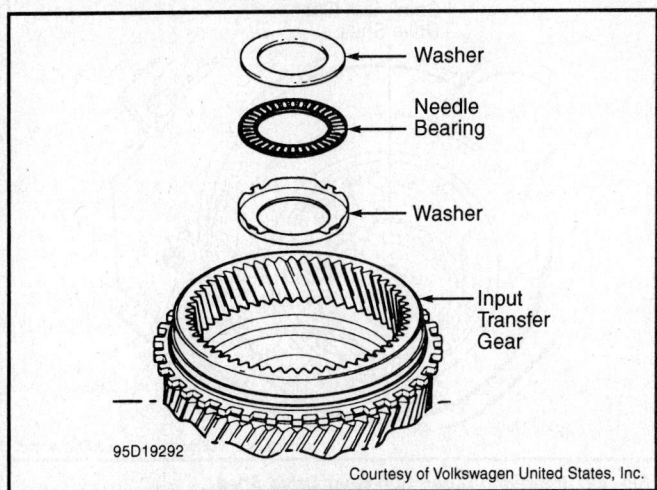

Fig. 53: **Installing Axial Needle Bearing To Input Transfer Gear**

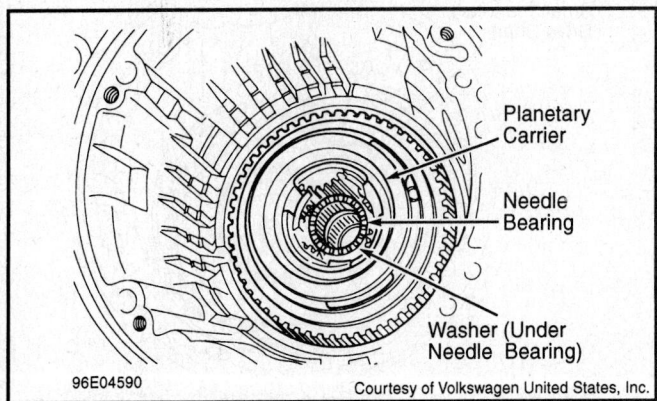

Fig. 54: **Installing Planetary Carrier & Axial Needle Bearing**

BRAKE CLUTCH PLATE APPLICATIONS

Application	Number Of Plates
Reverse Clutch	
Inner	5
Outer	5
2nd-4th Clutch	
Inner	6
Outer	7

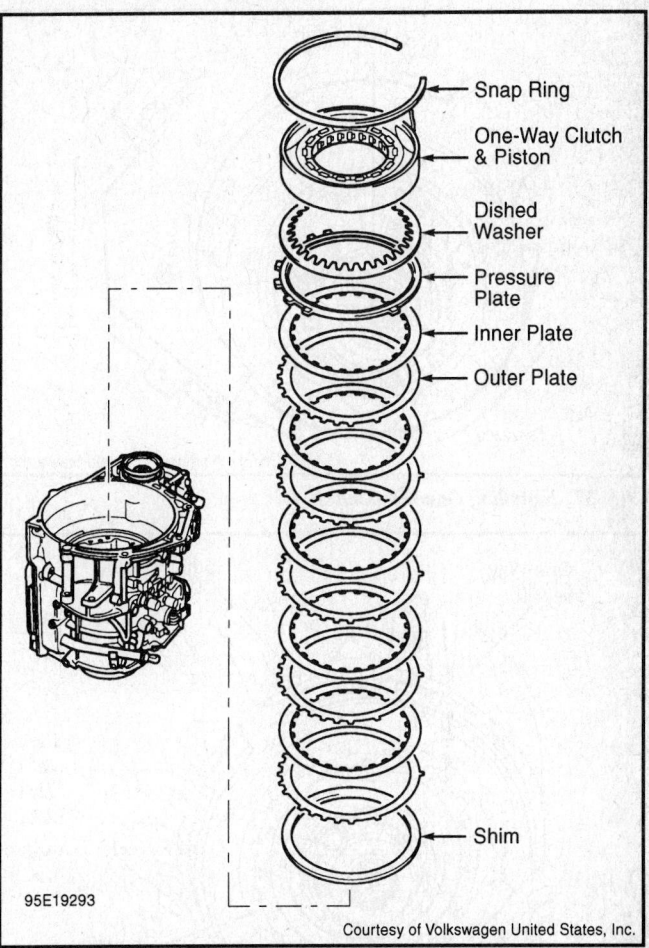

Fig. 55: **Exploded View Reverse Brake Clutch Assembly**

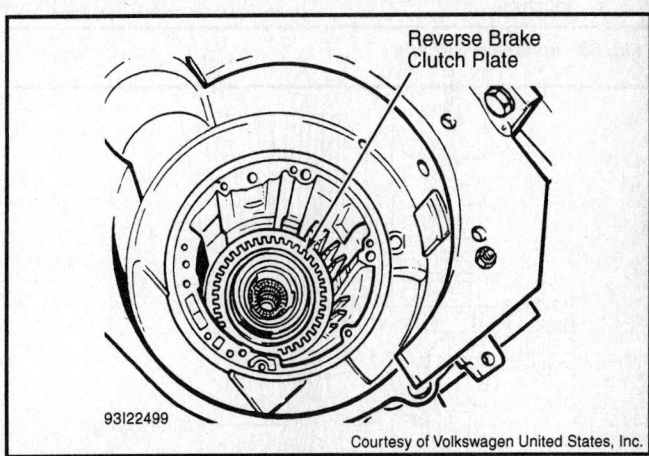

Fig. 56: **Installing Reverse Brake Clutch Plates**

4) Install upper circlip for support tube. *See Fig. 58.* Install washer and needle bearing into large sun gear drive shell. *See Fig. 17.* Install large sun gear drive shell. *See Fig. 60.*

5) Install small sun gear drive shell. Install small planetary drive shaft with needle bearings. *See Figs. 17, 61 and 62.* Using a screwdriver, lock small sun gear drive shell to large sun gear drive shell. *See Fig. 19.* Install adjustment shim, washer and bolt on end of small planetary drive shaft. Tighten bolt to 22 ft. lbs. (30 N.m).

6) Ensure end play is .009-.014" (.23-.37 mm). If end play is not as specified, recheck assembly or adjustment. See PLANETARY CARRIER under COMPONENT DISASSEMBLY & REASSEMBLY.

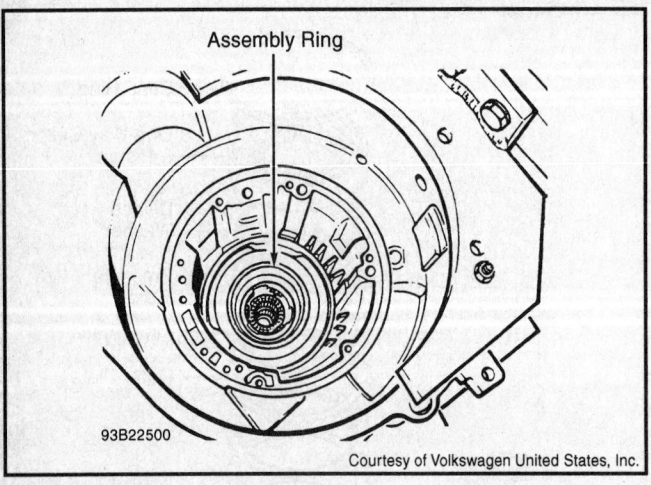

Fig. 57: **Installing One-Way Clutch**

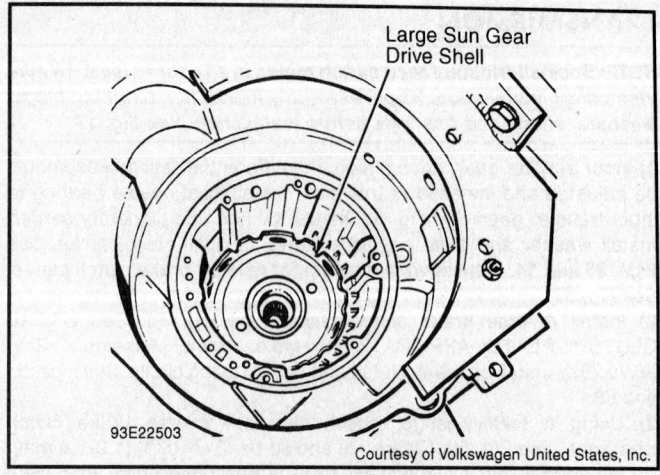

Fig. 60: **Installing Large Sun Gear Drive Shell**

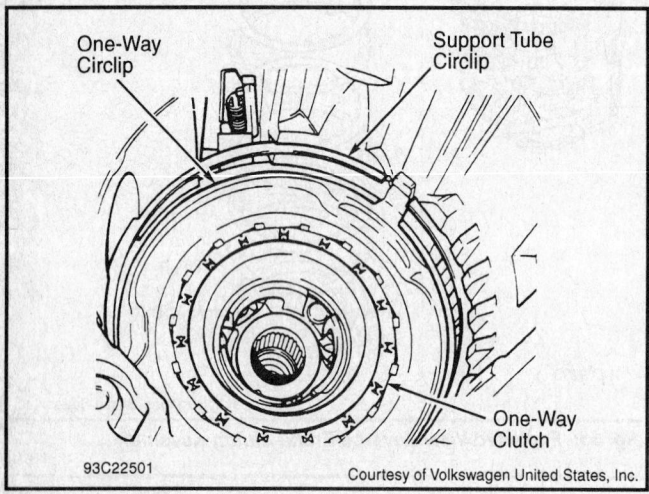

Fig. 58: **Installing Circlips**

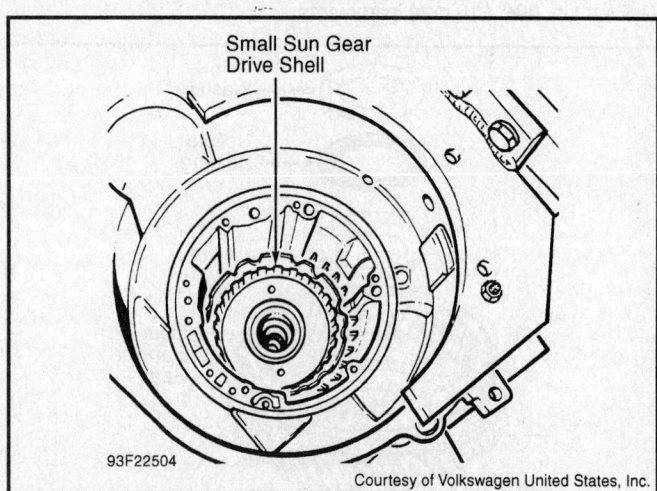

Fig. 61: **Installing Small Sun Gear Drive Shell**

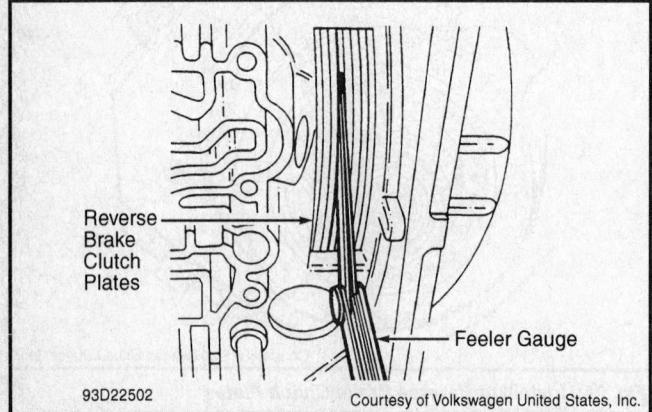

Fig. 59: **Checking Reverse Brake Clutch Clearance**

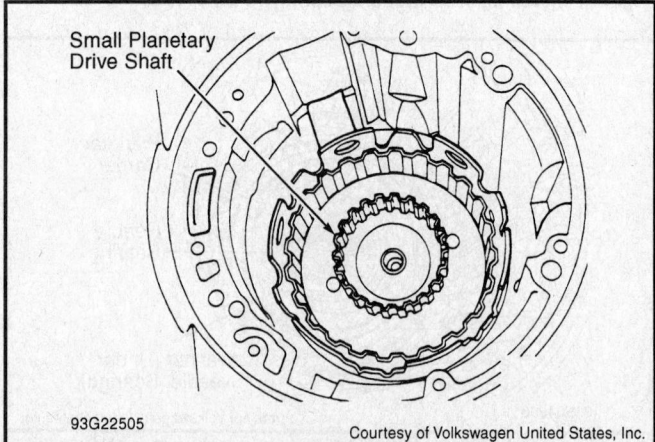

Fig. 62: **Installing Small Planetary Drive Shaft**

7) Install bearing, washer, and impeller shaft and 4th apply clutch. See Fig. 63. Install bearing, washer and 1st-3rd apply clutch with turbine shaft assembly. See Fig. 64. Install thrust shims on 1st-3rd apply clutch housing. Install reverse apply clutch and support tube. See Fig. 65.

NOTE: Turbine shaft end play was measured before disassembly. If end play is okay, use original thrust shims. If end play is not okay or new parts are installed, calculate end play and install required thrust shims.

8) For checking purposes, install oil pump gasket and oil pump. See Fig. 17. Position dial indicator and Support (VW 387) on transaxle case. See Fig. 66.

9) Press dial indicator on turbine shaft, and apply .040" (1.0 mm) preload. Move turbine shaft up and down. Turbine shaft end play should be .019-.047" (.50-1.20 mm).

10) If end play is okay, go to next step. If end play is not okay, install required thrust shims. Thrust shims are available in thicknesses ranging from .04" (1.0 mm) to .07" (1.8 mm) in .008" (.20 mm) increments. Recheck turbine shaft end play.

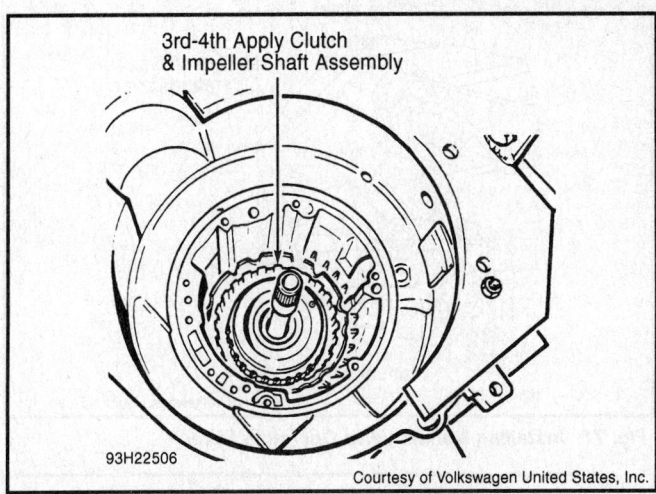

Fig. 63: Installing 4th Apply Clutch & Impeller Shaft

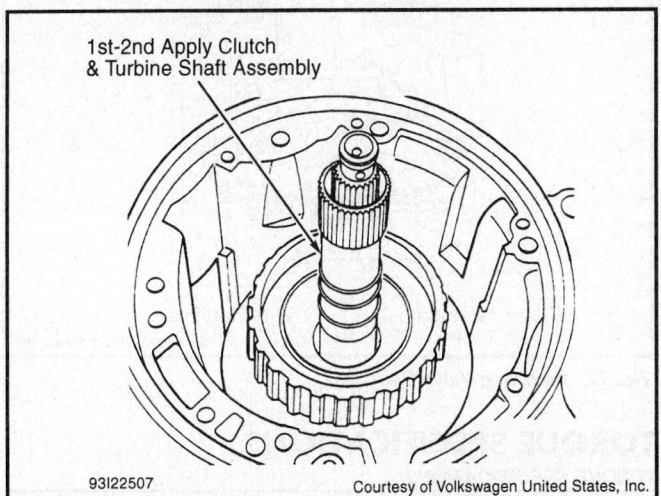

Fig. 64: Installing 1st-3rd Apply Clutch & Turbine Shaft

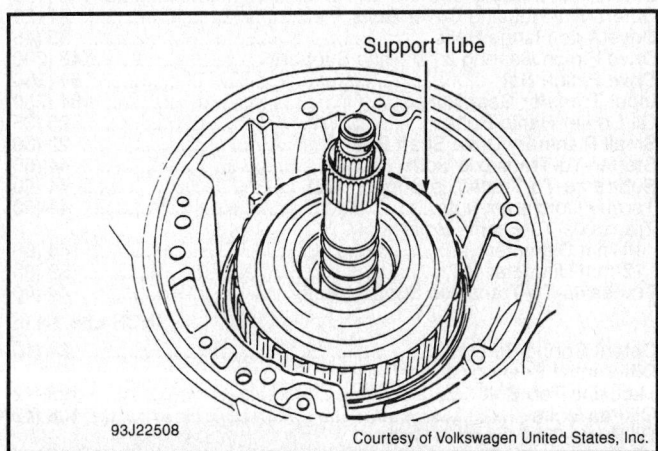

Fig. 65: Installing Support Tube

11) Remove oil pump and oil pump gasket. Install support tube and .118" (3.0 mm) thick outer splined plate for reverse apply clutch. Ensure groove on support tube engages wedge of one-way clutch. See Figs. 17 and 65.

12) Install friction plates and outer splined plates for reverse apply clutch into transaxle case. See Fig. 67. Install 3 caps and springs. Install 2nd-4th brake clutch plates. See Fig. 68. See BRAKE CLUTCH PLATE APPLICATIONS table. Install 3 spring caps to springs.

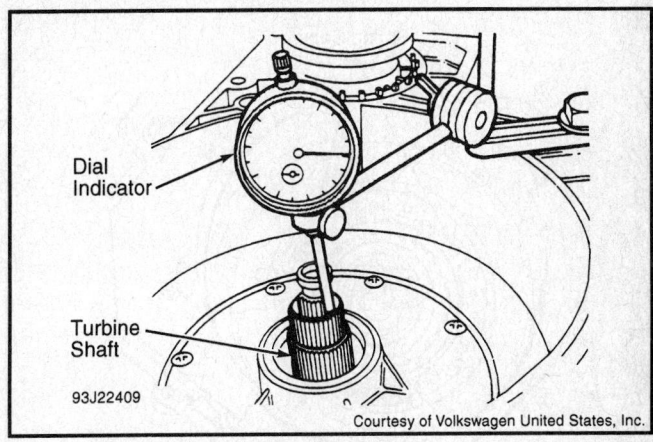

Fig. 66: Checking Turbine Shaft End Play

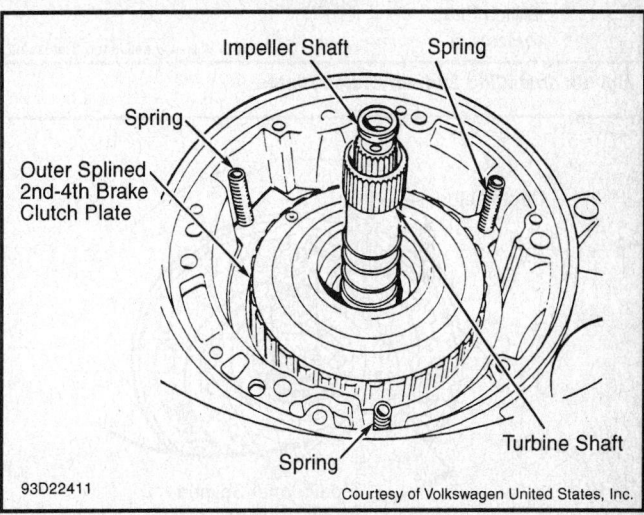

Fig. 67: Installing 2nd-4th Brake Clutch Plate & Springs

13) DO NOT install top outer splined clutch plate or waved spring washer. Determine clearance of 2nd-4th brake clutch. Press 2nd-4th brake clutch assembly down. Using a depth gauge, measure distance from top of oil pump flange to 2nd-4th brake clutch (inner splined). See Fig. 69.

14) Place a straightedge across top of piston. Place gasket on oil pump flange. Using depth gauge, measure distance from straightedge to oil pump flange gasket. See Fig. 70. Subtract thickness of straightedge.

15) Subtract distance measured in step 13) from distance calculated in step 14). This gives 2nd-4th brake clutch-to-piston distance.

16) Subtract .140" (3.6 mm) from value calculated in step 15). This determines thickness of last outer splined 2nd-4th brake clutch plate. Outer splined 2nd-4th brake clutch plates are available in thickness ranging from .080-.148" (2.00-3.75 mm), in .010" (.25 mm) increments.

NOTE: Manufacturer uses .140" (3.6 mm) value to allow for waved spring washer thickness installed with 2nd-4th brake clutch plates.

17) Install last outer 2nd-4th brake clutch plate. Install waved spring washer. Install oil pump gasket. Install "O" ring to oil pump, and install oil pump. Install cover for transfer gears.

18) Move gear change shaft to "P" position. Push manual valve operating lever with manual valve into valve body. Tighten set screw. Install sealing plug. See Figs. 14 and 36. Install valve body. Install oil filter screen and oil pan. See Figs. 14, 71 and 72. Install torque converter.

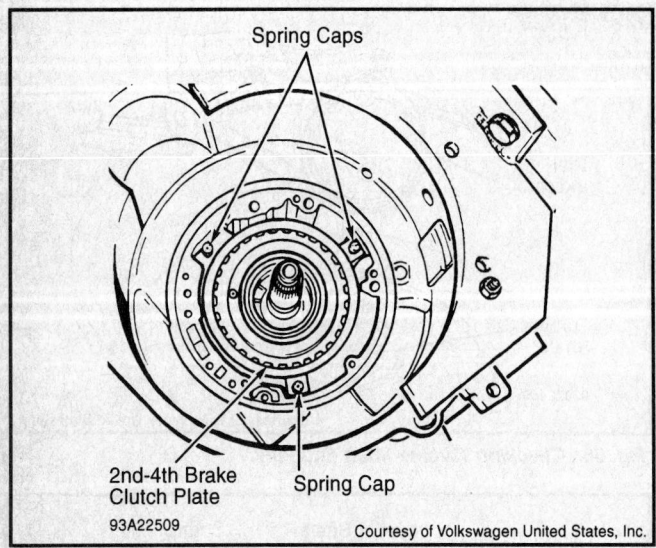

Fig. 68: *Installing 2nd-4th Clutch Plates*

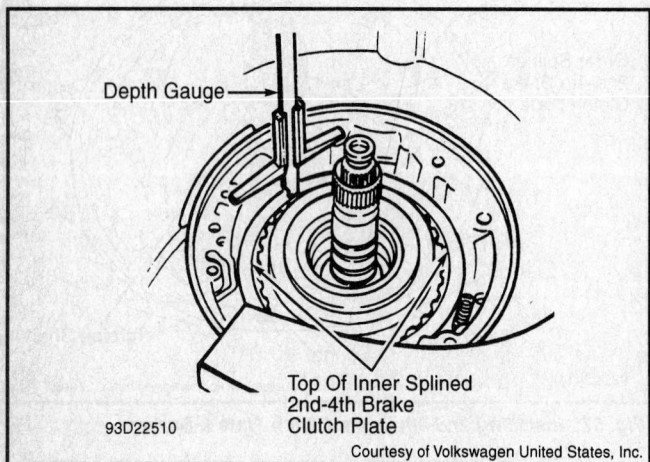

Fig. 69: *Measuring Oil Pump Flange-To-Clutch Plate*

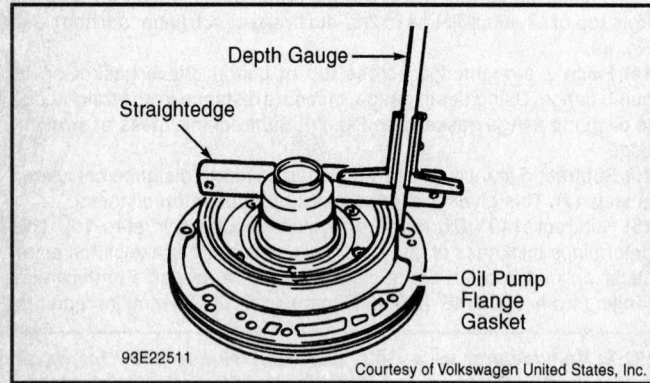

Fig. 70: *Measuring Height Of Piston*

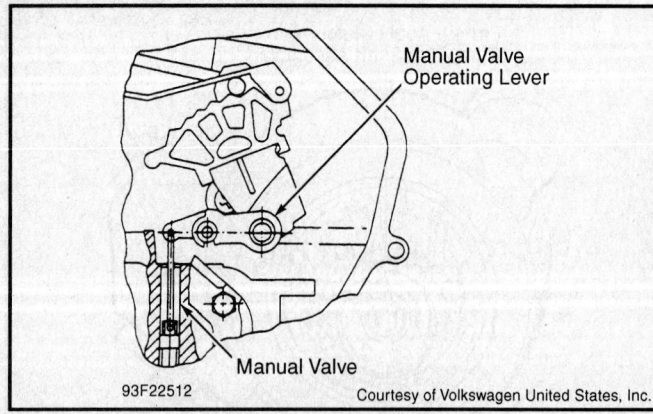

Fig. 71: *Installing Manual Valve Operating Lever*

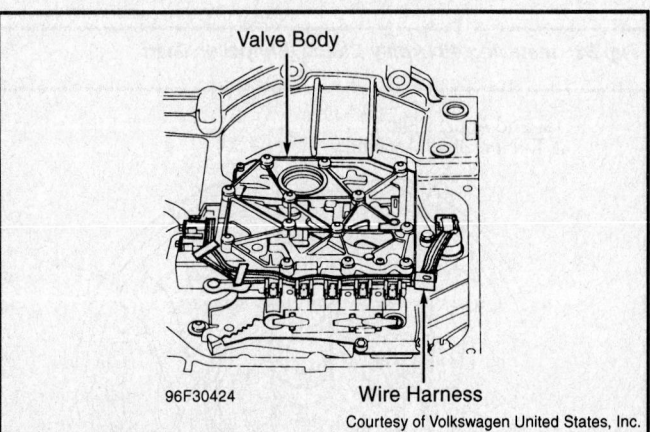

Fig. 72: *Installing Valve Body*

TORQUE SPECIFICATIONS
TORQUE SPECIFICATIONS

Application	Ft. Lbs. (N.m)
Differential Bearing Carrier	111 (150)
Differential Housing Cover Bolts	21 (28)
Drive Axle Flange Bolts	33 (45)
Drive Pinion Bearing & "O" Ring Support	148 (200)
Drive Pinion Nut	184 (250)
Input Transfer Gear Nut	184 (250)
Oil Cooler Banjo Bolts	26 (35)
Small Planetary Drive Shaft Bolt	22 (30)
Starter-To-Transaxle Bolts	44 (60)
Subframe-To-Transaxle Support Nut	44 (60)
Torque Converter Nuts	44 (60)
Transaxle-To-Engine Bolts	
10-mm Diameter	44 (60)
12-mm Diameter	59 (80)
Transaxle-To-Transaxle Support Bolts	44 (60)

	INCH Lbs. (N.m)
Detent Spring Screws	84 (10)
Differential Bearing Carrier/Adjuster	
Locking Tab Bolt	108 (12)
Oil Pan Bolts	108 (12)
Oil Pump-To-Transaxle Bolts	
Step 1	71 (8)
Step 2	Additional 90 Degrees
Transfer Gear Cover Bolts	71 (8)
Valve Body Bolts	44 (5)
Valve Body Conductor Strip Bolt	89 (10)

TRANSMISSION SPECIFICATIONS

TRANSMISSION SPECIFICATIONS

Application	In. (mm)
Clutch Clearance	
Apply Clutches	[1]
Brake Clutches	
2nd-4th	[2] .060-.068 (1.50-1.74)
Reverse	.047-.071 (1.2-1.8)
Gear & Shaft End Play	
Planetary Carrier	.009-.014 (.23-.37)
1st-3rd To Reverse Apply Clutch	.019-.047 (.50-1.20)
Turbine Shaft	.019-.047 (.50-1.20)

[1] – Assembled clutch clearance is not available.
[2] – See TRANSMISSION under TRANSAXLE REASSEMBLY.

TECHNICAL SERVICE BULLETINS

SHIFTING ERRATIC, HARSH OR DELAYED

1993-On Cabrio, Golf, GTI, Jetta & Passat (Group 01, TSB No. 97-01, 1-8-97) – Transaxle may shift erratic, harsh or hold shifts too long (delayed upshifts) with no trouble codes stored in memory. This condition is normally caused by improper throttle angle setting. If shifting quality is a concern, perform THROTTLE ANGLE SETTING procedure.

NOTE: On a newly installed TCM, basic settings must be set prior to performing the following procedure. Basic settings can be set with Scan Tool (VAG 1551) using Function "04", Display "OOO".

Throttle Angle Setting – 1) Connect scan tool. Turn ignition on. Press "1" to select RAPID DATA TRANSFER. Enter address word 02 "TRANSMISSION ELECTRONICS" and advance until "SELECT FUNCTION XX" appears in scan tool display.

2) Press buttons "0", then "8" to select function 08 "READ MEASURING VALUE BLOCK". Press "Q" button to confirm input. Press "Q" button once more, then enter group No. 001. Press "Q" button to confirm input.

3) Print screen. While observing scan tool display, slowly press accelerator pedal until display reads 25 percent. DO NOT release pedal. Print screen.

4) While observing scan tool display, slowly press accelerator pedal until display reads 50 percent. DO NOT release pedal. Print screen.

5) While observing scan tool display, slowly press accelerator pedal until display reads 75 percent. DO NOT release pedal. Print screen.

6) While observing scan tool display, slowly press accelerator pedal until display reads 99 percent. DO NOT release pedal (resistance of kickdown switch should be felt). Print screen.

7) Continue pressing accelerator pedal to its stop while observing fourth digit on right-side 8 digit display. Fourth digit must change from 0 to 1, indicating kickdown. Hold for 5 seconds to set throttle angle.

8) Release accelerator pedal, then press right arrow button on scan tool. Select function 06 "END OUTPUT". Repeat procedure from beginning.

9) Compare voltage readings and throttle angle percentages on printout from first test with that of second test. If readings do not match, throttle angle was set incorrectly.

10) If readings do match, road test vehicle and activate kickdown switch several times to ensure proper operation.

AUTOMATIC TRANSMISSIONS
Volkswagen Type 01M (Cont.)

WIRING DIAGRAMS

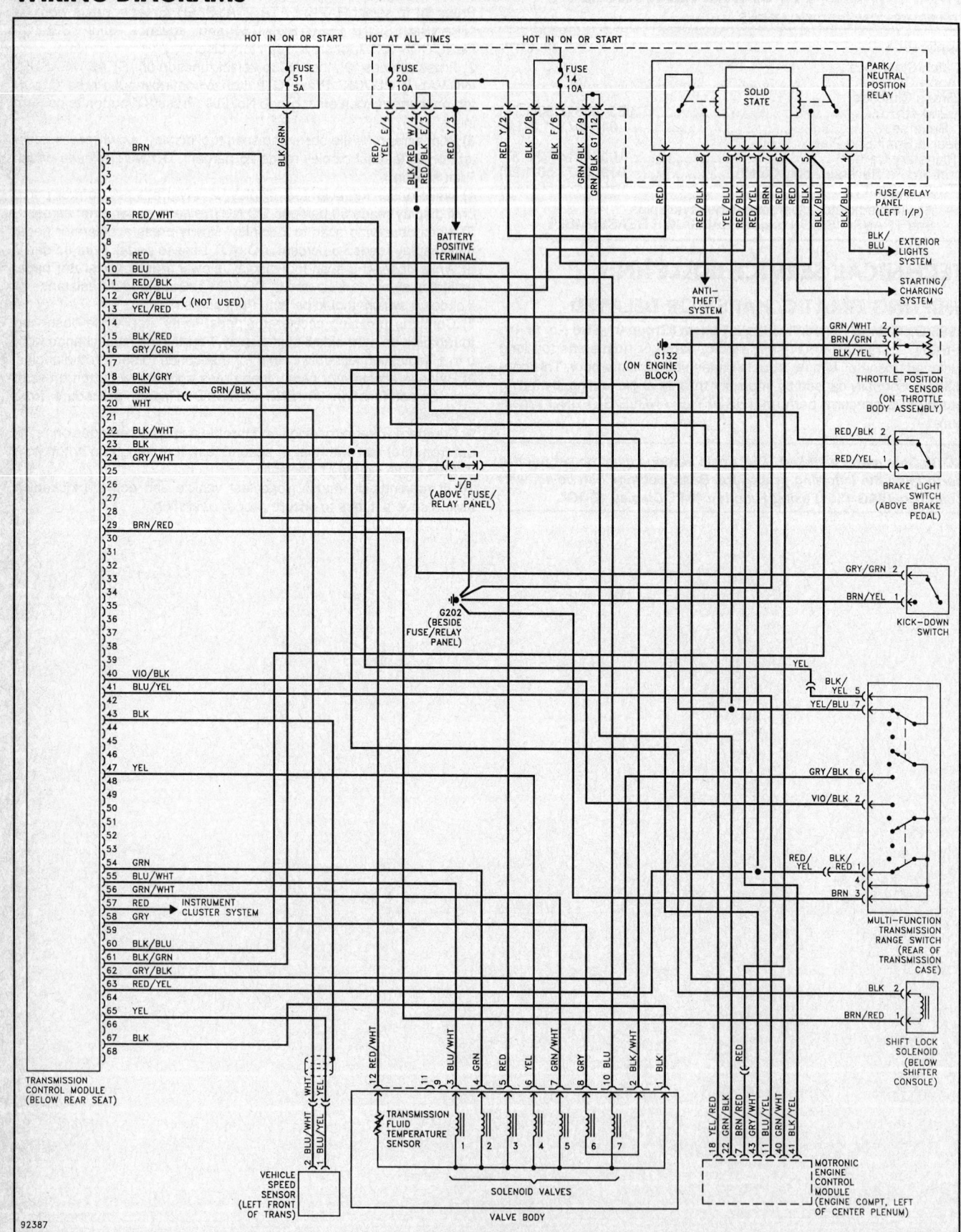

Fig. 73: 1995 Transaxle Wiring Diagram (Cabrio, Golf & Jetta 2.0L - Early Production)

92387

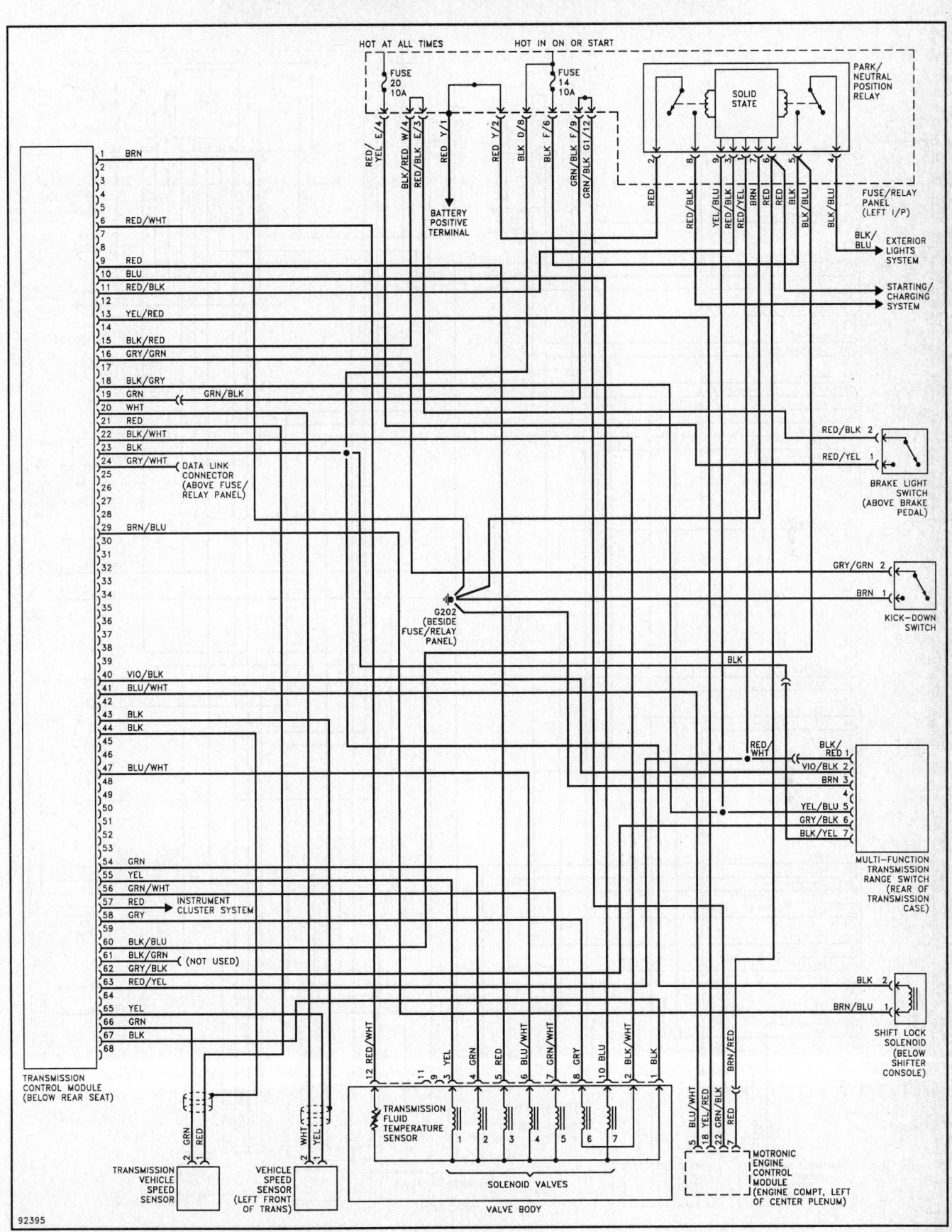

Fig. 74: 1995 Transaxle Wiring Diagram (Cabrio 2.0L – Late Production)

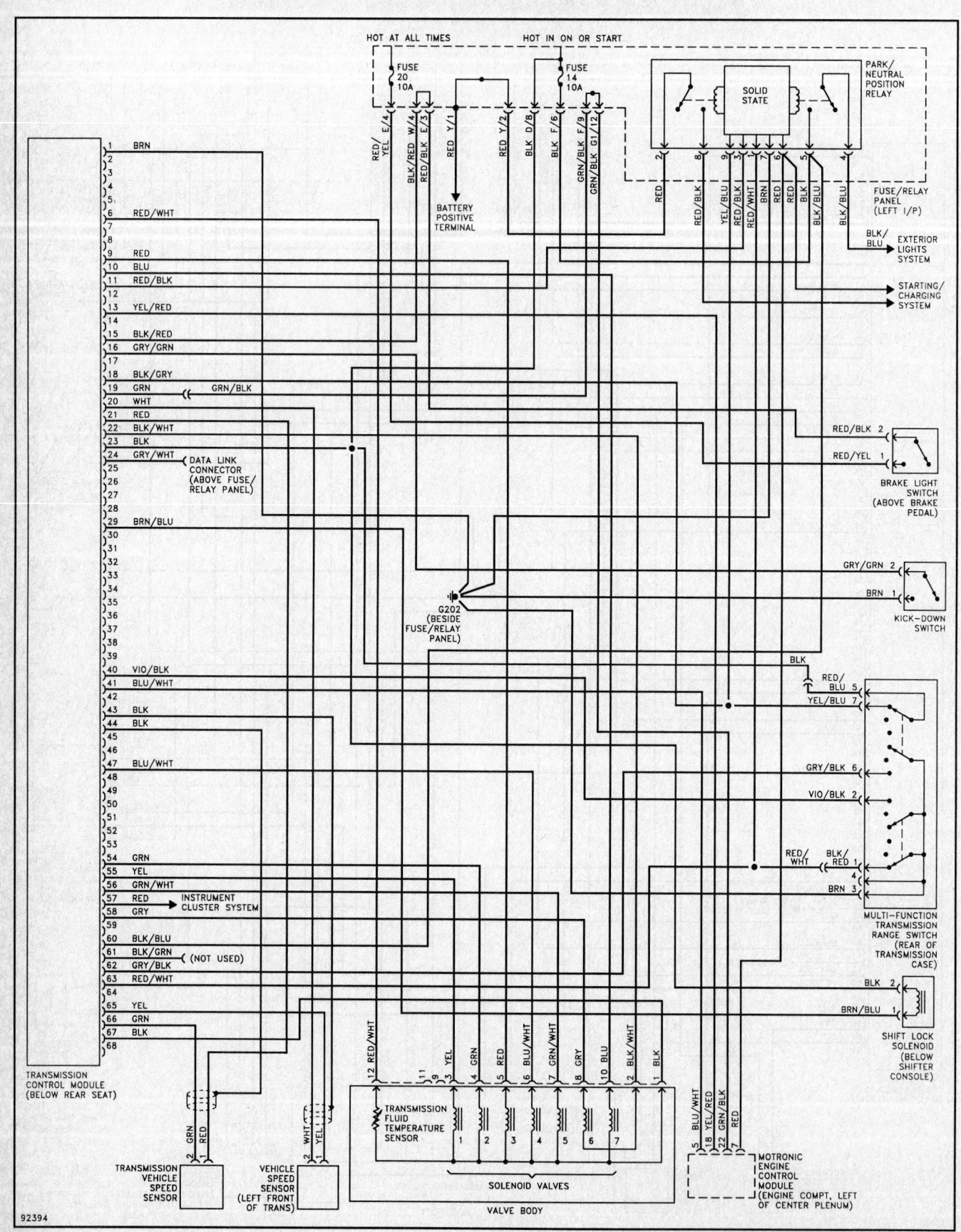

Fig. 75: 1995 Transaxle Wiring Diagram (Golf & Jetta 2.0L — Late Production)

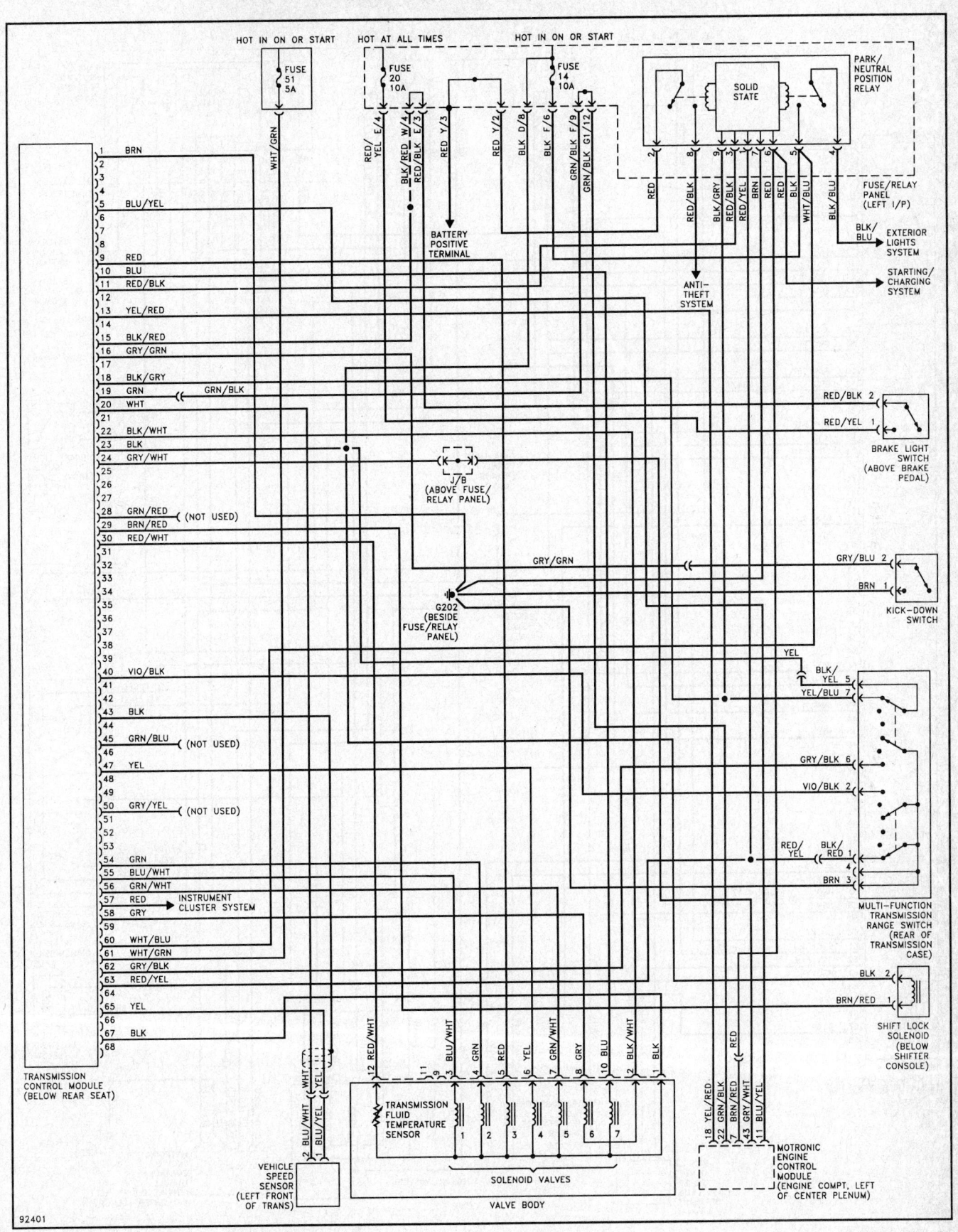

Fig. 76: 1995 Transaxle Wiring Diagram (Jetta 2.8L)

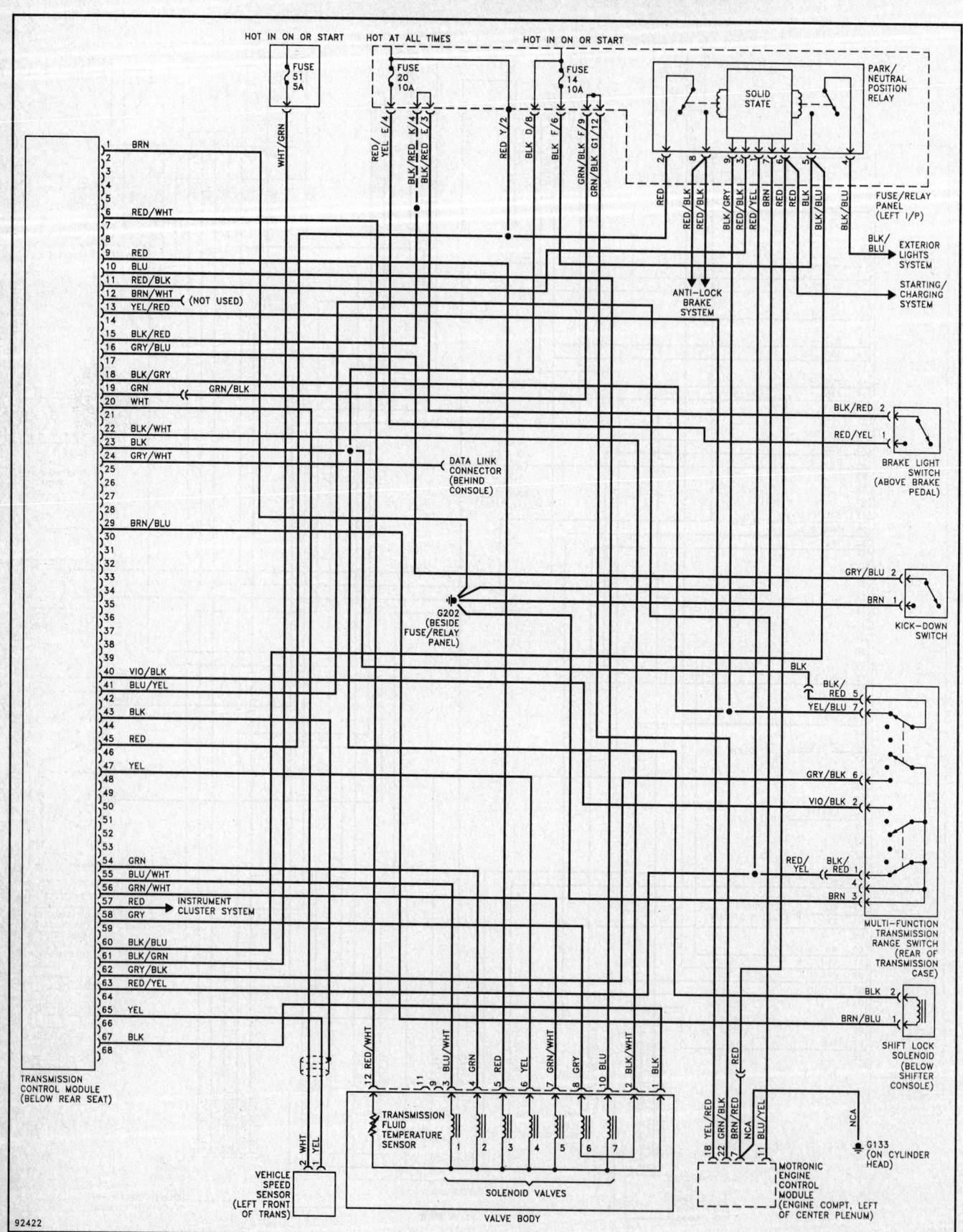

Fig. 77: 1995 Transaxle Wiring Diagram (Passat)

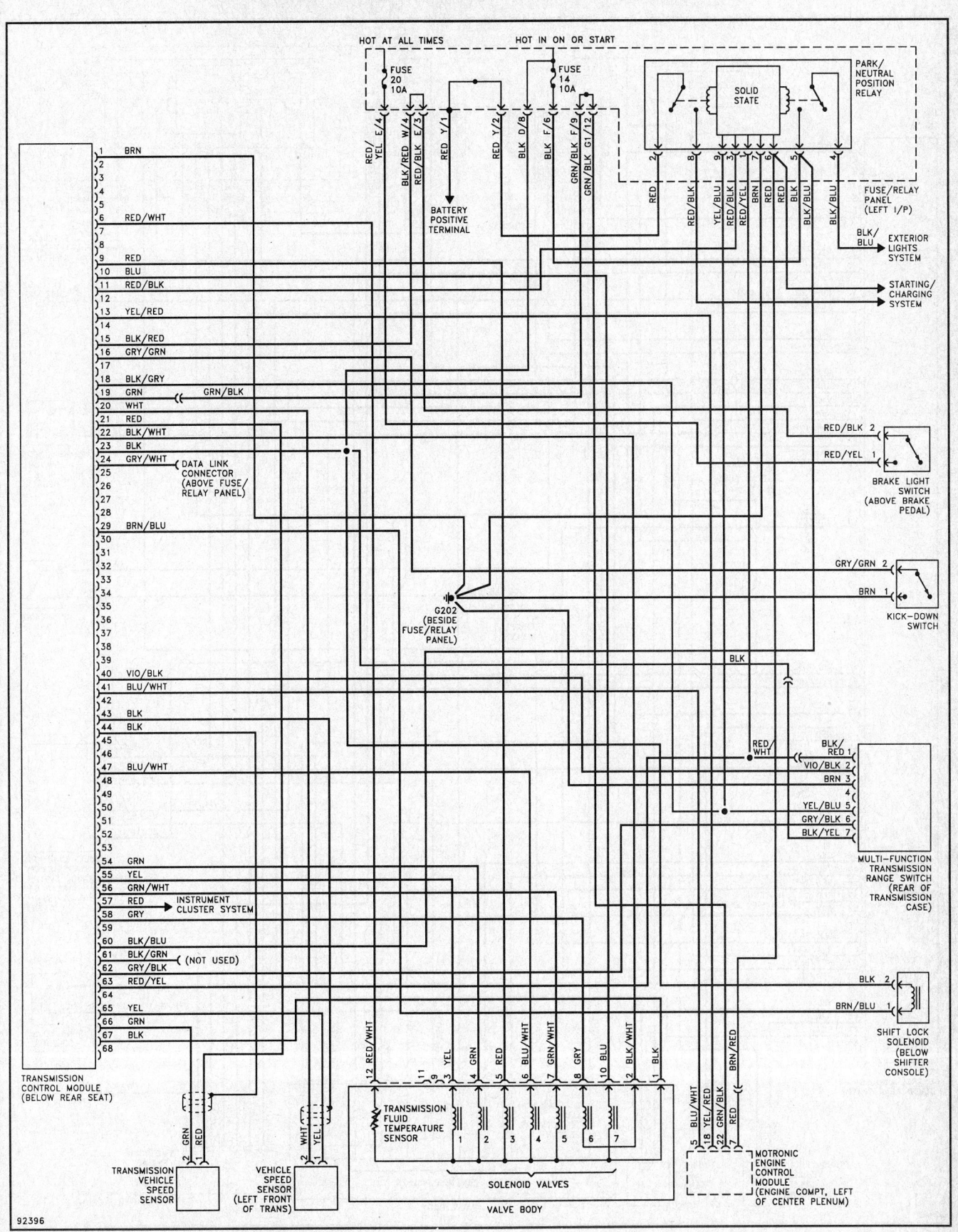

Fig. 78: 1996 Transaxle Wiring Diagram (Cabrio)

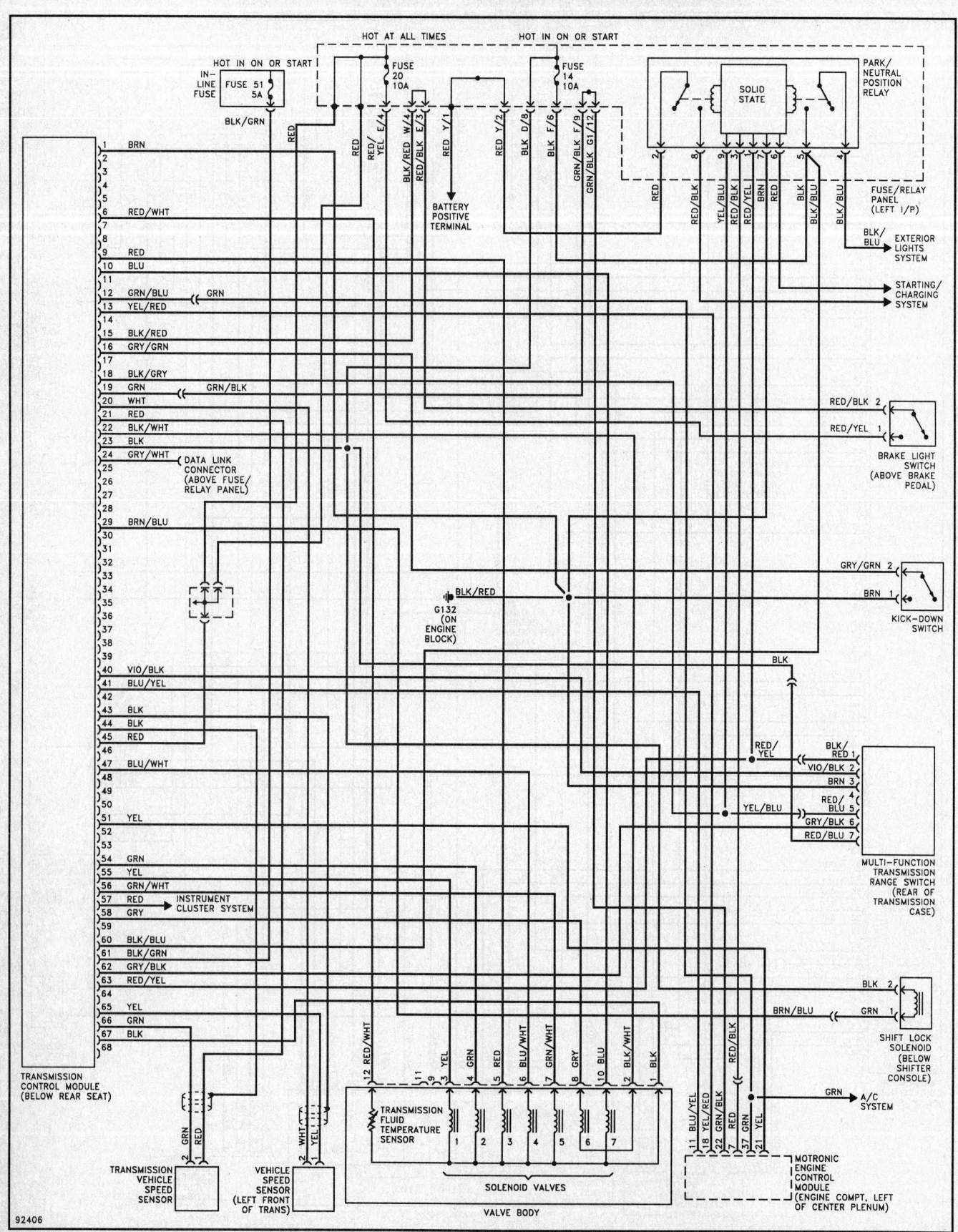

Fig. 79: 1996 Transaxle Wiring Diagram (Golf 2.0L & Jetta 2.0L & 2.8L)

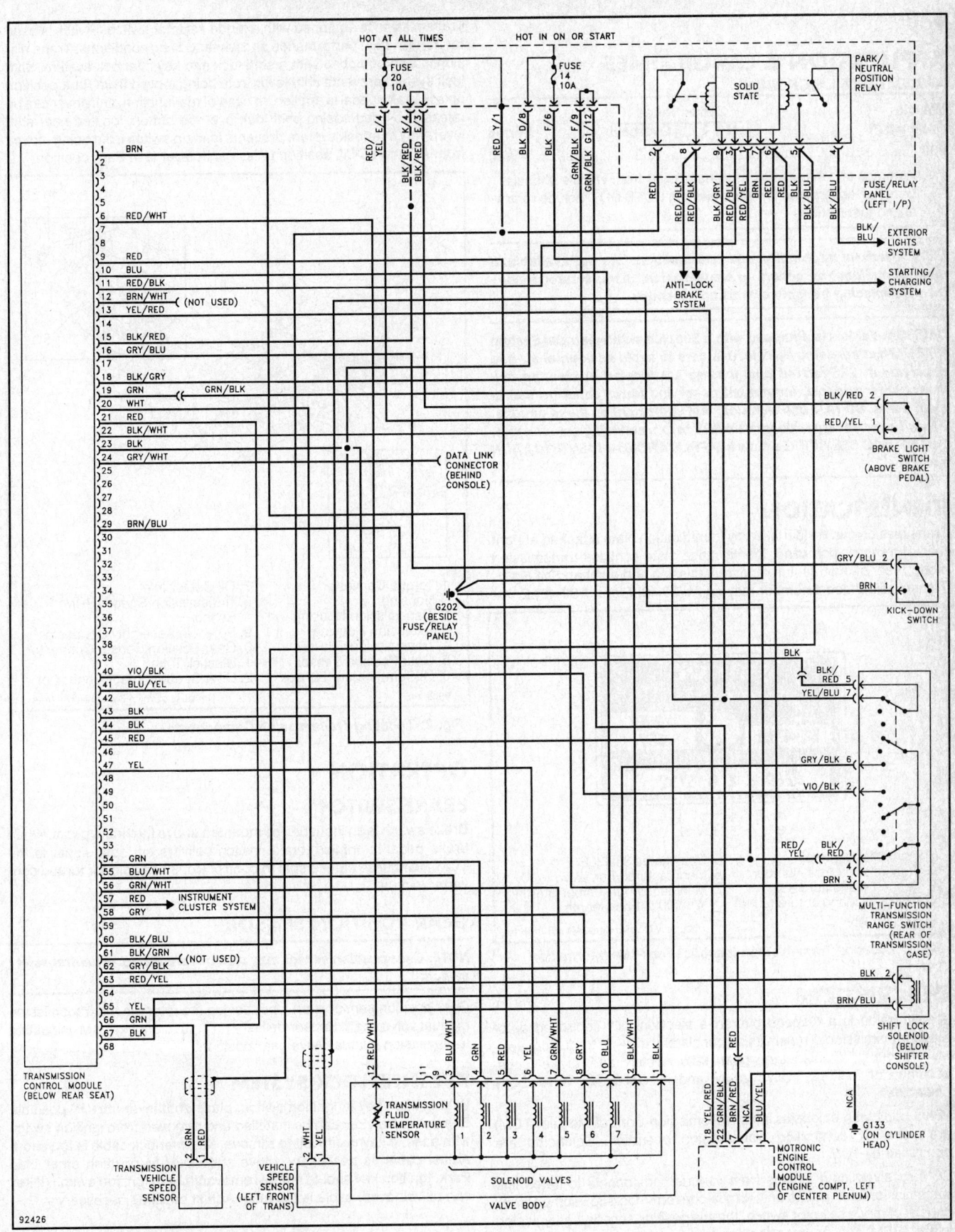

Fig. 80: 1996 Transaxle Wiring Diagram (Passat)

960

APPLICATION & LABOR TIMES

APPLICATION & LABOR TIMES

Vehicle Application	Labor Times		Series
	[1] R & I	[2] Overhaul	
960	4.3	10.3	AW40

[1] – Removal and installation of transmission from vehicle chassis.
[2] – Bench overhaul time for transmission. DOES NOT include removal and installation.

NOTE: Overhaul information and specifications are not available. If internal malfunction occurs to transmission, manufacturer recommends replacing transmission as an assembly.

CAUTION: Vehicle is equipped with a Supplemental Restraint System (SAS). When servicing vehicle, use care to avoid accidental air bag deployment. SRS-related components are located in steering column, center console, instrument panel and lower panel on instrument panel. DO NOT use electrical test equipment on these circuits. It may be necessary to deactivate SRS before servicing components. See AIR BAG SERVICING article in APPLICATIONS & IDENTIFICATION section.

IDENTIFICATION

Transmission can be identified by identification plate attached at right rear of transmission case. Identification plate contains transmission model, year of manufacture and transmission part number. *See Fig. 1.* Transmission model number may be AW30-40LE or AW30-43LE.

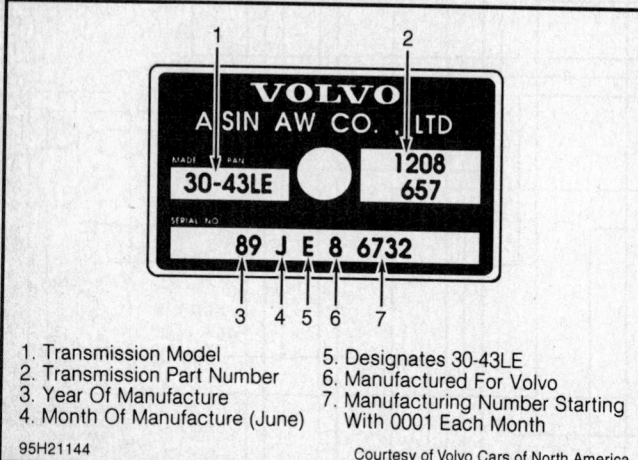

1. Transmission Model
2. Transmission Part Number
3. Year Of Manufacture
4. Month Of Manufacture (June)
5. Designates 30-43LE
6. Manufactured For Volvo
7. Manufacturing Number Starting With 0001 Each Month

95H21144   *Courtesy of Volvo Cars of North America.*

Fig. 1: Locating Transmission Identification Plate Information

DESCRIPTION

Transmission is a 4-speed overdrive electronically controlled automatic transmission. Transmission consists of lock-up torque converter, oil pump, 3 planetary gear sets, clutch and brake units, accumulator pistons, valve body and 4 electronic valve body solenoids.

Valve body with solenoids and Transmission Control Module (TCM) are used for controlling transmission operation. Solenoids are controlled by TCM.

TCM receives input signals from various components to determine transmission shift points and torque converter lock-up. Components consist of mode selector switch, throttle position sensor, transmission speed (RPM) sensor, gear position sensor, transmission oil temperature sensor, brake switch and kickdown switch. *See Fig. 2.*

Transmission is equipped with a mode selector switch. Switch is used for normal, high performance and winter driving conditions. Transmission is also equipped with a shift lock and key interlock system. Shift lock system prevents shift lever from being moved from Park position unless brake pedal is applied. In case of malfunction, shift lever can be released by depressing shift lock override button, located near shift lever. Key interlock system prevents ignition switch from being moved from ACC to LOCK position unless shift lever is in Park position.

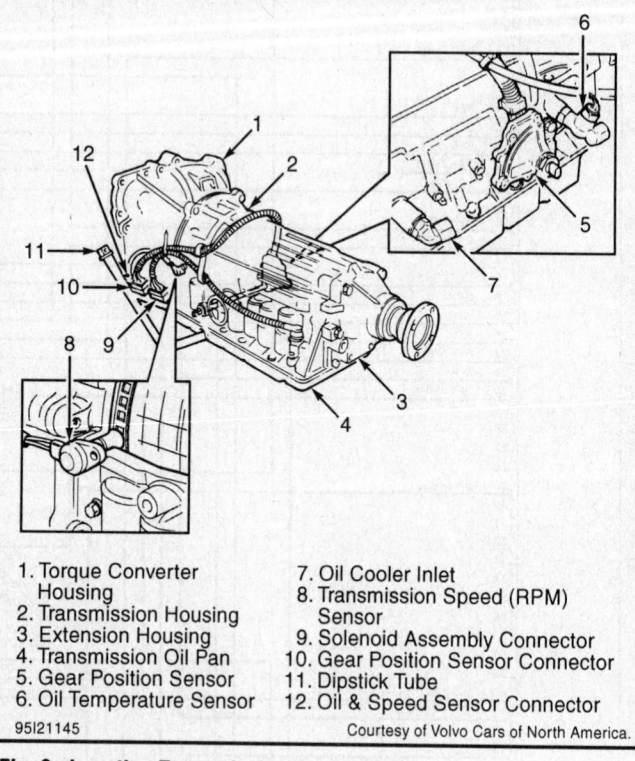

1. Torque Converter Housing
2. Transmission Housing
3. Extension Housing
4. Transmission Oil Pan
5. Gear Position Sensor
6. Oil Temperature Sensor
7. Oil Cooler Inlet
8. Transmission Speed (RPM) Sensor
9. Solenoid Assembly Connector
10. Gear Position Sensor Connector
11. Dipstick Tube
12. Oil & Speed Sensor Connector

95I21145   *Courtesy of Volvo Cars of North America.*

Fig. 2: Locating Transmission Components

OPERATION

BRAKE SWITCH

Brake switch is an input device mounted above the brake pedal. When brake pedal is applied, brake switch delivers an input signal to the TCM. TCM uses input signal to control No. 3 solenoid for torque converter lock-up.

GEAR POSITION SENSOR

NOTE: Gear position sensor may also be referred to as neutral safety switch.

Gear position sensor is an input device mounted on the transmission manual valve shaft. Sensor delivers an input signal to TCM, indicating transmission manual valve gear position.

KEY INTERLOCK SYSTEM

With ignition key in ignition switch, place shift lever into "P" position. Ensure ignition key can be installed and removed from ignition switch with ease. If key is difficult to remove, key interlock cable is too short. Adjust cable as necessary. Move shift lever to position other than Park. Ignition key should not be removable from ignition switch. If key can be removed, cable is too long. Adjust cable as necessary.

KICKDOWN SWITCH

Kickdown switch, located at firewall on accelerator cable, sends input signal to TCM when accelerator pedal is fully depressed. TCM uses input signal for controlling transmission downshifting and torque converter lock-up.

MODE SELECTOR SWITCH

Mode selector switch, located to left of shift lever, has 3 different modes which effect transmission shift points. Input signal from mode selector switch is sent to TCM. TCM uses input signal for controlling transmission shifting and torque converter lock-up.

"E" (Economy) mode, is for normal driving and provides early upshifts combined with lock-up as often as possible for top 3 gears. Transmission line pressure is modulated to provide smooth gear engagement.

In "S" (Sport) mode, transmission shift points are designed to provide the highest possible performance. Under normal acceleration, transmission shifts occur the same as in economy mode. During increased acceleration, TCM selects shift and lock-up points for best possible performance.

"W" (Winter) mode prevents wheel spin on slippery surfaces. Transmission starts out in high gear. When "W" mode is selected, warning light on dash is illuminated. This mode may also be used when driver wants to control gear selection.

OIL TEMPERATURE SENSOR

Oil temperature sensor, located on right side of transmission, forward of gear position sensor, measures transmission fluid temperature and delivers an input signal to TCM. TCM uses input signal for controlling transmission shifting and torque converter lock-up.

SHIFT LOCK OVERRIDE FUNCTION

Move shift lever to "P" position and turn ignition key to (I) or (II) position. Press override button. Shift lever should move from "P" position. Return shift lever to "P" position and remove ignition key. Press override button. Shift lever should not move from "P" position. Override function should operate only when ignition key is in (I) or (II) position.

TRANSMISSION CONTROL MODULE (TCM)

TCM is located under instrument panel, to right of steering column. *See Fig. 3.* TCM determines shift points and torque converter lock-up timing based on input signals received from various components. Components consist of mode selector switch, throttle position sensor, transmission speed (RPM) sensor, gear position sensor, transmission oil temperature sensor, brake switch and kickdown switch.

TCM contains a self-diagnostic system which stores a Diagnostic Trouble Code (DTC). If a transmission problem exists, DTC(s) can be retrieved to determine transmission problem area.

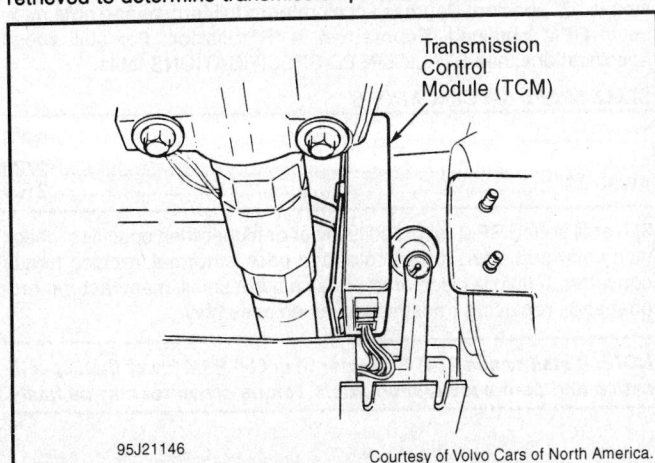

Transmission Control Module (TCM)

95J21146
Courtesy of Volvo Cars of North America.

Fig. 3: Locating Transmission Control Module (TCM)
(1995 960 Is Shown; 1996 960 Is Similar)

TRANSMISSION SPEED (RPM) SENSOR

Electromagnetic RPM sensor, mounted in transmission housing, is activated by a toothed impulse wheel. Sensor is an input device which delivers an RPM signal to the TCM. By comparing transmission RPM and vehicle speed, TCM calculates torque converter slippage.

THROTTLE POSITION (TP) SENSOR

Throttle position sensor, mounted on throttle body, determines throttle position and delivers an input signal to TCM. TCM uses input signal for controlling transmission upshifts and torque converter lock-up.

VALVE BODY SOLENOIDS

Valve body solenoids, mounted on the valve body, are output devices controlled by signals received from the TCM. The No. 1 and No. 2 solenoids are used to control transmission shifting. No. 3 solenoid is used to control torque converter lock-up. No. 4 solenoid is used to control transmission line pressure. For valve body solenoid usage, see VALVE BODY SOLENOID APPLICATION table.

VALVE BODY SOLENOID APPLICATION [1]

Shift Lever Position	No. 1 Solenoid	No. 2 Solenoid
"D" (Drive)		
1st	ON	OFF
2nd	ON	ON
3rd	OFF	ON
4th	OFF	OFF
"3"		
1st	ON	OFF
2nd	ON	ON
3rd	OFF	ON
"L"		
1st	ON	OFF
2nd	ON	ON
"R" (Reverse)	ON	OFF
"N" Or "P"	ON	OFF

[1] – Valve body contains 4 solenoids. No. 1 and No. 2 solenoids are used to control transmission shifts. No. 3 solenoid is used to control torque converter lock-up. No. 4 solenoid is used to control line pressure.

LUBRICATION & ADJUSTMENTS

See appropriate AUTOMATIC TRANSMISSION SERVICING article in TRANSMISSION SERVICING section.

TROUBLE SHOOTING

Preliminary Checks – Ensure fluid level is correct. Inspect throttle cable, kickdown cable and gear position sensor. Check idle speed RPM and adjust as necessary.

NOTE: Manufacturer recommends transmission assembly replacement only. Manufacturer does not provide mechanical trouble shooting or overhaul information.

TESTING

ROAD TEST

"D" & "3" Position – 1) Engine and transmission must be at normal operating temperature. Shift transmission into "D" position. Set mode selector switch to "E" position. Test drive vehicle and ensure all upshifts and downshifts occur at specified speeds. See SHIFT SPEED SPECIFICATIONS table.

2) Ensure lock-up occurs at appropriate speeds. See LOCK-UP SPEED SPECIFICATIONS table. Lightly depress accelerator. If excessive increase in engine RPM exists, lock-up did not occur.

NOTE: Lock-up in 2nd gear occurs when transmission oil temperature exceeds 257°F (125°C) on AW30-40 transmission or 239°F (115°C) on AW30-43 transmission. Lock-up in 3rd gear occurs when transmission oil temperature exceeds 140°F (60°C). Lock-up in 4th gear occurs when transmission oil temperature exceeds 86°F (30°C).

"L" Position – While driving vehicle in "L" position, check for failure to upshift to 2nd gear. Check engine braking effect when accelerator pedal is released.

"R" Position – Shift vehicle into "R" position. Accelerate vehicle and check for transmission slippage.

"P" Position – Stop vehicle on incline of 5 degrees or steeper. Shift vehicle into "P" position and release parking brake. Ensure parking pawl prevents vehicle from moving.

TIME LAG TEST

1) Engine and transmission must be at normal operating temperature. Start engine and ensure idle RPM is within specification with A/C off. Apply service and parking brakes. Using stop watch, measure time until engagement shock is felt when shift lever is shifted from "N" to "D" position.

2) Allow one minute intervals between tests. Perform time measurement several times and calculate average time. Time should be less than .7 seconds. Repeat test procedure to test time lag when shift lever is shifted from "N" to "R" position. Time lag should be less than 1.2 seconds. If test time is not as described, check transmission line pressure. See HYDRAULIC PRESSURE TEST.

SHIFT SPEED SPECIFICATIONS [1]

Application	MPH
AW30-40	
Economy Mode	
1st-2nd	20
2nd-3rd	45
3rd-4th	82
4th-3rd	61
3rd-2nd	28
2nd-1st	12
Sport Mode	
1st-2nd	25
2nd-3rd	59
3rd-4th	98
4th-3rd	67
3rd-2nd	40
2nd-1st	19
AW30-43	
Economy Mode	
1st-2nd	22
2nd-3rd	50
3rd-4th	92
4th-3rd	53
3rd-2nd	31
2nd-1st	12
Sport Mode	
1st-2nd	32
2nd-3rd	69
3rd-4th	108
4th-3rd	96
3rd-2nd	58
2nd-1st	19

[1] – With shift lever in "D" position and throttle valve open 60 percent.

LOCK-UP SPEED SPECIFICATIONS [1][2]

Application	MPH
AW30-40	
Economy Mode	
Lock-Up ON	
2nd Gear	25
3rd Gear	65
4th Gear	90
Lock-Up OFF	
2nd Gear	19
3rd Gear	59
4th Gear	82
Sport Mode	
Lock-Up ON	
2nd Gear	50
3rd Gear	76
4th Gear	127
Lock-Up OFF	
2nd Gear	40
3rd Gear	71
4th Gear	122
AW30-43	
Economy Mode	
Lock-Up ON	
2nd Gear	29
3rd Gear	50
4th Gear	92
Lock-Up OFF	
2nd Gear	19
3rd Gear	59
4th Gear	71
Sport Mode	
Lock-Up ON	
2nd Gear	43
3rd Gear	79
4th Gear	108
Lock-Up OFF	
2nd Gear	37
3rd Gear	68
4th Gear	100

[1] – With shift lever in "D" position and throttle valve open 60 percent.

[2] – Lock-up in 2nd gear occurs when transmission oil temperature exceeds 257°F (125°C) on AW30-40 transmission or 239°F (115°C) on AW30-43 transmission. Lock-up in 3rd gear occurs when transmission oil temperature exceeds 140°F (60°C). Lock-up in 4th gear occurs when transmission oil temperature exceeds 86°F (30°C).

STALL SPEED TEST

1) Operate engine and transmission at normal operating temperature. Connect tachometer to vehicle and ensure it is visible to driver. Apply parking brake and block all 4 wheels.

CAUTION: DO NOT maintain stall speed RPM for more than 5 seconds. Transmission damage may occur.

2) Ensure A/C is off. Start engine, apply brakes and place transmission in "D" position. Depress accelerator to full throttle and note maximum RPM obtained. Repeat test in "R" position. For stall speed specifications, see STALL SPEED SPECIFICATIONS table.

STALL SPEED SPECIFICATIONS

Transmission	RPM
AW30-40	2700
AW30-43	2100

3) If stall speed RPM recorded is lower or higher then specified, check fluid color and odor. If fluid color and odor is normal, replace torque converter. If fluid is discolored or has a burnt smell, manufacturer recommends replacing transmission as an assembly.

NOTE: If stall speed RPM is greater than 600 RPM lower than specification and poor acceleration exists, torque converter may be faulty.

HYDRAULIC PRESSURE TEST

1) Ensure transmission is at normal operating temperature. Connect pressure gauge to line pressure test port. *See Fig. 4.*
2) Connect tachometer to vehicle and ensure it is visible to driver. Block drive wheels and fully apply parking brake. Start engine and let idle.
3) Apply service brake and shift transmission into "D" position. Check line pressure at idle and record pressure reading. Accelerate engine to stall speed and record line pressure reading.
4) Repeat test procedure in "R" position. If line pressures are not as specified, check throttle cable adjustment. Adjust throttle cable as necessary, and repeat test procedure and record pressure readings. Compare all readings to specification. See LINE PRESSURE SPECIFICATIONS table.

LINE PRESSURE SPECIFICATIONS

Engine Speed	"D" Position psi (kg/cm²)	"R" Position psi (kg/cm²)
Idle Speed	59-65 (4.1-4.6)	88-98 (6.2-6.9)
Stall Speed	180-194 (12.6-13.6)	209-252 (14.7-17.7)

5) If line pressures are not as specified, internal components in transmission may be malfunctioning. Check self-diagnostic system for trouble codes. See SELF-DIAGNOSTIC SYSTEM. If no trouble codes are found, manufacturer recommends replacing transmission as an assembly.

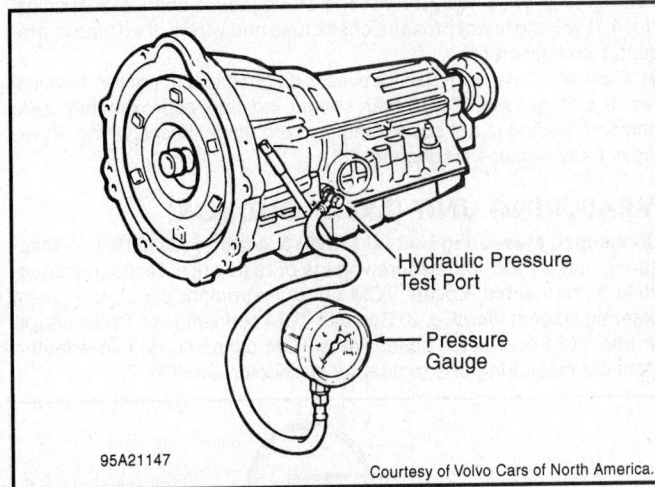

95A21147

Hydraulic Pressure Test Port

Pressure Gauge

Courtesy of Volvo Cars of North America.

Fig. 4: Locating Line Pressure Test Port

ON-VEHICLE SERVICE

EXTENSION HOUSING SEAL

Removal & Installation – 1) Raise and support vehicle. Mark drive shaft location at transmission flange for reassembly reference. Remove 4 nuts securing drive shaft to flange. Secure drive shaft aside. Free staked area of flange nut. Secure flange to prevent rotation. Remove flange nut and flange. Using appropriate puller, remove extension housing seal.
2) To install, reverse removal procedure. Lubricate seal lip prior to installation. Install NEW "O" ring on flange. Install NEW flange nut. Apply Loctite to flange nut threads prior to installation. Tighten flange nut to 91 ft. lbs. (123 N.m) and stake to secure. Install drive shaft. Tighten nuts to 37 ft. lbs. (50 N.m).

THROTTLE & KICKDOWN CABLES

Information is not available from manufacturer.

REMOVAL & INSTALLATION

TRANSMISSION

For transmission removal and installation procedure, see appropriate AUTOMATIC TRANSMISSION REMOVAL article in TRANSMISSION SERVICING section.

ACCUMULATOR PISTONS & SPRINGS

Removal & Installation – 1) Remove control valve assembly. See CONTROL VALVE ASSEMBLY. Remove retainers securing accumulator pistons and springs. Apply compressed air to transmission case oil ports to remove accumulator pistons and springs from transmission case. Note direction and location of springs and pistons for reassembly reference.
2) Measure accumulator piston spring free length and outside diameter. Replace springs if not within specification. See ACCUMULATOR SPRING SPECIFICATIONS table.
3) To install, reverse removal procedure. Replace accumulator piston seal rings prior to installation. Lubricate seal rings with ATF. Ensure components are installed in correct direction and location.

ACCUMULATOR SPRING SPECIFICATIONS

Piston Spring (Color)	Free Length In. (mm)	Diameter In. (mm)
2nd Brake (Blue)	2.78 (70.6)	.78 (19.8)
Direct Clutch		
Inner (Pink)	1.66 (42.2)	.58 (14.7)
Outer (Blue)	2.70 (68.6)	.80 (20.3)
OD Brake (Green)	2.40 (61.0)	.62 (15.7)
OD Clutch		
Inner (Yellow)	1.81 (46.0)	.55 (14.0)
Outer (Orange)	2.91 (73.9)	.81 (20.5)

CONTROL VALVE ASSEMBLY

CAUTION: Accumulator pistons, springs and non-return valve are secured in transmission case by control valve assembly. Components may fall from case when control valve assembly is removed. Secure components in case using retainers prior to removing control valve assembly.

Removal – 1) Raise and support vehicle. Remove transmission drain plug and drain fluid. Remove wiring harness from clips on oil pan. Remove oil pan bolts and remove oil pan. Remove 3 oil strainer bolts and oil strainer. Remove 2 bolts securing solenoid wire harness. Disconnect 4 valve body solenoid wire connectors, noting wire color and locations.
2) Loosen 18 control valve assembly bolts. Lower control valve assembly slightly. Secure accumulator pistons, springs and non-return valve in transmission case using retainers. Remove control valve assembly bolts, noting length and location of bolts for installation reference. Remove control valve assembly.
Installation – To install, reverse removal procedure. Ensure accumulator pistons, springs and non-return valve are installed in correct locations. Ensure control valve assembly bolts are installed in correct locations. Tighten oil strainer bolts and control valve assembly bolts to 89 INCH lbs. (10 N.m). Install .12" (3 mm) thick bead of sealing compound on oil pan and install pan. Tighten oil pan bolts to 62 INCH lbs. (7 N.m). Tighten drain plug to 15 ft. lbs. (21 N.m).

GEAR POSITION SENSOR

NOTE: Gear position sensor may also be referred to as neutral safety switch.

Removal & Installation – 1) Disconnect negative battery cable. Ensure transmission is in "N" position and parking brake is applied. Raise and support vehicle. Remove exhaust pipe and heat shield. Remove shift rod arm from manual shaft on left side of transmission. Disconnect 8-pin gear position sensor connector. Remove cooler inlet tube from transmission.

2) Note position of gear position sensor prior to removal. Remove nut with locking washer and rubber washer. Remove gear position sensor bolt and sensor. To install, reverse removal procedure. Tighten sensor bolt to 62 INCH lbs. (7 N.m). Tighten shift rod arm nut to 13 ft. lbs. (18 N.m). Ensure sensor is installed in correct position.

SELF-DIAGNOSTIC SYSTEM

DIAGNOSTIC PROCEDURE

When performing vehicle diagnosis;
- Ensure transmission fluid level is correct and fluid is neither contaminated nor aerated.
- Ensure battery is fully charged.
- Perform visual inspection, ensuring all electrical connections at transmission, TCM, throttle position sensor, gear position sensor, speed sensor and brake switch are clean and properly installed.
- Repair diagnostic trouble codes in order displayed.

NOTE: Volvo scan tool and Volvo diagnostic unit can be used in 6 different system test functions using manufacturer's instructions to activate system components and perform several tests on transmission. See SYSTEM TEST FUNCTIONS.

SELF-DIAGNOSTICS

Signals from various sensors are monitored continuously by TCM. If certain signals are lost or become faulty, TCM will cut off electrical signal to transmission components to protect transmission. TCM adopts fixed substitute values (limp-home mode) to enable vehicle to be driven when certain failures occur. Warning indicator light will illuminate. Transmission will not shift gears due to lack of electrical signal. Transmission will operate in 4th gear in "D", and in 3rd gear in "L" position. Manual shifting is possible into all other shift lever positions. When starting off in limp-home mode, shift lever should be in "L" position to minimize transmission wear.

Faults are recorded in TCM memory in the form of Diagnostic Trouble Codes (DTCs). On 1995 vehicles, codes can be displayed using LED on Volvo diagnostic unit or by using Volvo Diagnostic Key Scan Tool. On 1996 vehicles, codes can be displayed using Volvo Diagnostic Key Scan Tool or generic scan tool. Diagnostic unit is located in engine compartment at left strut tower. Diagnostic unit is equipped with an LED indicator, activation button and function select cable. *See Fig. 5.*

NOTE: Diagnostic unit is used on 1995 vehicles. Since 1996 vehicles no longer utilize diagnostic unit, a scan tool is necessary to retrieve DTCs on these vehicles.

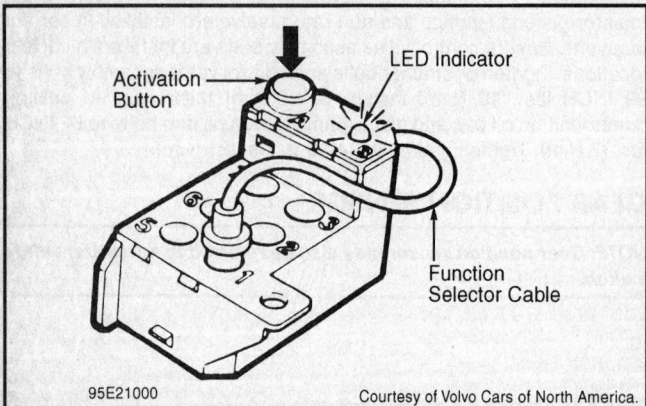

Fig. 5: Identifying Diagnostic Unit Components (1995 Vehicles Only)

Diagnostic unit output socket No. 1 is used to retrieve TCM diagnostic codes. Once function selector cable has been inserted in correct socket, depressing button 1-6 times selects from 1 to 6 control (system test) functions. Depress button and keep depressed for more than one second (but not more than 3 seconds). DTCs stored in memory are read by observing diagnostic unit LED flashes. Observe LED and count number of flashes to determine DTC. If LED does not flash, see DIAGNOSTIC UNIT LED DOES NOT FLASH.

All codes contain 3 digits (example: 213). Since all codes have 3 digits, each code requires 3 series of flashes. A 3-second interval separates each series of flashes. *See Fig. 6.* For DTC definition, see DIAGNOSTIC TROUBLE CODE DEFINITION table under TROUBLE CODE DEFINITION.

Fig. 6: Counting Red LED Flashes For Code 213

DIAGNOSTIC SYSTEM FAULTS

Diagnostic Unit LED Does Not Flash – 1) Disconnect diagnostic unit. Turn ignition on. Check for voltage at diagnostic connector terminal No. 4. If voltage is not present, check fuse and wiring. If voltage is present, turn ignition off.

2) Connect an ohmmeter between diagnostic connector terminal No. 8 and ground. Ohmmeter should indicate approximately zero ohms. If reading is not approximately zero ohms, check wiring. If wiring is okay, replace diagnostic unit.

MEASURING UNIT (BREAKOUT BOX)

Connecting Measuring Unit (9813190) & Adapter (9813194) – Measuring unit is used to measure voltage or resistance. Disconnect negative battery cable. Locate TCM under instrument panel, to right of steering column. *See Fig. 3.* Remove TCM connector(s). Press adapter into TCM connector base. Press TCM connector(s) into adapter. Connect measuring unit to adapter connector. *See Fig. 7.*

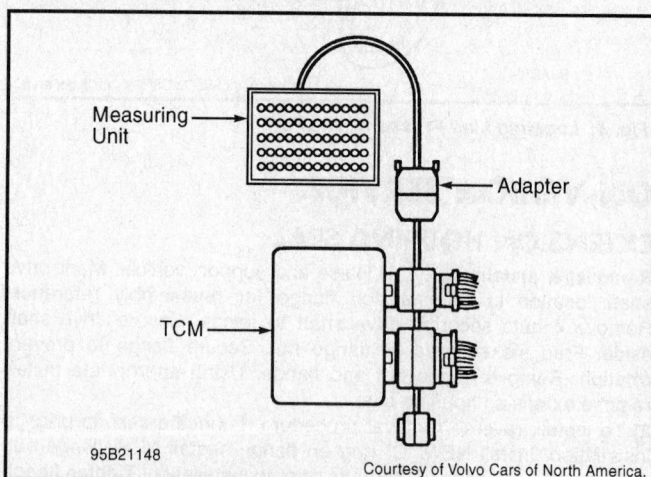

Fig. 7: Installing Measuring Unit & Adapter

CLEARING CODES

NOTE: Following procedure applies to 1995 vehicles which are equipped with a diagnostic unit.

1) Codes can be cleared only after all DTCs have been displayed and first DTC has been repeated at least once. To clear DTC, turn ignition on. Press test button on diagnostic unit and hold for more than 5 seconds. Wait for LED response.

2) Press button again and hold for more than 5 seconds. LED should go out when button is released. Ensure codes have been cleared by pressing button once. If LED displays code 111, codes have been cleared.

TCM LOCATION

TCM is located under instrument panel, to right of steering column. See Fig. 3.

SYSTEM TEST FUNCTIONS

CAUTION: Never disconnect or connect TCM connector with ignition on.

NOTE: Follow tool manufacturer's instructions if retrieving codes with Volvo Diagnostic Key Scan Tool or generic scan tool.

Volvo Self-Diagnostic System – 1) System is capable of self-diagnostic functions through the use of diagnostic unit in engine compartment, or manufacturer's scan tool. Access to diagnostic system is provided by socket No. 1 on diagnostic unit with ignition on. See Fig. 5. System has 6 test modes. Test mode No. 1 is used to display and clear codes. Test mode No. 2 is used to verify operation of system components. Test mode No. 3 operates components in a certain order.

2) Test mode No. 4 activates individual components to verify component operation when a specific code is input into diagnostic unit. Test mode No. 5 reads data values of various sensors. Values are for vehicle speed, throttle position, engine RPM and transmission oil temperature. Test mode No. 6 is used to enter data to reset adaptive values for throttle signal and shift speed adjustment function. Shift speed must be reset when transmission has been replaced.

NOTE: Manufacturer recommends use of scan tool when test modes No. 5 and 6 are performed. Follow manufacturer's instructions when performing these modes.

CAUTION: After displaying DTCs, ignition must be switched off BEFORE engine is started.

Test Mode No. 1 (Displaying Codes) – 1) To display DTCs, open diagnostic unit cover (located in engine compartment at left strut tower) and connect test lead to socket No. 1. Turn ignition on. Enter test mode No. 1 by pressing test button once for 1-3 seconds.

2) Observe LED, and count number of flashes in 3 digit series comprising a DTC. Because series are displayed at 3-second intervals, codes can be easily distinguished.

3) If a DTC is displayed, refer to DIAGNOSTIC TROUBLE CODES DEFINITION table under TROUBLE CODE DEFINITION. Depress button again, and check for additional codes. Depress button a third time if necessary. If first code repeats, no other codes are present.

Test Mode No. 1 (Clearing Codes) – 1) Codes can be cleared only after all DTCs have been displayed and first DTC has been repeated at least once. To clear DTCs, turn ignition on. Press button on diagnostic unit and hold for more than 5 seconds. Wait for LED response.

2) Press button again and hold for more than 5 seconds. LED should go out when button is released. Ensure codes have been cleared by pressing button once. If LED flashes code 111, codes have been cleared.

Test Mode No. 2 (Verifying Operation Of System Components) – 1) Sensors and switches are activated by diagnostic unit. When TCM receives a signal, a response code is displayed for each input signal. This function checks component operation, wiring and connections in each circuit. If response code is displayed, component and circuit are okay. If response code is not displayed, TCM has not received a signal. Check appropriate component or circuit and repair as necessary.

2) This test mode is activated by briefly pressing test button on diagnostic unit 2 times, causing LED to rapidly flash. TCM will flash a code indicating receipt of a signal from components.

3) Activate sensors or switches by operating appropriate component as described in RESPONSE CODE IDENTIFICATION table. Diagnostic unit LED should display appropriate response code.

NOTE: For optimum results, components should be activated in order given in RESPONSE CODE IDENTIFICATION table. Components may be tested individually if necessary.

RESPONSE CODE IDENTIFICATION

Component & Position	Circuit Tested	Response [1] Code
Gear Position Sensor		
"R" To "P"	Park	242
"P" To "R"	Reverse	144
"R" To "N"	Neutral	241
"N" To "D"	Drive	214
"D" To "3"	3rd Gear	224
"3" To "L"	Low Gear	234
Any Position	[2] Position Sensor	243
Mode Selector Switch		
"E"	Ecomomy Mode	244
"S"	Sport Mode	314
"W"	Winter Mode	324
Brake Pedal Depressed	Brake Switch	334
Acc. Pedal At WOT	Kickdown Switch	341

[1] – If response code is displayed, component and circuit tested are okay.

[2] – If response code 243 is present, gear position sensor is faulty.

Test Mode No. 3 (Operating Components In Specified Order) – 1) Output signals are checked at actuators to monitor component operation. Testing is performed in a cycle in which each component is activated 6 times with a short delay between each test. A longer delay occurs before next component is tested. The entire cycle is repeated 3 times, then test is exited automatically.

2) Test must be performed with shift lever in "P" or "N" position, and vehicle must be stopped. Test cannot be performed while driving vehicle. Output signals can be monitored by watching or listening to appropriate component to be activated.

3) Engine RPM will increase and decrease during tests. If any signal fails to activate a component, check electrical circuit and repair as necessary.

4) Test mode No. 3 is activated by briefly pressing test button on diagnostic unit 3 times. LED will flash each time component is activated. Components will be activated in the following order:

- No. 1 Shift Solenoid.
- No. 2 Shift Solenoid.
- Torque Converter Lock-Up Solenoid.
- Line Pressure Solenoid.
- Warning Indicator Light In Instrument Panel Flashes.
- Pause While Spare Output Terminal Is Tested.
- Drive Compensation For Idling.
- Torque Limiting Signal TC2 When Engine Idling.
- Torque Limiting Signal TC1 When Engine Idling.

NOTE: Engine idle speed will change during drive compensation, TC1 and TC2 activation.

Test Mode No. 4 (Activating Individual Components) – 1) Test mode No. 4 activates individual components to verify operation when a specific code is input into diagnostic unit. Components are activated 6 times in sequence. Shift lever must be in "P" or "N" position and vehicle must be stopped.

2) Rate of code transmission between TCM and diagnostic unit can be changed to 2 or 10 times the basic rate. Doubled rate can be used for reading codes from diagnostic unit LED. Highest rate is selected automatically when Volvo scan tool is used.

3) To activate test mode No. 4, push diagnostic unit button 4 times. Enter code for chosen component. See COMPONENT ACTIVATION CODES table. One digit is entered each time diagnostic unit LED is lit.

AUTOMATIC TRANSMISSIONS
Volvo AW40 Series Electronic Controls (Cont.)

NOTE: DTCs in TROUBLE CODE DEFINITION table do not necessarily apply to both 1995 and 1996 vehicles. To diagnose DTCs for 1995 vehicles, go to CIRCUIT & COMPONENT TESTING (1995). To diagnose DTCs for 1996 vehicles, go to DIAGNOSTIC TESTING (1996).

TROUBLE CODE DEFINITION

DIAGNOSTIC TROUBLE CODE DEFINITION

DTC/OBD-II DTC [1]	Warning Light On [2]	Fault/Repair
111	No	No Faults Recorded
112	Yes	Short To Voltage In No. 1 Shift Solenoid Circuit
113	Yes	TCM Fault
114	No	Mode Selector Switch Circuit Malfunction
121/P0750	Yes	Short To Ground In No. 1 Shift Solenoid Circuit
122/P0750	Yes	Open In No. 1 Shift Solenoid Circuit
123/P0745	Yes	Short To Voltage In Line Pressure Solenoid Circuit
124	No	Short To Ground In Mode Selector Switch Circuit
131	Yes	Open Or Short To Ground In Line Pressure Solenoid (STH) Circuit
132/P0745	Yes	TCM Fault
134	No	Incorrect Load Signal
141	No	Short Circuit In Oil Temperature Sensor Circuit
142	No	Open In Oil Temperature Sensor Circuit
143	No	Short To Ground In Kickdown Switch Circuit
211	Yes	TCM Fault
212	Yes	Short To Voltage In No. 2 Shift Solenoid Circuit
213/P0120	Yes	Throttle Position Sensor Signal Too High
221/P0755	Yes	Short To Ground In No. 2 Shift Solenoid Circuit
222/P0755	Yes	Open In No. 2 Shift Solenoid Circuit
223/P0120	Yes	Throttle Position Sensor Signal Too Low
231	Yes	Erratic Throttle Position Sensor Signal
232/P0500	Yes	Speedometer Signal Missing
233	Yes	Speedometer Signal Incorrect
235	[3] Yes	High Oil Temperature
245	Yes	Open Or Short In Torque Limiting Circuit
311	Yes	Transmission RPM/Speed Sensor Signal Missing
312	Yes	Transmission RPM Signal Incorrect
313/P0705	Yes	Gear Position Sensor Signal Incorrect
321/P0731, 322/P0732, 323/P0733	Yes	Incorrect Gear Ratio
331	No	Short To Voltage In Lock-Up Solenoid Circuit
332	No	Open In Lock-Up Solenoid Circuit
333	No	Short To Ground In Lock-Up Solenoid Circuit
341	No	Lock-Up Function Slips Or Disengages
411	No	Control Module EEPROM Memory Fault
421	No	Battery Voltage Too Low

[1] – OBD-II DTCs are emission-related codes.

[2] – Warning light is located in instrument panel. When a fault occurs, DTC is recorded and warning light comes on. If fault is intermittent, warning light will go out, but DTC will remain.

[3] – Only for as long as oil temperature remains high.

Diagnostic unit LED flashes when chosen component is activated. After testing components, system automatically exits test mode No. 4.

COMPONENT ACTIVATION CODES

Component	Code
No. 1 Shift Solenoid	342
No. 2 Shift Solenoid	343
Lock-Up Solenoid	344
Line Pressure Solenoid	411
Warning Indicator Light	412
Drive Compensation [1]	414
Torque Limiting TC2 [1]	422
Torque Limiting TC1 [1]	423
Basic Code Transmission Rate	311
2 Times Basic Code Transmission Rate	312
10 Times Basic Code Transmission Rate	313

[1] – Engine idle speed will change during activation.

CIRCUIT & COMPONENT TESTING (1995)

BRAKE SWITCH

1) Ensure ignition is off. Remove sound insulator to gain access to brake switch, located at top of brake lever. Connect a voltmeter between brake switch terminal No. 1 (Green/Yellow wire) and a good known ground. Battery voltage should be present. If battery voltage is not present, check for open circuit between terminal No. 1 and brake switch fuse.

2) Disconnect brake switch connector. Connect an ohmmeter between brake switch terminals No. 1 (Green/Yellow wire) and 2 (Yellow/Brown wire). With brake pedal released, resistance should be infinite. With brake pedal depressed, resistance should be zero ohms. If resistance is not as specified, replace brake switch.

KICKDOWN SWITCH

Ensure ignition switch is off. Disconnect kickdown switch connector, located left of brake booster assembly. Using a DVOM, measure resistance between switch terminals when accelerator pedal is in WOT position. Resistance should be zero ohms. While slowly releasing accelerator pedal continue to measure resistance. Resistance should be infinite in all other pedal positions. If kickdown switch does not test as described, replace switch.

MODE SELECTOR SWITCH

1) Perform test mode No. 2. See SYSTEM TEST FUNCTIONS. If response codes are correct, intermittent condition exists in wiring circuit. Visually inspect wiring. Ensure connectors fit tightly and are not corroded. If wiring is okay, go to next step.

2) Ensure ignition switch is off. Connect measuring unit to TCM. See Fig. 7. Turn ignition switch on. Using a DVOM, measure voltage between measuring unit terminals No. 12 and 39. With mode selector switch in "E" position, battery voltage should exist. With switch in any other position, voltage should exist.

3) Measure voltage between measuring unit terminals No. 12 and 41. With mode selector switch in "E" or "S" position, battery voltage should exist. With switch in any other position, voltage should not exist. If voltage is as specified, and each mode selector switch light illuminates in each position, wiring and switch are okay. If voltage is as specified, but vehicle does not function in all modes, replace TCM.

4) If voltage is not as specified, check appropriate circuit and repair as necessary. If mode selector switch lights illuminate but fault remains, check for open circuit and repair as necessary. If only one switch light illuminates, replace switch.

NOTE: DTC 124 will set if "W" button on mode selector switch is applied for more than 30 seconds.

OIL TEMPERATURE SENSOR

1) Ensure ignition switch is off. Connect measuring unit to TCM. See Fig. 7. Using a DVOM, measure resistance between measuring unit terminals No. 6 and 7. If resistance is as specified in OIL TEMPERATURE SENSOR RESISTANCE table, sensor and wiring are okay. If resistance is not as specified, go to next step.

2) Disconnect transmission 4-pin connector. See Fig. 2. Connect DVOM leads to 4-pin connector terminals No. 3 and 4. See Fig. 8. Measure resistance between connector terminals (oil temperature sensor terminals) as transmission fluid temperature gradually increases. See OIL TEMPERATURE SENSOR RESISTANCE table. If resistance is not as specified, replace oil temperature sensor.

OIL TEMPERATURE SENSOR RESISTANCE

Temperature °F (°C)	Resistance (Ohms)
32 (0)	2000
68 (20)	900
104 (40)	400
176 (80)	125
212 (100)	75
302 (150)	27

TRANSMISSION SPEED (RPM) SENSOR

1) Ensure ignition switch is off. Connect measuring unit to TCM. See Fig. 7. Using a DVOM, measure resistance between measuring unit terminals No. 16 and 17. Resistance should be 400-800 ohms. If resistance is as specified, sensor and wiring are okay. If resistance is not as specified, go to next step.

2) Measure resistance between transmission 4-pin connector terminals No. 1 and 2. See Fig. 8. Resistance should be 400-800 ohms. If resistance is as specified, sensor is okay. If resistance is not as specified, replace sensor.

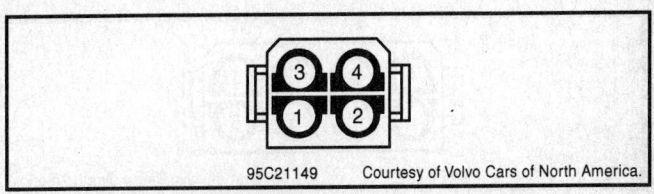

95C21149   Courtesy of Volvo Cars of North America.

Fig. 8: Identifying Oil & Transmission Speed (RPM) Sensor Connector Terminals

THROTTLE POSITION SENSOR (TPS)

1) Ensure ignition switch is off. Connect measuring unit to TCM. See Fig. 7. Turn ignition switch on. Using a DVOM, measure voltage between measuring unit terminals No. 12 and 31. Voltage should be .2 volt with throttle closed and up to 4.8 volts with Wide Open Throttle (WOT). If voltage is as specified, sensor is okay. If voltage is not as specified, replace sensor.

2) Using a DVOM, measure voltage between measuring unit terminal No. 12 and a good known ground. Voltage should be less than .7 volt. If voltage is as specified, TCM is properly grounded. If voltage is not as specified, check for poor ground connection.

TORQUE LIMITING SIGNAL VOLTAGE

1) Ensure ignition is off. Connect measuring unit to TCM. See Fig. 7. Turn ignition on. Check torque limiting signals using test mode No. 4. Using a DVOM, measure voltage at measuring unit terminals No. 12 and 35. Voltage should vary between zero and 5 volts.

2) If voltage is not as specified, fault is in wiring to TCM or TCM. Check appropriate circuits and repair as necessary. If voltage is correct, but fault is still present, replace TCM.

VALVE BODY SOLENOIDS

1) Remove transmission oil pan. Disconnect solenoid wire connector(s). For solenoid wire color identification, see SOLENOID WIRE COLOR IDENTIFICATION table. Using a DVOM, measure resistance between appropriate solenoid terminal and ground. Resistance should be 10-15 ohms for No. 1, No. 2 and torque converter lock-up solenoids. If resistance is not as specified, replace solenoid.

2) Using DVOM, measure resistance between line pressure solenoid terminals. Resistance should be 2-6 ohms. If resistance is not as specified, replace solenoid.

SOLENOID WIRE COLOR IDENTIFICATION

Solenoid	Wire Color
No. 1	Green
No. 2	Blue
Line Pressure	Pink & Brown
Torque Converter Lock-Up	Yellow

GEAR POSITION SENSOR CIRCUITS

Using a DVOM, check continuity between appropriate gear position sensor 8-pin connector terminal and TCM 30-pin connector terminal. See Figs. 9 and 11. Continuity should exist for each circuit. If continuity does not exist, repair circuit(s) as necessary. For gear position sensor connector terminal locations, See Fig. 9. For gear position sensor connector terminal identification, see SENSOR-TO-TCM CONNECTOR TERMINAL IDENTIFICATION table.

SENSOR-TO-TCM CONNECTOR TERMINAL IDENTIFICATION

Gear Position Sensor Terminal No. [1][2]	TCM Terminal No.
5	19
6	20
7	21
8	22

[1] – For terminal locations, See Figs. 9 and 11.
[2] – Terminals No. 1-4 do not send signal to TCM.

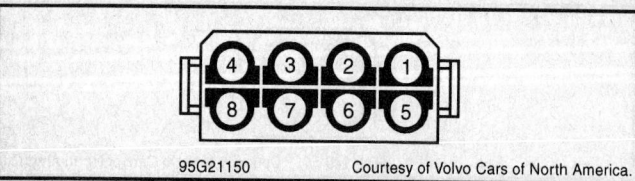

95G21150   Courtesy of Volvo Cars of North America.

Fig. 9: Identifying Gear Position Sensor Connector Terminals

VALVE BODY SOLENOID CIRCUITS

Using a DVOM, measure resistance between appropriate solenoid wire connector and appropriate terminal at transmission 8-pin connector. See Fig. 2. Resistance should be zero ohms for each solenoid wire. For transmission connector terminal locations, See Fig. 10. For transmission connector terminal identification, see TRANSMISSION CONNECTOR TERMINAL IDENTIFICATION table. If resistance is not as specified, repair appropriate circuit as necessary.

TRANSMISSION CONNECTOR TERMINAL IDENTIFICATION

Terminal No. [1] [2]	Component
1	No. 1 Shift Solenoid
2	No. 2 Shift Solenoid
3	Lock-Up Solenoid
4 & 5	Line Pressure Solenoid

[1] – For terminal locations, See Fig. 10.
[2] – Terminals No. 6-8 are blank.

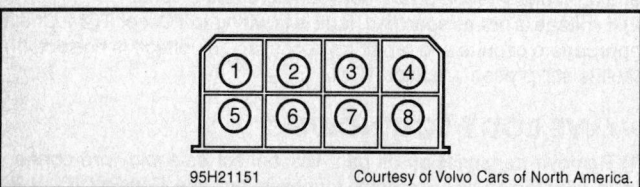

95H21151   Courtesy of Volvo Cars of North America.

Fig. 10: Identifying Solenoid Connector Terminals

DIAGNOSTIC TESTING (1996)

DTC 114: MODE SELECTOR SWITCH CIRCUIT MALFUNCTION

1) Turn ignition on. Set mode selector to "E". Wait about 30 seconds. Set mode selector to "S" position. Wait about 30 seconds. Read status of DTC. If status is PERMANENT FAULT, go to next step. If status is not PERMANENT FAULT, check all wiring and connectors for an intermittent open circuit or poor terminal contact. Repair as necessary.

2) Ensure ignition is off. Using a screwdriver, carefully pry off selector switch from console. Check wires at back of switch for poor terminal contact. Repair as necessary. If connection is okay, ensure Black wire is grounded. Repair as necessary. If Black wire at ground is okay, go to next step.

3) Disconnect driving mode selector. Turn ignition on. Connect test light between Green/Yellow and Black wires, then between Gray/Red and Black wires. If test light does not come on, go to next step. If test light comes on, check for short circuit to voltage in Gray/Red and Green/Yellow wires.

4) Connect voltmeter between selector switch Gray/Red and Black wires, then between selector switch Green/Yellow and Black wires. If about 10-12 volts are present, go to next step. If about 10-12 volts are not present, check TCM connector for poor terminal contact. Repair as necessary, and check voltage at switch again. If voltages are to specification, DTC was set because of poor terminal contact at switch selector. If voltages are not to specification, check for open circuit in Gray/Red and Green/Yellow wires. Repair as necessary.

5) Turn ignition off. Switch selector to "S" position. Connect ohmmeter between Green/Yellow and Black wires. Switch selector to "E" position. Connect ohmmeter between Gray/Red and Black wires. If ohmmeter does not read zero ohms in both cases, replace driving mode selector. If ohmmeter does read zero ohms, DTC was set because of poor terminal contact in mode selector connector.

DTC 121/P0750: SHORT TO GROUND IN NO. 1 SHIFT SOLENOID CIRCUIT

1) Turn ignition on. Set gearshift lever to "P" position. Activate shift solenoid No. 1. Read solenoid status. If status alternates between OFF/ON, check wiring and connectors for an intermittent open circuit. Repair as necessary. If status does not alternate between OFF/ON, go to next step.

2) Turn ignition off. Raise vehicle to access transmission. Clean around solenoid assembly connector. Disconnect solenoid assembly connector. Connect ohmmeter between solenoid assembly connector terminal No. 1 (Green wire) and ground. If ohmmeter does not read 12-18 ohms, go to next step. If ohmmeter reads 12-18 ohms, check for short circuit to ground in Green wire.

3) Access and disconnect shift solenoid No. 1. Connect ohmmeter between pin on solenoid and ground. If ohmmeter reads about 12-18 ohms, check for short circuit to ground in Green wire. If ohmmeter does not read about 12-18 ohms, replace solenoid.

DTC 122/P0750: OPEN IN NO. 1 SHIFT SOLENOID CIRCUIT

1) Turn ignition on. Set gearshift lever to "P" position. Activate shift solenoid No. 1. Read solenoid status. If status alternates between OFF/ON, check wiring and connectors for an intermittent open circuit. Repair as necessary. If status does not alternate between OFF/ON, go to next step.

2) Turn ignition off. Connect measuring unit to TCM connector. Using ohmmeter, check ground circuits. See WIRING DIAGRAM. If ohmmeter reads about zero ohms, go to next step. If ohmmeter does not read about zero ohms, repair ground circuit as necessary.

3) Connect ohmmeter between measuring unit terminals No. 1 and 17. If ohmmeter reads about 12-18 ohms, go to step **7)**. If ohmmeter does not read about 12-18 ohms, go to next step.

4) Raise vehicle to access transmission. Clean around solenoid assembly connector. Disconnect solenoid assembly connector. Connect ohmmeter between solenoid assembly connector terminal No. 1 (Green wire) and measuring unit terminal No. 17. If ohmmeter reads about zero ohms, go to next step. If ohmmeter does not read about zero ohms, check for open circuit in Green wire.

5) Connect ohmmeter between solenoid assembly connector terminal No. 1 (Green wire) and ground. If ohmmeter reads 12-18 ohms, repair poor terminal contact at TCM connector. If ohmmeter does not read 12-18 ohms, go to next step.

6) Access and disconnect shift solenoid No. 1. Connect ohmmeter between pin on solenoid and ground. If ohmmeter reads about 12-18 ohms, check for open circuit in Green wire. If ohmmeter does not read about 10-15 ohms, replace solenoid.

7) Connect voltmeter between measuring unit terminals No. 1 and 17. If voltmeter reads about zero volts, go to next step. If voltmeter does not read about zero volts, check for an open circuit in Green wire.

8) Turn on as many power consuming items as possible. Connect voltmeter between measuring unit terminals No. 1 and 15. If voltmeter reads less than .6 volt, go to next step. If voltmeter reads greater than .6 volts, check all TCM grounds for good terminal contact. Repair as necessary.

9) Disconnect measuring unit. Reconnect TCM. Erase DTC. Start engine. Wait about 15 seconds. If DTC resets, replace TCM. If DTC does not reset, check all connectors for poor terminal contact. Repair as necessary.

DTC 123/P0745: SHORT TO VOLTAGE IN LINE PRESSURE SOLENOID (STH) CIRCUIT

1) Turn ignition on. Using scan tool, select SCROLLING VALUES. Read current in solenoid circuit. Depress accelerator pedal slowly. If current decreases as accelerator pedal is depressed, go to step **5)**. If current does not decrease as accelerator pedal is depressed, go to next step.

2) Turn ignition off. Connect measuring unit to TCM connector. Connect ohmmeter between measuring unit terminals No. 4 and 16. If ohmmeter reads 2-6 ohms, repair short to voltage in control signal wiring. If control signal wiring is okay, replace TCM. If ohmmeter does not read 2-6 ohms, go to next step.

3) Raise vehicle to access transmission. Clean around solenoid assembly connector. Disconnect solenoid assembly connector. Connect ohmmeter between solenoid assembly connector terminals No. 4 (Pink wire) and No. 5 (Brown/Black wire). If ohmmeter reads about 2-6 ohms, check for short circuit in wiring. If ohmmeter does not read about 2-6 ohms, go to next step.

4) Access and disconnect solenoid STH. Connect ohmmeter between pins on solenoid connector. If ohmmeter reads about 2-6 ohms, check wiring between solenoid STH and transmission connector terminals No. 4 (Pink wire) and No. 5 (Brown/Black wire) for a short circuit. If ohmmeter does not read about 2-6 ohms, replace TCM.

5) Check for an intermittent short to voltage in Pink and Brown/Black wires. If wiring is okay, check system pressure. See HYDRAULIC PRESSURE TEST. If system pressure is okay, replace TCM.

DTC 124: SHORT TO GROUND IN MODE SELECTOR SWITCH CIRCUIT

1) Turn ignition on. Set mode selector to "E". Wait about 30 seconds. Set mode selector to "S". Wait about 30 seconds. If scan tool displays PERMANENT FAULT, go to next step. If scan tool does not display PERMANENT FAULT, to step **5)**.

2) Turn ignition off. Carefully pry driving mode selector from center console. Ensure controls for selector operate smoothly and do not stick. Ensure "W" button does not stick in depressed position and operates smoothly without catching. Shake driving mode selector to see if there are loose parts in the switch. Replace as necessary. If driving mode selector is okay, go to next step.

3) Disconnect driving mode selector connector. Put switch in mode "E". Connect ohmmeter between selector terminal Green/Yellow and Black wires. Put switch in mode "S". Connect ohmmeter between Gray/Red and Black wires. Ensure "W" button is up. Connect ohmmeter between Green/Yellow and Gray/Red wires. If ohmmeter reads infinite resistance for all tests, go to next step. If ohmmeter does not read infinite resistance for all tests, replace driving mode selector module.

4) Ensure ignition is off. Connect driving mode selector. Turn ignition on. Read mode selector sensor signal MS1. Set mode selector to "E". If mode selector sensor signal MS1 displays HIGH, check for short to ground in Gray/Red wire. If signal does not display HIGH, check for short circuit to ground in Green/Yellow wire.

5) Ensure "W" button does not stick down in depressed position and operates smoothly without catching. Check for an intermittent short circuit to ground in Gray/Red or Green/Yellow wires.

DTC 131: OPEN OR SHORT TO GROUND IN LINE PRESSURE SOLENOID (STH) CIRCUIT

1) Check for other DTCs. If DTC 123 is stored, perform diagnosis for that DTC first. See DTC 123: SHORT TO VOLTAGE IN LINE PRESSURE SOLENOID (STH) CIRCUIT. If DTC 123 is not stored, turn ignition on. Using scan tool, select SCROLLING VALUES and read current in solenoid circuit. Depress accelerator pedal slowly. If current decreases as accelerator pedal is depressed, fault is intermittent. Check wiring for an intermittent open or short circuit. If current does not decrease as accelerator pedal is depressed, connect measuring unit to TCM connector and check ground circuit. See WIRING DIAGRAM. Repair as necessary. If ground circuit is okay, go to next step.

2) Reconnect TCM. Turn on as many power consuming items as possible. Connect voltmeter between measuring unit terminals No. 1 and 15. If voltmeter reads less than .6 volt, go to next step. If voltmeter does not read less than .6 volt, check grounding points for an open circuit. Repair as necessary.

3) Ensure ignition is off. Disconnect ECM. Connect ohmmeter between measuring unit terminals No. 4 and 16. If ohmmeter reads 2-6 ohms, go to step **7)**. If ohmmeter does not read 2-6 ohms, raise vehicle to access solenoid assembly connector. Disconnect solenoid assembly connector. Connect ohmmeter between transmission

connector terminals No. 4 (Pink wire) and No. 5 (Brown/Black wire). If ohmmeter reads 2-6 ohms, go to step **5)**. If ohmmeter does not read 2-6 ohms, go to next step.

4) Ensure ignition is off. Open control system and disconnect solenoid STH. Connect ohmmeter between terminals on solenoid connector. If ohmmeter does not read 2-6 ohms, replace TCM. If ohmmeter reads 2-6 ohms, check for an open circuit in Pink and Brown/Black wires. Repair as necessary.

5) Ensure ignition is off. Disconnect solenoid assembly connector. Connect ohmmeter between solenoid assembly connector terminal No. 4 (Pink wire) and measuring unit connector terminal No. 16. If ohmmeter reads about zero ohms, go to next step. If ohmmeter does not read about zero ohms, check for open circuit in Pink wire. Repair as necessary.

6) Connect ohmmeter between solenoid assembly connector terminal No. 5 (Brown/Black wire) and measuring unit terminal No. 4. If ohmmeter does not read about zero ohms, check for open circuit in Brown/Black wire between solenoid assembly connector terminal No. 5 and TCM connector terminal No. 4. Repair as necessary. If ohmmeter reads about zero ohms, DTC was caused by poor terminal contact at TCM connector.

7) Ensure ignition is off and ECM is disconnected. Connect ohmmeter between measuring unit terminal No. 16 and ground. If ohmmeter reads infinite resistance, go to step **10)**. If ohmmeter does not read infinite resistance, raise vehicle to access solenoid assembly connector. Disconnect solenoid assembly connector. Connect ohmmeter between solenoid assembly connector terminal No. 4 (Pink wire) and ground. If ohmmeter reads infinite resistance, go to step **9)**. If ohmmeter does not read infinite resistance, go to next step.

8) Open control system and disconnect solenoid STH. Connect ohmmeter between ground and solenoid connector terminal. If ohmmeter does not read infinite resistance, replace TCM. If ohmmeter does read infinite resistance, check for short to ground in Pink or Brown/Black wires.

9) Connect ohmmeter between measuring unit terminal No. 16 and ground. If ohmmeter reads infinite resistance, check for short circuit to ground in Brown/Black wire. If ohmmeter does not read infinite resistance, check for short circuit to ground in Pink wire. Repair as necessary. Go to step **11)**.

10) Connect TCM to measuring unit. Turn ignition on. Connect voltmeter between measuring unit terminals No. 1 and 16. If voltmeter reads 0-6 volts, go to next step. If voltmeter does not read 0-6 volts, check for short circuit to voltage in Pink wire.

11) Ensure ignition is off. Reconnect all connectors. Reinstall all components. Turn ignition on. Using scan tool, select SCROLLING VALUES. Read current in solenoid circuit. Depress accelerator pedal slowly. If current decreases as accelerator pedal is depressed, DTC was caused by poor terminal contact in TCM or solenoid assembly connectors. If current does not decrease as accelerator pedal is depressed, replace TCM.

DTC 132/P0745: TCM FAULT

1) Turn ignition on. Using scan tool, select SCROLLING VALUES. Read current in solenoid circuit. Depress accelerator pedal slowly. If current decreases as accelerator pedal is depressed, go to next step. If current does not decrease as accelerator pedal is depressed, replace TCM.

2) Erase DTC. Turn ignition on. Using scan tool, select SCROLLING VALUES. Read current in solenoid circuit. Depress accelerator pedal slowly. If current decreases as accelerator pedal is depressed, system is okay. If current does not decrease as accelerator pedal is depressed, repeat step **1)**.

DTC 134: INCORRECT LOAD SIGNAL

1) Load signal from ECM provides information to TCM on torque being delivered by engine. If TCM does not register an incoming load signal when RPM sensor on transmission gives a signal that input shaft RPM is greater than about 600 RPM, DTC 134 will set.

2) If DTC 134 is set, check for poor terminal contact in connectors between TCM and ECM. Also check for an open, or short circuit to voltage, or short circuit to ground in signal wiring between ECM and TCM. If all circuits are okay, connect scan tool to DLC. Ensure engine is warm, transmission is in Neutral, and A/C is off. Select SCROLLING VALUES. Load signal should be about 35. If load signal is okay, replace TCM. If load signal is not okay, replace ECM.

DTC 141: SHORT CIRCUIT IN OIL TEMPERATURE SENSOR CIRCUIT

1) Check for short circuit to ground in oil temperature sensor signal wiring. Repair as necessary. If wiring is okay, go to next step.
2) Ensure ignition is off. Raise vehicle to access oil temperature sensor and speed (oil/speed) sensor connector. Disconnect oil/speed sensor connector. Connect ohmmeter between ground and oil/speed sensor connector terminal No. 3 (Red/White wire). See OIL TEMPERATURE SENSOR RESISTANCE table. If resistance is to specification, check Red/White wire for a short circuit to ground. If resistance is not to specification, replace oil temperature sensor.

OIL TEMPERATURE SENSOR RESISTANCE

°F (°C)	Ohms
0 (0)	1700-2300
68 (20)	765-1035
104 (40)	340-460
176 (80)	107-143
212 (100)	64-86
302 (150)	23-31

DTC 142: OPEN IN OIL TEMPERATURE SENSOR CIRCUIT

1) Check for open or short circuit to ground or voltage in oil temperature sensor signal wiring. Repair as necessary. If wiring is okay, go to next step.
2) Ensure ignition is off. Raise vehicle to access electrical connectors. Disconnect oil/speed sensor connector. Connect ohmmeter between oil/speed sensor connector terminal No. 4 (Orange/White wire) and ground. If ohmmeter reads about zero ohms, go to step 4). If ohmmeter does not read about zero ohms, go to next step.
3) Check TCM connector for poor terminal contact. Repair as necessary. Connect ohmmeter between oil/speed sensor connector terminal No. 4 (Orange/White wire) and ground. If ohmmeter reads about zero ohms, DTC was set because of poor terminal contact. If ohmmeter does not read about zero ohms, check Orange/White wire for an open circuit.
4) Turn ignition on. Connect voltmeter between oil/speed sensor connector terminal No. 3 (Red/White wire) and ground. If voltmeter reads about 5 volts, check oil temperature sensor resistance. See DTC 141: SHORT CIRCUIT IN OIL TEMPERATURE SENSOR CIRCUIT. If voltmeter reads less than 5 volts, go to next step. If voltmeter reads greater than 5 volts, check Red/White wire for a short circuit to voltage. If wire is okay, check oil temperature sensor resistance. See DTC 141: SHORT CIRCUIT IN OIL TEMPERATURE SENSOR CIRCUIT.
5) Turn ignition off. Check TCM connector for poor terminal contact. Repair as necessary. Connect voltmeter between oil/speed sensor connector terminal No. 3 (Red/White wire) and ground. If voltmeter reads about 5 volts, DTC set because of poor contact in TCM connector. If voltmeter does not read about 5 volts, check Red/White wire for an open circuit.

DTC 143: SHORT TO GROUND IN KICKDOWN SWITCH CIRCUIT

1) Connect scan tool. Turn ignition on. Ensure brake pedal is not depressed. Wait about 10 seconds. Push down accelerator pedal completely and keep it fully depressed in kickdown mode. Wait about 10 seconds. Read out DTC. If status indicates PERMANENT FAULT, go to next step. If status does not indicate PERMANENT FAULT, problem is intermittent. Check connectors and wiring for poor terminal contact.

2) Turn ignition on. Using scan tool, select SCROLLING VALUES. Read kickdown switch position. Reading should be ON if accelerator pedal is depressed to kickdown position. In any other accelerator pedal position reading should be OFF. If correct reading is displayed, go to step 5) If correct reading is not displayed, go to next step.
3) When accelerator pedal is fully depressed a circuit is made when sheath on throttle cable is pressed in to kickdown switch. Releasing accelerator pedal allows cable sheath to spring back and switch breaks circuit. If sheath operates to specification, go to next step. If sheath does not operate to specification, repair as necessary.
4) Ensure ignition is off. Disconnect kickdown switch connector. Connect ohmmeter between kickdown switch terminals No. 1 and 2. Fully depress accelerator pedal. If ohmmeter reads about zero ohms with accelerator pedal fully depressed and infinite resistance in all other positions, check for a short circuit to ground in wiring between kickdown switch terminal No. 1 (Violet/White wire) and TCM connector terminal No. 18. If ohmmeter does not read about zero ohms with accelerator pedal fully depressed and infinite resistance in all other positions, replace kickdown switch.
5) Ensure ignition is off. Connect measuring unit to ECM connector. Ensure ECM is connected. Turn ignition on. Turn on as many power consuming items as possible. Connect voltmeter between ground and measuring unit terminal No. 42. Note voltage reading, then turn ignition off. Disconnect measuring unit from ECM. Connect measuring unit to TCM connector and check grounds. See WIRING DIAGRAM. Go to next step.
6) Ensure ignition is off. Reconnect control modules. Turn ignition on. Turn on as many power consuming items as possible. Connect voltmeter between ground and test box terminal No. 15. Note voltage reading. Add both voltage readings together. Total of both readings should not be greater than .1 volt. If final voltage reading is okay, go to next step. If final reading is not okay, check TCM Brown ground wire located at base of left front strut tower for poor terminal contact. Repair as necessary.
7) Adapt wide open throttle position setting. Block all wheels. Start engine. Apply parking brake and press down hard on brake pedal. Shift gear selector to "D". Fully depress accelerator pedal so kickdown switch closes. Keep accelerator fully depressed for 5 seconds. Release accelerator pedal and move gear selector to "P". Wide open throttle position should be adapted.

DTC 213/P0120: THROTTLE POSITION SENSOR SIGNAL TOO HIGH

1) Check for engine performance DTCs. If engine performance DTCs are present, see appropriate SELF-DIAGNOSTICS article in ENGINE PERFORMANCE in appropriate MITCHELL® manual. Check throttle position sensor signal. See appropriate SENSOR OPERATING RANGE CHARTS and SELF-DIAGNOSTICS article in ENGINE PERFORMANCE in appropriate MITCHELL® manual. Check for a short circuit to voltage in signal wiring between TCM and ECM. See WIRING DIAGRAM. Repair as necessary. If all components and wiring are okay, go to next step.
2) Ensure ignition is off. Connect measuring unit to ECM connector. Ensure ECM is connected. Turn ignition on. Turn on as many power consuming items as possible. Connect voltmeter between ground and measuring unit terminal No. 42. Note voltage reading, then turn ignition off. Disconnect measuring unit from ECM. Connect measuring unit to TCM connector and check grounds. See WIRING DIAGRAM. Go to next step.
3) Ensure ignition is off. Reconnect control modules. Turn ignition on. Turn on as many power consuming items as possible. Connect voltmeter between ground and test box terminal No. 15. Note voltage reading. Add both voltage readings together. Total of both readings should not be greater than .1 volt. If final voltage reading is okay, go to next step. If final reading is not okay, check TCM Brown ground wire located at base of left front strut tower and TCM connector terminals for poor terminal contact. Repair as necessary.

4) Ensure ignition is on. Turn on as many power consuming items as possible. Connect voltmeter between measuring unit terminals No. 7 and 15. If voltmeter reads less than .6 volts, check throttle position sensor signal. See appropriate SENSOR OPERATING RANGE CHARTS and SELF-DIAGNOSTICS article in ENGINE PERFORMANCE in appropriate MITCHELL® manual. If voltmeter reads greater than .6 volts, check TCM Brown ground wire located at base of left front strut tower and TCM connector terminals for poor terminal contact. Repair as necessary.

DTC 221/P0755: SHORT TO GROUND IN NO. 2 SHIFT SOLENOID CIRCUIT

1) Turn ignition on. Set gearshift lever to "P" position. Activate solenoid. Read solenoid status. If status alternates between OFF/ON, problem is intermittent. Check connectors for poor terminal contact. If status does not alternate between OFF/ON, go to next step.

2) Turn ignition off. Raise vehicle to access electrical connectors. Disconnect solenoid assembly connector. Connect ohmmeter between solenoid assembly connector terminal No. 2 (Gray/Orange wire) and ground. If ohmmeter does not read 12-18 ohms, go to next step. If ohmmeter reads 12-18 ohms, check for short circuit to ground in Gray/Orange wire.

3) Access and disconnect shift solenoid No. 2. Connect ohmmeter between pin on solenoid and ground. If ohmmeter reads about 12-18 ohms, check for short circuit to ground in Gray/Orange wire. If ohmmeter does not read about 12-18 ohms, replace solenoid.

DTC 222/P0755: OPEN IN NO. 2 SHIFT SOLENOID CIRCUIT

1) Turn ignition on. Set gearshift lever to "P" position. Activate solenoid. Read solenoid status. If status alternates between OFF/ON, problem is intermittent. Check connectors for poor terminal contact. If status does not alternate between OFF/ON, go to next step.

2) Turn ignition off. Connect measuring unit to TCM. Check grounds. See WIRING DIAGRAM. Repair as necessary. If grounds are okay, connect ohmmeter between measuring unit terminals No. 15 and 31. If ohmmeter reads about 12-18 ohms, go to step **6)**. If ohmmeter does not read about 12-18 ohms, go to next step.

3) Raise vehicle to access electrical connectors. Disconnect solenoid assembly connector. Connect ohmmeter between solenoid assembly connector terminal No. 2 (Gray/Orange wire) and terminal No. 31 on measuring unit. If ohmmeter reads about zero ohms, go to next step. If ohmmeter does not read about zero ohms, check for open circuit in Gray/Orange wire.

4) Disconnect solenoid assembly connector. Connect ohmmeter between solenoid assembly connector terminal No. 2 (Gray/Orange wire) and ground. If ohmmeter reads 12-18 ohms, repair poor terminal contact at TCM connector. If ohmmeter does not read 12-18 ohms, go to next step.

5) Access and disconnect shift solenoid No. 2. Connect ohmmeter between pin on solenoid and ground. If ohmmeter reads about 12-18 ohms, check for short circuit to ground in Gray/Orange wire. If ohmmeter does not read about 10-15 ohms, replace solenoid.

6) Ensure ignition is off. Disconnect TCM. Turn ignition on. Connect voltmeter between measuring unit terminals No. 1 and 31. If voltmeter reads about zero volts, go to next step. If voltmeter does not read about zero volts, check for short to voltage in Gray/Orange wire.

7) Ensure ignition is off. Reconnect TCM. Turn ignition on. Turn on as many power consuming items as possible. Connect voltmeter between measuring unit terminals No. 1 and 15. If voltmeter reads less than .6 volt, go to next step. If voltmeter does not read less than .6 volt, check TCM Brown ground wire at base of left front strut tower, and Black ground wire located at left kick panel. Repair as necessary.

8) Ensure ignition is off. Disconnect measuring unit. Reconnect TCM. Turn ignition on. Erase DTCs. Move gear shift lever to "P" position. Start engine. Wait about 15 seconds and check whether DTC reoccurs. If DTC reoccurs, replace TCM. If DTC does not reoccur, check TCM connector for poor terminal contact.

DTC 223/P0120: THROTTLE POSITION SENSOR SIGNAL TOO LOW

1) Check for engine performance DTCs. If engine performance DTCs are present, see appropriate SELF-DIAGNOSTICS article in ENGINE PERFORMANCE in appropriate MITCHELL® manual. If engine performance DTCs are not present, check status message on scan tool. If status message indicates PERMANENT FAULT, go to next step. If status message does not indicate PERMANENT FAULT, problem is intermittent. Check wiring for an intermittent open circuit or connectors for poor terminal contact. Repair as necessary.

2) Ensure ignition is on. Using scan tool, select SCROLLING VALUES. Read throttle position sensor signal. Press accelerator pedal to floor. If throttle position signal increases, go to step **6)**. If throttle position signal does not increase, go to next step.

3) Ensure ignition is off. Disconnect TCM and ECM. Connect measuring unit to ECM connector. Connect ohmmeter between ground and measuring unit terminal No. 20. If ohmmeter reads about zero ohms, go to next step. If ohmmeter does not read about zero ohms, check for short circuit to ground in Gray/Black wire.

4) Ensure ignition is off. Reconnect ECM. Turn ignition on. Connect voltmeter between ground and measuring unit terminal No. 20. If voltmeter reads about .5 volt at closed throttle, go to next step. If voltmeter does not read about .5 volt at closed throttle, check throttle position sensor circuit. See appropriate SELF-DIAGNOSTICS article in ENGINE PERFORMANCE in appropriate MITCHELL® manual.

5) Ensure ignition is off. Connect measuring unit to TCM connector. Check ground points. See WIRING DIAGRAM. Reconnect ECM. Turn ignition on. Connect voltmeter between measuring unit terminals No. 7 and 15. If voltmeter reads about .5 volt at closed throttle, check control module connectors for poor terminal contact. If voltmeter does not read about .5 volt at closed throttle, check for open circuit in Gray/Black wire at TCM connector terminal No. B20.

6) Ensure ignition is off. Connect measuring unit to ECM connector. Ensure ECM is connected. Turn ignition on. Turn on as many power consuming items as possible. Connect voltmeter between ground and measuring unit terminal No. 42. Note voltage reading, then turn ignition off. Disconnect measuring unit from ECM. Connect measuring unit to TCM connector and check grounds. See WIRING DIAGRAM. Go to next step.

7) Ensure ignition is off. Reconnect control modules. Turn ignition on. Turn on as many power consuming items as possible. Connect voltmeter between ground and measuring unit terminal No. 1. Note voltage reading. Add both voltage readings together. Total of both readings should not be greater than .1 volt. If final voltage reading is okay, go to next step. If final reading is not okay, check TCM Brown ground wire located at base of left front strut tower, and TCM connector terminals for poor terminal contact. Repair as necessary.

8) Ensure ignition is on. Turn on as many power consuming items as possible. Connect voltmeter between measuring unit terminals No. 7 and 15. If voltmeter reads less than .6 volt, go to next step. If voltmeter reads greater than .6 volt, check TCM Brown ground wire located at base of left front strut tower, Black ground wire located at left kick panel, and TCM connector terminals for poor terminal contact. Repair as necessary.

9) Ensure ignition is on. Connect voltmeter between measuring unit terminals No. 7 and 15. If voltmeter does not read about .5 volt at closed throttle position, check throttle position sensor signal. See appropriate SENSOR OPERATING RANGE CHARTS and SELF-DIAGNOSTICS article in ENGINE PERFORMANCE in appropriate MITCHELL® manual. If voltmeter does read about .5 volt at closed throttle position, DTC was set because of poor terminal contact at TCM and ECM connectors. Repair as necessary.

DTC 232/P0500: SPEEDOMETER SIGNAL

1) Ensure ignition is off. Connect scan tool. Raise and support rear of vehicle. Turn ignition on. Using scan tool, select SCROLLING VALUES. Read speed. Move gear selector to "D" position so rear wheels begin to rotate. If speed increases with engine speed, problem is intermittent. Check connectors for poor terminal contact. If speed does not increase with engine speed, go to next step.

2) Turn ignition off. Connect test box to TCM connector. Check grounds. See WIRING DIAGRAM. Repair as necessary. If grounds are okay, reconnect TCM. Connect voltmeter between measuring unit terminals No. 8 and 15. If voltmeter reads 4-7 volts, go to step **4)**. If voltmeter reads less than 4-7 volts, go to next step. If voltmeter reads greater than 4-7 volts, check for a short circuit to voltage in Green/Gray wire between TCM terminal No. 8 and instrument cluster connector.

3) Ensure ignition is off. Disconnect TCM. Disconnect instrument panel cluster connector with speedometer Green/Gray wire. See appropriate INSTRUMENT PANELS article in ACCESSORIES & EQUIPMENT in appropriate MITCHELL® manual. Connect ohmmeter between measuring unit terminals No. 8 and 15. If ohmmeter reads infinite resistance, check for open circuit in Green/Gray wire. If ohmmeter does not read infinite resistance, check for short to ground in Green/Gray wire.

4) Check for contact resistance and oxidation at speedometer Black ground wire at instrument panel cluster connector "A" terminal No. 4. If terminal contact is okay, check ground connections for good terminal contact. Repair as necessary.

DTC 235: HIGH OIL TEMPERATURE

1) Check for other DTCs. If DTC 141 is stored, perform testing for that DTC first. See DTC 141: SHORT CIRCUIT IN OIL TEMPERATURE SENSOR CIRCUIT. If DTC 141 is not stored, turn ignition on. Using scan tool, select SCROLLING VALUES on scan tool. Read transmission oil temperature. If temperature is okay, check sensor wiring for a short circuit to ground. if temperature is not okay, go to next step.

2) Raise vehicle to access electrical connectors. Disconnect oil/speed sensor connector. Connect ohmmeter between oil/speed sensor connector terminal No. 3 (Red/White wire) and ground. If ohmmeter reads infinite resistance, go to next step. If ohmmeter does not read infinite resistance, check Red/White wire for a short circuit to ground. If wire is okay, replace oil temperature sensor.

3) Ensure ignition is off. Connect ohmmeter between oil/speed sensor connector terminals No. 3 (Red/White wire) and No. 4 (Orange/White wire). See OIL TEMPERATURE SENSOR RESISTANCE table. If resistance is to specification, check Red/White wire for a short circuit to ground. If resistance is not to specification, replace oil temperature sensor.

DTC 245: OPEN OR SHORT IN TORQUE LIMITING CIRCUIT

1) Engine torque is reduced to allow smoother shifting in some gear changes. Torque limiting process is controlled by signals sent from TCM to ECM. A receipt confirmation signal is sent from ECM to TCM. Signal indicates that torque limiting is taking place. If TCM fails to register a receipt signal after request for torque limiting, DTC 245 is set.

2) Ensure ignition is off. Connect measuring unit to TCM connector. Check grounds. See WIRING DIAGRAM. Repair as necessary. Reconnect TCM. Connect test light between measuring unit terminal No. 15 and No. 10, No. 25, and No. 39. If test light does not come on, go to next step. If test light comes on, check for short circuit to voltage in Green/Yellow, Yellow/Brown, and Violet wires. Repair as necessary.

3) Ensure ignition is off. Disconnect TCM and ECM. Connect ohmmeter between measuring unit terminal No. 15 and No. 10, No. 25, and No. 39. If ohmmeter reads infinite resistance, go to next step. If ohmmeter does not read infinite resistance, check wiring for a short circuit to ground. See WIRING DIAGRAM.

4) Ensure ignition is off. Disconnect measuring unit from TCM. Connect measuring unit to ECM. Ensure TCM and ECM are connected. Turn ignition on. Move gear selector to "P" position. Connect voltmeter between ground and measuring unit terminals No. 2 and 3. Using scan tool, activate TC/TC2. If voltmeter reading rapidly oscillates between about zero volts and 10-12 volts, go to next step. If voltmeter reading does not rapidly oscillate between about zero volts and 10-12 volts, check for an open circuit in wiring between TCM and ECM.

5) Ensure ignition is on. Move gear selector to "P" position. Using scan tool, activate torque limiting TC1/TC2. Read TCM torque limiting acknowledgment status. If status alternates between OFF/ON, problem is intermittent. Check wiring and connectors for an intermittent open circuit. If status does not alternate between OFF/ON, go to next step.

6) Check for an open circuit in Green/Yellow wire between TCM terminal No. 10 and ECM terminal B4. Repeat step **4)**. If signal does not oscillate, repeat test. If signal oscillates, system is okay.

DTC 311: TRANSMISSION SPEED SENSOR SIGNAL MISSING

1) Ensure ignition is off. Connect measuring unit to TCM. Measure resistance between measuring unit terminals No. 22 and 37. If resistance is 300-600 ohms, sensor and wiring are okay. If resistance is not 300-600 ohms, go to next step.

2) Raise vehicle and access oil/speed sensor connector. Disconnect oil/speed sensor connector. Measure resistance between connector terminals No. 1 (White/Black wire) and No. 2 (Green/Black wire). If resistance is not 300-600 ohms, check for open circuit in White/Black and Green/Black wires between speed sensor and TCM terminals No. 22 and 37. Repair wiring as necessary. If wiring is okay, replace speed sensor. If resistance is 300-600 ohms, speed sensor is okay. Check wiring for an open or short circuit. Repair as necessary.

DTC 313/P0705: GEAR POSITION SENSOR SIGNAL INCORRECT

1) If DTC 313 is set, check gear shift position sensor adjustment. Ensure gear shift is set to "N" position. Raise and support front of vehicle. Disconnect HO2S connectors. Remove front exhaust pipe. Remove front heat shield. Loosen gear position sensor adjusting bolt slightly so gear position sensor can be turned relative to shaft. Position Alignment Tool (999 5475) outside nut on gear selector shaft. Turn gear position sensor until groove on alignment tool aligns with lug on gear position sensor. Tighten adjusting bolt to 10 ft. lbs. (13 N.m). To complete installation, reverse removal procedure, then go to next step.

2) Ensure ignition is off. Connect ohmmeter between gear shift position sensor case and transmission housing. If ohmmeter reads about zero ohms, go to next step. If ohmmeter does not read about zero ohms, check gear shift position sensor ground. Repair as necessary.

3) Ensure ignition is off. Connect measuring unit to TCM connector. Check TCM grounds. See WIRING DIAGRAM. Repair as necessary. If grounds are okay, connect ohmmeter between measuring unit terminal No. 15 and terminal No. 27 ("A"), No. 41 ("B"), No. 26 ("C"), and No. 13 ("PA"). If ohmmeter reads infinite resistance, go to next step. If ohmmeter does not read infinite resistance, check for short circuit to ground in Blue/Gray, Brown/White, Green/Brown and Green/White wires between gear position sensor and TCM.

4) Ensure ignition is off. Disconnect gear position sensor connector. Connect ohmmeter between measuring unit terminal No. 15 and terminal No. 27 ("A"), No. 41 ("B"), No. 26 ("C"), and No. 13 ("PA"). If ohmmeter reads infinite resistance, go to next step. If ohmmeter does not read infinite resistance, check for short circuit to ground in Blue/Gray, Brown/White, Green/Brown and Green/White wires between gear position sensor and TCM.

5) Connect ohmmeter between gear position sensor terminals and measuring unit terminals. See GEAR POSITION SENSOR/MEASURING UNIT TERMINAL RESISTANCE table. If ohmmeter reads about zero ohms for all readings, go to next step. If ohmmeter does not read about zero ohms for all readings, check for open circuit in wiring between gear position sensor and TCM. Repair as necessary.

GEAR POSITION SENSOR/MEASURING UNIT TERMINAL RESISTANCE

Gear Position Sensor Connector Terminal	Measuring Unit Terminal
No. 5 (Blue/Gray wire)	No. 27
No. 6 (Brown/White wire)	No. 41
No. 7 (Green/Brown wire)	No. 26
No. 8 (Green/White wire)	No. 13

6) Ensure ignition is off. Reconnect TCM. Turn ignition on. Connect test light between measuring unit terminal No. 15 and terminals No. 27 (Blue/Gray wire), No. 41 (Brown/White wire), No. 26 (Green/Brown wire), and No. 13 (Green/White wire). If test light comes on, check wiring for a short circuit to voltage. If test light does not come on, go to next step.

7) Ensure ignition is off. Reconnect gear position sensor connector. Turn ignition on. Using scan tool, go into SCROLLING VALUES. Read gear shift sensor position. Move gear shift position sensor to all shift positions several times. Repeatedly select same position to check operation. If all values are okay, DTC was caused by poor terminal contact. If all values are not okay, replace gear shift position sensor.

DTC 321/P0731, 322/P0732, 323/P0733: INCORRECT GEAR RATIO

1) Check transmission oil level. If oil level is low, top off as necessary and check for leaks. Repair as necessary. If oil level is okay, turn ignition on and check DTCs. Test drive vehicle while observing automatic transmission warning light. If light begins to flash, note any unusual symptoms in transmission operation or function. If transmission does not show any mechanical fault or malfunction, go to next step. If transmission has a mechanical malfunction and DTCs are not reset, repair or replace transmission as necessary.

2) Ensure ignition is off. Disconnect TCM. Connect measuring unit to TCM connector. Leave TCM disconnected. Connect ohmmeter between measuring unit terminals No. 15 and 22. If ohmmeter reads infinite resistance, go to step **5)**. If ohmmeter does not read infinite resistance, go to next step.

3) Ensure ignition is off. Raise vehicle and disconnect oil/speed sensor connector. Connect ohmmeter connector terminal No. 2 (Green/Black wire) and ground. If ohmmeter reads infinite resistance, go to next step. If ohmmeter does not read infinite resistance, replace speed sensor.

4) Check for a short circuit to ground in Green/Black wire between oil/speed sensor connector terminal No. 2 and TCM terminal No. 22. Repair as necessary.

5) Turn ignition off. Connect measuring unit to TCM. Raise and support rear of vehicle. Turn A/C off. Idle engine. Set gear selector to "D" position so rear wheels begin to rotate. Increase and keep engine speed at 2000 RPM. Set DVOM to Hz scale, then connect DVOM between measuring unit terminals No. 22 and 37. If DVOM gives a stable Hz reading when engine speed is constant and transmission is not shifting, go to step **8)**. If Hz frequency reading shows wide fluctuations, go to next step.

6) Ensure ignition is off. Disconnect TCM. Connect ohmmeter between measuring unit terminals No. 22 and 37. If ohmmeter does not read 300-600 ohms, go to next step. If ohmmeter reads 300-600 ohms, ensure speed sensor wiring is not located near sources of interference such as electric motors or spark plugs.

7) Disconnect transmission connector. Check TCM connector for poor terminal contact. Repair as necessary. Reconnect transmission connector. Connect ohmmeter between measuring unit terminals No. 22 and 37. If ohmmeter reads about 300-600 ohms, DTC was set because of poor contact in transmission connector. If ohmmeter does not read about 300-600 ohms, replace RPM sensor.

8) Ensure ignition is off. Connect measuring unit to TCM and TCM connector. Raise and support rear of vehicle. Turn A/C off. Idle engine. Set gear selector to "D" position so rear wheels begin to rotate. Increase and hold engine speed at 2000 RPM. Set DVOM to Hz scale, then connect DVOM between measuring unit terminals No. 8 and 15. If DVOM gives a stable Hz reading when engine speed is constant and transmission is not shifting, go to next step. If Hz frequency reading shows wide fluctuations, check for a short to ground or voltage in wiring between speed sensor and TCM, and between TCM and speedometer. See WIRING DIAGRAM. Repair as necessary.

9) Ensure ignition is off. Disconnect TCM from measuring unit. Connect ohmmeter between measuring unit terminals No. 1 and 17 (solenoid S1) or No. 1 and 31 (solenoid S2). If ohmmeter reads 12-18 ohms, go to next step. If ohmmeter does not read 300-600 ohms, check transmission connector for poor terminal contact. Repair as necessary.

10) Ensure ignition is off. Check gear position sensor adjustment. See DTC 313: GEAR POSITION SENSOR SIGNAL INCORRECT. Repair as necessary. If adjustment is okay, go to next step.

11) Ensure ignition is off. Reconnect all connectors. Reinstall all components. Turn ignition on. Erase DTCs. Test drive vehicle. For DTC 321, put gear selector in "L" position. Accelerate evenly at an engine speed over 1400 RPM. For DTC 322, put gear selector in "3" position. Accelerate evenly at an engine speed over 1400 RPM. For DTC 323, put gear selector in "3" position. Maintain throttle opening at about 10 percent and accelerate evenly at an engine speed over 1400 RPM. If DTC resets, replace TCM. If DTC does not reset, system is okay.

DTC 331: SHORT TO VOLTAGE IN LOCK-UP SOLENOID CIRCUIT

Turn ignition on. Set gearshift lever to "P" position. Check solenoid function by using test mode No. 4 or Volvo scan tool. See TEST MODE NO. 4. If solenoid operates, check wiring for an intermittent short circuit. If solenoid does not operate, check for a short circuit to voltage in wiring between lock-up solenoid and TCM connector terminal A9. Repair as necessary.

DTC 332: OPEN IN LOCK-UP SOLENOID CIRCUIT

1) Turn ignition on. Set gearshift lever to "P" position. Using scan tool, activate lock-up solenoid. Read solenoid status. If status alternates between OFF/ON, problem is intermittent. Check connectors for poor terminal contact. If status does not alternate between OFF/ON, go to next step.

2) Ensure ignition is off. Connect measuring unit to TCM connector. Connect ohmmeter between measuring unit terminals No. 1 and 2. If ohmmeter reads 12-18 ohms, DTC was caused by poor terminal contact in TCM connector. Repair as necessary. If ohmmeter does not read 12-18 ohms, go to next step.

3) Ensure ignition is off. Raise vehicle to access solenoid assembly connector. Connect ohmmeter between connector terminal No. 3 (Yellow/White wire) and measuring unit terminal No. 2. If ohmmeter reads about zero ohms, go to next step. If ohmmeter does not read about zero ohms, check for an open circuit in Yellow/White wire between solenoid assembly connector terminal No. 3 and TCM terminal No. 2.

4) Ensure ignition is off. Connect ohmmeter between solenoid assembly connector terminal No. 3 (Yellow/White wire) and transmission housing. If ohmmeter does not read 12-18 ohms, go to next step. If ohmmeter reads 12-18 ohms, DTC set because of poor terminal contact at solenoid assembly connector. Repair as necessary.

5) Ensure ignition is off. Open control system and disconnect lock-up solenoid. Connect ohmmeter between lock-up solenoid terminal and transmission housing. If ohmmeter reads 12-18 ohms, check for an open circuit in Yellow/White wire between lock-up solenoid and transmission connector terminal No. 2. If ohmmeter does not read 12-18 ohms, replace lock-up solenoid.

DTC 333: SHORT TO GROUND IN LOCK-UP SOLENOID CIRCUIT

1) Turn ignition on. Set gearshift lever to "P" position. Using scan tool, activate lock-up solenoid. Read solenoid status. If status alternates between OFF/ON, check wiring for an intermittent short circuit. If solenoid does not alternate between OFF/ON, go to next step.

2) Ensure ignition is off. Raise vehicle to access solenoid assembly connector. Disconnect solenoid assembly connector. Connect ohmmeter between connector terminal No. 3 (Yellow/White wire) and transmission housing. If ohmmeter does not read 10-15 ohms, go to next step. If ohmmeter reads 10-15 ohms, check for a short circuit to ground in Yellow/White wire between solenoid assembly connector terminal No. 3 and TCM connector terminal No. 2.

3) Ensure ignition is off. Open control system and disconnect lock-up solenoid. Connect ohmmeter between lock-up solenoid terminal and transmission housing. If ohmmeter reads 12-18 ohms, check for an open circuit in Yellow/White wire between lock-up solenoid and solenoid assembly connector terminal No. 2. If ohmmeter does not read 12-18 ohms, replace lock-up solenoid.

DTC 341: LOCK-UP FUNCTION SLIPS OR DISENGAGES

1) Ensure ignition is off. Disconnect TCM. Connect measuring unit to TCM connector. Check TCM grounds. See WIRING DIAGRAM. If grounds are okay, connect ohmmeter between measuring unit terminals No. 2 and 15. If ohmmeter reads 12-18 ohms, go to next step. If ohmmeter does not read 12-18 ohms, check TCM connector for poor terminal contact, then go to next step.

2) Test drive vehicle. If DTC reoccurs, check transmission for mechanical fault.

DTC 411: CONTROL MODULE EEPROM MEMORY FAULT

1) Turn ignition off. Wait about 2 minutes. Turn ignition on. Carefully pry off driving mode selector from panel on center console. Disconnect driving mode selector to simulate a fault that would set a DTC. Wait about 45 seconds, then connect and reinstall driving mode selector. Go to next step.

2) Ensure ignition is off. Wait about 2 minutes. Turn ignition on. If DTC 114 is set, system is okay. If DTC 114 is not set, replace TCM.

DTC 421: BATTERY VOLTAGE TOO LOW

Check charging system. If charging system is okay, connect measuring unit to TCM connector and check ground and voltage. Check all connectors and wiring for poor terminal contact or open circuits. Repair as necessary.

TCM CONNECTOR TERMINAL IDENTIFICATION

If component and/or circuit fault is diagnosed, check appropriate circuit between component and TCM connector terminal(s) and repair as necessary. If component and circuits are okay, replace TCM. For TCM connector terminal locations, See Fig. 11. For TCM connector terminal identification, see WIRING DIAGRAMS.

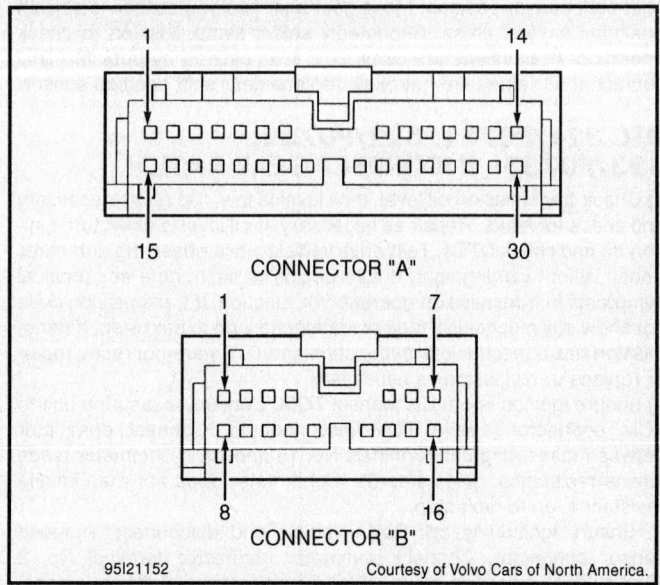

Fig. 11: *Identifying TCM Connector Terminals (1995 Vehicles)*

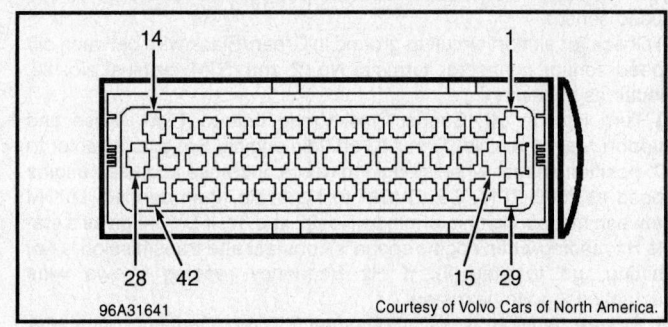

Fig. 12: *Identifying TCM Connector Terminals (1996 Vehicles)*

AUTOMATIC TRANSMISSIONS
Volvo AW40 Series Electronic Controls (Cont.)

WIRING DIAGRAMS

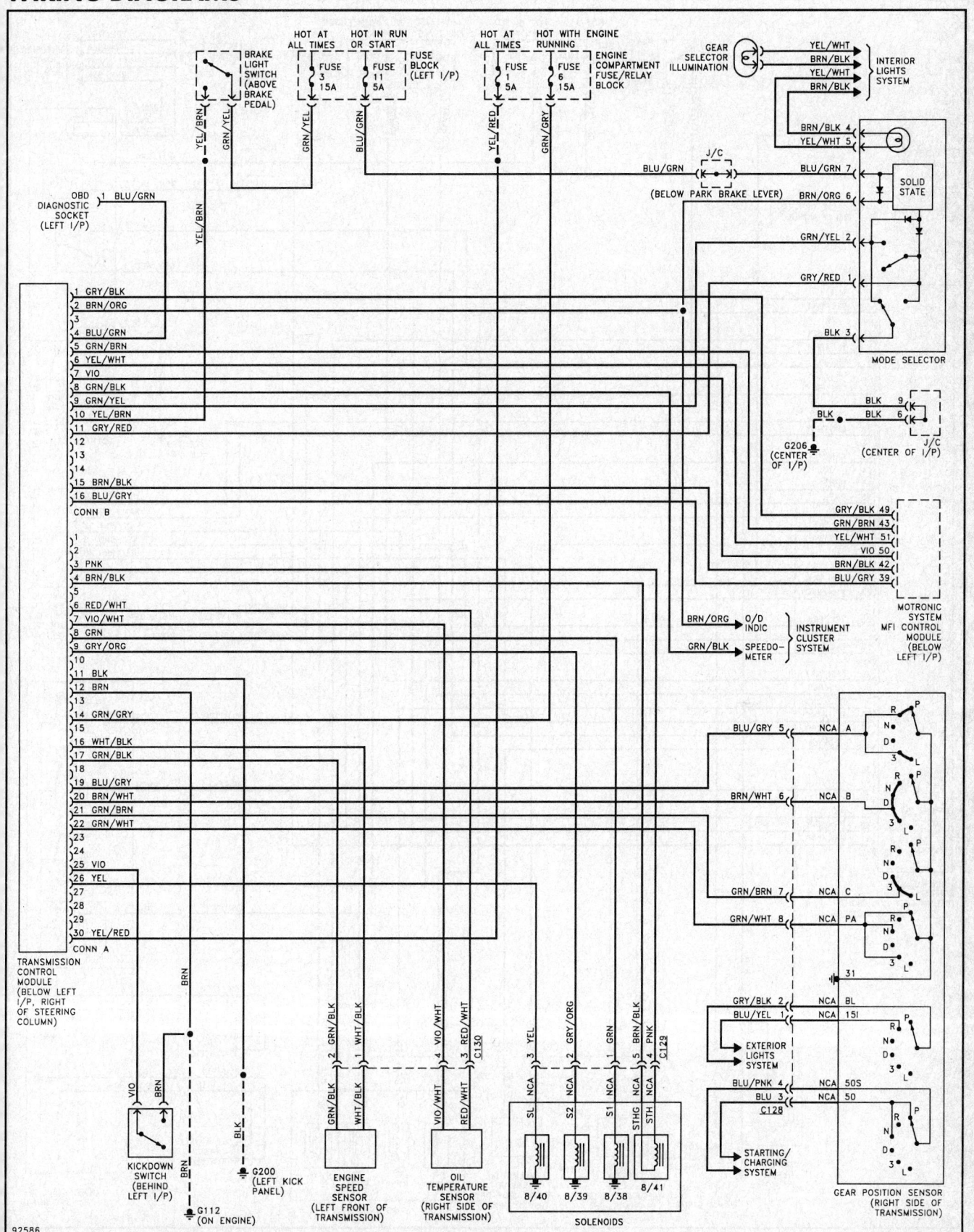

Fig. 13: 1995 Volvo 960 Transmission Wiring Diagram (AW40 Transmission)

92586

AUTOMATIC TRANSMISSIONS
Volvo AW40 Series Electronic Controls (Cont.)

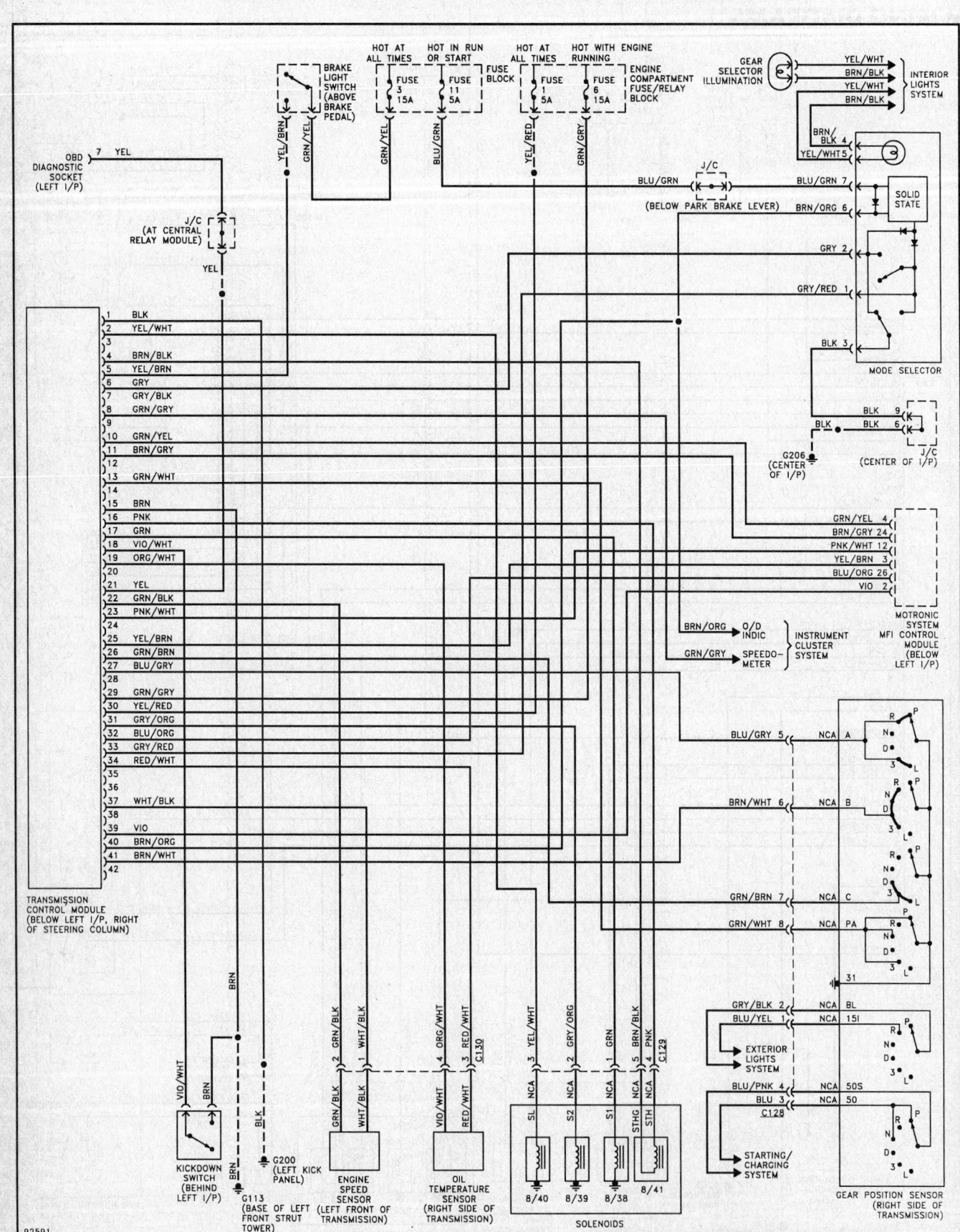

Fig. 14: 1996 Volvo 960 Transmission Wiring Diagram (AW40 Transmission)

850

APPLICATION & LABOR TIMES

APPLICATION & LABOR TIMES

Vehicle Application	Labor Times [1] R & I	[2] Overhaul	Series
850	7.2	9.0	AW50-42LE

[1] – Removal and installation of transaxle from vehicle chassis.
[2] – Bench overhaul time for transaxle. DOES NOT include removal and installation.

NOTE: Overhaul information or specifications are not available. In case of internal malfunction, manufacturer recommends replacing transaxle as an assembly.

CAUTION: Vehicle is equipped with a Supplemental Restraint System (SAS). When servicing vehicle, use care to avoid accidental air bag deployment. SRS-related components are located in steering column, center console, instrument panel and lower panel on instrument panel. DO NOT use electrical test equipment on these circuits. If may be necessary to deactivate SRS before servicing components. See AIR BAG SERVICING article in APPLICATIONS & IDENTIFICATION section.

IDENTIFICATION

Transaxle can be identified by identification plate attached to top of transaxle case. *See Fig. 1.* Identification plate contains transaxle model, year of manufacture and transaxle part number.

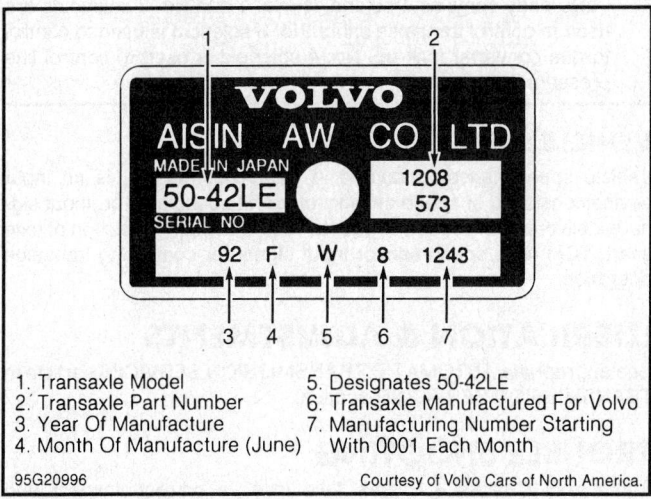

1. Transaxle Model
2. Transaxle Part Number
3. Year Of Manufacture
4. Month Of Manufacture (June)
5. Designates 50-42LE
6. Transaxle Manufactured For Volvo
7. Manufacturing Number Starting With 0001 Each Month

95G20996   Courtesy of Volvo Cars of North America.

Fig. 1: Locating Transaxle Identification Plate Information

DESCRIPTION

Transaxle is a 4-speed overdrive electronically controlled automatic transaxle. Transaxle consists of lock-up torque converter, oil pump, 3 planetary gear sets, clutch and brake units, accumulator pistons, valve body and 4 electronic valve body solenoids.

Valve body with solenoids and Transaxle Control Module (TCM) are used for controlling transaxle operation. Solenoids are controlled by TCM.

TCM receives input signals from various components to determine transaxle shift points and torque converter lock-up. Components consist of mode selector switch, throttle position sensor, engine speed (RPM) sensor, vehicle speed sensor, gear position sensor, transaxle oil temperature sensor, brake switch and kickdown switch. *See Fig. 2.*

Transaxle is equipped with a mode selector switch. Switch is used for normal, high performance and winter driving conditions. Transaxle is also equipped with a shift lock and key interlock system. Shift lock system prevents shift lever from being moved from Park position unless brake pedal is applied. In case of malfunction, shift lever can be released by depressing shift lock override button, located near shift lever. Key interlock system prevents ignition switch from being moved from ACC to LOCK position unless shift lever is in Park position.

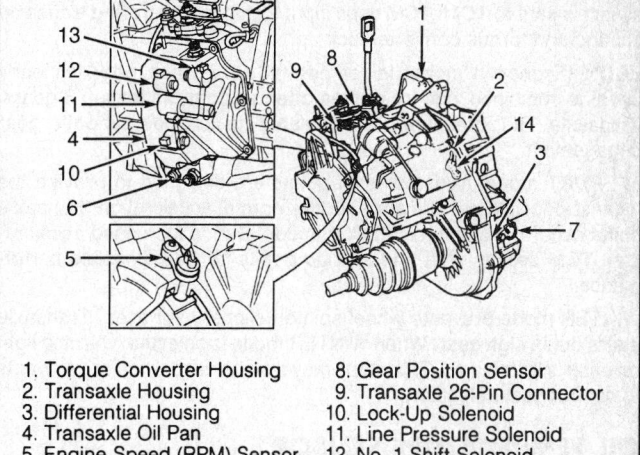

1. Torque Converter Housing
2. Transaxle Housing
3. Differential Housing
4. Transaxle Oil Pan
5. Engine Speed (RPM) Sensor
6. Oil Temperature Sensor
7. Vehicle Speed Sensor (1995)
8. Gear Position Sensor
9. Transaxle 26-Pin Connector
10. Lock-Up Solenoid
11. Line Pressure Solenoid
12. No. 1 Shift Solenoid
13. No. 2 Shift Solenoid
14. Vehicle Speed Sensor (1996)

96B31642   Courtesy of Volvo Cars of North America.

Fig. 2: Locating Transaxle Components

OPERATION

BRAKE SWITCH

Brake switch is an input device mounted above the brake pedal. When brake pedal is applied, brake switch delivers an input signal to the TCM. TCM uses input signal to control No. 3 solenoid for torque converter lock-up.

ENGINE SPEED (RPM) SENSOR

Electromagnetic RPM sensor, mounted in transaxle housing, is activated by a toothed impulse wheel. Sensor is an input device which delivers an engine RPM signal to the TCM. By comparing engine RPM and vehicle speed, TCM can determine amount of torque converter slippage.

GEAR POSITION SENSOR

NOTE: Gear position sensor may also be referred to as neutral safety switch.

Gear position sensor is an input device mounted on the transaxle manual valve shaft. Sensor delivers an input signal to TCM, indicating transaxle manual valve gear position.

KEY INTERLOCK SYSTEM

With ignition key in ignition switch, place shift lever into "P" position. Ensure ignition key can be installed and removed from ignition switch with ease. If key is difficult to remove, key interlock cable is too short. Adjust cable as necessary. Move shift lever to position other than Park. Ignition key should not be removable from ignition switch. If key can be removed, cable is too long. Adjust cable as necessary.

KICKDOWN SWITCH

Kickdown switch, located at firewall on accelerator cable, sends input signal to TCM when accelerator pedal is fully depressed. TCM uses input signal for controlling transaxle downshifting and torque converter lock-up.

MODE SELECTOR SWITCH

Mode selector switch, located to left of shift lever, has 3 different modes which effect transaxle shift points. Input signal from mode selector switch is sent to TCM. TCM uses input signal for controlling transaxle shifting and torque converter lock-up.

ECON (Economy) mode, is for normal driving and provides early upshifts combined with lock-up as often as possible for top 3 gears. Transaxle line pressure is modulated to provide smooth gear engagement.

In SPORT mode, transaxle shift points are designed to provide the highest possible performance. Under normal acceleration, transaxle shifts occur the same as in ECON mode. During increased acceleration, TCM selects shift and lock-up points for best possible performance.

WINTER mode prevents wheel spin on slippery surfaces. Transaxle starts out in high gear. When WINTER mode is selected, warning light on dash is illuminated. This mode may also be used when driver wants to control gear selection.

OIL TEMPERATURE SENSOR

Oil temperature sensor, located below transaxle oil pan, measures transaxle fluid temperature and delivers an input signal to TCM. TCM uses input signal for controlling transaxle shifting and torque converter lock-up.

SHIFT LOCK OVERRIDE FUNCTION

Move shift lever to "P" position and turn ignition key to (I) or (II) position. Press override button. Shift lever should move from "P" position. Return shift lever to "P" position and remove ignition key. Press override button. Shift lever should not move from "P" position. Override function should operate only when ignition key is in (I) or (II) position.

TRANSAXLE CONTROL MODULE (TCM)

TCM is located in control module box in engine compartment, between coolant recovery reservoir and washer fluid reservoir. TCM is in position No. 3 in module box. See Fig. 3. TCM determines shift points and torque converter lock-up timing based on input signals received from various components. Components consist of mode selector switch, throttle position sensor, engine speed (RPM) sensor, vehicle speed sensor, gear position sensor, transaxle oil temperature sensor, brake switch and kickdown switch.

TCM contains a self-diagnostic system which stores a Diagnostic Trouble Code (DTC). If a transaxle problem exists, DTC(s) can be retrieved to determine transaxle problem area.

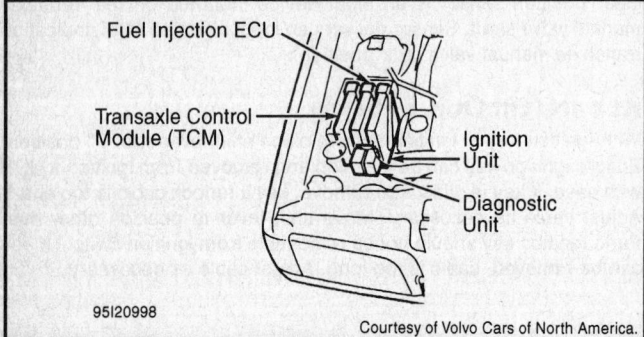

Fuel Injection ECU

Transaxle Control Module (TCM)

Ignition Unit

Diagnostic Unit

95I20998

Courtesy of Volvo Cars of North America.

Fig. 3: Locating Transaxle TCM & Diagnostic Unit

THROTTLE POSITION (TP) SENSOR

Throttle position sensor, mounted on throttle body, determines throttle position and delivers an input signal to TCM. TCM uses input signal for controlling transaxle upshifts and torque converter lock-up.

VALVE BODY SOLENOIDS

Valve body solenoids, mounted on the valve body, are output devices controlled by signals received from the TCM. The No. 1 and No. 2 solenoids are used to control transaxle shifting. No. 3 solenoid is used to control torque converter lock-up. No. 4 solenoid is used to control transaxle line pressure. For solenoid locations, See Fig. 2. For valve body solenoid usage, see VALVE BODY SOLENOID APPLICATION table.

VALVE BODY SOLENOID APPLICATION [1]

Shift Lever Position	No. 1 Solenoid	No. 2 Solenoid
"D" (Drive)		
1st Gear	OFF	ON
2nd Gear	ON	ON
3rd Gear	ON	OFF
4th Gear	OFF	OFF
"3"		
1st	OFF	ON
2nd	ON	ON
3rd	ON	OFF
"L"		
1st	OFF	ON
2nd	ON	ON
"R" (Reverse)	OFF	ON
"N" Or "P"	OFF	ON

[1] – Valve body contains 4 solenoids. No. 1 and No. 2 solenoids are used to control transaxle shifts. No. 3 solenoid is used to control torque converter lock-up. No. 4 solenoid is used to control line pressure.

VEHICLE SPEED SENSOR

Vehicle speed sensor, mounted in transaxle housing, is an input device consisting of speed sensor rotor and speed sensor. Input signal is delivered from speed sensor to TCM with each revolution of axle shaft. TCM uses speed sensor input signal for controlling transaxle operation.

LUBRICATION & ADJUSTMENTS

See appropriate AUTOMATIC TRANSMISSION SERVICING article in TRANSMISSION SERVICING section.

TROUBLE SHOOTING

Preliminary Checks – Ensure fluid level is correct. Inspect and adjust throttle cable, kickdown cable and gear position sensor (if necessary). Check idle speed RPM and adjust as necessary.

NOTE: Manufacturer recommends transaxle assembly replacement only. Manufacturer does not provide mechanical trouble shooting information.

TESTING

ROAD TEST

"D" & "3" Position – 1) Engine and transaxle must be at normal operating temperature. Shift transaxle into "D" position. Set mode selector switch to ECON position. Test drive vehicle and ensure all upshifts and downshifts occur at specified speeds. See SHIFT SPEED SPECIFICATIONS table.

2) Ensure lock-up occurs at appropriate speeds. See LOCK-UP SPEED SPECIFICATIONS table. Lightly depress accelerator. If excessive increase in engine RPM exists, lock-up did not occur.

NOTE: *Lock-up does not occur at coolant temperatures below 68°F (20°C). Lock-up in 2nd gear occurs when transaxle oil temperature exceeds 239°F (115°C).*

"L" Position – While driving vehicle in "L" position, check for failure to upshift to 2nd gear. Check engine braking effect when accelerator pedal is released.

"R" Position – Shift vehicle into "R" position. Accelerate vehicle and check for transaxle slippage.

"P" Position – Stop vehicle on incline of 5 degrees or steeper. Shift vehicle into "P" position and release parking brake. Ensure parking pawl prevents vehicle from moving.

TIME LAG TEST

1) Engine and transaxle must be at normal operating temperature. Start engine and ensure idle RPM is within specification with A/C off. Apply service and parking brakes. Using stop watch, measure time until engagement shock is felt when shift lever is shifted from "N" to "D" position.

2) Allow one minute intervals between tests. Perform time measurement several times and calculate average time. Time should be less than .7 seconds. Repeat test procedure to test time lag when shift lever is shifted from "N" to "R" position. Time lag should be less than 1.2 seconds. If test time is not as described, check transaxle line pressure. See HYDRAULIC PRESSURE TEST.

SHIFT SPEED SPECIFICATIONS [1]

Application	MPH
2.3L Turbo	
Economy Mode	
1st-2nd	25
2nd-3rd	51
3rd-4th	76
4th-3rd	53
3rd-2nd	31
2nd-1st	16
Sport Mode	
1st-2nd	36
2nd-3rd	69
3rd-4th	106
4th-3rd	62
3rd-2nd	47
2nd-1st	26
2.4L Non-Turbo	
Economy Mode	
1st-2nd	24
2nd-3rd	48
3rd-4th	75
4th-3rd	60
3rd-2nd	36
2nd-1st	15
Sport Mode	
1st-2nd	35
2nd-3rd	68
3rd-4th	101
4th-3rd	86
3rd-2nd	57
2nd-1st	24

[1] – With shift lever in "D" position and throttle valve open 60 percent.

STALL SPEED TEST

1) Operate engine and transaxle at normal operating temperature. Connect tachometer to vehicle and ensure it is visible to driver. Apply parking brake and block all 4 wheels.

CAUTION: DO NOT maintain stall speed RPM for more than 5 seconds. Transaxle damage may occur.

2) Ensure A/C is off. Start engine, apply brakes and place transaxle in "D" position. Depress accelerator to full throttle and note maximum RPM obtained. Repeat test in "R" position. For stall speed specifications, see STALL SPEED SPECIFICATIONS table.

LOCK-UP SPEED SPECIFICATIONS [1][2]

Application	MPH
2.3L Turbo [3]	
Economy & Sport Mode	
Lock-Up ON	
4th Gear	129
Lock-Up OFF	
4th Gear	124
2.4L Non-Turbo	
Economy Mode	
Lock-Up ON	
2nd Gear	25
3rd Gear	49
4th Gear	73
Lock-Up OFF	
2nd Gear	23
3rd Gear	44
4th Gear	68
Sport Mode	
Lock-Up ON	
2nd Gear	35
3rd Gear	65
4th Gear	96
Lock-Up OFF	
2nd Gear	33
3rd Gear	60
4th Gear	90

[1] – With shift lever in "D" position and throttle valve open 60 percent.
[2] – Lock-up does not occur in 2nd gear until fluid temperature exceeds 239°F (115°C).
[3] – Lock-up occurs in 4th gear only.

STALL SPEED SPECIFICATIONS

Engine Application	RPM
2.3L Turbo	2900
2.4L	2650

3) If stall speed RPM recorded is lower or higher then specified, check fluid color and odor. If fluid color and odor is normal, replace torque converter. If fluid is discolored or has a burnt smell, manufacturer recommends replacing transaxle as an assembly.

HYDRAULIC PRESSURE TEST

1) Ensure transaxle is at normal operating temperature. Connect pressure gauge to line pressure test port. See Fig. 4.

2) Connect tachometer to vehicle and ensure it is visible to driver. Block all 4 wheels and fully apply parking brake. Start engine and ensure idle speed is adjusted properly. Idle speed should be 850 RPM.

3) Apply service brake and shift transaxle into "D" position. Check line pressure at idle and record pressure reading. Accelerate engine to stall speed and record line pressure reading.

4) Repeat test procedure in "R" position. If line pressures are not as specified, check throttle cable adjustment. Adjust throttle cable as necessary, and repeat test procedure and record pressure readings. Compare all readings to specification. See LINE PRESSURE SPECIFICATIONS table.

LINE PRESSURE SPECIFICATIONS

Engine Speed	"D" Position psi (kg/cm²)	"R" Position psi (kg/cm²)
Idle Speed	57 (4)	85 (6)
Stall Speed	171 (12)	256 (18)

5) If line pressures are not as specified, internal components in transaxle may be malfunctioning. Check for Diagnostic Trouble Codes (DTCs). See SELF-DIAGNOSTIC SYSTEM. If no DTCs are found, manufacturer recommends replacing transaxle as an assembly.

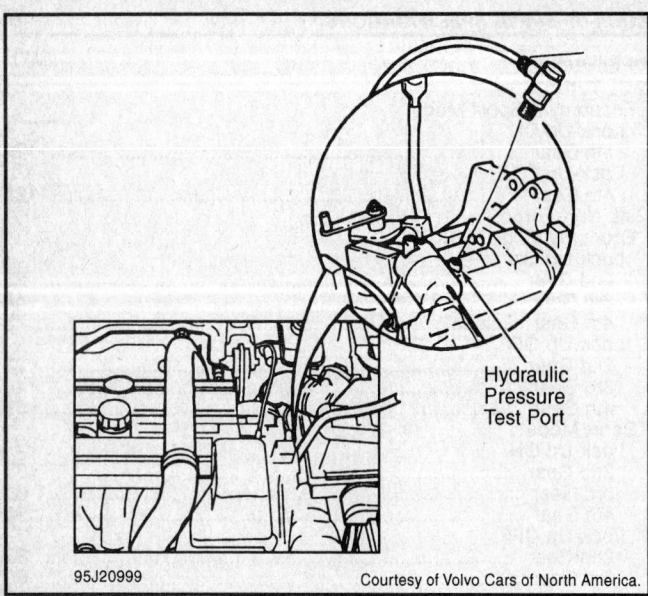

95J20999   Courtesy of Volvo Cars of North America.

Fig. 4: Locating Line Pressure Test Port

ON-VEHICLE SERVICE

AXLE SHAFTS

See appropriate AXLE SHAFTS article in AXLE SHAFTS & TRANSFER CASES section.

THROTTLE & KICKDOWN CABLES

For throttle and kickdown cable adjustments, see appropriate AUTOMATIC TRANSMISSION SERVICING article in TRANSMISSION SERVICING section.

REMOVAL & INSTALLATION

TRANSAXLE

For transaxle removal and installation procedure, see appropriate AUTOMATIC TRANSMISSION REMOVAL article in TRANSMISSION SERVICING section.

ACCUMULATOR PISTONS & SPRINGS

NOTE: Control valve assembly is equipped with 3 accumulator pistons and 6 modulator valves. Assembly has 2 cover plates on opposite sides of assembly.

Removal & Installation – 1) Remove control valve assembly. See CONTROL VALVE ASSEMBLY. Place control valve assembly on clean workbench. Remove gear selector valve ("S" shaped) from control valve assembly (transaxle side of assembly). Remove 6 cover plate bolts, cover plate and gasket. Remove 2 accumulator pistons and 3 springs, and 3 modulator valves and springs. Note location and direction of all components during removal. Lay all components on workbench exactly as removed from control valve assembly.
2) Rotate control valve assembly and remove 6 cover plate bolts, cover plate and gasket. Remove one accumulator piston and spring, and 3 modulator valves and springs. Note location and direction of all components during removal. Lay all components on workbench exactly as removed from control valve assembly.
3) Clean all components in solvent. Dry with compressed air. Ensure valve spools are not worn and that valves move easily in their bores. Valve spools may be dressed using extremely fine emery cloth if necessary. Measure accumulator valve spring free length and outside diameter. Replace springs if not within specification. See appropriate ACCUMULATOR SPRING SPECIFICATIONS table.

4) To install, reverse removal procedure. Replace accumulator piston seal rings prior to installation. Lubricate seal rings with ATF. Ensure components are installed in correct direction and location. Tighten cover plate bolts to 62 INCH lbs. (7 N.m).

ACCUMULATOR SPRING SPECIFICATIONS (1995)

Spring Color	Free Length In. (mm)	Outer Diameter In. (mm)
1-Piston Side		
Non-Turbo Engine		
No Color	.96 (24.4)	.28 (7.0)
Violet	1.12 (28.5)	.31 (8.0)
Blue	1.05 (26.6)	.28 (7.0)
Violet	1.89 (48.0)	.48 (12.3)
Turbo Engine		
Yellow	.90 (22.8)	.33 (8.3)
Violet	1.12 (28.5)	.31 (8.0)
Blue	1.05 (26.6)	.28 (7.0)
Violet	1.89 (48.0)	.48 (12.3)
2-Piston Side		
Non-Turbo Engine		
No Color	.86 (21.9)	.24 (6.0)
White	1.29 (32.8)	.28 (7.0)
Yellow	1.21 (30.7)	.28 (7.0)
Lt. Green [1]	1.38 (35.0)	.58 (14.8)
Violet	1.45 (37.0)	.44 (11.3)
Green	1.81 (46.0)	.60 (15.3)
Turbo Engine		
No Color	.86 (21.9)	.24 (6.0)
White	1.29 (32.8)	.28 (7.0)
Blue	1.04 (26.6)	.28 (7.0)
Lt. Green [1]	1.38 (35.0)	.58 (14.8)
No Color	1.81 (46.0)	.56 (14.2)

[1] – Not applicable to outer spring attached to piston.

ACCUMULATOR SPRING SPECIFICATIONS (1996)

Spring Color	Free Length In. (mm)	Outer Diameter In. (mm)
1-Piston Side		
Non-Turbo Engine		
No Color	.96 (24.4)	.28 (7.0)
Violet	1.12 (28.5)	.31 (8.0)
Blue	1.05 (26.6)	.28 (7.0)
Lt. Blue	1.81 (46.0)	.46 (11.8)
Turbo Engine		
Yellow	.90 (22.8)	.32 (8.3)
Violet	1.12 (28.5)	.31 (8.0)
Blue	1.05 (26.6)	.28 (7.0)
Violet	1.88 (48.0)	.48 (12.3)
2-Piston Side		
Non-Turbo Engine		
No Color	.86 (21.9)	.24 (6.0)
White	1.29 (32.8)	.28 (7.0)
Yellow	1.21 (30.7)	.28 (7.0)
Lt. Green [1]	1.38 (35.0)	.58 (14.8)
White	1.45 (37.0)	.34 (8.8)
Red	1.81 (46.0)	.55 (14.1)
Turbo Engine		
No Color	.86 (21.9)	.24 (6.0)
White	1.29 (32.8)	.28 (7.0)
Yellow	1.20 (30.7)	.28 (7.0)
Lt. Green [1]	1.38 (35.0)	.58 (14.8)
No Color	1.81 (46.0)	.56 (14.2)

[1] – Not applicable to outer spring attached to piston.

CONTROL VALVE ASSEMBLY

Removal & Installation – 1) Raise and support vehicle. Remove transaxle oil pipe and drain fluid. Undo clip securing oil temperature sensor harness. Remove oil pan Torx screws and remove oil pan. Disconnect 4 valve body solenoid wire connectors, noting wire color and locations. Remove 9 control valve assembly bolts, noting length and location of bolts for installation reference. Remove control valve assembly.

2) To install, reverse removal procedure. Ensure bolts are installed in correct locations. Tighten bolts to 89 INCH lbs. (10 N.m). Install .12" (3 mm) thick bead of sealing compound on oil pan and install pan. Tighten oil pan Torx screws to 18 ft. lbs. (25 N.m).

GEAR POSITION SENSOR

NOTE: Gear position sensor may also be referred to as neutral safety switch.

Removal & Installation – 1) Ensure transaxle is in "N" position and parking brake is applied. Remove battery, battery tray and air intake hose. Remove air cleaner assembly. Disconnect transaxle cable from shift rod arm. Remove shift rod arm from sensor. Note position of notch on sensor for installation reference.

2) Remove nut, washer and seal from sensor. Loosen dipstick bracket. Remove 2 bolts securing sensor to transaxle. Remove sensor from control shaft. To install, reverse removal procedure. Ensure notch on sensor is located in exact position as prior to removal. Tighten 2 sensor bolts to 18 ft. lbs (25 N.m).

SELF-DIAGNOSTIC SYSTEM

DIAGNOSTIC PROCEDURE

When performing vehicle diagnosis:

- Ensure transaxle fluid level is correct and fluid is neither contaminated nor aerated.
- Ensure throttle and kickdown cables are properly adjusted. See appropriate AUTOMATIC TRANSMISSION SERVICING article in TRANSMISSION SERVICING section.
- Ensure battery is fully charged.
- Perform visual inspection, ensuring all electrical connections at transaxle, TCM, throttle position sensor, gear position sensor, speed sensors and brake switch are clean and properly installed.
- Repair diagnostic trouble codes in order displayed.

NOTE: Volvo diagnostic unit (1995 vehicles) or scan tool (1995 and 1996 vehicles) can be used in 6 different system test functions using manufacturer's instructions to activate system components and perform several tests on transaxle. See SYSTEM TEST FUNCTIONS.

SELF-DIAGNOSTICS

Signals from various sensors are monitored continuously by TCM. If certain signals are lost or become faulty, TCM will cut off electrical signal to transaxle components to protect transaxle. TCM adopts fixed substitute values (limp-home mode) to enable vehicle to be driven when certain failures occur. Warning indicator light will illuminate. Transaxle will not shift gears due to lack of electrical signal. Transaxle will operate in 4th gear in "D", and in 3rd gear in "L" position. Manual shifting is possible into all other shift lever positions. When starting off in limp-home mode, shift lever should be in "L" position to minimize transaxle wear. Faults are recorded in TCM memory in the form of Diagnostic Trouble Codes (DTCs).

On 1995 vehicles, DTCs can be displayed using LED on Volvo diagnostic unit in engine compartment, using Volvo Diagnostic Key Scan Tool connected to Volvo Data Link Connector (DLC) in engine compartment, using Volvo System Tester Scan Tool connected to Volvo Data Link Connector (DLC) in engine compartment, or using an aftermarket scan tool connected to On-Board Diagnostics II (OBD-II) Data Link Connector (DLC). OBD-II DLC is located in center console in front of gear shift lever. Using OBD-II DLC and scan tool will only output OBD-II DTCs, and not entire range of DTCs. *See Figs. 5 and 6.* On 1996 vehicles, DTCs can only be accessed using scan tool connected to DLC located in front of gear shift lever. Scan tool will output entire range of DTCs.

On 1995 vehicles, on-board Volvo diagnostic unit for retrieving codes is located in right front of engine compartment. *See Fig. 3.* Diagnostic unit is equipped with an LED indicator, activation button and function select cable. *See Fig. 5.*

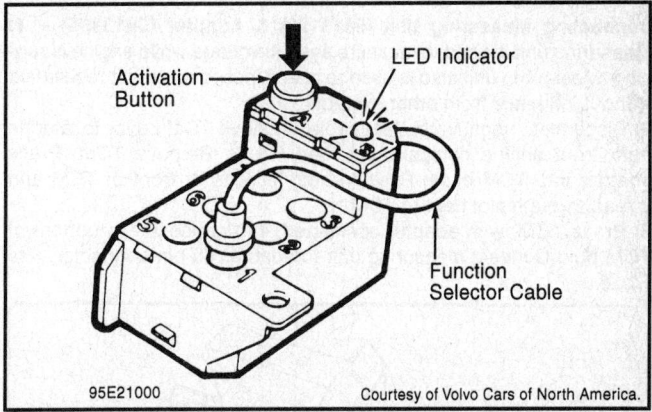

95E21000   Courtesy of Volvo Cars of North America.

Fig. 5: Identifying Diagnostic Unit Components (1995 Vehicles)

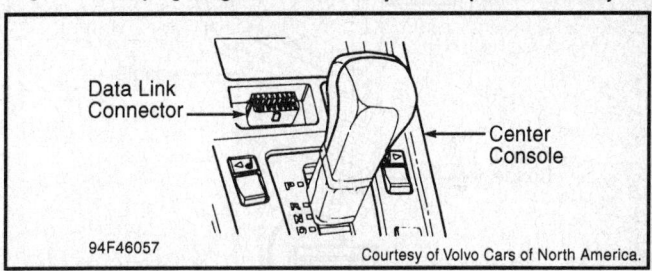

94F46057   Courtesy of Volvo Cars of North America.

Fig. 6: Locating Data Link Connector (DLC)

Diagnostic unit output socket No. 1 is used to retrieve TCM diagnostic codes. Once function selector cable has been inserted in correct socket, depressing button 1-6 times selects from 1 to 6 control (system test) functions. Depress button and keep depressed for more than one second (but not more than 3 seconds). DTCs stored in memory are read by observing diagnostic unit LED flashes. Observe LED and count number of flashes to determine DTC. If LED does not flash, see DIAGNOSTIC UNIT LED DOES NOT FLASH.

All codes contain 3 digits (example: 2-1-3). Since all codes have 3 digits, each code requires 3 series of flashes. A 3-second interval separates each series of flashes. *See Fig. 7.* For DTC definition, see appropriate DIAGNOSTIC TROUBLE CODE DEFINITION table under TROUBLE CODE DEFINITION.

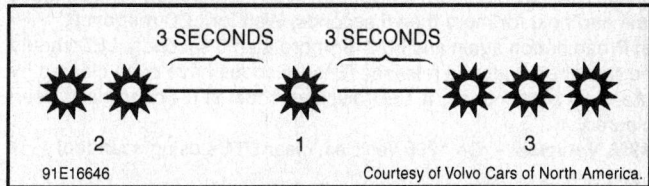

91E16646   Courtesy of Volvo Cars of North America.

Fig. 7: Counting Red LED Code Flashes For Code 213

DIAGNOSTIC SYSTEM FAULTS

Diagnostic Unit LED Does Not Flash – 1) Disconnect diagnostic unit. Turn ignition on. Check for voltage at diagnostic connector terminal No. 4. If voltage is not present, check fuse and wiring. If voltage is present, turn ignition off.

2) Connect an ohmmeter between diagnostic connector terminal No. 8 and ground. Ohmmeter should indicate approximately zero ohms. If reading is not approximately zero ohms, check wiring. If wiring is okay, replace diagnostic unit.

Diagnostic Unit LED Flashes But TCM Does Not Respond – Turn ignition on. Check for voltage at diagnostic connector terminal No. 2 and ground. Approximately 5 volts should be present. Check for voltage at diagnostic connector terminal No. 6 and ground. Approximately 5 volts should be present. If voltage is not as specified, check wiring and repair as necessary.

MEASURING UNIT

Connecting Measuring Unit (9813190) & Adapter (9813195) – 1) Measuring unit is used to measure system voltage while engine is running. Measuring unit also is used to check individual circuit resistance without influence from other systems.

2) Disconnect negative battery cable. Remove TCM cover located in right front engine compartment. *See Fig. 3.* Remove TCM. Press adapter into TCM base. Position adapter lead at front of TCM and thread through slot next to TCM.

3) Press TCM, with adapter connected, into connector in bottom of TCM box. Connect measuring unit to adapter 60-pin connector. *See Fig. 8.*

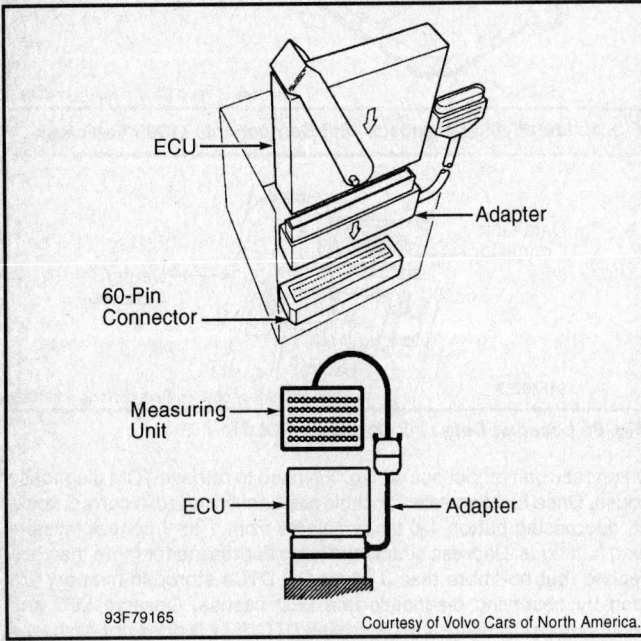

93F79165   Courtesy of Volvo Cars of North America.

Fig. 8: Installing Measuring Unit & Adapter

CLEARING CODES

1995 Vehicles – 1) On 1995 vehicles, codes can be cleared only after all DTCs have been displayed and first DTC has been repeated at least once. To clear DTC, turn ignition on. Press test button on diagnostic unit and hold for more than 5 seconds. Wait for LED response.

2) Press button again and hold for more than 5 seconds. LED should go out when button is released. Ensure codes have been cleared by pressing button once. If LED displays code 111, codes have been cleared.

1996 Vehicles – On 1996 vehicles, clear DTCs using scan tool.

TCM LOCATION

TCM is located in right front of engine compartment, between coolant recovery reservoir and washer fluid reservoir. *See Fig. 3.*

SYSTEM TEST FUNCTIONS

CAUTION: Never disconnect or connect TCM connector with ignition switch in ON position.

Follow tool manufacturer's instructions if retrieving codes with Volvo Diagnostic Key Scan Tool, Volvo System Tester Scan Tool or generic scan tool. Volvo Diagnostic Key Scan Tool and Volvo System Tester Scan Tool must be connected to Volvo DLC located in engine compartment. Generic scan tool must be connected to DLC located in console in front of gear shift lever. *See Fig. 6.*

NOTE: 1996 vehicles are not equipped with a diagnostic unit. DTCs on these vehicles can only be retrieved using scan tool.

Volvo Self-Diagnostic System – System is capable of self-diagnostic functions through the use of diagnostic unit in engine compartment, or manufacturer's scan tool. Access to diagnostic system is provided by socket No. 1 on diagnostic unit with ignition on. *See Fig. 5.* System has 6 test modes. Test mode No. 1 is used to display and clear codes. Test mode No. 2 is used to verify operation of system components. Test mode No. 3 operates components in a certain order.

Test mode No. 4 activates individual components to verify component operation when a specific code is input into diagnostic unit. Test mode No. 5 reads data values of various sensors. Values are for vehicle speed, throttle position, engine RPM and transaxle oil temperature. Test mode No. 6 is used to enter data to reset adaptive values for throttle signal and shift speed adjustment function. Shift speed must be reset when transaxle has been replaced.

NOTE: Manufacturer recommends use of scan tool when test modes No. 5 and 6 are performed. Follow manufacturer's instructions when performing these modes.

CAUTION: After displaying DTCs, ignition must be switched off BEFORE engine is started.

Test Mode No. 1 (Displaying Codes) – 1) To display DTCs, open diagnostic unit cover (located in right corner of engine compartment) and connect test lead to socket No. 1. Turn ignition on. Enter test mode No. 1 by pressing test button once for 1-3 seconds.

2) Observe LED, and count number of flashes in 3 digit series comprising a DTC. Because series are displayed at 3-second intervals, codes can be easily distinguished.

3) If a DTC is displayed, refer to appropriate DIAGNOSTIC TROUBLE CODES DEFINITION table under TROUBLE CODE DEFINITION. Depress button again, and check for additional codes. Depress button a third time if necessary. If first code repeats, no other codes are present.

Test Mode No. 1 (Clearing Codes) – 1) Codes can be cleared only after all DTCs have been displayed and first DTC has been repeated at least once. To clear DTCs, turn ignition on. Press button on diagnostic unit and hold for more than 5 seconds. Wait for LED response.

2) Press button again and hold for more than 5 seconds. LED should go out when button is released. Ensure codes have been cleared by pressing button once. If LED flashes code 1-1-1, codes have been cleared.

RESPONSE CODE IDENTIFICATION

Component & Position	Circuit Tested	Response [1] Code
Gear Position Sensor		
"R" To "P"	Park	242
"P" To "R"	Reverse	144
"R" To "N"	Neutral	241
"N" To "D"	Drive	214
"D" To "3"	3rd Gear	224
"3" To "L"	Low Gear	234
Any Position	[2] Position Sensor	243
Mode Selector Switch		
Economy	Ecomomy Mode	244
Sport	Sport Mode	314
Winter	Winter Mode	324
Brake Pedal Depressed	Brake Switch	334
Acc. Pedal At WOT	Kickdown Switch	341

[1] – If response code is displayed, component and circuit tested are okay.

[2] – If response code 2-4-3 is present, gear position sensor is faulty.

Test Mode No. 2 (Verifying Operation Of System Components) – 1) Sensors and switches are activated by diagnostic unit. When TCM receives a signal, a response code is displayed for each input signal. This function checks component operation, wiring and connections in each circuit. If response code is displayed, component and circuit are okay. If response code is not displayed, TCM has not received a signal. Check appropriate component or circuit and repair as necessary.

2) This test mode is activated by briefly pressing test button on diagnostic unit 2 times, causing LED to rapidly flash. TCM will flash a code indicating receipt of a signal from components.

3) Activate sensors or switches by operating appropriate component as described in RESPONSE CODE IDENTIFICATION table. Diagnostic unit LED should display appropriate response code.

NOTE: For optimum results, components should be activated in order given in RESPONSE CODE IDENTIFICATION table. Components may be tested individually if necessary.

Test Mode No. 3 (Operating Components In Specified Order) – 1) Output signals are checked at various actuators to determine component operation. Testing is performed in a cycle in which each component is activated 6 times with a short delay between each activation. A longer delay occurs prior to testing next component. The entire cycle is repeated 3 times, then test is exited automatically.

2) Test must be performed with shift lever in "P" or "N" position, and vehicle must be stopped. Test cannot be performed while driving vehicle. Output signals can be monitored by watching or listening to appropriate component to be activated. Engine RPM will increase during drive compensation activation and decrease during torque limiting activation. If any signal fails to activate a component, check wire circuit and repair as possible.

3) This test mode is activated by briefly pressing test button on diagnostic unit button 3 times. LED will flash each time component is activated. Components will be activated in the following order:
- No. 1 Shift Solenoid.
- No. 2 Shift Solenoid.
- Torque Converter Lock-Up Solenoid.
- Line Pressure Solenoid.
- Warning Indicator Light In Instrument Panel Flashes.
- Fault Indication Signal (OBD-II) Malfunction Indicator Light.
- Torque Limiting Signal (TCT).
- Drive Compensation For Idling.
- Torque Limiting Signal TC2 When Engine Idling.
- Torque Limiting Signal TC1 When Engine Idling.

NOTE: Engine idle speed will change during drive compensation, TC1 and TC2 activation.

TROUBLE CODE DEFINITION
DIAGNOSTIC TROUBLE CODE DEFINITION

DTC/OBD-II DTC	Warning Light On [1]	Fault/Repair
112/P0750	Yes	Short To Voltage In No. 1 Shift Solenoid Circuit
113/P0755	Yes	TCM Fault
114	No	Mode Selector Switch Circuit Malfunction
121/P0750	Yes	Short To Ground In No. 1 Shift Solenoid Circuit
122/P0750	Yes	Open In No. 1 Shift Solenoid Circuit
123/P0745	Yes	Short To Voltage In Line Pressure Solenoid (STH) Circuit
124	No	Short To Ground In Mode Selector Switch Circuit
131	Yes	Open Or Short To Ground In Line Pressure Solenoid (STH) Circuit
132/P0745	Yes	TCM Fault
134	No	Incorrect Load Signal
141	No	Short Circuit In Oil Temperature Sensor Circuit
142	No	Open In Oil Temperature Sensor Circuit
143	No	Short To Ground In Kickdown Switch Circuit
211/P0750	Yes	TCM Fault
212/P0755	Yes	Short To Voltage In No. 2 Shift Solenoid Circuit
213/P0120	Yes	Throttle Position Sensor Signal Too High
221/P0755	Yes	Short To Ground In No. 2 Shift Solenoid Circuit
222/P0755	Yes	Open In No. 2 Shift Solenoid Circuit
223/P0120	Yes	Throttle Position Sensor Signal Too Low
231	Yes	Erratic Throttle Position Sensor Signal
232/P0500	Yes	Speedometer Signal Missing Or Vehicle Speed Signal Missing
233	Yes	Speedometer Signal Incorrect
235	[2] Yes	High Oil Temperature
245	Yes	Open Or Short In Torque Limiting Circuit
311/P0715	Yes	RPM Signal Missing Or Transmission Speed Sensor Signal Missing
312	Yes	RPM Signal Incorrect
313/P0705	Yes	Gear Position Sensor Signal Incorrect
321/P0731, 322/P0732, 323/P0733 & 324/P0734	Yes	Incorrect Gear Ratio
322/P0730 [3]	Yes	Gear Ratio Information Incorrect
323 [3]	Yes	Lock-Up Slips Or Is Not Engaged
331	No	Short To Voltage In Lock-Up Solenoid Circuit
332	No	Open In Lock-Up Solenoid Circuit
333	No	Short To Ground In Lock-Up Solenoid Circuit
341	Yes	Lock-Up Function Slips Or Disengages
411	No	Control Module EEPROM Memory Fault
421	No	Battery Voltage Too Low

[1] – Warning light is located in instrument panel. When a fault occurs, DTC is recorded and warning light comes on. If fault is intermittent, warning light will go out, but DTC will remain.

[2] – Only for as long at oil temperature remains high.

[3] – If DTC is present, mechanical malfunction has occurred. Manufacturer recommends replacing transaxle assembly.

Test Mode No. 4 (Activating Individual Components) – **1)** Test mode No. 4 activates individual components to verify operation when a specific code is input into diagnostic unit. Components are activated 6 times in sequence. Shift lever must be in "P" or "N" position and vehicle must be stopped. Rate of code transmission between TCM and diagnostic unit can be changed to 2 or 10 times the basic rate. Doubled rate can be used for reading codes from diagnostic unit LED. Highest rate is selected automatically when Volvo scan tool is used.

2) To activate test mode No. 4, push diagnostic unit button 4 times. Enter code for chosen component. See COMPONENT ACTIVATION CODES table. One digit is entered each time diagnostic unit LED is lit. Diagnostic unit LED flashes when chosen component is activated. After testing components, system automatically exits test mode No. 4.

COMPONENT ACTIVATION CODES

Component	Code
No. 1 Shift Solenoid	342
No. 2 Shift Solenoid	343
Lock-Up Solenoid	344
Line Pressure Solenoid	411
Warning Indicator Light	412
Drive Compensation [1]	414
Torque Limiting TC2 [1]	422
Torque Limiting TC1 [1]	423
Basic Code Transmission Rate	311
2 Times Basic Code Transmission Rate	312
10 Times Basic Code Transmission Rate	313

[1] – Engine idle speed will change during activation.

CIRCUIT & COMPONENT TESTING

BRAKE SWITCH

1) Ensure ignition is off. Remove sound insulator to gain access to brake switch, located at top of brake lever. Connect a voltmeter between brake switch terminal No. 1 (Red wire) and a good known ground. Battery voltage should be present. If battery voltage is not present, check for open circuit between terminal No. 1 and brake switch fuse.

2) Disconnect brake switch connector. Connect an ohmmeter between brake switch terminals No. 1 (Red wire) and 2 (Yellow wire). With brake pedal released, resistance should be infinite. With brake pedal depressed, resistance should be zero ohms. If resistance is not as specified, replace brake switch.

KICKDOWN SWITCH

Ensure ignition switch is off. Disconnect kickdown switch connector from switch. Using a DVOM, measure resistance between switch terminals when accelerator pedal is in WOT position. Resistance should be zero ohms. While slowly releasing accelerator pedal continue to measure resistance. Resistance should be infinite in all other pedal positions. If kickdown switch does not test as described, replace switch.

MODE SELECTOR SWITCH

1) Ensure ignition switch is off. Disconnect mode selector switch from center bracket. Disconnect switch connector from switch. Using a DVOM, measure resistance between switch terminals No. 2 (Green/Orange wire) and 5 (Light Blue wire) when switch is in SPORT mode. Resistance should be infinite. When mode selector switch is moved to any other position, zero ohms should exist.

2) Measure resistance between switch terminals No. 3 (Brown/Gray wire) and 5 (Light Blue wire) when switch is in ECON mode. Resistance should be infinite. When mode selector switch is moved to any other position, zero ohms should exist. If resistance is not as specified, replace mode selector switch.

OIL TEMPERATURE SENSOR

1) Ensure ignition switch is off. Connect measuring unit to TCM. See Fig. 8. Using a DVOM, measure resistance between measuring unit terminals No. 14 and 15. If resistance is as specified in OIL TEMPERATURE SENSOR RESISTANCE table, sensor and wiring are okay. If resistance is not as specified, go to next step.

2) Disconnect transaxle 26-pin connector. See Fig. 2. Connect DVOM leads to 26-pin connector terminals No. 12 and 13. See Fig. 9. Measure resistance between 26-pin connector terminals (oil temperature sensor terminals) as transaxle fluid temperature gradually increases. See OIL TEMPERATURE SENSOR RESISTANCE table. If resistance is not as specified, replace oil temperature sensor.

OIL TEMPERATURE SENSOR RESISTANCE

Temperature °F (°C)	Resistance (Ohms)
32 (0)	2000
68 (20)	900
104 (40)	400
176 (80)	125
212 (100)	75
302 (150)	27

RPM SENSOR

1) Ensure ignition switch is off. Connect measuring unit to TCM. See Fig. 8. Using a DVOM, measure resistance between measuring unit terminals No. 1 and 2. Resistance should be 300-600 ohms. If resistance is as specified, sensor and wiring are okay. If resistance is not as specified, go to next step.

2) Measure resistance between transaxle 26-pin connector terminals No. 16 and 17. See Fig. 9. Resistance should be 300-600 ohms. If resistance is as specified, sensor is okay. If resistance is not as specified, replace sensor.

THROTTLE POSITION SENSOR (TPS)

1) Ensure ignition switch is off. Connect measuring unit to TCM. See Fig. 8. Turn ignition switch on. Using a DVOM, measure voltage between measuring unit terminals No. 20 and 50. Voltage should be .2 volt with throttle closed and up to 4.8 volts with wide open throttle (WOT). If voltage is as specified, sensor is okay. If voltage is not as specified, replace sensor.

2) Using a DVOM, measure voltage between measuring unit terminal No. 20 and a good known ground. Voltage should be less than .7 volt. If voltage is as specified, TCM is properly grounded. If voltage is not as specified, check for poor ground connection.

TORQUE LIMITING SIGNAL VOLTAGE

1) Ensure ignition is off. Connect measuring unit to TCM. See Fig. 8. Turn ignition on. Check torque limiting signals using test mode No. 4. Using a DVOM, measure voltage at measuring unit terminals No. 20 and 32 (TC1), terminals No. 20 and 33 (TC2) and between terminals No. 20 and 34 (acknowledged signal). Voltage should vary between zero and 5 volts at each pair of terminals.

2) If TC1 and/or TC2 voltage is not as specified, fault is in TCM. If TC1 voltage is correct, but TC2 voltage is not, fault is in wiring to TCM. If all voltage measurements are correct, but fault is still present, replace TCM.

VEHICLE SPEED SENSOR (VSS)

1) To check speed signal, connect measuring unit to TCM. See Fig. 8. Raise and support front wheels of vehicle. Set shift lever to "N" position. Turn ignition on.

2) Connect voltmeter between measuring unit terminals No. 20 and 48. Battery voltage should be present. Block one front wheel and spin other wheel rapidly. Voltage should be 4-7 volts. If voltage is consistently high or low, check wiring for an open or short circuit. If no fault is found, replace TCM.

3) To check speed signal wiring to instrument panel, connect measuring unit to instrument panel 30-pin connector. Ensure ignition is off. Using a DVOM, measure resistance between measuring unit terminal No. 6 and TCM connector "B" terminal No. 18. *See Fig. 10.*
4) Resistance should be zero ohms. If resistance is not as specified, check wiring circuit and repair as necessary. If resistance is as specified, check for incorrect installation of wiring which may cause interference, such as ignition wiring, mobile phone, etc.

VALVE BODY SOLENOIDS

1) Remove transaxle oil pan. Disconnect solenoid wire connector(s). For solenoid wire color identification, see SOLENOID WIRE COLOR IDENTIFICATION table. Using a DVOM, measure resistance between appropriate solenoid terminal and ground. Resistance should be 10-15 ohms for No. 1, No. 2 and torque converter lock-up solenoids. If resistance is not as specified, replace solenoid.
2) Using DVOM, measure resistance between line pressure solenoid terminals. Resistance should be 2-6 ohms. If resistance is not as specified, replace solenoid.

SOLENOID WIRE COLOR IDENTIFICATION

Solenoid	Wire Color
No. 1	White
No. 2	Black
Line Pressure	Blue & Brown
Torque Converter Lock-Up	Red

VALVE BODY SOLENOID CIRCUITS

Using a DVOM, measure resistance between appropriate solenoid wire connector and appropriate terminal at transaxle 26-pin connector. Resistance should be zero ohms for each solenoid wire. For transaxle connector terminal locations, *See Fig. 9.* For transaxle connector terminal identification, see TRANSAXLE CONNECTOR TERMINAL IDENTIFICATION table. If resistance is not as specified, repair appropriate circuit as necessary.

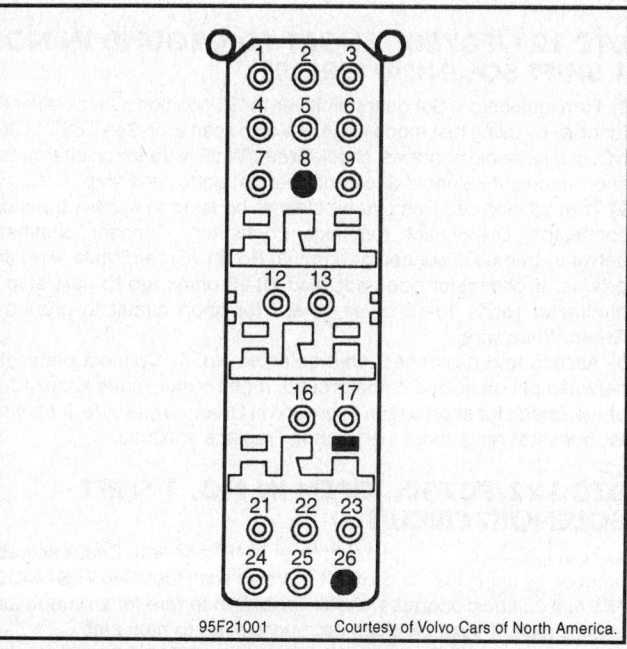

95F21001   Courtesy of Volvo Cars of North America.

Fig. 9: Identifying Transaxle Connector Terminals

TCM WIRING CIRCUITS

If component and/or circuit fault is diagnosed, check appropriate circuit between component and TCM connector terminal(s) and repair as necessary. If component and circuits are okay, replace TCM. For TCM connector terminal locations, *See Fig. 10.* For TCM connector terminal identification, see TCM CONNECTOR TERMINAL IDENTIFICATION table.

TRANSAXLE CONNECTOR TERMINAL IDENTIFICATION

Terminal No. [1] [2]	Component
1-9	Gear Position Sensor
12 & 13	Oil Temperature Sensor
16 & 17	RPM Sensor
21	No. 1 Shift Solenoid
22	No. 2 Shift Solenoid
23	Lock-Up Solenoid
24 & 25	Line Pressure Solenoid

[1] – For terminal locations, *See Fig. 9.*
[2] – Terminals No. 8 and 26 are blank.

TCM CONNECTOR TERMINAL IDENTIFICATION

Terminal No. [1] [2]	Component
Connector "A"	
1	RPM/Speed Sensor
2	RPM/Speed Sensor Ground
3	Gear Position Sensor
4	Gear Position Sensor
5	Gear Position Sensor
6	Gear Position Sensor
9	Lock-Up Solenoid
10	Battery Power
11	Speedometer (1996)
12	Speedometer (1996)
14	Oil Temperature Sensor
15	Oil Temperature Sensor Ground
20	Signal Ground
22	Line Pressure Solenoid
23	Line Pressure Solenoid Ground
27	No. 1 Shift Solenoid
28	No. 2 Shift Solenoid
29	Power Ground
30	Battery Voltage Via Ignition Switch
Connector "B"	
2	Torque Limiting
3	Torque Limiting
4	Torque Limiting Acknowledge Signal
5	Diagnostic Output
7	Warning Indicator Light
12	Engine Load
14	Gear Position Sensor
16	Mode Selector Switch
17	Mode Selector Switch
18	Speedometer
20	Throttle Position Sensor
26	Brake Switch
30	Kickdown Switch

[1] – For terminal locations, *See Fig. 10.*
[2] – Terminals not listed are blank.

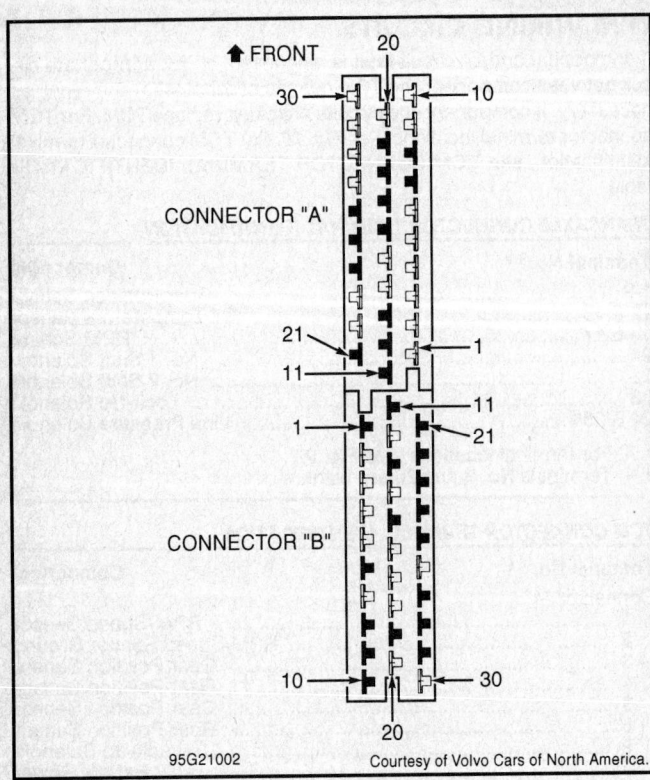

Fig. 10: Identifying TCM Connector Terminals

DIAGNOSTIC TESTING (1995)

DTC 112/P0750: SHORT TO VOLTAGE IN NO. 1 SHIFT SOLENOID CIRCUIT

1) Turn ignition on. Set gearshift lever to "P" position. Check solenoid function by using test mode No. 4 or Volvo scan tool. See TEST MODE NO. 4.

2) If solenoid operates, check wiring for an intermittent short circuit in Green/White wire. If solenoid does not operate, check Green/White wire for a short circuit. If wiring is okay, replace solenoid.

DTC 113/P0755: TCM FAULT

1) Turn ignition off. Turn off all equipment in the vehicle that uses battery power. Disconnect TCM. Connect measuring unit to TCM connector. Leave TCM disconnected. Connect ohmmeter between measuring unit terminal No. 20 and ground, and between measuring unit terminal No. 29 and ground. If ohmmeter reads zero ohms, go to next step. If ohmmeter does not read zero ohms, check grounds for an open circuit.

2) Reconnect TCM. Turn ignition on. Turn on as many power consuming items as possible. Connect voltmeter between measuring unit terminals No. 20 and 29. If voltmeter reads less than .6 volts, go to next step. If voltmeter does not read less than .6 volts, check grounds for an open circuit.

3) Ensure ignition is off. Connect measuring unit to TCM connector. Ensure TCM is connected. Connect an additional measuring unit to ECM connector. Ensure ECM is connected. Turn ignition on. Turn on as many power consuming items as possible. Connect voltmeter between TCM measuring unit terminal No. 20 and ECM measuring unit terminal No. 20 (non-turbo) or No. 42 (turbo). If voltmeter reads less than 10 volts, go to next step. If voltmeter does not read less than 10 volts, check ground points for an open circuit or poor terminal contact. Repair as necessary.

4) Ensure ignition is on. Connect voltmeter between TCM measuring unit terminals No. 29 and 30. If voltmeter reads about battery voltage, go to next step. If voltmeter does not read about battery voltage, check for an open circuit in Blue/Red wire between TCM terminal A30 and fuse No. 11-1. Repair as necessary.

5) Ensure ignition is on. Connect voltmeter between TCM measuring unit terminals No. 10 and 20. If voltmeter reads about battery voltage, go to next step. If voltmeter does not read about battery voltage, check for an open circuit in wiring between battery positive terminal and TCM terminal A30 (Blue/Red wire). Repair as necessary.

6) Ensure ignition is off. Disconnect measuring unit. Reconnect TCM. Turn ignition on. Clear DTCs. Test drive vehicle at a speed greater than 15 mph. If DTC resets, replace TCM.

DTC 114: MODE SELECTOR SWITCH CIRCUIT MALFUNCTION

1) Ensure ignition is off. Using a screwdriver, carefully pry off selector switch from console. Check wires at back of switch for poor terminal contact. Repair as necessary. If terminal contact is okay, check Black ground wire for good terminal contact. Repair as necessary. If Black ground wire is okay, go to next step.

2) Turn ignition on. Connect voltmeter between selector switch Brown/Green and Black wires. If about 11 volts are present, go to step **4)**. If zero voltage is present, go to next step. If battery voltage is present, check Brown/Green wire for a short circuit to voltage.

3) Check TCM connector for poor terminal contact. Repair as necessary. If TCM connector is okay, check for an open circuit in Brown/Green wire.

4) Connect voltmeter between selector switch Green/Orange and Black wires. If about 11 volts are present, go to step **6)**. If zero voltage is present, go to next step. If battery voltage is present, check Green/Orange wire for a short circuit to voltage.

5) Check TCM connector for poor terminal contact. Repair as necessary. If TCM connector is okay, check for an open circuit in Green/Orange wire.

6) Turn ignition off. Switch selector to position "S". Connect ohmmeter between Brown/Green and Black wires. Switch selector to position "E". Connect ohmmeter between Green/Orange and Black wires. If ohmmeter does not read zero ohms in both cases, replace driving mode selector module. If ohmmeter reads zero ohms, DTC was set because of poor terminal contact in mode selector connector.

DTC 121/P0750: SHORT TO GROUND IN NO. 1 SHIFT SOLENOID CIRCUIT

1) Turn ignition on. Set gearshift lever to "P" position. Check solenoid function by using test mode No. 4 or Volvo scan tool. See TEST MODE NO. 4. If solenoid operates, check Green/White wire for an intermittent short circuit. If solenoid does not operate, go to next step.

2) Turn ignition off. Remove air cleaner housing to access transaxle connector. Disconnect transaxle connector. Connect ohmmeter between transaxle connector terminal No. 21 (Green/White wire) and ground. If ohmmeter does not read 10-15 ohms, go to next step. If ohmmeter reads 10-15 ohms, check for short circuit to ground in Green/White wire.

3) Access and disconnect shift solenoid No. 1. Connect ohmmeter between pin on solenoid and ground. If ohmmeter reads about 10-15 ohms, check for short circuit to ground in Green/White wire. If ohmmeter does not read about 10-15 ohms, replace solenoid.

DTC 122/P0750: OPEN IN NO. 1 SHIFT SOLENOID CIRCUIT

1) Turn ignition on. Set gearshift lever to "P" position. Check solenoid function by using test mode No. 4 or Volvo scan tool. See TEST MODE NO. 4. If solenoid operates, check Green/White wire for an intermittent short circuit. If solenoid does not operate, go to next step.

2) Turn ignition off. Connect measuring unit to TCM. Connect ohmmeter between measuring unit terminals No. 20 and 27. If ohmmeter reads about 10-15 ohms, repair poor terminal contact at TCM connector. If ohmmeter does not read about 10-15 ohms, go to next step.

3) Remove air cleaner housing to access transaxle connector. Disconnect transaxle connector. Connect ohmmeter between transaxle connector terminal No. 21 (Green/White wire) and measuring unit terminal No. 27. If ohmmeter reads about zero ohms, go to next step. If ohmmeter does not read about zero ohms, check for open circuit in Green/White wire.

4) Disconnect transaxle connector. Connect ohmmeter between transaxle connector terminal No. 21 (Green/White wire) and ground. If ohmmeter reads 10-15 ohms, repair poor terminal contact at TCM connector. If ohmmeter does not read 10-15 ohms, go to next step.

5) Access and disconnect shift solenoid No. 1. Connect ohmmeter between pin on solenoid and ground. If ohmmeter reads about 10-15 ohms, check for short circuit to ground in Green/White wire. If ohmmeter does not read about 10-15 ohms, replace solenoid.

DTC 123/P0745: SHORT TO VOLTAGE IN LINE PRESSURE SOLENOID (STH) CIRCUIT

1) Turn ignition on. Set gearshift lever to "P" position. Check solenoid function by using test mode No. 4 or Volvo scan tool. See TEST MODE NO. 4. If solenoid operates, check Violet/White or Violet wire for an intermittent short circuit. If solenoid does not operate, go to next step.

2) Turn ignition off. Connect measuring unit to TCM. Connect ohmmeter between measuring unit terminals No. 22 and 23. If ohmmeter reads 2-6 ohms, repair short to voltage in control signal wiring. If control signal wiring is okay, replace TCM. If ohmmeter does not read 2-6 ohms, go to next step.

3) Remove air cleaner housing to access transaxle connector. Disconnect transaxle connector. Connect ohmmeter between transaxle connector terminals No. 24 (Violet wire) and No. 25 (Violet/White wire). If ohmmeter reads about 2-6 ohms, check for short circuit in Violet and Violet/White wiring. If ohmmeter does not read about 2-6 ohms, go to next step.

4) Access and disconnect solenoid STH. Connect ohmmeter between pins on solenoid connector. If ohmmeter reads about 2-6 ohms, check Violet and Violet/White wiring between solenoid STH and transaxle connector terminals No. 24 and 25 for a short circuit. If ohmmeter does not read about 2-6 ohms, replace TCM.

DTC 124: SHORT TO GROUND IN MODE SELECTOR SWITCH CIRCUIT

1) Turn ignition off. Carefully pry driving mode selector switch from center console. Ensure controls for selector operate smoothly and do not stick. Ensure "W" button does not stick in depressed position and operates smoothly without catching. Shake driving mode selector to see if there are loose parts in the switch. Replace as necessary. If driving mode selector is okay, go to next step.

2) Disconnect driving mode selector connector. Put switch in mode "E". Connect ohmmeter between selector terminal Brown/Green and Black wires. Put switch in mode "S". Connect ohmmeter between Green/Orange and Black wires. Ensure "W" button is up. Connect ohmmeter between Green/Orange and Brown/Green wires. If ohmmeter reads infinite resistance for all tests, go to next step. If ohmmeter does not read infinite resistance for all tests, replace driving mode selector module.

3) Disconnect TCM. Connect ohmmeter between TCM side of selector terminal Brown/Green and Black wires. If ohmmeter reads infinite resistance, check for short circuit to ground in Green/Orange wire. If ohmmeter does not read infinite resistance, check for short circuit to ground in Brown/Green wire.

DTC 131: OPEN OR SHORT TO GROUND IN LINE PRESSURE SOLENOID (STH) CIRCUIT

1) Check for open or short circuit to ground in control signal wiring or signal wiring. See DTC 113: TCM FAULT. If wiring is okay, check solenoid voltage supply. Repair as necessary. If voltage supply is okay, go to next step.

2) Ensure ignition is off. Open control system and access solenoid. Disconnect solenoid. Connect ohmmeter between terminals in solenoid connector. If ohmmeter reads 2-6 ohms, check Violet/White and Violet wires for an open circuit. If ohmmeter does not read 2-6 ohms, replace TCM.

DTC 132/P0745: TCM FAULT

Check TCM connector for poor terminal contact. Repair as necessary. Check for open circuit in TCM voltage supply or grounds. See DTC 113: TCM FAULT. Repair as necessary. If TCM connector and voltage/ground circuits are okay, replace TCM.

DTC 134: INCORRECT LOAD SIGNAL

1) Load signal from ECM provides information to TCM on torque being delivered by engine. If TCM does not register an incoming load signal when RPM sensor on transmission gives a signal that input shaft RPM is greater than about 600 RPM, DTC 134 will set.

2) If DTC 134 is set, check for poor terminal contact in connectors between TCM and ECM. Also check for an open, short circuit to voltage, or short circuit to ground in signal wiring between ECM and TCM. If all circuits are okay, connect scan tool to DLC. Ensure engine is warm, transmission is in neutral, and A/C is off. Select SCROLLING VALUES. Load signal should be about 35. If load signal is okay, replace TCM. If load signal is not okay, replace ECM.

DTC 141: SHORT CIRCUIT IN OIL TEMPERATURE SENSOR CIRCUIT

1) Check for short circuit to ground in oil temperature sensor signal wiring. Repair as necessary. If wiring is okay, go to next step.

2) Ensure ignition is off. Disconnect transaxle connector. Connect ohmmeter between transaxle connector terminals No. 12 (Blue/Green wire) and No. 13 (Blue/Black wire). See OIL TEMPERATURE SENSOR RESISTANCE table. If resistance is to specification, check Blue/Green wire for a short circuit to ground. If resistance is not to specification, replace oil temperature sensor.

OIL TEMPERATURE SENSOR RESISTANCE

°F (°C)	Ohms
0 (0)	1700-2300
68 (20)	765-1035
104 (40)	340-460
176 (80)	107-143
212 (100)	64-86
302 (150)	23-31

DTC 142: OPEN IN OIL TEMPERATURE SENSOR CIRCUIT

1) Check for open or short circuit to ground or voltage in oil temperature sensor signal wiring. Repair as necessary. If wiring is okay, go to next step.

2) Ensure ignition is off. Remove air cleaner housing to access transaxle connector. Disconnect transaxle connector. Connect ohmmeter between transaxle connector terminal No. 13 (Blue/Black wire) and ground. If ohmmeter reads about zero ohms, go to step **4)**. If ohmmeter does not read about zero ohms, go to next step.

3) Check TCM connector for poor terminal contact. Repair as necessary. Connect ohmmeter between transaxle connector terminal No. 13 and ground. If ohmmeter reads about zero ohms, DTC was set because of poor terminal contact. If ohmmeter does not read about zero ohms, check Blue/Black wire for an open circuit.

4) Turn ignition on. Connect voltmeter between transaxle connector terminal No. 12 (Blue/Green wire) and ground. If voltmeter reads about 5 volts, check oil temperature sensor resistance. See DTC 141: SHORT CIRCUIT IN OIL TEMPERATURE SENSOR CIRCUIT. If voltmeter reads less than 5 volts, go to next step. If voltmeter reads greater than 5 volts, check Blue/Green wire for a short circuit to voltage. If wire is okay, check oil temperature sensor resistance. See DTC 141: SHORT CIRCUIT IN OIL TEMPERATURE SENSOR CIRCUIT.

5) Turn ignition off. Check TCM connector for poor terminal contact. Repair as necessary. Connect voltmeter between transaxle connector terminal No. 12 (Blue/Green wire) and ground. If voltmeter reads about 5 volts, DTC set because of poor contact in TCM connector. If voltmeter does not read about 5 volts, check Blue/Green wire for an open circuit.

DTC 143: SHORT TO GROUND IN KICKDOWN SWITCH CIRCUIT

1) Check for short circuit to ground in signal wiring between TCM and ECM. Connect measuring unit to TCM and another measuring unit to ECM. Turn ignition on. Connect voltmeter between TCM measuring unit terminal No. 20 and ECM measuring unit terminal No. 20 (non-turbo) or No. 42 (turbo).

2) If voltage is less than .10 volt, check kickdown switch. Replace as necessary. If voltage is greater than .10 volt, check grounds and wiring for poor terminal contact. Repair as necessary.

DTC 211/P0750: TCM FAULT

Check voltage drop over signal ground and power ground. See DTC 113: TCM FAULT. If voltage drop and power ground are okay, check voltage supply to TCM. If voltage supply to TCM is okay, replace TCM.

DTC 212/P0755: SHORT TO VOLTAGE IN NO. 2 SHIFT SOLENOID CIRCUIT

Turn ignition on. Check solenoid using diagnostic test mode No. 4 or scan tool. See TEST MODE NO. 4. If solenoid operates, fault is intermittent. Check for loose wiring. If solenoid does not operate, check Brown/White wire for a short circuit to voltage.

DTC 213/P0120: THROTTLE POSITION SENSOR SIGNAL TOO HIGH

Check throttle position sensor signal. See appropriate SENSOR OPERATING RANGE CHARTS article in ENGINE PERFORMANCE in appropriate MITCHELL® manual. Repair as necessary. If sensor signal is okay, check voltage drop over signal ground and power ground. See DTC 113: TCM FAULT. Repair as necessary.

DTC 221/P0755: SHORT TO GROUND IN NO. 2 SHIFT SOLENOID CIRCUIT

1) Turn ignition on. Set gearshift lever to "P" position. Check solenoid function by using test mode No. 4 or Volvo scan tool. See TEST MODE NO. 4. If solenoid operates, check wiring for an intermittent short circuit. If solenoid does not operate, go to next step.

2) Turn ignition off. Remove air cleaner housing to access transaxle connector. Disconnect transaxle connector. Connect ohmmeter between transaxle connector terminal No. 22 (Violet wire) and ground. If ohmmeter does not read 10-15 ohms, go to next step. If ohmmeter reads 10-15 ohms, check for short circuit to ground in Violet wire.

3) Access and disconnect shift solenoid No. 2. Connect ohmmeter between pin on solenoid and ground. If ohmmeter reads about 10-15 ohms, check for short circuit to ground in Violet wire. If ohmmeter does not read about 10-15 ohms, replace solenoid.

DTC 222/P0755: OPEN IN NO. 2 SHIFT SOLENOID CIRCUIT

1) Turn ignition on. Set gearshift lever to "P" position. Check solenoid function by using test mode No. 4 or Volvo scan tool. See TEST MODE NO. 4. If solenoid operates, check wiring for an intermittent short circuit. If solenoid does not operate, go to next step.

2) Turn ignition off. Connect measuring unit to TCM. Connect ohmmeter between measuring unit terminals No. 20 and 28. If ohmmeter reads about 10-15 ohms, repair poor terminal contact at TCM connector. If ohmmeter does not read about 10-15 ohms, go to next step.

3) Remove air cleaner housing to access transaxle connector. Disconnect transaxle connector. Connect ohmmeter between transaxle connector terminal No. 22 (Violet wire) and measuring unit terminal No. 28. If ohmmeter reads about zero ohms, go to next step. If ohmmeter does not read about zero ohms, check for open circuit in Violet wire.

4) Disconnect transaxle connector. Connect ohmmeter between transaxle connector terminal No. 22 (Violet wire) and ground. If ohmmeter reads 10-15 ohms, repair poor terminal contact at TCM connector. If ohmmeter does not read 10-15 ohms, go to next step.

5) Access and disconnect shift solenoid No. 2. Connect ohmmeter between solenoid terminal and ground. If ohmmeter reads about 10-15 ohms, check for short circuit to ground in Violet wire. If ohmmeter does not read about 10-15 ohms, replace solenoid.

DTC 223/P0120: THROTTLE POSITION SENSOR SIGNAL TOO LOW

1) Throttle Position (TP) sensor signal is normally .5-4.2 volts. Opening throttle increases signal voltage. If TPS voltages are not to specification, check voltage drop over signal ground and power ground. See DTC 113: TCM FAULT. Repair as necessary. If voltage drop and power ground are okay, go to next step.

2) Ensure ignition is off. Disconnect TCM and ECM modules. Connect ohmmeter between TCM measuring unit terminal No. 20 and ECM measuring unit terminal No. 50 (non-turbo) or No. 20 (turbo). If ohmmeter reads about zero ohms, go to next step. If ohmmeter does not read about zero ohms, check Green/Brown wire between TCM and ECM for an open circuit.

3) Connect ohmmeter between TCM measuring unit terminals No. 50 and 20. If ohmmeter reads infinite resistance, go to next step. If ohmmeter does not read infinite resistance, check Green/Brown wire between TCM and ECM for a short circuit to ground.

4) Ensure ignition is off. Connect measuring unit to TCM. Connect ECM control modules. Turn ignition on. Measure voltage between measuring unit terminals No. 50 and 20. Press accelerator pedal. If voltmeter reads about .5 volt for closed throttle, and about 4.2 volts for wide open throttle, DTC was set due to poor terminal contact at ECM connector or ground. If voltmeter does not read about .5 volt for closed throttle, and about 4.2 volts for wide open throttle, check TP sensor. See appropriate SENSOR OPERATING RANGE CHARTS article in ENGINE PERFORMANCE in appropriate MITCHELL® manual.

DTC 231: ERRATIC THROTTLE POSITION SENSOR SIGNAL

1) Throttle Position (TP) sensor signal is normally .5-4.2 volts. Opening throttle increases signal voltage. If TPS voltages are not to specification, check voltage drop over signal ground and power ground. See DTC 113: TCM FAULT. Repair as necessary. If voltage drop and power ground are okay, go to next step.

2) Turn ignition off. Ensure TP sensor wiring and Brown/Green wire between TCM and ECM are not located near sources of interference, such as electric motors, spark plug wires, and mobile telephone wires. Repair as necessary.

DTC 232/P0500: SPEEDOMETER SIGNAL MISSING

1) Speedometer provides vehicle speed information to TCM. TCM uses signal to determine whether transmission changes gear at correct speeds. If DTC 232 is set, use scan tool and compare vehicle speed with speedometer. If reading is correct, go to step 3). If reading is incorrect, check for speedometer malfunction. See appropriate INSTRUMENT PANELS article in ACCESSORIES & EQUIPMENT in appropriate MITCHELL® manual. If speedometer is okay, check for an open circuit or short to voltage or ground in signal wiring. Repair as necessary. If wiring is okay, go to next step.

2) Ensure ignition is off. Connect measuring unit to TCM. Shift transmission to "N" position. Raise and support front of vehicle. Turn ignition on. Measure voltage between measuring unit terminals No. 20 and 48. Block one front wheel and spin other wheel rapidly. If voltmeter reads 4-7 volts, DTC was set because of poor terminal contact at TCM or speedometer connector. If voltmeter does not read 4-7 volts, replace speedometer.

3) Ensure ignition is off. Check that Vehicle Speed Sensor (VSS) is securely fastened to transmission. Ensure there is no dirt between sensor and mating surfaces. Repair as necessary. If VSS is okay, ensure all grounds are clean and tight. Repair as necessary.

DTC 233: SPEEDOMETER SIGNAL INCORRECT

If TCM registers an unusually large variation in speed signal from speedometer, DTC will set. Check for loose contact in wiring or splices, damaged insulation, or poor terminal contact. Repair as necessary.

DTC 235: HIGH OIL TEMPERATURE

1) Check for other DTCs. If DTC 141 is stored, perform testing for that DTC first. See DTC 141: SHORT CIRCUIT IN OIL TEMPERATURE SENSOR CIRCUIT. If DTC 141 is not stored, go to next step.

2) Remove air cleaner housing to access transaxle connector. Disconnect transaxle connector. Connect ohmmeter between transaxle connector terminal No. 12 (Blue/Green wire) and measuring unit terminal No. 28. If ohmmeter reads infinite resistance, go to next step. If ohmmeter does not read infinite resistance, check Blue/Green wire for a short circuit to ground.

3) Ensure ignition is off. Disconnect transaxle connector. Connect ohmmeter between transaxle connector terminals No. 12 (Blue/Green wire) and No. 13 (Blue/Black wire). See OIL TEMPERATURE SENSOR RESISTANCE table. If resistance is to specification, check Blue/Green wire for a short circuit to ground. If resistance is not to specification, replace oil temperature sensor.

DTC 245: OPEN OR SHORT IN TORQUE LIMITING CIRCUIT

1) Engine torque is reduced to allow smoother shifting in some gear changes. Torque limiting process is controlled by signals sent from TCM to ECM. A receipt confirmation signal is sent from ECM to TCM. Signal indicates that torque limiting is taking place. If TCM fails to register a receipt signal after request for torque limiting, DTC 245 is set.

2) Ensure ignition is off. Disconnect TCM. Connect measuring unit to TCM connector. Disconnect ECM. Connect ohmmeter between measuring unit terminal No. 20 and No. 32, 33, and 34. If ohmmeter reads infinite resistance, go to next step. If ohmmeter does not read infinite resistance, check wiring between TCM connector terminal B2 (Yellow/Red wire), B3 (Yellow/Violet wire), or B4 (Violet wire) and respective ECM connector terminal B2, B3, and B4.

3) Ensure ignition is off. Disconnect TCM. Connect measuring unit to ECM connector. Leave ECM disconnected. Connect ohmmeter between TCM measuring unit and ECM measuring unit. See TCM/ECM MEASURING UNIT RESISTANCE CHECK table. If ohmmeter reads about zero ohms, go to next step. If ohmmeter does not read about zero ohms, check for open circuit in Yellow/Red, Yellow/Violet, or Violet wire. Repair as necessary.

TCM/ECM MEASURING UNIT RESISTANCE CHECK

TCM Terminal No.	ECM Terminal No.
32	2
33	3
34	4

4) Ensure ignition is off. Reconnect TCM and ECM. Turn ignition on. Connect voltmeter between TCM measuring unit terminals No. 20 and 32. If voltmeter reads about 5 volts (non-turbo) or about 11 volts (turbo), go to next step. If voltmeter does not read about 5 volts (non-turbo) or about 11 volts (turbo), check for short to voltage in Yellow/Red wire.

5) Ensure ignition is on. Connect voltmeter between TCM measuring unit terminals No. 20 and 33. If voltmeter reads about 5 volts (non-turbo) or about 11 volts (turbo), go to next step. If voltmeter does not read about 5 volts (non-turbo) or about 11 volts (turbo), check for short to voltage in Yellow/Violet wire.

6) Ensure ignition is on. Connect voltmeter between TCM measuring unit terminals No. 20 and 34. If voltage is to specification, go to next step. If voltage is not to specification, check for short to voltage in Violet wire. See TCM VOLTAGE CIRCUIT CHECK table.

TCM VOLTAGE CIRCUIT CHECK

ECM Type	Voltage
Non-Turbo	5
Turbo	10

7) Ensure ignition is on. Connect voltmeter between TCM measuring unit terminals No. 20 and 32. Voltmeter should read about 5 volts (non-turbo) or about 10-11 volts (turbo). Check torque limiting (TC1) operation using scan tool or test mode No. 4. See TEST MODE NO. 4. If voltage drops rapidly to about zero volts when signal is activated, go to next step. If voltage does not drop, replace TCM.

8) Ensure ignition is on. Connect voltmeter between TCM measuring unit terminals No. 20 and 33. Voltmeter should read about 5 volts (non-turbo) or about 10-11 volts (turbo). Check torque limiting (TC2) operation using scan tool or test mode No. 4. See TEST MODE NO. 4. If voltage drops rapidly, go to next step. If voltage does not drop, replace TCM.

9) Ensure ignition is on. Connect voltmeter between TCM measuring unit terminals No. 20 and 34. See TCM VOLTAGE CIRCUIT CHECK table. Check TCM acknowledge signal and activate torque limiting (TC1/TC2) using scan tool or test mode No. 4. See TEST MODE NO. 4. If voltage drops, fault is intermittent. Check for poor terminal contact or open circuits in wiring. If voltage does not drop, replace ECM.

DTC 311/P0715: RPM SIGNAL MISSING

1) Ensure ignition is off. Connect measuring unit to TCM. Measure resistance between measuring unit terminals No. 1 and 2. If resistance is 300-600 ohms, sensor and wiring are okay. If resistance is not 300-600 ohms, go to next step.

2) Measure resistance between transmission 26-pin connector terminals No. 16 (Yellow/White wire) and No. 17 (Yellow/Brown wire). If resistance is 300-600 ohms, sensor is okay. Check wiring. If resistance is not 300-600 ohms, check wiring. If wiring is okay, replace sensor.

DTC 312: RPM SIGNAL INCORRECT

1) Check for additional DTCs. If DTC 311 is present, see DTC 311: RPM SIGNAL MISSING. If DTC 311 is not present, go to next step.

2) Ensure RPM sensor is correctly positioned. Check transmission and TCM connectors for poor terminal contact. Repair as necessary. Check Yellow/Brown and Yellow/White wires between RPM sensor and TCM. Repair as necessary. If all components are okay, ensure RPM sensor wiring is not located close to sources of interference, such as electric motors or spark plugs.

DTC 313/P0705: GEAR POSITION SENSOR SIGNAL INCORRECT

1) If DTC 313 is set, check gear shift position sensor adjustment. Ensure gear shift is set to position "N". Remove battery, battery shelf, and air intake manifold. Remove transmission cable from rod arm. Remove selector lever. Install gear position Alignment Tool (999 5475) on control shaft. If shaft is set correctly to position "N", indentation on alignment tool should align with mark on gear position sensor. If indentation aligns with mark on gear position sensor, go to step 3). If indentation does not align with mark, go to next step.

2) Remove dipstick pipe bracket and gear position sensor screws. Rotate gear position sensor so mark on switch aligns with indentation on tool. Tighten sensor screws to 37 ft. lbs. (25 N.m). To complete installation, reverse removal procedure.

3) Ensure ignition is off. Connect ohmmeter between gear shift position sensor case and transmission housing. If ohmmeter reads about zero ohms, go to next step. If ohmmeter does not read about zero ohms, check gear shift position sensor ground. Repair as necessary.

4) Ensure ignition is off. Check battery voltage at battery and note reading. Connect measuring unit to TCM. Turn ignition on. Check gear position sensor voltage specification by connecting voltmeter between measuring unit terminal No. 20 and gear position sensor terminal. See GEAR POSITION SENSOR VOLTAGE SPECIFICATIONS table. If voltages are to specification, DTC was set because of poor terminal contact in TCM connector. Repair as necessary. If voltmeter reads a steady zero volts for some or all terminals, regardless of selector position, go to step **7)**. If voltmeter reads a steady 12 volts for some or all terminals, regardless of selector position, check for short circuit to voltage in wiring for terminal with incorrect reading between gear position sensor and TCM, then go to step **8)**.

5) Ensure ignition is off. Check transaxle connector for poor terminal contact. Repair as necessary. Turn ignition on. Connect voltmeter between measuring unit terminal No. 20 and gear position sensor terminal. See GEAR POSITION SENSOR VOLTAGE SPECIFICATIONS table. If voltage readings are okay, DTC was set because of poor terminal contact. If voltage readings are not okay, go to next step.

6) Ensure ignition is off. Disconnect transaxle connector. Connect ohmmeter between transaxle connector terminal and measuring unit terminal. See TRANSAXLE CONNECTOR/MEASURING UNIT TERMINAL RESISTANCE table. If ohmmeter reads about zero ohms for all readings, replace gear position sensor. If ohmmeter does not read about zero ohms for all readings, check for open circuit in wiring between transaxle connector and TCM. Repair as necessary.

TRANSAXLE CONNECTOR/MEASURING UNIT TERMINAL RESISTANCE

Transaxle Connector Terminal	Measuring Unit Terminal
1 (White wire)	3
2 (Yellow wire)	4
3 (Green wire)	5
4 (Blue wire)	6

7) Ensure ignition is off. Disconnect transmission and TCM connectors. Connect ohmmeter between measuring unit terminal No. 20 and gear position sensor connector terminals No. 3 (Green wire), No. 4 (Blue wire), No. 5 (Blue wire), and No. 6 (Green/Red wire). If ohmmeter reads infinite resistance, replace gear position sensor. If ohmmeter does not read infinite resistance, check for short circuit to ground in wire between transaxle connector and TCM.

GEAR POSITION SENSOR VOLTAGE SPECIFICATIONS [1]

Gearshift Position & Measuring Unit Terminal	Specification
"P"	
A3	0-0.5 Volt
A4	Approx. 1 Volt Below Battery Voltage
A5	Approx. 1 Volt Below Battery Voltage
A6	0-0.5 Volt
"R"	
A3	0-0.5 Volt
A4	0-0.5 Volt
A5	Approx. 1 Volt Below Battery Voltage
A6	Approx. 1 Volt Below Battery Voltage
"N"	
A3	Approx. 1 Volt Below Battery Voltage
A4	0-0.5 Volt
A5	Approx. 1 Volt Below Battery Voltage
A6	0-0.5 Volt
"D"	
A3	Approx. 1 Volt Below Battery Voltage
A4	0-0.5 Volt
A5	0-0.5 Volt
A6	Approx. 1 Volt Below Battery Voltage
3	
A3	0-0.5 Volt
A4	0-0.5 Volt
A5	0-0.5 Volt
A6	0-0.5 Volt
"L"	
A3	0-0.5 Volt
A4	Approx. 1 Volt Below Battery Voltage
A5	0-0.5 Volt
A6	Approx. 1 Volt Below Battery Voltage

[1] – Measured between measuring unit terminal A20 and terminal in table.

8) Ensure ignition is off. Connect TCM and transaxle connectors. Turn ignition on. Connect voltmeter between measuring unit terminal No. 20 and gear position sensor terminal. See GEAR POSITION SENSOR VOLTAGE SPECIFICATIONS table. If voltage readings are okay, gear position sensor is okay. If voltage readings are not okay, replace gear position sensor.

DTC 322/P0730: GEAR RATIO INFORMATION INCORRECT

1) Check transmission oil level. If oil level is low, top off as necessary and check for leaks. Repair as necessary. If oil level is okay, turn ignition on and check DTCs. Test drive vehicle while observing automatic transmission warning light. If light begins to flash note any unusual symptoms in transmission operation or function. If transmission does not show any mechanical fault or malfunction, go to next step. If transmission has a mechanical malfunction and DTC 322 is not reset, repair or replace transmission as necessary.

2) Turn ignition off. Connect measuring unit to TCM. Raise and support front of vehicle. Turn A/C off. Idle engine. Set gear selector to position "D" so front wheels begin to rotate. Increase and keep engine speed at 2000 RPM. Set DVOM to Hz scale, then connect DVOM between measuring unit terminals No. 1 and 2. If DVOM gives a stable Hz reading when engine speed is constant and transmission is not shifting, go to step **5)**. If Hz frequency reading shows wide fluctuations, go to next step.

3) Ensure ignition is off. Disconnect TCM. Connect ohmmeter between measuring unit terminals No. 1 and 2. If ohmmeter does not read 300-600 ohms, go to next step. If ohmmeter reads 300-600 ohms, ensure RPM sensor wiring is not located near sources of interference such as electric motors or spark plugs.

4) Disconnect transaxle connector. Check TCM connector for poor terminal contact. Repair as necessary. Reconnect transaxle connector. Connect ohmmeter between measuring unit terminals No. 1 and 2. If ohmmeter reads about 300-600 ohms, DTC was set because of poor contact in transaxle connector. If ohmmeter does not read about 300-600 ohms, replace RPM sensor.

5) Connect DVOM between measuring unit terminals No. 20 and 48. Shift transmission to "D" so front wheels begin to rotate. Increase engine speed to 1800-2000 RPM. If DVOM displays a stable Hz reading when engine speed is constant, go to step **8)**. If DVOM does not display a stable Hz reading when engine speed is constant, go to next step.

6) Replace VSS. Connect DVOM between measuring unit terminals No. 20 and 48. Shift transmission to "D" so front wheels begin to rotate. Increase engine speed to 1800-2000 RPM. If DVOM displays a stable Hz reading when engine speed is constant, system is okay. If DVOM does not display a stable Hz reading when engine speed is constant, go to next step.

7) Ensure ignition is off. Ensure wiring between VSS and instrument cluster is not located near sources of interference such as electric motors or spark plugs. If wiring is okay, replace instrument cluster. See appropriate INSTRUMENT PANELS article in ACCESSORIES & EQUIPMENT in appropriate MITCHELL® manual.

8) Ensure ignition is off. Disconnect TCM. Connect ohmmeter between measuring unit terminals No. 20 and 27 (solenoid S1), then between measuring unit terminals No. 20 and 28 (solenoid S2). If ohmmeter reads 10-15 ohms, go to next step. If ohmmeter does not read 10-15 ohms, check transaxle connector for poor terminal contact. Repair as necessary.

9) Ensure ignition is off. Reconnect TCM. Turn ignition on. Set gearshift selector to "D" position. Connect voltmeter between measuring unit terminals No. 5 and 20. If voltmeter reads 0-.5 volt, twist gear position sensor lever/shaft up, down, and to side. If voltage reading remains constant, system is okay. If voltage reading does not remain constant, go to next step.

10) Turn ignition off. Check gear position sensor adjustment. Repair as necessary. See DTC 313: GEAR POSITION SENSOR SIGNAL INCORRECT. If adjustment is okay, replace gear position sensor.

DTC 323: LOCK-UP SLIPS OR IS NOT ENGAGED

1) Turn ignition on. Clear DTCs. Test drive vehicle. If transmission does not show any malfunction, go to next step. If transmission has a mechanical malfunction and DTC 323 is not reset, diagnose mechanical malfunction. If transmission has a mechanical malfunction and DTC 323 is reset, replace transmission.

2) Ensure ignition is on. Connect measuring unit to TCM connector. Connect ohmmeter between measuring unit terminals No. 9 and 20. If ohmmeter reads 10-15 ohms, transmission is probably okay. However, if problem persists, replace transmission. If ohmmeter does not read 10-15 ohms, check TCM connector for poor terminal contact. Repair as necessary.

DTC 331: SHORT TO VOLTAGE IN LOCK-UP SOLENOID CIRCUIT

Turn ignition on. Set gearshift lever to "P" position. Check solenoid function by using test mode No. 4 or Volvo scan tool. See TEST MODE NO. 4. If solenoid operates, check wiring for an intermittent short circuit. If solenoid does not operate, check for a short circuit to voltage in wiring between lock-up solenoid and TCM connector terminal A9. Repair as necessary.

DTC 332: OPEN IN LOCK-UP SOLENOID CIRCUIT

1) Turn ignition on. Set gearshift lever to "P" position. Check solenoid function by using test mode No. 4 or Volvo scan tool. See TEST MODE NO. 4. If solenoid operates, check wiring for an intermittent short circuit. If solenoid does not operate, go to next step.

2) Ensure ignition is off. Connect measuring unit to TCM connector. Connect ohmmeter between measuring unit terminals No. 9 and 20. If ohmmeter reads 10-15 ohms, DTC was caused by poor terminal contact in TCM connector. Repair as necessary. If ohmmeter does not read 10-15 ohms, go to next step.

3) Ensure ignition is off. Remove air cleaner housing to access transaxle connector. Connect ohmmeter between transaxle connector terminal No. 23 and measuring unit terminal No. 9. If ohmmeter reads about zero ohms, go to next step. If ohmmeter does not read about zero ohms, check for an open circuit in Brown/Black wire between transaxle connector terminal No. 23 and TCM terminal A9.

4) Ensure ignition is off and transaxle connector is disconnected. Connect ohmmeter between transaxle connector terminal No. 23 and transmission housing. If ohmmeter does not read 10-15 ohms, go to next step. If ohmmeter reads 10-15 ohms, DTC set because of poor terminal contact at transaxle connector. Repair as necessary.

5) Ensure ignition if off. Open control system and disconnect lock-up solenoid. Connect ohmmeter between lock-up solenoid terminal and transmission housing. If ohmmeter reads 10-15 ohms, check for an open circuit in Brown/Black wire between lock-up solenoid and transaxle connector terminal No. 23. If ohmmeter does not read 10-15 ohms, replace lock-up solenoid.

DTC 333: SHORT TO GROUND IN LOCK-UP SOLENOID CIRCUIT

1) Turn ignition on. Set gearshift lever to "P" position. Check solenoid function by using test mode No. 4 or Volvo scan tool. See TEST MODE NO. 4. If solenoid operates, check wiring for an intermittent short circuit. If solenoid does not operate, go to next step.

2) Ensure ignition is off. Remove air cleaner housing to access transaxle connector. Disconnect transaxle connector. Connect ohmmeter between transaxle connector terminal No. 23 (Brown/Black wire) and transmission housing. If ohmmeter does not read 10-15 ohms, go to next step. If ohmmeter reads 10-15 ohms, check for a short circuit to ground in Brown/Black wire between transaxle connector terminal No. 23 and TCM connector terminal A9.

3) Ensure ignition is off. Open control system and disconnect lock-up solenoid. Connect ohmmeter between lock-up solenoid terminal and transmission housing. If ohmmeter reads 10-15 ohms, check for an open circuit in Brown/Black wire between lock-up solenoid and transaxle connector terminal No. 23. If ohmmeter does not read 10-15 ohms, replace lock-up solenoid.

DIAGNOSTIC TESTING (1996)

DTC 114: MODE SELECTOR SWITCH CIRCUIT MALFUNCTION

1) Turn ignition on. Set mode selector to "E". Wait about 30 seconds. Set mode selector to "S". Wait about 30 seconds. Using scan tool, read status of DTC. If status is PERMANENT FAULT, go to next step. If status is not PERMANENT FAULT, check all wiring and connectors for an intermittent open circuit or poor terminal contact. Repair as necessary.

2) Ensure ignition is off. Using a screwdriver, carefully pry off selector switch from console. Check wires at back of switch for poor terminal contact. Repair as necessary. If connection is okay, ensure Black wire is grounded. Repair as necessary. If Black wire ground is okay, go to next step.

3) Disconnect driving mode selector. Turn ignition on. Connect test light between Brown/Green and Black wires, then between Green/Orange and Black wires. If test light does not come on, go to next step. If test light comes on, check for short circuit to voltage in Brown/Green wire.

4) Connect voltmeter between selector switch Brown/Green and Black wires, then between selector switch Green/Orange and Black wires. If about 10-12 volts are present, go to next step. If about 10-12 volts are not present, check TCM connector for poor terminal contact. Repair as necessary, then again check voltage at switch. If voltages are to specification, DTC was set because of poor terminal contact at switch selector. If voltages are not to specification, check for open circuit in Brown/Green and Green/Orange wires. Repair as necessary.

5) Turn ignition on. Switch selector to "S" position. Connect ohmmeter between Brown/Green and Black wires. Switch selector to "E" position. Connect ohmmeter between Green/Orange and Black wires. If ohmmeter does not read zero ohms in both cases, replace driving mode selector module. If ohmmeter does read zero ohms, DTC was set because of poor terminal contact in mode selector connector.

DTC 121/P0750: SHORT TO GROUND IN NO. 1 SHIFT SOLENOID CIRCUIT

1) Turn ignition on. Set gearshift lever to "P" position. Activate shift solenoid No. 1. Read solenoid status. If status alternates between OFF/ON, check wiring and connectors for an intermittent open circuit. Repair as necessary. If status does not alternate between OFF/ON, go to next step.

2) Turn ignition off. Remove air cleaner housing to access transaxle connector. Disconnect transaxle connector. Connect ohmmeter between transaxle connector terminal No. 21 (Green/White wire) and ground. If ohmmeter does not read 12-18 ohms, go to next step. If ohmmeter reads 12-18 ohms, check for short circuit to ground in Green/White wire.

3) Access and disconnect shift solenoid No. 1. Connect ohmmeter between pin on solenoid and ground. If ohmmeter reads about 12-18 ohms, check for short circuit to ground in Green/White wire. If ohmmeter does not read about 12-18 ohms, replace solenoid.

DTC 122/P0750: OPEN IN NO. 1 SHIFT SOLENOID CIRCUIT

1) Turn ignition on. Set gearshift lever to "P" position. Activate shift solenoid No. 1. Read solenoid status. If status alternates between OFF/ON, check wiring and connectors for an intermittent open circuit. Repair as necessary. If status does not alternate between OFF/ON, go to next step.

2) Turn ignition off. Connect measuring unit to TCM connector. Using ohmmeter, check ground circuits. See WIRING DIAGRAM. If ohmmeter reads about zero ohms, go to next step. If ohmmeter does not read about zero ohms, repair ground circuit as necessary.

3) Connect ohmmeter between measuring unit terminals No. 27 and 29. If ohmmeter reads about 10-15 ohms, go to step 7). If ohmmeter does not read about 10-15 ohms, go to next step.

4) Remove air cleaner housing to access transaxle connector. Disconnect transaxle connector. Connect ohmmeter between transaxle connector terminal No. 21 (Green/White wire) and measuring unit terminal No. 27. If ohmmeter reads about zero ohms, go to next step. If ohmmeter does not read about zero ohms, check for open circuit in Green/White wire.

5) Disconnect transaxle connector. Connect ohmmeter between transaxle connector terminal No. 21 (Green/White wire) and ground. If ohmmeter reads 12-18 ohms, repair poor terminal contact at TCM connector. If ohmmeter does not read 12-18 ohms, go to next step.

6) Access and disconnect shift solenoid No. 1. Connect ohmmeter between pin on solenoid and ground. If ohmmeter reads about 12-18 ohms, check for open circuit in Green/White wire. If ohmmeter does not read about 10-15 ohms, replace solenoid.

7) Connect voltmeter between measuring unit terminals No. 27 and 29. If voltmeter reads about zero volts, go to next step. If voltmeter does not read about zero volts, check for an open circuit in Green/White wire.

8) Turn on as many power consuming items as possible. Connect voltmeter between measuring unit terminals No. 20 and 29. If voltmeter reads less than .6 volt, go to next step. If voltmeter reads greater than .6 volt, check all TCM grounds for good terminal contact. Repair as necessary.

9) Disconnect measuring unit. Reconnect TCM. Erase DTC. Start engine. Wait about 15 seconds. If DTC resets, replace TCM. If DTC does not reset, check all connectors for poor terminal contact. Repair as necessary.

DTC 123/P0745: SHORT TO VOLTAGE IN LINE PRESSURE SOLENOID (STH) CIRCUIT

1) Turn ignition on. Using scan tool, select SCROLLING VALUES. Read current in solenoid circuit. Depress accelerator pedal slowly. If current decreases as accelerator pedal is depressed, go to step 5). If current does not decrease as accelerator pedal is depressed, go to next step.

2) Turn ignition off. Connect measuring unit to TCM connector. Connect ohmmeter between measuring unit terminals No. 22 and 23. If ohmmeter reads 2-6 ohms, repair short to voltage in control signal wiring. If control signal wiring is okay, replace TCM. If ohmmeter does not read 2-6 ohms, go to next step.

3) Remove air cleaner housing to access transaxle connector. Disconnect transaxle connector. Connect ohmmeter between transaxle connector terminals No. 24 (Violet wire) and No. 25 (Violet/White wire). If ohmmeter reads about 2-6 ohms, check for short circuit in wiring. If ohmmeter does not read about 2-6 ohms, go to next step.

4) Access and disconnect solenoid STH. Connect ohmmeter between pins on solenoid connector. If ohmmeter reads about 2-6 ohms, check wiring between solenoid STH and transaxle connector terminals No. 24 and 25 for a short circuit. If ohmmeter does not read about 2-6 ohms, replace TCM.

5) Check for an intermittent short to voltage in Violet and Violet/White wires. If wiring is okay, check system pressure. See HYDRAULIC PRESSURE TEST. If system pressure is okay, replace TCM.

DTC 124: SHORT TO GROUND IN MODE SELECTOR SWITCH CIRCUIT

1) Turn ignition on. Set mode selector to "E". Wait about 30 seconds. Set mode selector to "S". Wait about 30 seconds. If scan tool displays PERMANENT FAULT, go to next step. If scan tool does not display PERMANENT FAULT, to step 5).

2) Turn ignition off. Carefully pry driving mode selector from center console. Ensure controls for selector operate smoothly and do not stick. Ensure "W" button does not stick in depressed position and operates smoothly without catching. Shake driving mode selector to see if there are loose parts in the switch. Replace as necessary. If driving mode selector is okay, go to next step.

3) Disconnect driving mode selector connector. Put switch in mode "E". Connect ohmmeter between selector terminal Brown/Green and Black wires. Put switch in mode "S". Connect ohmmeter between Green/Orange and Black wires. Ensure "W" button is up. Connect ohmmeter between Green/Orange and Brown/Green wires. If ohmmeter reads infinite resistance for all tests, go to next step. If ohmmeter does not read infinite resistance for all tests, replace driving mode selector module.

4) Ensure ignition is off. Connect driving mode selector. Turn ignition on. Read mode selector sensor signal MS1. Set mode selector to "E". If mode selector sensor signal MS1 displays HIGH, check for open circuit in Green/Orange wire. If signal does not display HIGH, check for short circuit to ground in Brown/Green wire.

5) Ensure "W" button does not stick down in depressed position and operates smoothly without catching. Check for an intermittent short circuit to ground in Green/Orange or Brown/Green wires.

DTC 131: OPEN OR SHORT TO GROUND IN LINE PRESSURE SOLENOID (STH) CIRCUIT

1) Check for other DTCs. If DTC 123 is present, perform diagnosis for that DTC first. See DTC 123: SHORT TO VOLTAGE IN LINE PRESSURE SOLENOID (STH) CIRCUIT. If DTC 123 is not stored, turn ignition on. Using scan tool, select SCROLLING VALUES, Read current in solenoid circuit. Depress accelerator pedal slowly. If current decreases as accelerator pedal is depressed, fault is intermittent. Check wiring for an intermittent open or short circuit. If current does not decrease as accelerator pedal is depressed, connect measuring unit to TCM connector and check ground circuits. See WIRING DIAGRAM. Repair as necessary. If ground circuits are okay, go to next step.

2) Reconnect TCM. Turn on as many power consuming items as possible. Connect voltmeter between measuring unit terminals No. 20 and 29. If voltmeter reads less than .6 volt, go to next step. If voltmeter does not read less than .6 volt, check grounding points for an open circuit. Repair as necessary.

3) Ensure ignition is off. Disconnect TCM. Connect ohmmeter between measuring unit terminals No. 22 and 23. If ohmmeter reads 2-6 ohms, go to step 7). If ohmmeter does not read 2-6 ohms, remove air cleaner housing to access transaxle connector. Disconnect transaxle connector. Connect ohmmeter between transaxle connector terminals No. 24 and 25. If ohmmeter reads 2-6 ohms, go to step 5). If ohmmeter does not read 2-6 ohms, go to next step.

4) Ensure ignition is off. Open control system and disconnect solenoid STH. Connect ohmmeter between terminals on solenoid connector. If ohmmeter does not read 2-6 ohms, replace TCM. If ohmmeter reads 2-6 ohms, check for an open circuit in Violet and Violet/White wires. Repair as necessary.

5) Ensure ignition is off. Disconnect transaxle connector. Connect ohmmeter between transaxle connector terminal No. 24 (Violet/White wire) and measuring unit connector terminal No. 22. If ohmmeter reads about zero ohms, go to next step. If ohmmeter does not read about zero ohms, check for open circuit in Violet wire. Repair as necessary.

6) Connect ohmmeter between transaxle connector terminal No. 25 (Violet/White wire) and measuring unit terminal No. 23. If ohmmeter does not read about zero ohms, check for open circuit in Violet/White wire between transaxle connector terminal No. 25 and TCM connector terminal A23. Repair as necessary. If ohmmeter reads about zero ohms, DTC was caused by poor terminal contact at TCM connector.

7) Ensure ignition is off and TCM is disconnected. Connect ohmmeter between measuring unit terminal No. 22 and ground. If ohmmeter

reads infinite resistance, go to step 10). If ohmmeter does not read infinite resistance, remove air cleaner housing to access transaxle connector. Disconnect transaxle connector. Connect ohmmeter between transaxle connector terminal No. 24 (Violet wire) and ground. If ohmmeter reads infinite resistance, go to step 9). If ohmmeter does not read infinite resistance, go to next step.

8) Open control system and disconnect solenoid STH. Connect ohmmeter between ground and solenoid connector terminal. If ohmmeter does not read infinite resistance, replace TCM. If ohmmeter does read infinite resistance, check for short to ground in Violet or Violet/White wires.

9) Connect ohmmeter between measuring unit terminal No. 23 and ground. If ohmmeter reads infinite resistance, check for short circuit to ground in Violet/White wire. If ohmmeter does not read infinite resistance, check for short circuit to ground in Violet wire. Repair as necessary. Go to step 11).

10) Connect TCM to measuring unit. Turn ignition on. Connect voltmeter between measuring unit terminals No. 22 and 29. If voltmeter reads 0-6 volts, go to next step. If voltmeter does not read 0-6 volts, check for short circuit to voltage in Violet wire.

11) Ensure ignition is off. Reconnect all connectors. Reinstall all components. Turn ignition on. Using scan tool, select SCROLLING VALUES. Read current in solenoid circuit. Depress accelerator pedal slowly. If current decreases as accelerator pedal is depressed, DTC was caused by poor terminal contact in TCM or transaxle connector. If current does not decrease as accelerator pedal is depressed, replace TCM.

DTC 132/P0745: TCM FAULT

1) Turn ignition on. Using scan tool, select SCROLLING VALUES. Read current in solenoid circuit. Depress accelerator pedal slowly. If current decreases as accelerator pedal is depressed, go to next step. If current does not decrease as accelerator pedal is depressed, replace TCM.

2) Erase DTC. Turn ignition on. Using scan tool, select SCROLLING VALUES. Read current in solenoid circuit. Depress accelerator pedal slowly. If current decreases as accelerator pedal is depressed, system is okay. If current does not decrease as accelerator pedal is depressed, repeat test.

DTC 134: INCORRECT LOAD SIGNAL

1) Load signal from ECM provides information to TCM on torque being delivered by engine. If TCM does not register an incoming load signal when RPM sensor on transmission gives a signal that input shaft RPM is greater than about 600 RPM, DTC 134 will set.

2) If DTC 134 is set, check for poor terminal contact in connectors between TCM and ECM. Also check for an open, short circuit to voltage, or short circuit to ground in signal wiring between ECM and TCM. If all circuits are okay, connect scan tool to DLC. Ensure engine is warm, transmission is in Neutral, and A/C is off. Select SCROLLING VALUES. Load signal should be about 35. If load signal is okay, replace TCM. If load signal is not okay, replace ECM.

DTC 141: SHORT CIRCUIT IN OIL TEMPERATURE SENSOR CIRCUIT

1) Check for short circuit to ground in oil temperature sensor signal wiring. Repair as necessary. If wiring is okay, go to next step.

2) Ensure ignition is off. Remove air cleaner housing to access transaxle connector. Disconnect transaxle connector. Connect ohmmeter between ground and transaxle connector terminal No. 12 (Blue/Green wire) and No. 13 (Blue/Black wire). See OIL TEMPERATURE SENSOR RESISTANCE table. If resistance is to specification, check Blue/Green wire for a short circuit to ground. If resistance is not to specification, replace oil temperature sensor.

OIL TEMPERATURE SENSOR RESISTANCE

°F (°C)	Ohms
0 (0)	1700-2300
68 (20)	765-1035
104 (40)	340-460
176 (80)	107-143
212 (100)	64-86
302 (150)	23-31

DTC 142: OPEN IN OIL TEMPERATURE SENSOR CIRCUIT

1) Check for open or short circuit to ground or voltage in oil temperature sensor signal wiring. Repair as necessary. If wiring is okay, go to next step.

2) Ensure ignition is off. Remove air cleaner housing to access transaxle connector. Disconnect transaxle connector. Connect ohmmeter between transaxle connector terminal No. 13 (Blue/Black wire) and ground. If ohmmeter reads about zero ohms, go to step 4). If ohmmeter does not read about zero ohms, go to next step.

3) Check TCM connector for poor terminal contact. Repair as necessary. Connect ohmmeter between transaxle connector terminal No. 13 and ground. If ohmmeter reads about zero ohms, DTC was set because of poor terminal contact. If ohmmeter does not read about zero ohms, check Blue/Black wire for an open circuit.

4) Turn ignition on. Connect voltmeter between transaxle connector terminal No. 12 (Blue/Green wire) and ground. If voltmeter reads about 5 volts, check oil temperature sensor resistance. See DTC 141: SHORT CIRCUIT IN OIL TEMPERATURE SENSOR CIRCUIT. If voltmeter reads less than 5 volts, go to next step. If voltmeter reads greater than 5 volts, check Blue/Green wire for a short circuit to voltage. If wire is okay, check oil temperature sensor resistance. See DTC 141: SHORT CIRCUIT IN OIL TEMPERATURE SENSOR CIRCUIT.

5) Turn ignition off. Check TCM connector for poor terminal contact. Repair as necessary. Connect voltmeter between transaxle connector terminal No. 12 (Blue/Green wire) and ground. If voltmeter reads about 5 volts, DTC set because of poor contact in TCM connector. If voltmeter does not read about 5 volts, check Blue/Green wire for an open circuit.

DTC 143: SHORT TO GROUND IN KICKDOWN SWITCH CIRCUIT

1) Connect scan tool. Turn ignition on. Ensure brake pedal is up. Wait about 10 seconds. Push down accelerator pedal completely and keep it fully depressed in kickdown mode. Wait about 10 seconds. Read out DTC. If status indicates PERMANENT FAULT, go to next step. If status does not indicate PERMANENT FAULT, problem is intermittent. Check connectors and wiring for poor terminal contact.

2) Turn ignition on. Using scan tool, select SCROLLING VALUES. Read kickdown switch position. Reading should be ON if accelerator pedal is depressed to kickdown position. In any other accelerator pedal position reading should be OFF. If correct reading is displayed, go to step 5) If correct reading is not displayed, go to next step.

3) When accelerator pedal is fully depressed a circuit is made when sheath on throttle cable is pressed in to kickdown switch. Releasing accelerator pedal allows cable sheath to spring back and switch breaks circuit. If sheath operates to specification, go to next step. If sheath does not operate to specification, repair as necessary.

4) Ensure ignition is off. Disconnect kickdown switch connector. Connect ohmmeter between kickdown switch terminals No. 1 and 2. Fully depress accelerator pedal. If ohmmeter reads about zero ohms with accelerator pedal fully depressed and infinite resistance in all other positions, check for short circuit to ground in wiring between kickdown switch terminal No. 2 (Blue/Black wire) and control module terminal B30. If ohmmeter does not read about zero ohms with accelerator pedal fully depressed and infinite resistance in all other positions, replace kickdown switch.

5) Ensure ignition is off. Connect measuring unit to ECM connector. Ensure ECM is connected. Turn ignition on. Turn on as many power consuming items as possible. Connect voltmeter between ground and measuring unit terminal No. 42. Note voltage reading, then turn ignition off. Disconnect measuring unit from ECM. Connect measuring unit to TCM connector and check grounds. See WIRING DIAGRAM. Go to next step.

6) Ensure ignition is off. Reconnect control modules. Turn ignition on. Turn on as many power consuming items as possible. Connect voltmeter between ground and measuring unit terminal No. 20. Note voltage reading. Add both voltage readings together. Total of both readings should not be greater than .1 volt. If final voltage reading is okay, go to next step. If final reading is not okay, check TCM (Brown ground wire) located in front left corner of engine compartment and TCM connector terminals for poor terminal contact. Repair as necessary.

7) Perform wide open throttle relearn setting by blocking all wheels. Start engine. Apply parking brake and press down hard on brake pedal. Shift gear selector to "D". Fully depress accelerator pedal so kickdown switch closes. Keep accelerator fully depressed for 5 seconds. Release accelerator pedal and move gear selector to "P". Wide open throttle setting should be relearned.

DTC 213/P0120: THROTTLE POSITION SENSOR SIGNAL TOO HIGH

1) Check for engine performance DTCs. If engine performance DTCs are present, see appropriate SELF-DIAGNOSTICS article in ENGINE PERFORMANCE in appropriate MITCHELL® manual. Check throttle position sensor signal. See appropriate SENSOR OPERATING RANGE CHARTS and SELF-DIAGNOSTICS article in ENGINE PERFORMANCE in appropriate MITCHELL® manual. Check for a short circuit to voltage in signal wiring between TCM and ECM. See WIRING DIAGRAM. Repair as necessary. If all components and wiring are okay, go to next step.

2) Ensure ignition is off. Connect measuring unit to ECM connector. Ensure ECM is connected. Turn ignition on. Turn on as many power consuming items as possible. Connect voltmeter between ground and measuring unit terminal No. 42. Note voltage reading, then turn ignition off. Disconnect measuring unit from ECM. Connect measuring unit to TCM connector and check grounds. See WIRING DIAGRAM. Go to next step.

3) Ensure ignition is off. Reconnect control modules. Turn ignition on. Turn on as many power consuming items as possible. Connect voltmeter between ground and measuring unit terminal No. 20. Note voltage reading. Add both voltage readings together. Total of both readings should not be greater than .1 volt. If final voltage reading is okay, go to next step. If final reading is not okay, check TCM Brown ground wire located in front left corner of engine compartment and TCM connector terminals for poor terminal contact. Repair as necessary.

4) Ensure ignition is on. Turn on as many power consuming items as possible. Connect voltmeter between measuring unit terminals No. 20 and 29. If voltmeter reads less than .6 volt, check throttle position sensor signal. See appropriate SENSOR OPERATING RANGE CHARTS and SELF-DIAGNOSTICS article in ENGINE PERFORMANCE in appropriate MITCHELL® manual. If voltmeter reads greater than .6 volt, check TCM Brown ground wire located in front left corner of engine compartment and TCM connector terminals for poor terminal contact. Repair as necessary.

DTC 221/P0755: SHORT TO GROUND IN NO. 2 SHIFT SOLENOID CIRCUIT

1) Turn ignition on. Set gearshift lever to "P" position. Activate solenoid. Read solenoid status. If status alternates between OFF/ON, problem is intermittent. Check connectors for poor terminal contact. If status does not alternate between OFF/ON, go to next step.

2) Turn ignition off. Remove air cleaner housing to access transaxle connector. Disconnect transaxle connector. Connect ohmmeter between transaxle connector terminal No. 22 (Violet wire) and ground. If ohmmeter does not read 12-18 ohms, go to next step. If ohmmeter reads 12-18 ohms, check for short circuit to ground in Violet wire.

3) Access and disconnect shift solenoid No. 2. Connect ohmmeter between pin on solenoid and ground. If ohmmeter reads about 12-18 ohms, check for short circuit to ground in Violet wire. If ohmmeter does not read about 12-18 ohms, replace solenoid.

DTC 222/P0755: OPEN IN NO. 2 SHIFT SOLENOID CIRCUIT

1) Turn ignition on. Set gearshift lever to "P" position. Activate solenoid. Read solenoid status. If status alternates between OFF/ON, problem is intermittent. Check connectors for poor terminal contact. If status does not alternate between OFF/ON, go to next step.

2) Turn ignition off. Connect measuring unit to TCM. Check grounds. See WIRING DIAGRAM. Repair as necessary. If grounds are okay, connect ohmmeter between measuring unit terminals No. 28 and 29. If ohmmeter reads about 12-18 ohms, go to step **6)**. If ohmmeter does not read about 12-18 ohms, go to next step.

3) Remove air cleaner housing to access transaxle connector. Disconnect transaxle connector. Connect ohmmeter between transaxle connector terminal No. 22 (Violet wire) and terminal No. 28 on measuring unit. If ohmmeter reads about zero ohms, go to next step. If ohmmeter does not read about zero ohms, check for open circuit in Violet wire.

4) Disconnect transaxle connector. Connect ohmmeter between transaxle connector terminal No. 22 (Violet wire) and ground. If ohmmeter reads 12-18 ohms, repair poor terminal contact at TCM connector. If ohmmeter does not read 10-15 ohms, go to next step.

5) Access and disconnect shift solenoid No. 2. Connect ohmmeter between pin on solenoid and ground. If ohmmeter reads about 12-18 ohms, check for short circuit to ground in Violet wire. If ohmmeter does not read about 10-15 ohms, replace solenoid.

6) Ensure ignition is off. Disconnect TCM. Turn ignition on. Connect voltmeter between measuring unit terminals No. 28 and 29. If voltmeter reads about zero volts, go to next step. If voltmeter does not read about zero volts, check for short to voltage in Brown/White wire.

7) Ensure ignition is off. Reconnect TCM. Turn ignition on. Turn on as many power consuming items as possible. Connect voltmeter between measuring unit terminals No. 20 and 29. If voltmeter reads less than .6 volt, go to next step. If voltmeter does not read less than .6 volt, check TCM Brown and Black ground wires located in front of engine compartment above starter, and TCM connector terminals for poor terminal contact. Repair as necessary.

8) Ensure ignition is off. Disconnect measuring unit. Reconnect TCM. Turn ignition on. Erase DTCs. Move gear shift lever to "P" position. Start engine. Wait about 15 seconds and check whether DTC reoccurs. If DTC reoccurs, replace TCM. If DTC does not reoccur, check TCM connector for poor terminal contact.

DTC 223/P0120: THROTTLE POSITION SENSOR SIGNAL TOO LOW

1) Check for engine performance DTCs. If engine performance DTCs are present, see appropriate SELF-DIAGNOSTICS article in ENGINE PERFORMANCE in appropriate MITCHELL® manual. If engine performance DTCs are not present, check status message on scan tool. If status message indicates PERMANENT FAULT, go to next step. If status message does not indicate PERMANENT FAULT, problem is intermittent. Check for an intermittent open circuit or poor terminal contact. Repair as necessary.

2) Ensure ignition is on. Using scan tool, select SCROLLING VALUES. Read throttle position sensor signal. Press accelerator pedal to floor. If throttle position signal increases, go to step **6)**. If throttle position signal does not increase, go to next step.

3) Ensure ignition is off. Disconnect TCM and ECM. Connect measuring unit to ECM connector. Connect ohmmeter between ground and measuring unit terminal No. 20. If ohmmeter reads about zero ohms, go to next step. If ohmmeter does not read about zero ohms, check for short circuit to ground in Green/Brown wire.

4) Ensure ignition is off. Reconnect ECM. Turn ignition on. Connect voltmeter between ground and measuring unit terminal No. 20. If voltmeter reads about .5 volt at closed throttle, go to next step. If voltmeter does not read about .5 volt at closed throttle, check throttle position sensor circuit. See appropriate SELF-DIAGNOSTICS article in ENGINE PERFORMANCE in appropriate MITCHELL® manual.

5) Ensure ignition is off. Connect measuring unit to TCM connector. Check ground points. See WIRING DIAGRAM. Reconnect ECM. Turn ignition on. Connect voltmeter between measuring unit terminals No. 20 and 50. If voltmeter reads about .5 volt at closed throttle, check control module connectors for poor terminal contact. If voltmeter does not read about .5 volt at closed throttle, check for open circuit in Green/Brown wire at TCM connector terminal No. B20.

6) Ensure ignition is off. Connect measuring unit to ECM connector. Ensure ECM is connected. Turn ignition on. Turn on as many power consuming items as possible. Connect voltmeter between ground and measuring unit terminal No. 42. Note voltage reading, then turn ignition off. Disconnect measuring unit from ECM. Connect measuring unit to TCM connector and check grounds. See WIRING DIAGRAM. Go to next step.

7) Ensure ignition is off. Reconnect control modules. Turn ignition on. Turn on as many power consuming items as possible. Connect voltmeter between ground and measuring unit terminal No. 20. Note voltage reading. Add both voltage readings together. Total of both readings should not be greater than .1 volt. If final voltage reading is okay, go to next step. If final reading is not okay, check TCM Brown ground wire located in front left corner of engine compartment and TCM connector terminals for poor terminal contact. Repair as necessary.

8) Ensure ignition is on. Turn on as many power consuming items as possible. Connect voltmeter between measuring unit terminals No. 20 and 29. If voltmeter reads less than .6 volt, go to next step. If voltmeter reads greater than .6 volt, check TCM Brown and Black ground wires located in front left corner of engine compartment and TCM connector terminals for poor terminal contact. Repair as necessary.

9) Ensure ignition is on. Connect voltmeter between measuring unit terminals No. 20 and 50. If voltmeter does not read about .5 volt at closed throttle position, check throttle position sensor signal. See appropriate SENSOR OPERATING RANGE CHARTS and SELF-DIAGNOSTICS article in ENGINE PERFORMANCE in appropriate MITCHELL® manual. If voltmeter does read about .5 volt at closed throttle position, DTC was set because of poor terminal contact at TCM and ECM connectors. Repair as necessary.

DTC 232/P0500: VEHICLE SPEED SIGNAL (VSS)

1) Ensure ignition is off. Connect scan tool. Raise and support front of vehicle. Turn ignition on. Using scan tool, select SCROLLING VALUES. Move gear selector to "D" position so front wheels begin to rotate. Read speed signal. If speed signal increases with engine speed, problem is intermittent. Check connectors for poor terminal contact. If speed does not increase with engine speed, go to next step.

2) Turn ignition off. Connect measuring unit to TCM connector. Check grounds. See WIRING DIAGRAM. Repair as necessary. If grounds are okay, connect ohmmeter between measuring unit terminals No. 11 and 12. If ohmmeter reads 300-600 ohms, go to step 7). If ohmmeter does not read 300-600 ohms, go to next step.

3) Remove air cleaner housing to access VSS connector. Disconnect VSS connector. Connect ohmmeter between VSS connector terminals No. 1 and 2. If ohmmeter reads 300-600 ohms, go to next step. If ohmmeter does not read 300-600 ohms, replace VSS.

4) Ensure ignition is off. Connect ohmmeter between VSS connector terminal No. 1 (Yellow/Brown wire) and measuring unit terminal No. 11. If ohmmeter reads about zero ohms, go to next step. If ohmmeter does not read about zero ohms, check for an open circuit in Yellow/Brown wire. Repair as necessary.

5) Connect ohmmeter between VSS connector terminal No. 2 (Green/Yellow wire) and measuring unit terminal No. 12. If ohmmeter reads about zero ohms, go to next step. If ohmmeter does not read about zero ohms, check for an open circuit in Green/Yellow wire. Repair as necessary.

6) Connect ohmmeter between measuring unit terminals No. 11 and 12. If ohmmeter does not read infinite resistance, check for a short circuit between VSS Yellow/Brown and Green/Yellow wires. If ohmmeter reads infinite resistance, DTC was caused by poor terminal contact at TCM. Repair as necessary.

7) Ensure ignition is off. Connect measuring unit to TCM connector. Ensure TCM is connected. Turn ignition on. Connect voltmeter between measuring unit terminals No. 11 and 12. If voltmeter reads about 2.5 volts, DTC was caused by poor terminal contact at TCM connector. If voltmeter reads less than 2.5 volts, check for a short circuit to ground in Yellow/Brown and Green/Yellow wires. If voltmeter reads greater than 2.5 volts, check for a short circuit to voltage in Yellow/Brown and Green/Yellow wires. Repair as necessary.

DTC 235: HIGH OIL TEMPERATURE

1) Check for other DTCs. If DTC 141 is present, perform testing for that DTC first. See DTC 141: SHORT CIRCUIT IN OIL TEMPERATURE SENSOR CIRCUIT. If DTC 141 is not present, turn ignition on. Select SCROLLING VALUES on scan tool. Read transmission oil temperature. If temperature is okay, check sensor wiring for a short circuit to ground. if temperature is not okay, go to next step.

2) Remove air cleaner housing to access transaxle connector. Disconnect transaxle connector. Connect ohmmeter between transaxle connector terminal No. 12 (Blue/Green wire) and ground. If ohmmeter reads infinite resistance, go to next step. If ohmmeter does not read infinite resistance, check Blue/Green wire for a short circuit to ground.

3) Ensure ignition is off. Disconnect transaxle connector. Connect ohmmeter between transaxle connector terminals No. 12 (Blue/Green wire) and No. 13 (Blue/Black wire). See OIL TEMPERATURE SENSOR RESISTANCE table. If resistance is to specification, check Blue/Green wire for a short circuit to ground. If resistance is not to specification, replace oil temperature sensor.

DTC 245: OPEN OR SHORT IN TORQUE LIMITING CIRCUIT

1) Engine torque is reduced to allow smoother shifting in some gear changes. Torque limiting process is controlled by signals sent from TCM to ECM. A receipt confirmation signal is sent from ECM to TCM. Signal indicates that torque limiting is taking place. If TCM fails to register a receipt signal after request for torque limiting, DTC 245 is set.

2) Ensure ignition is off. Reconnect TCM. Connect test light between measuring unit terminal No. 20 and No. 32, 33, and 34. If test light does not come on, go to next step. If test light comes on, check for short circuit to voltage is Yellow/Red, Yellow/Violet, and Violet wires. Repair as necessary.

3) Ensure ignition is off. Disconnect TCM and ECM. Connect measuring unit to TCM and ECM connectors. Connect ohmmeter between TCM measuring unit and ECM measuring unit. See TCM/ECM MEASURING UNIT RESISTANCE CHECK table. If ohmmeter reads infinite resistance, go to next step. If ohmmeter does not read infinite resistance, check for short to ground in Yellow/Red, Yellow/Violet, or Violet wire. Repair as necessary.

TCM/ECM MEASURING UNIT RESISTANCE CHECK

TCM Terminal No.	ECM Terminal No.
32	2
33	3
34	4

4) Ensure ignition is off. Disconnect measuring unit from TCM. Connect measuring unit to ECM. Turn ignition on. Move gear selector to "P" position. Connect voltmeter between ground and ECM measuring unit terminals No. 2 and 3. Using scan tool, activate TC1/TC2. Voltmeter should vary between -2 to zero volts. If oscillation is rapid (about one second), go to next step. If oscillation is not rapid, check for open circuit in Yellow/Red, Yellow/Violet, or Violet wires between TCM and ECM.

5) Ensure ignition is on. Move gear selector to "P" position. Using scan tool, activate torque limiting (TC1/TC2) signal. Read TCM status. If status alternates between OFF/ON, go to next step. If status does not alternate between OFF/ON, check Violet wire between TCM and ECM for an open circuit. Repair as necessary, then repeat step **4)**.

DTC 311/P0715: TRANSMISSION SPEED SENSOR SIGNAL MISSING

1) Ensure ignition is off. Connect measuring unit to TCM. Measure resistance between measuring unit terminals No. 1 and 2. If resistance is 300-600 ohms, sensor and wiring are okay. If resistance is not 300-600 ohms, go to next step.

2) Measure resistance between transmission 26-pin connector terminals No. 16 (Yellow/White wire) and No. 17 (Yellow/Brown wire). If resistance is not 300-600 ohms, check for open circuit in wiring between transmission speed sensor and transaxle connector terminals No. 16 (Yellow/White wire) and No. 17 (Yellow/Brown wire). Repair wiring as necessary. If wiring is okay, replace transmission speed sensor. If resistance is 300-600 ohms, speed sensor is okay. Check wiring for an open or short circuit. Repair as necessary.

DTC 313/P0705: GEAR POSITION SENSOR SIGNAL INCORRECT

1) If DTC 313 is set, check gear shift position sensor adjustment. Ensure gear shift is set to "N" position. Remove battery, battery shelf, and air intake manifold. Remove transmission cable from rod arm. Remove selector lever. Install gear position Alignment Tool (999 5475) on control shaft. If shaft is set correctly to "N" position and indentation on alignment tool aligns with mark on gear position sensor, go to step **3)**. If indentation does not align with mark, go to next step.

2) Remove dipstick pipe bracket and gear position sensor screws. Rotate gear position sensor so mark on switch aligns with indentation on tool. Tighten sensor screws to 37 ft. lbs. (25 N.m). To complete installation, reverse removal procedure.

3) Ensure ignition is off. Connect ohmmeter between gear shift position sensor case and transmission housing. If ohmmeter reads about zero ohms, go to next step. If ohmmeter does not read about zero ohms, check gear shift position sensor ground. Repair as necessary.

4) Ensure ignition is off. Connect measuring unit to TCM connector. Check TCM grounds. See WIRING DIAGRAM. Repair as necessary. If grounds are okay, connect ohmmeter between measuring unit terminal No. 20 and terminals No. 3 ("A"), No. 4 ("B"), No. 5 ("C"), and No. 6 (PA). If ohmmeter reads infinite resistance, go to next step. If ohmmeter does not read infinite resistance, check for short circuit to ground in White, Yellow, Green, and Blue wires between gear position sensor and TCM.

5) Ensure ignition is off. Disconnect transaxle connector. Connect ohmmeter between transaxle connector terminals and measuring unit terminals. See TRANSAXLE CONNECTOR/MEASURING UNIT TERMINAL RESISTANCE table. If ohmmeter reads about zero ohms for all readings, go to next step. If ohmmeter does not read about zero ohms for all readings, check for open circuit in wiring between transaxle connector and TCM. Repair as necessary.

TRANSAXLE CONNECTOR/MEASURING UNIT TERMINAL RESISTANCE

Transaxle Connector Terminal	Measuring Unit Terminal
1 (White wire)	3
2 (Yellow wire)	4
3 (Green wire)	5
4 (Blue wire)	6

6) Ensure ignition is off. Disconnect transmission and TCM connectors. Turn ignition on. Connect test light between measuring unit terminal No. 20 and gear position sensor connector terminals No. 1 (White wire), No. 2 (Yellow wire), No. 3 (Green wire), and No. 4 (Blue wire). If test light comes on, check wiring for a short circuit to voltage. If test light does not come on, go to next step.

7) Ensure ignition is off. Connect TCM and transaxle connectors. Turn ignition on. Using scan tool, go into SCROLLING VALUES. Read gear shift sensor position. Move gear shift position sensor to all shift positions several times. Repeatedly select same position to check operation. If all values are okay, DTC was caused by poor terminal contact. If all values are not okay, replace gear shift position sensor.

DTC 321/P0731, 322/P0732, 323/P0733 & 324/P0734: INCORRECT GEAR RATIO

1) Check transmission oil level. If oil level is low, top off as necessary and check for leaks. Repair as necessary. If oil level is okay, turn ignition on and check DTCs. Test drive vehicle while observing automatic transmission warning light. If light begins to flash, note any unusual symptoms in transmission operation or function. If transmission does not show any mechanical fault or malfunction, go to next step. If transmission has a mechanical malfunction and DTCs are not reset, repair transmission as necessary.

2) Ensure ignition is off. Disconnect TCM. Connect measuring unit to TCM connector. Leave TCM disconnected. Connect ohmmeter between measuring unit terminals No. 2 and 20. If ohmmeter reads infinite resistance, go to step **5)**. If ohmmeter does not read infinite resistance, go to next step.

3) Ensure ignition is off. Disconnect transaxle connector. Connect ohmmeter between transaxle connector terminal No. 17 (Yellow/Brown wire) and ground. If ohmmeter reads infinite resistance, go to next step. If ohmmeter does not read infinite resistance, replace transmission speed sensor.

4) Check for a short circuit to ground in Yellow/Brown wire between transaxle connector terminal No. 17 and TCM terminal A2. Repair as necessary.

5) Turn ignition off. Connect measuring unit to TCM. Raise and support front of vehicle. Turn A/C off. Idle engine. Set gear selector to "D" position so front wheels begin to rotate. Increase and keep engine speed at 2000 RPM. Set DVOM to Hz scale, then connect DVOM between measuring unit terminals No. 1 and 2. If DVOM gives a stable Hz reading when engine speed is constant and transmission is not shifting, go to step **8)**. If Hz frequency reading shows wide fluctuations, go to next step.

6) Ensure ignition is off. Disconnect TCM. Connect ohmmeter between measuring unit terminals No. 1 and 2. If ohmmeter does not read 300-600 ohms, go to next step. If ohmmeter reads 300-600 ohms, ensure RPM sensor wiring is not located near sources of interference such as electric motors or spark plugs.

7) Disconnect transaxle connector. Check TCM connector for poor terminal contact. Repair as necessary. Reconnect transaxle connector. Connect ohmmeter between measuring unit terminals No. 1 and 2. If ohmmeter reads about 300-600 ohms, DTC was set because of poor contact in transaxle connector. If ohmmeter does not read about 300-600 ohms, replace RPM sensor.

8) Ensure ignition is off. Disconnect TCM. Connect ohmmeter between measuring unit terminals No. 12 and 20. If ohmmeter reads infinite resistance, go to step **10)**. If ohmmeter does not read infinite resistance, go to next step.

9) Ensure ignition is off. Disconnect transmission speed sensor. Connect ohmmeter between speed sensor connector terminal No. 2 (Green/Yellow wire) and ground. If ohmmeter reads infinite resistance, check for short circuit to ground in Green/Yellow wire. If ohmmeter does not read infinite resistance, replace transmission speed sensor.

10) Ensure ignition is off. Connect measuring unit to TCM and TCM connector. Raise and support front of vehicle. Turn A/C off. Idle engine. Set gear selector to "D" position so front wheels begin to rotate. Increase and keep engine speed at 2000 RPM. Set DVOM to Hz scale, then connect DVOM between measuring unit terminals No.

11 and 12. If DVOM gives a stable Hz reading when engine speed is constant and transmission is not shifting, go to step **12)**. If Hz frequency reading shows wide fluctuations, go to next step.

11) Ensure ignition is off. Disconnect TCM from measuring unit. Connect ohmmeter between measuring unit terminals No. 11 and 12. If ohmmeter reads 300-600 ohms, check that speed sensor wires are not close to sources of interference. Ensure speed sensor is not loose. Repair as necessary. If ohmmeter does not read 300-600 ohms, go to next step.

12) Ensure ignition is off. Check transmission speed sensor connector for poor terminal contact. Repair as necessary. Connect ohmmeter between measuring unit terminals No. 11 and 12. If ohmmeter reads 300-600 ohms, cause of DTC was poor terminal contact at transmission speed sensor. If ohmmeter does not read 300-600 ohms, replace transmission speed sensor.

13) Ensure ignition is off. Disconnect TCM. Connect ohmmeter between measuring unit terminals No. 27 and 29 (solenoid S1) and terminals No. 28 and 29 (solenoid S2). If ohmmeter reads 12-18 ohms, go to next step. If ohmmeter does not read 12-18 ohms, check transaxle connector for poor terminal contact. Repair as necessary.

14) Ensure ignition is off. Check gear position sensor adjustment. See DTC 313: GEAR POSITION SENSOR SIGNAL INCORRECT. Repair as necessary. If adjustment is okay, go to next step.

15) Ensure ignition is off. Reconnect all connectors. Reinstall all components. Turn ignition on. Erase DTCs. Test drive vehicle. For DTC 321, put gear selector in "L" position. Accelerate evenly at an engine speed over 1400 RPM. For DTC 322, put gear selector in "3" position. Accelerate evenly at an engine speed over 1400 RPM. For DTC 323, put gear selector in "3" position. Maintain throttle opening at about 10 percent and accelerate evenly at an engine speed over 1400 RPM. For DTC 324, put gear selector in "D" position. Maintain throttle opening at about 10 percent and accelerate evenly at an engine speed over 1400 RPM. If DTC resets, replace TCM. If DTC does not reset, system is okay.

DTC 331: SHORT TO VOLTAGE IN LOCK-UP SOLENOID CIRCUIT

Turn ignition on. Set gearshift lever to "P" position. Check solenoid function by using test mode No. 4 or Volvo scan tool. See TEST MODE NO. 4. If solenoid operates, check wiring for an intermittent short circuit. If solenoid does not operate, check for a short circuit to voltage in wiring between lock-up solenoid and TCM connector terminal A9. Repair as necessary.

DTC 332: OPEN IN LOCK-UP SOLENOID CIRCUIT

1) Turn ignition on. Set gearshift lever to "P" position. Using scan tool, activate lock-up solenoid. Read solenoid status. If status alternates between OFF/ON, problem is intermittent. Check connectors for poor terminal contact. If status does not alternate between OFF/ON, go to next step.

2) Ensure ignition is off. Connect measuring unit to TCM connector. Connect ohmmeter between measuring unit terminals No. 9 and 29. If ohmmeter reads 12-18 ohms, DTC was caused by poor terminal contact in TCM connector. Repair as necessary. If ohmmeter does not read 12-18 ohms, go to next step.

3) Ensure ignition is off. Remove air cleaner housing to access transaxle connector. Connect ohmmeter between transaxle connector terminal No. 23 and measuring unit terminal No. 9. If ohmmeter reads about zero ohms, go to next step. If ohmmeter does not read about zero ohms, check for an open circuit in Brown/Black wire between transaxle connector terminal No. 23 and TCM terminal A9.

4) Ensure ignition is off and transaxle connector is disconnected. Connect ohmmeter between transaxle connector terminal No. 23 and transmission housing. If ohmmeter does not read 12-18 ohms, go to next step. If ohmmeter reads 12-18 ohms, DTC set because of poor terminal contact at transaxle connector. Repair as necessary.

5) Ensure ignition is off. Open control system and disconnect lock-up solenoid. Connect ohmmeter between lock-up solenoid terminal and transmission housing. If ohmmeter reads 12-18 ohms, check for an open circuit in Brown/Black wire between lock-up solenoid and transaxle connector terminal No. 23. If ohmmeter does not read 12-18 ohms, replace lock-up solenoid.

DTC 333: SHORT TO GROUND IN LOCK-UP SOLENOID CIRCUIT

1) Turn ignition on. Set gearshift lever to "P" position. Using scan tool, activate lock-up solenoid. Read solenoid status. If status alternates between OFF/ON, check wiring for an intermittent short circuit. If solenoid does not alternate, go to next step.

2) Ensure ignition is off. Remove air cleaner housing to access transaxle connector. Disconnect transaxle connector. Connect ohmmeter between transaxle connector terminal No. 23 (Brown/Black wire) and transmission housing. If ohmmeter does not read 10-15 ohms, go to next step. If ohmmeter reads 10-15 ohms, check for a short circuit to ground in Brown/Black wire between transaxle connector terminal No. 23 and TCM connector terminal A9.

3) Ensure ignition is off. Open control system and disconnect lock-up solenoid. Connect ohmmeter between lock-up solenoid terminal and transmission housing. If ohmmeter reads 10-15 ohms, check for an open circuit in Brown/Black wire between lock-up solenoid and transaxle connector terminal No. 23. If ohmmeter does not read 10-15 ohms, replace lock-up solenoid.

DTC 341: LOCK-UP FUNCTION SLIPS OR DISENGAGES

1) Ensure ignition is off. Disconnect TCM. Connect measuring unit to TCM connector. Check TCM grounds. See WIRING DIAGRAM. If grounds are okay, connect ohmmeter between measuring unit terminals No. 9 and 20. If ohmmeter reads 10-15 ohms, go to next step. If ohmmeter does not read 10-15 ohms, check TCM connector for poor terminal contact, then go to next step.

2) Test drive vehicle. If DTC reoccurs, check transmission for mechanical fault.

DTC 411: CONTROL MODULE EEPROM MEMORY FAULT

1) Turn ignition off. Wait about 2 minutes. Turn ignition on. Carefully pry off driving mode selector from panel on center console. Disconnect driving mode selector to simulate a fault that would set a DTC. Wait about 45 seconds, then connect and reinstall driving mode selector. Go to next step.

2) Ensure ignition is off. Wait about 2 minutes. Turn ignition on. If DTC 114 is set, system is okay. If DTC 114 is not set, replace TCM.

DTC 421: BATTERY VOLTAGE TOO LOW

Check charging system. If charging system is okay, connect measuring unit to TCM connector and check ground and voltage. Check all connectors and wiring for poor terminal contact or open circuits. Repair as necessary.

AUTOMATIC TRANSMISSIONS
Volvo AW50-42LE Electronic Controls (Cont.)

WIRING DIAGRAM

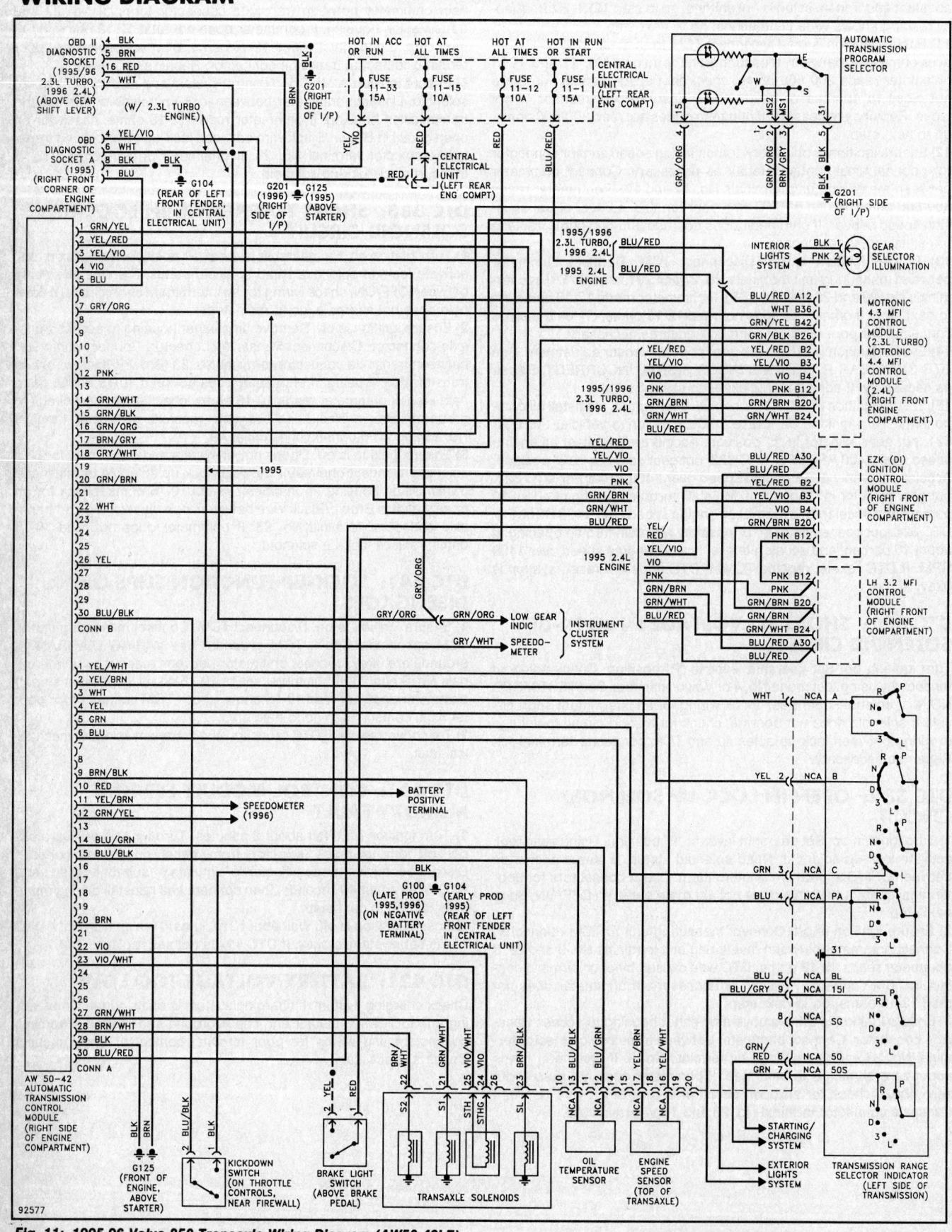

Fig. 11: 1995-96 Volvo 850 Transaxle Wiring Diagram (AW50-42LE)

AUTOMATIC TRANSMISSIONS
Volvo AW-71

940, 940 Turbo

APPLICATION & LABOR TIMES

APPLICATION & LABOR TIMES

Vehicle Application	Labor Times [1] R & I	[2] Overhaul	Series
1995			
940	3.0	10.3	AW-71
940 Turbo	3.0	10.3	AW-71

[1] – Removal and installation of transmission from vehicle chassis.

[2] – Bench overhaul time for transmission. DOES NOT include removal and installation.

IDENTIFICATION

Transmission identification plate is located on driver's side of transmission, above oil pan, near shift lever.

DESCRIPTION & OPERATION

Transmission is a fully automatic 4-speed transmission consisting of clutches, brakes, one-way clutches, planetary gear sets and lock-up torque converter. *See Fig. 1.* Transmissions with model number ending in "L" use a lock-up torque converter.

An Overdrive (OD) switch is mounted on shift lever. When overdrive switch is released to the ON position, transmission will automatically upshift to overdrive and overdrive indicator light on instrument panel will be off.

When overdrive switch is depressed to the OFF position, transmission will not upshift to overdrive and overdrive indicator light on instrument panel will come on. Overdrive switch provides voltage through overdrive relay to overdrive solenoid.

Transmission is equipped with shift and key lock systems. Shift lock system prevents shift lever from being moved from "P" position unless brake pedal is depressed, ignition is on and release button on shift lever is depressed. If shift lever fails to moved from "P" position with brake pedal depressed (ignition on and release button on shift lever is depressed), shift lock system release button may be depressed to allow shift lever movement. Shift lock system release button is located on console, near shift lever.

Key lock system prevents ignition switch from being placed in LOCK (O) position unless shift lever is in "P" position. A shift control cable is connected between shift lever and ignition switch. When shift lever is placed in "P" position, shift control cable moves lock on ignition switch so ignition switch may be placed in LOCK (O) position.

LUBRICATION & ADJUSTMENTS

See appropriate AUTOMATIC TRANSMISSION SERVICING article in TRANSMISSION SERVICING section.

TROUBLE SHOOTING

Transmission malfunctions may be caused by poor engine performance, improper adjustments, or failure of hydraulic or mechanical components. Always begin by checking fluid level, fluid condition, linkage and cable adjustments. Perform road test to determine if problem has been corrected. If problem still exists, several tests must be performed on transmission. See TRANSMISSION TESTING.

Grinding Noise From Transmission With Shift Lever In "N" Or "P" Position
- Defective Flexplate Or Loose Torque Converter Bolts
- Defective Planetary Gear
- Internal Transmission Failure

Groaning Noise After Torque Converter Lock-Up
- Sticking Lock-Up Or Lock-Up Relay Valve In Valve Body

Harsh Gear Engagement Or Noisy Gear Disengagement
- Defective Accumulator Piston Or Seal Rings
- Defective Or Improperly Adjusted Shift Linkage
- Defective Or Improperly Adjusted Kickdown Cable
- Improper Fluid Level
- Improper Line Pressure
- Internal Transmission Failure
- Valve Body Malfunction

Harsh Torque Converter Lock-Up
- Defective Torque Converter
- Sticking Lock-Up Relay Valve In Valve Body

No Engine Braking In 1st Gear
- Defective Brake No. 3
- Defective Overdrive Clutch

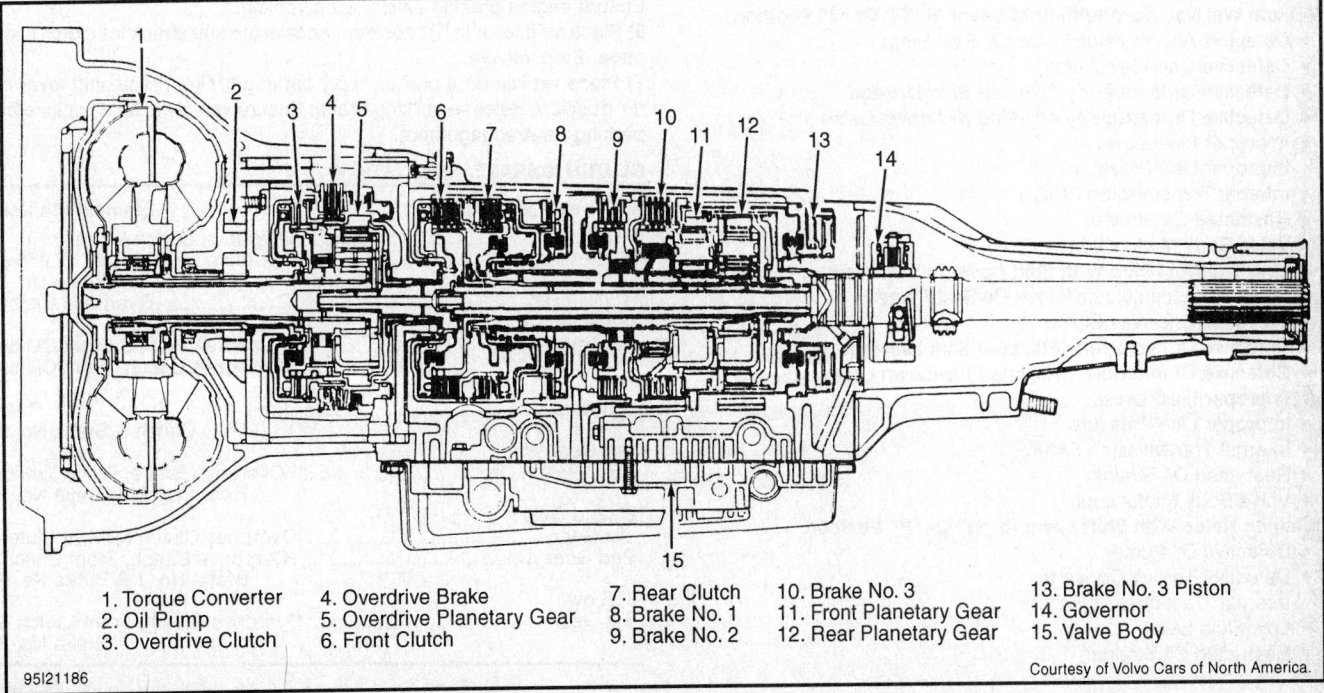

1. Torque Converter	4. Overdrive Brake	7. Rear Clutch	10. Brake No. 3	13. Brake No. 3 Piston
2. Oil Pump	5. Overdrive Planetary Gear	8. Brake No. 1	11. Front Planetary Gear	14. Governor
3. Overdrive Clutch	6. Front Clutch	9. Brake No. 2	12. Rear Planetary Gear	15. Valve Body

95I21186

Courtesy of Volvo Cars of North America.

Fig. 1: Identifying Transmission Component Locations

No Engine Braking In 2nd Gear
- Defective Brake No. 1
- Defective Overdrive Clutch

No Shift Or Delayed Shift
- Defective Governor
- Defective Or Improperly Adjusted Shift Linkage
- Defective Or Improperly Adjusted Kickdown Cable
- Improper Fluid Level
- Improper Line Pressure
- Internal Transmission Failure
- Valve Body Malfunction

No 3-4 Upshift
- Defective Governor
- Defective Overdrive Brake
- Defective Overdrive Switch, Wiring Or Solenoid

No 4-3 Downshift
- Defective Governor
- Defective Overdrive Switch, Wiring Or Solenoid
- Defective Or Improperly Adjusted Kickdown Cable
- Valve Body Malfunction

Squeeking Noise From Transmission With Shift Lever In "N" Or "P" Position
- Worn Torque Converter Bushing In Oil Pump

Torque Converter Lock-Up Inoperative
- Defective Torque Converter
- Transmission Is Not In 4th Gear
- Valve Body Malfunction

Torque Converter Lock-Up Operates At Incorrect Speed
- Incorrect Governor Pressure
- Sticking Lock-Up Valve In Valve Body

Vehicle Does Not Hold With Shift Lever In "P" Position
- Defective Or Improperly Adjusted Shift Linkage
- Defective Parking Pawl Or Components

Vehicle Will Not Move In Any Forward Gear
- Defective Accumulator Piston Or Seal Rings
- Defective One-Way Clutch
- Defective Or Improperly Adjusted Shift Linkage
- Defective Or Improperly Adjusted Kickdown Cable
- Improper Fluid Level
- Improper Line Pressure
- Internal Transmission Failure
- Restricted Oil Strainer
- Valve Body Malfunction

Vehicle Will Not Move With Shift Lever In "D" Or "2" Position
- Defective Accumulator Piston Or Seal Rings
- Defective One-Way Clutch
- Defective Or Improperly Adjusted Shift Linkage
- Defective Or Improperly Adjusted Kickdown Cable
- Improper Fluid Level
- Improper Line Pressure
- Internal Transmission Failure
- Restricted Oil Strainer
- Valve Body Malfunction

Vehicle Will Not Move With Shift Lever In "R" Position
- Defective Accumulator Piston Or Seal Rings
- Defective One-Way Clutch
- Defective Or Improperly Adjusted Shift Linkage
- Defective Or Improperly Adjusted Kickdown Cable
- Improper Fluid Level
- Improper Line Pressure
- Internal Transmission Failure
- Restricted Oil Strainer
- Valve Body Malfunction

Whining Noise With Shift Lever In "N" Or "P" Position
- Defective Oil Pump
- Defective Torque Converter
- Internal Transmission Failure
- Low Fluid Level
- Restricted Oil Strainer

ELECTRICAL SYSTEM COMPONENT TESTING

OVERDRIVE SOLENOID

1) Disconnect electrical connector at overdrive solenoid located on side of transmission. *See Fig. 2.* Using ohmmeter, measure resistance between electrical terminal on overdrive solenoid and body of overdrive solenoid. Replace overdrive solenoid if resistance is not 13 ohms.

2) To check overdrive solenoid operation, remove overdrive solenoid from transmission. Apply battery voltage to overdrive solenoid by connecting positive battery terminal to electrical terminal on overdrive solenoid and negative battery terminal to body on overdrive solenoid.

3) Apply air pressure to small hole on bottom side of overdrive solenoid where solenoid mounts on transmission. Air pressure should flow from remaining small hole on bottom side of overdrive solenoid.

4) Disconnect battery voltage from overdrive solenoid. Air pressure should not flow through overdrive solenoid with battery voltage disconnected. Replace overdrive solenoid if defective.

OVERDRIVE (OD) SWITCH

Overdrive switch is located on shift lever. Testing information is not available from manufacturer.

TRANSMISSION TESTING

ROAD TEST

1) Before performing road test, warm engine to normal operating temperature. Ensure fluid level is correct and in good condition. Ensure shift linkage and kickdown cable are properly adjusted.

2) Road test vehicle and check for abnormal noise, vibration and clutch slippage. Specified clutch and brake are applied in designated gear. See CLUTCH & BRAKE APPLICATION table.

3) Drive vehicle. Ensure upshift and downshift speeds are correct in relation to vehicle speed and throttle opening. See SHIFT SPEED SPECIFICATIONS table. Stop vehicle.

4) Place shift lever in "2" position. Drive vehicle and ensure a 1-2 upshift exists. Release accelerator. Ensure transmission downshifts and engine braking exists. Stop vehicle.

5) Place shift lever in "1" position. Drive vehicle and ensure no upshift exists and transmission remains in 1st gear. Release accelerator. Ensure engine braking exists. Stop vehicle.

6) Place shift lever in "R" position. Accelerate and check for clutch slippage. Stop vehicle.

7) Place vehicle on a grade. Apply parking brake. Place shift lever in "P" position. Release parking brake. Ensure vehicle is held in place by parking pawl engagement.

CLUTCH & BRAKE APPLICATION

Shift Lever Position	Elements In Use
"P" (Park)	Overdrive Clutch & Brake No. 3
"R" (Reverse)	Overdrive Clutch, Rear Clutch & Brake No. 3
"N" (Neutral)	Overdrive Clutch
"D" (Drive)	
1st Gear	Overdrive Clutch & Front Clutch
2nd Gear	Overdrive Clutch, Front Clutch & Brake No. 2
3rd Gear	Overdrive Clutch, Front Clutch, Rear Clutch & Brake No. 2
3rd Gear With OD Switch ON	Overdrive Brake, Front Clutch, Rear Clutch & Brake No. 2
"2" (2nd Gear)	
1st Gear	Overdrive Clutch & Front Clutch
2nd Gear	Overdrive Clutch, Front Clutch, Brake No. 1 & Brake No. 2
"L" (Low)	
1st Gear	Overdrive Clutch, Front Clutch & Brake No. 3

SHIFT SPEED SPECIFICATIONS

Application	[1] MPH
940	
1-2	[2] 36
2-3	[2] 63
3-4	[3] 70
4-3	[4] 23
3-2	[2] 59
2-1	[2] 28
940 Turbo	
1-2	[2] 41
2-3	[2] 73
3-4	[3] 85
4-3	[4] 18
3-2	[2] 68
2-1	[2] 30

[1] – Approximate shift speed listed.
[2] – Shift speed at full throttle.
[3] – Shift speed at 3/4 throttle.
[4] – Shift speed at closed throttle.

TORQUE CONVERTER STALL SPEED TEST

CAUTION: Ensure line pressure is within specification before performing torque converter stall speed test. See LINE PRESSURE TEST under HYDRAULIC PRESSURE TEST. DO NOT perform torque converter stall speed test if line pressure is not within specification. DO NOT perform torque converter stall speed test for more than 5 seconds or transmission may be damaged.

1) Apply parking brake. Block all wheels. Connect tachometer. Start and warm engine to normal operating temperature. Ensure transmission fluid level is correct. Ensure A/C is off. Place shift lever in "D" position.
2) Fully depress brake pedal. Fully depress accelerator for no more than 5 seconds and note maximum RPM. This is the torque converter stall speed.
3) Place shift lever in "N" position and allow engine to idle for 30 seconds to cool transmission. Repeat test procedure with shift lever in "R" position. Torque converter stall speed should be within specification with shift lever in both "D" and "R" positions. See TORQUE CONVERTER STALL SPEED SPECIFICATIONS table.

TORQUE CONVERTER STALL SPEED SPECIFICATIONS

Application	RPM
940	2000
940 Turbo	2000-2700

4) If torque converter stall speed is not within specification, see TORQUE CONVERTER STALL SPEED TROUBLE SHOOTING table for possible causes.

TORQUE CONVERTER STALL SPEED TROUBLE SHOOTING

Torque Converter Stall Speed Test Results	Probable Cause
Stall Speed RPM Low In "D" Or "R" Position	Engine Output Low, Defective Torque Converter
Stall Speed RPM High In "D" Position	Incorrect Fluid Level, Restricted Oil Strainer, Slipping Front Clutch
Stall Speed RPM High In "R" Position	Incorrect Fluid Level, Restricted Oil Strainer, Slipping Rear Clutch Or Brake No. 3

HYDRAULIC PRESSURE TEST

Pressure Test Preparation – Warm engine to normal operating temperature. Ensure transmission fluid level is correct.

Line Pressure Test – 1) With engine off, remove pressure tap plug from line pressure tap on transmission. *See Fig. 2.* Install pressure gauge on line pressure tap.

2) Apply parking brake. Block all wheels. Connect tachometer. Start engine. Ensure idle speed is within specification. Fully depress brake pedal. Place shift lever in "D" position. Note and record line pressure with engine idling.
3) Fully depress brake pedal. Fully depress accelerator for no more than 5 seconds until torque converter stall speed is obtained and note line pressure. Repeat line pressure test with shift lever in "R" position.
4) Line pressure should be within specification. See LINE PRESSURE SPECIFICATIONS table. If line pressure is not within specification, check and adjust kickdown cable. Recheck line pressure.
5) If line pressure still is not within specification, see HYDRAULIC PRESSURE TEST TROUBLE SHOOTING table. Shut engine off. Remove pressure gauge. Install pressure tap plug.

LINE PRESSURE SPECIFICATIONS (940 & 940 TURBO)

Application	psi (kg/cm²)
At Idle Speed	
"D" Position	65-77 (4.6-5.4)
"R" Position	99-116 (7.0-8.2)
At Torque Converter Stall Speed	
"D" Position	142-170 (10.0-12.0)
"R" Position	213-269 (15.0-18.9)

Governor Pressure Test – 1) Ensure line pressure is correct before checking governor pressure. See LINE PRESSURE TEST under HYDRAULIC PRESSURE TEST.
2) With engine off, remove pressure tap plug from governor pressure tap. *See Fig. 2.* Install pressure gauge on governor pressure tap. Start engine.
3) Ensure no governor pressure exists with engine idling with shift lever in "D" and "R" positions. Position pressure gauge so governor pressure may be monitored while driving vehicle.
4) Drive vehicle and note governor pressure at specified speeds. See GOVERNOR PRESSURE SPECIFICATIONS table. Governor pressure should be within specification.
5) If governor pressure is not within specification, see HYDRAULIC PRESSURE TEST TROUBLE SHOOTING table. Shut engine off. Remove pressure gauge. Install pressure tap plug.

GOVERNOR PRESSURE SPECIFICATIONS (940 & 940 TURBO)

Vehicle Speed	psi (kg/cm²)
With 3.54:1 Final Drive Ratio	
21 MPH	16-24 (3.9-1.7)
34 MPH	24-32 (1.7-2.3)
68 MPH	54-71 (3.8-5.0)
With 3.73:1 Final Drive Ratio	
19 MPH	13-21 (.9-1.5)
34 MPH	23-31 (1.6-2.2)
67 MPH	58-75 (4.1-5.3)
With 3.91:1 Final Drive Ratio	
18 MPH	13-21 (.9-1.5)
33 MPH	23-31 (1.6-2.2)
64 MPH	58-75 (4.1-5.3)
With 4.10:1 Final Drive Ratio	
17 MPH	13-21 (.9-1.5)
45 MPH	23-31 (1.6-2.2)
61 MPH	58-75 (4.1-5.3)

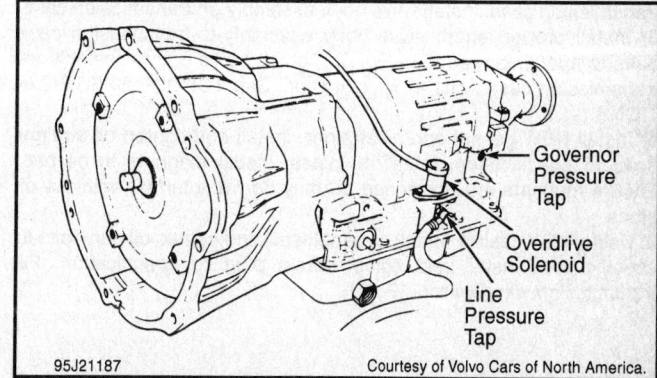

95J21187   Courtesy of Volvo Cars of North America.

Fig. 2: Identifying Overdrive Solenoid & Pressure Taps

HYDRAULIC PRESSURE TEST TROUBLE SHOOTING

Application	Probable Cause
Line Pressure	
Low Line Pressure	Primary Regulator Valve Or Throttle Valve Sticking, Defective Oil Pump Or Relief Valve, Restricted Oil Strainer, Defective Accumulator Piston
No Line Pressure & Vehicle Will Not Move In "R"	Defective Primary Regulator, 2-3 Shift Valve Or Reverse Clutch Sequence Valve, Defective Rear Clutch Accumulator Piston, Loose Center Support Assembly Bolts
High Line Pressure In All Ranges	Defective Or Improperly Adjusted Kickdown Cable, Throttle Valve Sticking, Primary Regulator Valve Sticking, Sticking Shift Or Cut-Back Valves
Line Pressure Is Correct But Drops After A Few Seconds	Defective Secondary Regulator Valve
Governor Pressure	
Pressure Not Within Specification	Incorrect Line Pressure, Oil Pressure Leakage In Governor Hydraulic Circuit, Faulty Governor

ON-VEHICLE SERVICE

VALVE BODY ASSEMBLY

Valve body may be serviced on the vehicle. See VALVE BODY ASSEMBLY under REMOVAL & INSTALLATION.

REMOVAL & INSTALLATION

TRANSMISSION

See appropriate AUTOMATIC TRANSMISSION REMOVAL article in TRANSMISSION SERVICING section.

VALVE BODY ASSEMBLY

Removal – 1) Raise and support vehicle. Remove drain plug from oil pan and drain transmission fluid. Remove bolts, oil pan and gasket. Note oil pipe location for reassembly reference. Note valve body assembly-to-transmission case bolt location for reassembly reference, as different bolt lengths are used. *See Fig. 3.*
2) Using screwdriver, carefully pry oil pipes from valve body and transmission case. Use care not to damage oil pipe. Remove oil strainer.
3) Remove valve body assembly-to-transmission case bolts. Slightly lower valve body assembly. DO NOT allow accumulator pistons and springs to come out of transmission case when removing valve body assembly.
4) Disconnect kickdown cable from throttle cam on valve body assembly. Remove valve body assembly.
Installation – 1) Ensure accumulator pistons and springs are installed in transmission case. Install kickdown cable on throttle cam.
2) Align manual valve on valve body assembly with detent lever in transmission case. Install valve body assembly on transmission case.
3) Install proper length valve body assembly-to-transmission case bolts in specified area. *See Fig. 3.* Tighten valve body assembly-to-transmission case bolts to specification. See TORQUE SPECIFICATIONS.
4) Install NEW gasket and oil strainer. Install and tighten oil strainer bolts to specification. Install oil pipes. Install magnets in oil pan. Ensure magnets are positioned so they do not interfere with the oil pipes.
5) Using NEW gasket, install oil pan. Install and tighten oil pan bolts to specification. Install and tighten drain plug to specification. Fill transmission with Dexron-IIE ATF.

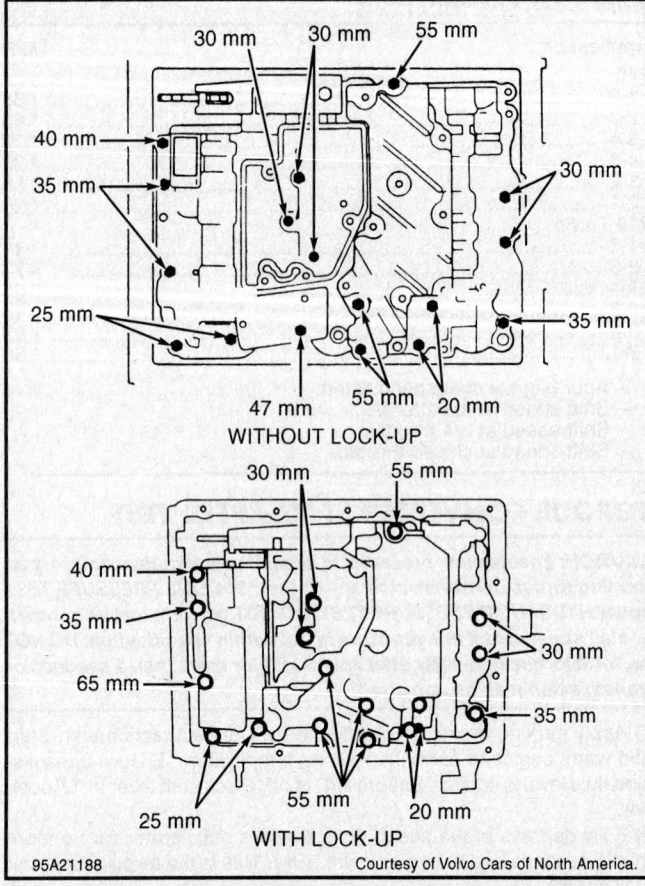

WITHOUT LOCK-UP

WITH LOCK-UP

95A21188   Courtesy of Volvo Cars of North America.

Fig. 3: Identifying Valve Body Assembly-To-Transmission Case Bolt Length

TORQUE CONVERTER

NOTE: Torque converter is a sealed unit and cannot be serviced and must be replaced if defective. For torque converter stall speed test, see TORQUE CONVERTER STALL SPEED TEST under TRANSMISSION TESTING.

TRANSMISSION DISASSEMBLY

VALVE BODY ASSEMBLY & INTERNAL COMPONENTS

1) Remove torque converter. Remove overdrive solenoid and "O" ring from transmission case. Remove shift lever from end of manual shaft.
2) Remove companion flange from output shaft. Remove bolts, rear cover assembly, gasket, spacer or speedometer drive gear with spacer as equipped from output shaft. *See Fig. 4.*
3) Bend over tabs on bolt lock and remove governor assembly bolt. Using screwdriver, raise governor retaining ring located at governor assembly. Remove governor assembly. Remove filter cover plate, gasket and filter from rear of transmission case, near output shaft. *See Fig. 5.*
4) Remove bolts, oil pan and gasket. Note oil pipe location for reassembly reference. Note valve body assembly-to-transmission case bolt location for reassembly reference, as different bolt lengths are used. *See Fig. 3.*
5) Using screwdriver, carefully pry oil pipes from valve body and transmission case. Use care not to damage oil pipe. Remove oil strainer.
6) Remove valve body assembly-to-transmission case bolts. Slightly lower valve body assembly. Disconnect kickdown cable from throttle cam on valve body assembly. Remove valve body assembly. Remove kickdown cable from transmission case.

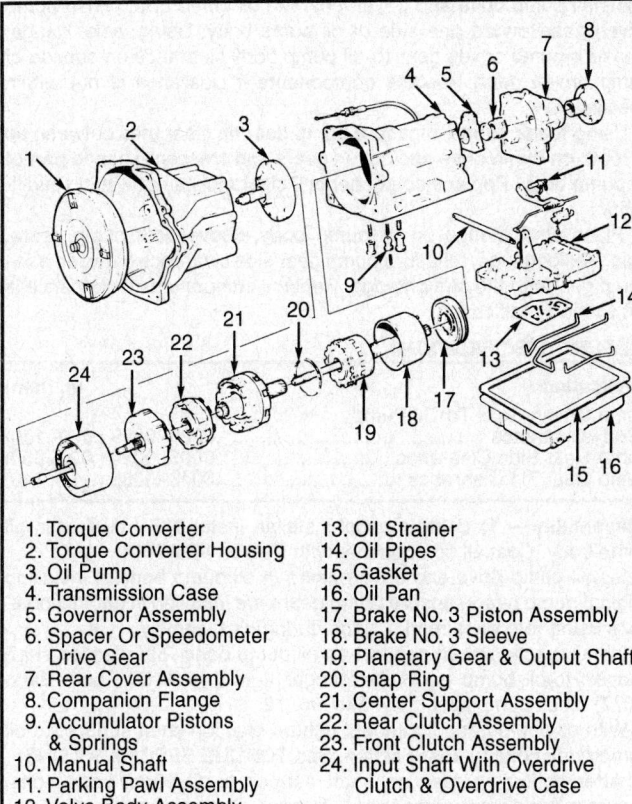

1. Torque Converter
2. Torque Converter Housing
3. Oil Pump
4. Transmission Case
5. Governor Assembly
6. Spacer Or Speedometer Drive Gear
7. Rear Cover Assembly
8. Companion Flange
9. Accumulator Pistons & Springs
10. Manual Shaft
11. Parking Pawl Assembly
12. Valve Body Assembly
13. Oil Strainer
14. Oil Pipes
15. Gasket
16. Oil Pan
17. Brake No. 3 Piston Assembly
18. Brake No. 3 Sleeve
19. Planetary Gear & Output Shaft
20. Snap Ring
21. Center Support Assembly
22. Rear Clutch Assembly
23. Front Clutch Assembly
24. Input Shaft With Overdrive Clutch & Overdrive Case

95B21189   Courtesy of Volvo Cars of North America.

Fig. 4: Exploded View Of Transmission Case & Components

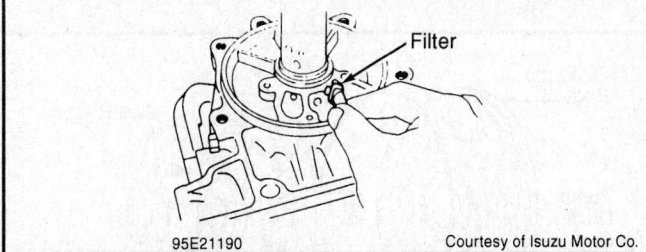

95E21190   Courtesy of Isuzu Motor Co.

Fig. 5: Identifying Filter Location

7) Remove accumulator pistons by applying air pressure on passages in transmission case. *See Fig. 6.* Remove accumulator springs. Mark accumulator piston and spring locations for reassembly reference.

8) Remove bolts, parking pawl bracket, pivot pin, parking pawl spring and parking pawl. *See Fig. 7.* Slide lock ring back from end of manual shaft in transmission case for access to retaining pin. Remove retaining pin from manual shaft. Remove manual shaft with detent lever and parking rod from transmission case.

NOTE: For reassembly reference, note if there are washers on the oil pump assembly bolts. If bolts are equipped with washers, NEW washers must be installed during installation. If bolts do not have washers, sealant must be applied to lower side of bolt head before installation.

---

9) Remove oil pump bolts. Install 2 guide pins to hold oil pump in alignment. Using Oil Pump Puller (5071), remove oil pump assembly. *See Fig. 8.*

10) Remove bolts and torque converter housing. Remove input shaft with overdrive clutch and overdrive case. *See Fig. 4.*

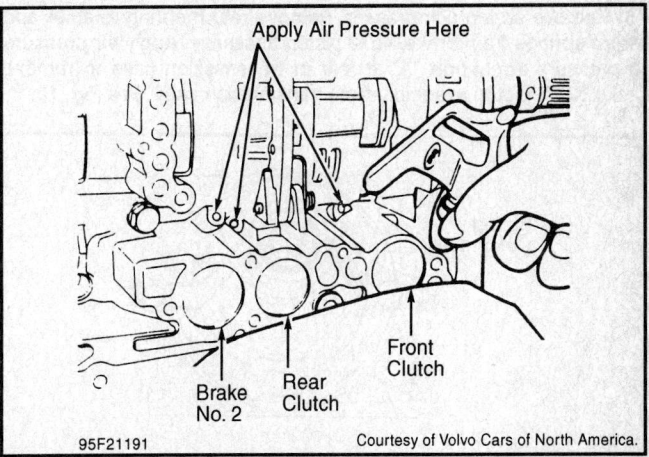

95F21191   Courtesy of Volvo Cars of North America.

Fig. 6: Removing Accumulator Pistons

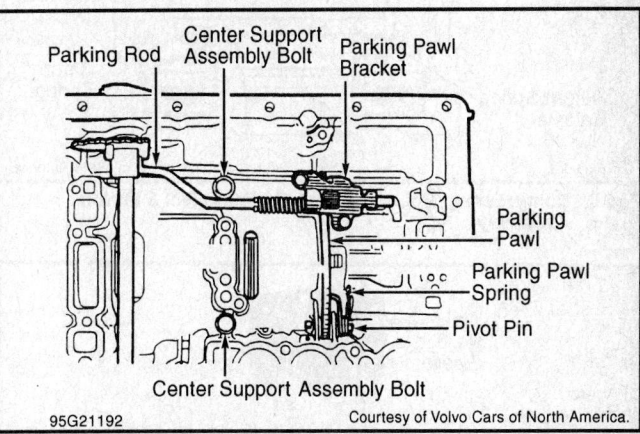

95G21192   Courtesy of Volvo Cars of North America.

Fig. 7: Identifying Parking Pawl Components & Center Support Assembly Bolts

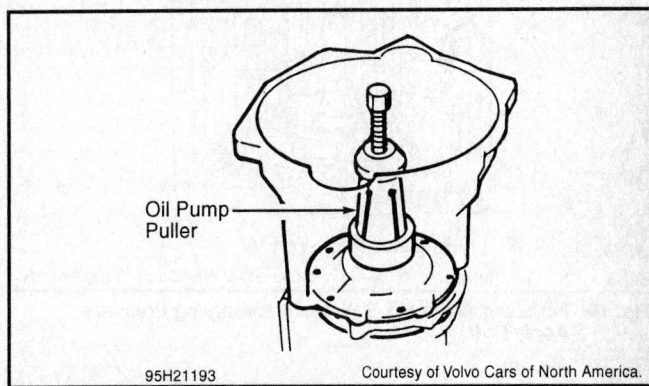

95H21193   Courtesy of Volvo Cars of North America.

Fig. 8: Removing Oil Pump Assembly

11) Remove front clutch assembly with thrust bearing and thrust bearing race from transmission case. Remove thrust bearing and thrust bearing races from front of rear clutch assembly. Remove rear clutch assembly from transmission case.

12) Remove center support assembly bolts from transmission case. *See Fig. 7.* Remove center support assembly from transmission case.

13) From inside transmission case, remove snap ring that retains planetary gear and output shaft in transmission case. Remove planetary gear and output shaft with brake No. 3 clutch discs and clutch plates. Remove brake No. 3 sleeve.

14) Remove thrust bearing and thrust bearing race for output shaft from inside of transmission case. Using Spring Compressor (5073), compress return springs on brake No. 3 piston. *See Fig. 9.* Remove retaining ring from inside of transmission case.

15) Remove spring compressor. Remove return spring retainer and return springs from brake No. 3 piston assembly. Apply air pressure to pressure apply port "A" at rear of transmission case to remove brake No. 3 piston assembly from transmission case. See Fig. 10.

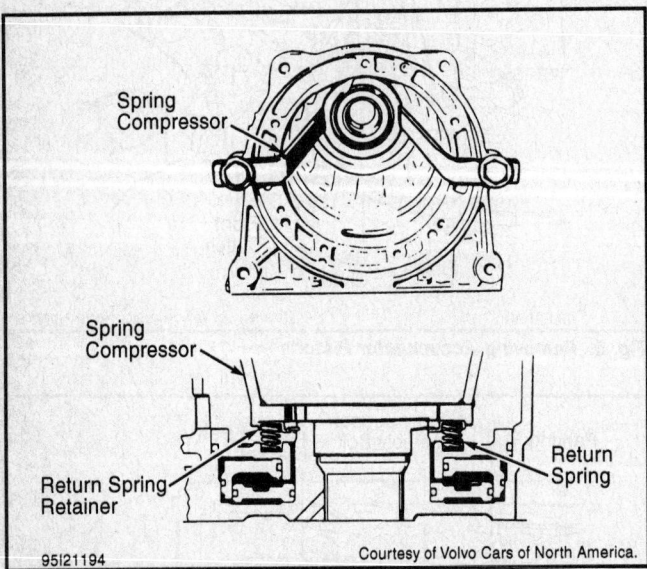

Fig. 9: Compressing Return Springs On Brake No. 3 Piston Assembly

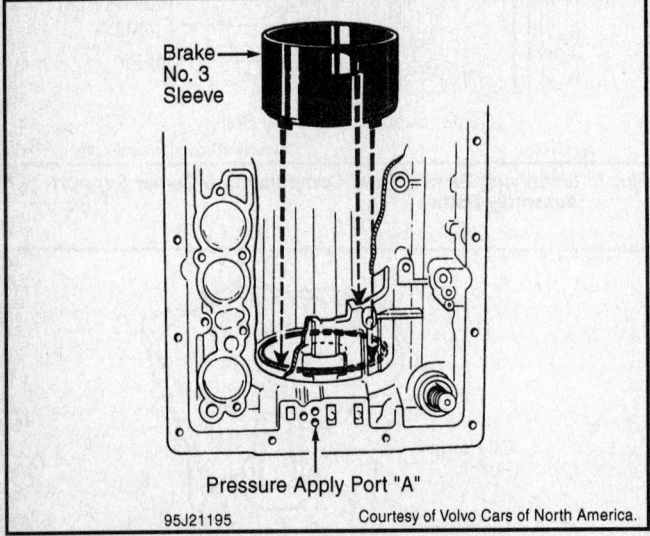

Fig. 10: Installing Brake No. 3 Sleeve & Identifying Pressure Apply Port

COMPONENT DISASSEMBLY & REASSEMBLY

OIL PUMP ASSEMBLY

Disassembly – 1) Remove seal rings from reaction shaft support. Remove "O" ring from oil pump body. Remove reaction shaft support-to-oil pump body bolts. Remove reaction shaft support from oil pump body. See Fig. 11.

2) Use felt pin, place reference mark on pump drive and driven gears for reassembly reference to ensure gears are installed in original direction. Remove pump drive and driven gears from oil pump body. Remove oil seal from oil pump body.

Cleaning & Inspection – 1) Clean components with solvent and dry with compressed air. DO NOT wash reference marks off of drive and driven gears. Inspect components for damage or signs of wear. Replace components as required.

2) Install pump drive and driven gears in oil pump body. Push pump driven gear toward one side of oil pump body. Using feeler gauge, measure pump driven gear-to-oil pump body clearance on outside of pump driven gear. Replace components if clearance is not within specification.

3) Using feeler gauge, measure pump gear tip clearance between tip of tooth on pump drive and driven gears and crescent-shaped part of oil pump body. Replace components if clearance is not within specification.

4) Place straightedge on oil pump body, above both pump gears. Using feeler gauge, measure pump gear side clearance between each pump gear and the straightedge. Replace components if clearance is not within specification.

OIL PUMP SPECIFICATIONS

Application	In. (mm)
Pump Driven Gear-To-Oil Pump Body Clearance	.0028-.0059 (.070-.150)
Pump Gear Side Clearance	.0008-.0020 (.020-.050)
Pump Gear Tip Clearance	.0043-.0055 (.110-.140)

Reassembly – 1) Using oil seal installer, install NEW oil seal in oil pump body. Coat all components with Dexron-IIE ATF.

2) Install pump drive and driven gears in oil pump body. If installing original pump gears, ensure pump gears are installed in original positions using reference marks made during disassembly.

3) Install reaction shaft support on oil pump body with reaction shaft support-to-oil pump body bolts finger tight. Install Oil Pump Band (5077) on oil pump assembly. See Fig. 12.

4) With oil pump band tightened, tighten reaction shaft support-to-oil pump body bolts to specification. See TORQUE SPECIFICATIONS.

5) After tightening reaction shaft support-to-oil pump body bolts, ensure pump gears rotate freely. Remove oil pump band.

6) Install NEW "O" ring on outside circumference of oil pump body. Install NEW seal rings on reaction shaft support. Ensure ends of seal rings are fastened together and seal rings move freely in grooves. Coat "O" ring and seal rings with petroleum jelly.

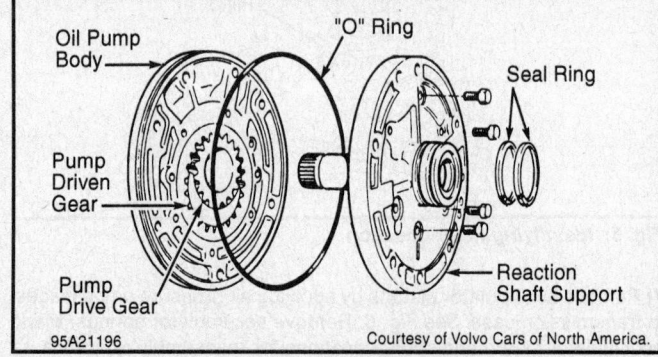

Fig. 11: Exploded View Of Oil Pump Assembly

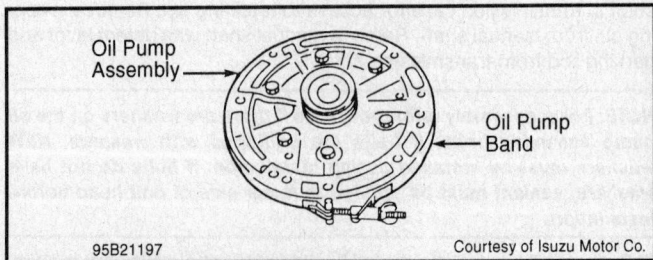

Fig. 12: Installing Oil Pump Band

INPUT SHAFT & OVERDRIVE CLUTCH ASSEMBLY

Disassembly – 1) Remove thrust washer from rear of planetary gear. *See Fig. 13.*

2) Remove thrust bearing race and thrust bearing from input shaft. Remove clutch assembly from input shaft and planetary gear.

3) Remove retaining ring and brake hub. Remove retaining ring, chamfered clutch plate, clutch disc and flat clutch plate for overdrive clutch from clutch drum.

4) Using spring compressor, compress return springs on clutch piston. Remove snap ring from center of clutch drum. Release and remove spring compressor. Remove spring retainer and return springs from clutch piston.

CAUTION: When removing clutch piston from clutch drum, DO NOT apply excessive air pressure on oil passage on clutch drum when removing clutch piston.

5) Apply light air pressure on oil passage at center of clutch drum to remove clutch piston from clutch drum. *See Fig. 13.* It may be necessary to block other oil passage at center of clutch drum for clutch piston removal. Remove "O" rings from clutch piston.

6) Remove retaining ring, pressure plate, one-way clutch assembly, thrust washer, thrust bearing and thrust bearing race from input shaft and planetary gear. *See Fig. 13.*

7) Remove retainers from one-way clutch assembly. Note direction of one-way clutch installation in one-way clutch outer race for reassembly reference.

NOTE: One-way clutch assembly may be referred to as overdrive one-way clutch assembly.

Cleaning & Inspection – 1) Clean metal components with solvent and dry with compressed air. Inspect components for damage or signs of wear. Replace components as required.

2) Shake clutch piston to ensure check ball movement exists. Check ball is located in clutch piston. Replace clutch piston if free movement of check ball cannot be obtained.

Reassembly – 1) Install NEW "O" rings on clutch piston. Lubricate all components with Dexron-IIE ATF. Install clutch piston in clutch drum, using care not to damage "O" rings.

2) Install return springs and spring retainer. Using spring compressor, compress return springs. Install snap ring. Remove spring compressor.

3) Install flat clutch plate (thin clutch plate), clutch disc, chamfered clutch plate (thick clutch plate) and retaining ring in clutch drum. Ensure chamfered area on tang of chamfered clutch plate is facing outward, away from clutch drum. *See Fig. 13.* Ensure ends of retaining ring are not positioned in recessed area on clutch drum.

4) Using feeler gauge, measure overdrive clutch clearance between chamfered clutch plate and retaining ring. Overdrive clutch clearance should be .012-.035" (.30-.90 mm).

5) Install brake hub and retaining ring in clutch drum. Ensure ends of retaining ring are not positioned in recessed area on clutch drum.

6) To check clutch piston operation, apply light air pressure on oil passage at center of clutch drum while blocking remaining oil passage at center of clutch drum. Operating sound should be heard and clutch piston should move when air pressure is applied. Install oil passage plugs in planetary gear.

CAUTION: Thrust washer must be installed in planetary gear with oil groove on thrust washer facing toward shaft end of planetary gear.

7) Install thrust bearing, thrust bearing race and thrust washer in planetary gear. Ensure thrust washer is installed with oil groove on thrust washer facing toward shaft end of planetary gear.

CAUTION: One-way clutch must be installed in planetary gear with collar area on one-way clutch toward shaft end of overdrive planetary gear. See Fig. 13.

8) Install one-way clutch in one-way clutch outer race. Install retainers on one-way clutch assembly. Install one-way clutch with one-way clutch outer race in overdrive planetary gear. Ensure one-way clutch is installed in proper direction with collar area on one-way clutch toward shaft end of planetary gear. *See Fig. 13.*

9) Install pressure plate and snap ring. Install clutch assembly on planetary gear. To check one-way clutch operation, hold clutch drum and rotate input shaft clockwise. *See Fig. 14.* Input shaft should rotate clockwise and lock when rotated counterclockwise. Install thrust washer on rear of planetary gear. Install thrust bearing race and thrust bearing on input shaft.

1. Clutch Drum
2. Flat Clutch Plate
3. Clutch Disc
4. Retaining Ring
5. Brake Hub
6. Pressure Plate
7. One-Way Clutch Assembly
8. Thrust Washer
9. Thrust Bearing
10. Thrust Bearing Race
11. Input Shaft & Planetary Gear
12. Oil Passage Plug
13. Retainer
14. One-Way Clutch
15. One-Way Clutch Outer Race
16. Chamfered Clutch Plate
17. Oil Passage Located Here
18. Chamfered Area
19. Collar Area

95C21198

Courtesy of Volvo Cars of North America.

Fig. 13: Exploded View Of Typical Input Shaft & Overdrive Clutch Assembly

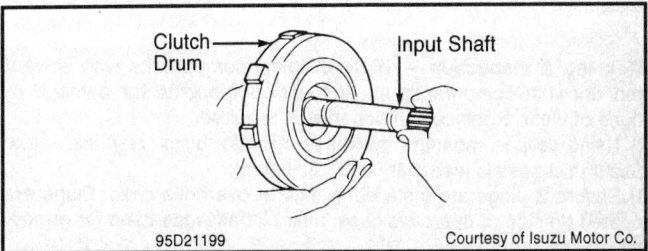

95D21199

Courtesy of Isuzu Motor Co.

Fig. 14: Checking One-Way Clutch Operation

OVERDRIVE CASE & OVERDRIVE BRAKE ASSEMBLY

Disassembly – 1) Remove retaining ring, pressure plate, brake discs and brake plates. *See Fig. 15.* Note direction of spring plate installation for reassembly reference. Remove spring plate.

2) Remove thrust washer, ring gear, thrust bearing races and thrust bearing from front of overdrive case. *See Fig. 15.*

CAUTION: When removing brake piston from overdrive case, DO NOT apply excessive air pressure on oil passage on overdrive case.

---

3) Compress return springs. Remove snap ring that retains spring retainer. Remove spring retainer and return springs. Apply air pressure on oil passage on rear of overdrive case to remove brake piston. *See Fig. 16.*

4) Remove "O" rings from brake piston. Remove seal rings from rear of overdrive case. If replacing needle bearing at center of overdrive case, tap needle bearing from overdrive case.

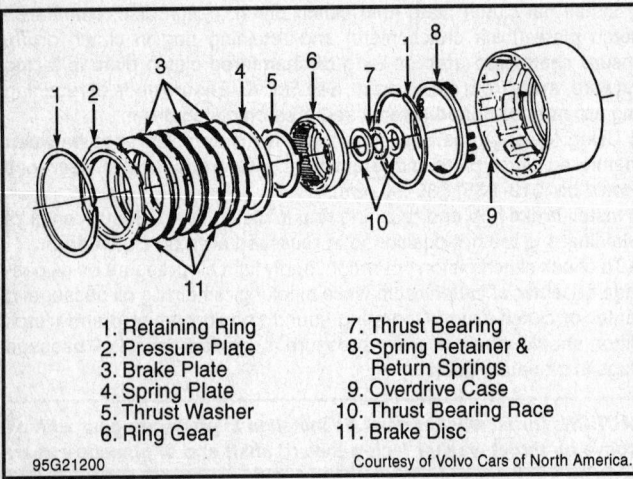

1. Retaining Ring	7. Thrust Bearing
2. Pressure Plate	8. Spring Retainer &
3. Brake Plate	Return Springs
4. Spring Plate	9. Overdrive Case
5. Thrust Washer	10. Thrust Bearing Race
6. Ring Gear	11. Brake Disc

95G21200   Courtesy of Volvo Cars of North America.

Fig. 15: Exploded View Of Overdrive Case & Overdrive Brake Assembly

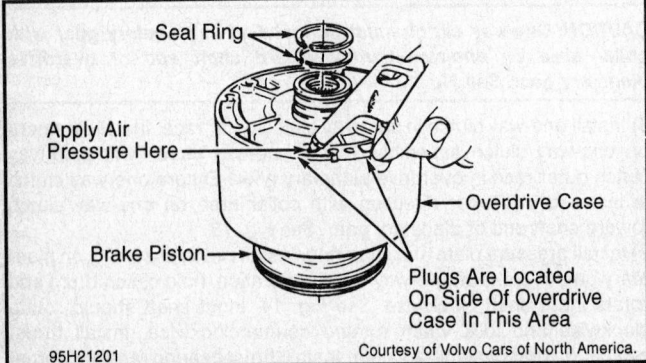

95H21201   Courtesy of Volvo Cars of North America.

Fig. 16: Removing Brake Piston Or Checking Brake Operation & Identifying Plug Locations

Cleaning & Inspection – 1) Clean metal components with solvent and dry with compressed air. Inspect components for damage or signs of wear. Replace components as required.

2) Using caliper, measure thickness of brake discs. Replace brake disc if thickness is less than .083" (2.10 mm).

3) Ensure 2 plugs are installed in side of overdrive case. Plugs are located on side of overdrive case, near oil passages used for removing brake piston. *See Fig. 16.*

Reassembly – 1) Install NEW "O" rings on brake piston. Lubricate all components with Dexron-IIE ATF.

2) If replacing needle bearing at center of overdrive case, press NEW needle bearing into overdrive case. Install NEW seal rings on rear of overdrive case. Ensure ends of seal rings are hooked together and seal rings move freely in groove on overdrive case.

3) Install brake piston in overdrive case, using care not to damage "O" rings. Install return springs and spring retainer.

4) Compress return springs. Install retaining ring to retain spring retainer. Ensure retaining ring is properly seated in overdrive case and ends of retaining ring are not in recessed area on overdrive case.

5) Install thrust bearing race, thrust bearing and thrust bearing race on inside of ring gear. When installing inner thrust bearing race on ring gear, ensure flat side of thrust bearing race is against ring gear. When installing outer thrust bearing race on thrust bearing, ensure flat side of thrust bearing race is against thrust bearing.

6) Install ring gear in overdrive case. Install thrust washer at center of ring gear. Ensure thrust washer fully seats in ring gear.

CAUTION: Spring plate must be installed in overdrive case with large dished side on spring plate facing upward, toward the brake plate.

---

7) Install spring plate in overdrive case with large dished side on spring plate facing upward, toward the brake plate. Install brake plates, brake discs, pressure plate and retaining ring. Ensure components are installed in correct sequence. *See Fig. 15.*

8) Ensure retaining ring is properly seated in overdrive case and ends of retaining ring are not in recessed area on overdrive case. Overdrive brake clearance must be checked.

9) Using feeler gauge, measure overdrive brake clearance between retaining ring and pressure plate. Overdrive brake clearance should be .014-.063" (.35-1.60 mm).

10) To check overdrive brake operation, apply air pressure on oil passage on rear of overdrive case and check for movement of brake piston. *See Fig. 16.* If brake piston movement does not exists, check for damaged "O" rings on brake piston.

FRONT CLUTCH ASSEMBLY

Disassembly – 1) Remove thrust bearing race and thrust bearing from shaft on clutch housing. Remove retaining ring, rear clutch hub and front clutch hub from clutch housing. *See Fig. 17.*

2) Remove thrust bearing races and thrust bearing from inside of clutch housing. Remove clutch disc and retaining ring from clutch housing.

3) Remove clutch discs and clutch plates from clutch housing. Note direction of component installation for reassembly reference.

4) Using spring compressor, compress return springs. Remove retaining ring from center of clutch housing. Remove spring compressor. Remove spring retainer and return springs.

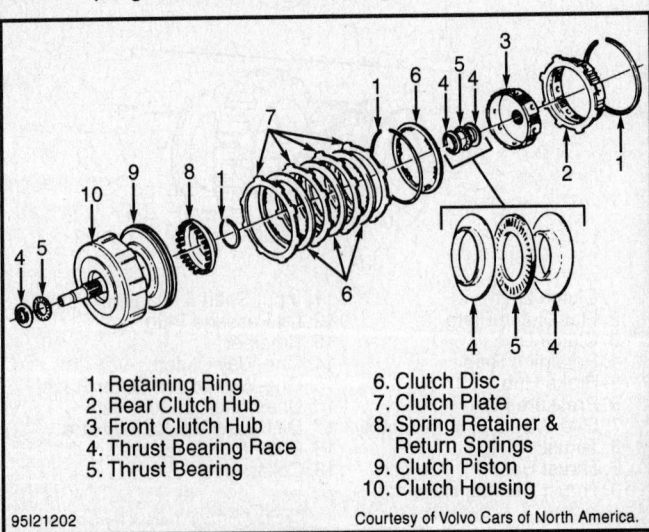

1. Retaining Ring	6. Clutch Disc
2. Rear Clutch Hub	7. Clutch Plate
3. Front Clutch Hub	8. Spring Retainer &
4. Thrust Bearing Race	Return Springs
5. Thrust Bearing	9. Clutch Piston
	10. Clutch Housing

95I21202   Courtesy of Volvo Cars of North America.

Fig. 17: Exploded View Of Front Clutch Assembly

CAUTION: *When removing clutch piston from clutch housing, DO NOT apply excessive air pressure to oil passage on clutch housing.*

5) Note location of oil passages at center of clutch housing, near shaft end of clutch housing. Some models may have 2 oil passages or 4 oil passages.

6) Place fingers over 2 oil passages on 4 oil passage applications or over one oil passage on 2 oil passage applications. Apply air pressure to remaining oil passage(s) to remove clutch piston from clutch housing. Remove "O" rings from clutch piston.

Cleaning & Inspection – 1) Clean metal components with solvent and dry with compressed air. Inspect components for damage or signs of wear. Replace components as required.

2) Using caliper, measure thickness of clutch discs. Replace clutch disc if thickness is less than .083" (2.10 mm).

3) Shake clutch piston to ensure check ball movement exists. Check ball is located in clutch piston. Replace clutch piston if free movement of check ball cannot be obtained.

Reassembly – 1) Install NEW "O" rings on clutch piston. Lubricate all components with Dexron-IIE ATF.

2) Install clutch piston in clutch housing using care not to damage "O" rings. Install return springs and spring retainer.

3) Using spring compressor, compress return springs. Install retaining ring at center of clutch housing. Remove spring compressor. Ensure retaining ring is properly seated in clutch housing.

4) Apply air pressure to oil passages on clutch housing and check for movement of clutch piston. Operating sound should be heard and clutch piston should move when air pressure is applied.

5) Install clutch plates, clutch discs and retaining ring in clutch housing. Ensure components are installed in correct sequence. See Fig. 17. Install remaining clutch disc in clutch housing.

6) Install thrust bearing races and thrust bearing in clutch housing. Ensure thrust bearing races are installed with shoulder facing toward clutch housing.

7) Install front clutch hub, rear clutch hub and retaining ring in clutch housing. Install thrust bearing and thrust bearing race on shaft of clutch housing. Ensure shoulder on thrust bearing race is facing outward, away from thrust bearing and flat side on thrust bearing race is against thrust bearing.

REAR CLUTCH ASSEMBLY

Disassembly – 1) Remove retaining ring, pressure plate, clutch discs and clutch plates from clutch drum. See Fig. 18. Note direction of component installation for reassembly reference.

2) Using spring compressor, compress return springs. Remove retaining ring from center of clutch drum. Remove spring compressor. Remove spring retainer and return springs.

CAUTION: *When removing clutch piston from clutch drum, DO NOT apply excessive air pressure on oil passage on clutch drum.*

3) Note location of oil passages located on rear side of clutch drum at shaft opening area on clutch drum. Apply air pressure on oil passage on clutch drum to remove clutch piston from clutch drum. Remove "O" rings from clutch piston.

NOTE: *Clutch piston is a one-piece design.*

Cleaning & Inspection – 1) Clean metal components with solvent and dry with compressed air. Inspect components for damage or signs of wear. Replace components as required.

2) Using caliper, measure thickness of clutch discs. Replace clutch disc if thickness is less than .091" (2.30 mm).

3) Shake clutch piston to ensure check ball moves. Check ball is located in clutch piston. Replace clutch piston if free movement of check ball cannot be obtained.

Reassembly – 1) Install NEW "O" rings on clutch piston. Lubricate all components with Dexron-IIE ATF.

2) Install clutch piston in clutch drum, using care to damage "O" rings. Install return springs and spring retainer.

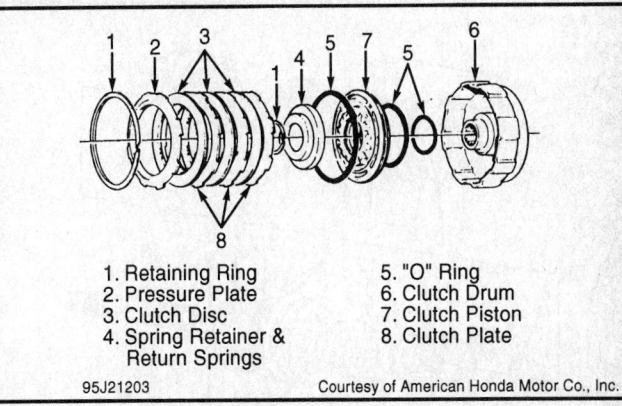

1. Retaining Ring	5. "O" Ring
2. Pressure Plate	6. Clutch Drum
3. Clutch Disc	7. Clutch Piston
4. Spring Retainer &	8. Clutch Plate
Return Springs	

95J21203   Courtesy of American Honda Motor Co., Inc.

Fig. 18: Exploded View Of Rear Clutch Assembly

3) Using spring compressor, compress return springs. Install retaining ring at center of clutch drum. Remove spring compressor. Ensure retaining ring is properly seated in clutch drum.

4) Install clutch plates and clutch discs in clutch drum. Ensure components are installed in correct sequence. See Fig. 18.

NOTE: *Some models may have a pressure plate that is flat and does not have a chamfered side. If pressure plate has a chamfered side, ensure pressure plate is installed so chamfered side is facing upward, toward retaining ring.*

5) Install pressure plate in clutch drum with chamfered side (if equipped) of pressure plate facing upward, toward retaining ring. Install retaining ring. Ensure ends of retaining ring are not positioned in recessed area on clutch drum.

6) Using feeler gauge, measure rear clutch clearance between pressure plate and retaining ring. Rear clutch clerance should be .012-.047" (.30-1.20 mm).

CENTER SUPPORT ASSEMBLY

Disassembly – 1) Remove retaining ring, sun gear shaft with one-way clutch assembly and brake hub from center support assembly. See Fig. 19. Remove brake hub with one-way clutch assembly from sun gear shaft if necessary.

NOTE: *One-way clutch assembly may be referred to as one-way clutch F1 assembly.*

2) Remove retaining ring for brake No. 1 from front of center support assembly. Note direction of pressure plate installation for reassembly reference. Remove pressure plate, brake disc and brake plate for brake No. 1 from front of center support assembly.

3) Remove retaining ring for brake No. 2 from rear of center support assembly. Note direction of pressure plate installation for reassembly reference. Remove pressure plate, brake discs and brake plates for brake No. 2 from rear of center support assembly.

4) Using spring compressor, compress return springs on brake piston for brake No. 1 on front of center support assembly. Remove retaining ring from center of center support assembly. Remove spring compressor. Remove spring retainer and return springs from brake piston.

5) Using spring compressor, compress return springs on brake piston for brake No. 2 on rear of center support assembly. Remove retaining ring from center of center support assembly. Remove spring compressor. Remove spring retainer and return springs from brake piston.

CAUTION: *When removing brake piston from center support, DO NOT apply excessive air pressure on oil passage on center support assembly.*

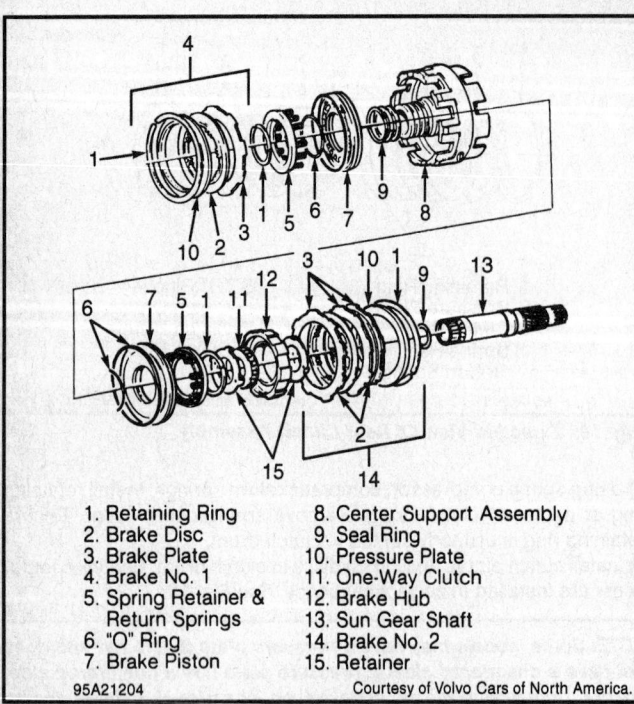

1. Retaining Ring
2. Brake Disc
3. Brake Plate
4. Brake No. 1
5. Spring Retainer & Return Springs
6. "O" Ring
7. Brake Piston
8. Center Support Assembly
9. Seal Ring
10. Pressure Plate
11. One-Way Clutch
12. Brake Hub
13. Sun Gear Shaft
14. Brake No. 2
15. Retainer

95A21204   Courtesy of Volvo Cars of North America.

Fig. 19: Exploded View Of Center Support Assembly

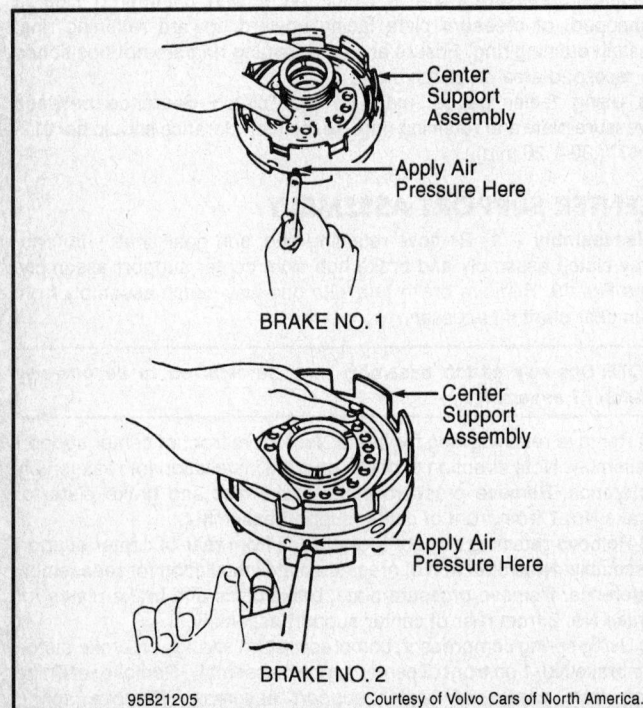

Center Support Assembly

Apply Air Pressure Here

BRAKE NO. 1

Center Support Assembly

Apply Air Pressure Here

BRAKE NO. 2

95B21205   Courtesy of Volvo Cars of North America.

Fig. 20: Removing Brake Pistons Or Checking Brake Piston Operation

6) Apply air pressure to oil passage on center support assembly to remove appropriate brake piston from center support assembly. See Fig. 20. Remove "O" rings from brake pistons. Remove "O" ring and seal rings from center support assembly. Remove seal rings from sun gear shaft.

Cleaning & Inspection – 1) Clean metal components with solvent and dry with compressed air. Inspect components for damage or signs of wear. Replace components as required.

2) Using caliper, measure thickness of brake discs. Replace brake disc if thickness is less than .083" (2.10 mm).

3) Install brake hub with one-way clutch assembly on sun gear shaft if removed. Ensure brake hub is installed with one-way clutch facing the correct direction. See Fig. 19.

4) Hold brake hub with your left hand so one-way clutch is on your left side. Using your right hand, rotate sun gear shaft. Sun gear shaft should rotate freely counterclockwise (toward you) and lock when rotated clockwise (away from you). Ensure no grinding in one-way clutch exists. Replace one-way clutch if defective.

Reassembly – 1) Lubricate all components with Dexron-IIE ATF. Install NEW seal rings on sun gear shaft and center support assembly. Ensure ends of seal rings are hooked together and seal rings move freely in groove.

2) Install NEW "O" rings on brake pistons and center support assembly. Install brake pistons in center support assembly, using care not to damage "O" rings. Install spring retainer and return springs on brake piston for brake No. 1.

3) Using spring compressor, compress return springs on brake piston for brake No. 1. Install retaining ring at center of center support assembly. Remove spring compressor. Ensure retaining ring is properly seated in center support assembly.

4) Install spring retainer and return springs on brake piston for brake No. 2. Using spring compressor, compress return springs on brake piston for brake No. 2. Install retaining ring at center of center support assembly. Remove spring compressor. Ensure retaining ring is properly seated in center support assembly.

CAUTION: When checking brake piston operation, DO NOT apply more than 14 psi (.98 kg/cm²) air pressure on oil passage on center support assembly or brake piston may be dislocated.

5) Apply 14 psi (.98 kg/cm²) air pressure to oil passage on center support assembly to check operation of appropriate brake piston. See Fig. 20. Operating sound should be heard and brake piston should move when air pressure is applied.

NOTE: Some models may have a pressure plate for brake No. 1 or No. 2 that is flat and does not have a chamfered side. If pressure plate has a chamfered side, ensure pressure plate is installed so chamfered side is facing upward, toward retaining ring.

6) Install brake plate (thin plate), brake disc and pressure plate for brake No. 1 in front of center support assembly. If pressure plate has a chamfered side, ensure chamfered side is facing upward, toward retaining ring. Install retaining ring. Ensure ends of retaining ring are not positioned in open area on center support assembly.

7) Install brake plate (thin plate), brake discs, brake plates and pressure plate for brake No. 2 in rear of center support assembly. If pressure plate has a chamfered side, ensure chamfered side is facing upward, toward retaining ring. Install retaining ring. Ensure ends of retaining ring are not positioned in open area on center support assembly.

8) Using feeler gauge, measure brake clearance between pressure plate and retaining ring on both brake No. 1 and brake No. 2. Brake No. 1 and brake No. 2 clerance should be .012-.047" (.30-1.20 mm).

9) Install sun gear shaft with one-way clutch assembly and brake hub in center support assembly. Ensure splines on brake hub align with all brake discs. Install retaining ring on end of sun gear shaft.

REAR PLANETARY GEAR & OUTPUT SHAFT

Disassembly – 1) Remove reaction plate, brake discs, brake plates, pressure plate, one-way clutch assembly and front planetary gear from intermediate shaft. See Fig. 21.

2) Remove thrust washer from rear of front planetary gear. Note sequence and number of brake discs and brake plates for reassembly reference. Remove brake discs and brake plates from front planetary gear.

3) Remove front planetary gear from reaction plate. For servicing of one-way clutch assembly and front planetary gear, see FRONT PLANETARY GEAR & ONE-WAY CLUTCH ASSEMBLY under COMPONENT DISASSEMBLY & REASSEMBLY.

4) Compress retaining ring and lift front ring gear from rear ring gear. Lift intermediate shaft with rear ring gear from output shaft. Remove rear planetary gear, thrust bearing race and thrust bearing from output shaft.

5) Remove rear planetary gear, thrust bearing race and thrust bearing from rear ring gear. Remove retaining ring from end of intermediate shaft. Remove rear ring gear, thrust bearing race and thrust bearing from intermediate shaft. Remove seal rings from output shaft and intermediate shaft.

Cleaning & Inspection – **1)** Clean metal components with solvent and dry with compressed air. Inspect components for damage or signs of wear. Replace components as required. Ensure oil passages in intermediate shaft and output shaft are not restricted.

2) Using caliper, measure thickness of brake discs discs. Replace brake disc if thickness is less than .091" (2.30 mm).

Reassembly – **1)** Lubricate all components with Dexron-IIE ATF. Install front planetary gear on reaction plate.

2) To check one-way clutch assembly operation, hold reaction plate. Front planetary gear should rotate freely counterclockwise and lock when rotated clockwise. *See Fig. 22.* If operation is not as specified, check for improperly installed one-way clutch assembly.

3) Install brake discs and brake plates on reaction plate, starting with brake disc and alternating with brake plate. Ensure original number of components are installed. Install pressure plate.

4) Install NEW seal rings on output shaft. Ensure ends of seal rings are fastened together and seal rings move freely in groove on output shaft. Install thrust bearing race on intermediate shaft. Ensure flat side of thrust bearing race is facing toward rear ring gear.

5) Install rear ring gear on intermediate shaft. Install retaining ring on end of intermediate shaft. Install thrust bearing and thrust bearing race on intermediate shaft at inside of rear ring gear. Ensure flat side of thrust bearing race is against thrust bearing.

6) Install rear planetary gear in rear ring gear. Install thrust bearing and thrust bearing race on output shaft. Ensure thrust bearing race is installed with flat side toward rear ring gear. *See Fig. 21.*

7) Install intermediate shaft with rear ring gear on output shaft. Install front ring gear on rear ring gear. Ensure end of retaining ring on front ring gear aligns with opening between teeth on output shaft.

8) Compress retaining ring until front ring gear fully seats on rear ring gear. Release retaining ring. Ensure retaining ring is fully seated.

9) Install thrust washer on front of rear planetary gear. Ensure tabs on thrust washer engage with slots on rear planetary gear. Install thrust washer on rear of front planetary gear. Ensure tabs on thrust washer engage with slots on front planetary gear.

10) Install front planetary gear with brake components on rear planetary gear. Ensure thrust washers remain in position and front planetary gear fully engages front ring gear.

FRONT PLANETARY GEAR & ONE-WAY CLUTCH ASSEMBLY

Disassembly – Remove retaining ring and outer retainer from front planetary gear. *See Fig. 23.* Note direction of one-way clutch assembly installation in front planetary gear for reassembly reference. Remove one-way clutch assembly, inner retainer and thrust washer from front planetary gear.

Cleaning & Inspection – Clean components with solvent and dry with compressed air. Inspect components for damage or signs of wear. Replace components as required.

Reassembly – **1)** Lubricate all components with Dexron-IIE ATF. Install thrust washer in front planetary gear. Ensure tabs on thrust washer engage with grooves in front planetary gear.

CAUTION: One-way clutch assembly must be installed in front planetary gear with arrow on one-way clutch assembly facing toward front planetary gear. See Fig. 23.

---

2) Install inner retainer and one-way clutch assembly in front planetary gear. Ensure arrow on one-way clutch assembly is facing toward front planetary gear. *See Fig. 23.* This positions flange area on one-way clutch facing upward.

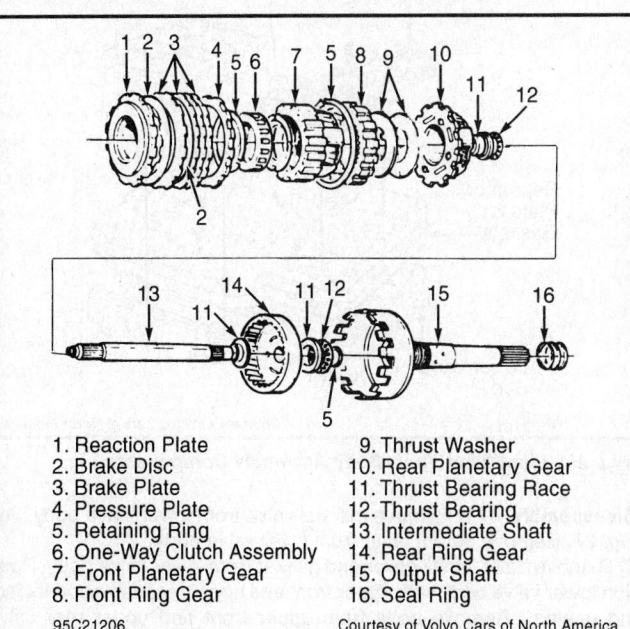

1. Reaction Plate	9. Thrust Washer
2. Brake Disc	10. Rear Planetary Gear
3. Brake Plate	11. Thrust Bearing Race
4. Pressure Plate	12. Thrust Bearing
5. Retaining Ring	13. Intermediate Shaft
6. One-Way Clutch Assembly	14. Rear Ring Gear
7. Front Planetary Gear	15. Output Shaft
8. Front Ring Gear	16. Seal Ring

95C21206 — Courtesy of Volvo Cars of North America.

Fig. 21: Exploded View Of Rear Planetary Gear & Output Shaft

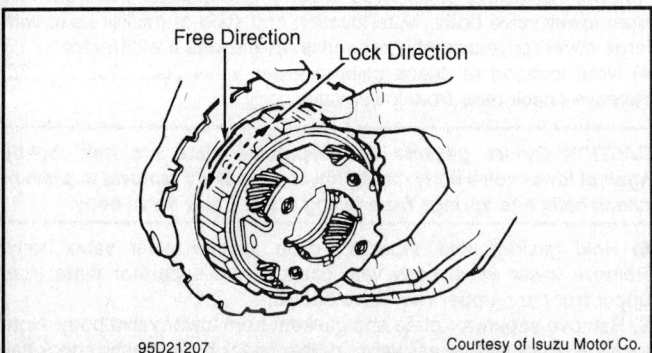

95D21207 — Courtesy of Isuzu Motor Co.

Fig. 22: Checking One-Way Clutch Assembly Operation

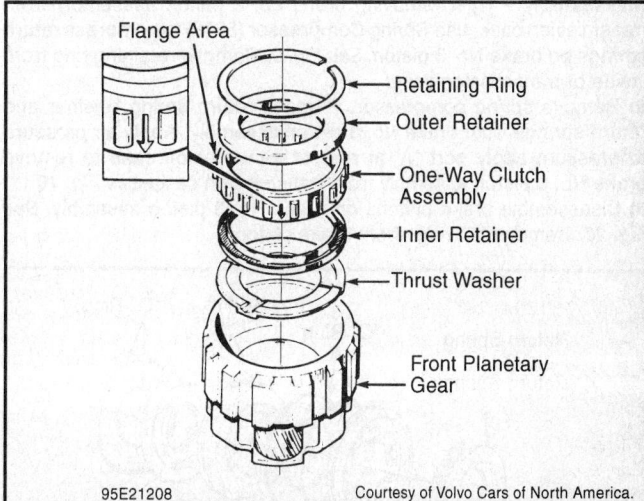

95E21208 — Courtesy of Volvo Cars of North America.

Fig. 23: Exploded View Of Front Planetary Gear & One-Way Clutch Assembly

3) Install outer retainer and retaining ring. To check one-way clutch assembly operation, install front planetary gear with one-way clutch assembly on reaction plate. Hold reaction plate.

4) Front planetary gear should rotate freely counterclockwise and lock when rotated clockwise. *See Fig. 22.* If operation is not as specified, check for improperly installed one-way clutch assembly.

CAUTION: Ensure front planetary gear rotates freely counterclockwise and locks when rotated clockwise if one-way clutch assembly is properly installed.

GOVERNOR ASSEMBLY

Disassembly – Remove ring and components from governor body. *See Fig. 24.*

Cleaning & Inspection – Clean components with solvent and dry with compressed air. Inspect components for damage. Replace components as required.

Reassembly – Lubricate all components with Dexron-IIE ATF. To reassemble, reverse disassembly procedure. Ensure retaining clip is fully seated on valve stem and governor valve moves smoothly.

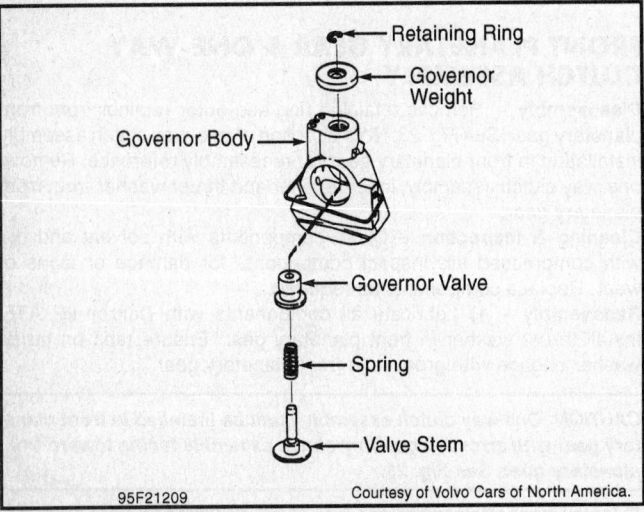

95F21209   Courtesy of Volvo Cars of North America.

Fig. 24: Exploded View Of Governor Assembly

BRAKE NO. 3 PISTON ASSEMBLY

Disassembly – **1)** If removing brake no. 3 piston assssembly from transmission case, use Spring Compressor (5073) to compress return springs on brake No. 3 piston. *See Fig. 9.* Remove retaining ring from inside of transmission case.

2) Remove spring compressor. Remove return spring retainer and return springs from brake No. 3 piston assembly. Apply air pressure to pressure apply port "A" at rear of transmission case to remove brake No. 3 piston assembly from transmission case. *See Fig. 10.*

3) Disassemble brake pistons on brake No. 3 piston assembly. *See Fig. 25.* Remove "O" rings from brake pistons.

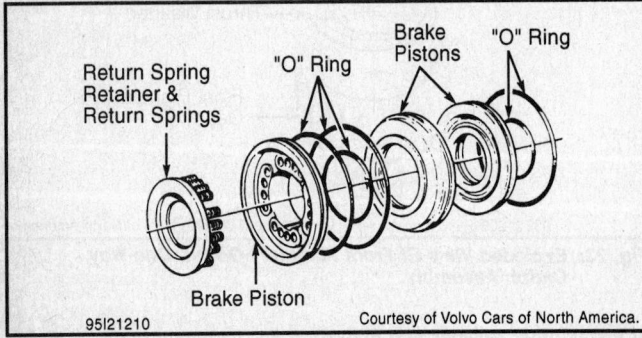

95I21210   Courtesy of Volvo Cars of North America.

Fig. 25: Exploded View Of Brake No. 3 Assembly

Cleaning & Inspection – Clean components with solvent and dry with compressed air. Inspect components for damage. Replace components as required.

Reassembly – **1)** Lubricate all components with Dexron-IIE ATF. Install NEW "O" rings on brake pistons. Assemble brake pistons for brake No. 3 piston assembly.

2) If installing brake No. 3 piston assembly in transmission case, install brake No. 3 piston assembly, using care not to damage "O" rings. Install return spring retainer and return springs on brake No. 3 piston assembly.

3) Using spring compressor, compress return springs on brake No. 3 piston assembly. Install retaining ring in transmission case. Ensure retaining ring is fully seated. Remove spring compressor.

VALVE BODY ASSEMBLY

NOTE: Valve body assembly consists of upper front valve body, upper rear valve body and lower valve body. See Fig. 26.

CAUTION: When disassembling valve bodies, place components in order and mark spring locations for reassembly reference. DO NOT use force to remove components from valve body. Note location of check ball for reassembly befor removing, as check ball locations may vary.

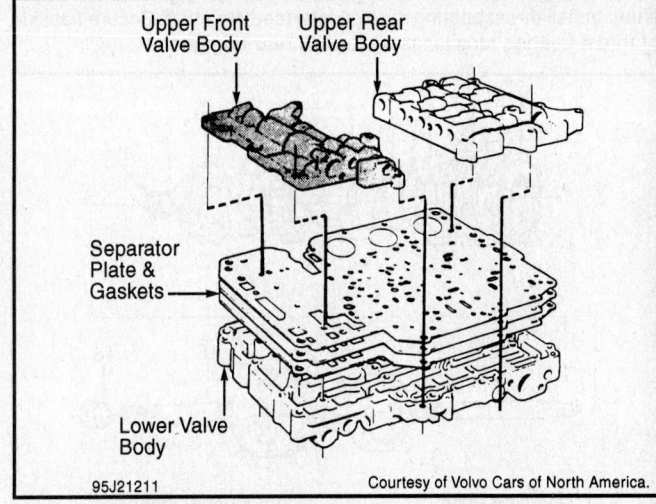

95J21211   Courtesy of Volvo Cars of North America.

Fig. 26: Identifying Valve Body Assembly Components

Disassembly – **1)** Remove manual valve from lower valve body. *See Fig. 27.* Remove detent lever from lover valve body.

2) Remove bolts, small cover and gasket from lower valve body. Position lower valve body with upper front and upper rear valve bodies facing upward. Remove bolts from upper front and upper rear valve bodies.

3) Turn lower valve body over so lower valve body is facing upward. Remove remaining bolts, large cover with separator plate gaskets from lower valve body. Note location and style of gasket used with large cover for reassembly reference, as gaskets are different.

4) Note location of check balls in lower valve body. *See Fig. 28.* Remove check balls from lower valve body.

CAUTION: Ensure gaskets and separator plate are held tightly against lower valve body during lower valve body removal to prevent check balls and springs from falling out of lower valve body.

---

5) Hold gaskets and separator plate against lower valve body. Remove lower valve body with gaskets and separator plate from upper front and upper rear valve bodies.

6) Remove separator plate and gaskets from lower valve body. Note location of cooler by-pass valve, rubber check balls, plastic check ball and springs in lower valve body. *See Fig. 28.*

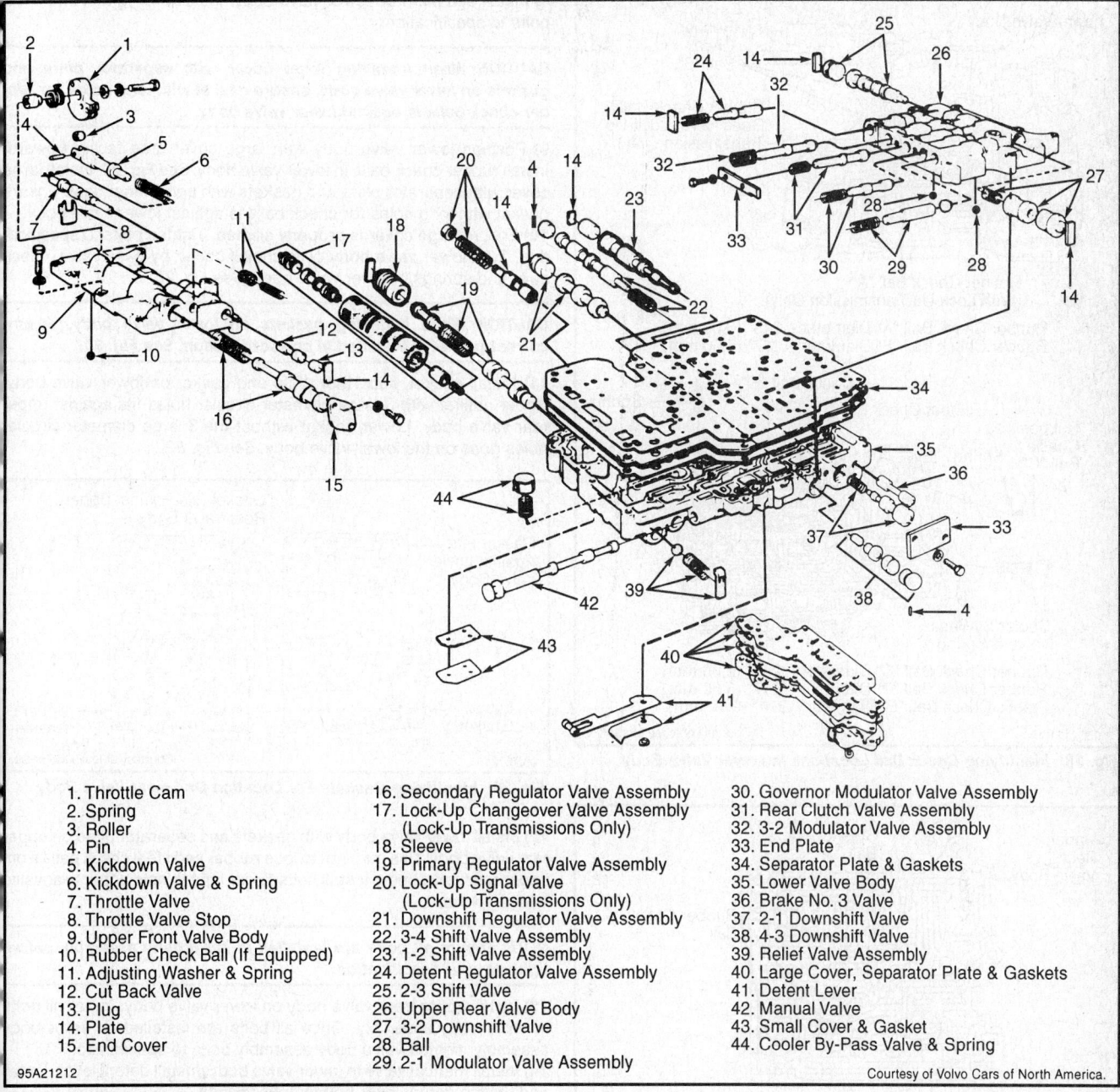

Fig. 27: Exploded View Of Valve Body Assembly

1. Throttle Cam
2. Spring
3. Roller
4. Pin
5. Kickdown Valve
6. Kickdown Valve & Spring
7. Throttle Valve
8. Throttle Valve Stop
9. Upper Front Valve Body
10. Rubber Check Ball (If Equipped)
11. Adjusting Washer & Spring
12. Cut Back Valve
13. Plug
14. Plate
15. End Cover

16. Secondary Regulator Valve Assembly
17. Lock-Up Changeover Valve Assembly (Lock-Up Transmissions Only)
18. Sleeve
19. Primary Regulator Valve Assembly
20. Lock-Up Signal Valve (Lock-Up Transmissions Only)
21. Downshift Regulator Valve Assembly
22. 3-4 Shift Valve Assembly
23. 1-2 Shift Valve Assembly
24. Detent Regulator Valve Assembly
25. 2-3 Shift Valve
26. Upper Rear Valve Body
27. 3-2 Downshift Valve
28. Ball
29. 2-1 Modulator Valve Assembly

30. Governor Modulator Valve Assembly
31. Rear Clutch Valve Assembly
32. 3-2 Modulator Valve Assembly
33. End Plate
34. Separator Plate & Gaskets
35. Lower Valve Body
36. Brake No. 3 Valve
37. 2-1 Downshift Valve
38. 4-3 Downshift Valve
39. Relief Valve Assembly
40. Large Cover, Separator Plate & Gaskets
41. Detent Lever
42. Manual Valve
43. Small Cover & Gasket
44. Cooler By-Pass Valve & Spring

95A21212

Courtesy of Volvo Cars of North America.

7) Remove cooler by-pass valve, check balls and springs from lower valve body. Remove components from lower valve body. *See Fig. 27.* Use care when removing end cover, pins and rollers, as components are under spring tension.

8) Note location of check ball in upper front valve body on nonlock-up transmissions. *See Fig. 29.* Remove components from upper front and upper rear valve body assemblies. *See Fig. 27.* Use care when removing end plates, end cover and plates, as components are under spring tension.

Cleaning & Inspection – Clean components with solvent and dry with compressed air. Inspect components for damage or signs of wear. Replace components as required. Ensure valves slide freely in bores on valve body.

Reassembly – 1) Lubricate all components with Dexron-IIE ATF before reassembly. Install all components in upper rear valve body. Ensure components are installed in correct location. *See Fig. 27.*

2) Install end plate on upper rear valve body. Install and tighten end plate bolts to specification. See TORQUE SPECIFICATIONS. Install rubber and steel check balls in rear upper valve body assembly. *See Fig. 29.*

3) Install all components in upper front valve body. Ensure components are installed in correct location. *See Fig. 27.* Ensure original number of adjusting washers on upper front valve body.

4) Install end cover on upper front valve body. Install and tighten end cover bolts to specification.

5) Install spring and throttle cam. Ensure spring is hooked on upper valve body and throttle cam. Install and tighten throttle cam bolt to specification. Ensure throttle cam operates smoothly.

6) Install throttle valve plate and check ball (non-lockup transmissions) in upper front valve body. Ensure throttle valve plate and check ball are installed in correct location. *See Fig. 29.*

7) Install all components in lower valve body. Ensure components are installed in correct location. *See Fig. 27.*

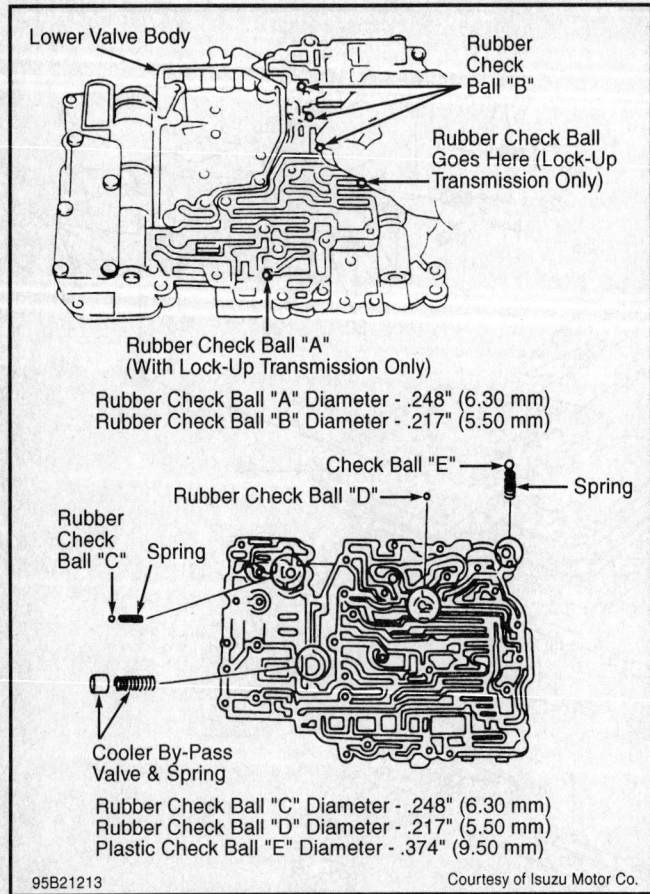

Rubber Check Ball "A" Diameter - .248" (6.30 mm)
Rubber Check Ball "B" Diameter - .217" (5.50 mm)

Rubber Check Ball "C" Diameter - .248" (6.30 mm)
Rubber Check Ball "D" Diameter - .217" (5.50 mm)
Plastic Check Ball "E" Diameter - .374" (9.50 mm)

95B21213   Courtesy of Isuzu Motor Co.

Fig. 28: Identifying Check Ball Locations In Lower Valve Body

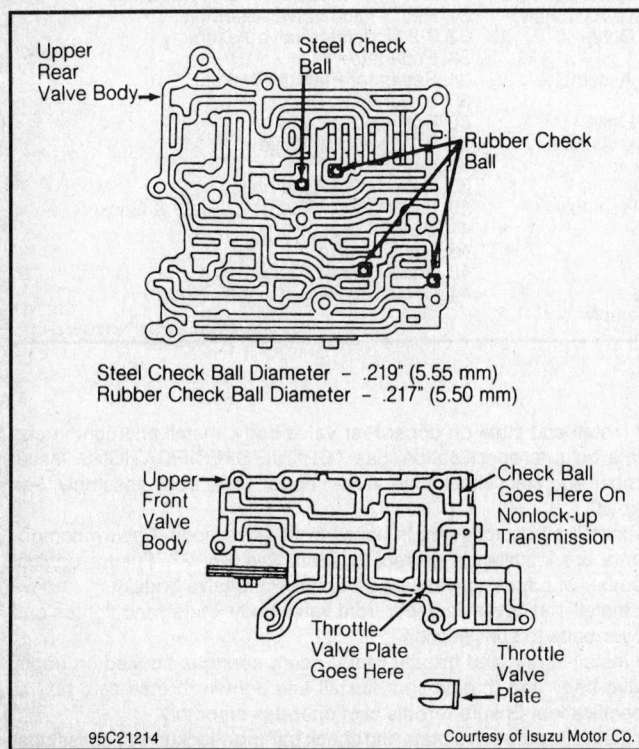

Steel Check Ball Diameter - .219" (5.55 mm)
Rubber Check Ball Diameter - .217" (5.50 mm)

95C21214   Courtesy of Isuzu Motor Co.

Fig. 29: Identifying Check Ball Locations In Upper Valve Bodies & Throttle Valve Plate Location

8) Install end plate on lower valve body. Install and tighten end plate bolts to specification.

CAUTION: When installing large cover with separator plate and gaskets on lower valve body, ensure gasket with long holes for rubber check balls is against lower valve body.

9) Position lower valve body with large cover area facing upward. Install rubber check balls in lower valve body. *See Fig. 28.* Install large cover with seperator plate and gaskets with bolts finger tight. Ensure gasket with long holes for check balls is against lower valve body.
10) Ensure large cover is properly aligned. Tighten bolts to specification. Turn lower valve body over. Install cooler by-pass valve, check balls and springs in lower valve body. *See Fig. 28.*

CAUTION: When installing gaskets on lower valve body, ensure correct gasket is installed in correct location. See Fig. 30.

11) Install gasket, separator plate and gasket on lower valve body. Upper gasket with 3 large diameter circular holes fits against upper rear valve body. Lower gasket without the 3 large diameter circular holes goes on the lower valve body. *See Fig. 30.*

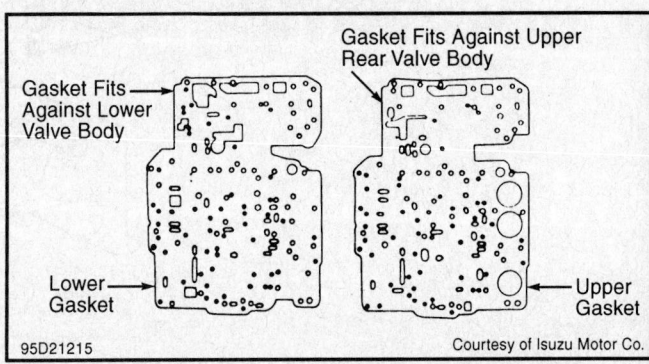

95D21215   Courtesy of Isuzu Motor Co.

Fig. 30: Identifying Gaskets For Location On Lower Valve Body

12) Install lower valve body with gaskets and separator plate on upper rear valve body. Use care not to lose rubber and steel check balls from upper rear valve body. Install bolts finger tight to hold upper rear valve body in place.

NOTE: Ensure all bolts are installed in valve body assembly before tightening to specification.

13) Install upper front valve body on lower valve body. Install all bolts in valve body assembly. Once all bolts are installed on valve body assembly, tighten valve body assembly bolts to specification.
14) Install manual valve in lower valve body. Install detent lever. Install and tighten detent lever bolt to specification.

TRANSMISSION REASSEMBLY

VALVE BODY ASSEMBLY & INTERNAL COMPONENTS

NOTE: Lubricate all components with Dexron-IIE ATF before reassembly. Clutch and brake discs should be soaked in Dexron-IIE ATF before reassembly. Coat all thrust bearings, thrust bearing races and thrust washers with petroleum jelly before installing.

1) Install brake No. 3 piston assembly in transmission case, using care not to damage "O" rings on piston assembly. Install return spring retainer and return springs on brake No. 3 piston assembly.
2) Using spring compressor, compress return springs on brake No. 3 piston. *See Fig. 9.* Install retaining ring on inside of transmission case. Ensure retaining ring is fully seated.

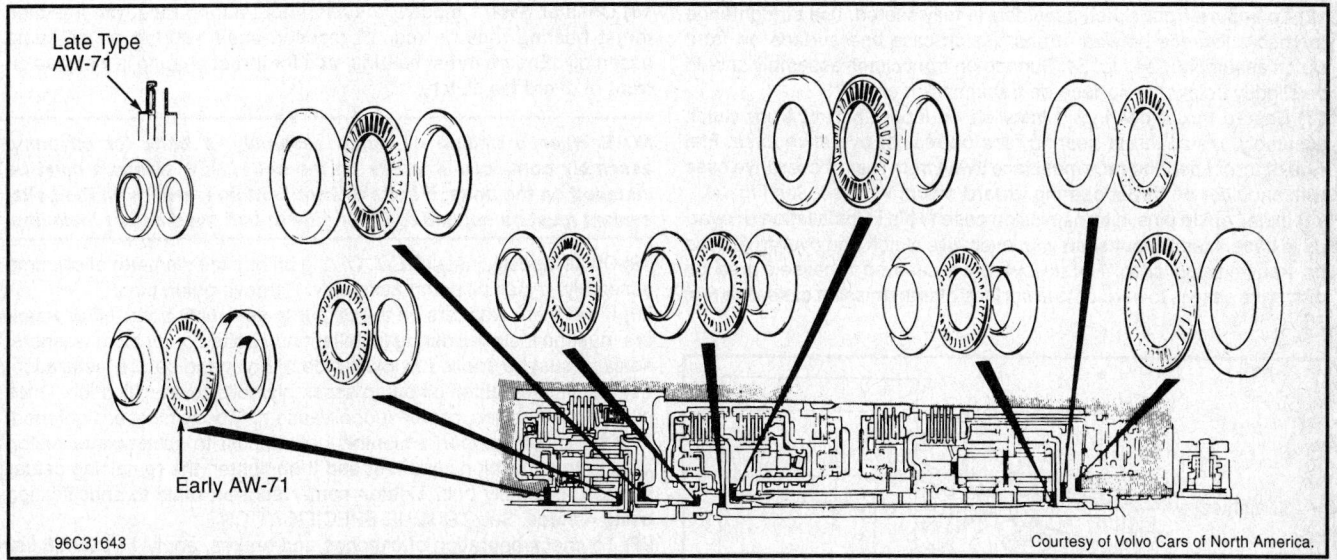

Fig. 31: Positioning Thrust Bearings & Thrust Bearing Races

3) Install thrust bearing race and thrust bearing for output shaft in rear of transmission case. Flat side of thrust bearing race must face upward, toward front of transmission. *See Fig. 31.*

4) Install brake No. 3 sleeve in transmission case. Ensure flanage on brake No. 3 sleeve fully engages with brake No. 3 piston assembly. *See Fig. 10.* Ensure opening in brake No. 3 sleeve is properly aligned for installation of parking pawl components.

5) Install planetary gear and output shaft with brake No. 3 clutch discs and clutch plates in transmission case. Ensure recessed area at edge of reaction plates is toward oil pan surface of transmission case. *See Fig. 32.*

6) Install snap ring that retains planetary gear and output shaft in transmission case. Ensure ends of snap ring are located at recessed area at edge of reaction plate.

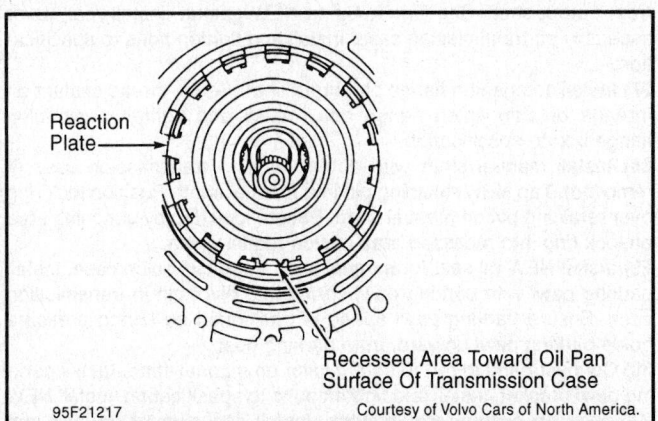

Fig. 32: Identifying Recessed Area On Reaction Plate & Positioning Reaction Plate

---

CAUTION: When checking brake No. 3 piston assembly operation, DO NOT apply more than 14 psi (.98 kg/cm²) air pressure on brake No. 3 pressure apply port.

---

7) To check operation of brake No. 3 piston assembly, apply 14 psi (.98 kg/cm²) air pressure to brake No. 3 pressure apply port at rear of transmission case. *See Fig. 33.* Operating sound should be heard with movement of brake No. 3 piston assembly when air pressure is applied. If no piston movement exists, check for damaged components on brake No. 3 piston assembly.

8) Install center support assembly in transmission case. When installing center support assembly, hold sun gear shaft to prevent brake hub from slipping out of position. Loosely install center support assembly bolts in transmission case. *See Fig. 7.* DO NOT tighten center support assembly bolts at this time.

9) Align splines on brake discs in center support assembly. Install rear clutch assembly in transmission case. When rear clutch assembly is fully seated, splines at center of rear clutch should be even or slightly below surface on end of sun gear shaft.

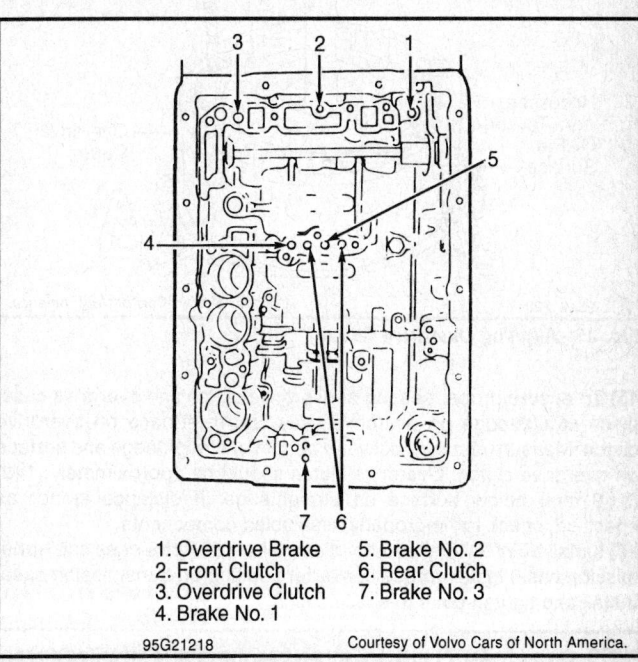

1. Overdrive Brake   5. Brake No. 2
2. Front Clutch   6. Rear Clutch
3. Overdrive Clutch   7. Brake No. 3
4. Brake No. 1

Fig. 33: Identifying Pressure Apply Ports

10) Install thrust bearing races and thrust bearing on front of rear clutch assembly. Ensure thrust bearing races and thrust bearing are installed in proper direction. *See Fig. 31.*

11) Align splines on clutch discs in rear clutch assembly. Install front clutch assembly on rear clutch assembly. When installing front clutch assembly on rear clutch assembly, it may be neceesary to lock clutch discs in rear clutch assembly by applying 14 psi (.98 kg/cm²) air pressure to rear clutch pressure apply port on transmission case. *See Fig. 33.*

12) To ensure front clutch assembly is fully seated, use straightedge to check distance between transmission case and surface on front clutch assembly. *See Fig. 34.* Surface on front clutch assembly should be slightly below the surface on transmission case.

13) Ensure thrust bearing is installed on input shaft at front clutch assembly. Install thrust bearing race on rear of overdrive case. Flat side of thrust bearing race must face away from rear of overdrive case with shoulder on thrust bearing toward overdrive case. *See Fig. 31.*

14) Install guide pins in transmission case to aid in installation of overdrive case. Install input shaft with overdrive clutch and overdrive case on transmission case. Rotate overdrive case so recessed area on overdrive case is toward oil pan surface of transmission case. *See Fig. 35.*

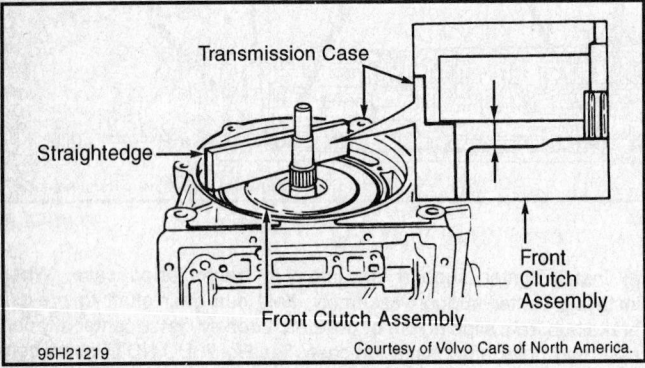

Fig. 34: Checking Front Clutch Installation

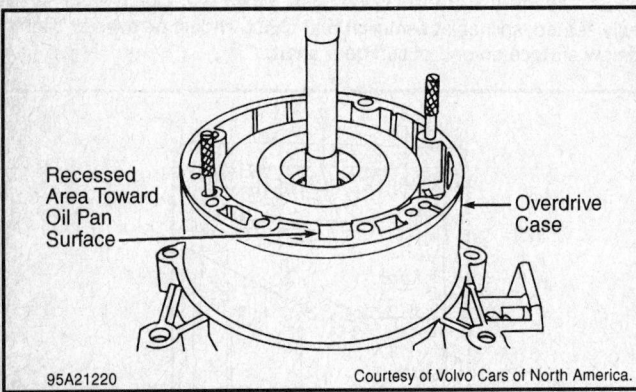

Fig. 35: Aligning Overdrive Case

15) To ensure proper seating of overdrive clutch and overdrive case, place straightedge on overdrive case, above surface on overdrive clutch. Measure distance between bottom of straightedge and surface on overdrive clutch. Overdrive clutch should be approximately .140" (3.50 mm) below surface on straightedge. If distance is not as specified, check for improperly assembled components.

16) Install NEW "O" ring at outer diameter of overdrive case and transmission case. Install torque converter housing on transmission case. Install and tighten bolts to specification.

NOTE: On early AW-71 models, thrust bearing race is installed on rear of reaction shaft support on oil pump assembly. Thrust bearing and remaining thrust bearing race is installed on front of overdrive clutch. On later AW-71 models, thrust bearing is attached to thrust bearing race and must be installed on rear of reaction shaft support on oil pump assembly. Remaining thrust bearing race for thrust bearing is installed on front of overdrive clutch. See Fig. 31.

17) On early AW-71 models, install thrust bearing race on rear of reaction shaft support on oil pump assembly. Ensure thrust bearing and remaining thrust bearing race are installed on front of overdrive clutch.

18) On later AW-71 models, install thrust bearing race with attached thrust bearing race on rear of reaction shaft support on oil pump assembly. Ensure thrust bearing race for thrust bearing is installed on front of overdrive clutch.

NOTE: When installing oil pump assembly, if bolts for oil pump assembly contained washers on the bolts, NEW washers must be installed on the bolts. If bolts did not contain washers on the bolts, sealant must be applied to lower side of bolt head before installing.

19) On all models, install NEW "O" ring on outside diameter of oil pump assembly. Install oil pump assembly. Remove guide pins.

20) If there are washers on the oil pump assembly bolts, NEW washers must be installed during installation. If bolts do not have washers, sealant must be applied to lower side of bolt head before installation.

21) Install and tighten oil pump assembly bolts to specification. Once oil pump is installed, center support assembly bolts must be tightened. Tighten center support assembly bolt closest to accumulator piston area in transmission case first and then tighten the remaining center support assembly bolt. Tighten center support bolts to specification using 4 steps. See TORQUE SPECIFICATIONS.

22) To check operation of clutches and brakes, apply 14 psi (.98 kg/cm²) air pressure to appropriate pressure apply port at rear of transmission case. *See Fig. 33.* Operating sound should be heard to indicate component operation when air pressure is applied. If operating sound is not heard, check for damaged on improperly assembly clutch or brake components.

23) Using dial indicator, check end play on input and output shafts. Input and output shaft end play should be .012-.035" (.30-.90 mm). Ensure input and output shafts rotate smoothly.

24) Install filter at rear of transmission case, near output shaft. *See Fig. 5.* Install gasket and filter cover plate. Install and tighten bolts to specification.

25) Install governor assembly on output shaft. Install and tighten governor assembly bolt to specification. Bend over tabs of bolt lock on governor assembly bolt. Using screwdriver, raise governor retaining ring located at governor assembly so retaining ring is seated against governor assembly.

26) Install spacer or speedometer drive gear with spacer as equipped from output shaft. *See Fig. 4.* Using NEW gasket, install rear cover assembly on transmission case. Install and tighten bolts to specification.

27) Install companion flange on output shaft. Apply thread sealant on threads of companion flange bolt. Install and tighten companion flange bolt to specification.

28) Install manual shaft with detent lever in transmission case (if removed). Tap NEW retaining pin into manual shaft. Position lock ring over retaining pin on manual shaft. Secure lock ring by punching area on lock ring into recessed area beside retaining pin.

29) Install NEW oil seal for manual shaft in transmission case. Install parking pawl with parking pawl spring and pivot pin in transmission case. Ensure parking pawl spring is positioned so spring pressure holds parking pawl upward, from parking gear.

30) Connect parking rod to detent lever on manual shaft. Install parking pawl bracket. Install and tighten bolts to specification. Install NEW "O" rings on accumulator pistons. Install accumulator springs and accumulator pistons in transmission case. Smallest accumulator piston fits in the (center) rear clutch accumulator.

31) Install kickdown cable in transmission case. Install kickdown cable on throttle cam on valve body assembly. Align manual valve on valve body assembly with detent lever in transmission case. Install valve body assembly on transmission case.

32) Install proper length valve body assembly-to-transmission case bolts in specified area. *See Fig. 3.* Tighten valve body assembly-to-transmission case bolts to specification.

33) Install NEW gasket and oil strainer. Install and tighten oil strainer bolts to specification. Install oil pipes. Install magnets in oil pan. Ensure magnets are positioned so they do not interfere with the oil pipes.

34) Using NEW gasket, install oil pan. Install and tighten oil pan bolts to specification. Install and tighten drain plug to specification.

35) Install torque converter. To ensure torque converter is fully seated, place straightedge across front of torque converter housing. Measure distance from surface on torque converter housing to surface on torque converter bolt mounting lug. Distance should be .64-.77" (16.2-19.6 mm). If distance is not as specified, check for improperly seated torque converter.

TORQUE SPECIFICATIONS

TORQUE SPECIFICATIONS

Application	Ft. Lbs. (N.m)
Center Support Assembly Bolt [1]	
Step 1	[2]
Step 2	[3]
Step 3	15 (20)
Step 4	19 (26)
Companion Flange Bolt	33 (45)
Drain Plug	17 (23)
Oil Pump Assembly Bolt	16 (22)
Rear Cover Assembly Bolt	26 (35)
Torque Converter Housing Bolt	
10-mm Bolt	26 (35)
12-mm Bolt	44 (60)
	INCH Lbs. (N.m)
Detent Lever Bolt	53 (6.0)
End Cover Bolt	53 (6.0)
End Plate Bolt	53 (6.0)
Filter Cover Plate Bolt	71 (8.0)
Governor Assembly Bolt	35 (4.0)
Large Cover Bolt	53 (6.0)
Oil Pan Bolt	44 (5.0)
Oil Strainer Bolt	44 (5.0)
Parking Pawl Bracket Bolt	62 (7.0)
Reaction Shaft Support-To-Oil	
Pump Body Bolt	71 (8.0)
Throttle Cam Bolt	71 (8.0)
Valve Body Assembly Bolt	53 (6.0)
Valve Body Assembly-To-Transmission Case Bolt	89 (10.0)

[1] – Tighten center support assembly bolt closest to accumulator piston area in transmission case first and then tighten the remaining center support assembly bolt.
[2] – Tighten bolt to 62 INCH lbs. (7.0 N.m).
[3] – Tighten bolt to 124 INCH lbs. (14.0 N.m).

TRANSMISSION SPECIFICATIONS

TRANSMISSION SPECIFICATIONS

Application	In. (mm)
Clutch & Brake Clearances	
Brake No. 1 Clearance	.012-.047 (.30-1.20)
Brake No. 2 Clearance	.012-.047 (.30-1.20)
Overdrive Brake Clearance	.014-.063 (.35-1.60)
Overdrive Clutch Clearance	.012-.035 (.30-.90)
Rear Clutch Clearance	.012-.047 (.30-1.20)
Input Shaft End Play	.012-.035 (.30-.90)
Oil Pump Assembly Clearances	
Gear Tip Clearance	.0043-.0055 (.110-.140)
Pump Driven Gear-To-Oil Pump	
Body Clearance	.0028-.0059 (.070-.150)
Pump Gear Side Clearance	.0008-.0020 (.020-.050)
Pump Gear Tip Clearance	.0043-.0055 (.110-.140)
Output Shaft End Play	.012-.035 (.30-.90)

WIRING DIAGRAMS

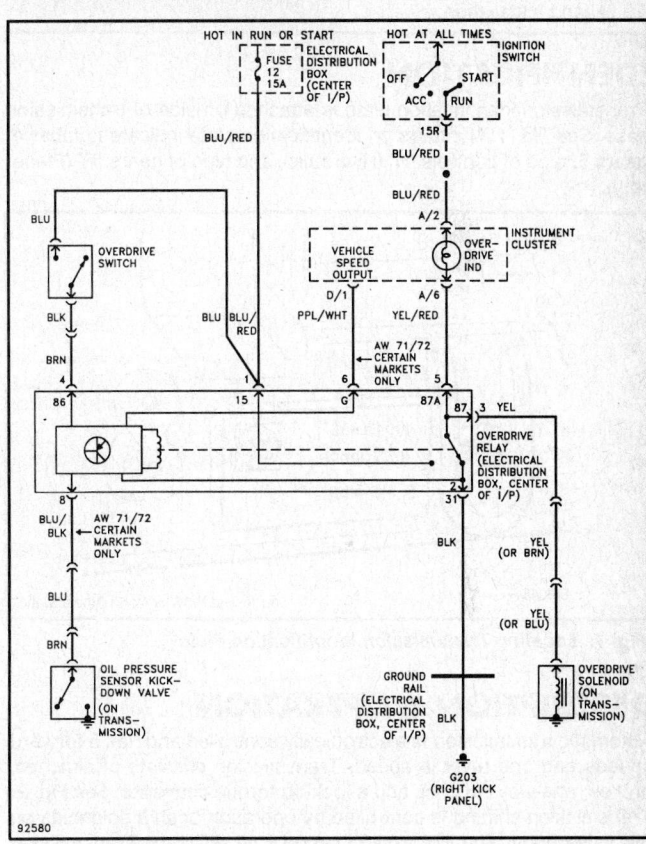

Fig. 36: 1995 940 & 940 Turbo Transmission Wiring Diagram (AW-71)

AUTOMATIC TRANSMISSIONS
ZF 5HP18 & ZF 5HP30

BMW: M3, 5-Series, 7-Series, 8-Series

APPLICATION & LABOR TIMES

APPLICATION & LABOR TIMES

Vehicle Application	Labor Times [1] R & I	[2] Overhaul	Trans. Model
1995			
M3	7.2	8.0	ZF 5HP18
530i & 530iT	6.5	8.0	ZF 5HP18
540i	6.0	8.0	ZF 5HP18
740i	5.7	8.0	ZF 5HP30
840Ci	7.0	8.0	ZF 5HP30
1996			
740i	5.7	8.0	ZF 5HP30
840Ci	7.0	8.0	ZF 5HP30

[1] – Removal and installation of transmission from vehicle chassis.
[2] – Bench overhaul time for transmission. DOES NOT include removal and installation.

IDENTIFICATION

Transmission identification plate is attached on side of transmission case. *See Fig. 1.* Numbers on identification plate indicate number of gears 5, type of controls "H" (Hydraulic), and type of gears "P" (Planetary).

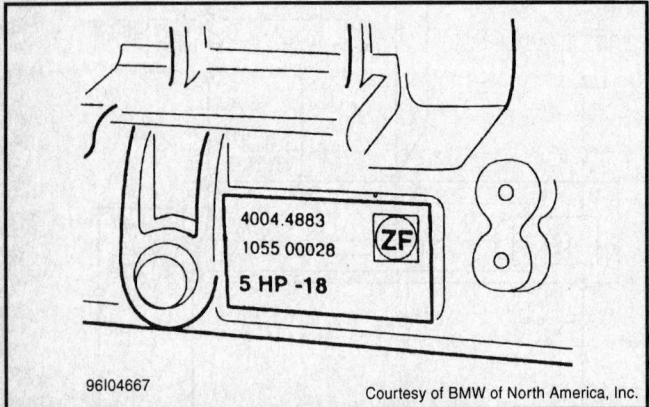

Fig. 1: Locating Transmission Identification Plate

DESCRIPTION & OPERATION

Automatic transmission is electronically controlled and has 5 forward speeds and one reverse speed. Transmission consists of clutches, brakes, one-way clutches and a lock-up torque converter. *See Fig. 2.* Transmission shifting is controlled by operation of shift solenoids on the valve body. The Electronic Control Unit (ECU) or Transmission Control Unit (TCU) controls shift solenoid operation by information supplied by various inputs. Transmissions are equipped with various shift modes. See SHIFT MODES under DESCRIPTION & OPERATION.

SHIFT MODES

1) Transmission is equipped with 2 different shift modes, Manual ("M") mode and Economy ("A") mode. Economy ("A") mode may be used to provide maximum fuel efficiency. When in Economy mode, torque converter lock-up will activate.
2) Manual ("M") mode is for single gear driving. When in Manual mode, transmission will remain in the selected gear. For example, if shift lever is in "D" range, transmission will remain in 3rd gear. Manual or Economy mode may be selected by using shift mode switch, located near shift lever on console.

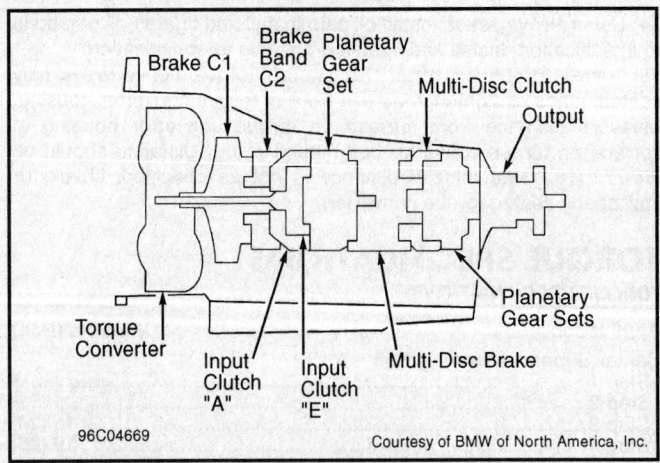

Fig. 2: Identifying Transmission Components
(5HP18 Is Shown; 5HP30 Is Similar)

LUBRICATION & ADJUSTMENTS

See appropriate AUTOMATIC TRANSMISSION SERVICING article in TRANSMISSION SERVICING section.

TROUBLE SHOOTING

NOTE: Following trouble shooting procedures apply to 5HP18 transmission. Trouble shooting procedures for 5HP30 transmission are not available.

Transmission malfunctions may be caused by poor engine performance, improper adjustments, or failure of hydraulic or mechanical components. Always begin by checking fluid level, fluid condition, linkage and cable adjustments. Perform road test to determine if problem has been corrected. If problem still exists, several tests must be performed on transmission. See TESTING.

SHIFT LEVER IN POSITION "P"

Park Will Not Engage Or Does Not Hold – Selector linkage between selector lever and transmission improperly adjusted. Excessive friction in parking lock mechanism. Defective parking pawl mechanism.
Engine Cannot Be Started In "P" – Transmission switch faulty.

SHIFT LEVER IN POSITION "R"

No Reverse Gear – Selector linkage between selector lever and transmission improperly adjusted. Defective clutch "B". Brake "D" defective; also no engine braking in 1st gear. Brake "G" defective. Signal wire to solenoid No. 3 grounded. Valve piston for reverse gear lock not in parked position.
Hard Engaging Jolt "P"-"R" Or "N"-"R" – Idle speed too high. Brake "G" defective. Modulation pressure too high. Open in pressure regulator circuit. Pressure regulator defective.
Back-Up Lights Do Not Come On (Electrical System Okay) – Transmission switch faulty.

SHIFT LEVER IN POSITION "N"

Car Moves Or Creeps – Selector linkage between selector lever and transmission improperly adjusted. Defective clutch "A".

SHIFT LEVER IN POSITION "D"

No Forward Gear Engagement – Defective damper "A". Signal wire to solenoid No. 5 grounded.
Hard Engaging Jolt "N"-"D" – Idle speed too high. Clutch "A" damper defective. Open in pressure regulator circuit. Pressure regulator defective. Modulation valve defective. Defective valve body.

No 1-2 Or 2-1 Shift (Warm Or Cold) – Brakes C1 and C2 defective. Insufficient oil supply to brakes C1 and C2. Open in output speed sensor circuit. Output speed sensor defective. Signal or other wiring to solenoid No. 1 grounded or open. Solenoid No. 1 defective. Shift valve No. 1 seized in parked or pushed position. Damper C2 or clutch valve C1 seized. Shift valve No. 3 seized in parked position.

No 2-3 Or 3-2 Shift – Clutch "F" defective. Insufficient oil supply to clutch "F". Signal wire to solenoid No. 2 defective. Solenoid No. 2 defective. Shift valve No. 2 seized in pushed position. Pulling valve 2-3 seized in parked position. Signal or positive wire to solenoid No. 2 defective. Shift valve seized in parked position. Pulling valve 2-3 seized in pushed position.

No 3-4 Or 4-3 Shift – Clutch "E" defective. Insufficient oil supply to clutch "E". Brake band C2 defective (shift 1-2 also not okay). Insufficient oil supply to brake C2. Signal or positive wire to solenoid No. 3 grounded. Solenoid No. 3 defective. Shift valve seized in pushed or parked position.

No 4-5 Or 5-4 Shift – Defective valve body. Clutch "A" defective. Signal or positive lead to solenoid valve No. 1 defective. Shift valve No. 4 seized in parked position. Damper C2 blocked. Solenoid No. 1 faulty. Shift valve No. 4 seized in pushed position.

Car Starts Off In 2nd Gear – Signal or positive wire to solenoid No. 1 defective. Shift valve No. 1 seized in parked position.

Car Starts Off In 3rd Gear – Signal or positive wire to solenoids No. 1 and 2 defective. Shift valves No. 1 and 2 seized in parked position.

Car Starts Off In 4th Gear – Open circuit in transmission voltage supply (transmission without current). Shift valves No. 1, 2, and 3 seized in parked position.

SHIFT POINTS

No-Load Shift Incorrect – Modulator valve defective. Wire to pressure regulator defective. Pressure regulator defective. Damper malfunction.

Full-Load Shift To Kickdown Too Long – Plates broken, Valve body defective. Pressure reducing valves No. 1 and 2 defective. Modulation valve function defective. Pressure regulator defective.

No Kickdown Shifts, Only Partial Load/Full Load Shifts – Open or short circuit in wiring. Kickdown switch defective. Kickdown switch misadjusted.

Shift Speed & Shift Quality Poor – Defective temperature sensor.

Engine "Flares" In Shift 2-1 – Poor friction torque at plates. First gear one way gear defective.

Engine "Flares" In Shift 2-3/3-2 – Poor friction torque at plates.

Engine "Flares" In Shift 4-3 – Poor friction torque at plates. Third gear one way gear defective.

Engine "Flares" In Shift 4-5/5-4 – Poor friction torque at plates.

Engine Dies From Shift 2-3/3-2 (Overlapped Condition) – Signal or positive lead to solenoid valve No. 4 defective. Solenoid No. 4 defective. Pull/push valve No. 1 moves too hard. Aperture for damper "G" clogged. Damper "F" moves too hard. Pull valve 2-3/3-2 moves too hard.

Engine Dies From Shift 4-5/5-4 (Overlapped Condition) – Signal or positive lead to solenoid valve No. 5 defective. Solenoid No. 5 defective. Pull/push valve No. 2 moves too hard. Damper C2 defective. Pull valve 4-5/5-4 moves too hard. Damper "A" moves too hard.

Wrong Shift Points Or Oscillating Shifts – Idle speed too high or low. Idle speed control valve defective.

No Engine Braking Effect/No Manual Downshift 5-4 – Clutch "A" damaged. Valve body defective.

No Engine Braking Effect/No Manual Downshift 4-3/3-2 – Valve body defective.

No First Gear/No Braking Action – Brake "D" defective. Valve body defective.

No Engagement In Forward Or Reverse – Driver pressed off impeller.

PROGRAM SWITCH

"A" Or "M" Program Always On Or Off – Open circuit in signal wire to program switch. Switch faulty.

SELECTOR LEVER POSITION SWITCH

Vehicle Remains In Shifted Gear – No voltage supply/fuse blown. Open circuit in signal wire. Switch defective.

TORQUE CONVERTER CLUTCH OPERATION

Torque Converter Lock-Up Clutch Engagement Too Hard – Defective converter clutch function. Torque converter defective.

No Converter Lock-Up Clutch – Defective torque converter. Signal or positive wire to solenoid No. 6 defective. Solenoid No. 6 defective.

Engine Dies When Stopping Car In Drive (Converter Lock-Up Clutch Always Engaged) – Signal wire to solenoid No. 6 grounded. Converter lock-up clutch valve seized in pushed position. Solenoid No. 6 defective.

NOISE FROM TRANSMISSION

Loud Oil Pump Intake Noise – Oil level too low. Valve body leaks. Oil strainer dirty. Round seal on oil filter missing or defective.

Noisy & No Gear Engagement After Long Trip – Oil filter screen dirty.

TRANSMISSION LEAKS

Oil Dripping From Converter Bellhousing – Round seal on oil pump body leaks. Round seal on pump body leaks. Radial oil seal for converter leaks.

Leak Between Transmission Case & Oil Sump – Mounting bolts loose. Gasket defective.

Output Leaks – Radial oil seal for output flange leaks. "O" ring for transmission extension leaks.

TESTING

HYDRAULIC PRESSURE TEST

Main Pressure – Connect Pressure Gauge (13 3 061) and Hose (24 0 021). Unscrew and remove plug from right side of transmission case. *See Fig. 3.* Install Adapter (24 0 022). Install pressure gauge and hose to adapter. Start and run engine at idle. Main pressure should be 78-92 psi (5.4-6.4 kg/cm²).

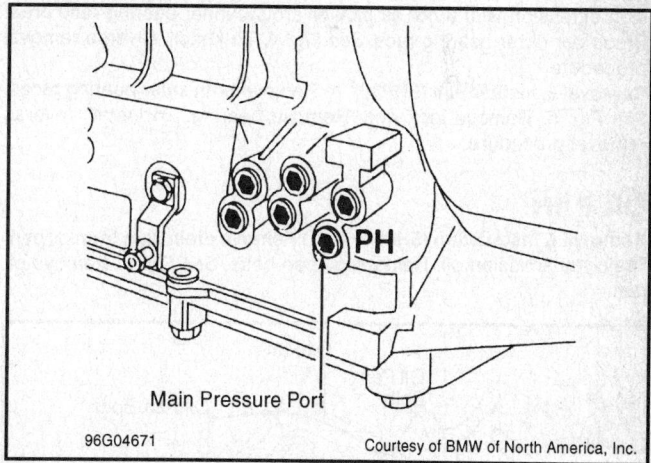

Main Pressure Port

96G04671   Courtesy of BMW of North America, Inc.

Fig. 3: Locating Pressure Test Port

REMOVAL & INSTALLATION

TRANSMISSION

See appropriate AUTOMATIC TRANSMISSION REMOVAL article in TRANSMISSION SERVICING section.

EXTENSION HOUSING BEARING

Removal & Installation (5HP18) – Remove output flange. See OUTPUT FLANGE SEAL. Remove lock ring and bearing. Heat transmis-

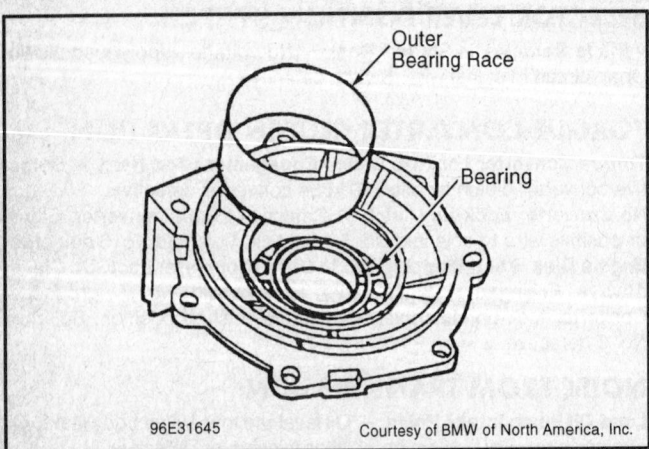

Fig. 4: Removing Outer Bearing Race (5HP18)

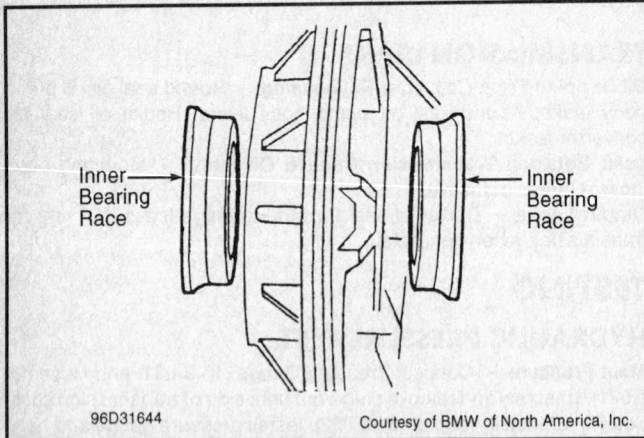

Fig. 5: Removing Inner Bearing Races (5HP30)

sion extension with a hot air blower around inner bearing race area. Press out outer bearing race. See Fig. 4. To install, reverse removal procedure.

Removal & Installation (5HP30) – Remove both inner bearing races. See Fig. 5. Remove lock ring. Remove bearing. To install, reverse removal procedure.

OIL PAN

Removal & Installation (5HP18) – **1)** Remove drain plug from oil pan. Drain transmission oil. Remove oil pan bolts. See Fig. 6. Remove oil pan.

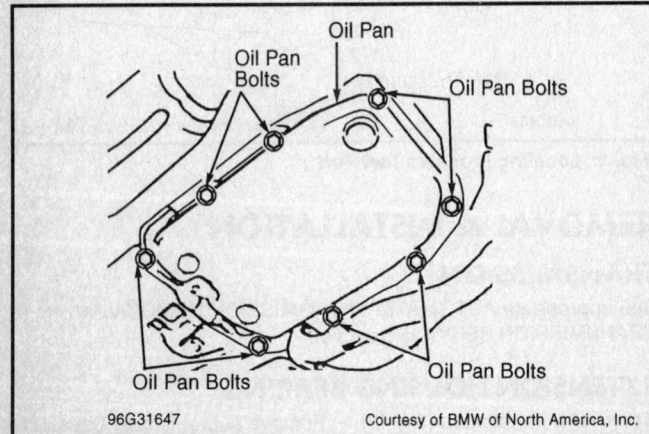

Fig. 6: Removing Oil Pan Bolts (5HP18)

2) To install, reverse removal procedure. Clean oil pan and magnetic washers. Install rounded bracket on edges of oil pan. Install new gasket. Tighten oil pan bolts to specification. See TORQUE SPECIFICATIONS.

Removal & Installation (5HP30) – **1)** Remove drain plug from oil pan. Drain transmission oil. Remove oil pan bolts. Lift expansion tank off oil pan. Remove clips and magnets.

2) To install, reverse removal procedure. Clean oil pan and magnets. Install magnets. See Fig. 7. Install new gasket. Tighten oil pan bolts to specification. See TORQUE SPECIFICATIONS.

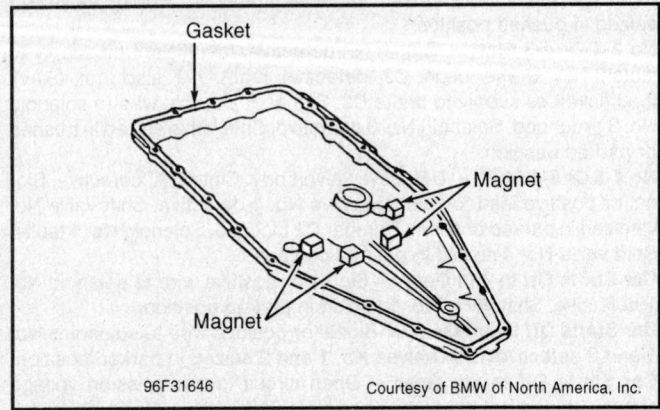

Fig. 7: Installing Magnets In Oil Pan (5HP30)

OIL PUMP

Removal – **1)** Remove transmission. See appropriate AUTOMATIC TRANSMISSION REMOVAL article in TRANSMISSION SERVICING section. Remove torque converter. See TORQUE CONVERTER. Set transmission upright. Mark oil pump mounting location for reassembly reference. Remove 9 oil pump-to-transmission housing bolts.

2) Install Extractor (24180) on converter support shaft. Turn spindle on extractor and press out oil pump. Lift out oil pump housing. Pry out oil seal. Remove "O" ring from around oil pump.

Installation – **1)** Lubricate sealing lip of oil seal with ATF. Firmly seat oil seal using Seal Installer (240110) and Supplementary Ring (240111). Install new "O" ring from around oil pump. Ensure thrust washer, needle bearing, and additional thrust washer are correctly installed before installing oil pump housing. See Fig. 8.

2) Coat "O" ring with ATF. Align marks made during removal. Install oil pump-to-transmission housing bolts with new sealing rings.

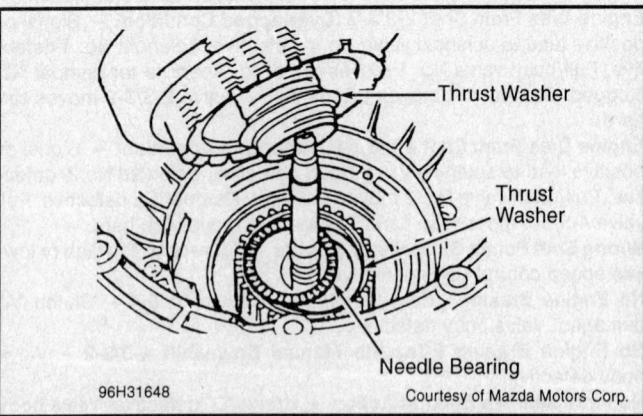

Fig. 8: Checking Thrust Washers & Needle Bearing Installation

OUTPUT FLANGE SEAL

Removal – **1)** Remove exhaust assembly. Remove center heat shield. Remove left and right splash guard heat shields. Support transmission with transmission jack. Disconnect HO2S wiring from transmission crossmember. Remove crossmember.

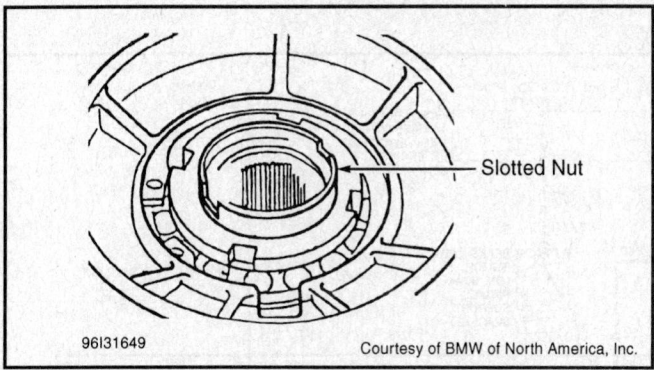

Fig. 9: Locating Slotted Nut

2) Disconnect propeller shaft from transmission and secure to one side. Remove 7 (5HP18) or 5 (5HP30) transmission extension housing bolts. Remove extension housing. Knock back peened lock of slotted nut in extension housing. *See Fig. 9.* Loosen slotted nut. Pull output flange out of bearings. Pry out output flange seal.

Installation – Install new output flange seal flush with output shaft groove. Coat sealing lip on output flange seal with ATF. Install grooved nut. Secure grooved nut by peening edge. Install extension housing. To complete installation, reverse removal procedure.

POSITION SWITCH SEAL

Removal & Installation (5HP30) – Move shift lever to "P" position. Remove rear splash guard. Using Wrench (245240), loosen shift lever nut. Remove retaining plate and cable. Remove shift lever nut. *See Fig. 10.* Remove shift lever. Using Seal Remover (245260), remove seal. To install, reverse removal procedure.

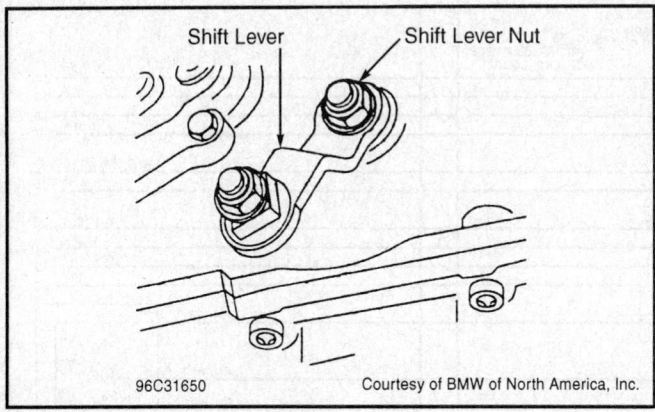

Fig. 10: Removing Shift Lever Nut

POSITION SWITCH SHAFT SEAL

Removal & Installation (5HP30) – Remove 2 heat shield bolts. Remove heat shield. Remove position switch bolt. *See Fig. 11.* Remove position switch from manual shift valve shaft. Using Seal Remover (245260), remove seal. To install, reverse removal procedure.

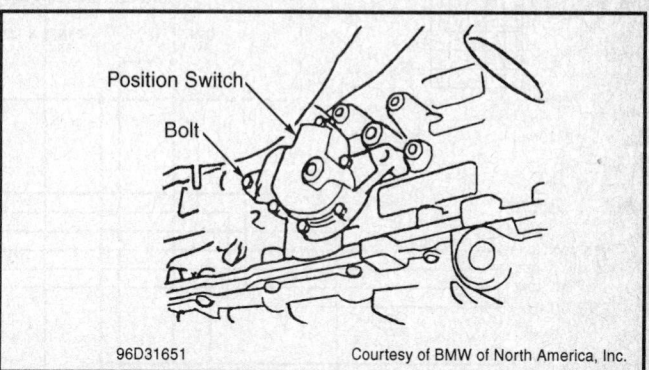

Fig. 11: Removing Position Switch Bolt

TORQUE CONVERTER

Removal & Installation – 1) Remove transmission. See appropriate AUTOMATIC TRANSMISSION REMOVAL article in TRANSMISSION SERVICING section. Once transmission is removed, lift torque converter from transmission.
2) To install, reverse removal procedure. Slide torque converter into transmission and rotate while applying slight pressure. Ensure recesses in torque converter align with primary pump. Use care to avoid damaging seal and bearing.

TORQUE SPECIFICATIONS
TORQUE SPECIFICATIONS

Application	Ft. Lbs. (N.m)
Extension Housing Bolt	17-19 (23-26)
Torque Converter Bellhousing-To-Transmission	
Case Bolt	34 (46)

	INCH Lbs. (N.m)
Oil Filter Bolt	62-80 (7.0-9.0)
Oil Pan Bolt	62-80 (7.0-9.0)
Oil Pan Drain Plug	115 (13.0)
Oil Pump Bolt	84-97 (9.5-11.0)

WIRING DIAGRAMS

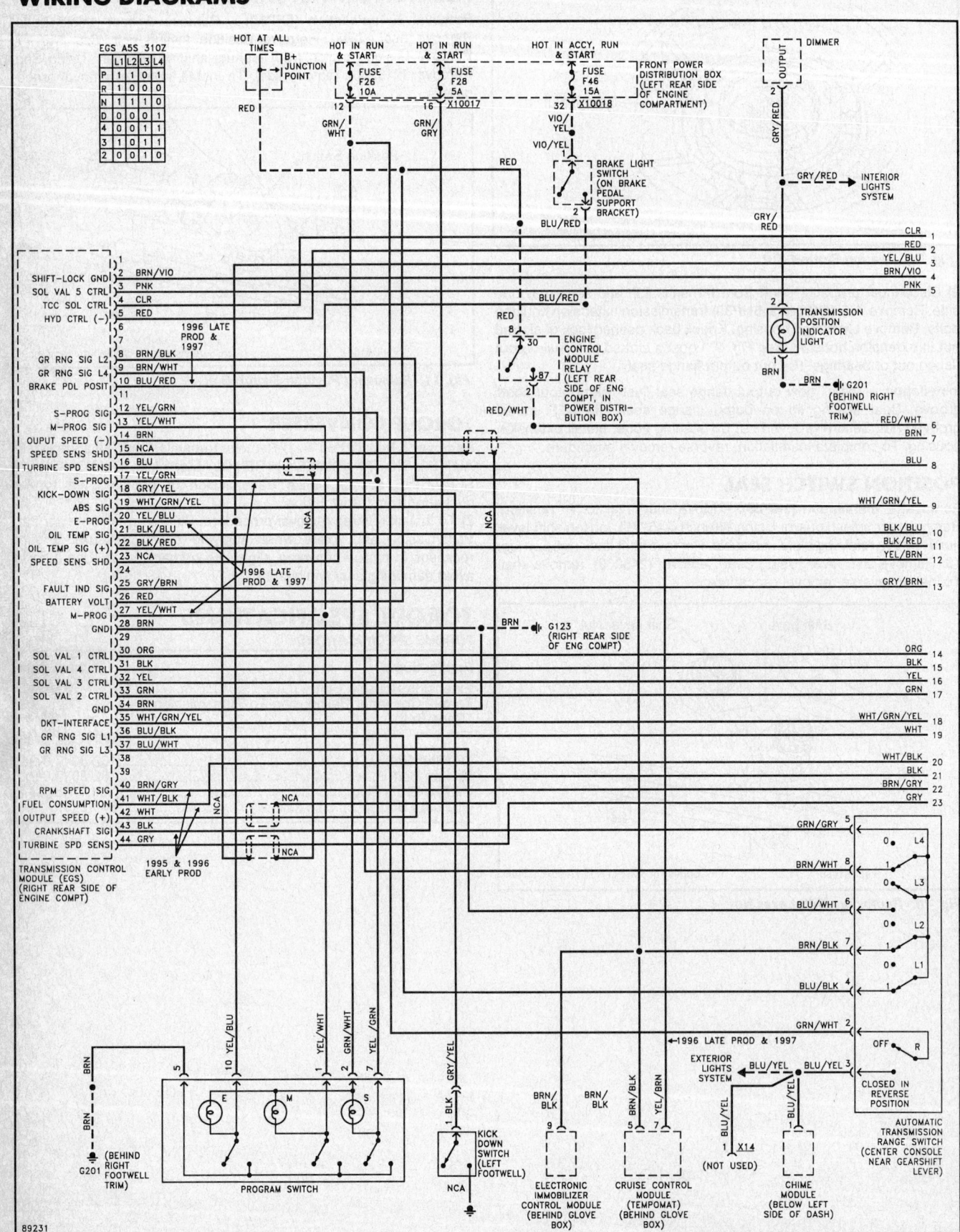

Fig. 12: Transmission Wiring Diagram (1995-96 M3 — 1 Of 2)

89231

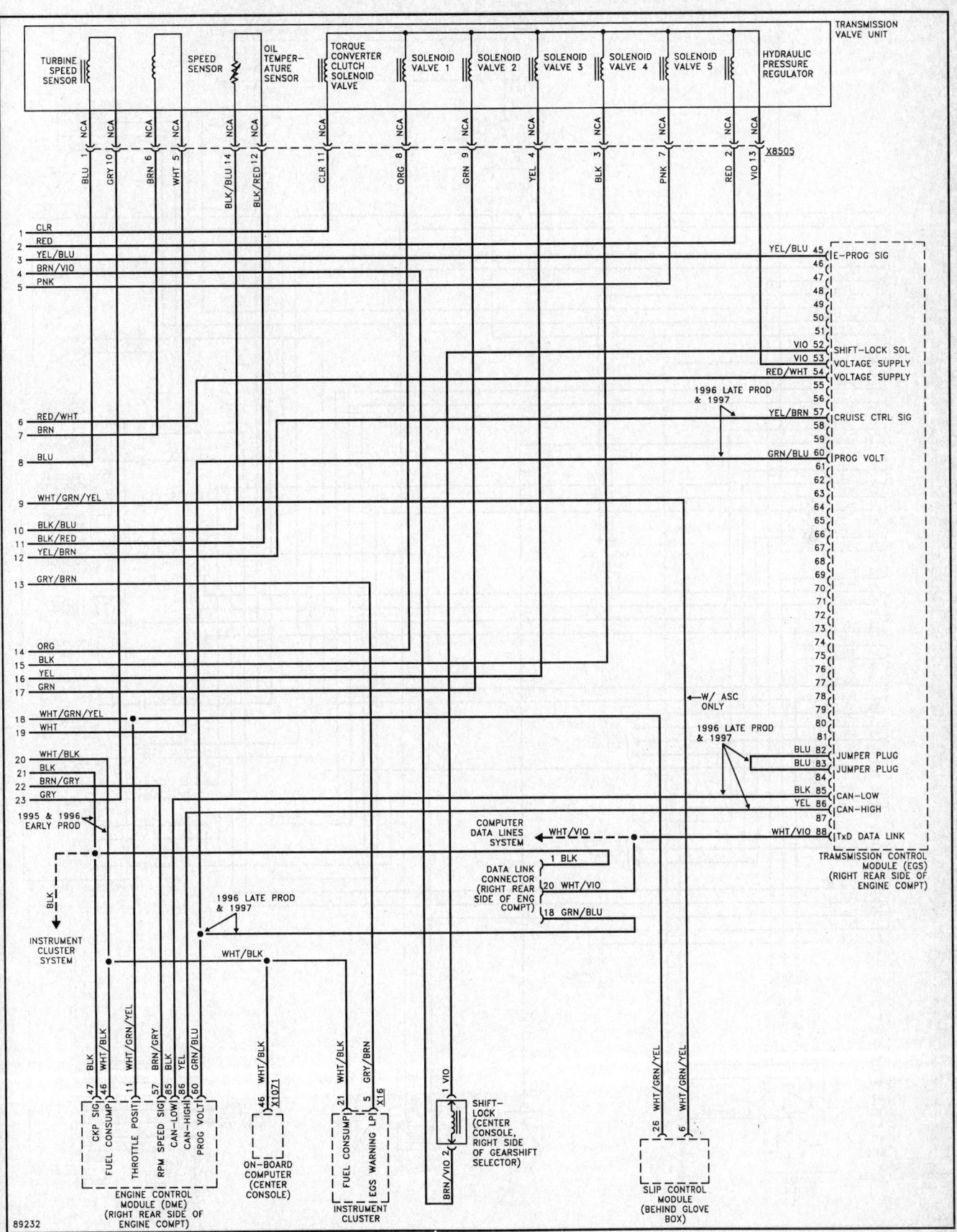

Fig. 13: Transmission Wiring Diagram (1995-96 M3 – 2 Of 2)

89232

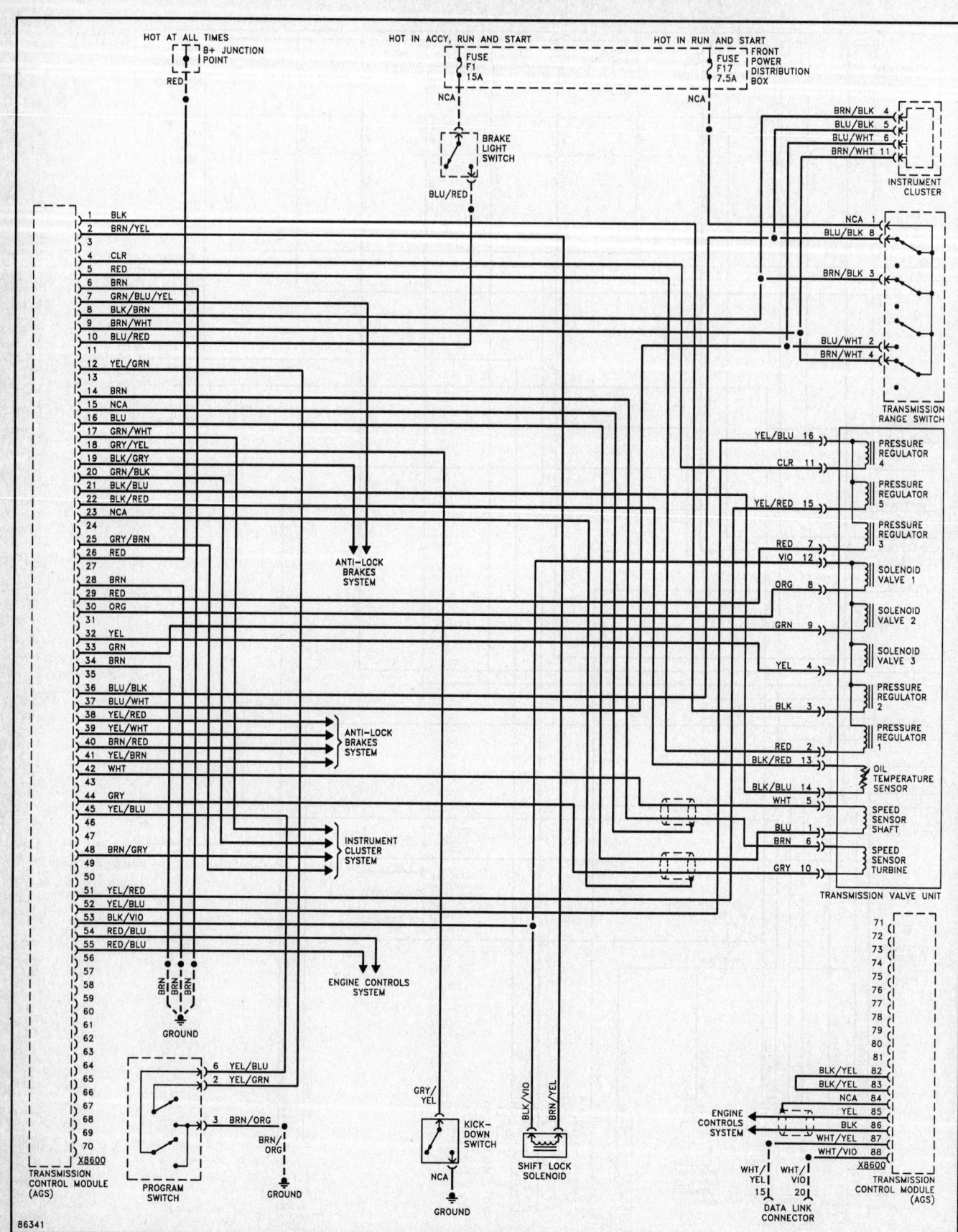

Fig. 14: Transmission Wiring Diagram (1995 525i, 525iT, 530i, 530iT & 540i)

86341

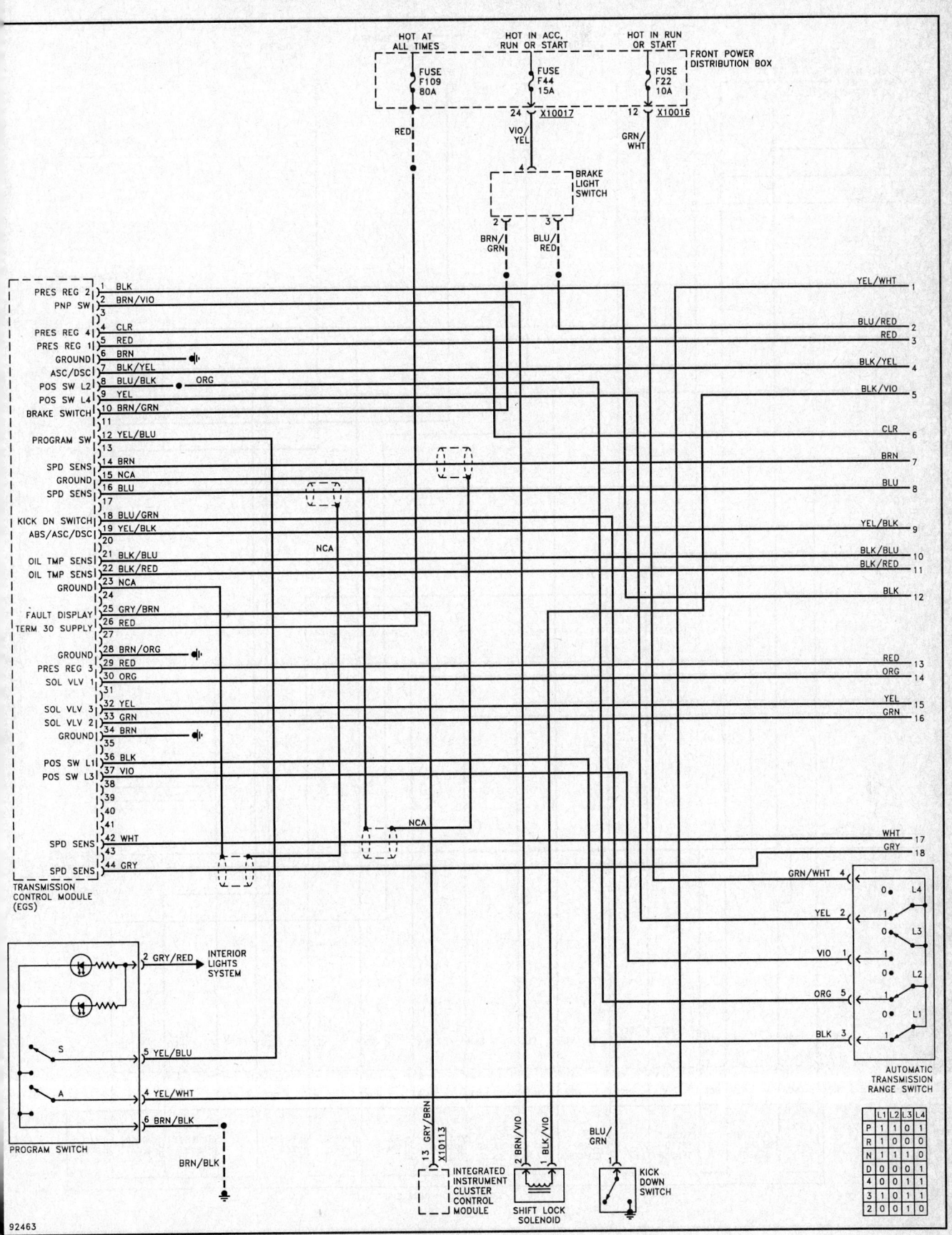

Fig. 15: Transmission Wiring Diagram (1995 740i & 740iL – 1 Of 2)

92463

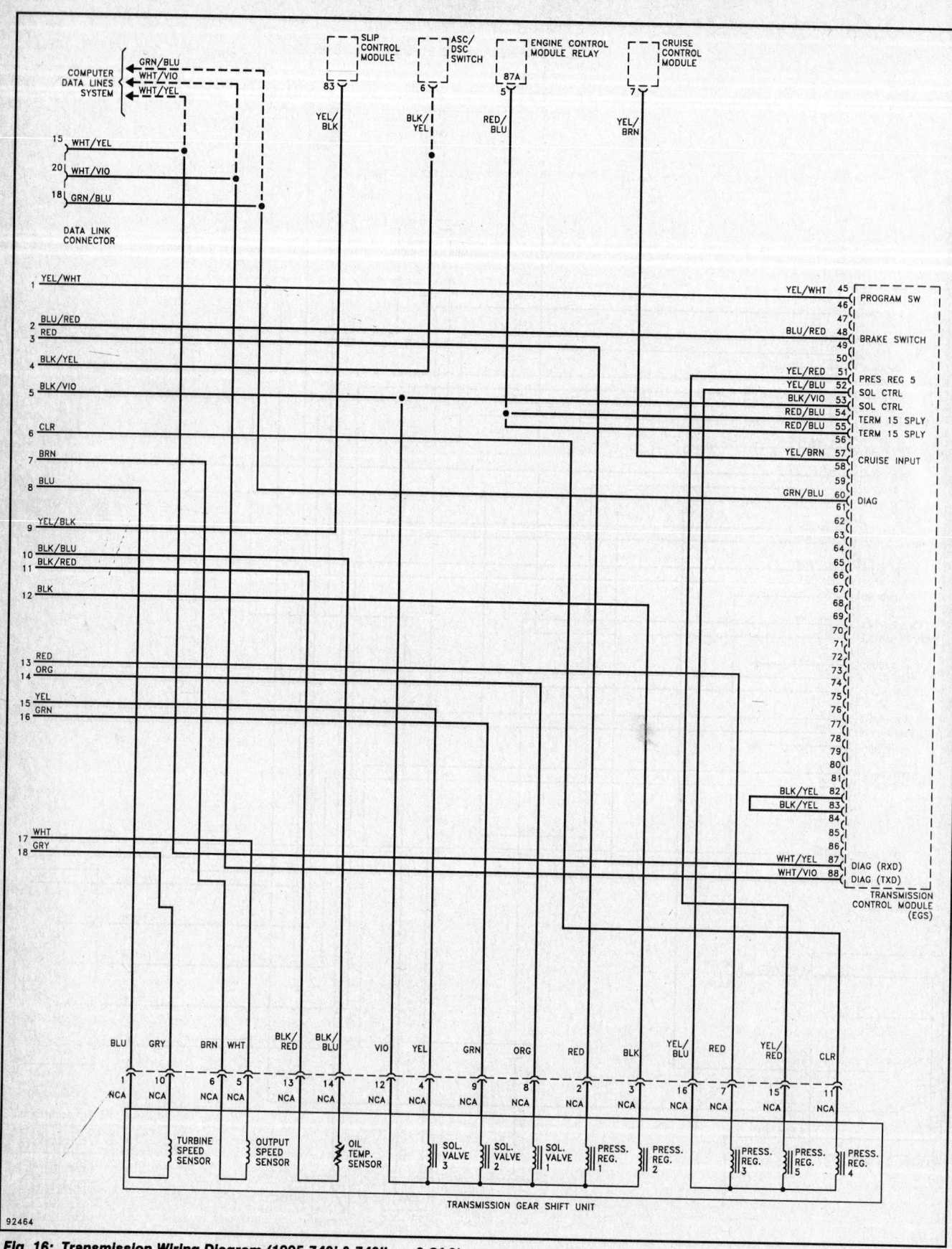

Fig. 16: Transmission Wiring Diagram (1995 740i & 740iL – 2 Of 2)

92464

MANUAL TRANSMISSIONS

MANUFACTURER & MODEL   Page

General Trouble Shooting 4-2
Acura K4A6 & K4F6 4-3
Acura/Honda Y21, Y80, S21 & S80 4-19
Audi Type 01A 4-32
Audi Type 01E 4-43
Audi Type 012 4-54
Geo Metro & Suzuki Swift 4-64
Geo Tracker & Suzuki Sidekick 4-72
Honda M2F4, M2L5, M2S4, P2A5 & P2U5 4-78
Honda S20 4-86
Honda S40 & S8G 4-95
Hyundai M5A Series 5-Speed 4-104
Isuzu MUA Series 5-Speed 4-110
Kia (Getrag) 5-Speed 4-116
Mazda F25M-R & G25M-R 4-122
Mazda M15M-D 4-131
Mazda R15M-D 4-135
Mitsubishi F5MC1 4-141
Mitsubishi F5M20, F5M30 & KM200 Series 4-145
Mitsubishi R5M21 5-Speed 4-152
Mitsubishi V5MT1 4-156
Mitsubishi W5M33 & W6MG1 4-160
Nissan FS5R30A & RS5R30A 4-168
Nissan FS5W71C 5-Speed 4-173
Nissan RS5F31A, RS5F32A & RS5F32V 4-178
Nissan RS5F50A & RS5F50V 5-Speed 4-184
Porsche G50/20 6-Speed 4-190
Rover R380 5-Speed 4-201
Saab FM5 5-Speed 4-207
Subaru Impreza & Legacy 5-Speed 4-216
Suzuki Samurai 5-Speed 4-229
Suzuki Sidekick & X90 .... See Geo Tracker
Suzuki Swift .... See Geo Metro
Toyota "C" Series – 4 & 5 Speed 4-233
Toyota E153 5-Speed 4-238
Toyota G58 5-Speed 4-248
Toyota RAV4 E250F 5-Speed 4-254
Toyota R150 & R150F 5-Speed 4-265
Toyota S51 & S54 5-Speed 4-273
Toyota "W" Series 5-Speed 4-279
Volkswagen Type 02A 4-287
Volkswagen Type 020 4-293

MANUAL TRANSMISSIONS
General Trouble Shooting

INTRODUCTION

There are many times when the transmission is incorrectly blamed for shifting problems or noises that are actually caused by other reasons. Shift difficulties are frequently caused by conditions outside the transmission or transaxle. Typical conditions include: shift linkage, shift cables, alignment of engine to transmission, worn engine mounts, or clutch problems.

Drive train noises may come from many sources such as tires, road surfaces, wheel bearings, differentials, engine, or exhaust system. Repairing or overhauling the transmission will not cure these problems.

No manufacturer makes a perfectly quiet transmission. Gear rollover noise is present in most constant mesh transmissions and will tend to disappear when the clutch is disengaged or the transmission is placed in gear. Clutch release bearing noise will disappear when the release bearing is moved enough to slide the release bearing away from the pressure plate, if clutch is properly adjusted.

Trouble shooting can be helped by driving the vehicle on a smooth level road to help eliminate tire and body noises. Note whether noise occurs on acceleration, coasting, deceleration, or steady driving conditions. Some problems may only occur when transmission is either hot or cold. Gear lubricant that is too thick can cause hard shifting on cold mornings before the engine is warm and vehicle has been driven.

MANUAL TRANSMISSION/TRANSAXLE TROUBLE SHOOTING

Condition	Possible Cause
Noisy In Forward Gears	Low Gear Oil Level, Loose Bellhousing Bolts, Worn Bearings Or Gears
Clunk On Deceleration (FWD Only)	Loose Engine Mounts, Worn Inboard CV Joints, Worn Differential Pinion Shaft Side Gear Hub Counterbore In Case Worn Oversize
Gear Clash When Shifting Forward Gears	Clutch Out Of Adjustment, Shift Linkage Damaged Or Out Of Adjustment, Gears Or Synchronizers Damaged, Low Gear Oil Level
Transmission Noisy When Moving (RWD Only) Quiet In Neutral With Clutch Engaged	Worn Rear Output Shaft Bearing
Gear Rattle	Worn Bearings, Wrong Gear Oil, Low Gear Oil, Worn Gears
Steady Ticking At Idle (Increases With RPM)	Broken Tooth On A Gear
Gear Clash When Shifting Forward Gears	Worn Or Broken Synchronizers, Faulty Clutch
Loud Whine In Reverse	[1] Normal Condition
Noise When Stepping On Clutch	Faulty Release Bearing, Worn Pilot Bearing
Ticking Or Screeching As Clutch Is Engaged	Faulty Release Bearing, Uneven Pressure Plate Fingers
Click Or Snap When Clutch Is Engaged	Worn Clutch Fork, Worn Pivot Ball, Worn Or Broken Front Bearing Retainer
Transmission Shifts Hard	Clutch Not Releasing, Incorrect Gear Oil, Shift Mechanism Binding, Clutch Installed Backward
Will Not Shift Into One Gear, Shifts Into All Others	Bent Shift Fork, Worn Detent Balls
Locked Into Gear, Cannot Shift	Clutch Adjustment, Worn Detent Balls
Transmission Jumps Out Of Gear	Pilot Bearing Worn, Bent Shift Fork, Worn Gear Teeth Or Face, Excessive Gear Train End Play, Worn Synchronizers, Missing Detent Ball Spring, Shift Mechanism Worn Or Out Of Adjustment Engine Or Transmission Mount Bolts Loose, Transmission Not Aligned
Shift Lever Rattle	Worn Detents Or Shift Lever, Worn Shift Fork, Worn Synchronizer Sleeves
Shift Lever Hops Under Acceleration	Worn Engine Or Transmission Mounts

[1] – Most units use spur cut gears in Reverse and are naturally noisy.

Legend

APPLICATION & LABOR TIMES

APPLICATION & LABOR TIMES

Vehicle Application	Labor Times		Series
	[1] R & I	[2] Overhaul	
1995 Legend			
5-Speed	7.5	8.8	K4A6
6-Speed	7.5	8.8	K4F6

[1] – Removal and installation of transmission from vehicle chassis.
[2] – Bench overhaul time for transaxle/differential. DOES NOT include removal and installation.

IDENTIFICATION

Transmission identification is stamped on a metal pad on top of transmission. First 4 numbers indicate model. *See Fig. 1.*

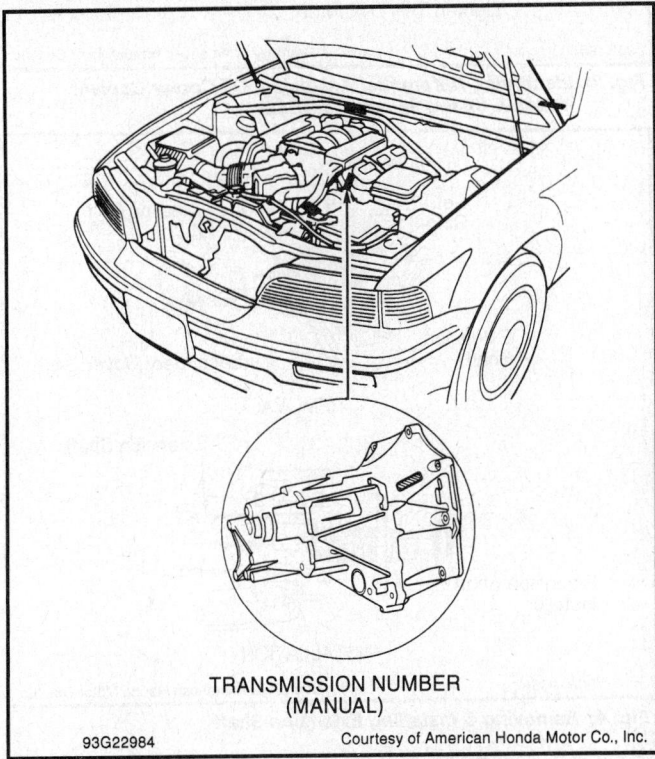

TRANSMISSION NUMBER
(MANUAL)

93G22984   Courtesy of American Honda Motor Co., Inc.

Fig. 1: Locating Transmission Identification Number

DESCRIPTION

The Acura Legend "L" and "LS" model are equipped with 5-speed K4A6 model transmission. "GS" models are equipped with 6-speed K4F6 model transmission. The K4F6 is equipped with a reverse lockout system. At vehicle speed above 12 MPH the reverse lockout solenoid is activated causing select lock pin to block interlock rotation to reverse shift piece.

LUBRICATION & ADJUSTMENT

See appropriate MANUAL TRANSMISSION SERVICING article in TRANSMISSION SERVICING.

TROUBLE SHOOTING

See GENERAL TROUBLE SHOOTING article.

ON-VEHICLE SERVICE

DIFFERENTIAL ASSEMBLY

Differential assembly may be removed from vehicle with transaxle in the vehicle. See DIFFERENTIAL ASSEMBLY under REMOVAL & INSTALLATION.

AXLE SHAFTS

See AXLE SHAFTS article in AXLE SHAFTS & TRANSFER CASES.

ELECTRONIC TESTING

REVERSE LOCKOUT SYSTEM

Reverse Lockout System Inoperative – 1) Check for any PGM-FI system DTCs. See appropriate SELF-DIAGNOSTICS article in ENGINE PERFORMANCE of appropriate MITCHELL® manual. If no DTCs are present, go to next step. If any DTCs are present, repair DTCs first and recheck system.
2) Check fuse No. 13 (7.5 amp) in under dash fuse/relay panel. Under dash fuse/relay panel is located under left side of instrument panel. If fuse is okay, go to next step. If fuse is blown, replace fuse and recheck system.
3) Remove reverse lockout relay from under hood fuse/relay panel. Test reverse lockout relay. See REVERSE LOCKOUT RELAY TEST. If relay is okay, go to next step. If relay is defective, replace fuse and recheck system.
4) Turn ignition on. Using DVOM, measure voltage between Yellow wires at reverse lockout relay and ground. If battery voltage is present at both wires, go to next step. If battery voltage is not present at both wires, repair open Yellow wire between under hood fuse/relay panel reverse lockout relay connector and under dash fuse/relay panel fuse No. 13 (7.5 amp).

NOTE: Test terminals are identified on test harness connector.

---

5) Turn ignition off. Reinstall reverse lockout relay. Connect ECM Test Harness (07LAJ-PT3010A) between ECM and ECM connectors. ECM is located under right side of instrument panel. Turn ignition on. Measure voltage between test harness connector terminal No. A8 and ground. If battery voltage is present, go to next step. If battery voltage is not present, go to step 9).
6) Disconnect reverse lockout solenoid connector. Reverse lockout solenoid is located at rear of transmission near back-up light and neutral position switches. Connect jumper between test harness connector terminal No. A8 and reverse lockout solenoid connector 3-pin Green/White wire. If battery voltage is present, go to next step. If battery voltage is not present, repair open Green/White wire between reverse lockout solenoid and under hood fuse/relay panel.
7) Turn ignition off. Reconnect reverse lockout solenoid connector. Turn ignition on. If transmission can be shifted into reverse, go to next step. If transmission cannot be shifted into reverse, go to step 10).
8) Turn ignition off. Remove reverse lockout solenoid. Test reverse lockout solenoid. See REVERSE LOCKOUT SOLENOID TEST. If solenoid is okay, transmission has internal problem. See TRANSMISSION DISASSEMBLY. If solenoid is defective, replace solenoid.
9) Disconnect ECM 26-pin connector "A". If battery voltage is present, check and repair poor connection at ECM. If connections are okay, replace with known good ECM and retest. If battery voltage is not present, repair open or short to ground in Red/White wire between under hood fuse/relay panel reverse lockout relay connector and ECM.
10) Remove jumper wire. If transmission cannot be shifted into reverse, go to next step. If transmission can be shifted into reverse, check and repair poor connection at ECM. If connections are okay, replace with known good ECM and retest.
11) Turn ignition off. Remove reverse lockout solenoid. If transmission can be shifted into reverse, replace reverse lockout solenoid. If transmission cannot be shifted into reverse, transmission has internal problem. See TRANSMISSION DISASSEMBLY.

Reverse Lockout Relay Test – Remove reverse lockout relay from under hood fuse/relay panel. Continuity should exist between Red/White wire terminal and Yellow wire terminal. Continuity should exist between Green/White wire terminal and Yellow wire terminal when power and ground are applied to Red/White wire terminal and Yellow wire terminal. If continuity is not as described, replace reverse lockout relay.

Reverse Lockout Solenoid – **1)** Disconnect reverse lockout solenoid sub-harness connector. Reverse lockout solenoid sub-harness connector is located at rear of engine near bellhousing.

2) Using DVOM, measure resistance between reverse lockout solenoid sub-harness connector outside terminals. If resistance is 9-13.6 ohms, solenoid is okay, go to step **4)**. If resistance is not 9-13.6 ohms, go to next step.

3) Disconnect reverse lockout solenoid connector. Reverse lockout solenoid connector is located at rear of transmission near back-up light and neutral position switches. Measure resistance between reverse lockout solenoid connector outside terminals. If resistance is 9-13.6 ohms, replace reverse lockout solenoid sub-harness. If resistance is not 9-13.6 ohms, replace reverse lockout solenoid.

4) To test reverse lockout solenoid, apply power and ground to outside terminals of reverse lockout solenoid connector. A clicking sound should be heard. If no clicking sound is heard, replace reverse lockout solenoid.

REMOVAL & INSTALLATION

NOTE: For transmission removal, see appropriate MANUAL TRANS-MISSION REMOVAL article in TRANSMISSION SERVICING.

DIFFERENTIAL ASSEMBLY

NOTE: Before disconnecting negative battery cable, ensure radio anti-theft code is obtained from customer. Radio anti-theft code must be re-entered into radio for radio operation.

Removal – **1)** Obtain radio anti-theft code from customer. Disconnect negative battery cable. Raise and support vehicle. Drain differential assembly gear oil. Drain cooling system.

2) Remove axle shafts and intermediate shaft. See appropriate article in AXLE SHAFTS & TRANSFER CASES.

3) Remove bolts and lower plate, located below differential assembly. See Fig. 2. Reinstall bolts to hold steering gear in place, as bolts must be removed for lower plate removal.

4) Remove bolt, speed sensor assembly and "O" ring from differential assembly. See Fig. 3. Speed sensor assembly contains the Vehicle Speed Sensor (VSS) and power steering speed sensor. DO NOT disconnect the 2 hoses for the power steering at speed sensor assembly.

5) Disconnect oil cooler hoses at pipes on differential assembly. See Fig. 3. Remove sealing bolt from transaxle. See Fig. 9.

6) Place shift lever in 1st gear. Using Puller (07LAC-PW50101), remove extension shaft from differential assembly. See Fig. 4.

7) Remove differential assembly mounting bolts, shim and differential assembly. See Fig. 3.

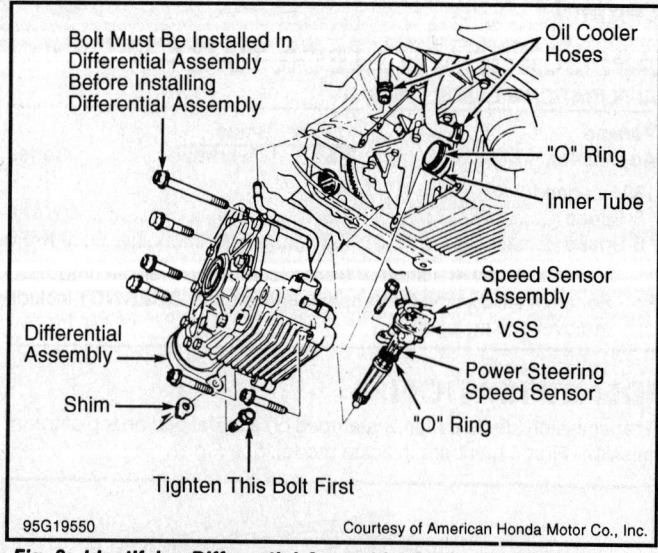

Fig. 3: *Identifying Differential Assembly, Oil Cooler Coolant Hoses & Speed Sensor Assembly*

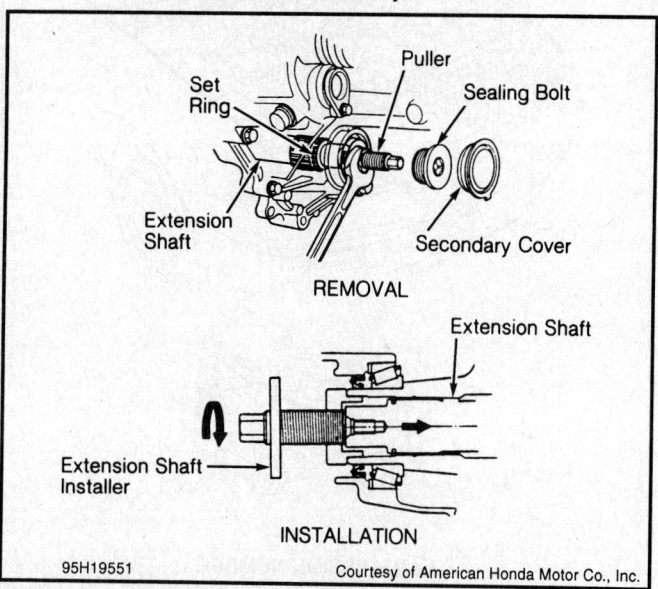

Fig. 4: *Removing & Installing Extension Shaft*

Installation – **1)** Thickness of shim must be checked. Install differential assembly. Ensure upper mounting bolt is installed on differential assembly, as bolt must be installed before installing differential assembly. See Fig. 3. Install and tighten differential assembly mounting bolts to specification. See TORQUE SPECIFICATIONS.

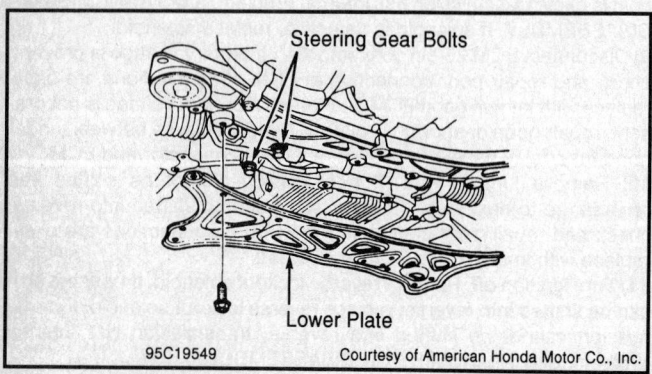

Fig. 2: *Identifying Lower Plate*

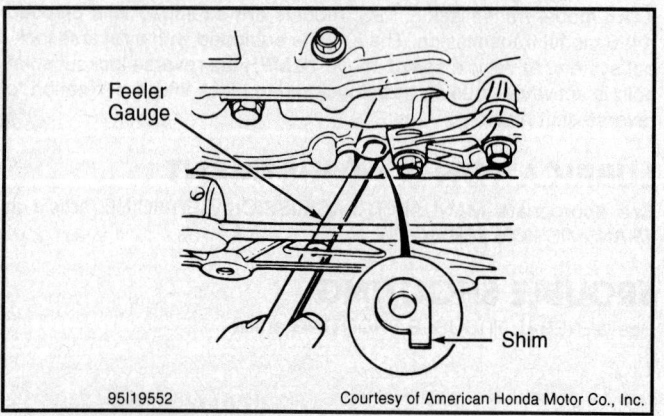

Fig. 5: *Determining Shim Thickness*

2) Using feeler gauge, measure clearance between differential case and torque converter housing where the shim fits. See Fig. 5.

3) Select proper thickness shim. Shims are available in .004" (.1 mm) increments ranging from .075" (1.9 mm) to .118" (3.0 mm). Remove differential assembly.

4) Ensure upper mounting bolt is installed on differential assembly, as bolt must be installed before installing differential assembly. See Fig. 3. Install differential assembly using NEW "O" ring on end of inner tube at the oil pan.

5) Install shim and differential assembly mounting bolts. Tighten differential assembly mounting bolt at the shim area first. Tighten all differential assembly mounting bolts to specification.

6) Apply high-temperature grease on splines on extension shaft. Install NEW set ring on end of extension shaft so ends of set ring are at 12 o'clock position.

7) Using Extension Shaft Installer (07MAF-PY40100), install extension shaft. See Fig. 4. Ensure extension shaft locks into the secondary gear. Fill cavity on secondary gear around extension shaft with high-temperature grease.

8) Apply thread sealant on threads of sealing bolt. Install and tighten sealing bolt to specification.

9) Install lower plate. Install and tighten lower plate and steering gear bolts to specification.

10) Using NEW "O" ring, install speed sensor assembly. Install and tighten speed sensor assembly bolt to specification. Reconnect oil cooler coolant hoses and speed sensor assembly electrical connector.

11) Install axle shafts and intermediate shaft using proper procedure. See appropriate article in AXLE SHAFTS & TRANSFER CASES.

12) Fill differential assembly with 80W-90 hypoid gear oil with API GL5 rating. Use NEW seal washer when installing differential assembly oil filler plug. Tighten differential assembly oil filler plug to specification.

13) When refilling cooling system, open air bleeder bolt, located on upper radiator hosing housing on the engine. Fill cooling system until coolant flows from air bleeder bolt. Tighten air bleeder bolt to specification. Finish filling cooling system.

14) Reconnect negative battery cable. To enter radio anti-theft code, turn radio on. When CODE is displayed on radio re-enter anti-theft code by using the radio station preset buttons.

TRANSMISSION DISASSEMBLY

NOTE: Place clutch housing on supports high enough to keep mainshaft from hitting workbench.

1) Remove extension stay. Remove set bolts, springs and steel detent balls from transmission cover. Remove sealing bolt (sealing bolt has square hole). Remove all housing bolts. Access mainshaft bearing snap ring through sealing bolt opening. Spread snap ring, lift and remove cover. See Figs. 6-9.

2) Remove oil/reverse guide tube assembly. Raise lock nut tab from mainshaft and countershaft. Pry tab up and remove nut from each shaft.

3) Using a 5-mm pin punch and hammer, drive out pin from 5th gear shift fork.

4) On 5-speed model, remove 5th gear components from mainshaft and countershaft. See Figs. 6 and 7.

5) On 6-speed model, remove 5th and 6th gear components from mainshaft and countershaft. See Figs. 8 and 9.

6) Remove oil pump pipes. Remove back-up and neutral safety switches. Remove all set bolts, springs and steel detent balls in transmission housing. Disassemble and remove strainer assembly. Remove all housing bolts. Lift and remove housing. See Figs. 6-9.

7) Inspect reverse shift holder and shift fork. See Fig. 10. Measure clearance between reverse shift holder and 5th/reverse shift fork shaft (5-speed) or reverse shift piece (6-speed). See Fig. 11. Clearance should be .008-.020" (.20-.50 mm). Service limit is .032" (.80 mm). If clearance exceeds service limit, measure end width of reverse shift holder. Width of end of reverse shift holder should be .504-.512" (12.80-13.00 mm). If width is less than minimum, replace reverse shift holder.

8) Measure clearance between reverse shift holder and reverse shift fork. Clearance should be .008-.020" (.20-.50 mm). Service limit is .032" (.80 mm). If clearance exceeds service limit, measure end width of reverse shift holder. Width of end of reverse shift holder should be .504-.512" (12.80-13.00 mm). If width is less than minimum, replace reverse shift holder.

9) Measure clearance between reverse shift fork and reverse synchro sleeve. See Fig. 12. Clearance should be .014-.026" (.35-.65 mm). Service limit is .039" (1.0 mm). If clearance exceeds service limit, measure thickness of reverse shift fork fingers. Thickness should be .252-.260" (6.4-6.6 mm). If thickness is less than specification, replace reverse shift fork.

10) Inspect change holder and shift forks. See Fig. 13. Measure clearance between shift fork shafts, shift fork and shift piece. See Fig. 14. Clearance should be .010-.022" (.25-.55 mm). Service limit is .034" (.85 mm). If clearance exceeds service limit, measure thickness of shift piece. Thickness should be .467-.471" (11.85-11.95 mm). If thickness is less than specification, replace shift piece.

11) Measure clearance between shift forks and synchro sleeves. See Fig. 15. Clearance should be .014-.026" (.35-.65 mm). Service limit is .394" (1.0 mm). If clearance exceeds service limit, measure thickness of shift fork. Thickness should be .292-.299" (7.4-7.6 mm). If thickness is less than standard, replace shift fork.

12) Remove reverse shift holder. Remove oil guide pipe and change holder assembly. Remove reverse gear set on shaft with reverse shift fork as one assembly. Lift and remove both mainshaft and countershaft with shift forks as one assembly. Remove secondary gear. See Figs. 6-9.

COMPONENT DISASSEMBLY & REASSEMBLY

MAINSHAFT

Measurements – 1) For all mainshaft measurement specifications, refer to MAINSHAFT SPECIFICATIONS table. Measure clearance between 3rd gear and mainshaft. If clearance exceeds service limit, measure thickness of 3rd gear. If thickness of 3rd gear is less than service limit, replace 3rd gear. See Fig. 18.

2) Measure clearance between 4th gear and distance collar. If clearance exceeds service limit, measure thickness of 4th gear. If thickness of 4th gear is less than service limit, replace 4th gear.

3) Measure clearance between 5th gear and distance collar. If clearance exceeds service limit, measure thickness of 5th gear. If thickness of 5th gear is less than service limit, replace 5th gear.

MAINSHAFT SPECIFICATIONS

Application	Specification
3rd Gear-to-Mainshaft Clearance	
Design Clearance	.0024-.0075" (.06-.19 mm)
Service Limit	.012" (.30 mm)
4th Gear/Distance Collar Clearance	
Design Clearance	.0024-.0075" (.06-.19 mm)
Service Limit	.012" (.30 mm)
5th Gear/Distance Collar Clearance	
Design Clearance	.0024-.0075" (.06-.19 mm)
Service Limit	.012" (.30 mm)
6th Gear/Distance Collar Clearance	
Design Clearance	.0024-.0075" (.06-.19 mm)
Service Limit	.012" (.30 mm)
3rd Gear Thickness	
Thickness	1.236-1.239" (31.39-31.47 mm)
Service Limit	1.233" (31.32 mm)
4th Gear Thickness	
Thickness	1.157-1.160" (29.39-29.47 mm)
Service Limit	1.154" (29.32 mm)
5th Gear Thickness	
Thickness	1.157-1.160" (29.39-29.47 mm)
Service Limit	1.154" (29.32 mm)
6th Gear Thickness	
Thickness	1.157-1.160" (29.39-29.47 mm)
Service Limit	1.154" (29.32 mm)

MANUAL TRANSMISSIONS
Acura K4A6 & K4F6 (Cont.)

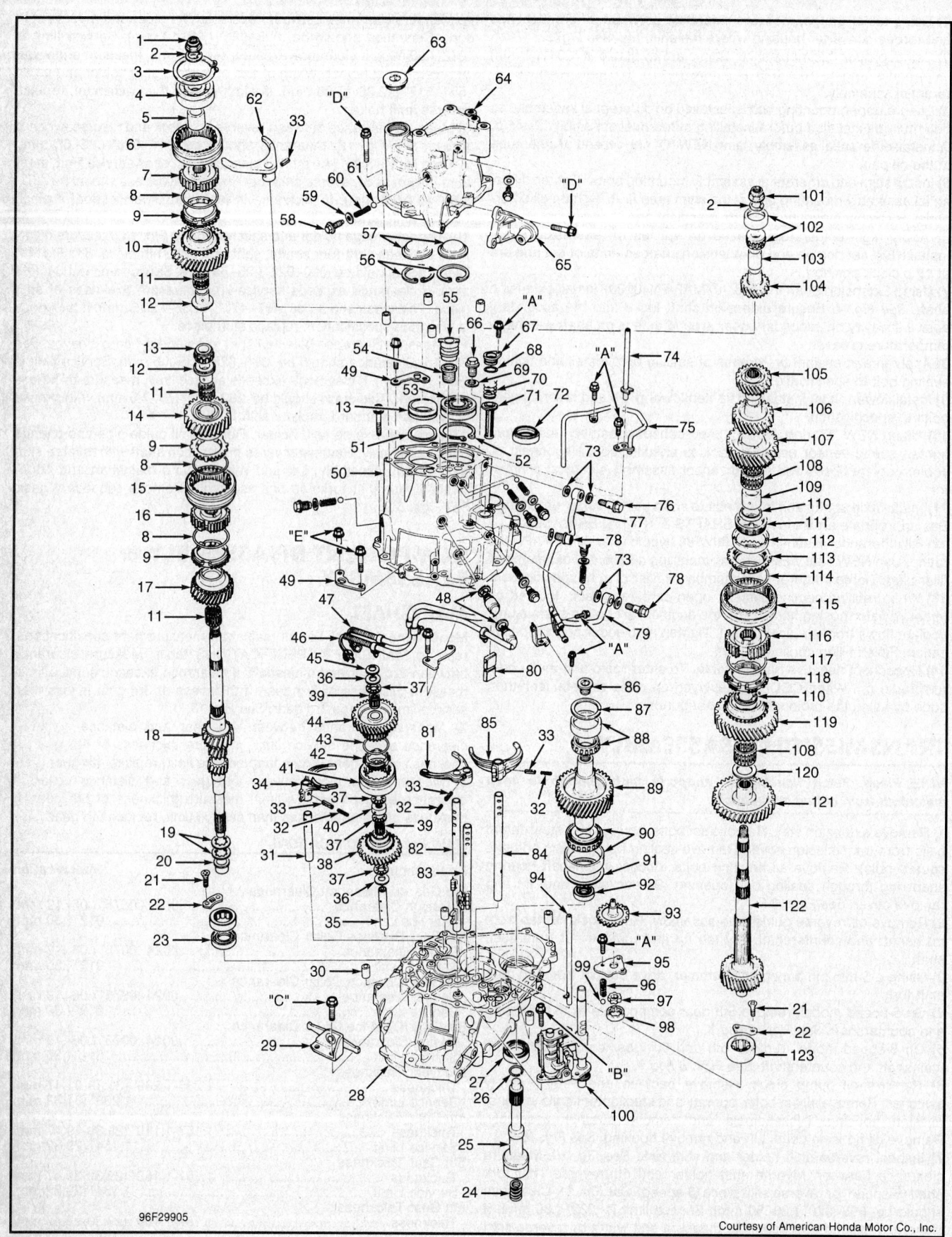

96F29905

Courtesy of American Honda Motor Co., Inc.

Fig. 6: Exploded View Of 5-Speed Transmission (1 Of 2)

TORQUE VALUE

"A" - 108 INCH lbs. (12 N.m)
"B" - 11 ft. lbs. (15 N.m)
"C" - 19 ft. lbs. (26 N.m)
"D" - 21 ft. lbs. (28 N.m)
"E" - 33 ft. lbs. (45 N.m)

1. Lock Nut
2. Spring Washer
3. Snap Ring
4. Bearing
5. Spacer
6. Distance Collar
7. 5th Synchro Sleeve
8. Synchro Spring
9. Synchro Ring
10. 5th Gear
11. Needle Bearing
12. Distance Collar
13. Needle Bearing
14. 4th Gear
15. 3rd/4th Synchro Sleeve
16. 3rd/4th Synchro Hub
17. 3rd Gear
18. Mainshaft
19. Mainshaft Washer
20. Needle Bearing
21. Flat Screw
22. Needle Set Plate
23. Oil Seal
24. Secondary Spring
25. Extension Shaft

26. Set Ring
27. Oil Seal
28. Clutch Housing
29. Reverse Shift Holder
30. Dowel Pin
31. Reverse Shift Fork Shaft
32. Spring Pin
33. Spring Pin
34. Reverse Shift Fork
35. Reverse Gear Shaft
36. Thrust Washer
37. Needle Bearing
38. Reverse Drive Gear
39. Needle Bearing
40. Distance Collar
41. Reverse Synchro Sleeve
42. Synchro Ring
43. Synchro Spring
44. Reverse Synchro Hub
45. Spring Washer
46. Back-Up Light Switch
47. Neutral Safety Switch
48. Washer
49. Transmission Hanger
50. Transmission Housing
51. Snap Ring
52. Snap Ring
53. Bearing
54. Oil Seal
55. Shift Rod Boot
56. Snap Ring
57. Oil Guide Plate
58. Sealing Bolt

59. Washer
60. Spring
61. Steel Ball
62. 5th Shift Fork
63. Sealing Bolt
64. Transmission Cover
65. Extension Stay
66. Oil Filler Plug
67. Strainer Cover
68. "O" Ring
69. Washer
70. Strainer Set Spring
71. Oil Pump Strainer
72. Oil Seal
73. Washer
74. Oil Guide Pipe
75. Reverse Pipe
76. Joint Bolt
77. Oil Pump Pipe "B"
78. Drain Plug
79. Oil Pump Pipe "A"
80. Magnet
81. 3rd/4th Shift Fork
82. 5th/Reverse Shift Fork Shaft
83. 3rd/4th Shift Fork Shaft
84. 1st/2nd Shift Fork Shaft
85. 1st/2nd Shift Fork
86. Sealing Bolt
87. Thrust Shim
88. Bearing
89. Secondary Gear
90. Bearing
91. Thrust Washer

92. Oil Seal
93. Oil Pump Shaft
94. Oil Guide Pipe "C"
95. Oil Pump Plate
96. Relief Valve Spring
97. Oil Pump Inner
98. Oil Pump Outer
99. Steel Ball
100. Change Holder
101. Lock Nut
102. Needle Bearing
103. Distance Collar
104. 5th Gear
105. 4th Gear
106. 3rd Gear
107. 2nd Gear
108. Needle Bearing
109. Spacer Collar
110. Friction Damper
111. Inner Synchro Ring
112. Synchro Cone
113. Outer Synchro Ring
114. Synchro Spring
115. 1st/2nd Synchro Sleeve
116. 1st/2nd Synchro Hub
117. Synchro Spring
118. Synchro Ring
119. Low Gear
120. Thrust Shim
121. Reverse Gear
122. Countershaft
123. Needle Bearing

96G29906

Courtesy of American Honda Motor Co., Inc.

Fig. 7: Legend For Fig. 2 (2 Of 2)

Disassembly & Inspection – 1) Use puller to remove bearing. Support 4th gear on steel blocks and press mainshaft out of 5th synchro hub. Support 3rd gear on steel blocks and press mainshaft out of 3rd/4th synchro hub. Remove remaining components. *See Figs. 16 and 17.* Inspect all parts for damage and wear. Replace if necessary. Clean all parts in new solvent. Dry and lubricate all parts.
2) Measure mainshaft at points "A", "B", "C" and "D". Using dial indicator to measure runout, rotate mainshaft 2 complete revolutions. *See Fig. 19.* Replace countershaft if runout or any part of shaft is not within service limit. See MAINSHAFT BEARING SURFACE SPECIFICATIONS table.

MAINSHAFT BEARING SURFACE SPECIFICATIONS

Application [1]	Standard In. (mm)	Service Limits In. (mm)
"A" Needle Bearing Surface ...	1.1015-1.1020 (27.977-27.990)	1.0996 (27.930)
"B" Needle Bearing Surface ...	1.4956-1.4961 (37.989-38.000)	1.4935 (37.935)
"C" Ball Bearing Surface	1.2200-1.2205 (30.987-31.000)	1.2181 (30.940)
"D" Ball Bearing Surface	1.1018-1.1024 (27.987-28.000)	1.0999 (27.937)
Runout Limits	.001 (.02)	.002 (.05)

[1] – "A", "B", "C" and "D" refer to measuring points indicated in *Fig. 19.*

Reassembly – To reassemble, install components on countershaft in reverse order of removal. *See Figs. 16 and 17.*

COUNTERSHAFT

Measurements – Measure clearance between 1st gear and thrust shim. *See Fig. 20.* Clearance should be .002-.004" (.04-.10 mm). If clearance exceeds specification, select appropriate shim from following chart.

60 MM THRUST SHIM CHART

Thickness	Part Number
.056" (1.42 mm)	23971-PY5-000
.058" (1.46 mm)	23972-PY5-000
.059" (1.50 mm)	23973-PY5-000
.061" (1.54 mm)	23974-PY5-000

Measure clearance between 2nd gear and 3rd gear. *See Fig. 20.* Clearance should be .002-.004" (.040-.10 mm). If clearance exceeds specification, select appropriate shim from following chart.

SPACER COLLAR CHART

Thickness	Part Number
1.4201-1.4209" (36.07-36.09 mm)	23911-PY5-000
1.4185-1.4193" (36.03-36.05 mm)	23912-PY5-000

Disassembly – Remove components in order of assembly. Use bearing puller to remove top ball bearing. Use bearing splitter or appropriate blocks, support 4th gear. Press countershaft out of 4th gear and 5th gear. Support 1st gear and press countershaft out of 3rd gear. Remove remaining parts. *See Figs. 20 and 21.*
Inspection – 1) Inspect all parts for damage and wear. Replace if necessary. Clean all parts in new solvent. Dry and lubricate all parts.
2) Measure mainshaft at points "A", "B" and "C". Using dial indicator to measure runout, rotate countershaft 2 complete revolutions. *See Fig. 21.* Replace countershaft if runout or any part of shaft is not within service limit. See COUNTERSHAFT BEARING SURFACE SPECIFICATIONS table.

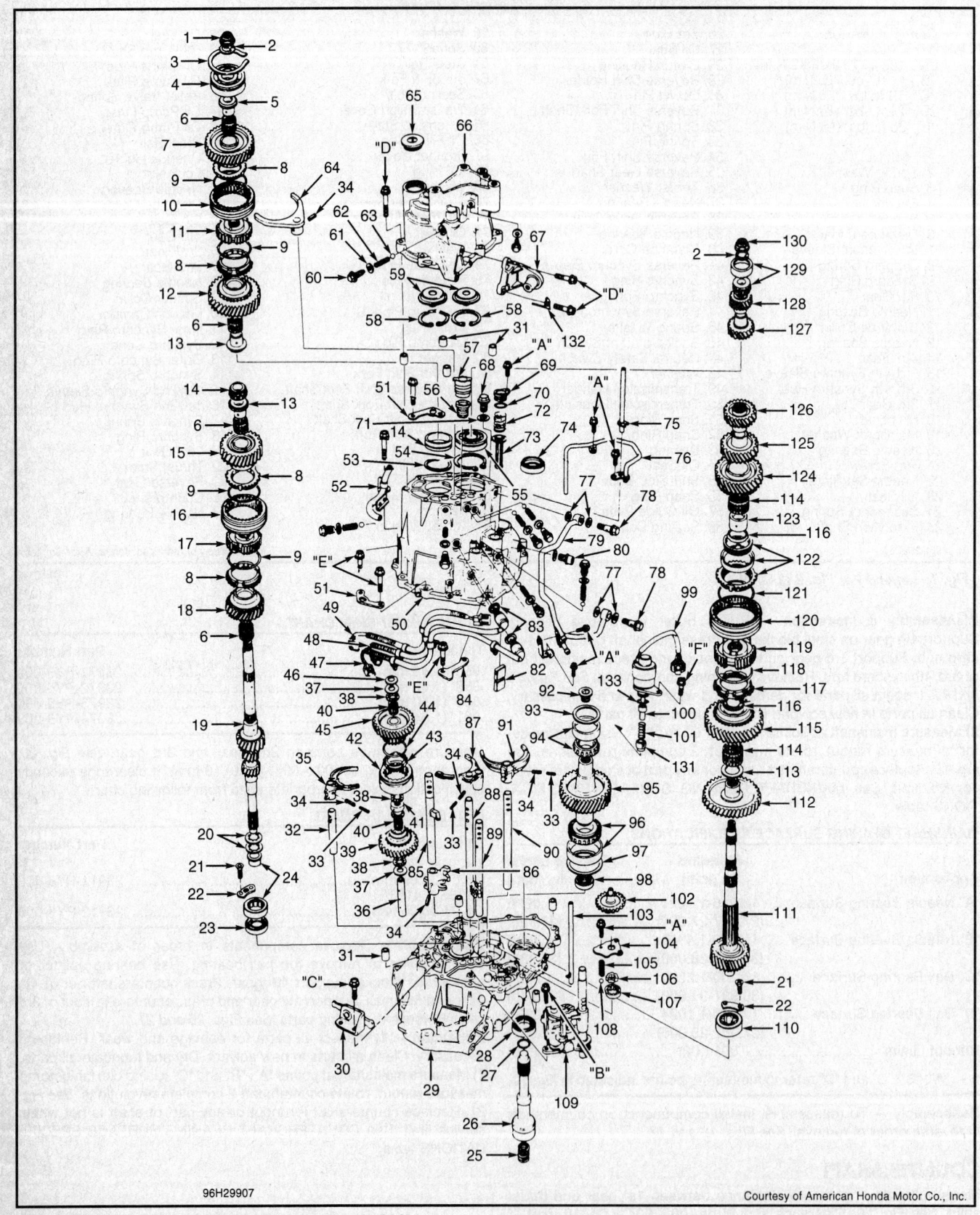

96H29907

Courtesy of American Honda Motor Co., Inc.

Fig. 8: Exploded View Of 6-Speed Transmission (1 Of 2)

TORQUE VALUE

"A" - 108 INCH lbs. (12 N.m)
"B" - 11 ft. lbs. (15 N.m)
"C" - 19 ft. lbs. (26 N.m)
"D" - 21 ft. lbs. (28 N.m)
"E" - 33 ft. lbs. (45 N.m)
"F" - 10 ft. lbs. (14 N.m)

1. Lock Nut
2. Spring Washer
3. Snap Ring
4. Bearing
5. Spacer Collar
6. Needle Bearing
7. 6th Gear
8. Synchro Ring
9. Synchro Spring
10. 5th/6th Synchro Sleeve
11. 5th/6th Synchro Hub
12. 5th Gear
13. Spacer Collar
14. Needle Bearing
15. 4th Gear
16. 3rd/4th Synchro Sleeve
17. 3rd/4th Synchro Hub
18. 3rd Gear
19. Mainshaft
20. Mainshaft Washer
21. Flat Screw
22. Needle Set Plate
23. Oil Seal
24. Needle Bearing
25. Secondary Spring
26. Extension Shaft
27. Set Ring
28. Oil Seal
29. Clutch Housing
30. Reverse Shift Holder
31. Dowel Pin
32. Reverse Shift Fork Shaft
33. Spring Pin
34. Spring Pin
35. Reverse Shift Fork
36. Reverse Gear Shaft
37. Thrust Washer
38. Needle Bearing
39. Reverse Drive Gear
40. Needle Bearing
41. Spacer
42. Reverse Synchro Sleeve
43. Synchro Ring
44. Synchro Spring
45. Reverse Synchro Hub
46. Spring Washer
47. Neutral Position Switch
48. Back-Up Light Switch
49. Reverse Lock-Out Subharness
50. Transmission Housing
51. Transmission Hanger
52. Tube Clamp
53. Snap Ring
54. Snap Ring
55. Bearing
56. Oil Seal
57. Shift Rod Boot
58. Snap Ring
59. Oil Guide Plate
60. Sealing Bolt
61. Sealing Washer
62. Spring
63. Steel Ball
64. 5th/6th Shift Fork
65. Sealing Bolt
66. Transmission Cover
67. Extension Stay
68. Oil Filler Plug
69. Strainer Cover
70. "O" Ring
71. Washer
72. Strainer Set Spring
73. Oil Pump Strainer
74. Oil Seal
75. Oil Guide Pipe
76. Reverse Pipe
77. Washer
78. Joint Bolt
79. Oil Pump Pipe "B"
80. Drain Plug
81. Oil Pump Pipe "A"
82. Magnet
83. Washer
84. Transmission Stay
85. Reverse Shift Shaft
86. Reverse Shift Piece
87. 3rd/4th Shift Fork
88. 5th/6th Shift Fork Shaft
89. 3rd/4th Shift Fork Shaft
90. 1st/2nd Shift Fork Shaft
91. 1st/2nd Shift Fork
92. Sealing Bolt
93. Thrust Shim
94. Bearing
95. Secondary Gear
96. Bearing
97. Thrust Washer
98. Oil Seal
99. Reverse Lock-Out Solenoid
100. Select Lock Pin
101. Select Lock Return Spring
102. Oil Pump Shaft
103. Oil Guide Pipe "C"
104. Oil Pump Plate
105. Relief Valve Spring
106. Oil Pump Inner Rotor
107. Oil Pump Outer Rotor
108. Steel Ball
109. Change Holder
110. Needle Bearing
111. Countershaft
112. Reverse Gear
113. Thrust Shim
114. Needle Bearing
115. 1st Gear
116. Friction Damper
117. Synchro Ring
118. Synchro Spring
119. 1st/2nd Synchro Hub
120. 1st/2nd Synchro Sleeve
121. Synchro Spring
122. Double Cone Synchro
123. Spacer
124. 2nd Gear
125. 3rd Gear
126. 4th Gear
127. 5th Gear
128. 6th Gear
129. Needle Bearing
130. Lock Nut
131. Select Lock Collar
132. Solenoid Connector Clamp
133. "O" Ring

96I29908

Courtesy of American Honda Motor Co., Inc.

Fig. 9: Legend For Fig. 4 (2 Of 2)

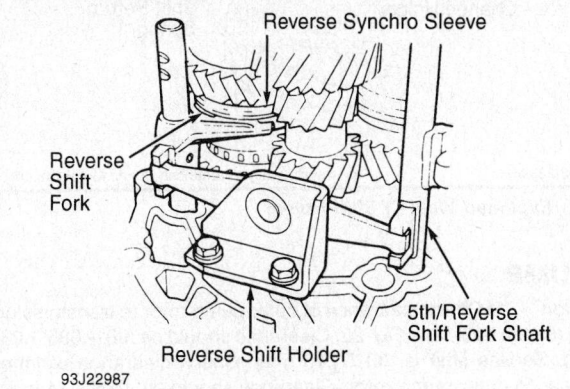

Reverse Synchro Sleeve

Reverse Shift Fork

Reverse Shift Holder

5th/Reverse Shift Fork Shaft

93J22987

Fig. 10-1: 5-Speed

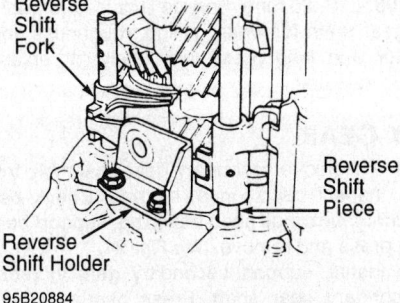

Reverse Shift Fork

Reverse Shift Holder

Reverse Shift Piece

95B20884

Fig. 10-2: 6-Speed

Courtesy of American Honda Motor Co., Inc.

Fig. 10: View Of Reverse Shift Mechanism

COUNTERSHAFT BEARING SURFACE SPECIFICATIONS

Application [1]	Standard In. (mm)	Service Limit In. (mm)
"A" Needle Bearing Surface	1.299-1.300	1.297
	(33.000-33.015)	(32.950)
"B" Ball Bearing Surface	1.2589-1.2594	1.2570
	(31.975-31.988)	(31.928)
"C" Needle Bearing Surface	1.1018-1.1024	1.0999
	(27.99-28.00)	(27.94)
Runout Limits	.001 (.02)	.002 (.05)

[1] – "A", "B" and "C" refer to measuring points indicated in *Fig. 21*.

Reassembly – To reassemble, install components on countershaft in reverse order of removal. See *Figs. 20 and 21*.

SYNCHRO RING & GEAR

Disassembly – Separate synchro ring and gear. Lubricate and install synchro spring on synchro ring and set aside.

Inspection – 1) Inspect gear teeth for wear, galling, roughness and cracks. Ensure ring and gear turn freely. If replacement is necessary, replace as a unit.

2) Measure clearance between ring and gear all the way around. Ensure ring is held evenly against gear while measuring. Ring to gear clearance should be .033-.043" (.85-1.10 mm). Service limit is .016" (.40 mm). If clearance exceeds limit, replace as a unit. See *Fig. 22*.

3) For double cone synchro, outer synchro ring to synchro cone clearance, "A", should be .0197-.0394" (.50-1.0 mm). Service limit is .0118" (.30 mm). Synchro cone to gear clearance, "B", should be .0197-.0394" (.50-1.0 mm). Service limit is .0118" (.30 mm). Outer synchro ring to gear clearance, "C", should be .0374-.0661 (.95-1.68 mm). Service limit is .0236 (.60 mm).

Reassembly – Each synchro sleeve has 3 sets of longer teeth (120 degrees apart) that must be matched with 3 sets of deeper grooves when hub is assembled. See *Fig. 22*.

MANUAL TRANSMISSIONS
Acura K4A6 & K4F6 (Cont.)

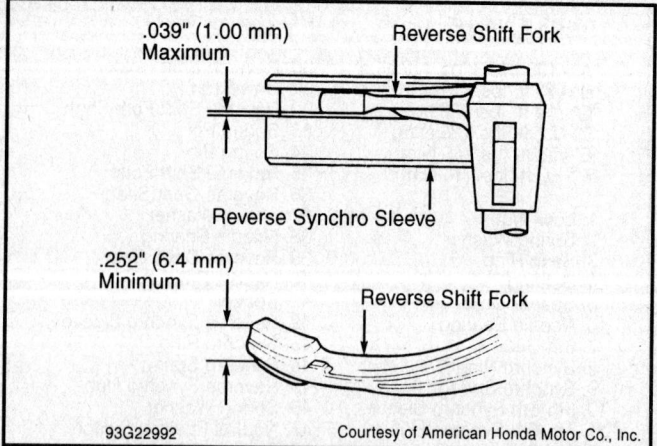

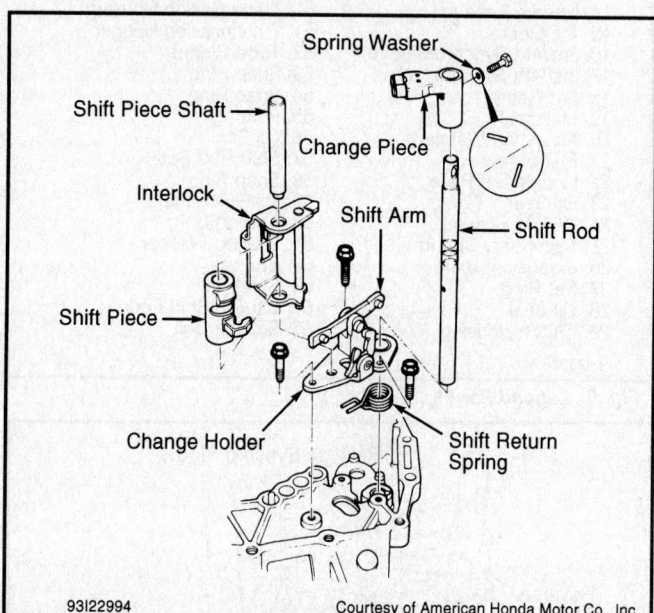

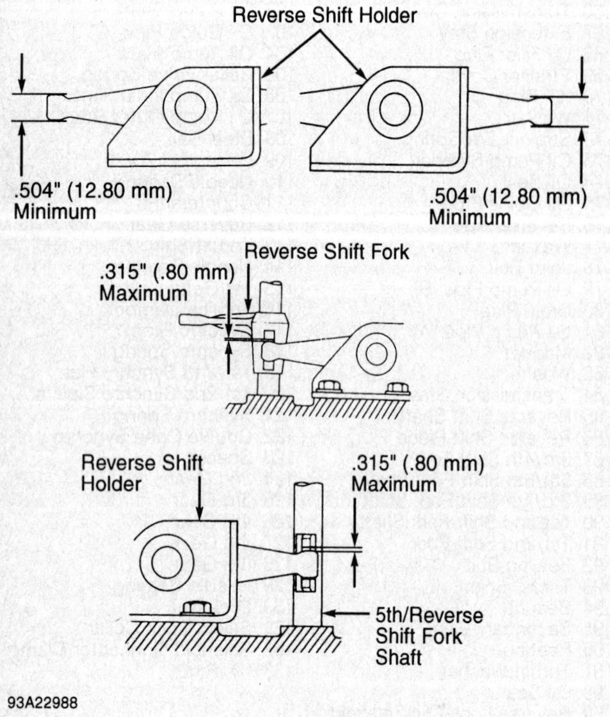

Fig. 11-1: 5-Speed

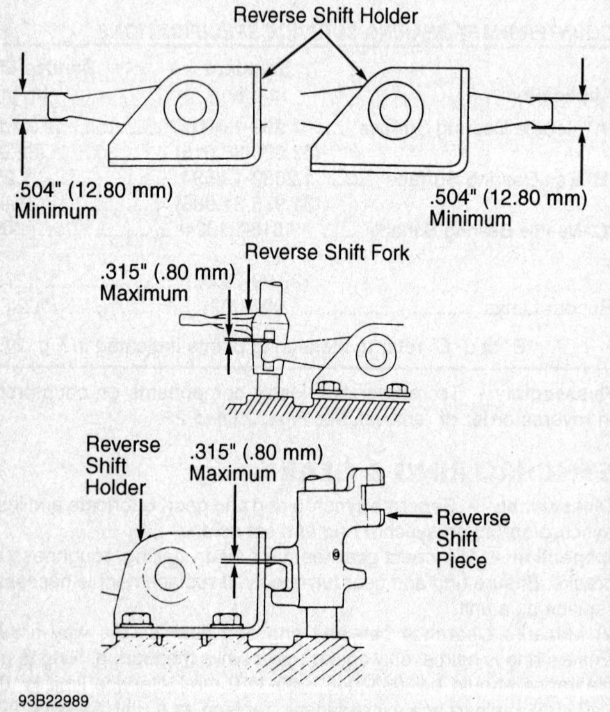

Fig. 11-2: 6-Speed

Courtesy of American Honda Motor Co., Inc.

Fig. 11: Measuring Reverse Shift Components

Courtesy of American Honda Motor Co., Inc.

Fig. 12: Measuring Reverse Shift Fork

Courtesy of American Honda Motor Co., Inc.

Fig. 13: Exploded View Of Shift Holder

OIL PUMP

Inspection – 1) Check clearance of outer pump rotor to transmission housing (clutch half). *See Fig. 23*. Clearance should be .001-.005" (.03-.13 mm). Service limit is .007" (.18 mm). Check clearance of inner pump gear to outer pump rotor. Clearance should be .006" (.14 mm). Service limit is .008" (.20 mm). Check clearance between top of pump rotor and housing using a straightedge and feeler gage. Clearance should be .004-.008" (.10-.20 mm). Service limit is .009" (.22 mm).
2) Inspect rotor/gear teeth for wear, galling, roughness and cracks. Ensure outer rotor and inner gear turn freely. If replacement is necessary, replace as a unit.

SECONDARY GEAR

Bearing Removal – Remove secondary gear assembly from transmission housing. Inspect condition of bearing. Check bearing for wear, rough rotation. If bearings need replacing, support bearing with bearing splitter in press and remove. *See Fig. 24*.
Installation – To install, support secondary gear in press. Press bearing onto secondary gear shaft. Press bearing squarely until bottomed against shaft lip.

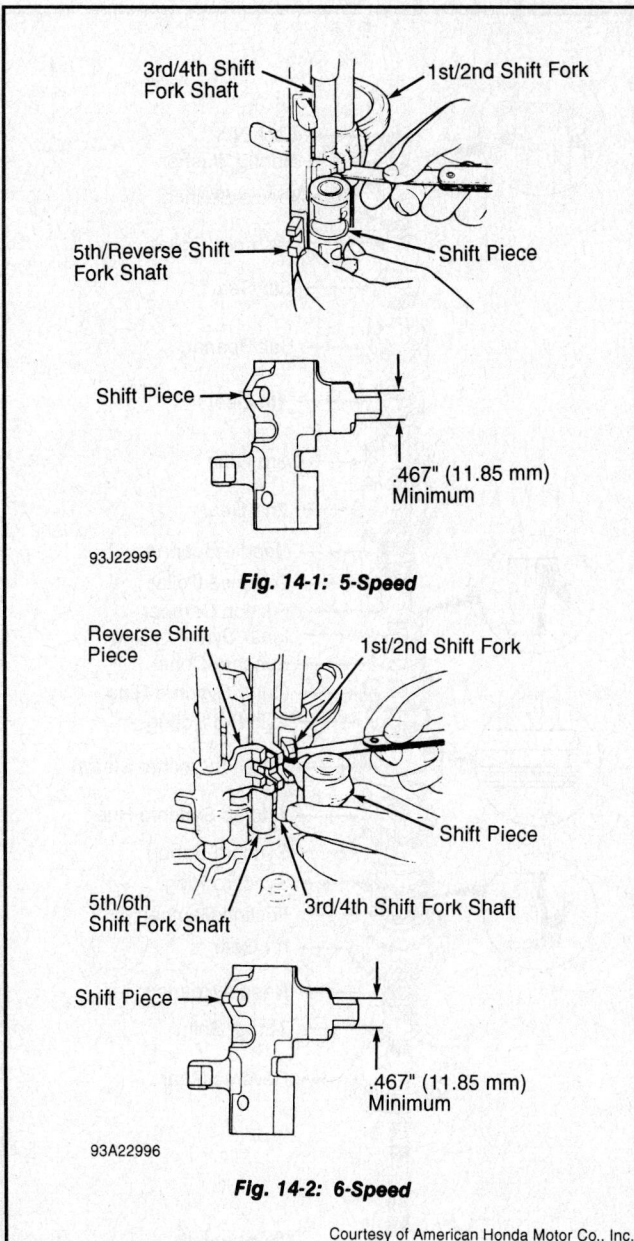

Fig. 14-1: 5-Speed

Fig. 14-2: 6-Speed

Courtesy of American Honda Motor Co., Inc.

Fig. 14: Measuring Shift Piece

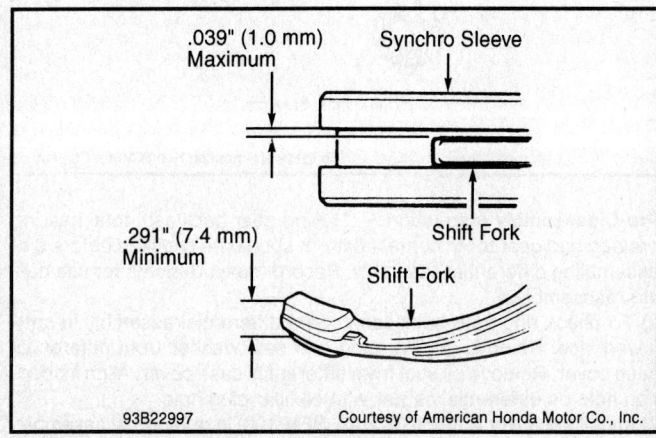

Fig. 15: Measuring Change Holder Shift Fork

Courtesy of American Honda Motor Co., Inc.

NOTE: Bearing preload must be adjusted if any of the following items are replaced: transmission housing (both halves), secondary gear, bearings, 75 mm thrust shim and/or 90 mm washer. The 75 mm washer is installed in transmission half of housing. The 90 mm washer is installed in clutch half of housing

Bearing Preload – **1)** Remove bearing outer race and 75-mm thrust shim from transmission housing by prying up on bearing outer race or by heating housing. Do not exceed 100°F (212°C).

CAUTION: Do not reuse thrust shim if outer race was pried out.

2) Select new thrust shim of same thickness as one removed and install. Install new outer bearing race in housing. Ensure there is no clearance between race and shim. Install 36 mm sealing bolt in end of secondary gear. Install secondary gear assembly in clutch housing.
3) Without installing mainshaft, countershaft or reverse gear assembly, install transmission housing and install all housing bolts and tighten to 36 ft. lbs. (50 N.m).
4) Rotate secondary gear in both directions to seat bearings. Install INCH lb. torque wrench into head of 36-mm sealing bolt and measure bearing preload force in both directions. Rotating torque specification is 12-23 INCH lbs. (1.4-2.6 N.m). If the bearing preload is beyond specification, select shim that will provide correct preload.

NOTE: Changing shim to next size will increase or decrease preload 2.6-3.5 INCH lbs. (.29-.40 N.m).

5) DO NOT use more than one shim. Shims are available at .03 mm increments in sizes from .061-.096 (1.56-2.43 mm). Part numbers are (23941-PY5-000 to 23970-PY5-000).

TRANSMISSION REASSEMBLY

1) Install components in reverse order of disassembly. *See Figs. 6-9.* Install secondary gear assembly. Install mainshaft, countershaft and shift forks as an assembly. Install change holder and reverse shift holder. Apply liquid gasket to mating surface of clutch housing. Install housing. Follow tightening sequence. *See Fig. 25.* Tighten bolts to specifications. See TORQUE SPECIFICATIONS table.

NOTE: This transmission uses no gasket between major housings; use Honda Genuine Liquid Gasket (08178-0001). Assemble housing within 20 minutes after applying liquid gasket. Allow 30 minutes curing time before filling with oil.

2) Install all detent balls, springs, bolts. Install oil pump tubes. Install back-up, neutral safety switches.
3) On 5-Speed models, install 5th gear components in reverse order of disassembly.
4) On 6-Speed models, install 5th and 6th gear components in reverse order of disassembly and reverse lockout solenoid.
5) On all models, install new lock nut and stake lock nut tab into shaft groove.
6) Apply liquid gasket to mating surface of housing. Through opening in cover, hold snap ring expanded and set snap ring in groove of mainshaft bearing while lowering cover into position. Install cover. Ensure snap ring is securely seated in groove of countershaft bearing. Snap ring opening clearance should be .106-.209" (2.69-5.32 mm). Follow tightening sequence. *See Fig. 25.* Tighten bolts to specifications. See TORQUE SPECIFICATIONS table.

NOTE: Refer to Figs. 6-9 for torque specifications not listed in TORQUE SPECIFICATIONS table. Apply liquid gasket to all threads.

MANUAL TRANSMISSIONS
Acura K4A6 & K4F6 (Cont.)

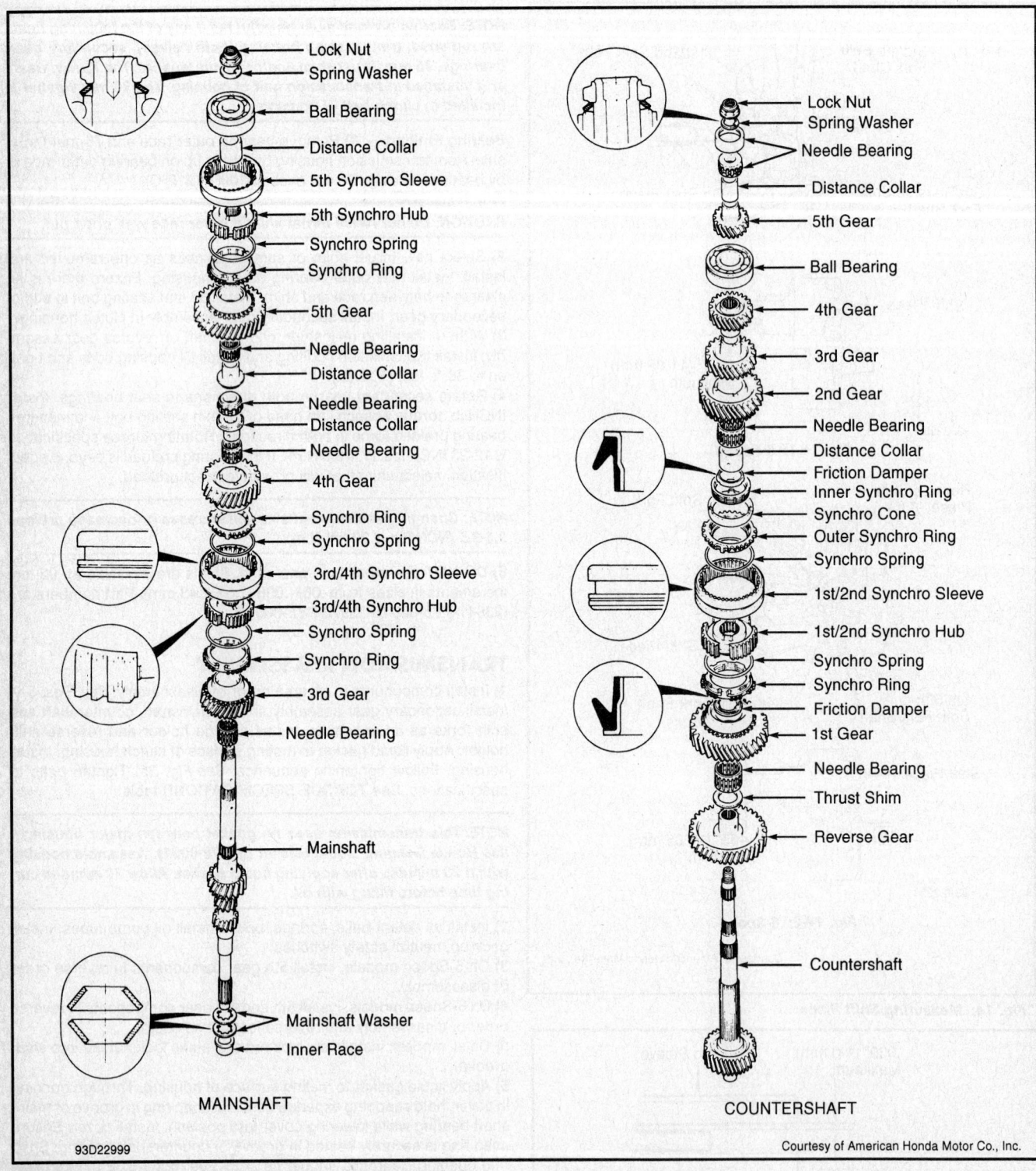

MAINSHAFT

- Lock Nut
- Spring Washer
- Ball Bearing
- Distance Collar
- 5th Synchro Sleeve
- 5th Synchro Hub
- Synchro Spring
- Synchro Ring
- 5th Gear
- Needle Bearing
- Distance Collar
- Needle Bearing
- Distance Collar
- Needle Bearing
- 4th Gear
- Synchro Ring
- Synchro Spring
- 3rd/4th Synchro Sleeve
- 3rd/4th Synchro Hub
- Synchro Spring
- Synchro Ring
- 3rd Gear
- Needle Bearing
- Mainshaft
- Mainshaft Washer
- Inner Race

COUNTERSHAFT

- Lock Nut
- Spring Washer
- Needle Bearing
- Distance Collar
- 5th Gear
- Ball Bearing
- 4th Gear
- 3rd Gear
- 2nd Gear
- Needle Bearing
- Distance Collar
- Friction Damper
- Inner Synchro Ring
- Synchro Cone
- Outer Synchro Ring
- Synchro Spring
- 1st/2nd Synchro Sleeve
- 1st/2nd Synchro Hub
- Synchro Spring
- Synchro Ring
- Friction Damper
- 1st Gear
- Needle Bearing
- Thrust Shim
- Reverse Gear
- Countershaft

93D22999

Courtesy of American Honda Motor Co., Inc.

Fig. 16: Exploded View Of 5-Speed Mainshaft & Countershaft

DIFFERENTIAL ASSEMBLY

OVERHAUL

NOTE: Differential carrier assembly components (excluding ring gear) are not serviced separately. If any components exhibit wear, damage or are not within specifications, the assembly must be replaced as a unit. Pre-disassembly inspection should be performed before disassembly of differential assembly. This will indicate if proper thrust shims and thrust washers are used.

Pre-Disassembly Inspection – 1) Ring gear backlash, total bearing preload and gear tooth contact pattern should be checked before disassembling differential assembly. Record measurements for use during reassembly.

2) To check ring gear backlash, mount differential assembly in soft-jawed vice. Remove oil filler plug and seal washer from differential case cover. Remove oil seal from differential case cover. Align inspection hole on differential carrier with oil filler plug hole.

3) Install Lock Nut Wrench (07HAA-SF10100) in differential assembly. *See Fig. 26.* Mount dial indicator on differential case.

4) Measure ring gear backlash on differential carrier. Ring gear backlash should be .002-.006" (.06-.14 mm).

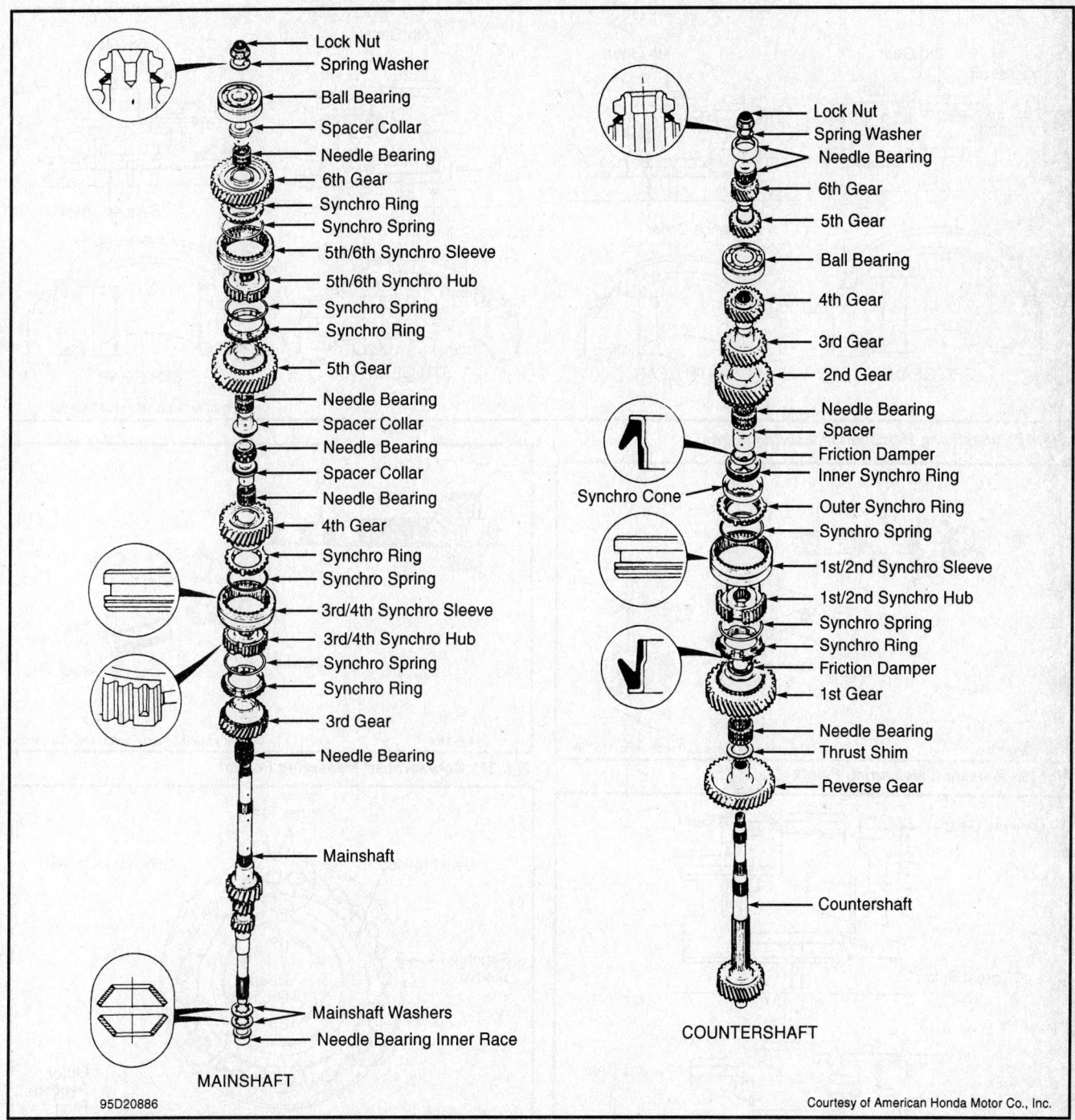

Lock Nut
Spring Washer
Ball Bearing
Spacer Collar
Needle Bearing
6th Gear
Synchro Ring
Synchro Spring
5th/6th Synchro Sleeve
5th/6th Synchro Hub
Synchro Spring
Synchro Ring
5th Gear
Needle Bearing
Spacer Collar
Needle Bearing
Spacer Collar
Needle Bearing
4th Gear
Synchro Ring
Synchro Spring
3rd/4th Synchro Sleeve
3rd/4th Synchro Hub
Synchro Spring
Synchro Ring
3rd Gear
Needle Bearing
Mainshaft
Mainshaft Washers
Needle Bearing Inner Race
MAINSHAFT

Lock Nut
Spring Washer
Needle Bearing
6th Gear
5th Gear
Ball Bearing
4th Gear
3rd Gear
2nd Gear
Needle Bearing
Spacer
Friction Damper
Inner Synchro Ring
Synchro Cone
Outer Synchro Ring
Synchro Spring
1st/2nd Synchro Sleeve
1st/2nd Synchro Hub
Synchro Spring
Synchro Ring
Friction Damper
1st Gear
Needle Bearing
Thrust Shim
Reverse Gear
Countershaft
COUNTERSHAFT

95D20886

Courtesy of American Honda Motor Co., Inc.

Fig. 17: Exploded View Of 6-Speed Mainshaft & Countershaft

5) If ring gear backlash is within specification, proper thickness thrust shims are installed behind bearing races for differential carrier bearings, provided no components are changed. If ring gear backlash is not within specification, different thickness thrust shim must be installed during reassembly.

6) To measure total bearing preload, install a dial-type INCH-lb. torque wrench on end of drive pinion. Rotate drive pinion and note total bearing preload. Total bearing preload should be 12-17 INCH-lbs. (1.4-2.0 N.m) with used bearings.

NOTE: *If total bearing preload is not within specification, different thickness shim must be installed behind bearing race for differential carrier bearings.*

7) To check gear tooth contact pattern, remove differential case cover bolts in a crisscross pattern. Remove differential case cover. *See Fig. 27.* Clean and paint both sides of ring gear teeth with Prussian Blue.

8) Install differential case cover. Install and tighten bolts in a crisscross pattern to 33 ft.lbs. (45 N.m). Install Lock Nut Wrench (07HAA-SF10100) in differential assembly. *See Fig. 26.*

9) Rotate ring gear both directions while applying resistance on drive pinion. Remove differential case cover and inspect ring gear tooth contact pattern. Correct gear tooth contact should be centered on the ring gear. See GEAR TOOTH CONTACT PATTERNS article in APPLICATIONS & IDENTIFICATION.

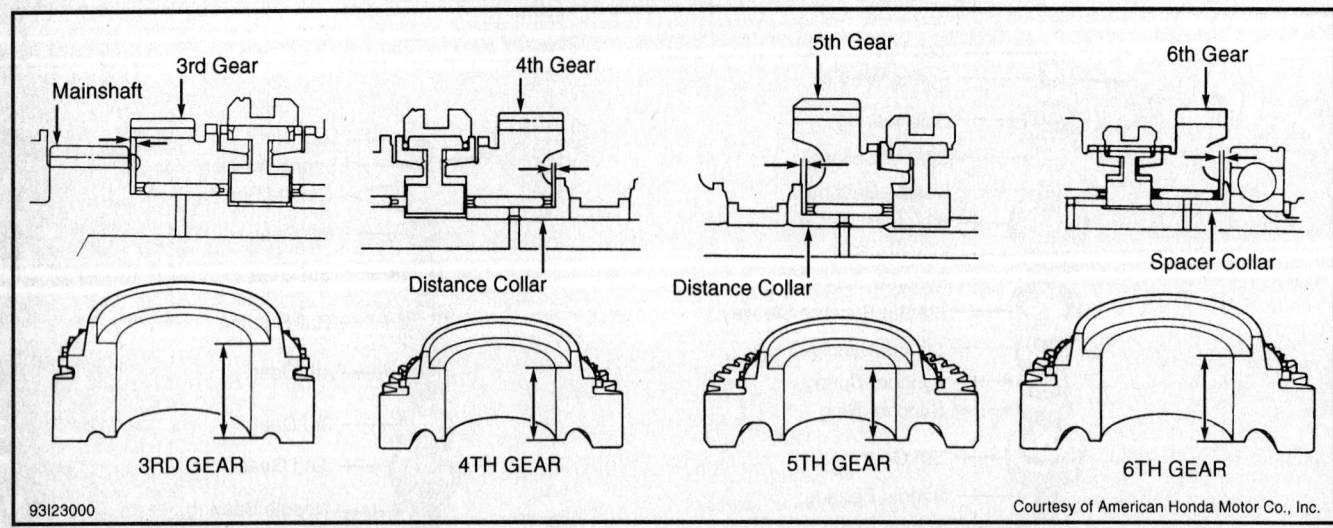

93I23000   Courtesy of American Honda Motor Co., Inc.

Fig. 18: Identifying Mainshaft Measuring Points

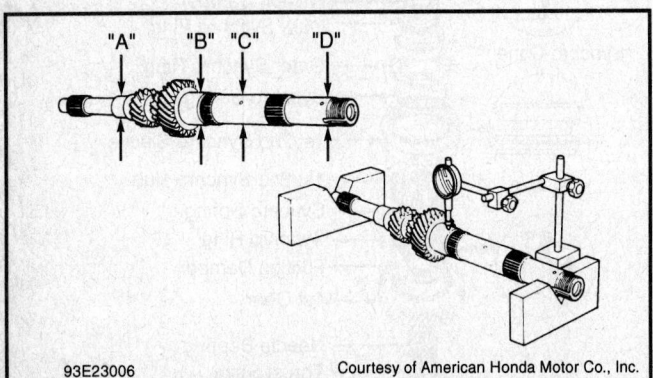

93E23006   Courtesy of American Honda Motor Co., Inc.

Fig. 19: Mainshaft Measuring Points

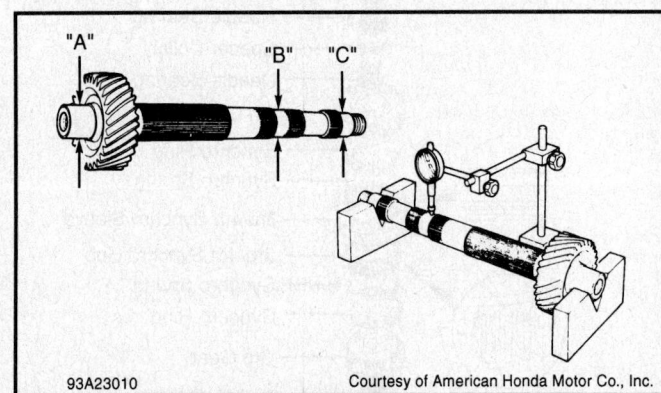

93A23010   Courtesy of American Honda Motor Co., Inc.

Fig. 21: Countershaft Measuring Points

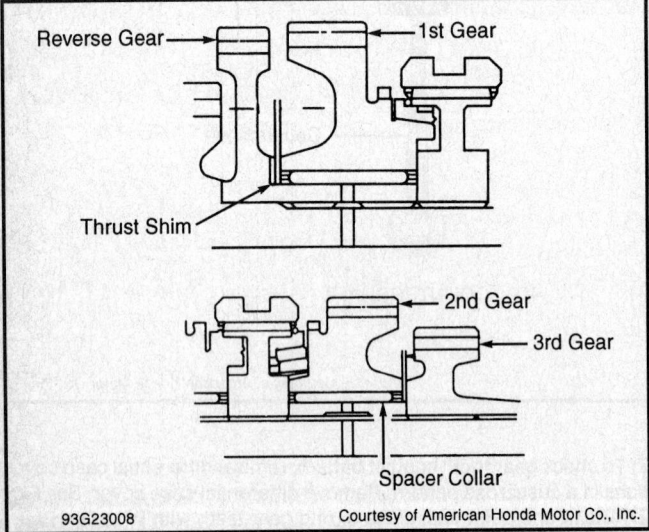

93G23008   Courtesy of American Honda Motor Co., Inc.

Fig. 20: Identifying Countershaft Measuring Points

Disassembly – 1) Remove bolts, speed sensor assembly and "O" ring. Remove differential case cover bolts in a crisscross pattern. Remove differential case cover. Remove breather plate from differential case cover (if necessary). *See Fig. 27.*

2) Remove differential carrier assembly from differential case. Remove coolant pipe joint bolts, seal washers and coolant pipes. Remove oil cooler nuts, oil cooler, "O" rings and oil guide pipe.

3) Using hammer and chisel, cut lock nut tab and pry away from drive pinion. Insert 17-mm Allen wrench into gear end of drive pinion. Secure long end of Allen wrench in vise.

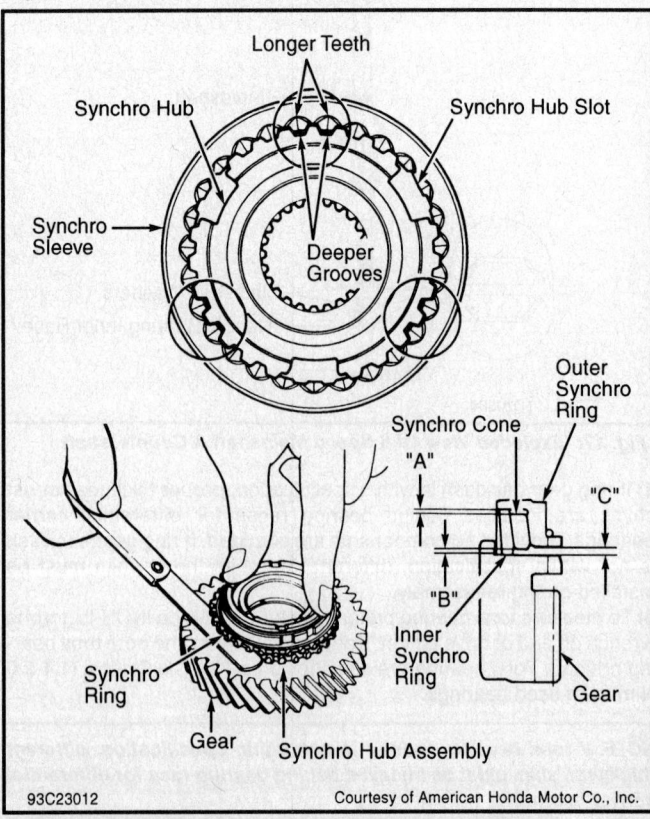

93C23012   Courtesy of American Honda Motor Co., Inc.

Fig. 22: Measuring Synchro Hub Clearance & Assembly

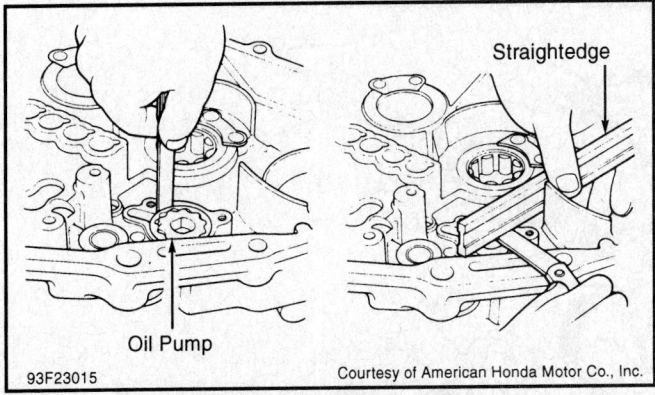

Fig. 23: Measuring Oil Pump Clearance

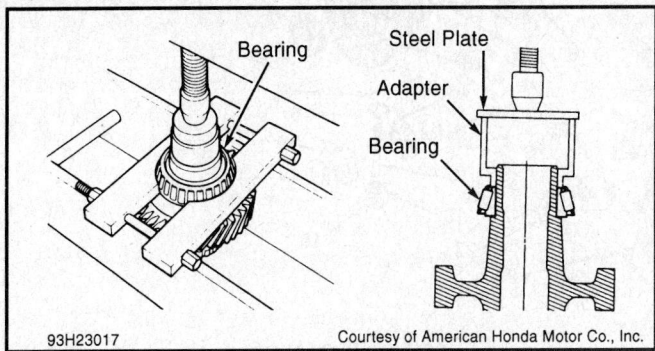

Fig. 24: Secondary Gear Bearing Removal & Assembly

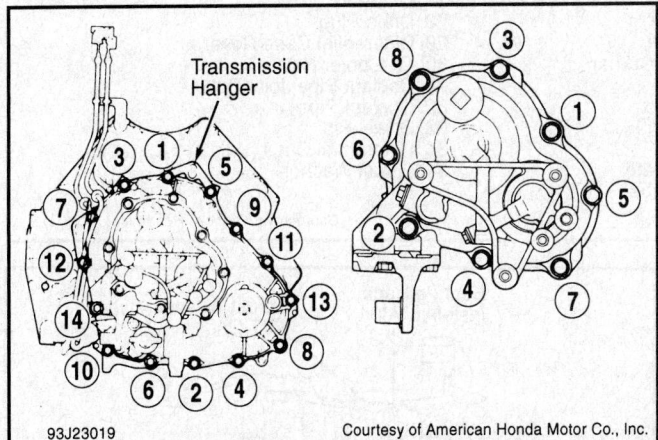

Fig. 25: Transmission Assembly Tightening Sequence

4) Remove lock nut, thrust washer and drive pinion hub. Remove oil seal and thrust washer. Using soft-faced hammer, tap drive pinion from pinion bearing on front of drive pinion. Remove drive pinion, pinion spacer and thrust washers.

5) Inspect pinion bearings. Ensure bearings are free of burrs, chips or scoring. Rotate bearing by hand to check for smooth operation. If replacing pinion bearing on drive pinion, use press and bearing remover to press bearing from drive pinion. Remove drive pinion thrust shim from drive pinion.

NOTE: If pinion bearings are replaced, bearing races must also be replaced.

6) To remove pinion bearing races from differential case, using hammer and brass drift, tap bearing races from differential case. Inspect differential carrier bearings. Ensure bearings are free of burrs, chips or scoring. Rotate bearing by hand to check for smooth operation. If replacing differential carrier bearings, use press and bearing remover to press bearing from differential carrier.

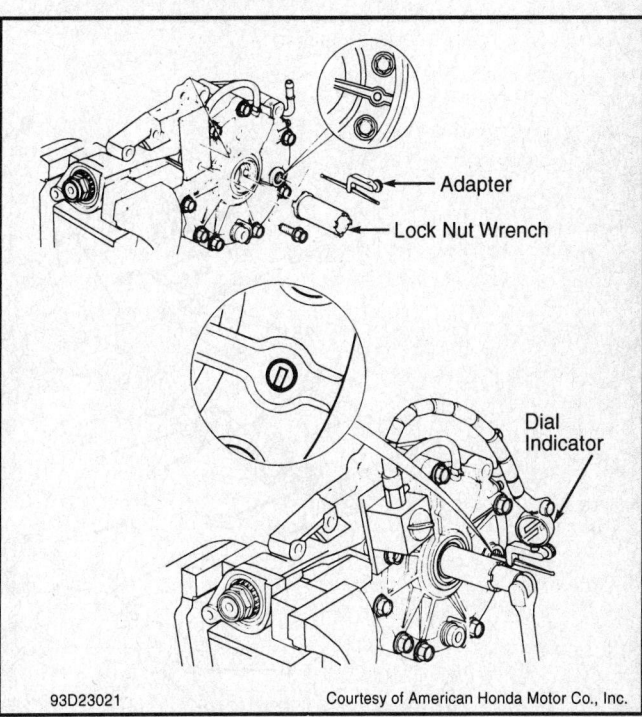

Fig. 26: Rotating Ring Gear & Checking Ring Gear Backlash

NOTE: If differential carrier bearings are replaced, bearing races must also be replaced.

7) To remove differential carrier bearing races, use hammer and brass drift to tap bearing race from differential case or differential case cover. Remove thrust shim(s), located below bearing races, from differential case or differential case cover.

NOTE: Thrust shim must be replaced if bearing race was removed from differential case or differential case cover.

NOTE: Pinion gear backlash must be checked to determine if differential carrier assembly must be replaced. Differential carrier bearings must be removed from differential carrier to measure pinion gear backlash.

8) Mount differential carrier in "V" blocks with axle shaft and intermediate shaft inserted into side gears. *See Fig. 28.* Using dial indicator, check pinion gear backlash. Pinion gear backlash should be .002-.012" (.05-.30 mm).

9) Replace differential carrier assembly if pinion gear backlash is not within specification. Remove ring gear (if necessary).

Cleaning & Inspection – Clean components with solvent and dry with compressed air. Inspect components for damage. Replace components if damaged.

Reassembly – **1)** Install ring gear. Install and tighten ring gear bolts to specification in a crisscross pattern. See TORQUE SPECIFICATIONS. Using press, install differential carrier bearings on differential carrier (if removed). Ensure bearings are fully seated.

2) Use Shaft (07MAF-SPOO13A), Bearing Race Installer "A" (07MAF-SPOO11A) and Bearing Race Installer "B" (07MAF-SPOO12A) to install bearing races. *See Fig. 29.* Install drive pinion bearing races in differential case starting with outer bearing race (lock nut side) and then inner bearing race.

3) If installing bearing races for differential carrier bearings, install NEW thrust shim(s) in differential case or differential case cover. Ensure thrust shim is the same thickness as thrust shim that was removed. Using hammer and bearing race installer, drive bearing race into differential case and differential case cover.

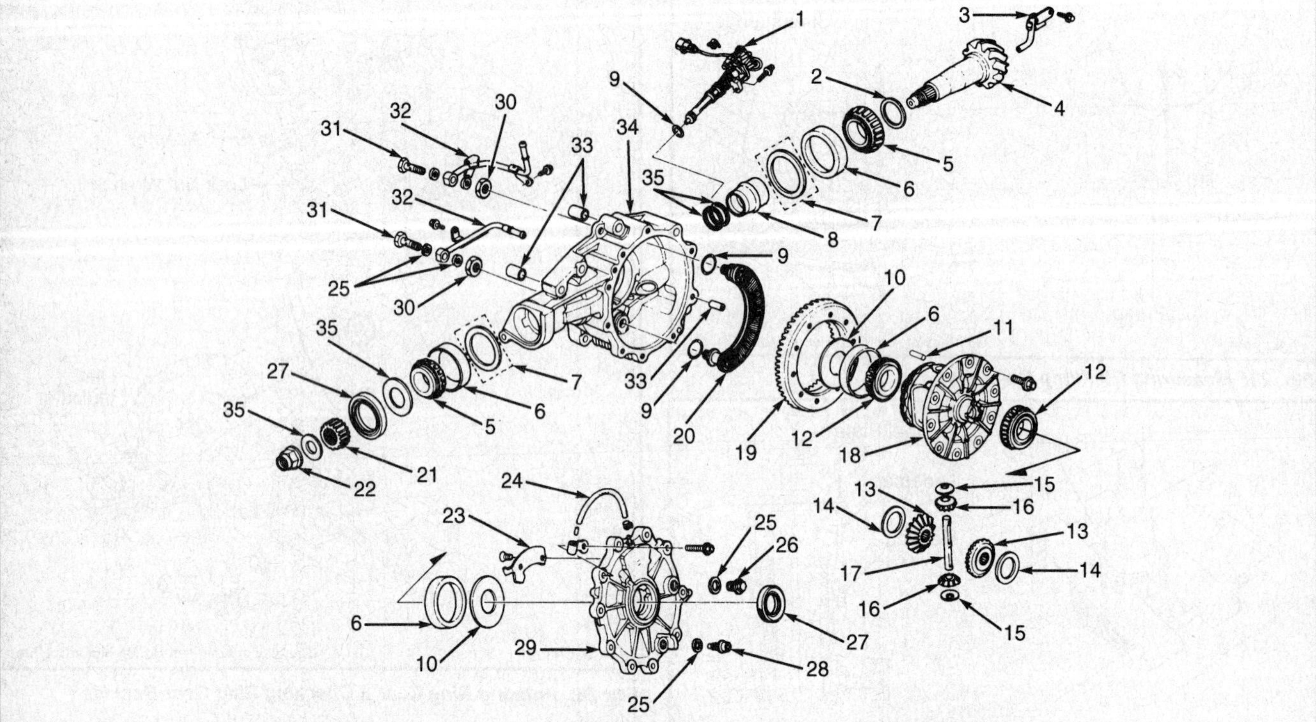

95C19564

1. Speed Sensor Assembly	13. Side Gear	25. Seal Washer
2. Drive Pinion Thrust Shim	14. Side Gear Thrust Washer	26. Oil Filler Plug
3. Oil Guide Pipe	15. Pinion Gear Thrust Washer	27. Oil Seal
4. Drive Pinion	16. Pinion Gear	28. Drain Plug
5. Pinion Bearing	17. Pinion Shaft	29. Differential Case Cover
6. Bearing Race	18. Differential Carrier	30. Oil Cooler Nut
7. Thrust Washer (A/T Only)	19. Ring Gear	31. Coolant Pipe Joint Bolt
8. Pinion Spacer	20. Oil Cooler	32. Coolant Pipe
9. "O" Ring	21. Drive Pinion Hub	33. Dowel Pin
10. Thrust Shim	22. Lock Nut	34. Differential Case
11. Pin	23. Breather Plate	35. Thrust Washer
12. Differential Carrier Bearing	24. Breather Tube	

Courtesy of American Honda Motor Co., Inc.

Fig. 27: Exploded View Of Differential Assembly

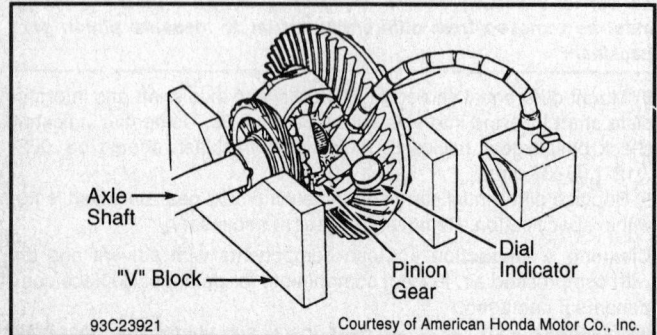

93C23921   Courtesy of American Honda Motor Co., Inc.

Fig. 28: Checking Pinion Gear Backlash

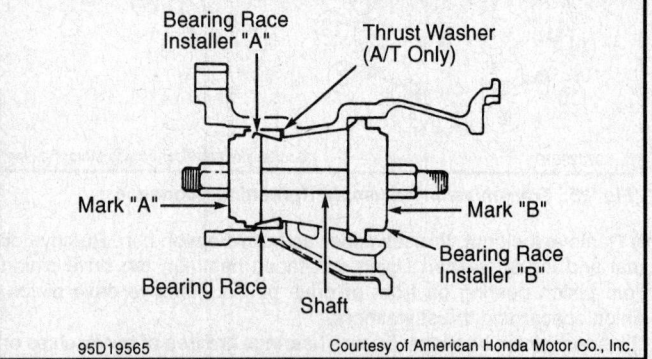

95D19565   Courtesy of American Honda Motor Co., Inc.

**Fig. 29: Installing Bearing Race For Drive Pinion
(Outer Bearing Shown; Inner Bearing Race Is Similar)**

4) If original drive pinion and ring gear are being installed, install original thickness drive pinion thrust shim on drive pinion (if removed). If NEW drive pinion and ring gear are being installed, proper thickness drive pinion thrust shim must be determined to obtain correct drive pinion height. See DRIVE PINION HEIGHT under ADJUSTMENTS.

5) If installing pinion bearing on drive pinion, use press, old spacer and bearing installer to press pinion bearing onto drive pinion. Lubricate all pinion bearings and threads on drive pinion with oil.

6) Install drive pinion in differential case. DO NOT install pinion spacer and thrust washers at this time. Install pinion bearing on drive pinion. Using hammer and bearing installer, drive outer pinion bearing onto drive pinion while supporting drive pinion. Install thrust washer, drive pinion hub, thrust washer and lock nut.

7) Tighten lock nut to 15 ft. lbs. (20 N.m). DO NOT overtighten lock nut or pinion bearings may be damaged, as pinion spacer and thrust washers are not installed. Clean drive pinion and ring teeth and coat with Prussian Blue. Lubricate differential carrier bearings with oil.

8) Install differential carrier into differential case. Install differential case cover. Install and tighten differential case cover bolts in a crisscross pattern to 33 ft.lbs. (45 N.m).

9) Install Lock Nut Wrench (07HAA-SF10100) in differential assembly. See Fig. 26. Rotate ring gear on full revolution in both directions while applying resistance (on drive pinion). Remove differential cover and inspect ring gear tooth contact pattern. Correct gear tooth contact should be centered on the ring gear. See GEAR TOOTH CONTACT PATTERNS article in APPLICATIONS & IDENTIFICATION.

10) If gear tooth contact pattern is incorrect, drive pinion height must be changed to correct gear tooth contact pattern. Change drive pinion thrust shim located below bearing on drive pinion to adjust drive pinion height.

11) If gear tooth contact pattern is correct, remove components from drive pinion for installation of pinion spacer. Install NEW pinion spacer and thrust washers on drive pinion.

12) Install outer pinion bearing on drive pinion. Using hammer and bearing installer, drive outer pinion bearing onto drive pinion while supporting drive pinion.

13) Install thrust washer, drive pinion hub, thrust washer and NEW lock nut on drive pinion. Check pinion bearing preload. See PINION BEARING PRELOAD under ADJUSTMENTS.

14) Once correct pinion bearing preload is obtained, stake lock nut against drive pinion. Clean drive pinion and ring teeth and coat with Prussian Blue. Lubricate differential carrier bearings with oil.

15) Install differential carrier into differential case. Install differential case cover. Install and tighten differential case cover bolts in a crisscross pattern to 33 ft.lbs. (45 N.m).

16) Check TOTAL BEARING PRELOAD. See TOTAL BEARING PRELOAD under ADJUSTMENTS. Once correct total bearing preload is correct, check ring gear backlash. See RING GEAR BACKLASH under ADJUSTMENTS.

17) Once correct ring gear backlash is obtained, remove differential case cover and differential assembly. Check gear tooth contact pattern. Correct gear tooth contact should be centered on the ring gear. See GEAR TOOTH CONTACT PATTERNS article in APPLICATIONS & IDENTIFICATION.

18) Install breather plate on differential case cover (if removed). Install breather plate bolts and tighten to specification. Stake heads of breather plate bolts against differential case cover.

19) Install oil guide pipe, oil cooler and NEW "O" rings. Tighten oil guide pipe bolt and oil cooler nuts to specification. Using NEW seal washers, install coolant pipes and coolant pipe joint bolts. Tighten coolant pipe joint bolts to specification.

20) Install differential assembly. Apply Liquid Gasket (08718-0001) on sealing surface of differential case cover. Install differential case cover. Install and tighten bolts to specification in a crisscross pattern.

21) Using hammer and oil seal installer, install NEW oil seal in differential case cover. Using hammer and oil seal installer, install NEW oil seal for drive pinion.

22) Oil seal must be installed so installation distance on oil seal is below surface of differential case .22-.24" (5.5-6.0 mm). *See Fig. 30.* Using NEW "O" ring, install speed sensor assembly. Install and tighten bolt to specification.

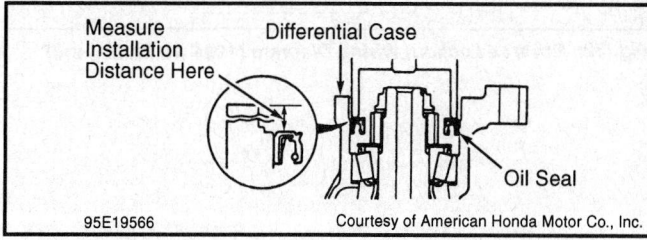

95E19566　　Courtesy of American Honda Motor Co., Inc.

Fig. 30: Measuring Drive Pinion Oil Seal Installation Distance

ADJUSTMENTS

NOTE: If drive pinion and ring gear are replaced, drive pinion height must be set. Drive pinion height may also need to be set if incorrect gear tooth contact pattern exists.

Drive Pinion Height – 1) Drive pinion height is controlled by thickness of drive pinion thrust shim located between pinion bearing and drive pinion shaft. When installing used drive pinion and ring gear

and gear tooth contact pattern is incorrect, see GEAR TOOTH CONTACT PATTERN in APPLICATIONS & IDENTIFICATION to determine if thrust shim should be thicker or thinner.

2) When installing NEW drive pinion and ring gear, calculate drive pinion thrust shim thickness by noting etched mark located on side of drive pinion. *See Fig. 31.*

3) Etched mark is a (+) positive or (–) negative mark along with a numerical digit indicating drive pinion size. Etched mark is positive or negative in thousandths of a millimeter.

NOTE: Etched mark is indicated in thousandths of a millimeter. If etched mark is -20, this is a negative .02 mm.

4) If etched mark on old drive pinion is positive (+), add it to the old drive pinion thrust shim thickness. If etched mark on old drive pinion is negative (–), subtract it from the old drive pinion thrust shim thickness.

5) If etched mark on NEW drive pinion is positive (+), subtract it from drive pinion thrust shim thickness obtained in step **4)**. If etched mark on NEW drive pinion is negative (–), add it to drive pinion thrust shim thickness obtained in step **4)**.

6) For example, if old drive pinion thrust shim thickness is 2.00 mm and old drive pinion etched mark is +20 (.02 mm) and NEW drive pinion etched mark is -10 (.01 mm), replacement drive pinion thrust shim thickness should be 2.03 mm.

7) Select drive pinion thrust shim that is closest to but not more than the determined drive pinion thrust shim thickness. Drive pinion thrust shims are available in thicknesses of .064-.089" (1.64-2.27 mm) in .001" (.03 mm) increments. Part numbers are 41410-PY4-000 to 41431-PY4-000 in numerical sequence.

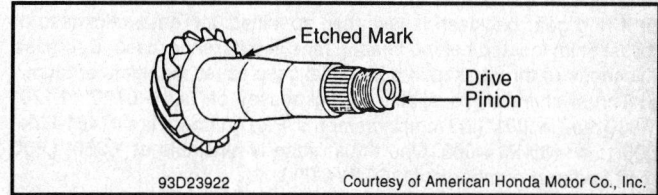

Etched Mark — Drive Pinion

93D23922　　Courtesy of American Honda Motor Co., Inc.

Fig. 31: Identifying Drive Pinion Etched Mark Location

Pinion Bearing Preload – 1) Tighten drive pinion lock nut to 162 ft. lbs. (220 N.m). Rotate drive pinion several revolutions to seat bearings.

2) Install a dial-type INCH-lb. torque wrench on end of drive pinion. Rotate drive pinion and note pinion bearing preload. Pinion bearing preload should be within specification. See PINION BEARING PRELOAD SPECIFICATIONS table.

PINION BEARING PRELOAD SPECIFICATIONS

Application	INCH Lbs. (N.m)
New Bearings	8-14 (.9-1.5)
Used Bearings	6-11 (.7-1.2)

3) If pinion bearing preload exceeds specification, replace pinion spacer. If pinion bearing preload is less than specified, slightly tighten lock nut until correct pinion bearing preload is obtained.

CAUTION: DO NOT tighten lock nut to more than 237 ft. lbs. (320 N.m). If pinion bearing preload is still less than specified with lock nut tightened to 236 ft. lbs. (320 N.m), replace pinion spacer.

Total Bearing Preload – 1) With differential fully assembled, without oil seals, install Wrench (07HAA-SF10100) in differential assembly. *See Fig. 26.*

2) Rotate ring gear one full revolution in both directions while applying resistance on drive pinion. Remove wrench from differential assembly.

3) Install a dial-type INCH-lb. torque wrench on end of drive pinion. Rotate drive pinion several times and note total bearing preload. Total bearing preload should be within specification. See TOTAL BEARING PRELOAD SPECIFICATIONS table.

MANUAL TRANSMISSIONS
Acura K4A6 & K4F6 (Cont.)

TOTAL BEARING PRELOAD SPECIFICATIONS

Application	INCH Lbs. (N.m)
New Bearings	
All New Bearings	13-20 (1.5-2.3)
Differential Carrier Bearings Only	
Outer Bearing (Ring Gear Side) Only	11-18 (1.3-1.9)
Inner Bearing (Drive Pinion Side) Only	14-21 (1.6-2.4)
Used Bearings	12-17 (1.4-2.0)

4) If total bearing preload is not within specification, increase preload by increasing thickness of thrust shim located below bearing races in differential case and differential case cover. Decreasing shim thickness will decrease total bearing preload.

NOTE: Ensure thrust shim thickness is increased the same amount on both thrust shims.

Ring Gear Backlash – 1) Mount differential assembly in soft-jawed vice. Remove oil filler plug and seal washer from differential case cover. Remove oil seal from differential case cover. Align inspection hole on differential carrier with oil filler plug hole.
2) Install Wrench (07HAA-SF10100) in differential assembly. See Fig. 26. Mount dial indicator on differential case cover. Measure ring gear backlash on differential carrier. Ring gear backlash should be .002-.006" (.06-.14 mm).
3) If ring gear backlash is within specification, proper thickness thrust shims are installed behind bearing races for differential carrier bearings, provided no components are changed.
4) If ring gear backlash exceeds specification, decrease thickness of thrust shim located behind bearing race in differential case. Increase thickness of thrust shim in differential case cover the same amount.
5) If ring gear backlash is less than specified, increase thickness of thrust shim located behind bearing race in differential case. Decrease thickness of thrust shim in differential case cover the same amount.
6) Thrust shims are available in thicknesses of .0461-.0720" (1.170-1.830 mm) in .001" (.03 mm) increments. Part numbers are 41461-PY4-000 to 41483-PY4-000. One thrust shim is available at .0260" (.660 mm) and part number is 41460-PY4-000.

AXLE ASSEMBLY SPECIFICATIONS

AXLE ASSEMBLY SPECIFICATIONS

Application	Specification
Nominal Pinion Shim Thickness	.030" (.76 mm)
Pinion Seal-To-Top Of Diff. Housing	.24" (6 mm)
Ring Gear Backlash	.002-.006" (.06-.14 mm)

TORQUE SPECIFICATIONS

TORQUE SPECIFICATIONS

Application	Ft. Lbs. (N.m)
Transmission	
Back-Up Light Switch Bolt	18 (25)
Change Holder Outer Bolt	11 (15)
Countershaft Lock Nut	118 (160)
Mainshaft Lock Nut	118 (160)
Neutral Safety Switch Bolt	18 (25)
Oil Filler Plug	33 (45)
Oil Drain Plug	29 (40)
Oil Pump Pipe Bolt	21 (29)
Reverse Shift Holder	19 (26)
Transmission Cover Bolt	20 (28)
Transmission Housing Bolt	20 (28)
36-mm Sealing Bolt	18 (25)

	INCH Lbs. (N.m)
Bearing Retainer Plate Bolt	89 (10)
Change Holder Inner Bolt	106 (12)
Release Bearing Guide Bolt	106 (12)

Application	Ft. Lbs. (N.m)
Differential	
Cooler Line Joint Bolt	21 (29)
Cover Bolt	33 (45)
Drain Plug	29 (40)
Oil Filler Plug	33 (45)
Pinion Nut	162 (220)
Ring Gear Bolt	87 (118)

	INCH Lbs. (N.m)
Breather Plate	106 (12)

WIRING DIAGRAMS

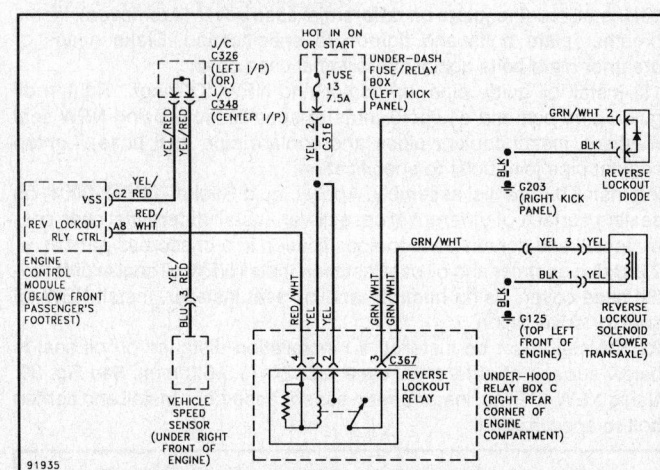

Fig. 32: Reverse Lockout Wiring Diagram (1995 Acura Legend)

Acura: Integra
Honda: Civic Del Sol (1995)

APPLICATION & LABOR TIMES

APPLICATION & LABOR TIMES

Vehicle Application	Labor Times		Series
	[1] R & I	[2] Overhaul	
Acura			
Integra			
1995	3.6	5.5	Y80
1996	3.6	5.5	S80
Honda			
1995 Civic Del Sol [3]	3.7	4.1	Y21 & S21

[1] – Removal and installation of transmission from vehicle chassis.
[2] – Bench overhaul time for transaxle/differential. DOES NOT include removal and installation.
[3] – If cruise control interferes add .3 hr. If power steering interferes add .3 hr.

IDENTIFICATION

NOTE: On Integra, determine engine size: 1.8L (B18B1) or 1.8L VTEC (B18C1), before disassembling transmission or components.

Transmission identification is stamped on a metal pad on top of transmission. First 3 numbers indicate model. *See Fig. 1.*

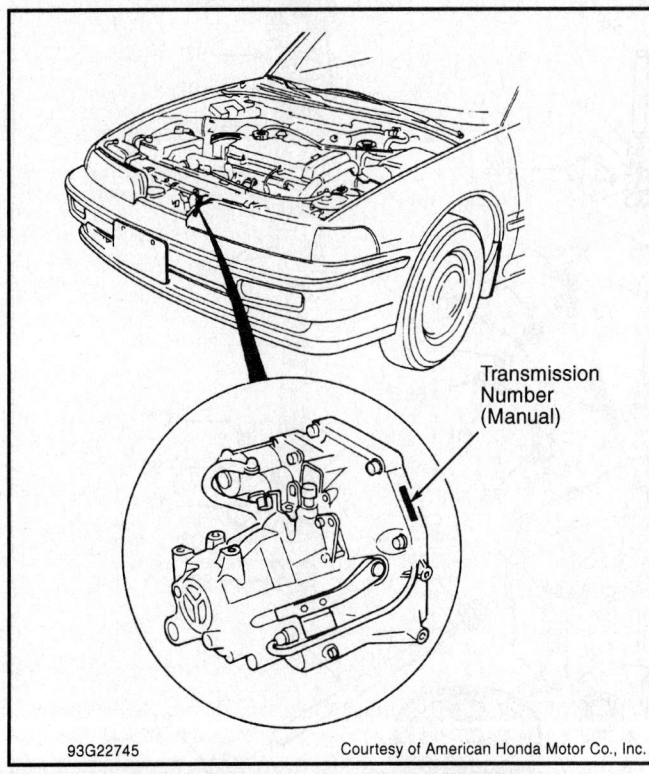

Transmission Number (Manual)

93G22745   Courtesy of American Honda Motor Co., Inc.

Fig. 1: Locating Transmission Identification Number

LUBRICATION & ADJUSTMENT

See appropriate MANUAL TRANSMISSION SERVICING article in TRANSMISSION SERVICING section.

TROUBLE SHOOTING

See GENERAL TROUBLE SHOOTING article in this section.

ON-VEHICLE SERVICE

AXLE SHAFTS

See appropriate AXLE SHAFTS article in AXLE SHAFTS & TRANSFER CASES section.

REMOVAL & INSTALLATION

See appropriate MANUAL TRANSMISSION REMOVAL article in TRANSMISSION SERVICING section.

TRANSMISSION DISASSEMBLY

NOTE: If equipped with B18C1 VTEC engine, when replacing either transmission housing, bearing preload must be reset.

NOTE: Place clutch housing on supports high enough to keep mainshaft from hitting workbench.

1) Remove back-up light switch. Remove bolts, springs and steel balls from transmission cover. Remove reverse idler gear shaft bolt. Remove all housing bolts in crisscross pattern and 32-mm sealing bolt (32-mm bolt has square hole).

2) Remove snap ring under 32-mm bolt. Separate transmission housings. Remove thrust shim and oil guide plate from housing. *See Figs. 2-5 .* Remove 16-mm sealing bolt (bolt has hex hole). Remove oil gutter plate.

3) Measure clearance between reverse shift fork and 5th/reverse shift piece pin. *See Fig. 6.* Clearance for reverse side (top of "L" groove) should be .002"-.018" (.05-.45 mm). Clearance for 5th gear side should be .016-.035" (.40-.90 mm).

4) If clearance exceeds specification, measure width of groove in reverse shift fork. Width for reverse side should be .278-.285" (7.05-7.25 mm). Width for 5th gear side should be .291-.303" (7.40-7.70 mm). If width of groove exceeds specification, replace reverse shift fork. If width of groove is within specification, replace 5th/reverse shift piece.

5) Measure clearance between reverse idler gear and reverse shift fork. *See Fig. 7.* Clearance should be .020-.043" (.50-1.10 mm). Service limit is .071" (1.80 mm). If clearance exceeds service limit, measure width of reverse shift fork pawl groove. Opening should be .512-.524" (13.0-13.3 mm). If width exceeds specification, replace reverse shift arm. If width is within specification, replace reverse shift fork.

6) Remove reverse shift fork. Shift 3rd/4th shift fork to the 4th side. Remove reverse idler gear, shaft and washer, if equipped. Measure clearance between shift piece and shift arm. Clearance should be .004-.012" (.10-.30 mm). Service limit is .024" (.60 mm). If clearance exceeds service limit, measure width of groove in shift piece. *See Fig. 8.* Width should be .319-.323" (8.10-8.20 mm). If width of groove exceeds specification, replace shift piece. If width of groove is within specification, replace shift arm.

7) Measure clearance between select arm and interlock. Clearance should be .002-.010" (.05-.25 mm). Service limit is .020" (.50 mm). If clearance exceeds service limit, measure width of interlock. *See Fig. 9.* Width should be .390-.394" (9.90-10.00 mm). If width exceeds specification, replace select arm. If width is within specification, replace interlock.

8) Measure clearance between select arm and shim. Clearance should be .004-.008" (.08-.20 mm). *See Fig. 10.* If clearance exceeds specification, select appropriate thrust shim for correct clearance. See THRUST SHIM table.

THRUST SHIM

Part Number	Thickness
24435-689-000	.031" (.80 mm)
24436-689-000	.039" (1.00 mm)
24437-689-000	.047" (1.20 mm)
24438-689-000	.055" (1.40 mm)
24439-689-000	.063" (1.60 mm)

MANUAL TRANSMISSIONS
Acura/Honda Y21, Y80, S21 & S80 (Cont.)

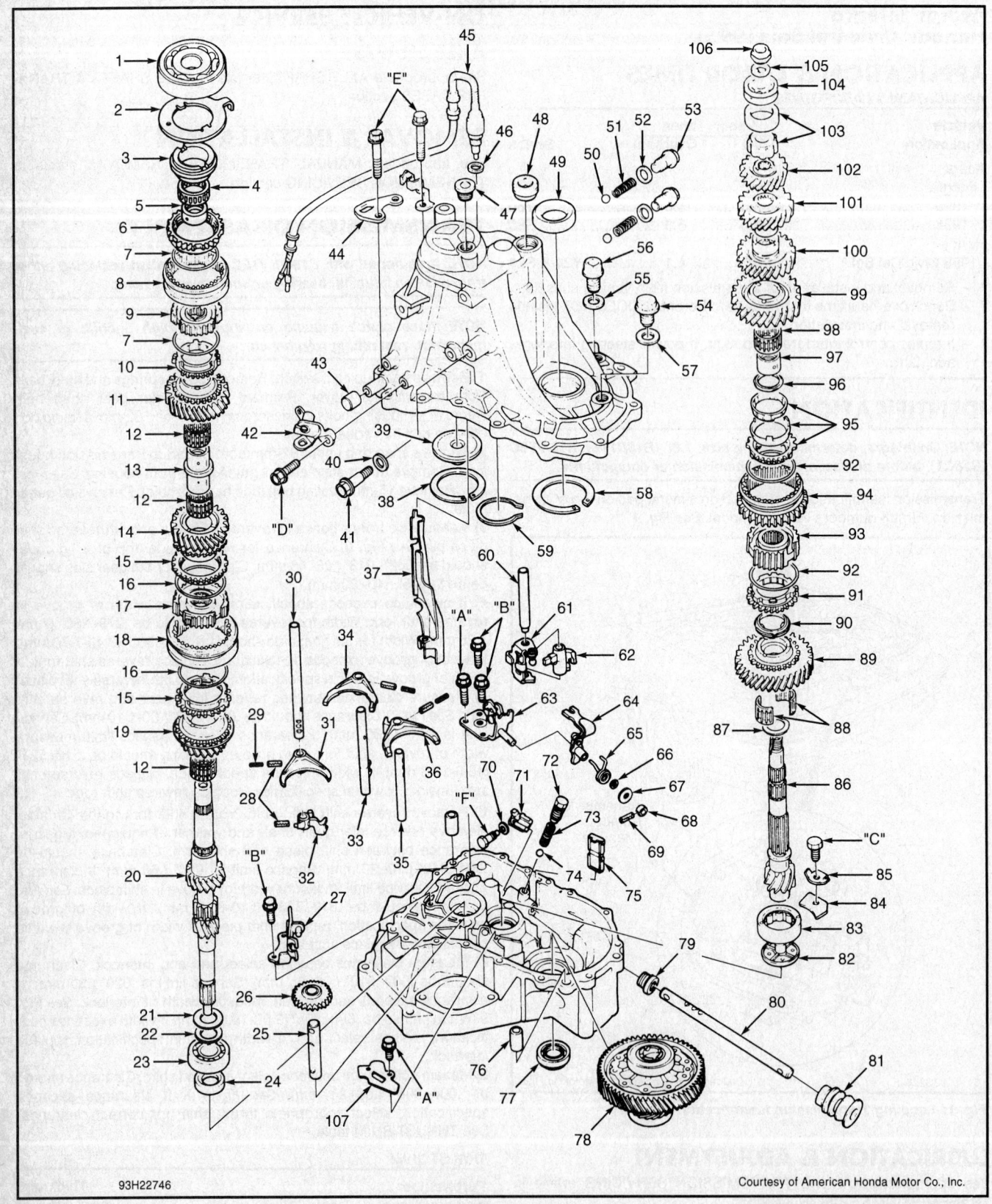

93H22746

Courtesy of American Honda Motor Co., Inc.

Fig. 2: Exploded View Of S21 & Y21 Transmission Assembly (1 Of 2)

Torque Value
"A" – 106 INCH Lbs. (12 N.m)
"B" – 11 Ft. Lbs. (15 N.m)
"C" – 11 Ft. Lbs. (15 N.m)
"D" – 17 Ft. Lbs. (24 N.m)
"E" – 20 Ft. Lbs. (28 N.m)
"F" – 23 Ft. Lbs. (32 N.m)

1. Ball Bearing
2. Stopper Ring
3. Taper Ring
4. Needle Bearing
5. Collar
6. Synchro Ring
7. Synchro Spring
8. 5th/Reverse Synchro Sleeve
9. 5th/Reverse Synchro Hub
10. Synchro Ring
11. 5th Gear
12. Needle Bearing
13. Spacer Collar
14. 4th Gear
15. Synchro Ring
16. Synchro Spring
17. 3-4 Synchro Hub
18. 3-4 Synchro Sleeve
19. 3rd Gear
20. Mainshaft
21. Washer
22. Spring Washer

23. Ball Bearing
24. Oil Seal
25. Reverse Idler Gear Shaft
26. Reverse Idler Gear
27. Reverse Shift Fork
28. Spring Pin
29. Spring Pin
30. 5th/Reverse Shift Fork Shaft
31. 5th/Reverse Shift Fork
32. 5th/Reverse Shift Piece
33. 3rd/4th Shift Fork Shaft
34. 3rd/4th Shift Fork
35. 1st/2nd Shift Fork Shaft
36. 1st/2nd Shift Fork
37. Oil Gutter Plate
38. Thrust Shim (72 mm)
39. Oil Guide Plate
40. Washer
41. Reverse Idler Gear Shaft Bolt
42. Transmission Hanger
43. Breather Cap
44. Transmission Hanger
45. Back-Up Light Switch
46. Washer
47. Sealing Bolt
48. Sealing Bolt
49. Oil Seal
50. Steel Ball
51. Spring
52. Washer

53. Set Bolt
54. Oil Filler Plug
55. Washer
56. Oil Drain Plug
57. Washer
58. Thrust Shim
59. Snap Ring
60. Shift Piece Shaft
61. Interlock
62. Shift Piece
63. Shift Arm Holder
64. Select Arm
65. Select Return Spring
66. Thrust Shim
67. Washer
68. Lock Collar
69. Spring Pin
70. Spring Pin
71. Change Piece
72. Sealing Bolt
73. Spring
74. Steel Ball
75. Magnet
76. Dowel Pin
77. Oil Seal
78. Differential Assembly
79. Oil Seal
80. Shift Rod
81. Boot
82. Oil Guide Plate

83. Needle Bearing
84. Bearing Retainer Plate
85. Lock Washer
86. Countershaft
87. Thrust Shim
88. Needle Bearing
89. 1st Gear
90. Friction Damper
91. Synchro Ring
92. Synchro Spring
93. 1st/2nd Synchro Hub
94. Reverse Gear
95. Double Cone Synchro
96. Friction Damper
97. Distance Collar
98. Needle Bearing
99. 2nd Gear
100. 3rd Gear
101. 4th Gear
102. 5th Gear
103. Needle Bearing
104. Ball Bearing
105. Spring Washer
106. Lock Nut
107. Oil Chamber Plate

Courtesy of American Honda Motor Co., Inc.

96D29903

Fig. 3: Legend For Fig. 2 (2 Of 2)

9) Measure clearance between shift arm holder and change piece. Clearance should be .002-.014" (.05-.35 mm). Service limit is .031" (.80 mm). See Fig. 11. Width should be .474-.478" (12.05-12.15 mm). If clearance exceeds service limit, measure groove of change piece. If groove exceeds specification, replace change piece. If groove is within specification, replace change piece.

10) Measure clearance between select arm and change piece. Clearance should be .002-.010" (.05-.25 mm) on Civic Del Sol models and 002-.014" (.05-.35 mm) on Integra models. Service limit is .020" (.50 mm). See Fig. 11. If clearance exceeds service limit, measure width of select arm. Width should be .474-.478" (12.05-12.15 mm). If width exceeds specification, replace select arm. If width is within specification, replace change piece.

11) Remove shift piece shaft, then remove shift piece and interlock. Remove change holder assembly. Tape mainshaft spline for protection. Remove mainshaft and countershaft assemblies with shift fork from clutch housing. Remove differential assembly. Remove camber plate. Remove shift rod change piece bolt and spring washer. Remove set bolt, spring and steel ball. Remove shift rod, then remove change piece.

12) Measure clearance between synchro sleeve and shift fork. Clearance should be .014-.026" (.35-.65 mm). Service limit is .039" (1.0 mm). If clearance exceeds service limit, measure width of shift fork fingers. Clearance should be .291-.299" (7.4-7.6 mm). If width of shift fork fingers exceeds specification, replace shift fork. If width of shift fork fingers is within specification, replace synchro sleeve. Synchro sleeve and synchro hub should ALWAYS be replaced together.

13) Measure clearance between shift piece and shift fork shafts. Clearance should be .008-.020" (.20-.50 mm). Service limit is .031" (.80 mm). See Fig. 12. If clearance exceeds service limit, measure width of shift piece. Clearance should be .469-.472" (11.9-12.0 mm). If width of shift piece exceeds specification, replace shift fork. If width is within specification, replace shift fork shaft.

COMPONENT DISASSEMBLY & REASSEMBLY

MAINSHAFT

NOTE: On Integra, determine engine size: 1.8L (B18B1) or 1.8L VTEC (B18C1), before disassembling transmission or components.

CAUTION: Install 3rd/4th and 5th synchro hubs using a press. Do not lubricate parts before installation. ALWAYS replace synchro sleeves and hubs as sets.

Measurements – 1) For all mainshaft measurement specifications, refer to MAINSHAFT SPECIFICATIONS table. Measure clearance between 2nd and 3rd gears. See Figs. 13 and 14. If clearance exceeds service limit, measure thickness of 3rd gear. If thickness of 3rd gear is less than service limit, replace 3rd gear.

2) Measure clearance between 4th gear and spacer collar. If clearance exceeds service limit, measure height "A" on spacer collar. If height "A" is greater than clearance specification, replace spacer collar. If height "A" is within specification, measure thickness of 4th gear. If thickness

MAINSHAFT SPECIFICATIONS

Application	Specification
2nd-3rd Gear Clearance	
Design Clearance	.002-.008" (.06-.21 mm)
Service Limit	.12" (.30 mm)
4th Gear/Spacer Collar Clearance	
Design Clearance	.002-.008" (.06-.21 mm)
Service Limit	.12" (.30 mm)
5th Gear/Spacer Collar Clearance	
Design Clearance	.002-.008" (.06-.21 mm)
Service Limit	.12" (.30 mm)
3rd Gear Thickness	
Integra (VTEC) & Civic Del Sol	
Design Thickness	1.375-1.377" (34.92-34.97 mm)
Service Limit	1.370" (34.8 mm)
Integra (Except VTEC)	
Design Thickness	1.355-1.357" (34.42-34.47 mm)
Service Limit	1.350" (34.3 mm)
4th Gear Thickness	
Integra (VTEC) & Civic Del Sol	
Design Thickness	1.237-1.239" (31.42-31.47 mm)
Service Limit	1.232" (31.3 mm)
Integra (Except VTEC)	
Design Thickness	1.217-1.219" (30.92-30.97 mm)
Service Limit	1.213" (30.8 mm)
5th Gear Thickness	
Design Thickness	1.237-1.239" (31.42-31.47 mm)
Service Limit	1.232" (31.3 mm)
Spacer Collar Height "A"	
Height	1.025-1.027 (26.03-26.08 mm)
Spacer Collar Height "B"	
Height	1.025-1.027 (26.03-26.08 mm)

of 4th gear is less than service limit, replace 4th gear. If thickness of 4th gear is within service limit, replace 3rd/4th synchro hub.

3) Measure clearance between 5th gear and spacer collar. If clearance exceeds service limit, measure height "B" on spacer collar. If height "B" is greater than specification, replace spacer collar. If height "B" is within specification, measure thickness of 5th gear. If thickness of 5th gear is less than service limit, replace 5th gear. If thickness of 5th gear is within service limit, replace 5th/reverse synchro hub.

CAUTION: *Remove synchro hub using a press and steel block. Use of jaw-type puller can cause damage to gear teeth.*

Disassembly – Remove roller bearing using bearing puller. Support 5th gear on steel blocks and press shaft out of 5th synchro hub. Support 3rd gear on steel blocks and press shaft out of 3rd/4th synchro hub. *See Fig. 16.*

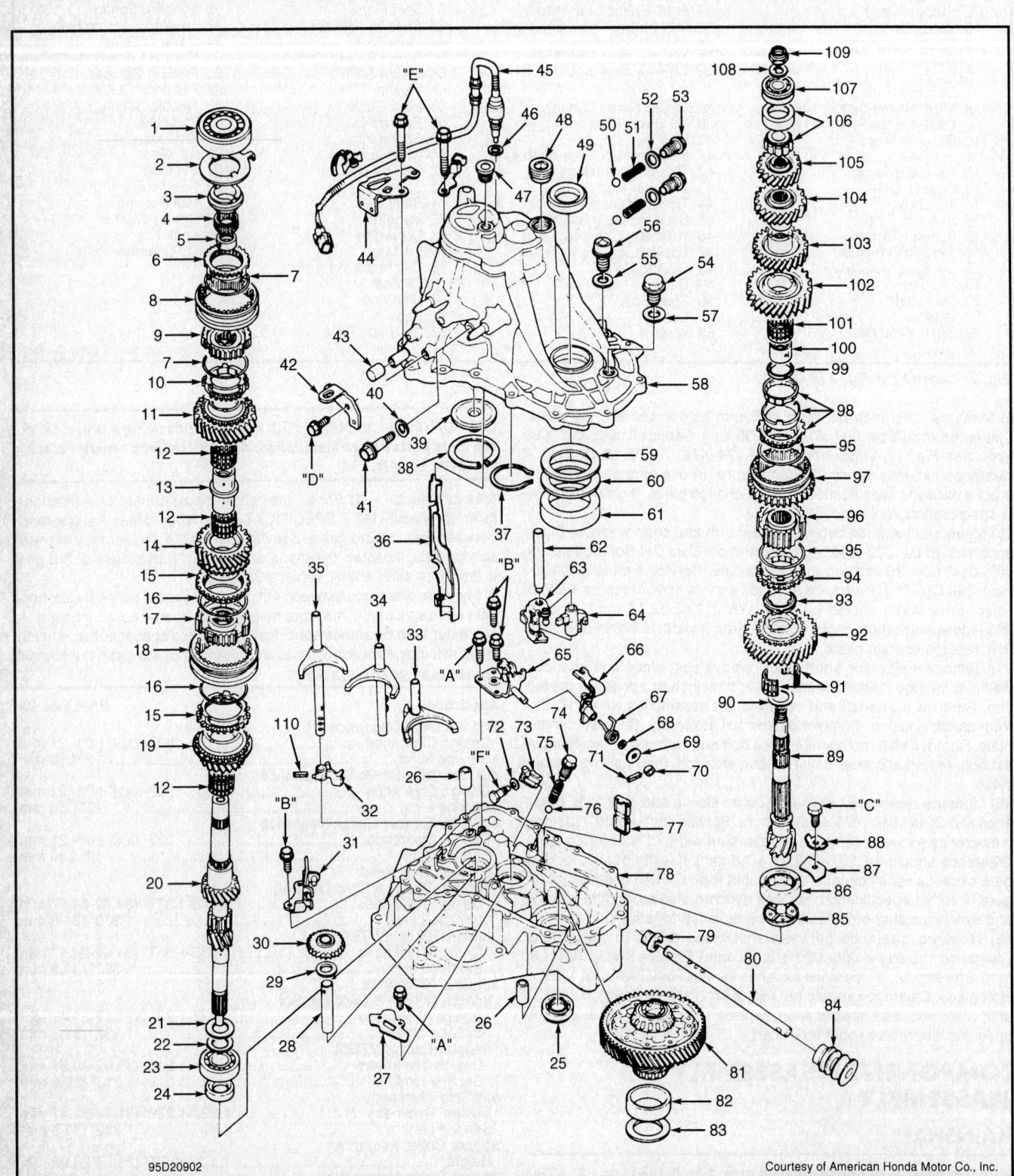

95D20902

Courtesy of American Honda Motor Co., Inc.

Fig. 4: Exploded View Of S80 & Y80 Transmission Assembly (1 Of 2)

Torque Value
"A" – 106 INCH Lbs. (12 N.m)
"B" – 11 Ft. Lbs. (15 N.m)
"C" – 11 Ft. Lbs. (15 N.m)
"D" – 17 Ft. Lbs. (24 N.m)
"E" – 20 Ft. Lbs. (28 N.m)
"F" – 23 Ft. Lbs. (32 N.m)

1. Ball Bearing
2. Stopper Ring
3. Taper Ring
4. Needle Bearing
5. Spacer
6. Synchro Ring
7. Synchro Spring
8. 5th/Reverse Synchro Sleeve
9. 5th/Reverse Synchro Hub
10. Synchro Ring
11. 5th Gear
12. Needle Bearing
13. Spacer Collar
14. 4th Gear
15. Synchro Ring
16. Synchro Spring
17. 3-4 Synchro Hub
18. 3-4 Synchro Sleeve
19. 3rd Gear
20. Mainshaft
21. Washer
22. Spring Washer
23. Ball Bearing
24. Oil Seal
25. Oil Seal
26. Dowel Pin
27. Oil Chamber Plate
28. Reverse Idler Gear Shaft
29. Washer (VTEC)
30. Reverse Idler Gear
31. Reverse Change Holder
32. 5th/Reverse Shift Piece
33. 1st/2nd Shift Fork
34. 3rd/4th Shift Fork
35. 5th/Reverse Shift Fork
36. Oil Gutter Plate
37. Snap Ring
38. Thrust Shim (72 mm)
39. Oil Guide Plate
40. Washer
41. Reverse Idler Gear Shaft Bolt
42. Transmission Hanger
43. Breather Cap
44. Transmission Hanger
45. Back-Up Light Switch
46. Washer
47. Sealing Bolt
48. Sealing Bolt
49. Oil Seal
50. Steel Ball
51. Spring
52. Washer
53. Set Bolt
54. Oil Filler Plug
55. Washer
56. Oil Drain Plug
57. Washer
58. Transmission Housing
59. Shim 80 mm
    Shim 79.5 mm (VTEC)
60. Shim 2.0 mm (VTEC)
61. Bearing Outer Race (VTEC)
62. Shift Piece Shaft
63. Interlock
64. Shift Piece
65. Shift Arm Holder
66. Select Arm
67. Select Return Spring
68. Shim
69. Washer
70. Lock Collar
71. Spring Pin
72. Spring Washer
73. Change Piece
74. Set Screw
75. Spring
76. Steel Ball
77. Magnet
78. Clutch Housing
79. Oil Seal
80. Shift Rod
81. Differential Assembly
82. Bearing Outer Race (VTEC)
83. Shim (VTEC)
84. Shift Rod Boot
85. Oil Guide Plate
86. Needle Bearing
87. Bearing Retainer Plate
88. Lock Washer
89. Countershaft
90. Thrust Shim
91. Needle Bearing
92. 1st Gear
93. Friction Damper
94. Synchro Ring
95. Synchro Spring
96. 1st/2nd Synchro Hub
97. Reverse Gear
98. Synchro Ring
    Double Cone Synchro (VTEC)
99. Friction Damper
100. Spacer
101. Needle Bearing
102. 2nd Gear
103. 3rd Gear
104. 4th Gear
105. 5th Gear
106. Needle Bearing
107. Ball Bearing
108. Spring Washer
109. Lock Nut
110. Spring Pin

96E29904

Courtesy of American Honda Motor Co., Inc.

Fig. 5: Legend For Fig. 4 (2 Of 2)

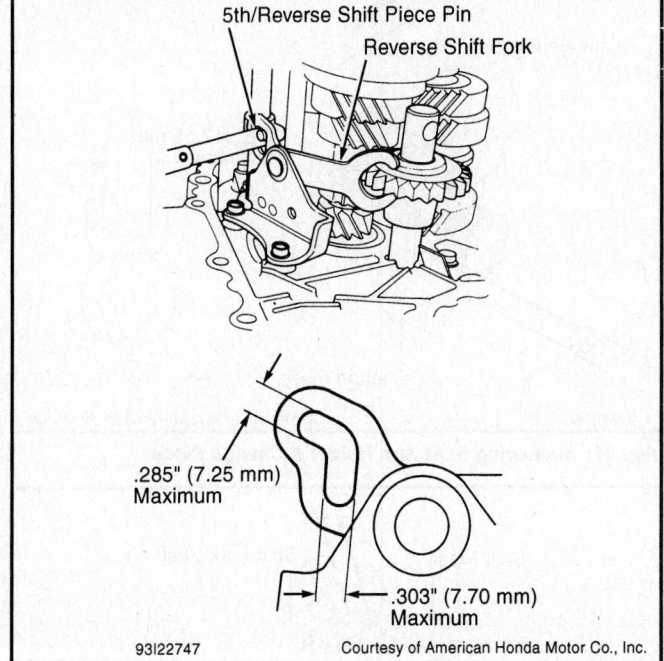

93I22747   Courtesy of American Honda Motor Co., Inc.

Fig. 6: Measuring Reverse Shift Fork Pin Groove

Inspection – 1) Inspect all parts for damage and wear. Replace if necessary. Clean all parts in new solvent, dry and lubricate all parts. Install 3rd/4th, and 5th synchro hubs with a press before lubricating them.
2) Measure mainshaft at points "A", "B" and "C". Support mainshaft in "V" blocks. Using dial indicator to measure runout, rotate mainshaft 2 complete revolutions. Replace mainshaft if runout or any part is not within service limit. See MAINSHAFT BEARING SURFACE SPECIFICATIONS table.

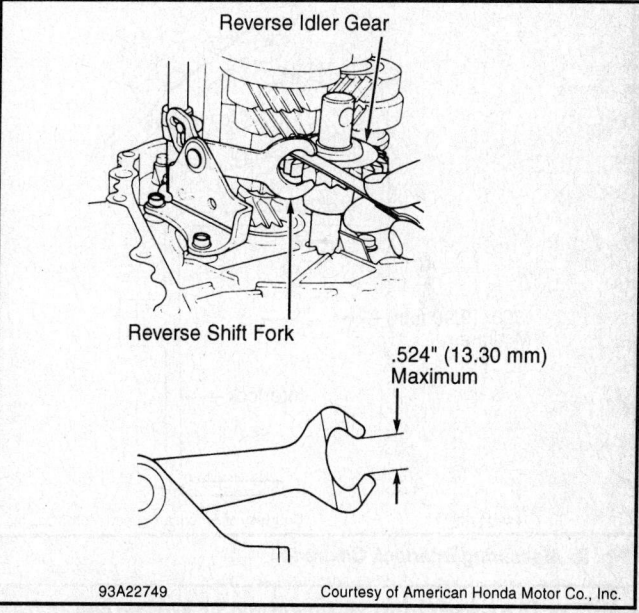

93A22749   Courtesy of American Honda Motor Co., Inc.

Fig. 7: Measuring Reverse Shift Fork

MAINSHAFT BEARING SURFACE SPECIFICATIONS

Application [1]	Standard In. (mm)	Service Limits In. (mm)
"A" Ball Bearing Surface	1.1019-1.1024	1.100
	(27.987-28.000)	(27.94)
"B" Needle Bearing Surface	1.495-1.496	1.493
	(37.98-38.00)	(37.93)
"C" Ball Bearing Surface	1.1019-1.1024	1.100
	(27.987-28.000)	(27.94)
Runout Limits	.0008 (.020)	.0020 (.050)

[1] – "A", "B" and "C" refer to measuring points indicated in *Fig. 13*.

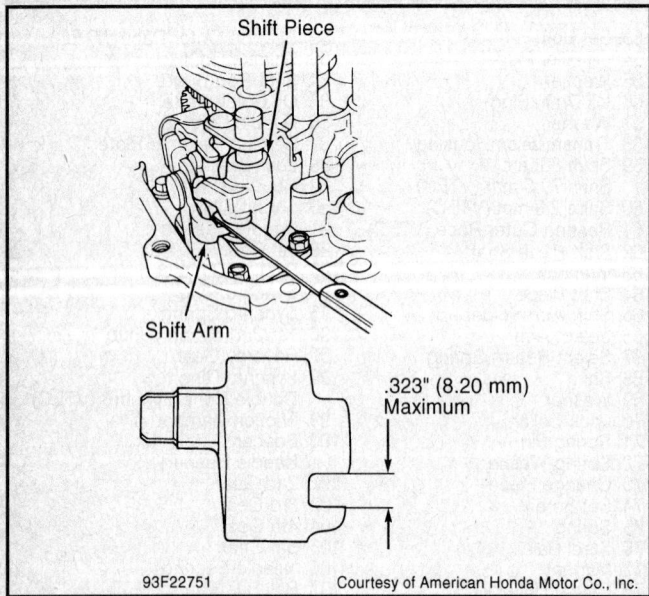

Fig. 8: *Measuring Shift Piece*

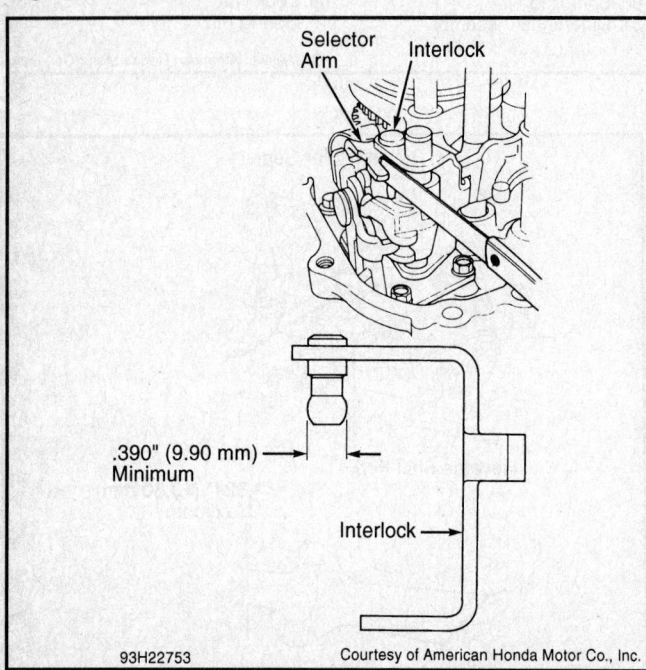

Fig. 9: *Measuring Interlock Clearance*

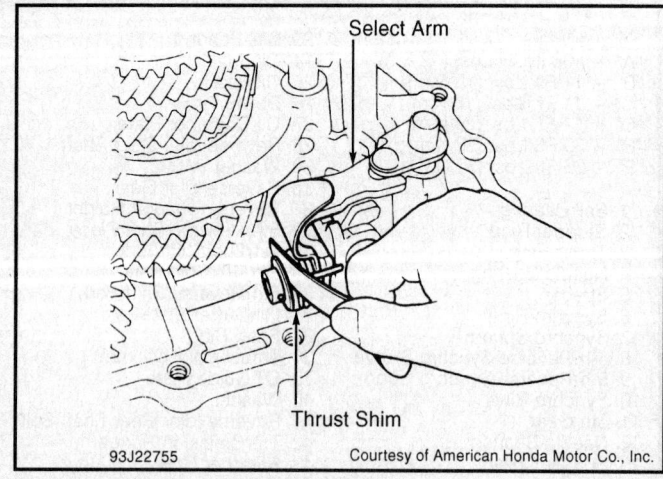

Fig. 10: *Measuring Select Arm Clearance*

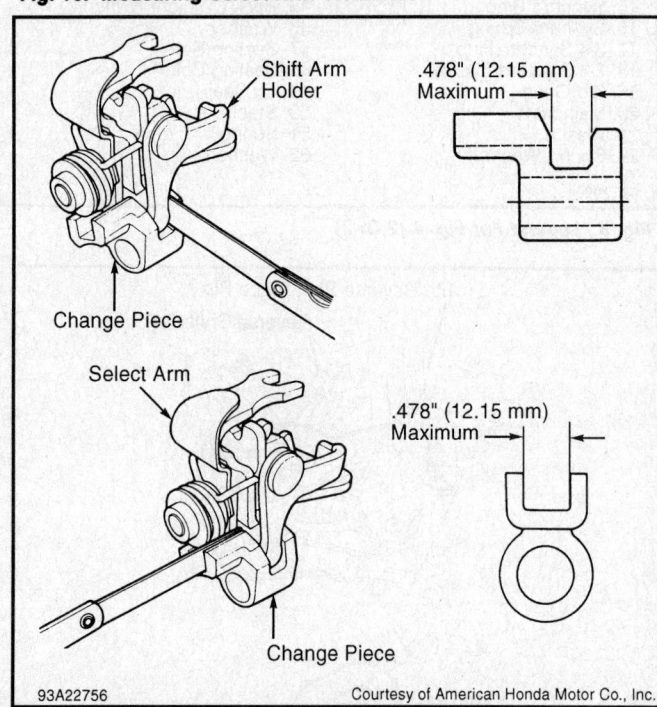

Fig. 11: *Measuring Shift Arm Holder & Change Piece*

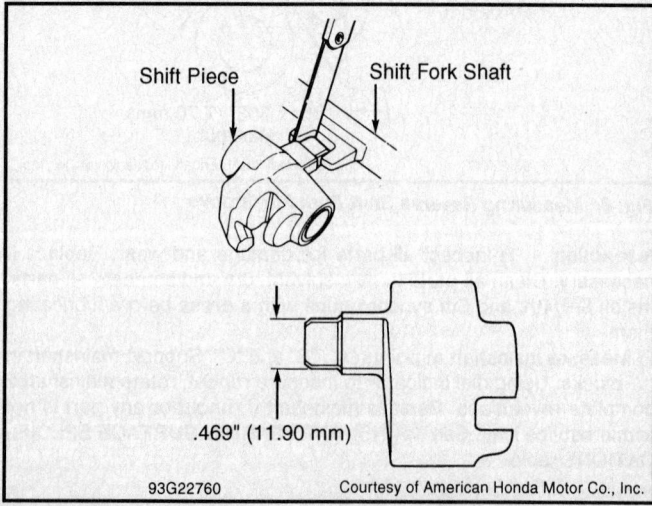

Fig. 12: *Measuring Shift Piece & Shift Fork Shaft*

CAUTION: Use a press to install 3rd/4th and 5th synchro hub. DO NOT exceed a maximum of 4410 lbs. pressure while supporting mainshaft on blocks. Lubricate all parts only after mainshaft is complete.

Reassembly – 1) Supporting 2nd gear on steel blocks, install 3rd/4th synchro hub using 35-mm adapter and press. Ensure synchro hub installation direction is correct. *See Fig. 13.* On Integra (VTEC) and Civic Del Sol models, assemble 3rd/4th synchro hub and sleeve before installation on mainshaft. On all models, check operation of 3rd/4th synchro hub set.

2) Install 5th/reverse synchro hub using 35-mm adapter and press. Install ball bearing with tapered end facing down using, 30-mm adapter and press. *See Fig. 15.*

Mainshaft Thrust Shim Measurement – 1) Remove 72-mm thrust shim and oil guide plate from transmission housing. Install assembled mainshaft in transmission housing.

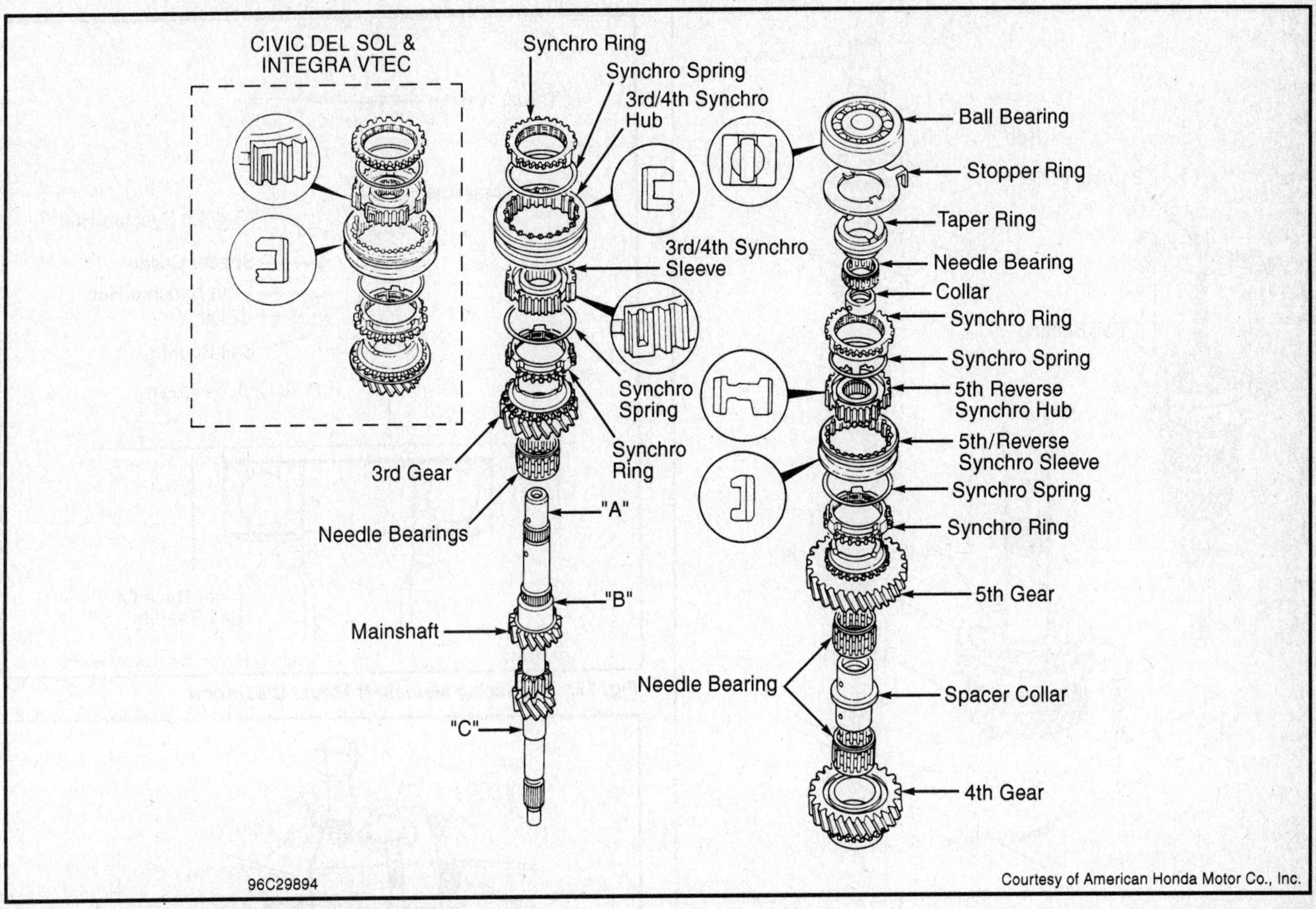

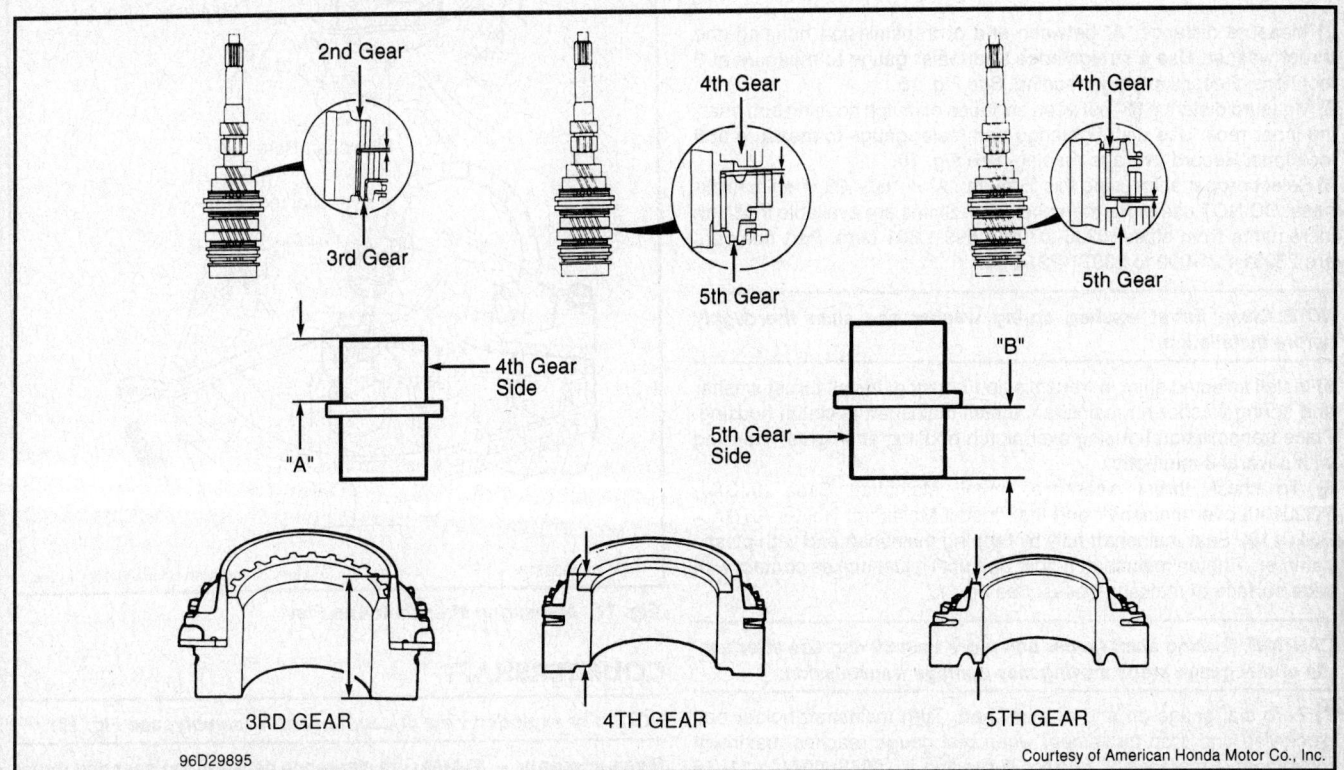

Fig. 13: Exploded View Of Mainshaft Assemblies

Fig. 14: Identifying Mainshaft Measuring Points

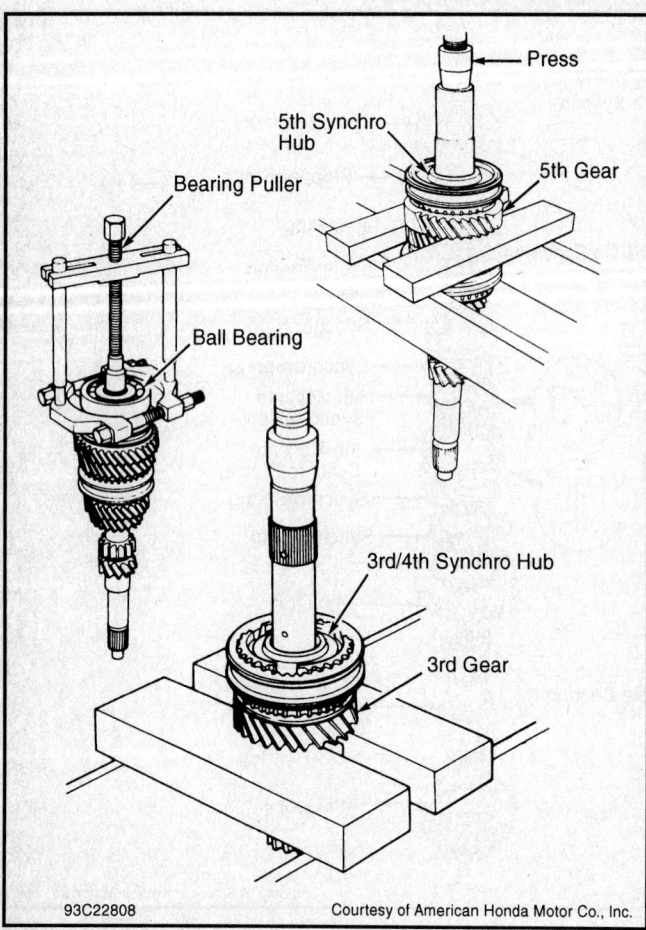

Fig. 15: Disassembling Mainshaft

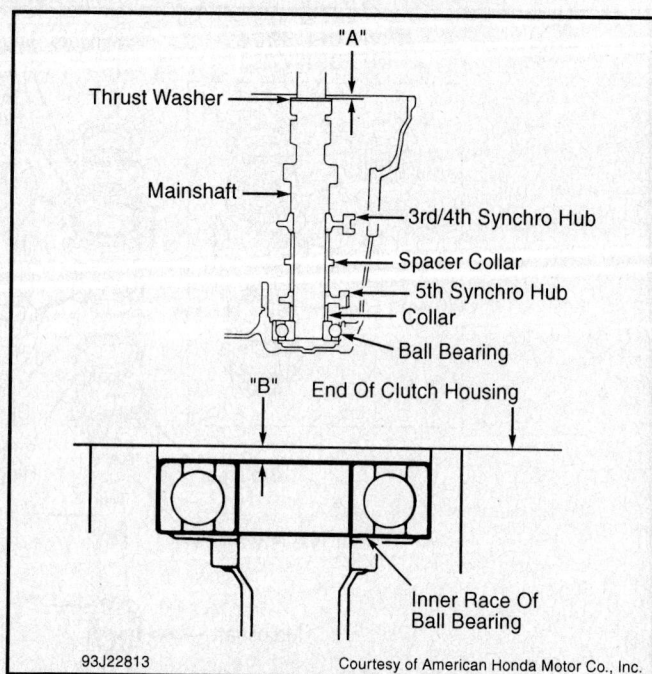

Fig. 16: Measuring Mainshaft Thrust Clearance

2) Measure distance "A" between end of transmission housing and thrust washer. Use a straightedge and feeler gauge to measure at 3 locations. Record average reading. See Fig. 16.

3) Measure distance "B" between surfaces of clutch housing and bearing inner race. Use a straightedge and feeler gauge to measure at 3 locations. Record average reading. See Fig. 16.

4) Select proper shim using this formula: "A" + "B" − .93 = shim thickness. DO NOT use more than one shim. Shims are available in .3 mm increments from sizes .0236-.0709" (.599-1.801 mm). Part numbers are 23931-P21-000 to 23971-P21-000.

NOTE: Clean thrust washer, spring washer and shim thoroughly before installation.

5) Install selected shim in transmission housing. Install thrust washer and spring washer on mainshaft. Install mainshaft in clutch housing. Place transmission housing over clutch housing and tighten housing with several 8-mm bolts.

6) To check thrust clearance, install Mainshaft Base (07GAJ-PG20130) over mainshaft and then install Mainshaft Holder (07GAJ-PG20110). Seat mainshaft fully by tapping mainshaft end with plastic hammer. Tighten mainshaft holder bolt until it just makes contact with wide surface of mainshaft base. See Fig. 17.

CAUTION: Turning shaft holder bolt more than 60 degrees after needle of dial gauge stops moving may damage transmission.

7) Zero dial gauge on end of mainshaft. Turn mainshaft holder bolt clockwise and stop movement when dial gauge reaches maximum movement. Clearance is correct if reading is .0043-.0071" (.11-.18 mm). If reading is not within limits, replace thrust shim with correct thickness. See Fig. 17.

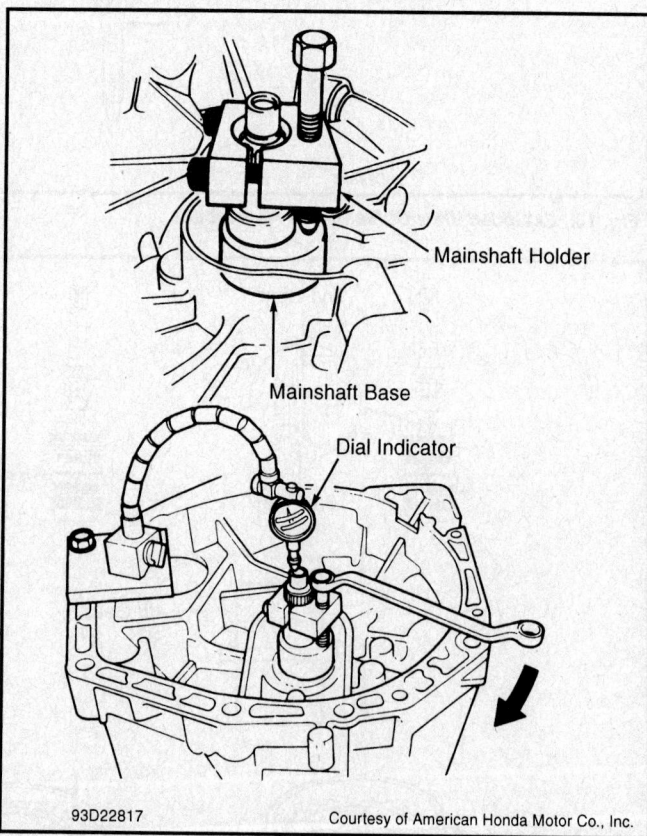

Fig. 17: Measuring Mainshaft End Play

COUNTERSHAFT

NOTE: For exploded view of countershaft assembly, see Fig. 18.

Measurements – 1) Measure clearance between 1st gear and thrust shim. See Fig. 19. Clearance should be .0018-.0081" (.045-.205 mm). Service limit is .0104" (.265 mm). If clearance exceeds service limits,

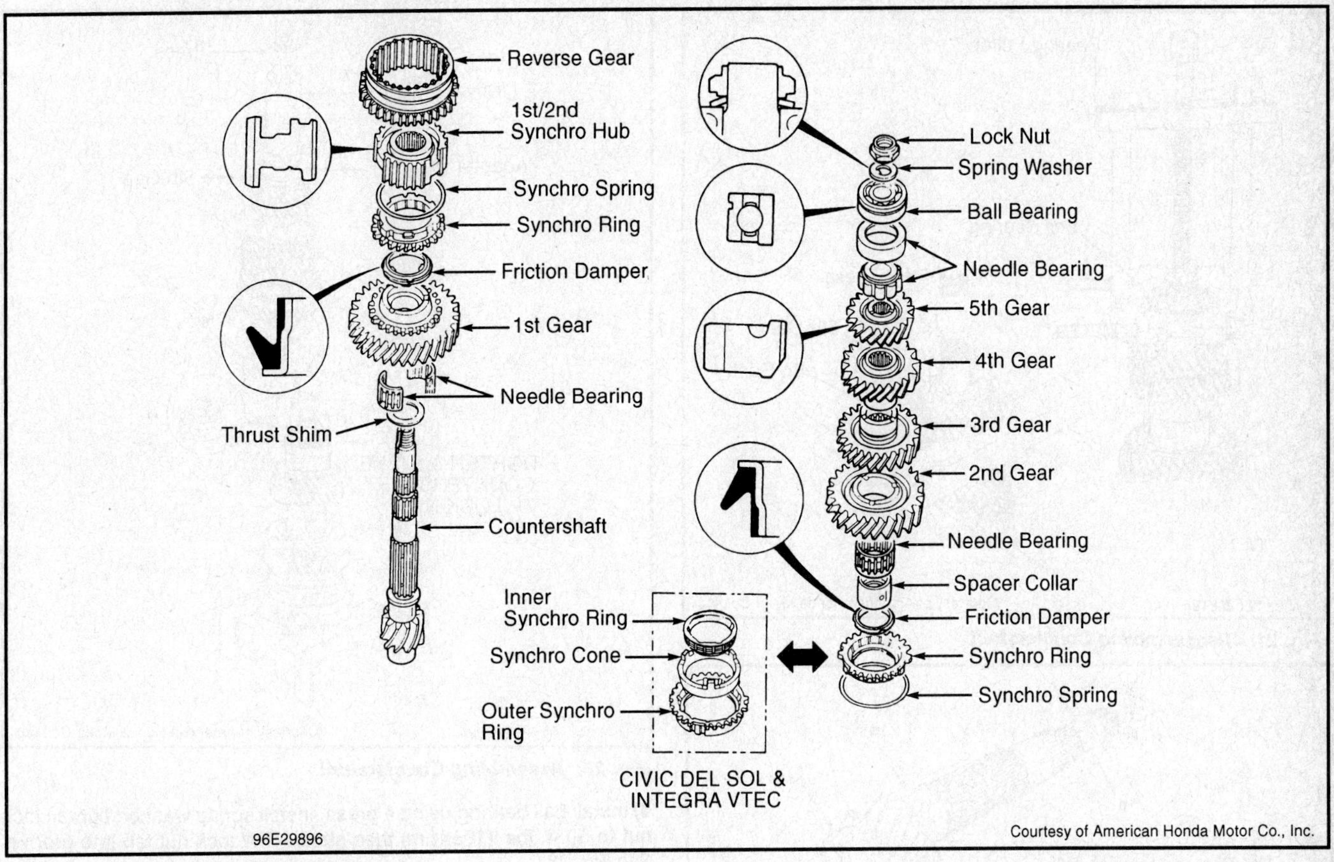

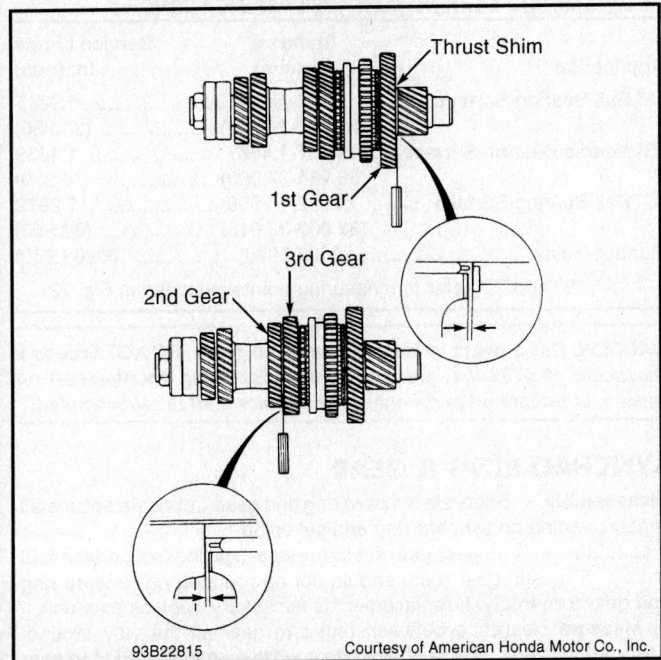

Fig. 18: Exploded View Of Countershaft

Fig. 19: Measuring Countershaft Gear Clearances

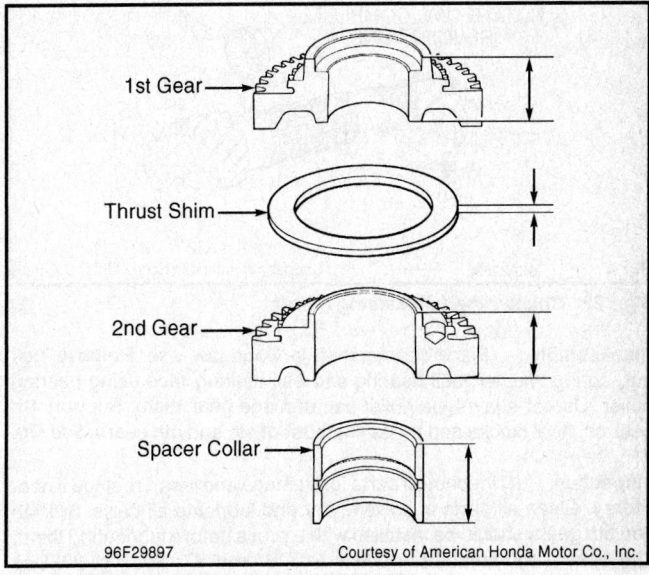

Fig. 20: Measuring Countershaft Components

19. If clearance exceeds service limits, measure thickness of 2nd and 3rd gear. See Fig. 20. If 2nd and 3rd gear thickness is not within specification, replace as necessary. See COUNTERSHAFT COMPONENT SPECIFICATIONS table. If 2nd and 3rd gear thickness is within specification, replace 1st/2nd synchro hub.

COUNTERSHAFT COMPONENT SPECIFICATIONS

Component	Thickness
1st Gear	1.238-1.240" (31.45-31.50 mm)
Thrust Shim	.0767-.0770" (1.945-1.955 mm)
2nd Gear	1.139-1.141" (28.92-28.97 mm)
Spacer Collar	1.144-1.145" (29.07-29.09 mm)

measure thickness of 1st gear and thrust shim. See Fig. 20. If 1st gear and thrust shim thickness is not within specification, replace as necessary. See COUNTERSHAFT COMPONENT SPECIFICATIONS table. If 1st gear and thrust shim thickness is within specification, replace 1st/2nd synchro hub.

2) Measure clearance between 2nd and 3rd gear. Clearance should be .0028-.0055" (.070-.140 mm). Service limit is .0079" (.200 mm). See Fig.

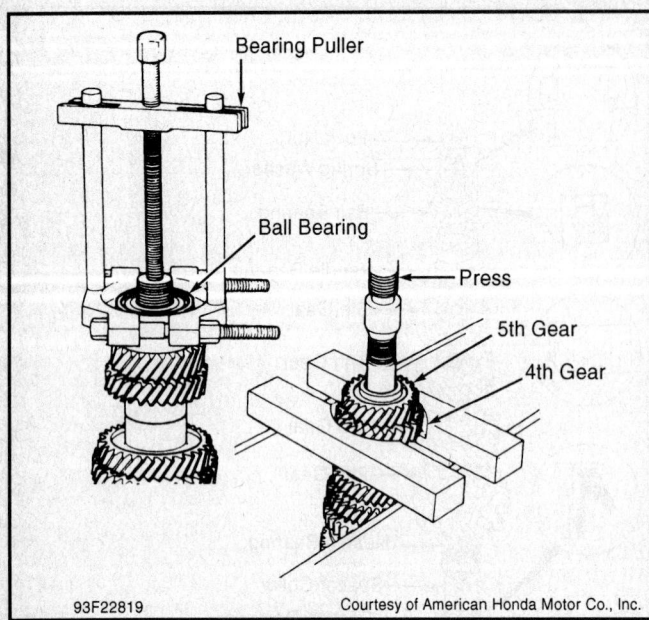

Fig. 21: Disassembling Countershaft

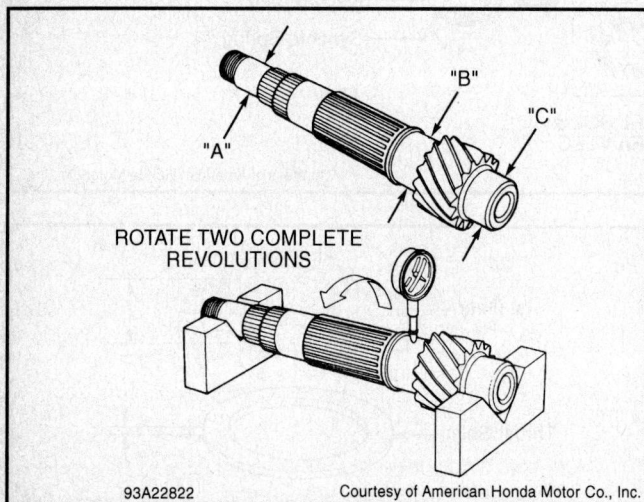

Fig. 22: Countershaft Measuring Points

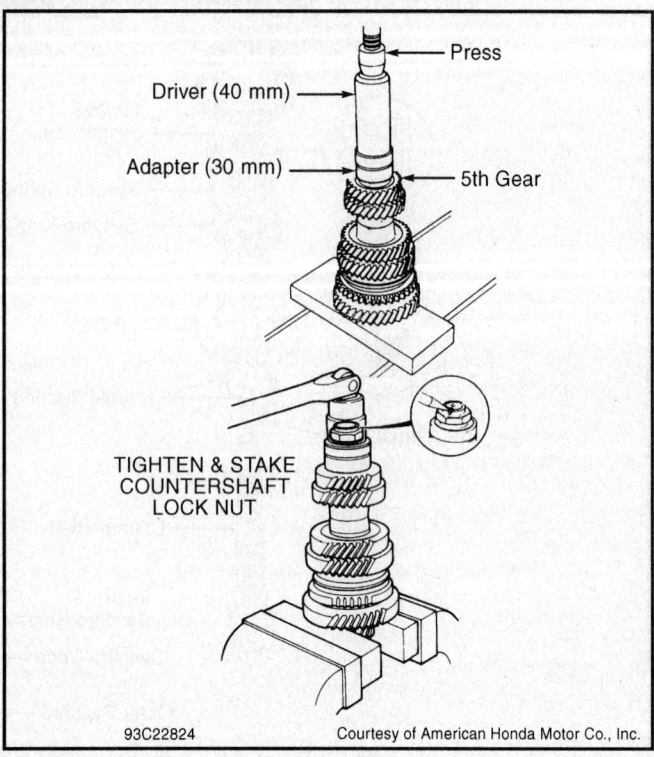

Fig. 23: Assembling Countershaft

3) Install ball bearing using a press. Install spring washer; tighten lock nut to 80 ft. lbs. (108 N.m) then stake NEW lock nut tab into groove. See Fig. 23.

COUNTERSHAFT BEARING SURFACE SPECIFICATIONS

Application [1]	Standard In. (mm)	Service Limits In. (mm)
"A" Ball Bearing Surface	.9835-.9840	.9815
	(24.980-24.993)	(24.930)
"B" Needle Bearing Surface	1.4561-1.4567	1.4539
	(36.984-37.000)	(36.930)
"C" Ball Bearing Surface	1.2992-1.2998	1.2972
	(33.000-33.015)	(32.950)
Runout Limits	.0008 (.020)	.0020 (.050)

[1] – "A", "B" and "C" refer to measuring points indicated in Fig. 22.

CAUTION: Use a press to install 4th and 5th gears. DO NOT exceed a maximum of 5732 lbs. pressure while supporting countershaft on blocks. Lubricate all parts only after countershaft is reassembled.

SYNCHRO RING & GEAR

Disassembly – Separate synchro ring and gear. Lubricate and install synchro spring on synchro ring and set aside.

Inspection – 1) Inspect gear teeth for wear, galling, roughness and cracks. Ring and gear teeth should not be rounded off. Ensure ring and gear turn freely. If replacement is necessary, replace as a unit.

2) Measure clearance between ring and gear all the way around. Ensure ring is held evenly against gear while measuring. Ring to gear clearance should be .033-.043" (.85-1.10 mm). Service limit is .016" (.40 mm). If clearance exceeds limit, replace as a unit. See Fig. 24.

3) For Integra (VTEC) and Civic Del Sol, double cone synchro, outer synchro ring to synchro cone clearance should be .008-.016" (.20-.40 mm). Service limit is .012 (.30 mm). Synchro cone to gear clearance should be .008-.016" (.20-.40 mm). Service limit is .012" (.30 mm). Outer Synchro ring to gear clearance should be .037-.066" (.95-1.68 mm). Service limit is .024" (.60 mm).

Disassembly – Place countershaft in wood jaw vise. Remove lock nut, spring washer, ball bearing and ball bearing race using bearing puller. Use of a jaw-type puller can damage gear teeth. Support 4th gear on steel blocks and press shaft out of 4th and 5th gears. See Fig. 21.

Inspection – 1) Inspect all parts for damage and wear, replace if necessary. Clean all parts in solvent; dry and lubricate all parts. 3rd/4th and 5th gears should be installed with a press before lubricating them.

2) Measure countershaft at points "A", "B" and "C". See Fig. 22. Use dial indicator to measure runout. Rotate countershaft 2 complete revolutions. Replace countershaft if runout or any part is not within service limit. See COUNTERSHAFT BEARING SURFACE SPECIFICATIONS table.

Reassembly – 1) Install thrust shim and 1st gear needle bearings. In the following order, install: 1st gear, friction damper, synchro ring and spring. Install 1st/2nd hub and reverse gear. Install synchro ring. On Integra (VTEC) and Civic Del Sol, install 3-piece ring set. Install friction damper, spacer collar, needle bearing, 2nd and 3rd gear. Ensure friction dampers are properly indexed to mating grooves.

2) Support countershaft on a steel block. Using driver and 35-mm adapter, press on 4th gear. Press 5th gear on countershaft with driver and 30-mm adapter. Install needle bearing.

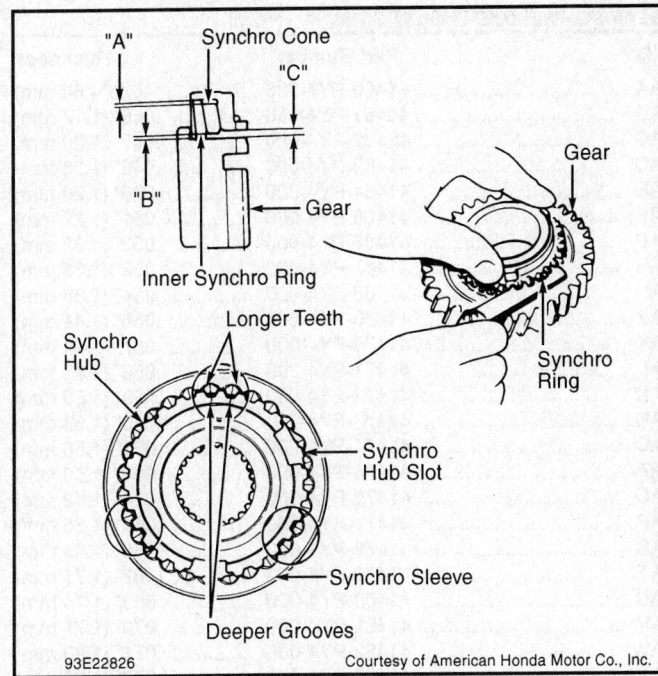

Fig. 24: *Measuring Synchro Hub Clearance & Assembly*

Reassembly – Each synchro sleeve has 3 sets of longer teeth (120 degrees apart) that must be matched with 3 sets of deeper grooves when hub is assembled. *See Fig. 24.*

DIFFERENTIAL

CAUTION: Ring gear bolts have LEFT-HAND threads.

Disassembly – **1)** Check bearings for wear and rough rotation. If bearings need replacing, use bearing puller and remove bearings from differential carrier. To install bearings, use bearing driver.
2) Remove ring gear. Differential carrier assembly is not serviceable. DO NOT disassemble. *See Fig. 25.*
Inspection – Inspect ring gear teeth for excessive wear. Wash parts in solvent and dry with compressed air. Replace any worn or damaged parts.
Reassembly – **1)** Coat all parts with molylube before reassembly. To check backlash of both pinion gears, place differential assembly on blocks and install both axles. Backlash should be .002-.006" (.05-.15 mm). *See Fig. 26.*
2) If backlash exceeds limit, replace carrier assembly. After final backlash check and with all tolerances correct, install ring gear. Ensure chamfer on inside diameter of ring gear is facing the carrier.

TRANSMISSION ADJUSTMENTS

NOTE: If vehicle is an Integra (VTEC) or Civic Del Sol, see DIFFERENTIAL PRELOAD ADJUSTMENT. If vehicle is an Integra (Except VTEC), see DIFFERENTIAL SIDE CLEARANCE ADJUSTMENT.

DIFFERENTIAL SIDE CLEARANCE ADJUSTMENT

1) Install differential assembly in clutch housing. Ensure differential assembly is bottomed in housing. Install thrust shim and snap ring. Install transmission housing. Do NOT apply sealer at this time.
2) Install and torque housing bolts. See TORQUE SPECIFICATIONS. Measure clearance between thrust shim and outer race in housing. Maximum clearance is .004" (.10 mm). If not within limits, select proper thrust shim from DIFFERENTIAL THRUST SHIM THICKNESS table. Disassemble transmission housing and replace original thrust shim with selected thrust shim. Reassemble transmission housing and recheck side clearance.

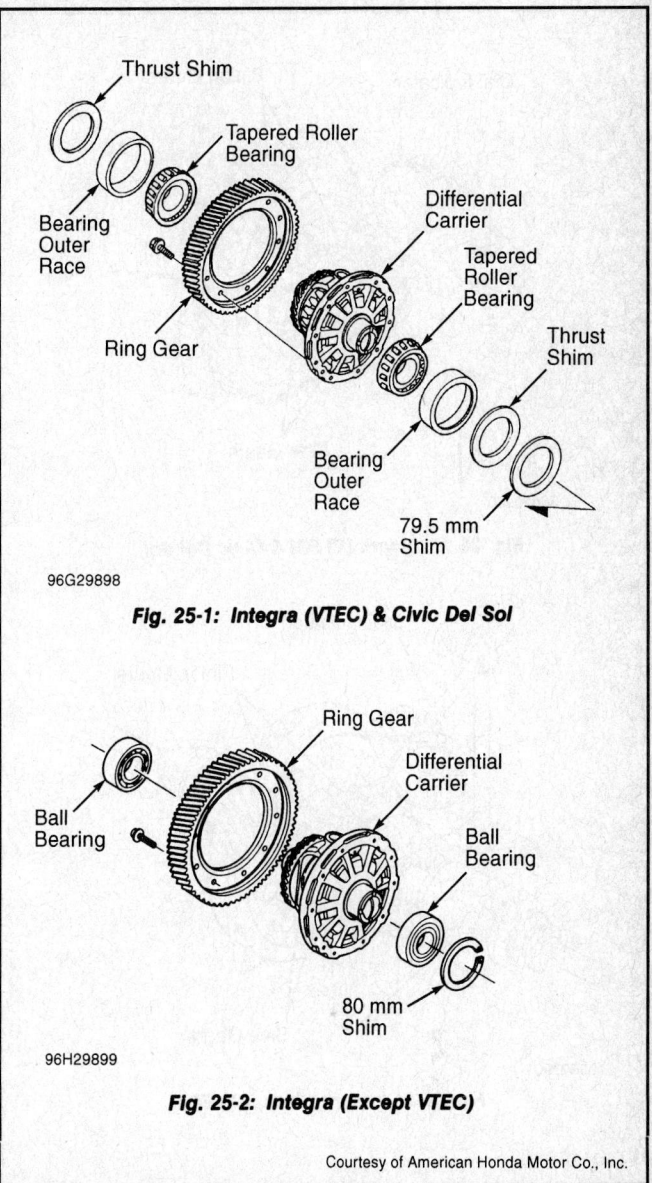

Fig. 25-1: *Integra (VTEC) & Civic Del Sol*

Fig. 25-2: *Integra (Except VTEC)*

Courtesy of American Honda Motor Co., Inc.

Fig. 25: *Exploded View Of Differential Assembly*

3) If differential side clearance is not within specifications, repeat step 2). If differential side clearance is okay, adjustment is complete.

DIFFERENTIAL THRUST SHIM THICKNESS

Part Number	Thickness
41441-PL3-B00	.039" (1.00 mm)
41442-PL3-B00	.043" (1.10 mm)
41443-PL3-B00	.047" (1.20 mm)
41444-PL3-B00	.051" (1.30 mm)
41445-PL3-B00	.055" (1.40 mm)
41446-PL3-B00	.059" (1.50 mm)
41447-PL3-B00	.063" (1.60 mm)
41448-PL3-B00	.067" (1.70 mm)
41449-PL3-B00	.071" (1.80 mm)
41450-PL3-B00	.041" (1.05 mm)
41451-PL3-B00	.045" (1.15 mm)
41452-PL3-B00	.049" (1.25 mm)
41453-PL3-B00	.053" (1.35 mm)
41454-PL3-B00	.057" (1.45 mm)
41455-PL3-B00	.061" (1.55 mm)
41456-PL3-B00	.065" (1.65 mm)
41457-PL3-B00	.069" (1.75 mm)
41441-P21-000	.073" (1.85 mm)
41442-P21-000	.075" (1.90 mm)
41443-P21-000	.077" (1.95 mm)

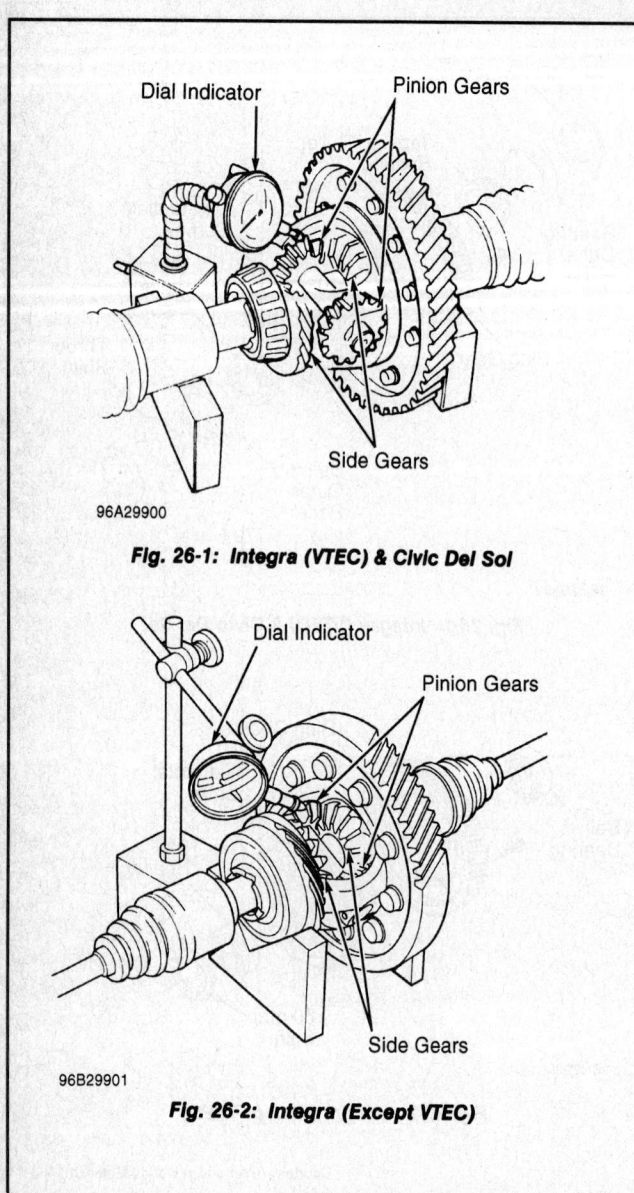

Fig. 26-1: Integra (VTEC) & Civic Del Sol

96A29900

Fig. 26-2: Integra (Except VTEC)

96B29901

Courtesy of American Honda Motor Co., Inc.

Fig. 26: Measuring Pinion Gear Backlash

DIFFERENTIAL PRELOAD ADJUSTMENT

NOTE: If tapered roller bearing, transmission housing, differential carrier or thrust shim is replaced, bearing preload MUST be adjusted.

1) Install differential assembly in clutch housing. Install transmission housing. Do NOT apply sealer at this time. Install and torque housing bolts. See TORQUE SPECIFICATIONS. Rotate differential assembly in both directions to seat bearings.

2) Using torque wrench and Preload Inspection Tool (07HAJ-PK40201), measure bearing preload in both directions. Preload should be 18.7-26.9 INCH lbs. (2.11-3.04 N.m). If bearing preload is not within specifications, select appropriate 79.5 mm shim. See BEARING PRELOAD THRUST SHIM table. *See Fig. 25-1.* One shim size change will adjust preload approximately 2.6-3.5 INCH lbs. (.3-.4 N.m).

BEARING PRELOAD THRUST SHIM

I.D.	Part Number	Thickness
AA	41460-PY4-000	.026" (.66 mm)
AB	41461-PY4-000	.046" (1.17 mm)
AC	41462-PY4-000	.047" (1.20 mm)
AD	41463-PY4-000	.048" (1.23 mm)
AE	41464-PY4-000	.050" (1.26 mm)
AF	41465-PY4-000	.051" (1.29 mm)
AG	41466-PY4-000	.052" (1.32 mm)
AH	41467-PY4-000	.053" (1.35 mm)
AI	41468-PY4-000	.054" (1.38 mm)
AJ	41469-PY4-000	.056" (1.41 mm)
AK	41470-PY4-000	.057" (1.44 mm)
AL	41471-PY4-000	.058" (1.47 mm)
AM	41472-PY4-000	.059" (1.50 mm)
AN	41473-PY4-000	.060" (1.53 mm)
AO	41474-PY4-000	.061" (1.56 mm)
AP	41475-PY4-000	.063" (1.59 mm)
AQ	41476-PY4-000	.064" (1.62 mm)
AR	41477-PY4-000	.065" (1.65 mm)
AS	41478-PY4-000	.066" (1.68 mm)
AT	41479-PY4-000	.067" (1.71 mm)
AU	41480-PY4-000	.069" (1.74 mm)
AV	41481-PY4-000	.070" (1.77 mm)
AW	41482-PY4-000	.071" (1.80 mm)
AX	41483-PY4-000	.072" (1.83 mm)

3) After shim is installed, reinstall differential. Install transmission housing and torque to specifications. Recheck bearing preload. If bearing preload is not within specifications, repeat step 2). If bearing preload is okay, adjustment is complete.

TRANSMISSION REASSEMBLY

1) Drive oil seal into clutch housing. Set change piece into clutch housing. Install shift rod with detent hole facing up. Grease and install steel detent ball, spring and set screw. Tighten change piece bolt to 22 ft. lbs. (30 N.m).

2) Install shift rod boots so that hole faces downward when transmission is mounted on vehicle. Install oil chamber plate. Perform differential preload or side clearance adjustment. If vehicle is an Integra (VTEC) or Civic Del Sol, see DIFFERENTIAL PRELOAD ADJUSTMENT under TRANSMISSION ADJUSTMENTS. If vehicle is an Integra (Except VTEC), see DIFFERENTIAL SIDE CLEARANCE ADJUSTMENT under TRANSMISSION ADJUSTMENTS.

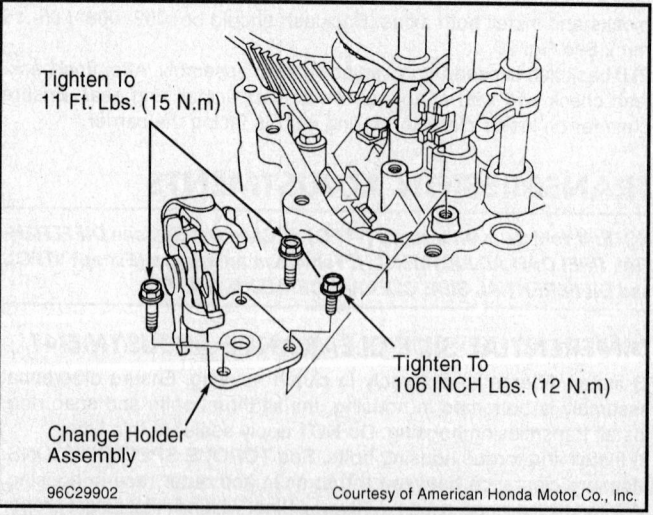

Tighten To 11 Ft. Lbs. (15 N.m)

Tighten To 106 INCH Lbs. (12 N.m)

Change Holder Assembly

96C29902

Courtesy of American Honda Motor Co., Inc.

Fig. 27: Installing Change Holder Assembly Bolts

3) Install differential assembly. Insert mainshaft spring washer and thrust washer with angle against clutch housing. Tape mainshaft splines before installation, then insert mainshaft and countershaft into shift forks and install them as an assembly.

4) Install change holder assembly in clutch housing. Tighten bolts to appropriate torque. *See Fig. 27.* Assemble shift piece and interlock and insert shift guide shaft.

5) Measure distance from top of shift piece shaft to top of interlock after mounting shift guide shaft. Clearance should be .468-.484" (11.90-12.30 mm). If clearance is not correct, check installation. Install reverse idler gear and idler gear shaft in clutch housing. Install reverse shift fork in clutch housing. Install oil guide plate and 72-mm thrust shim into housing. Install oil gutter plate and 16-mm sealing bolt.

NOTE: This transmission uses no gaskets between major housings; use Honda Genuine Liquid Gasket (08178-550000-OE). Assemble housing within 20 minutes after applying liquid gasket. Allow 30 minutes curing time before filling with oil.

6) Apply liquid gasket to transmission mating surface of clutch housing. Install dowel pins on clutch housing; place transmission housing over clutch housing, ensuring shafts are aligned.

7) Lower transmission housing with snap ring expanded and set snap ring in groove of countershaft bearing. Ensure snap ring is securely seated in groove of countershaft bearing. Snap ring opening clearance should be .180-.327" (4.57-8.30 mm).

8) Place transmission hanger between bolts No. 11 and 15. Tighten transmission housing bolts to 21 ft. lbs. (28 N.m) in sequence. *See Fig. 28.*

9) Apply liquid gasket to 32-mm bolt threads. Tighten sealing bolt to 18 ft. lbs. (25 N.m). Install and tighten reverse idler gear shaft bolt. Install clutch cable bracket and tighten bolt to 16 ft. lbs. (22 N.m). Install back-up light switch and tighten bolt to 18 ft. lbs. (25 N.m). Install harness and harness clamp; tighten bolt to 106 INCH lbs. (12 N.m).

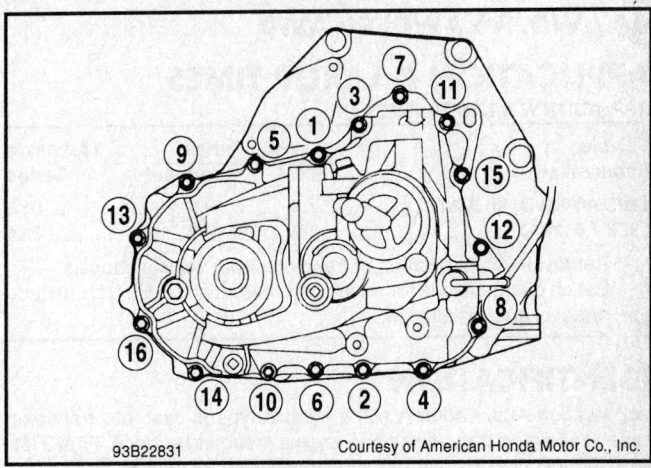

93B22831   Courtesy of American Honda Motor Co., Inc.

Fig. 27: Bolt Tightening Sequence

TORQUE SPECIFICATIONS

NOTE: Refer to Figs. 2, 3, 4 and 5 for torque specifications not listed in TORQUE SPECIFICATIONS.

TORQUE SPECIFICATIONS

Application	Ft. Lbs. (N.m)
Back-Up Light Switch Bolt	18 (25)
Bearing Retainer Plate Bolt	11 (15)
Countershaft Lock Nut	80 (108)
Clutch Cable Bracket Bolt	18 (25)
Oil Drain Plug	30 (40)
Oil Filler Plug	33 (45)
Reverse Idler Gear Shaft Bolt	41 (55)
Reverse Shift Lock Bolt	11 (15)
Shift Arm Special Bolt	11 (15)
Shift Rod Guide Bolt	22 (30)
Transmission Housing Bolt	21 (28)
32-mm Sealing Bolt	18 (25)

	INCH Lbs. (N.m)
Harness Clamp Bolt	106 (12)
Shift Arm Bolt 6-mm	106 (12)

MANUAL TRANSMISSIONS
Audi Type 01A 5-Speed

A4 AWD, A6 AWD, 90 AWD

APPLICATION & LABOR TIMES

APPLICATION & LABOR TIMES

Vehicle Application	Labor Times		Transaxle Series
	¹ R & I	² Overhaul	
1995 A6 AWD, 90 AWD	7.4	9.8	01A
1996 A4 AWD	7.4	9.8	01A

¹ – Removal and installation of transaxle from vehicle chassis.
² – Bench overhaul time for transaxle/differential. DOES NOT include removal and installation.

IDENTIFICATION

Volkswagon Audi Group (VAG) transaxle type is cast into transaxle case flange near transmission-to-engine mounting surface. First 3 letters of transmission code identify transmission for vehicle application. Remaining identification code numbers identify build day, month, and year.

Transmission identification model number is located on side of transmission case flange near transmission-to-engine mounting surface. First 3 numbers of identification model number will be 01A, identifying transmission as a 5-speed manual gearbox used on vehicles with selectable 2 Wheel Drive (2WD) or All Wheel Drive (AWD).

LUBRICATION & ADJUSTMENTS

See appropriate MANUAL TRANSMISSION SERVICING article in TRANSMISSION SERVICING section.

TROUBLE SHOOTING

See GENERAL TROUBLE SHOOTING article in this section.

ON-VEHICLE SERVICE

AXLE SHAFTS

See appropriate AXLE SHAFTS article in AXLE SHAFTS & TRANSFER CASES section.

REMOVAL & INSTALLATION

NOTE: For transaxle removal, see appropriate MANUAL TRANSMISSION REMOVAL article in TRANSMISSION SERVICING section.

TRANSAXLE DISASSEMBLY

1) Mount transmission on stand and drain fluid. Remove clutch return lever, clutch release bearing, guide sleeve and spring washer. Remove snap ring in front of ball bearing, and measure and record snap ring thickness. Remove roller bearing from gearbox housing. DO NOT damage roller bearing cage with puller.

2) Remove snap ring behind roller bearing, and measure and record snap ring thickness. Remove Torsen differential bolts, Torsen differential and compression spring. Remove gearbox cover bolts and gearbox cover.

3) Remove multi-function sensor and transmission breather sleeve. Remove relay arm bolts. Using a slide hammer, remove 3rd/4th shift rod bushing. Remove bolt for shift detent and remove shift detent. Remove mainshaft, pinion/hollow shaft assembly, relay shaft, relay shaft selector rods and shift forks together. *See Fig. 13.* Remove 5th/Reverse gear detent assembly.

4) Remove drive flange from front differential gear. Remove front differential cover. Remove sealing ring and carefully pry out speedometer drive at drive pins using a screwdriver. Remove taper roller bearing outer race from front differential cover using commercial puller. Remove differential from gearbox housing. *See Figs. 1 and 16.*

COMPONENT DISASSEMBLY & REASSEMBLY

GEARBOX COVER

Disassembly – Remove gearbox cover from gearbox housing. Remove pinion and hollow shaft gear assembly, mainshaft gear assembly and shift selector assembly together, as an assembly. Pry out oil collector using screwdriver. Remove inner shift rod sealing ring.
Cleaning & Inspection – Clean gearbox cover with solvent. Dry with compressed air. Inspect for cracks and distortion, and replace as necessary.
Reassembly – Push oil tray into gearbox cover until oil tray locking tabs snap into cover. Tray cup faces upward in gearbox cover. Install inner shift rod sealing ring .04" (1.0 mm) below cover lip. Install assembled mainshaft, pinion/hollow shaft and shift selector assemblies together into gearbox housing. Install gearbox cover on gearbox housing. Tighten Torx bolts to 18 ft. lbs. (25 N.m).

MAINSHAFT

NOTE: Snap rings are of different thicknesses and should be measured as they are removed. Record measurements for reassembly reference. If a gear or shaft is replaced, snap ring clearance must be checked. If only a snap ring is being replaced, replacement must be same thickness.

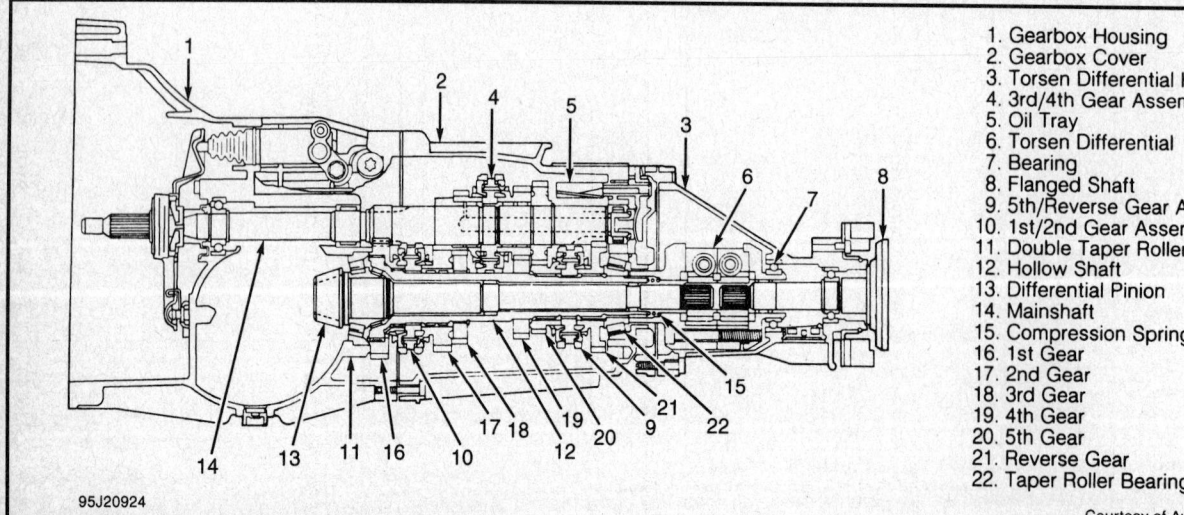

1. Gearbox Housing
2. Gearbox Cover
3. Torsen Differential Housing
4. 3rd/4th Gear Assembly
5. Oil Tray
6. Torsen Differential
7. Bearing
8. Flanged Shaft
9. 5th/Reverse Gear Assembly
10. 1st/2nd Gear Assembly
11. Double Taper Roller Bearing
12. Hollow Shaft
13. Differential Pinion
14. Mainshaft
15. Compression Spring
16. 1st Gear
17. 2nd Gear
18. 3rd Gear
19. 4th Gear
20. 5th Gear
21. Reverse Gear
22. Taper Roller Bearing

95J20924

Courtesy of Audi of America, Inc.

Fig. 1: Cross Sectional View Of Type 01A Transmission

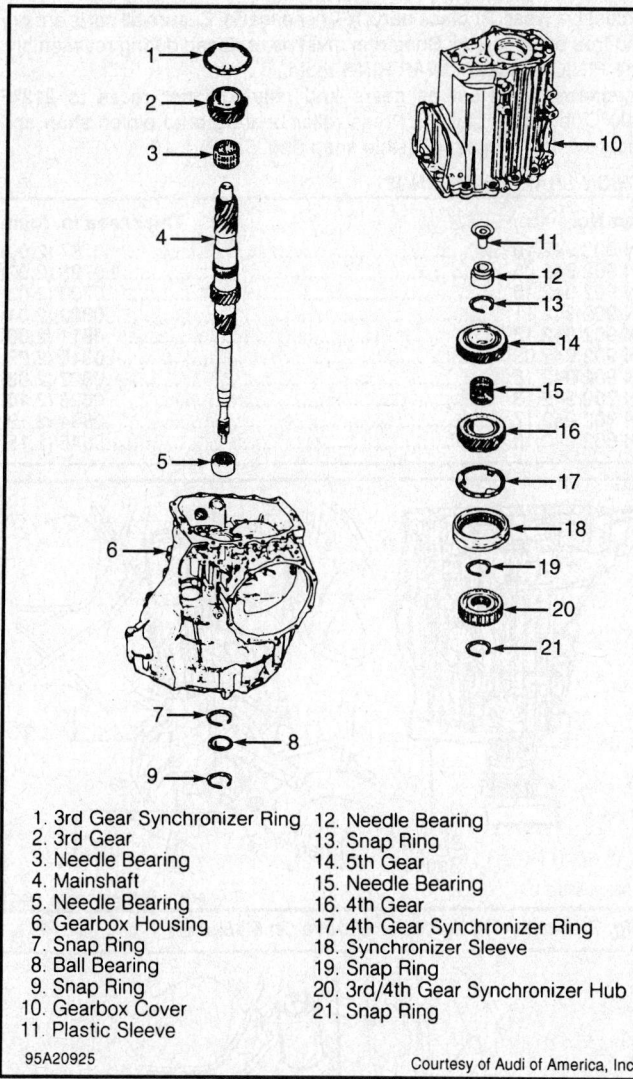

1. 3rd Gear Synchronizer Ring
2. 3rd Gear
3. Needle Bearing
4. Mainshaft
5. Needle Bearing
6. Gearbox Housing
7. Snap Ring
8. Ball Bearing
9. Snap Ring
10. Gearbox Cover
11. Plastic Sleeve
12. Needle Bearing
13. Snap Ring
14. 5th Gear
15. Needle Bearing
16. 4th Gear
17. 4th Gear Synchronizer Ring
18. Synchronizer Sleeve
19. Snap Ring
20. 3rd/4th Gear Synchronizer Hub
21. Snap Ring

95A20925   Courtesy of Audi of America, Inc.

Fig. 2: Exploded View Of Mainshaft

Disassembly – 1) Disassemble transaxle. See TRANSAXLE DISASSEMBLY step **1)** through step **3)**. Remove 5th gear snap ring (No.5) and press off 5th gear.
2) Remove 4th gear, 4th synchro ring and operating sleeve. Remove snap ring No. 4, 3rd/4th synchro hub, snap ring No. 3, 3rd gear and 3rd gear synchro ring.
Cleaning & Inspection – Clean all parts with solvent and dry with compressed air. Inspect for chipped gears, galling and scoring on gears and shaft. Replace any damaged or broken parts. *See Fig. 2.*

NOTE: *Prior to reassembly, replace seals and bearings as necessary in gearbox housing and gearbox cover. See GEARBOX HOUSING and GEARBOX COVER. Heat all gears and bearing inner races to 212°F (100°C) before installing.*

Reassembly – 1) Install spring on third gear. *See Fig. 12.* Slide gear and bearing on mainshaft *See Fig. 2.* Inspect synchro wear by installing 3rd and 4th gear rings in sleeve and measuring gap "a" in positions "A", "B" and "C". *See Fig. 5.* Add measurements and divide by 3 to obtain average. Measurement must not be less than .02" (.5 mm).
2) Install third gear synchro ring and No. 3 snap ring. Press 3-4 synchro hub on mainshaft, then install No. 4 snap ring, using thickest snap ring that fits. See MAIN SHAFT SNAP RING TABLE.

NOTE: *Snap ring thickness is critical. Measure thickness during disassembly and replace with new snap rings. No. 3 snap ring thickness is always the same. Thickness of snap rings No. 1 and 2 are used to adjust mainshaft. See Fig. 6.*

---

3) Install 3-4 synchro with chamfer toward 4th gear on mainshaft and 4th gear synchro ring. Install spring on 4th gear and install bearing and gear on main shaft. Press 5th gear on main shaft with higher collar facing reverse gear and install No. 5 snap ring, using thickest snap ring that fits.
4) Install needle bearing in gearbox housing. Needle bearing installed depth should be 1.56" (39.5 mm) from lower edge of straightedge to upper edge of bearing. *See Fig. 3.*

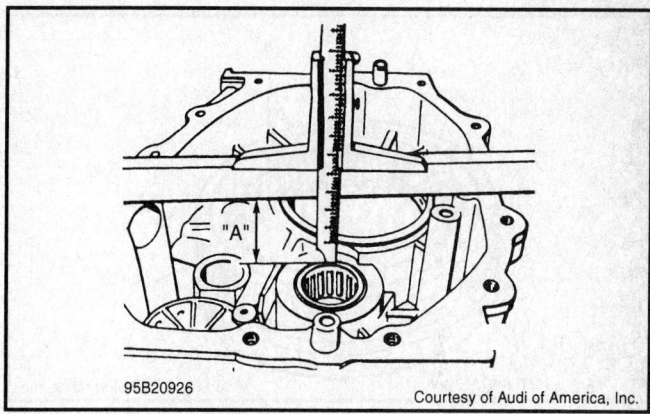

95B20926   Courtesy of Audi of America, Inc.

Fig. 3: Measuring Needle Bearing Installation Depth

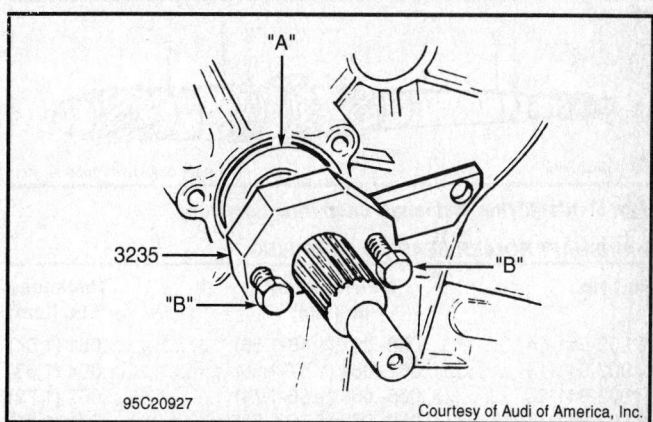

95C20927   Courtesy of Audi of America, Inc.

Fig. 4: Installing Roller Bearing In Final Drive Housing

MAINSHAFT SNAP RINGS

Part No.	Thickness In. (mm)
Snap Ring No. 3 (Brown)	
N 902 945.01	.078 (2.00)
Snap Ring No. 4 (Blue)	
N 902 944.01	.075 (1.90)
N 902 944.02	.076 (1.93)
N 902 944.03	.077 (1.96)
N 902 944.04	.078 (1.99)
N 902 944.05	.079 (2.02)
N 902 944.06	.080 (2.05)
Snap Ring No. 5	
N 902 942.02	.075 (1.90)
N 902 942.03	.076 (1.93)
N 902 942.04	.077 (1.96)
N 902 942.05	.078 (1.99)
N 902 942.06	.079 (2.02)

5) Install plastic sleeve and needle bearing into gearbox cover. Plastic sleeve is used on mainshaft with oil passages for 3rd/4th gear. Place mainshaft in a soft-jawed vise, and clamp securely. Place Spacer Gauge (3167) on 3rd gear. Install gearbox housing onto spacer gauge via mainshaft. Place depth gauge on housing and measure to lower groove in shaft, dimension "a". *See Fig. 7.*

Example: 1.12" (28.5 mm)

6) Place depth gauge on gearbox housing and measure roller bearing seat, dimension "b". Example: 1.05" (26.8 mm). *See Fig. 8.* Use the following formula to find roller bearing snap ring thickness:

X = a - b

Example: 28.5 mm - 26.8 mm = 1.70 mm. See MAINSHAFT ROLLER BEARING SNAP RING table.

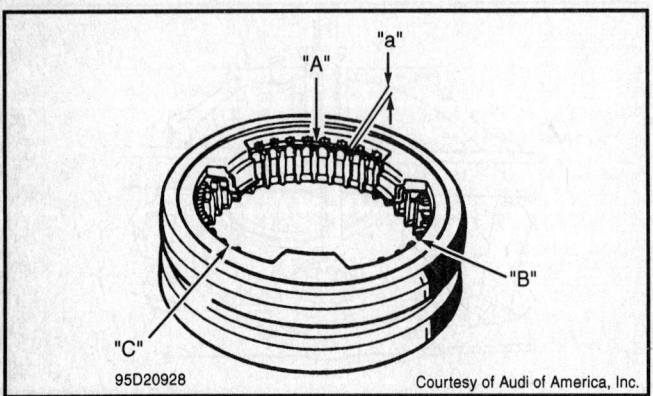

95D20928   Courtesy of Audi of America, Inc.

Fig. 5: Identifying Synchro Ring Measuring Points

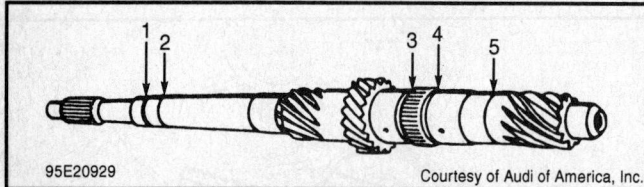

95E20929   Courtesy of Audi of America, Inc.

Fig. 6: Identifying Mainshaft Snap Ring Locations

MAINSHAFT ROLLER BEARING SNAP RING

Part No.	Measurement In. (mm)	Thickness In. (mm)
N 902-941-14	.058-.061 (1.48-1.56)	.061 (1.54)
N 902-941-15	.062-.064 (1.57-1.65)	.064 (1.63)
N 902-941-16	.065-.068 (1.66-1.74)	.067 (1.72)
N 902-941-17	.069-.072 (1.75-1.83)	.071 (1.81)
N 902-941-18	.073-.075 (1.84-1.92)	.074 (1.90)
N 902-941-19	.076-.079 (1.93-2.01)	.078 (1.99)
N 902-941-20	.080-.082 (2.02-2.10)	.081 (2.08)
N 902-941-11	.083-.086 (2.12-2.19)	.085 (2.17)
N 902-941-12	.087-.089 (2.20-2.27)	.088 (2.25)
N 902-941-13	.090-.092 (2.28-2.35)	.091 (2.33)

PINION SHAFT

NOTE: DO NOT damage seal lips between taper roller bearings. If pinion bearings are to be replaced, record and measure clearances. See PINION DEPTH under ADJUSTMENTS. Snap rings are different in thickness and diameter and should be measured as removed. If shaft is replaced, measure snap ring for correct size and fit.

Disassembly – 1) Disassemble transaxle. See TRANSAXLE DISASSEMBLY step 1) through step 3). *See Fig. 7.* Remove double taper roller bearing outer race.

2) Separate pinion shaft from hollow shaft. Remove hollow shaft needle bearing. Remove snap ring and press off double taper roller bearing inner race using outer race removed in Step 1).

Cleaning & Inspection – Clean all parts in solvent and dry with compressed air. Inspect for chipped gear teeth, galling, scoring and excessive wear. Replace parts (as necessary). Ensure all parts are dry and free of lubricants. Snap ring must be replaced during reassembly. See PINION SHAFT SNAP RING table.

Reassembly – Heat all gears and bearing inner races to 212°F (100°C) before installing. Press roller bearing onto pinion shaft and secure using thickest possible snap ring. *See Fig. 10.*

PINION SHAFT SNAP RINGS

Part No.	Thickness In. (mm)
N 902 942.10	.0787 (2.00)
N 902 942.06	.0795 (2.02)
N 902 942.15	.0799 (2.03)
N 902 942.11	.0803 (2.04)
N 902 942.12	.0811 (2.06)
N 902 942.08	.0818 (2.08)
N 902 942.16	.0822 (2.09)
N 902 942.13	.0826 (2.10)
N 902 942.17	.0834 (2.12)
N 902 942.18	.0846 (2.15)

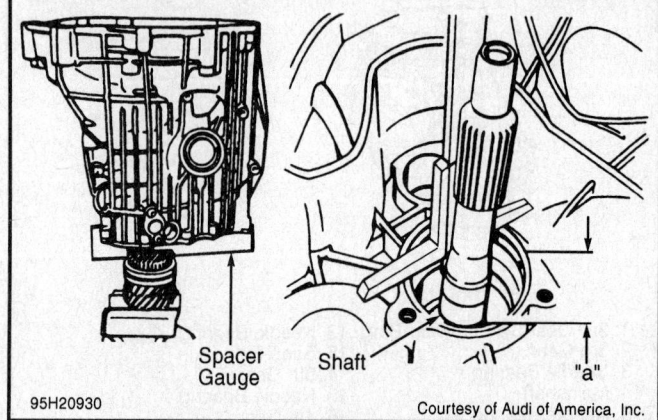

95H20930   Courtesy of Audi of America, Inc.

Fig. 7: Measuring To Lower Groove On Mainshaft

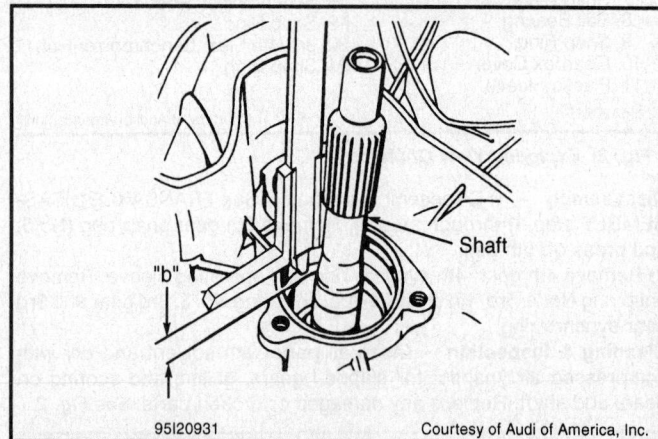

95I20931   Courtesy of Audi of America, Inc.

Fig. 8: Measuring To Ball Bearing Seat

HOLLOW SHAFT

NOTE: DO NOT damage seal lips between taper roller bearings. If bearings are to be replaced, record and measure clearances. See PINION DEPTH under ADJUSTMENTS. Snap rings are different in thickness and diameter and should be measured as removed. If gears or hollow shaft is replaced, determine shim thicknesses and measure snap rings for correct size and fit.

Disassembly – 1) Disassemble transaxle. See TRANSAXLE DISASSEMBLY step 1) through step 3). *See Fig. 7.* Separate pinion shaft from hollow shaft. Press off taper roller bearing inner race with Reverse gear. Remove No. 6 snap ring and press off synchro hub with 5th gear.

2) Remove No. 4 snap ring and press off 4th gear. Remove No. 3 snap ring and press off 2nd and 3rd gears. Remove No. 1 snap ring and press off synchro hub with 1st gear. *See Fig. 9.*

3) Remove locking bushing and outer race for taper roller bearing from gearbox cover.

NOTE: Bushing reinstallation is not necessary once outer race is replaced. Bushing is only required during production.

Cleaning & Inspection – Clean all parts in cleaning solvent and dry with compressed air. Inspect for chipped gear teeth, galling, scoring and excessive wear. Replace parts as necessary. Ensure all parts are dry and free of any lubricants. All snap rings must be replaced during reassembly. See HOLLOW SHAFT SNAP RING table.

Reassembly – 1) Heat all gears and bearing inner races to 212°F (100°C) before installing. Install needle bearing and 1st gear, ensuring spring angled end is in gear bore. *See Fig. 12.* Inspect syncro wear by installing 1st and 2nd gear rings in sleeve and measuring gap "a" in positions "A", "B" and "C". *See Fig. 5.* Add measurements and divide by 3 to obtain average. Measurement must not be less than .02" (.5 mm). Install synchro ring onto 1st/2nd gear synchro hub, ensuring recessed side faces 1st gear and chamfered edge faces 2nd gear. Press hub on hollow shaft.

2) Install No. 1 snap ring and 2nd gear needle bearing. *See Fig. 11.* Install 1st/2nd gear operating sleeve, synchro ring and spring on 2nd gear. *See Fig. 12.* Press 2nd gear hollow shaft and install No. 2 snap ring. Press on 3rd gear with groove facing 4th gear and install No. 3 snap ring. Press on 4th gear with shoulder facing 3rd gear and install No. 4 snap ring. *See Figs. 9 and 11.*

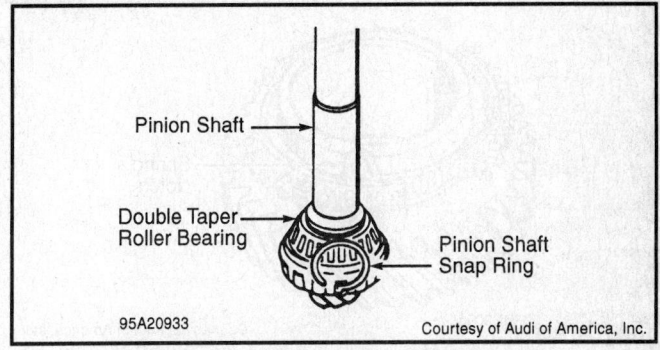

95A20933   Courtesy of Audi of America, Inc.

Fig. 10: Identifying Snap Ring On Pinion Shaft

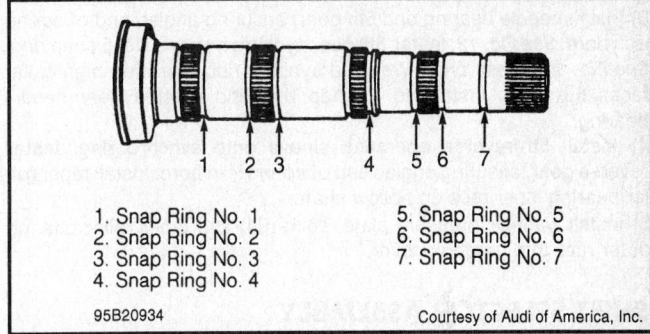

1. Snap Ring No. 1	5. Snap Ring No. 5
2. Snap Ring No. 2	6. Snap Ring No. 6
3. Snap Ring No. 3	7. Snap Ring No. 7
4. Snap Ring No. 4	

95B20934   Courtesy of Audi of America, Inc.

Fig. 11: Identifying Snap Rings On Hollow Shaft

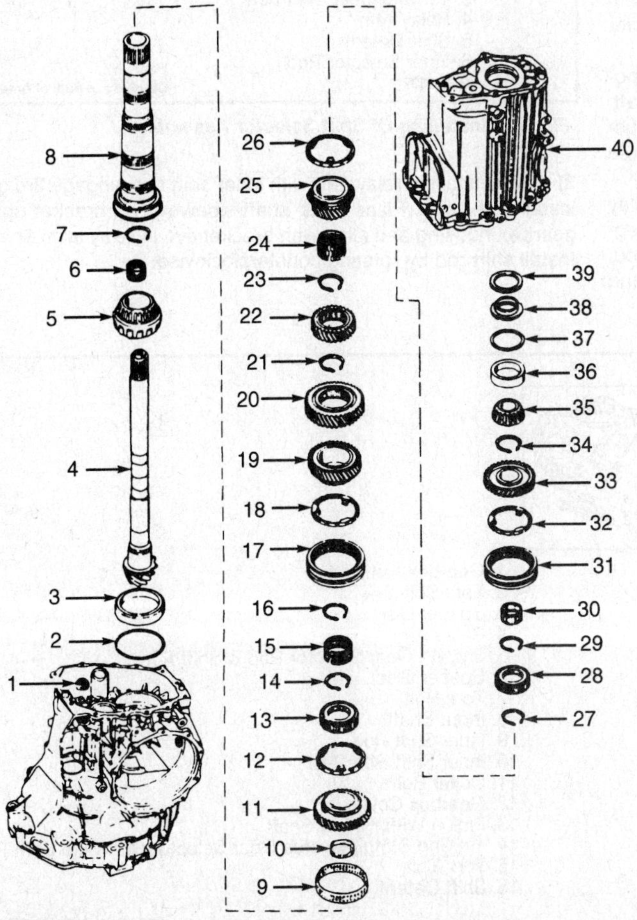

1. Gearbox Housing
2. Shim "S_3"
3. Double Taper Roller Bearing – Outer Race
4. Pinion
5. Double Taper Roller Bearing – Inner Race
6. Needle Bearing – Hollow Shaft
7. Snap Ring
8. Hollow Shaft
9. Needle Bearing – 1st Gear
10. Needle Bearing – 1st Gear
11. 1st Gear
12. Synchronizer Ring – 1st Gear
13. Synchronizer Hub – 1st/2nd Gear
14. Snap Ring
15. Needle Bearing – 2nd Gear
16. Snap Ring
17. Synchronizer Sleeve – 1st/2nd Gear
18. Synchronizer Ring – 2nd Gear
19. 2nd Gear
20. 3rd Gear
21. Snap Ring
22. 4th Gear
23. Snap Ring
24. Needle Bearing – 5th Gear
25. 5th Gear
26. Synchronizer Ring – 5th Gear
27. Snap Ring
28. Synchronizer Hub – 5th/Reverse
29. Snap Ring
30. Needle Bearing – Reverse Gear
31. Synchronizer Sleeve – 5th/Reverse Gear
32. Synchronizer Ring – Reverse Gear
33. Reverse Gear
34. Snap Ring
35. Taper Roller Bearing – Inner Race
36. Taper Roller Bearing – Outer Race
37. Shim "S_4"
38. Pressure Plate
39. Washer
40. Gearbox Cover

95J20932   Courtesy of Audi of America, Inc.

Fig. 9: Exploded View Of Pinion & Hollow Shaft Assembly

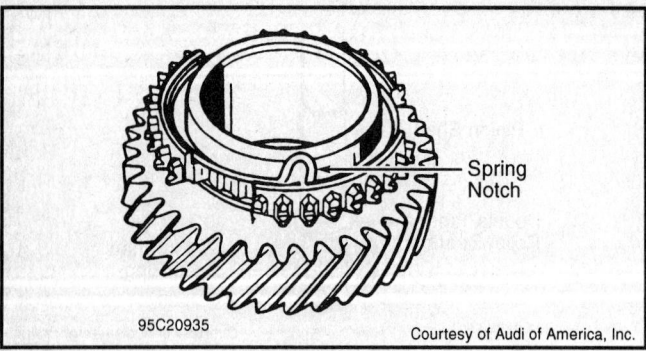

Fig. 12: Identifying Spring & Notch In Gear

3) Install needle bearing and 5th gear, ensuring angled end of spring is in bore. *See Fig. 12.* Install 5th gear synchro ring and No. 5 snap ring. *See Fig. 11.* Press on 5th/reverse synchro hub, ensuring high collar faces 5th gear. Install No. 6 snap ring and reverse gear needle bearing.

4) Install 5th/reverse operating sleeve onto synchro ring. Install reverse gear, ensuring angled end of spring is in bore. Install taper roller bearing inner race on hollow shaft.

5) Install washer, pressure plate, shim (S4) and taper roller bearing outer race into gearbox cover.

SHIFT SELECTOR ASSEMBLY

Disassembly – For disassembly, see exploded view of components. *See Fig. 13.*

Cleaning & Inspection – Clean all parts in solvent and dry with compressed air. Inspect for damaged or excessively worn parts. All components can be replaced individually except 5th/reverse gear shift fork which must be replaced together with selector ring and selector shaft.

Reassembly – 1) For reassembly, see exploded view of components. *See Fig. 13.* Assembly must be assembled with main shaft, pinion shaft and hollow shaft in gearbox housing. Place gearbox housing on work table with open end up. *See Fig. 14.* Install 5th/reverse gear selector shaft with swinging fork.

2) Install 3rd/4th selector shaft and 1st/2nd gear shift fork. Install relay shaft and tighten Torx bolts to 30 ft. lbs. (40 N.m). Install locking segment and tighten Torx bolt to 18 ft. lbs. (25 N.m). Install inner shift rod, assembled mainshaft, pinion with hollow shaft, selector shafts and shift forks together.

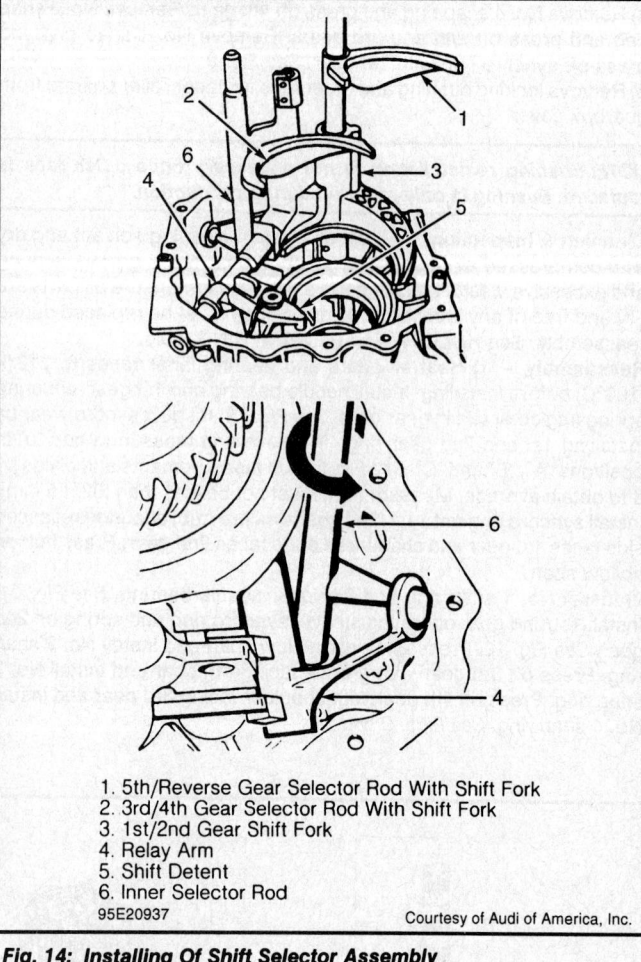

1. 5th/Reverse Gear Selector Rod With Shift Fork
2. 3rd/4th Gear Selector Rod With Shift Fork
3. 1st/2nd Gear Shift Fork
4. Relay Arm
5. Shift Detent
6. Inner Selector Rod

Fig. 14: Installing Of Shift Selector Assembly

3) When installing relay arm with inner shift rod, engage 3rd gear and install relay arm. Place inner shaft sideways on bracket opening in gearbox housing and align with bracket eye in relay arm. *See Fig. 14.* Install shift rod by rotating counterclockwise.

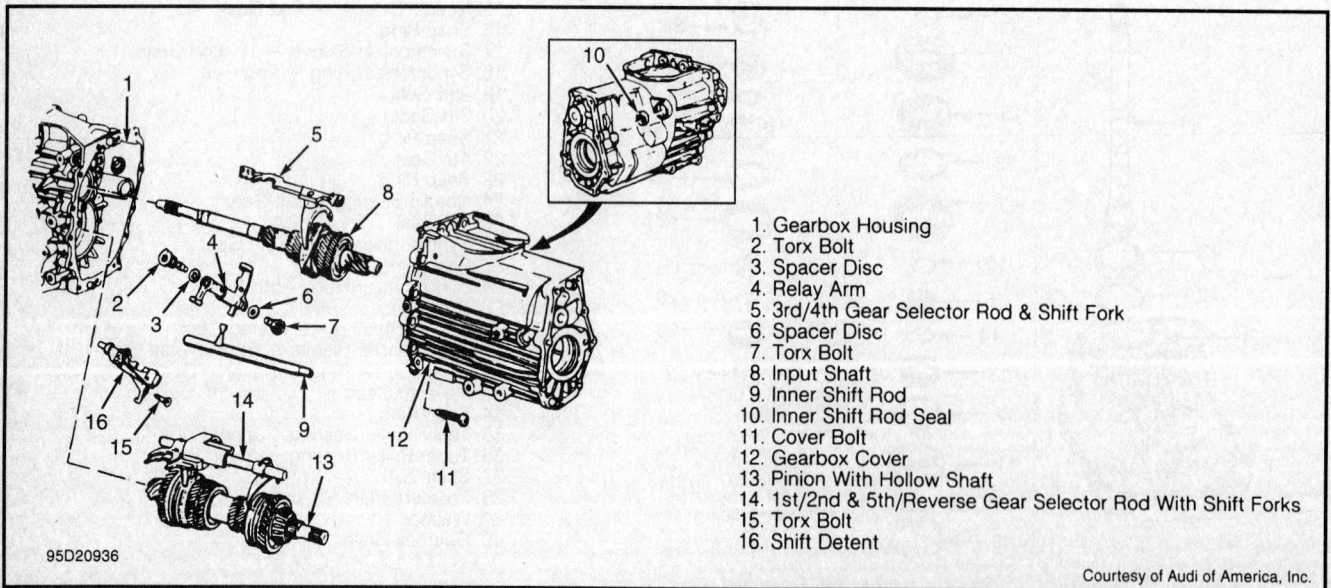

1. Gearbox Housing
2. Torx Bolt
3. Spacer Disc
4. Relay Arm
5. 3rd/4th Gear Selector Rod & Shift Fork
6. Spacer Disc
7. Torx Bolt
8. Input Shaft
9. Inner Shift Rod
10. Inner Shift Rod Seal
11. Cover Bolt
12. Gearbox Cover
13. Pinion With Hollow Shaft
14. 1st/2nd & 5th/Reverse Gear Selector Rod With Shift Forks
15. Torx Bolt
16. Shift Detent

Fig. 13: Exploded View Of Shift Selector Assembly

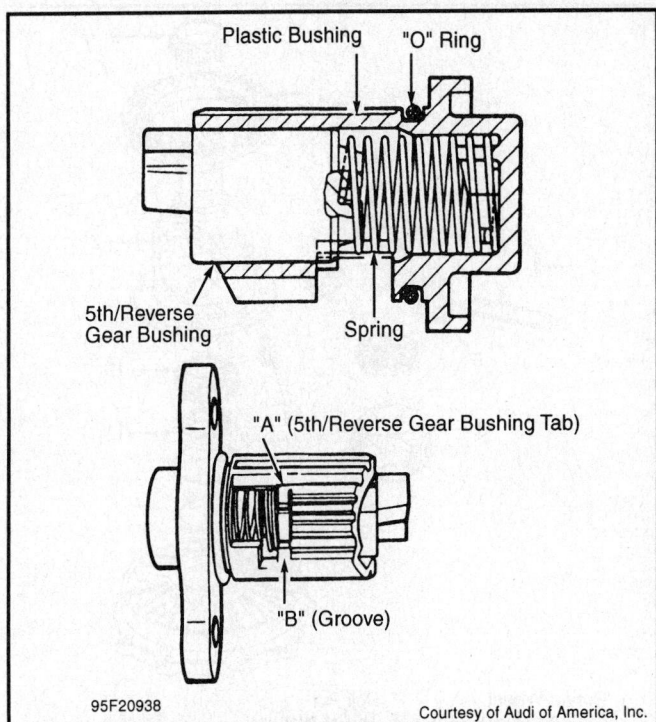

Fig. 15: Identifying Correct Procedure To Assemble 5th/Reverse Gear Detent Assembly

5TH/REVERSE GEAR DETENT ASSEMBLY

NOTE: If there is any catching or hanging up in 5th gear or Reverse gear, remove, check and reassemble 5th/Reverse gear detent assembly prior to removing transmission.

Disassembly & Reassembly – 1) Place spring in plastic bushing. Turn spring counterclockwise using light pressure until spring snaps in place in base of plastic bushing. Place 5th/Reverse gear detent bushing in spring so bent end of spring lies in groove. See Fig. 15.

2) Press spring together using 5th/Reverse gear detent bushing. Twist 5th/Reverse gear detent bushing about one turn counterclockwise

HOLLOW SHAFT SNAP RING

Part No.	Thickness In. (mm)
Snap Ring No. 1 (Blue)	
N 902 947.01	.075 (1.90)
N 902 947.02	.076 (1.93)
N 902 947.03	.077 (1.96)
N 902 947.04	.078 (1.98)
N 902 947.05	.079 (2.02)
Snap Ring No. 2 (Blue)	
N 902 947.06	.098 (2.50)
Snap Ring No. 3	
N 902 946.02	.075 (1.90)
N 902 946.09	.076 (1.94)
N 902 946.10	.078 (1.98)
N 902 946.06	.079 (2.02)
N 902 946.11	.081 (2.06)
Snap Ring No. 4	
N 902 952.07	.073 (1.86)
N 902 952.02	.074 (1.90)
N 902 952.08	.076 (1.94)
N 902 952.09	.077 (1.96)
Snap Ring No. 5 (Brown)	
N 902 945.01	.078 (1.98)
Snap Ring No. 6 (Blue)	
N 902 944.01	.075 (1.90)
N 902 944.02	.076 (1.93)
N 902 944.03	.077 (1.96)
N 902 944.04	.078 (1.99)
N 902 944.05	.079 (2.02)
N 902 944.06	.080 (2.03)
Snap Ring No. 7	
N 902 944.07	.098 (2.50)

until tab on 5th/Reverse gear detent bushing lines up on groove in plastic bushing. Press 5th/Reverse gear detent bushing tab into groove in plastic bushing until it stops.

3) Turn 5th/Reverse gear detent bushing clockwise and release 5th/Reverse gear detent bushing into final installed position. To ensure installation is correct, 5th/Reverse gear detent bushing tab "A" must always come to stop opposite groove "B" on plastic bushing.

GEARBOX COVER

Disassembly – Remove mainshaft needle bearing and plastic sleeves. Remove Torx bolt for reverse gear shaft. Pry out oil tray using screwdriver and remove inner shift rod sealing ring.

Cleaning & Inspection – Clean all parts with cleaning solvent and dry with compressed air. Inspect housing for cracks or damage. Replace as necessary.

Reassembly – 1) Install inner shaft rod sealing ring .04" (1.0 mm) below housing lip. Push oil tray into gearbox cover until oil tray locking tab snaps into cover. Ensure tray cup points upward in gearbox cover. Install reverse gear shaft.

2) Install mainshaft needle bearing into gearbox cover 8.50" (216.0 mm) measured from gearbox cover face. On mainshaft with oil holes, insert plastic sleeve into end of mainshaft.

FRONT DIFFERENTIAL & GEARBOX HOUSING

NOTE: Differential can be removed and installed without disassembling transmission. If adjustments are necessary, transmission must be disassembled to access pinion.

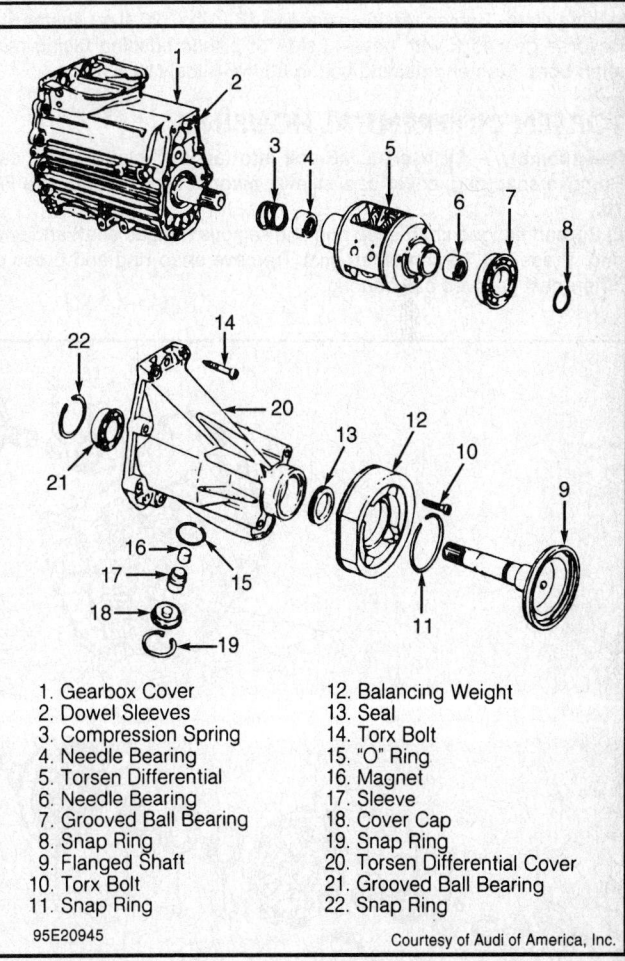

1. Gearbox Cover	12. Balancing Weight
2. Dowel Sleeves	13. Seal
3. Compression Spring	14. Torx Bolt
4. Needle Bearing	15. "O" Ring
5. Torsen Differential	16. Magnet
6. Needle Bearing	17. Sleeve
7. Grooved Ball Bearing	18. Cover Cap
8. Snap Ring	19. Snap Ring
9. Flanged Shaft	20. Torsen Differential Cover
10. Torx Bolt	21. Grooved Ball Bearing
11. Snap Ring	22. Snap Ring

Fig. 16: Exploded View Of Torsen Differential Housing

Disassembly – 1) To remove drive flange, position chisel or spacer under drive flange and extract drive flange from gear by tightening flange bolt against spacer. Remove flange cover with sealing ring. Remove differential. *See Figs. 17 and 18.*

2) Remove differential bearing inner and outer race using puller. Remove all bolts, and use punch to remove ring gear from differential. Use puller to remove differential large inner race. Use puller to remove differential bearing large outer race from flange cover.

3) Rotate side gears to bring pinion gears to an opening in case. Remove pinion gears, thrust washers and side gears.

4) Remove final drive flange sealing ring and transmission breather. Remove tapered roller bearing outer race and 3rd/4th gear shift rod bushing. Remove pinion shaft needle bearing. Remove speedometer drive multifunction sender and connector.

Cleaning & Inspection – Clean all parts with cleaning solvent and dry with compressed air. Inspect all parts for chipped gears, scoring and damage. Replace as necessary. Inspect housing for cracks and damage, and replace as necessary. Lubricate parts with transmission fluid prior to reassembly.

Reassembly (Differential) – 1) Heat all gears and bearing inner races to 212°F (100°C) before installing. Install one-piece thrust washer coated with gear oil. Install differential side gears and flange shafts without lock ring. Install differential pinion gears about 180 degrees apart and pivot into place by turning flange shaft clockwise.

2) Align thrust washers and pinion gears. Drive in differential pinion shaft, and secure it using new roll pin. To complete assembly, reverse removal procedure and see ADJUSTMENTS.

Reassembly (Gearbox Housing) – Install sealing ring for drive flange .02" (.5 mm) below housing edge. Install multifunction sender with locking plate. Tighten retaining plate to 18 ft. lbs. (25 N.m). Install 5th/Reverse gear lock with beveled side of plastic bushing facing relay shaft bore. Tighten retaining bolt to 89 INCH lbs. (10 N.m).

TORSEN DIFFERENTIAL HOUSING

Disassembly – 1) Insert a M8 bolt into tapped hole of cover cap. Remove snap ring, cover cap, sleeve, magnet and "O" ring. *See Fig. 16.*

2) Spread flanged shaft snap ring and remove flanged shaft and snap ring. Press out Torsen differential. Remove snap ring and press off differential grooved ball bearing.

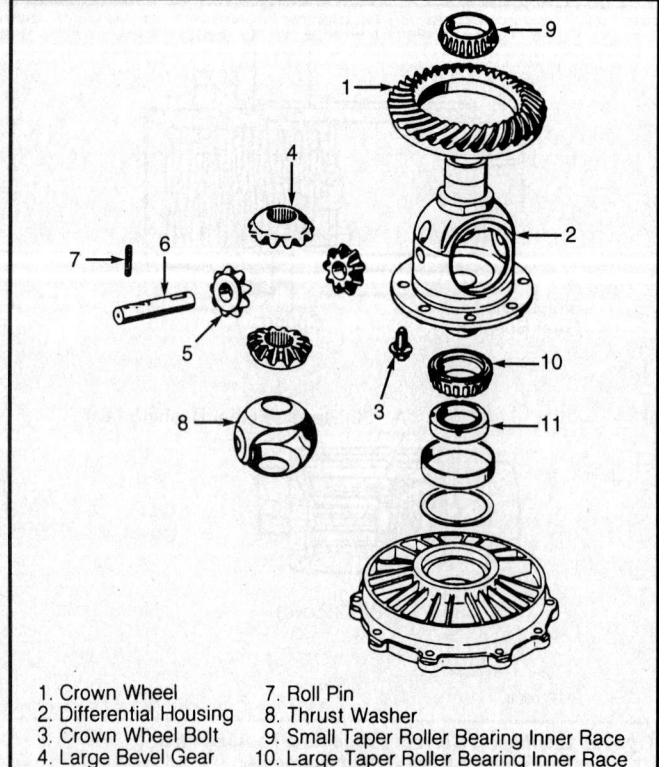

1. Crown Wheel	7. Roll Pin
2. Differential Housing	8. Thrust Washer
3. Crown Wheel Bolt	9. Small Taper Roller Bearing Inner Race
4. Large Bevel Gear	10. Large Taper Roller Bearing Inner Race
5. Small Bevel Gear	11. Speedometer Gear
6. Bevel Gear Shaft	
95J20940	Courtesy of Audi of America, Inc.

Fig. 18: Exploded View Of Differential Assembly

3) Remove snap ring and press out flanged shaft grooved ball bearing from differential cover. Pull out needle bearings for pinion/hollow shaft and flanged shaft from differential.

NOTE: DO NOT disassemble Torsen differential. Replace as a unit.

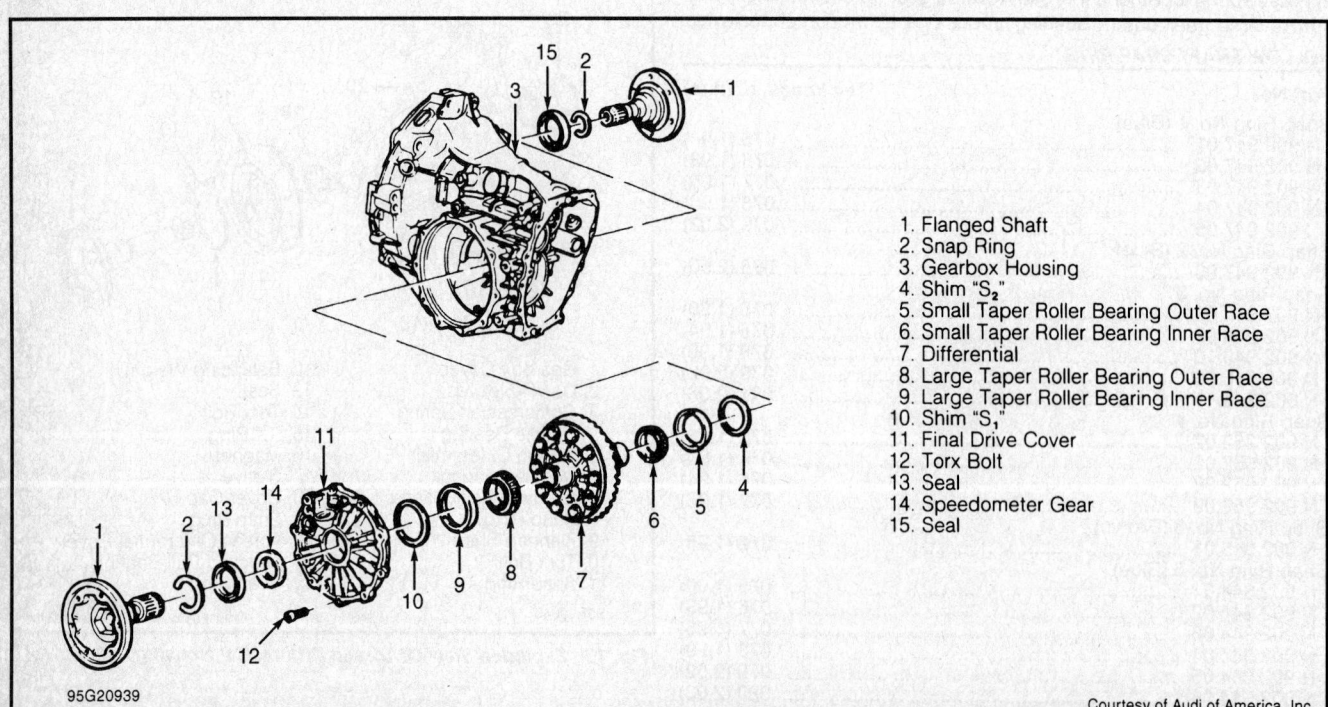

1. Flanged Shaft
2. Snap Ring
3. Gearbox Housing
4. Shim "S_2"
5. Small Taper Roller Bearing Outer Race
6. Small Taper Roller Bearing Inner Race
7. Differential
8. Large Taper Roller Bearing Outer Race
9. Large Taper Roller Bearing Inner Race
10. Shim "S_1"
11. Final Drive Cover
12. Torx Bolt
13. Seal
14. Speedometer Gear
15. Seal

95G20939

Courtesy of Audi of America, Inc.

Fig. 17: Exploded View Of Gearbox Housing

ADJUSTMENT TABLE

ADJUSTMENT TABLE

Replaced Part \ To Be Adjusted	Ring Gear "S₁" + "S₂"	Pinion "S₃" Using Deviation r	Pinion "S₃" Using Actual Measurement	Pinion (shim "S₄" only)
Gearbox Housing ¹	X		X	
Gearbox Cover				X
Differential Housing	X			
Pinion Bearings			X	
Differential Bearings	X			
Ring Gear & Pinion	X	X		
Cover On Gearbox Housing	X			

¹ – When gearbox housing is replaced, adjust mainshaft.

96I19362   Courtesy of Audi of America, Inc.

ADJUSTMENTS

NOTE: *When assembling final drive, it is necessary to adjust ring gear, pinion or both. See ADJUSTMENT TABLE.*

4) Remove balancing weight snap ring, bolts and balancing weight. Remove flanged shaft seal.

Cleaning & Inspection – Clean all parts with cleaning solvent and dry with compressed air. Inspect housing for cracks or damage. Replace as necessary.

Reassembly – **1)** Press in pinion/hollow shaft needle bearing to a depth of 1.28" (32.5 mm). Press in flanged shaft needle bearing to a depth of .55" (14 mm). *See Fig. 16.*

2) Press on differential grooved ball bearing and install snap ring. Press in flanged shaft grooved ball bearing and install snap ring. Press in flanged shaft seal to a depth of .08" (2 mm) below inner edge of cover.

3) Install balancing weight and torque bolts to 26 ft. lbs. (35 N.m). Install balancing weight snap ring.

4) Press Torsen differential into housing. Install flanged shaft and flanged shaft snap ring. Install "O" ring, magnet, sleeve, cover cap and cover cap snap ring.

PINION DEPTH

NOTE: *Always install shims and pressure plate to determine "S₄" shim. Pressure plate thickness is .58-.60" (14.8-15.3 mm).*

1) Install bearing outer races in gearbox housing and gearbox cover without shims. Install pinion and hollow shaft bearing inner races. Seat lower bearing securely. Install assembled pinion and hollow shaft into gearbox housing.

2) Install gearbox cover, and tighten bolts to 18 ft. lbs. (25 N.m). Turn final drive so gear housing faces down. Press pinion head on using Special Tool (VW296) until pinion bearing outer race contacts housing. Turn pinion manually until pinion bearing is seated.

3) Install dial indicator, and set .04" (1.0 mm) preload. Turn gearbox so cover faces up. Turn pinion several times before measuring so pinion bearing seats, or readings will be inaccurate. Read and record measurement.

4) To determine "S" total (total shim thickness), use the following formula: "S$_{tot}$" = **Dial Indicator Reading + Preload**

Example:

Dial Indicator Reading	.057" (1.45 mm)
Preload (Constant Value)	+ .006" (.15 mm)
"S$_{tot}$"	= .063" (1.60 mm)

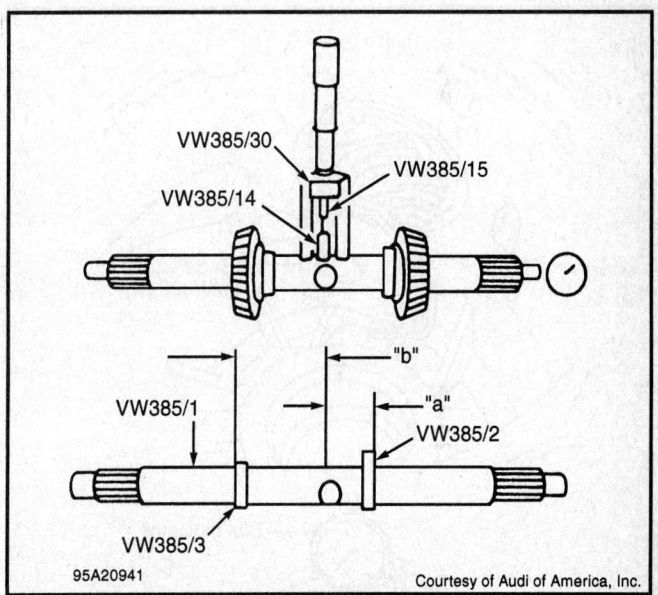

95A20941   Courtesy of Audi of America, Inc.

Fig. 19: Identifying Universal Measuring Bar

5) To determine pinion bearing preload, select shims with combined thickness of "S$_{tot}$", e.g., .063" (1.60 mm). Install shims behind pinion bearings outer race in gearbox cover (S4 position). *See Fig. 22.* See appropriate SHIM THICKNESS table. Install gearbox cover. Turn pinion in both directions several times to seat bearings.

6) Install dial indicator using Special Tool (VW792/1) on gearbox housing and zero with .04" (1.0 mm) preload at S4 end of shaft. Loosen bolts on gearbox cover. Dial indicator will display value of .003-.006" (.08-.15 mm) with selection of proper shim.

7) Leave shim behind bearing in transmission (S4 side). Lube bearings with gear lube and install gearbox cover. Using Special Tool (3182) measure turning torque. Used bearings should have 3-5 INCH Lbs. (.3-.6 Nm), New bearings should have 13-27 INCH Lbs. (1.5-3.0 Nm) turning torque.

8) To determine dimension "E", install selected "S$_{tot}$" e.g., .063" (1.60 mm) behind pinion bearing outer race in gear carrier housing (S4 position). *See Fig. 22.* Install gear carrier housing. Turn pinion several times in both directions to seat bearing. Set Universal Bar (VW385/1) centering ring to dimension "a" (1.38"/35.0 mm) and sliding ring to dimension "b" (2.95"/75.0 mm). *See Fig. 19.*

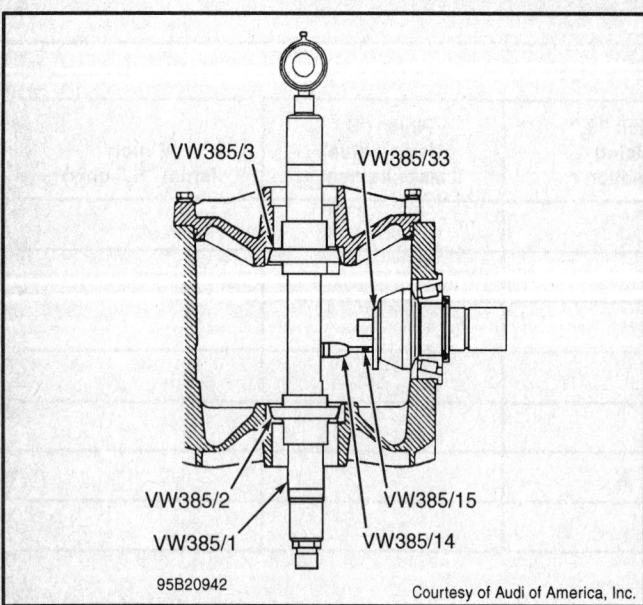

Fig. 20: Measuring Pinion Depth

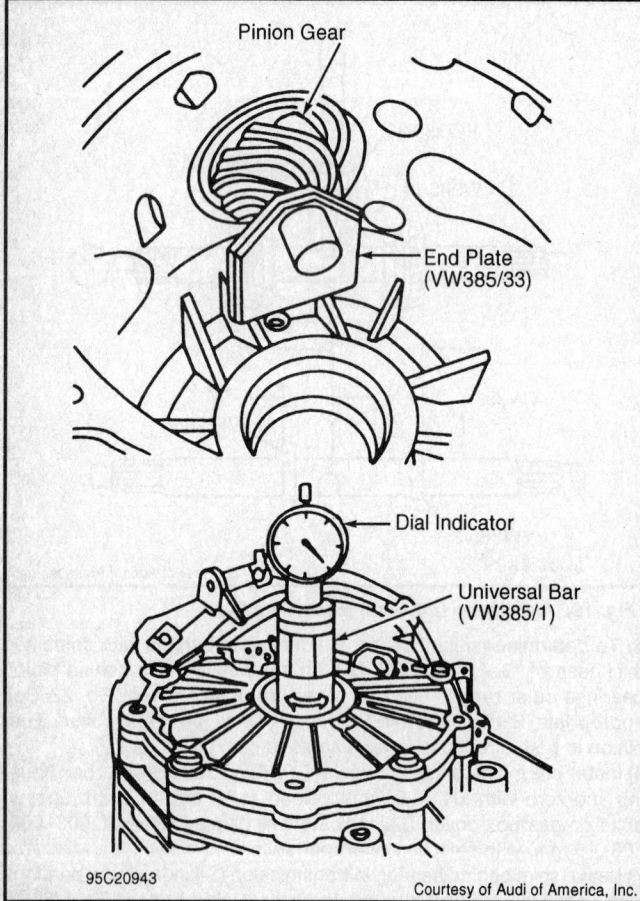

Fig. 21: Identifying Dimension "E" Measuring Points

9) Assemble and adjust measuring bar using the following specifications. See Fig. 17:

With 6.7" (170 mm) Ring Gear
- Set Universal Master Gauge (VW385/30) dimension "Ro" to 2.200" (54.95 mm).
- Set Indicator Extension (VW385/15) to .260" (6.50 mm)

With 7.1" (180 mm) Ring Gear
- Set Universal Master Gauge (VW385/30) dimension "Ro" to 2.348" (59.65 mm).
- Set Indicator Extension (VW385/15) to .366" (9.30 mm)

10) Place master gauge on measuring bar and set dial indicator with .12" (3.0 mm) range to zero with .04" (1.0 mm) preload. Place End Plate (VW385/33) on pinion end face. See Fig. 21. Remove master gauge and install measuring bar in housing. Ensure Centering Disc (VW385/3) faces final drive cover. See Fig. 20.

11) Install cover for final drive housing, and tighten bolts. Pull 2nd centering ring outward until measuring bar can just be turned by hand. Turn measuring bar slightly until dial indicator contacts end face of pinion and indicates maximum deflection (return point). Measured readings equal dimension "E". See Fig. 21.

12) To determine "S_3" shim thickness, use the following formula and see S_3 SHIM THICKNESS table: "S_3" = "E" + "R"
- "E" = dial indicator reading maximum deflection,
- "R" = deviation (marked on ring gear) or determined by actual measurement.

Example:

Dial Indicator Reading "E"	.020"	(.51 mm)
Deviation "R"	+ .007"	(.18 mm)
Shim Thickness "S_3"	= .027"	(.69 mm)

13) To determine "S_4" shim thickness, use the following formula and see "S_4" SHIM THICKNESS table: "S_4" = "S" total - "S_3"

Example:

Total Shim Thickness	.063"	(1.60 mm)
"S_3" Shim Thickness	- .027"	(.69 mm)
"S_4" Shim Thickness	= .036"	(.91 mm)

S_3 SHIM THICKNESS

Part No.	Thickness In. (mm)
012-311-391 A	.017 (.45)
012-311-391 B	.019 (.50)
012-311-391 C	.022 (.55)
012-311-391 D	.024 (.60)
012-311-391 E	.026 (.65)
012-311-391 F	.028 (.70)
012-311-391 G	.030 (.75)
012-311-391 H	.031 (.80)
012-311-391 J	.033 (.85)
012-311-391 K	.035 (.90)
012-311-391 L	.037 (.95)
012-311-391 M	.039 (1.00)
012-311-391 N	.041 (1.05)

S_4 SHIM THICKNESS

Part No.	Thickness In. (mm)
01A-311-393	.017 (.45)
01A-311-393 A	.019 (.50)
01A-311-393 B	.021 (.55)
01A-311-393 C	.023 (.60)
01A-311-393 D	.025 (.65)
01A-311-393 E	.027 (.70)
01A-311-393 F	.029 (.75)
01A-311-393 G	.031 (.80)
01A-311-393 H	.033 (.85)
01A-311-393 J	.035 (.90)

NOTE: If required thickness is more than thickest shim, 2 shims that equal total required thickness may be installed.

14) To ensure settings are correct, install pinion with measured shims "S_3" and "S_4" and turn several times in both directions. Install measuring bar in position and verify measurements. Adjustment shims are correct if dial indicator, reading counterclockwise (Red reading), shows deviation "R" within .001" (.04 mm) tolerance.

GEARBOX COVER

1) If gearbox cover is to be replaced, only "S_4" shim must be remeasured. Install pinion in old gearbox cover and turn pinion several times to seat bearing. Place dial indicator on cover and zero with .04" (1.02 mm) preload. Turn pinion several times and record reading.

2) Remove dial indicator from cover. Remove pinion and bearing outer race with pressure plate adjustment shim and washer. Install in new cover and repeat measurements. Select correct shim from S_4 SHIM THICKNESS table.

Example:

Preload	.04" (1.02 mm)
Dial Indicator Reading	- .034" (.88 mm)
	"X" = .005" (.12 mm)
Shim Thickness "S_4"	.030" (.77 mm)
Value "X"	+ .005" (.12 mm)
	= .035" (.89 mm)

3) If reading is greater than .04" (1.0 mm), "S_4" shim must be reduced by value "X". Install shim and gearbox cover, and recheck preload of pinion bearing.

RING GEAR ADJUSTMENT

1) Ring gear must be adjusted if any of following parts were replaced:
- Gearbox housing
- Final Drive cover
- Differential bearings
- Differential gear housing
- Ring and pinion set

2) To adjust differential bearing preload (pinion removed) remove oil seals and outer races of differential bearings. Install bearing outer races without shims and seat into stop. Install differential gear into housing without speedometer gear. Install ring gear on left side.

3) Install cover and tighten bolts to 18 ft. lbs. (25 N.m). Attach dial indicator. Zero indicator with .04" (1.0 mm) preload. Ensure dial indicator extension is 1.2" (30 mm) long. Install Special Tools (VW521/4 and VW521/8) on gearbox housing. Move differential up and down and record end play.

NOTE: While taking measurements, DO NOT turn differential; bearing will settle, resulting in an incorrect reading.

---

4) Example: Dial Indicator Reading .05" (1.27 mm).

"S_{tot}" = Dial Indicator Reading	.05" (1.27 mm)
+ Preload (constant)	+ .02" (.51 mm)
	= .07" (1.78 mm)

Install shim of correct size behind bearing outer race in gearbox housing ("S_2" side). See S_2 SHIM THICKNESS table under RING GEAR BACKLASH. *See Fig. 22.*

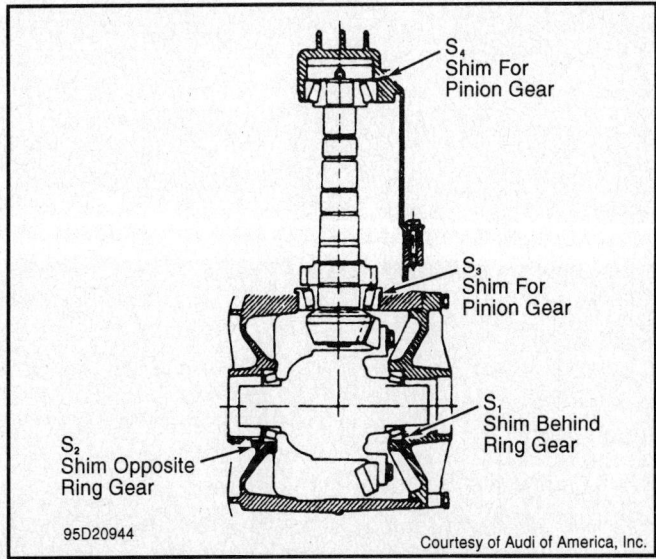

Fig. 22: Identifying Shim Points For Pinion & Ring Gear

95D20944 — Courtesy of Audi of America, Inc.

5) Check rotation torque using INCH-lb. torque wrench and Adapters (VW521/4 and VW521/8). Lubricate bearings with transmission oil prior to measuring torque. Torque should be:
- New bearing – 22-31 INCH lbs. (2.5-3.5 N.m).
- Used bearing – 3-5 INCH lbs. (.33-.56 N.m).

RING GEAR BACKLASH

1) Install pinion with shim "S_3" and "S_4" installed. Install "S_{tot}" shims on housing side of differential and turn differential several times to seat bearings. Install dial indicator and adjust Measuring Lever (VW388) to:

A = 2.6" (67 mm) on 6.7" (170 mm) ring gear
2.8" (72 mm) on 7.1" (180 mm) ring gear

2) To hold pinion from moving, install lock bolt on locking sleeve and tighten lock bolt. Turn ring gear to stop and set indicator to zero. Turn ring gear back. Note and record backlash.

NOTE: If pinion turning torque is too low, install Bracket "A" (3177) to measure backlash precisely. Differential must be installed so opening for installation of gears faces pinion.

---

3) Loosen lock bolt on locking sleeve, rotate ring gear 90 degrees, tighten lock bolt and measure backlash again. Repeat this procedure at least 2 more times. Add all 4 readings together and divide by 4 to determine average backlash.

Example: Average Backlash = .13" divided by 4 = .03"

4) If measurements differ by more than .002" (.06 mm) from each other, ring gear/pinion installation is incorrect. Check ring and pinion, and replace if necessary.

5) To determine "S_2" shim (side opposite ring gear), use the following formula: "S_2" = "S_{tot}" - Average Backlash + Lift Constant Value of .006" (.15 mm). Select appropriate shim from S_2 SHIM THICKNESS table.

Example:

"S_{tot}"	.07" (1.78 mm)
Minus Backlash	- .03" (.76 mm)
	= .04" (1.02 mm)
Plus Lift (constant)	+ .006" (.15 mm)
"S_2"	= .046" (1.17 mm)

Select appropriate shim from S_2 SHIM THICKNESS table.

S_2 SHIM THICKNESS

Part No.	Thickness In. (mm)
012 409 386	.017 (.45)
012 409 386 A	.019 (.50)
012 409 386 B	.021 (.55)
012 409 386 C	.023 (.60)
012 409 386 D	.025 (.65)
012 409 386 E	.027 (.70)
012 409 386 F	.029 (.75)
012 409 386 G	.031 (.80)
012 409 386 H	.033 (.85)
012 409 386 J	.035 (.90)
012 409 386 K	.037 (.95)
012 409 386 L	.039 (1.00)

6) To determine "S_1" shim thickness (ring gear side), use the following formula: "S_1" = "S_{tot}" - "S_2". Select appropriate shim from S_1 SHIM THICKNESS table.

Example:

"S_{tot}"	.07" (1.78 mm)
"S_2"	- .05" (1.27 mm)
"S_1"	= .02" (.51 mm)

S, SHIM THICKNESS

Part No.	Thickness In. (mm)
012 409 385	.017 (.45)
012 409 385 A	.019 (.50)
012 409 385 B	.021 (.55)
012 409 385 C	.023 (.60)
012 409 385 D	.025 (.65)
012 409 385 E	.027 (.70)
012 409 385 F	.029 (.75)
012 409 385 G	.031 (.80)
012 409 385 H	.033 (.85)
012 409 385 J	.035 (.90)
012 409 385 K	.037 (.95)
012 409 385 L	.039 (1.00)

NOTE: If required thickness is more than thickest shim, 2 shims that equal total required thickness may be installed.

7) To ensure correct backlash, measure backlash 4 times around circumference of ring gear. Acceptable values can range from .004-.008" (.12-.22 mm). No two values can deviate from each other by more than .002" (.05 mm).

TRANSMISSION REASSEMBLY

1) Assemble mainshaft, pinion with hollow shaft, relay shaft, selector rods and shift rods. All components must be installed together as one unit into gearbox cover. Install relay shaft and locking segment. Tighten relay shaft bolts to 30 ft. lbs. (40 N.m). Tighten locking segment bolt to 18 ft. lbs. (25 N.m).

2) Install multifunction sender with new "O" ring, and tighten retaining plate bolt to 18 ft. lbs. (25 N.m). Install 5th/reverse lock bolt and tighten to 89 INCH lbs. (10 N.m). Install roller bearing on mainshaft and use selected snap rings that are installed before and after roller bearing.

3) Lightly coat sealing face on gearbox housing with sealing compound. Install new gasket and dowel pins. Attach gearbox cover to gearbox housing. Tighten Torx bolt to 18 ft. lbs. (25 N.m).

4) Install guide sleeve with new sealing ring, and tighten new Torx bolts 26 ft. lbs. (35 N.m). Install assembled differential gear and differential cover. Tighten differential cover bolts in crisscross pattern to 18 ft. lbs. (25 N.m). Install drive flanges with new snap rings. Install speedometer drive. Ensure speedometer drive has not been dropped or damaged.

5) Install transmission breather sleeve so sleeve extends .8" (21 mm) above vent lip. Install clutch return lever and clutch release bearing. Install Compression spring and Torsen differential. Tighten bolts to 18 ft. lbs. (25 N.m).

TORQUE SPECIFICATIONS
TORQUE SPECIFICATIONS

Application	Ft. Lbs. (N.m)
Differential Cover Bolts	18 (25)
Gearbox Cover Bolts	18 (25)
Guide Sleeve Bolt	26 (35)
Locking Segment Bolt	18 (25)
Multifunction Sender Retaining Plate Bolt	18 (25)
Relay Shaft Bolt	30 (40)
Reverse Gear Shaft Bolt	26 (35)
Ring Gear Bolt	66 (90)
Torsen Differential Housing Bolts	18 (25)

	INCH Lbs. (N.m)
Multifunction Connector Bolt	89 (10)
5th/Reverse Gear Lock Bolt	89 (10)

S6

NOTE: The metric dimensions listed in this article are the preferred service measurement. Inch conversions are given to the 3rd or 4th decimal place for reference.

APPLICATION & LABOR TIMES

APPLICATION & LABOR TIMES

Vehicle Application	Labor Times		Trans. Type (Code)
	[1] R & I	[2] Overhaul	
1995-96			
S6	8.4	9.3	01E (CBD)

[1] – Removal and installation of transmission from vehicle chassis.
[2] – Bench overhaul time for transaxle/differential. DOES NOT include removal and installation.

IDENTIFICATION

Transmission identification code is located on top of transmission case flange near transmission-to-engine mounting surface. First 3 letters of transmission code identify transmission for vehicle application. Remaining identification code numbers identify consecutive serial number.

Transmission identification model number is located on side of transmission case flange near transmission-to-engine mounting surface. First 3 characters of identification model number will be 01E, identifying transmission as a 5-speed manual gearbox used on vehicles with All Wheel Drive (AWD).

LUBRICATION

See appropriate MANUAL TRANSMISSION SERVICING article in TRANSMISSION SERVICING section.

TROUBLE SHOOTING

See GENERAL TROUBLE SHOOTING article in this section.

ON-VEHICLE SERVICE

Front differential can be removed and installed without removing transmission. See DIFFERENTIAL in COMPONENT DISASSEMBLY & REASSEMBLY.

AXLE SHAFTS

See appropriate AXLE SHAFTS article in AXLE SHAFTS & TRANSFER CASES section.

REMOVAL & INSTALLATION

NOTE: For transaxle removal, see appropriate MANUAL TRANSMISSION REMOVAL article in TRANSMISSION SERVICING section.

TRANSAXLE DISASSEMBLY

1) Mount transmission on stand and drain fluids. Remove clutch return lever, clutch release bearing and guide sleeve. Remove rear bearing housing, recording thickness of shims. Remove Torsen differential. *See Fig. 1.* Slide oil retainer back, then down and forward to remove. *See Fig. 2.* Remove locking bolts for shift rod, shift rod cover and shift rod.

2) Lock input shaft by moving 2 shift rails to engage 2 gears. *See Fig. 3.* Remove input shaft end screw through hole in differential cover. Remove support plate and magnets. Remove differential cover and bearing plate. Remove bearing from input shaft.

3) Pull 5th gear off input shaft. Remove synchronizer ring. Remove circlip. Pull 5th gear off pinion shaft. Remove and record thickness of shim. Remove spacer sleeve.

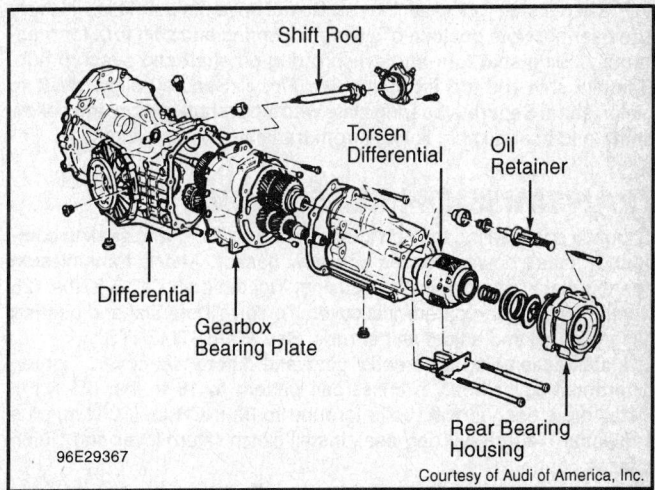

Fig. 1: *Exploded View Of Type 01E Subassemblies*

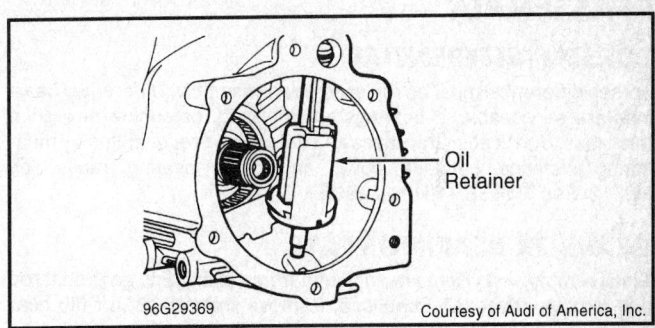

Fig. 2: *Removing Oil Retainer*

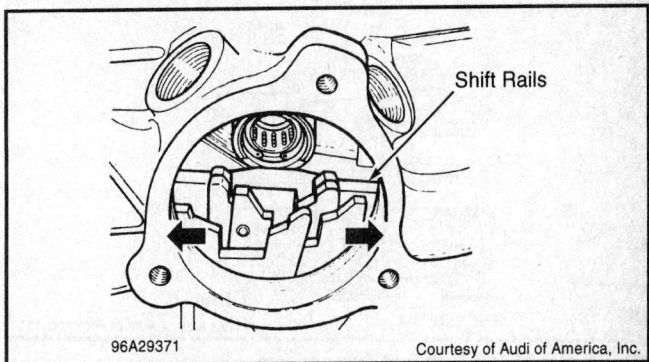

Fig. 3: *Locking Input Shaft*

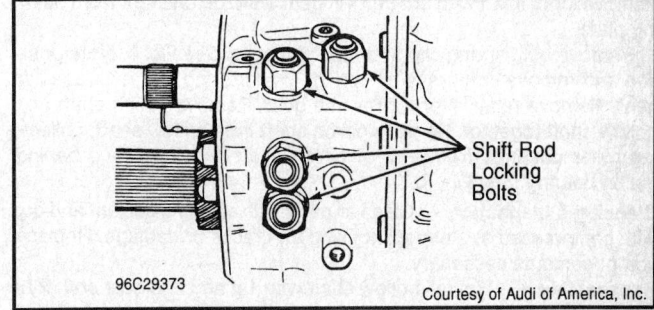

Fig. 4: *Identifying Shift Rod Locking Bolts*

4) Press out shift fork retaining pin. Do not drive pin out. This will damage bearing. Note position of synchronizer ring and shift fork for reassembly. Slide shift fork and synchro ring off shaft and synchro hub. Remove shift rod locking bolts. See Fig. 4. Secure hollow shaft to pinion shaft. Separate bearing plate with input shaft, pinion and hollow shaft, and internal shift linkage from transmission housing.

TRANSMISSION REASSEMBLY

1) Lightly coat sealing face on transmission housing with sealing compound. Install dowel sleeves and new gasket. Attach transmission bearing plate to transmission housing. Tighten bolts to 18 ft. lbs. (25 N.m). Install Torsen differential cover, Torsen differential and bearing flange. Install and adjust shifter rods. See ADJUSTMENTS.
2) Install assembled differential gear and differential cover. Tighten differential cover bolts in crisscross pattern to 18 ft. lbs. (25 N.m). Install drive flanges with bolts torqued to 89 INCH lb. (10 N.m) plus additional 1/4 turn (90 degrees). Install clutch return lever and clutch release bearing.

COMPONENT DISASSEMBLY & REASSEMBLY

TORSEN DIFFERENTIAL

Torsen differential must be replaced as an assembly. Differential bearings are serviceable. If bearings are replaced, determine new shim thickness. Check shim thickness and determine proper shims by measuring distance between cover and outer bearing race. See Fig. 12. See TORSEN SHIM TABLE.

GEARBOX BEARING PLATE

Disassembly – 1) Remove snap ring from 1st and 2nd gear shift rod and remove driver "A". See Fig. 5. Remove shift rod "B" for 5th gear and driver "C" for reverse gear.

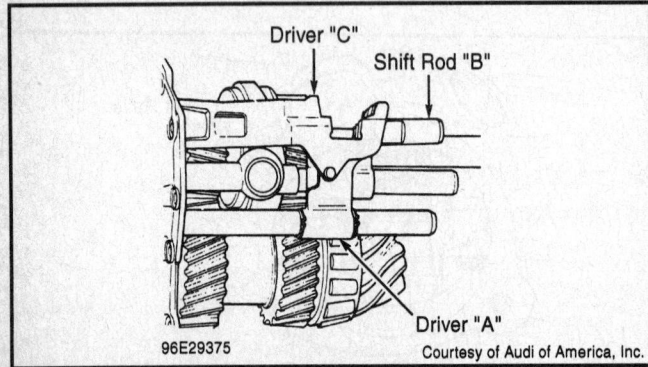

Fig. 5: Identifying Shift Rod Components

2) Remove snap ring for inner race of bearing and bearing inner race. Remove input shaft with 3rd and 4th gear shift rod and fork from bearing plate.
3) Remove bolt, spring clip and retaining plate. See Fig. 6. Note position and remove compression spring, synchro ring and reverse idler gear. Remove relay lever for reverse gear. Remove pinion shaft and hollow shaft together. Remove pinion shaft from hollow shaft, collecting roller bearings from end of pinion shaft and from race behind pinion bearing. See Fig. 7.

Cleaning & Inspection – Clean all parts with cleaning solvent and dry with compressed air. Inspect housing for cracks or damage. Replace components as necessary.
Reassembly – 1) Install hollow shaft with 1st and 2nd gear shift fork and shift rod into bearing plate. Grease pinion/hollow shaft tapered roller bearing, oil needle bearing and install in bearing plate.
2) Install reverse gear relay lever onto screw for relay lever. See Fig. 8. Install reverse gear and mesh relay lever into groove in gear. Install synchro ring with flat on circumference facing input shaft (not yet installed).

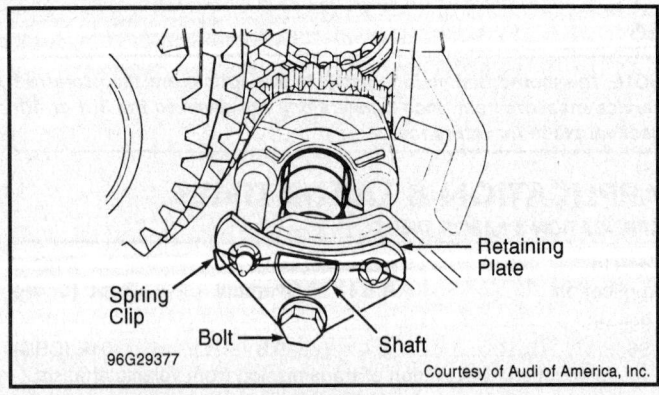

Fig. 6: Identifying Reverse Components

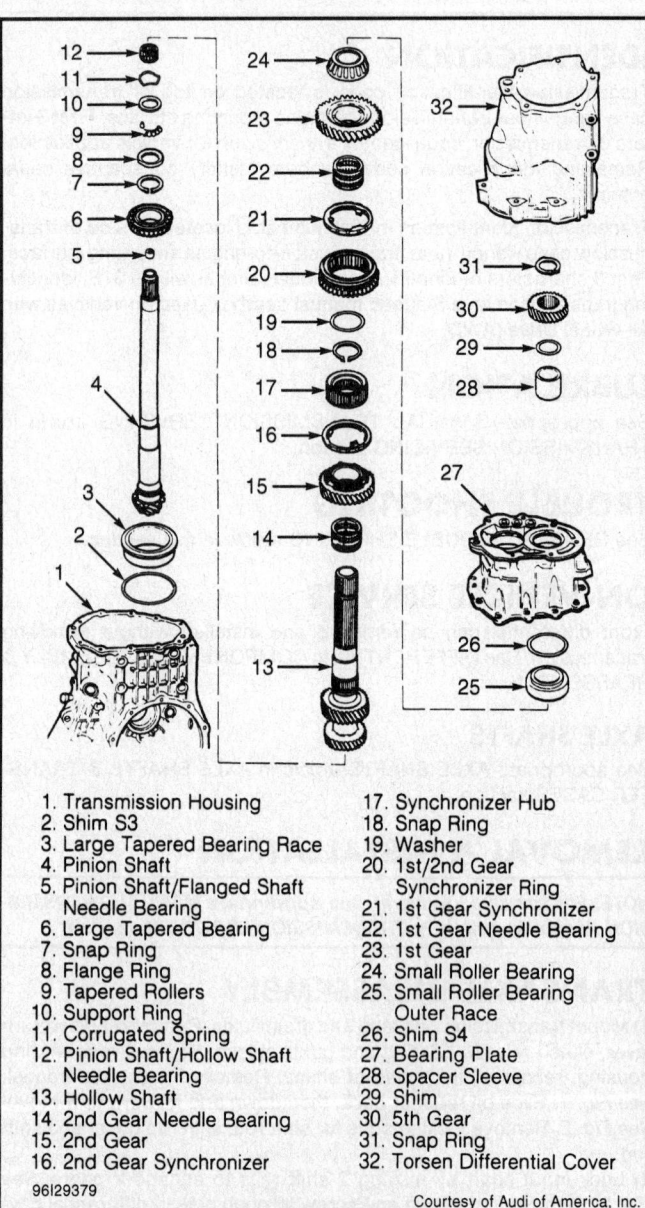

1. Transmission Housing
2. Shim S3
3. Large Tapered Bearing Race
4. Pinion Shaft
5. Pinion Shaft/Flanged Shaft Needle Bearing
6. Large Tapered Bearing
7. Snap Ring
8. Flange Ring
9. Tapered Rollers
10. Support Ring
11. Corrugated Spring
12. Pinion Shaft/Hollow Shaft Needle Bearing
13. Hollow Shaft
14. 2nd Gear Needle Bearing
15. 2nd Gear
16. 2nd Gear Synchronizer
17. Synchronizer Hub
18. Snap Ring
19. Washer
20. 1st/2nd Gear Synchronizer Ring
21. 1st Gear Synchronizer
22. 1st Gear Needle Bearing
23. 1st Gear
24. Small Roller Bearing
25. Small Roller Bearing Outer Race
26. Shim S4
27. Bearing Plate
28. Spacer Sleeve
29. Shim
30. 5th Gear
31. Snap Ring
32. Torsen Differential Cover

96I29379

Courtesy of Audi of America, Inc.

Fig. 7: Exploded View Of Pinion Shaft

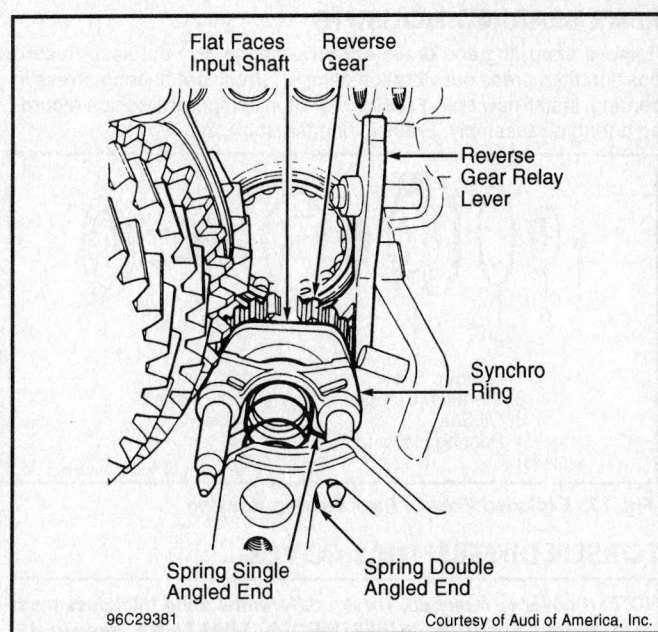

Fig. 8: Installing Reverse Components

3) Insert compression spring with single angled end in recess on synchro ring. Turn doubled end counterclockwise and insert into opening on bearing plate. See Fig. 8.

4) Insert shaft and retaining plate with chamfered hole side facing bearing plate. See Fig. 6. Install spring clip and tighten bolt.

5) Install input shaft with 3rd and 4th gear shift rod and fork into bearing plate. Install inner race of roller bearing onto main shaft at flange for differential cover. Install snap ring.

6) Mesh recess in reverse gear driver with free end of relay lever. See Fig. 9. Install 5th gear shift rod through reverse gear driver. Install 1st and 2nd gear driver onto shift rod and install snap rings. Oil all bearings and shift rods. Replace input shaft seal in transmission housing. Coat mating surfaces with sealant and ensure internal shift rod bushings are in place. Install complete bearing plate into transmission housing, while ensuring shift rods align in housing.

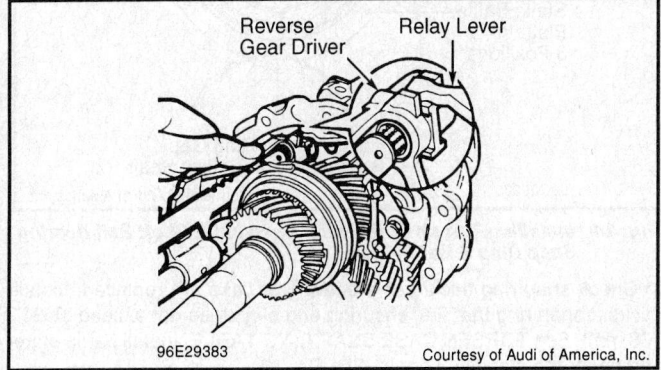

Fig. 9: Meshing Reverse Gear Driver

7) Support input shaft with Tool (30-211A). See Fig. 10. Align 5th gear synchro hub on input shaft with projecting face towards shaft end and oil groove on inner diameter of hub aligned with oil hole in shaft. Heat hub to 248ºF (120ºC) and drive onto shaft.

8) Install spacer disc with large face toward bearing on shift rod. Install 5th gear synchro ring and shift fork on synchro hub and driver on shift rod together, ensuring synchro ring and shift fork are positioned correctly and holes for retaining pin in driver and rod align. Press in retaining pin. If using split pin, install with split toward fork.

9) Install spacer sleeve (72.5 mm) and snap ring on hollow shaft. Measure between sleeve and installed snap ring to determine shim thickness. See Fig. 11. See 5TH GEAR SHIM TABLE.

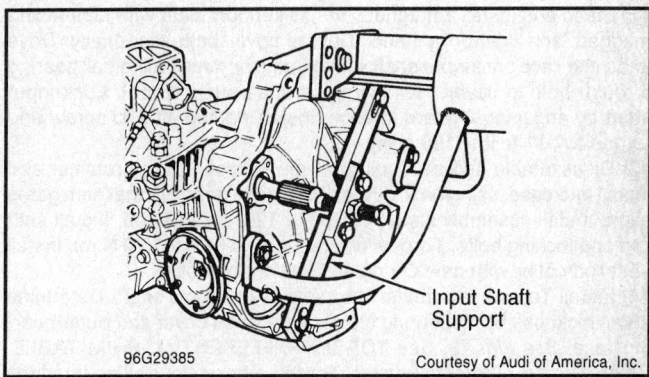

Fig. 10: Installing Input Shaft Support Tool

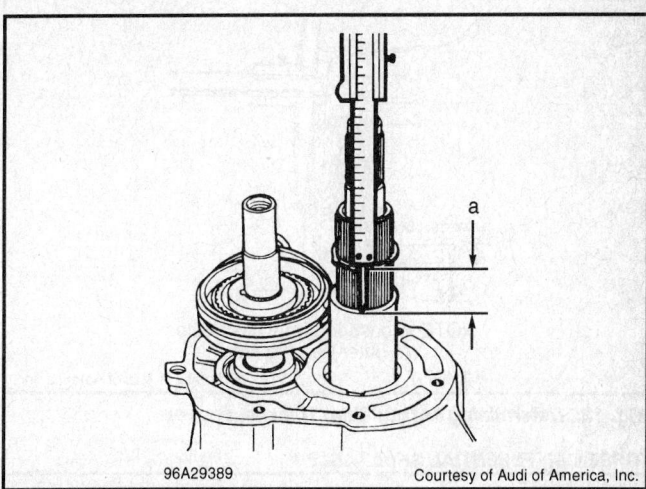

Fig. 11: Measuring For 5th Gear Shim

5TH GEAR SHIM TABLE

Measurement In. (mm)	Shim Thickness In. (mm)	Part No.
.1221-.1224 (31.01-31.11)	.0413 (1.05)	016 311 391 P
.1224-.1228 (31.11-31.21)	.0452 (1.15)	016 311 391 Q
.1228-.1232 (31.21-31.31)	.0492 (1.25)	016 311 391 R
.1232-.1236 (31.31-31.41)	.0531 (1.35)	016 311 391 S

10) Remove snap ring and install shim on hollow shaft. Heat 5th gear to 248ºF (120ºC) and drive on hollow shaft. Select thickest snap ring that will fit. See 5TH GEAR SNAP RING TABLE.

5TH GEAR SNAP RING TABLE

Thickness In. (mm)	Part No.
.091 (2.32)	N 905 138 01
.092 (2.34)	N 905 138 02
.093 (2.36)	N 905 138 03
.094 (2.38)	N 905 138 04
.094 (2.40)	N 905 138 05
.095 (2.42)	N 905 138 06
.096 (2.44)	N 905 138 07
.097 (2.46)	N 905 138 08
.098 (2.48)	N 905 138 09
.098 (2.50)	N 905 138 10

11) Drive inner race of 5th gear on input shaft, oil needle bearing and install. Install 5th gear synchro ring and 5th gear with spring. Heat inner race of input shaft ball bearing to 212ºF (100ºC) and drive on input shaft. Ensure 5th gear axial play is .0059-.0138 in. (.15-.35 mm). Install internal shift rod bushings and new gasket on bearing plate. Install differential cover and bolts on bearing plate. Do not tighten bolts.

12) Clean and install 2 magnets. Install support plate with lugs facing magnets and tighten by hand. Tighten cover bolts diagonally. Drive 2nd inner race onto input shaft with bearing surface facing ball bearing through hole in cover. Remove input shaft support tool. Lock input shaft by engaging 2 gears at once. Install input shaft end screw and torque to 111 ft. lbs (150 N.m).

13) Disassemble and clean oil retainer. Reassemble oil retainer and install into case, using new O-ring. Disengage gears so that shift gates align. Install assembly sleeve (01E 311 120) on shift rod. Install shift rod and locking bolts. Torque locking bolts to 52 ft lb. (70 N.m). Install shift rod cover with new O-ring and sealant on bolts.

14) Install Torsen differential onto splines of hollow shaft. Determine shim thickness by measuring distance between cover and outer bearing race. *See Fig. 12.* See TORSEN DIFFERENTIAL SHIM TABLE. When Torsen differential cover, Torsen differential and/or bearings have been replaced, shim thickness must be determined.

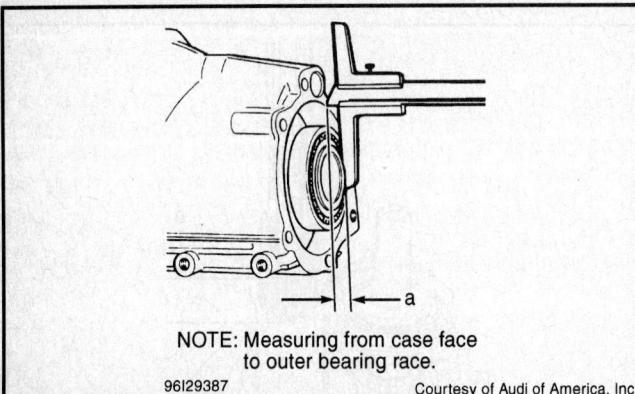

NOTE: Measuring from case face to outer bearing race.

96I29387   Courtesy of Audi of America, Inc.

Fig. 12: Determining Torsen Shim Thickness

TORSEN DIFFERENTIAL SHIM TABLE [1]

Measured Range In. (mm)	Shim Thickness In. (mm) [2]	Part No.
.2775-.2874 (7.05-7.30)	.0649 (1.65)	01A 311 393AF
	.0570 (1.45)	01A 311 393AB
	.0649 (1.65)	01A 311 393Q
.2874-.2972 (7.30-7.55)	.0649 (1.65)	01A 311 393AF
	.0570 (1.45)	01A 311 393AB
	.0374 (0.95)	01A 311 393K
.2972-.3070 (7.55-7.80)	.0649 (1.65)	01A 311 393AF
	.0570 (1.45)	01A 311 393AB
	.0275 (0.70)	01A 311 393E
.3070-.3169 (7.80-8.05)	.0649 (1.65)	01A 311 393AF
	.0570 (1.45)	01A 311 393AB
	.0177 (0.45)	01A 311 393
.3169-.3248 (8.05-8.25)	[3] .0649 (1.65)	01A 311 393AF
.3248-.3346 (8.25-8.50)	.0649 (1.65)	01A 311 393AF
	.0570 (1.45)	01A 311 393AB
.3346-.3444 (8.50-8.75)	.0649 (1.65)	01A 311 393AF
	.0472 (1.20)	01A 311 393Q
.3444-.3543 (8.75-9.00)	.0649 (1.65)	01A 311 393AF
	.0374 (0.95)	01A 311 393K
.3543-.3641 (9.00-9.25)	.0649 (1.65)	01A 311 393AF
	.0275 (0.70)	01A 311 393E
.3641-.3740 (9.25-9.50)	.0649 (1.65)	01A 311 393AF
	.0177 (0.45)	01A 311 393

[1] – All measurements in mm.
[2] – Use all shims listed for Measured Range
[3] – 2 shims required

15) Put shims and spring on shaft. Put dished washer in rear bearing housing, concave side facing shims, oil needle bearing and install bearing housing on differential housing.

16) Install clutch release parts and shifter. Adjust shifter. See ADJUSTMENTS. Ensure transmission can be shifted through all gears. Fill with gear oil.

REAR BEARING HOUSING

Remove snap ring and press out drive flange. Pry out seal. Record position then press out vibration damper. Press out bearing. Press in bearing. Install new seal. Press in vibration damper to position recorded during disassembly. Press in flanged shaft. *See Fig. 13.*

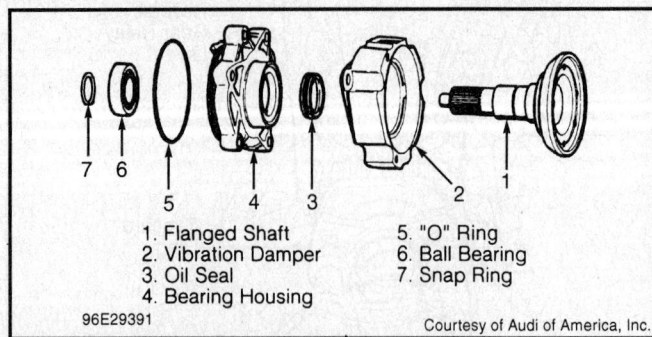

1. Flanged Shaft
2. Vibration Damper
3. Oil Seal
4. Bearing Housing
5. "O" Ring
6. Ball Bearing
7. Snap Ring

96E29391   Courtesy of Audi of America, Inc.

Fig. 13: Exploded View Of Rear Bearing Housing

TORSEN DIFFERENTIAL COVER

NOTE: If cover is replaced, Torsen differential shim thickness must be measured. See TORSEN DIFFERENTIAL SHIM TABLE. See Fig. 12.

Disassembly & Reassembly – **1)** Press input shaft roller bearing out of case. Remove snap ring and pry input shaft ball bearing from case. Pull Torsen needle bearing from case.

2) Press Torsen needle bearing into case. Press input shaft roller bearing into case. Install input shaft ball bearing and snap ring with snap ring ends positioned as shown. *See Fig. 14.*

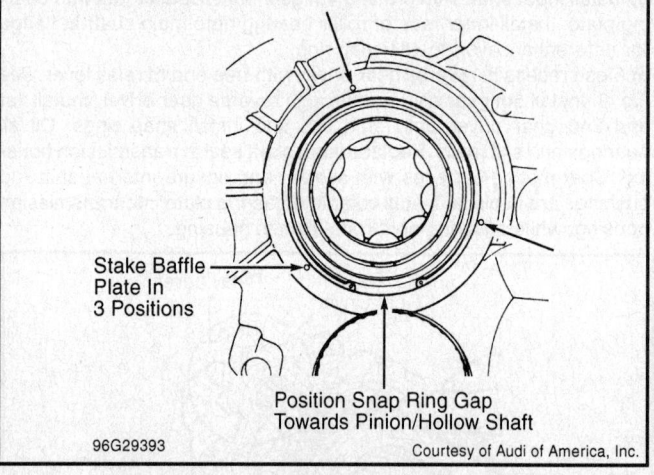

Stake Baffle Plate In 3 Positions

Position Snap Ring Gap Towards Pinion/Hollow Shaft

96G29393   Courtesy of Audi of America, Inc.

Fig. 14: Installing Torsen Differential Case Input Shaft Ball Bearing Snap Ring & Baffle Plate

3) Check snap ring thickness if bearing or case are replaced. Install thickest snap ring that fits, ensuring end play does not exceed .0031 (.08 mm). See TORSEN CASE SNAP RING TABLE. Install baffle plate and peen into place in 3 spots. *See Fig. 14.*

TORSEN CASE SNAP RING TABLE

Thickness In. (mm)	Part No.
.100 (2.55)	N 905 140.01
.102 (2.60)	N 905 140.02
.104 (2.65)	N 905 140.03
.106 (2.70)	N 905 140.04

TRANSMISSION BEARING PLATE

NOTE: If replacing bearing plate, shafts, bearings or pinion shaft, determine shim and snap ring thickness.

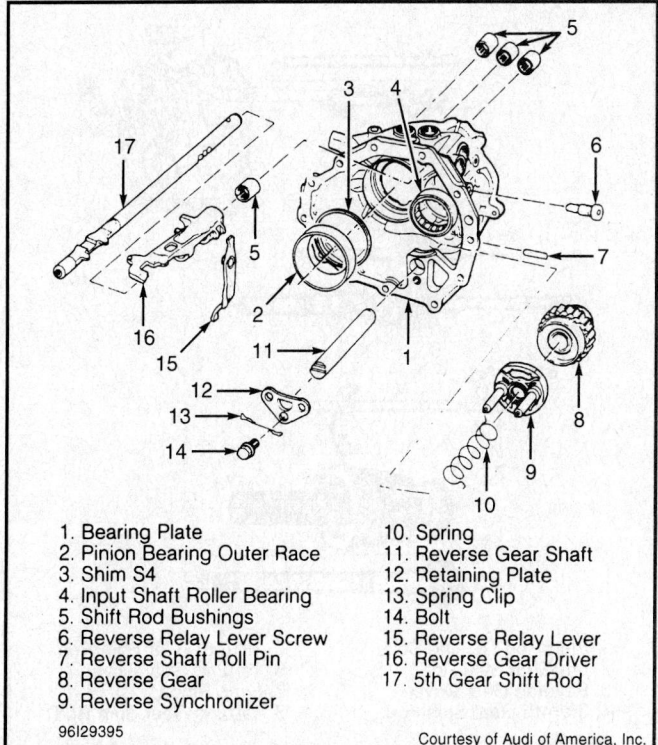

1. Bearing Plate
2. Pinion Bearing Outer Race
3. Shim S4
4. Input Shaft Roller Bearing
5. Shift Rod Bushings
6. Reverse Relay Lever Screw
7. Reverse Shaft Roll Pin
8. Reverse Gear
9. Reverse Synchronizer
10. Spring
11. Reverse Gear Shaft
12. Retaining Plate
13. Spring Clip
14. Bolt
15. Reverse Relay Lever
16. Reverse Gear Driver
17. 5th Gear Shift Rod

96I29395   Courtesy of Audi of America, Inc.

Fig. 15: Exploded View Of Transmission Bearing Plate

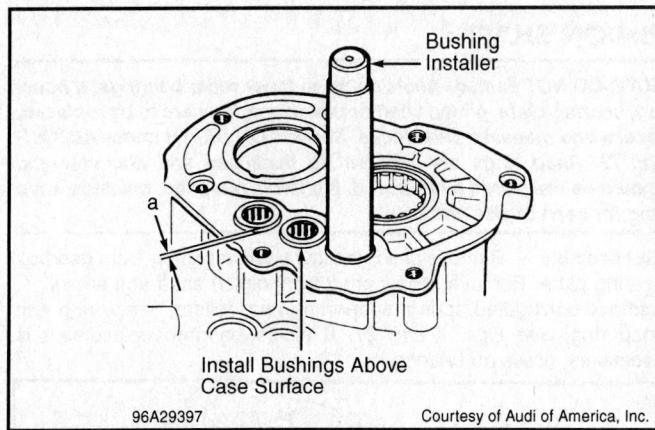

Bushing Installer

a

Install Bushings Above Case Surface

96A29397   Courtesy of Audi of America, Inc.

Fig. 16: Installing Shift Rod Bushings

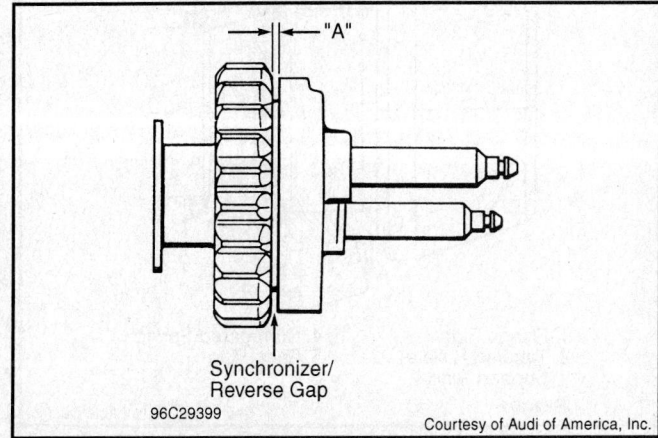

"A"

Synchronizer/ Reverse Gap

96C29399   Courtesy of Audi of America, Inc.

Fig. 17: Checking Synchronizer/Reverse Gap

Press input shaft roller bearing outer race and shift rod bushings out of bearing case. See Fig. 15. Always replace shift rod bushings. Install bushings in bearing case to .098" (2.5 mm) above case surface. See Fig. 16. Install bushings in reverse gear driver flush. Press synchro on gear and measure gap "A". See Fig. 17. New part tolerance is .0295-.0906" (.75-2.3 mm). If gap is less than .008" (0.2 mm), replace worn parts. Press in input shaft roller bearing outer race.

INPUT SHAFT

Disassembly – Remove snap ring, thrust washer, 4th gear and needle bearing. See Fig. 18. Remove snap ring and press off synchronizer hub. Remove 3rd gear and needle bearing.

Cleaning & Inspection – Clean all parts in cleaning solvent and dry with compressed air. Inspect for chipped gear teeth, galling, scoring and excessive wear. Check for synchronizer wear. Push synchro ring into sleeve and measure gap at 3 points. See Fig. 19. Replace synchronizer if measurement is less than .020" (.5 mm). Replace worn or broken parts. All snap rings must be replaced during reassembly.

Reassembly – Lube all bearings. Install needle bearing and 3rd gear. Heat synchronizer hub to 212°F (100° C). Press synchronizer hub on input shaft with oil groove in hub aligned with oil hole in shaft. Install thickest snap ring that will fit. See SYNCHRONIZER SNAP RING TABLE. Install snap ring with opening aligned with slot in synchronizer hub. Install needle bearing, 4th gear, thrust washer and snap ring.

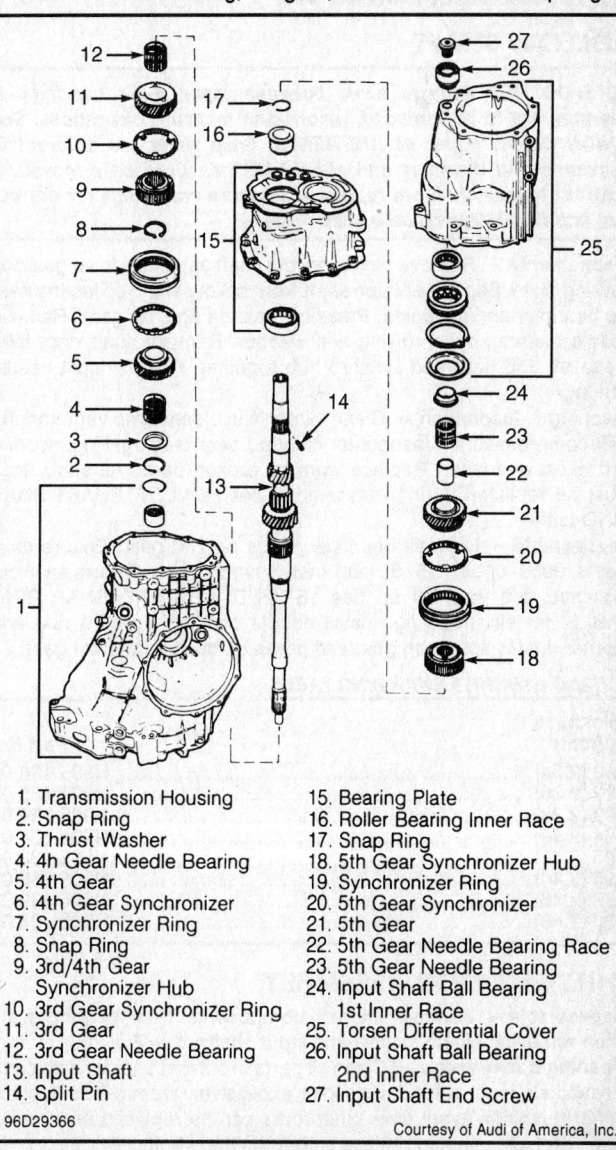

1. Transmission Housing
2. Snap Ring
3. Thrust Washer
4. 4h Gear Needle Bearing
5. 4th Gear
6. 4th Gear Synchronizer
7. Synchronizer Ring
8. Snap Ring
9. 3rd/4th Gear Synchronizer Hub
10. 3rd Gear Synchronizer Ring
11. 3rd Gear
12. 3rd Gear Needle Bearing
13. Input Shaft
14. Split Pin
15. Bearing Plate
16. Roller Bearing Inner Race
17. Snap Ring
18. 5th Gear Synchronizer Hub
19. Synchronizer Ring
20. 5th Gear Synchronizer
21. 5th Gear
22. 5th Gear Needle Bearing Race
23. 5th Gear Needle Bearing
24. Input Shaft Ball Bearing 1st Inner Race
25. Torsen Differential Cover
26. Input Shaft Ball Bearing 2nd Inner Race
27. Input Shaft End Screw

96D29366   Courtesy of Audi of America, Inc.

Fig. 18: Exploded View Of Input Shaft Components

SYNCHRONIZER SNAP RING TABLE

Thickness In. (mm)	Part No.
.074 (1.90)	N 902 944 01
.075 (1.93)	N 902 944 02
.077 (1.96)	N 902 944 03
.078 (1.99)	N 902 944 04
.079 (2.02)	N 902 944 05
.080 (2.05)	N 902 944 06

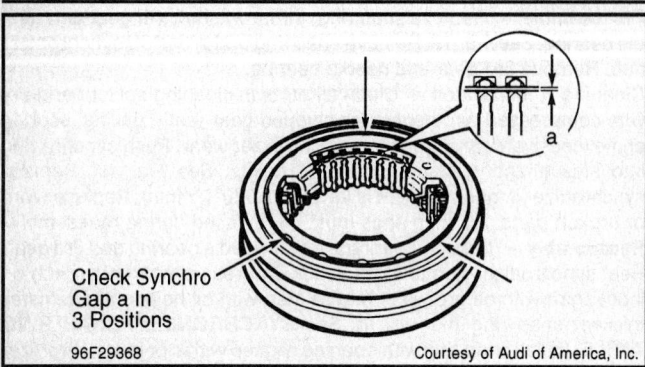

Check Synchro
Gap a In
3 Positions

96F29368   Courtesy of Audi of America, Inc.

Fig. 19: Checking Synchronizer Wear

HOLLOW SHAFT

NOTE: DO NOT damage seals between taper roller bearings. If bearings are to be replaced, record and measure clearances. See PINION DEPTH under ADJUSTMENTS. Snap rings are different in thickness and diameter and should be measured as removed. If gears or hollow shaft are replaced, measure snap rings for correct size and fit. Always replace snap rings.

Disassembly – Remove pinion/hollow shaft assembly from gearbox bearing plate. Separate pinion shaft from hollow shaft, collecting needle bearings and set aside. Press off bearing and 1st gear. Remove needle bearing, synchro ring and washer. Remove snap ring, then press off 2nd gear and synchro hub together. Remove split needle bearing.

Cleaning & Inspection – Clean all parts in cleaning solvent and dry with compressed air. Inspect for chipped gear teeth, galling, scoring and excessive wear. Replace worn or broken parts. All snap rings must be replaced during reassembly. See HOLLOW SHAFT SNAP RING table.

Reassembly – Lube all bearings. Press on 2nd gear. Ensure axial play is .0059-.0138" (.15-.35 mm). Install synchro hub. Determine thickest snap ring that will fit. See 1ST/2ND SYNCHRO SNAP RING TABLE. Install snap ring. Install needle bearing, synchro ring and washer. Install spring on gear and press on bearing and 1st gear.

1ST/2ND SYNCHRO SNAP RING TABLE

Thickness In. (mm)	Part No.
.092 (2.34)	N905 138 02
.092 (2.36)	N905 138 03
.093 (2.38)	N905 138 04
.094 (2.40)	N905 138 05
.095 (2.42)	N905 138 06
.096 (2.44)	N905 138 07
.097 (2.46)	N905 138 08
.098 (2.48)	N905 138 09

SHIFT SELECTOR ASSEMBLY

Disassembly – Remove internal components from bearing plate when removing pinion, hollow and input shafts. See Fig. 20.

Cleaning & Inspection – Clean all parts in solvent and dry with compressed air. Inspect for damaged or excessively worn parts. Replace shifter bushings every time. Shift forks can be replaced separately. When replacing shafts, replace shift forks and shafts.

Reassembly – To install, reverse removal procedure. Ensure shafts move freely without binding.

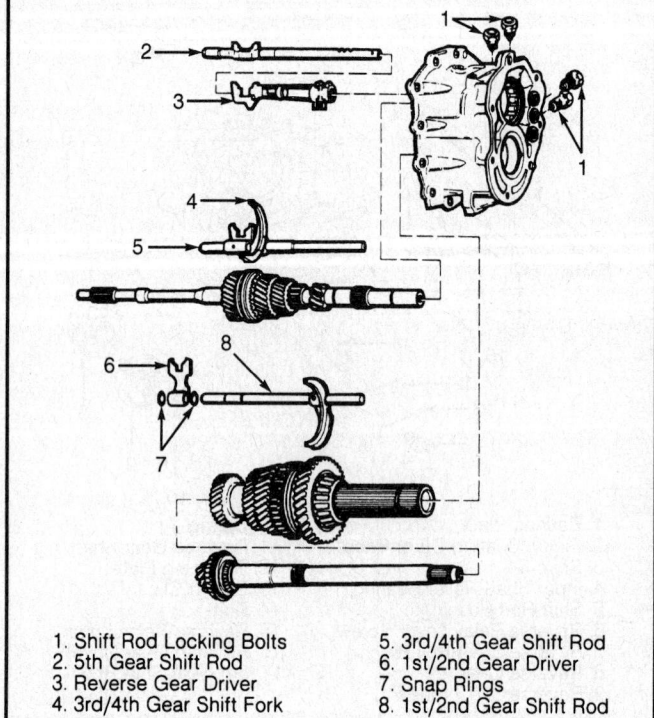

1. Shift Rod Locking Bolts
2. 5th Gear Shift Rod
3. Reverse Gear Driver
4. 3rd/4th Gear Shift Fork
5. 3rd/4th Gear Shift Rod
6. 1st/2nd Gear Driver
7. Snap Rings
8. 1st/2nd Gear Shift Rod

96J29370   Courtesy of Audi of America, Inc.

Fig. 20: Internal Shift Components

PINION SHAFT

NOTE: DO NOT damage seals between taper roller bearings. If housing, bearing plate, pinion shaft or pinion bearings are to be replaced, record and measure clearances. See PINION DEPTH under ADJUSTMENTS. Snap rings are different in thickness and diameter and should be measured as removed. If shaft is replaced, measure snap ring for correct size and fit.

Disassembly – Remove pinion/hollow shaft assembly from gearbox bearing plate. Remove hollow shaft from pinion shaft and set aside. Remove corrugated spring, supporting ring, rollers, flange ring and snap ring. See Figs. 7 and 21. If pinion bearing replacement is necessary, press off bearing.

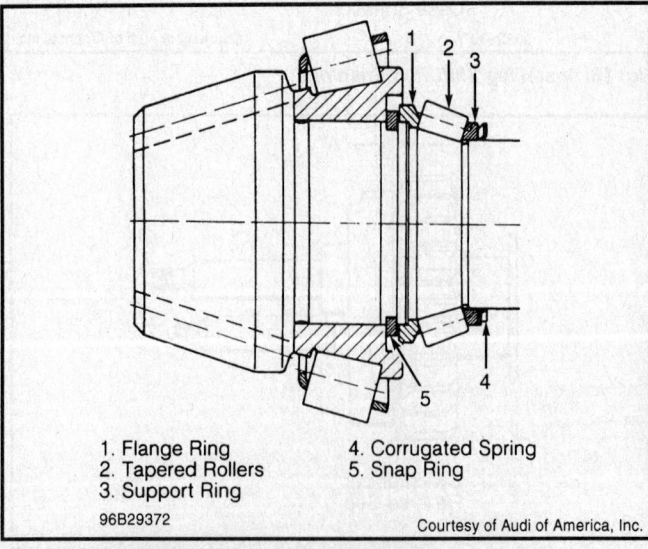

1. Flange Ring
2. Tapered Rollers
3. Support Ring
4. Corrugated Spring
5. Snap Ring

96B29372   Courtesy of Audi of America, Inc.

Fig. 21: Identifying Pinion Shaft Components

Cleaning & Inspection – Clean all parts in solvent and dry with compressed air. Inspect for chipped gear teeth, galling, scoring and excessive wear. Replace parts as necessary. Snap ring must be replaced during reassembly.

Reassembly – Heat bearing inner race to 212ºF (100ºC). Press bearing on pinion shaft. Determine thickest snap ring that will fit. Install snap ring. Install flange ring, rollers, supporting ring and corrugated spring on shaft. *See Fig. 21.*

DIFFERENTIAL

Removal & Installation – Using punch to prevent rotation, remove drive flange bolts. Remove drive flanges from front differential. Remove front differential cover Remove differential from gearbox housing. To reassemble, reverse removal procedure.

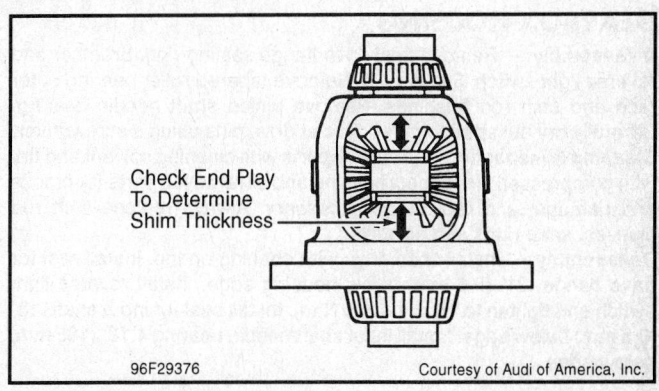

96F29376   Courtesy of Audi of America, Inc.

Fig. 23: Checking Bevel Gear Play

Reassembly – **1)** Install large bevel gears with thinnest shims available, then install small bevel gears and shaft. Check play of large gears by hand. *See Fig. 23.* Adjust play using various shims to maximum of .0039 " (.10 mm) with gears turning freely. See BEVEL GEAR SHIM TABLE.

BEVEL GEAR SHIM TABLE

Part Number	Thickness In. (mm)
011 519 215	.0059 (.15)
088 409 249	.0236 (.6)
088 409 249A	.0275 (.7)
088 409 249B	.0314 (.8)
088 409 249C	.0354 (.9)
088 409 249D	.0393 (1.0)

2) Install thrust washers coated with transmission oil. Install large differential bevel gears with selected shims. Install small bevel gears about 180 degrees apart and pivot into place by turning one large bevel gear. Install threaded inserts in ends of large bevel gears. Install shaft and roll pin.

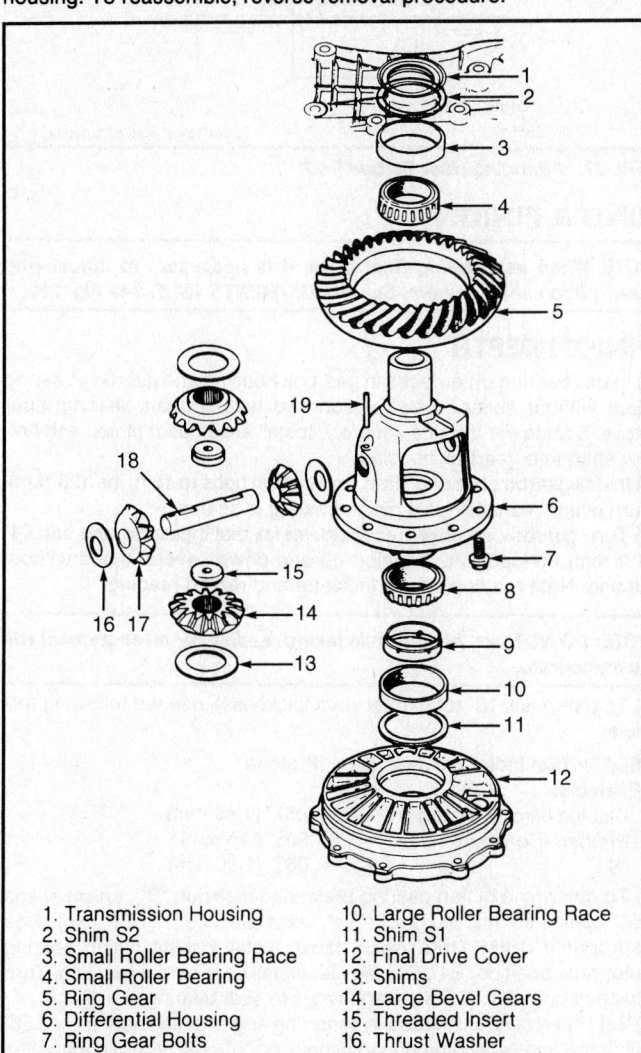

1. Transmission Housing
2. Shim S2
3. Small Roller Bearing Race
4. Small Roller Bearing
5. Ring Gear
6. Differential Housing
7. Ring Gear Bolts
8. Large Roller Bearing
9. Speedometer Gear
10. Large Roller Bearing Race
11. Shim S1
12. Final Drive Cover
13. Shims
14. Large Bevel Gears
15. Threaded Insert
16. Thrust Washer
17. Small Bevel Gears
18. Bevel Gear Shaft
19. Roll Pin

96D29374   Courtesy of Audi of America, Inc.

Fig. 22: Exploded View Of Differential Assembly

Disassembly & Reassembly – **1)** Remove differential bearing inner and outer races using puller. *See Fig. 22.* Remove all bolts, and use punch to remove ring gear from differential.

2) Remove roll pin and small bevel gear shaft. Rotate large bevel gear to bring small bevel gears to an opening in case and remove. Remove large bevel gears, thrust washers and threaded inserts.

Cleaning & Inspection – Clean all parts with cleaning solvent and dry with compressed air. Inspect all parts for chipped gears, scoring and damage. Replace as necessary. Lubricate parts with transmission fluid prior to reassembly.

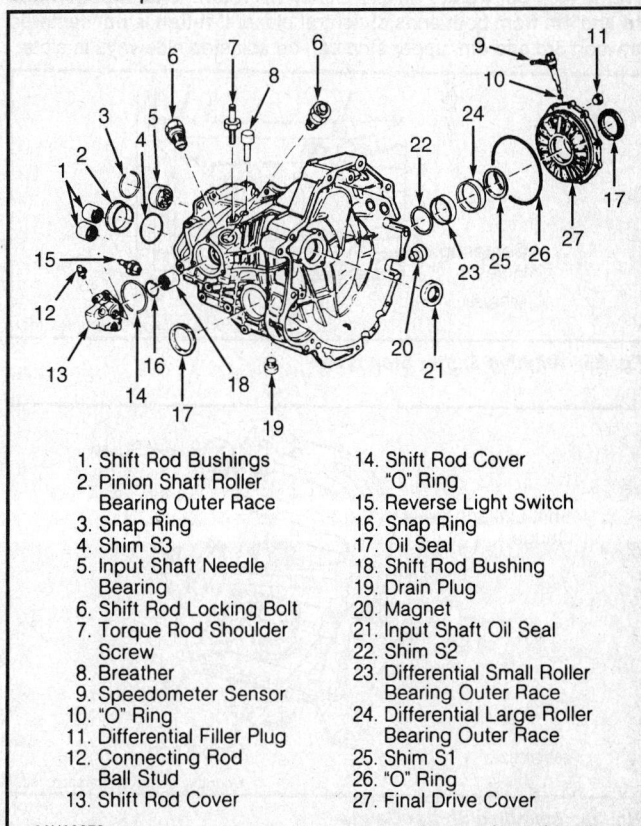

1. Shift Rod Bushings
2. Pinion Shaft Roller Bearing Outer Race
3. Snap Ring
4. Shim S3
5. Input Shaft Needle Bearing
6. Shift Rod Locking Bolt
7. Torque Rod Shoulder Screw
8. Breather
9. Speedometer Sensor
10. "O" Ring
11. Differential Filler Plug
12. Connecting Rod Ball Stud
13. Shift Rod Cover
14. Shift Rod Cover "O" Ring
15. Reverse Light Switch
16. Snap Ring
17. Oil Seal
18. Shift Rod Bushing
19. Drain Plug
20. Magnet
21. Input Shaft Oil Seal
22. Shim S2
23. Differential Small Roller Bearing Outer Race
24. Differential Large Roller Bearing Outer Race
25. Shim S1
26. "O" Ring
27. Final Drive Cover

96H29378   Courtesy of Audi of America, Inc.

Fig. 24: Exploded View Of Gearbox Housing

GEARBOX HOUSING

Disassembly – Remove final drive flange sealing ring, breather and reverse light switch. *See Fig. 24.* Remove tapered roller bearing outer race and shift rod bushings. Remove pinion shaft needle bearing. Carefully pry out speedometer drive at drive pins using a screwdriver.

Cleaning & Inspection – Clean all parts with cleaning solvent and dry with compressed air. Inspect housing and all removed parts for cracks and damage, and replace as necessary. Always replace shift rod sleeves, snap rings and all seals.

Reassembly – Install snap rings with opening on top. Install seal for drive flange .21" (5.5 mm) below housing edge. Install reverse light switch and tighten to 15 ft. lbs. (20 N.m). Install seal for input shaft .13" (3.5 mm) below edge. Install input shaft needle bearing 4.13" (105 mm) below edge.

ADJUSTMENTS

SHIFTER

1) Adjust connecting rod length to 6.63" (168.5 mm) center-to-center with rod ends aligned. Remove shifter knob and boot. Align centering holes on upper and lower sections of stop and tighten bolts to 89 INCH lbs. (10 N.m). *See Fig. 25.* Place shifter in neutral between 3rd and 4th. loosen clamp connection of shift and torque rods to allow free movement. Adjust shift lever, then rear torque rod.

2) To adjust shifter, install Shift Linkage Gauge (3286) on shift lever. *See Fig. 26.* Place left then right side of gauge into holes of stop until seated. Carefully tighten knurled screw until stop knob is touching shift linkage gauge.

3) To adjust rear torque rod, check and adjust measurement "d1" and "d2" to within .04" (1.0 mm), aligning shift lever bearing and shifter upper stop. *See Fig. 27.* Tighten clamp connection of shift and torque rods. Loosen knurled screw and remove shift linkage gauge.

4) Check adjustment by placing shifter in 2nd and holding shifter to the left. Allow shifter to spring back toward center. Travel should be .12-.35" (3-9 mm) at knob. Ensure shifter engages all gears. Ensure reverse lock out works. Ensure shifter will return to neutral between 3rd and 4th from both ends of neutral plane. If return is not centered between 3rd and 4th, upper stop can be adjusted sideways in slots.

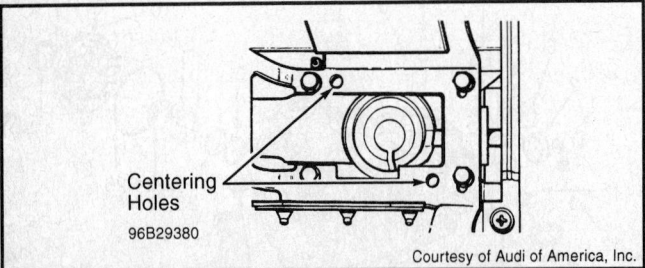

Centering Holes

96B29380

Courtesy of Audi of America, Inc.

Fig. 25: Aligning Shifter Stop Holes

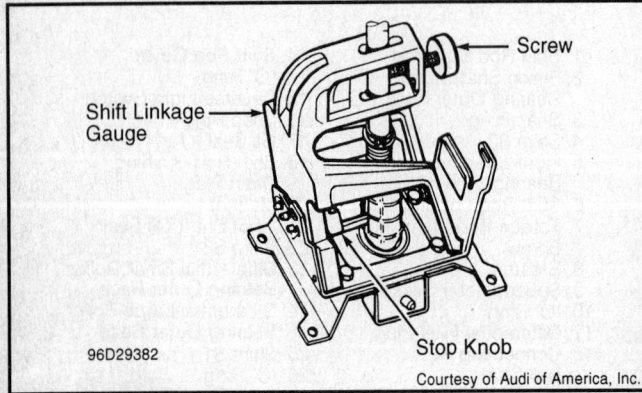

Screw

Shift Linkage Gauge

Stop Knob

96D29382

Courtesy of Audi of America, Inc.

Fig. 26: Installing Shifter Gauge

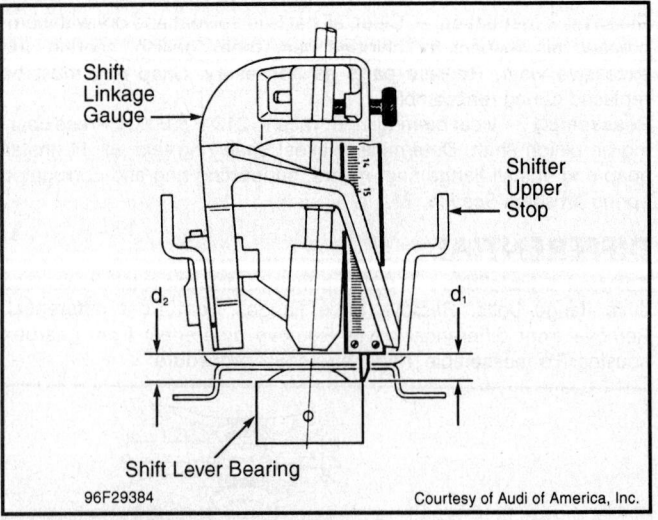

Shift Linkage Gauge

Shifter Upper Stop

d_2 d_1

Shift Lever Bearing

96F29384

Courtesy of Audi of America, Inc.

Fig. 27: Adjusting Rear Torque Rod

RING & PINION

NOTE: When assembling final drive, it is necessary to adjust ring gear, pinion shaft or both. See ADJUSTMENT TABLE. See Fig. 28.

PINION DEPTH

1) Install bearing outer races in gearbox housing and gearbox bearing plate without shims. Install pinion and hollow shaft bearing inner races. Seat lower bearing securely. Install assembled pinion and hollow shaft into gearbox housing.

2) Install gearbox bearing plate, and tighten bolts to 18 ft. lbs. (25 N.m). Turn pinion manually until pinion bearing is seated.

3) Turn gearbox so cover faces up. Install dial indicator, and set .04" (1.0 mm) preload. Move pinion up and down several times without turning. Note reading on dial indicator and record reading.

NOTE: DO NOT turn pinion while taking reading, or measurement will be inaccurate.

4) To determine "S" total (total shim thickness), use the following formula:

"S_{tot}" = Dial Indicator Reading + Preload
  Example:
  Dial Indicator Reading   .057" (1.45 mm)
  Preload (Constant Value)   + .006" (.15 mm)
  "S_{tot}"   = .063" (1.60 mm)

5) To determine pinion bearing preload (dimension "B"), select shims with combined thickness of "S_{tot}", example: .063" (1.60 mm). See appropriate SHIM THICKNESS table. Install behind pinion bearing outer race position "S4". *See Fig. 32.* Install gear carrier housing. Turn pinion in both directions several times to seat bearings.

6) Set Universal Bar (VW385/1) centering ring to dimension "a" = 2.56" (65.0mm) and set sliding ring to dimension "b" = 2.17" (55.0 mm). *See Fig. 29.*

7) Assemble measuring bar in following procedure:
  • Indicator Extension (VW385/15) = .366" (9.30 mm)
  • Master Gauge (VW 385/30) to RO = 2.348" (59.65 mm)
Master Gauge (VW 385/30) may be replaced with Gauge (VW 385/27).

8) Place master gauge on measuring bar and set dial indicator with .12" (3.0 mm) range to zero with .04" (1.0 mm) preload. Place End Plate (VW385/17) on pinion end face. Remove master gauge and install measuring bar in housing. Ensure Centering Disc (VW385/3) faces final drive cover. *See Fig. 30.*

9) Install cover for final drive housing, and tighten bolts. Pull 2nd centering ring outward until measuring bar can just be turned by hand. Turn measuring bar slightly until dial indicator contacts end face of pinion and indicates maximum deflection (return point). Measured reading equals dimension "E". *See Fig. 30.*

ADJUSTMENT TABLE

Replaced Part	To Be Adjusted	Ring Gear "S₁" + "S₂"	Pinion "S₃" Using Deviation r	Pinion "S₃" Using Actual Measurement	Pinion (shim "S₄" only)
Gearbox Housing ¹		X		X	
Gearbox Cover					X
Differential Housing		X			
Pinion Bearings				X	
Differential Bearings		X			
Ring Gear & Pinion		X	X		
Cover On Gearbox Housing		X			

¹ – When gearbox housing is replaced, adjust mainshaft.

96I19362

Courtesy of Audi of America, Inc.

Fig. 28: Ring & Pinion Adjusting Table

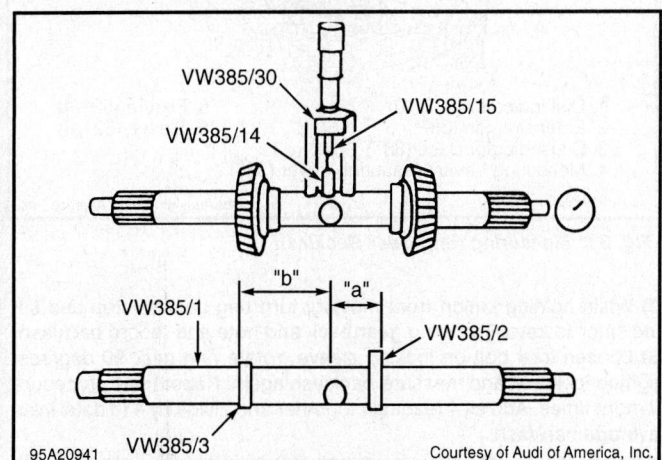

Fig. 29: Identifying Universal Measuring Bar

VW385/30
VW385/15
VW385/14
"b"   "a"
VW385/1
VW385/2
VW385/3
95A20941   Courtesy of Audi of America, Inc.

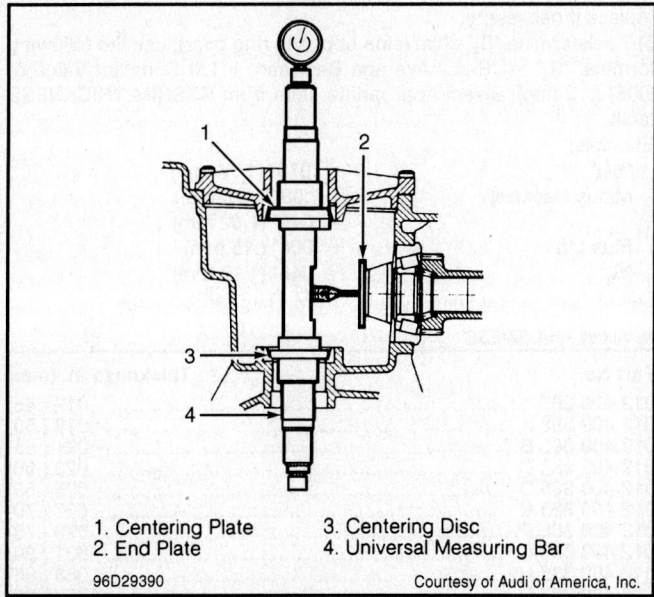

1. Centering Plate   3. Centering Disc
2. End Plate   4. Universal Measuring Bar

96D29390   Courtesy of Audi of America, Inc.

Fig. 30: Measuring Pinion Depth

10) To determine "S₃" shim thickness, use the following formula and then refer to S₃ SHIM THICKNESS table:

"S₃" = "E" + "R"

- "E" = dial indicator reading maximum deflection,
- "R" = deviation (marked on ring gear) or determined by actual measurement.

Example:

Dial Indicator Reading "E"	.020" (.51 mm)
Deviation "R"	+ .007" (.18 mm)
Shim Thickness "S₃"	= .027" (.69 mm)

11) To determine "S₄" shim thickness, use following formula and then refer to "S₄" SHIM THICKNESS table:

"S₄" = "S" total - "S₃"

Example:

Total Shim Thickness	.063" (1.60 mm)
"S₃" Shim Thickness	- .027" (.69 mm)
"S₄" Shim Thickness	= .036" (.91 mm)

S₃ SHIM THICKNESS

Part No.	Thickness In. (mm)
01E-311-391	.017 (.45)
01E-311-391 A	.019 (.50)
01E-311-391 B	.021 (.55)
01E-311-391 C	.023 (.60)
01E-311-391 D	.025 (.65)
01E-311-391 E	.027 (.70)
01E-311-391 F	.029 (.75)
01E-311-391 G	.031 (.80)
01E-311-391 H	.033 (.85)

S₄ SHIM THICKNESS

Part No.	Thickness In. (mm)
01A-311-393	.017 (.45)
01E-311-393 A	.019 (.50)
01E-311-393 B	.021 (.55)
01E-311-393 C	.023 (.60)
01E-311-393 D	.025 (.65)
01E-311-393 E	.027 (.70)
01E-311-393 F	.029 (.75)
01E-311-393 G	.031 (.80)
01E-311-393 H	.033 (.85)
01E-311-393 J	.048 (1.25)

12) To ensure settings are correct, install pinion with measured shims "S₃" and "S₄" and turn several times in both directions. Install measuring bar in position and verify measurements. Adjustment shims are correct if dial indicator, reading counterclockwise (Red reading), shows deviation "R" within .001" (.04 mm) tolerance.

RING GEAR

1) Ring gear must be adjusted if any of following parts were replaced:
- Gearbox bearing plate
- Differential bearings
- Differential cover
- Differential gear housing
- Ring and pinion set

2) To adjust differential bearing preload (pinion removed) remove oil seals and outer races of differential bearings. Install bearing outer races without shims and seat fully. Install differential gear into housing without speedometer gear. Install ring gear on left side (opposite cover side).

3) Install cover and tighten bolts to 18 ft. lbs. (25 N.m). Rotate differential to seat bearings. Attach dial indicator. Zero indicator .04" (1.0 mm) preload. Ensure dial indicator extension is 1.2" (30 mm) long. *See Fig. 31.* Move differential up and down and record end play.

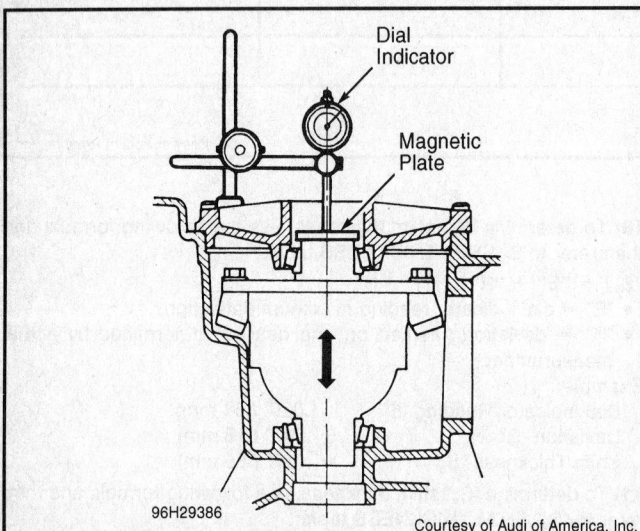

Fig. 31: Checking Ring Gear Preload

NOTE: While taking measurements, DO NOT turn differential. This will result in an incorrect reading.

---

4) Example: Dial Indicator Reading .05" (1.27 mm).

"S_{tot}" = Dial Indicator Reading		.05" (1.27 mm)
+ Preload		+ .02" (.51 mm)
		= .07" (1.78 mm)

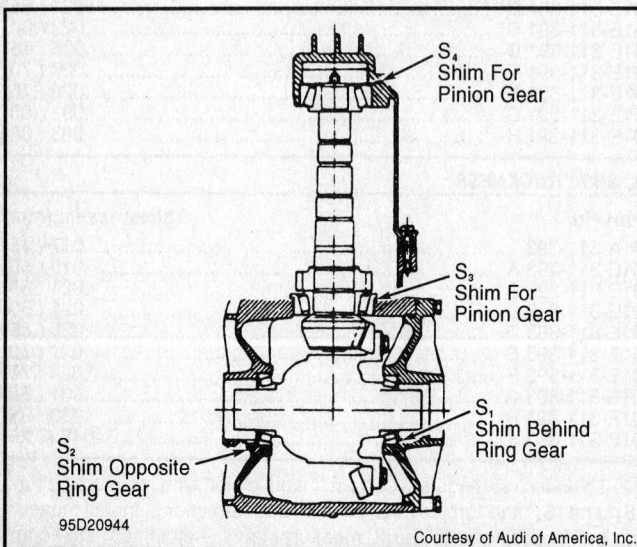

Fig. 32: Identifying Shim Points For Pinion & Ring Gear

Install shim of correct size behind bearing outer race in gearbox housing ("S_2" side). See S_2 SHIM THICKNESS table under RING GEAR BACKLASH. *See Fig. 32.*

5) Check rotation torque using INCH-lb. torque wrench and Adapters (VW521/4 and VW521/8). Lubricate bearings with transmission oil prior to measuring torque. Torque should be:
- New bearing – 22-31 INCH lbs. (2.5-3.5 N.m).
- Used bearing – 3-5 INCH lbs. (.33-.56 N.m).

RING GEAR BACKLASH

1) Install pinion with shim "S_3" and "S_4" installed. Install "S_{tot}" shims on housing side of differential and turn differential several times to seat bearings. Install dial indicator and adjust Measuring Lever (VW388) to A = 3.11" (79 mm). *See Fig. 33.*

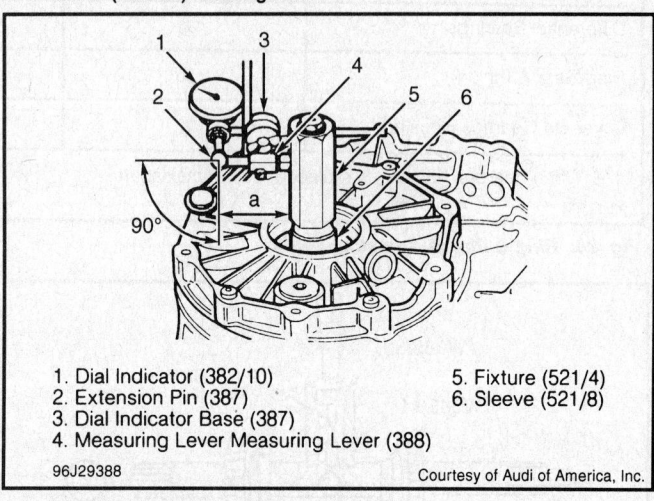

1. Dial Indicator (382/10)
2. Extension Pin (387)
3. Dial Indicator Base (387)
4. Measuring Lever Measuring Lever (388)
5. Fixture (521/4)
6. Sleeve (521/8)

Fig. 33: Measuring Ring Gear Backlash

2) While holding pinion from moving, turn ring gear to stop and set indicator to zero. Turn ring gear back and note and record backlash.

3) Loosen lock bolt on locking sleeve, rotate ring gear 90 degrees, tighten lock bolt and measure backlash again. Repeat this procedure 2 more times. Add all 4 readings together and divide by 4 to determine average backlash.

Example: Average Backlash = .13" (.33 mm) divided by 4 = .03" (.08 mm).

4) If measurements differ by more than .002" (.06 mm) from each other, ring gear/pinion installation is incorrect. Check ring and pinion, replace if necessary.

5) To determine "S_2" shim (side opposite ring gear), use the following formula: "S_2" = "S_{tot}" - Average Backlash + Lift Constant Value of .006" (.15 mm). Select appropriate shim from S_2 SHIM THICKNESS table.

Example:

"S_{tot}"	.070" (1.78 mm)
Minus Backlash	- .030" (.76 mm)
	= .040" (1.02 mm)
Plus Lift	+ .006" (.15 mm)
"S_2"	= .046" (1.17 mm)

Select appropriate shim from S_2 SHIM THICKNESS table.

S_2 SHIM THICKNESS

Part No.	Thickness In. (mm)
012 409 385	.017 (.45)
012 409 385 A	.019 (.50)
012 409 385 B	.021 (.55)
012 409 385 C	.023 (.60)
012 409 385 D	.025 (.65)
012 409 385 E	.027 (.70)
012 409 385 F	.029 (.75)
012 409 385 G	.031 (.80)
012 409 385 H	.033 (.85)
012 409 385 R	.049 (1.25)

6) To determine "S₁" shim thickness (ring gear side), use the following formula, and then select appropriate shim from S₁ SHIM THICKNESS table:

$$\text{"}S_1\text{"} = \text{"}S_{tot}\text{"} - \text{"}S_2\text{"}$$

Example:

"S$_{tot}$"	.07" (1.78 mm)	
"S$_2$"	- .05" (1.27 mm)	
"S$_1$"	= .02" (.51 mm)	

S₁ SHIM THICKNESS

Part No.	Thickness In. (mm)
012 409 386	.017 (.45)
012 409 386 A	.019 (.50)
012 409 386 B	.021 (.55)
012 409 386 C	.023 (.60)
012 409 386 D	.025 (.65)
012 409 386 E	.027 (.70)
012 409 386 F	.029 (.75)
012 409 386 G	.031 (.80)
012 409 386 H	.033 (.85)
012 409 386 R	.049 (1.25)

7) If required thickness is greater than the largest shim listed, two shims that total required thickness may be used. Check final backlash in 4 places as before. Final backlash should be .12mm-.22mm.

TORQUE SPECIFICATIONS
TORQUE SPECIFICATIONS

Application	Ft. Lbs. (N.m)
Differential Cover Bolts	18 (25)
Gearbox Cover Bolts	18 (25)
Clutch Slave Cylinder Bolts	18 (25)
Transmission Support To Subframe	33 (45)
Crossmember To Body	18 (25)
Engine To Transmission Bolts	
M8	18 (25)
M10	33 (45)
M12	48 (65)
Guide Sleeve Bolt	26 (35)
Shift Rod Locking Bolts	52 (70)
Ring Gear Bolt	66 (90)
Torsen Differential Housing Bolts	18 (25)
Input Shaft End Screw	111 (150)
Reverse Light Switch	15 (20)
Oil Filler And Drain Plugs	26 (35)

MANUAL TRANSMISSIONS
Audi Type 012 5-Speed

A4, A6, A90

APPLICATION & LABOR TIMES

APPLICATION & LABOR TIMES

Vehicle Application	Labor Times		Type & Series
	[1] R & I	[2] Overhaul	
1995 A4, A6 & A90	6.5	8.9	.... 012.CAC
			012.CUZ
1996 A4	6.5	8.9	.... 012.CTJ[3]
			012.CUZ[4]

[1] – Removal and installation of transmission from vehicle chassis.
[2] – Bench overhaul time for transaxle and differential. DOES NOT include removal and installation.
[3] – 1.842 2nd gear ratio, from 11/94.
[4] – 1.994 2nd gear ratio, from 1/95.

IDENTIFICATION

Transmission identification code is located on top of transmission case flange near transmission-to-engine mounting surface. First 3 letters of transmission code identify transmission for vehicle application. Remaining identification code numbers identify build day, month, and year.

Transmission identification model number is located on side of transmission case flange near transmission-to-engine mounting surface. First 3 numbers of identification model number will be 012, identifying transmission as a 5-speed manual gearbox used on front wheel drive vehicles.

LUBRICATION & ADJUSTMENTS

See appropriate MANUAL TRANSMISSION SERVICING article in TRANSMISSION SERVICING section.

TROUBLE SHOOTING

See GENERAL TROUBLE SHOOTING article in this section.

ON-VEHICLE SERVICE

AXLE SHAFTS

See appropriate AXLE SHAFTS article in AXLE SHAFTS & TRANSFER CASES section.

REMOVAL & INSTALLATION

NOTE: For transaxle removal, see appropriate MANUAL TRANSMISSION REMOVAL article in TRANSMISSION SERVICING section.

TRANSAXLE DISASSEMBLY

1) Drain fluid and remove clutch release lever, clutch release bearing and guide sleeve. Remove snap ring in front of ball bearing, and measure and record snap ring thickness. Remove roller bearing from final drive using Puller (VAG 1582) and Gripper (VAG 1582/2). DO NOT damage roller bearing cage with puller.

2) Remove snap ring behind roller bearing, and measure and record snap ring thickness. Remove gear carrier housing bolts. Remove gear carrier housing.

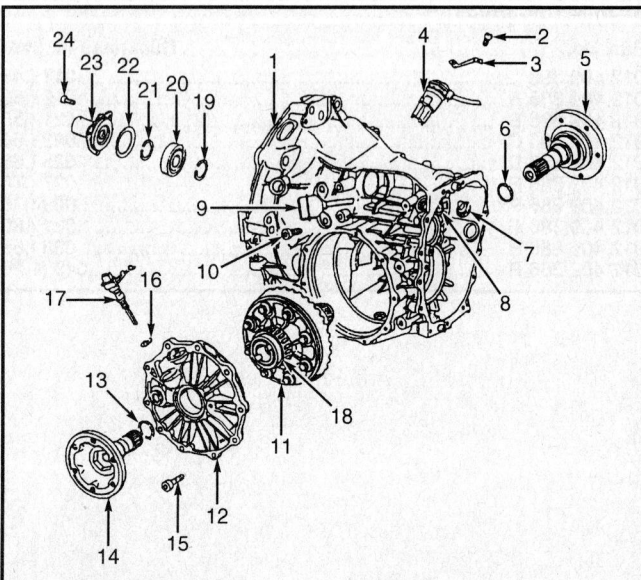

1. Transmission Housing
2. Screw
3. Locking Plate
4. Multifunction Switch
5. Right Drive Flange Shaft
6. Snap Ring
7. 5th/Reverse Gear Lock
8. Shift Shaft Cover
9. Multifunction Switch Connector
10. Torx Bolt
11. Differential
12. Final Drive Cover
13. Snap Ring
14. Left Drive Flange
15. Torx Bolt
16. Vehicle Speed Sensor Seal
17. Vehicle Speed Sensor
18. Speedometer Drive Gear
19. Snap Ring
20. Input Shaft Bearing
21. Snap Ring
22. Belleville Spring Washer
23. Guide Sleeve With Seal
24. Torx Belt

96B04777   Courtesy of Audi of America, Inc.

Fig. 2: Exploded View Of Transaxle Assembly

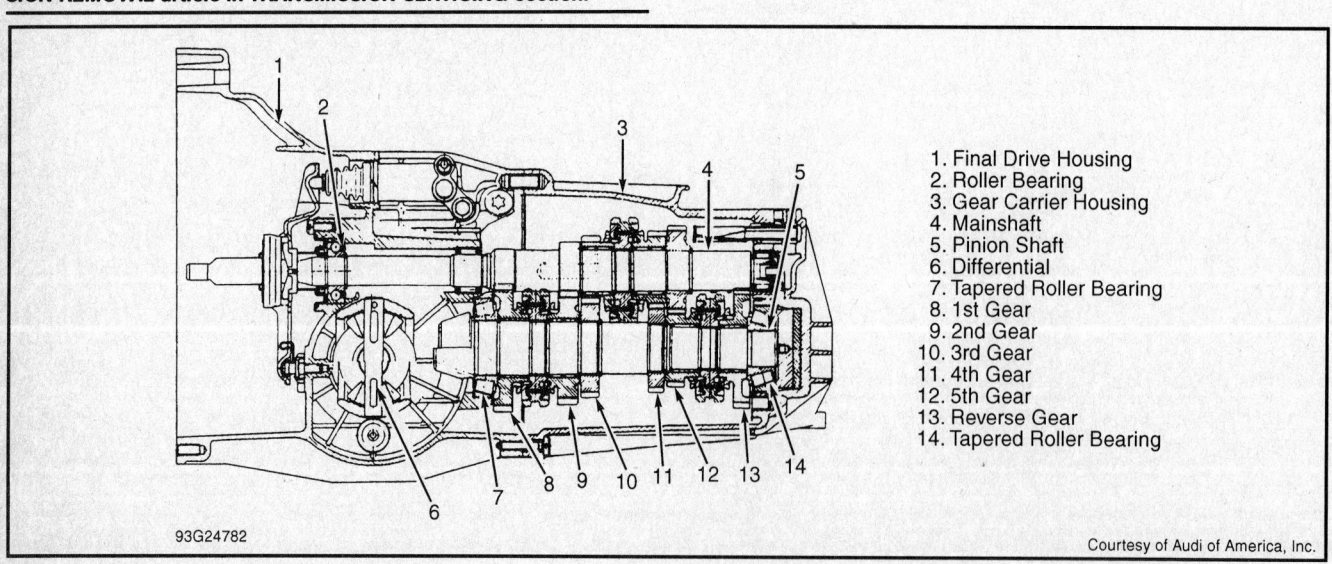

1. Final Drive Housing
2. Roller Bearing
3. Gear Carrier Housing
4. Mainshaft
5. Pinion Shaft
6. Differential
7. Tapered Roller Bearing
8. 1st Gear
9. 2nd Gear
10. 3rd Gear
11. 4th Gear
12. 5th Gear
13. Reverse Gear
14. Tapered Roller Bearing

93G24782   Courtesy of Audi of America, Inc.

Fig. 1: Cut-Away View Of 012 Transmission

3) Remove multi-function switch and transmission breather sleeve. Remove relay shaft bolts. Remove bolt and shift detent. Using a slide hammer, remove 3rd/4th shift rod bushing (if necessary). Remove input shaft, pinion shaft, relay shaft selector rods and shift forks as an assembly.

4) Remove drive flange from differential gear. Remove flange shaft seal and carefully pry out speedometer drive at drive pins. Remove taper roller bearing outer race from final drive cover. Remove differential from final drive housing. *See Fig. 2.*

COMPONENT DISASSEMBLY & REASSEMBLY

GEAR CARRIER

Disassembly – Remove gear carrier from final drive housing. Remove pinion shaft gear assembly, input shaft gear assembly and shift selector assembly together, as an assembly. Pry out oil retainer using screwdriver. Remove inner shift rod sealing ring.

Cleaning & Inspection – Clean gear carrier housing with solvent. Dry with compressed air. Inspect for cracks and distortion, and replace as necessary.

Reassembly – Push oil retainer into gear carrier housing until oil retainer detent engages into housing. Retainer faces upward in gear carrier housing. Install inner shift rod sealing ring .04" (1.0 mm) below housing lip. Install assembled input shaft, pinion shaft and shift selector assemblies into gear carrier housing. Install gear carrier on final drive housing. Tighten Torx bolts to 18 ft. lbs. (25 N.m).

INPUT SHAFT

NOTE: Snap rings are of different thicknesses and should be measured as they are removed. If a gear or shaft is replaced, snap ring must be measured and replacement snap rings must be same size.

Disassembly – **1)** Remove snap ring, roller bearing and snap ring from input shaft. Remove input shaft from final drive housing and gear carrier housing. Remove 5th gear snap ring and press off 5th gear.
2) Remove 4th gear, 4th synchro ring and operating sleeve. Remove 3rd/4th synchro hub, 3rd gear and 3rd gear synchro ring.

Cleaning & Inspection – Clean all parts with cleaning solvent and dry with compressed air. Inspect for chipped gears, galling and scoring on gears and shaft. Replace any damaged or broken parts. *See Fig. 3.*

Reassembly – **1)** Install needle bearing in final drive housing. Needle bearing installed depth "A" should be 1.56" (39.5 mm) from lower edge of straightedge to upper edge of bearing. *See Fig. 4.*
2) Install snap ring on input shaft. Slide roller bearing on input shaft up to stop. Install shaft on roller bearing, and insert it into final drive housing opening. Install snap ring on input shaft and pull shaft into housing and roller bearing using Special Tool (3235 A-B). Evenly press in bearing as far as possible. Ensure open side of plastic cage faces guide sleeve. *See Fig. 5.*
3) Install spring in 4th gear with angled end of spring into hole. Press synchronizer ring in operating sleeve and measure gap "a" using with a feeler gauge in positions "A", "B" and "C". *See Fig. 6.* Add measured values and divide by 3. Value obtained must not be less than .02" (.5 mm). Install 3rd/4th gear, ensuring recessed side of operating sleeve faces 3rd gear. When pressing on 5th gear assembly, ensure higher collar faces reverse gear and oil pocket faces 4th gear.

NOTE: Thickness of snap rings No. 1, 2, 4 and 5 must always be measured. Snap ring No. 3 size is always same. Snap rings No. 1 and 2 size is determined during input shaft adjustment. See Fig. 7.

4) Replace input shaft needle bearing using a slide hammer and puller. Install bearing to a depth of 8.5" (216.0 mm) as measured from housing face. Install 4th gear snap ring ensuring thickest snap ring possible is installed, (position 4). *See Fig. 7.* Select 5th gear snap ring in same manner, (position 5). See INPUT SHAFT SNAP RINGS table.

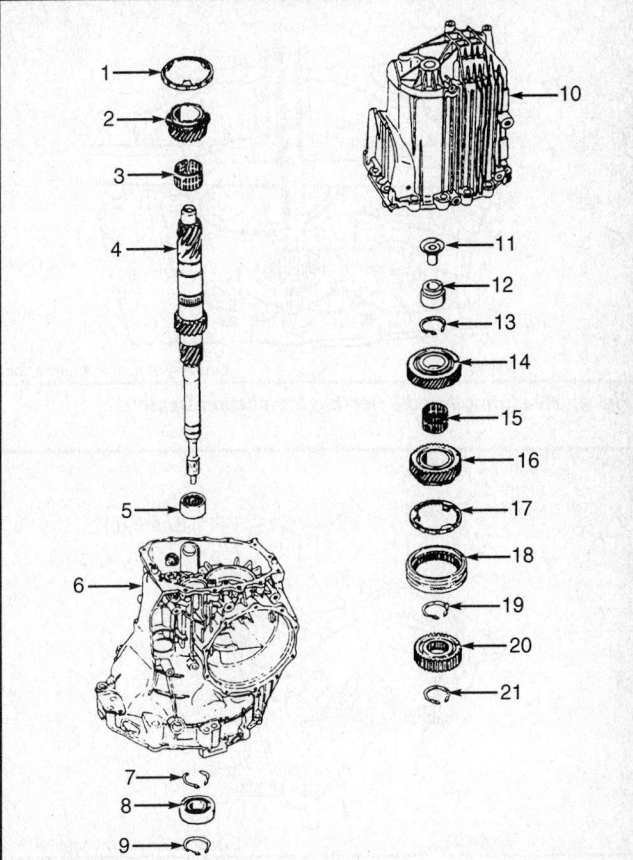

1. Synchronizer Ring – 3rd Gear
2. 3rd Gear
3. Needle Bearing – 3rd Gear
4. Mainshaft
5. Needle Bearing – Mainshaft
6. Final Drive Housing
7. Snap Ring
8. Ball Bearing – Mainshaft
9. Snap Ring
10. Gear Carrier Housing
11. Plastic Sleeve
12. Needle Bearing – Mainshaft
13. Snap Ring
14. 5th Gear
15. Needle Bearing – 4th Gear
16. 4th Gear
17. Synchronizer Ring – 4th Gear
18. Operating Sleeve – 3rd/4th Gear
19. Snap Ring
20. Synchronizer Hub – 3rd/4th Gear
21. Snap Ring

93H24783   Courtesy of Audi of America, Inc.

Fig. 3: Exploded View Of Input shaft

INPUT SHAFT SNAP RINGS

Part No.	Thickness In. (mm)
Snap Ring No. 3 (Brown)	
N 902 945.01	.080 (2.03)
Snap Ring No. 4 (Blue)	
N 902 944.01	.075 (1.90)
N 902 944.02	.076 (1.93)
N 902 944.03	.077 (1.96)
N 902 944.04	.078 (1.99)
N 902 944.05	.079 (2.02)
N 902 944.06	.080 (2.03)
Snap Ring No. 5	
N 902 942.02	.075 (1.90)
N 902 942.03	.076 (1.93)
N 902 942.04	.077 (1.96)
N 902 942.05	.078 (1.99)
N 902 942.06	.080 (2.03)

5) Install plastic sleeve and needle bearing into gear carrier housing. Plastic sleeve is used on input shaft with oil passages for 3rd/4th gear. Place input shaft in vise with soft jaws, and clamp securely. Place Spacer Gauge (3167) on 3rd gear. Install housing onto spacer gauge via input shaft. Place depth gauge on housing and measure to lower groove in shaft, dimension "A". Example: Dimension "A" = 1.12" (28.5 mm). *See Fig. 8.*

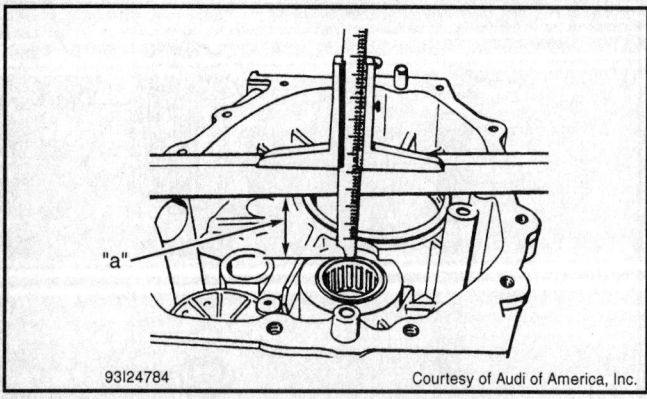

Fig. 4: Measuring Needle Bearing Installation Depth

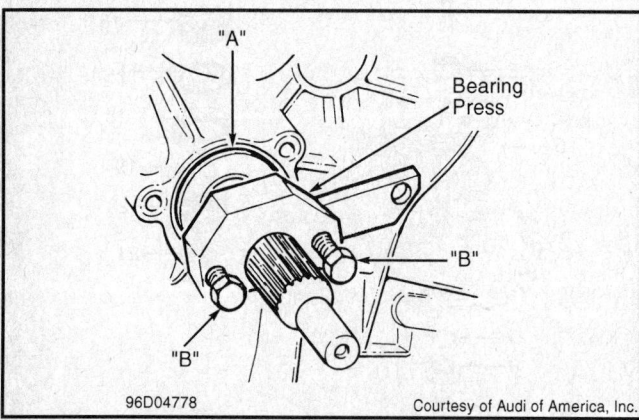

Fig. 5: Installing Roller Bearing In Final Drive Housing

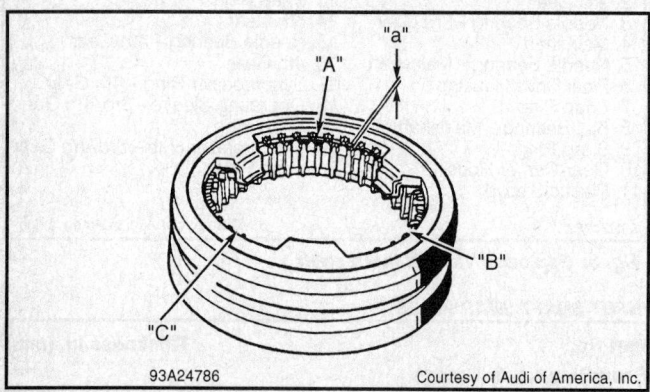

Fig. 6: Identifying Synchro Ring Measuring Points

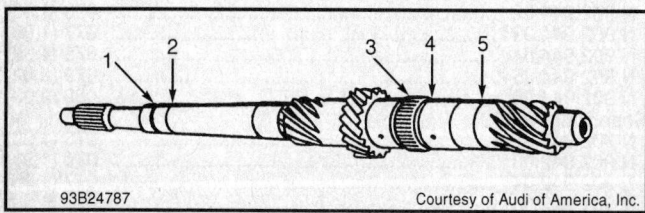

Fig. 7: Identifying Snap Ring Locations

6) Place depth gauge on housing and measure roller bearing seat, dimension "B". Example: Dimension "B" = 1.05" (26.8 mm). See Fig. 9. Use formula to find roller bearing snap ring thickness. X = a - b. Example: 28.5 mm - 26.8 mm = 1.70 mm. See INPUT SHAFT ROLLER BEARING SNAP RING table.

INPUT SHAFT ROLLER BEARING SNAP RING

Part No.	Measurement In. (mm)	Thickness In. (mm)
N 902-941-14	.058-.061 (1.48-1.56)	.061 (1.54)
N 902-941-15	.062-.064 (1.57-1.65)	.064 (1.63)
N 902-941-16	.065-.068 (1.66-1.74)	.067 (1.72)
N 902-941-17	.069-.072 (1.75-1.83)	.071 (1.81)
N 902-941-18	.073-.075 (1.84-1.92)	.074 (1.90)
N 902-941-19	.076-.079 (1.93-2.01)	.078 (1.99)
N 902-941-20	.080-.082 (2.02-2.10)	.081 (2.08)
N 902-941-11	.083-.086 (2.12-2.19)	.085 (2.17)
N 902-941-12	.087-.089 (2.20-2.27)	.088 (2.25)
N 902-941-13	.090-.092 (2.28-2.35)	.091 (2.33)

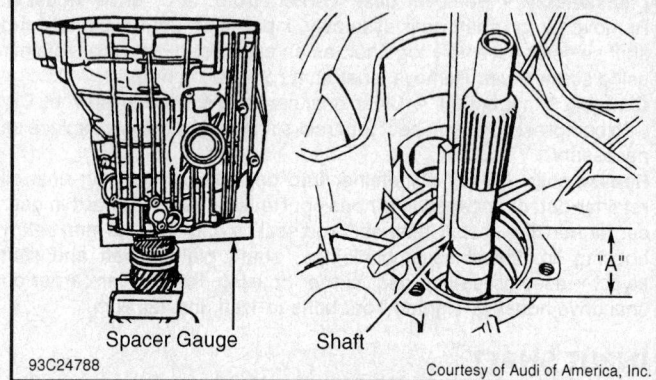

Fig. 8: Measuring To Lower Groove On Input shaft

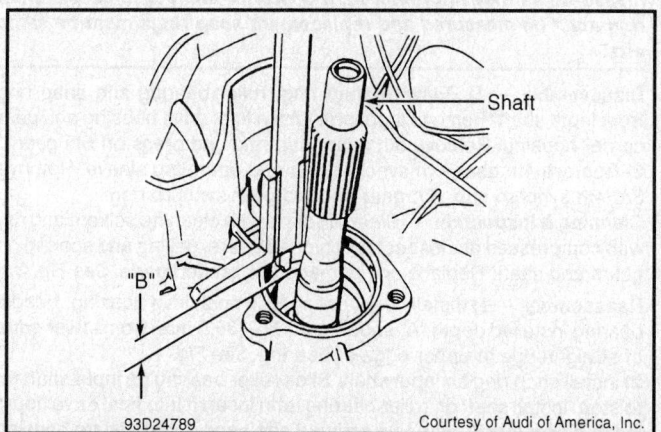

Fig. 9: Measuring To Ball Bearing Seat

PINION SHAFT

NOTE: DO NOT damage seal lips between taper roller bearings. If pinion bearings are to be replaced, record and measure clearances. See PINION DEPTH under ADJUSTMENTS. Snap rings are different in thickness and diameter and should be measured as removed. If gear or shaft is replaced, measure snap rings for correct size and fit.

Disassembly – 1) Remove pinion shaft from final drive housing and gear carrier housing. Remove outer race. Press off 3rd and 4th gear assembly. Remove synchronizer hub with 5th gear using .87-4.50" (22.0-115.0 mm) separating tool and Kukko Tool (17/2).
2) Remove taper roller bearing inner race using .87-4.50" (22.0-115.0 mm) separating tool and Kukko Tool (17/2). Remove locking bushing and outer race for taper roller bearing. See Fig. 10.

NOTE: Bushing is not necessary once outer race is replaced. Bushing is only required during production.

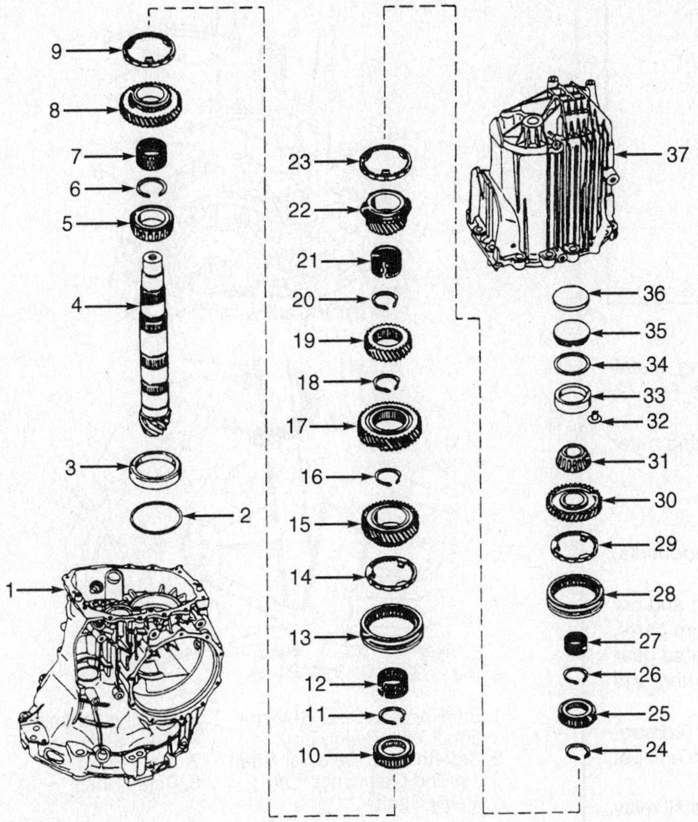

1. Final Drive Housing
2. Shim "S_3"
3. Double Taper Roller Bearing – Outer Race
4. Pinion
5. Double Taper Roller Bearing – Inner Race
6. Snap Ring
7. Needle Bearing – 1st Gear
8. 1st Gear
9. Synchronizer Ring – 1st Gear
10. Synchronizer Hub – 1st/2nd Gear
11. Snap Ring
12. Needle Bearing – 2nd Gear
13. Operating Sleeve – 1st/2nd Gear
14. Synchronizer Ring – 2nd Gear
15. 2nd Gear
16. Snap Ring
17. 3rd Gear
18. Snap Ring
19. 4th Gear
20. Snap Ring
21. Needle Bearing – 5th Gear
22. 5th Gear
23. Synchronizer Ring – 5th Gear
24. Snap Ring
25. Synchronizer Hub – 5th/Reverse
26. Snap Ring
27. Needle Bearing – Reverse Gear
28. Operating Sleeve – 5th/Reverse Gear
29. Synchronizer Ring – Reverse Gear
30. Reverse Gear
31. Taper Roller Bearing – Inner Race
32. Locking Bushing
33. Taper Roller Bearing – Outer Race
34. Shim "S_4"
35. Pressure Plate
36. Washer
37. Gear Carrier Housing

Courtesy of Audi of America, Inc.

93G24790

Fig. 10: Exploded View Of Pinion Shaft Assembly

Cleaning & Inspection – Clean all parts in cleaning solvent and dry with compressed air. Inspect for chipped gear teeth, galling, scoring and excessive wear. Replace parts (as necessary). Ensure all parts are dry and free of any lubricants. All snap rings must be replaced during reassembly. See PINION SHAFT SNAP RING table.

Reassembly – 1) Press roller bearing onto pinion shaft and secure using snap ring. See Fig. 11. Install needle bearing and 1st gear, ensuring spring angled end is in gear bore. See Fig. 12. Install synchronizer ring onto 1st/2nd gear synchronizer hub, ensuring higher shoulder faces 1st gear.

2) Install snap ring and 2nd gear needle bearing. See Fig. 11. Install 1st/2nd gear synchronizer hub, synchronizer ring, 2nd gear and snap ring. Install 3rd gear with groove facing 4th gear. Install 4th gear with shoulder facing 3rd gear and snap ring. See Fig. 10.

3) Install needle bearing and 5th gear, ensuring angled end of spring is in bore. See Fig. 12. Install 5th gear synchro ring and snap ring. See Fig. 11. Press on 5th/reverse synchronizer hub, ensuring inner shoulder faces 5th gear. Install snap ring and reverse gear needle bearing.

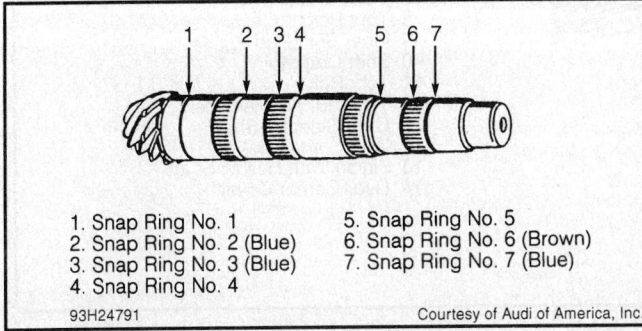

1. Snap Ring No. 1
2. Snap Ring No. 2 (Blue)
3. Snap Ring No. 3 (Blue)
4. Snap Ring No. 4
5. Snap Ring No. 5
6. Snap Ring No. 6 (Brown)
7. Snap Ring No. 7 (Blue)

93H24791

Courtesy of Audi of America, Inc.

Fig. 11: Identifying Snap Rings On Pinion Shaft

PINION SHAFT SNAP RING

Part No.	Thickness In. (mm)
Snap Ring No. 1	
N 902 950.01	.079 (2.00)
N 902 950.08	.080 (2.03)
N 902 950.04	.081 (2.06)
N 902 950.09	.082 (2.09)
N 902 950.10	.083 (2.12)
N 902 950.11	.084 (2.15)
Snap Ring No. 2 (Blue)	
N 902 947.01	.075 (1.90)
N 902 947.02	.076 (1.93)
N 902 947.03	.077 (1.96)
N 902 947.04	.078 (1.98)
N 902 947.05	.079 (2.02)
Snap Ring No. 3 (Blue)	
N 902 947.06	.098 (2.50)
Snap Ring No. 4	
N 902 946.02	.075 (1.90)
N 902 946.09	.076 (1.94)
N 902 946.10	.078 (1.98)
N 902 946.06	.079 (2.02)
N 902 946.11	.081 (2.06)
Snap Ring No. 5	
N 902 952.07	.073 (1.86)
N 902 952.02	.074 (1.90)
N 902 952.08	.076 (1.94)
N 902 952.09	.077 (1.98)
Snap Ring No. 6 (Brown)	
N 902 945.01	.078 (1.98)
Snap Ring No. 7 (Blue)	
N 902 944.01	.075 (1.90)
N 902 944.02	.076 (1.93)
N 902 944.03	.077 (1.96)
N 902 944.04	.078 (1.99)
N 902 944.05	.079 (2.02)
N 902 944.06	.080 (2.03)

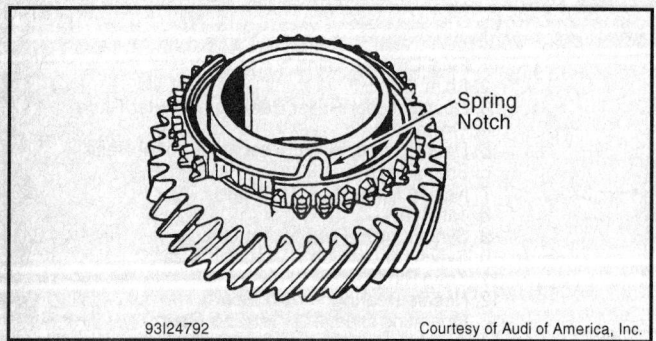

Fig. 12: Identifying Spring & Notch In Gear

4) Install 5th/reverse synchronizer hub onto synchronizer ring. Install reverse gear, ensuring angled end of spring is in bore. *See Fig. 12.* Install taper roller bearing inner race on pinion shaft.

5) Install washer, pressure plate, shim and taper roller bearing outer race into gear carrier housing.

SHIFT SELECTOR ASSEMBLY

Disassembly – For disassembly, see exploded view of components. *See Fig. 12.*

Cleaning & Inspection – Clean all parts in cleaning solvent and dry with compressed air. Inspect for damaged or excessively worn parts. All components can be replaced individually except 5th/reverse gear shift fork which must be replaced together with selector ring and selector shaft.

Reassembly – **1)** For reassembly, see exploded view of components. *See Fig. 13.* Place gear carrier on work table with open end up. Install 5th reverse gear selector shaft with shift fork.

2) Install 3rd/4th selector shaft and 1st/2nd gear shift fork. Install relay shaft and tighten Torx bolts to 30 ft. lbs. (40 N.m). Install locking segment and tighten Torx bolt to 18 ft. lbs. (25 N.m). Install inner shift rod, assembled input shaft, pinion with hollow shaft, selector shafts and shift forks together.

3) When installing relay shaft with inner shift rod, engage 3rd gear and install relay shaft. Place inner shaft sideways on bracket opening in final drive housing and align with bracket eye in relay shaft. *See Fig. 14.* Install shift rod by rotating counterclockwise.

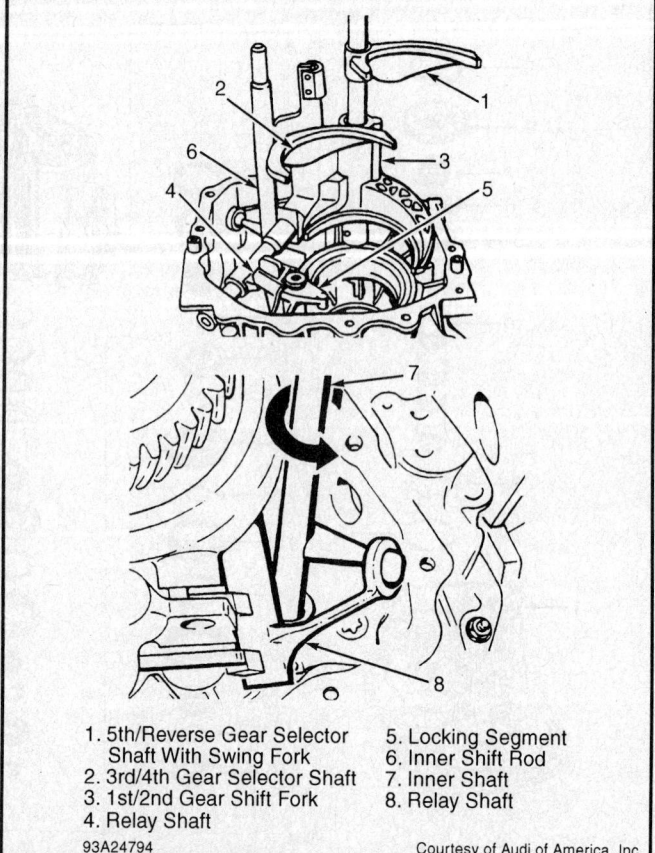

1. 5th/Reverse Gear Selector Shaft With Swing Fork
2. 3rd/4th Gear Selector Shaft
3. 1st/2nd Gear Shift Fork
4. Relay Shaft
5. Locking Segment
6. Inner Shift Rod
7. Inner Shaft
8. Relay Shaft

Fig. 14: Installing Of Shift Selector Assembly

REVERSE IDLER GEAR

Disassembly & Reassembly – **1)** Remove snap ring, washer and reverse idler gear from reverse idler gear shaft. Remove reverse idler gear needle bearings and thrust washer. Remove reverse idler gear shaft Torx bolt and remove shaft.

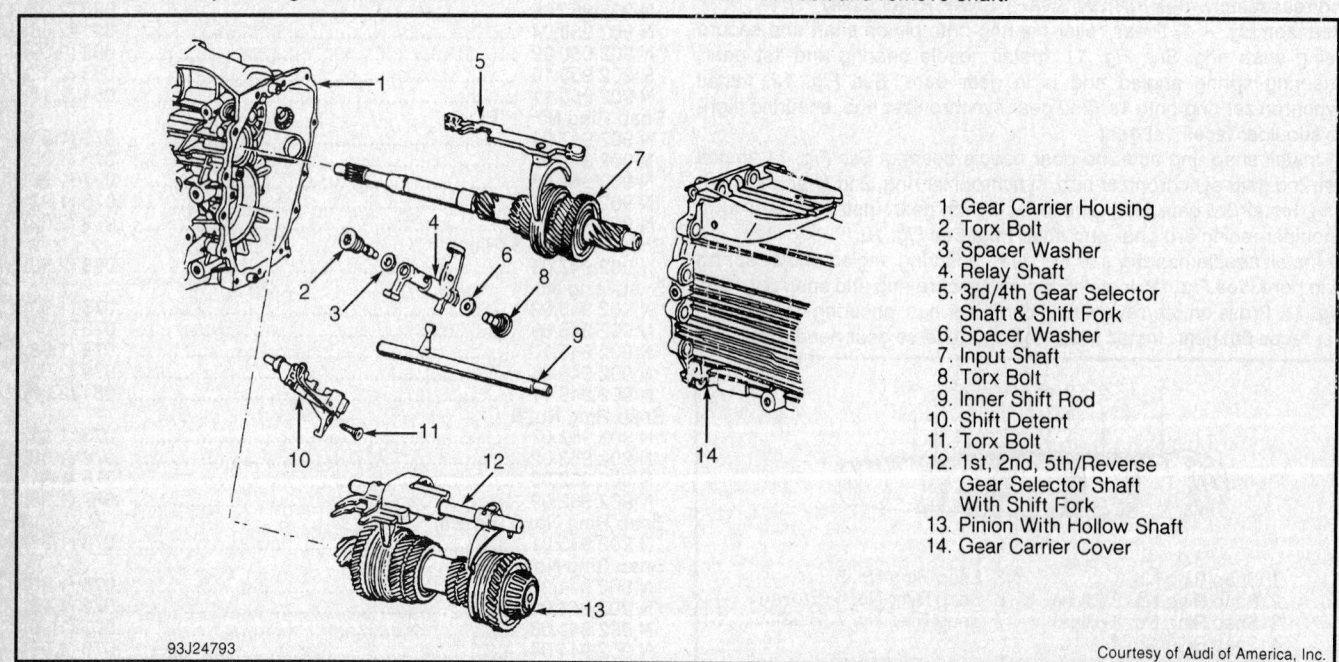

1. Gear Carrier Housing
2. Torx Bolt
3. Spacer Washer
4. Relay Shaft
5. 3rd/4th Gear Selector Shaft & Shift Fork
6. Spacer Washer
7. Input Shaft
8. Torx Bolt
9. Inner Shift Rod
10. Shift Detent
11. Torx Bolt
12. 1st, 2nd, 5th/Reverse Gear Selector Shaft With Shift Fork
13. Pinion With Hollow Shaft
14. Gear Carrier Cover

Fig. 13: Exploded View Of Shift Selector Assembly

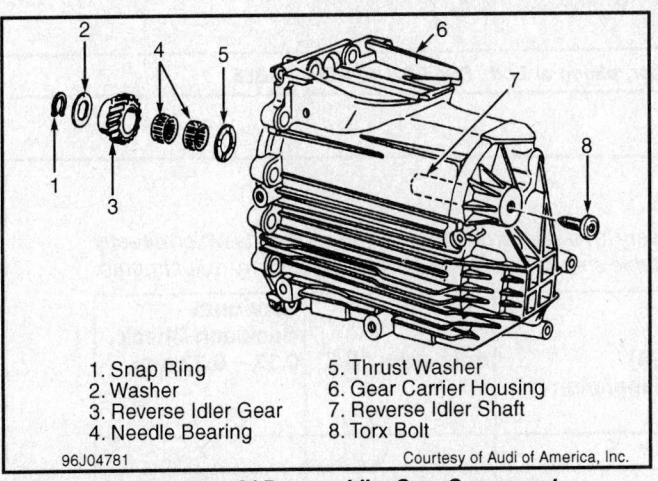

1. Snap Ring
2. Washer
3. Reverse Idler Gear
4. Needle Bearing
5. Thrust Washer
6. Gear Carrier Housing
7. Reverse Idler Shaft
8. Torx Bolt

96J04781   Courtesy of Audi of America, Inc.

Fig. 15: *Exploded View Of Reverse Idler Gear Components*

2) Clean all parts in cleaning solvent and dry with compressed air. Inspect for damaged or excessively worn parts. Replace as necessary.

3) Install Reverse idler gear shaft to gear carrier housing. Torque Torx bolt to 26 ft.lbs. (35 N.m). Install thrust washer and needle bearings. Install reverse idler gear, washer and snap ring. *See Fig. 15.*

5TH/REVERSE GEAR DETENT

NOTE: If there is any catching or hanging up in 5th gear or reverse gear, remove, check and reassemble 5th reverse gear assembly as necessary.

Disassembly & Reassembly – 1) Place spring in plastic bushing. Turn counterclockwise using light pressure until spring snaps in place in base of plastic bushing. Place 5th/reverse gear bushing in spring so bent end of spring lies in groove. *See Fig. 16.*

2) Press spring together using 5th/reverse gear bushing. Twist 5th/reverse gear bushing about one turn counterclockwise until tab on 5th/reverse gear bushing lines up on groove in plastic bushing. Press 5th/reverse gear bushing tab into groove in plastic bushing to stop surface.

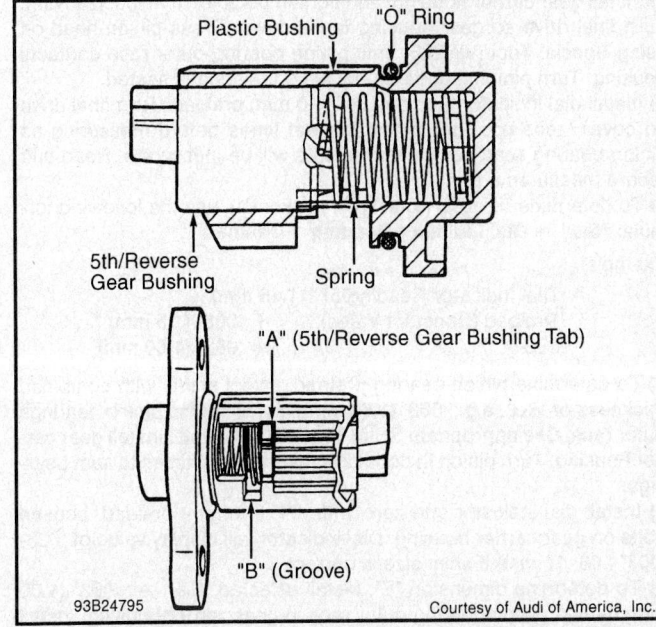

Plastic Bushing   "O" Ring

5th/Reverse Gear Bushing   Spring

"A" (5th/Reverse Gear Bushing Tab)

"B" (Groove)

93B24795   Courtesy of Audi of America, Inc.

Fig. 16: *Identifying Correct Procedure To Assemble 5th/Reverse Gear*

3) Turn 5th/reverse gear bushing clockwise and release 5th/reverse gear bushing into assembly end position. To ensure installation si correct, 5th/reverse gear bushing tab "A" must always come to stop opposite groove "B" on plastic bushing.

FINAL DRIVE HOUSING

Disassembly – Remove final drive flange seal and transmission breather. Remove tapered roller bearing outer race and 3rd/4th gear shift rod bushing. Remove pinion shaft needle bearing. Remove speedometer drive and multifunction switch and connector.

Cleaning & Inspection – Clean all parts with cleaning solvent and dry with compressed air. Inspect housing for cracks and damage, and replace as necessary.

Reassembly – Install seal for drive flange .02" (.5 mm) below housing edge. Install multifunction switch with locking plate. Tighten retaining plate to 18 ft. lbs. (25 N.m). Install 5th/reverse gear lock with beveled side of plastic bushing facing relay shaft bore. Tighten retaining bolt to 89 INCH lbs. (10 N.m).

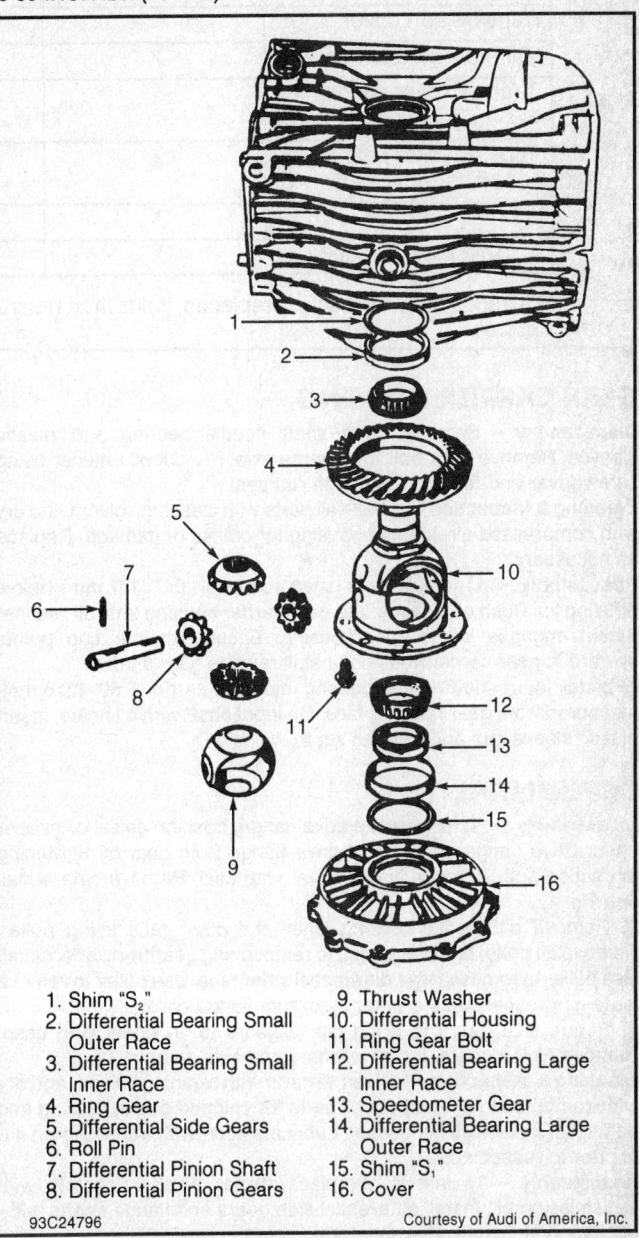

1. Shim "S₂"
2. Differential Bearing Small Outer Race
3. Differential Bearing Small Inner Race
4. Ring Gear
5. Differential Side Gears
6. Roll Pin
7. Differential Pinion Shaft
8. Differential Pinion Gears
9. Thrust Washer
10. Differential Housing
11. Ring Gear Bolt
12. Differential Bearing Large Inner Race
13. Speedometer Gear
14. Differential Bearing Large Outer Race
15. Shim "S₁"
16. Cover

93C24796   Courtesy of Audi of America, Inc.

Fig. 17: *Exploded View Of Differential Assembly*

ADJUSTMENTS

NOTE: When assembling final drive, it is necessary to adjust ring gear, pinion or both. See ADJUSTMENT TABLE.

ADJUSTMENT TABLE

Adjustment Table

When removing and installing transmission, it is only necessary to re–adjust pinion or pinion set if parts which directly affect adjustment of final drive are replaced. The following table should be used to avoid unnecessary adjustments.

To be adjusted: replaced part	Ring gear (S1 + S2)	Pinion (S3 + S4) Over dimension "r"	Pinion only shim "S4"	Torsional Backlash Check 0.12 – 0.22 mm
Transmission housing [1]	X	X		X
Transmission cover			X	X
Differential gear housing	X			X
Tapered roller bearing for pinion		X		X
Tapered roller bearing for differential gear	X			X
Gear set	X	X		X
Cover for final drive	X			X

[1] If transmission housing is replaced, input shaft must also be adjusted

96E30472

Courtesy of Audi of America, Inc.

GEAR CARRIER HOUSING

Disassembly – Remove input shaft needle bearing and plastic sleeves. Remove Torx bolt for reverse axle. Pry out oil retainer using screwdriver and remove inner shift rod seal.
Cleaning & Inspection – Clean all parts with cleaning solvent and dry with compressed air. Inspect housing for cracks or damage. Replace as necessary.
Reassembly – 1) Install inner shaft rod seal .04" (1.0 mm) below housing lip. Push oil retainer into gear carrier housing until oil retainer detent engages into carrier housing. Ensure retainer cup points upward in gear carrier housing. Install reverse gear shaft.
2) Install input shaft needle bearing into gear carrier 8.50" (216 mm) measured from gear housing face. On input shaft with oil holes, insert plastic sleeve into end of input shaft.

DIFFERENTIAL

Disassembly – 1) To remove drive flange, position chisel or spacer under drive flange and extract drive flange from gear by tightening extraction bolt. Remove flange cover with seal. Remove differential. See Fig. 17.
2) Remove differential bearing inner and outer race using puller. Remove all bolts, and use punch to remove ring gear from differential. Use puller to remove large differential inner race. Use puller to remove large differential bearing outer race from flange cover.
3) Rotate side gears to bring pinion gears to an opening in case. Remove pinion gears, thrust washers and side gears.
Cleaning & Inspection – Clean all parts with cleaning solvent and dry with compressed air. Inspect all parts for chipped gears, scoring and damage. Replace as necessary. Lubricate parts with transmission fluid prior to reassembly.
Reassembly – 1) Install one-piece thrust washer coated with transmission oil. Install differential side gears and flange shafts without lock ring. Install differential pinion gears about 180 degrees apart and pivot into place by turning flange shaft clockwise.
2) Align thrust washers and pinion gears. Drive in differential pinion shaft, and secure it using roll pin.

PINION DEPTH

NOTE: Always install rubber shims and pressure plate to determine "S4" shim. Pressure plates of .58-.60" (14.8-15.3 mm) can be installed.

1) Install bearing outer races in housing and gear carrier without shims. Install pinion bearing inner races. Seat lower bearing securely. Install assembled pinion into final drive housing.
2) Install gear carrier housing, and tighten bolts to 18 ft. lbs. (25 N.m). Turn final drive so gear housing faces down. Press pinion head on using Special Tool (VW296) until pinion bearing outer race contacts housing. Turn pinion manually until pinion bearing is seated.
3) Install dial indicator, and set .04" (1.0 mm) preload. Turn final drive so cover faces up. Turn pinion several times before measuring so pinion bearing seats, or measurements will be inaccurate. Read and record measurement.
4) To determine "S" total (total shim thickness), use the following formula: **"Stot" = Dial Indicator Reading + Preload**

Example:

Dial Indicator Reading	.057" (1.45 mm)
Preload (Constant Value)	+ .006" (.15 mm)
"Stot"	= .063" (1.60 mm)

5) To determine pinion bearing preload, select shims with combined thickness of "Stot", e.g., .063" (1.60 mm). Install behind pinion bearings outer race. See appropriate SHIM THICKNESS table. Install gear carrier housing. Turn pinion in both directions several times to seat bearings.
6) Install dial indicator and zero with .04" (1.0 mm) preload. Loosen bolts on gear carrier housing. Dial indicator will display value of .003-.006" (.08-.15 mm) if shim size is correct.
7) To determine dimension "E", install selected "Stot" i.e., .063" (1.60 mm) behind pinion bearing outer race in gear carrier housing. Install gear carrier housing. Turn pinion several times in both directions to seat bearing. Set Universal Bar (VW385/1) centering ring to dimension "a" = 1.38" (35.0 mm) and sliding ring to dimension "b" = 2.95" (75.0 mm). See Fig. 18.

8) Assemble measuring bar with following specifications:
- Indicator Extension (VW385/20) = .366" (9.30 mm), with RO = 2.348" (59.65 mm)
- Indicator Extension (VW385/20) = .26" (6.5 mm) with RO = 2.2" (54.95 mm). Set Universal Master Gauge (VW385/30) for RO.
- 7.09" (180.0 mm) diameter ring gear = 2.348" (59.65 mm)
- 6.7" (170 mm) diameter ring gear = 2.163" (54.95 mm). *See Fig. 18.*

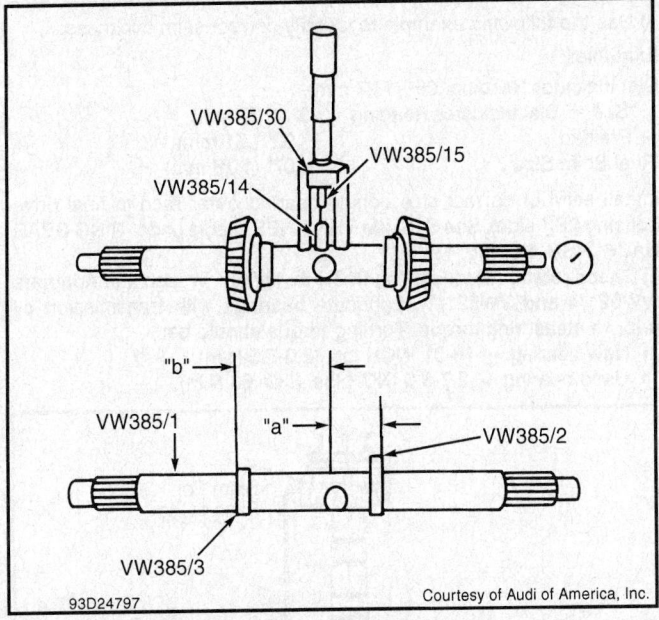

93D24797   Courtesy of Audi of America, Inc.

Fig. 18: Identifying Universal Measuring Bar

9) Place master gauge on measuring bar and set dial indicator with .12" (3.0 mm) range to zero with .04" (1.0 mm) preload. Place End Plate (VW385/33) on pinion end face. Remove master gauge and install measuring bar in housing. Ensure Centering Disc (VW385/3) faces final drive cover. *See Fig. 19.*

10) Install cover for final drive housing, and tighten bolts. Pull 2nd centering ring outward until measuring bar can just be turned by hand. Turn measuring bar slightly until dial indicator contacts end face of pinion and indicates maximum deflection (return point). Measured readings equal dimension "E". *See Fig. 19.*

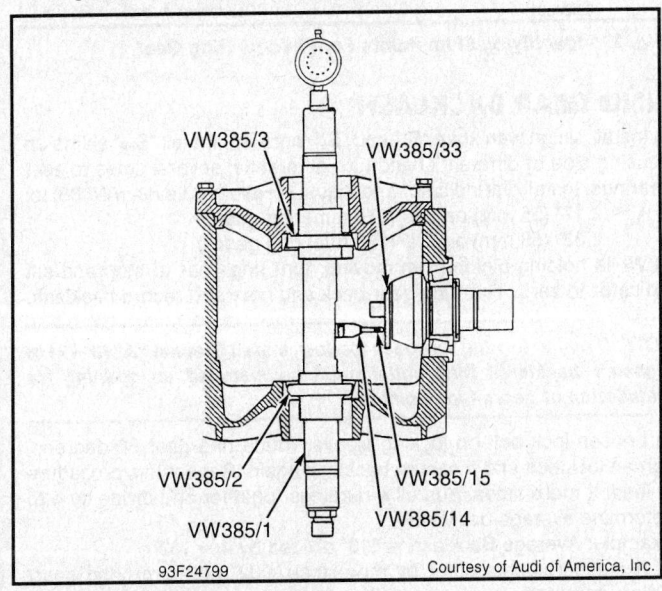

93F24799   Courtesy of Audi of America, Inc.

Fig. 19: Measuring Pinion Depth

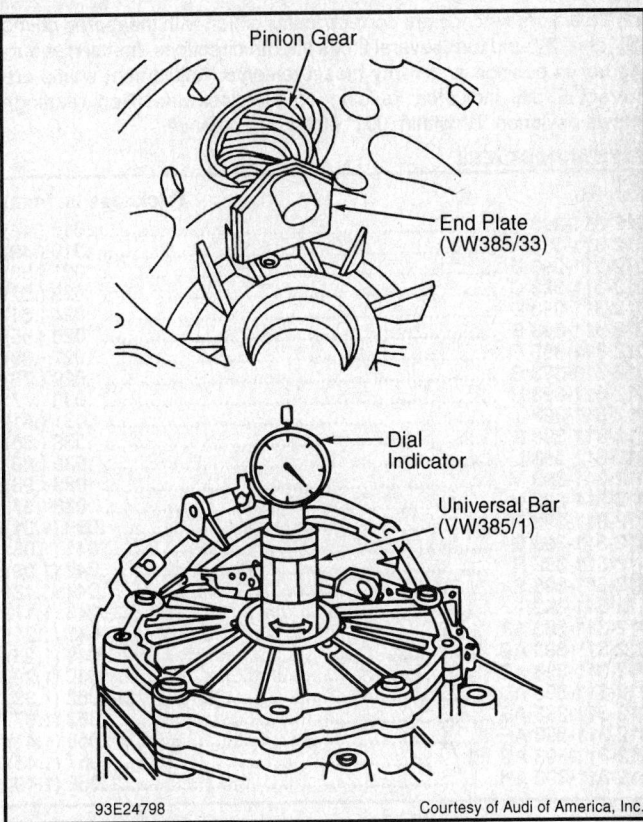

93E24798   Courtesy of Audi of America, Inc.

Fig. 20: Identifying Dimension "E" Measuring Points

11) To determine "S_3" shim thickness, use the following formula:
"S_3" = "E" + "R"
- "E" = dial indicator reading maximum deflection,
- "R" = deviation (marked on ring gear) or determined by actual measurement.

Example:

Dial Indicator Reading "E"	.020" (.51 mm)
Deviation "R"	+ .007" (.18 mm)
Shim Thickness "S_3"	= .027" (.69 mm)

See S_3 SHIM THICKNESS table.

12) To determine "S_4" shim thickness, use the following formula:
"S_4" = "S" total - "S_3"

Example:

Total Shim Thickness	.063" (1.60 mm)
"S_3" Shim Thickness	- .027" (.69 mm)
"S_4" Shim Thickness	= .036" (.91 mm)

See S_4 SHIM THICKNESS table.

S_3 SHIM THICKNESS

Part No.	Thickness In. (mm)
012-311-391 A	.018 (.45)
012-311-391 B	.020 (.50)
012-311-391 C	.022 (.55)
012-311-391 D	.024 (.60)
012-311-391 E	.026 (.65)
012-311-391 F	.028 (.70)
012-311-391 G	.030 (.75)
012-311-391 H	.031 (.80)
012-311-391 J	.033 (.85)
012-311-391 K	.035 (.90)
012-311-391 L	.037 (.95)
012-311-391 M	.039 (1.00)
012-311-391 N	.041 (1.05)

13) To ensure settings are correct, install pinion with measured shims "S₃" and "S₄" and turn several times in both directions. Install measuring bar in position and verify measurements. Adjustment shims are correct if dial indicator, reading counterclockwise (Red reading), shows deviation "R" within .001" (.04 mm) tolerance.

S₄ SHIM THICKNESS

Part No.	Thickness In. (mm)
012-311-393	.018 (.45)
012-311-393 A	.019 (.49)
012-311-393 B	.021 (.53)
012-311-393 C	.022 (.57)
012-311-393 D	.024 (.61)
012-311-393 E	.026 (.65)
012-311-393 F	.027 (.69)
012-311-393 G	.029 (.73)
012-311-393 H	.030 (.77)
012-311-393 J	.031 (.81)
012-311-393 K	.033 (.85)
012-311-393 L	.035 (.89)
012-311-393 M	.036 (.93)
012-311-393 N	.038 (.97)
012-311-393 P	.039 (1.01)
012-311-393 Q	.041 (1.05)
012-311-393 R	.042 (1.09)
012-311-393 S	.044 (1.13)
012-311-393 T	.046 (1.17)
012-311-393 AA	.046 (1.21)
012-311-393 AB	.049 (1.25)
012-311-393 AC	.050 (1.29)
012-311-393 AD	.052 (1.33)
012-311-393 AE	.053 (1.37)
012-311-393 AF	.055 (1.41)
012-311-393 AG	.057 (1.45)
012-311-393 AH	.058 (1.49)

GEAR CARRIER HOUSING

1) If gear carrier housing is to be replaced, "S₄" shim must be remeasured. Install pinion in old gear carrier housing and turn pinion several times to seat bearing. Place dial indicator on housing and zero with .04" (1.02 mm) preload. Turn pinion several times and record reading.

2) Remove dial indicator from housing. Remove pinion and bearing outer race with pressure plate adjustment shim and washer. Install in new housing. Use the following example to find correct shim thickness:

Example:

Preload	.04" (1.02 mm)
Dial Indicator Reading	- .88" (22.35 mm)
	X = .005" (.12 mm)
Shim Thickness "S₄"	.030" (.77 mm)
Value "X"	+ .005" (.12 mm)
	= .035" (.89 mm)

Select correct shim from S₄ SHIM THICKNESS table.

3) If reading is greater than .04" (1.0 mm), "S₄" shim must be reduced by value "X". Install gear carrier housing and check preload of pinion bearing.

RING GEAR ADJUSTING

1) Ring gear must be adjusted if any of following parts were replaced:
- Final drive housing
- Gear carrier housing
- Differential bearings
- Differential gear housing
- Ring and pinion set

2) To adjust differential bearing preload (pinion removed) remove oil seals and outer races of differential bearings. Install bearing outer races without shims and seat into stop. Install differential gear into housing without speedometer gear. Install ring gear on left side (opposite cover side).

3) Install cover and tighten bolts to 16 ft. lbs (22 N.m). Attach dial indicator. Zero indicator with .04" (1.0 mm) preload. Ensure dial indicator

extension is 1.2" (30 mm) long. Install Special Tools (VW521/4 and VW521/8) on final drive housing. Place Measuring Plate (VW385/17) on differential gear. Move differential up and down and record end play.

NOTE: While taking measurements, DO NOT turn differential; bearing will settle, resulting in an incorrect reading.

4) Use the following example to identify correct shim thickness:

Example:

Dial Indicator Reading .05" (1.27 mm).

"S_tot" = Dial Indicator Reading	.05"	(1.27 mm)
+ Preload	+ .02"	(.51 mm)
Final Shim Size	= .07"	(1.78 mm)

Install shim of correct size behind bearing outer race in final drive housing ("S₂" side). See S₂ SHIM THICKNESS table under RING GEAR BACKLASH. *See Fig. 19.*

5) Check rotation torque using INCH-lb. tighten wrench and Adapters (VW521/4 and VW521/8). Lubricate bearings with transmission oil prior to measuring torque. Turning torque should be:
- New bearing – 18-31 INCH lbs. (2.0-3.5 N.m).
- Used bearing – 2.7-5.3 INCH lbs. (.30-.60 N.m).

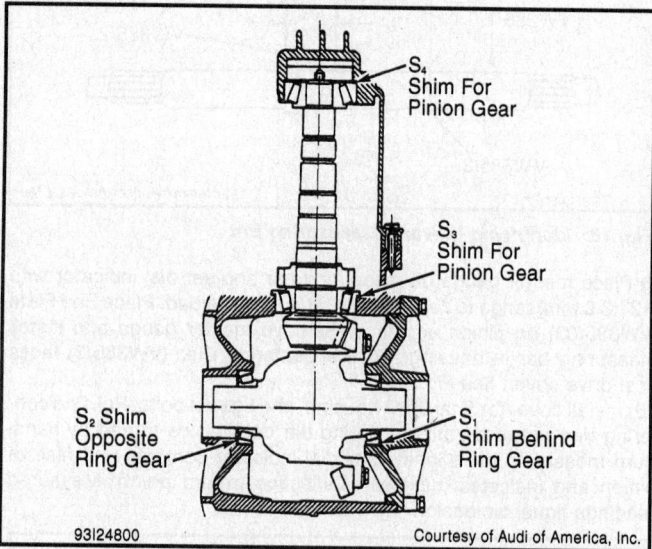

93124800   Courtesy of Audi of America, Inc.

Fig. 21: Identifying Shim Points For Pinion & Ring Gear

RING GEAR BACKLASH

1) Install pinion with shim "S₃" and "S₄" installed. Install "S_tot" shims on housing side of differential and turn differential several times to seat bearings. Install dial indicator and adjust Measuring Lever (VW388) to:

A = 2.17" (55 mm) on 6.7" (170 mm) ring gear
2.32" (59 mm) on 7.1" (180 mm) ring gear

2) While holding pinion from moving, turn ring gear to stop and set indicator to zero. Turn ring gear back and note and record backlash.

NOTE: If pinion turning torque is too low, install Bracket "A" (3177) to measure backlash. Differential must be installed so opening for installation of gears faces pinion.

3) Loosen lock bolt on locking sleeve, rotate ring gear 90 degrees, tighten lock bolt and measure backlash again. Repeat this procedure at least 2 more times. Add all 4 readings together and divide by 4 to determine average backlash.

Example: Average Backlash = .13" divided by 4 = .03"

4) If measurements differ by more than .002" (.06 mm), ring gear/pinion installation is incorrect. Check ring and pinion, and replace if necessary.

5) To determine "S_2" shim (side opposite ring gear), use the following formula:

"S_2" = "S_{tot}" - Average Backlash + Lift Constant of .006" (.15mm)

Example:

"S_{tot}"	.07" (1.78 mm)
Minus Backlash	- .03" (.76 mm)
	= .04" (1.02 mm)
Plus Lift	+ .006" (.15 mm)
"S_2"	= .046" (1.17 mm)

Select appropriate shim from S_2 SHIM THICKNESS table.

S_2 SHIM THICKNESS

Part No.	Thickness In. (mm)
012 409 386	.017 (.45)
012 409 386 A	.019 (.50)
012 409 386 B	.021 (.55)
012 409 386 C	.023 (.60)
012 409 386 D	.025 (.65)
012 409 386 E	.027 (.70)
012 409 386 F	.029 (.75)
012 409 386 G	.031 (.80)
012 409 386 H	.033 (.85)
012 409 386 J	.035 (.90)
012 409 386 K	.037 (.95)
012 409 386 L	.039 (1.00)

6) To determine "S_1" shim thickness (ring gear side), use the following formula: "S_1" = "S_{tot}" - "S_2"

Example:

"S_{tot}"	.07" (1.78 mm)
"S_2"	- .05" (1.27 mm)
"S_1"	= .02" (.51 mm)

Select appropriate shim from S_1 SHIM THICKNESS table.

S_1 SHIM THICKNESS

Part No.	Thickness In. (mm)
012 409 385	.017 (.45)
012 409 385 A	.019 (.50)
012 409 385 B	.021 (.55)
012 409 385 C	.023 (.60)
012 409 385 D	.025 (.65)
012 409 385 E	.027 (.70)
012 409 385 F	.029 (.75)
012 409 385 G	.031 (.80)
012 409 385 H	.033 (.85)
012 409 385 J	.035 (.90)
012 409 385 K	.037 (.95)
012 409 385 L	.039 (1.00)

7) To ensure correct backlash, measure backlash 4 times around circumference of ring gear. Acceptable values can range from .004-.008" (.12-.22 mm). No 2 values can deviate from each other more than .002" (.05 mm).

TRANSMISSION REASSEMBLY

1) Lightly coat sealing face on final drive housing with sealing compound. Install new gasket and dowel pins. Attach gear carrier housing to final drive housing. Tighten Torx bolt to 18 ft. lbs. (25 N.m).

2) Assemble input shaft, pinion with hollow shaft, relay shaft, selector rods and shift forks. All must be installed together as one unit into gear carrier housing. Install relay shaft and locking segment. Tighten relay shaft bolts to 30 ft. lbs. (40 N.m). Tighten locking segment bolt to 18 ft. lbs. (25 N.m).

3) Install multifunction switch, and tighten retaining plate bolt to 18 ft. lbs. (25 N.m). Install 5th/reverse lock bolt and tighten to 89 INCH lbs. (10 N.m). Install roller bearing on input shaft and use selected snap rings that are installed before and after roller bearing.

4) Install guide sleeve with sealing ring, and tighten bolts to 26 ft. lbs. (35 N.m). Install assembled differential gear and final drive cover. Tighten final drive cover bolts in crisscross pattern to 18 ft. lbs. (25 N.m). Install drive flanges with proper snap rings. Install speedometer drive.

5) Install transmission breather sleeve so sleeve extends .8" (21 mm) above vent lip. Install clutch return lever and clutch release bearing. Install multifunction connector, and tighten bolt to 89 INCH lbs. (10 N.m).

TORQUE SPECIFICATIONS
TORQUE SPECIFICATIONS

Application	Ft. Lbs. (N.m)
Final Drive Cover Bolts	18 (25)
Gear Carrier Housing Bolts	18 (25)
Guide Sleeve Bolt	26 (35)
Locking Segment Bolt	18 (25)
Multifunction Sender Retaining Plate Bolt	18 (25)
Oil Filler Plug	18 (25)
Relay Shaft Bolt	30 (40)
Reverse Gear Axle Bolt	26 (35)
Ring Gear Bolt	66 (90)
Shift Cover Bolt	15 (20)
Shift Detent Bolt	18 (25)

	INCH Lbs. (N.m)
Multifunction Connector Bolt	89 (10)
5th/Reverse Gear Lock Bolt	89 (10)

Geo: Metro
Suzuki: Swift

APPLICATION & LABOR TIMES

APPLICATION & LABOR TIMES

Vehicle Application	Labor Times		Series
	[1] R & I	[2] Overhaul	
Geo Metro			
1.0L Engine	3.2	3.7	5-Speed
1.3L Engine	4.3	3.7	5-Speed
Suzuki Swift			
1.0L	3.2	3.7	5-Speed
1.3L	4.3	3.7	5-Speed

[1] – Removal and installation of transaxle from vehicle chassis.
[2] – Bench overhaul time for transaxle/differential. DOES NOT include removal and installation.

IDENTIFICATION

Transaxle identification number plate is located on upper surface of transaxle case. See Fig. 1.

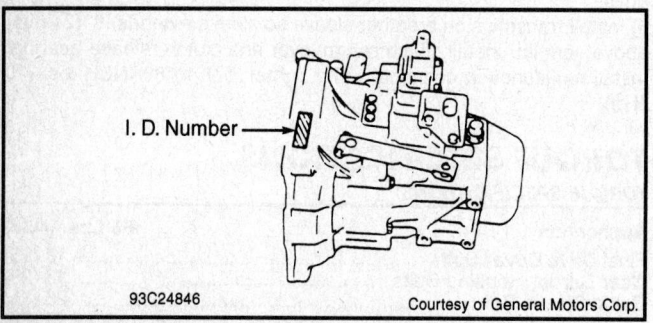

I. D. Number

93C24846   Courtesy of General Motors Corp.

Fig. 1: Identification Number Plate Location

DESCRIPTION

Transaxle provides 5 forward speeds and one reverse speed by means of 3 synchronizers and 3 shafts: input shaft, countershaft and reverse shaft.

LUBRICATION & ADJUSTMENTS

See appropriate MANUAL TRANSMISSION SERVICING article in TRANSMISSION SERVICING section.

TROUBLE SHOOTING

See GENERAL TROUBLE SHOOTING article in this section.

ON-VEHICLE SERVICE

DRIVE AXLE SHAFTS

See appropriate AXLE SHAFTS article in AXLE SHAFTS & TRANSFER CASES section.

SPEEDOMETER DRIVEN GEAR ASSEMBLY

Removal – Pull up speedometer cable boot. Remove speedometer case clip and disconnect speedometer cable from case. Remove bolt and speedometer driven gear case assembly.
Disassembly – Drive out spring pin and remove speedometer driven gear. See Fig. 2. Hold driven gear case with camshaft sprocket holder and remove oil seal. Remove "O" ring.
Reassembly – Install oil seal with spring side down. Install speedometer driven gear into case and drive in spring pin. Check driven gear for smooth rotation. Install "O" ring.

Installation – Apply grease to "O" ring and install case assembly to transaxle. Install bolt and torque to 53 INCH lbs. (6 N.m). Connect cable and install clip and boot.

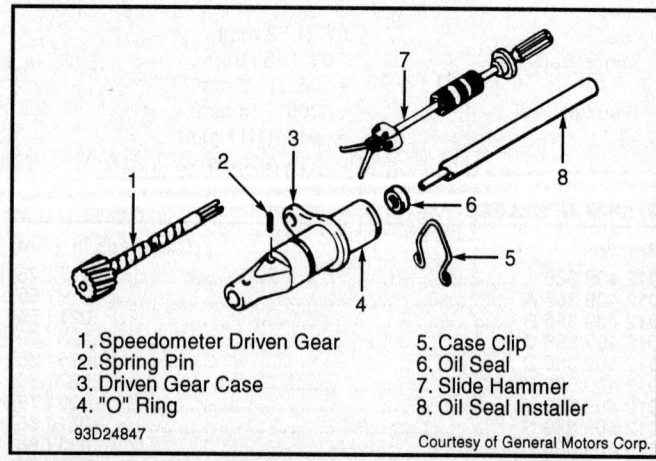

1. Speedometer Driven Gear
2. Spring Pin
3. Driven Gear Case
4. "O" Ring
5. Case Clip
6. Oil Seal
7. Slide Hammer
8. Oil Seal Installer

93D24847   Courtesy of General Motors Corp.

Fig. 2: Exploded View Of Speedometer Driven Gear Assembly

REMOVAL & INSTALLATION

See appropriate MANUAL TRANSMISSION REMOVAL article in TRANSMISSION SERVICING section.

TRANSAXLE DISASSEMBLY

1) Remove bolts and transaxle side cover. Remove snap ring and hub plate. See Fig. 3. Engage transaxle by pushing in on gear shift shaft. Engage 5th gear by sliding 5th speed sleeve down to lock transaxle in 2 gears. This allows countershaft nut removal.

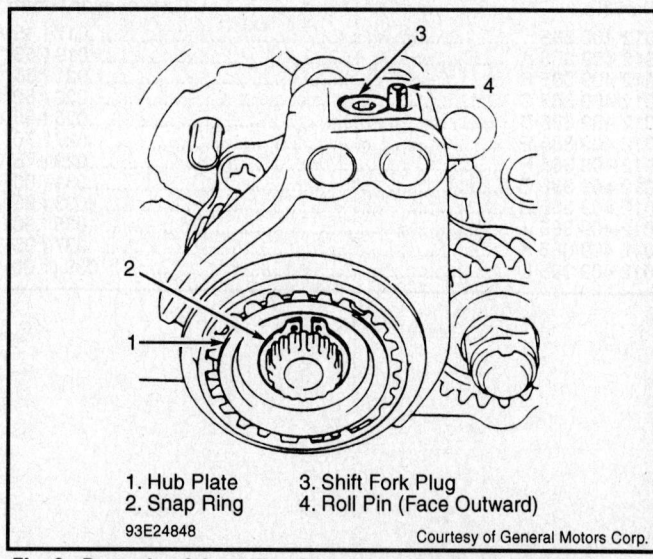

1. Hub Plate
2. Snap Ring
3. Shift Fork Plug
4. Roll Pin (Face Outward)

93E24848   Courtesy of General Motors Corp.

Fig. 3: Removing & Installing Snap Ring, Hub Plate, Roll Pin & Ball Plug

2) Unstake countershaft lock nut and remove. Remove shift fork plug and guide ball. Move transaxle gear shift shaft to Neutral position. Drive out roll pin from shift fork.
3) Using a 2-jaw puller, remove 5th speed shift fork, 5th speed sleeve and hub, synchronizer unit, input shaft 5th gear and bearing as an assembly. Remove 5th speed shift fork from 5th speed sleeve and hub assembly. Remove synchronizer ring spring and 5th speed hub from 5th speed sleeve.
4) Using a 2-jaw gear puller, remove countershaft 5th gear from countershaft. Remove 6 screws, bearing set shim and left case plate from

left-side case. Remove 3 bolts, left case cap and "O" ring from left-side case. Remove gear shift yoke bolt and 3 gear shift fork shaft bolts with washers, springs and steel balls. *See Fig. 4.*

NOTE: Springs are color coded. Note which spring goes into each hole to aid in reassembly.

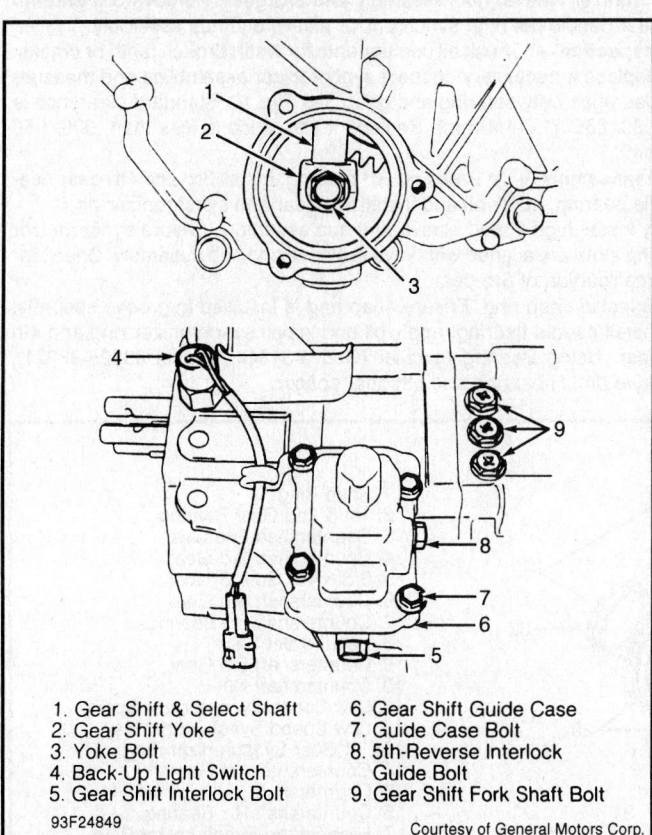

1. Gear Shift & Select Shaft
2. Gear Shift Yoke
3. Yoke Bolt
4. Back-Up Light Switch
5. Gear Shift Interlock Bolt
6. Gear Shift Guide Case
7. Guide Case Bolt
8. 5th-Reverse Interlock Guide Bolt
9. Gear Shift Fork Shaft Bolt

93F24849

Courtesy of General Motors Corp.

Fig. 4: Identifying Gear Shift Bolt Locations

5) Remove 4 bolts, wiring harness clamp and gear shift guide case. Remove gear shift interlock bolt with washer. Remove back-up light switch. Remove gear shift and select shaft assembly.
6) Remove reverse shaft bolt with washer. *See Fig. 5.* Remove 11 case bolts from outside of transaxle and 2 bolts from clutch housing side. Separate case halves with right-side case (clutch housing) facing downward.
7) Remove gear shift yoke, reverse idler gear shaft with washer and reverse idler gear. *See Fig. 6.* Remove 5th and reverse gear shift guide shaft together with 5th and reverse gear shift shaft by pushing up high speed gear shift shaft and shifting to 4th gear.
8) Remove differential gear assembly by lifting upward. Remove input shaft assembly, countershaft assembly, high and low speed gear shift shafts together.
9) Remove high and low speed shift shafts from input shaft and countershaft assemblies. Separate input shaft assembly from countershaft assembly.
10) Remove speedometer driven gear from right-side case. Using a slide hammer, remove input shaft oil seal from right-side case. Remove 2 bolts and reverse shift lever from right-side case. Remove countershaft RH bearing race. Remove magnet.
11) Remove one bolt, then remove gear shift arm from gear shift shaft. Remove gear shift shaft bolt with washer, spring and steel ball. *See Fig. 7.* Remove gear shift shaft, boot and oil seal. Remove differential side RH oil seal from right-side case.
12) Remove bolts and reverse gear shift lever. *See Fig. 6.* Remove bolt and oil gutter. *See Fig. 8.*

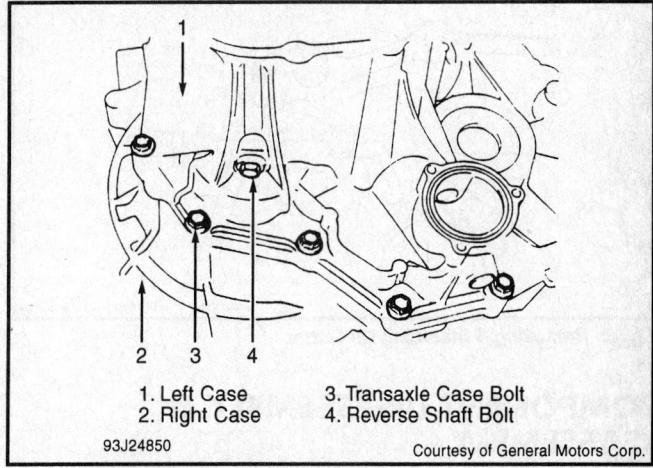

1. Left Case
2. Right Case
3. Transaxle Case Bolt
4. Reverse Shaft Bolt

93J24850

Courtesy of General Motors Corp.

Fig. 5: Removing & Installing Case Bolts

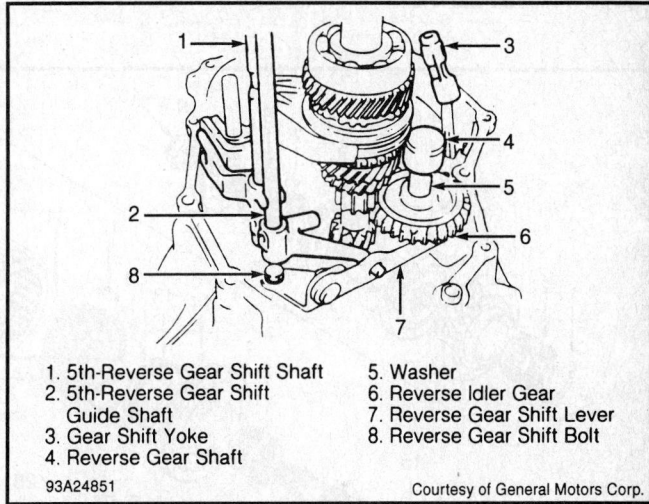

1. 5th-Reverse Gear Shift Shaft
2. 5th-Reverse Gear Shift Guide Shaft
3. Gear Shift Yoke
4. Reverse Gear Shaft
5. Washer
6. Reverse Idler Gear
7. Reverse Gear Shift Lever
8. Reverse Gear Shift Bolt

93A24851

Courtesy of General Motors Corp.

Fig. 6: Removing Reverse Idler Gear

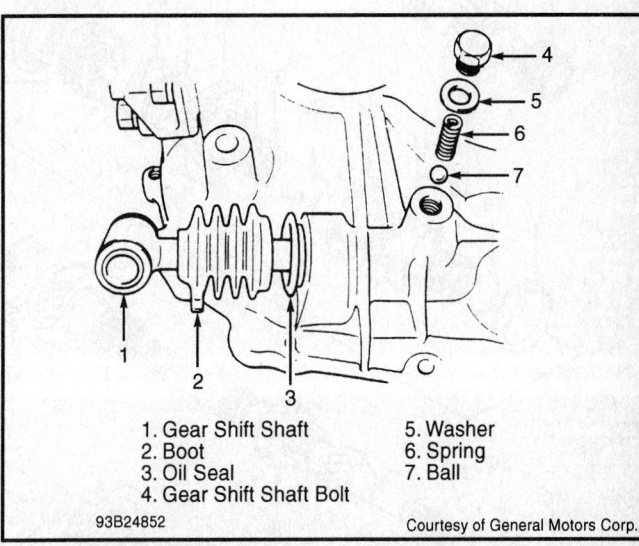

1. Gear Shift Shaft
2. Boot
3. Oil Seal
4. Gear Shift Shaft Bolt
5. Washer
6. Spring
7. Ball

93B24852

Courtesy of General Motors Corp.

Fig. 7: Removing & Installing Gear Shift Shaft

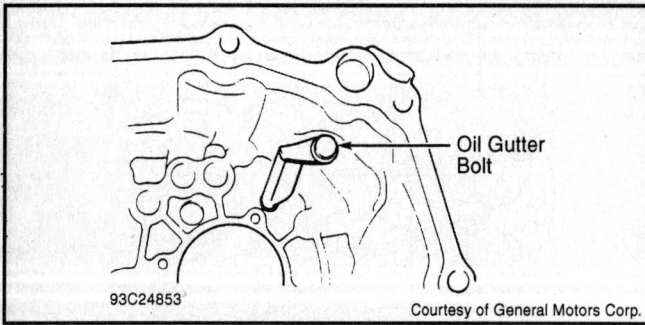

Fig. 8: Removing & Installing Oil Gutter

COMPONENT DISASSEMBLY & REASSEMBLY

SPEEDOMETER DRIVEN GEAR ASSEMBLY

See ON-VEHICLE SERVICE.

INPUT SHAFT ASSEMBLY

Disassembly – 1) Using a split plate and press, remove RH bearing. *See Fig. 9.* Press off 5th gear spacer, LH bearing and 4th gear as an assembly. Remove 3rd and 4th gear needle bearing, high speed synchronizer ring and snap ring.

2) Using a split plate (flat side up) and press, remove high speed synchronizer sleeve, hub assembly and 3rd gear. Remove 3rd and 4th gear needle bearing, synchronizer sleeve and hub assembly.

Inspection – Check all components for wear, broken teeth or cracks. Replace if necessary. Inspect synchronizer assemblies and measure clearance between ring and gear. *See Fig. 10.* Standard clearance is .039-.055" (1.0-1.4 mm). Replace if clearance is less than .020" (.50 mm).

Reassembly – 1) Press on RH bearing. Install 3rd and 4th gear needle bearing, apply oil and install 3rd gear and synchronizer ring.

2) Install high speed sleeve and hub assembly. Ensure synchronizer ring slots are aligned with keys in sleeve and hub assembly. Check for free rotation of 3rd gear.

3) Install snap ring. Ensure snap ring is installed in groove securely. Install needle bearing, apply oil and install synchronizer ring and 4th gear. Using Bearing Installer (Geo J-34844, Suzuki 09925-98221), drive on LH bearing and 5th gear spacer.

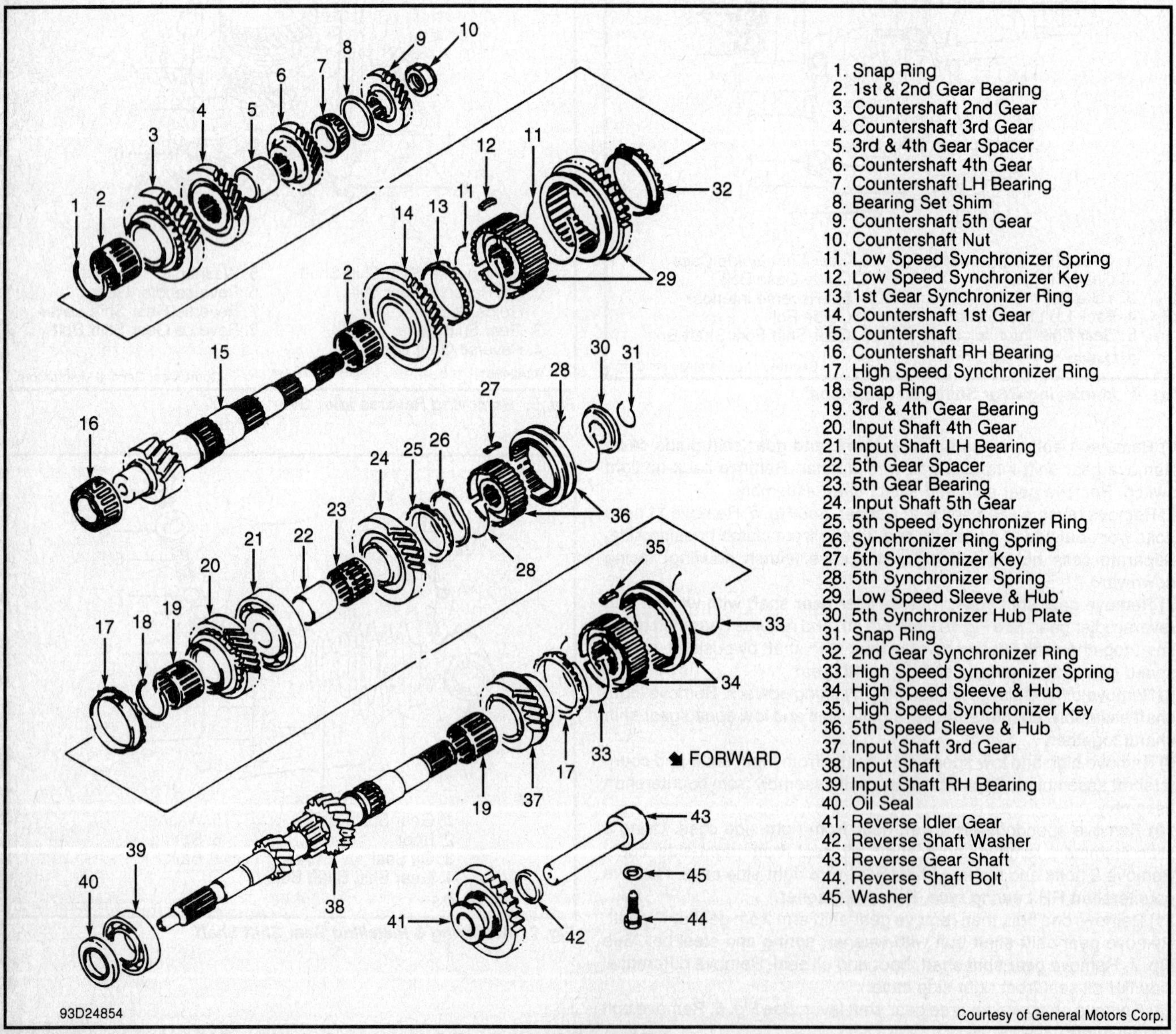

1. Snap Ring
2. 1st & 2nd Gear Bearing
3. Countershaft 2nd Gear
4. Countershaft 3rd Gear
5. 3rd & 4th Gear Spacer
6. Countershaft 4th Gear
7. Countershaft LH Bearing
8. Bearing Set Shim
9. Countershaft 5th Gear
10. Countershaft Nut
11. Low Speed Synchronizer Spring
12. Low Speed Synchronizer Key
13. 1st Gear Synchronizer Ring
14. Countershaft 1st Gear
15. Countershaft
16. Countershaft RH Bearing
17. High Speed Synchronizer Ring
18. Snap Ring
19. 3rd & 4th Gear Bearing
20. Input Shaft 4th Gear
21. Input Shaft LH Bearing
22. 5th Gear Spacer
23. 5th Gear Bearing
24. Input Shaft 5th Gear
25. 5th Speed Synchronizer Ring
26. Synchronizer Ring Spring
27. 5th Synchronizer Key
28. 5th Synchronizer Spring
29. Low Speed Sleeve & Hub
30. 5th Synchronizer Hub Plate
31. Snap Ring
32. 2nd Gear Synchronizer Ring
33. High Speed Synchronizer Spring
34. High Speed Sleeve & Hub
35. High Speed Synchronizer Key
36. 5th Speed Sleeve & Hub
37. Input Shaft 3rd Gear
38. Input Shaft
39. Input Shaft RH Bearing
40. Oil Seal
41. Reverse Idler Gear
42. Reverse Shaft Washer
43. Reverse Gear Shaft
44. Reverse Shaft Bolt
45. Washer

♦ FORWARD

93D24854

Courtesy of General Motors Corp.

Fig. 9: Exploded View Of Input Shaft, Countershaft & Reverse Shaft Assemblies

COUNTERSHAFT ASSEMBLY

Disassembly – **1)** Using a split plate and press, press off LH bearing and 4th gear. See Fig. 9. Press off 3rd and 4th gear spacer with countershaft 3rd gear and 2nd gear from countershaft. Remove 2nd synchronizer ring and snap ring.

2) Using a split plate and press, press off low speed synchronizer sleeve and hub with 1st gear. Remove needle bearing. Press off 1st and second gear bearing from countershaft.

3) Remove low speed sleeve and synchronizer spring from low speed hub. Remove 1st and 2nd gear bearing from countershaft. Press off RH countershaft bearing.

Inspection – Check all components for wear, broken teeth or cracks. Replace if necessary. Inspect synchronizer assemblies and measure clearance between ring and gear. See Fig. 10. Standard clearance is .039-.055" (1.0-1.4 mm). Replace if less than .020" (.50 mm).

Reassembly – **1)** Using Bearing Installer (Geo J-34846, Suzuki 09923-78210) and a hammer, drive on RH bearing. Install 1st and 2nd gear needle bearing, apply oil and install 1st gear and 1st gear synchronizer ring. Ensure proper synchronizer ring is used. See Fig. 11.

NOTE: Key slot width of 1st gear synchronizer ring is smaller than that of the 2nd gear synchronizer ring.

---

2) Support countershaft in bearing installer and press on low speed sleeve and hub assembly. Ensure synchronizer key slots are aligned with keys. Check for free rotation of 1st gear.

3) Install snap ring. Ensure snap ring is installed securely in groove. Install needle bearing, apply oil and install 2nd gear synchronizer ring and 2nd gear.

4) Support countershaft in bearing installer. Press on 3rd gear and spacer. Press on 4th gear. With countershaft still supported in bearing installer, install LH bearing.

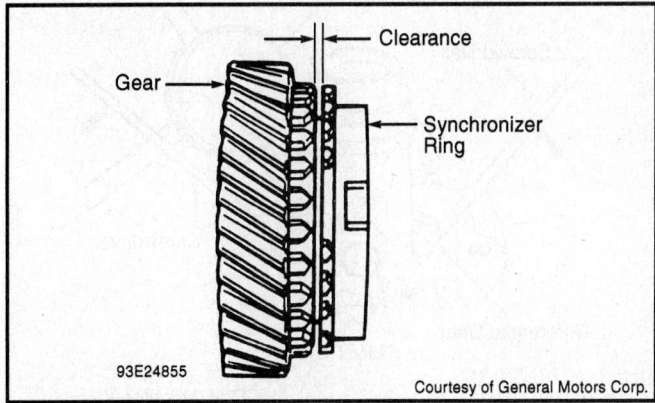

Fig. 10: Checking Gear & Synchronizer Ring

GEAR SHIFT & SELECT SHAFT ASSEMBLY

Disassembly – Remove "E" rings. Drive out spring pins with standard punch. See Fig. 12.

Reassembly – Install components, "E" rings and drive in spring pins. Assemble 5th and reverse gear shift cam by winding cam guide return spring half to one full turn before driving in spring pin. Support shaft with wood block to prevent bending shaft.

HIGH SPEED & LOW SPEED GEAR SHIFT SHAFTS

Disassembly – Drive out spring pins. Remove forks and yokes from shaft. See Fig. 13.

Reassembly – Install forks and yokes on shaft. Drive in spring pins. Support shafts with wood block to prevent bending shafts.

5TH & REVERSE GEAR SHIFTER

Disassembly – Drive out spring pins. Remove yoke, arm, steel balls and springs. See Fig. 14.

Reassembly – Reverse disassembly procedure. Ensure 2 steel balls are installed in reverse gear shift arm, and that spring pin slit "A" is installed toward front.

DIFFERENTIAL ASSEMBLY

Disassembly – **1)** Using a 2-jaw puller, remove both RH and LH bearings. Remove speedometer drive gear.

2) Remove 8 bolts and ring gear from differential carrier. Drive out pinion shaft roll pin. Remove pinion shaft, pinion gears with thrust washers and side gears with thrust washers.

Reassembly – **1)** Install thrust washers and side gears. Install pinion gears and thrust washers. Install pinion shaft.

2) Install differential carrier in a soft-jawed vise. Apply measuring tip of dial indicator to top surface of side gears. Move side gears up and down. See Fig. 15. Thrust play should be .002-.013" (.05-.33 mm). Select and install suitable thrust washers to obtain specified thrust play. Thrust washers are available in thicknesses of .035-.047" (.90-1.20 mm) in .002" (.05) increments.

3) Drive in pinion shaft roll pin until flush with case. Install speedometer drive gear. Using appropriate bearing installer, press on both LH and RH bearings. Apply Loctite to ring gear bolts. Install ring gear on differential carrier and torque bolts to 63 ft. lbs. (85 N.m).

TRANSAXLE REASSEMBLY

1) Install reverse gear shift lever. Apply Loctite to bolts and install bolts loosely. Measure and set lever end .2" (5 mm) from reverse gear shaft bore. See Fig. 16. Torque bolts to 17 ft. lbs. (23 N.m).

2) Install input shaft oil seal with spring side upward. Install countershaft RH bearing race. See Fig. 16.

3) Apply grease to gear shift shaft oil seal lip and install, spring side toward case. Install gear shift shaft, boot, steel ball, spring and washer. See Fig. 7. Apply sealant to bolt and torque to 10 ft. lbs. (14 N.m).

4) Install boot over oil seal. Install gear shift shaft inner oil seal with spring side toward case. Install differential RH oil seal and torque bolt with washer flush with case. Apply grease to seal lip.

5) Install gear shift arm onto gear shift shaft. Drive in roll pin coated with Loctite. Install magnet to case. Install oil gutter. See Fig. 8. Coat bolt threads with Loctite and torque to 102 INCH lbs. (12 N.m).

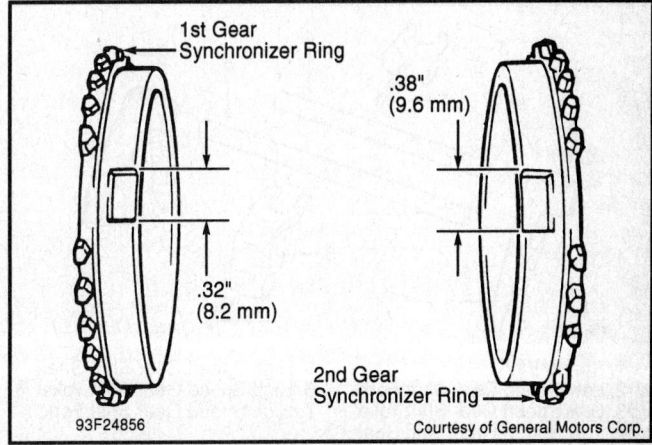

Fig. 11: Identifying 1st & 2nd Synchronizer Ring

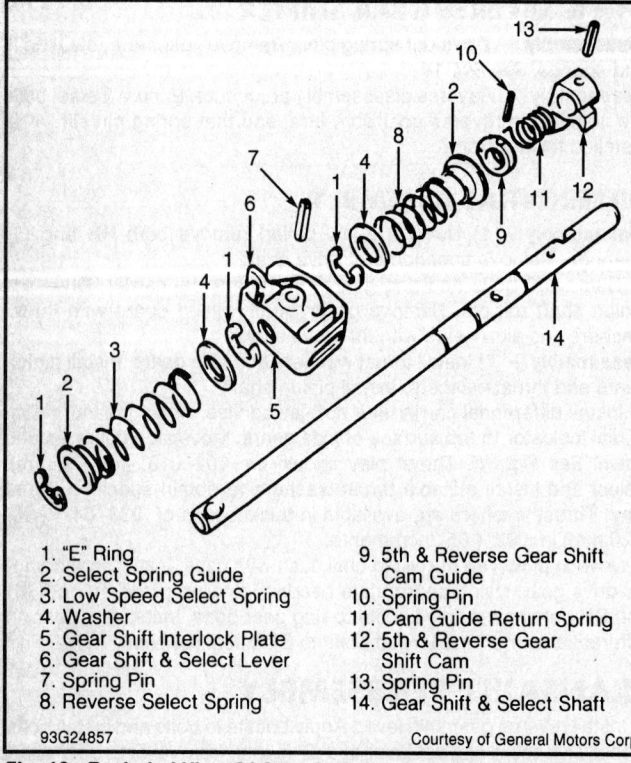

1. "E" Ring
2. Select Spring Guide
3. Low Speed Select Spring
4. Washer
5. Gear Shift Interlock Plate
6. Gear Shift & Select Lever
7. Spring Pin
8. Reverse Select Spring
9. 5th & Reverse Gear Shift Cam Guide
10. Spring Pin
11. Cam Guide Return Spring
12. 5th & Reverse Gear Shift Cam
13. Spring Pin
14. Gear Shift & Select Shaft

93G24857 Courtesy of General Motors Corp.

Fig. 12: Exploded View Of Gear Shift & Select Shaft Assembly

6) Apply grease to differential side LH oil seal lip. Install seal with spring side toward case. Install countershaft LH bearing race by tapping lightly with plastic hammer.

7) Assemble input shaft and countershaft together with high and low speed gear shift shaft assemblies. Install into right-side case. *See Fig. 17.* Ensure countershaft is engaged to final gear.

8) Coat speedometer driven gear case assembly "O" ring with oil and install to case. Torque bolt to 53 INCH lbs. (6 N.m). Install differential assembly flush into right-side case. Rotate differential assembly to ensure speedometer drive gear meshes with speedometer driven gear.

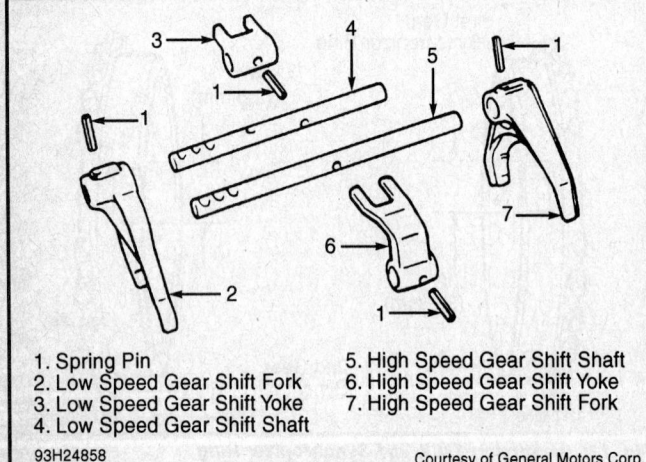

1. Spring Pin
2. Low Speed Gear Shift Fork
3. Low Speed Gear Shift Yoke
4. Low Speed Gear Shift Shaft
5. High Speed Gear Shift Shaft
6. High Speed Gear Shift Yoke
7. High Speed Gear Shift Fork

93H24858 Courtesy of General Motors Corp.

Fig. 13: Exploded View Of Low & High Speed Shifter Assemblies

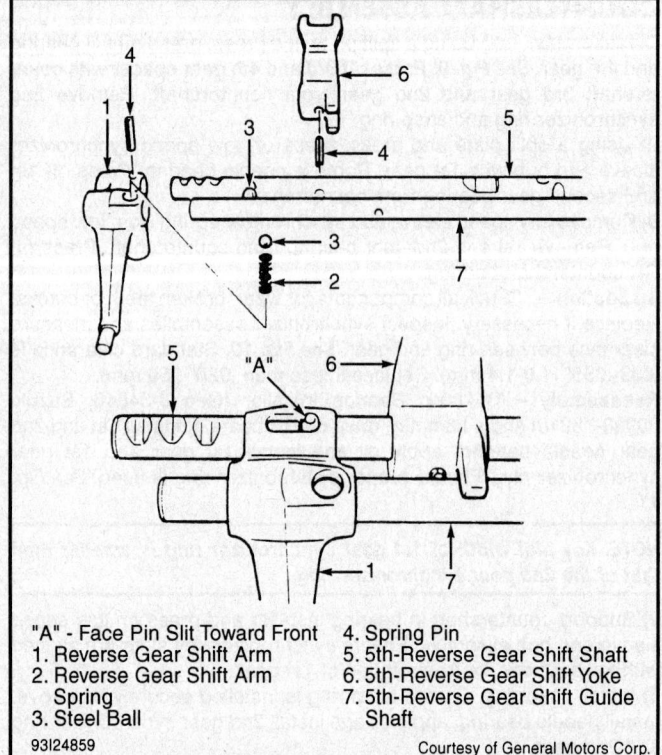

"A" - Face Pin Slit Toward Front
1. Reverse Gear Shift Arm
2. Reverse Gear Shift Arm Spring
3. Steel Ball
4. Spring Pin
5. 5th-Reverse Gear Shift Shaft
6. 5th-Reverse Gear Shift Yoke
7. 5th-Reverse Gear Shift Guide Shaft

93I24859 Courtesy of General Motors Corp.

Fig. 14: Exploded View Of 5th & Reverse Shifter Assembly

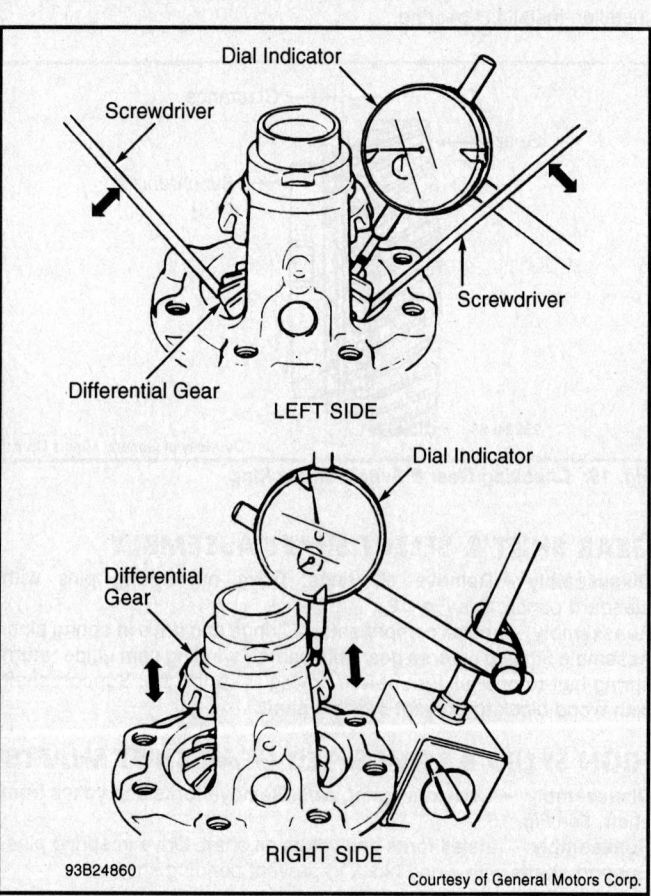

93B24860 Courtesy of General Motors Corp.

Fig. 15: Measuring Side Gear Thrust Play

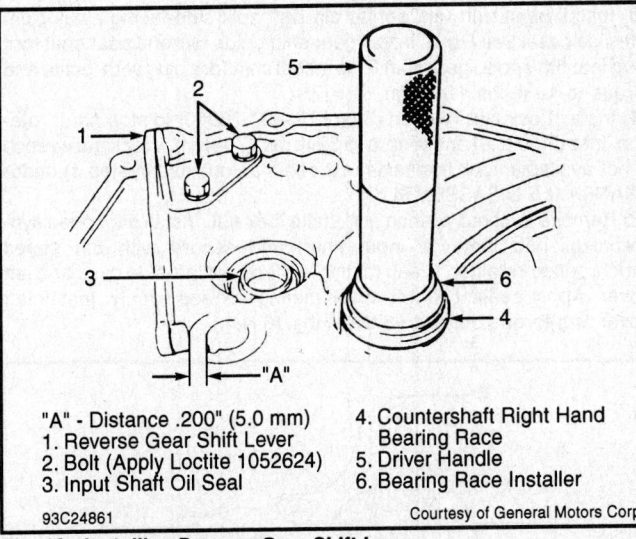

"A" - Distance .200" (5.0 mm)
1. Reverse Gear Shift Lever
2. Bolt (Apply Loctite 1052624)
3. Input Shaft Oil Seal
4. Countershaft Right Hand Bearing Race
5. Driver Handle
6. Bearing Race Installer

93C24861
Courtesy of General Motors Corp.

Fig. 16: Installing Reverse Gear Shift Lever

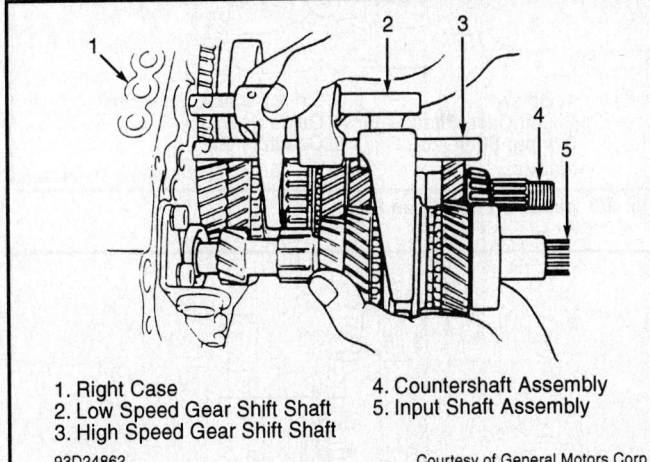

1. Right Case
2. Low Speed Gear Shift Shaft
3. High Speed Gear Shift Shaft
4. Countershaft Assembly
5. Input Shaft Assembly

93D24862
Courtesy of General Motors Corp.

Fig. 17: Installing Input Shaft & Countershaft

9) Install 5th and reverse gear shift shaft with 5th and reverse gear shift guide shaft into right-side case. *See Fig. 6.* Join reverse gear shift arm to reverse gear shift lever.

10) Install reverse idler gear with reverse gear shift lever and insert reverse gear shaft with washer into case through idler gear. Align shaft mark "A" with case mark "B". *See Fig. 18.* Install gear shift yoke to gear shift arm. Clean mating surfaces of left and right-side cases.

11) Coat mating surface of left-side case with sealant and install to right-side case. Install 2 case bolts inside right-side case (clutch housing) and 11 case bolts to outside of left-side case and torque to 16 ft. lbs. (22 N.m). *See Fig. 5.* Install reverse shaft bolt with Loctite and aluminum washer and torque to 10 ft. lbs. (14 N.m).

12) Install gear shift and select shaft assembly into left-side case, inserting bottom of gear shift and select shaft into gear shift yoke. Install gear shift interlock bolt and washer into left-side case. Torque to specification. See TORQUE SPECIFICATIONS.

13) Install back-up light switch into left-side case. Apply silicone sealer to gear shift guide case mating surface. Install gear shift guide case, retaining clamp and secure with 4 bolts. Torque to 89 INCH lbs. (10 N.m). *See Fig. 19.*

14) Inspect shift shaft detent springs for deterioration or deformation. See SHIFT SHAFT DETENT SPRINGS LENGTH table. Replace with new springs as necessary. Install steel balls, spring, washers and bolts. *See Fig. 20.* Torque gear shift shaft bolts to 10 ft. lbs. (14 N.m).

SHIFT SHAFT DETENT SPRINGS LENGTH

Spring	Length In. (mm)
Low Speed Spring	
Standard Length	1.028 (26.10)
Service Limit	.984 (25.00)
High Speed Spring	
Standard Length	1.579 (40.10)
Service Limit	1.535 (39.00)

15) Install gear shift yoke bolt with loctite and torque to 26 ft. lbs. (35 N.m). *See Fig. 4.* Install left case cap "O" ring and left case cap to left-side case. Torque to 89 INCH lbs. (10 N.m).

16) Install countershaft LH bearing race to bearing. Select suitable shim to adjust clearance "A". *See Fig. 21.* Install shim on bearing race. Place Flat Gauge Bar (Geo J34673) over it and compress. Measure "A" using feeler gauge. Clearance should be .0031-.0047" (.08-.12 mm).

17) Install left case plate, inserting end in groove of shift guide shaft. *See Fig. 22.* Apply Loctite to screws and torque to 102 INCH lbs. (12 N.m). Ensure countershaft can be rotated by hand.

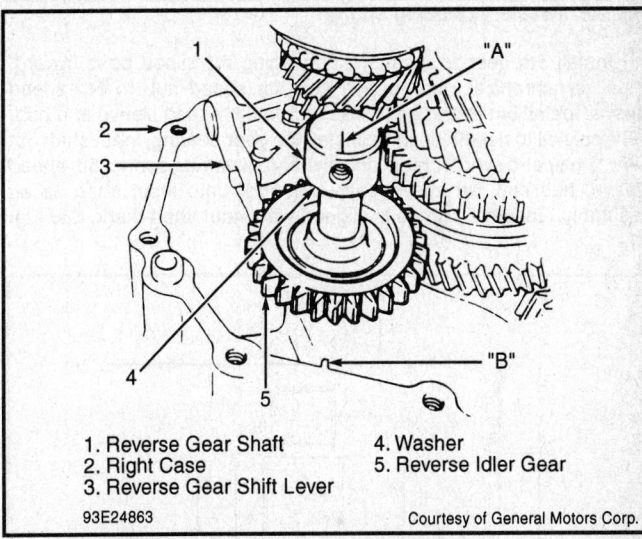

1. Reverse Gear Shaft
2. Right Case
3. Reverse Gear Shift Lever
4. Washer
5. Reverse Idler Gear

93E24863
Courtesy of General Motors Corp.

Fig. 18: Installing & Aligning Reverse Gear Shaft

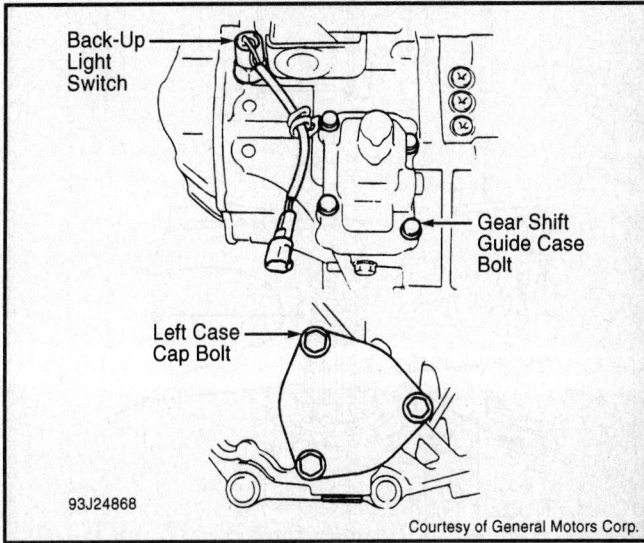

Back-Up Light Switch

Gear Shift Guide Case Bolt

Left Case Cap Bolt

93J24868
Courtesy of General Motors Corp.

Fig. 19: Installing Gear Shift Guide Case

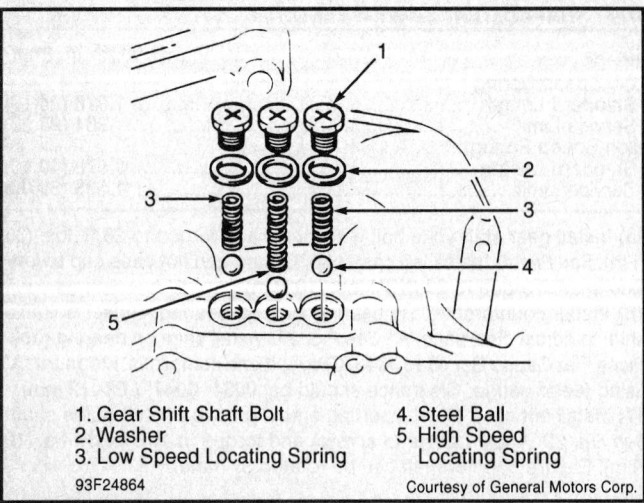

1. Gear Shift Shaft Bolt
2. Washer
3. Low Speed Locating Spring
4. Steel Ball
5. High Speed Locating Spring

93F24864   Courtesy of General Motors Corp.

Fig. 20: Installing Locating Spring

18) Install 5th gear to countershaft, facing machined boss inward. Install synchronizer ring springs and 5th speed hub to 5th speed sleeve. Install 5th speed gear shift fork to 5th speed sleeve and hub.
19) Apply oil to needle bearing. Install 5th gear bearing, input shaft 5th gear, 5th speed synchronizer ring, synchronizer ring spring, 5th speed sleeve, hub and 5th speed gear shift fork onto input shaft as an assembly. Ensure oil grove is aligned with input shaft mark. See Fig. 23.

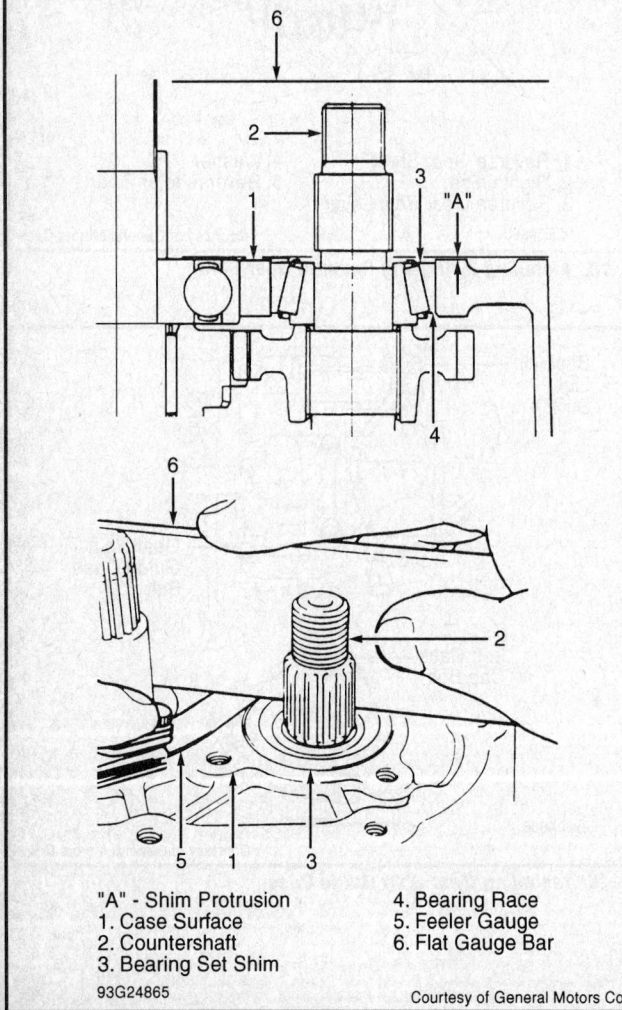

"A" - Shim Protrusion
1. Case Surface
2. Countershaft
3. Bearing Set Shim
4. Bearing Race
5. Feeler Gauge
6. Flat Gauge Bar

93G24865   Courtesy of General Motors Corp.

Fig. 21: Selecting Bearing Set Shim

20) Install gear shift fork spring pin with split side facing away from left-side case. See Fig. 3. Install gear shift guide ball and gear shift fork plug into 5th speed gear shift fork. Install shift fork plug with loctite and torque to 10 ft. lbs. (14 N.m).
21) Install Lock Nut Wrench (Suzuki 09927-76010) to stop shaft rotation. Install lock nut and torque to 52 ft. lbs. (70 N.m). If lock nut wrench is not available, lock transaxle in 2 gears as outlined in step 1) under TRANSAXLE DISASSEMBLY.
22) Remove lock nut wrench and stake lock nut. Install 5th speed synchronizer hub plate to input shaft and secure with 5th speed synchronizer retainer. Clean mating surfaces of left-side case and left cover. Apply sealant to left cover mating surface evenly. Install left cover and torque bolts to 53 INCH lbs. (6 N.m).

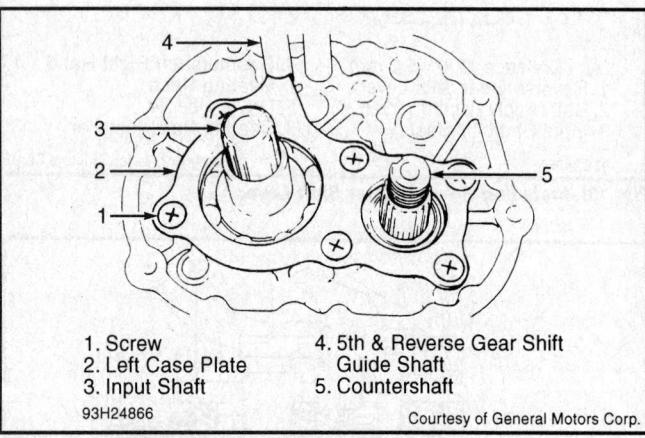

1. Screw
2. Left Case Plate
3. Input Shaft
4. 5th & Reverse Gear Shift Guide Shaft
5. Countershaft

93H24866   Courtesy of General Motors Corp.

Fig. 22: Installing Left Case Plate

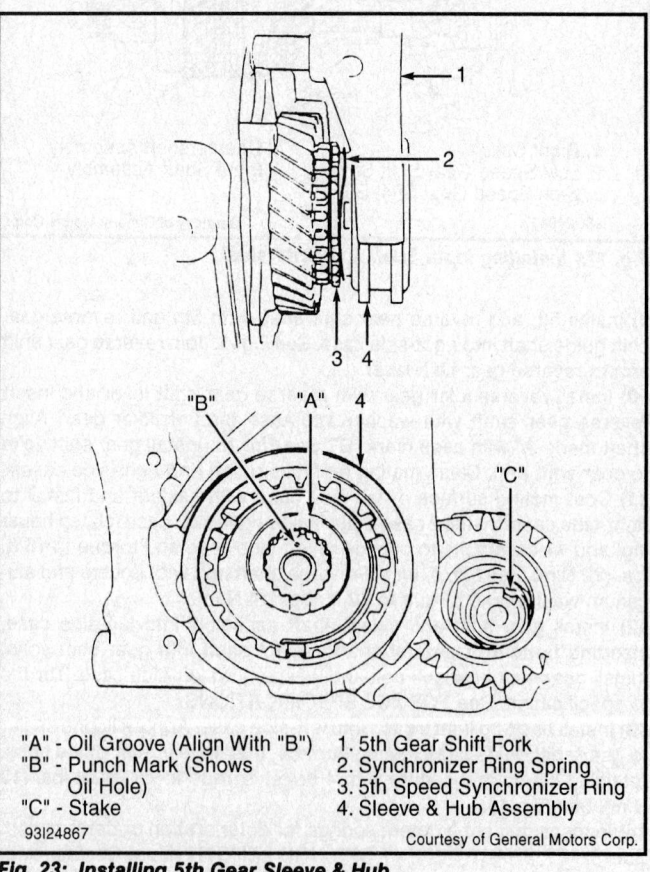

"A" - Oil Groove (Align With "B")
"B" - Punch Mark (Shows Oil Hole)
"C" - Stake
1. 5th Gear Shift Fork
2. Synchronizer Ring Spring
3. 5th Speed Synchronizer Ring
4. Sleeve & Hub Assembly

93I24867   Courtesy of General Motors Corp.

Fig. 23: Installing 5th Gear Sleeve & Hub

TRANSMISSION SPECIFICATIONS

TRANSMISSION SPECIFICATIONS

Application	In. (mm)
Reverse Gear Shift Lever-To-Idler Shaft Clearance	.20 (5.0)
Synchronizer Ring-To-Gear Clearance	.039-055 (1.0-1.4)
High/Low Speed Gear Shift Fork-To-	
Synchronizer Sleeve Clearance (Maximum)	.039 (1.0)
Differential Side Gear End Play	
Standard	.002-.013 (.05-.33)
Minimum	.002 (.05)
Low Speed & 5th Speed Locating Spring Length	
Standard	1.028 (26.1)
Minimum	.984 (25.0)
High Speed Locating Spring Length	
Standard	1.597 (40.1)
Minimum	1.535 (39.0)
Bearing Set Shim Clearance	.0032-.0047 (.081-.119)

TORQUE SPECIFICATIONS

TORQUE SPECIFICATIONS

Application	Ft. Lbs. (N.m)
Back-Up Light Switch	15 (20)
Countershaft Lock Nut	52 (70)
Gear Shift Interlock Bolts	
Strength 7	17 (23)
Strength 9	25 (34)
Gear Shift Shaft Bolts	10 (14)
Left-To-Right Case Bolts	16 (22)
Reverse Gear Shift Lever Bolts	17 (23)
Reverse Idler Shaft Bolt	10 (14)
Ring Gear Bolts	63 (85)
Yoke & Shaft Bolt	26 (35)
5th Gear Shift Fork Plug	10 (14)

Application	INCH Lbs. (N.m)
Gear Shift Guide Case Bolts	89 (10)
Left Case Cap Bolts	89 (10)
Left Case Plate Screws	102 (12)
Left Cover Bolts	53 (6)
Oil Gutter Bolt	102 (12)
Speedometer Case Bolt	53 (6)

MANUAL TRANSMISSIONS
Geo Tracker & Suzuki Sidekick 5-Speed

Geo: Tracker
Suzuki: Sidekick, X-90

APPLICATION & LABOR TIMES

APPLICATION & LABOR TIMES

Vehicle Application	¹ R & I	² Overhaul	Series
Geo Tracker			
2WD	3.5	5.7	5-Speed
4WD	4.5	5.7	5-Speed
Suzuki Sidekick			
2WD	3.5	5.7	5-Speed
4WD	4.5	5.7	5-Speed
Suzuki X-90			
2WD	3.5	5.7	5-Speed
4WD	4.5	5.7	5-Speed

¹ – Removal and installation of transmission from vehicle chassis.
² – Bench overhaul time for transmission. DOES NOT include removal and installation.

IDENTIFICATION

Transmission identification number is stamped on top of transmission clutch housing. *See Fig. 1.*

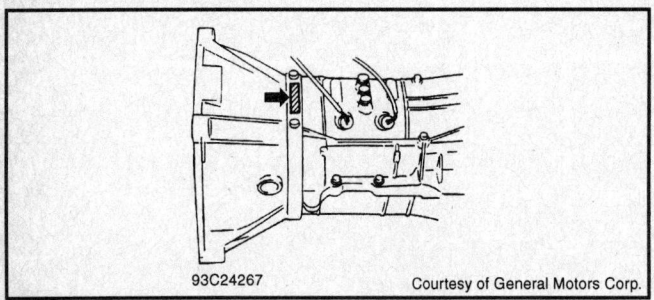

93C24267   Courtesy of General Motors Corp.

Fig. 1: Identification Number Plate Location

DESCRIPTION

Transmission consists of an input shaft, mainshaft, countershaft and reverse gear which are installed in an aluminum case. It has 5 forward speeds in synchromesh and one reverse speed in constant-mesh. *See Fig. 2.*

LUBRICATION & ADJUSTMENTS

See appropriate MANUAL TRANSMISSION SERVICING article in TRANSMISSION SERVICING section.

TROUBLE SHOOTING

See GENERAL TROUBLE SHOOTING article in this section.

ON-VEHICLE SERVICE

SPEEDOMETER DRIVEN GEAR

Removal – Disconnect speedometer cable from extension case (2WD), or transmission case (4WD). Remove ground wire if equipped. Remove gear case bolt and speedometer gear case.
Disassembly – Remove oil seal from speedometer gear case. *See Fig. 3.* Drive out spring pin and remove speedometer driven gear. Remove "O" ring.
Reassembly – Install speedometer driven gear and drive in spring pin. Apply oil to "O" ring and install. Install new oil seal. *See Fig. 3.*
Installation – Install gear case to extension case or transmission and torque bolt to 106 INCH lbs. (12 N.m). Connect speedometer cable to case.

REMOVAL & INSTALLATION

For transmission removal procedure, see appropriate MANUAL TRANSMISSION REMOVAL article in TRANSMISSION SERVICING section.

TRANSMISSION DISASSEMBLY

1) Remove clutch release bearing from input shaft. Remove 8 clutch housing bolts and clutch housing from upper and lower case. Remove 10 gear shift lever case bolts and gear shift lever case. Remove 12 extension case (2WD) or 12 rear case (4WD) bolts, case and case seal.
2) On 2WD extension case, remove oil seal, select return spring bolts, return springs and guide pins. *See Fig. 4.* On all models, remove 8 input shaft bearing retainer bolts. Using two 6 mm bolts, remove input shaft bearing retainer. *See Fig 5.*
3) Remove 10 upper case-to-lower case bolts. Using Case Separator (Geo J37637, or Suzuki 09912-34510), separate case halves. *See Fig. 6.* Remove mainshaft and input shaft assembly.

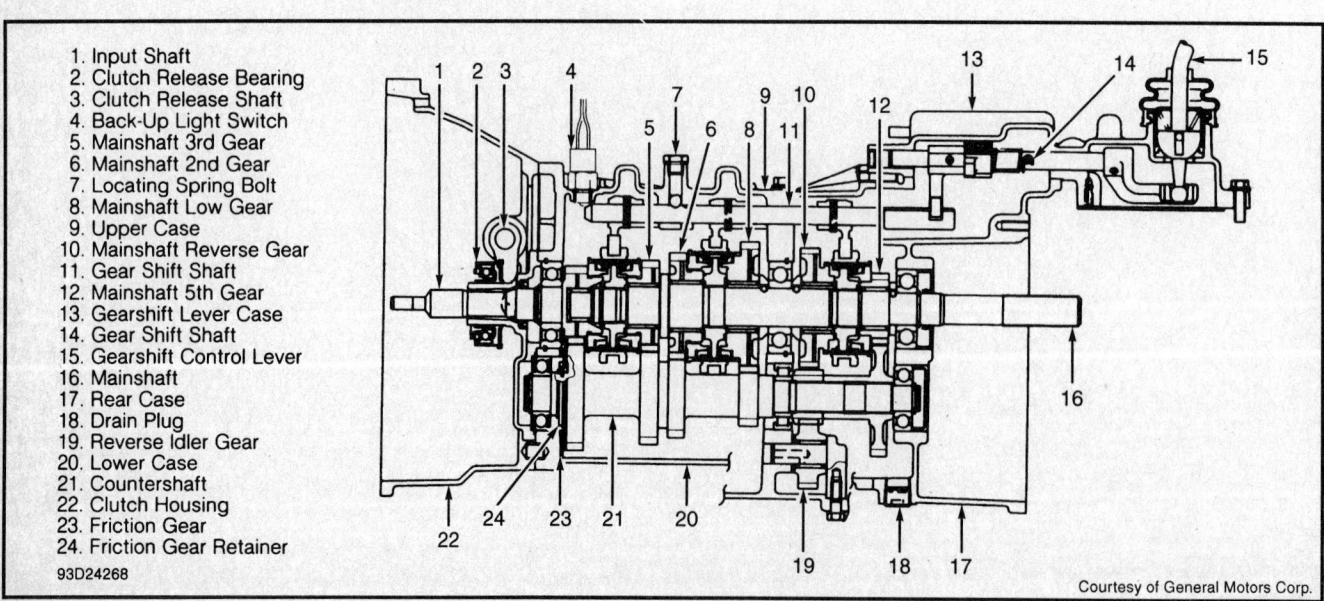

1. Input Shaft
2. Clutch Release Bearing
3. Clutch Release Shaft
4. Back-Up Light Switch
5. Mainshaft 3rd Gear
6. Mainshaft 2nd Gear
7. Locating Spring Bolt
8. Mainshaft Low Gear
9. Upper Case
10. Mainshaft Reverse Gear
11. Gear Shift Shaft
12. Mainshaft 5th Gear
13. Gearshift Lever Case
14. Gear Shift Shaft
15. Gearshift Control Lever
16. Mainshaft
17. Rear Case
18. Drain Plug
19. Reverse Idler Gear
20. Lower Case
21. Countershaft
22. Clutch Housing
23. Friction Gear
24. Friction Gear Retainer

93D24268   Courtesy of General Motors Corp.

Fig. 2: Transmission Cut-Away View (4WD Shown; 2WD Is Similar)

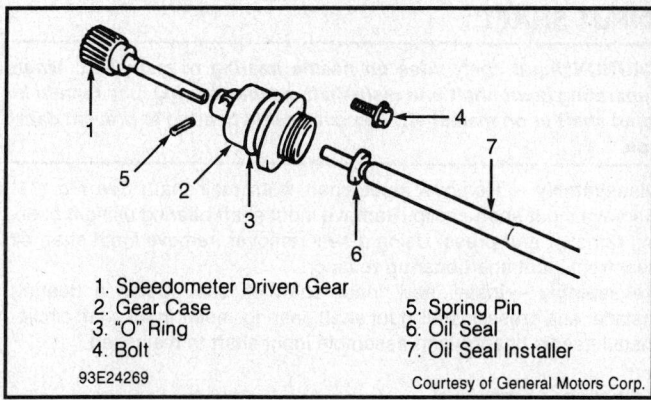

1. Speedometer Driven Gear
2. Gear Case
3. "O" Ring
4. Bolt
5. Spring Pin
6. Oil Seal
7. Oil Seal Installer

93E24269

Courtesy of General Motors Corp.

Fig. 3: Exploded View Of Speedometer Driven Gear Assembly

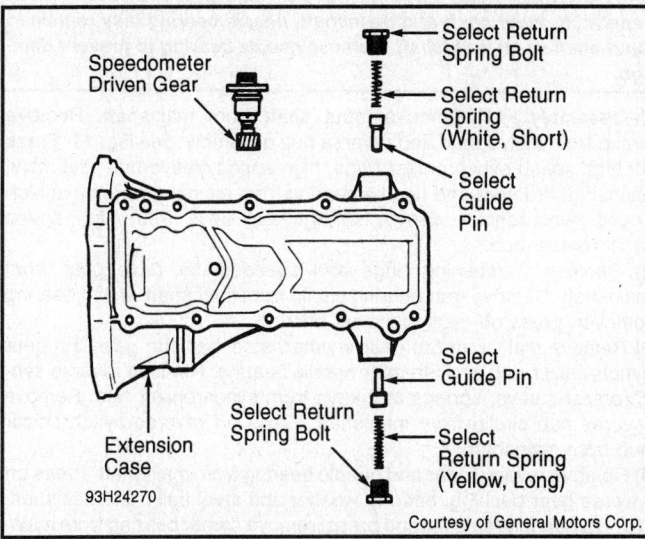

Speedometer Driven Gear

Select Return Spring Bolt

Select Return Spring (White, Short)

Select Guide Pin

Select Guide Pin

Select Return Spring Bolt

Select Return Spring (Yellow, Long)

Extension Case

93H24270

Courtesy of General Motors Corp.

Fig. 4: Exploded View Of Extension Case Components (2WD)

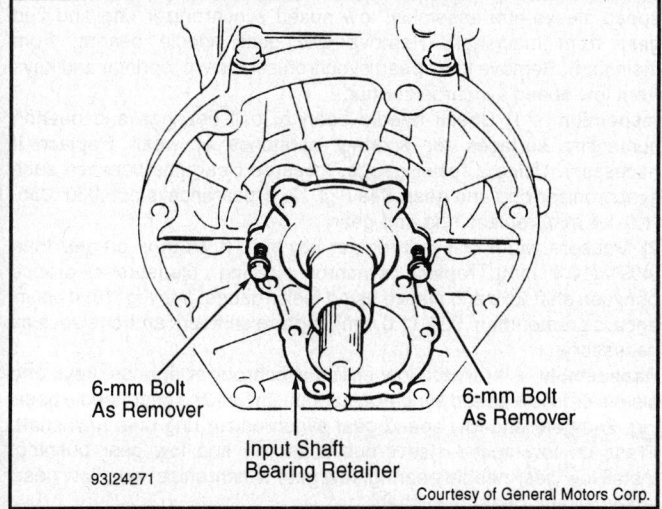

6-mm Bolt As Remover

6-mm Bolt As Remover

Input Shaft Bearing Retainer

93I24271

Courtesy of General Motors Corp.

Fig. 5: Removing Input Shaft Bearing Retainer

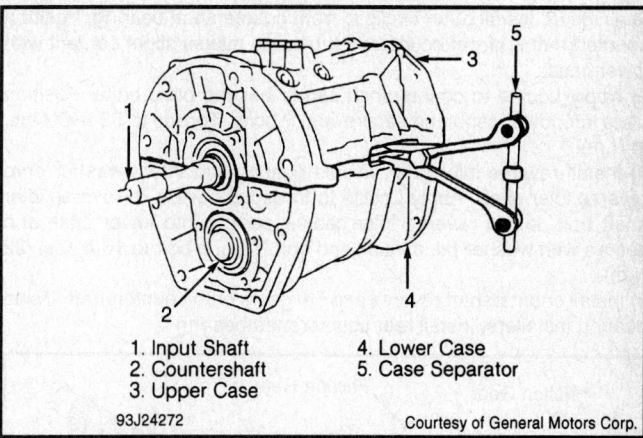

1. Input Shaft
2. Countershaft
3. Upper Case
4. Lower Case
5. Case Separator

93J24272

Courtesy of General Motors Corp.

Fig. 6: Separating Upper & Lower Case

COMPONENT DISASSEMBLY & REASSEMBLY

LOWER CASE ASSEMBLY

Disassembly – 1) Remove rear countershaft circlip. *See Fig. 7.* Using a 2-jaw puller, remove rear bearing. Remove countershaft 5th gear and reverse gear from countershaft. Remove reverse idler shaft bolt, reverse idler shaft and idler gear from lower case. Remove reverse idler gear thrust washer, needle bearing and gear from reverse idler shaft.

2) Remove 2 bolts and countershaft center bearing plate from lower case. Remove front countershaft bearing "C" ring. Tap countershaft rearward with a plastic hammer to remove center bearing from lower case. Pull countershaft forward and remove from lower case. Remove front countershaft bearing circlip from countershaft. Using a 2-jaw puller, remove front bearing from countershaft.

3) Remove friction gear circlip, retainer, pin, spring and friction gear from countershaft. *See Fig. 8.*

Reassembly – 1) Install friction gear, spring, pin, retainer and circlip to countershaft. Install front countershaft bearing and circlip onto countershaft. *See Fig. 9.* Install countershaft center bearing onto countershaft. Press countershaft and center bearing into lower case.

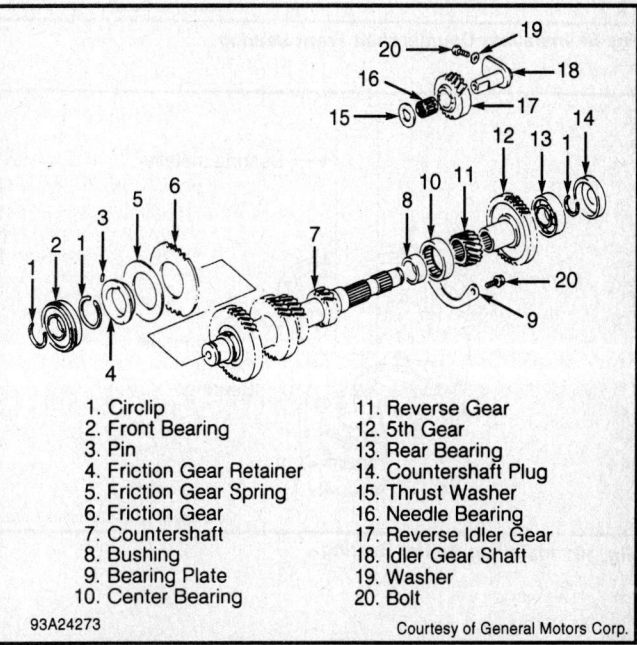

1. Circlip
2. Front Bearing
3. Pin
4. Friction Gear Retainer
5. Friction Gear Spring
6. Friction Gear
7. Countershaft
8. Bushing
9. Bearing Plate
10. Center Bearing
11. Reverse Gear
12. 5th Gear
13. Rear Bearing
14. Countershaft Plug
15. Thrust Washer
16. Needle Bearing
17. Reverse Idler Gear
18. Idler Gear Shaft
19. Washer
20. Bolt

93A24273

Courtesy of General Motors Corp.

Fig. 7: Exploded View Of Countershaft & Reverse Shaft Assemblies

See Fig. 10. Install outer circlip to front countershaft bearing. Position countershaft so front countershaft bearing makes slight contact with lower case.

2) Apply Loctite to countershaft center bearing plate bolts. Position plate into lower case and secure with 2 bolts. Torque to 53 INCH lbs. (6 N.m).

3) Install reverse idler gear, needle bearing and thrust washer onto reverse idler shaft. Apply Loctite to threaded portion of reverse idler shaft bolt. Install reverse idler gear assembly into lower case and secure with washer (aluminum) and bolt. Torque bolt to 16 ft. lbs. (22 N.m).

4) Install countershaft reverse and 5th gears onto countershaft. Using bearing installers, install rear countershaft bearing.

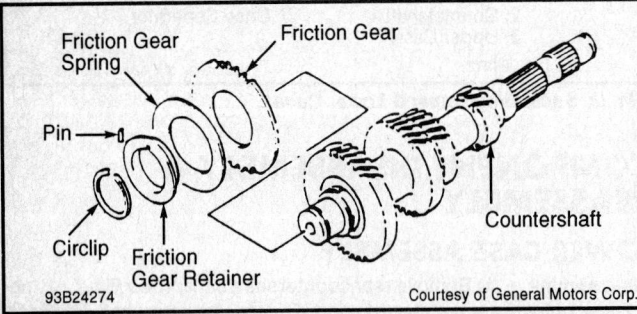

Fig. 8: **Exploded View Of Countershaft Friction Gear Assembly**

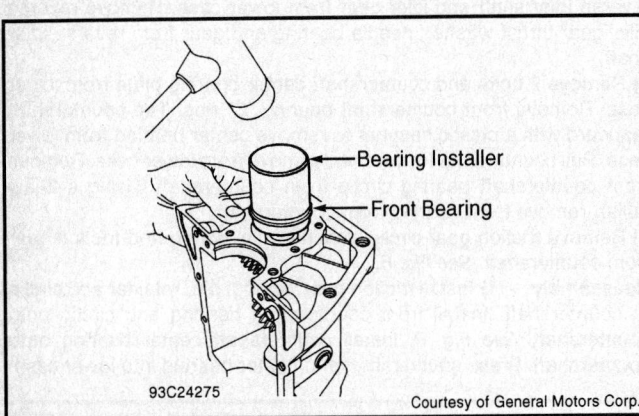

Fig. 9: **Installing Countershaft Front Bearing**

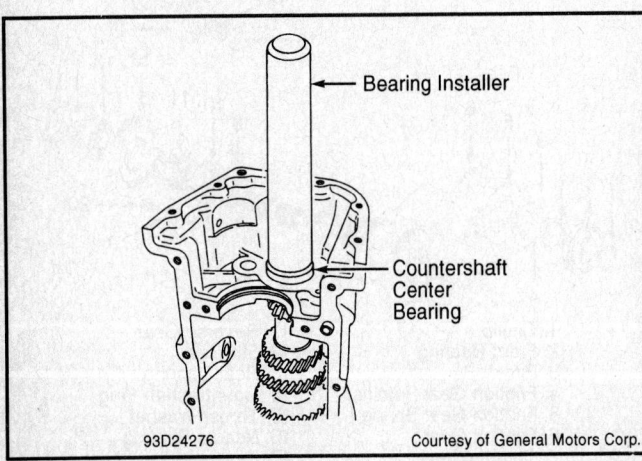

Fig. 10: **Installing Center Bearing**

INPUT SHAFT

CAUTION: Input shaft rides on needle bearing of mainshaft. When separating input shaft and mainshaft, needle bearing may remain in input shaft or on mainshaft. Remove needle bearing to prevent damage.

Disassembly – Remove input shaft from mainshaft. *See Fig. 11.* Remove input shaft circlip. Remove input shaft bearing using a bearing remover and press. Using a seal remover, remove input shaft oil seal from input shaft bearing retainer.

Reassembly – Install new input shaft oil seal. Using a bearing installer and press, install input shaft bearing. Install input shaft circlip. Install needle bearing and assemble input shaft to mainshaft.

MAINSHAFT

CAUTION: Input shaft rides on needle bearing of mainshaft. When separating input shaft and mainshaft, needle bearing may remain in input shaft or on mainshaft. Remove needle bearing to prevent damage.

Disassembly – 1) Remove input shaft from mainshaft. Remove circlip from high speed and reverse hub assembly. *See Fig. 11.* Press off high speed synchronizer rings, high speed sleeve-hub assembly, mainshaft 3rd gear and needle bearing from mainshaft. Remove high speed synchronizer sleeve, springs and keys from high speed synchronizer hub.

2) Remove 2 retaining rings and speedometer drive gear from mainshaft. Remove rear bearing circlip from mainshaft. Using bearing remover, press off mainshaft rear bearing.

3) Remove mainshaft 5th gear washer, steel ball, 5th gear, 5th gear synchronizer ring and 5th gear needle bearing. Remove reverse synchronizer sleeve, springs and keys from synchronizer hub. Remove reverse hub circlip from mainshaft. Press off reverse synchronizer hub from mainshaft.

4) Remove reverse gear and needle bearing from mainshaft. Press off reverse gear bushing, bearing washer and steel ball from mainshaft. Using a bearing remover and press, remove center bearing from mainshaft. Remove bearing washer, steel ball, low gear, low gear needle bearing and synchronizer ring from mainshaft.

5) Using a bearing remover and press, press off low gear bushing, low speed sleeve-hub assembly, low speed synchronizer ring and 2nd gear from mainshaft. Remove 2nd gear needle bearing from mainshaft. Remove low speed synchronizer sleeve, springs and keys from low speed synchronizer hub.

Inspection – 1) Check needle bearing, ball bearings and bearing contacting surfaces for scoring, scratches or wear. Replace if necessary. Using a feeler gauge, measure clearance between each synchronizer ring and gear. *See Fig. 12.* If clearance is not .039-.055" (1.0-1.4 mm) replace ring and gear.

2) Measure width of synchronizer key slot. If width is greater than .409" (10.4 mm), replace synchronizer ring. Measure clearance between shift fork and sleeve using feeler gauge. *See Fig. 13.* If clearance is greater than .039" (1.0 mm), replace shift fork and/or sleeve as necessary.

Reassembly – 1) Install low speed synchronizer springs, keys and sleeve onto low speed synchronizer hub. Install 2nd gear needle bearing, 2nd gear and low speed gear synchronizer ring onto mainshaft. Press on low speed sleeve-hub assembly and low gear bushing. Install low gear needle bearing, low gear synchronizer ring, low gear, steel ball and bearing washer.

2) Press on mainshaft center bearing. Install reverse synchronizer springs and keys to synchronizer hub (thick side of keys and sleeve should face toward 5th gear). Install reverse synchronizer sleeve to reverse synchronizer hub. Install steel ball and bearing washer onto mainshaft. Tap on reverse gear bushing using bearing installers and a hammer. Install reverse gear needle bearing and reverse gear.

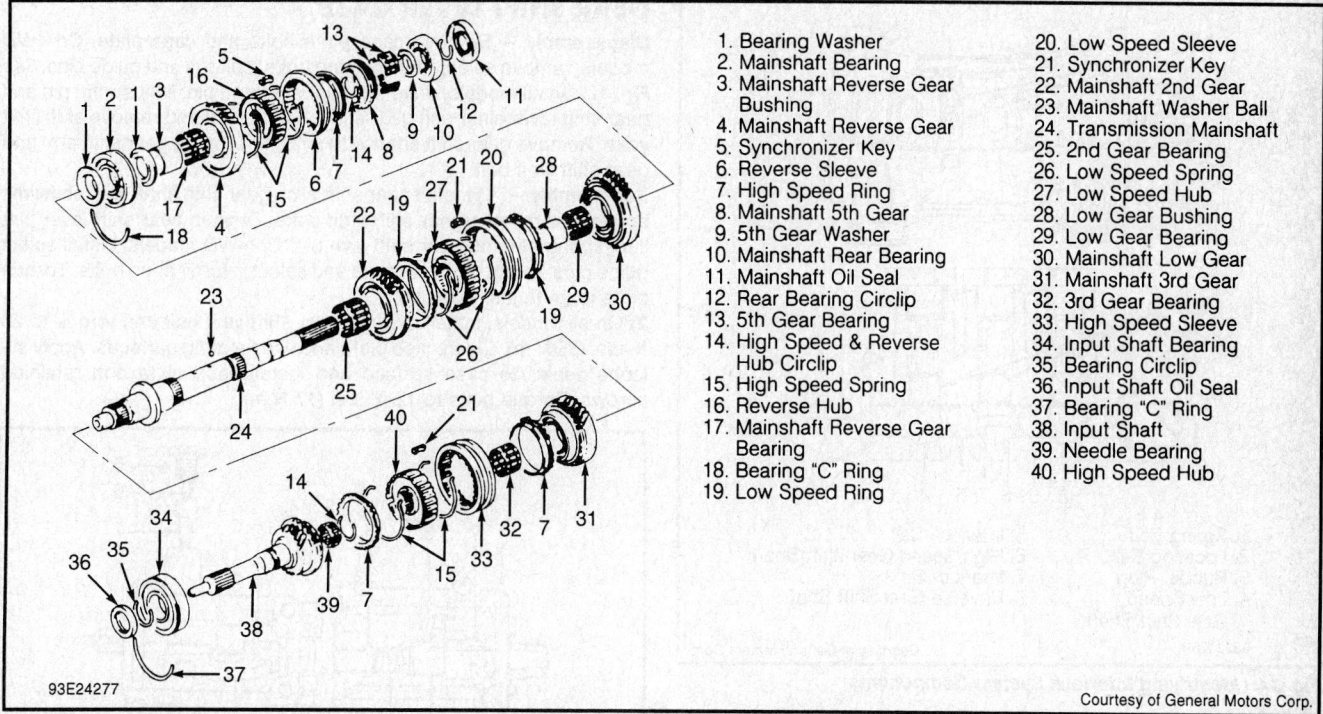

1. Bearing Washer
2. Mainshaft Bearing
3. Mainshaft Reverse Gear Bushing
4. Mainshaft Reverse Gear
5. Synchronizer Key
6. Reverse Sleeve
7. High Speed Ring
8. Mainshaft 5th Gear
9. 5th Gear Washer
10. Mainshaft Rear Bearing
11. Mainshaft Oil Seal
12. Rear Bearing Circlip
13. 5th Gear Bearing
14. High Speed & Reverse Hub Circlip
15. High Speed Spring
16. Reverse Hub
17. Mainshaft Reverse Gear Bearing
18. Bearing "C" Ring
19. Low Speed Ring
20. Low Speed Sleeve
21. Synchronizer Key
22. Mainshaft 2nd Gear
23. Mainshaft Washer Ball
24. Transmission Mainshaft
25. 2nd Gear Bearing
26. Low Speed Spring
27. Low Speed Hub
28. Low Gear Bushing
29. Low Gear Bearing
30. Mainshaft Low Gear
31. Mainshaft 3rd Gear
32. 3rd Gear Bearing
33. High Speed Sleeve
34. Input Shaft Bearing
35. Bearing Circlip
36. Input Shaft Oil Seal
37. Bearing "C" Ring
38. Input Shaft
39. Needle Bearing
40. High Speed Hub

Courtesy of General Motors Corp.

Fig. 11: Exploded View Of Input Shaft & Mainshaft Assemblies

3) Tap on reverse sleeve-hub assembly using bearing installers and a hammer. Install high speed and reverse hub circlip, high speed synchronizer ring, 5th gear needle bearing, 5th gear, steel ball and 5th gear washer. Ensure oil slot on washer faces 5th gear.

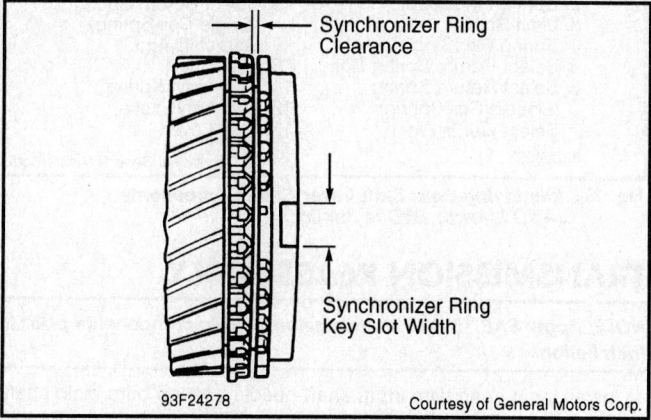

Courtesy of General Motors Corp.

Fig. 12: Measuring Synchronizer Ring Clearances

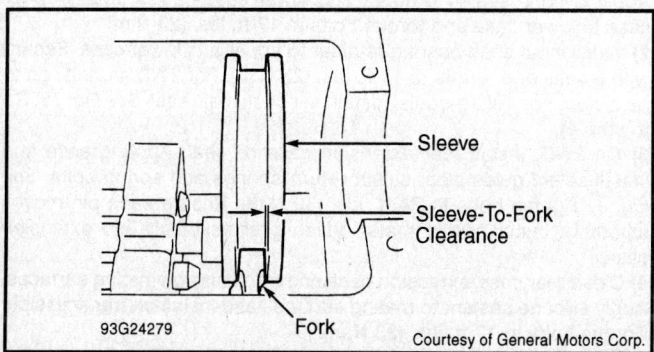

Courtesy of General Motors Corp.

Fig. 13: Measuring Sleeve-To-Fork Clearance

4) Press on rear bearing. Install rear bearing circlip and speedometer drive gear. Install high speed synchronizer springs, keys and sleeve onto high speed synchronizer hub. Install 3rd gear needle bearing, 3rd gear and high speed sleeve-hub assembly onto mainshaft. Install high speed and reverse hub circlip.

UPPER CASE & SHIFTER ASSEMBLY

Disassembly – 1) Remove back-up light switch, 3 locating spring bolts and set washers, locating springs and locating balls from upper case. See Fig. 14. Place all shift shafts in Neutral position.
2) Drive out spring pin and remove low speed gear shift fork and shaft. Drive out spring pin and remove high speed gear shift fork and shaft. Remove reverse gear shift shaft from upper case.
3) Drive out spring pin and remove reverse gear shift fork from shaft. Remove 2 rubber plugs and interlock balls from upper case. Drive out interlock pin from high speed gear shift shaft. See Figs. 14 and 15.
Inspection – Using a dial caliper, measure free length of locating springs. Length should be .945-1.063" (24.0-27.0 mm). Replace spring if length is less than .945" (24.0 mm).

NOTE: On some models, shift fork pins may be different lengths. If one pin is longer than the other two, use longer pin on the reverse gear shift fork only. When installing the longer reverse gear shift fork pin, press pin into fork until .138-.177" (3.5-4.5 mm) protrudes from top of fork. See Fig. 16.

Reassembly – 1) Install reverse gear shift shaft and interlock ball into upper case. Place reverse gear shift shaft in Neutral position. Install interlock pin into high speed gear shift shaft.
2) Install high speed gear shift shaft and high speed gear shift fork into upper case. Drive in spring pin and install interlock ball. Place high speed gear shift shaft in Neutral position.
3) Install low speed gear shift shaft and low speed gear shift fork into upper case. Drive in spring pin. Apply silicone sealer to rubber plugs and install into upper case.
4) Install locating balls, springs, washers and spring bolts. Torque bolts to 21 ft. lbs. (28 N.m). Install back-up light switch. Torque switch to 15 ft. lbs. (20 N.m). Inspect interlock system for proper operation.

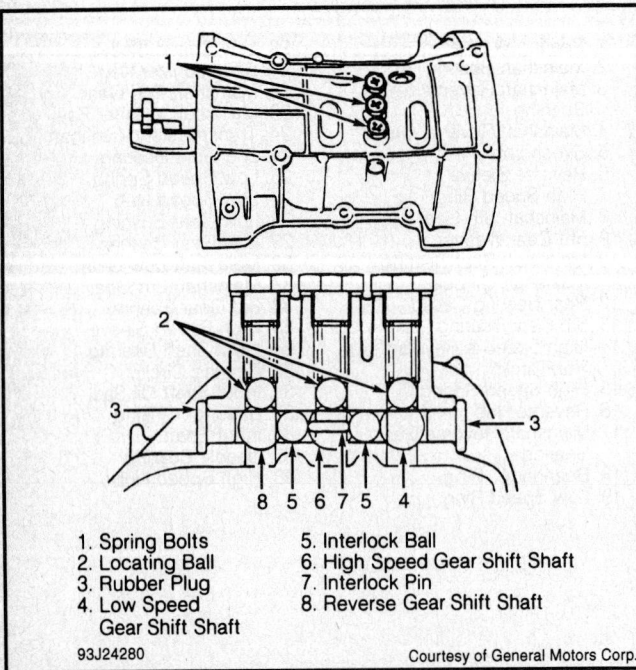

1. Spring Bolts
2. Locating Ball
3. Rubber Plug
4. Low Speed Gear Shift Shaft
5. Interlock Ball
6. High Speed Gear Shift Shaft
7. Interlock Pin
8. Reverse Gear Shift Shaft

93J24280   Courtesy of General Motors Corp.

Fig. 14: Identifying Interlock System Components

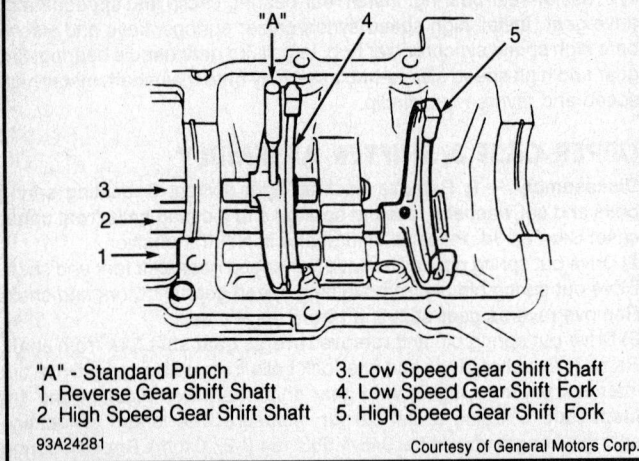

"A" - Standard Punch
1. Reverse Gear Shift Shaft
2. High Speed Gear Shift Shaft
3. Low Speed Gear Shift Shaft
4. Low Speed Gear Shift Fork
5. High Speed Gear Shift Fork

93A24281   Courtesy of General Motors Corp.

Fig. 15: Removing & Installing Gear Shift Shaft & Fork

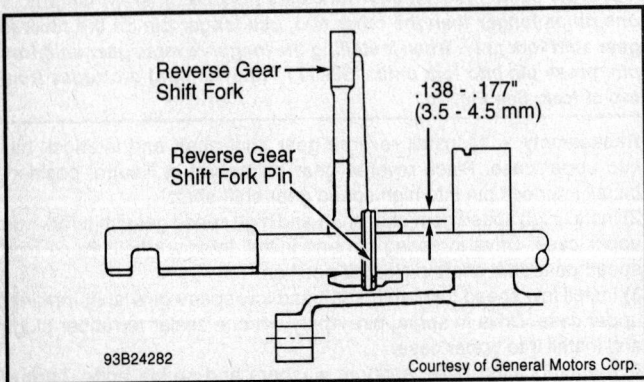

Reverse Gear Shift Fork

Reverse Gear Shift Fork Pin

.138 - .177" (3.5 - 4.5 mm)

93B24282   Courtesy of General Motors Corp.

Fig. 16: Installing Longer Reverse Gear Shift Fork Pin

GEAR SHIFT LEVER CASE

Disassembly – Remove case plate bolts and case plate. On 4WD models, remove select return spring bolts, springs and guide pins. See Fig. 17. On all models, drive out gear shift arm pin, limit spring pin and gear shift lever pin. Push gear shift shaft inward and remove shift limit yoke. Remove gear shift shaft with shift limit spring, gear shift arm and gear shift limit bolt.

Reassembly – **1)** Install gear shift arm, gear shift shaft with shift limit spring and reverse gear shift limit yoke. Drive in gear shift lever pin, limit spring pin and gear shift arm pin. On 4WD models, install select guide pins, select return springs and select return spring bolts. Torque bolts to 24 ft. lbs. (32 N.m).

2) On all models, install reverse gear shift limit bolt and torque to 26 ft. lbs. (35 N.m). Clean case plate and case mating surfaces. Apply silicone sealer to case surface and install case plate and retaining screws. Torque bolts to 12 ft. lbs. (17 N.m).

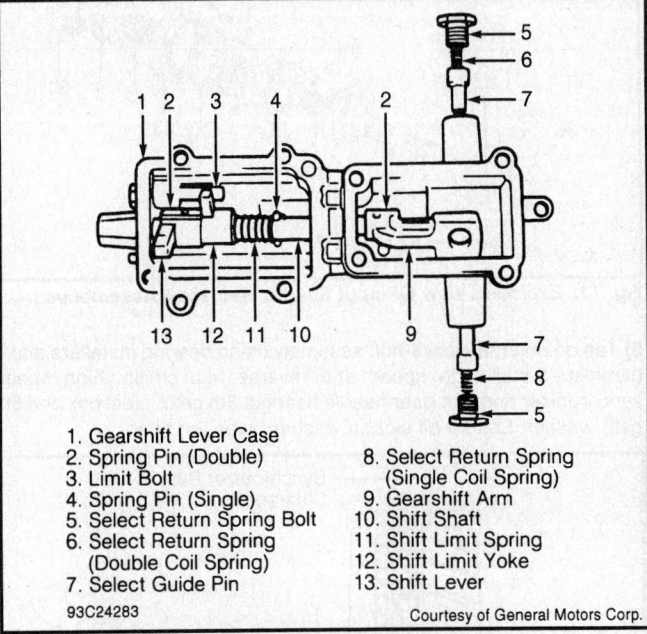

1. Gearshift Lever Case
2. Spring Pin (Double)
3. Limit Bolt
4. Spring Pin (Single)
5. Select Return Spring Bolt
6. Select Return Spring (Double Coil Spring)
7. Select Guide Pin
8. Select Return Spring (Single Coil Spring)
9. Gearshift Arm
10. Shift Shaft
11. Shift Limit Spring
12. Shift Limit Yoke
13. Shift Lever

93C24283   Courtesy of General Motors Corp.

Fig. 17: Identifying Gear Shift Lever Case Components (4WD Shown; 2WD Is Similar)

TRANSMISSION REASSEMBLY

NOTE: Apply SAE 75W-85 transmission fluid to components prior to installation.

1) Install input shaft with input shaft needle bearing onto main shaft. Install mainshaft and input shaft assembly into lower case. Ensure smooth engagement with countershaft. Shift all gears to neutral. Apply silicone sealer to upper and lower case halves. Install upper case to lower case and torque bolts to 17 ft. lbs. (23 N.m).

2) Install input shaft bearing retainer to upper and lower case. Secure with 8 bolts and torque to 17 ft. lbs. (23 N.m). For 2WD models, go to next step. For 4WD models, install rear case main seal. See Fig. 18. Go to step **4)**.

3) On 2WD, install rear extension case oil seal. Apply grease and install select guide pins, select return springs and spring bolts. See Fig. 4. Tighten bolts to 24 ft. lbs. (32 N.m). Ensure each pin moves smoothly. Install speedometer driven gear assembly into extension case.

4) Clean rear case/extension case and transmission mating surfaces. Apply silicone sealant to mating surfaces and install on transmission. Torque bolts to 17 ft. lbs. (23 N.m).

5) Clean gear shift lever case and rear case/extension case mating surfaces. Apply silicone sealant to shift lever case. Install and torque bolts to 12 ft. lbs. (17 N.m). Install clutch housing and bolts. Torque to 33 ft. lbs. (45 N.m). Install clutch release bearing.

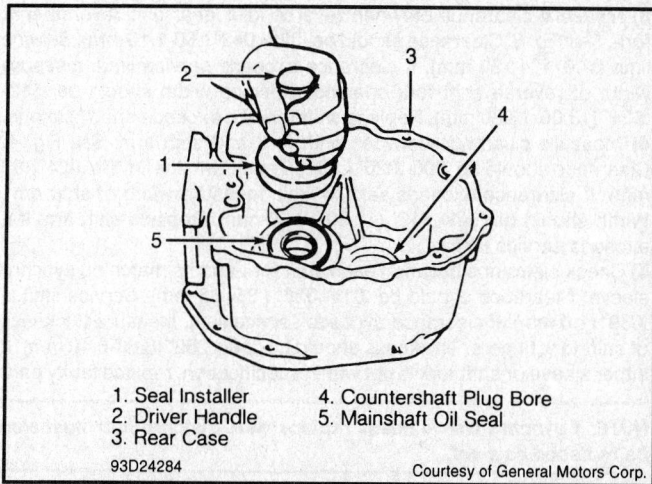

1. Seal Installer
2. Driver Handle
3. Rear Case
4. Countershaft Plug Bore
5. Mainshaft Oil Seal

93D24284

Courtesy of General Motors Corp.

**Fig. 18: Installing Rear Case Oil Seal
(4WD Shown; 2WD Extension Case Oil Seal Is Similar)**

TORQUE SPECIFICATIONS
TORQUE SPECIFICATIONS

Application	Ft. Lbs. (N.m)
Back-Up Light Switch	15 (20)
Clutch Housing Bolts	33 (45)
Gear Shift Lever Case-To-Rear Case Bolts	12 (17)
Input Shaft Retainer Bolts	17 (23)
Rear Case/Extension Case Bolts	17 (23)
Reverse Gear Shift Limit Bolt	26 (35)
Reverse Idler Gear Shaft Bolt	16 (22)
Select Return Spring Bolts	24 (32)
Shift Shafts Locating Spring Bolts	21 (28)
Upper Case-To-Lower Case Bolts	17 (23)
5th Gear Switch (If Equipped)	15 (20)

	INCH Lbs. (N.m)
Counter Shaft Center Bearing Plate Bolts	53 (6)
Speedometer Driven Gear Case Bolts	106 (12)

MANUAL TRANSMISSIONS
Honda M2F4, M2L5, M2S4, P2A5 & P2U5

Accord, Prelude

APPLICATION & LABOR TIMES

APPLICATION & LABOR TIMES

Vehicle Application	[1][3] R & I	[2] Overhaul	Series
Accord			
F22B1 Engine	5.0	4.3	P2U5
F22B2 Engine	5.0	4.3	P2A5
Prelude			
F22A1 Engine	5.0	4.3	M2L5
H22A2 Engine (VTEC)	5.0	4.3	M2F4
H23A1 Engine	5.0	4.3	M2S4

[1] – Removal and installation of transmission from vehicle chassis.

[2] – Bench overhaul time for transaxle/differential. DOES NOT include removal and installation.

[3] – Where air pump interferes add .4 hr.
Where cruise control interferes add .3 hr.
Where power steering interferes add .3 hr.

IDENTIFICATION

Transmission identification number is stamped on metal pad on top of transmission. First 4 numbers indicate transmission model.

LUBRICATION & ADJUSTMENT

See appropriate MANUAL TRANSMISSION SERVICING article in TRANSMISSION SERVICING section.

TROUBLE SHOOTING

See GENERAL TROUBLE SHOOTING article in APPLICATIONS & IDENTIFICATION section.

ON-VEHICLE SERVICE

AXLE SHAFTS

See appropriate AXLE SHAFTS article in AXLE SHAFTS & TRANSFER CASES section.

REMOVAL & INSTALLATION

See appropriate MANUAL TRANSMISSION REMOVAL article in TRANSMISSION SERVICING section.

TRANSMISSION DISASSEMBLY

NOTE: *Place clutch housing on supports high enough to keep mainshaft from hitting workbench.*

CAUTION: *If it is necessary to heat transmission case for component removal, DO NOT exceed 212°F (100°C).*

1) Remove shift arm cover and shift arm lever. Remove shift arm and interlock. Remove reverse idler shaft bolt. Remove all bolts, springs and steel detent balls. Remove bolts attaching transmission housing to clutch housing. Remove 32-mm sealing bolt (bolt has square hole). Expand snap ring on countershaft bearing. Lift and remove transmission housing from clutch housing. See Fig. 1.

2) Measure clearance between reverse shift fork and 5th/reverse shift piece pin. See Fig. 2. Clearance for dimension "A" should be .002-.014" (.05-.35 mm), service limit is .020" (.50 mm). Clearance for dimension "B" should be .016-.031" (.40-.80 mm), service limit is .039" (1.0 mm). If clearance exceeds service limit, measure width of "L" groove in reverse shift fork. Width for dimension "A" should be .278-.285" (7.05-7.25 mm). Width for dimension "B" should be .291-.303" (7.40-7.70 mm). Replace reverse shift fork if "L" shaped groove exceeds specifications.

3) Measure clearance between reverse idler gear and reverse shift fork. See Fig. 3. Clearance should be .020-.043" (.50-1.10 mm). Service limit is .071" (1.80 mm). If clearance exceeds service limit, measure width of reverse shift fork opening. Opening width should be .512-.524" (13.00-13.30 mm). Replace shift fork if it exceeds specifications.

4) Measure clearance between shift fork and shift arm. See Fig. 4. Clearance should be .008-.020" (.20-.50 mm). Service limit is .024" (.60 mm). If clearance exceeds service limit, measure width of shift arm. Width should be .508-.512" (12.90-13.00 mm). Replace shift arm if it exceeds service limit.

5) Check clearance between each shift fork and its matching synchro sleeve. Clearance should be .014-.026" (.35-.65 mm). Service limit is .039" (1.0 mm). If clearance exceeds service limit, measure thickness of shift fork fingers. Thickness should be .244-.252" (6.20-6.40 mm). If either sleeve or shift fork is not within specification, replace faulty part.

NOTE: *If synchro sleeve needs replacement, synchro hub must also be replaced as a set.*

---

6) Remove reverse shift fork from clutch housing. See Fig. 1. Remove reverse idler shaft and gear from clutch housing. Tape mainshaft spline. Remove mainshaft and countershaft with shift forks as single assembly from clutch housing. Remove shift fork shaft by removing roll pin from 5th/reverse shift piece. Remove differential assembly. If differential is to be overhauled, see DIFFERENTIAL under COMPONENT DISASSEMBLY & REMOVAL. Disassemble remaining components. Inspect all components for wear or damage.

COMPONENT DISASSEMBLY & REASSEMBLY

MAINSHAFT

Measurements – 1) For all mainshaft measurement specifications refer to MAINSHAFT SPECIFICATIONS table. Using socket or appropriate adapter, support ball bearing inner race. Push down on mainshaft. See Fig. 6. Measure clearance between 3rd and 2nd gears. If measurement is not within specification, measure thickness of 3rd gear. If thickness is within specifications, replace synchro hub. If thickness of 3rd gear is less than service limit, replace gear.

2) Measure clearance between 4th gear and spacer collar. If clearance is not within specification, measure distance "A" on spacer collar. See Fig. 6. If distance "A" is within specification, measure thickness of 4th gear. If thickness is not within specification, replace 4th gear. If thickness is within specification, replace 4th gear synchro hub.

MAINSHAFT SPECIFICATIONS

Application	Specification In. (mm)
2nd-3rd Gear Clearance	
Standard	.002-.008 (.06-.21)
Service Limit	.12 (.30)
4th Gear-To-Spacer Collar Clearance	
Standard	.002-.008 (.06-.21)
Service Limit	.12 (.30)
5th Gear-To-Spacer Collar Clearance	
Standard	.002-.008 (.06-.21)
Service Limit	.12 (.30)
3rd Gear Thickness	
Standard	1.276-1.278 (32.42-32.47)
Service Limit	1.272 (32.3)
4th Gear Thickness	
Standard	1.217-1.219 (30.92-30.97)
Service Limit	1.213 (30.8)
5th Gear Thickness	
Standard	1.198-1.200 (30.42-30.47)
Service Limit	1.193 (30.3)
Spacer Collar Height "A"	
Standard	1.025-1.027 (26.03-26.08)
Service Limit	1.024 (26.01)
Spacer Collar Height "B"	
Standard	1.025-1.027 (26.03-26.08)
Service Limit	1.024 (26.01)

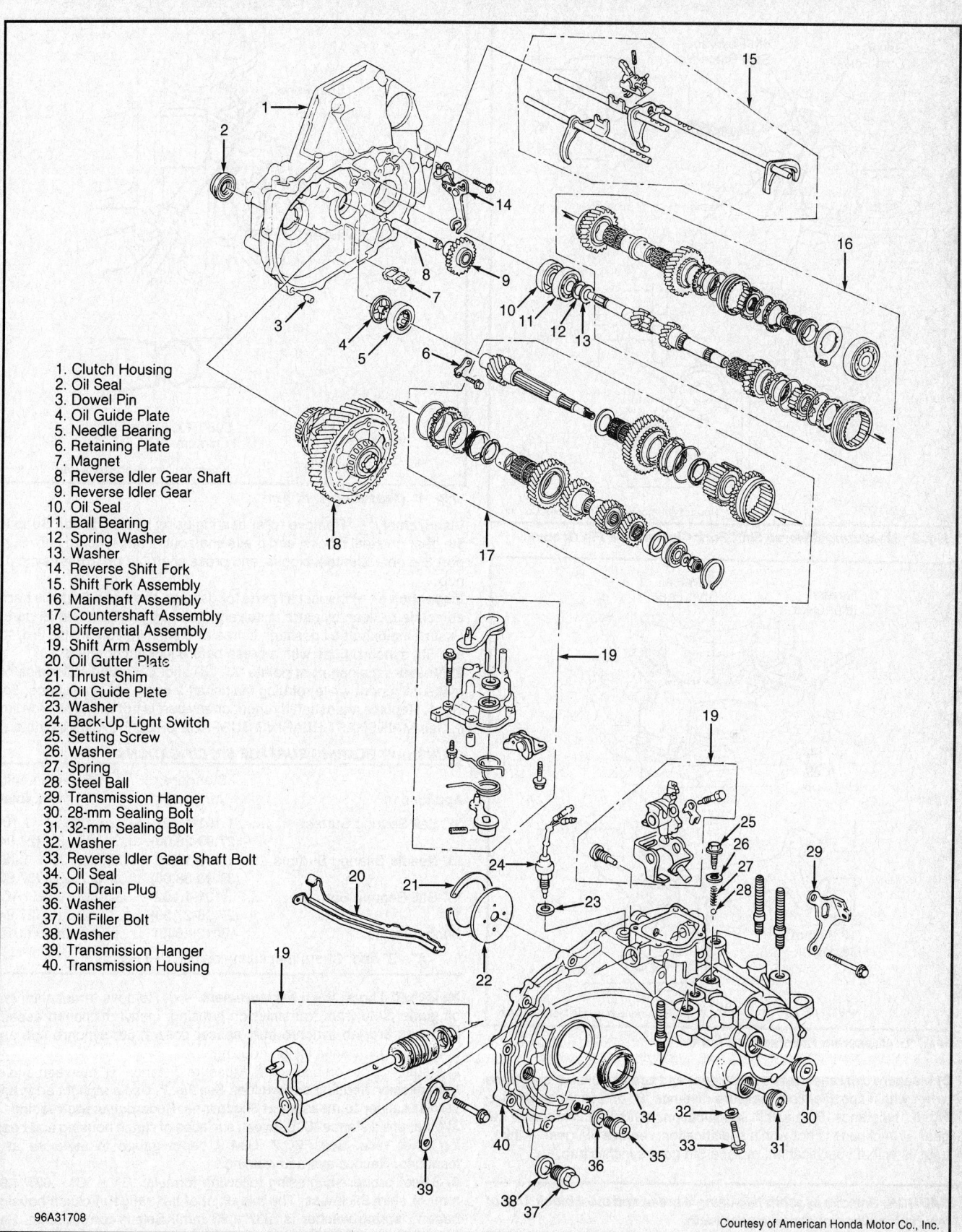

1. Clutch Housing
2. Oil Seal
3. Dowel Pin
4. Oil Guide Plate
5. Needle Bearing
6. Retaining Plate
7. Magnet
8. Reverse Idler Gear Shaft
9. Reverse Idler Gear
10. Oil Seal
11. Ball Bearing
12. Spring Washer
13. Washer
14. Reverse Shift Fork
15. Shift Fork Assembly
16. Mainshaft Assembly
17. Countershaft Assembly
18. Differential Assembly
19. Shift Arm Assembly
20. Oil Gutter Plate
21. Thrust Shim
22. Oil Guide Plate
23. Washer
24. Back-Up Light Switch
25. Setting Screw
26. Washer
27. Spring
28. Steel Ball
29. Transmission Hanger
30. 28-mm Sealing Bolt
31. 32-mm Sealing Bolt
32. Washer
33. Reverse Idler Gear Shaft Bolt
34. Oil Seal
35. Oil Drain Plug
36. Washer
37. Oil Filler Bolt
38. Washer
39. Transmission Hanger
40. Transmission Housing

96A31708

Courtesy of American Honda Motor Co., Inc.

Fig. 1: Exploded View Of Transmission Assembly

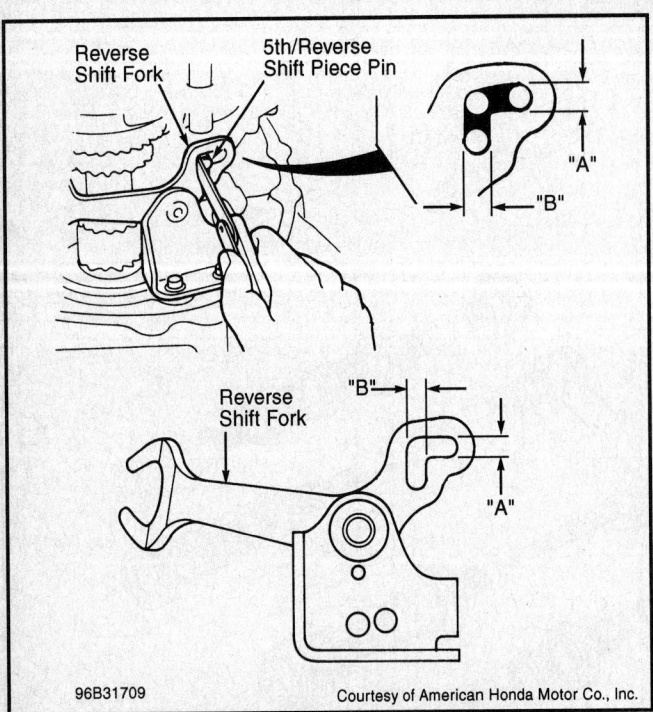

96B31709   Courtesy of American Honda Motor Co., Inc.

Fig. 2: Measuring Reverse Shift Fork Clearance & Pin Groove

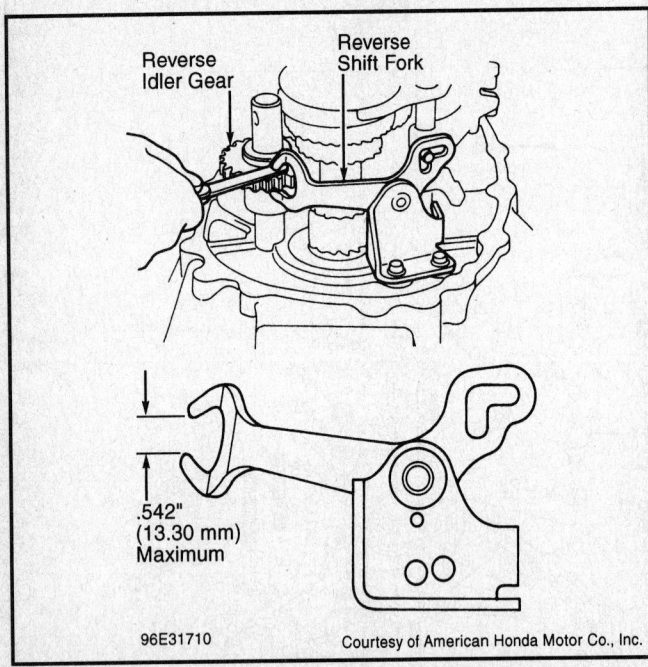

96E31710   Courtesy of American Honda Motor Co., Inc.

Fig. 3: Measuring Reverse Shift Fork

3) Measure clearance between 5th gear and spacer collar. If clearance is not within specification, measure distance "B" on spacer collar. See Fig. 6. If distance "B" is within specification, measure thickness of 5th gear. If thickness is not within specification, replace 5th gear. If thickness is within specification, replace 5th gear synchro hub.

CAUTION: Remove synchro hub using a press and steel block. Use of jaw-type puller can damage gear teeth.

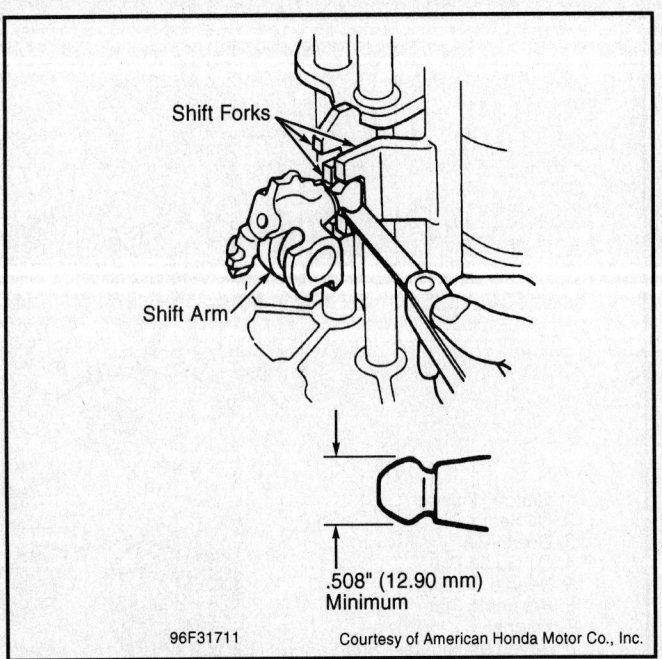

96F31711   Courtesy of American Honda Motor Co., Inc.

Fig. 4: Measuring Shift Arm

Disassembly – Remove roller bearing using bearing puller. Support 5th gear on steel blocks, and press shaft out of 5th synchro hub. Support 3rd gear on steel blocks, and press shaft out of 3rd/4th synchro hub.

Inspection – 1) Inspect all parts for damage and wear. Replace parts as needed. Clean all parts in solvent, then dry and lubricate all parts. Ensure mainshaft oil passage is free of contamination. Install 3rd/4th and 5th synchro hubs with a press before lubricating them.

2) Measure mainshaft at points "A", "B" and "C". Using dial indicator, measure runout while rotating mainshaft 2 complete revolutions. See Fig. 5. Replace mainshaft if runout or any part is not within service limit. See MAINSHAFT BEARING SURFACE SPECIFICATIONS table.

MAINSHAFT BEARING SURFACE SPECIFICATIONS

Application [1]	Standard In. (mm)	Service Limits In. (mm)
"A" Ball Bearing Surface	1.101-1.102	1.100
	(27.99-28.00)	(27.94)
"B" Needle Bearing Surface	1.495-1.496	1.493
	(37.98-38.00)	(37.93)
"C" Ball Bearing Surface	1.101-1.102	1.100
	(27.98-27.99)	(27.94)
Runout Limits	.0016 (.040)	.0040 (.010)

[1] – "A", "B" and "C" are measuring points. See Fig. 5.

Mainshaft Thrust Shim Measurement – 1) Remove thrust shim and oil guide plate from transmission housing. Install mainshaft assembled with 3rd/4th synchro hub, spacer collars, 5th synchro hub and ball bearing in transmission housing.

2) Install washer on mainshaft. Measure distance "B" between end of transmission housing and washer. See Fig. 7. Use a straight edge and vernier caliper to measure at 3 locations. Record average reading.

3) Measure distance "C" between surfaces of clutch housing and bearing inner race. See Fig. 7. Use a depth gauge to measure at 3 locations. Record average reading.

4) Select proper shim using following formula: "B" + "C" - .037" (.93 mm) = shim thickness. The mid point of flex range of clutch housing bearing spring washer is .037" (.93 mm). Select correct shim. See MAINSHAFT THRUST SHIM IDENTIFICATION table. DO NOT use more than one shim.

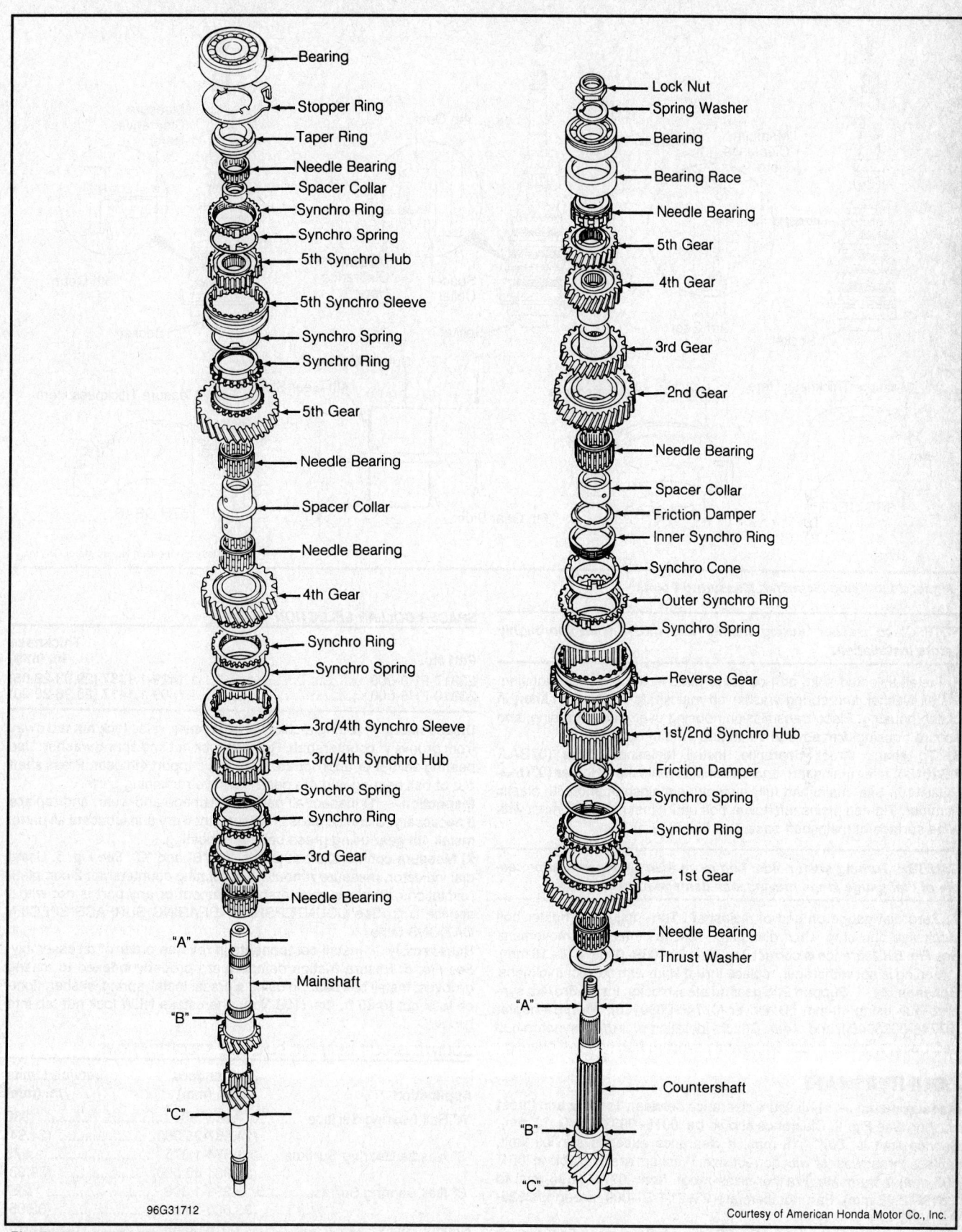

Fig. 5: Exploded View Of Mainshaft & Countershaft

96G31712

Courtesy of American Honda Motor Co., Inc.

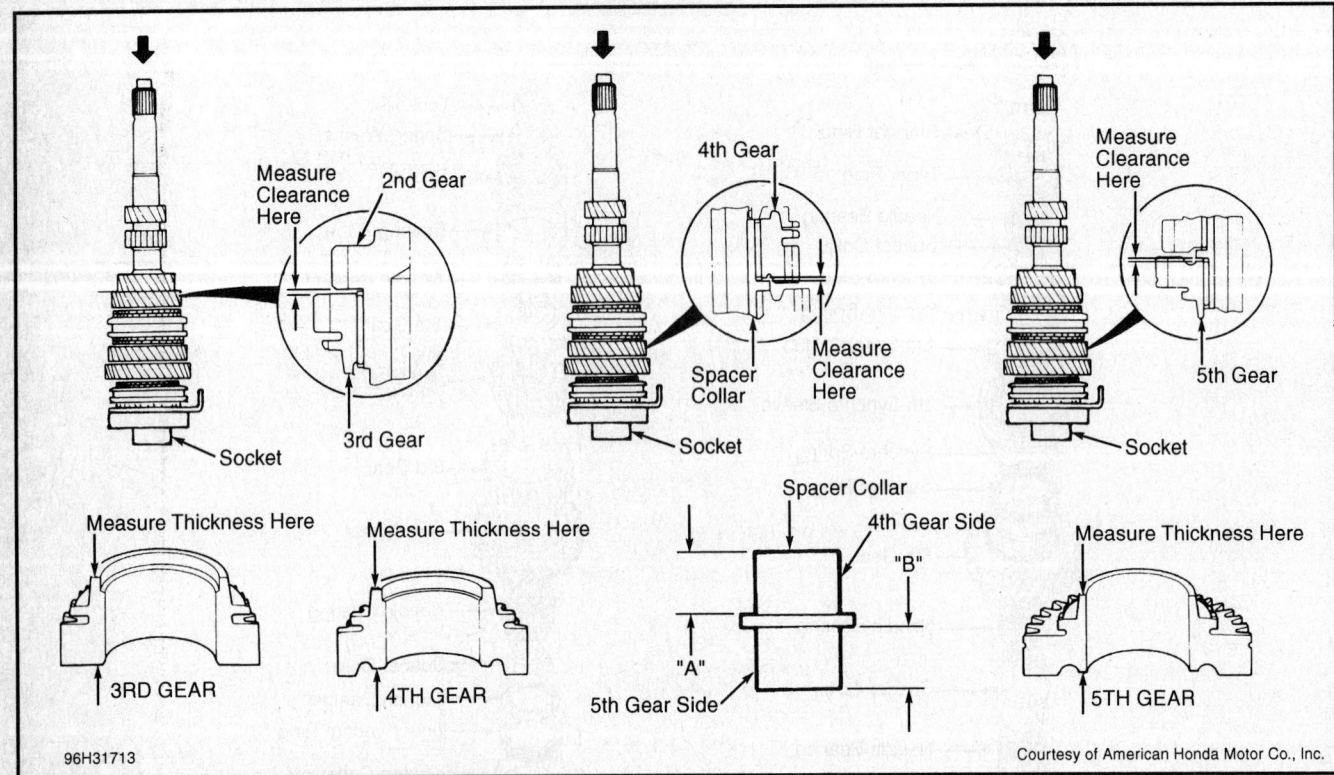

96H31713   Courtesy of American Honda Motor Co., Inc.

Fig. 6: Identifying Mainshaft Measuring Points

NOTE: Clean washer, spring washer and thrust shim thoroughly before installation.

5) Install selected shim and oil guide plate in transmission housing. Install washer and spring washer on mainshaft. Install mainshaft in clutch housing. Place transmission housing over clutch housing, and secure housing with several 8-mm and 10-mm bolts.

6) To check thrust clearance, install Mainshaft Base (07GAJ-PG20130) over mainshaft, and then install Mainshaft Holder (07GAJ-PG20110). Seat mainshaft fully by tapping mainshaft end with plastic hammer. Tighten mainshaft holder bolt until it just makes contact with wide surface of mainshaft base. *See Fig. 8.*

CAUTION: Turning shaft holder bolt more than 60 degrees after needle of dial gauge stops moving may damage transmission.

7) Zero dial gauge on end of mainshaft. Turn mainshaft holder bolt clockwise and stop when dial gauge reaches maximum movement. *See Fig. 8.* Clearance is correct if reading is .0039-.0063" (.10-.16 mm). If reading is not within limit, replace thrust shim with correct thickness.

Reassembly – Support 2nd gear on steel blocks. Install 3rd/4th synchro hub using 40-mm I.D. Driver (07746-0030100), 35-mm Adapter (07746-00330400) and press. Check operation of 3rd/4th synchro hub set. Using a press, install 5th/reverse synchro hub and ball bearing.

COUNTERSHAFT

Measurements – **1)** Measure clearance between 1st gear and thrust washer. *See Fig. 9.* Clearance should be .0016-.0039" (.040-.10 mm). Service limit is .007" (.18 mm). If clearance exceeds service limit, replace thrust washer with correct size. Washers are available in .001" (.03 mm) increments. Washer sizes range from .0771" (1.96 mm) to .0819" (2.08 mm). Part numbers are 23921-PG1-000 through 23925-PG1-000.

2) Measure clearance between 2nd and 3rd gear. *See Fig. 9.* Clearance should be .0016-.0039" (.040-.10 mm). Service limit is .007" (.18 mm). If clearance exceeds service limit, replace spacer collar with correct size. See SPACER COLLAR SELECTION table.

SPACER COLLAR SELECTION

Part No.	Thickness In. (mm)
23917-PH8-000	1.1429-1.1437 (29.03-29.05)
23918-PH8-000	1.1409-1.1417 (28.98-29.00)

Disassembly – Using a chisel and hammer, raise lock nut tab away from groove in countershaft. Remove lock nut and spring washer. Use bearing splitter or appropriate blocks to support 4th gear. Press shaft out of ball bearing and 4th gear. Remove remaining parts.

Inspection – **1)** Inspect all parts for damage and wear, and replace if necessary. Clean all parts in solvent, then dry and lubricate all parts. Install 4th gear using press before lubricating.

2) Measure countershaft at points "A", "B" and "C". *See Fig. 5.* Using dial indicator, measure runout while rotating countershaft 2 complete revolutions. Replace countershaft if runout or any part is not within service limit. See COUNTERSHAFT BEARING SURFACE SPECIFICATIONS table.

Reassembly – Install components in reverse order of disassembly. *See Fig. 5.* Ensure friction dampers are properly indexed to mating grooves. Install ball bearing using a press. Install spring washer, tighten lock nut to 80 ft. lbs. (108 N.m), then stake NEW lock nut tab into groove.

COUNTERSHAFT BEARING SURFACE SPECIFICATIONS

Application [1]	Standard In. (mm)	Service Limits In. (mm)
"A" Ball Bearing Surface	.983-.984 (24.987-25.000)	.982 (24.94)
"B" Needle Bearing Surface	1.574-1.575 (39.984-40.000)	1.575 (39.93)
"C" Ball Bearing Surface	1.299-1.300 (33.000-33.015)	1.297 (32.95)
Runout Limits	.0016 (.040)	.0040 (.010)

[1] – "A", "B" and "C" are measuring points. *See Fig. 5.*

MAINSHAFT THRUST SHIM IDENTIFICATION

ID Number	Part Number	Thickness In. (mm)
A	23941-PK5-000	.0472 (1.20)
B	23942-PK5-000	.0484 (1.23)
C	23943-PK5-000	.0496 (1.26)
D	23944-PK5-000	.0508 (1.29)
E	23945-PK5-000	.0520 (1.32)
F	23946-PK5-000	.0531 (1.35)
G	23947-PK5-000	.0543 (1.38)
H	23948-PK5-000	.0555 (1.41)
I	23949-PK5-000	.0567 (1.44)
J	23950-PK5-000	.0579 (1.47)
K	23951-PK5-000	.0591 (1.50)
L	23952-PK5-000	.0602 (1.53)
M	23953-PK5-000	.0614 (1.56)
N	23954-PK5-000	.0626 (1.59)
O	23955-PK5-000	.0638 (1.62)
P	23956-PK5-000	.0650 (1.65)
Q	23957-PK5-000	.0661 (1.68)
R	23958-PK5-000	.0673 (1.71)
S	23959-PK5-000	.0685 (1.74)
T	23960-PK5-000	.0697 (1.77)
U	23961-PK5-000	.0709 (1.80)
V	23962-PK5-000	.0720 (1.83)
W	23963-PK5-000	.0732 (1.86)
X	23964-PK5-000	.0744 (1.89)
Y	23965-PK5-000	.0756 (1.92)
Z	23966-PK5-000	.0768 (1.95)
AA	23967-PK5-000	.0780 (1.98)
AB	23968-PK5-000	.0791 (2.01)
AC	23969-PK5-000	.0803 (2.04)
AD	23970-PK5-000	.0815 (2.07)
AE	23971-PK5-000	.0827 (2.10)
AF	23972-PK5-000	.0839 (2.13)
AG	23973-PK5-000	.0850 (2.16)
AH	23974-PK5-000	.0862 (2.19)
AI	23975-PK5-000	.0874 (2.22)
AJ	23976-PK5-000	.0886 (2.25)
AK	23977-PK5-000	.0898 (2.28)
AL	23978-PK5-000	.0909 (2.31)
AM	23979-PK5-000	.0921 (2.34)
AN	23980-PK5-000	.0933 (2.37)

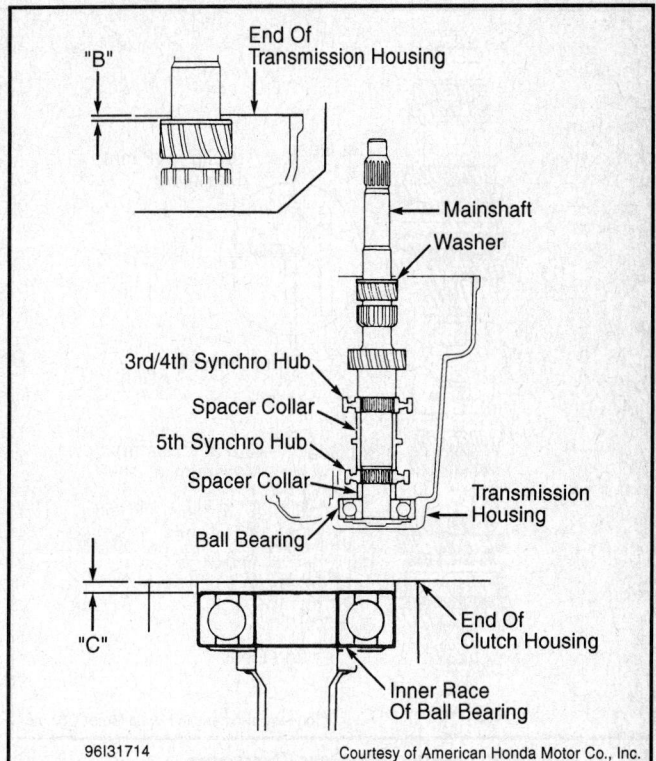

Fig. 7: **Measuring Mainshaft Thrust Clearance**

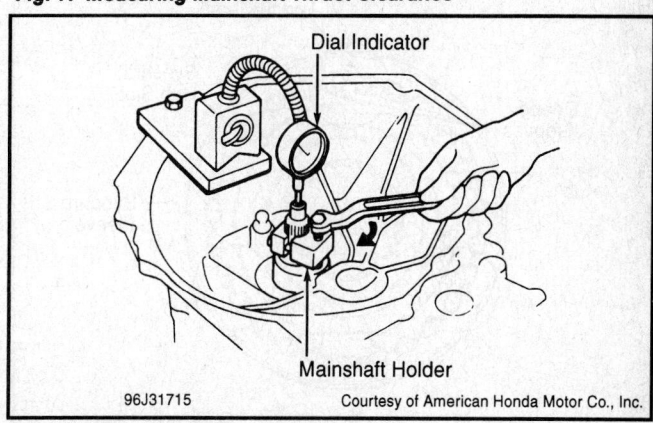

Fig. 8: **Measuring Mainshaft End Play**

SYNCHRO RING & GEAR

Disassembly – Separate synchro ring and gear. Lubricate and install synchro spring on synchro ring and set aside.

Inspection – 1) Inspect gear teeth for wear, galling, roughness and cracks. Ensure ring and gear turn freely. If replacement is necessary, replace ring and gear as a unit.

2) Measure clearance between ring and gear all the way around. See Fig. 10. Ensure ring is held evenly against gear while measuring. Ring-to-gear clearance should be .033-.043" (.85-1.10 mm). Service limit is .016" (.40 mm). If clearance exceeds limit, replace ring and gear as a unit.

3) On double-cone synchro, outer synchro ring-to-synchro cone clearance, "A", should be .0197-.0394" (.50-1.0 mm). Service limit is .0118" (.30 mm). Synchro cone-to-gear clearance, "B", should be .0197-.0394" (.50-1.0 mm). Service limit is .0118" (.30 mm). Outer Synchro ring-to-gear clearance, "C", should be .0374-.0661" (.95-1.68 mm). Service limit is .0236" (.60 mm).

Reassembly – Each synchro sleeve has 3 sets of longer teeth (120 degrees apart) that must be matched with 3 sets of deeper grooves when hub is assembled. See Fig. 10.

DIFFERENTIAL

CAUTION: Ring gear bolts have left-hand threads.

Disassembly – 1) Check bearings for wear and rough rotation. If bearings need replacing, use bearing puller to remove bearings from differential carrier. Remove ring gear.

2) Drive out roll pin from ring gear side of carrier assembly. Remove pinion shaft, side gears, thrust washers and thrust shims. Clean and inspect all parts for damage and wear. Replace any worn parts as needed. See Fig. 11.

Reassembly – 1) After inspecting condition of carrier assembly, coat all parts with molylube. Install side gears and thrust washers in differential carrier. Place pinion gears exactly opposite each other, in mesh with side gears. Install thrust washers behind pinion gears. Install pinion shaft and roll pin.

2) Mount carrier assembly in V-blocks with axles inserted into carrier side gears. Mount dial indicator to measure backlash. See Fig. 12. Backlash should be .002-.006" (.05-.15 mm). If backlash exceeds specification, select correct pinion washers. See PINION WASHER table.

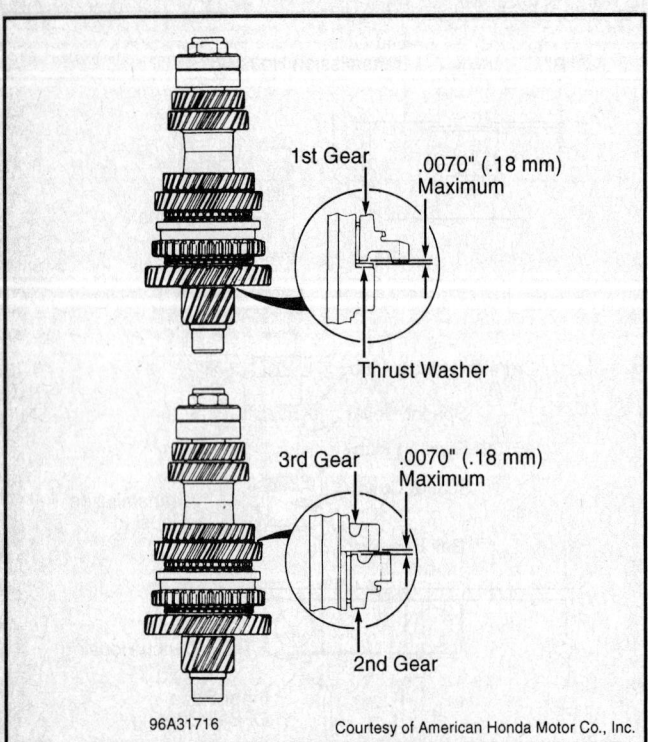

Fig. 9: Measuring Countershaft Gear Clearances

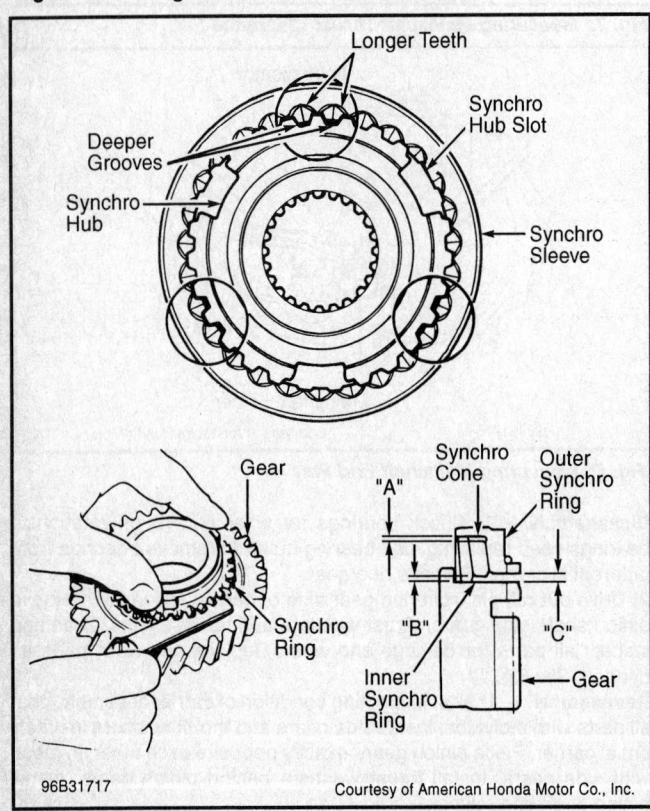

Fig. 10: Measuring Synchro Hub Assembly Clearance

PINION WASHER

Part Number	Thickness In. (mm)
41351-PG1-000	.0276 (.70)
41352-PG1-000	.0295 (.75)
41353-PG1-000	.0315 (.80)
41354-PG1-000	.0335 (.85)
41355-PG1-000	.0354 (.90)
41356-PG1-000	.0374 (.95)
41357-PG1-000	.0394 (1.00)
41358-PG1-000	.0413 (1.05)

TRANSMISSION REASSEMBLY

Differential Carrier Bearing Preload – 1) Check and adjust bearing preload if either half of transmission case, carrier assembly, carrier bearings and/or thrust shims have been replaced.

2) Install standard .085" (2.17 mm) shim in transmission housing. Install bearing race and carrier assembly. Install clutch housing without installing mainshaft or countershaft. Tighten all housing bolts to specifications. See TORQUE SPECIFICATIONS.

3) Rotate differential in both directions to seat bearing. Using an INCH-lb. torque wrench and Preload Socket (07HAJ-PK40201), measure starting torque of differential assembly. Starting torque should be 12-23 INCH lbs. (1.4-2.6 N.m). If starting torque is not within specifications, select correct shim. Recheck preload. Changing shim to the next size will change preload approximately 2.60-3.47 INCH lbs. (.3-.4 N.m).

Reassembly – 1) After adjusting differential carrier bearing preload to specifications, disassemble housing. Install shift fork, then drive in spring pin through shift pieces. Install spring washer with angle against clutch housing. Tape mainshaft spline. Insert mainshaft and countershaft into shift forks and install as an assembly.

2) Install reverse idler gear and idler gear shaft into clutch housing. Install reverse shift fork in clutch housing with 5th/reverse shift piece pin positioned in slot of reverse shift fork. Tighten bolt to 11 ft. lbs. (15 N.m). Install oil guide plate and mainshaft thrust shim into transmission housing. Install oil gutter plate in transmission housing.

3) Install 28-mm sealing bolt. Tighten bolt to 32 ft. lbs. (45 N.m). Apply Liquid Gasket (08718-0001) to mating surface of clutch housing. Ensure stopper ring is aligned to mating slots in transmission housing. Place transmission housing over clutch housing. Ensure shafts line up properly.

4) With snap ring pliers inserted through 32-mm sealing bolt hole, spread snap ring while lowering transmission housing into place. Install snap ring on countershaft ball bearing. Snap ring end clearance should be .142-.249" (3.60-6.32 mm). Install 32-mm sealing bolt and tighten to 18 ft. lbs. (25 N.m). Tighten all housing bolts in sequence. See Fig. 13. Install reverse idler shaft bolt and tighten to 41 ft. lbs. (55 N.m). Install all detent steel balls, springs and washers. Install shift arm assembly. Assemble all remaining components. Tighten all bolts to specifications. See TORQUE SPECIFICATIONS.

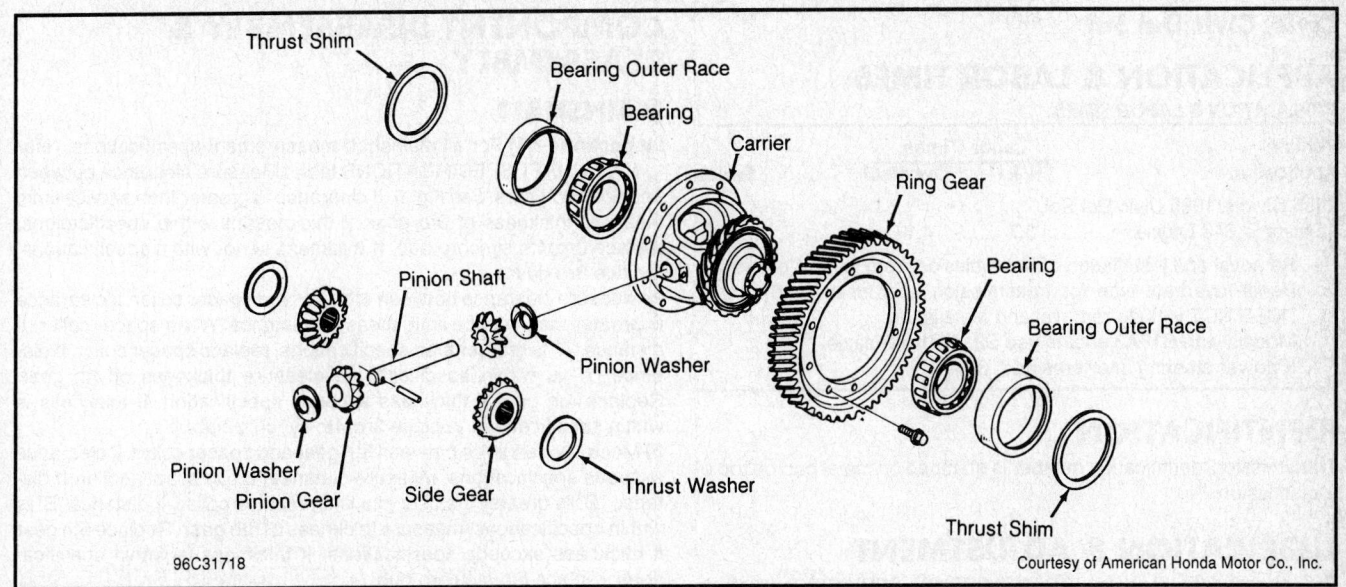

Fig. 11: Exploded View Of Differential Assembly

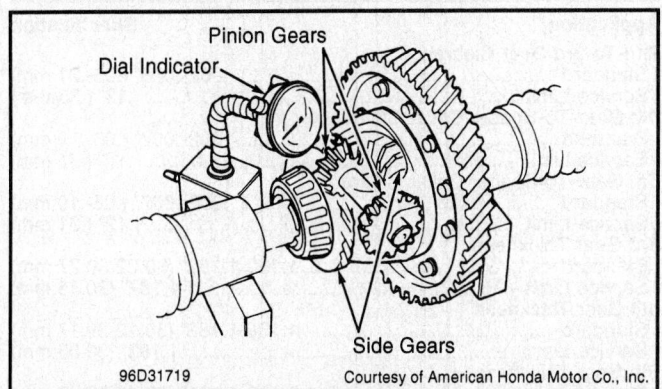

Fig. 12: Measuring Pinion Gear Backlash

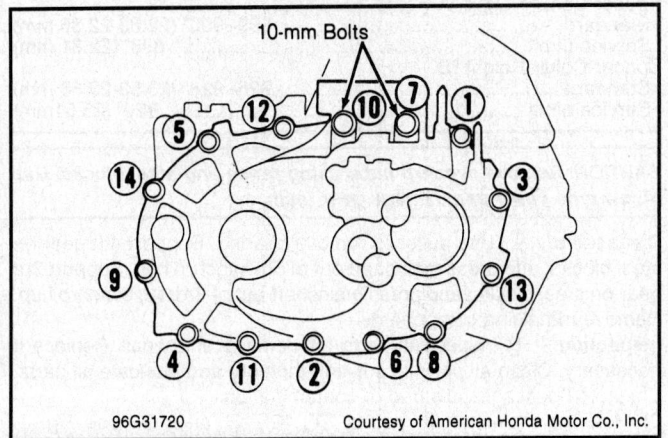

Fig. 13: Bolt Tightening Sequence

TORQUE SPECIFICATIONS
TORQUE SPECIFICATIONS

Application	Ft. Lbs. (N.m)
Countershaft Lock Nut	81 (110)
Housing Bolt	
8 mm	21 (28)
10 mm	33 (45)
Reverse Idler Shaft Bolt	41 (55)
Reverse Shift Fork Bracket Bolt	11 (15)
Ring Gear Bolt	76 (103)
Setting Screw	16 (22)
Shift Arm Lever Bolt	21 (29)
Sealing Bolt	
28 mm	33 (45)
32 mm	18 (25)
	INCH Lbs. (N.m)
Shift Arm Cover Assembly Bolts	106 (12)

Civic, Civic Del Sol

APPLICATION & LABOR TIMES

APPLICATION & LABOR TIMES

Vehicle Application	Labor Times [1] R & I	[2] Overhaul	Series
1995 Civic & 1995 Civic Del Sol Except B16A3 Engine [3] [4]	3.7	4.1	S20

[1] – Removal and installation of transmission from vehicle chassis.
[2] – Bench overhaul time for transmission or transaxle/differential. DOES NOT include removal and installation.
[3] – Models with B16A3 engine use S21/Y21 transaxle.
[4] – If power steering interferes add .3 hr.

IDENTIFICATION

Transmission identification number is stamped on metal pad on top of transmission.

LUBRICATION & ADJUSTMENT

See appropriate MANUAL TRANSMISSION SERVICING article in TRANSMISSION SERVICING section.

TROUBLE SHOOTING

See GENERAL TROUBLE SHOOTING article in APPLICATIONS & IDENTIFICATION section.

ON-VEHICLE SERVICE

AXLE SHAFTS

See appropriate AXLE SHAFTS article in AXLE SHAFTS & TRANSFER CASES section.

REMOVAL & INSTALLATION

See appropriate MANUAL TRANSMISSION REMOVAL article in TRANSMISSION SERVICING section.

TRANSMISSION DISASSEMBLY

NOTE: Place clutch housing on supports high enough to keep mainshaft from hitting workbench.

CAUTION: If it is necessary to heat transmission case for component removal, DO NOT exceed 212°F (100°C).

1) Remove back-up light switch and cable bracket. Remove transmission attaching bolts, and disconnect breather tube. Remove 32-mm sealing plug (plug has square hole). Expand snap ring on countershaft ball bearing. Separate transmission housing from clutch housing. *See Figs. 1 and 2.*
2) Measure clearance between reverse shift fork and shift piece pin. *See Fig. 3.* Clearance should be .002-.014" (.05-.35 mm). Service limit is .020" (.50 mm). If clearance exceeds limit, measure width of "L" groove in reverse shift fork. *See Fig. 3.* Width should be .278-.285" (7.05-7.25 mm). Replace reverse shift fork if width exceeds specification.
3) Measure clearance between reverse idler gear and reverse shift fork. *See Fig. 4.* Clearance should be .020-.043" (.50-1.10 mm). Service limit is .071" (1.80 mm). If clearance exceeds service limit, measure width of reverse shift fork pawl opening. Width should be .500-.512" (12.70-13.00 mm). If width exceeds limit, replace shift fork.
4) Remove reverse shift fork. Remove reverse idler gear shaft and gear. Remove interlock guide bolt from under clutch housing. Remove shift arm "B" bolt. Tape mainshaft splines for protection. Remove mainshaft and countershaft with shift forks as an assembly from clutch housing. Remove differential assembly.

COMPONENT DISASSEMBLY & REASSEMBLY

MAINSHAFT

Inspection – 1) For all mainshaft measurement specifications, refer to MAINSHAFT SPECIFICATIONS table. Measure clearance between 2nd and 3rd gears. *See Fig. 5.* If clearance is greater than service limit, measure thickness of 3rd gear. If thickness is within specifications, replace 3rd/4th synchro hub. If thickness is not within specifications, replace 3rd gear.
2) Measure clearance between 4th gear and spacer collar. If clearance is greater than service limit, measure distance "A" on spacer collar. If distance "A" is greater than specifications, replace spacer collar. If distance "A" is within specifications, measure thickness of 4th gear. Replace 4th gear if thickness exceeds specification. If thickness is within specifications, replace 3rd/4th synchro hub.
3) Measure clearance between 5th gear and spacer collar. If clearance exceeds specifications, measure distance "B" on spacer collar. If distance "B" is greater than service limit, replace collar. If distance "B" is within specifications, measure thickness of 5th gear. Replace 5th gear if thickness exceeds specifications. If thickness is within specifications, replace 5th synchro hub.

MAINSHAFT SPECIFICATIONS

Application	Specification
2nd-To-3rd Gear Clearance	
Standard	.002-.008" (.06-.21 mm)
Service Limit	.13" (.33 mm)
4th Gear-To-Spacer Collar Clearance	
Standard	.002-.007" (.06-.19 mm)
Service Limit	.12" (.31 mm)
5th Gear-To-Spacer Collar Clearance	
Standard	.002-.007" (.06-.19 mm)
Service Limit	.12" (.31 mm)
3rd Gear Thickness	
Standard	1.190-1.192" (30.22-30.27 mm)
Service Limit	1.187" (30.15 mm)
4th Gear Thickness	
Standard	1.186-1.188" (30.12-30.17 mm)
Service Limit	1.183" (30.05 mm)
5th Gear Thickness	
Standard	1.119-1.121" (28.42-28.47 mm)
Service Limit	1.116" (28.35 mm)
Spacer Collar Height "A"	
Standard	.899-.900" (22.83-22.86 mm)
Service Limit	.898" (22.81 mm)
Spacer Collar Height "B"	
Standard	.926-.928" (23.53-23.56 mm)
Service Limit	.926" (23.51mm)

CAUTION: Remove synchro hubs using press and steel blocks. Use of jaw-type puller can damage gear teeth.

Disassembly – Use puller to remove bearing. Support 4th gear on steel blocks, and press mainshaft out of 5th synchro hub. Support 3rd gear on steel blocks, and press mainshaft out of 3rd/4th synchro hub. Remove remaining components.
Inspection – 1) Inspect all parts for damage and wear. Replace if necessary. Clean all parts in solvent, then dry and lubricate all parts. Ensure oil passages are free of contamination.
2) Measure mainshaft at points "D", "E", "F" and "G". *See Fig. 1.* Support mainshaft on "V" blocks. Using dial indicator, measure runout while rotating mainshaft 2 complete revolutions. Replace mainshaft if runout or any part of shaft is not within service limit. See MAINSHAFT BEARING SURFACE SPECIFICATIONS table.

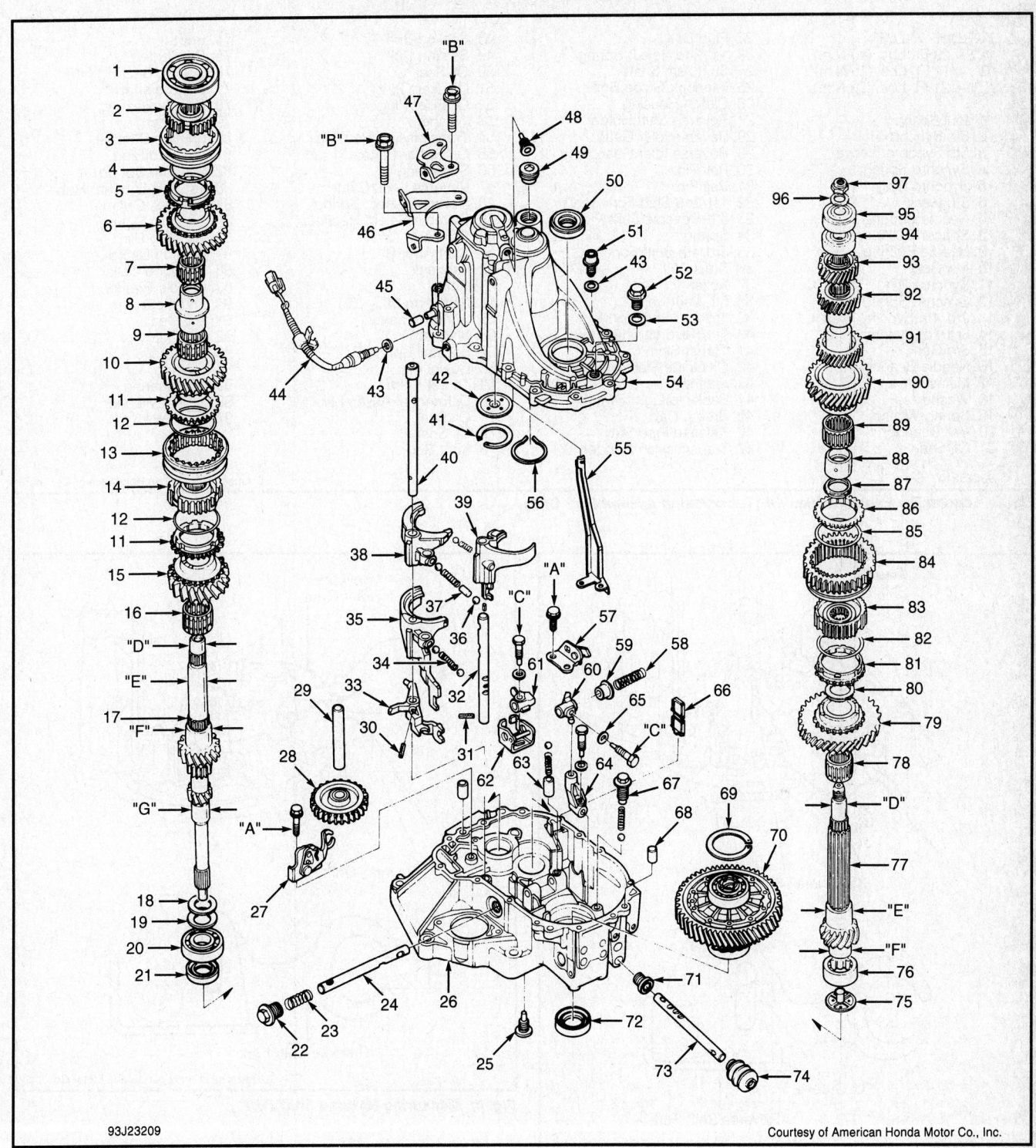

93J23209

Courtesy of American Honda Motor Co., Inc.

Fig. 1: Exploded View Of Transmission Assembly (1 Of 2)

TORQUE VALUE
"A" – 29 Ft. Lbs. (40 N.m)
"B" – 11 Ft. Lbs. (15 N.m)
"C" – 21 Ft. Lbs. (28 N.m)

1. Ball Bearing
2. 5th Synchro Hub
3. 5th Synchro Sleeve
4. Synchro Spring
5. Synchro Ring
6. 5th Gear
7. Needle Bearing
8. Spacer Collar
9. Needle Bearing
10. 4th Gear
11. Synchro Ring
12. Synchro Spring
13. 3rd/4th Synchro Sleeve
14. 3rd/4th Synchro Hub
15. 3rd Gear
16. Needle Bearing
17. Mainshaft
18. Washer
19. Spring Washer
20. Ball Bearing
21. Oil Seal

22. Plug Bolt
23. 1st/2nd Select Spring
24. Shift Arm Shaft
25. Interlock Guide Bolt
26. Clutch Housing
27. Reverse Shift Holder
28. Reverse Idler Gear
29. Reverse Idler Gear Shaft
30. Roll Pin
31. Roll Pin
32. 1st/2nd Shift Fork Shaft
33. 5th/Reverse Shift Piece
34. Spring
35. 3rd/4th Shift Fork
36. Steel Ball
37. Roller
38. 5th Shift Fork
39. 1st/2nd Shift Fork
40. 5th/Reverse Shift Fork
41. Thrust Shim
42. Oil Guide Plate
43. Washer
44. Back-Up Light Switch
45. Breath Cap
46. Release Pipe Stay
47. Transmission Hanger "B"

48. Sealing Bolt
49. Sealing Bolt
50. Oil Seal
51. Oil Drain Plug
52. Oil Filler Plug
53. Washer
54. Transmission Housing
55. Oil Gutter Plate
56. Snap Ring
57. Reverse Lock Cam
58. Reverse Select Spring
59. Reverse Select Retainer
60. Shift Arm "C"
61. Shift Arm "B"
62. Interlock
63. Collar
64. Shift Arm "A"
65. Spring Washer
66. Magnet
67. Set Ball Spring Bolt
68. Dowel Pin
69. Thrust Shim
70. Differential Assembly
71. Oil Seal
72. Oil Seal
73. Shift Rod

74. Boot
75. Oil Guide Plate
76. Needle Bearing
77. Countershaft
78. Needle Bearing
79. 1st Gear
80. Friction Damper
81. Synchro Ring
82. Synchro Spring
83. 1st/2nd Synchro Hub
84. Reverse Gear
85. Synchro Spring
86. Synchro Ring
87. Friction Damper
88. Distance Collar
89. Needle Bearing
90. 2nd Gear
91. 3rd Gear
92. 4th Gear
93. 5th Gear
94. Bearing
95. Ball Bearing
96. Spring Washer
97. Lock Nut

93C23210

Courtesy of American Honda Motor Co., Inc.

Fig. 2: Legend For Exploded View Of Transmission Assembly (2 Of 2)

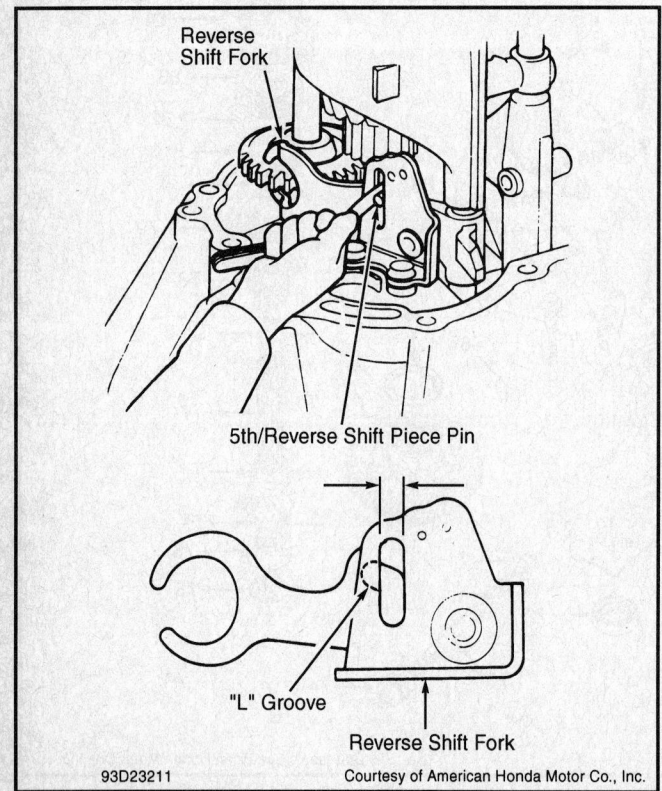

93D23211   Courtesy of American Honda Motor Co., Inc.

Fig. 3: Measuring Reverse Shift Fork Pin Groove

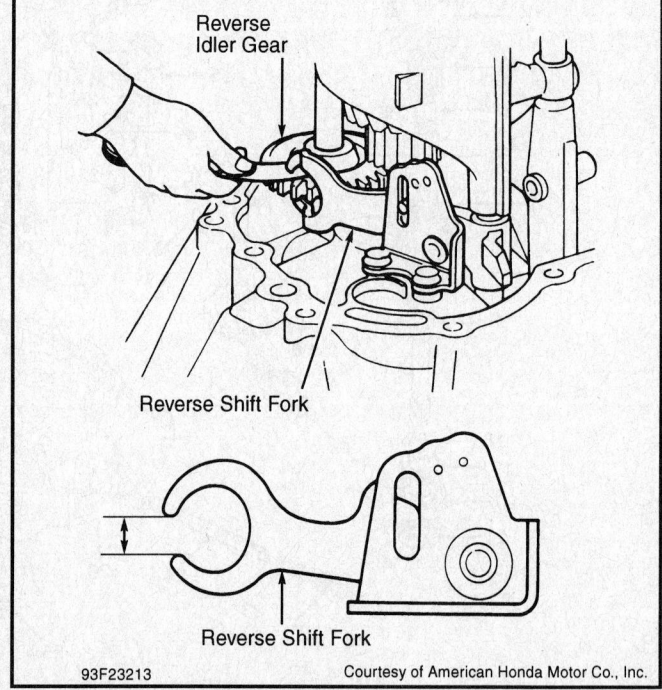

93F23213   Courtesy of American Honda Motor Co., Inc.

Fig. 4: Measuring Reverse Shift Fork

MAINSHAFT BEARING SURFACE SPECIFICATIONS

Application [1]	Standard In. (mm)	Service Limit In. (mm)
"D" Ball Bearing Surface	.8657-.8661 (21.99-22.00)	.8634 (21.93)
"E" Needle Bearing Surface	1.062-1.063 (26.98-26.99)	1.060 (26.93)
"F" Needle Bearing Surface	1.338-1.339 (33.98-34.00)	1.336 (33.93)
"G" Ball Bearing Surface	1.022-1.023 (25.98-25.99)	1.020 (25.92)
Runout Limits	.001 (.02)	.002 (.05)

[1] – "D", "E", "F" and "G" are measuring points. *See Fig. 1.*

Reassembly – Assemble components on mainshaft in reverse order of disassembly. Ensure proper installation of synchro hub, synchro sleeves and ball bearing. *See Fig. 6.*

Mainshaft Thrust Shim Adjustments – 1) Remove thrust shim and oil guide plate from transmission housing. Install 3rd/4th synchro hub, spacer collar, 5th synchro hub (5-speed) or collar (4-speed), and ball bearing on mainshaft. Install mainshaft in transmission housing.

2) Measure distance "B" between transmission housing end and thrust washer using straight edge and feeler gauge. Measure at 3 locations, and average readings. *See Fig. 7.*

3) Measure distance "C" between clutch housing surface and bearing inner race using straight edge and feeler gauge. Measure at 3 locations, and average readings.

4) Calculate shim thickness as follows: "B" + "C" – .95 = shim thickness. The number .93 is mid point of flex range of clutch housing bearing spring washer. DO NOT use more than 2 shims. Shims are available in 0.3-mm increments. Shim thickness ranges from .0236" (.60 mm) to .0709" (1.80 mm). On 1.5L engines, shim diameter is 2.55" (65 mm). On 1.6L engines, shim diameter is 2.75" (70 mm). Shim thickness is the same for both shim sizes. Part numbers for 1.5L engines are 23931-PL3-A10 through 23971-PL3-A10. Part numbers for 1.6L engines are 23931-PL3-B00 through 23971-PL3-B00.

5) Install selected shim in transmission housing. Install spring washer on mainshaft. Clean spring washer and shim thoroughly before installation. Install mainshaft in clutch housing.

6) Install transmission housing onto clutch housing. Install and tighten bolts. Tap mainshaft with a plastic hammer. Attach Mainshaft Base (07GAJ-PG20130) and Collar (07GAJ-PG20120). Attach Mainshaft Holder (07GAJ-PG20110) to mainshaft. Attach magnetic base to clutch housing, and set dial gauge on top of mainshaft. *See Fig. 8.* Turn bolt clockwise, and measure clearance.

CAUTION: DO NOT turn shaft holder more than 60 degrees after needle of dial indicator stops moving.

---

7) Clearance should be .004-.007" (.11-.18 mm). If reading is not correct, recheck shim thickness.

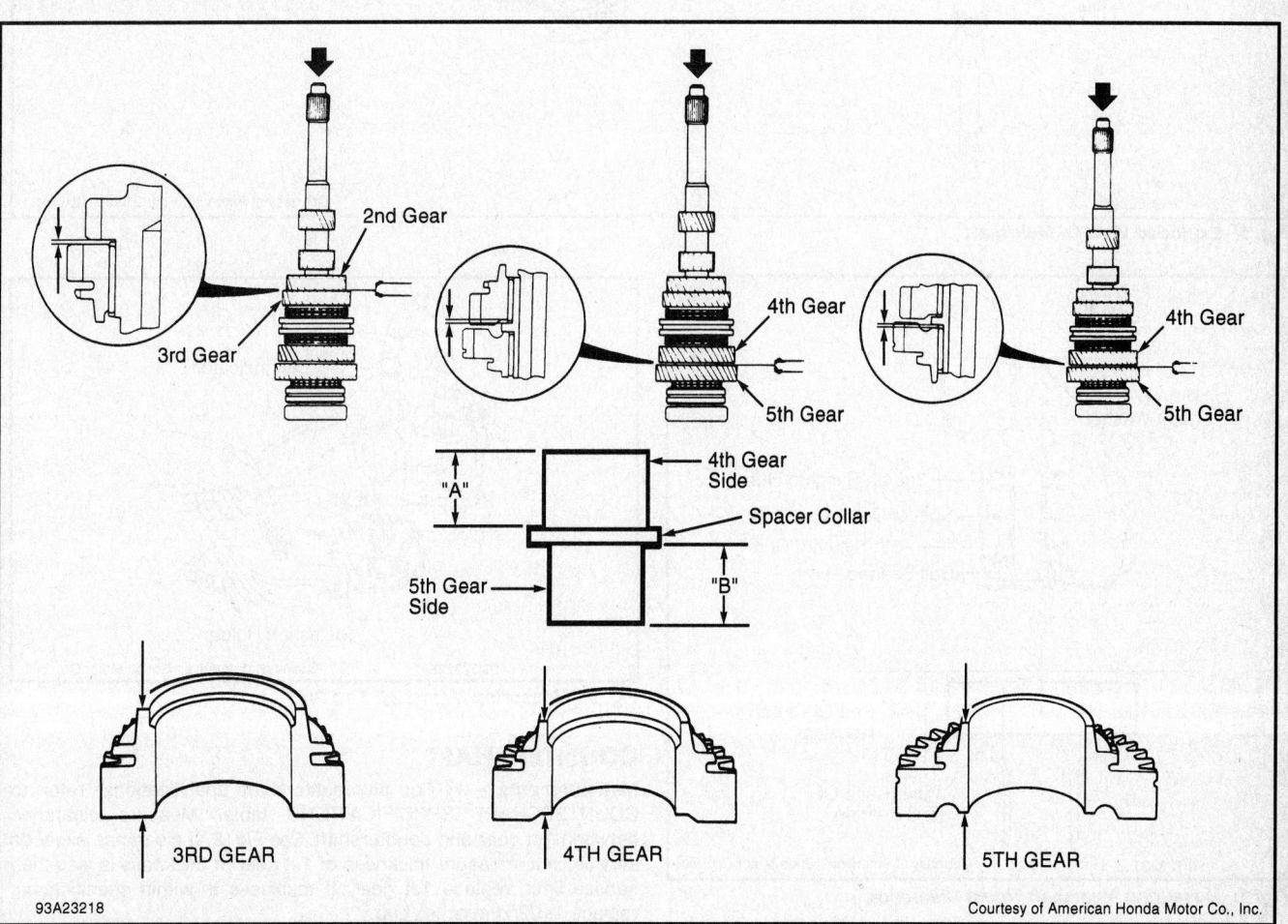

93A23218
Courtesy of American Honda Motor Co., Inc.

Fig. 5: Identifying Mainshaft Measuring Points

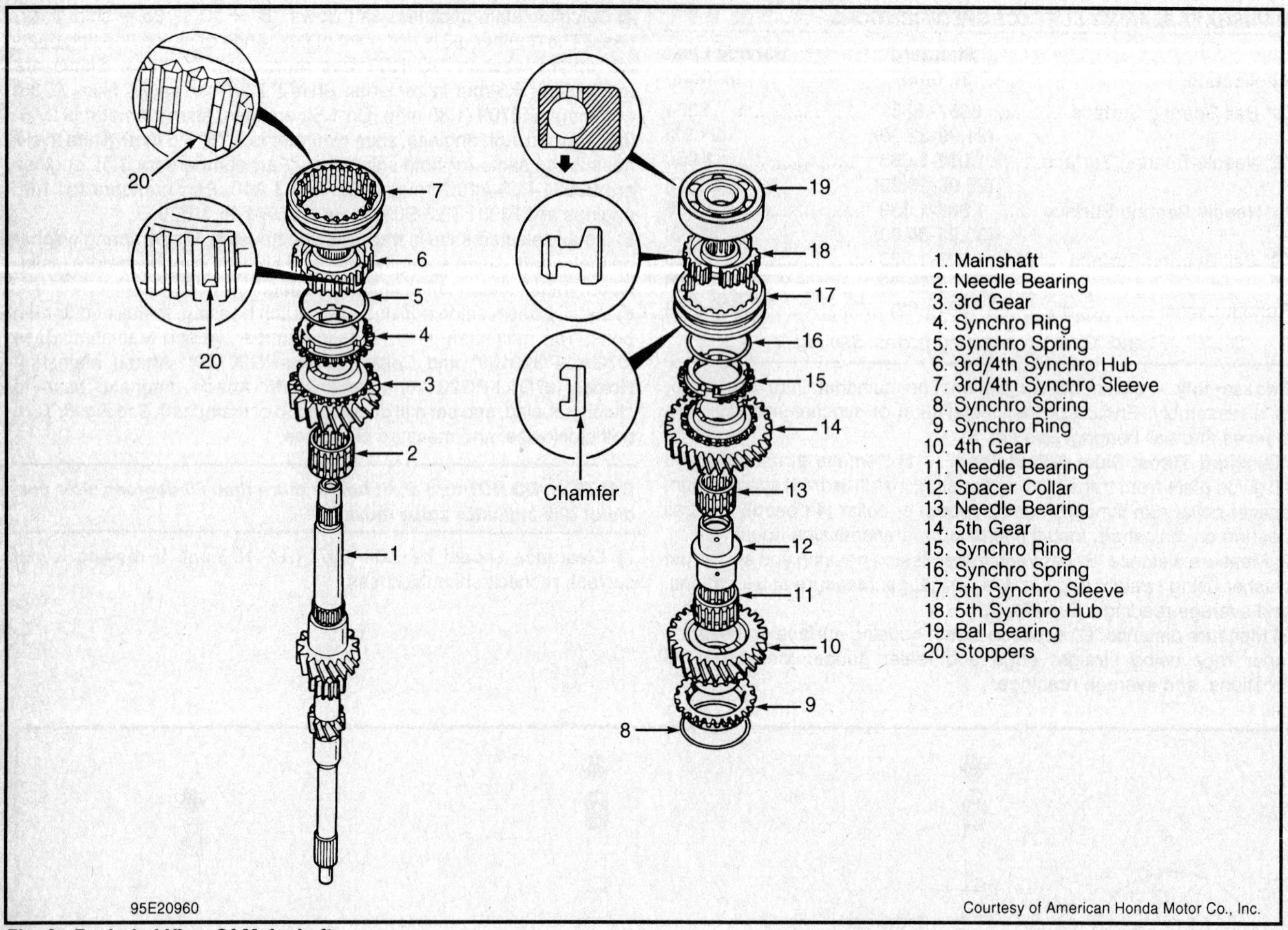

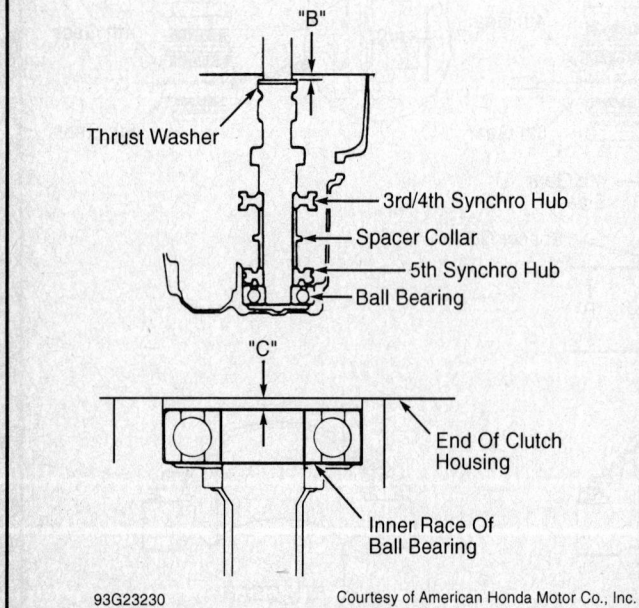

20
7
6
5
4
20
3
2
1
Chamfer
19
18
17
16
15
14
13
12
11
10
9
8
1. Mainshaft
2. Needle Bearing
3. 3rd Gear
4. Synchro Ring
5. Synchro Spring
6. 3rd/4th Synchro Hub
7. 3rd/4th Synchro Sleeve
8. Synchro Spring
9. Synchro Ring
10. 4th Gear
11. Needle Bearing
12. Spacer Collar
13. Needle Bearing
14. 5th Gear
15. Synchro Ring
16. Synchro Spring
17. 5th Synchro Sleeve
18. 5th Synchro Hub
19. Ball Bearing
20. Stoppers
95E20960
Courtesy of American Honda Motor Co., Inc.

Fig. 6: Exploded View Of Mainshaft

"B"
Thrust Washer
3rd/4th Synchro Hub
Spacer Collar
5th Synchro Hub
Ball Bearing
"C"
End Of Clutch Housing
Inner Race Of Ball Bearing
93G23230
Courtesy of American Honda Motor Co., Inc.

Fig. 7: Measuring Mainshaft Thrust Clearance

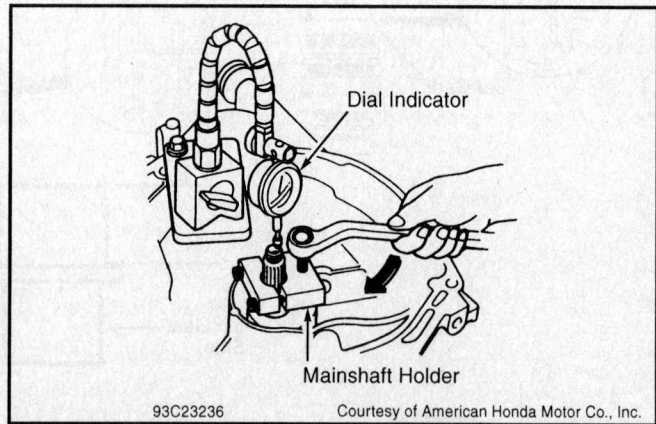

Dial Indicator
Mainshaft Holder
93C23236
Courtesy of American Honda Motor Co., Inc.

Fig. 8: Measuring Mainshaft End Play

COUNTERSHAFT

Measurements – 1) For all countershaft specifications, refer to COUNTERSHAFT SPECIFICATIONS table. Measure clearance between 1st gear and countershaft. *See Fig. 9*. If clearance exceeds service limit, measure thickness of 1st gear. If thickness is less than service limit, replace 1st gear. If thickness is within specification, replace 1st/2nd synchro hub.

2) Measure clearance between 2nd gear and 3rd gear. If clearance exceeds service limit, measure distance "A" on spacer collar. If distance "A" is less than service limit, replace collar. If distance "A" is within specification, measure thickness of 2nd gear. Replace 2nd gear if thickness is less than service limit. If thickness is within specification, replace spacer collar.

COUNTERSHAFT SPECIFICATIONS

Application	Specification
1st Gear-To-Countershaft Clearance	
Standard	.001-.004" (.03-.10 mm)
Service Limit	.009" (.22 mm)
2nd Gear-To-3rd Gear Clearance	
Standard	.001-.004" (.03-.11 mm)
Service Limit	.009" (.23 mm)
1st Gear Thickness	
Standard	1.197-1.198" (30.41-30.44 mm)
Service Limit	1.195" (30.36mm)
2nd Gear Thickness	
Standard	1.257-1.259" (31.92-31.97 mm)
Service Limit	1.254" (31.85 mm)
Spacer Collar Height "A"	
Standard	1.261-1.262 (32.03-32.06 mm)
Service Limit	1.260" (32.01 mm)

CAUTION: Remove synchro hubs using press and steel blocks. Use of jaw-type puller can damage gear teeth.

Disassembly – Using chisel and hammer, raise lock nut tab away from groove in countershaft. Remove lock nut and spring washer. Use bearing puller to remove top ball bearing. Use bearing splitter or appropriate blocks to support 4th gear. Press countershaft out of 4th gear and 5th gear. Support 1st gear, and press countershaft out of 3rd gear. Remove remaining parts.

Inspection – **1)** Inspect all parts for damage and wear. Replace if necessary. Clean all parts in solvent, then dry and lubricate all parts. Using press, install 3rd, 4th and 5th gears before lubricating.
2) Measure countershaft at points "D", "E" and "F". See Fig. 1. Support countershaft on "V" blocks. Using dial indicator, measure runout while Rotating countershaft 2 complete revolutions. Replace countershaft if runout or any part of countershaft is not within service limit. See COUNTERSHAFT BEARING SURFACE SPECIFICATIONS table.

COUNTERSHAFT BEARING SURFACE SPECIFICATIONS

Application [1]	Standard In. (mm)	Service Limits In. (mm)
"D" Ball Bearing Surface	.983-.984 (24.98-24.99)	.981 (24.93)
"E" Needle Bearing Surface	1.416-1.417 (35.98-36.00)	1.415 (35.93)
"F" Ball Bearing Surface	1.181-1.182 (30.00-30.02)	1.179 (29.95)
Runout Limits	.0008 (.020)	.0020 (.050)

[1] – "D", "E" and "F" are measuring points. See Fig. 1.

Reassembly – Assemble components in reverse order of disassembly. See Fig. 10. Ensure friction dampers are properly indexed to mating grooves. Install ball bearing using a press. Install spring washer. Tighten lock nut to 80 ft. lbs. (108 N.m), then stake NEW lock nut tab into groove.

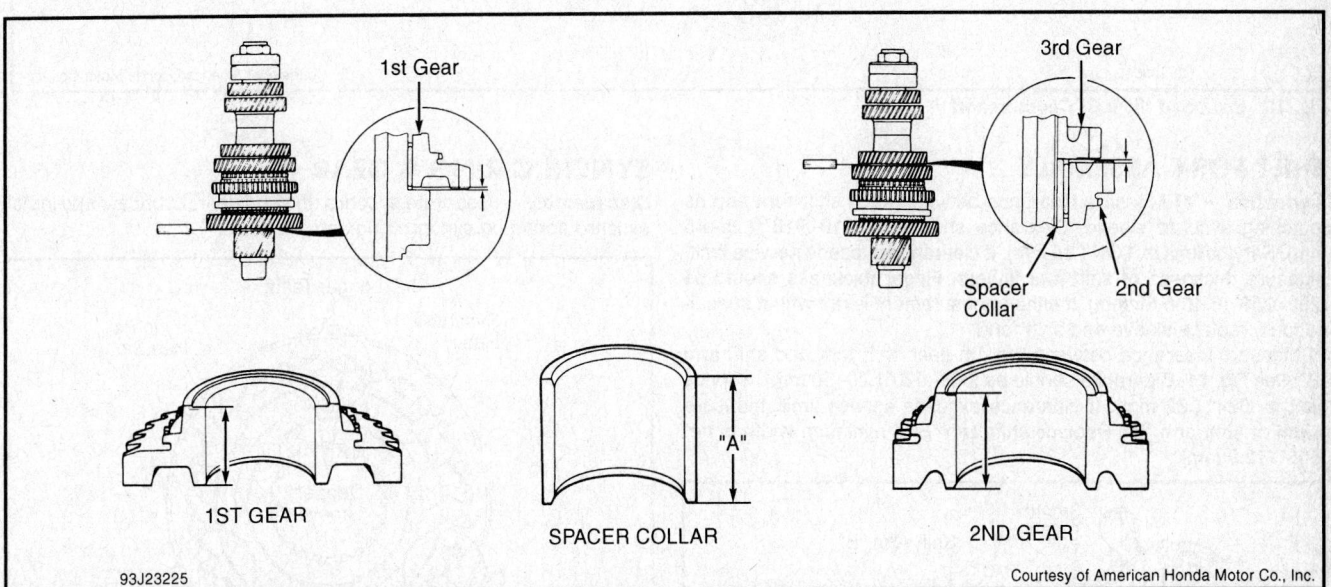

93J23225   Courtesy of American Honda Motor Co., Inc.

Fig. 9: Identifying Countershaft Measuring Points

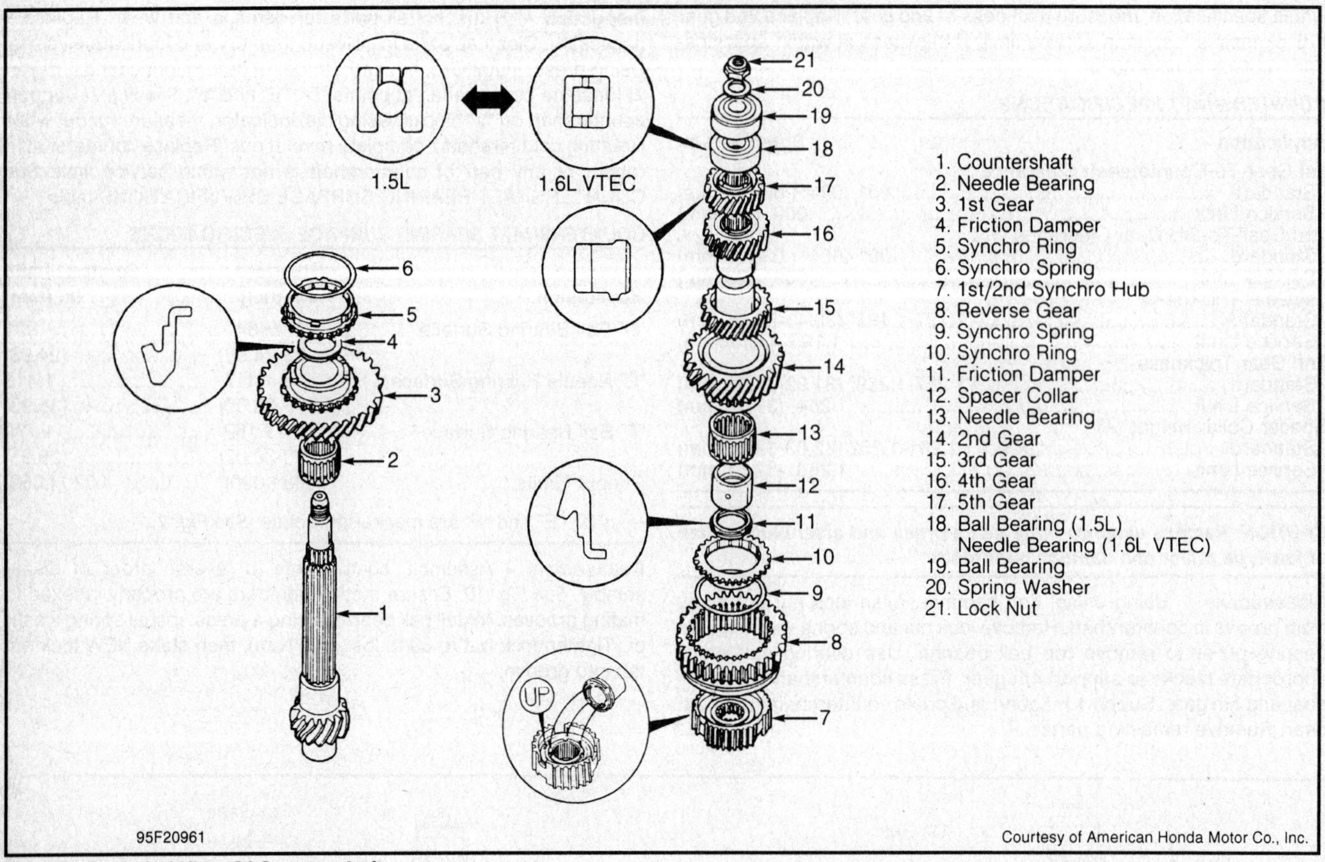

1.5L ↔ 1.6L VTEC

1. Countershaft
2. Needle Bearing
3. 1st Gear
4. Friction Damper
5. Synchro Ring
6. Synchro Spring
7. 1st/2nd Synchro Hub
8. Reverse Gear
9. Synchro Spring
10. Synchro Ring
11. Friction Damper
12. Spacer Collar
13. Needle Bearing
14. 2nd Gear
15. 3rd Gear
16. 4th Gear
17. 5th Gear
18. Ball Bearing (1.5L)
    Needle Bearing (1.6L VTEC)
19. Ball Bearing
20. Spring Washer
21. Lock Nut

95F20961

Courtesy of American Honda Motor Co., Inc.

Fig. 10: Exploded View Of Countershaft

SHIFT FORK ASSEMBLY

Inspection – 1) Measure clearance between each shift fork and its matching synchro sleeve. Clearance should be .010-.018" (.25-.45 mm). Service limit is .031" (.80 mm). If clearance exceeds service limit, measure thickness of shift fork fingers. Finger thickness should be .252-.256" (6.40-6.50 mm). If either measurement is not within specifications, replace sleeve and shift fork.

2) Measure clearance between 3rd/4th gear shift fork and shift arm "B". See Fig. 11. Clearance should be .008-.020" (.20-.50 mm). Service limit is .024" (.62 mm). If clearance exceeds service limit, measure width of shift arm "B". Replace shift arm "B" if minimum width is not .508" (12.9 mm).

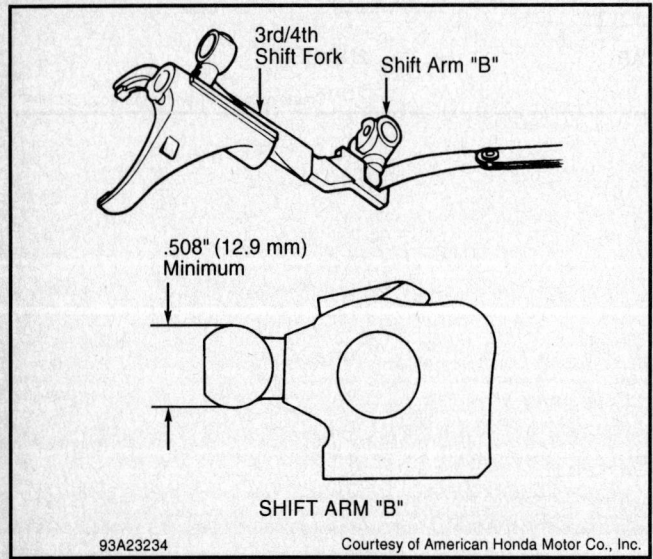

3rd/4th Shift Fork

Shift Arm "B"

.508" (12.9 mm) Minimum

SHIFT ARM "B"

93A23234

Courtesy of American Honda Motor Co., Inc.

Fig. 11: Measuring Shift Arm Clearance

SYNCHRO RING & GEAR

Disassembly – Separate synchro ring and gear. Lubricate and install synchro spring on synchro ring and set aside.

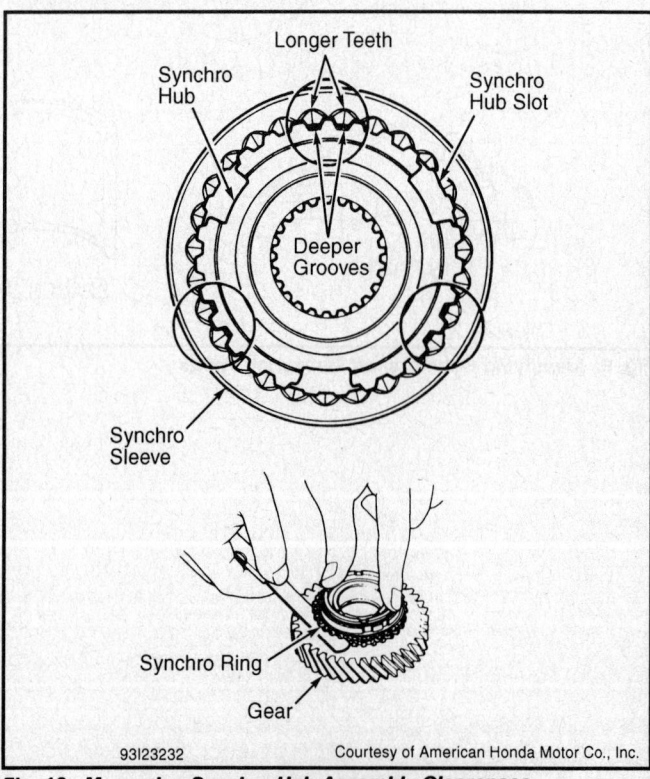

Longer Teeth

Synchro Hub

Synchro Hub Slot

Deeper Grooves

Synchro Sleeve

Synchro Ring

Gear

93I23232

Courtesy of American Honda Motor Co., Inc.

Fig. 12: Measuring Synchro Hub Assembly Clearances

Inspection – 1) Inspect gear teeth for wear, galling, roughness and cracks. Ensure ring and gear turn freely. If replacement is necessary, replace ring and gear as a unit.
2) Measure ring-to-gear clearance all the way around. *See Fig. 12.* Ensure ring is held evenly against gear while measuring. Ring-to-gear clearance should be .033-.043" (.85-1.10 mm). Service limit is .016" (.40 mm). If clearance exceeds limit, replace ring and gear as a unit.
Reassembly – Each synchro sleeve has 3 sets of longer teeth (120 degrees apart) that must be matched with 3 sets of deeper grooves when hub is assembled. *See Fig. 12.*

NOTE: Installing synchro sleeve with its longer teeth in 1st/2nd synchro hub slots will damage spring ring.

DIFFERENTIAL

CAUTION: Ring gear bolts have left-hand threads.

Disassembly – 1) Check bearings for wear and rough rotation. If bearings need replacing, use bearing puller to remove bearings from differential carrier.
2) Remove ring gear. Differential carrier assembly is not serviceable. DO NOT disassemble. If carrier assembly is damaged or backlash is not .002-.006" (.05-.15 mm), replace assembly. *See Fig. 13.*
Reassembly – After inspecting condition of carrier assembly, coat all parts with molylube. Mount carrier assembly in V-blocks, with axles inserted into carrier side gears. Mount dial indicator to measure backlash. *See Fig. 14.* Backlash should be .002-.006" (.05-.15 mm). If backlash exceeds specification, replace differential carrier assembly.

NOTE: Before differential assembly can be adjusted perform step 1) under TRANSMISSION REASSEMBLY.

Adjustments – 1) Using 40 mm I.D. driver, ensure differential assembly is seated in clutch housing. Install original thrust shim in transmission housing. *See Fig. 1.* Install transmission housing. Do NOT apply sealer at this time.
2) Install and torque housing bolts. See TORQUE SPECIFICATIONS. Measure clearance between thrust shim and outer race in housing. Maximum clearance is .004" (.10 mm). If not within limits, select proper thrust shim from appropriate DIFFERENTIAL THRUST SHIM THICKNESS table. Disassemble transmission housing and replace original thrust shim with selected thrust shim. Reassemble transmission housing and recheck side clearance.
3) If differential side clearance is not within specifications, repeat step **2)**. If differential side clearance is okay, adjustment is complete.

DIFFERENTIAL THRUST SHIM THICKNESS (D16Z6 ENGINE)

Part Number	Thickness
41441-PL3-B00	.039" (1.00 mm)
41442-PL3-B00	.043" (1.10 mm)
41443-PL3-B00	.047" (1.20 mm)
41444-PL3-B00	.051" (1.30 mm)
41445-PL3-B00	.055" (1.40 mm)
41446-PL3-B00	.059" (1.50 mm)
41447-PL3-B00	.063" (1.60 mm)
41448-PL3-B00	.067" (1.70 mm)
41449-PL3-B00	.071" (1.80 mm)
41450-PL3-B00	.041" (1.05 mm)
41451-PL3-B00	.045" (1.15 mm)
41452-PL3-B00	.049" (1.25 mm)
41453-PL3-B00	.053" (1.35 mm)
41454-PL3-B00	.057" (1.45 mm)
41455-PL3-B00	.061" (1.55 mm)
41456-PL3-B00	.065" (1.65 mm)
41457-PL3-B00	.069" (1.75 mm)

DIFFERENTIAL THRUST SHIM THICKNESS (EXCEPT D16Z6 ENGINE)

Part Number	Thickness
41441-PL3-A00	.039" (1.00 mm)
41442-PL3-A00	.043" (1.10 mm)
41443-PL3-A00	.047" (1.20 mm)
41444-PL3-A00	.051" (1.30 mm)
41445-PL3-A00	.055" (1.40 mm)
41446-PL3-A00	.059" (1.50 mm)
41447-PL3-A00	.063" (1.60 mm)
41448-PL3-A00	.067" (1.70 mm)
41449-PL3-A00	.071" (1.80 mm)
41450-PL3-A00	.041" (1.05 mm)
41451-PL3-A00	.045" (1.15 mm)
41452-PL3-A00	.049" (1.25 mm)
41453-PL3-A00	.053" (1.35 mm)
41454-PL3-A00	.057" (1.45 mm)
41455-PL3-A00	.061" (1.55 mm)
41456-PL3-A00	.065" (1.65 mm)
41457-PL3-A00	.069" (1.75 mm)

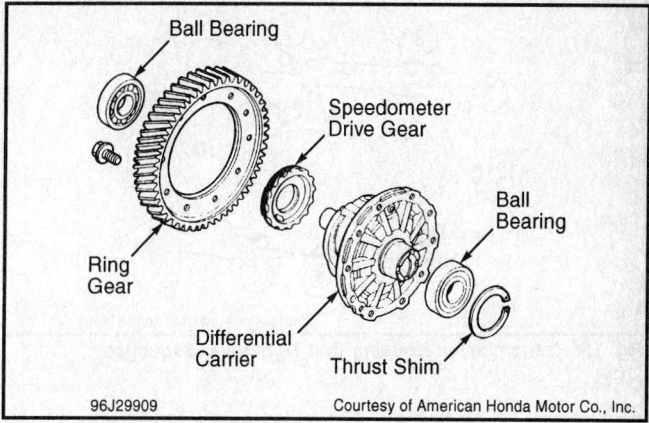

Fig. 13: Exploded View Of Differential Assembly

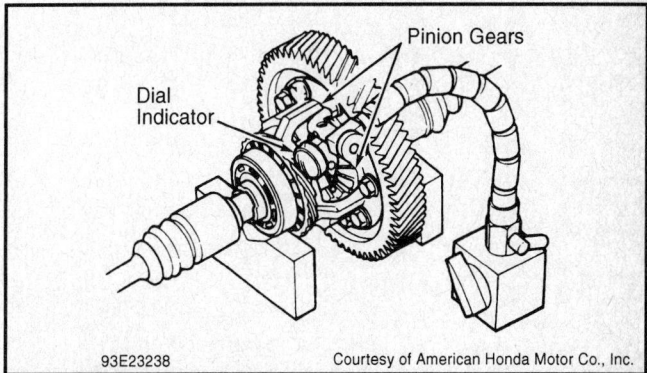

Fig. 14: Measuring Pinion Gear Backlash

TRANSMISSION REASSEMBLY

1) Install magnet and reverse lock cam. Place shift arm "A" in clutch housing, then push shift rod through . Install spring washer and shift arm "A" bolt. Install steel ball, spring and spring bolt. Install shift arm "B" into interlock, and set interlock in clutch housing. Insert shift arm shaft "B" in clutch housing. Install shift arm "C" in shift arm "A", then insert shift arm shaft. Install reverse select retainer and reverse select spring. Install differential assembly.
2) Insert mainshaft and countershaft into shift forks, and install them as an assembly. Fit tab of interlock assembly into notches of shift forks. Lower mainshaft and countershaft into clutch housing. Install shift arm "B" attaching bolt. Install 1st-2nd select spring and plug bolt. Install interlock guide bolt under clutch housing.

3) Install reverse idler shaft. Install reverse shift holder. Install oil guide plate and mainshaft thrust shim into transmission housing. Apply sealant to transmission mating surface of clutch housing. Install dowel pins.

NOTE: This transmission uses no gaskets between major housings. Use Sealant (08718-550000). Assemble housings within 20 minutes after applying sealant, and allow it to cure for at least 30 minutes after assembly before filling it with oil.

---

4) Insert snap ring pliers into 32-mm sealing plug hole. Spread snap ring and install onto countershaft ball bearing, then install transmission housing over clutch housing. Ensure to line up shafts. Install 32-mm sealing plug. Install transmission housing bolts in sequence. *See Fig. 15.* Install back-up light switch.

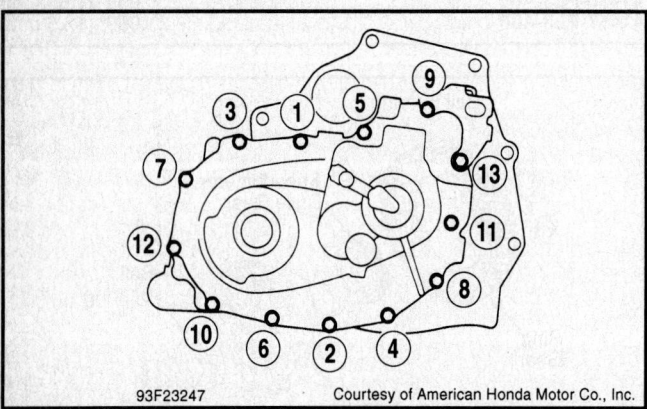

93F23247   Courtesy of American Honda Motor Co., Inc.

Fig. 15: Transmission Housing Bolt Tightening Sequence

TORQUE SPECIFICATIONS
TORQUE SPECIFICATIONS

Application	Ft. Lbs. (N.m)
Back-Up Light Switch	18 (25)
Breather Tube Bolt	21 (28)
Countershaft Lock Nut	81 (110)
Interlock Guide Bolt	30 (40)
Oil Drain Plug	30 (40)
Oil Filler Plug	33 (45)
Plug Bolt	41 (55)
Reverse Lock Cam Bolt	11 (15)
Set Ball Spring Bolt	16 (22)
"A", "B" & "C" Bolts	21 (28)
Transmission Housing Bolts	21 (28)
32-mm Sealing Bolt	18 (25)
	INCH lbs.
10-mm Sealing Bolt	96 (11)

Civic, Civic Del Sol

APPLICATION & LABOR TIMES

APPLICATION & LABOR TIMES

Vehicle	Labor Times		
Application	[1] R & I	[2] Overhaul	Series
1996 Civic & 1996 Civic Del Sol			
Except B16A2 Engine [3]	4.1	6.2	S20 & S8G

[1] – Removal and installation of transmission from vehicle chassis.

[2] – Bench overhaul time for transmission or transaxle/differential. DOES NOT include removal and installation.

[3] – Models with B16A2 engine use S21 transaxle.

IDENTIFICATION

Transmission identification number is stamped on metal pad on top of transmission.

LUBRICATION & ADJUSTMENT

See appropriate MANUAL TRANSMISSION SERVICING article in TRANSMISSION SERVICING section.

TROUBLE SHOOTING

See GENERAL TROUBLE SHOOTING article in APPLICATIONS & IDENTIFICATION section.

ON-VEHICLE SERVICE

AXLE SHAFTS

See appropriate AXLE SHAFTS article in AXLE SHAFTS & TRANSFER CASES section.

REMOVAL & INSTALLATION

See appropriate MANUAL TRANSMISSION REMOVAL article in TRANSMISSION SERVICING section.

TRANSMISSION DISASSEMBLY

NOTE: Place clutch housing on supports high enough to keep mainshaft from hitting workbench.

1) Remove back-up light switch and cable bracket. Remove transmission hanger. Remove set screws, washers, springs and steel balls. See Fig. 1. Loosen transmission housing bolts in crisscross pattern.

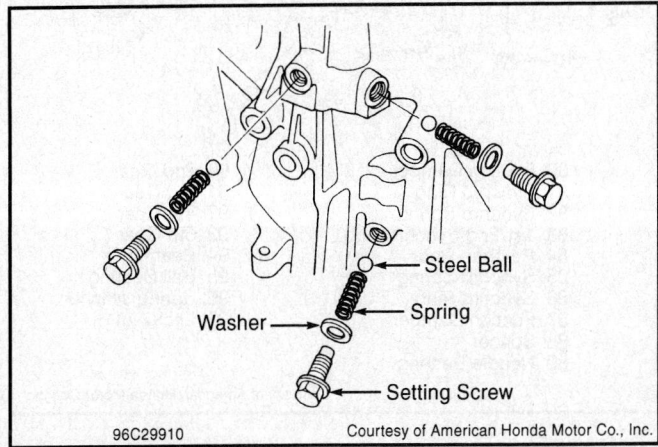

96C29910 — Courtesy of American Honda Motor Co., Inc.

Fig. 1: Removing Set Screws

2) Remove 32-mm sealing plug (plug has square hole). Expand snap ring on countershaft ball bearing. Separate transmission housing from clutch housing. See Fig. 2. Remove thrust shim, oil guide plate and oil gutter plate from transmission housing.

3) Measure clearance between reverse shift fork and 5th/reverse shift piece pin. See Fig. 3. Clearance should be .002-.014" (.05-.35 mm). Service limit is .020" (.50 mm). If clearance exceeds limit, measure width of "L" groove in reverse shift fork. See Fig. 3. Width should be .278-.285" (7.05-7.25 mm). Replace reverse shift fork if width exceeds specification.

4) Measure clearance between reverse idler gear and reverse shift fork. See Fig. 4. Clearance should be .020-.043" (.50-1.10 mm). Service limit is .071" (1.80 mm). If clearance exceeds service limit, measure width of reverse shift fork pawl opening. Width should be .500-.512" (12.70-13.00 mm). If width exceeds limit, replace shift fork.

5) Remove reverse shift holder. Remove reverse idler gear shaft and gear. Remove interlock guide bolt from under clutch housing. See Fig. 5. Remove shift arm "B" bolt. Tape mainshaft splines for protection. Remove mainshaft and countershaft with shift forks as an assembly from clutch housing. Remove differential assembly.

COMPONENT DISASSEMBLY & REASSEMBLY

MAINSHAFT

Inspection – **1)** For all mainshaft measurement specifications, refer to MAINSHAFT SPECIFICATIONS table. Measure clearance between 2nd and 3rd gears. See Fig. 6. If clearance is greater than service limit, measure thickness of 3rd gear. If thickness is within specifications, replace 3rd/4th synchro hub. If thickness is not within specifications, replace 3rd gear.

2) Measure clearance between 4th gear and spacer collar. If clearance is greater than service limit, measure distance "A" on spacer collar. If distance "A" is greater than specifications, replace spacer collar. If distance "A" is within specifications, measure thickness of 4th gear. Replace 4th gear if thickness exceeds specification. If thickness is within specifications, replace 3rd/4th synchro hub.

3) Measure clearance between 5th gear and spacer collar. If clearance exceeds specifications, measure distance "B" on spacer collar. If distance "B" is greater than service limit, replace collar. If distance "B" is within specifications, measure thickness of 5th gear. Replace 5th gear if thickness exceeds specifications. If thickness is within specifications, replace 5th synchro hub.

MAINSHAFT SPECIFICATIONS

Application	Specification
2nd-To-3rd Gear Clearance	
Standard	.002-.008" (.06-.21 mm)
Service Limit	.13" (.33 mm)
4th Gear-To-Spacer Collar Clearance	
Standard	.002-.007" (.06-.19 mm)
Service Limit	.12" (.31 mm)
5th Gear-To-Spacer Collar Clearance	
Standard	.002-.007" (.06-.19 mm)
Service Limit	.12" (.31 mm)
3rd Gear Thickness	
Standard	1.190-1.192" (30.22-30.27 mm)
Service Limit	1.187" (30.15 mm)
4th Gear Thickness	
Standard	1.186-1.188" (30.12-30.17 mm)
Service Limit	1.183" (30.05 mm)
5th Gear Thickness	
Standard	1.119-1.121" (28.42-28.47 mm)
Service Limit	1.116" (28.35 mm)
Spacer Collar Height "A"	
Standard	.899-.900" (22.83-22.86 mm)
Service Limit	.898" (22.81 mm)
Spacer Collar Height "B"	
Standard	.926-.928" (23.53-23.56 mm)
Service Limit	.926" (23.51mm)

MANUAL TRANSMISSIONS
Honda S40 & S8G (Cont.)

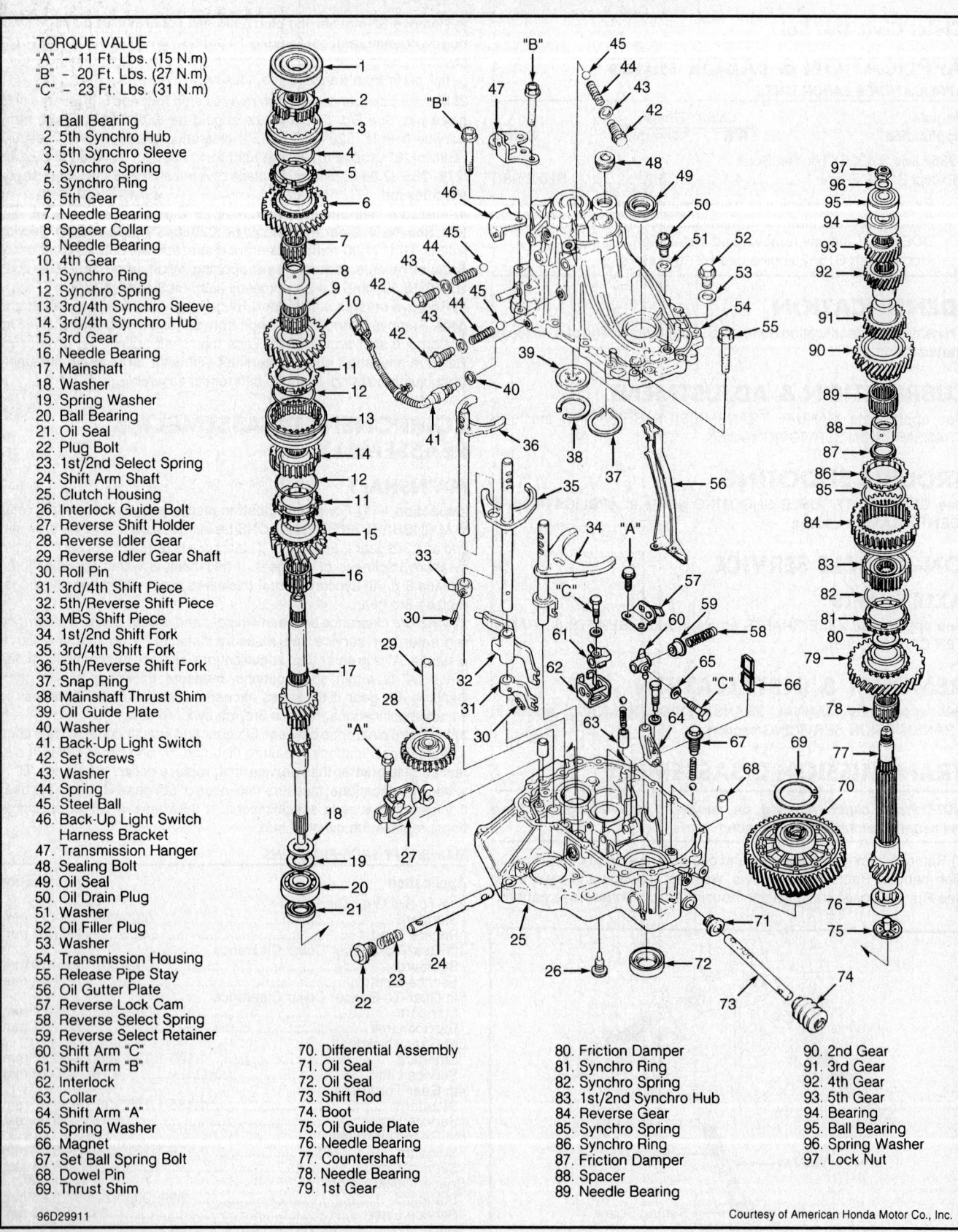

TORQUE VALUE
"A" – 11 Ft. Lbs. (15 N.m)
"B" – 20 Ft. Lbs. (27 N.m)
"C" – 23 Ft. Lbs. (31 N.m)

1. Ball Bearing
2. 5th Synchro Hub
3. 5th Synchro Sleeve
4. Synchro Spring
5. Synchro Ring
6. 5th Gear
7. Needle Bearing
8. Spacer Collar
9. Needle Bearing
10. 4th Gear
11. Synchro Ring
12. Synchro Spring
13. 3rd/4th Synchro Sleeve
14. 3rd/4th Synchro Hub
15. 3rd Gear
16. Needle Bearing
17. Mainshaft
18. Washer
19. Spring Washer
20. Ball Bearing
21. Oil Seal
22. Plug Bolt
23. 1st/2nd Select Spring
24. Shift Arm Shaft
25. Clutch Housing
26. Interlock Guide Bolt
27. Reverse Shift Holder
28. Reverse Idler Gear
29. Reverse Idler Gear Shaft
30. Roll Pin
31. 3rd/4th Shift Piece
32. 5th/Reverse Shift Piece
33. MBS Shift Piece
34. 1st/2nd Shift Fork
35. 3rd/4th Shift Fork
36. 5th/Reverse Shift Fork
37. Snap Ring
38. Mainshaft Thrust Shim
39. Oil Guide Plate
40. Washer
41. Back-Up Light Switch
42. Set Screws
43. Washer
44. Spring
45. Steel Ball
46. Back-Up Light Switch
    Harness Bracket
47. Transmission Hanger
48. Sealing Bolt
49. Oil Seal
50. Oil Drain Plug
51. Washer
52. Oil Filler Plug
53. Washer
54. Transmission Housing
55. Release Pipe Stay
56. Oil Gutter Plate
57. Reverse Lock Cam
58. Reverse Select Spring
59. Reverse Select Retainer
60. Shift Arm "C"
61. Shift Arm "B"
62. Interlock
63. Collar
64. Shift Arm "A"
65. Spring Washer
66. Magnet
67. Set Ball Spring Bolt
68. Dowel Pin
69. Thrust Shim

70. Differential Assembly
71. Oil Seal
72. Oil Seal
73. Shift Rod
74. Boot
75. Oil Guide Plate
76. Needle Bearing
77. Countershaft
78. Needle Bearing
79. 1st Gear

80. Friction Damper
81. Synchro Ring
82. Synchro Spring
83. 1st/2nd Synchro Hub
84. Reverse Gear
85. Synchro Spring
86. Synchro Ring
87. Friction Damper
88. Spacer
89. Needle Bearing

90. 2nd Gear
91. 3rd Gear
92. 4th Gear
93. 5th Gear
94. Bearing
95. Ball Bearing
96. Spring Washer
97. Lock Nut

96D29911

Courtesy of American Honda Motor Co., Inc.

Fig. 2: Exploded View Of Transmission Assembly

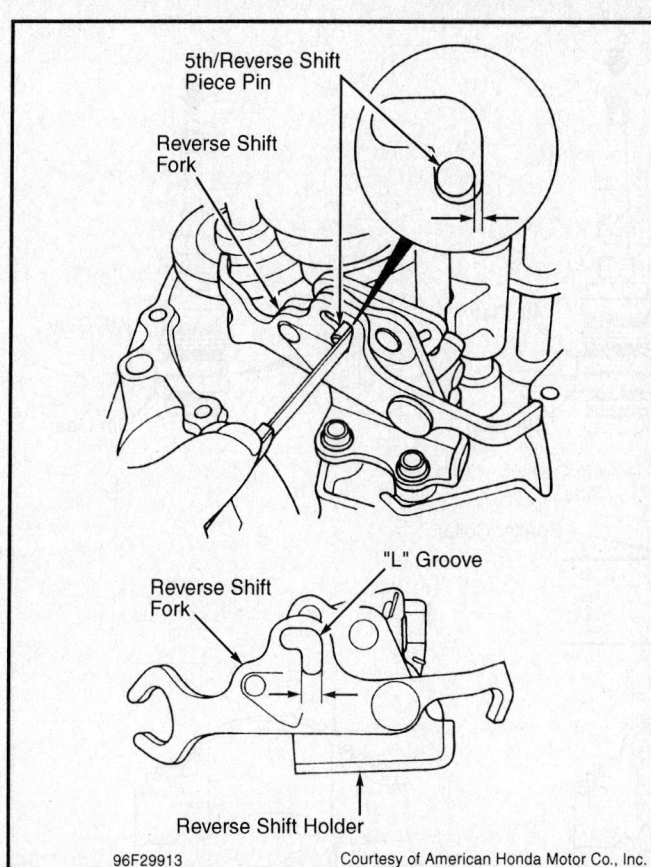

Fig. 3: Measuring Reverse Shift Fork Pin Groove

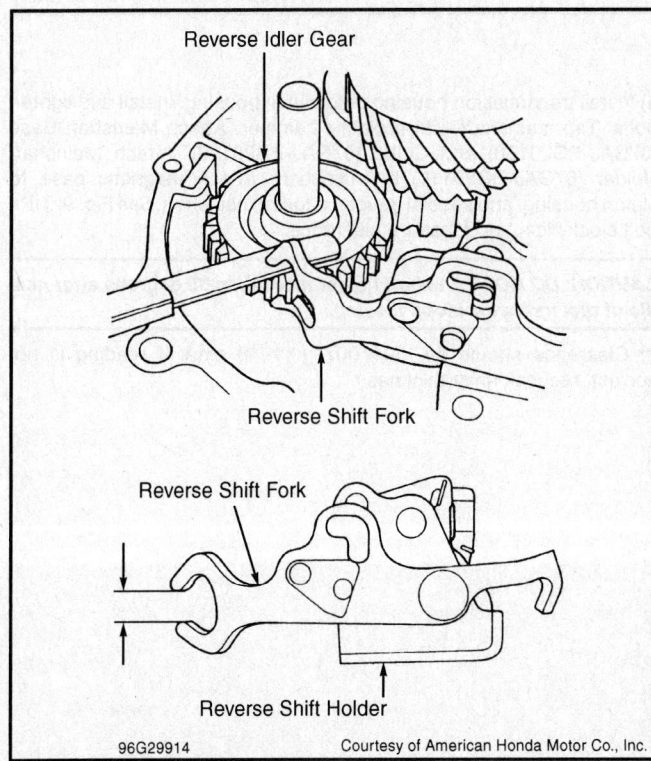

Fig. 4: Measuring Reverse Shift Fork

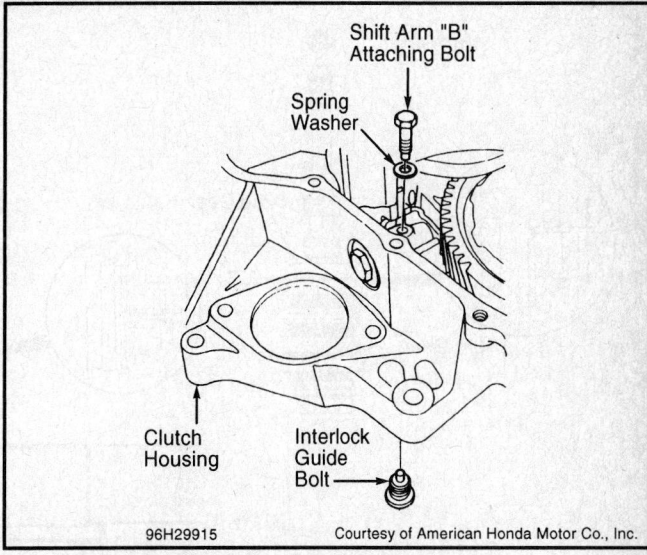

Fig. 5: Removing Clutch Housing Components

CAUTION: Remove synchro hubs using press and steel blocks. Use of jaw-type puller can damage gear teeth.

Disassembly – Use puller to remove bearing. Support 4th gear on steel blocks, and press mainshaft out of 5th synchro hub. Support 3rd gear on steel blocks, and press mainshaft out of 3rd/4th synchro hub. Remove remaining components.

Inspection – 1) Inspect all parts for damage and wear. Replace if necessary. Clean all parts in solvent, then dry and lubricate all parts. Ensure oil passages are free of contamination.

2) Measure mainshaft at points "D", "E", "F" and "G". *See Fig. 2.* Support mainshaft on "V" blocks. Using dial indicator, measure runout while rotating mainshaft 2 complete revolutions. Replace mainshaft if runout or any part of shaft is not within service limit. See MAINSHAFT BEARING SURFACE SPECIFICATIONS table.

MAINSHAFT BEARING SURFACE SPECIFICATIONS

Application [1]	Standard In. (mm)	Service Limit In. (mm)
"D" Ball Bearing Surface	.8657-.8661	.8634
	(21.99-22.00)	(21.93)
"E" Needle Bearing Surface	1.062-1.063	1.060
	(26.98-26.99)	(26.93)
"F" Needle Bearing Surface	1.338-1.339	1.336
	(33.98-34.00)	(33.93)
"G" Ball Bearing Surface	1.022-1.023	1.020
	(25.98-25.99)	(25.92)
Runout Limits	.001 (.02)	.002 (.05)

[1] – "D", "E", "F" and "G" are measuring points. *See Fig. 2.*

Reassembly – Assemble components on mainshaft in reverse order of disassembly. Ensure proper installation of synchro hub, synchro sleeves and ball bearing. *See Fig. 7.*

Mainshaft Thrust Shim Adjustments – 1) Remove thrust shim and oil guide plate from transmission housing. Install 3rd/4th synchro hub, spacer collar, 5th synchro hub (5-speed) or collar (4-speed), and ball bearing on mainshaft. Install mainshaft in transmission housing.

2) Measure distance "B" between transmission housing end and thrust washer using straight edge and feeler gauge. Measure at 3 locations, and average readings. *See Fig. 8.*

3) Measure distance "C" between clutch housing surface and bearing inner race using straight edge and feeler gauge. Measure at 3 locations, and average readings.

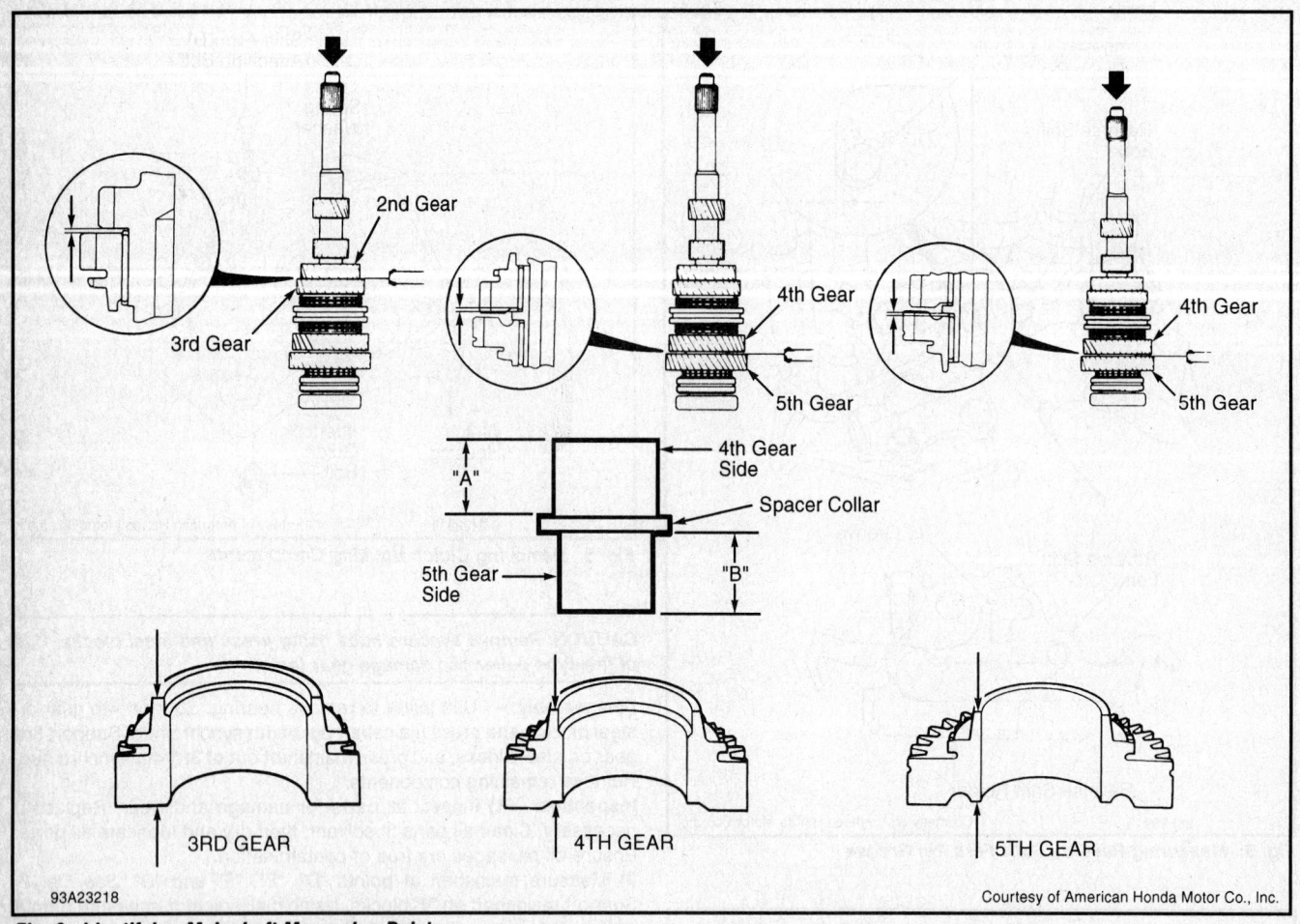

93A23218   Courtesy of American Honda Motor Co., Inc.

Fig. 6: Identifying Mainshaft Measuring Points

4) Calculate shim thickness as follows: "B" + "C" – .95 = shim thickness. The number .93 is mid point of flex range of clutch housing bearing spring washer. DO NOT use more than 2 shims. Shims are available in 0.3-mm increments. Shim thickness ranges from .0236" (.60 mm) to .0709 (1.80 mm). On non-VTEC engines, shim diameter is 2.55" (65 mm). On VTEC engines, shim diameter is 2.75" (70 mm). Shim thickness is the same for both shim sizes. Part numbers for non-VTEC engines are 23931-PL3-A10 through 23971-PL3-A10. Part numbers for VTEC engines are 23931-PL3-B00 through 23971-PL3-B00.

5) Install selected shim in transmission housing. Install spring washer on mainshaft. Clean spring washer and shim thoroughly before installation. Install mainshaft in clutch housing.

6) Install transmission housing onto clutch housing. Install and tighten bolts. Tap mainshaft with a plastic hammer. Attach Mainshaft Base (07GAJ-PG20130) and Collar (07GAJ-PG20120). Attach Mainshaft Holder (07GAJ-PG20110) to mainshaft. Attach magnetic base to clutch housing, and set dial gauge on top of mainshaft. *See Fig. 9.* Turn bolt clockwise, and measure clearance.

CAUTION: DO NOT turn shaft holder more than 60 degrees after needle of dial indicator stops moving.

7) Clearance should be .004-.007" (.11-.18 mm). If reading is not correct, recheck shim thickness.

20
7
6
5
4
20
3
2
1
Chamfer
19
18
17
16
15
14
13
12
11
10
9
8
1. Mainshaft
2. Needle Bearing
3. 3rd Gear
4. Synchro Ring
5. Synchro Spring
6. 3rd/4th Synchro Hub
7. 3rd/4th Synchro Sleeve
8. Synchro Spring
9. Synchro Ring
10. 4th Gear
11. Needle Bearing
12. Spacer Collar
13. Needle Bearing
14. 5th Gear
15. Synchro Ring
16. Synchro Spring
17. 5th Synchro Sleeve
18. 5th Synchro Hub
19. Ball Bearing
20. Stoppers
95E20960
Courtesy of American Honda Motor Co., Inc.

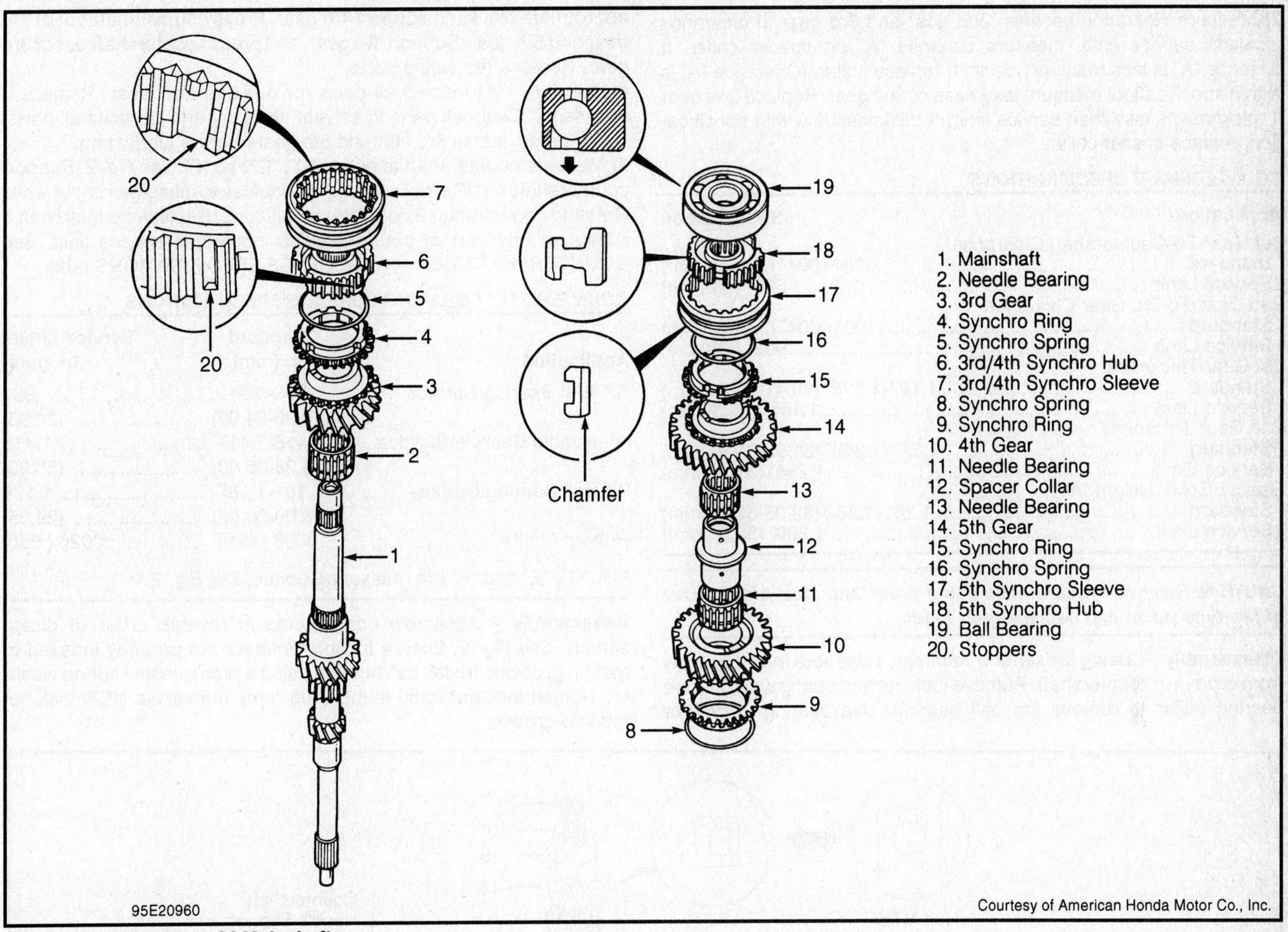

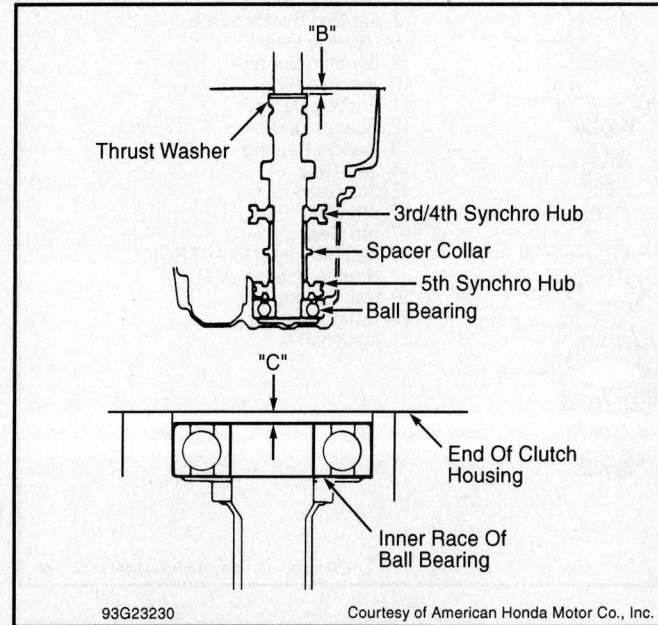

Fig. 7: Exploded View Of Mainshaft

"B"
Thrust Washer
3rd/4th Synchro Hub
Spacer Collar
5th Synchro Hub
Ball Bearing
"C"
End Of Clutch Housing
Inner Race Of Ball Bearing
93G23230
Courtesy of American Honda Motor Co., Inc.

Fig. 8: Measuring Mainshaft Thrust Clearance

Dial Indicator
Mainshaft Holder
93C23236
Courtesy of American Honda Motor Co., Inc.

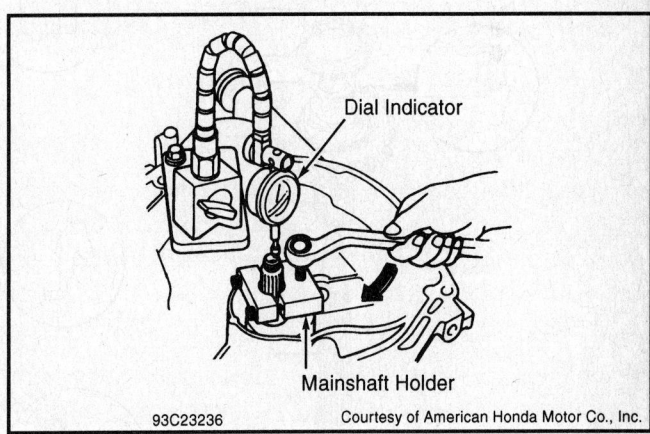

Fig. 9: Measuring Mainshaft End Play

COUNTERSHAFT

Measurements – 1) For all countershaft specifications, refer to COUNTERSHAFT SPECIFICATIONS table. Measure clearance between 1st gear and countershaft. *See Fig. 10.* If clearance exceeds service limit, measure thickness of 1st gear. If thickness is less than service limit, replace 1st gear. If thickness is within specification, replace 1st/2nd synchro hub.

2) Measure clearance between 2nd gear and 3rd gear. If clearance exceeds service limit, measure distance "A" on spacer collar. If distance "A" is less than service limit, replace collar. If distance "A" is within specification, measure thickness of 2nd gear. Replace 2nd gear if thickness is less than service limit. If thickness is within specification, replace spacer collar.

COUNTERSHAFT SPECIFICATIONS

Application	Specification
1st Gear-To-Countershaft Clearance	
Standard	.001-.004" (.03-.10 mm)
Service Limit	.009" (.22 mm)
2nd Gear-To-3rd Gear Clearance	
Standard	.001-.004" (.03-.11 mm)
Service Limit	.009" (.23 mm)
1st Gear Thickness	
Standard	1.197-1.198" (30.41-30.44 mm)
Service Limit	1.195" (30.36mm)
2nd Gear Thickness	
Standard	1.257-1.259" (31.92-31.97 mm)
Service Limit	1.254" (31.85 mm)
Spacer Collar Height "A"	
Standard	1.261-1.262 (32.03-32.06 mm)
Service Limit	1.260" (32.01 mm)

CAUTION: Remove synchro hubs using press and steel blocks. Use of jaw-type puller can damage gear teeth.

Disassembly – Using chisel and hammer, raise lock nut tab away from groove in countershaft. Remove lock nut and spring washer. Use bearing puller to remove top ball bearing. Use bearing splitter or appropriate blocks to support 4th gear. Press countershaft out of 4th gear and 5th gear. Support 1st gear, and press countershaft out of 3rd gear. Remove remaining parts.

Inspection – 1) Inspect all parts for damage and wear. Replace if necessary. Clean all parts in solvent, then dry and lubricate all parts. Using press, install 3rd, 4th and 5th gears before lubricating.

2) Measure countershaft at points "D", "E" and "F". See Fig. 2. Support countershaft on "V" blocks. Using dial indicator, measure runout while Rotating countershaft 2 complete revolutions. Replace countershaft if runout or any part of countershaft is not within service limit. See COUNTERSHAFT BEARING SURFACE SPECIFICATIONS table.

COUNTERSHAFT BEARING SURFACE SPECIFICATIONS

Application [1]	Standard In. (mm)	Service Limits In. (mm)
"D" Ball Bearing Surface	.983-.984	.981
	(24.98-24.99)	(24.93)
"E" Needle Bearing Surface	1.416-1.417	1.415
	(35.98-36.00)	(35.93)
"F" Ball Bearing Surface	1.181-1.182	1.179
	(30.00-30.02)	(29.95)
Runout Limits	.0008 (.020)	.0020 (.050)

[1] – "D", "E" and "F" are measuring points. See Fig. 2.

Reassembly – Assemble components in reverse order of disassembly. See Fig. 9. Ensure friction dampers are properly indexed to mating grooves. Install ball bearing using a press. Install spring washer. Tighten lock nut to 80 ft. lbs. (108 N.m), then stake NEW lock nut tab into groove.

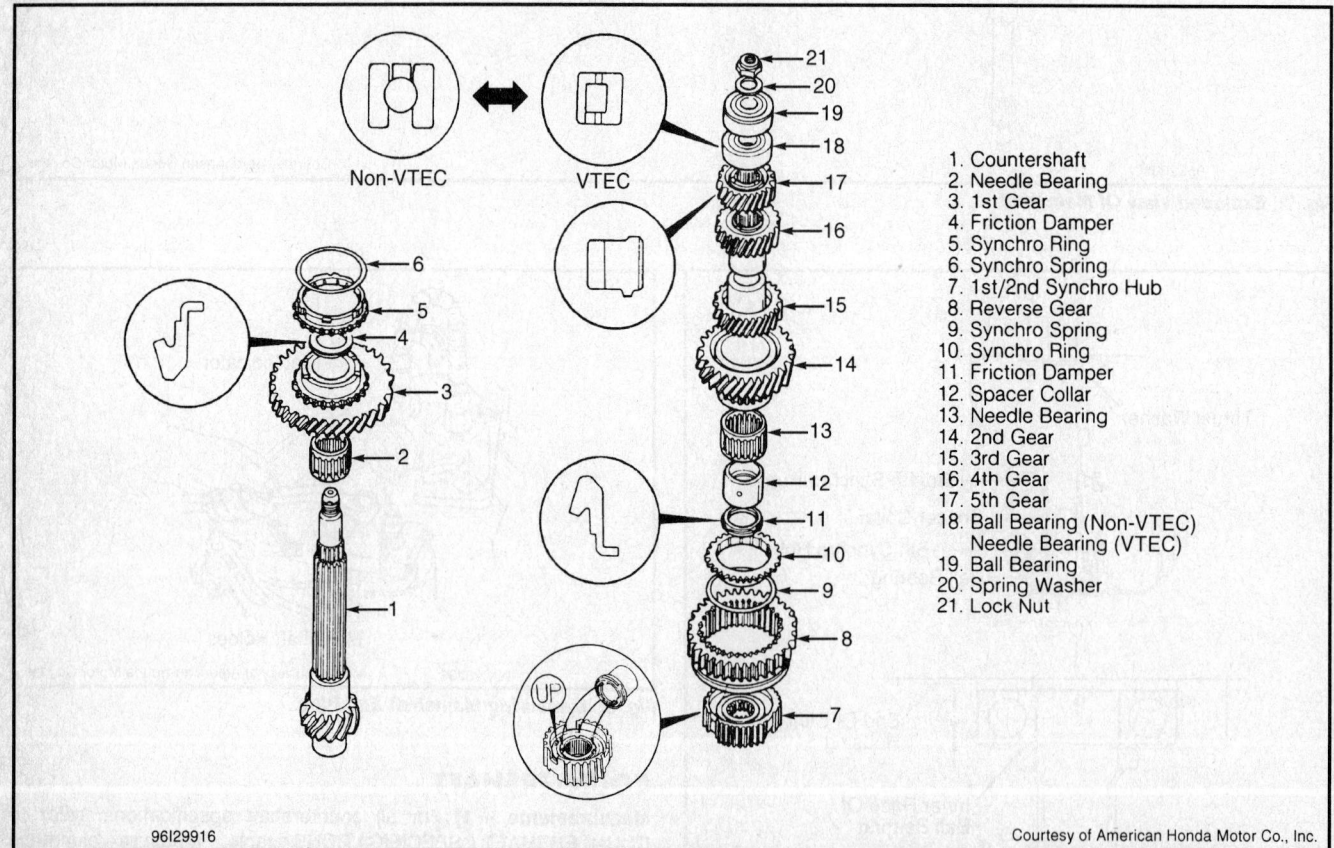

Non-VTEC   VTEC

1. Countershaft
2. Needle Bearing
3. 1st Gear
4. Friction Damper
5. Synchro Ring
6. Synchro Spring
7. 1st/2nd Synchro Hub
8. Reverse Gear
9. Synchro Spring
10. Synchro Ring
11. Friction Damper
12. Spacer Collar
13. Needle Bearing
14. 2nd Gear
15. 3rd Gear
16. 4th Gear
17. 5th Gear
18. Ball Bearing (Non-VTEC)
    Needle Bearing (VTEC)
19. Ball Bearing
20. Spring Washer
21. Lock Nut

96I29916

Courtesy of American Honda Motor Co., Inc.

Fig. 10: Identifying Countershaft Measuring Points

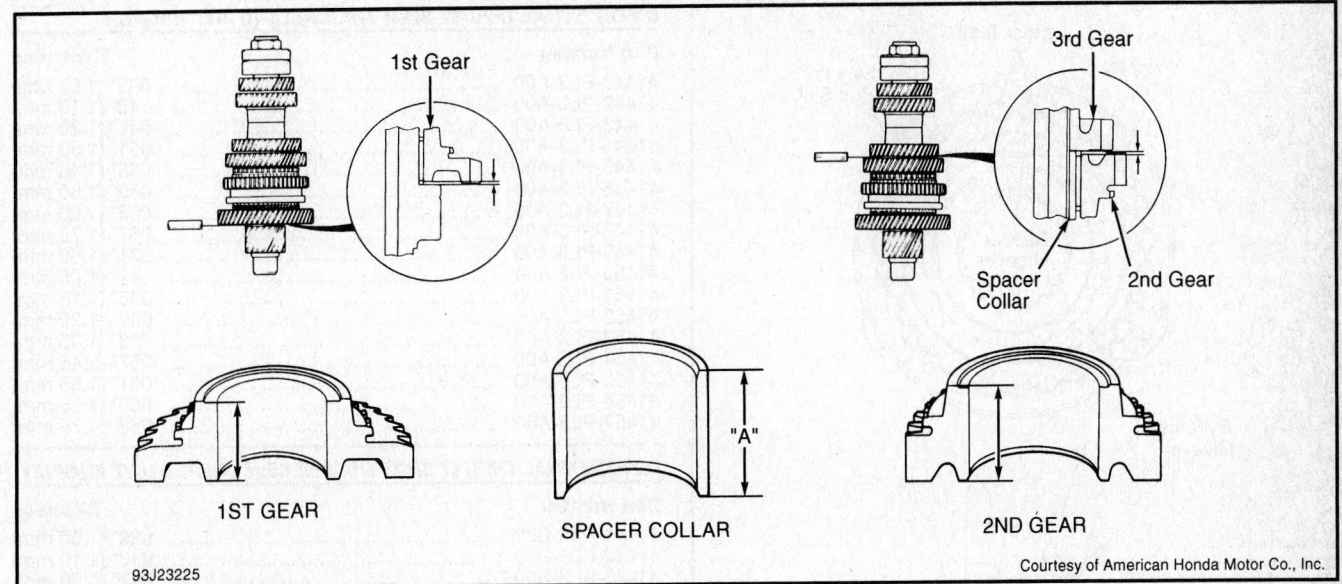

Fig. 11: Exploded View Of Countershaft

SHIFT FORK ASSEMBLY

Inspection – 1) Measure clearance between each shift fork and its matching synchro sleeve. Clearance should be .014-.026" (.35-.65 mm). Service limit is .039" (1.00 mm). If clearance exceeds service limit, measure thickness of shift fork fingers. Finger thickness should be .291-.299" (7.40-7.60 mm) for 3rd/4th shift fork and .244-.252" (6.20-6.40 mm) for 11st/2nd and 5th shift fork. If either measurement is not within specifications, replace sleeve and shift fork.

2) Measure clearance between shift piece or shift fork and shift arm "B". See Fig. 12. Clearance should be .008-.020" (.20-.50 mm). Service limit is .031" (.80 mm). If clearance exceeds service limit, measure

groove in shift piece or shift fork. Groove width should be .520-.528" (13.2-13.4 mm). If groove width is outside specification, replace shift piece or shift fork. mm). If groove width is within specification, replace shift arm "B".

3) Measure width of MBS shift piece. MBS shift piece width should be .272-.280" (6.90-7.10 mm). See Fig. 13. Replace MBS shift piece if minimum width is not as specified.

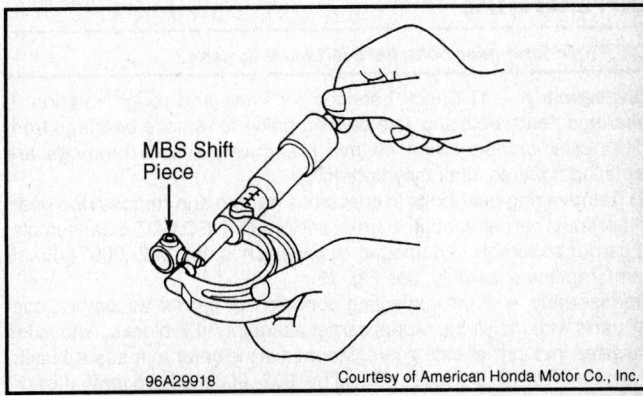

Fig. 13: Measuring MBS Shift Piece

SYNCHRO RING & GEAR

Disassembly – Separate synchro ring and gear. Lubricate and install synchro spring on synchro ring and set aside.

Inspection – 1) Inspect gear teeth for wear, galling, roughness and cracks. Ensure ring and gear turn freely. If replacement is necessary, replace ring and gear as a unit.

2) Measure ring-to-gear clearance all the way around. See Fig. 14. Ensure ring is held evenly against gear while measuring. Ring-to-gear clearance should be .033-.043" (.85-1.10 mm). Service limit is .016" (.40 mm). If clearance exceeds limit, replace ring and gear as a unit.

Reassembly – Each synchro sleeve has 3 sets of longer teeth (120 degrees apart) that must be matched with 3 sets of deeper grooves when hub is assembled. See Fig. 13.

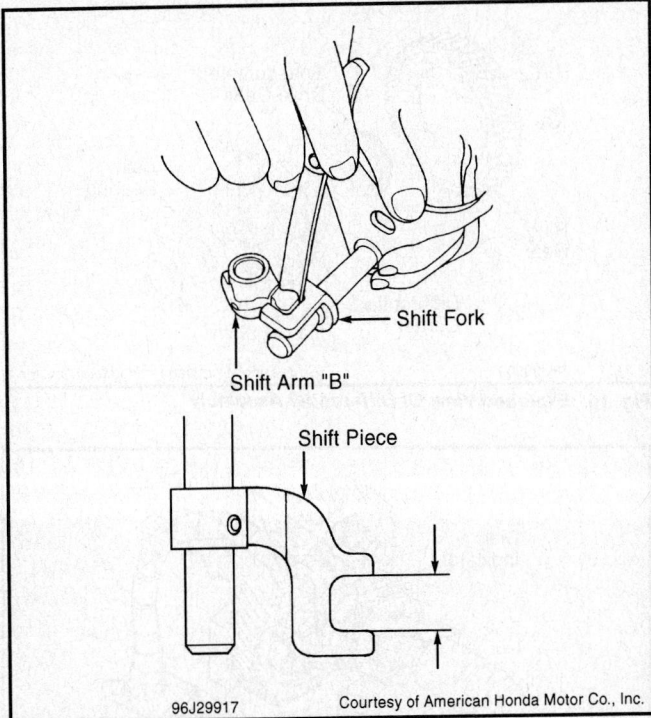

Fig. 12: Measuring Shift Arm Clearance

NOTE: Installing synchro sleeve with its longer teeth in 1st/2nd synchro hub slots will damage spring ring.

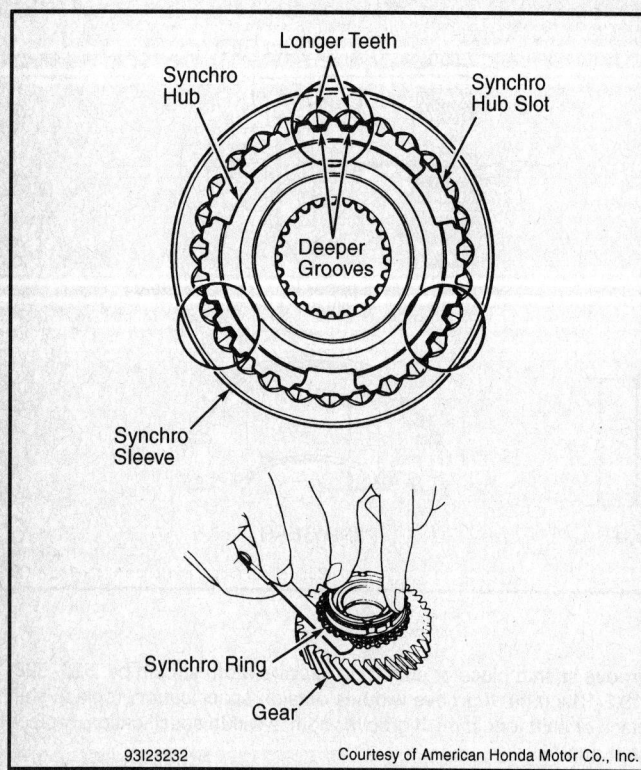

Fig. 14: *Measuring Synchro Hub Assembly Clearances*

DIFFERENTIAL

CAUTION: *Ring gear bolts have left-hand threads.*

Disassembly – 1) Check bearings for wear and rough rotation. If bearings need replacing, use bearing puller to remove bearings from differential carrier. Using 40 mm I.D. driver, ensure bearings are installed squarely until they bottom.

2) Remove ring gear bolts in crisscross pattern and remove ring gear. Differential carrier assembly is not serviceable. DO NOT disassemble. If carrier assembly is damaged or backlash is not .002-.006" (.05-.15 mm), replace assembly. *See Fig. 15.*

Reassembly – After inspecting condition of carrier assembly, coat all parts with molylube. Mount carrier assembly in V-blocks, with axles inserted into carrier side gears. Mount dial indicator to measure backlash. *See Fig. 16.* Backlash should be .002-.006" (.05-.15 mm). If backlash exceeds specification, replace differential carrier assembly.

NOTE: *Before differential assembly can be adjusted perform steps 1) and 2) under TRANSMISSION REASSEMBLY.*

Adjustments – 1) Using 40 mm I.D. driver, ensure differential assembly is seated in clutch housing. Install original thrust shim in transmission housing. *See Fig. 2.* Install transmission housing. Do NOT apply sealer at this time.

2) Install and torque housing bolts to specification. See TORQUE SPECIFICATIONS. Measure clearance between thrust shim and outer race in housing. Maximum clearance is .004" (.10 mm). If not within limits, select proper thrust shim from appropriate DIFFERENTIAL THRUST SHIM THICKNESS table. Disassemble transmission housing and replace original thrust shim with selected thrust shim. Reassemble transmission housing and recheck side clearance.

3) If differential side clearance is not within specifications, repeat step **2)**. If differential side clearance is okay, adjustment is complete.

DIFFERENTIAL THRUST SHIM THICKNESS (D16Y7 ENGINE)

Part Number	Thickness
41441-PL3-A00	.039" (1.00 mm)
41442-PL3-A00	.043" (1.10 mm)
41443-PL3-A00	.047" (1.20 mm)
41444-PL3-A00	.051" (1.30 mm)
41445-PL3-A00	.055" (1.40 mm)
41446-PL3-A00	.059" (1.50 mm)
41447-PL3-A00	.063" (1.60 mm)
41448-PL3-A00	.067" (1.70 mm)
41449-PL3-A00	.071" (1.80 mm)
41450-PL3-A00	.041" (1.05 mm)
41451-PL3-A00	.045" (1.15 mm)
41452-PL3-A00	.049" (1.25 mm)
41453-PL3-A00	.053" (1.35 mm)
41454-PL3-A00	.057" (1.45 mm)
41455-PL3-A00	.061" (1.55 mm)
41456-PL3-A00	.065" (1.65 mm)
41457-PL3-A00	.069" (1.75 mm)

DIFFERENTIAL THRUST SHIM THICKNESS (EXCEPT D16Y7 ENGINE)

Part Number	Thickness
41441-PL3-B00	.039" (1.00 mm)
41442-PL3-B00	.043" (1.10 mm)
41443-PL3-B00	.047" (1.20 mm)
41444-PL3-B00	.051" (1.30 mm)
41445-PL3-B00	.055" (1.40 mm)
41446-PL3-B00	.059" (1.50 mm)
41447-PL3-B00	.063" (1.60 mm)
41448-PL3-B00	.067" (1.70 mm)
41449-PL3-B00	.071" (1.80 mm)
41450-PL3-B00	.041" (1.05 mm)
41451-PL3-B00	.045" (1.15 mm)
41452-PL3-B00	.049" (1.25 mm)
41453-PL3-B00	.053" (1.35 mm)
41454-PL3-B00	.057" (1.45 mm)
41455-PL3-B00	.061" (1.55 mm)
41456-PL3-B00	.065" (1.65 mm)
41457-PL3-B00	.069" (1.75 mm)

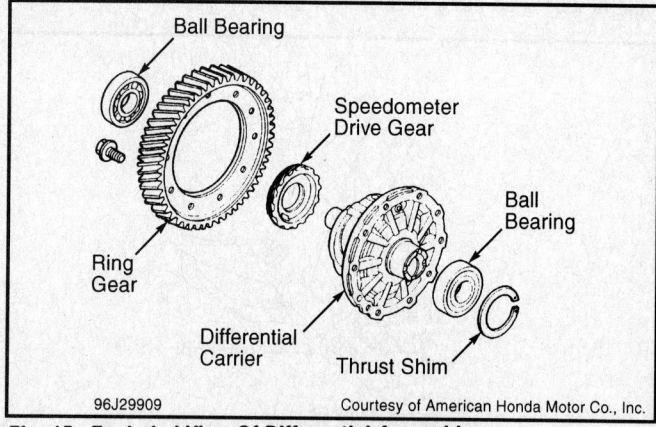

Fig. 15: *Exploded View Of Differential Assembly*

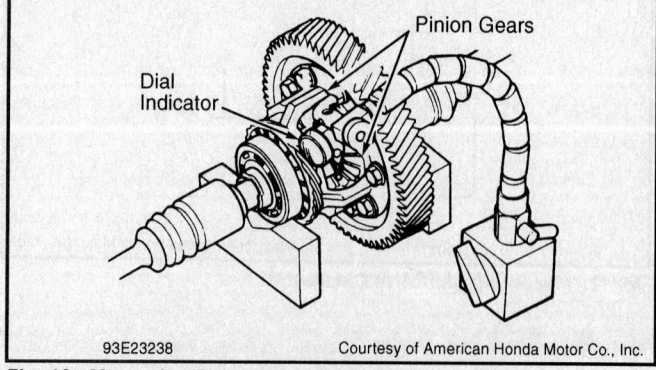

Fig. 16: *Measuring Pinion Gear Backlash*

TRANSMISSION REASSEMBLY

1) Install magnet and reverse lock cam. Place shift arm "A" in clutch housing, then push shift rod through . Install spring washer and shift arm "A" bolt. Install steel ball, spring and spring bolt.

2) Install shift arm "B" into interlock, and set interlock in clutch housing. Insert shift arm shaft "B" in clutch housing Install collar, spring and steel ball and insert shift arm shaft. Install reverse select retainer and reverse select spring. Install differential assembly.

3) Install spring washer and washer onto mainshaft bearing. *See Fig. 2.* Insert mainshaft and countershaft into shift forks, and install them as an assembly. Fit finger of interlock assembly into notches of shift forks. Lower mainshaft and countershaft into clutch housing. Install spring washer and shift arm "B" attaching bolt. Install 1st-2nd select spring and plug bolt. Install interlock guide bolt under clutch housing.

4) Install reverse idler gear and shaft. Install reverse shift holder. Install oil guide plate and mainshaft thrust shim into transmission housing. Apply sealant to transmission mating surface of clutch housing. Install dowel pins.

NOTE: This transmission uses no gaskets between major housings. Use Sealant (08718-550000). Assemble housings within 20 minutes after applying sealant, and allow it to cure for at least 30 minutes after assembly before filling it with oil.

---

5) Insert snap ring pliers into 32-mm sealing plug hole. Spread snap ring and install onto countershaft ball bearing, then install transmission housing over clutch housing. Ensure to line up shafts. Install 32-mm sealing plug. Install transmission housing bolts in sequence. *See Fig. 17.* Install back-up light switch.

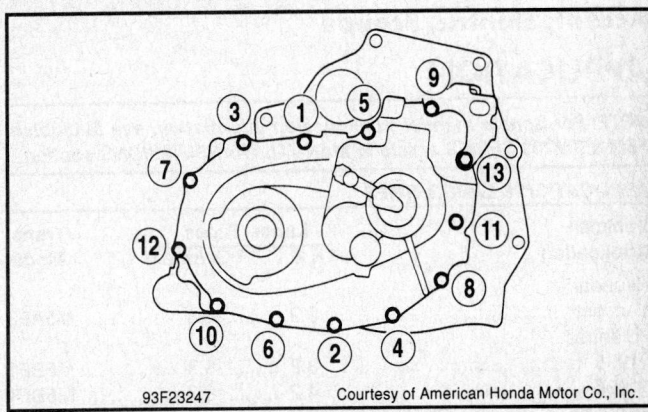

93F23247   Courtesy of American Honda Motor Co., Inc.

Fig. 17: Transmission Housing Bolt Tightening Sequence

TORQUE SPECIFICATIONS

TORQUE SPECIFICATIONS

Application	Ft. Lbs. (N.m)
Back-Up Light Switch	18 (25)
Breather Tube Bolt	21 (28)
Countershaft Lock Nut	81 (110)
Interlock Guide Bolt	30 (40)
Oil Drain Plug	30 (40)
Oil Filler Plug	33 (45)
Plug Bolt	41 (55)
Reverse Lock Cam Bolt	11 (15)
Set Ball Spring Bolt	16 (22)
"A", "B" & "C" Bolts	21 (28)
Transmission Housing Bolts	21 (28)
32-mm Sealing Bolt	18 (25)
	INCH lbs.
10-mm Sealing Bolt	96 (11)

Accent, Elantra, Scoupe

APPLICATION

NOTE: For Sonata manual transmission information, see Mitsubishi F5M & KM200 SERIES article in MANUAL TRANSMISSIONS section.

APPLICATION & LABOR TIMES

Vehicle Application	Labor Times [1] R & I	[2] Overhaul	Trans. Model
Hyundai			
Accent	3.2	8.3	M5AF3
Elantra			
1995	3.2	8.3	M5BF1
1996	4.2	8.3	M5BF1
Scoupe	3.2	8.3	M5AF

[1] – Removal and installation of transaxle from vehicle chassis.

[2] – Bench overhaul time for transaxle and differential. DOES NOT include removal and installation.

IDENTIFICATION

Transaxle can be identified by information code plate, located on transaxle case. *See Fig. 1.*

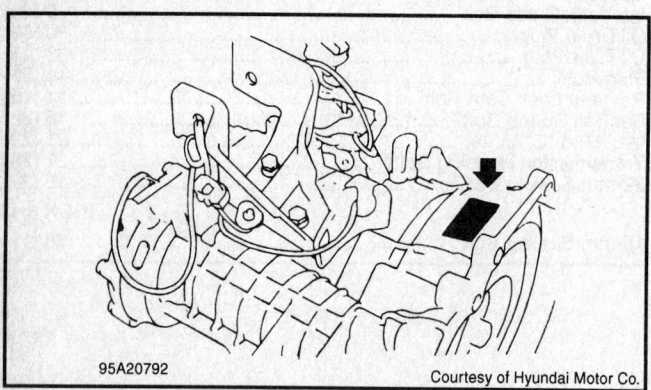

95A20792   Courtesy of Hyundai Motor Co.

Fig. 1: Locating Transaxle Identification Number

LUBRICATION & ADJUSTMENTS

See appropriate MANUAL TRANSMISSION SERVICING article in TRANSMISSION SERVICING section.

TROUBLE SHOOTING

See GENERAL TROUBLE SHOOTING article in this section.

ON-VEHICLE SERVICE

DRIVE AXLE SHAFTS

See appropriate AXLE SHAFTS article in AXLE SHAFTS & TRANSFER CASES section.

REMOVAL & INSTALLATION

For transaxle removal procedure, see appropriate MANUAL TRANSMISSION REMOVAL article in TRANSMISSION SERVICING section.

TRANSAXLE DISASSEMBLY

1) Remove back-up light switch, gasket, mounting bracket, restrict ball assembly and mounting bracket. Remove bolts and rear cover. Remove seal bolts, spring cases, poppet springs and poppet balls. *See Fig. 2.*

2) Drive out 5th gear shift fork spring pin. Unstake input shaft and output shaft lock nuts. Engage transaxle into 1st gear using control lever and select lever. *See Fig. 3.* Shift 5th gear synchronizer into 5th gear. Remove input shaft and output shaft lock nuts.

3) Remove 5th gear synchronizer sleeve and shift fork. Pull 5th gear synchronizer hub and ring with 5th gear from input shaft. Pull 5th driven gear from output shaft.

4) Remove select lever assembly, select lever shoe, control shaft mounting bolts, interlock plate fixed bolt, air breather and control shaft assembly.

5) Remove reverse gear shaft bolt, 2 transaxle case fixing bolts (inside clutch housing) and transaxle case bolts. Remove transaxle case.

6) Remove oil guides. Pull out left and right drive shaft bearing outer races and spacers. Pull out input shaft bearing race and spacer.

7) Remove reverse shift lever assembly and reverse shift lever shoe. Remove reverse idler gear shaft and reverse idler gear.

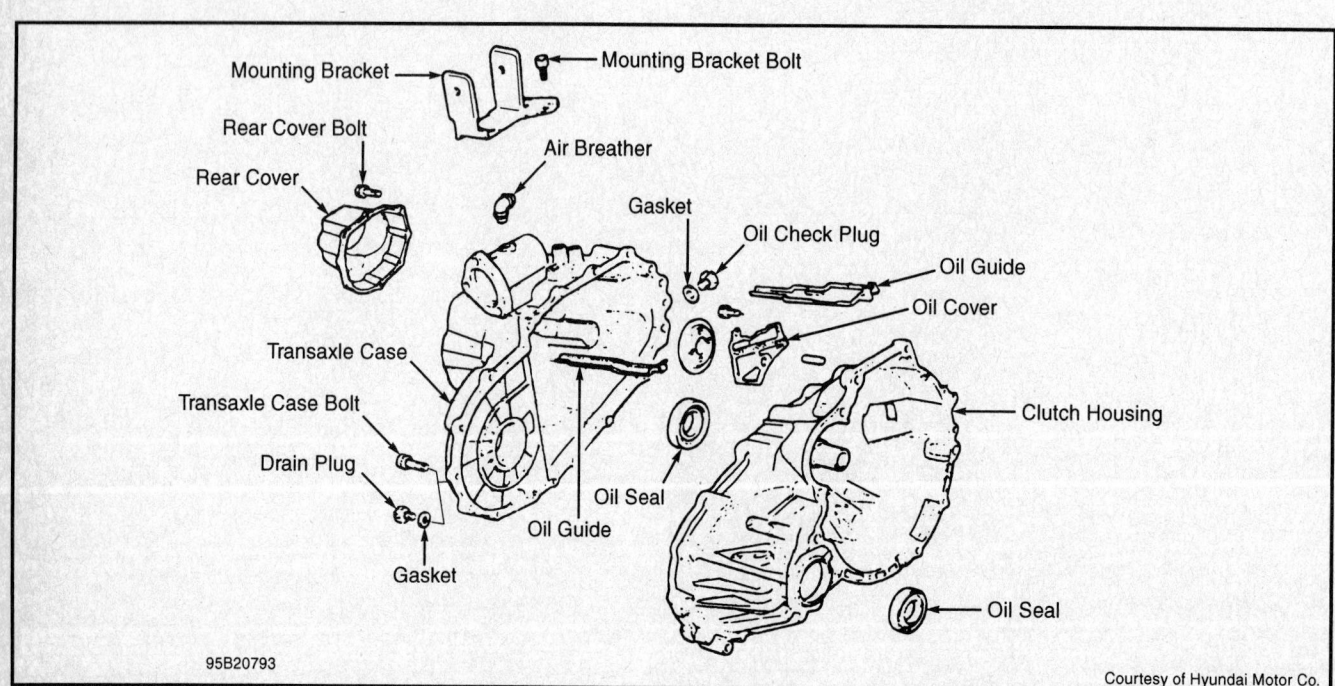

95B20793

Courtesy of Hyundai Motor Co.

Fig. 2: Exploded View Of Transaxle Case

8) Drive out shift forks spring pins. Detach and remove shift rail and fork assemblies. Remove input shaft and output shaft as a unit. Remove differential gear assembly, speedometer driven gear assembly and cable support bracket.

9) Pull input shaft bearing outer race and output shaft bearing outer race. Pull drive shaft bearing outer race. Remove oil cover, differential side oil seal, output shaft oil guide and input shaft front oil seal.

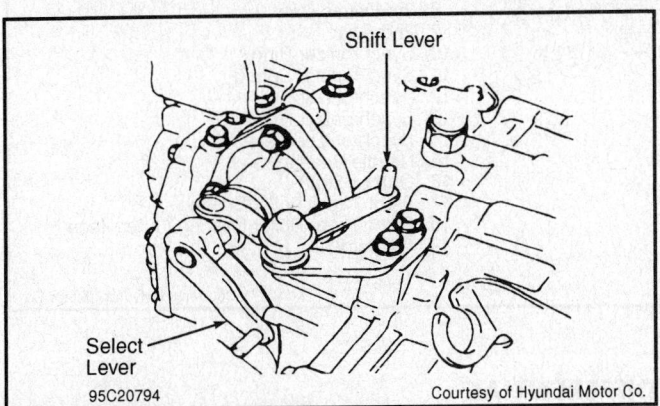

Fig. 3: *Location Of Select & Shift Levers*

COMPONENT DISASSEMBLY & REASSEMBLY

INPUT SHAFT

Disassembly – Press off front taper roller bearing. *See Fig. 4.* Press off 5th gear sleeve, rear taper roller bearing, 4th gear, 4th gear synchronizer ring , 3rd/4th gear synchronizer hub/sleeve assembly, 3rd gear synchronizer ring, 3rd gear and needle roller bearing.

Inspection – **1)** Check splines and outer surface of input shaft for damage or wear. Inspect needle bearings for smooth rotation and bearing cage distortion.

2) Inspect synchronizer rings for damaged teeth and internal surface damage, wear or broken grooves. Install synchronizer ring onto gear and measure clearance "A". *See Fig. 5.* If clearance is less than .02" (.5 mm) replace synchronizer ring.

3) Install synchronizer sleeve on hub and check for smooth movement. Inspect surfaces for wear or damage. If synchronizer sleeve or hub is damaged, replace both as a set. Check synchronizer keys for wear and synchronizer springs for weakness, deformation and breakage.

4) Inspect gears for tooth damage or wear. Check gear cones and bores for rough surfaces, damage or wear.

Reassembly – **1)** Install needle roller bearing, 3rd gear and 3rd gear synchronizer ring. Press on 3rd/4th synchronizer hub/sleeve assembly. Ensure synchronizer assembly is installed correctly positioned and synchronizer keys are seated in grooves in synchronizer ring. *See Fig. 6.* Check that 3rd gear rotates smoothly.

2) Press on 4th gear sleeve. Install needle bearing and 4th gear. Press on rear taper roller bearing and 5th gear sleeve. Press on front taper roller bearing.

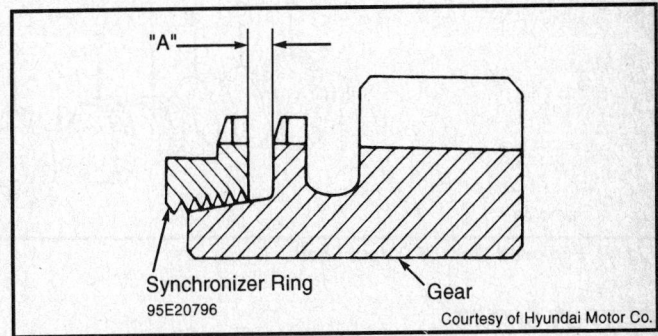

Fig. 5: *Measuring Synchronizer Ring Clearance*

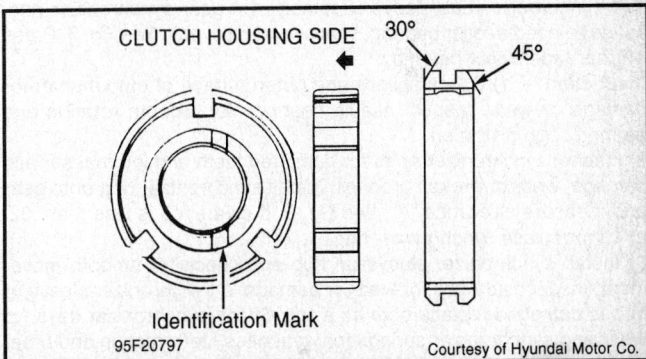

Fig. 6: *3rd/4th Synchronizer Hub & Sleeve*

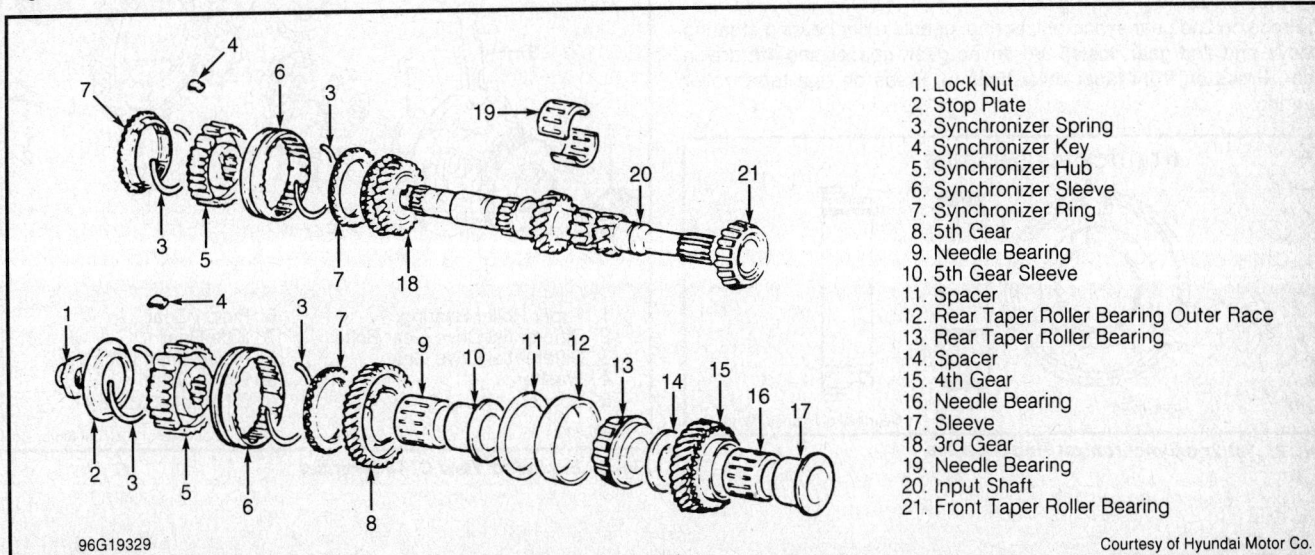

1. Lock Nut
2. Stop Plate
3. Synchronizer Spring
4. Synchronizer Key
5. Synchronizer Hub
6. Synchronizer Sleeve
7. Synchronizer Ring
8. 5th Gear
9. Needle Bearing
10. 5th Gear Sleeve
11. Spacer
12. Rear Taper Roller Bearing Outer Race
13. Rear Taper Roller Bearing
14. Spacer
15. 4th Gear
16. Needle Bearing
17. Sleeve
18. 3rd Gear
19. Needle Bearing
20. Input Shaft
21. Front Taper Roller Bearing

Courtesy of Hyundai Motor Co.

Fig. 4: *Exploded View Of Input Shaft*

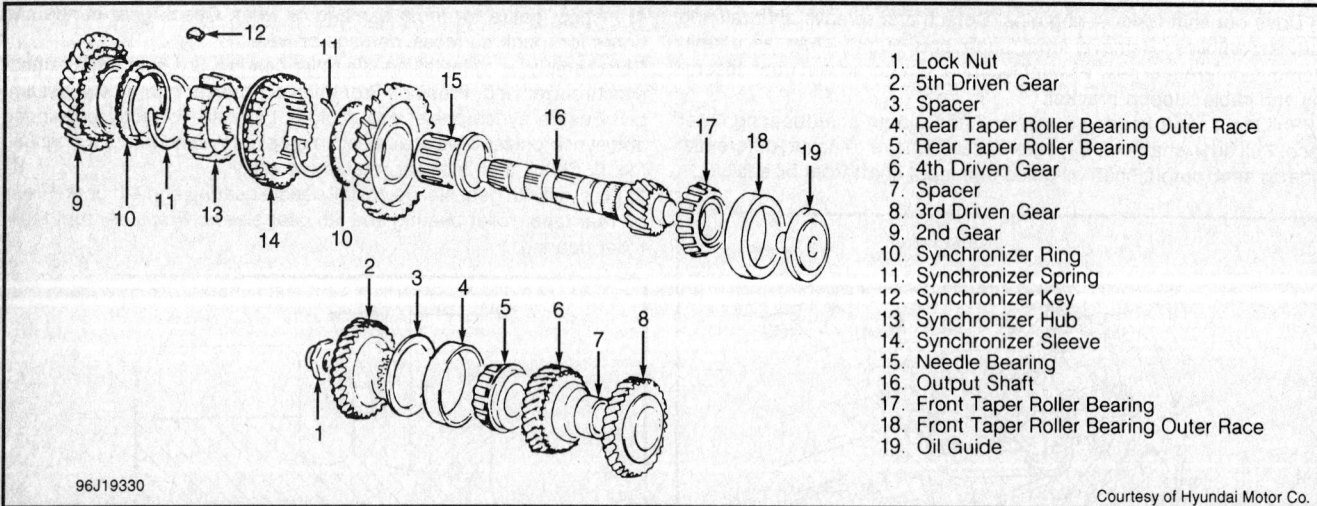

1. Lock Nut
2. 5th Driven Gear
3. Spacer
4. Rear Taper Roller Bearing Outer Race
5. Rear Taper Roller Bearing
6. 4th Driven Gear
7. Spacer
8. 3rd Driven Gear
9. 2nd Gear
10. Synchronizer Ring
11. Synchronizer Spring
12. Synchronizer Key
13. Synchronizer Hub
14. Synchronizer Sleeve
15. Needle Bearing
16. Output Shaft
17. Front Taper Roller Bearing
18. Front Taper Roller Bearing Outer Race
19. Oil Guide

96J19330

Courtesy of Hyundai Motor Co.

Fig. 7: Exploded View Of Output Shaft

OUTPUT SHAFT

Disassembly – Press off front taper roller bearing 4th driven gear, spacer, 3rd driven gear, 2nd gear, 2nd gear synchronizer ring, 1st/2nd synchronizer hub/sleeve assembly, 1st gear synchronizer ring, 1st gear, needle roller bearing, spacer and steel ball. *See Fig. 7*. Press off rear taper roller bearing.

Inspection – 1) Check splines and outer surface of output shaft for damage or wear. Inspect needle bearings for smooth rotation and bearing cage distortion.

2) Inspect synchronizer rings for damaged teeth and internal surface damage, wear or broken grooves. Install synchronizer ring onto gear and measure clearance "A". *See Fig. 5*. If clearance is less than .02" (.5 mm) replace synchronizer ring.

3) Install synchronizer sleeve on hub and check for smooth movement. Inspect surfaces for wear or damage. If synchronizer sleeve or hub is damaged replace both as a set. Check synchronizer keys for wear and synchronizer springs for weakness, deformation and breakage.

4) Inspect gears for tooth damage or wear. Check gear cones and bores for rough surfaces, damage or wear.

Reassembly – 1) Install steel ball and spacer to output shaft. Install needle bearing, 1st gear and 1st gear synchronizer ring. Press on 1st/2nd synchronizer hub/sleeve assembly. Ensure synchronizer assembly is installed correctly and synchronizer keys are seated in grooves of synchronizer ring. *See Fig. 8*.

2) Press on 2nd gear synchronizer ring, needle roller bearing, bearing sleeve and 2nd gear. Install 3rd driven gear, spacer and 4th driven gear. Press on front taper roller bearing. Press on rear taper roller bearing.

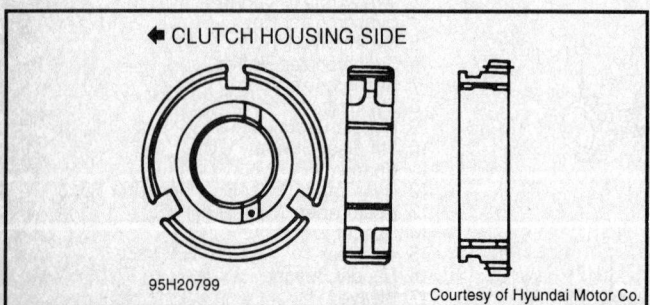

◄ CLUTCH HOUSING SIDE

95H20799

Courtesy of Hyundai Motor Co.

Fig. 8: 1st/2nd Synchronizer Hub & Sleeve

DIFFERENTIAL

Disassembly – Place differential in a soft jaw vice. Remove differential drive gear bolts and drive gear. *See Fig. 9*. Press off differential ball bearings. Drive out pinion shaft lock pin. Drive out pinion shaft. Remove pinion gears, washers, side gears and spacers.

Reassembly – 1) Install spacers to back of side gears and install in differential case. Install washers to pinions and install in differential case while engaging with side gears. Install pinion shaft.

2) Measure backlash between side gears and pinions. If backlash is not .001-.006" (.025-.150 mm) disassemble and install selective spacers, reassemble and remeasure.

NOTE: Adjust backlash of both side gears to same specification.

---

3) Align pinion shaft lock pin hole with case lock pin hole and drive in NEW lock pin. Ensure lock pin head does not protrude more than .118" (3.0 mm). Press on differential ball bearings. Install differential drive gear and bolts. Torque bolts to specification in sequence. See TORQUE SPECIFICATIONS. *See Fig. 10*.

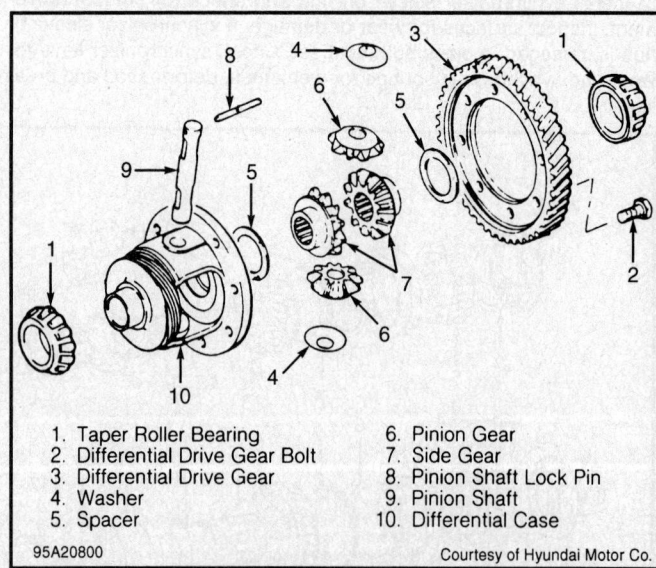

1. Taper Roller Bearing
2. Differential Drive Gear Bolt
3. Differential Drive Gear
4. Washer
5. Spacer
6. Pinion Gear
7. Side Gear
8. Pinion Shaft Lock Pin
9. Pinion Shaft
10. Differential Case

95A20800

Courtesy of Hyundai Motor Co.

Fig. 9: Exploded View Of Differential

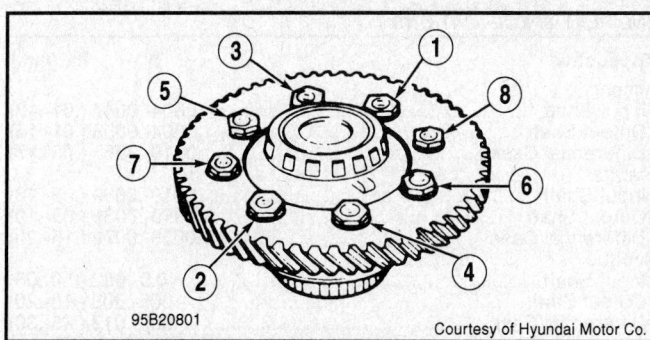

95B20801

Courtesy of Hyundai Motor Co.

Fig. 10: Differential Drive Gear Bolt Torque Sequence

5th GEAR SYNCHRONIZER

Inspection – Install synchronizer sleeve on hub and check for smooth movement. Inspect surfaces for wear or damage. If synchronizer sleeve or hub is damaged replace both as a set. Check synchronizer keys for wear and synchronizer springs for weakness, deformation and breakage.

Reassembly – Install synchronizer sleeve and keys onto synchronizer hub. Ensure proper orientation of parts. See Fig. 11. Install sleeve on hub so that center tooth between 2 missing teeth will touch synchronizer key. Install synchronizer springs and ensure protrusion engages groove of keys.

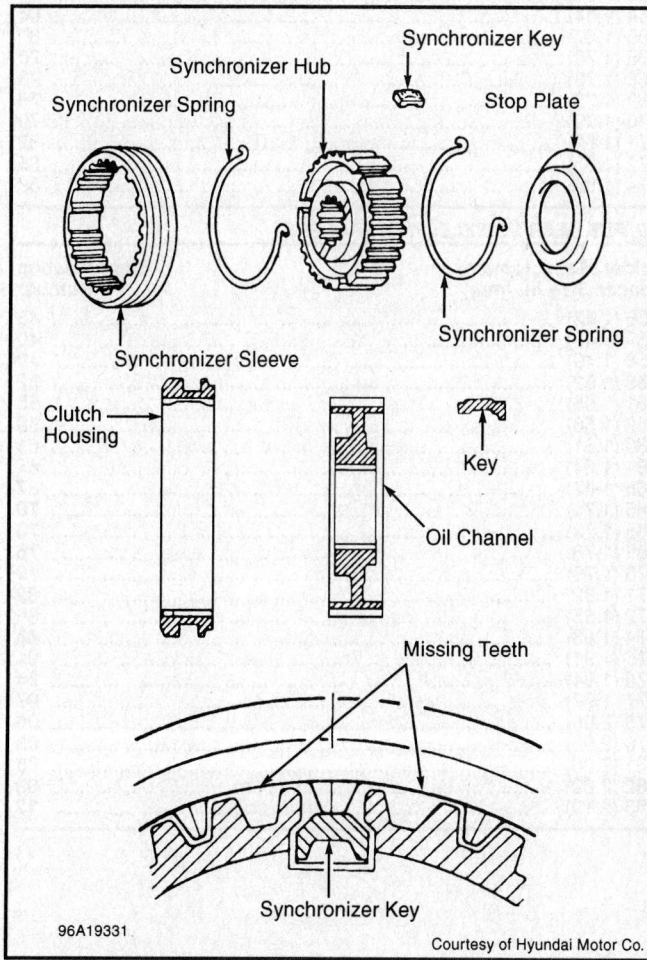

96A19331

Courtesy of Hyundai Motor Co.

Fig. 11: 5th Gear Synchronizer

TRANSAXLE REASSEMBLY

1) Install drive shaft oil seal, input shaft front oil seal, output shaft oil guide, input shaft bearing outer race, output shaft bearing outer race and drive shaft bearing race. Ensure proper output shaft oil guide position. See Fig. 12. Install oil cover and differential gear assembly. Install input shaft and output shaft as a unit. See Fig. 13

2) Place 1st/2nd gear synchronizer sleeve and 3rd/4th gear synchronizer sleeve to neutral. Install shift rail and fork assembly. Drive in NEW shift fork spring pins. Ensure slit of spring pin is aligned with center line of shift rail. See Fig. 14.

3) Install reverse idler gear and reverse idler gear shaft. Ensure reverse idler gear shaft is positioned correctly. See Fig. 15. Install reverse shift lever assembly and reverse shift lever shoe.

4) Install drive shaft oil seal, input shaft roller bearing outer race, output shaft bearing outer race and drive shaft bearing outer race. Place 2 pieces of rosin-core solder about 1/8" diameter on bearing outer races. See Fig. 16. Install transaxle case, torque bolts to specification and then remove transaxle case. Remove and measure crushed solder. Select and install spacers to set proper end play. See END PLAY SPECIFICATIONS table.

5) Install oil guides. Apply Three Bond (1216) sealant to clutch housing mating surface. Install transaxle case and torque bolts to specifications. See TORQUE SPECIFICATIONS. Using a screw driver, center reverse idler gear shaft hole with case. Install reverse idler gear shaft bolt and torque to specification.

6) Install poppet balls, poppet springs, spring cases and seal bolts. Install control shaft assembly and torque bolts to specification. Install interlock plate fixed bolt and washer. Apply sealant to air breather and install it.

7) Install 5th driven gear to output shaft. Install 5th gear sleeve, needle roller bearing, 5th gear and 5th gear synchronizer ring. Install 5th gear synchronizer hub. Install 5th gear shift fork and 5th gear synchronizer sleeve together.

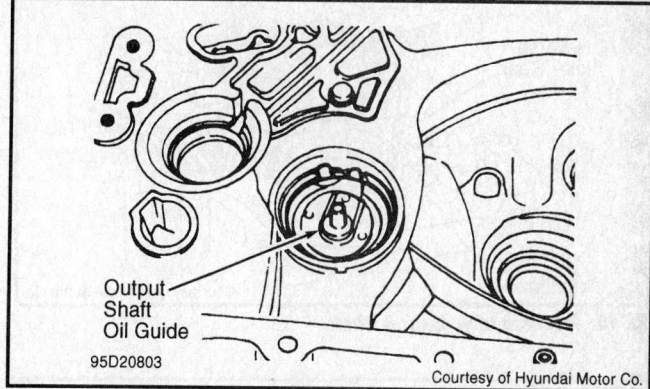

95D20803

Courtesy of Hyundai Motor Co.

Fig. 12: Output Shaft Oil Guide Position

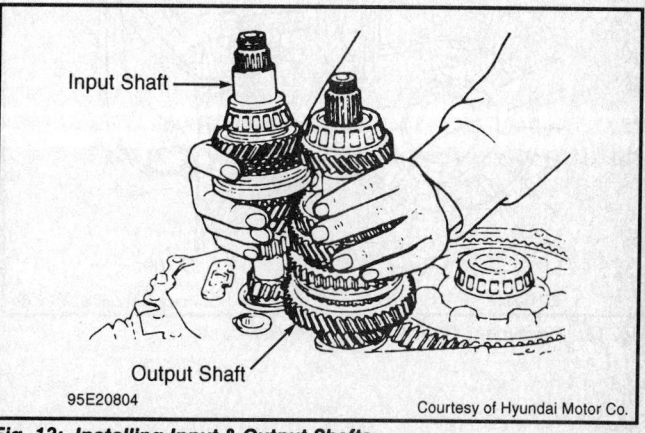

95E20804

Courtesy of Hyundai Motor Co.

Fig. 13: Installing Input & Output Shafts

8) Shift transaxle into 1st gear using control lever and select lever. Engage 5th gear synchronizer sleeve to 5th gear. Install lock nuts and torque to specifications. See TORQUE SPECIFICATIONS. Stake lock nuts. Disengage 5th gear synchronizer ring from 5th gear and drive in NEW spring pin into 5th gear shift fork. ensure slit in spring pin is aligned with center line of shift rail.

9) Apply Three Bond (1216) sealant to mating surface of rear cover and install. Torque bolts to specifications. Install speedometer driven gear assembly and shift control cable bracket. Install back up light switch, gasket and restrict ball assembly. Install mounting bracket and select lever assembly.

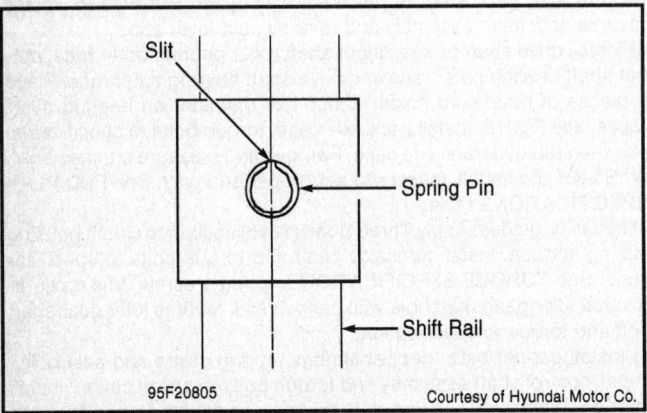

Fig. 14: Spring Pin & Shift Rail Alignment

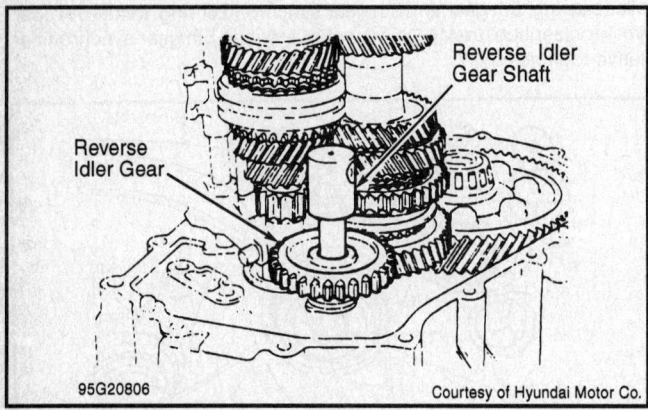

Fig. 15: Reverse Idler Gear & Shaft

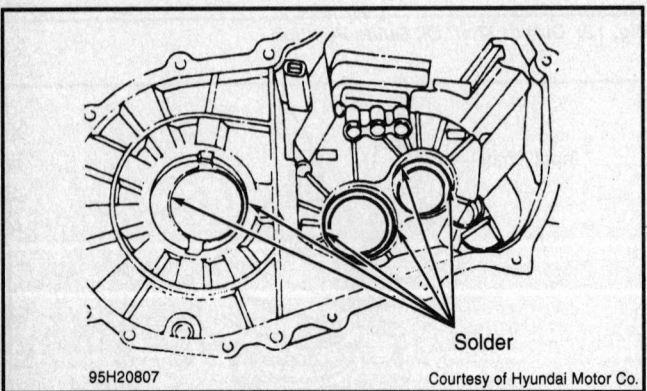

Fig. 16: Placement Of Solder In Transaxle Case

END PLAY SPECIFICATIONS

Application	In. (mm)
Accent	
Input Shaft	.0004-.0047 (.01-.12)
Output Shaft	.0004-.0059 (.01-.15)
Differential Case	.0019-.0067 (.05-.17)
Elantra	
Input Shaft	.0019-.0039 (.05-.10)
Output Shaft	.0019-.0039 (.05-.10)
Differential Case	.0059-.0078 (.15-.20)
Scoupe	
Input Shaft	0.0-.002 (0.0-.05)
Output Shaft	.005-.008 (.15-.20)
Differential Case	.009-.012 (.25-.30)

INPUT BEARING SELECTIVE SPACERS

Solder Measurement/ Spacer Size In. (mm)	Identification Number
.049 (1.25)	25
.050 (1.28)	28
.051 (1.31)	31
.052 (1.34)	34
.053 (1.37)	37
.055 (1.40)	40
.056 (1.43)	43
.057 (1.46)	46
.058 (1.49)	49
.059 (1.52)	52
.061 (1.55)	55
.062 (1.58)	58
.063 (1.61)	61
.064 (1.64)	64
.065 (1.67)	67
.066 (1.70)	70
.068 (1.73)	73
.069 (1.76)	76
.070 (1.79)	79
.071 (1.82)	82
.072 (1.85)	85
.074 (1.88)	88

OUTPUT BEARING SELECTIVE SPACERS

Solder Measurement/ Spacer Size In. (mm)	Identification Number
.056 (1.43)	43
.057 (1.46)	46
.058 (1.49)	49
.059 (1.52)	52
.061 (1.55)	55
.062 (1.58)	58
.063 (1.61)	61
.064 (1.64)	64
.065 (1.67)	67
.066 (1.70)	70
.068 (1.73)	73
.069 (1.76)	76
.070 (1.79)	79
.071 (1.82)	82
.072 (1.85)	85
.074 (1.88)	88
.075 (1.91)	91
.076 (1.94)	94
.077 (1.97)	97
.078 (2.00)	00
.079 (2.03)	03
.081 (2.06)	06
.082 (2.09)	09
.083 (2.12)	12

DIFFERENTIAL BEARING SELECTIVE SPACERS

Solder Measurement/ Spacer Size In. (mm)	Identification Number
.031 (.80)	80
.032 (.83)	83
.033 (.86)	86
.035 (.89)	89
.036 (.92)	92
.037 (.95)	95
.038 (.98)	98
.039 (1.01)	01
.040 (1.04)	04
.042 (1.07)	07
.043 (1.10)	10
.044 (1.13)	13
.045 (1.16)	16
.046 (1.19)	19
.048 (1.22)	22
.049 (1.25)	25
.050 (1.28)	28

TORQUE SPECIFICATIONS

TORQUE SPECIFICATIONS

Application	Ft. Lbs. (N.m)
Transaxle Mounting Bracket Bolts	43-58 (60-80)
Transaxle Mounting Bolts	32-39 (43-53)
Rear Cover Bolts	11-15 (15-22)
Backup Light Switch	22-25 (30-35)
Poppet Spring Plug	18-22 (25-30)
Input Shaft Lock Nut	102-115 (140-160)
Output Shaft Lock Nut	102-115 (140-160)
Reverse Idler Gear Shaft Bolt	32-39 (43-53)
Transaxle Case Tightening Bolt	25-30 (35-42)
Stopper Bracket Bolt	11-15 (15-22)
Restrict Ball Assembly	22-25 (30-35)
Reverse Shift Lever Attaching Bolt	11-15 (15-22)
Bearing Retainer Bolt	11-15 (15-22)
Differential Drive Gear Bolts	94-101 (130-140)
Interlock Plate Bolt	15-19 (20-27)
	INCH Lbs. (N.m)
Speedometer Sleeve Bolt	24-48 (3-5)

TECHNICAL SERVICE BULLETINS

REPAIRING GEAR CLASH

All Hyundai Vehicles With Manual Transmissons (Hyundai TSB 95-40-007) – **1)** Confirm gear clash exists, and which gears are affected. If gear clash exists, remove and diassemble transaxle. Remove affected gear and synchronizer ring.

2) Place synchronizer ring onto gear. With light pressure applied, measure gap between top of gear and bottom of synchronizer ring. See Fig. 5. If gap is less than .02" (.5 mm), replace synchronizer ring and go to next step.

3) Place new or original synchronizer ring onto gear. Rotate synchronizer ring with light pressure to seat ring on gear. Grab synchronizer ring 120 degrees from previous location and attempt to rock synchronizer ring back and forth on gear. Repeat again grasping ring at an additional 120 degrees. If synchronizer ring is not seating properly, go to next step. If synchronizer ring seats properly, reassemble and reinstall tranaxle.

4) Clamp gear into soft jaw vise. Apply fine lapping compound to synchronizer ring seating surface. See Fig. 17. Place synchronizer ring onto gear. Applying light pressure, rotate synchronizer ring back and forth about 10 times. See Fig. 18. Repeat step 3).

5) Continue repeating steps 3) and 4) until synchronizer ring seats properly onto gear. Remove all lapping compound from synchronizer ring and gear. Reassemble and reinstall transaxle.

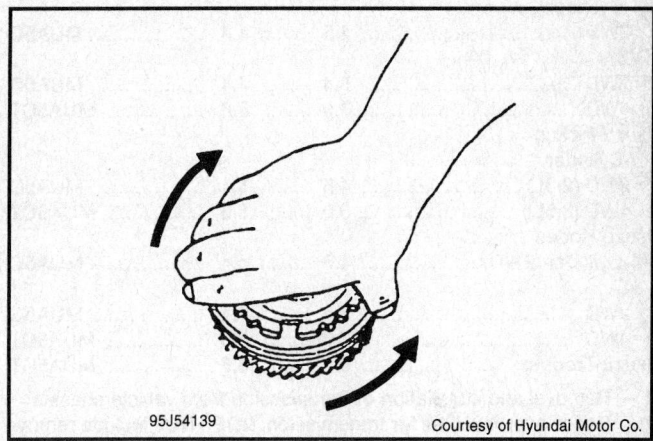

95J54139   Courtesy of Hyundai Motor Co.

Fig. 17: Applying Lapping Compound

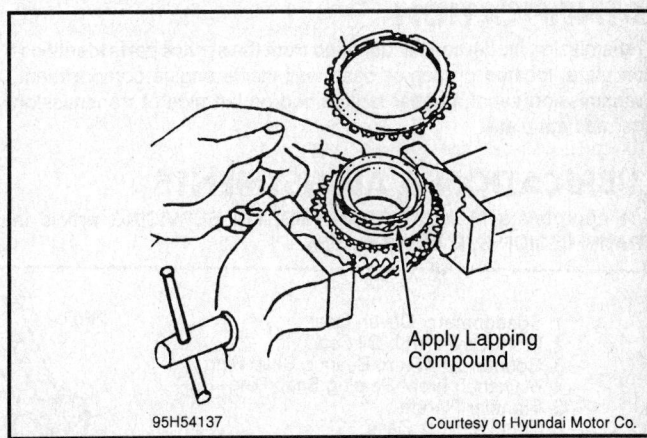

Apply Lapping Compound

95H54137   Courtesy of Hyundai Motor Co.

Fig. 18: Rotating Synchronizer Ring On Gear

MANUAL TRANSMISSIONS
Isuzu MUA Series 5-Speed

Acura: SLX
Honda: Passport
Isuzu: Pickup, Rodeo, Trooper

APPLICATION & LABOR TIMES

APPLICATION & LABOR TIMES

Vehicle Application	Labor Times [1] R & I	[2] Overhaul	Transmission Series
Acura SLX	6.5	8.6	MUA5CT
Honda Passport			
4-Cylinder			
2WD	4.5	4.4	MUA5C
V6			
2WD	5.4	4.4	MUA5C
4WD	7.0	8.6	MUA5CT
Isuzu Pickup			
4-Cylinder			
2WD (2.3L)	4.5	4.4	MUA5C
4WD (2.6L)	6.0	8.6	MUA5CT
Isuzu Rodeo			
4-Cylinder (2WD)	4.5	4.4	MUA5C
V6			
2WD	5.4	4.4	MUA5C
4WD	7.0	8.6	MUA5CT
Isuzu Trooper	6.5	8.6	MUA5CT

[1] – Removal and installation of transmission from vehicle chassis.
[2] – Bench overhaul time for transmission. DOES NOT include removal and installation.

IDENTIFICATION

Transmission model can be identified from the service parts identification plate, located on center dash wall inside engine compartment. Transmission serial number is stamped on left side of transmission intermediate plate.

LUBRICATION & ADJUSTMENTS

See appropriate MANUAL TRANSMISSION SERVICING article in TRANSMISSION SERVICING section.

TROUBLE SHOOTING

See GENERAL TROUBLE SHOOTING article in this section.

ON-VEHICLE SERVICE

EXTENSION HOUSING OIL SEAL (2WD)

Removal & Installation – Remove rear drive shaft. Pry out oil seal using a flat-blade screwdriver. Install NEW oil seal. Apply engine oil to oil seal lip and install rear drive shaft.

TRANSFER CASE FRONT & REAR OIL SEAL (4WD)

Removal & Installation – Remove appropriate drive shaft and transfer case companion flange. Using a flat-blade screwdriver, pry out oil seal. Install NEW oil seal. Apply engine oil to oil seal lip and install transfer case companion flange and nut. Torque nut to specification. See TORQUE SPECIFICATIONS. Install drive shaft.

REMOVAL & INSTALLATION

See appropriate MANUAL TRANSMISSION REMOVAL article in TRANSMISSION SERVICING section.

TRANSMISSION DISASSEMBLY

1) On all models, remove speedometer driven gear assembly and front cover with oil seal. See Fig. 1. Using snap ring pliers, remove countergear front bearing snap ring and mainshaft front bearing snap ring. On 4WD models, remove transfer case companion flange and transfer rear case assembly. On 2WD models, remove extension housing and intermediate plate with gear assembly.

2) On 4WD models, remove detent plugs, springs and balls. See Fig. 2. Remove transfer switch, bridge and 2nd-4th shift rod-to-shift arm spring. Engage 2nd-4th sleeve with front output gear. Drive spring pin from 2nd-4th block. Remove 2nd-4th shift rod, 2nd-4th shift arm and 2nd-4th block.

3) Remove interlock pin and interlock pin spring. See Fig. 2. Drive out high-low shift arm spring pin and remove high-low shift rod, high-low shift arm and high-low block.

4) Remove mainshaft end bearing snap ring. See Fig. 2. Remove mainshaft end ball bearing. Engage 3rd-4th synchronizer with 3rd gear and

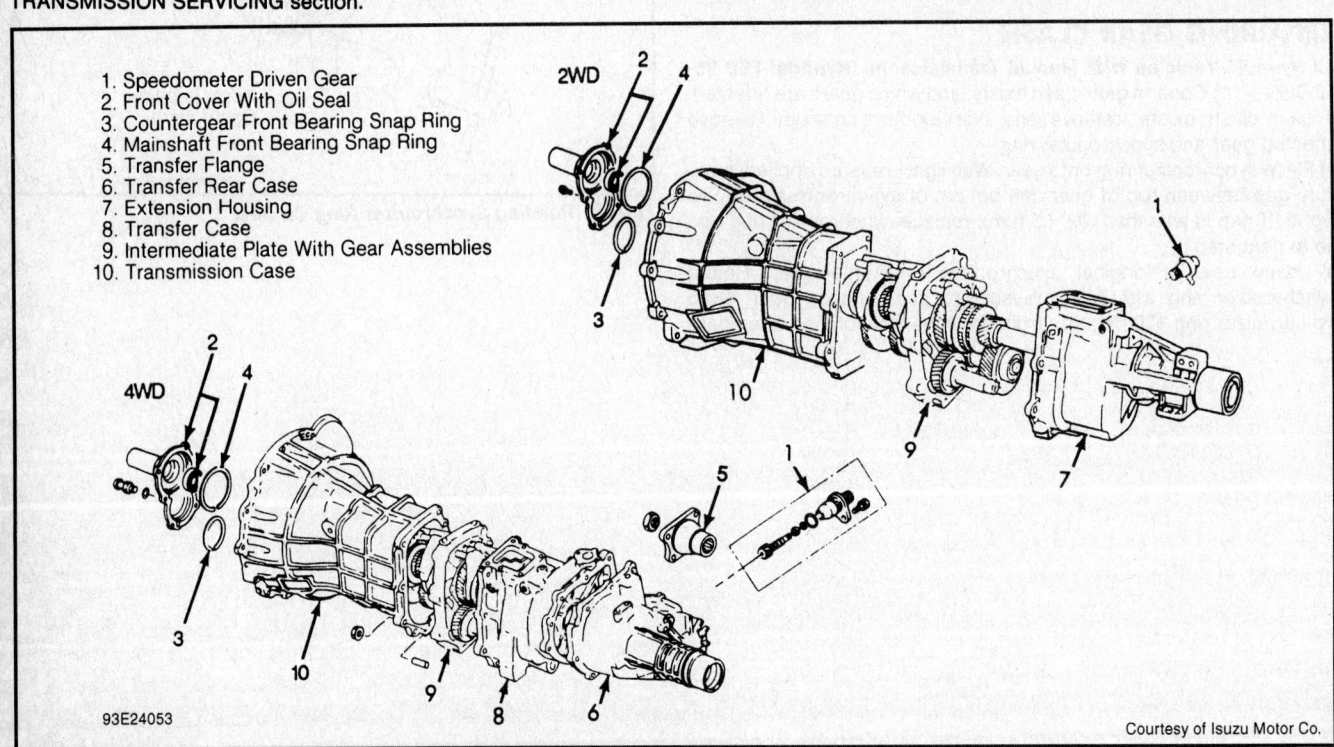

1. Speedometer Driven Gear
2. Front Cover With Oil Seal
3. Countergear Front Bearing Snap Ring
4. Mainshaft Front Bearing Snap Ring
5. Transfer Flange
6. Transfer Rear Case
7. Extension Housing
8. Transfer Case
9. Intermediate Plate With Gear Assemblies
10. Transmission Case

Courtesy of Isuzu Motor Co.

93E24053

Fig. 1: Exploded Views Of Transmission Major Components (Typical)

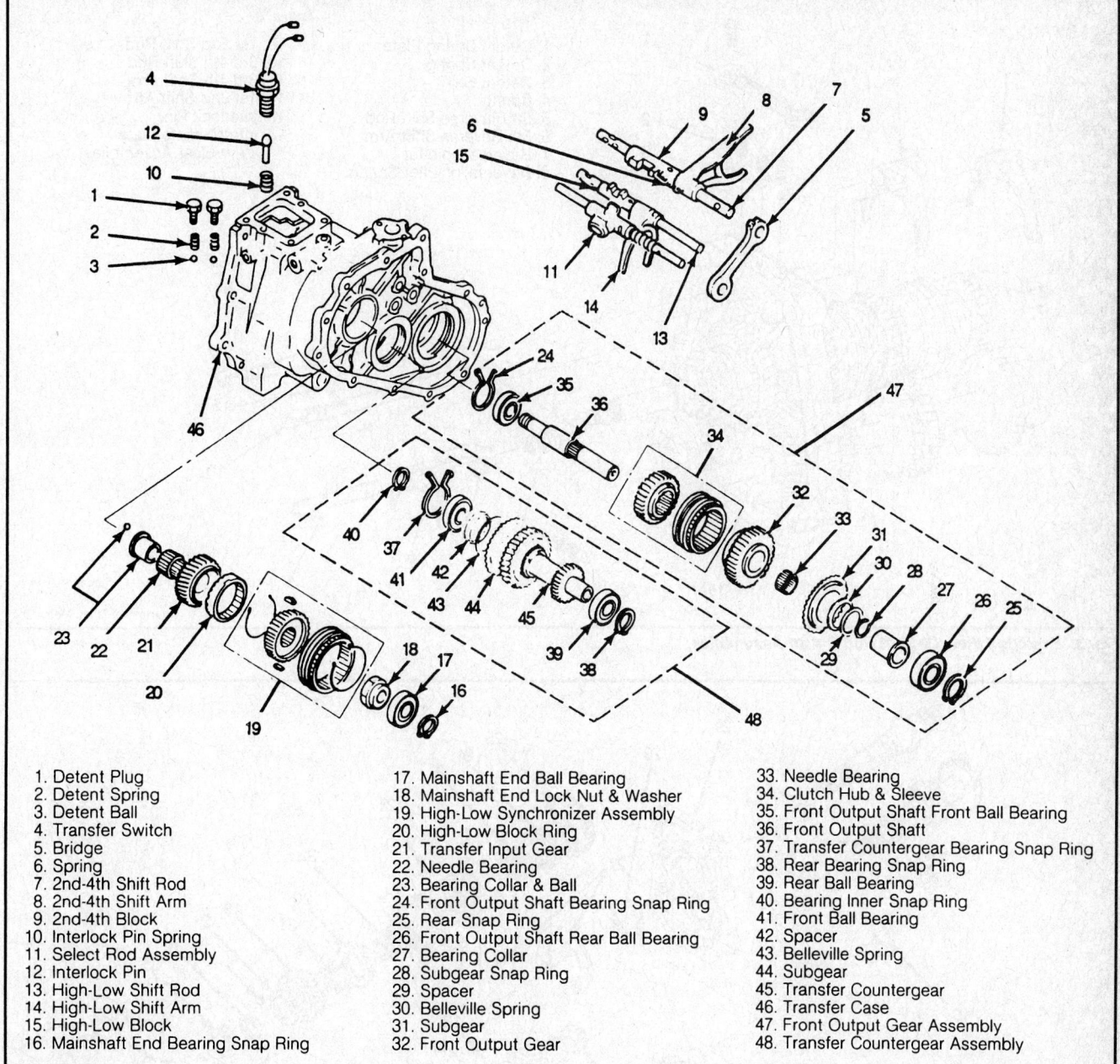

1. Detent Plug	17. Mainshaft End Ball Bearing	33. Needle Bearing
2. Detent Spring	18. Mainshaft End Lock Nut & Washer	34. Clutch Hub & Sleeve
3. Detent Ball	19. High-Low Synchronizer Assembly	35. Front Output Shaft Front Ball Bearing
4. Transfer Switch	20. High-Low Block Ring	36. Front Output Shaft
5. Bridge	21. Transfer Input Gear	37. Transfer Countergear Bearing Snap Ring
6. Spring	22. Needle Bearing	38. Rear Bearing Snap Ring
7. 2nd-4th Shift Rod	23. Bearing Collar & Ball	39. Rear Ball Bearing
8. 2nd-4th Shift Arm	24. Front Output Shaft Bearing Snap Ring	40. Bearing Inner Snap Ring
9. 2nd-4th Block	25. Rear Snap Ring	41. Front Ball Bearing
10. Interlock Pin Spring	26. Front Output Shaft Rear Ball Bearing	42. Spacer
11. Select Rod Assembly	27. Bearing Collar	43. Belleville Spring
12. Interlock Pin	28. Subgear Snap Ring	44. Subgear
13. High-Low Shift Rod	29. Spacer	45. Transfer Countergear
14. High-Low Shift Arm	30. Belleville Spring	46. Transfer Case
15. High-Low Block	31. Subgear	47. Front Output Gear Assembly
16. Mainshaft End Bearing Snap Ring	32. Front Output Gear	48. Transfer Countergear Assembly

93F24054

Courtesy of Isuzu Motor Co.

Fig. 2: *Exploded View Of Transfer Case Assembly (4WD)*

1st-2nd synchronizer with low gear. Remove mainshaft end lock nut. Remove washer.

5) Remove high-low synchronizer assembly, high-low block ring and transfer input gear. *See Fig. 2.* Remove needle bearing, bearing collar and ball. Using snap ring pliers, expand front output shaft bearing snap ring and tap out front output gear assembly with a plastic hammer. Using snap ring pliers, expand transfer countergear bearing snap ring and remove transfer countergear assembly. Remove transfer case and intermediate plate with gear assemblies.

6) On all models, remove detent spring plate, detent springs and detent balls from intermediate plate. *See Fig. 3.* Remove spring, 5th-reverse shift rod, 5th-reverse shift arm, reverse inhibitor and reverse inhibitor spring. Drive out spring pins and remove 1st-2nd shift rod, 3rd-4th shift rod, 3rd-4th shift arm, 1st-2nd shift arm and interlock pins.

7) On 4WD models, remove oil seal collar, ball bearing and retainer. *See Fig. 4.* On 2WD models, remove bearing snap ring and ball bearing using bearing remover with bearing plate, snap ring, clip, speedometer drive gear, retainer snap ring and retainer.

8) On all models, remove thrust plate, thrust washer and lock ball. Remove reverse gear shaft snap ring and countergear bearing snap ring. Engage 5th-reverse synchronizer with 5th gear. Using universal puller, remove countergear ball bearing and counter 5th gear while also removing reverse shaft, reverse idler thrust washer gear, and reverse shaft pin.

9) Remove counter reverse gear, 5th gear, 5th block ring and needle bearing. Engage 3rd-4th synchronizer with 3rd gear and 1st-2nd synchronizer with 1st gear. Attach Holding Fixture (J37224) and Holding Base (J3289-20) to mainshaft front bearing and countergear front bearing. Remove mainshaft nut.

MANUAL TRANSMISSIONS
Isuzu MUA Series 5-Speed (Cont.)

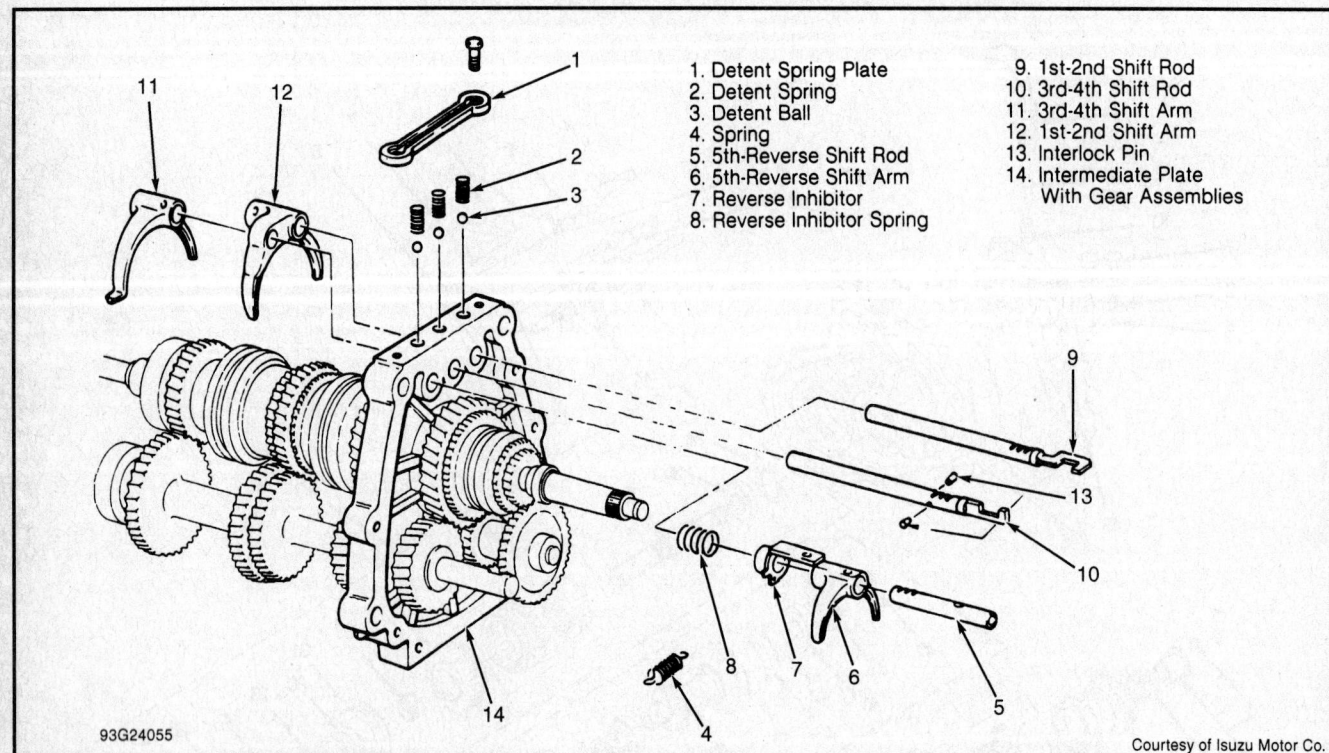

1. Detent Spring Plate
2. Detent Spring
3. Detent Ball
4. Spring
5. 5th-Reverse Shift Rod
6. 5th-Reverse Shift Arm
7. Reverse Inhibitor
8. Reverse Inhibitor Spring
9. 1st-2nd Shift Rod
10. 3rd-4th Shift Rod
11. 3rd-4th Shift Arm
12. 1st-2nd Shift Arm
13. Interlock Pin
14. Intermediate Plate With Gear Assemblies

93G24055

Courtesy of Isuzu Motor Co.

Fig. 3: Exploded View Of Shift Rod & Arm Assemblies

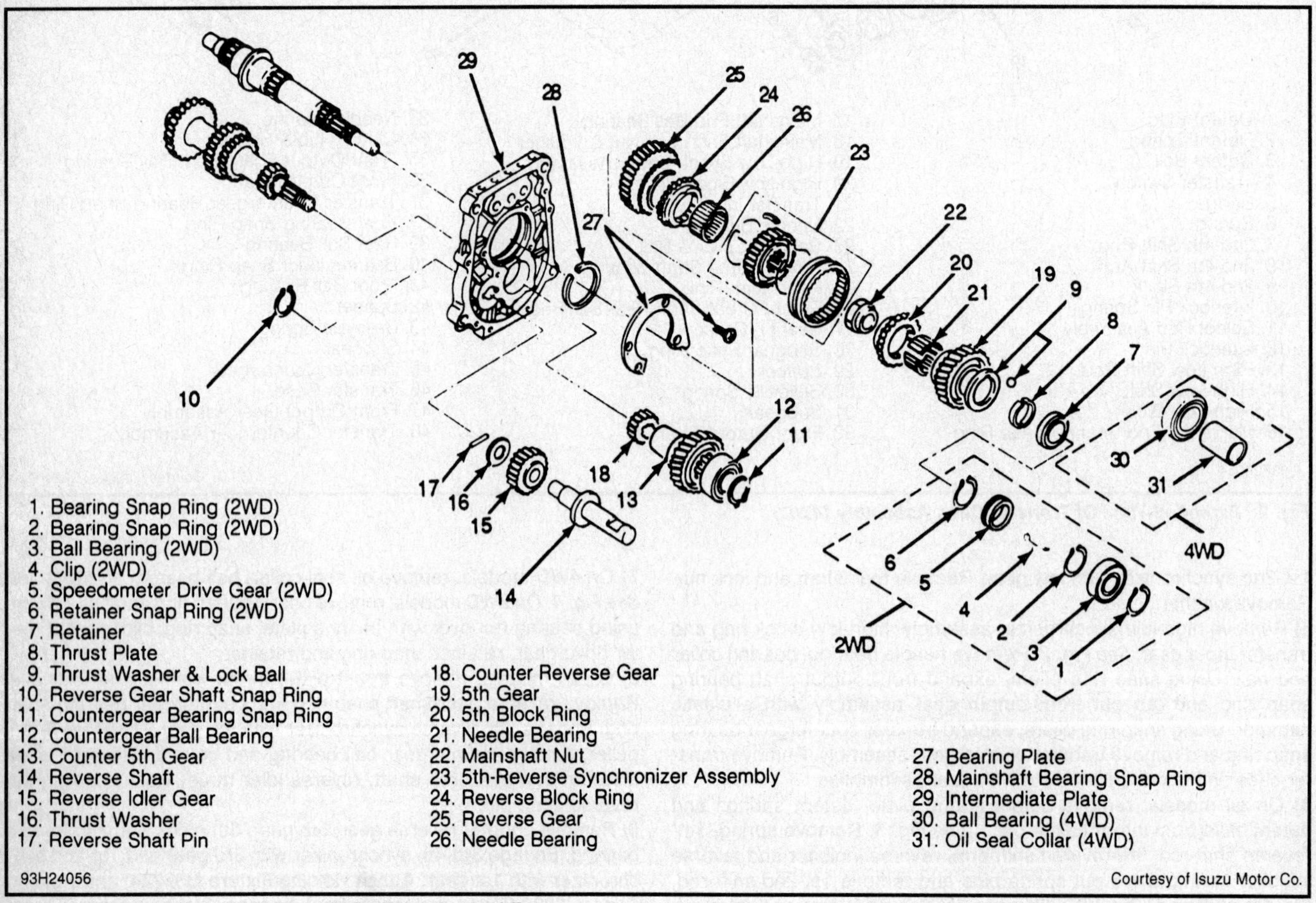

1. Bearing Snap Ring (2WD)
2. Bearing Snap Ring (2WD)
3. Ball Bearing (2WD)
4. Clip (2WD)
5. Speedometer Drive Gear (2WD)
6. Retainer Snap Ring (2WD)
7. Retainer
8. Thrust Plate
9. Thrust Washer & Lock Ball
10. Reverse Gear Shaft Snap Ring
11. Countergear Bearing Snap Ring
12. Countergear Ball Bearing
13. Counter 5th Gear
14. Reverse Shaft
15. Reverse Idler Gear
16. Thrust Washer
17. Reverse Shaft Pin
18. Counter Reverse Gear
19. 5th Gear
20. 5th Block Ring
21. Needle Bearing
22. Mainshaft Nut
23. 5th-Reverse Synchronizer Assembly
24. Reverse Block Ring
25. Reverse Gear
26. Needle Bearing
27. Bearing Plate
28. Mainshaft Bearing Snap Ring
29. Intermediate Plate
30. Ball Bearing (4WD)
31. Oil Seal Collar (4WD)

93H24056

Courtesy of Isuzu Motor Co.

Fig. 4: Exploded View Of Reverse & 5th Gear Assemblies

10) Remove 5th-reverse synchronizer assembly, reverse block ring and reverse gear together. Remove bearing plate and screws using Torx Bit Wrench No. 45. Using snap ring pliers, hold open mainshaft bearing snap ring and remove mainshaft assembly. Using snap ring pliers, hold open countergear bearing snap ring and remove countergear assembly.

COMPONENT DISASSEMBLY & REASSEMBLY

4TH GEAR SHAFT

CAUTION: The 4th gear shaft rides on needle bearing on front end of mainshaft. Needle bearing may come off mainshaft with top shaft when removed. Remove needle bearing to prevent it from damage.

Disassembly & Reassembly – Remove 4th gear shaft snap ring using snap ring pliers. Press off ball bearing. Press on ball bearing and install snap ring. *See Fig. 5.*

MAINSHAFT ASSEMBLY

CAUTION: The 4th gear shaft rides on needle bearing on front end of mainshaft. Needle bearing may come off mainshaft with top shaft when removed. Remove needle bearing to prevent it from damage.

Disassembly – 1) Remove needle bearing and 4th block ring. *See Fig. 5.* Remove mainshaft snap ring. Press off 3rd-4th synchronizer assembly. Remove 3rd block ring and 3rd gear needle bearing.
2) Using bearing remover, press off needle bearing collar, mainshaft ball bearing, 1st gear thrust bearing and 1st gear. Remove 1st block ring, needle bearing and 1st-2nd synchronizer snap ring. Press off 1st-2nd synchronizer assembly, 2nd block ring and 2nd gear together using bearing remover. Remove needle bearing.
Inspection – 1) Measure clearance between block rings and their respective gear dog teeth. *See Fig. 6.* Standard clearance is .059" (1.50 mm). Wear limit is .031" (.80 mm). If clearance exceeds specification, replace block ring.
2) Place mainshaft onto "V" blocks and measure center portion runout. *See Fig. 6.* Mainshaft runout should not exceed .002" (.05 mm). Replace as necessary.

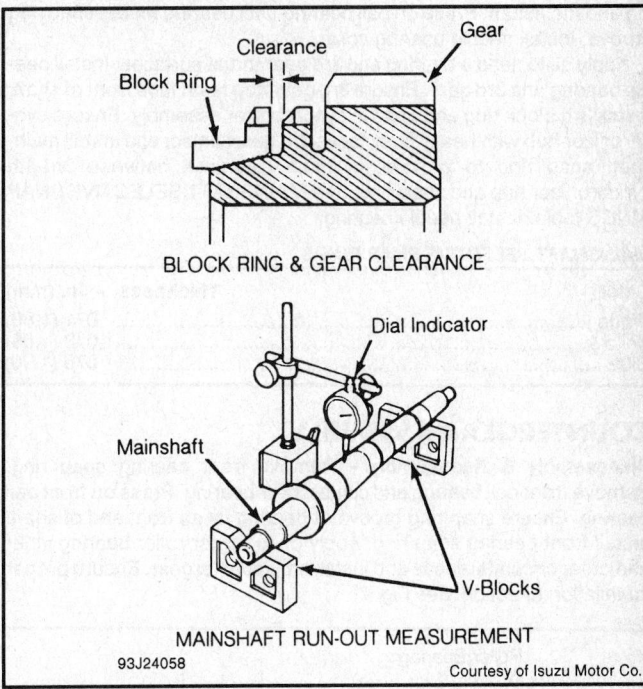

BLOCK RING & GEAR CLEARANCE

MAINSHAFT RUN-OUT MEASUREMENT

93J24058   Courtesy of Isuzu Motor Co.

Fig. 6: Measuring Block Ring Clearance & Mainshaft Run-Out

Reassembly – 1) Apply oil to needle bearing and 2nd gear thrust surfaces and install onto mainshaft. Ensure 2nd gear dog teeth face rear of shaft. Install 2nd block ring and 1st-2nd synchronizer assembly. Ensure synchronizer hub with heavy boss faces 2nd gear. Select and install snap ring to provide minimum clearance between 1st-2nd synchronizer hub and snap ring. See MAINSHAFT SELECTIVE SNAP RINGS table.
2) Apply oil to needle bearing and 1st gear thrust surfaces. Install 1st block ring, needle bearing and 1st gear. Ensure 1st gear dog teeth face front of shaft. Install 1st gear thrust bearing. Apply oil to ball bear-

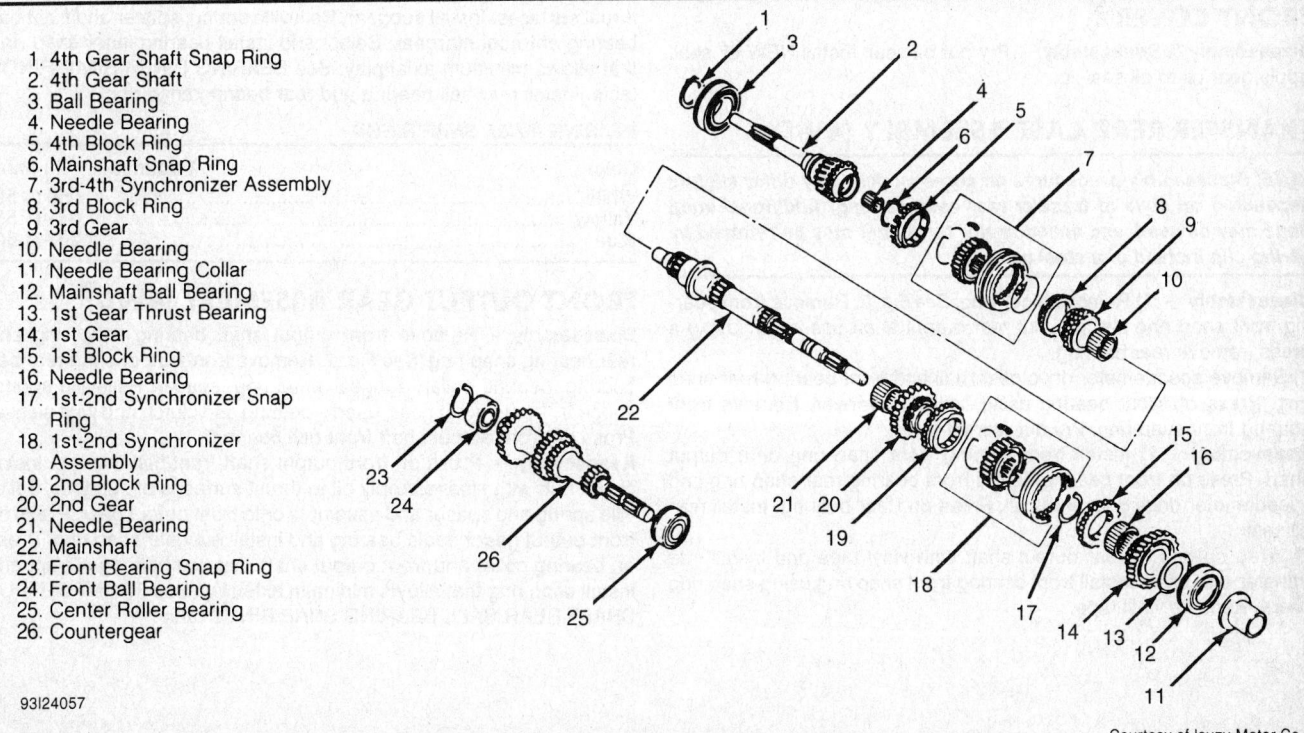

1. 4th Gear Shaft Snap Ring
2. 4th Gear Shaft
3. Ball Bearing
4. Needle Bearing
5. 4th Block Ring
6. Mainshaft Snap Ring
7. 3rd-4th Synchronizer Assembly
8. 3rd Block Ring
9. 3rd Gear
10. Needle Bearing
11. Needle Bearing Collar
12. Mainshaft Ball Bearing
13. 1st Gear Thrust Bearing
14. 1st Gear
15. 1st Block Ring
16. Needle Bearing
17. 1st-2nd Synchronizer Snap Ring
18. 1st-2nd Synchronizer Assembly
19. 2nd Block Ring
20. 2nd Gear
21. Needle Bearing
22. Mainshaft
23. Front Bearing Snap Ring
24. Front Ball Bearing
25. Center Roller Bearing
26. Countergear

93I24057

Courtesy of Isuzu Motor Co.

Fig. 5: Exploded View Of 4th Gear Shaft, Mainshaft & Countergear Assemblies

ing and mainshaft. Press on ball bearing until bearing meets snap ring groove. Install needle bearing collar.

3) Apply oil to needle bearing and 3rd gear thrust surfaces. Install needle bearing and 3rd gear. Ensure 3rd gear dog teeth face front of shaft. Install 3rd block ring and 3rd-4th synchronizer assembly. Ensure synchronizer hub with heavy boss faces 3rd gear. Select and install mainshaft snap ring to provide minimum clearance between 3rd-4th synchronizer hub and snap ring. See MAINSHAFT SELECTIVE SNAP RINGS table. Install needle bearing.

MAINSHAFT SELECTIVE SNAP RINGS

Color	Thickness – In. (mm)
White	.071 (1.80)
Yellow	.073 (1.85)
Blue	.075 (1.90)

COUNTERGEAR ASSEMBLY

Disassembly & Reassembly – Remove front bearing snap ring. Remove front ball bearing and center roller bearing. Press on front ball bearing. Ensure snap ring groove of bearing faces front end of shaft. Install front bearing snap ring. Apply oil to center roller bearing inner and outer circumferences and install onto countergear. Ensure proper installation direction. *See Fig. 7.*

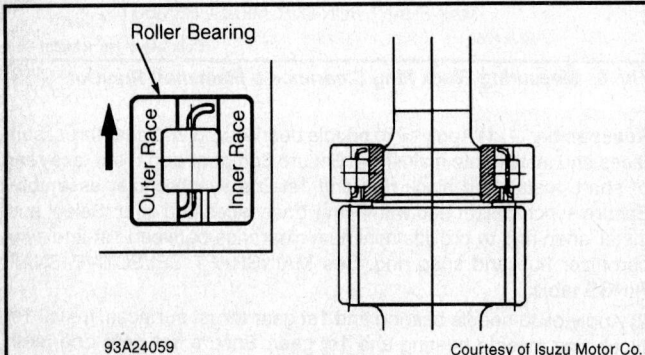

Fig. 7: Installing Center Roller Bearing

FRONT COVER

Disassembly & Reassembly – Pry out oil seal. Install NEW oil seal. Apply gear oil to oil seal lip.

TRANSFER REAR CASE ASSEMBLY (4WD)

NOTE: Disassembly procedures on some models may differ slightly depending on style of transfer rear case casting. Additional snap rings may be used, and speedometer drive gear may be retained by spring clip instead of a steel ball.

Disassembly – 1) Remove block ring. *See Fig. 8.* Remove front bearing front snap ring and pull out rear output shaft assembly. Using a press, remove rear bearing.
2) Remove speedometer drive gear, ball and front bearing rear snap ring. Press off front bearing using bearing remover. Remove front bearing front snap ring. Pry out rear oil seal.
Reassembly – 1) Install front bearing front snap ring onto output shaft. Press on front bearing. Install front bearing rear snap ring and speedometer drive gear with ball. Press on Rear bearing. Install rear oil seal.
2) Wrap splines of rear output shaft with vinyl tape and install into transfer rear case. Install front bearing front snap ring using snap ring pliers. Remove vinyl tape.

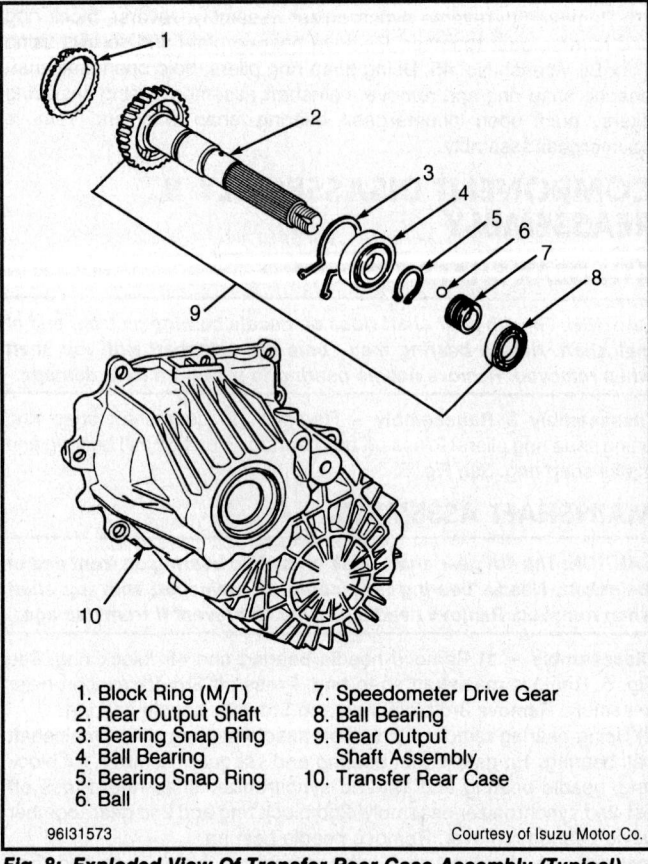

1. Block Ring (M/T)
2. Rear Output Shaft
3. Bearing Snap Ring
4. Ball Bearing
5. Bearing Snap Ring
6. Ball
7. Speedometer Drive Gear
8. Ball Bearing
9. Rear Output Shaft Assembly
10. Transfer Rear Case

Fig. 8: Exploded View Of Transfer Rear Case Assembly (Typical)

TRANSFER COUNTERGEAR (4WD)

Disassembly – Remove transfer countergear rear bearing snap ring and front bearing inner snap ring. *See Fig. 2.* Remove front and rear ball bearings. Remove spacer, Belleville spring and subgear.
Reassembly – Apply chassis grease to subgear and countergear thrust surfaces. Install subgear, Belleville spring, spacer and front ball bearing onto countergear. Select and install bearing inner snap ring that allows minimum axial play. See BEARING INNER SNAP RINGS table. Install rear ball bearing and rear bearing snap ring.

BEARING INNER SNAP RINGS

Color	Thickness - In. (mm)
White	.059 (1.50)
Yellow	.061 (1.55)
Blue	.063 (1.60)

FRONT OUTPUT GEAR ASSEMBLY (4WD)

Disassembly – Remove front output shaft bearing snap ring and rear bearing snap ring. *See Fig. 2.* Remove front output shaft rear ball bearing, bearing collar, subgear snap ring, spacer, Belleville spring, subgear, front output gear, needle bearing and clutch hub with sleeve. Press off front output shaft front ball bearing.
Reassembly – Press on front output shaft front ball bearing. Install clutch hub with sleeve. Apply oil to thrust surfaces of subgear, Belleville spring and spacer and assemble onto front output gear. Press on front output gear needle bearing and install subgear snap ring. Press on bearing collar and front output shaft rear ball bearing. Select and install snap ring that allows minimum axle play. See FRONT OUTPUT SHAFT REAR BALL BEARING SNAP RINGS table.

FRONT OUTPUT SHAFT REAR BALL BEARING SNAP RINGS

Color	Thickness In. (mm)
White	.061 (1.55)
Yellow	.063 (1.60)
Blue	.065 (1.65)
Pink	.067 (1.70)
Green	.069 (1.75)
Brown	.071 (1.80)
Red	.073 (1.85)
Orange	.075 (1.90)

TRANSMISSION REASSEMBLY

1) Mesh countergear assembly with mainshaft and 4th gear shaft assemblies and install into Holding Fixture (J37224) and Holding Base (J3289-20). Install intermediate plate and mainshaft bearing snap ring. See Fig. 4. Install bearing plate. Apply Loctite to bearing plate screws and torque to 11 ft. lbs. (15 N.m) using Torx Bit Wrench No. 45.

2) Install needle bearing, mainshaft reverse gear and reverse block ring. Install 5th-reverse synchronizer assembly with hub facing reverse gear. Mesh 1st-2nd synchronizer with 1st gear and 3rd-4th synchronizer with 3rd gear. Install mainshaft nut and torque to 101 ft. lbs. (137 N.m). Stake nut in one place.

3) Install needle bearing, 5th block ring and 5th gear. See Fig. 4. Install counter reverse gear with projection towards intermediate plate. Assemble reverse shaft pin, thrust washer, reverse idler gear and reverse shaft. Install counter 5th gear and reverse shaft assembly together onto intermediate plate. Install countergear ball bearing. Select and install countergear bearing snap ring that will allow minimum clearance between bearing and snap ring. See COUNTERGEAR BEARING SNAP RINGS table.

COUNTERGEAR BEARING SNAP RINGS

Color	Thickness - In. (mm)
White	.043 (1.10)
Yellow	.047 (1.20)
Blue	.051 (1.30)
Pink	.055 (1.40)
Green	.059 (1.50)
Brown	.063 (1.60)

4) Select and install reverse gear shaft snap ring that allows minimum clearance between intermediate plate and snap ring. See REVERSE GEAR SHAFT SNAP RINGS table.

REVERSE GEAR SHAFT SNAP RINGS

Color	Thickness - In. (mm)
White	.047 (1.20)
Yellow	.051 (1.30)
Blue	.055 (1.40)

5) Install thrust washer and lock ball onto mainshaft. Measure clearance between 5th gear and thrust washer. Clearance should be .004-.010" (.10-.25 mm). If clearance is not to specification, select a NEW thrust washer to bring clearance to specification. See SELECTIVE THRUST WASHERS table. Apply grease to thrust washer and lock ball and install onto mainshaft.

SELECTIVE THRUST WASHERS

Color	Thickness - In. (mm)
White	.311 (7.90)
Yellow	.315 (8.00)
Green	.319 (8.10)
Blue	.323 (8.20)

6) Install thrust plate and retainer. On 2WD models, install retainer snap ring, speedometer drive gear, clip and bearing snap ring. On all models, press on ball bearing. On 2WD models, install bearing snap ring. On 4WD models, install oil seal collar.

7) On all models, install 1st-2nd shift arm onto 1st-2nd synchronizer sleeve and 3rd-4th shift arm onto 3rd-4th synchronizer sleeve. See Fig. 3. Install interlock pins into 3rd-4th shift rod and install 3rd-4th shift rod into intermediate plate. Install 1st-2nd shift rod and drive in 1st-2nd and 3rd-4th shift rod into intermediate plate. Install 1st-2nd shift rod and drive in 1st-2nd and 3rd-4th shift arm spring pins.

8) Assemble reverse inhibitor spring, reverse inhibitor, 5th-reverse shift arm and 5th-reverse shift rod and install assembly into intermediate plate. Drive in spring pin and install spring. Install detent balls, springs and detent spring plate. Torque bolts to 15 ft. lbs. (20 N.m).

9) On 2WD models, clean transmission case, intermediate plate and extension housing mating surfaces. Apply liquid gasket to transmission case and extension housing mating surfaces. Install intermediate plate to transmission case and extension housing to intermediate plate. Install extension housing bolts and torque to 27 ft. lbs. (37 N.m).

10) On 4WD models, clean transmission case, intermediate plate and transfer case mating surfaces. Apply liquid gasket to transmission case and transfer case mating surfaces. Install intermediate plate to transmission case and transfer case to intermediate plate. Install transfer case bolts and torque to 27 ft. lbs. (37 N.m).

11) Install transfer countergear bearing snap ring. See Fig. 2. Expand snap ring using snap ring pliers and tap in transfer countergear assembly. Install front output shaft bearing snap ring. Expand snap ring and tap in front output shaft assembly.

12) Install ball, bearing collar, needle bearing, transfer input gear high-low block ring and high-low synchronizer assembly. Install washer and mainshaft end lock nut. Torque nut to 101 ft. lbs. (137 N.m) using mainshaft nut wrench. Install mainshaft end ball bearing and mainshaft end bearing snap ring.

13) Install high-low shift arm onto high-low synchronizer sleeve. Install high-low block, high-low shift rod and select rod assembly. Drive in high-low shift arm spring pin. Engage high-low synchronizer with rear output gear and install interlock pin spring and interlock pin.

14) Assemble 2nd-4th block, 2nd-4th shift arm, and spring onto 2nd-4th shift rod. Push down interlock pin and install 2nd-4th shift rod into transfer case. Drive in 2nd-4th block spring pin. Install bridge, detent balls, detent springs and detent plugs. Torque plugs to 18 ft. lbs. (25 N.m).

15) Install transfer switch and torque to 29 ft. lbs. (39 N.m). Clean transfer case and transfer rear case mating surfaces. Apply liquid gasket to transfer rear case mating surfaces and install onto transfer case. Torque bolts to 27 ft. lbs. (37 N.m).

16) Install transfer flange and nut. See Fig. 1. Using Transfer Flange Holder (J27221) and socket wrench, torque nut to specification.

17) On all models, install speedometer driven gear and torque bolt to specification. Install countergear front bearing snap ring and mainshaft front bearing snap ring. See Fig. 1. Install front cover with oil seal. Coat bolt threads with liquid gasket and torque to specification.

TORQUE SPECIFICATIONS
TORQUE SPECIFICATIONS

Application	Ft. Lbs. (N.m)
Bearing Plate Screws	11 (15)
Detent Spring Plate Bolts	15 (20)
Extension Housing Bolts (2WD)	27 (37)
Front Cover Bolts	18 (25)
Mainshaft End Lock Nut (4WD)	101 (137)
Speedometer Driven Gear Bolt	11 (15)
Transfer Case Bolts (4WD)	27 (37)
Transfer Case Detent Plugs (4WD)	18 (25)
Transfer Flange Nut (4WD)	
Front	101 (137)
Rear	123 (167)
Transfer Rear Case Bolts (4WD)	27 (37)
Transfer Switch (4WD)	29 (39)

MANUAL TRANSMISSIONS
Kia (Getrag) 5-Speed

Sportage

APPLICATION & LABOR TIMES

APPLICATION & LABOR TIMES

Vehicle Application	Labor Times		Series
	¹ ³ R & I	² ³ Overhaul	
1995-96 Sportage	4.2	5.3	5-Speed

¹ – Removal and installation of transmission from vehicle chassis.
² – Bench overhaul time for transmission. DOES NOT include removal and installation.

IDENTIFICATION

Transmission identification number is located on front of transmission case. *See Fig. 1.* Number identifies transmission model.

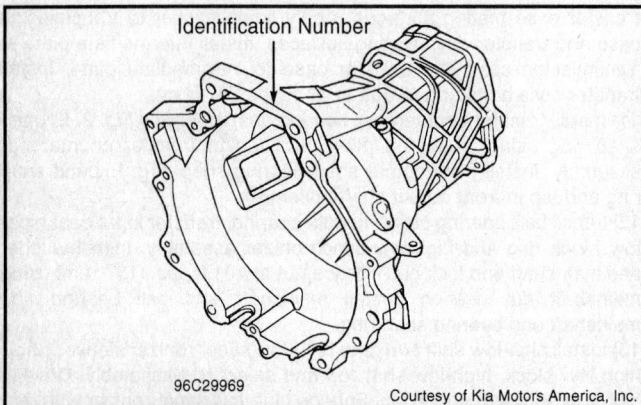

Fig. 1: Locating Transmission Identification Number

DESCRIPTION

Transmission is a 5-speed unit with fully synchronized forward gears. Reverse gear is a selective sliding type with a reverse idler.

LUBRICATION & ADJUSTMENT

See appropriate MANUAL TRANSMISSION SERVICING article in TRANSMISSION SERVICING section.

TROUBLE SHOOTING

See GENERAL TROUBLE SHOOTING article in this section.

REMOVAL & INSTALLATION

See appropriate MANUAL TRANSMISSION REMOVAL article in TRANSMISSION SERVICING section.

TRANSMISSION DISASSEMBLY

1) Remove 10 bolts and separate either transfer case or extension housing from transmission case. Remove clutch release lever and bearing from front housing.
2) Remove shift control rod extension. Using appropriate pliers, slide back spring clamp. Pry spring sleeve open and slide off coupling with snap ring pliers. Drive out roll pin. Remove back-up light switch from right side of rear cover.
3) Using chisel, carefully remove shift control rod detent plug from front housing. Remove spring and detent. *See Fig. 2.* Remove 6 bolts and separate bearing support with shim from clutch housing. Remove retaining snap ring and control washer from input shaft.
4) Remove 8 transmission housing bolts that secure case halves. Note bolt length and location. Remove forward of two reverse idler shaft mounting bolts, located on driver's side of front housing (clutch housing). Install appropriate puller to front housing and separate rear housing and gearshaft assemblies from front housing.

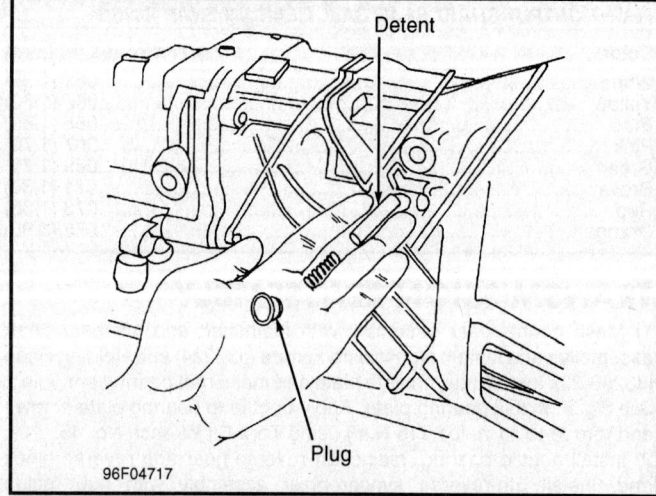

Fig. 2: Removing Shift Control Rod Detent

5) Place rear housing with gearshaft assemblies on end with output shaft facing down. Remove reverse idler gear shaft bolt, located on left side of rear cover. Remove reverse idler gear locking plate. Remove reverse idler gear shaft and gear. Remove roller bearing from end of countershaft.
6) Remove threaded plug located on right side of rear cover and remove 5th/reverse return spring. Remove control rod bearing support retaining bolt, located on top front of rear housing. Drive out roll pin from control lever assembly.
7) Break contact between control rod and transmission seal by tapping ball end of control rod with soft-faced mallet. Raise control rod. Lift control rod support block and pull spring towards front of rear cover with needle-nosed pliers. Pull spring clip and bearing support with pliers to remove from rear cover. Ensure 4 small rollers from control lever or selector arm roller are removed.
8) Remove spring cover. Remove 3 springs and steel balls. *See Fig. 3.* Using hammer and pin punch, drive out roll pin from 3rd/4th shift fork. *See Fig. 4.* Remove 3rd/4th shift rod and interlock pin at end of shift rod. Ensure syncro hub is not moved or hub keys, steel balls and springs will be released.
9) Using magnet, remove 2 steel balls of 1st/2nd and 5th/reverse shift rods. Steel balls are removed through 3rd/4th shift rod hole.
10) Place transmission housing horizontal. Remove 3 bearing support block bolts from back of rear housing. Remove gearshaft assemblies (shift rods, mainshaft, coutershaft) as a single unit from rear housing.

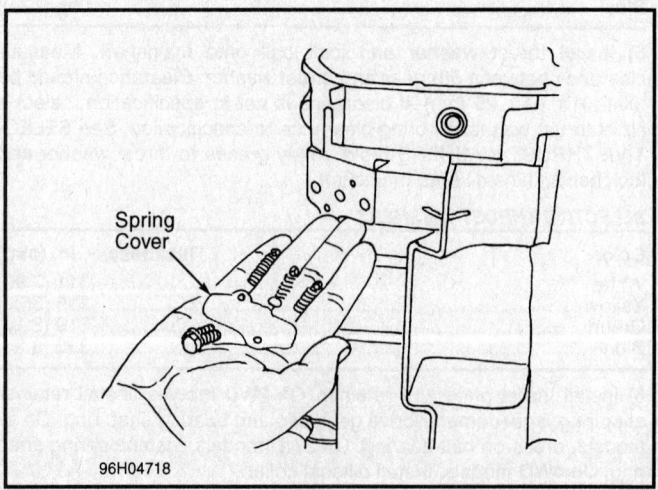

Fig. 3: Removing Spring Cover

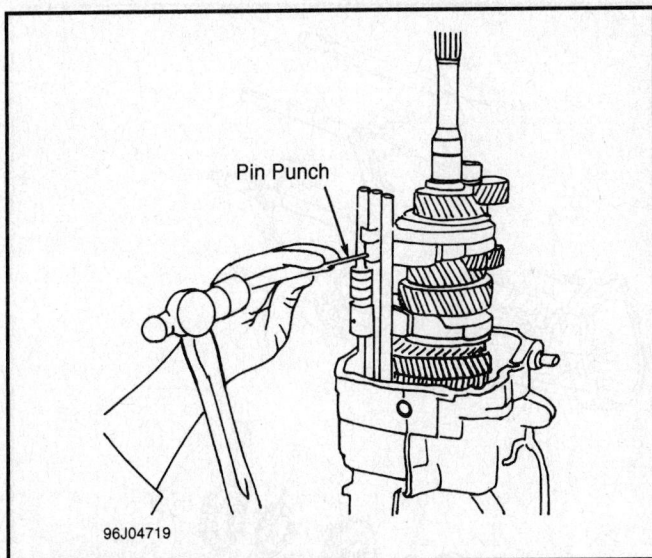

Pin Punch

96J04719

Fig. 4: Removing 3rd/4th Shift Fork

COMPONENT DISASSEMBLY & REASSEMBLY

MAINSHAFT

NOTE: Remove each gear, bearing and clutch hub assembly in order given. Do not attempt to remove more than one group of parts at a time unless directed to do so in disassembly step. For exploded view of internal components, see Fig. 5.

NOTE: Synchronizer hub assemblies must remain together until removed. Steel balls and springs may be lost if hub sleeve is removed prematurely.

NOTE: Before disassembling mainshaft, measure synchronizing ring clearance. Clearance should be .04-.06" (.9-1.6 mm). Replace rings as needed.

Disassembly – 1) Separate countershaft and shift rods with their forks from mainshaft. Remove shim from lower end of mainshaft. Support mainshaft in vise with input shaft assembly pointing up. Lift input shaft assembly and 4th gear synchronizer ring off. Remove needle bearing from mainshaft.
2) Remove 3rd/4th clutch hub retaining snap ring and washer using snap ring pliers. Using press and appropriate bearing splitter, remove 3rd/4th clutch hub assembly, 3rd gear synchronizer ring and 3rd gear from mainshaft. Remove 3rd gear needle bearing.
3) Using press and appropriate bearing splitter, remove 2nd gear and 3rd gear inner race. Remove indexing steel ball from shaft. Remove 2nd gear needle bearing and synchronizer ring. Remove 1st/2nd hub sleeve retaining snap ring.
4) Using press and appropriate bearing splitter, remove 1st/2nd clutch hub assembly, 1st gear synchronizer ring and 1st gear. Remove 1st gear needle bearing.
5) Turn over mainshaft and clamp in vise. Remove retaining snap ring. Remove adjusting washer. Remove snap ring and control washer. Press off rear bearing. Remove locking spacer and roll pin. Remove support plate. Remove 5th gear adjusting nut.
6) Using press and appropriate bearing splitter, remove 5th gear and synchronizer ring. Remove 5th gear split needle bearing from mainshaft. Remove retaining snap ring. Remove 5th/reverse clutch hub assembly, reverse synchronizer ring and reverse gear.
Inspection – Inspect mainshaft for lateral runout. Maximum runout is .002" (.05 mm). Inspect for wear or cracks. Check gears for cracks,

wear and damage. Measure thickness of guide on all shift forks. Thickness should be .19-.20" (4.90-4.96 mm). Replace as needed. Check all bearings for rough operation.

NOTE: Manufacturer recommends use of Synchronizer Assembly Tool (K95B-4110-MT).

NOTE: For exploded view of internal components, see Fig. 5.

Reassembly – 1) To reassemble clutch hub and synchronizer ring assemblies, place hub sleeve on workbench with grooves facing down. Insert inner synchronizer spacer ring of tool into hub sleeve.
2) Place correct hub sleeve on spacer tool. Align 3 key tabs in ring with 3 flat teeth on hub sleeve. Hub sleeves are identified by number of machined lines on outside of sleeve. *See Fig. 6.* 1st/2nd sleeve has one line. 3rd/4th sleeve has 2 lines and 5th/reverse sleeve has 3 lines.
3) Locate clutch hub on hub sleeve with hub's identification markings facing up. Align 3 hub key seat areas to key tabs on ring. Slide outer ring of tool over assembly. Three set screws should align with 3 key seat areas in hub.
4) Insert 3 keys with stepped sides facing out. Remove set screw and insert spring and ball. Reinsert screw and finger tighten. Repeat procedure for remaining 2 springs and steel balls.
5) Place appropriate synchronizer ring onto hub assembly. For synchronizer ring identification, *see Fig. 7.* Align 3 key tabs on synchronizer ring to key seat areas on hub. Carefully lift entire assembly, leaving inner spacer ring on bench.
6) Apply pressure to hub sleeve while loosening 3 screws enough to allow sleeve and outer ring of tool to slide down. Slide assembly to edge of bench. Push up on bottom synchronizer ring until balls and keys click into place. Inspect assembly for properly aligned and seated springs, steel balls and keys.
7) Align key groove of 1st gear synchronizer ring with key groove of 1st/2nd clutch hub. Ensure grooves on outer surface of hub sleeve face to rear in assembly. Apply grease to 1st gear needle bear. On press, assembly 1st/2nd clutch hub assembly, synchronizer ring, 1st gear and needle bearing onto appropriate support tube. Insert mainshaft into assembly. Press shaft into 1st/2nd clutch hub assembly.
8) Install original retaining snap ring. Using a feeler gauge, measure end play (gap) between retaining snap ring and 1st gear. End play should be .004-.008" (.10-.20 mm). Install correct retaining snap ring to achieve end play. Snap rings range in thickness from .065" (1.65 mm) to .077" (1.95 mm) in .002" (.05 mm) increments.
9) Install selected retaining snap ring. Install 2nd gear synchronizer assembly and 2nd gear. Grease needle bearing and install onto mainshaft. Install indexing steel ball and spacer (stepped side facing down). Press 3rd gear inner race into place. Measure end play of 2nd gear. End play should be .004-.010" (.10-.25 mm). If end play is not correct, check installation of 2nd gear components.
10) Apply grease to 3rd gear needle bearing. Align key groove of 3rd gear synchronizer ring with key groove of clutch hub. Place mainshaft on press platform. Install 3rd/4th clutch hub assembly, 3rd gear synchronizer ring, 3rd gear and needle bearing.
11) Press mainshaft into assembly. Install original retaining snap ring. Using a feeler gauge, measure 3rd gear end play (gap) between 3rd gear and 2nd gear. End play should be .002-.006" (.05-.015 mm). Install correct retaining snap ring to achieve end play. Snap rings range in thickness from .091" (2.30 mm) to .104" (2.65 mm) in .002" (.05 mm) increments.
12) Assemble 5th/reverse clutch hub assembly, reverse synchronizer ring, reverse gear and needle bearing onto appropriate support tube. Press mainshaft into 5th/reverse clutch hub assembly.
13) Align key groove of 5th gear synchronizer ring with key groove of clutch hub. Assembly synchronizer ring, needle bearing and 5th gear onto mainshaft.
14) Install adjusting nut with orientation mark facing upward. Hand tighten nut to set end play of 5th gear. End play should be .002-.004" (.05-.10 mm). Install locking spacer and roller. Recheck 5th gear end play and reset adjusting nut as needed.

MANUAL TRANSMISSIONS
Kia (Getrag) 5-Speed (Cont.)

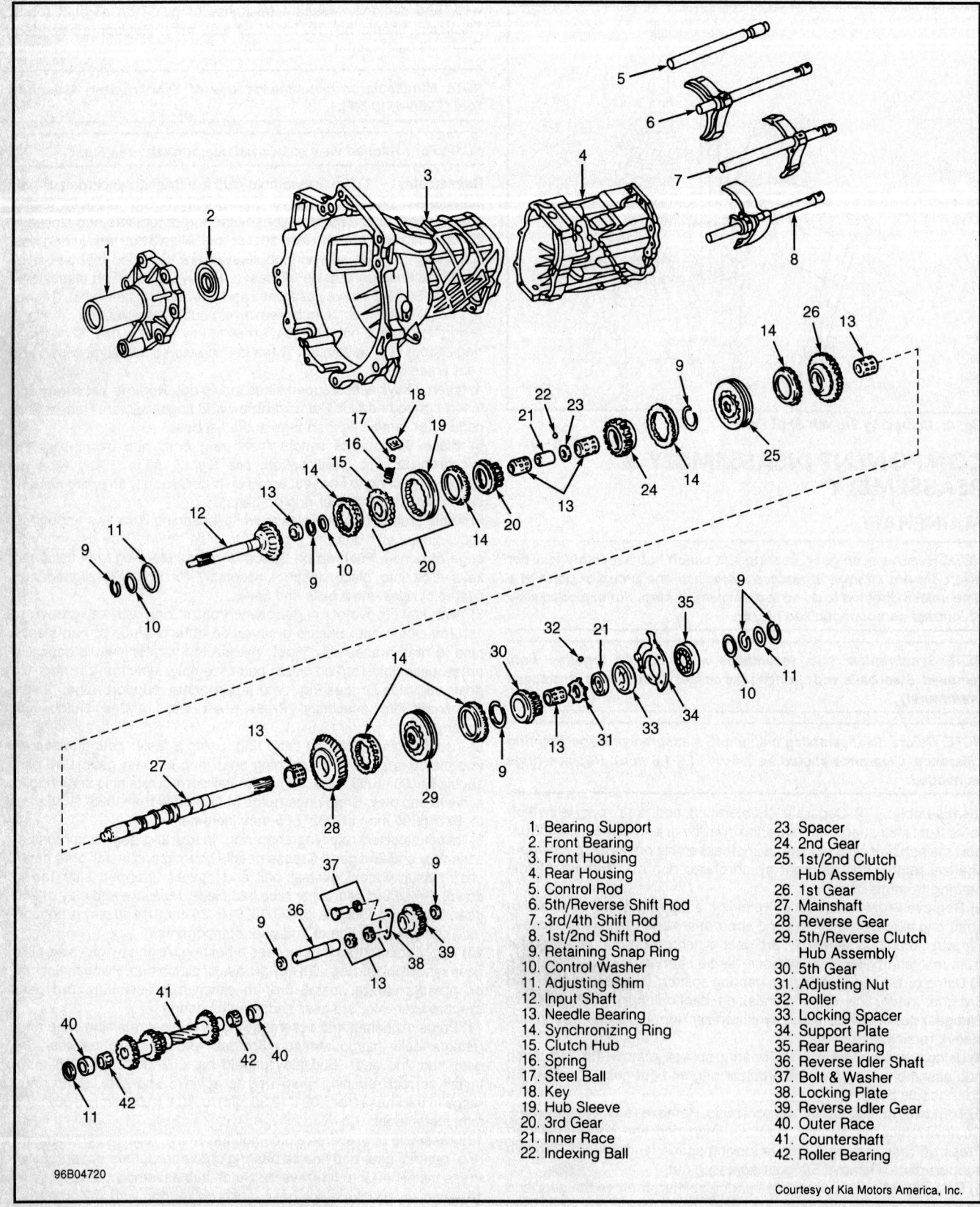

1. Bearing Support
2. Front Bearing
3. Front Housing
4. Rear Housing
5. Control Rod
6. 5th/Reverse Shift Rod
7. 3rd/4th Shift Rod
8. 1st/2nd Shift Rod
9. Retaining Snap Ring
10. Control Washer
11. Adjusting Shim
12. Input Shaft
13. Needle Bearing
14. Synchronizing Ring
15. Clutch Hub
16. Spring
17. Steel Ball
18. Key
19. Hub Sleeve
20. 3rd Gear
21. Inner Race
22. Indexing Ball

23. Spacer
24. 2nd Gear
25. 1st/2nd Clutch
    Hub Assembly
26. 1st Gear
27. Mainshaft
28. Reverse Gear
29. 5th/Reverse Clutch
    Hub Assembly
30. 5th Gear
31. Adjusting Nut
32. Roller
33. Locking Spacer
34. Support Plate
35. Rear Bearing
36. Reverse Idler Shaft
37. Bolt & Washer
38. Locking Plate
39. Reverse Idler Gear
40. Outer Race
41. Countershaft
42. Roller Bearing

96B04720

Courtesy of Kia Motors America, Inc.

Fig. 5: Exploded View Of Kia (Getrag) 5-Speed

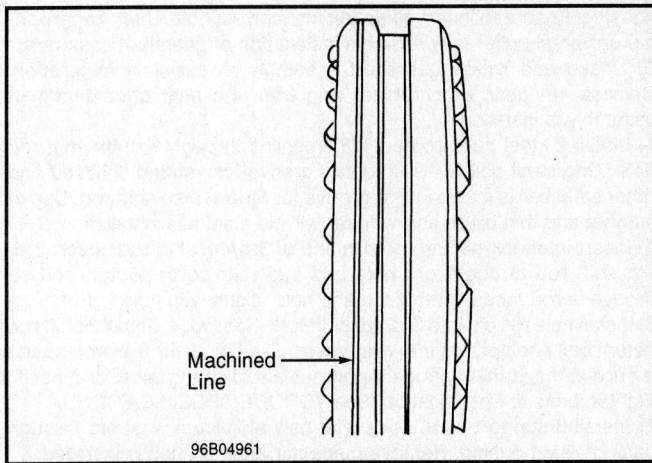

Fig. 6: Identifying 1st/2nd Clutch Hub Sleeve

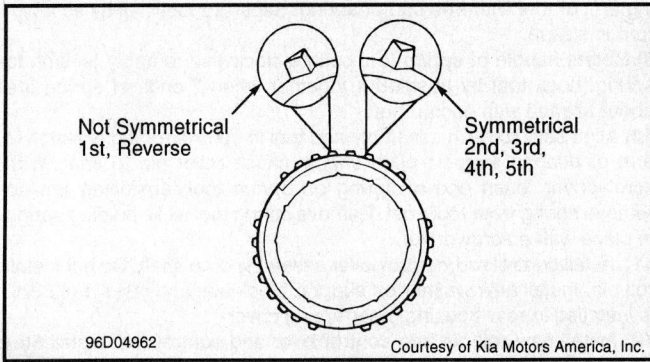

Fig. 7: Identifying Synchronizer Rings

Courtesy of Kia Motors America, Inc.

15) Hold bearing support plate with arm side facing up. Rotate arm fully counterclockwise against stop pin. Holding arm in place, install bearing support plate onto mainshaft with arm facing toward gears.

16) Install rear bearing onto mainshaft. Press support plate and bearing onto shaft using appropriate universal handle driver. Install control washer and retaining snap ring. Install an adjusting shim (cup side down) that will minimize bearing end play. Adjusting shims range in thickness from .087" (2.20 mm) to .104" (2.65 mm) in .002" (.05 mm). Install retaining snap ring.

17) Apply grease to mainshaft needle bearing and install on front end of mainshaft. Install 4th gear synchronizer ring on front of 3rd clutch hub assembly. Install input shaft on front of mainshaft.

ADJUSTMENTS

COUNTERSHAFT

NOTE: Countershaft bearing preload adjustment is necessary if countershaft is replaced.

1) Using appropriate puller, remove countershaft bearing outer race from front housing. Remove adjusting shim. Reinstall outer race. Install countershaft with bearings in front housing. Place outer race on rear of countershaft.

2) Set double post portion of Countershaft Shim Gauge (K95B-4106-MT) on countershaft. *See Fig. 8.* Measure distance between upper face of bearing outer race and sealing surface of rear housing. Apply pressure to gauge's cross bar where it contacts bearing race. Loosen knurled screws and let posts rest on sealing surface of housing. Tighten screws.

3) Remove countershaft from front housing. Set single post portion of Countershaft Shim Gauge (K95B-4106-MT) in front housing. *See Fig. 9.* Measure distance between bottom of countershaft bearing outer race and sealing surface of front housing. Apply pressure to gauge's cross bar where it contacts sealing surface. Loosen knurled screw and let post rest on bearing race. Tighten screw.

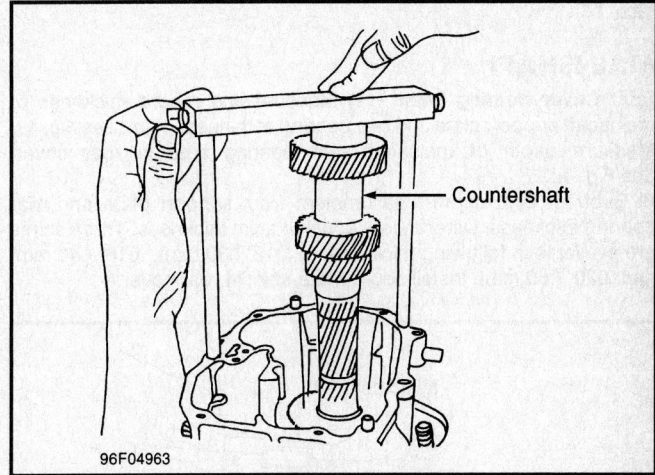

Fig. 8: Measuring Countershaft Install Height

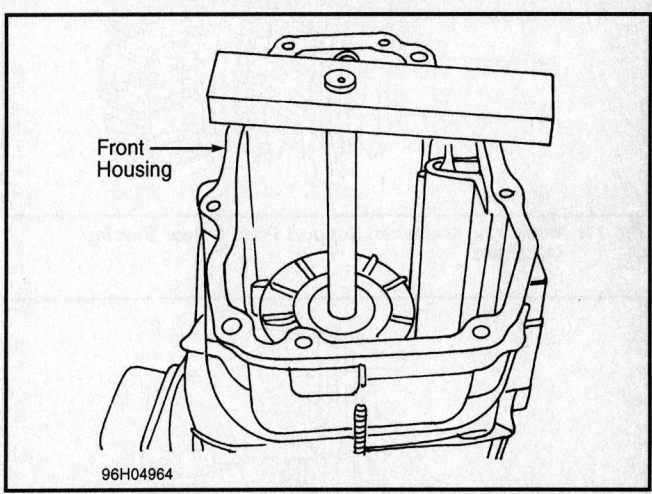

Fig. 9: Measuring Countershaft Bearing Outer Race Depth

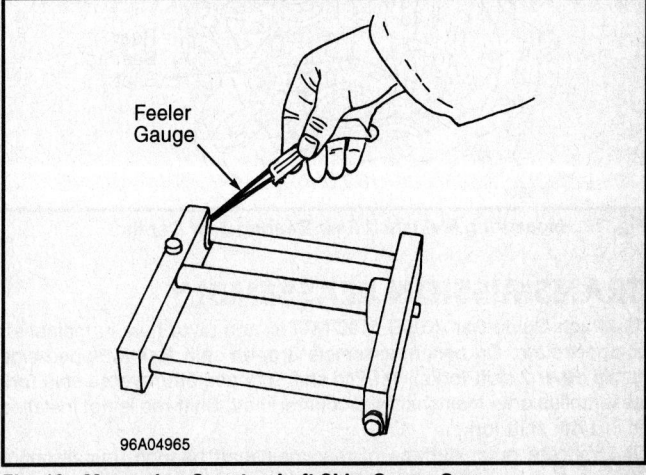

Fig. 10: Measuring Countershaft Shim Gauge Gap

4) Assemble gauge set and measure gap between posts and cross bar with feeler gauge. *See Fig. 10*. Subtract end play .005-.009" (.13-.23 mm) from measured gap. Select shim that is equal to figure. A variety of shims are available and range in thickness from .020" (.50 mm) to .093" (2.35 mm).

5) Using appropriate puller, remove countershaft bearing outer race from front housing. Install selected adjusting shim. Reinstall outer race.

MAINSHAFT

Rear Cover Bearing Shim – **1)** Measure and record thickness of mainshaft support plate and rear bearing at thinnest point. *See Fig. 11*. Measure depth of mainshaft rear bearing seat in rear cover. *See Fig. 12*.

2) Subtract seat depth measurement from support plate and rear bearing thickness. Difference is equal to shim thickness. Three shims are available in following thicknesses; .012" (.30 mm), .016" (.40 mm) and .020" (.50 mm). Install appropriate shim in rear cover.

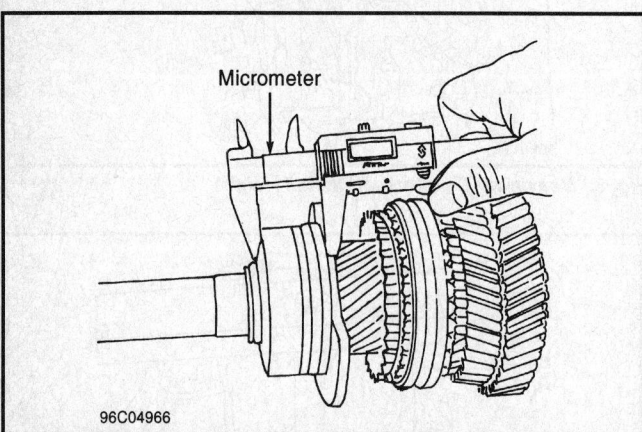

Fig. 11: *Measuring Mainshaft Support Plate & Rear Bearing Thickness*

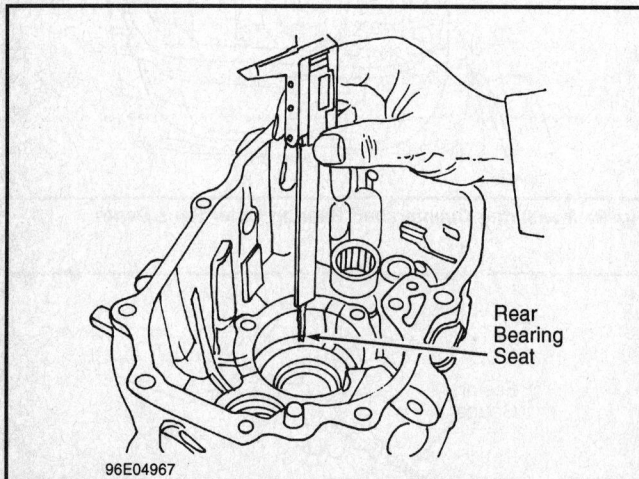

Fig. 12: *Measuring Mainshaft Rear Bearing Seat Depth*

TRANSMISSION REASSEMBLY

1) Attach Guide Bar (K95B-4100-MT) to arm pivot hole in mainshaft support plate. On bench, assemble 3rd/4th shift fork (stepped side faces other 2 shift forks), 1st/2nd shift fork and 5th/reverse shift fork assemblies onto mainshaft and countershaft. Shift rod is not installed in 3rd/4th shift fork.

2) Lubricate outer surface of rear mainshaft bearing. Install entire gearshaft assembly with shift forks and countershaft into rear

housing. Ensure to insert guide bar into correct hole. Use of appropriate universal puller may assist in installation of gearshaft assembly.

3) Shake and rotate gearshaft assembly to assist in installation. Release 4th gear synchronizer ring from 4th gear after gearshaft assembly is installed.

4) Install 2 steel balls coated with vasoline through 3rd/4th shift rod hole. One steel ball is inserted into groove for 1st/2nd shift rod and other steel ball is inserted into groove for 5th/reverse shift rod. Use of magnet and thin blade screwdriver will aid steel ball installation.

5) Insert interlock pin into hole in end of 3rd/4th shift rod. Insert 3rd/4th shift rod through fork hole and into rear cover. Rotate rod so groove in rod faces control rod and hole aligns with hole in fork.

6) Install new roll pin into 3rd/4th shift fork. *See Fig. 4*. Install 3 shift rod detent ball and springs into rear cover. *See Fig. 3*. 5th/reverse spring is shorter than other springs. Apply sealant to spring cover and install. Tighten bolts to specification. See TORQUE SPECIFICATIONS.

7) Install 3 support plate bolts with new aluminum washers through back of rear housing. Remove guide bar after 1st bolt is installed.

8) Install roller onto shift selector arm. Insert spring, sleeve and selector arm into Spring Tool (K95B-4103-MT). Align spring tensioning arm of tool with free end of spring. Separate tool slightly so it can turn in sleeve.

9) Rotate handle of spring tool counterclockwise to apply tension to spring. Lock tool by pushing it together when 2 ends of spring are about aligned with each other.

10) Align selector arm assembly and tool in control rod hole. Notch in arm of bearing support plate should cause roller pin to seat. With screwdriver, push end of spring off spring tool tensioning arm to remove spring from tool post. Remove spring tool while holding spring in place with a screwdriver.

11) Install control rod/control lever assembly onto shaft. Do not install roll pin. Install new washer on support block bolt and install bolt. Bolt is installed in rear housing, near spring cover.

12) Install new roll pin into control lever and control rod. Install 5th/reverse return spring. Apply sealant to return spring plug threads. Install plug. Tighten plug to specification. See TORQUE SPECIFICATIONS.

13) Install backup light switch with new washer into rear housing. Install reverse idler gear into rear cover. Ensure chamfered side faces down and grooved side faces up. Install reverse idler gear shaft into gear.

14) Place new washer and thread sealant on reverse idler gear shaft retaining bolt. Install bolt into rear housing. Install new helical spring washer onto locking plate bolt. Install locking plate and tighten bolt to specification. See TORQUE SPECIFICATIONS.

15) Lubricate countershaft front bearing and install in front housing. Ensure stepped collar of bearing faces housing. Apply sealant to front housing sealing surface. Install front housing to rear housing.

16) Install 8 bolts securing case halves. Install control rod detent and spring. Slot in detent rod faces top of case. Apply sealant to new plug and install. *See Fig. 2*. Place new washer and thread sealant on reverse idler gear shaft retaining bolt. Install bolt into front housing.

17) Drive front bearing into place using appropriate driver. Install washer and retaining snap ring on input shaft. Use depth gauge, measure and record amount that front bearing protrudes from front housing (measurement "A"). Measure and record bearing seat depth in bearing support (measurement "B"). Measure and record height of lip on bearing support from sealing surface (measurement "C").

18) Shim thickness is determined by formula: "B" – "C" – "A" = shim thickness. Select appropriate shim and install with bearing support. Shims range in thickness from .020" (.50 mm) to .039" (1.0 mm) in .002" (.05 mm) increments. Apply sealant to bearing support and install. Tighten bolts to specification. See TORQUE SPECIFICATIONS.

19) Install shift control rod extension. Install new roll pin. Slide on coupling with snap ring pliers. Slide back spring clamp. Install clutch release lever and bearing from front housing. Install either transfer case or extension housing to transmission case. Install 10 bolts and tighten to specification.

TORQUE SPECIFICATIONS

TORQUE SPECIFICATIONS

Application	Ft. Lbs. (N.m)
Backlight Switch	15 (20)
Extension Housing Bolt	18 (24)
5th/Reverse Spring Plug	44 (60)
Housing Bolt	18 (24)
Reverse Idler Gear Shaft Bolt	18 (24)
Reverse Idler Gear Locking Plate Bolt	18 (24)
Support Block Bolt	18 (24)
Support Plate Bolt	18 (24)
Transfer Case Housing Bolt	18 (24)
	INCH Lbs.
Bearing Support Bolt	62 (7)
Spring Cover Bolt	62 (7)

MANUAL TRANSMISSIONS
Mazda F25M-R & G25M-R

Kia: Sephia
Mazda: MX-3, MX-6, Protege, 626

APPLICATION & LABOR TIMES

APPLICATION & LABOR TIMES

Vehicle Application	Labor Times [1] R & I	[2] Overhaul	Series
1995-96 Kia			
Sephia			
1.6L	3.5	5.0	F25M-R
1.8L	3.5	5.0	G25M-R
1995-96 Mazda			
MX-3	3.9	4.8	F25M-R
MX-6 & 626			
4-Cylinder	4.5	5.0	G25M-R
V6	4.8	5.0	G25M-R
Protege			
1.5L	3.5	5.0	F25M-R
1.8L	4.3	5.0	G25M-R

[1] – Removal and installation of transmission from vehicle chassis.
[2] – Bench overhaul time for transmission or transaxle/differential. DOES NOT include removal and installation.

LUBRICATION & ADJUSTMENTS

See appropriate MANUAL TRANSMISSION SERVICING article in TRANSMISSION SERVICING section.

TROUBLE SHOOTING

See GENERAL TROUBLE SHOOTING article in this section.

ON-VEHICLE SERVICE

DRIVE AXLE SHAFTS

See appropriate AXLE SHAFTS article in AXLE SHAFTS & TRANSFER CASES section.

REMOVAL & INSTALLATION

See appropriate MANUAL TRANSMISSION REMOVAL article in TRANSMISSION SERVICING section.

TRANSAXLE DISASSEMBLY

NOTE: Refer to appropriate exploded view for disassembly reference. See Figs. 1 and 2.

1) Remove clutch release bearing and release fork. *See Fig. 1 or 2.* Remove rear cover. Secure primary shaft with Holder (49 F401 440). Shift to 1st or 2nd gear to lock rotation of primary shaft. Remove and discard lock nuts from primary and secondary shafts. Remove sleeve, primary reverse synchronizer cone assembly, synchronizer ring.
2) Remove 5th/reverse gear shift fork, 5th/reverse synchronizer hub assembly with synchronizer ring, 5th gear and gear sleeve from secondary shaft. *See Fig. 1.*
3) Remove secondary 5th gear. Remove guide bolt from outside of case. *See Fig. 3.* Remove back-up light switch, neutral switch and lock bolt. Remove bolts securing transaxle case to converter housing. Using soft-faced hammer, strike case to loosen and remove.
4) Remove reverse idler gear with shaft. Holding primary shaft assembly, secondary shaft assembly and shift forks as an assembly, lift and remove from clutch housing. Separate shift fork assemblies from shaft assemblies.

COMPONENT DISASSEMBLY & REASSEMBLY

TRANSAXLE CASE

Disassembly – **1)** Lift mainshaft oil funnel from clutch housing and remove funnel and outer race bearing as a unit. Remove 3 bolts retaining shifter guide plate. Remove shifter guide plate, reverse gate and spring. *See Fig. 4.*
2) Drive out spring pin retaining selector arm to change rod and withdraw change rod from clutch housing. Remove boot from change rod and oil seal from rod bore. Remove vent cover and vent from top of clutch housing.
3) Remove speedometer driven gear assembly. Remove differential and input shaft oil seals. Drive out reverse lever shaft roll pin. Remove spring and ball (if equipped).
4) Remove reverse lever set spring and reverse lever. Drive out differential bearing races. Remove 5th gear outer bearing races from transaxle.
5) Remove diaphragm spring and adjusting shims from transaxle case. Remove differential oil seal from transaxle case.

NOTE: Check and adjust bearing preload before reassembling case. See BEARING PRELOAD under adjustments.

Reassembly – To reassemble, reverse disassembly procedure. Smaller diameter of diaphragm spring, located behind bearing race, should face toward inside of transaxle case.

PRIMARY SHAFT

NOTE: When disassembling synchronizer assemblies, note cut-outs in some blocking rings for reassembly reference. Cut-out rings MUST be installed in original position.

Disassembly – Remove snap rings as necessary and refer to appropriate figure. *See Fig. 5.* On G25M-R, press off bearing next to 4th gear. On F25M-R, press off 4th gear and bearing together. Press off 4th gear. Press off 3rd gear with clutch hub assembly. Press off bearing on clutch end.

Inspection – Inspect synchronizer cones for wear. Inspect gear teeth for damage, wear and cracks. Inspect synchronizer ring matching teeth for damage and wear. Inspect synchronizer ring teeth for damage, wear and cracks. Measure clearance between synchronizer ring and teeth on matching gear. See TRANSAXLE COMPONENT CLEARANCE SPECIFICATIONS table. Inspect clutch hub sleeve and hub operation. Inspect gear teeth for damage, wear and cracks. Inspect synchronizer keys for damage, wear and cracks.
Reassembly – **1)** To reassemble, reverse disassembly procedure. Measure clearance after each component is installed. See TRANSAXLE COMPONENT CLEARANCE SPECIFICATIONS table. *See Fig. 5.*
2) Select correct synchronizer keys. See SYNCHRONIZER KEY DIMENSIONS table. *See Fig. 6.* Install keys and spring in synchronizer hub. Install synchronizer assembly with bevel facing away from input end of primary shaft. Locate synchronizer rings on correct clutch assembly.

SYNCHRONIZER KEY DIMENSIONS

Synchro	Dimension 1	Dimension 2	Dimension 3
1st/2nd	0.748 (19.00)	0.167 (4.25)	0.197 (5.00)
3rd/4th	0.669 (17.00)	0.167 (4.25)	0.197 (5.00)
5th/Rev.	0.669 (17.00)	0.167 (4.25)	0.197 (5.00)

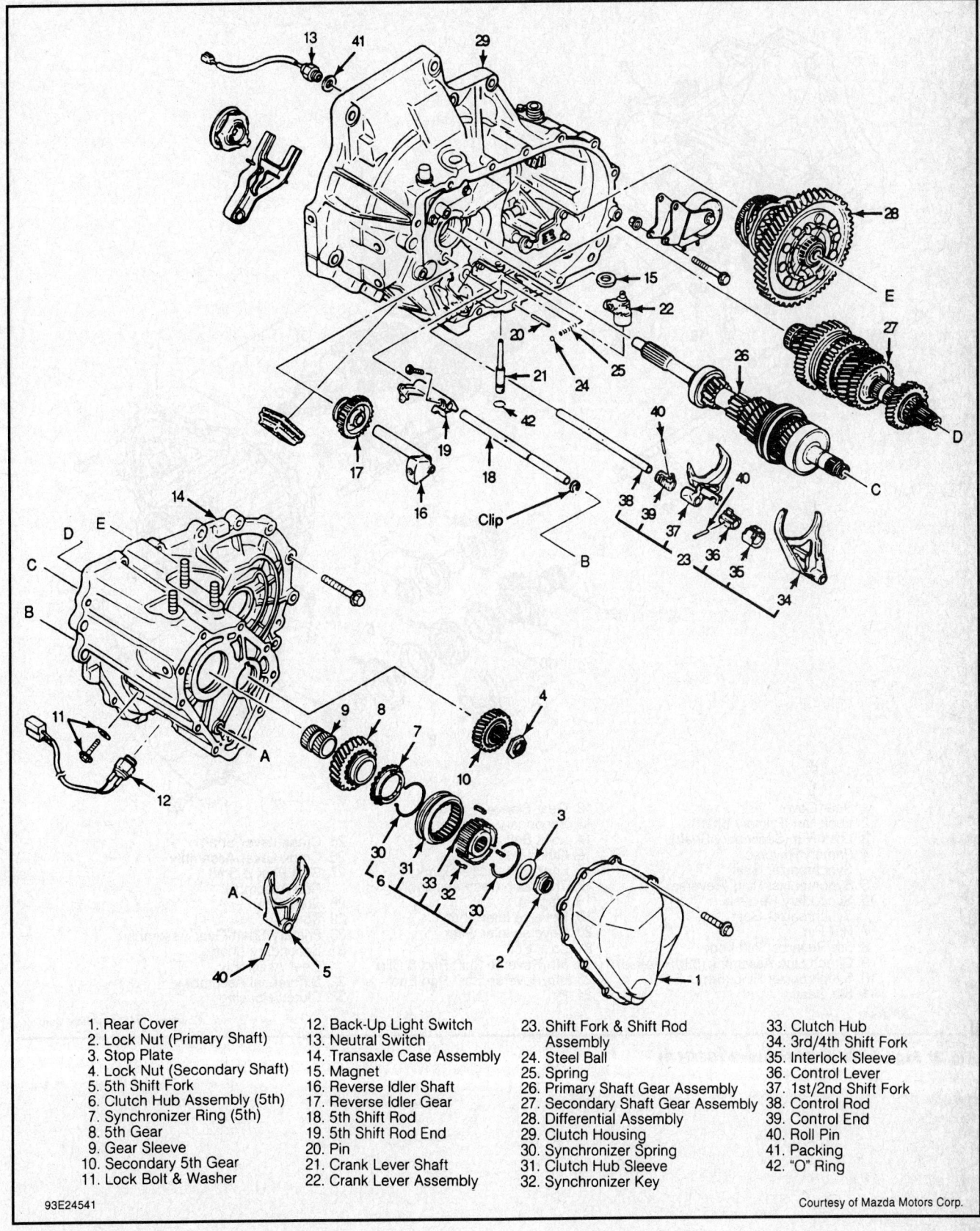

1. Rear Cover	12. Back-Up Light Switch	23. Shift Fork & Shift Rod Assembly	33. Clutch Hub
2. Lock Nut (Primary Shaft)	13. Neutral Switch	24. Steel Ball	34. 3rd/4th Shift Fork
3. Stop Plate	14. Transaxle Case Assembly	25. Spring	35. Interlock Sleeve
4. Lock Nut (Secondary Shaft)	15. Magnet	26. Primary Shaft Gear Assembly	36. Control Lever
5. 5th Shift Fork	16. Reverse Idler Shaft	27. Secondary Shaft Gear Assembly	37. 1st/2nd Shift Fork
6. Clutch Hub Assembly (5th)	17. Reverse Idler Gear	28. Differential Assembly	38. Control Rod
7. Synchronizer Ring (5th)	18. 5th Shift Rod	29. Clutch Housing	39. Control End
8. 5th Gear	19. 5th Shift Rod End	30. Synchronizer Spring	40. Roll Pin
9. Gear Sleeve	20. Pin	31. Clutch Hub Sleeve	41. Packing
10. Secondary 5th Gear	21. Crank Lever Shaft	32. Synchronizer Key	42. "O" Ring
11. Lock Bolt & Washer	22. Crank Lever Assembly		

93E24541

Courtesy of Mazda Motors Corp.

Fig. 1: Exploded View Of Transaxle (F25M-R)

MANUAL TRANSMISSIONS
Mazda F25M-R & G25M-R (Cont.)

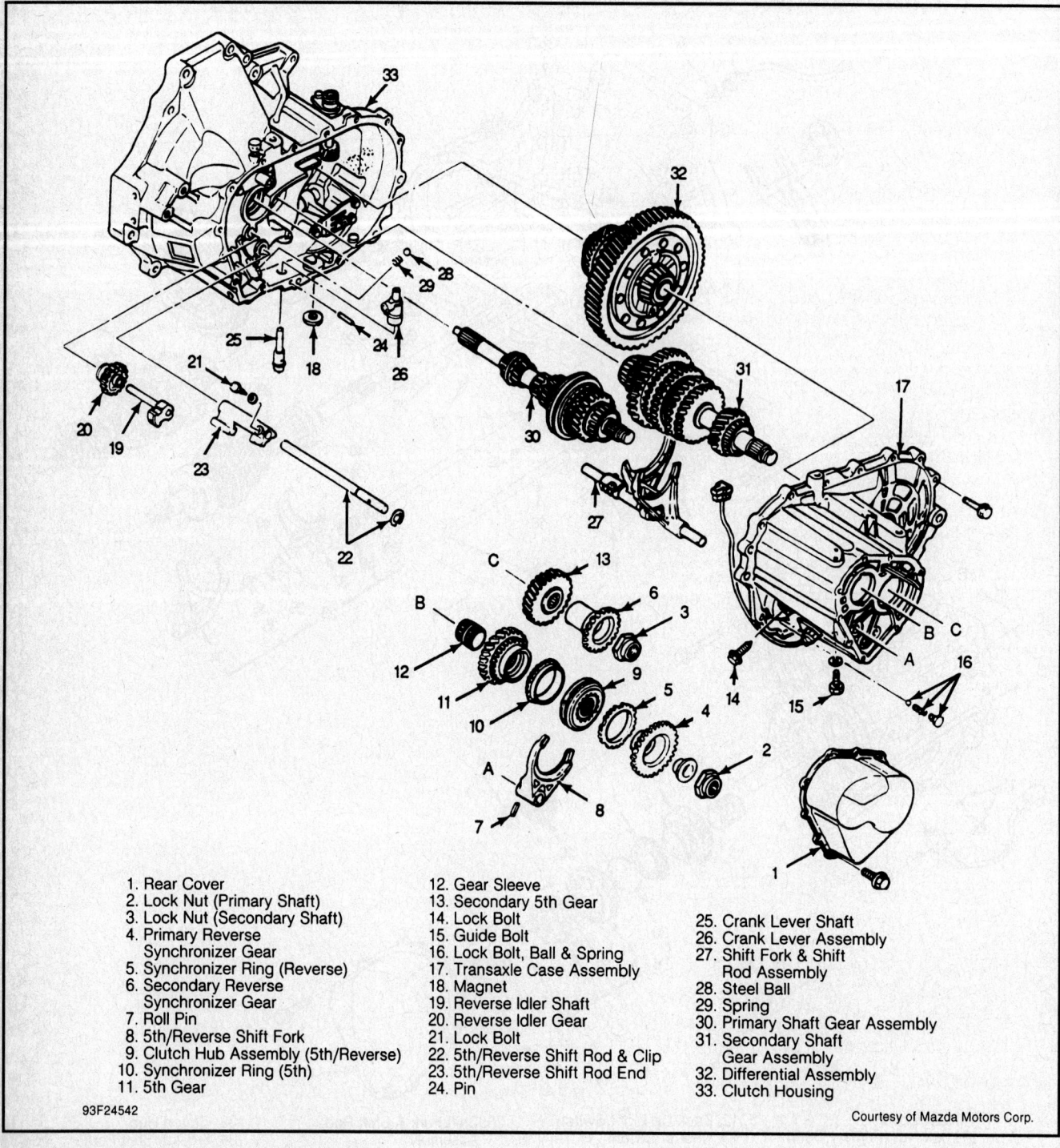

1. Rear Cover
2. Lock Nut (Primary Shaft)
3. Lock Nut (Secondary Shaft)
4. Primary Reverse
   Synchronizer Gear
5. Synchronizer Ring (Reverse)
6. Secondary Reverse
   Synchronizer Gear
7. Roll Pin
8. 5th/Reverse Shift Fork
9. Clutch Hub Assembly (5th/Reverse)
10. Synchronizer Ring (5th)
11. 5th Gear

12. Gear Sleeve
13. Secondary 5th Gear
14. Lock Bolt
15. Guide Bolt
16. Lock Bolt, Ball & Spring
17. Transaxle Case Assembly
18. Magnet
19. Reverse Idler Shaft
20. Reverse Idler Gear
21. Lock Bolt
22. 5th/Reverse Shift Rod & Clip
23. 5th/Reverse Shift Rod End
24. Pin

25. Crank Lever Shaft
26. Crank Lever Assembly
27. Shift Fork & Shift
   Rod Assembly
28. Steel Ball
29. Spring
30. Primary Shaft Gear Assembly
31. Secondary Shaft
   Gear Assembly
32. Differential Assembly
33. Clutch Housing

93F24542

Courtesy of Mazda Motors Corp.

Fig. 2: Exploded View Of Transaxle (G25M-R)

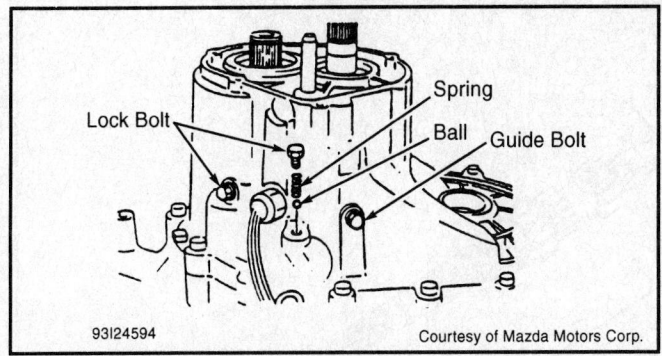

93I24594   Courtesy of Mazda Motors Corp.

Fig. 3: Removing Guide, Lock Bolts, Ball & Spring

SECONDARY SHAFT

Disassembly – Press off 4th gear with bearing. Remove retaining ring. Shift clutch hub sleeve to 1st gear. Press off 3rd and 2nd gears. Remove retaining ring. Press off 1st gear with 1-2 clutch hub assembly. Press off bearing on differential drive gear end of shaft. *See Fig. 8 or 9.*

Inspection – See INSPECTION under PRIMARY SHAFT.

Reassembly – To reassemble, reverse disassembly procedure. Measure clearance after pressing on each component. See TRANS-AXLE COMPONENT CLEARANCE SPECIFICATIONS table. *See Fig. 5.*

DIFFERENTIAL

Pre-Disassembly Backlash Inspection – Install left and right axle shafts into differential. Support axle shafts on V-blocks. *See Fig. 7.* Measure backlash of both pinion gears. Backlash should be .002-.006" (.05-.15 mm). Rebuild or replace differential assembly if backlash is not as specified.

TRANSAXLE COMPONENT CLEARANCE SPECIFICATIONS

Application/Clearance	Standard In. (mm)	Maximum In. (mm)
Primary Shaft		
3rd-To-2nd Gear		
F25M-R & G25M-R	.002-.008 (.05-.20)	.010 (.25)
4th Gear-To-Bearing		
F25M-R	.008-.024 (.21-.61)	.026 (.66)
G25M-R	.006-.015 (.17-.37)	.017 (.42)
Secondary Shaft		
1st Gear Thrust		
F25M-R & G25M-R	.002-.011 (.05-.28)	.013 (.33)
2nd-To-3rd Gear		
F25M-R	.007-.020 (.18-.51)	.22 (.56)
G25M-R	.007-.018 (.18-.46)	.020 (.50)
1st/2nd Hub-To-Shift Fork		
F25M-R	.004-.014 (.10-.36)	.036 (.86)
G25M-R	.004-.018 (.10-.45)	.029 (.73)
3rd/4th Hub-To-Shift Fork		
F25M-R	.008-.020 (.20-.50)	.039 (1.0)
G25M-R	.004-.016 (.10-.40)	.039 (1.00)
5th/Reverse		
Hub-To-Shift Fork		
F25M-R	.016-.030 (.40-.75)	.049 (1.24)
G25M-R	.004-.014 (.10-.36)	.038 (.96)
Synchronizer-To-Gear	.059 (1.50)	.031 (.80)
Reverse Idler		
Gear-To-Shift Lever	.004-.013 (.10-.32)	.015 (.37)
Primary Shaft Run Out		.002 (.05)
Secondary Shaft Run Out		.0006 (.015)
Oil Clearance		
Between Shafts & Gears	.001-.003 (.03-.08)	.003 (.08)

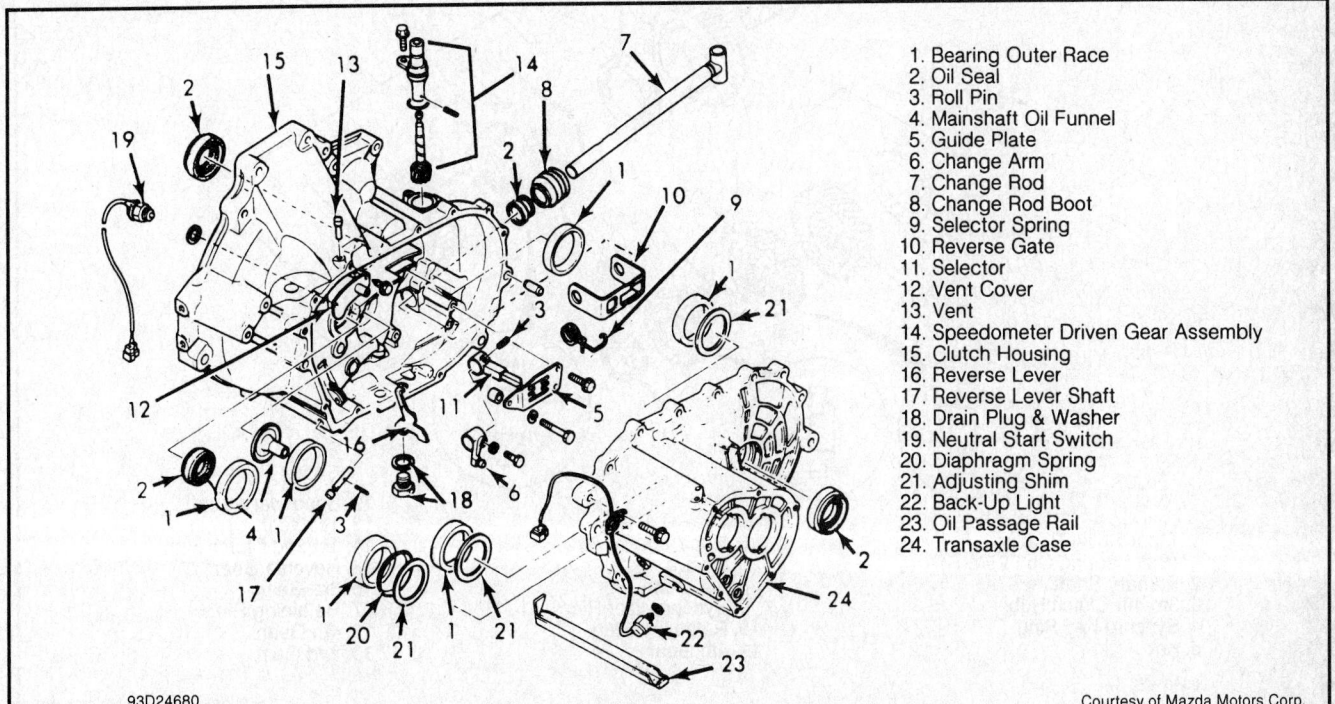

1. Bearing Outer Race
2. Oil Seal
3. Roll Pin
4. Mainshaft Oil Funnel
5. Guide Plate
6. Change Arm
7. Change Rod
8. Change Rod Boot
9. Selector Spring
10. Reverse Gate
11. Selector
12. Vent Cover
13. Vent
14. Speedometer Driven Gear Assembly
15. Clutch Housing
16. Reverse Lever
17. Reverse Lever Shaft
18. Drain Plug & Washer
19. Neutral Start Switch
20. Diaphragm Spring
21. Adjusting Shim
22. Back-Up Light
23. Oil Passage Rail
24. Transaxle Case

93D24680   Courtesy of Mazda Motors Corp.

Fig. 4: Exploded View Of Transaxle Case & Components (G25M-R Shown; F25M-R Similar)

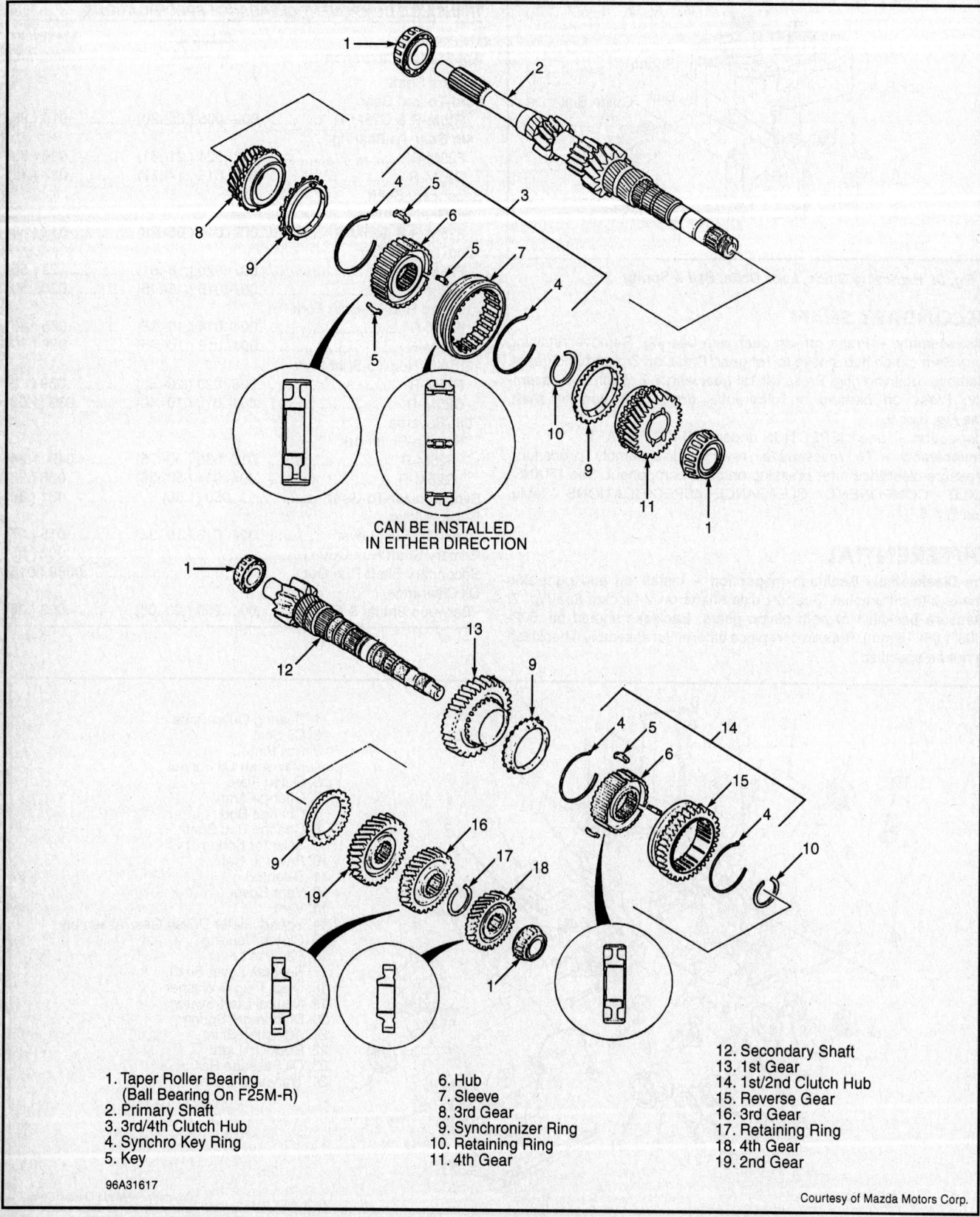

CAN BE INSTALLED
IN EITHER DIRECTION

1. Taper Roller Bearing
   (Ball Bearing On F25M-R)
2. Primary Shaft
3. 3rd/4th Clutch Hub
4. Synchro Key Ring
5. Key

6. Hub
7. Sleeve
8. 3rd Gear
9. Synchronizer Ring
10. Retaining Ring
11. 4th Gear

12. Secondary Shaft
13. 1st Gear
14. 1st/2nd Clutch Hub
15. Reverse Gear
16. 3rd Gear
17. Retaining Ring
18. 4th Gear
19. 2nd Gear

96A31617

Courtesy of Mazda Motors Corp.

Fig. 5: Exploded View Of Primary & Secondary Shafts (G25M-R Shown, F25M-R Similar)

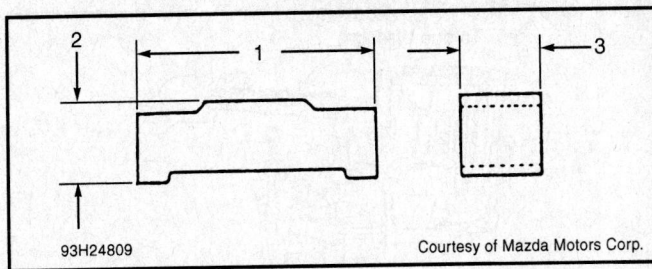

Fig. 6: Measuring Synchronizer Key

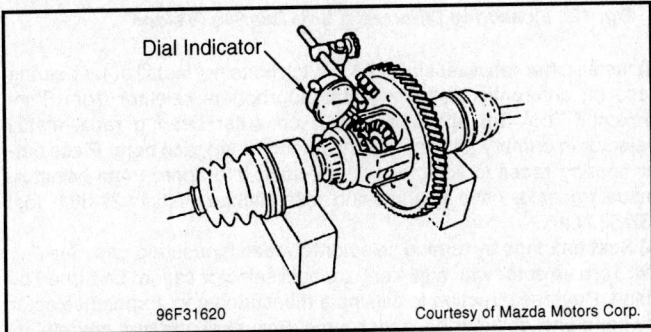

Fig. 7: Checking Pinion Gear Backlash

Disassembly – 1) Remove roll pin and pinion shaft. *See Fig. 8.* Remove pinion gears and rotate thrust washers out of differential housing.

2) Remove side gears and thrust washers. Using appropriate bearing puller, remove side bearings. DO NOT remove speedometer drive gear unless damaged.

Reassembly – Install speedometer drive gear (if removed) and bearings. Install thrust washers, pinion gears and side gears. Install pinion shaft. Install and crimp roll pin.

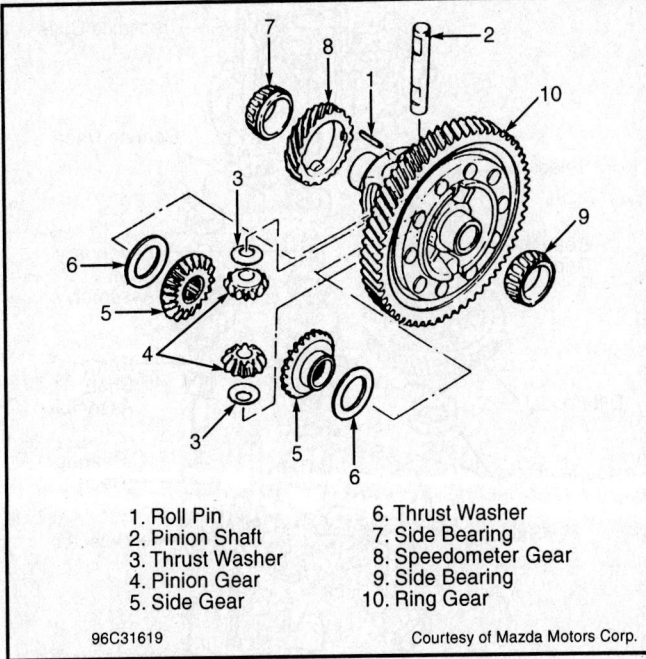

1. Roll Pin
2. Pinion Shaft
3. Thrust Washer
4. Pinion Gear
5. Side Gear
6. Thrust Washer
7. Side Bearing
8. Speedometer Gear
9. Side Bearing
10. Ring Gear

Fig. 8: Exploded View Of Differential

ADJUSTMENTS

BEARING PRELOAD (F25M-R)

Primary Shaft – 1) Install primary shaft assembly into clutch housing. Install transaxle case to clutch housing and tighten bolts to 14-18 ft. lbs. (19-25 N.m).

2) Mount dial indicator to clutch housing and place plunger on end of primary shaft. *See Fig. 9.* Zero out dial indicator. Pull primary shaft upward and record measurement.

3) Thrust clearance should be .0002-.0039" (.005-.100 mm). Select appropriate shim to adjust clearance. Shims are available in following thicknesses; .004-.024" (.1-.6 mm) in .004 (.1 mm) increments.

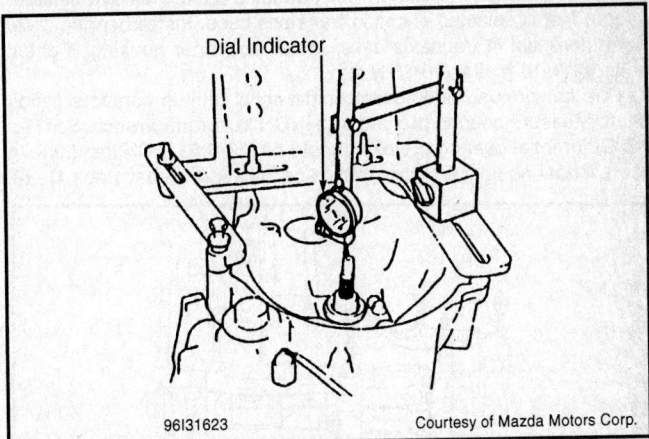

Fig. 9: Measuring Primary Shaft Thrust Clearance (F25M-R)

Secondary Shaft – 1) Disassemble transmission case from clutch housing. Remove primary shaft. Install funnel and secondary bearing race in clutch housing. *See Fig. 4.* Install secondary shaft into transaxle case. Install transaxle case to clutch housing and tighten bolts to 14-18 ft. lbs. (19-25 N.m).

2) Mount dial indicator to clutch housing and place plunger on end of secondary shaft. *See Fig. 10.* Zero out dial indicator. Pull secondary shaft upward and record measurement.

3) Bearing preload is measured shaft movement plus .003" (.08 mm). Select appropriate shim to adjust preload. Shims are available in following thicknesses; .006-.020" (.15-.50 mm) in .002" (.05 mm) increments.

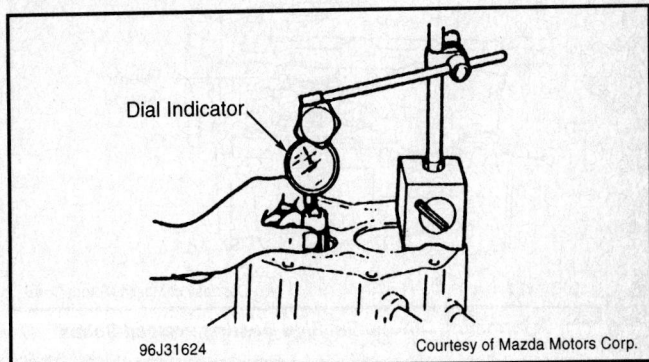

Fig. 10: Measuring Secondary Shaft Thrust Clearance (F25M-R)

Differential Assembly – 1) Remove bearing outer race and adjustment shims from transaxle case. Mount differential assembly in converter housing (with race installed). Install bearing outer race onto selector gauge (49 D017 2A2A-Shim Selector Tool Set). Set selector gauge on differential. Set transaxle case on selector gauge.

2) Eliminate gap on selector gauge by turning collars of selector gauge. Mount spacing collars between transaxle case and clutch housing. *See Fig. 11.* Tighten bolts to 14-18 ft. lbs. (19-25 N.m).

3) Using rods on collars of selector, turn selector in a direction which widens the gap between collars of selector. Turn selector (to widen gap) until it will no longer turn. This will seat bearing race.

4) Turn selector collars in opposite direction until gap is closed. Mount preload adapter into differential until it contacts pinion shaft. Using INCH-lb. torque wrench, rotate differential. See Fig. 12. Turn selector collars until turning torque is .26-6.59 INCH lbs. (.03-.74 N.m).

5) Using feeler gauge, measure clearance of gap between selector collars. See Fig. 11. Measure around entire circumference of selector. Select shims equal to maximum clearance measured. Shims range in thickness from .008" (.20 mm) to .022" (.55 mm) in increments of .002" (.5 mm).

6) Unbolt converter housing from transaxle case. Remove selector gauge. Install selected shims in transaxle case. Install bearing race. Set differential in transaxle case. Install converter housing. Tighten bolts to 14-18 ft. lbs. (19-25 N.m).

7) Position preload adapter into differential until in contacts pinion shaft. Measure bearing preload with INCH-lb. torque wrench. See Fig. 12. Differential bearing preload should be .26-6.59 INCH lbs. (.03-.74 N.m). If bearing preload is not within specification, repeat steps 1) - 5).

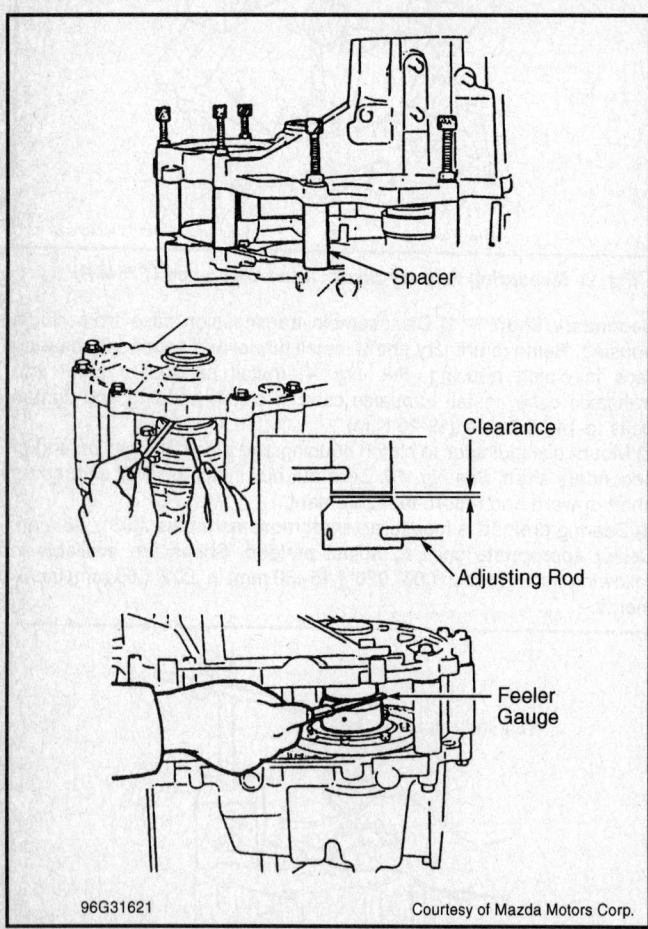

Fig. 11: Determining Differential Side Bearing Preload Shims

BEARING PRELOAD (G25M-R)

1) Remove differential seals from transaxle case and clutch housing. Remove input shaft seal from clutch housing. Install differential bearing outer race in clutch housing.

2) Remove primary and secondary shaft outer race from clutch housing. Install primary and secondary shaft bearing outer race into transaxle case. Remove differential bearing outer race from transaxle case. Note selector arrangement. See Fig. 13.

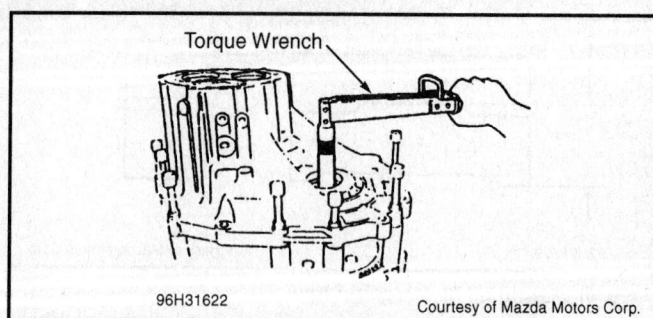

Fig. 12: Measuring Differential Side Bearing Preload

3) Install differential assembly into clutch housing. Install outer bearing race on differential bearing. Install appropriate selector from Shim Selector Tool Set (49 G030 380D) on outer bearing race. Install selector in primary and secondary outer bearing race bore. Place outer bearing races in selector and set shaft into appropriate selector. Install transaxle case, spacers and bolts. Tighten bolts to 27-38 ft. lbs. (37-52 N.m).

4) Seat bearings by turning selector to widen measuring gap. See Fig. 14. Turn selector with adjuster bars until selector cannot be turned by hand. Reverse direction to eliminate measuring gap. Expand selector by hand until selector no longer turns. Ensure shafts turn smoothly.

5) Measure gap with feeler gauge. See Fig. 15. Measure around entire circumference of selector. Select thinnest allowable shim to obtain standard clearance (primary shaft) or bearing preload (secondary shaft).

6) Primary shaft bearing clearance is 0-.002" (0-.05 mm). Shims range in thickness from .008" (.20 mm) to .028" (.70 mm) in increments of .002" (.05 mm).

7) Secondary shaft bearing preload is selector clearance plus .001" (.03 mm) - .003" (.08 mm). Shims range in thickness from .008" (.20 mm) to .028" (.70 mm) in increments of .002" (.5 mm).

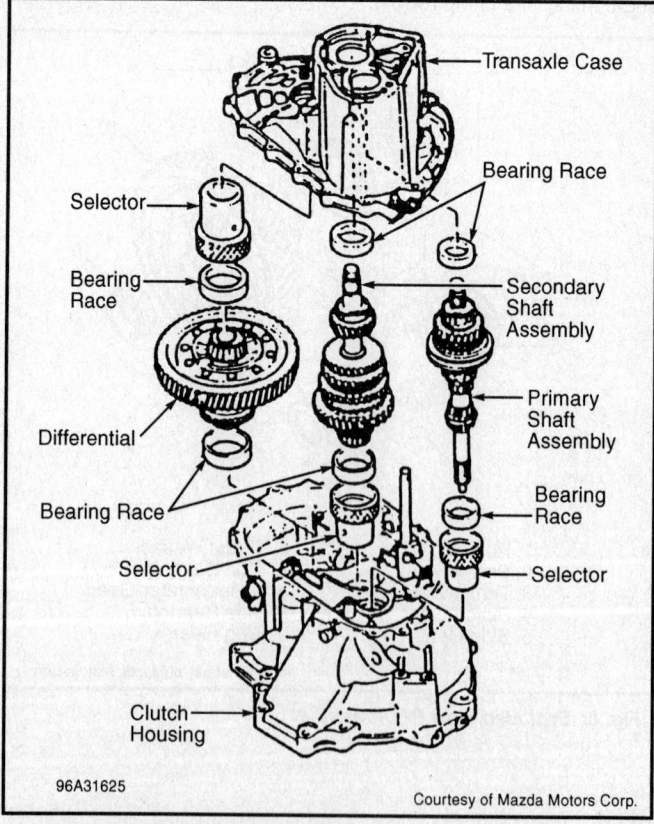

Fig. 13: Identifying Selector Location

8) Turn differential selector collars in opposite direction until gap is closed. Mount preload adapter into differential until in contacts pinion shaft. Using INCH lb. torque wrench, rotate differential. See Fig. 12. Turn selector collars until turning torque is 4.3 INCH lbs. (.50 N.m).

9) Using feeler gauge, measure clearance of gap between selector collars. See Fig. 11. Measure around entire circumference of selector. Select shims equal to maximum clearance measured plus .006" (.15 mm). Shims range in thickness from .004" (.10 mm) to .047" (1.20 mm) in increments of .002" (.05 mm).

10) Disassemble transmission case. Remove selectors. Remove bearing races and install selected shims. See Fig. 4. Install primary shaft and differential. Install transaxle case to clutch housing. Tighten bolts in crisscross pattern to 28-38 ft. lbs (38-51 N.m).

11) Using INCH-lb. torque wrench and appropriate adapter, measure turning torque (preload) of differential and primary shaft. See Fig. 12 and 16. Differential preload should be 13-17 INCH lbs. (1.4-1.0 N.m). Primary shaft preload should be .9-2.1 INCH lbs. (.1-.2 N.m). If preload is not as specified, repeat adjustment procedure.

12) Disassemble transmission case. Remove primary shaft and differential. Install secondary shaft. Install transaxle case to clutch housing. Tighten bolts in crisscross pattern to 28-38 ft. lbs (38-51 N.m).

13) Using INCH lb. torque wrench and appropriate adapter, measure turning torque (preload) of secondary shaft. See Fig. 16. Secondary shaft preload should be 1.8-3.4 INCH lbs. (.2-.3 N.m). If preload is not as specified, repeat adjustment procedure.

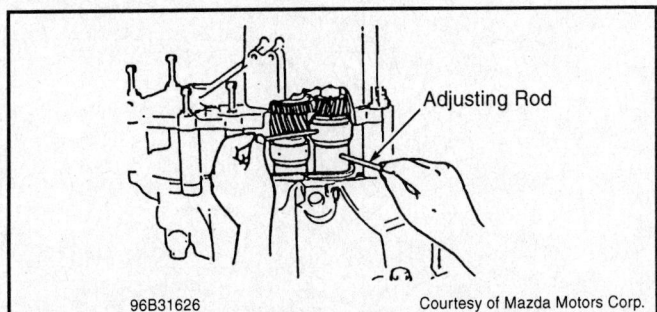

96B31626   Courtesy of Mazda Motors Corp.

Fig. 14: Expanding Selector Tool

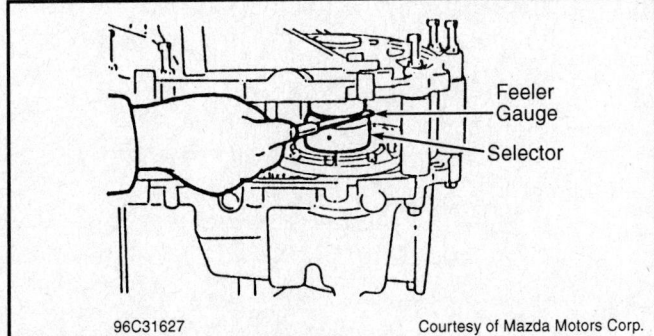

96C31627   Courtesy of Mazda Motors Corp.

Fig. 15: Measuring Selector Gap

TRANSAXLE REASSEMBLY

Reassembly – 1) To reassemble, reverse disassembly procedure. Place primary and secondary shaft assemblies into clutch housing. Install shift fork and shift rod assembly.

2) Insert spring seat and spring into reverse lever shaft. Install steel ball and place scraper so that ball contacts steel ball. See Fig. 17. With edge of control end against scraper the rod will line up with shift rod coupling hole in clutch housing.

3) Set each clutch hub sleeve to neutral position, and tap shift rod from above so steel ball goes into center groove. Pull steel ball section of control end forward so that steel ball goes into detent in groove.

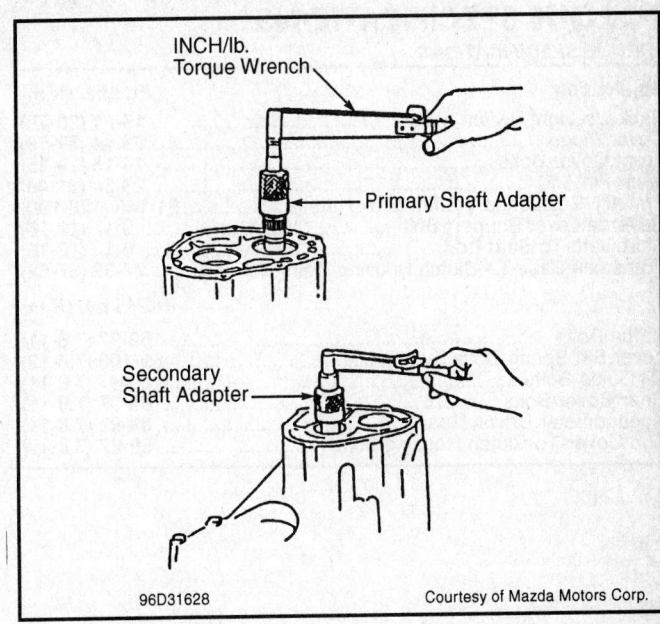

96D31628   Courtesy of Mazda Motors Corp.

Fig. 16: Measuring Primary & Secondary Turning Torque (G25M-R)

4) Fit crank lever between change arm and control end. Connect crank lever shaft and clutch housing. Align pin holes of crank lever shaft and clutch housing. Insert new retaining pin. See Fig. 18.

5) Install 5th gear and reverse clutch fork. Shift transmission to 1st gear and 5th clutch fork to 5th gear to lock transmission. Tighten lock nuts on primary and secondary shafts and stake into place.

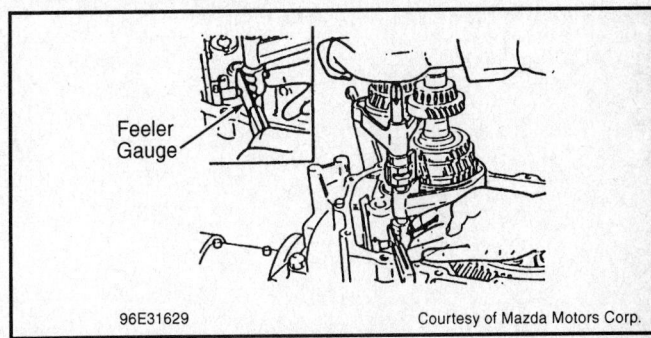

96E31629   Courtesy of Mazda Motors Corp.

Fig. 17: Installing Shift Shaft Assembly

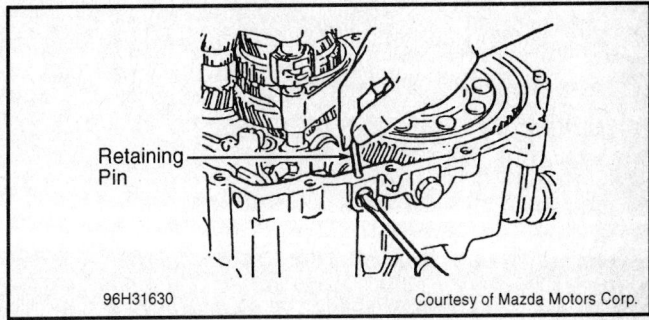

96H31630   Courtesy of Mazda Motors Corp.

Fig. 18: Install Crank Lever Shaft Retaining Pin

TORQUE SPECIFICATIONS

TORQUE SPECIFICATIONS

Application	Ft. Lbs. (N.m)
Back-Up Light Switch	15-21 (20-29)
Cover Plugs	29-44 (39-59)
Front Cover Bolts	14-18 (19-25)
Pivot Pin	23-34 (31-46)
Primary & Secondary Shaft Lock Nuts	94-140 (128-190)
Reverse Lever Support Bolt	9-12 (12-16)
Shift Gate-To-Shift Rod	9-12 (12-16)
Transaxle Case-To-Clutch Housing Bolts	27-38 (37-52)

	INCH Lbs. (N.m)
Baffle Bolts	69-97 (7.8-11)
Lever Set Spring Bolts	69-106 (7.8-12)
Oil Guide Bolts	69-97 (7.8-11)
Rear Cover Bolts	69-97 (7.8-11)
Speedometer Driven Gear	69-97 (7.8-11)
Top Cover-To-Clutch Housing Bolts	69-97 (7.8-11)

Miata

APPLICATION & LABOR TIMES

APPLICATION & LABOR TIMES

Vehicle	Labor Times		
Application	[1] R & I	[2] Overhaul	Series
Miata	3.0	4.5	M15M-D

[1] – Removal and installation of transmission from vehicle chassis.
[2] – Bench overhaul time for transmission. DOES NOT include removal and installation.

LUBRICATION & ADJUSTMENTS

See appropriate MANUAL TRANSMISSION SERVICING article in TRANSMISSION SERVICING section.

TROUBLE SHOOTING

See GENERAL TROUBLE SHOOTING article in this section.

REMOVAL & INSTALLATION

See appropriate MANUAL TRANSMISSION REMOVAL article in TRANSMISSION SERVICING section.

TRANSMISSION DISASSEMBLY

1) Remove clutch release bearing, release fork and dust boot. See Fig. 1. Remove front cover bolts, front cover (bearing support), gasket, adjustment shim(s), snap ring and oil seal.

2) Remove snap ring, cover, bolt, spring and lock ball from extension housing. Remove extension housing attaching bolts. Rotate extension housing clockwise and separate extension housing from intermediate housing.

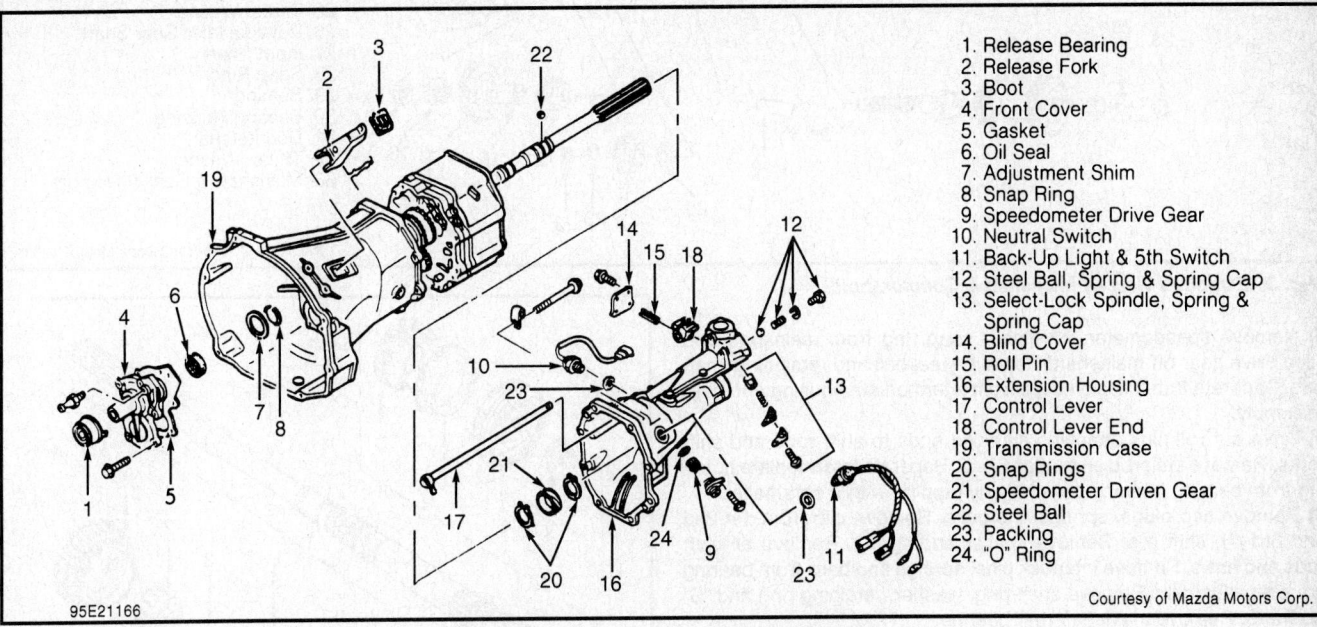

1. Release Bearing
2. Release Fork
3. Boot
4. Front Cover
5. Gasket
6. Oil Seal
7. Adjustment Shim
8. Snap Ring
9. Speedometer Drive Gear
10. Neutral Switch
11. Back-Up Light & 5th Switch
12. Steel Ball, Spring & Spring Cap
13. Select-Lock Spindle, Spring & Spring Cap
14. Blind Cover
15. Roll Pin
16. Extension Housing
17. Control Lever
18. Control Lever End
19. Transmission Case
20. Snap Rings
21. Speedometer Driven Gear
22. Steel Ball
23. Packing
24. "O" Ring

Courtesy of Mazda Motors Corp.

95E21166

Fig. 1: Exploded View Of Transmission Case, Intermediate Housing & Extension Housing

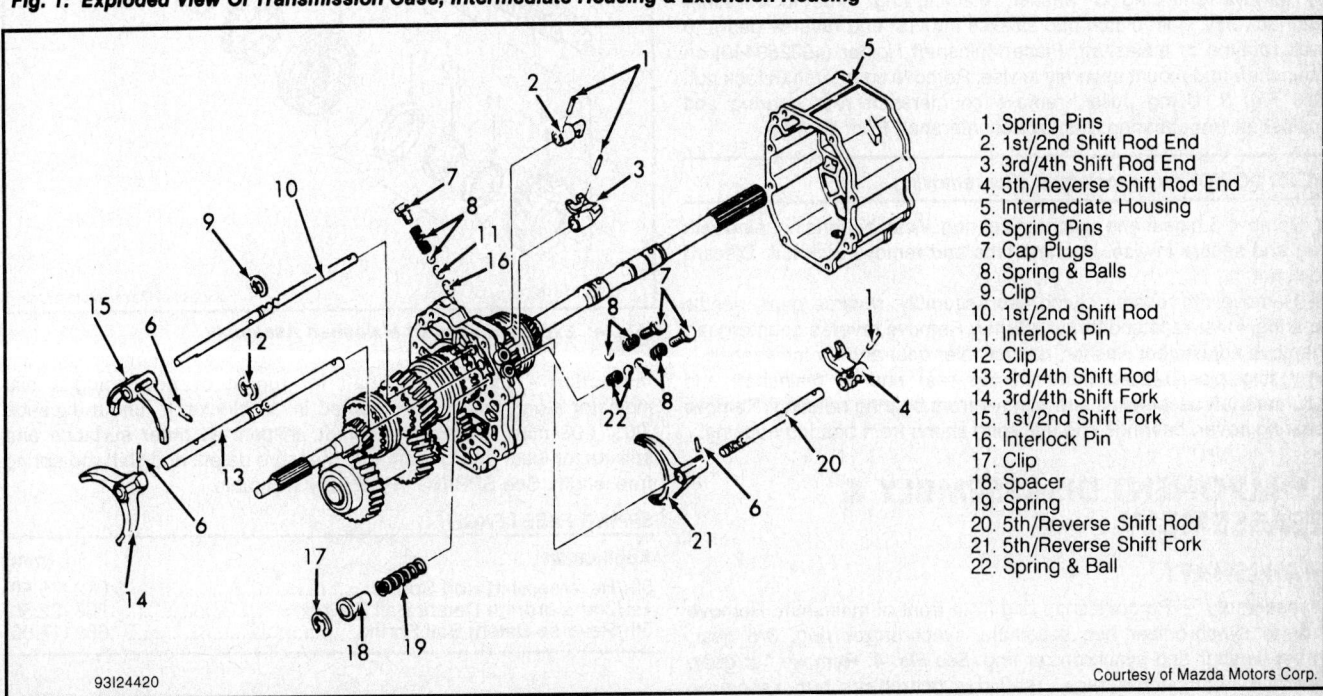

1. Spring Pins
2. 1st/2nd Shift Rod End
3. 3rd/4th Shift Rod End
4. 5th/Reverse Shift Rod End
5. Intermediate Housing
6. Spring Pins
7. Cap Plugs
8. Spring & Balls
9. Clip
10. 1st/2nd Shift Rod
11. Interlock Pin
12. Clip
13. 3rd/4th Shift Rod
14. 3rd/4th Shift Fork
15. 1st/2nd Shift Fork
16. Interlock Pin
17. Clip
18. Spacer
19. Spring
20. 5th/Reverse Shift Rod
21. 5th/Reverse Shift Fork
22. Spring & Ball

Courtesy of Mazda Motors Corp.

93I24420

Fig. 2: Exploded View Of Mainshaft, Countershaft & Shift Linkage

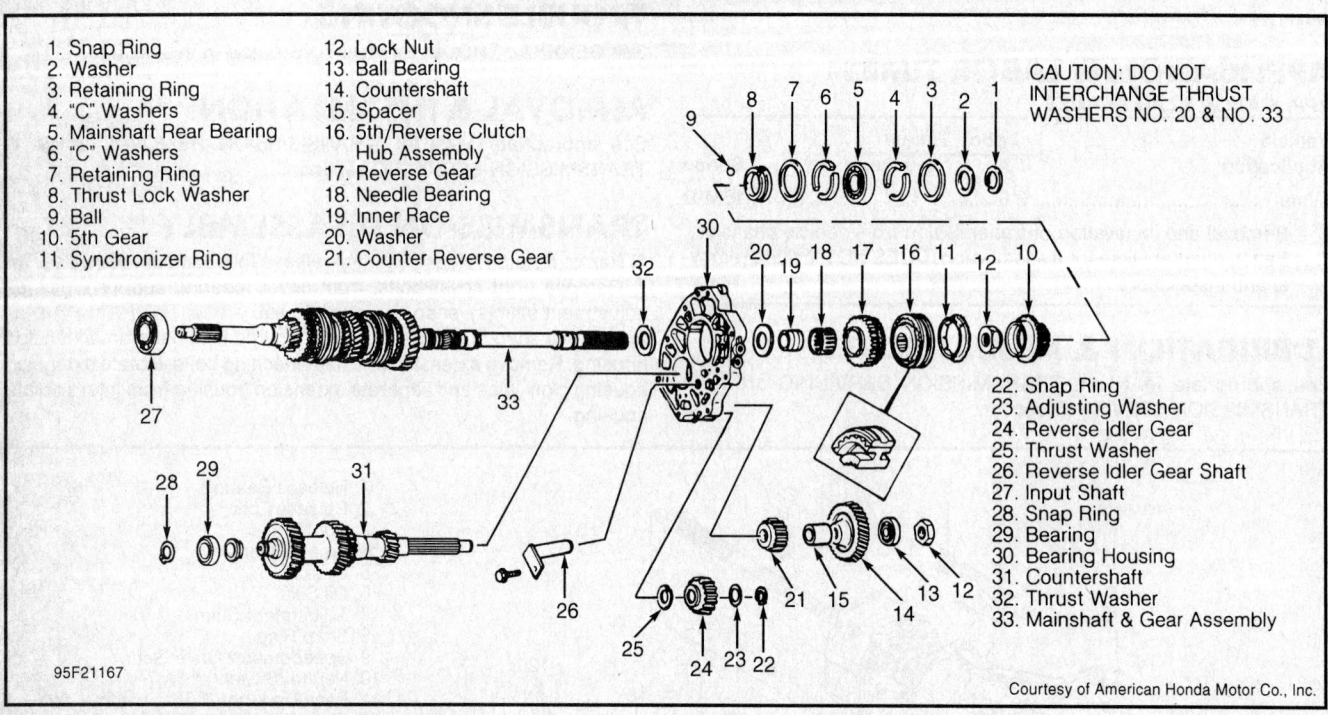

1. Snap Ring
2. Washer
3. Retaining Ring
4. "C" Washers
5. Mainshaft Rear Bearing
6. "C" Washers
7. Retaining Ring
8. Thrust Lock Washer
9. Ball
10. 5th Gear
11. Synchronizer Ring
12. Lock Nut
13. Ball Bearing
14. Countershaft
15. Spacer
16. 5th/Reverse Clutch Hub Assembly
17. Reverse Gear
18. Needle Bearing
19. Inner Race
20. Washer
21. Counter Reverse Gear

CAUTION: DO NOT INTERCHANGE THRUST WASHERS NO. 20 & NO. 33

22. Snap Ring
23. Adjusting Washer
24. Reverse Idler Gear
25. Thrust Washer
26. Reverse Idler Gear Shaft
27. Input Shaft
28. Snap Ring
29. Bearing
30. Bearing Housing
31. Countershaft
32. Thrust Washer
33. Mainshaft & Gear Assembly

95F21167

Courtesy of American Honda Motor Co., Inc.

Fig. 3: Exploded View Of Mainshaft & Countershaft

3) Remove speedometer drive gear snap ring from mainshaft and slide drive gear off mainshaft. Remove steel ball and remaining snap ring. Separate transmission case from intermediate housing and gear assembly.

4) Drive out roll pins attaching shift rod ends to shift rods and shift forks. Remove shift rod ends. See Fig. 2. Separate intermediate housing from bearing housing assembly by tapping with a soft mallet.

5) Remove cap plugs, springs and balls. Remove clip from 1st-2nd and 3rd-4th shift rod. Remove spacer and spring. Remove all shift rods and forks. Remove interlock pins, springs and balls from bearing housing assembly. Remove snap ring, washer, retaining ring and "C" washers. Remove mainshaft rear bearing.

6) Remove remaining "C" washer, retaining ring, thrust lock washer and lock ball. Shift clutch hub sleeves into 1st and reverse gears to lock rotation of mainshaft. Place Mainshaft Holder (490259440) on mainshaft and mount securely in vise. Remove countershaft lock nut. See Fig. 3. Using puller, remove countershaft rear bearing and mainshaft front bearing. Remove countershaft front bearing.

NOTE: DO NOT reuse lock nuts after removing.

---

7) Remove 5th gear and synchronizer ring. Wrap bearing housing with rag and secure in vise. Uncrimp tabs and remove lock nut. Discard lock nut.

8) Remove 5th-reverse clutch hub assembly, reverse gear, needle bearing, inner race and thrust washer. Remove reverse countergear. Remove adjustment washer, reverse idler gear and thrust washer.

9) Using plastic-faced hammer, tap rear end of mainshaft and countershaft assemblies and remove from bearing housing. Remove bearing cover, bearings and adjusting shims from bearing housing.

COMPONENT DISASSEMBLY & REASSEMBLY

MAINSHAFT

Disassembly – Remove snap ring from front of mainshaft. Remove 3rd/4th synchronizer hub assembly, synchronizer ring, 3rd gear, thrust washer and synchronizer ring. See Fig. 4. Remove 1st gear, needle bearing, inner race, 1st-2nd synchronizer hub assembly, synchronizer ring and 2nd gear.

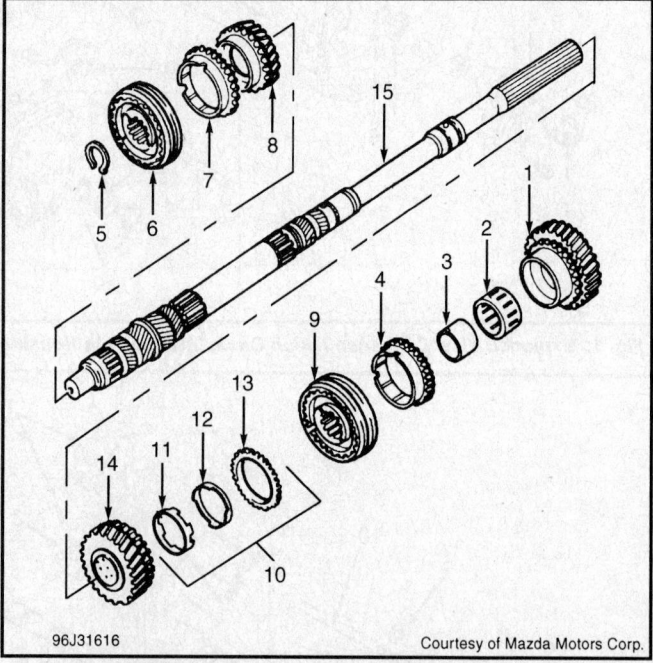

96J31616

Courtesy of Mazda Motors Corp.

Fig. 4: Exploded View Of Mainshaft Assembly

Inspection – Inspect mainshaft for runout by positioning a dial indicator along the shaft, mounted in "V" blocks. If runout exceeds .001" (.03 mm), replace mainshaft. Inspect all other surfaces and splines for wear and/or damage. Measure detent and shift rod spring free length. See SPRING FREE LENGTH table.

SPRING FREE LENGTH

Application	In. (mm)
5th/Reverse Shift Rod Spring	3.012 (76.50)
1st/2nd & 3rd/4th Detent Ball Spring	.886 (22.50)
5th/Reverse Detent Ball Spring	.669 (17.00)

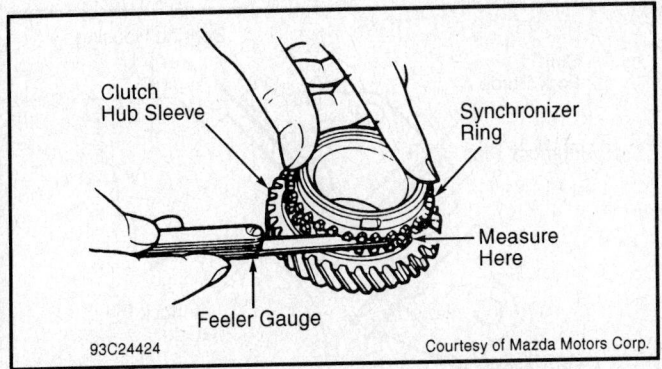

93C24424   Courtesy of Mazda Motors Corp.

Fig. 5: Checking Synchro Ring & Hub Sleeve Clearance

Synchronizer Inspection – 1) Inspect unit for worn or damaged parts. Install synchronizer ring evenly to gear cone and measure clearance between side faces of ring and gear with feeler gauge. Standard clearance is .059" (1.50 mm). Minimum clearance is .031" (.80 mm), replace synchronizer ring or gear if not within specifications. See Fig. 5.

2) Inspect contact between ring and gear. Check synchronizer key spring for tension. Ensure clutch sleeve slides easily on clutch hub. Check clearance between hub sleeve and release fork groove using feeler gauge. Standard clearance is .008-.012" (.20-.30 mm). Clearance limit is .020" (.51 mm). Replace if not within specifications. Ensure intermediate housing dowel pins are fully seated.

NOTE: Ensure synchronizer ring and clutch hub are aligned during assembly.

Reassembly – 1) Place 3rd gear and synchronizer ring on mainshaft. Press 3rd and 4th clutch hub assembly. Install snap ring. Install 2nd gear, synchronizer ring, 1st/2nd clutch hub and sleeve assembly on mainshaft using arbor press.

2) Ensure clutch hubs are facing correct direction. See Fig. 7. Install gear sleeve, 1st gear and washer to mainshaft. Install needle bearing, synchronizer ring and input shaft. Reverse disassembly procedures to complete reassembly.

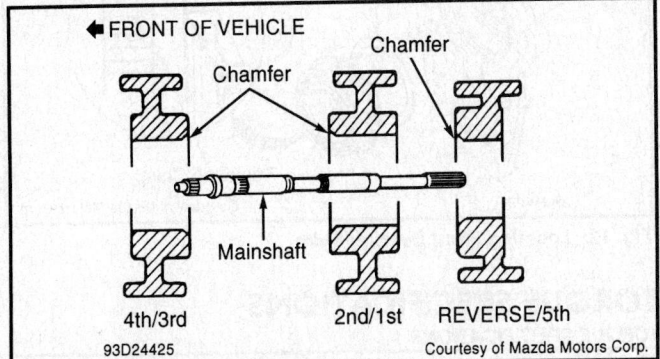

93D24425   Courtesy of Mazda Motors Corp.

Fig. 6: Checking Hub Alignment

TRANSMISSION REASSEMBLY

1) Press countershaft and mainshaft rear bearings into bearing plate. Check bearing height above bearing plate with straight edge and feeler gauge. Bearing height should be .004" (.10 mm). If clearance exceeds specifications, replace adjusting shim. See CENTER BEARING SELECTIVE SHIM table. See Fig. 7. Install and tighten bearing cover to bearing housing. Using arbor press, install countershaft and mainshaft assembly into bearing plate.

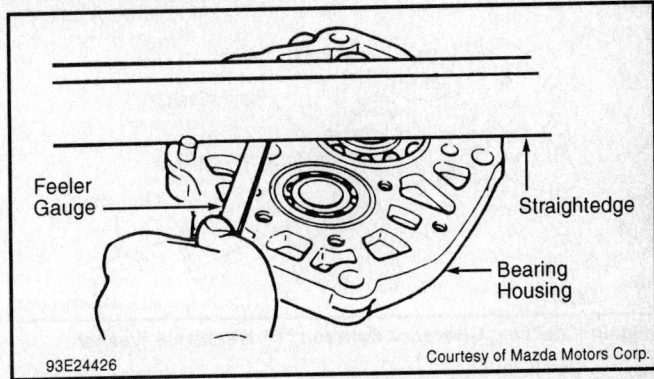

93E24426   Courtesy of Mazda Motors Corp.

Fig. 7: Checking Bearing-To-Bearing Housing Clearance

CENTER BEARING SELECTIVE SHIM

Application	In. (mm)
Countershaft	.004, .012 (.10 & .30)
Mainshaft	.004, .006, .012 (.10, .15 & .30)

2) Secure reverse idler gear and 2 washers to reverse idler gear shaft. Install counter reverse gear, washer, inner race, needle bearing, reverse gear and 5th-reverse clutch hub assembly. Install reverse idler gear shaft into bearing housing and install lock plate. Install thrust washer, reverse idler gear, adjusting washer and snap ring. Measure clearance between adjusting washers and snap ring. Standard clearance should be .004" (.10 mm). Adjusting washers are available in thicknesses of .102" (2.60 mm), .110" (2.80 mm) and .118" (3.00 mm).

3) Secure bearing housing in vise with protector covers in place. Slide clutch hub sleeves into 1st and reverse gear to lock mainshaft. Tighten lock nut. Bend lock washer tab. Install 5th gear and synchronizer ring on mainshaft. Install ball and thrust lock washer for 5th gear. Install "C" washers and hold them with retaining ring. Check clearance between 5th gear thrust lock washer and "C" washers using feeler gauge. See Fig. 8. If clearance exceeds .004-.012" (.10-.30 mm), replace thrust lock washer. Thrust washers are available in thicknesses of .244" (6.20 mm), .252" (6.40 mm), .256" (6.50 mm) and .260" (6.60 mm).

CAUTION: Use .118" (3.00 mm) "C" washers to begin clearance adjustment procedure; otherwise the rear "C" washer may not be able to be installed. When clearance adjustment is complete, the two "C" washers must be the same thickness or bearing failure will result. See "C" WASHER THICKNESS table.

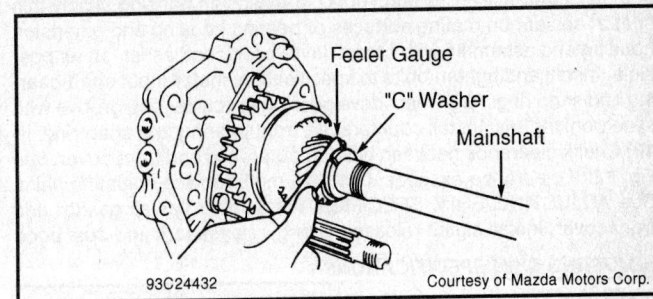

93C24432   Courtesy of Mazda Motors Corp.

Fig. 8: Checking Clearance Between "C" Washer & Thrust Washer

4) Tighten mainshaft drive gear bearing. Install "C" washers, retaining ring, washer and snap ring. Check clearance between mainshaft "C" washers and washer using feeler gauge. See Fig. 9. If clearance exceeds .004" (.10 mm), replace "C" washer. Washers are available in following thicknesses; .114" (2.90 mm), .118" (3.00 mm), .122" (3.10 mm) and .126" (3.20 mm).

NOTE: Ensure no clearance exists between mainshaft bearing washer and "C" washers.

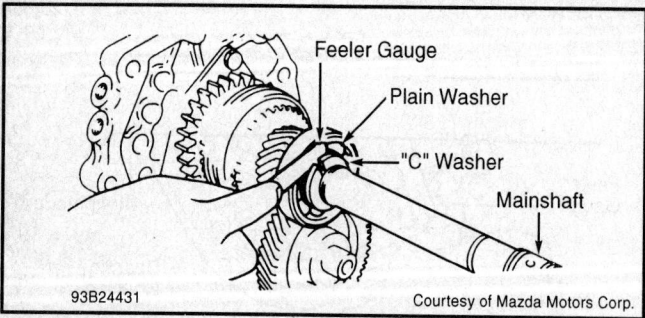

Fig. 9: Checking Clearance Between "C" Washers & Washer

5) Install countershaft rear bearing. Shift clutch hub sleeves to 1st gear and reverse, to lock mainshaft. Install and tighten lock nut. Press 5th/reverse spring and ball with interlock pin assembly and screwdriver to install shift rod. See Fig. 10. Install 5th/reverse shift fork and rod into bearing housing. Position interlock pin into bearing housing with Shift Fork Guide (490862350) and Interlock Pin Guide (490187451A).

NOTE: *There are 2 types of springs; be sure to install them correctly. The looser wound spring is for the 5th/reverse shift rod.*

6) Install 3rd/4th and 1st/2nd shift forks onto clutch sleeves. Install each shift fork rod and interlock pin. Ensure interlock pin is installed correctly. See Fig. 10. Align holes in both shift forks and rods. Install roll pins. Install shift rod locking balls and springs into respective bores in bearing plate. Install and tighten spring cap bolts. Install 5th/reverse spacer, spring and clip. Install clips on 1st/2nd and 3rd/4th shift rods.

7) Ensure shift fork-to-synchronizer hub sleeve is aligned correctly. Adjust position of shift fork as shown. See Fig. 11. Install proper thrust washer between 1st gear and mainshaft bearing or between reverse gear and mainshaft bearing. Thrust washers are available in .087" (2.20 mm), .106" (2.70 mm), .118" (3.00 mm), .126" (3.20 mm) and .146" (3.70 mm) sizes.

NOTE: *Total thrust washer thickness should be .232-.236" (5.90-6.00 mm).*

8) Apply sealer on bearing housing and intermediate housing contact surface and assemble. Install shift rod ends to shift rods and install roll pins. See Figs. 2 and 3. Install speedometer drive gear, lock ball and snap ring on mainshaft. Apply sealer on bearing housing and transmission case contact surface and assemble.

9) Install control lever through holes in extension housing. Apply thin coat of sealant on mating surfaces of bearing housing and extension housing and assemble with control lever positioned as far left as possible. Install and tighten bolts to specification. Install input shaft bearing and snap ring. Align main drive gear synchronizer ring groove with synchronizer key. Install countershaft front bearing and snap ring.

10) Check clearance between bearing outer race and front cover. See Fig. 12. If clearance exceeds .004" (.10 mm), replace adjusting shim. See ADJUSTING SHIM SPECIFICATIONS table. Install gasket and front cover. Install clutch release bearing, release fork and dust boot.

ADJUSTING SHIM SPECIFICATIONS

Washer No.	In. (mm)
1	.004 (.10)
2	.006 (.15)
3	.012 (.30)

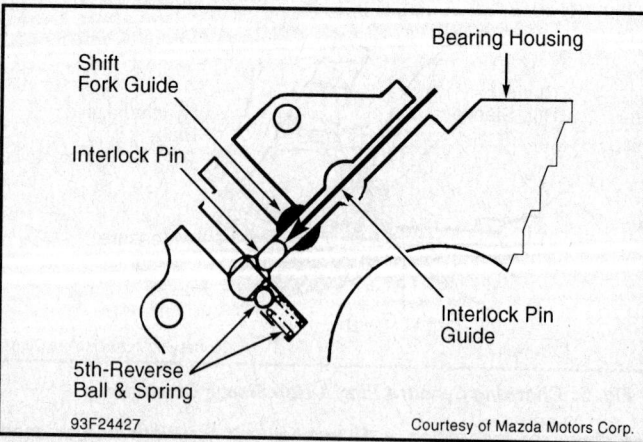

Fig. 10: Identifying Correct Positioning Of Interlock Pin

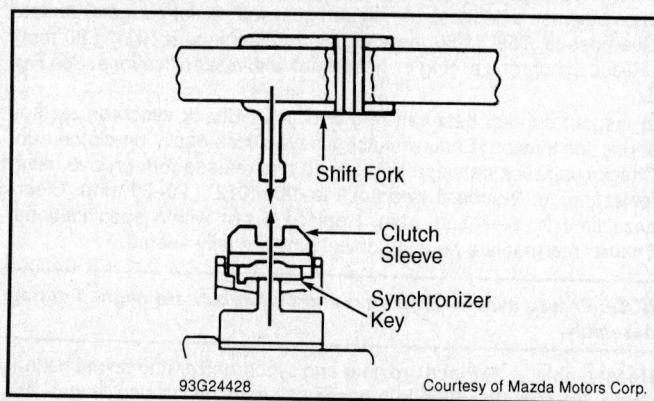

Fig. 11: Adjusting Shift Fork-To-Synchronizer Hub Sleeve

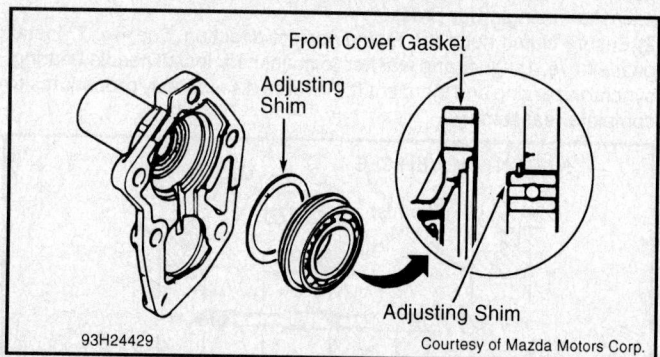

Fig. 12: Locating Front Bearing Shim

TORQUE SPECIFICATIONS
TORQUE SPECIFICATIONS

Application	Ft. Lbs. (N.m)
Bearing Cover	13-19 (18-26)
Cap Plug	13-19 (18-26)
Countershaft Lock Nut	94-145 (128-197)
Dynamic Balancer Lock Nut	116-152 (157-206)
Extension Housing	12-17 (16-23)
Input Shaft Front Cover	13-19 (18-26)
Mainshaft Lock Nut	94-173 (128-235)

	INCH Lbs. (N.m)
Interlock Pin Plug	89-133 (10-15)
Reverse Idler Gear	71-97 (8-11)
Shift Fork Bolts	106-142 (12-16)
Spring Cap Bolts	89-133 (10-15)
Shift Rod End Bolts	71-106 (8-12)
Speedometer Driven Gear Bolt	69-97 (7.8-11)

RX-7

APPLICATION & LABOR TIMES

APPLICATION & LABOR TIMES

Vehicle Application	Labor Times		Series
	[1] R & I	[2] Overhaul	
RX7 .... 3.8 .... 5.0			R15M-D

[1] – Removal and installation of transmission from vehicle chassis.

[2] – Bench overhaul time for transmission. DOES NOT include removal and installation.

CAUTION: Vehicle is equipped with Supplemental Restraint System (SRS). When servicing vehicle, use care to avoid accidental air bag deployment. SRS-related components are located in steering column, center console and instrument panel. DO NOT use electrical test equipment on these circuits. If necessary, deactivate SRS before servicing components. See AIR BAG SERVICING article in APPLICATIONS & IDENTIFICATIONS section.

CAUTION: Disconnecting battery on models equipped with anti-theft radio require canceling of anti-theft operation. See appropriate AUTOMATIC TRANSMISSION SERVICING article in TRANSMISSION SERVICING section. Refer to vehicle owner's manual to identify radio type.

LUBRICATION & ADJUSTMENTS

See appropriate MANUAL TRANSMISSION SERVICING article in TRANSMISSION SERVICING section.

TROUBLE SHOOTING

See GENERAL TROUBLE SHOOTING article in this section.

REMOVAL & INSTALLATION

See appropriate MANUAL TRANSMISSION REMOVAL article in TRANSMISSION SERVICING section.

TRANSMISSION DISASSEMBLY

1) Remove release bearing, clutch release fork and dust boot. Remove front cover bolts, front cover (bearing support), gasket, oil seal, clutch housing and adjustment shim(s). *See Figs. 1 and 2.* Remove control case cover and select lock spindle.

2) Remove extension housing attaching bolts. Move control rod to Neutral position. Separate extension housing from transmission case. Remove undercover and gasket.

3) Remove speedometer drive gear snap ring from mainshaft and slide drive gear off mainshaft. Remove steel ball and remaining snap ring. *See Figs. 1 and 2.*

4) Drive out roll pins attaching shift rod ends to shift rods. Remove shift rod ends. *See Fig. 3.* Separate transmission case from bearing housing assembly by prying gently with a pry bar. Remove snap ring, washer retaining ring and "C" washers.

5) Using appropriate puller, remove mainshaft rear bearing. Remove remaining "C" washer, retaining ring, thrust lock washer and lock ball. Shift clutch hub assemblies into 1st and reverse gears to lock rotation of mainshaft. Remove countershaft rear lock nut. Using bearing puller, remove countershaft rear bearing. Remove counter 5th gear and spacer from countershaft. Remove center housing mounting bolts. Tap housing with a soft mallet to remove. Remove mainshaft front bearing snap ring from case.

6) Install Synchronizer Ring Holder (49F017101) between 4th gear synchronizer ring and synchromesh gear on mainshaft. Turn bearing snap rings so gap is at a 90 degree angle to case grooves. Remove input shaft bearing using bearing puller. Remove countershaft bearing snap ring from front of countershaft. Remove countershaft front bearing using bearing puller.

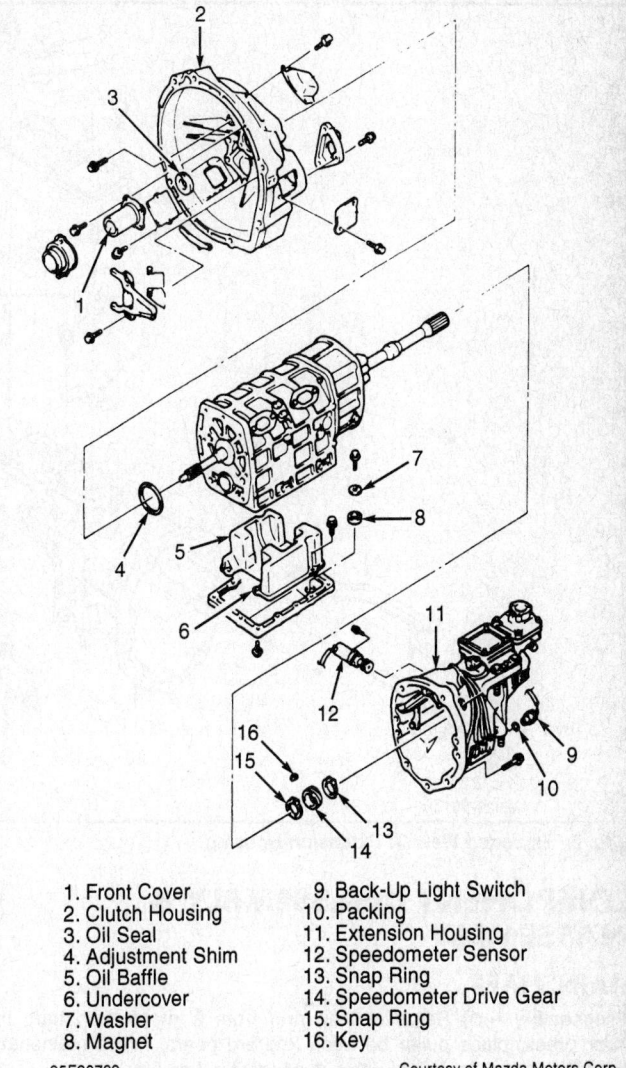

1. Front Cover
2. Clutch Housing
3. Oil Seal
4. Adjustment Shim
5. Oil Baffle
6. Undercover
7. Washer
8. Magnet
9. Back-Up Light Switch
10. Packing
11. Extension Housing
12. Speedometer Sensor
13. Snap Ring
14. Speedometer Drive Gear
15. Snap Ring
16. Key

95F20789   Courtesy of Mazda Motors Corp.

Fig. 1: Exploded View Of Transmission

NOTE: DO NOT reuse lock nuts after removing.

7) Remove 5th/reverse shift fork. Remove blind covers and gaskets. Remove 3 spring cap bolts, springs and balls for shift rod. Drive roll pin from 3rd/4th shift fork and slide 3rd/4th shift rod out rear of transmission case. Drive roll pin from 1st/2nd shift fork and slide 1st/2nd shift rod out of transmission. *See Fig. 3.*

8) From end of mainshaft, remove thrust lock washer, lock ball, 5th gear, needle bearings and synchronizer ring. Uncrimp tabs of lock nut, shift into 1st and reverse gear to lock mainshaft and remove. Discard lock nut.

9) Remove bearing cover. Remove assembly containing 5th/reverse hub assembly, synchronizer ring, needle bearing, inner race, reverse gear and thrust washers. Remove thrust washers, reverse idler gear shaft, reverse idler gear and remaining thrust washers.

10) Remove mainshaft center bearing using bearing puller. Remove 1st gear. *See Fig. 4.* Remove countershaft center bearing using bearing puller. Remove countershaft from transmission case. Remove input shaft from transmission case. Remove mainshaft and gear assembly from transmission case.

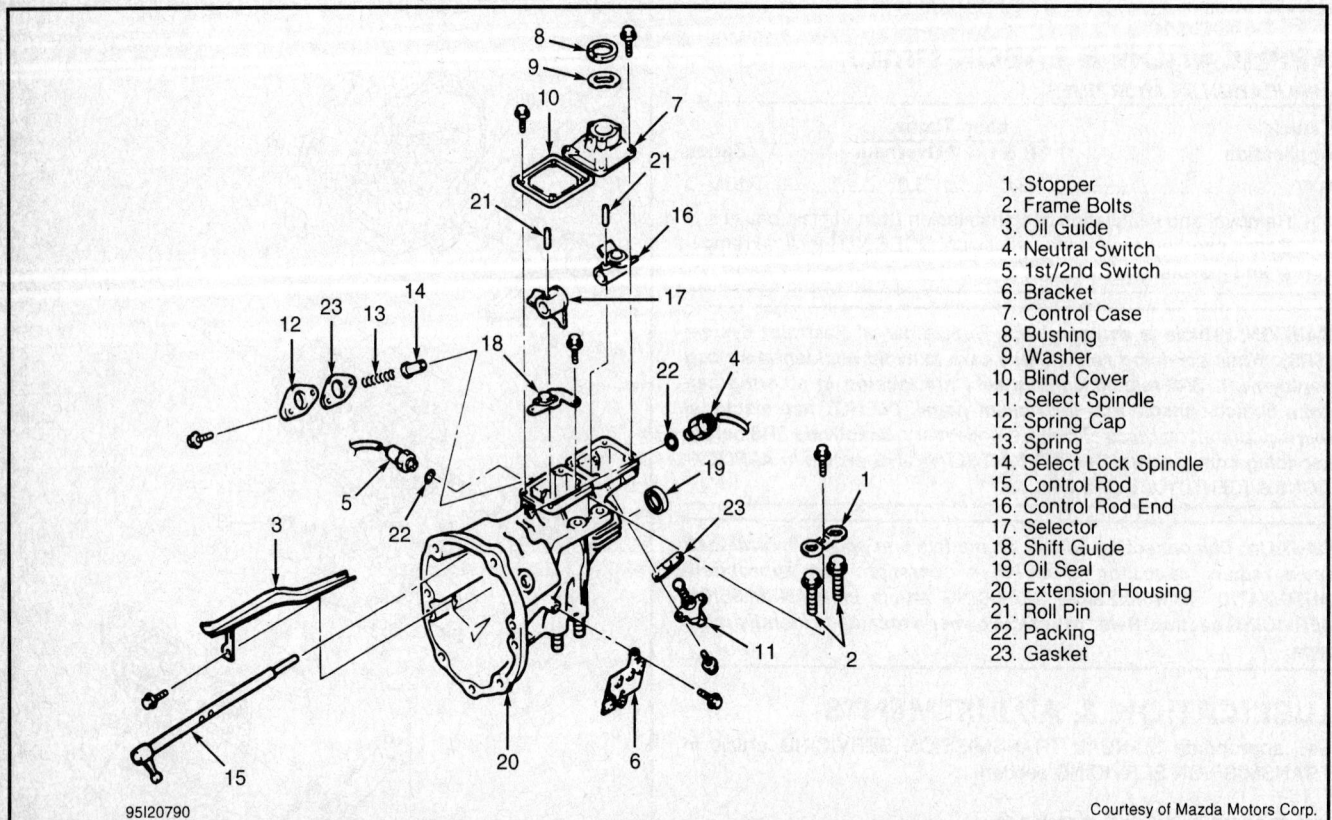

1. Stopper
2. Frame Bolts
3. Oil Guide
4. Neutral Switch
5. 1st/2nd Switch
6. Bracket
7. Control Case
8. Bushing
9. Washer
10. Blind Cover
11. Select Spindle
12. Spring Cap
13. Spring
14. Select Lock Spindle
15. Control Rod
16. Control Rod End
17. Selector
18. Shift Guide
19. Oil Seal
20. Extension Housing
21. Roll Pin
22. Packing
23. Gasket

95I20790

Courtesy of Mazda Motors Corp.

Fig. 2: Exploded View Of Extension Housing

COMPONENT DISASSEMBLY & REASSEMBLY

MAINSHAFT

Disassembly – 1) Remove snap ring from front of mainshaft. In arbor press, place puller between 2nd/3rd gears. Press mainshaft through 3rd and 3rd/4th clutch hub assembly. See Fig. 4.

2) Reposition mainshaft in press and remove 1st/2nd clutch hub and sleeve assembly. Remove 1st gear sleeve from rear of mainshaft. Remove inner race of countershaft bearing from countershaft.

Inspection – Place disassembled mainshaft in "V" blocks. Position a dial indicator on a smooth bearing surface and zero indicator. Rotate mainshaft and note reading. If mainshaft exceeds maximum runout, replace mainshaft. Inspect all gears, synchronizers, splines and surfaces for wear and/or damage. See TRANSMISSION SPECIFICA-TIONS table.

Reassembly – Position mainshaft in arbor press. Install 2nd gear with needle bearings installed and 1st/2nd clutch hub assembly over mainshaft and press into place. Install 3rd gear, needle bearing and 3rd/4th clutch hub assembly and press into place. Install snap ring in front of mainshaft. Install inner race, needle bearing, 1st gear and thrust washer.

TRANSMISSION SPECIFICATIONS

Application	In. (mm)
Mainshaft Runout	.001 (.03)
Control Lever-To-Shift Rod Clearance	.031 (.80)
Clutch Hub Sleeve-To-Shift Fork Clearance	.008-.012 (.20-.30)
Synchronizer-To-Gear Clearance	.031-.059 (.80-1.50)
Reverse Idler Gear-To-Shaft Clearance	.0008-.006 (.020-.15)

SYNCHRONIZERS

Disassembly – Synchronizers were disassembled during mainshaft disassembly. The synchronizers all have similar shapes. Measure each component to ensure correct reassembly. See SYNCHRONIZER DIMENSIONS. See Fig. 5.

SYNCHRONIZER DIMENSIONS

Dimension No.	1st/2nd In. (mm)	3rd/4th In. (mm)	5th/Reverse In. (mm)
"1"	.709 (18.00)	.669 (17.00)	.669 (17.00)
"2"	.215 (5.45)	.167 (4.25)	.167 (4.25)
"3"	.236 (6.00)	.197 (5.00)	.197 (5.00)

Inspection – 1) Inspect synchronizer unit for worn or damaged parts. Install synchronizer ring evenly to gear cone and measure clearance between side faces of ring and gear with feeler gauge. See Fig. 6. Standard clearance is .059" (1.5 mm). Minimum clearance is .031" (.8 mm), replace synchronizer ring or gear if not within specifications. Check clearance between control lever and gate of shift rod with a feeler gauge. Maximum clearance should be .031" (.8 mm).

2) Check synchronizer key springs for tension. Ensure that clutch sleeve slides easily on clutch hub. Check clearance between hub sleeve and release fork groove using feeler gauge. See Fig. 6. Standard clearance is .008-.012" (.20-.30 mm). Clearance limit is .020" (.50 mm). Replace if not within specifications. Inspect reverse idler gear and shaft for wear and damage. Standard clearance is .001-.002" (.03-.05 mm). Limit is .006" (.15 mm).

NOTE: Ensure synchronizer ring and clutch hub are properly aligned on press during reassembly procedure.

Reassembly – Ensure clutch hubs are facing correct direction. See Fig. 7.

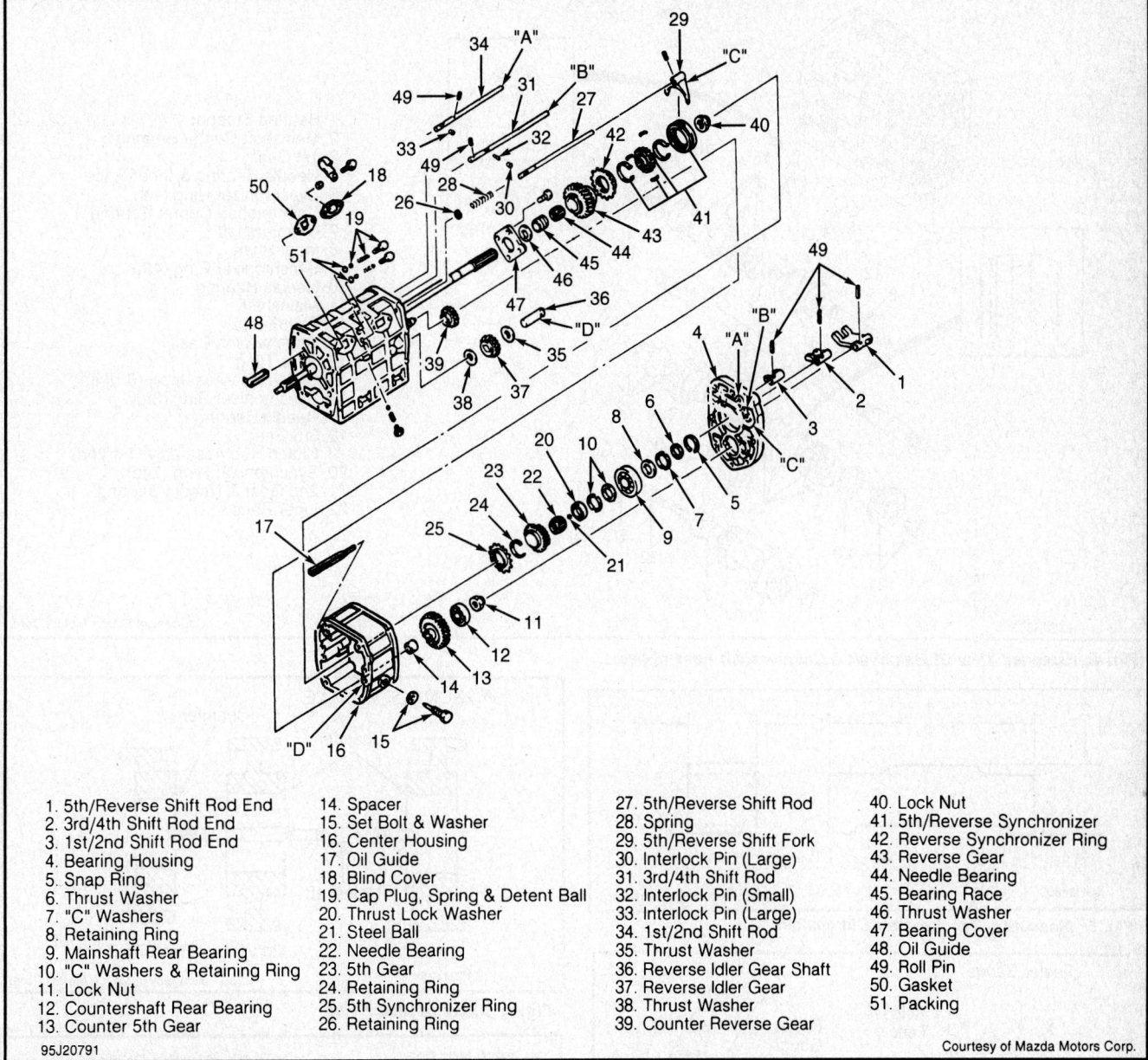

1. 5th/Reverse Shift Rod End	14. Spacer	27. 5th/Reverse Shift Rod	40. Lock Nut
2. 3rd/4th Shift Rod End	15. Set Bolt & Washer	28. Spring	41. 5th/Reverse Synchronizer
3. 1st/2nd Shift Rod End	16. Center Housing	29. 5th/Reverse Shift Fork	42. Reverse Synchronizer Ring
4. Bearing Housing	17. Oil Guide	30. Interlock Pin (Large)	43. Reverse Gear
5. Snap Ring	18. Blind Cover	31. 3rd/4th Shift Rod	44. Needle Bearing
6. Thrust Washer	19. Cap Plug, Spring & Detent Ball	32. Interlock Pin (Small)	45. Bearing Race
7. "C" Washers	20. Thrust Lock Washer	33. Interlock Pin (Large)	46. Thrust Washer
8. Retaining Ring	21. Steel Ball	34. 1st/2nd Shift Rod	47. Bearing Cover
9. Mainshaft Rear Bearing	22. Needle Bearing	35. Thrust Washer	48. Oil Guide
10. "C" Washers & Retaining Ring	23. 5th Gear	36. Reverse Idler Gear Shaft	49. Roll Pin
11. Lock Nut	24. Retaining Ring	37. Reverse Idler Gear	50. Gasket
12. Countershaft Rear Bearing	25. 5th Synchronizer Ring	38. Thrust Washer	51. Packing
13. Counter 5th Gear	26. Retaining Ring	39. Counter Reverse Gear	

95J20791 | | Courtesy of Mazda Motors Corp.

Fig. 3: Exploded View Of 5th/Reverse Gear & Housing Components

TRANSMISSION REASSEMBLY

1) Press inner race of countershaft rear bearings onto countershaft. Using Vernier calipers, measure depth of input shaft bearing bore in clutch housing (View "A"). Measure mainshaft bearing snap ring height (View "B"). See Fig. 8. Difference between 2 measurements is required adjusting shim thickness.

2) Standard input shaft thrust play is .004" (.10 mm). Adjusting shims (5) are available from .012-.028" (.30-.70 mm) in .004" (.10 mm) increments. Measure depth of mainshaft center bearing in bore of transmission case using Vernier calipers (View "A"). See Fig. 9. Measure mainshaft center bearing height (View "B"). Difference between 2 measurements is required adjusting shim thickness. Standard mainshaft thrust play is .004" (.10 mm). Adjusting shims are available in sizes of .004 and .012" (.10 and .30 mm).

3) Using Vernier calipers, measure depth of countershaft front bearing in bore of transmission case ("A"). Measure countershaft front bearing height ("B"). See Fig. 10. Select adjusting shim for difference ("A" - "B" + shim) to equal bearing height .035-.039" (.90-1.00 mm). Adjusting shims are available in sizes of .004 and .012" (.10 and .30 mm).

4) Install mainshaft in transmission case. Install 1st/2nd and 3rd/4th shift forks into grooves of clutch hub and sleeve assemblies. Apply molybdenum grease to needle bearings in input shaft. Install needle bearing and input shaft on front of the mainshaft. Install countershaft into case. Ensure all gears mesh correctly.

5) Using suitable pipe, drive on countershaft center bearing. Install predetermined mainshaft center bearing adjusting shim into bore of transmission case. Drive mainshaft center bearing onto mainshaft using suitable driver. Install bearing cover.

6) Install Synchronizer Holder (49F017101) between 4th gear synchronizer and synchromesh gear on main drive gear. Drive on input shaft bearing. Install snap ring to secure input shaft bearing. Place predetermined countershaft front bearing adjusting shim into bore of transmission case. Drive on countershaft front bearing.

7) Install reverse idler gear and shaft with a spacer on each side of the shaft. Install counter reverse gear (chamfer toward front) and spacer onto countershaft. Install thrust washer, reverse gear, synchronizer ring, inner race, needle bearing and clutch hub assembly. Shift transmission into 1st and reverse gear to lock rotation of mainshaft and install a NEW lock nut on mainshaft using Lock Nut Wrench (491243465A).

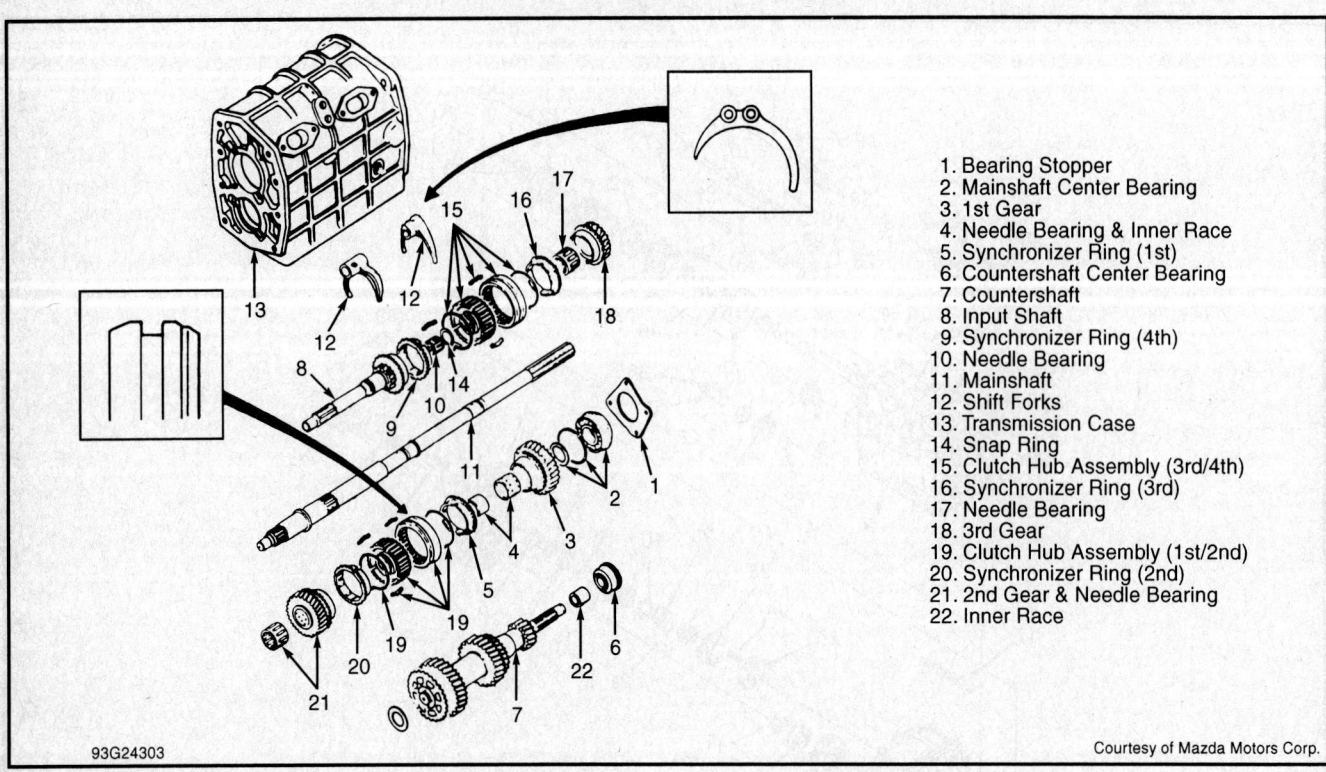

1. Bearing Stopper
2. Mainshaft Center Bearing
3. 1st Gear
4. Needle Bearing & Inner Race
5. Synchronizer Ring (1st)
6. Countershaft Center Bearing
7. Countershaft
8. Input Shaft
9. Synchronizer Ring (4th)
10. Needle Bearing
11. Mainshaft
12. Shift Forks
13. Transmission Case
14. Snap Ring
15. Clutch Hub Assembly (3rd/4th)
16. Synchronizer Ring (3rd)
17. Needle Bearing
18. 3rd Gear
19. Clutch Hub Assembly (1st/2nd)
20. Synchronizer Ring (2nd)
21. 2nd Gear & Needle Bearing
22. Inner Race

Courtesy of Mazda Motors Corp.

Fig. 4: Exploded View Of Mainshaft & Countershaft Assemblies

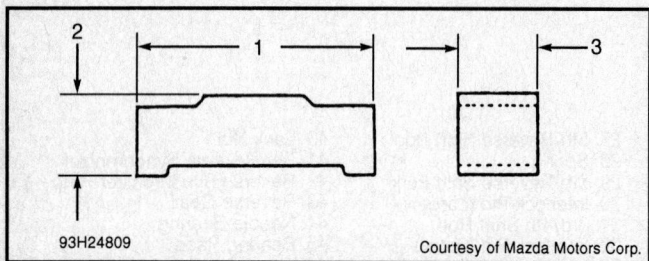

Courtesy of Mazda Motors Corp.

Fig. 5: Measuring Synchronizer Dimensions

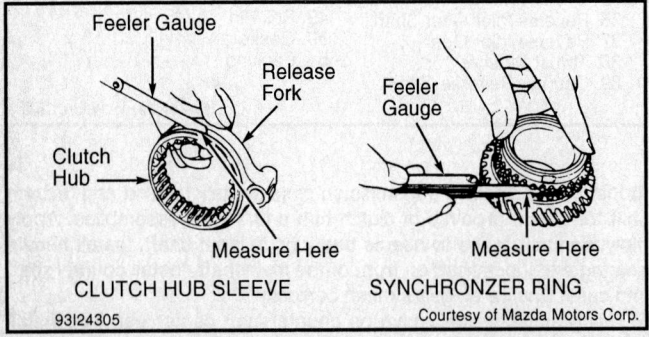

CLUTCH HUB SLEEVE   SYNCHRONZER RING

Courtesy of Mazda Motors Corp.

Fig. 6: Checking Synchro Ring & Hub Sleeve Clearance

8) Check clearance between synchronizer key and exposed edge of the synchronizer ring. If clearance is not .079" (2.00 mm), install a selective thrust washer between mainshaft front and rear bearing. Selective thrust washers are available in sizes of .098" (2.50 mm), .118" (3.00 mm) and .138" (3.50 mm). Stake lock nut in place on mainshaft.

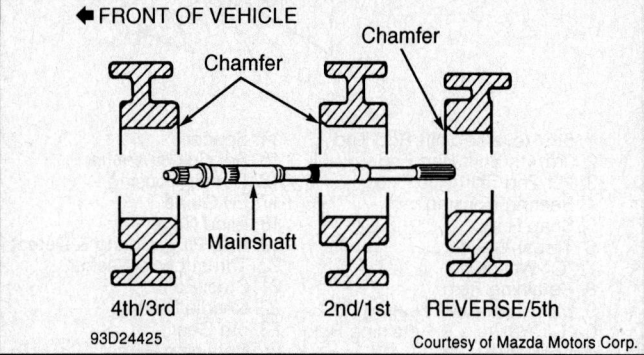

Fig. 7: Aligning Clutch Hub

Courtesy of Mazda Motors Corp.

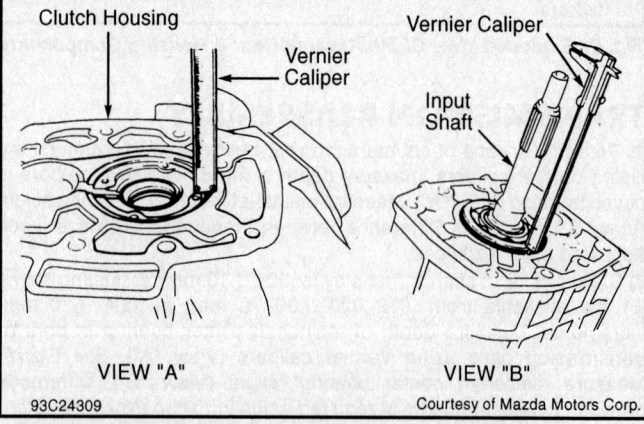

VIEW "A"   VIEW "B"

Courtesy of Mazda Motors Corp.

Fig. 8: Determining Input Shaft Bearing Shim Thickness

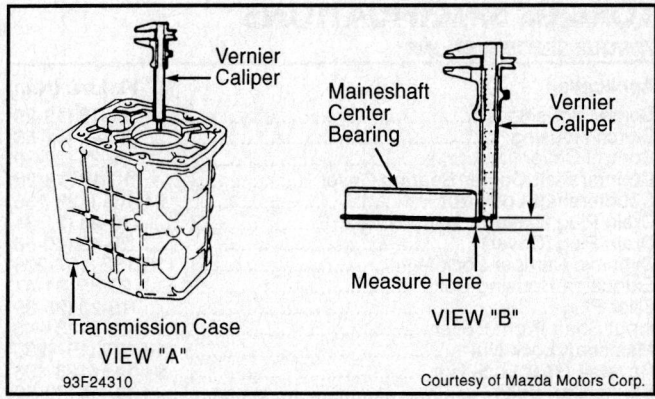

Fig. 9: *Determining Mainshaft Center Bearing Shim Thickness*

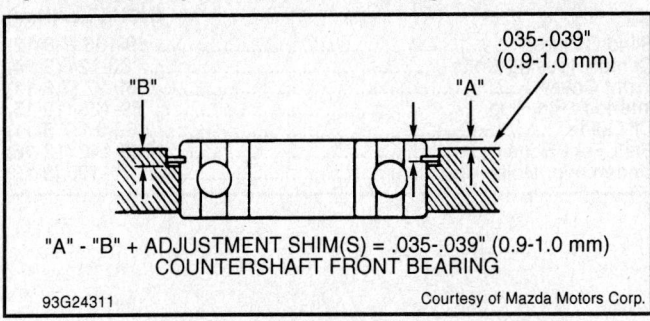

Fig. 10: *Determining Countershaft Bearing Shim Thickness*

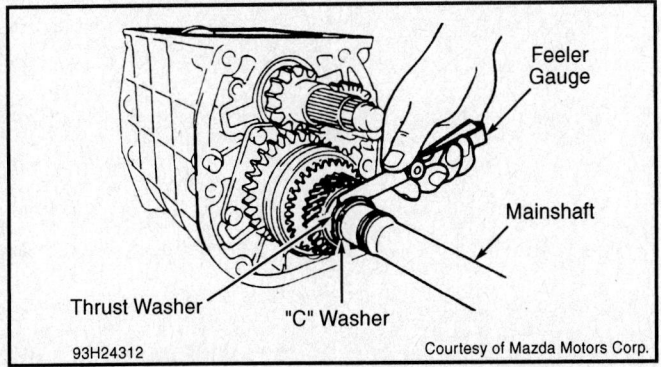

Fig. 11: *Measuring Between Thrust Washer & "C" Washer*

9) Install synchronizer ring, 5th gear and needle bearing. Install steel ball and thrust washer. *See Fig. 3.* Install .118" (3.00 mm) thick "C" washer and hold them with retaining ring on mainshaft. Using a feeler gauge, measure clearance between "C" washer and thrust washer. Standard clearance is .004-.008" (.10-.20 mm). If clearance is not within specification, select proper thrust washer. *See Fig. 11.* Thrust washers are available from .244-.264" (6.20-6.70 mm) in .004" (.10 mm) increments.

10) Identify shift rods for proper location. *See Fig. 12.* Slide 1st/2nd shift rod into transmission case. Secure 1st/2nd shift forks to shift rods with NEW spring pins. Slide 2 Shift Fork Guides (490862350) into transmission case. Insert interlock 1st pin. Remove 3rd/4th shift fork guide. Slide 3rd/4th shift rod into transmission case. Secure 3rd/4th shift rod with NEW spring pins. Insert interlock pin and remove shift fork guide. Install 5th/reverse shift fork on clutch hub and slide shift rod into transmission case. Secure with NEW spring pins. Install shift rod ends on proper shift rods. Secure shift rod ends with NEW spring pins.

11) Install 2 blind covers and gaskets. Install 3 detent balls, springs and cap bolts. Apply sealant to transmission case and center housing. Install center housing, ensuring to align reverse idler gear shaft boss with hold bolt hole and install hold bolt with gasket. Install oil guide.

Install spacer and counter 5th gear. Install rear countershaft bearing. Lock transmission into gear and install countershaft lock nut. Stake lock nut into countershaft keyway. Drive in mainshaft rear bearing using suitable driver.

12) Install "C" washers and retaining ring. Measure clearance between mainshaft "C" washers and groove in mainshaft using feeler gauge. *See Fig. 13.* If clearance exceeds .004" (.10 mm), replace "C" washer. See "C" WASHER THICKNESS table.

"C" WASHER THICKNESS

"C" Washer No.	In. (mm)
1	.114 (2.90)
2	.118 (3.00)
3	.122 (3.10)
4	.126 (3.20)

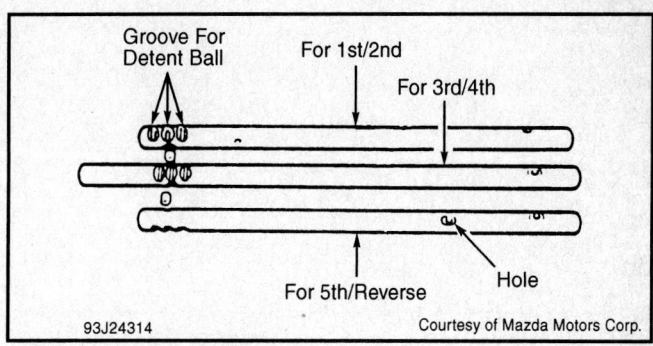

Fig. 12: *Identifying Shift Rods*

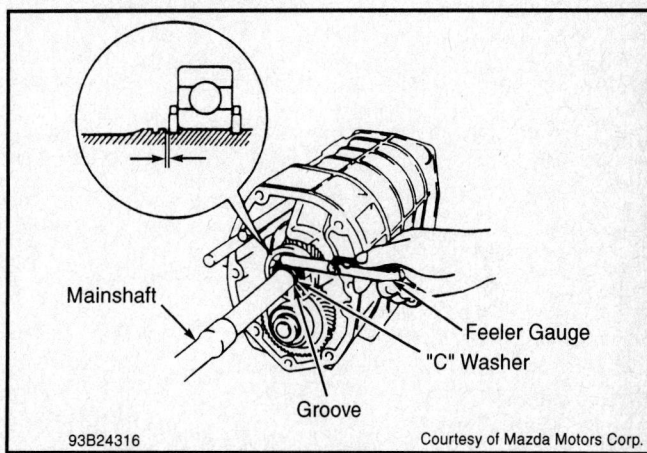

Fig. 13: *Checking Clearance Between "C" Washer & Groove*

13) Apply thin coat of sealer on mating surfaces of bearing housing and center housing. Assemble using a soft mallet. Install shift rod ends to shift rods and install spring pins. Install speedometer drive gear, lock ball and snap ring on mainshaft. Apply thin coat of sealer on mating surfaces of clutch housing and transmission case. Install predetermined shim on input shaft and countershaft front bearings. Install clutch housing and torque bolts to specification.

14) Install oil seal into extension housing. Install control rod into extension housing. On 4WD, apply sealant to contact surfaces of bearing housing and extension housing. Install extension housing on bearing housing.

15) Install input sleeve. Coat mating surfaces of transfer case and extension housing with sealant. Guide control lever into position when transfer case is installed on extension housing. Install control lever end and secure with spring pin. Coat bolts with sealant, install bolts and torque to specifications. Apply sealant to control cover and transfer case. Install control cover to transfer case. Apply sealant to threads of bolts, install and torque to specifications.

16) Apply thin coat of sealant on mating surfaces of bearing housing and extension housing. Assemble with control lever positioned as far left as possible. Install and tighten bolts. Install select lock spindle, spring and cap by pushing select lock spindle down with control rod. Install gasket and under cover. See Fig. 1. Torque mounting bolts to specification. Install clutch release bearing, clutch release fork and dust cover.

TORQUE SPECIFICATIONS
TORQUE SPECIFICATIONS

Application	Ft. Lbs. (N.m)
Center Housing	14-18 (19-25)
Clutch Housing	30-41 (41-55)
Control Cover	16-22 (22-30)
Countershaft Center Bearing Cover	13-19 (18-26)
Countershaft Lock Nut	94-145 (128-196)
Drain Plug (Case)	16-23 (21-31)
Drain Plug (Cover)	29-43 (40-58)
Dynamic Damper Lock Nut	116-152 (157-206)
Extension Housing Bolts	23-35 (31-47)
Filler Plug	19-28 (25-39)
Input Shaft Front Cover	23-34 (31-46)
Mainshaft Lock Nut	116-173 (157-235)
Reverse Gear Lock Nut	94-145 (128-196)
Spring Cap Bolts	29-44 (39-59)
Transfer Case-To-Extension Housing	27-35 (36-47)

Application	INCH Lbs. (N.m)
Blind Covers	69-106 (7.8-12)
Center Housing Bolts	80-124 (9-14)
Front Cover	69-97 (7.8-11)
Interlock Pin Plug	89-133 (10-15)
Oil Guide	69-97 (7.8-11)
Shift Fork Bolts	106-142 (12-16)
Undercover Bolts	71-106 (8-12)

Eclipse

APPLICATION & LABOR TIMES

APPLICATION & LABOR TIMES

Vehicle Application	Labor Times		Series
	[1] R & I	[2] Overhaul	
Eclipse			
2.0L Non-Turbo	4.3	8.3	F5MC1

[1] – Removal and installation of transmission from vehicle chassis.
[2] – Bench overhaul time for transaxle/differential. DOES NOT include removal and installation.

IDENTIFICATION

Transaxle can be identified by vehicle information code plate, located on firewall in engine compartment.

DESCRIPTION

F5MC1 5-speed transaxle is a fully synchronized, manual, front wheel drive transmission. *See Fig. 1.* Transmission features a final drive ratio of 3.55:1. Output shaft overhaul is not possible and should be replaced as an assembly if determined to have excess wear or damage.

LUBRICATION & ADJUSTMENTS

See appropriate MANUAL TRANSMISSION SERVICING article in TRANSMISSION SERVICING section.

TROUBLE SHOOTING

See GENERAL TROUBLE SHOOTING article in this section.

ON-VEHICLE SERVICE

AXLE SHAFTS

See appropriate AXLE SHAFTS article in AXLE SHAFTS & TRANSFER CASES section.

REMOVAL & INSTALLATION

For transaxle removal procedure, see appropriate MANUAL TRANSMISSION REMOVAL article in TRANSMISSION SERVICING section.

TRANSAXLE DISASSEMBLY

1) Place transaxle on bench with clutch housing facing upward. Remove shift levers and transaxle case bolts. Insert prybar into slots provided and separate case halves. *See Fig. 2.*

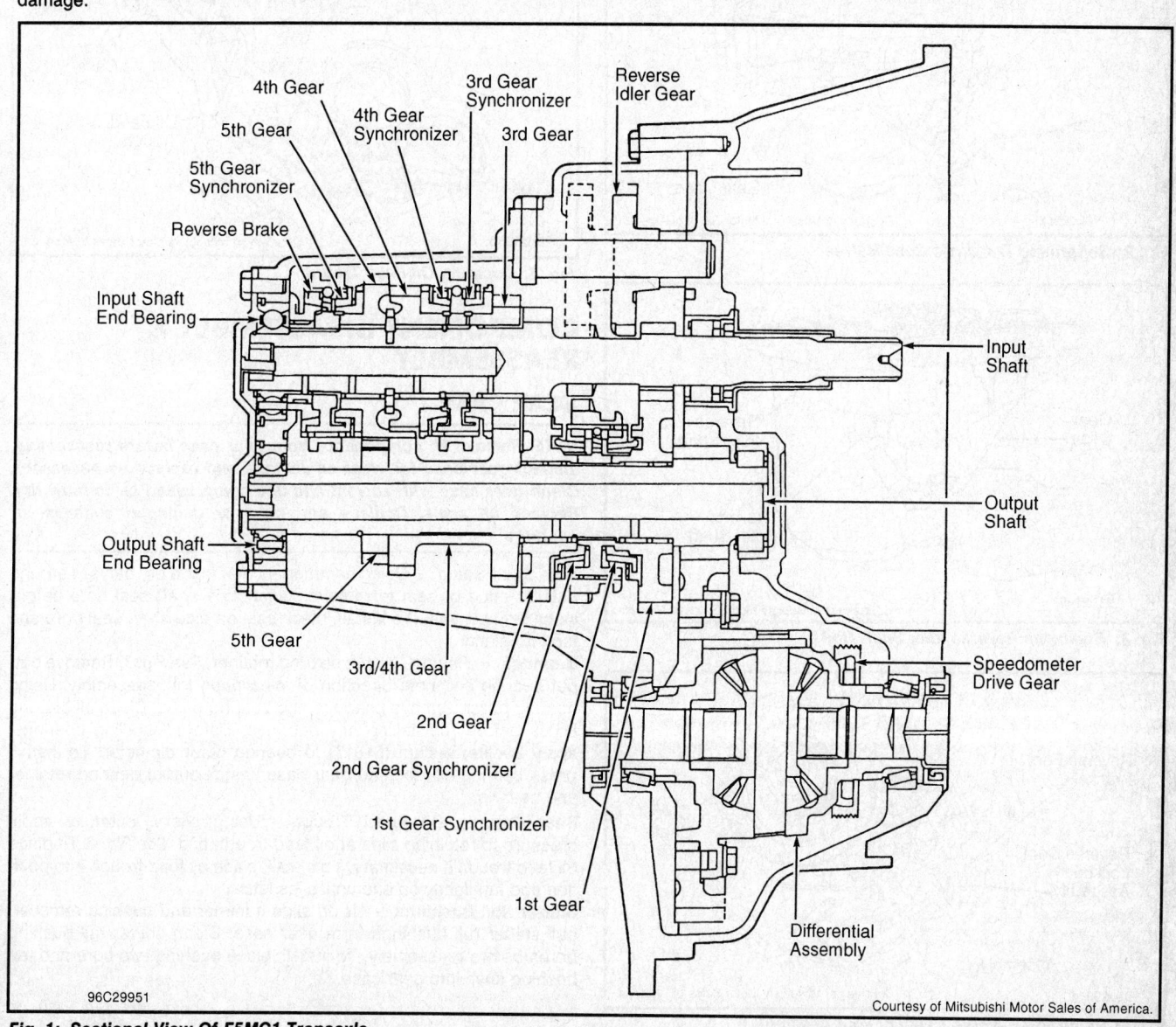

96C29951

Courtesy of Mitsubishi Motor Sales of America.

Fig. 1: Sectional View Of F5MC1 Transaxle

2) Remove output shaft bearing and differential assembly. Remove reverse idler shaft bolt and reverse idler gear. *See Fig. 3.* Remove reverse fork bracket retaining screws and reverse fork bracket. Remove reverse cam lockout assembly. *See Fig. 4.*

3) Using snap ring pliers, remove selector shaft spacer. Pull selector shaft free from shift lock assembly and rotate upwards. Lay transaxle on its bottom and prop up end. Remove transaxle end cover. Using snap ring pliers, remove 2 snap rings holding output shaft and input shaft bearings.

4) Turn transaxle over and place down on Transaxle Holder (MB995025) and Shims (MB995023, MB995024). *See Fig. 5.* Using Bearing Remover (MB995056) and suitable press, press input and output shafts from transaxle.

CAUTION: Ensure transaxle is aligned with bearing remover. Damage to input and output shaft assemblies oil dams may result if bearing remover is not properly aligned.

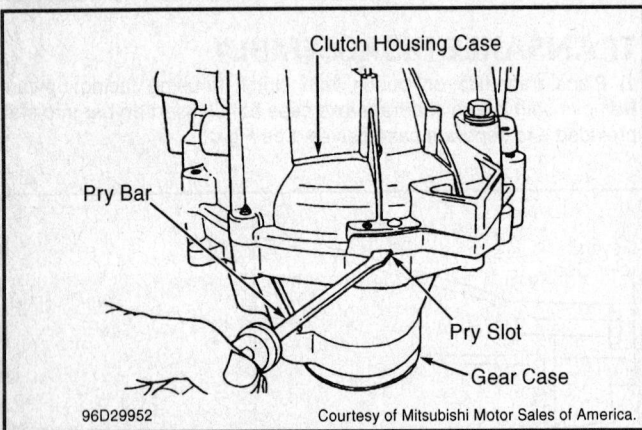

96D29952   Courtesy of Mitsubishi Motor Sales of America.

Fig. 2: Separating Transaxle Case Halves

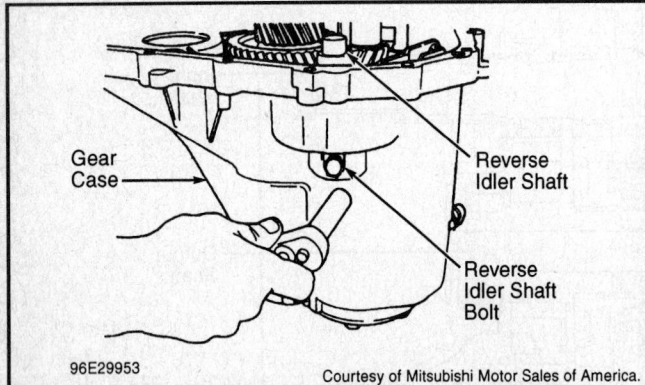

96E29953   Courtesy of Mitsubishi Motor Sales of America.

Fig. 3: Removing Reverse Idler Shaft Bolt

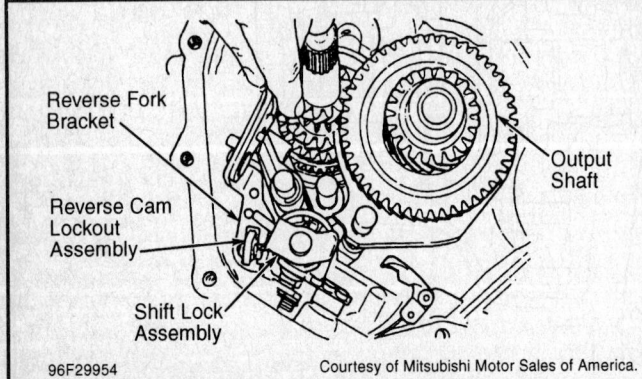

96F29954   Courtesy of Mitsubishi Motor Sales of America.

Fig. 4: Removing Reverse Cam Lockout Assembly

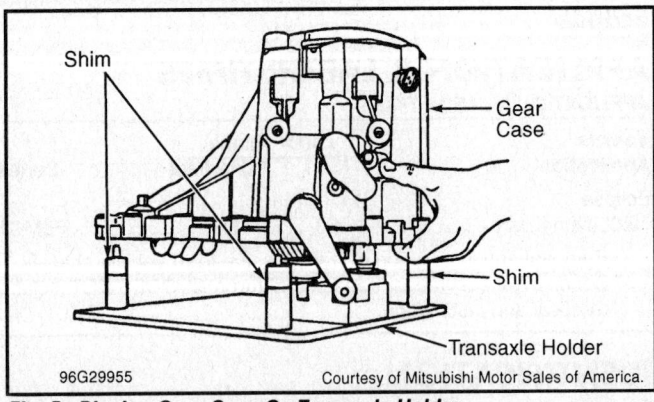

96G29955   Courtesy of Mitsubishi Motor Sales of America.

Fig. 5: Placing Gear Case On Transaxle Holder

5) Remove transaxle case from input and output shaft assemblies. Ensure end bearings oil feed trough is not damaged. *See Fig. 6.* Remove shift lock assembly and 1-2 shift fork.

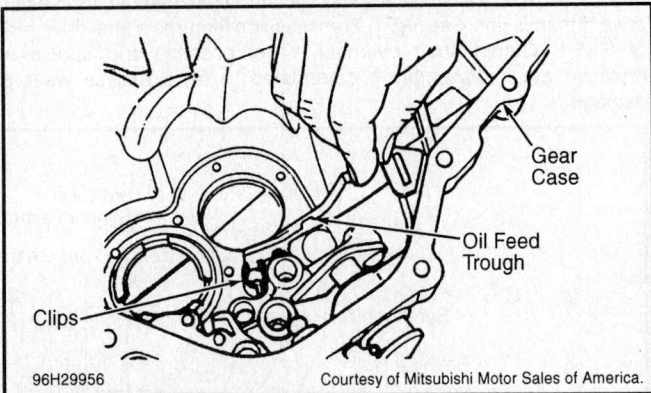

96H29956   Courtesy of Mitsubishi Motor Sales of America.

Fig. 6: Locating Oil Feed Trough

COMPONENT DISASSEMBLY & REASSEMBLY

GEAR CASE

NOTE: Remove all components from gear case before reassembly. Inspect gear case for wear or damage and replace as necessary. Clean gear case with solvent and use compressed air to blow dry. Replace all seals. Replace any worn or damaged bushings or bearings.

Axle Shaft Seals – Using hammer and flat blade pry bar, tap around outside edge of seal to remove. Clean axle shaft seal bore before installing new seal. To install, place seal on axle shaft seal bore and tap into place.

Bearings – Remove output bearing retainer. *See Fig. 7.* Remove output bearing and note direction of installation for reassembly. Using bearing puller, remove bearings and bearing races. Clean all bearing bores before reinstalling any bearings. Before installing bearings, apply Loctite Sealant (51817) to bearing outer diameter. To install, press bearing or race into gear case. Install output bearing retainer and bearing.

Rear Bearing Oil Feed Trough – Using pliers, carefully apply pressure to retaining clips at oil feed trough end. *See Fig. 6.* Replace oil feed trough if necessary. To install, place oil feed trough into position and tap lightly on end until clips latch.

Shifter Rail Bushings – Using slide hammer and bushing remover, pull shifter rail bushings from gear case. Clean shifter rail bushing bores before reassembly. To install, place bushing into bore and tap bushing flush into gear case.

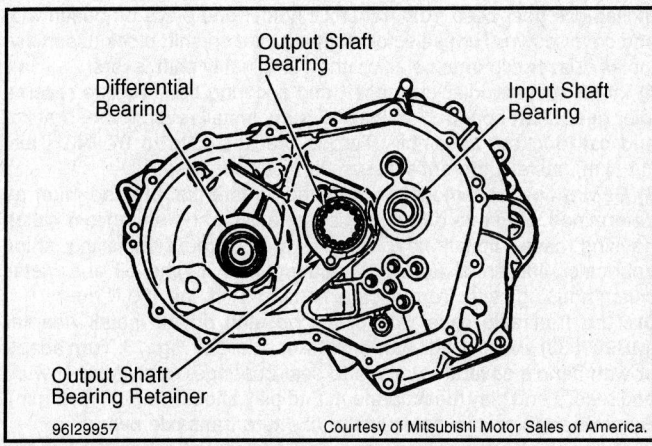

Fig. 7: Locating Output Shaft Bearing Retainer & Bearings

Shifter Shafts – Using snap ring pliers, remove snap ring from shifter crossover shaft. Push shifter selector and crossover shafts from gear case. To install, reverse removal procedure.

Shifter Shaft Seals – Using pick tool, pry up and out on seal to remove. To install, place seal on edge of bore and tap in with an appropriate deep well socket.

INPUT & OUTPUT SHAFT INSPECTION

Before disassembly, measure synchronizer stop ring gaps. *See Figs. 8 and 9.* See SYNCHRONIZER STOP RING CLEARANCE SPECIFICATIONS table. Measure clearance between synchronizer stop ring and gear. If stop ring is not within specifications, replace stop ring. If output shaft clearances are not within specifications, replace output shaft as an assembly.

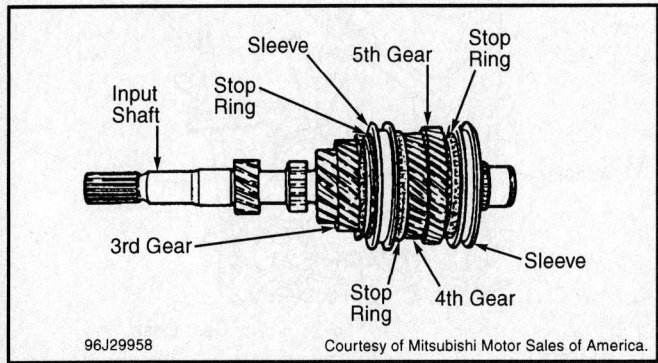

Fig. 8: Identifying Input Shaft Components

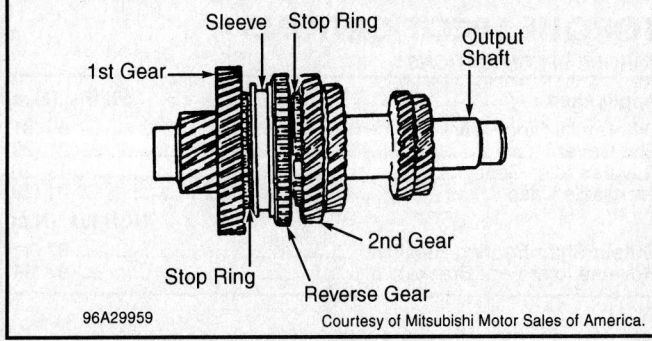

Fig. 9: Identifying Output Shaft Components

SYNCHRONIZER STOP RING CLEARANCE SPECIFICATIONS

Gear [1]	Clearance in. (mm)
1st	.041-.068 (1.04-1.72)
2nd	.037-.068 (.94-1.72)
3rd	.054-.076 (1.37-1.93)
4th	.056-.078 (1.41-1.97)
5th	.054-.076 (1.37-1.93)

[1] – Measure clearance between specified gear and adjacent stop ring.

INPUT SHAFT

Disassembly – 1) Install bearing remover behind 5th gear and remove snap ring from 5th synchronizer hub. Press input shaft from 5th gear and synchronizer assembly. Remove needle bearing, split thrust washer and ring.

2) Using pliers, remove split thrust washer separation pin. Remove 4th gear and needle bearing. Ensure needle bearing retention spring is not damaged. Remove snap ring and install bearing remover behind 3rd gear. Press input shaft from 3rd gear and synchronizer assembly.

3) Remove needle bearing and ensure needle bearing retention spring is not damaged. Inspect input shaft bearing races and gear teeth for damage or wear. Replace as necessary.

Reassembly – 1) Install bearing remover. *See Fig. 10.* Install 3rd gear needle bearing. Using a press, install 3rd gear and synchronizer assembly. Synchronizer hub is stamped with a "U". Install synchronizer assembly with "U" stamp upward.

2) Install thickest snap ring that will fit into slot. Install 4th gear needle bearing and 4th gear onto input shaft. Install split thrust washer separation pin, split thrust washer and ring.

3) Install 5th gear needle bearing. Using press, install 5th gear and synchronizer assembly. Synchronizer hub is stamped with a "S". Install synchronizer assembly with "S" stamp facing upward. Install thickest snap ring that will fit into slot.

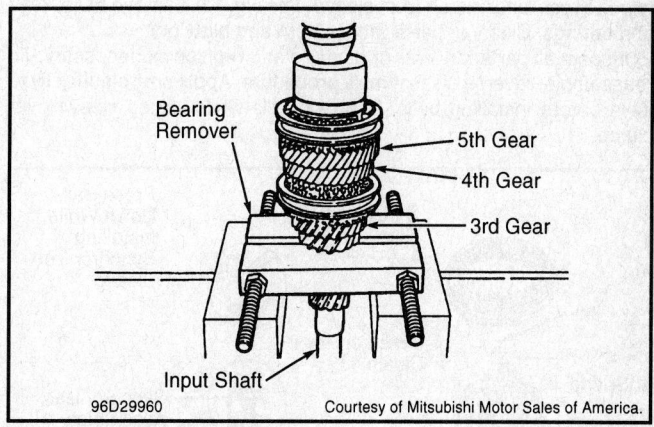

Fig. 10: Installing Bearing Remover

OUTPUT SHAFT

NOTE: Check output shaft stop ring clearances. See SYNCHRONIZER STOP RING CLEARANCE SPECIFICATIONS table under INPUT & OUTPUT SHAFT INSPECTION. See Fig. 9. If clearances are not within specification or damage to output shaft has occurred, replace output shaft as an assembly.

DIFFERENTIAL ASSEMBLY

Disassembly & Reassembly – 1) Using bearing puller, remove both differential end bearings. Remove ring gear bolts and ring gear. Using flat blade pry bar, remove speedometer drive gear.

2) Remove pinion shaft pin and pinion shaft. Rotate side gears to differential opening. Remove pinion gears, side gears and thrust washers.

3) To reassemble, reverse disassembly procedure. Stake pinion shaft pin into place. Rotate pinion gears and side gears 2 full revolutions clockwise and counterclockwise. Using dial indicator and Adapter (MB995039), measure side gear end play. *See Fig. 11.*

4) Side gear end play should be .001-.013" (.25-.33 mm). If end play is not within specification, replace thrust washer to obtain specified end play. Repeat procedure for opposite side gear.

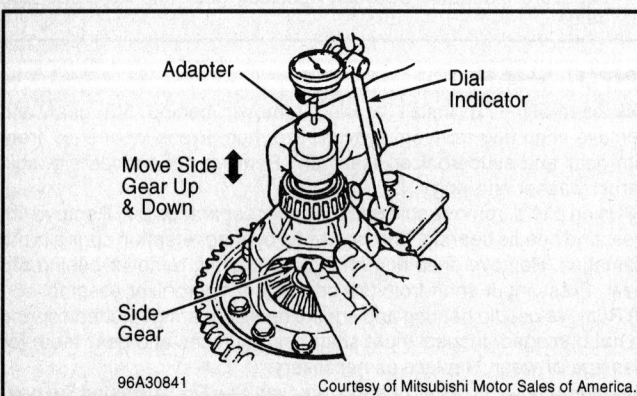

Fig. 11: Measuring Side Gear End Play

SHIFT SHAFTS

NOTE: Manufacturer does not provide any disassembly or overhaul procedures for transaxle shift shafts. Inspect forks and shafts for wear or damage and replace as necessary.

SYNCHRONIZER ASSEMBLY

Disassembly & Reassembly – 1) Place synchronizer assembly in towel. Press inner clutch from sleeve. *See Fig. 12.* Remove balls, keys and springs. Clean all parts with solvent and blow dry.

2) Inspect all parts for wear or damage and replace as necessary. To reassemble, reverse disassembly procedure. Apply pretroleum jelly to keys before installing balls. Depress balls while sliding sleeve over clutch.

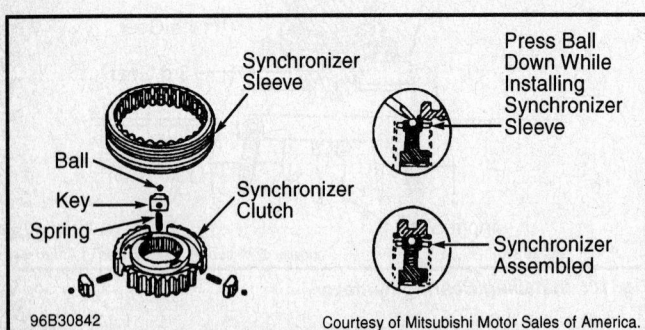

Fig. 12: Exploded View Of Synchronizer Assembly

TRANSAXLE REASSEMBLY

1) Place assembled input and output shafts onto Transaxle Holder (MB995025). Install shift rails and shift forks onto shafts. Put shift lock into place and lower gear case onto transaxle holder.

2) Install reverse brake shim and ensure it is alligned properly. Place input and ouput end bearings on shaft ends and press into case until flush. Install bearing retainer snap rings on input and ouput shafts. Apply Loctite Sealant (18718) to end cover outer edge and install end cover to case. Torque end cover bolts to 21 ft. lbs. (29 N.m).

3) Remove gear case from transaxle holder and place on bench with end cover down. Turn selector shaft into slot on shift block assembly. Install spacer clip onto selector shaft and install shift levers.

4) Install reverse idler gear shaft and securing bolt. Torque reverse idler gear shaft bolt to 19 ft. lbs. (26 N.m). Install reverse fork bracket and cam lockout assembly. Torque bracket bolts to 97 INCH lbs. (11 N.m). Install differential assembly into gear case.

5) Before final assembly is completed, differential preload must be determined. Remove differential bearing race and shim from clutch housing case. Install new bearing race without installing shim. Lubricate differential assembly bearing with engine oil and install clutch housing case. Torque case bolts to 21 ft. lbs. (29 N.m).

6) Turn transaxle case with clutch housing down. Install Adapter (MB995038) and dial indicator onto transaxle. *See Fig. 13.* Turn adapter with handle several rotations to seat bearings. Apply load upward and record end play measurement. End play should be .007" (.18 mm). Remove adapter and dial indicator and turn transaxle over.

7) Remove clutch housing case and differential assembly bearing race. Use the following formula to determine shim selection:

$$\text{“A”} - .007" (.18 \text{ mm}) = \text{“B”}$$

"A" = Recorded end play measurement.
"B" = Shim thickness required for proper preload.
.007" (.18 mm) = Standard end play value.

8) Install shim, bearing race and clutch housing case. Torque transaxle case bolts to 21 ft. lbs. (29 N.m). Using Adapter (MB995038) and an INCH lb. torque wrench, turn differential assembly. Turning torque should be 6-12 INCH lbs. (.7-1.4 N.m). If turning torque is more than specified, reduce shim thickness by .020" (.5 mm). If turning torque is less than specified, increase shim thickness by .020" (.5 mm). Recheck turning torque is shim replacement is made.

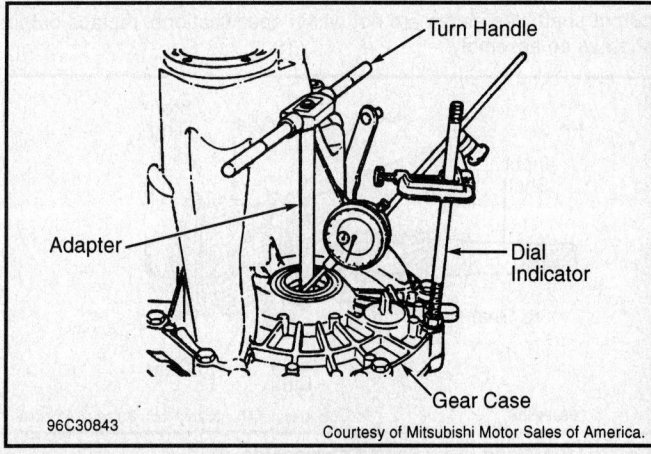

Fig. 13: Measuring Differential End Play

TORQUE SPECIFICATIONS

TORQUE SPECIFICATIONS

Application	Ft. lbs. (N.m)
Differential Ring Gear	60 (81)
End Cover	21 (29)
Reverse Idler Gear	19 (26)
Transaxle Case	21 (29)

	INCH lbs. (N.m)
Output Shaft Bearing Retainer	97 (11)
Reverse Idler Fork Bracket	97 (11)

Hyundai: Sonata
Mitsubishi: Eclipse, Expo, Galant
Mirage, 3000GT

APPLICATION & LABOR TIMES

APPLICATION & LABOR TIMES

Vehicle Application	Labor Times		Series
	[1] R & I	[2] Overhaul	
Hyundai			
Sonata	3.2	8.3	KM210
Mitsubishi			
Eclipse			
2.0L Turbo	4.3	8.3	F5M33
2.4L	4.3	8.3	F5M31
Expo			
FWD			
1.8L	4.3	8.3	F5M22
2.4L	4.3	8.3	F5M31
Galant	6.0	8.3	F5M31
Mirage			
1.5L	4.3	8.3	F5M21
1.8L	4.3	8.3	F5M22
3000GT			
FWD	4.3	8.3	F5M33

[1] – Removal and installation of transmission from vehicle chassis.
[2] – Bench overhaul time for transmission or transaxle/differential. DOES NOT include removal and installation.

IDENTIFICATION

Transaxle can be identified by vehicle information code plate, located on firewall in engine compartment.

LUBRICATION & ADJUSTMENTS

See appropriate MANUAL TRANSMISSION SERVICING article in TRANSMISSION SERVICING section.

TROUBLE SHOOTING

See GENERAL TROUBLE SHOOTING article in this section.

ON-VEHICLE SERVICE

AXLE SHAFTS

See appropriate AXLE SHAFTS article in AXLE SHAFTS & TRANSFER CASES section.

REMOVAL & INSTALLATION

For transaxle removal procedure, see appropriate MANUAL TRANSMISSION REMOVAL article in TRANSMISSION SERVICING section.

TRANSAXLE DISASSEMBLY

1) On F5M21 models, remove transaxle switch and gasket. On all models, remove rear cover. *See Fig. 1 or 2.* Remove back-up light switch and gasket. Remove wave spring, screw bolts and reverse brake cone. Remove poppet plugs, poppet springs and poppet balls.

2) Remove speedometer driven gear assembly from clutch housing. Remove air breather from clutch housing. Remove spring pin from 5th gear shift fork. Unstake lock nuts on input shaft and intermediate shaft.

3) Shift transaxle into Reverse using control and select levers. Install splined socket and breaker bar on input shaft. Install 10 mm bolt in clutch housing and position breaker bar against bolt to prevent input shaft from rotating. Remove lock nuts.

4) Remove 5th gear synchronizer assembly and shift fork. Remove synchronizer ring, and 5th gear. On F5M21 models, remove needle bearing, spacer, bearing sleeve, snap ring and roller bearing.

5) On all models, remove intermediate 5th gear. Remove reverse idler gear shaft bolt and gasket. Remove transaxle case and oil guide. Remove stopper bracket bolt and spring washer. Remove restrict ball assembly and gasket.

6) On F5M21 models, remove outer ring. On all models, remove oil seal. On F5M21 models, remove 3 spacers and one bearing outer race. On all other models, remove 3 spacers and 3 bearing outer races.

7) Remove reverse shift lever assembly, reverse shift lever shoe, reverse idler gear shaft and reverse idler gear.

8) Remove spring pins for 1st-2nd and 3rd-4th gear shift forks. Shift 1st-2nd gear shift fork to 2nd gear. Shift 3rd-4th gear shift fork to 4th gear.

9) On F5M21, F5M22 and KM210 models, rotate shift rails as necessary to free shift lugs from control finger and interlock plate. Pull shift rails upward to extract rail ends from clutch housing. Remove shift rails and forks.

10) On F5M31 and F5M33 models, remove shift rail assembly. On all models, remove bearing retainer. Lift up on input shaft and remove intermediate gear assembly.

11) Remove input shaft and output shaft assemblies. Remove differential assembly. Remove bearing outer races from input shaft, output shaft and differential bores in clutch housing (if equipped). Remove oil guide and oil seals from clutch housing. Remove magnet and magnet holder. *See Fig. 1 or 2.*

COMPONENT DISASSEMBLY & REASSEMBLY

5TH GEAR SYNCHRONIZER ASSEMBLY

Disassembly – Remove reverse brake ring, stop plate, synchronizer spring, synchronizer sleeve, synchronizer keys and hub. *See Fig. 3.*
Inspection – Insert synchronizer hub into sleeve. Ensure they slide smoothly. Ensure sleeve is not damaged or worn at inside front and rear edges. Inspect for wear on 5th gear mating surface of hub. Inspect for wear of synchronizer key center protrusion. Inspect spring for weakness, deformation and breakage.

NOTE: Replace synchronizer sleeve and hub as a set.

Reassembly – 1) Assemble synchronizer hub, sleeve and keys. *See Fig. 3.* Synchronizer sleeve has a tooth missing at 6 places. Assemble hub to sleeve so center tooth is between 2 missing teeth and touches synchronizer key.
2) Install synchronizer springs so synchronizer keys rest in stepped portions in springs. Ensure synchronizer springs are not installed in same direction. Install stop plate and reverse brake ring.

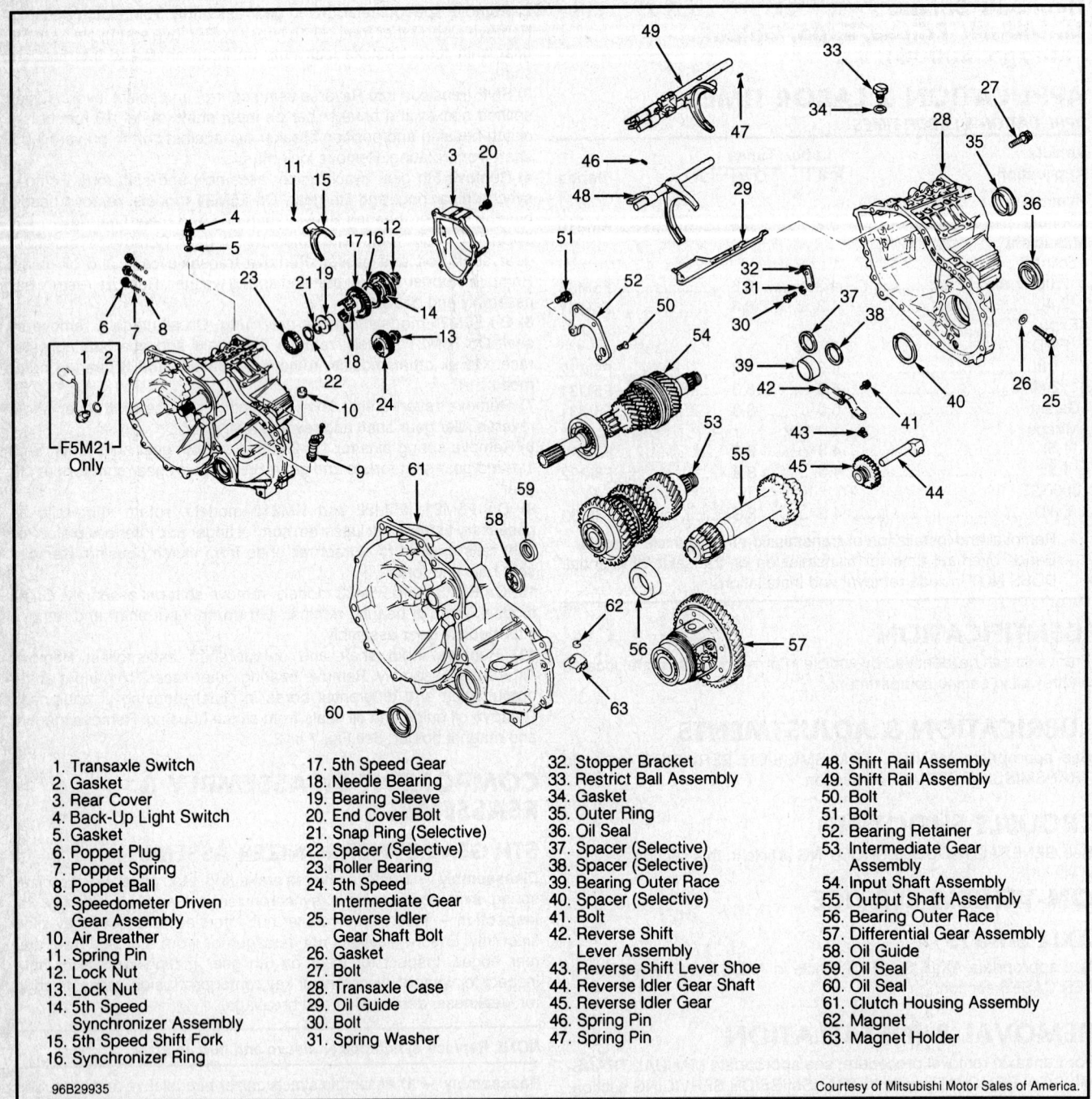

1. Transaxle Switch	17. 5th Speed Gear	32. Stopper Bracket	48. Shift Rail Assembly
2. Gasket	18. Needle Bearing	33. Restrict Ball Assembly	49. Shift Rail Assembly
3. Rear Cover	19. Bearing Sleeve	34. Gasket	50. Bolt
4. Back-Up Light Switch	20. End Cover Bolt	35. Outer Ring	51. Bolt
5. Gasket	21. Snap Ring (Selective)	36. Oil Seal	52. Bearing Retainer
6. Poppet Plug	22. Spacer (Selective)	37. Spacer (Selective)	53. Intermediate Gear
7. Poppet Spring	23. Roller Bearing	38. Spacer (Selective)	Assembly
8. Poppet Ball	24. 5th Speed	39. Bearing Outer Race	54. Input Shaft Assembly
9. Speedometer Driven	Intermediate Gear	40. Spacer (Selective)	55. Output Shaft Assembly
Gear Assembly	25. Reverse Idler	41. Bolt	56. Bearing Outer Race
10. Air Breather	Gear Shaft Bolt	42. Reverse Shift	57. Differential Gear Assembly
11. Spring Pin	26. Gasket	Lever Assembly	58. Oil Guide
12. Lock Nut	27. Bolt	43. Reverse Shift Lever Shoe	59. Oil Seal
13. Lock Nut	28. Transaxle Case	44. Reverse Idler Gear Shaft	60. Oil Seal
14. 5th Speed	29. Oil Guide	45. Reverse Idler Gear	61. Clutch Housing Assembly
Synchronizer Assembly	30. Bolt	46. Spring Pin	62. Magnet
15. 5th Speed Shift Fork	31. Spring Washer	47. Spring Pin	63. Magnet Holder
16. Synchronizer Ring			

96B29935

Courtesy of Mitsubishi Motor Sales of America.

Fig. 1: Exploded View Of Transaxle (F5M21, F5M22 & KM210)

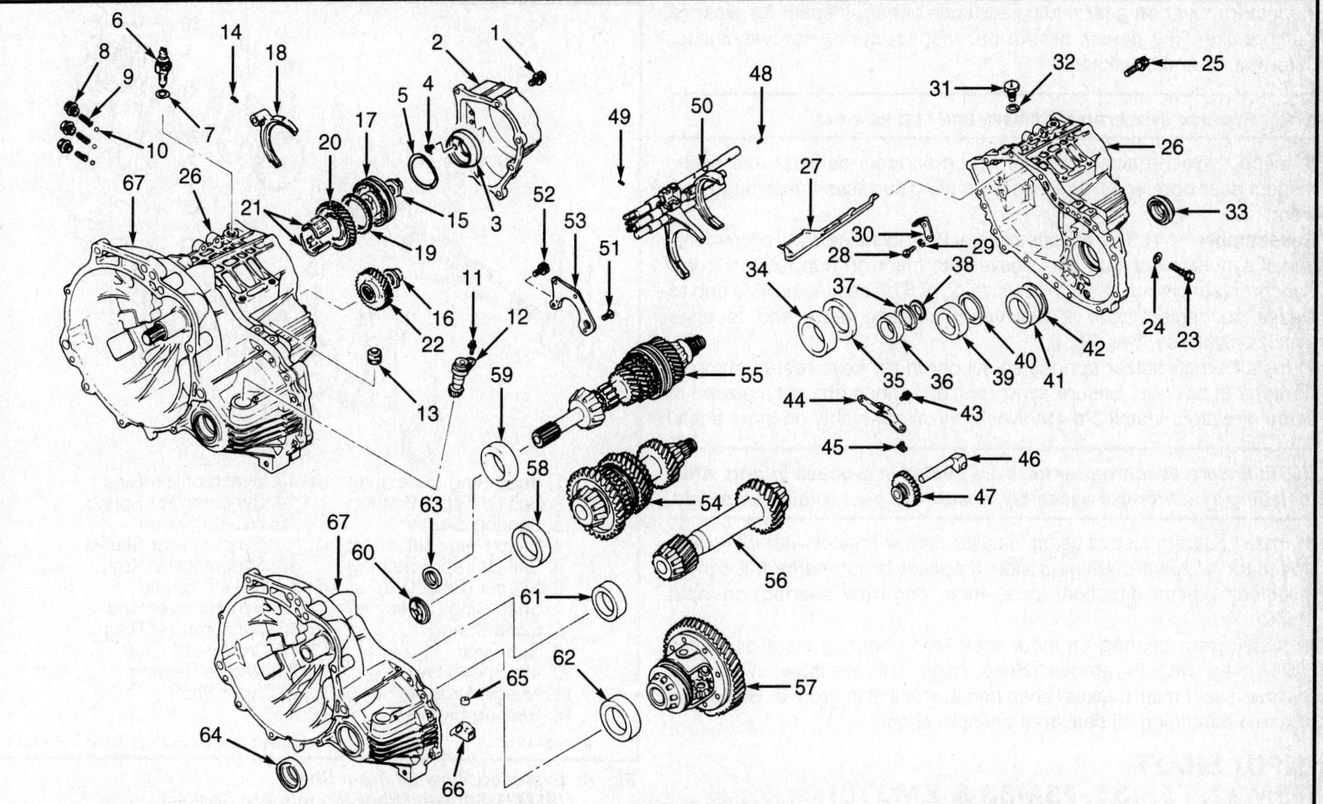

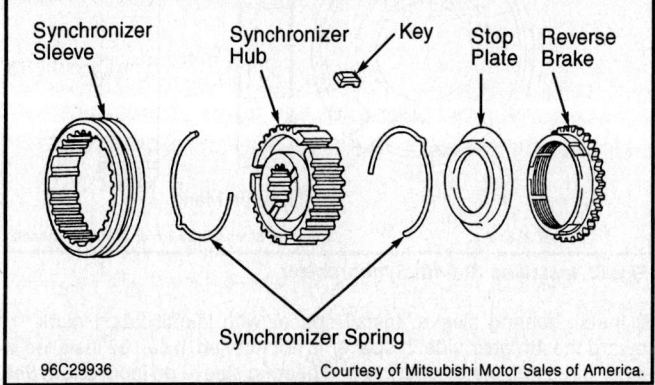

1. Bolt	18. 5th Speed Shift Fork	34. Bearing Outer Race	49. Spring Pin
2. Rear Cover	19. Synchronizer Ring	35. Spacer (Selective)	50. Shift Rail Assembly
3. Reverse Brake Cone	20. 5th Speed Gear	36. Bearing Outer Race	51. Bolt
4. Wave Spring	21. Needle Bearing	37. Spacer (Selective)	52. Bolt
5. Machine Screw	22. 5th Speed	38. Filter (F5M33 Only)	53. Bearing Retainer
6. Back-Up Light Switch	Intermediate Gear	39. Bearing Outer Race	54. Intermediate Gear Assembly
7. Gasket	23. Reverse Idler	(F5M33 Only)	55. Input Shaft Assembly
8. Poppet Plug	Gear Shaft Bolt	40. Spacer (Selective/F5M33 Only)	56. Output Shaft Assembly
9. Poppet Spring	24. Gasket	41. Bearing Outer Race	57. Differential Gear Assembly
10. Poppet Ball	25. Bolt	42. Spacer (Selective)	58. Bearing Outer Race
11. Bolt	26. Transaxle Case	43. Bolt	59. Bearing Outer Race
12. Speedometer Driven	27. Oil Guide	44. Reverse Shift	60. Oil Guide
Gear Assembly	28. Bolt	Lever Assembly	61. Bearing Outer Race
13. Air Breather	29. Spring Washer	45. Reverse Shift	62. Bearing Outer Race
14. Spring Pin	30. Stopper Bracket	Lever Shoe	63. Oil Seal
15. Lock Nut	31. Restrict Ball Assembly	46. Reverse Idler Gear Shaft	64. Oil Seal
16. Lock Nut	32. Gasket	47. Reverse Idler Gear	65. Magnet
17. 5th Speed	33. Oil Seal	48. Spring Pin	66. Magnet Holder
Synchronizer Assembly			67. Clutch Housing Assembly

93B24308

Courtesy of Mitsubishi Motor Sales of America.

Fig. 2: Exploded View Of Transaxle (F5M31 & F5M33)

96C29936   Courtesy of Mitsubishi Motor Sales of America.

Fig. 3: Exploded View Of 5th Synchronizer Assembly

INPUT SHAFT (F5M21)

Disassembly – Remove snap ring. Press front bearing from input shaft. Press inner ring (rear bearing), spacer and 4th gear from input shaft. Press 3rd gear, 3rd-4th synchronizer assembly and bearing sleeve from input shaft. See Fig. 4.

Inspection – 1) Inspect input shaft bearing surfaces for wear, seizure and damage. Inspect shaft splines for damage and wear. Assemble needle bearing to shaft and ensure it rotates smoothly without abnormal noise, roughness or play. Inspect bearing cage for deformation.

2) Inspect synchronizer ring for damaged or broken teeth. Inspect inner surface for damage, wear and broken threads. Force synchronizer ring toward clutch gear and check clearance between gear and synchronizer ring. Replace synchronizer ring if clearance is not at least .020" (.5 mm). See Fig. 5.

3) Insert synchronizer hub into sleeve. Ensure they slide smoothly. Ensure sleeve is not damaged or worn at inside front and rear edges.

Inspect for wear on gear mating surfaces of hub. Inspect for wear of synchronizer key center protrusion. Inspect spring for weakness, deformation and breakage.

NOTE: Replace synchronizer sleeve and hub as a set.

4) Inspect synchronizer cone for rough surface, damage and wear. Inspect gear bore and front and rear mating surfaces for damage and wear.

Reassembly – 1) To reassemble, reverse disassembly procedure. Install synchronizer hub and sleeve with mark on hub toward front. Synchronizer sleeve has a tooth missing at 6 places. Assemble hub to sleeve so center tooth is between 2 missing teeth and touches synchronizer key. *See Fig. 6.*

2) Install synchronizer springs so synchronizer keys rest in stepped portions of springs. Ensure synchronizer springs are not installed in same direction. Install 3rd-4th synchronizer assembly on input shaft.

NOTE: Ensure synchronizer keys are seated in grooves in ring. After installing synchronizer assembly, ensure 3rd gear rotates smoothly.

3) Install bearing sleeve using installer. Install spacer with identification mark "1" toward 4th gear side. If spacer is not marked, it can be installed in either direction. Install inner ring (rear bearing) on input shaft.

4) Install front bearing on input shaft using bearing installer. Install NEW snap ring in groove. Snap rings are available in various thicknesses. Install thickest snap ring that will fit in groove. Be careful to avoid damaging oil seal area on input shaft.

INPUT SHAFT
(F5M22, F5M31, F5M33 & KM210)

Disassembly – Remove snap ring. Press front bearing from input shaft. Press rear bearing and bearing sleeve from input shaft. Remove spacer, 4th gear and bearing. Press bearing sleeve, 3rd-4th synchronizer assembly and 3rd gear from input shaft. Remove needle bearing. *See Fig. 4.*

Inspection – 1) Inspect input shaft bearing surfaces for wear, seizure and damage. Inspect shaft splines for damage and wear. Assemble needle bearing to shaft and ensure it rotates smoothly without abnormal noise, roughness or play. Inspect bearing cage for deformation.

2) Inspect synchronizer ring for damaged or broken teeth and inner surface for damage, wear and broken threads. Force synchronizer ring toward clutch gear and check clearance between gear and synchronizer ring. Replace synchronizer ring if clearance is not at least .020" (.5 mm). *See Fig. 5.*

3) Insert synchronizer hub into sleeve. Ensure they slide smoothly. Ensure sleeve is not damaged or worn at inside front and rear edges. Inspect for wear on gear mating surfaces of hub. Inspect for wear of synchronizer key center protrusion. Inspect spring for weakness, deformation and breakage.

NOTE: Replace synchronizer sleeve and hub as a set.

4) Inspect synchronizer cone for rough surface, damage and wear. Inspect gear bore and front and rear mating surfaces for damage and wear. Inspect bevel gear and clutch gear teeth for damage and wear.

Reassembly – 1) To reassemble, reverse disassembly procedure. Install synchronizer hub and sleeve with mark on hub toward front. Synchronizer sleeve has a tooth missing at 6 places. Assemble hub to sleeve so center tooth is between 2 missing teeth and touches synchronizer key.

2) Install synchronizer springs so synchronizer keys rest in stepped portions in springs. Ensure synchronizer springs are not installed in same direction. Install 3rd-4th synchronizer assembly on input shaft using installer.

NOTE: Ensure synchronizer keys are seated in grooves in ring. After installing synchronizer assembly, ensure 3rd gear rotates smoothly.

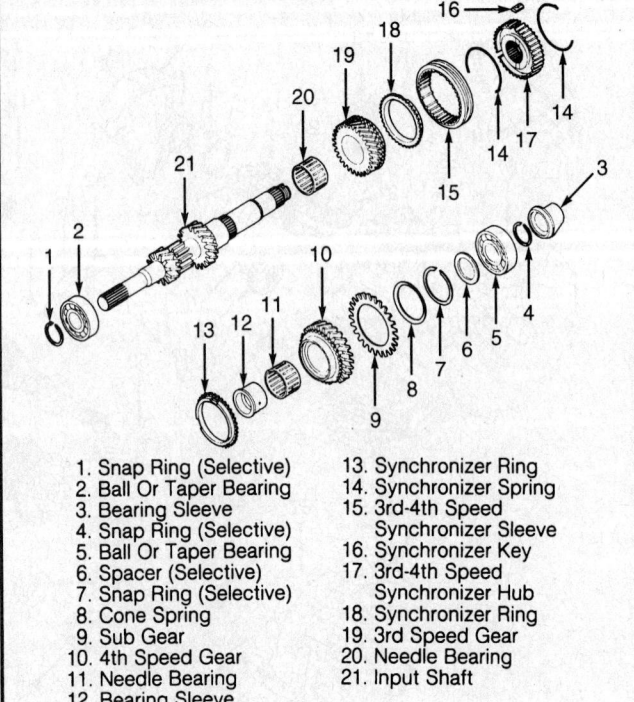

1. Snap Ring (Selective)	13. Synchronizer Ring
2. Ball Or Taper Bearing	14. Synchronizer Spring
3. Bearing Sleeve	15. 3rd-4th Speed
4. Snap Ring (Selective)	Synchronizer Sleeve
5. Ball Or Taper Bearing	16. Synchronizer Key
6. Spacer (Selective)	17. 3rd-4th Speed
7. Snap Ring (Selective)	Synchronizer Hub
8. Cone Spring	18. Synchronizer Ring
9. Sub Gear	19. 3rd Speed Gear
10. 4th Speed Gear	20. Needle Bearing
11. Needle Bearing	21. Input Shaft
12. Bearing Sleeve	

93I24313   Courtesy of Mitsubishi Motor Sales of America.

Fig. 4: Exploded View Of Input Shaft (F5M31 Shown; Other Models Are Similar)

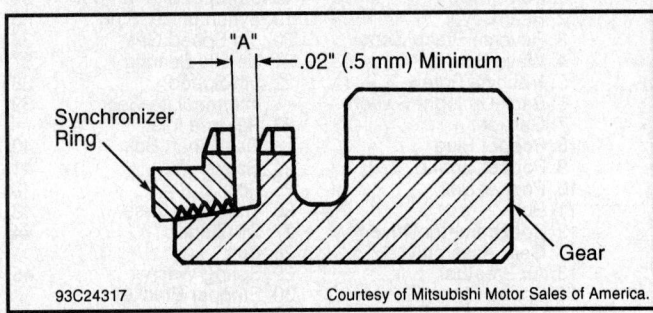

93C24317   Courtesy of Mitsubishi Motor Sales of America.

Fig. 5: Checking Synchronizer-To-Gear Clearance

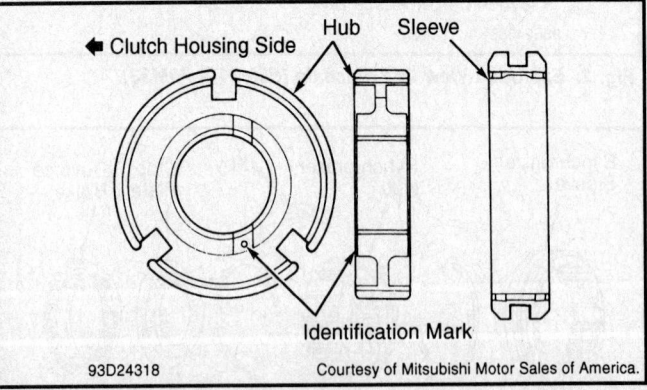

93D24318   Courtesy of Mitsubishi Motor Sales of America.

Fig. 6: Installing 3rd-4th Synchronizer

3) Install bearing sleeve. Install spacer with identification mark "1" toward the 4th gear side. If spacer is not marked, it can be installed in either direction. Install bearing and bearing sleeve on input shaft. *See Fig. 6.*

4) Install front bearing on input shaft. Install NEW snap ring in groove. Snap rings are available in various thicknesses. Install thickest snap ring that will fit in groove. Be careful to avoid damaging oil seal area on input shaft.

INTERMEDIATE GEAR ASSEMBLY

Disassembly – Remove snap ring. Press bearing, bearing sleeve, needle bearing and 1st gear from intermediate gear. DO NOT reuse bearing. Press 1st-2nd synchronizer assembly, 2nd gear and needle bearing from intermediate gear. Press bearing from rear of intermediate gear. See Fig. 7.

Inspection – **1)** Inspect intermediate gear bearing surfaces for damage, wear and seizure. Assemble needle bearing to shaft and ensure it rotates smoothly without abnormal noise, roughness or play. Check bearing cage for deformation.

2) Inspect synchronizer ring for damaged or broken teeth and inner surface for damage, wear and broken threads. Force synchronizer ring toward clutch gear and measure clearance between gear and synchronizer ring. Replace synchronizer ring if clearance is not at least .020" (.5 mm). See Fig. 5.

3) Insert synchronizer hub into sleeve. Ensure they slide smoothly. Ensure sleeve is not damaged or worn at inside front and rear edges. Inspect for wear on gear mating surfaces of hub. Inspect for wear of synchronizer key center protrusion. Inspect spring for weakness, deformation and breakage.

NOTE: Replace synchronizer sleeve and hub as a set.

---

4) Inspect synchronizer cone for rough surface, damage and wear. Inspect gear bore and front and rear mating surfaces for damage and wear. Inspect bevel gear and clutch gear teeth for damage and wear.

Reassembly – **1)** To reassemble, reverse disassembly procedure. Install bearing on intermediate gear using bearing installer. Ensure installer pushes on bearing inner race only.

2) The 1st-2nd synchronizer rings have an identification mark. See Fig. 6. Install synchronizer hub and sleeve with mark on hub toward front. The synchronizer sleeve has a tooth missing at 6 places. Assemble hub to sleeve so center tooth is between 2 missing teeth and touches synchronizer key.

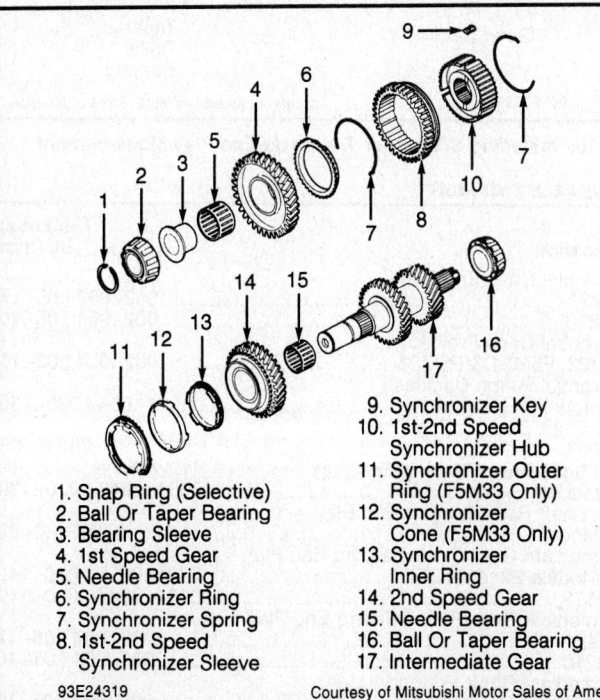

1. Snap Ring (Selective)
2. Ball Or Taper Bearing
3. Bearing Sleeve
4. 1st Speed Gear
5. Needle Bearing
6. Synchronizer Ring
7. Synchronizer Spring
8. 1st-2nd Speed Synchronizer Sleeve
9. Synchronizer Key
10. 1st-2nd Speed Synchronizer Hub
11. Synchronizer Outer Ring (F5M33 Only)
12. Synchronizer Cone (F5M33 Only)
13. Synchronizer Inner Ring
14. 2nd Speed Gear
15. Needle Bearing
16. Ball Or Taper Bearing
17. Intermediate Gear

93E24319   Courtesy of Mitsubishi Motor Sales of America.

Fig. 7: Exploded View Of Intermediate Gear Assembly (F5M33 Shown; Other Models Are Similar)

NOTE: Ensure synchronizer keys are seated in grooves in ring. After installing synchronizer assembly, ensure 3rd gear rotates smoothly.

---

3) Install synchronizer springs so synchronizer keys rest in stepped portions in springs. Ensure synchronizer springs are not installed in same direction. Install 1st-2nd synchronizer assembly on intermediate shaft.

4) Install bearing sleeve. Install 1st gear and bearing sleeve together. Install bearing on intermediate shaft.

OUTPUT SHAFT

Disassembly, Inspection & Reassembly – Press bearings from output shaft. DO NOT reuse bearings. Replace inner and outer bearing races as a set. Inspect output shaft for damage or wear. Press NEW bearings on output shaft. See Fig. 1 or 2.

SHIFT FORK ASSEMBLY (F5M21, F5M22, F5M31, F5M33 & KM210)

Disassembly & Reassembly – Remove 1st-2nd gear shift fork. Remove 1st-2nd gear shift rail. Remove 3rd-4th gear shift fork. Remove 5th-reverse gear shift rail. Remove interlock plunger. Remove 3rd-4th gear shift rail. Remove reverse shift lug. To reassemble, reverse disassembly procedure. Insert interlock plunger in reverse shift lug in 3rd-4th gear shift rail notch. See Fig. 1 or 2.

DIFFERENTIAL ASSEMBLY

Disassembly & Inspection – Remove drive gear. Press bearings from differential case. DO NOT reuse bearings. Remove and discard lock pin from drive gear side of differential case. Remove pinion shaft, pinion gears, washers, side gears and spacers from differential case. See Fig. 8. Inspect all parts for wear and damage. Replace as necessary.

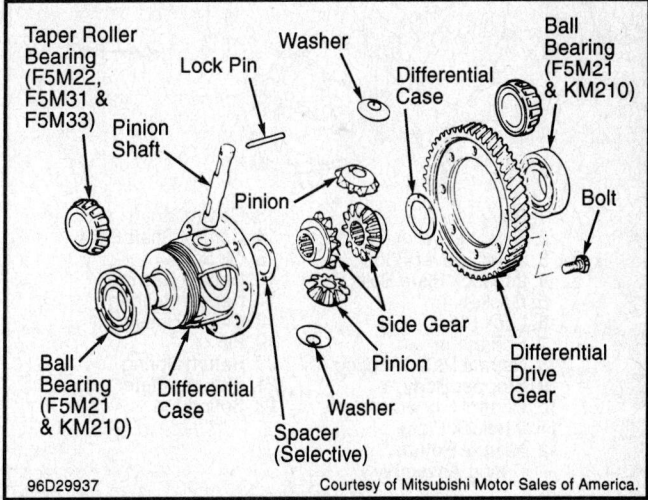

96D29937   Courtesy of Mitsubishi Motor Sales of America.

Fig. 8: Exploded View Of Differential Assembly

Reassembly – **1)** Install spacers on backs of side gears and install side gears in case. Install washers on back of pinion gears. Position pinion gears opposite each other on side gears and rotate them into case. Install pinion shaft. Measure backlash between side and pinion gears. If backlash is not .001-.006" (.025-.150 mm), disassemble and install spacers of correct thickness.

NOTE: If installing new side gears, install spacers of a medium thickness .037-.039" (.93-1.00 mm). Install same thickness spacer on each side gear.

---

2) Align pinion shaft lock pin hole with lock pin hole in case. Install NEW lock pin. Lock pin must not protrude more than .118" (3.00 mm) from differential case.

3) Press NEW bearings on differential case. When installing bearings, press on bearing inner race only. If reusing drive gear bolts, clean thread locking compound from threads. Apply fresh thread locking compound to bolts and torque to specification in a crisscross pattern. See TORQUE SPECIFICATIONS.

CLUTCH HOUSING

Disassembly – **1)** Remove select lever assembly and select lever shoe. Remove interlock plate bolt and gasket. Position control finger so that spring pin will not contact clutch housing. Drive spring pin from control finger using a punch.

2) Remove spacer, control finger, neutral return spring and interlock plate. Using a 13 mm socket and extension bar, remove needle bearings. Remove control shaft, dust boot, oil seal and needle bearing from clutch housing. See Fig. 9.

Reassembly – To reassemble, reverse disassembly procedure. Install needle bearings flush with clutch housing surface using a 14 mm socket and extension bar. Install new oil seal and spring pins. Install lock pins with slit perpendicular to center line of control shaft.

1. Bolt
2. Select Lever Assembly
3. Select Lever Shoe
4. Interlock Plate Bolt
5. Gasket
6. Lock Pin
7. Spring Pin
8. Neutral Return Spring
9. Stopper Body
10. Control Finger
11. Interlock Plate
12. Neutral Return Spring Assembly
13. Control Shaft
14. Control Shaft Boot
15. Oil Seal
16. Needle Bearing
17. Needle Bearing
18. Clutch Housing
19. Pin
20. Return Spring
21. Stopper Plate
22. Spring Pin

96E29938 Courtesy of Mitsubishi Motor Sales of America.

Fig. 9: Exploded View Of Clutch Housing

TRANSAXLE REASSEMBLY

NOTE: Spacers used for preload adjustments and snap rings are available in selective sizes.

1) To reassemble, reverse disassembly procedure. Install drive shaft oil seals. Install input shaft oil seal. Install intermediate shaft and input shaft simultaneously.

2) Apply 3M STUD Locking Sealant (4170) to threads of input shaft bearing retainer bolt closest to differential. DO NOT apply sealant to bolt head. Torque bolts to specification. See TORQUE SPECIFICATIONS.

3) Position 1st-2nd gear shift sleeve in 2nd gear. Position 3rd-4th gear shift sleeve in 4th gear. Fit shift forks of shift rail assembly to groove of sleeves. Insert shift rails into shift rail holes of clutch housing. Rotate shift rails to engage shift lugs to control finger and interlock plate.

4) Using a punch, install NEW spring pins with slit of spring pin on center line of shift rail. Install reverse idler gear shaft with threaded hole in head facing differential case.

5) On KM210 models, place 2 pieces of solder measuring .400" (10 mm) long and .120" (3 mm) diameter on gear shaft outer bearing races and on differential at spacer mounting positions. On all other models, place 2 pieces of solder measuring .400" (10 mm) long and .060" (1.6 mm) diameter at spacer mounting positions. See Fig. 10.

6) Install transaxle case and torque bolts to specification. See TORQUE SPECIFICATIONS. Remove transaxle case. Remove outer races and take out crushed solder. Measure thickness of crushed solder with a micrometer. Select and install spacer that gives correct end play. See TRANSAXLE END PLAY table.

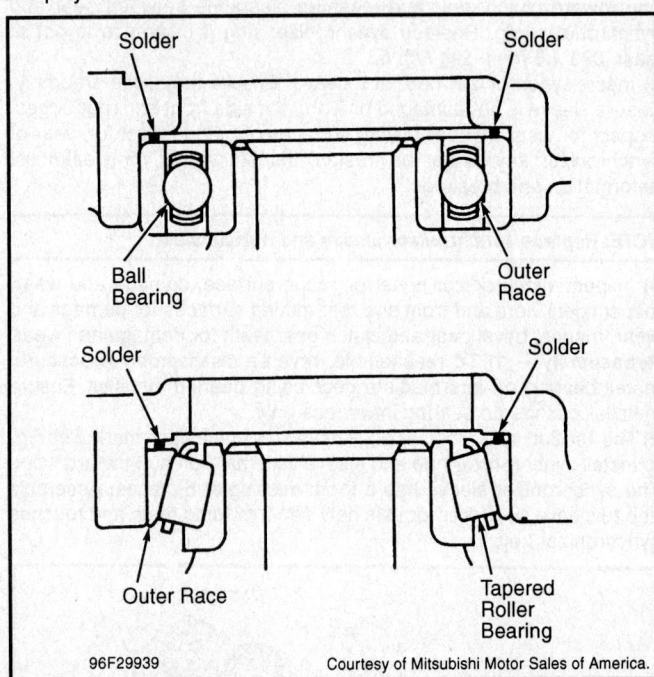

96F29939 Courtesy of Mitsubishi Motor Sales of America.

Fig. 10: Installing Solder For Transaxle End Play Measurement

TRANSAXLE END PLAY

Application	Thickness In. (mm)
Differential Case End Play	
F5M21	.002-.007 (.05-.17)
KM210	.002-.004 (.05-.10)
Differential Case Preload	
F5M22, F5M31 & F5M33	.002-.004 (.05-.10)
Differential Pinion Backlash	
All Models	.001-.006 (.025-.150)
Input Shaft Bearing End Play	
F5M33	0-.002 (0-.05)
Input Shaft Front Bearing End Play	
All Models Except F5M33	.0004-.0047 (.010-.120)
Input Shaft Rear Bearing End Play	
All Models	0-.0035 (0-.09)
Intermediate Gear Front Bearing End Play	
All Models Except F5M31	.0004-.0055 (.010-.140)
F5M31	.0004-.0044 (.010-.110)
Intermediate Gear Rear Bearing End Play	
F5M21	.002-.007 (.05-.17)
KM210	.002-.004 (.05-.10)
Intermediate Shaft Preload	
F5M22, F5M31 & F5M33	.002-.004 (.05-.10)
Output Shaft	
All Models	.002-.004 (.05-.10)

7) Install oil guide into transaxle case. Position selected spacers on intermediate gear and differential bearing outer race. Insert selected spacer between output shaft bearing outer race and transaxle case. Ensure threaded hole of reverse idler gear shaft head is facing correct direction before installing transaxle case.

8) Apply .039-.079" (1.0-2.0 mm) bead of Mitsubishi Sealant (MD997740) or Three Bond (1216) to clutch housing side of transaxle case. Apply an even bead of sealer. Install transaxle case to clutch housing.

9) Using a Phillips screwdriver (or suitable drift pin) with a .315" (8.0 mm) diameter, align threaded hole in reverse idler gear shaft with bolt hole in transaxle case. Install reverse idler gear shaft bolt and tighten to specifications. Torque all transaxle case bolts to specification. See TORQUE SPECIFICATIONS.

10) On models with snap rings, select thickest snap ring available that will fit in groove. DO NOT reuse old snap ring. Install bearing sleeve on input shaft. Ensure sleeve flange fits tightly against bearing.

11) Install 5th gear shift fork and synchronizer simultaneously. Install splined socket and breaker bar on input shaft. Install 10 mm bolt in clutch housing and position breaker bar against 10 mm bolt to keep input shaft from rotating.

12) Shift transaxle into reverse using control and select levers. Install NEW lock nuts and torque to specification. Stake lock nuts. Install NEW spring pin in 5th gear shift fork. Align slit in spring pin with shift rail center line.

13) Apply 3M Super Weatherstrip sealant (8001) to air breather mounting portion and install in clutch housing. Apply Mitsubishi Sealant (MD997740) or Three Bond (1216) to rear cover. Apply sealer bead uniformly, without excess or discontinuity, approximately .04-.08" (1-2 mm) in diameter. Install rear cover.

TORQUE SPECIFICATIONS
TORQUE SPECIFICATIONS

Application	Ft. Lbs. (N.m)
Back-Up Light Switch	22-26 (30-35)
Bearing Retainer Bolt	12-16 (16-22)
Differential Drive Gear Bolt	96-103 (130-140)
Drain Plug	22-26 (30-35)
Filler Plug	22-26 (30-35)
Input Shaft Lock Nut	103-118 (140-160)
Interlock Plate Bolt	15-20 (20-27)
Intermediate Shaft Lock Nut	103-118 (140-160)
Lower Control Arm Ball Joint-To-Knuckle	44-53 (60-72)
Poppet Plug	22-31 (30-42)
Rear Cover Bolt	11-16 (15-22)
Restrict Ball Assembly	22-26 (30-35)
Reverse Idler Gear Shaft Bolt	32-41 (43-55)
Reverse Shift Lever Assembly Attaching Bolt	11-16 (15-22)
Stopper Bracket Bolt	11-16 (15-22)
Transaxle Bracket-To-Transaxle	44-59 (60-80)
Transaxle Mount Bolt	
12 mm	32-39 (43-53)
10 mm	22-26 (30-35)
6-8 mm	7-9 (10-12)
Transaxle Mounting Bracket-To-Transaxle	44-59 (60-80)
Transaxle Case Tightening Bolt	26-31 (35-42)
Transaxle Switch	24 (33)

Application	INCH Lbs. (N.m)
Bellhousing Cover-To-Transaxle	71-89 (8-10)
Clutch Tube Flare Nut (1.6L)	115-150 (13-17)
Lever Assembly-To-Body	84-124 (9-14)
Select & Shift Cable Guide	84-124 (9-14)
Speedometer Sleeve Bolt	27-44 (3-5)

MANUAL TRANSMISSIONS
Mitsubishi R5M21 5-Speed

Pickup

APPLICATION & LABOR TIMES

APPLICATION & LABOR TIMES

Vehicle Application	Labor Times		Series
	[1] R & I	[2] Overhaul	
Pickup	3.6	3.4	R5M21

[1] – Removal and installation of transmission from vehicle chassis.
[2] – Bench overhaul time for transmission. DOES NOT include removal and installation.

IDENTIFICATION

Transmission is identified by vehicle information code plate riveted to firewall in engine compartment.

LUBRICATION & ADJUSTMENTS

See appropriate MANUAL TRANSMISSION SERVICING article in TRANSMISSION SERVICING section.

TROUBLE SHOOTING

See GENERAL TROUBLE SHOOTING article in this section.

ON-VEHICLE SERVICE

REMOVAL & INSTALLATION

For transmission removal procedure, see appropriate MANUAL TRANSMISSION REMOVAL article in TRANSMISSION SERVICING section.

TRANSMISSION DISASSEMBLY

1) Remove bolt, sleeve clamp and speedometer assembly. *See Fig. 1.* Remove back-up light switch, gasket and ball. Remove spring, ball, plugs, springs, neutral plungers "A" and "B". Remove bolts, extension housing and extension gasket. Remove snap ring, mainshaft rear bearing and snap ring.

2) Remove bolts, undercover and undercover gasket. Remove poppet plugs, poppet springs and balls. *See Fig. 2.* Drive out shift fork spring pins. Remove OD-R shift rail, 3rd-4th shift rail and OD-R shift fork.

3) Unstake countershaft lock nut. Shift OD-R synchronizer sleeve to reverse side and 1st-2nd synchronizer sleeve to 2nd gear side. Remove countershaft lock nut. Remove counter overdrive gear and ball bearing. Remove 1st-2nd shift rail and interlock plungers.

4) Unstake mainshaft lock nut and remove lock nut. Remove spacer, reverse idler gear, spacer, sleeve, ball, overdrive gear and needle bearing. *See Fig. 3.*

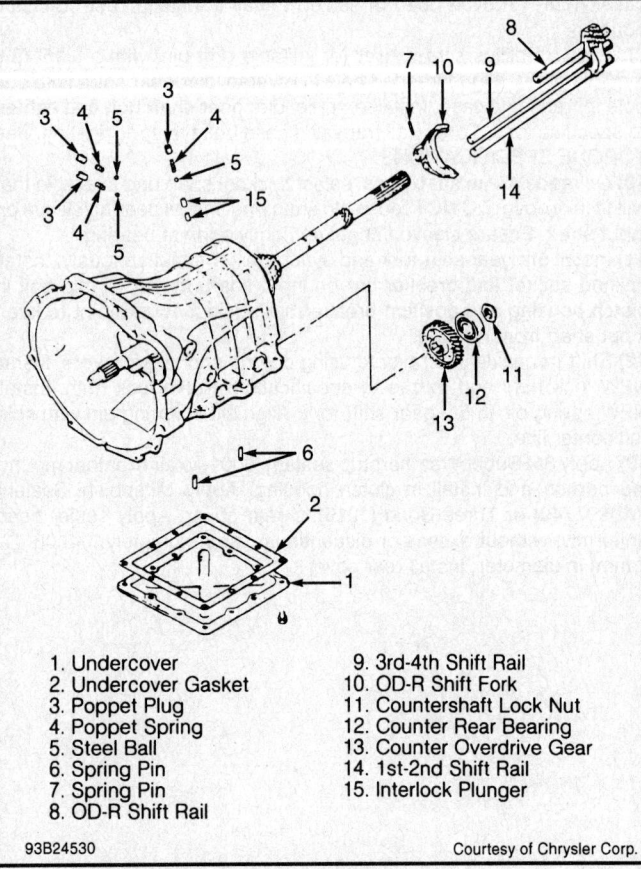

1. Undercover	9. 3rd-4th Shift Rail
2. Undercover Gasket	10. OD-R Shift Fork
3. Poppet Plug	11. Countershaft Lock Nut
4. Poppet Spring	12. Counter Rear Bearing
5. Steel Ball	13. Counter Overdrive Gear
6. Spring Pin	14. 1st-2nd Shift Rail
7. Spring Pin	15. Interlock Plunger
8. OD-R Shift Rail	

93B24530   Courtesy of Chrysler Corp.

Fig. 2: Disassembling Transmission Case

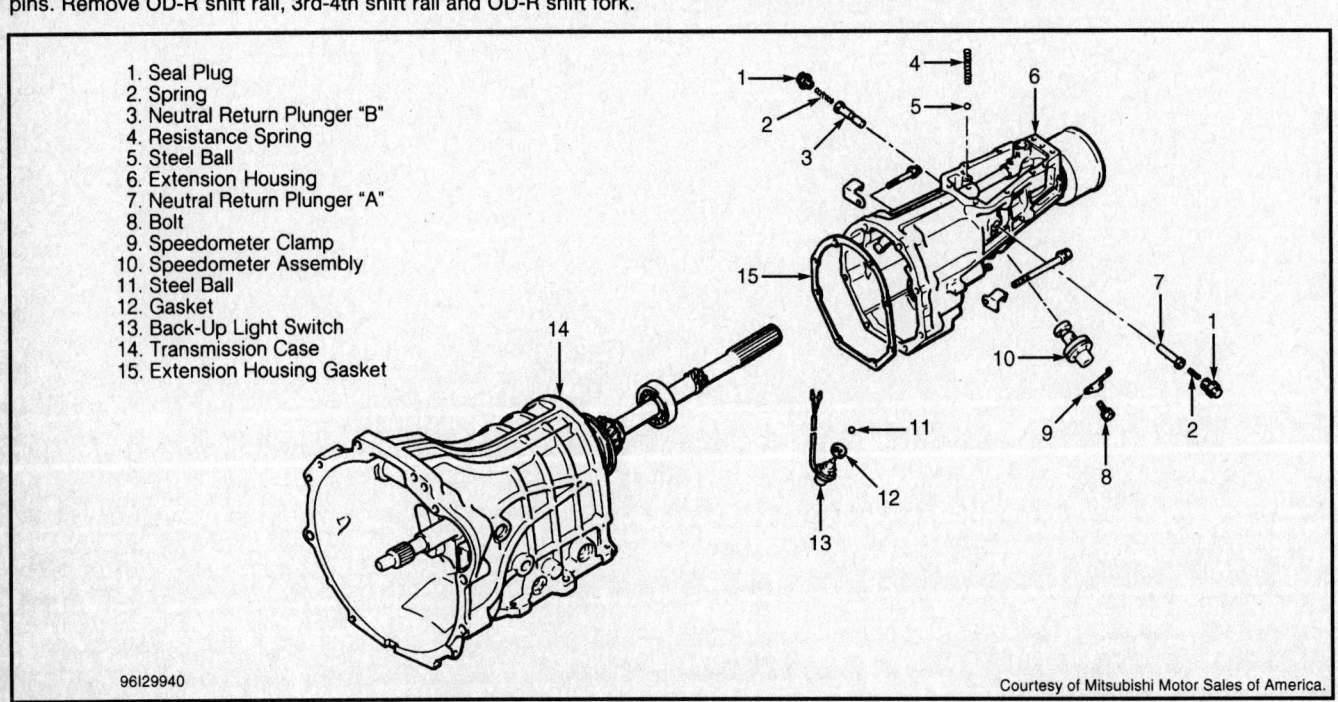

1. Seal Plug
2. Spring
3. Neutral Return Plunger "B"
4. Resistance Spring
5. Steel Ball
6. Extension Housing
7. Neutral Return Plunger "A"
8. Bolt
9. Speedometer Clamp
10. Speedometer Assembly
11. Steel Ball
12. Gasket
13. Back-Up Light Switch
14. Transmission Case
15. Extension Housing Gasket

96I29940   Courtesy of Mitsubishi Motor Sales of America.

Fig. 1: Removing & Installing Extension Housing

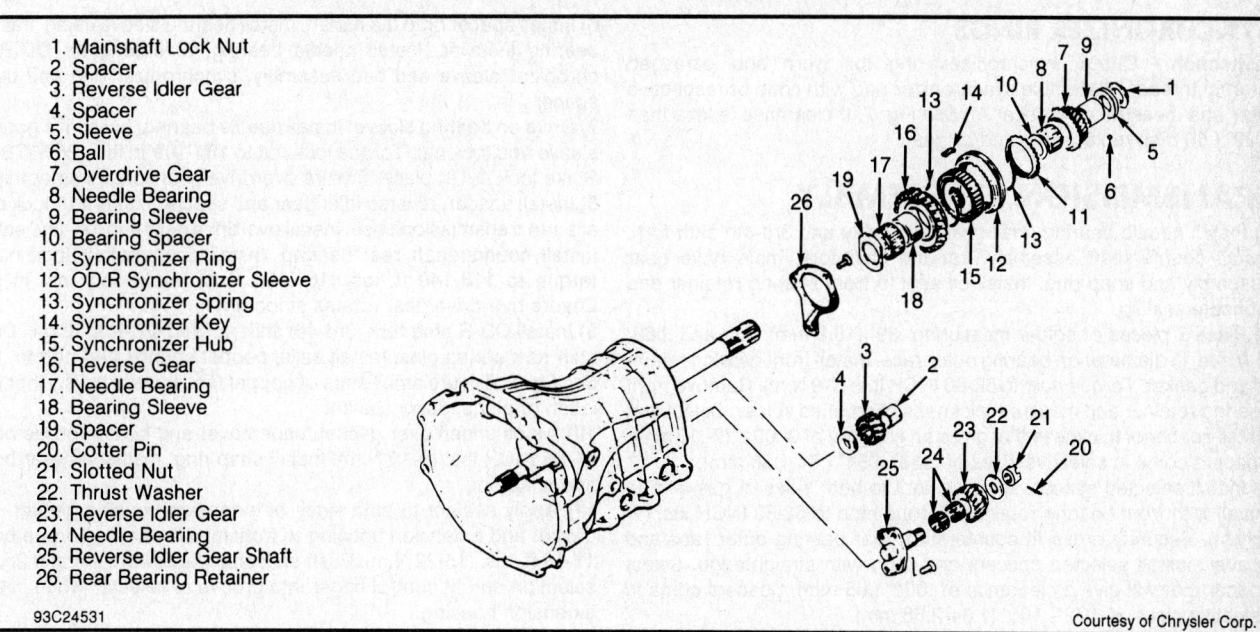

1. Mainshaft Lock Nut
2. Spacer
3. Reverse Idler Gear
4. Spacer
5. Sleeve
6. Ball
7. Overdrive Gear
8. Needle Bearing
9. Bearing Sleeve
10. Bearing Spacer
11. Synchronizer Ring
12. OD-R Synchronizer Sleeve
13. Synchronizer Spring
14. Synchronizer Key
15. Synchronizer Hub
16. Reverse Gear
17. Needle Bearing
18. Bearing Sleeve
19. Spacer
20. Cotter Pin
21. Slotted Nut
22. Thrust Washer
23. Reverse Idler Gear
24. Needle Bearing
25. Reverse Idler Gear Shaft
26. Rear Bearing Retainer

93C24531   Courtesy of Chrysler Corp.

Fig. 3: Removing & Installing Mainshaft Gear

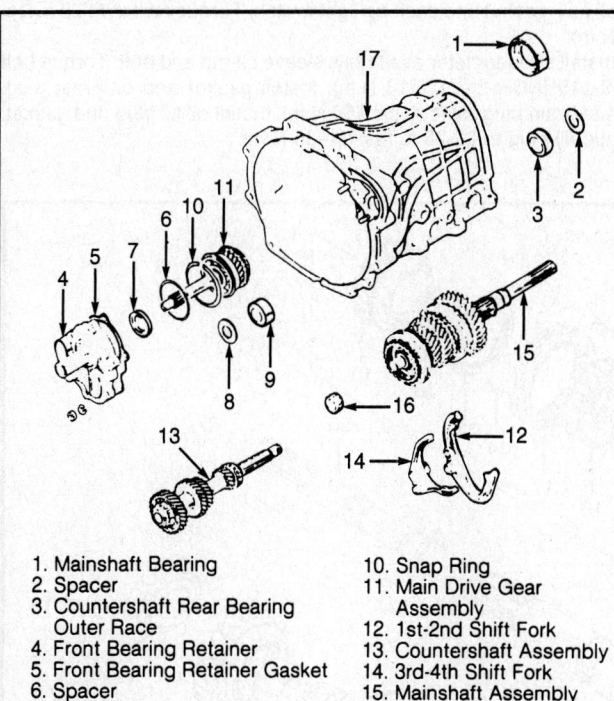

1. Mainshaft Bearing
2. Spacer
3. Countershaft Rear Bearing Outer Race
4. Front Bearing Retainer
5. Front Bearing Retainer Gasket
6. Spacer
7. Oil Seal
8. Spacer
9. Countershaft Front Bearing Outer Race
10. Snap Ring
11. Main Drive Gear Assembly
12. 1st-2nd Shift Fork
13. Countershaft Assembly
14. 3rd-4th Shift Fork
15. Mainshaft Assembly
16. Needle Bearing
17. Transmission Case

93D24532   Courtesy of Chrysler Corp.

Fig. 4: Removing & Installing Main Drive Gear Assembly

5) Remove bearing sleeve, bearing spacer, synchronizer ring, OD-R synchronizer sleeve and hub assembly and reverse gear. Remove needle bearing, bearing sleeve and spacer.
6) Remove cotter pin, slotted nut, thrust washer, reverse idler gear and needle bearings. Remove reverse idler gear shaft mounting bolts and drive out reverse idler gear shaft from inside case. Remove bolts and rear bearing retainer.

7) Remove mainshaft bearing snap ring. Remove mainshaft rear bearing. See Fig. 4. Remove spacer and countershaft rear bearing outer race. Remove nuts, front bearing retainer, front bearing retainer gasket, spacer, oil seal, spacer and countershaft front bearing outer race.
8) Remove snap ring and main drive gear assembly, 1st-2nd shift fork and countershaft assembly. Remove 3rd-4th shift fork, mainshaft assembly and needle bearing.

COMPONENT DISASSEMBLY & REASSEMBLY

MAIN DRIVE GEAR ASSEMBLY

Disassembly & Reassembly – Remove snap ring. Remove bearing from main drive gear. Install bearing onto main drive gear. Select and install thickest snap ring that will fit into snap ring groove. Standard clearance between bearing and snap ring is 0-.002" (0-.06 mm).

MAINSHAFT ASSEMBLY

Disassembly – 1) Remove as an assembly ball bearing inner race, 1st gear, bearing sleeve, needle bearing, 1st-2nd synchronizer sleeve with hub assembly and 2nd gear. See Fig. 5. Remove needle bearing.
2) Remove snap ring, synchronizer ring, 3rd-4th synchronizer sleeve and hub assembly, synchronizer ring, needle bearing and 3rd gear from mainshaft.

Reassembly – To reassemble, reverse disassembly procedure. Install ball bearing inner race. Select and install thickest snap ring that will fit in snap ring groove.

COUNTERSHAFT ASSEMBLY

Disassembly & Reassembly – Remove countershaft front bearing and countershaft center bearing. Install countershaft front bearing. Install countershaft center bearing.

SYNCHRONIZER SLEEVE & HUB ASSEMBLIES

Disassembly & Reassembly – Remove synchronizer springs, keys and synchronizer sleeves from synchronizer hubs. Install synchronizer sleeves to synchronizer hubs. Ensure position is correct. See Fig. 6. Install keys and synchronizer springs. Ensure steps of springs are positioned on keys, but not on same key.

SYNCHRONIZER RINGS

Inspection – Check synchronizer ring for worn and damaged internal threads. Assemble synchronizer ring with cone of respective gear and measure clearance "A". *See Fig. 7.* If clearance is less than .020" (.50 mm) replace ring and/or gear.

TRANSMISSION REASSEMBLY

1) Install needle bearing, mainshaft assembly and 3rd-4th shift fork. Install countershaft assembly, 1st-2nd shift fork, main drive gear assembly and snap ring. Install oil seal to front bearing retainer and lubricate seal lip.

2) Place 2 pieces of solder measuring .39" (10.0 mm) long and .063" (1.0 mm) in diameter on bearing outer race. Install front bearing retainer and gasket. Torque nuts to 62-80 INCH lbs. (7-9 N.m). Remove front bearing retainer and measure thickness of crushed solder. Select and install spacer of thickness that gives an end play of 0-.004" (0-.10 mm). Spacers come in selective sizes of .033"-.054" (.84-1.38 mm).

3) Install selected spacer, apply sealant to both sides of gasket and install with front bearing retainer. Torque nuts to 62-80 INCH lbs. (7-9 N.m). Securely press fit countershaft rear bearing outer race and spacer. Install selected spacers and align with straightedge. Select spacer that will give a clearance of .002" (.05 mm). Spacers come in selective sizes of .072"-.106" (1.84-2.68 mm).

4) Install snap ring onto mainshaft bearing and drive bearing into transmission case. Apply sealant to both sides of front bearing retainer gasket and affix to front bearing retainer. Install rear bearing retainer and apply locking compound to threads of bolts. Torque bolts to 11-15 ft. lbs. (15-20 N.m).

5) Use bolt as guide and tap in reverse idler gear shaft. Apply locking compound to threads of bolts and torque to 11-15 ft. lbs. (15-20 N.m). Install needle bearings, reverse idler gear, thrust washer and slotted nut. Torque slotted nut to 15-44 ft. lbs. (20-60 N.m). Install cotter pin.

6) Install spacer onto mainshaft. Install bearing sleeve using mainshaft bearing installer. Install needle bearing, reverse gear, OD-R synchronizer sleeve and hub assembly, synchronizer ring and bearing spacer.

7) Drive on bearing sleeve. Install needle bearing, overdrive gear, ball, sleeve and lock nut. Torque lock nut to 184-199 ft. lbs. (250-270 N.m). Stake lock nut in place. Ensure overdrive gear rotates smoothly.

8) Install spacer, reverse idler gear and spacer. Install interlock plungers into transmission case. Install overdrive gear and 1st-2nd shift rail. Install countershaft rear bearing. Install countershaft lock nut and torque to 118-140 ft. lbs. (160-190 N.m). Stake lock nut in place. Ensure overdrive gear rotates smoothly.

9) Install OD-R shift fork, 3rd-4th shift rail and OD-R shift rail. Drive in shift fork spring pins. Install balls, poppet springs and poppet plugs. *See Fig. 8.* Ensure small ends of poppet face toward balls. After installation of plugs, apply sealant.

10) Install undercover gasket, undercover and bolts. Torque bolts to 71-89 INCH lbs. (8-10 N.m). Install snap ring, mainshaft rear bearing and snap ring.

11) Apply sealant to both sides of extension housing gasket. Install gasket and extension housing to transmission case. Torque bolts to 11-16 ft. lbs. (15-22 N.m). Push shift changer toward 1st and 2nd gear selection and fit control finger into groove in selector when installing extension housing.

12) Install neutral return plungers "A" and "B", springs and seal plugs. Torque plugs to 15 ft. lbs. (20 N.m). Install ball and resistance spring. Install ball, gasket and back-up light switch. Torque switch to 22 ft. lbs. (30 N.m).

13) Install speedometer assembly, sleeve clamp and bolt. Torque bolt to 89-115 INCH lbs. (10-13 N.m). Install gasket and oil drain plug. Torque drain plug to 44 ft. lbs. (60 N.m). Install oil fill plug and gasket. Torque fill plug to 22-26 ft. lbs. (30-35 N.m).

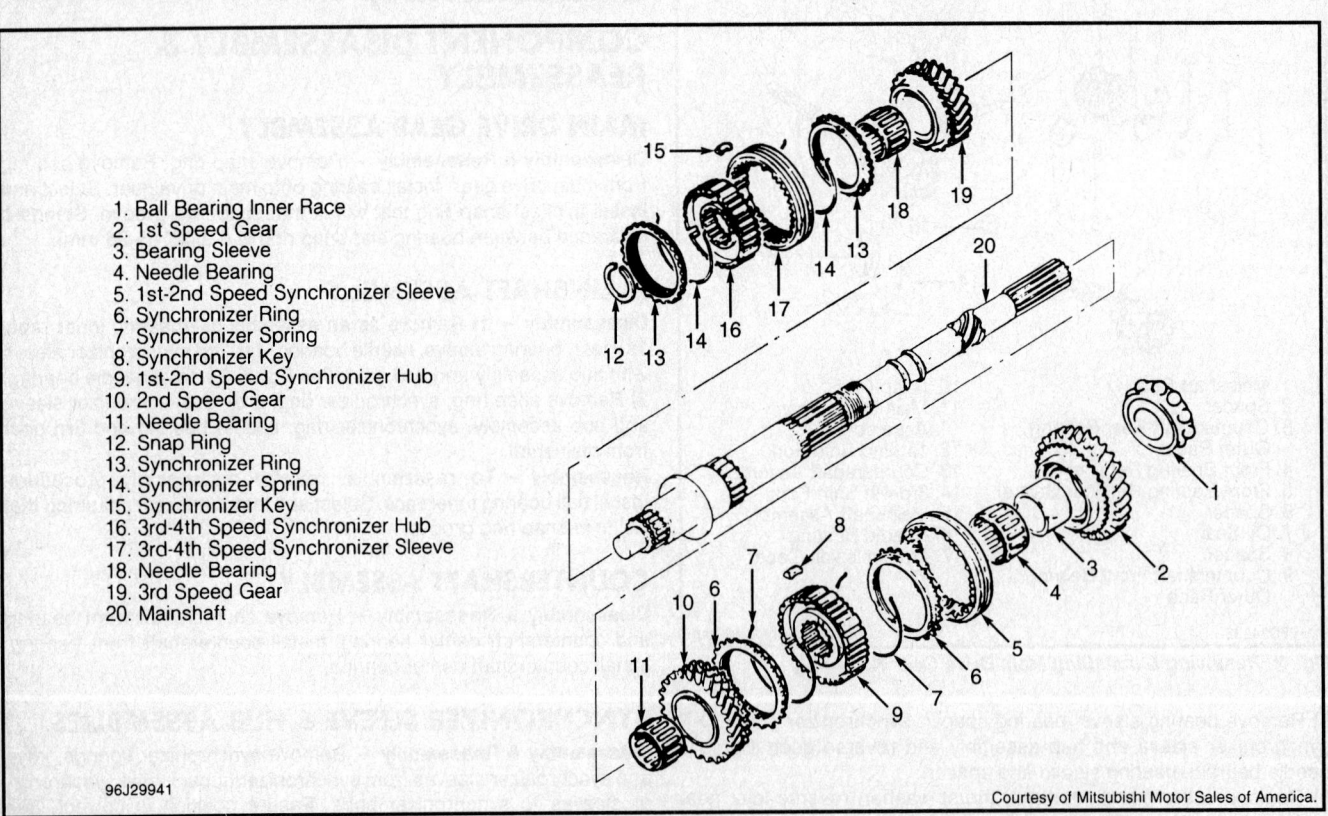

1. Ball Bearing Inner Race
2. 1st Speed Gear
3. Bearing Sleeve
4. Needle Bearing
5. 1st-2nd Speed Synchronizer Sleeve
6. Synchronizer Ring
7. Synchronizer Spring
8. Synchronizer Key
9. 1st-2nd Speed Synchronizer Hub
10. 2nd Speed Gear
11. Needle Bearing
12. Snap Ring
13. Synchronizer Ring
14. Synchronizer Spring
15. Synchronizer Key
16. 3rd-4th Speed Synchronizer Hub
17. 3rd-4th Speed Synchronizer Sleeve
18. Needle Bearing
19. 3rd Speed Gear
20. Mainshaft

96J29941

Courtesy of Mitsubishi Motor Sales of America.

Fig. 5: Exploded View Of Mainshaft Assembly

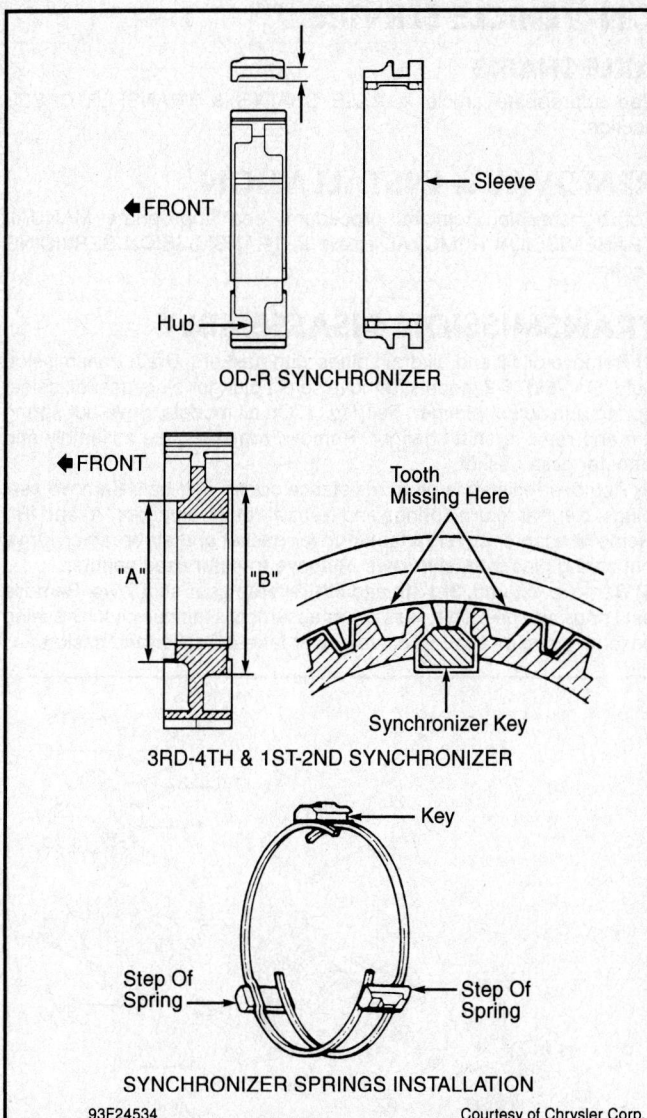

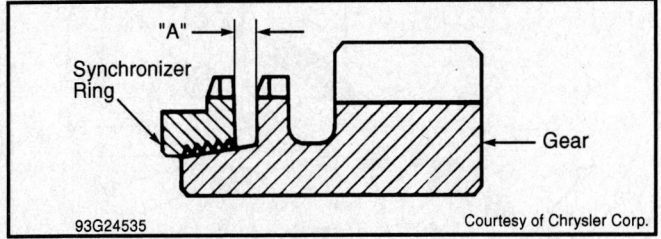

Fig. 6: *Identifying Synchronizer Sleeve & Hub Assembly*

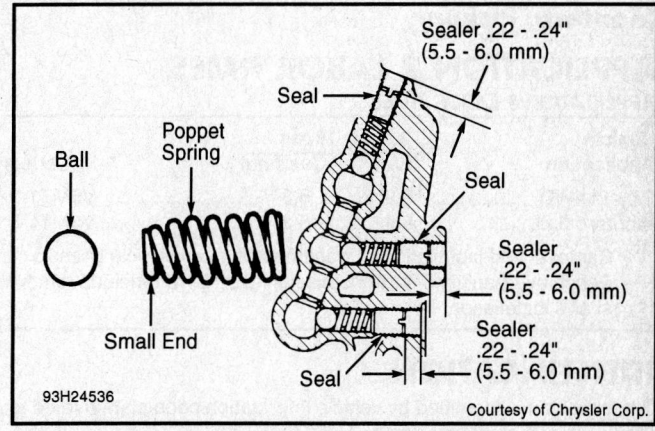

Fig. 8: *Installing Ball, Poppet Spring & Poppet Plug*

TORQUE SPECIFICATIONS

TORQUE SPECIFICATIONS

Application	Ft. Lbs. (N.m)
Back-Up Light Switch	22 (30)
Countershaft Lock Nut	118-140 (160-190)
Extension Housing Bolts	11-16 (15-22)
Mainshaft Lock Nut	184-199 (250-270)
Neutral Return Seal Plugs	15 (20)
Oil Drain Plug	44 (60)
Oil Fill Plug	22-26 (30-35)
Rear Bearing Retainer Bolts	11-15 (15-20)
Reverse Idler Gear Shaft Bolts	11-15 (15-20)
Reverse Idler Gear Slotted Nut	15-32 (20-44)
Select Plug	22-26 (30-35)
	INCH Lbs. (N.m)
Front Bearing Retainer Nuts	62-80 (7-9)
Speedometer Sleeve Clamp Bolt	89-115 (10-13)
Undercover Bolts	71-89 (8-10)

Fig. 7: *Measuring Synchronizer Ring Clearance*

MANUAL TRANSMISSIONS
Mitsubishi V5MT1 5-Speed

Montero, Pickup

APPLICATION & LABOR TIMES

APPLICATION & LABOR TIMES

Vehicle Application	Labor Times		Series
	¹ R & I	² Overhaul	
Pickup 4WD	5.9	5.3	V5MT1-2
Montero 3.0L	8.9	5.3	V5MT1-6

¹ – Removal and installation of transmission from vehicle chassis.
² – Bench overhaul time for transmission. DOES NOT include removal and installation.

IDENTIFICATION

Transmission is identified by vehicle information code plate riveted to firewall in engine compartment.

LUBRICATION & ADJUSTMENTS

See appropriate MANUAL TRANSMISSION SERVICING article in TRANSMISSION SERVICING section.

TROUBLE SHOOTING

See GENERAL TROUBLE SHOOTING article in this section.

ON-VEHICLE SERVICE

AXLE SHAFTS

See appropriate article in AXLE SHAFTS & TRANSFER CASES section.

REMOVAL & INSTALLATION

For transmission removal procedure, see appropriate MANUAL TRANSMISSION REMOVAL article in TRANSMISSION SERVICING section.

TRANSMISSION DISASSEMBLY

1) Remove oil fill and oil drain plugs with gaskets. Drain transmission fluid. On V5MT1-2 models, remove select plunger plug, gasket, select spring and select plunger. *See Fig. 1.* On all models, drive out spring pin and remove shift changer. Remove transfer case assembly and transfer case gasket.

2) Remove resistance plug, resistance spring and ball. Remove seal plugs, Neutral return springs and Neutral return plungers "A" and "B". Remove adapter cover, adapter cover gasket and air breather. Drive out spring pins from shift jaws. Remove transfer case adapter.

3) Remove 1st-2nd, 3rd-4th and 5th-reverse gear shift jaws. Remove seal rings and gear shift case cover assembly. Remove clutch housing assembly and oil seal. Remove power take-off cover and gasket.

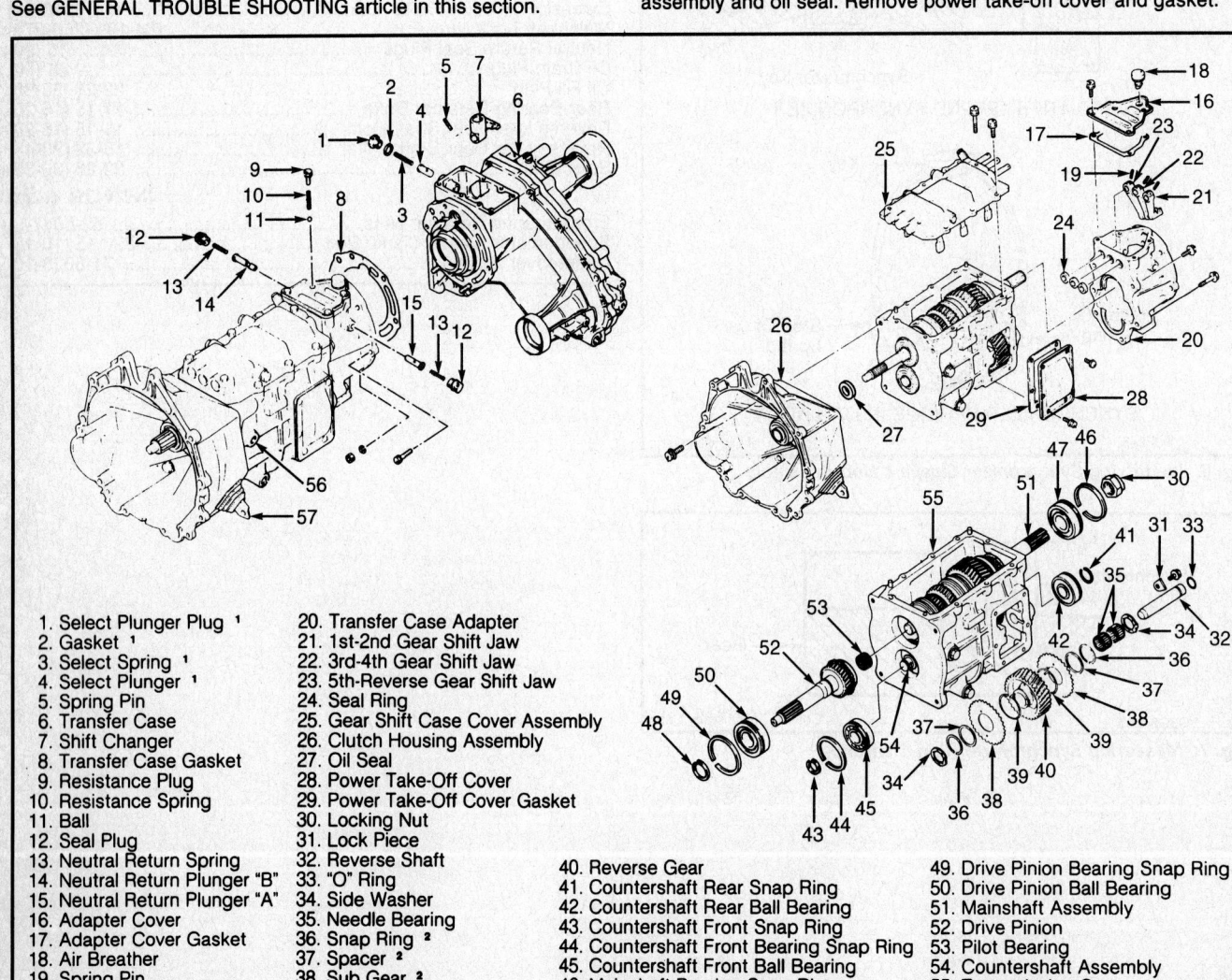

1. Select Plunger Plug ¹	20. Transfer Case Adapter
2. Gasket ¹	21. 1st-2nd Gear Shift Jaw
3. Select Spring ¹	22. 3rd-4th Gear Shift Jaw
4. Select Plunger ¹	23. 5th-Reverse Gear Shift Jaw
5. Spring Pin	24. Seal Ring
6. Transfer Case	25. Gear Shift Case Cover Assembly
7. Shift Changer	26. Clutch Housing Assembly
8. Transfer Case Gasket	27. Oil Seal
9. Resistance Plug	28. Power Take-Off Cover
10. Resistance Spring	29. Power Take-Off Cover Gasket
11. Ball	30. Locking Nut
12. Seal Plug	31. Lock Piece
13. Neutral Return Spring	32. Reverse Shaft
14. Neutral Return Plunger "B"	33. "O" Ring
15. Neutral Return Plunger "A"	34. Side Washer
16. Adapter Cover	35. Needle Bearing
17. Adapter Cover Gasket	36. Snap Ring ²
18. Air Breather	37. Spacer ²
19. Spring Pin	38. Sub Gear ²
	39. Spring ²
¹ – V5MT1-2 Only.	
	² – V5MT1-6 Only.

40. Reverse Gear	49. Drive Pinion Bearing Snap Ring
41. Countershaft Rear Snap Ring	50. Drive Pinion Ball Bearing
42. Countershaft Rear Ball Bearing	51. Mainshaft Assembly
43. Countershaft Front Snap Ring	52. Drive Pinion
44. Countershaft Front Bearing Snap Ring	53. Pilot Bearing
45. Countershaft Front Ball Bearing	54. Countershaft Assembly
46. Mainshaft Bearing Snap Ring	55. Transmission Case
47. Mainshaft Ball Bearing	56. Oil Fill Hole
48. Drive Pinion Snap Ring	57. Oil Drain Hole

Courtesy of Mitsubishi Motor Sales of America

96B29943

Fig. 1: Exploded View Of Transmission With Transfer Case

4) Slide 1st-2nd synchronizer sleeve to 1st gear side and 5th-reverse synchronizer sleeve to reverse gear side to lock mainshaft. Remove mainshaft lock nut. Remove reverse shaft lock piece. Install slide hammer to reverse shaft and remove reverse shaft. Remove "O" ring from shaft and side washers and needle bearings. On V5MT1-6 models, remove snap ring, spacer, sub gear and spring. On all models, remove reverse gear.

5) Remove countershaft rear snap ring and countershaft rear ball bearing. Remove countershaft front snap ring and countershaft front bearing.

6) Remove mainshaft bearing snap ring and mainshaft ball bearing. Remove drive pinion snap ring and drive pinion bearing snap ring. Remove drive pinion ball bearing.

7) Pull drive pinion to front of case. *See Fig. 2.* Remove mainshaft assembly from case. Remove drive pinion from inside of case.

8) Move snap ring from groove toward countershaft reverse gear. Move overdrive gear toward countershaft reverse gear. Move countershaft assembly toward rear of case, lift front of countershaft up and out to remove.

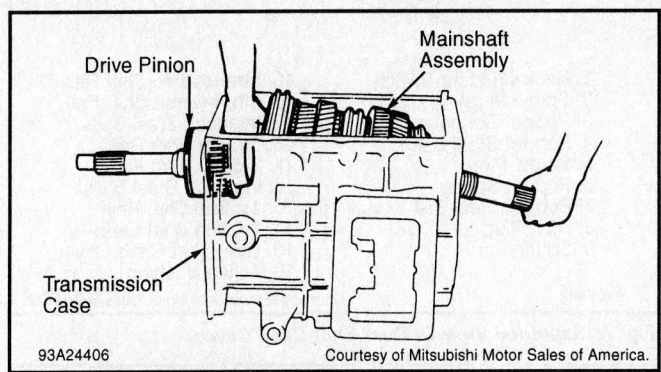

Fig. 2: Removal & Installation Of Drive Pinion & Mainshaft Assembly

COMPONENT DISASSEMBLY & REASSEMBLY

MAINSHAFT ASSEMBLY

Disassembly – **1)** Remove thrust washer No. 3, overdrive gear, needle bearing, synchronizer ring, snap ring, 5th-reverse synchronizer sleeve and hub assembly, reverse gear and needle bearing. *See Fig. 3.*

2) Remove front snap ring and synchronizer ring. Remove 3rd-4th synchronizer sleeve and hub assembly. Remove 3rd gear, needle bearing, thrust washer No. 1 and steel ball. Remove snap ring, thrust washer No. 2, 2nd gear, needle bearing and snap ring. Remove synchronizer ring, 1st-2nd synchronizer sleeve and hub assembly, 1st gear and needle bearing.

NOTE: Use transmission fluid to clean synchro ring composite lining.

Inspection – On V5MT1-2 models, check synchronizer rings for worn and damaged internal threads. Measure clearance "A" of each synchronizer ring and respective gear. *See Fig. 4.* If clearance is less than .008" (.20 mm) replace synchronizer ring and/or gear. On V5MT1-6 models, install inner and outer synchronizer rings and cone to gear. Measure clearance "B" of synchronizer rings. *See Fig. 5.* If clearance is less than .012" (.30 mm), replace synchronizer rings and cone as a unit.

Reassembly – To reassemble mainshaft, reverse disassembly procedure. *See Fig. 3.* Ensure thrust washers are installed with oil grooves facing gears. Replace all snap rings.

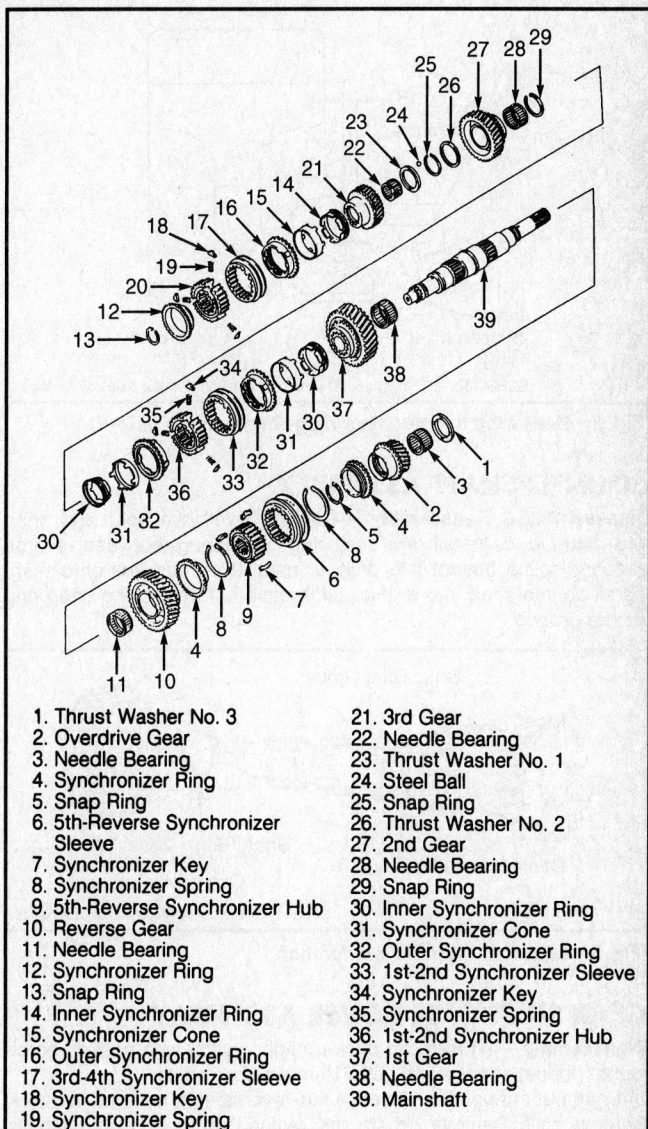

1. Thrust Washer No. 3	21. 3rd Gear
2. Overdrive Gear	22. Needle Bearing
3. Needle Bearing	23. Thrust Washer No. 1
4. Synchronizer Ring	24. Steel Ball
5. Snap Ring	25. Snap Ring
6. 5th-Reverse Synchronizer Sleeve	26. Thrust Washer No. 2
7. Synchronizer Key	27. 2nd Gear
8. Synchronizer Spring	28. Needle Bearing
9. 5th-Reverse Synchronizer Hub	29. Snap Ring
10. Reverse Gear	30. Inner Synchronizer Ring
11. Needle Bearing	31. Synchronizer Cone
12. Synchronizer Ring	32. Outer Synchronizer Ring
13. Snap Ring	33. 1st-2nd Synchronizer Sleeve
14. Inner Synchronizer Ring	34. Synchronizer Key
15. Synchronizer Cone	35. Synchronizer Spring
16. Outer Synchronizer Ring	36. 1st-2nd Synchronizer Hub
17. 3rd-4th Synchronizer Sleeve	37. 1st Gear
18. Synchronizer Key	38. Needle Bearing
19. Synchronizer Spring	39. Mainshaft
20. 3rd-4th Synchronizer Hub	

Fig. 3: Exploded View Of Mainshaft (V5MT1-6 Shown; V5MT1-2 Is Similar)

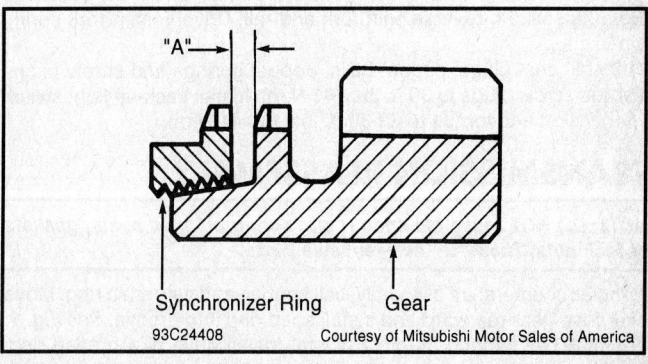

Fig. 4: Measuring Synchronizer Ring Clearance (V5MT1-2)

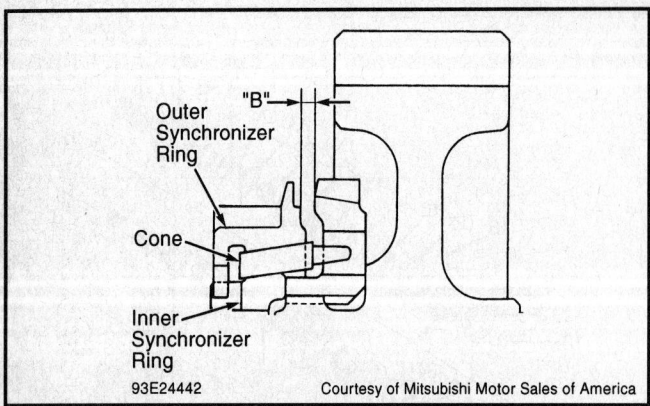

Fig. 5: Measuring Synchronizer Ring Clearance (V5MT1-6)

COUNTERSHAFT ASSEMBLY

Disassembly & Reassembly – Remove overdrive gear and snap ring. See Fig. 6. Install new snap ring on bearing, between reverse gear and spline, but not in its groove. Install overdrive gear onto shaft. Install countershaft into transmission case before moving snap ring into its groove.

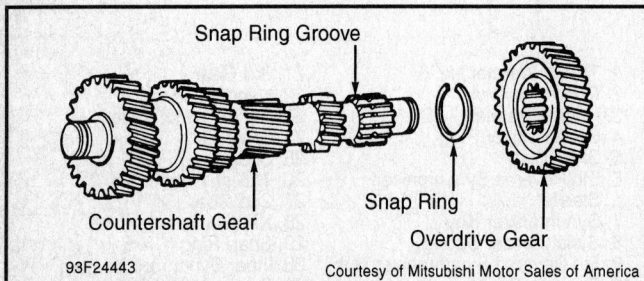

Fig. 6: Exploded View Of Countershaft

GEAR SHIFT CASE COVER ASSEMBLY

Disassembly – 1) Remove back-up light switch with gasket, screw plugs, poppet springs and balls. Remove dust plugs.
2) Drive out spring pins. Remove 5th-reverse shift rail and shift fork. Remove balls. Remove 3rd-4th shift rail and shift fork. Remove balls. Remove 1st-2nd shift rail and shift fork. See Fig. 7.
Inspection – Check Teflon bushings in case cover for damage. DO NOT remove bushing except when defective. See Fig. 8.
Reassembly – 1) Install 1st-2nd shift fork and shift rail. Install 2 interlock balls. Install 3rd-4th shift fork and rail. Install 2 interlock balls. See Fig. 9. Install 5th-reverse shift fork and rail. Drive in shift fork spring pins.
2) Install dust plugs, poppet balls, poppet springs and screw plugs. Torque screw plugs to 30 ft. lbs. (41 N.m). Install back-up light switch with gasket and torque to 22-30 ft. lbs. (30-41 N.m).

TRANSMISSION REASSEMBLY

NOTE: DO NOT reuse old snap rings, spring pins, oil seals, gaskets or lock nuts. These are non-reusable parts.

1) Install countershaft assembly, ball bearing and new snap ring. Move overdrive gear rearward and install snap ring into groove. See Fig. 1.
2) Install ball bearing on drive pinion. Install drive pinion snap ring. Install drive pinion into case from inside. Tap drive pinion with soft hammer until drive pinion ball bearing comes out of transmission case. Install drive pinion ball bearing snap ring and pilot bearing.
3) Install mainshaft assembly into case and insert mainshaft into pilot bearing on drive pinion. Tap drive pinion bearing into case until bearing snap ring contacts case. Install mainshaft bearing snap ring and tap ball bearing until snap ring contacts case.

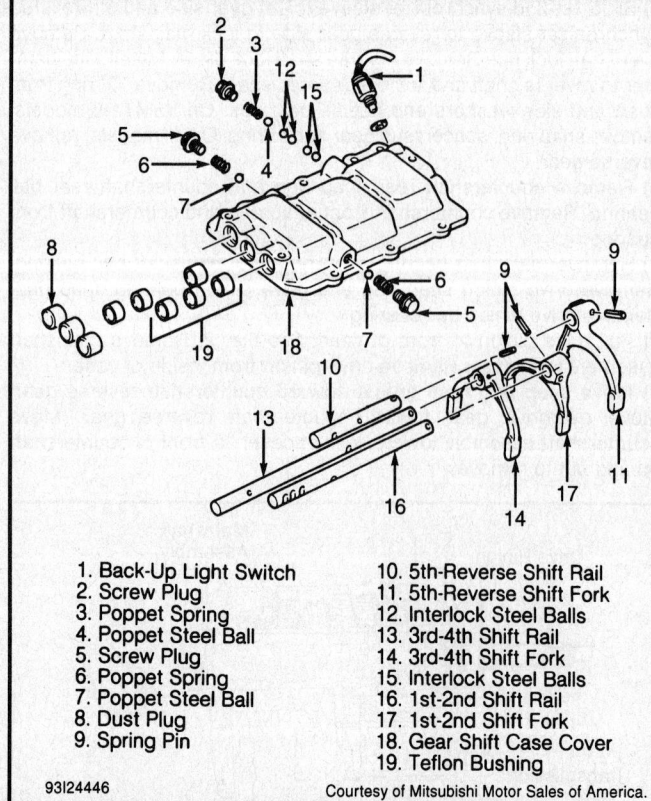

1. Back-Up Light Switch
2. Screw Plug
3. Poppet Spring
4. Poppet Steel Ball
5. Screw Plug
6. Poppet Spring
7. Poppet Steel Ball
8. Dust Plug
9. Spring Pin
10. 5th-Reverse Shift Rail
11. 5th-Reverse Shift Fork
12. Interlock Steel Balls
13. 3rd-4th Shift Rail
14. 3rd-4th Shift Fork
15. Interlock Steel Balls
16. 1st-2nd Shift Rail
17. 1st-2nd Shift Fork
18. Gear Shift Case Cover
19. Teflon Bushing

Fig. 7: Exploded View Of Gear Shift Case Cover

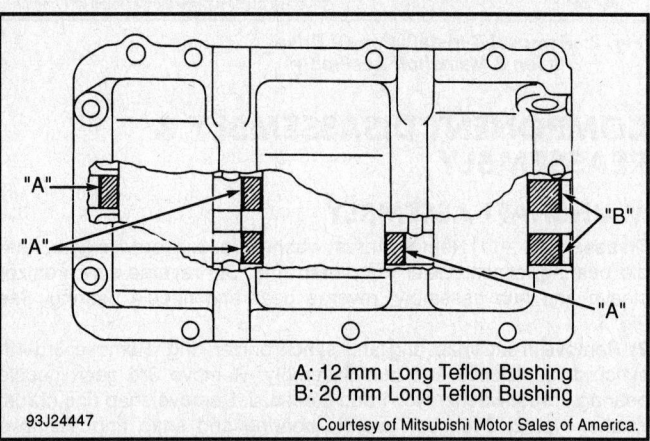

A: 12 mm Long Teflon Bushing
B: 20 mm Long Teflon Bushing

Fig. 8: Identifying Teflon Bushings

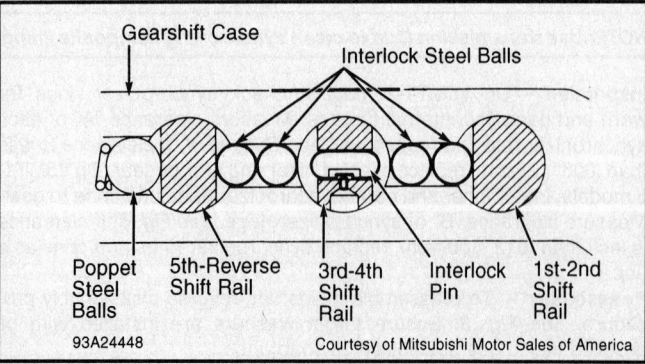

Fig. 9: Installation Of Steel Balls

4) Install snap rings onto countershaft front and rear ball bearings. Install front countershaft bearing and front countershaft snap ring. Install rear countershaft bearing and rear countershaft snap ring. On V5MT1-6 models, assemble reverse gear, spring, spacers, snap rings and sub gears. Position long end of spring towards reverse gear with sub gears, spacers and snap rings. *See Fig. 1.* Turn reverse gear and sub gears to align all through-holes and install into transmission case.

5) On V5MT1-2 models, install reverse gear and needle bearings into transmission case. On all models, install side washers, ensuring bent sections of side washers are installed into grooves. Install "O" ring onto reverse shaft and tap reverse shaft into case. Install lock piece and bolt. Torque bolt to 30 ft. lbs. (41 N.m).

6) Slide 1st-2nd synchronizer sleeve to 1st gear side and 5th-reverse synchronizer sleeve to reverse gear side to lock mainshaft. Install mainshaft lock nut and torque to 184-199 ft. lbs. (250-270 N.m). Stake lock nut at 2 grooves of mainshaft.

7) Install power take off cover and gasket. Torque bolts to 14 ft. lbs. (19 N.m). Install oil seal onto clutch housing. Apply Mitsubishi Sealant (MD997740) to clutch housing mating surface and wrap drive pinion shaft splined portions with vinyl tape. Install clutch housing to transmission case and torque bolts to 88 ft. lbs. (119 N.m). Remove vinyl tape.

8) Apply sealant to gear shift case cover mating surface and install to transmission case. Torque bolts to 18 ft. lbs. (24 N.m). Apply sealant to mating surface of transfer adapter and install adapter partway onto case. Install shift jaws to respective shift rails. Push transfer adapter into contact with case and torque bolts to 30 ft. lbs. (41 N.m). Drive in gear shift jaw spring pins.

9) Apply 3M Super Weatherstrip (8001) to air breather and install on adapter cover. Install gasket and cover. Torque bolts to 18 ft. lbs. (24 N.m).

10) Install control shaft into transfer adapter. Apply multipurpose grease to Neutral return plungers "A" and "B" and install with Neutral return springs and seal plugs. *See Fig. 1.* Torque seal plugs to 22-26 ft. lbs. (30-35 N.m). Install ball, resistance spring and resistance plug. Torque resistance plug to 22-31 ft. lbs. (30-42 N.m).

11) Apply Mitsubishi Sealant (MD997740) to both sides of transfer case gasket and affix to transfer adapter. Install transfer case and torque nuts and bolts to 22-31 ft. lbs. (30-42 N.m). Install shift changer onto control shaft and drive in spring pin leaving .12-.14" (3.0-3.5 mm) protruding.

12) Install select plunger, select spring and select plunger plug with gasket. Torque select plunger plug to 22-31 ft. lbs. (30-42 N.m). Install oil drain plug with gasket and oil fill plug with gasket. See TORQUE SPECIFICATIONS.

TORQUE SPECIFICATIONS

TORQUE SPECIFICATIONS

Application	Ft. Lbs. (N.m)
Adapter Cover Bolts	18 (24)
Back-Up Light Switch	22-30 (30-41)
Clutch Housing Bolts	88 (119)
Gear Shift Case Cover Bolts	18 (24)
Mainshaft Lock Nut	184-199 (250-270)
Neutral Return Plunger Seal Plugs	22-26 (30-35)
Oil Drain Plug	41-63 (55-85)
Oil Fill Plug	22-26 (30-35)
Poppet Screw Plugs	30 (41)
Power Takeoff Cover Bolts	14 (19)
Resistance Plug	35 (48)
Reverse Shaft Lock Piece Bolt	30 (41)
Select Plunger Plug	22-31 (30-42)
Transfer Adapter Bolts	30 (41)
Transfer Case Nuts & Bolts	22-31 (30-42)

MANUAL TRANSMISSIONS
Mitsubishi W5M33 & W6MG1

Eclipse, Expo, 3000GT

APPLICATION & LABOR TIMES

APPLICATION & LABOR TIMES

Vehicle	Labor Times		
Application	[1] R & I	[2] Overhaul	Series
Eclipse AWD	5.8	8.3	W5M33
Expo AWD	5.3	8.3	W5M33
3000GT AWD	5.3	8.3	W6MG1

[1] – Removal and installation of transmission from vehicle chassis.

[2] – Bench overhaul time for transaxle/differential. DOES NOT include removal and installation.

IDENTIFICATION

Transaxle model can be identified by vehicle information code plate located on bulkhead in engine compartment.

DESCRIPTION

Mitsubishi manual transaxle W5M33 is equipped with 3 shift rails, 3 synchronizer assemblies and 3 shafts. See Fig. 1. Transmission features limited slip AWD using 2 differential assemblies and a viscous coupling. Rear wheel drive consists of transfer assembly directing power to a separate differential at rear axle. Transfer assembly attaches externally to clutch housing, allowing transfer assembly to be serviced as a separate unit.

NOTE: Overhaul procedures for W6MG1 transaxle are not available. There are 6 external seals and 2 air breather caps that are serviceable. See Fig. 2. This transaxle must be replaced as an assembly.

LUBRICATION & ADJUSTMENTS

See appropriate MANUAL TRANSMISSION SERVICING article in TRANSMISSION SERVICING section.

TROUBLE SHOOTING

See GENERAL TROUBLE SHOOTING article in this section.

ON-VEHICLE SERVICE

AXLE SHAFT OIL SEAL REPLACEMENT

Removal & Installation – 1) Disconnect axle shaft from transaxle. See appropriate article in AXLE SHAFTS & TRANSFER CASES section.

2) Disconnect front exhaust pipe connection and remove transfer assembly. Remove oil seal(s) from transaxle case.

3) There are 2 different types of axle shaft oil seals for right and left sides. See Fig. 1 or 2. Install NEW oil seals in transaxle case. Ensure oil seals are installed in proper locations.

4) Lubricate oil seal with gear oil and install in transaxle case. Reinstall transfer assembly and reconnect axle shaft(s). Fill transaxle with API GL-4 or GL-5, SAE 75W-85W or 75W-90 hypoid gear oil.

TRANSFER OIL SEAL REPLACEMENT

Removal & Installation – 1) Remove drive shaft from transfer unit output shaft, then remove oil seal. See appropriate article in AXLE SHAFTS & TRANSFER CASES section.

2) Lubricate oil seal with gear oil and reinstall in transaxle case. Install drive shaft and fill transaxle with API GL-4 or GL-5, SAE 75W-85W or 75W-90 hypoid gear oil.

REMOVAL & INSTALLATION

See appropriate MANUAL TRANSMISSION REMOVAL article in TRANSMISSION SERVICING section.

TRANSAXLE DISASSEMBLY

1) Remove rear cover. Remove reverse brake cone and wave spring. See Fig. 1. Remove back-up light switch and gasket from transaxle case adapter.

2) Remove restrict ball assembly and gasket. Remove poppet (detent) balls, springs, and plugs. Remove speedometer driven gear assembly and air breather.

3) Remove 5th speed gear shift fork spring pin. Unstake input shaft and intermediate gear lock nuts. Using control lever and select lever, shift transaxle into reverse. Install splined socket and breaker bar on input shaft. Install 10 mm bolt in clutch housing and position breaker against bolt to prevent input shaft from rotating. Remove lock nuts. Remove 5th gear synchronizer assembly with 5th gear shift fork.

4) Remove 5th speed gear needle bearing and 5th speed intermediate gear. Remove viscous coupling snap ring. Remove viscous coupling from shaft and steel ball from splines of shaft. See Fig. 1.

5) Remove center shaft from clutch housing end of transaxle. Stand transaxle assembly on clutch housing and remove transaxle case adapter. Remove 3 bearing outer race and spacer pairs.

6) Remove center differential assembly. Remove reverse idler gear shaft bolt and gasket from transaxle case.

7) Remove bolts attaching transaxle case to clutch housing. Separate cases. Remove both oil guides.

8) Remove outer bearing race and shims from front differential. Remove bolt and stopper bracket from transaxle case.

9) Remove bolt and reverse shift lever assembly with reverse shift lever shoe from clutch housing. Lift reverse idler gear and shaft.

10) Lift front output shaft assembly and needle bearing out of clutch housing. Lift front differential assembly out of clutch housing.

11) Shift 1st-2nd speed shift fork into 2nd speed. Shift 3rd-4th shift fork into 4th speed. Rotate shift controls in direction of arrows in numerical order to remove. See Fig. 10.

12) Remove shift lugs from control finger and interlock plate. Raise each shift rail upward and out of clutch housing. Remove all shift rails and forks.

13) Lift input shaft assembly and remove intermediate gear assembly. Remove outer bearing race from clutch housing. See Fig. 1.

COMPONENT DISASSEMBLY & REASSEMBLY

5TH SPEED SYNCHRONIZER

Disassembly & Inspection – 1) Slide synchronizer sleeve off synchronizer hub and remove springs and keys. Reassemble synchronizer hub and sleeve to ensure smooth operation with no binding.

2) Remove sleeve and inspect inside diameter for wear or damage. Synchronizer hub and sleeve should be replaced as a set only.

3) Inspect center protrusion of synchronizer keys for wear. Inspect both springs for deformation or damage.

Reassembly – Reassemble hub and sleeve with oil groove of hub facing 5th gear. Install keys and springs and ensure spring protrusions in front and rear springs are not in same key.

CENTER DIFFERENTIAL

Disassembly – 1) Remove taper roller bearings from each side of differential assembly. Remove bolts and output gear from differential case.

2) Remove side gear, spacer and then pinion shaft from differential case. Remove washers, pinions, spacers, and side gear from case.

Inspection & Reassembly – 1) DO NOT reuse taper roller bearings and races if bearing has been removed from shaft.

2) Install spacer, side gear, pinion gear, washer, and pinion shaft into differential case after inspection. Select and install thickest spacer that ensures smooth rotation of pinion gear when holding pinion shaft.

3) Install side gear, spacer, and output gear. Apply Stud Locking Compound (3M 4170) to output gear bolts and torque to 52-59 ft. lbs. (70-80 N.m). See Fig. 3.

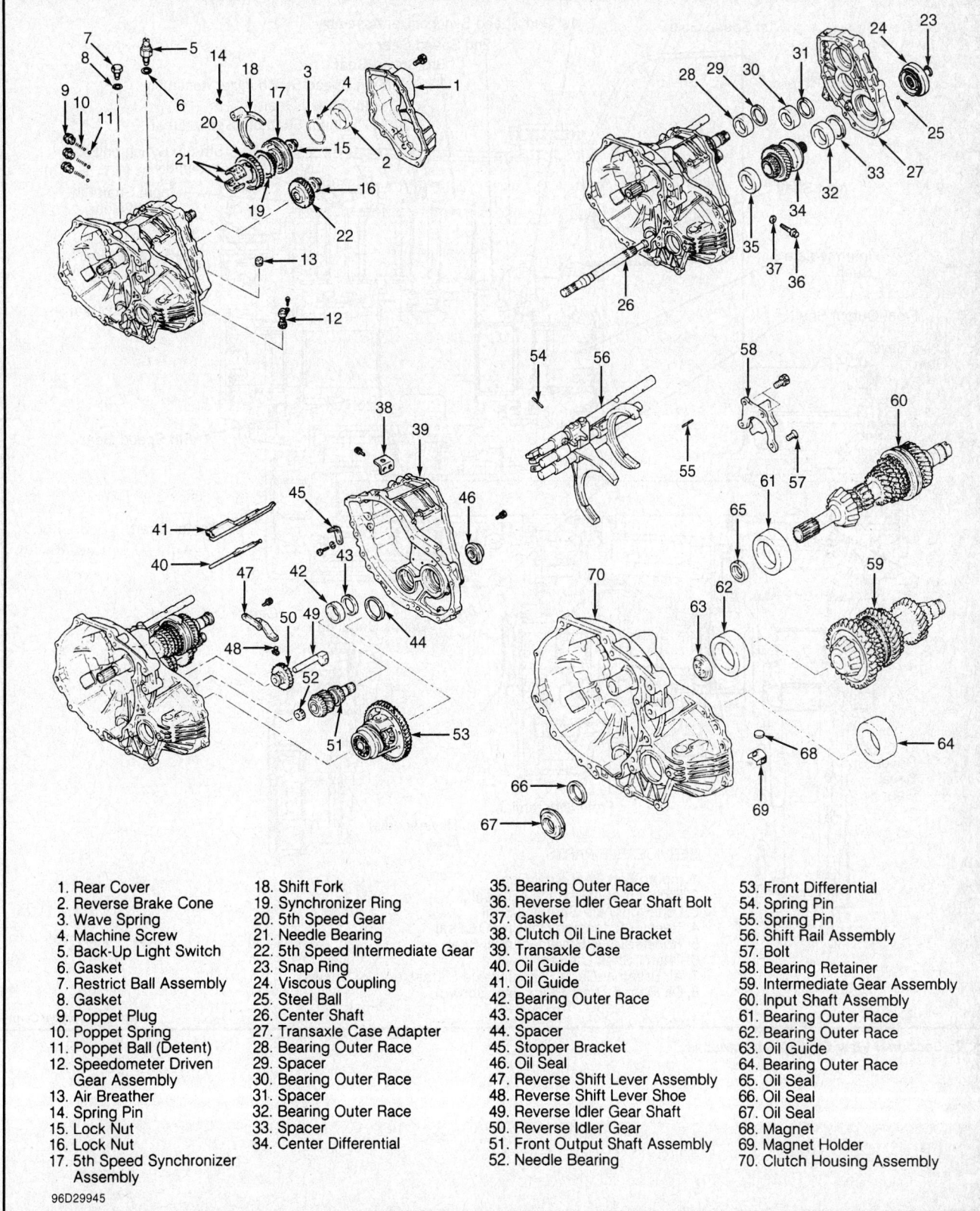

1. Rear Cover	18. Shift Fork	35. Bearing Outer Race	53. Front Differential
2. Reverse Brake Cone	19. Synchronizer Ring	36. Reverse Idler Gear Shaft Bolt	54. Spring Pin
3. Wave Spring	20. 5th Speed Gear	37. Gasket	55. Spring Pin
4. Machine Screw	21. Needle Bearing	38. Clutch Oil Line Bracket	56. Shift Rail Assembly
5. Back-Up Light Switch	22. 5th Speed Intermediate Gear	39. Transaxle Case	57. Bolt
6. Gasket	23. Snap Ring	40. Oil Guide	58. Bearing Retainer
7. Restrict Ball Assembly	24. Viscous Coupling	41. Oil Guide	59. Intermediate Gear Assembly
8. Gasket	25. Steel Ball	42. Bearing Outer Race	60. Input Shaft Assembly
9. Poppet Plug	26. Center Shaft	43. Spacer	61. Bearing Outer Race
10. Poppet Spring	27. Transaxle Case Adapter	44. Spacer	62. Bearing Outer Race
11. Poppet Ball (Detent)	28. Bearing Outer Race	45. Stopper Bracket	63. Oil Guide
12. Speedometer Driven Gear Assembly	29. Spacer	46. Oil Seal	64. Bearing Outer Race
13. Air Breather	30. Bearing Outer Race	47. Reverse Shift Lever Assembly	65. Oil Seal
14. Spring Pin	31. Spacer	48. Reverse Shift Lever Shoe	66. Oil Seal
15. Lock Nut	32. Bearing Outer Race	49. Reverse Idler Gear Shaft	67. Oil Seal
16. Lock Nut	33. Spacer	50. Reverse Idler Gear	68. Magnet
17. 5th Speed Synchronizer Assembly	34. Center Differential	51. Front Output Shaft Assembly	69. Magnet Holder
		52. Needle Bearing	70. Clutch Housing Assembly

96D29945

Fig. 1: Exploded View Of Transaxle Assembly (W5M33)

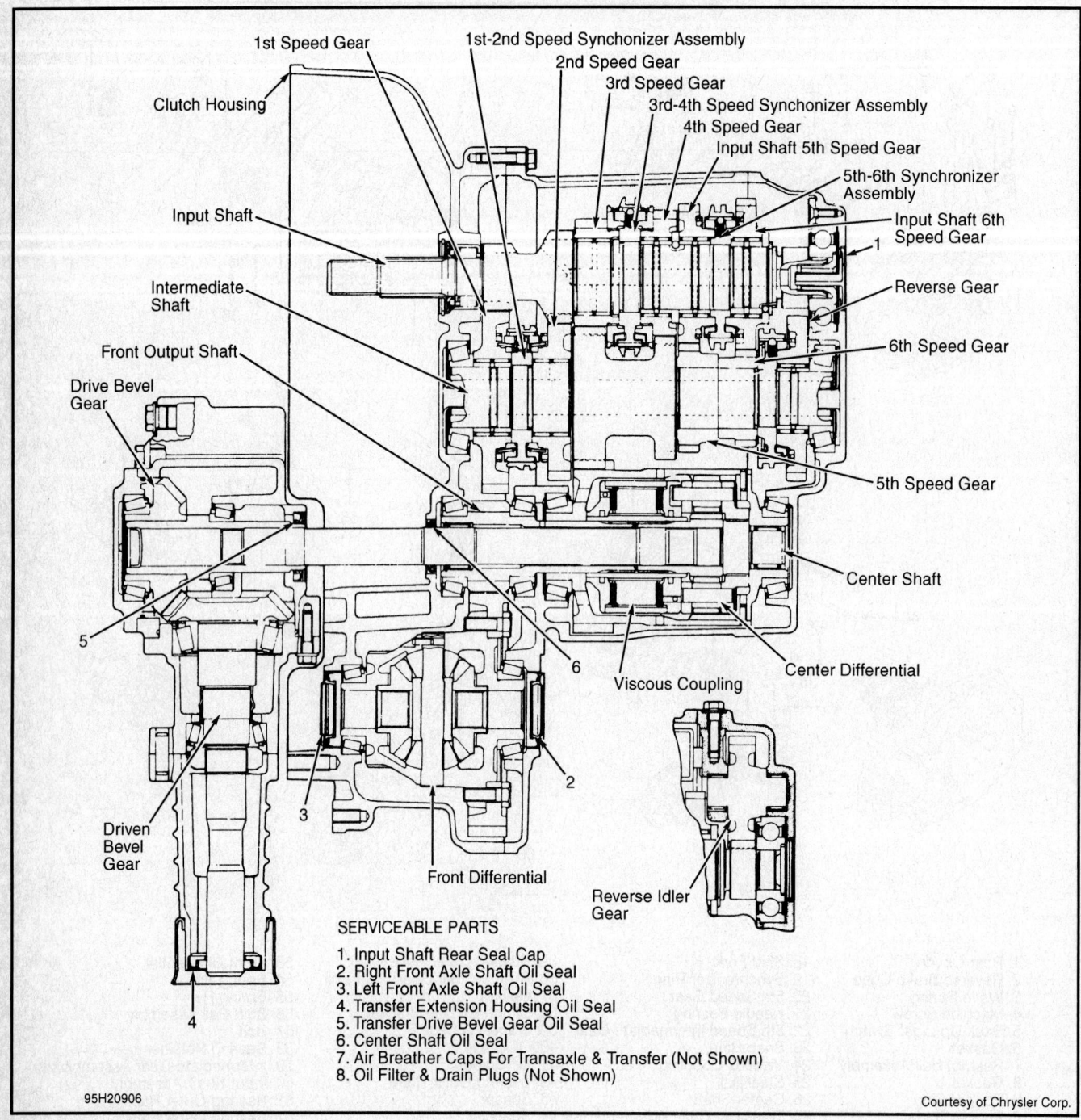

1st Speed Gear
Clutch Housing
1st-2nd Speed Synchonizer Assembly
2nd Speed Gear
3rd Speed Gear
3rd-4th Speed Synchronizer Assembly
4th Speed Gear
Input Shaft 5th Speed Gear
5th-6th Synchronizer Assembly
Input Shaft
Input Shaft 6th Speed Gear
Intermediate Shaft
Reverse Gear
Front Output Shaft
6th Speed Gear
Drive Bevel Gear
5th Speed Gear
Center Shaft
Center Differential
Viscous Coupling
Driven Bevel Gear
Front Differential
Reverse Idler Gear

SERVICEABLE PARTS
1. Input Shaft Rear Seal Cap
2. Right Front Axle Shaft Oil Seal
3. Left Front Axle Shaft Oil Seal
4. Transfer Extension Housing Oil Seal
5. Transfer Drive Bevel Gear Oil Seal
6. Center Shaft Oil Seal
7. Air Breather Caps For Transaxle & Transfer (Not Shown)
8. Oil Filter & Drain Plugs (Not Shown)

95H20906

Courtesy of Chrysler Corp.

Fig. 2: Sectional View Of W6MG1 Transaxle

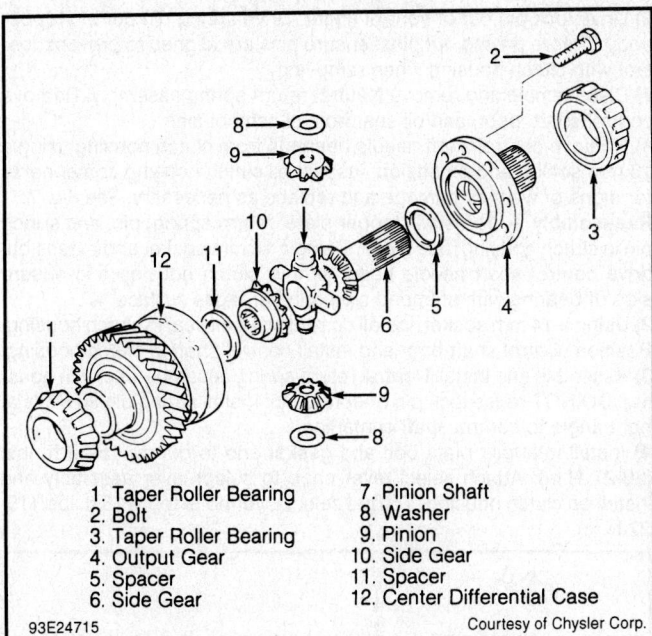

1. Taper Roller Bearing
2. Bolt
3. Taper Roller Bearing
4. Output Gear
5. Spacer
6. Side Gear
7. Pinion Shaft
8. Washer
9. Pinion
10. Side Gear
11. Spacer
12. Center Differential Case

93E24715   Courtesy of Chysler Corp.

Fig. 3: Exploded View Of Center Differential (W5M33)

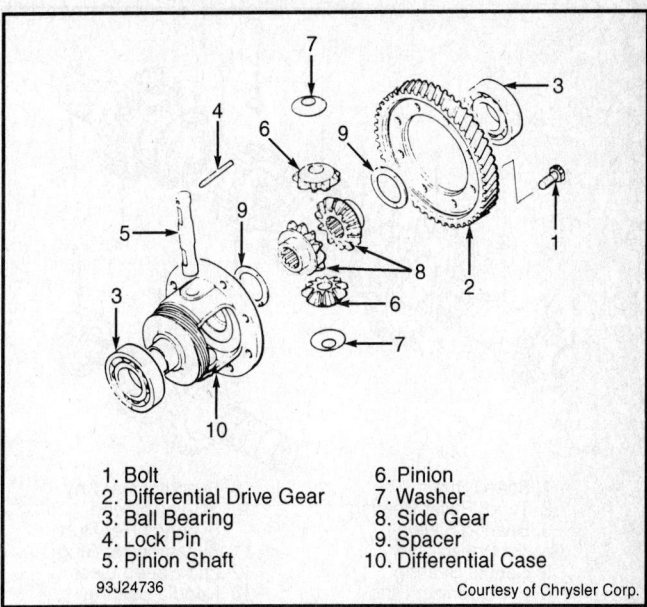

1. Bolt
2. Differential Drive Gear
3. Ball Bearing
4. Lock Pin
5. Pinion Shaft
6. Pinion
7. Washer
8. Side Gear
9. Spacer
10. Differential Case

93J24736   Courtesy of Chrysler Corp.

Fig. 4: Exploded View Of Front Differential

4) Ensure side gears turn smoothly. Measure pinion backlash. Center differential pinion backlash should be .0001-.0060" (.025-.150 mm). Press taper roller bearings in place at ends of differential assembly.

FRONT OUTPUT SHAFT

Disassembly, Inspection & Reassembly – 1) Remove taper roller bearings from front output shaft. Inspect bearings for wear or damage. See Fig. 1.

2) Inspect gear teeth and splines of shaft for wear or damage. Press taper roller bearings in place on front output shaft. See TRANSAXLE SPECIFICATIONS for end play specifications.

FRONT DIFFERENTIAL

Disassembly – 1) Remove bolts and differential drive gear from differential case. Remove ball bearings from ends of differential assembly. DO NOT reuse bearings removed from shaft.

2) Drive pinion shaft lock pin from case. See Fig. 4. Remove pinion shaft, pinions, washers, side gears and spacers from case.

Reassembly – 1) Install spacers on back of side gears and install into differential case. Install washers on back of pinions and install into case while turning side gears. Install pinion shaft. Measure backlash between pinion and side gears.

2) Adjustments to pinion backlash should provide equal backlash for both side gears. Front differential pinion backlash should be .001-.006" (.025-.150 mm).

3) Install NEW pinion shaft lock pin and ensure lock pin head is lower than case flange surface. Press ball bearings on ends of differential.

4) Apply Stud Locking Compound (3M 4170) to bolts and install differential drive gear. Torque drive gear bolts to 96-103 ft. lbs. (130-140 N.m) in crisscross pattern. See Fig. 4.

INTERMEDIATE GEAR

Disassembly – 1) Remove snap ring, taper roller bearing, bearing sleeve and 1st gear. Remove needle bearing with synchronizer ring and spring. Remove 1st-2nd gear synchronizer sleeve, key, hub and ring.

2) Remove 2nd gear, needle bearing, taper roller bearing and intermediate gear. DO NOT reuse ball bearings if they have been removed from shaft. See Fig. 5.

Inspection – 1) Inspect needle bearing surface of intermediate gear for wear or damage. Inspect splines for damage. Inspect bearings for wear.

2) Inspect synchronizer ring gear teeth and inside surface for wear or damage. Measure synchronizer ring-to-gear clearance. Synchronizer ring minimum clearance limit is .020" (.50 mm). Ensure synchronizer sleeve and hub slide together smoothly. Inspect sleeve inside front and rear ends for damage. Inspect hub end surface for wear at gear contact points. If necessary, replace synchronizer hub and sleeve as a set.

3) Inspect synchronizer key center protrusions for wear. Check springs for deformation. Inspect speed gear clutch teeth, cone, and gear bore for wear or damage.

Reassembly – 1) Press taper roller bearing in place on threaded end of intermediate gear. Assemble 1st-2nd synchronizer and install synchronizer assembly with 2nd gear and needle bearing on intermediate gear.

2) Install 1st gear with needle bearing and sleeve on intermediate gear. Press taper roller bearing in place, install snap ring, and measure end play between snap ring and bearing. Intermediate gear end play should be .0004-.0055" (.010-.140 mm). End play is adjustable with various thickness snap rings.

INPUT SHAFT

Disassembly – 1) Remove snap ring and taper bearing from splined end of input shaft. Press bearing sleeve off threaded end of input shaft.

2) Remove snap ring and rear taper bearing from input shaft. Remove spacer and 4th gear, with needle bearing and sleeve, from input shaft. See Fig. 6. Remove 3rd-4th synchronizer assembly and 3rd gear from input shaft.

Inspection – 1) Inspect needle bearings and needle bearing surfaces of input shaft for wear or damage. Ensure needle bearings rotate smoothly on shaft without abnormal noise or play. Check splines for signs of wear or damage.

2) Inspect synchronizer rings for wear or damage and measure synchronizer ring-to-gear clearances. Synchronizer ring to gear clearance should be no less than .020" (.50 mm).

3) Inspect synchronizer hub and sleeve condition and operation. Inspect synchronizer keys and springs for wear or damage. Inspect gear teeth, cone, and bore of speed gears for wear or damage.

Reassembly – 1) Install 3rd gear with needle bearing and 3rd-4th synchronizer assembly on input shaft. Press bearing sleeve on input shaft from threaded end.

2) Install needle bearing and 4th gear on input shaft. Press ball bearing on input shaft after installing spacer. Spacers with identification mark "1" are installed with identification mark facing 4th gear. Spacers without identification marks may be installed in either direction.

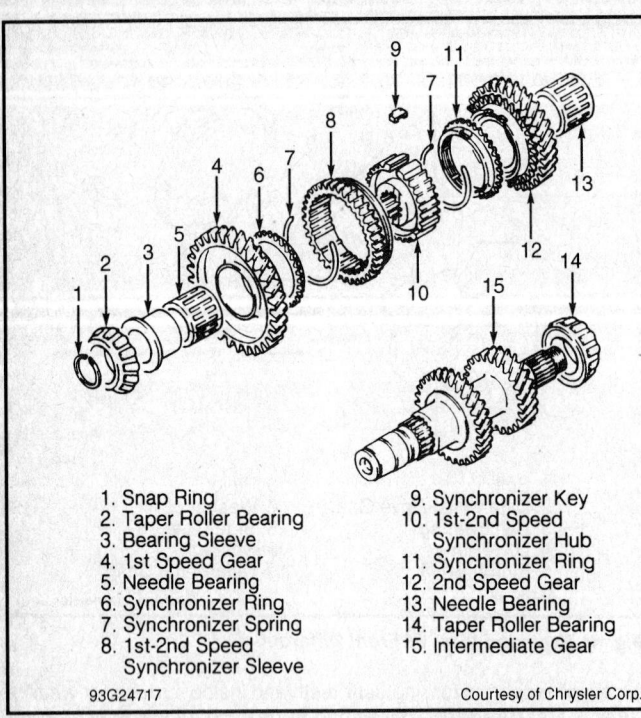

1. Snap Ring
2. Taper Roller Bearing
3. Bearing Sleeve
4. 1st Speed Gear
5. Needle Bearing
6. Synchronizer Ring
7. Synchronizer Spring
8. 1st-2nd Speed Synchronizer Sleeve
9. Synchronizer Key
10. 1st-2nd Speed Synchronizer Hub
11. Synchronizer Ring
12. 2nd Speed Gear
13. Needle Bearing
14. Taper Roller Bearing
15. Intermediate Gear

93G24717   Courtesy of Chrysler Corp.

Fig. 5: Exploded View Of Intermediate Gear Assembly

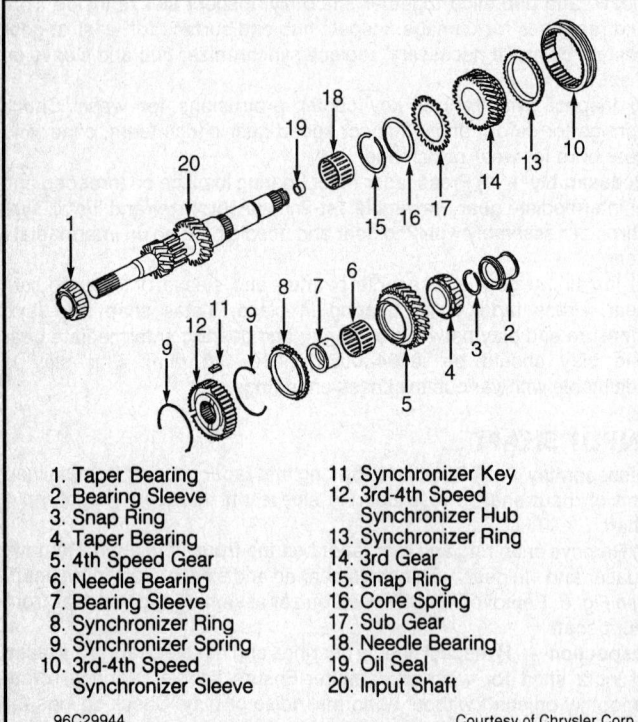

1. Taper Bearing
2. Bearing Sleeve
3. Snap Ring
4. Taper Bearing
5. 4th Speed Gear
6. Needle Bearing
7. Bearing Sleeve
8. Synchronizer Ring
9. Synchronizer Spring
10. 3rd-4th Speed Synchronizer Sleeve
11. Synchronizer Key
12. 3rd-4th Speed Synchronizer Hub
13. Synchronizer Ring
14. 3rd Gear
15. Snap Ring
16. Cone Spring
17. Sub Gear
18. Needle Bearing
19. Oil Seal
20. Input Shaft

96C29944   Courtesy of Chrysler Corp.

Fig. 6: Exploded View Of Input Shaft Assembly

3) After NEW ball bearing is pressed in place, install NEW snap ring. Press bearing sleeve on input shaft. Install front ball bearing and NEW snap ring. Install thickest snap ring that fits into snap ring groove. Snap rings are available in 3 sizes.

CLUTCH HOUSING

Disassembly & Inspection – 1) Remove bolt and select lever assembly with select lever shoe. Remove interlock plate bolt and gasket.

2) Drive lock pin out of control finger. Drive spring pin out of stopper body. Before driving out pins, ensure pins are aligned to prevent contact with clutch housing when removing.

3) Disassemble and remove Neutral return spring assembly. Remove control shaft, boot, and oil seal from clutch housing.

4) Remove control shaft needle bearings from clutch housing using a 13 mm socket and extension. Inspect all clutch housing components for signs of wear or damage and replace as necessary. *See Fig. 7.*

Reassembly – 1) Install stopper plate, return spring, pin, and spring pin in clutch housing. *See Fig. 7.* Using a 14 mm socket and extension, drive control shaft needle bearings into clutch housing and ensure side of bearing with stamped type number faces surface "A".

2) Using a 14 mm socket, install control shaft oil seal in clutch housing. Position control shaft boot and install control shaft in clutch housing.

3) Assemble and install Neutral return spring assembly in clutch housing. DO NOT reuse lock pin or spring pin. Install spring pin so slit is at right angle to control shaft centerline.

4) Install interlock plate bolt and gasket and torque to 15-20 ft. lbs. (20-27 N.m). Attach select lever shoe to select lever assembly and install on clutch housing. Torque select lever bolts to 11-16 ft. lbs. (15-22 N.m).

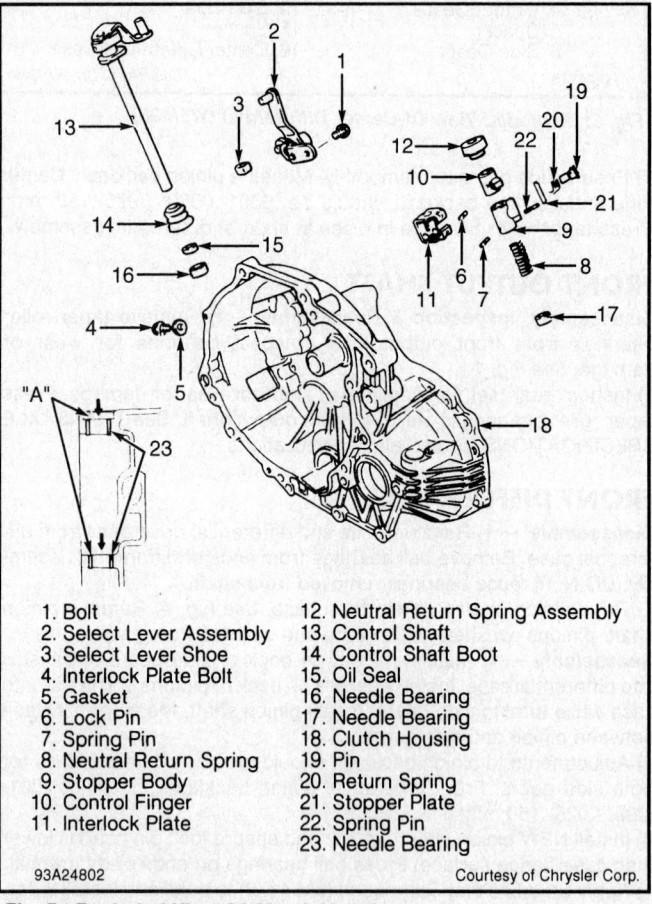

1. Bolt
2. Select Lever Assembly
3. Select Lever Shoe
4. Interlock Plate Bolt
5. Gasket
6. Lock Pin
7. Spring Pin
8. Neutral Return Spring
9. Stopper Body
10. Control Finger
11. Interlock Plate
12. Neutral Return Spring Assembly
13. Control Shaft
14. Control Shaft Boot
15. Oil Seal
16. Needle Bearing
17. Needle Bearing
18. Clutch Housing
19. Pin
20. Return Spring
21. Stopper Plate
22. Spring Pin
23. Needle Bearing

93A24802   Courtesy of Chrysler Corp.

Fig. 7: Exploded View Of Clutch Housing

TRANSFER CASE

Disassembly – 1) Remove cover and gasket from transfer case sub-assembly. Remove extension housing from transfer case adapter. *See Fig. 8.*

2) Separate transfer case from transfer case adapter. Remove spacer and "O" ring from between transfer case and adapter subassemblies.

Reassembly – 1) To ensure proper bevel gear tooth contact pattern, brush on a thin even coat of machine Blue or Red lead to both surfaces of driven bevel gear. Using old spacer, assemble transfer case and adapter subassemblies and torque bolts to 26-31 ft. lbs. (35-42 N.m). Install transfer case and transfer adapter with gear mating marks aligned.

2) Attach preload socket and side gear holder to drive bevel gear shaft and rotate one turn in direction of normal rotation and one turn in reverse rotation. Ensure mating marks of driven bevel gear and transfer case are aligned when viewed through cover opening. Separate transfer case and adapter subassemblies and inspect tooth contact pattern. *See Fig. 9.* To adjust drive bevel gear tooth contact, replace driven bevel gear mount adjusting spacer. See BEVEL GEAR BACKLASH ADJUSTMENT.

3) If tooth contact pattern is normal, complete transfer case and transfer adapter assembly. Ensure drive bevel gear and driven bevel gear backlash is .0031-.0051" (.080-.130 mm). If backlash is not as specified, see BEVEL GEAR BACKLASH ADJUSTMENT.

4) Use a NEW "O" ring between transfer case and transfer case adapter for final assembly. Apply sealant to extension housing in a uniform and continuous bead. Install extension housing and tighten bolts to 11-16 ft. lbs. (15-22 N.m). Apply Sealant (3M ATD 8660) to both sides of transfer case cover gasket. Install transfer case cover and tighten bolts to 80 INCH lbs. (9 N.m).

Cleaning & Inspection – Inspect all splines for wear or damage. Check bearing surfaces for scoring, scratches or excessive wear. Spacers should be replaced with NEW spacers of same thickness. Replace all "O" rings. Clean all surfaces with solvent and dry with compressed air.

Transfer Case Subassembly – 1) Remove transfer case cover, bolts, spacer and "O" ring from side of transfer case. Slide drive bevel gear assembly with outer races and spacers out of transfer case and inspect for wear or damage.

2) If necessary, use a press to remove and install drive bevel gear bearings or drive bevel gear. When installing drive bevel gear, ensure mating marks on drive bevel gear shaft and gear are aligned.

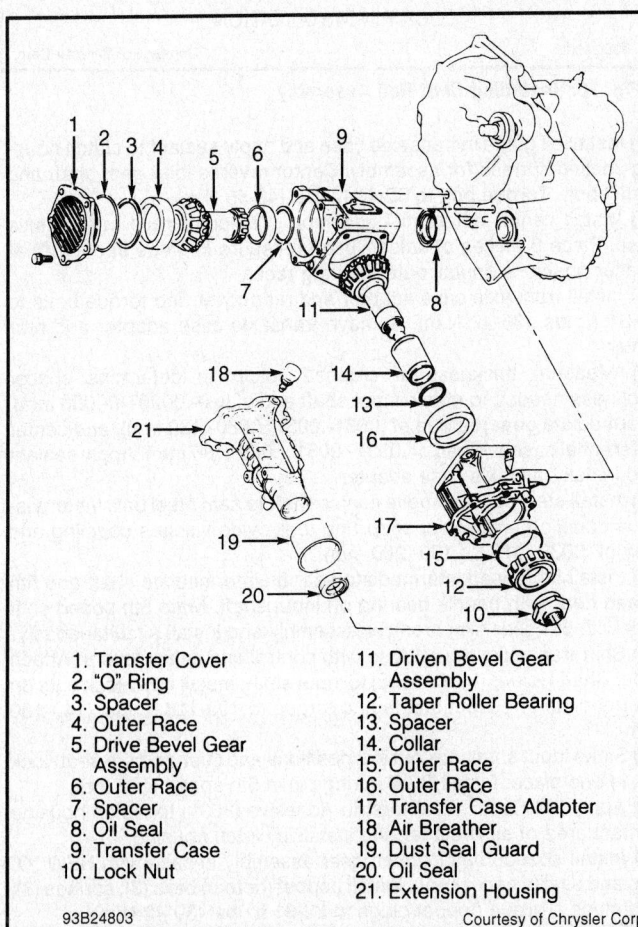

1. Transfer Cover
2. "O" Ring
3. Spacer
4. Outer Race
5. Drive Bevel Gear Assembly
6. Outer Race
7. Spacer
8. Oil Seal
9. Transfer Case
10. Lock Nut
11. Driven Bevel Gear Assembly
12. Taper Roller Bearing
13. Spacer
14. Collar
15. Outer Race
16. Outer Race
17. Transfer Case Adapter
18. Air Breather
19. Dust Seal Guard
20. Oil Seal
21. Extension Housing

93B24803   Courtesy of Chrysler Corp.

Fig. 8: Exploded View Of Transfer Assembly

3) To complete transfer case assembly, replace seal. Install bearing races and drive bevel gear assembly with mating marks on transfer case and drive bevel gear shaft aligned. Tighten transfer case cover bolts to 26-31 ft. lbs. (35-42 N.m).

4) Ensure bevel gear rotating drive torque is 15-22 INCH lbs (1.7-2.5 N.m). Replace adjusting spacers if rotating torque is not as specified. When replacing adjusting spacers, use spacers of similar thickness.

Transfer Case Adapter Subassembly – 1) Unstake lock nut and remove from driven bevel gear assembly. Remove driven bevel gear assembly, bearing, spacer, collar and bearing races. Inspect all components for wear or damage. Replace as necessary.

2) Assemble driven bevel gear, taper roller bearing, collar, existing spacer, and outer bearing race in transfer case adapter and align mating marks. Install outer bearing race, taper roller bearing, and lock nut in transfer case adapter. Tighten lock nut to 103-118 ft. lbs (140-160 N.m). Ensure turning torque is 9-15 INCH lbs. (1.0-1.7 N.m). Driven bevel gear turning torque can be adjusted by replacing driven bevel gear spacer. Stake lock nut in 2 positions.

BEVEL GEAR BACKLASH ADJUSTMENT

1) On a standard tooth contact pattern, wear is distributed evenly between small end side "A" and large end side "C". Drive side tooth face "B" is side on which force acts when running forward. Coast side tooth face "D" is side on which force acts when reversing. *See Fig. 9.*

2) If contact pattern is at "C" end of "B" and "A" end of "D", driven bevel is too close to drive bevel gear. Use a thicker bevel drive gear spacer to separate bevel driven gear from bevel drive gear.

3) If contact pattern is at "C" end of "D" and "A" end of "B", bevel driven gear is too far from drive bevel gear. Use a thinner driven gear mounting spacer to bring bevel driven gear closer to drive gear.

4) If correct tooth contact pattern cannot be obtained by changing driven bevel gear mounting spacer, change drive gear preload adjusting spacer and mounting spacer. *See Fig. 9.*

5) Bevel driven gear spacers are available in sizes from .0051" to .0205" (.13 mm to .52 mm). Bevel drive gear spacers are available in various sizes from .0528" to .0657" (1.34 mm to 1.67 mm). Bevel drive gear preload spacers are available in various sizes from .0504" to .0728" (1.28 mm to 1.85 mm).

6) If driven bevel gear height is too small, replace bevel drive gear adjusting spacer with spacer one size thicker and replace drive gear preload spacer with one size thinner. If bevel driven gear height is too large, replace bevel drive gear spacer with one size thinner and bevel drive gear preload adjusting spacer with one size thicker. *See Fig. 9.*

7) Repeat step 6) until tooth contact pattern is equal to or close to standard pattern. If tooth contact pattern cannot be adjusted close to standard pattern, replace drive bevel gear and driven bevel gear as a set and readjust tooth contact.

TRANSAXLE REASSEMBLY

1) Install magnet and magnet holder in clutch housing and ensure proper installation direction. Install rear output shaft oil seal.

2) Install drive shaft oil seals. See AXLE SHAFT OIL SEAL REPLACEMENT under ON-VEHICLE SERVICE. Ensure notch in left side drive shaft oil seal is facing up. Install input shaft front oil seal.

3) Install front differential outer race, oil guide, and intermediate gear outer race in clutch housing. Install input shaft assembly with intermediate gear assembly in clutch housing.

4) Install input shaft front bearing retainer and torque hex bolts and countersunk bolt to 11-16 ft. lbs. (15-22 N.m). Apply Stud Locking Compound (3M 4170) to first 5 mm of threads.

5) To install shift rail assembly, shift 1st-2nd synchronizer sleeve to 2nd speed. Shift 3rd-4th synchronizer sleeve to 4th speed.

6) Fit shift forks to synchronizer sleeves and install shift rails through forks and reverse lug into clutch housing. Turn shift rails and engage shift lugs to control finger and interlock plate. Install new spring pins. *See Fig. 10.*

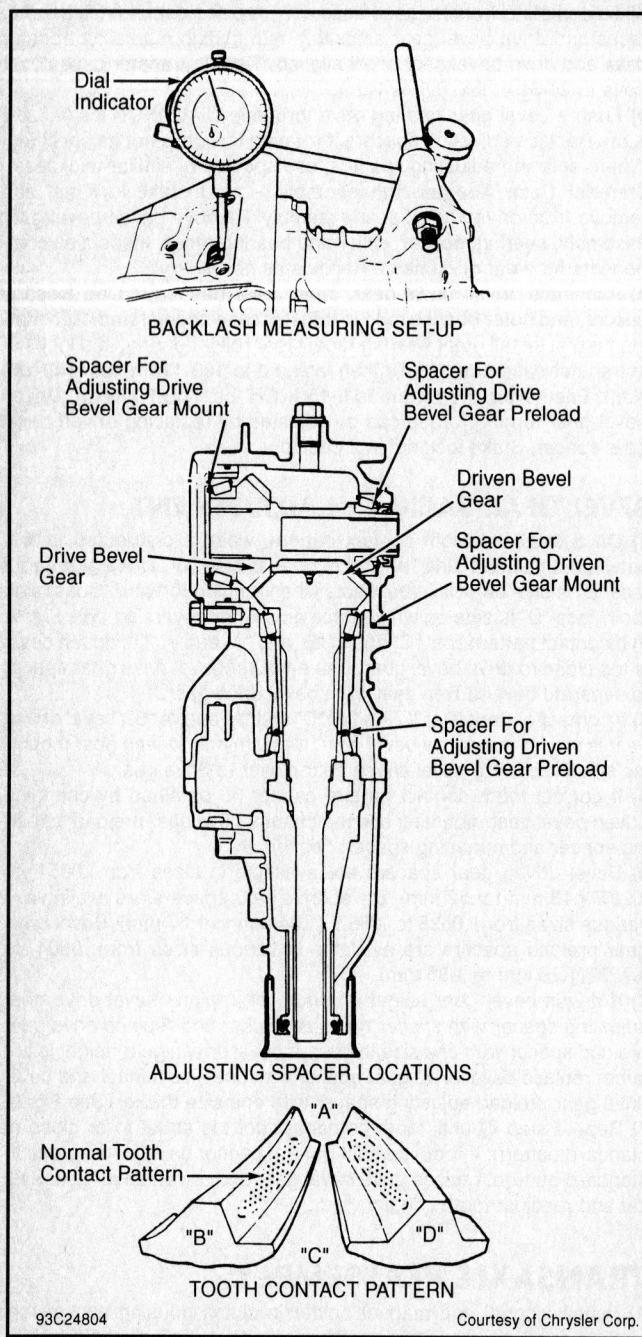

Fig. 9: Measuring Bevel Gear Backlash

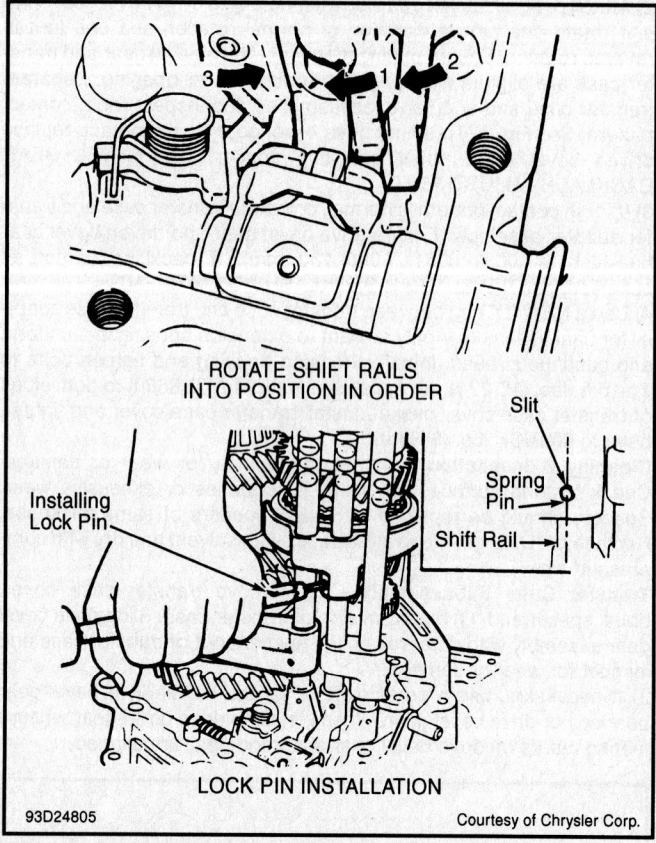

Fig. 10: Installing Shift Rail Assembly

7) Install front differential assembly in clutch housing and front differential spacer in transaxle case. Install front output shaft assembly and needle bearing in clutch housing. Install front output shaft spacer and outer race in transaxle case.

8) Install reverse idler gear and shaft in clutch housing. Install reverse shift lever and shoe. Torque bolts to 11-16 ft. lbs. (15-22 N.m).

9) Install stopper bracket and torque bolt to 11-16 ft. lbs. (15-22 N.m). Measure front output shaft preload and front differential case end play by placing 2 pieces of solder measuring approximately .40" (10 mm) long, .12" (3 mm) diameter at spacer locations.

10) Place 2 more pieces of solder (same size) on front differential bearing outer race. Install transaxle case and torque bolts to 26-31 ft. lbs. (35-42 N.m). Remove transaxle case from clutch housing.

11) Measure thickness of crushed solder to determine spacer thickness needed to obtain front differential end play of .0020-.0067" (.050-.170 mm) and front output shaft preload of .0031-.0051" (.080-.130 mm).

12) Install oil guide in transaxle case and apply sealant to clutch housing sealing surface for assembly. Center reverse idler gear shaft and install bolt. Torque bolt to 32-41 ft. lbs. (43-55 N.m).

13) Install center differential assembly with outer race in transaxle case. Place 6 pieces of solder (use procedure in steps 9) and 10) at spacer positions. Install outer bearing race.

14) Install transaxle case adapter and rear cover and torque bolts to 26-31 ft. lbs. (35-42 N.m). Remove transaxle case adapter and rear cover.

15) Measure thickness of crushed solder to determine spacer thickness needed to obtain input shaft end play 0-.0020" (0-.050 mm), intermediate gear preload of .0031-.0051" (.080-.130 mm), and center differential case preload of .0031-.0051" (.080-.130 mm). Apply sealant and install transaxle case adapter.

16) Install steel ball and move center shaft to seat steel ball. Install viscous coupling and select snap ring to provide viscous coupling end play of .0039-.0102" (.100-.260 mm).

17) Install 5th speed intermediate gear on intermediate shaft and 5th speed gear with needle bearing on input shaft. Mate 5th speed shift fork with 5th gear synchronizer assembly and install simultaneously.

18) Shift transaxle into reverse with control and select levers. Attach Input Shaft Holder (MD998802) to input shaft. Install NEW lock nuts on intermediate and input shafts and torque to 103-118 ft. lbs. (140-160 N.m).

19) Stake input shaft lock nut in 2 positions and intermediate shaft lock nut in one place. Install NEW spring pin in 5th speed shift fork.

20) Apply 3M Super Weatherstrip Adhesive (8001) to clutch housing contact area of air breather and install in clutch housing.

21) Install speedometer driven gear assembly in case with NEW "O" ring and seal (if necessary). Install poppet (detent) balls (3), springs (3), and plugs. Torque poppet plugs to 22-31 ft. lbs. (30-42 N.m).

22) Install restrict ball assembly and back-up light switch and torque both to 22-26 ft. lbs. (30-35 N.m). Apply Stud Locking Compound (3M 4170) to countersunk bolt threads. Install reverse brake cone. Torque bolts to 35-49 INCH lbs. (4.0-5.5 N.m).

23) Position NEW wave spring on 5th gear synchronizer. Apply Mitsubishi Sealant (MD997740) in a uniform and continuous bead, .04-.08" (1-2 mm) in diameter, to rear cover and install. Torque rear cover bolts to 26-31 ft. lbs. (35-42 N.m). *See Fig. 1.*

TORQUE SPECIFICATIONS
TORQUE SPECIFICATIONS

Application	Ft. Lbs. (N.m)
Back-Up Light Switch	22-26 (30-35)
Bearing Retainer Bolt	11-16 (15-22)
Center Differential Drive Gear Bolts	52-59 (70-80)
Driven Bevel Gear Lock Nut	103-118 (140-160)
Front Differential Drive Gear Bolts	52-59 (70-80)
Input Shaft Lock Nut	103-118 (140-160)
Interlock Plate Bolt	11-16 (15-22)
Intermediate Shaft Lock Nut	103-118 (140-160)
Oil Drain Plug	22-26 (30-35)
Oil Filler Plug	22-26 (30-35)
Poppet Plug	22-31 (30-42)
Rear Cover Bolts	26-31 (35-42)
Restrict Ball	22-26 (30-35)
Reverse Idler Shaft Bolt	32-41 (43-55)
Reverse Shift Lever Bolt	11-16 (15-22)
Select Lever Assembly Bolt	11-16 (15-22)
Stopper Bracket Bolt	11-16 (15-22)
Transaxle Case Bolts	26-31 (35-42)
Transfer Assembly Mounting Bolts	41-44 (55-60)
Transfer Case Adapter Bolts	26-31 (35-42)
Transfer Cover Bolts	26-31 (35-42)
Transfer Driven Bevel Gear Lock Nut	103-118 (140-160)
Transfer Extension Housing Bolts	11-16 (15-22)

	INCH Lbs. (N.m)
Transaxle Reverse Brake Cone Screws	35-49 (4.0-5.5)
Transaxle Speedometer Mounting Bolt	27-44 (3-5)
Transfer Case Cover	71-89 (8-10)

TRANSAXLE SPECIFICATIONS
TRANSAXLE SPECIFICATIONS

Application	In. (mm)
Center Differential	
Differential Case Preload	.0031-.0051 (.080-.130)
Viscous Coupling End Play	.0039-.0102 (.100-.260)
Differential Side Gear End Play	.0020-.0100 (.05-.25)
Front Differential	
Differential Case End Play	.0020-.0067 (.050-.170)
Differential Pinion Backlash	.001-.006 (.025-.150)
Front Output Shaft Preload	.0031-.0051 (.080-.130)
Input Shaft Rear Bearing End Play	.0004-.0035 (.010-.090)
Intermediate Gear Preload	.0031-.0051 (.080-.130)
Transaxle	
Input Shaft End Play	0-.0020 (0-.050)
Intermediate Gear Bearing End Play	.0004-.0055 (.010-.140)
Synchronizer Ring Clearance Limit	.020 (.50)
Transfer Case	
Bevel Gear Set Backlash	.0031-.0051 (.080-.130)

	INCH Lbs. (N.m)
Transfer Case Turning Torque	
Drive Bevel Gear	15-22 (1.7-2.5)
Driven Bevel Gear	9-15 (1.0-1.7)

MANUAL TRANSMISSIONS
Nissan FS5R30A & RS5R30A

Pathfinder, Pickup & 300ZX

APPLICATION & LABOR TIMES

APPLICATION & LABOR TIMES

Vehicle Application	Labor Times [1] R & I	[2] Overhaul	Transmission Series
Pathfinder & Pickup (3.0L)			
2WD	3.5	4.5	FS5R30A
4WD	7.5	4.5	FS5R30A
300ZX	4.2	4.5	RS5R30A

[1] – Removal and installation of transmission from vehicle chassis.
[2] – Bench overhaul time for transmission. DOES NOT include removal and installation.

IDENTIFICATION

Transmission serial number is stamped on top of bellhousing.

LUBRICATION & ADJUSTMENTS

See appropriate MANUAL TRANSMISSION SERVICING article in TRANSMISSION SERVICING section.

TROUBLE SHOOTING

See GENERAL TROUBLE SHOOTING article in this section.

REMOVAL & INSTALLATION

See appropriate MANUAL TRANSMISSION REMOVAL article in TRANSMISSION SERVICING section.

TRANSMISSION DISASSEMBLY

1) Remove interlock check plug, spring and detent ball. Remove interlock stopper. Interlock stopper assembly MUST be disassembled before removal to prevent detent ball from falling into case. Remove control housing check ball and spring. See Fig. 1.
2) Using a punch, remove retaining roll pin from shifting arm. Remove control rod. Remove rear extension housing with striking arm from main case. Remove front cover and gasket. Remove stopper ring and main bearing snap ring. Separate and remove intermediate plate from transmission case.
3) Install Mounting Adapter Plate (ST23810001) to intermediate plate and mount assembly in vise. Remove overdrive/reverse fork rod. Remove retaining roll pin from shift lever. Remove shift rod, lever and interlock. Remove 1st/2nd, 3rd/4th and reverse shift forks. Remove retaining roll pin from overdrive shift fork. Remove overdrive shift rod with shift fork.
4) Measure thrust clearance of each gear. See Fig. 3. See MAINSHAFT & COUNTERSHAFT GEAR THRUST CLEARANCES table. If thrust clearance is not within specification, check condition of gear, bushings, washers, shaft and synchronizer hub for wear or damage during disassembly.

MAINSHAFT & COUNTERSHAFT GEAR THRUST CLEARANCES

Application	Clearance - In. (mm)
1st Main Gear	.009-.013 (.23-.33)
2nd Main Gear	.009-.013 (.23-.33)
3rd Main Gear	.009-.013 (.23-.33)
O.D. Counter Gear	.009-.013 (.23-.33)
Counter Gear	.004-.010 (.10-.25)
Reverse Main Gear (FS5R30A)	.013-.017 (.33-.43)
Reverse Main Gear (RS5R30A)	0-.004 (0-.11)
Reverse Idler Gear (FS5R30A)	.012-.021 (.30-.53)
Reverse Idler Gear (RS5R30A)	.013-.017 (.33-.43)

5) Remove reverse coupling sleeve. Remove mainshaft and countershaft rear snap ring. Remove "C" ring holder. Remove "C" ring from mainshaft. Using 2-jaw puller, remove countershaft rear bearing. See Fig. 2.

6) Remove reverse idler gear and thrust washers. On 300ZX model, remove sub-gear from reverse idler gear. On 2WD models, remove mainshaft rear bearing using 2-jaw puller. On all models, remove reverse gear, mainshaft spacer and reverse synchronizer hub as an assembly. Remove reverse gear needle bearings.
7) Using bearing splitter with puller, remove reverse counter gear. Remove overdrive coupling sleeve, overdrive synchronizer ring, reverse synchronizer ring and spring inserts as an assembly. Using bearing splitter with puller, remove reverse gear bushing. Remove overdrive gear and reverse cone as an assembly.
8) Using a press, remove mainshaft and countershaft from intermediate plate. Alternate between mainshaft and countershaft. Shafts must be removed together.

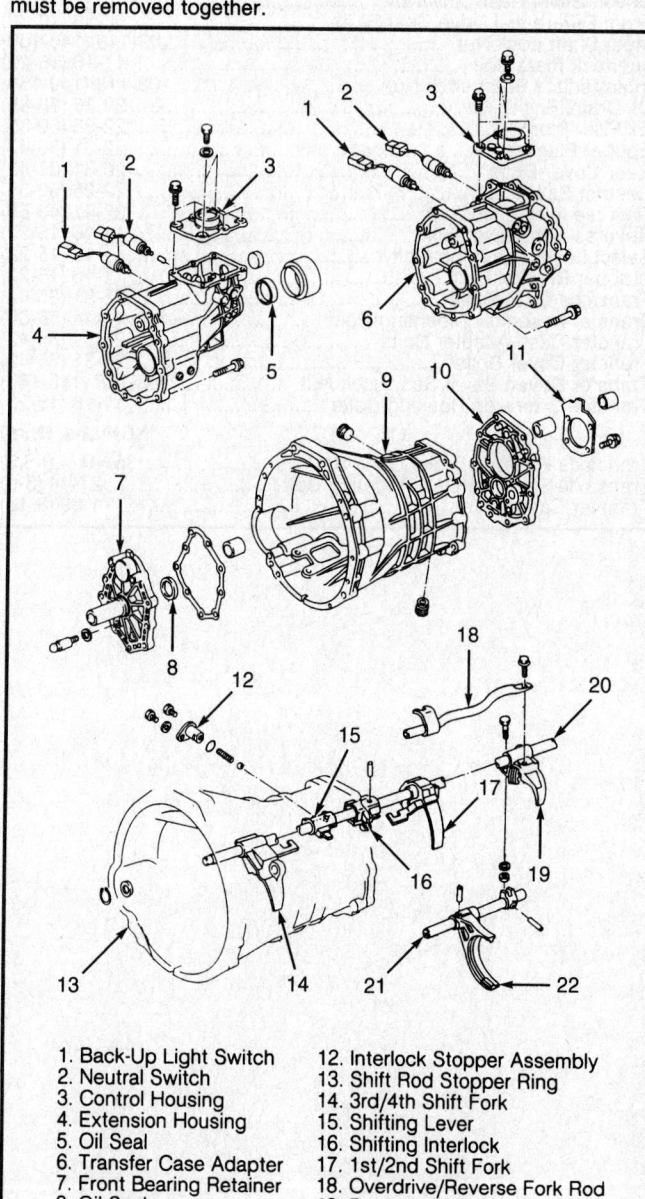

1. Back-Up Light Switch	12. Interlock Stopper Assembly
2. Neutral Switch	13. Shift Rod Stopper Ring
3. Control Housing	14. 3rd/4th Shift Fork
4. Extension Housing	15. Shifting Lever
5. Oil Seal	16. Shifting Interlock
6. Transfer Case Adapter	17. 1st/2nd Shift Fork
7. Front Bearing Retainer	18. Overdrive/Reverse Fork Rod
8. Oil Seal	19. Reverse Shift Fork
9. Transmission Case	20. Shift Rod
10. Intermediate Plate	21. Overdrive Fork Rod
11. Rear Bearing Retainer	22. Overdrive Shift Fork

93J23993   Courtesy of Nissan Motor Co., U.S.A.

Fig. 1: Exploded View Of Case & Shifting Assemblies

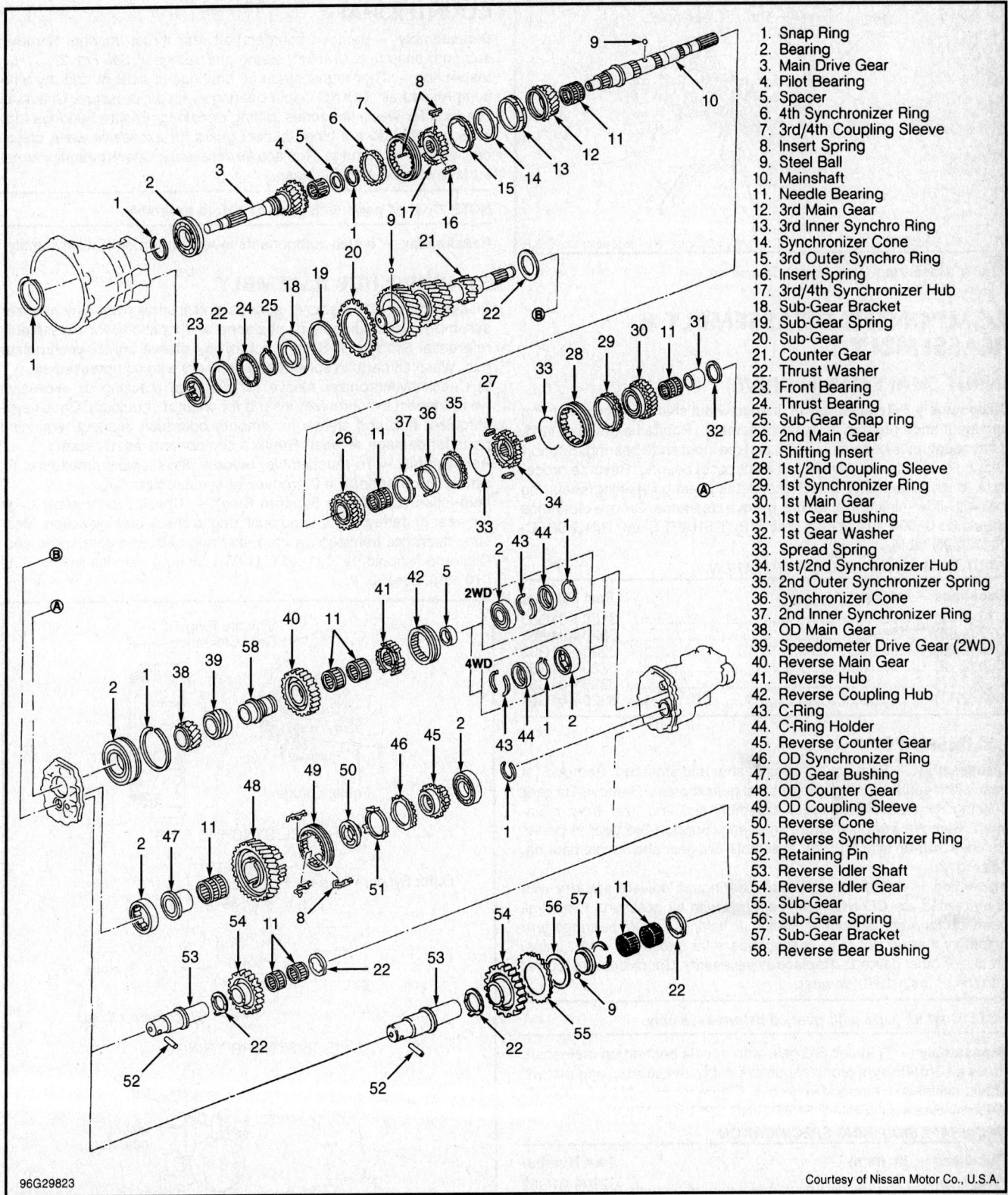

1. Snap Ring
2. Bearing
3. Main Drive Gear
4. Pilot Bearing
5. Spacer
6. 4th Synchronizer Ring
7. 3rd/4th Coupling Sleeve
8. Insert Spring
9. Steel Ball
10. Mainshaft
11. Needle Bearing
12. 3rd Main Gear
13. 3rd Inner Synchro Ring
14. Synchronizer Cone
15. 3rd Outer Synchro Ring
16. Insert Spring
17. 3rd/4th Synchronizer Hub
18. Sub-Gear Bracket
19. Sub-Gear Spring
20. Sub-Gear
21. Counter Gear
22. Thrust Washer
23. Front Bearing
24. Thrust Bearing
25. Sub-Gear Snap ring
26. 2nd Main Gear
27. Shifting Insert
28. 1st/2nd Coupling Sleeve
29. 1st Synchronizer Ring
30. 1st Main Gear
31. 1st Gear Bushing
32. 1st Gear Washer
33. Spread Spring
34. 1st/2nd Synchronizer Hub
35. 2nd Outer Synchronizer Spring
36. Synchronizer Cone
37. 2nd Inner Synchronizer Ring
38. OD Main Gear
39. Speedometer Drive Gear (2WD)
40. Reverse Main Gear
41. Reverse Hub
42. Reverse Coupling Hub
43. C-Ring
44. C-Ring Holder
45. Reverse Counter Gear
46. OD Synchronizer Ring
47. OD Gear Bushing
48. OD Counter Gear
49. OD Coupling Sleeve
50. Reverse Cone
51. Reverse Synchronizer Ring
52. Retaining Pin
53. Reverse Idler Shaft
54. Reverse Idler Gear
55. Sub-Gear
56. Sub-Gear Spring
57. Sub-Gear Bracket
58. Reverse Bear Bushing

96G29823

Courtesy of Nissan Motor Co., U.S.A.

Fig. 2: Exploded View Of Mainshaft & Countershaft Assemblies

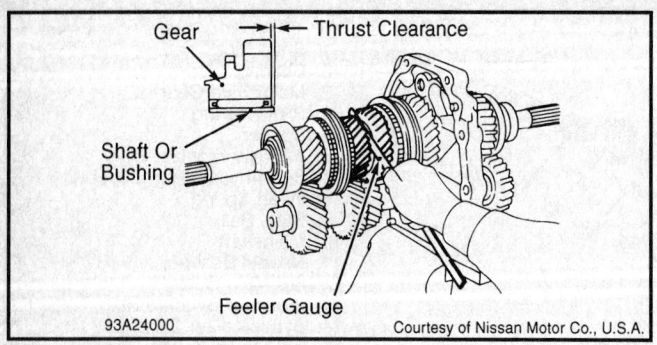

Fig. 3: Measuring Gear Thrust Clearance

COMPONENT DISASSEMBLY & REASSEMBLY

INPUT SHAFT (MAIN DRIVE)

Disassembly & Reassembly – Inspect input shaft, synchronizer ring and input shaft bearing for wear or damage. Rotate bearing by hand. If any roughness or binding is felt, replace input shaft bearing. Support bearing in blocks and press input shaft out of bearing. Reverse procedure to install bearing. Select and install bearing retaining snap ring that will allow minimum snap ring groove clearance. Groove clearance should be 0-.004" (0-.10 mm). See INPUT SHAFT SNAP RING SPECIFICATION table.

INPUT SHAFT SNAP RING SPECIFICATION

Thickness – In. (mm)	Part Number
.074 (1.89)	32204-01G60
.077 (1.95)	32204-01G61
.078 (2.05)	32204-01G62
.080 (2.12)	32204-01G63
.082 (2.07)	32204-01G64
.083 (2.11)	32204-01G65

MAINSHAFT

Disassembly – Remove 1st gear washer and steel ball. Remove 1st gear with needle bearing. Support 2nd gear in press. Remove 1st gear bushing, 1st/2nd synchronizer assembly and 2nd gear from mainshaft. Remove front mainshaft snap ring. Support 3rd gear in press. Remove 3rd/4th synchronizer assembly, 3rd gear and needle bearing. See Fig. 2.
Inspection – Thoroughly clean all bearings in solvent and dry with compressed air. DO NOT spin bearings with air pressure. Check all bearings for wear, scratches, pitting or flaking. Ensure bearings turn smoothly and do not bind. Inspect gears for excessive wear, chips, cracks or other damage. Replace as necessary. Check bearing journal surface of mainshaft for wear.

NOTE: Coat all parts with gear oil before assembly.

Reassembly – 1) Install 3rd gear with needle bearing on mainshaft. Press on 3rd/4th synchronizer hub assembly. Install snap ring that will obtain minimum clearance in groove. Clearance should be 0-.004" (0-.10 mm). See MAINSHAFT SNAP RING SPECIFICATION table.

MAINSHAFT SNAP RING SPECIFICATION

Thickness – In. (mm)	Part Number
.074 (1.99)	32204-01G62
.078 (2.03)	32204-01G63
.081 (2.07)	32204-01G64
.083 (2.11)	32204-01G65
.085 (2.15)	32204-01G66
.086 (2.19)	32204-01G67

2) Install 2nd gear with needle bearing. Press on 1st/2nd synchronizer hub assembly. Press on 1st gear bushing using 1st gear washer. Install 1st gear with needle bearing. Install steel ball and 1st gear washer. See Fig. 2.

COUNTERSHAFT

Disassembly – Remove countershaft rear thrust bearing. Remove sub-gear snap ring, bracket, spring and sub-gear. See Fig. 2.
Inspection – Thoroughly clean all bearings in solvent and dry with compressed air. DO NOT spin bearings with air pressure. Check all bearings for wear, scratches, pitting or flaking. Ensure bearings turn smoothly and do not bind. Inspect gears for excessive wear, chips, cracks or other damage. Replace as necessary. Check bearing journal surface of mainshaft for wear.

NOTE: Coat all parts with gear oil before assembly.

Reassembly – Install components in reverse order of disassembly.

SYNCHRO HUB ASSEMBLY

Disassembly – 1) Remove springs and inserts from synchronizer assembly. Note component positions and locations for reassembly reference. See Fig. 4. Slide synchronizer sleeve off of synchronizer hub. Wash all parts in solvent and blow dry with compressed air.
2) Check synchronizer sleeve for damage, cracking or excessive wear. Inspect synchronizer inserts for wear at shoulders. Check synchronizer hub and sleeve for smooth operation. Inspect remaining parts for damage or wear. Replace components as necessary.
Reassembly – To reassemble, reverse disassembly procedure. Fit synchronizer springs in 3 grooves of synchronizer hub.
Inspection (One-Piece Synchro Ring) – Check synchronizer rings for wear or damage. Turn and push ring to check braking action. Measure clearance between synchronizer ring back and gear spline end. Clearance should be .041-.051" (1.05-1.30 mm). Service limit is .028" (.70 mm). See Fig. 4.

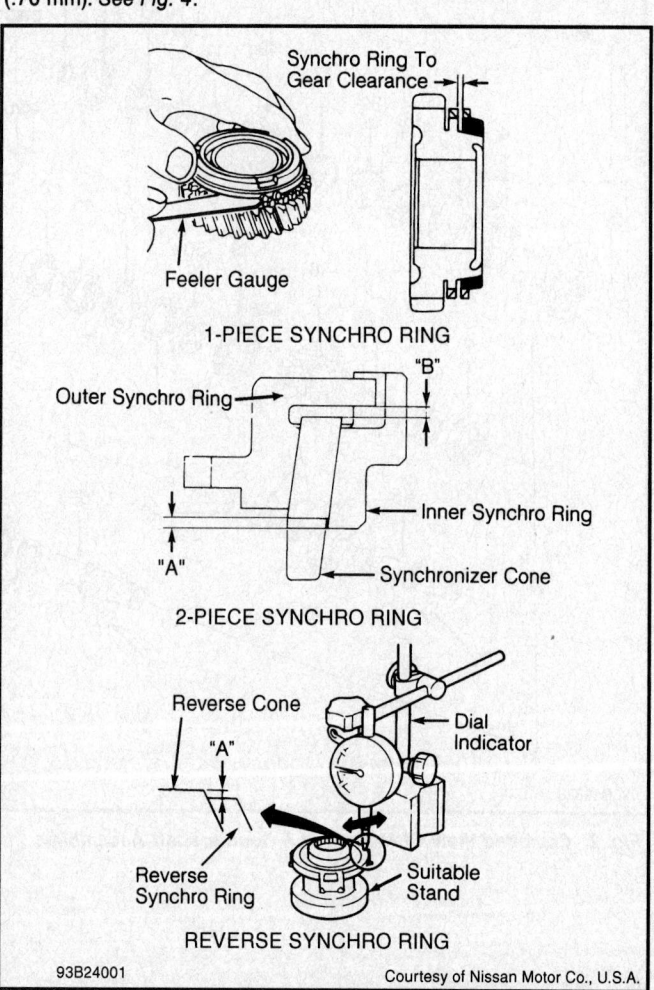

Fig. 4: Identifying Synchro Assembly Measuring Points

Inspection (3rd/4th gear 2-Piece Synchro Ring) – The 3rd/4th hub assembly uses a 2-piece synchronizer ring assembly. Apply pressure on inner and outer synchronizer ring against synchronizer cone. Measure clearance "A" between inner synchronizer ring and synchronizer cone. *See Fig. 4.* Clearance should be .024-.043" (.60-1.1 mm). Measure clearance "B" between outer synchronizer ring and synchronizer cone. Clearance should be .028-.035" (.70-.90 mm). Service limit for both measurements is .008" (.20 mm).

Inspection (Reverse Synchro Ring) – Apply pressure between inner synchronizer cone and outer ring. Measure distance "A". *See Fig. 4.* Height should be .004"-.014" (.1-.35 mm). Service limit is .028" (.70 mm).

TRANSMISSION ADJUSTMENTS

NOTE: Check countershaft thrust clearance if transmission case, countershaft, countershaft thrust bearing and/or sub-gear components have been replaced.

Countershaft Thrust Clearance – **1)** Install countershaft with sub-gear components and front thrust bearing in intermediate plate. Install transmission case. Do not install countershaft front bearing shim. Install 2 bolts to secure case to intermediate plate. Mount dial indicator and measure countershaft thrust clearance. *See Fig. 5.*

2) Thrust clearance (end play) should be .004-.010" (.10-.25 mm). Select correct countershaft thrust shim. See COUNTERSHAFT FRONT BEARING THRUST WASHER SPECIFICATION table.

COUNTERSHAFT FRONT BEARING THRUST WASHER SPECIFICATION

Dial Indication Deflection In. (mm)	Thickness In. (mm)	Part Number
.037-.040 (.93-1.02)	.032 (.80)	32218-01G00
.040-.043 (.101-1.10)	.035 (.88)	32218-01G11
.043-.047 (1.09-1.18)	.038 (.96)	32218-01G12
.046-.049 (1.17-1.26)	.041 (1.04)	32218-01G13
.049-.053 (1.25-1.34)	.044 (1.12)	32218-01G14
.052-.060 (1.33-1.42)	.050 (1.28)	32218-01G15
.059-.062 (1.49-1.58)	.054 (1.36)	32218-01G16
.061-.065 (1.57-1.66)	.057 (1.44)	32218-01G17

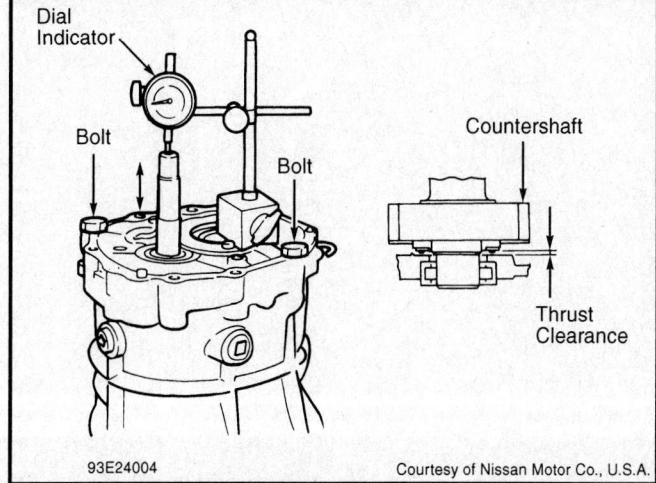

93E24004   Courtesy of Nissan Motor Co., U.S.A.

Fig. 5: Measuring Countershaft Thrust Clearance

NOTE: Check reverse idler gear thrust clearance if rear extension housing (2WD), transfer adapter (4WD), reverse idler gear, reverse idler shaft and/or reverse idler thrust washer have been replaced.

Reverse Idler Gear Thrust Clearance – **1)** Install original reverse idler gear rear thrust washer with reverse idler gear, needle bearings, front thrust washer and idler shaft into extension housing or transfer adapter.

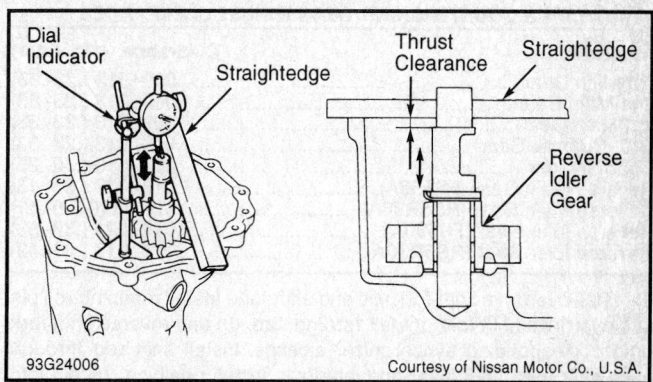

93G24006   Courtesy of Nissan Motor Co., U.S.A.

Fig. 6: Measuring Reverse Idler Gear Thrust Clearance

2) Mount dial indicator on front end of reverse idler shaft. *See Fig. 6.* Place straightedge on front surface of extension housing or transfer adapter. Straightedge acts as a stop for reverse idler shaft. Move reverse idler shaft up until it contacts straightedge and measure movement. Reverse idler gear thrust clearance should be .012-.021" (.30-.53 mm).

3) If thrust clearance is not within specification, replace reverse idler rear thrust washer. Thrust washers are available in .078" (1.97 mm) and .082" (2.07 mm) sizes. Part numbers are 32284-01G10 and 32284-01G11.

TRANSMISSION REASSEMBLY

1) Install mainshaft and countershaft into intermediate plate. Install Mounting Adapter Plate (ST23810001) to intermediate plate and mount assembly in vise. Apply multipurpose grease to countershaft rear bearing to hold bearing rollers in place. Partially install mainshaft into intermediate plate. Install countershaft into intermediate plate while installing input shaft with bearing and spacer onto mainshaft. *See Fig. 2.*

2) Install Mainshaft Puller (J26349-3) onto mainshaft. Install "C" ring and "C" holder onto mainshaft behind Puller. Pull mainshaft until seated in bearing. Guide countershaft into intermediate plate as mainshaft is being installed.

3) Install overdrive bushing onto countershaft. Install overdrive gear onto mainshaft. Ensure wide shoulder of overdrive gear faces backward. Place transmission housing on end. Remove mounting adapter from intermediate plate. Install intermediate plate with gear assemblies into transmission housing.

4) Install reverse idler shaft while installing overdrive counter gear with needle bearing onto countershaft. Install reverse gear bushing with speedometer drive gear (2WD) on mainshaft. Install reverse inner synchronizer cone on countershaft. Install overdrive coupling sleeve with synchronizer ring on overdrive countergear. *See Fig. 2.*

5) Install reverse counter gear. Install reverse gear with needle bearing. Install sub-gear onto reverse idler gear. Install reverse idler gear with thrust washers and needle bearings. Install reverse synchronizer hub on mainshaft. On 2WD models, install mainshaft spacer and rear bearing. Install countershaft rear bearing.

6) On all models, remove intermediate plate with gear assemblies from transmission housing. Mount intermediate plate with mounting adapter in vise. Select and install "C" ring that will obtain minimum groove clearance. Groove clearance should be 0-.004" (0-.10 mm). "C" rings are available in .003" (.07 mm) increments. Rings range in thickness from .104" (2.63 mm) to .145" (3.68 mm). Part numbers are 32348-01G00 through 32348-01G15. *See Fig. 2.*

7) Install "C" ring holder and snap ring on mainshaft. Install spacer and snap ring on countershaft. Select and install snap ring that will obtain minimum groove clearance. Groove clearance should be 0-.004" (0-.10 mm). Snap rings are available in .002 (.06 mm) increments. Snap rings range in thickness from .050" (1.26 mm) to .069" (1.74 mm). Part numbers are 32236-01G00 through 32236-01G08.

8) Install reverse synchronizer hub sleeve. Recheck all gear thrust clearances. See MAINSHAFT & COUNTERSHAFT GEAR THRUST CLEARANCES table.

MAINSHAFT & COUNTERSHAFT GEAR THRUST CLEARANCES

Application	Clearance - In. (mm)
1st Main Gear	.009-.013 (.23-.33)
2nd Main Gear	.009-.013 (.23-.33)
3rd Main Gear	.009-.013 (.23-.33)
O.D. Counter Gear	.009-.013 (.23-.33)
Counter Gear	.004-.010 (.10-.25)
Reverse Main Gear (FS530A)	.013-.017 (.33-.43)
Reverse Main Gear (RS5R30A)	0-.004 (0-.11)
Reverse Idler Gear (FS530A)	.012-.021 (.30-.53)
Reverse Idler Gear (RS5R30A)	.013-.017 (.33-.43)

9) Install overdrive shift fork rod and shift fork. Install retaining roll pin into overdrive shift fork. Install 1st/2nd, 3rd/4th and reverse shift fork onto corresponding synchronizer sleeves. Install shift rod through each shift fork, shift lever and interlock. Install retaining roll pin into shift lever. Ensure shift rod operates smoothly. *See Fig. 1.*

10) Remove intermediate plate from vise. Remove mounting adapter plate from intermediate plate. Apply sealant to intermediate plate. Install countershaft front thrust bearing and selected thrust shim. Install intermediate plate to transmission case. Install check spring and detent ball into interlock stopper. Install interlock stopper assembly. Tighten detent ball plug.

11) Install shift rod stopper ring and snap ring. Install front bearing snap ring. Install front bearing retainer. Install extension housing (2WD) or transfer adapter (4WD) with shift arm. Install retaining roll pin into shift arm. Install return spring and check ball. Apply sealant to control housing and install.

TORQUE SPECIFICATIONS
TORQUE SPECIFICATIONS

Application	Ft. Lbs. (N.m)
Control Housing bolt	12-15 (16-21)
Detent Ball Plug	14-18 (19-25)
Drain & Fill Plug	18-25 (25-34)
Extension Housing-To-Case Bolt	23-31 (31-42)
Front Bearing Retainer Bolt	12-15 (16-21)
Housing Bolt	12-15 (16-21)
Interlock Stopper Bolt	23-31 (31-42)
Neutral Safety Switch	14-22 (19-29)
Overdrive/Reverse Fork Rod Bolt	18-22 (25-29)
Overdrive/Reverse Shift Fork Bolt	21-25 (29-34)
Reverse Lamp Switch	14-22 (19-29)
Select Check Plug	14-22 (19-29)

Application	INCH Lbs. (N.m)
Guide Plate-To-Extension Housing Bolt	53-71 (6-8)
Reverse Check Sleeve Bolt	53-71 (6-8)
Vehicle Speed Sensor	35-44 (4-5)

Pickup (2.4L) & 240SX

APPLICATION & LABOR TIMES

APPLICATION & LABOR TIMES

Vehicle Application	Labor Times		Series
	[1] R & I	[2] Overhaul	
Pickup (2.4L 4-Cylinder)			
2WD	3.5	4.5	FS5W71C
4WD	7.5	4.5	FS5W71C
240SX	3.0	4.5	FS5W71C

[1] – Removal and installation of transmission from vehicle chassis.
[2] – Bench overhaul time for transmission. DOES NOT include removal and installation.

IDENTIFICATION

Transmission serial number is stamped on top of bellhousing.

LUBRICATION & ADJUSTMENTS

See appropriate MANUAL TRANSMISSION SERVICING article in TRANSMISSION SERVICING section.

TROUBLE SHOOTING

See GENERAL TROUBLE SHOOTING article in this section.

REMOVAL & INSTALLATION

See appropriate MANUAL TRANSMISSION REMOVAL article in TRANSMISSION SERVICING section.

TRANSMISSION DISASSEMBLY

1) Remove control housing, reverse check ball and spring. Remove shift restrict spring plugs, springs and plungers. Use pin punch to remove shift arm retaining roll pin. Remove shift arm. Using plastic hammer, remove extension housing (2WD) or transfer case adapter (4WD). Remove front cover and gasket. Remove countershaft front bearing shim and mainshaft bearing snap ring. Remove oil seal from front cover. See Figs. 1 and 2.

2) Separate transmission case from intermediate plate. Install mounting Adapter Plate (ST23810001) to intermediate plate. Remove shift rod from intermediate plate. Remove all check ball plugs, springs and check balls from intermediate plate.

3) Drive out all retaining roll pins from shift forks. Remove fork rods and interlock balls. Draw out 3rd/4th and OD/reverse fork rods.

4) Measure thrust clearance of each gear. See Fig. 2 and 3. For specifications, see MAINSHAFT GEAR THRUST CLEARANCES table. If thrust clearances are not within specifications, check condition of gears, bushings, washers, shaft and/or synchronizer hub for wear or damage during disassembly.

MAINSHAFT GEAR THRUST CLEARANCES

Application	Clearance In. (mm)
1st Main Gear	.012-.016 (.31-.41)
2nd Main Gear	.004-.008 (.11-.21)
3rd Main Gear	.004-.008 (.11-.21)
Overdrive Gear	.009-.016 (.24-.41)

5) Engage 2nd and reverse gear to lock transmission shafts. Using 2-jaw puller, remove countershaft front bearing. Remove countershaft front snap ring. Remove sub-gear bracket, spring and gear. Using 2-jaw puller, remove counter drive gear with input shaft assembly. Remove snap ring and 3rd and 4th synchronizer assembly. Remove 3rd main gear. Unstake mainshaft and countershaft lock nuts and remove. See Fig. 2 and 3.

NOTE: Mainshaft lock nut has left-hand thread.

6) Using 2-jaw puller, remove overdrive counter gear with bearing. Remove reverse counter gear with spacer. On 1995 models, remove snap rings from reverse idler shaft and draw out reverse idler gear, thrust washers and reverse idler gear bearing. Remove speedometer drive gear and steel ball. On 1996 models, remove reverse idler gear assembly with shaft. On both models, remove snap ring and pull out overdrive mainshaft bearing. Remove snap ring, (2WD model). Remove mainshaft nut. Remove speedometer drive gear with steel ball, (1996 2WD models).

7) Remove thrust washer, steel roller bearing and washer. Remove overdrive (5th) main gear, needle bearing and synchronizer ring. On 1995 models, remove OD coupling sleeve and shifting inserts. Press out mainshaft and counter gear alternately. Ensure gears do not hit each other. On 1996 models, Remove counter gear by tapping on rear end of counter gear. Press out overdrive gear bushing and overdrive and reverse synchronizer assembly. Remove reverse main gear and needle bearing.

8) Press out reverse gear bushing. Reverse thrust washer, steel ball, 1st main gear needle bearing. Press out 1st gear bushing together with 2nd main gear. Remove 2nd gear needle bearing. Remove main drive snap ring and ball bearing.

9) Drive out mainshaft ball bearing and counter rear bearing from adaptor plate. Remove oil gutter.

COMPONENT DISASSEMBLY & REASSEMBLY

MAINSHAFT, COUNTERSHAFT & MAIN DRIVE GEAR

Disassembly – Remove 1st gear washer and steel ball. Remove 1st main gear and needle bearing. Press out 2nd main gear together with 1st gear bushing and 1st/2nd synchronizer assembly. Remove mainshaft front snap ring. Press out 3rd/4th synchronizer assembly and 3rd gear needle bearing. Remove main drive gear snap ring and spacer. Press out main drive gear bearing.

Inspection – Inspect mainshaft, synchronizer ring, gears and mainshaft for wear or damage.

SYNCHRO HUB ASSEMBLY

Disassembly – 1) Slide synchronizer sleeve off of synchronizer hub. Remove springs and/or keys from synchronizer assembly. Note component positions and locations for reassembly reference. Wash all parts in solvent and blow dry with compressed air.

2) Check synchronizer sleeve for damage, cracking or excessive wear. Inspect synchronizer key or insert key for wear at shoulders. Check synchronizer hub and sleeve for smooth operation. Inspect remaining parts for damage or wear. Replace components as necessary.

Reassembly – To reassemble, reverse disassembly procedure. Fit synchronizer springs in 3 grooves of synchro hub. Ensure synchronizer key spring openings are offset.

Inspection (1-Piece Synchro Ring) – Check synchronizer rings for wear or damage. Turn and push ring to check braking action. Measure clearance between synchronizer ring back and gear spline end. See Fig. 5. Clearance for 1st, 3rd/main drive and OD, should be .047-.063" (1.2-1.6 mm). Service limit is .031" (.80 mm). For reverse synchronizer, clearance should be .043-.061" (1.10-1.55 mm). Service limit is .028" (.70 mm).

Inspection (2-Piece Synchro Ring) – The 2nd (4WD), 3rd/4th (2WD) hub assembly uses a 2-piece synchronizer ring assembly. Apply pressure on inner and outer synchronizer ring against synchronizer cone. Measure clearance "A" between inner synchronizer ring and synchronizer cone. See Fig. 5. Clearance "A" should be .028-.035" (.70-.90 mm). Measure clearance "B" between outer synchronizer ring and synchronizer cone. Clearance "B" should be .024-.043" (.60-1.10 mm). Service limit for both measurements is .008" (.20 mm).

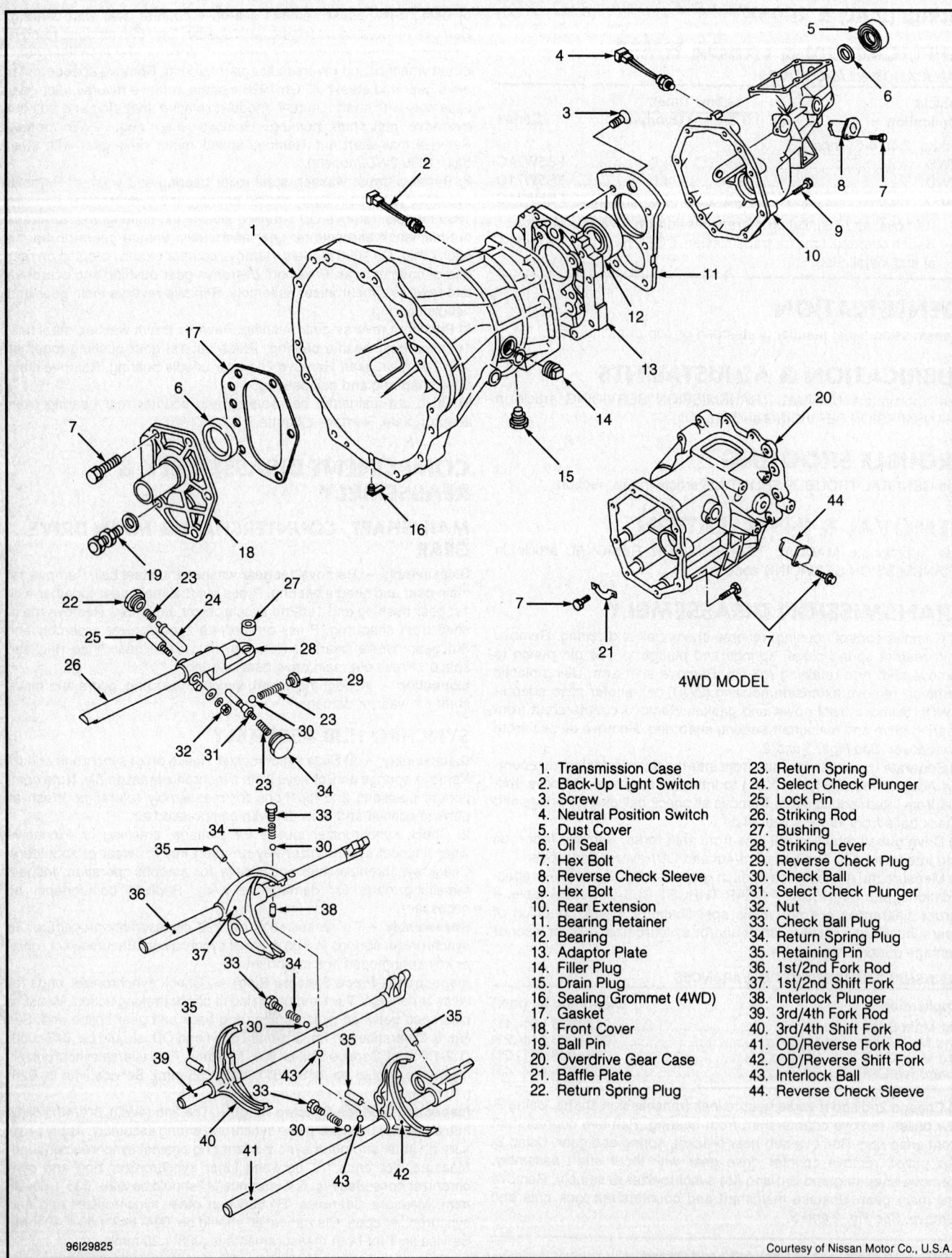

1. Transmission Case
2. Back-Up Light Switch
3. Screw
4. Neutral Position Switch
5. Dust Cover
6. Oil Seal
7. Hex Bolt
8. Reverse Check Sleeve
9. Hex Bolt
10. Rear Extension
11. Bearing Retainer
12. Bearing
13. Adaptor Plate
14. Filler Plug
15. Drain Plug
16. Sealing Grommet (4WD)
17. Gasket
18. Front Cover
19. Ball Pin
20. Overdrive Gear Case
21. Baffle Plate
22. Return Spring Plug
23. Return Spring
24. Select Check Plunger
25. Lock Pin
26. Striking Rod
27. Bushing
28. Striking Lever
29. Reverse Check Plug
30. Check Ball
31. Select Check Plunger
32. Nut
33. Check Ball Plug
34. Return Spring Plug
35. Retaining Pin
36. 1st/2nd Fork Rod
37. 1st/2nd Shift Fork
38. Interlock Plunger
39. 3rd/4th Fork Rod
40. 3rd/4th Shift Fork
41. OD/Reverse Fork Rod
42. OD/Reverse Shift Fork
43. Interlock Ball
44. Reverse Check Sleeve

4WD MODEL

96l29825

Courtesy of Nissan Motor Co., U.S.A.

Fig. 1: Identifying Transmission Components

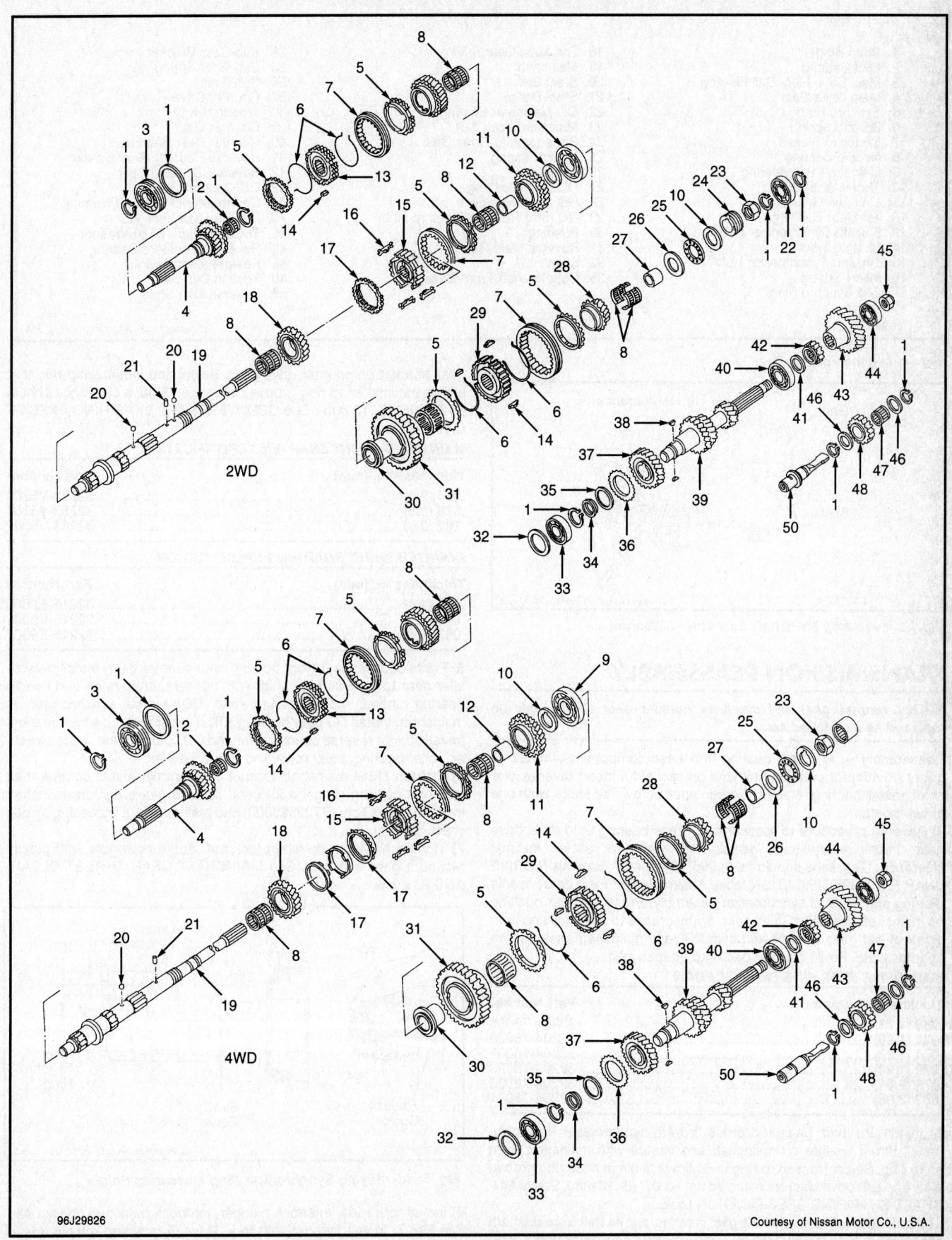

Fig. 2: Identifying Gear Components (1996 2WD & 4WD Shown, 1995 Similar)(1 Of 2)

96J29826

Courtesy of Nissan Motor Co., U.S.A.

1. Snap Ring	18. 2nd Main Gear	34. Sub-Gear Bracket
2. Pilot Bearing	19. Mainshaft	35. Sub-Gear Spring
3. Main Drive Gear Ball Bearing	20. Steel Ball	36. Sub-Gear
4. Main Drive Gear	21. Steel Roller	37. Counter Drive
5. Synchro Ring	22. OD Mainshaft Bearing	38. Woodruff Key
6. Spread Spring	23. Mainshaft Lock Nut	39. Counter Gear
7. Coupling Sleeve	24. Speedometer Drive Gear	40. Counter Rear Bearing
8. Needle Bearing	25. Roller Bearing	41. Reverse Counter Gear Spacer
9. Mainshaft Ball Bearing	26. Washer	42. Reverse Counter Gear
10. Thrust Washer	27. OD Gear Bushing	43. OD Counter Gear
11. 1st Main Gear	28. OD (5th) Main Gear	44. Countershaft Rear End Bearing
12. 1st Gear Bushing	29. OD (5th)/Reverse Synchro Hub	45. Countershaft Lock Nut
13. 3rd/4th Synchronizer Hub	30. Bushing	46. Reverse Idler Thrust Washer
14. Shifting Insert	31. Reverse Main Gear	47. Reverse Idler Gear Bearing
15. 1st/2nd Synchronizer Hub	32. Shim	48. Reverse Idler Gear
16. Insert Spring	33. Countershaft Front Bearing	49. Friction Damper
17. 2nd Synchro Ring		50. Reverse Idler Shaft

96J30477

Courtesy of Nissan Motor Co., U.S.A.

Fig. 3: Legend For Fig. 2

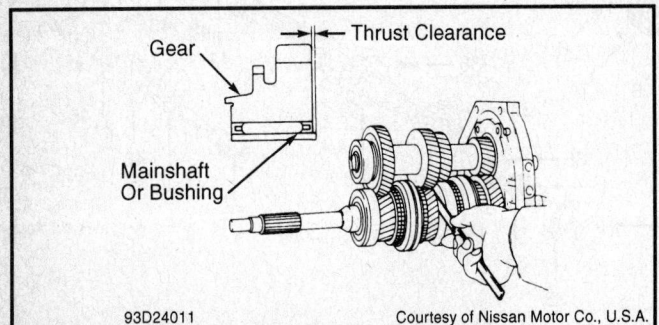

93D24011   Courtesy of Nissan Motor Co., U.S.A.

Fig. 4: Measuring Mainshaft Gear Thrust Clearance

TRANSMISSION REASSEMBLY

NOTE: Overdrive gear and overdrive counter gear should only be replaced as a matched set.

Reassembly – 1) Install bearing into case components. Install oil gutter on adaptor plate and expand on rear side. Insert reverse idler shaft. Install bearing retainer. Tighten each screw and stake each one at two points.

2) Reverse procedure to reassemble. Press bearing onto main drive gear. Install washer and select snap ring that allows minimal clearance. Clearance should be 0-.005" (0-.13 mm). See MAIN DRIVE SNAP RING SPECIFICATION table. Assemble 2nd main gear, needle bearing and 1st/2nd synchronizer assembly. Press 1st gear bushing on mainshaft. Install 1st main gear. Apply grease to steel ball and both sides of 1st gear washer and install. Press mainshaft assembly to adaptor plate. Press counter gear into adaptor plate.

MAIN DRIVE SNAP RING SPECIFICATION

Thickness In. (mm)	Part Number
.068 (1.73)	32204-78005
.071 (1.80)	32204-78000
.074 (1.87)	32204-78001
.076 (1.94)	32204-78002
.079 (2.01)	32204-78003
.082 (2.08)	32204-78004

3) Install 3rd main gear and press 3rd/4th synchronizer assembly. Install thrust washer on mainshaft and secure with mainshaft front snap ring. Select front snap ring that allows minimal snap ring groove clearance. Groove clearance should be 0-.007" (0-.18 mm). See MAINSHAFT SNAP RING SPECIFICATION table.

4) Apply gear oil to mainshaft pilot bearing and install to mainshaft. Press counter drive gear with main drive gear. Ensure side with shoulder of counter drive gear are facing to front. Install sub-gear and sub-

gear bracket on counter drive gear. Select and install snap ring that allows minimal snap ring groove clearance. Groove clearance should be 0-.005" (0-.13 mm). See COUNTERSHAFT SNAP RING SPECIFICATION table.

MAINSHAFT FRONT SNAP RING SPECIFICATION

Thickness In. (mm)	Part Number
.094 (2.4)	32263-V5200
.098 (2.5)	32263-V5201
.102 (2.6)	32263-V5202

COUNTER SHAFT SNAP RING SPECIFICATION

Thickness In. (mm)	Part Number
.055 (1.4)	32215-E9000
.059 (1.5)	32215-E9001
.063 (1.6)	32215-E9002

5) Press counter gear front bearing onto counter gear. Install reverse idler gear to reverse idler shaft with spacers, snap rings and needle bearing. Install insert retainer and OD/reverse synchronizer to mainshaft. Install OD gear bushing, OD main gear and needle bearing. Install spacer reverse counter gear and OD counter gear. Install washer, roller bearing, steel roller and thrust washer.

6) Tighten NEW mainshaft locknut temporarily. Install countershaft rear end bearing. Engage 2nd and reverse gears tighten mainshaft lock nut using Tool (ST22520000) and mainshaft nut tightening torque chart. *See Fig. 6.*

7) Tighten NEW countershaft lock nut. Stake both nuts with punch. Measure gear end play. See MAINSHAFT GEAR THRUST CLEARANCES table.

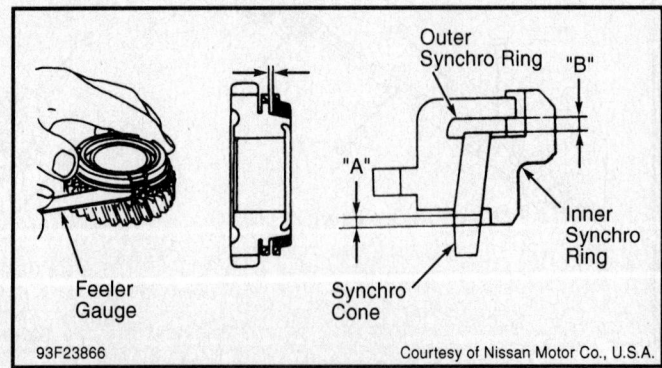

93F23866   Courtesy of Nissan Motor Co., U.S.A.

Fig. 5: Identifying Synchronizer Ring Measuring Points

8) Install fork rods, interlock plunger, interlock balls and check balls. *See Fig. 7.* Install 1st/2nd shift fork. Drive in retaining roll pin. Install 3rd/4th shift fork. Drive in retaining roll pin. Install overdrive and reverse shift fork. Drive in retaining roll pin.

9) Install front cover oil seal. Apply grease to lip of seal. Apply liquid gasket Loctite (51813) or equivalent. Install gear assembly onto adaptor plate by lightly tapping with plastic hammer. Install main drive gear ball bearing snap ring. Apply sealant to mating surface of adaptor plate. Place shift forks in neutral position. Install shift lever and rod onto adaptor plate and align shifting lever with shift brackets. Install rear extension housing. Install shift arm retaining roll pin. Measure distance ("A") from front of transmission case to front of countershaft bearing. *See Fig. 7.* Clearance should be .178" (4.52 mm) to .185" (4.71 mm). If clearance is less than specifications, select and install correct shim. To determine correct shim, subtract measurement ("A") from specification. Match difference to shims available. See COUNTERSHAFT ADJUSTING SHIM SPECIFICATION table.

10) Install front bearing retainer. Install shifter restrict pin assemblies. Install reverse check ball and spring. Install shifter control housing.

COUNTERSHAFT ADJUSTING SHIM SPECIFICATION

Shim Thickness In. (mm)	Part Number
.004 (.10)	32218-V5000
.008 (.20)	32218-V5001
.012 (.30)	32218-V5002
.016 (.40)	32218-V5003
.020 (.50)	32218-V5004
.024 (.60)	32218-V5005

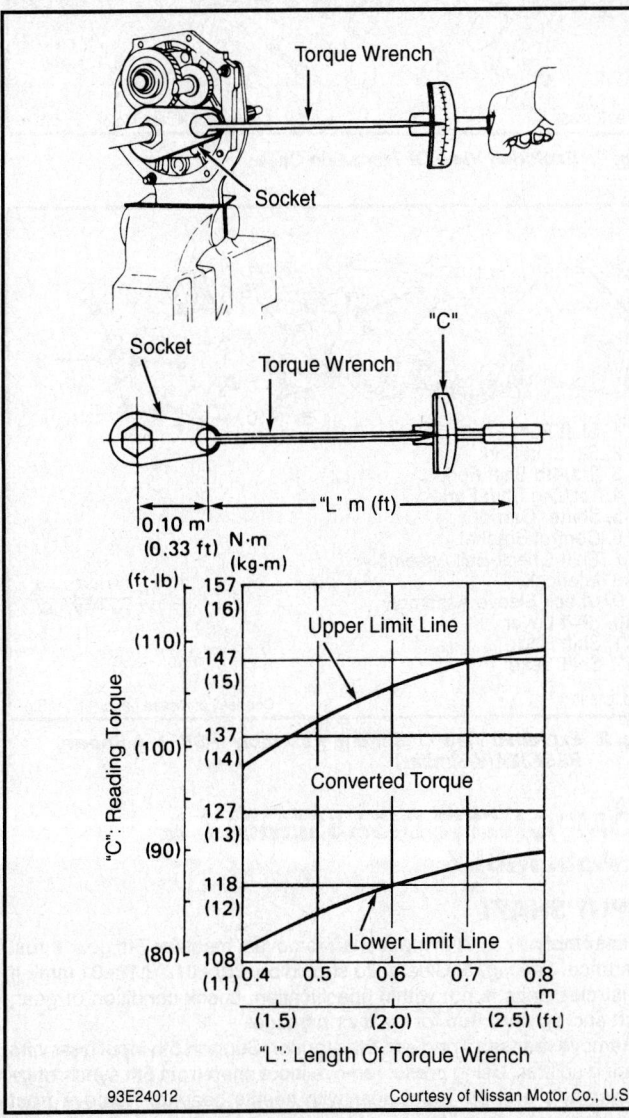

93E24012   Courtesy of Nissan Motor Co., U.S.A.

Fig. 6: *Measuring Mainshaft Nut Tightening Torque*

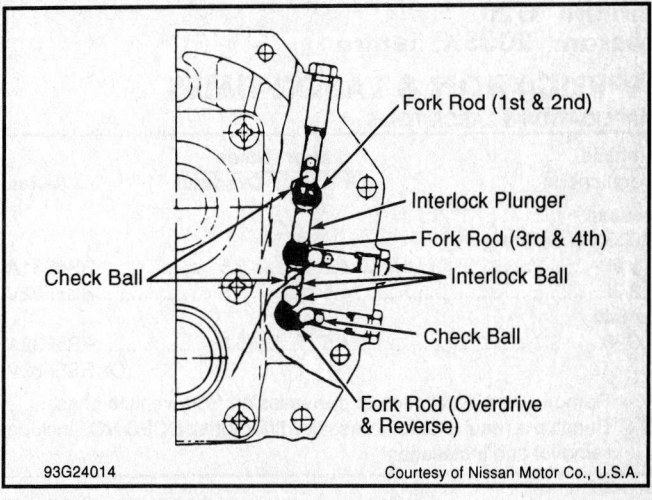

93G24014   Courtesy of Nissan Motor Co., U.S.A.

Fig. 7: *Location Of Interlock Plunger & Balls*

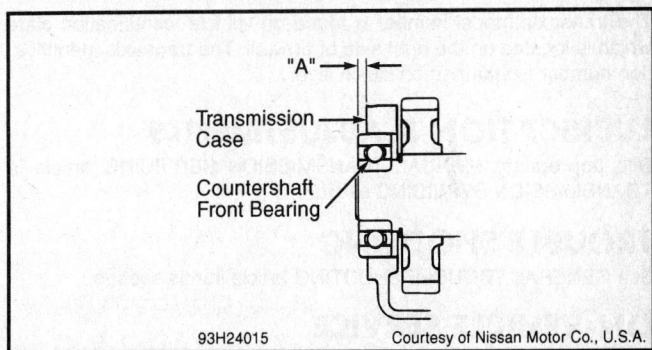

93H24015   Courtesy of Nissan Motor Co., U.S.A.

Fig. 8: *Measuring Countershaft Front Bearing Clearance*

TORQUE SPECIFICATIONS

TORQUE SPECIFICATIONS

Application	Ft. Lbs. (N.m)
Back-Up Light Switch	14-21 (19-29)
Check Ball Plug	14-18 (19-25)
Control Housing Bolt	10-13 (14-18)
Counter Gear Lock Nut	72-94 (98-128)
Drain/Filler Plugs	18-25 (25-34)
Front Bearing Retainer Bolt	12-15 (16-21)
Lever Bracket Securing Bolt	36-44 (49-59)
Mainshaft Lock Nut	See Fig. 4.
Rear Bearing Retainer Bolt	14-18 (19-25)
Rear Extension Housing Bolt	14-18 (19-25)
Shift Restrict Plug	15-21 (20-29)
Transfer Adapter Bolt	12-14 (16-19)
Overdrive Position Switch	14-22 (19-29)
	INCH Lbs. (N.m)
Reverse Check Sleeve	35-44 (4-5)
Shift Lever Pin	80-106 (9-12)

MANUAL TRANSMISSIONS
Nissan RS5F31A, RS5F32A & RS5F32V

Infiniti: G20
Nissan: 200SX, Sentra

APPLICATION & LABOR TIMES

APPLICATION & LABOR TIMES

Vehicle Application	¹ R & I	Labor Times ² Overhaul	Series
Nissan			
200SX & Sentra			
1.6L	4.2	5.5	RS5F31A
2.0L	4.5	5.5	RS5F32V
Infiniti			
G20	4.5	5.5	RS5F32A
			Or RS5F32V

¹ – Removal and installation of transmission from vehicle chassis.
² – Bench overhaul time for transaxle/differential. DOES NOT include removal and installation.

IDENTIFICATION

The transaxle model number is found on vehicle identification plate which is located on the right side of firewall. The transaxle identification number is stamped on clutch lever.

LUBRICATION & ADJUSTMENTS

See appropriate MANUAL TRANSMISSION SERVICING article in TRANSMISSION SERVICING section.

TROUBLE SHOOTING

See GENERAL TROUBLE SHOOTING article in this section.

ON-VEHICLE SERVICE

AXLE SHAFTS

See appropriate AXLE SHAFTS article in AXLE SHAFTS & TRANSFER CASES section.

SHIFT ROD SEAL

Removal – Remove shifter control rod from yoke. Drive out roll pin from yoke. Remove yoke from shift rod. Remove seal.
Installation – To install, reverse removal procedure. Apply multipurpose grease on seal prior to installation. Check transaxle oil level. See appropriate MANUAL TRANSMISSION SERVICING article in TRANSMISSION SERVICING section.

REMOVAL & INSTALLATION

See appropriate MANUAL TRANSMISSION REMOVAL article in TRANSMISSION SERVICING section.

TRANSAXLE DISASSEMBLY

1) On RS5F32A and RS5F32V, remove transaxle case cover. Remove mainshaft bearing snap ring. On all models, unbolt and remove transaxle case. Tilt transaxle case away from differential during removal to prevent 5th shift fork from contacting case. Remove reverse idler gear spacer. Remove 5th shift fork and 3rd/4th shift fork. Ensure shifting caps are not misplaced. *See Figs. 1 and 2.*
2) Remove shifter control bracket with 1st/2nd shift fork. On RS5F31A, remove mainshaft and differential assembly. Remove mainshaft by pulling straight up. Remove input shaft bearing retainer bolts. Using plastic hammer, tap input shaft and remove with reverse idler gear. On 1RS5F32A and RS5F32V, unbolt bearing retainer and remove input shaft, mainshaft and reverse idler gear as single assembly. Remove differential assembly. *See Figs. 1 and 2.*
3) On all models, remove shift check ball, check spring and check ball plug. Drive roll pin out of shift rod. Remove shift rod, shift lever trand shift interlock. Remove reverse check plug. Remove reverse check spring and check balls. Remove check sleeve assembly.

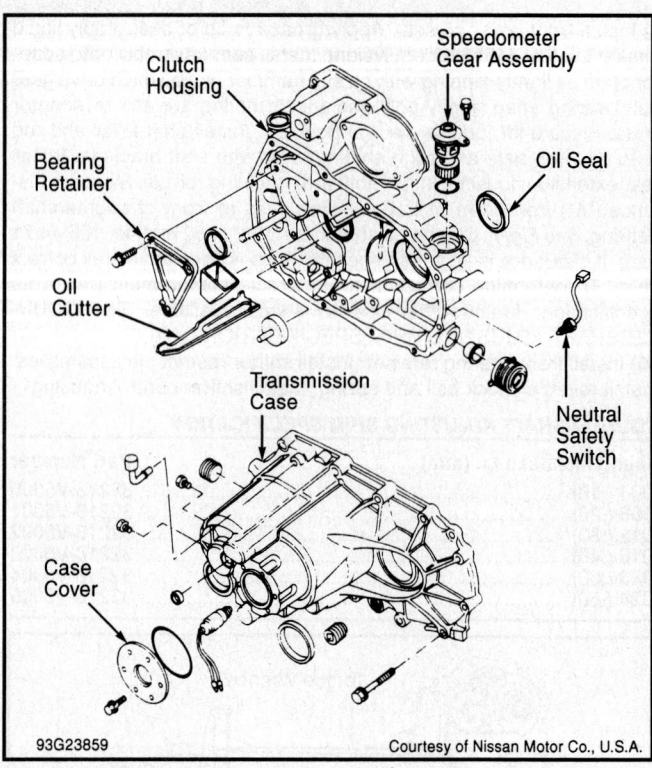

Fig. 1: *Exploded View Of Transaxle Case*

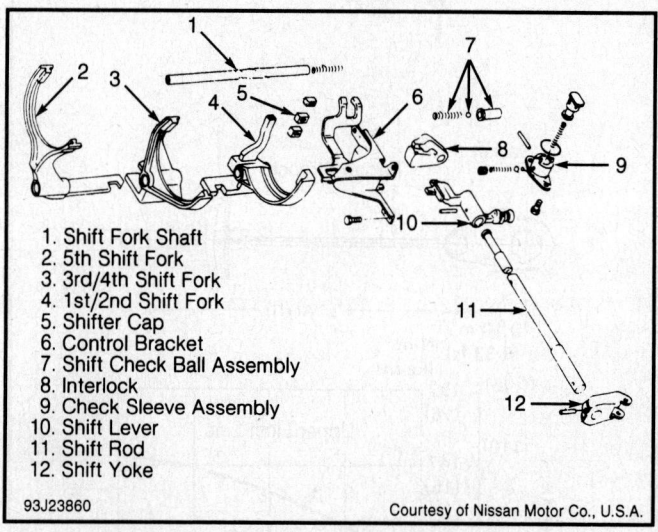

1. Shift Fork Shaft
2. 5th Shift Fork
3. 3rd/4th Shift Fork
4. 1st/2nd Shift Fork
5. Shifter Cap
6. Control Bracket
7. Shift Check Ball Assembly
8. Interlock
9. Check Sleeve Assembly
10. Shift Lever
11. Shift Rod
12. Shift Yoke

Fig. 2: *Exploded View Of Shifting Assembly (RS5F31A Shown, RS5F32A/V Similar)*

COMPONENT DISASSEMBLY & REASSEMBLY

INPUT SHAFT

Disassembly – 1) With input shaft removed, measure 5th gear thrust clearance. *See Fig. 3.* Clearance should be .007-.012" (.18-.31 mm). If thrust clearance is not within specification, check condition of gear, shaft and synchro hub for wear or damage.
2) Remove rear snap ring and 5th stopper. Support 5th input gear with bearing splitter. Using press, remove input shaft from 5th synchronizer assembly and 5th input gear with needle bearing. Remove front snap ring and spacer. Press off front input shaft bearing and remove bearing retainer. *See Fig. 4.*

Inspection – Thoroughly clean all bearings in solvent and dry with compressed air. DO NOT spin bearings with air pressure. Check tapered roller bearings for wear, scratches, pitting or flaking. Ensure bearings turn smoothly and do not bind. Inspect gears for excessive wear, chips, cracks or other damage. Replace as necessary. Check bearing journal surface of input shaft for wear.

NOTE: Coat all parts with gear oil before assembly.

Reassembly – 1) Install bearing retainer. Press on front bearing. Install spacer and snap ring. Select snap ring that will allow minimum axial play. Clearance should be .0-.004" (.0-.10 mm). See INPUT SHAFT FRONT SNAP RING IDENTIFICATION table.

INPUT SHAFT FRONT SNAP RING IDENTIFICATION

Thickness – In. (mm)	Part Number
.050 (1.27)	32204-M8004
.052 (1.33)	32204-M8005
.055 (1.39)	32204-M8006
.057 (1.45)	32204-M8007

2) Install 5th input gear with needle bearing and synchro ring. Press on synchro hub assembly. Recheck 5th gear thrust clearance. Clearance should be .007-.012" (.18-.31 mm). Install 5th stopper and snap ring. Select snap ring that will allow minimum axial play. Clearance should be .0-.004" (.0-.10 mm). See INPUT SHAFT REAR SNAP RING IDEN-TIFICATION table.

INPUT SHAFT REAR SNAP RING IDENTIFICATION

Thickness – In. (mm)	Part Number
.079 (2.00)	32311-M8812
.081 (2.05)	32311-M8813
.083 (2.10)	32311-M8814
.085 (2.15)	32311-M8815
.087 (2.25)	32311-M8816
.089 (2.30)	32311-M8817
.091 (2.35)	32311-M8818

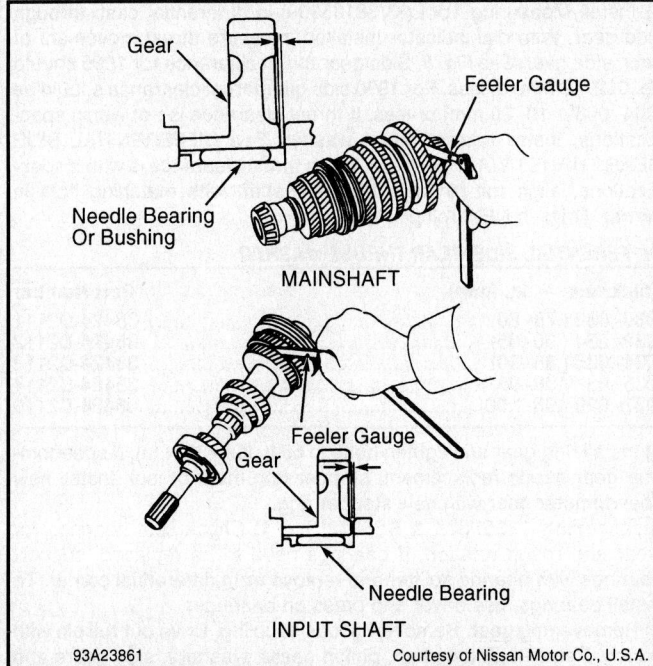

Fig. 3: Identifying Input & Mainshaft Measuring Points

93A23861   Courtesy of Nissan Motor Co., U.S.A.

MAINSHAFT

Disassembly – 1) With mainshaft removed from transaxle, measure thrust clearance of 1st, 2nd, 3rd and 4th gears. *See Fig. 3.* Clearance for 1st gear should be .007-.012" (.18-.31 mm). Clearance for 2nd, 3rd and 4th gears should be .008-.012" (.20-.30 mm). If thrust clearance is

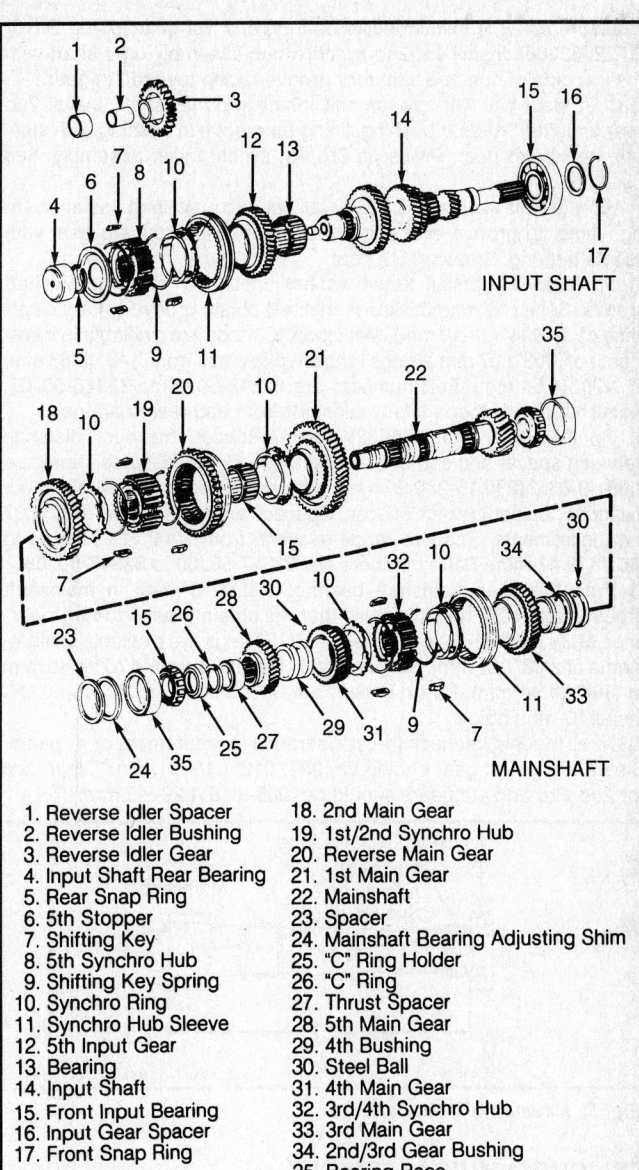

1. Reverse Idler Spacer
2. Reverse Idler Bushing
3. Reverse Idler Gear
4. Input Shaft Rear Bearing
5. Rear Snap Ring
6. 5th Stopper
7. Shifting Key
8. 5th Synchro Hub
9. Shifting Key Spring
10. Synchro Ring
11. Synchro Hub Sleeve
12. 5th Input Gear
13. Bearing
14. Input Shaft
15. Front Input Bearing
16. Input Gear Spacer
17. Front Snap Ring
18. 2nd Main Gear
19. 1st/2nd Synchro Hub
20. Reverse Main Gear
21. 1st Main Gear
22. Mainshaft
23. Spacer
24. Mainshaft Bearing Adjusting Shim
25. "C" Ring Holder
26. "C" Ring
27. Thrust Spacer
28. 5th Main Gear
29. 4th Bushing
30. Steel Ball
31. 4th Main Gear
32. 3rd/4th Synchro Hub
33. 3rd Main Gear
34. 2nd/3rd Gear Bushing
35. Bearing Race

93C23863   Courtesy of Nissan Motor Co., U.S.A.

Fig. 4: Exploded View Of Input & Mainshaft Assemblies (RS5F32V Is Shown; RS5F32A & RS5F31A Are Similar)

not within specification, check condition of gears, shaft and synchro hubs for wear or damage during disassembly.

2) On RS5F31A, remove mainshaft front and rear bearings, using press. Remove "C" rings, "C" ring holder and thrust washer. On RS5F32A and RS5F32V, remove rear snap ring, "C" ring holder and "C" rings. Press off bearing and remove spacer.

3) On all models, locate bearing splitter under 5th gear flange and remove 5th gear. Remove 4th gear, 4th gear bushing and steel ball. Support 3rd/4th synchro hub assembly and remove. Remove 3rd gear, 2nd/3rd gear bushing, steel ball and 2nd gear. Support 1st gear and remove 1st/2nd synchro assembly and 1st gear with needle bearing. *See Fig. 4.*

Inspection – Thoroughly clean all bearings in solvent and dry with compressed air. DO NOT spin bearings with air pressure. Check tapered roller bearings for wear, scratches, pitting or flaking. Ensure bearings turn smoothly and do not bind. Inspect gears for excessive wear, chips, cracks or other damage. Replace as necessary. Check bearing journal surface of input shaft for wear.

NOTE: Coat all parts with gear oil before assembly.

Reassembly – 1) Install needle bearing and 1st gear. Using Driver (ST22452000), install 1st/2nd synchro hub assembly onto shaft with shallow side of hub and shift fork groove facing toward 1st gear.

2) Coat steel ball with grease and install into mainshaft. Install 2nd gear and 2nd/3rd gear bushing, lining up groove in bushing with steel ball. Install 3rd gear. Press on 3rd/4th synchronizer assembly. *See Fig. 4.*

3) Apply grease to steel ball and install ball into mainshaft. Install bushing, lining up groove in bushing with steel ball. Install 4th gear with needle bearing. Press on 5th gear.

4) On RS5F31A, install thrust washer. Install "C" ring in mainshaft groove. Select "C" ring thickness that will obtain groove-to-ring clearance of .0-.004" (.0-.10 mm). Mainshaft "C" rings are available in increments of .003" (.07 mm.) Rings range in thickness from .143" (3.63 mm) to .179" (4.54 mm). Part numbers are 32348-50J00 to 32348-50J07. Install "C" ring holder. Install mainshaft front and rear bearings.

5) On RS5F32A and RS5F32V, install spacer. Measure distance between spacer and end of mainshaft. *See Fig. 5.* Distance should be 9.061-9.065" (230.15-230.25 mm). If measurement is not within specifications, select correct spacer. Spacers are available in .003" (.07 mm) increments. Spacers range in width from .744" (18.91 mm) to .767" (19.47 mm). Parts numbers are 32347-50J00 to 32347-50J08.

6) Press on rear mainshaft bearing. Install "C" ring in mainshaft groove. Select "C" ring thickness that will obtain groove-to-ring clearance of .0-.004" (.0-.10 mm). Mainshaft "C" rings are available in increments of .003" (.07 mm). Rings range in thickness from .175" (4.45 mm) to .194" (4.94 mm). Part numbers are 32348-50J00 to 32348-50J07. Install "C" ring holder.

7) On all models, recheck thrust clearance measurement of all gears. Clearance for 1st gear should be .007-.012" (.18-.31 mm). Clearance for 2nd, 3rd and 4th gears should be .008-.016" (.20-.40 mm).

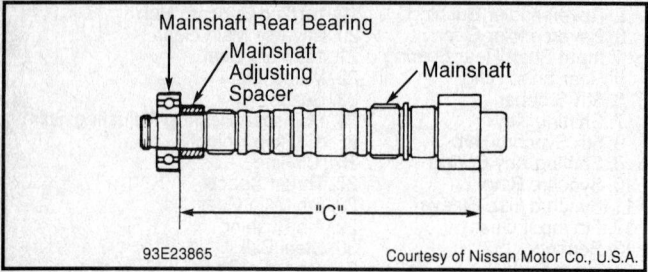

Fig. 5: Measuring Mainshaft

93E23865 — Courtesy of Nissan Motor Co., U.S.A.

SYNCHRO HUB ASSEMBLY

Disassembly – 1) Remove springs and keys from synchro assembly. Note component positions and locations for reassembly reference. *See Fig. 4.* Slide synchro sleeve off of synchro hub. Wash all parts in solvent and blow dry with compressed air.

2) Check synchro sleeve for damage, cracking or excessive wear. Inspect synchro key for wear at shoulders. Check synchro hub and sleeve for smooth operation. Inspect remaining parts for damage or wear. Replace components as necessary.

Measuring Procedure (2-Piece Synchro Ring) – The 2nd/3rd hub assembly uses a 2-piece synchro ring assembly. Apply pressure on inner and outer synchro ring against synchro cone. Measure clearance "A" between inner synchro ring and synchro cone. *See Fig. 6.* Clearance should be .028-.035" (.70-.90 mm). Measure clearance "B" between outer synchro ring and synchro cone. Clearance should be .024-.043" (.60-1.10 mm). Service limit for both measurements is .008" (.20 mm).

Measuring Procedure (One-Piece Synchro Ring) – Check synchronizer rings for wear or damage. Turn and push ring to check braking action. Measure clearance between synchronizer ring back and gear spline end. Clearance should be .035-.059" (.90-1.5 mm). Service limit is .028" (.70 mm). *See Fig. 6.*

Reassembly – To reassemble, reverse disassembly procedure. Fit synchro keys in 3 grooves of synchro hub. Insert shifting key springs into groove of shifting keys. DO NOT hook ends of springs to the same synchro key. Ensure that open portion of springs are offset.

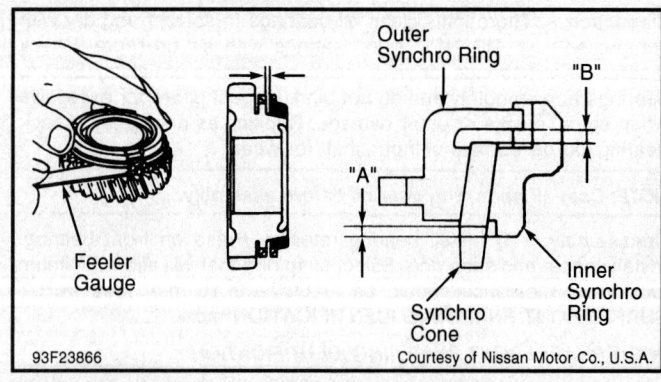

Fig. 6: Identifying Synchro Ring Measuring Points

93F23866 — Courtesy of Nissan Motor Co., U.S.A.

DIFFERENTIAL

Disassembly (RS5F31A) – 1) Check side bearings for wear and rough rotation. If bearings need to be replaced, support bearings with bearing splitter and remove from differential carrier. To install bearings, use driver and press on bearings.

2) Remove ring gear. Cut and remove speedometer drive gear. Drive out roll pin with punch. Remove pinion shaft, pinion gears, side gears and thrust washers. *See Fig. 7.*

Inspection – Inspect ring gear teeth for excessive wear. Inspect pinion shaft for scoring and burrs. Wash parts in solvent and dry with compressed air. Replace any worn or damaged parts.

Reassembly – 1) Coat all parts with gear oil before reassembly. Install side gears with original thrust washers. Set pinion gears in place exactly opposite each other, in mesh with side gears. Install thrust washers behind each pinion gear. Washers must be of equal thickness. *See Fig. 7.*

2) Rotate gears until holes in pinion gears line up with shaft holes in carrier. Insert pinion shaft. measure clearance between side gear and differential case.

3) Install Measuring Tool (KV38105900) in differential case through side gear. With dial indicator installed, measure thrust movement of each side gear. *See Fig. 8.* Side gear thrust clearance for 1995 should be .012" (.3 mm) or less. For 1996 side gear thrust clearance should be .004-.008" (.10-.20 mm) or less. If thrust clearance is not within specifications, install correct thrust washer. See DIFFERENTIAL SIDE GEAR THRUST WASHER table. When thrust clearance is within specifications, align roll pin hole in pinion shaft with matching hole in carrier. Drive in NEW roll pin.

DIFFERENTIAL SIDE GEAR THRUST WASHER

Thickness – In. (mm)	Part Number
.030-.032 (.75-.80)	38424-D2111
.032-.034 (.80-.85)	38424-D2112
.034-.035 (.85-.90)	38424-D2113
.035-.037 (.90-.95)	38424-D2114
.037-.039 (.95-1.00)	38424-D2115

4) Install ring gear and tighten bolts to 65 ft. lbs. (88 N.m). If speedometer gear needs replacement, stopper ring must be cut. Install new speedometer gear with new stopper ring.

Disassembly (RS5F32A & RS5F32V) – 1) Check side bearings for wear and rough rotation. If bearings need to be replaced, support bearings with bearing splitter and remove from differential carrier. To install bearings, use driver and press on bearings.

2) Remove ring gear. Remove viscous coupling. Drive out roll pin with punch. Remove pinion shaft, pinion gears, washers, side gears and thrust washers. *See Fig. 7.*

Inspection – Inspect ring gear teeth for excessive wear. Inspect pinion shaft for scoring and burrs. Wash parts in solvent and dry with compressed air. Replace any worn or damaged parts. Inspect viscous coupling for any leaks or damage to case.

Reassembly – 1) Coat all parts with gear oil before reassembly. Install side gears with original thrust washers. Set pinion gears in place exactly opposite each other, in mesh with side gears. Install thrust washer behind each pinion gear. Washers must be of equal thickness. Rotate gears until holes in pinion gears line up with shaft holes in carrier. Insert pinion shaft. Measure clearance between side gear and differential case.

2) Install Measuring Tool (KV38107700) in differential case through side gear. With dial indicator installed, measure thrust movement of side gear. See Fig. 8. Side gear thrust clearance for 1995 (RS5F32V) should be .004-.008" (.1-.2 mm). Side gear thrust clearance for 1996 (RS5F32A-RS5F32V) should be 0-.004" (0-.10 mm). If thrust clearance is not within specifications, install correct thrust washer. See DIFFER-ENTIAL SIDE GEAR THRUST WASHER table. When thrust clearance is within specifications, align roll pin hole in pinion shaft with matching hole in carrier. Drive in NEW roll pin.

3) Install opposite side gear with thrust washer in differential case. Using 2 height gauges (parallel gauges) of equal measurement, mea-sure and record dimension "X". See Fig. 9. Place height gauges on vis-cous coupling half of differential. Measure and record dimension "Y".

4) Clearance between side gear and viscous coupling is determined by adding dimension "X" of differential case half to dimension "Y" of viscous coupling half. Multiply dimension "A" (height gauge) by 2 and subtract from sum of dimensions "X" and "Y".

5) 1995-1996 NISSAN specification for thrust clearance is .004-.008" (.10-.20 mm). 1995-1996 INFINITI specification for thrust clearance is 0-.004" (0-.1 mm). If clearance is not within specification, install correct side gear thrust washer. Side gear thrust washers are available in .002" (.05) mm increments. Washers range in thickness from .028-.030" (.70-.75 mm) to .051-.053" (1.30-1.35 mm). Part numbers are 38424-D2110 through 38424-D2122.

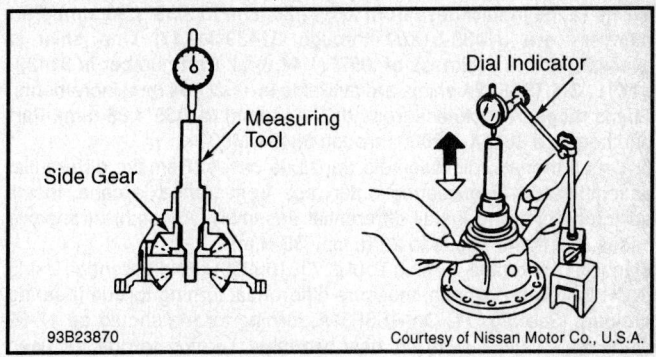

Fig. 8: Measuring Side Gear Thrust Clearance

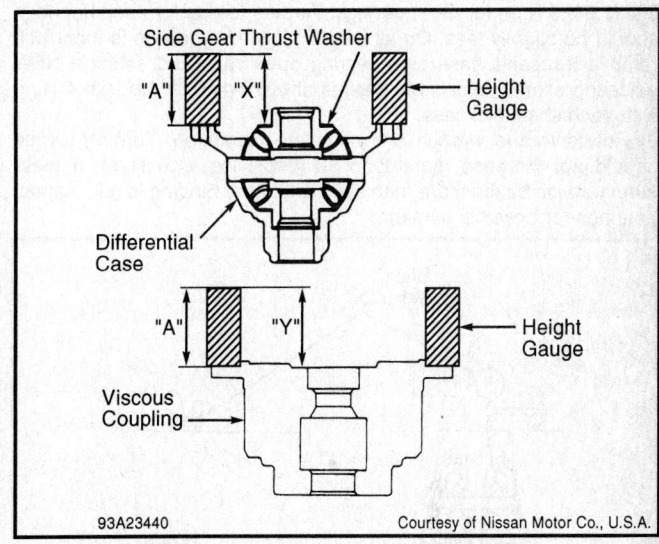

Fig. 9: Measuring Side Gear-To-Viscous Coupling Thrust Clearance

6) Install viscous coupling to differential. Install ring gear and tighten bolts for 1995-1996 RS5F32V to 50 ft. lbs. (68 N.m). For 1995-1996 RS5F32A tighten bolts to 80 ft. lbs. (108 mm). If speedometer gear needs replacement, stopper ring must be cut. Install NEW speedome-ter gear with NEW stopper ring. See Fig. 7.

TRANSMISSION ADJUSTMENTS

NOTE: Transmission adjustments are performed as part of transaxle assembly procedure. See TRANSMISSION REASSEMBLY.

DIFFERENTIAL BEARING PRELOAD

NOTE: Check differential bearing preload if differential case, differen-tial bearings, clutch housing and/or transaxle case have been replaced.

1) Preload is set by adjusting shim thickness. Using 2-jaw puller, remove side bearing outer race and shim from transaxle case. Using driver, replace race in transaxle case without shim. Install differential assembly into transaxle case. Install clutch housing and tighten bolts to 22 ft. lbs. (30 N.m).

2) Rotate differential to seat bearing. Mount dial indicator on clutch housing side to measure thrust clearance. See Fig. 10. Insert appropri-ate tool into transaxle housing end of differential and move assembly up and down. Measure thrust clearance and record. Bearing preload should be 0098-.0018" (.25-.30 mm). Shim thickness for RS5F31A, is determined by adding .08-.010" (.20-.25 mm) to thrust clearance mea-surement.

3) On RS5F32A and RS5F32V, shim thickness is determined by add-ing .010-.012" (.25-.30 mm) to thrust clearance measurement. Select

Fig. 7: Exploded View Of Differential Assemblies

RS5F31A & RS5F32A

RS5F32V

1. Thrust Shim
2. Bearing Race
3. Ring Gear
4. Differential Housing
5. Speedometer Gear
6. Stopper Ring
7. Bearing
8. Pinion Gear
9. Side Gear
10. Pinion Shaft
11. Viscous Coupling

Courtesy of Nissan Motor Co., U.S.A.

correct shim. Use combination of 2 shims if necessary. On RS5F31A, shims are available in .002" (.04 mm) increments. Shims range in thickness from .017" (.44 mm) to .035" (.88 mm). Part numbers are 38454-M8000 through 38454-M8011.

4) On RS5F32V, shims are available in .002" (.04 mm) increments. Shims range in thickness from .011" (.28 mm) to .038" (.96 mm). Part numbers are 31439-31X00 through 31439-31X17. One shim is available with a thickness of .057" (1.44 mm). Part number is 31439-31X18. On RS5F32A shims are available in .002" (.04 mm) increments. Shims range in thickness from .017" (.44 mm) to .035" (.88 mm). Part numbers are 38454-M8000 through 38454-M8011.

5) On all models, disassemble transaxle cases. Remove differential assembly and side bearing outer race from transaxle case. Install selected shim and install differential assembly. Assemble transaxle cases and tighten bolts to 22 ft. lbs. (30 N.m).

6) Insert Differential Turning Tool (KV38105900) into differential. Using INCH lb. torque wrench, measure differential turning torque (bearing preload). See Fig. 11. On RS5F31A, turning torque should be 17-69 INCH lbs. (2.0-7.8 N.m) for new bearings. Turning torque for used bearings should be slightly less.

7) On RS5F32A and RS5F32V, turning torque should be 26-61 INCH lbs. (2.9-6.9 N.m) for new bearings. Turning torque for used bearings should be slightly less. On all models, if turning torque is incorrect, remove transaxle case side bearing outer race and select a NEW adjusting shim. Preload will change about 3-4 INCH lbs. (.3-.4 N.m) with each shim thickness.

8) Rotate torque wrench one complete revolution. Turning torque should not increase more than 8.7 INCH lbs. (1.0 N.m). If measurement increases more than specification or binding is felt, inspect bearings for possible damage.

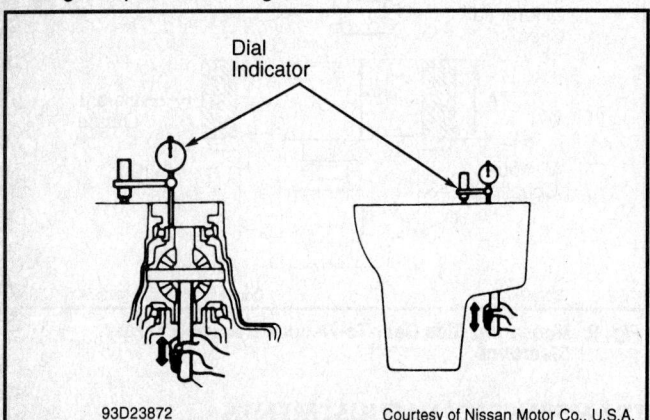

93D23872   Courtesy of Nissan Motor Co., U.S.A.

Fig. 10: Measuring Differential Side Gear Thrust Clearance

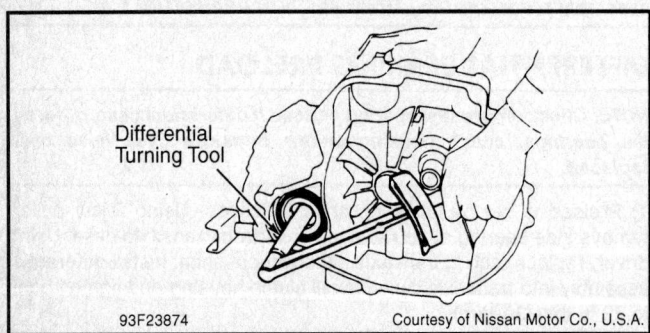

93F23874   Courtesy of Nissan Motor Co., U.S.A.

Fig. 11: Measuring Turning Torque

MAINSHAFT BEARING PRELOAD (RS5F31A)

NOTE: Check mainshaft bearing preload if mainshaft, mainshaft bearings, clutch housing and/or transaxle case have been replaced.

1) Mainshaft bearing preload is adjusted by thickness of shim under transaxle case cover. Install mainshaft into clutch housing. Ensure differential assembly is installed. Install transaxle case and tighten bolts to 22 INCH lbs. (30 N.m). Using Differential Turning Tool (KV38105900), rotate differential assembly to ensure mainshaft bearings are properly seated. Remove case cover, "O" ring, spacer and adjusting shim.

2) Using depth micrometer, measure distance from transaxle case to bearing outer race. If distance measured is .093-.094" (2.35-2.40 mm), required shim thickness is .004" (.10 mm). For each increase of .002" (.05 mm) in depth, shim thickness will increase equal amount to a maximum of .128-.129" (3.25-3.30 mm) in depth. Shims are available in .002 (.05 mm) increments. Shims range in thickness from .004" (.10 mm) to .039" (1.00 mm). Part numbers are 32137-M8000 through 32137-M8018.

3) Install selected shim, spacer and cover. Tighten cover to 70 INCH lbs. (7.9 N.m). Using Differential Turning Tool (KV38105900), rotate differential assembly and measure total turning torque (total preload). See Fig. 11. Total turning torque should be 35-122 INCH lbs. (3.9-13.7 N.m).

MAINSHAFT BEARING THRUST CLEARANCE (RS5F32A & RS5F32V)

1) Mainshaft bearing thrust clearance is adjusted by thickness of transaxle case cover. Install mainshaft into clutch housing. Ensure differential assembly is installed. Install transaxle case and tighten bolts to 22 INCH lbs. (30 N.m). Using Differential Turning Tool (KV38105900), rotate differential assembly to ensure mainshaft bearings are properly seated. Remove case cover and "O" ring.

2) Using depth micrometer, measure distance from transmission case to mainshaft bearing. See Fig. 12. Mainshaft thrust clearance is calculated by subtracting .004" (.10 mm) from depth measurement. Select matching thickness case cover. Case covers are available in .05mm increments. Covers range in thickness from .424" (10.78 mm) to .434" (11.03 mm). Part numbers are 32131-50J00 through 32131-50J05.

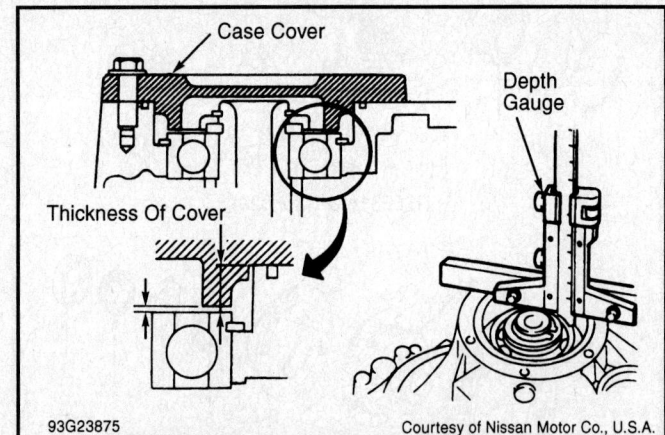

93G23875   Courtesy of Nissan Motor Co., U.S.A.

Fig. 12: Measuring Mainshaft Thrust Clearance (RS5F32V Is Shown; RS5F32A & RS5F31A Are Similar)

SHIFT CONTROL COMPONENTS (RS5F32A & RS5F32V)

Inspection – 1) Install shift rod, shift lever, interlock and control assembly. Ensure mounting hole protrusion on control bracket is properly installed in mounting hole. Measure maximum height of 1st/2nd shifter (height "H") when shifting from Neutral to Reverse position. See Fig. 13. Maximum height should be 2.6441-2.6630" (67.16-67.64 mm).

2) Measure clearance "C" between reverse brake cam and shift lever while shifting to Reverse position. See Fig. 13. Clearance should be .002-.008" (.05-.20 mm). If either measurement is not within specification, replace shift lever assembly, shift interlock assembly and control bracket assembly as a set.

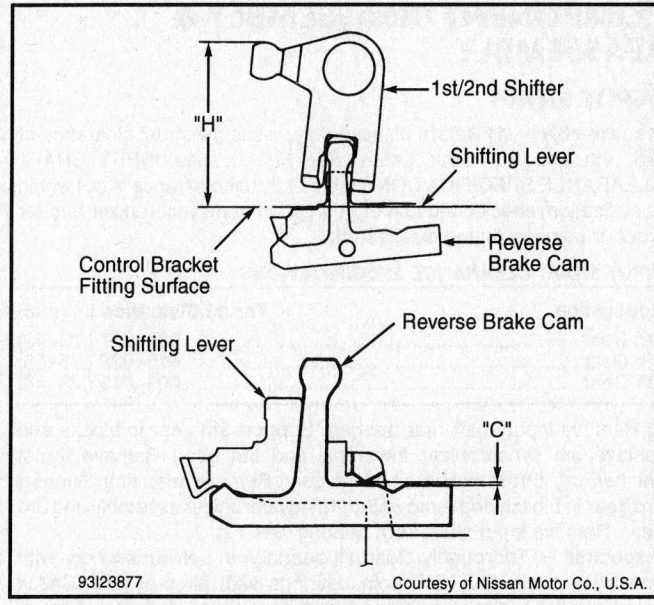

Control Bracket Fitting Surface

1st/2nd Shifter

Shifting Lever

Reverse Brake Cam

"H"

Shifting Lever

Reverse Brake Cam

"C"

93I23877 — Courtesy of Nissan Motor Co., U.S.A.

Fig. 13: Identifying Shift Component Measuring Points

TRANSAXLE REASSEMBLY

1) Install shift rod into clutch housing, shift lever and interlock. Install roll pin into shift lever. Install check sleeve assembly. Install both check balls, reverse check spring and plug. Install check ball plug, shift check ball and check spring.

2) On RS5F31A, install input shaft and reverse idler gear. Install mainshaft and differential assembly. On RS5F32A and RS5F32V, install input shaft, mainshaft and reverse idler gear together as single assembly. On all models, ensure not to damage oil gutter when installing mainshaft. Secure shifting caps to control bracket with grease. Install control bracket with 1st/2nd shift fork. Ensure mounting hole protrusion on bracket is properly installed in mounting hole. Install 3rd/4th and 5th shift fork.

3) Install shift fork shaft spring and shaft. Apply grease to spring before installation. Install reverse idler spacer. Apply appropriate sealant to clutch housing and install transaxle case. Tighten housing bolts to 22 ft. lbs. (30 N.m). On RS5F32A and RS5F32V, install mainshaft bearing snap ring. Install selected transaxle case cover with "O" ring. See MAINSHAFT BEARING THRUST CLEARANCE section. On all models, recheck total turning torque (total preload). Total turning torque should be 35-122 INCH lbs. (3.9-13.7 N.m).

TORQUE SPECIFICATIONS
TORQUE SPECIFICATIONS

Application	Ft. Lbs. (N.m)
Back-Up Light Switch	22 (30)
Clutch Housing-To-Transmission Case Bolt	22 (30)
Drain Plug	25 (34)
Filler Plug	25 (34)
Input Shaft Bearing Retainer Bolt	15 (21)
Neutral Switch	22 (30)
Reverse light Plug	22 (29)
Ring Gear Mount Bolt	65 (88)
	INCH Lbs. (N.m)
Differential Case Bolt	52 (5.9)
Speedometer Gear Mount Bolt	33 (3.7)
Transmission Case Cover Bolt	73 (8.3)
Vehicle Speed Sensor Bolt	44 (5.0)

MANUAL TRANSMISSIONS
Nissan RS5F50A & RS5F50V 5-Speed

Nissan: Altima, Maxima
Infiniti: I30

APPLICATION & LABOR TIMES

APPLICATION & LABOR TIMES

Vehicle Application	Labor Times ¹ R & I	² Overhaul	Transaxle Series
Nissan			
Altima	6.6	9.0	RS5F50A/V
Maxima	6.8	9.0	RS5F50A/V
Infiniti			
I30	6.8	9.0	RS5F50A/V

¹ – Removal and installation of transmission from vehicle chassis.
² – Bench overhaul time for transaxle/differential. DOES NOT include removal and installation.

IDENTIFICATION

The transaxle model number is found on vehicle identification plate which is located on the right side of firewall. The transaxle identification number is stamped on clutch housing.

LUBRICATION & ADJUSTMENTS

See appropriate MANUAL TRANSMISSION SERVICING article in TRANSMISSION SERVICING section.

TROUBLE SHOOTING

See GENERAL TROUBLE SHOOTING article in this section.

ON-VEHICLE SERVICE

AXLE SHAFTS

See appropriate AXLE SHAFTS article in AXLE SHAFTS & TRANSFER CASES section.

SHIFT ROD SEAL

Removal – Remove shifter control rod from yoke. Drive out roll pin from yoke. Remove yoke from shift rod. Remove seal.
Installation – To install, reverse removal procedure. Apply multipurpose grease on seal prior to installation. Check transaxle for proper oil level. See appropriate MANUAL TRANSMISSION SERVICING article in TRANSMISSION SERVICING section.

REMOVAL & INSTALLATION

See appropriate MANUAL TRANSMISSION REMOVAL article in TRANSMISSION SERVICING section.

TRANSAXLE DISASSEMBLY

1) Remove transaxle case housing bolts. Remove all plugs, springs and detent balls from case. Remove transaxle case by lifting and tilting away from clutch housing. Remove position switch. Remove shift position switch and oil gutter from case. Engage 4th gear and remove reverse idler shaft and reverse idler gear. See Figs. 1 and 2.
2) Remove retaining pin from reverse arm shaft. Remove reverse lever spring and reverse lock spring from reverse lever assembly. Using a screwdriver to rotate shaft in both directions, push shaft out of case. Remove reverse lever assembly. Remove 5th and reverse check plug, spring and ball. Remove snap rings and retaining pins from 5th/reverse and 3rd/4th shift rods. Remove 5th/reverse and 3rd/4th shift rods. Remove shift forks and brackets. See Figs. 1 and 2
3) Remove both input and mainshaft with 1st/2nd fork and rod as a single assembly. Remove differential assembly. Remove reverse check assembly. Remove retaining pin from selector shaft and remove shaft. Remove drain plug. Remove retaining pin which holds shifting lever to shifting rod. Shifting rod retaining pin is accessed through drain plug hole. Remove shifting lever and shifting rod.

COMPONENT DISASSEMBLY & REASSEMBLY

INPUT SHAFT

Disassembly – 1) Before disassembly, measure thrust clearance of 3rd, 4th and 5th input gears. See Fig. 3. See INPUT SHAFT CLEARANCE SPECIFICATIONS table. If thrust clearance is not within specification, check condition of gear, shaft and synchronizer hub for wear or damage during disassembly.

INPUT SHAFT CLEARANCE SPECIFICATIONS

Application	Thrust Clearance In. (mm)
3rd Gear	.009-.017 (.23-.43)
4th Gear	.010-.022 (.25-.55)
5th Gear	.009-.019 (.23-.48)

2) Remove input shaft rear bearing. Support 5th gear in blocks and remove 5th synchronizer assembly and 5th gear. Remove thrust washer ring, thrust washers and 4th gear. Remove snap ring. Support 3rd gear in blocks and remove 3rd/4th synchronizer assembly and 3rd gear. Remove input shaft front bearing. See Fig. 1.
Inspection – Thoroughly clean all bearings in solvent and dry with compressed air. DO NOT spin bearings with air pressure. Check tapered roller bearings for wear, scratches, pitting or flaking. Ensure bearings turn smoothly and do not bind. Inspect gears for excessive wear, chips, cracks or other damage. Replace as necessary. Check bearing journal surface of input shaft for wear.

NOTE: Coat all parts with gear oil before assembly

Reassembly – 1) Install 3rd gear and synchronizer ring. Press on 3rd/4th synchronizer hub assembly with shallow side of hub facing 4th gear. Install snap ring that will obtain snap ring groove clearance of 0-.004" (0-.10 mm). Snap rings for 3rd/4th synchronizer hub are available in the following sizes: .077" (1.95 mm), .079" (2.00 mm), .081" (2.05 mm) and .083" (2.10 mm). See Fig. 1.
2) Install 4th gear, thrust washers and thrust washer ring. Install thickness of thrust washers that will obtain groove clearance of 0-.002" (0-.06 mm). Input shaft thrust washers are available in the following sizes: .177" (4.50 mm), .178" (4.53 mm), .179" (4.55 mm) and .180" (4.58 mm). Part numbers 32278-03E01 through 32278-03E04
3) Install 5th gear. Press on 5th gear synchronizer assembly. Press on front and rear bearings. Recheck 3rd, 4th and 5th gear thrust clearance. See INPUT SHAFT CLEARANCE SPECIFICATIONS table.

MAINSHAFT

Disassembly – 1) Before disassembly, measure thrust clearance of 1st and 2nd mainshaft gears. See Fig. 3. See MAINSHAFT CLEARANCE SPECIFICATIONS table. If thrust clearance is not within specification, check condition of gear, shaft and synchronizer hub for wear or damage during disassembly.

MAINSHAFT CLEARANCE SPECIFICATIONS

Application	Thrust Clearance In. (mm)
1st Gear	.009-.017 (.23-.43)
2nd Gear	.009-.023 (.23-.58)

2) Remove mainshaft rear bearing. Remove thrust washer and snap ring. Support 4th gear and press 5th gear and 4th gear off of mainshaft. Support 2nd gear and press 3rd and 2nd gears off of mainshaft. Remove snap ring. Support 1st gear and remove 1st/2nd synchronizer and 1st gear off of mainshaft. Remove mainshaft front bearing. See Fig. 1.
Inspection – Thoroughly clean all bearings in solvent and dry with compressed air. DO NOT spin bearings with air pressure. Check tapered roller bearings for wear, scratches, pitting or flaking. Ensure bearings turn smoothly and do not bind. Inspect gears for excessive wear, chips, cracks or other damage. Replace as necessary. Check bearing journal surface of input shaft for wear.

MANUAL TRANSMISSIONS
Nissan RS5F50A & RS5F50V 5-Speed (Cont.)

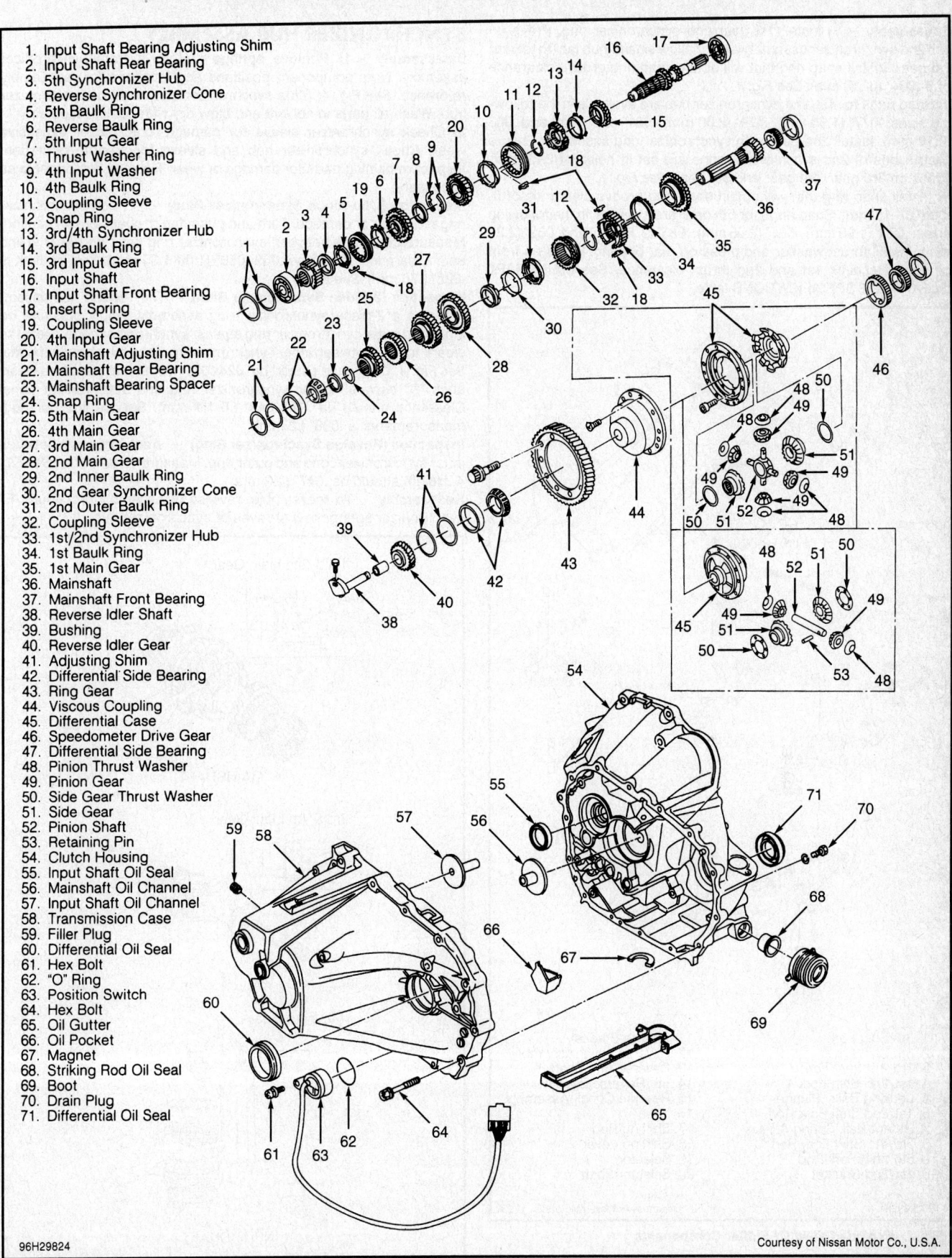

1. Input Shaft Bearing Adjusting Shim
2. Input Shaft Rear Bearing
3. 5th Synchronizer Hub
4. Reverse Synchronizer Cone
5. 5th Baulk Ring
6. Reverse Baulk Ring
7. 5th Input Gear
8. Thrust Washer Ring
9. 4th Input Washer
10. 4th Baulk Ring
11. Coupling Sleeve
12. Snap Ring
13. 3rd/4th Synchronizer Hub
14. 3rd Baulk Ring
15. 3rd Input Gear
16. Input Shaft
17. Input Shaft Front Bearing
18. Insert Spring
19. Coupling Sleeve
20. 4th Input Gear
21. Mainshaft Adjusting Shim
22. Mainshaft Rear Bearing
23. Mainshaft Bearing Spacer
24. Snap Ring
25. 5th Main Gear
26. 4th Main Gear
27. 3rd Main Gear
28. 2nd Main Gear
29. 2nd Inner Baulk Ring
30. 2nd Gear Synchronizer Cone
31. 2nd Outer Baulk Ring
32. Coupling Sleeve
33. 1st/2nd Synchronizer Hub
34. 1st Baulk Ring
35. 1st Main Gear
36. Mainshaft
37. Mainshaft Front Bearing
38. Reverse Idler Shaft
39. Bushing
40. Reverse Idler Gear
41. Adjusting Shim
42. Differential Side Bearing
43. Ring Gear
44. Viscous Coupling
45. Differential Case
46. Speedometer Drive Gear
47. Differential Side Bearing
48. Pinion Thrust Washer
49. Pinion Gear
50. Side Gear Thrust Washer
51. Side Gear
52. Pinion Shaft
53. Retaining Pin
54. Clutch Housing
55. Input Shaft Oil Seal
56. Mainshaft Oil Channel
57. Input Shaft Oil Channel
58. Transmission Case
59. Filler Plug
60. Differential Oil Seal
61. Hex Bolt
62. "O" Ring
63. Position Switch
64. Hex Bolt
65. Oil Gutter
66. Oil Pocket
67. Magnet
68. Striking Rod Oil Seal
69. Boot
70. Drain Plug
71. Differential Oil Seal

96H29824

Courtesy of Nissan Motor Co., U.S.A.

Fig. 1: Exploded View Of Transmission Assembly

Reassembly – 1) Install 1st gear and synchronizer ring. Press on 1st/2nd synchronizer assembly with shallow side of hub facing toward 1st gear. Install snap ring that will obtain snap ring groove clearance of 0-.004" (0-.10 mm). See Fig. 1.

2) Snap rings for 1st/2nd synchronizer hub are available in the following sizes: .077" (1.95 mm), .079" (2.00 mm), .081" (2.05 mm) and .083 (2.10 mm). Install 2nd gear with synchronizer ring assembly. Ensure protrusions of 2nd synchronizer cone are set in holes of 2nd gear. Press on 3rd gear, 4th gear and 5th gear. See Fig. 1.

3) Install snap ring that will obtain snap ring groove clearance of 0-.006" (0-.15 mm). Snap rings for 5th gear are available in the following sizes: .077" (1.95 mm), .081" (2.05 mm), .085" (2.15 mm) and .089" (2.25 mm). Install thrust washer and press on rear bearing. Press on front bearing. Recheck 1st and 2nd thrust clearance. See MAINSHAFT CLEARANCE SPECIFICATIONS table.

SYNCHRONIZER HUB ASSEMBLY

Disassembly – 1) Remove springs and keys from synchronizer assembly. Note component positions and locations for reassembly reference. See Fig. 4. Slide synchronizer sleeve off of synchronizer hub. Wash all parts in solvent and blow dry with compressed air.

2) Check synchronizer sleeve for damage, cracking or excessive wear. Check synchronizer hub and sleeve for smooth operation. Inspect remaining parts for damage or wear. Replace components as necessary.

Inspection (One-Piece Synchronizer Ring) – Check synchronizer rings for wear or damage. Turn and push ring to check braking action. Measure clearance between synchronizer ring back and gear spline end. Clearance should be .039-.053" (1.00-1.35 mm). Service limit is .028" (.70 mm). See Fig. 4.

Inspection (2-Piece Synchronizer Ring) – The 1st/2nd hub assembly uses a 2-piece synchronizer ring assembly. Apply pressure on inner and outer synchronizer ring against synchronizer cone. Measure clearance "A" between inner synchronizer ring and synchronizer cone. See Fig. 4. Clearance should be .024-.031" (.6-.8 mm). Measure clearance "B" between outer synchronizer ring and synchronizer cone. Clearance should be .024-.043" (.6-1.1 mm). Service limit for both measurements is .008" (.2 mm).

Inspection (Reverse Synchronizer Ring) – Apply pressure between inner synchronizer cone and outer ring. Measure distance "A". See Fig. 4. Height should be .047" (1.2 mm)

Reassembly – To reassemble, reverse disassembly procedure. Fit synchronizer springs in 3 grooves of synchronizer hub.

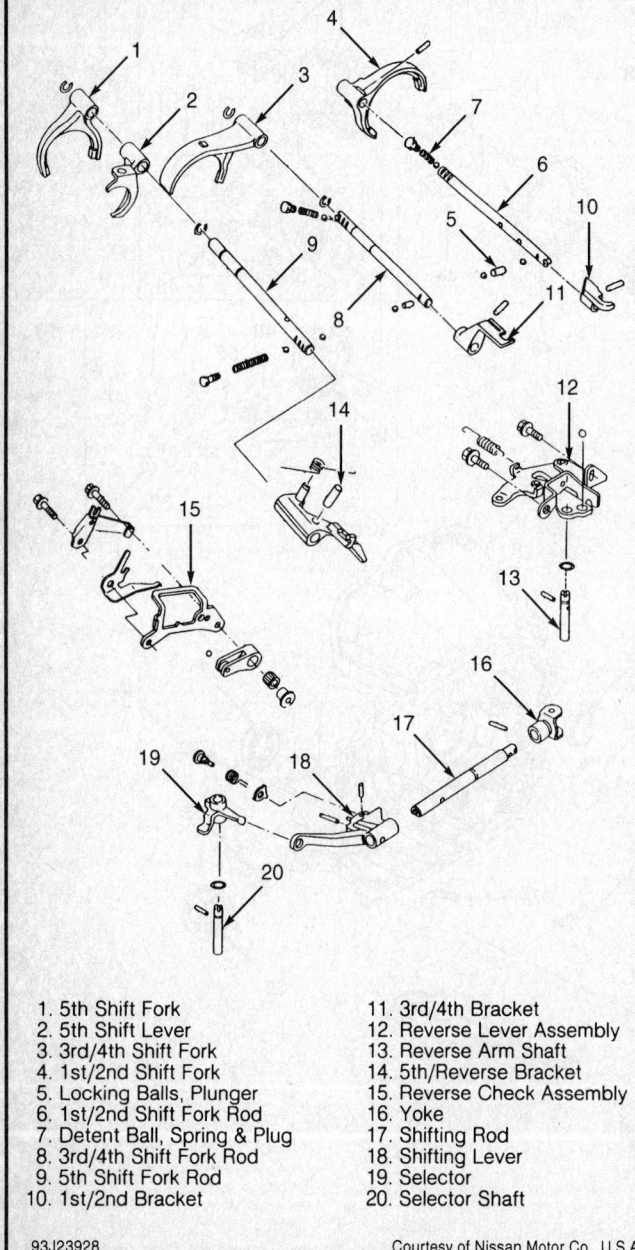

1. 5th Shift Fork
2. 5th Shift Lever
3. 3rd/4th Shift Fork
4. 1st/2nd Shift Fork
5. Locking Balls, Plunger
6. 1st/2nd Shift Fork Rod
7. Detent Ball, Spring & Plug
8. 3rd/4th Shift Fork Rod
9. 5th Shift Fork Rod
10. 1st/2nd Bracket
11. 3rd/4th Bracket
12. Reverse Lever Assembly
13. Reverse Arm Shaft
14. 5th/Reverse Bracket
15. Reverse Check Assembly
16. Yoke
17. Shifting Rod
18. Shifting Lever
19. Selector
20. Selector Shaft

93J23928   Courtesy of Nissan Motor Co., U.S.A.

Fig. 2: Exploded View Of Shifter Components

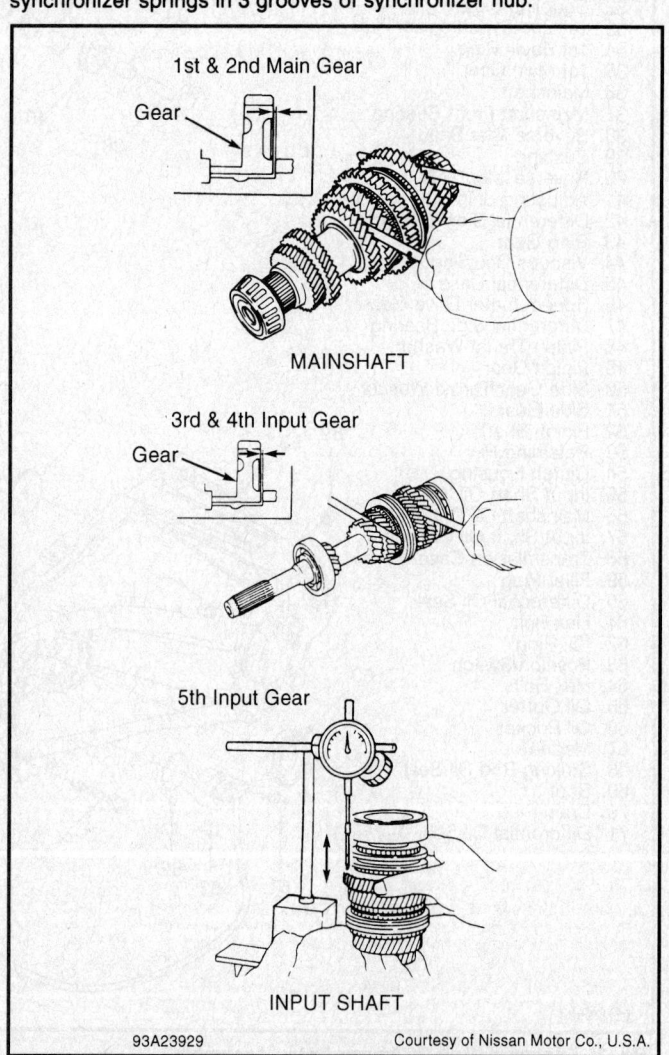

1st & 2nd Main Gear

Gear

MAINSHAFT

3rd & 4th Input Gear

Gear

5th Input Gear

INPUT SHAFT

93A23929   Courtesy of Nissan Motor Co., U.S.A.

Fig. 3: Identifying Input & Mainshaft Measuring Points

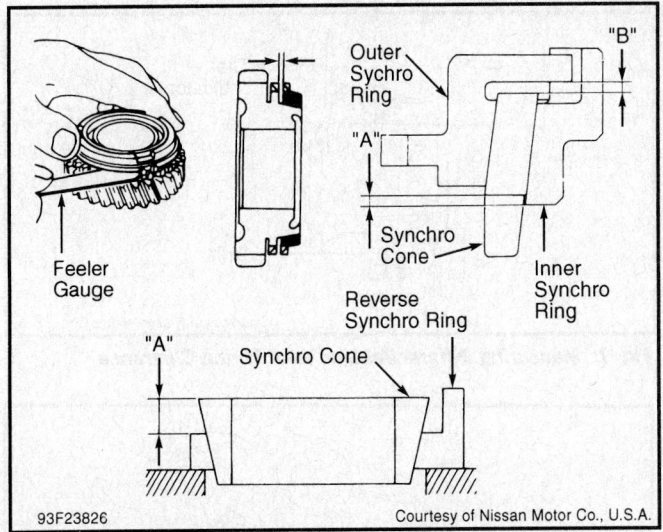

Fig. 4: *Identifying Synchronizer Assembly Measuring Points*

DIFFERENTIAL

NOTE: There are 2 designs of differentials used: conventional non-limited slip (RS5F50A) and viscous coupling limited slip (RS5F50V).

Disassembly (RS5F50A) – 1) Remove final gear. Remove speedometer drive gear by cutting. Press off differential side bearings. Check side bearings for wear and rough rotation.

2) Remove ring gear. Drive out roll pin with punch. Remove pinion shaft, pinion gears, side gears and thrust washers.

Inspection – Inspect ring gear teeth for excessive wear. Inspect pinion shaft for scoring and burrs. Wash parts in solvent and dry with compressed air. Replace any worn or damaged parts.

Reassembly (RS5F50A) – 1) Coat all parts with gear oil before reassembly. Install side gears with original thrust washers. Set pinion gears in place exactly opposite each other, in mesh with side gears. Install thrust washers behind each pinion gear. Washers must be of equal thickness.

2) Rotate gears until holes in pinion gears line up with shaft holes in carrier. Insert pinion shaft. Measure clearance between side gear and differential case.

3) Install Measuring Tool (KV38106500) in differential case through side gear. With dial indicator installed, measure thrust movement of each side gear. *See Fig. 5.* Side gear thrust clearance should be .004-.008" (.10-.20 mm). If thrust clearance is not within specifications, install correct thrust washer. See DIFFERENTIAL SIDE GEAR THRUST WASHER table. When thrust clearance is within specifications, align roll pin hole in pinion shaft with matching hole in carrier. Drive in NEW roll pin. Ensure pin is flush with case. Install ring gear and tighten bolts to 65-76 ft. lbs. (88-103 N.m). Install speedometer drive gear. Press on differential side bearings.

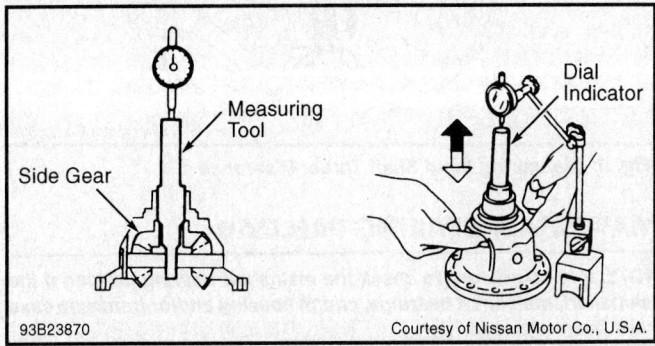

Fig. 5: *Measuring Side Gear Thrust Clearance (RS5F50V Model Shown; RS5F50A Model Similar)*

DIFFERENTIAL SIDE GEAR THRUST WASHER

Thickness In. (mm)	Part Number
.030-.032 (.75-.80)	38424-E3020
.032-.034 (.80-.85)	38424-E3021
.034-.035 (.85-.90)	38424-E3022
.035-.037 (.90-.95)	38424-E3023

Disassembly (RS5F50V) – Remove ring gear. Using 2-jaw puller and adapter, remove differential side bearings. Remove speedometer drive gear. Remove viscous coupling. Mark differential case halves for reassembly reference. Remove differential case bolts and separate differential case halves. Remove pinion spider with pinion gears and thrust washers from differential case. *See Fig. 1.*

Inspection – Check mating surfaces of differential case, gears and pinion shaft for wear, scoring or damage. Check thrust washers for wear or damage. Check tapered roller bearings for wear, scratches, pitting or flaking. Ensure bearings turn smoothly and do not bind. Check viscous coupling case for cracks or silicone oil leakage. Replace bearings as a set (if necessary).

Reassembly (RS5F50V) – 1) Install Gauging Tool (J34291) on outer differential case (speedometer gear half of case), and lock Gauging Cylinder in place (STEP "A"). *See Fig. 6.* Install Gauging Plunger (J34290-6) into Gauging Cylinder. Install pinion and side gears with thrust washers in viscous coupling half of differential case. Install Gauging Tool on case and allow Gauging Plunger to rest on side gear thrust washer.

2) Using a feeler gauge, measure gap between Gauging Plunger and Gauging Cylinder (STEP "B"). *See Fig. 6.* Clearance should be .004-.008" (.10-.20 mm). If clearance is not within specifications, adjust clearance by changing thrust washer thickness. See DIFFERENTIAL CASE SIDE GEAR THRUST WASHER table.

DIFFERENTIAL CASE SIDE GEAR THRUST WASHER

Thickness In. (mm)	Part Number
.030-.032 (.75-.80)	38424-E3000
.032-.034 (.80-.85)	38424-E3001
.034-.035 (.85-.90)	38424-E3002
.035-.037 (.90-.95)	38424-E3003

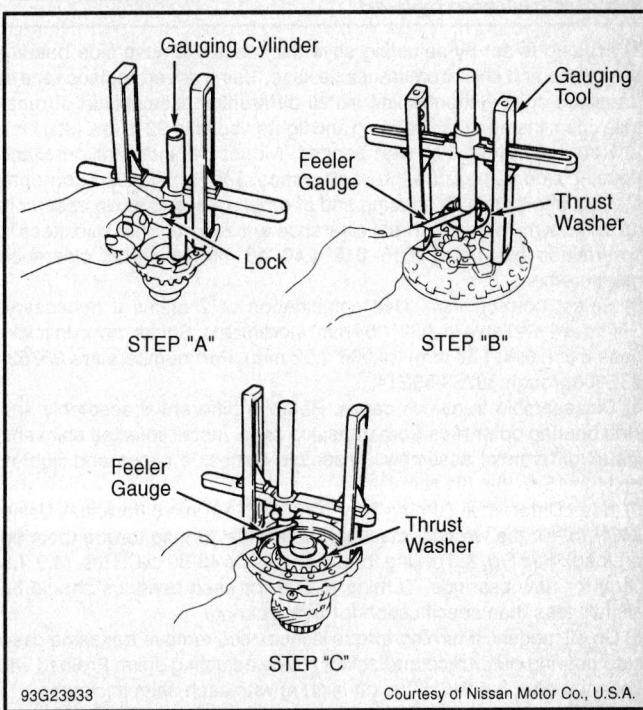

Fig. 6: *Measuring Side Gear Clearance*

3) Install Gauging Tool (J34291) on differential case side of viscous coupling and lock Gauging Cylinder in place. Remove Gauging Cylinder. Install speedometer drive gear side of differential case to viscous coupling side of differential case, matching marks made during disassembly. Tighten case bolts to 27-30 ft. lbs. (36-40 N.m). Install Gauging Tool (J34291) on viscous coupling side of differential case and allow Gauging Plunger to rest on thrust washer. See Fig. 6.

4) Using a feeler gauge, measure gap between Gauging Plunger and Gauging Cylinder (STEP "C"). Measurement should be exact clearance between side gear thrust washer and differential case. Clearance should be .004-.008" (.10-.20 mm). If clearance is not within specifications, adjust clearance by changing thrust washer thickness. See VISCOUS COUPLING SIDE GEAR THRUST WASHER table.

VISCOUS COUPLING SIDE GEAR THRUST WASHER

Thickness In. (mm)	Part Number
.017-.018 (.43-.45)	38424-51E10
.021-.021 (.52-.54)	38424-51E11
.024-.025 (.61-.63)	38424-51E12
.028-.028 (.70-.72)	38424-51E13
.031-.032 (.79-.81)	38424-51E14

5) Install viscous coupling onto differential case. Tighten bolts to 34-44 INCH Lbs. (4-5 N.m). Install speedometer drive gear on differential case. Align projections of speedometer drive gear with groove in differential case. Press differential side bearings on differential case. Install ring gear and tighten bolts in crisscross pattern to 65-76 ft. lbs. (88-103 N.m).

TRANSAXLE ADJUSTMENTS

NOTE: Transaxle adjustments are performed as part of transaxle assembly procedure. See TRANSAXLE REASSEMBLY.

DIFFERENTIAL BEARING PRELOAD

NOTE: It is mandatory to check differential bearing preload if differential case, differential bearings, clutch housing and/or transaxle case have been replaced.

1) Preload is set by adjusting shim thickness. Remove side bearing outer race and shim from transaxle case. Using driver, replace race in transaxle case without shim. Install differential assembly into transaxle case. Install clutch housing and tighten bolts to 22 ft. lbs. (30 N.m).

2) Rotate differential to seat bearing. Mount dial indicator on clutch housing side to measure thrust clearance. See Fig. 7. Insert appropriate tool into transaxle housing end of differential and move assembly up and down. Measure thrust clearance and record. Shim thickness is determined by adding .016-.018" (.40-.46 mm) to thrust clearance measurement.

3) Select correct shim. Use combination of 2 shims if necessary. Shims are available in .002" (.04 mm) increments. Shims range in thickness from .014" (.36 mm) to .036" (.92 mm). Part numbers are 38753-56E00 through 38753-56E14.

4) Disassemble transaxle cases. Remove differential assembly and side bearing outer race from transaxle case. Install selected shim and install differential assembly. Assemble transaxle cases and tighten bolts to 15 ft. lbs. (21 N.m).

5) Insert Differential Turning Tool (KV38105210) into differential. Using INCH lb. torque wrench, measure differential turning torque (bearing preload). See Fig. 8. Turning torque should be 43-69 INCH lbs. (4.9-7.8 N.m) for new bearings. Turning torque for used bearings should be slightly less than specification for new bearings.

6) On all models, if turning torque is incorrect, remove transaxle case side bearing outer race and select a new adjusting shim. Preload will change about 3-4 INCH lbs. (.3-.4 N.m) with each shim thickness.

7) Rotate torque wrench one complete revolution. Turning torque should not increase more than 8.7 INCH lbs. (1.0 N.m). If measurement increases more than specification or binding is felt, inspect bearings for possible damage.

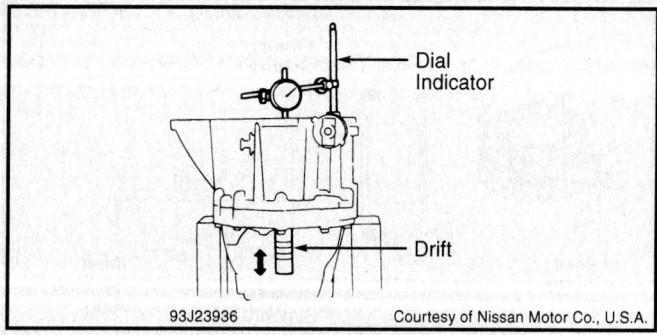

Fig. 7: Measuring Differential Side Gear Thrust Clearance

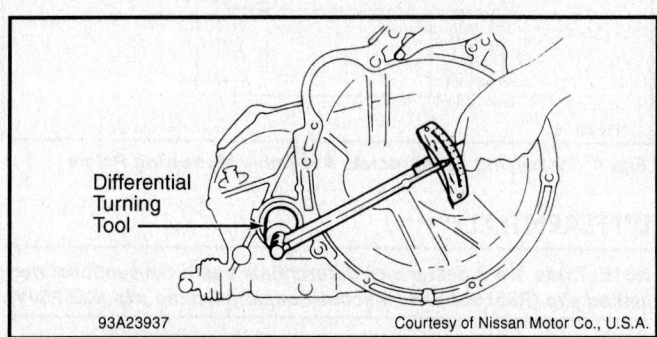

Fig. 8: Measuring Turning Torque

INPUT SHAFT THRUST CLEARANCE

NOTE: It is mandatory to check input shaft thrust clearance (end play) if the input shaft, input shaft bearing, clutch housing and/or transaxle case have been replaced.

1) Disassemble clutch housing from transaxle housing and install input shaft. Install clutch housing and tighten bolts to 15 ft. lbs. (21 N.m). Mount dial indicator and measure input thrust clearance. See Fig. 9. Clearance should be .0004-.002" (.010-.05 mm).

2) If thrust clearance is not within specifications, dissemble transaxle case. Remove input shaft and install correct shim or combination of shims. Shims are available in .002" (.04 mm) increments. Shims range in thickness from .016" (.40 mm) to .032" (.80 mm). Part numbers are 32225-08E00 through 32225-08E10. One shim is available in thickness of .047" (1.20 mm). Part number is 32225-08E11.

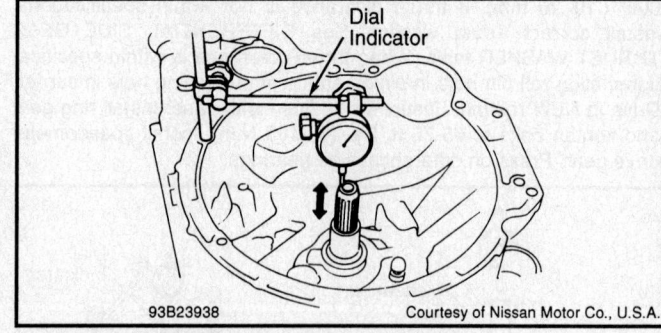

Fig. 9: Measuring Input Shaft Thrust Clearance

MAINSHAFT BEARING PRELOAD

NOTE: It is mandatory to check the mainshaft bearing preload if the mainshaft, mainshaft bearings, clutch housing and/or transaxle case have been replaced.

1) Remove any components in transaxle housing before measuring mainshaft bearing preload. Disassemble transaxle case and remove input shaft and differential assembly. Mainshaft bearing preload is adjusted by changing thickness of shims located behind the rear mainshaft bearing race.

2) Remove mainshaft rear bearing outer race and shim(s). Install rear bearing outer race without shims. Install mainshaft into transaxle case. Place front bearing outer race onto front bearing. Turn mainshaft while holding bearing race to ensure bearings are properly seated.

3) Place Gauging Bridge (J-34290-1) with Gauging Cylinder (J-34290-2) onto machined surface of transaxle case (STEP "A"). *See Fig. 10.* Gauging Cylinder should rest on front bearing outer race surface. Turn screw in bridge to lock Cylinder in place.

4) Turn bridge over and insert Mainshaft Gauging Plunger (J-34290-8) into Gauging Cylinder (STEP "B"). *See Fig. 10.* Place bridge, with legs up onto machined surface of clutch housing. Allow Gauging Plunger to rest on mating surface where front bearing outer race is positioned.

5) Using a feeler gauge, measure the distance between Gauging Cylinder and shoulder of Gauging Plunger. *See Fig. 10.* Mainshaft bearing preload is determined by adding .010-.012" (.25-.31 mm) to measurement taken.

6) Mainshaft bearing adjusting shims are available in .002" (.04 mm) increments. Shims range in thickness from .016" (.40 mm) to .032" (.80 mm). Part numbers are 32139-03E11 through 32139-03E08. One shim is available in a thickness of .047" (1.20 mm). Part number is 32139-03E13. Remove rear bearing race from case and install selected shim(s). Using driver, install bearing race.

TRANSAXLE REASSEMBLY

1) Using driver, install mainshaft front bearing race into clutch housing. Install shifting rod and shift lever. Install retaining pin through shifting lever. Access retaining pin hole through drain hole in case. Install drain plug. Install selector and shaft. Drive in selector shaft retaining pin.

2) Install differential assembly. Install input shaft, mainshaft with 1st/2nd shift fork and rod as single assembly. Ensure input shaft oil seal is not damaged. Install interlock balls and plunger. *See Fig. 2.* Install 3rd/4th shift fork and bracket. Install 3rd/4th shift rod, snap rings and retaining roll pin. Install interlock balls.

3) Install 5th shift fork and bracket. Install shift rod, snap ring and retaining roll pin. Install locking ball, spring and check plug. Install reverse lock spring on 5th/Reverse bracket. Install loop of spring facing upward. Install check ball and reverse lever spring on reverse lever assembly.

4) Install reverse lever assembly on clutch housing. Install reverse arm shaft and retaining pin. Hook reverse lock spring and reverse lever spring on reverse lever assembly. Engage 4th gear and install reverse idler gear and reverse idler shaft. To assist in installation of transaxle case, place shift selector in 1st/2nd shift bracket. Install magnet on clutch housing. *See Figs. 1 and 2.*

5) Apply appropriate sealant to transaxle case and install case. Install shift position switch. Install all detent balls, springs and plugs. Once assembly is completed, ensure transaxle can be shifted into all gears smoothly. Measure total turning torque (total preload). *See Fig. 8.*

NOTE: Specifications provided for total turning torque (total preload), are for new bearings only. Total turning torque for used bearings will be slightly less.

---

6) Install Differential Turning Tool (KV38105210) into differential and measure turning torque. Total turning torque should be 78-191 INCH lbs. (8.8-21.6 N.m). If total turning torque is not within specifications, recheck mainshaft bearing preload.

TORQUE SPECIFICATIONS
TORQUE SPECIFICATIONS

Application	Ft. Lbs. (N.m)
Check Plug (All)	12-16 (16-22)
Drain Plug	15-22 (20-29)
Differential Case Bolt	15-19 (21-25)
Filler Plug	19-25 (25-35)
Reverse Check Assembly	12-15 (16-21)
Reverse Idler Shaft Bolt	12-15 (16-21)
Reverse Lever Assembly Bolt	12-15 (16-21)
Ring Gear Mount Bolts	54-65 (74-88)
Transaxle Housing Bolt	15-19 (21-25)

	INCH Lbs. (N.m)
Shift Position Switch Bolt	33-44 (4-5)
Speedometer Gear Assembly Bolt	33-44 (4-5)
Viscous Coupling Bolt	33-52 (4-6)

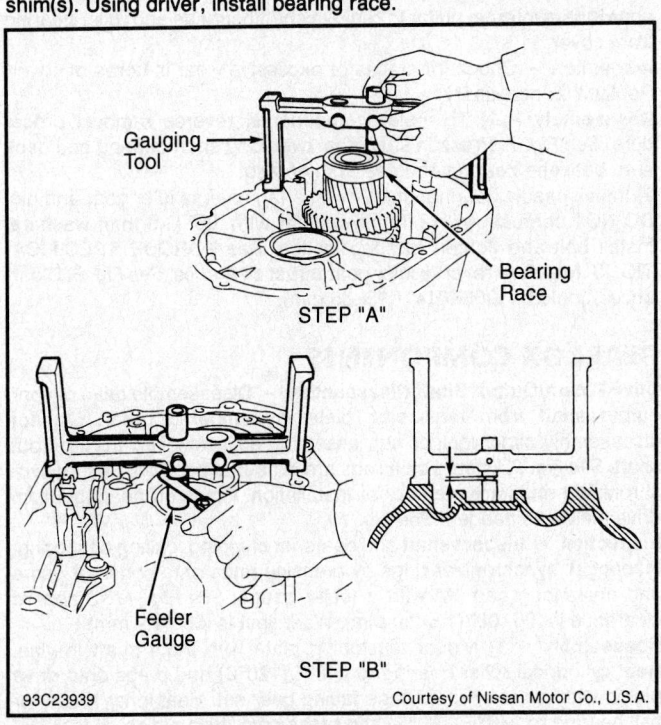

Gauging Tool

Bearing Race

STEP "A"

Feeler Gauge

STEP "B"

93C23939   Courtesy of Nissan Motor Co., U.S.A.

Fig. 10: Measuring Mainshaft Bearing Clearance

MANUAL TRANSMISSIONS
Porsche G50/20 6-Speed

911 Carrera 2

NOTE: The metric dimensions listed in this article are the preferred service measurement. Inch conversions are given to the fourth decimal place for reference.

APPLICATION & LABOR TIMES

APPLICATION & LABOR TIMES

Vehicle Application	[1][3] R & I	[2][3] Overhaul	Series
911 Carrera 2 (2WD)	11.0	14.4	G50/20

[1] – Removal and installation of transmission from vehicle chassis.
[2] – Bench overhaul time for transaxle/differential. DOES NOT include removal and installation.
[3] – Add .4 hr. if equipped with A/C.

IDENTIFICATION

The G50/20 Transaxle is identified by a transaxle number stamped in transaxle case at case joint near drain plug. The 12 digits identify transaxle type, variations within assembly number and serial number. For example, transaxle number G5021-1-05641 is broken down as follows: G5021-transaxle type, 1-index for variations (1 = normal differential, 2 = limited-slip differential) and 05641 - serial number. See Fig. 1.

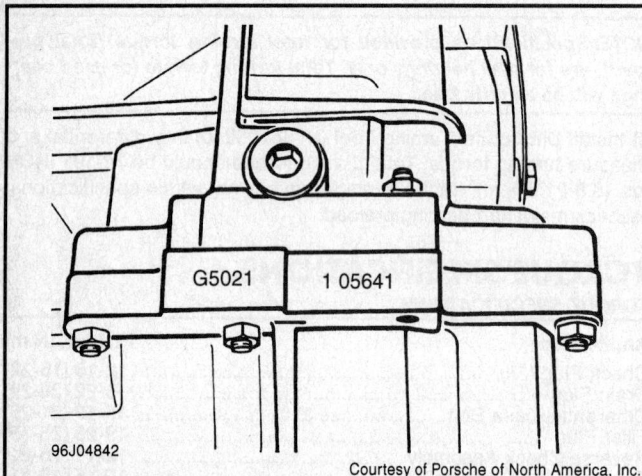

96J04842

Courtesy of Porsche of North America, Inc.

Fig. 1: Locating Transaxle Identification Number

DESCRIPTION

The G50/20 transaxle is a 6 speed, fully synchronized, manual transaxle. Transaxle features an overdrive 6th gear ratio of .82:1 and a final drive ratio 3.44:1. Transaxle controls consist of a remote, floor mounted shifter using a selector rod for gear actuation. Clutch hydraulic system consists of a pedal actuated clutch master cylinder, a case mounted slave actuating cylinder, hydraulic lines and a reservoir tank.

LUBRICATION & ADJUSTMENT

See appropriate MANUAL TRANSMISSION SERVICING article in TRANSMISSION SERVICING section.

TROUBLE SHOOTING

See GENERAL TROUBLE SHOOTING article in this section.

REMOVAL & INSTALLATION

See appropriate MANUAL TRANSMISSION REMOVAL article in TRANSMISSION SERVICING section.

TRANSAXLE DISASSEMBLY

1) Remove eccentric bushing, seal, pressure spring and locking bushing from transaxle front cover. Remove transaxle cover bolts and remove cover. See Fig. 2. Install Holder (9253) and engage 6th gear. See Fig. 3.
2) Remove remaining components in numbered order. See Fig. 2. Ensure synchronizing rings are marked for installation reference. Remove 6th gear, needle cage and bearing inner race using a bearing puller. See Fig. 4.
3) Remove back-up light switch and plunger. Remove 4 brackets from gearbox. Remove gearbox and gasket from transaxle housing. Remove remaining components in numbered order. See Fig. 5.
4) Remove bolts securing both stub axles to differential area of clutch housing. See Fig. 6. Remove remaining components in numbered order. Do not disassembly synchronizer hub assembly until removed from output shaft.

COMPONENT DISASSEMBLY & REASSEMBLY

NOTE: Information for limited slip differential is not available from manufacturer.

FRONT TRANSAXLE COVER

Disassembly – Remove front transaxle cover components in numbered order. See Fig. 7. Mark thrust washer(s) for reassembly. Use appropriate internal puller to remove shaft bearings and roller bearing from cover.
Inspection – Check for cracks or excessive wear in bores of cover. Replace as necessary.
Reassembly – 1) To install components, reverse removal procedure. See Fig. 7. Press in shaft seal over long shaft bearing and pack area between bearing and seal with grease.
2) Install needle bearing, thrust washer(s), reverse idler gear and pin. DO NOT confuse .07" (2.0 mm) washer with .06" (1.5 mm) washers. Install bolt and tighten to specification. See TORQUE SPECIFICATIONS. Measure reverse idler gear thrust clearance. See Fig. 8. Clearance should be .006-.014" (.15-.35 mm).

GEARBOX COMPONENTS

Drive Pinion/Output Shaft Disassembly – Disassemble drive pinion/output shaft from tensioning plate in numbered order. Do not disassembly synchronizer hub assembly until removed from output shaft. See Fig. 9. Ensure shift rods are in neutral position. Ensure synchronizing rings are marked for installation. Press off bearings from drive pinion as needed. See Fig. 10.
Inspection – Inspect shaft and gears for chipping, galling or scoring. Inspect all synchronizer rings by pressing rings onto cones of gears and measuring gap "A" with a feeler gauge. See Fig. 11. Standard clearance is .06-.08" (1.5-2.0 mm). Wear limit is .05" (1.2 mm).
Reassembly – 1) Mount tensioning plate with input shaft in vise. Heat cylindrical roller bearing to 248°F (120°C) and press onto drive pinion with collar of roller cage facing gear set. Heat inner races for ball bearing to 248°F (120°C) and press onto drive pinion.

NOTE: Drive pinion and ring gear are marked with pairing number which must correspond when components are assembled.

2) Install remaining components in reverse order of disassembly. See Fig. 9. Heat all interference fit bearings to 248°F (120°C) before assembling. Ensure 1st/2nd shift sleeve is installed with groove facing 2nd gear. See Figs. 12 and 13. Ensure shift hub is properly aligned with oil hole of drive pinion/output shaft.

Input Shaft Disassembly – Clamp Holder (9282) in vise and install input shaft. See Fig. 14. Unscrew input shaft nut with Socket (9105). Pull off roller bearing, ball bearing and inner races. Remove tensioning plate. Remove remaining components in numbered order. Install synchronizer hub components as an assembly. See Fig. 15.

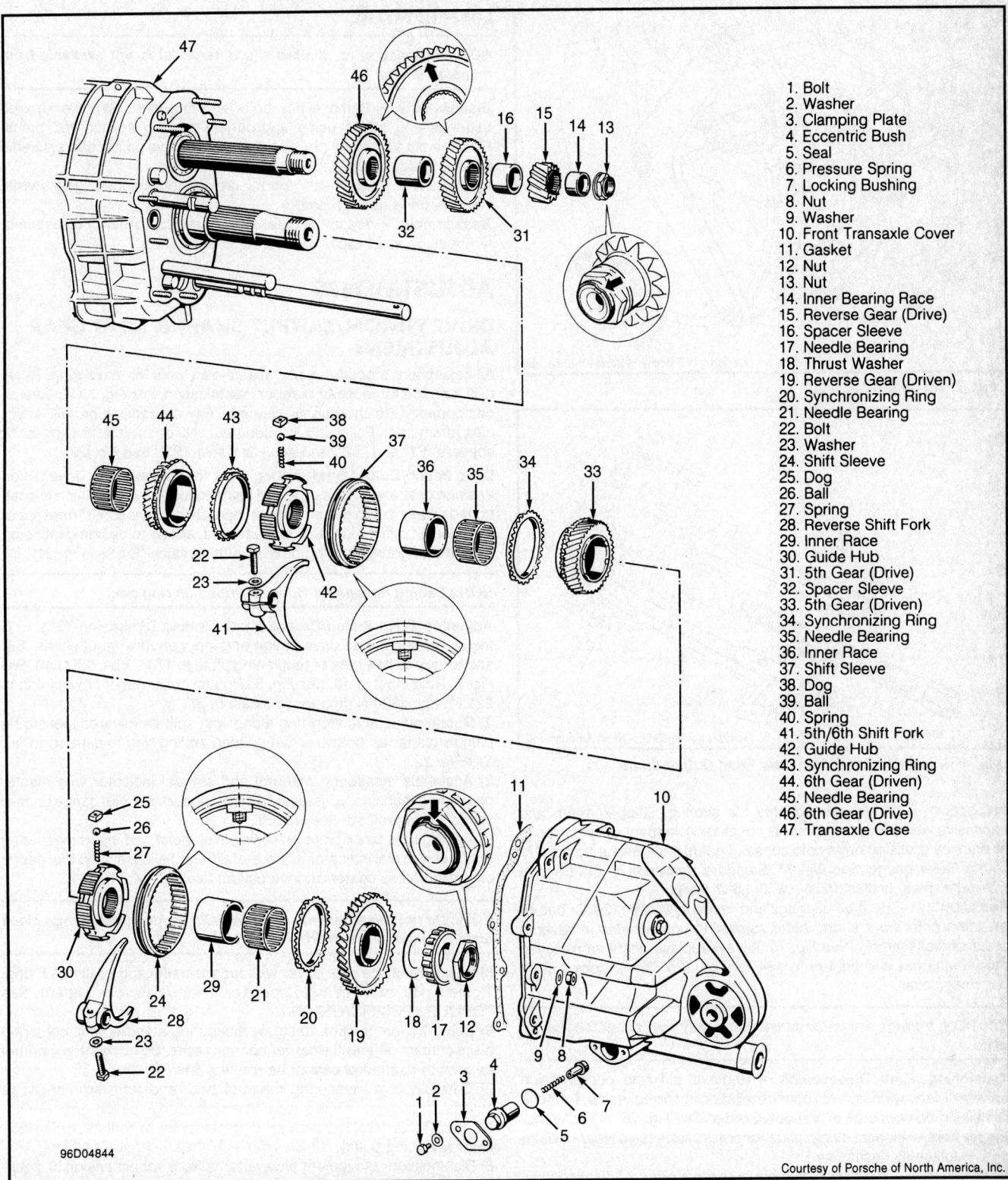

1. Bolt
2. Washer
3. Clamping Plate
4. Eccentric Bush
5. Seal
6. Pressure Spring
7. Locking Bushing
8. Nut
9. Washer
10. Front Transaxle Cover
11. Gasket
12. Nut
13. Nut
14. Inner Bearing Race
15. Reverse Gear (Drive)
16. Spacer Sleeve
17. Needle Bearing
18. Thrust Washer
19. Reverse Gear (Driven)
20. Synchronizing Ring
21. Needle Bearing
22. Bolt
23. Washer
24. Shift Sleeve
25. Dog
26. Ball
27. Spring
28. Reverse Shift Fork
29. Inner Race
30. Guide Hub
31. 5th Gear (Drive)
32. Spacer Sleeve
33. 5th Gear (Driven)
34. Synchronizing Ring
35. Needle Bearing
36. Inner Race
37. Shift Sleeve
38. Dog
39. Ball
40. Spring
41. 5th/6th Shift Fork
42. Guide Hub
43. Synchronizing Ring
44. 6th Gear (Driven)
45. Needle Bearing
46. 6th Gear (Drive)
47. Transaxle Case

96D04844

Courtesy of Porsche of North America, Inc.

Fig. 2: Exploded View Of 5th, 6th & Reverse Gear Assemblies

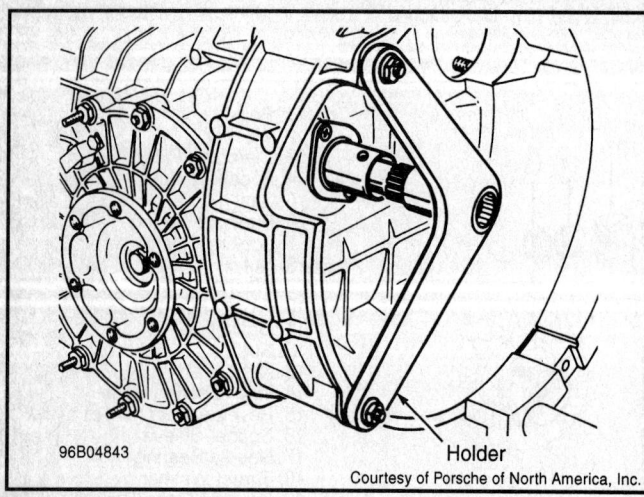

96B04843   Holder
Courtesy of Porsche of North America, Inc.

Fig. 3: Holding Input Shaft

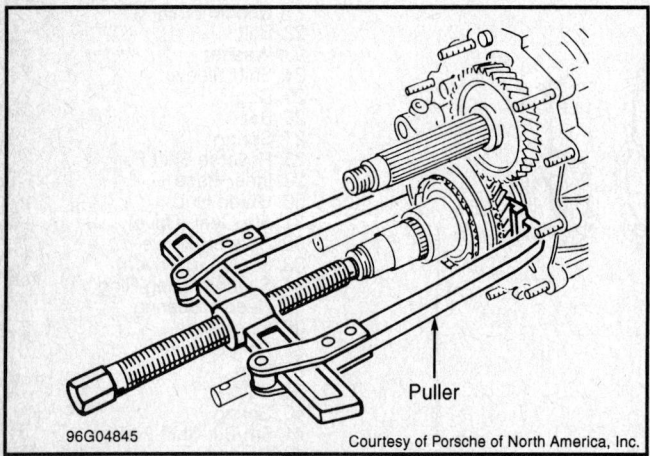

96G04845   Puller
Courtesy of Porsche of North America, Inc.

Fig. 4: Removing 6th Driven Gear From Output Shaft

Inspection – Inspect components for scoring, chipped teeth and excessive wear. Replace parts (as necessary). Inspect all synchronizer rings by pressing rings onto cones of gears and measuring gap "A" with a feeler gauge. See Fig. 11. Standard clearance is .04" (.9 mm) minimum. Wear limit is .0236-.0276" (.6-.7 mm).

Reassembly – Heat all bearings and races to 248°F (120°C) before pressing onto input shaft. Install remaining components in reverse order of disassembly. See Fig. 15. Always replace gears as matched pair. Install nut and tighten to 184 Ft. Lbs. (250 N.m). Lock nut by punching collar.

CAUTION: Springs are under tension and may pop out of tensioning plate.

Tensioning Plate Disassembly – Remove pin and compression springs. Mark springs for proper installation in correct holes. Remove remaining components in numbered order. See Fig. 16.

Inspection – Inspect clamp plate for cracks excessive wear or damage. Replace as necessary.

Reassembly – Install components in reverse order of disassembly. See Figs. 16 and 17. Ensure deflection lever springs are installed in original locations. See DEFLECTION LEVER THRUST SPRING SPECIFICATIONS table.

DEFLECTION LEVER THRUST SPRING SPECIFICATIONS

Application	Free Length In. (mm)	Thickness In. (mm)
Lower Spring	2.17-12.28 (50.8-51.8)	.059 (1.1)
Upper Spring	1.33-11.35 (33.9-34.4)	.063 (1.60)

DIFFERENTIAL

NOTE: Information for limited slip differential is not available from manufacturer.

Disassembly – Remove hex bolts and ring gear. Remove tapered bearings and shims using appropriate bearing splitter and press. Remove pin and spiral pin. See Fig. 18. Remove pinion gears, needle bearings, side gears and threaded nuts.

Inspection – Inspect for worn, broken or chipped gear teeth. Replace parts (as necessary).

Reassembly – Assemble differential in reverse order of disassembly. Press on inner races of tapered roller bearing.

ADJUSTMENTS

DRIVE PINION/OUTPUT SHAFT & RING GEAR ADJUSTMENT

All adjustment procedures use specialized tools for measuring. Refer to illustration for tool part number identification. See Fig. 19. Ensure all components are thoroughly cleaned. Any contamination will affect measurements. Following procedures will determine thickness of spacers "S1" and "S2", and adjusting shim "S3". See Fig. 20.

Drive Pinion/Output Shaft & Ring Gear Identification – Drive pinion and ring gear are always replaced as matched set. Drive pinion is positioned axially to achieve smoothest operation. Deviation "r" from specified design dimension "Ro" is measured, added to design dimension "Ro" and engraved on ring gear as setting value "E". See Fig. 21.

NOTE: Setting dimension "E" is stamped on ring gear.

Adjusting Drive Pinion/Output Shaft (Setting Dimension "E") – 1) Install preassembled drive pinion and input shaft without shims "S3" and torque all hex nuts of tensioning plate to 17 Ft. Lbs. (23 N.m). See Fig. 5. Hold input shaft. See Fig. 3. Tighten collar nut of drive pinion to 221 Ft. Lbs. (300 N.m) prior to measuring.

2) Rotate adjustable stop ring along with spindle towards measuring plunger as far as possible. Set second setting ring to dimension "a". See Fig. 22.

3) Assemble measuring mandrel and set dial indicator with master gauge to dimension "E" (stamped on ring gear). Set dial gauge to zero with a 1 mm preload. See Fig. 23.

4) Place gauge block plate on drive pinion head and insert measuring mandrel with dial indicator in place of differential assembly. Dial gauge extension faces center of drive pinion. See Fig. 24.

NOTE: Do not use a hammer when installing side cover. Gauge block plate is magnetically held to drive pinion.

5) Install transaxle side cover without shaft seal and sealing "O" ring. Tighten side cover bolts to specification in crisscross pattern. See TORQUE SPECIFICATIONS.

6) Using 24 mm socket, unscrew measuring mandrel until centering discs contact differential carrier bearing races. Do not tighten mandrel to point that mandrel cannot be rotated. See Fig. 25.

7) Carefully turn measuring mandrel back and forth so dial gauge extension (plunger) sweeps on either side of drive pinion vertical (center) line. Record dial indicator reading at maximum deflection (dial indicator reversing point).

8) Dial indicator movement always turns from set dimension in clockwise direction. If dial indicator needle movement from zero is taken as shim thickness "S3" to be installed. Round off dial indicator reading to nearest .05 mm.

9) Remove drive pinion and install selected shim. Recheck drive pinion dimension "E". A 0 – .03 mm tolerance is allowed.

Adjusting Differential Bearing Preload – 1) Ensure drive pinion is removed. Remove shims "S1" and "S2" from differential. See Fig. 20. Install .0984" (2.5 mm) shims in place of shims "S1" and "S2". Press on bearings. Install differential assembly in transaxle case. Install side cover without seals. Tighten bolts in crisscross pattern to 17 ft. lbs. (23 N.m).

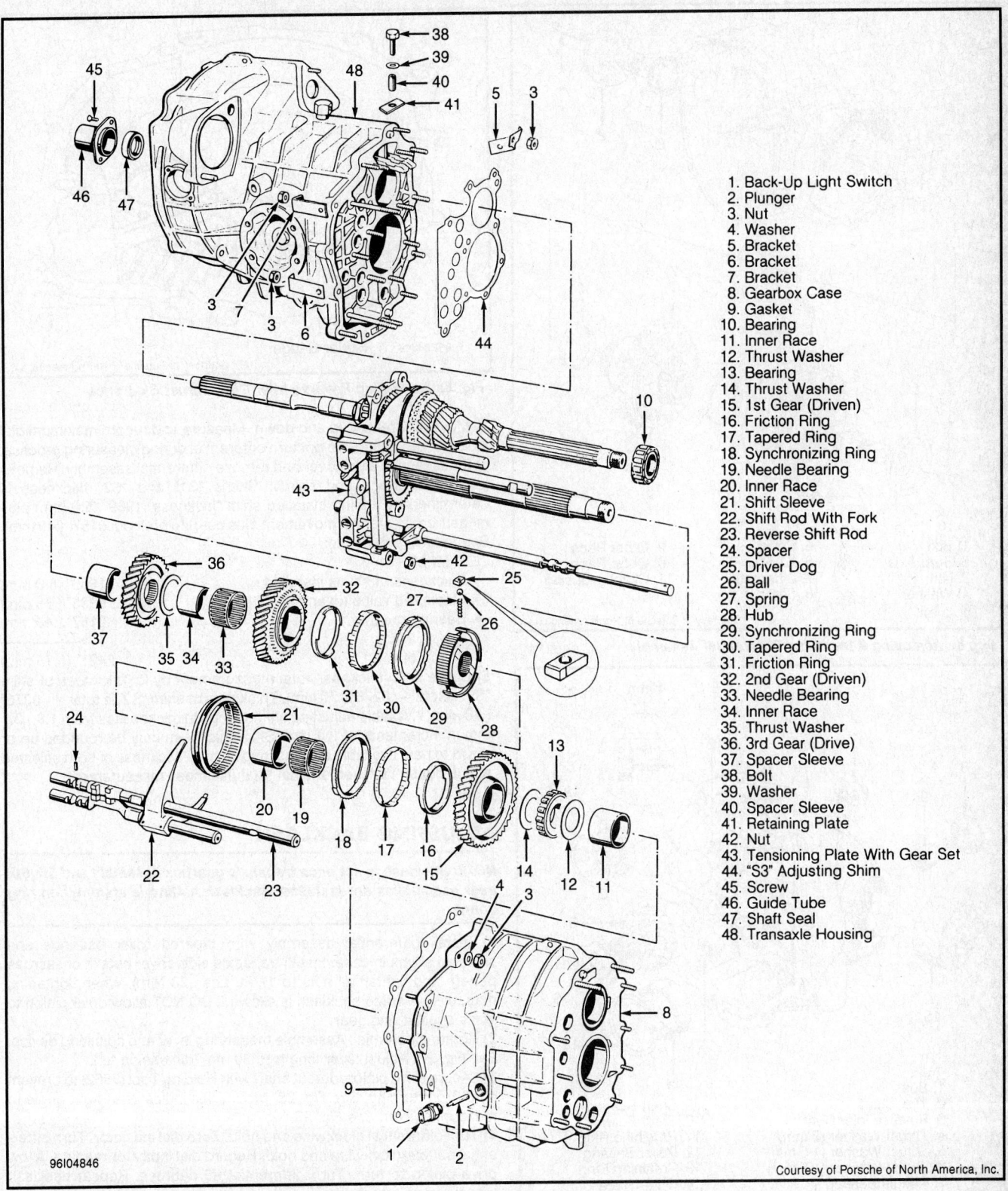

1. Back-Up Light Switch
2. Plunger
3. Nut
4. Washer
5. Bracket
6. Bracket
7. Bracket
8. Gearbox Case
9. Gasket
10. Bearing
11. Inner Race
12. Thrust Washer
13. Bearing
14. Thrust Washer
15. 1st Gear (Driven)
16. Friction Ring
17. Tapered Ring
18. Synchronizing Ring
19. Needle Bearing
20. Inner Race
21. Shift Sleeve
22. Shift Rod With Fork
23. Reverse Shift Rod
24. Spacer
25. Driver Dog
26. Ball
27. Spring
28. Hub
29. Synchronizing Ring
30. Tapered Ring
31. Friction Ring
32. 2nd Gear (Driven)
33. Needle Bearing
34. Inner Race
35. Thrust Washer
36. 3rd Gear (Drive)
37. Spacer Sleeve
38. Bolt
39. Washer
40. Spacer Sleeve
41. Retaining Plate
42. Nut
43. Tensioning Plate With Gear Set
44. "S3" Adjusting Shim
45. Screw
46. Guide Tube
47. Shaft Seal
48. Transaxle Housing

96I04846

Courtesy of Porsche of North America, Inc.

Fig. 5: Exploded View Of Gearbox Components

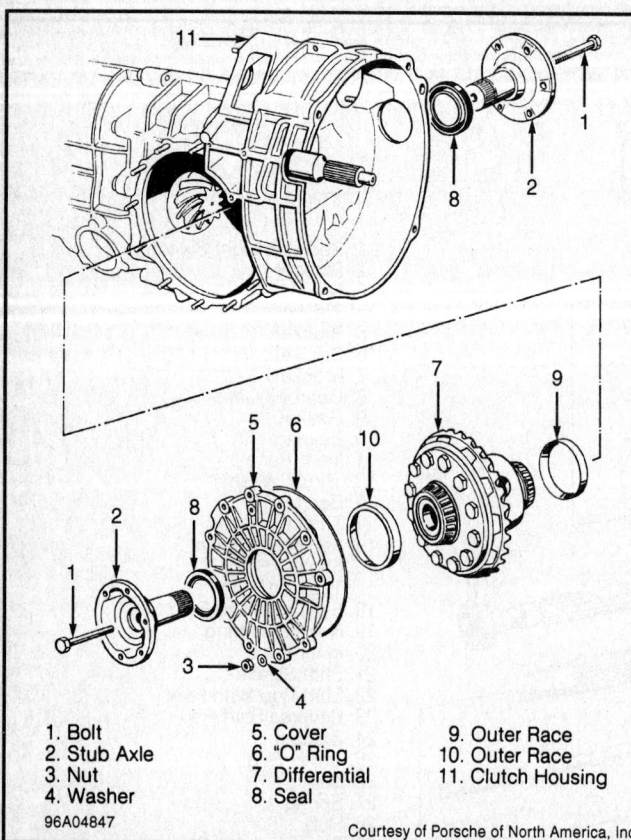

1. Bolt
2. Stub Axle
3. Nut
4. Washer
5. Cover
6. "O" Ring
7. Differential
8. Seal
9. Outer Race
10. Outer Race
11. Clutch Housing

96A04847

Courtesy of Porsche of North America, Inc.

Fig. 6: Removing & Installing Differential Assembly

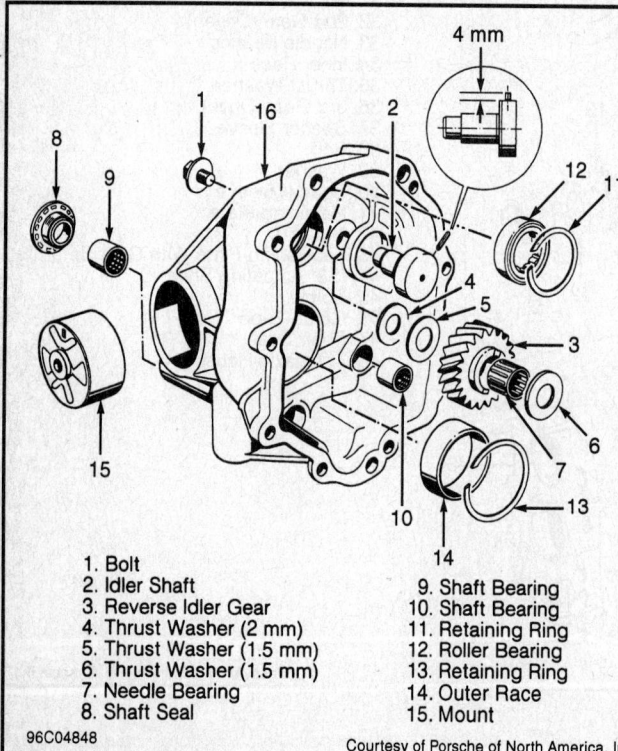

1. Bolt
2. Idler Shaft
3. Reverse Idler Gear
4. Thrust Washer (2 mm)
5. Thrust Washer (1.5 mm)
6. Thrust Washer (1.5 mm)
7. Needle Bearing
8. Shaft Seal
9. Shaft Bearing
10. Shaft Bearing
11. Retaining Ring
12. Roller Bearing
13. Retaining Ring
14. Outer Race
15. Mount

96C04848

Courtesy of Porsche of North America, Inc.

Fig. 7: Exploded View Of Front Transaxle Cover

2) Rotate differential to seat bearings. Place gauge block plate on differential collar. *See Fig. 26.* Mount dial indicator with 30 mm extension. Set dial indicator to zero with 2 mm preload.

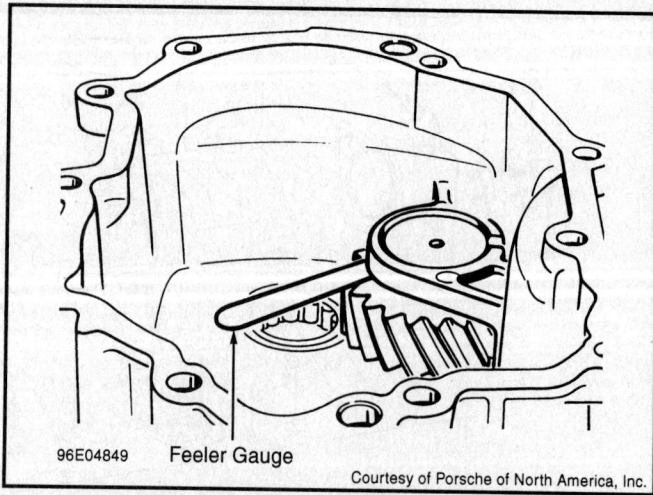

96E04849   Feeler Gauge

Courtesy of Porsche of North America, Inc.

Fig. 8: Measuring Reverse Idler Gear Thrust Clearance

3) Move differential up and down. Measure and record maximum dial indicator deflection. Do not turn differential during measuring process.
4) Disassemble side cover and remove differential assembly. Remove tapered bearings and shims. Shims "S1" and "S2" thickness is determined by adding installed shim thickness .1969" (5.0 mm) plus measured differential movement plus bearing preload .0157" (.40 mm). See following example:

EXAMPLE

- Thickness of shims installed   .1969" (5.0 mm)
- Measured value (example)   .0295" (.75 mm)
- Bearing preload   +   .0157" (.40 mm)

- Shim Total   .2421" (6.15 mm)

5) Divide shim thickness total measurement by 2. Thickness of shim "S1" is total – .0276" (.70 mm). Thickness of shim "S2" is total + .0276" (.70 mm). Available adjusting shims range in thicknesses from 1.6 - 3.1 mm in increments of .10 mm. Shim thickness may be rounded up or down to next available shim as long as total thickness of both selected shims doesn't exceed original total thickness measurement.

ADJUSTING BACKLASH

NOTE: Backlash is set once transaxle gearbox assembly and 5th/6th gear assemblies are installed. Backlash setting is stamped on ring gear.

1) Install differential assembly with tapered roller bearings and selected shims in case. Install transaxle side cover nuts in crisscross pattern and tighten all nuts to 17 Ft. Lbs. (23 N.m). When tightening nuts, ensure some backlash is allowed. DO NOT allow drive pinion to seize against ring gear.
2) Rotate differential. Assemble measuring lever and adjusting device. *See Fig. 27.* Adjust lever length to 80 mm (dimension "a").
3) Secure drive pinion/output shaft with Holding Tool (9562) to prevent shaft from turning. *See Fig. 28.* Mount dial indicator at right angle to measuring lever. *See Fig. 27.*
4) Turn differential clockwise and hold. Zero dial indicator. Turn differential counterclockwise and hold. Record dial indicator reading. Allow drive pinion to turn. Turn differential 90 degrees. Repeat backlash measurement procedure.
5) Turn differential 90 degrees 2 more times while repeating backlash measurement procedure. Recorded readings should not vary by more than .03 mm. Preferred backlash figure is stamped on ring gear.
6) Backlash is adjusted by changing shims "S1" and "S2". A shim thickness change of .05 mm will result in backlash change of approximately .1 mm. DO NOT change total thickness of both selected shims determined in ADJUSTING RING GEAR procedure.

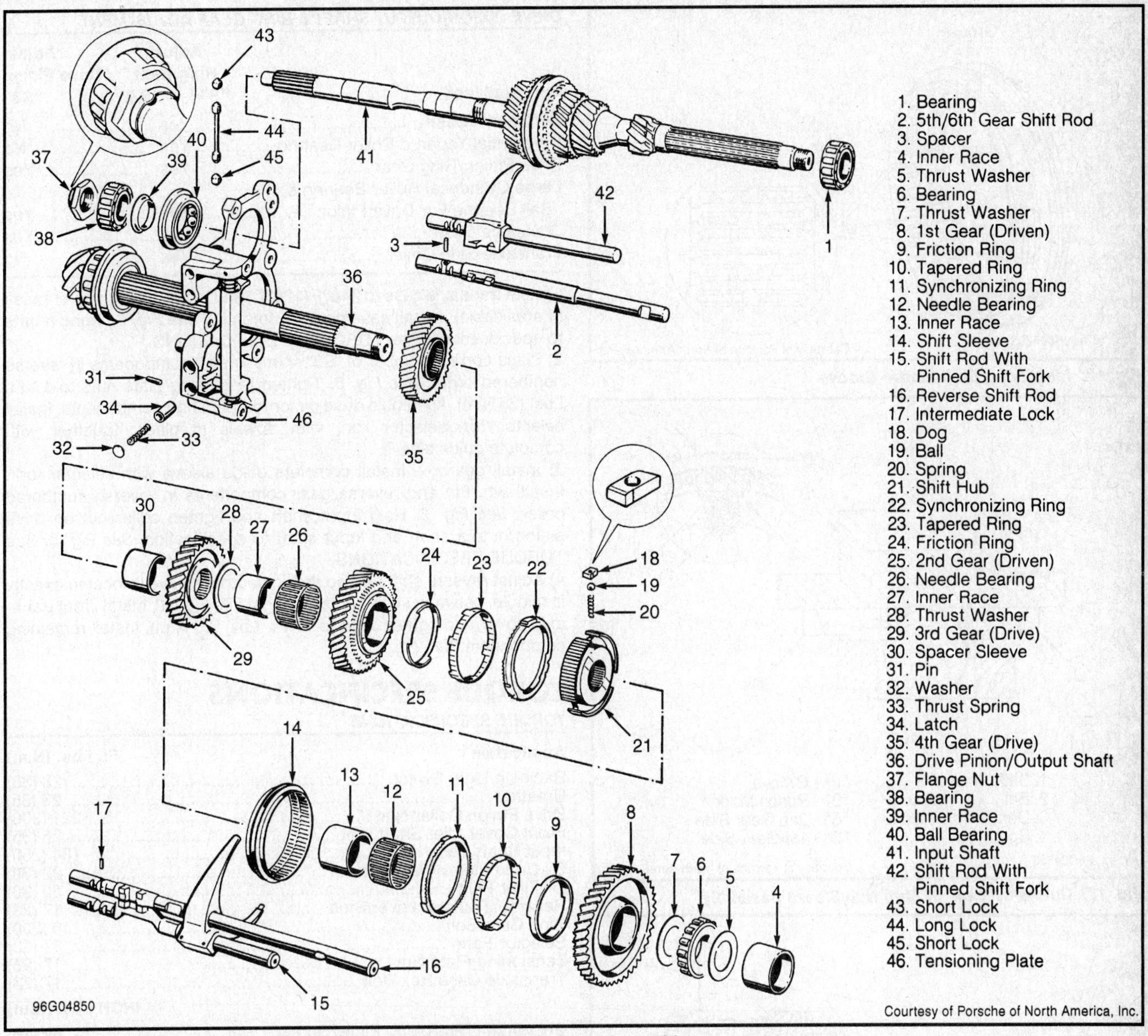

1. Bearing
2. 5th/6th Gear Shift Rod
3. Spacer
4. Inner Race
5. Thrust Washer
6. Bearing
7. Thrust Washer
8. 1st Gear (Driven)
9. Friction Ring
10. Tapered Ring
11. Synchronizing Ring
12. Needle Bearing
13. Inner Race
14. Shift Sleeve
15. Shift Rod With Pinned Shift Fork
16. Reverse Shift Rod
17. Intermediate Lock
18. Dog
19. Ball
20. Spring
21. Shift Hub
22. Synchronizing Ring
23. Tapered Ring
24. Friction Ring
25. 2nd Gear (Driven)
26. Needle Bearing
27. Inner Race
28. Thrust Washer
29. 3rd Gear (Drive)
30. Spacer Sleeve
31. Pin
32. Washer
33. Thrust Spring
34. Latch
35. 4th Gear (Drive)
36. Drive Pinion/Output Shaft
37. Flange Nut
38. Bearing
39. Inner Race
40. Ball Bearing
41. Input Shaft
42. Shift Rod With Pinned Shift Fork
43. Short Lock
44. Long Lock
45. Short Lock
46. Tensioning Plate
96G04850
Courtesy of Porsche of North America, Inc.

Fig. 9: Exploded View Of Drive Pinion, Output Shaft & Tensioning Plate Assembly

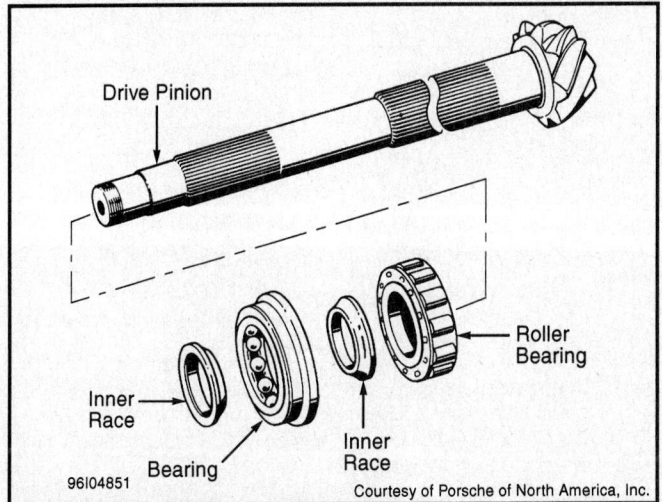

Drive Pinion
Roller Bearing
Inner Race
Bearing
Inner Race
96I04851
Courtesy of Porsche of North America, Inc.

Fig. 10: Exploded View Of Drive Pinion

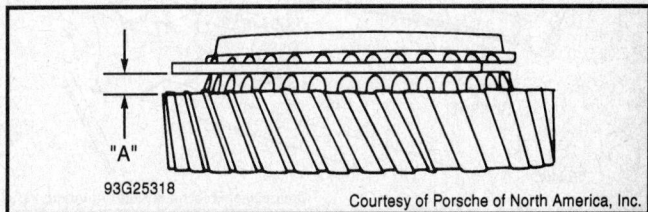

"A"
93G25318
Courtesy of Porsche of North America, Inc.

Fig. 11: Measuring Synchronizer Ring Gap "A"

TRANSMISSION REASSEMBLY

NOTE: Drive pinion/output shaft, ring gear backlash or differential bearing preload need to be readjusted only if repair to final drive involves replacement of parts directly affecting setting. See DRIVE PINION/OUTPUT SHAFT & RING GEAR ADJUSTMENT table. See ADJUSTMENTS.

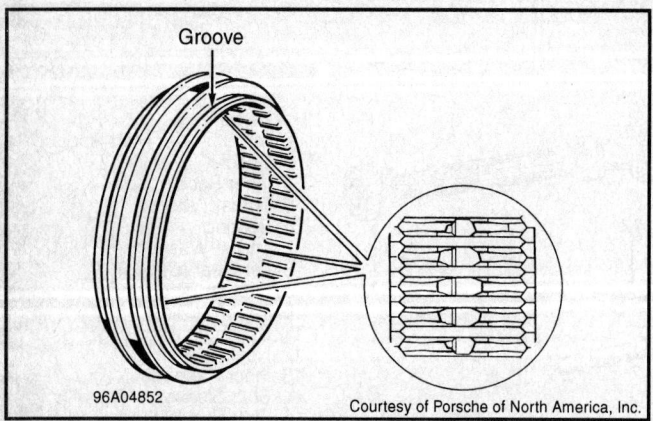

Fig. 12: Identifying Shift Sleeve Groove

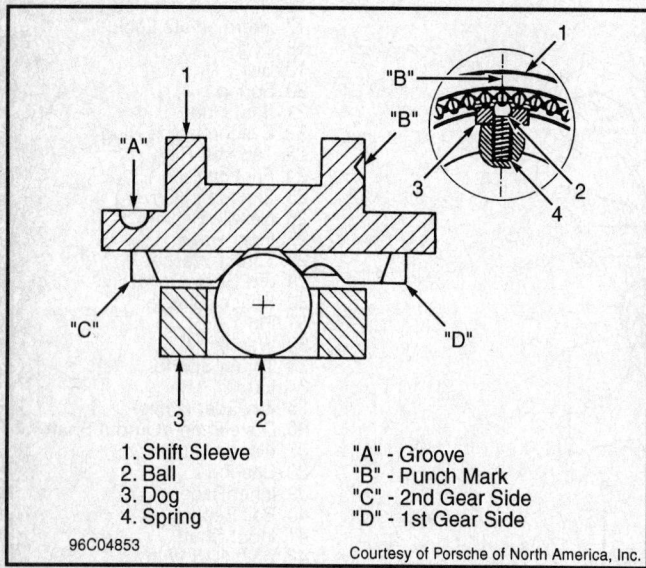

1. Shift Sleeve
2. Ball
3. Dog
4. Spring

"A" - Groove
"B" - Punch Mark
"C" - 2nd Gear Side
"D" - 1st Gear Side

96C04853   Courtesy of Porsche of North America, Inc.

Fig. 13: Cut-Away View Of Shift Hub/Sleeve Assembly

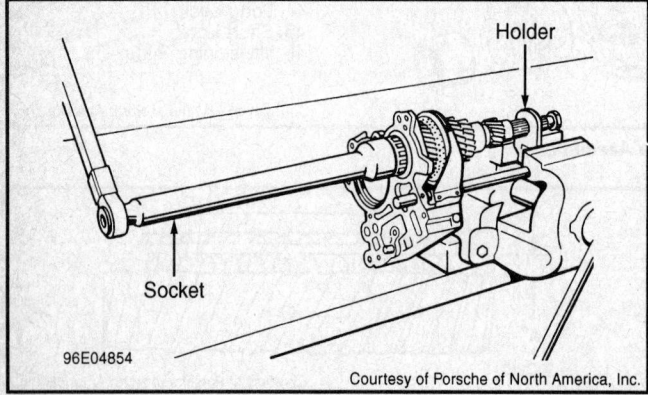

Fig. 14: Removing Input Shaft Nut

DRIVE PINION/OUTPUT SHAFT & RING GEAR ADJUSTMENT

Part Replaced	Adjust Ring Gear "S1" + "S2"	Adjust Drive Pinion "S3"
Differential Case	Yes	No
Differential Tapered Roller Bearing	Yes	No
Drive Pinion/Ring Gear	Yes	Yes
Large Cylindrical Roller Bearing & Ball Bearing For Drive Pinion	Yes	Yes
Transaxle Case	Yes	Yes
Transaxle Side Cover	Yes	No

1) Heat transaxle case to 248°F (120°C) and install bearing outer races (if applicable). Install assembled differential. *See Fig. 6.* Tighten nuts to specifications. See TORQUE SPECIFICATIONS.

2) Place correct number of "S3" shims. Install components in reverse numbered order. *See Fig. 5.* Tighten tensioning plate nuts to 17 Ft. Lbs. (23 N.m). Assemble drive pinion/output shaft components. Install selector fork/selector rod, with dowels in place, together with complete guide sleeve.

3) Install gearbox. Install complete guide sleeve with selector fork. Install 5th, 6th and reverse gear components in reverse numbered order. *See Fig. 2.* Hold input shaft and tighten collar nut on drive pinion/output shaft and input shaft to specification. *See Fig. 3.* See TORQUE SPECIFICATIONS.

4) Adjust reverse shift fork so that in neutral, sleeve is located exactly in middle, between synchronizing rings. *See Fig. 29.* Install front transaxle cover and tighten nuts to 17 Ft. Lbs. (23 N.m). Install remaining components. *See Fig. 2.*

TORQUE SPECIFICATIONS
TORQUE SPECIFICATIONS

Application	Ft. Lbs. (N.m)
Back-Up Light Switch	26 (35)
Breather	26 (35)
Drive Pinion Collar Nut	221 (300)
Front Cover Idler Shaft Bolt	26 (35)
Input Shaft Collar Nut	184 (250)
Oil Drain Plug W/Magnet	22 (30)
Oil Filler Plug	22 (30)
Reverse/Transfer Lever Stud	17 (23)
Ring Gear Bolt	148 (200)
Selector Fork	17 (23)
Tensioning Plate Nut	17 (23)
Transaxle Case Hex Bolt	17 (23)

	INCH Lbs. (N.m)
Gearshaft (Tensioning Plate) Screw	89 (10)
Oval Head Countersunk Screw	89 (10)

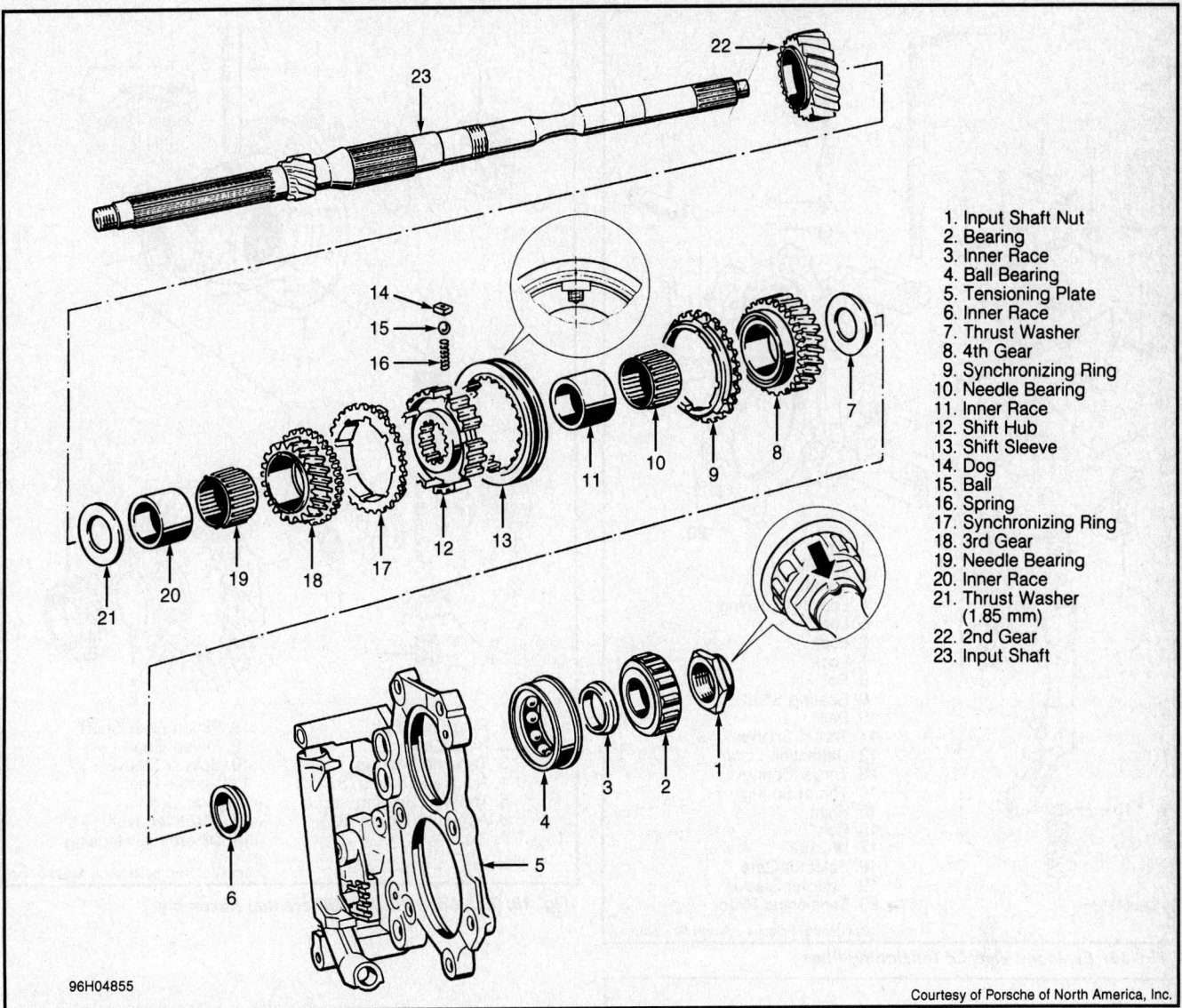

1. Input Shaft Nut
2. Bearing
3. Inner Race
4. Ball Bearing
5. Tensioning Plate
6. Inner Race
7. Thrust Washer
8. 4th Gear
9. Synchronizing Ring
10. Needle Bearing
11. Inner Race
12. Shift Hub
13. Shift Sleeve
14. Dog
15. Ball
16. Spring
17. Synchronizing Ring
18. 3rd Gear
19. Needle Bearing
20. Inner Race
21. Thrust Washer
    (1.85 mm)
22. 2nd Gear
23. Input Shaft

96H04855

Courtesy of Porsche of North America, Inc.

Fig. 15: Exploded View Of Input Shaft

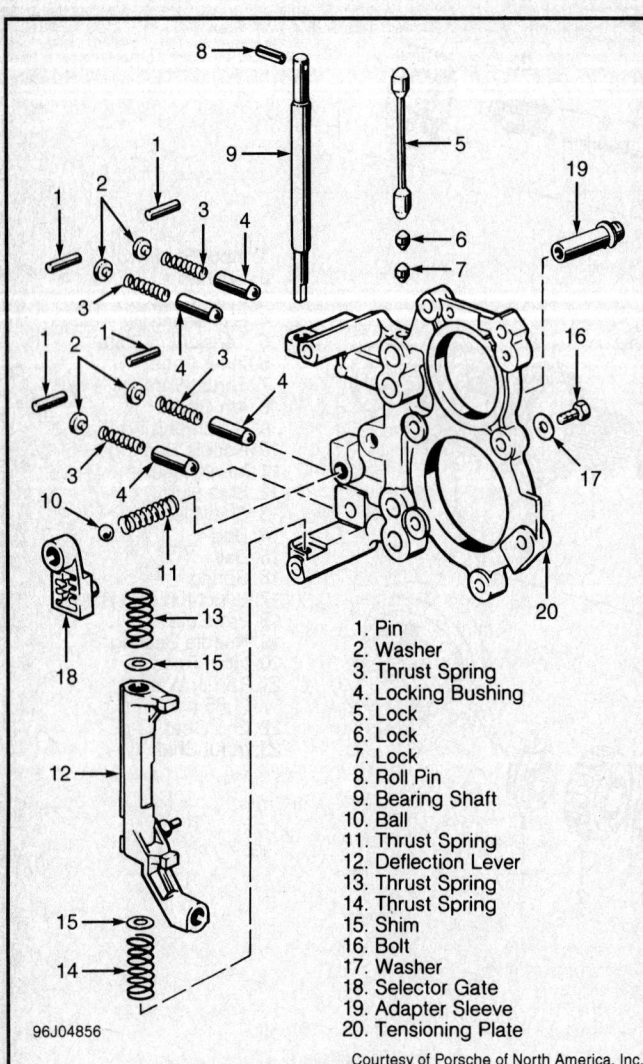

1. Pin
2. Washer
3. Thrust Spring
4. Locking Bushing
5. Lock
6. Lock
7. Lock
8. Roll Pin
9. Bearing Shaft
10. Ball
11. Thrust Spring
12. Deflection Lever
13. Thrust Spring
14. Thrust Spring
15. Shim
16. Bolt
17. Washer
18. Selector Gate
19. Adapter Sleeve
20. Tensioning Plate

96J04856

Courtesy of Porsche of North America, Inc.

Fig. 16: Exploded View Of Tensioning Plate

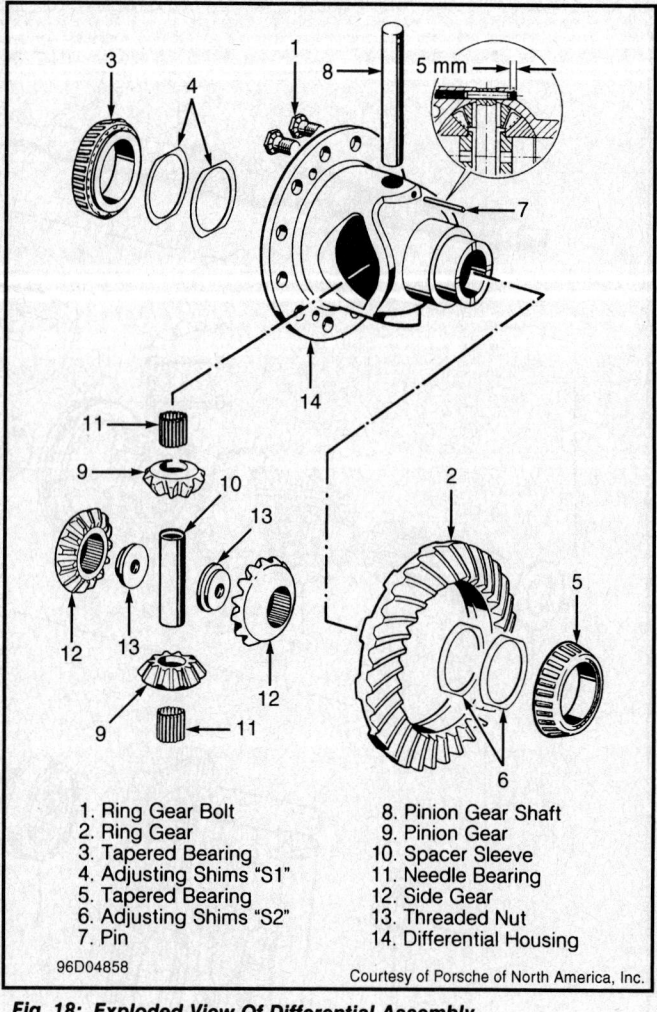

1. Ring Gear Bolt
2. Ring Gear
3. Tapered Bearing
4. Adjusting Shims "S1"
5. Tapered Bearing
6. Adjusting Shims "S2"
7. Pin
8. Pinion Gear Shaft
9. Pinion Gear
10. Spacer Sleeve
11. Needle Bearing
12. Side Gear
13. Threaded Nut
14. Differential Housing

96D04858

Courtesy of Porsche of North America, Inc.

Fig. 18: Exploded View Of Differential Assembly

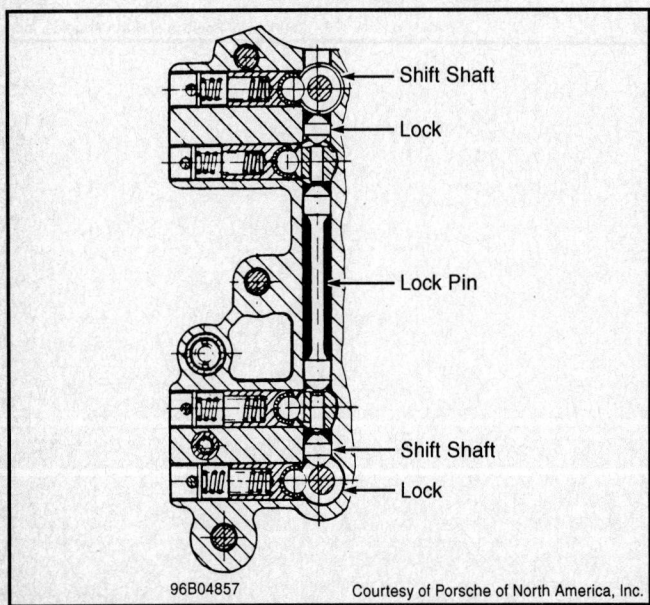

Shift Shaft

Lock

Lock Pin

Shift Shaft

Lock

96B04857

Courtesy of Porsche of North America, Inc.

Fig. 17: Cut-Away View Of Tensioning Plate Assembly

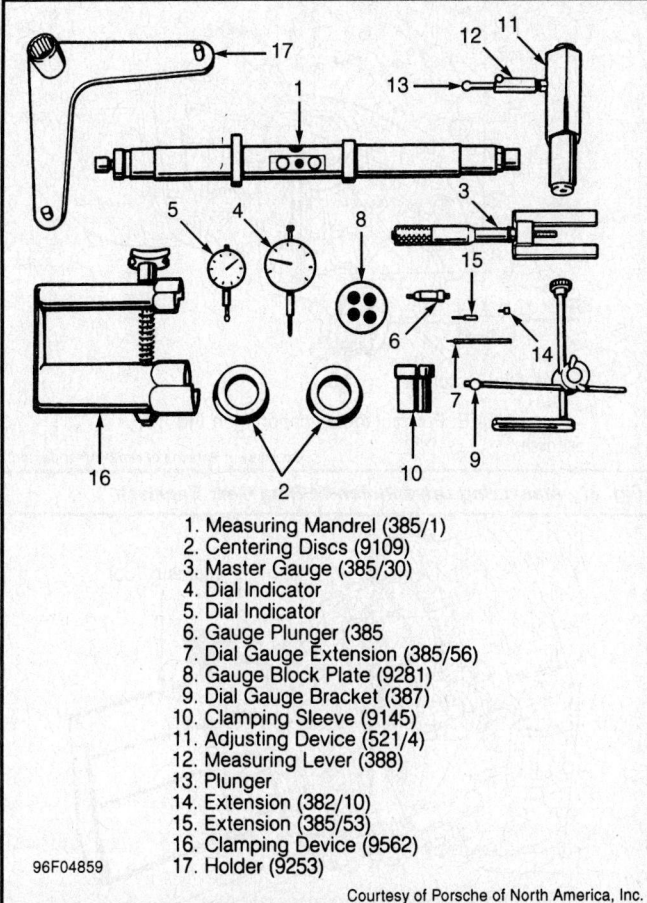

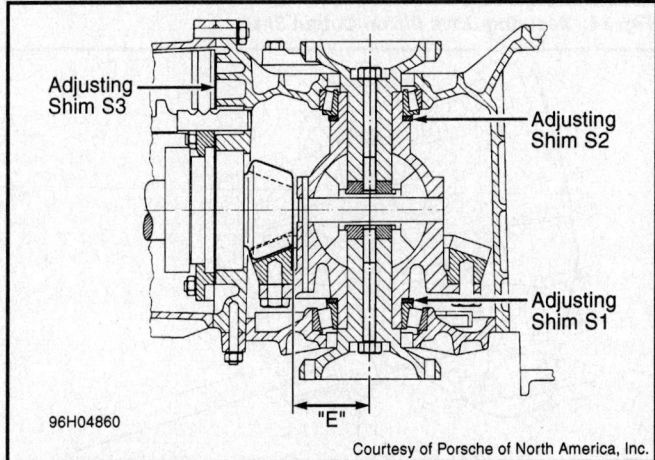

1. Measuring Mandrel (385/1)
2. Centering Discs (9109)
3. Master Gauge (385/30)
4. Dial Indicator
5. Dial Indicator
6. Gauge Plunger (385
7. Dial Gauge Extension (385/56)
8. Gauge Block Plate (9281)
9. Dial Gauge Bracket (387)
10. Clamping Sleeve (9145)
11. Adjusting Device (521/4)
12. Measuring Lever (388)
13. Plunger
14. Extension (382/10)
15. Extension (385/53)
16. Clamping Device (9562)
17. Holder (9253)

96F04859

Courtesy of Porsche of North America, Inc.

Fig. 19: Identifying Final Drive Assembly Measuring Tool Set

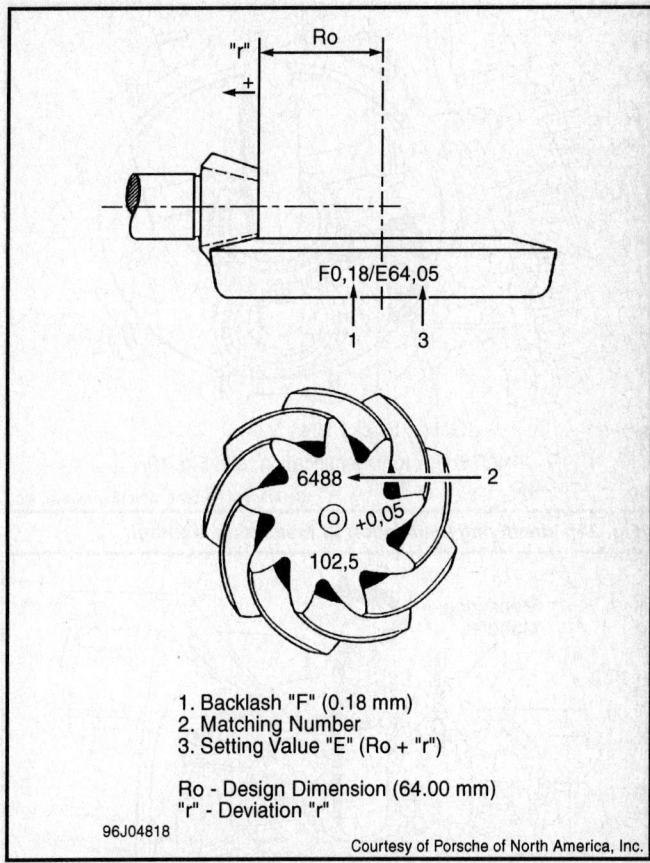

1. Backlash "F" (0.18 mm)
2. Matching Number
3. Setting Value "E" (Ro + "r")

Ro - Design Dimension (64.00 mm)
"r" - Deviation "r"

96J04818

Courtesy of Porsche of North America, Inc.

Fig. 21: Identifying Ring Gear & Drive Pinion Stamping

Adjusting Shim S3
Adjusting Shim S2
Adjusting Shim S1

96H04860

Courtesy of Porsche of North America, Inc.

Fig. 20: Cut-Away View Of Final Drive Assembly

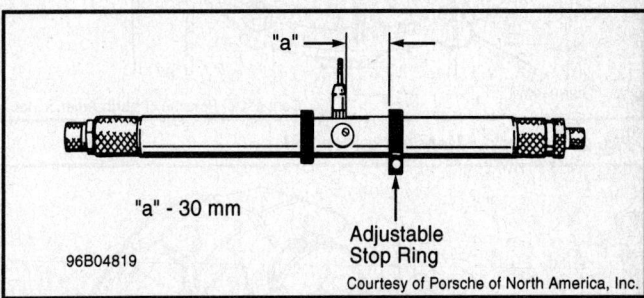

"a" - 30 mm

Adjustable Stop Ring

96B04819

Courtesy of Porsche of North America, Inc.

Fig. 22: Setting Dimension "a" On Measuring Mandrel (385/1)

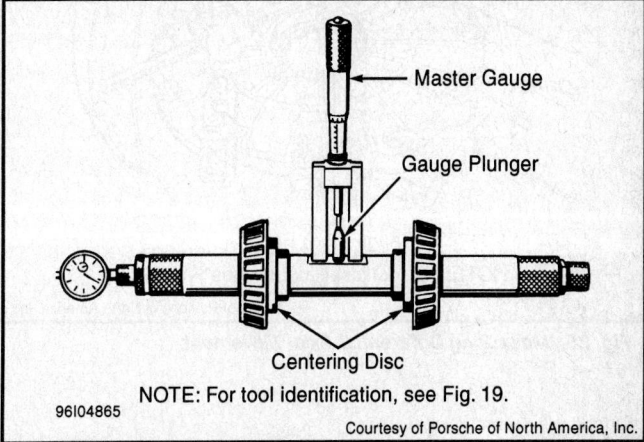

Master Gauge

Gauge Plunger

Centering Disc

NOTE: For tool identification, see Fig. 19.

96I04865

Courtesy of Porsche of North America, Inc.

Fig. 23: Setting Measuring Mandrel (385/1) For Dimension "E" Measurement

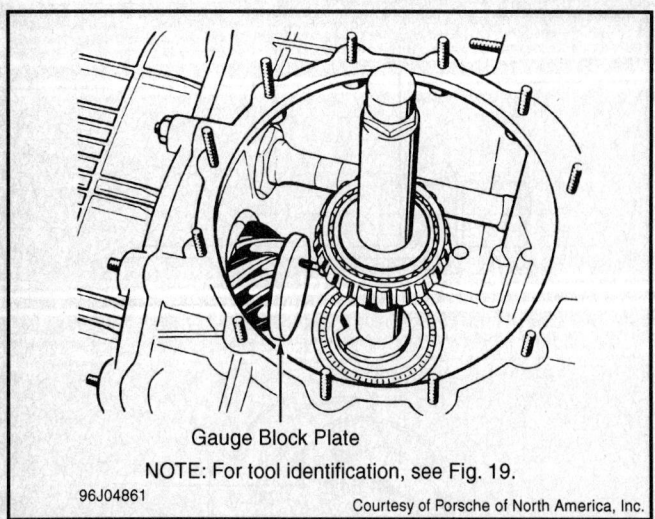

Gauge Block Plate

NOTE: For tool identification, see Fig. 19.

96J04861

Courtesy of Porsche of North America, Inc.

Fig. 24: Identifying Installation Of Measuring Mandrel

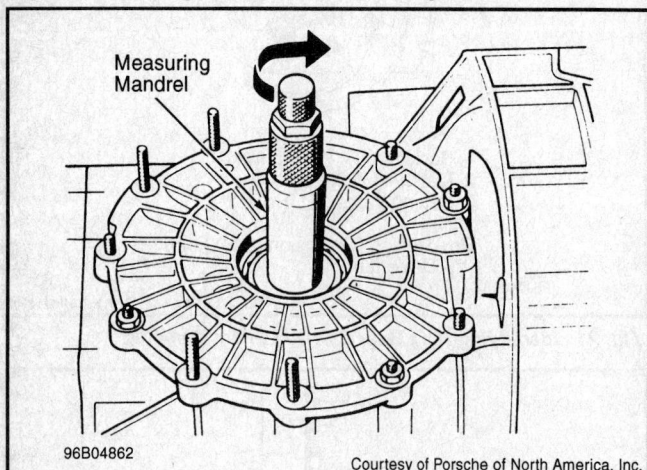

Measuring Mandrel

96B04862

Courtesy of Porsche of North America, Inc.

Fig. 25: Rotating Measuring Mandrel

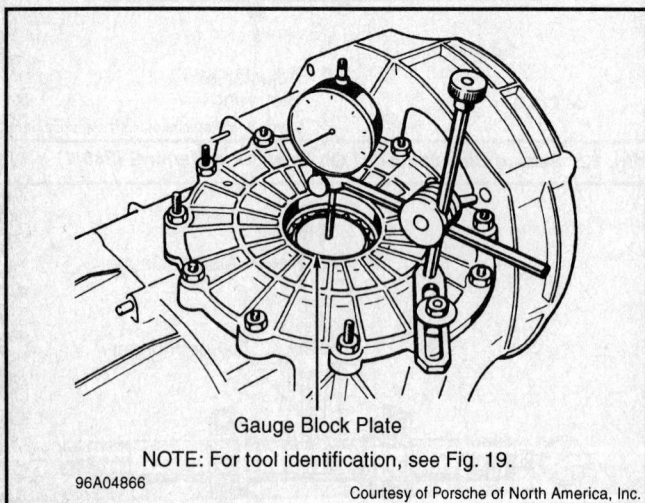

Gauge Block Plate

NOTE: For tool identification, see Fig. 19.

96A04866

Courtesy of Porsche of North America, Inc.

Fig. 26: Measuring Differential Axial Movement

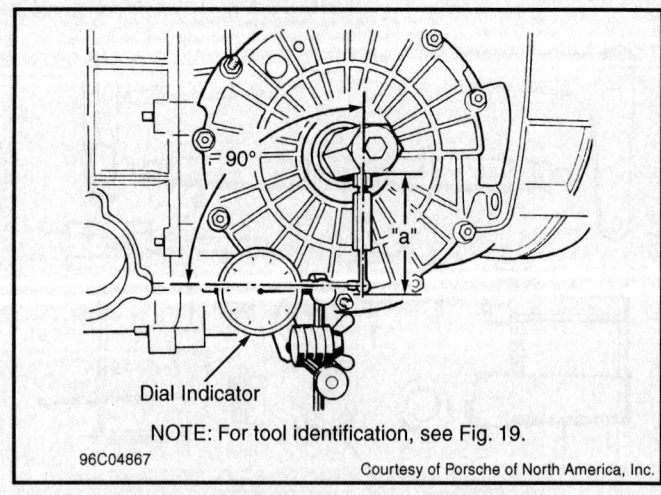

= 90°

"a"

Dial Indicator

NOTE: For tool identification, see Fig. 19.

96C04867

Courtesy of Porsche of North America, Inc.

Fig. 27: Measuring Drive Pinion-To-Ring Gear Backlash

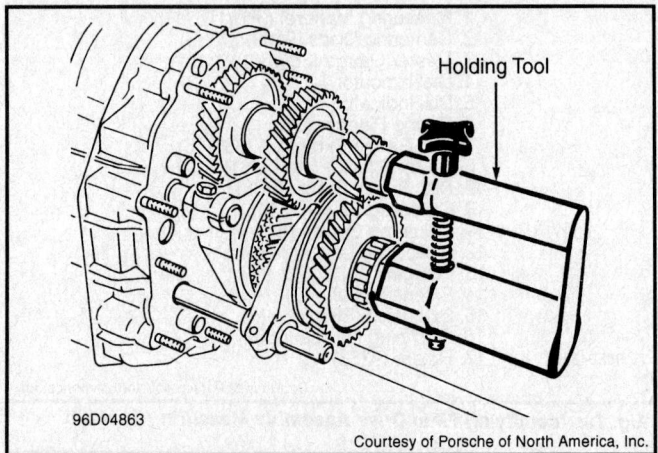

Holding Tool

96D04863

Courtesy of Porsche of North America, Inc.

Fig. 28: Securing Drive Pinion/Output Shaft

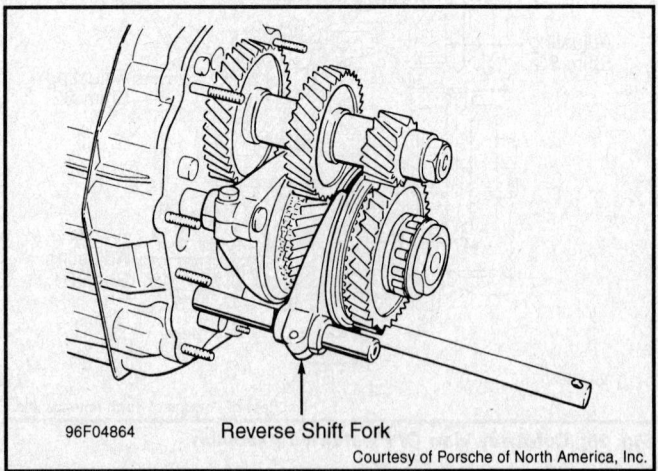

96F04864

Reverse Shift Fork

Courtesy of Porsche of North America, Inc.

Fig. 29: Identifying Reverse Shift Fork Position

MANUAL TRANSMISSIONS
Rover R380 5-Speed

Defender 90, Discovery

APPLICATION & LABOR TIMES

APPLICATION & LABOR TIMES

Vehicle Application	Labor Times [1] R & I	[2] Overhaul	Transmission Series
1995			
Defender 90	8.4	7.2	R380/60A
Discovery	8.4	7.2	R380/53A
1996			
Discovery	7.9	7.2	R380/53A

[1] – Removal and installation of transmission from vehicle chassis.
[2] – Bench overhaul time for transmission. DOES NOT include removal and installation.

IDENTIFICATION

Transmission series (serial number prefix) is stamped on right side of transmission case. Defender 90 prefix is 60A. Discovery prefix is 53A.

LUBRICATION & ADJUSTMENTS

See appropriate MANUAL TRANSMISSION SERVICING article in TRANSMISSION SERVICING section.

TROUBLE SHOOTING

See GENERAL TROUBLE SHOOTING article in this section.

REMOVAL & INSTALLATION

See appropriate MANUAL TRANSMISSION REMOVAL article in TRANSMISSION SERVICING section.

TRANSMISSION DISASSEMBLY

1) Remove clutch release bearing. Remove clutch release lever. Remove clutch housing from transmission. Remove retaining bolts and gear change housings. See Fig. 1 or 2.

2) On 60A transmission, remove remote housing. Remove and discard shift quadrant set screw. See Fig. 3. Move shift rod forwards and remove shift quadrant. On 53A transmission, remove and discard shift yoke set screw. See Fig. 4. Move shift rod forwards and remove shift yoke.

3) On all transmissions, using Oil Seal Collar Remover (LRT-37-009), remove oil seal collar from mainshaft. See Fig. 5. Remove 5th gear spool retainer. Place drain pan underneath extension housing. Remove extension housing bolts noting location of longer bolts for installation reference.

4) Using a soft faced mallet, remove extension housing from transmission case. Remove oil filter. See Fig. 5. Using two 8 x 35 mm bolts, secure center plate to transmission case.

5) Using bearing puller, remove countershaft rear support bearing track. See Fig. 6. Remove 5th gear retaining nut. Remove 5th gear segment retaining ring and 5th gear segments from mainshaft. Remove mainshaft thrust collar roll pin.

6) Remove 5th gear from countershaft. Using puller, remove mainshaft rear support bearing track. Remove 5th gear and 5th gear synchro ring from mainshaft. Remove needle roller bearing from mainshaft. Remove circlip securing 5th gear synchro hub to mainshaft.

7) Rotate interlock spool clear of shift fork, and remove 5th/reverse gear synchro hub assembly with shift fork and spool. Remove reverse gear, needle roller bearing, bushing and washer from mainshaft. Remove reverse gear from countershaft. Remove selector plug, outer detent ball and spring. See Fig. 5.

8) Remove 2 center plate-to-transmission case bolts installed in step 4). Align shift rod pin with slot in center plate. Using a soft faced mallet, remove center plate from transmission case. Remove inner detent ball and spring from center plate. Remove bearings and shims. Remove countershaft, mainshaft and shift rod as an assembly. Remove input shaft and 4th gear synchro ring.

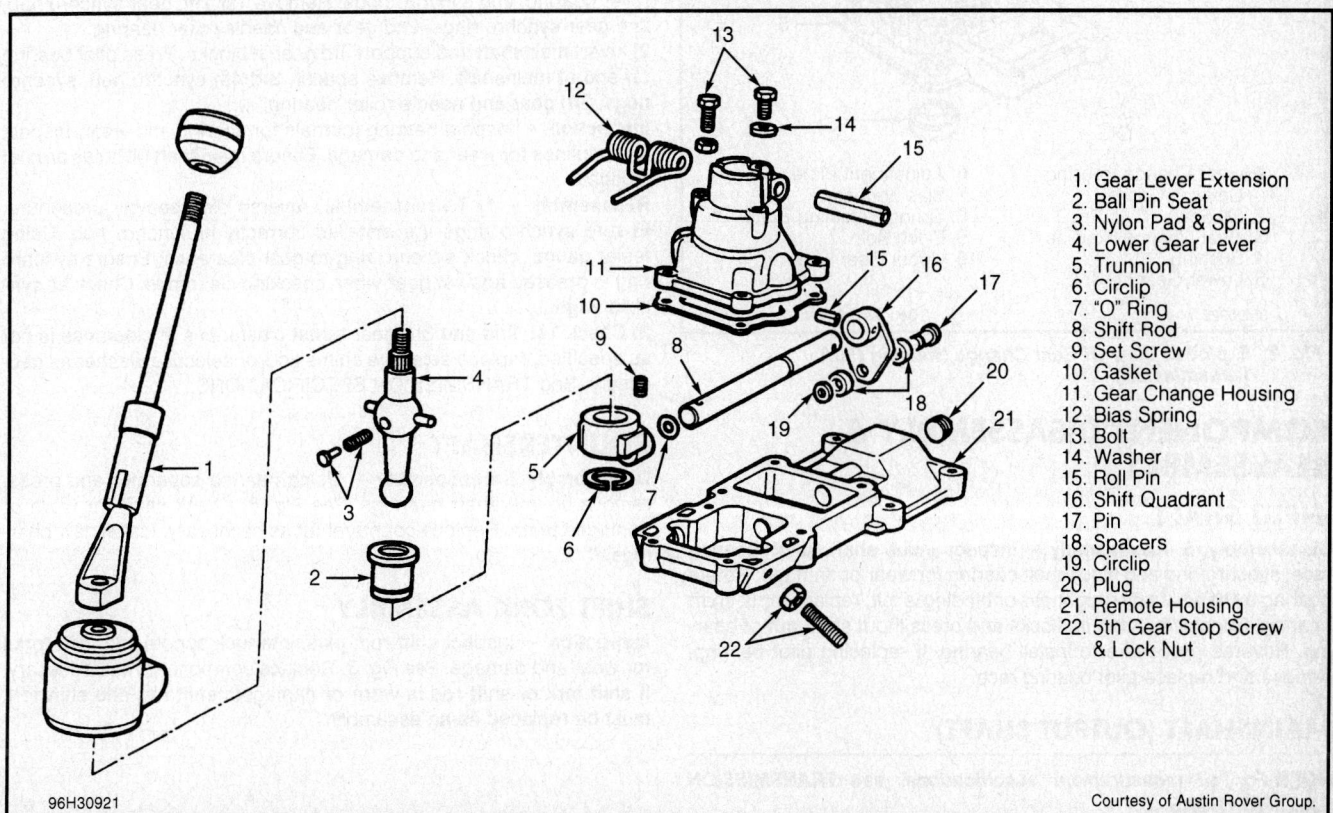

1. Gear Lever Extension
2. Ball Pin Seat
3. Nylon Pad & Spring
4. Lower Gear Lever
5. Trunnion
6. Circlip
7. "O" Ring
8. Shift Rod
9. Set Screw
10. Gasket
11. Gear Change Housing
12. Bias Spring
13. Bolt
14. Washer
15. Roll Pin
16. Shift Quadrant
17. Pin
18. Spacers
19. Circlip
20. Plug
21. Remote Housing
22. 5th Gear Stop Screw & Lock Nut

96H30921

Courtesy of Austin Rover Group.

Fig. 1: Exploded View Of Gear Change Housing (60A Transmission)

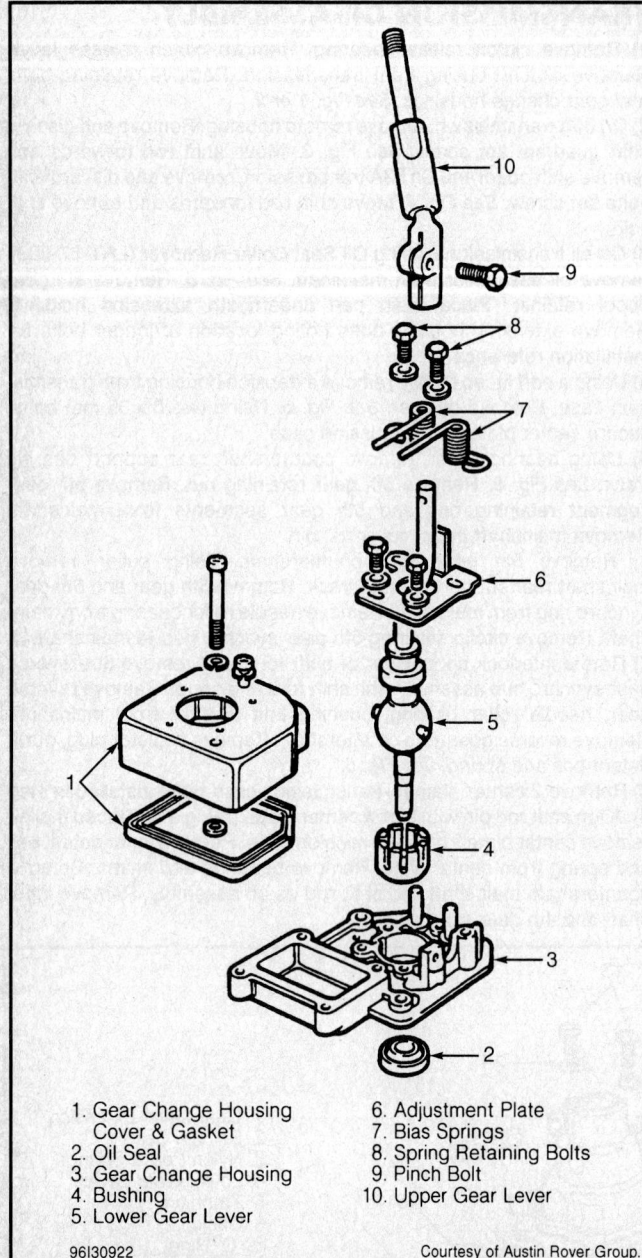

1. Gear Change Housing
   Cover & Gasket
2. Oil Seal
3. Gear Change Housing
4. Bushing
5. Lower Gear Lever
6. Adjustment Plate
7. Bias Springs
8. Spring Retaining Bolts
9. Pinch Bolt
10. Upper Gear Lever

96I30922   Courtesy of Austin Rover Group.

Fig. 2: Exploded View Of Gear Change Housing (53A Transmission)

COMPONENT DISASSEMBLY & REASSEMBLY

INPUT SHAFT

Disassembly & Reassembly – Inspect input shaft, pilot bearing race, synchro ring and input shaft bearing for wear or damage. Rotate bearing by hand. If any roughness or binding is felt, replace input shaft bearing. Support bearing in blocks and press input shaft out of bearing. Reverse procedure to install bearing. If replacing pilot bearing, remove and replace pilot bearing race.

MAINSHAFT (OUTPUT SHAFT)

NOTE: For all measurement specifications, see TRANSMISSION SPECIFICATIONS.

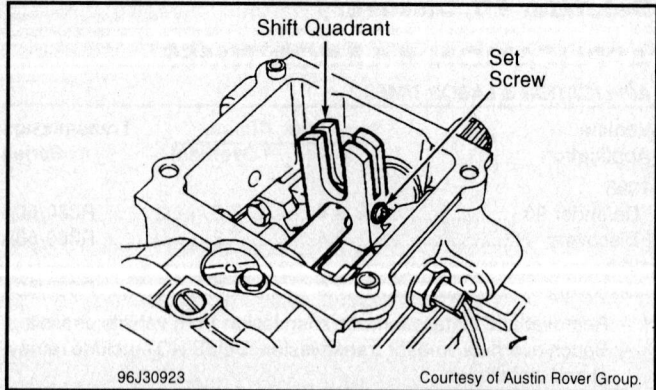

Fig. 3: Removing Shift Quadrant (60A Transmission)

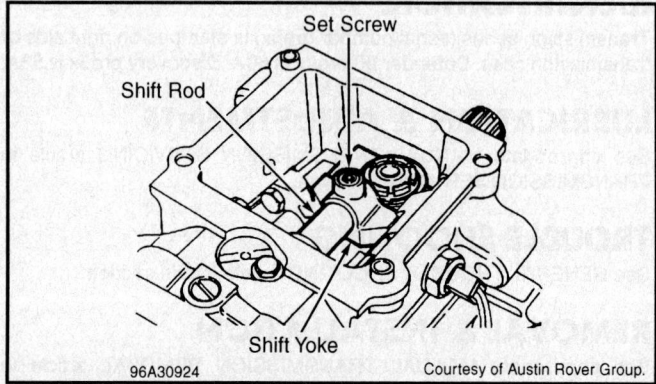

Fig. 4 Removing Shift Yoke (53A Transmission)

Disassembly – 1) Support 1st gear in blocks. Press mainshaft rear support bearing from mainshaft. See Fig. 6. Remove 1st gear, needle roller bearing, and synchro rings. Remove 1st/2nd gear synchro hub, 2nd gear synchro rings, 2nd gear and needle roller bearing.

2) Invert mainshaft and support 3rd gear in blocks. Press pilot bearing off end of mainshaft. Remove spacer, 3rd/4th synchro hub, synchro rings, 3rd gear and needle roller bearing.

Inspection – Inspect bearing journals for scoring and wear. Inspect shaft splines for wear and damage. Ensure mainshaft oil holes are not plugged.

Reassembly – 1) To reassemble, reverse disassembly procedure. Ensure synchro rings are installed correctly in synchro hub. Using feeler gauge, check synchro ring-to-gear clearance. Ensure synchro ring is pressed against gear when checking clearance. Check all synchro rings.

2) Check 1st, 2nd and 3rd gear thrust clearances. If clearance is not as specified, replace selective shims and/or selective washer as necessary. See TRANSMISSION SPECIFICATIONS.

COUNTERSHAFT

Disassembly & Reassembly – Using bearing separator and press, remove countershaft bearings. See Fig. 6. Check shaft for worn or damaged teeth. Replace countershaft as necessary. Install new bearings.

SHIFT FORK ASSEMBLY

Inspection – Inspect shift rod, pins, interlock spools and shift forks for wear and damage. See Fig. 8. Replace components as necessary. If shift fork or shift rod is worn or damaged, shift rod and shift fork must be replaced as an assembly.

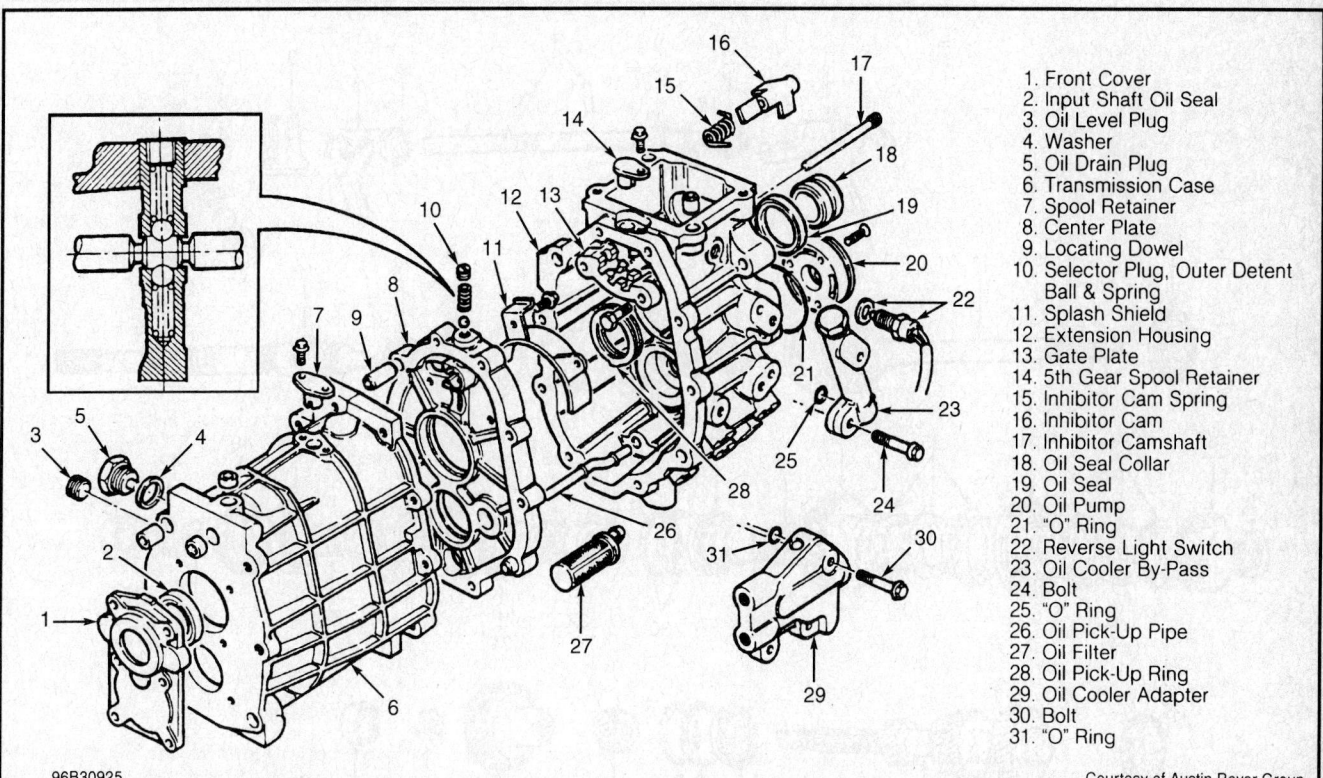

1. Front Cover
2. Input Shaft Oil Seal
3. Oil Level Plug
4. Washer
5. Oil Drain Plug
6. Transmission Case
7. Spool Retainer
8. Center Plate
9. Locating Dowel
10. Selector Plug, Outer Detent Ball & Spring
11. Splash Shield
12. Extension Housing
13. Gate Plate
14. 5th Gear Spool Retainer
15. Inhibitor Cam Spring
16. Inhibitor Cam
17. Inhibitor Camshaft
18. Oil Seal Collar
19. Oil Seal
20. Oil Pump
21. "O" Ring
22. Reverse Light Switch
23. Oil Cooler By-Pass
24. Bolt
25. "O" Ring
26. Oil Pick-Up Pipe
27. Oil Filter
28. Oil Pick-Up Ring
29. Oil Cooler Adapter
30. Bolt
31. "O" Ring

96B30925

Courtesy of Austin Rover Group.

Fig. 5: Exploded View Of Transmission

SYNCHRO HUB

Disassembly – Remove spring clips from both sides of synchro hub. Remove keys and separate hub from sleeve. *See Fig. 7.* Inspect all components for wear and damage. Replace hub assembly as necessary.

Reassembly – To reassemble, reverse disassembly procedure. Hub and sleeve has a master spline combination that can only be assembled one way. Sleeves are further identified with a series of half-moon notches that identify which side of hub assembly faces which gear. See SYNCHRO SLEEVE IDENTIFICATION table.

NOTE: 5th/reverse synchro hub spring clips differ from other synchro hub assemblies and are colored Yellow.

SYNCHRO SLEEVE IDENTIFICATION

Hub Assembly	Sleeve	Against Gear
1st/2nd	One Notch	1st
3rd/4th	3 Notches	3rd
5th/Reverse	5 Notches	5th

EXTENSION HOUSING

Disassembly – 1) Remove 3 screws and oil pump. *See Fig. 8.* Remove oil pick-up pipe. Using a punch, remove countershaft support bearing. Remove mainshaft rear oil seal. Using a punch, remove mainshaft support bearing and oil pick-up ring.

2) Remove reverse inhibit shaft, inhibit cam and spring. Remove reverse light switch and washer. Remove gate plate. Check all components and replace as necessary.

Reassembly – 1) Apply a light coat of Vaseline into oil pump recess. Install new "O" ring and press oil pump firmly into recess. Ensure TOP marking on oil pump is installed at top of housing. Lightly tap on oil pump edges to fully seat pump.

2) Install and tighten oil pump to specification. See TORQUE SPECIFICATIONS. Install new mainshaft support bearing and oil seal. Install new countershaft bearing. Install new oil pick-up ring, ensuring tag on ring is aligned with center of drain slot. To complete reassembly, reverse disassembly procedure.

CENTER PLATE

Disassembly – Remove bearing races and shims. Remove splash shield. *See Fig. 5.* Using a press, remove reverse idler shaft. Remove idler gear, needle roller bearing and spacer.

Inspection – Check idler gear and spacer for wear and damage. Check shift rod bore for wear. Check center plate gasket mating surfaces for nicks, burrs and damage. Repair or replace components as necessary.

Reassembly – Assemble needle roller bearing, idler gear and spacer onto reverse idler shaft. Press shaft into center plate. Check idler gear end play. End play should be .0016-.015" (.04-.38 mm). To complete reassembly, reverse disassembly procedure.

REMOTE HOUSING

Disassembly (60A Transmission) – Remove set screw and trunnion. *See Fig. 1.* Remove circlip and ball pin seat. Loosen lock nut and remove 5th gear stop screw. Remove plug from end of remote housing. Remove set screw and shift quadrant. Remove shift rod and "O" ring from housing. Remove and discard circlip from shift quadrant pin. Remove pin and spacers.

Inspection – Check shift rod bore for wear. Check remote housing gasket mating surfaces for nicks, burrs and damage. Check shift quadrant spacers and pin for wear. Check ball pin seat for wear. Replace components as necessary.

Reassembly – 1) Apply a light coat of oil to shift rod and new "O" ring. Install "O" ring on shift rod. Install shift rod into remote housing. Position spacers and pin to shift quadrant. Secure pin with new circlip. Install shift quadrant to shift rod.

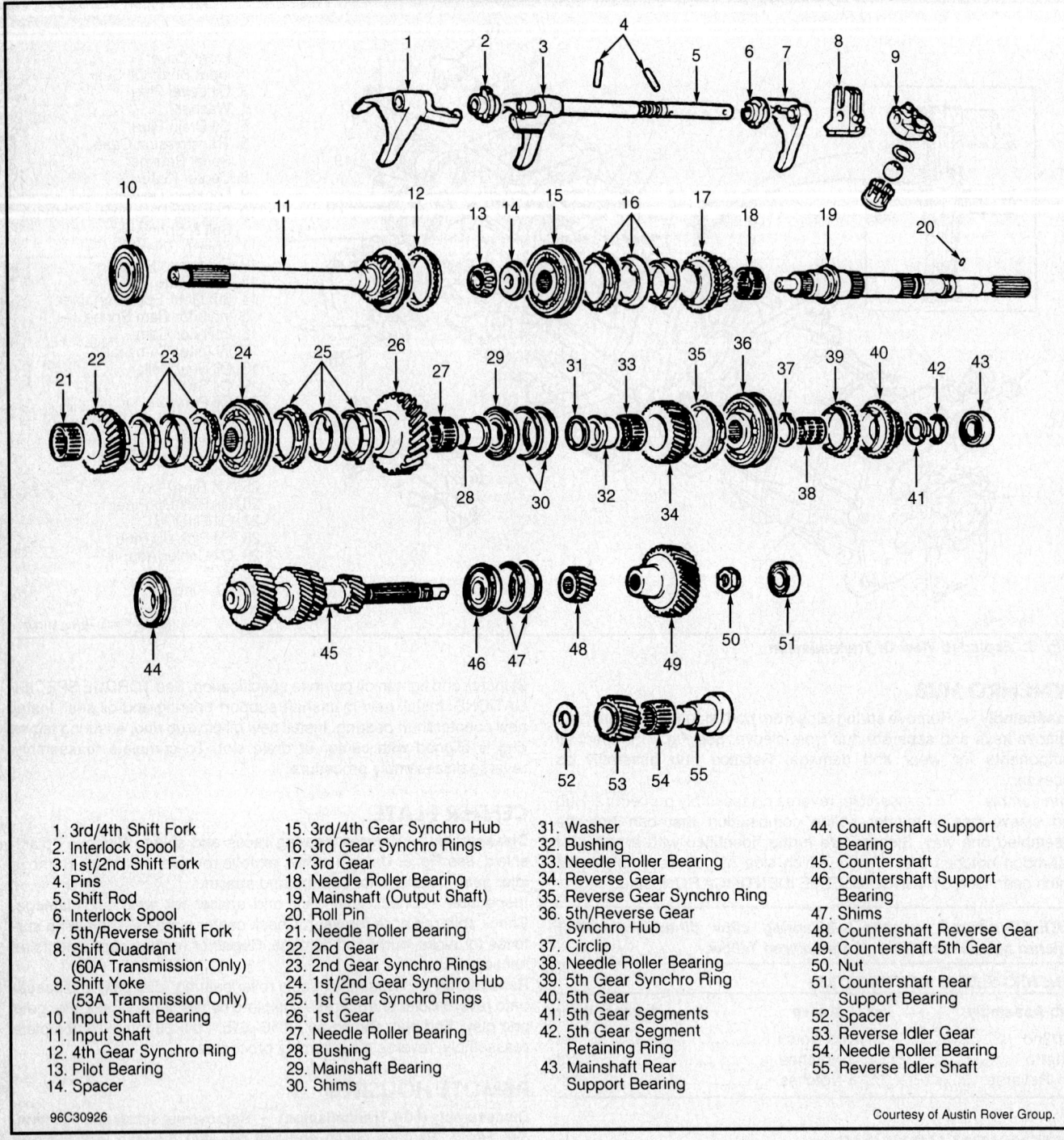

Fig. 6: Exploded View Of Mainshaft & Countershaft Assemblies

1. 3rd/4th Shift Fork
2. Interlock Spool
3. 1st/2nd Shift Fork
4. Pins
5. Shift Rod
6. Interlock Spool
7. 5th/Reverse Shift Fork
8. Shift Quadrant (60A Transmission Only)
9. Shift Yoke (53A Transmission Only)
10. Input Shaft Bearing
11. Input Shaft
12. 4th Gear Synchro Ring
13. Pilot Bearing
14. Spacer
15. 3rd/4th Gear Synchro Hub
16. 3rd Gear Synchro Rings
17. 3rd Gear
18. Needle Roller Bearing
19. Mainshaft (Output Shaft)
20. Roll Pin
21. Needle Roller Bearing
22. 2nd Gear
23. 2nd Gear Synchro Rings
24. 1st/2nd Gear Synchro Hub
25. 1st Gear Synchro Rings
26. 1st Gear
27. Needle Roller Bearing
28. Bushing
29. Mainshaft Bearing
30. Shims
31. Washer
32. Bushing
33. Needle Roller Bearing
34. Reverse Gear
35. Reverse Gear Synchro Ring
36. 5th/Reverse Gear Synchro Hub
37. Circlip
38. Needle Roller Bearing
39. 5th Gear Synchro Ring
40. 5th Gear
41. 5th Gear Segments
42. 5th Gear Segment Retaining Ring
43. Mainshaft Rear Support Bearing
44. Countershaft Support Bearing
45. Countershaft
46. Countershaft Support Bearing
47. Shims
48. Countershaft Reverse Gear
49. Countershaft 5th Gear
50. Nut
51. Countershaft Rear Support Bearing
52. Spacer
53. Reverse Idler Gear
54. Needle Roller Bearing
55. Reverse Idler Shaft

96C30926

Courtesy of Austin Rover Group.

2) Apply Loctite to threads and install shift quadrant set screw. Apply Loctite to threads and install remote housing plug. Apply a light coat of grease to ball pin seat. Position ball pin seat in trunnion. Install new circlip. Position trunnion on shift rod.

3) Apply Loctite to threads and install trunnion set screw. Install, but DO NOT tighten 5th gear stop screw at this time. Fifth gear stop screw adjustment is performed during transmission reassembly. See TRANSMISSION REASSEMBLY.

GEAR CHANGE HOUSING

Disassembly (60A Transmission) – 1) Release both ends of bias spring from ball pins. See Fig. 1. Loosen lock nuts and remove spring adjusting bolts. Using a punch, remove bias spring roll pin.

2) Remove gear lever extension from lower gear lever. Remove bolt and washer securing lower gear lever. Ensuring nylon pad and spring does not shoot out, carefully lift and remove lower gear lever from housing. Remove nylon pad and spring from lower gear lever.

Inspection – Clean all components. Check bias spring for distortion. Check lower gear lever ball pin for wear. If lower gear lever is replaced, ball pin seat in remote housing must also be replaced. Check remaining parts for wear and damage. Replace as necessary.

Reassembly – Apply a light coat of grease to lower gear lever ball pin. Position spring and nylon pad into lower gear lever. Depress nylon pad and lower gear lever into housing. To complete reassembly, reverse disassembly procedure. DO NOT adjust bias spring at this time. Bias spring is adjusted during transmission reassembly. See TRANSMISSION REASSEMBLY.

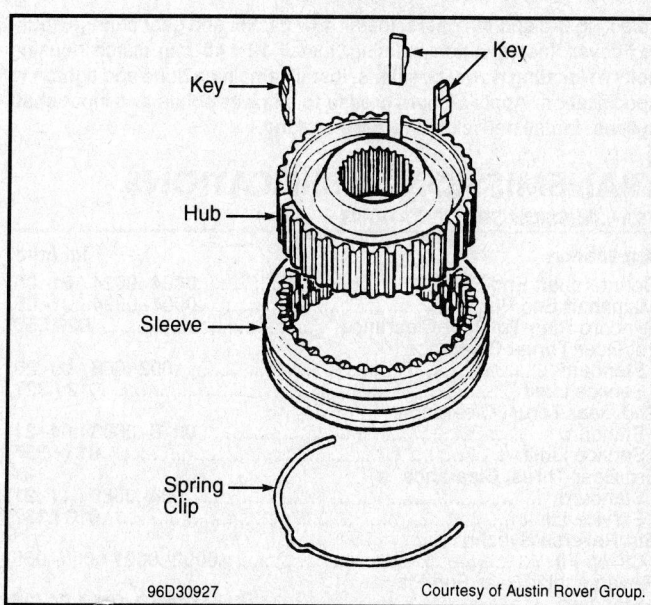

Fig. 7: Exploded View Of Synchro Hub Assembly

96D30927   Courtesy of Austin Rover Group.

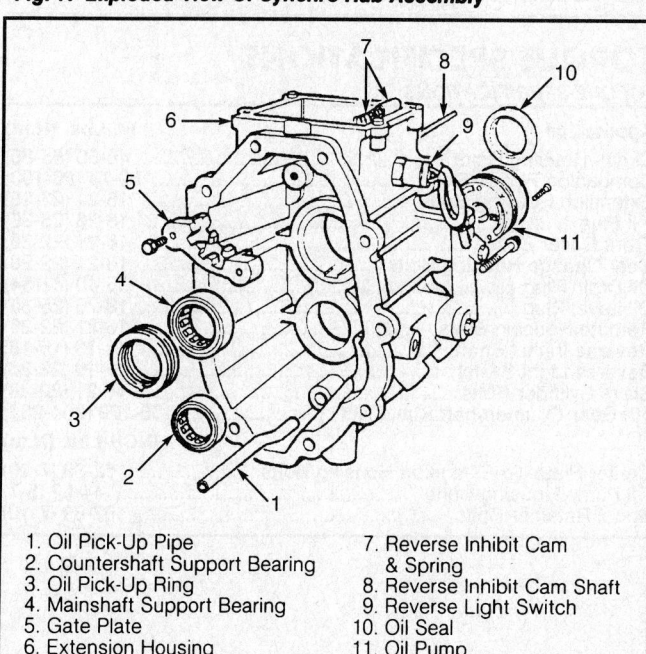

1. Oil Pick-Up Pipe
2. Countershaft Support Bearing
3. Oil Pick-Up Ring
4. Mainshaft Support Bearing
5. Gate Plate
6. Extension Housing
7. Reverse Inhibit Cam & Spring
8. Reverse Inhibit Cam Shaft
9. Reverse Light Switch
10. Oil Seal
11. Oil Pump

96E30928   Courtesy of Austin Rover Group.

Fig. 8: Exploded View Of Extension Housing

Disassembly (53A Transmission) – Secure bias springs with vise grips and remove both bias spring retaining bolts. See Fig. 2. Remove bias springs. Remove adjustment plate bolts. Remove lower gear lever and bushing. Remove and discard oil seal.

Inspection – Clean all components. Check bias springs for distortion. Check lower gear lever ball pin for wear. Check remaining parts for wear and damage. Replace as necessary.

Reassembly – Apply a light coat of oil to new oil seal and install seal. Install new lower gear lever bushing. Apply a light coat of grease to lower gear lever ball pin. Install lower gear lever into housing. To complete reassembly, reverse disassembly procedure.

ADJUSTMENTS

CAUTION: End play for mainshaft and countershaft must be determined before gear box is reassembled.

MAINSHAFT & COUNTERSHAFT END PLAY

1) Install new bearing race in transmission front cover. Install front cover to transmission case, without front oil seal. Clamp transmission case in vise with front cover facing downward. Install input shaft. DO NOT install 4th gear synchro ring.

2) Install mainshaft assembly. Install mainshaft bearing shim and race to center plate. Position center plate on transmission case. Using 8 x 35 mm bolts, install and tighten center plate bolts. Install mainshaft rear bearing. Mount base of dial indicator on rear of transmission case. Adjust dial indicator so tip of indicator gauge touches end of mainshaft.

3) Rotate mainshaft to seat bearings. Zero dial indicator. Lift mainshaft and note reading. End play should be .0004-.0024" (.01-.06 mm). If end play is not as specified, disassemble and replace shims as necessary. Repeat steps 2) and 3).

4) With end play set to specification, remove mainshaft assembly and repeat procedure for countershaft. Countershaft end play should be .0004-.0024" (.01-.06 mm). With both mainshaft and countershaft end play set, disassemble components in preparation for transmission reassembly.

TRANSMISSION REASSEMBLY

NOTE: Mainshaft and countershaft end play must be determined before gear box is reassembled. See ADJUSTMENTS. Coat all parts with gear oil before assembly.

1) Secure center plate to workstand. Install selected shims and bearing races. Install spring and inner detent ball in center plate, using a dummy shift rod to temporarily hold ball in place. See Fig. 5. Ensure synchro hubs are in Neutral position and fit shift rod assembly to mainshaft assembly. Install mainshaft and shift rod as an assembly to center plate, aligning roll pin with slot in center plate.

2) Install outer detent ball, spring and selector plug. Install 4th gear synchro ring. While slightly lifting mainshaft to clear countershaft rear bearing, install countershaft. Lubricate pilot bearing and install input shaft. Install new front cover oil seal. Ensure seal is fully seated. Using Sealant (Hylogrip 2000 or equivalent), apply a continuous bead of sealant to front cover mating surface.

3) Install transmission case bearing races and clips. Install front cover. Apply a continuous bead of sealant to rear of transmission case gasket mating surface. Position center plate on rear of transmission case. Using 8 x 35 mm bolts, temporarily secure center plate to transmission case. Using new "O" ring, install spool retainer.

4) Remove transmission from stand. With front of transmission case facing downward, secure case in a vise. Install mainshaft reverse gear washer, bushing and needle roller bearing. Install mainshaft reverse gear and synchro ring.

5) Install countershaft reverse gear. Assemble interlock spool, shift fork and 5th/reverse gear synchro hub. Install as an assembly to mainshaft splines and shift rod. Ensure synchro ring is seated properly in synchro hub. Install new circlip.

NOTE: Circlip fit is controlled by a selectable washer located behind mainshaft reverse gear. Adjust to .0002-.0021" (.005-.055 mm)

6) Install mainshaft 5th gear needle roller bearing. Install mainshaft 5th gear and synchro ring. Install countershaft 5th gear. Install new mainshaft thrust collar roll pin. Install mainshaft 5th gear segments and retaining ring. Install new countershaft 5th gear retaining nut and tighten to specification. See TORQUE SPECIFICATIONS. Stake nut closed.

7) Install mainshaft rear support bearing track. Install countershaft rear support bearing track (it may be necessary to apply small amount of heat). Remove center plate-to-transmission case retaining bolts installed in step 3). Install oil filter. Apply a continuous bead of sealant to extension housing mating surface. Install extension housing ensuring oil pick-up pipe and bearings are align properly. Tighten extension housing bolts to specification.

CAUTION: DO NOT use force to install extension housing. If extension housing is difficult to install, remove housing and re-align oil pump drive.

8) Apply sealant and install 5th gear spool retainer into extension housing. Using Oil Seal Collar Installer (LRT-37-015 and LRT-37-21), install mainshaft oil seal collar. On 53A transmission, go to step 14). On 60A transmission, install selector quadrant on shift rod. *See Fig. 3.* Ensure hole in shift rod aligns with set screw hole on selector quadrant. Apply Loctite and install new set screw. Move shift rod to Neutral position.

9) Apply sealant to mating surfaces and position remote housing onto extension housing. Install new gaskets and install gear change housings. Tighten remote housing, transfer case gear change housing and transmission gear change housing bolts in that order.

10) To adjust 5th gear stop screw, shift transmission into Reverse position. Lightly press shift lever towards right side of transmission, and turn stop screw until it contacts yoke. Turn screw counterclockwise until 1" (25 mm) of free play can be felt at shift knob. Tighten lock nut. Ensure transmission can be shifted into all gears.

11) To adjust bias spring tension, shift transmission into 3rd gear. Turn both adjusting bolts until clearance between both spring legs and cross pin on lower gear lever is about .002" (.50 mm). Lightly press shift lever towards left side of transmission and tighten adjusting bolt until right leg of spring just makes contact with cross pin on lower gear lever.

12) Lightly press shift lever towards right side of transmission and tighten adjusting bolt until left leg of spring just makes contact with cross pin. Tighten both adjusting screws equal amounts until radial play is removed. Tighten lock nuts. Shift transmission into Neutral.

13) Rock shifter several times across shift gate. Gear lever should return to 3rd/4th gate. Install clutch housing. Install 12 x 45 mm clutch housing bolts at locating dowel positions. Install remaining bolts and tighten to specification. Apply Lithium grease to all pivot points and input shaft splines. Install new clutch release bearing.

14) On 53A transmission, position shift yoke on shift rod with ball facing towards mainshaft. *See Fig. 4.* Ensure hole in shift rod aligns with set screw hole on shift yoke. Apply Loctite and install new set screw. Using new gasket, install transfer gear change housing. Apply a continuous bead of sealant to extension housing mating surface and install transmission gear change housing. Ensure gear lever passes through center of gear change lever yoke and engages in gate plate.

15) To adjust bias spring tension, loosen adjustment plate bolts. *See Fig. 1.* Shift transmission into 4th gear and move shifter to right as far as possible. Tighten adjustment plate bolts. Check adjustment by selecting 3rd and 4th gears. Install new gasket and gear change housing cover. Install clutch housing. Install 12 x 45 mm clutch housing bolts at locating dowel positions. Install remaining bolts and tighten to specification. Apply Lithium grease to all pivot points and input shaft splines. Install new clutch release bearing.

TRANSMISSION SPECIFICATIONS
TRANSMISSION SPECIFICATIONS

Application	In. (mm)
Countershaft End Play	.0004-.0024 (.01-.06)
Mainshaft End Play	.0004-.0024 (.01-.06)
Synchro Ring-To-Gear Clearance	.020 (.50)
1st Gear Thrust Clearance	
Standard	.002-.008 (.05-.20)
Service Limit	.012 (.327)
2nd Gear Thrust Clearance	
Standard	.0016-.0083 (.04-.21)
Service Limit	.013 (.337)
3rd Gear Thrust Clearance	
Standard	.004-.0083 (.11-.21)
Service Limit	.013 (.337)
5th/Reverse Synchro Hub	
Circlip Fit	.0002-.0021 (.005-.055)
Reverse Idler Gear End Play	
Standard	.0016-.015 (.04-.38)
Service Limit	.013 (.337)

TORQUE SPECIFICATIONS
TORQUE SPECIFICATIONS

Application	Ft. Lbs. (N.m)
Clutch Housing Bolts	48-59 (65-80)
Companion Flange Bolt	59-74 (80-100)
Extension Housing Bolts	16-21 (22-28)
Fill Plug	18-26 (25-35)
Front Cover Bolts	16-21 (22-28)
Gear Change Housing Bolts	16-21 (22-28)
Oil Drain Plug	35-40 (47-54)
Oil Level Plug	18-26 (25-35)
Remote Housing Bolts	16-21 (22-28)
Reverse Inhibit Shaft	11-13 (15-18)
Reverse Light Switch	16-19 (22-26)
Slave Cylinder Bolts	16-21 (22-28)
5th Gear Countershaft Stake Nut	150-170 (204-231)

Application	INCH Lbs. (N.m)
Center Plate-To-Extension Housing Bolts	62-89 (7-10)
Oil Pump Housing Bolts	44-62 (5-7)
Spool Retainer Bolts	62-89 (7-10)

900 Series, 9000 Series

APPLICATION & LABOR TIMES

APPLICATION & LABOR TIMES

Vehicle Application	Labor Times [1] R & I	[2] Overhaul	Series
900 Series			
Non-Turbo	4.4	9.3	FM-5
Turbo	4.4	9.3	FM-5
9000 Series			
Non-Turbo	5.4	9.3	FM-5
Turbo	5.4	9.3	FM-5

[1] – Removal and installation of transmission from vehicle chassis.

[2] – Bench overhaul time for transaxle/differential. DOES NOT include removal and installation.

IDENTIFICATION

Identification plate is located on top of transaxle, near bellhousing. Serial and model number are found on this plate. For explaination of model codes, see appropriate MANUAL TRANSMISSION SERVICING article in TRANSMISSION SERVICING section.

LUBRICATION & ADJUSTMENTS

See appropriate MANUAL TRANSMISSION SERVICING article in TRANSMISSION SERVICING section.

TROUBLE SHOOTING

See GENERAL TROUBLE SHOOTING article in this section.

ON-VEHICLE SERVICE

DRIVE AXLE SHAFTS

See appropriate AXLE SHAFTS article in AXLE SHAFTS & TRANSFER CASES section.

REMOVAL & INSTALLATION

See appropriate MANUAL TRANSMISSION REMOVAL article in TRANSMISSION SERVICING section.

TRANSAXLE DISASSEMBLY

1) Mount transaxle on stand. On 900 models, remove clutch bearing fork screw. Pull out shaft and clutch bearing. *See Fig. 1.* On 9000 models, remove screws and inner actuator shaft. *See Fig. 2.* On all models, remove rear cover. Engage transaxle into 3rd gear. Remove dowel and 5th gear selector fork with 5th gear synchronizer sleeve. *See Fig. 3.*

2) Place 5th gear synchronizer sleeve back on shaft. Press down on sleeve until 1st and 5th gears are locked. Ensure 2 deep slots in gears are aligned. Remove locking flange from lock nut. Remove lock nut. Remove snap ring. Using a puller, remove 5th gear synchronizer sleeve and 5th gear.

3) Remove reverse gear shaft support screw from gear case. Remove clutch case-to-gear case screws and tap down guide sleeves. *See Fig. 4.* Press out gear case with gears and bearings. Remove fork shaft and reverse gear selector fork. Remove screws and reverse gear lever.

4) Engage reverse gear on gear change mechanism to gain access to screw for gear selector shaft. Remove screw for carrier on gear selector shaft. Pull out shaft and remove carrier. Disengage reverse and engage 4th gear on gear change mechanism. *See Fig. 5.* Remove screw, guide sleeves and gear change mechanism. Lift up input shaft and remove reverse gear shaft and reverse gear assembly.

5) Install puller on output shaft and pull up 1st gear aproximately .59" (15 mm). Remove input shaft assembly. Continue pulling until gears on

output shaft come loose. Remove 4th gear, clamping sleeve, spacer sleeve and 3rd gear. Remove 1st gear and 2nd gear. Remove synchronizer rings, sleeve and hub as a unit. Remove screws and output shaft bearing support. Pull out output shaft. Align notch in differential with bulge in output shaft bearing support and lift out differential.

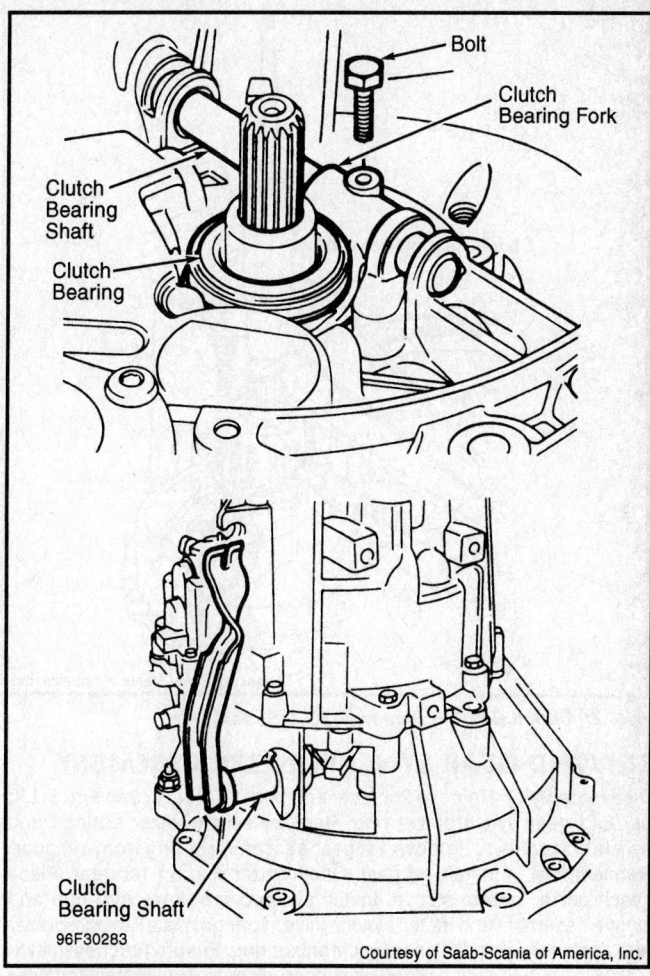

Fig. 1: Clutch Bearing Removal (900 Series)

COMPONENT DISASSEMBLY & REASSEMBLY

INPUT SHAFT

Disassembly – 1) Place input shaft in a soft-jaw vise and remove snap ring. *See Fig. 6.* Press bearing off shaft. Remove 4th gear, synchronizer ring and needle bearing.

2) Lift up synchronizer sleeve slightly and remove spring loaded rollers from synchronizer hub. Remove all springs and plungers from hub.

3) Remove snap ring and synchronizer hub. Remove 3rd gear synchronizer ring, 3rd gear and needle bearing.

Reassembly – 1) Place input shaft in a soft-jaw vice. Install 3rd gear needle bearing, 3rd gear and 3rd gear synchronizer ring. Install synchronizer hub and NEW snap ring. Ensure sharper edge faces upward. Measure axial play between 2nd and 3rd gears. *See Fig. 7.* Axial play should be .002-.016" (.05-.40 mm).

2) Install springs, plungers and synchronizer sleeve. Using a feeler gauge, press in springs and plungers and install rollers into synchronizer assembly. Install 4th gear synchronizer ring needle bearing and 4th gear.

3) Press on NEW bearing ensuring beveled edge faces upward. Install snap ring and tap carefully into groove of shaft with a drift. Measure end play between bearing and 4th gear. End play should be .002-.016" (.05-.40 mm).

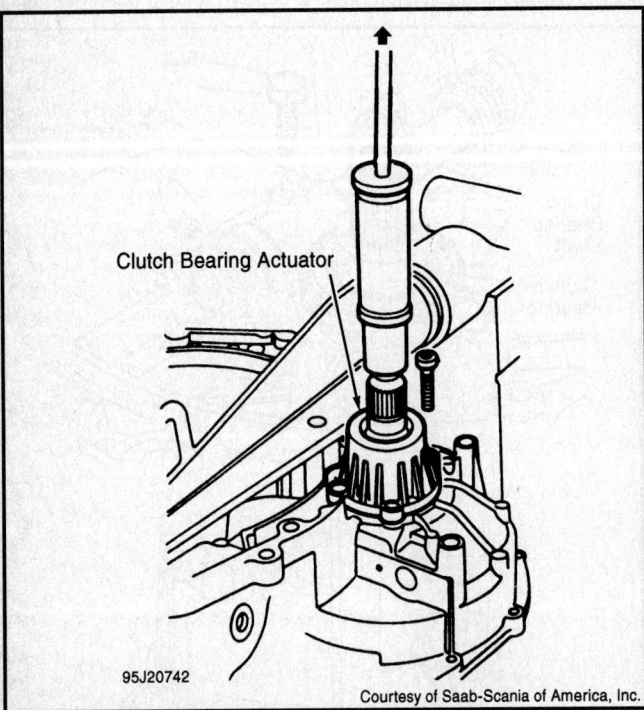

Clutch Bearing Actuator

95J20742

Courtesy of Saab-Scania of America, Inc.

Fig. 2: Clutch Bearing Removal (9000 Series)

1ST/2ND GEAR SYNCHRONIZER ASSEMBLY

Disassembly – Remove 2nd gear and bearing sleeve. *See Fig. 8*. Lift out 2nd gear synchronizer ring. Remove synchronizer springs and synchronizer keys. Remove 1st gear synchronizer ring from 1st gear.

Reassembly – Install 1st gear synchronizer ring on 1st gear. Place synchronizer hub in sleeve. Install synchronizer keys into hub and sleeve assembly and install synchronizer springs. Install synchronizer hub assembly onto 1st gear synchronizer ring. Ensure notches in synchronizer hub fit over bosses on synchronizer sleeve. Install 2nd gear synchronizer ring, bearing sleeve and 2nd gear.

5TH GEAR SYNCHRONIZER ASSEMBLY

Disassembly – Remove synchronizer sleeve, synchronizer hub and 5th gear synchronizer ring. *See Fig. 9*. Remove needle bearing from 5th gear.

Reassembly – Install needle bearing into 5th gear. Ensure wire coil on synchronizer ring is fitted and install synchronizer ring on 5th gear. Install synchronizer hub with 3 notches over heels of synchronizer ring. Ensure flat side of sleeve faces upward and that bosses on sleeve fit into deep notches of synchronizer hub.

REVERSE GEAR ASSEMBLY

Disassembly – Place reverse gear in a soft-jaw vise and mark position of bearing support on reverse gear shaft. Drive out reverse gear shaft from bearing support. *See Fig. 10*. Remove bearing support, reverse gear, sleeve, synchronizer ring, wire coil, reverse driven gear and needle bearing.

Reassembly – **1)** Place reverse gear shaft in a soft-jaw vise. Install needle bearing, reverse driven gear, synchronizer ring and wire coil. *See Fig. 11*. Ensure wire coil is fitted on synchronizer. Install synchronizer sleeve and ensure bosses of sleeve fit into deep notches in synchronizer ring and notches in sleeve face downwards.

2) Install reverse gear and ensure 3 notches in synchronizer hub fit over 3 holes in synchronizer ring. *See Fig. 13*. Install bearing washer

and reverse gear shaft support. Ensure tab on washer is between bosses of reverse gear shaft support.

3) Align marks on reverse gear shaft and bearing support and press bearing support onto reverse gear shaft. Ensure screw hole in reverse gear shaft support is in line with shaft's lubrication holes. Using a feeler guage, measure end play between upper reverse gear and washer. End play should be .004-.008" (.10-.20 mm).

GEAR CHANGE MECHANISM

Disassembly – **1)** Place gear change mechanism in a soft-jaw vise. Drive out gear change lever shaft spring pin and tap out gear change lever shaft. *See Fig. 12*. Remove gear change lever.

2) Place a finger in front of catch ball seat and pull out reverse gear shift shaft. *See Fig. 14*. Remove catch balls and springs. Remove 5th gear shift shaft, 3rd/4th gear shift shaft and 1st/2nd gear shift shaft in same manner. Remove pins from 5th gear shift shaft and 3rd/4th gear shift shaft.

3) If forks or actuators need to be replaced, drive out spring pins and remove forks and actuators.

Reassembly – **1)** Assemble forks and actuators on their respective shafts and drive in NEW spring pins. Install spring and ball into bearing support and compress spring with a drift pin. *See Fig. 15*. Install 1st/2nd shift shaft.

2) Install double position catch ball in 3rd/4th gear shift shaft catch ball seat. *See Fig. 15*. Install pin in 3rd/4th gear shift shaft and spring and ball in bearing support. Compress spring and install 3rd/4th gear shift shaft. Ensure 1st/2nd gear shift shaft fits through hole in 3rd/4th gear shift fork.

3) Install double position catch ball in 5th gear shift shaft catch ball seat. *See Fig. 15*. Install pin in 5th gear shift shaft and spring and ball in bearing support. Compress spring and install 5th gear shift shaft.

4) Install double position catch ball in Reverse gear shift shaft catch ball seat. *See Fig. 15*. Install spring and ball in bearing support. Compress spring and install Reverse gear shift shaft.

5) Install selector lever with springs and sleeves in bearing support. Press in shaft and drive in a NEW spring pin.

DIFFERENTIAL

Disassembly & Reassembly – Place differential in a soft-jaw vice. Remove bolts and ring gear. *See Figs. 16 and 17*. Pull off differential bearings using puller. On 9000 series, cut speedometer drive gear to remove it. On all models, remove pinion shaft dowel and pinion shaft. Remove differential gears and wear discs. To reassemble, reverse disassembly procedure. Tighten NEW ring gear bolts to specification.

TRANSAXLE REASSEMBLY

1) Install differential in clutch case. Install output shaft in its seat and install bearing race using a plastic hammer. Install bearing support and tap down. Install bearing support screws and tighten 3 middle screws alternately. Tighten outermost screw. See TORQUE SPECIFICATIONS.

2) Install 1st/2nd driven gears with their synchronizer assembly onto output shaft. Install 3rd driven gear and spacing sleeve onto output shaft. Install input shaft assembly into case and output shaft. Ensure gear teeth are properly engaged. Press gears onto output shaft until clamping sleeve and 4th driven gear can be installed. Install 4th driven gear with machining marks facing upwards. Press 4th driven gear down until its even with 4th gear.

3) Lift input shaft and install reverse gear assembly. *See Fig. 18*. Ensure hole in reverse gear shaft is facing channel in clutch case. Install gear change mechanism in clutch case. Ensure 1st gear fork is in 1st gear position on mechanism and push up sleeve to 2nd gear position on output shaft. Push up sleeve into 4th gear position on input shaft.

4) Fit 1st/2nd gear and 3rd/4th gear forks in their sleeves. *See Fig. 5*. Turn and push mechanism into place. Lift up fork and disengage 1st gear. Install guide sleeves and bolt. Install reverse gear lever with 2 remaining bolts. Torque bolts to specification. See TORQUE SPECIFICATIONS.

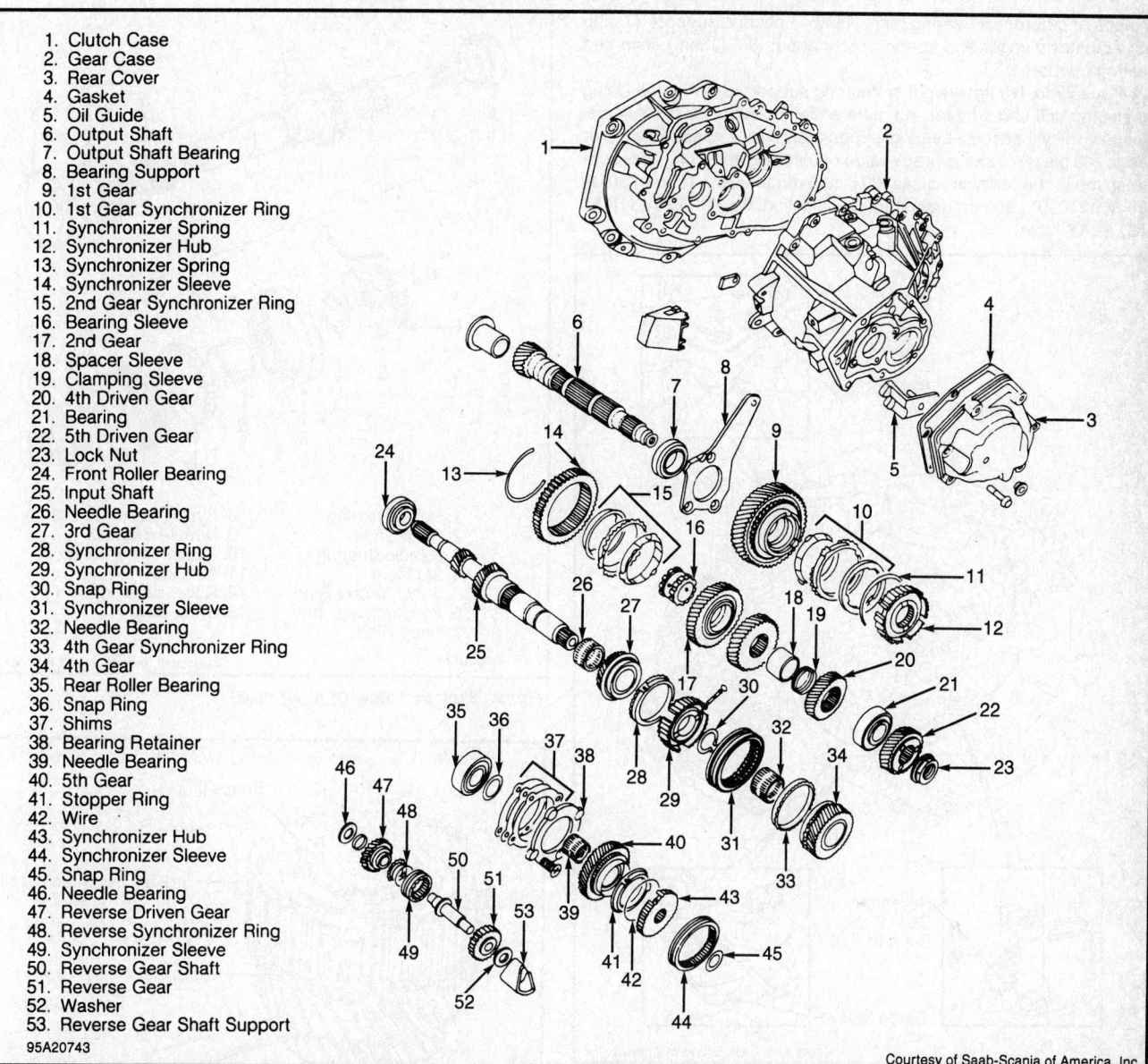

1. Clutch Case
2. Gear Case
3. Rear Cover
4. Gasket
5. Oil Guide
6. Output Shaft
7. Output Shaft Bearing
8. Bearing Support
9. 1st Gear
10. 1st Gear Synchronizer Ring
11. Synchronizer Spring
12. Synchronizer Hub
13. Synchronizer Spring
14. Synchronizer Sleeve
15. 2nd Gear Synchronizer Ring
16. Bearing Sleeve
17. 2nd Gear
18. Spacer Sleeve
19. Clamping Sleeve
20. 4th Driven Gear
21. Bearing
22. 5th Driven Gear
23. Lock Nut
24. Front Roller Bearing
25. Input Shaft
26. Needle Bearing
27. 3rd Gear
28. Synchronizer Ring
29. Synchronizer Hub
30. Snap Ring
31. Synchronizer Sleeve
32. Needle Bearing
33. 4th Gear Synchronizer Ring
34. 4th Gear
35. Rear Roller Bearing
36. Snap Ring
37. Shims
38. Bearing Retainer
39. Needle Bearing
40. 5th Gear
41. Stopper Ring
42. Wire
43. Synchronizer Hub
44. Synchronizer Sleeve
45. Snap Ring
46. Needle Bearing
47. Reverse Driven Gear
48. Reverse Synchronizer Ring
49. Synchronizer Sleeve
50. Reverse Gear Shaft
51. Reverse Gear
52. Washer
53. Reverse Gear Shaft Support

95A20743

Courtesy of Saab-Scania of America, Inc.

Fig. 3: Exploded View Of Transaxle

NOTE: Oil plate of reverse gear lever fits under edge of gear change mechanism.

5) Install reverse gear fork onto reverse gear synchronizer sleeve. Ensure reverse gear lever is in grooves of reverse gear fork. Install reverse gear fork shaft. Install gear selector shaft with beveled hole facing upwards. Thread in and fit carrier in place. Push in gear selector shaft and install bolt. Torque bolt to specifications. See TORQUE SPECIFICATIONS.

6) Apply Loctite 518 to contact surfaces of gear box case and clutch case. Ensure sintered plug is not blocked and that reverse gear shaft is correctly positioned so that its bolt can be installed after gear case installation.

7) Install gear case and secure lightly with 2 bolts. Tap up guide sleeves. *See Fig. 4.* Install bolt for reverse shaft and remaining case bolts. Torque to specifications. See TORQUE SPECIFICATIONS.

8) Install output shaft bearing and pull it down to, but not against, outer bearing race. Install 5th driven gear and NEW nut. Install 5th gear, needle bearing, synchronizer ring, hub and sleeve on input shaft.

9) Engage 3rd gear and 5th gears. Install dial indicator on output shaft and a M8 bolt to case. *See Fig. 19.* Tighten nut and measure output shaft end play until it is .006-.008" (.15-.20 mm). Remove M8 bolt. Dis-

engage 5th and 3rd gears. Use an electric drill to run gear box for about 20 revolutions, while pressing down and pulling up to settle bearings. Measure and record output shaft end play. *See Fig. 20.* Add output shaft end play nominal value to measured end play value. See OUTPUT SHAFT END PLAY table.

OUTPUT SHAFT END PLAY

Application	Specification in. (mm)
Old Case & Bearing	
Over (50,000 km)	.005 (.12)
Up to (50,000 km)	.006 (.15)
Old Case & New Bearing	
Case (Up to & over (50,000 km)	.008 (.20)
New Case & Bearing	.010 (.26)

10) Engage 3rd and 5th gears. Install MM Disc (87 92 061) onto output shaft nut. *See Fig. 21.* Mark tooth on gear at value calculated in step **9).** Tighten in 2 or 3 stages until tool's zero reading is opposite marked tooth. Remove tool and stake nut in 3 places. Remove 5th gear, needle bearing, synchronizer ring, hub and sleeve from input shaft.

11) If output shaft bearings or differential bearings have been replaced, differential's prestressing must be adjusted. If prestressing is not required, go to step **14).** Install Milled Bearing Race (87 92 137) in place of differential bearing race. Remove bearing support "O" ring and actuator plunger and spring. Install about .08" (2 mm) shim and bearing support.

12) Place 22 lb. (10 kg) weight on bearing support. *See Fig. 22.* Using an electric drill and adapter, run differential for about 20 revolutions. Measure play between bearing support and gear case with feeler gauge in 3 places. Take average value of readings and using appropriate shims in the following sizes .004" (.10 mm), .006" (.15 mm), .012" (.30 mm), .020" (.50 mm) adjust to specification. See DIFFERENTIAL END PLAY table.

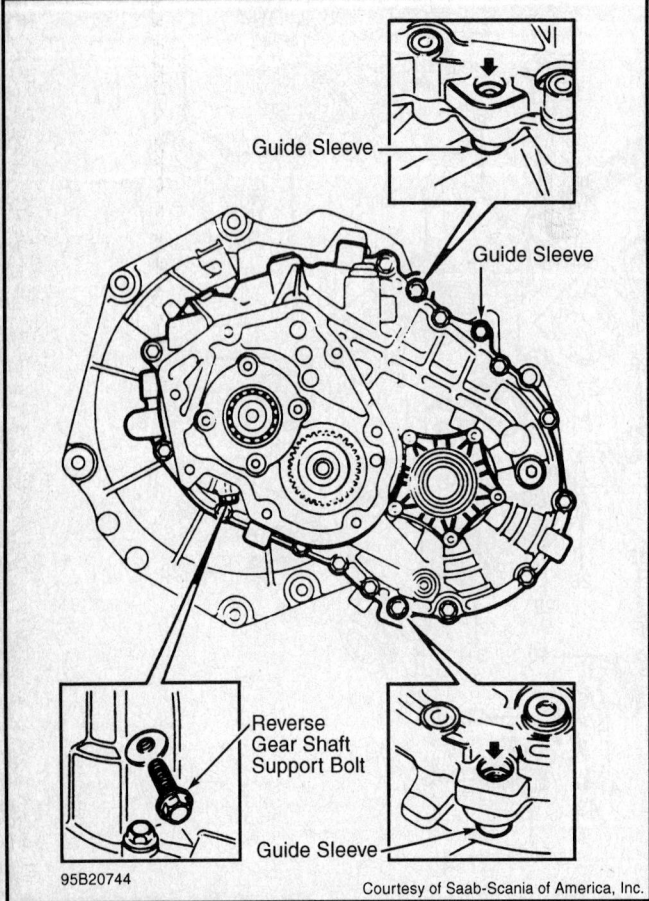

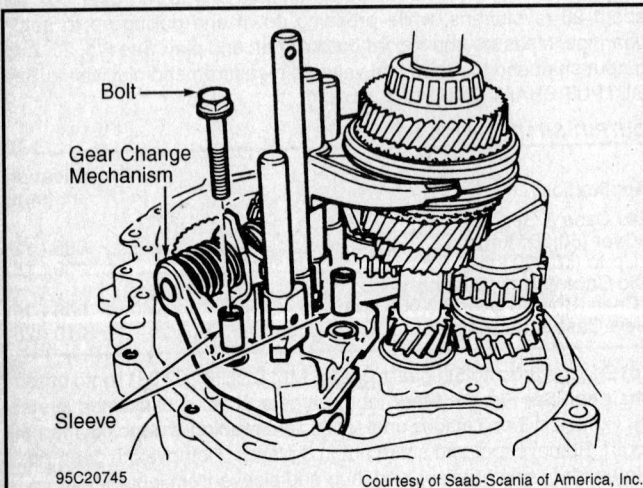

Fig. 4: **Transaxle Case Bolt Locations**

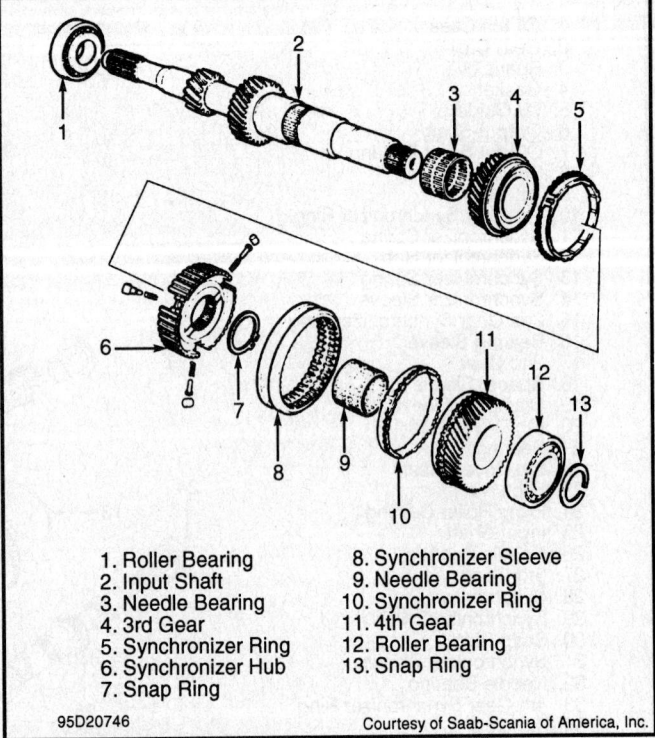

1. Roller Bearing
2. Input Shaft
3. Needle Bearing
4. 3rd Gear
5. Synchronizer Ring
6. Synchronizer Hub
7. Snap Ring
8. Synchronizer Sleeve
9. Needle Bearing
10. Synchronizer Ring
11. 4th Gear
12. Roller Bearing
13. Snap Ring

95D20746   Courtesy of Saab-Scania of America, Inc.

Fig. 6: **Exploded View Of Input Shaft**

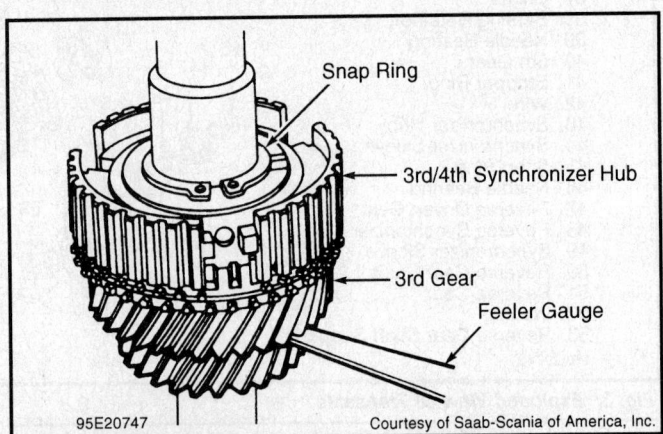

Fig. 7: **Measuring Axial Play**

DIFFERENTIAL END PLAY

Application	Specification in. (mm)
Old Case & Bearing (50,000 km)	.008 (.20)
Old Case & New Case (50,000 km)	.012 (.30)
New Case & Bearing	.014 (.35)

13) Remove weight, differential bearing support, and milled bearing race tool. Install differential bearing race. *See Fig. 23.* Lubricate and install "O" ring on bearing support. Install plunger and spring. Install shims and bearing support. Torque bolts alternately to specification. See TORQUE SPECIFICATIONS.

14) Place dial indicator on input shaft bearing. *See Fig. 24.* Using an electric drill an adapter run gear box to settle bearings. Press drill up and down while operating for about 20 revolutions. Measure end play. Input shaft end play should be .002-.004" (.04-.11 mm). Adjust end play using shims under bearing support. Shims are avialable in sizes of .004" (.10 mm), .006" (.15 mm) and .012" (.30 mm).

Fig. 5: **Gear Change Mechanism**

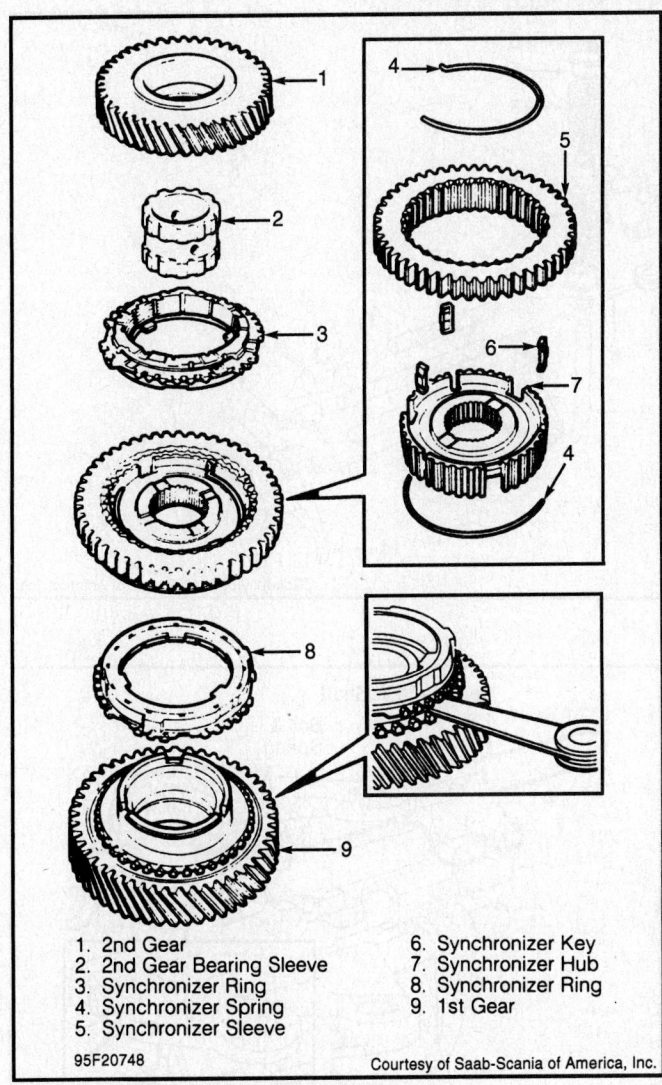

1. 2nd Gear
2. 2nd Gear Bearing Sleeve
3. Synchronizer Ring
4. Synchronizer Spring
5. Synchronizer Sleeve
6. Synchronizer Key
7. Synchronizer Hub
8. Synchronizer Ring
9. 1st Gear

95F20748   Courtesy of Saab-Scania of America, Inc.

Fig. 8: 1st/2nd Gear Synchronizer Assembly

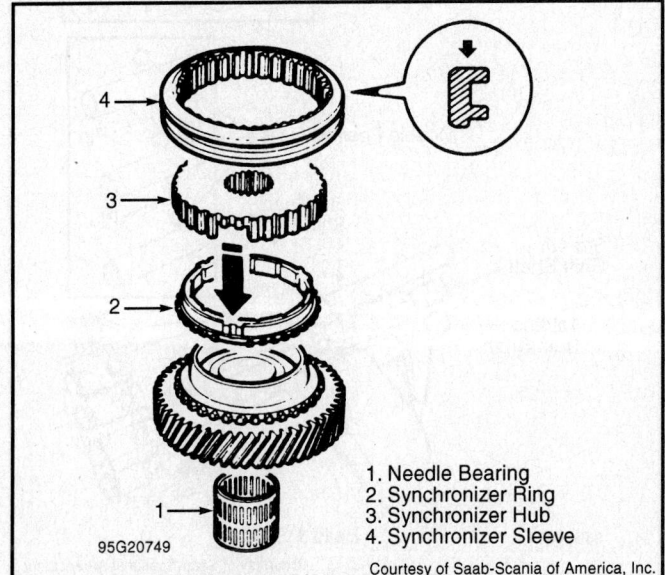

1. Needle Bearing
2. Synchronizer Ring
3. Synchronizer Hub
4. Synchronizer Sleeve

95G20749   Courtesy of Saab-Scania of America, Inc.

Fig. 9: 5th Gear Synchronizer Assembly

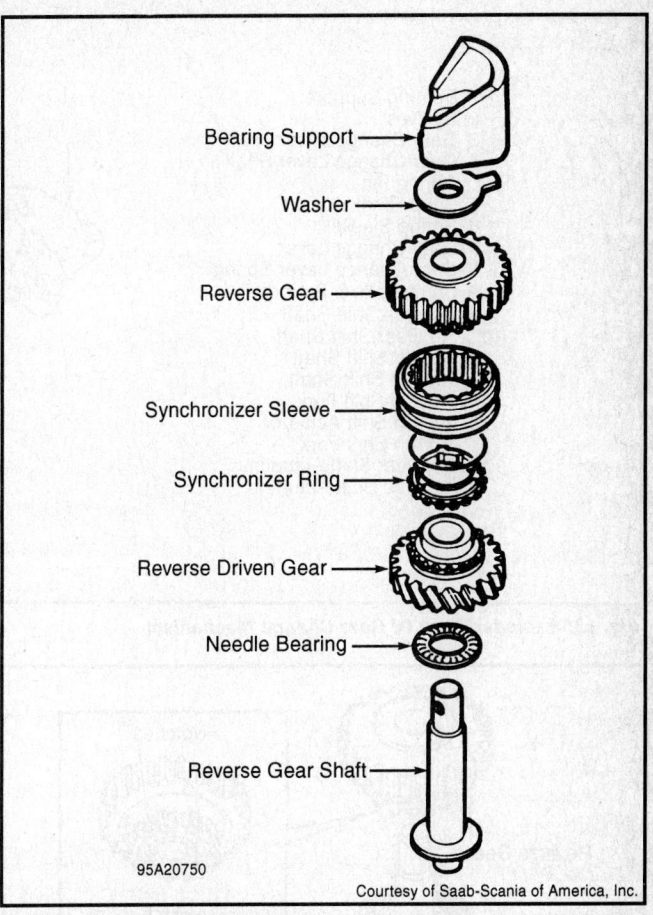

Bearing Support
Washer
Reverse Gear
Synchronizer Sleeve
Synchronizer Ring
Reverse Driven Gear
Needle Bearing
Reverse Gear Shaft

95A20750   Courtesy of Saab-Scania of America, Inc.

Fig. 10: Reverse Gear Assembly

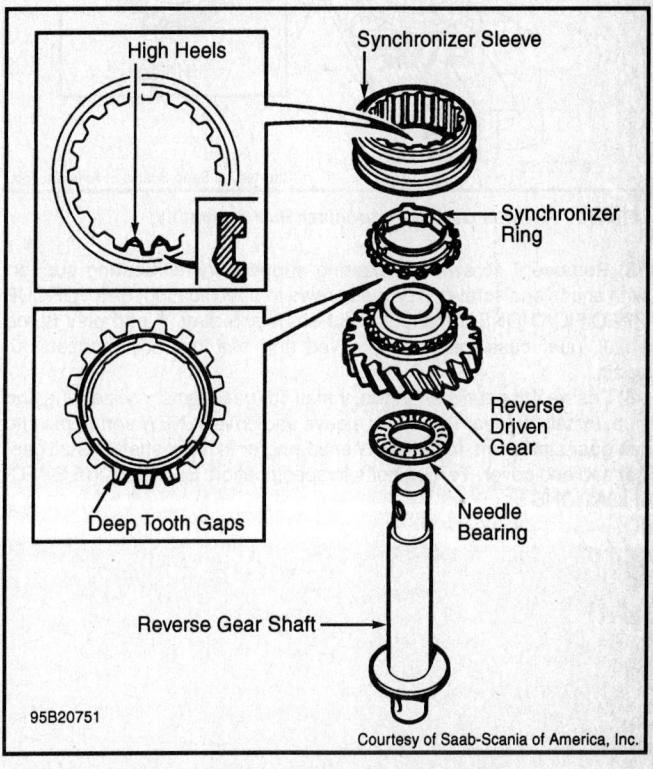

High Heels
Synchronizer Sleeve
Synchronizer Ring
Deep Tooth Gaps
Reverse Driven Gear
Needle Bearing
Reverse Gear Shaft

95B20751   Courtesy of Saab-Scania of America, Inc.

Fig. 11: Reverse Gear Synchronizer Sleeve Assembly

MANUAL TRANSMISSIONS
Saab FM5 5-Speed (Cont.)

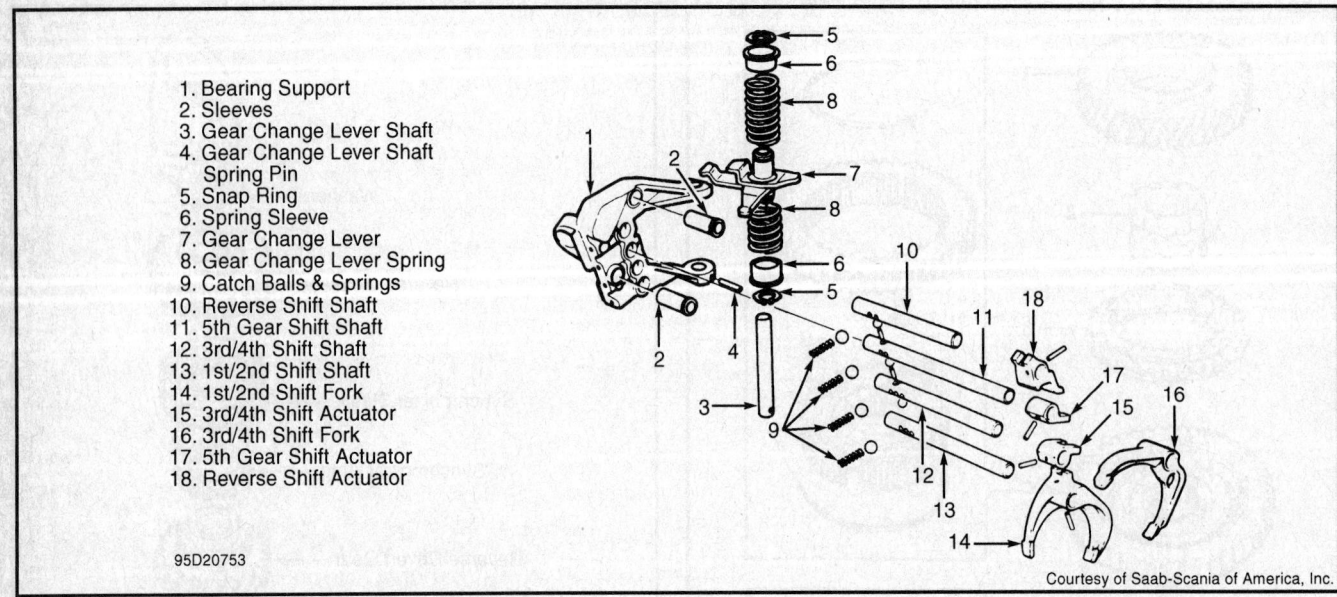

1. Bearing Support
2. Sleeves
3. Gear Change Lever Shaft
4. Gear Change Lever Shaft
   Spring Pin
5. Snap Ring
6. Spring Sleeve
7. Gear Change Lever
8. Gear Change Lever Spring
9. Catch Balls & Springs
10. Reverse Shift Shaft
11. 5th Gear Shift Shaft
12. 3rd/4th Shift Shaft
13. 1st/2nd Shift Shaft
14. 1st/2nd Shift Fork
15. 3rd/4th Shift Actuator
16. 3rd/4th Shift Fork
17. 5th Gear Shift Actuator
18. Reverse Shift Actuator

95D20753

Courtesy of Saab-Scania of America, Inc.

Fig. 12: Exploded View Of Gear Change Mechanism

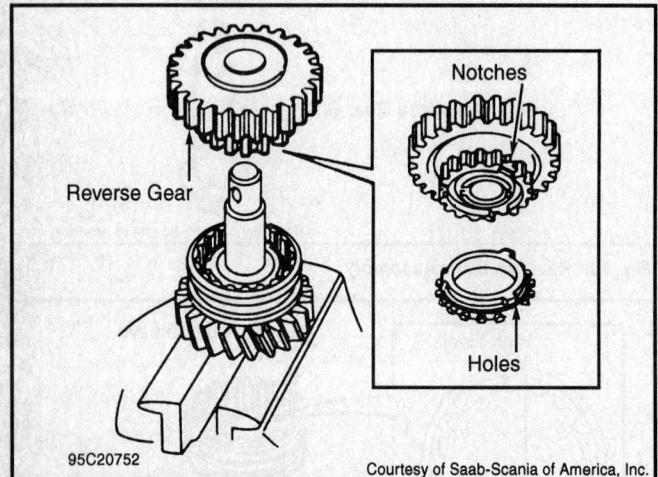

95C20752

Courtesy of Saab-Scania of America, Inc.

Fig. 13: Reverse Gear Synchronizer Hub Assembly

15) Remove 4 screws and bearing support. Install bearing support with shims and screws. Torque screws to specification. See TORQUE SPECIFICATIONS. Measure input shaft end play. If end play is too small, gear case must be removed and bearing race pressed out again.

16) Ensure 4th gear is engaged. Install 5th gear, synchronizer ring and hub. Install 5th gear fork on its sleeve and drive in NEW spring pin into 5th gear shift shaft. Install NEW snap ring onto input shaft. Install gasket and end cover. Torque bolts to specification. See TORQUE SPECIFICATIONS.

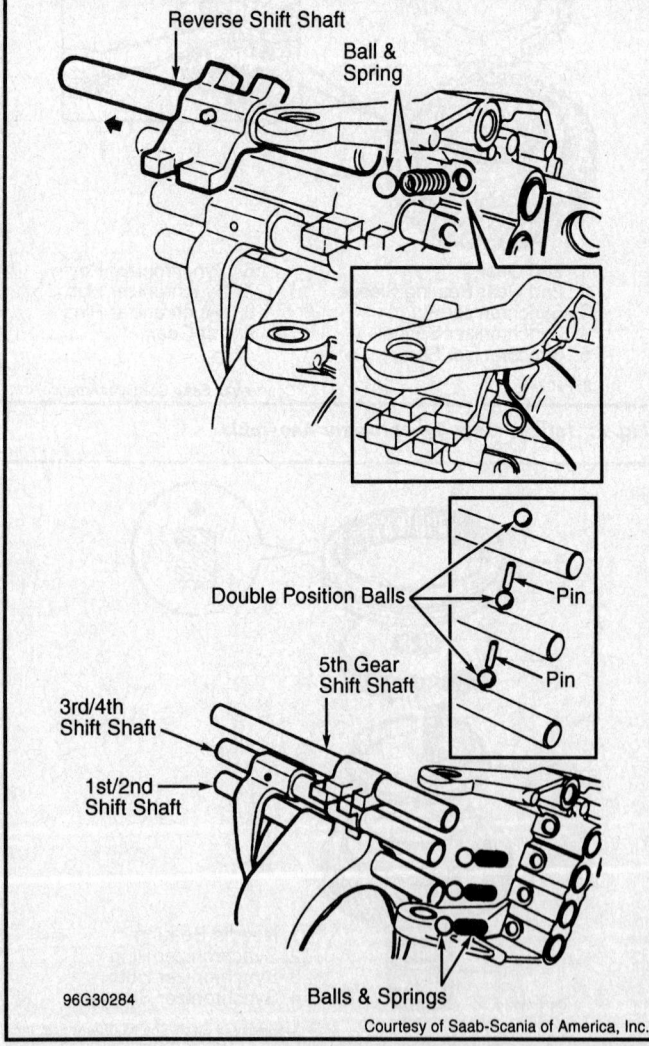

96G30284

Courtesy of Saab-Scania of America, Inc.

Fig. 14: Removal Of Shift Shafts, Balls & Springs

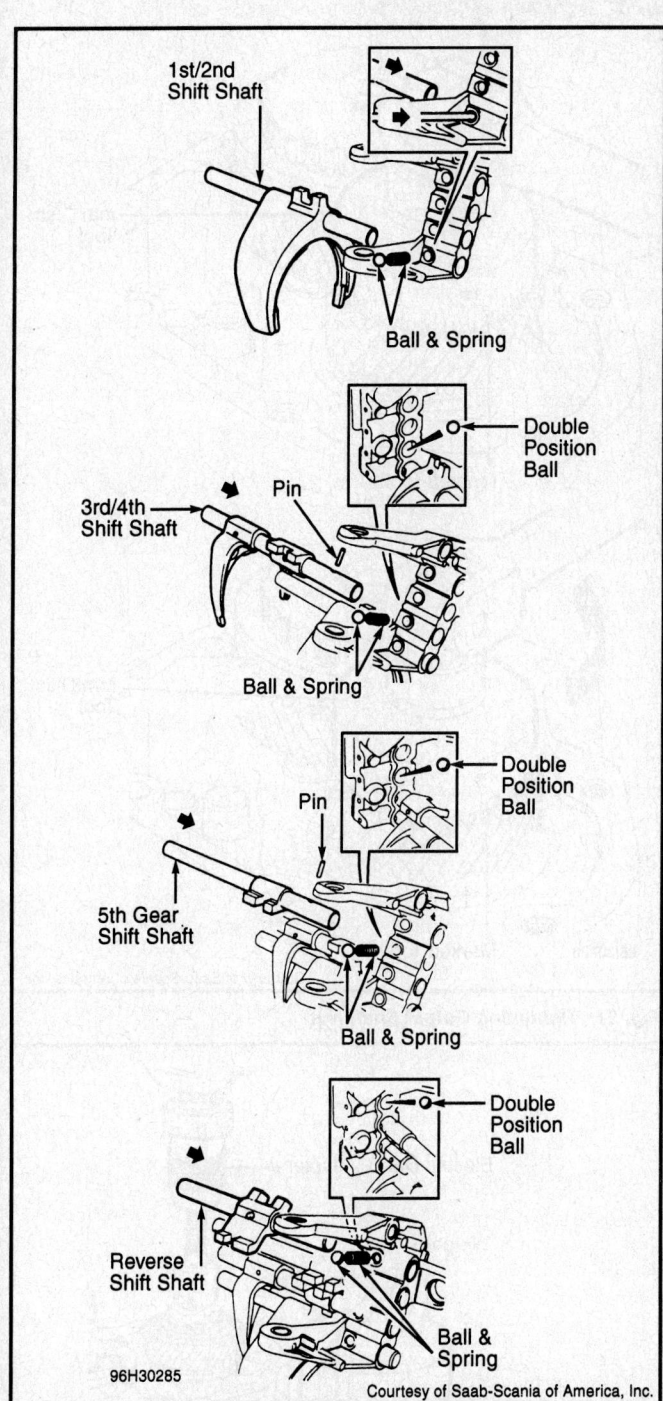

Fig. 15: Installation Of Shift Shafts, Balls & Springs

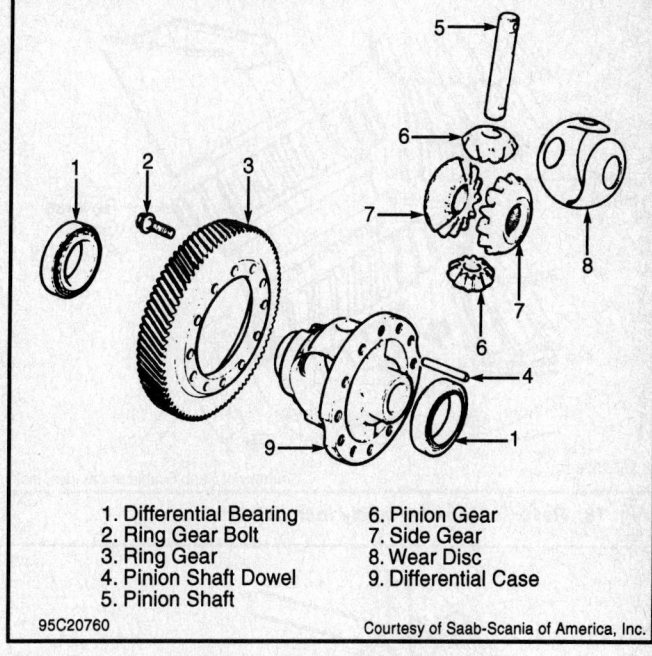

1. Differential Bearing
2. Ring Gear Bolt
3. Ring Gear
4. Pinion Shaft Dowel
5. Pinion Shaft
6. Pinion Gear
7. Side Gear
8. Wear Disc
9. Differential Case

Courtesy of Saab-Scania of America, Inc.

Fig. 16: Exploded View Of Differential (900 Series)

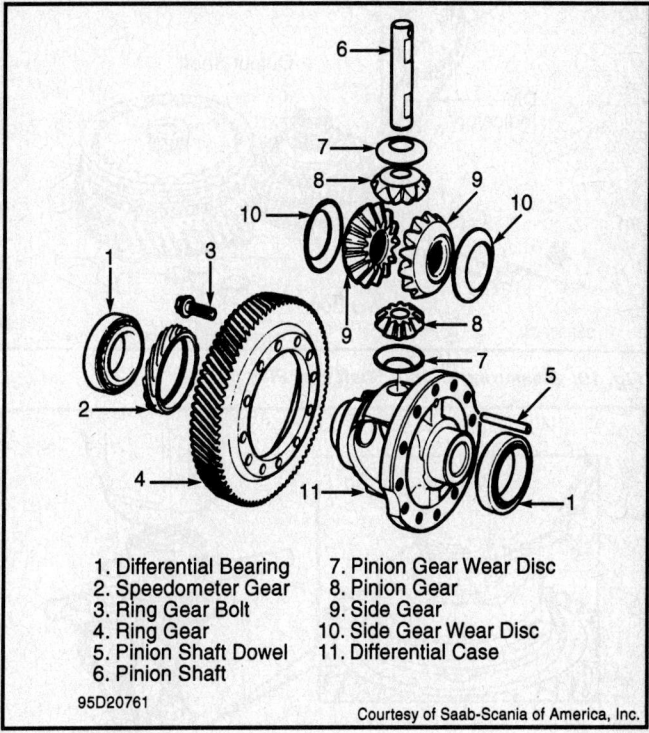

1. Differential Bearing
2. Speedometer Gear
3. Ring Gear Bolt
4. Ring Gear
5. Pinion Shaft Dowel
6. Pinion Shaft
7. Pinion Gear Wear Disc
8. Pinion Gear
9. Side Gear
10. Side Gear Wear Disc
11. Differential Case

Courtesy of Saab-Scania of America, Inc.

Fig. 17: Exploded View Of Differential (9000 Series)

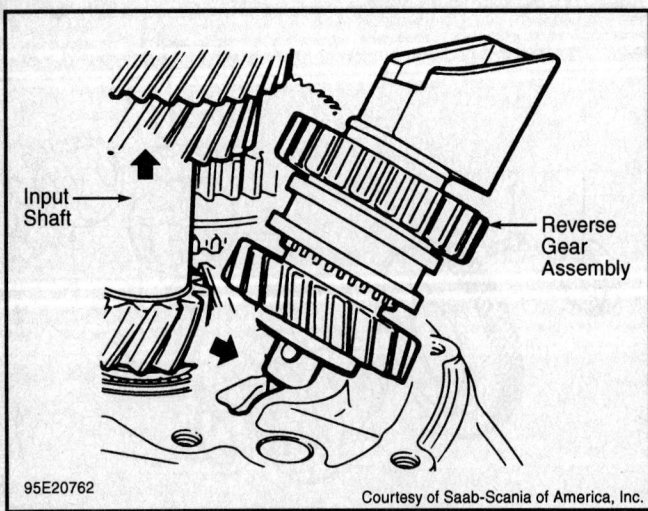

Fig. 18: Reverse Gear Assembly Installation

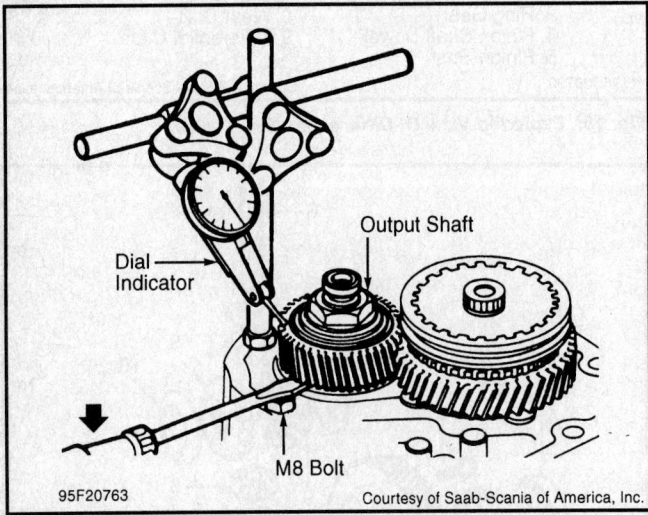

Fig. 19: Measuring Output Shaft End Play

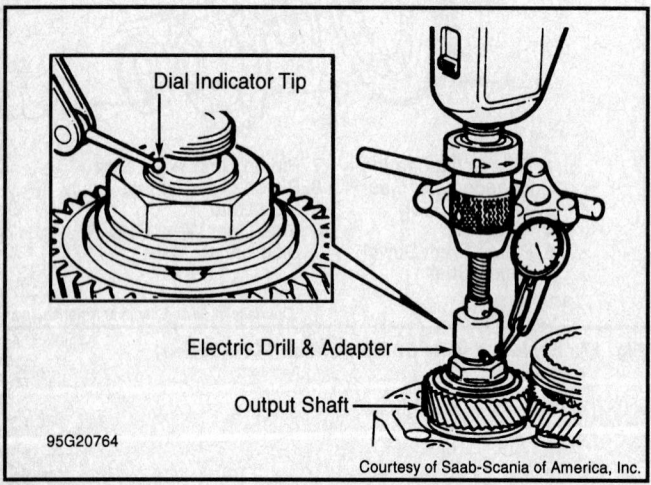

Fig. 20: Measuring Output Shaft End Play

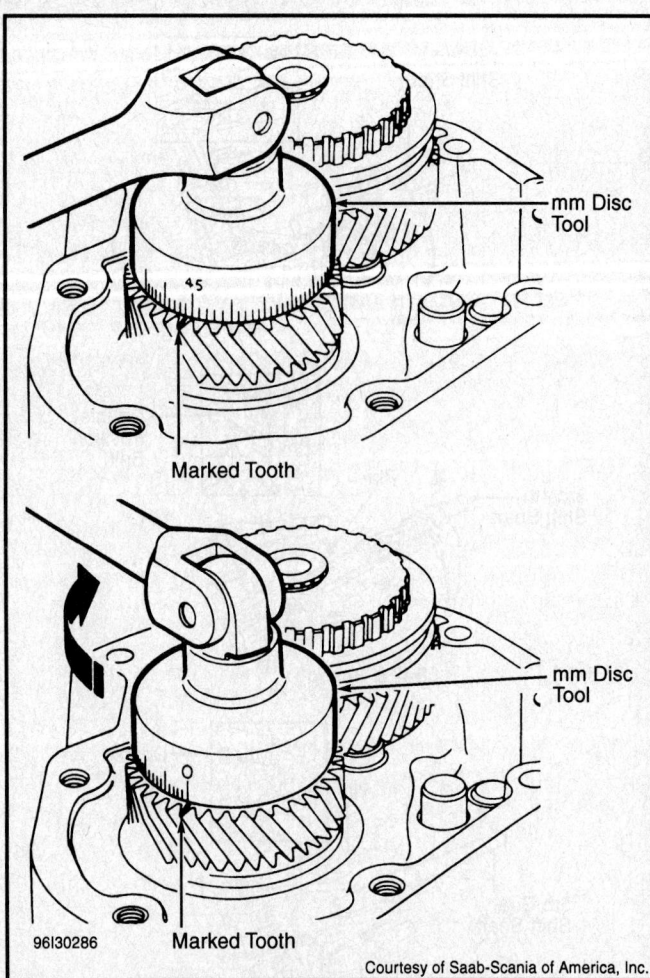

Fig. 21: Tightening Output Shaft Nut

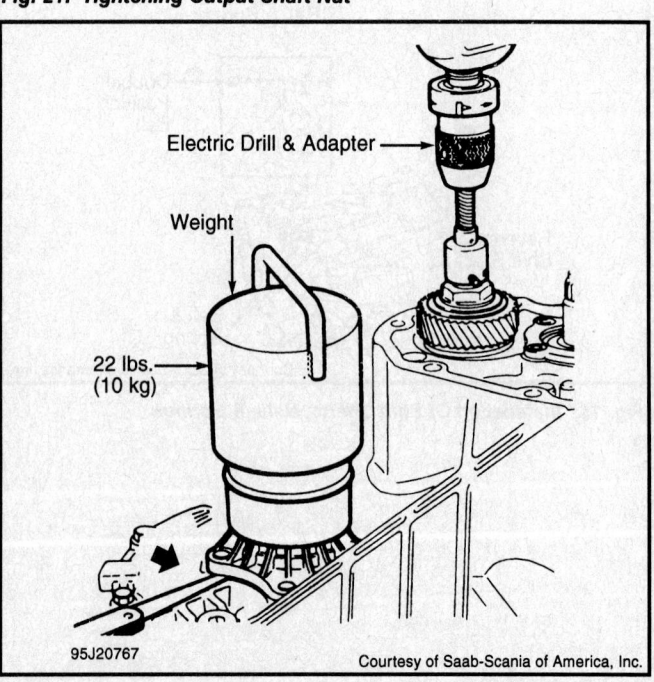

Fig. 22: Measuring Differential bearing Support End Play

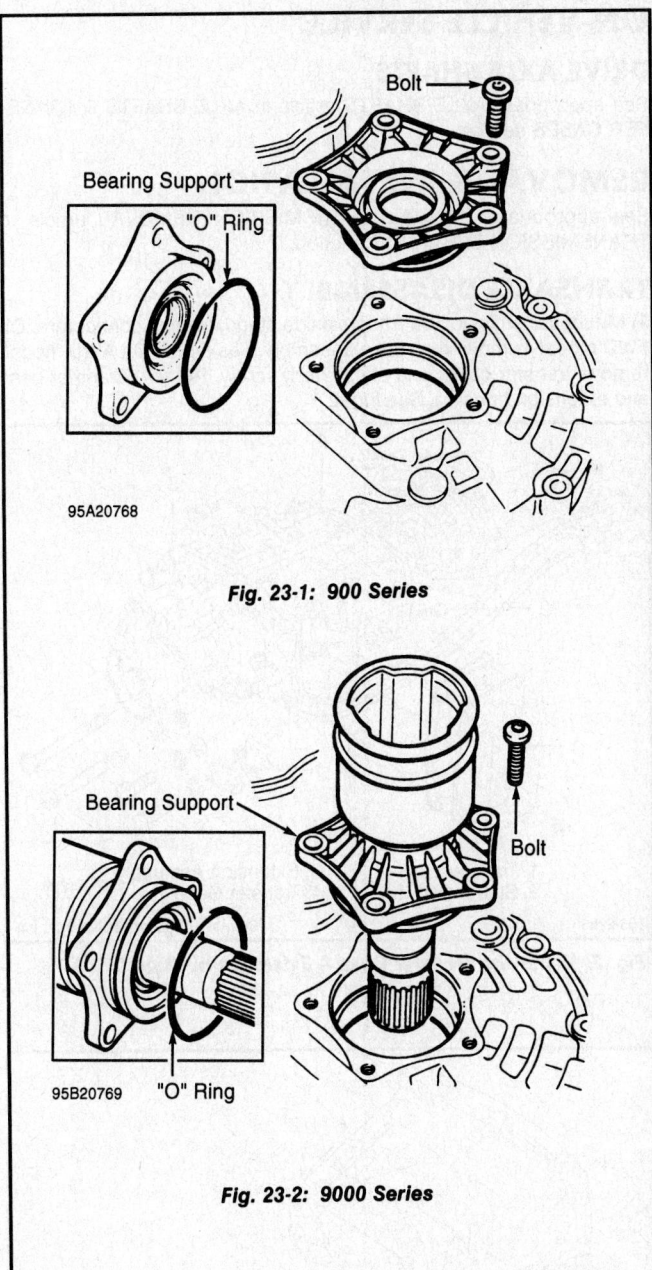

Fig. 23-1: 900 Series

95A20768

Fig. 23-2: 9000 Series

95B20769

Courtesy of Saab-Scania of America, Inc.

Fig. 23: Differential Bearing Support Installation

Bolt

Bearing Retainer

Shims

95E20770

Courtesy of Saab-Scania of America, Inc.

Fig. 24: Measuring Input Shaft End Play

TORQUE SPECIFICATIONS

TORQUE SPECIFICATIONS

Application	Ft. Lbs. (N.m)
Actuator Set Screw	15-18 (20-24)
Back-up Light Switch Bolts	15-18 (20-24)
Bearing Bracket Torx Screws	18-21 (24-28)
End Cover Bolts	15-18 (20-24)
Oil Fill Plug	30-45 (40-60)
Output Shaft Bearing Bracket Bolts	18-21 (24-28)
Reverse Selector Fork Bolt	15-18 (20-24)
Ring Gear Bolt	59-74 (80-100)
Selector Shaft Securing Bolt	15-18 (20-24)
Transmission Housing Bolt	15-18 (20-24)
Triangular Plate Torx Screws	18-21 (24-28)

MANUAL TRANSMISSIONS
Subaru Impreza & Legacy 5-Speed

Impreza, Legacy

APPLICATION & LABOR TIMES

APPLICATION & LABOR TIMES

Vehicle Application	Labor Times		Series
	¹ R & I	² Overhaul	
1995-96 Impreza			
FWD	3.1	5.3	5MT-1
AWD	3.6	6.7	5MT-2
1995-96 Legacy			
FWD	3.1	5.3	5MT-1
AWD	3.6	6.7	5MT-2

¹ – Removal and installation of transaxle from vehicle chassis.
² – Bench overhaul time for transaxle/differential. DOES NOT include removal and installation.

IDENTIFICATION

Transmission identification label is located on upper surface of main case. 5MT-1 is a 5-forward gears with synchromesh and one reverse gear transmission. 5MT-2 is a 5-forward gears with synchromesh and one reverse gear with a center differential and viscous coupling.

DESCRIPTION

FWD

Transmission provides one reverse and 5 forward speeds. Forward gears are synchronized.

AWD

Transmission is similar to that on FWD models. It is a full-time 4WD transmission with a center differential and a viscous coupling.

LUBRICATION & ADJUSTMENTS

See appropriate MANUAL TRANSMISSION SERVICING article in TRANSMISSION SERVICING section.

TROUBLE SHOOTING

See GENERAL TROUBLE SHOOTING article in this section.

ON-VEHICLE SERVICE

DRIVE AXLE SHAFTS

See appropriate AXLE SHAFTS article in AXLE SHAFTS & TRANSFER CASES section.

REMOVAL & INSTALLATION

See appropriate MANUAL TRANSMISSION REMOVAL article in TRANSMISSION SERVICING section.

TRANSAXLE DISASSEMBLY

1) Mount transmission on transmission stand. Unplug connectors. On FWD model, remove rear case assembly. *See Fig. 1.* On AWD model, remove transfer cover and shifter fork screw. Remove transfer case and extension housing. *See Fig. 2.*

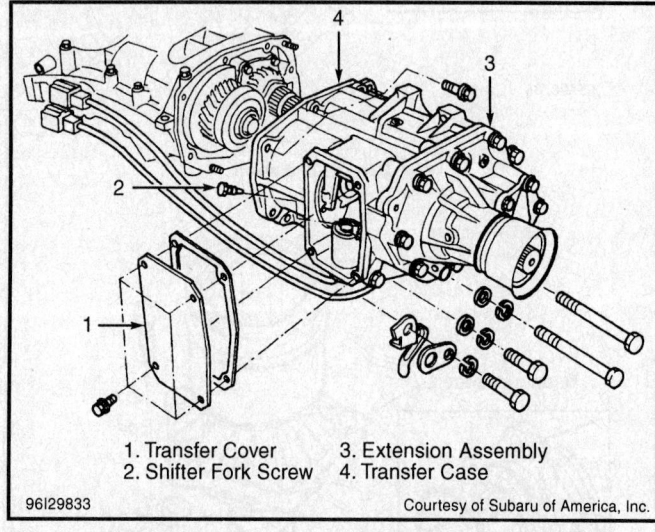

1. Transfer Cover	3. Extension Assembly
2. Shifter Fork Screw	4. Transfer Case

96I29833   Courtesy of Subaru of America, Inc.

Fig. 2: Removing Transfer Case & Extension Housing (AWD)

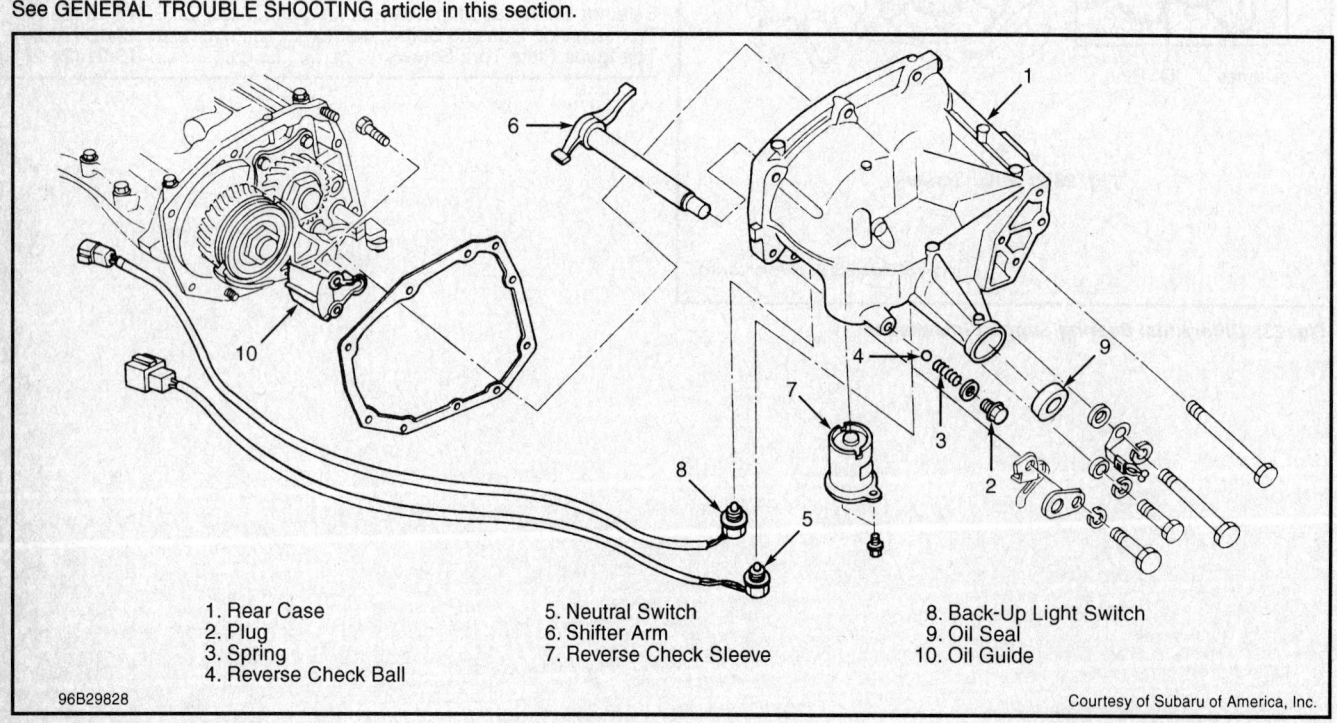

1. Rear Case	5. Neutral Switch	8. Back-Up Light Switch
2. Plug	6. Shifter Arm	9. Oil Seal
3. Spring	7. Reverse Check Sleeve	10. Oil Guide
4. Reverse Check Ball		

96B29828   Courtesy of Subaru of America, Inc.

Fig. 1: Removing Rear Case (FWD)

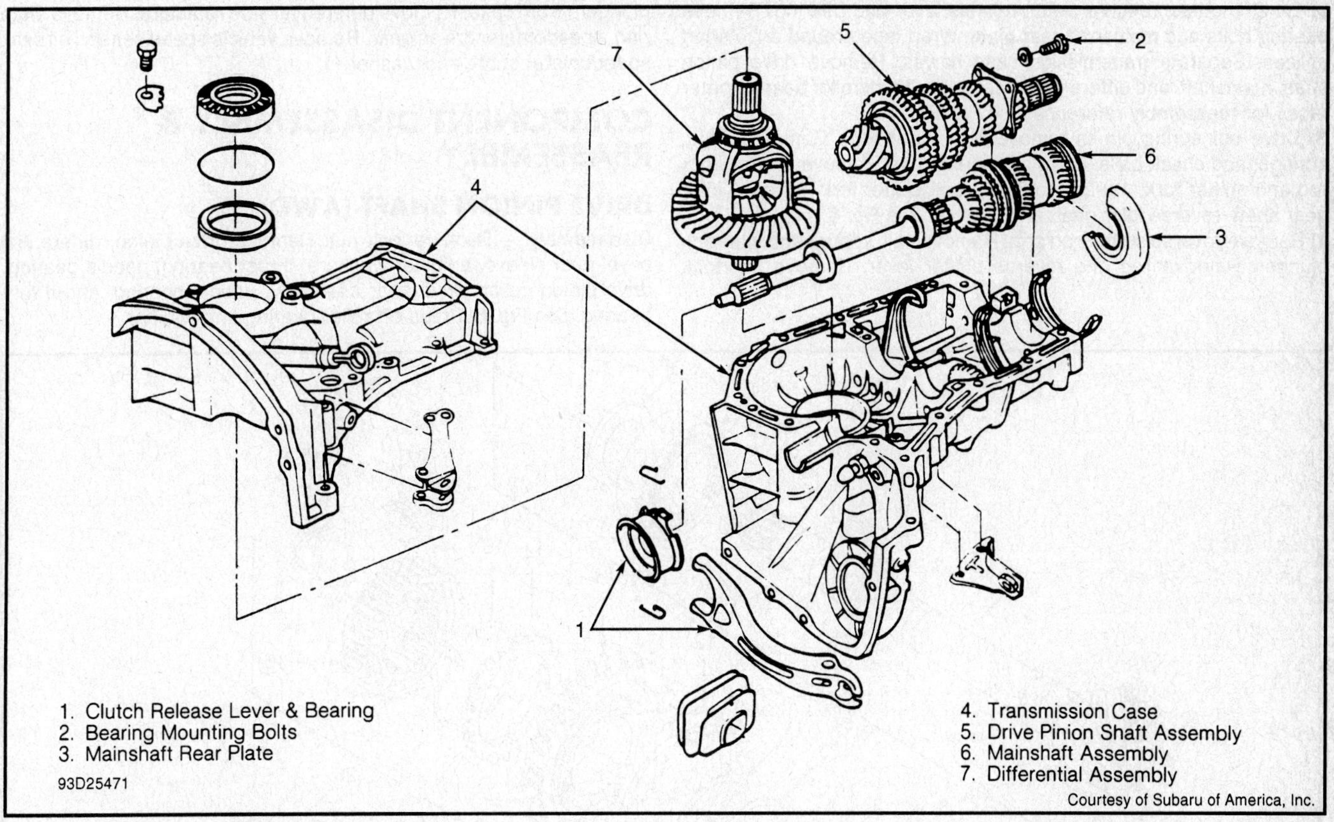

1. Clutch Release Lever & Bearing
2. Bearing Mounting Bolts
3. Mainshaft Rear Plate

4. Transmission Case
5. Drive Pinion Shaft Assembly
6. Mainshaft Assembly
7. Differential Assembly

93D25471

Courtesy of Subaru of America, Inc.

Fig. 3: Exploded View Of Transmission Case

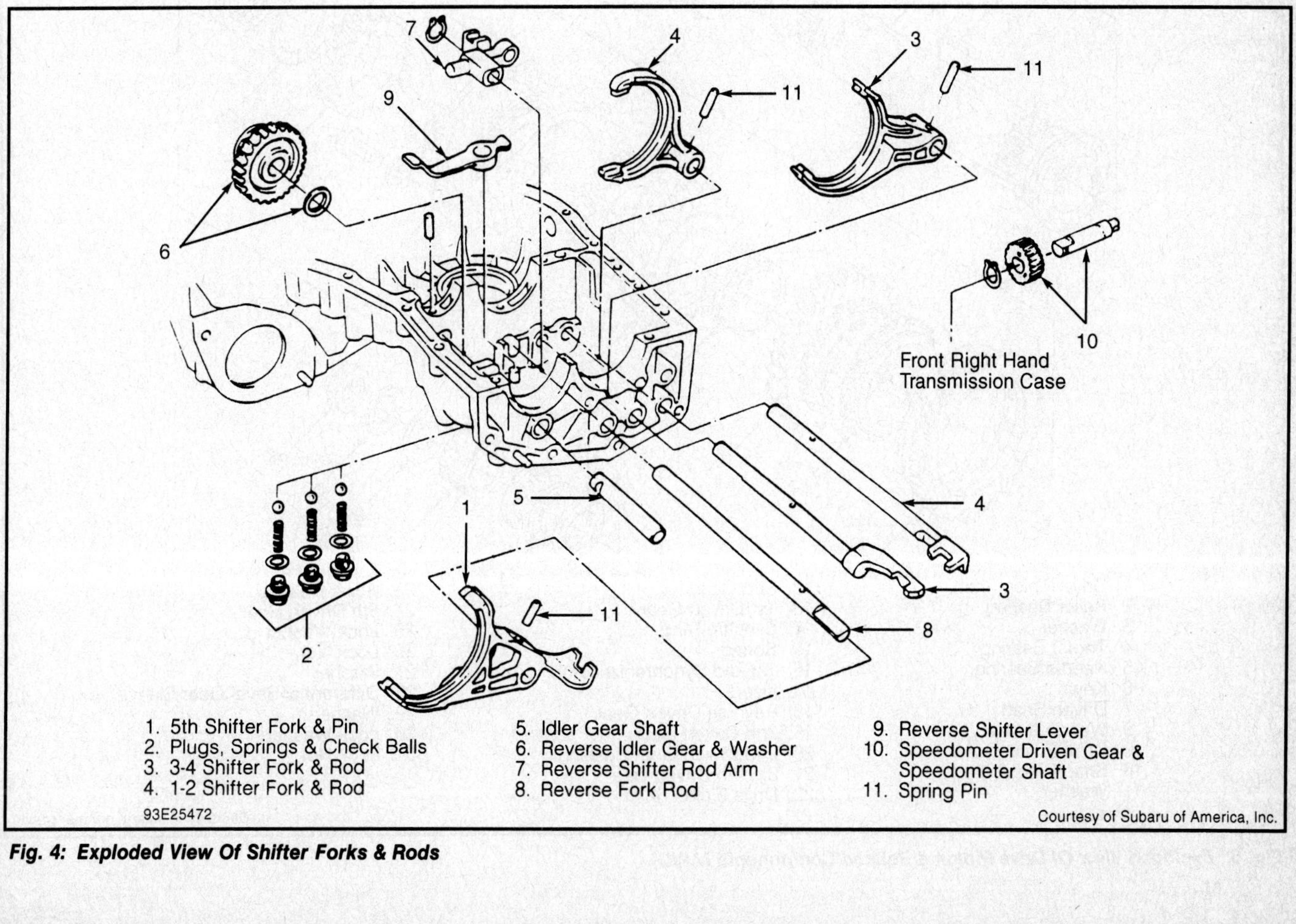

Front Right Hand
Transmission Case

1. 5th Shifter Fork & Pin
2. Plugs, Springs & Check Balls
3. 3-4 Shifter Fork & Rod
4. 1-2 Shifter Fork & Rod

5. Idler Gear Shaft
6. Reverse Idler Gear & Washer
7. Reverse Shifter Rod Arm
8. Reverse Fork Rod

9. Reverse Shifter Lever
10. Speedometer Driven Gear &
    Speedometer Shaft
11. Spring Pin

93E25472

Courtesy of Subaru of America, Inc.

Fig. 4: Exploded View Of Shifter Forks & Rods

2) On all models, remove clutch release lever and bearing. Remove bearing bolts and mainshaft rear plate. Wrap tape around drive shaft splines. Separate transmission case halves. Remove drive pinion shaft, mainshaft, and differential assemblies. Mark roller bearing outer races for reassembly reference. *See Fig. 3.*

3) Drive out spring pin to remove 5th shifter fork. Remove plugs, springs, and check balls. Drive out spring pins. Remove 3rd-4th fork rod and shifter fork, 1st-2nd fork rod, and shifter fork. Remove idler gear shaft, reverse idler gear, and washer. *See Fig. 4.*

4) Remove reverse shifter rod arm. Remove ball, spring, and interlock plunger. Remove rod and reverse shifter lever. Remove interlock plungers from case. Remove differential side retainers. Remove snap ring, speedometer driven gear. Remove vehicle speed sensor, oil seal, speedometer shaft, and washer.

COMPONENT DISASSEMBLY & REASSEMBLY

DRIVE PINION SHAFT (AWD)

Disassembly – Remove lock nut. Remove drive pinion, differential bevel gear sleeve, adjuster washers, thrust bearing, needle bearing, drive pinion collar, drive gear assembly, needle bearing, and thrust bearing. *See Fig. 5.* Press off roller bearing and washer.

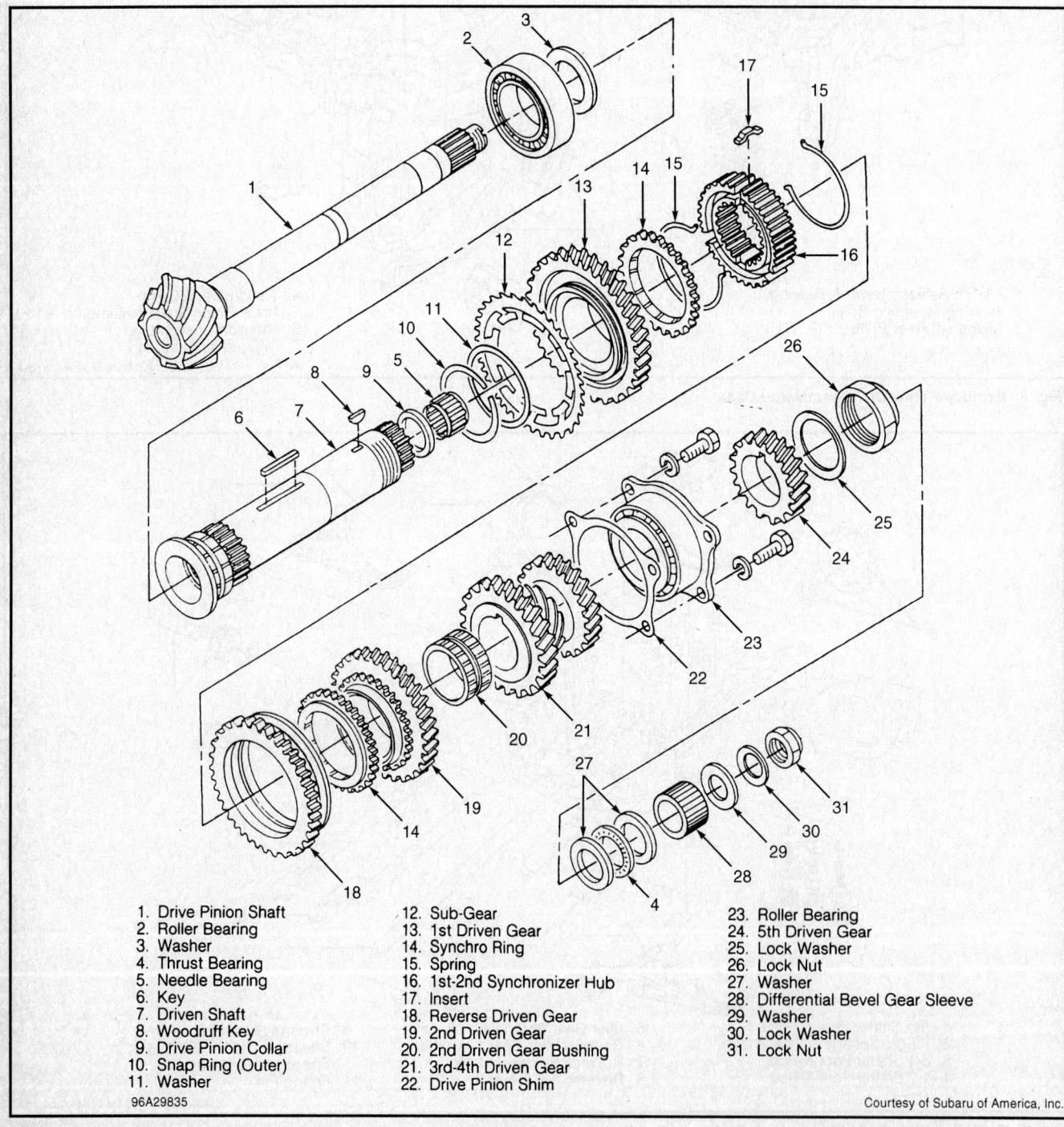

1. Drive Pinion Shaft	12. Sub-Gear	23. Roller Bearing
2. Roller Bearing	13. 1st Driven Gear	24. 5th Driven Gear
3. Washer	14. Synchro Ring	25. Lock Washer
4. Thrust Bearing	15. Spring	26. Lock Nut
5. Needle Bearing	16. 1st-2nd Synchronizer Hub	27. Washer
6. Key	17. Insert	28. Differential Bevel Gear Sleeve
7. Driven Shaft	18. Reverse Driven Gear	29. Washer
8. Woodruff Key	19. 2nd Driven Gear	30. Lock Washer
9. Drive Pinion Collar	20. 2nd Driven Gear Bushing	31. Lock Nut
10. Snap Ring (Outer)	21. 3rd-4th Driven Gear	
11. Washer	22. Drive Pinion Shim	

96A29835

Courtesy of Subaru of America, Inc.

Fig. 5: *Exploded View Of Drive Pinion & Related Components (AWD)*

Reassembly – **1)** Press roller bearing and washer onto drive pinion. Position hole in outer race so it engages locating pin.

2) Install thrust bearing and needle bearing. Install driven gear assembly, drive pinion collar, needle bearing, adjuster washer No. 2, thrust bearing, adjuster washer No. 1, and differential bevel gear sleeve.

3) Select adjuster washer No. 2 so dimension "H" is zero as estimated visually. See Fig. 6. Install washer, lock washer, and lock nut. Tighten lock nut to 81-93 ft. lbs. (110-126 N.m).

4) Measure starting torque. If starting torque is not 2-13 INCH lbs. (.1-1.5 N.m), select and install new adjuster washer No. 1. Recheck starting torque. See ADJUSTER WASHER No. 1 table.

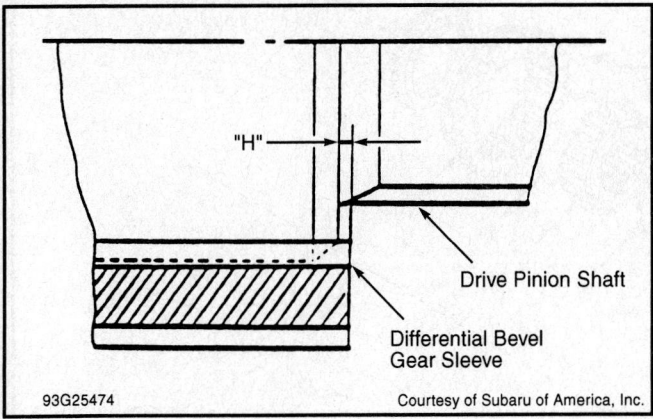

Fig. 6: Selecting Adjuster Washer

ADJUSTER WASHER NO. 1

Part No.	Thickness In. (mm)
803025051	.1545 (3.925)
803025052	.1555 (3.950)
803025053	.1565 (3.975)
803025054	.1575 (4.000)
803025055	.1585 (4.025)
803025056	.1594 (4.050)
803025057	.1604 (4.075)

5) If starting torque is not within specification with new adjuster washer No. 1 installed, select another adjuster washer No. 2. See ADJUSTER WASHER No. 2 table. Recheck starting torque. When starting torque is correct, stake lock nut in 4 places.

ADJUSTER WASHER NO. 2

Part No.	Thickness In. (mm)
803025059	.1516 (3.850)
803025054	.1575 (4.000)
803025058	.1634 (4.150)

DRIVEN GEAR SHAFT (AWD)

NOTE: Cover end of driven shaft with shop towel to prevent damage to needle bearing.

Disassembly – **1)** Unstake and remove lock nut. Remove lock washer. Press off 5th driven gear. Remove key. Press off roller bearing and 3rd-4th driven gear. Remove key.

2) Remove 2nd gear assembly. Press off 1st driven gear and 2nd gear bushing, gear, and hub. Replace gear and hub if necessary. DO NOT disassemble gear and hub unless necessary. If disassembly is required, mark engagement points on all components before disassembly.

Reassembly – **1)** Press 1st driven gear, 1st-2nd synchro ring, gear, and hub onto driven shaft. Note installation orientation for hub. See Fig. 7. Press 2nd driven gear bushing onto driven shaft.

2) Install 2nd driven gear, 1st-2nd synchro ring, and shifting insert onto driven shaft. Align groove in synchro ring with insert. Install key. Press 3rd-4th driven gear onto shaft.

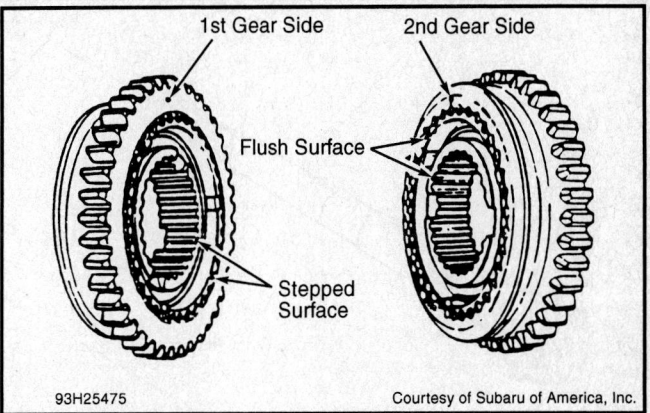

Fig. 7: Installing Hub

3) Press roller bearing onto shaft. Install key. Press 5th driven gear onto shaft. Install lock washer and lock nut. Tighten lock nut to 173-188 ft. lbs. (235-255 N.m). Stake lock nut in 2 places. Using spring scale, verify starting torque is 1-13 INCH lbs. (.1-1.5 N.m). See Fig. 8.

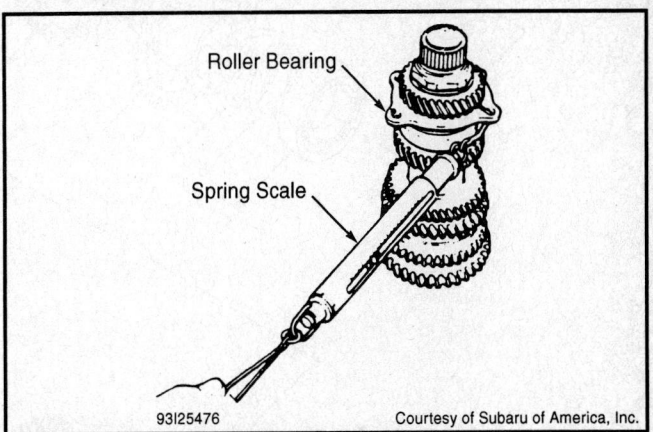

Fig. 8: Measuring Starting Torque

DRIVE PINION ASSEMBLY (FWD)

Disassembly – **1)** Remove lock nut. Press off 5th driven gear. Remove key. See Fig. 9. Press off ball bearing and 3rd-4th driven gear. Remove 2nd driven gear and 3rd-4th driven gear key.

2) Press off 1st driven gear, 2nd gear bushing, gear, and hub assembly. Press off 1st gear bushing, 1st driven gear thrust plate, and roller bearing.

Reassembly – **1)** Press NEW roller bearing and 1st driven gear thrust washer onto shaft. Install 1st-2nd driven gear bushing. Measure outside diameter of 1st-2nd driven gear bushing to select 1st-2nd driven gear. See 1ST-2ND DRIVEN GEAR SELECTION table.

1ST-2ND DRIVEN GEAR SELECTION

1st-2nd Driven Gear Part No.	Bushing Outside Diameter In. (mm)
32230AA120	1.6529-1.6534 (41.983-41.996)
32231AA330	1.6523-1.6528 (41.968-41.982)
32230AA140	1.6517-1.6522 (41.954-41.967)

2) Install 1st driven gear, 1st-2nd synchro ring, insert, gear, and hub assembly. Press on 1st-2nd driven gear bushing. Install 2nd driven gear, 1st-2nd synchro ring, and key. Install 3rd-4th driven gear and ball bearing.

3) Install Woodruff key. Press on 5th driven gear, taking care not to dislocate key. Side of 5th driven gear with groove goes toward rear. Install NEW lock washer and lock nut. Tighten lock nut to 83-91 ft. lbs. (112-124 N.m). Stake lock nut in 2 places.

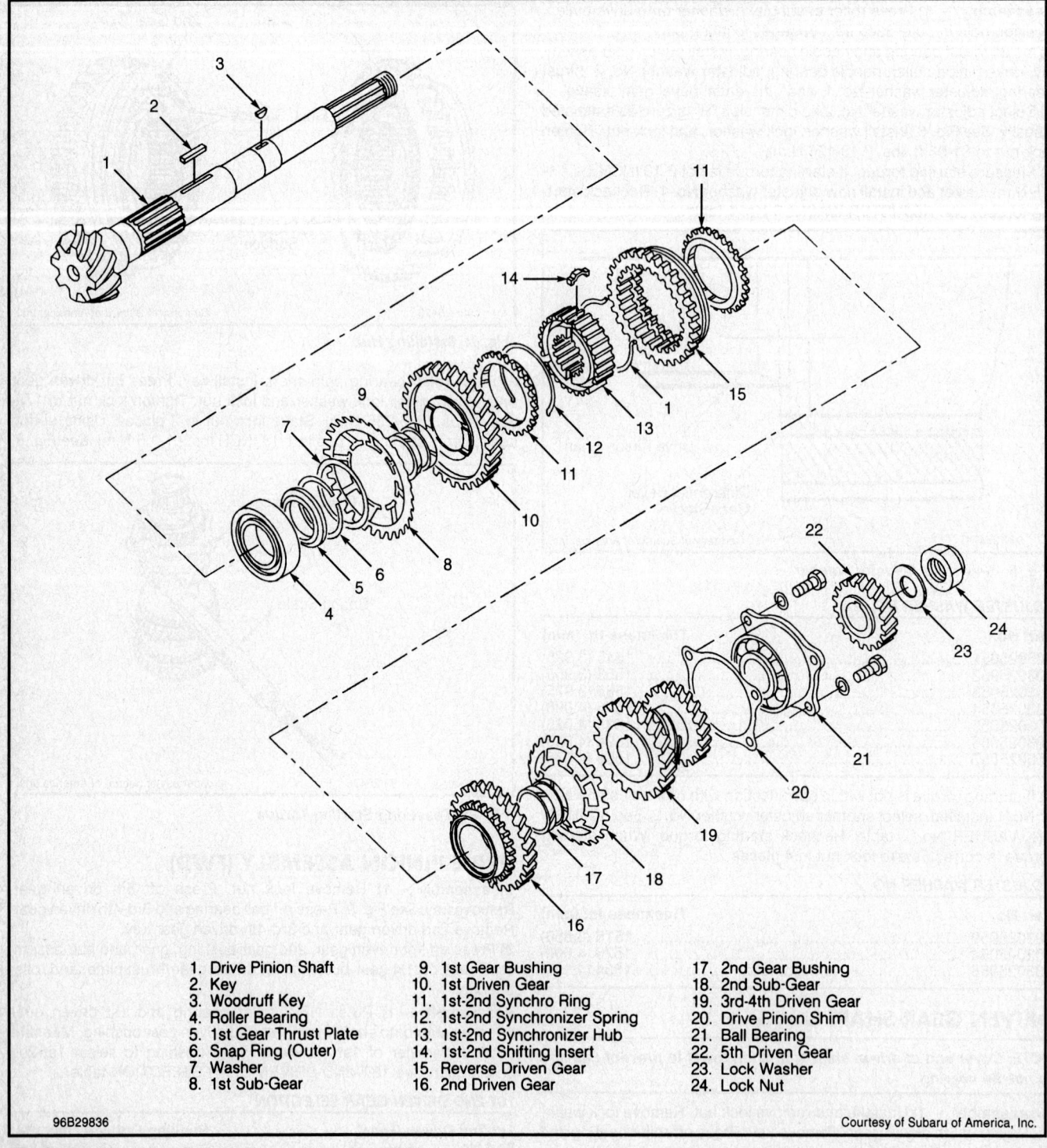

1. Drive Pinion Shaft	9. 1st Gear Bushing	17. 2nd Gear Bushing
2. Key	10. 1st Driven Gear	18. 2nd Sub-Gear
3. Woodruff Key	11. 1st-2nd Synchro Ring	19. 3rd-4th Driven Gear
4. Roller Bearing	12. 1st-2nd Synchronizer Spring	20. Drive Pinion Shim
5. 1st Gear Thrust Plate	13. 1st-2nd Synchronizer Hub	21. Ball Bearing
6. Snap Ring (Outer)	14. 1st-2nd Shifting Insert	22. 5th Driven Gear
7. Washer	15. Reverse Driven Gear	23. Lock Washer
8. 1st Sub-Gear	16. 2nd Driven Gear	24. Lock Nut

96B29836 · Courtesy of Subaru of America, Inc.

Fig. 9: Exploded View Of Drive Pinion Assembly (FWD)

MAINSHAFT

Disassembly – 1) Wrap tape around mainshaft splines. Remove oil seal and needle bearing. *See Fig. 10.* Remove lock nut. Remove lock washer, insert stopper plate, sleeve and hub assembly, No. 2 synchro ring, 5th drive gear, and needle bearing.

2) Press off 5th needle bearing inner race, 5th gear thrust washer, ball bearing, 4th gear thrust washer, 4th drive gear, 5th hub and sleeve assembly, synchro ring, needle bearing, bearing inner race, 3rd drive gear, and 3rd-4th hub and sleeve assembly.

NOTE: Replace hubs and sleeves if necessary. Avoid disassembly of hubs, because they must engage at specific points. If disassembly is required, mark engagement point on splines beforehand.

Reassembly – 1) Install 3rd drive gear, synchro ring, and 3rd-4th hub and sleeve assembly onto main shaft. Align groove on synchro ring with shifting insert. Press 4th needle bearing race onto shaft.

2) Install synchro ring, needle bearing, 4th drive gear, and 4th gear thrust washer. Install thrust washer with grooves toward 4th gear.

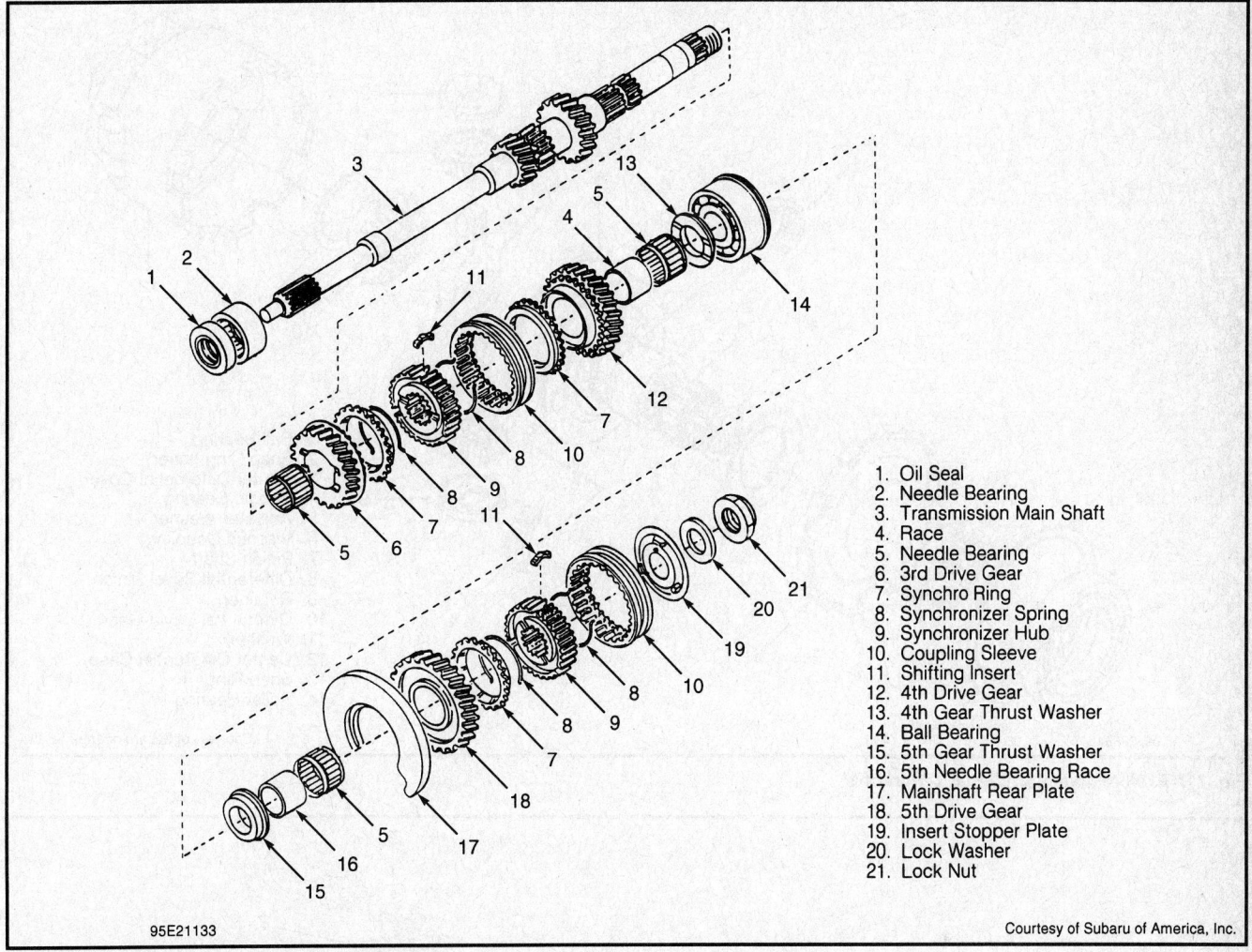

1. Oil Seal
2. Needle Bearing
3. Transmission Main Shaft
4. Race
5. Needle Bearing
6. 3rd Drive Gear
7. Synchro Ring
8. Synchronizer Spring
9. Synchronizer Hub
10. Coupling Sleeve
11. Shifting Insert
12. 4th Drive Gear
13. 4th Gear Thrust Washer
14. Ball Bearing
15. 5th Gear Thrust Washer
16. 5th Needle Bearing Race
17. Mainshaft Rear Plate
18. 5th Drive Gear
19. Insert Stopper Plate
20. Lock Washer
21. Lock Nut

95E21133

Courtesy of Subaru of America, Inc.

Fig. 10: Exploded View Of Mainshaft Assembly

Press ball bearing, 5th gear thrust washer, and 5th needle bearing race onto shaft. Install thrust washer with grooves toward 5th gear.
3) Install needle bearing, 5th drive gear, synchro ring, 5th hub and sleeve assembly, insert stopper plate, and lock washer. Align groove in synchro ring with shifting insert. Ensure pawl of insert stopper plate fits into hole in boss section of 5th hub. Install and tighten lock nut to 83-91 ft. lbs. (112-124 N.m). Stake lock nut in 2 places.

CENTER DIFFERENTIAL (AWD MODELS)

Disassembly – Remove snap ring, center differential cover, snap ring, roller bearing, and viscous coupling. Remove needle bearings, adjuster washer, pinion shaft, bevel pinions, and retainers. Remove side gear and thrust washer. See Fig. 11. Press ball bearing from cover.

Reassembly – 1) Install NEW ball bearing into cover. Install thrust washer with chamfered side facing side gear. Install side gear, pinion shaft, bevel pinions, and retainers. Install viscous coupling and needle bearings. Install adjuster washer with chamfered side facing viscous coupling. Install cover and snap ring.
2) Measure clearance between snap ring and cover. If clearance is not 0-.006" (0-.15 mm), select and install appropriate snap ring. See SNAP RING CLEARANCE table.
3) Measure axial play. If axial play is not .0244-.0339" (.62-.86 mm), select and install appropriate adjuster washer. See ADJUSTER WASHER SELECTION table.

SNAP RING CLEARANCE

Part No.	Thickness – In. (mm)
805100061	.0827 (2.10)
805100062	.0870 (2.21)
805100063	.0913 (2.32)

ADJUSTER WASHER SELECTION

Part No.	Thickness – In. (mm)
803045041	.063 (1.60)
803045042	.071 (1.80)
803045043	.079 (2.00)
803045044	.087 (2.20)
803045045	.094 (2.40)

FRONT DIFFERENTIAL

Disassembly – 1) Remove drive shafts. During reassembly, reinstall each axle drive shaft in same place from which it was removed. See Fig. 12. Remove bolts and hypoid driven gear. Drive pin from differential assembly.
2) Remove pinion shaft, differential bevel pinions, differential bevel gears, and washers. Remove roller bearings.

Reassembly – 1) Install pinions, bevel gears, and washers. Insert pinion shaft. Install washers with chamfered side toward gears.
2) Measure backlash between bevel gears and pinions. Ensure pinion gear tooth contacts adjacent gear teeth during measurement. If backlash is not .005-.007" (.13-.18 mm), select and install appropriate washer. See BEVEL GEAR WASHER SELECTION table.

MANUAL TRANSMISSIONS
Subaru Impreza & Legacy 5-Speed (Cont.)

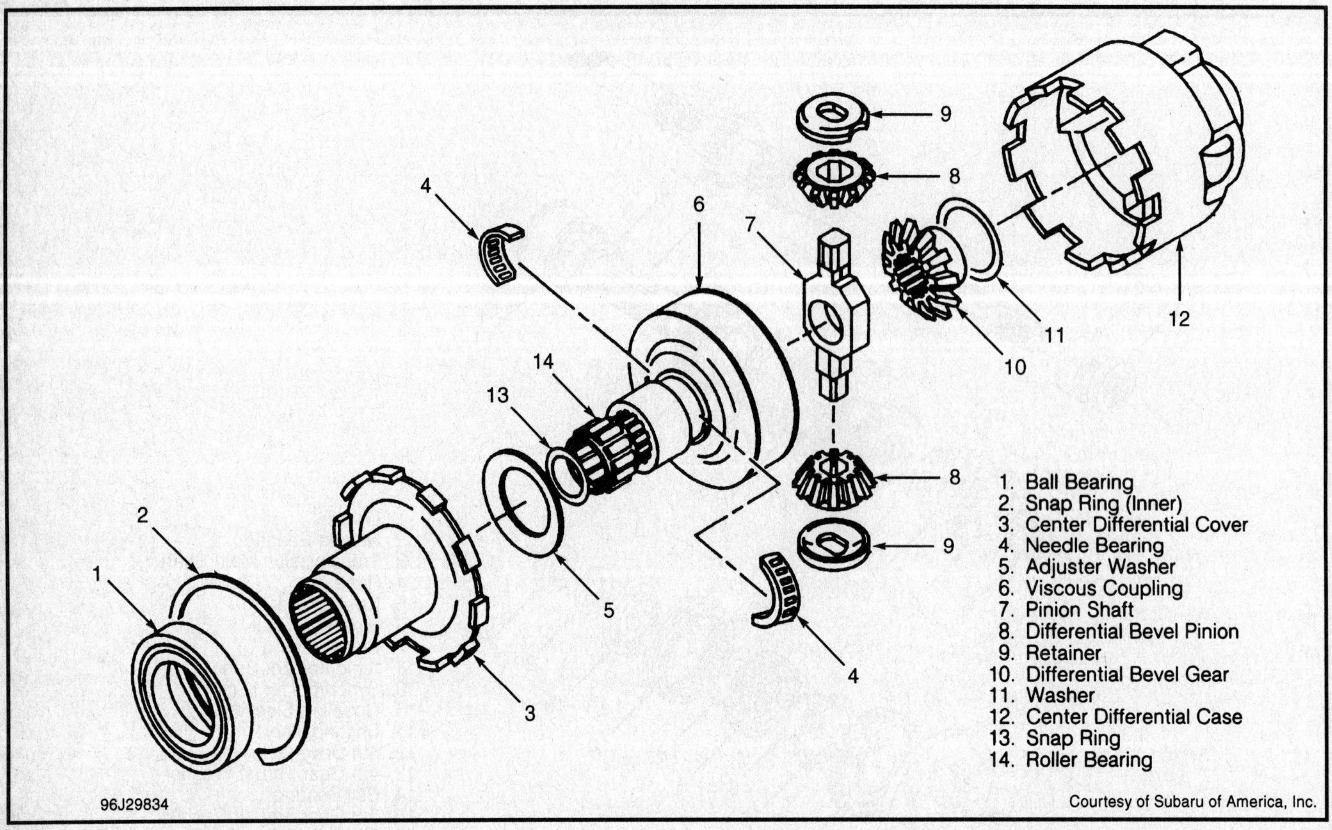
1. Ball Bearing
2. Snap Ring (Inner)
3. Center Differential Cover
4. Needle Bearing
5. Adjuster Washer
6. Viscous Coupling
7. Pinion Shaft
8. Differential Bevel Pinion
9. Retainer
10. Differential Bevel Gear
11. Washer
12. Center Differential Case
13. Snap Ring
14. Roller Bearing
96J29834
Courtesy of Subaru of America, Inc.

Fig. 11: Exploded View Of Center Differential

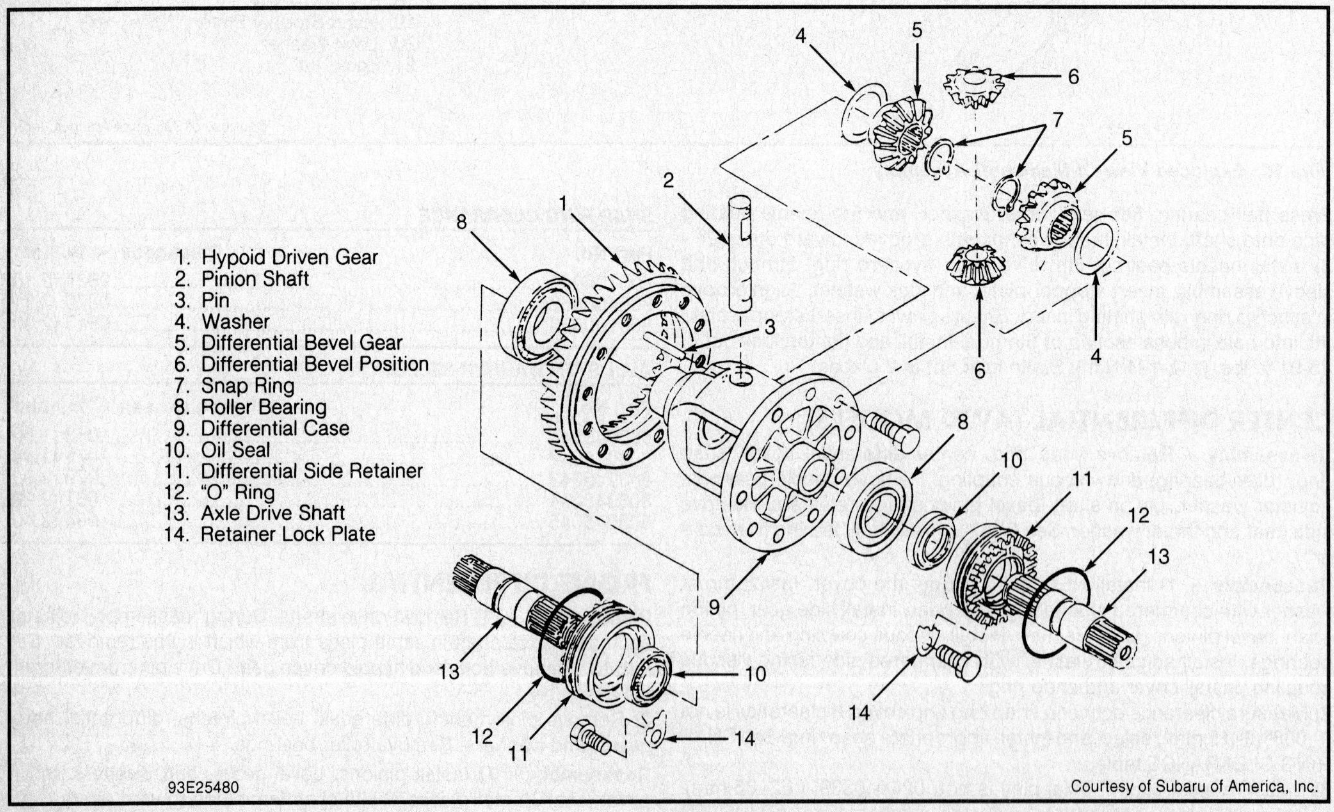
1. Hypoid Driven Gear
2. Pinion Shaft
3. Pin
4. Washer
5. Differential Bevel Gear
6. Differential Bevel Position
7. Snap Ring
8. Roller Bearing
9. Differential Case
10. Oil Seal
11. Differential Side Retainer
12. "O" Ring
13. Axle Drive Shaft
14. Retainer Lock Plate
93E25480
Courtesy of Subaru of America, Inc.

Fig. 12: Exploded View Of Front Differential

BEVEL GEAR WASHER SELECTION

Part No.	Thickness In. (mm)
803038021	.0364-.0374 (.925-.95)
803038022	.0384-.0394 (.975-1.00)
803038023	.0404-.0413 (1.025-1.05)

3) Align pinion shaft hole with differential case hole. Drive and stake pin into position. Press roller bearings into differential case. Install hypoid driven gear. Tighten bolts to 42-49 ft. lbs. (57-67 N.m). Install drive shafts and snap rings. Measure clearance between shafts and case. *See Fig. 13.* If clearance is not 0-.008" (0-.20 mm), select and install appropriate snap ring. See SNAP RING SELECTION table.

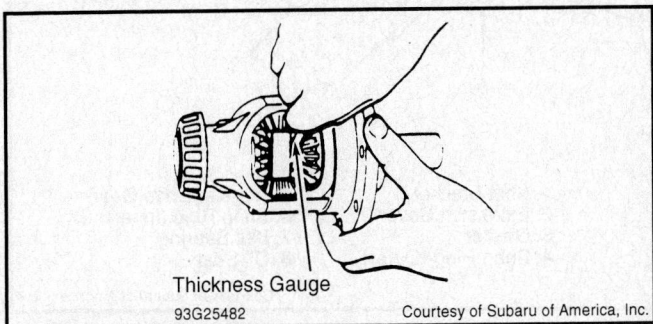

Thickness Gauge

93G25482   Courtesy of Subaru of America, Inc.

Fig. 13: Measuring Drive Shaft Clearance

SNAP RING SELECTION

Part No.	Thickness In. (mm)
805028011	.0413 (1.05)
805028012	.0472 (1.20)

TRANSFER CASE (AWD) & EXTENSION HOUSING

Disassembly – Remove extension housing. *See Fig. 14.* Remove transfer driven gear and center differential as a unit. Remove thrust washer.

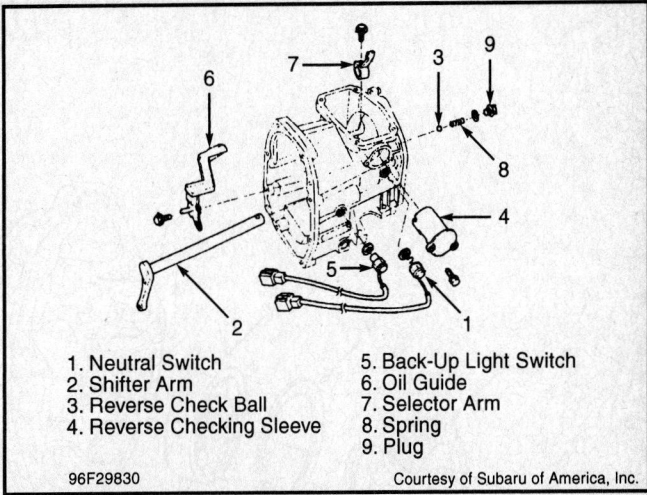

1. Neutral Switch
2. Shifter Arm
3. Reverse Check Ball
4. Reverse Checking Sleeve
5. Back-Up Light Switch
6. Oil Guide
7. Selector Arm
8. Spring
9. Plug

96F29830   Courtesy of Subaru of America, Inc.

Fig. 15: Exploded View Of Transfer Case

Transfer Case Disassembly – Remove neutral switch. Remove shifter arm and selector arm. *See Fig. 15.* Remove plug, spring, and reverse check ball. Remove reverse check sleeve, back-up light switch, and oil guide.

Extension Housing Disassembly – Remove extension cover, gasket, and shift bracket. *See Fig. 16.* Remove outer snap ring, transfer drive shaft, inner snap ring, ball bearing, and oil seal.

Extension Housing Reassembly – **1)** Install NEW oil seal, NEW ball bearing and inner snap ring. Measure clearance between snap ring and outer race of ball bearing. If clearance is not 0-.006" (0-.15 mm), select and install another inner snap ring. See INNER SNAP RING table.

INNER SNAP RING

Part No.	Thickness – In. (mm)
805172071	.070 (1.78)
805172072	.075 (1.90)
805172073	.080 (2.02)

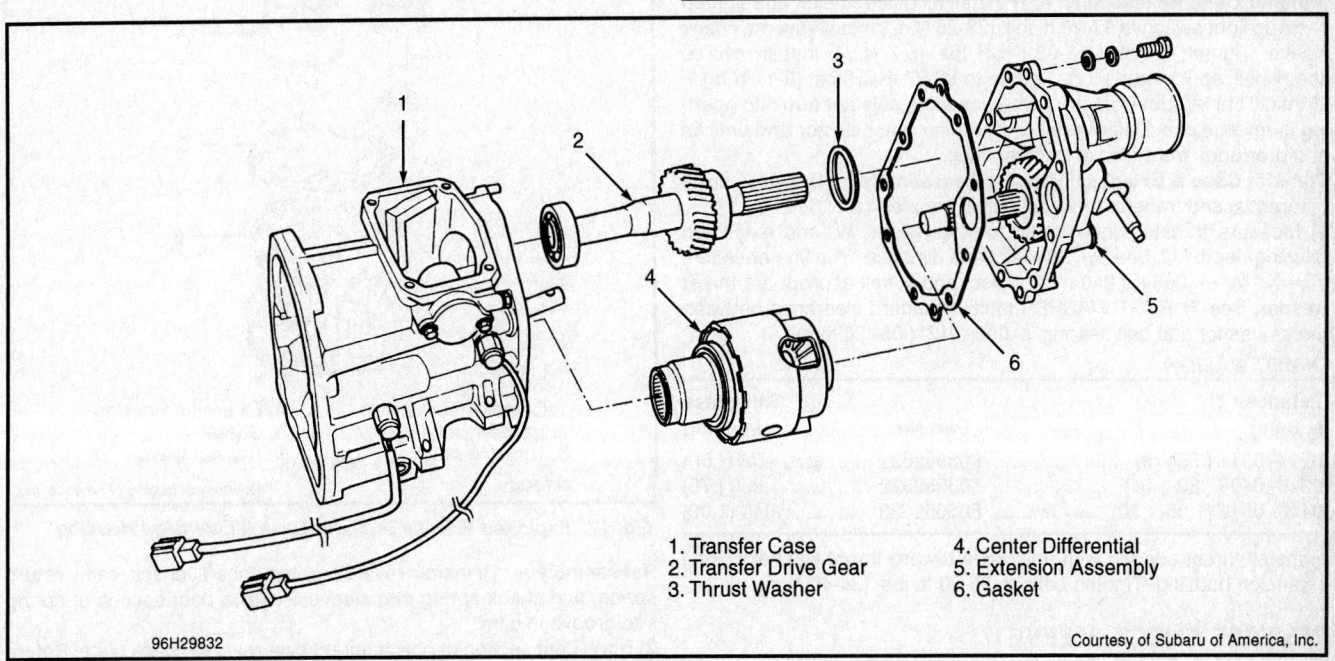

1. Transfer Case
2. Transfer Drive Gear
3. Thrust Washer
4. Center Differential
5. Extension Assembly
6. Gasket

96H29832   Courtesy of Subaru of America, Inc.

Fig. 14: Removing Extension Housing

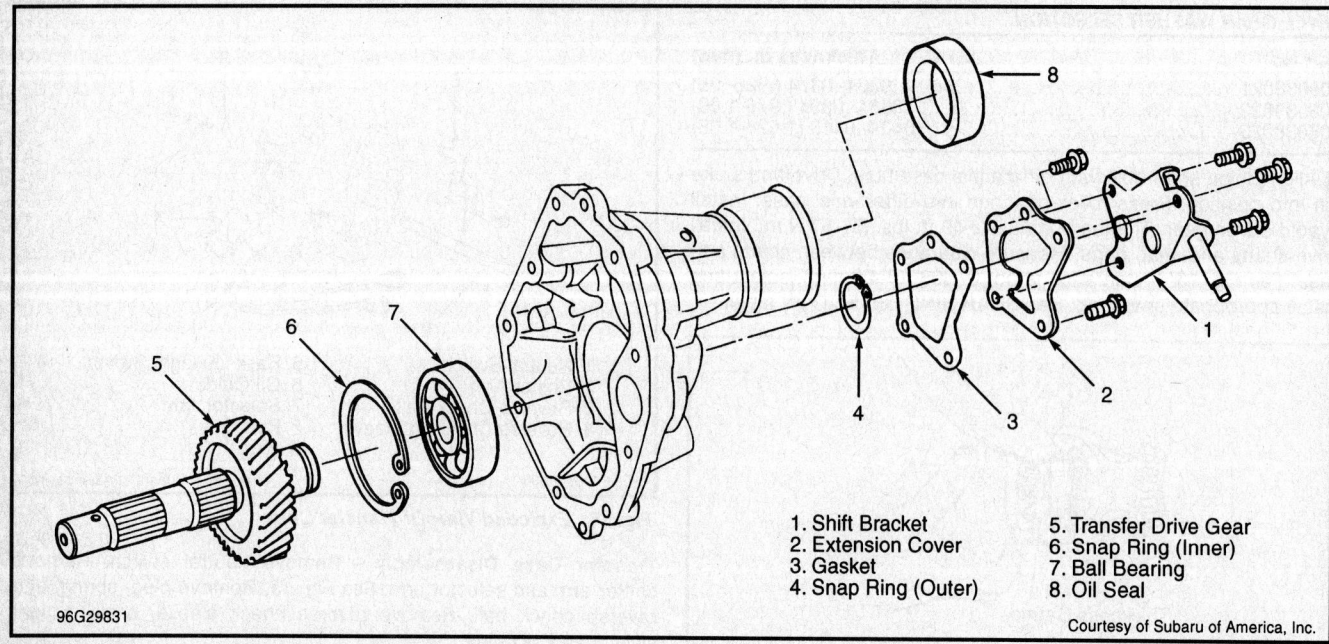

1. Shift Bracket
2. Extension Cover
3. Gasket
4. Snap Ring (Outer)
5. Transfer Drive Gear
6. Snap Ring (Inner)
7. Ball Bearing
8. Oil Seal

96G29831

Courtesy of Subaru of America, Inc.

Fig. 16: Exploded View Of Extension Housing

2) Press transfer drive gear into ball bearing. Install outer snap ring. Measure clearance between snap ring and bearing inner race. If clearance is not 0-.006" (0-.15 mm), select and install another outer snap ring. See OUTER SNAP RING table.

OUTER SNAP RING

Part No.	Thickness – In. (mm)
805030041	.060 (1.53)
805030042	.065 (1.65)
805030043	.070 (1.77)

3) Install NEW gasket, extension cover, and shift bracket. Tighten bolts to 17-20 ft. lbs. (23-26 N.m). Install NEW oil seal.

Transfer Case Reassembly – 1) Install oil guide. Install and tighten back-up light switch to 17-20 ft. lbs. (23-26 N.m). Install reverse check sleeve. Tighten bolts to 53-62 INCH lbs. (6-7 N.m). Install reverse check ball, spring, and plug. Tighten to 80-97 INCH lbs. (9-11 N.m).

2) Install shifter arm from front while inserting selector arm into opening in reverse check sleeve. Insert shaft through selector arm until its end protrudes from rear of transfer case.

Transfer Case & Extension Housing Reassembly – 1) Install center differential and transfer drive shaft into transfer case. See Fig. 17.

2) Measure transfer driven gear bearing height "W" and extension housing depth "X". See Fig. 18. Calculate distance "Y" using equation: $Y = X - W + .0094$ (.240 mm). Select and install appropriate thrust washer. See THRUST WASHER table. Standard clearance between thrust washer and ball bearing is .002-.012" (.05-.30 mm).

THRUST WASHER

Distance "Y" In. (mm)	Part No.	Thickness In. (mm)
.0217-.0311 (.55-.79)	803052021	.020 (.50)
.0315-.0409 (.80-1.04)	803052022	.030 (.75)
.0413-.0512 (1.05-1.30)	803052023	.040 (1.00)

4) Install thrust bearing with roller side toward thrust washer. Install extension housing. Tighten bolts to 25-30 ft. lbs. (34-40 N.m).

REVERSE CHECK SLEEVE

Disassembly – Remove snap ring, reverse check plate, and reverse check spring with cam. See Fig. 19. Remove reverse return spring, reverse detent shaft, and "O" ring.

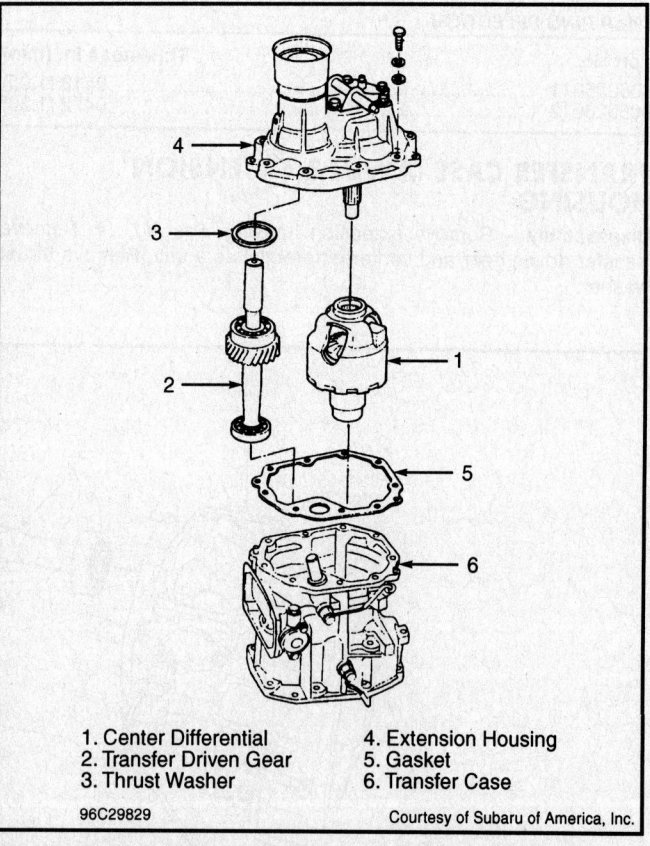

1. Center Differential
2. Transfer Driven Gear
3. Thrust Washer
4. Extension Housing
5. Gasket
6. Transfer Case

96C29829

Courtesy of Subaru of America, Inc.

Fig. 17: Exploded View Of Transfer Case & Extension Housing

Reassembly – 1) Install reverse detent shaft, check cam, return spring, and check spring into sleeve. Position bent section of spring into groove in cam.

2) Hook bent section of check spring over reverse check plate. Rotate cam so that protrusion on cam is at opening in plate. Install plate onto reverse check sleeve. Install snap ring. Install "O" ring into sleeve groove.

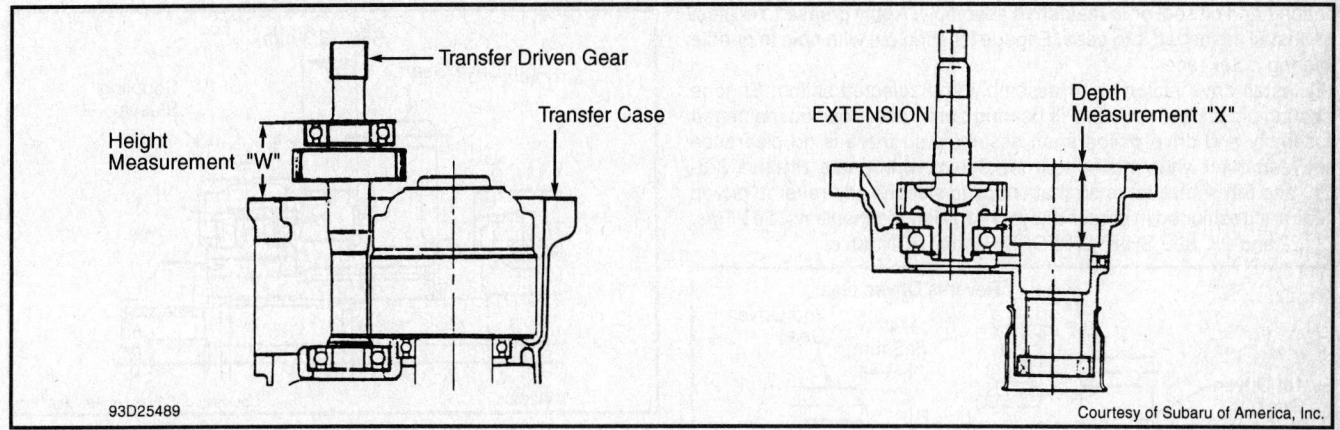

Fig. 18: Determining Thrust Washer Thickness

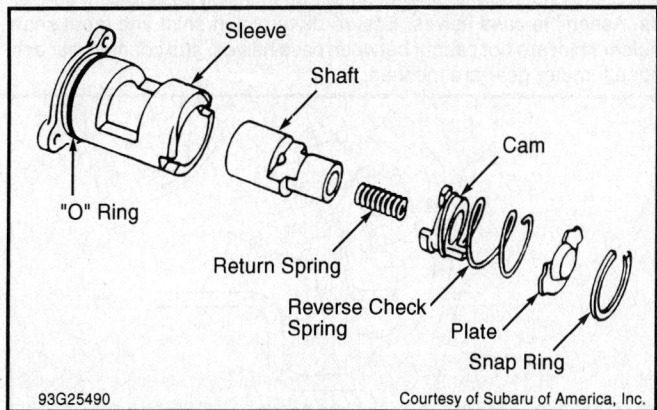

Fig. 19: Exploded View Of Reverse Check Sleeve

TRANSAXLE REASSEMBLY

1) Install interlock plungers between 1st-2nd and 3rd-4th fork rod holes, and between 3rd-4th and reverse fork rod holes. Install reverse shifter lever, reverse idler gear, and reverse idler shaft. Drive in pin.

2) Install reverse arm fork spring, ball, and interlock plunger into reverse fork rod arm. Insert reverse fork rod into hole in reverse fork rod arm. Install snap ring. Install check ball, spring, gasket, and plug. Tighten to 13-15 ft. lbs. (18-21 N.m).

3) Position reverse shifter rod toward reverse side. Measure clearance between reverse idler gear and transmission case. If clearance is not .236-.295" (6.0-7.5 mm), select and install appropriate reverse shifter lever. See REVERSE SHIFTER LEVER SELECTION table.

REVERSE SHIFTER LEVER SELECTION

Part No.	Number	Remarks
32820AA000	0	Farther From Case
32820AA010	-	Standard
32820AA020	2	Closer To Case Wall

4) Set reverse shifter rod to Neutral position. Measure clearance between reverse idler gear and case. If clearance is not 0-.020" (0-.50 mm), select and install washer(s). See WASHER SELECTION table.

WASHER SELECTION

Part No.	Thickness – In. (mm)
803020151	.016 (0.40)
803020152	.043 (1.10)
803020153	.059 (1.50)
803020154	.075 (1.90)
803020155	.091 (2.30)

5) Install 1st-2nd shifter fork and fork rod into case. Align holes in rod and fork. Drive in pin. Install interlock plunger into 3rd-4th fork rod. Install together with 3rd-4th shifter fork into case. Align holes in rod and fork. Drive in pin.

6) Install 5th shifter fork onto reverse fork rod. Align holes. Drive in pin. Install check balls, springs, gaskets, and plugs. Tighten to 13-15 ft. lbs. (18-21 N.m). Install washer, speedometer shaft, vehicle speed sensor, oil seal, speedometer driven gear, and snap ring.

7) Upper number on drive pinion is match number for mating gear. Lower number is for shim adjustment. If no lower number is shown, value is zero.

8) Loosen bolts on Gauge Assembly (499917500). Adjust until scale indicates 0.5 when plate end and scale end are even.

9) Install drive pinion shaft assembly, without shim, into right case. Tighten bearing bolts to 19-24 ft. lbs. (26-32 N.m). Position gauge by inserting gauge pin into case hole. Slide gauge toward pinion. Measure distance at point where it matches with end of drive pinion. See Fig. 20.

10) Determine thickness of drive pinion shim by adding or subtracting value on drive pinion shaft to value indicated on gauge. Add if pinion shaft value is prefixed with (+), or subtract if prefixed with (–). Select one to 3 shims for value determined. See DRIVE PINION SHIM table. Remove drive pinion shaft from case.

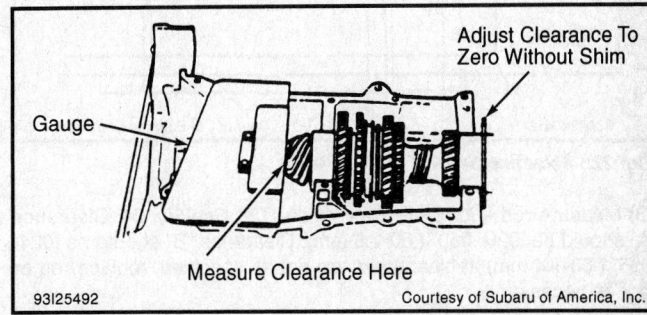

Fig. 20: Determining Drive Pinion Shim Thickness

DRIVE PINION SHIM

Part No.	Thickness – In. (mm)
32295AA031	.006 (0.15)
32295AA041	.007 (0.17)
32295AA051	.008 (0.20)
32295AA061	.009 (0.22)
32295AA071	.010 (0.25)
32295AA081	.011 (0.27)
32295AA091	.012 (0.30)
32295AA101	.020 (0.50)

11) Wrap tape around drive axle splines. Install differential assembly into left hand case. Wrap tape around mainshaft splines. Install needle bearing and oil seal onto mainshaft assembly. Apply grease to oil seal lip. Install mainshaft into case. Engage locating pin with hole in needle bearing outer race.

12) Install drive pinion shaft assembly and selected shims. Engage locating pin of case with hole in bearing outer race. Position mainshaft assembly and drive pinion shaft assembly so there is no clearance between them when moved to front. Select appropriate 1st-2nd, 3rd-4th, and 5th shifter forks so that coupling sleeves and reverse driven gear are positioned in center of synchronizing mechanisms. *See Figs. 21, 22 and 23.* See SHIFTER FORK SELECTION table.

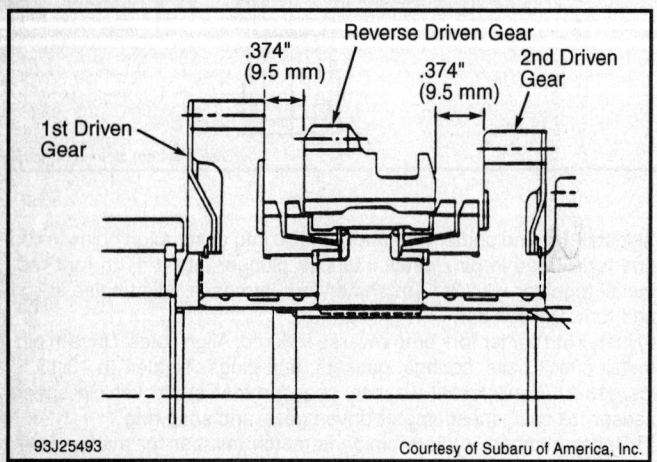

Fig. 21: Selecting 1st-2nd Shifter Fork

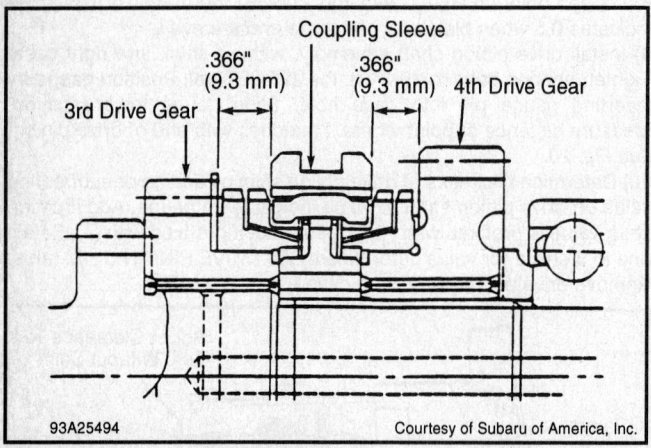

Fig. 22: Selecting 3rd-4th Shifter Fork

13) Measure rod end clearances "A" and "B". *See Fig. 24.* Clearance "A" should be .020-.059" (.50-1.5 mm). Clearance "B" should be .024-.055" (.60-1.4 mm). If clearances are not as specified, replace rod or fork as necessary.

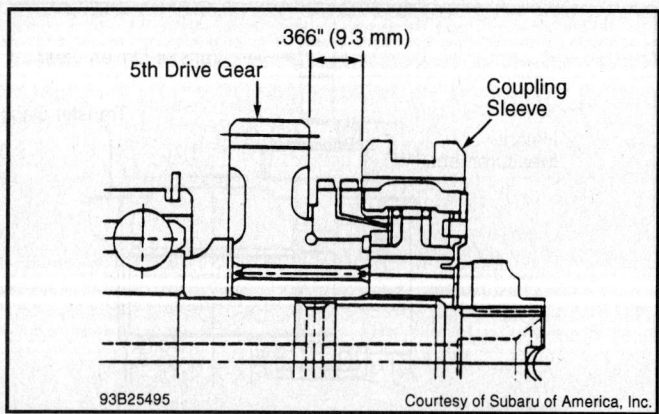

Fig. 23: Selecting 5th Shifter Fork

14) Clean and apply liquid gasket to transmission case mating surfaces. Assemble case halves. Ensure drive pinion shim and input shaft holder shim are not caught between case halves, and countergear and speedometer gear are meshed.

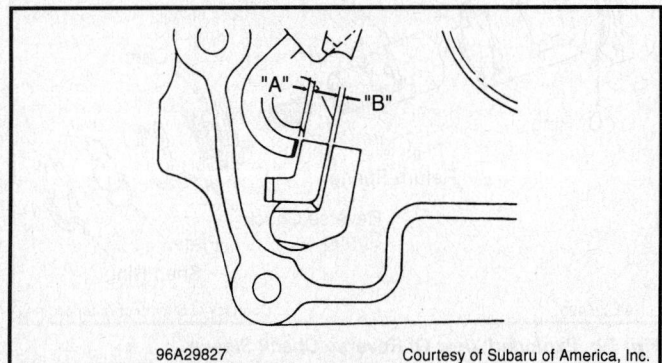

Fig. 24: Measuring Rod End Clearance

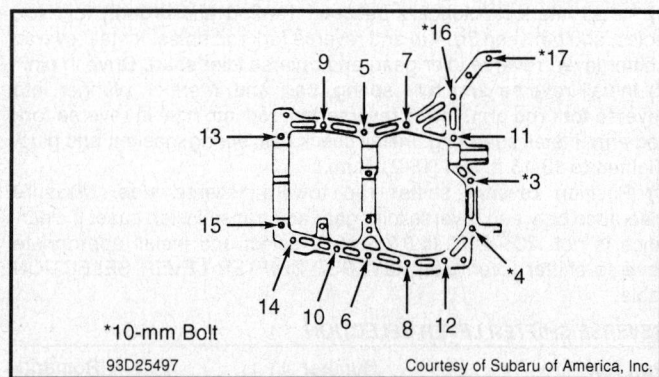

Fig. 25: Case Bolt Tightening Sequence

SHIFTER FORK SELECTION

1st-2nd Shifter Fork			3rd-4th Shifter Fork			5th Shifter Fork		
Part No.	No.	Remarks	Part No.	No.	Remarks	Part No.	No.	Remarks
32804AA060	1	Moves .008 (.20 mm) in closer to 1st gear	32810AA060	1	Moves .008 (.20 mm) in closer to 4th gear	32812AA060	1	Moves .008 (.20 mm) in closer to 5th gear
32804AA070	-	Positions in the center	32810AA070	-	Positions in the center	32812AA070	-	Positions in the center
32804AA080	3	Moves .008 (.20 mm) in closer to 2nd gear	32810AA100	3	Moves .008 (.20 mm) in closer to 3rd gear	32812AA100	3	Moves .008 (.20 mm) in closer to 5th gear

15) Insert transmission case bolts from bottom. Tighten nuts on top. Tighten 8-mm bolts to 17-19 ft. lbs. (23-26 N.m), and 10-mm bolts to 27-31 ft. lbs. (36-42 N.m) in sequence. *See Fig. 25.* Tighten ball bearing bolts to 19-24 ft. lbs. (26-32 N.m).

16) Mount transmission with left side down. Install Weight (399780104) onto bearing cup. Screw retainer into left case from bottom. Install Handle (499927100) onto main shaft.

17) Shift transmission into 4th or 5th gear. Rotate shaft several times. Screw in retainer while turning handle until resistance occurs. This is contact point of hypoid gear and drive pinion shaft.

18) Remove weight. Screw in retainer, without "O" ring, into upper side. Stop when resistance occurs. Backlash between hypoid gear and drive pinon is now zero. Install lock plates. Loosen retainer on lower side by 1 1/2 notches. Tighten upper side retainer by same amount to adjust backlash.

19) Tighten upper side retainer one notch to apply preload to roller bearing. Temporarily tighten upper and lower lock plates. Rotate mainshaft 12-15 times while tapping retainer lightly to seat bearings.

20) Install dial gauge through oil drain hole so plunger contacts tooth surface at right angle. Backlash should be .005-.007" (.13-.18 mm). If backlash is outside specified range, rotate upper retainer to adjust.

21) Apply thin coat of Red lead to both tooth surfaces of 3 or 4 teeth of hypoid gear. Rotate mainshaft until definite contact pattern appears. *See Fig. 26.*

22) Mark retainers and lock plates. Loosen retainers until "O" ring grooves appear. Install "O" rings into grooves. Retighten retainers to marked positions. Tighten lock plate bolts to 16-20 ft. lbs. (22-27 N.m).

23) Tap end of mainshaft lightly to ensure zero clearance between main case and bearing. Measure bearing protrusion "A" from surface. *See Fig. 27.* Select and install mainshaft rear plate. See MAINSHAFT REAR PLATE table. Install clutch release lever and bearing.

Condition	Contact Pattern	Adjustment
Proper contact	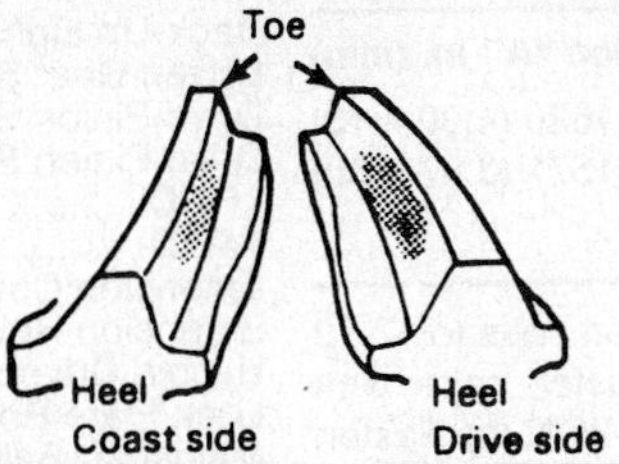	
Backlash is too large.	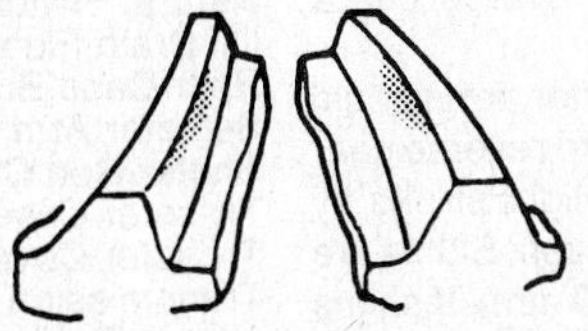	Reduce the backlash.
Backlash is too small.	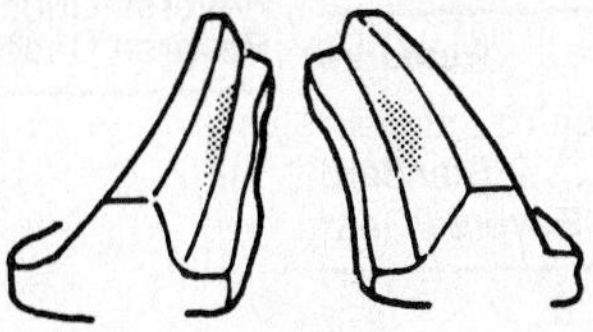	Increase the backlash.
Adjusting shim (drive gear shim) thickness is too large.	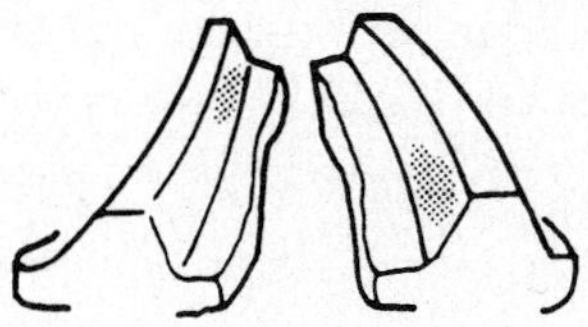	Reduce the thickness of drive gear shim.
Adjusting shim (drive gear shim) thickness is too small.	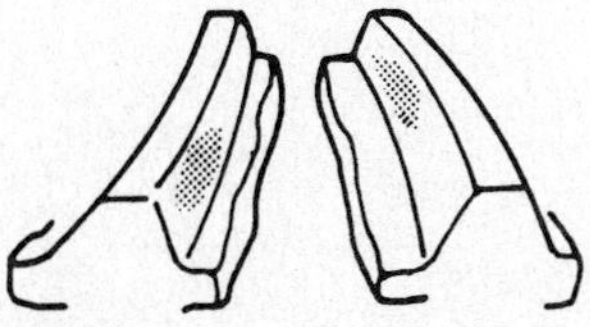	Increase the thickness of drive gear shim.

93E25498

Courtesy of Subaru of America, Inc.

Fig. 26: Determining Gear Tooth Contact Pattern

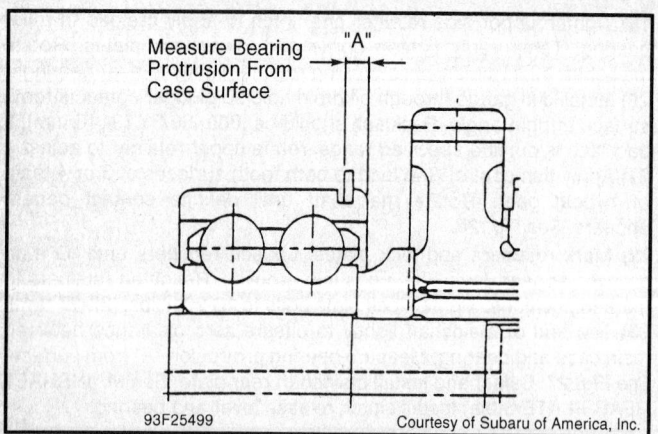

Fig. 27: Measuring Ball Bearing Protrusion

MAINSHAFT REAR PLATE [1]

Part No.	Ident.	Dimension "A" In. (mm)
32294AA040	1	.1575-.1626 (4.00-4.13)
32294AA050	2	.1524-.1571 (3.87-4.00)

[1] – Use appropriate plate for measured dimension "A".

24) On FWD model, install rear case assembly. Tighten bolts to 17-19 ft. lbs. (23-26 N.m). On AWD model, install transfer case with extension housing. Tighten bolts to 17-19 ft. lbs. (23-26 N.m). Fasten selector arm to shifter arm with shifter fork screw. Ensure shifter arm engages rod pawl, and selector arm engages with reverse check sleeve.

25) On all models, shift transmission into 3rd gear. Shifter arm should move easily toward 1st-2nd gear side, but heavily toward reverse gear side. Adjust so that heavy stroke is a little more than light stroke by installing adjuster shim between sleeve assembly and case. Shims are available in thicknesses of .006" (.15 mm) and .012" (.30 mm). If shims alone do not adjust clearance, replace reverse detent shaft. See REVERSE DETENT SHAFT table.

REVERSE DETENT SHAFT

Part No.	Mark	Remarks
32188AA020	"A"	Closer To 1st Gear
32188AA002	None Or "B"	Standard
32188AA030	"C"	Closer To Reverse Gear

26) Set shifter arm to 5th gear position, and then to reverse gear to verify operation of reverse check mechanism. Verify arm returns to Neutral when released from Reverse position. If arm does not return to Neutral, replace reverse check plate. See REVERSE CHECK PLATE table. Install transfer cover. Tighten bolts to 10.5-12.7 ft. lbs. (14.2-17.2 N.m).

REVERSE CHECK PLATE

Part No.	Number	Angle "B"	Remarks
32189AA000	0	28°	Closer To 5th
32189AA010	1	31°	Closer To 5th
32189AA020	2	34°	Standard
32189AA030	3	37°	Closer To Reverse
32189AA040	4	40°	Closer To Reverse

TORQUE SPECIFICATIONS
TORQUE SPECIFICATIONS

Application	Ft. Lbs. (N.m)
Back-Up Light Switch	17-19 (23-26)
Driven Gear Shaft Lock Nut (4WD)	173-188 (235-255)
Drive Pinion Shaft Bearing Bolts	19-24 (26-32)
Drive Pinion Shaft Lock Nut	
FWD	83-91 (112-124)
4WD	81-93 (110-126)
Extension Cover Bolts	17-19 (23-26)
Extension Housing Bolts	25-30 (34-40)
Hypoid Driven Gear Bolts	42-49 (57-67)
Lock Plate Bolts	16-19 (22-26)
Mainshaft Ball Bearing Bolts	19-24 (26-32)
Mainshaft Lock Nut	83-91 (112-124)
Neutral Switch	17-19 (23-26)
Oil Drain Plug	30-35 (41-47)
Rear Case Bolts	17-19 (23-26)
Selector Arm Bolt	14-16 (18-21)
Shifter Rod Check Ball Plugs	13-15 (18-21)
Transfer Case Bolts (4WD)	17-19 (23-26)
Transfer Cover Bolts (4WD)	10-13 (14-18)
Transmission Main Case	
8-mm Bolts	17-19 (23-26)
10-mm Bolts	27-31 (36-42)
	INCH Lbs. (N.m)
Reverse Check Ball Plug	80-97 (9-11)
Reverse Check Sleeve Bolts	53-62 (6-7)

Samurai

APPLICATION & LABOR TIMES

APPLICATION & LABOR TIMES

Vehicle Application	Labor Times		Series
	[1] R & I	[2] Overhaul	
1995 Samurai	3.3	5.7	5-Speed

[1] – Removal and installation of transmission from vehicle chassis.
[2] – Bench overhaul time for transmission. DOES NOT include removal and installation.

IDENTIFICATION

An identification tag is attached to the side of the transmission case.

LUBRICATION & ADJUSTMENTS

See appropriate MANUAL TRANSMISSION SERVICING article in TRANSMISSION SERVICING section.

TROUBLE SHOOTING

See GENERAL TROUBLE SHOOTING article in this section.

REMOVAL & INSTALLATION

See appropriate MANUAL TRANSMISSION REMOVAL article in TRANSMISSION SERVICING section.

TRANSMISSION DISASSEMBLY

1) Remove clutch release bearing and spring. Remove clutch release shaft. Remove clutch release bushings from housing. Using 3 bolts (6 mm), remove input shaft retainer. Remove shifter housing bolts. Remove reverse shift rim bolt. Remove shifter housing.
2) Remove bolts and separate case halves. Remove mainshaft assembly. Remove reverse gear shaft and gear. Remove countershaft rear bearing. Remove countershaft 5th gear and reverse gear. Remove snap ring from countershaft. Remove countershaft with a hydraulic press. *See Fig. 1.*

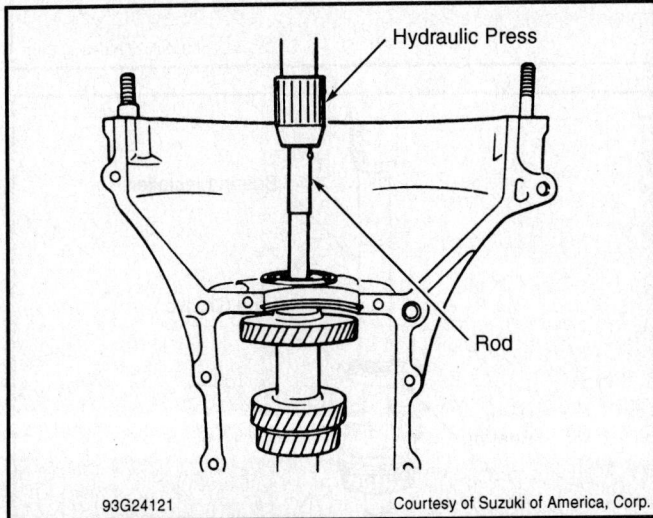

93G24121   Courtesy of Suzuki of America, Corp.

Fig. 1: Removing Countershaft

3) Using puller, remove bearing. Carefully remove input shaft from mainshaft. DO NOT allow high-speed hub assembly synchronizer to fall. Remove high-speed synchronizer sleeve retaining snap ring. Remove sleeve hub, 3rd driven gear and needle bearing from mainshaft. Remove rear bearing retaining snap ring from mainshaft. *See Fig. 2.*

4) Using puller, remove rear bearing. Remove 5th gear washer, ball and 5th gear. Remove 5th gear synchronizer ring and needle bearing. Remove reverse synchronizer hub retaining snap ring. Remove reverse synchronizer hub, reverse gear and needle bearing. Using a hydraulic press, remove bearing washer and reverse gear bushing. Remove ball and press center bearing from mainshaft.

NOTE: Be careful not to lose ball during disassembly. DO NOT remove ball bearing with bearing washer and reverse gear bushing.

5) Remove 1st gear, needle bearing and washer (DO NOT lose ball during disassembly), synchronizer ring and spring from mainshaft. Using a hydraulic press, remove 1st gear bushing, synchronizer hub, ring, spring, 2nd gear and 2nd gear bearing.
6) Ensure all shift fork shafts are in neutral position. Remove yoke pin from each shift fork. DO NOT drive pin out too far or case damage could occur. Carefully remove each shaft from case. Remove yoke pin from each shift yoke. DO NOT allow locating balls and springs to jump out of holes. Remove forks and shaft.

CLEANING & INSPECTION

1) Check all parts for wear or damage. Replace any damaged or worn parts. Ensure all mating parts engage and disengage smoothly. Check clearance between each shift fork and sleeve. If clearance exceeds .039" (1.00 mm), replace worn part. Check clearance between synchronizer ring and cone.
2) Fit synchronizer ring to cone of each gear and measure clearance between bordering teeth. See SYNCHRONIZER CLEARANCE SPECIFICATIONS table. If clearance is not as specified, replace worn or damaged synchronizer. Check synchronizer ring key slot width. If width is not .398-.409" (10.11-10.39 mm), replace synchronizer ring.

SYNCHRONIZER CLEARANCE SPECIFICATIONS

Application	In. (mm)
Low & High-Speed	
Standard	.039-.055 (1.00-1.40)
Service Limit (Minimum)	.020 (.51)
5th Speed	
Standard	.047-.063 (1.19-1.60)
Service Limit (Minimum)	.020 (.51)

3) Install synchronizer assembly on mainshaft. Push in and twist each synchronizer. If 1/3 mesh between ring and gear cone does not occur, replace entire synchronizer assembly. *See Fig. 3.*
4) Check fork shaft locating springs. Free length should be .826-1.004" (21.00-25.50 mm). If not, replace springs. Check radial clearance between sliding yoke and bushing bore. If standard clearance is not .0010-.0035" (.025-.089 mm) or service limit of .0078" (.198 mm) is not met, replace bushing and sliding yoke together. DO NOT replace bushing only.

TRANSMISSION REASSEMBLY

NOTE: Apply recommended lubricant to each part before installing. Install NEW snap rings. DO NOT reuse old snap rings.

1) Install 2nd gear bearing, gear, spring, synchronizer ring, low-speed synchronizer hub and sleeve onto mainshaft. Ensure synchronizer sleeve is properly installed and keys fit snugly in slots. Using a hydraulic press, install low gear bushing.
2) Install low gear needle bearing, spring, synchronizer ring, low gear ball and washer on mainshaft. Ensure ball fits into hole and slot in washer is positioned over ball. Using Bearing Installer (09925-18010), place center bearing onto mainshaft with ring groove facing up. *See Fig. 4.*
3) Install ball and washer with chamfered side facing center bearing. Ensure slot in washer is over ball. While preventing ball from falling out, press reverse gear bushing on shaft with bearing installer. Install reverse gear bearing, reverse gear, reverse synchronizer hub and sleeve.

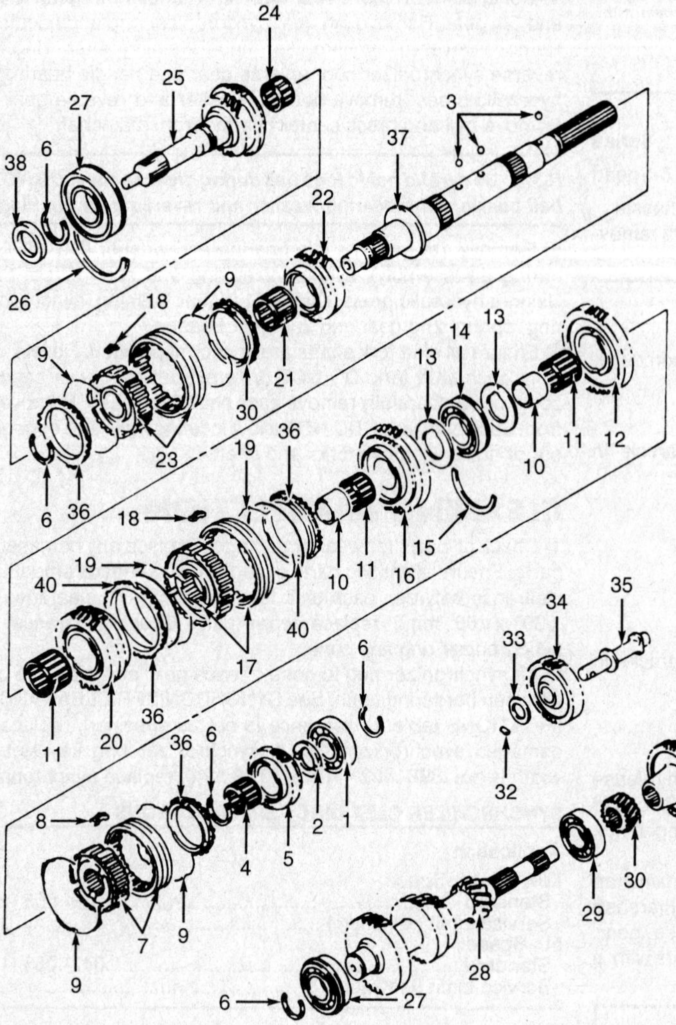

1. Mainshaft Rear Bearing
2. 5th Gear Washer
3. Mainshaft Washer Ball
4. 5th Gear Needle Bearing
5. 5th Gear
6. Snap Ring
7. Synchronizer Reverse Hub
8. Synchronizer Key
9. Synchronizer Spring
10. Gear Bushing
11. Needle Bearing
12. Reverse Gear
13. Mainshaft Bearing Washer
14. Mainshaft Bearing
15. "C" Ring
16. Low Gear
17. Synchronizer Low-Speed Hub
18. Synchronizer Key
19. Synchronizer Spring
20. 2nd Gear
21. 3rd Gear Needle Bearing
22. 3rd Gear
23. High-Speed Synchronizer Hub
24. Input Shaft Bearing
25. Input Shaft
26. "C" Ring
27. Front Bearing
28. Countershaft
29. Center Bearing
30. Reverse Gear
31. Countershaft 5th Gear
32. Pin
33. Washer
34. Reverse Idler Gear
35. Reverse Gear Shaft
36. Ring
37. Mainshaft
38. Oil Seal
39. Rear Bearing
40. Spring

93H24122

Courtesy of Suzuki of America, Corp.

Fig. 2: Exploded View Of Suzuki 5-Speed Transmission

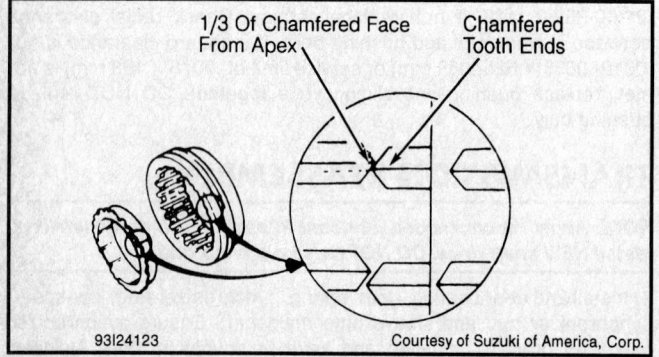

93I24123   Courtesy of Suzuki of America, Corp.

Fig. 3: Checking Mesh Between Synchronizer Ring & Cone

4) Ensure hub is installed so smaller diameter and longer boss face mainshaft rear bearing. Sleeve should be installed so that stepped-side faces mainshaft rear bearing. See Fig. 5.

5) Install reverse hub snap ring. Install 5th gear bearing, synchronizer ring and gear. Install ball and washer, ensuring oil groove faces 5th gear. Using bearing installer, press rear bearing onto mainshaft. Install snap ring. Install 3rd gear bearing and gear. Install synchronizer ring, hub and sleeve.

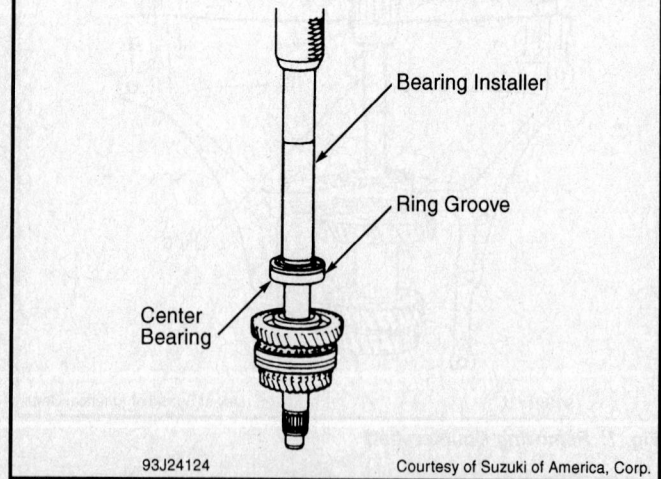

93J24124   Courtesy of Suzuki of America, Corp.

Fig. 4: Installing Center Bearing

6) Ensure hub is positioned so side with larger outer diameter boss faces 3rd gear. Install synchronizer ring, needle bearing and input shaft. Drive countershaft front bearing into case. Using a plastic hammer, tap countershaft partially into front bearing.

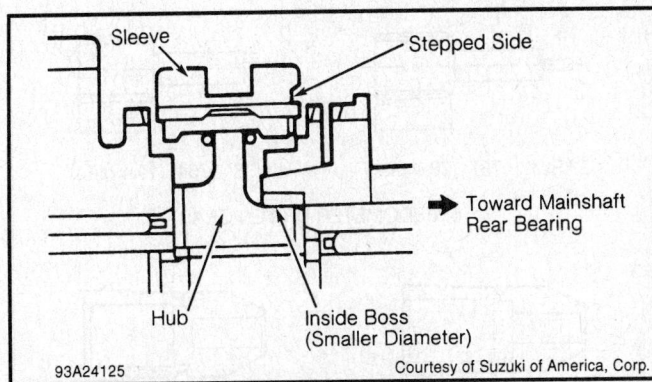

Fig. 5: Identifying Correct Sleeve Position

7) With countershaft in this position, use Bearing Installer (09925-18010) to drive center bearing onto countershaft and into case. Install countershaft front snap ring. Install countershaft reverse gear and 5th gear on countershaft. Drive rear bearing onto countershaft. Install idler gear and washer onto reverse gear shaft. Install pin. Ensure pin and washer tongue are aligned.

8) Install 3 locating springs into holes in upper case. Position locating balls on top of springs. Install low-speed gearshift shaft and low-speed shift fork in case. *See Fig. 6.* Push down on locating ball and spring to allow shaft to pass through case.

9) Install shift yoke pin. Install remaining shift shafts using the same procedure. Ensure shift forks are positioned correctly. Install gear shift yokes on each shaft. *See Fig. 7.* Ensure springs are positioned correctly. Ensure assemblies are positioned correctly.

10) Install bearing stopper rings in both bearing saddles of lower case. Install alignment bushings in diagonal corners of lower case (if removed). *See Fig. 6.* Install mainshaft and input shaft assembly in lower case. Apply Sealant (99000-31110) to mating surfaces of case halves. Position upper case half over lower case half. Align 3 shift forks with 3 grooves in synchronizer sleeve. Install case halve retaining bolts and torque to 13-21 ft. lbs. (18-29 N.m). Ensure shift shafts are in neutral position.

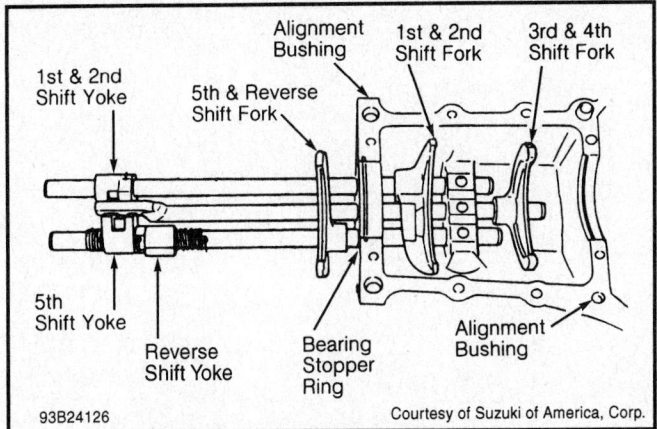

Fig. 6: Identifying Correct Shift Fork Positions

11) Install shifter housing. Torque bolts to 13-21 ft. lbs. (18-29 N.m). Apply Loctite to reverse gear shift rim bolt threads. Install rim bolt and torque to 10-13 ft. lbs. (14-18 N.m). Apply grease to input shaft oil seal. Apply sealant to input shaft bearing retainer mating surface.

12) Check operation of transmission by rotating input shaft by hand. Ensure transmission shifts into each gear easily and smoothly. Apply grease to release bearing inner surface. Install release bearing and springs. Install 2.75 pints (1.3L) SAE 80W-90 or SAE 75W-90 (recommended) gear oil in transmission and check for leakage. Recheck level with transmission installed in vehicle.

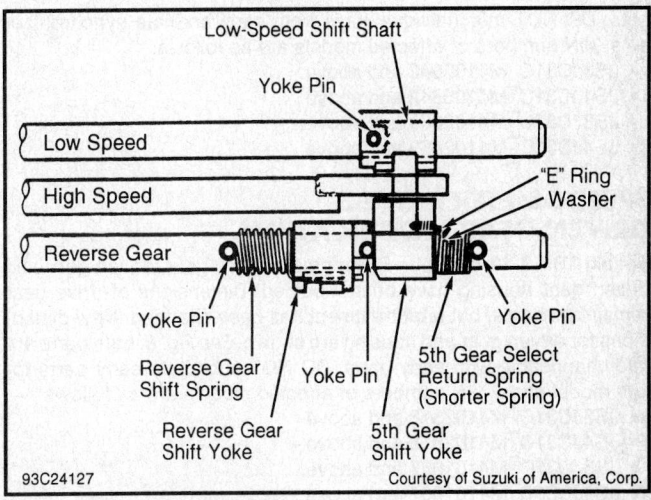

Fig. 7: Installing Shift Yokes

TORQUE SPECIFICATIONS
TORQUE SPECIFICATIONS

Application	Ft. Lbs. (N.m)
Case Halve Retaining Bolts	13-21 (18-29)
Control Lever Locating Bolt	10-13 (14-18)
Drain & Filler Plug[1]	13-21 (18-29)
Gearshift Lever Case Bolt	13-21 (18-29)
Input Shaft Bearing Retainer Bolt	13-21 (18-29)
Reverse Gearshift Rim Bolt	10-13 (14-18)
Reverse Select Pin Screw	18-26 (24-35)
Shifter Housing Bolt	13-21 (18-29)

	INCH Lbs. (N.m)
Clutch Release Arm Nut	89-142 (10-16)
Gearshift Boot Cover Bolt	35-62 (4-7)
Gearshift Lever Case Bolt	35-62 (4-7)
Low-Speed Select Pin Bolt	35-62 (4-7)
Oil Level Plug[1]	89-142 (10-16)

[1] – Sealant applied.

TECHNICAL SERVICE BULLETINS

SQUEALING NOISE FROM TRANSMISSION/TRANSFER CASE

Suzuki TSB 3-07 12070 – A high pitched squealing coming from transmission or transfer case area may be caused by a dry oil seal. Possible sources are transmission extension case oil seal, transfer gearbox input shaft oil seal, transfer gearbox output front shaft oil seal or transfer gearbox rear case oil seal. Support vehicle by both axles and operate in gear at speeds which duplicate noisy conditions. Spray each oil seal with silicone lubricant until noise disappears, indicating dry seal. Lubricate or replace as necessary to correct.

CHANGE IN CLUTCH PEDAL FEEL AFTER CLUTCH COVER REPLACEMENT

Suzuki TSB 3-09 02081 – On 1990 and later models, a change in clutch pedal feel after replacing clutch cover is normal. The pressure characteristics of the clutch have been changed. Service life of the clutch will not be affected.

MODIFICATION OF 5TH GEAR SYNCHRONIZER KEYS

Suzuki TSB 3-11 10031 – On models produced since June 1991, the synchronizer keys for 5th gear have been modified. Old (early) key set part No. is 09422-05012 and new (late) key set part No. is 24473-90D00. Early and late parts can be interchanged only as complete sets. DO NOT mix individual keys from early and late synchronizer sets. VIN numbers of affected models are as follows:

- JS3JC31C‾M4103842 and above.
- JS4JC31C‾M4103842 and above.
- JS3JD31C‾M4102039 and above.
- JS4JD31C‾M4102039 and above.

SPEEDOMETER DRIVE & DRIVEN GEAR MODIFICATION

Suzuki TSB 3-12 12131 – Speedometer drive gear, driven gear and driven gear housing have been modified. Dimensions of drive gear remain the same, but heat treatment has been changed. New dimensions for driven gear and housing are shown. See Fig. 8. Late parts are interchangeable with early parts. DO NOT substitute early parts for late model parts. VIN numbers of affected models are as follows:

- JS3JC31C‾M4102618 and above.
- JS4JC31C‾M4102618 and above.
- JS3JD31C‾M4101667 and above.
- JS4JD31C‾M4101667 and above.

MODIFIED SPEEDOMETER COMPONENT IDENTIFICATION

Application	Early Part No.	Late Part No.
Drive Gear	29411-83050	29411-83051
Driven Gear	29421-80450	29421-80451
Driven Gear Housing	29431-80051	29431-80052

NOTE: Late model speedometer driven gear and gear housing are interchangeable with early parts only if both are replaced as a set.

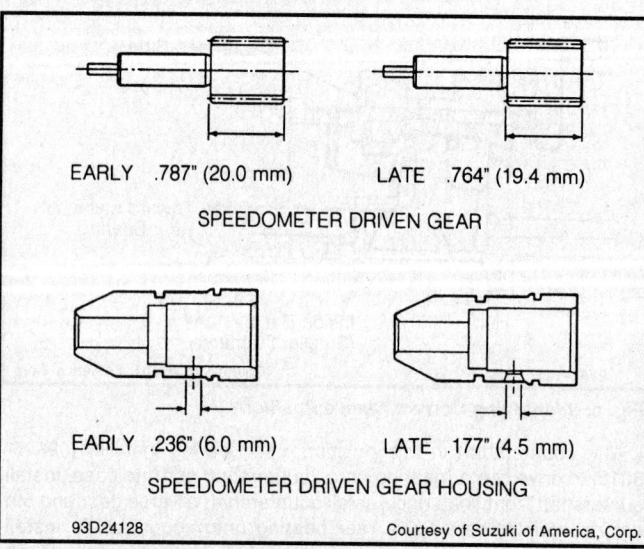

EARLY .787" (20.0 mm)   LATE .764" (19.4 mm)

SPEEDOMETER DRIVEN GEAR

EARLY .236" (6.0 mm)   LATE .177" (4.5 mm)

SPEEDOMETER DRIVEN GEAR HOUSING

93D24128   Courtesy of Suzuki of America, Corp.

Fig. 8: Identifying Early & Late Speedometer Driven Gear & Driven Gear Housing

APPLICATION & LABOR TIMES

Geo: Prizm
Toyota: Celica, Corolla, Paseo, Tercel

APPLICATION & LABOR TIMES

Vehicle Application	Labor Times		Series
	[1] R & I	[2] Overhaul	
Geo			
Prizm	5.0	6.3	C52 5-Speed
Toyota			
Celica			
1.8L	5.8	6.3	C52 5-Speed
Corolla			
1.6L	5.0	6.3	C50 5-Speed
1.8L	5.0	6.3	C52 5-Speed
Paseo			
1.5L	4.6	4.4	C150 5-Speed
Tercel			
1.5L	4.6	4.4	C151 5-Speed
	4.6	4.9	C141 4-Speed

[1] – Removal and installation of transmission from vehicle chassis.
[2] – Bench overhaul time for transaxle/differential. DOES NOT include removal and installation.

IDENTIFICATION

Transmission series is notated on ID label, located on driver door post.

LUBRICATION & ADJUSTMENTS

See appropriate MANUAL TRANSMISSION SERVICING article in TRANSMISSION SERVICING section.

TROUBLE SHOOTING

See GENERAL TROUBLE SHOOTING article in APPLICATIONS & IDENTIFICATION section.

ON-VEHICLE SERVICE

DRIVE AXLE SHAFTS

See appropriate AXLE SHAFTS article in AXLE SHAFT & TRANSFER CASES section.

REMOVAL & INSTALLATION

See appropriate MANUAL TRANSMISSION REMOVAL article in TRANSMISSION SERVICING section.

TRANSMISSION DISASSEMBLY

1) Remove release fork and bearing. Remove speedometer driven gear. Remove back-up light switch. Remove control lever housing support bracket. Remove selecting bell crank. On C50 and C52, remove bearing retainer. Remove transmission case cover. *See Fig. 1.*
2) On 5-speed models, measure 5th gear clearance. *See Fig. 2.* Using a dial indicator, measure thrust clearance. Standard clearance should be .004-.022" (.10-.57 mm). Service limit is .026" (.65 mm). Record clearance for reassembly reference. Remount dial indicator to measure radial clearance (gear oil clearance) of 5th gear. Standard clearance should be .0006-.0023" (.015-.058 mm). Service limit is .0028" (.070 mm).
3) On all models, remove shift and select lever assembly lock bolt. Remove shift and select lever shaft assembly. Lock transmission in 2 gears. Using chisel, lift staked section of output shaft (countershaft) nut. Remove lock nut. Unlock transmiaaion from 2 gears.

4) Remove spacer from 4-speed model. On 5-speed models, remove input shaft (mainshaft) snap ring. Remove bolt from No. 3 shift fork. Remove No. 3 hub sleeve and shift fork. Using 2-jaw puller, remove 5th gear, No. 3 hub, synchronizer ring, needle bearings and spacer. Remove 5th driven gear from output shaft using puller.
5) On all models, remove rear bearing retainer. Remove bearing snap rings. Pull up on both shafts to assist in snap ring removal. Remove reverse idler gear shaft lock bolt. Remove snap ring from No. 2 shift fork shaft. Remove all plugs, lock balls, seats and springs. Remove straight screw plug (4-speed), or lock ball assembly (5-speed). Remove attaching bolts from transmission housing. Use soft-faced hammer to loosen and remove housing. Remove reverse idler gear, thrust washer and shaft. Remove reverse shift arm bracket.
6) On 4-speed model, remove 2 snap rings and roll pin from reverse shift fork. Remove No. 2 shift fork shaft and shift head. On 5-speed models, remove 3 snap rings from shift fork shafts.
7) Remove 2 balls from reverse shift fork. Remove No. 3 shift fork shaft and reverse shift fork. Remove No. 1 shift fork shaft. Remove No. 1 and No. 2 shift forks. Remove input and output shafts together from transaxle case. Remove magnet and oil receiver. Remove No. 3 hub sleeve, shifting keys and springs from No. 3 clutch hub.
8) Remove transaxle case receiver. Remove input shaft front bearing and replace with new bearing if necessary. Remove bearing lock plate. Pull out bearing, replace with new bearing if necessary. Install bearing lock plate. Install transaxle case receiver. Replace input shaft front seal. If necessary, replace reverse restrict pin. Remove straight screw pin. Using pin punch and hammer, drive out roll pin. Replace reverse restrict pin. Drive in roll pin. Apply Three Bond (1344), or equivalent, install and tighten to specification. See TORQUE SPECIFICATIONS table.

COMPONENT DISASSEMBLY & REASSEMBLY

INPUT SHAFT (MAINSHAFT)

Disassembly – 1) For all clearance specifications, refer to INPUT SHAFT SPECIFICATIONS table. Using feeler gauge, measure 3rd gear and 4th gear thrust clearances. Secure input shaft in soft jaw vise. Using dial indicator, measure 3rd gear and 4th gear radial clearance (gear oil clearance). If clearance exceeds service limit, replace gear, needle bearing and/or shaft.
2) Remove input shaft snap ring. Using bearing splitter or blocks, press out ball bearing. Remove 4th gear, needle bearings, spacer and synchronizer ring from input shaft. Remove No. 2 hub sleeve snap ring. Support 3rd gear, and press No. 2 hub and sleeve, 3rd gear, synchronizer ring and needle bearings from input shaft. Remove No. 2 hub sleeve, shifting keys and springs. *See Fig. 3.*

INPUT SHAFT SPECIFICATIONS

Application	Specification
3rd Gear Thrust Clearance	
Standard	.004-.014" (.10-.35 mm)
Service Limit	.016" (.40 mm)
4th Gear Thrust Clearance	
Standard	.004-.022" (.10-.55 mm)
Service Limit	.024" (.60 mm)
3rd & 4th Gear Radial Clearance	
Standard	.006-.0023" (.015-.058 mm)
Service Limit	.029" (.070 mm)

Inspection – 1) Inspect all parts for damage and wear. Replace if necessary. Clean all parts in new solvent, then dry and lubricate all parts. Ensure oil passages are free of contamination.
2) Measure input shaft at points "A", "B", "C" and "D". *See Fig. 3.* Support input shaft on "V" blocks. Using dial indicator, measure runout while rotating input shaft 2 complete revolutions. Replace input shaft if runout or any part of shaft is not within specification. See INPUT SHAFT BEARING SURFACE SPECIFICATIONS table.

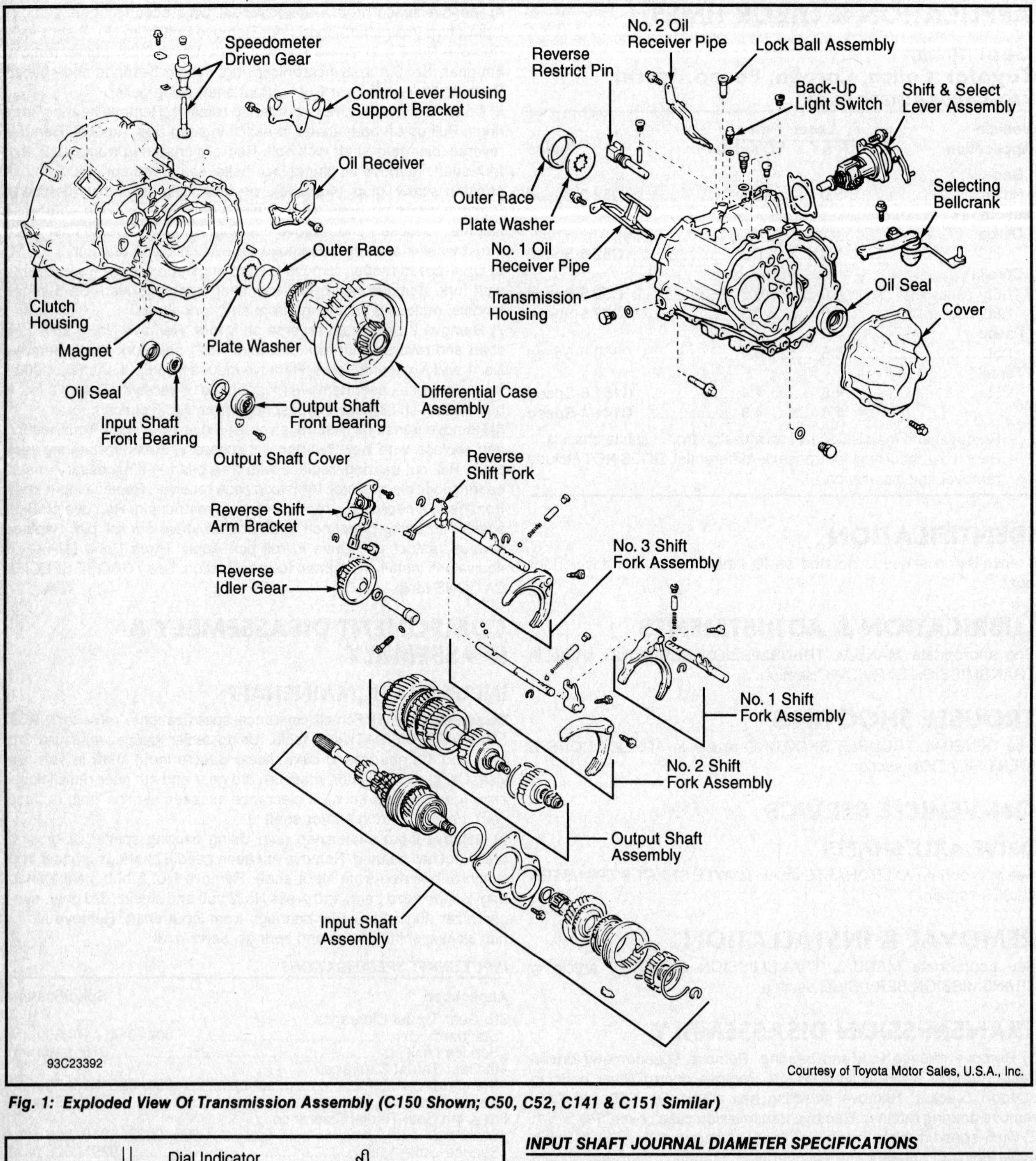

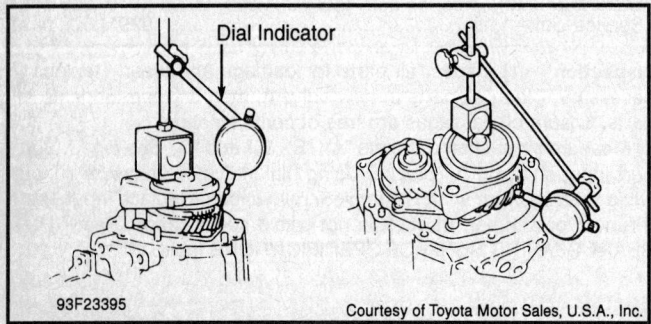

Speedometer Driven Gear

Control Lever Housing Support Bracket

Oil Receiver

Outer Race

Clutch Housing

Magnet

Oil Seal

Input Shaft Front Bearing

Plate Washer

Output Shaft Cover

Output Shaft Front Bearing

Differential Case Assembly

No. 2 Oil Receiver Pipe

Reverse Restrict Pin

Lock Ball Assembly

Back-Up Light Switch

Shift & Select Lever Assembly

Outer Race

Plate Washer

No. 1 Oil Receiver Pipe

Transmission Housing

Selecting Bellcrank

Oil Seal

Cover

Reverse Shift Fork

Reverse Shift Arm Bracket

Reverse Idler Gear

No. 3 Shift Fork Assembly

No. 1 Shift Fork Assembly

No. 2 Shift Fork Assembly

Output Shaft Assembly

Input Shaft Assembly

93C23392

Courtesy of Toyota Motor Sales, U.S.A., Inc.

Fig. 1: Exploded View Of Transmission Assembly (C150 Shown; C50, C52, C141 & C151 Similar)

Dial Indicator

93F23395

Courtesy of Toyota Motor Sales, U.S.A., Inc.

Fig. 2: Measuring 5th Gear Clearances

INPUT SHAFT JOURNAL DIAMETER SPECIFICATIONS

Application [1]	Minimum Diameter In. (mm)
"A" Journal Diameter	.979 (24.87)
"B" Journal Diameter	
C52 (Prizm)	1.040 (28.97)
C50, C52, C141, C150 and C151	1.141 (28.97)
"C" Journal Diameter	1.219 (30.97)
"D" Journal Diameter	.983 (24.97)
Runout Limit	.002 (.05)

[1] – "A", "B", "C" and "D" are measuring points. *See Fig. 3.*

Reassembly – 1) Reassemble components in reverse order of disassembly. Support No. 2 hub assembly when pressing input shaft into 3rd gear and hub. Select snap ring that allows minimum axial movement. Snap rings are available in .002 (.06 mm) increments. Snap rings range in thickness from .091" (2.30 mm) to .102" (2.60 mm). Snap rings are marked "0" through "5".

2) Recheck 3rd gear thrust clearance. See INPUT SHAFT SPECIFICATION table. Install remaining components. Use press to install ball bearing. Select snap ring that allows minimum axial movement. Recheck 4th gear thrust clearance. Snap rings range in thickness from .090" (2.29 mm) to .102" (2.59 mm). Snap rings are marked "A" through "F".

OUTPUT SHAFT (COUNTERSHAFT)

Disassembly – 1) For all clearance specifications, refer to OUTPUT SHAFT SPECIFICATIONS table. Using feeler gauge, measure 1st and 2nd gear thrust clearances. Secure input shaft in soft jaw vise. Using dial indicator, measure 1st and 2nd gear radial clearance (gear oil clearance). If clearance exceeds maximum, replace gear, needle bearing and/or shaft.

OUTPUT SHAFT SPECIFICATIONS

Application	Specification
1st Gear Thrust Clearance	
Standard	.004-.016" (.10-.40 mm)
Service Limit	.018" (.45 mm)
2nd Gear Thrust Clearance	
Standard	.004-.018" (.10-.45 mm)
Service Limit	.020" (.50 mm)
1st & 2nd Gear Radial Clearance	
Standard	.0006-.0023" (.015-.058 mm)
Service Limit	.003" (.07 mm)

2) Using bearing splitter or appropriate blocks, support 4th gear and press output shaft out of ball bearing and 4th driven gear. Remove spacer. Shift No. 1 hub sleeve into 1st gear. Support 2nd gear and press output shaft out of 3rd driven gear and 2nd gear. Remove needle bearing and synchronizer ring. Remove snap ring. See Fig. 4.

3) Support 1st gear, and press output shaft out of No. 1 hub sleeve, 1st gear and synchronizer ring. Remove needle roller bearing, thrust washer and locking ball.

Inspection – 1) Inspect all parts for damage and wear. Replace if necessary. Clean all parts in new solvent, then dry and lubricate all parts. Ensure oil passages are free of contamination.

2) Measure output shaft at points "A", "B", and "C". See Fig. 4. Support output shaft on "V" blocks. Using dial indicator, measure runout while rotating output shaft 2 complete revolutions. Replace output shaft if runout on any part of shaft is not within specification. See OUTPUT SHAFT MEASUREMENT SPECIFICATIONS table.

OUTPUT SHAFT JOURNAL DIAMETER SPECIFICATIONS

Application [1]	Minimum Diameter In. (mm)
"A" Journal Diameter	1.298 (32.97)
"B" Journal Diameter	1.495 (37.97)
"C" Journal Diameter	1.259 (31.97)
Runout Limit	.002 (.05)

[1] – "A", "B", and "C" are measuring points. See Fig. 4.

Reassembly – 1) If output shaft was replaced, drive roll pin into new output shaft to a depth of .236" (6.0 mm). Apply gear oil to needle bearings. Assemble components in reverse order of disassembly. Install No. 1 clutch hub and shifting keys to No. 1 hub sleeve. Install shifting key springs under shifting keys, ensure key springs end gaps are not in line. Install ball to shaft. Install thrust washer groove securely over locking ball. Place synchronizer on gear aligning ring slots with shifting keys. Support No. 1 hub and press output shaft into 1st gear and No. 1 hub sleeve onto output shaft. See Fig. 4.

2) Select snap ring that allows minimum axial movement. Snap rings are available in .002 (.06 mm) increments. Snap rings range in thickness from .098" (2.50 mm) to .110" (2.80 mm). Snap rings are marked "A" through "F".

3) Recheck 1st gear thrust clearance. Refer to OUTPUT SHAFT SPECIFICATIONS table. Install 2nd gear. Press 3rd driven gear onto output shaft. Recheck 2nd gear thrust clearance. Install spacer. Press 4th driven gear and ball bearing onto output shaft.

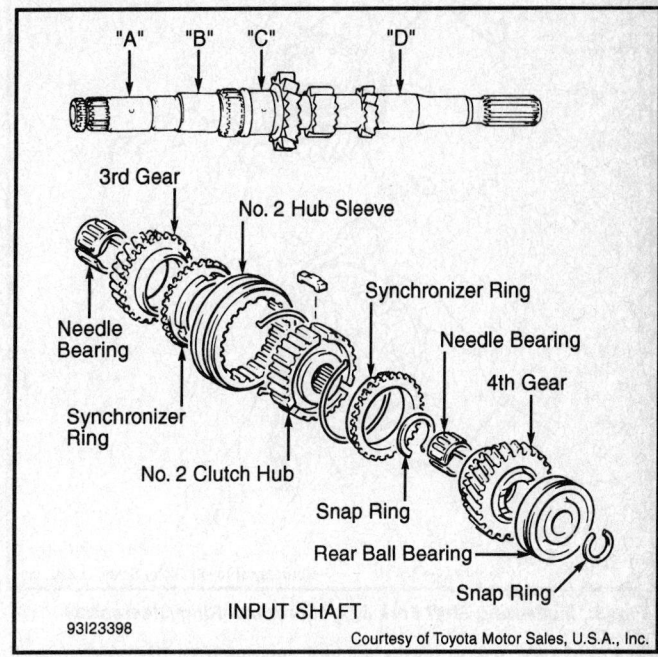

Fig. 3: Identifying Input Shaft Components

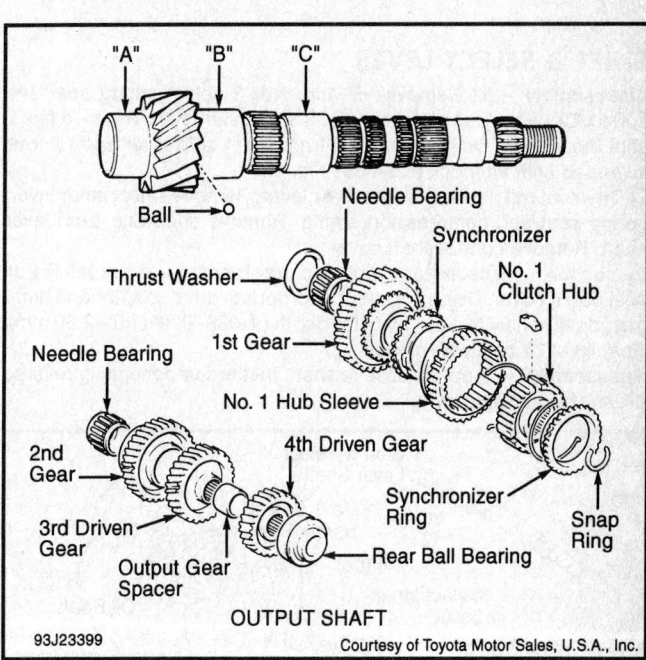

Fig. 4: Identifying Output Shaft Components

SHIFT FORK ASSEMBLY

Measure clearance between hub sleeve and shift fork. Maximum clearance is .039" (1.00 mm). If clearance exceeds specification, replace shift fork or hub sleeve. See Fig. 5.

SYNCHRO RING & GEAR

Check synchronizer rings for wear or damage. Turn and push ring to check braking action. Measure clearance between synchronizer ring

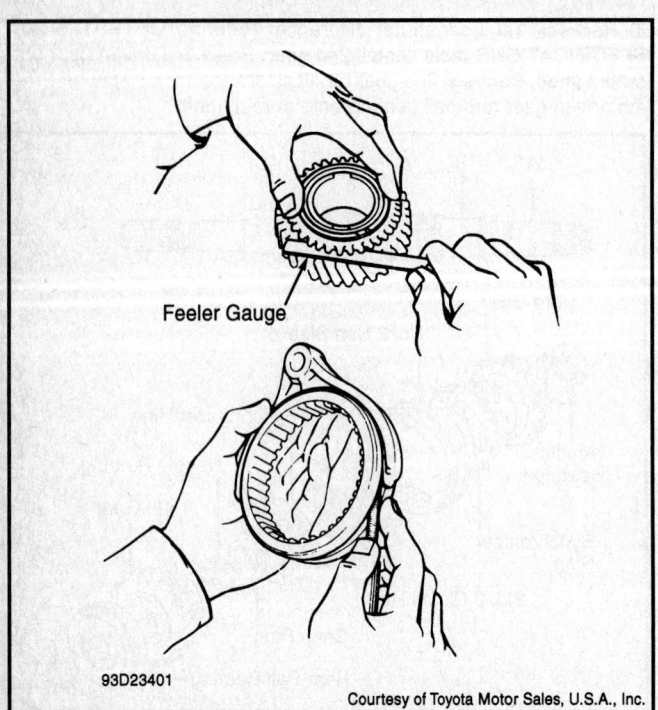

Fig. 5: **Measuring Shift Fork & Synchronizer Ring Clearances**

back and gear spline end. Minimum clearance is .024" (.60 mm). If clearance is less than specification, replace synchronizer ring. See Fig. 5.

SHIFT & SELECT LEVER

Disassembly – 1) Remove "E" ring, No. 2 select spring seat and spring. Drive out roll pins from No. 2 shift inner lever. Remove No. 2 shift inner lever. Drive out roll pin from No. 1 shift lever and remove lever and shift interlock plate. See Fig. 6.

2) Drive out roll pin from select inner lever. Remove select inner lever, spring seat and compression spring. Remove snap ring from lever shaft. Remove control shaft cover.

Inspection – If necessary, replace control shaft cover oil seal. Pry oil seal out of cover. Using socket or appropriate drive adapter and hammer, drive in new oil seal. Install to depth of .039-.079" (1.00-2.00 mm). Coat lip of oil seal with grease.

Reassembly – Apply grease to shaft. Install components in reverse order of disassembly.

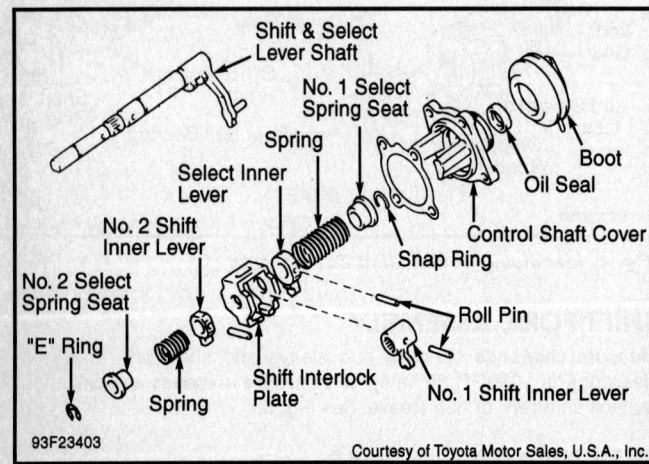

Fig. 6: **Exploded View Of Shift & Select Lever Assembly**

DIFFERENTIAL

Disassembly – 1) Fasten 2-jaw puller under bearing above cutouts on speedometer drive gear. Remove bearing from front differential case. Remove bearing from opposite side of differential case. Mark ring gear and case for reassembly reference. Remove bolts. Using a copper hammer, tap ring gear and remove from differential case.

2) Measure backlash of one side gear while holding one pinion toward case. See Fig. 8. Backlash should be .002-.008" (.05-.20 mm). If backlash is incorrect, drive out pinion shaft roll pin from ring gear side of case. Remove pinion shaft from case. Remove pinion gears, side gears and thrust washers from case. See Fig. 7.

Reassembly – 1) If backlash is incorrect, select thrust washer to correct backlash. Install thrust washers to side gears. Install side gear thrust washers, pinion thrust washers and pinion gears. Install pinion shaft. If backlash is correct, use thrust washer removed during disassembly.

2) Recheck side gear backlash while holding one pinion gear toward case. See Fig. 8. Backlash should be .002-.008" (.20-.50 mm). If backlash is incorrect, disassemble case and install new thrust washers. Install washer of equal size. Side gear thrust washers are available in .002 (.05 mm) increments. For C141, C150 and C151, washers range in thickness from .059" (1.50 mm) to .689" (1.75 mm). For C50 and C52, washers range in thickness from .037" (.95 mm) to .047" (1.42 mm).

3) Drive lock pin through case and into pinion shaft. Stake differential case to hold pin in place. Clean ring gear contact surface of case. Heat ring gear to 212°F (100°C) in boiling water.

4) Clean contact surface of ring gear with cleaning solvent. Align ring gear with differential case and install. Install bolts. After ring gear has cooled sufficiently, tighten bolts to specifications. See TORQUE SPECIFICATIONS. Press new bearings on differential case.

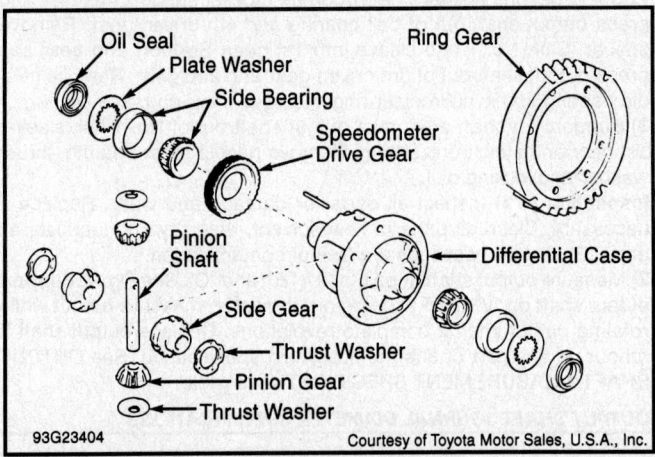

Fig. 7: **Exploded View Of Differential Assembly**

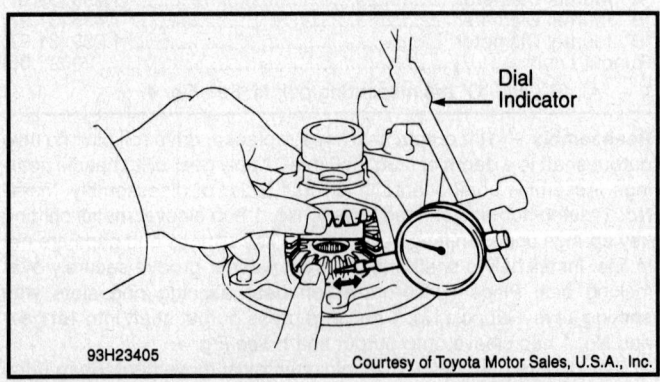

Fig. 8: **Measuring Backlash**

TRANSMISSION REASSEMBLY

Differential Bearing Preload – **1)** Install magnet. Install oil receiver. Install differential in transmission housing. Install clutch housing and tighten bolts to 22 ft. lbs. (29 N.m).

2) Using Differential Preload Adapter (09564-32011) and an INCH-lb. torque wrench, measure differential side bearing starting torque. *See Fig. 9.* Starting torque should be 7-14 INCH lbs. (.8-1.6 N.m) for new bearing and 4.3-8.7 INCH lbs. (.5-1.0 N.m) for used bearing. If preload is incorrect, remove transmission case side bearing outer race, and select new adjusting shim. Preload will change about 3-4 INCH lbs. (.3-.4 N.m) with each shim thickness change. Shims are available in .002 (.05 mm) increments. Shims range in thickness from .083" (2.10 mm) to .118" (3.0 mm). Shims are marked "A" through "U", depending on thickness.

Reassembly – **1)** Install 3 shifting keys and 2 springs to No. 3 clutch hub. Install No. 3 hub sleeve. Install magnet to transaxle case. Install differential case. Install input and output shaft together as an assembly. Install No. 1 and No. 2 shift forks. Install No. 1 shift fork shaft. Install No. 3 shift fork shaft and reverse shift fork. Install 2 ball to reverse shift fork. On 141 models, install No.2 shift fork shaft and shift head. Drive in slotted spring pin to reverse shift fork. Install 3 set bolts and tighten to specification. See TORQUE SPECIFICATIONS table. Install 2 snap rings. On all other models, install 3 snap rings.

2) Install reverse shift arm bracket. Install reverse idler gear, thrust washer and shaft. Align marking on reverse idler gear shaft with marking on case. Apply Three Bond (1281), or equivalent, sealant to transaxle case. Install transmission case. Install 13 bolts to transmission side, 3 bolts to transaxle case side. Tighten to specification. See TORQUE SPECIFICATIONS table.

NOTE: This transmission uses no gasket between major housings; use Three Bond (1281) sealant. Assemble housing within 10 minutes after applying liquid gasket. Allow 30 minutes curing time before filling with oil.

---

3) On C141 models, apply Three Bond (1344), or equivalent, to straight screw plug and install and tighten to specifications. On other models, apply sealant to lock ball assembly threads and install. Tighten to specifications. Insert balls, springs and seats into holes. Apply Three Bond (1344) sealant to plug threads. Install and tighten to specifications. On C141, install plug. *See Fig. 1.*

4) On all models, install reverse idler gear shaft. Install bearing snap rings. Install snap ring on No. 2 fork shaft. Install rear bearing retainer. Install 5th driven gear onto shaft. Install spacer. Apply gear oil to needle roller bearings. Install 5th gear, needle roller bearing and synchronizer ring.

5) Install No. 3 clutch hub and shifting keys to No. 3 hub sleeve. Install shifting key springs under shifting keys. Ensure key spring end gaps are not in line. Support tip of input shaft with spacer to raise transaxle assembly. Drive in No. 3 hub sleeve with shift fork. Align synchronizer ring slots with shifting keys.

6) Measure 5th gear thrust clearance. Standard clearance should be .004-.022" (.10-.57 mm). Select 5th gear snap ring that will allow minimum axial play, and install snap ring. Snap rings are available in .002 (.06 mm) increments. Snap rings range in thickness from .089" (2.25 mm) to .103" (2.61 mm).

7) Engage 2 gears to lock transmission. On C141, install spacer. On all models, install and tighten lock nut to 87 ft. lbs. (118 N.m). Disengage gears. Stake lock nut. On C50, C52, C150 and C151, install shift and select lever shaft assembly with new gasket. Install shift and select lever lock bolt.

8) On all models, apply Three Bond Sealant (1281), or equivalent, to transmission case cover. Install transmission case cover. Install selecting bellcrank assembly. Install control lever housing support bracket. Install back-up light switch. Install speedometer driven gear. Install release fork and bearing.

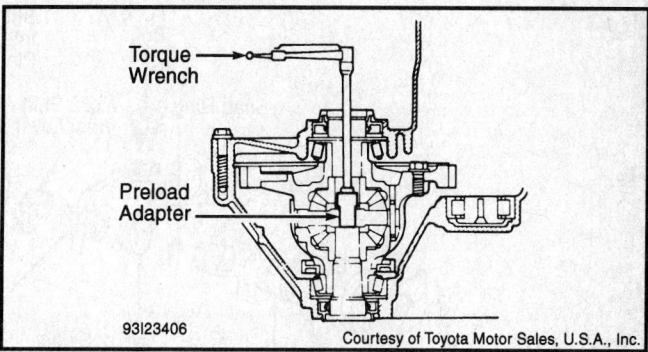

93123406   Courtesy of Toyota Motor Sales, U.S.A., Inc.

Fig. 9: Measuring Bearing Preload

TORQUE SPECIFICATIONS
TORQUE SPECIFICATIONS

Application	Ft. Lbs. (N.m)
Back-Up Light Switch	30 (40)
Differential Ring Gear Bolt (C50 & C52)	61 (83)
Differential Ring Gear Bolt (C141, 150, & C151)	91 (124)
Drain & Filler Plugs	29 (39)
Lock Ball Assembly Bolt	18 (25)
Rear Bearing Retainer Bolt	20 (27)
Reverse Idler Shaft Lock Bolt	22 (29)
Reverse Restrict Pin Straight Screw Plug	14 (19)
Reverse Shift Arm Bracket Bolt	13 (17)
Selecting Bellcrank Assembly	18 (25)
Shift Fork Shaft Straight Screw Plug	18 (25)
Shift Fork-To-Shift Fork Shaft Bolt	13 (17)
Shift Interlock Plate Lock Bolt	21 (29)
Shift & Select Lever Assembly Bolt	14 (19)
Transaxle Case-To-Transmission Case Bolt	22 (29)
Transmission Case Cover Bolt	13 (18)
5th Driven Gear Lock Nut	87 (118)
	INCH Lbs. (N.m)
Output Shaft Front Bearing Lock Plate Bolt	97 (11)
Vehicle Speed Sensor	97 (11)

MANUAL TRANSMISSIONS
Toyota E153 5-Speed

MR2 Turbo (1995)

APPLICATION & LABOR TIMES

APPLICATION & LABOR TIMES

Vehicle Application	Labor Times		Series
	¹ R & I	² Overhaul	
MR2 Turbo (1995))	5.4	6.6	E153

¹ – Removal and installation of transaxle from vehicle chassis.
² – Bench overhaul time for transaxle/differential. DOES NOT include removal and installation.

IDENTIFICATION

Transmission series is notated on ID label. ID label is located on driver-side door post.

LUBRICATION & ADJUSTMENTS

See appropriate MANUAL TRANSMISSION SERVICING article in TRANSMISSION SERVICING section.

TROUBLE SHOOTING

See GENERAL TROUBLE SHOOTING article in this section.

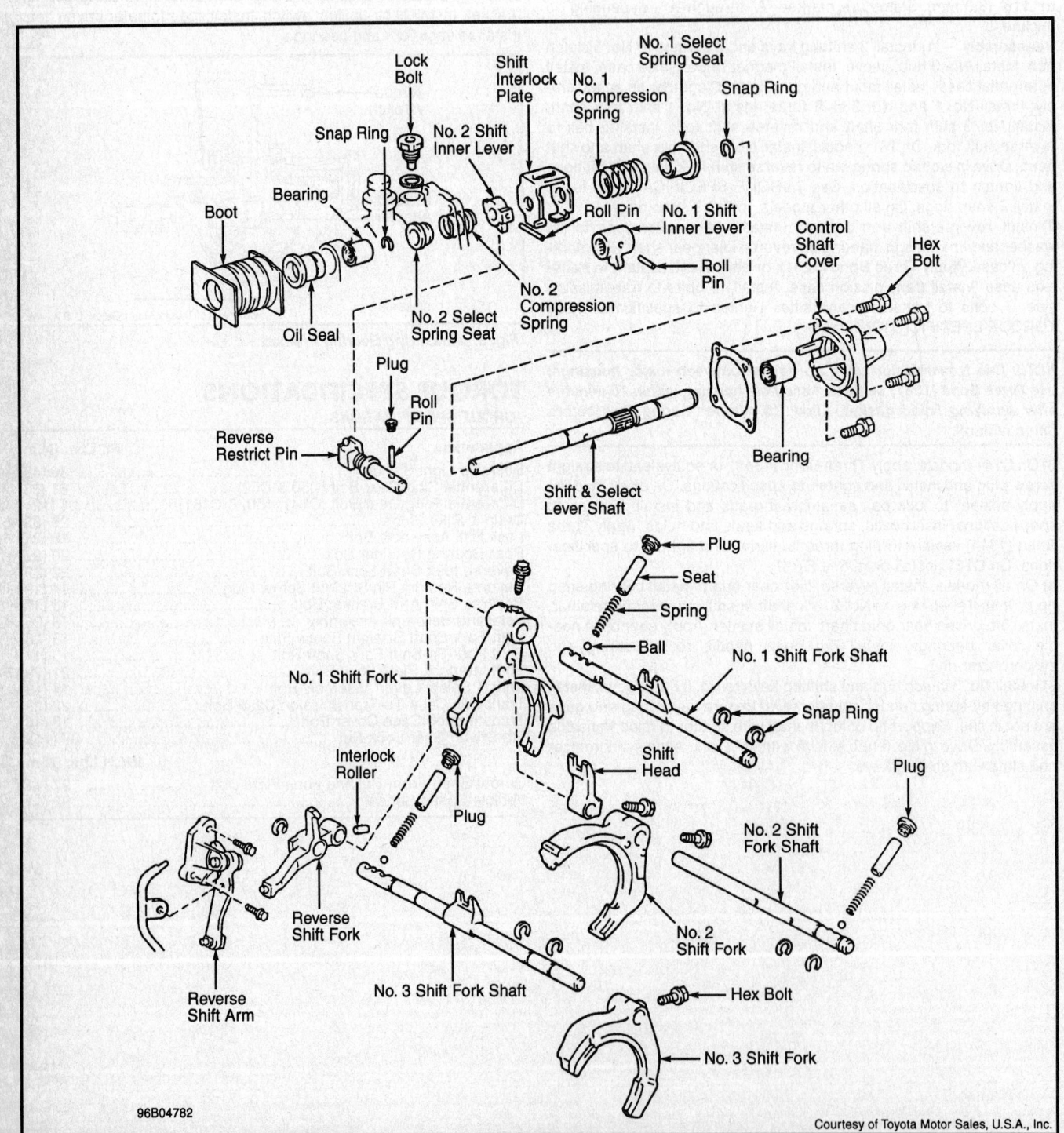

96B04782

Courtesy of Toyota Motor Sales, U.S.A., Inc.

Fig. 1: Exploded View Of Shift Fork & Select Lever Shaft Assemblies

ON-VEHICLE SERVICE

DRIVE AXLE SHAFTS

See appropriate AXLE SHAFTS article in AXLE SHAFT & TRANSFER CASES section.

REMOVAL & INSTALLATION

See appropriate MANUAL TRANSMISSION REMOVAL article in TRANSMISSION SERVICING section.

TRANSAXLE DISASSEMBLY

1) Remove back-up light switch. Remove vehicle speed sensor adapter. Remove speed sensor drive gear. Remove selecting bellcrank. Remove shift and select lever lock bolt. Remove shift lever set nut. Using a punch, drive out shift lever lock pin. Remove control shaft cover. Remove shift and select lever shaft assembly. Replace shift control shaft oil seal if necessary. If needed, replace reverse restrict pin. *See Figs. 1 and 2.*

2) Remove case cover. Remove breather plug. Unstake output shaft lock nut. Lock transmission in 2 gears. Remove output shaft lock nut. Unlock transmission.

3) Remove No. 3 shift fork set bolt. Remove No. 3 hub sleeve and the No. 3 shift fork. Using puller, remove 5th driven gear.

4) Measure 5th gear clearances. Record for reassembly reference. Using dial indicator, measure 5th gear thrust clearance. *See Fig. 4.* Standard clearance should be .004-.022" (.10-.57 mm). Service limit is .026" (.65 mm). Remount dial indicator to measure radial clearance (gear oil clearance) of 5th gear. Standard clearance should be .0004-.002" (.009-.05 mm). Service limit is .0028" (.070 mm).

5) Remove input shaft snap ring. Using Puller (09950-30010), remove No. 3 clutch hub with synchronizer ring and 5th gear. Remove needle bearing and spacer. Remove 7 Torx screws (T45) and rear bearing retainer. Remove adjusting shim.

6) Remove input shaft rear bearing snap ring. Remove shift fork shaft snap rings. Remove plug, seat, spring and detent ball with a magnet. Remove reverse idler gear shaft bolt.

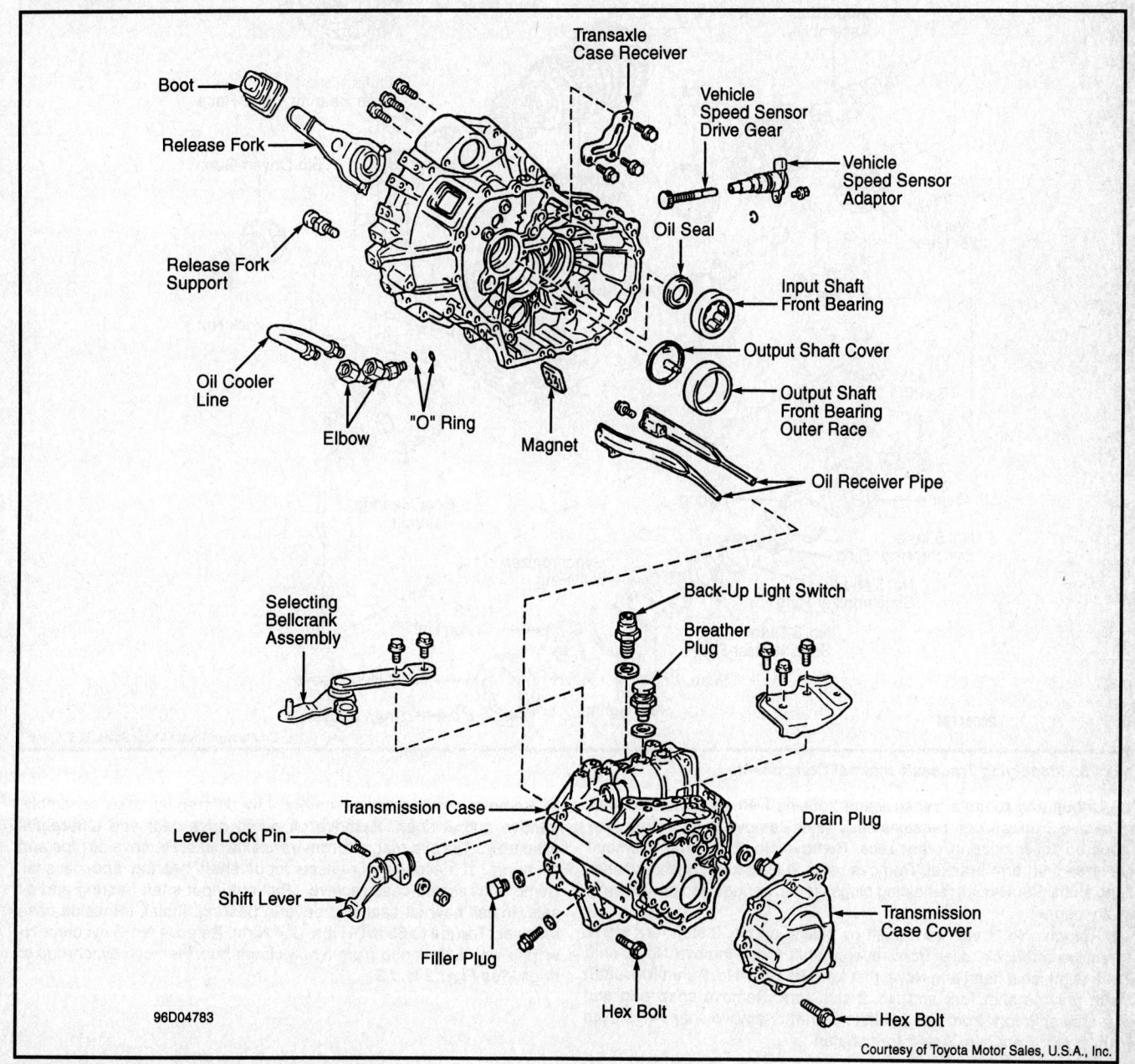

Boot

Release Fork

Release Fork Support

Oil Cooler Line

Elbow

"O" Ring

Magnet

Transaxle Case Receiver

Vehicle Speed Sensor Drive Gear

Vehicle Speed Sensor Adaptor

Oil Seal

Input Shaft Front Bearing

Output Shaft Cover

Output Shaft Front Bearing Outer Race

Oil Receiver Pipe

Selecting Bellcrank Assembly

Back-Up Light Switch

Breather Plug

Transmission Case

Lever Lock Pin

Shift Lever

Filler Plug

Hex Bolt

Drain Plug

Transmission Case Cover

Hex Bolt

96D04783

Courtesy of Toyota Motor Sales, U.S.A., Inc.

Fig. 2: Identifying Transaxle Case Components

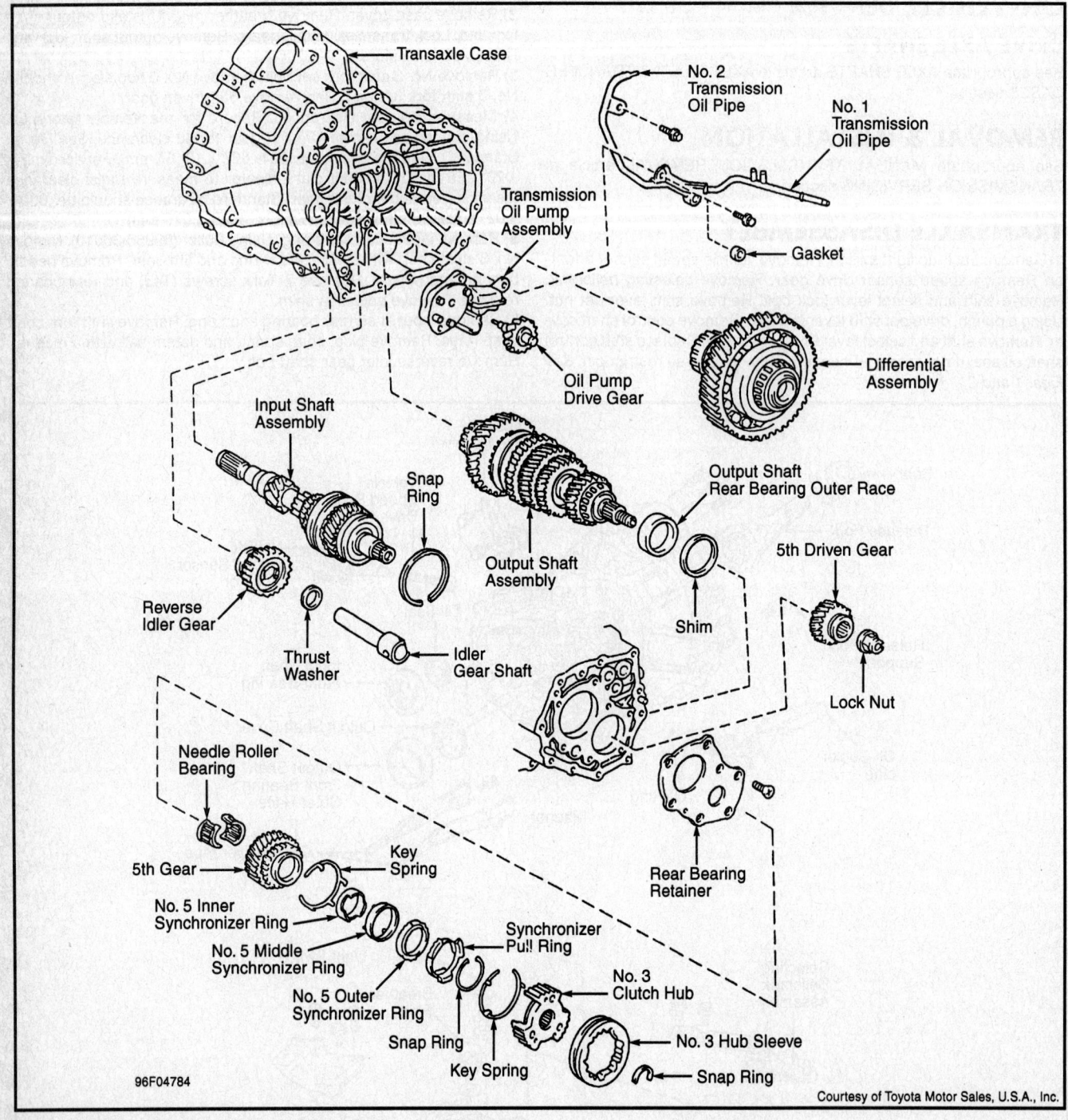

96F04784

Courtesy of Toyota Motor Sales, U.S.A., Inc.

Fig. 3: Identifying Transaxle Internal Components

7) Unbolt and remove transmission housing with a plastic hammer. Remove 3 bolts from transaxle case side. Remove output shaft rear tapered roller bearing outer race. Remove No. 2 oil pipe. Remove reverse shift arm bracket. Remove reverse idler gear, thrust washer and shaft. Remove all remaining plugs, seats, springs and detent balls with magnet.

8) Remove No. 1 shift fork shaft by pulling up No. 3 shift fork shaft. Remove interlock roller from reverse shift fork. Remove No. 2 shift fork shaft, shift head and No. 1 shift fork. Remove No. 3 shift fork shaft with reverse shift fork and No. 2 shift fork. Remove snap ring and reverse shift fork from No. 3 shift fork shaft. Remove snap rings from No. 1, No. 2 and No. 3 shift fork shafts.

9) Remove input shaft assembly. Lift differential case assembly, remove output shaft. Remove oil pump drive gear and differential assembly. Remove magnet from transaxle case. Remove oil pipe and oil pump. If necessary, replace input shaft bearing and oil seal. Remove transaxle case receiver. Pull out input shaft bearing and oil seal. Install new oil seal and drive in bearing. Install transaxle case receiver. Torque to 65 INCH lbs. (7.4 N.m). Remove No. 5 synchronizer ring with key spring from No. 3 clutch hub. Remove synchronizer rings. *See Figs. 2 and 3.*

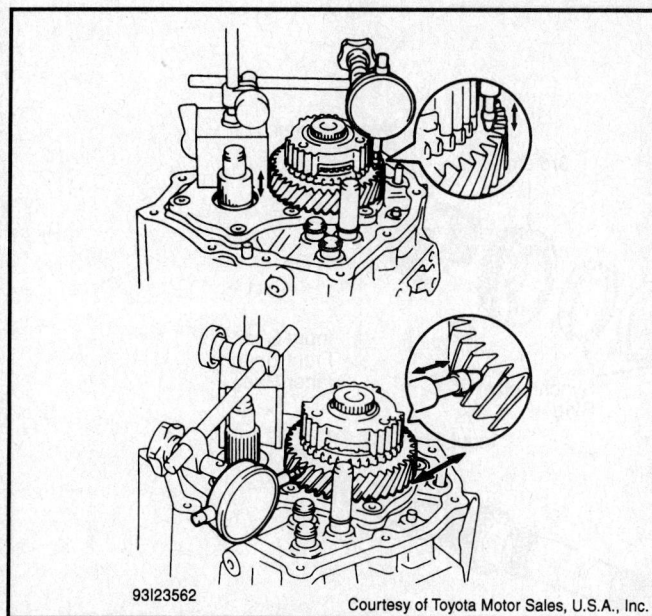

93I23562

Courtesy of Toyota Motor Sales, U.S.A., Inc.

Fig. 4: Measuring 5th Gear Clearances

COMPONENT DISASSEMBLY & REASSEMBLY

INPUT SHAFT (MAINSHAFT)

Disassembly – 1) For all measurement specifications, refer to INPUT SHAFT SPECIFICATIONS table. Using feeler gauge, measure 3rd and 4th gear thrust clearances. *See Fig. 5.* Secure input shaft in soft-jaw vise. Using dial indicator, measure 3rd and 4th gear lateral movement (gear oil clearance). If clearance exceeds maximum specification, replace gear, needle bearing and/or shaft.

INPUT SHAFT SPECIFICATIONS

Application	In. (mm)
3rd Gear Thrust Clearance	
Standard Clearance	.004-.018 (.10-.45)
Service Limit	.020 (.50)
4th Gear Thrust Clearance	
Standard Clearance	.004-.022 (.10-.55)
Service Limit	.024 (.60)
3rd & 4th Gear Lateral Movement	
Standard Clearance	.0004-.002 (.009-.05)
Service Limit	.003 (.07)

2) Remove snap ring from input shaft. Using bearing splitter or appropriate blocks, support 4th gear and press input shaft out of rear bearing and 4th gear. Remove needle bearings, spacer and synchronizer ring. Remove snap ring. Supporting 3rd gear, press input shaft out of No. 2 hub sleeve, synchronizer ring, needle bearing and 3rd gear. Remove needle bearing. Press input shaft out of front bearing inner race. *See Fig. 6.*

Inspection – 1) Inspect all parts for damage and wear. Replace if necessary. Clean all parts in solvent, dry and lubricate all parts. Ensure oil passages are free of contamination.

2) Measure input shaft at points "A", "B" and "C". *See Fig. 7.* Support input shaft on "V" blocks. Using dial indicator to measure runout, rotate input shaft 2 complete revolutions. Replace input shaft if runout or any part of shaft is not within service limit. See INPUT SHAFT BEARING SURFACE SPECIFICATIONS table.

Reassembly – 1) Install clutch hub and shifting keys to No. 2 hub sleeve. Ensure key spring end-gaps are not in line.

2) Apply multipurpose grease to needle bearings. Install bearing in 3rd gear. Place synchronizer ring on 3rd gear and align ring slots with shifting keys. Using press, install 3rd gear and No. 2 hub sleeve. *See Fig. 6.*

3) Select snap ring that will allow minimum axial play on shaft. See SNAP RING APPLICATION CHART NO. 1.

INPUT SHAFT BEARING SURFACE SPECIFICATIONS

Application [1]	Minimum Diameter In. (mm)
"A" Journal Diameter	1.1004 (27.95)
"B" Journal Diameter	1.415 (35.95)
"C" Journal Diameter	1.415 (35.95)
Runout Limit	.002 (.05)

[1] – "A", "B", and "C" refer to measuring points indicated in *Fig. 7.*

SNAP RING APPLICATION CHART NO. 1

Thickness In. (mm)	Stamped Letter
.091 (2.30)	H
.093 (2.35)	J
.095 (2.40)	K
.097 (2.45)	L
.098 (2.50)	M
.100 (2.55)	N
.102 (2.60)	P

4) Install selected snap ring. Recheck 3rd gear thrust clearance. Standard clearance should be .004-.018" (.10-.45 mm). Maximum clearance is .020" (.50 mm). Install spacer. Place synchronizer ring on 4th gear and align ring slots with shifting keys. Install 4th gear. Press on ball bearing. *See Fig. 6.*

5) Select 4th gear snap ring that will allow minimum axial play on shaft. See SNAP RING APPLICATION CHART NO. 2.

SNAP RING APPLICATION CHART NO. 2

Thickness In. (mm)	Stamped Number
.093 (2.35)	1
.095 (2.40)	2
.097 (2.45)	3
.098 (2.50)	4
.100 (2.55)	5
.102 (2.60)	6
.104 (2.65)	7
.106 (2.70)	8

6) Install snap ring. Recheck 4th gear thrust clearance. Standard clearance should be .004-.022" (.10-.55 mm). Maximum clearance is .024" (.60 mm). Using press, install input shaft front bearing inner race.

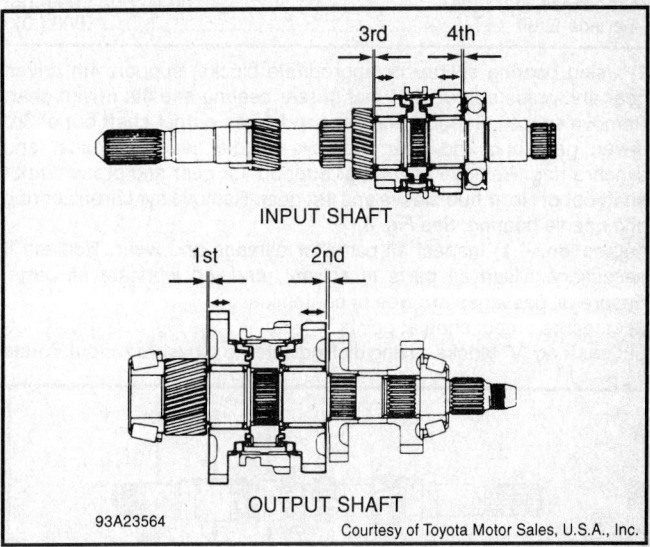

93A23564

Courtesy of Toyota Motor Sales, U.S.A., Inc.

Fig. 5: Measuring Input & Output Shaft Clearances

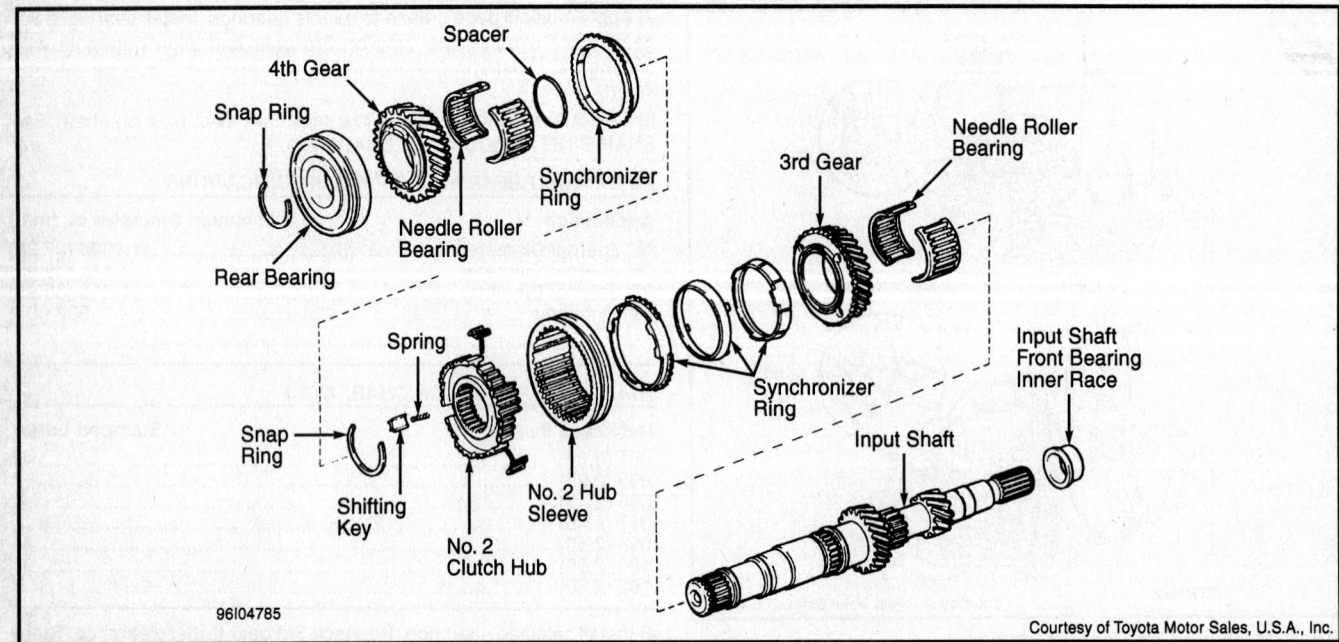

96I04785

Courtesy of Toyota Motor Sales, U.S.A., Inc.

Fig. 6: Exploded View Of Input Shaft

OUTPUT SHAFT (COUNTERSHAFT)

Disassembly – 1) For all measurement specifications, refer to OUTPUT SHAFT SPECIFICATIONS table. Using feeler gauge, measure 1st and 2nd gear thrust clearances. See Fig. 5. Secure output shaft in soft-jaw vise. Using dial indicator, measure 1st and 2nd gear lateral movement (gear oil clearance). If clearance exceeds maximum, replace gear, needle bearing and/or shaft.

OUTPUT SHAFT SPECIFICATIONS

Application	In. (mm)
1st Gear Thrust Clearance	
Standard Clearance	.004-.014 (.10-.35)
Service Limit	.016 (.40)
2nd Gear Thrust Clearance	
Standard Clearance	.004-.018 (.10-.45)
Service Limit	.020 (.50)
1st & 2nd Gear Lateral Movement	
Standard Clearance	.0004-.002 (.009-.05)
Service Limit	.003 (.07)

2) Using bearing splitter or appropriate blocks, support 4th driven gear and press output shaft out of rear bearing and 4th driven gear. Remove spacer. Support 2nd gear and press output shaft out of 3rd driven gear and 2nd gear. Remove needle bearing, spacer and synchro ring. Remove snap ring. Support 1st gear and press output shaft out of No. 1 hub sleeve and 1st gear. Remove synchronizer ring and needle bearing. See Fig. 8.

Inspection – 1) Inspect all parts for damage and wear. Replace if necessary. Clean all parts in solvent, dry and lubricate all parts. Ensure oil passages are free of contamination.

2) Measure output shaft at points "A" and "B". See Fig. 9. Support output shaft on "V" blocks. Using dial indicator to measure runout, rotate

output shaft 2 complete revolutions. Replace output shaft if runout or any part of shaft is not within service limit. See OUTPUT SHAFT MEASUREMENT SPECIFICATIONS table.

OUTPUT SHAFT MEASUREMENT SPECIFICATIONS

Application [1]	Minimum Diameter In. (mm)
"A" Journal Diameter	1.534 (38.95)
"B" Journal Diameter	1.534 (38.95)
Runout Limit	.002 (.05)

[1] – "A", and "B" refer to measuring points indicated in Fig. 9.

Reassembly – 1) If front output shaft bearing replacement is necessary, support bearing with bearing splitter or appropriate blocks. Press output shaft out of bearing. To replace, support bearing with Adapter (09316-60010), press shaft onto bearing. Use 2-jaw puller to remove bearing race from clutch housing. To replace, use appropriate race driver.

2) Install components in reverse order of disassembly. Install No. 1 clutch hub and shifting keys to No. 1 hub sleeve. Install shifting key springs under shifting keys. Ensure key spring end-gaps are not in line. Apply multipurpose grease to needle bearings. Install bearing in 1st gear. Place synchronizer ring on gear and align ring slots with shifting keys. Press 1st gear and No. 1 hub sleeve onto output shaft. See Fig. 8.

3) Select 1st gear snap ring that will allow minimum axial play on shaft. Snap rings are available in .002" (.05 mm) increments. Snap ring range in thickness from .110" (2.80 mm) to .122" (3.10 mm). Snap rings are stamped "A" Through "G".

4) Recheck 1st gear thrust clearance. Standard clearance should be .004-.014" (.10-.35 mm). Maximum clearance is .016" (.40 mm). Install spacer. Apply multipurpose grease to needle bearing. Place synchronizer ring on 2nd gear and align ring slots with shifting keys. Install 2nd gear. Using press, install 3rd driven gear on output shaft. Recheck 2nd gear thrust clearance. Standard clearance should be .004-.018" (.10-.45 mm). Maximum clearance is .02" (.50 mm). Install spacer. Using press, install 4th driven gear on output shaft. Press on output shaft rear bearing.

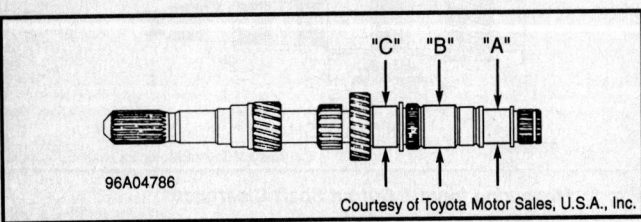

96A04786

Courtesy of Toyota Motor Sales, U.S.A., Inc.

Fig. 7: Measuring Input Shaft Bearing Journals

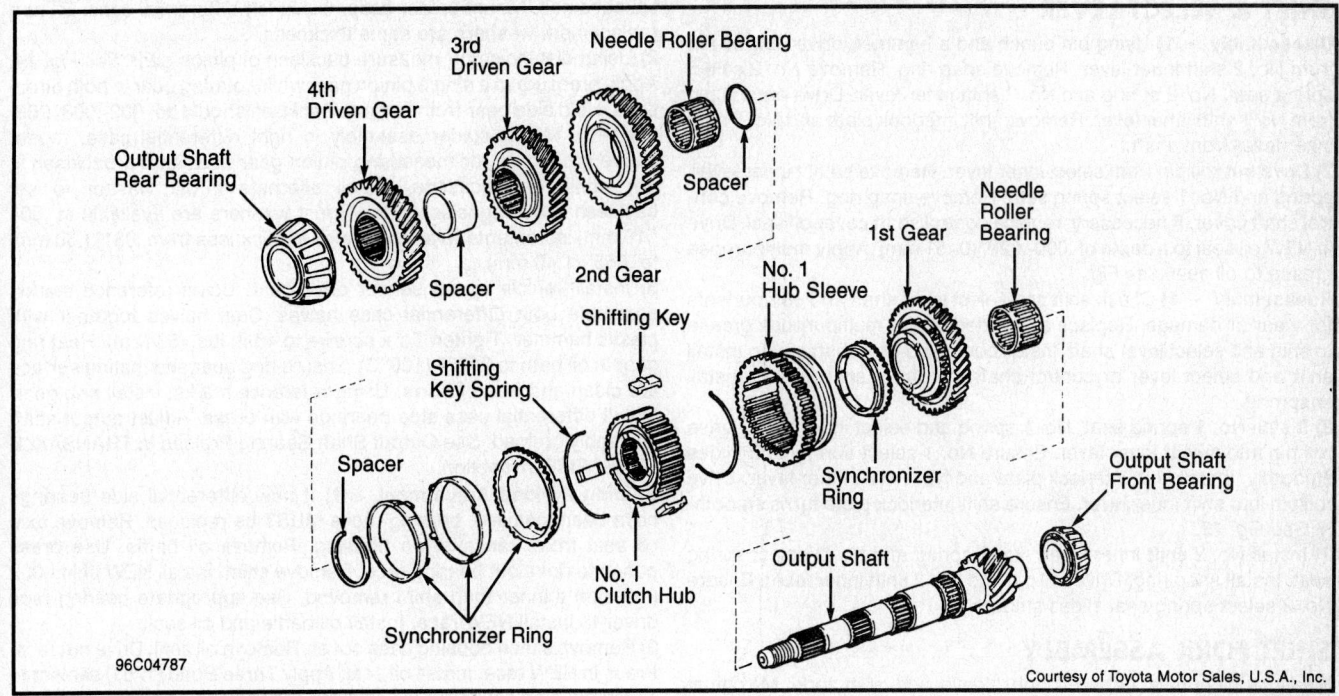

96C04787

Courtesy of Toyota Motor Sales, U.S.A., Inc.

Fig. 8: Exploded View Of Output Shaft

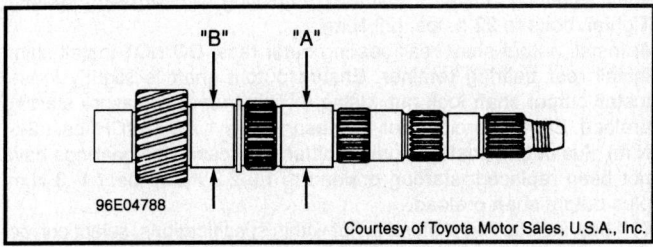

96E04788

Courtesy of Toyota Motor Sales, U.S.A., Inc.

Fig. 9: Output Shaft Measuring Points

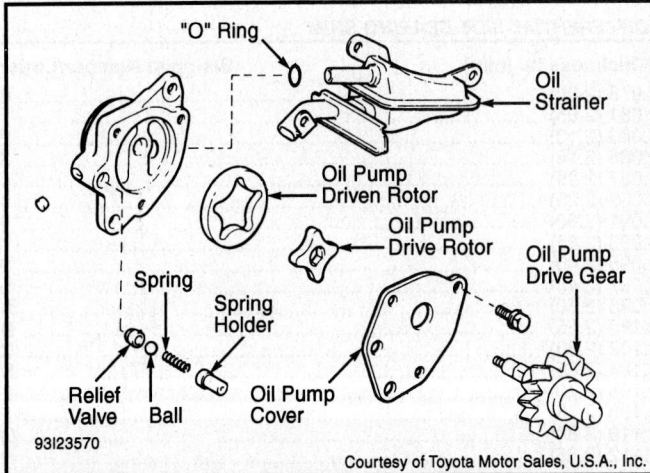

93I23570

Courtesy of Toyota Motor Sales, U.S.A., Inc.

Fig. 10: Exploded View Of Oil Pump Assembly

OIL PUMP

Disassembly – 1) Install oil pump drive gear to drive rotor. Ensure drive rotor turns smoothly. Remove gasket from oil pump case. Remove bolt and pull out oil strainer. Hold oil pump cover. Unbolt and remove cover. Remove spring holder, spring, ball and relief valve seat. See Fig. 10.

2) Install oil pump drive gear to drive rotor. Measure body clearance between drive rotor and oil pump case. See Fig. 11. Standard clearance should be .004-.006" (.10-.16 mm). Service limit is .012" (.30 mm). Measure tip clearance between drive and drive rotors. Standard clearance should be .003-.006" (.08-.15 mm). Service limit is .012" (.30 mm).

3) Remove oil pump drive gear. Using straightedge and feeler gauge, measure side clearance of both rotors. Standard clearance should be .001-.003" (.03-.08 mm). Maximum clearance is .006" (.15 mm). Remove oil pump drive rotor and driven rotor. Replace "O" ring in oil pump case.

Reassembly – Install driven rotor and drive rotor. Install relief valve, ball, spring and spring holder to oil pump case. Install oil strainer to oil pump case. Tighten oil pump cover bolts to 96 INCH lbs. (10 N.m). Insert oil pump drive gear to drive rotor. Ensure drive rotor turns smoothly. Install NEW gasket to oil pump case.

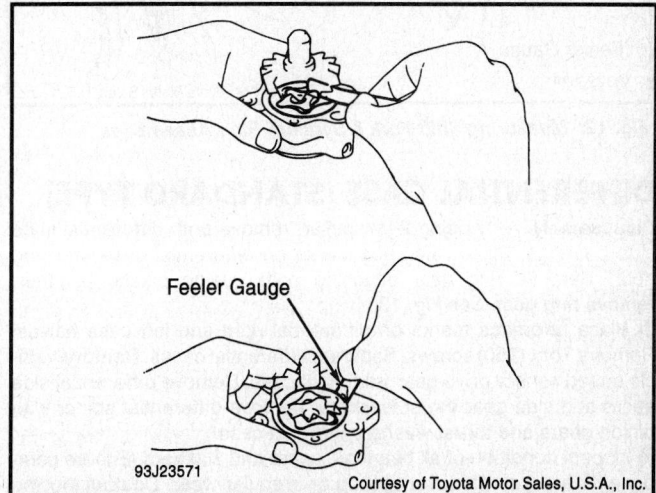

93J23571

Courtesy of Toyota Motor Sales, U.S.A., Inc.

Fig. 11: Measuring Oil Pump Clearances

SHIFT & SELECT LEVER

Disassembly – 1) Using pin punch and a hammer, drive out roll pin from No. 2 shift inner lever. Remove snap ring. Remove No. 2 select spring seat, No. 2 spring and No. 2 shift inner lever. Drive out roll pin from No.1 shift inner lever. Remove shift interlock plate and No. 1 shift inner lever from shaft.

2) Drive out roll pin from select inner lever. Remove select inner lever, spring and No. 1 select spring seat. Remove snap ring. Remove control shaft cover. If necessary, replace control shaft cover oil seal. Drive in NEW oil seal to a depth of .000-.020" (0-.51 mm). Apply multipurpose grease to oil seal. See Fig. 1.

Reassembly – 1) Check shift and select lever shaft and components for wear or damage. Replace as needed. Apply multipurpose grease to shift and select lever shaft. Install boot to control shaft cover. Install shift and select lever or control shaft to control shaft cover. Install snap ring.

2) Install No. 1 spring seat, No. 1 spring and select inner lever. Drive roll pin into select inner lever. Ensure No. 1 select spring seat slides smoothly. Install shift interlock plate and No. 1 shift inner lever. Drive roll pin into shift inner lever. Ensure shift interlock plate turns smoothly. See Fig. 12.

3) Install No. 2 shift inner lever, No. 2 spring and No. 2 select spring seat. Install snap ring. Drive roll pin into No. 2 shift inner lever. Ensure No. 2 select spring seat slides smoothly.

SHIFT FORK ASSEMBLY

Measure clearance between hub sleeve and shift fork. Maximum clearance is .039" (1.00 mm). If clearance exceeds specification, replace shift fork or hub sleeve. See Fig. 12.

SYNCHRONIZER RING & GEAR

Check synchronizer rings for wear or damage. Turn and push ring to check braking action. Measure clearance between synchronizer ring back and gear spline end. 1st and 4th synchronizer and ring gear minimum clearance is .024" (.60 mm). 2nd and 3rd synchronizer gear minimum clearance is .028" (.70 mm). If clearance is less than specification, replace synchronizer ring. See Fig. 12.

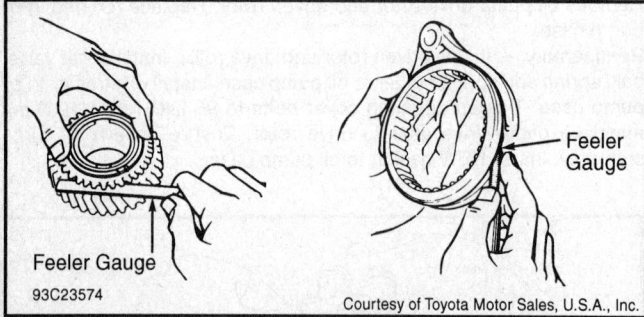

Feeler Gauge

Feeler Gauge

93C23574

Courtesy of Toyota Motor Sales, U.S.A., Inc.

Fig. 12: Measuring Shift Fork & Synchro Ring Assemblies

DIFFERENTIAL CASE (STANDARD TYPE)

Disassembly – 1) Using 2-jaw puller, remove both differential case side bearings. Place reference marks on differential case and ring gear. Remove ring gear attaching bolts. Using plastic hammer, remove ring gear. See Fig. 13.

2) Place reference marks on differential right and left case halves. Remove Torx (T50) screws. Separate differential cases. Remove vehicle speed sensor drive gear from right case. Remove differential side gears and side gear thrust washers. Remove differential spider with pinion gears and thrust washers from left case.

3) Inspect condition of all bearings, gears and washers. Ensure components are free of burrs, scoring or irregular wear. Coat all moving parts with gear oil before reassembly.

Reassembly – 1) Install thrust washers to side gears. Install pinion gears with thrust washers to spider. Install side gears in each differen-

tial case half. Mount spider assembly in left differential case. Ensure replacement washers are same thickness.

2) Using dial indicator, measure backlash of pinion gear. See Fig. 14. Apply pressure to a single pinion gear while rotating gear in both directions. Hold side gear from turning. Backlash should be .002-.008" (.05-.20 mm). Mount spider assembly in right differential case, repeat above procedure for measuring pinion gear backlash. If backlash is not within specifications, install alternate thrust washer to set backlash within specifications. Thrust washers are available in .004 (.10 mm) increments. Washers range in thickness from .031" (.80 mm) to .055" (1.40 mm).

3) Install vehicle speed sensor drive gear. Using reference marks, assemble both differential case halves. Seat halves together with plastic hammer. Tighten Torx screws to 46 ft. lbs. (63 N.m). Heat ring gear in oil bath to 212°F (100°C). Ensure ring gear and mating surface are clean and free of burrs. Using reference marks, install ring gear. Install differential case side bearings with press. Adjust output shaft assembly preload. See Output Shaft Bearing Preload in TRANSAXLE REASSEMBLY section.

Bearing Preload Adjustment – 1) If new differential side bearings have been installed, bearing races MUST be replaced. Remove axle oil seal from transmission housing. Remove oil baffle. Use brass punch to drive out bearing race. Remove shim. Install NEW shim .002 (.05 mm) thinner than shim removed. Use appropriate bearing race driver to install NEW race. Install oil baffle and oil seal.

2) Remove clutch housing case cover. Remove oil seal. Drive out race. Press in NEW race. Install oil seal. Apply Three Bond (1281) sealant to clutch housing cover. Install cover to clutch housing.

3) Install differential case assembly in clutch housing. Install output shaft assembly. Install transmission housing without using sealant. Tighten bolts to 22 ft. lbs. (29 N.m).

4) Install output shaft rear bearing outer race. DO NOT install shim. Install rear bearing retainer. Ensure output shaft is slightly loose. Install output shaft lock nut. Using torque wrench, measure starting preload. Starting preload for new bearings is 1.7-3.6 INCH lbs. (.2-.4 N.m) plus output shaft preload. If differential case side bearings have not been replaced, starting preload is 1.9-2.2 INCH lbs. (.1-.3 N.m) plus output shaft preload.

5) If bearing starting preload is not within specifications, select correct thrust shim for correction. See DIFFERENTIAL SIDE BEARING SHIM table. The total preload will change approximately .9-1.7 INCH lbs. (.1-.2 N.m) with each .05mm change in shim thickness.

DIFFERENTIAL SIDE BEARING SHIM

Thickness In. (mm)	Stamped Number/Letter
.079 (2.00)	0
.081 (2.05)	1
.083 (2.10)	2
.085 (2.15)	3
.087 (2.20)	4
.089 (2.25)	5
.091 (2.30)	6
.093 (2.35)	7
.095 (2.40)	8
.097 (2.45)	9
.098 (2.50)	A
.100 (2.55)	B
.102 (2.60)	C
.104 (2.65)	D
.106 (2.70)	E
.108 (2.75)	F
.110 (2.80)	G
.112 (2.85)	H

6) Remove output shaft lock nut. Remove bearing retainer. Remove case bolts and disassemble transmission case. Remove differential and output shaft assembly. Install correct shim in transmission housing. Recheck differential side bearing starting preload. Once starting preload is within specifications, disassemble transmission.

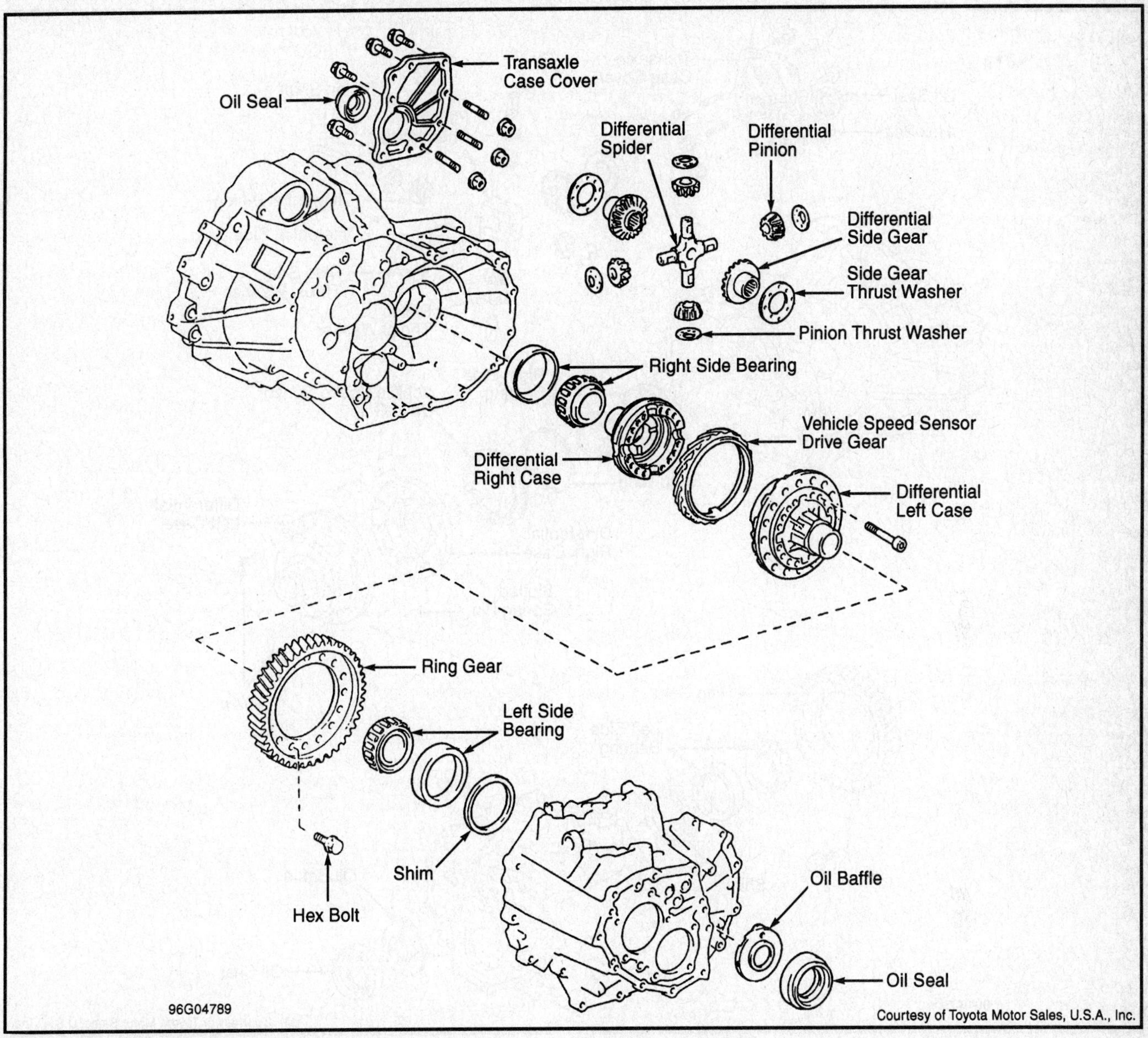

Oil Seal

Transaxle Case Cover

Differential Spider

Differential Pinion

Differential Side Gear

Side Gear Thrust Washer

Pinion Thrust Washer

Right Side Bearing

Differential Right Case

Vehicle Speed Sensor Drive Gear

Differential Left Case

Ring Gear

Left Side Bearing

Shim

Hex Bolt

Oil Baffle

Oil Seal

96G04789

Courtesy of Toyota Motor Sales, U.S.A., Inc.

Fig. 13: Exploded View Of Differential Case (Standard Type)

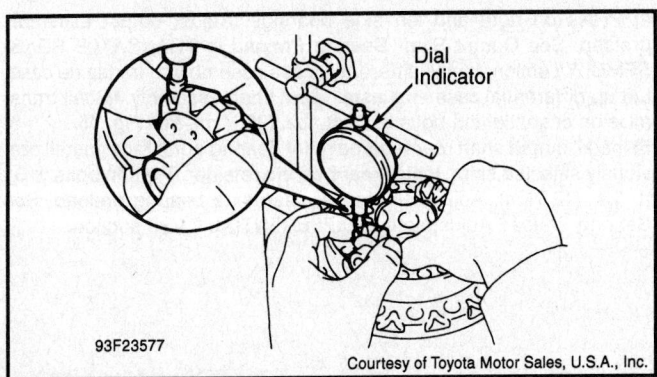

Dial Indicator

93F23577

Courtesy of Toyota Motor Sales, U.S.A., Inc.

Fig. 14: Measuring Differential Backlash

DIFFERENTIAL CASE (VISCOUS COUPLING)

Disassembly – 1) Remove side bearings. Place reference marks on both differential case and ring gear. Remove ring gear. Remove snap ring and vehicle speed sensor drive gear.

2) Place reference marks on differential right and left case. Remove 2 screws, disassemble differential case, side gear and thrust washer. Using a pin punch, drive out 3 roll pins. Remove pinion shafts, pinion gears, pinion washers and shaft holder. Remove side gear and thrust washer from differential right case. See Fig. 15.

3) Inspect condition of all bearings, gears and washers. Ensure components are free of burrs, scoring or irregular wear. Coat all moving parts with gear oil before reassembly.

Reassembly – 1) Install thrust washer and differential side gear to differential right case. Install pinion washers, pinions, pinion shafts and shaft holder. Using a pin punch, drive in 3 roll pins to differential right case.

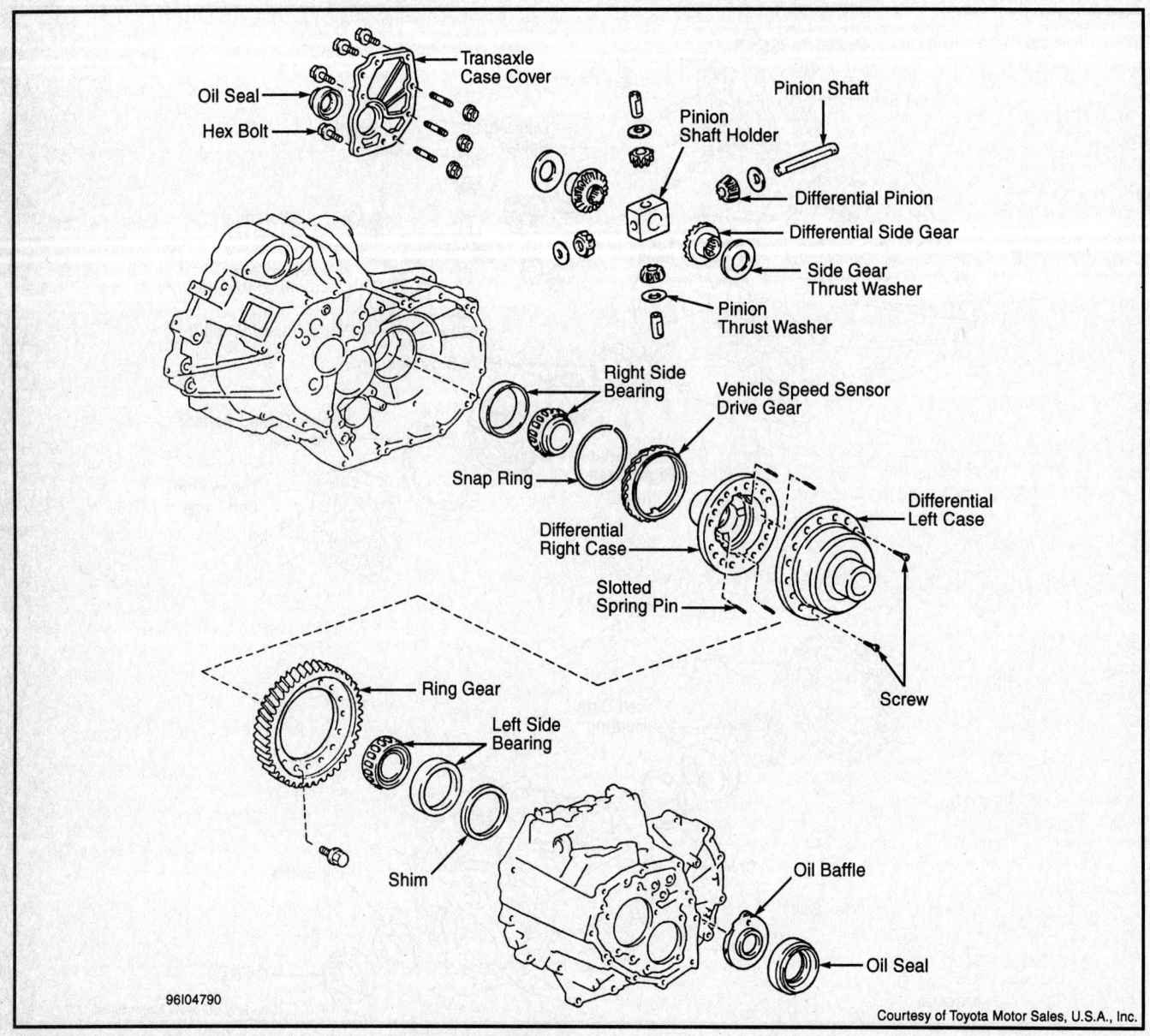

Fig. 15: Exploded View Of Differential Case (Viscous Coupling LSD)

2) Using a dial indicator, measure pinion gear backlash while holding No. 2 differential case. Standard backlash is .0020-.0079" (.05-.20 mm). Install side gear, pinion shafts and shaft holder with 4 pinions to right side of differential case. Check side gear backlash. Ensure backlash is within specification. If backlash is not in specification, select appropriate thrust washer to set backlash to specification. Thrust washer thicknesses are available in .004" (.10 mm) increments ranging from .0315" (.80 mm) to .0551" (1.40 mm).

3) Assemble differential, aligning reference marks, side gear and thrust washers. Install and tighten 2 screws. Install vehicle speed sensor drive gear to differential right case. Install snap ring. Heat ring gear in oil bath to 212°F (100°C). Ensure ring gear and mating surface are clean and free of burrs. Using reference marks, install ring gear. Allow ring gear to cool sufficiently before tightening set bolts. Torque to 91 ft. lbs. (134 N.m).

4) Press on right and left side bearings. Adjust output assembly preload. See Output Shaft Bearing Preload in TRANSAXLE REASSEMBLY section. Install differential case assembly to transaxle case. Lift up differential case and install input shaft assembly. Install transmission case, tighten bolts to 21 ft. lbs. (29 N.m). See Fig. 15.

5) Install output shaft rear tapered roller bearing outer race. Install previously selected shim. Install rear bearing retainer. Tighten bolts to 31 ft. lbs. (42 N.m). Adjust differential case side bearing preload. See Bearing Preload Adjustment in DIFFERENTIAL CASE section.

TRANSAXLE REASSEMBLY

Output Shaft Bearing Preload (Standard & Viscous Coupling LSD) –

1) Install magnet to transaxle case. Install oil pump and gasket. Install oil pipe. Install output shaft in clutch housing. Install transmission housing. Install and tighten bolts to 21 ft. lbs. (29 N.m). Install output shaft rear taper roller bearing outer race. Install original adjusting shim if output shaft bearing has not been replaced. If new bearing has been installed, install .002" (.05 mm) thinner adjusting shim. Install bearing retainer.

2) Install lock nut to output shaft. Rotate output shaft both directions to ensure bearings are seated. Using torque wrench, measure output shaft starting preload. Starting preload should be 6.9-13.9 INCH lbs. (.8-1.6 N.m) for a new bearing. If bearing has not been replaced, starting preload is 4.3-8.7 INCH lbs. (.5-1.0 N.m).

3) If starting preload is not within specifications, select alternate adjusting shim. Starting preload changes about 3.5-4.4 INCH lbs. (.4-.5 N.m) with each shim thickness. Shims are available in .002" (.05 mm) increments. Shims range in thickness from .051" (1.30 mm) to .098" (2.50 mm). Shims are stamped 0-9 and A-Q. Install correct shim. Disassemble transmission.

Reassembly – **1)** Remove output shaft. Install oil pump drive gear. Install input and output shaft assemblies and shift fork assemblies as single unit. Install shift fork shaft locking balls, springs, seats and plugs. Install reverse idler gear and shaft. Align referencing marks on idler gear and clutch housing. Place reverse shift fork pivot into reverse shift arm and install reverse shift arm bracket to clutch housing. Install No. 2 oil pipe. Install NEW gasket to oil pipe. See Fig. 3.

NOTE: *This transmission uses no gasket between major housings; use Three Bond (1281) sealant. Assemble housing within 10 minutes after applying liquid gasket. Allow 30 minutes curing time before filling with oil.*

---

2) Apply Three Bond (1281) sealant to transmission housing. Install transmission housing to clutch housing. Install reverse idler gear shaft retaining bolt. Install shift shaft locking ball, spring, seat and plug. Install snap rings to shift fork shafts.

3) Install output shaft rear bearing outer race. Install correct adjusting shim. Install snap ring to input shaft rear bearing. Install rear bearing retainer. Install spacer, needle bearing and 5th gear. Install synchronizer ring and key spring to No. 3 clutch hub. Install No. 3 clutch hub with synchronizer ring and key spring.

4) Select a snap ring that will allow minimum axial play and install snap ring on shaft. Snap rings are available in .002" (.05 mm) increments.

Snap rings range in thickness from .089" (2.25 mm) to .104" (2.65 mm). Shims are stamped Q-Y. See Fig. 3.

5) Recheck 5th gear thrust clearance. Standard clearance is .004-.022" (.10-.57 mm). Install 5th driven gear. Install No. 3 hub sleeve and No. 3 shift fork. Tighten No. 3 hub sleeve set bolt to 14 ft. lbs. (24 N.m). Lock transmission in 2 gears. Install and tighten NEW lock nut to 91 ft. lbs. (123 N.m). Stake lock nut. Unlock transmission.

6) Apply Three Bond (1281) sealant to transmission case cover. Install cover. Install shift and select lever shaft. Install control shaft cover. Install lock bolt. Install boot to control shaft oil seal. Ensure boot is installed in correct direction. Position air bleed of boot downward. Align shaft notch with pin groove and install pin. Install and tighten nut to 106 INCH lbs. (12 N.m). Install selecting bellcrank. Install back-up light switch and speedometer driven gear.

TORQUE SPECIFICATIONS
TORQUE SPECIFICATIONS

Application	Ft. Lbs. (N.m)
Back-Up Light Switch	30 (40)
Breather Plug	36 (49)
Control Shaft Cover Bolt	14 (19)
Differential Ring Gear Bolt	91 (123)
Differential Case Bolt	46 (63)
Drain & Filler Plug	36 (49)
Elbow-To-Transaxle	20 (27)
Oil Cooler Tube-To-Elbow	25 (34)
Oil Pipe Clamp	13 (18)
Rear Bearing Retainer Bolt	31 (42)
Reverse Idler Shaft Lock Bolt	21 (29)
Reverse Shaft Arm Bracket Bolt	13 (18)
Selecting Bellcrank Support Set Bolt	14 (19)
Shift Fork Lock Bolt	18 (25)
Shift & Select Lever Lock Bolt	36 (49)
Straight Screw Plug	18 (25)
Transaxle Case Cover Bolt	40 (54)
Transaxle Case-To-Oil Pump Bolt	13 (18)
Transaxle Case-To-Transmission Case Bolt	21 (29)
Transmission Case Cover Bolt	21 (29)
Vehicle Speed Sensor	13 (17)
5th Driven Gear Lock Nut	91 (123)

	INCH Lbs. (N.m)
Oil Pump-To-Cover Bolt	96 (10)
Reverse Restrict Pin Holder	115 (13)
Selecting Bellcrank Set Bolt	106 (12)
Shift Lever Lock Nut	106 (12)
Transaxle Case Receiver	65 (7.4)

MANUAL TRANSMISSIONS
Toyota G58 5-Speed

1995 Pickup & 4Runner (4-Cylinder)

APPLICATION & LABOR TIMES

APPLICATION & LABOR TIMES

Vehicle Application	Labor Times		Series
	[1] R & I	[2] Overhaul	
1995 Pickup & 4Runner			
4-Cylinder (22R-E)	4.8	4.4	G58

[1] – Removal and installation of transmission from vehicle chassis.
[2] – Bench overhaul time for transmission. DOES NOT include removal and installation.

IDENTIFICATION

Transmission model is identified on ID label. ID label is located on driver's side door post.

LUBRICATION & ADJUSTMENTS

See appropriate MANUAL TRANSMISSION SERVICING article in TRANSMISSION SERVICING section.

TROUBLE SHOOTING

See GENERAL TROUBLE SHOOTING article in this section.

ON-VEHICLE SERVICE

DRIVE AXLE SHAFTS

See appropriate AXLE SHAFTS article in AXLE SHAFT & TRANSFER CASES section.

REMOVAL & INSTALLATION

See appropriate MANUAL TRANSMISSION REMOVAL article in TRANSMISSION SERVICING section.

TRANSMISSION DISASSEMBLY

1) Remove back-up light switch. Remove clutch housing from transmission case. Remove straight screw plug from transfer adapter. Remove spring and detent ball. Remove transfer shift lever control retainer and select return spring. Remove 2 restrict pins. See Fig. 1.
2) Remove transfer adapter bolts. Remove shift lever housing set bolt. Remove transfer adapter. Remove shift lever housing and shift and select lever. Remove front bearing retainer. Remove input and countershaft front bearing snap rings. Using plastic hammer, remove transmission case and separate from intermediate plate.
3) Mount intermediate plate in vise. Use 2 bolts with nuts and washers in bottom holes of intermediate plate to prevent damage to sealing surface of intermediate plate. DO NOT apply pressure on intermediate plate. Using Torx (T40) socket, remove straight screw plugs, springs and locking balls. Remove 3 shift fork shaft snap rings. Drive out roll pin from reverse shift head. Remove No. 5 shift fork shaft. See Fig. 2.
4) Remove set bolt from No. 3 shift fork. Remove No. 3 shift fork, No. 4 shift fork shaft, reverse shift head and 2 balls. Remove interlock pin No. 2 from No. 3 shift fork shaft. Drive out roll pin from reverse shift fork. Remove No. 3 shift fork shaft. Remove No. 1 interlock pin. See Fig. 2.
5) Remove reverse shift arm and fork. Remove No. 2 interlock pin from No. 2 shift fork shaft. Remove No. 1 shift fork set bolt. Remove No. 1 shift fork shaft. Remove No. 1 interlock pin. See Fig. 8. Remove No. 2 shift fork set bolt. Remove No. 1 and 2 shift fork and No. 2 shift fork shaft. See Fig. 2.
6) Measure countershaft 5th gear thrust clearance. See Fig. 4. Standard clearance should be .004-.012" (.10-.30 mm). Maximum clearance is .012" (.30 mm). Remove countershaft snap ring. Using Puller (09950-50010), remove No. 5 gear spline piece, synchronizer ring, needle bearings and countershaft 5th gear. See Figs. 1 and 3.

7) Remove spacer and ball. Remove reverse shift arm bracket. Remove reverse idler gear shaft set bolt and stopper. Remove reverse idler gear and shaft. Remove rear bearing retainer. Remove countershaft rear bearing snap ring. Remove countershaft rear bearing. Remove countershaft. Remove input shaft with 13 needle bearings and synchronizer from output shaft. See Fig. 1.
8) Remove output shaft center bearing snap ring. Remove output shaft from intermediate plate by pulling on output shaft and tapping intermediate plate with plastic hammer.

COMPONENT DISASSEMBLY & REASSEMBLY

INPUT SHAFT

Inspect input shaft, synchronizer ring and input shaft bearing for wear or damage. Rotate bearing by hand. If any roughness or binding is felt, replace input shaft bearing. Support bearing in blocks and press input shaft out of bearing. Reverse procedure to install bearing. Select and install bearing retaining snap ring that will allow minimum axial play. See INPUT SHAFT SNAP RING table.

INPUT SHAFT SNAP RING

Thickness – In. (mm)	ID Stamp
.081-.083 (2.05-2.10)	0
.083-.085 (2.10-2.15)	1
.085-.087 (2.15-2.20)	2
.087-.089 (2.20-2.25)	3
.089-.091 (2.25-2.30)	4
.091-.093 (2.30-2.35)	5

OUTPUT SHAFT (MAINSHAFT)

Disassembly – 1) Using feeler gauge, measure 1st, 2nd and 3rd gear thrust clearances. See Fig. 4. Standard clearance should be .004-.010" (.10-.25 mm). Maximum clearance is .010" (.25 mm). Secure output shaft in soft-jawed vise. Using dial indicator, measure 1st, 2nd and 3rd gear radial movement (gear oil clearance). See Fig. 5. Standard clearance should be .0004-.0013" (.009-.032 mm). Maximum clearance is .0013" (.032 mm). If clearance exceeds maximum, replace gear, needle bearing and/or shaft.
2) Using 2-jaw puller, remove sleeve from output shaft. Support 1st gear in blocks, press output shaft out of 5th gear, rear bearing and 1st gear.
3) Remove synchronizer ring. Remove locking ball with a magnet. Support 2nd gear, press output shaft out of No. 1 hub sleeve, synchronizer ring and 2nd gear. Remove three shifting keys and springs from clutch hub No. 1. Remove needle bearing. Remove front snap ring. Support 3rd gear in blocks, press No. 2 hub sleeve, synchronizer ring and 3rd gear from output shaft. Remove needle bearing. Remove 3 shifting keys and 2 springs from clutch hub No. 2. See Fig. 3.
Inspection – 1) Measure output shaft flange thickness "A" and shaft diameter "B" and "C", inner race flange thickness "D" and outer diameter of inner race "E". See Fig. 3. Support output shaft on "V" blocks. Using dial indicator to measure runout, rotate output shaft 2 complete revolutions. Replace output shaft if runout or any part of shaft is not within service limit. See OUTPUT SHAFT MEASUREMENT SPECIFICATIONS table.

OUTPUT SHAFT MEASUREMENT SPECIFICATIONS

Application [1]	Minimum Diameter In. (mm)
"A" Shaft Flange Minimum Thickness	.189 (4.80)
"B" Journal Diameter	1.495 (37.98)
"C" Journal Diameter	1.377 (34.98)
"D" Inner Race Flange Thickness	.157 (3.99)
"E" Inner Race Diameter	1.535 (34.98)
Runout Limits	.002 (.05)

[1] – "A", "B", "C", "D" and "E" refer to measuring points indicated in Fig. 3.

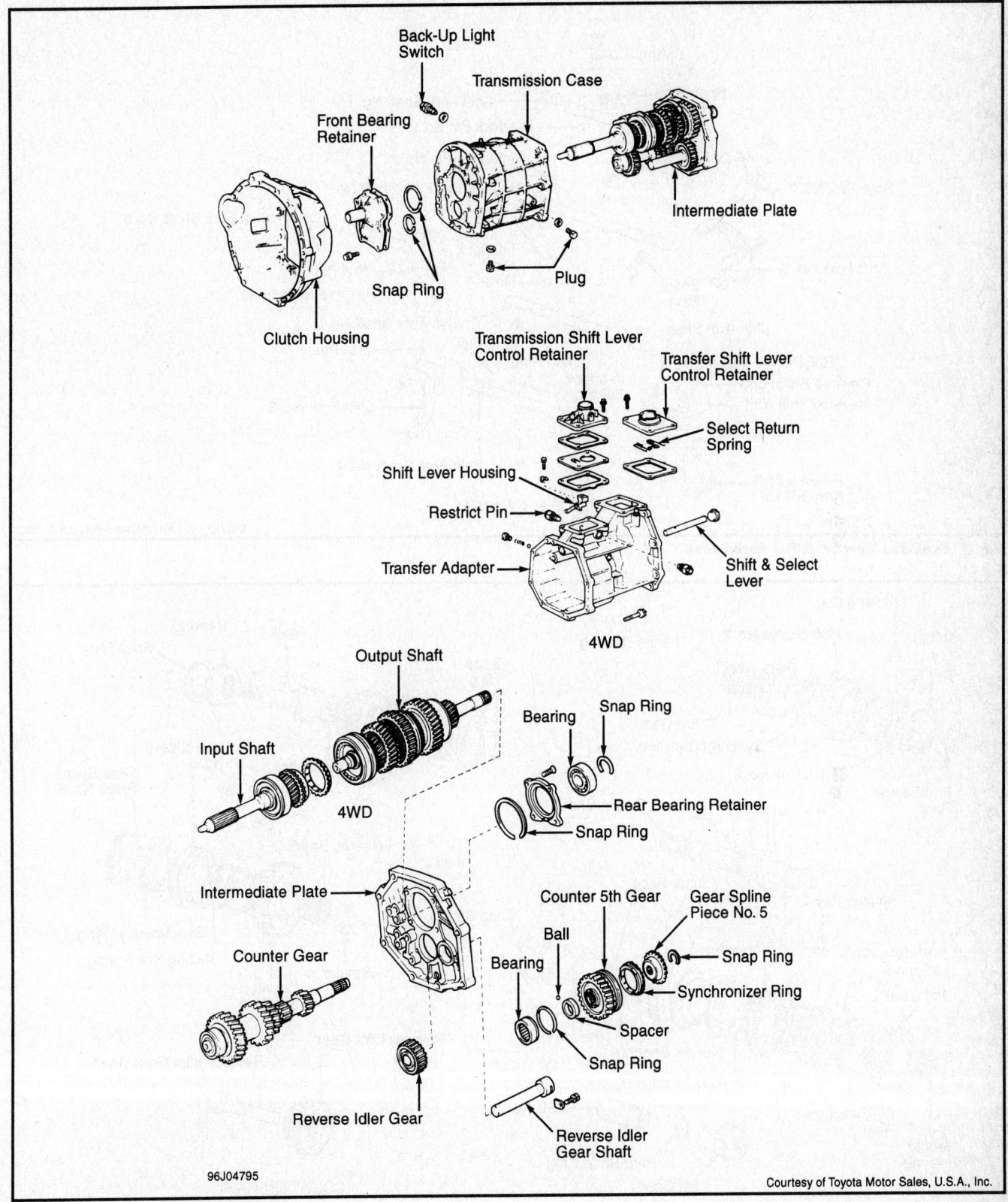

96J04795

Courtesy of Toyota Motor Sales, U.S.A., Inc.

Fig. 1: Exploded View Of Transmission

MANUAL TRANSMISSIONS
Toyota G58 5-Speed (Cont.)

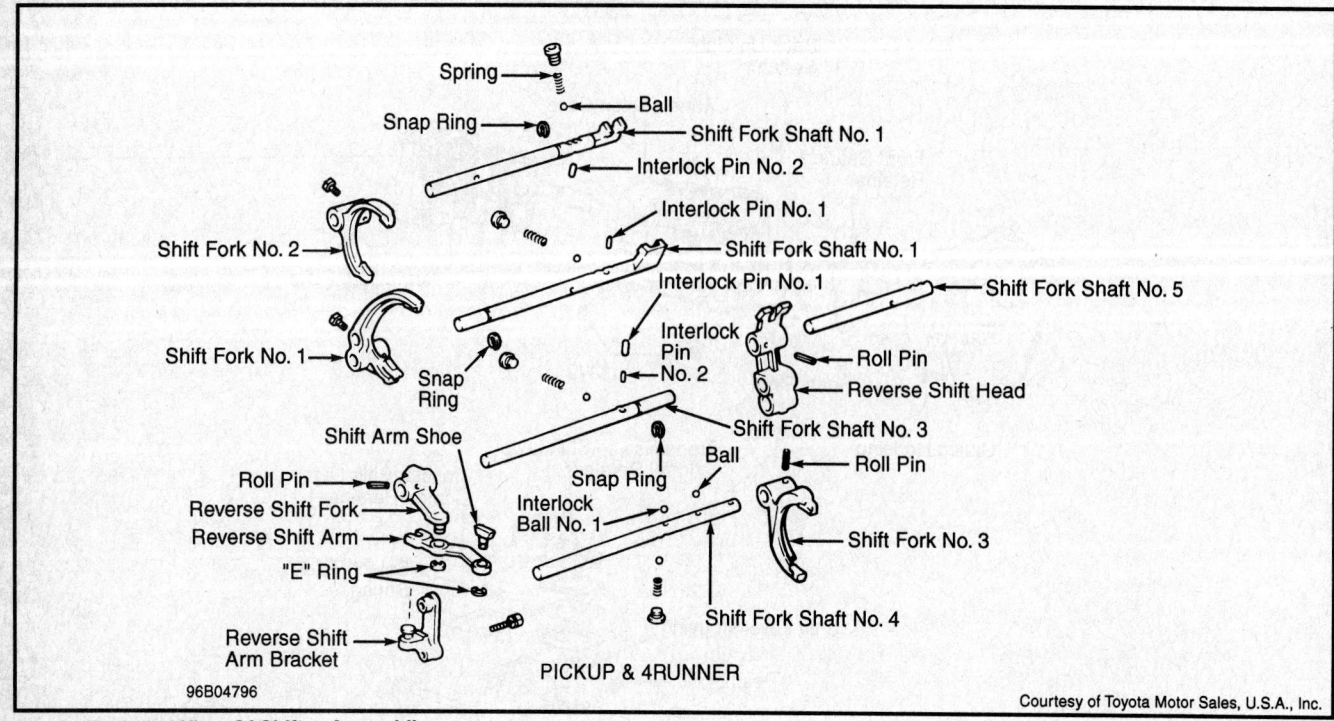

Fig. 2: Exploded View Of Shifter Assemblies

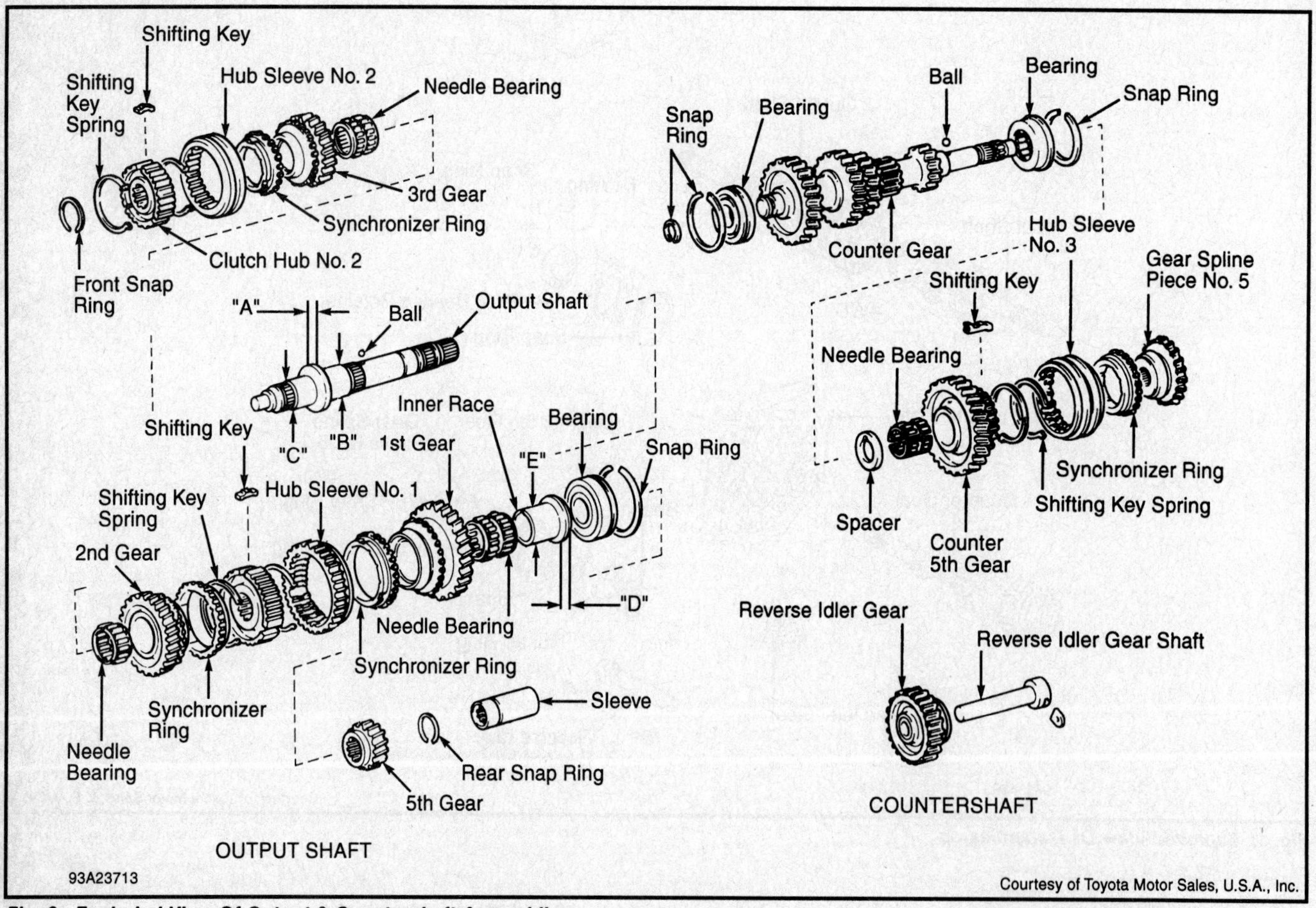

Fig. 3: Exploded View Of Output & Countershaft Assemblies

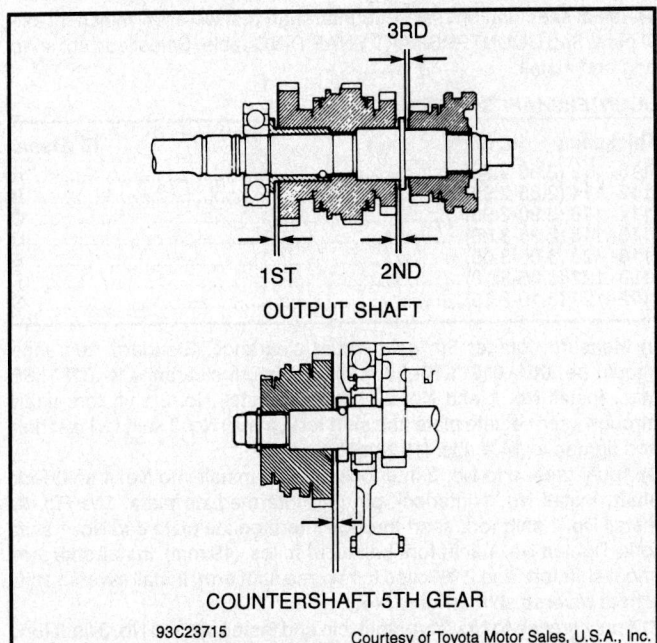

Fig. 4: Identifying Output & Countershaft Measuring Points

Reassembly – 1) Apply gear oil to shaft and needle roller bearing. Place synchronizer ring on gear and align ring slots with shifting keys. Install needle bearing in 3rd gear. Support No. 2 clutch hub, press 3rd gear and No. 2 hub assembly on output shaft. Select No. 2 hub snap ring that will allow minimum axial play and install. See OUTPUT SHAFT FRONT SNAP RING table.

OUTPUT SHAFT FRONT SNAP RING

Thickness – In. (mm)	ID Stamp
.069-.071 (1.75-1.80)	C-1
.071-.073 (1.80-1.85)	D
.073-.075 (1.85-1.90)	D-1
.075-.077 (1.90-1.95)	E
.077-.079 (1.95-2.00)	E-1
.079-.081 (2.00-2.05)	F
.081-.083 (2.05-2.10)	F-1

2) Recheck 3rd gear thrust clearance. Standard clearance should be .004-.010" (.10-.25 mm). Maximum clearance is .010" (.25 mm). Place synchronizer ring on 2nd gear and align ring slots with shifting keys. Apply gear oil to needle roller bearing and shaft. Install needle roller bearing in 2nd gear. Support No. 1 hub, press 2nd gear and No. 1 hub assembly on shaft. Recheck 2nd gear thrust clearance. Standard clearance should be .004-.010" (.10-.25 mm). Maximum clearance is .010" (.25 mm).

3) Install locking ball in output shaft. Apply gear oil to needle roller bearings. Assemble 1st gear, synchronizer ring, needle bearing and bearing inner race. Install 1st gear assembly on output shaft with synchronizer ring slots aligned with shifting keys. Ensure inner race is aligned with locking ball. See Fig. 3.

OUTPUT SHAFT REAR SNAP RING

Thickness – In. (mm)	ID Stamp
.105-.107 (2.67-2.72)	A
.108-.109 (2.73-2.78)	B
.110-.112 (2.79-2.84)	C
.112-.114 (2.85-2.90)	D
.115-.117 (2.91-2.96)	E
.117-.119 (2.97-3.02)	F
.119-.121 (3.03-3.08)	G
.122-.124 (3.09-3.14)	H
.124-.126 (3.15-3.20)	J
.126-.128 (3.21-3.26)	K
.129-.131 (3.27-3.32)	L

4) Press rear bearing on output shaft with outer race snap ring groove toward rear. Hold 1st gear inner race to prevent race from moving. Press 5th gear on end of output shaft. Select 5th gear rear snap ring that will allow minimum axial play and install. See OUTPUT SHAFT REAR SNAP RING table.

5) Measure 1st gear thrust clearance. Standard clearance should be .004-.010" (.10-.25 mm). Maximum clearance is .010" (.25 mm). Install sleeve onto output shaft. See Figs. 1 and 3.

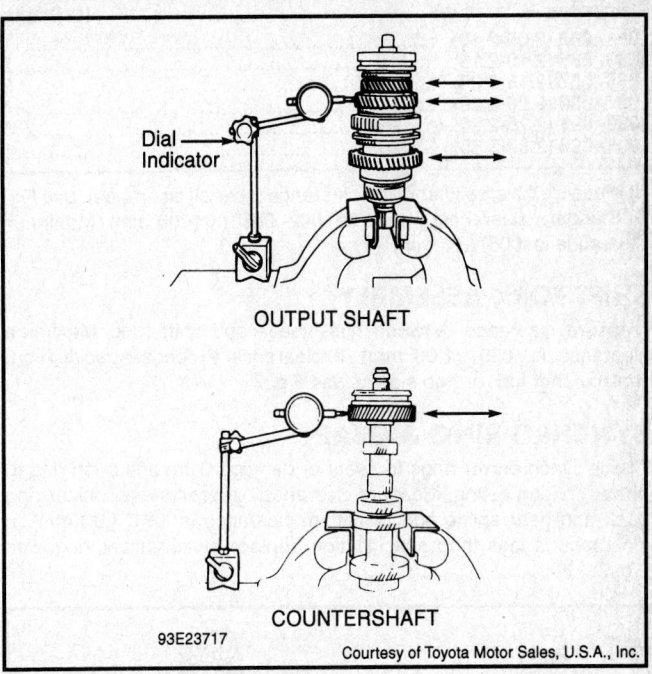

Fig. 5: Measuring Radial Movement

COUNTERSHAFT & REVERSE IDLER GEAR

Inspection – 1) Install spacer, needle roller bearing and 5th gear on countershaft. Measure countershaft 5th gear radial movement (gear oil clearance). See Fig. 5. Standard clearance should be .0004-.0013" (.009-.032 mm). Maximum clearance is .0013" (.032 mm). Measure outer diameter of countershaft needle bearing surface. Standard diameter should be 1.023-1.024" (25.98-26.00 mm). Minimum diameter is 1.018" (25.86 mm).

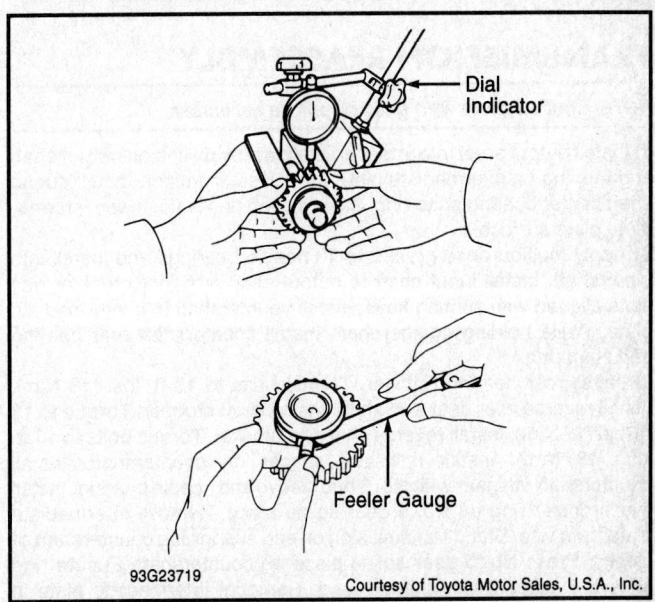

Fig. 6: Identifying Reverse Idler Gear Measuring Points

2) Rotate countershaft front bearing by hand. If any roughness or binding is felt, replace countershaft bearing. Support bearing in blocks and press countershaft out of bearing. Reverse procedure to install bearing. Select and install bearing retaining snap ring that will allow minimum axial play. See COUNTERSHAFT FRONT BEARING SNAP RING table.

COUNTERSHAFT FRONT BEARING SNAP RING

Thickness – In. (mm)	ID Stamp
.081-.083 (2.05-2.10)	1
.083-.085 (2.10-2.15)	2
.085-.087 (2.15-2.20)	3
.087-.089 (2.20-2.25)	4
.089-.091 (2.25-2.30)	5
.091-.093 (2.30-2.35)	6

3) Measure reverse idler radial clearance (gear oil clearance). *See Fig. 6.* Standard clearance should be .002"-.003" (.04-.08 mm). Maximum clearance is .005" (.13 mm).

SHIFT FORK ASSEMBLY

Measure clearance between hub sleeve and shift fork. Maximum clearance is .039" (1.00 mm). If clearance exceeds specification, replace shift fork or hub sleeve. *See Fig. 7.*

SYNCHRO RING & GEAR

Check synchronizer rings for wear or damage. Turn and push ring to check braking action. Measure clearance between synchronizer ring back and gear spline end. Minimum clearance is .031" (.80 mm). If clearance is less than specification, replace synchronizer ring. *See Fig. 7.*

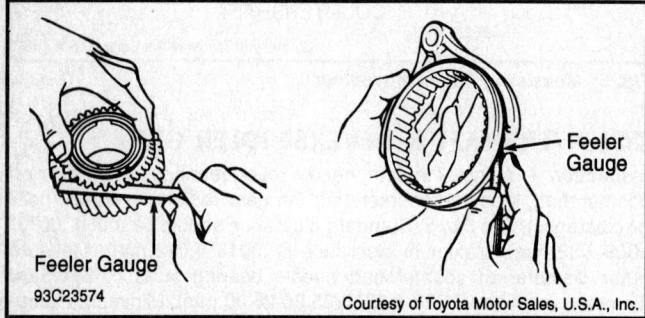

Feeler Gauge

Feeler Gauge

93C23574

Courtesy of Toyota Motor Sales, U.S.A., Inc.

Fig. 7: Measuring Shift Fork & Synchro Ring Assemblies

TRANSMISSION REASSEMBLY

NOTE: Coat all parts with gear oil before assembly.

1) Install output shaft into intermediate plate by pulling on output shaft and tapping on intermediate plate with plastic hammer. Install output shaft center bearing snap ring. Ensure snap ring is flush with intermediate plate surface.

2) Apply multipurpose grease to 13 needle bearings and install into input shaft. Install input shaft to output shaft with synchronizer ring slots aligned with shifting keys. Install countershaft into intermediate plate. While holding countershaft, install countershaft rear bearing and snap ring.

3) Install rear bearing retainer. Torque bolts to 13 ft. lbs. (18 N.m). Install reverse idler gear and shaft. Install shaft stopper. Torque to 13 ft. lbs. (18 N.m). Install reverse shift arm bracket. Torque bolts to 13 ft. lbs. (18 N.m). Install ball and spacer on countershaft. Install countershaft 5th gear with No. 3 hub sleeve and needle bearing. Install synchronizer ring on No. 5 gear spline piece. Remove intermediate plate from vise. Stand transmission on end supporting countershaft of blocks. Press No. 5 gear spline piece on countershaft. Ensure ring slots are aligned with shifting keys. Remount intermediate plate in vise.

4) Select snap ring on rear of countershaft that will allow minimum axial play. See COUNTERSHAFT SNAP RING table. Select correct snap ring and install.

COUNTERSHAFT SNAP RING

Thickness – In. (mm)	ID Stamp
.110-.112 (2.80-2.85)	A
.112-.114 (2.85-2.90)	B
.114-.116 (2.90-2.95)	C
.116-.118 (2.95-3.00)	D
.118-.120 (3.00-3.05)	E
.120-.122 (3.05-3.10)	F
.122-.124 (3.10-3.15)	G

5) Measure counter 5th gear thrust clearance. Standard clearance should be .004-.012" (.10-.30 mm). Maximum clearance is .012" (.30 mm). Install No. 1 and No. 2 shift fork. Install No. 2 shift fork shaft through intermediate plate and shift fork. Install No. 2 shift fork set bolt and tighten to 14 ft. lbs. (19 N.m).

6) Apply grease to No. 2 interlock pin and install into No. 1 shift fork shaft. Install No. 1 interlock pin into intermediate plate. *See Fig. 8.* Install No. 1 shift fork shaft through intermediate plate and No. 1 shift fork. Tighten No. 1 shift fork bolt to 14 ft. lbs. (19 mm). Install shift arm shoe, shift fork and 2 "E" clips to reverse shift arm. Install reverse shift arm to reverse shift arm bracket.

7) Apply grease to No. 2 interlock pin and install pin into No. 3 shift fork shaft. Install No. 1 interlock pin to intermediate plate. Install No. 3 shift fork shaft through intermediate plate and reverse shift fork. Drive roll pin in reverse shift fork.

8) Install reverse shift head to No. 3 shift fork shaft. Install No. 3 shift fork. Install ball into reverse shift head. Install No. 4 shift fork shaft. Install No. 1 interlock ball into intermediate plate. Install No. 4 shift fork shaft. Install set bolt into No. 3 shift fork. Torque to 14 ft. lbs. (19 N.m). Install No. 5 shift fork shaft through reverse shift head and intermediate plate. Drive roll pin into reverse shift head.

9) Install three shift fork shaft snap rings. Install locking balls and springs. Apply sealant to plug threads. Install and torque to 14 ft. lbs. (19 N.m). Apply Three Bond (1281) sealant to transmission case. Stand intermediate plate on end. Install transmission case to intermediate plate. Install 2 snap rings to input shaft front bearing and countershaft front bearing. Replace front bearing retainer oil seal, if necessary. Install bearing retainer with a new gasket. Torque bolts to 12 ft. lbs. (17 N.m).

NOTE: This transmission uses no gasket between major housings; use Three Bond (1281) sealant. Assemble housing immediately after applying liquid gasket. Allow 30 minutes curing time before filling with oil.

10) Install shift lever shaft and shift lever housing. Apply sealant to transfer adapter. Install transfer adapter. Insert shift lever housing to transfer adapter and connect fork shafts. Insert shift lever shaft to transfer adapter and shift lever housing. Install shift lever housing bolt. Torque bolts to 28 ft. lbs. (38 N.m). Install and tighten plug to 27 ft. lbs. (37 N.m).

11) Install locking ball, spring and plug. Torque plug to 14 ft. lbs. (19 N.m). After installing extension housing or transfer adapter ensure input and output shafts rotate smoothly. Ensure shifting can be made smoothly to all positions. Install Black shifter restrict pin on reverse gear/5th gear side. Install second restrict pin. Torque pins to 20 ft. lbs. (27 N.m).

12) Install transmission shift lever control retainer. Torque bolts to 13 ft. lbs. (18 N.m). Install transfer shift lever control retainer. Torque bolts to 13 ft. lbs. (18 N.m). Install select return spring in retainer. Install clutch housing. Torque bolts to 27 ft. lbs. (37 N.m). Install back-up light. Torque to 27 ft. lbs. (37 N.m).

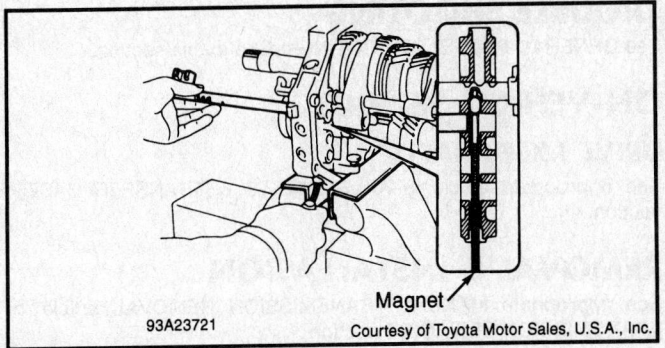

Magnet

93A23721

Courtesy of Toyota Motor Sales, U.S.A., Inc.

Fig. 8: View Of No. 1 Interlock Pin

TORQUE SPECIFICATIONS

TORQUE SPECIFICATIONS

Application	Ft. Lbs. (N.m)
Back-Up Light Switch	27 (37)
Clutch Housing Bolts	27 (37)
Front Bearing Retainer Bolts	13 (18)
Rear Bearing Retainer Bolts	13 (18)
Restrict Pin	20 (27)
Reverse Idler Gear Shaft Stopper Bolt	13 (18)
Reverse Shift Arm Bracket Bolt	13 (18)
Shift Fork Bolt	14 (19)
Shift Lever Housing Bolt	28 (38)
Shaft Stopper Bolt	13 (18)
Straight Screw Plug	14 (19)
Transfer Adapter	27 (37)
Transmission Housing Bolt	27 (37)

MANUAL TRANSMISSIONS
Toyota RAV4 E250F 5-Speed

APPLICATION & LABOR TIMES

APPLICATION & LABOR TIMES

Vehicle	Labor Times		
Application	[1] R & I	[2] Overhaul	Series
1996 RAV4			
With A/C	12.8	10.6	E250F
Without A/C	12.5	10.6	E250F

[1] – Removal and installation of transmission from vehicle chassis.
[2] – Bench overhaul time for transaxle/differential. DOES NOT include removal and installation.

IDENTIFICATION

Transmission type is identified by ID label located on driver's side door post.

DESCRIPTION

Transaxle design incorporates transmission, center differential, front differential and transfer case. Transmission is shifted by a pair of push-pull cables. These cables provide positive shift feel and absorb transmission and engine vibrations.

The E250F model utilizes a full-time transfer case with a limited slip viscous coupling. Both units have a center differential, which compensates for difference between the rotational speed of the front and rear wheels. *See Fig. 1.*

LUBRICATION & ADJUSTMENTS

See appropriate MANUAL TRANSMISSION SERVICING article in TRANSMISSION SERVICING section.

TROUBLE SHOOTING

See GENERAL TROUBLE SHOOTING article in this section.

ON-VEHICLE SERVICE

DRIVE AXLE SHAFTS

See appropriate article in AXLE SHAFTS & TRANSFER CASES section.

REMOVAL & INSTALLATION

See appropriate MANUAL TRANSMISSION REMOVAL article in TRANSMISSION SERVICING section.

TRANSAXLE DISASSEMBLY

1) Unbolt transfer case from transaxle housing. Using a plastic hammer, remove transfer case from transaxle. Screw in appropriate bolt and washer into differential side gear intermediate shaft. Using slide hammer type puller, remove shaft.

2) Remove back-up light switch. Remove speedometer adapter. Remove speedometer driven gear or speed sensor, if equipped. Remove gear selecting bellcrank. Remove shift and select lever lock bolt. Remove control shaft cover. Remove shift and select lever shaft assembly. *See Fig. 2.*

3) Remove case cover. Unstake output shaft lock nut. Lock transmission in 2 gears. Remove output shaft lock nut. Unlock transmission. *See Fig. 3.*

4) Remove No. 3 shift fork set bolt. Remove No. 3 hub sleeve and No. 3 shift fork. Using puller, remove 5th driven gear. *See Fig. 3.* Measure 5th gear clearances. Record for reassembly reference. Using dial indicator, measure 5th gear thrust clearance. *See Fig. 4.* Standard

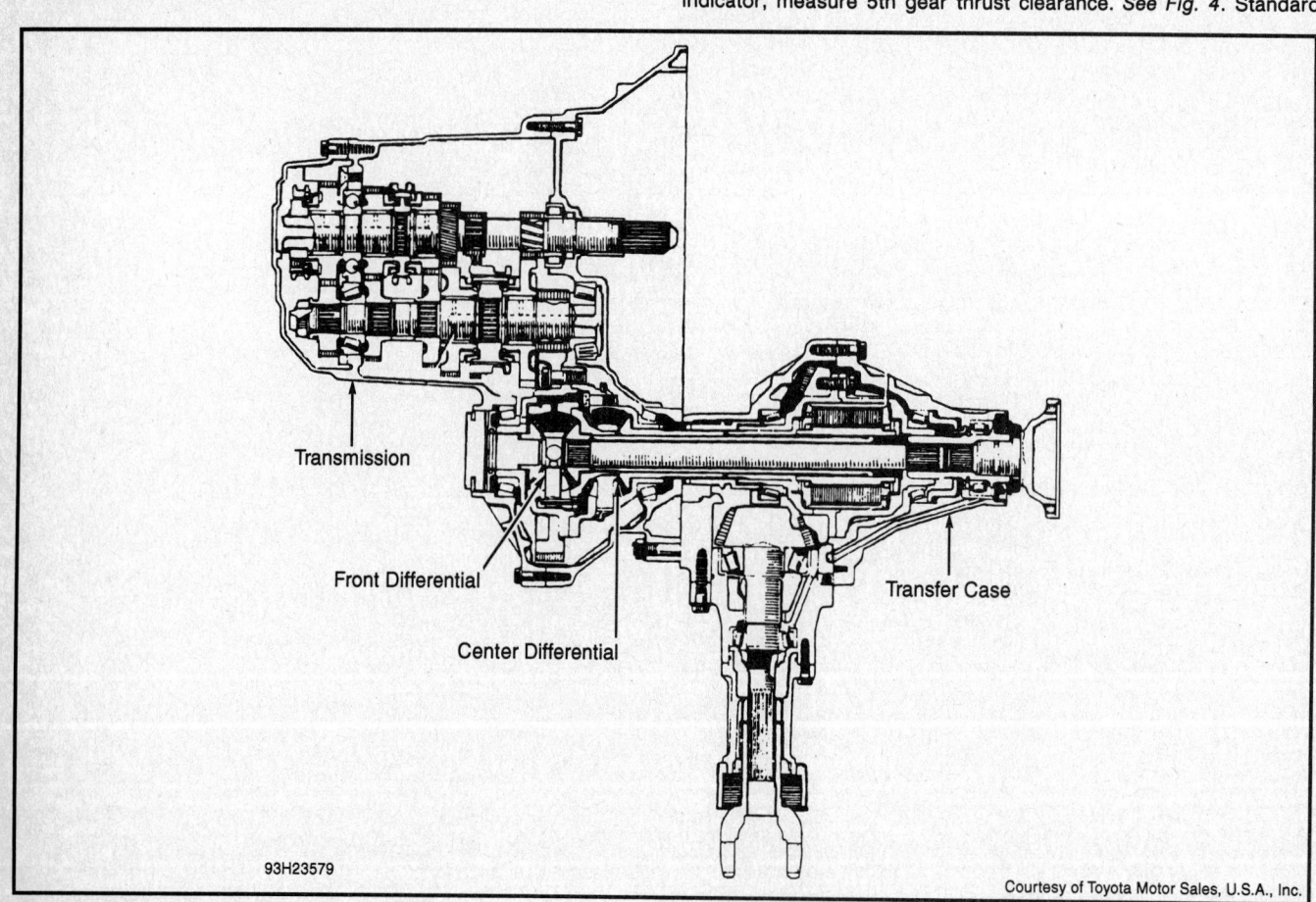

93H23579

Courtesy of Toyota Motor Sales, U.S.A., Inc.

Fig. 1: Cut-Away View Of Transaxle Assembly

Labels in figure: Transmission, Front Differential, Center Differential, Transfer Case clearance should be .004-.022" (.10-.57 mm). Service limit is .026" (.65 mm). Remount dial indicator to measure lateral movement (oil clearance) of 5th gear. Standard clearance should be .0004-.002" (.009-.05 mm). Service limit is .0028" (.070 mm).

5) Remove input shaft snap ring. Using puller, remove No. 3 clutch hub with synchronizer ring and 5th gear. Remove needle bearing and spacer. Remove 7 Torx (T45) screws and rear bearing retainer. Remove adjusting shim.

6) Remove input shaft rear bearing snap ring. Remove shift fork shaft snap rings. Remove plug. Remove seat, spring and detent ball with a magnet. Remove reverse idler gear shaft retaining bolt.

7) Remove transmission housing. Remove No. 2 oil pipe. Remove reverse shift arm bracket. Remove reverse idler gear, thrust washer and shaft. Remove all remaining plugs, seats, springs and detent balls with magnet.

8) To remove No. 1 shift fork shaft, pull up No. 3 shift fork shaft. Using magnetic finger, remove interlock roller. Remove No. 2 shift fork shaft, shift head and No. 1 shift fork. Pull out No. 3 shift fork shaft with the reverse shift fork.

9) Remove output and input shaft assemblies. Remove oil pump drive gear. Remove differential case assembly. Remove oil pipe and oil pump. *See Fig. 2.*

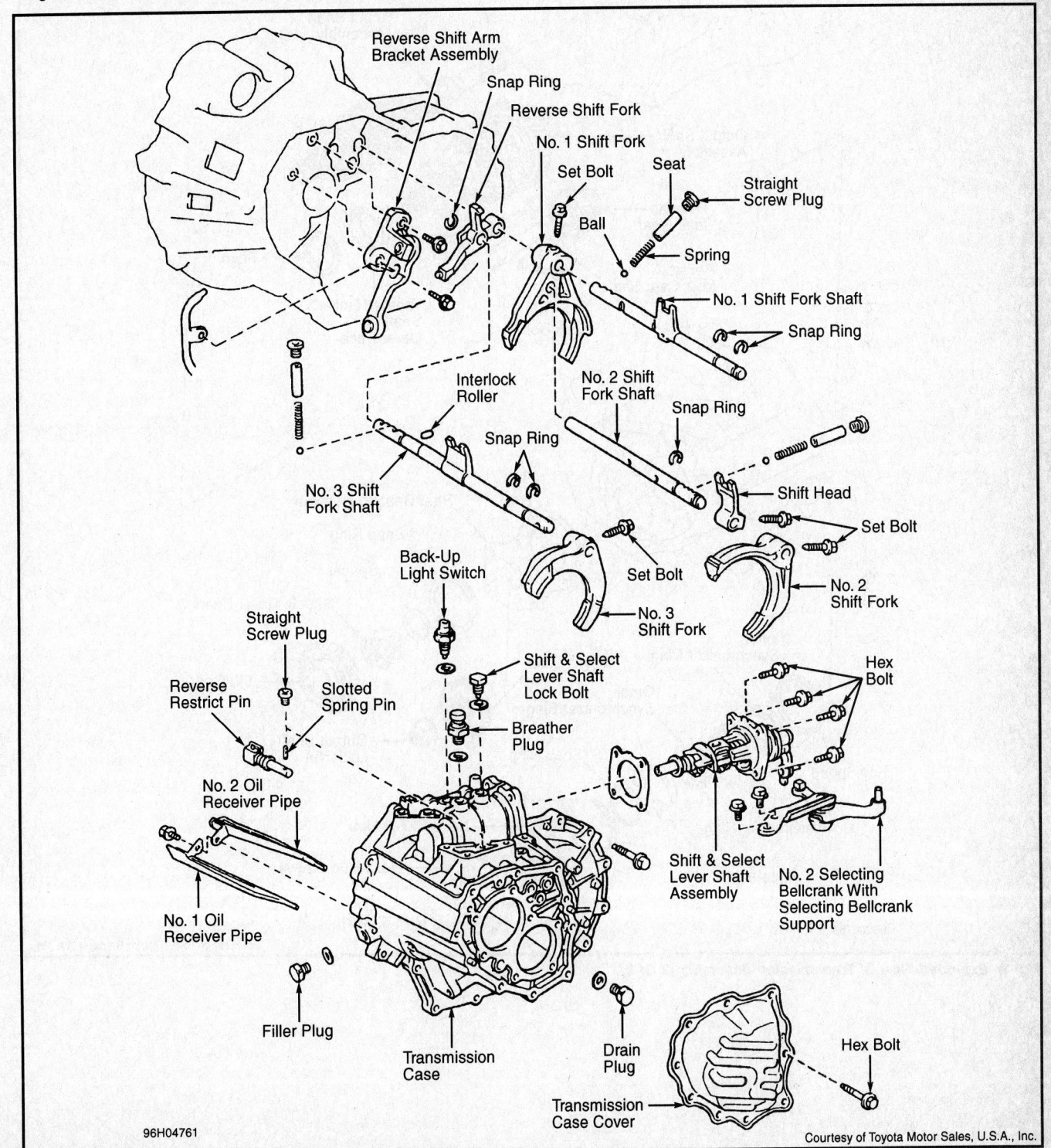

96H04761

Courtesy of Toyota Motor Sales, U.S.A., Inc.

Fig. 2: Exploded View Of Transmission Assembly (1 Of 2)

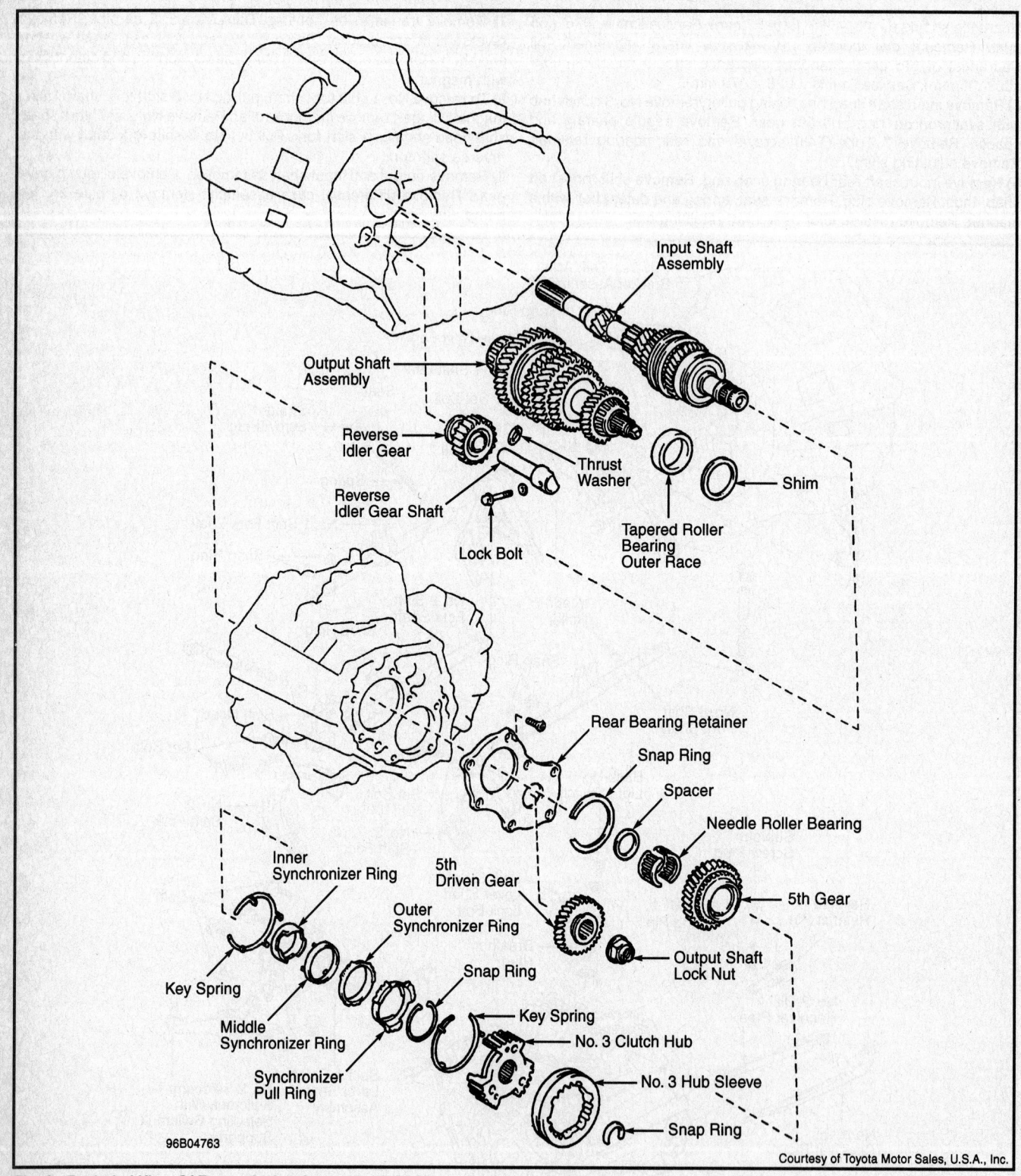

Input Shaft Assembly

Output Shaft Assembly

Reverse Idler Gear

Reverse Idler Gear Shaft

Thrust Washer

Lock Bolt

Shim

Tapered Roller Bearing Outer Race

Rear Bearing Retainer

Snap Ring

Spacer

Needle Roller Bearing

Inner Synchronizer Ring

5th Driven Gear

Outer Synchronizer Ring

5th Gear

Key Spring

Snap Ring

Output Shaft Lock Nut

Middle Synchronizer Ring

Key Spring

No. 3 Clutch Hub

Synchronizer Pull Ring

No. 3 Hub Sleeve

Snap Ring

96B04763

Courtesy of Toyota Motor Sales, U.S.A., Inc.

Fig. 3: Exploded View Of Transmission Assembly (2 Of 2)

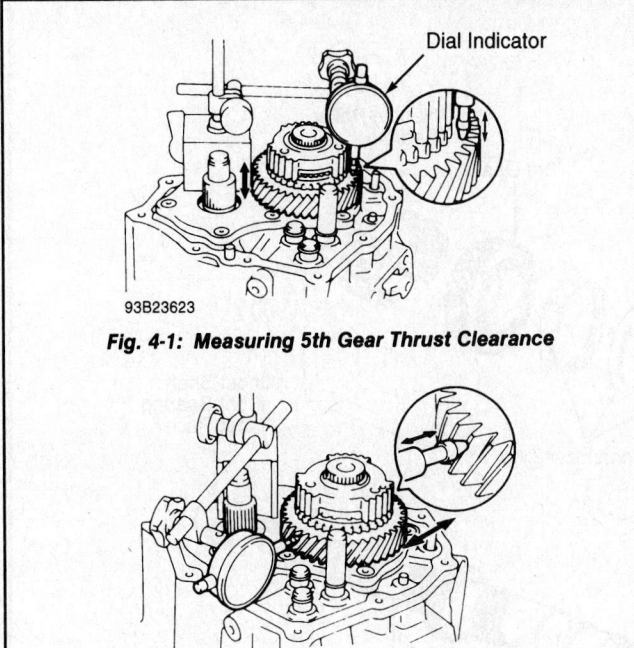

Fig. 4-1: Measuring 5th Gear Thrust Clearance

93B23623

93C23624

Fig. 4-2: Measuring 5th Gear Lateral Movement

Courtesy of Toyota Motor Sales, U.S.A., Inc.

Fig. 4: Measuring 5th Gear clearances

COMPONENT DISASSEMBLY & REASSEMBLY

INPUT SHAFT (MAINSHAFT)

Disassembly – 1) For all measurement specifications, refer to INPUT SHAFT SPECIFICATIONS table. Using feeler gauge, measure 3rd and 4th gear thrust clearances. *See Fig. 5.* Secure input shaft in soft-jawed vise. Using dial indicator, measure 3rd and 4th gear lateral movement (gear oil clearance). If clearance exceeds maximum specification, replace gear, needle bearing and/or shaft.

INPUT SHAFT SPECIFICATIONS

Application	Specification In. (mm)
3rd Gear Thrust Clearance	
Standard Clearance	.004-.014 (.10-.35)
Service Limit	.016 (.40)
4th Gear Thrust Clearance	
Standard Clearance	.004-.022 (.10-.55)
Service Limit	.024 (.60)
3rd & 4th Gear Lateral Movement	
Standard Clearance	.0004-.002 (.009-.05)
Service Limit	.003 (.07)

2) Remove snap ring from input shaft. Using bearing splitter or appropriate blocks, support 4th gear and press input shaft out of rear bearing and 4th gear. Remove needle bearings, spacer and synchronizer ring. Remove snap ring. Supporting 3rd gear, press input shaft out of No. 2 hub sleeve. Remove synchronizer ring, needle bearing and 3rd gear. Remove needle bearing. Press input shaft out of front bearing inner race. *See Fig. 6.*

NOTE: Input shaft inner bearing race is non-reusable and should be replaced.

Inspection – 1) Inspect all parts for damage and wear. Replace if necessary. Clean all parts in new solvent, dry and lubricate all parts. Ensure oil passages are free of contamination.

2) Measure input shaft at points "A", "B" and "C". *See Fig. 7.* Support input shaft on "V" blocks. Using dial indicator to measure runout, rotate input shaft 2 complete revolutions. Replace input shaft if runout or any part of shaft is not within service limit. See INPUT SHAFT JOURNAL DIAMETERS table.

INPUT SHAFT JOURNAL DIAMETERS

Application [1]	Minimum Diameter In. (mm)
"A" Shaft Journal Diameter	1.100 (27.95)
"B" Shaft Journal Diameter	1.415 (35.95)
"C" Shaft Journal Diameter	1.415 (35.95)
Runout Limits	.002 (.05)

[1] – "A", "B", and "C" refer to measuring points indicated in *Fig. 7.*

NOTE: Input shaft front inner bearing race is non-reusable and should be replaced.

Reassembly – 1) Install clutch hub and shifting keys to No. 2 hub sleeve. Ensure key spring end-gaps are not in line.

2) Apply multipurpose grease to needle bearings. Install bearing in 3rd gear. Place synchronizer ring on 3rd gear and align ring slots with shifting keys. Using press, install 3rd gear and No. 2 hub sleeve. *See Fig. 6.*

3) Select snap ring that will allow minimum axial play on shaft. See SNAP RING APPLICATION CHART NO. 1.

SNAP RING APPLICATION CHART NO. 1

Thickness – In. (mm)	Stamped Letter
.091-.093 (2.30-2.35)	H
.093-.095 (2.35-2.40)	J
.095-.097 (2.40-2.45)	K
.097-.098 (2.45-2.50)	L
.098-.100 (2.50-2.55)	M
.100-.102 (2.55-2.60)	N
.102-.104 (2.60-2.65)	P

4) Install selected snap ring. Recheck 3rd gear thrust clearance. Clearance should be .004-.014" (.10-.35 mm). Install spacer. Place synchronizer ring on 4th gear and align ring slots with shifting keys. Install 4th gear. Press on ball bearing. *See Fig. 6.*

5) Select 4th gear snap ring that will allow minimum axial play on shaft. See SNAP RING APPLICATION CHART NO. 2.

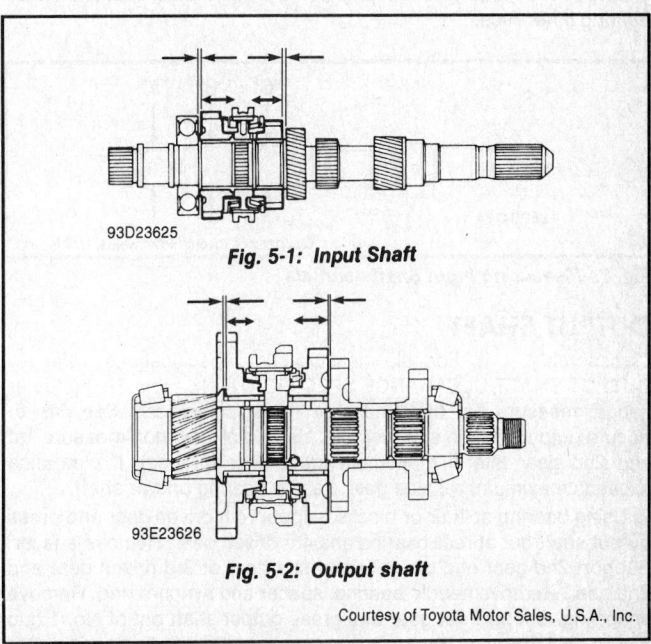

93D23625

Fig. 5-1: Input Shaft

93E23626

Fig. 5-2: Output shaft

Courtesy of Toyota Motor Sales, U.S.A., Inc.

Fig. 5: Measuring Shaft Thrust Clearances

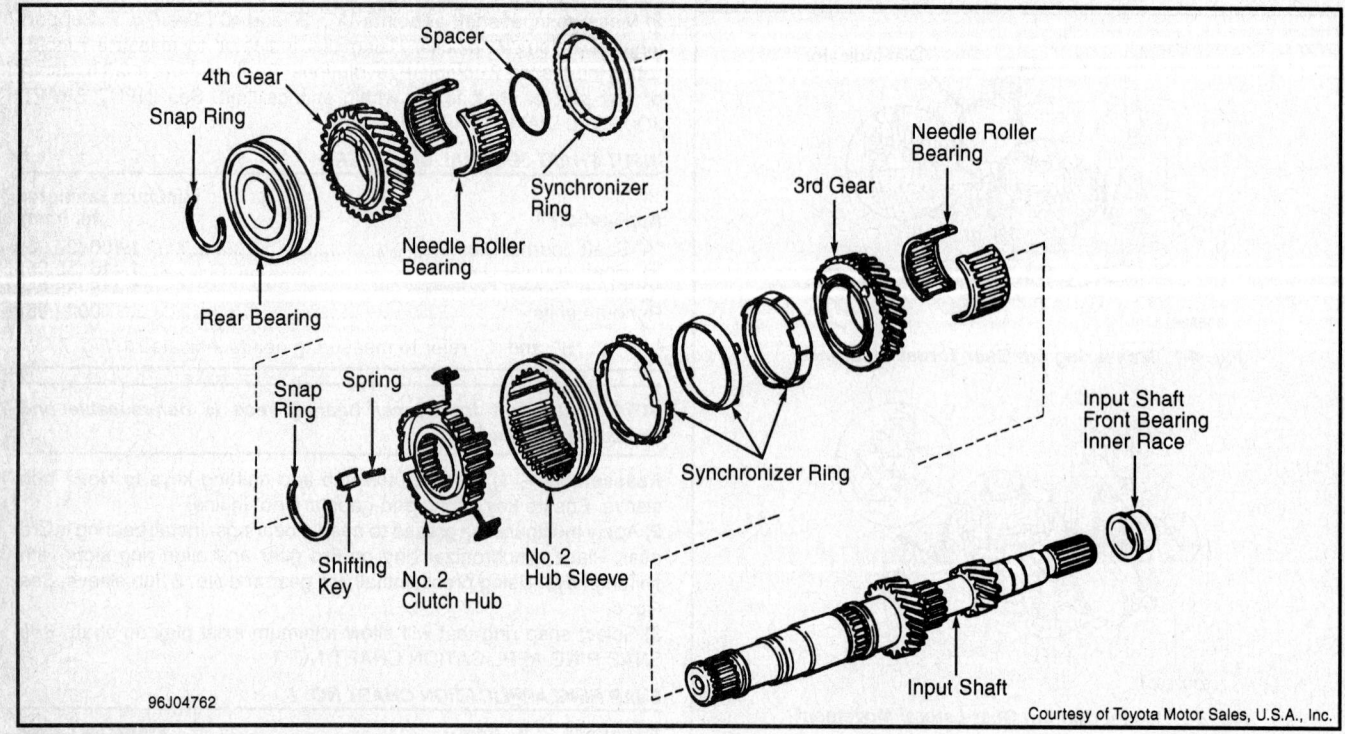

96J04762

Courtesy of Toyota Motor Sales, U.S.A., Inc.

Fig. 6: Identifying Input Shaft Components

SNAP RING APPLICATION CHART NO. 2

Thickness – In. (mm)	Stamped Number
.093-.095 (2.35-2.40)	1
.095-.097 (2.40-2.45)	2
.097-.098 (2.45-2.50)	3
.098-.100 (2.50-2.55)	4
.100-.102 (2.55-2.60)	5
.102-.104 (2.60-2.65)	6
.104-.106 (2.65-2.70)	7
.106-.108 (2.70-2.75)	8

6) Install snap ring. Recheck 4th gear thrust clearance. Clearance should be .004-.022" (.10-.55 mm). Using press, install input shaft front bearing inner race.

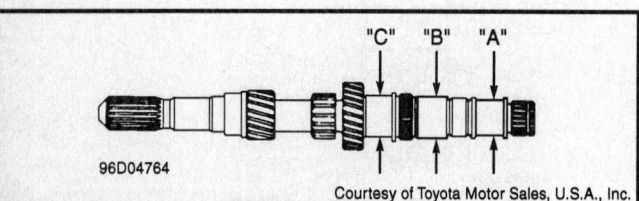

96D04764

Courtesy of Toyota Motor Sales, U.S.A., Inc.

Fig. 7: Measuring Input Shaft Journals

OUTPUT SHAFT

Disassembly – 1) For all measurement specifications refer to OUTPUT SHAFT CLEARANCE SPECIFICATIONS table. Using feeler gauge, measure 1st and 2nd gear thrust clearances. *See Fig. 5.* Secure output shaft in soft-jaw vise. Using dial indicator, measure 1st and 2nd gear lateral movement (gear oil clearance). If clearance exceeds maximum, replace gear, needle bearing and/or shaft.

2) Using bearing splitter or blocks, support 4th driven gear and press output shaft out of rear bearing and 4th driven gear. Remove spacer. Support 2nd gear and press output shaft out of 3rd driven gear and 2nd gear. Remove needle bearing, spacer and synchro ring. Remove snap ring. Support 1st gear and press output shaft out of No. 1 hub sleeve and 1st gear. Remove synchro ring and needle bearing. *See Fig. 8.*

OUTPUT SHAFT CLEARANCE SPECIFICATIONS

Application	Specification In. (mm)
1st Gear Thrust Clearance	
Standard Clearance	.004-.014 (.10-.35)
Service Limit	.016 (.40)
2nd Gear Thrust Clearance	
Standard Clearance	.004-.018 (.10-.45)
Service Limit	.020 (.50)
1st & 2nd Gear Lateral Movement	
Standard Clearance	.0004-.002 (.009-.05)
Service Limit	.003 (.07)

Inspection – 1) Inspect all parts for damage and wear. Replace if necessary. Clean all parts in new solvent, dry and lubricate all parts. Ensure oil passages are free of contamination.
2) Measure output shaft at points "A" and "B". *See Fig. 9.* Support output shaft on "V" blocks. Using a dial indicator to measure runout, rotate output shaft 2 complete revolutions. Replace output shaft if runout or any part of shaft is not within service limit. See OUTPUT SHAFT JOURNAL DIAMETERS table.

OUTPUT SHAFT JOURNAL DIAMETERS

Application [1]	Minimum Diameter In. (mm)
"A" Shaft Journal Diameters	1.48 (37.53)
"B" Shaft Journal Diameter	1.36 (34.51)
Runout Limits	.002 (.06)

[1] – "A" and "B" refer to measuring points indicated in *Fig. 9.*

NOTE: *Output shaft inner bearing race is non-reusable and should be replaced.*

Reassembly – 1) If output shaft rear bearing replacement is necessary, support bearing with bearing splitter or blocks. Press output shaft out of bearing. To replace, support bearing with Adapter (09316-60010), press shaft onto bearing. Use 2-jaw puller to remove bearing race from clutch housing. To replace, use driver.

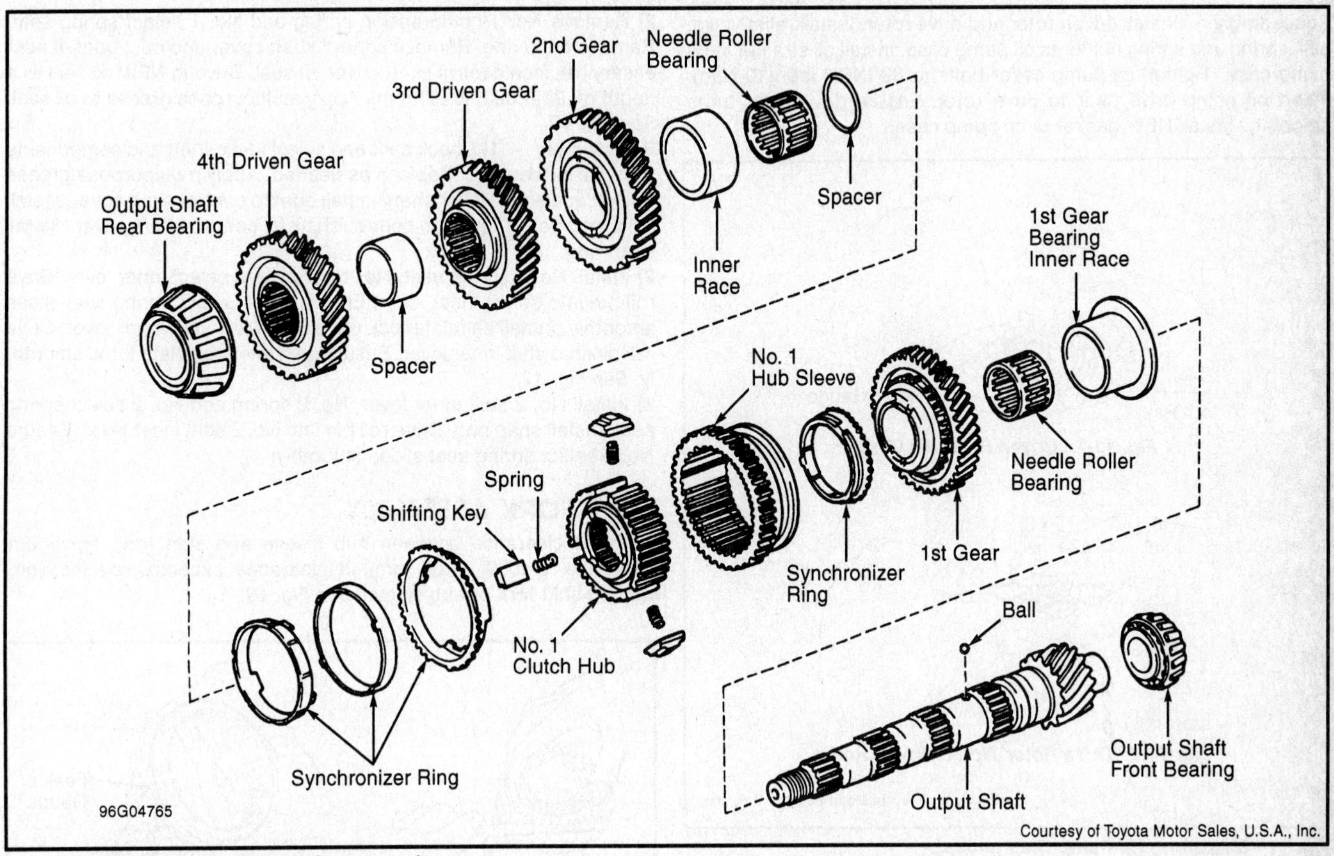

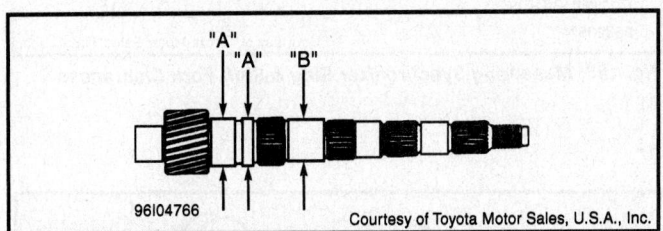

Fig. 8: Identifying Output Shaft Components

96G04765

Courtesy of Toyota Motor Sales, U.S.A., Inc.

Fig. 9: Measuring Output Shaft Journals

96I04766

Courtesy of Toyota Motor Sales, U.S.A., Inc.

2) Install components in reverse order of disassembly. Install ball, 1st gear bearing inner race, align hole in bearing to shaft. Install No. 1 clutch hub and shifting keys to No. 1 hub sleeve. Install shifting key springs under shifting keys. Ensure key spring end gaps are not in line. Apply multipurpose grease to needle bearings. Install bearing in 1st gear. Place synchronizer ring on gear and align ring slots with shifting keys. Press 1st gear and No. 1 hub sleeve onto output shaft. See Fig. 8.

3) Select 1st gear snap ring that allows minimum axial play on shaft. Snap rings are available in thicknesses of .110" (2.80 mm) to .122" (3.10 mm) in .05 mm increments. Snap rings are stamped "A" thorough "G", depending on thickness.

4) Recheck 1st gear thrust clearance. Clearance should be .004-.014" (.10-.35 mm). Install spacer. Apply multipurpose grease to needle bearing. Place synchronizer ring on 2nd gear and align ring slots with shifting keys. Install 2nd gear. Using press, install 3rd driven gear on output shaft. Recheck 2nd gear thrust clearance. Standard clearance should be .004-.018" (.10-.45 mm). Install spacer. Using press, install 4th driven gear on output shaft. Press on output shaft rear bearing.

OIL PUMP

Disassembly – 1) Install oil pump drive gear to drive rotor. Ensure drive rotor turns smoothly. Remove gasket from oil pump case.

Remove bolt and pull out oil strainer. Hold oil pump cover. Unbolt and remove cover. Remove spring holder, spring, ball and relief valve seat. See Fig. 10.

2) Install oil pump drive gear to drive rotor. Measure clearance between driven rotor and oil pump case. See Fig. 11. Clearance should be .004-.006" (.10-.16 mm). Service limit is .012" (.30 mm). Measure tip clearance between drive rotor and driven rotor. See Fig. 11. Standard clearance should be .003-.006" (.08-.15 mm). Service limit is .012" (.30 mm).

3) Remove oil pump drive gear. Using straightedge and feeler gauge, measure side clearance of both rotors. Standard clearance should be .001-.003" (.03-.08 mm). Maximum clearance is .006" (.16 mm). Remove oil pump drive rotor and driven rotor. Replace "O" ring in oil pump case.

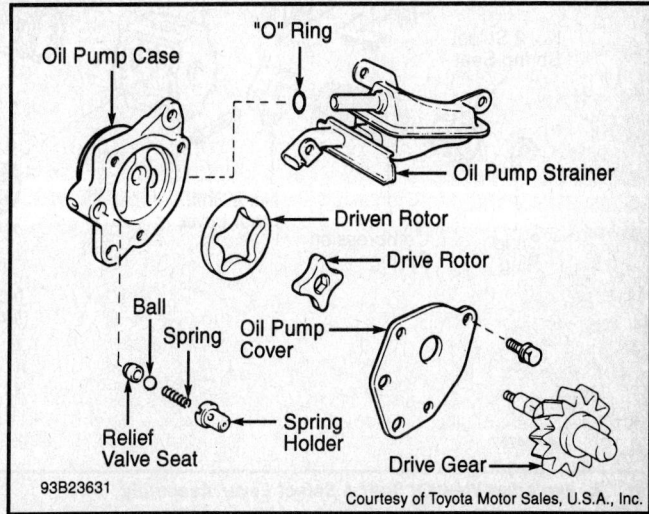

93B23631

Courtesy of Toyota Motor Sales, U.S.A., Inc.

Fig. 10: Exploded View Of Oil Pump Assembly

Reassembly – Install driven rotor and drive rotor. Install relief valve, ball, spring and spring holder to oil pump case. Install oil strainer to oil pump case. Tighten oil pump cover bolts to 89 INCH lbs. (10 N.m). Insert oil pump drive gear to drive rotor. Ensure drive rotor turns smoothly. Install NEW gasket to oil pump case.

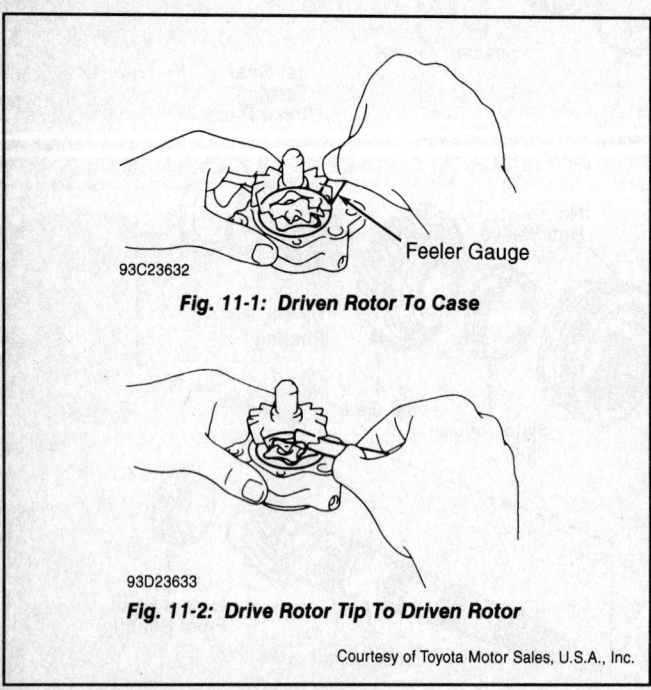

Fig. 11-1: **Driven Rotor To Case**

Fig. 11-2: **Drive Rotor Tip To Driven Rotor**

Courtesy of Toyota Motor Sales, U.S.A., Inc.

Fig. 11: **Measuring Oil Pump Clearances**

SHIFT & SELECT LEVER SHAFT

Disassembly – **1)** Using pin punch and a hammer, drive out roll pin from No. 2 shift inner lever. Remove snap ring. Remove No. 2 select spring seat, No. 2 spring and No. 2 shift inner lever. Drive out roll pin from No.1 shift inner lever. Remove shift interlock plate and No. 1 shift inner lever from shaft. *See Fig. 12.*

2) Remove No. 1 compression spring and No. 1 select spring seat. Remove snap ring. Remove control shaft cover and dust boot. If necessary, replace control shaft cover oil seal. Drive in NEW oil seal to a depth of .000-.020" (0-.51 mm). Apply multipurpose grease to oil seal. *See Fig. 12.*

Reassembly – **1)** Check shift and select lever shaft and components for wear or damage. Replace as needed. Apply multipurpose grease to shift and select lever shaft. Install boot to control shaft cover. Install shift and select lever or control shaft to control shaft cover. Install snap ring.

2) Install No. 1 spring seat, No. 1 spring and select inner lever. Drive roll pin into select inner lever. Ensure No. 1 select spring seat slides smoothly. Install shift interlock plate and No. 1 shift inner lever. Drive roll pin into shift inner lever. Ensure shift interlock plate turns smoothly. *See Fig. 12.*

3) Install No. 2 shift inner lever, No. 2 spring and No. 2 select spring seat. Install snap ring. Drive roll pin into No. 2 shift inner lever. Ensure No. 2 select spring seat slides smoothly.

SHIFT FORK ASSEMBLY

Measure clearance between hub sleeve and shift fork. Maximum clearance is .039" (1.00 mm). If clearance exceeds specification, replace shift fork or hub sleeve. *See Fig. 13.*

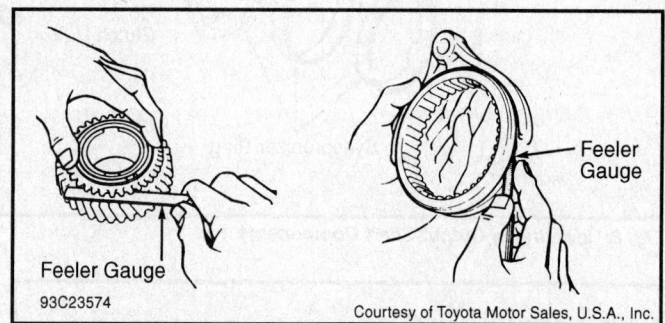

Courtesy of Toyota Motor Sales, U.S.A., Inc.

Fig. 13: **Measuring Synchronizer Ring & Shift Fork Clearances**

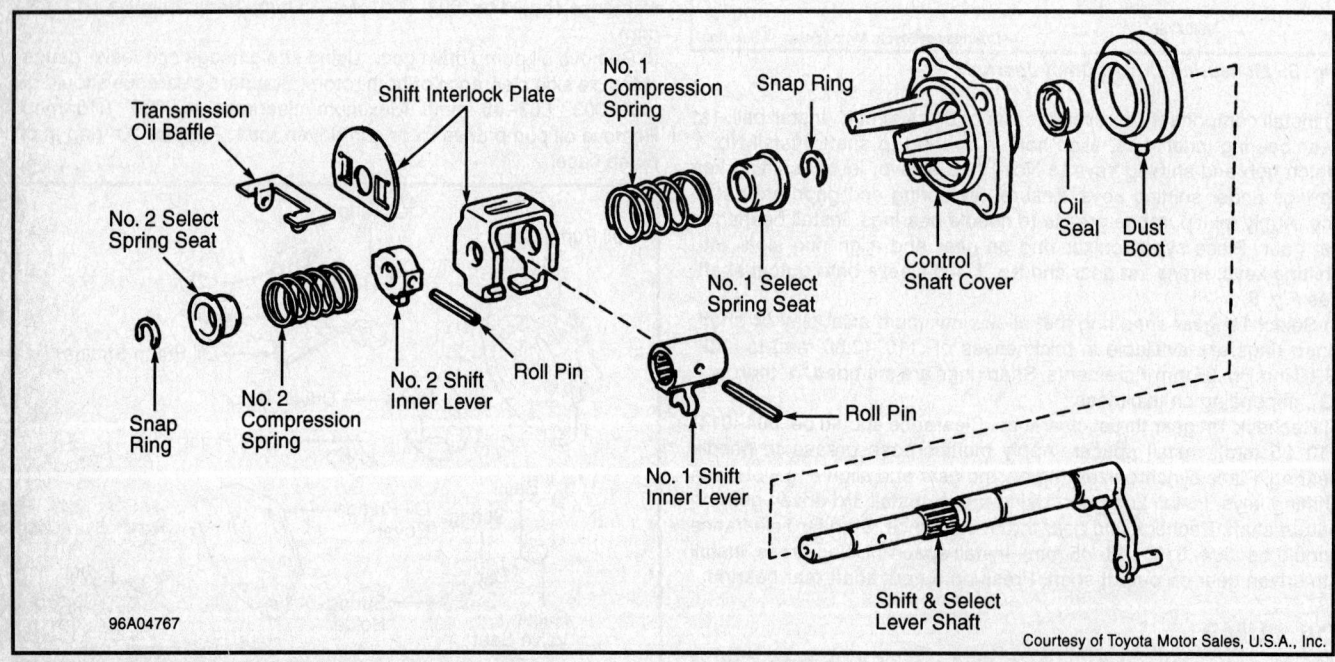

Fig. 12: **Exploded View Of Shift & Select Lever Assembly**

Courtesy of Toyota Motor Sales, U.S.A., Inc.

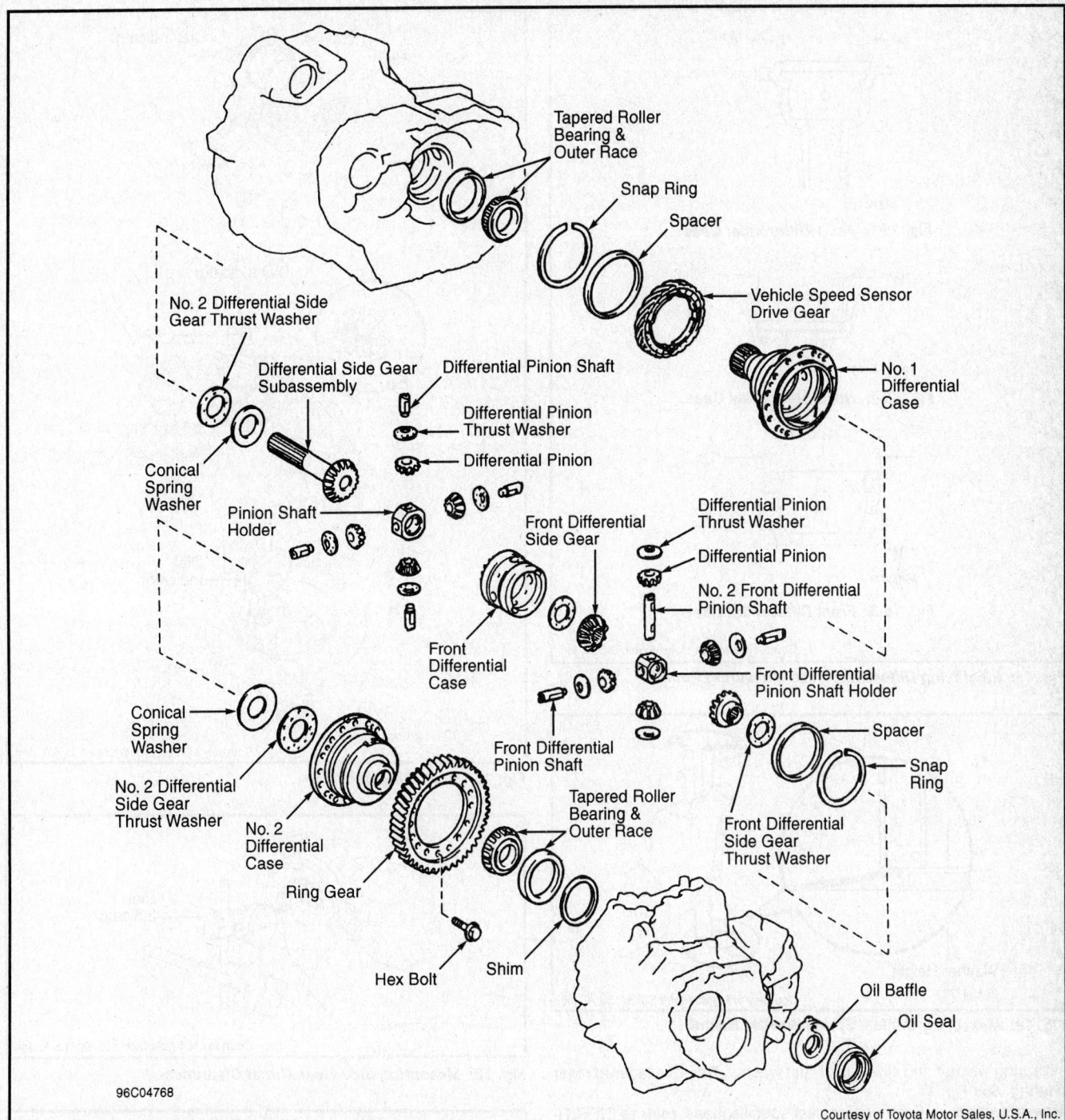

Fig. 14: Exploded View Of Differential Assemblies

96C04768

Courtesy of Toyota Motor Sales, U.S.A., Inc.

SYNCHRO RING & GEAR

Check synchronizer rings for wear or damage. Turn and push ring to check braking action. Measure clearance between synchronizer ring back and gear spline end. First and fourth gear synchronizer minimum clearance is 0.03" (0.8 mm). Second gear synchronizer minimum clearance is 0.028" (0.7 mm). If clearance is less than specification, replace synchronizer ring. *See Fig. 13.*

DIFFERENTIAL

NOTE: Measure differential bearing preload prior to transmission disassembly.

Disassembly – **1)** Remove No. 2 differential case. Matchmark differential case and ring gear. Remove ring gear. Remove No. 2 differential side gear thrust washer and conical spring washer. *See Fig. 14.*
2) Remove front differential case assembly. Remove front differential side gear and thrust washer. Remove snap ring and spacer.

NOTE: Wrap vinyl tape around case to prevent damage.

Remove front differential pinion shafts, No. 2 front pinion shaft, shaft holder, pinions, pinion thrust washers, front differential side gear and front differential thrust washer. Remove snap ring, spacer and vehicle speed sensor drive gear. Remove tapered roller bearing.
3) From No. 1 differential case, remove pinion shafts, shaft holder, pinions and thrust washers, differential side gear subassembly, coni-

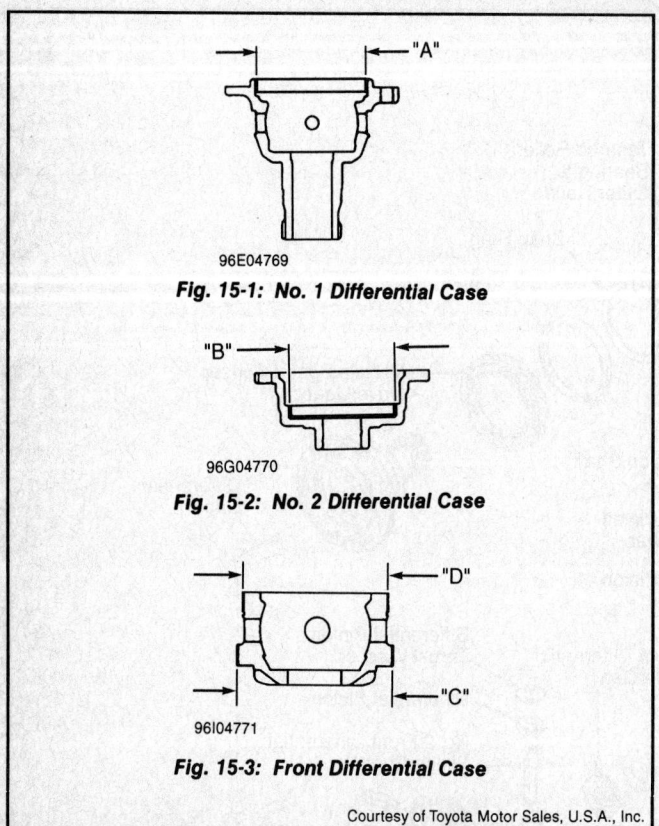

Fig. 15-1: No. 1 Differential Case

Fig. 15-2: No. 2 Differential Case

Fig. 15-3: Front Differential Case

Courtesy of Toyota Motor Sales, U.S.A., Inc.

Fig. 15: Identifying Differential Case Measuring Points

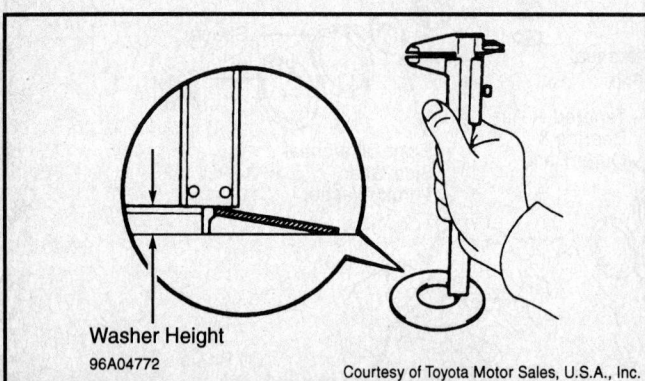

Courtesy of Toyota Motor Sales, U.S.A., Inc.

Fig. 16: Measuring Conical Spring Washer Height

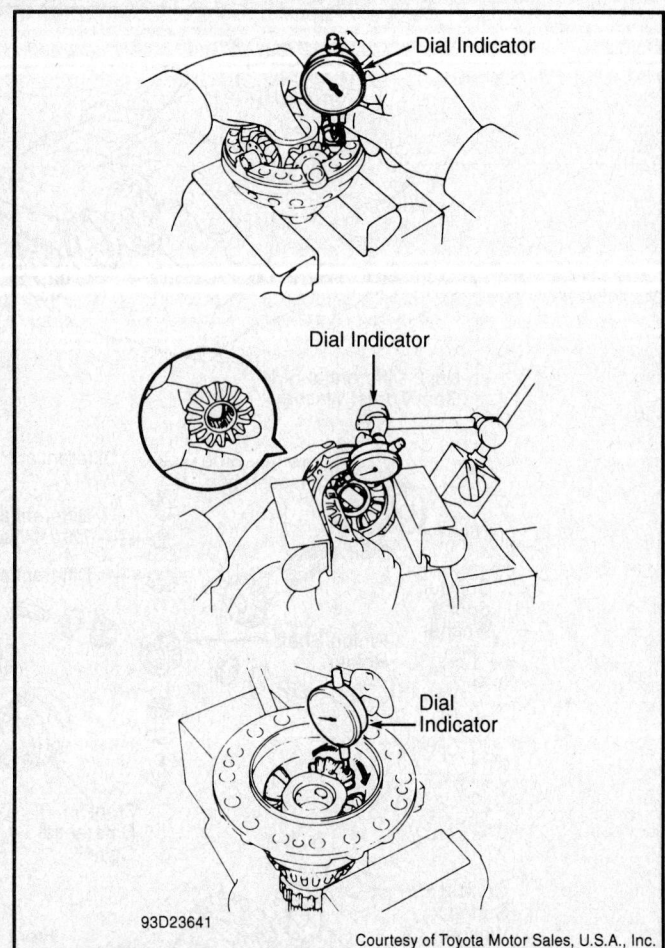

Courtesy of Toyota Motor Sales, U.S.A., Inc.

Fig. 17: Measuring Backlash

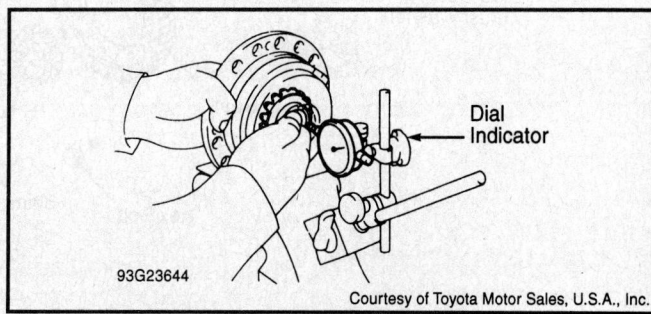

Courtesy of Toyota Motor Sales, U.S.A., Inc.

Fig. 18: Measuring Side Gear Thrust Clearance

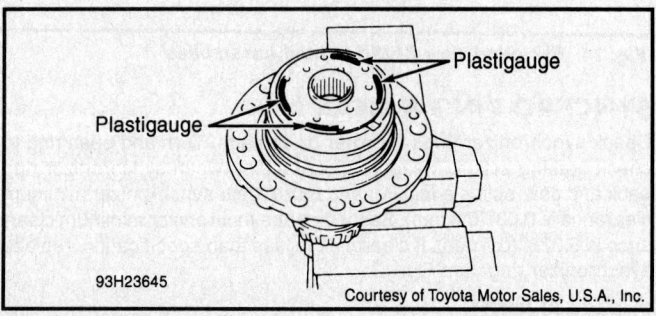

Courtesy of Toyota Motor Sales, U.S.A., Inc.

Fig. 19: Location Of Plastigauge

cal spring washer and side gear thrust washer. Remove tapered roller bearing. *See Fig. 14.*

Measurements – For measurement specifications, refer to DIFFERENTIAL CASE SPECIFICATIONS table. Using a dial bore gauge, measure inner diameters of No. 1 differential case and No. 2 differential case. Measure outer diameters of No. 2 differential case. Measure height of conical spring washer. *See Figs. 15 and 16.*

Reassembly – **1)** Replace transmission case oil seal and outer bearing race. Adjust bearing race with shims as necessary. Install adjust shim, tapered outer bearing race, oil baffle and oil seal. On transaxle case side replace tapered roller bearing outer race if needed. Install tapered roller bearing to No. 1 differential case side. Reassemble differential side gear subassembly. Measure backlash of one pinion gear while holding differential side gear subassembly toward case. Using dial indicator, measure backlash. Ensure backlash is .002-.008" (.05-.20 mm). *See Fig. 17.* If backlash is out of specifications, select a thrust washer to adjust. Thrust washers are available in thicknesses of .031" (.80 mm) to .055" (1.40 mm) in .002" (.05 mm) increments.

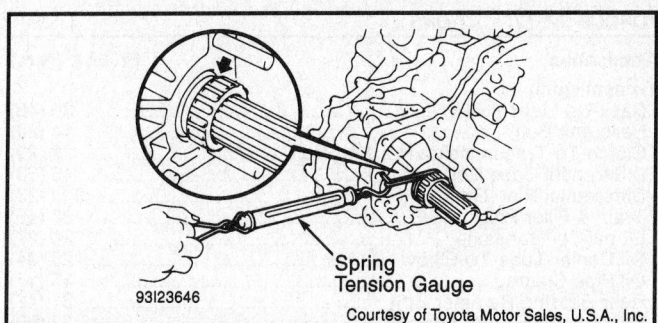

Fig. 20: Measuring Differential Side Bearing Preload

DIFFERENTIAL CASE SPECIFICATIONS

Application	In. (mm)
No. 1 Differential Case [1]	
"A" Standard Diameter	4.095-4.096 (104.0-104.3)
"A" Maximum Diameter	4.097 (104.60)
No. 2 Differential Case [1]	
"B" Standard Diameter	3.819-3.820 (97.00-97.04)
"B" Maximum Diameter	3.821 (97.06)
Front Differential Case [1]	
"C" Standard Diameter	4.092-4.093 (103.93-103.96)
"C" Minimum Diameter	4.089 (103.85)
"D" Standard Diameter	3.816-3.818 (96.93-96.96)
"D" Minimum Diameter	3.813 (96.85)
Conical Spring Washer	
No. 2 Case Washer	
Standard Height	.102-.110 (2.60-2.80)
Minimum Height	.098 (2.50)
No. 1 Case Washer	
Standard Height	.067-.078 (1.70-1.90)
Minimum Height	.063 (1.60)

[1] – "A", "B", "C" and "D" refer to measuring points in Fig. 16.

2) Reassemble No. 1 differential case. Install No. 2 side gear thrust washer, conical spring washer and differential side gear subassembly. Install pinions, pinion thrust washers and pinion shafts. Install spacer, vehicle speed sensor drive gear and snap ring. To front differential case side, Install front differential side gear thrust washer, front differential side gear. Install pinion shaft holder, pinions, pinion thrust washers, No. 2 differential pinion shaft and 2 front differential pinion shafts. Using dial indicator, measure backlash. Ensure backlash is .002-.008" (.05-.20 mm). See Fig. 17. Front differential side gear thrust washers are available in thicknesses of .039" (1.0 mm) to .049" (1.25 mm) in .002" (.05 mm) increments. Washers are stamped "B" through "G".

NOTE: Do not mount surface of front differential case, which contacts with bushing, in vise.

3) Install to No. 2 differential case, No. 2 side gear thrust washer, front differential side gear thrust washer, front differential side gear and front differential case assembly. Using dial indicator, measure thrust clearance of front differential side gear. Standard clearance is .007-.010" (.17-.26 mm). See Fig. 18. If backlash is out of specification select appropriate thrust washer to ensure backlash is within specification. Thrust washers are available in thicknesses of .037" (.95 mm) to .056" (1.40 mm) in .002" (.05 mm) increments. Washers are stamped "A" through "K". Disassemble No. 2 differential case.

4) Clean contact surface of differential left case. Heat ring gear to approximately 212°F (100°C) in boiling water. Carefully remove ring gear from water, clean contact surface of ring gear with cleaning solvent. Quickly install ring gear on differential case, aligning matchmarks.

5) Check and adjust center differential side gear thrust clearance. Install to front differential case side, front differential case assembly, front differential side gear, front differential side gear thrust washer. Install (temporarily, for reference when checking back lash) .039" (1.0 mm) size No. 2 differential side gear thrust washer. Clean contact surface of No. 2 side gear thrust washer and No. 2 differential case. Apply plastigage to No. 2 thrust washer. See Fig. 19. Install No. 2 differential case aligning matchmarks. Install bolts and torque to 91 ft. lbs. (124 N.m). Remove bolts and No. 2 differential case. Measure plastigage at widest point. Standard clearance is .006-.010" (.16-.25 mm). Select No. 2 thrust washer which will ensure backlash specification. Thrust washers are available in thicknesses of .031" (.80 mm) to .055" (1.40 mm) in .020" (.05 mm) increments. Remove No. 2 differential case, No. 2 side gear thrust washer and temporarily install .039 " (1.0 mm) No. 2 side gear thrust washer.

6) Assemble No. 2 differential case. Install previously selected No. 2 side gear thrust washer and conical spring washer to front differential case. Install No. 2 differential case to No. 1 differential case, aligning matchmarks. Install and torque bolt to 91 ft. lbs. (124 N.m).

7) Adjust differential case side bearing preload. Install differential case assembly to transaxle case. Install transmission case. Torque bolts to specifications. See TORQUE SPECIFICATIONS. Rotate differential case assembly right and left 2 or 3 times to allow bearings to settle. Using spring tension gauge, measure preload. See Fig. 20. If preload is not within specification, select appropriate adjusting shim. Adjusting shims are available in thicknesses of .079" (2.0 mm) to .096" (2.45 mm) in .02" (.05 mm) increments. Washers are stamped "1"-"9", also "A"-"K" measuring from .098" (2.50 mm) to .112" (2.85 mm) in .02" (.05 mm) increments.

PRELOAD SPECIFICATIONS

Application	Lbs. (kg)
Starting Preload[1]	
New Bearing	7-14 (3.2-6.3)
Used Bearing	4-9 (2.0-4.0)

[1] – Plus Output Shaft Preload

NOTE: Total preload will change approximately 1.1 lb. (.5 kg) for every .02" (.05 mm) change in adjusting shim thickness.

TRANSAXLE REASSEMBLY

Output Shaft Bearing Preload – **1)** Install oil pump and gasket. Install oil pipe. Install output shaft in clutch housing. Install transmission housing. Install and tighten bolts to 22 ft. lbs. (29 N.m). Install output shaft rear taper roller bearing outer race. Install original adjusting shim if output shaft bearing has not been replaced. If NEW bearing has been installed, install .002" (.05 mm) thinner adjusting shim. Install bearing retainer. Install rear bearing retainer, torque to 31 ft. lbs. (42 N.m).

2) Install lock nut to output shaft. Rotate output shaft both directions to ensure bearings are seated. Using torque wrench, measure output shaft starting preload. Starting preload should be 6.9-13.9 INCH lbs. (8-16 N.m) for a NEW bearing. If bearing has not been replaced, starting preload should be 4.3-8.7 INCH lbs. (5-10 N.m). If starting preload is not within specifications, select alternate adjusting shim. Starting preload changes about 3.5-4.3 Lbs. (4-5 kg) with each shim thickness. Shims are available in .002" (.05 mm) increments. Shims range in thickness from .051" (1.30 mm) to .098" (2.50 mm). Shims are stamped "0"-"9" and "A" through "Q". Install correct shim. Disassemble transmission.

Reassembly – **1)** Assemble is reverse order of separation. Remove output shaft. Install oil pump drive gear. Install input and output shaft assemblies, and shift fork assemblies as single unit. Install shift fork shaft locking balls, springs, seats and plugs. Install reverse idler gear and shaft. Align referencing marks on idler gear and clutch housing. Place reverse shift fork pivot into reverse shift arm and install reverse shift arm bracket to clutch housing. Install No. 2 oil pipe. Install NEW gasket to oil pipe. See Fig. 2.

NOTE: This transmission does not use gaskets between major housings; use Three Bond (1281) sealant. Assemble housing within 20 minutes after applying liquid gasket. Allow 30 minutes curing time before filling with oil.

2) Apply Three Bond (1281) sealant to transmission housing. Install transmission housing to clutch housing. Install reverse idler gear shaft retaining bolt. Install shift shaft locking ball, spring, seat and plug. Install snap rings to shift fork shafts.

3) Install output shaft rear bearing outer race. Install correct adjusting shim. Install snap ring to input shaft rear bearing. Install rear bearing retainer. Install spacer, needle bearing and 5th gear. Install synchro ring and key spring to No. 3 clutch hub. Using Installer (09310-17010), install No. 3 clutch hub with synchronizer ring and key spring. *See Fig. 3.*

4) Select a snap ring that will allow minimum axial play and install snap ring on shaft. Snap rings are available in thicknesses of .089" (2.25 mm) to .104" (2.65 mm) in .002" (.05 mm) increments. Shims are stamped "A" through "J". *See Fig. 3.*

5) Recheck 5th gear thrust clearance. Standard clearance is .004-.022" (.10-.57 mm). Install 5th driven gear. Install No. 3 hub sleeve and No. 3 shift fork. Lock transmission in 2 gears. Install and tighten NEW lock nut to 91 ft. lbs. (123 N.m). Stake lock nut. Unlock transmission.

6) Apply Three Bond (1281) sealant to transmission case cover. Install cover. Install shift and select lever shaft. Install control shaft cover. Install lock bolt. Install boot to control shaft oil seal. Ensure boot is installed in correct direction. Position air bleed of boot downward. Install selecting bellcrank. Install back-up light switch and speedometer driven gear. Install side gear intermediate shaft. Distance from end of shaft to clutch housing should be 10.06" (255.5 mm).

TORQUE SPECIFICATIONS

Application	Ft. Lbs. (N.m)
Transmission	
Back-Up Light Switch	30 (40)
Bellcrank Bolt	14 (20)
Clutch-To-Transmission Housing Bolt	22 (29)
Differential Case Bolt	46 (63)
Differential Ring Gear Bolt	91 (123)
Drain & Filler Plug	36 (49)
Elbow-To-Transaxle	20 (27)
Oil Cooler Tube-To-Elbow	25 (34)
Oil Pipe Clamp	13 (17)
Rear Bearing Retainer Bolt	31 (42)
Reverse Idler Shaft Lock Bolt	22 (29)
Reverse Shaft Arm Bracket Bolt	13 (17)
Selecting Bellcrank Support Set Bolt	14 (20)
Selector Shaft Lock Bolt	36 (49)
Shift Forks & Head Set Bolts	17 (24)
Shift Lever Lock Nut	12 (16)
Shift & Select Lever Cover Bolt	14 (20)
Stiffener Plate-To-Transaxle Bolt	27 (37)
Straight Screw Plug	18 (25)
Transaxle Case Cover Bolt	22 (29)
Transmission Case Cover Bolt	22 (29)
Vehicle Speed Sensor Bolt	13 (17)
5th Driven Gear Lock Nut	91 (123)
	INCH Lbs. (N.m)
Oil Pump-To-Cover Bolt	108 (12)
Oil Tube	108 (12)
Reverse Restrict Pin Holder	115 (13)
Selecting Bellcrank Set Bolt	108 (12)
Transaxle Case Receiver	65 (7.4)

MANUAL TRANSMISSIONS
Toyota R150 & R150F 5-Speed

Pickup, Tacoma, T100, 4Runner

APPLICATION & LABOR TIMES

APPLICATION & LABOR TIMES

Vehicle Application	Labor Times [1] R & I	[2] Overhaul	Series
1995			
Pickup (3.0L)			
2WD	4.1	4.4	R150
4WD	5.3	4.4	R150F
Tacoma			
2.4L (2WD)			
Manual Steering			
With A/C	10.2 [3]	4.4	R150
Without A/C	9.8 [3]	4.4	R150
Power Steering			
With A/C	10.8 [3]	4.4	R150
Without A/C	10.4 [3]	4.4	R150
2.7L (4WD)	4.8	4.4	R150F
3.4L (4WD)	5.0	4.4	R150F
T100			
3.4L			
2WD			
With A/C	11.2 [3]	4.4	R150
Without A/C	10.8 [3]	4.4	R150
4WD	5.3	4.4	R150F
4Runner			
3.4L (4WD)	5.3	4.4	R150F
1996			
Tacoma			
3.4L			
2WD			
Manual Steering			
With A/C	12.2 [3]	4.4	R150
Without A/C	11.8 [3]	4.4	R150
Power Steering			
With A/C	12.8 [3]	4.4	R150
Without A/C	12.4 [3]	4.4	R150
4WD	5.0	4.4	R150F
T100 (3.4L)			
2WD			
With A/C	11.2 [3]	4.4	R150
Without A/C	10.8 [3]	4.4	R150
4WD	5.3	4.4	R150F
4Runner 4WD (3.4L)	5.3	4.4	R150F

[1] – Removal and installation of transmission from vehicle chassis.
[2] – Bench overhaul time for transmission or transaxle/differential. DOES NOT include removal and installation.
[3] – Requires engine removal.

IDENTIFICATION

Transmission series is identified on ID label. ID label is located on driver-side door post.

LUBRICATION & ADJUSTMENTS

See appropriate MANUAL TRANSMISSION SERVICING article in TRANSMISSION SERVICING section.

TROUBLE SHOOTING

See GENERAL TROUBLE SHOOTING article in this section.

ON-VEHICLE SERVICE

DRIVE AXLE SHAFTS

See appropriate AXLE SHAFTS article in AXLE SHAFTS & TRANSFER CASES section.

REMOVAL & INSTALLATION

See appropriate MANUAL TRANSMISSION REMOVAL article in TRANSMISSION SERVICING section.

TRANSMISSION DISASSEMBLY

1) Remove back-up light switch. Remove driven gear lock plate and speedometer driven gear (2WD). Remove clutch housing from transmission case. Remove shift lever retainer, gasket (2WD) or oil deflector (4WD) and restrict pins. Remove shift lever housing set bolt. Remove extension housing-to-case bolts, Remove extension housing (2WD). Remove transfer adaptor-to-case bolts, remove transfer adaptor (4WD). Remove front bearing retainer and two snap rings. Remove transmission housing from intermediate plate. See Figs. 1 and 2.

2) Mount intermediate plate in vise. Use 2 bolts with nuts and washers in bottom holes of intermediate plate to prevent damage to sealing surface of intermediate plate. DO NOT apply pressure on intermediate plate. Using Torx (T40) socket, remove 4 straight screw plugs, locking balls and springs. Remove set bolts from shift forks No. 1 and No. 2. Drive out slotted pin from shift fork No. 3. Remove snap rings from each fork shaft. Remove shift fork shaft No. 2 from shift fork No. 1, No. 2 and intermediate plate. Remove shift fork No. 2 from groove of hub sleeve No. 2. Remove the interlock pin from intermediate plate. See Fig. 3.

3) Pull out shift fork shaft No. 1 with straight pin from shift fork No. 1 and intermediate plate. Remove shift fork No. 1 from groove of reverse gear. Using a magnet, remove interlock pin from intermediate plate. Remove shift fork shaft No. 3 from shift fork No. 3, reverse shift fork and intermediate plate. Remove shift fork No. 3 from groove of hub sleeve No. 3. Remove interlock pin from intermediate plate.

4) Using magnet, remove ball. Remove shift fork shaft No. 4 from reverse shift fork shaft and intermediate plate. Ball in reverse shift fork is under spring tension and will come out when shaft is removed. Remove spring from reverse shift fork. Remove reverse shift fork and arm. Remove "E"-ring, separate reverse shift fork and arm. Remove reverse shift arm bracket. See Fig. 3.

5) On 2WD, remove rear snap ring and drive gear and ball. Remove front snap ring and remove drive gear. Remove snap ring. Using puller, remove rear bearing and remove spacer. Using feeler gauge, measure the counter 5th gear thrust clearance. Standard clearance is .0039-.0138" (.10-.35 mm). Maximum clearance is .0157" (.40 mm). See Fig. 4.

6) Remove snap ring. Using puller, remove gear spline piece No. 5. Remove counter 5th gear with hub sleeve No. 3. Remove thrust washer and ball from counter gear. Remove rear bearing retainer. Pull out reverse idler gear and shaft. Remove output shaft bearing snap ring. Remove output shaft, counter gear and input shaft assembly by pulling on counter gear and tapping on intermediate plate.

7) Remove input shaft with needle bearing from the output shaft. Remove counter rear bearing. On 2WD, replace speedometer driven gear oil seal, if needed.

MANUAL TRANSMISSIONS
Toyota R150 & R150F 5-Speed (Cont.)

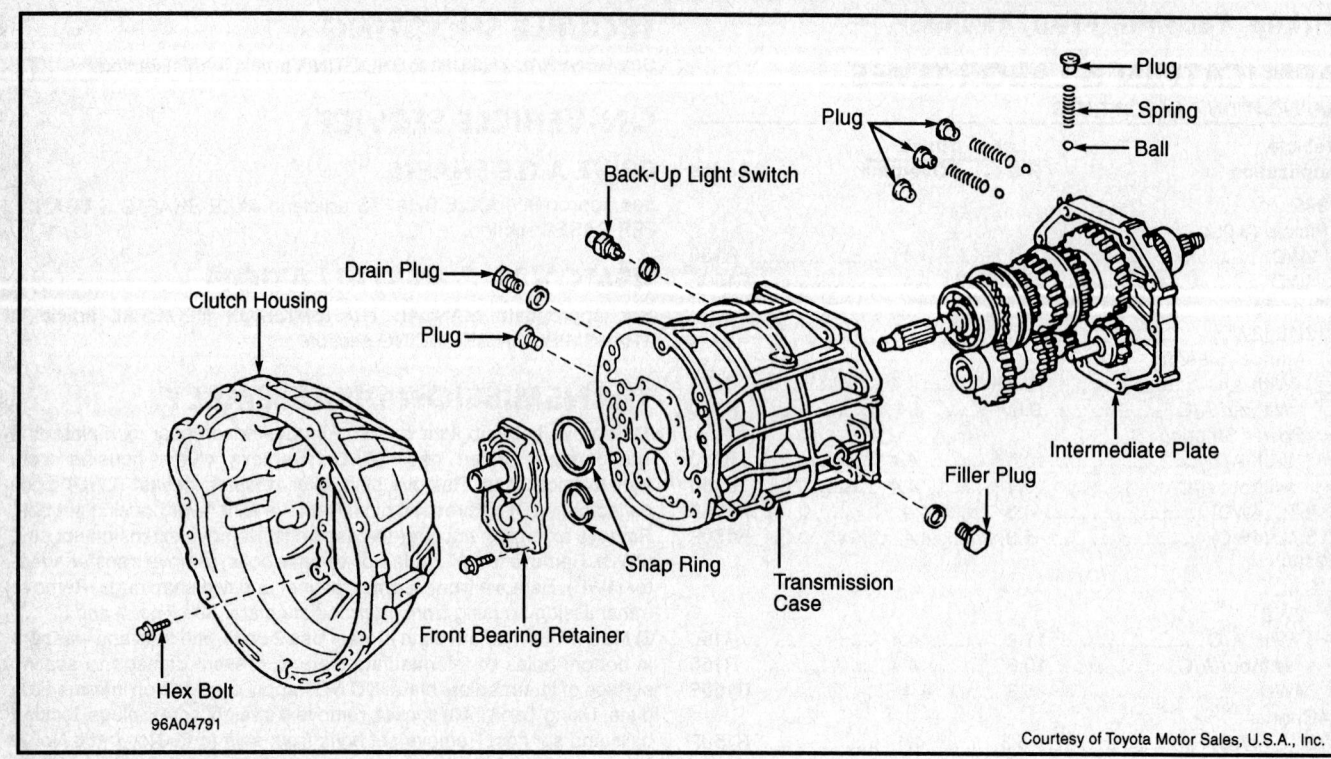

Fig. 1: Exploded View Of 2WD Transmission Components

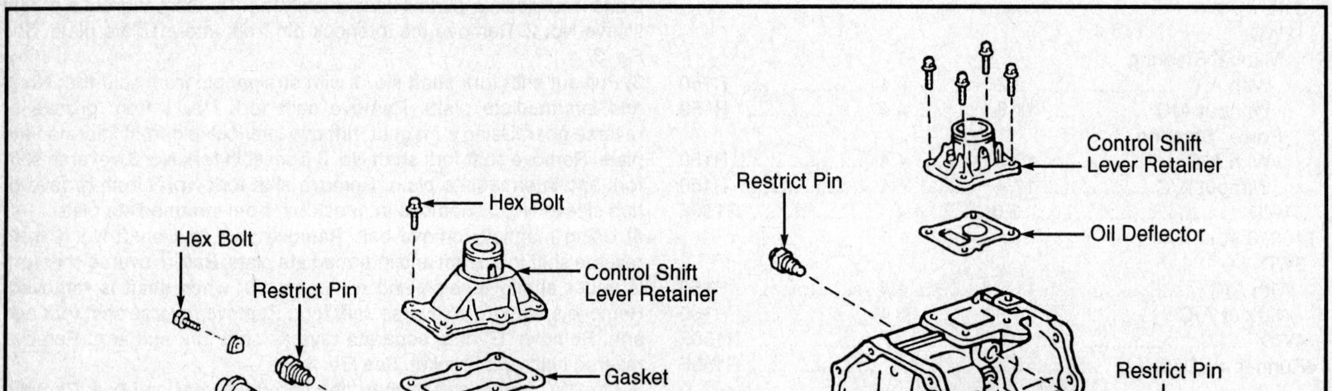

Fig. 2: Exploded View Of 4WD Transmission Components

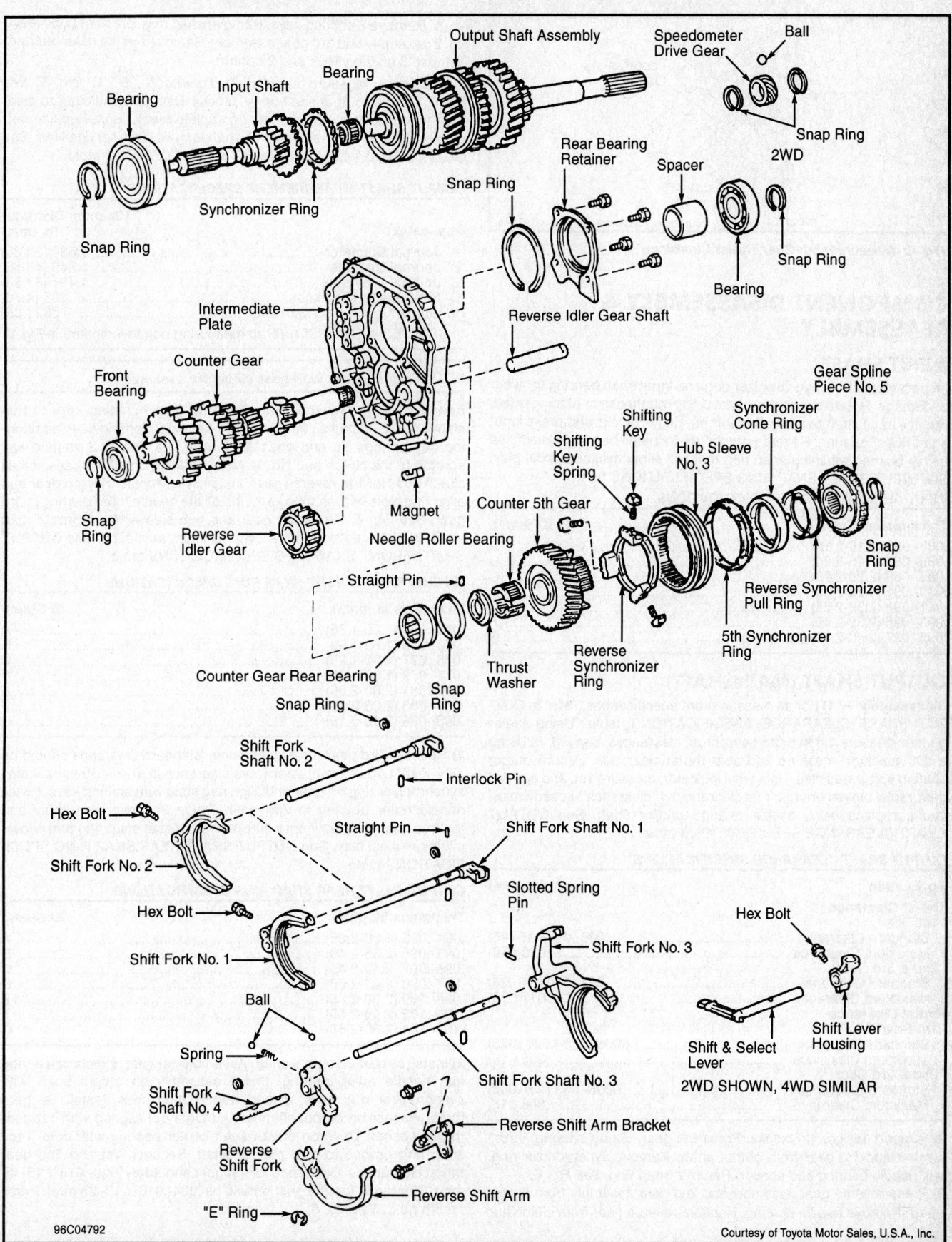

96C04792

Courtesy of Toyota Motor Sales, U.S.A., Inc.

Fig. 3: Exploded View Of Transmission Assemblies

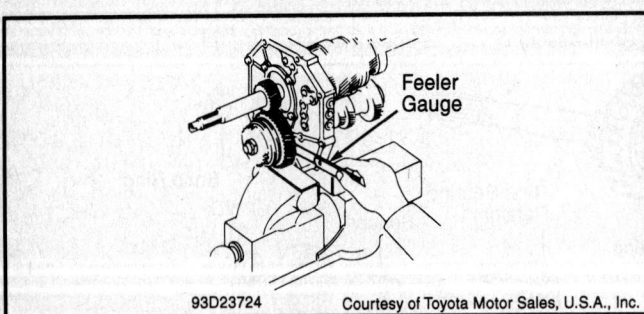

93D23724   Courtesy of Toyota Motor Sales, U.S.A., Inc.

Fig. 4: Measuring 5th Gear Thrust Clearance

COMPONENT DISASSEMBLY & REASSEMBLY

INPUT SHAFT

Inspect input shaft, synchronizer ring and input shaft bearing for wear or damage. Rotate bearing by hand. If any roughness or binding is felt, replace input shaft bearing. Support bearing in blocks and press input shaft out of bearing. Reverse procedure to install bearing. Select and install bearing retaining snap ring that will allow minimum axial play. See INPUT SHAFT SNAP RING SPECIFICATIONS table.

INPUT SHAFT SNAP RING SPECIFICATIONS

Thickness In. (mm)	ID Stamp
.083-.085 (2.10-2.15)	A
.085-.087 (2.15-2.20)	B
.087-.089 (2.20-2.25)	C
.089-.091 (2.25-2.30)	D
.091-.093 (2.30-2.35)	E
.093-.095 (2.35-2.40)	F
.095-.097 (2.40-2.45)	G

OUTPUT SHAFT (MAINSHAFT)

Disassembly – **1)** For all measurement specifications, refer to OUTPUT SHAFT CLEARANCE SPECIFICATIONS table. Using feeler gauge, measure 1st and 3rd gear thrust clearances. See Fig. 5. Using a dial indicator, measure 2nd gear thrust clearance. Secure output shaft in soft-jawed vise. Using dial indicator, measure 1st, 2nd and 3rd gear radial movement (gear oil clearance). If clearance exceeds maximum, replace gear, needle bearing and/or shaft. See OUTPUT SHAFT CLEARANCE SPECIFICATIONS table.

OUTPUT SHAFT CLEARANCE SPECIFICATIONS

Application	In. (mm)
Thrust Clearance	
1st Gear	
Standard Clearance	.006-.018 (.15-.45)
Maximum Clearance	.020 (.50)
2nd & 3rd Gear	
Standard Clearance	.004-.010 (.10-.25)
Maximum Clearance	.012 (.30)
Radial Clearance	
1st Gear	
Standard Clearance	.0008-.003 (.020-.073)
Maximum Clearance	.006 (.16)
2nd & 3rd Gear	
Standard Clearance	.0006-.003 (.15-.068)
Maximum Clearance	.006 (.16)

2) Support 1st gear in blocks. Press 5th gear, center bearing, thrust washer and 1st gear from output shaft. Remove synchronizer ring, pin, needle bearing and spacer. Remove snap ring. See Fig. 6.
3) Press reverse gear assembly and 2nd gear assembly from output shaft. Remove needle bearing. Remove reverse gear from clutch hub

No. 1. Remove 3 shifting keys. Remove snap ring, press of hub sleeve No. 2 assembly and 3rd gear assembly. Remove needle roller bearing. Remove 3 shifting keys and 2 springs.

Inspection – Measure output shaft at points "A", "B", "C" and "D". See Fig. 6. Support output shaft on "V" blocks. Using dial indicator to measure runout, rotate output shaft 2 complete revolutions. Replace output shaft if runout or any part of shaft is not within service limit. See OUTPUT SHAFT MEASUREMENT SPECIFICATIONS table.

OUTPUT SHAFT MEASUREMENT SPECIFICATIONS

Application [1]	Minimum Diameter In. (mm)
"A" Journal Diameter	1.530 (38.86)
"B" Journal Diameter	1.845 (46.86)
"C" Journal Diameter	1.491 (37.86)
"D" Shaft Flange Thickness	.185 (4.70)
Runout Limit	.002 (.05)

[1] – "A", "B", "C" and "D" refer to measuring points indicated in Fig. 6.

NOTE: Coat all parts with gear oil before assembly.

Reassembly – **1)** Install clutch hub No. 2 and shifting keys to hub sleeve No. 2. Install shifting key springs under shifting keys positioning key springs so end gaps are not in line. Install 3 shifting key springs to the clutch hub No. 1. While pushing 3 shifting keys, install clutch hub No. 1 to reverse gear. Install synchronizer ring on gear and align ring slots with shifting keys. Install the needle roller bearing in 3rd gear. See Fig. 6. Press 3rd gear and hub sleeve No. 2 onto output shaft. Install snap ring that allows minimum axial play. See OUTPUT SHAFT FRONT SNAP RING SPECIFICATIONS table.

OUTPUT SHAFT FRONT SNAP RING SPECIFICATIONS

Thickness In. (mm)	ID Stamp
.071-.073 (1.80-1.85)	A
.073-.075 (1.85-1.90)	B
.075-.077 (1.90-1.95)	C
.077-.079 (1.95-2.00)	D
.079-.081 (2.00-2.05)	E
.081-.083 (2.05-2.10)	F
.083-.085 (2.10-2.15)	G

2) Recheck 3rd gear thrust clearance. Standard clearance should be .004-.010" (.10-.25 mm). Maximum clearance is .012" (.30 mm). Install synchronizer ring on gear and align ring slots with shifting keys. Install needle roller bearing in 2nd gear. Press 2nd gear assembly and reverse gear assembly onto output shaft. Install snap ring that allows minimum axial play. See OUTPUT SHAFT REAR SNAP RING SPECIFICATIONS table.

OUTPUT SHAFT REAR SNAP RING SPECIFICATIONS

Thickness In. (mm)	ID Stamp
.091-.093 (2.30-2.35)	A
.093-.095 (2.35-2.40)	B
.095-.097 (2.40-2.45)	C
.097-.098 (2.45-2.50)	D
.098-.100 (2.50-2.55)	E
.100-.102 (2.55-2.60)	F
.102-.104 (2.60-2.65)	G

3) Install spacer on output shaft. Assemble 1st gear, synchronizer ring and needle roller bearing. Install assembly on output shaft with synchronizer ring slots aligned with shifting keys. Install 1st gear thrust washer on output shaft with straight pin aligned with 1st gear thrust washer. Drive on output shaft center bearing with outer race snap ring groove toward rear of shaft. Recheck 1st and 2nd gear thrust clearances. Clearance for 1st gear should be .006-.018" (.15-.45 mm). Clearance for 2nd gear should be .004-.010" (.10-.25 mm). Press on 5th gear. See Fig. 6.

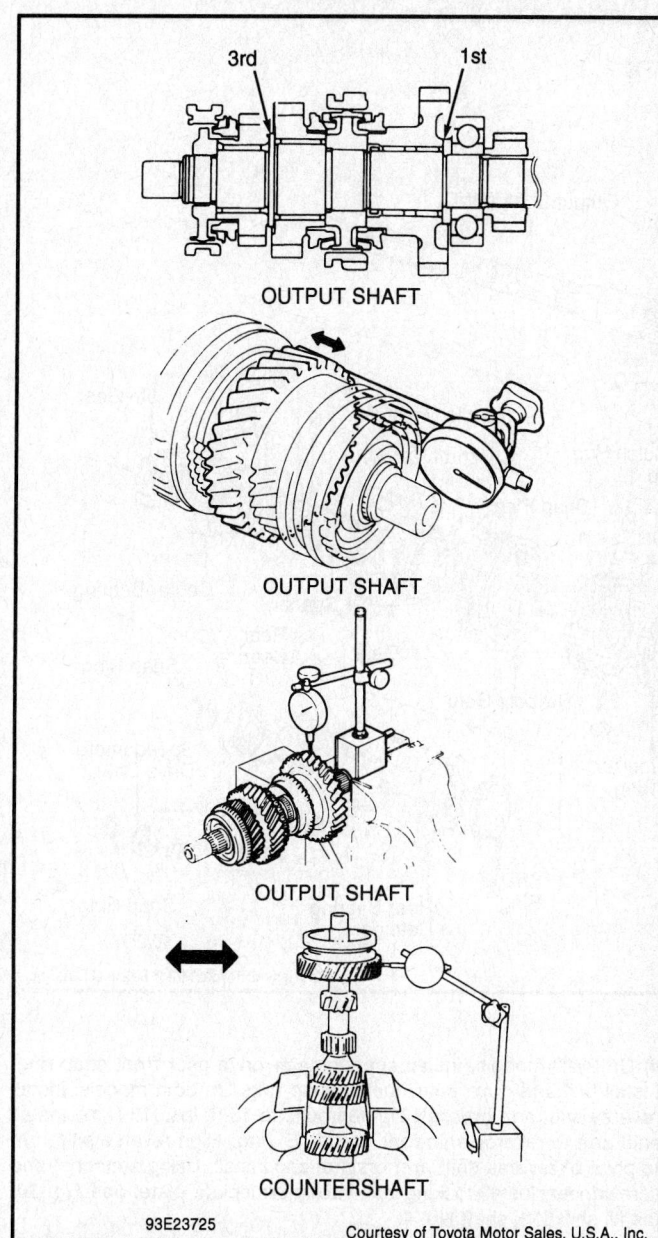

Fig. 5: Identifying Output & Countershaft Measuring Points

COUNTERSHAFT & REVERSE IDLER GEAR

Disassembly – 1) Remove synchronizer ring assembly from hub sleeve No. 3. Turn reverse synchronizer ring. Remove reverse synchronizer and 5th synchronizer from synchronizer pull ring and cone ring. Turn reverse synchronizer pull ring, separate pull ring and cone ring. Push shifting key and spring and remove 3 shifting keys and springs from reverse synchronizer ring. *See Fig. 7* .

Inspection – 1) Install spacer, needle roller bearing and 5th gear on countershaft. Measure countershaft 5th gear radial movement (gear oil clearance). *See Fig. 8*. Standard clearance should be .0006-.003" (.015-.068 mm). Maximum clearance is .006" (.16 mm). Measure outer diameter of countershaft needle bearing surface. Minimum diameter is 1.097" (27.86 mm).

2) Rotate countershaft front bearing by hand. If any roughness or binding is felt, replace countershaft bearing. Support bearing in blocks

and press countershaft out of bearing. Reverse procedure to install bearing. Select and install bearing retaining snap ring that allows minimum axial play. See COUNTERSHAFT FRONT BEARING SNAP RING SPECIFICATIONS table.

COUNTERSHAFT FRONT BEARING SNAP RING SPECIFICATIONS

Thickness In. (mm)	ID Stamp
.079-.081 (2.00-2.05)	A
.081-.083 (2.05-2.10)	B
.083-.085 (2.10-2.15)	C
.085-.087 (2.15-2.20)	D
.087-.089 (2.20-2.25)	E
.089-.090 (2.25-2.30)	F

3) Measure reverse idler gear radial clearance. *See Fig. 8*. Standard clearance should be .002-.003" (.04-.08 mm). Maximum clearance is .005" (.13 mm). Measure clearance between reverse idler gear and shift arm shoe. *See Fig. 8*. Standard clearance should be .002-.010" (.05-.25 mm). Maximum clearance is .020" (.50 mm).

Assembly – 1) Install key springs and shifting keys to reverse synchronizer ring. Install synchronizer cone ring to reverse synchronizer pull ring and turn pull ring. Install 5th synchronizer ring, and reverse synchronizer ring. Turn reverse synchronizer pull ring. While pushing 3 shifting keys, install synchronizer ring assembly to hub sleeve No. 3. *See Fig. 7*.

SHIFT FORK ASSEMBLY

Measure clearance between hub sleeve and shift fork. Maximum clearance is .039" (1.00 mm). If clearance exceeds specification, replace shift fork or hub sleeve. *See Fig. 9*.

SYNCHRO RING & GEAR

Check synchronizer rings for wear or damage. Turn and push ring to check braking action. Measure clearance between synchronizer ring back and gear spline end. Minimum clearance is .024" (.60 mm). If clearance is less than specification, replace synchronizer ring. *See Fig. 9*.

EXTENSION HOUSING & TRANSFER ADAPTOR

Disassembly – 1) Using Torx (T40) socket wrench, remove screw plug. Using pin punch, drive out slotted spring pin. Remove reverse restrict pin. Inspect for smooth operation. Reinstall reverse restrict pin to extension housing, drive in spring pin. Apply sealant, (Loctite 242 or equivalent) to screw plug threads and install. Tighten to 14 ft. lbs. (19 N.m).

2) On 2WD models, If necessary, replace extension housing oil seal. Remove dust deflector, pry out seal. Drive in new seal, reinstall dust deflector. On 4WD models, replace transfer adaptor oil seal. Pry out and drive in new oil seal. On both models, replace oil seal in front bearing retainer if necessary.

TRANSMISSION REASSEMBLY

NOTE: Coat all parts with gear oil before assembly.

1) Install counter rear bearing. Install input shaft with needle roller bearing to output shaft. Install output shaft, counter gear and input shaft assemblies to intermediate shaft. Install output shaft center snap ring. Align reverse shift arm to reverse idler gear shaft and install to intermediate plate. Install rear bearing retainer and bolts. Torque bolts to 13 ft. lbs. (18 N.m). Install counter 5th gear with hub sleeve No. 2. Install rear gear spline piece No. 5 with synchronizer ring slots aligned with shifting keys.

2) Install snap ring that will allow minimum axial play. Using feeler gauge, measure counter gear thrust clearance. Standard clearance is .004"-.014" (.10-.35 mm). Maximum clearance is .016" (.40 mm). See OUTPUT SHAFT REAR BEARING SNAP RING SPECIFICATIONS table.

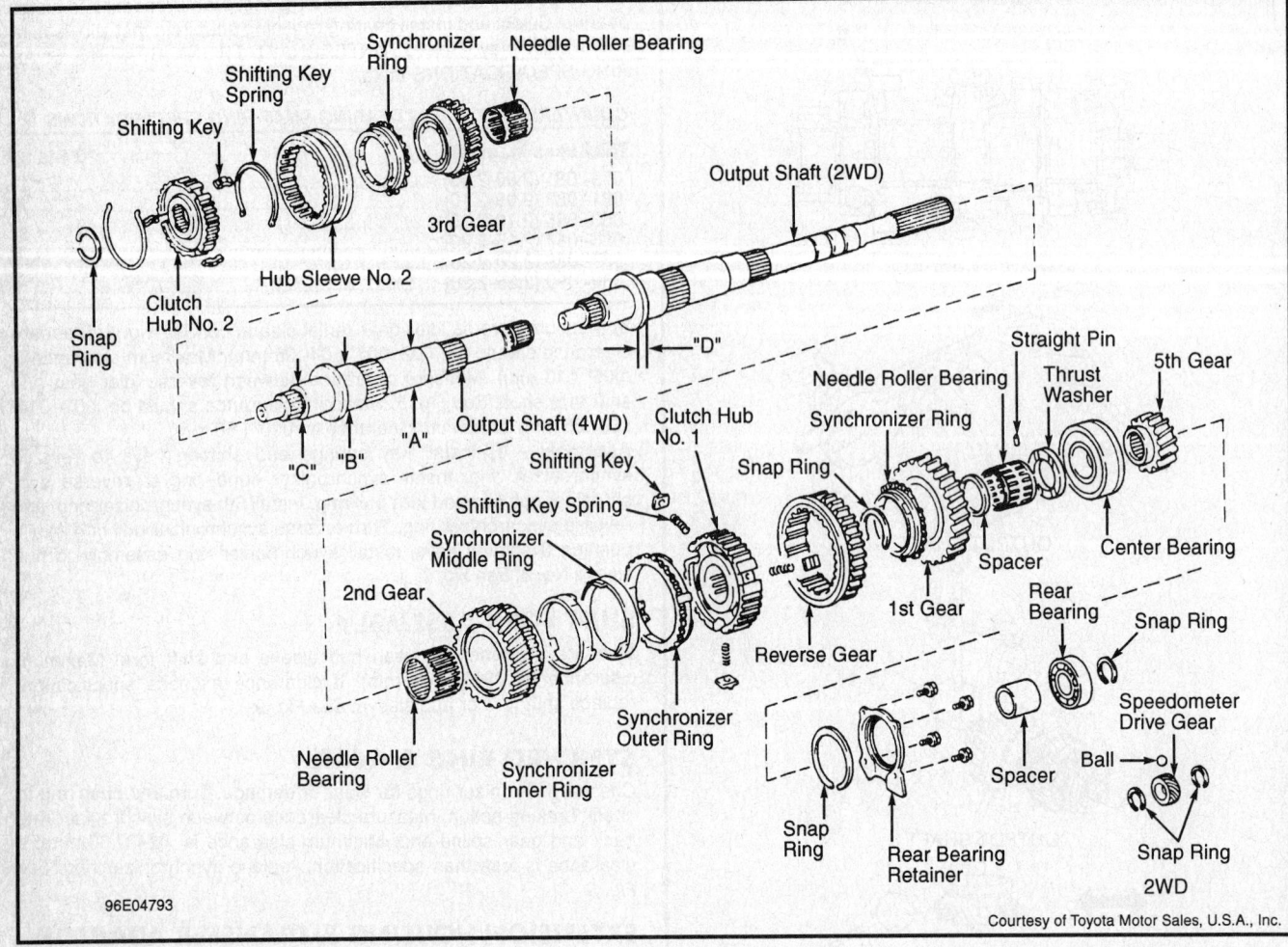

Fig. 6: Exploded View Of Output Shaft

COUNTERSHAFT 5TH GEAR SNAP RING SPECIFICATIONS

Thickness In. (mm)	ID Stamp
.110-.112 (2.80-2.85)	A
.112-.114 (2.85-2.90)	B
.114-.116 (2.90-2.95)	C
.116-.118 (2.95-3.00)	D
.118-.120 (3.00-3.05)	E
.120-.122 (3.05-3.10)	F
.122-.124 (3.10-3.15)	G

3) Install spacer and rear bearing. Select and install snap ring that will allow minimum axial play. See OUTPUT SHAFT REAR BEARING SNAP RING SPECIFICATIONS table.

OUTPUT SHAFT REAR BEARING SNAP RING SPECIFICATIONS

Thickness In . (mm)	ID Stamp
.104-.106 (2.65-2.70)	A
.106-.108 (2.70-2.75)	B
.108-.110 (2.75-2.80)	C
.110-.112 (2.80-2.85)	D
.112-.114 (2.85-2.90)	E
.114-.116 (2.90-2.95)	F
.116-.118 (2.95-3.00)	G
.118-.120 (3.00-3.05)	H
.120-.122 (3.05-3.10)	J
.122-.124 (3.10-3.15)	K
.124-.126 (3.15-3.20)	L
.126-.128 (3.20-3.25)	M
.128-.130 (3.25-3.30)	N
.130-.132 (3.30-3.35)	P
.132-.134 (3.35-3.40)	Q
.134-.136 (3.40-3.45)	R
.136-.138 (3.45-3.50)	S

4) On 2WD models, install speedometer drive gear front snap ring. Install ball and drive gear. Install snap ring. On both models, install reverse shift arm bracket. Tighten bolts to 13 ft. lbs. (18 N.m). Install shift arm to reverse shift fork. Install "E" ring. Align reverse shift arm to pivot of reverse shift arm bracket and install. Using a magnet and screwdriver, install locking ball into intermediate plate. See Fig. 10. Install shift fork shaft No. 4.

5) Install interlock for No. 3 shift fork shaft into intermediate plate. Install shift fork No. 3 to groove of hub sleeve No. 3. Install No. 3 shift fork shaft into intermediate plate, No. 3 shift fork and reverse shift fork.

6) Install interlock pin for No. 1 shift fork shaft into intermediate plate. Install shift fork No. 1 to groove of reverse gear. Install shift fork shaft No. 1 with straight pin to shift fork No. 1 and intermediate plate. Install interlock pin for shift fork shaft No. 2 into intermediate plate. Install shift fork No. 2 to groove of hub sleeve No. 2. Install shift fork shaft No. 2 through intermediate plate and shift forks No. 1 and No. 2. Install snap rings to each shift fork shaft. Install slotted spring pin to shift fork No. 3. Install shift fork set bolts to shift fork No. 1 and shift fork No. 2. Tighten to 14 ft. lbs. (19 N.m). See Fig. 3.

NOTE: This transmission uses no gasket between major housings; use Three Bond (1281 or 1344) sealant. Assemble housing immediately after applying liquid gasket. Allow 30 minutes curing time before filling with oil.

7) Install 3 balls and springs into intermediate plate. Apply sealer (Loctite 242 or equivalent) to 4 straight screw plug threads and install. Torque to 14 ft. lbs. (19 N.m). Install magnet. Apply Three Bond (1281) or equivalent to transmission case. Install transmission case to inter-

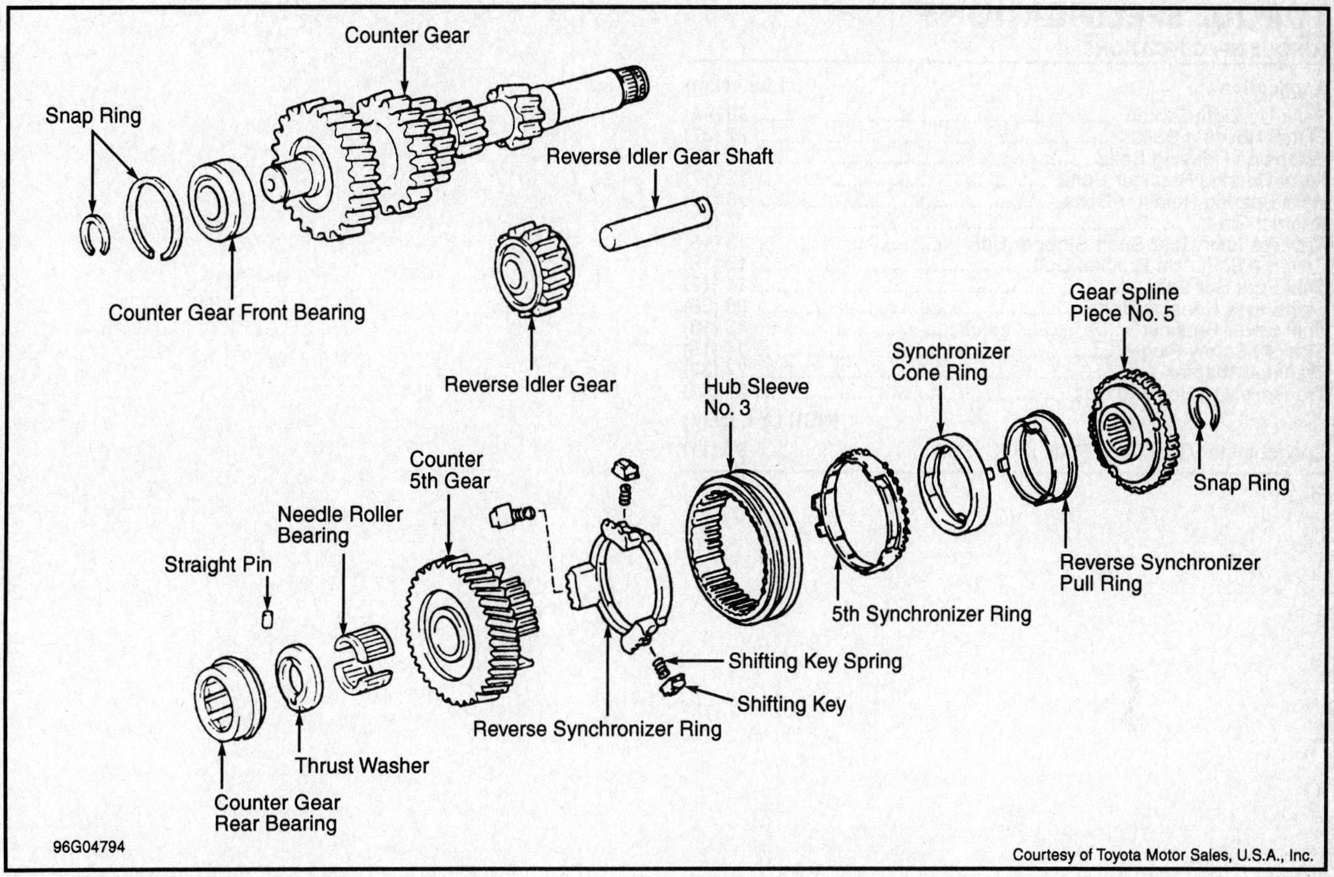

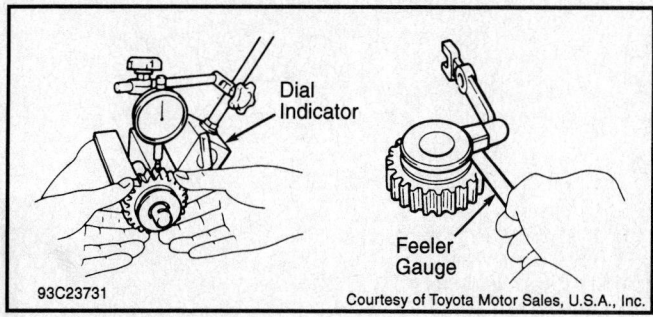

Fig. 7: **Exploded View Of Countershaft Assemblies**

mediate plate. Install 2 snap rings. Apply Three Bond (1344) or equivalent to front bearing retainer. Install bolts and tighten bolts 12 ft. lbs. (17 N.m).

8) On 2WD models, apply Three Bond (1281) or equivalent to shift lever housing and install. Tighten bolts to 27 ft. lbs. (27 N.m). Install shift lever housing set bolt. Tighten to 28 ft. lbs. (38 N.m).

9) On 4WD models, apply Three Bond (1281) or equivalent to transfer adaptor and install. Tighten bolts to 27 ft. lbs. (37 N.m). Install shift lever housing set bolt. Tighten to 28 ft. lbs. (38 N.m).

10) On both models, Install restrict pins. Tighten to 27 ft. lbs. (37 N.m). Install retainer and gasket (2WD) or oil deflector (4WD). Tighten bolts to 13 ft. lbs. (18 N.m). Install clutch housing to transmission case. Tighten bolts to 27 ft. lbs. (36 N.m). Install speedometer driven gear and lock plate (2WD). Tighten to 97 INCH lbs. (11 N.m). Install backup light switch. Tighten to 32 ft. lbs. (44 N.m). *See Figs. 1 and 2.*

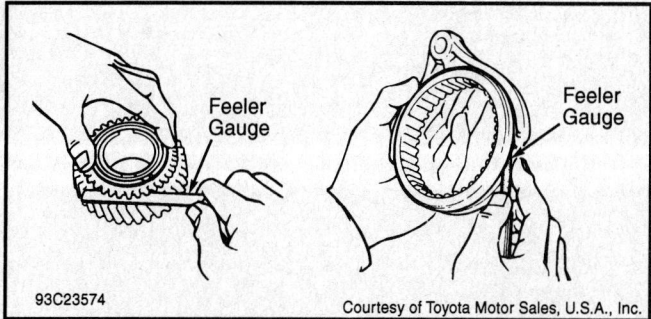

Fig. 8: *Identifying Reverse Idler Gear Measuring Points*

Fig. 9: *Measuring Shift Fork & Synchro Ring Assemblies*

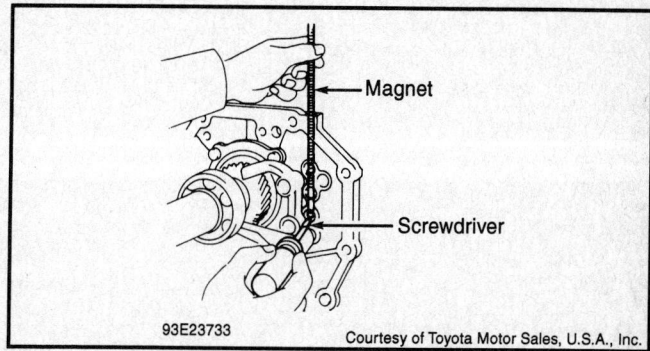

Fig. 10: *Installing Locking Ball In Intermediate Plate*

TORQUE SPECIFICATIONS

TORQUE SPECIFICATIONS

Application	Ft. Lbs. (N.m)
Back-Up Light Switch	32 (44)
Clutch Housing Bolts	27 (37)
Extension Housing Bolts	27 (37)
Front Bearing Retainer Bolts	12 (17)
Rear Bearing Retainer Bolts	13 (18)
Restrict Pin	27 (37)
Reverse Idler Gear Shaft Stopper Bolt	13 (18)
Reverse Shift Arm Bracket Bolt	13 (18)
Shift Fork Set Bolt	14 (19)
Shift Lever Housing Bolt	28 (38)
Shift Lever Retainer	13 (18)
Straight Screw Plug	14 (19)
Transfer Adapter	27 (37)
Transmission Housing Bolt	27 (37)
	INCH Lbs. (N.m)
Speedometer Gear Lock Plate (2WD) Bolt	97 (11)

MANUAL TRANSMISSIONS
Toyota S51 & S54 5-Speed

Camry, Celica, MR2 Non-Turbo

APPLICATION & LABOR TIMES

APPLICATION & LABOR TIMES

Vehicle Application	Labor Times		Series
	[1] R & I	[2] Overhaul	
Camry 2.2L	6.3	6.3	S51
Celica 2.2L	5.8	6.3	S54
MR2 Non-Turbo (1995)	5.4	6.3	S54

[1] – Removal and installation of transmission from vehicle chassis.
[2] – Bench overhaul time for transaxle/differential. DOES NOT include removal and installation.

IDENTIFICATION

Transmission series is identified on ID label. ID label is located on driver-side door post.

LUBRICATION & ADJUSTMENTS

See appropriate MANUAL TRANSMISSION SERVICING article in TRANSMISSION SERVICING section.

TROUBLE SHOOTING

See GENERAL TROUBLE SHOOTING article in this section.

ON-VEHICLE SERVICE

DRIVE AXLE SHAFTS

See appropriate AXLE SHAFTS article in AXLE SHAFT & TRANSFER CASES section.

REMOVAL & INSTALLATION

See appropriate MANUAL TRANSMISSION REMOVAL article in TRANSMISSION SERVICING section.

TRANSAXLE DISASSEMBLY

1) Remove release fork and bearing. Remove vehicle speed sensor. Remove back-up light switch. Remove release bearing retainer. Remove engine mount bracket and selecting bellcrank. Remove transmission case cover. Remove lock ball assembly, shift and select lever assembly. See Fig. 1.

2) Lock transmission in 2 gears. Using a chisel, lift staked section of output shaft lock nut. Remove lock nut. Lock nut has left-hand threads. Unlock transmission gears. Remove No. 3 shift fork set bolt, No. 3 hub sleeve and No. 3 shift fork. Remove 5th driven gear. Measure 5th gear clearance. See Fig. 3. Using a dial indicator, measure thrust clearance. Standard clearance should be .008-.016" (.20-.40 mm). Service limit is .018" (.45 mm). Record for reassembly reference. Remount dial indicator to measure radial clearance (gear oil clearance) of 5th gear. Standard clearance should be .0004-.0020" (.009-.050 mm). Service limit is .0028" (.070 mm). If clearance exceeds maximum, replace gear, roller bearing or input shaft.

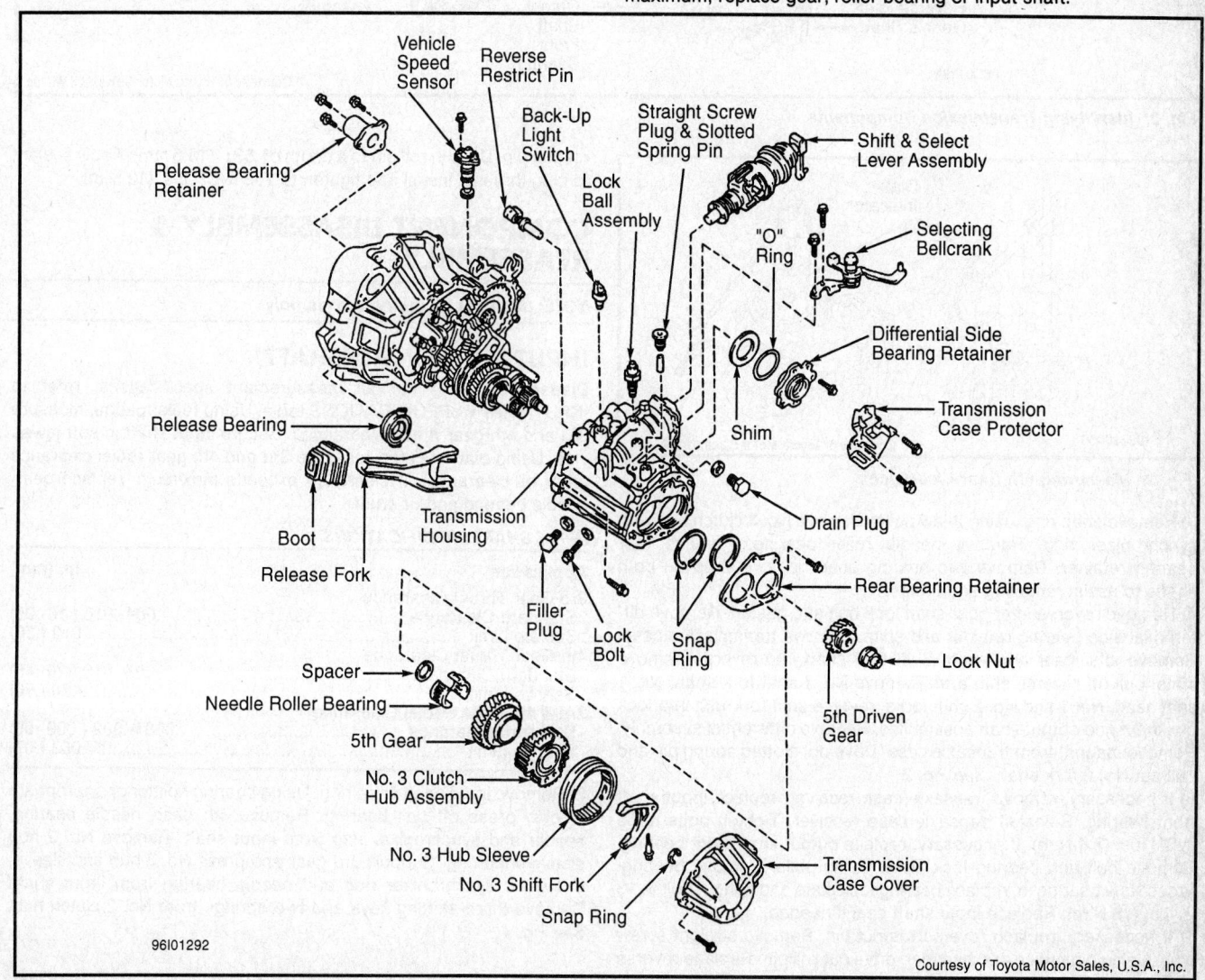

96I01292

Courtesy of Toyota Motor Sales, U.S.A., Inc.

Fig. 1: Exploded View Of Transmission Assemblies

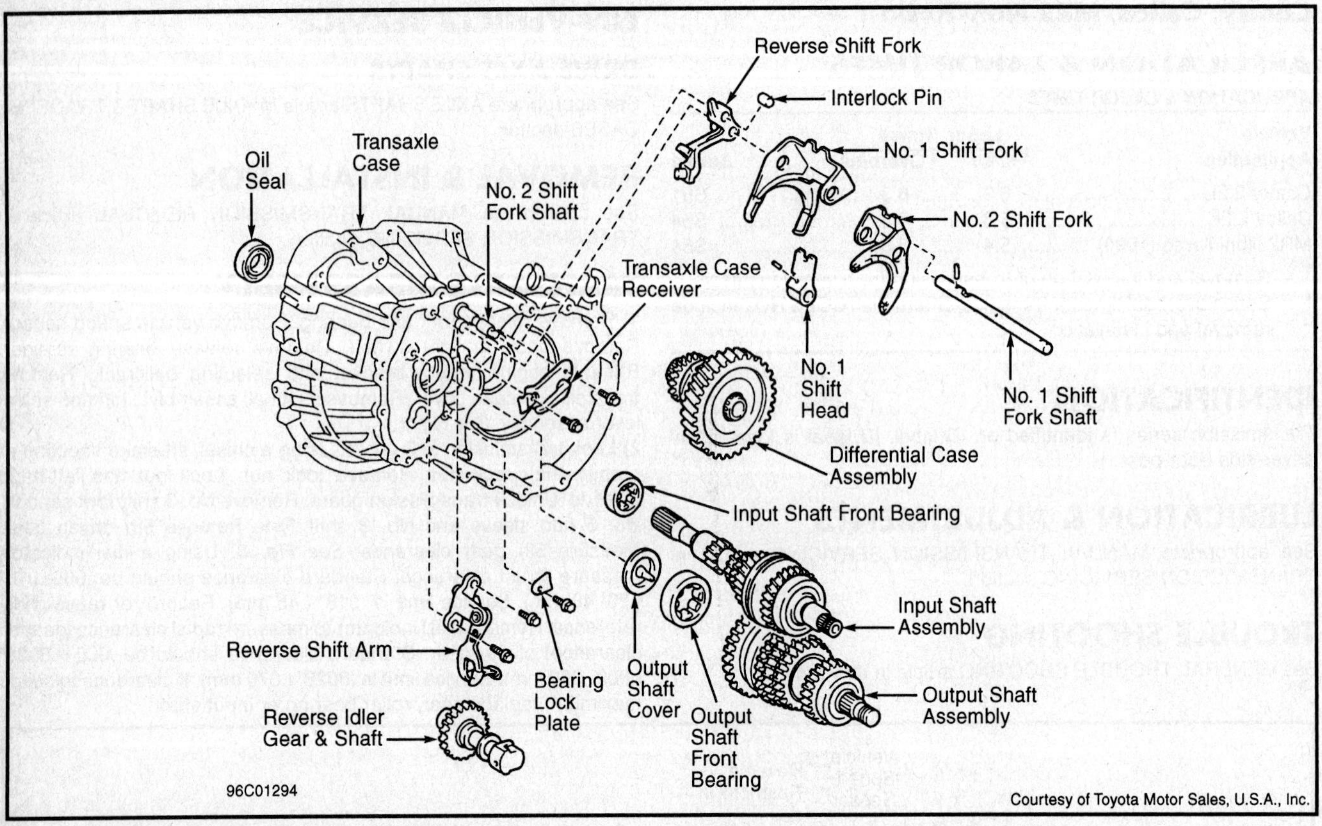

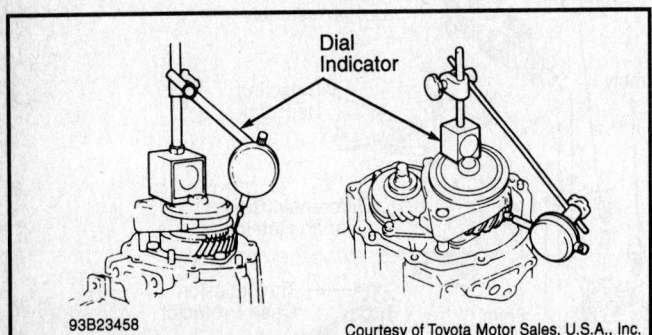

Fig. 2: Identifying Transmission Components

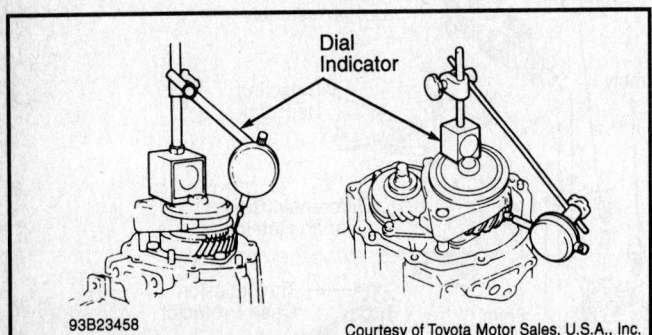

Fig. 3: Measuring 5th Gear Clearances

3) Remove snap ring, using 2-jaw puller, remove No. 3 clutch hub with synchronizer ring. Remove needle roller bearing. Remove rear bearing retainer. Remove two bearing snap rings. Pull up on both shafts to assist removing snap rings.

4) Remove reverse idler gear shaft lock bolt and gasket. Remove differential side bearing retainer and shim. Remove transmission case. Remove idler gear and shaft. Shift fork shaft into reverse, remove bolts, pull off reverse shift arm. Remove No. 1 shift fork shaft, No. 1 shift head, No. 1 and No. 2 shift forks, reverse shift fork with interlock pin, input and output shaft assemblies. Remove differential assembly. Remove magnet from transaxle case. Drive out slotted spring pin and pull out No. 2 fork shaft. See Fig. 2.

5) If necessary, remove transaxle case receiver, replace input shaft front bearing. Reinstall transaxle case receiver. Tighten bolts to 65 INCH lbs. (7.4 N.m). If necessary, replace output shaft front bearing. Remove bolt and bearing lock plate. Using puller, remove bearing. Press New bearing in, replace bearing lock plate and tighten bolt to 13 ft. lbs. (18 N.m). Replace input shaft seal if needed.

6) If necessary, replace reverse restrict pin. Remove straight screw plug. Using pin punch and hammer, drive out roll pin. Replace reverse

restrict pin. Drive in roll pin to a depth of .531" (13.5 mm). Apply sealant to plug threads, install and tighten to 108 INCH lbs. (12 N.m).

COMPONENT DISASSEMBLY & REASSEMBLY

NOTE: Use gear oil during reassembly.

INPUT SHAFT (MAINSHAFT)

Disassembly – 1) For all measurement specifications, refer to INPUT SHAFT SPECIFICATIONS table. Using feeler gauge, measure 3rd and 4th gear thrust clearances. Secure input shaft in soft-jawed vise. Using dial indicator, measure 3rd and 4th gear radial clearance (gear oil clearance). If clearance exceeds maximum, replace gear, needle bearing and/or shaft.

INPUT SHAFT SPECIFICATIONS

Application	In. (mm)
3rd Gear Thrust Clearance	
Standard Clearance	.004-.010 (.10-.25)
Service Limit	.012 (.30)
4th Gear Thrust Clearance	
Standard Clearance	.008-.018 (.20-.45)
Service Limit	.020 (.50)
3rd & 4th Gear Radial Clearance	
Standard Clearance	.0004-.002 (.009-.05)
Service Limit	.003 (.07)

2) Remove input shaft snap ring. Using bearing splitter or appropriate blocks, press off ball bearing. Remove 4th gear, needle bearing, spacer and synchronizer ring from input shaft. Remove No. 2 hub sleeve snap ring. Support 3rd gear and press No. 2 hub and sleeve, 3rd gear, synchronizer ring and needle bearing from input shaft. Remove three shifting keys and two springs from No. 2 clutch hub. See Fig. 4.

Inspection – 1) Inspect all parts for damage and wear. Replace if necessary. Clean all parts in new solvent, dry and lubricate all parts. Ensure oil passages are free of contamination.

2) Measure input shaft at points "A", "B", "C" and "D". See Fig. 4. Support input shaft on "V" blocks. Using dial indicator to measure runout, rotate input shaft 2 complete revolutions. Replace input shaft if runout or any part of shaft is not within service limit. See INPUT SHAFT MEASUREMENT SPECIFICATIONS table.

INPUT SHAFT MEASUREMENT SPECIFICATIONS

Application [1]	Minimum Diameter In. (mm)
"A" Journal Diameter	1.062 (26.97)
"B" Journal Diameter	1.278 (32.47)
"C" Journal Diameter	1.303 (33.09)
"D" Journal Diameter	1.180 (29.97)
Runout Limits	.002 (.05)

[1] – "A", "B", "C" and "D" refer to measuring points indicated in Fig. 4.

Reassembly – 1) Install clutch hub and shifting keys to hub sleeve. Install shifting key springs under shifting keys. Ensure key springs end gaps are not in line. Install synchronizer ring to 3rd gear and align ring slots with shifting keys. Using a press, install 3rd gear and No. 2 hub sleeve. Select and install snap ring that will allow minimum axial movement. See SNAP RING APPLICATION CHART NO. 1

SNAP RING APPLICATION CHART NO. 1

Snap Ring Thickness In. (mm)	Stamped Number
.077-.079 (1.95-2.00)	1
.079-.081 (2.00-2.05)	2
.081-.083 (2.05-2.10)	3
.083-.085 (2.10-2.15)	4
.085-.087 (2.15-2.20)	5
.087-.089 (2.20-2.25)	6

2) Recheck 3rd gear thrust clearance. See INPUT SHAFT SPECIFICATIONS table for clearance. Install spacer and needle bearings. Install synchronizer ring on gear, aligning ring slots with shifting keys and ring projections with hub slots. Use press to install ball bearing. Select snap ring that allows minimum axial movement. See SNAP RING APPLICATION CHART NO. 2

SNAP RING APPLICATION CHART NO. 2

Snap Ring Thickness In. (mm)	Stamped Letter
.085-.087 (2.15-2.20)	A
.087-.089 (2.20-2.25)	B
.089-.091 (2.25-2.30)	C
.091-.093 (2.30-2.35)	D
.093-.095 (2.35-2.40)	E

OUTPUT SHAFT (COUNTERSHAFT)

Disassembly – 1) For all measurement specifications, refer to OUTPUT SHAFT SPECIFICATIONS table. Using feeler gauge, measure 1st and 2nd gear thrust clearances. Secure output shaft in soft-jawed vise. Using dial indicator, measure 1st and 2nd gear radial clearance (gear oil clearance). If clearance exceeds maximum, replace gear, needle bearing and/or shaft.

OUTPUT SHAFT SPECIFICATIONS

Application	In. (mm)
1st Gear Thrust Clearance	
Standard Clearance	.004-.012 (.10-.29)
Service Limit	.014 (.35)
2nd Gear Thrust Clearance	
Standard Clearance	.008-.017 (.20-.44)
Service Limit	.020 (.50)
1st & 2nd Gear Radial Clearance	
Standard Clearance	.0004-.002 (.009-.06)
Service Limit	.003 (.07)

2) Using bearing splitter or appropriate blocks, support 4th gear and press output shaft out of ball bearing and 4th driven gear. Remove spacer. Shift No. 1 hub sleeve into 1st gear. Support 2nd gear and press output shaft out of 3rd driven gear and 2nd gear. Remove needle bearing and synchronizer ring. See Fig. 5.

3) Support 1st gear and press output shaft out of No. 1 hub sleeve, 1st gear and synchronizer ring from output shaft. Remove needle roller bearing, thrust washer and locking ball. Remove No. 1 hub sleeve, 3 shifting keys and springs from No. 1 clutch hub.

Inspection – 1) Inspect all parts for damage and wear. Replace if necessary. Clean all parts in new solvent, dry and lubricate all parts. Ensure oil passages are free of contamination.

2) Measure output shaft at points "A", "B", and "C". See Fig. 5. Support output shaft on "V" blocks. Using dial indicator to measure runout, rotate output shaft 2 complete revolutions. Replace output shaft if runout or any part of shaft is not within service limit. See OUTPUT SHAFT MEASUREMENT SPECIFICATIONS table.

OUTPUT SHAFT MEASUREMENT SPECIFICATIONS

Application [1]	Minimum Diameter In. (mm)
"A" Journal Diameter	1.259 (31.97)
"B" Journal Diameter	1.495 (37.97)
"C" Journal Diameter	1.259 (31.99)
Runout Limits	.002 (.05)

[1] – "A", "B", and "C" refer to measuring points indicated in Fig. 5.

Reassembly – 1) Install 3 springs and shifting keys to clutch hub No. 1. Install hub sleeve to clutch hub, positioning identification groove of hub sleeve to front of transmission. Press thrust washer to output shaft. Install needle roller bearing. Place synchronizer ring on gear aligning ring slots with shifting keys. Using a press, install 1st gear and No. 1 hub sleeve. Measure 1st gear thrust clearance. Refer to OUTPUT SHAFT SPECIFICATIONS table. See Fig. 5.

2) Install ball. Install synchronizer rings on 2nd gear. Install needle roller bearing. Install 2nd gear, aligning clutch hub grooves with projections of synchronizer ring. Ensure 2nd gear bushing groove is securely over ball. Press 3rd driven gear onto output shaft. Recheck

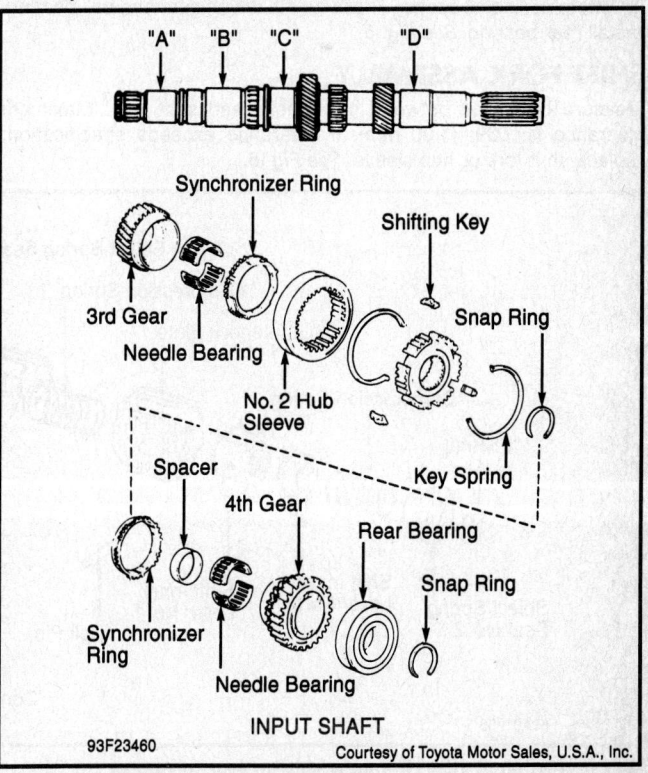

93F23460
Courtesy of Toyota Motor Sales, U.S.A., Inc.

Fig. 4: Identifying Input Shaft Components

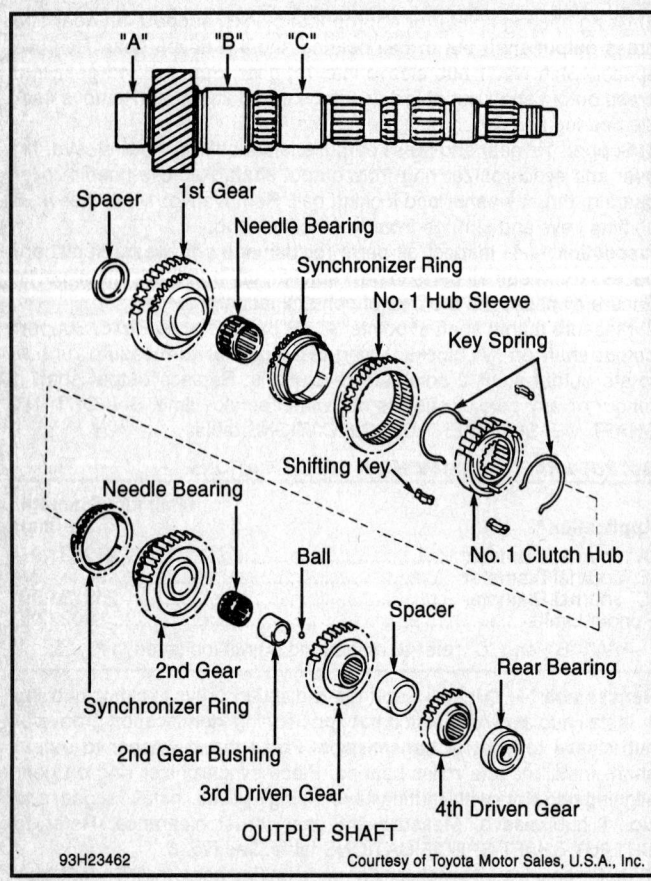

Fig. 5: Identifying Output Shaft Components

2nd gear thrust clearance. Refer to OUTPUT SHAFT SPECIFICATIONS table. Install spacer. Press on 4th driven gear and ball bearing. Install rear bearing. See Fig. 5.

SHIFT FORK ASSEMBLY

Measure clearance between hub sleeve and shift fork. Maximum clearance is .039" (1.00 mm). If clearance exceeds specification, replace shift fork or hub sleeve. See Fig. 6.

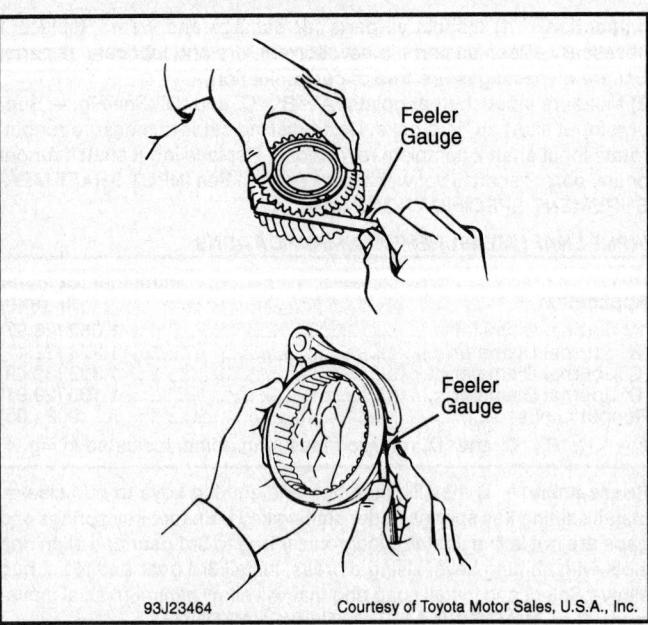

Fig. 6: Measuring Shift Fork & Synchro Ring Assemblies

SYNCHRO RING & GEAR

Check synchronizer rings for wear or damage. Turn and push ring to check braking action. Measure clearance between synchronizer ring back and gear spline end. Minimum clearance for No. 1 and No. 3 is .024" (.60 mm). No. 2 is .028" (.70 mm). If clearance is less than specification, replace synchronizer ring. See Fig. 6.

SHIFT & SELECT LEVER

Disassembly – 1) Unbolt and remove control shift lever lock bolt. Remove lever. Remove dust boot and control shaft cover. On opposite end of shaft, remove "E" ring. Remove select spring seat No. 2, spring and No. 2 shift inner lever. See Fig. 7.

2) Drive out roll pin from shift inner lever No.1. Remove shift inner lever No. 2, shift interlock plate, spring and shift interlock plate. Remove "E" ring from lever shaft.

Inspection – If necessary, replace control shaft cover oil seal. Pry oil seal out of cover. Using socket or appropriate drive adapter and ham-

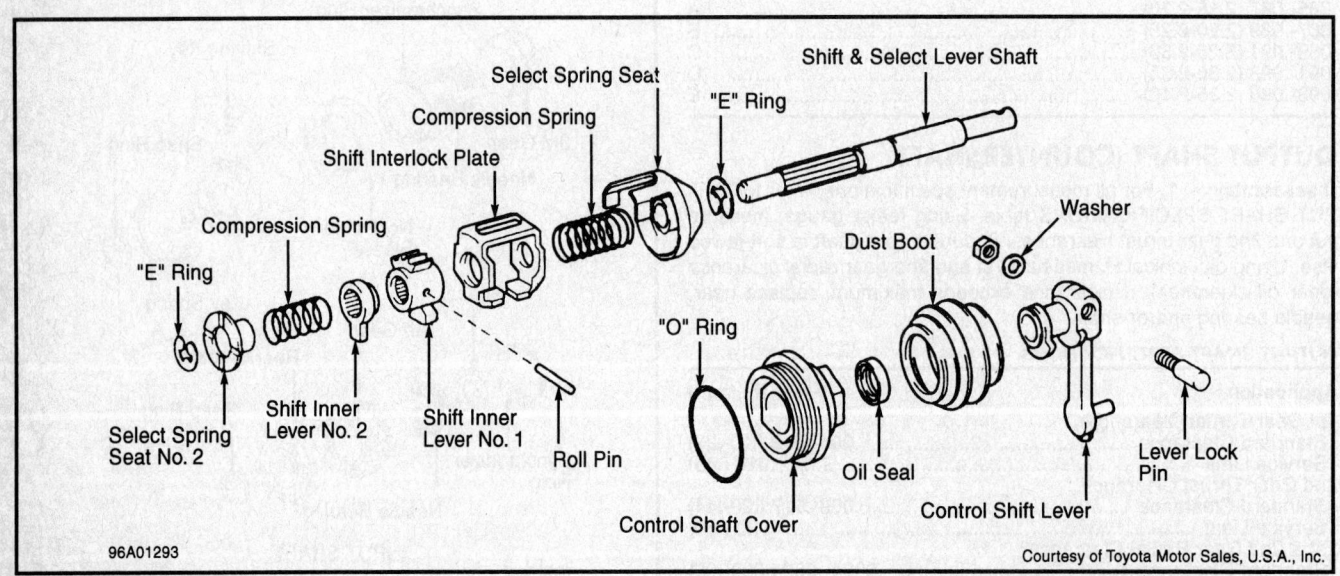

Fig. 7: Exploded View Of Shift & Select Lever Assembly

mer, drive in NEW oil seal. Install seal flush with surface of cover. Coat lip of oil seal with grease.

Reassembly – Apply MP grease to shaft. Install components in reverse order of disassembly.

DIFFERENTIAL

Disassembly – **1)** Remove bearing from drive gear side of differential case. Remove vehicle speed sensor drive gear. Place matchmarks on ring gear and differential case for reassembly reference. Remove ring gear. Remove side bearing from ring gear side of differential case. Unstake lock plates. Remove ring gear bolts. Using a soft faced hammer, tap ring gear and remove from differential case.

2) Measure backlash of one side gear while holding one pinion toward case. See Fig. 9. Backlash should be .002-.008 (.05-.20 mm). Drive out pinion shaft roll pin from ring gear side of case. Remove pinion shaft from case. Remove pinion gears, side gears and thrust washers from case. See Fig. 8. If necessary, replace oil seal in differential side bearing retainer and transaxle case.

Reassembly – **1)** If backlash is incorrect, select thrust washers that will ensure correct backlash. Install washers of equal thickness. Install thrust washers to side gears. Install side gear thrust washers, pinion thrust washers and pinion gears. Install pinion shaft. If backlash is correct, use thrust washers removed during disassembly.

2) Recheck side gear backlash while holding one pinion gear toward case. See Fig. 9. Backlash should be .002-.008 (.20-.50 mm). If backlash is incorrect, disassemble case and install new thrust washers. Install washers of equal size. Side gear thrust washers are available in .002 (.05 mm) increments. Washers range in thickness from .037" (.95 mm) to .047" (1.20 mm).

3) Drive lock pin through case and into pinion shaft. Stake differential case to hold pin in place. Clean ring gear contact surface of case. Heat ring gear to 212°F (100°C) in boiling water.

4) Clean contact surface of ring gear with cleaning solvent. Align matchmarks on ring gear with differential case and install. Install bolts.

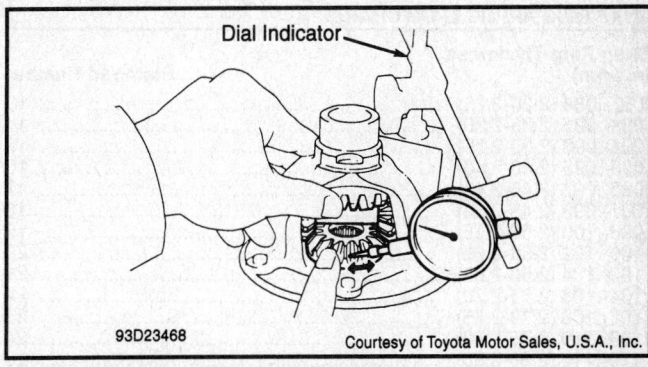

Fig. 9: **Measuring Differential Backlash**

After ring gear has cooled sufficiently, tighten bolts to 61 ft. lbs. (83 N.m). Press NEW side bearing on transmission side of differential case. Install vehicle speed sensor drive gear to transaxle case side. Press NEW bearing (Black cage) to transaxle case side.

TRANSMISSION REASSEMBLY

Differential Bearing Preload – **1)** Install differential in transaxle case. Install transmission case, tighten bolts to 22 ft. lbs. (29 N.m). Install original side bearing shim. Install bearing retainer without "O" ring. Tighten bolts to 13 ft. lbs. (18 N.m).

2) Using Differential Preload Adapter (09564-32011) and an INCH lb. torque wrench, measure differential side bearing starting torque. See Fig. 10. Starting torque preload should be 7-14 INCH lbs. (.8-1.6 N.m). If preload is incorrect, remove case side bearing retainer and select a NEW adjusting shim.

3) Preload will change about 2.6-3.5 INCH lbs. (.3-.4 N.m) with each shim thickness. Shims are available in .05 mm increments. Shims range in thickness from .075" (1.90 mm) to .110" (2.80 mm). Shims are marked "1" through "19" depending on thickness.

Reassembly – **1)** Disassemble transmission case. Remove bearing retainer and install NEW "O" ring. Reverse disassembly procedure. Install input and output shafts with shift fork assemblies as a single unit.

2) Install No. 2 fork shaft. Drive in slotted spring pin. Install straight screw plug, tighten to 108 INCH lbs. (12 N.m). Install magnet to transaxle case. Install differential case, input and output shaft assemblies. Install No. 1 shift fork shaft, No. 1 shift head, No. 1 and No. 2 shift forks and reverse shift fork with interlock pin. Install reverse shift arm. Tighten bolts to 13 ft. lbs. (18 N.m). Install reverse idler gear, thrust washer and shaft. Apply Three Bond (1281) or equivalent, to transaxle case. Install transmission housing. Tighten bolts to 22 ft. lbs. (29 N.m).

NOTE: This transmission uses no gasket between major housings; use Three Bond (1281) sealant. Assemble housing within 10 minutes after applying liquid gasket. Allow 30 minutes curing time before filling with oil.

---

3) Apply Three Bond (1344) or equivalent, to differential side bearing retainer bolts. Install differential side bearing retainer and shim. Tighten bolts to 13 ft. lbs. (18 N.m). Install reverse idler gear shaft lock bolt. Tighten to 22 ft. lbs. (29 N.m). Install bearing snap rings. Install rear bearing retainer. Tighten bolts to 31 ft. lbs. (42 N.m). Install needle roller bearing and 5th gear. Using press, install No. 3 clutch assembly with synchronizer. Select and install snap ring that will allow minimum axial play. Measure 5th gear thrust clearance. Standard clearance should be .008-.016" (.20-.40 mm). See SNAP RING APPLICATION CHART.

4) Install 5th driven gear. Install No. 3 hub and No. 3 shift fork. Install set bolt. Tighten to 13 ft. lbs. (18 N.m). Lock transmission in 2 gears. Install and tighten lock nut to 90 ft. lbs. (123 N.m). Disengage gears. Stake lock nut. Install shift and select lever shaft assembly with new gasket. Tighten bolts to 27 ft. lbs. (37 N.m). Apply Three Bond (1281) or equivalent, to lock ball assembly threads, install lock ball assembly. Tighten to 22 ft. lbs. (29 N.m).

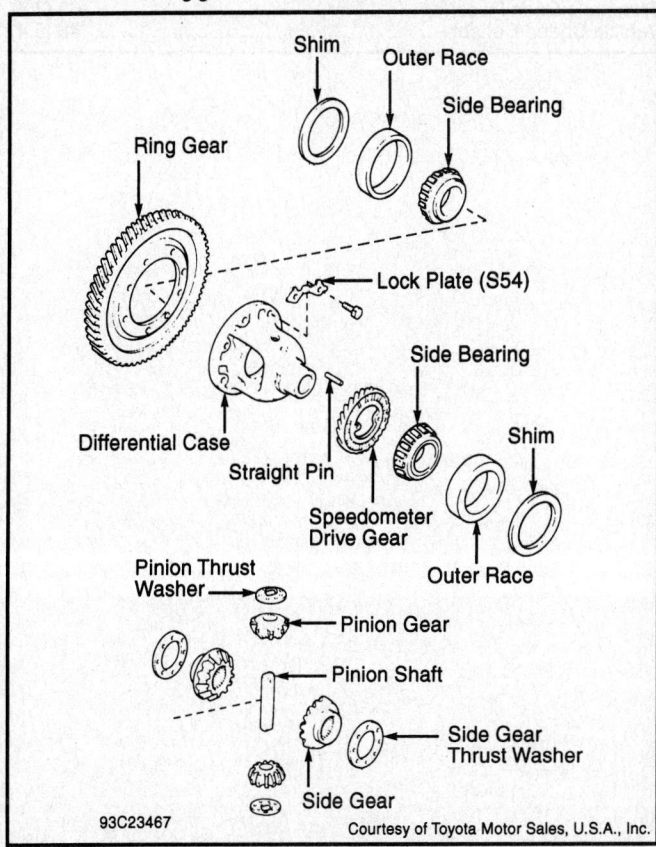

Fig. 8: **Exploded View Of Differential Assembly**

Labels in figure:
Shim, Outer Race, Side Bearing, Ring Gear, Lock Plate (S54), Side Bearing, Shim, Differential Case, Straight Pin, Speedometer Drive Gear, Outer Race, Pinion Thrust Washer, Pinion Gear, Pinion Shaft, Side Gear Thrust Washer, Side Gear

93C23467 Courtesy of Toyota Motor Sales, U.S.A., Inc.

MANUAL TRANSMISSIONS
Toyota S51 & S54 5-Speed (Cont.)

SNAP RING APPLICATION CHART

Snap Ring Thickness In. (mm)	Stamped Number
.087-.089 (2.20-2.25)	13
.089-.091 (2.25-2.30)	14
.091-.093 (2.30-2.35)	15
.093-.095 (2.35-2.40)	16
.095-.097 (2.40-2.45)	17
.097-.098 (2.45-2.50)	18
.098-.100 (2.50-2.55)	19
.100-.102 (2.55-2.60)	20
.102-.104 (2.60-2.65)	21
.104-.106 (2.65-2.70)	22
.106-.108 (2.70-2.75)	23
.108-.110 (2.75-2.80)	24
.110-.112 (2.80-2.85)	25
.112-.114 (2.85-2.90)	26
.114-.116 (2.90-2.95)	27

5) Apply Three Bond (1281) or equivalent, sealant to transmission case cover. Install transmission case cover. Apply Three Bond (1344) or equivalent, to transmission case cover bolts, install and tighten to 22 ft. lbs. (29 N.m). Install engine mount bracket and selecting bellcrank. Install bearing release retainer. Install vehicle speed sensor. Install back-up light switch. Install release fork and bearing.

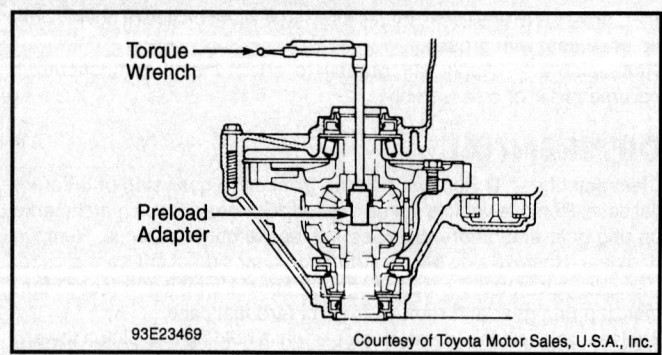

93E23469   Courtesy of Toyota Motor Sales, U.S.A., Inc.

Fig. 10: Measuring Bearing Preload

TORQUE SPECIFICATIONS
TORQUE SPECIFICATIONS

Application	Ft. Lbs. (N.m)
Back-Up Light Switch	32 (44)
Differential Ring Gear	61 (83)
Drain & Fill Plugs	36 (49)
Engine Mount Bracket	38 (52)
Lock Ball Assembly	22 (29)
Rear Bearing Retainer	31 (42)
Reverse Idler Shaft Lock Bolt	22 (29)
Reverse Shift Arm Bracket	13 (18)
Selecting Bellcrank	27 (37)
Shift & Select Lever Assembly	27 (37)
Side Gear Bearing Retainer	13 (18)
Transaxle Case	22 (29)
Transaxle Case Cover	22 (29)
5th Gear Driven Gear Lock Nut	91 (123)

Application	INCH Lbs. (N.m)
Release Bearing Retainer	62 (7)
Transaxle Case Receiver	65 (7.4)
Vehicle Speed Sensor	48 (5.4)

MANUAL TRANSMISSIONS
Toyota "W" Series 5-Speed

Lexus: SC300
Toyota: Pickup, Supra, Tacoma, T100, 4Runner

APPLICATION & LABOR TIMES

APPLICATION & LABOR TIMES

Vehicle Application	Labor Times [1] R & I	[2] Overhaul	Series
Lexus			
1995-96 SC300	4.5	4.4	W58
Toyota			
Pickup			
1995			
2WD			
2.4L	8.0	4.4	W55
4WD			
2.4L	9.2	4.4	W56
Supra			
1995-1996			
3.0L	3.5	4.4	W58
Tacoma			
1996			
2WD (2.4L)			
Manual Steering			
With A/C	10.2 [3]	4.4	W59
Without A/C	9.8 [3]	4.4	W59
Power Steering			
With A/C	10.8 [3]	4.4	W59
Without A/C	10.4	4.4	W59
4WD (2.7L)	4.8	4.4	W59
T100 (2.7L)			
1995			
With A/C	12.5 [3]	4.4	W56
Without A/C	12.1 [3]	4.4	W56
1996			
With A/C	12.5	4.4	W59
Without A/C	12.1	4.4	W59
4Runner			
1996			
2WD & 4WD			
2.7L	9.2	4.4	W59

[1] – Removal and installation of transmission from vehicle chassis.
[2] – Bench overhaul time for transmission. DOES NOT include removal and installation.
[3] – Requires engine removal.

IDENTIFICATION

Transmission type is identified on ID label located on driver's side door post.

LUBRICATION & ADJUSTMENTS

See appropriate MANUAL TRANSMISSION SERVICING article in TRANSMISSION SERVICING section.

TROUBLE SHOOTING

See GENERAL TROUBLE SHOOTING article in this section.

ON-VEHICLE SERVICE

DRIVE AXLE SHAFTS

See appropriate AXLE SHAFTS article in AXLE SHAFT & TRANSFER CASES section.

REMOVAL & INSTALLATION

See appropriate MANUAL TRANSMISSION REMOVAL article in TRANSMISSION SERVICING section.

TRANSMISSION DISASSEMBLY

1) Remove back-up light switch and vehicle speed sensor driven gear. On all models, remove clutch housing from transmission case. On W58 models, remove 3 bolts, nut and control shift lever arm. Remove dust boot, nut and No. 1 control shift yoke. Remove control shift lever retainer assembly and oil deflector. On 4WD models, Remove shift lever retainer and gasket or oil baffle plate. Remove shift lever housing set bolt. On all models, remove 2 restrict pins. Remove extension housing or transfer adaptor (4WD). See Fig. 1.

2) Using plastic hammer, tap housing or adaptor. Disengage shift and select lever from shift head. Remove housing or adaptor. Remove front bearing retainer and bearing snap rings. Using plastic hammer, tap transmission case and remove from intermediate plate.

3) On all models, mount intermediate plate in vise. Use 2 bolts with nuts and washers in bottom holes of intermediate plate to prevent damage to sealing surface of intermediate plate. DO NOT apply pressure on intermediate plate. Remove oil separator. Remove front magnet. Remove all plugs from intermediate plate. Using magnet, remove springs and detent balls.

4) On all models, remove shift fork set bolts. Remove bolt and reverse idler gear shaft stopper. Remove reverse idler gear and shaft. Remove No. 1 shift fork and shaft. Using a magnet, remove No. 1 and No. 2 interlock pins. Remove snap ring from No. 2 shift fork shaft. Remove No. 2 shift fork shaft. Remove No. 3 interlock pin. Remove snap ring from No. 3 shift fork shaft. Remove No. 3 shift fork roll pin. Remove screw plug, spring and ball. See Figs. 2 and 3.

5) Remove No. 4 shift fork shaft. Remove pin from reverse shift head. Remove No. 3 shift fork, fork shaft and reverse shift arm with snap ring. On 2WD models, remove speedometer drive gear from shaft.

6) Measure counter 5th gear thrust clearance. See Fig. 4. Standard clearance is .004-.016" (.10-.41 mm). Maximum clearance is .018" (.46 mm). Remove 5th gear snap ring on countershaft. Using 2-jaw puller, remove countershaft rear bearing, spacer, 5th gear, needle bearing and spacer. See Fig. 2.

7) Ensure output shaft rear bearing roller and counter 5th gear do not contact each other when removing gear. Remove synchronizer ring assembly with No. 3 hub sleeve from No. 3 clutch hub. Remove spacer and snap ring. Using puller, remove No. 3 clutch hub. Remove rear magnet. Remove output shaft snap ring. Remove rear bearing and 5th gear. See Fig. 2.

8) Remove output shaft reverse gear snap ring. Using puller, remove reverse gear. Using Torx (T40) socket, remove bearing retainer bolts and retainer. Remove bearing snap rings. Using plastic hammer, tap intermediate plate and remove output shaft with input shaft, and countergear as a unit. Remove input shaft from output shaft.

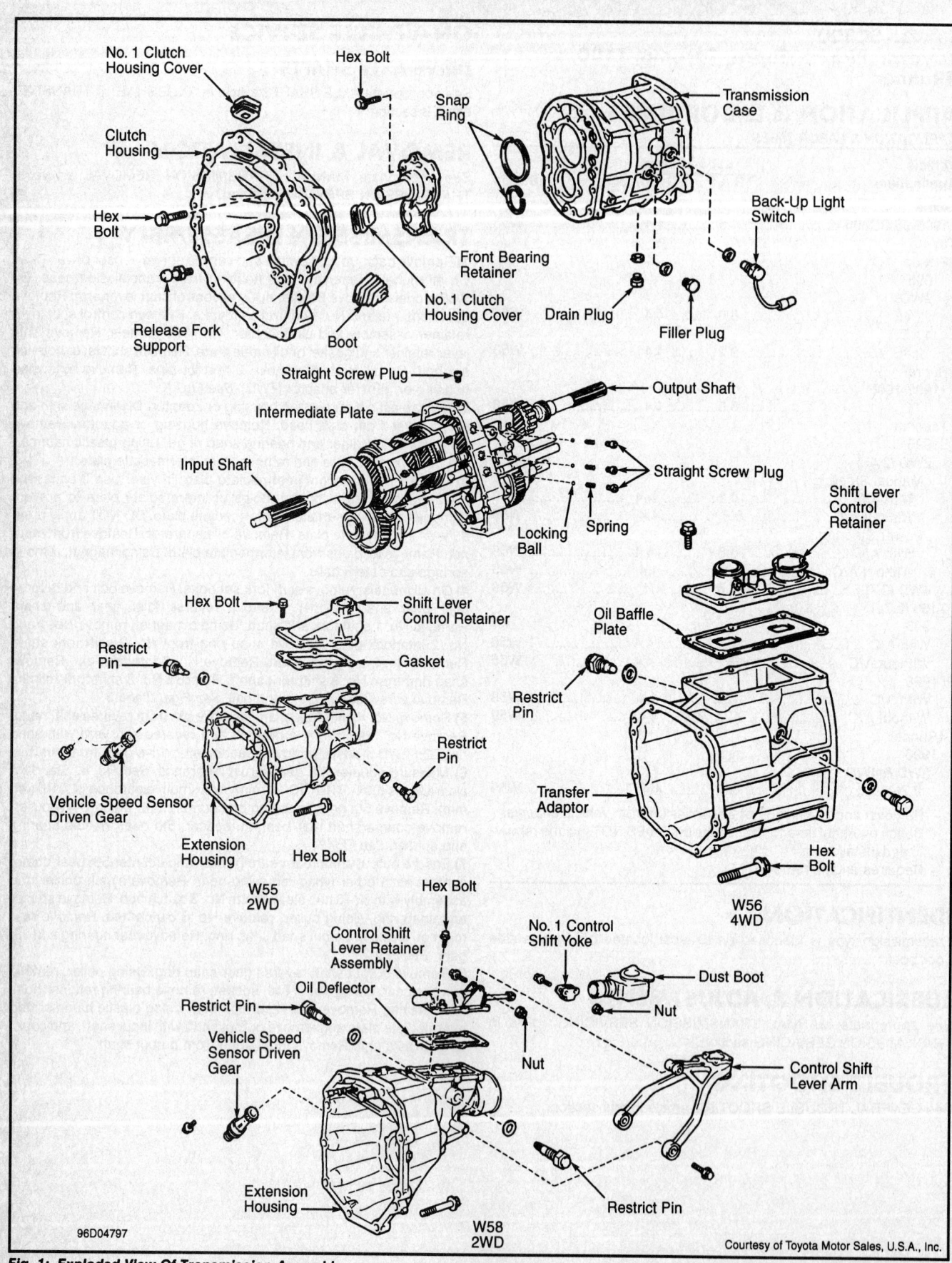

Fig. 1: *Exploded View Of Transmission Assembly*

96D04797

Courtesy of Toyota Motor Sales, U.S.A., Inc.

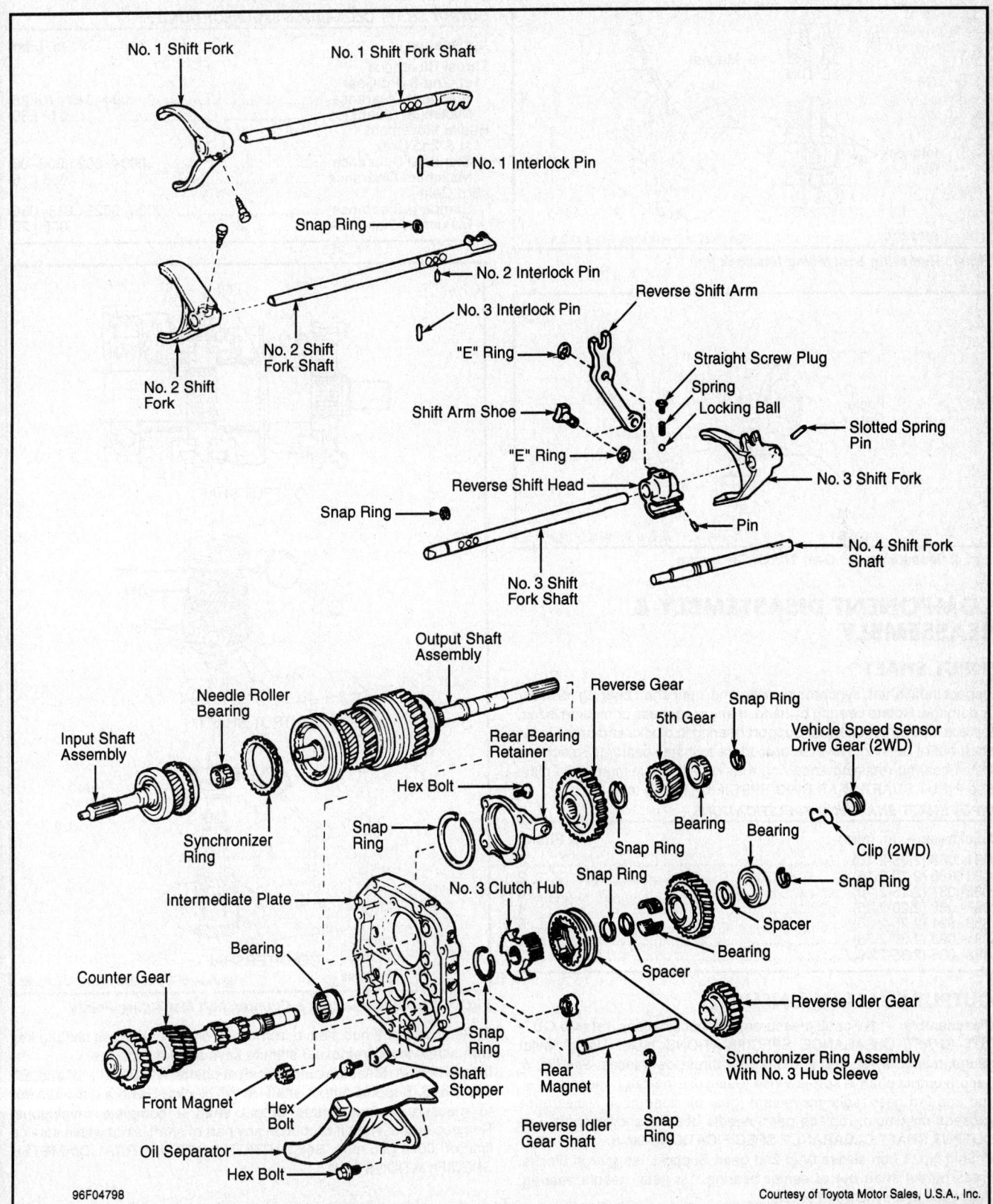

96F04798

Courtesy of Toyota Motor Sales, U.S.A., Inc.

Fig. 2: Exploded View Of Shifter & Intermediate Plate

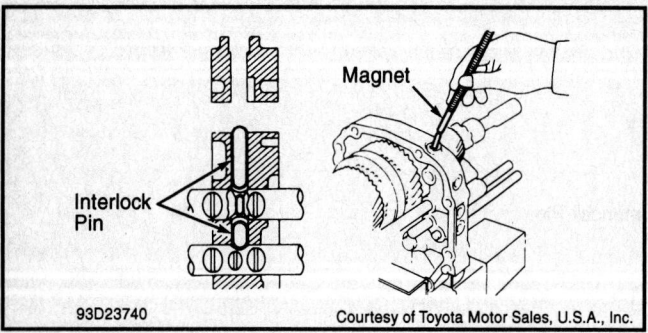

Fig. 3: Removing & Installing Interlock Pin

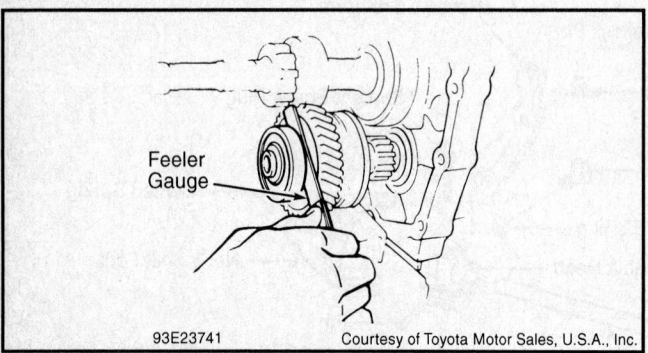

Fig. 4: Measuring 5th Gear Thrust Clearance

COMPONENT DISASSEMBLY & REASSEMBLY

INPUT SHAFT

Inspect input shaft, synchronizer ring and input shaft bearing for wear or damage. Rotate bearing by hand. If any roughness or binding is felt, replace input shaft bearing. Support bearing in blocks and press input shaft out of bearing. Reverse procedure to install bearing. Select and install bearing retaining snap ring that will allow minimum axial play. See INPUT SHAFT SNAP RING SPECIFICATIONS table.

INPUT SHAFT SNAP RING SPECIFICATIONS

Thickness – In. (mm)	ID Stamp
.081-.083 (2.05-2.10)	1
.083-.085 (2.10-2.15)	2
.085-.087 (2.15-2.20)	3
.087-.089 (2.20-2.25)	4
.089-.091 (2.25-2.30)	5
.091-.093 (2.30-2.35)	11
.093-.095 (2.35-2.40)	12

OUTPUT SHAFT (MAINSHAFT)

Disassembly – **1)** For all measurement specifications, refer to OUTPUT SHAFT CLEARANCE SPECIFICATIONS table. Using feeler gauge, measure 1st, 2nd and 3rd gear thrust clearances. *See Fig. 5.* Secure output shaft in soft-jaw vise. Using dial indicator, measure 1st, 2nd and 3rd gear radial movement (gear oil clearance). If clearance exceeds maximum, replace gear, needle bearing and/or shaft. See OUTPUT SHAFT CLEARANCE SPECIFICATIONS table.

2) Shift No. 1 hub sleeve onto 2nd gear. Support 1st gear in blocks. Press output shaft out of center bearing, 1st gear, needle bearing, inner race and synchronizer ring.

3) Remove locking ball with a magnet. Supporting 2nd gear, remove No. 1 hub sleeve assembly, 2nd gear and needle roller bearing. Remove No. 1 hub sleeve from No. 1 clutch hub. Push shifting key spring with a screwdriver, remove 3 shifting keys and key springs. Remove snap ring. Supporting 3rd gear, remove No. 2 hub sleeve, synchronizer ring and 3rd gear.

OUTPUT SHAFT CLEARANCE SPECIFICATIONS

Application	In. (mm)
Thrust Clearance	
1st, 2nd & 3rd Gear	
Standard Clearance	.004-.010 (.10-.25)
Maximum Clearance	.012 (.30)
Radial Movement	
1st & 2nd Gear	
Standard Clearance	.0004-.002 (.009-.06)
Maximum Clearance	.006 (.15)
3rd Gear	
Standard Clearance	.0006-.0026 (.015-.066)
Maximum Clearance	.008 (.20)

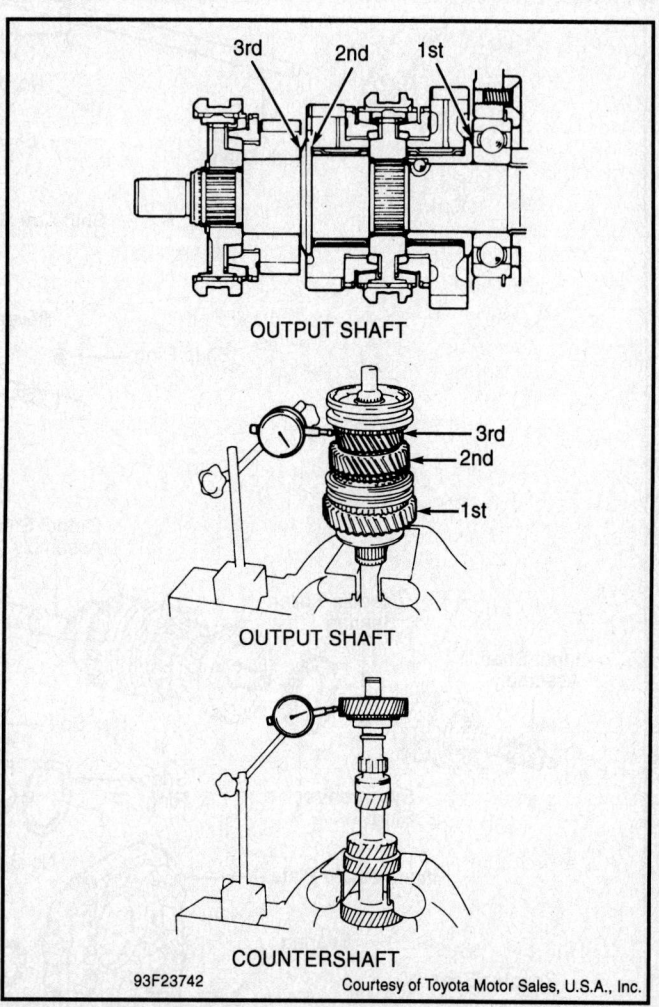

Fig. 5: Identifying Output & Countershaft Measuring Points

4) Remove No. 2 hub sleeve from No. 2 clutch hub. Push shifting key with screwdriver, remove 3 shifting keys and key springs.

Inspection – Measure output shaft at points "A", "B", "C", "D" and "E". *See Fig. 6.* Support output shaft on "V" blocks. Using a dial indicator to measure runout, rotate output shaft 2 complete revolutions. Replace output shaft if runout on any part of shaft is not within service limit of .0024 (.06 mm). See OUTPUT SHAFT JOURNAL DIAMETER SPECIFICATIONS table.

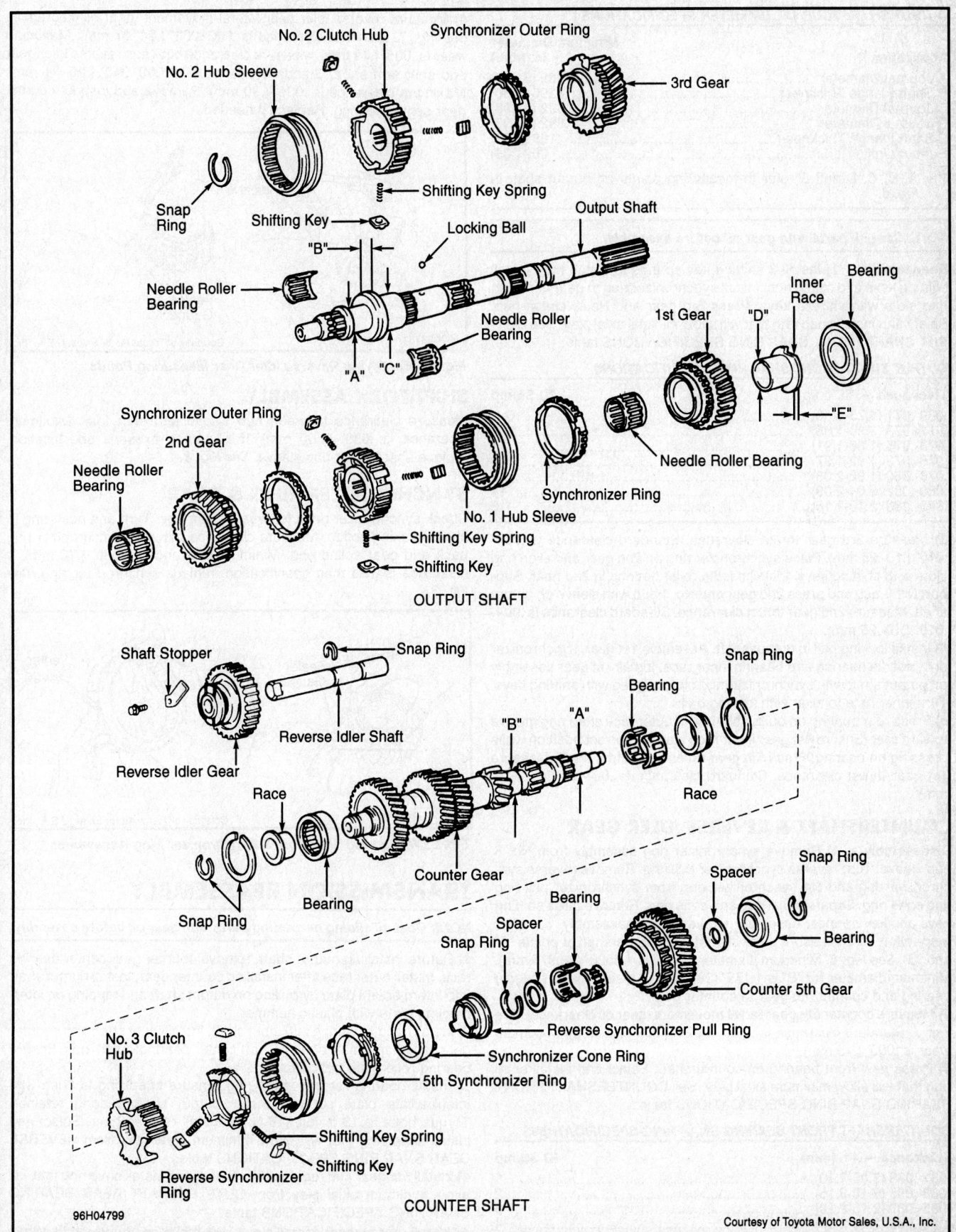

OUTPUT SHAFT

COUNTER SHAFT

96H04799

Courtesy of Toyota Motor Sales, U.S.A., Inc.

Fig. 6: Exploded View Of Output & Countershaft Assemblies

OUTPUT SHAFT JOURNAL DIAMETER SPECIFICATIONS

Application [1]	Minimum Diameter In. (mm)
A Journal Diameter	1.259 (31.97)
B Shaft Flange Thickness	.2205 (5.60)
C Journal Diameter	1.692 (42.98)
D Journal Diameter	1.692 (42.98)
E Shaft Flange Thickness	.188 (4.78)
Runout Limits	.002 (.05)

[1] – A, B, C, D and E refer to measuring points on output shaft in *Fig. 6.*

NOTE: Coat all parts with gear oil before assembly.

Reassembly – **1)** Install 3 shifting key springs to clutch hub. Install shifting keys and clutch hub. Install synchronizer ring to gear and align ring slots with shifting keys. Press 3rd gear and No. 2 clutch hub. Select and install snap ring that will allow minimal axial play. See OUTPUT SHAFT FRONT SNAP RING SPECIFICATIONS table.

OUTPUT SHAFT FRONT SNAP RING SPECIFICATIONS

Thickness – In. (mm)	ID Stamp
.069-.071 (1.75-1.80)	C-1
.071-.073 (1.80-1.85)	D
.073-.075 (1.86-1.91)	11
.076-.078 (1.92-1.97)	12
.078-.080 (1.98-2.03)	13
.080-.082 (2.04-2.09)	14
.083-.085 (2.10-2.15)	15

3) Measure 3rd gear thrust clearance. Standard clearance is .004-.010" (.10-.25 mm). Place synchronizer ring on 2nd gear and align ring slots with shifting keys. Install needle roller bearing in 2nd gear. Support No. 1 hub and press 2nd gear and No. 1 hub with sleeve on output shaft. Measure 2nd gear thrust clearance. Standard clearance is .004-.010" (.10-.25 mm).

4) Install locking ball in output shaft. Assemble 1st gear, synchronizer ring, needle bearing and bearing inner race. Install 1st gear assembly on output shaft with synchronizer ring slots aligned with shifting keys. Turn inner race to align with locking ball.

5) Press rear bearing on output shaft with outer race snap ring groove toward rear. Ensure 1st gear inner race stays in correct position while pressing on bearing. Press 5th gear on end of output shaft. Measure 1st gear thrust clearance. Standard clearance is .004-.010" (.10-.25 mm).

COUNTERSHAFT & REVERSE IDLER GEAR

Disassembly – **1)** Remove synchronizer ring assembly from No. 3 hub sleeve. Turn reverse synchronizer pull ring. Remove reverse synchronizer ring and 5th synchronizer ring from synchronizer pull ring and cone ring. Separate pull ring and cone ring. Remove three shifting keys and key springs. Assembly is reverse of disassembly.

Inspection – **1)** Measure outer diameter of countershaft at points "A" and "B". See Fig. 6. Minimum diameter for "A" is 1.0620" (26.975 mm). Minimum diameter for "B" is 1.179" (29.95 mm). Install spacer, needle bearing and counter 5th gear to counter gear.

2) Measure counter 5th gear radial movement (gear oil clearance). See Fig. 5. Standard clearance is .0004-.0024" (.009-.060 mm). Maximum wear is .006" (.15 mm).

3) Press new front bearing on countershaft. Select and install snap ring that will allow minimum axial play. See COUNTERSHAFT FRONT BEARING SNAP RING SPECIFICATIONS table.

COUNTERSHAFT FRONT BEARING SNAP RING SPECIFICATIONS

Thickness – In. (mm)	ID Stamp
.081-.083 (2.05-2.10)	1
.083-.085 (2.10-2.15)	2
.085-.087 (2.15-2.20)	3
.087-.089 (2.20-2.25)	4
.089-.091 (2.25-2.30)	5
.091-.093 (2.30-2.35)	6
.093-.095 (2.35-2.40)	7

4) Measure reverse idler gear lateral movement (gear oil clearance). See Fig. 7. Standard clearance is .002-.003" (.04-.07 mm). Maximum wear is .008" (.19 mm). Measure clearance between reverse idler gear and shift arm shoe. Standard clearance is .008-.016" (.20-.41 mm). Maximum clearance is .035" (.90 mm). Remove and inspect counter gear center bearing. Replace if needed.

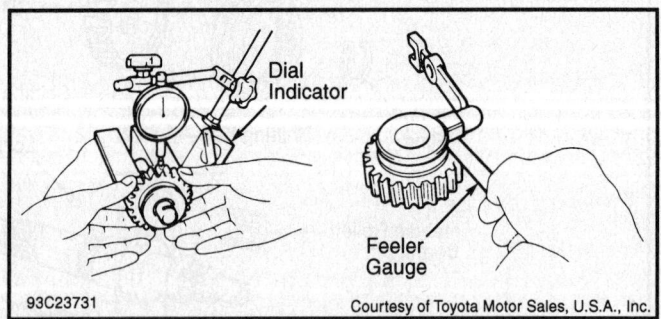

93C23731   Courtesy of Toyota Motor Sales, U.S.A., Inc.

Fig. 7: Identifying Reverse Idler Gear Measuring Points

SHIFT FORK ASSEMBLY

Measure clearance between hub sleeve and shift fork. Maximum clearance is .039" (1.00 mm). If clearance exceeds specification, replace shift fork or hub sleeve. See Fig. 8.

SYNCHRONIZER RING & GEAR

Check synchronizer rings for wear or damage. Turn and push ring to check braking action. Measure clearance between synchronizer ring back and gear spline end. Minimum clearance is .028" (.70 mm). If clearance is less than specification, replace synchronizer ring. See Fig. 8.

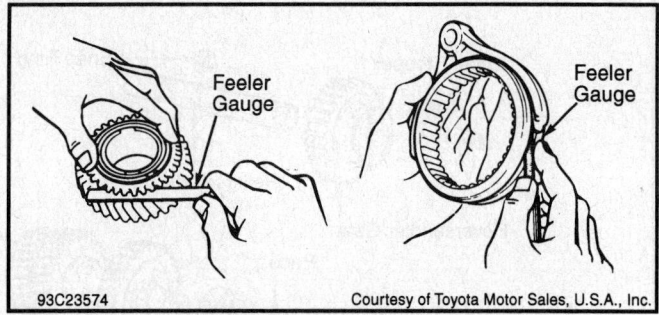

93C23574   Courtesy of Toyota Motor Sales, U.S.A., Inc.

Fig. 8: Measuring Shift Fork & Synchronizer Ring Assemblies

TRANSMISSION REASSEMBLY

NOTE: Coat all sliding or rotating parts with gear oil before assembly.

1) Before installing output shaft, remove counter gear center bearing race. Install outer race after installing counter gear. Install output shaft into intermediate plate by pulling on output shaft and tapping on intermediate plate with plastic hammer.

2) Install needle bearing into input shaft. Install input shaft and counter gear together. Install countershaft center bearing outer race. Ensure bearing rollers are not damaged.

3) Install bearing retainer snap ring. Ensure snap ring is flush with intermediate plate surface. Install output shaft bearing retainer. Torque bolts to 13 ft. lbs. (18 N.m). Install reverse gear. Select and install snap ring that will allow minimum axial play from REVERSE GEAR SNAP RING SPECIFICATIONS table.

4) Install 5th gear and rear bearing. Select and install snap ring that will allow minimum axial play from OUTPUT SHAFT REAR BEARING SNAP RING SPECIFICATIONS table.

5) Install rear magnet. Install No. 3 clutch hub on countershaft. When installing clutch hub, support countershaft with 3-5 lb. hammer. Select and install snap ring that will allow minimum axial play from NO. 3 CLUTCH HUB SNAP RING SPECIFICATIONS table.

REVERSE GEAR SNAP RING SPECIFICATIONS

Thickness – In. (mm)	ID Stamp
.089-.091 (2.25-2.30)	5
.091-.093 (2.30-2.35)	11
.093-.095 (2.35-2.40)	12
.095-.097 (2.40-2.45)	13
.097-.099 (2.45-2.50)	14
.098-.100 (2.50-2.55)	15
.100-.102 (2.55-2.60)	16
.103-.105 (2.61-2.66)	17
.105-.107 (2.67-2.72)	18
.108-.109 (2.73-2.78)	19
.110-.112 (2.79-2.84)	20
.112-.114 (2.85-2.90)	21
.115-.117 (2.91-2.96)	22
.117-.119 (2.97-3.02)	23

OUTPUT SHAFT REAR BEARING SNAP RING SPECIFICATIONS

Thickness – In. (mm)	ID Stamp
.091-.093 (2.31-2.36)	8
.093-.095 (2.37-2.42)	9
.096-.098 (2.43-2.48)	10
.098-.100 (2.49-2.54)	11
.100-.102 (2.55-2.60)	12
.103-.105 (2.61-2.66)	13
.106-.108 (2.68-2.73)	14
.108-.110 (2.74-2.79)	15

NO. 3 CLUTCH HUB SNAP RING SPECIFICATIONS

Thickness – In. (mm)	ID Stamp
.081-.083 (2.06-2.11)	2
.083-.085 (2.12-2.17)	3
.086-.088 (2.18-2.23)	4
.088-.090 (2.24-2.29)	5

6) Install bearing spacer on countershaft. Assemble 5th counter gear, synchronizer ring and needle bearings. Install 5th gear with 5th gear gaps aligned with synchronizer cone ring pin. Install spacer and bearing with bearing shield toward rear of shaft. Support front of countershaft and drive in bearing with 3-5 lb. hammer. Select and install snap ring that will allow minimum axial play. See COUNTER 5TH GEAR SHAFT SNAP RING SPECIFICATIONS table .

COUNTER 5TH GEAR SHAFT SNAP RING SPECIFICATIONS

Thickness – In. (mm)	ID Stamp
.075-.077 (1.90-1.95)	1
.077-.079 (1.96-2.01)	2
.080-.082 (2.02-2.07)	3
.082-.084 (2.08-2.13)	4
.085-.086 (2.14-2.19)	5
.087-.089 (2.20-2.25)	6
.089-.091 (2.26-2.31)	7

7) Measure counter 5th gear thrust clearance. Standard clearance is .004-.016" (.10-.41 mm). Maximum clearance is .019" (.46 mm). On 2WD models, install vehicle speed sensor drive gear clip into slot on output shaft. Slide drive gear with clip and fit clip into holes. Install reverse idler gear and shaft. Coat interlock pin with MP grease and install into reverse shift head hole. Install No. 3 shift fork shaft with snap ring through No. 3 shift fork and reverse shift arm. Align No. 3 shift fork with No. 3 hub sleeve groove, put reverse shift arm the pivot bearing retainer and align reverse shift arm shoe with reverse idler groove. Install No. 3 shift fork shaft to intermediate plate.

8) Install No. 4 shift fork shaft into intermediate plate. Install ball and spring. Install and tighten plug to 18 ft. lbs. (25 N.m). Install slotted spring pin until flush with No. 3 shift fork. Install snap ring to No. 3 fork shaft. Apply MP grease to No. 2 and No. 3 interlock pin and install to intermediate plate hole. Place No. 2 shift fork into groove of No. 2 hub sleeve. Install No. 2 fork shaft through intermediate plate. Install snap ring to No. 2 fork shaft.

9) Place No. 1 shift fork onto groove of No. 1 hub sleeve. Install No. 1 fork shaft to No. 1 shift fork through intermediate plate. Install two new bolts to No. 1 and No. 2 shift fork. Tighten bolts to 14 ft. lbs. (20 N.m).

NOTE: This transmission uses no gasket between major housings; use Three Bond (1281) sealant. Assemble housing immediately after applying liquid gasket. Allow 30 minutes curing time before filling with oil.

10) Install 3 locking balls and springs. Apply Locktite 242 or equivalent, to straight screw plugs and install. Note length and position of plugs. *See Fig. 9.* Tighten to 18 ft. lbs. (25 N.m). Install reverse idler gear shaft stopper. Tighten bolt to 18 ft. lbs. (25 N.m). Install front magnet and oil separator. Tighten bolts to 13 ft. lbs. (18 N.m). Dismount intermediate plate from vise. Using Three Bond (1281), or equivalent, install transmission case.

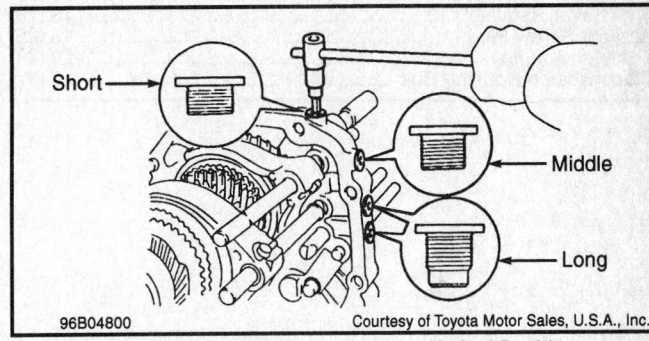

Short — Middle — Long

96B04800   Courtesy of Toyota Motor Sales, U.S.A., Inc.

Fig. 9: Identifying Straight Screw Plug Length And Position.

11) Install 2 bearing snap rings. Apply Three Bond (1281), or equivalent, to front bearing retainer. Apply Locktite (242), or equivalent, to front bearing retainer bolts, install and tighten to 18 ft. lbs. (25 N.m). On 2WD, Apply Three Bond (1281), or equivalent, to extension housing. Align each bearing outer race and shift fork shaft end with case holes. Install case using plastic hammer.

12) Connect shift and select lever to shift fork shaft. Install shift lever housing to shift and select lever shaft. Install new bolt and tighten to 29 ft. lbs. (37 N.m). Apply Locktite (242), or equivalent, to bolts, install and tighten bolts to 27 ft. lbs. (37 N.m).

13) On 4WD models, install shift and select lever into transfer adaptor. Apply Three Bond (1281), or equivalent, to transfer adaptor, connect shift and select lever to shift fork shaft. Install the shift lever housing to shift and select lever shaft. Push in transfer adaptor. Install new bolt and tighten to 29 ft. lbs. (39 N.m). Install bolts to transfer adaptor and tighten to 27 ft. lbs. (37 N.m).

14) Ensure input and output shafts rotate smoothly and shifting is smooth in all positions. Install restrict pins with gasket. Install Black restrict pin on reverse gear/5th gear side. Tighten pins to 30 ft. lbs. (40 N.m).

15) On 2WD models, install shift lever control retainer with new gasket. Apply Three Bond (1281), or equivalent, to bolts, install and tighten to 13 ft. lbs. (18 N.m). On 4WD models, install shift lever control retainer with oil baffle plate. Apply Three Bond (1281), or equivalent, to bolts, install and tighten to 13 ft. lbs. (18 N.m).

16) On both models, install clutch housing. Tighten bolts to 27 ft. lbs. Install vehicle speed sensor driven gear (2WD). Install and tighten back-up light switch to 30 ft. lbs. (40 N.m). Install wire clamp.

TORQUE SPECIFICATIONS

TORQUE SPECIFICATIONS

Application	Ft. Lbs. (N.m)
Back-Up Light Switch	30 (40)
Clutch Housing Bolts	27 (37)
Control Shift Lever Arm Bolts	14 (19)
Control Shift Lever Arm Nut	18 (25)
Extension Housing Bolts	29 (39)
Front Bearing Retainer Bolts	18 (25)
No. 1 Control Shift Yoke Nut	14 (20)
Rear Bearing Retainer Bolts	14 (20)
Restrict Pin	30 (40)
Reverse Idler Gear Shaft Stopper Bolt	18 (25)
Reverse Shift Arm Bracket Bolt	13 (18)
Speed Sensor Bolt	10 (14)
Vehicle Speed Sensor Lock Plate (2WD) Bolt	9 (13)
Shift Fork Set Bolt	14 (20)
Shift Lever Housing Bolt	29 (39)
Shift Lever Retainer	13 (18)
Straight Screw Plug	18 (25)
Transfer Adapter	29 (39)
Transmission Housing Bolt	27 (37)

Golf, GTI VR6, Jetta, Jetta III, Passat

APPLICATION & LABOR TIMES

APPLICATION & LABOR TIMES

Vehicle Application	Labor Times		Series
	[1] R & I	[2] Overhaul	
1995			
GTI VR6	3.8	4.9	02A
Jetta III [3]	3.8	4.9	02A
Passat [3]	5.9	4.9	02A
1996			
GTI VR6	3.8	4.9	02A
Jetta [3]	3.8	4.9	02A
Passat [3]	5.9	4.9	02A

[1] – Removal and installation of transmission from vehicle chassis.

[2] – Bench overhaul time for transaxle/differential. DOES NOT include removal and installation.

[3] – Equipped with 2.8L V6 engine.

IDENTIFICATION

Volkswagen Audi Group (VAG) transaxle is identified by a type number cast into transaxle case. Code letter and production date information is stamped on a machined surface located on upper portion of transaxle clutch housing surface.

DESCRIPTION

Type 02A is a 5-speed transaxle consisting of an input shaft, mainshaft/drive pinion shaft and a differential assembly which transfers power to front wheels.

LUBRICATION

Use hypoid oil API GL4, MIL-L2105 SAE 80 or G50 SAE 75W90 synthetic lubricant.

TROUBLE SHOOTING

See GENERAL TROUBLE SHOOTING article in this section.

ON-VEHICLE SERVICE

SHIFT LINKAGE ADJUSTMENT

1) Place gear selector lever in "N" position. Remove knob and boot. Remove balance weight. Loosen bolt "A" and nut "B" sufficiently so that operating cables move freely in centering holes. See Fig 1. Install Shift Linkage Gauge (3192). Loosen bolt "C". See Fig 2.

2) Pivot locating pin under bearing plate. Tighten nut "D". Place gearshift lever into left detent of slide. Move gearshift lever and slide together to left stop. Tighten slide with bolt "D". Move gearshift lever to right detent. Tighten bolt "E". Move gearshift lever to right detent. Tighten bolt "C".

DRIVE AXLE SHAFTS

See appropriate AXLE SHAFTS article in AXLE SHAFTS & TRANSFER CASES section.

REMOVAL & INSTALLATION

See appropriate MANUAL TRANSMISSION REMOVAL article in TRANSMISSION SERVICING section.

TRANSAXLE DISASSEMBLY & REASSEMBLY

Disassembly – 1) Mount transaxle in mounting fixture and drain oil from transaxle. Loosen and remove gearbox housing cover bolts and remove cover. Loosen and remove 5th gear selector fork. See Fig. 3.

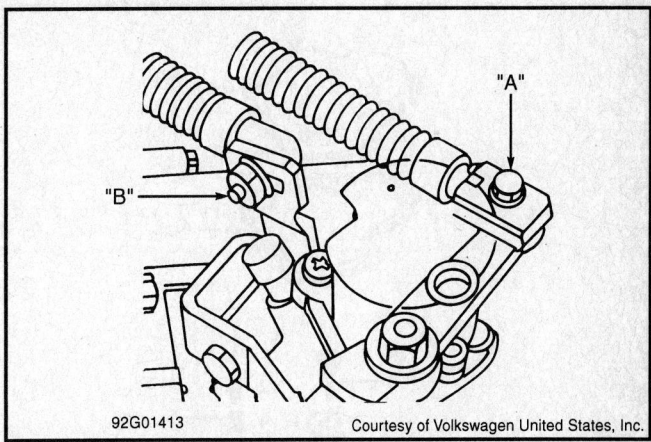

92G01413   Courtesy of Volkswagen United States, Inc.

Fig. 1: Identifying Centering Holes

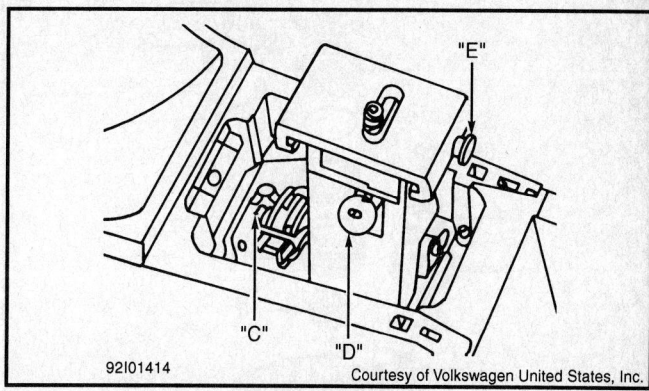

92I01414   Courtesy of Volkswagen United States, Inc.

Fig. 2: Installing Shift Linkage Gauge

2) To facilitate removal of gears, engage transaxle 2nd gear. Remove 5th gear synchronizer assembly retaining bolt and diaphragm spring. Using a puller, remove synchronizer assembly, synchronizer ring and 5th gear. Remove 5th gear needle bearing from shaft. Remove fixed 5th gear retaining bolt and diaphragm spring. Using a puller, pull off fixed 5th gear. Return transaxle to Neutral.

3) From gearbox side of transaxle, remove drive flange using two bolts as a puller tool. Make certain to line up bolts with oil drain plug so they will bear on reinforced portion of gearbox. Failure to do so could result in a damaged gearbox. Remove shift fork locating pins.

4) Remove bearing sleeve cover. Remove oil drain plug if necessary. Remove gearshift selector mechanism. Loosen and remove gearbox to clutch housing mounting bolts from both sides of cover. Carefully remove gearbox housing.

5) Remove guide sleeve, locating dowels, oil drain plug and magnet from case. See Fig. 4. Remove shift fork assembly. Loosen and remove 4 output shaft retaining nuts on clutch side of clutch housing. Discard seals. Remove bolts for reverse shaft support.

6) Remove reverse gear, input shaft and output shaft assembly, in that order. See Fig. 5. Remove speedometer drive gear. Remove left hand drive flange. Remove differential assembly.

Reassembly – 1) Install bearing housing to clutch cover housing. Place differential assembly into clutch housing. Install speedometer drive gear.

2) Install input shaft, output shaft and reverse shaft into clutch cover housing as an assembly. Install reverse shaft mounting bolts finger tight. Install new oil seals and nuts on output shaft retaining bracket studs. Install guide sleeve, locating dowels, oil drain plug and magnet. Tighten reverse shaft bolts.

NOTE: Once output shaft retaining bracket stud nuts are tightened to specification, they must be turned an additional 90 degrees.

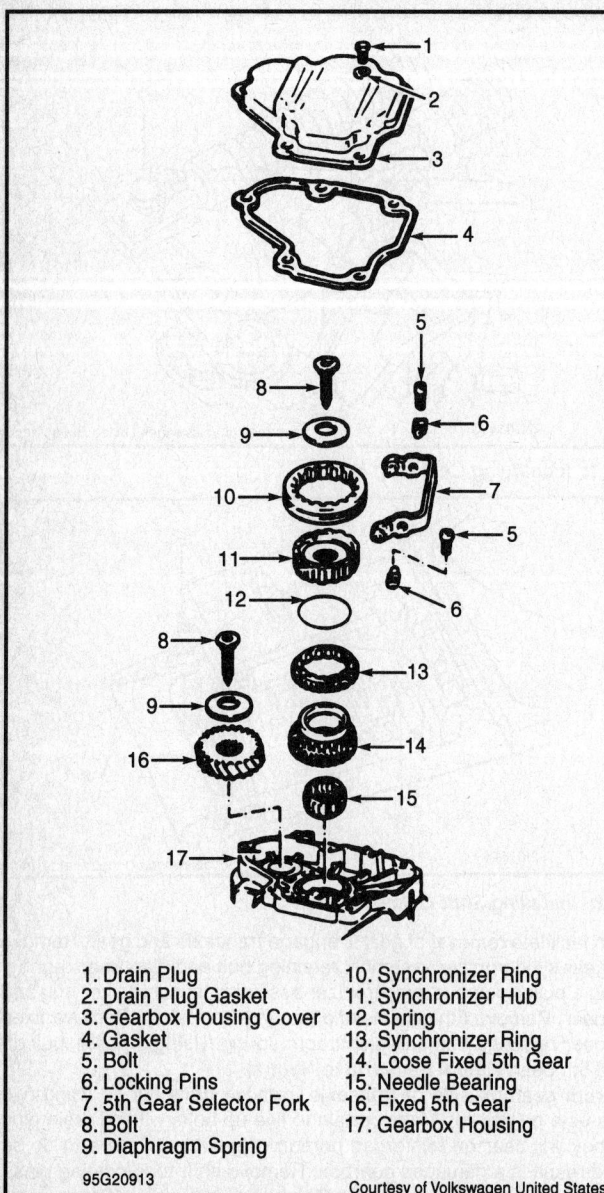

1. Drain Plug
2. Drain Plug Gasket
3. Gearbox Housing Cover
4. Gasket
5. Bolt
6. Locking Pins
7. 5th Gear Selector Fork
8. Bolt
9. Diaphragm Spring
10. Synchronizer Ring
11. Synchronizer Hub
12. Spring
13. Synchronizer Ring
14. Loose Fixed 5th Gear
15. Needle Bearing
16. Fixed 5th Gear
17. Gearbox Housing

95G20913   Courtesy of Volkswagen United States, Inc.

Fig. 3: Exploded View Of Gearbox Housing Cover & 5th Gears

3) Install gearbox housing onto clutch cover. Align shift forks with shift fork locating pins by using a screwdriver or similar tool to move forks. Insert 4 pins and tighten mounting bolts. Install bearing sleeve cover, shift shaft selector assembly and drive flange.

4) Install fixed 5th gear, diaphragm spring and mounting bolt onto output shaft. Install needle bearing, free 5th gear, 5th gear synchronizer ring, 5th gear synchronizer assembly, diaphragm spring and mounting bolt onto input shaft. Install 5th gear selector fork, locating dowels and bolts. Install gearbox housing cover and gasket.

COMPONENT DISASSEMBLY & REASSEMBLY

CLUTCH HOUSING

Disassembly – **1)** Remove oil drain plug, locating dowels, differential bearing outer race and shim, magnet, output shaft outer bearing race and adjusting shim. Using puller, extract input shaft needle bearing.
2) Unbolt relay lever brackets, relay lever and springs. Extract bushing for starter shaft. Remove threaded plug, input shaft oil seal, drive flange sleeve and oil seal.

Inspection – Inspect clutch housing for cracks, worn or galled bearing race bores, stripped threads or damaged case machined surfaces.
Reassembly – **1)** Install drive flange sleeve and oil seal. Install threaded plug and bushing for starter. Install relay lever, brackets and springs.
2) Install input shaft needle bearing using bearing driver. Install shim and bearing outer race for differential assembly. Install selected adjusting shim and outer bearing race for output shaft. Install locating dowels and oil drain plug. Install magnet on case (secured in place by surface of mating housing).

GEARBOX HOUSING

Disassembly – Using a press, remove output shaft needle bearing. Remove differential outer bearing race, adjustment shim and drive flange oil seal. Remove input shaft outer bearing race and shim.
Inspection – Inspect clutch housing for cracks, worn or galled bearing race bores, stripped threads or damaged case machined surfaces.
Reassembly – Using a press, install output shaft needle bearing. Install outer bearing races and selected adjusting shims for differential and input shaft. Install output flange oil seal(s).

GEARBOX HOUSING COVER

Disassembly – Remove gearbox housing cover. Remove clutch lever clip, clutch lever and lever return spring. Remove release bearing, oil seal and release shaft clip. Remove oil filler plug, needle bearing and bearing retainer bolt.
Inspection – Inspect clutch housing for cracks, worn or galled bearing race bores, stripped threads or damaged case machine surfaces.
Reassembly – Install oil filler plug, needle bearing and bearing retainer bolt. Install release bearing, release shaft oil seal, release shaft and shaft clip. Install clutch lever, clutch lever return spring, and lever retaining clip.

INPUT ASSEMBLY

Disassembly – Remove thrust washer from 5th gear end of input shaft. Using a press, remove inner bearing from clutch end of shaft and inner bearing race and fixed 4th gear. Remove circlip and remove free 3rd gear. See Fig. 6.
Inspection – Inspect all bearing surfaces for wear. Inspect gears for damage to teeth, bearing surfaces and synchronizer tabs. Check synchronizer rings for wear by installing ring on respective gear and measuring thickness between ring teeth and gear teeth. All synchronizer rings except 2nd gear should have a clearance of .043-.066" (1.1-1.7 mm), and a wear limit minimum thickness of .020" (.5 mm). Second gear synchronizer should have a clearance of .030-.049" (.75-1.25 mm), and a minimum wear thickness of .010" (.3 mm).
Reassembly – Install free 3rd gear and circlip onto input shaft. Using a press, install fixed 4th gear, and tapered bearing onto input shaft. Invert shaft in press and install tapered bearing on clutch end of shaft. Place thrust washer on end of shaft and hold in place with grease.

OUTPUT SHAFT ASSEMBLY

Disassembly – **1)** Using a separator plate, position under 2nd gear and press off components No. 19 (2nd gear) through No. 30 (4th gear) from output shaft. See Fig. 7.
2) Remove circlip. Using a 2-jaw puller, position under bearing carrier and pull off synchronizer sleeve along with 1st/2nd gear synchro-hub assembly. See Fig. 7. Using appropriate puller, remove tapered roller bearing from output shaft.
Inspection – Inspect output shaft and gears for scoring and wear marks. Check gear and synchronizer teeth for wear and chipping. Check synchronizer rings for clearance.
Reassembly – **1)** Install tapered bearings on output shaft. Using a press and bearing saddle, install thrust washer, 1st gear, 1st gear synchronizer ring, needle bearing, 1st/2nd gear synchronizer hub assembly, 2nd gear, 2nd gear synchronizer ring, needle bearing and bearing race.

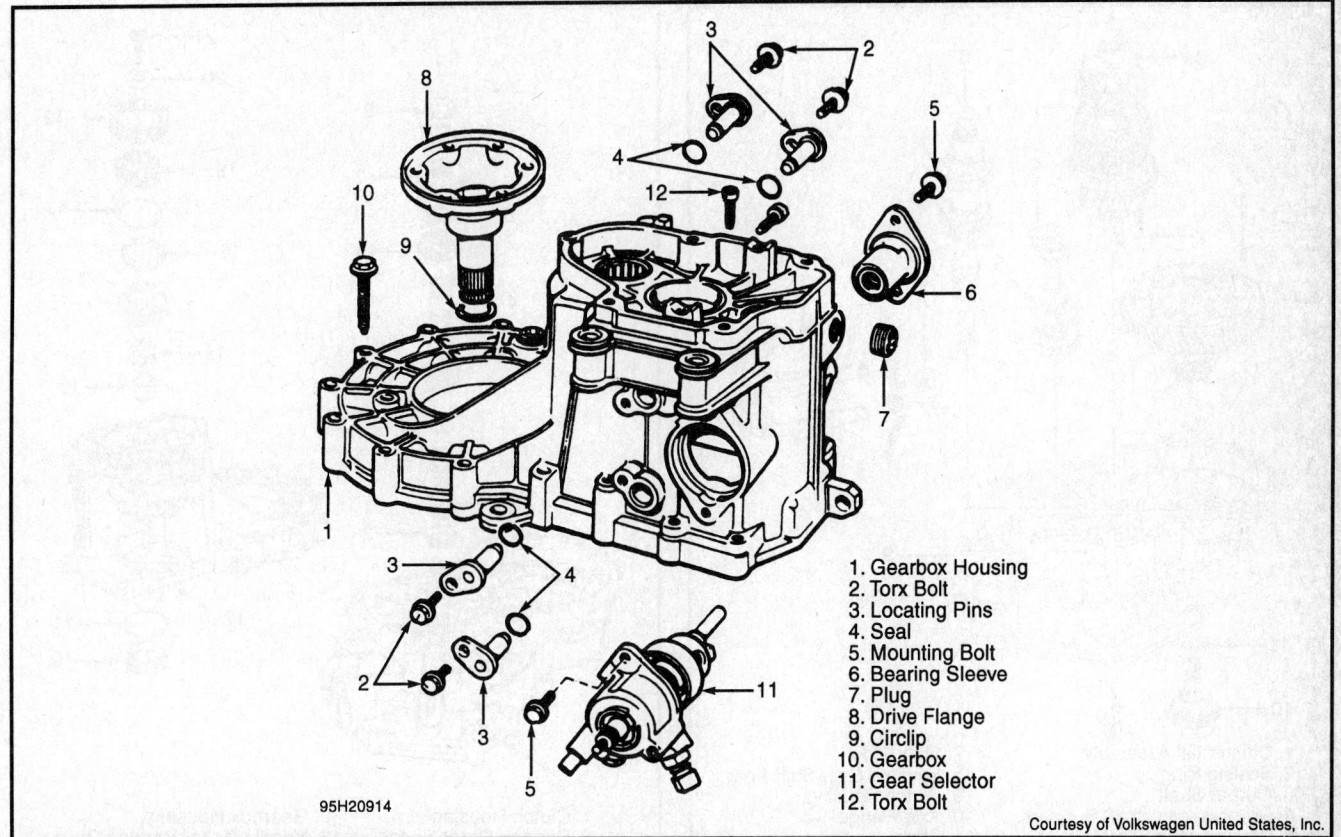

95H20914

1. Gearbox Housing
2. Torx Bolt
3. Locating Pins
4. Seal
5. Mounting Bolt
6. Bearing Sleeve
7. Plug
8. Drive Flange
9. Circlip
10. Gearbox
11. Gear Selector
12. Torx Bolt

Courtesy of Volkswagen United States, Inc.

Fig. 4: Exploded View Of Gearbox Housing

2) Install thrust washer, 3rd gear, 3rd gear synchronizer ring, needle bearing and needle bearing inner race, 3rd/4th synchronizer hub assembly, 4th gear, 4th gear synchronizer ring, needle bearing and race. Place thrust washer on shaft assembly and hold in place with grease.

REVERSE GEAR SHAFT ASSEMBLY

Disassembly – Following removal of both mounting bolts, remove reverse gear shaft support and needle bearing. Remove helical cut reverse gear, circlip and straight cut reverse gear. See Fig. 8.
Inspection – Inspect reverse gear shaft for galling or wear. Inspect reverse gears for wear, chipping or other damage.
Reassembly – Install straight cut reverse gear onto reverse gear shaft. Install circlip and helical cut reverse gear. Install needle bearing and gear shaft support.

DIFFERENTIAL ASSEMBLY

Disassembly – **1)** Press tapered roller bearings off both ends of differential housing. Remove ring gear from differential housing if ring gear or housing needs replacement. See Fig. 9.
2) Remove spring pin. Remove pinion shaft, pinion gears and one piece thrust washer.
Inspection – Inspect gears and pinion shaft for wear, chipping or galling. Inspect thrust washer for wear. Replace components as needed.
Reassembly – **1)** If differential ring gear is being replaced, heat gear to approximately 212°F (100°C) and press onto differential housing using several bolts as guide pins during installation. Torque nuts to 44 ft. lbs. (60 N.m) and turn an additional 90 degrees.
2) Install one piece thrust washer, pinion gears and pinion shaft into differential case and secure with spring pin. Press tapered bearings onto each end of differential carrier.

NOTE: If installing a new ring gear or pinion, be sure both components are a matched set. Use NEW ring gear retaining Bolt Kit (02A 498 088A).

ADJUSTING INPUT SHAFT PRELOAD

NOTE: The input shaft must be readjusted if the gearbox housing, clutch housing, input shaft, 4th speed gear or tapered roller bearings are replaced.

1) Press tapered roller bearing race into gearbox housing without shim. Install outer bearing race for opposite end of input shaft in gearbox housing. Place input shaft into clutch housing and install gearbox. Torque gearbox to clutch housing bolts to 18 ft. lbs. (25 N.m) and turn each bolt an additional 90 degrees.
2) Install a dial indicator to measure end play of the input shaft. See Fig. 10. Select a shim from the table based on dial indicator measurement. See INPUT SHAFT SHIM SELECTION CHART.

ADJUSTING OUTPUT SHAFT PRELOAD

NOTE: Resetting is not necessary unless replacing output shaft bearings, differential assembly or clutch housing.

1) Install output shaft roller bearing outer races into their respective clutch and gearbox housings. Insert a .025" (.65 mm) shim behind clutch housing race. Insert output shaft into clutch housing and install gearbox housing. Torque plate to 18 ft. lbs. (25 N.m), then turn each bolt an additional 90 degrees. Set up a dial indicator and measure up and down movement of output shaft. See Fig. 11.
2) The specified shim size is obtained by adding a constant of .008" (.20 mm) to recorded dial indicator reading and .025" (.65 mm) shim value. The sum of these three figures will determine shim size to be installed. Shims are available in sizes from .025" (.65 mm) to .055" (1.40 mm) in increments of .002" (.05 mm). Output shaft preload should be 12-18 INCH lbs. (130-180 N.m).

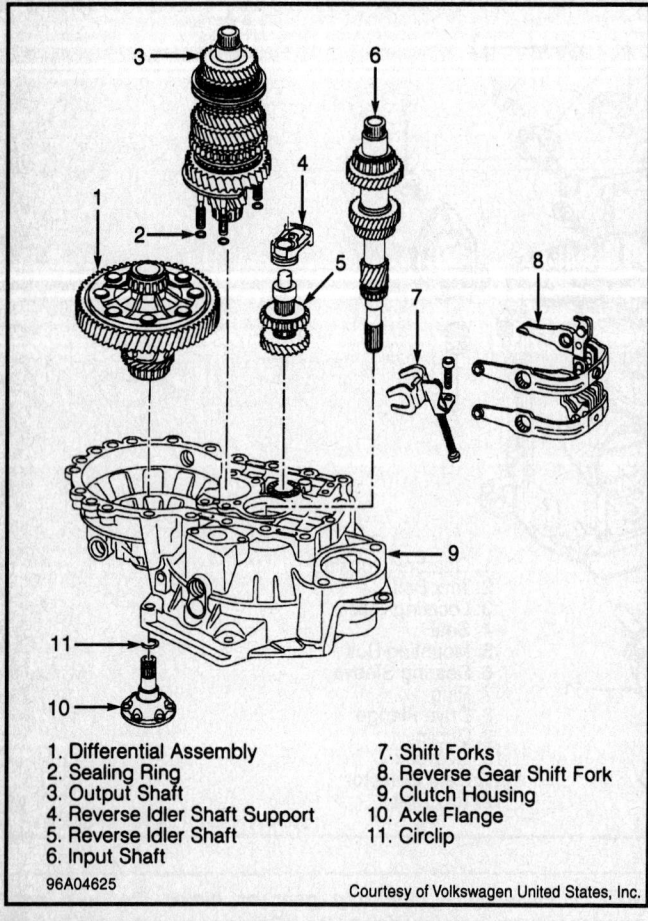

1. Differential Assembly
2. Sealing Ring
3. Output Shaft
4. Reverse Idler Shaft Support
5. Reverse Idler Shaft
6. Input Shaft
7. Shift Forks
8. Reverse Gear Shift Fork
9. Clutch Housing
10. Axle Flange
11. Circlip

96A04625

Courtesy of Volkswagen United States, Inc.

Fig. 5: Exploded View Of Geartrain & Differential

ADJUSTING DIFFERENTIAL PRELOAD

NOTE: Resetting is not necessary unless replacing gearbox housing, clutch housing, differential housing or differential bearings.

1) Install differential outer bearing race into their respective clutch and gearbox housing. Install differential into clutch housing case and install gearbox housing. Torque gearbox-to-clutch housing bolts to 18 ft. lbs. (25 N.m) and turn each bolt an additional 90 degrees.
2) Set up dial indicator to measure differential end play. *See Fig. 12.* The specified bearing shim is obtained by adding a constant value for preload of .015" (.40 mm) to dial indicator measurement. This sum is equal to the needed shim size. Shims are available is various sizes from .025" (.65 mm) to .049" (1.25 mm) in increments of .002" (.05 mm).
3) Differential bearing preload should be 10-28 INCH lbs. (120-320 N.m) for new bearings and at least 3 INCH lbs. (30 N.m) for used bearings.

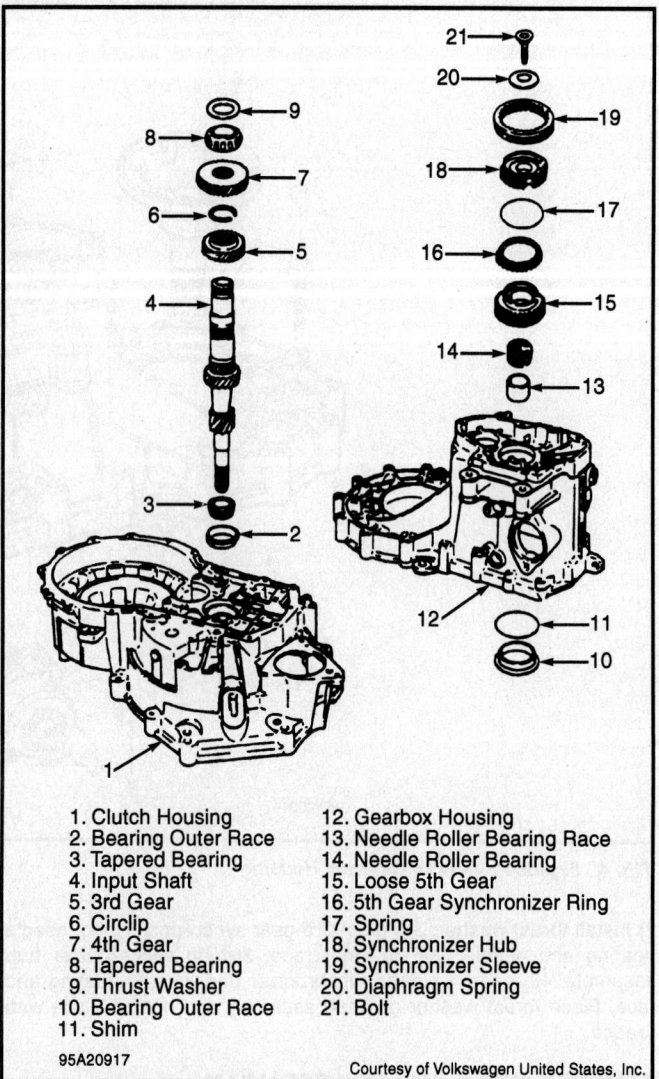

1. Clutch Housing
2. Bearing Outer Race
3. Tapered Bearing
4. Input Shaft
5. 3rd Gear
6. Circlip
7. 4th Gear
8. Tapered Bearing
9. Thrust Washer
10. Bearing Outer Race
11. Shim
12. Gearbox Housing
13. Needle Roller Bearing Race
14. Needle Roller Bearing
15. Loose 5th Gear
16. 5th Gear Synchronizer Ring
17. Spring
18. Synchronizer Hub
19. Synchronizer Sleeve
20. Diaphragm Spring
21. Bolt

95A20917

Courtesy of Volkswagen United States, Inc.

Fig. 6: Exploded View Of Input Shaft

MANUAL TRANSMISSIONS
Volkswagen Type 02A (Cont.)

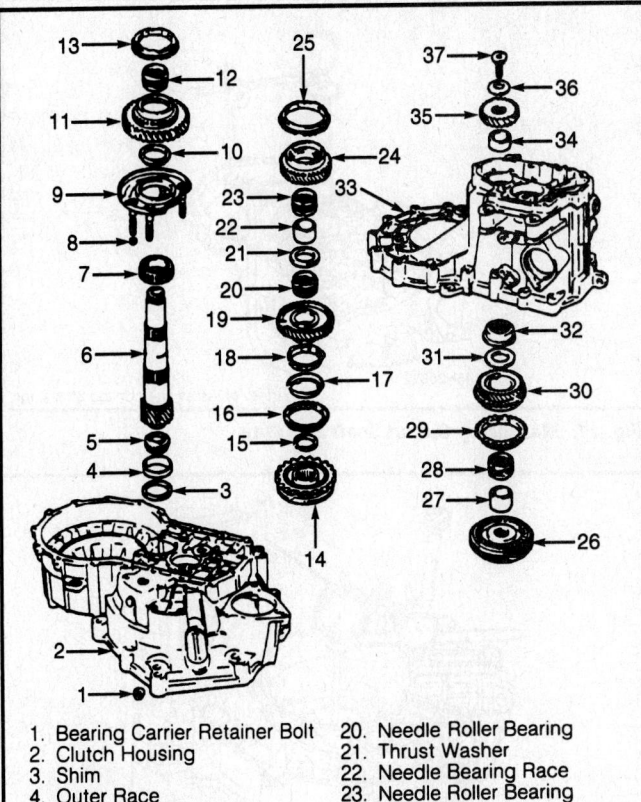

1. Bearing Carrier Retainer Bolt
2. Clutch Housing
3. Shim
4. Outer Race
5. Tapered Bearing
6. Output Shaft
7. Tapered Bearing
8. "O" Ring
9. Bearing Carrier
10. Thrust Washer
11. 1st Gear
12. Needle Bearing
13. 1st Gear Synchronizer Ring
14. Synchronizer Sleeve
15. Circlip
16. Synchronizer Ring
17. Outer Ring
18. Synchronizer Ring
19. 2nd Speed Gear
20. Needle Roller Bearing
21. Thrust Washer
22. Needle Bearing Race
23. Needle Roller Bearing
24. 3rd Gear
25. 3rd Gear Synchronizer Ring
26. Synchronizer Hub Assembly
27. Needle Bearing Race
28. Needle Bearing
29. Synchronizer Ring
30. 4th Gear
31. Thrust Washer
32. Needle Roller Bearing
33. Gearbox Housing
34. Needle Roller Bearing
35. 5th Gear
36. Diaphragm Spring
37. Bolt

95B20918

Courtesy of Volkswagen United States, Inc.

Fig. 7: Exploded View Of Output Shaft

INPUT SHAFT SHIM SELECTION CHART

Measured End Play – In. (mm)	Specified Shim Size
.026-.027(.671-.699)	025 (.650)
.027-.028 (.700-.724)	026 (.675)
.028-.029 (.725-.749)	027 (.700)
.029-.030 (.750-.774)	028 (.725)
.030-.031 (.775-.799)	029 (.750)
.031-.032 (.800-.824)	030 (.775)
.032-.033 (.825-.849)	031 (.800)
.033-.034 (.850-.874)	032 (.825)
.034-.035 (.875-.899)	033 (.850)
.035-.036 (.900-.924)	034 (.875)
.036-.037 (.925-.949)	035 (.900)
.037-.038 (.950-.974)	036 (.925)
.038-.039 (.975-.999)	037 (.950)
.039-.040 (1.0-1.024)	038 (.975)
.040-.041 (1.025-1.049)	039 (1.000)
.041-.042 (1.050-1.074)	040 (1.025)
.042-.043 (1.075-1.099)	041 (1.050)
.043-.044 (1.100-1.124)	042 (1.075)
.044-.045 (1.125-1.149)	043 (1.100)
.045-.046 (1.150-1.174)	044 (1.125)
.046-.047 (1.175-1.199)	045 (1.150)
.047-.048 (1.200-1.224)	046 (1.175)
.048-.049 (1.225-1.249)	047 (1.200)
.049-.050 (1.250-1.299)	048 (1.225)

INPUT SHAFT SHIM SELECTION CHART (Cont.)

Measured End Play – In. (mm)	Specified Shim Size
.050-.051 (1.275-1.299)	049 (1.250)
.051-.052 (1.300-1.324)	050 (1.275)
.052-.053 (1.325-1.349)	051 (1.300)
.053-.054 (1.350-1.374)	052 (1.325)
.054-.055 (1.375-1.399)	053 (1.350)
.055-.056 (1.400-1.424)	054 (1.375)
.056-.057 (1.425-1.449)	055 (1.400)
.057-.058 (1.450-1.474)	056 (1.425)
.058-.059 (1.475-1.499)	057 (1.450)
.059-.060 (1.500-1.524)	058 (1.475)
.060-.061 (1.525-1.549)	059 (1.500)
.061-.062 (1.550-1.574)	060 (1.525)
.062-.063 (1.575-1.599)	061 (1.550)
.063-.064 (1.600-1.624)	062 (1.575)
.064-.065 (1.625-1.649)	063 (1.600)
.065-.066 (1.650-1.674)	064 (1.625)
.066-.067 (1.675-1.699)	065 (1.650)
.067-.068 (1.700-1.724)	066 (1.675)
.068-.069 (1.725-1.749)	067 (1.700)
.069-.070 (1.750-1.774)	068 (1.725)
.070-.071 (1.775-1.791)	069 (1.750)

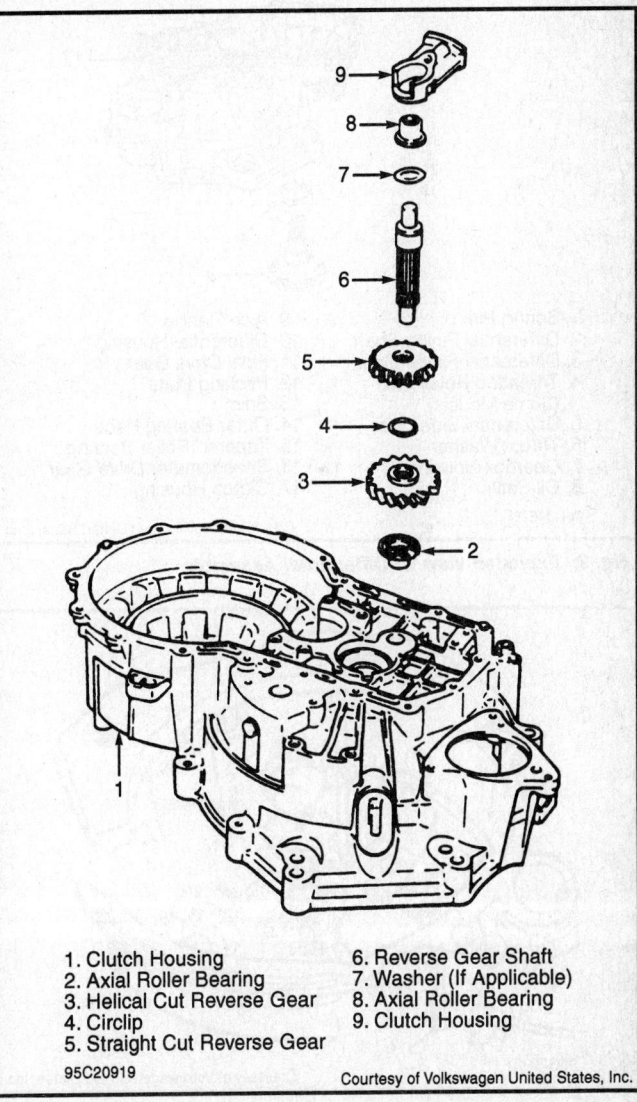

1. Clutch Housing
2. Axial Roller Bearing
3. Helical Cut Reverse Gear
4. Circlip
5. Straight Cut Reverse Gear
6. Reverse Gear Shaft
7. Washer (If Applicable)
8. Axial Roller Bearing
9. Clutch Housing

95C20919

Courtesy of Volkswagen United States, Inc.

Fig. 8: Exploded View Of Reverse Gear Assembly

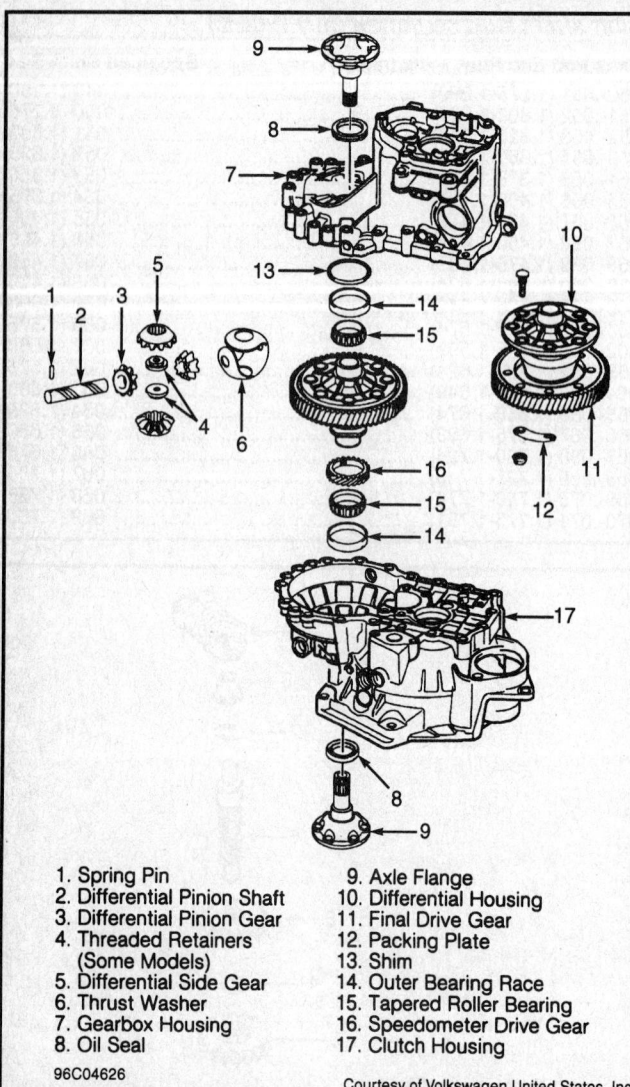

1. Spring Pin
2. Differential Pinion Shaft
3. Differential Pinion Gear
4. Threaded Retainers (Some Models)
5. Differential Side Gear
6. Thrust Washer
7. Gearbox Housing
8. Oil Seal
9. Axle Flange
10. Differential Housing
11. Final Drive Gear
12. Packing Plate
13. Shim
14. Outer Bearing Race
15. Tapered Roller Bearing
16. Speedometer Drive Gear
17. Clutch Housing

96C04626

Courtesy of Volkswagen United States, Inc.

Fig. 9: Exploded View Of Differential Assembly

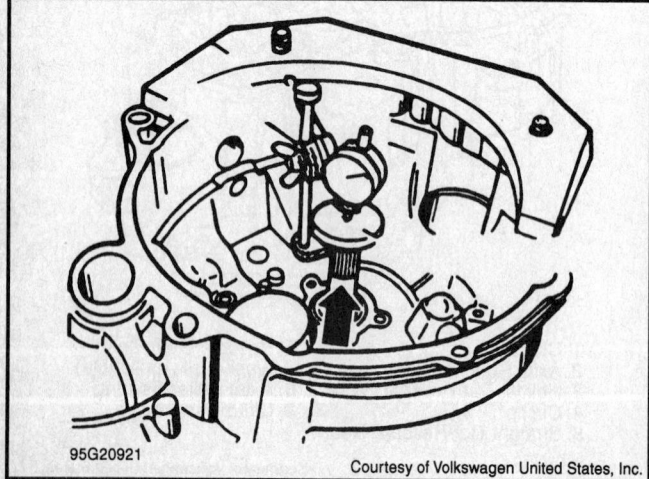

95G20921

Courtesy of Volkswagen United States, Inc.

Fig. 10: Measuring Input Shaft End Play

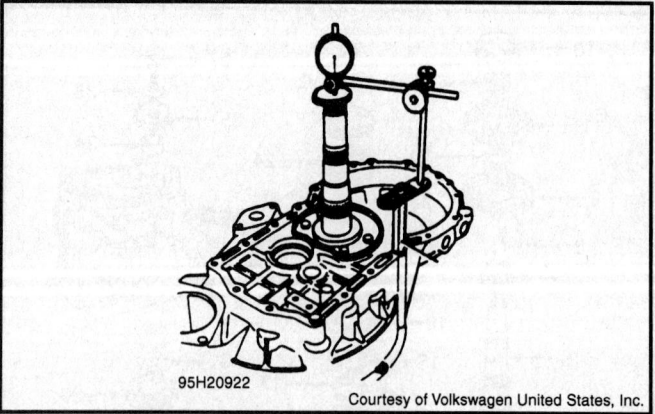

95H20922

Courtesy of Volkswagen United States, Inc.

Fig. 11: Measuring Output Shaft End Play

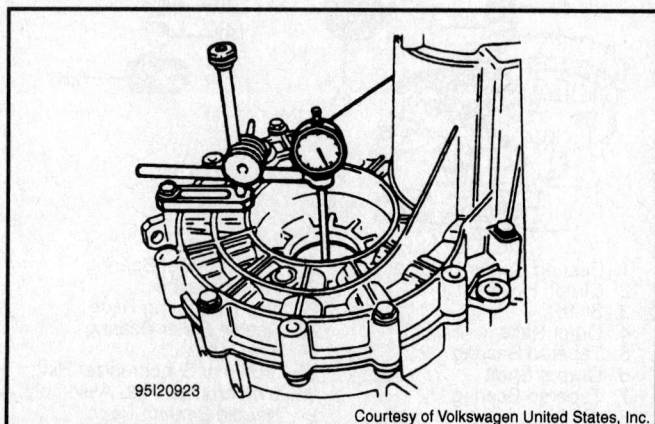

95I20923

Courtesy of Volkswagen United States, Inc.

Fig. 12: Measuring Differential Assembly Clearance

TORQUE SPECIFICATIONS
TORQUE SPECIFICATIONS

Application	Ft. Lbs. (N.m)
Bearing Retainer Bolts	[1] 18 (25)
Fifth Gear Retaining Bolts	59 (80)
Gearbox-To-Clutch Housing Bolts	[1] 18 (25)
Oil Fill & Drain Plugs	18 (25)
Reverse Shaft Support Bolts	22 (30)
Ring Gear Nut	[1] 44 (60)
Shift Fork Locating Pin Bolts	18 (25)
Shift Selector Mounting Bolts	18 (25)
Shift Selector Stop Bolt	30 (40)
Shift Shaft Lock Bolt	18 (25)
Speedometer Drive	22 (30)

	INCH lbs. (N.m)
Housing Cover Bolts	7 (10)
Needle Bearing Retainer Bolt	5 (44)

[1] – Turn fastener an additional 90 degrees.

Cabrio, Golf III, GTI, Jetta III

APPLICATION & LABOR TIMES

APPLICATION & LABOR TIMES

Vehicle Application	Labor Times		Series
	¹ R & I	² Overhaul	
1995			
Cabrio & Golf III	3.8	4.9	020 (CHE)
Jetta III			
4-Cylinder	3.8	4.9	020 (CHE)
1996			
Cabrio	3.8	4.9	020 (DFQ)
Golf & Jetta			
4-Cylinder			
Gas Engine	3.8	4.9	020 (DFQ)

¹ – Removal and installation of transaxle from vehicle chassis.
² – Bench overhaul time for transaxle and differential. DOES NOT include removal and installation.

IDENTIFICATION

Transaxles are identified by a type number as well as a 2 letter suffix. Transmission type is cast into transmission case. Code letter and production date information is stamped on a machined surface located on upper portion of engine-to-transaxle mating surface.

DESCRIPTION

Type 020 is a 5-speed transaxle consisting of an input shaft, mainshaft/drive pinion shaft and a differential assembly which transfers power to front wheels.

LUBRICATION & ADJUSTMENTS

Use hypoid oil API GL4, MIL-L2105 SAE 75 or G50 SAE 75W90 synthetic lubricant. See appropriate MANUAL TRANSMISSION SERVICING article in TRANSMISSION SERVICING section for adjustments.

TROUBLE SHOOTING

See GENERAL TROUBLE SHOOTING article in this section.

ON-VEHICLE SERVICE

CHECKING SHIFT LINKAGE ADJUSTMENT

Shift into 1st gear, push gearshift lever to left stop. Release lever. Lever should spring back to right. Shift lever should rest in 3rd/4th gear plane. To adjust position, transmission in neutral and loosen clamp at selector shaft. Insert Position Gauge (VW 3104) on shift lever housing. Align selector rod/lever. Retighten clamp. If gear fails to engage smoothly during repeated shifting, engage 1st gear. Press shift lever gently to left to remove play. Distance between gearshift housing to travel stop must be .04-.06" (1-1.5 mm). Adjust by turning eccentric adjuster in shifter housing. Torque clamping bolt to 18 INCH lbs. (2 N.m).

DRIVE FLANGE OIL SEAL

Remove axle shaft from mounting flange. Remove drive flange cover, circlip and dished washer. Remove axle flange using puller. Pry seal out of transaxle case. To install, drive new seal in using Driver (30-212). Fill lips of new seal with lubricant. Install flange into differential case. Install dished washer, circlip and flange cover. Install axle shaft and tighten to 30 ft. lbs. (40 N.m). Check transaxle oil level.

DRIVE AXLE SHAFTS

See appropriate AXLE SHAFTS article in AXLE SHAFTS & TRANSFER CASES section.

REMOVAL & INSTALLATION

See appropriate MANUAL TRANSMISSION REMOVAL article in TRANSMISSION SERVICING section.

TRANSAXLE DISASSEMBLY

Disassembly – 1) Mount transaxle in Mounting Fixture (VW 309 and 353), if available. Install input shaft support bridge Special Tool (VW 295a and 30-211a), if available. Drain gearbox oil. Remove clutch push rod from input shaft.

2) Remove bolts from transmission housing cover. Remove entire assembly. Remove selector shaft lock nut and vehicle speed sensor. Remove selector shaft cover together with spring. Bring shift forks to neutral position and remove selector shaft. Remove Torx bolt to remove reverse idler gear shaft.

3) From gearbox side of transaxle, remove drive flange cover, circlip, and dished washer. Using a puller, remove drive flange. *See Fig. 1.*

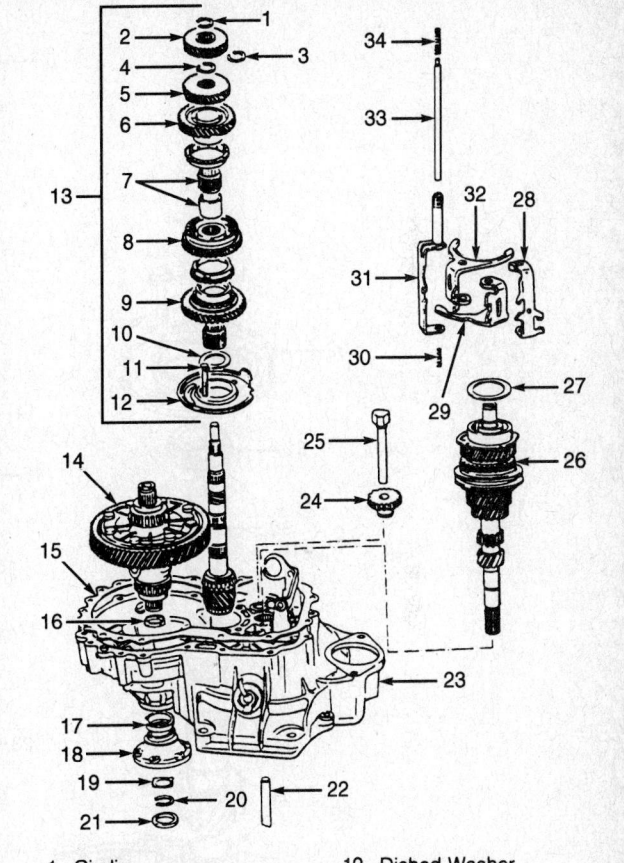

1. Circlip	19. Dished Washer
2. 4th Gear	20. Circlip
3. 4th Gear Circlip	21. Cover
4. 3rd Gear Circlip	22. Clutch Push Rod
5. 3rd Gear	23. Clutch Housing
6. 2nd Gear	24. Reverse Idler Gear
7. 2nd Gear Needle Bearing	25. Reverse Gear Shaft
8. 1st/2nd Gear Synchronizer	26. Input Shaft
9. 1st Gear	27. Adjustment Shim
10. Thrust Washer	28. Reverse Gear Shift Fork
11. Bolt	29. 1st/2nd Gear Shift Fork
12. Bearing Cover	30. Spring
13. Output Shaft Assembly	31. 5th Gear Selector
14. Differential	Bridge & Tube
15. Gasket	32. 3rd/4th Gear Shift Fork
16. Tapered Ring	33. Selector Rod
17. Spring With Thrust Washer	34. Spring
18. Drive Flange	

96F04779   Courtesy of Volkswagen United States, Inc.

Fig. 1: Identifying Internal Components

4) Engage 5th gear and reverse gear. Remove synchronizer hub retaining bolt. Remove selector tube securing plate. Turn selector tube counter-clockwise, DO NOT pull, to remove from shift fork. Remove synchronizer hub together with 5th gear and shift fork using 2 levers to pry free. Use caution to avoid damage to housing sealing surfaces. Remove circlip and thrust washer for 5th gear. On vehicles with 2.0L engine, 5th gear circlip is replaced by a securing plate. Remove 5th gear using puller if necessary.

5) Remove tension bracket on input shaft deep groove ball bearing. Pull off transmission housing. Pull selector rod from bore and remove

shift fork. Remove 4th gear circlip from output shaft. Vehicles using 2.0L engine are equipped with a second circlip. Remove 4th gear using puller if necessary. Ensure reverse gear is not engaged, remove input shaft assembly. Remove 3rd and 2nd gear, using puller if necessary. Remove synchronizer ring and needle bearings. Drive out reverse gear shaft with bolt using plastic hammer. Remove reverse gear from relay lever. Pull off synchronizer hub and 1st gear together with 2nd gear needle bearing inner race. *See Fig. 2.*

6) Remove bearing cover bolts, thrust washer and cover. Remove output shaft Remove right side drive flange, thrust washer, tapered ring and differential assembly.

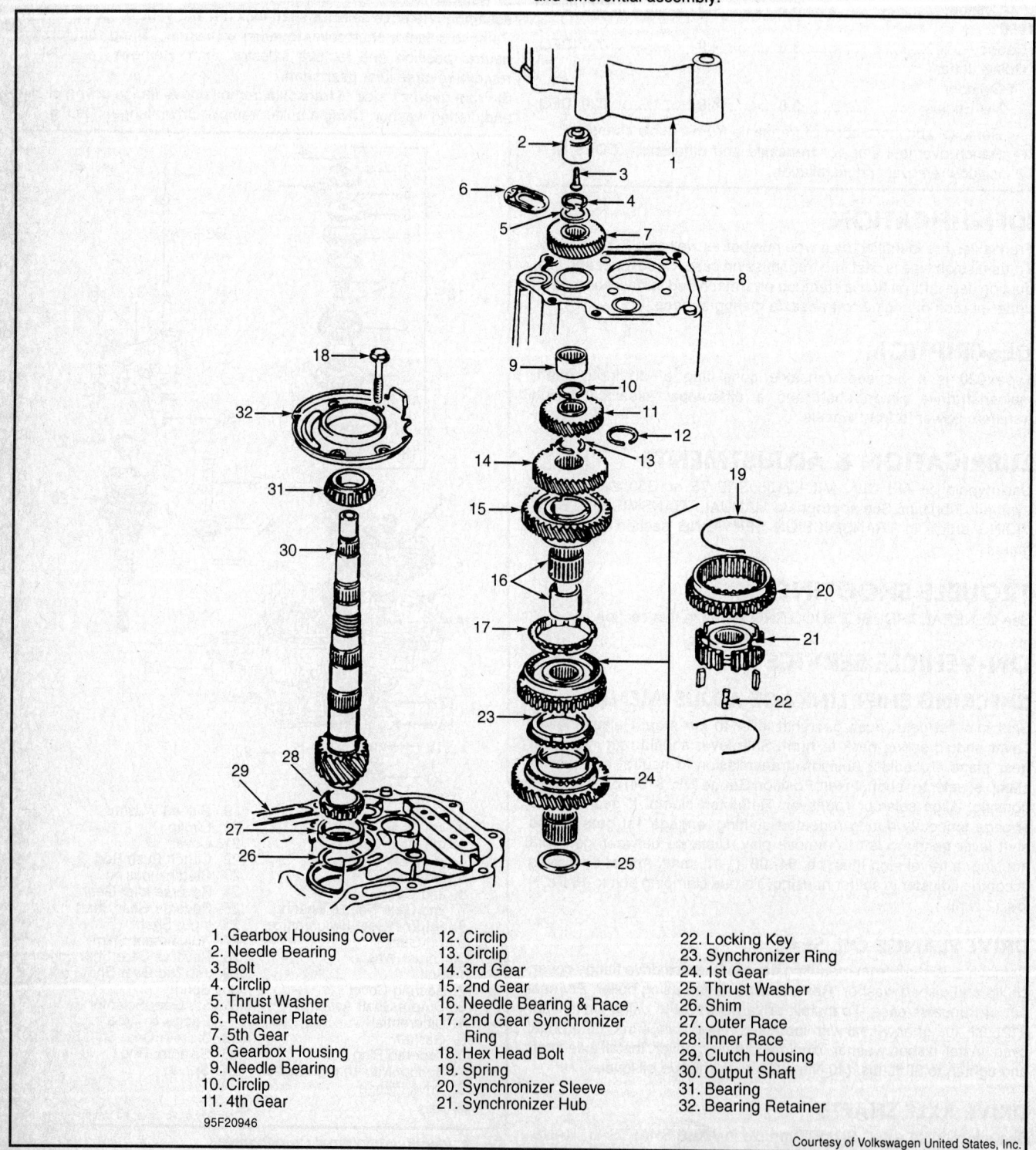

1. Gearbox Housing Cover
2. Needle Bearing
3. Bolt
4. Circlip
5. Thrust Washer
6. Retainer Plate
7. 5th Gear
8. Gearbox Housing
9. Needle Bearing
10. Circlip
11. 4th Gear
12. Circlip
13. Circlip
14. 3rd Gear
15. 2nd Gear
16. Needle Bearing & Race
17. 2nd Gear Synchronizer Ring
18. Hex Head Bolt
19. Spring
20. Synchronizer Sleeve
21. Synchronizer Hub
22. Locking Key
23. Synchronizer Ring
24. 1st Gear
25. Thrust Washer
26. Shim
27. Outer Race
28. Inner Race
29. Clutch Housing
30. Output Shaft
31. Bearing
32. Bearing Retainer

95F20946

Courtesy of Volkswagen United States, Inc.

Fig. 2: Exploded View Of Output Shaft

Reassembly – 1) Install differential assembly into clutch housing. Install output shaft and bearing cover. Torque to specifications. See TORQUE SPECIFICATIONS. With shoulder on inner diameter facing bearing cover, install thrust washer. Install synchronizer hub, 1st gear with 2nd gear needle bearing inner race, to output shaft with groove on face and outside teeth on operating sleeve facing 1st gear. Heat 1st/2nd gear synchronizer hub to approximately 212° F (100° C), drive firmly into place aligning grooves in synchronizer ring with keys. Install reverse idler gear.

2) Install 2nd gear needle bearing race. Ensure race is firmly seated. Install needle bearings, synchronizer ring, 2nd gear and 3rd gear with shoulder facing 2nd gear. Install new circlip which allows for minimal amount of axial play. Circlips are available in sizes from .098" (2.5 mm) to .0118" (3.0 mm) in increments of .004" (.1 mm).

3) Install input shaft, without bearing, into clutch housing. Install 4th gear, with shoulder facing toward spline of 5th gear, and install circlip(s). Press in deep groove ball bearing with wide shoulder facing outward. Install tension bracket. Insert selector rod lower spring into clutch housing. Install 3rd/4th gear shift fork, 1st/2nd gear shift fork, reverse gear shift fork and 5th gear selector bridge and tube. 1st/2nd gear shift fork is recessed to clear bridge. Slide selector rod into position. Align reverse idler gear shaft. *See Figs. 1 and 3.*

4) Install transmission housing making sure Support Bridge (30-211a) and (VW 295a) Needle Bearing Drift provide input shaft with satisfactory support. Install torx bolt to idler gear shaft. Torque to 15 ft. lbs (20 N.m). Install hex head bolts to secure housing. Torque to 18 ft. lbs. (25 N.m). Torque bolts to deep groove bearing tension bracket to 11 ft. lbs. (15 N.m). Heat 5th gear to approximately 212° F (100° C) and install (circular groove facing upward on vehicles with 2.0L engines). Install thrust washer and circlip. On vehicles with 2.0L engines securing plate is used in place of circlip. *See Fig. 4.*

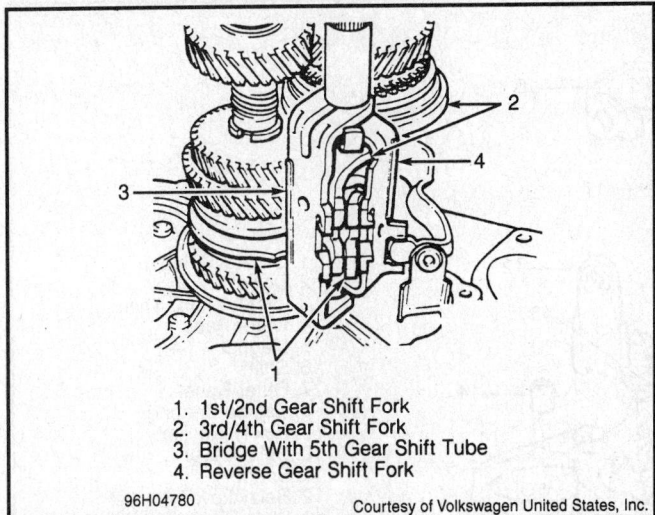

1. 1st/2nd Gear Shift Fork
2. 3rd/4th Gear Shift Fork
3. Bridge With 5th Gear Shift Tube
4. Reverse Gear Shift Fork

96H04780　　　　Courtesy of Volkswagen United States, Inc.

Fig. 3: Shift Fork Alignment

5) Using Tube Wrench (VW 3059), screw shift tube clockwise into shift lock. Thread shift tube back out to adjust shift tube height "A". *See Fig. 5.*

CAUTION: Do not extract selector rod from shift tube. It may cause shift fork to come apart inside, making it necessary to disassemble transmission again. If necessary, insert screwdriver through slot to hold selector rod while removing tube wrench.

6) Engage 5th gear and reverse. Coat threads of new synchronizer hub bolt (M17) with locktite, install, torque to 111 ft. lbs (150 N.m). Move shift fork to neutral position. Insert selector shaft, selector shaft spring and cover with new seal ring. Torque to 47 ft lbs. (50 N.m). Install selector shaft lock bolt with sealant. Torque to 30 ft. lbs. (40 N.m).

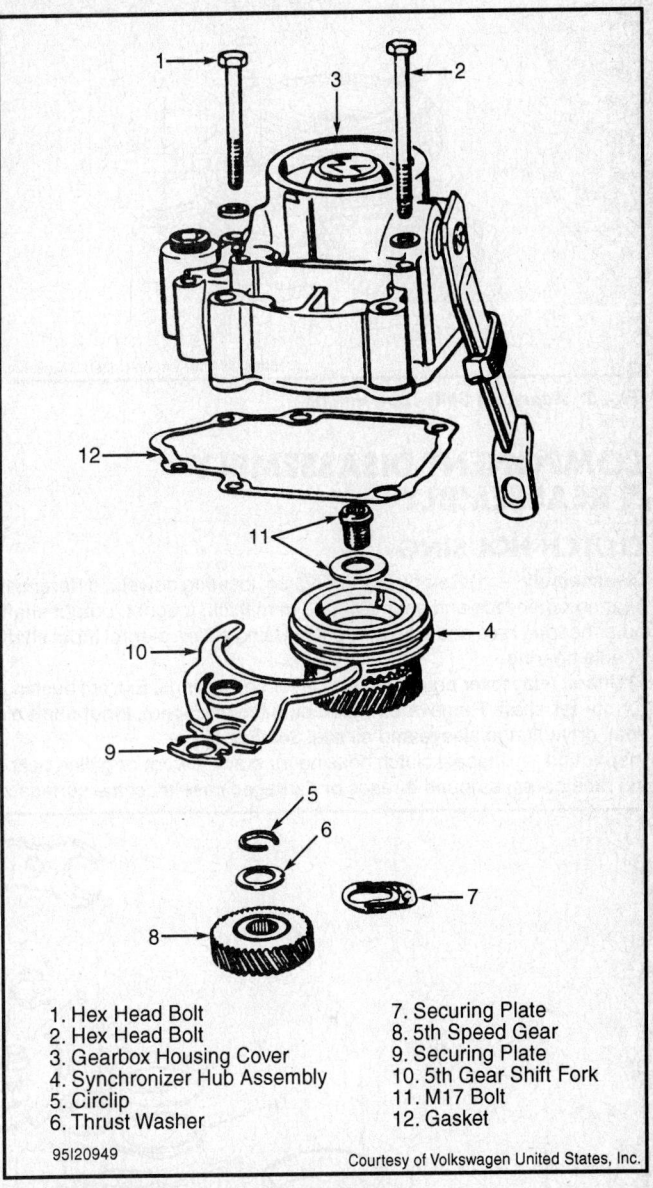

1. Hex Head Bolt	7. Securing Plate
2. Hex Head Bolt	8. 5th Speed Gear
3. Gearbox Housing Cover	9. Securing Plate
4. Synchronizer Hub Assembly	10. 5th Gear Shift Fork
5. Circlip	11. M17 Bolt
6. Thrust Washer	12. Gasket

95I20949　　　　Courtesy of Volkswagen United States, Inc.

Fig. 4: Exploded View Of 5th Gear Cover

7) Adjust 5th gear selector fork. Use caution in performing this adjustment to prevent transmission from jumping out of gear. Check height "A" of shift tube. *See Fig. 5.* Adjust if necessary. Bolt gear selector shaft lever onto selector shaft and engage 5th gear. Raise operating sleeve together with shift fork to compensate for free play in linkage components. Align operating sleeve with selector fork so there is no free play to 5th gear. Clearance between 5th gear and synchronizer hub should be .197" (5.0 mm). If necessary, adjust clearance by turning selector tube. Ensure synchronizer ring moves freely. Support shift fork, drive on new securing plate.

8) Release tension on input shaft support bridge. Starting at 5th gear end, install clutch pushrod into input shaft. Install clutch release bearing on clutch push rod. Install new gasket to housing cover. Install cover. Shift through all gears to ensure correct engagement. Install drive flanges, dished washers, circlips, and new drive flange covers.

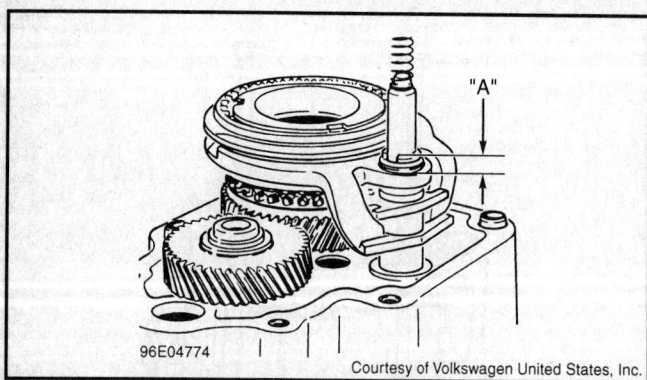

96E04774

Courtesy of Volkswagen United States, Inc.

Fig. 5: Adjusting Shift Tube Height

COMPONENT DISASSEMBLY & REASSEMBLY

CLUTCH HOUSING

Disassembly – 1) Remove oil drain plug, locating dowels, differential bearing outer race and shim .04" (1.0 mm) thick, magnet, output shaft outer bearing race and adjusting shim. Using puller, extract input shaft needle bearing.

2) Unbolt relay lever brackets, relay lever and springs. Extract bushing for starter shaft. Remove threaded plug (color coded), input shaft oil seal, drive flange sleeve and oil seal. See Fig. 6.

Inspection – Inspect clutch housing for cracks, worn or galled bearing race bores, stripped threads or damaged case machine surfaces.

Reassembly – 1) Install drive flange sleeve and oil seal. Install threaded plug (Green) and bushing for starter. Install relay lever, brackets and springs.

CAUTION: It is essential that threaded plug installed is correct for specific application. Green: for 1.8L, 1.9L Turbo Diesel and 2.0L engine with 210 mm clutch. White plug available for engines with 200 mm clutch. (not applicable for U.S.A./Canada). If White plug is installed in place of Green, damage to TDC sensor and flywheel markings will result.

2) Install input shaft needle bearing using bearing driver. Install shim and bearing outer race for differential assembly. Install selected adjusting shim and outer bearing race for output shaft. Install locating dowels and oil drain plug. Install magnet on case using Sealant (AMV 188 200 03 or equivalent).

GEARBOX HOUSING

Disassembly – Remove locating dowels, backup light switch, vent sleeve and cover. Using a suitable driver, remove output shaft needle bearing. Remove selector shaft, stop cover, spring, retaining plate and circlip. Remove ball sleeve, oil seal and protective cover. Remove differential outer bearing race, selected adjustment shim and drive flange oil seal. Remove tensioner plate, input shaft bearing and shim. See Fig. 7.

Inspection – Inspect clutch housing for cracks, worn or galled bearing race bores, stripped threads or damaged case machine surfaces.

Reassembly – Install drive flange sealing ring. Install differential adjustment shim, outer bearing race and drive flange oil seal. Using driver, install output shaft needle bearing, stop cover with ball sleeve, ball sleeve shaft and oil seal. Install protective cover. Install input shaft

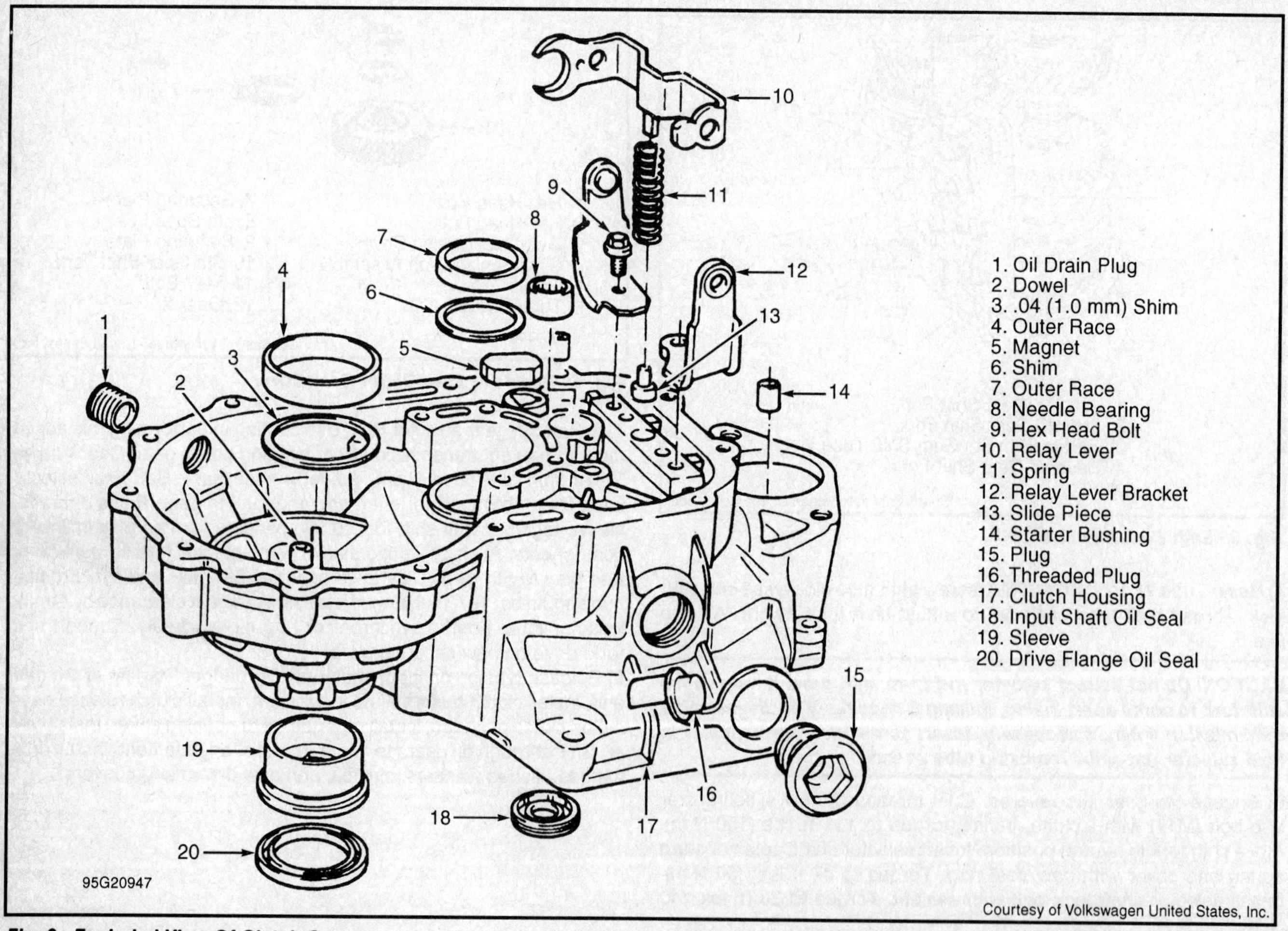

1. Oil Drain Plug
2. Dowel
3. .04 (1.0 mm) Shim
4. Outer Race
5. Magnet
6. Shim
7. Outer Race
8. Needle Bearing
9. Hex Head Bolt
10. Relay Lever
11. Spring
12. Relay Lever Bracket
13. Slide Piece
14. Starter Bushing
15. Plug
16. Threaded Plug
17. Clutch Housing
18. Input Shaft Oil Seal
19. Sleeve
20. Drive Flange Oil Seal

95G20947

Courtesy of Volkswagen United States, Inc.

Fig. 6: Exploded View Of Clutch Cover

bearing and shim and secure in place with tensioning plate. Install vent sleeve, cover, back-up light switch with new seal and locating dowels.

GEARBOX HOUSING COVER

Disassembly – Remove gearbox housing cover. Remove release shaft. Remove clutch lever clip, clutch lever and lever return spring. Remove release bearing, oil seal and release shaft clip. Remove oil filler plug, needle bearing and bearing retainer bolt. *See Fig. 8.*

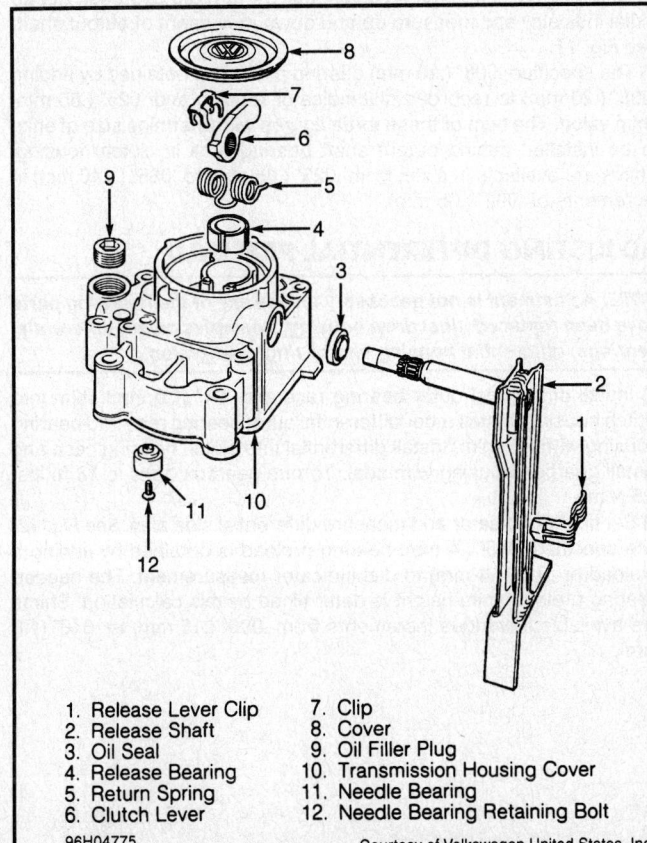

1. Transmission Housing
2. Dowel Sleeves
3. Oil Seal
4. Back-Up Light Switch
5. Cover
6. Vent Sleeve
7. Selector Shaft
8. Stop Cover
9. Spring
10. Retaining Plate
11. Circlip
12. Output Shaft Needle Bearing
13. Selector Shaft Ball Sleeve
14. Selector Shaft Oil Seal
15. Protective Cover
16. Outer Race For Differential Tapered Roller Bearing
17. Shim S1
18. Sealing Ring

96J04776

Courtesy of Volkswagen United States, Inc.

Fig. 7: Exploded View Of Gearbox Housing

1. Release Lever Clip
2. Release Shaft
3. Oil Seal
4. Release Bearing
5. Return Spring
6. Clutch Lever
7. Clip
8. Cover
9. Oil Filler Plug
10. Transmission Housing Cover
11. Needle Bearing
12. Needle Bearing Retaining Bolt

96H04775

Courtesy of Volkswagen United States, Inc.

Fig. 8: Exploded View Of Transmission Housing Cover

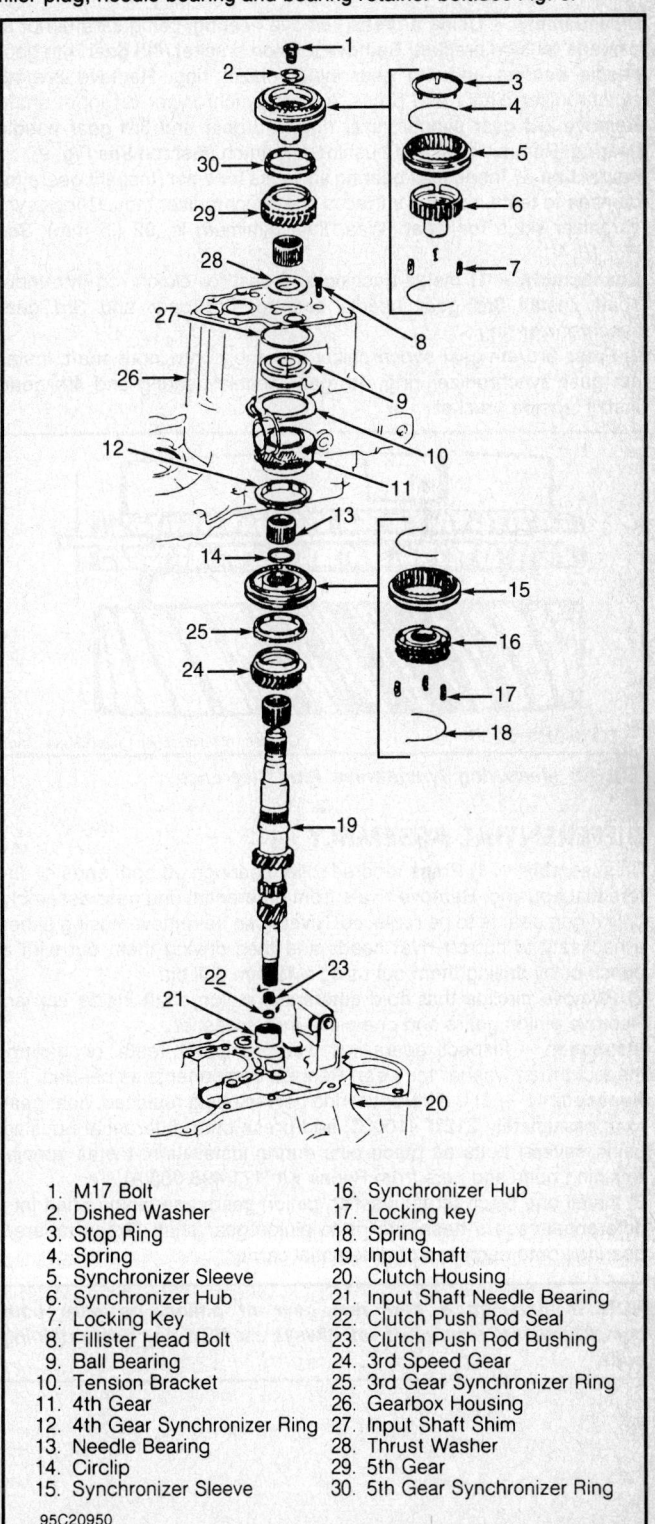

1. M17 Bolt
2. Dished Washer
3. Stop Ring
4. Spring
5. Synchronizer Sleeve
6. Synchronizer Hub
7. Locking Key
8. Fillister Head Bolt
9. Ball Bearing
10. Tension Bracket
11. 4th Gear
12. 4th Gear Synchronizer Ring
13. Needle Bearing
14. Circlip
15. Synchronizer Sleeve
16. Synchronizer Hub
17. Locking key
18. Spring
19. Input Shaft
20. Clutch Housing
21. Input Shaft Needle Bearing
22. Clutch Push Rod Seal
23. Clutch Push Rod Bushing
24. 3rd Speed Gear
25. 3rd Gear Synchronizer Ring
26. Gearbox Housing
27. Input Shaft Shim
28. Thrust Washer
29. 5th Gear
30. 5th Gear Synchronizer Ring

95C20950

Courtesy of Volkswagen United States, Inc.

Fig. 9: Exploded View Of Input Shaft

Inspection – Inspect clutch housing for cracks, worn or galled bearing race bores, stripped threads or damaged case machine surfaces.

Reassembly – Install oil filler plug, needle bearing and bearing retainer bolt. Install release bearing, release shaft oil seal, release shaft and shaft clip. Install clutch lever, clutch lever return spring, and lever retaining clip.

INPUT ASSEMBLY

Disassembly – Using a press, remove bearing, being careful not to damage tension bracket. Remove tension bracket, 4th gear, 4th gear needle bearing and 4th gear synchronizer ring. Remove 3rd/4th synchronizer circlip and press 3rd/4th synchronizer off input shaft. Remove 3rd gear synchronizer ring, 3rd gear and 3rd gear needle bearing. Remove seal and bushing for clutch pushrod. See Fig. 9.

Inspection – Inspect all bearing surfaces for wear. Inspect gears for damage to teeth, bearing surfaces and synchronizer tabs. Check synchronizer rings for wear. Wear limit minimum is .02 (.5 mm). See Fig. 10.

Reassembly – **1)** Install bushing and seal for clutch rod into input shaft. Install 3rd gear needle bearing, 3rd gear and 3rd gear synchronizer ring.

2) Press 3rd/4th gear synchronizer assembly onto input shaft. Install 4th gear synchronizer ring, 4th gear needle bearing and 4th gear. Install tension bracket

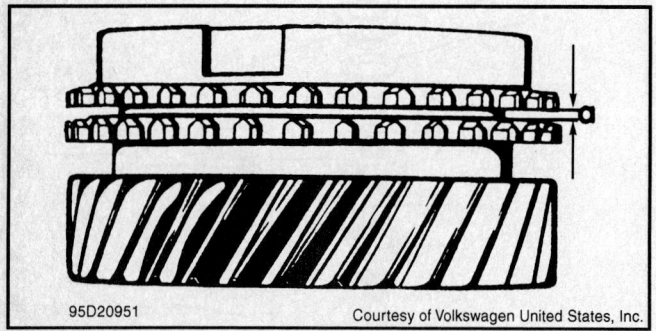

95D20951   Courtesy of Volkswagen United States, Inc.

Fig. 10: Measuring Synchronizer Ring Clearance

DIFFERENTIAL ASSEMBLY

Disassembly – **1)** Press tapered roller bearings off both ends of differential housing. Remove rivets from differential ring gear assembly only if ring gear is to be replaced. Rivets can be removed using either a hacksaw to cut off rivet heads and then driving them out with a punch or by drilling them out using a 12 mm drill bit.

2) Remove circlips that hold differential pinion shaft inside carrier. Remove pinion gears and one piece thrust washer.

Inspection – Inspect gears for wear, chipped teeth or galling. Inspect thrust washer for wear. Replace components as needed.

Reassembly – **1)** If differential ring gear is being replaced, heat gear to approximately 212°F (100°C) and press onto differential housing using several bolts as guide pins during installation. Install special retaining bolts and nuts from Repair Kit (171 498 088 A).

2) Install one piece thrust washer, pinion gears and pinion shaft into differential case. Attach circlips to pinion gear shaft. Press tapered bearings onto each end of differential carrier.

NOTE: If installing a new ring gear or pinion, be sure both components are a matched set. Always use NEW ring gear retaining bolts.

ADJUSTING OUTPUT SHAFT PRELOAD

NOTE: Adjustment is not necessary unless any of the following parts have been replaced: output shaft bearings, differential or pinion gears.

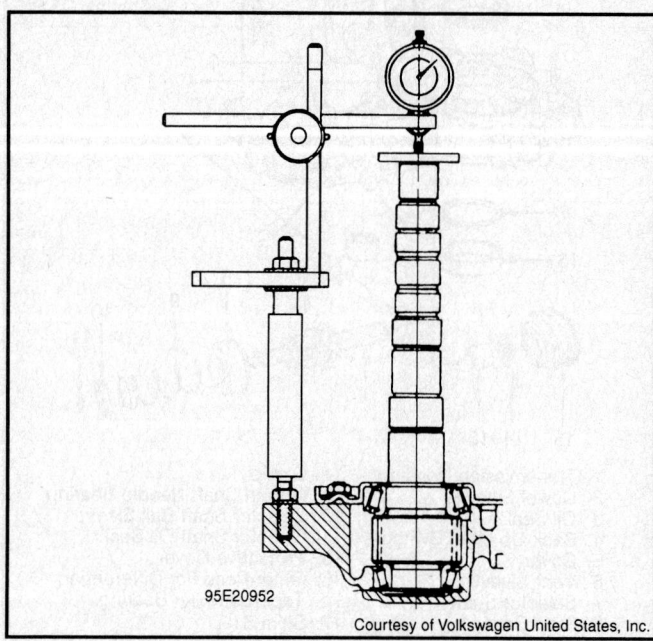

95E20952

Courtesy of Volkswagen United States, Inc.

Fig. 11: Measuring Output Shaft End Play

1) Install roller bearing outer race into clutch housing with a .025" (.65 mm) shim. Install output shaft and bearing retainer plate. Torque plate to 18 ft. lbs. (25 N.m) plus an additional 1/4 turn (90 degrees). Set up a dial indicator and measure up and down movement of output shaft. See Fig. 11.

2) The specified .008" (.20 mm) bearing preload is obtained by adding .008" (.20 mm) to recorded dial indicator reading and .025" (.65 mm) shim value. The sum of these three figures will determine size of shim to be installed behind output shaft bearing race in clutch housing. Shims are available in sizes from .025" (.65 mm) to .055" (1.40 mm) in increments of .002" (.05 mm).

ADJUSTING DIFFERENTIAL PRELOAD

NOTE: Adjustment is not necessary unless any of the following parts have been replaced: final drive housing, final drive cover, differential bearings, differential housing and/or ring gear/pinion.

1) Install differential outer bearing race and .04" (1.0 mm) shim into clutch housing. Install other differential outer bearing race into bearing housing without shim. Install differential into clutch housing case and install gearbox housing with seal. Torque gearbox bolts to 18 ft. lbs. (25 N.m).

2) Set up dial indicator and measure differential side play. See Fig. 12. The specified .015" (.4 mm) bearing preload is obtained by adding a preload of .015" (.4 mm) to dial indicator measurement. The needed bearing preload shim height is determined by this calculation. Shims are available in various increments from .006" (.15 mm) to .040" (1.0 mm).

95F20953

Courtesy of Volkswagen United States, Inc.

Fig. 12: Measuring Differential Side Play

TORQUE SPECIFICATIONS
TORQUE SPECIFICATIONS

Application	Ft. Lbs. (N.m)
Back-Up Light Switch	15 (20)
Deep Groove Bearing Tension	11 (15)
Fifth Gear Cover Bolts	18 (25)
Fillister Head Screws	18 (25)
Gearbox To Clutch Housing	18 (25)
Idler Gear Shaft Bolt	15 (20)
Oil Fill and Drain Plugs	18 (25)
Output Shaft Bearing Cover	30 (40)
Shift Relay Bracket	18 (25)
Shift Shaft Cover	37 (50)
Shift Shaft Lock Bolt	30 (40)
Synchronizer Hub Bolt (M17)	111 (150)

	INCH lbs. (N.m)
Needle Bearing Retainer Bolt	44 (5)
Shifter Housing Clamp Bolt	18 (2)
Speedometer Drive Retainer Bolt	44 (5)
Vehicle Speed Sensor	44 (5)

AXLE SHAFTS & TRANSFER CASES

GENERAL INFORMATION   Page

Drive Axle Noise Diagnosis 5-2

AXLE SHAFTS

Acura 5-3
Audi 5-5
BMW 5-6
Geo 5-7
Honda 5-9
Hyundai 5-12
Infiniti FWD 5-14
Infiniti RWD 5-17
Isuzu 5-20
Kia 5-21
Lexus FWD 5-22
Lexus RWD 5-24
Mazda FWD 5-28
Mazda RWD 5-32
Mitsubishi FWD 5-36
Mitsubishi RWD 5-39
Nissan FWD 5-42
Nissan RWD 5-46
Nissan 4WD 5-48
Porsche RWD 5-50
Saab 5-52
Subaru FWD 5-53
Subaru AWD Rear Shafts 5-55
Suzuki 5-57
Toyota FWD 5-61
Toyota RWD 5-66
Toyota 4WD Front Shafts 5-71
Toyota RAV4 5-74
Volkswagen 5-79
Volvo 5-80

TRANSFER CASES

Acura, Honda, Isuzu 5-82
Geo & Suzuki 5-90
Mazda MPV 5-93
Mitsubishi 5-107
Nissan Pathfinder & Pickup 5-116
Suzuki Samurai 5-120
Toyota Land Cruiser & Lexus LX450 5-123
Toyota Pickup, T100, Tacoma & 4Runner 5-130
Toyota Previa 5-159
Toyota RAV4 – With Automatic Transmission 5-163
Toyota RAV4 – With Manual Transmission 5-169

GENERAL INFORMATION
Drive Axle Noise Diagnosis

UNRELATED NOISES

Some driveline trouble symptoms are also common to the engine, transmission, wheel bearings, tires, and other parts of the vehicle. Make sure that cause of trouble actually is in the drive axle before adjusting, repairing, or replacing any of its parts.

NON-DRIVE AXLE NOISES

A few conditions can sound just like drive axle noise and have to be considered in pre-diagnosis. The 4 most common noises are exhaust, tires, CV/universal joints and trim moldings.

In certain conditions, the pitch of the exhaust gases may sound like gear whine. At other times, it may be mistaken for a wheel bearing rumble.

Tires, especially radial and snow tires, can have a high-pitched tread whine or roar, similar to gear noise. Also, some non-standard tires with an unusual tread construction may emit a roar or whine.

Defective CV/universal joints may cause clicking noises or excessive driveline play that can be improperly diagnosed as drive axle problems.

Trim and moldings also can cause a whistling or whining noise. Ensure that none of these components are causing the noise before disassembling the drive axle.

GEAR NOISE

A "howling" or "whining" noise from the ring and pinion gear can be caused by an improper gear pattern, gear damage, or improper bearing preload. It can occur at various speeds and driving conditions, or it can be continuous.

Before disassembling axle to diagnose and correct gear noise, make sure that tires, exhaust, and vehicle trim have been checked as possible causes.

CHUCKLE

This is a particular rattling noise that sounds like a stick against the spokes of a spinning bicycle wheel. It occurs while decelerating from 40 MPH and usually can be heard until vehicle comes to a complete stop. The frequency varies with the speed of the vehicle.

A chuckle that occurs on the driving phase is usually caused by excessive clearance due to differential gear wear, or by a damaged tooth on the coast side of the pinion or ring gear. Even a very small tooth nick or a ridge on the edge of a gear tooth is enough to cause the noise.

This condition can be corrected simply by cleaning the gear tooth nick or ridge with a small grinding wheel. If either gear is damaged or scored badly, the gear set must be replaced. If metal has broken loose, the carrier and housing must be cleaned to remove particles that could cause damage.

KNOCK

This is very similar to a chuckle, though it may be louder, and occur on acceleration or deceleration. Knock can be caused by a gear tooth that is damaged on the drive side of the ring and pinion gears. Ring gear bolts that are hitting the carrier casting can cause knock. Knock can also be due to excessive end play in the axle shafts.

CLUNK

Clunk is a metallic noise heard when an automatic transmission is engaged in Reverse or Drive, or when throttle is applied or released. It is caused by backlash somewhere in the driveline, but not necessarily in the axle. To determine whether driveline clunk is caused by the axle, check the total axle backlash as follows:

1) Raise vehicle on a frame or twinpost hoist so that drive wheels are free. Clamp a bar between axle companion flange and a part of the frame or body so that flange cannot move.

2) On conventional drive axles, lock the left wheel to keep it from turning. On all models, turn the right wheel slowly until it is felt to be in drive condition. Hold a chalk marker on side of tire about 12" from center of wheel. Turn wheel in the opposite direction until it is again felt to be in drive condition.

3) Measure the length of the chalk mark, which is the total axle backlash. If backlash is one inch or less, clunk will not be eliminated by overhauling drive axle.

BEARING WHINE

Bearing whine is a high-pitched sound similar to a whistle. It is usually caused by malfunctioning pinion bearings. Pinion bearings operate at driveshaft speed. Roller wheel bearings may whine in a similar manner if they run completely dry of lubricant. Bearing noise will occur at all driving speeds. This distinguishes it from gear whine, which usually comes and goes as speed changes.

BEARING RUMBLE

Bearing rumble sounds like marbles being tumbled. It is usually caused by a malfunctioning wheel bearing. The lower pitch is because the wheel bearing turns at only about 1/3 of driveshaft speed.

CHATTER ON TURNS

This is a condition where the whole front or rear vibrates when the vehicle is moving. The vibration is plainly felt as well as heard. Extra differential thrust washers installed during axle repair can cause a condition of partial lock-up that creates this chatter.

AXLE SHAFT NOISE

Axle shaft noise is similar to gear noise and pinion bearing whine. Axle shaft bearing noise will normally distinguish itself from gear noise by occurring in all driving modes (drive, cruise, coast and float), and will persist with transmission in neutral while vehicle is moving at problem speed.

If vehicle displays this noise condition, remove suspect axle shafts, replace wheel seals and install a new set of bearings. Re-evaluate vehicle for noise before removing any internal components.

VIBRATION

Vibration is a high-frequency trembling, shaking or grinding condition (felt or heard) that may be constant or variable in level and can occur during the total operating speed range of the vehicle.

The types of vibrations that can be felt in the vehicle can be divided into 3 main groups:
- Vibrations of various unbalanced rotating parts of the vehicle.
- Resonance vibrations of the body and frame structures caused by rotating of unbalanced parts.
- Tip-in moans of resonance vibrations from stressed engine or exhaust system mounts or driveline flexing modes.

Integra, Legend, 2.5TL, 3.2TL, 3.5RL

NOTE: For Acura SLX models, see Isuzu Trooper 4WD in appropriate ISUZU AXLE SHAFTS article.

DESCRIPTION & OPERATION

Each axle shaft consists of a shaft and a Constant Velocity (CV) joint at each end. Inner CV joint is splined to transaxle. Outer CV joint is splined to hub assembly and secured by a spindle nut. Inner and outer CV joints are enclosed by boots. Inner CV joints can be repaired; outer CV joints can be serviced only as an assembly.

TROUBLE SHOOTING

NOTE: See DRIVE AXLE NOISE DIAGNOSIS in GENERAL INFORMATION at beginning of this section.

REMOVAL, DISASSEMBLY, REASSEMBLY & INSTALLATION

AXLE SHAFTS

Removal – 1) Pry lock tab away from spindle nut. Loosen spindle nut and wheel lug nuts. Raise and support vehicle. Drain transaxle fluid. On Integra and Legend, draining transaxle fluid is not necessary if removing only left axle shaft. On 2.5TL, drain differential fluid when only right axle is removed. On all models, remove front wheels and spindle nut. Remove damper pinch bolt and damper fork bolt. Remove damper fork. *See Fig. 1.*

2) Remove lower ball joint cotter pin. Back off castle nut until outer surface is flush with end of stud. Using ball joint puller, separate ball joint from lower control arm. Remove ball joint castle nut and ball joint from lower control arm. Pull steering knuckle outward. Remove axle shaft from hub assembly. If necessary, use plastic mallet to drive axle from hub.

NOTE: DO NOT pull on inner CV joint; it may come apart. Be careful not to damage seals.

3) On 2.5TL, using a plastic hammer, remove right driveshaft from bearing support. On all other models, using a large screwdriver, carefully pry inner CV joint and shaft assembly outward to disengage retaining ring from groove at end of inner drive axle. Grip both sides of inner CV joint, and remove axle shaft and CV joint from vehicle.

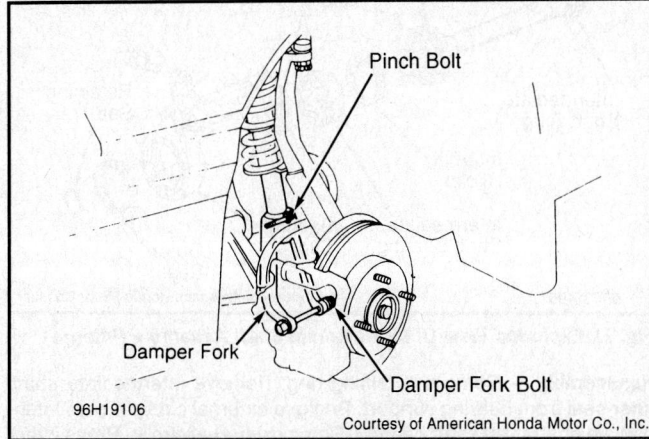

96H19106   Courtesy of American Honda Motor Co., Inc.

Fig. 1: Locating Damper Fork & Pinch Bolts

NOTE: DO NOT disassemble outer CV joint. If service is necessary, replace it as an assembly. On inner CV joint, mark rollers and roller grooves for reassembly reference.

Disassembly – 1) Remove axle shaft from vehicle, and place on work bench. Remove and discard inner CV joint boot clamps. Slide boot toward outer CV joint for access to inner CV joint. *See Fig. 2.*

2) Mark axle shaft, inner CV joint housing, and spider roller for reassembly reference. Remove housing from spider assembly. Mark rollers and spider for reassembly reference. Remove rollers from spider.

3) Remove snap ring retaining spider to axle shaft. Remove spider. Remove stopper ring. Tape splines of axle shaft to prevent damage to boots and dynamic balancer (if equipped). Slide inboard boot from axle shaft. On Integra and 2.5TL models, remove dynamic balancer. On all models, remove outer CV joint boot clamps. Slide boot from axle shaft inner CV joint end.

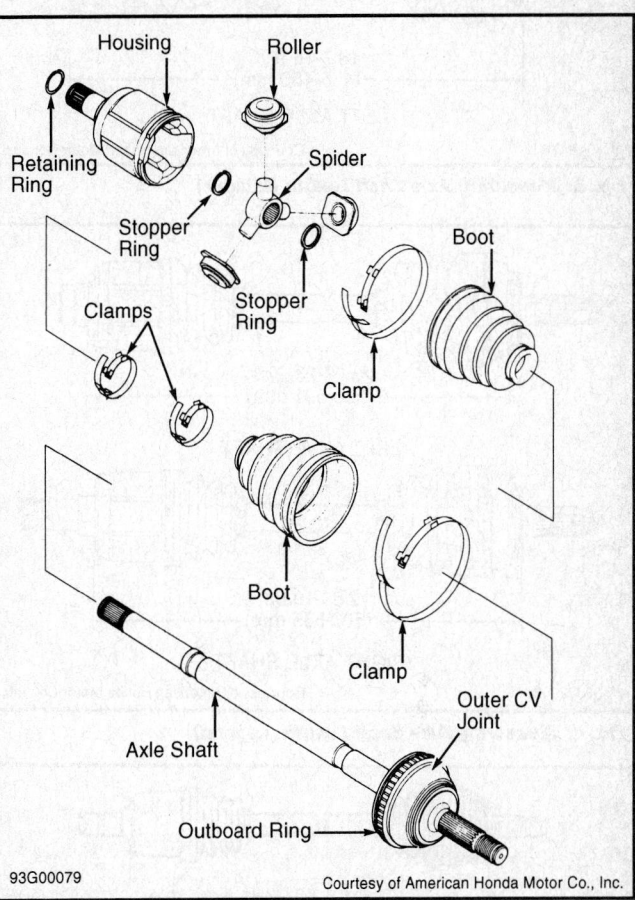

93G00079   Courtesy of American Honda Motor Co., Inc.

Fig. 2: Exploded View Of Axle Shaft (Typical)

Reassembly – 1) Using solvent and compressed air, thoroughly clean axle shaft, and inspect for wear. Replace all defective parts. Wrap axle shaft splines with vinyl tape to prevent damage to CV joint boots.

2) Install outer CV joint boot, dynamic balancer (if equipped) and inner CV joint boot. Remove vinyl tape from axle shaft. DO NOT install CV joint boot clamps yet.

3) Install stopper ring into groove on axle shaft. Install spider onto axle shaft with reference marks aligned. Install snap ring into groove. Pack outer CV joint boot with grease supplied with joint kit. Lubricate spider and inner bore of rollers.

4) Align rollers with marks made at disassembly. Ensure high sides of rollers face outward. Install rollers. Pack inner CV joint and boot with grease. Install housing onto spider assembly. Align reference marks made at disassembly while installing housing onto spider assembly. Adjust length of axle shaft. *See Figs. 3-6.*

5) Position boots halfway between full compression and full extension. Install new boot clamps. Lightly tap boot clamp to reduce clamp height. Install new retaining ring onto end of inner CV joint. Install axle shaft.

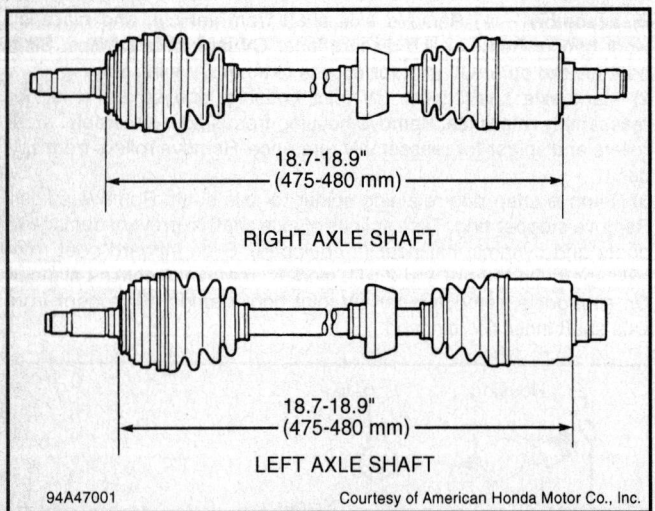

Fig. 3: *Measuring Axle Shaft Length (Integra)*

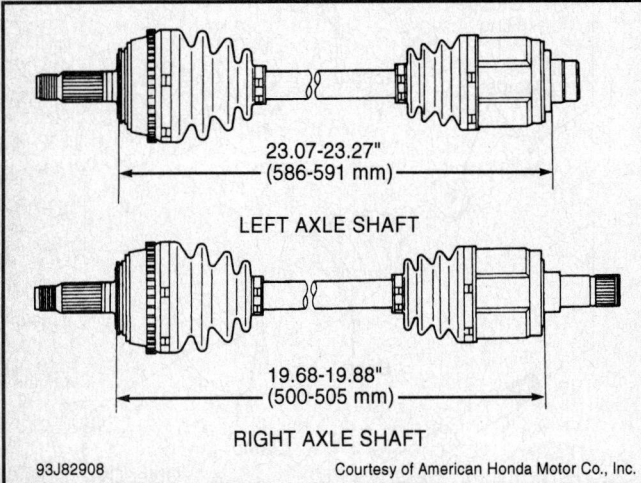

Fig. 4: *Measuring Axle Shaft Length (Legend)*

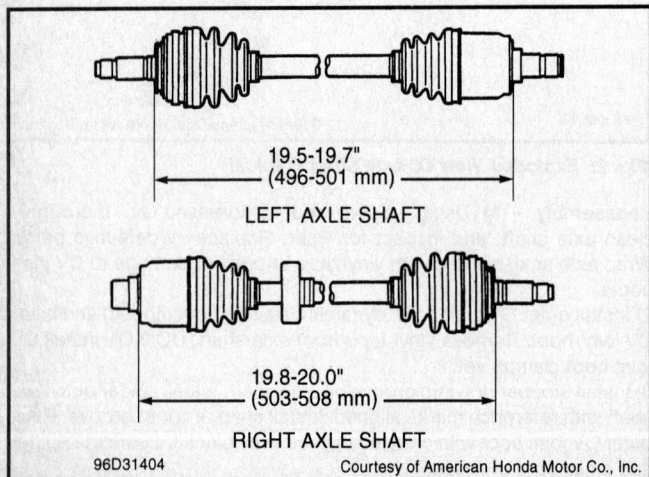

Fig. 5: *Measuring Axle Shaft Length (2.5TL)*

CAUTION: *Always use a NEW retaining ring when installing axle shaft.*

Installation – **1)** Ensure length of assembled axle shaft is within specification. *See Figs. 3-6.* Install new retaining ring into groove at end of axle shaft. Install new clamps onto boots.

2) Slide axle into transaxle or intermediate shaft. Seat retaining ring fully into groove. Check installation by attempting to pull axle out of installed position.
3) Pull hub assembly away from axle shaft. Slide axle into hub assembly. Install and lightly tighten spindle nut. Position ball joint into hub. Raise lower control arm with floor jack. Install ball joint nut. Tighten ball joint nut to specification. See TORQUE SPECIFICATIONS.
4) Install and secure cotter pin. Remove floor jack. Tighten spindle nut to specification. To complete installation, reverse removal procedure.

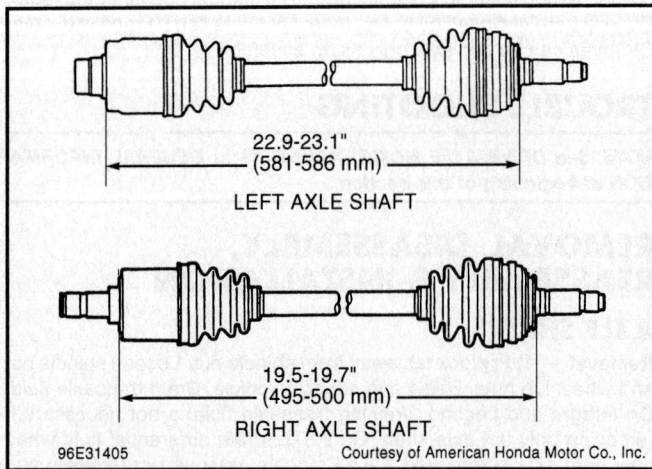

Fig. 6: *Measuring Axle Shaft Length (3.2TL & 3.5RL)*

INTERMEDIATE SHAFT

Removal (Integra) – **1)** Drain fluid from transaxle. Remove left axle shaft. See AXLE SHAFTS. Remove bearing support bolts. *See Fig. 7.*

CAUTION: *To prevent damaging oil seal when removing intermediate shaft, hold shaft in horizontal position until shaft is clear of seal.*

---

2) Lower bearing support. Remove intermediate shaft from differential. To prevent damage to seal, hold intermediate shaft in horizontal position when removing.

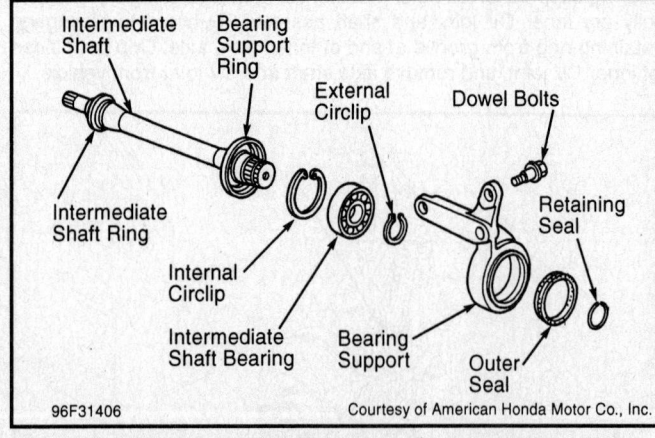

Fig. 7: *Exploded View Of Intermediate Shaft Assembly (Integra)*

Disassembly – Remove retaining ring. Remove intermediate shaft outer seal from bearing support. Remove external circlip. Press intermediate shaft from shaft bearing. Remove internal circlip. Press intermediate shaft bearing from bearing support. Inspect all components for wear or damage. Replace as necessary.
Reassembly – **1)** Press intermediate shaft bearing into bearing support. Seat internal circlip into groove of bearing support. Install circlip so tapered end faces outward.

2) Press intermediate shaft into shaft bearing. Install external circlip into intermediate shaft groove so tapered end faces outward. Press outer seal into bearing support until flush.

Installation – To install, reverse removal procedure. Ensure intermediate shaft is held horizontal to prevent damaging new seal. Refill transaxle.

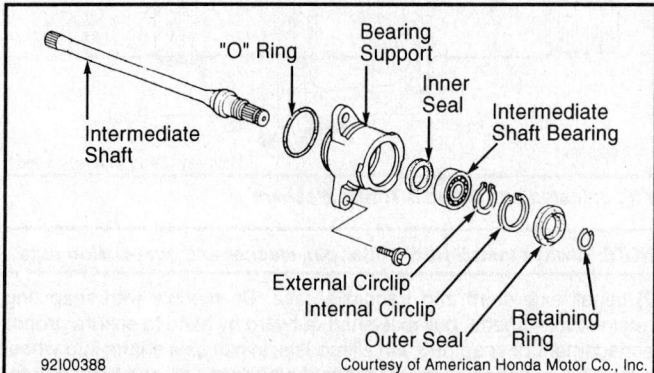

Fig. 8: **Exploded View Of Intermediate Shaft (Legend, 2.5TL, 3.2TL & 3.5RL)**

Labels: Intermediate Shaft, "O" Ring, Bearing Support, Inner Seal, Intermediate Shaft Bearing, External Circlip, Internal Circlip, Outer Seal, Retaining Ring

92I00388   Courtesy of American Honda Motor Co., Inc.

CAUTION: Bearing support is made of aluminum. DO NOT overstress when servicing intermediate shaft.

Removal (Legend, 2.5TL, 3.2TL & 3.5RL) – Drain fluid from transaxle. Remove left axle shaft. See AXLE SHAFTS. Remove bearing support bolts. See Fig. 8. Remove intermediate shaft assembly from oil pan.

Disassembly – Remove intermediate shaft outer seal from bearing support. Remove external and internal circlips. Press intermediate shaft from shaft bearing. Press intermediate shaft bearing from bearing support. Remove intermediate shaft inner seal from bearing support. Remove "O" ring. Inspect all components for wear or damage. Replace as necessary.

Reassembly – **1)** Press intermediate shaft inner seal into bearing support. Seat internal circlip into bearing support groove so tapered end faces outward.

2) Press intermediate shaft into shaft bearing. Install external circlip into intermediate shaft groove so tapered end faces outward. On Legend, press in seal until it is flush with bearing support. On Vigor, press seal into bearing support until seal is .28" (7 mm) from end of bearing support.

Installation – To install, reverse removal procedure. Refill transaxle.

TORQUE SPECIFICATIONS

TORQUE SPECIFICATIONS

Application	Ft. Lbs. (N.m)
Integra	
Ball Joint Nut	41 (55)
Damper Fork Bolt	47 (64)
Damper Pinch Bolt	32 (43)
Intermediate Shaft Bearing Support Bolts	29 (39)
Spindle Nut	134 (181)
Wheel Lug Nut	80 (108)
Legend	
Ball Joint Nut	52-59 (70-80)
Damper Fork Bolt	52 (70)
Damper Pinch Bolt	37 (50)
Intermediate Shaft Bearing Support Bolts	16 (22)
Spindle Nut	240 (325)
Wheel Lug Nut	81 (110)
2.5TL	
Ball Joint Nuts	36-43 (49-59)
Damper Fork Bolt	47 (64)
Damper Fork Pinch Bolt	32 (43)
Intermediate Shaft Bearing Support Bolts	16 (22)
Spindle Nut	181 (245)
Wheel Lug Nut	80 (108)
3.2TL	
Ball Joint Nuts	36-43 (49-59)
Damper Fork Bolt	51 (69)
Damper Fork Pinch Bolt	37 (50)
Intermediate Shaft Bearing Support Bolts	16 (22)
Spindle Nut	181 (245)
Wheel Lug Nut	80 (108)
3.5RL	
Ball Joint Nuts	51-58 (69-78)
Damper Fork Bolt	51 (69)
Damper Fork Pinch Bolt	32 (43)
Intermediate Shaft Bearing Support Bolts	16 (22)
Spindle Nut	181 (245)
Wheel Lug Nut	80 (108)

Audi

A4, A6, S6, 90, Cabriolet

DESCRIPTION

Axle shafts transfer power from transaxle to drive wheels. Axle shafts consist of a shaft and flexible Constant Velocity (CV) joint at each end. Inner CV joint is bolted to transaxle. Outer CV joint is splined to hub assembly and secured by axle shaft nut/bolt.

TROUBLE SHOOTING

NOTE: See DRIVE AXLE NOISE DIAGNOSIS in GENERAL INFORMATION at beginning of this section.

REMOVAL, DISASSEMBLY, REASSEMBLY & INSTALLATION

AXLE SHAFTS

Removal – **1)** Remove hub cap. Loosen axle shaft nut/bolt. Raise and support vehicle. Remove axle nut/bolt and wheel. Mark suspension to align during reassembly. Remove Allen bolts connecting inner CV joint to transaxle case flange. See Fig. 1.

NOTE: On ABS models, pull speed sensor out slightly before removing drive axle.

2) Remove suspension strut tie rod. Remove nut and bolt and separate ball joint from control arm. Press out axle shaft from hub and swing suspension strut outward. Remove axle shaft.

NOTE: Disassemble axle shafts to replace defective boots. If boots are replaced, check all components for wear or damage and replace as necessary.

Disassembly – **1)** On inner CV joint, remove circlip from axle shaft and drive protective cap from CV joint. Place axle shaft in Holder (VW 402) and press CV joint from shaft with Adapter (VW 408a) while supporting hub to prevent damage.

NOTE: CV joints may be removed from axle to replace boots. Inner and outer CV joints cannot be disassembled. Replace as an assembly.

2) Remove and discard inner boot clamp and boot. On outer CV joint, spread circlip inside ball hub. Using a brass drift, tap on hub to drive CV joint off axle shaft.

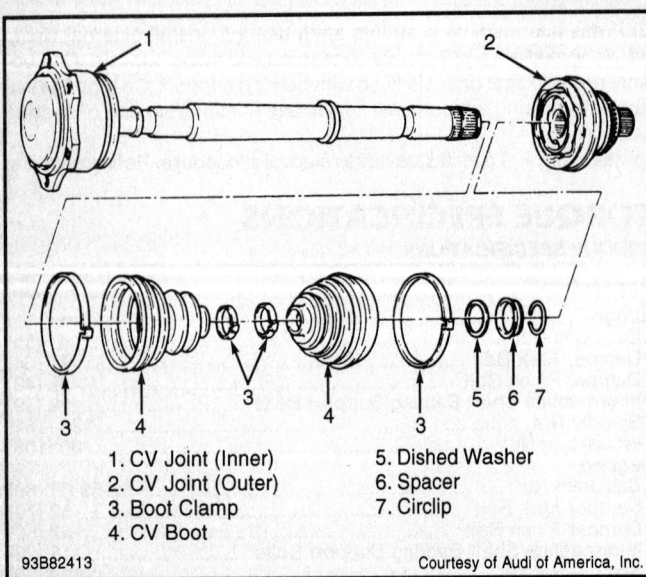

1. CV Joint (Inner)
2. CV Joint (Outer)
3. Boot Clamp
4. CV Boot
5. Dished Washer
6. Spacer
7. Circlip

93B82413   Courtesy of Audi of America, Inc.

Fig. 1: Exploded View Of Axle Shaft Assembly (Typical)

Reassembly – 1) To reassemble, reverse disassembly procedure. Lubricate inner CV joints with 3 ounces of molybdenum disulfide grease.

2) Replace dust boots and clamps. Install CV joints onto axle shaft with inside ball hub chamfer facing shaft.

3) Install outer CV joint with concave side of dished washer facing thrust washer and convex side of thrust washer facing CV joint. *See Fig. 2.*

4) Assemble inner CV joints with concave side of dished washer facing CV joint when installed on shaft. Install boot clamps with open end facing opposite direction of normal rotation. Use NEW circlips to retain CV joints on shafts.

Installation – 1) To install, reverse removal procedure. Check seals at both sides of transaxle and replace prior to installation (if necessary). Lubricate transaxle seal lip with transaxle oil.

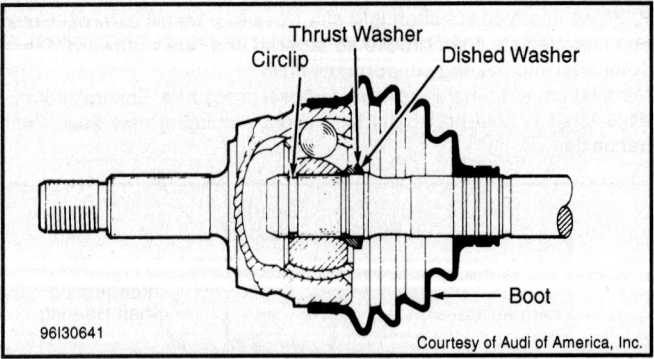

Fig. 2: Installing Dished & Thrust Washers

NOTE: Always install NEW cotter pin, washer and suspension nuts.

2) Install axle shaft into transaxle case. On models with snap ring retained axle shafts, pull axle shaft outward by hand to ensure proper engagement of snap ring. On all models, install axle shafts into wheel hub. Align suspension marks made during removal, and tighten nuts. Apply locking compound (D6) to splines.

3) Check camber setting and adjust if necessary. Install NEW bolt or stake NEW axle shaft nut in place with a punch or install NEW cotter pin after tightening. Bleed brake system and replace transaxle fluid, if required.

TORQUE SPECIFICATIONS
TORQUE SPECIFICATIONS

Application	Ft. Lbs. (N.m)
Axle Shaft Bolt	148 (200) Plus 1/4 Turn
Ball Joint Nut	48 (65)
Brake Caliper Bolts	92 (125)
CV Joint Bolt To Axle Flange	33 (45)
3 Way CV Joint Bolt To Axle Flange	59 (80)
Stabilizer Bar Bracket Bolt	26 (35)
Stabilizer Bar End Nut	30 (40)
Suspension Strut Tie Rod	37 (50)
Wheel Bearing Housing-To-Strut	81 (110) Plus 1/4 Turn

BMW

3-Series, 5-Series, 7-Series, 8-Series
TROUBLE SHOOTING

NOTE: See DRIVE AXLE NOISE DIAGNOSIS in GENERAL INFORMATION at beginning of this section.

REMOVAL, DISASSEMBLY, REASSEMBLY & INSTALLATION

RWD AXLE SHAFTS

Removal – Raise and support vehicle. Remove inner CV joint axle flange bolts, and separate axle shaft from final drive flange. Remove CV joint axle flange bolts. Disconnect and remove axle shaft from vehicle.

Disassembly – 1) Remove sealing plate cover from end of shaft. Remove snap ring from shaft, and index mark CV joint assembly to axle shaft. Press dust cover and boot from bearing assembly.

2) Separate boot from joint assembly, and remove snap ring. Press CV joint assembly off axle shaft (press on inner race surface only), and note direction of inner race collar. DO NOT disassemble CV joint.

3) Inspect boot for deterioration and cracking, and replace if necessary. Check bearing assembly for smooth operation. Inspect assembly for abnormal wear, scoring and pitting. Replace as an assembly.

Reassembly – 1) Clean splines of axle shaft to remove grease. Install boot and dust cover assembly over shaft. Apply coat of Loctite to splines and press joint onto shaft. Keep Loctite from entering ball passages.

2) Install snap ring. Pack joint and boot with grease supplied in joint kit. Coat large diameter end of boot with an adhesive, and press on cover.

Installation – To install, reverse removal procedure.

TORQUE SPECIFICATIONS
TORQUE SPECIFICATIONS

Application	Ft. Lbs. (N.m)
Axle Flange Bolts	
10 mm	43 (58)
12 mm	81 (110)

Metro, Prizm, Tracker

DESCRIPTION & OPERATION

Axle shaft assembly consists of inner and outer Constant Velocity (CV) joint assemblies joined by an axle shaft. The inner (differential-side) joint may be of a tripot or double-offset design, depending on application. See CV JOINT APPLICATION table. Outer (wheel-side) joint is of the ball and socket design.

Tripot and Double-Offset Joint (DOJ) types are both flexible and have in-and-out movement capability, while ball and socket type joints provide flexible movement only.

CV JOINT APPLICATION

Application	Inner Joint	Outer Joint
Metro (A/T)	Tripot	Ball & Socket
Metro (M/T)		
Left Side	[1] DOJ	Ball & Socket
Right Side	Tripot	Ball & Socket
Prizm	Tripot	Ball & Socket
Tracker	[1] DOJ	Ball & Socket

[1] – DOJ is double-offset joint.

TROUBLE SHOOTING

NOTE: See DRIVE AXLE NOISE DIAGNOSIS in GENERAL INFORMATION at beginning of this section.

REMOVAL & INSTALLATION

AXLE SHAFT

CAUTION: DO NOT pull outward on inner joint assembly housing. If inner joint housing is pulled outward, joint may overextend and separate from axle shaft.

Removal & Installation (Metro) – 1) Disconnect negative battery cable. Raise and support vehicle. Remove front wheels. Remove one retaining bolt and ABS speed sensor from steering knuckle (if equipped). Set aside. Unstake axle shaft nut. Remove nut and washer from axle shaft.
2) Remove ball joint-to-steering knuckle bolt, nut and washer. Separate ball joint from steering knuckle. On sedan models, right-side inner joint may be removed from center support bearing by gently tapping with a plastic hammer. On all other models, use 2 screwdrivers to gently pry axle shaft from transaxle case. Separate axle shaft from steering knuckle assembly and remove axle shaft.

NOTE: If vehicle is to be lowered and moved, front wheel bearings must be supported. Install a 9/16" (14 mm) bolt and nut through axle shaft opening in hub with a 1 3/4" (44.5 mm) washer on each side. Tighten bolt and nut to 40 ft. lbs. (54 N.m).

3) To install, reverse removal procedure. When installing axle shaft in differential, ensure snap ring seats fully in differential assembly. Tighten all fasteners to specification. See TORQUE SPECIFICATIONS (METRO) table.
Removal & Installation (Prizm) – 1) Disconnect negative battery cable. Raise and support vehicle. Remove lower splash shields. Remove one bolt and ABS speed sensor from steering knuckle (if equipped). Set aside. Remove front wheels.
2) Remove axle shaft cotter pin, hub nut cap, hub nut and washer. Remove tie rod nut from steering knuckle. Separate tie rod from steering knuckle.
3) Remove lower ball joint-to-control arm bolts. Separate lower control arm from ball joint. Separate outer joint from hub assembly.
4) Remove inner joint from transaxle by gently prying joint away from transaxle case with a pry bar or large screwdriver. Pull axle shafts from transaxle.

NOTE: If vehicle is to be lowered and moved, front wheel bearings must be supported. Install a 9/16" (14 mm) bolt and nut through axle shaft opening in hub with a 1 3/4" (44.5 mm) washer on outside and a 2" (50.8 mm) washer on inside. Tighten bolt and nut to 40 ft. lbs. (54 N.m).

5) To install, reverse removal procedure. Tighten all fasteners to specification. See TORQUE SPECIFICATIONS (PRIZM) table.
Removal & Installation (Tracker) – 1) Raise and support vehicle. Remove skid plate (if equipped). Remove front wheels. Remove locking hub caps, retaining bolts, locking hubs and "O" rings. Remove snap ring and washer from end of axle shafts.
2) Using a floor jack, support lower control arm. Remove 3 ball joint-to-control arm bolts. Slowly lower floor jack until coil spring tension is relieved. Swing steering knuckle outward. Pull outer CV joint from steering knuckle.
3) To remove right axle shaft from differential housing, use Shaft Removal Fork (J-37780) and a soft faced mallet. Tap on shaft removal fork and remove right axle shaft.
4) To remove left axle shaft from differential housing, place index marks on flanges, remove left axle shaft flange bolts, then remove axle shaft.
5) To install left axle shaft, reverse removal procedure. Align index marks and tighten axle shaft-to-inner axle shaft flange bolts to specification. See TORQUE SPECIFICATIONS (TRACKER) table.
6) To install right axle shaft, reverse removal procedure. Ensure snap ring on axle shaft seats in differential carrier. Tighten bolts to specification. See TORQUE SPECIFICATIONS (TRACKER) table. When installing locking hub, use a NEW "O" ring.

INNER AXLE SHAFT BEARING

Removal & Installation (Tracker) – 1) Raise and support vehicle. Remove left axle shaft. See AXLE SHAFT. Using Shaft Removal Fork (J-37780) and a soft faced mallet, remove left inner axle shaft from differential housing. Place shaft removal fork on inner axle shaft flange and tap axle shaft out of differential housing.
2) Using Seal Hook Adapter (J-26941) and a slide hammer, pull seal from differential housing. Remove axle bearing snap ring. See Fig. 1. Using Bearing Removal Adapter (J-29369-1) and a slide hammer, pull bearing from differential housing.
Inspection – Check axle shaft bearing for roughness or wear. Replace as necessary. Inspect differential housing at sealing surface for scratches.
Installation – 1) Using Bearing Installer (J-8092), install bearing into axle housing. Install axle bearing snap ring. Using Seal Installer (J-37770), install inner axle shaft seal.
2) To complete installation, reverse removal procedure. Tighten bolts to specification. See TORQUE SPECIFICATIONS (TRACKER) table. Fill differential with 75W-85 GL-4 synthetic gear lubricant.

OVERHAUL

CAUTION: DO NOT attempt to disassemble ball & socket (outer) CV joint or tripot joint spider assembly on inner joint. If components are worn or damaged, replace entire joint assembly. DO NOT use solvents or degreasers to clean CV boots or tripot joint spider assembly.

NOTE: Manufacturer recommends disassembly of Double-Offset Joint (DOJ) for CV boot replacement only.

BALL & SOCKET JOINT

Disassembly – 1) To disassemble outer ball and socket type CV joint, remove both CV boot clamps. Place index marks on axle shaft and joint for reassembly reference. Expand outer joint snap ring. See Fig. 2. Pull outer joint from axle shaft.
Inspection – Inspect CV boots for cracks and deterioration. Inspect components for damage. Replace damaged components.

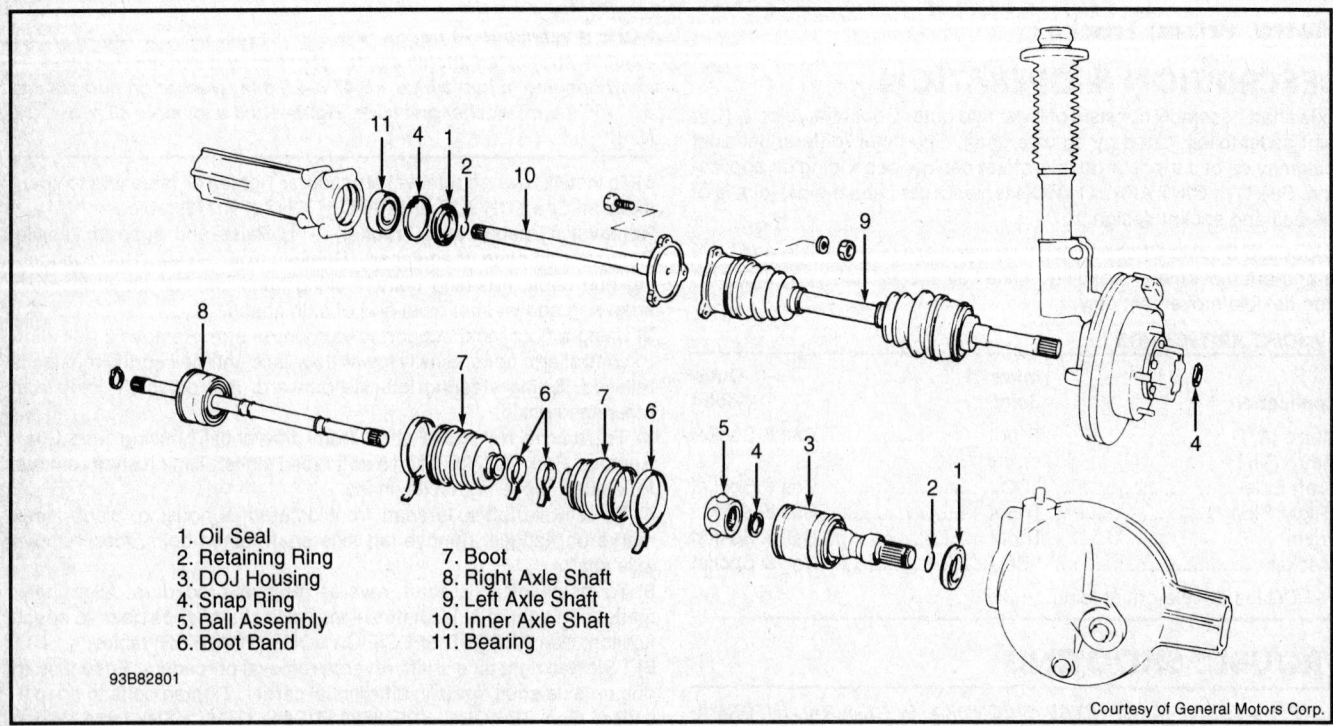

93B82801

Courtesy of General Motors Corp.

1. Oil Seal
2. Retaining Ring
3. DOJ Housing
4. Snap Ring
5. Ball Assembly
6. Boot Band
7. Boot
8. Right Axle Shaft
9. Left Axle Shaft
10. Inner Axle Shaft
11. Bearing

Fig. 1: Exploded View Of Front Axle Shaft (Tracker)

Reassembly – Pack CV boot with specified amount of CV joint grease. See BALL & SOCKET JOINT GREASE SPECIFICATIONS table. Install outer joint assembly to axle shaft. Ensure index marks are aligned. Secure with snap ring. Using CV boot clamp pliers, install CV boot clamps.

BALL & SOCKET JOINT GREASE SPECIFICATIONS

Application	Ozs. (g)
Metro	2.1-2.8 (60-79)
Prizm	4.6-5.3 (130-150)
Tracker	2.5 (71)

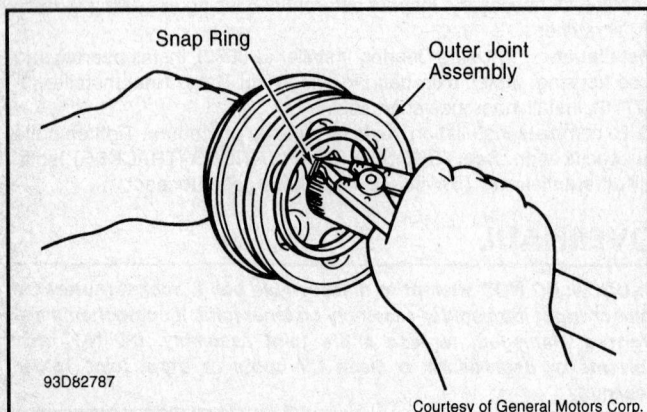

93D82787

Courtesy of General Motors Corp.

Fig. 2: Expanding Outer Joint Snap Ring

DOUBLE-OFFSET JOINT (DOJ)

Disassembly – **1)** Place an index mark on DOJ housing and axle shaft. Remove CV boot bands and slide CV boot away from joint. Remove snap ring and housing from joint. *See Fig. 3.*
2) Place an index mark on roller ball guide and axle shaft. Remove snap ring from end of axle shaft. Remove roller ball guide, 6 balls and roller cage from axle shaft. Remove CV boot.

Inspection – Inspect CV boots for cracks or deterioration. Inspect components for damage. Replace components as necessary. Ensure outer CV joint turns smoothly.
Reassembly – **1)** Install CV boot, then joint assembly onto axle shaft. Ensure index marks are aligned. Secure with snap ring. Pack joint assembly (Metro), or CV boot (Tracker) with specified amount of CV joint grease. See DOJ GREASE SPECIFICATIONS table.
2) Install housing onto joint assembly. Ensure index marks are aligned. Secure with snap ring. Install CV boot onto housing and secure with CV boot band.

DOJ GREASE SPECIFICATIONS

Application	Ozs. (g)
Metro	[1] 1.0-1.4 (28-40)
Tracker	3.2 (91)

[1] – Pack remainder of grease supplied in CV boot kit into CV boot before completion of assembly.

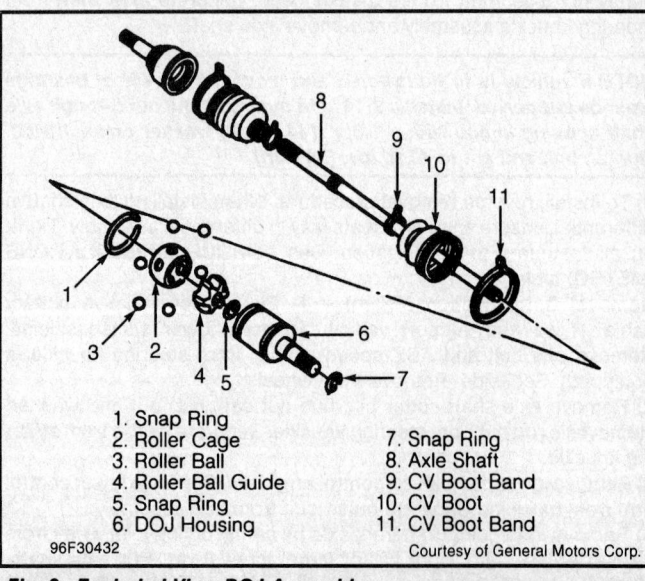

96F30432

1. Snap Ring
2. Roller Cage
3. Roller Ball
4. Roller Ball Guide
5. Snap Ring
6. DOJ Housing
7. Snap Ring
8. Axle Shaft
9. CV Boot Band
10. CV Boot
11. CV Boot Band

Courtesy of General Motors Corp.

Fig. 3: Exploded View DOJ Assembly

TRIPOT JOINT

Disassembly – 1) Place an index mark on axle shaft and tripot joint housing. Remove CV boot band from tripot joint housing. *See Fig. 4.* Remove housing from tripot joint spider.

2) Place an additional index mark on tripot joint spider and axle shaft. Remove snap ring and tripot joint spider from axle shaft. Remove inner CV boot band and CV boot from axle shaft.

Inspection – Inspect CV boots for cracks and deterioration. Clean all components. DO NOT clean tripot joint spider assembly using solvent; grease will be removed from needle bearings. Inspect components for damage. Replace components as necessary.

Reassembly – 1) Install CV boot and CV boot band onto axle shaft. Align index mark on tripot joint spider with that of axle shaft and install. Secure with snap ring.

2) Pack tripot joint housing with specified amount of CV joint grease. See TRIPOT JOINT GREASE SPECIFICATIONS table. Install housing onto tripot joint spider. Install CV boot onto housing and secure with CV boot band.

TRIPOT JOINT GREASE SPECIFICATIONS

Application	Ozs. (g)
Metro	2.8-3.5 (79-99)
Prizm	8.1-8.8 (230-250)

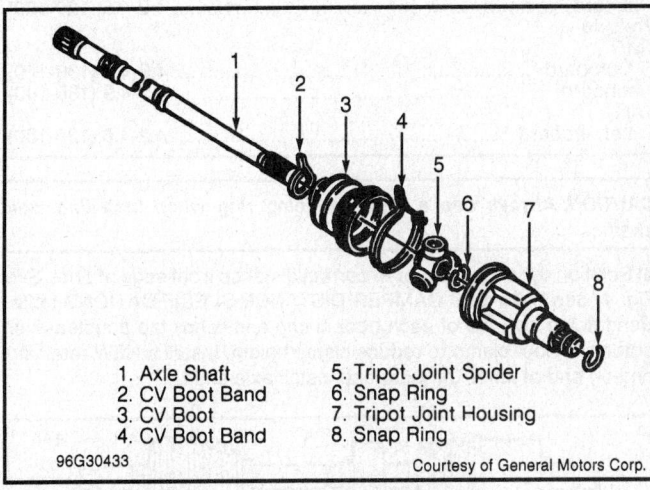

1. Axle Shaft
2. CV Boot Band
3. CV Boot
4. CV Boot Band
5. Tripot Joint Spider
6. Snap Ring
7. Tripot Joint Housing
8. Snap Ring

96G30433   Courtesy of General Motors Corp.

Fig. 4: Exploded View Of Tripot Joint Assembly

TORQUE SPECIFICATIONS

TORQUE SPECIFICATIONS (METRO)

Application	Ft. Lbs. (N.m)
Axle Shaft Nut	129 (175)
Ball Joint Nut	44 (60)
Center Support Bearing Arbor Bolts	44 (60)
Transaxle Drain Plug	
A/T	17 (23)
M/T	21 (28)
Wheel Bearing Support Bolt & Nut	40 (54)
Wheel Lug Nut	44 (60)
	INCH Lbs. (N.m)
ABS Speed Sensor Retaining Bolt	71 (8)

TORQUE SPECIFICATIONS (PRIZM)

Application	Ft. Lbs. (N.m)
Axle Shaft Nut	159 (216)
Ball Joint-To-Lower Control Arm Bolt	105 (142)
Tie Rod-To-Steering Knuckle Bolt	40 (54)
Transaxle Drain Plug	
A/T	29 (39)
M/T	¹
Wheel Lug Nut	76 (103)
	INCH Lbs. (N.m)
ABS Speed Sensor Retaining Bolt	71 (8)
Splash Shield Bolts	71 (8)

¹ – Tighten to 97 INCH lbs. (11 N.m)

TORQUE SPECIFICATIONS (TRACKER)

Application	Ft. Lbs. (N.m)
Front Axle Drain Plug	17 (23)
Front Skid Plate Bolts (If Equipped)	40 (54)
Left Axle Shaft-To-Inner Flange Bolt	
1995	44 (60)
1996	41 (55)
Locking Hub Cover Bolt (Tracker)	18 (25)
Lower Ball Joint Bolts & Nuts	63 (85)
Wheel Lug Nut	70 (95)

Honda

Accord, Civic, Civic Del Sol, Odyssey, Prelude

NOTE: For Honda Passport models, see appropriate AXLE SHAFTS – ISUZU article.

DESCRIPTION & OPERATION

Axle shafts transfer power from the transaxle to the driving wheels. Axle shafts consist of a shaft with a flexible Constant Velocity (CV) joint at each end. Inner CV joint is splined to transaxle. Outer CV joint is splined to hub assembly and secured by spindle shaft nut.

CV joint boots protect CV joints by maintaining proper lubrication and preventing contaminants from entering joint. Boots must be replaced when leakage or cracks are present. Inner CV joint can be repaired without replacing the assembly. Outer CV joint must be replaced as an assembly.

Inner CV joint is a plunging Tripod Joint (TJ), sometimes referred to as a tripod. The plunging action allows axle shaft length to change as suspension moves up and down. Outer CV joint, which is either a Double-Offset Joint (DOJ) or Birfield Joint (BJ), cannot be rebuilt.

TROUBLE SHOOTING

NOTE: See DRIVE AXLE DIAGNOSIS in GENERAL INFORMATION at beginning of this section.

REMOVAL, DISASSEMBLY, REASSEMBLY & INSTALLATION

AXLE SHAFT

Removal – 1) Raise and support vehicle. Remove front wheels. Drain transaxle if removing right or both axle shafts. Draining transaxle is unnecessary if removing left axle shaft only. Spread locking tab on spindle nut and remove nut. Remove damper fork bolt and damper pinch bolt. Remove damper fork. *See Fig. 1.*

2) Remove lower ball joint cotter pin, and loosen castle nut half length of ball joint threads. Using a ball joint puller, separate ball joint from front hub. Remove ball joint castle nut. Lower control arm and steering knuckle. Pull steering knuckle outward and remove axle shaft from hub assembly. If necessary, use a plastic hammer to drive axle shaft out of hub.

NOTE: DO NOT pull on inner CV joint or disassembly may occur. Be careful not to damage seals.

3) Using a large screwdriver, carefully pry inner CV joint and shaft assembly about .5" (12.7 mm) out of transaxle, dislodging retaining ring from its groove at end of drive axle. Grip both sides of inner CV joint and remove axle shaft and CV joint from vehicle.

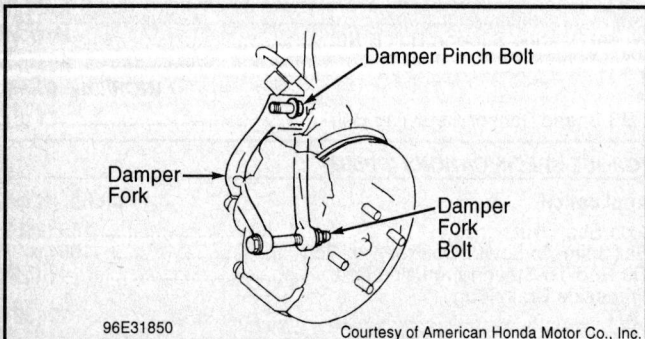

96E31850   Courtesy of American Honda Motor Co., Inc.

Fig. 1: Locating Damper Fork & Pinch Bolts

NOTE: DO NOT attempt to disassemble outer CV joint; it must be replaced as an assembly. On inner CV joint, mark rollers and roller grooves for reassembly reference.

Disassembly – 1) Remove axle shaft from vehicle, and place it on work bench. Remove and discard inner CV joint boot clamps. Slide boot toward outer CV joint to access inner CV joint. See Fig. 2.
2) Index axle shaft, inner CV joint housing and spider roller to ensure reassembly in original positions. Remove housing from spider assembly. Index rollers and spider to ensure reassembly to original locations. Remove rollers from spider.
3) Remove snap ring securing spider to axle shaft, and remove spider. Remove snap ring, and slide boot off axle shaft. Remove outer CV joint boot clamps. Slide boot off axle shaft inner CV joint end. DO NOT attempt to disassemble outer CV joint. Replace outer CV joint as an assembly only.

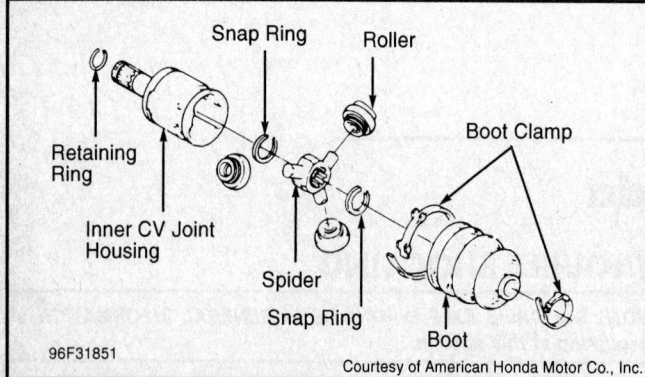

96F31851   Courtesy of American Honda Motor Co., Inc.

Fig. 2: Exploded View Of Inboard CV Joint Assembly (Typical)

Reassembly – 1) Thoroughly clean and inspect axle shaft for wear. Replace all defective parts. Wrap axle shaft splines using vinyl tape to prevent damage to dynamic damper and CV joint boots.
2) Install outer CV joint boot, dynamic damper and inner CV joint boot. Remove vinyl tape from axle shaft. DO NOT install CV joint boot clamps yet.
3) Install snap ring in groove on axle shaft. Install spider on axle shaft by aligning marks made at disassembly. Install snap ring into groove. Pack outer CV joint boot with molybdenum disulfide grease. Lube spider and inside bores of rollers.
4) Ensure rollers are aligned with marks made at disassembly and high side of rollers face outward. Install rollers. Pack inner CV joint and

boot with molybdenum disulfide grease. See BOOT & JOINT GREASE CAPACITY table. Align housing marks made at disassembly and install housing on spider assembly.
5) Adjust standard length of axle shaft. See Fig. 3. See AXLE SHAFT LENGTH SPECIFICATIONS table. Position boots halfway between full compression and full extension and install NEW boot clamps.

BOOT & JOINT GREASE CAPACITY

Application	Oz. (g)
Accord	
Outboard	4.6-4.9 (130-140)
Inboard	4.2-4.6 (120-130)
Civic & Del Sol	
Outboard	
1995	3.2-3.5 (90-100)
1996 Japan Produced (Civic)	2.5-2.8 (70-80)
1996 Except Japan Produced (Civic)	4.0-4.8 (115-135)
1996 B16A2 Engine (Del Sol)	3.2-3.5 (90-100)
1996 Except B16A2 Engine	2.5-2.8 (70-80)
Inboard	
1995	4.2-4.6 (120-130)
1996 Japan Produced	3.9-4.2 (110-120)
Except Japan Produced	4.2-4.6 (120-130)
1996 B16A2 Engine (Del Sol)	4.2-4.6 (120-130)
1996 Except B16A2 Engine	3.9-4.2 (110-120)
Odyssey	
Outboard	4.6-4.9 (130-140)
Inboard	4.2-4.6 (120-130)
Prelude	
M/T	
Outboard	4.6-4.9 (130-140)
Inboard	4.2-4.9 (130-140)
A/T	
Left Inboard	4.2-4.6 (120-130)

CAUTION: Always use a NEW retaining ring when installing axle shaft.

6) Position dynamic damper to correct distance from edge of boot. See Fig. 4. See DYNAMIC DAMPER DISTANCE SPECIFICATIONS table. Bend down lock tab of each boot clamp and lightly tap doubled-over portion of boot clamp to reduce clamp height. Install a NEW retaining ring on end of inner CV joint, and install axle shaft.

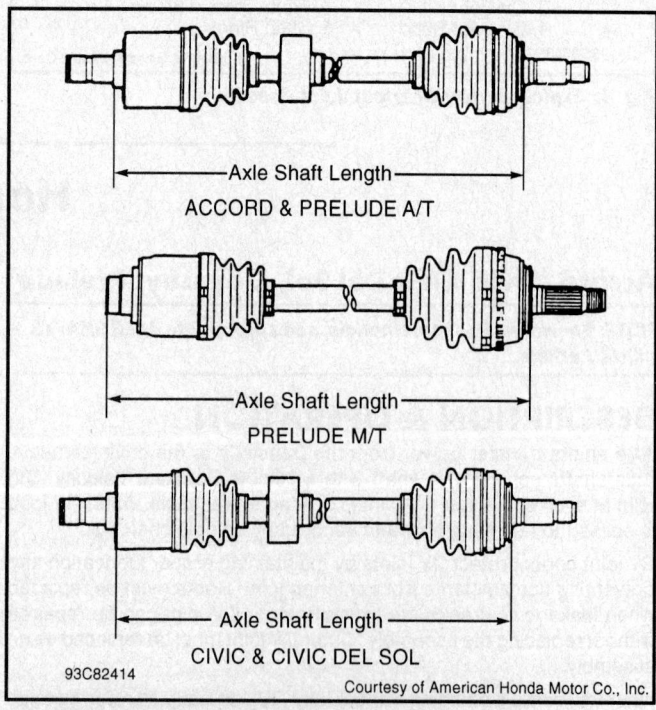

Axle Shaft Length
ACCORD & PRELUDE A/T

Axle Shaft Length
PRELUDE M/T

Axle Shaft Length
CIVIC & CIVIC DEL SOL

93C82414   Courtesy of American Honda Motor Co., Inc.

Fig. 3: Measuring Drive Axle Shaft Assembled Length

1995-96 AXLE SHAFT LENGTH SPECIFICATIONS

Application	In. (mm)
Accord	
A/T	
Left	33.3-33.5 (845-850)
Right	19.1-19.3 (486-491)
M/T	
Left & Right	19.1-19.3 (486-491)
Civic	
Left	30.50-30.70 (774-779)
Right	19.70-19.90 (501-506)
Del Sol	
Left & Right	18.7-18.9 (475-480)
Odyssey	
Left	18.5-18.7 (471-476)
Right	18.9-19.1 (481-486)
Prelude	
Left	
M/T	20.50-20.70 (520.9-525.9)
A/T	33.97-34.17 (862.9-867.9)
Right	20.00-20.20 (507.9-512.9)

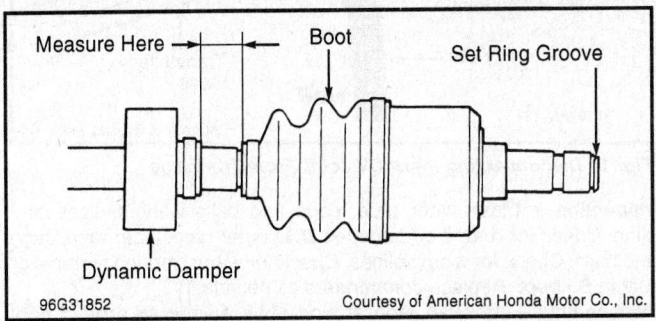

Fig. 4: Measuring Distance Between CV Boot & Dynamic Damper

1995-96 DYNAMIC DAMPER DISTANCE SPECIFICATIONS

Application	In. (mm)
Accord	
Left (A/T)	6.6-6.8 (169.0-173.0)
Civic & Civic Del Sol	
Left	
1995	2.9-3.1 (73-77)
1996 With "SR1" Mark	3.60-3.80 (92.0-96.0)
1996 Without "SR1" Mark	2.8-3.0 (73-77)
Right 1995-96	2.10-2.30 (53.0-57.0)
Del Sol (B16A3 & B16A2 Engine)	
Left & Right	1.0-1.2 (27-31)
Prelude	6.80-7.00 (173.0-177.0)

Installation – 1) Slide axle into transaxle or intermediate shaft. Ensure inner joint housing locks into differential side gear groove and joint sub-axle bottoms in differential or intermediate shaft.
2) Install damper fork over drive shaft and onto lower control arm. Install damper in damper fork so aligning tab aligns with slot in damper fork. Loosely install damper pinch bolt using NEW damper fork nut.
3) Pull hub assembly away from axle shaft, and slide axle into hub assembly. Install and lightly tighten spindle shaft nut. Position ball joint in hub. Raise lower control arm using floor jack, and install ball joint nut. Tighten ball joint nut to specification. See TORQUE SPECIFICATIONS.
4) Install and secure cotter pin. Remove floor jack. Tighten spindle nut to specification. Install wheels. Lower vehicle. With vehicle weight on damper, tighten damper pinch bolt to specification. Refill transaxle.

INTERMEDIATE SHAFT

Removal – 1) Drain fluid from transaxle. Remove outer axle shaft assembly from intermediate shaft assembly. See FWD AXLE SHAFT. Remove bolts attaching intermediate shaft bearing support.
2) Remove intermediate shaft from transaxle assembly. Use care not to damage seal in transaxle by holding shaft in a horizontal position when removing.
Disassembly – 1) Remove set ring. Remove intermediate shaft outer seal. Remove external circlip. Press intermediate shaft out of shaft bearing and support.
2) Remove intermediate shaft inner seal, and remove internal circlip. Press intermediate shaft bearing out of bearing support. Inspect all components for wear and damage, and replace components if necessary. See Fig. 5.

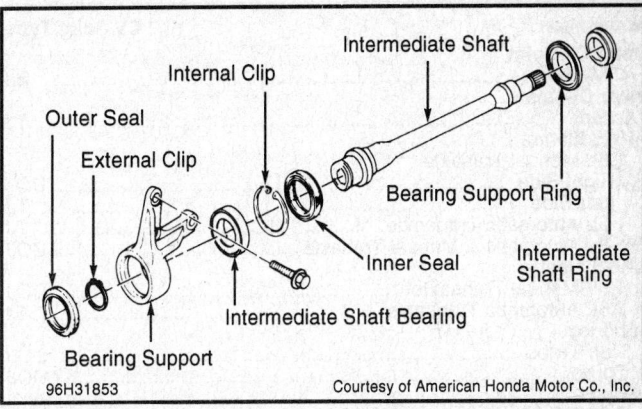

Fig. 5: Exploded View Of Intermediate Shaft Assembly (Typical)

CAUTION: Ensure internal circlip is installed with tapered end facing out.

NOTE: Pack interior of inner and outer seal.

Reassembly – 1) Press intermediate shaft bearing into bearing support. Seat internal circlip in groove of bearing support with tapered end facing out.
2) Press intermediate shaft inner seal into bearing support. Press intermediate shaft into shaft bearing. Seat external circlip in groove of intermediate shaft with tapered end facing out. Press outer seal into bearing support.
Installation – To install intermediate shaft assembly, reverse removal procedure. Add fluid to transaxle.

TORQUE SPECIFICATIONS
TORQUE SPECIFICATIONS

Application	Ft. Lbs. (N.m)
Damper Fork Nut	47 (64)
Damper Pinch Bolt	32 (43)
Intermediate Bearing Support Bolts	28 (38)
Lower Ball Joint Nut	36-43 (49-59)
Spindle Nut	
Accord, Odyssey & Prelude	181 (245)
Civic	134 (181)
Wheel Lug Nuts	80 (108)

Accent, Elantra, Scoupe, Sonata

DESCRIPTION & OPERATION

Axle shafts transfer power from transaxle to driving wheels. Axle shafts consist of a center shaft with a flexible Constant Velocity (CV) joint at each end. Inner CV joint is either a Double Offset Joint (DOJ) or a Tripod Joint (TJ) that is splined into transaxle. Outer CV joint is a Birfield Joint (BJ) that is splined into wheel hub assembly and secured by an axle nut.

CV joint boots protect CV joints by maintaining proper lubrication and preventing contaminants from entering joint. To prevent premature CV joint failure, boots must be replaced if signs of leakage or cracks are present.

CV JOINT APPLICATION

Application	[1] CV Joint Type
Outer CV Joint	
All Models	BJ
Inner CV Joint	
Accent	TJ
1995 Elantra	
1.6L Manual Trasaxle	
Right Side	DOJ
Left Side	TJ
1.6L Automatic Transaxle	TJ
1.8L Automatic & Manual Trasaxle	DOJ
1996 Elantra	
1.8L Manual Transaxle	DOJ
1.8L Automatic Transaxle	TJ
Scoupe	
Non-Turbo	DOJ
Turbo	[2] DOJ
Sonata	
2.0L Engine	DOJ
3.0L Engine	[2] DOJ

[1] – CV joint types are: Birfield Joint (BJ); Double Offset Joint (DOJ); Tripod Joint (TJ).
[2] – CV joint is connected to an intermediate shaft.

TROUBLE SHOOTING

NOTE: *See DRIVE AXLE NOISE DIAGNOSIS in GENERAL INFORMATION at beginning of this section.*

REMOVAL, DISASSEMBLY, REASSEMBLY & INSTALLATION

AXLE SHAFTS

Removal (All Models) – **1)** Raise and support vehicle. Remove front wheel. Remove axle nut cotter pin, and loosen axle nut. Remove engine undercover (if equipped). Drain transaxle fluid.
2) Remove lower ball joint-to-lower control arm mounting bolts or separate lower ball joint from steering knuckle. Remove tie rod from steering knuckle. Remove stabilizer bar self-locking nut.
3) Using care not to damage oil seal, insert pry bar between transaxle case and inner CV joint housing. *See Fig. 1.* Pry axle shaft assembly from transaxle. On Scoupe Turbo and Sonata 3.0L left axle shaft, insert pry bar between center bearing bracket and CV joint housing.
4) Using a universal puller, press outer CV joint axle shaft through wheel hub. Prevent hub spacer from falling out when removing shaft.

NOTE: *Outer CV joint assembly is not repairable and should not be disassembled. Remove large boot band and check for foreign substances in grease. If necessary, clean assembly and repack with proper CV joint grease. Always install new boot bands.*

Disassembly (Double Offset Joint) – **1)** Measure distance between CV joint boot bands for reassembly reference. *See Fig. 2.* Remove CV joint boot bands and slide boots from joint assemblies. Remove large circlip from inner joint housing. *See Fig. 3, 4 or 5.*

2) Remove axle shaft from joint assembly. Remove snap ring. Remove inner race, cage, and balls as an assembly. If reusing CV joint boots, wrap tape around axle shaft to protect boot. Remove CV joint boots. If dynamic damper is to be removed, mark location of damper on shaft for reinstallation.

NOTE: *Inner and outer boots are NOT interchangeable. Mark boots before removal to ensure proper location of boots when installing.*

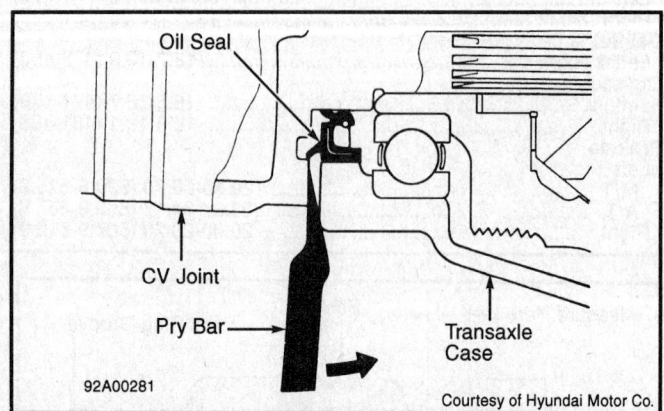

Fig. 1: Disconnecting Inner CV Joint From Transaxle

Inspection – Clean inner race, cage and balls without disassembling. Check for rusted or damaged DOJ outer race, inner race, cage and balls. Check for worn splines. Check for water, foreign material or rust in BJ boot. Replace components as necessary.
Reassembly – **1)** Wrap tape around shaft splines to protect boot during installation. Install boots and bands, but do not tighten bands. Install dynamic damper, if removed. Ensure damper is installed in same location.
2) Pack joint inner race, cage and ball bearings with 2.0-2.1 ounces of grease. Install assembly on axle shaft with chamfered side (small end) of cage facing away from shaft end. *See Fig. 6.* Install snap ring.
3) Install large circlip into joint assembly. Apply 1.1-1.3 ounces of grease into inner CV joint boot. Position boot and boot band over joint housing. Ensure distance between bands is same as measurement made before disassembly. Tighten boot bands.

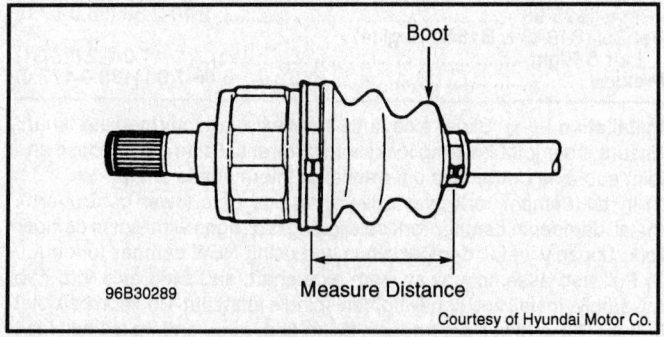

Fig. 2: Measuring Boot Band Distance

Disassembly Of Tripod Joint – **1)** Measure distance between CV joint boot bands for reassembly reference. *See Fig. 2.* If dynamic damper is to be removed, mark location of damper on shaft to maintain distance from center of inner CV joint housing to center of dynamic damper.
2) Remove inner CV joint boot bands and slide boot from joint assembly. *See Fig. 7.* Remove remove snap ring and spider assembly from shaft. Do not disassemble spider assembly. Remove outer CV joint boot bands and slide boot from joint assembly.

3) If reusing CV joint boots, wrap tape around axle shaft to protect boots. Remove inner CV joint boot. Loosen dynamic damper band, and remove damper (if necessary). Remove outer CV joint boot and bands, if necessary.

NOTE: *Inner and outer boots are NOT interchangeable. Mark boots before removal to ensure proper location of boots when installing.*

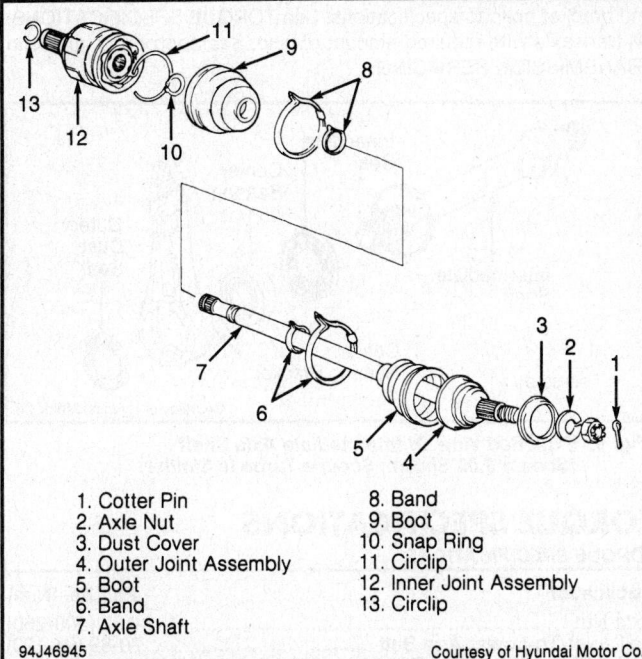

1. Cotter Pin
2. Axle Nut
3. Dust Cover
4. Outer Joint Assembly
5. Boot
6. Band
7. Axle Shaft
8. Band
9. Boot
10. Snap Ring
11. Circlip
12. Inner Joint Assembly
13. Circlip

94J46945   Courtesy of Hyundai Motor Co.

Fig. 3: *Exploded View Of Axle Shaft Assembly (Elantra & Sonata 2.0L)*

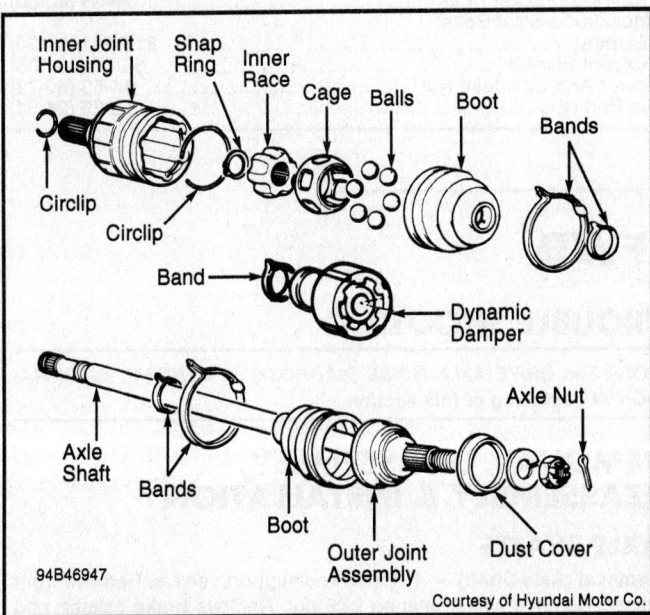

94B46947   Courtesy of Hyundai Motor Co.

Fig. 4: *Exploded View Of Axle Shaft Assembly (Scoupe Non-Turbo)*

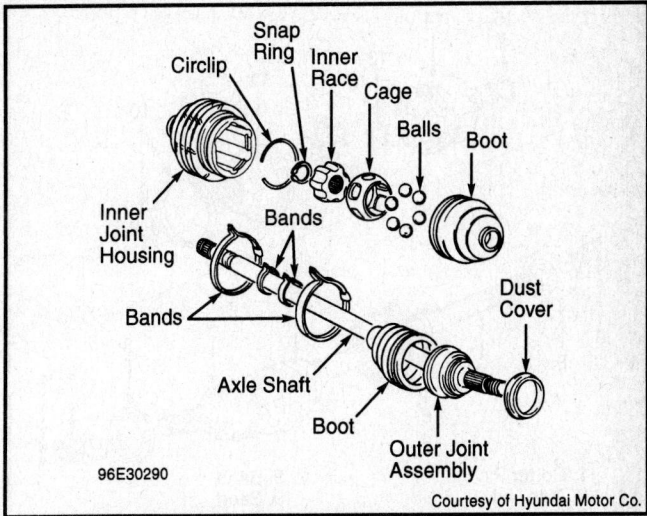

96E30290   Courtesy of Hyundai Motor Co.

Fig. 5: *Exploded View Of Axle Shaft Assembly (Scoupe Turbo & Sonata 3.0L)*

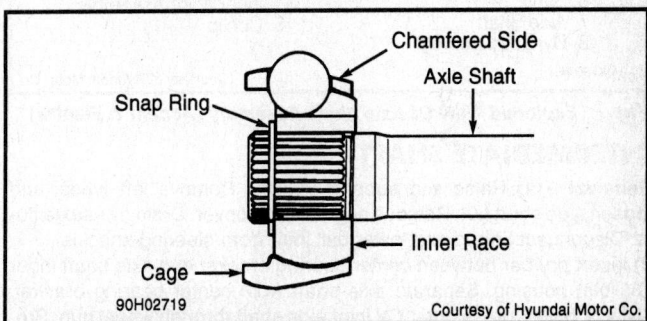

90H02719   Courtesy of Hyundai Motor Co.

Fig. 6: *Installing Inner Race Assembly (Double Offset Joint)*

Inspection – Clean axle shaft splines for wear and damage. Check spider assembly for roller rotation, wear or corrosion. Check groove inside TJ housing for wear or corrosion. Check dynamic damper for cracking or damage. Check for water, foreign material or rust in BJ boot. Replace components as necessary.

Reassembly – **1)** Wrap tape around shaft splines to protect boot during installation. Install outer CV joint boot and bands, but do not tighten bands. Pack outer joint assembly and boot with same amount of grease that was wiped away at time of inspection.

2) Install dynamic damper, if removed. Ensure distance from center of inner CV joint housing to center of dynamic damper is same as measurement made before disassembly. Install inner CV joint boot and bands, but do not tighten bands. Pack inner CV joint boot with 1.3-1.5 ounces of grease.

3) Pack spider assembly with 2.2-2.4 ounces of grease. Install spider assembly onto axle shaft. Install snap ring. Position boot and boot band over joint housing. Ensure distance between bands is same as measurement made before disassembly. Tighten boot bands.

Installation (All Models) – To install, reverse removal procedure. Install NEW circlip (retainer ring) on inner CV joint splined shaft before installation. Install axle nut convex washer with outside beveled edge toward nut. Tighten nut to specification. See TORQUE SPECIFICATIONS. Fill transaxle with required amount of fluid. See appropriate article in TRANSMISSION SERVICING.

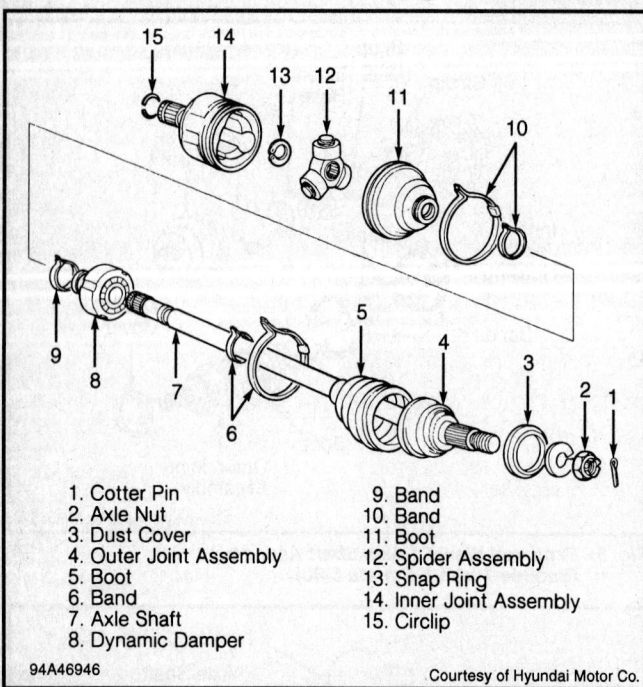

1. Cotter Pin
2. Axle Nut
3. Dust Cover
4. Outer Joint Assembly
5. Boot
6. Band
7. Axle Shaft
8. Dynamic Damper
9. Band
10. Band
11. Boot
12. Spider Assembly
13. Snap Ring
14. Inner Joint Assembly
15. Circlip

94A46946

Courtesy of Hyundai Motor Co.

Fig. 7: Exploded View Of Axle Shaft Assembly (Accent & Elantra)

INTERMEDIATE SHAFT

Removal – 1) Raise and support vehicle. Remove left wheel and loosen axle shaft nut. Remove engine undercover. Drain transaxle fluid. Disconnect tie rod and lower ball joint from steering knuckle.

2) Insert pry bar between center bearing bracket and axle shaft inner CV joint housing. Separate axle shaft from center bearing bracket. Using a puller, press outer CV joint axle shaft through wheel hub. Prevent inner spacer from falling out when removing axle shaft from hub.

3) Remove oxygen sensor connector from center bearing bracket. Remove center bearing bracket mounting bolts. Insert pry bar between intermediate shaft assembly and transaxle. *See Fig. 1.* Remove center bearing bracket and intermediate shaft assembly. *See Fig. 8.*

Disassembly – Using suitable puller, remove center bearing bracket from intermediate shaft. Remove outer dust seal from bracket. Press bearing from center bearing bracket.

NOTE: *Center bracket bearing can only be removed and installed from one side of bracket.*

Reassembly – Apply multipurpose grease to center bearing and to inside of bracket. Press center bearing into center bearing bracket. Apply grease to inside of seals, and install dust seals flush with edge of center bearing bracket.

Installation – To install, reverse removal procedure. Install axle nut convex washer with outside beveled edge toward nut. Tighten axle nut and bracket bolts to specifications. See TORQUE SPECIFICATIONS. Fill transaxle with required amount of fluid. See appropriate article in TRANSMISSION SERVICING.

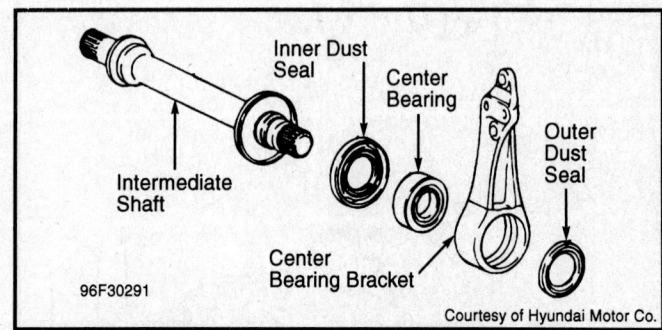

96F30291

Courtesy of Hyundai Motor Co.

Fig. 8: Exploded View Of Intermediate Axle Shaft (Sonata 3.0L Shown; Scoupe Turbo Is Similar)

TORQUE SPECIFICATIONS
TORQUE SPECIFICATIONS

Application	Ft. Lbs. (N.m)
Axle Nut	148-192 (200-260)
Ball Joint-To-Lower Arm Bolt	70-89 (95-120)
Brake Caliper Mounting Bolts	
Except Sonata	48-55 (65-75)
Sonata	51-63 (69-85)
Intermediate Center	
Bearing Bracket Bolts	29-36 (40-50)
Knuckle-To-Strut Bolts	
Elantra	81-96 (110-130)
Except Elantra	66-77 (90-105)
Lower Arm Ball Joint Nut	44-53 (60-72)
Tie Rod Nut	18-25 (24-34)

Infiniti FWD

G20, I30

DESCRIPTION

Axle shafts transfer power from transaxle to drive wheels. Axle shafts consist of a shaft and flexible Constant Velocity (CV) joint at each end. *See Fig. 1.* Inner CV joint is splined to transaxle. Outer CV joint is splined to hub assembly and secured by wheel bearing lock nut.

Inner CV joint is a plunging tripod joint. The plunging action allows for axle shaft length change as suspension moves up and down.

Inner and outer CV joints are enclosed by CV boots. The boot retains lubrication in the joint and prevents contamination of CV lubricant. Boots must be replaced when leakage or cracks are present. The inner CV joint can be repaired without replacing assembly. The outer CV joint must be replaced as an assembly.

TROUBLE SHOOTING

NOTE: *See DRIVE AXLE NOISE DIAGNOSIS in GENERAL INFORMATION at beginning of this section.*

REMOVAL, DISASSEMBLY, REASSEMBLY & INSTALLATION

AXLE SHAFTS

Removal (Axle Shaft) – 1) Raise and support vehicle. Remove front wheel. Remove wheel bearing lock nut. Remove brake caliper, and support aside. Remove brake rotor.

NOTE: *DO NOT allow brake caliper to hang from brake hose.*

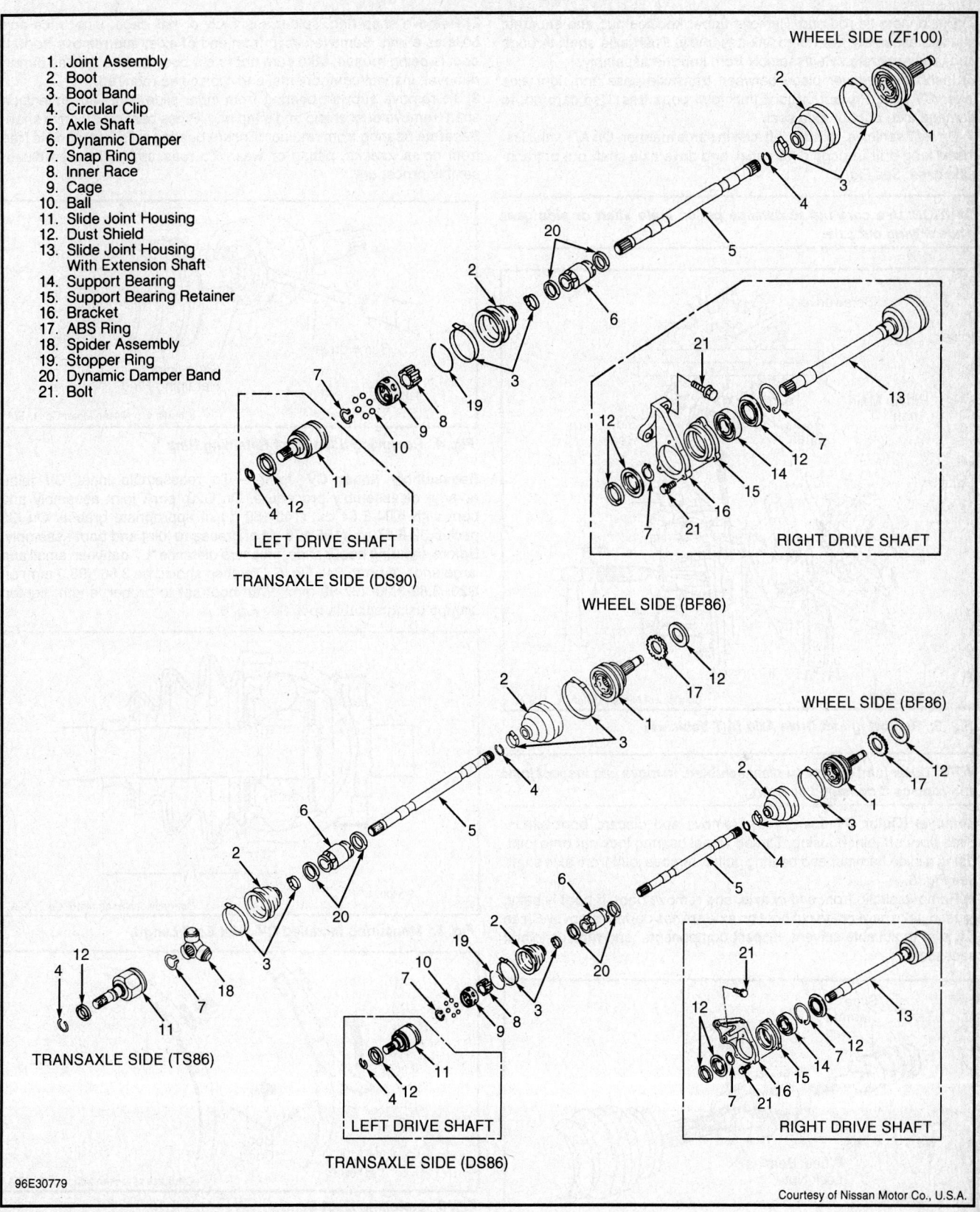

1. Joint Assembly
2. Boot
3. Boot Band
4. Circular Clip
5. Axle Shaft
6. Dynamic Damper
7. Snap Ring
8. Inner Race
9. Cage
10. Ball
11. Slide Joint Housing
12. Dust Shield
13. Slide Joint Housing
    With Extension Shaft
14. Support Bearing
15. Support Bearing Retainer
16. Bracket
17. ABS Ring
18. Spider Assembly
19. Stopper Ring
20. Dynamic Damper Band
21. Bolt

WHEEL SIDE (ZF100)

LEFT DRIVE SHAFT
TRANSAXLE SIDE (DS90)

RIGHT DRIVE SHAFT
WHEEL SIDE (BF86)

WHEEL SIDE (BF86)

TRANSAXLE SIDE (TS86)

LEFT DRIVE SHAFT
TRANSAXLE SIDE (DS86)

RIGHT DRIVE SHAFT

96E30779

Courtesy of Nissan Motor Co., U.S.A.

Fig. 1: Exploded View Of Axle Shafts

2) Disconnect tie rod end. Remove upper knuckle nut, and separate knuckle assembly from third link assembly. Push axle shaft through hub, and separate axle assembly from knuckle assembly.

3) Insert screwdriver blade between transaxle case and right axle inner CV joint. Pry out on joint until joint pops free. Use care not to damage axle boot or axle seal.

4) On M/T vehicles, remove left axle in same manner. On A/T vehicles, insert long drift through differential, and drive axle shaft out of transaxle case. *See Fig. 2.*

CAUTION: Use care not to damage pinion mate shaft or side gear while driving out axle.

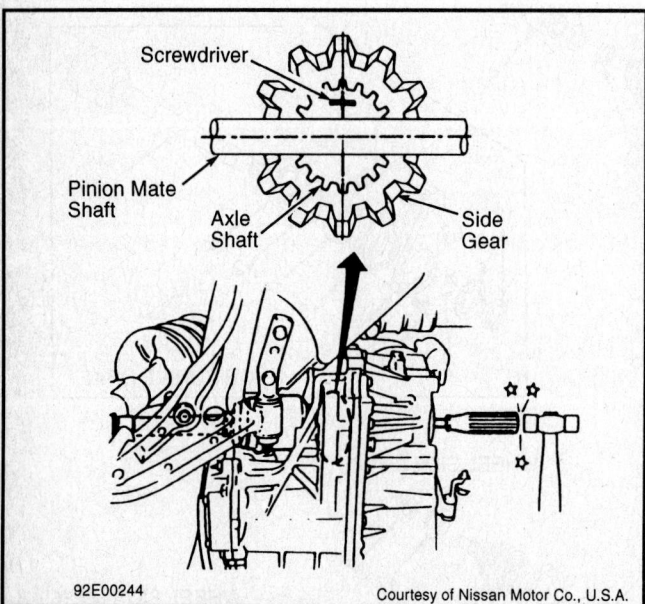

Fig. 2: Removing Left Drive Axle (A/T Vehicles)

NOTE: Outer joint cannot be disassembled. Remove and inspect joint and replace if damaged or worn.

Removal (Outer CV Joint) – **1)** Remove and discard boot bands. Slide boot off joint housing. Thread wheel bearing lock nut onto joint. Using a slide hammer and bearing puller, remove joint from axle shaft. *See Fig. 3.*

2) Remove circlip from end of axle, and remove boot. If boot is being reused, take care not to cut boot on axle splines during removal. Clean CV joint in suitable solvent. Inspect components, and replace joint if necessary.

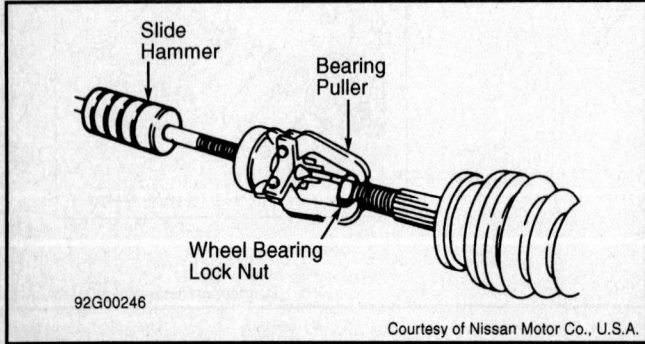

Fig. 3: Removing Outer CV Joint

Disassembly (Inner CV Joint) – **1)** Remove and discard boot bands. Slide boot off slide joint housing. Mark slide joint housing, inner race and axle shaft for reassembly reference. Using a screwdriver, pry out slide joint retaining ring. *See Fig. 4.*

2) Remove snap ring, spider assembly or ball cage, inner race and balls as a unit. Remove circlip from end of axle, and remove boot. If boot is being reused, take care not to cut boot on axle splines during removal. Inspect components, and replace as required.

3) To remove support bearing from inner slide joint with extension shaft, remove dust shield and snap ring. Press bearing off drive shaft. Separate bearing from retainer. Ensure bearing rolls freely and is free from noise, cracks, pitting or wear. To reassemble, reverse disassembly procedure

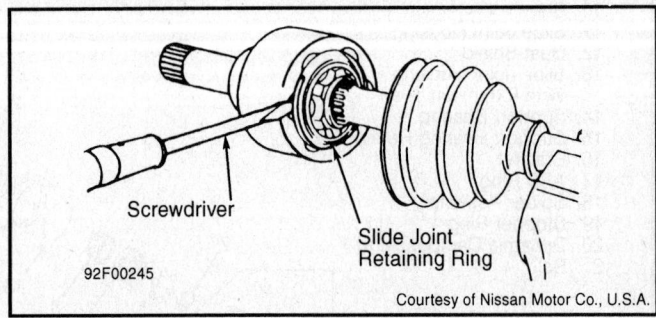

Fig. 4: Removing Slide Joint Retaining Ring

Reassembly (Inner CV Joint) – To reassemble inner CV joint, reverse disassembly procedure. On G20, pack joint assembly and boot with 4.94-5.64 oz. (140-160 g.) of appropriate grease. On I30 pack 5.82-6.17 oz. (165-175 g.) of grease to joint and boot assembly. Before securing boot bands, measure distance "L," between small and large ends of boot. *See Fig. 5.* Distance should be 3.86" (98.0 mm) on G20, 3.82-3.90" (97-99 mm). With boot set to proper length, tighten clamps using suitable tool. *See Fig. 6.*

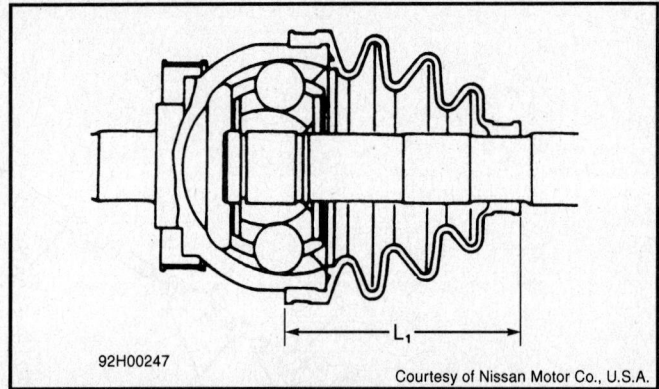

Fig. 5: Measuring Installed CV Joint Boot Length

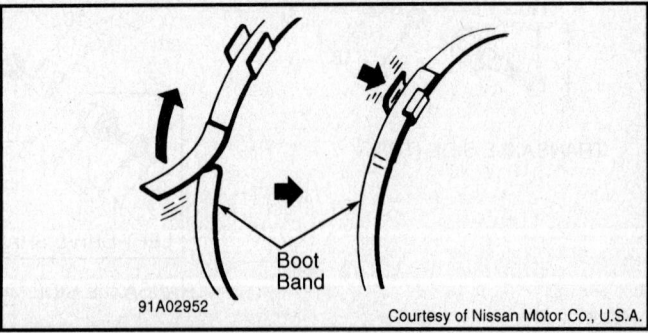

Fig. 6: Installing Boot Bands

Installation (Outer CV Joint) – Install boot and circlip onto axle shaft. Thread bearing lock nut onto joint, and install joint onto axle shaft. *See Fig. 7.* On G20, pack joint assembly and boot with 3.70-4.41 oz. (105-125 g.) of appropriate grease. On I30, pack 4.76-5.11 oz. (135-145 g.) of appropriate grease. Before securing boot bands, measure distance

"L₁" between small and large ends of boot. *See Fig. 5.* Distance should be 3.96" (100.5 mm) on G20, 3.78-3.86" (96-98 mm) on I30. With boot set to proper length, tighten clamps using suitable tool. *See Fig. 6.*

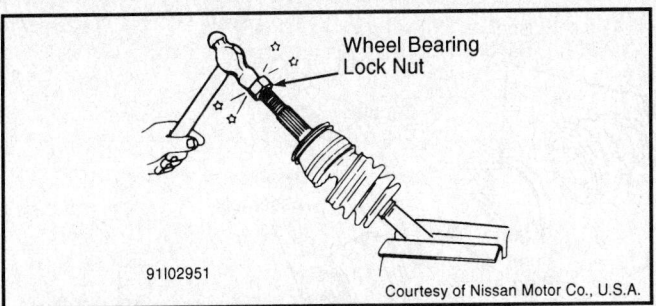

Fig 7: *Installing Outer CV Joint*

91I02951

Courtesy of Nissan Motor Co., U.S.A.

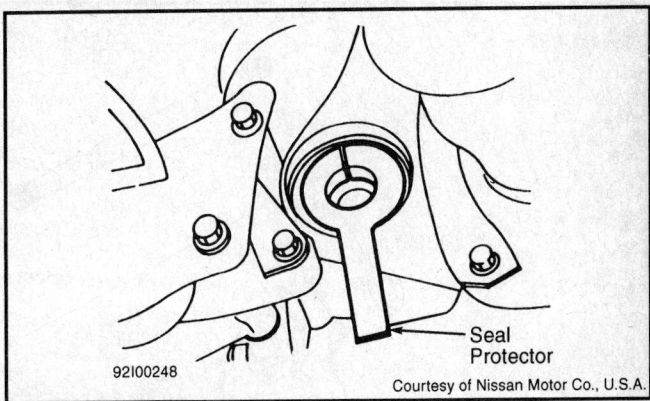

Fig. 8: *Installing Seal Protector*

92I00248

Courtesy of Nissan Motor Co., U.S.A.

Installation (Axle Shaft) – 1) Install NEW oil seal in transaxle (if required). Install Seal Protector (KV38106800 or J34297) into seal. *See Fig. 8.* Insert axle shaft into transaxle and engage splines into side gear. Remove seal protector.

2) Seat axle fully into transaxle, ensuring circlip engages groove in side gear. Test for proper installation by pulling outward on CV joint. DO NOT pull on axle shaft. Axle is properly seated if CV joint will not pull free. To complete installation, reverse removal procedure. Tighten bolts and nuts to specification. See TORQUE SPECIFICATIONS. Check transaxle fluid level. Add fluid as necessary.

TORQUE SPECIFICATIONS

TORQUE SPECIFICATIONS

Application	Ft. Lbs. (N.m)
Bearing Lock Nut	174-231 (235-314)
Brake Caliper Bolt	53-72 (72-98)
Support Bearing Retainer-To-Bracket Bolt	9-14 (13-19)
Support Bearing Bracket	19-26 (25-35)
Tie Rod End Nut	21-29 (28-39)
Upper Knuckle Nut	72-87 (98-118)
Wheel Lug Nut	72-87 (98-118)

Infiniti RWD

J30, Q45

DESCRIPTION

Axle shafts consist of a shaft and a flexible Constant Velocity (CV) joint at each end. Each inner CV joint is bolted to a side flange which is splined to differential. On all models, outer CV joint is splined to hub assembly and secured by wheel bearing lock nut. The CV joints are enclosed by boots, which maintain and prevent contamination of lubricant. Boots must be replaced if leakage or cracks exists. *See Fig. 1.*

TROUBLE SHOOTING

NOTE: See DRIVE AXLE NOISE DIAGNOSIS in GENERAL INFORMATION at beginning of this section.

REMOVAL, DISASSEMBLY, REASSEMBLY & INSTALLATION

AXLE SHAFTS

Removal – When removing axle shaft, use shop towels to cover boots to prevent damage. Remove wheel bearing lock nut. At final drive side, remove side flange mounting bolts. Separate axle shaft from final drive side. At wheel side, tap axle shaft lightly with brass mallet. If axle shaft is difficult to remove, use puller.

Disassembly – Remove boot bands. Mark wheel side housing, axle shaft, and inner race for reassembly reference. Pry snap ring from housing. Remove cage, inner race, and balls as an assembly. Remove boot. Mark axle shaft and wheel side joint for reassembly reference. Separate joint from axle shaft with slide hammer and puller.

Inspection – Clean parts. Inspect for deformation or other damage. Replace axle shaft if twisted or cracked. Replace boot if cracked or worn. Use NEW boot bands when replacing boot. Replace assembly if necessary. If housing is defective, replace housing and internal components as a set.

Reassembly (Final Drive Side) – 1) Install boot and NEW boot band onto axle shaft. Cover axle shaft serrations with tape to prevent dam-

age to boot during installation. Install ball cage, inner race, and balls as an assembly, with reference marks aligned. Install NEW snap ring. Pack joint with 5.47-6.17 ozs. (155-175 g) of grease. Install slide joint housing. Install NEW snap ring.

2) Install boot, ensuring it does not swell or deform. Distance (L₁) between boot ends should be 3.80" (96.5 mm). *See Fig. 2.* Install boot into grooves provided, and secure with NEW boot bands.

Reassembly (Wheel Side) – 1) Install boot and NEW small boot band. Cover axle shaft serrations with tape to prevent damage to boot during installation. Tap joint onto axle shaft, with reference marks aligned.

2) Pack joint with 4.41-5.11 ozs. (125-145 g) of grease. Install boot, ensuring it does not swell or deform. Distance between boot ends should be 4.02" (102.0 mm). Install boot into grooves provided, and secure with NEW boot bands.

Installation – To install, reverse removal procedure. Tighten flange bolts to specification. See TORQUE SPECIFICATIONS.

REAR HUB & CARRIER ASSEMBLY

Removal – 1) Remove wheel bearing lock nut. Separate axle shaft from housing by tapping lightly. If axle shaft is difficult to remove, use puller. Remove brake caliper and rotor. Suspend caliper with wire. Remove axle housing.

2) Remove wheel bearing with flange and wheel hub from axle housing. Remove baffle plate and grease seal.

Inspection – Inspect wheel hub and axle housing for cracks. Press off wheel bearing. Inspect for damage, seizure, rust, or rough operation. *See Fig. 3 or 4.* Inspect rubber bushing for wear and other damage. Replace as necessary.

NOTE: Wheel bearing must be replaced as an assembly.

Installation – To install, reverse removal procedure. Tighten wheel bearing lock nut to specification. See TORQUE SPECIFICATIONS. Measure wheel bearing end play. Maximum end play should be .002" (.05 mm).

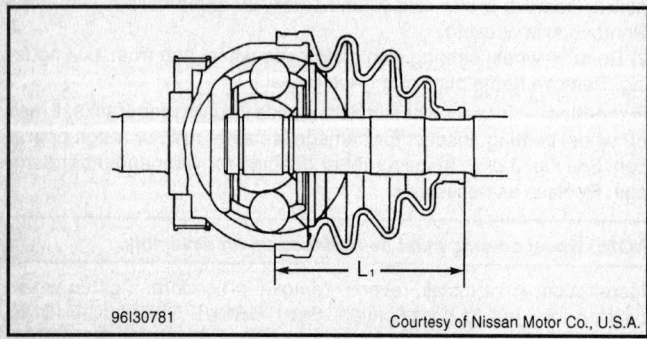

96A30783

Courtesy of Nissan Motor Co., U.S.A.

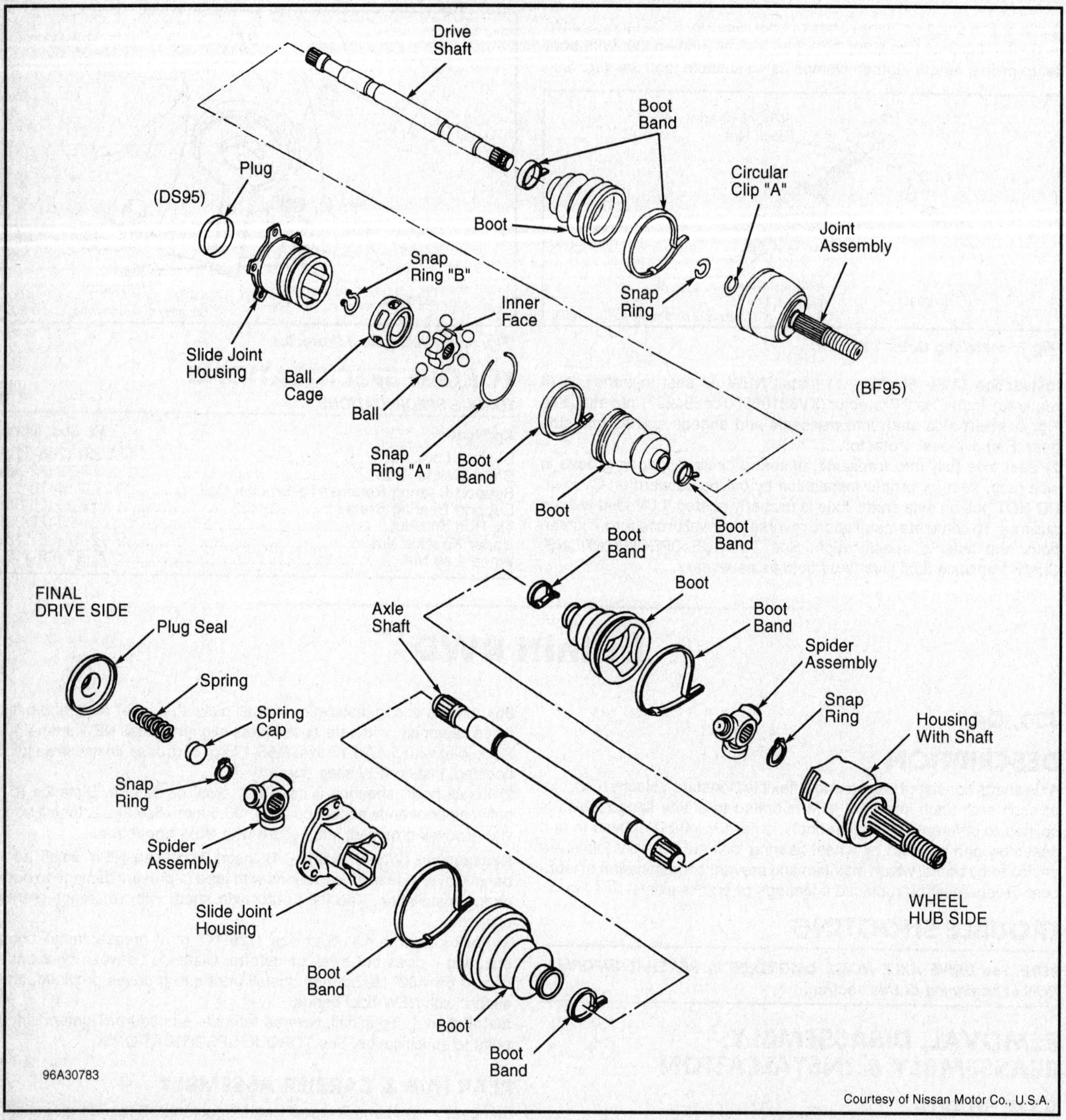

Fig. 1: Exploded View Of Rear Axle Shaft

96I30781

Courtesy of Nissan Motor Co., U.S.A.

Fig. 2: Measuring Installed CV Joint Boot Length

TORQUE SPECIFICATIONS
TORQUE SPECIFICATIONS

Application	Ft. Lbs. (N.m)
Anchor Pin	53-72 (72-97)
Axle Shaft Slide Joint	
Housing-To-Side Flange Bolt (Q45)	61-69 (83-94)
Axle Shaft-To-Companion Flange Nut (J30)	25-33 (34-44)
Caliper-To-Carrier Bolt	23-30 (31-41)
Wheel Bearing Lock Nut	152-203 (206-275)
Wheel Lug Nut	
J30	76-90 (103-122)
Q45	72-87 (98-118)

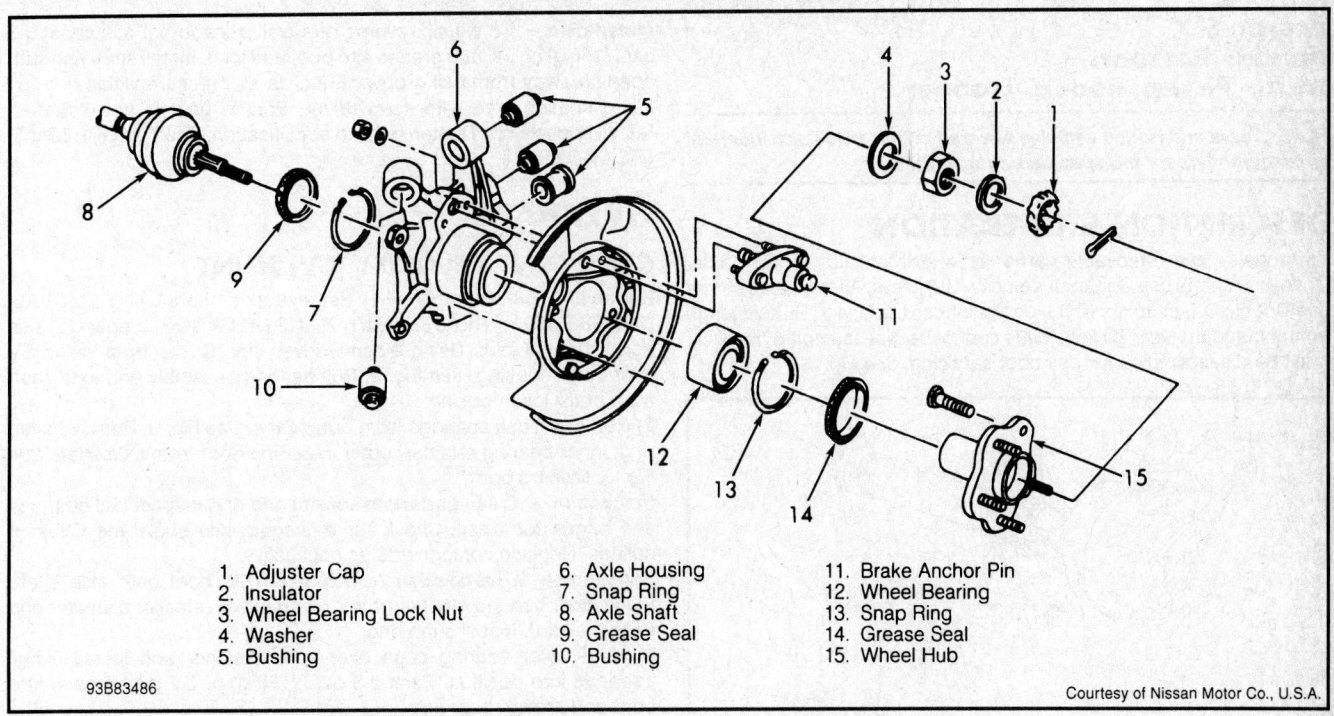

1. Adjuster Cap
2. Insulator
3. Wheel Bearing Lock Nut
4. Washer
5. Bushing
6. Axle Housing
7. Snap Ring
8. Axle Shaft
9. Grease Seal
10. Bushing
11. Brake Anchor Pin
12. Wheel Bearing
13. Snap Ring
14. Grease Seal
15. Wheel Hub

93B83486

Courtesy of Nissan Motor Co., U.S.A.

Fig. 3: Exploded View Of Axle Housing & Hub Assembly (J30)

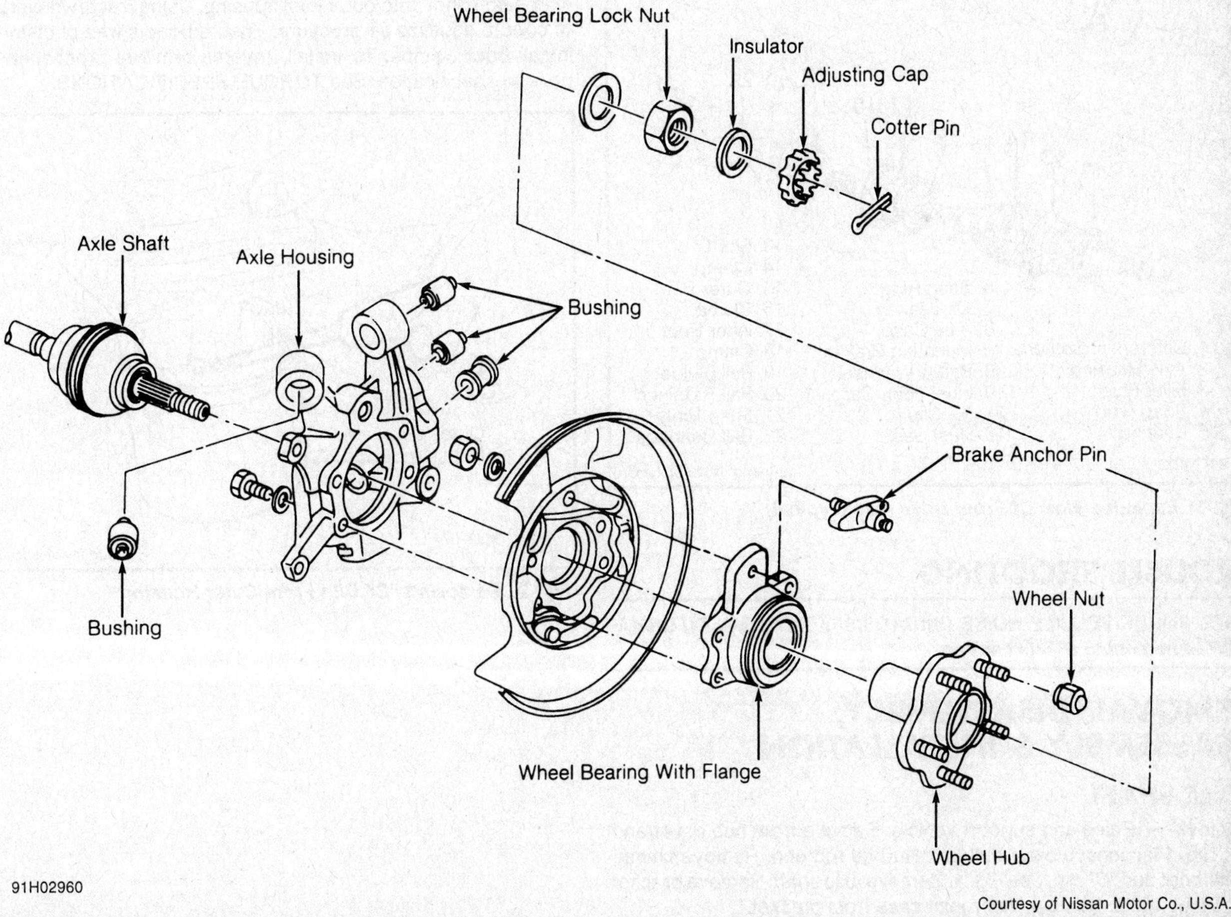

Wheel Bearing Lock Nut

Insulator

Adjusting Cap

Cotter Pin

Axle Shaft

Axle Housing

Bushing

Brake Anchor Pin

Bushing

Wheel Nut

Wheel Bearing With Flange

Wheel Hub

91H02960

Courtesy of Nissan Motor Co., U.S.A.

Fig. 4: Exploded View Of Axle Housing & Hub Assembly (Q45)

Acura: SLX
Honda: Passport
Isuzu: Pickup, Rodeo, Trooper

NOTE: Acura and Honda vehicles covered in this article are identical to Isuzu models for the specified components.

DESCRIPTION & OPERATION

All models have removable carrier type differentials on front axle. Drive axle shafts use Constant Velocity (CV) joints. All front axle shafts use Double Offset Joints (DOJ) on the inboard side, and Birfield joints on the outboard side. Birfield joints cannot be disassembled, the DOJ must be disassembled for any boot servicing. *See Fig. 1.*

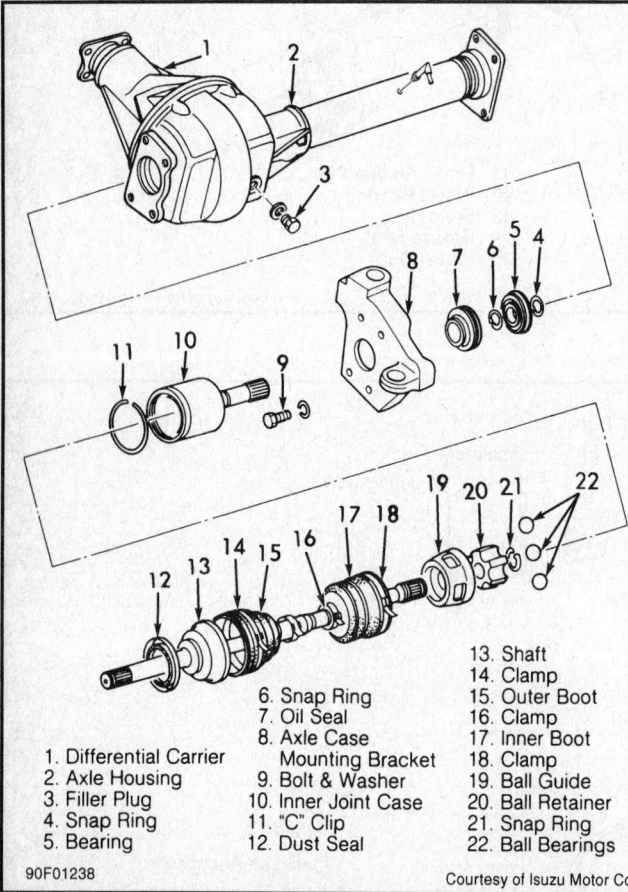

13. Shaft
14. Clamp
6. Snap Ring   15. Outer Boot
7. Oil Seal   16. Clamp
8. Axle Case   17. Inner Boot
   Mounting Bracket   18. Clamp
1. Differential Carrier   9. Bolt & Washer   19. Ball Guide
2. Axle Housing   10. Inner Joint Case   20. Ball Retainer
3. Filler Plug   11. "C" Clip   21. Snap Ring
4. Snap Ring   12. Dust Seal   22. Ball Bearings
5. Bearing

90F01238   Courtesy of Isuzu Motor Co.

Fig. 1: Exploded View Of Front Drive Axle (Typical)

TROUBLE SHOOTING

NOTE: See DRIVE AXLE NOISE DIAGNOSIS in GENERAL INFORMATION at beginning of this section.

REMOVAL, DISASSEMBLY, REASSEMBLY & INSTALLATION

AXLE SHAFT

Removal – Raise and support vehicle. Remove front hub cover and "C" clip. Disconnect lower ball joint and tie rod end. Remove clamp, inner boot and "C" clip. *See Fig. 1.* Remove axle shaft. Remove bracket mounting bolts. Remove inner joint case from bracket.

Installation – To install, reverse removal procedure. Pack about 5.3 ozs. (150 g) of CV joint grease into boot and joint. Install snap ring with opening away from ball groove. Equalize air pressure within boot by lifting seating area with screwdriver. Ensure boot is not distorted. Install boot clamp. Tighten bolts to specification. See TORQUE SPECIFICATIONS.

OVERHAUL

CONSTANT VELOCITY (CV) JOINT

Removal & Disassembly – 1) Remove axle shaft. See REMOVAL, DISASSEMBLY, REASSEMBLY & INSTALLATION. Separate axle boot from CV joint. Using a screwdriver, pry "C" clip from inside CV joint outer housing. *See Fig. 2.* Pull bearing assembly and axle shaft from outer joint housing.

2) Remove 6 ball bearings from outer cage. *See Fig. 3.* Remove snap ring, inner bearing retainer, outer cage and boot from axle shaft. *See Fig. 3.* Discard boot.

Inspection – Clean parts with solvent and dry. Inspect ball bearings and cages for wear. Check for damaged axle shaft and CV joint splines. Replace components as necessary.

Reassembly & Installation – 1) Install NEW boot onto axle shaft. Place inner bearing retainer onto axle shaft with smaller diameter end facing inward. Install snap ring.

2) Hold outer bearing cage over inner retainer and install 6 ball bearings into position. Pack 5.3 ozs. (150 g) of CV joint grease into boot and around bearings.

3) Carefully slide bearing assembly into outer housing. Install "C" clip into groove of outer housing so ends of "C" clip are not visible (away from bearing groove).

4) Position boot onto outer joint housing. Using a screwdriver, lift edge of boot to equalize air pressure. Ensure boot is free of distortion and install boot clamps. To install, reverse removal procedure. Tighten bolts to specification. See TORQUE SPECIFICATIONS.

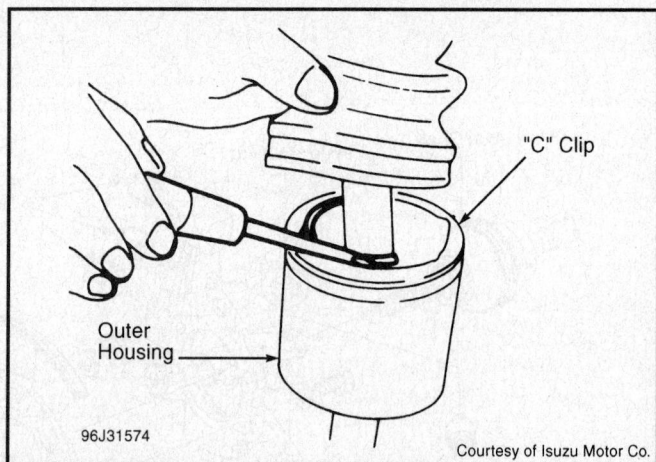

"C" Clip

Outer Housing

96J31574   Courtesy of Isuzu Motor Co.

Fig. 2: Removing "C" Clip From Outer Housing

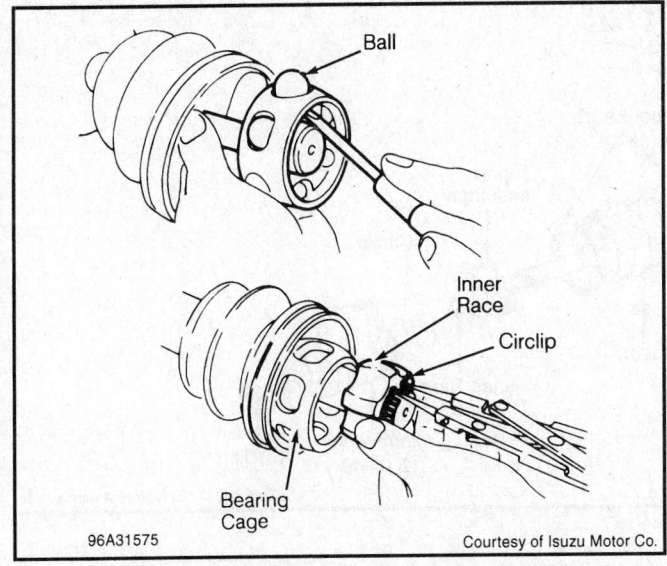

96A31575   Courtesy of Isuzu Motor Co.

Fig. 3: Disassembling Double Offset Joint (DOJ) Assembly

TORQUE SPECIFICATIONS

TORQUE SPECIFICATIONS

Application	Ft. lbs. (N.m)
Axle Bracket-To-Body Bolt & Nut	112 (152)
Axle Bracket-To-Carrier Bolt	85 (115)
Lower Ball Joint Nut	108 (146)
Tie Rod End Nut	72 (98)
Wheel Lug Nut [1]	87 (118)

[1] – Torque aluminum wheels to 118 ft. lbs. (160 N.m).

Kia

Sephia

DESCRIPTION

Sephia uses inner and outer CV joints. Inner joint is a Tripod type joint. Outer joint is a Birfield type joint. CV joints are enclosed by CV boots, which maintain lubrication and prevent contaminants from entering joints.

TROUBLE SHOOTING

NOTE: See DRIVE AXLE NOISE DIAGNOSIS in GENERAL INFORMATION at beginning of this section.

REMOVAL, DISASSEMBLY, REASSEMBLY & INSTALLATION

FWD AXLE SHAFT

Removal – 1) Raise and support vehicle. Remove front wheels. Remove inner fender shield. Unstake axle shaft lock nut. Apply brakes and remove axle shaft lock nut.

2) Using appropriate puller, separate tie rod end from steering knuckle. Disconnect stabilizer bar from lower control arm. Disconnect lower control arm ball joint from steering knuckle.

3) Carefully insert pry bar between inner CV joint and transaxle ensuring no damage to boot or oil seal occurs. Using hammer, lightly tap end of pry bar to unseat inner CV joint assembly from transaxle

4) Remove axle shaft assembly from hub. If axle shaft is frozen to hub, reinstall axle shaft lock nut until flush with end of axle shaft and tap end of axle shaft with brass or plastic hammer.

NOTE: DO NOT disassemble outer CV joint. Replace outer axle shaft and CV joint as an assembly. Service outer boot only after inner CV joint has been removed.

NOTE: BEFORE disassembling right axle shaft assembly, measure and record dynamic damper position from axle shaft end for reassembly reference.

Disassembly – 1) Place axle shaft assembly in soft-jawed vise. Keep axle shaft assembly clean during disassembly and reassembly. Remove CV joint boot bands and slide boot away from CV joint housing. Index mark CV joint housing, tripod assembly and axle shaft for reassembly reference.

2) Using screwdriver, remove large circlip ring from inner race groove in CV joint housing. See Fig. 1. Remove CV joint housing from tripod assembly. Remove snap ring retaining tripod assembly to axle shaft. Using a hammer and soft drift, drive tripod assembly from axle shaft.

3) Wrap axle shaft end with tape. Remove inner CV joint boot. Index mark and remove dynamic damper as necessary. Remove outer CV joint boot bands and remove boot by sliding it off inner CV joint end. Clean and inspect all parts. Ensure axle shaft is not bent, twisted or damaged.

4) Check splines for wear. Inspect tripod bearings for abnormal wear, excessive looseness, seizure, rust or other damage. Replace as necessary.

NOTE: Inner and outer CV joint boots look similar but differ in diameter. Ensure correct boot is installed at proper end when reassembling axle shaft. See Fig. 2. See FRONT AXLE SHAFT BOOT IDENTIFICATION table.

Reassembly – 1) Pack outer CV joint assembly with grease. Wrap tape around axle shaft end and slide outer boot on axle shaft (if removed). Install dynamic damper and band (if removed). Slide inner CV joint boot on axle shaft.

2) Align marks on tripod assembly and axle shaft. Install tripod assembly on axle shaft using hammer and soft drift. Install snap ring. Apply grease to CV joint housing. Align marks on tripod assembly, axle shaft and CV joint housing. Position housing onto tripod assembly and install circlip ring.

3) Remove trapped air by lifting boot off housing with a dull screwdriver. Ensure boot is properly seated. Using NEW boot bands, position bands so when folded down, the direction is opposite axle shaft direction of rotation. Fold boot band back by pulling on end of band with pliers. Lock end of band by bending locking clip.

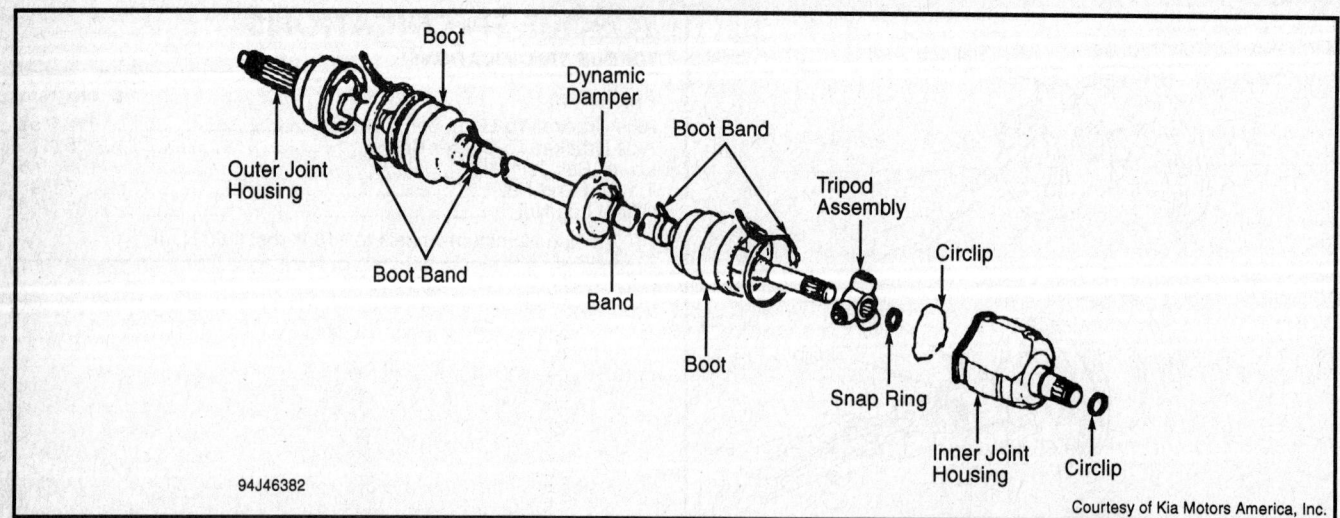

94J46382

Courtesy of Kia Motors America, Inc.

Fig. 1: Exploded View Of Axle Shaft Assembly

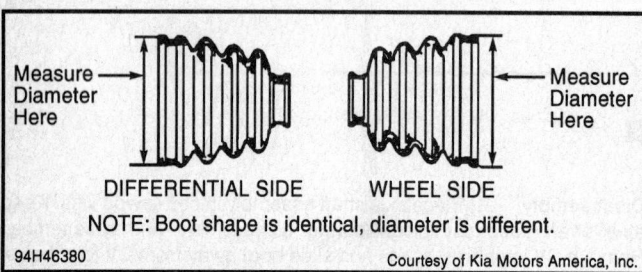

DIFFERENTIAL SIDE   WHEEL SIDE

NOTE: Boot shape is identical, diameter is different.

94H46380   Courtesy of Kia Motors America, Inc.

Fig. 2: Identifying CV Joint Boot Dimensions

FRONT AXLE SHAFT BOOT IDENTIFICATION

Application	In. (mm)
Axle Boot	
Differential Side Diameter	3.26 (82.8)
Wheel Side Diameter	3.36 (85.5)

Installation – 1) Install NEW circlip ring on inner end of axle shaft. Inspect oil seals and sealing surfaces to ensure proper sealing. Replace seals as necessary.

2) Carefully install axle shaft assembly into transaxle so as not to damage oil seal. Pull axle shaft assembly outward to ensure axle shaft assembly is properly seated in transaxle. Pull outward on hub assembly and insert axle shaft into hub. Install NEW axle shaft lock nut.

3) Install lower control arm ball joint on steering knuckle. Install stabilizer bar and tie rod end. Install engine undercover or inner fender shield as equipped. Tighten bolts and nuts to specification. See TORQUE SPECIFICATIONS. Apply brakes and tighten axle shaft lock nut to specification. Stake axle shaft lock nut. Add transaxle fluid or differential fluid as necessary.

TORQUE SPECIFICATIONS
TORQUE SPECIFICATIONS

Application	Ft. Lbs. (N.m)
Axle Shaft Lock Nut	158-206 (214-279)
Lower Control Arm Ball Joint-To-	
Steering Knuckle Nut	32-40 (43-54)
Tie Rod End Nut	21-32 (29-43)
Wheel Lug Nuts	65-87 (88-118)

Lexus FWD

ES300

DESCRIPTION

ES300 uses inner and outer CV joints with a center shaft on right side of vehicle. See Fig. 1. The inner CV joint is a cross-groove type joint. The outer CV joint is a Rzeppa type joint. The CV joints are enclosed by CV joint boots, which maintain lubrication and prevent contaminants from entering joints.

TROUBLE SHOOTING

NOTE: See DRIVE AXLE NOISE DIAGNOSIS in GENERAL INFORMATION at beginning of this section.

REMOVAL, DISASSEMBLY, REASSEMBLY & INSTALLATION

AXLE SHAFTS

Removal – 1) Remove axle shaft lock nut, cap and cotter pin for axle(s) to be removed. Raise and support vehicle. Remove front wheel(s). Remove engine undercover(s) and side cover(s). Drain out gear oil fluid.

2) Disconnect tie rod end from steering knuckle. Disconnect stabilizer bar link from lower arm. Disconnect steering knuckle from lower ball joint. Mark differential, axle shaft and center shaft for reassembly reference. Remove differential-to-axle shaft mounting bolts. Using plastic hammer, disconnect axle shaft from axle hub.

3) Push front axle hub outward, away from axle shaft. Using pry bar, remove left axle shaft. See Fig. 2. Remove right axle shaft bearing lock bolt and snap ring. Remove right axle shaft.

CAUTION: To prevent damage to axle hub bearing, DO NOT subject hub bearing to vehicle weight with axle shaft removed. If vehicle must be moved with axle shaft removed, install a bolt, nut, a small washer (outboard) and a large washer/bearing retainer (inboard) in place of axle shaft.

Disassembly – 1) Check for and record any play or roughness in axle shaft assembly. Using Socket (09923-00020), remove bolts attaching center shaft to axle shaft. Remove joint end cover gasket.

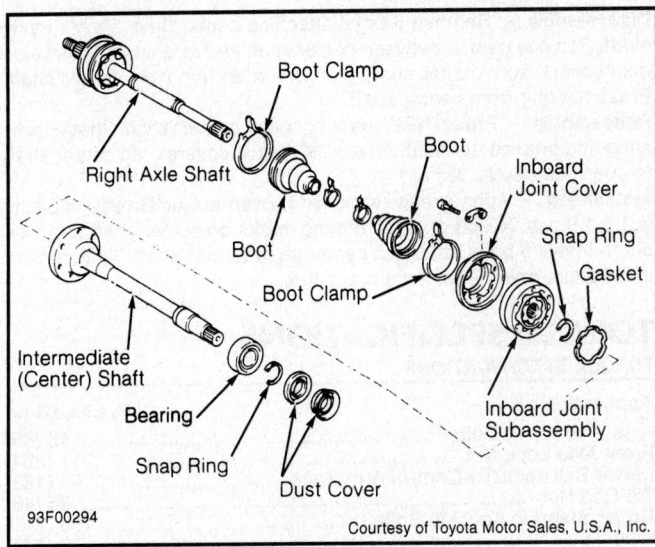

Fig. 1: Exploded View Of FWD Axle Shafts (Right Side Shown; Left Side Is Similar)

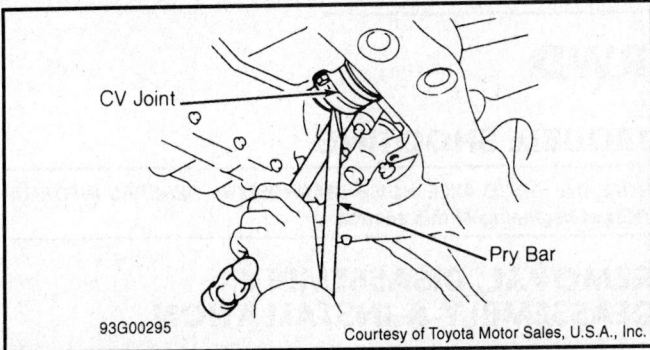

Fig. 2: Removing Left Axle Shaft Assembly From Differential

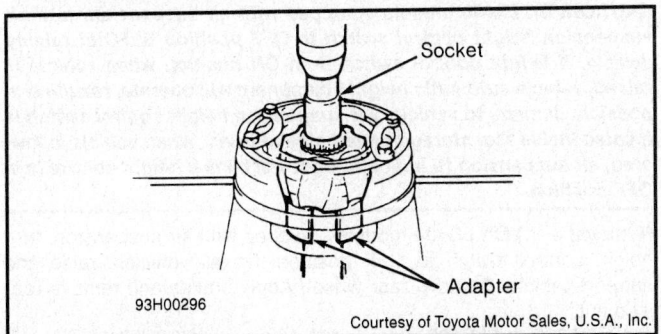

Fig. 3: Pressing Inboard CV Joint From Axle Shaft

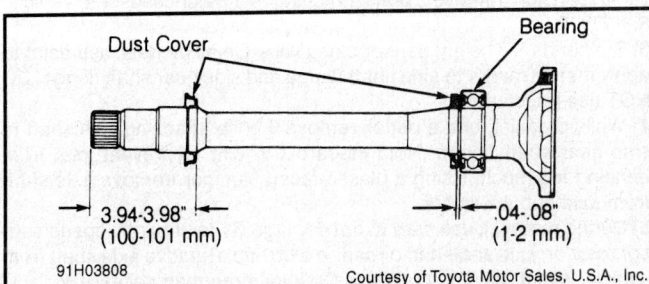

Fig. 4: Installing Bearing & Dust Boot On Center Shaft

2) Install, but do not tighten, nuts to hold inboard joint together. Using a screwdriver, remove inboard and outboard CV joint boot clamps. Use paint to apply mating marks to inboard CV joint and axle shaft. Remove snap ring on end of axle shaft.

3) Using Adapter (SST09726-10010) press inboard CV joint from axle shaft. See Fig. 3. Using a screwdriver and hammer, remove inboard joint from inboard CV joint cover.

4) On left axle shaft, use screwdriver to remove dust cover. On right axle shaft, use press to remove transaxle side dust cover. On all axle shafts, remove snap ring. Use press to remove bearing.

Reassembly – **1)** On right axle shaft, install NEW snap ring on center axle shaft. Using a press, install bearing and dust cover on axle shaft. Ensure clearance between dust cover and bearing is .04-.08" (1-2 mm). See Fig. 4.

2) On left axle shaft assembly, use press to install dust cover. On all axle shafts, wrap axle shaft splines using vinyl tape to protect boot from damage during reassembly. Slide NEW boots and clamps onto axle shaft.

3) Apply grease supplied in overhaul kit. Grease capacity is 4.2-4.6 ozs. (120-130 g). Assemble outboard boot onto outboard joint. Temporarily install 2 boot clamps and inboard CV joint.

4) Apply Sealant (08826-00801) to inboard CV joint cover. See Fig. 5. Align bolt holes and place cover on inboard CV joint. Using a star pattern, tap cover into place using a plastic-faced hammer.

5) Use bolts and nuts to hold inboard joint together. Tighten bolts by hand to prevent scratching flange surface. Align mating marks on axle shaft with inner CV joint. Using a brass bar and hammer, tap inboard CV joint onto axle shaft.

6) Ensure brass bar is touching inner race, not cage. Remove bolts and nuts used to hold CV joint assembly together. Install a NEW snap ring onto end of axle shaft. Use care so outer race does not come off.

7) Assemble inboard CV joint. Apply grease supplied in overhaul kit. Grease capacity is 3.2-3.5 ozs. (90-100 g). Assemble boot clamps on both boots. DO NOT tighten boot clamps at this time. Ensure boots are on shaft groove.

8) Ensure boots are not stretched or contracted when axle shaft is at standard length. See Fig. 6. Standard axle shaft length for left and right axle shaft is 17.80" (452 mm).

Installation – **1)** To install axle shaft, reverse removal procedure. If side gear shaft was removed, install NEW side gear shaft snap ring. Ensure axle shaft end play is same as measured during removal.

2) Check seals at both ends of axle shaft and if necessary replace prior to installation. Lubricate transaxle seal lip with transaxle oil. Install axle shaft into transaxle case.

3) To ensure proper engagement of snap ring, attempt to pull axle shaft out of differential by hand. Install axle shafts into wheel hub. Align reference marks made at removal and tighten nuts. Check wheel alignment.

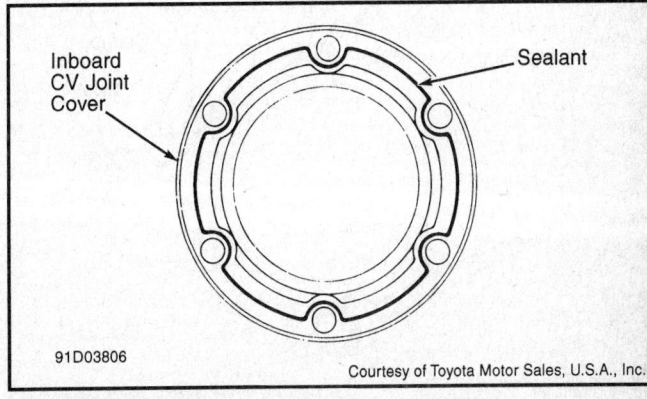

Fig. 5: Applying Sealant To Inboard CV Joint Cover

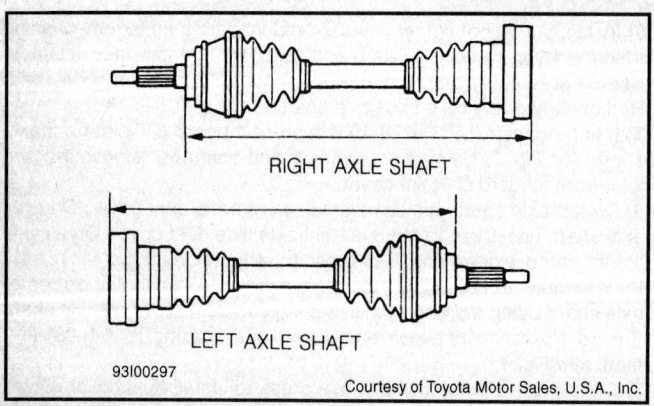

Fig. 6: Measuring Axle Shaft Length

CENTER DRIVE SHAFT

Removal – Raise and support vehicle. Drain some fluid from transaxle. Remove right axle shaft from vehicle. See FWD AXLE SHAFT under REMOVAL, DISASSEMBLY, REASSEMBLY & INSTALLATION.

Disassembly – Remove 6 bolts attaching center drive shaft to axle shaft. Remove gasket between center shaft and axle shaft. Press side dust covers from center shaft. Remove snap ring from center shaft. Press bearing from center shaft.

Reassembly – Press NEW bearing onto center shaft. Install new snap ring onto center shaft. Press NEW dust covers onto center shaft to specified depth. See Fig. 4.

Installation – Apply grease supplied in overhaul kit. Grease capacity is 1.5-1.9 ozs. (43-53 g). Align mating marks on center shaft and axle shaft. Install 6 bolts attaching center shaft to axle shaft. To complete installation, reverse removal procedure.

TORQUE SPECIFICATIONS
TORQUE SPECIFICATIONS

Application	Ft. Lbs. (N.m)
Axle Shaft Joint Bolts	48 (65)
Front Axle Lock Nut	217 (294)
Lower Ball Joint-To-Control Arm Bolts	91 (123)
Tie Rod Nut	36 (49)
Upper Steering Knuckle Bolts	156 (211)
Wheel Lug Nuts	76 (103)

Lexus RWD

GS300, LS400, SC300, SC400
DESCRIPTION

Axle shafts transfer power from differential to driving wheels. All axle shafts consist of a shaft and flexible Constant Velocity (CV) joint at each end. Inboard CV joint is bolted to differential. Outboard CV joint is splined to hub assembly and secured by axle shaft nut. See Fig. 1.

Inboard and outboard CV joints are enclosed by a rubber joint boot. Boot maintains lubrication in the joint and prevents contamination of CV lubricant. Boots must be replaced if leaking or cracked. Inboard CV joint can be repaired without replacing assembly; outboard CV joint must be replaced as an assembly.

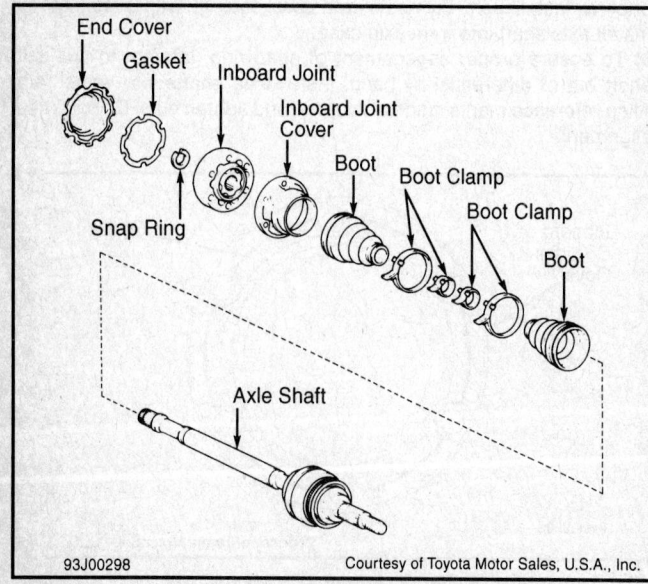

Fig. 1: Exploded View Of RWD Axle Shaft (Typical)

TROUBLE SHOOTING

NOTE: See DRIVE AXLE NOISE DIAGNOSIS in GENERAL INFORMATION at beginning of this section.

REMOVAL, DISASSEMBLY, REASSEMBLY & INSTALLATION

AXLE SHAFTS

CAUTION: On LS400 models equipped with air suspension, turn air suspension height control switch to OFF position BEFORE raising vehicle. If height control switch is in ON position when vehicle is raised, vehicle automatic height adjustment will operate, resulting in possible damage to vehicle. Air suspension height control switch is located inside tool storage on left side of trunk. When vehicle is lowered, air suspension HI indicator light will blink if height control is in OFF position.

Removal – **1)** On LS400 models equipped with air suspension, turn height control switch to OFF position. On all vehicles, raise and support vehicle. Remove rear wheel. Apply brakes and remove rear axle nut.

2) On GS300 and LS400, remove "O" rings supporting tailpipe assembly. Support tailpipe assembly using wire. On models equipped with air suspension, remove 2 bolts attaching rear height sensor to vehicle. See Fig. 2.

3) Suspend rear height sensor using wire. On all models, use paint to apply mating marks to axle shaft flange and side gear shaft flange. DO NOT use punch marks.

4) While pressing brake pedal, remove 6 bolts attaching axle shaft to side gear shaft flange. Hold inboard CV joint to prevent joint from bending too much. Using a plastic-faced hammer, remove axle shaft from axle hub assembly.

5) During removal, use care to not damage CV joint boots, speed sensor rotor on axle shaft and oil seal in axle hub. Remove axle shaft from vehicle. Avoid bending outboard CV joint more than necessary.

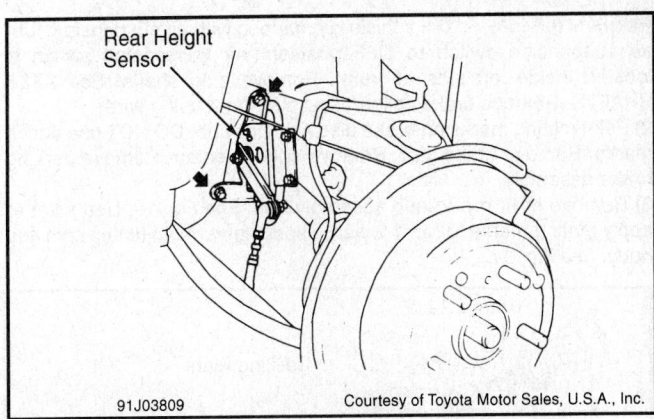

Fig. 2: Locating Rear Air Suspension Height Control Sensor

Disassembly – 1) Place inboard CV joint flange in a soft-jawed vise. Using a screwdriver and hammer, remove end cover gasket. Install bolts, nuts and washers to inboard CV joint to keep it together. Tighten bolts and nuts by hand and avoid scratching flange surface. Using a screwdriver, remove boot clamps. Use paint to apply mating marks on inboard CV joint and axle shaft. DO NOT use punch marks.

2) Remove snap ring on inboard end of axle shaft. Press inboard CV joint from axle shaft. Place inboard CV joint into a soft-jawed vise. Remove CV joint cover from inboard CV joint. Remove CV joint boots.

Reassembly – 1) Assemble inboard CV joint. If mating marks are present, ensure cage and races are correctly aligned. If mating marks are not present, install inner race to cage so that beveled areas are in contact.

2) Install outer race so indented side of outer race is facing in same direction as beveled surface of cage. Align inner race narrow projection with cage wide projection. See Fig. 3.

3) Wrap vinyl tape over axle shaft splines to protect CV joint boots. Temporarily install CV boots and boot clamps. Remove grease from inboard joint-to-cover surface. Apply a .04" (1.0 mm) bead of Sealant (08826-00801) to inboard CV joint cover.

4) Place new gasket on inboard CV joint. Align bolt holes and place cover on inboard CV joint. Loosely install cover bolts. Using a star pattern, tap cover into place using a plastic-faced hammer. See Fig. 4.

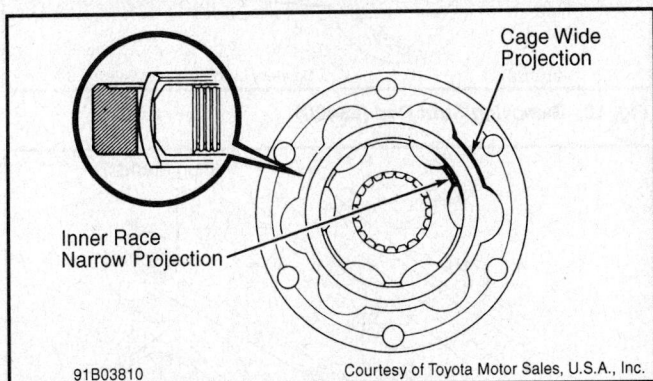

Fig. 3: Assembling Inboard CV Joint

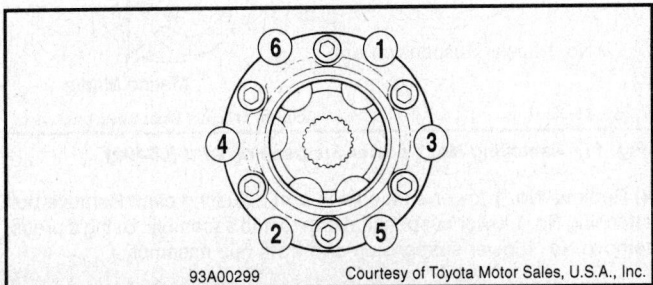

Fig. 4: Inboard Joint Cover Tightening Sequence

5) Align mating marks on axle shaft with inboard CV joint. If mating marks are not present, use alignment procedure described in step **1)**. Using a brass bar and a hammer, tap inboard CV joint onto axle shaft. Ensure brass bar is touching inner race (not cage).

6) Remove bolts and nuts used to hold CV joint assembly together. Install a new snap ring onto end of axle shaft. Use care so outer race does not come off.

7) Install CV boots using grease supplied in overhaul kit. Grease capacity is 3.5-3.9 ozs. (100-110 g). Assemble boot clamps on both boots. DO NOT tighten boot clamps yet. Ensure boots are on shaft groove.

8) Measure axle shaft. See Fig. 5. Ensure axle shaft is correct length. See AXLE SHAFT STANDARD LENGTH table. Ensure boots are not stretched or contracted when axle shaft is at standard length. On SC300, SC400 and GS300, pinch boot clamp using Boot Clamp Tool (09521-24010). Tighten boot clamp until there is .031" (.8 mm) or less clearance. On LS400, bend and lock boot clamp band.

9) On all models, pack end cover with 1.8-1.9 ozs. (50-55 g) of grease. Install end cover with new gasket. Install 6 nuts to boot side of inboard joint. Tighten bolts in a star pattern several times. See Fig. 5. Ensure end cover claw touches inboard joint.

NOTE: End cover may be loose until axle shaft is bolted to differential.

AXLE SHAFT STANDARD LENGTH

Application	Left Side	Right Side
GS300	21.79" (553.5 mm)	23.56" (598.5 mm)
LS400	22.58" (573.5 mm)	24.39" (619.5 mm)
SC300 & SC400	21.79" (553.5 mm)	23.56" (598.5 mm)

Installation – 1) During installation, use care to not damage CV joint boots, speed sensor rotor on axle shaft and oil seal in axle hub. Insert outboard CV joint side into axle hub assembly. Align mating marks made during removal.

2) Lubricate 6 axle shaft bolts. Tighten bolts to specification using a star pattern. See Fig. 4. See TORQUE SPECIFICATIONS. To complete installation, reverse removal procedure.

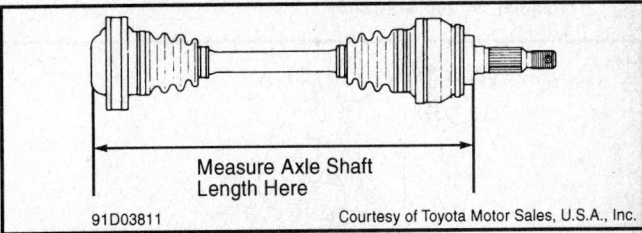

Fig. 5: Measuring Axle Shaft Length

REAR HUB & BEARING ASSEMBLY

Inspection (All Models) – 1) On LS400 models equipped with air suspension, turn height control switch to OFF position. Height control switch is located in tool compartment on left side of trunk. On all vehicles, raise and support vehicle. Remove rear wheel. Remove brake caliper, and support it using wire. Paint match marks on disc brake rotor and axle hub and remove disc brake rotor.

2) Position a dial indicator near center of axle hub and measure backlash in bearing shaft direction. If backlash is greater than .002" (.05 mm) replace bearing.

3) Position a dial indicator on axle hub face near outside of hub bolt and measure axle hub deviation. If axle hub deviation is greater than .0028" (.071 mm), replace axle hub.

Removal (GS300, SC300 & SC400) – 1) Remove axle shafts. See AXLE SHAFTS. Remove brake caliper, and support it using wire.

2) Paint mating marks on brake disc and axle hub. DO NOT use punch marks. Remove parking brake shoe. Remove ABS sensor. Remove 4 outer hub bolts. Remove inner hub bolt.

3) Slide hub and backing plate outward and disconnect parking brake. Remove strut rod. Disconnect parking brake cable and exhaust support brackets. Paint match marks on adjusting cam and rear suspension crossmember. Using Puller (09628-10011), remove No. 1 lower suspension arm. See Fig. 6.

4) Using Puller (09610-20012), remove No. 2 lower suspension arm. See Fig. 7. Using Puller (09628-62011), disconnect upper arm from axle carrier. See Fig. 8. Remove hub assembly.

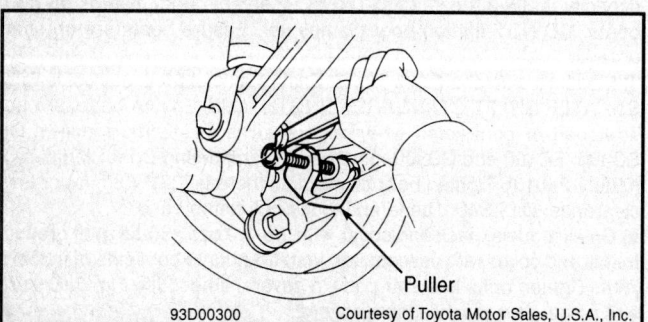

93D00300   Courtesy of Toyota Motor Sales, U.S.A., Inc.

Fig. 6: Removing No. 1 Lower Suspension Arm (GS300, SC300 & SC400)

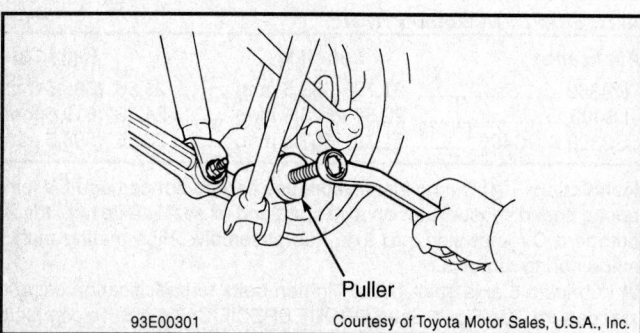

93E00301   Courtesy of Toyota Motor Sales, U.S.A., Inc.

Fig. 7: Removing No. 2 Lower Suspension Arm (GS300, SC300 & SC400)

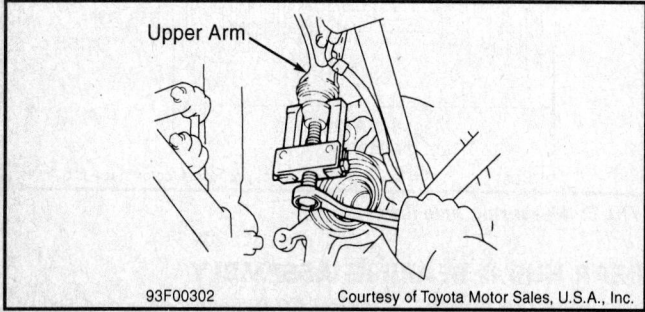

93F00302   Courtesy of Toyota Motor Sales, U.S.A., Inc.

Fig. 8: Removing Upper Arm From Axle Carrier (GS300, SC300 & SC400)

Disassembly – 1) Using a screwdriver, remove dust shield from hub assembly. See Fig. 9. Secure hub assembly in vise. Using Seal Puller (09308-00010) and slide hammer, remove inner oil seal. See Fig. 14. Using bearing puller, remove axle hub. Remove backing plate.

2) Using puller, remove inner race. Remove outer oil seal. Remove bearing snap ring. Temporarily install inner race from axle hub inside bearing assembly. Press bearing from hub assembly.

Reassembly – 1) Using Bearing Replacer (09309-36010) and Seal Installer (09608-32010), press bearing into hub assembly. See Fig. 15. Install bearing snap ring. Install snap ring and outer seal.

2) Temporarily install backing plate onto hub assembly. Install inner bearing race. Press axle hub into hub assembly. Using seal installer, install inner oil seal and dust shield.

Installation – To install, reverse removal procedure. Before tightening suspension bolts to specification, lower vehicle. After tightening suspension bolts to specification, check rear wheel alignment.

Removal (LS400) – 1) If vehicle is equipped with air suspension, turn air suspension switch to OFF position. Air suspension switch is located inside left side of trunk. Remove axle shafts. See AXLE SHAFTS. Remove brake caliper, and support it using wire.

2) Paint mating marks on brake disc and axle hub. DO NOT use punch marks. Remove brake disc. Remove speed sensor. Remove parking brake assembly.

3) Remove strut rod-to-hub assembly bolt. See Fig. 10. Use paint to apply mating marks to No. 1 lower suspension arm adjusting cam and body. See Fig. 11.

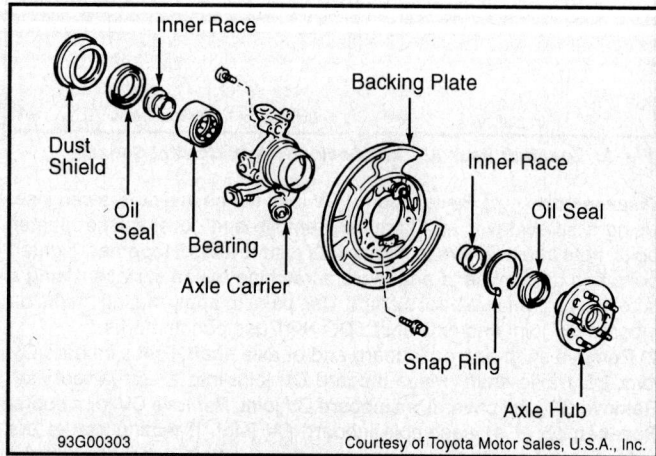

93G00303   Courtesy of Toyota Motor Sales, U.S.A., Inc.

Fig. 9: Exploded View Of Hub Assembly (GS300, SC300 & SC400 Shown; LS400 Is Similar)

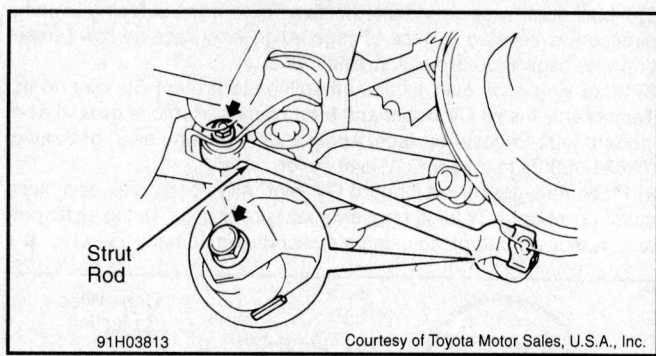

91H03813   Courtesy of Toyota Motor Sales, U.S.A., Inc.

Fig. 10: Removing Strut Rod (LS400)

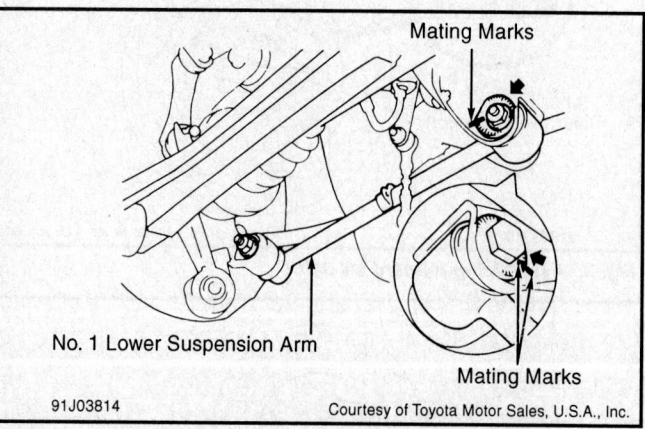

91J03814   Courtesy of Toyota Motor Sales, U.S.A., Inc.

Fig. 11: Removing No. 1 Lower Suspension Arm (LS400)

4) Remove No. 1 lower suspension arm adjusting cam. Remove bolt attaching No. 1 lower suspension arm to hub assembly. Using a press, remove No. 1 lower suspension arm from hub assembly.

5) Disconnect stabilizer bar link from No. 2 lower suspension arm. *See Fig. 12.* Use paint to apply mating marks to No. 2 lower suspension arm adjusting cam and body. Remove No. 2 lower suspension arm adjusting cam. *See Fig. 13.*

6) Loosen, but DO NOT remove, lower shock absorber mounting bolt. Remove 2 upper suspension arm mounting bolts. Remove lower shock absorber mounting bolt. Remove hub assembly with upper suspension arm.

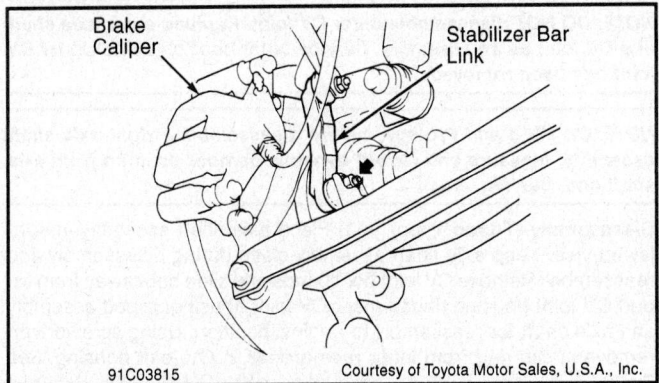

Fig. 12: *Removing Stabilizer Bar Link (LS400)*

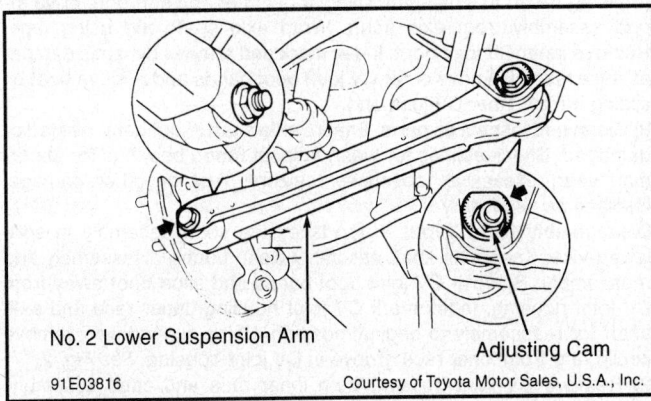

Fig. 13: *Removing No. 2 Lower Suspension Arm (LS400)*

Disassembly – 1) Install 2 nuts and bolt into hub assembly. Secure hub assembly in a vise. Loosen nut attaching upper suspension arm to hub assembly. Loosen nut to end of threads on bolt.

2) Using a hammer, tap end of nut to loosen bolt from hub assembly. Remove upper suspension arm from hub assembly. Using a screwdriver, remove dust shield from hub assembly.

3) Secure hub assembly in a vise. Using a slide hammer, remove inner oil seal. *See Fig. 14.* Remove 2 bolts and nuts from backing plate. Press axle hub from hub assembly. Remove backing plate.

4) Press inner race from axle hub. Using a slide hammer, remove outer oil seal. Remove bearing snap ring. Temporarily install inner race from axle hub inside bearing assembly. Press bearing from hub assembly.

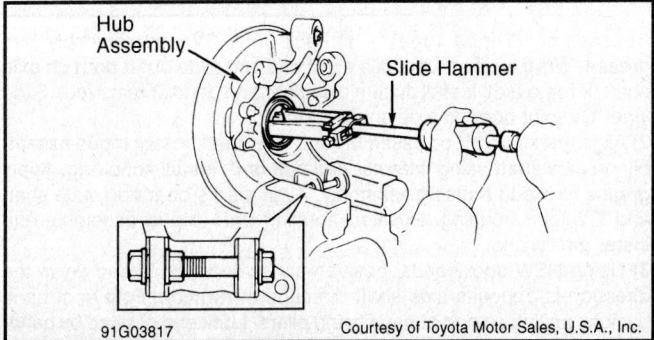

Fig. 14: *Removing Inner Oil Seal*

Reassembly – 1) Place Bearing Replacer (09309-36010) on inboard side of hub assembly. *See Fig. 15.* Press bearing into hub assembly. Install bearing snap ring. Install backing plate onto hub assembly.

2) Install inner bearing race. Install outer bearing race. Install outer oil seal. Press axle hub into hub assembly. Install inner oil seal.

3) Align hole in dust cover with hole in hub assembly. Install dust cover. Secure hub assembly in a vise. Install upper suspension arm to hub assembly. Install a NEW upper suspension nut.

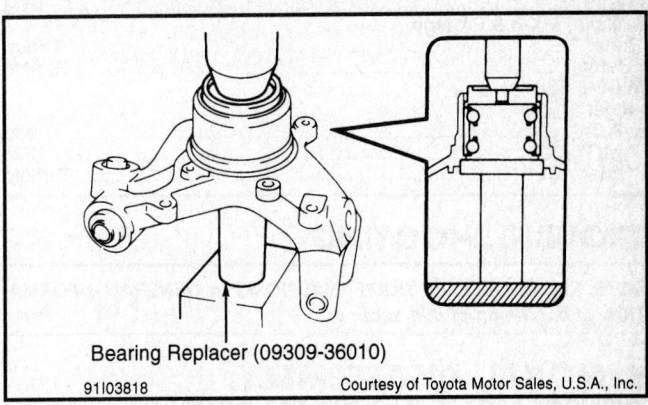

Fig. 15: *Installing Hub Bearing*

Installation – To install, reverse removal procedure. Before tightening suspension bolts to specification, lower vehicle, and turn height control switch to ON position. Bounce vehicle up and down several times to stabilize suspension. Turn height control switch to OFF position and raise vehicle. Tighten suspension nuts and bolts to specification. Check rear wheel alignment.

TORQUE SPECIFICATIONS

TORQUE SPECIFICATIONS

Application	Ft. Lbs. (N.m)
Backing Plate Nuts	
GS300, SC300 & SC400	19 (26)
LS400	43 (58)
Brake Caliper Bolts	77 (104)
Lower Shock Absorber Bolt	101-105 (137-143)
No. 1 Lower Suspension Arm	
Adjusting Cam Nut	
GS300, SC300 & SC400	136 (184)
LS400	58 (78)
No. 1 Lower Suspension	
Arm-To-Hub Assembly Nut	43 (58)
No. 2 Lower Suspension Arm	
Adjusting Cam Nut	
GS300, SC300 & SC400	136 (184)
LS400	58 (78)
No. 2 Lower Suspension	
Arm-To-Hub Assembly Bolt	
GS300, SC300 & SC400	111 (150)
LS400	121 (164)
Rear Axle Lock Nut	213 (289)
Side Gear Shaft-To-Axle Shaft Bolts	61-64 (83-87)
Stabilizer Bar Link Nut	
GS300, SC300 & SC400	32 (44)
LS400	48 (65)
Strut Rod Nuts	136 (184)
Upper Suspension Arm-To-Hub Assembly Nut	80 (108)
Upper Suspension Arm-To-Vehicle Body Nuts	121 (164)
Wheel Lug Nuts	76 (103)
	INCH Lbs. (N.m)
ABS Speed Sensor Bolts	69 (8)
Backing Plate-To-Parking Brake Bolts	69 (8)
Rear Height Sensor Bolts	45 (5)

AXLE SHAFTS
Mazda FWD

Millenia, MPV 4WD, MX-3, MX-6, Protege, 626

DESCRIPTION

CV JOINT IDENTIFICATION

Application	Joint Type
MPV 4WD	
Front	DOJ
Millenia, MX-3 & Protege	
Inner	Tripod
Outer	Birfield
MX-6 & 626	
Inner	
A/T	Tripod
M/T	DOJ
Outer	Birfield

TROUBLE SHOOTING

NOTE: See DRIVE AXLE NOISE DIAGNOSIS in GENERAL INFORMATION at beginning of this section.

REMOVAL, DISASSEMBLY, REASSEMBLY & INSTALLATION

FWD AXLE SHAFT

Removal (MPV 4WD) – 1) Raise vehicle on hoist or support vehicle using stands. Drain differential gear oil. Remove wheel and tire assembly. Remove engine undercover. Raise lock tab on axle shaft lock nut. Apply brakes and remove axle shaft lock nut. Separate tie rod end from steering knuckle using appropriate puller. Remove bolts holding lower control arm ball joint to lower control arm.

2) Carefully insert pry bar between inner CV joint and differential so as not to damage boot or oil seal. Using hammer, lightly tap end of pry bar to unseat inner CV joint assembly from differential. *See Fig. 1.*

3) Remove left axle shaft assembly; then, remove right axle shaft assembly from hub. If axle shaft is stuck to hub, reinstall axle shaft lock nut until flush with end of axle shaft and tap end of axle shaft with brass or plastic hammer.

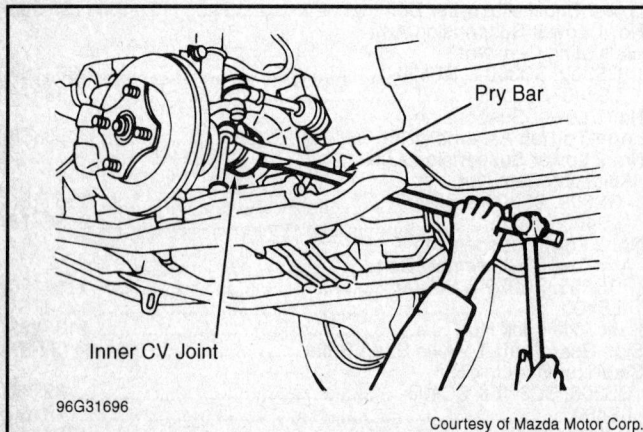

Pry Bar

Inner CV Joint

96G31696

Courtesy of Mazda Motor Corp.

Fig. 1: Prying Axle Shaft From Transaxle, Intermediate Shaft Or Differential

Removal (Except MPV 4WD) – 1) Raise vehicle on hoist or support vehicle with stands. Drain transaxle fluid. Remove wheel and tire assembly. Remove inner fender shield. Raise lock tab on axle shaft lock nut. Apply brakes and remove axle shaft lock nut.

2) Using appropriate puller, separate tie rod end from steering knuckle. On Protege, remove stabilizer bar bushing assembly and disconnect stabilizer bar from lower control arm. On Millenia, MX-3, MX-6 and 626, remove stabilizer bar from stabilizer link and remove stabilizer link from lower control arm. On all models, remove lower control arm ball joint from steering knuckle.

3) Carefully insert pry bar between inner CV joint and transaxle or intermediate shaft so as not to damage boot or oil seal. Using hammer, lightly tap end of pry bar to unseat inner CV joint assembly from transaxle or intermediate shaft. *See Fig. 1.*

4) Remove axle shaft assembly from hub. If axle shaft is stuck to hub, use appropriate bearing puller to push axle shaft assembly from hub or reinstall axle shaft lock nut until flush with end of axle shaft and tap end of axle shaft with brass or plastic hammer.

NOTE: DO NOT disassemble outer CV joint. Replace outer axle shaft and CV joint as an assembly. Service outer boot only after inner CV joint has been removed.

NOTE: On MX-3 and Protege, before disassembling right axle shaft assembly, measure and record dynamic damper position from axle shaft end. See Fig. 4 and 5.

Disassembly (Tripod Type) – 1) Place axle shaft assembly in soft-jawed vise. Keep axle shaft assembly clean during disassembly and reassembly. Remove CV joint boot bands and slide boot away from tripod CV joint housing. Index mark CV joint housing, tripod assembly and axle shaft for reassembly to original position. Using screwdriver, remove circlip ring from inner race groove in CV joint housing. *See Fig. 2.*

2) Remove CV joint housing from tripod assembly. Remove snap ring retaining tripod to axle shaft. Using a hammer and soft drift, drive tripod assembly from axle shaft. Wrap axle shaft end using tape. Remove inner CV joint boot. Index mark and remove dynamic damper as necessary. Remove outer CV joint boot bands and remove boot by sliding it from inner CV joint end.

3) Clean and inspect all parts. Ensure axle shaft is not bent, twisted or damaged. Check splines for wear. Inspect tripod bearings for abnormal wear, excessive looseness, seizure, rust or other damage. Replace as necessary.

Disassembly (DOJ Type) – 1) Place axle shaft assembly in soft-jawed vise. Keep axle shaft assembly clean during disassembly and reassembly. Remove CV joint boot bands and slide boot away from CV joint housing. Index mark CV joint housing, inner race and axle shaft for reassembly to original position. Using screwdriver, remove circlip ring from inner race groove in CV joint housing. *See Fig. 2.*

2) Remove CV joint housing from inner race and cage assembly. Remove snap ring retaining ball, inner race and cage assembly to axle shaft. Insert screwdriver between inner race and cage, and remove balls. Index mark inner race and cage for reassembly to original position. Turn cage approximately 30 degrees to inner race and separate cage from inner race.

3) Wrap axle shaft end with tape. Remove inner CV joint boot. Remove outer CV joint boot bands, and remove boot by sliding it off inner CV joint end. Clean and inspect all parts. Ensure axle shaft is not bent, twisted or damaged. Check splines for wear. Inspect bearing inner race, cage and balls for abnormal wear and replace as an assembly as necessary.

NOTE: Inner and outer CV joint boots differ in design and/or diameter. Ensure correct boot is installed at proper end when reassembling axle shaft. See Fig. 3. See FRONT AXLE BOOT IDENTIFICATION table.

Reassembly (Tripod Type) – 1) Pack outer CV joint assembly with grease. Wrap tape around axle shaft end and slide outer boot on axle shaft (if removed). Install dynamic damper and band (if removed). Slide inner CV joint boot on axle shaft.

2) Align marks on tripod assembly and axle shaft. Install tripod assembly on axle shaft using hammer and soft drift. Install snap ring. Apply grease to tripod housing assembly. Align marks on tripod, axle shaft and CV joint housing. Position housing onto tripod assembly and install circlip ring.

3) Using NEW boot bands, position bands so when folded down the direction is opposite axle shaft direction of rotation. Fold boot band back by pulling on end of band using pliers. Lock end of band by bending locking clip.

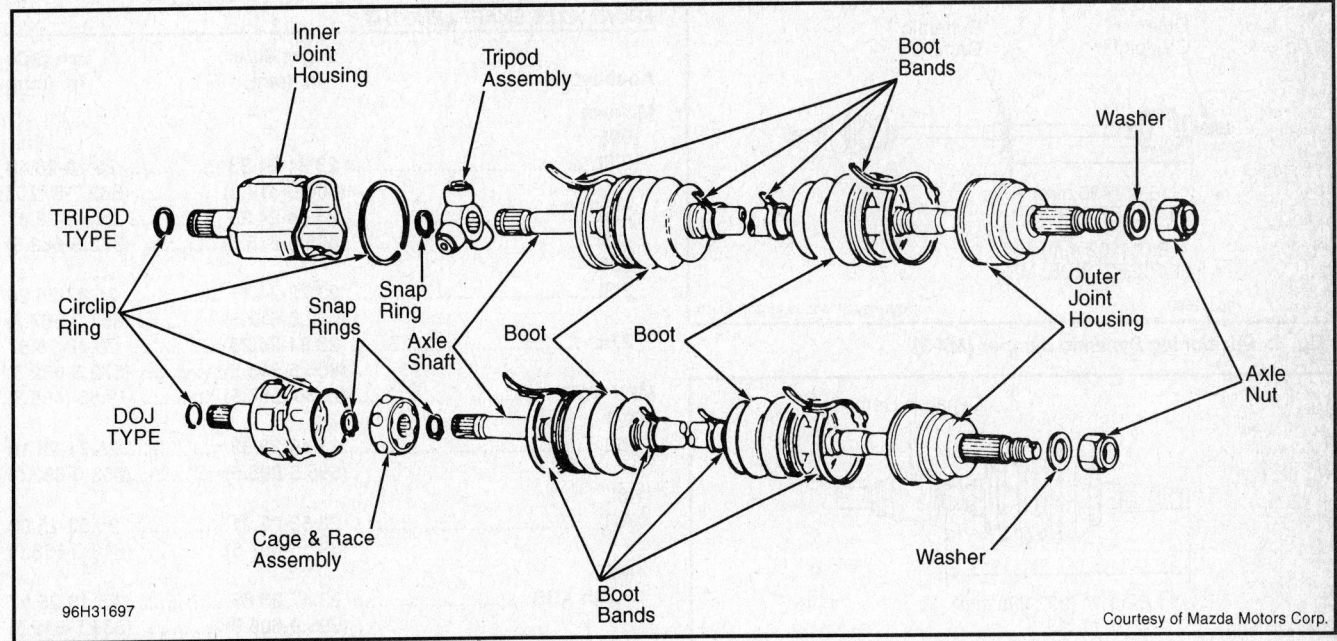

96H31697

Courtesy of Mazda Motors Corp.

Fig. 2: Exploded View Of Axle Assemblies (DOJ & Tripod)

Reassembly (DOJ Type) – 1) Pack outer CV joint assembly with grease. Wrap tape around axle shaft end and slide outer boot on axle shaft (if removed). Slide inner CV joint boot on axle shaft.

2) Install inner race into cage and turn cage approximately 30 degrees to inner race aligning marks made during disassembly. Insert balls through cage and seat in grooves of inner race. Pack ball, inner race and cage assembly with grease. Align marks on inner race and axle shaft. Install ball, inner race and cage assembly on axle shaft with large side of cage facing axle shaft end. Install snap ring.

3) Align marks on inner race, axle shaft and CV joint housing. Position housing onto ball, inner race and cage assembly and install circlip ring. Using NEW boot bands, position bands so when folded down, the direction is opposite axle shaft direction of rotation. Fold boot band back by pulling on end of band with pliers. Lock end of band by bending locking clip.

NOTE: For front axle shaft lengths, see FRONT AXLE SHAFT LENGTHS table.

NOTE: Before installing right axle shaft assembly on MX-3 or Protege, ensure dynamic damper is installed in proper position and at proper distance from CV joint end. See Fig. 4 or 5.

Installation (All Models) – 1) Install NEW circlip ring on inner end of axle shafts. Inspect oil seals and sealing surfaces to ensure proper sealing. Replace seals as necessary.

2) Carefully install axle shaft assembly into transaxle, intermediate shaft or differential so as not to damage oil seal. Pull axle shaft assembly outward to ensure axle shaft assembly is properly seated in transaxle, intermediate shaft or differential. Pull outward on hub assembly and insert axle shaft into hub. Install NEW axle shaft lock nut.

3) Install lower control arm ball joint on steering knuckle. Install stabilizer bar and tie rod end. Install engine undercover or inner fender shield as equipped. Tighten bolts and nuts to specification. See TORQUE SPECIFICATIONS. Apply brakes and tighten axle shaft lock nut to specification. Stake axle shaft lock nut. Add transaxle fluid or differential gear oil as necessary.

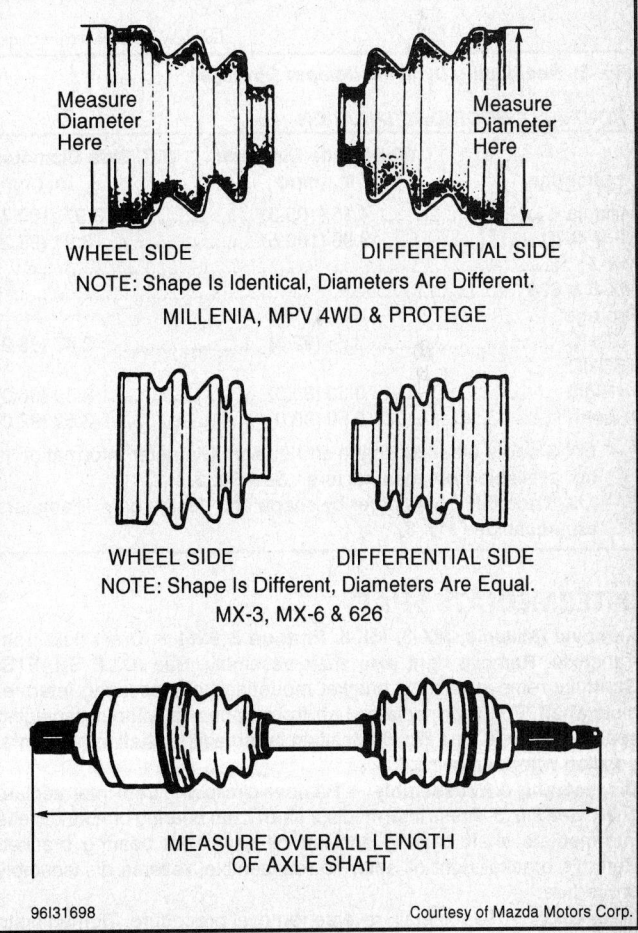

96I31698

Courtesy of Mazda Motors Corp.

Fig. 3: Identifying Axle & Boot Dimensions

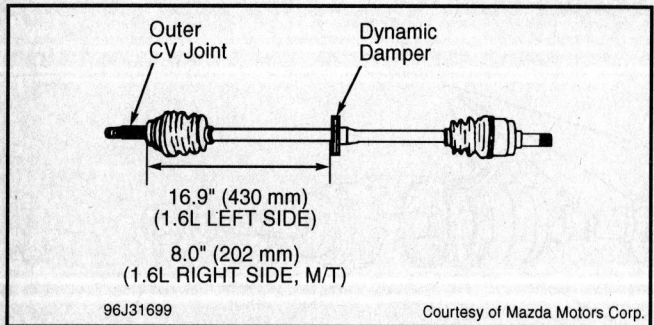

Fig. 4: Positioning Dynamic Damper (MX-3)

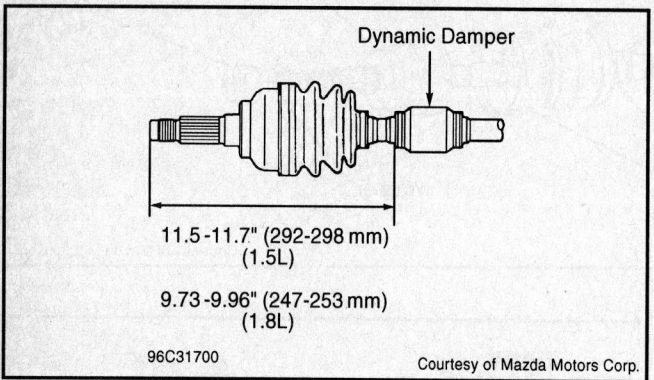

Fig. 5: Positioning Dynamic Damper (Protege)

FRONT AXLE BOOT IDENTIFICATION

Application	Wheel Side Diameter In. (mm)	Diff. Side Diameter In. (mm)
Millenia	4.15 (105.3)	3.97 (100.7)
MPV 4WD	3.96 (100.5)	3.91 (99.2)
MX-3	[1]	[1]
MX-6 & 626	[2]	[3]
Protege		
DOHC	3.64 (92.4)	3.47 (88.2)
SOHC		
Right	3.50 (89.0)	3.39 (86.0)
Left	3.50 (89.0)	3.62 (92.0)

[1] – MX-3 boots differ by shape and design. Diameter information is not available from manufacturer. *See Fig. 3.*

[2] – MX-6 and 626 boots differ by shape and design only. Diameters are equal. *See Fig. 3.*

INTERMEDIATE SHAFT

Removal (Millenia, MX-3, MX-6, Protege & 626) – Drain fluid from transaxle. Remove right axle shaft assembly. See AXLE SHAFTS. Carefully remove bearing bracket mounting bolts securing intermediate shaft. Pull intermediate shaft from transaxle without damaging seal in transaxle. *See Fig. 6.* Maintain intermediate shaft in horizontal position when removing.

Disassembly & Reassembly – Remove circlip ring from intermediate shaft. *See Fig. 5.* Press intermediate shaft from bearing bracket. Press intermediate shaft bearing and left oil seal from bearing bracket. Remove bracket right oil seal. To reassemble, reverse disassembly procedure.

Installation – To reinstall, reverse removal procedure. Tighten bolts to specification. See TORQUE SPECIFICATIONS table.

FRONT AXLE SHAFT LENGTHS [1]

Application	Right Side In. (mm)	Left Side In. (mm)
Millenia		
1995		
2.3L	23.94-24.33 (608.0-618.0)	26.10-26.48 (662.7-672.7)
2.5L	23.84-24.23 (605.5-615.5)	26.48-26.87 (672.5-682.5)
1996		
2.3L	23.72-24.11 (602.5-612.5)	25.87-26.26 (657.2-667.2)
2.5L	23.84-24.23 (605.5-615.5)	26.48-26.87 (672.5-682.5)
MPV 4WD	22.30 (566.5)	19.63 (498.5)
MX-3		
1.6L	23.45-23.83 (595.5-605.5)	25.71-26.10 (653.0-663.0)
1.8L		
A/T	23.53-23.91 (597.5-607.5)	25.52-25.90 (648.0-658.0)
M/T		
With ABS	23.47-23.85 (595.9-605.9)	25.18-25.57 (639.5-649.5)
Without ABS	23.47-23.85 (595.9-605.9)	25.02-25.41 (635.5-645.5)
MX-6 & 626		
Automatic Transaxle		
2.0L Engine	23.75-24.13 (603.1-613.1)	27.39-27.77 (695.5-705.5)
2.5L Engine	23.75-24.13 (603.1-613.1)	25.74-26.12 (653.6-663.6)
Manual Transaxle		
2.0L Engine	23.63-24.02 (600.2-610.2)	25.56-25.95 (649.2-659.2)
2.5L Engine	23.65-24.04 (600.7-610.7)	25.62-26.01 (650.7-660.7)
Protege		
Automatic Transaxle		
1.5L Engine	23.44-23.84 (595.5-605.5)	25.57-25.96 (649.5-659.5)
1.8L Engine	25.22-25.61 (640.5-650.5)	25.48-25.88 (647.3-657.3)
Manual Transaxle		
1.5L Engine	23.44-23.84 (595.5-605.5)	25.73-26.12 (653.5-663.5)
1.8L Engine	25.22-25.61 (640.5-650.5)	24.94-25.33 (633.4-643.4)

[1] – Measurement is overall length of drive axle shaft. *See Fig. 3.*

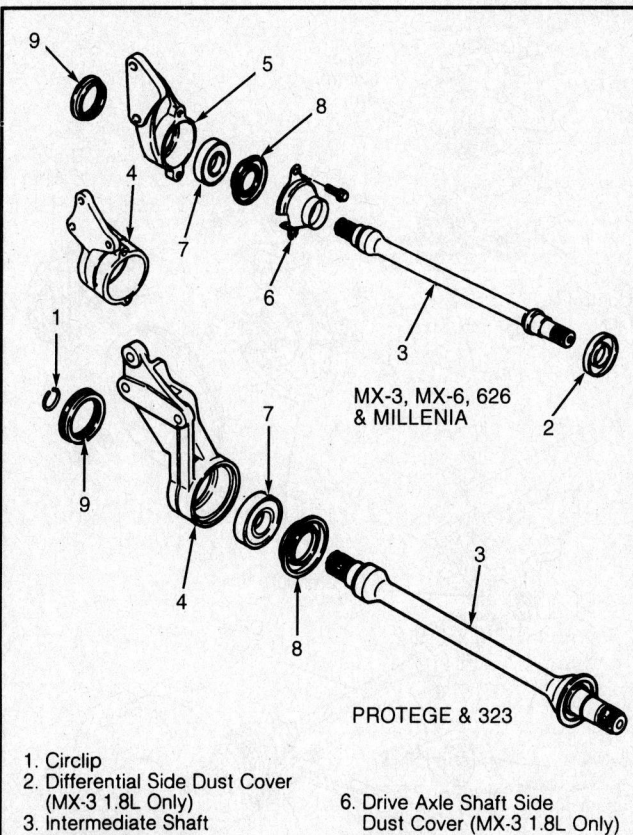

1. Circlip
2. Differential Side Dust Cover (MX-3 1.8L Only)
3. Intermediate Shaft
4. Bearing Bracket
5. Bearing Bracket (MX-3 1.8L Only)
6. Drive Axle Shaft Side Dust Cover (MX-3 1.8L Only)
7. Bearing
8. Differential Side Oil Seal
9. Drive Axle Shaft Side Oil Seal

94I46191

Courtesy of Mazda Motors Corp.

Fig. 6: Exploded View Of Intermediate Shaft

TORQUE SPECIFICATIONS
TORQUE SPECIFICATIONS

Application	Ft. Lbs. (N.m)
Millenia	
Axle Shaft Lock Nut	174-235 (235-319)
Intermediate Shaft Bearing Bracket Bolts	31-46 (42-62)
Upper Lateral Link Ball Joint Nut	41-59 (50-80)
Lower Control Arm Ball Joint-To Steering Knuckle Nut	58-86 (79-116)
Stabilizer Bar-To-Stabilizer Link Nut	32-45 (43-61)
Tie Rod End Nut	31-42 (42-57)
Wheel Lug Nuts	65-87 (88-118)
MPV 4WD	
Axle Shaft Lock Nut	174-231 (236-314)
Engine Undercover Bolts	12-17 (16-23)
Lower Control Arm	
Ball Joint-To-Control Arm Bolts (2)	75-101 (102-137)
Ball Joint-To-Control Arm Through Bolt Nut	94-127 (128-172)
Ball Joint-To-Steering Knuckle Nut	116-138 (157-187)
Stabilizer Bar Nut	[3]
Tie Rod End Nut	43-58 (58-78)
Wheel Lug Nuts	65-87 (88-118)
MX-3	
Axle Shaft Lock Nut	174-235 (235-319)
Intermediate Shaft Bearing Bracket Bolts	31-46 (42-62)
Lower Control Arm Ball Joint-To Steering Knuckle Nut	32-43 (43-58)
Stabilizer Bar-To-Stabilizer Link Nut	32-45 (43-61)
Stabilizer Link-To-Lower Control Arm Nut	31-42 (42-57)
Tie Rod End Nut	31-42 (42-57)
Wheel Lug Nuts	65-87 (88-118)
MX-6 & 626	
Axle Shaft Lock Nut	174-235 (236-319)
Intermediate Shaft Bearing Bracket	31-46 (42-62)
Lower Control Arm Ball Joint-To Steering Knuckle Nut	27-40 (37-54)
Stabilizer Bar-To-Stabilizer Nut	27-39 (37-53)
Stabilizer Link-To-Lower Control Arm Nut	27-39 (37-53)
Tie Rod End Nut	24-32 (32-43)
Wheel Lug Nut	65-87 (88-118)
Protege	
Axle Shaft Lock Nut	174-235 (235-319)
Intermediate Shaft Bearing Bracket Bolts	31-46 (42-62)
Lower Control Arm Ball Joint-To Steering Knuckle Nut	32-43 (43-58)
Stabilizer Bar Nut	[4]
Tie Rod End Nut	31-42 (42-57)
Wheel Lug Nuts	65-87 (88-118)
	INCH Lbs. (N.m)
Inner Fender Shield Bolts (MX-3, MX-6, Protege & 626)	69-95 (7.8-11)

[1] – Tighten axle shaft lock nut during wheel bearing preload adjustment.
[2] – Tighten stabilizer bolt until distance from top of bolt to top of nut is .55-.73" (14.0-18.5 mm).
[3] – Tighten stabilizer bolt until distance from top of bolt to top of nut is .24" (6.0 mm).
[4] – Tighten stabilizer bolt until distance from top of bolt to top of nut is .67-.75" (17.0-19.0 mm).

AXLE SHAFTS
Mazda RWD

Miata, RX7, 929

NOTE: Information in this article applies only to models with independent rear suspension.

DESCRIPTION

CV JOINT IDENTIFICATION

Application	Joint Type
Miata & 929	DOJ
RX7	Tripod

TROUBLE SHOOTING

NOTE: See DRIVE AXLE NOISE DIAGNOSIS in GENERAL INFORMATION at beginning of this section.

REMOVAL, DISASSEMBLY, REASSEMBLY & INSTALLATION

AXLE SHAFTS

Removal (Miata) – **1)** Raise vehicle and support with safety stands. Remove wheel and tire assembly. Loosen drive axle shaft lock nut until flush with end of drive axle shaft. Mark differential and drive axle shaft flanges for installation reference.

2) Remove lower control arm bolt at knuckle, and pull knuckle/hub assembly outward. Using pry bar between differential housing and inner CV joint, remove inner CV joint from differential. Remove drive axle shaft from knuckle/hub assembly. If drive axle shaft is stuck in knuckle/hub assembly, use plastic or soft-faced hammer to tap drive axle shaft from knuckle/hub assembly. Remove drive axle shaft lock nut.

Removal (RX7) – **1)** Raise vehicle and support with safety stands. Remove wheel and tire assembly. Loosen drive axle shaft lock nut until flush with end of drive axle shaft.

2) Remove I-arm bolt, and pull knuckle/hub assembly outward. *See Fig. 1.* Remove inner CV joint from differential. Remove drive axle shaft from knuckle/hub assembly. If drive axle shaft is stuck in knuckle/hub assembly, use plastic or soft-faced hammer to tap drive axle shaft from knuckle/hub assembly. Remove drive axle shaft lock nut and washer.

Removal (929) – **1)** Raise vehicle and support with safety stands. Remove wheel and tire assembly. Loosen drive axle shaft lock nut until flush with end of drive axle shaft.

2) Remove exhaust pipe. *See Fig. 2.* Using appropriate ball joint puller, separate rear lower lateral link from hub support assembly. Remove drive shaft from differential. Remove upper and lower lateral links from subframe. Remove stabilizer bar from stabilizer link.

3) Mark differential and drive axle shaft flanges for installation reference. Support differential and subframe using jack. Remove drive axle shaft flange nuts. Remove subframe mounting nuts and washers. Lower subframe and differential about 4" (102 mm).

4) Remove inner CV joint from differential flange. Remove drive axle shaft from hub assembly. If drive axle shaft is stuck in hub assembly, use plastic or soft-faced hammer to tap drive axle shaft from hub assembly. Remove drive axle shaft lock nut and washer.

NOTE: DO NOT disassemble outer CV joint. Replace drive axle shaft and outer CV joint as an assembly. Service outer boot only after inner CV joint has been removed.

Disassembly (DOJ Type) – **1)** Place drive axle shaft assembly in soft-jawed vise. Keep drive axle shaft assembly clean during disassembly and reassembly. Remove CV joint boot bands and slide boot away from CV joint housing. Index mark CV joint housing, inner race and drive axle shaft for reassembly reference. Using screwdriver, remove large circlip ring from inner race groove in CV joint housing. *See Fig. 3.*

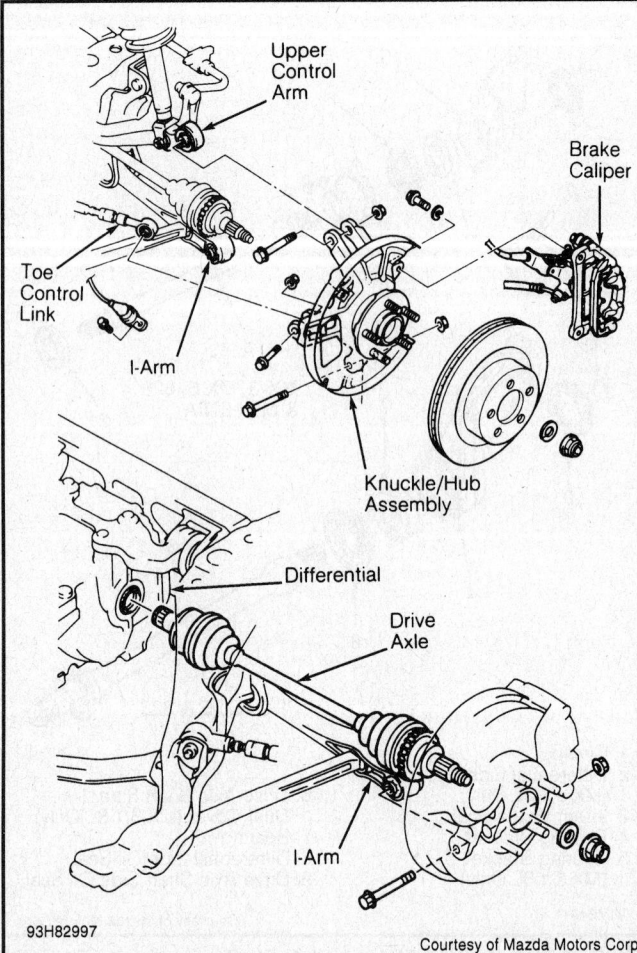

Fig. 1: Removing Rear Drive Axle & Knuckle/Hub Assembly (RX7)

2) Remove CV joint housing from ball, inner race and cage assembly. Remove snap ring retaining ball, inner race and cage assembly to drive axle shaft. Remove ball, inner race and cage assembly from drive axle shaft. Insert screwdriver between inner race and cage, and remove balls. Index mark inner race and cage for reassembly reference. Turn cage about 30 degrees to inner race and separate cage from inner race.

3) Wrap drive axle shaft end with tape. Remove inner CV joint boot. Remove outer CV joint boot bands and remove boot by sliding it off inner CV joint end. Clean and inspect all parts. Ensure drive axle shaft is not bent, twisted or damaged. Check splines for wear. Inspect bearing inner race, cage and balls for abnormal wear and replace as an assembly if necessary.

Disassembly (Tripod Type) – **1)** Place drive axle shaft assembly in soft-jawed vise. Keep drive axle shaft assembly clean during disassembly and reassembly. Remove CV joint boot bands and slide boot away from CV joint housing. Index mark CV joint housing, tripod assembly and drive axle shaft for reassembly reference. Using screwdriver, remove large circlip ring from inner race groove in CV joint housing. *See Fig. 3.*

2) Remove CV joint housing from tripod assembly. Remove snap ring retaining tripod assembly to drive axle shaft. Using a hammer and soft drift, drive tripod assembly from drive axle shaft. Wrap drive axle shaft end with tape. Remove inner CV joint boot. Remove outer CV joint boot bands and remove boot by sliding it off inner CV joint end.

3) Clean and inspect all parts. Ensure drive axle shaft is not bent, twisted or damaged. Check splines for wear. Inspect tripod bearings for abnormal wear, excessive looseness, seizure, rust or other damage. Replace as necessary.

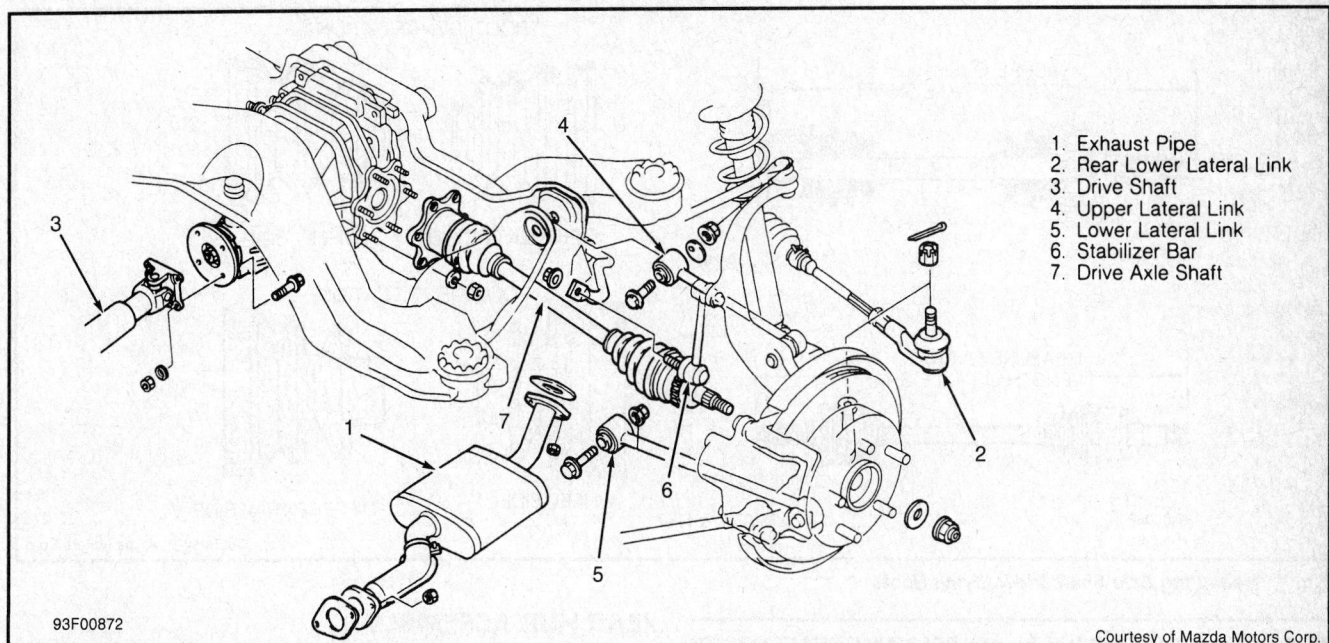

1. Exhaust Pipe
2. Rear Lower Lateral Link
3. Drive Shaft
4. Upper Lateral Link
5. Lower Lateral Link
6. Stabilizer Bar
7. Drive Axle Shaft

93F00872

Courtesy of Mazda Motors Corp.

Fig. 2: Removing Rear Drive Axle Shaft (929)

NOTE: Inner and outer CV joint boots differ in design and/or diameter. Ensure correct boot is installed at proper location when reassembling drive axle shaft. See Fig. 4. See REAR AXLE SHAFT BOOT IDENTIFICATION table.

Reassembly (DOJ Type) – 1) Pack outer CV joint assembly with grease. Wrap tape around drive axle shaft end and slide outer boot onto drive axle shaft (if removed). Slide inner CV joint boot onto drive axle shaft.
2) Install inner race into cage and turn cage approximately 30 degrees to inner race aligning marks made during disassembly. Insert balls through cage and seat them in grooves of inner race. Pack ball, inner race and cage assembly with grease. Align marks on inner race and drive axle shaft. Install ball, inner race and cage assembly on drive axle shaft with large side of cage facing drive axle shaft end. Install snap ring.

3) Apply grease to CV joint housing. Align marks on inner race, drive axle shaft and CV joint housing. Position housing onto ball, inner race and cage assembly and install large circlip ring. Using NEW boot bands, position bands so when folded down, the direction is opposite drive axle shaft direction of rotation. Fold boot band back by pulling on end of band with pliers. Lock end of band by bending locking clip.
Reassembly (Tripod Type) – 1) Pack outer CV joint assembly with grease. Wrap tape around drive axle shaft end and slide outer boot on drive axle shaft (if removed). Slide inner CV joint boot on drive axle shaft.
2) Align marks on tripod assembly and drive axle shaft. Install tripod assembly on drive axle shaft using hammer and soft drift. Install snap ring. Apply grease to CV joint housing. Align marks on tripod assembly, drive axle shaft and CV joint housing. Position housing onto tripod assembly and install circlip ring.
3) Using NEW boot bands, position bands so when folded down, the direction is opposite drive axle shaft direction of rotation. Fold boot band back by pulling on end of band with pliers. Lock end of band by bending locking clip.

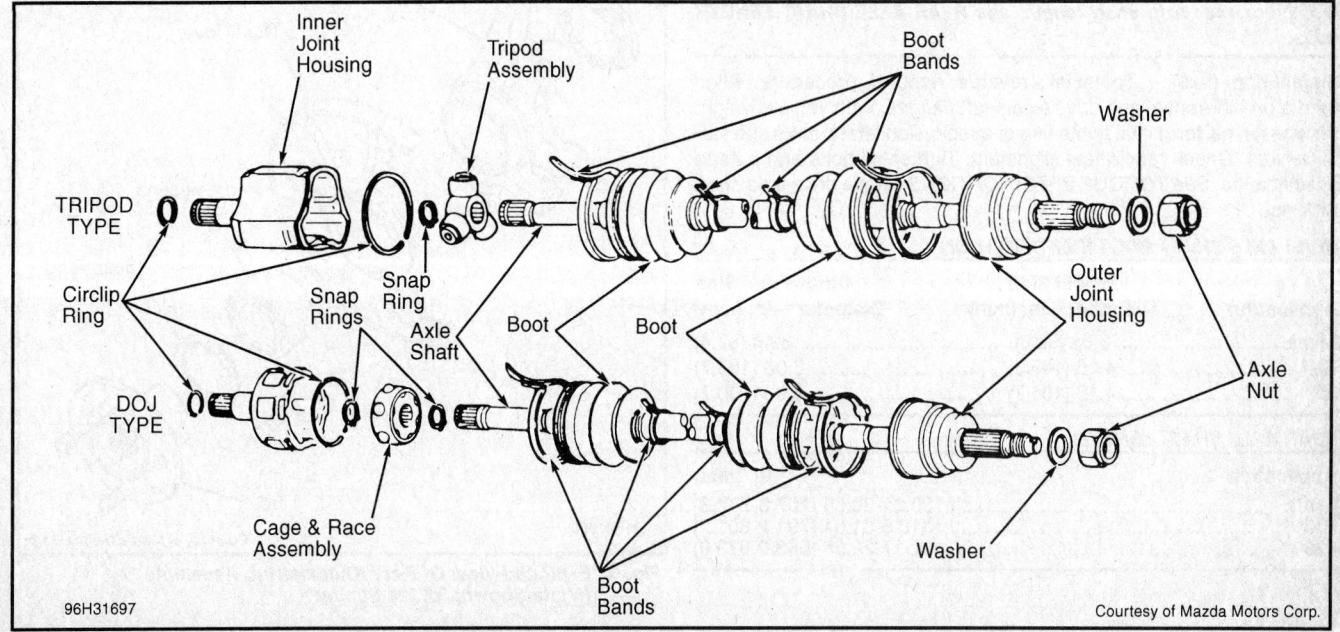

96H31697

Courtesy of Mazda Motors Corp.

Fig. 3: Exploded View Of Axle Shaft Assemblies (DOJ & Tripod)

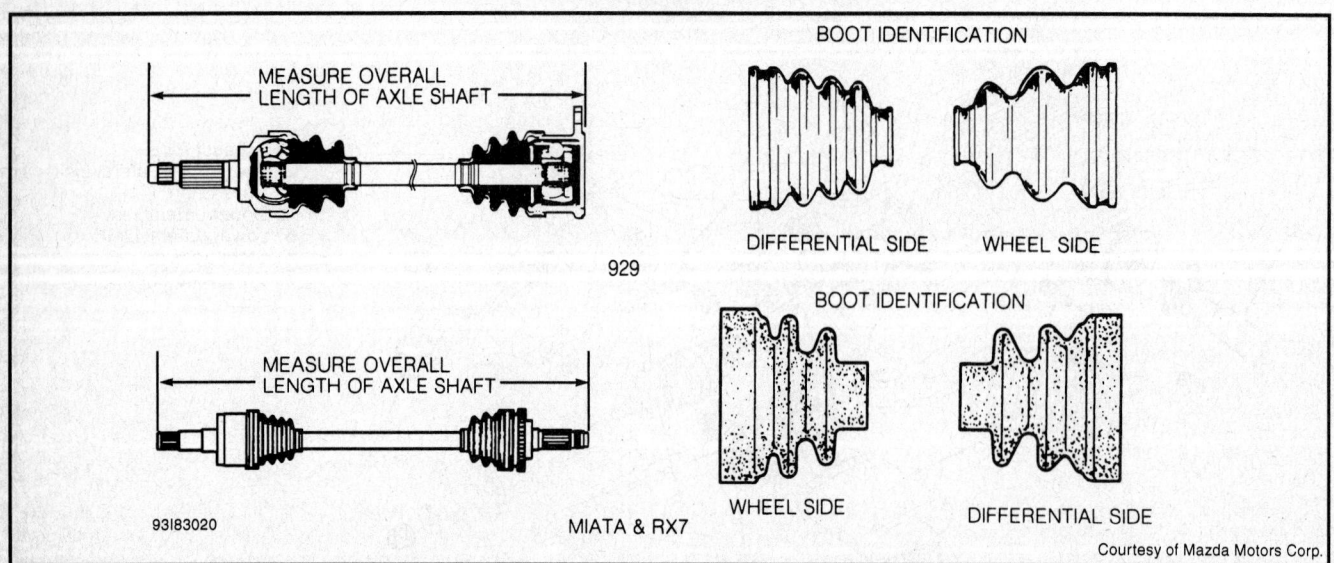

MEASURE OVERALL
LENGTH OF AXLE SHAFT

929

BOOT IDENTIFICATION

DIFFERENTIAL SIDE   WHEEL SIDE

BOOT IDENTIFICATION

MEASURE OVERALL
LENGTH OF AXLE SHAFT

93I83020   MIATA & RX7

WHEEL SIDE   DIFFERENTIAL SIDE

Courtesy of Mazda Motors Corp.

Fig. 4: Measuring Axle Shaft & Identifying Boots

NOTE: For rear axle shaft lengths, see REAR AXLE SHAFT LENGTH table.

Installation (Miata) – To install, reverse removal procedure. Check rear wheel alignment. Tighten all bolts and nuts to specification. See TORQUE SPECIFICATIONS. Stake drive axle shaft lock nut.

NOTE: For rear axle shaft length, see REAR AXLE SHAFT LENGTH table.

Installation (RX7) – 1) To install, reverse removal procedure. Measure outside diameter of snap ring on inner drive axle shaft. Diameter should be a maximum of 1.26" (32 mm). Replace snap ring if measurement exceeds specification. Ensure ends of snap ring are facing upward when installing drive axle shaft into differential.
2) Carefully install drive axle shaft assembly into differential so as not to damage oil seal. Pull drive axle shaft assembly outward to ensure drive axle shaft assembly is properly seated in differential. Check rear wheel alignment. Tighten all bolts and nuts to specification. See TORQUE SPECIFICATIONS. Stake drive axle shaft lock nut.

NOTE: For rear axle shaft length, see REAR AXLE SHAFT LENGTH table.

Installation (929) – To install, reverse removal procedure. Align marks on differential and drive axle shaft flanges. With vehicle weight on wheels, perform final tightening of suspension lateral links and stabilizer bar. Check rear wheel alignment. Tighten all bolts and nuts to specification. See TORQUE SPECIFICATIONS. Stake drive axle shaft lock nut.

REAR AXLE SHAFT BOOT IDENTIFICATION

Application	Wheel Side Diameter – In. (mm)	Differential Side Diameter – In. (mm)
Miata	3.58 (90.8)	3.44 (87.4)
RX7	4.15 (105.3)	3.96 (100.7)
929	4.16 (105.7)	3.96 (100.7)

REAR AXLE SHAFT LENGTH

Application	In. (mm)
Miata	30.21-30.60 (767.3-777.3)
RX7	31.15-31.54 (791.2-801.2)
929	22.17-22.55 (563.0-573.0)

REAR HUB ASSEMBLY

Removal & Disassembly (Miata) – 1) Raise vehicle and support with safety stands. Remove wheel and tire assembly. Remove brake caliper and support aside. Remove rotor from hub.
2) Mount dial indicator on hub and measure wheel bearing play by pulling and pushing on hub. Wheel bearing play should be a maximum of .002" (.05 mm). Check and adjust drive axle shaft lock nut torque or replace wheel bearing if measurement exceeds specification.
3) Remove drive axle shaft lock nut. Remove ABS speed sensor and bracket from knuckle/hub assembly. Remove upper and lower control arm bolts retaining knuckle/hub assembly. Remove knuckle/hub assembly from vehicle. If drive axle shaft is stuck in hub, use plastic or soft-faced hammer to tap drive axle shaft from hub assembly.
4) Pry inner seal from knuckle/hub assembly. See Fig. 5. Using puller, remove hub from knuckle. Remove snap ring retaining bearing. Using Press bearing from knuckle.

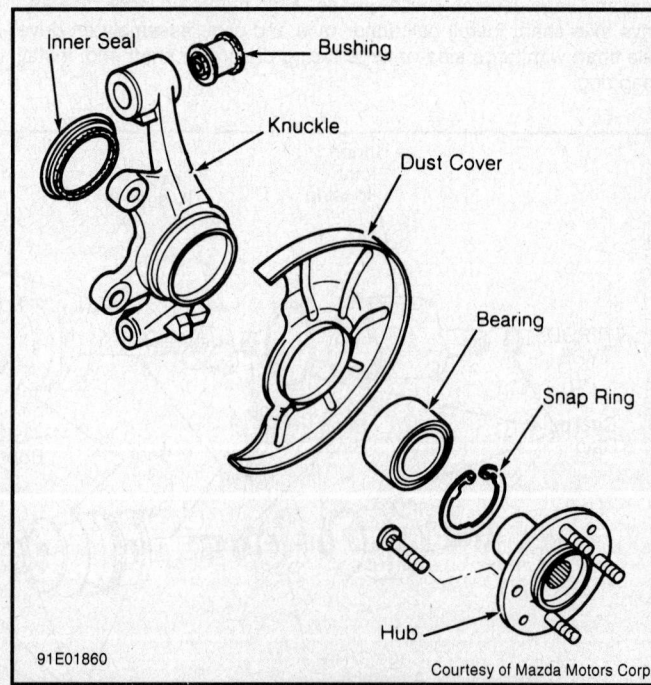

Inner Seal   Bushing   Knuckle   Dust Cover   Bearing   Snap Ring   Hub

91E01860   Courtesy of Mazda Motors Corp.

Fig. 5: Exploded View Of Rear Knuckle/Hub Assembly (Miata Shown; RX7 Is Similar)

5) Move inner bearing race away from hub using chisel and hammer. Using puller, press inner bearing race from hub. DO NOT reuse wheel bearing.

6) Inspect all components for cracks, wear and damage. Replace components as necessary. DO NOT reuse dust cover (if removed). If replacing dust cover, mark location on knuckle and original dust cover for NEW dust cover installation reference.

NOTE: Never press or chisel brake dust cover from knuckle/hub unless replacing cover. DO NOT reuse wheel bearing if it is removed from knuckle/hub.

Reassembly & Installation (Miata) – 1) Press NEW dust cover onto knuckle (align reference marks made from original dust cover). Press NEW wheel bearing into knuckle. Install snap ring.

2) Apply grease to inner bearing race. Press hub into knuckle and install inner seal. Lubricate inner seal lip. Reverse removal procedure to install knuckle/hub assembly. Check rear wheel alignment. Tighten all bolts and nuts to specification. See TORQUE SPECIFICATIONS. Stake drive axle shaft lock nut.

Removal & Disassembly (RX7) – 1) Raise vehicle and support with safety stands. Remove wheel and tire assembly. Remove brake caliper and support aside. *See Fig. 1.* Remove rotor from hub.

2) Mount dial indicator on hub and measure wheel bearing play by pulling and pushing on hub. Wheel bearing play should be a maximum of .002" (.05 mm). Check and adjust drive axle shaft lock nut torque or replace wheel bearing if measurement exceeds specification.

3) Remove drive axle shaft lock nut and washer. Remove ABS speed sensor from knuckle/hub assembly. Remove upper control arm, I-arm and toe control link bolts retaining knuckle/hub assembly. Remove knuckle/hub assembly from vehicle. If drive axle shaft is stuck in hub, use plastic or soft-faced hammer to tap drive axle shaft from hub assembly.

4) Using puller, remove hub from knuckle. *See Fig. 5.* Remove snap ring retaining bearing. Press bearing from knuckle.

5) Grind inner bearing race to a thickness of .02" (0.5 mm). Using chisel, cut remaining inner bearing race from hub. DO NOT reuse wheel bearing. Inspect all components for cracks, wear and damage. Replace components as necessary.

Reassembly & Installation (RX7) – Press NEW wheel bearing into knuckle using. Install snap ring. Apply grease to inner bearing race. Press hub into knuckle. Reverse removal procedure to install knuckle/hub assembly. Check rear wheel alignment. Tighten all bolts and nuts to specification. See TORQUE SPECIFICATIONS. Stake drive axle shaft lock nut.

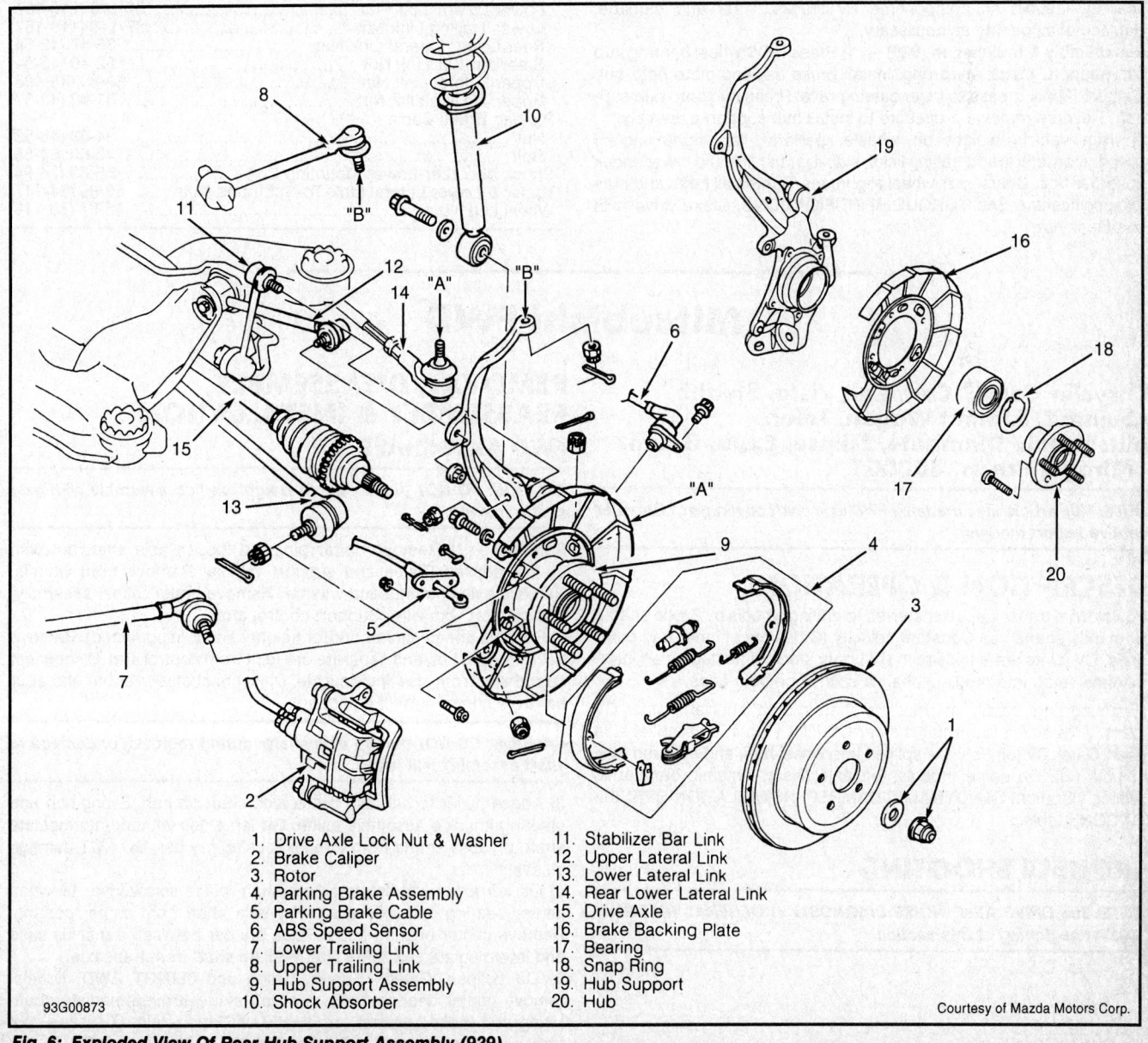

1. Drive Axle Lock Nut & Washer	11. Stabilizer Bar Link
2. Brake Caliper	12. Upper Lateral Link
3. Rotor	13. Lower Lateral Link
4. Parking Brake Assembly	14. Rear Lower Lateral Link
5. Parking Brake Cable	15. Drive Axle
6. ABS Speed Sensor	16. Brake Backing Plate
7. Lower Trailing Link	17. Bearing
8. Upper Trailing Link	18. Snap Ring
9. Hub Support Assembly	19. Hub Support
10. Shock Absorber	20. Hub

93G00873   Courtesy of Mazda Motors Corp.

Fig. 6: Exploded View Of Rear Hub Support Assembly (929)

Removal & Disassembly (929) – 1) Raise vehicle and support with safety stands. Remove wheel and tire assembly. Remove brake caliper and support aside. See Fig. 6. Remove rotor from hub.

2) Mount dial indicator on hub and measure wheel bearing play by pulling and pushing on hub. Wheel bearing play should be a maximum of .002" (.05 mm). Check and adjust drive axle shaft lock nut torque or replace wheel bearing if measurement exceeds specification.

3) Remove drive axle shaft lock nut and washer. Remove ABS speed sensor from hub support assembly. Remove parking brake shoes and mechanism. Remove parking brake cable. Remove upper and lower trailing links from hub support assembly. Remove shock absorber lower mounting bolt. Remove stabilizer bar link-to-hub support assembly mounting nuts.

4) Remove upper, lower and rear lower lateral links from hub support assembly. Remove drive axle shaft from hub support assembly. If drive axle shaft is stuck in hub assembly, use plastic or soft-faced hammer to tap drive axle shaft from hub assembly. Remove hub support assembly from vehicle.

5) Loosen brake backing plate. Using puller, remove hub from hub support. See Fig. 6. Remove brake backing plate from hub support. Remove snap ring retaining bearing. Press bearing from hub support.

6) Grind inner bearing race to a thickness of .02" (0.5 mm). Using chisel, cut remaining inner bearing race from hub. DO NOT reuse wheel bearing. Inspect all components for cracks, wear and damage. Replace components as necessary.

Reassembly & Installation (929) – 1) Press NEW wheel bearing into hub support. Install snap ring. Install brake backing plate onto hub support. Apply grease to inner bearing race. Press hub onto hub support. Reverse removal procedure to install hub support assembly.

2) With vehicle weight on wheels, perform final tightening of suspension lateral and trailing links, stabilizer bar link and lower shock absorber bolt. Check rear wheel alignment. Tighten all bolts and nuts to specification. See TORQUE SPECIFICATIONS. Stake drive axle shaft lock nut.

TORQUE SPECIFICATIONS
TORQUE SPECIFICATIONS

Application	Ft. Lbs. (N.m)
Miata	
ABS Speed Sensor Bolt	12-17 (16-23)
Brake Caliper Mounting Bolts	36-51 (49-69)
Differential-To-Drive Axle Flange Nuts (4)	40-47 (54-64)
Drive Axle Shaft Lock Nut	159-217 (216-294)
Lower Control Arm Bolt/Nut	46-55 (62-75)
Upper Control Arm Bolt/Nut	34-49 (46-66)
Wheel Lug Nuts	65-87 (88-118)
RX7	
ABS Speed Sensor Bolt	14-18 (19-25)
Brake Caliper Mounting Bolts	34-49 (46-66)
Drive Axle Shaft Lock Nut	174-231 (236-313)
I-Arm Bolt/Nut	44-55 (59-74)
Toe Control Link Bolt/Nut	47-57 (64-77)
Upper Control Arm Bolt/Nut	44-55 (59-74)
Wheel Lug Nuts	65-87 (88-118)
929	
ABS Speed Sensor Bolt	12-17 (16-23)
Brake Caliper Mounting Bolt	33-50 (45-68)
Differential-To-Drive Axle Flange Nuts (6)	40-47 (54-64)
Differential-To-Drive Shaft Flange Nuts (4)	36-44 (49-59)
Drive Axle Shaft Lock Nut	174-231 (236-313)
Hub Support Assembly-To-	
Lower Lateral Link Nut	87-116 (118-157)
Lower Trailing Link Nut	87-116 (118-157)
Rear Lower Lateral Link Nut	36-47 (49-64)
Stabilizer Bar Link Nut	32-40 (43-54)
Upper Lateral Link Nut	58-80 (78-108)
Upper Trailing Link Nut	31-42 (42-57)
Parking Brake Cable	
Nut	34-39 (46-53)
Bolt	40-50 (54-68)
Shock Absorber Lower Mounting Bolt	55-69 (74-94)
Upper & Lower Lateral Link-To-Subframe Nuts	69-86 (94-117)
Wheel Lug Nuts	65-87 (88-118)

Mitsubishi FWD

**Chrysler Corp.: Colt, Colt Vista, Stealth
  Summit, Summit Wagon, Talon
Mitsubishi: Diamante, Eclipse, Expo, Galant
  Mirage, Precis, 3000GT**

NOTE: This article also contains FWD axle shaft coverage of Chrysler captive import models.

DESCRIPTION & OPERATION

Power from transaxle is transferred to driving wheels by 2 axle shafts. Both axle shafts use Constant Velocity (CV) joints at inner and outer ends. CV joints are enclosed in CV boots, and connected by an intermediate shaft. Intermediate shaft is splined on both ends.

Retaining rings retain intermediate shaft in both inner and outer CV joints. A retaining ring retains inner CV joint stub in differential side gear. Outer CV joint stub is splined into wheel hub, and secured by a spindle nut. On some models, left axle has a dynamic damper to reduce vibration. See DYNAMIC DAMPER INSTALLATION SPECIFICATIONS table.

TROUBLE SHOOTING

NOTE: See DRIVE AXLE NOISE DIAGNOSIS in GENERAL INFORMATION at beginning of this section.

REMOVAL, DISASSEMBLY, REASSEMBLY & INSTALLATION
FWD AXLE SHAFT

CAUTION: DO NOT place vehicle weight on hub assembly with axle shaft removed.

Removal – 1) Remove cotter pin, and loosen axle shaft nut with brakes applied. Raise and support vehicle. Remove front wheels. Remove axle shaft nut and washer. Remove brake caliper assembly, and support with wire. Support control arm.

2) Remove speed sensor and/or height sensor (if equipped). Remove ball joint stud nut, and separate ball joint from control arm. Disconnect tie rod end from steering knuckle. Disconnect stabilizer bar and strut bar from control arm (if equipped).

CAUTION: DO NOT pull on axle shafts during removal, or damage to shaft assembly will result.

3) Attach puller to hub and press axle shaft off hub. Swing hub and steering knuckle assembly aside. On left axles without intermediate shaft, pry axle shafts from transaxle using pry bar. DO NOT damage oil seals.

4) On left axles with intermediate shaft, place screwdriver between center bearing and axle shaft. Pry axle shaft from center bearing. Remove center bearing bolts. Place pry bar between transaxle case and intermediate shaft. Pry intermediate shaft from transaxle.

5) On Eclipse, Galant, Stealth, Talon and 3000GT AWD models, remove center bearing bolts from left axle with intermediate shaft. Using soft-faced hammer, tap lightly on Tripod Joint (TJ) case, and remove axle shaft from transaxle. See Fig. 1.

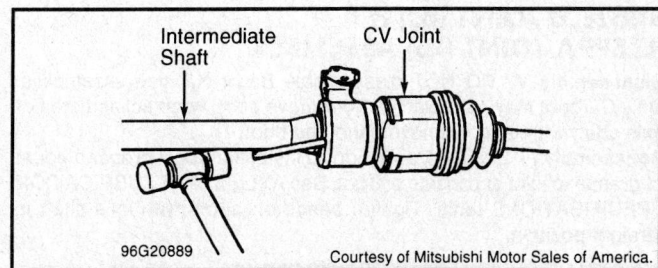

Fig. 1: Removing Left Axle Shaft (AWD Models)

Installation – Position dynamic damper properly on axle shaft (if equipped). See DYNAMIC DAMPER. To complete installation, reverse removal procedure. *See Fig. 2.* On all models, when installing axle shaft nut, washer must be installed with chamfered edge (raised side) toward axle shaft nut. Tighten axle shaft nut to specification. See TORQUE SPECIFICATIONS.

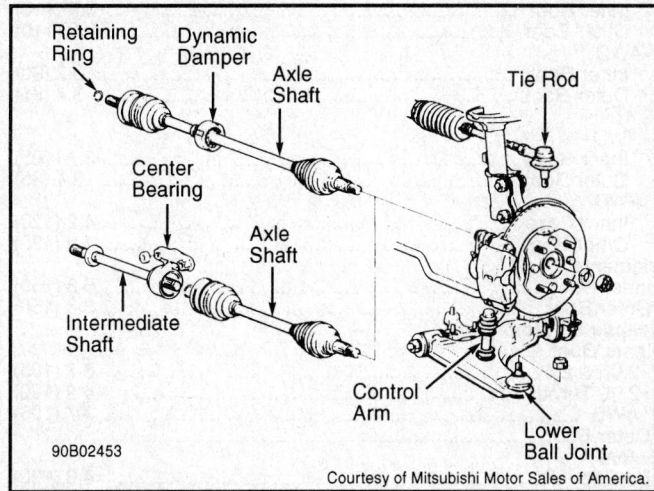

Fig. 2: Installing Axle Shafts (Typical)

AXLE SHAFT SPECIFICATIONS

Application [1]	[2] Inner Joint	[2] Outer Joint	Length In. (mm)
Colt, Mirage & Summit			
1.5L			
Left	TJ	BJ Or RJ	27.5 (698)
Right	TJ	RJ	14.9 (407)
1.8L			
Left	TJ	BJ Or RJ	27.5 (698)
Right	TJ	RJ	14.4 (365)
Colt Vista, Expo & Summit Wagon (1.8L)			
FWD			
Left	TJ	RJ	27.9 (709)
Right	TJ	RJ	14.5 (368)
AWD			
Left	DOJ	BJ	14.6 (371)
Right	DOJ	BJ	14.8 (377)

[1] – Right indicates passenger's side, and left indicates driver's side.
[2] – Type of CV joint used is identified by letters as follows: BJ – Birfield Joint, DOJ – Double Offset Joint, RJ – Rzeppa Joint, and TJ – Tripod Joint.

AXLE SHAFT SPECIFICATIONS (Cont.)

Application [1]	[2] Inner Joint	[2] Outer Joint	Length In. (mm)
Colt Vista, Expo & Summit Wagon (2.4L)			
FWD (A/T)			
Left	TJ	BJ	27.7 (703)
Right	TJ	BJ	14.6 (371)
FWD (M/T)			
Left	TJ	BJ	27.8 (706)
Right	TJ	BJ	14.5 (368)
AWD			
Left	TJ	BJ	14.4 (366)
Right	TJ	BJ	14.6 (371)
Diamante			
Left	TJ	BJ	16.1 (409)
Right	TJ	BJ	15.0 (381)
Eclipse & Talon			
FWD			
2.0L (A/T Turbo)			
Left	TJ	BJ	27.6 (701)
Right	TJ	BJ	14.5 (368)
2.0L & 2.4L			
Left	TJ	BJ	27.8 (706)
Right	TJ	BJ	14.4 (366)
AWD (A/T)			
Left	TJ	BJ	14.4 (366)
Right	TJ	BJ	14.6 (371)
AWD (M/T)			
Left	TJ	BJ	14.5 (368)
Right	TJ	BJ	14.5 (368)
Galant			
Left	TJ	BJ	27.8 (706)
Right	TJ	BJ	14.4 (366)
Stealth & 3000GT			
FWD			
SOHC (A/T)			
Left	TJ	BJ	16.5 (419)
Right	TJ	BJ	15.5 (394)
SOHC (M/T)			
Left	TJ	BJ	16.5 (419)
Right	TJ	BJ	16.0 (406)
DOHC (A/T)			
Left	TJ	BJ	16.4 (417)
Right	TJ	BJ	15.5 (394)
DOHC (M/T)			
Left	TJ	BJ	16.4 (417)
Right	TJ	BJ	15.9 (404)
AWD			
Left	TJ	BJ	16.5 (419)
Right	TJ	BJ	15.4 (391)

[1] – Right indicates passenger's side, and left indicates driver's side.
[2] – Type of CV joint used is identified by letters as follows: BJ – Birfield Joint, DOJ – Double Offset Joint, RJ – Rzeppa Joint, and TJ – Tripod Joint.

DYNAMIC DAMPER

Dynamic damper must be properly positioned on axle shaft. Position damper so proper distance exists between damper and end of boot with axle shaft in a straight position. *See Fig. 3.* Distance must be within specification. See DYNAMIC DAMPER INSTALLATION SPECIFICATIONS table.

DYNAMIC DAMPER INSTALLATION SPECIFICATIONS

Application	[1] Damper-To-Boot End Distance In. (mm)
Colt, Mirage & Summit (1.5L)	
A/T	13.70-13.94 (348-354)
M/T	18.82-19.06 (434-439)
Colt, Mirage & Summit (1.8L)	
Left (M/T)	14.25-14.49 (362-368)
Right (A/T)	7.77-8.01 (197-203)
Colt Vista, Expo & Summit Wagon (FWD)	
1.8L	
Left [2]	16.89-17.13 (429-435)
Right [3]	7.77-8.01 (197-203)
2.4L	
Left [3]	14.25-14.49 (362-368)
Right [3]	7.72-7.96 (197-203)
Colt Vista, Expo & Summit Wagon (AWD)	
1.8L & 2.4L	
Both Sides [3]	7.72-7.96 (197-203)
Eclipse & Talon	
2.0L	
Left [3]	7.52-7.76 (191-197)
Right [3]	14.60-14.84 (371-377)
2.0L Turbo	
Left [3]	14.60-14.84 (371-377)
2.4L	
Left [3]	14.25-14.49 (362-368)
Right [3]	8.58-8.82 (218-224)
Galant	
Left [2]	14.25-14.49 (362-368)
Right [2]	8.58-8.82 (218-224)

[1] – Ensure axle shaft is in straight position.
[2] – Measure at width "A".
[3] – Measure at width "B".

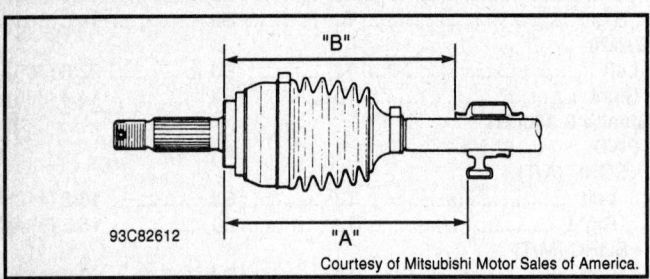

93C82612

Courtesy of Mitsubishi Motor Sales of America.

Fig. 3: Installing Dynamic Damper

INTERMEDIATE SHAFT

Disassembly – On Colt Vista, Eclipse, Expo, Stealth, Summit, Talon and 3000GT AWD models, press intermediate shaft and bearing assembly from TJ case with Intermediate Shaft Remover (MB991248 or MD998801). On all models, press out intermediate shaft from center bearing assembly with Bearing Puller (MB990938). Remove center bearing from bracket with appropriate bearing remover. See Fig. 4.

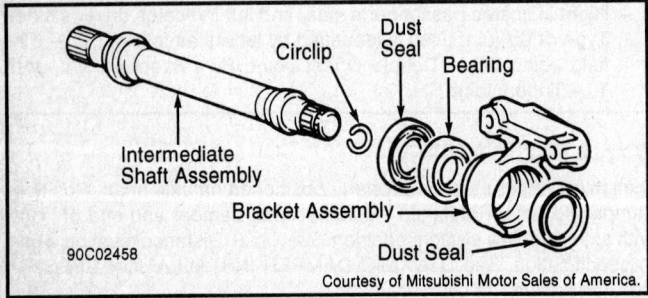

90C02458

Courtesy of Mitsubishi Motor Sales of America.

Fig. 4: Assembling Intermediate Shaft (Typical)

Reassembly – Grease center bearing and inside center bearing bracket. Press bearing into bearing bracket assembly with appropriate bearing installer. Press dust seals into bearing with handle and installer. Lubricate assembly with grease. Press intermediate shaft into center bearing assembly.

BIRFIELD JOINT (BJ) & RZEPPA JOINT (RJ) ASSEMBLY

Disassembly – DO NOT disassemble BJ or RJ type assemblies. Only CV boot may be replaced. To remove boot, wrap splined area of axle shaft with tape. Remove band and boot.

Reassembly – Ensure proper boot is installed. Apply proper amount of grease to joint and inside of boot. See AXLE SHAFT LUBRICATION SPECIFICATIONS table. Tighten bands on boots with axle shaft in straight position.

AXLE SHAFT LUBRICATION SPECIFICATIONS

Application	Ozs. (g)
Colt, Mirage & Summit	
Outer Boot	3.9 (110)
TJ Boot	
Inner-RJ Type Axle	4.4 (125)
Inner-BJ Type Axle	3.4 (95)
Colt Vista, Expo & Summit Wagon	
1.8L	
FWD	
Inner Boot	3.9 (110)
Outer Boot	3.9 (110)
4WD	
Inner Boot	3.2 (90)
Outer Boot	3.4 (95)
2.4L	
AWD	
Inner Boot	3.7 (105)
Outer Boot	3.4 (95)
FWD	
Inner Case	4.2 (120)
Outer Boot	4.6 (130)
Diamante	
Inner Boot	5.3 (150)
Outer Boot	5.3 (150)
Eclipse & Talon	
Inner Boot	
2.0L & 2.4L	3.7 (105)
2.0L Turbo	4.2 (120)
AWD	3.7 (105)
Outer Boot	[1]
Galant	
BJ Boot	4.6 (130)
TJ Boot	4.2 (120)
Stealth & 3000GT	
Outer Boot	[1]
Inner Boot	
SOHC	5.3 (151)
DOHC & AWD	5.6 (160)

[1] – Apply same amount of grease as removed. No specification available from manufacturer.

DOUBLE OFFSET JOINT (DOJ) ASSEMBLY

Disassembly – 1) Note type of boot and location prior to removal. Remove bands and boot from DOJ housing. See Fig. 5. Remove circlip and remove DOJ housing.

2) Place reference marks on axle shaft, DOJ inner race and DOJ outer race for reassembly reference. Remove snap ring. Remove DOJ cage, balls and DOJ inner race. Wrap splined area of axle shaft with tape, and remove boot.

Reassembly – 1) To reassemble, reverse disassembly procedure. Ensure reference marks are aligned on DOJ inner race and axle shaft. Apply one half of proper lubricant amount in balls and inner race, and other half in DOJ boot. See AXLE SHAFT LUBRICATION SPECIFICATIONS table.

2) Install boot and bands. Position boots so bands are spaced 3.42-3.66" (87.0-93.0 mm) apart. Tighten bands with axle shaft in straight position.

TRIPOD JOINT (TJ) ASSEMBLY

Disassembly – 1) Note type of boot and location prior to removal. Remove bands and boot from TJ case. See Fig. 6. Place reference mark on TJ case and spider assembly. Pull axle shaft and spider assembly from TJ case.

AXLE SHAFTS
Mitsubishi FWD (Cont.)

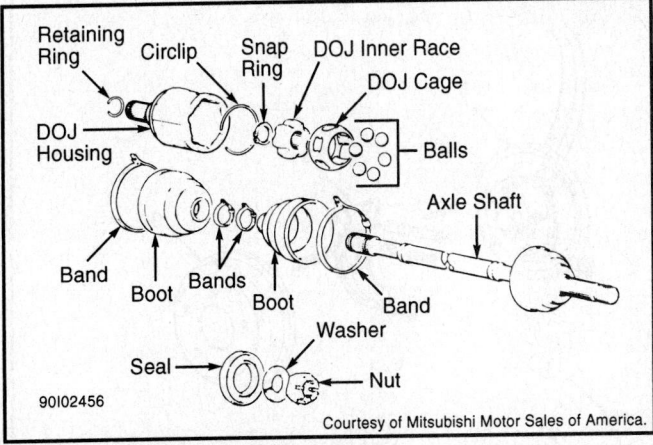

Fig. 5: Exploded View Of DOJ Assembly

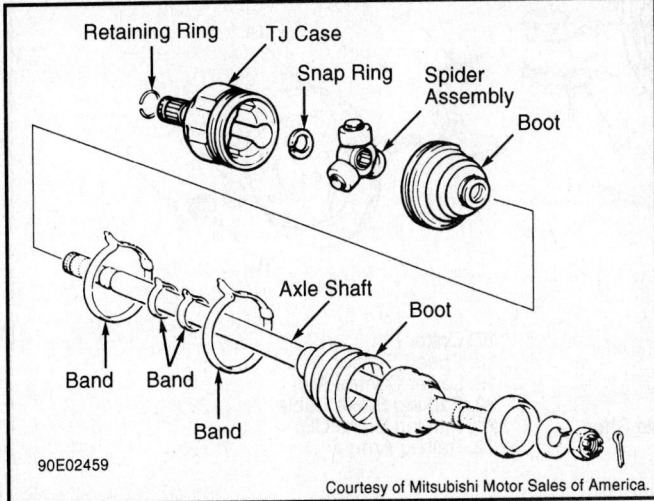

Fig. 6: Exploded View Of TJ Assembly

2) Remove snap ring and pull spider assembly from axle shaft. Clean, but DO NOT disassemble spider assembly. Wrap splined area of axle shaft with tape, and remove boot. Dynamic damper (if equipped) and outer boots can be serviced at this time.

Reassembly – 1) To reassemble, reverse disassembly procedure. Use new snap ring to retain spider assembly. Ensure reference marks are aligned on spider assembly and TJ case. Using proper lubricant, apply one half of grease in TJ case and other half TJ boot. See AXLE SHAFT LUBRICATION SPECIFICATIONS table.

2) Install boot and bands. Tighten bands on boots with axle shaft in straight position. Position boots so bands are positioned at specified distance and secure. See TJ BOOT BAND INSTALLATION SPECIFICATIONS table.

TJ BOOT BAND INSTALLATION SPECIFICATIONS

Application	Distance Between Bands In. (mm)
Colt, Mirage & Summit	3.23-3.47 (82.0-88.1)
Colt Vista, Expo & Summit Wagon	
1.8L	3.11-3.35 (79.0-85.0)
2.4L	
FWD	3.03-3.27 (77.0-83.0)
AWD	3.23-3.47 (82.0-88.1)
Diamante	2.83-3.07 (72.0-78.0)
Eclipse & Talon	3.03-3.27 (77.0-83.0)
Galant	3.03-3.27 (77.0-83.0)

TORQUE SPECIFICATIONS
TORQUE SPECIFICATIONS

Application	Ft. Lbs. (N.m)
Axle Shaft Nut	145-188 (197-255)
Center Bearing Bracket Bolt	
Galant, Eclipse, Stealth & 3000GT	26-33 (35-45)
Control Arm Ball Joint Nut	43-53 (58-72)
Tie Rod Nut	17-25 (23-34)
Wheel Lug Nut	
Eclipse, Stealth, Talon & 3000GT	87-101 (118-137)
All Others	65-80 (88-108)

Mitsubishi RWD

Chrysler Corp.: Colt Vista, Stealth, Summit Wagon, Talon
Mitsubishi: Eclipse, Expo, 3000GT

NOTE: Information in this article applies only to RWD axle shafts of AWD models with independent rear suspension. This article includes coverage for Chrysler import models.

DESCRIPTION & OPERATION

Power from differential is transferred to rear wheels by 2 axle shafts. Both axle shafts use CV joints at inner and outer ends. CV joints are enclosed in CV boots, and are connected by an interconnecting shaft. Interconnecting shaft is splined on both ends. A retaining ring retains inner CV joint in differential side gear. Outer CV joint is attached to stub axle shaft.

TROUBLE SHOOTING

NOTE: See DRIVE AXLE NOISE DIAGNOSIS in GENERAL INFORMATION at beginning of this section.

REMOVAL, DISASSEMBLY, REASSEMBLY & INSTALLATION

RWD AXLE SHAFT

CAUTION: DO NOT place vehicle weight on hub assembly with axle shaft removed.

Removal & Installation (Colt Vista, Expo & Summit Wagon) – 1) Raise and support vehicle. Remove wheels. Remove side flange-to-differential bolts and separate axle shaft.

2) Remove brake drum or caliper and rotor. Remove speed sensor (if equipped). Remove axle shaft nut and washer. Attach puller to hub and press axle shaft from hub. To install, reverse removal procedure.

Removal & Installation (Eclipse & Talon) – 1) Raise and support vehicle. Remove rear wheels. Remove speed sensor (if equipped). See Fig. 1. Remove brake caliper (if equipped). Remove brake disc or drum. Remove brake shoes. Remove parking brake clip and cable.

2) On vehicles with rear drum brakes, remove brake line from wheel cylinder. Remove lower shock bolt and disconnect shock. Disconnect trailing arm from knuckle. Remove lower control arm and tie rod from knuckle. Remove cotter pin, drive shaft nut and washer. Remove differential support.

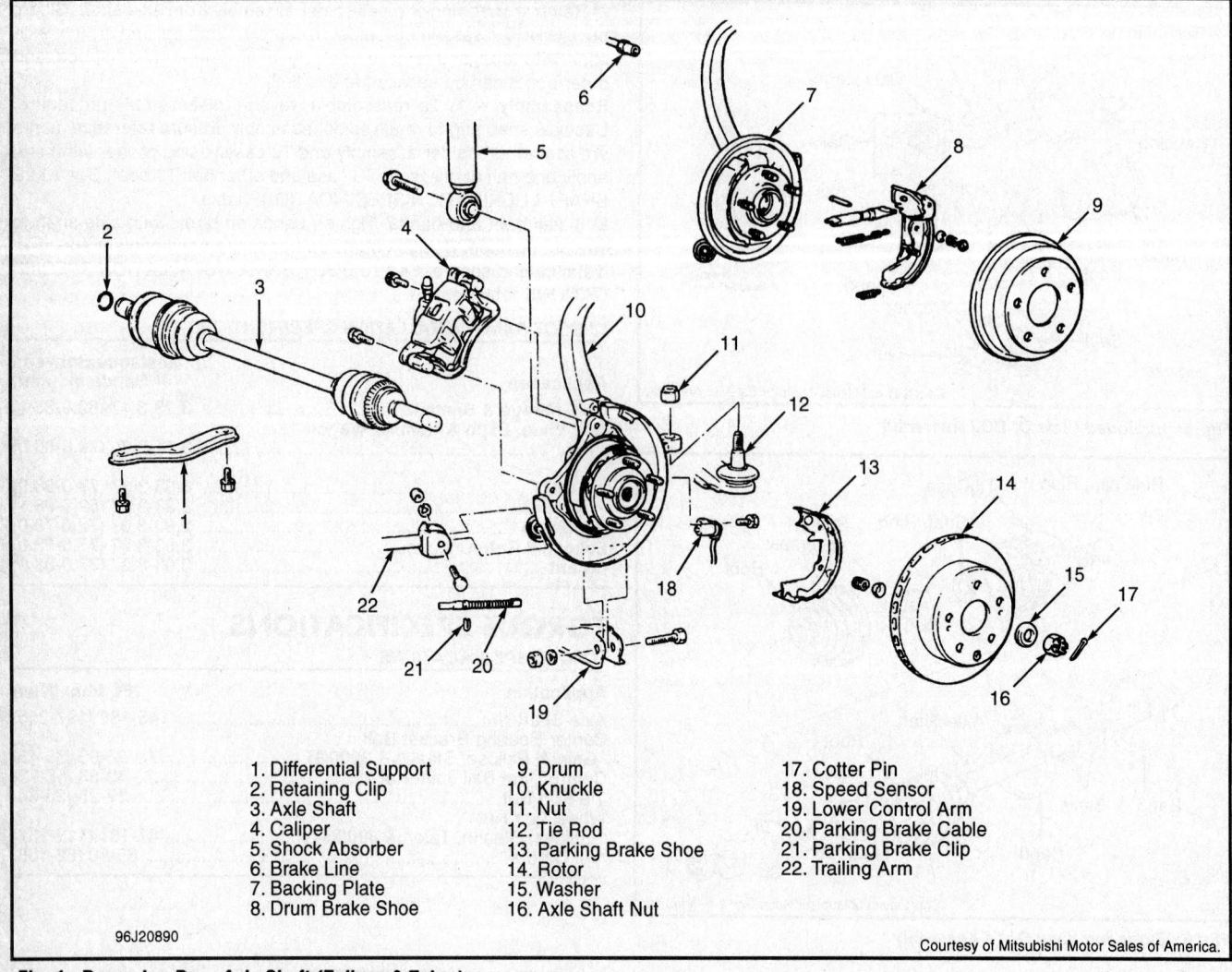

1. Differential Support
2. Retaining Clip
3. Axle Shaft
4. Caliper
5. Shock Absorber
6. Brake Line
7. Backing Plate
8. Drum Brake Shoe
9. Drum
10. Knuckle
11. Nut
12. Tie Rod
13. Parking Brake Shoe
14. Rotor
15. Washer
16. Axle Shaft Nut
17. Cotter Pin
18. Speed Sensor
19. Lower Control Arm
20. Parking Brake Cable
21. Parking Brake Clip
22. Trailing Arm

96J20890

Courtesy of Mitsubishi Motor Sales of America.

Fig. 1: Removing Rear Axle Shaft (Eclipse & Talon)

3) Push knuckle away from vehicle and remove drive shaft from knuckle. Remove drive shaft from differential. To install, reverse removal procedure. On vehicles with rear drum brakes, bleed brake lines.

Removal & Installation (Stealth & 3000GT) – 1) Raise and support vehicle. Unbolt axle shaft from stub axle shaft. Pry axle shaft from differential using flat-blade screwdriver. Ensure seal is not damaged by axle shaft splines during removal. Remove oil seal from differential carrier (if necessary).

2) To install, reverse removal procedure. Using Seal Installer (C-3893), install oil seal in differential. Coat seal lip with grease. Install new retaining clip on axle shaft. Install axle shaft in differential carrier. Install companion flange bolts.

NOTE: Always replace retaining clip when axle shaft has been removed.

DOUBLE OFFSET JOINT (DOJ) ASSEMBLY

NOTE: Birfield Joint (BJ) and shaft assembly cannot be disassembled. DO NOT attempt to disassemble.

Disassembly (Colt Vista, Expo & Summit Wagon) – 1) Remove axle shaft. Note type of band and boot location prior to removal. Remove bands and boot from DOJ housing. Remove circlip and remove DOJ housing. *See Fig. 2.*

2) Place reference marks on axle shaft, DOJ inner race and DOJ outer race for reassembly reference. Remove snap ring. Remove DOJ cage,

balls and DOJ inner race. Wrap splined area of axle shaft with tape, and remove boot.

Reassembly – 1) To reassemble, reverse disassembly procedure. Ensure reference marks are aligned on DOJ inner race and axle shaft. Apply one half of proper lubricant amount to balls and inner race, and other half in DOJ boot. See DOUBLE OFFSET JOINT (DOJ) ASSEMBLY SPECIFICATIONS table.

2) Install boot and bands. Tighten large band with axle shaft in straight position. Position boots so bands are positioned at specified distance and tighten small band. *See Fig. 3.* See DOUBLE OFFSET JOINT (DOJ) ASSEMBLY SPECIFICATIONS table. Install axle shaft.

DOUBLE OFFSET JOINT (DOJ) ASSEMBLY SPECIFICATIONS

Application	In. (mm)
Axle Shaft Dimensions	
Colt Vista, Expo & Summit Wagon	
Length (Both Shafts)	
With ABS	18.62 (473)
Without ABS	19.60 (498)
DOJ Boot Length	
Colt Vista, Expo & Summit Wagon	2.72-3.18 (69-81)
CV Joint Grease Capacity	**Ozs. (g)**
DOJ	[1] 3.0 (85)
BJ	
With ABS	[1] 4.4 (125)
Without ABS	[1] 2.6 (75)
[1] – Split grease equally between boot and joint.	

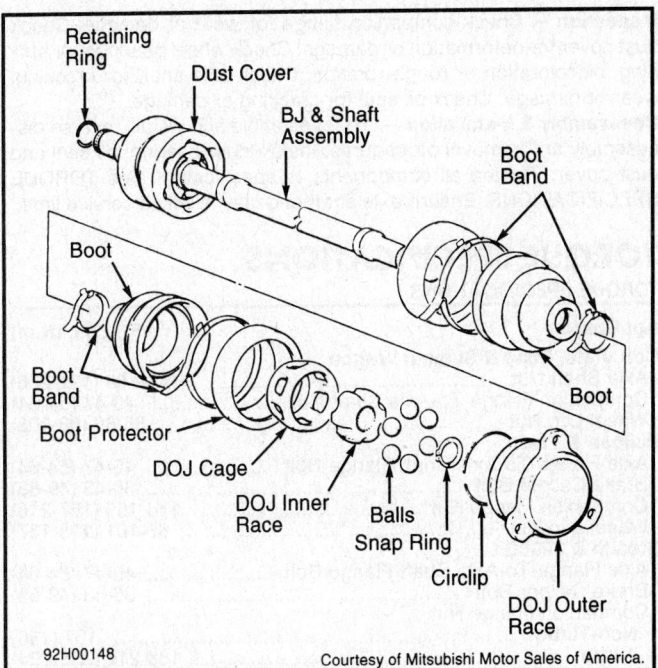

Fig. 2: Exploded View Of Axle Shaft Assembly (Colt Vista, Expo & Summit Wagon)

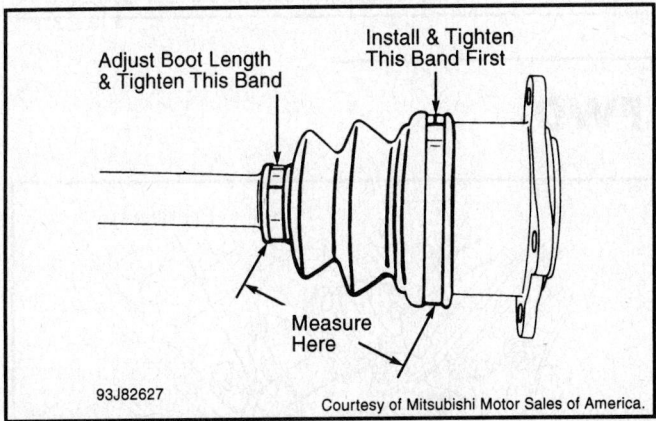

Fig. 3: Installing DOJ Or TJ Boot

TRIPOD JOINT (TJ) ASSEMBLY

NOTE: BJ and shaft assembly cannot be disassembled. DO NOT attempt to disassemble.

Disassembly (Eclipse, Stealth & 3000GT) – Remove axle shaft. Remove boot bands from inner Tripod Joint (TJ). Scribe alignment marks (for reassembly reference) on shaft, TJ case and spider assembly. Remove TJ case, snap ring and spider assembly. Remove boot bands from outer Birfield Joint (BJ). Wrap axle shaft splines with tape and remove CV boots. *See Fig. 4.*

Reassembly – 1) To reassemble, reverse disassembly procedure. If reusing BJ and shaft assembly, pack BJ with specified quantity of CV joint grease. See TRIPOD JOINT (TJ) ASSEMBLY SPECIFICATIONS table. Install CV joint boots and clamps on axle shaft. Lubricate and assemble TJ.

2) Align reference marks made during disassembly and install TJ assembly. Install snap ring. Pack TJ and boot with specified quantity of CV joint grease. See TRIPOD JOINT (TJ) ASSEMBLY SPECIFICATIONS table.

3) Tighten large CV boot band in straight position. Set CV boot length to specification. *See Fig. 3.* See TRIPOD JOINT (TJ) ASSEMBLY SPECIFICATIONS table. Tighten small CV boot band. Install axle shaft.

TRIPOD JOINT (TJ) ASSEMBLY SPECIFICATIONS

Application	In. (mm)
Drive Axle Shaft Dimensions	
Eclipse	
Length (Both Shafts)	15.2 (385)
Stealth & 3000GT	
Length (Both Shafts)	15.6 (396.2)
TJ Boot Length	
Eclipse & Talon	
With LSD [1]	3.19-3.43 (81-87)
Without LSD [1]	2.99-3.23 (76-82)
Stealth & 3000GT	3.23-3.47 (82-88)
CV Joint Grease Capacity	**Ozs. (g)**
Eclipse & Talon	
BJ	[2] 2.6 (75)
TJ	
With LSD [1]	[2] 3.7 (105)
Without LSD [1]	[2]3.4 (95)
Stealth & 3000GT	
BJ	[2] 4.4 (125)
TJ	[2] 4.8 (135)

[1] – Vehicles equipped with or without Limited Slip Differential (LSD).
[2] – Split grease equally between boot and joint.

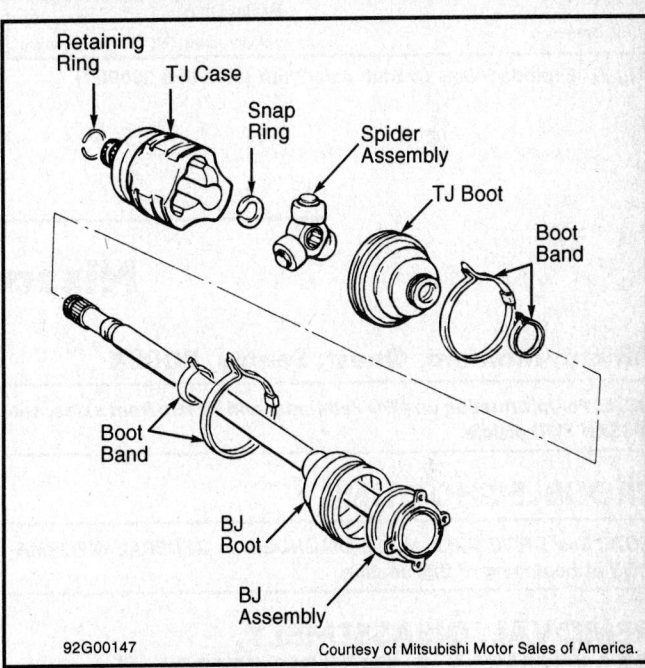

Fig. 4: Exploded View Of Axle Shaft Assembly (Eclipse, Stealth, Talon & 3000GT)

STUB AXLE SHAFTS

End Play Check (Stealth & 3000GT) – Place dial indicator stem on rear axle flange near lug nut. Check stub axle shaft end play. If end play is greater than .031" (.8 mm), check torque of companion flange nut. See TORQUE SPECIFICATIONS. If torque is as specified, replace inner and outer bearings.

Removal – 1) Raise and support vehicle on safety stands. Remove rear wheels. Remove rear speed sensor (if equipped). *See Fig. 5.* Disconnect parking brake cable from rear brake caliper assembly. Remove rear caliper assembly and rotor. Support caliper assembly away from work area with wire.

2) Scribe index marks on flange yoke and companion flange. Remove axle shaft mounting bolts. Remove self-locking nut and separate axle from flange.

3) Remove axle shaft from trailing arm using slide hammer. Attach slide hammer attachment must fit on outboard side of axle shaft flange.

NOTE: When removing axle shaft spline, DO NOT damage oil seal.

Disassembly – Remove rear speed sensor rotor (if equipped). See Fig. 5. Remove outer bearing and dust cover from axle shaft. Remove axle shaft. Remove oil seal and inner bearing.

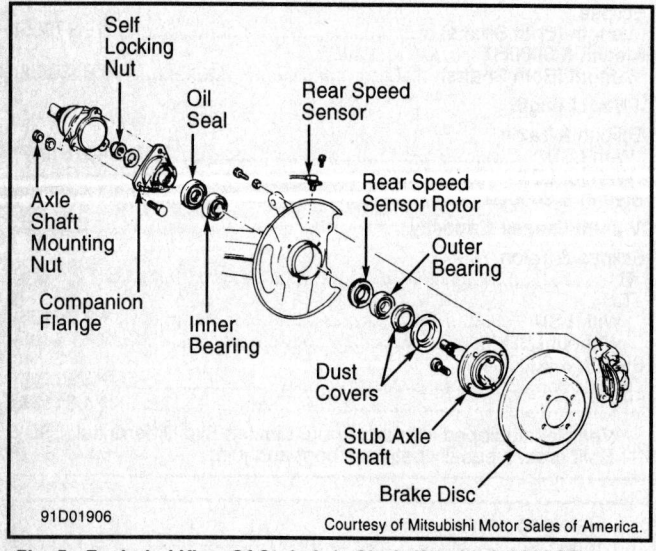

91D01906   Courtesy of Mitsubishi Motor Sales of America.

Fig. 5: Exploded View Of Stub Axle Shaft (Stealth & 3000GT)

Inspection – Check companion flange for wear or damage. Check dust cover for deformation or damage. Check wheel bearings for burning, discoloration or rough rotation. Check axle shaft for cracking, wear or damage. Check oil seal for cracking or damage.

Reassembly & Installation – To reassemble and install, reverse disassembly and removal procedures. Install inner bearing, oil seal and dust cover. Tighten all components to specification. See TORQUE SPECIFICATIONS. Ensure axle shaft end play is within service limit.

TORQUE SPECIFICATIONS

TORQUE SPECIFICATIONS	
Application	**Ft. Lbs. (N.m)**
Colt Vista, Expo & Summit Wagon	
Axle Shaft Nut	145-188 (197-255)
Companion Flange-To-Axle Shaft Nut	40-47 (54-64)
Wheel Lug Nut	65-80 (88-108)
Eclipse & Talon	
Axle Flange-To-Axle Shaft Flange Bolt	40-47 (54-64)
Brake Caliper Bolt	36-43 (49-58)
Companion Flange Nut	116-159 (157-216)
Wheel Lug Nut	87-101 (118-137)
Stealth & 3000GT	
Axle Flange-To-Axle Shaft Flange Bolt	40-47 (54-64)
Brake Caliper Bolt	36-43 (49-58)
Companion Flange Nut	
Non-Turbo	137 (186)
Turbo	188-217 (255-294)
Wheel Lug Nut	87-101 (118-137)
	INCH Lbs. (N.m)
Rear Speed Sensor Bolts	80-124 (9-14)

Nissan FWD

Altima, Maxima, Quest, Sentra, 200SX

NOTE: For information on 4WD Pathfinder and Pickup front axles, see NISSAN 4WD article.

TROUBLE SHOOTING

NOTE: See DRIVE AXLE NOISE DIAGNOSIS in GENERAL INFORMATION at beginning of this section.

REMOVAL, DISASSEMBLY, REASSEMBLY & INSTALLATION

FWD AXLE SHAFT

NOTE: On A/T models, right axle shaft must be removed to remove left axle shaft. On all models, cover axle shaft boots with shop towel to prevent damaging boots. Always use NEW snap rings, circular clips and boot clamps during reassembly and installation. Replace axle shaft oil seal in differential before installing axle shaft.

Removal – 1) Raise and support vehicle. Remove wheel. Remove wheel bearing hub nut from end of drive axle. Remove disc brake caliper and suspend out of way. DO NOT allow caliper to hang by hydraulic hose.

2) On Altima and Maxima, separate tie rod end from steering knuckle. On Quest, Sentra and 200SX, separate ball joint from steering knuckle. On all models, remove axle shaft from steering knuckle hub using a soft mallet. On models with ball and cage type right axle shaft, remove support bearing retainer-to-block bolts. See Fig. 5.

3) On all models, pry right axle shaft from transaxle using screwdriver. See Fig. 1. On M/T models, pry left axle shaft from transaxle using screwdriver. On A/T models, insert screwdriver through right axle shaft hole in differential, and drive out left axle shaft. See Fig. 2.

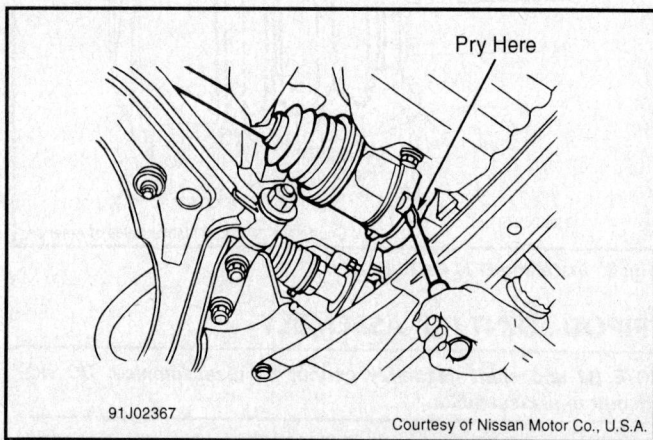

Pry Here

91J02367   Courtesy of Nissan Motor Co., U.S.A.

Fig. 1: Removing Axle Shaft (Except A/T Left Shaft)

Disassembly (Inner Joint – Ball & Cage Type) – 1) Place axle shaft in soft-jawed vise with inner joint facing up. Remove boot clamps. See Fig. 5. Mark slide joint housing and inner race in relation to axle shaft for reassembly reference.

2) Remove and discard snap ring "A". See Figs. 3, 4 and 5. Remove slide joint housing. Remove snap ring "C". Remove cage, inner race and balls as an assembly. Remove snap ring "B". Cover axle shaft splines with tape. Remove boot.

3) To disassemble support bearing and retainer assembly on right axle shaft, remove dust shield and snap ring "D". See Fig. 5. Press axle shaft out of support bearing and retainer assembly. Remove snap ring and dust shield from retainer. Using bearing driver and hammer, drive support bearing out of retainer.

Disassembly (Inner Joint – Spider Assembly Type) – 1) Place axle shaft in soft jawed vise with inner joint facing up. Remove boot clamps. See Fig. 4. Mark side joint housing and spider assembly in relation to axle shaft for reassembly reference.

2) Remove slide joint housing. Remove snap ring. Remove spider assembly, DO NOT disassemble spider assembly. Cover axle splines with tape. Remove boot.

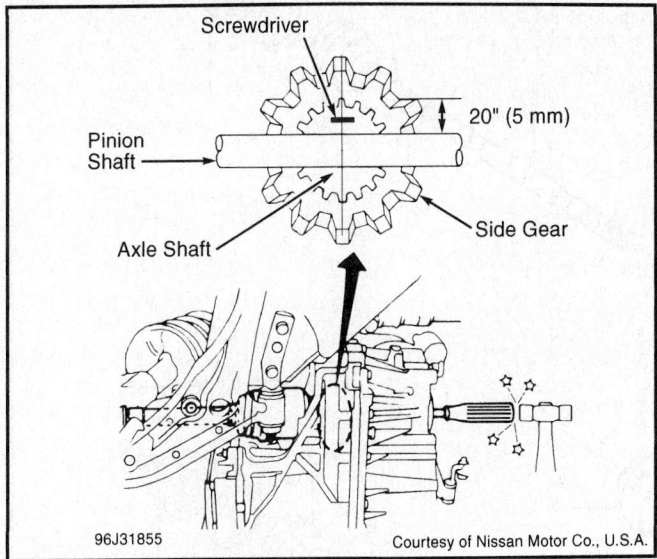

Fig. 2: Removing Axle Shaft (A/T Left Shaft)

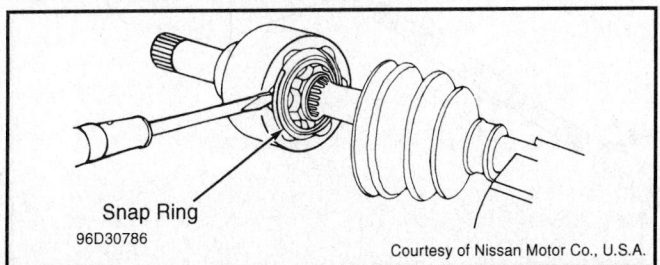

Fig. 3: Removing Snap Ring "A" (Inner Joint – Ball & Cage Type)

NOTE: Outer joint can be removed from axle shaft but cannot be disassembled.

Disassembly (Outer Joint) – Place axle shaft in soft-jawed vise with outer joint facing up. Remove boot clamps. See Figs. 4 and 5. Mark slide joint housing and inner race in relation to axle shaft for reassembly reference. Remove joint assembly from axle shaft using slide hammer. See Fig. 5.

Inspection – Replace axle shaft if twisted or cracked. Check boots for fatigue, cracks or wear. Replace joint components that are scorched, rusted, worn or loose. Check axle shaft splines for deformation. Inspect slide joint housing for damage. Ensure support bearing rolls freely and is not noisy, cracked, pitted or worn.

Reassembly (Inner Joint – Ball & Cage Type) – 1) Mount axle shaft in soft-jawed vise with inner joint facing up. Wrap tape around shaft splines. Install boot and clamp on shaft. Install snap ring "B". See Fig. 5.

2) Install ball cage, inner race and balls as an assembly, aligning marks made during disassembly. Install snap ring "C". Pack joint with specific amount of grease. See BOOT GREASE CAPACITY table. Install slide joint housing, aligning marks made during disassembly. Install snap ring "A".

3) Position boot to correct length. See AXLE SHAFT BOOT LENGTH table. See Fig. 7. Lock boot clamps in place using hammer and punch. See Fig. 8.

Reassembly (Inner Joint – Spider Assembly Type) – 1) Mount axle shaft in soft-jawed vise with inner joint facing up. Wrap tape around shaft splines. Install boot and clamp on shaft. See Fig 4. Install spider assembly, aligning marks made during disassembly. Install snap ring.

2) Pack joint with grease. See BOOT GREASE CAPACITY table. Install slide joint housing, aligning marks made during disassembly. Position boot to correct length. See AXLE SHAFT BOOT LENGTH table. See Fig. 7. Lock boot clamps in place using hammer and punch. See Fig. 8.

BOOT GREASE CAPACITY

Application	Ozs. (g)
Altima	
Inner	5.11-5.82 (145-165)
Outer	3.53-4.23 (100-120)
Maxima	
Inner	5.82-6.17 (165-175)
Outer (1995)	6.70-7.05 (190-200)
Outer (1996)	4.76-5.11 (135-145)
Quest	
Inner	7.41-8.11 (210-230)
Outer	6.17-6.88 (175-195)
Sentra & 200SX	
Inner	
TS79C [1]	5.47-5.82 (155-165)
TS83 [1]	4.59-5.29 (130-150)
Outer	
ZF90 [1]	4.06-4.41 (115-125)
BF83 [1]	3.70-4.41 (105-125)
[1] – See Fig. 4. to identify axle type.	

AXLE SHAFT BOOT LENGTH

Model	Outboard Boot In. (mm)	Inboard Boot In. (mm)
Altima	3.3-3.4 (85-87)	3.8-3.9 (97-99)
Maxima	3.8-3.9 (97-99)	3.8-3.9 (97-99)
Sentra & 200SX		
ZF90/TS79C	3.8-3.9 (97-99)	4.6-4.1 (101-103)
BF83/TS83	3.74 (95)	3.90 (99)
Quest	3.4-3.5 (87-89)	4.0-4.1 (101-103)

Dynamic damper – Install dynamic damper and clamps to specific length. See DYNAMIC DAMPER MEASUREMENT SPECIFICATION table.

NOTE: Refer to Fig. 9 for measurement specifications.

DYNAMIC DAMPER MEASUREMENT SPECIFICATION

Application	"A" In. (mm)	"B" In. (mm)
Altima		
RE4F04A A/T		
Right Side	8.00 (203.1)	2.76 (70)
Left Side	7.31 (185.6)	1.97 (50)
RE4F04V A/T		
Right Side	8.00 (203.1)	2.76 (70)
Left Side	6.87 (174.6)	1.97 (50)
RS5F50A M/T		
Right Side	8.00 (203.1)	2.76 (70)
Left Side	7.31 (185.6)	1.97 (50)
RS5F50V M/T		
Right Side	8.00 (203.1)	2.76 (70)
Left Side	7.09 (180.1)	1.97 (50)
Maxima		
Left Side	8.07-8.46 (205-215)	1.97 (50)
Quest		
Left Side	7.83-8.07 (199-205)	2.76 (70)
Sentra & 200SX		
ZF90/TS79C [1]		
Right Side	17.01-17.40 (432-442)	2.60 (66)
Left Side	6.90-7.30 (175-185)	2.28 (58)
BF83/TS83, DS83 [1]		
Right Side	6.65-6.89 (169-175)	2.76 (70)
Left Side		
A/T	6.09-6.33 (155-101)	1.97 (50)
M/T	6.09-6.33 (155-101)	2.76 (70)
[1] – See Fig. 4. to identify axle type.		

AXLE SHAFTS
Nissan FWD (Cont.)

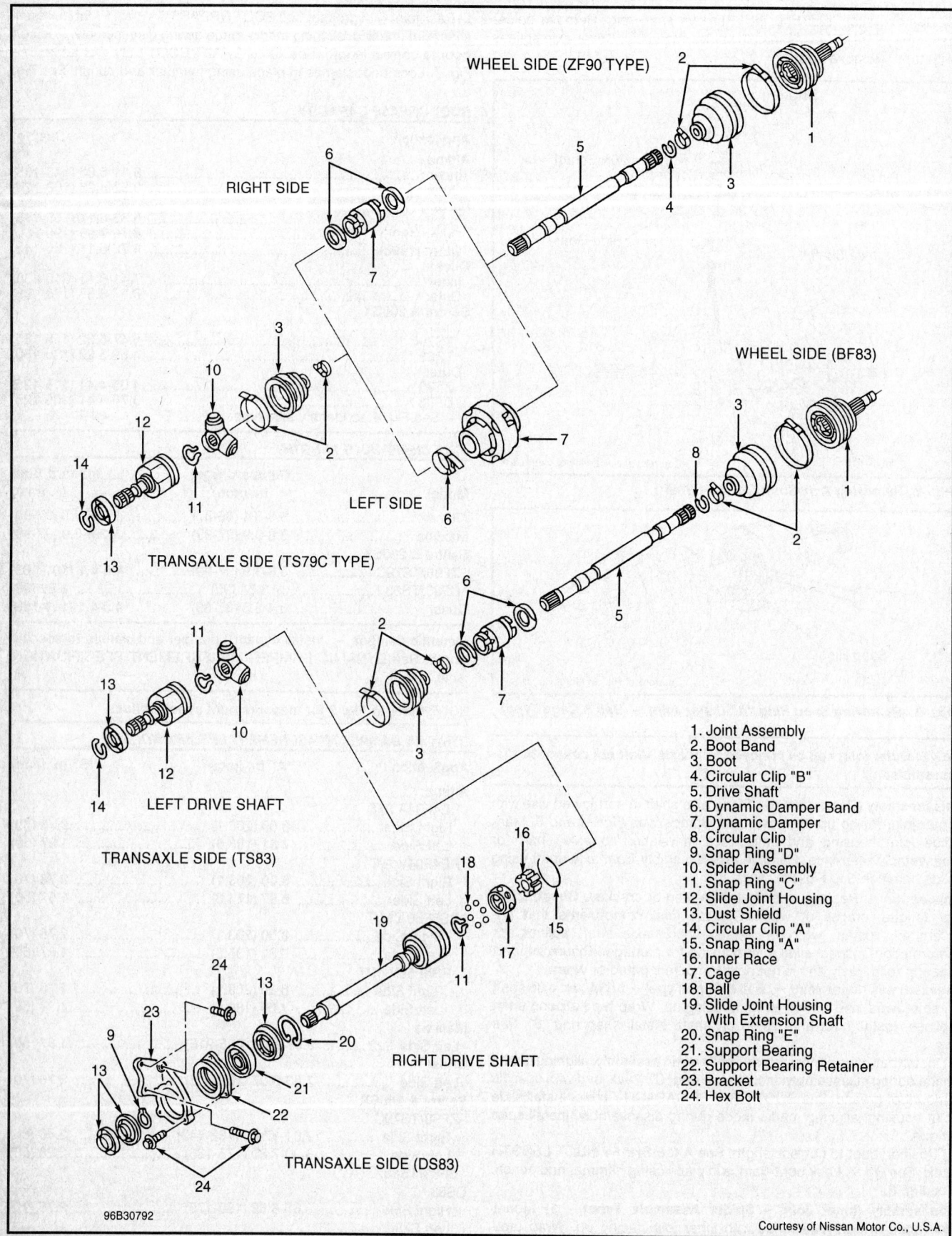

WHEEL SIDE (ZF90 TYPE)

RIGHT SIDE

WHEEL SIDE (BF83)

LEFT SIDE

TRANSAXLE SIDE (TS79C TYPE)

LEFT DRIVE SHAFT

TRANSAXLE SIDE (TS83)

RIGHT DRIVE SHAFT

TRANSAXLE SIDE (DS83)

1. Joint Assembly
2. Boot Band
3. Boot
4. Circular Clip "B"
5. Drive Shaft
6. Dynamic Damper Band
7. Dynamic Damper
8. Circular Clip
9. Snap Ring "D"
10. Spider Assembly
11. Snap Ring "C"
12. Slide Joint Housing
13. Dust Shield
14. Circular Clip "A"
15. Snap Ring "A"
16. Inner Race
17. Cage
18. Ball
19. Slide Joint Housing
    With Extension Shaft
20. Snap Ring "E"
21. Support Bearing
22. Support Bearing Retainer
23. Bracket
24. Hex Bolt

96B30792

Courtesy of Nissan Motor Co., U.S.A.

Fig. 4: Exploded View Of Front Axle Shaft (Spider Assembly Type)

NOTE: Replace all snap rings, circlips & boot clamps when overhauling axle shaft.

Boot Clamp

OUTBOARD SIDE

Joint Assembly

Axle Shaft

Boot

Circlip

Boot

Snap Ring "A"

Cage

Ball

Snap Ring "C"

Boot Clamp

Snap Ring "B"

Inner Race

Slide Joint Housing With Extension Shaft

Support Bearing

Dust Shield

Snap Ring

Support Bearing Retainer

Bracket

Dust Shield

Slide Joint Housing

Circlip

Dust Shield

Snap Ring "D"

LEFT AXLE SHAFT

RIGHT AXLE SHAFT

90I09429

Courtesy of Nissan Motor Co., U.S.A.

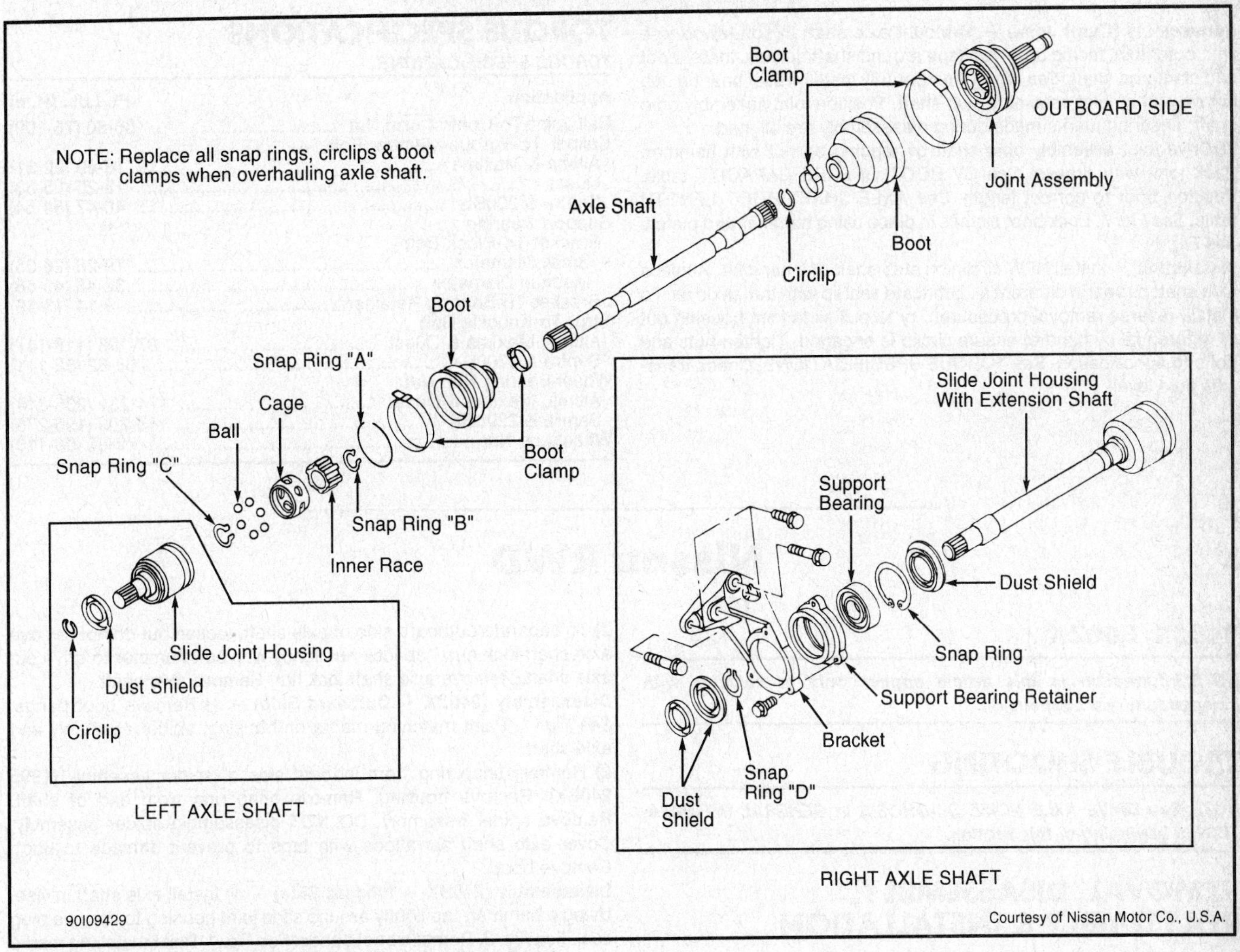

Fig. 5: Exploded View Of Front Axle Shaft (Ball & Cage Type)

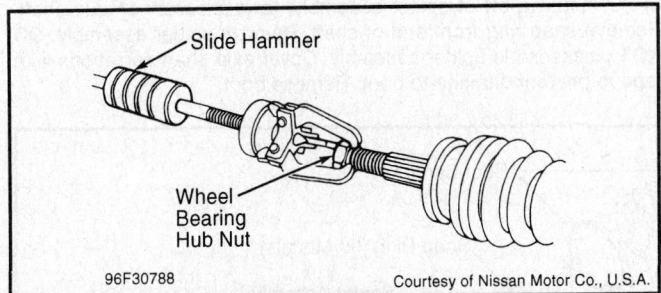

Slide Hammer

Wheel Bearing Hub Nut

96F30788

Courtesy of Nissan Motor Co., U.S.A.

Fig. 6: Removing Outer Joint Assembly

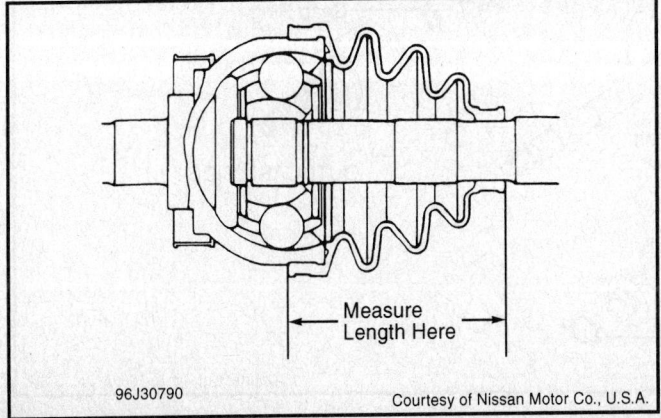

Measure Length Here

96J30790

Courtesy of Nissan Motor Co., U.S.A.

Fig. 7: Setting Boot Length

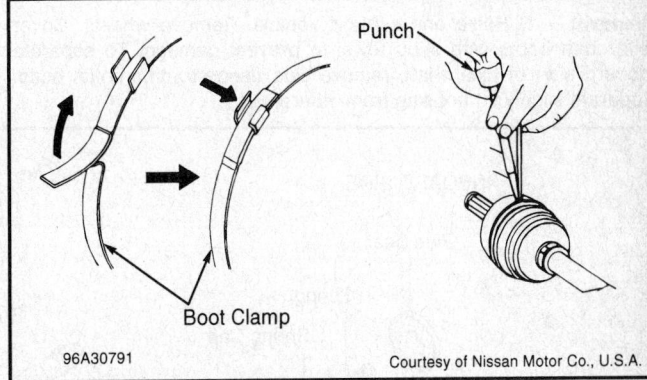

Punch

Boot Clamp

96A30791

Courtesy of Nissan Motor Co., U.S.A.

Fig. 8: Installing Boot Clamps

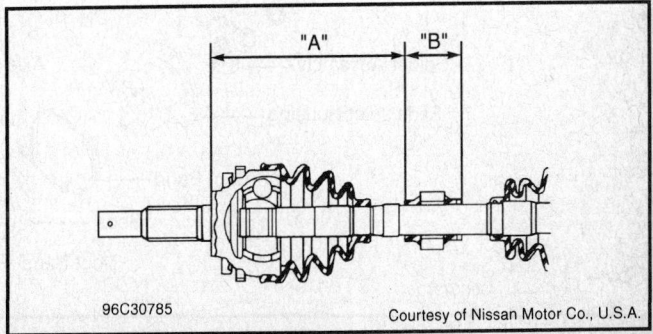

"A"

"B"

96C30785

Courtesy of Nissan Motor Co., U.S.A.

Fig. 8: Locating Dynamic Damper

AXLE SHAFTS
Nissan FWD (Cont.)

Reassembly (Outer Joint) – **1)** Mount axle shaft in soft-jawed vise with outer joint facing up. Wrap tape around shaft splines. Install boot and clamp on shaft. See Fig. 5. Temporarily install wheel bearing hub nut on end of joint assembly stub shaft. Position joint assembly onto shaft, ensuring marks made during disassembly are aligned.

2) Drive joint assembly onto shaft by tapping on nut with hammer. Pack joint with grease. See CV BOOT GREASE CAPACITY table. Position boot to correct length. See AXLE SHAFT BOOT LENGTH table. See Fig. 7. Lock boot clamps in place using hammer and punch. See Fig. 8.

Installation – Install NEW circlip on stub shaft of inner joint. Replace axle shaft oil seal in differential. Lubricate seal lip with transaxle oil. To install, reverse removal procedure. Try to pull slide joint housing out of differential by hand to ensure circlip is engaged. Tighten nuts and bolts to specification. See TORQUE SPECIFICATIONS. Check transaxle fluid level.

TORQUE SPECIFICATIONS
TORQUE SPECIFICATIONS

Application	Ft. Lbs. (N.m)
Ball Joint-To-Control Arm Nut	56-80 (76-109)
Caliper-To-Torque Member Bolt	
Altima & Maxima	16-23 (22-31)
Quest	18-25 (25-33)
Sentra & 200SL	40-47 (54-64)
Support Bearing	
Bracket-To-Block Bolt	
Small Diameter	19-26 (26-35)
Medium Diameter	32-43 (43-58)
Bracket-To-Bearing Retainer	9-14 (13-19)
Strut-To-Knuckle Bolt	
Altima, Maxima & Quest	87-108 (118-147)
Sentra & 2200SX	68-82 (92-111)
Wheel Bearing Hub Nut	
Altima, Maxima & Quest	174-231 (235-314)
Sentra & 2200SX	145-203 (196-275)
Wheel Lug Nut	72-87 (98-118)

Nissan RWD

240SX, 300ZX

NOTE: Information in this article applies only to vehicles with independent rear suspension.

TROUBLE SHOOTING

NOTE: See DRIVE AXLE NOISE DIAGNOSIS in GENERAL INFORMATION at beginning of this section.

REMOVAL, DISASSEMBLY, REASSEMBLY & INSTALLATION

AXLE SHAFTS

Removal – **1)** Raise and support vehicle. Remove wheels. Cover axle shaft boots with shop towel to prevent damage. To separate inboard side of axle shaft, remove side flange-to-differential bolts. Separate slide joint housing from differential.

2) To separate outboard side of axle shaft, loosen but do not remove axle shaft lock nut. Tap lock nut lightly with soft hammer to drive out axle shaft. Remove axle shaft lock nut. Remove axle shaft.

Disassembly (240SX – Outboard Side) – **1)** Remove boot bands. See Fig. 1. Paint matching marks on housing, spider assembly and axle shaft.

2) Remove snap ring from inboard side of spider assembly (1995 240SX). Remove housing. Remove snap ring from end of shaft. Remove spider assembly. DO NOT disassemble spider assembly. Cover axle shaft serrations with tape to prevent damage to boot. Remove boot.

Disassembly (240SX – Inboard Side) – **1)** Install axle shaft in vise. Using a hammer, tap lightly around slide joint housing to remove plug seal. See Fig. 2. Remove boot bands. See Fig. 1. Paint matching marks on slide joint housing, spider assembly and axle shaft.

2) Pull housing off of spider assembly, toward center of axle shaft. Remove snap ring from end of shaft. Remove spider assembly. DO NOT disassemble spider assembly. Cover axle shaft serrations with tape to prevent damage to boot. Remove boot.

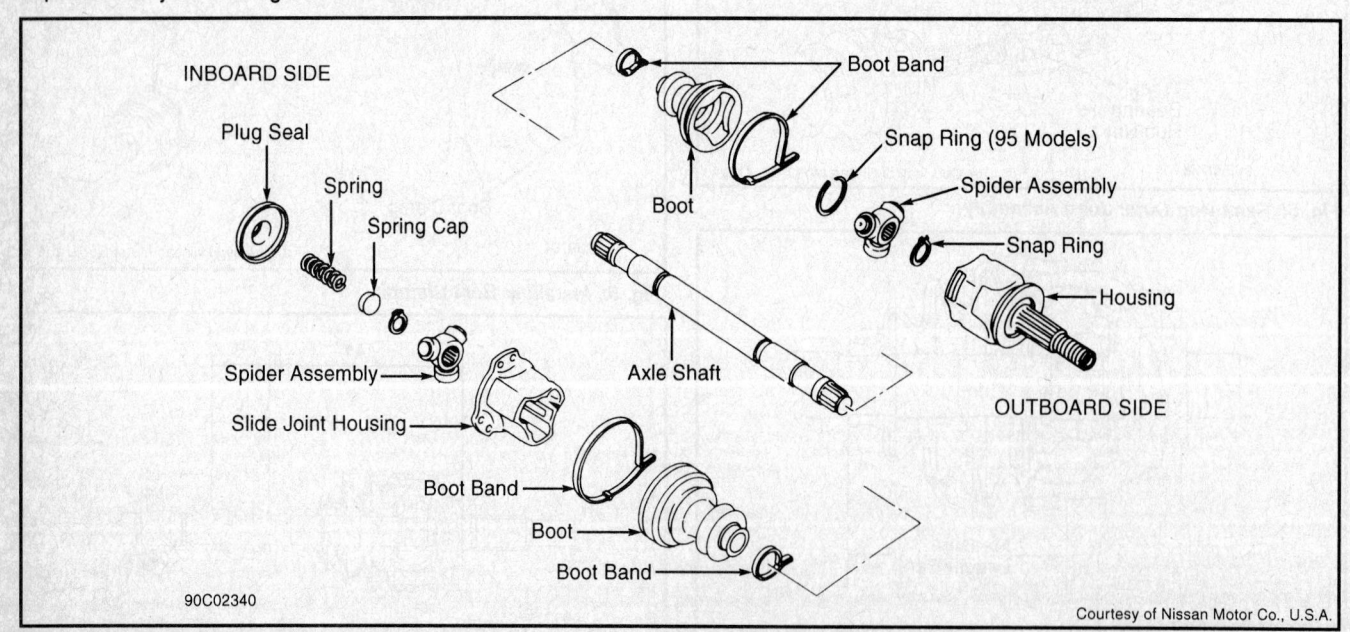

90C02340

Courtesy of Nissan Motor Co., U.S.A.

Fig. 1: Exploded View Of Axle Shaft (240SX, 1995 Shown 1996 Similar)

CAUTION: On 300ZX, outboard joint cannot be disassembled.

Disassembly (300ZX – Outboard Side) – Remove boot bands. Paint matching marks on joint assembly and axle shaft. *See Fig. 3*. Install axle shaft in vise. Temporarily install wheel bearing lock nut on end of shaft. Grasping nut with slide hammer, pull joint assembly off of shaft. Cover axle shaft serration with tape to prevent boot damage. Remove boot.

Disassembly (300ZX – Inboard Side) – 1) Remove boot bands. *See Fig. 3*. Mark slide joint housing in relation to inner race. Remove snap ring from outboard side of slide joint housing. Remove slide joint housing.

2) Mark inner race in relation to axle shaft. Remove snap ring from end of shaft. Remove ball cage, inner race and balls as a unit. Cover axle shaft serration with tape to prevent boot damage. Remove boot.

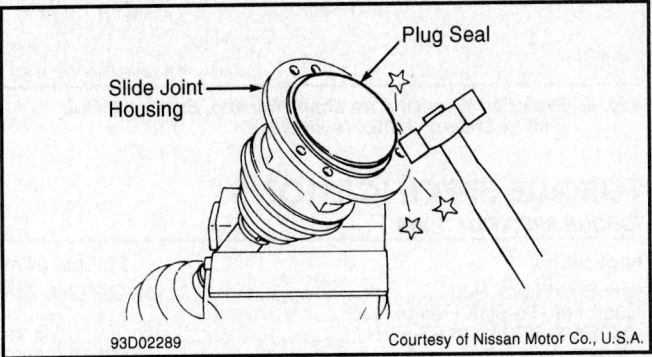

Fig. 2: Removing Plug Seal (240SX)

Reassembly (240SX – Outboard Side) – 1) Cover axle shaft serrations with tape to prevent damage to boot. Install NEW small boot band and boot onto axle shaft. Install spider assembly, ensuring chamfered side of spider assembly faces axle shaft. Ensure marks made during disassembly are aligned. Lightly tap spider assembly to seat it on shaft.

2) Install NEW snap ring at outboard end of shaft. Pack CV joint with specific amount of grease. See BOOT GREASE CAPACITY table. Install housing. Install NEW snap ring on inboard side of spider assembly. Set boot to specified length. See AXLE SHAFT BOOT LENGTH table. Ensure boot is fully installed on axle shaft groove. Lock boot bands securely with punch.

Reassembly (240SX – Inboard Side) – 1) Cover axle shaft serrations with tape to prevent boot damage. Install NEW small boot band and boot onto axle shaft. Install spider assembly, ensuring marks made during disassembly are aligned and chamfered edge of assembly faces axle shaft. Install NEW snap ring.

2) Install slide joint housing. Apply sealer to outer edge of NEW plug seal. Install spring cap, spring and plug seal, holding plug seal horizontally to ensure spring remains in position. After plug seal is installed, move shaft in axial direction to ensure spring stayed in position. If shaft drags or spring did not remain in position, remove plug seal, correctly position spring and install NEW plug seal.

3) Pack CV joint with specified amount of grease. See BOOT GREASE CAPACITY table. Install slide joint housing. Set boot to specified length. See AXLE SHAFT BOOT LENGTH table. Ensure boot is properly installed on axle shaft groove. Lock boot bands securely using punch.

AXLE SHAFT BOOT LENGTH

Application	Outboard Boot In. (mm)	Inboard Boot In. (mm)
240SX	3.74-3.82 (95-97)	3.74-3.82 (95-97)
300ZX		
Non-Turbo	3.66-3.74 (93-95)	3.78-3.86 (96-98)
Turbo	3.76-3.84 (96-97)	3.98-4.06 (101-103)

BOOT GREASE CAPACITY

Application	Ozs. (g)
240SX	
1995	
Inner	5.47-5.82 (155-165)
Outer	4.76-5.11 (135-145)
1996	
Inner	3.60-3.77 (102-107)
Outer	4.06-4.41 (115-125)
300ZX	
1995 (Non-Turbo)	
Inner	5.82-6.17 (165-175)
Outer	3.99-4.34 (113-123)
1995 (Turbo)	
Inner	6.35-7.05 (180-200)
Outer	6.00-6.70 (170-190)
1996 (Non-Turbo)	
Inner	5.82-6.17 (165-175)
Outer	3.99-4.34 (113-123)
1996 (Turbo)	
Inner	5.47-6.17 (155-175)
Outer	3.98-4.06 (101-103)

Reassembly (300ZX – Outboard Side) – 1) Cover axle shaft serrations with tape to prevent boot damage. Install NEW small boot band and boot onto axle shaft. Temporarily install nut on end of axle shaft. Install housing by lightly tapping on nut at end of axle shaft, ensuring marks made during disassembly are aligned.

2) Pack CV joint with Specified amount of grease. Set boot to specified length. See AXLE SHAFT BOOT LENGTH table. Ensure boot is properly installed on axle shaft groove. Lock boot bands securely using punch.

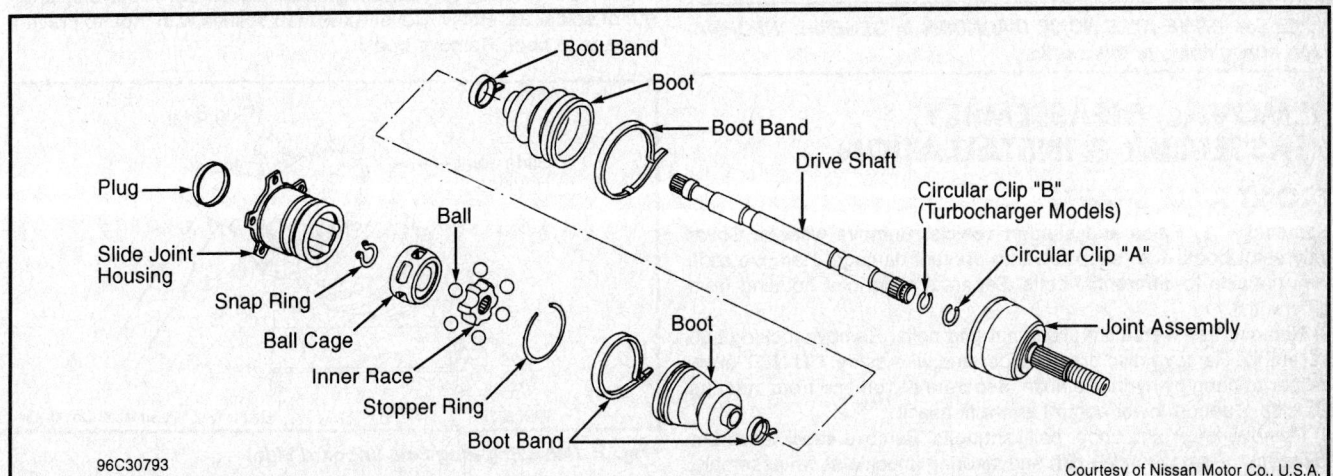

Fig. 3: Exploded View Of Axle Shaft (300ZX)

Reassembly (300ZX – Inboard Side) – 1) Cover axle shaft serrations with tape to prevent boot damage. Install boot and NEW small boot band onto axle shaft. Install ball cage, inner race and balls as an assembly. Ensure marks made during disassembly are aligned.

2) Install NEW snap ring on end of shaft. Pack CV joint with specified amount grease. Install slide joint housing. Install NEW snap ring on slide joint housing. Set boot to specified length. See AXLE SHAFT BOOT LENGTH table. Ensure boot is properly installed on axle shaft groove. Lock boot bands securely using punch.

Installation – 1) Install axle shafts into wheel hub and temporarily tighten wheel hub lock nut. Install axle shaft onto differential side flange. Try to pull axle shaft out of differential by hand to ensure proper engagement of snap rings.

2) Tighten wheel hub lock nut to specification. See TORQUE SPECIFICATIONS. Replace differential fluid (if required). To complete installation, reverse removal procedure.

REAR HUB ASSEMBLY

Removal – While applying parking brake or pressing brake pedal, remove lock nut from end of axle stub shaft. *See Fig. 4.* Release brakes. Remove brake caliper and rotor. Suspend caliper aside. Remove axle shaft. See AXLE SHAFTS under REMOVAL, DISASSEMBLY, REASSEMBLY & INSTALLATION. Remove wheel bearing/hub assembly from axle housing.

Disassembly – Press wheel bearing assembly out of hub. Using bearing puller, remove bearing race from hub.

Reassembly – Press wheel bearing assembly over hub. Use care not to damage grease seal.

Installation – To install, reverse removal procedure. Tighten wheel bearing lock nut to specification. See TORQUE SPECIFICATIONS. If wheel bearing is noisy, or if hub axial play exceeds .002 (.05 mm), replace rear hub assembly.

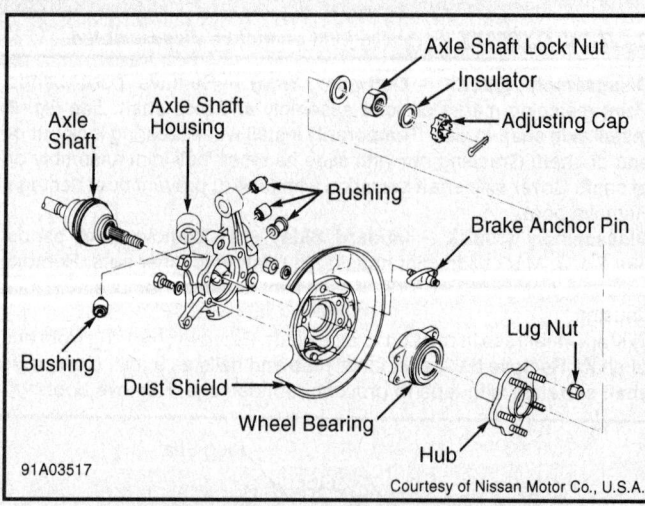

Fig. 4: Exploded View Of Axle Shaft Housing, Bearing & Hub (300ZX Shown; 240SX Is Similar)

TORQUE SPECIFICATIONS

TORQUE SPECIFICATIONS

Application	Ft. Lbs. (N.m)
Axle Shaft Lock Nut	152-203 (206-275)
Axle Shaft-To-Side Flange Nut	
240SX & 300ZX Non-Turbo	47-58 (64-78)
300ZX Turbo (Bolt)	50-58 (68-78)
Drive Shaft-To-Companion Flange Bolt	25-32 (34-44)
Strut-To-Axle Housing Bolt	
240SX	58-72 (78-98)
300ZX	57-72 (77-98)
Wheel Bearing Hub-To-Axle Housing Nut	58-72 (79-98)
Wheel Lug Nuts	72-87 (98-118)

Nissan 4WD

Pathfinder, Pickup

NOTE: Only front wheel shafts with CV type drive joints are covered in this article.

TROUBLE SHOOTING

NOTE: See DRIVE AXLE NOISE DIAGNOSIS in GENERAL INFORMATION at beginning of this section.

REMOVAL, DISASSEMBLY, REASSEMBLY & INSTALLATION

FRONT AXLE SHAFTS

Removal – 1) Raise and support vehicle. Remove wheels. Cover axle shaft boots with shop towel to prevent damage. Remove slide joint housing-to-differential bolts. Separate slide joint housing from differential.

2) Remove transverse link fixing nut and bolts. Remove locking hub assembly. Remove disc brake caliper and wire aside. DO NOT allow caliper to hang by hydraulic hose. Separate tie rod end from steering knuckle. Support lower control arm with a jack.

3) Remove lower and upper ball joint bolts. Remove shock absorber lower bolt. Remove axle shaft and steering knuckle as an assembly. Protect end of axle shaft with block of wood. Lightly tap end of axle shaft to separate axle shaft from steering knuckle.

Disassembly (Inboard Side – 1) Mount axle shaft in vise. Using a hammer, tap lightly around slide joint housing to remove plug seal. *See Fig. 1.* Remove boot clamps. *See Fig. 2.* Mark slide joint housing in relation to axle shaft for reassembly reference. Pull boot and housing off of spider assembly, toward center of axle shaft.

2) Mark spider assembly in relation to axle shaft for reassembly reference. Remove snap ring securing spider assembly. Press axle shaft out of spider assembly. Cover axle shaft splines with tape to prevent damage to boot. Remove boot.

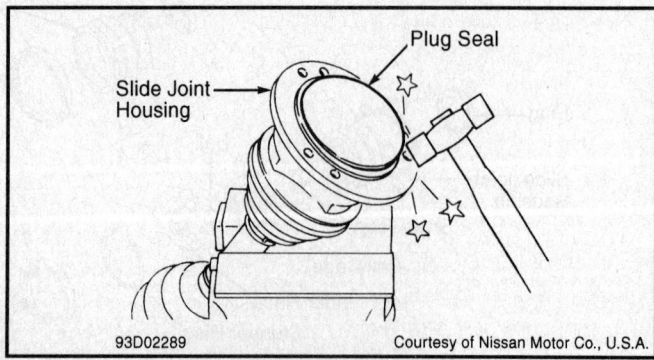

Fig. 1: Removing Plug Seal (Inboard Side)

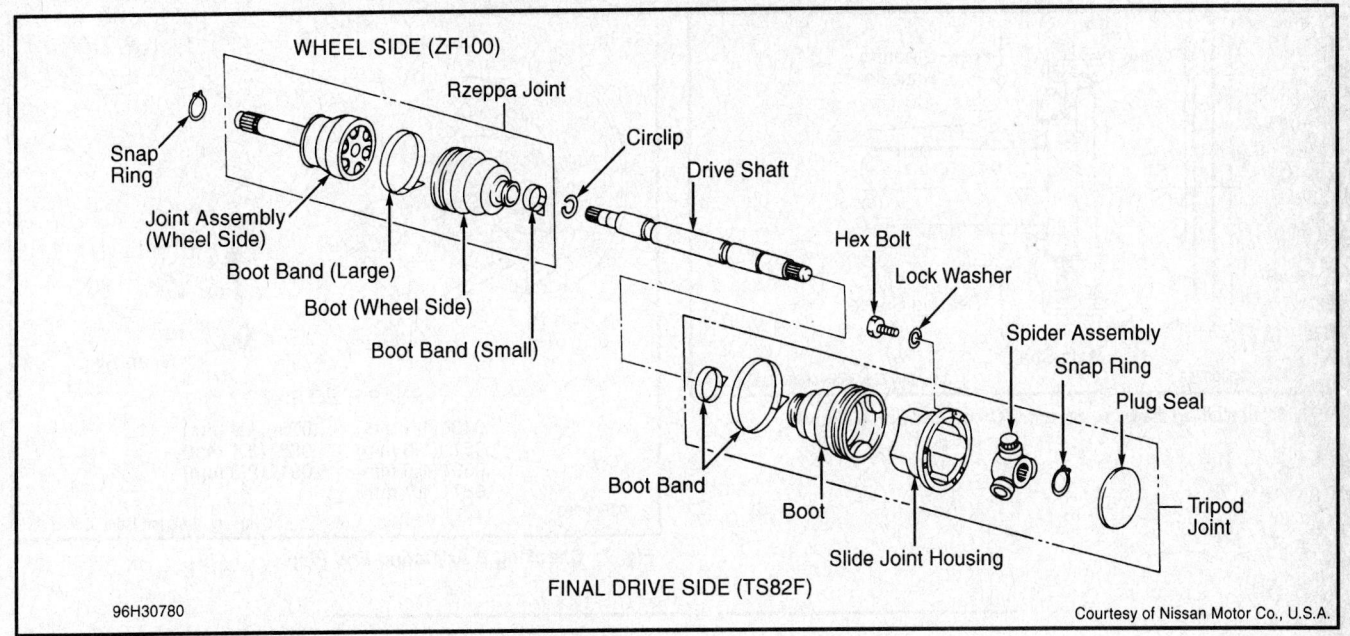

Fig. 2: Exploded View Of Axle Shaft (Pathfinder & Pickup 3.0L)

NOTE: Outer joint can be removed from axle shaft but cannot be disassembled.

Disassembly (Outboard Side) – Mount axle shaft in vise. Remove boot clamps. *See Fig. 2.* Slide boot away from joint assembly. Mark joint assembly in relation to axle shaft. To remove joint assembly, pull stub shaft and tap joint assembly with brass mallet. *See Fig. 3.* Cover axle shaft splines with tape to prevent boot damage. Remove boot.

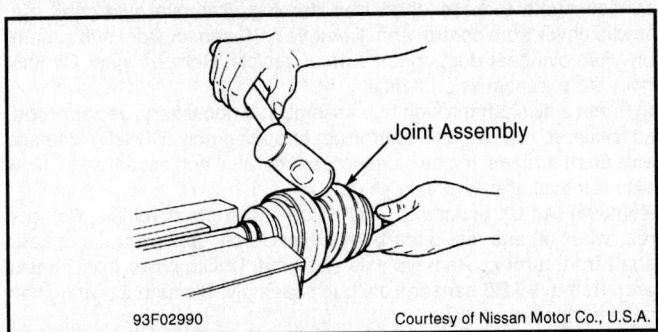

Fig. 3: Removing Outer Joint Assembly

Inspection – **1)** Thoroughly clean all parts in cleaning solvent and dry with compressed air. Check for deformation or damage. Replace driveshaft of twisted or cracked. Inspect boot for fatigue, cracks or wear.

2) Inspect inner joint for signs of scoring, rust, wear or excessive play. Inspect splines for deformation or damage. Inspect slide joint housing for any damage. Inspect outer joint assembly for deformation or damage. Replace parts an necessary.

Reassembly (Inboard Side – **1)** Mount axle shaft in vise. Wrap tape around shaft splines. Install small clamp, boot and slide joint housing on shaft. Install spider assembly, with chamfer facing shaft, aligning matchmarks made during disassembly. Install NEW snap ring.

2) Pack joint with 3.35-3.70 ozs. (95-105 g) of grease. Install slide joint housing, aligning marks made during disassembly. Position boot to correct length. Inboard boot length should be 3.74-3.82" (95-97 mm). Outboard boot length should be 3.78-3.86" (96-98 mm) *See Fig. 4.* Lock boot clamps in place using hammer and punch. *See Fig. 5.*

Installation – Ensure chamfered side of bearing spacer is facing inboard. *See Fig. 6.* Install axle shaft into wheel bearing hub. To complete installation, reverse removal procedure. If axle shaft end play is not .004-.012" (.1-.3 mm), replace snap ring with snap ring of appropri-

ate size. *See Fig. 7.* Attach inboard to slide joint housing to differential final drive. Install transverse link. Install locking hub assembly. Install disc brake caliper. Tighten nuts and bolt to specification. See TORQUE SPECIFICATIONS.

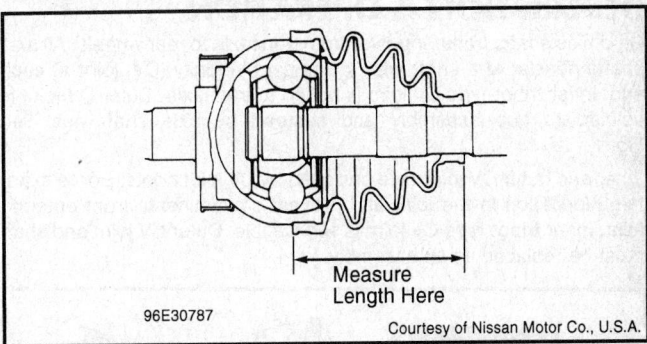

Fig. 4: Setting Boot Length

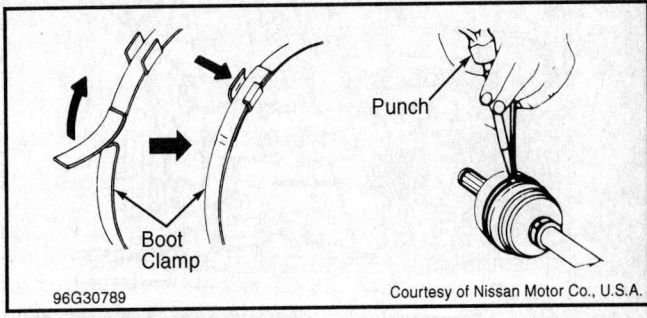

Fig. 5: Installing Boot Clamps

TORQUE SPECIFICATIONS
TORQUE SPECIFICATIONS

Application	Ft. Lbs. (N.m)
Ball Joint-To-Control Arm Bolt	
Lower	87-123 (118-167)
Upper	58-108 (78-147)
Caliper-To-Torque Member Bolt	53-72 (72-97)
Free-Running Hub Bolts	18-25 (25-34)
Shock Absorber Lower Mount Bolt	87-108 (118-147)
Tie Rod End Ball Joint Nut	47-80 (64-108)
Wheel Lug Nuts	87-108 (118-146)

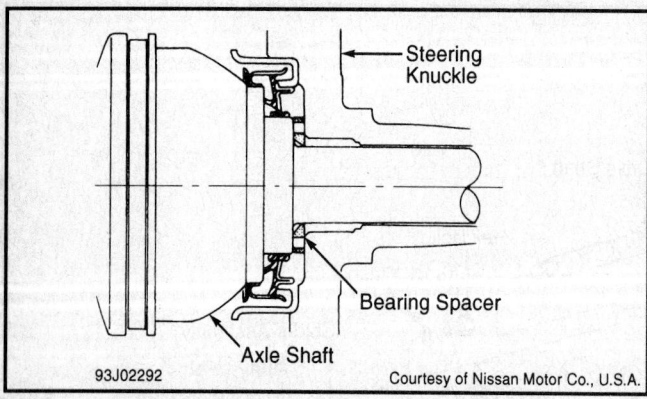

Fig. 6: Installing Bearing Spacer (Cross-Sectional View)

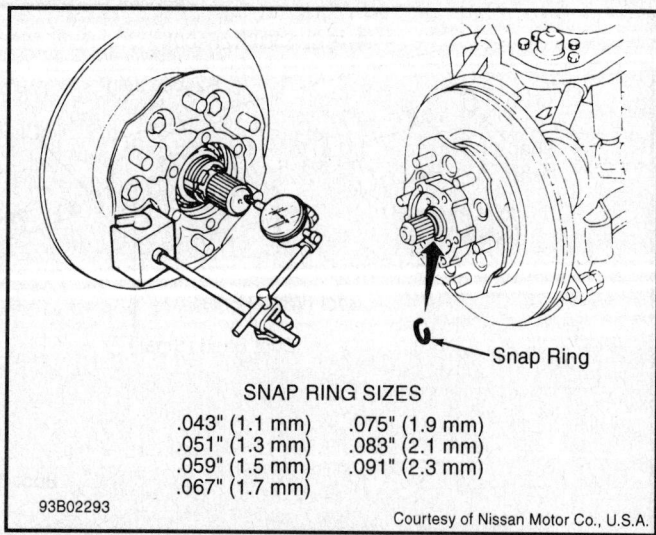

SNAP RING SIZES

.043" (1.1 mm)	.075" (1.9 mm)
.051" (1.3 mm)	.083" (2.1 mm)
.059" (1.5 mm)	.091" (2.3 mm)
.067" (1.7 mm)	

Fig. 7: Checking & Adjusting End Play

Porsche RWD

911 Carrera 2
DESCRIPTION & OPERATION

Rear axle shafts transfer power from transaxle to rear wheels. All axle shafts consist of a shaft with a Constant Velocity (CV) joint at each end. Inner tripot-type CV joint is bolted to transaxle. Outer CV joint is splined to hub assembly and secured by axle shaft nut. See Fig. 1.

Inner and outer CV joints are enclosed by CV joint boots. Boots maintain lubrication in the joint and prevent contaminants from entering joint. Inner tripot-type CV joint is serviceable, Outer CV joint and shaft must be replaced as an assembly.

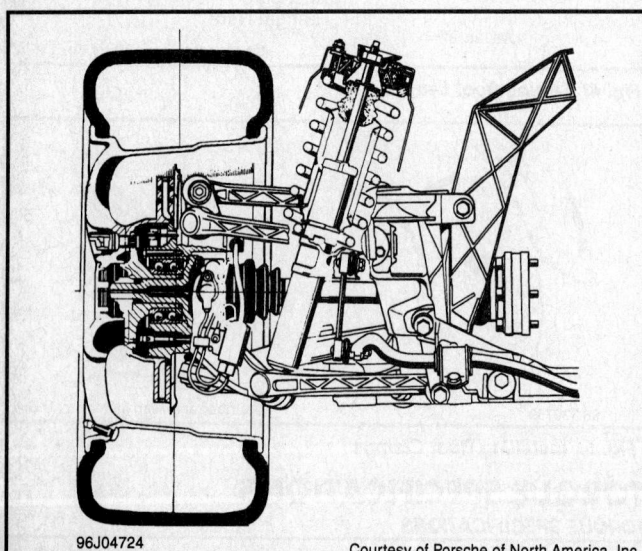

Fig. 1: Cut-Away View Of Rear Suspension

TROUBLE SHOOTING

NOTE: See DRIVE AXLE NOISE DIAGNOSIS in GENERAL INFORMATION at beginning of this section.

REMOVAL, DISASSEMBLY, REASSEMBLY & INSTALLATION

DRIVE AXLE SHAFTS

Removal (Left Axle – Manual Transmission) – 1) Raise and support vehicle. Remove rear wheel(s) and rear underbody cover. Apply service brake to keep shaft from turning. Remove axle shaft nut. Unclip cover from control arm. Remove ABS sensor from hub assembly. Remove heat duct on left side of vehicle. Remove inner CV joint bolts from transmission flange.

2) Press axle shaft through hub assembly. If necessary, use appropriate puller to remove axle shaft from hub assembly. DO NOT damage axle shaft threads. It may be necessary to raise hub assembly to allow axle removal. Remove axle shaft.

Removal (All Other Axles) – 1) Raise and support vehicle. Remove rear wheel(s) and rear underbody cover. Apply service brake to keep shaft from turning. Remove axle shaft nut. Unclip cover from control arm. Remove ABS sensor from hub assembly. Disconnect wiring harness and move aside.

2) Unbolt oil line from transmission on right side of vehicle. Unbolt brake caliper and move aside, supporting with wire. Remove heat duct on left side of vehicle. Disconnect sway bar link from sway bar.

3) Disconnect parking brake cable in interior of vehicle. Remove center console. Remove adjusting nut. See Fig. 2. Remove retaining clip and remove pin. Remove brake handle. Unhook tab washer. Unhook parking brake cable and pull out cable housing.

4) Disconnect 3 lower control arms from undercarriage mounts. See Fig. 3. Place reference marks on lower control arm eccentric adjusters for reassembly reference.

5) Remove inner CV joint bolts from transmission flange. Attach lever to wheel studs. Using helper, lift hub assembly. See Fig. 4. Press axle shaft through hub assembly. If necessary, use appropriate puller to remove axle shaft from hub assembly. DO NOT damage axle shaft threads. Remove axle shaft toward center of vehicle.

Disassembly – Remove circlip from inboard end of axle shaft. Remove inner CV joint. Cut boot clamps. Slide inboard and outboard boots off inboard end of axle shaft. See Fig. 5.

NOTE: DO NOT disassemble outboard CV joint. If outboard CV joint is defective, replace axle shaft as an assembly.

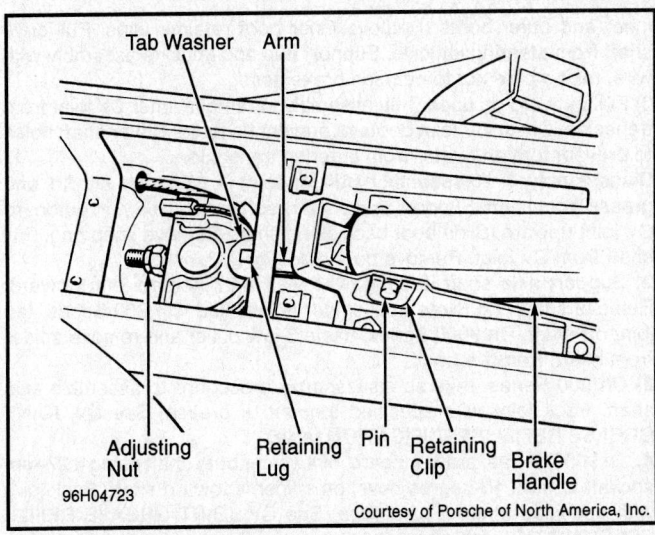

Fig. 2: Identifying Parking Brake Components

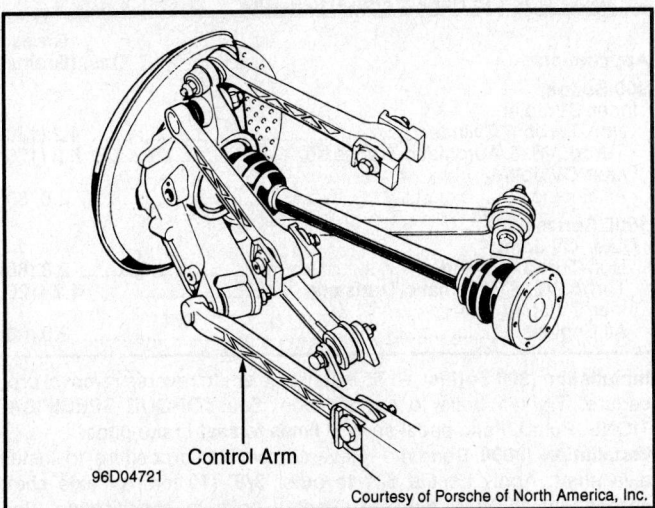

Fig. 3: View Of Rear Suspension & Axle Assembly

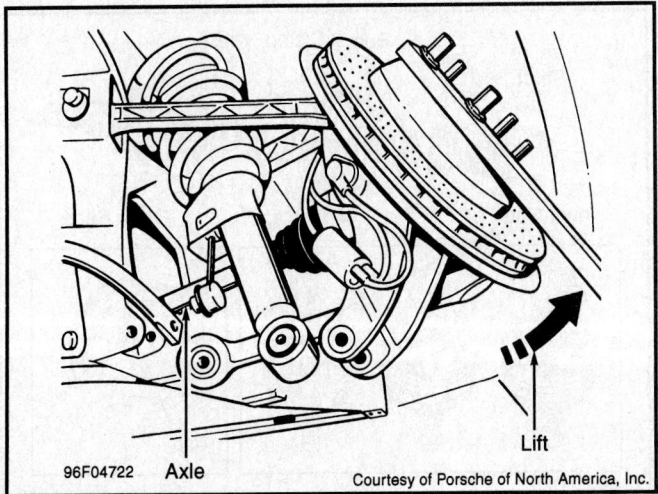

Fig. 4: Removing Rear Axle Assembly

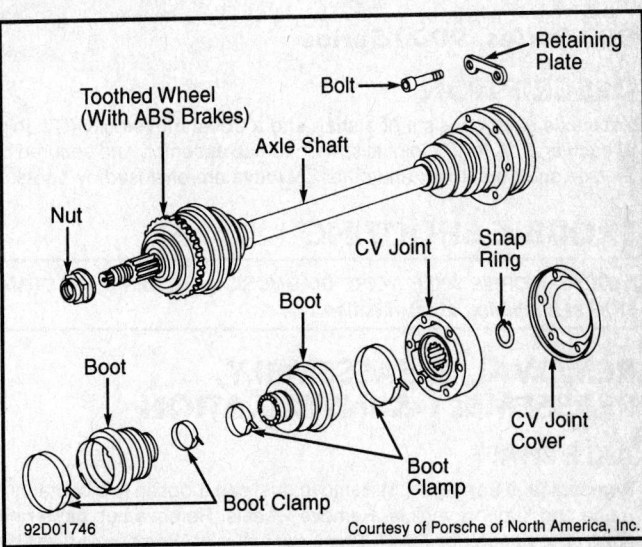

Fig. 5: Exploded View Of RWD Axle Assembly

Reassembly & Installation – Clean all components and inspect for wear and/or damage. To reassemble axle shaft, reverse disassembly procedure. Pack CV boots with new grease supplied with boot kit. Install clamps. To complete installation, reverse removal procedure. Ensure lower control arm eccentric adjusters are installed in original position. Install new axle nut. Tighten axle nut and flange bolts to specification. See TORQUE SPECIFICATIONS. Once parking brake is assembled, adjust handle free play to 4 "clicks" when handle is lifted.

TORQUE SPECIFICATIONS

TORQUE SPECIFICATIONS

Application	Ft. Lbs. (N.m)
Axle Shaft Hub Nut	340 (460)
Axle Shaft-To-Transaxle Bolt	
8-mm Bolt	31 (42)
10-mm Bolt	59 (80)
Brake Caliper Bolt	63 (85)
Control Arm Bolt	148 (200)
Retaining Plate Bolt	15 (20)
Stabilizer Bar-To-Stabilizer Link Nut	34 (46)
Strut-To-Control Arm Bolt	63 (85)
Wheel Lug Nut	96 (130)
	INCH Lbs. (N.m)
Speed Sensor Bolt	89 (10)

AXLE SHAFTS
Saab

900 Series, 9000 Series

DESCRIPTION

Each axle shaft consists of a shaft and a Constant Velocity (CV) joint at each end. Outer CV joint is splined to hub assembly and secured by an axle shaft nut. Inner and outer CV joints are enclosed by boots.

TROUBLE SHOOTING

NOTE: See DRIVE AXLE NOISE DIAGNOSIS in GENERAL INFORMATION at beginning of this section.

REMOVAL, DISASSEMBLY, REASSEMBLY & INSTALLATION

AXLE SHAFT

Removal (900 Series) – 1) Remove dust cap. Loosen hub center nut. Raise and support vehicle. Remove wheels. Remove hub center nut and ball joint nut. *See Fig. 1.* Press out ball joint. Remove anti-roll bar nut, using care to save washer and rubber bushing.
2) Press lower control arm down. Tap axle shaft out of hub with a rubber mallet. Move strut aside and remove drive shaft. Disconnect axle shaft joint from intermediate shaft.

NOTE: Use care to avoid stretching brake hoses and sensor cables.

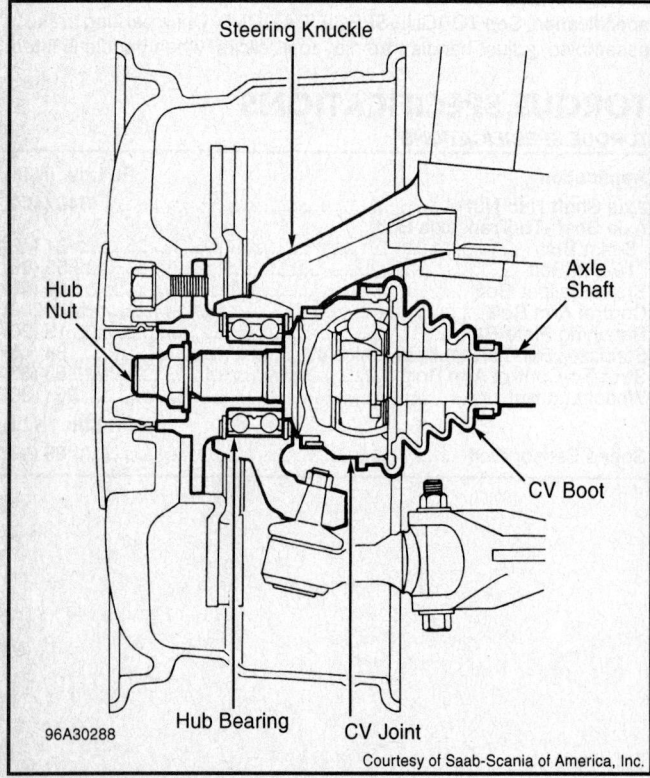

96A30288

Courtesy of Saab-Scania of America, Inc.

Fig. 1: Sectional View Of Steering Knuckle (900 Series Shown, 9000 Series Is Similar)

Removal (9000 Series) – 1) Raise and support vehicle. Remove wheels. Remove and discard hub nut. Using puller, press axle shaft into hub assembly no more than .79" (20 mm). Disconnect brake hose from strut.
2) Disconnect strut from steering knuckle. Disconnect ABS sensor and wiring. Clean all dirt from work area, paying particular attention to

inner and outer boots. Remove inner boot retainer clips. Pull drive shaft from steering knuckle. Support hub and knuckle assembly with wire, taking care not to damage brake hose.
3) Pull outward on upper hub assembly to remove inner CV joint from transaxle. Cover CV joint boots to prevent damage. Cover shaft holes to prevent foreign matter from entering transaxle.
Disassembly & Reassembly (All Models) – 1) Clean all dirt and grease from shaft. Support axle shaft in soft-jawed vise with outboard CV joint upward. Slide boot back along shaft. Remove snap ring. Pull shaft from CV joint. Remove boot. *See Fig. 2, 3, or 4.*
2) Support axle shaft in soft-jawed vise with inboard joint upward. Remove snap ring. Note how spider is installed. On 900 Series, tap joint off shaft. On 9000 Series, use a 3-jaw puller and remove spider from shaft. Remove boot.
3) On 900 Series, reverse disassembly procedure to assemble axle shaft. Pack joint with specified amount of grease. See CV JOINT GREASE REFILL SPECIFICATION table.
4) On 9000 Series, press inboard joint spider onto shaft using a 27-mm socket. Ensure 45-degree bevel on spider is toward shaft. Pack joint with specified amount of grease. See CV JOINT GREASE REFILL SPECIFICATION table.

CV JOINT GREASE REFILL SPECIFICATION

Application	Grease Ozs. (Grams)
900 Series	
Inner CV Joint	
Non-Turbo 4 Cylinder	4.2 (120)
Turbo, V6, & Automatic Transaxle	6.2 (175)
Outer CV Joint	
All Engines	2.8 (80)
9000 Series	
Outer CV Joint	
Non-Turbo 4 Cylinder	2.8 (80)
Turbo, V6, & Automatic Transaxle	4.2 (120)
Inner CV Joint	
All Engines	2.0 (60)

Installation (900 Series) – To install axle shaft, reverse removal procedure. Tighten bolts to specification. See TORQUE SPECIFICATIONS. Pump brake pedal several times to seat brake pads.
Installation (9000 Series) – Reverse removal procedure to install axle shaft. Apply Loctite 641 to outer 3/8" (10 mm) of axle shaft splines. Install NEW hub nut. Tighten bolts to specification. See TORQUE SPECIFICATIONS.

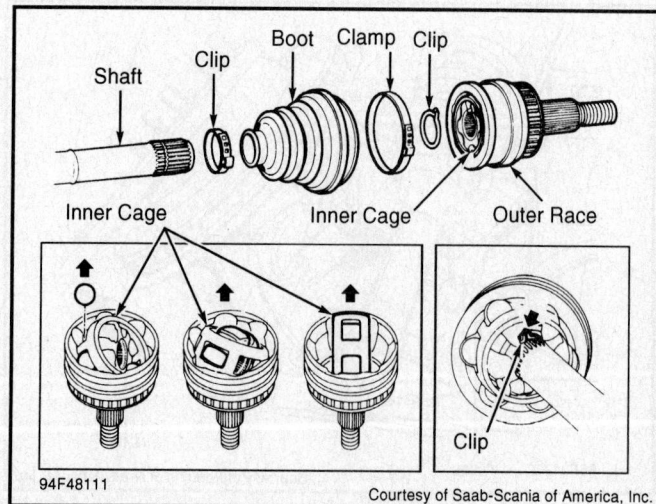

94F48111

Courtesy of Saab-Scania of America, Inc.

Fig. 2: Disassembling Outer CV Joint (All Models)

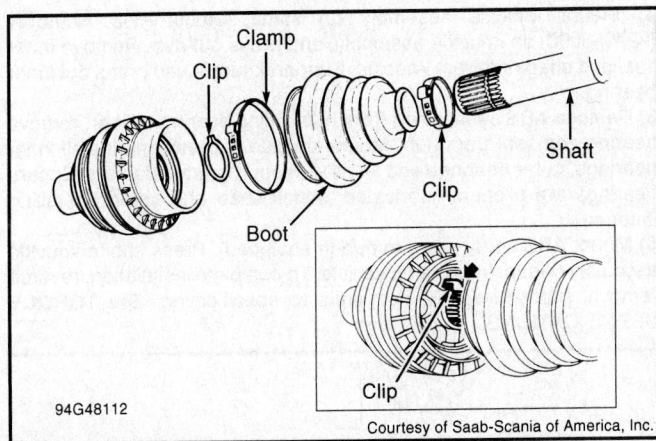

Fig. 3: Disassembling Inner CV Joint (Non-Turbo 4-Cylinder)

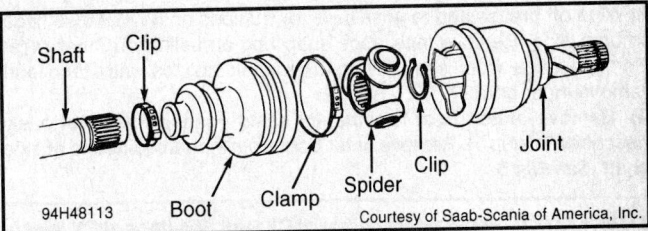

Fig. 4: Disassembling Inner CV Joint
(Turbo, V6, & Automatic Transaxle)

TORQUE SPECIFICATIONS

TORQUE SPECIFICATIONS

Application	Ft. Lbs. (N.m)
Axle Shaft Hub Nut	207-222 (280-300)
Ball Joint Nut	52-66 (70-90)
Lower Strut Bolts	58-77 (78-105)
Wheel Lug Bolts	77-92 (105-125)

Subaru FWD

Impreza, Legacy, SVX

DESCRIPTION & OPERATION

Axle shafts transfer power from transaxle to driving wheels. All axle shafts consist of a shaft with a flexible Constant Velocity (CV) joint at each end. Inner tripod type CV joint is secured to transaxle stub shaft by a roll pin. Outer CV joint is splined to hub assembly and secured by axle shaft nut.

Inner and outer CV joints are enclosed by CV joint boots. Boots maintain lubrication in the joint and prevents contaminants from entering joint. Boots must be replaced when signs of leakage or cracks are present. Inner tripod type CV joint can be repaired, but outer CV joint and shaft must be replaced as an assembly. Three types are used, identified by number of rings on shaft. See Fig. 1. All types have a spline ID of 1.055" (26.8 mm) diameter with 25 spline teeth on inboard joint.

TROUBLE SHOOTING

NOTE: See DRIVE AXLE NOISE DIAGNOSIS in GENERAL INFORMATION at beginning of this section.

REMOVAL, DISASSEMBLY, REASSEMBLY & INSTALLATION

NOTE: For information on rear axle shafts for AWD vehicles, see Subaru AWD Rear Shafts article.

FWD AXLE SHAFT

Removal – 1) Raise and support vehicle. Remove front wheels. Unstake axle shaft nut and remove. Remove stabilizer link. Disconnect ABS sensor from housing. Remove brake caliper assembly from steering knuckle without disconnecting hydraulic line. Suspend caliper out of way.

2) Remove brake rotor. On inboard side of axle shaft, drive out roll pin securing axle shaft to transaxle.

3) Remove tie rod cotter pin and nut. Using a puller, disconnect tie rod end from steering knuckle. Remove steering knuckle-to-strut retaining bolt(s). Remove pinch bolt and separate ball joint from lower control arm.

4) Using Puller (926470000) and Plate (927140000), remove axle shaft from steering knuckle. See Fig. 2.

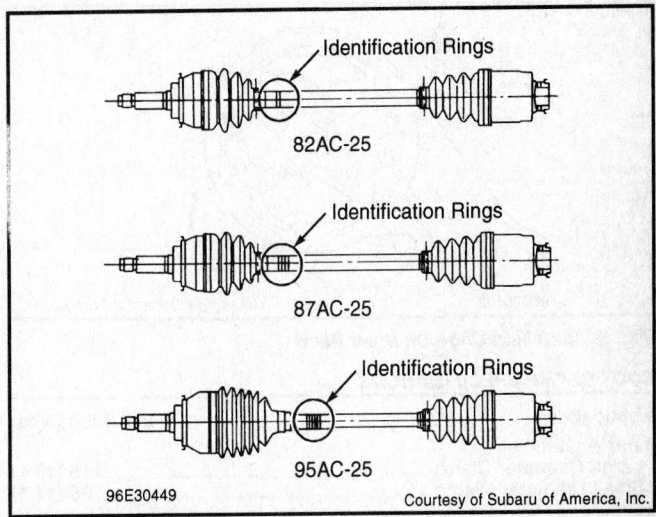

Fig. 1: Identifying Axle Shafts

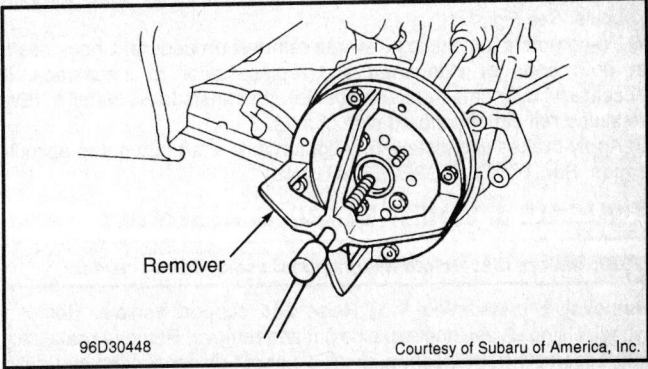

Fig. 2: Removing Axle Shaft From Steering Knuckle

Disassembly – 1) Straighten bent end of boot clamps on inner boot of axle shaft. Loosen clamps with screwdriver or pliers, taking care not to damage boot.

2) Slide boot from larger end of inboard joint. Pry out and remove round snap ring located at neck of outer race of inboard joint. Slide outer race from shaft assembly.

3) Wipe off grease and remove balls (or trunions on SVX). Move cage to boot side. Remove inner race snap ring and slide off inner race. Remove cage from shaft. Wrap axle shaft splines with tape and remove inner boot.

4) Remove outer boot clamps in same manner as previously described in step **1)**. Remove outer boot from inboard joint end of axle shaft. *See Fig. 5*

NOTE: DO NOT disassemble outboard CV joint. If outboard CV joint is defective, replace axle shaft as an assembly.

Reassembly – **1)** To reassemble axle shaft, reverse disassembly procedure. Apply 2.82-3.17 oz. (80-90 g) of grease (NTG2218) to outer joint and boot. Install and tighten boot clamps to specifications. See BOOT CLAMP TORQUE SPECIFICATIONS table.

2) Ensure cage is installed onto shaft with cut-out side facing end of shaft. When installing cage over inner race, align inner race protrusions with tracks on cage, then rotate cage one-half turn. *See Fig. 3.* Apply 2.82-3.17 oz.(80-90 g) of grease, Molylex No. 2 for M/T, Yellow VU-3A702 for A/T grease into outer race. Fit over cage and balls, install circlip. Evenly apply .71-1.06 oz (20-30 g) of appropriate grease to inner surface of boot. Ensure inside of larger end of boot and boot groove of outer race is free of grease. Before tightening inner boot clamps, ensure inboard joint is at center of its travel. Distance between inner and outer boots on SVX models should be 11.28" (286.5 mm)

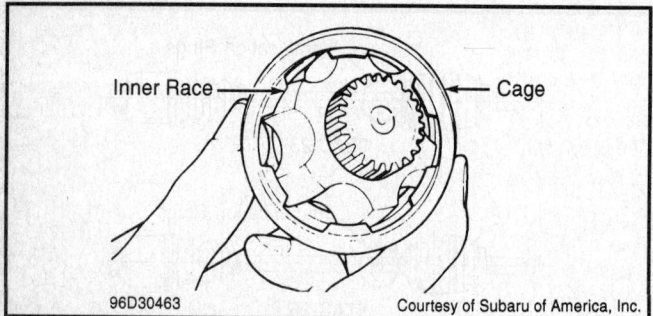

Fig. 3: Installing Cage On Inner Race

BOOT CLAMP SPECIFICATIONS

Application	INCH lbs (N.m)
Inner & Outer	
Large Diameter Clamp	116 (13.1)
Small Diameter Clamp	98 (11.1)

Installation – **1)** To install axle shaft, insert outboard end of shaft in steering knuckle. Use Installer (92243000) to insert shaft through knuckle. *See Fig. 4.*

2) To complete installation, reverse removal procedure. Check seals at both ends of axle shaft and replace prior to installation, if necessary. Lubricate transaxle seal lip with transaxle oil. Install a NEW retaining roll pin on inboard side of axle.

3) Apply brakes and install NEW tighten axle shaft hub nut to specification. See TORQUE SPECIFICATIONS.

KNUCKLE & WHEEL BEARING ASSEMBLY

NOTE: Always discard old bearings and seals. Do not reuse.

Removal & Installation – **1)** Raise and support vehicle. Remove wheel. Using chisel, unstake axle nut and remove. Remove brake caliper assembly from steering knuckle without disconnecting hydraulic line. Wire caliper out of way. Disconnect ABS speed sensor.

2) Remove brake rotor. Disconnect ball joint from knuckle. Remove tie rod cotter pin and nut. Using a puller, disconnect tie rod end from steering knuckle. Scribe reference mark on strut-to-knuckle retaining bolts. Remove steering knuckle-to-strut retaining bolt(s).

3) Remove axle shaft from steering knuckle. *See Fig. 5.* Remove steering knuckle from vehicle.

4) Mount knuckle assembly on stand. Mount Hub Remover (927060000) on knuckle assembly, and press out hub. Remove inner seal and snap ring from knuckle. Support knuckle and press out inner bearing.

5) Remove ABS sensor ring from hub. Using bearing splitter, remove bearing and seal from hub. Mount knuckle in press and install inner bearings, outer bearings and seals with appropriate adapters. Ensure bearings are properly lubricated. Install snap ring before installing inner seal.

6) Mount ABS sensor ring to hub (if equipped). Press hub in knuckle assembly. Mount knuckle on vehicle. To complete installation, reverse removal procedures. Tighten bolts to specification. See TORQUE SPECIFICATIONS.

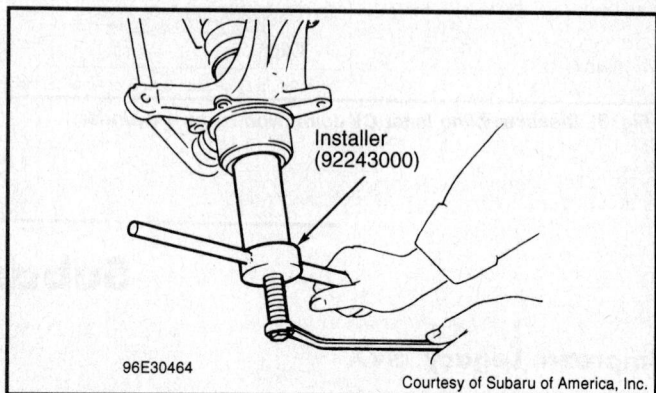

Fig. 4: Installing Axle Shaft In Steering Knuckle

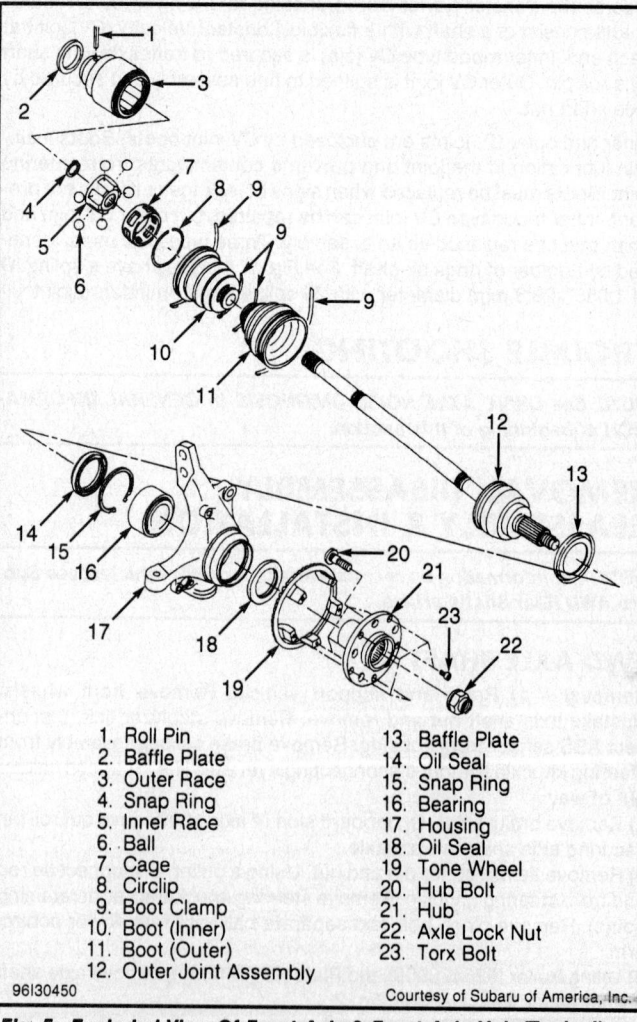

1. Roll Pin	13. Baffle Plate
2. Baffle Plate	14. Oil Seal
3. Outer Race	15. Snap Ring
4. Snap Ring	16. Bearing
5. Inner Race	17. Housing
6. Ball	18. Oil Seal
7. Cage	19. Tone Wheel
8. Circlip	20. Hub Bolt
9. Boot Clamp	21. Hub
10. Boot (Inner)	22. Axle Lock Nut
11. Boot (Outer)	23. Torx Bolt
12. Outer Joint Assembly	

Fig. 5: Exploded View Of Front Axle & Front Axle Hub (Typical)

AXLE SHAFTS
Subaru FWD (Cont.)

TORQUE SPECIFICATIONS

TORQUE SPECIFICATIONS

Application [1]	Ft. Lbs. (N.m)
Impreza & Legacy	
Axle Nut	122-152 (166-206)
Ball Joint-To-Control Arm Nut	29 (39)
Ball Joint-To-Knuckle Nut	28-37 (38-50)
Caliper-To-Knuckle Bolt	36-51 (49-69)
Strut-To-Knuckle Bolt	97-119 (132-162)
Tie Rod End Nut	18-22 (25-30)

[1] – Use NEW self-locking nuts.

Subaru AWD Rear Shafts

Impreza, Legacy, SVX

DESCRIPTION & OPERATION

Axle shafts transfer power from rear differential to rear wheels. Axle shafts consist of a shaft with a flexible Constant Velocity (CV) joint at each end. Inner and outer CV joints are enclosed by CV joint boots. Boot maintains lubrication in the joint and prevents contaminants from entering joint. Boots must be replaced when signs of leakage or cracks are present. Inner tripod type CV joint can be repaired, but outer CV joint and shaft must be replaced as an assembly. Shafts are identified by rings on shafts and marked as follows: Impreza and Legacy (79AC-RH and 79AC-LH). SVX (87AC-RH and 87AC-LH). See Fig. 1.

TROUBLE SHOOTING

NOTE: See DRIVE AXLE NOISE DIAGNOSIS in GENERAL INFORMATION at beginning of this section.

REMOVAL, DISASSEMBLY, REASSEMBLY & INSTALLATION

AWD AXLE SHAFTS

NOTE: Disassembly and reassembly procedures for rear axle shafts are same as front shafts. See appropriate AXLE SHAFTS article.

Removal – 1) Remove rear hub cap. Apply brakes, unstake and loosen axle shaft nut. Raise and support vehicle. Remove wheel. Remove axle shaft nut. Remove disc rotor.

2) On vehicles with anti-lock brakes (ABS), remove rear speed sensor from backing plate. On all vehicles, remove brake assembly from backing plate and wire aside. Disconnect end of parking brake. With drum brakes, remove brake line to wheel cylinder.

3) Remove nut and bolt attaching lateral link assembly to rear housing. Remove nut and bolt attaching trailing link assembly to rear housing. Use a pin punch to drive out spring pin retaining inboard joint to differential. Remove outboard joint from rear housing. Remove axle shaft.

Disassembly – 1) Straighten bent end of boot clamps on inner boot of axle shaft. Loosen clamps with screwdriver or pliers, taking care not to damage boot.

2) Slide boot from larger end of inboard joint. Pry out and remove round snap ring located at neck of outer race of inboard joint. Slide outer race from shaft assembly.

3) Wipe off grease and remove balls. Move cage to boot side. Remove inner race snap ring and slide off inner race. Remove cage from shaft. Wrap axle shaft splines with tape and remove inner boot.

4) Remove outer boot clamps in same manner as previously described in step **1)**. Remove outer boot from inboard joint end of axle shaft. See Fig. 2

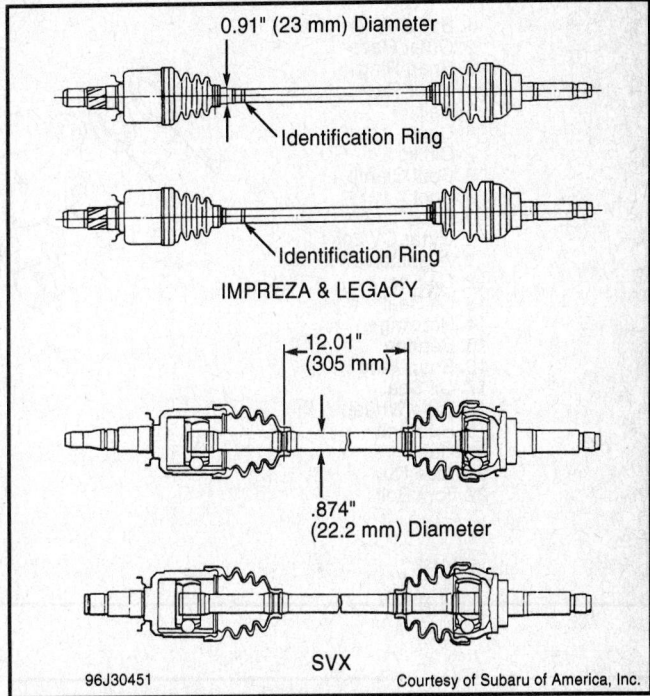

Fig. 1: Identifying Rear Axle Shafts

NOTE: DO NOT disassemble outboard CV joint. If outboard CV joint is defective, replace axle shaft as an assembly.

Reassembly – 1) To reassemble axle shaft, reverse disassembly procedure. Apply 2.12-2.47 oz. (60-70 g) of Molylex No. 2 grease to outer joint and boot. Install and tighten boot clamps to specifications. See BOOT CLAMP TORQUE SPECIFICATIONS table.

2) Ensure cage is installed onto shaft with cut-out side facing end of shaft. When installing cage over inner race, align inner race protrusions with tracks on cage, then rotate cage one-half turn. See Fig. 3. Apply 2.82-3.17 oz. (80-90 g) of Molylex No. 2 (M/T), VU-3A702 Yellow (A/T) grease into outer race. Fit over cage and balls, install circlip. Evenly apply .71-1.06 oz (20-30 g) of grease to inner surface of boot. Ensure inside of larger end of boot and boot groove of outer race is free of grease. Install boot and clamp. Before tightening inner boot clamps, ensure inboard joint is at center of its travel. Distance between inner and outer boots on SVX models should be 12.081 (305 mm)

BOOT CLAMP SPECIFICATIONS

Application	INCH lbs (N.m)
Inner & Outer	
Large Diameter Clamp	116 (13.1)
Small Diameter Clamp	98 (11.1)

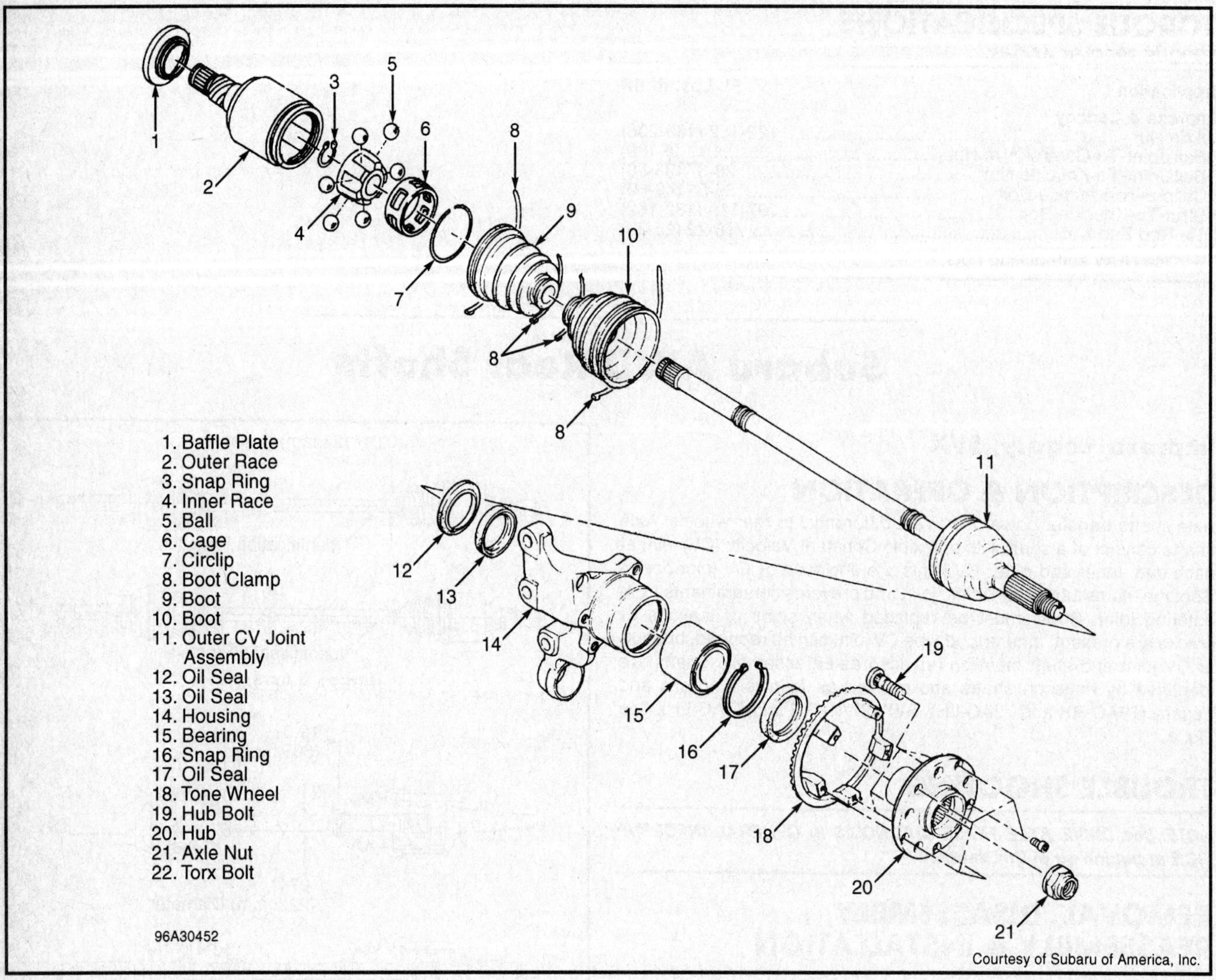

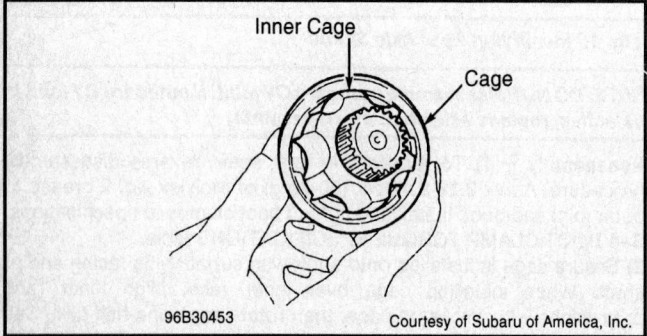

1. Baffle Plate
2. Outer Race
3. Snap Ring
4. Inner Race
5. Ball
6. Cage
7. Circlip
8. Boot Clamp
9. Boot
10. Boot
11. Outer CV Joint
    Assembly
12. Oil Seal
13. Oil Seal
14. Housing
15. Bearing
16. Snap Ring
17. Oil Seal
18. Tone Wheel
19. Hub Bolt
20. Hub
21. Axle Nut
22. Torx Bolt

96A30452

Courtesy of Subaru of America, Inc.

Inner Cage

Cage

96B30453   Courtesy of Subaru of America, Inc.

Fig. 3: Installing Race On Inner Race

Installation – Using Installer (9224310000) and Adapter (927390000), install outboard joint into rear housing. *See Fig. 4.* Install, but DO NOT tighten new axle shaft nut. Using caution not to damage oil seal, install inboard joint to differential using NEW retaining spring pin. To complete installation, reverse removal procedure. Tighten all nuts and bolts to specification. See TORQUE SPECIFICATIONS.

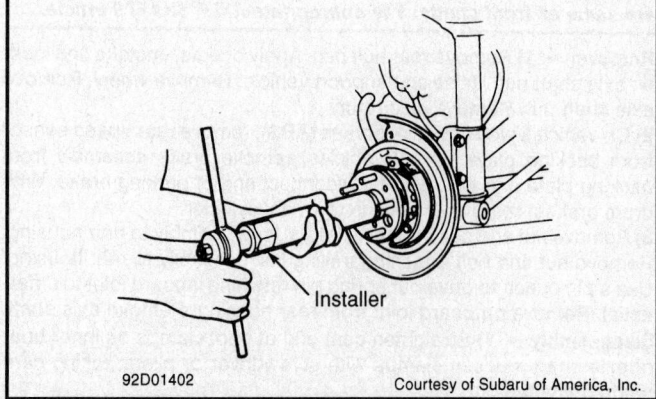

Installer

92D01402   Courtesy of Subaru of America, Inc.

Fig. 4: Installing Axle Shaft In Rear Housing

REAR HUB ASSEMBLY

CAUTION: On vehicles with Anti-Lock Brake System (ABS), DO NOT damage toothed wheel.

NOTE: DO NOT remove hub bearing unless damaged. DO NOT re-use bearing after removal.

Removal & Disassembly – 1) Remove axle shaft. See AWD AXLE SHAFTS under REMOVAL, DISASSEMBLY, REASSEMBLY & INSTALLATION. Remove nuts and bolts attaching lower strut assembly to rear housing. Remove rear housing.

2) Remove backing plate from rear housing. Press hub from rear housing. Use a screwdriver to remove inner and outer oil seals. Remove snap ring from rear housing. *See Fig. 2.* Press bearing assembly out of rear housing.

Reassembly & Installation – Clean housing before installing bearing assembly. Lubricate and install new bearing assembly and oil seals. Ensure snap ring fits properly into groove. To complete reassembly, reverse disassembly procedure. Tighten nuts and bolts to specification. See TORQUE SPECIFICATIONS.

TORQUE SPECIFICATIONS

TORQUE SPECIFICATIONS

Application	Ft. Lbs. (N.m)
Axle/Spindle Nut	
Legacy & Loyale	123-151 (167-206)
SVX	123-152 (167-207)
Backing Plate-To-Rear Housing	34-43 (46-58)
Backing Plate-To-Inner Arm Bolt	34-43 (46-58)
Disc Brake Caliper	34-43 (46-58)
Strut-To-Axle Housing Bolt	97-127 (132-172)
Strut-To-Body Bolt	10-18 (14-25)
Lateral Link To Rear Housing	87-115 (117-157)
Trailing Link Bolt	72-94 (98-127)
Wheel Lug Nuts	58-72 (78-98)
	INCH lbs. (N.m)
Tone Wheel	86-139 (10-16)

Suzuki

Esteem, Sidekick, Swift, X-90

DESCRIPTION

Axle shafts transfer power from transaxle or differential to drive wheels. All axle shafts consist of a shaft and flexible Constant Velocity (CV) joint at each end. Inner CV joint is splined or bolted to transaxle. On Esteem and Swift, outer CV joint is splined to hub assembly and secured by axle shaft nut.

Inner and outer CV joints are enclosed in CV joint boots. Boots maintain lubrication and prevent contaminants from entering the joint. Boots must be replaced when signs of leakage or cracks are present. Inner CV joint can be repaired, but outer CV joint must be replaced as an assembly.

NOTE: Vehicles equipped with automatic transmissions use Tripod type joints on the inside of the axle shaft and Double Offset Joint (DOJ) type joints on the outside. Vehicles equipped with manual transmissions use DOJ type joints on both ends of the axle shafts.

TROUBLE SHOOTING

NOTE: See DRIVE AXLE NOISE DIAGNOSIS in GENERAL INFORMATION at beginning of this section.

REMOVAL, DISASSEMBLY, REASSEMBLY & INSTALLATION

NOTE: When removing or overhauling FWD axle shafts, refer to appropriate illustration. See Figs. 1-6.

ESTEEM & SWIFT

Removal (Left-Side Shaft) – 1) Unstake axle shaft nut. Remove nut. Raise and support vehicle. Drain transaxle fluid. Use large screwdrivers or pry bars to pry inner joint from transaxle to release retaining circlip. Disconnect stabilizer bar from suspension arm.

2) Remove lower suspension ball stud and nut. Disconnect lower suspension control arm. To remove axle shaft assembly, pull inboard CV joint from differential, and then remove outer CV joint from axle hub.

Removal (Right-Side Shaft) – 1) Unstake axle shaft nut. Remove nut. Raise and support vehicle. Use a plastic hammer to drive CV joint from center shaft. Disconnect stabilizer bar from suspension arm. Remove lower suspension ball stud and nut. Disconnect lower suspension control arm.

2) To remove axle shaft assembly, pull inboard CV joint from differential, and then remove outer joint from axle hub. To remove center

shaft, drain transaxle fluid. Remove center bearing support bolts, and remove center shaft from differential gear.

NOTE: DO NOT disassemble outboard CV joints. If joint is faulty, replace as an assembly.

Disassembly – 1) Remove boot band from differential-side CV joint. Remove circlip. Remove CV joint housing. Remove circlip from axle shaft. Remove CV joint from axle shaft. Remove inner and outer boots from axle shaft.

2) To disassemble center shaft and bearing, remove right-side oil seal and circlip. Pull center shaft from center bearing. Remove left-side oil seal and circlip. Remove center bearing from support.

Inspection & Cleaning – Check boots for breakage or deterioration. Replace as necessary. Check circlip, snap ring and boot bands. Replace as necessary. Clean disassembled parts (except boots), in degreaser. Dry components with compressed air. Clean boots with cloth. DO NOT wash boots in degreaser.

Reassembly – 1) Grease outer CV joint fully. Position boot on shaft and fill inside of boot with about 3 ozs. (90 g) of grease. Install inner CV joint boot onto axle shaft. Install inner CV joint onto shaft, ensuring smaller outside diameter of cage faces outer CV joint.

2) Install snap ring into shaft groove. Fill inside of boot with grease. Attach boots using boot bands. Ensure boot band clamp end is bent in a reverse direction of rotation. If boots are distorted or dented, correct before installing on vehicle.

3) To install center bearing and shaft, reverse removal procedure. Install circlip securely into groove of bearing support. Apply grease to oil seals.

Installation – Clean and lubricate axle shaft oil seals. To install right-side axle shaft, push into differential until circlip locks into groove and axle shaft is held in position. To complete installation, reverse removal procedures.

SIDEKICK & X90

Removal – 1) Raise and support vehicle. Remove front wheels. Drain transaxle fluid. Remove locking hub, if equipped. Remove circlip from axle shaft. Remove stabilizer ball joint nut. Remove castle nut from tie rod end. Remove mounting bolts from brake caliper. Remove caliper from steering knuckle, and suspend using wire. Remove stud nut from steering knuckle.

2) Support lower suspension arm with a jack. Remove lower strut bracket bolts. Lower jack and disconnect knuckle from lower suspension control arm. Pull outer axle shafts from hubs. To remove right-side inner joint, use large screwdrivers or pry bars to pry inner joint from transaxle to release retaining circlip. To remove left side-inner joint, remove mounting bolts from inner joint.

AXLE SHAFTS
Suzuki (Cont.)

NOTE: DO NOT disassemble CV joints. If joint is faulty, replace as an assembly. DO NOT disassemble differential side joint assembly.

Disassembly – Remove CV boot band. Remove circlip from CV joint housing. Remove CV joint from housing. Remove circlip from axle shaft. Remove CV joint from shaft. Remove inner and outer boots from axle shaft.

Inspection & Cleaning – Check boots for breakage or deterioration. Replace as necessary. Check circlip, snap ring and boot bands. Replace as necessary. Clean disassembled parts (except boots), in degreaser. Dry components with compressed air. Clean boots with cloth. DO NOT wash boots in degreaser.

Reassembly – **1)** Grease outer CV joint fully. Position boot on shaft, and fill inside of boot with about 3 ozs. (90 g) of grease. Install inner CV joint boot onto axle shaft. Install inner CV joint onto shaft, ensuring flat side of joint faces outer CV joint.

2) Install snap ring into shaft groove. Fill inside of boot with grease. Attach boots with boot bands. Ensure boot band clamp end is bent in a reverse direction of rotation. If boots are distorted or dented, correct prior to installation on vehicle.

Installation – Clean and lubricate axle shaft oil seals. To install right-side axle shaft, push into differential until circlip locks into groove and axle is held in position. Install mounting bolts to left-side axle shaft. To complete installation, reverse removal procedure.

TORQUE SPECIFICATIONS
TORQUE SPECIFICATIONS

Application	Ft. lbs. (N.m)
Esteem	
Center Bearing Support Bolt	37 (50)
Axle Shaft Outer Nut	129 (175)
Lower Ball Joint Stud	44 (60)
Oil Drain Plug	
Automatic Transaxle	30 (40)
Manual Transaxle	15 (21)
Oil Filler & Level Plug	15 (21)
Stabilizer Joint Nut	21 (28)
Wheel Lug Nut	63 (85)
Sidekick & X90	
Ball Joint Nut	21 (28)
Ball Joint Stud Castle Nut	43 (58)
Caliper Mounting Bolts	63 (85)
Left-Side Inner CV Bolt	37 (50)
Lower Strut Bracket Bolt	66 (90)
Oil Drain Plug	17 (23)
Tie Rod End Castle Nut	32 (43)
Wheel Lug Nut	70 (95)
Swift	
Center Bearing Support Bolt	30-44 (40-60)
Axle Shaft Outer Nut	111-148 (150-200)
Lower Ball Joint Stud	37-52 (50-70)
Oil Drain Plug	
Automatic Transaxle	13-17 (18-23)
Manual Transaxle	13-17 (18-23)
Oil Filler & Level Plug	13-17 (18-23)
Stabilizer Joint Nut	17-24 (23-33)
Wheel Lug Nut	37-59 (50-80)

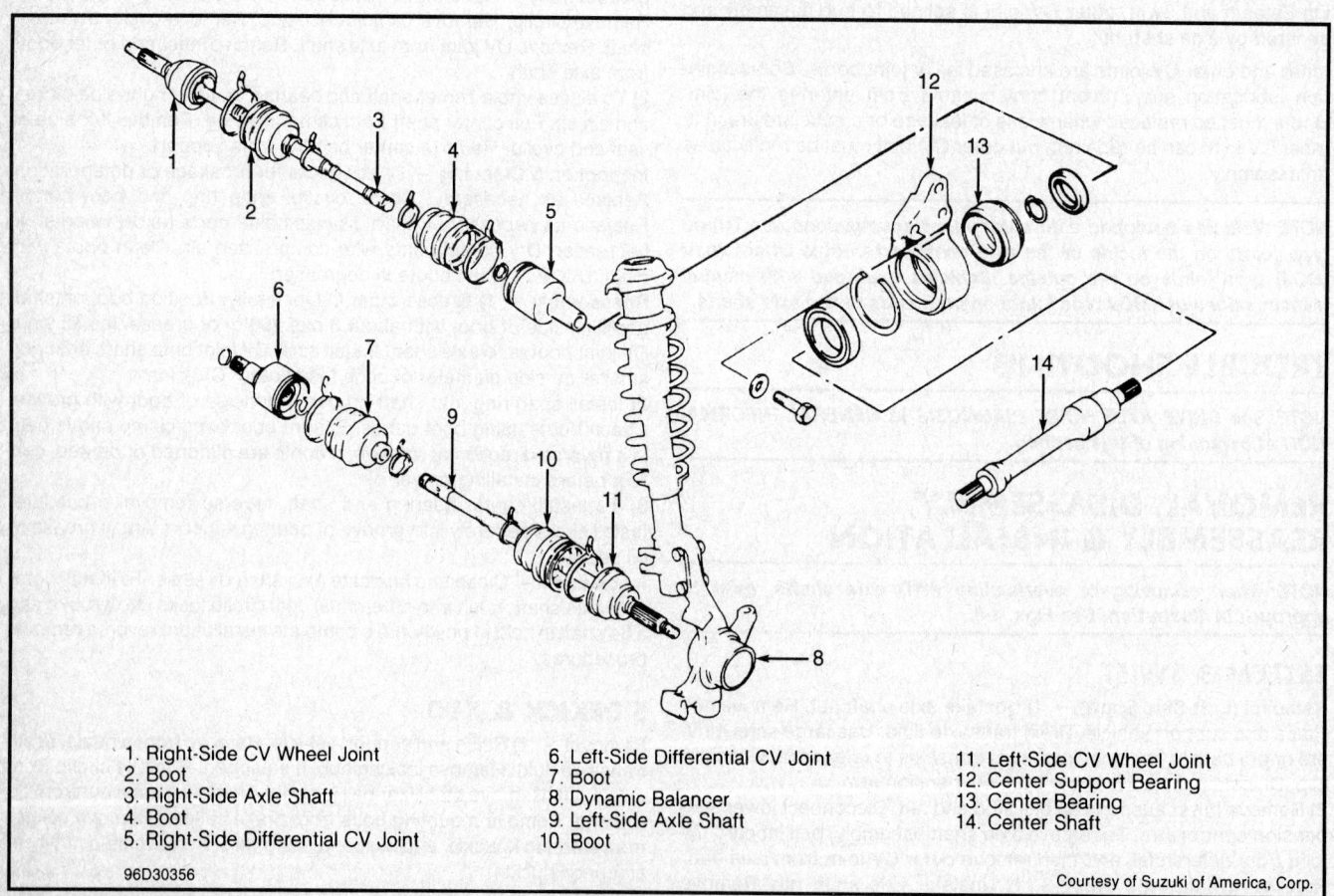

96D30356

Courtesy of Suzuki of America, Corp.

1. Right-Side CV Wheel Joint
2. Boot
3. Right-Side Axle Shaft
4. Boot
5. Right-Side Differential CV Joint
6. Left-Side Differential CV Joint
7. Boot
8. Dynamic Balancer
9. Left-Side Axle Shaft
10. Boot
11. Left-Side CV Wheel Joint
12. Center Support Bearing
13. Center Bearing
14. Center Shaft

Fig. 1: Exploded View Of FWD Axle Components (Esteem & Swift)

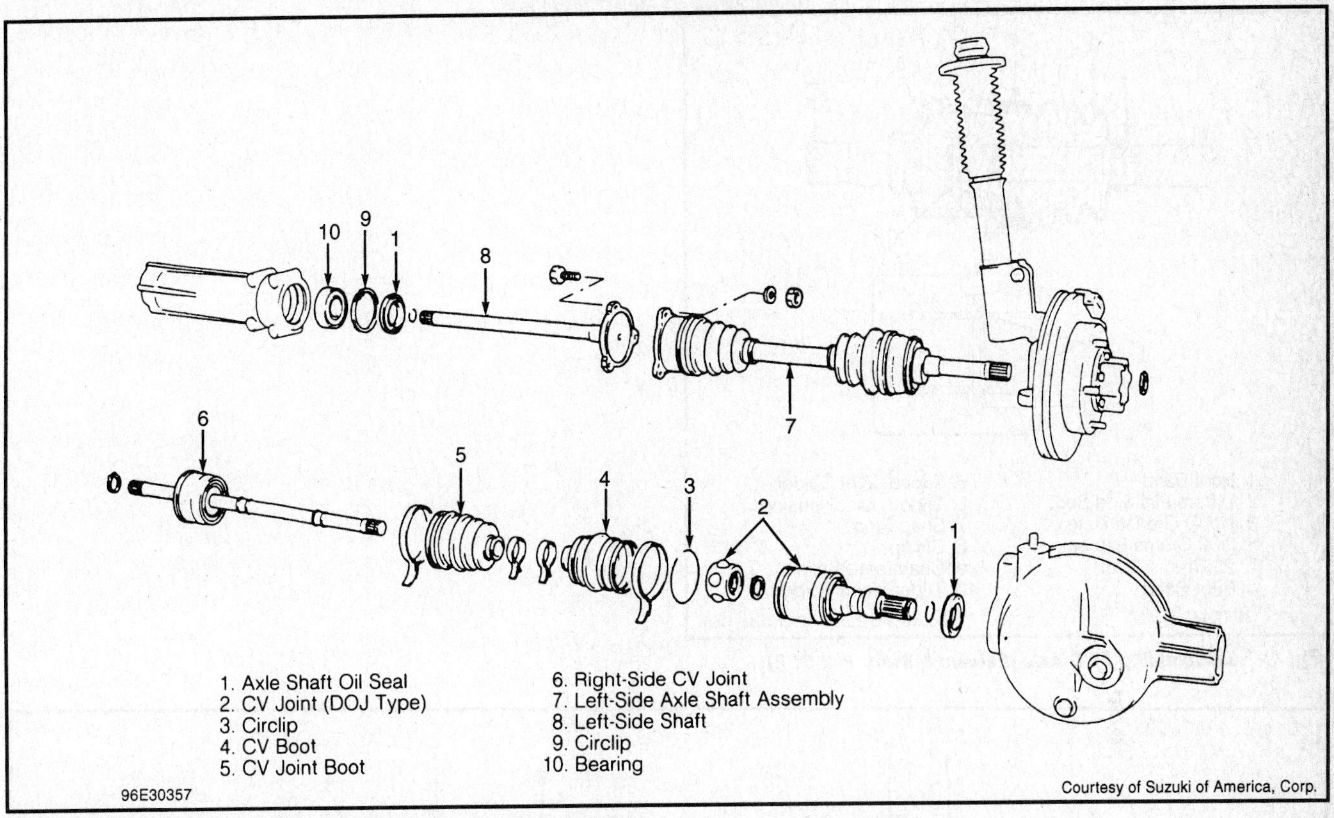

1. Axle Shaft Oil Seal
2. CV Joint (DOJ Type)
3. Circlip
4. CV Boot
5. CV Joint Boot
6. Right-Side CV Joint
7. Left-Side Axle Shaft Assembly
8. Left-Side Shaft
9. Circlip
10. Bearing

96E30357

Courtesy of Suzuki of America, Corp.

Fig. 2: Exploded View Of FWD Axle Components (Sidekick & X90)

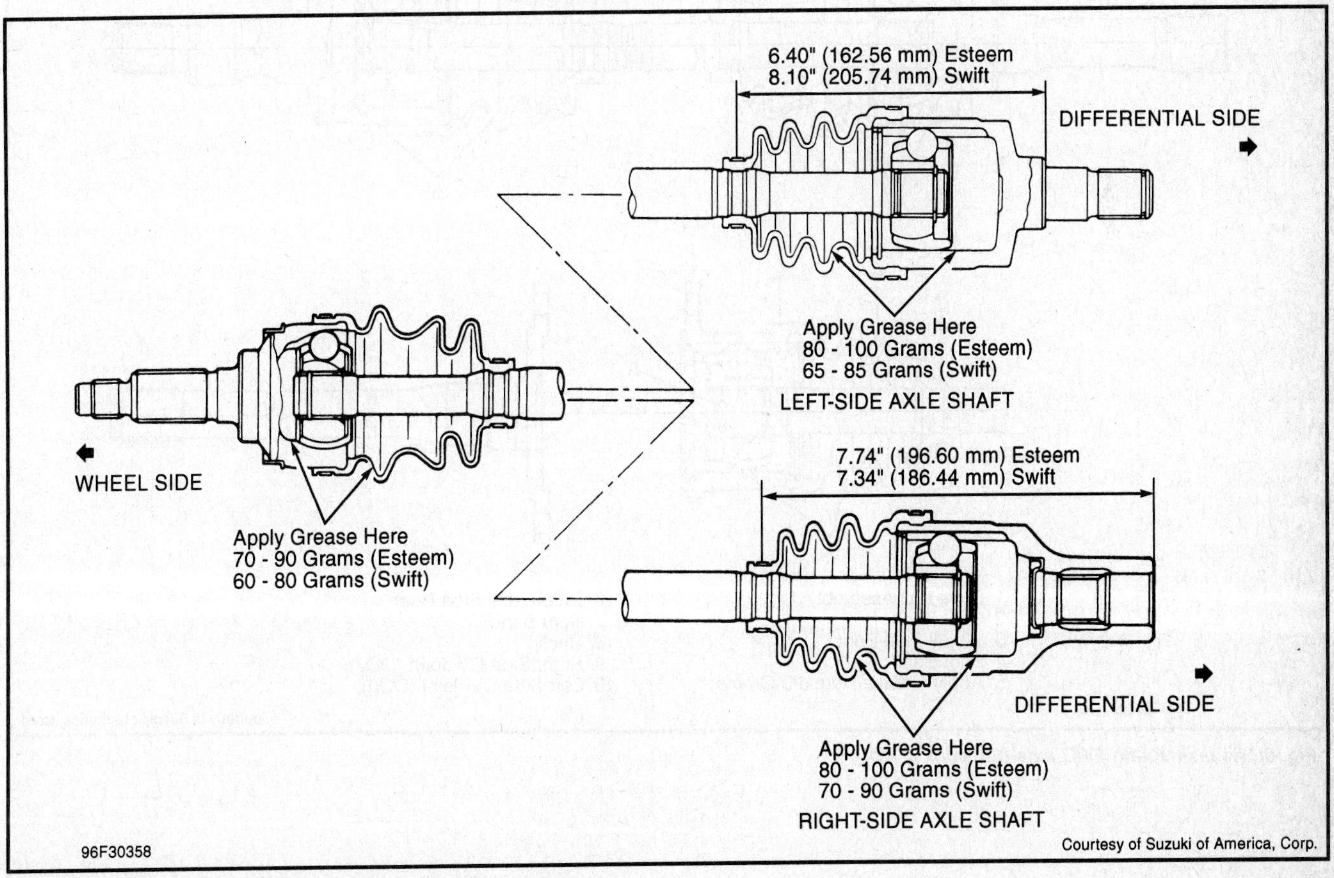

6.40" (162.56 mm) Esteem
8.10" (205.74 mm) Swift

DIFFERENTIAL SIDE →

Apply Grease Here
80 - 100 Grams (Esteem)
65 - 85 Grams (Swift)
LEFT-SIDE AXLE SHAFT

7.74" (196.60 mm) Esteem
7.34" (186.44 mm) Swift

← WHEEL SIDE

Apply Grease Here
70 - 90 Grams (Esteem)
60 - 80 Grams (Swift)

Apply Grease Here
80 - 100 Grams (Esteem)
70 - 90 Grams (Swift)
RIGHT-SIDE AXLE SHAFT

DIFFERENTIAL SIDE →

96F30358

Courtesy of Suzuki of America, Corp.

Fig. 3: Reassembling FWD Axle (Esteem & Swift – 1 Of 2)

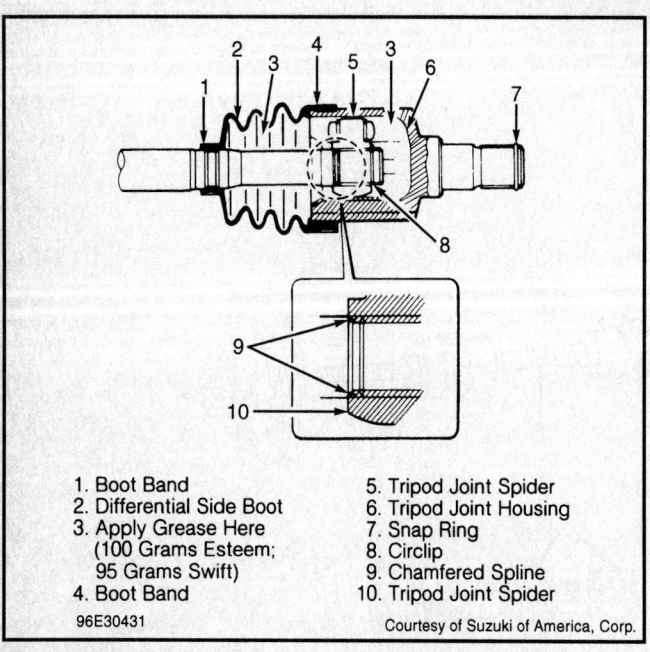

1. Boot Band
2. Differential Side Boot
3. Apply Grease Here
   (100 Grams Esteem;
   95 Grams Swift)
4. Boot Band
5. Tripod Joint Spider
6. Tripod Joint Housing
7. Snap Ring
8. Circlip
9. Chamfered Spline
10. Tripod Joint Spider

96E30431

Courtesy of Suzuki of America, Corp.

Fig. 4: Reassembling FWD Axle (Esteem & Swift – 2 Of 2)

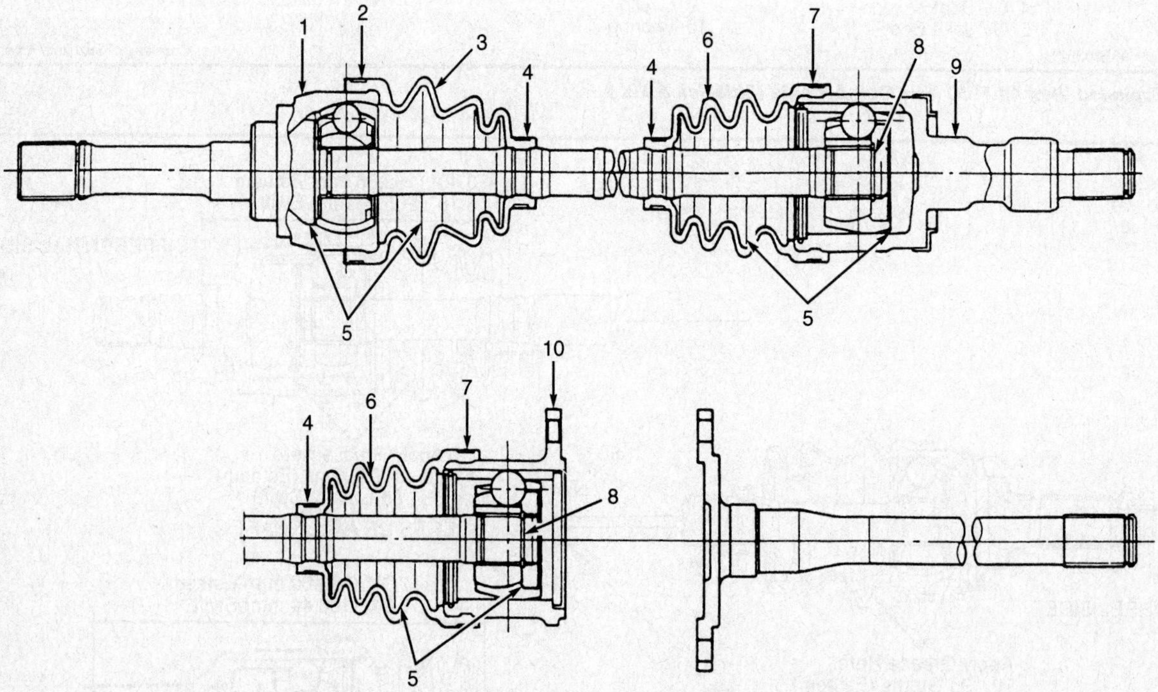

1. Drive Ball Assembly
2. Boot Band
3. Wheel Side Boot
4. Boot Band
5. Apply Grease Here (90 Grams)
6. Differential Side Boot
7. Boot Band
8. Circlip
9. Right-Side CV Joint (DOJ)
10. Left-Side CV Joint (DOJ)

96G30359

Courtesy of Suzuki of America, Corp.

Fig. 5: Reassembling FWD Axle (Sidekick & X90)

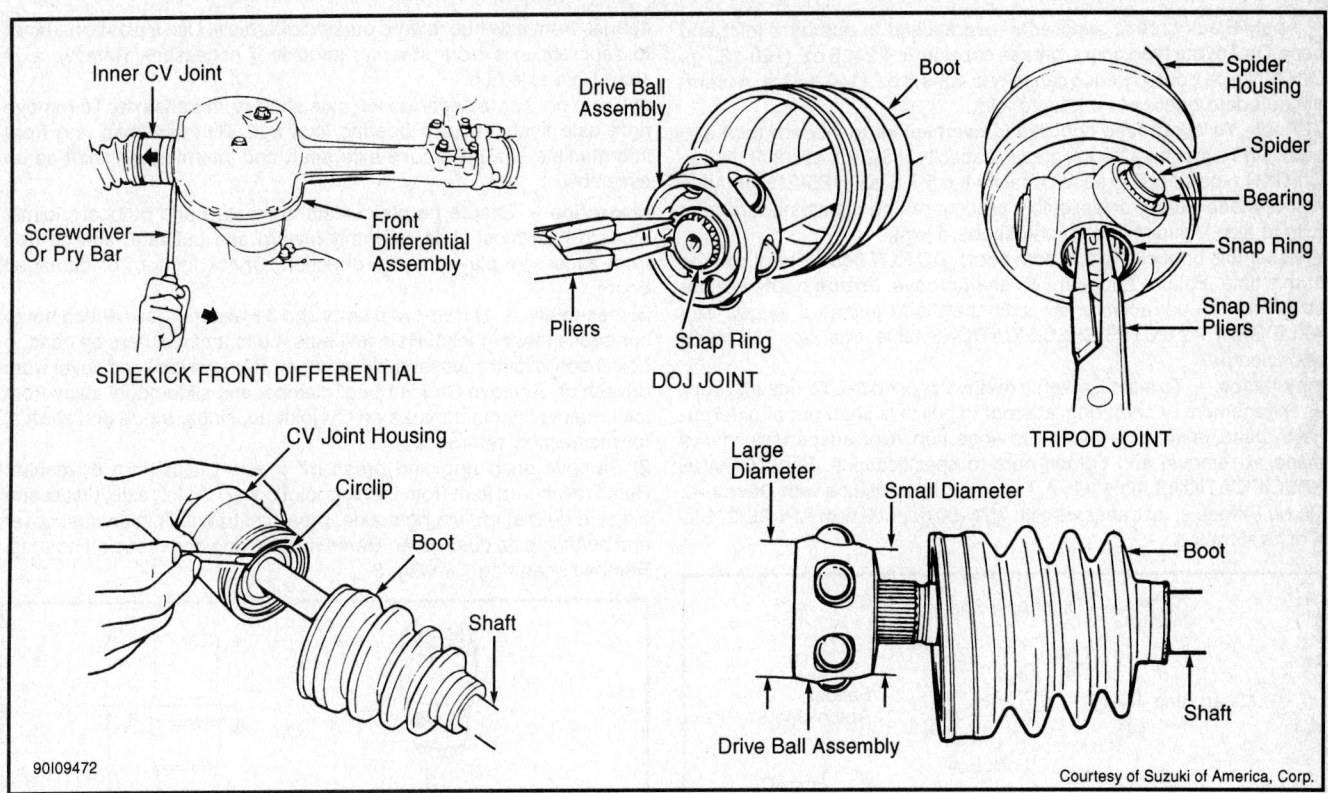

90I09472   Courtesy of Suzuki of America, Corp.

Fig. 6: Overhauling CV Joints

Toyota FWD

Avalon, Camry, Celica, Corolla, Paseo, Tercel

DESCRIPTION

Axle shafts transfer power from transaxle to front wheels. All axle shafts consist of a shaft and flexible Constant Velocity (CV) joint at each end. Inner CV joint is splined or bolted to transaxle. Outer CV joint is splined to hub assembly and secured by axle shaft nut.

The inner CV joint is a plunging tripod joint. The plunging action allows for axle shaft length change as suspension moves up and down.

The inner and outer CV joints are enclosed by a CV joint boot. The boot maintains lubrication in the joint and prevents contamination of CV lubricant. Boots must be replaced when signs of leakage or cracks are present. The inner CV joint can be repaired without replacing assembly. The outer CV joint must be replaced as an assembly.

REMOVAL, DISASSEMBLY, REASSEMBLY & INSTALLATION

NOTE: Manufacturer recommends removing right axle shaft and intermediate shaft as an assembly

CAMRY (4-CYLINDER)

Removal – 1) Raise and support vehicle. Remove front wheels. Remove front fender apron seal. *See Fig. 1.* Remove cotter pin, lock nut cap and lock nut. Apply brake and remove lock nut from wheel bearing. Drain transaxle fluid. Remove cotter pin and nut from tie rod end.
2) Disconnect tie rod end from steering knuckle. Disconnect stabilizer from lower control arm. Remove bolts, and disconnect steering knuckle from lower control arm.

3) Using a plastic hammer, tap axle shaft out of bearing hub. To remove left axle shaft, using a pry bar, pry axle shaft from transaxle and remove axle. To remove right axle shaft, remove bearing lock bolt from bearing bracket. *See Fig. 1.* Using pliers, remove snap ring, and remove axle shaft.

Inspection – Ensure no play exists in outboard joint. Inboard joint must slide smoothly in thrust direction and be free from excessive play in radial direction. Check for torn or damaged boots.

Disassembly – Remove CV joint boot clamps and slide boots away from joint. Paint alignment marks on CV joint housings, tripod and shaft(s) for reassembly reference. Remove inboard joint tulip or center drive shaft. Remove snap ring and tripod from driveshaft. Remove inboard and outboard boots. Do not disassemble outboard joint. Using appropriate adaptor and press, remove dust cover from inboard tulip. On center drive shaft, remove dust cover, snap ring and bearing. Remove snap ring. *See Fig. 1.*

Reassembly – 1) On right axle shaft, install NEW snap ring on center axle shaft. Using a press, install bearing and NEW dust cover on axle shaft. Ensure clearance between dust cover and bearing is .04-.08" (1-2 mm). *See Fig. 2.* Use press to install NEW dust cover on right axle shaft.
2) Ensure dust cover is 3.39-3.43" (86-87 mm) from end of shaft (splined end). *See Fig. 2.* On all axle shafts, wrap axle shaft splines using vinyl tape to protect boot from damage during reassembly. Slide NEW boots and clamps onto axle shaft.
3) Install NEW snap ring. Align marks made during disassembly procedure and install tripod joint with beveled side towards outboard joint. Align mating marks on axle shaft with tripod joint. Using a brass bar and a hammer, tap tripod joint onto axle shaft. DO NOT tap on roller. Install a NEW snap ring onto end of axle shaft.

4) Apply Black grease supplied in overhaul kit to outboard joint and boot. On Toyota type boots, grease capacity is 4.2-4.6 oz. (120-130 g). On GKN type boots, grease capacity is 4.9-5.6 oz. (140-160 g). Assemble outboard boot onto outboard joint.

5) Apply Yellow grease supplied in overhaul kit to inboard joint and boot. On Toyota type boots, grease capacity is 8.2-8.5 oz. (232-242 g). On GKN type boots, grease capacity it 6.5-7.6 oz. (185-215 g). Align marks made during disassembly procedure and install inboard joint tulip to axle. Assemble boot onto inboard joint.

6) Assemble boot clamps on both boots. DO NOT tighten boot clamps at this time. Ensure boots are on shaft groove. Ensure boots are not stretched or contracted when axle shaft is at standard length. See AXLE SHAFT LENGTH SPECIFICATIONS table. See Fig. 9. Tighten boot clamps.

Installation – To install, reverse removal procedure. To ensure proper engagement of snap ring, attempt to pull axle shaft out of differential by hand. Install axle shafts into wheel hub. Align suspension marks made at removal and tighten nuts to specifications. See TORQUE SPECIFICATIONS table. On A/T models, fill transaxle with Dexron-II. On M/T models, fill transaxle with 75W-90 gear oil with API GL-3, GL-4 or GL-5 rating.

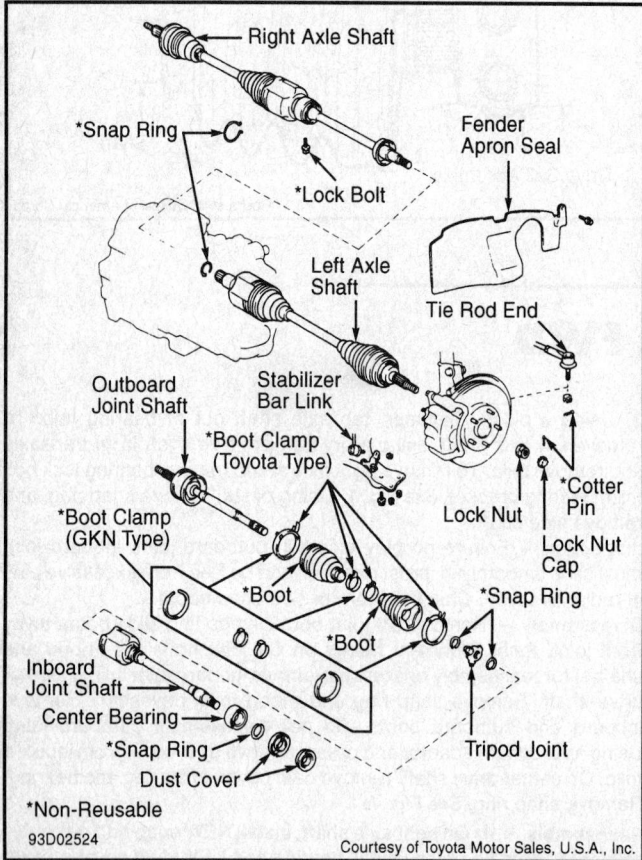

Fig. 1: Exploded View Of Front Axle Shafts (Camry 4-Cylinder)

AVALON & CAMRY (V6)

Removal – **1)** Raise and support vehicle. Remove fender apron seal. Remove cotter pin, lock nut cap and lock nut. Apply brake and remove lock nut from wheel bearing. Remove engine undercover. Remove cotter pin and nut from tie rod end.

2) Disconnect tie rod end from steering knuckle. Drain transaxle fluid. Disconnect stabilizer bar link from lower control arm. Remove bolts, and disconnect steering knuckle from lower control arm.

3) Paint mating marks on axle shaft flange and side gear shaft flange. DO NOT use punch to make mating marks. Apply brakes and loosen, but DO NOT remove, 6 retaining nuts on each inboard axle shaft flange.

4) Push front axle hub toward outside of vehicle. Use a plastic hammer to separate axle from steering knuckle if necessary. Remove axle shaft from axle hub.

5) Use a pry bar to separate left axle shaft from transaxle. To remove right axle shaft, remove bearing lock bolt. Remove snap ring from intermediate shaft. Remove axle shaft and intermediate shaft as an assembly.

Inspection – Ensure no play exists in inboard and outboard joints. Inboard joint must slide smoothly inward and outward, and be free from excessive play in radial direction. Check for torn or damaged boots.

Disassembly – 1) Remove 6 bolts and 3 washers. Use caution not to compress inboard joint. Reinstall nuts, bolts and washers by hand to hold inboard joint subassembly together. Remove joint end cover from driveshaft. Remove CV joint boot clamps, and slide boots away from joint. Paint alignment marks on CV joint housings, tripod and shaft(s) for reassembly reference.

2) Remove snap ring and press off inboard joint from driveshaft. Remove inboard joint from inboard joint cover. On left axle, disassemble side gear shaft. On right axle, press off transaxle side dust cover and bearing side dust cover. Remove snap ring and press off bearing. Remove snap ring. See Fig. 3.

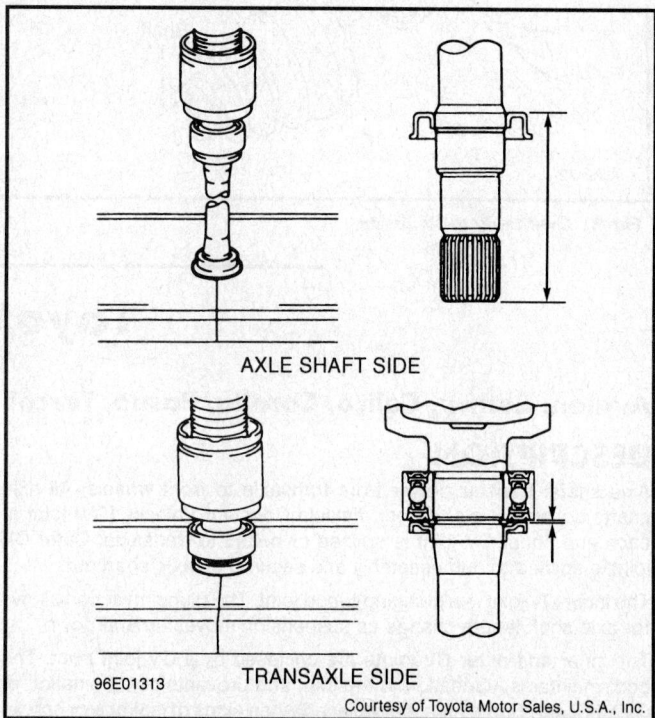

96E01313   Courtesy of Toyota Motor Sales, U.S.A., Inc.

Fig. 2: Installing Axle Shaft Dust Cover

Reassembly – 1) To reassemble axle shafts, reverse disassembly procedure. Tighten inboard CV joint cover bolts as shown. See Fig. 4. Ensure center drive shaft dust cover is 4.33-4.37 (110-111 mm) from end of shaft (splined end). See Fig. 2. Ensure clearance between dust cover and bearing is .04-.08" (1-2 mm). Press new dust cover to left axle side gear shaft. Apply seal packing to inboard joint cover, align holes to inboard joint and install bolts using nuts and washers to hold in place. Install inboard joint onto driveshaft, aligning matchmarks, and install snap ring.

2) Wrap splines on axle shaft with tape to prevent damaging boots during installation. Ensure dust boots are not collapsed or stretched. Pack joints and boots with grease supplied in overhaul kit. Outboard boot grease capacity is 4.8-5.5 oz. (135-155 g). Inboard boot capacity is 5.0-5.3 oz. (142-150). Set axle shaft to standard length. See AXLE SHAFT LENGTH SPECIFICATIONS table. Install and tighten boot clamps. Pack side gear shaft with grease. Capacity is 1.8-2.1 oz. (50-60 g). Connect side gear shaft to drive shaft.

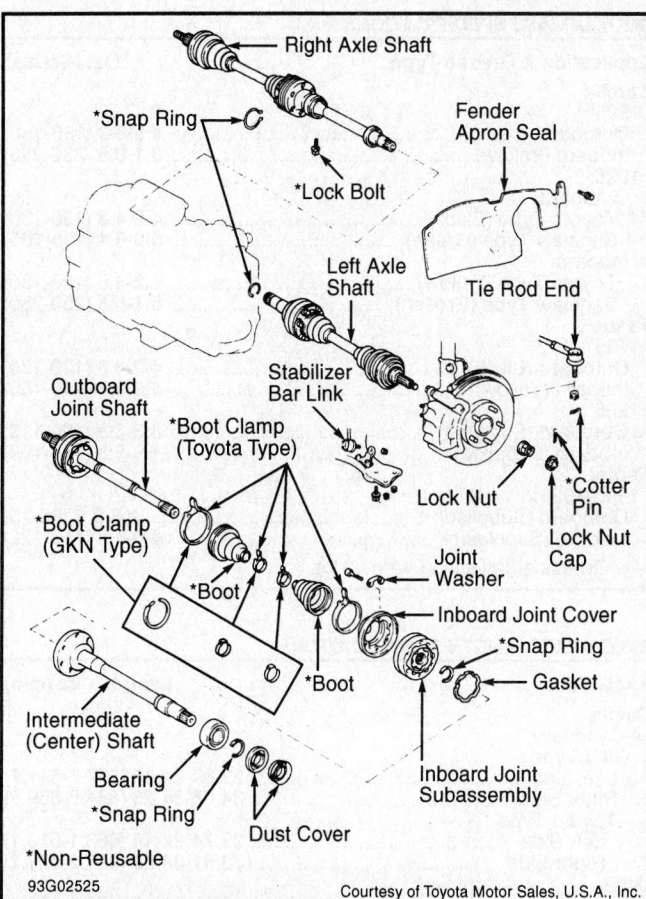

Fig. 3: Exploded View Of Front Drive Axle Shafts (Avalon & Camry V6)

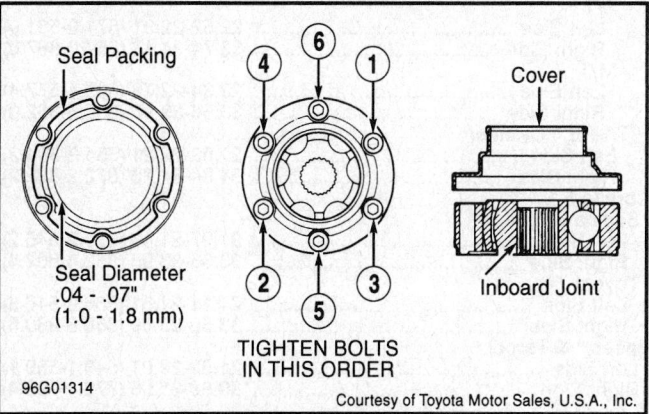

Fig. 4: Tightening Inboard CV Joint Cover Bolts (Avalon & Camry V6)

Installation – To install, reverse removal procedure. Ensure there is no free play in inboard and outboard joint. Before installing axle shafts, install NEW snap ring on end of left axle shaft. Coat axle shaft seals in transaxle with grease. Coat axle shaft splines and sliding surfaces with Dexron-II. To ensure proper engagement of snap ring, attempt to pull axle shaft out of differential by hand. Install axle shafts into wheel hub. Align suspension marks made at removal and tighten nuts to specifications. See TORQUE SPECIFICATIONS table.

CELICA

Removal – 1) Raise and support vehicle. Remove front wheels. Remove cotter pin and lock nut cap. Apply brakes and remove axle shaft bearing lock nut. Remove lower engine undercover.

2) Drain transaxle fluid. Remove nut and disconnect tie rod end from steering knuckle. Disconnect lower control arm from steering knuckle. Using universal puller, separate axle shaft from steering knuckle. Using a pry bar, remove left axle shaft from transaxle case.

3) Remove 2 bolts from center bearing bracket. Remove right axle shaft and center drive shaft as an assembly.

Inspection – Ensure no play exists in inboard and outboard joints. Inboard joint must slide smoothly in thrust direction and be free from excessive play in radial direction. Check for torn or damaged boots.

Disassembly – 1) Remove CV joint boot clamps, and slide boots away from joint. Paint alignment marks on CV joint housings, tripod and shaft(s) for reassembly reference.

2) Remove center driveshaft from driveshaft assembly. Remove snap ring. Place reference marks on driveshaft and tripod. Remove tripod and snap ring. Remove inboard joint boot with dynamic damper. Remove outboard joint boot. Remove dust covers from inboard tulip and center driveshaft. Remove snap ring, bearing case, dust cover, 2nd snap ring and bearing. Remove snap ring. Using pin punch and hammer, remove straight pin.

3) Mount outboard shaft in soft jawed vise. Using a hammer and screwdriver, remove No. 2 dust cover. Using caution not to damage ABS speed sensor ring, if applicable. See Fig. 6.

Reassembly – 1) To reassemble, reverse disassembly procedure. Right axle shaft dust cover must be located 3.39-3.43" (86-87 mm) from end of shaft (splined end).

2) Clearance between center drive shaft dust cover and bearing should be .04" (1 mm). See Fig. 2. Locate damper on right axle shaft. See Fig. 5. Distance should be 7.68-8.07" (195-205 mm).

3) On all models, ensure boots are not collapsed or stretched. Set axle shaft to standard length. See AXLE SHAFT LENGTH SPECIFICATIONS table. Pack inboard joint tulip and boot with Yellow grease supplied with boot kit. Capacity is 8.2-8.5 oz. (232-242 g) for M/T, and 6.3-6.7 oz. (180-190 g) for A/T. Pack outboard joint and boot with Black grease supplied with kit. Capacity is 4.2-4.6 oz (120-130 g) for both M/T and A/T. Install and tighten boot clamps.

Installation – To install, reverse removal procedure. Before installing axle shafts, install NEW snap ring on end axle shaft. Coat axle shaft seals in transaxle with grease. Coat axle shaft splines and sliding surfaces with gear oil (M/T models) or Dexron-II (A/T models). Torque bolts to specifications. See TORQUE SPECIFICATIONS table. Fill transaxle with Dexron-II (A/T models) or 75W-90 gear oil with API GL-4 or GL-5 rating (M/T models).

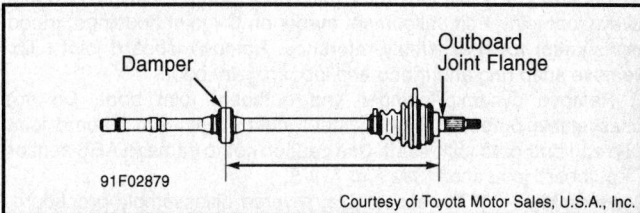

Fig. 5: Locating Axle Shaft Damper

COROLLA, PASEO & TERCEL

Removal – 1) Raise and support vehicle. Remove front wheels. On Corolla, disconnect ABS speed sensor. On all models, remove cotter pin and axle shaft lock nut cap. Apply brakes and remove axle shaft/ bearing lock nut. Remove engine undercover. Drain transaxle fluid. Disconnect tie rods from steering knuckle.

2) Disconnect steering knuckle from lower control arm. Using a plastic hammer or universal puller, separate axle shaft from bearing hub. On Paseo, use a brass drift and hammer to separate axle shafts from transaxle.

3) On Corolla and Tercel, use a pry bar to separate left axle shaft from transaxle. Use a brass drift and hammer to separate right axle shaft from transaxle. On Corolla, use caution to prevent damage to speed sensor serrations on axle shaft.

Inspection – Ensure no play exists in inboard and outboard joints. Inboard joint must slide smoothly in thrust direction and be free from excessive play in radial direction. Check for torn or damaged boots.

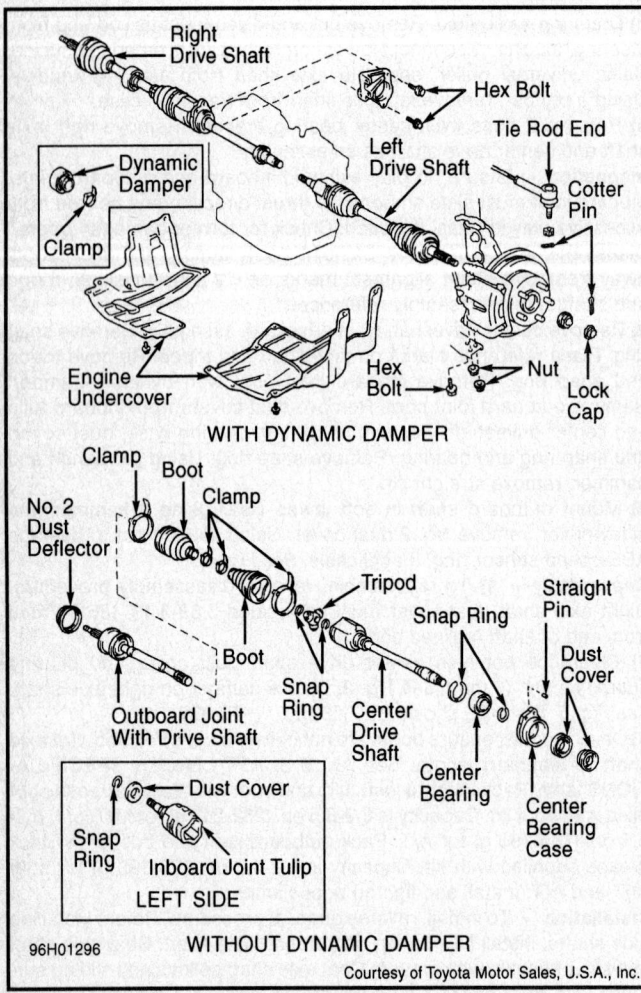

Fig. 6: Exploded View Of Axle Shafts (Celica – 5A-SE Shown, 7A-FE Is Similar)

Disassembly – 1) Remove CV joint boot clamps, and slide boots away from joint. Paint alignment marks on CV joint housings, tripod and shaft(s) for reassembly reference. Remove inboard joint tulip. Remove snap ring and tripod and inboard joint boot.

2) Remove dynamic damper and outboard joint boot. Do not disassemble outboard joint. Remove dust cover from inboard joint tulip and outboard joint shaft. Use caution not to damage ABS sensor on outboard joint shaft. See Fig. 7 or 8.

Reassembly – 1) To reassemble, reverse disassembly procedure. Wrap vinyl tape on splines to prevent damage to boots. Ensure beveled side of tripod joint axial spline is toward outboard joint.

2) On all models, install grease to outboard and inboard joints and boots. See BOOT GREASE SPECIFICATIONS table for grease capacities. On 1996 Corolla, Locate damper on right axle shaft, position damper on axle shaft so damper installation distance on axle shaft is 15.26-15.65" (387.6-397.5 mm). See Fig. 13.

3) On all models, ensure dust boots are not collapsed or stretched. Set axle shaft to standard length. See AXLE SHAFT LENGTH SPECIFICATIONS table. Install and tighten boot clamps.

Installation – To install, reverse removal procedure. Ensure there is .08-.12" (2-3 mm) play in shaft in axial direction and that shaft cannot be pulled out by hand. Tighten all fasteners to specification. See TORQUE SPECIFICATIONS table. Fill transaxle with Dexron-II (A/T models) or 75W-90 gear oil with API GL-4 or GL-5 rating (M/T models).

BOOT GREASE SPECIFICATIONS

Application & Grease Type	Oz. (Grams)
Corolla	
1995	
Outboard (Black)	4.6-5.3 (130-150)
Inboard (Yellow)	8.1-8.8 (230-250)
1996	
Outboard	
Toyota Type (Black)	4.2-4.6 (120-130)
Saginaw Type (Green)	5.8-6.4 (165-185)
Inboard	
Toyota Type (Yellow)	4.2-4.6 (120-130)
Saginaw Type (Greeen)	8.1-8.8 (230-250)
Paseo	
1995	
Outboard (Black)	4.2-4.6 (120-130)
Inboard (Yellow)	4.9-5.3 (140-150)
1996	
Outboard (Supplied) [1]	3.5-3.9 (100-110)
Inboard (Supplied) [1]	4.9-5.3 (140-150)
Tercel	
1995-1996	
Outboard (Supplied) [1]	2.3-2.6 (65-75)
Inboard (Supplied) [1]	4.0-4.3 (112-122)

[1] – Grease supplied in overhaul kit.

AXLE SHAFT LENGTH SPECIFICATIONS

Application	Length – In. (mm)
Camry	
4-Cylinder [1]	
GKN Type	
Left Side	23.89-24.08 (607.7-611.7)
Right Side	34.05-34.25 (864.8-869.8)
Toyota Type	
Left Side	23.74-24.14 (603.1-613.1)
Right Side	33.91-34.30 (861.2-871.2)
V6 [2]	
Standard	17.73-17.89 (450.4-454.4)
Celica [3]	
1995-1996	
5S-FE 4 Cylinder	
A/T	
Left Side	22.52-22.91 (571.9-581.9)
Right Side	33.74-34.13 (857.0-867.0)
M/T	
Left Side	22.34-22.73 (569.4-577.4)
Right Side	33.56-33.96 (852.5-862.0)
7A-FE 4 Cylinder	
Left Side	21.82-22.21 (554.2-564.2)
Right Side	34.34-34.73 (872.2-882.2)
Corolla [4]	
Saginaw Type	
Left Side	21.07-21.46 (535.2-545.2)
Right Side	33.56-33.95 (852.4-862.4)
Toyota Type	
Left Side	21.11-21.51 (536.2-546.3)
Right Side	33.50-33.89 (850.8-860.8)
Paseo [4] **& Tercel** [4]	
Left Side	21.62-22.01 (549.1-559.1)
Right Side	30.68-31.08 (779.4-790.4)

[1] – See Fig. 9.
[2] – See Fig. 11.
[3] – See Fig. 10.
[4] – See Fig. 12.

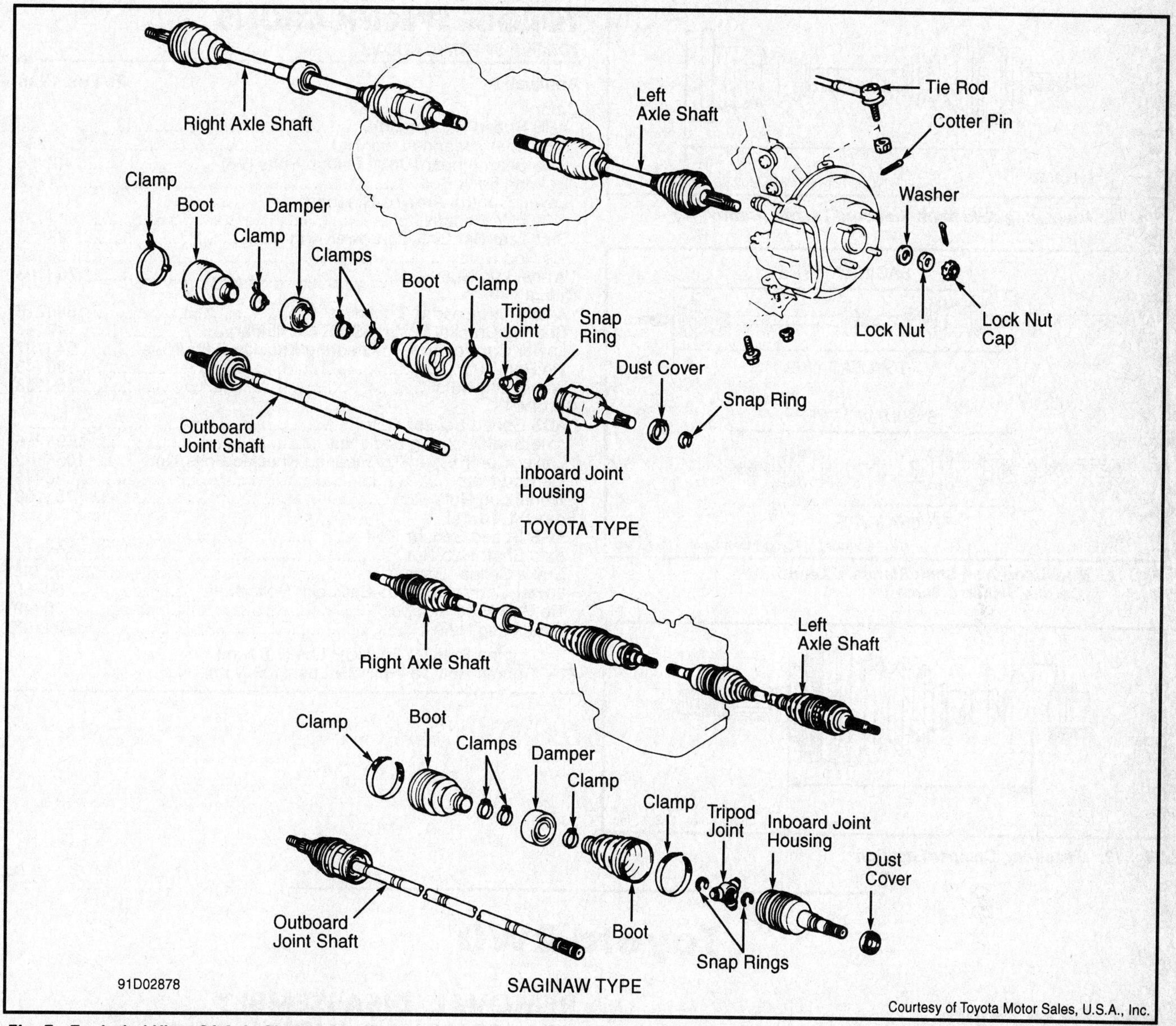

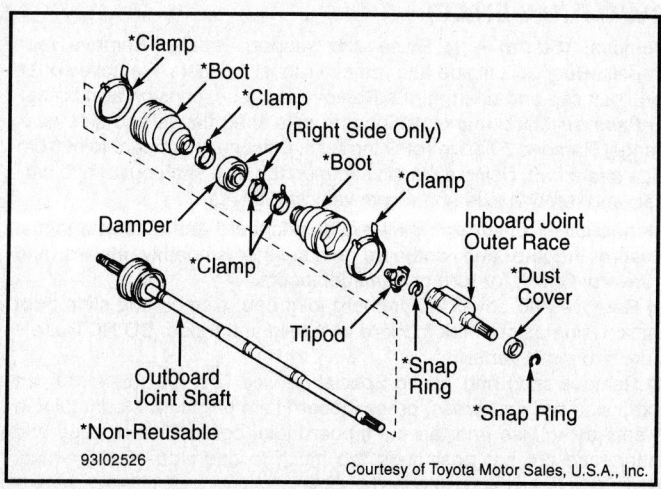

Right Axle Shaft

Clamp
Boot
Clamp
Damper
Clamps
Boot
Clamp
Tripod Joint
Snap Ring
Dust Cover
Snap Ring

Outboard Joint Shaft

Inboard Joint Housing

Left Axle Shaft

Tie Rod
Cotter Pin
Washer
Lock Nut
Lock Nut Cap

TOYOTA TYPE

Right Axle Shaft

Clamp
Boot
Clamps
Damper
Clamp
Boot
Clamp
Tripod Joint
Inboard Joint Housing
Dust Cover

Outboard Joint Shaft

Snap Rings

Left Axle Shaft

SAGINAW TYPE

91D02878

Courtesy of Toyota Motor Sales, U.S.A., Inc.

Fig. 7: Exploded View Of Axle Shafts (Corolla)

*Clamp
*Boot
*Clamp
(Right Side Only)
*Boot
*Clamp
Damper
*Clamp
Inboard Joint Outer Race
*Dust Cover
Tripod
*Snap Ring
*Snap Ring

Outboard Joint Shaft

*Non-Reusable

93I02526

Courtesy of Toyota Motor Sales, U.S.A., Inc.

Fig. 8: Exploded View Of Axle Shaft (Paseo & Tercel)

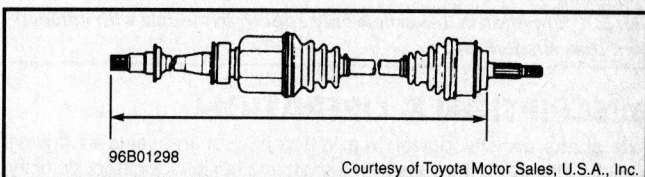

96B01298

Courtesy of Toyota Motor Sales, U.S.A., Inc.

Fig. 9: Measuring Axle Shaft Length (Camry)

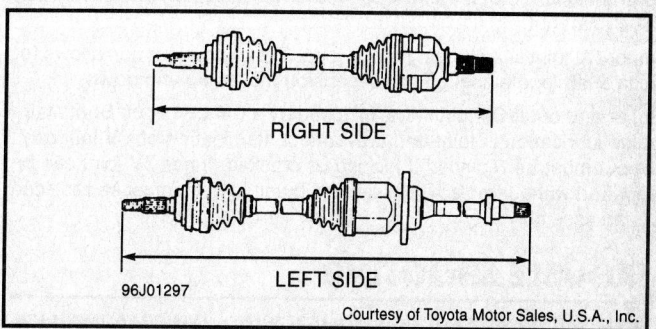

RIGHT SIDE

LEFT SIDE

96J01297

Courtesy of Toyota Motor Sales, U.S.A., Inc.

Fig. 10: Measuring Axle Shaft Standard Length (Celica)

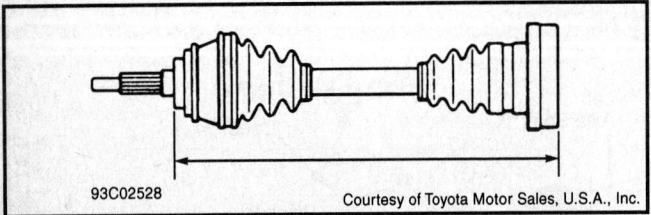

Fig. 11: Measuring Axle Shaft Standard Length (Camry V6)

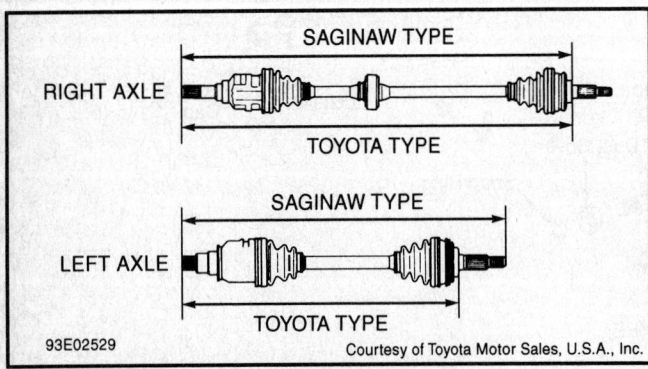

Fig. 12: Measuring Axle Shaft Standard Length (Corolla, Paseo & Tercel)

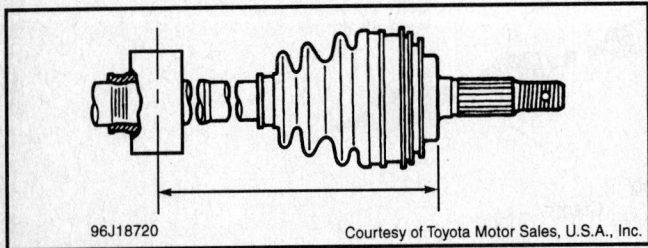

Fig. 13: Measuring Damper Location

TORQUE SPECIFICATIONS
TORQUE SPECIFICATIONS

Application	Ft. Lbs. (N.m)
Camry	
ABS Speed Sensor Bolt	[1]
Axle Shaft/Bearing Lock Nut	217 (294)
Axle Shaft Inboard Joint Flange Bolts (V6)	48 (65)
Bearing Lock Bolt	24 (32)
Lower Control Arm-To-Steering	
Knuckle Bolts/Nuts	94 (127)
Stabilizer Bar Link-To-Lower Arm	29 (39)
Tie Rod Nuts	36 (49)
Wheel Lug Nuts	76 (103)
Celica	
Axle Shaft/Bearing Lock Nut	159 (216)
Bearing Bracket Bolts (5S-FE 4 Cylinder)	47 (64)
Lower Control Arm-To-Steering Knuckle Bolts/Nuts	94 (127)
Tie Rod Nuts	36 (49)
Wheel Lug Nuts	76 (103)
Corolla	
ABS Speed Sensor Bolt	[2]
Axle Shaft/Bearing Lock Nut	159 (216)
Lower Control Arm-To-Steering Knuckle Bolts/Nuts	105 (142)
Tie Rod Nuts	36 (49)
Wheel Lug Nuts	76 (103)
Paseo & Tercel	
ABS Speed Sensor Bolt	[1]
Axle Shaft Hub Nut	159 (216)
Brake Caliper Bolts	65 (88)
Lower Control Arm-To-Ball Joint Bolts/Nuts	59 (80)
Tie Rod Nuts	36 (49)
Wheel Lug Nuts	76 (103)

[1] – Tighten Bolt TO 69 INCH Lbs.(7.8 N.m).
[2] – Tighten Bolt To 76 INCH Lbs. (103 N.m).

Toyota RWD

MR2, RAV4, Supra

NOTE: Information in this article only applies to models with independent rear suspension.

DESCRIPTION & OPERATION

Axle shafts transfer power from differential or transaxle to driving wheels. All axle shafts consist of a shaft and flexible Constant Velocity (CV) joint at each end. Inner CV joint is bolted or splined to differential or transaxle. Outer CV joint is splined to hub assembly and secured by axle shaft nut.

Inner CV joint is a plunging tripod joint. The plunging action allows for axle shaft length change as suspension moves up and down.

Inner and outer CV joints are enclosed by a CV joint boot. Boot maintains lubrication in joint and prevents contamination of CV lubricant. Boots must be replaced if leaking or cracked. Inner CV joint can be repaired without replacing assembly; outer CV joint must be replaced as an assembly.

TROUBLE SHOOTING

NOTE: See DRIVE AXLE NOISE DIAGNOSIS in GENERAL INFORMATION at beginning of this section.

REMOVAL, DISASSEMBLY, REASSEMBLY & INSTALLATION

RWD AXLE SHAFT

Removal (Supra) – 1) Raise and support vehicle. Remove rear wheels. Support tailpipe and remove rubber hangers. Remove cotter pin, lock cap and bearing nut. Remove lower suspension arm brace. **2)** Paint matching marks on inboard axle shaft flange and side gear flange. Remove 6 flange retaining nuts. Disconnect inboard joint from side gear shaft. Using a plastic hammer, tap axle shaft out of hub carrier, and remove axle shaft from vehicle. *See Fig. 1.*

Inspection – Ensure no play exists in inboard and outboard joints. Ensure inboard and outboard joints slide smoothly inward and outward. Check for torn or damaged boots.

1) Remove end cover and inboard joint boot clamps and slide boot back. Using paint, mark inboard joint tulip and tripod. DO NOT use a punch to mark parts.

2) Remove snap ring. Using Special Service Tool (09726-10130), an extension bar and press, press inboard joint off shaft. Mount joint in a soft-jawed vise and tap out inboard joint cover. Ensure cage and inner race are not positioned too much to one side of outer race. Remove inboard and outboard boots.

NOTE: Manufacturer does not recommend overhaul of outboard CV joint assembly.

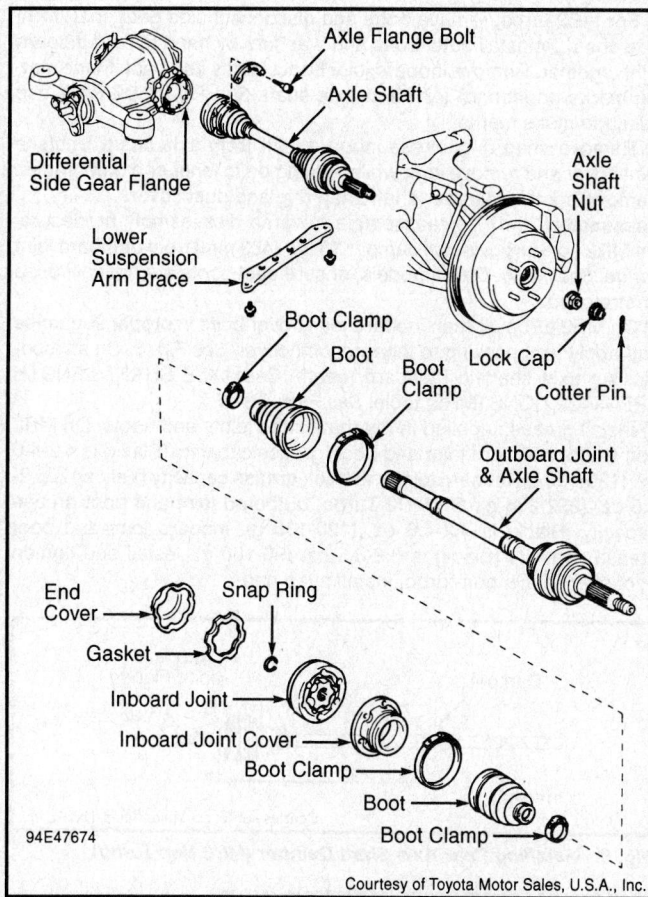

Fig. 1: *Identifying Rear Axle Shaft Components (Supra)*

Reassembly – 1) Wrap shaft splines with tape. Temporarily install outboard and inboard joint boots. Apply seal packing (Three Bond or equivalent), to inboard joint end cover. Align bolt holes and install joint end cover. Align marks made during disassembly and install joint onto axle shaft. Install snap ring on joint side of axle shaft. Apply CV joint grease, supplied in overhaul kit, to inboard and outboard joint and boot. Grease capacity is 3.5-3.7 oz. (100-105 g) for both inboard and outboard joints and boots.

2) Install boots and clamps. Tighten clamps until clamp opening clearance is .031" (.80 mm) or less. Set axle shaft to standard lengths. See AXLE SHAFT LENGTH SPECIFICATIONS (Supra) table. *See Fig. 2.*

3) Pack 1.8-1.9 oz. (50-55 g) of grease into end cover. Glue on a new gasket with adhesive side facing outer race. Align bolt holes and install cover. Install bolts. Attach nuts and tighten bolts in sequence to specification. *See Fig. 3.* Ensure claw of end cover touches inboard joint and that joint moves smoothly.

AXLE SHAFT LENGTH SPECIFICATIONS (SUPRA)

Application	In. (mm)
Turbo With Man. Trans.	
Right Axle Shaft	[1] 22.77-24.35 (578.5-618.5)
Left Axle Shaft	[1] 20.76-22.34 (527.5-567.5)
All Others	
Right Axle Shaft	[1] 22.77-24.35 (578.5-618.5)
Left Axle Shaft	[1] 21.00-22.57 (533.5-573.5)

[1] – Measured from outboard joint flange to end of inboard joint splines. *See Fig. 2.*

Installation – Insert outboard joint into axle hub. connect inboard joint to side gear shaft. Align match marks on side gear shaft and axle shaft. Install attaching bolts. To complete installation, reverse removal procedure. Tighten hub nut and axle flange nuts to specification. See TORQUE SPECIFICATIONS.

Removal (MR2) – 1) Raise and support vehicle. Remove rear wheels and engine undercover. Drain transaxle fluid. Remove cotter pin and lock nut cap. *See Fig. 4 or 5.* Apply parking brake and remove bearing lock nut.

2) On MR2 turbo, paint mating marks on axle shaft flange and side gear shaft flange. *See Fig. 5.* DO NOT use punch to make mating marks. Loosen, but DO NOT remove, 6 bolts connecting axle shaft flange to differential side gear shaft flange.

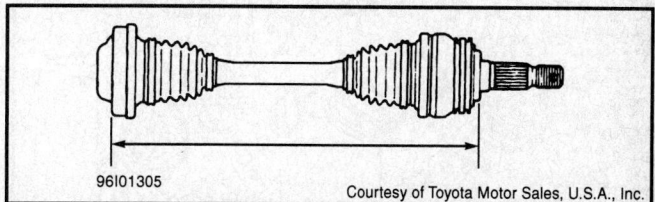

Fig. 2: *Measuring Rear Axle Shaft Standard Length (Supra)*

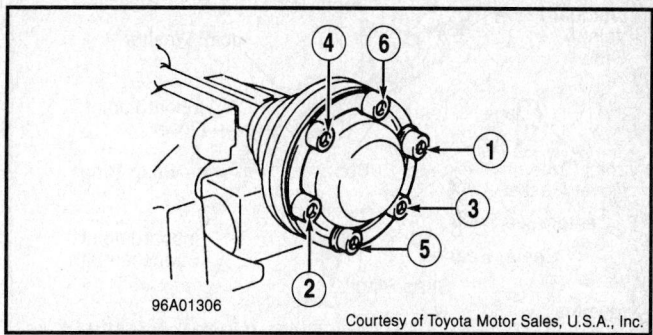

Fig. 3: *Tightening Inboard End Cover Sequence (Supra)*

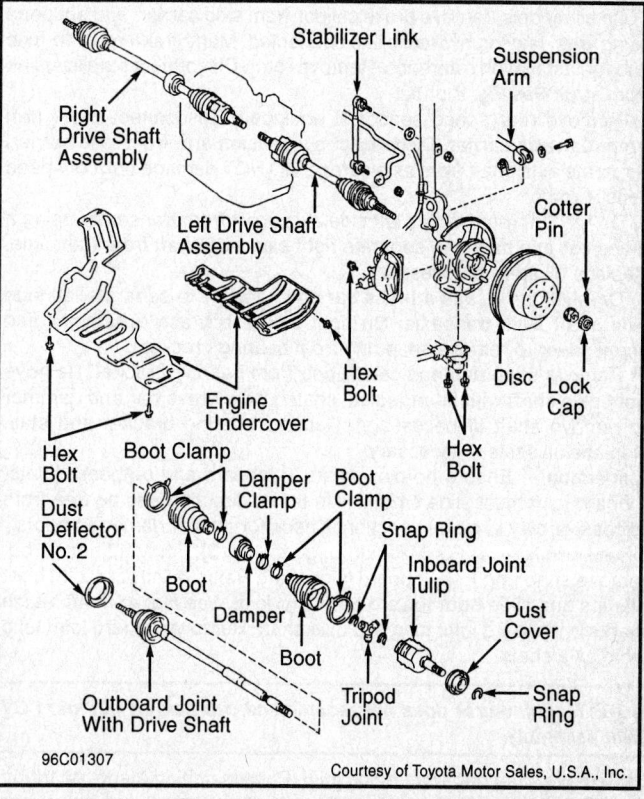

Fig. 4: *Identifying Rear Axle Shaft Components (MR2 Non-Turbo)*

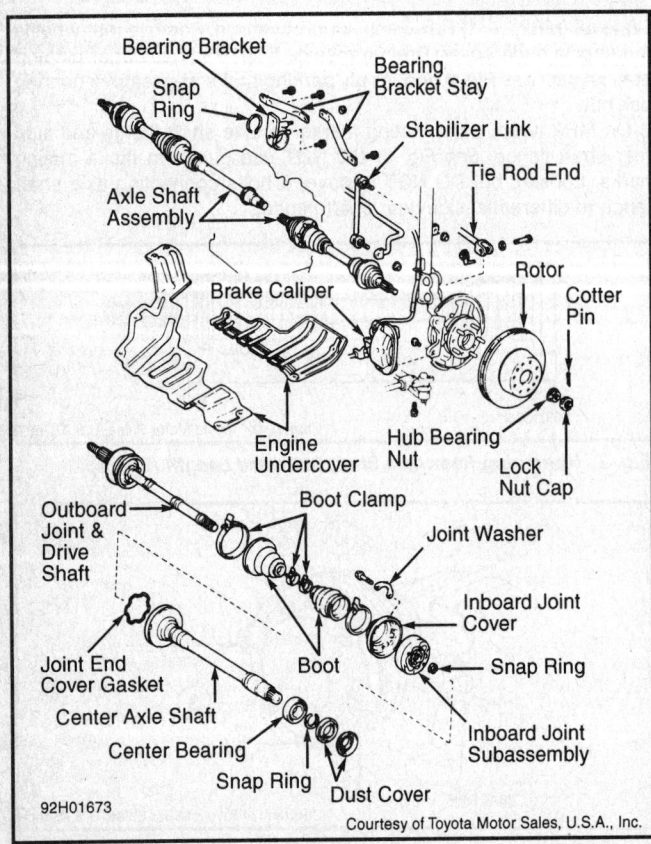

Fig. 5: Identifying Rear Axle Shaft Components (MR2 Turbo)

3) On all models, remove brake caliper from axle carrier, and suspend using wire, leaving hydraulic line connected. Mark brake rotor-to-axle hub for installation reference. Remove rotor. Disconnect stabilizer link from strut. *See Fig. 4 or 5.*

4) Remove rear speed sensor (if equipped). Disconnect lower arm from rear axle carrier. Disconnect suspension arm from axle carrier. Separate axle shaft from axle carrier. DO NOT damage boot or speed sensor rotor.

5) On MR2 non-turbo, pry left side axle shaft from transaxle. Using a brass bar and hammer, separate right side axle shaft from transaxle. Replace oil seals if necessary.

6) On MR2 turbo, use a brass bar and hammer to separate left side axle shaft from transaxle. On right axle shaft, use a hammer and screwdriver to remove snap ring from bearing bracket.

7) Remove snap ring and center bolt from bearing bracket. Remove right axle shaft with intermediate shaft. Use a brass bar and hammer to remove shaft (if necessary). Remove bearing bracket and stay. Replace oil seals if necessary.

Inspection – Ensure no play exists in inboard and outboard joints. Inboard joint must slide smoothly in thrust direction and be free from excessive play in radial direction. Check for torn or damaged boots.

Disassembly – **1)** For MR2 turbo, go to step **3)**. For MR2 non-turbo, remove snap ring from inboard joint shaft. Remove inboard joint boot clamps and slide boot toward outboard joint. *See Fig. 4.* Paint match marks on inboard joint tulip and axle shaft. Remove inboard joint tulip from axle shaft.

NOTE: Manufacturer does not recommend overhaul of outboard CV joint assembly.

---

2) Remove snap ring from tripod joint. Paint matching marks on tripod joint and axle shaft. Drive tripod joint from axle shaft using hammer and brass drift. Remove inboard boot. Remove damper clamp and damper. Remove outboard boot clamps, and slide boot from joint. Remove dust cover. Remove dust deflector No. 2.

3) For MR2 turbo, remove bolts and disconnect side gear shaft from axle shaft. Reinstall nuts, bolts and washers by hand to hold inboard joint together. Remove inboard joint boot clamps and boot. Place mating marks on inboard joint and axle shaft. *See Fig. 5.* DO NOT use punch to make marks.

4) Remove snap ring. Press inboard joint from axle shaft. Unstake joint cover and remove joint while holding on to inner and outer races. Remove boots, side gear shaft snap ring and dust cover.

Reassembly – 1) To reassemble, reverse disassembly procedure. On MR2 non-turbo, install damper 18.22" (463 mm) from outboard joint flange. *See Fig. 6.* On all models, ensure dust boots are not collapsed or stretched.

2) On MR2 turbo, tighten inboard joint cover bolts in proper sequence and apply seal packing to inboard joint cover. *See Fig. 3.* On all models, set axle shaft to standard length. See AXLE SHAFT LENGTH SPECIFICATIONS (MR2) table. *See Figs. 7 and 8.*

3) Install grease supplied in overhaul kit to joints and boots. On MR2 non-turbo, outboard joint and boot, grease capacity (Black) is 4.2-4.6 oz. (120-130 g). Inboard joint and boot, grease capacity (Yellow) is 8.2-8.5 oz. (232-234 g). On MR2 Turbo, outboard joint and boot grease capacity (Black) is 4.2-4.6 oz. (120-130 g). Inboard joint and boot grease capacity (Black) is 3.2-3.5 oz. (90-100 g). Install and tighten boot clamps. On non-turbo, install snap ring.

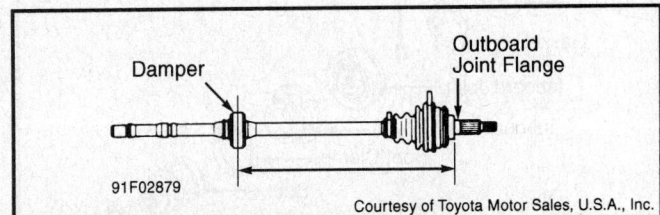

Fig. 6: Installing Rear Axle Shaft Damper (MR2 Non-Turbo)

AXLE SHAFT LENGTH SPECIFICATIONS (MR2)

Application	In. (mm)
Non-Turbo	
Right Axle Shaft	[1] 32.54-32.93 (826.4-836.4)
Left Axle Shaft	[1] 21.08-21.47 (535.3-545.3)
Turbo	
Right & Left Axle Shafts	[2] 15.15-15.54 (384.7-394.7)

[1] – Measured from outboard joint flange to end of inboard joint splines. *See Fig. 7.*

[2] – Measured from outboard joint flange to end of inboard joint flange. *See Fig. 8.*

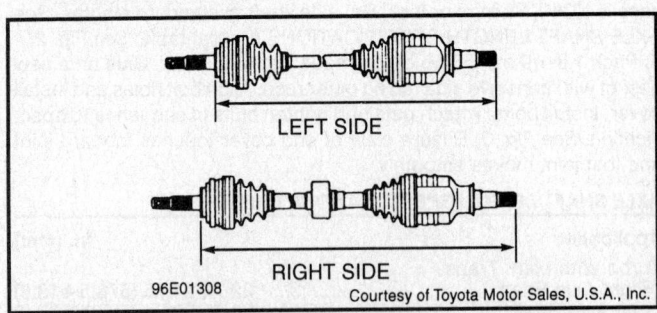

LEFT SIDE

RIGHT SIDE

Fig. 7: Measuring Rear Axle Shaft Standard Length (MR2)

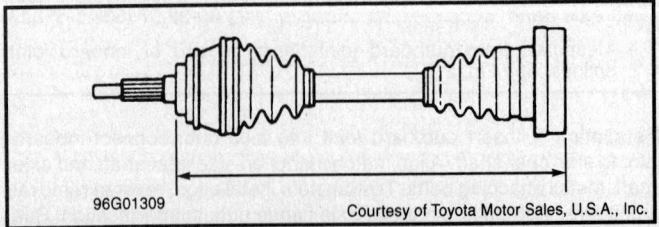

Fig. 8: Measuring Rear Axle Shaft Standard Length (MR2 Turbo)

Installation – 1) To install, reverse removal procedure. Before installing axle shaft, ensure NEW snap ring is installed on end of axle shaft. Coat axle shaft seals in transaxle with grease. DO NOT damage speed sensor rotor or joint boots. On MR2 non-turbo, ensure axial play is .08-.12" (2.0-3.0 mm) after installing axle shaft to transaxle. Ensure axle shaft cannot be pulled out by hand.

2) On all models, tighten bolts/nuts to specification. Tighten suspension arm-to-axle carrier bolt/nut to specification after vehicle is lowered to ground and bounced several times to stabilize suspension components. Check rear wheel alignment. Fill transaxle with Dexron-II (A/T models) or 75W-90 gear oil with API GL-3 or GL-4 rating (M/T models). See TORQUE SPECIFICATIONS.

Removal RAV4 – Raise and support vehicle. Remove rear wheels. Remove ABS speed sensor, if applicable. Remove drive shaft lock nut. Place matchmarks on drive shaft and differential side gear shaft. Remove 4 nuts and washers. Remove driveshaft from axle carrier. See Fig. 9.

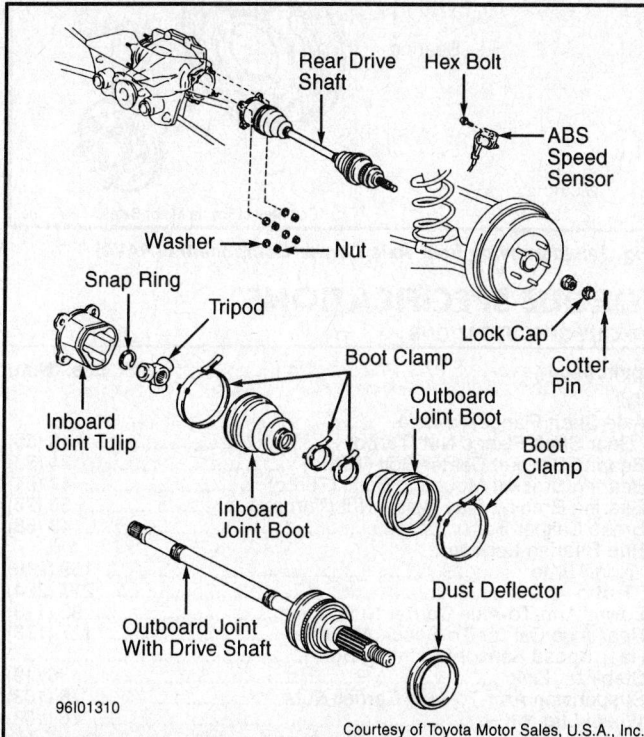

Fig. 9: Identifying Rear Axle Shaft Components (RAV4)

Inspection – Ensure no play exists in inboard and outboard joints. Inboard joint must slide smoothly in thrust direction and be free from excessive play in radial direction. Check for torn or damaged boots.

Disassembly – Remove inboard and outboard boot clamps. Paint matchmarks on inboard joint tulip and drive. DO NOT use punch to make marks. Remove inboard joint tulip. Remove snap ring. Paint matchmarks on shaft and tripod. If necessary, use a brass bar and hammer to remove tripod from drive shaft. DO NOT tap roller. Slide off inboard and outboard boots. Remove No. 2 dust deflector.

NOTE: Manufacturer does not recommend overhaul of outboard CV joint assembly.

Reassembly – To reassemble, reverse disassembly procedure. Install grease to inboard joint tulip and boot with Yellow grease supplied in overhaul kit. Grease capacity is 6.3-6.7 oz. (180-190 g). Install grease to outboard joint and boot with Black grease supplied in overhaul kit. Grease capacity is 3.5-3.9 oz. (100-110 g). Ensure boots are not stretched or contracted, set to standard length. See AXLE SHAFT LENGTH SPECIFICATION (RAV4). See Fig. 10. Install and tighten boot clamps.

Installation – To install, reverse removal procedure. Align matchmarks and tighten fasteners to specifications. See TORQUE SPECIFICATIONS table.

AXLE SHAFT LENGTH SPECIFICATIONS (MR2)

Application	In. (mm)
Right Side	23.40-23.80 (594.4-604.4)
Left Side	21.60-21.98 (548.4-558.4)

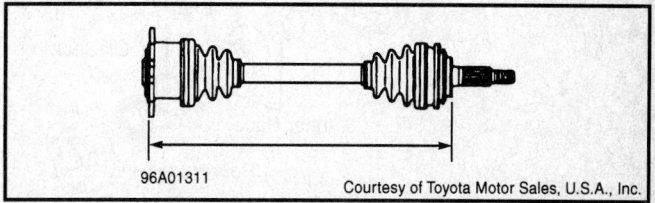

Fig. 10: Measuring Rear Axle Shaft Standard Length (RAV4)

REAR AXLE HUB & CARRIER

Removal (Supra) – 1) Raise and support vehicle. Remove rear wheel. Remove caliper and support out of way, without disconnecting brakeline. Mark brake rotor-to-axle hub for installation reference. Release parking brake and remove rotor. See Fig. 12.

2) Check bearing end play and axle hub runout. See Fig. 11. If bearing end play is greater than .002" (.05 mm), replace bearing. If hub runout is greater than .002" (.05 mm), replace hub. Remove axle shaft from vehicle. See RWD AXLE SHAFT.

3) Disconnect ABS sensor. Remove parking brake assembly. Remove strut rod. Place mating marks on adjusting cam and subframe, and remove lower suspension arm No. 1. Disconnect shock absorber and stabilizer bar link from suspension arm No. 2. Disconnect upper and lower suspension arms from axle carrier and remove carrier.

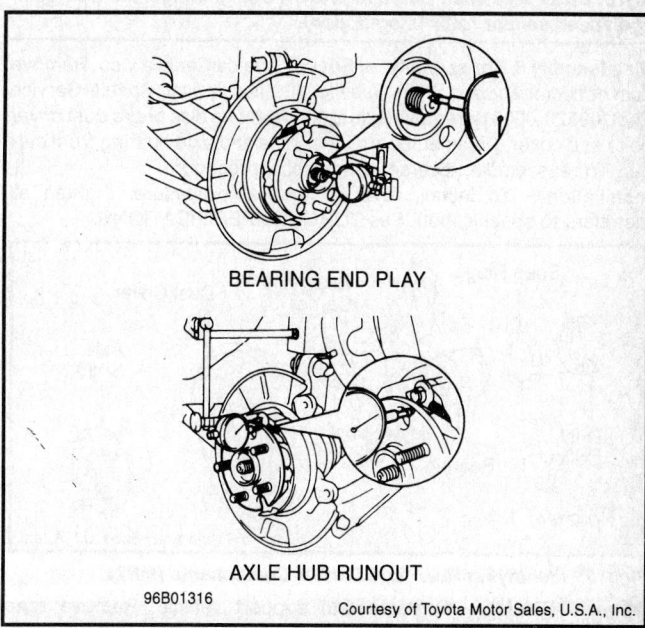

Fig. 11: Checking Axle Hub & Bearings

Disassembly – Remove dust reflector. Mount carrier in a vise and remove axle hub. Remove backing plate. Remove inner race from axle hub. Remove inner and outer oil seals. Remove snap ring and press bearing outer race from axle carrier.

Reassembly & Installation – 1) To reassemble axle carrier, reverse disassembly procedure. Coat bearings, races and interior of hub with multipurpose grease.

2) Reverse removal procedure to complete installation. Use NEW nut on upper control arm ball joint. DO NOT final tighten strut rod, No. 2 suspension arm and upper control arm nuts until suspension is at normal riding height. Check rear wheel alignment.

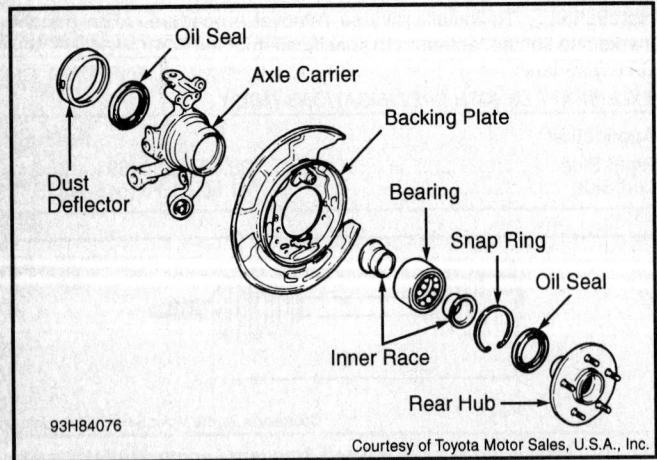

Fig. 12: Identifying Rear Axle Carrier Components (Supra)

Removal (MR2) – **1)** Raise and support rear of vehicle. Remove rear wheels. Remove disc brake caliper without disconnecting hydraulic line. Place matching marks on rotor and axle hub, and remove disc brake rotor.

2) Check bearing end play and axle hub runout. *See Fig. 11.* If bearing end play is greater than .002" (.05 mm), replace bearing. If hub runout is greater than .002" (.05 mm), replace hub. Remove cotter pin and lock nut cap. Apply parking brake and remove axle shaft hub nut. Release parking brake.

3) Disconnect stabilizer link. Remove rear speed sensor (if equipped). Disconnect lower arm and suspension arm from axle carrier. Remove steering knuckle-to-strut bolts, and remove axle carrier with axle shaft.

NOTE: Cover axle shaft boots to protect from damage. DO NOT damage speed sensor rotor (if equipped).

Disassembly & Reassembly – Secure axle carrier in a vise. Remove dust deflector and snap ring. *See Fig. 13.* Using puller, Special Service Tool (09520-00031), remove axle shaft. Remove disc brake dust cover bolts and cover. Press outboard inner race and axle bearing from carrier. To reassemble, reverse disassembly procedure.

Installation – To install, reverse removal procedure. Tighten all fasteners to specification. See TORQUE SPECIFICATIONS.

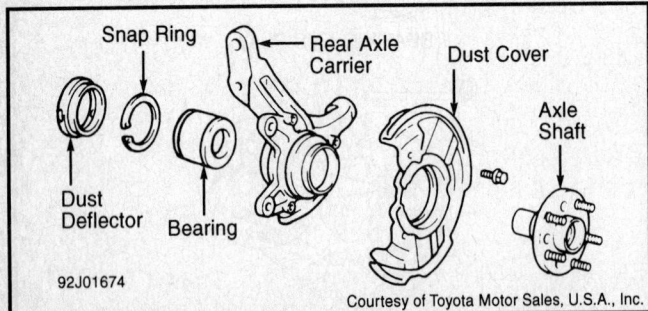

Fig. 13: Identifying Rear Axle Carrier Components (MR2)

Removal (RAV4) – **1)** Raise and support vehicle. Remove rear wheels. Remove brake drum. Check bearing end play and axle hub runout. If bearing end play is greater than .002" (.05 mm), replace bearing. If hub runout is greater than .003" (.07 mm), replace bearing. Remove ABS sensor, if equipped. On 2WD models, remove cotter pin and lock cap. While applying brakes, remove axle lock nut. Remove axle shaft.

2) On 4WD models, Remove rear drive shaft. See RWD AXLE SHAFT removal. Remove rear brakes. Disconnect brake line. Remove two bolts and disconnect parking brake. Remove rear axle hub with backing plate. *See Fig. 13.*

Disassembly) – Using Special Service Tool (09950-00370) with appropriate adaptor, remove axle hub from bearing. Remove inner race from axle hub.

Reassembly – To reassemble, reverse order of disassembly. Bleed brake system and check for leaks. Tighten all fasteners to specifications.

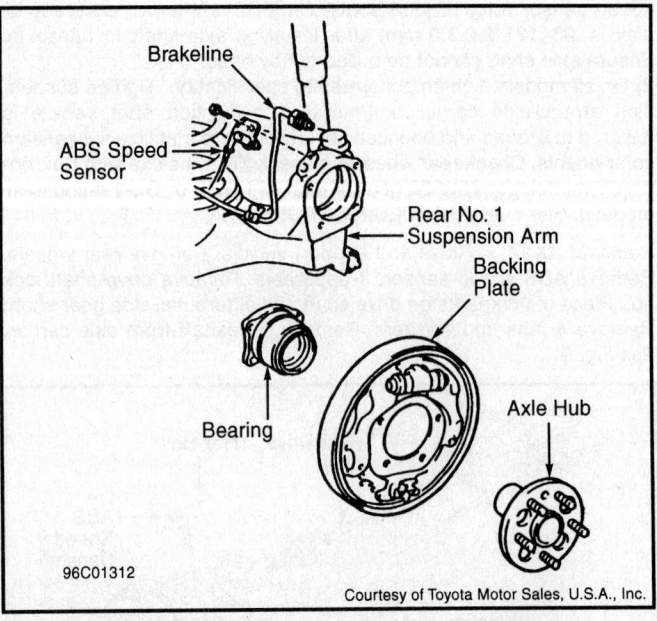

Fig. 14: Identifying Rear Axle Carrier Components (RAV4)

TORQUE SPECIFICATIONS
TORQUE SPECIFICATIONS

Application	Ft. Lbs. (N.m)
MR2	
Axle Shaft Flange-To-Side	
Gear Shaft Flange Nut (Turbo)	48 (65)
Bearing Bracket Center Bolt (Turbo)	24 (33)
Bearing Bracket Mounting Bolts (Turbo)	47 (64)
Bearing Bracket Stay Bolt & Nut (Turbo)	56 (76)
Brake Caliper Bolts	43 (58)
Hub Bearing Lock Nut	
Non-Turbo	159 (216)
Turbo	217 (294)
Lower Arm-To-Axle Carrier Nuts	83 (113)
Rear Axle Carrier-To-Shock Absorber	127 (173)
Rear Speed Sensor Mounting Bolt	[1]
Stabilizer Link	36 (49)
Suspension Arm-To-Axle Carrier Nuts	76 (103)
Wheel Lug Nut	76 (103)
Supra	
Adjusting Cam Nut	136 (184)
Axle Shaft Inner Flange Nuts	61 (83)
Axle Shaft Outer Hub Nut	213 (289)
Backing Plate Bolt	19 (26)
Bolt And Shoe Guide Plate	13 (18)
Disc Brake Caliper Bolts	77 (104)
No. 1 Suspension Arm-To-Axle Carrier Nut	43 (58)
No. 2 Suspension Arm-To-Axle Carrier Nut [4] [5]	111 (150)
Parking Brake Cable-To-Backing Plate Bolt	133 (180)
Parking Brake Cable Set Bolt	[1]
Shock Absorber-To-Lower Arm Bolt	101 (137)
Stabilizer Bar Link	54 (74)
Strut Rod-To-Axle Carrier Bolt & Nut [4]	136 (184)
Upper Control Arm Ball Joint Nut [5]	80 (108)
Wheel Lug Nuts	76 (103)
RAV4	
ABS Sensor Bolt	[1]
Brake Line	[3]
Differential Side Gear & Drive Shaft Bolt	41 (56)
Drive Shaft Lock Nut	152 (206)
Parking Brake Cable	[2]
Wheel Lug Nuts	76 (103)

[1] – Tighten to 74 INCH lbs. (8.3 N.m).
[2] – Tighten to 69 INCH lbs. (7.8 N.m).
[3] – Tighten to 132 INCH lbs. (14.9)
[4] – Tighten fasteners with vehicle suspension at normal riding height.
[5] – Always replace nut. Old nut should not be reused.

Pickup, Previa, Tacoma, T100, 4Runner

NOTE: For RAV4 models, see TOYOTA RAV4 axle shaft article.

DESCRIPTION

Axle shafts transfer power from transaxle to driving wheels. All axle shafts consist of a shaft and flexible Constant Velocity (CV) joint at each end. Inner CV joint is bolted or splined to transaxle. Outer CV joint is splined to hub assembly and secured by axle shaft nut.

The inner CV joint is a plunging tripod joint. The plunging action allows for axle shaft length change as suspension moves up and down.

The inner and outer CV joints are enclosed by a CV joint boot. The boot maintains lubrication in the joint and prevents contamination of CV lubricant. Boots must be replaced if leaking or cracked. The inner CV joint can be repaired. The outer CV joint must be replaced as an assembly.

TROUBLE SHOOTING

NOTE: See DRIVE AXLE NOISE DIAGNOSIS in GENERAL INFORMATION at beginning of this section.

REMOVAL, DISASSEMBLY, REASSEMBLY & INSTALLATION

4WD AXLE SHAFTS

Removal (Pickup, Tacoma, T100 & 4Runner) – **1)** Raise and support vehicle. Remove front wheels. On 1996 Tacoma and 4Runner, drain differential oil. Apply brakes and loosen 6 inboard CV joint flange-to-front differential nuts. If vehicle is equipped with free-wheeling hubs, go to next step. If vehicle is not equipped with free-wheeling hubs, go to step **3)**.

2) On models equipped with free-wheeling hubs, place free-wheeling hub cover in FREE position. Remove 6 cover mounting bolts and cover. On 1996 Tacoma and 4Runner, remove grease cap, cotter pin and locknut. Remove center hub body bolt and washer. Remove hub body mounting nuts and washers. Remove cone washers by tapping on bolt heads using brass drift and hammer. Remove hub body. Go to step **4)**.

3) On models not equipped with free-wheeling hubs, remove dust cap from flange. Remove center flange bolt. Remove 6 flange mounting nuts. Remove cone washers by tapping on bolt heads using brass drift and hammer. Install 2 bolts into flange. Tighten bolts and remove flange. Go to next step.

4) On all models except 1996 Tacoma and 4Runner, remove snap ring and spacer from outboard end of axle shaft. *See Fig. 1.* Remove 6 inboard CV joint flange-to-front differential nuts and slide axle shaft toward steering knuckle until it is free of differential. Pull axle shaft down and away, out of steering knuckle.

5) On 1996 Tacoma and 4Runner, disconnect lower suspension arm. Push steering knuckle outward and remove driveshaft. Remove snap ring from inboard shaft. *See Fig. 2.*

Inspection – Ensure no play exists in outboard joint. Inboard joint must slide smoothly in thrust direction and be free from excessive play in radial direction. Check for torn or damaged boots.

Disassembly – **1)** Remove CV joint boot clamps, and slide boots from joint. Paint alignment marks on CV joint housings, tripod and shaft(s) for reassembly reference. *See Fig. 1 or 2.*

NOTE: Manufacturer does not recommend overhaul of outer joint assembly.

2) Remove inner housing from tripod joint and axle shaft. Remove snap ring from end of axle shaft retaining tripod joint. Paint reference marks on tripod joint and axle shaft for reassembly reference.

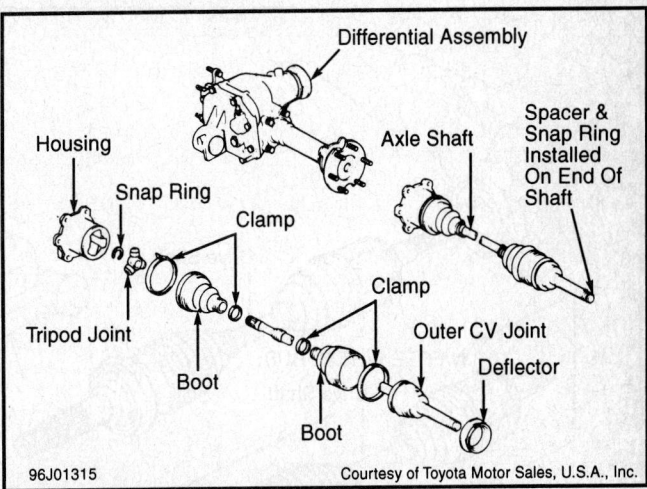

Fig. 1: Exploded View Of Front Axle Shaft (Pickup, T100 & 1995 4Runner)

3) Using a hammer and brass drift, tap tripod joint from axle shaft. DO NOT tap on roller of tripod joint during removal. Remove boots from axle shaft. Using a screwdriver and hammer, tap deflector from axle shaft.

Reassembly – **1)** To reassemble, reverse disassembly procedure. Install NEW deflector on axle shaft. Wrap splines on axle shaft with tape to prevent damaging boots during installation.

2) Install NEW boots and NEW boot clamps on axle shaft. Install tripod joint on axle shaft with beveled side toward outer joint. Ensure alignment marks align. Using Black grease supplied in overhaul kit, apply 6.2-6.5 oz. (176-186 g) of grease to outboard joint and boot. For Tacoma, outboard joint and boot grease capacity is 7.58-8.29 oz. (215-235 g). Assemble outboard boot onto outboard joint.

2) Using Brown grease supplied in overhaul kit, apply 9.5-9.9 oz. (270-280 g) of grease to inboard joint and boot. For Tacoma, inboard joint and boot, grease capacity is 8.11-8.82 oz. (230-250 g). For 1996 4Runner, inboard joint and boot grease capacity is 8.99-9.34 oz. (255-265 g). Assemble outboard boot onto inboard joint. Set axle shaft to standard length. See AXLE SHAFT LENGTH SPECIFICATIONS table. *See Fig. 3.* Install and tighten boot clamps.

Installation – To install, reverse removal procedure using NEW gaskets. Coat surfaces of shaft at outer joint with grease before installing axle shaft. Ensure reference marks on axle shaft flange and differential assembly flange are aligned. To ensure proper engagement of snap ring, attempt to pull axle shaft out of differential by hand. Tighten bolts/nuts to specifications. See TORQUE SPECIFICATIONS table.

Removal (Previa) – **1)** Raise and support vehicle. Remove front wheel. Remove hub cap, cotter pin and lock nut. Apply brake and remove wheel bearing lock nut. Loosen lower ball joint bolts. Remove cotter pin and nut from tie rod end. Using Tie Rod Remover (09628-10011), disconnect tie rod end from steering knuckle.

CAUTION: DO NOT damage oil seal, axle shaft boots or ABS speed sensor rotor (if equipped) during axle shaft removal or installation.

2) Paint mating marks on axle shaft flange and side gear shaft flange. DO NOT use punch to make mating marks. Apply brakes and remove retaining nuts on each inboard axle shaft flange. Remove bolts, disconnect steering knuckle from lower control arm. Separate steering knuckle from axle shaft.

Inspection – Ensure no play exists in outboard joint. Inboard joint must slide smoothly in thrust direction and be free from excessive play in radial direction. Check for torn or damaged boots.

Disassembly – **1)** Remove CV joint boot clamps, and slide boots from joint. Paint alignment marks on CV joint housings, tripod and shaft(s) for reassembly reference. *See Fig. 5.*

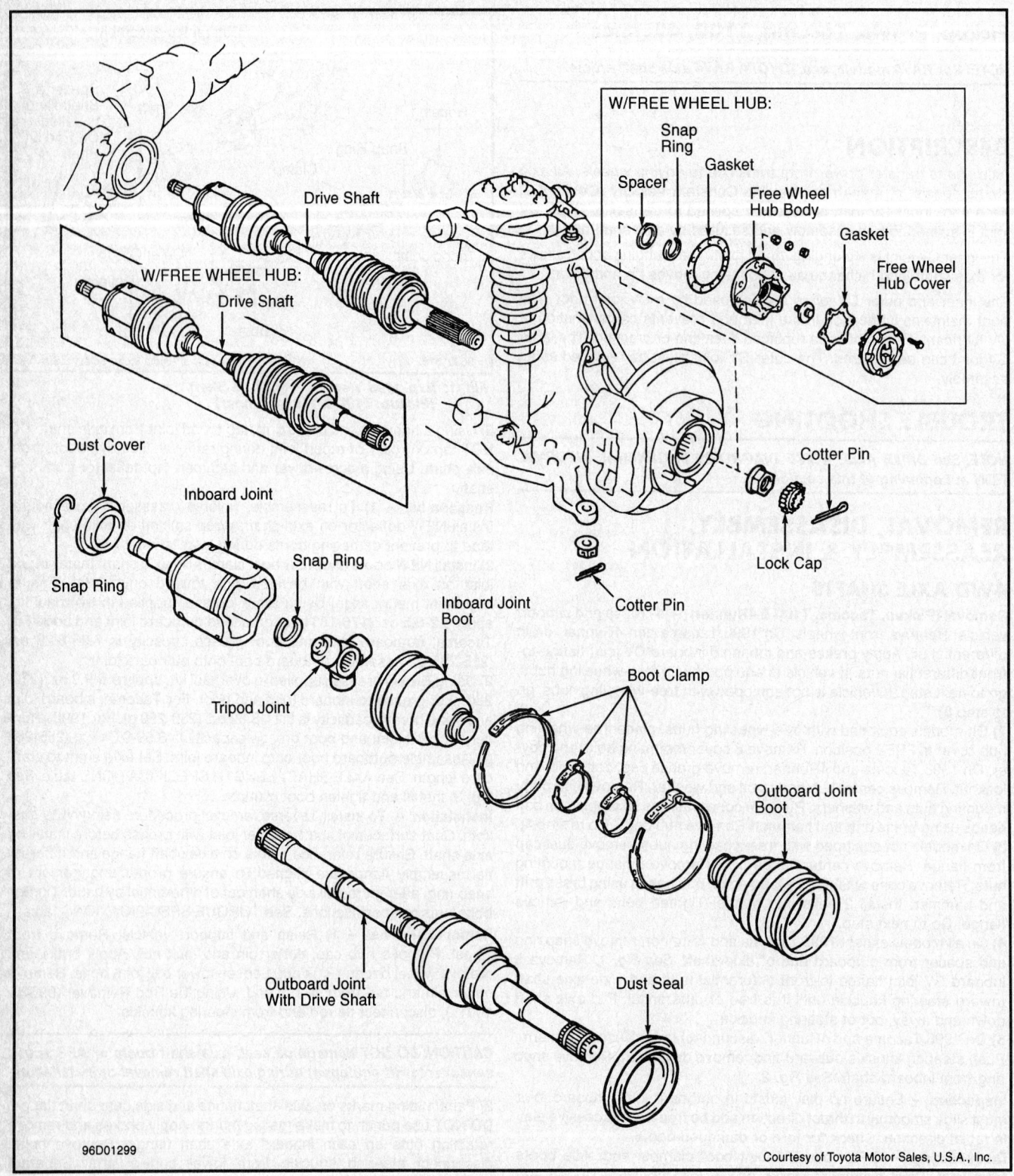

Drive Shaft

W/FREE WHEEL HUB:
Drive Shaft

W/FREE WHEEL HUB:
Snap Ring
Spacer
Gasket
Free Wheel Hub Body
Gasket
Free Wheel Hub Cover

Dust Cover

Inboard Joint

Cotter Pin

Lock Cap

Snap Ring

Snap Ring

Inboard Joint Boot

Cotter Pin

Tripod Joint

Boot Clamp

Outboard Joint Boot

Outboard Joint With Drive Shaft

Dust Seal

96D01299

Courtesy of Toyota Motor Sales, U.S.A., Inc.

Fig. 2: Exploded View Of Front Axle Shaft (1995-1996 Tacoma & 1996 4Runner)

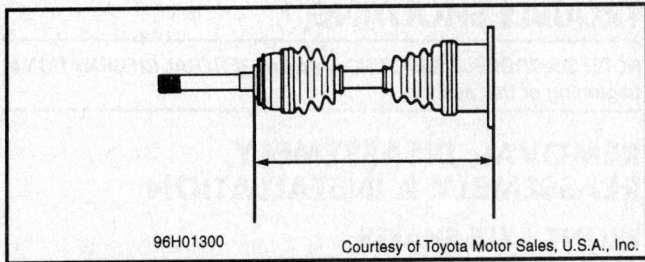

96H01300 — Courtesy of Toyota Motor Sales, U.S.A., Inc.

Fig. 3: Measuring Axle Shaft Standard Length (Pickup, T100, & 1995 4Runner)

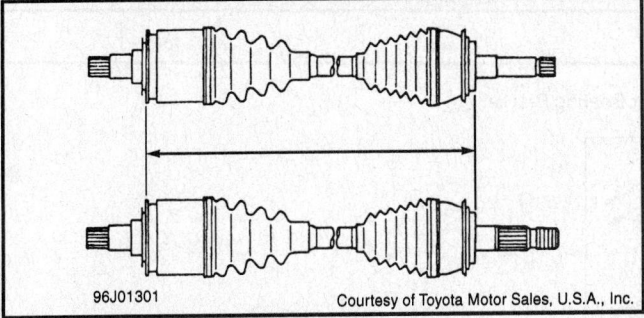

96J01301 — Courtesy of Toyota Motor Sales, U.S.A., Inc.

Fig. 4: Measuring Axle Shaft Standard Length (1995-1996 Tacoma & 1996 4Runner)

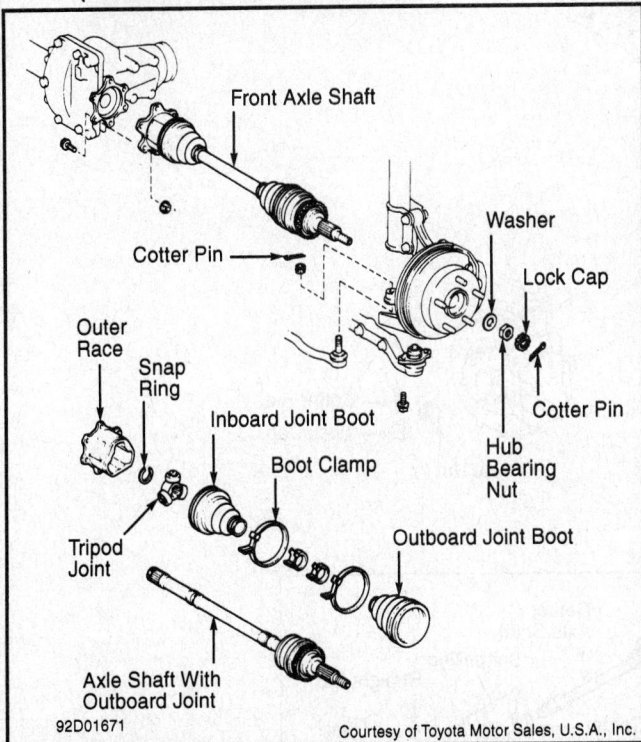

92D01671 — Courtesy of Toyota Motor Sales, U.S.A., Inc.

Fig. 5: Exploded View Of Front Axle Shaft (Previa)

NOTE: Manufacturer does not recommend overhaul of outer joint assembly.

2) Remove outer race from tripod joint and axle shaft. Remove snap ring from end of axle shaft retaining tripod joint. Paint reference marks on tripod joint and axle shaft for reassembly reference.

3) Using a hammer and brass drift, tap tripod joint from axle shaft. DO NOT tap on roller of tripod joint during removal. Remove boots from axle shaft.

Reassembly – To assemble, wrap splines on axle shaft with tape to prevent damaging boots during installation. Install NEW boots and NEW boot clamps on axle shaft. Install tripod joint on axle shaft. Ensure reference mark on tripod joint and axle shaft are aligned.

2) Using a hammer and brass drift, tap tripod joint on axle shaft. Tap on center of tripod joint. DO NOT tap on rollers on tripod joint.

3) Install NEW snap ring that retains tripod joint on axle shaft. Pack 7.6-7.9 ounces of grease supplied with overhaul kit into inner joint and outer race. Install outer race on inner joint and axle shaft so reference marks are aligned.

4) Using grease supplied in overhaul kit, apply same amount of grease that was removed in disassembly procedure on outer joint and boot. Grease capacity for outboard boot and joint is 4.2-4.6 oz. (120-130 g). Install boots on outer race and outer joint.

5) Ensure boots are seated in grooves on axle shaft. Adjust axle shaft to standard axle shaft length of 19.15-19.55" (486.30-496.47 mm). Install and tighten boot clamps.

Set axle shaft to standard length. See AXLE SHAFT LENGTH SPECIFICATIONS table. *See Fig. 3.* Install and tighten boot clamps.

Installation – To install, reverse removal procedure using NEW gaskets. Coat surfaces of shaft at outer joint with grease before installing axle shaft. Ensure reference marks on axle shaft flange and differential assembly flange are aligned. To ensure proper engagement of snap ring, attempt to pull axle shaft out of differential by hand. Tighten bolts/nuts to specifications. See TORQUE SPECIFICATONS table.

AXLE SHAFT LENGTH SPECIFICATIONS

Application	[1] Length – In. (mm)
Pickup	15.51-15.90 (393.9-403.9)
4Runner	
1995	15.51-15.90 (393.9-403.9)
1996	20.70-21.10 (525.8-535.8)
Previa	19.15-19.54 (486.4-496.4)
T100	18.94-19.34 (481.2-491.2)
Tacoma	17.09-17.25 (434.2-438.8)

[1] – Measured between axle shaft inboard joint flange and outboard joint flange. *See Fig. 3 or 4.*

TORQUE SPECIFICATIONS

TORQUE SPECIFICATIONS

Application	Ft. Lbs. (N.m)
Pickup, T100 & 4Runner (1995)	
Axle Shaft-To-Differential Drive Flange Nuts	61 (83)
Drive Shaft Lock Nut	174 (235)
Flange-To-Axle Hub Nuts	23 (31)
Free-Wheeling Hub Body Center Bolt	13 (18)
Free-Wheeling Hub Body-To-Axle Hub Nuts	23 (31)
Free-Wheeling Hub Bearing Lock Nut	35 (47)
Wheel Lug Nuts (T100)	76 (103)
Wheel Lug Nuts (Pickup & 1995 4Runner)	101 (137)
Tacoma & 4Runner (1996)	
Drive Shaft Lock Nut	174 (235)
Free-Wheeling Hub Body Center Bolt	13 (18)
Free-Wheeling Hub Body-To-Axle Hub Nuts	23 (31)
Lower Suspension Arm To Ball Joint	112 (152)
Wheel Lug Nuts	83 (110)
Previa	
Axle Shaft Hub Nut	152 (206)
Axle Shaft-To-Differential Drive Flange Nuts	51 (69)
Steering Knuckle-To-Lower Arm Bolts	94 (127)
Tie Rod Nuts	36 (49)
Wheel Lug Nuts	76 (103)
	INCH Lbs. (N.m)
Pickup, T100 Tacoma & 4Runner	
Free-Wheeling Hub Cover-To-Hub Body Bolts	89 (10)
Previa	
ABS Sensor Bolt	69 (7.8)

AXLE SHAFTS
Toyota RAV4

RAV4

DESCRIPTION

Axle shafts transfer power from transaxle to the front wheels (2WD), or front and rear wheels (4WD). Axle shaft consists of axle shaft and flexible Constant Velocity (CV) joint at each end. Front inner CV joint is splined to transaxle. Rear inner CV joint is bolted to differential. Outer CV joint is splined to front or rear hub assembly.

Inner and outer CV joints are enclosed by a CV joint boot. Boot maintains lubrication in CV joint and prevents contamination of CV lubricant. Boots must be replaced if cracked, torn or damaged. Inner CV joint can be repaired without replacing assembly as outer CV joint must be replaced as an assembly.

TROUBLE SHOOTING

NOTE: See TROUBLE SHOOTING article in GENERAL INFORMATION at beginning of this section.

REMOVAL, DISASSEMBLY, REASSEMBLY & INSTALLATION

FRONT AXLE SHAFTS

NOTE: Use care not to damage oil seal, axle shaft boots or Anti-Lock Brake System (ABS) speed sensor rotor when removing axle shaft.

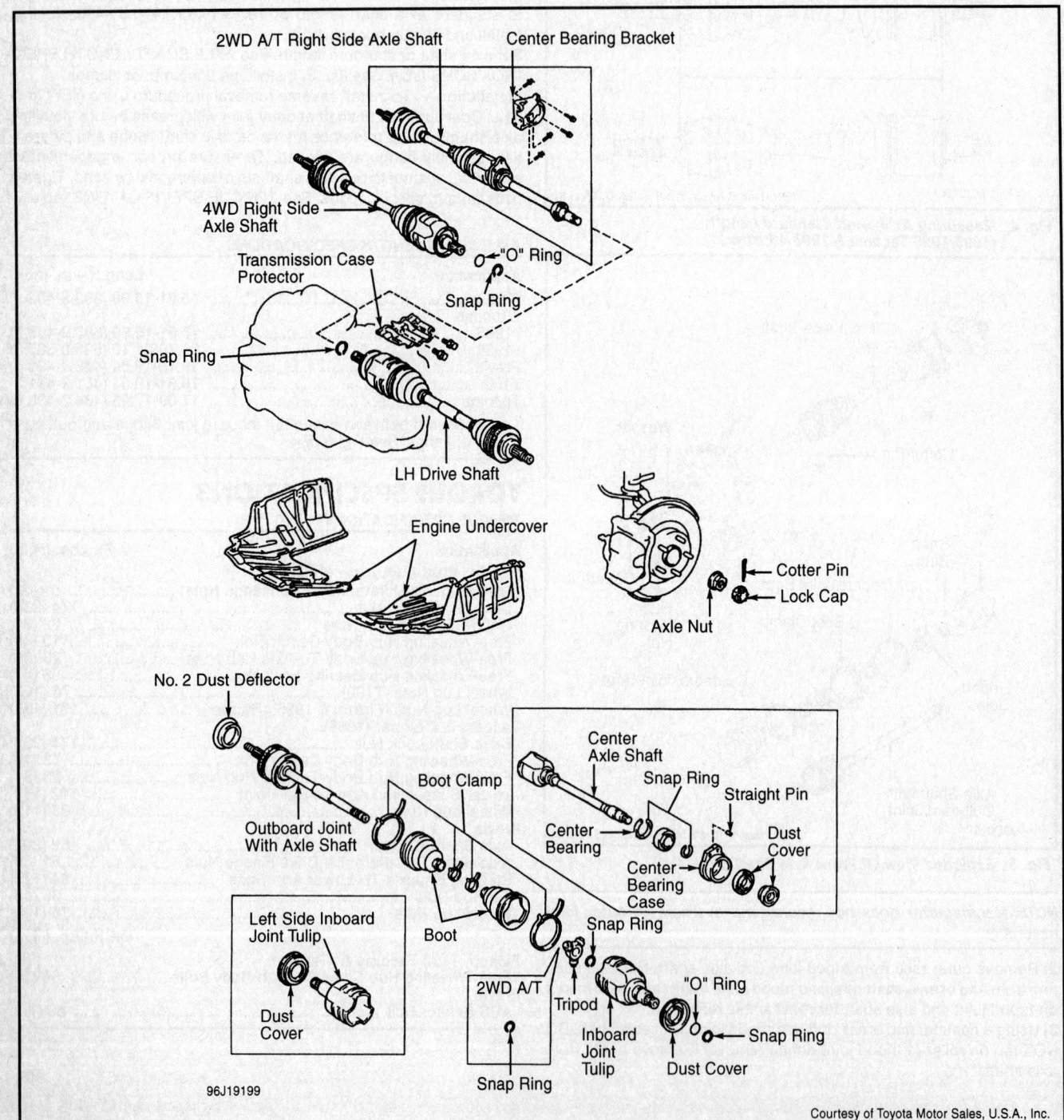

96J19199

Courtesy of Toyota Motor Sales, U.S.A., Inc.

Fig. 1: Exploded View Of Front Axle Shaft (2WD A/T & 4WD)

Removal – 1) Raise and support vehicle. Remove front wheel. Remove engine undercover. Drain gear oil from transaxle. Remove ABS speed sensor (if equipped). Remove cotter pin and lock cap. *See Fig. 1 or 2.* Apply brakes and remove axle shaft nut from end of axle shaft. Release brakes.

2) Remove cotter pin and nut from tie rod end. Using Tie Rod End Remover (SST 09610-20012), disconnect tie rod end from steering knuckle. Disconnect stabilizer bar link from lower suspension arm. Remove bolt and 2 nuts and separate lower ball joint from suspension arm.

3) Using a soft-faced hammer, tap axle shaft from hub. Pull steering knuckle outward and disconnect axle shaft from steering knuckle.

NOTE: On 2WD vehicles, removal of right-side axle shaft requires disassembly of center bearing axle support. See Fig. 3.

4) To remove axle shaft (except left side on 4WD), use a brass drift and hammer and tap on inner joint to separate from transaxle. Slide axle shaft toward steering knuckle until free of transaxle assembly.

5) To remove left-side axle shaft on 4WD, remove air cleaner and transaxle case protector. Using an appropriate pry bar, pry axle from transaxle assembly. *See Fig. 4.* Slide axle shaft toward steering knuckle until free of transaxle assembly.

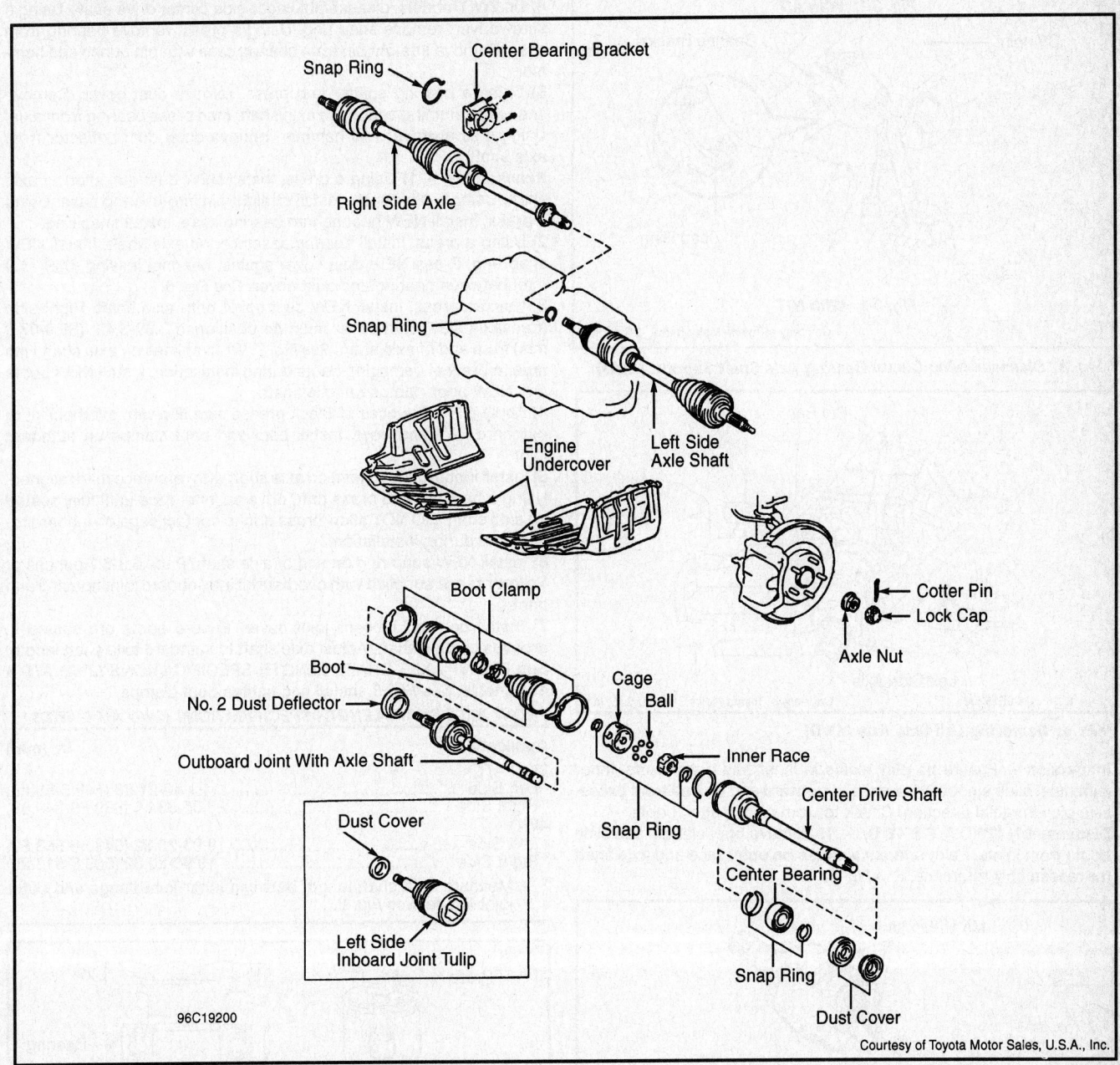

96C19200

Courtesy of Toyota Motor Sales, U.S.A., Inc.

Fig. 2: Exploded View Of Front Axle Shaft (2WD M/T)

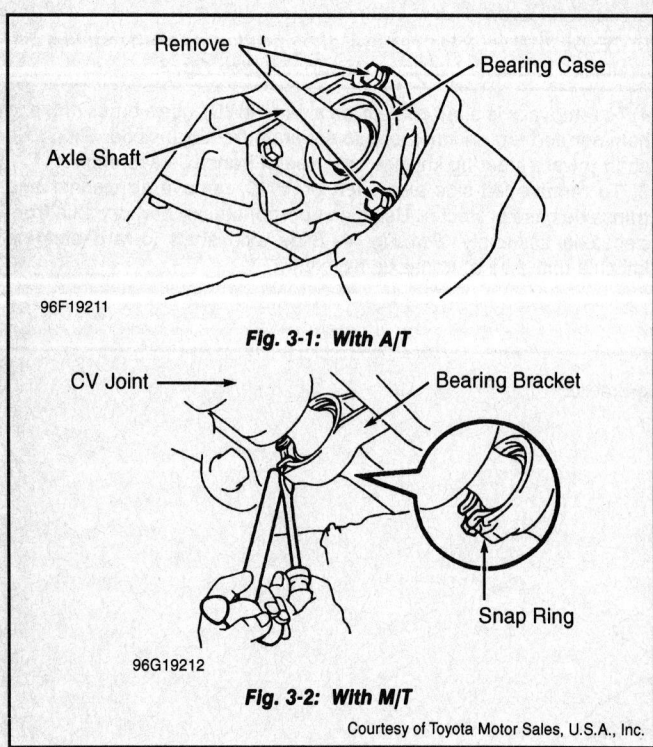

Fig. 3-1: With A/T

Fig. 3-2: With M/T

Courtesy of Toyota Motor Sales, U.S.A., Inc.

Fig. 3: Disassembling Center Bearing Axle Shaft Support (2WD)

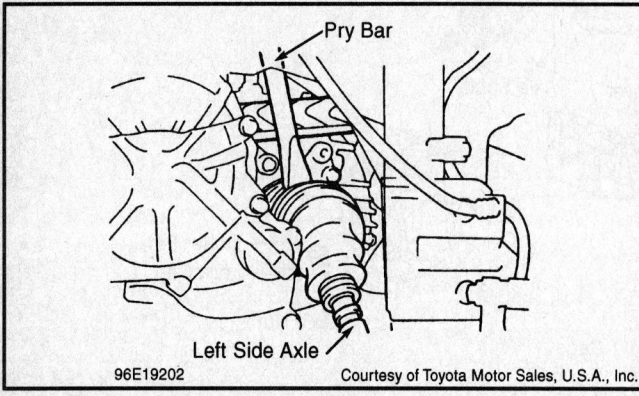

96E19202   Courtesy of Toyota Motor Sales, U.S.A., Inc.

Fig. 4: Removing Left-Side Axle (4WD)

Inspection – Ensure no play exists in inner and outer joints. Inner joint must slide smoothly inward and outward and be free from excessive play in radial direction. Check for torn or damaged boots.

Disassembly (2WD A/T & 4WD) – 1) Remove boot clamps and slide boots from joints. Paint reference marks on outer race and axle shaft for reassembly reference. See Fig. 5.

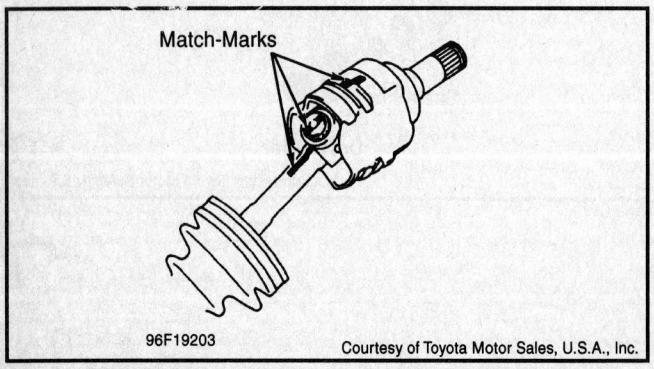

96F19203   Courtesy of Toyota Motor Sales, U.S.A., Inc.

Fig. 5: Match-Marking Components For Reassembly Reference (Typical)

NOTE: Manufacturer does not recommend overhaul of outer joint assembly.

2) Remove outer joint tulip from inboard tripod joint and axle shaft. Remove snap ring from end of axle shaft retaining inboard tripod joint. Paint reference marks on tripod joint and axle shaft for reassembly reference.

3) Using a hammer and brass drift, tap inboard tripod joint from axle shaft. DO NOT tap on roller of tripod joint during removal. Remove boots from axle shaft. Using a press, remove dust cover from right-side axle (2WD). Using a press and bearing splitter, remove dust cover from left-side inboard joint tulip (2WD and 4WD).

4) On 2WD models, disassemble right-side center drive shaft. Using a screwdriver, remove snap ring. Using a press, remove bearing from case. Remove straight pin from bearing case with pin punch and hammer.

5) Using a bearing splitter and press, remove dust cover. Remove snap ring retaining bearing to axle shaft, then press bearing from axle. Using a screwdriver and hammer, remove outer dust deflector from axle shaft.

Reassembly – **1)** Using a press, install NEW dust deflector on axle shaft. Using a pin punch, install straight pin into bearing case. Using a press, install NEW bearing into bearing case. Install snap ring.

2) Using a press, install bearing assembly on axle shaft. Install NEW snap ring. Press NEW dust cover against bearing, leaving .039" (1.0 mm) between bearing and dust cover. See Fig. 6.

3) Using a press, install NEW dust cover onto axle shaft. Right-side (transaxle side) dust cover must be positioned 3.39-3.43" (86.0-87.0 mm) from end of axle shaft. See Fig. 7. Wrap splines on axle shaft with tape to prevent damaging boots during installation. Install NEW boots and NEW boot clamps on axle shaft.

4) Apply 4.2-4.6 ounces of Black grease supplied with overhaul kit to outboard joint and boot. Install boot and boot clamps on outboard joint.

5) Install inboard tripod joint on axle shaft with reference mark aligned. Using a hammer and brass drift, drive on inner race until fully seated on axle shaft. DO NOT allow brass drift to contact cage on inboard tripod joint during installation.

6) Install NEW snap ring on end of axle shaft. Pack 6.3-6.7 ounces of Yellow grease supplied with overhaul kit into inboard joint housing and boot.

7) Install boot on inboard joint cover. Ensure boots are seated in grooves on axle shaft. Adjust axle shaft to standard axle shaft length. See FRONT AXLE SHAFT LENGTH SPECIFICATIONS (2WD A/T & 4WD) table. See Fig. 8. Install and tighten boot clamps.

FRONT AXLE SHAFT LENGTH SPECIFICATIONS (2WD A/T & 4WD) [1]

Application	In. (mm)
2WD A/T	
Left Side	21.40-21.80 (543.5-553.5)
Right Side	33.05-33.45 (839.60-849.60)
4WD	
Left Side	19.93-20.32 (543.50-553.50)
Right Side	19.93-20.32 (503.0-513.20)

[1] – Measure axle shaft length between inner joint flange and outer joint flange. See Fig. 8.

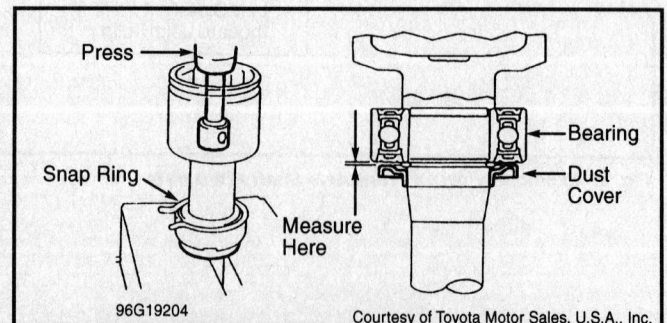

96G19204   Courtesy of Toyota Motor Sales, U.S.A., Inc.

Fig. 6: Positioning Dust Cover (Bearing Side)

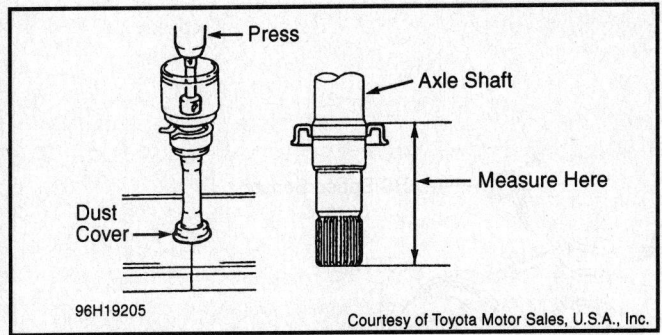

Fig. 7: Positioning Dust Cover (Transaxle Side)

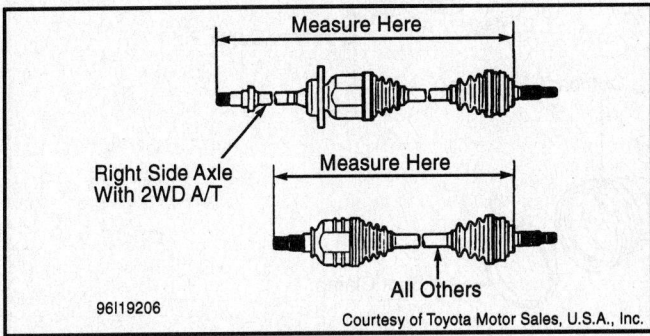

Fig. 8: Measuring Axle Shaft Length (Front)

Installation – 1) To install, reverse removal procedure. Before installing axle shafts, install NEW snap ring on end of axle shaft (except right side on 2WD). Coat axle shaft seals in transaxle with grease. Coat axle shaft splines and sliding surfaces with Dexron-II. Position snap ring on end of axle shaft with opening facing downward.

2) Install axle shaft by lightly tapping axle shaft into transaxle. Ensure axle shaft will move inward and outward approximately .079-.120" (2.00-3.00 mm) and cannot be pulled from transaxle.

3) To install remaining components, reverse removal procedure. Tighten remaining bolts/nuts to specification. See TORQUE SPECIFICATIONS. Fill transaxle with Dexron-II (A/T models), or 75W-90 gear oil with API GL-3, GL-4 or GL-5 rating (M/T models).

Disassembly (2WD M/T) – 1) Remove boot clamps and slide boots from joints. Paint reference marks on outer race and axle shaft for reassembly reference. See Fig. 5.

NOTE: Manufacturer does not recommend overhaul of outer joint assembly.

2) Using a screwdriver, remove snap ring from outer tulip race. Remove outer tulip race from inner joint and axle shaft. Remove snap ring from end of axle shaft retaining inner joint. Paint reference marks on inner joint, outer cage and axle shaft for reassembly reference.

3) Remove 6 balls and cage. Using a hammer and brass drift, tap inner joint from axle shaft. Remove inner snap ring. Remove boots from axle shaft. Using a press, remove dust cover from right-side axle. Using a press and bearing splitter, remove dust cover from left-side inner joint tulip.

4) Disassemble right-side center drive shaft. Using a screwdriver, remove snap ring. Using a press, remove bearing from axle. Using a screwdriver and hammer, remove outer dust deflector from axle shaft.

Reassembly – 1) Using a press, install NEW dust deflector on outboard end of axle shaft. Install NEW snap ring, then press center bearing on axle shaft. Press NEW dust cover against bearing, leaving .039" (1.0 mm) between bearing and dust cover. See Fig. 6.

2) Using a press, install NEW dust cover on axle shaft. Right-side (transaxle side) dust cover must be positioned 4.134-4.173" (105.0-106.0 mm) from end of axle shaft. See Fig. 7. Wrap splines on axle shaft with tape to prevent damaging boots during installation.

3) Install NEW boots and NEW boot clamps on axle shaft. Install NEW snap ring on axle shaft. Install inboard joint on axle shaft with small diameter side facing outboard joint. Ensure reference mark on inner joint and axle shaft are aligned. Install NEW snap ring that retains inner joint on axle shaft.

4) Position outer cage and 6 balls on inner joint and hold in place with grease. Apply 4.1-4.8 ounces of Yellow grease supplied with overhaul kit to inner joint and boot. Install inboard joint tulip (center shaft) on inner joint. Ensure match-marks are aligned. Install NEW snap ring.

5) Pack 4.1-4.8 ounces of Black grease supplied with overhaul kit into outer joint and boot. Install boot on inner housing and outer joint. Ensure boots are seated in grooves on axle shaft. Adjust axle shaft to standard axle shaft length. See FRONT AXLE SHAFT LENGTH SPECIFICATIONS (2WD M/T) table. See Fig. 8. Install and tighten boot clamps.

FRONT AXLE SHAFT LENGTH SPECIFICATIONS (2WD M/T) [1]

Application	In. (mm)
2WD M/T	
Left Side	21.165-21.559 (537.59-547.60)
Right Side	32.988-33.382 (837.90-847.90)

[1] – Measure axle shaft length between inner joint flange and outer joint flange. See Fig. 8.

Installation – 1) To install, reverse removal procedure. Before installing axle shafts, install NEW snap ring on end of axle shaft (except right side). Coat axle shaft seals in transaxle with grease. Coat axle shaft splines and sliding surfaces with Dexron-II. Position snap ring on end of axle shaft with opening facing downward.

2) Install axle shaft by lightly tapping axle shaft into transaxle. Ensure axle shaft will move inward and outward approximately .079-.120" (2.00-3.00 mm) and cannot be pulled from transaxle.

3) To install remaining components, reverse removal procedure. Tighten remaining bolts/nuts to specification. See TORQUE SPECIFICATIONS. Fill transaxle with 75W-90 gear oil with API GL-3, GL-4 or GL-5 rating.

REAR AXLE SHAFTS

NOTE: Use care not to damage oil seal, axle shaft boots or Anti-Lock Brake System (ABS) speed sensor rotor when removing axle shaft.

1) Raise and support vehicle. Remove rear wheels. Remove ABS speed sensor (if equipped). Apply brakes. Remove cotter pin, lock cap and axle nut. Release brakes.

2) Place match-marks on axle shaft flange and differential flange for installation reference. Remove 4 nuts and washers. Using a soft-faced hammer, tap axle from rear hub. Remove rear axle. See Fig. 9.

Inspection – Ensure no play exists in inner and outer joints. Inner joint must slide smoothly inward and outward and be free from excessive play in radial direction. Check for torn or damaged boots.

Disassembly – 1) Remove boot clamps and slide boots from joints. Paint reference marks on outer race and axle shaft for reassembly reference. See Fig. 5.

NOTE: Manufacturer does not recommend overhaul of outer joint assembly.

2) Remove outer race from inboard tripod joint and axle shaft. Remove snap ring from end of axle shaft retaining inboard tripod joint. Paint reference marks on tripod joint and axle shaft for reassembly reference.

3) Using a hammer and brass drift, tap inboard tripod joint from axle shaft. DO NOT tap on roller of tripod joint during removal. Remove boots from axle shaft. Using a screwdriver and hammer, remove dust deflector from axle shaft.

Reassembly – 1) Using a press, install NEW dust deflector on axle shaft. Wrap splines on axle shaft with tape to prevent damaging boots during installation.

Rear Axle Shaft

ABS Speed Sensor

Inboard Joint Tulip

Axle Nut

Boot Clamp

Boot Clamp

Snap Ring

Cotter Pin

Outboard Joint Boot

Lock Cap

Tripod Joint

Inboard Joint Boot

Boot Clamp

Outboard Joint
With Axle Shaft

Dust Deflector

96A19208

Courtesy of Toyota Motor Sales, U.S.A., Inc.

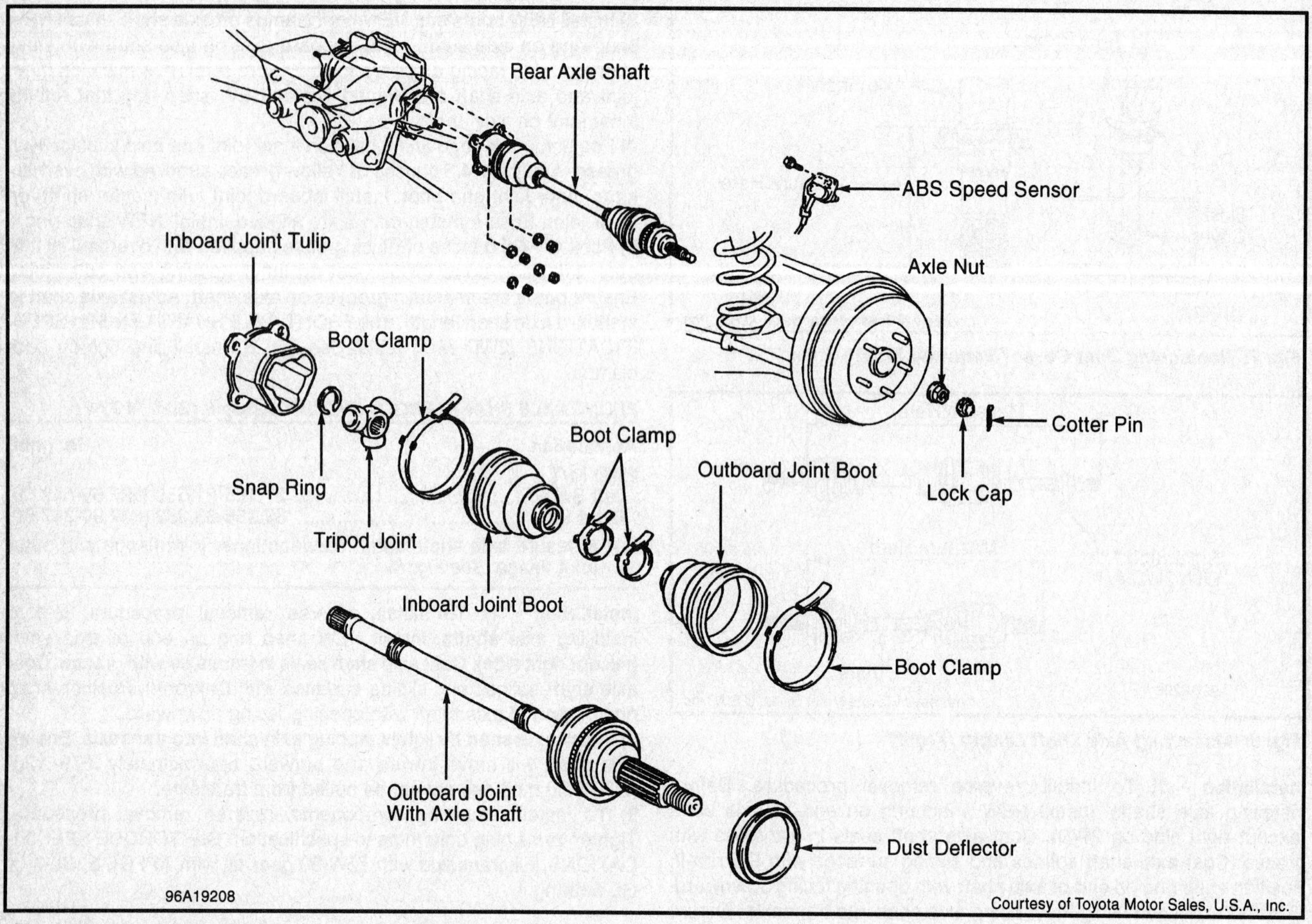

Fig. 9: Exploded View Of Rear Axle Shaft (4WD)

2) Install NEW boots and NEW boot clamps on axle shaft. Install NEW snap ring on axle shaft. Install inboard tripod joint on axle shaft with small diameter side facing outboard joint. Ensure reference mark on inboard joint and axle shaft are aligned. Install NEW snap ring that retains inboard tripod joint on axle shaft.

3) Apply 6.3-6.7 ounces of Yellow grease supplied with overhaul kit to inner joint and boot. Install outer joint tulip on inner joint. Ensure match-marks are aligned.

4) Pack 3.5-3.9 ounces of Black grease supplied with overhaul kit into outer joint and boot. Install boot on inner housing and outer joint. Ensure boots are seated in grooves on axle shaft. Adjust axle shaft to standard axle shaft length. See REAR AXLE SHAFT LENGTH SPEC-IFICATIONS table. See Fig. 10. Install and tighten boot clamps.

REAR AXLE SHAFT LENGTH SPECIFICATIONS [1]

Application	In. (mm)
4WD (Rear)	
Left Side	21.590-21.984 (548.39-558.39)
Right Side	23.401-23.795 (594.39-604.39)

[1] – Measure axle shaft length between inner joint flange and outer joint flange. See Fig. 10.

Installation – To install, reverse removal procedure. Tighten bolts and nuts to specification. See TORQUE SPECIFICATIONS. After installation, check ABS speed sensor signal and wheel alignment.

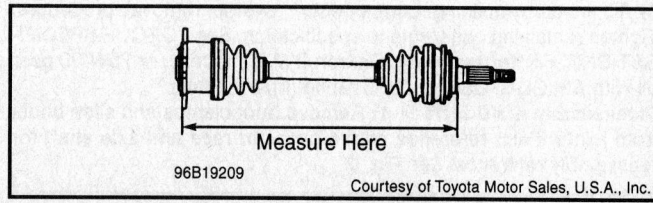

Measure Here

96B19209

Courtesy of Toyota Motor Sales, U.S.A., Inc.

Fig. 10: Measuring Axle Shaft Length (Rear)

TORQUE SPECIFICATIONS
TORQUE SPECIFICATIONS

Application	Ft. Lbs. (N.m)
ABS Speed Sensor Bolt	[1]
Axle Shaft Flange Bolt (Rear)	41 (56)
Axle Shaft Nut	
Front	159 (216)
Rear	152 (206)
Bearing Bracket Bolt	47 (64)
Lower Control Arm-To-Ball Joint Bolt/Nut	94 (127)
Stabilizer Bar Link-To-Lower Control Arm Nut	
3-Door	47 (64)
5-Door	83 (113)
Tie Rod End Nut	36 (49)
Wheel Lug Nut	76 (103)

[1] – Tighten bolt to 71 INCH lbs. (8.0 N.m).

Cabrio, Golf, Golf III, GTI VR6, Jetta, Jetta III, Passat

TROUBLE SHOOTING

NOTE: See DRIVE AXLE NOISE DIAGNOSIS in GENERAL INFORMATION at beginning of this section.

REMOVAL, DISASSEMBLY, REASSEMBLY & INSTALLATION

AXLE SHAFT

NOTE: Two different types of joints may be used on axle shaft. Types used are: Constant Velocity (CV) type joint, or tripod-type joint. CV joint uses a 6 ball and cage design, while tripod joint uses a triple-roller design. Three methods may be used to assemble axle shaft to hub assembly depending on hub spline type. Later model design and new replacement parts are revised, and require an updated installation procedure. See TORQUE SPECIFICATIONS.

NOTE: Tripod-type joints are used on models equipped with a 4-cylinder engine with an automatic transaxle. Engine/transaxle assembly must be raised to remove left-side axle shaft. It is not required to raise engine/transaxle assembly for right-side axle shaft removal.

Removal – 1) Remove axle shaft nut. Raise and support vehicle. Remove wheel. Remove air deflector plate from lower control arm (if equipped). On models equipped with tripod-type joint, remove bolt for rear transaxle mount, and bolt for front engine mount.
2) Using Engine Support Bridge (10-222A) and Adapter (10-222 A/1), raise and support engine/transaxle assembly. On all models, Disconnect axle shaft(s) from transaxle drive flange. Mark position of lower control arm-to-ball joint bolts.
3) Remove both outer control arm-to-ball joint bolts. Loosen, but DO NOT remove inner control arm-to-ball joint bolt. On models equipped with compressed hub splines, use Press (3283) to press axle shaft from wheel hub. On all models, swing wheel assembly outward and support if necessary. Remove axle shaft assembly.
Disassembly & Reassembly (CV-Type Joint) – 1) Remove axle shaft boot(s). Using a drift, remove protective cap from CV joint (if equipped). Remove circlip from transaxle-side CV joint. *See Fig. 1.* Support CV joint with axle assembly on Support Stand (VW 402).
2) Using Driver (VW 408A), press inner CV joint off axle shaft. Using a soft mallet, drive off outer CV joint from axle shaft. DO NOT disassemble outer CV joint. Outer CV joint is not serviceable, and must be replaced as an assembly if worn.

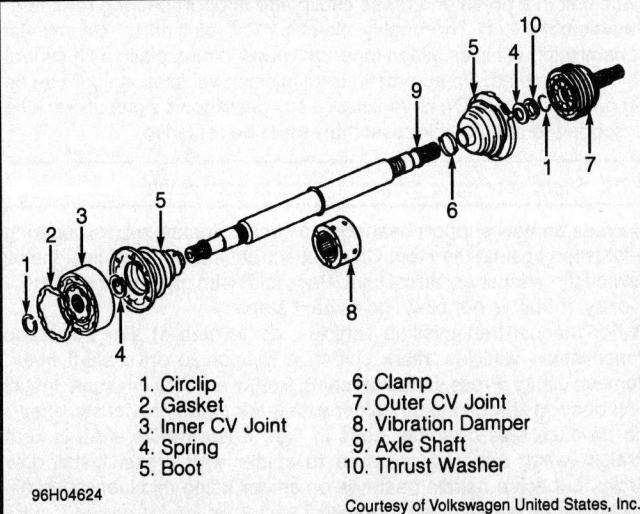

1. Circlip
2. Gasket
3. Inner CV Joint
4. Spring
5. Boot
6. Clamp
7. Outer CV Joint
8. Vibration Damper
9. Axle Shaft
10. Thrust Washer

96H04624

Courtesy of Volkswagen United States, Inc.

Fig. 1: Exploded View Of Axle Shaft With CV-Type Joint (Typical)

3) Mark position of ball hub in relation to ball cage and housing for installation reference of inner joint. Rotate inner race and remove balls. Clean and inspect parts for galling or wear. Cover balls with grease and reinstall in race.
4) To reassemble, reverse disassembly procedure. See AXLE SHAFT LENGTH table. Use NEW circlips and boot clamps during assembly.
Disassembly & Reassembly (Tripod-Type Joint) – 1) Remove axle shaft boot(s). Using a drift, remove protective cap from tripod joint. Remove circlip from tripod joint. Remove joint from axle shaft. Mark position of tripod-roller assembly in relation to housing for installation reference.
2) Remove tripod-roller assembly from housing. Clean and inspect parts for galling or wear. Install housing with a NEW boot on axle shaft. Cover tripod-roller assembly with grease and install into housing using reference marks made during disassembly.
3) Push triple-roller assembly onto axle shaft with chamfered side of splines first. *See Fig. 2.* Install a NEW circlip. Fasten boot using a NEW clamp. Measure axle shaft length. See AXLE SHAFT LENGTH table.

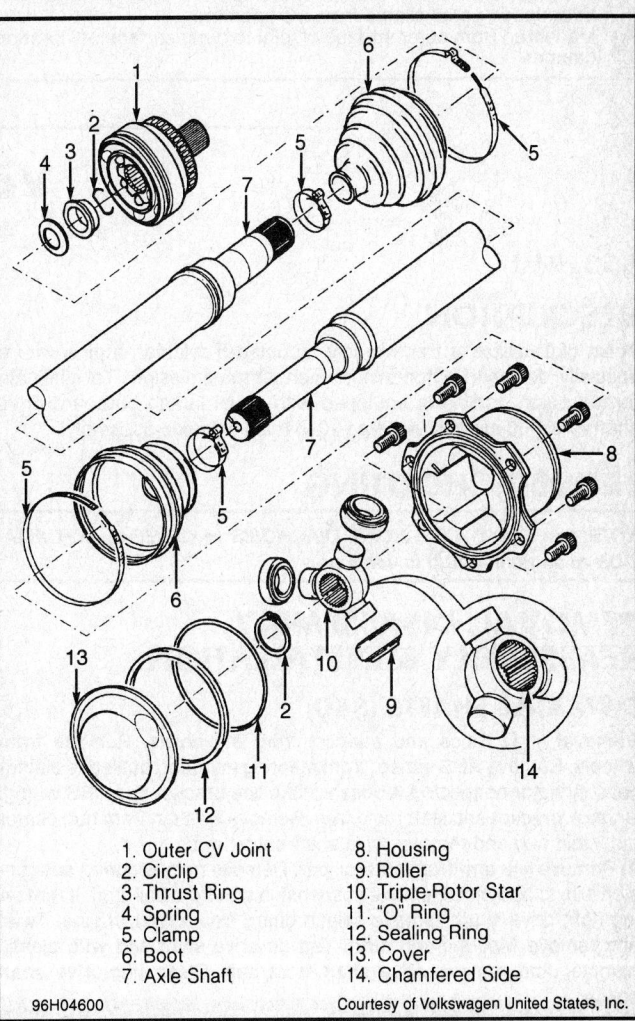

1. Outer CV Joint
2. Circlip
3. Thrust Ring
4. Spring
5. Clamp
6. Boot
7. Axle Shaft
8. Housing
9. Roller
10. Triple-Rotor Star
11. "O" Ring
12. Sealing Ring
13. Cover
14. Chamfered Side

96H04600

Courtesy of Volkswagen United States, Inc.

Fig. 2: Exploded View Of Axle Shaft With Tripod-Type Joint

NOTE: Bonded-type axle shafts use a locking fluid on mating axle shaft and hub splines. If reusing original hub assembly, apply Locking Fluid (D 185 400 A2) to axle shaft splines. Locking fluid is not needed if replacing hub assembly with revised part, since hub is a compress-fit design.

Installation – To install, reverse removal procedure. Clean bolts and nuts to ensure tightening torque is correct. Install a NEW axle shaft nut. See TORQUE SPECIFICATIONS.

AXLE SHAFTS
Volkswagen (Cont.)

AXLE SHAFT LENGTH

Application	In. (mm)
Passat	[1]
All Other Models	
Automatic Transaxle (096)	
Left Axle	17.6 (447.4)
Right Axle	26.8 (681.5)
Automatic Transaxle (01M)	[1]
Manual Transaxle (02A)	
Left Axle	17.6 (447.4)
Right Axle	26.8 (681.5)
Manual Transaxle (020)	
Left Axle	17.9 (455.5)
Right Axle	27.1 (691.5)
Vibration Dampener Position	
Passat	
Left Axle	[2] 20.47-20.55 (520.0-522.0)
Right Axle	[2] 10.35-10.43 (263.0-265.0)
All Other Models	
1.9L Engine	[2] 20.63-20.71 (524.0-526.0)
2.0L Engine	[2] 21.26-21.34 (540.0-542.0)

[1] – Information not available from manufacturer.
[2] – Measured from outer surface of joint to outer surface of vibration damper.

TORQUE SPECIFICATIONS
TORQUE SPECIFICATIONS

Application	Ft. Lbs. (N.m)
Axle Shaft Nut	
With Tripod-Type Joint	195 (265)
With Bonded Axle Shaft Splines	66 (90) Plus 1/8 Turn
With Compressed Hub Splines	[1]
Axle Shaft-To-Transaxle Flange Bolt	
CV-Type Joint	33 (45)
Tripod-Type Joint	
Except Passat	59 (80)
Passat	33 (45)
Lower Control Arm-To-Ball Joint Bolt	26 (35)
Wheel Lug Nut	81 (110)

[1] – Tighten to 148 ft. lbs. (200 N.m), then back off one turn. Retighten to 37 ft. lbs. (50 N.m), plus an additional 30 degrees.

Volvo

850, 960

DESCRIPTION

Volvo 850 utilizes a transversely mounted 5-cylinder engine with a specially designed automatic or manual transmission. To eliminate torque steer, vehicle is equipped with equal length outboard drive shafts. All 960 models use type 1045 multi-link axle assembly.

TROUBLE SHOOTING

NOTE: See DRIVE AXLE NOISE DIAGNOSIS in GENERAL INFORMATION at beginning of this section.

REMOVAL, DISASSEMBLY, REASSEMBLY & INSTALLATION

FWD AXLE SHAFTS (850)

Removal – 1) Raise and support front of vehicle. Remove front wheels. Remove ABS sensor from steering member, but leave electrical connector connected. Loosen brake line bracket and ABS wiring. Unhook bracket and let it hang free. Remove split pin from hub center nut. Hold hub and remove drive shaft center nut.

2) Remove link arm from anti-roll bar. Remove nuts securing suspension arm to ball joint. Remove suspension arm from ball joint. If removing right drive shaft, remove splash guard from under engine. Twist and remove MacPherson strut. Tap on drive shaft end with plastic hammer and remove drive shaft from hub. Clean hub-drive shaft splines.

3) On right drive shaft, remove bearing cap from drive shaft support bearing. Using care to avoid damage to drive shaft seal and boot, remove drive shaft from gearbox. On left drive shaft, use Lever (999 5462) to apply leverage between gearbox and inside of drive shaft. Using care to avoid damage to drive shaft seal and boot, remove drive shaft from gearbox.

Disassembly – 1) Remove clips from outer boot. Remove outer boot from outer CV joint. Wipe grease from outer CV joint. Clamp drive shaft in vise with gap in circlip at top. Open circlip to free it from groove. Insert an 8 mm diameter drift between circlip lugs. Tap inner race a few times along shaft to hold circlip open. Use a brass drift and tap CV joint off shaft.

NOTE: To avoid damaging cage or outer race, tap inner race only.

2) Remove clips from inboard boot and slide both boots off shaft. Ensure grease inside joints is not contaminated by water or dirt. For reassembly reference, scribe positions of outer race, cage, and inner race in CV joint.

3) For reassembly reference, mark location where balls will first be removed. Tilt inner race and cage and remove balls one at a time, moving in a clockwise direction. Put balls in order so they can be installed in original location. Rotate inner race 90 degrees relative to cage. Remove inner race. Remove circlip from inner race.

4) Remove clips from inner boot. Slide boot off inner universal joint. On manual transmission vehicles, use a rag and remove grease from inboard universal joint. Mount drive shaft in a vise, with gap in circlip facing upward. Open circlip to free it from groove and insert an 8 mm drift between circlip lugs. Tap inner race a few times along shaft to hold circlip open. Using a brass drift, tap inner universal joint off shaft.

5) On automatic transmission vehicles, mark position of drive shaft relative to joint housing. Pry up tabs on housing and remove spider from housing. On all vehicles, if support bearing requires replacement, place unit in a press and press circlip and support bearing off shaft.

Reassembly – 1) Thoroughly clean all CV joint parts. On manual transmission vehicles, clean inner universal joint in place as it cannot be disassembled. On automatic transmission vehicles, spider can be left on end of shaft. On all vehicles, if any part shows signs of cracking or scoring, entire CV joint assembly must be replaced.

NOTE: Slight scoring or pitting in races is acceptable.

2) Press on new support bearing and circlip. Ensure support bearing is installed against the stop. On manual transmission vehicles, Install new circlip in inner universal joint. Pack joint with grease. Ensure boot is okay. If boot is not okay, go to next step.

3) For manual transmission vehicles, go to step 4). For automatic transmission vehicles, mark spider in relation to drive shaft mark. Remove circlip. Press spider off shaft. Remove boot from shaft. Install new boot on shaft. Line up spider with mark made previously, ensuring bevelled side of spider goes in first. Ensure drive shaft is kept straight when applying pressure to spider with press. Install new circlip. Lubricate needle bearings on spider using thin lubricating oil. Pack bearing housing with grease.

4) For manual transmission vehicles, mount outboard drive shaft in a vise, ensuring inner race is square inside joint. Tap shaft into joint, ensuring circlip is properly seated in groove. Pack remaining grease into joint, using care not to get any grease on part of boot that makes contact with joint. Clean off all excess grease. Slide boot over joint, ensuring it is correctly positioned on shaft. Install new circlip on boot.

5) For all vehicles, install new circlip in inner race and place race inside cage. Line up scored marks and put first ball in position. Turn inner race and cage. Put balls back in their original position, one at a time.

6) Thoroughly lubricate joint. Apply grease to back of joint through opening for shaft in inner race. If joint has not been dismantled, remove old circlip and replace. Mount shaft in vise and slide new boot onto shaft. Install CV joint on shaft, ensuring inner race is square inside joint. Use a plastic hammer and tap joint onto shaft. Ensure circlip sits correctly in its groove.

7) Apply remaining grease to inner race and cage. Use care to not get any grease on part of boot that comes in contact with joints. Wipe off excess grease with mineral spirits. Slide boot over joints, ensuring they are correctly positioned on shaft. Install new circlip on boot.

Installation – 1) For right drive shaft installation, install bearing cap and tighten to 18 ft. lbs. (25 N.m). For left drive shaft installation, ensure ABS sensor wheel on drive shaft is free of dirt. Push drive shaft in so it engages with differential. Ensure drive shaft circlip snaps into place. *See Fig. 1.* Use care not to damage gearbox seals or bellows.

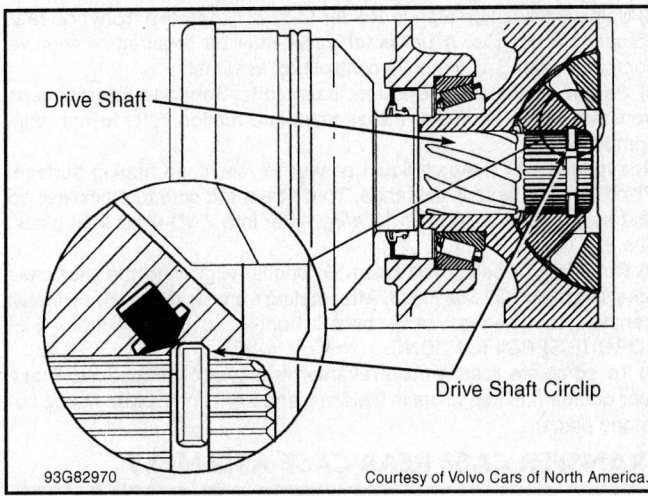

Drive Shaft

Drive Shaft Circlip

93G82970   Courtesy of Volvo Cars of North America.

Fig. 1: Installing Left Drive Shaft

2) Apply Metal Glue (1161370-0) to drive shaft splines. Use a socket wrench to hold suspension arm down. Twist and remove MacPherson strut and insert drive shaft into hub. Oil new drive shaft center nut threads and flange. Hand tighten new drive shaft center nut. Using new nuts, install suspension arm to ball joint.

NOTE: Ensure ball joint and suspension arm faces are clean and free of grease.

3) Tighten nuts to 13 ft. lbs. (18 N.m), plus an additional 120 degrees. Apply rust proofing to area between ball joint, suspension arm, and nuts. Using new nuts, install suspension arm to anti-roll bar. Tighten nuts to 37 ft. lbs. (50 N.m). Tighten center nut to 80 ft. lbs (120 N.m), plus an additional 120 degrees. Lock drive shaft center nut by using a chisel and tapping nut locking flange into drive shaft slot.

4) Install brake line bracket and ABS cable, ensuring ABS sensor is perfectly clean. Tighten ABS sensor to 7 ft. lbs. (10 N.m). Ensure brake disc and pad surfaces are clean. Lubricate hub center locating pin in front of pad with Rust Proofing Agent (1161038-3). Install, but do not tighten, lug nuts. Tighten lug nuts in opposite pairs to 81 ft. lbs. (110 N.m).

RWD AXLE SHAFTS (960)

Removal – Remove support arms and lower axle beam. See AXLE ASSEMBLY (960). Remove large nut holding drive shaft to wheel bearing housing. Remove 6 bolts holding drive shaft to final drive. Remove drive shaft. Repeat procedure for other side.

Disassembly – Using a hammer and drift, carefully tap off outer cover from drive shaft joint. Remove inner cover. Push boot over drive shaft. Remove grease to access circlip at end of drive shaft. Remove circlip. Press joint off shaft.

Reassembly – Install new boot and inner cover. Press joint into drive shaft. Install new circlip. Install new gasket in recess in joint. Pack joint and outer cover with grease. Press cover into place. Press new grease into joint and boot. Coat inner cover with Sealer (1 161 099-5). Press cover into place. Position boot on cover and on drive shaft.

Installation – Install drive shaft in position. Install bolts securing drive shaft to final drive. See TORQUE SPECIFICATIONS. To complete installation, reverse removal procedure.

AXLE ASSEMBLY (960)

Removal – 1) Raise vehicle and remove rear wheels. Remove anti-roll bar links-to-rear axle beam nuts. Remove support arm bolts. Remove anti-roll bar. Apply Compression Tool (999 5577) lightly against control arm. Remove damper lower bolt. Remove damper from support arm.

2) Lock compression tool with locking pin. Remove bolts in front and rear edges of support arm. Loosen nut in front edge. Tap support arm off wheel bearing housing. Remove nut. Remove support arm. Remove track rod bolt. Tap off rod from wheel bearing housing. Remove nut from wheel bearing housing link bolt. Using a brass drift, tap out bolt. Release compression tool and remove. Repeat this procedure for the other side.

3) Loosen 10 lower rear axle beam bolts. Remove 2 front bolts and spacers. Install Retainer (999 5580) to front edge of differential. Install Retainer (999 5579) to rear edge of differential. Position a transmission jack under rear axle beam. Remove remaining rear axle beam bolts. Lower rear axle beam.

4) Remove 2 bolts at drive shaft intermediate bearing. Position transmission jack and Fixture (999 5972) under differential. Adjust supporting arms and raise lift until it contacts differential. Remove Retainers (999 5580 and 999 5579) from differential.

5) Carefully lower differential housing about 2 inches. Remove large nut holding drive shaft to wheel bearing housing. Remove 6 bolts holding drive shaft to final drive. Remove drive shaft. Repeat procedure for other side. Carefully lower axle assembly.

Installation – Move axle assembly under vehicle on transmission jack and raise into position. Hold axle assembly in place with Retainers (999 5580 and 999 579). Remove transmission jack. Reinstall left and right drive shafts. Position rear axle beam on transmission jack and press up beam. Ensure bushing is outside guide flanges on rear axle beam. To complete installation, reverse removal procedure.

TORQUE SPECIFICATIONS
TORQUE SPECIFICATIONS

Application	Ft. Lbs. (N.m)
ABS Sensor	7 (10)
Bearing Cap Bolts	18 (25)
Drive Shaft-To-Final Drive Bolts	[2] 22 (30)
Lug Nuts	81 (110)
Rear Axle Beam Bolts	63 (80)
Rear Cover Bolts	18 (25)
Suspension Arm Nuts	[1] 13 (18)
Suspension Arm To Anti-Roll Bar	37 (50)
Suspension Arm To Anti-Roll Bar Center Nut	[1] 89 (120)

[1] – Tighten an additional 60 degrees.
[2] – Tighten an additional 90 degrees.

TRANSFER CASES
Acura, Honda & Isuzu

Acura: SLX
Honda: Passport
Isuzu: Rodeo, Trooper

DESCRIPTION & OPERATION

The transfer case is a manually operated gear driven type that provides 3 gear ranges; 2H, 4L and 4H. On 1995 models, front axle is engaged by automatic locking hubs. When 4WD operation is selected on 1996 models, front axle is engaged automatically by Shift-On-The-Fly system. Shift-On-The-Fly system consists of an actuator assembly mounted on front axle and a clutch gear attached to left-side axle shaft. Actuator assembly contains a vacuum diaphragm and a shift position switch. *See Fig. 1.* See appropriate wiring diagram to aid in diagnosis of Shift-On-The-Fly system. See WIRING DIAGRAMS.

Transfer case may be shifted from 2H to 4H and back while vehicle is moving straight ahead at speeds less than 60 MPH. Vehicle must be stopped with transmission in Neutral to shift transfer case from 4H to 4L and back.

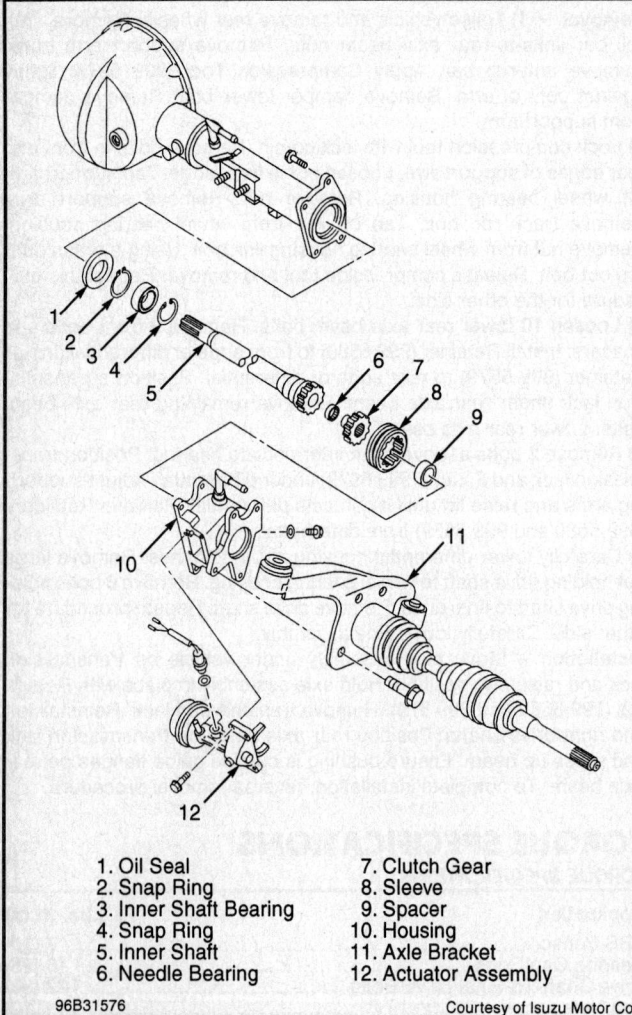

1. Oil Seal	7. Clutch Gear
2. Snap Ring	8. Sleeve
3. Inner Shaft Bearing	9. Spacer
4. Snap Ring	10. Housing
5. Inner Shaft	11. Axle Bracket
6. Needle Bearing	12. Actuator Assembly

96B31576   Courtesy of Isuzu Motor Co.

Fig. 1: Exploded View Of Shift-On-The-Fly System

REMOVAL & INSTALLATION

TRANSFER CASE

Removal – 1) Disconnect negative battery cable. Drain transfer case fluid. Remove skid plate. Place reference marks on drive shafts and companion flanges for installation reference.

2) Remove drive shafts. Disconnect 4 oxygen sensor harness connectors from transmission harness. Remove both right and left-side catalytic converters.

3) Remove transfer case gearshift lever knob. Remove front console and disconnect necessary harness connectors. Disconnect shift lock cable and shift control rod. Remove gearshift lever assembly.

4) Disconnect transfer case control lever. Disconnect 4WD switch and speed sensor harness connectors. Using a transmission jack, support transfer case. Remove transfer case-to-transmission bolts and nuts. Lower transfer case from vehicle.

Installation – 1) Apply a thin coat of grease to input shaft splines. To complete installation, reverse removal procedure. Tighten fasteners to specifications. See TORQUE SPECIFICATIONS.

2) Fill transfer case with SAE 5W-30 engine oil for operational temperature range up to 95°F (35°C). Use SAE 15W-40, 20W-40 or 20W-50 engine oil for operational temperatures greater than 50°F (10°C).

TRANSFER CASE DISASSEMBLY & REASSEMBLY

TRANSFER CASE HALVES

Disassembly – 1) Apply reference marks on speedometer driven gear bushing for reference during reassembly. Remove speedometer sensor and driven gear assembly with bushing.

2) Using Companion Flange Holder (J-37221), remove front and rear companion flanges. A universal puller may be required to remove companion flanges. Remove control box assembly.

3) Remove transfer case-to-rear case bolts. Separate transfer case from rear case. For further disassembly information, refer to individual components.

Reassembly – 1) Apply liquid gasket to rear case mating surface. Place transfer case in 4H range. Turn select rod counterclockwise so that select block projection "A" may enter into 2WD-4WD shift block. *See Fig. 2.*

2) Cut-away of select rod head "B" should align with the rear case hole's stopper "C". *See Fig. 3.* After mating transfer case halves, install transfer case-to-rear case bolts. Tighten to specification. See TORQUE SPECIFICATIONS.

3) To complete reassembly, reverse disassembly procedure. Stake rear companion flange nut in 2 places, and front companion flange nut in one place.

TRANSFER CASE REAR CASE ASSEMBLY

NOTE: Disassembly procedures on some models may differ slightly depending on style of transfer case rear case casting. Additional snap rings may be used, and speedometer drive gear may be retained by spring clip instead of a steel ball.

Disassembly – 1) Remove block ring. *See Fig. 4.* Remove front bearing front snap ring and pull out rear output shaft assembly. Using a press, remove rear bearing.

2) Remove speedometer drive gear, ball and front bearing rear snap ring. Press off front bearing using bearing remover. Remove front bearing front snap ring. Pry out rear oil seal.

Cleaning & Inspection – Clean all parts with cleaning solvent and dry with compressed air. Inspect all parts for damage or excessive wear. See TRANSFER CASE COMPONENT SPECIFICATIONS table under TRANSFER CASE. Replace parts as necessary.

Reassembly – 1) Install front bearing front snap ring onto output shaft. Press on front bearing. Install front bearing rear snap ring and speedometer drive gear with ball. Press on rear bearing. Install rear oil seal.

2) Wrap splines of rear output shaft with vinyl tape and install into transfer rear case. Install front bearing front snap ring using snap ring pliers. Remove vinyl tape.

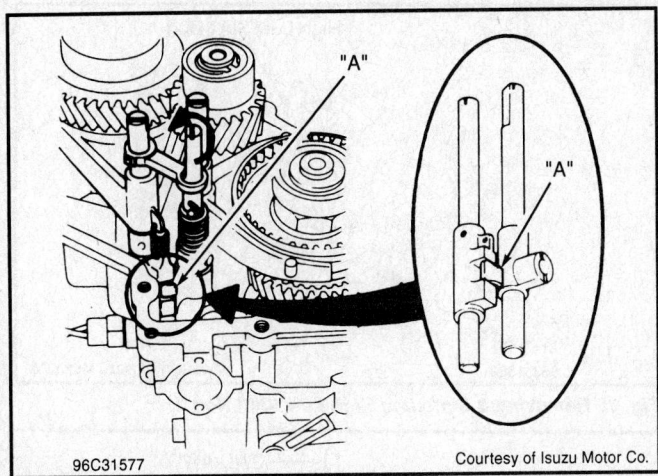

96C31577   Courtesy of Isuzu Motor Co.

Fig. 2: Aligning Shift Blocks

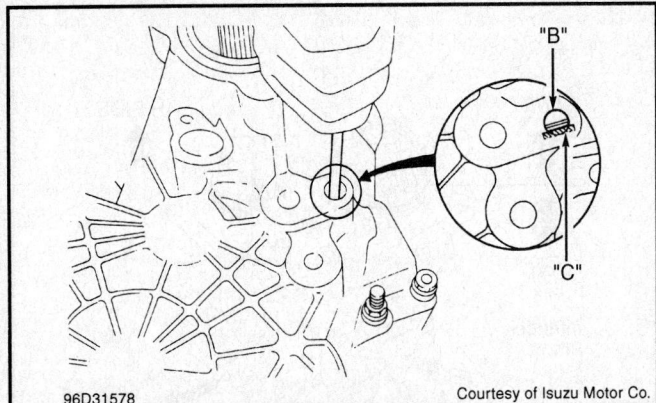

96D31578   Courtesy of Isuzu Motor Co.

Fig. 3: Shift Rod Head/Bolt Hole Alignment

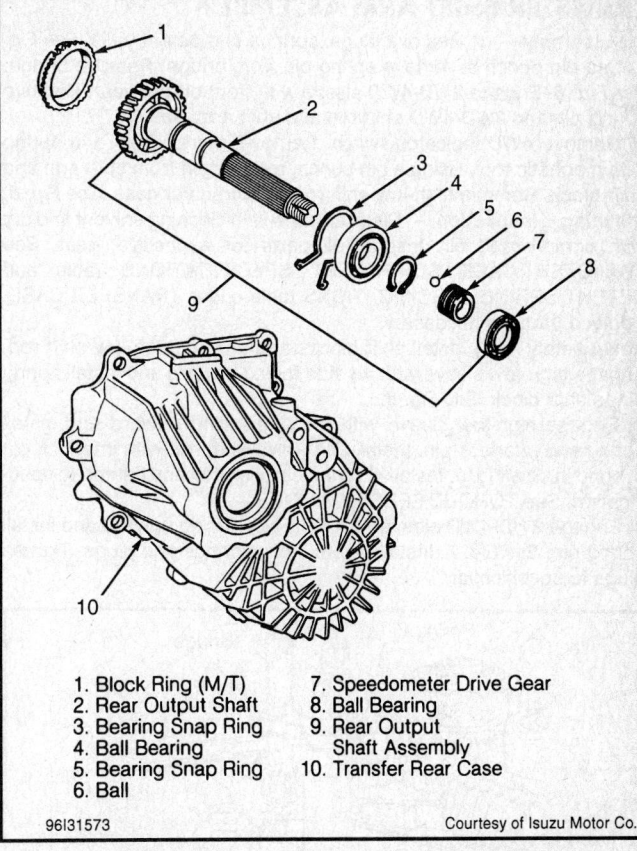

1. Block Ring (M/T)
2. Rear Output Shaft
3. Bearing Snap Ring
4. Ball Bearing
5. Bearing Snap Ring
6. Ball
7. Speedometer Drive Gear
8. Ball Bearing
9. Rear Output
   Shaft Assembly
10. Transfer Rear Case

96I31573   Courtesy of Isuzu Motor Co.

**Fig. 4: Exploded View Of Transfer Case Rear Case Assembly
(Typical)**

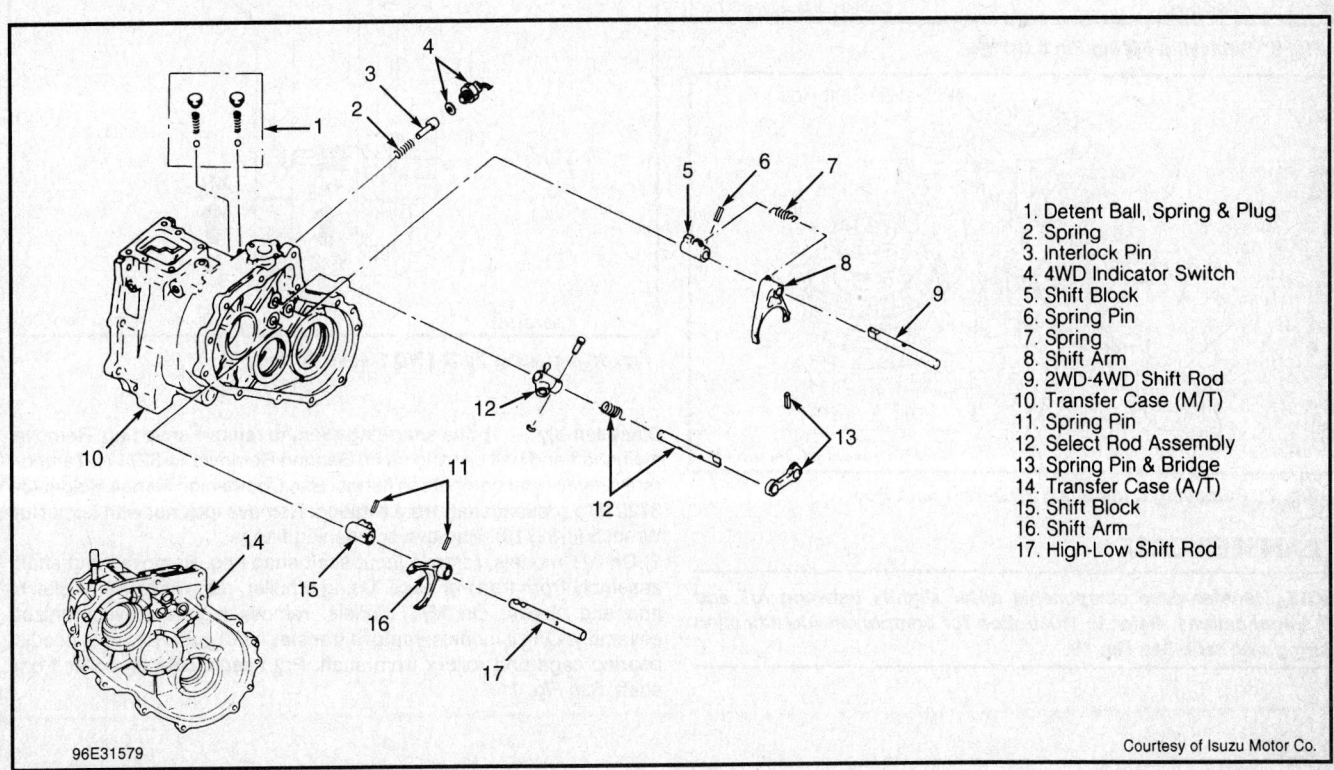

1. Detent Ball, Spring & Plug
2. Spring
3. Interlock Pin
4. 4WD Indicator Switch
5. Shift Block
6. Spring Pin
7. Spring
8. Shift Arm
9. 2WD-4WD Shift Rod
10. Transfer Case (M/T)
11. Spring Pin
12. Select Rod Assembly
13. Spring Pin & Bridge
14. Transfer Case (A/T)
15. Shift Block
16. Shift Arm
17. High-Low Shift Rod

96E31579   Courtesy of Isuzu Motor Co.

Fig. 5: Exploded View Of Transfer Shift Arm Assembly

TRANSFER SHIFT ARM ASSEMBLY

Disassembly – **1)** Remove plugs, springs and detent balls. *See Fig. 5.* Use pin punch to remove spring pin from bridge. Remove bridge. *See Fig. 6.* Engage 2WD-4WD sleeve with front output gear. Remove spring pin and 2WD-4WD shift rod and shift arm. *See Fig. 7.*

2) Remove 4WD indicator switch. Remove interlock pin and spring with magnetic tool. Using a pin punch, remove pin from shift arm and shift block. Remove high-low shift rod from transfer case. *See Fig. 8.*

Cleaning & Inspection – Clean all parts with cleaning solvent and dry with compressed air. Inspect all parts for excessive wear. See TRANSFER CASE COMPONENT SPECIFICATIONS table and DETENT SPRING SPECIFICATIONS table under TRANSFER CASE. Replace parts as necessary.

Reassembly – **1)** Install shift blocks and arm on high-low shift rod. Engage high-low sleeve with 4H side facing upward and install spring pin to shift block. *See Fig. 8.*

2) Engage high-low sleeve with 4H side facing upward and install spring and interlock pin. Install 2WD-4WD shift rod with interlock pin pushed in. *See Fig. 9.* Install 4WD indicator switch and tighten to specification. See TORQUE SPECIFICATIONS.

3) Engage 2WD-4WD sleeve with 4WD side facing upward and install spring pin. *See Fig. 7.* Install detent balls, springs and plugs. Tighten plugs to specification.

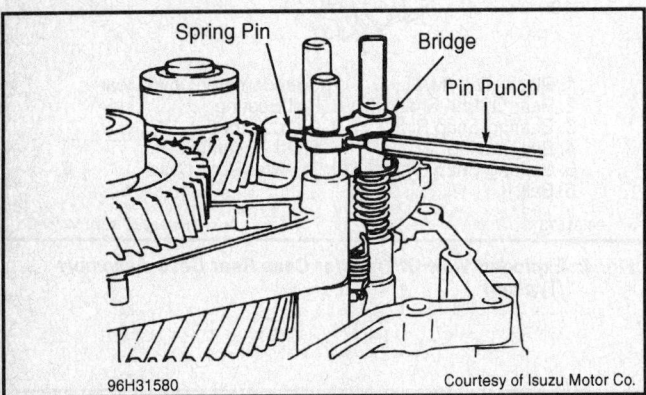

96H31580   Courtesy of Isuzu Motor Co.

Fig. 6: Removing Spring Pin & Bridge

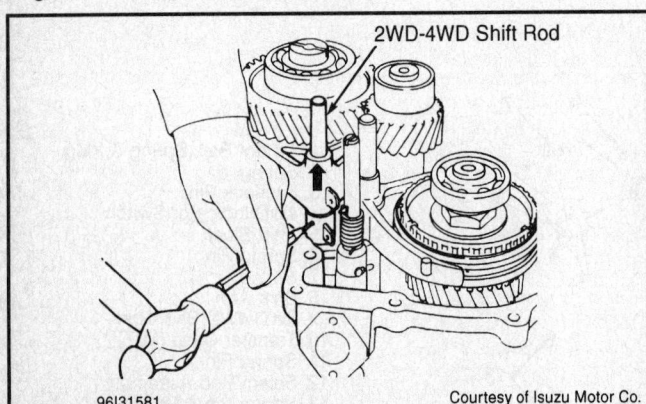

96I31581   Courtesy of Isuzu Motor Co.

Fig. 7: Removing & Installing 2WD-4WD Shift Rod

TRANSFER CASE

NOTE: Transfer case components differ slightly between A/T and M/T applications. Refer to illustration for component identification during overhaul. See Fig. 10.

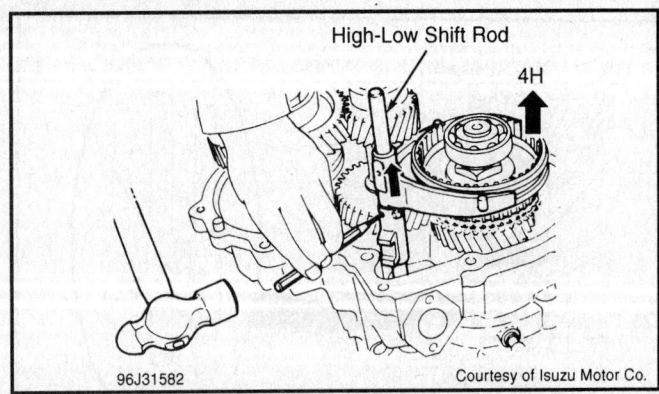

96J31582   Courtesy of Isuzu Motor Co.

Fig. 8: Removing & Installing High-Low Shift Rod

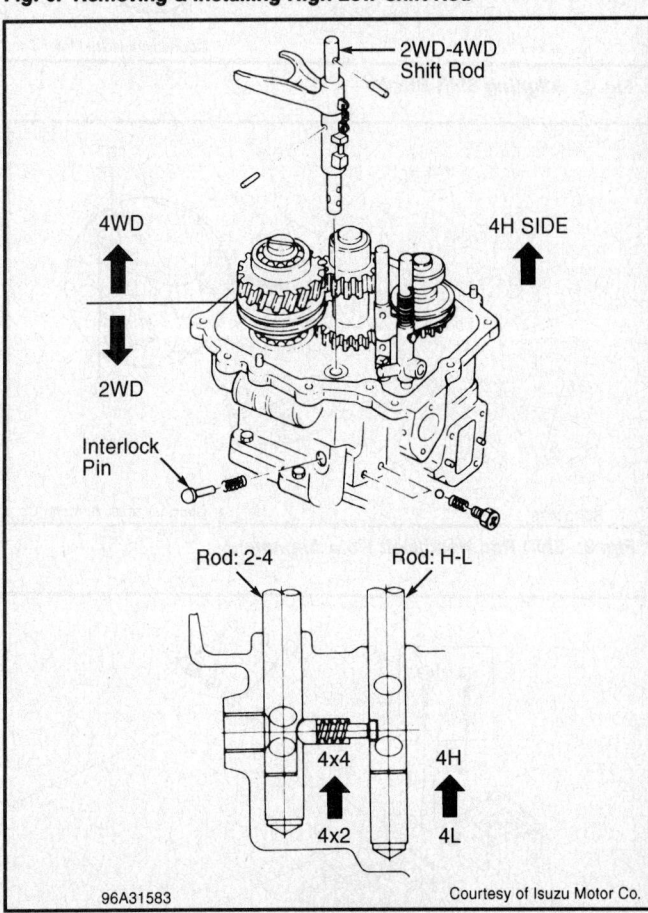

96A31583   Courtesy of Isuzu Motor Co.

Fig. 9: Installing 2WD-4WD Sleeve Spring Pin

Disassembly – **1)** Use snap-ring pliers to remove snap ring. Remove mainshaft end ball bearing using Bearing Remover (J-32717). Temporarily install front companion flange. Use Companion Flange Holder (J-37221) to prevent shaft from rotating. Remove lock nut with Lock Nut Wrench (J-32719). Remove companion flange.

2) On A/T models, remove input shaft snap ring. Remove input shaft assembly from transfer case. Using a puller, remove high-low clutch hub and sleeve. On M/T models, remove high-low synchronizer assembly. On all models, remove transfer input gear. Remove needle bearing cage and rollers from shaft. Pry needle bearing collar from shaft. *See Fig. 11.*

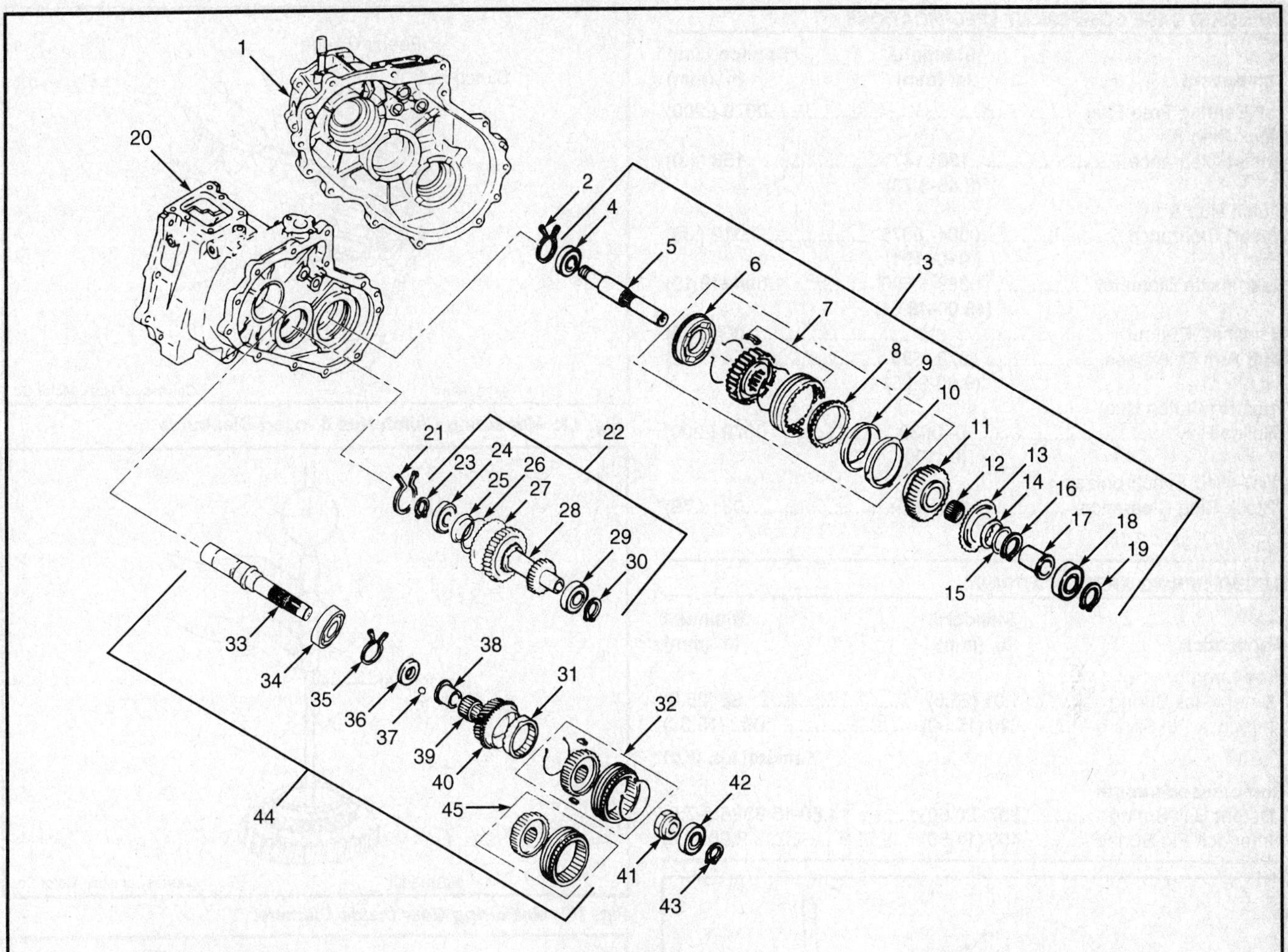

96B31584

1. Transfer Case (A/T)	16. Subgear Snap Ring (M/T)	31. High-Low Block Ring (M/T)
2. Bearing Snap Ring	17. Bearing Collar	32. High-Low Synchronizer (M/T)
3. Front Output Gear Assembly	18. Ball Bearing	33. Input Shaft (A/T)
4. Ball Bearing	19. Bearing Snap Ring	34. Ball Bearing (A/T)
5. Front Output Shaft	20. Transfer Case (M/T)	35. Snap Ring (A/T)
6. Stopper Plate	21. Bearing Snap Ring	36. Plate
7. Clutch Sleeve & Hub Assembly	22. Counter Gear Assembly	37. Ball
8. Block Ring	23. Snap Ring	38. Bearing Collar
9. Outside Ring	24. Ball Bearing	39. Needle Bearing
10. Inside Ring	25. Spacer	40. Transfer Input Gear
11. Front Output Gear	26. Belleville Spring	41. Lock Nut
12. Needle Bearing	27. Subgear	42. Ball Bearing
13. Subgear (M/T)	28. Counter Gear	43. Bearing Snap Ring
14. Belleville Spring (M/T)	29. Ball Bearing	44. Input Shaft Assembly (A/T)
15. Spacer (M/T)	30. Snap Ring	45. High-Low Sleeve & Hub (A/T)

Courtesy of Isuzu Motor Co.

Fig. 10: Exploded View Of Transfer Case Components

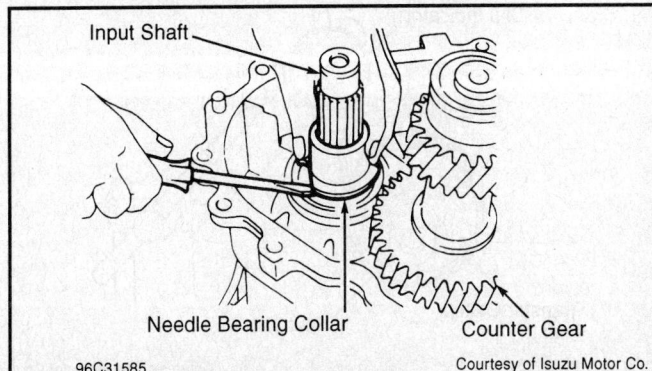

Input Shaft

Needle Bearing Collar

Counter Gear

Courtesy of Isuzu Motor Co.

96C31585

Fig. 11: Removing Needle Bearing Collar

3) On A/T models, remove ball bearing from input shaft using a press. On all models, remove snap ring. Remove front output gear assembly from case by tapping out with a plastic mallet. Remove bearing snap ring and collar. Install front output gear in press with remover, and press ball bearing from shaft. Ensure snap rings are removed, and press off components as necessary.

4) Remove and disassemble clutch sleeve and hub assembly. Remove countergear assembly from transfer case. Remove snap rings and press off necessary ball bearings. Disassemble countergear assembly. Remove transfer case input shaft oil seal. Remove transfer case front output shaft oil seal.

Cleaning & Inspection – Clean all parts with cleaning solvent and dry with compressed air. Inspect all parts for excessive wear. See TRANSFER CASE COMPONENT SPECIFICATIONS table and DETENT SPRING SPECIFICATIONS table under TRANSFER CASE. Replace parts as necessary.

TRANSFER CASE COMPONENT SPECIFICATIONS [1]

Component	Standard In. (mm)	Service Limit In. (mm)
Ball Bearing Free Play		.0079 (.200)
Block Ring & Insert Clearance	.136-.147 (3.45-3.73)	.158 (4.0)
Clutch Hub & Insert Clearance	.0004-.0075 (.010-.191)	.012 (.30)
Gear Inside Diameter	1.889-1.890 (48.00-48.01)	1.894 (48.10)
Mainshaft Runout		.002 (.05)
Shift Arm Thickness	.378-.388 (9.60-9.85)	.354 (9.00)
Transfer Clutch Hub Spline Play	0-.0039 (0-.100)	.0079 (.200)
2WD-4WD Synchronizer Block Ring Clearance	.059 (1.5)	.031 (.79)

[1] – See Figs. 12-18.

DETENT SPRING SPECIFICATIONS

Application	Standard In. (mm)	Minimum In. (mm)
Free Length		
Detent Ball Spring	1.01 (25.6)	.98 (25.0)
Interlock Pin Spring	.626 (15.90)	.602 (15.30)

Application	Standard In. (mm)	Tension Lb. (Kg)
Compressed Length		
Detent Ball Spring	.807 (20.50)	14.60-16.80 (6.6-7.6)
Interlock Pin Spring	.453 (11.50)	2.20 (1.0)

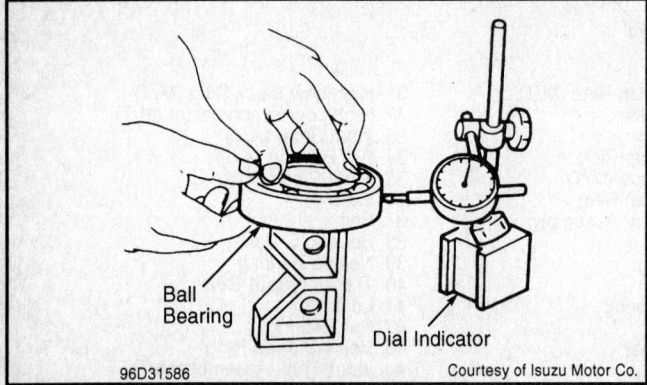

Fig. 12: Measuring Ball Bearing Free Play

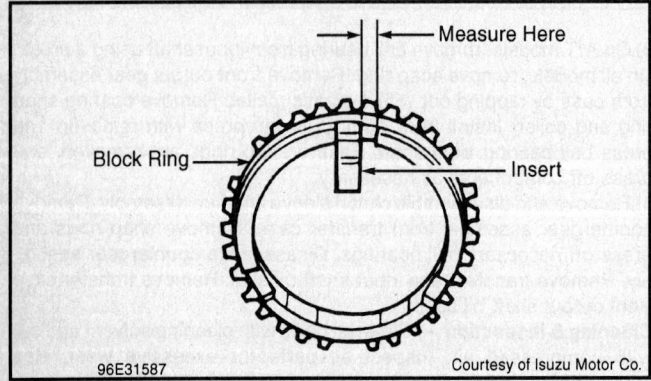

Fig. 13: Measuring Block Ring & Insert Clearance

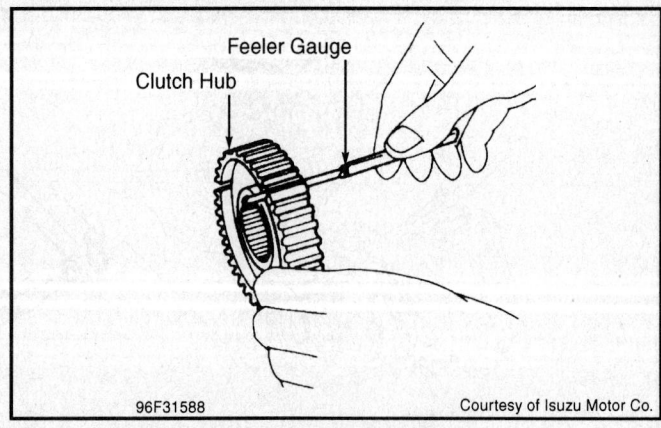

Fig. 14: Measuring Clutch Hub & Insert Clearance

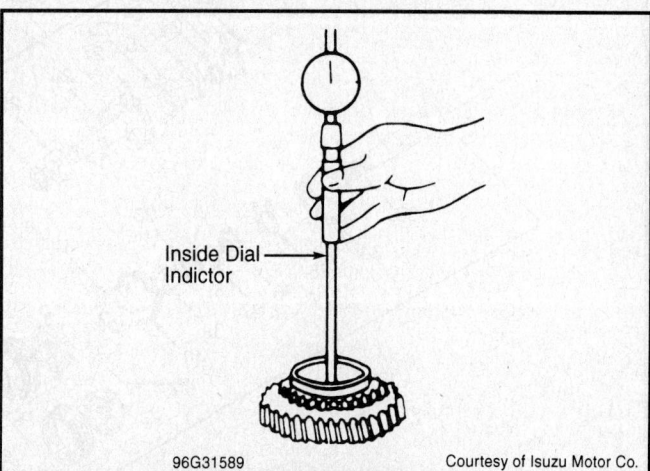

Fig. 15: Measuring Gear Inside Diameter

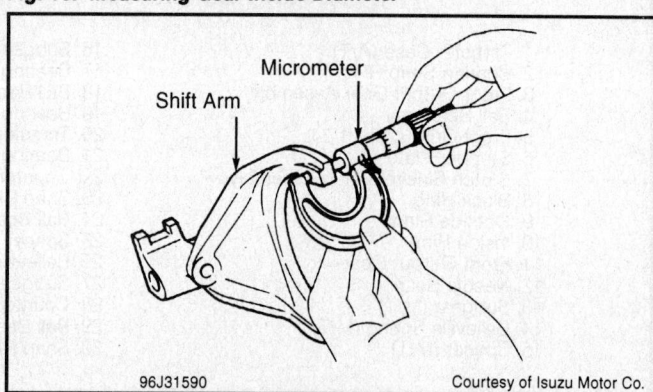

Fig. 16: Measuring Shift Arm Thickness

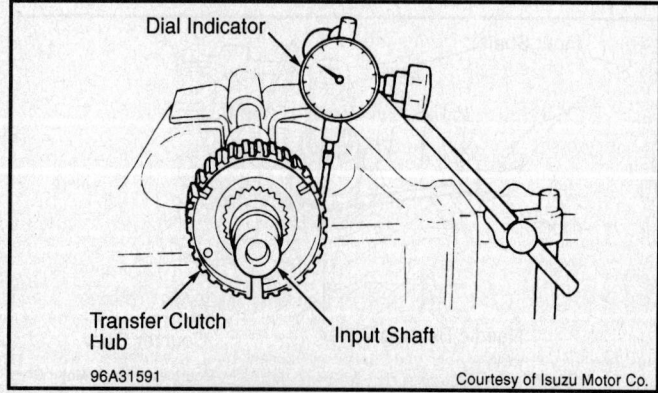

Fig. 17: Measuring Transfer Clutch Hub Spline Play

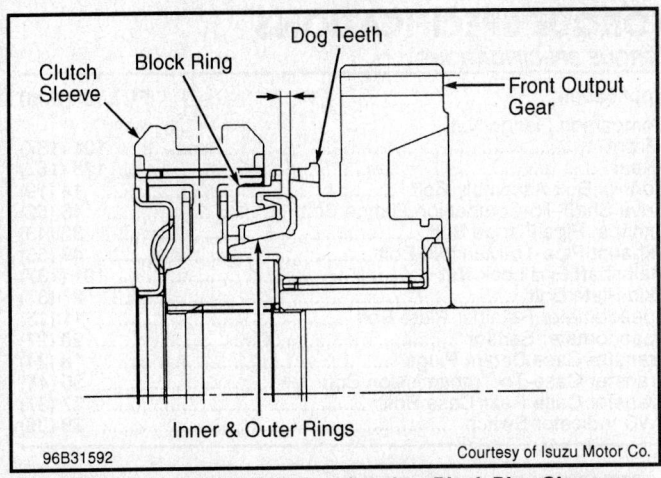

96B31592   Courtesy of Isuzu Motor Co.

Fig. 18: Measuring 2WD-4WD Synchronizer Block Ring Clearance

Reassembly – 1) On all models, apply engine oil to seals outer diameter. Install transfer case input shaft oil seal with Oil Seal Installer (J-38592). Install transfer case front output shaft oil seal with Oil Seal Installer (J-38594). Apply light multipurpose grease to seal lips.

2) Apply grease to gear thrust surfaces. Assemble countergear and subgear assembly. Using press, install ball bearing onto countergear shaft. Select and install a snap ring that allows minimal axial play. See COUNTERGEAR SNAP RING SPECIFICATIONS table.

COUNTERGEAR SNAP RING SPECIFICATIONS

Application	In. (mm)
Snap Ring Clearance	0-.0039 (0-.100)
Snap Ring Thickness	
White	.059 (1.50)
Yellow	.061 (1.55)
Blue	.063 (1.60)

3) Using a spring pull type gauge, check subgear preload. See Fig. 19. Preload should be 13-22 lbs. (58-98 N.). Install countergear assembly into transfer case. Install bearing snap ring into transfer case.

4) Press ball bearing onto front output shaft. DO NOT reuse stopper plate. Coat all clutch sleeve and hub assembly parts with transmission oil. Assemble clutch sleeve and hub assembly. Engage springs in insert with ends away from each other. See Fig. 20.

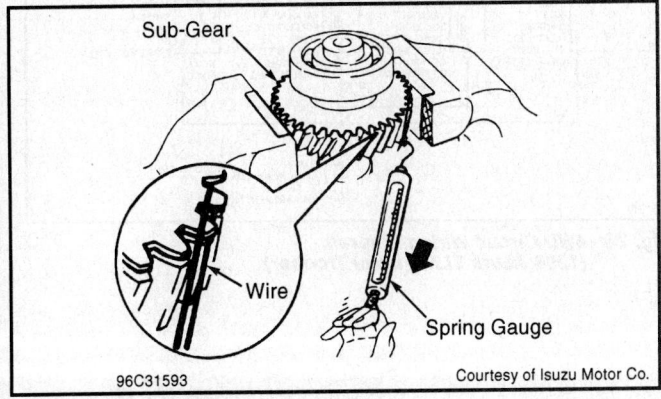

96C31593   Courtesy of Isuzu Motor Co.

Fig. 19: Measuring Subgear Preload

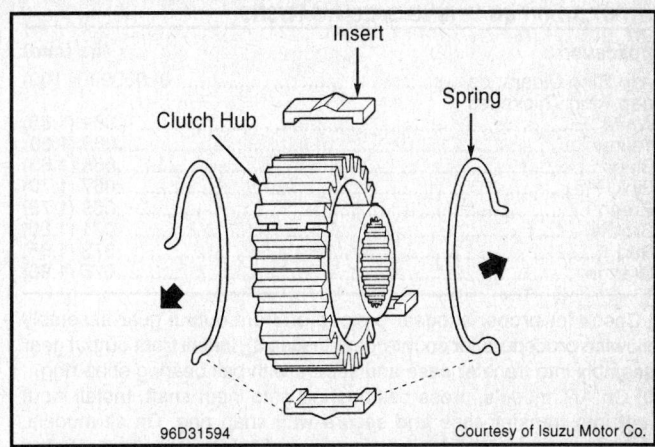

96D31594   Courtesy of Isuzu Motor Co.

Fig. 20: Assembling Clutch Sleeve & Hub Assembly

5) Install a NEW stopper plate and the clutch sleeve and hub assembly onto front output shaft. Ensure heavy boss of clutch hub face is toward front output gear side. See Fig. 21. Using a press, slowly force clutch sleeve and hub assembly together with stopper plate into place.

6) Align inserts with block ring insert grooves and install onto clutch sleeve and hub assembly. Install outside ring, inside ring and needle bearing onto front output gear and bearing collar. See Fig. 18.

7) On M/T models, assemble subgear, Belleville spring, spacer and snap ring to front output gear. Coat all parts with transmission fluid. On all models insert needle bearing into front output gear.

8) Press needle bearing collar and front output gear onto front output shaft. Press ball bearing onto front output shaft and secure with snap ring. See Fig. 22. Select and install a snap ring that allows minimal axial play. See OUTPUT SHAFT SNAP RING SPECIFICATIONS table.

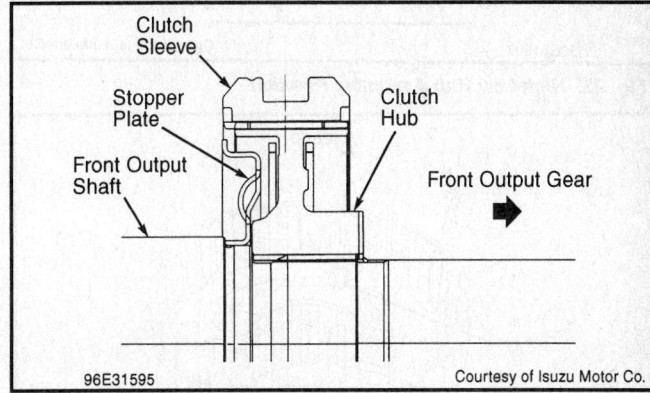

96E31595   Courtesy of Isuzu Motor Co.

Fig. 21: Installing Clutch Hub & Stopper Plate

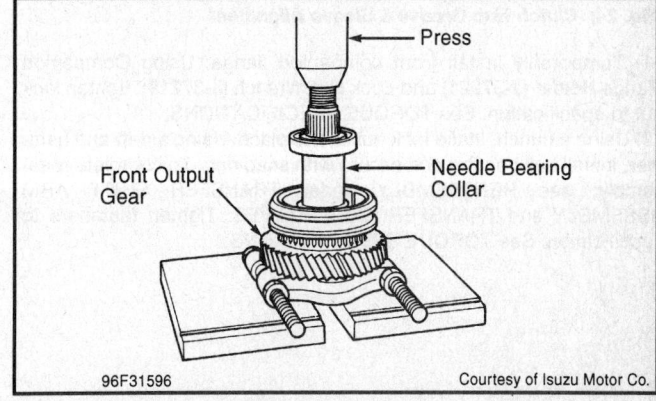

96F31596   Courtesy of Isuzu Motor Co.

Fig. 22: Assembling Needle Bearing Collar & Front Output Gear

OUTPUT SHAFT SNAP RING SPECIFICATIONS

Application	In. (mm)
Snap Ring Clearance	0-.0039 (0-.100)
Snap Ring Thickness	
White	.061 (1.55)
Yellow	.063 (1.60)
Blue	.065 (1.65)
Pink	.067 (1.70)
Green	.069 (1.75)
Brown	.071 (1.80)
Red	.073 (1.85)
Orange	.075 (1.90)

9) Check for proper subgear preload on front output gear assembly following procedure for countergear in step **3)**. Install front output gear assembly into transfer case and secure with ball bearing snap ring.

10) On A/T models, press ball bearing onto input shaft. Install input shaft into transfer case and secure with snap ring. On all models, assemble and install synchronizer assembly into transfer case and secure with lock nut.

NOTE: Clutch hub face with heavy boss must face transfer input gear side. See Fig. 23. On M/T models, clutch hub groove "A" must align with key groove of sleeve. See Fig. 24.

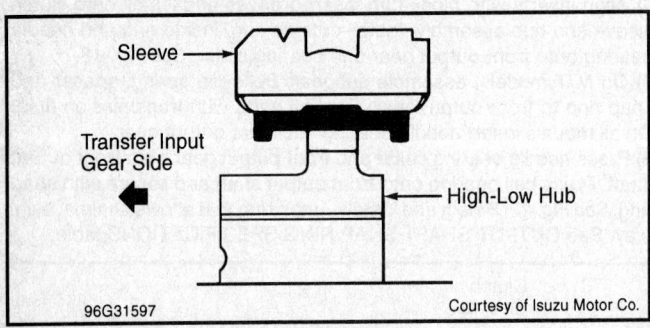

Fig. 23: High-Low Hub Assembly Position

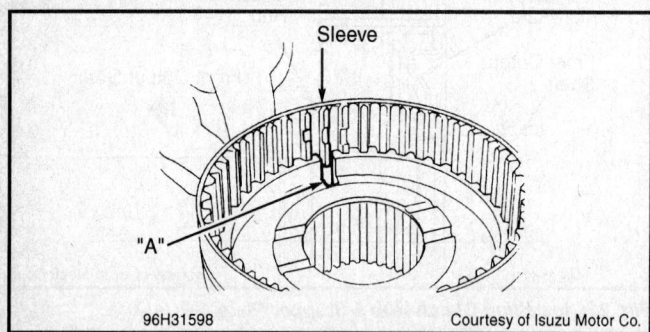

Fig. 24: Clutch Hub Groove & Sleeve Alignment

11) Temporarily install front companion flange. Using Companion Flange Holder (J-37221) and Lock Nut Wrench (J-37219), tighten lock nut to specification. See TORQUE SPECIFICATIONS.

12) Using a punch, stake lock nut in one place. Using a drift and hammer, install ball bearing and secure with snap ring. To complete reassembly, see REASSEMBLY under TRANSFER SHIFT ARM ASSEMBLY and TRANSFER CASE HALVES. Tighten fasteners to specification. See TORQUE SPECIFICATIONS.

TORQUE SPECIFICATIONS
TORQUE SPECIFICATIONS

Application	Ft. Lbs. (N.m)
Companion Flange Nut	
Front	101 (137)
Rear	123 (167)
Control Box Assembly Bolt	14 (19)
Drive Shaft-To-Companion Flange Bolt	46 (62)
Exhaust Pipe Flange Bolt	32 (43)
Exhaust Pipe-To-Manifold Bolt	49 (66)
Mainshaft End Lock Nut	101 (137)
Skid Plate Bolt	27 (37)
Speedometer Retainer Plate Bolt	11 (15)
Speedometer Sensor	20 (27)
Transfer Case Detent Plugs	18 (24)
Transfer Case-To-Transmission Bolt	30 (41)
Transfer Case Rear Case Bolt	27 (37)
4WD Indicator Switch	29 (39)

WIRING DIAGRAMS

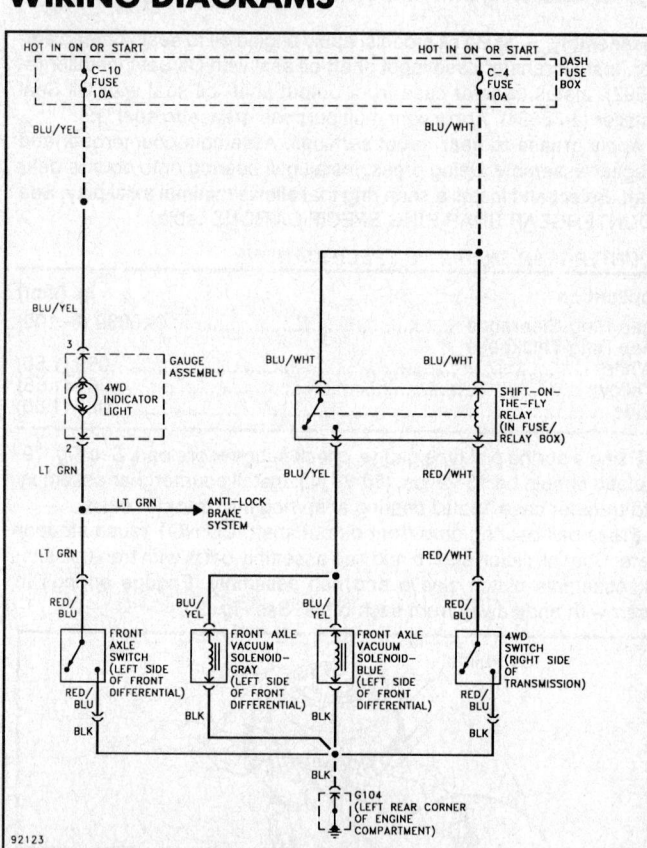

Fig. 25: 4WD Circuit Wiring Diagram (1996 Acura SLX & Isuzu Trooper)

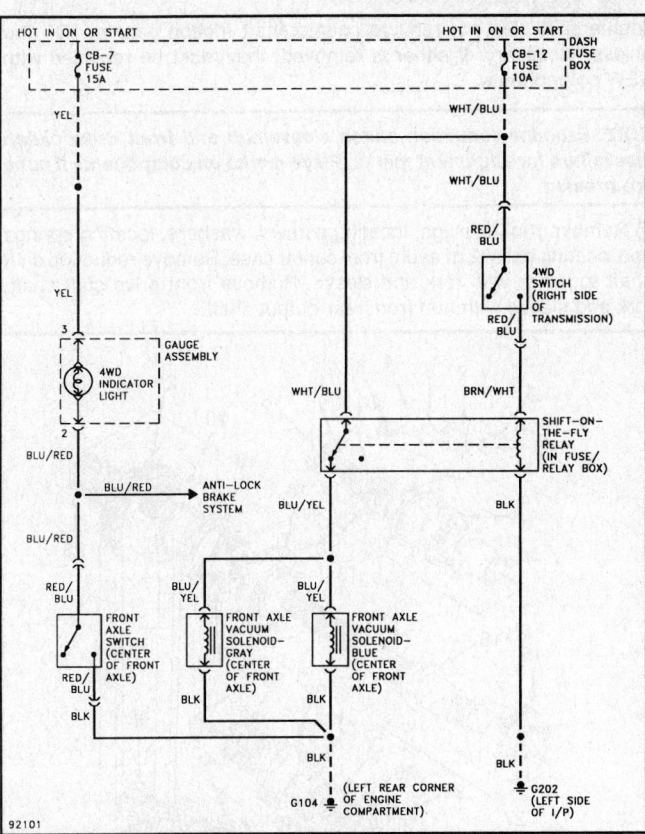

**Fig. 26: 4WD Circuit Wiring Diagram
(1996 Honda Passport & Isuzu Rodeo)**

Geo: Tracker
Suzuki: Sidekick, X-90

NOTE: Geo and Suzuki do not identify the transfer case application with a specific model number.

REMOVAL & INSTALLATION

TRANSFER CASE

Removal – 1) Disconnect negative battery cable. Remove both front and rear console boxes. On 4WD models, remove gear shift control lever knob, boot cover, lever boot and case boot. Remove gear shift control lever from gear shift lever case by pushing down and turning counterclockwise 1/4 turn, then pulling up.

2) Disconnect both 4WD electrical harness connectors. On all models, remove 4 bolts from radiator fan shroud. Raise and support vehicle. Remove transfer case skid plate. Drain transaxle oil. On 4WD models, place an index mark on front drive shaft flange and yoke for installation reference. Remove front drive shaft.

3) On all models, place an index mark on rear drive shaft flange and yoke for installation reference. Remove rear drive shaft. Disconnect speedometer cable. Remove one bolt, speedometer cable clip and ground wire from torque stopper housing. Remove Three-Way Catalytic Converter (TWC) and muffler/tailpipe assembly.

4) Support transfer case with jack. Remove 2 bolts from torque stopper bracket, and 6 bolts from transfer case crossmember. Remove crossmember. Place a wood block (1.8" x 5" x 8") between distributor gear housing and bulkhead to prevent damage to components while lowering transfer case.

5) Slowly lower transfer case. Remove breather hoses from gear shift lever case and cover (if equipped). On models equipped with manual transmission, remove gear shift lever case from rear of transmission. Remove 12 transfer case-to-transmission bolts. Separate transfer case from transmission, lower and remove from vehicle.

Installation – To install, reverse removal procedure. Tighten all fasteners to specification. See TORQUE SPECIFICATIONS. Ensure reference marks are aligned on drive shaft flanges and yokes. Fill and check fluid levels.

OVERHAUL

TRANSFER CASE

NOTE: Use illustration to identify transfer case internal components. See Fig. 1.

Disassembly – 1) Remove 4WD switch and steel ball. Remove 4WD low switch and steel ball (if equipped). Remove speedometer driven gear case. Remove gear shift lever housing. Remove select return spring bolt, washer, spring, steel ball and pin.

2) Drive out reduction shift yoke roll pin. Slide reduction shift yoke rearward and remove from reduction shift shaft. Remove 15 rear case-to-center case bolts. Using Case Separator (J-37637), separate rear case from center case.

3) Remove and save shim from top of rear output shaft rear bearing. Using Output Shaft Ring Remover (J-34757), remove speedometer drive gear "C" clip, speedometer drive gear and rear output shaft rear bearing "C" clip. Using a 2-jaw puller with bearing splitter, remove rear bearing from output shaft.

4) Remove sprocket bushing, needle bearing, sprocket and drive chain from rear output shaft. DO NOT lose steel ball when removing sprocket bushing. Using Needle Bearing Puller (J-26941) with a slide hammer, remove output shaft oil seal and needle bearing from rear case. Remove countershaft case plate from front case.

5) Remove 9 front case-to-center case bolts. Using Case Separator (J-37637), separate front and center cases. Remove countershaft assembly from center case. Remove washers and washer balls from countershaft. Remove countergear, needle bearings and spacer from

countershaft. Do not remove countershaft friction gear or "O" ring unless necessary. If either is removed, they must be replaced with NEW components.

NOTE: Examine reduction clutch sleeve/hub and front drive clutch sleeve/hub for alignment marks. Place marks on components if none are present.

6) Remove rubber plugs, locating screws, washers, locating springs and locating balls (2 of each) from center case. Remove reduction shift shaft together with fork and sleeve. Remove front drive shift shaft, fork and sleeve with hub from rear output shaft.

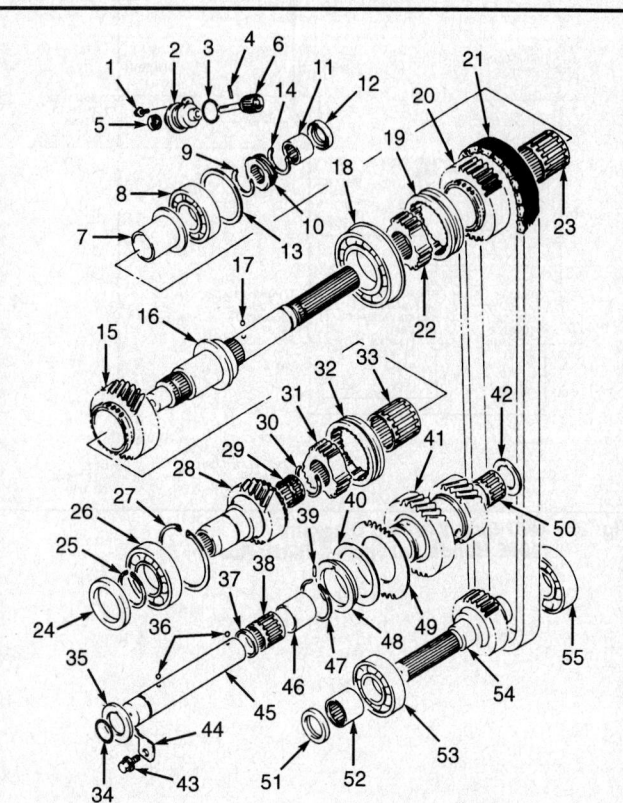

1. Retaining Bolt	29. Needle Bearing
2. Speedometer Gear Housing	30. "C" Clip
3. "O" Ring	31. Clutch Hub
4. Roll Pin	32. Clutch Sleeve
5. Seal	33. Needle Bearing
6. Speedometer Driven Gear	34. "O" Ring
7. Bushing	35. Countershaft Washer
8. Bearing	36. Steel Ball
9. "C" Clip	37. Friction Ring
10. Speedometer Drive Gear	38. Needle Bearing
11. Needle Bearing	39. Roll Pin
12. Seal	40. Friction Gear Spring
13. Shim	41. Countergear
14. "C" Clip	42. Countershaft Washer
15. Low Output Gear	43. Retaining Bolt
16. Rear Output Shaft	44. Case Retaining Plate
17. Steel Ball	45. Countershaft
18. Bearing	46. Spacer
19. Clutch Sleeve	47. Snap Ring
20. Drive Sprocket	48. Friction Gear
21. Drive Chain	49. Sub-Gear
22. Clutch Hub	50. Needle Bearing
23. Needle Bearing	51. Seal
24. Seal	52. Needle Bearing
25. Snap Ring	53. Bearing
26. Bearing	54. Front Output Shaft
27. Snap Ring	55. Bearing
28. Input Gear	

93D24870

Courtesy of Suzuki of America, Corp.

Fig. 1: Exploded View Of Internal Components

7) Remove interlock ball from center case passage. Remove "C" clip from rear output shaft and remove reduction clutch hub, low output gear and needle bearing. Using a plastic hammer, drive output shaft from center case. Press bearing off shaft. Remove front output shaft with bearings from center case.

8) Remove case gutter, oil seal and needle bearing from center case. Using a press, remove bearings from front output shaft. Remove input gear bearing "C" clip from front input gear. Using a plastic hammer, drive input gear from front case.

9) Remove oil guide from rear case. Remove oil seal from front case. Remove 'C' clip from input gear and press bearing from input gear. Remove roll pin from reduction shift fork. Remove reduction shift fork from shift shaft. Remove 2 "C" clips, shaft stop washer, shift fork and fork spring from front drive shift shaft.

Inspection – Replace any worn or damaged parts. Measure detent ball spring length. Standard spring length is .768" (19.5 mm). Replace any spring that measures less than .709" (18.0 mm) in length. Replace all seals and "O" rings. Measure shift fork-to-sleeve clearance. See Fig. 2. Replace shift fork if clearance exceeds .039" (1.0 mm).

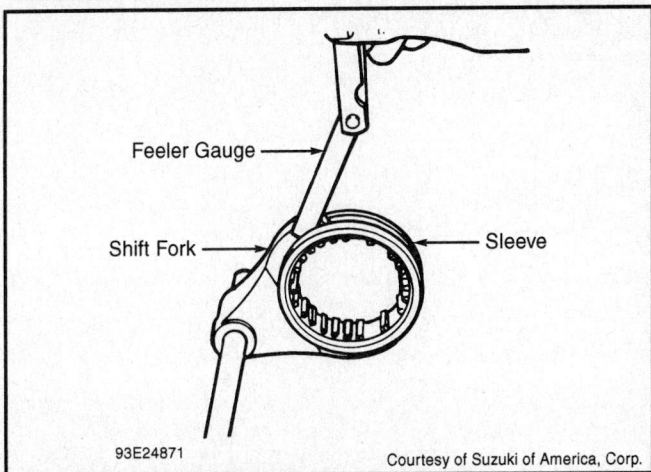

Fig. 2: Measuring Shift Fork-To-Sleeve Clearance

Reassembly – **1)** Install "C" clip, stop washer, shift fork spring, shift fork and stop washer onto front drive shift shaft. Secure with "C" clip. Install reduction shift fork onto reduction shift shaft and secure with roll pin. Press bearing onto input gear. Secure with "C" clip.

2) Install oil seal into front case. Apply Loctite to oil guide bolt and install with oil guide into rear case. Torque to specification. See TORQUE SPECIFICATIONS. Press input gear into front case and secure with "C" clip. Press bearings onto front output shaft. Press needle bearing into center case.

3) Seat oil seal flush with case surface and lubricate seal. Install case gutter into center case. Torque to specification. See TORQUE SPECIFICATIONS. Using a plastic hammer, drive front output shaft into center case. Press front bearing onto rear output shaft.

4) Drive output shaft into center case. Apply assembly lube to low output gear needle bearing. Install needle bearing, low output gear and reduction clutch hub onto rear output shaft. Place interlock ball into center case passage and push against interlock notch of front drive shift shaft.

5) Assemble front drive shift shaft, shift fork, clutch sleeve and clutch hub onto rear output shaft in rear of center case, aligning marks on front drive clutch hub and sleeve. Assemble reduction shift shaft, shift fork and clutch sleeve onto rear output shaft in front of center case, aligning marks on reduction clutch hub and sleeve.

6) Apply silicone sealer to both rubber plugs. Apply sealant to both locating screws. Install balls, locating springs, rubber plugs, washers and locating screws into center case. Torque to specification. See TORQUE SPECIFICATIONS. Install NEW countershaft friction ring and "O" ring onto countershaft (if removed).

NOTE: Friction ring MUST be installed 1.560" (3.95 mm) from end of countershaft.

7) Apply assembly lube to "O" ring and countershaft needle bearings. Install spacer, needle bearings and countergear onto countershaft. Install washer balls and washer onto countershaft. Install countershaft assembly into center case. Apply silicone sealer to front and center case mating surfaces. Assemble case halves and secure with 9 bolts. Torque to specification. See TORQUE SPECIFICATIONS.

8) Apply Loctite to countershaft plate bolt. Install countershaft case plate to front case. Torque to specification. See TORQUE SPECIFICATIONS. Press rear output shaft needle bearing and oil seal into rear case. Install shaft ball on rear output shaft. See Fig. 1. Use a small amount of assembly lube to help keep in place.

9) Install rear output shaft washer ball, drive sprocket and chain onto front and rear output shaft. Apply assembly lube to drive sprocket needle bearing. Press needle bearing and drive sprocket onto rear output shaft. Press rear bearing onto rear output shaft. Install speedometer drive gear and secure with "C" clip.

10) Using a straightedge and depth gauge, measure rear case dimension "A" (from mating surface to bottom of bearing bore), plus dimension "B" (straightedge). See Fig. 3. Place straight edge on bearing and measure bearing height "D" (from center case mating surface to bearing top) plus dimension "C" (straightedge). To prevent false measurements, DO NOT bridge straightedge between bearing and output front shaft bearing. See Fig. 3.

11) Use the formula, CLEARANCE "C" SHIM = A + B − C + D to select correct selective shim to install in bearing bore or rear case. See CLEARANCE "C" SHIM table.

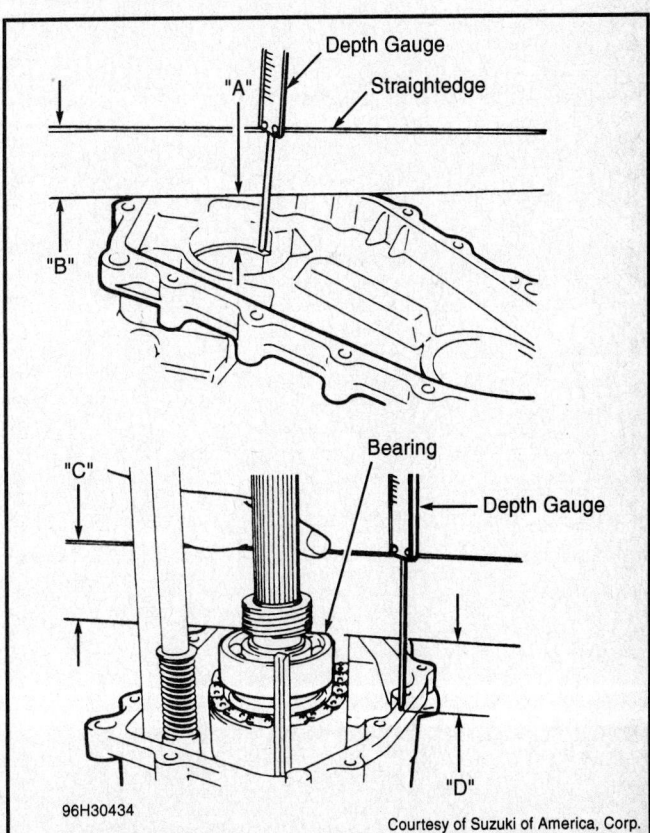

Fig. 3: Measuring Output Shaft Rear Bearing Clearance

CLEARANCE "C" SHIM

Clearance "C" In. (mm)	Shim Size In. (mm)
0-.005 (0-.13)	None
.005-.009 (.13-.23)	.004 (.10)
.009-.013 (.23-.33)	.008 (.20)
.013-.017 (.33-.43)	.012 (.30)
.017-.021 (.43-.53)	.016 (.40)
.021-.023 (.53-.58)	.020 (.50)

12) Apply assembly lube to selective shim and place on top of rear output shaft rear bearing. Apply silicone sealer to rear case mating surface. Assemble rear case to center case and secure with 15 bolts. Install reduction shift yoke onto shift shaft in rear case and secure with roll pin.

13) Apply Loctite to select return spring bolt. Install select return pin, ball, washer, spring and spring bolt into rear case. Torque to specification. See TORQUE SPECIFICATIONS. Apply silicone sealer to gear shift lever housing and secure to rear case with 5 bolts. Torque to specification.

14) Install speedometer driven gear case with "O" ring. Install steel balls and 4WD switches into rear case. Torque to specification.

TORQUE SPECIFICATIONS
TORQUE SPECIFICATIONS

Application	Ft. Lbs. (N.m)
Countershaft Case Plate Bolt	17 (23)
Drain Plug	21 (28)
Filler Plug	17 (23)
Front Case Bolts	17 (23)
Gearshift Lever Case Bolts	17 (23)
Locating Screws	19 (26)
Rear Case Bolts	17 (23)
Select Return Spring Bolt	25 (35)
Transfer Case Crossmember Bolts	37 (50)
Transfer Case Rear Mount Bolts	37 (50)
Transfer Case-To-Transmission Bolts	21 (28)
4WD Low Switch (If Equipped)	14 (19)
4WD Switch	14 (19)

	INCH Lbs. (N.m)
Case Gutter Bolt	106 (12)
Oil Guide Bolt	89 (10)
Speedometer Driven Gear Case Bolt	89 (10)

MPV 4WD

APPLICATION

MAZDA TRANSFER CASE APPLICATION

Application	Transfer Case Model
Mazda	
1995-96 MPV	R4AX-EL

DESCRIPTION & OPERATION

The Mazda R4AX-EL transfer case is an electronically controlled unit with mode changes (2WD-4WD) made by an electric motor operating the linkage. Mode selection is made through 4WD/2WD switch and center differential lock switch.

The 4WD control unit is a microprocessor unit which controls functions and warns driver of malfunction, but does not retain memory. The 4WD control unit is located behind driver's seat, next to door pillar. The Automatic Free Wheel (AFW) mechanism engages and disengages front drive axle during 2WD-4WD mode shifts.

NOTE: AFW is also known as Remote Free Wheel (RFW), but will be referred to as AFW in this article.

REMOVAL & INSTALLATION

Removal – 1) Drain transfer case oil. Match mark drive shaft with companion flange. Push a rag into double-offset joint to hold rear drive shaft straight to prevent boot damage. Remove rear drive shaft. Remove front drive shaft.

2) Support transmission with suitable support and remove transmission lower mount. Remove transmission upper mount. Remove exhaust pipe, heat insulator, speedometer cable and electrical connectors. Support transfer case with transmission jack, remove transfer case-to-adapter bolts and remove transfer case. Lower transfer case from vehicle.

Installation – Reverse removal procedure to install. Apply sealant around transfer case-to-adapter housing surface. Tighten all bolts to specifications.

DIAGNOSTIC TESTING

NOTE: The 4WD control unit retains no memory. When ignition is turned off warning alarm is canceled unless problem still exists when ignition is turned on.

Transfer case malfunctions may be caused by engine, driving conditions, transfer case or electrical control system. When diagnosing symptoms, begin with area that can be inspected quickly and easily. Recommended sequence is as follows:

Self Diagnosis – Check warning alarm operation.
Control Module Terminal Voltage Inspection – Check signals to and from 4WD control unit.
System Operation – Check operation of multimode 4WD system.
Symptom Trouble Shooting – Check multimode 4WD system for malfunction.

SELF-DIAGNOSIS

Fail Mode Function – A warning alarm will sound approximately 5 times in 8 seconds if a malfunction occurs in change motor or electrical circuit. Inspect change motor and circuit. Repair or replace faulty parts.

NOTE: While in fail mode, a warning alarm (same as above) will sound each time 4WD-2WD shift switch or center differential lock switch is activated.

- Fail mode function is canceled when ignition is turned off.
- If a problem of either position switch occurs in change motor while it is operating, 4WD control unit selects 2WD mode.
- If a problem of either limit switch occurs while shifting, 4WD control unit sets motor stop position.

Caution Mode Function – A caution alarm will sound 3 times if 4WD-2WD switch is activated while driving in 4WD center differential lock mode. Proper sequence is to set center differential lock switch to free mode and then set 4WD-2WD shift switch to 2WD mode.

CONTROL MODULE TERMINAL VOLTAGE INSPECTION

4WD Control Unit – Check electrical signals to and from 4WD control unit by turning ignition on and measuring 4WD control unit terminal voltage. See PIN VOLTAGE chart. See Figs. 1, 2, 3. If voltage is not as specified, check, repair or replace components, wiring and/or 4WD control unit.

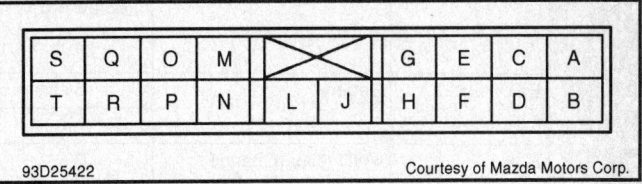

93D25422   Courtesy of Mazda Motors Corp.

Fig. 1: Identifying 4WD Control Unit Terminals

SYSTEM OPERATION

2WD To 4WD (Center Differential Free) Mode Shift – 1) Raise and support vehicle. Place transmission in "N". Start engine and let idle. Turn center differential lock switch to OFF position. Ensure center differential lock indicator light is off and 4WD indicator light is off.

2) Activate 4WD/2WD shift switch. If shift alarm sounds, go to next step. If shift alarm does not sound, inspect 4WD/2WD shift switch. See COMPONENT TESTING.

3) Monitor 4WD indicator light. If light is flashing, go to next step. If light does not flash, inspect indicator light.

4) Check if 4WD indicator light is illuminated. If light is not illuminated, go to next step. If light is illuminated, vehicle is in 4WD (center differential free) mode or vehicle is still in 4WD (center differential locked) mode. Go to next step.

5) Turn engine off. Turn front wheels clockwise. If rear tires rotate counterclockwise, check AFW switch. See AUTOMATIC FREE-WHEELING SYSTEM article in DRIVE AXLES in appropriate MITCHELL® manual. If rear tires rotate clockwise, check lock solenoid, actuator, change motor, change motor relay No. 1 and 4WD control module. See COMPONENT TESTING.

4WD (Center Differential Free) To 2WD Mode Shift – 1) Raise and support front of vehicle. Shift transmission to "N". Start engine and let it idle. Ensure center differential lock switch is in OFF position and 4WD indicator lamp is on.

2) Activate 4WD/2WD shift switch. If shift alarm sounds, go to next step. If shift alarm does not sound, inspect 4WD/2WD shift switch. See COMPONENT TESTING.

3) Monitor 4WD indicator light. If light is flashing, go to next step. If light does not flash, inspect indicator light.

4) Turn engine off. Rotate left front wheel clockwise. If right front wheel rotates, check free solenoid, actuator, change motor, change motor relay No. 2 and 4WD control module. See COMPONENT TESTING. If right front wheel does not rotate, vehicle is in 2WD mode. Test is complete.

4WD (Center Differential Free) To 4WD (Center Differential Lock) Mode Shift – 1) Raise and support vehicle. Set transmission in "N" with engine idling. Turn center differential lock switch to OFF position. Verify that indicator light is OFF and 4WD indicator light is on.

B+: Battery positive voltage

Terminal	Connected to	Voltage	Condition

A	Free solenoid	B+	Solenoid: OFF
			  Vehicle in 4WD (Free) mode
			  Vehicle in 4WD (Locked) mode

		Below 1.5 V	Solenoid: ON Vehicle in 2WD mode
B	Body	0 V	—

C	4WD relay (Change motor relay No.2)	B+	4WD relay (Change motor relay No.2): ON
			  During 4WD (Free) mode to 2WD mode
			  During 4WD (Free) mode to 4WD (Locked) mode shift

		Below 1.5 V	4WD relay (Change motor relay No.2): OFF Other than above conditions
D	Lock solenoid	B+	Solenoid: OFF Vehicle in 2WD mode

		Below 1.5 V	Solenoid: ON
			  Vehicle in 4WD (Free) mode
			  Vehicle in 4WD (Locked) mode

E	Battery	B+	Ignition switch ON
		0 V	Ignition switch OFF

F	4WD relay (Change motor relay No.1)	B+	4WD relay (Change motor relay No.1): ON
			  During 2WD to 4WD (Free) mode shift
			  During 2WD to 4WD (Locked) mode shift
			  During 4WD (Locked) mode to 4WD (Free) mode shift

		Below 1.5 V	4WD relay (Change motor relay No.1): OFF Other than above conditions
G	Buzzer	B+	Buzzer: OFF Normal condition

		Below 1.5 V	Buzzer: ON
			  4WD/2WD shift switch activated
			  Caution mode function
			  Fail mode function (System failure)

H	4WD indicator light	B+	4WD indicator light: OFF Vehicle in 2WD mode
		Below 1.5 V	4WD indicator light: ON Vehicle in either 4WD mode
J	CENTER DIFF. LOCK indicator light	B+	CENTER DIFF. LOCK indicator light: OFF Vehicle in 2WD or 4WD (Free) mode
		Below 1.5 V	CENTER DIFF. LOCK indicator light: ON Vehicle in 4WD (Locked) mode
L	—	—	—

96I31631

Courtesy of Mazda Motors Corp.

Fig. 2: 4WD Control Unit Pin Voltage Chart (1 Of 2)

2) Turn center differential lock switch to ON position. If indicator light is illuminated, go to next step. If indicator light is not on, check center differential lock switch and indicator light. See COMPONENT TESTING.

3) Turn engine off. Rotate front wheels clockwise. If rear wheels rotate, vehicle is in 4WD (center differential locked) mode. Test is complete. If rear wheels do not rotate, check actuator, change motor, change motor relay No. 2 and 4WD control module. See COMPONENT TESTING.

4WD (Center Differential Lock) To 4WD (Center Differential Free) Mode Shift – 1) Raise and support vehicle. Set transmission to "N" with engine idling. Turn center differential lock switch to ON position. Verify indicator light is on and 4WD indicator lamp is on.

2) Turn center differential lock switch to ON position. If indicator light is no longer illuminated, go to next step. If center differential lock indicator light is illuminated, check center differential lock switch and indicator light. See COMPONENT TESTING.

3) Turn engine off. Rotate front wheels clockwise. If rear wheels rotate, vehicle is in 4WD (center differential free) mode. Test is complete. If rear wheels do not rotate, check actuator, change motor, change motor relay No. 1 and 4WD control module. See COMPONENT TESTING.

2WD To 4WD (Center Differential Lock) Mode Shift – 1) Raise and support vehicle. Set transmission to "N" with engine idling. Turn center differential lock switch to OFF position. Verify indicator light is off and 4WD indicator light is off.

2) Activate center differential lock switch. If 4WD and center differential lock indicator lights flash, go to next step. If 4WD and center differential lock indicator lights do not flash, check center differential lock switch and indicator light. See COMPONENT TESTING.

3) Verify that 4WD and center differential lock indicator lights remain illuminated. If lights are illuminated, vehicle is in 4WD (center differential locked) mode. Test is complete. If lights are not illuminated, go to next step.

B+: Battery positive voltage

Terminal	Connected to	Voltage	Condition
M	Position switch A (In change motor)	B+	Position switch A: OFF Vehicle in 2WD mode Vehicle between 2WD mode and 4WD (Locked) mode
		0 V	Position switch A: ON Vehicle in 4WD (Free) mode Vehicle in 4WD (Locked) mode Vehicle between 4WD (Free) mode and 4WD (Locked) mode
N	AFW (Remote freewheel) switch	B+	RFW switch: OFF Vehicle in 2WD mode (AFW unit disengaged)
		0 V	RFW switch: ON Vehicle in either 4WD mode (AFW unit engaged)
O	Position switch B (In change motor)	B+	Position switch B: OFF Vehicle between 2WD mode and 4WD (Locked) mode Vehicle in 4WD (Locked) mode Vehicle between 4WD (Free) mode and 4WD (Locked) mode
		0 V	Position switch B: ON Vehicle in 2WD mode Vehicle in 4WD (Free) mode
P	Limit switch 1 (In change motor)	B+	Limit switch 1: OFF Normal condition
		0 V	Limit switch 1: ON High shift torque when shifting from 2WD to 4WD (Free) mode or vice-versa High shift torque when shifting from 2WD to 4WD (Locked) mode High shift torque when shifting from 4WD (Free) mode to 4WD (Locked) mode or vice-versa
Q	Position switch C (In change motor)	B+	Position switch C: OFF Vehicle between 4WD (Free) mode and 4WD (Locked) mode Vehicle in 4WD (Free) mode
		0 V	Position switch C: ON Vehicle in 2WD mode Vehicle between 2WD mode and 4WD (Locked) mode Vehicle in 4WD (Locked) mode
R	Limit switch 2 (In change motor)	B+	Limit switch 2: OFF Normal condition
		0 V	Limit switch 2: ON High shift torque when shifting from 2WD to 4WD (Free) mode or vice-versa High shift torque when shifting from 2WD to 4WD (Locked) mode High shift torque when shifting from 4WD (Free) mode to 4WD (Locked) mode or vice-versa
S	4WD/2WD shift switch	B+	4WD/2WD shift switch: OFF (released)
		0 V	4WD/2WD shift switch: ON (activated)
T	Center differential lock switch	B+	Center differential lock switch: OFF Bottom of rocker (Free position)
		0 V	Center differential lock switch: ON Top of rocker (Lock position)

96J31632

Courtesy of Mazda Motors Corp.

Fig. 3: 4WD Control Unit Pin Voltage Chart (2 Of 2)

4) Turn engine off. Turn front wheels clockwise. If rear tires rotate, check AFW switch. See AUTOMATIC FREE-WHEELING SYSTEM article in DRIVE AXLES in appropriate MITCHELL® manual. If rear tires do not rotate, check free solenoid, actuator, change motor, change motor relay No. 1 and 4WD control module. See COMPONENT TESTING.

SYMPTOM TROUBLE SHOOTING

NOTE: For 4WD control module terminal identification, see Fig. 1.

No Shift From 2WD To 4WD (Center Differential Free) – 1) Test drive vehicle to perform following trouble shooting procedure. Activate 4WD/2WD shift switch. If shift alarm sounds, go to next step. If shift alarm does not sound, check Light Green/White wire between terminal "S" on 4WD control module connector and 4WD/2WD shift switch connector. Repair as needed. If circuit is okay, check switch and switch ground circuit. Repair or replace as needed.

2) Activate 4WD/2WD shift switch. If warning alarm does not sound, go to step **4)**. If warning alarm does sound, check Blue wire between terminal "F" on 4WD control module connector and change motor relay No. 1 connector. Relay is mounted on left side of engine bulkhead. Repair as needed. If circuit is okay, go to next step.

3) Check change motor, change motor relay No. 1 and related circuits. Repair as needed. See appropriate wiring diagram in WIRING DIAGRAMS. If components and related circuits are okay, inspect transfer case for mechanical malfunction.

4) Monitor 4WD indicator light. If light is flashing, go to next step. If light is not flashing, inspect indicator light and related wiring. Repair as needed.

5) Monitor 4WD indicator light during test drive. If light is illuminated after .25-.50 miles, vehicle is in 4WD (center differential free) mode. Test is completed. If light is not illuminated after .25-.50 miles, go to next step.

6) Stop test drive. Turn ignition off. Using ohmmeter, check continuity between terminals "M", "O" and "Q" on 4WD control module connector and appropriate terminal on transfer case position switch. See appropriate wiring diagram in WIRING DIAGRAMS. Repair as needed. If all circuits are okay, go to next step.

7) Turn ignition on. Determine change motor position by measuring voltage between specified terminals on 4WD control module and ground. Battery voltage indicates position. *See Fig. 4.*

8) If position is 2H or "a", go to next step. If position is 4HL or "b", go to step **11)**. If position is 4HF, replace change motor or 4WD control module.

9) Measure voltage between ground and terminal "O" on 4WD control module. If voltage is present, go to next step. If no voltage is present, inspect Brown/White wire between terminal "P" on 4WD control module and change motor. See appropriate wiring diagram in WIRING DIAGRAMS. Repair as needed. If circuit is okay, check change motor, change motor relay No. 1 and related circuits. Repair as needed. If no problems are found, inspect transfer case for mechanical malfunction.

10) Measure voltage between ground and terminal "F" on 4WD control module. If battery voltage is present, check change motor, change motor relay No. 1 and related circuits. Repair as needed. If battery voltage is not present, replace 4WD control module.

11) Measure voltage between ground and terminal "N" on 4WD control module. If no voltage is present, go to step **13)**. If voltage is present, go to next step.

12) Measure voltage between ground and terminal "D" on 4WD control module. If voltage is present, replace 4WD control module. If no voltage is present, check Yellow/White wire between terminal "D" on 4WD control module and lock solenoid. Repair as needed. If circuit is okay, inspect lock solenoid. See COMPONENT TESTING. If lock solenoid is okay, inspect AFW unit. See AUTOMATIC FREE-WHEELING SYSTEM article in DRIVE AXLES in appropriate MITCHELL® manual.

13) Measure voltage between terminals "R" and "P" on 4WD control module. If voltage is present, go to next step. If no voltage is present, inspect circuits between terminals "Q" and "P" on 4WD control module and change motor. Repair as needed. If circuits are okay, go to step **16)**.

14) Check Blue wire between terminal "F" on 4WD control module and change motor relay No. 1. Repair as needed. See appropriate wiring diagram in WIRING DIAGRAMS. If circuit is okay, go to next step.

15) Measure voltage between ground and terminal "F" on 4WD control module. If battery voltage is present, go to next step. If battery voltage is not present, replace 4WD control module.

16) Check change motor, change motor relay No. 1 and related circuits. Repair as needed. If no problems are found, inspect transfer case for mechanical malfunction.

NOTE: For 4WD control module terminal identification, see Fig. 1.

No Shift From 4WD (Center Differential Free) To 2WD – 1) Test drive vehicle to perform following trouble shooting procedure. Activate 4WD/2WD shift switch. If shift alarm sounds, go to next step. If shift alarm does not sound, check Light Green/White wire between

	Position	2H	α	4HL	β	4HF
Terminal						B+: Battery positive voltage
M and ground (V)		B+	B+	0 V	0 V	0 V
O and ground (V)		0 V	B+	B+	B+	0 V
Q and ground (V)		0 V	0 V	0 V	B+	B+

96A31633   Courtesy of Mazda Motors Corp.

Fig. 4: Change Motor Position Voltage Chart

terminal "S" on 4WD control module connector and 4WD/2WD shift switch connector. Repair as needed. If circuit is okay, check switch and switch ground circuit. Repair or replace as needed.

2) Activate 4WD/2WD shift switch. If warning alarm does not sound, go to step **4)**. If warning alarm does sound, check Blue/Yellow wire between terminal "C" on 4WD control module connector and change motor relay No. 2 connector. Relay is mounted on left side of engine bulkhead. Repair as needed. If circuit is okay, go to next step.

3) Check change motor, change motor relay no. 2 and related circuits. Repair as needed. See appropriate wiring diagram in WIRING DIAGRAMS.

4) Monitor 4WD indicator light. If light is flashing, go to next step. If light is not flashing, inspect indicator light and related wiring. Repair as needed.

5) Stop test drive. Turn ignition off. Raise and support front of vehicle. Turn left front wheel clockwise. If right front wheel rotates, go to next step. If right front wheel does not rotate, vehicle is in 2WD mode. Test is complete.

6) Resume test drive. Drive vehicle .25-.50 miles. Repeat step **5)**. If right front wheel rotates, go to next step. If right front wheel does not rotate, vehicle is in 2WD mode. Test is complete.

7) Stop test drive. Turn ignition off. Using ohmmeter, check continuity between terminals "M", "O" and "Q" on 4WD control module connector and appropriate terminal on transfer case position switch. See appropriate wiring diagram in WIRING DIAGRAMS. Repair as needed. If all circuits are okay, go to next step.

8) Turn ignition on. Determine change motor position by measuring voltage between specified terminals on 4WD control module and ground. Battery voltage indicates position. *See Fig. 4.*

9) If position is 2H or "a", go to next step. If position is 4HL or "b", go to step **13)**. If position is 4HF, replace change motor or 4WD control module.

10) Measure voltage between ground and terminal "P" on 4WD control module. If voltage is present, go to next step. If no voltage is present, inspect Brown/White wire between terminal "P" on 4WD control module and change motor. See appropriate wiring diagram in WIRING DIAGRAMS. Repair as needed. If circuit is okay, check change motor, change motor relay No. 2 and related circuits. Repair as needed. If no problems are found, inspect transfer case for mechanical malfunction.

11) Measure voltage between ground and terminal "C" on 4WD control module. If battery voltage is present, go to next step. If battery voltage is not present, replace 4WD control module.

12) Check Blue/Yellow wire between terminal "C" on 4WD control module and change motor relay No. 2. Repair as needed. If circuit is okay, check change motor, change motor relay No. 2 and related circuits. Repair as needed. If no problems are found, inspect transfer case for mechanical malfunction.

13) Measure voltage between terminals "R" and "P" on 4WD control module. If voltage is present, go to next step. If no voltage is present, inspect circuits between terminals "R" and "P" on 4WD control module and change motor. If circuit is okay, check change motor, change motor relay No. 2 and related circuits. Repair as needed. If no problems are found, inspect transfer case for mechanical malfunction.

14) Measure voltage between ground and terminal "C" on 4WD control module. If no voltage is present, replace 4WD control module. If battery voltage is present, go to next step.

15) Check Blue/Yellow wire between terminal "C" on 4WD control module and change motor relay No. 2. Repair as needed. If circuit is okay, If circuit is okay, check change motor, change motor relay No. 2 and related circuits. Repair as needed. If no problems are found, inspect transfer case for mechanical malfunction.

16) Measure voltage between ground and terminal "A" on 4WD control module. If battery voltage is present, replace 4WD control module. If battery voltage is not present, go to next step.

17) Check White wire between terminal "A" on 4WD control module and free solenoid. See appropriate wiring diagram in WIRING DIAGRAMS. Repair as needed. If circuit is okay, inspect free solenoid and related wiring. See COMPONENT TESTING. Replace or repair as needed. If solenoid and related wiring are okay, check AFW unit. See AUTOMATIC FREE-WHEELING SYSTEM article in DRIVE AXLES in appropriate MITCHELL® manual.

NOTE: For 4WD control module terminal identification, see Fig. 1.

No Shift From 4WD (Center Differential Free) To 4WD (Center Differential Lock) – 1) Test drive vehicle to perform following trouble shooting procedure. Activate center differential switch. If warning alarm does not sound, go to next step. If warning alarm sounds, inspect circuits between terminals "P" and "R" on 4WD control module connector and change motor. See appropriate wiring diagram in WIRING DIAGRAMS. Repair as needed. If circuits are okay, check change motor, change motor relay No. 2 and related circuits. Repair as needed. If no problems are found, inspect transfer case for mechanical malfunction.

2) Turn ignition off. Check continuity of Green/Blue wire between terminal "T" on 4WD control module and center differential lock switch. Repair as needed. If circuit is okay, go to next step.

3) Resume test drive. Activate center differential switch. If indicator light illuminates, go to next step. If indicator light does not illuminate, inspect light and related circuits. Repair as needed.

4) Stop test drive. Turn ignition off. Raise and support vehicle. Rotate front wheels clockwise. If rear wheels rotate clockwise, vehicle is in 4WD (center differential locked) mode. Test is complete. If rear wheels rotate counterclockwise, go to next step.

5) Resume test drive. Drive vehicle .25-.50 miles. Repeat step 4). If rear wheels rotate counterclockwise, go to next step.

6) Stop test drive. Turn ignition off. Using ohmmeter, check continuity between terminals "M", "O" and "Q" on 4WD control module connector and appropriate terminal on transfer case position switch. See appropriate wiring diagram in WIRING DIAGRAMS. Repair as needed. If all circuits are okay, go to next step.

7) Turn ignition on. Determine change motor position by measuring voltage between specified terminals on 4WD control module and ground. Battery voltage indicates position. *See Fig. 4.*

8) If position is 4HF, go to next step. If position is "b", go to step 12). If position is 2H, "a" or 4HL, replace change motor or 4WD control module.

9) Measure voltage between ground and terminal "P" on 4WD control module. If voltage is present, go to next step. If no voltage is present, inspect Brown/White wire between terminal "P" on 4WD control module and change motor. See appropriate wiring diagram in WIRING DIAGRAMS. Repair as needed. If circuit is okay, check change motor, change motor relay No. 2 and related circuits. Repair as needed. If no problems are found, inspect transfer case for mechanical malfunction.

10) Measure voltage between ground and terminal "F" on 4WD control module. If battery voltage is present, go to next step. If battery voltage is not present, replace 4WD control module.

11) Check Blue wire between terminal "F" on 4WD control module and change motor relay No. 1. Repair as needed. If circuit is okay, check change motor, change motor relay No. 2 and related circuits. Repair as needed.

12) Measure voltage between terminals "R" and "P" on 4WD control module. If voltage is present, go to next step. If no voltage is present, inspect circuits between terminals "R" and "P" on 4WD control module and change motor. If circuit is okay, check change motor, change motor relay No. 2 and related circuits. Repair as needed. If no problems are found, inspect transfer case for mechanical malfunction.

13) Measure voltage between ground and terminal "F" on 4WD control module. If battery voltage is present, go to next step. If battery voltage is not present, replace 4WD control module.

14) Check Blue wire between terminal "F" on 4WD control module and change motor relay No. 1. Repair as needed. If circuit is okay, check change motor, change motor relay No. 2 and related circuits. Repair as needed. If no problems are found, inspect transfer case for mechanical malfunction.

NOTE: For 4WD control module terminal identification, see Fig. 1.

No Shift From 4WD (Center Differential Lock) To 4WD (Center Differential Free) – 1) Test drive vehicle to perform following trouble shooting procedure. Activate center differential switch. If warning alarm sounds, inspect Blue wire between terminals "F" on 4WD control module connector and change motor relay No. 1. See appropriate wiring diagram in WIRING DIAGRAMS. Repair as needed. If circuits are okay, check change motor, change motor relay No. 1 and related circuits. Repair as needed. If no problems are found, inspect transfer case for mechanical malfunction.

2) Turn ignition off. Check continuity of Green/Blue wire between terminal "T" on 4WD control module and center differential lock switch. Repair as needed. If circuit is okay, go to next step.

3) Resume test drive. Deactivate center differential switch. If indicator light goes off, go to next step. If indicator light is illuminated, inspect center differential lock switch, light and related circuits. Repair as needed.

4) Stop test drive. Turn ignition off. Raise and support vehicle. Rotate front wheels clockwise. If rear wheels rotate counterclockwise, vehicle is in 4WD (center differential free) mode. Test is complete. If rear wheels do not rotate counterclockwise, go to next step.

5) Resume test drive. Drive vehicle .25-.50 miles. Repeat step 4). If rear wheels do not rotate counterclockwise, go to next step.

6) Measure voltage between terminals "R" and "P" on 4WD control module. If no voltage is present, go to next step. If voltage is present, inspect circuits between terminals "R" and "P" on 4WD control module and change motor. If circuit is okay, check change motor, change motor relay No. 1 and related circuits. Repair as needed. If no problems are found, inspect transfer case for mechanical malfunction.

7) Measure voltage between ground and terminal "C" on 4WD control module. If battery voltage is present, go to next step. If battery voltage is not present, replace 4WD control module.

8) Check Blue/Yellow wire between terminal "C" on 4WD control module and change motor relay No. 1. Repair as needed. If circuit is okay, check change motor, change motor relay No. 1 and related circuits. Repair as needed. If no problems are found, inspect AFW unit. See AUTOMATIC FREE-WHEELING SYSTEM article in DRIVE AXLES in appropriate MITCHELL® manual.

NOTE: For 4WD control module terminal identification, see Fig. 1.

No Shift From 2WD To 4WD (Center Differential Lock) – 1) Test drive vehicle to perform following trouble shooting procedure. Activate center differential lock switch. If warning alarm does not sound, go to step 3). If warning alarm sounds, check Blue wire between terminal "F" on 4WD control module connector and change motor relay No. 1 connector. Repair as needed. Relay is mounted on left side of engine bulkhead. If circuit is okay, go to next step.

2) Check change motor, change motor relay no. 1 and related circuits. Repair as needed. See appropriate wiring diagram in WIRING DIAGRAMS. If components and related circuits are okay, inspect transfer case for mechanical malfunction.

3) Turn ignition off. Check continuity of Green/Blue wire between terminal "T" on 4WD control module and center differential lock switch. Repair as needed. If circuit is okay, go to next step.

4) Monitor 4WD indicator light and center differential indicator light. If lights are flashing, go to next step. If lights are not flashing, inspect indicator lights and related wiring. Repair as needed.

5) Monitor indicator lights during test drive. If both indicator lights are illuminated after .25-.50 mile, vehicle is in 4WD (center differential locked) mode. Test is completed. If lights are not illuminated after .25-.50 mile, go to next step.

6) Stop test drive. Turn ignition off. Using ohmmeter, check continuity between terminals "M", "O" and "Q" on 4WD control module connector and appropriate terminal on transfer case position switch. See appropriate wiring diagram in WIRING DIAGRAMS. Repair as needed. If all circuits are okay, go to next step.

7) Turn ignition on. Determine change motor position by measuring voltage between specified terminals on 4WD control module and ground. Battery voltage indicates position. See Fig. 4.

8) If position is 2H or "a", go to next step. If position is 4HL, go to step 11). If position is 4HF or "b", replace change motor or 4WD control module.

9) Measure voltage between ground and terminal "P" on 4WD control module. If voltage is present, go to next step. If no voltage is present, inspect Brown/White wire between terminal "P" on 4WD control module and change motor. See appropriate wiring diagram in WIRING DIAGRAMS. Repair as needed. If circuit is okay, check change motor, change motor relay No. 1 and related circuits. Repair as needed. If no problems are found, inspect transfer case for mechanical malfunction.

10) Measure voltage between ground and terminal "F" on 4WD control module. If battery voltage is present, go to next step. If battery voltage is not present, replace 4WD control module.

11) Inspect Blue wire between terminal "F" on 4WD control module and change motor. See appropriate wiring diagram in WIRING DIAGRAMS. Repair as needed. If circuit is okay, check change motor, change motor relay No. 1 and related circuits. Repair as needed. If no problems are found, inspect transfer case for mechanical malfunction.

12) Measure voltage between ground and terminal "N" on 4WD control module. If no voltage is present, go to step 14). If voltage is present, go to next step.

13) Measure voltage between ground and terminal "D" on 4WD control module. If voltage is present, replace 4WD control module. If no voltage is present, check Yellow/White wire between terminal "D" on 4WD control module and lock solenoid. Repair as needed. If circuit is okay, inspect lock solenoid. See COMPONENT TESTING. If lock solenoid is okay, inspect AFW unit. See AUTOMATIC FREE-WHEELING SYSTEM article in DRIVE AXLES in appropriate MITCHELL® manual.

14) Check Red/Yellow wire between terminal "N" on 4WD control module and AFW switch. Repair as needed. See appropriate wiring diagram in WIRING DIAGRAMS. If switch is okay, inspect AFW unit. See AUTOMATIC FREE-WHEELING SYSTEM article in DRIVE AXLES in appropriate MITCHELL® manual. Repair as needed.

COMPONENT TESTING

CHANGE MOTOR

On-Vehicle Inspection – Turn ignition on. Using voltmeter, backprobe change motor connector as specified. See Fig. 5. Check voltages during indicated mode shift operation. If voltage is not as specified, inspect change motor relays.

Mode shift	Terminal voltage	
	B+: Battery positive voltage	
	2A	2B
2WD→4WD FREE	Momentary B+	Ground 0 V
4WD FREE→2WD	Ground 0 V	Momentary B+
4WD FREE→4WD LOCKED	Ground 0 V	Momentary B+
4WD LOCKED→4WD FREE	Momentary B+	Ground 0 V
2WD→4WD LOCKED	Momentary B+	Ground 0 V

96B31634   Courtesy of Mazda Motors Corp.

Fig. 5: Change Motor Terminal Voltage Chart

Motor Inspection – **1)** Connect 12 volts to change motor connector terminals. Positive wire from battery to terminal 2A and negative wire from battery to terminal 2B. Ensure motor rotates clockwise. See Fig. 6.

2) Reverse battery leads to change motor connector terminals and ensure change motor rotates counterclockwise.

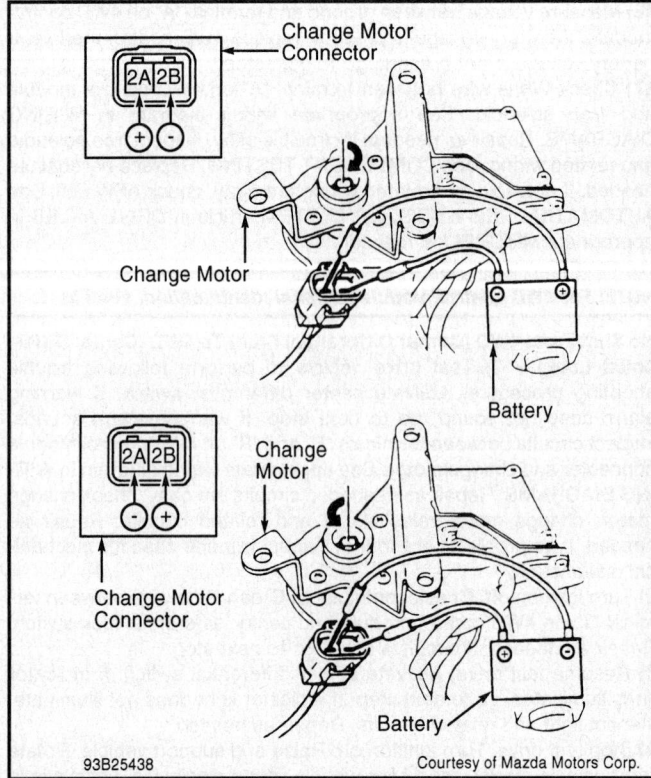

93B25438   Courtesy of Mazda Motors Corp.

Fig. 6: Testing Change Motor

CHANGE MOTOR LIMIT SWITCH

1) Remove change motor from transfer case and secure in vise. Ensure no continuity exists between terminals "F" and "H".

2) Turn change motor shaft clockwise with Change Motor Adapter (49L017302) and INCH lb. torque wrench until continuity is shown between terminals "F" and "H". Allow shaft to turn counterclockwise and note torque when continuity is lost. Torque should be 22-43 INCH lbs. (2.5-4.9 N.m).

3) Turn shaft counterclockwise as in step **2)** and check for continuity and torque reading. See Fig. 7.

4) Connect ohmmeter between terminals "E" and "H". Ensure no continuity exists. Turn change motor shaft clockwise with change motor adapter and torque wrench until continuity is shown. Allow change motor to turn counterclockwise and note torque when continuity is lost. Torque should be 61-113 INCH lbs. (6.9-13 N.m).

5) Turn change motor shaft counterclockwise as in step **4)** and check for continuity and torque reading. If not as specified in step **4)** above, replace change motor.

CHANGE MOTOR POSITION SWITCH

1) Connect ohmmeter to terminals "A" and "D" of change motor. Connect 12 volts to terminal 2A (+) and 2B (–). See Fig. 8. Check for continuity once per motor revolution.

2) Move ohmmeter leads to terminals "B" and "D" and repeat continuity check as in step **1)**. Move ohmmeter leads to terminals "C" and "D" and repeat continuity check. If any continuity test fails, replace change motor.

Change Motor Installation – **1)** Align mark on change drum groove with 2H mark. See Fig. 9. Ensure marks on change motor shaft and body are aligned. If not aligned, turn shaft by applying 12 volts to change motor connector terminals 2A (+) and 2B (–).

2) Lubricate new "O" ring and install on change motor. Install change motor and tighten bolts to 14-19 ft. lbs. (19-25 N.m). Install protector plate and tighten bolts to 32-41 ft. lbs. (43-55 N.m).

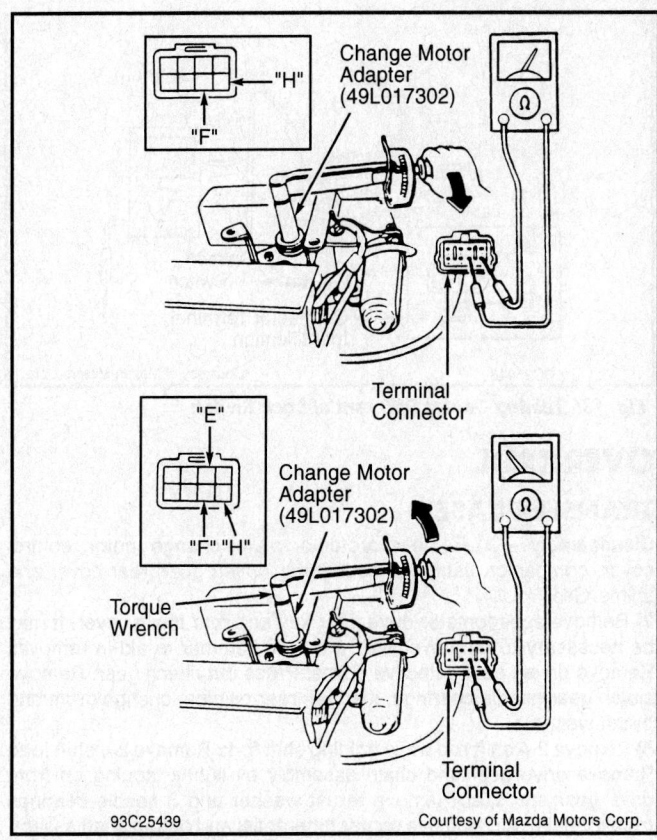

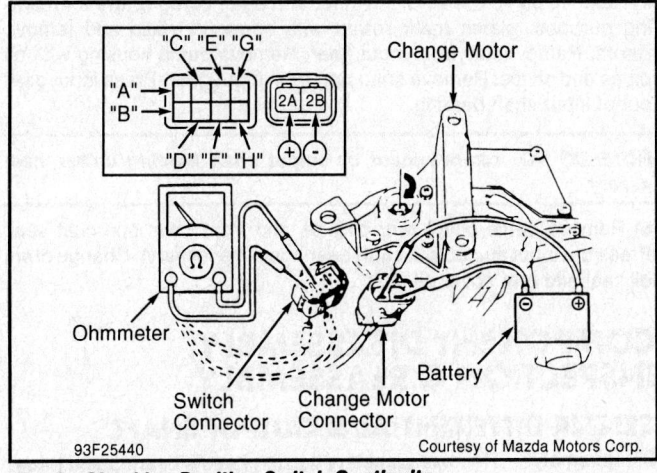

Fig. 7: Measuring Change Motor Torque

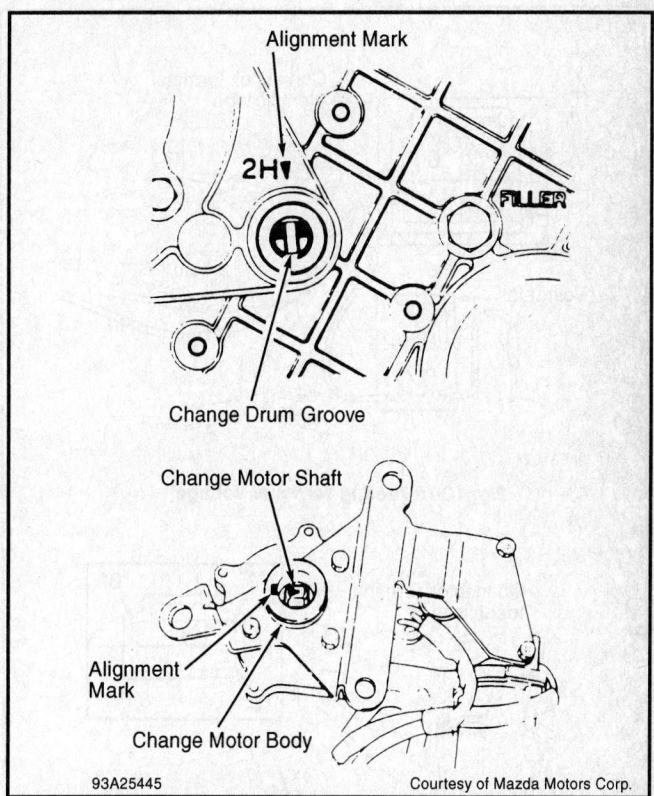

Fig. 9: Installing Change Motor

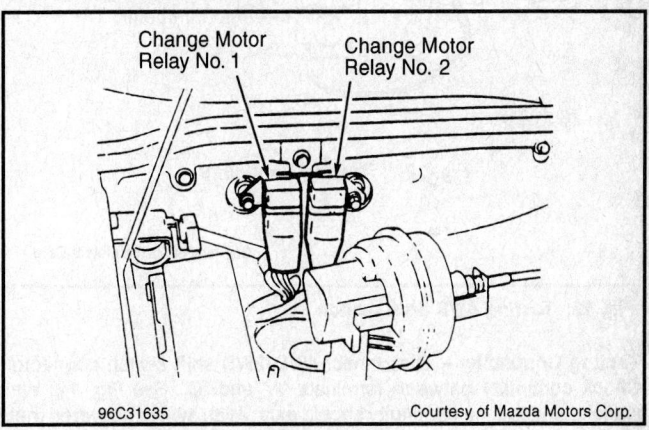

Fig. 10: Locating Change Motor Relay(s)

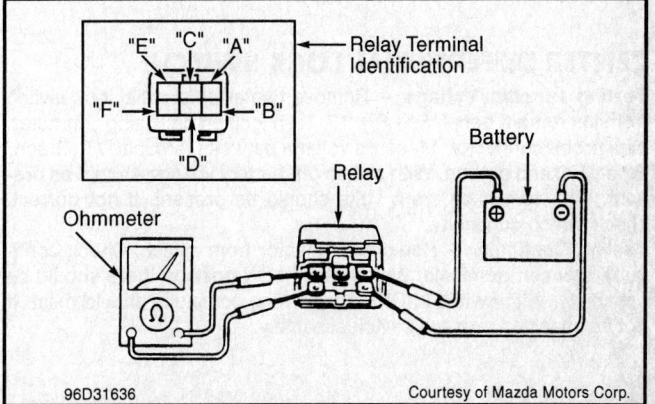

Fig. 8: Checking Position Switch Continuity

CHANGE MOTOR RELAY(S)

Remove change motor relay(s). See Fig. 10. Check for continuity between terminals "A" and "B". Move ohmmeter leads to terminals "C" and "E". Connect 12 volts to terminals "A" (+) and "B" (−). Check for continuity between terminal "C" and "E". See Fig. 11. If not as specified, replace change motor relay(s).

4WD/2WD SHIFT SWITCH

Testing Terminal Voltage – Remove column covers. Turn ignition on. Using voltmeter, backprobe shift switch connector. Measure voltage between terminal "C" (Light Green/White wire) and ground. See Fig. 12. With 4WD/2WD shift switch released, battery voltage should be present. With 4WD/2WD shift switch activated (held to left), zero volts should be present. If not as specified test 4WD/2WD shift switch for continuity.

Fig. 11: Testing Change Motor Relay(s)

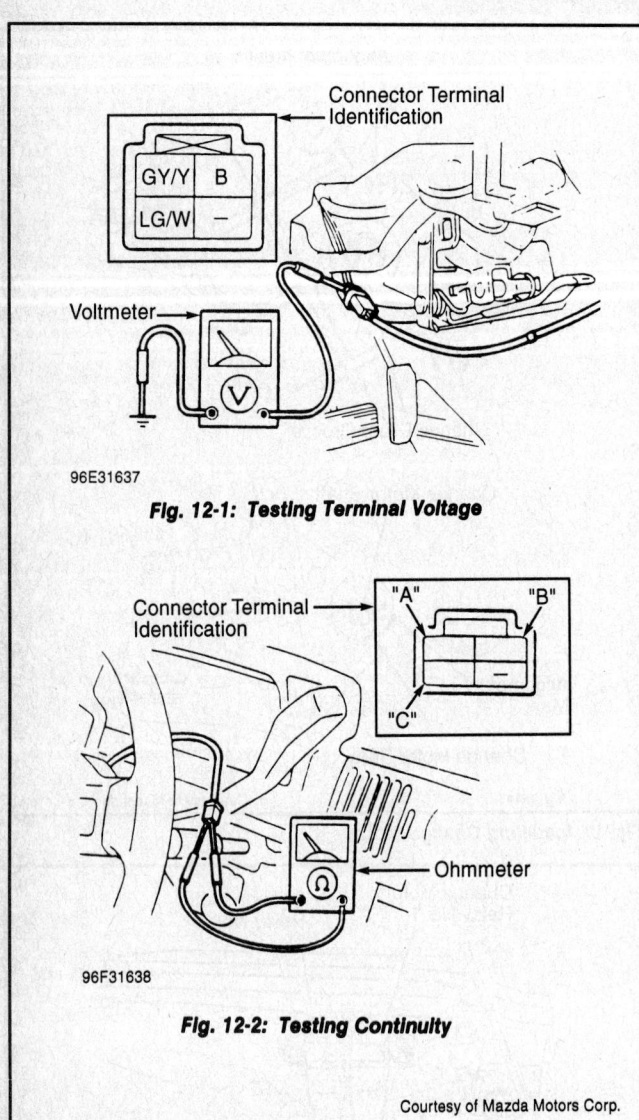

Fig. 12-1: *Testing Terminal Voltage*

Fig. 12-2: Testing Continuity

Courtesy of Mazda Motors Corp.

Fig. 12: Testing 4WD Shift Switch

Testing Continuity – Disconnect 4WD/2WD shift switch connector. Check continuity between terminals "A" and "C". See Fig. 12. With switch released, no continuity should exist. With switch activated (held to left), there should be continuity. If not as specified, replace switch assembly.

CENTER DIFFERENTIAL LOCK SWITCH

Testing Terminal Voltage – Remove center differential lock switch from instrument panel. See Fig. 13. Turn ignition on. Using voltmeter, backprobe connector. Measure voltage between terminal "A" (Green/Blue wire) and ground. With switch off, battery voltage should be present. With switch on, zero volts should be present. If not correct, check switch continuity.

Testing Continuity – Remove connector from switch. Check continuity between terminals. With switch in ON position there should be continuity. With switch in OFF position, no continuity should exist. If not as specified, replace switch assembly.

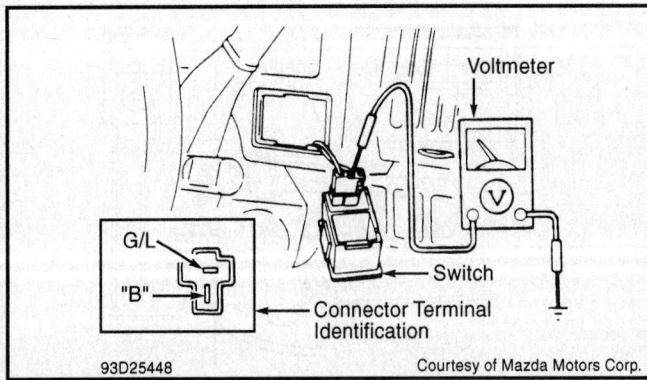

Fig. 13: Testing Center Differential Lock Switch

OVERHAUL

TRANSFER CASE

Disassembly – 1) Remove protector plate, change motor, control cover, companion flange, speedometer driven gear, rear cover and shims. See Fig. 14.

2) Remove speedometer drive gear key and rear chain cover. It may be necessary to tap cover with a plastic hammer to aid in removal. Remove driven gear selective shims. Press out clutch gear. Remove clutch gear needle bearings, magnet, rear oil pipe, change drum and thrust washers.

3) Remove 2-4 shift rod while holding shift fork. Remove 2-4 shift fork. Remove drive gear and chain assembly by lightly tapping on front drive gear sprocket. Remove thrust washer and 3 needle bearings from output shaft. Remove center differential and output shaft assembly. See Fig. 14.

4) Remove pump cover. Clean inner and outer pump rotors for marking purpose. Match mark rotors with correction fluid and remove rotors. Remove key from input gear. Remove pump housing with oil pipes and shims. Remove snap ring from input gear. Press input gear out of input shaft bearing.

NOTE: DO NOT remove input or output shaft bearing unless necessary.

---

5) Remove baffle plate, rear oil pipe and front drive sprocket seal. Press out input and output shaft bearings (if necessary). Change drum oil seal and rear cover oil seal.

COMPONENT DISASSEMBLY, INSPECTION & REASSEMBLY

CENTER DIFFERENTIAL & OUTPUT SHAFT

Disassembly – Remove planetary carrier, needle bearing and thrust washer. See Fig. 15. Remove retaining ring. Install companion flange on output shaft. Hold companion flange with Flange Holder (495120710) and remove lock nut with Universal Wrench (49F0171A0). See Fig. 16. Remove sun gear, ring gear, needle bearing and rear output shaft.

Inspection – 1) Measure clearance between pinion washer and planetary pinion carrier. See Fig. 17. Standard clearance is .008-.028" (.20-.70 mm). Maximum clearance is .031" (.80 mm).

2) Measure inner diameter of ring gear bushing. Standard diameter is 2.1268-2.1281" (54.021-54.055 mm). Maximum diameter 2.13" (54.1 mm). See Fig. 18.

3) Measure rear output shaft, making 3 measurements and figure average value. See Fig. 19. Measure output shaft runout. See Fig. 20. Maximum runout is .0012" (.030 mm).

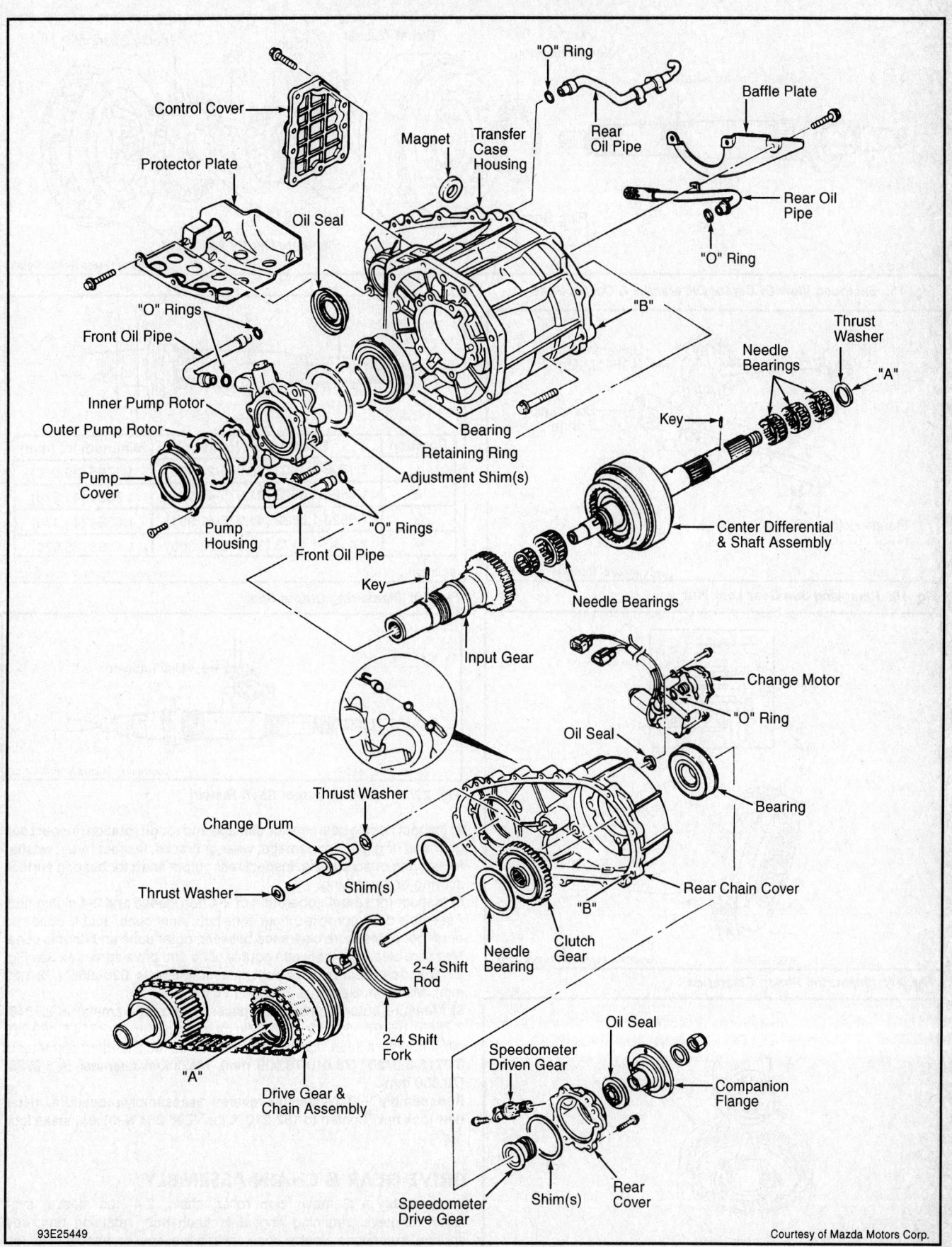

Courtesy of Mazda Motors Corp.

Fig. 14: Exploded View Of R4AX-EL Transfer Case (MPV)

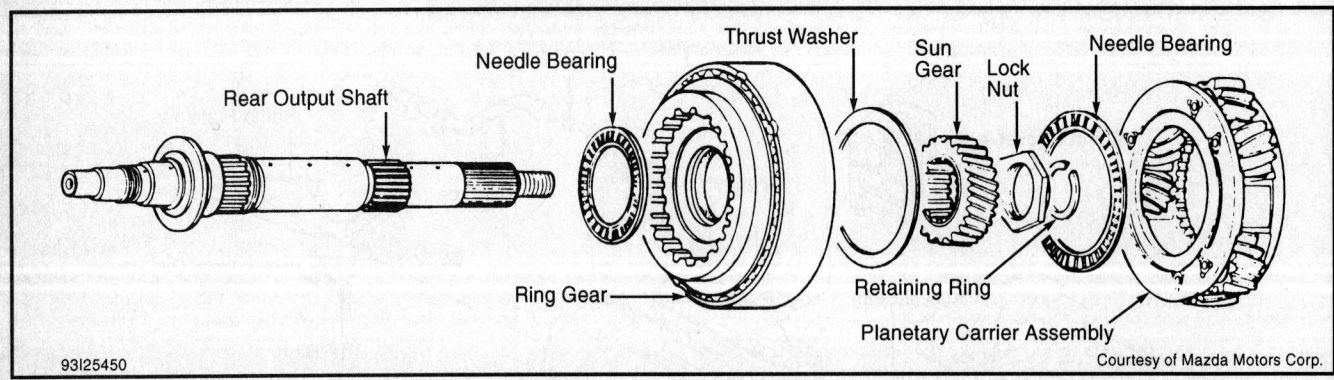

Fig. 15: Exploded View Of Center Differential & Output Shaft

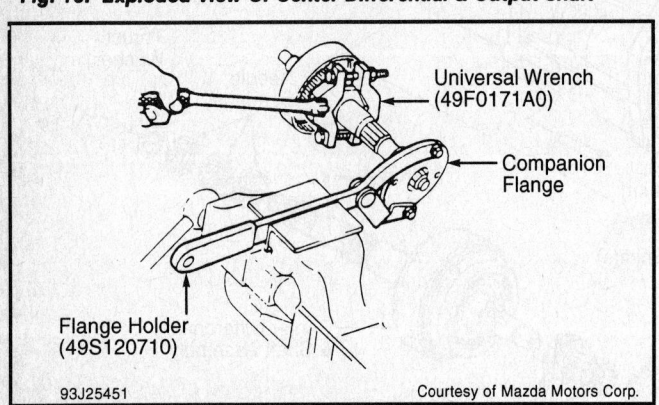

Fig. 16: Removing Sun Gear Lock Nut

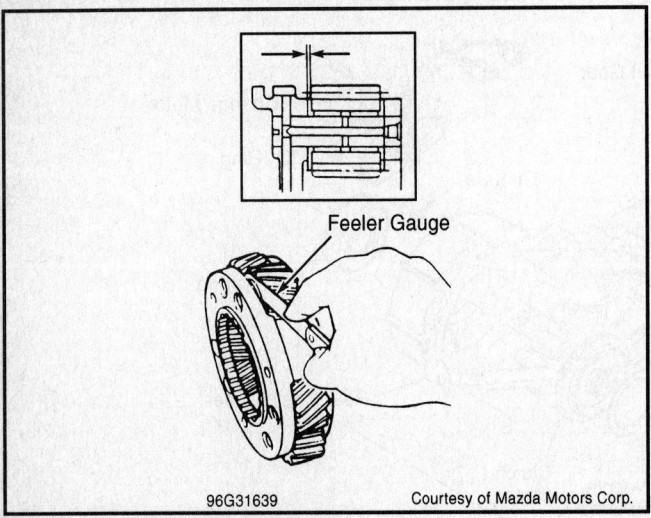

Fig. 17: Measuring Pinion Clearance

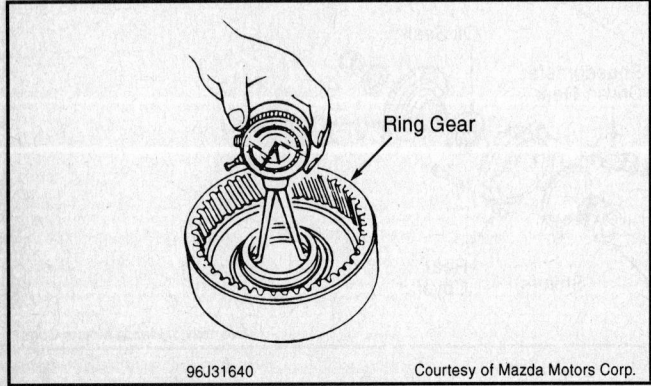

Fig. 18: Measuring Ring Gear Bushing

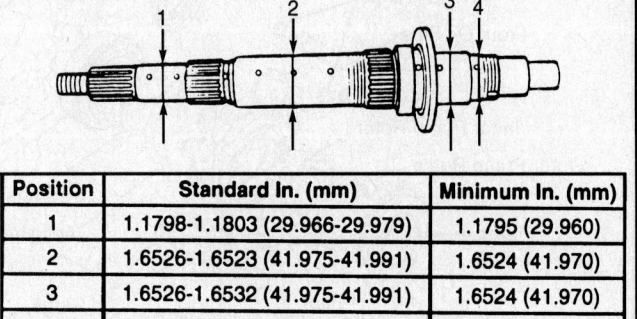

Position	Standard In. (mm)	Minimum In. (mm)
1	1.1798-1.1803 (29.966-29.979)	1.1795 (29.960)
2	1.6526-1.6523 (41.975-41.991)	1.6524 (41.970)
3	1.6526-1.6532 (41.975-41.991)	1.6524 (41.970)
4	1.4163-1.4173 (35.975-36.000)	1.4161 (35.970)

Fig. 19: Measuring Output Shaft

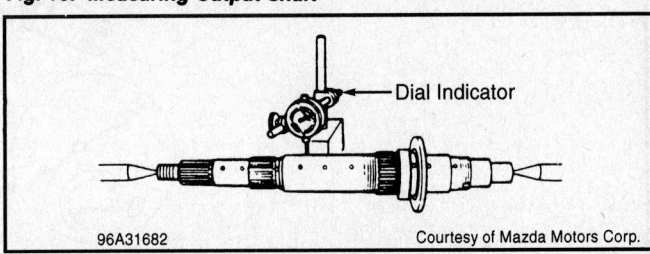

Fig. 20: Measuring Output Shaft Runout

4) Inspect needle bearings for damage and rough rotation. Inspect sun gear and ring gear for damage, wear or cracks. Inspect thrust washer for scoring or scratching. Inspect rear output shaft for bearing surface scoring or scratching.

5) Inspect for smooth operation of 2-4 hub sleeve and 2-4 clutch hub. Assemble drive sprocket, inner cone hub, inner cone, double cone and outer cone. Measure clearance between outer cone and double cone. Measure clearance between double cone and drive sprocket. See Fig. 21. Standard clearance for both measurements is .028-.055" (.72-1.39 mm). Minimum clearance is .027" (.70 mm).

6) Measure outer diameter of spacer. Standard diameter is 2.7548-2.7555" (69.971-69.990 mm). Minimum diameter is 2.7547" (69.970 mm). Measure inner diameter of drive sprocket. Standard diameter is 3.0713-3.0720" (78.010-78.029 mm). Maximum diameter is 3.0720" (78.030 mm).

Reassembly – To assemble reverse disassembly procedure. Install new lock nut. Tighten to 152-210 ft. lbs. (206-284 N.m) and stake lock nut.

DRIVE GEAR & CHAIN ASSEMBLY

Disassembly – Remove cam roller, chain, 2-4 hub sleeve, synchronizer keys, retaining ring, 2-4 clutch hub, retaining ring, key springs, outer cone, double cone, inner cone, spacer, needle bearings and spacer. Remove rear and front bearings. See Fig. 22.

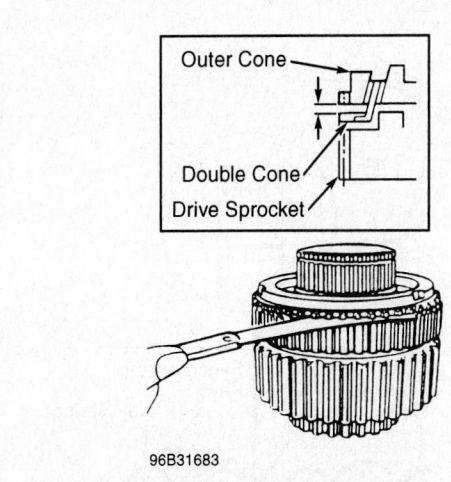

Fig. 21-1: *Measuring Outer Cone-To-Double Cone Clearance*

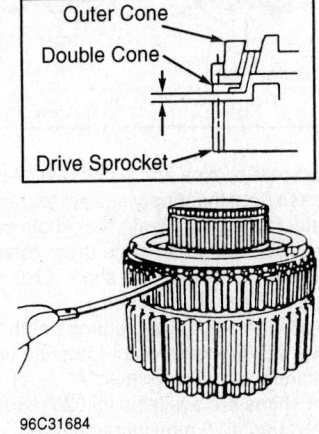

Fig. 21-2: *Measuring Double Cone-To-Drive Sprocket Clearance*

Courtesy of Mazda Motors Corp.

Fig. 21: *Measuring Outer Cone, Double Cone & Drive Sprocket Clearance*

NOTE: *DO NOT remove front or rear bearing on front drive sprocket unless necessary.*

Inspection – 1) Inspect cam roller, needle bearings and front and rear bearings for damage or rough rotation. Inspect synchronizer keys, 2-4 clutch hub, inner cone, inner cone hub and front drive sprocket for damage, wear and cracks. Inspect key springs for fatigue or damage. Inspect spacer for damage, worn or cracked splines.

2) Assemble 2-4 shift fork and rod. Ensure shift fork moves smoothly on rod. Measure inner diameter of shift fork bushing. Standard diameter is .5522-.5550" (14.025-14.096 mm). Maximum diameter is .5551" (14.100 mm). Measure clearance between 2-4 shift fork and hub sleeve. Standard clearance is .004-.022" (.10-.57 mm). Maximum clearance is .031" (.80 mm).

Reassembly – To assemble, reverse disassembly procedure.

PUMP HOUSING

Disassembly & Reassembly – Remove spring cap, gasket, pressure spring and steel ball. Measure spring free length. Spring free length specification is .787" (20.00 mm). Inspect pump housing for signs of wear and repair or replace as necessary. To assemble, reverse disassembly procedure.

TRANSFER CASE REASSEMBLY

1) Install oil seal in rear bearing cover. If bearing was removed install new bearing into rear chain cover. Install seal in rear chain cover. If bearing was removed, install new bearing into transfer case housing. Install oil seal into transfer case housing. See Fig. 14.

2) Install "O" ring on rear oil pipe and install rear oil pipe in transfer case housing. Install baffle plate. Press input gear into case and install new retaining ring on input gear.

3) Measure depth "A" of input shaft bearing bore in pump housing. Measure input shaft bearing height "B". See Fig. 23. Select proper adjustment shim by formula "A" – "B" = 0-.004" (0-.10 mm). Six adjustment shims are available from .020" (.50 mm) to .039" (1.00 mm) in .004" (.10 mm) increments.

4) Assemble inner and outer pump rotors and measure tooth clearance. Standard clearance is .001-.007" (.02-.18 mm). Maximum clearance is .008" (.20 mm). Measure outer rotor-to-pump cover clearance. Standard clearance is .007-.010" (.17-.26 mm). Maximum clearance is .012" (.30 mm). Measure inner and outer rotors-to-pump cover mating surface with a straightedge and feeler gauge. Standard clearance is .001-.003" (.02-.08 mm). Maximum clearance is .004" (.10 mm). See Fig. 14.

5) Install "O" rings on oil pipes and install oil pipes into pump housing. Install adjustment shim(s) in position, guide oil pipes to holes in transfer case housing and install pump housing. Install key in output gear. If reusing inner and outer pump rotors, align match marks. Install inner and outer pump rotors and pump cover. Ensure input shaft rotates smoothly. If not, reinstall pump cover.

6) Install needle bearing on center differential assembly and install center differential into output shaft. Adjust center differential end play by placing needle bearings onto 2-4 clutch hub. Measure height "A". See Fig. 24. Place straightedge on clutch gear and make measurement "B" with feeler gauge. Install needle bearing and thrust washer over output shaft. Install 2-4 clutch hub, needle bearing and clutch gear. Measure clearance "C" between 2-4 clutch hub and clutch gear. Select proper thrust washer(s) by using formula "C" – "A" – "B" = .004-.012" (.10-.30 mm). Seven thrust washers are available from .213" (5.40 mm) to .260" (6.60 mm) in approximately .008" (.20 mm) increments.

7) Remove clutch gear and 2-4 clutch hub. Install proper thrust washers. Assemble 2-4 clutch hub assembly, front drive sprocket and chain. Expand chain with Expansion Tool (495231395). DO NOT overtighten. Install drive gear and chain assembly into transfer case by lightly tapping front drive sprocket with a plastic hammer, keeping chain horizontal. Ensure chain rotates smoothly. See Fig. 14.

8) Install 2-4 shift fork into 2-4 hub sleeve and install 2-4 shift rod. Measure change drum thrust washers thickness. Standard thickness is .0768-.0787" (1.950-2.000 mm). Minimum thickness is .0748" (1.900 mm). Install thrust washers on change drum with grooves facing change drum. Align change drum groove and cam roller of 2-4 shift fork. Install change drum. See Fig. 14.

9) Press clutch gear into rear chain cover with seal driver. Adjust front drive sprocket end play by measuring depth "A" of bearing bore in rear chain cover. See Fig. 25. Install front sprocket into transfer case by tapping lightly with plastic hammer. Measure height "B" between transfer case and front sprocket rear bearing. Select proper adjustment shim by using formula "A" – "B" = 0-.004" (0-.10 mm). Twelve adjustment shims are available from .020" (.50 mm) to .063" (1.60 mm) in approximately .004" (.10 mm) increments. Shims will be installed later.

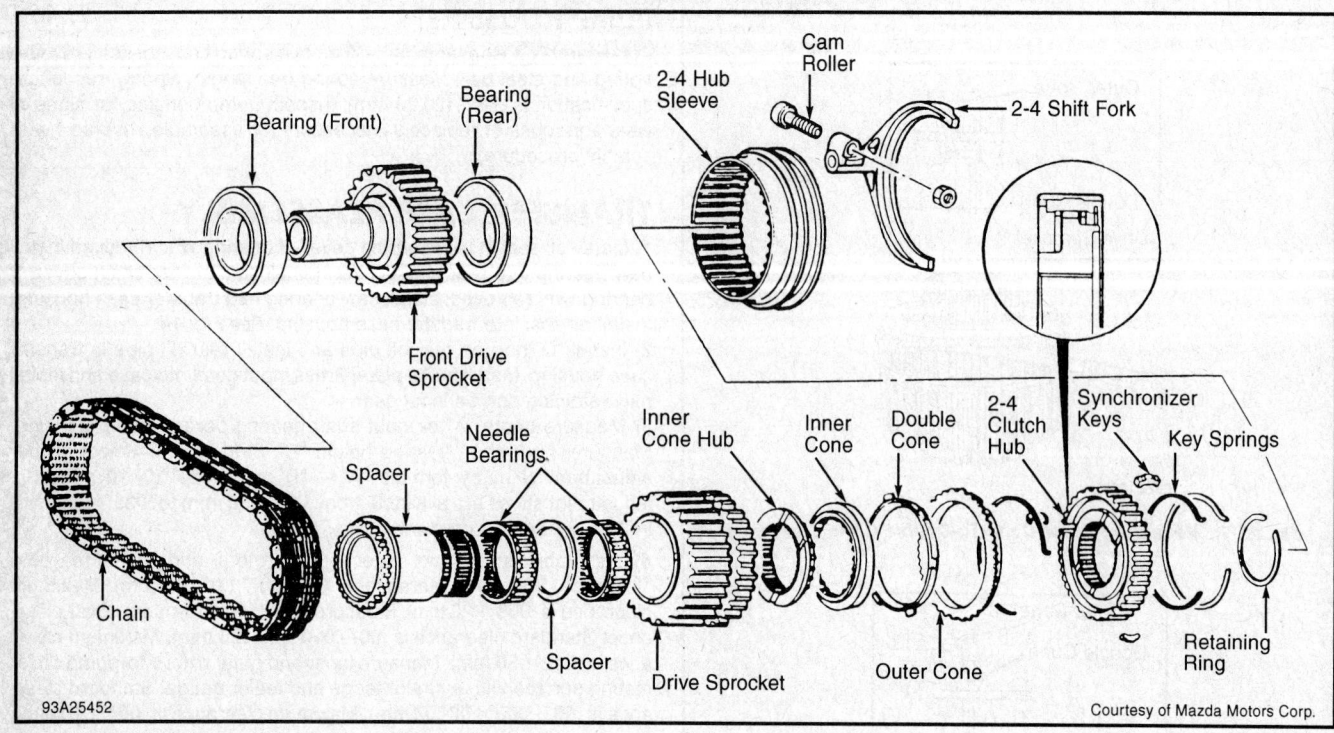

93A25452

Courtesy of Mazda Motors Corp.

Fig. 22: Exploded View Of Drive Gear & Chain Assembly

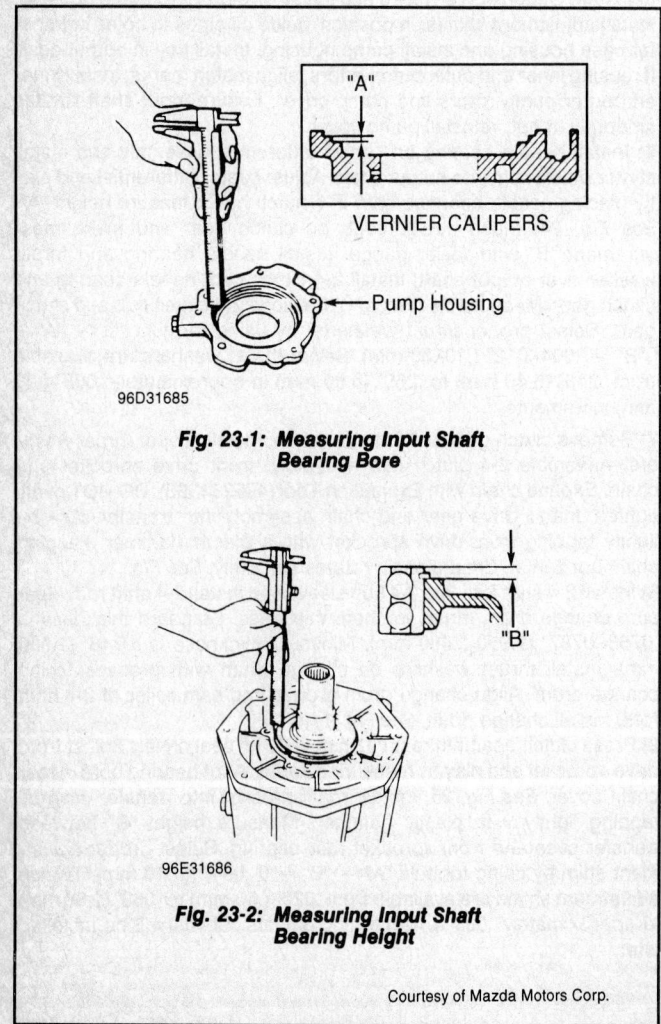

96D31685

Fig. 23-1: Measuring Input Shaft Bearing Bore

96E31686

Fig. 23-2: Measuring Input Shaft Bearing Height

Courtesy of Mazda Motors Corp.

Fig. 23: Measuring Oil Pump Housing

10) Install "O" rings on rear oil pipe and install rear oil pipe. Set magnet into slot in transfer case housing. Apply sealant to transfer case housing. Set shims as selected in step 9) into rear chain cover. Install rear chain cover and brackets. Ensure change drum rotates smoothly by using a screwdriver to turn change drum shaft. If chain drum does not rotate smoothly, reinstall rear chain cover.

11) Adjust output shaft end play by measuring depth "A" in rear cover bearing bore. See Fig. 26. Measure output bearing height "B". Select proper adjustment shim(s) by using formula "A" – "B" = 0-.004" (0-.10 mm). Six adjustment shims are available in .020" (.50 mm) .039" (1.00 mm) in approximately .004" (.10 mm) increments.

12) Install speedometer drive gear key and speedometer drive gear onto output shaft. Set adjustment shim(s) selected in step 11) into rear cover. Apply sealant to rear cover and install rear cover. Install speedometer driven gear. Apply sealant to output shaft splines and install companion flange.

13) Apply sealant to control cover and install control cover and brackets. Align mark on change drum groove with 2H mark. Ensure marks on change motor shaft and body are aligned. See Fig. 9. If not, see Change Motor Installation in CHANGE MOTOR POSITION SWITCH. Install "O" ring on change motor and install change motor. Install protector plate.

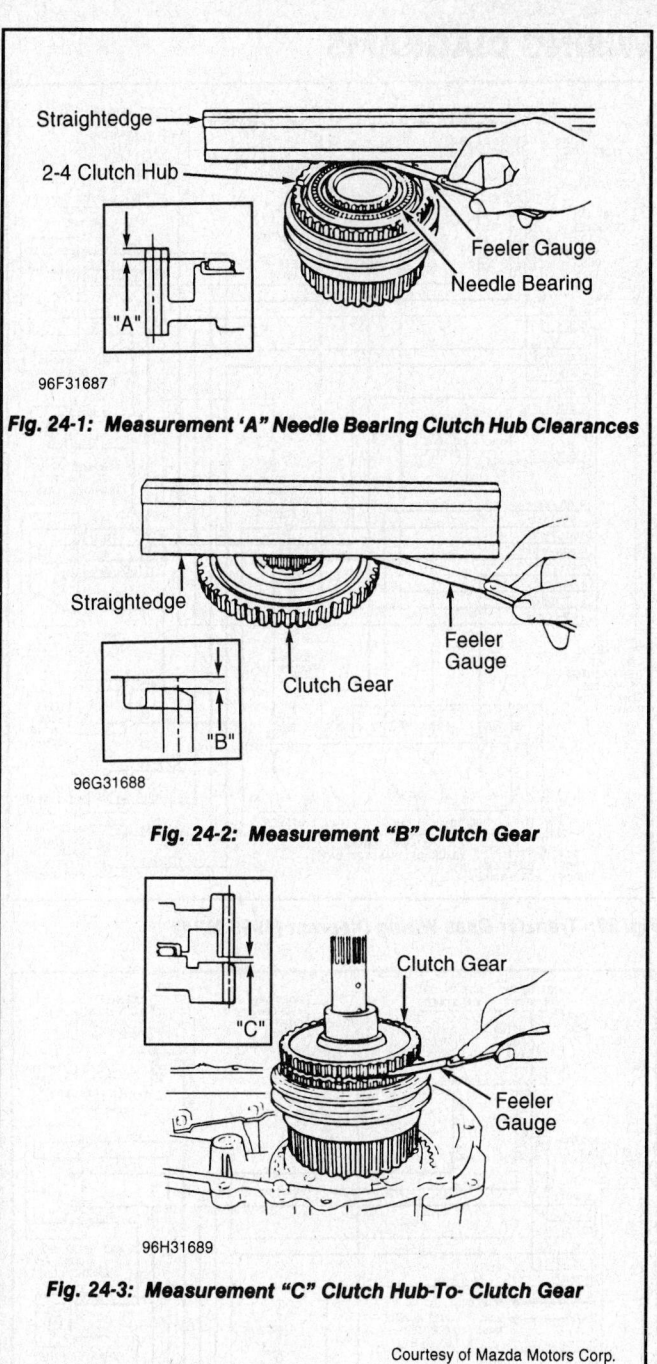

Fig. 24-1: *Measurement 'A" Needle Bearing Clutch Hub Clearances*

Fig. 24-2: *Measurement "B" Clutch Gear*

Fig. 24-3: *Measurement "C" Clutch Hub-To- Clutch Gear*

Courtesy of Mazda Motors Corp.

Fig. 24: *Measuring Clutch Hub Clearances*

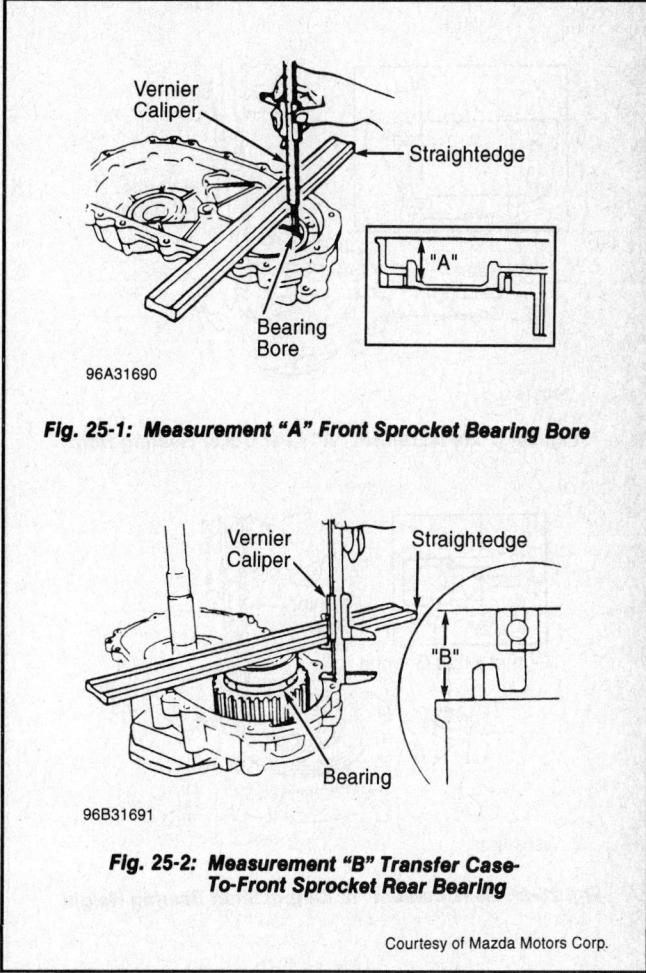

Fig. 25-1: *Measurement "A" Front Sprocket Bearing Bore*

Fig. 25-2: *Measurement "B" Transfer Case-To-Front Sprocket Rear Bearing*

Courtesy of Mazda Motors Corp.

Fig. 25: *Measuring Front Drive Sprocket End Play*

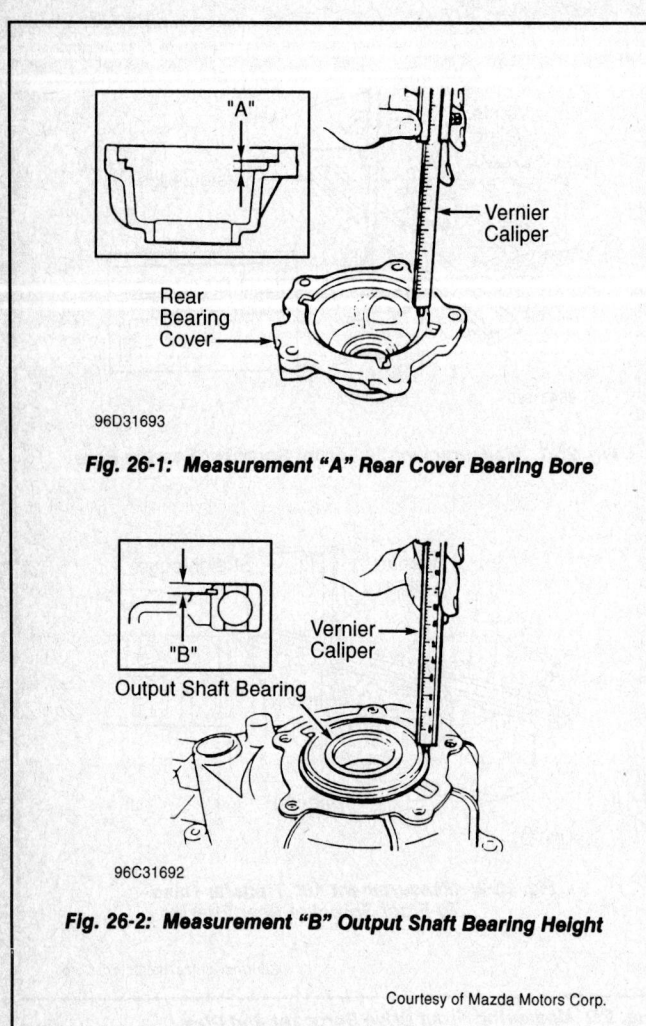

Fig. 26-1: Measurement "A" Rear Cover Bearing Bore

Fig. 26-2: Measurement "B" Output Shaft Bearing Height

Courtesy of Mazda Motors Corp.

Fig. 26: Measuring Output Shaft End Play

TORQUE SPECIFICATIONS
TORQUE SPECIFICATIONS

Application	Ft. Lbs. (N.m)
Case-To-Adapter Bolts	27-40 (36-54)
Case-To-Rear Chain Housing Bolts	23-34 (31-46)
Center Support Bearing Bolts	27-39 (36-53)
Change Motor Bolts	14-18 (19-25)
Companion Flange Nut	94-130 (128-177)
Control Cover Bolts	14-18 (19-25)
Drain Plug	29-44 (39-59)
Drive Shaft Bolts	36-44 (49-59)
Exhaust Pipe-To-Manifold Bolts	15-20 (21-27)
Exhaust Pipe-To-Manifold Nut	25-36 (34-49)
Filler Plug	29-44 (39-59)
Level Plug	14-18 (19-25)
Lower Mount-To-Upper Mount Bolt	23-34 (31-46)
Muffler-To-Exhaust Pipe Nut	23-34 (31-46)
Protector Plate Bolts	32-41 (43-55)
Pump Housing Bolts	14-18 (19-25)
Pump Housing Spring Cap	18-25 (25-34)
Rear Cover Bolts	24-33 (32-46)
Sun Gear Nut	152-209 (206-284)
Sun Gear Nut With Tool (49F0171A0)	137-188 (186-255)
Transmission Lower Mount Bolts	32-45 (43-61)
Transmission Upper Mount Bolts	23-34 (31-46)
	INCH Lbs. (N.m)
Baffle Plate Bolts	69-97 (7.8-11.0)
Cam Roller Lock Nut	69-106 (7.8-12.0)
Heat Insulator Bolts	69-97 (7.8-11.0)
Speedometer Gear-To-Case Bolt	69-97 (7.8-11.0)

WIRING DIAGRAMS

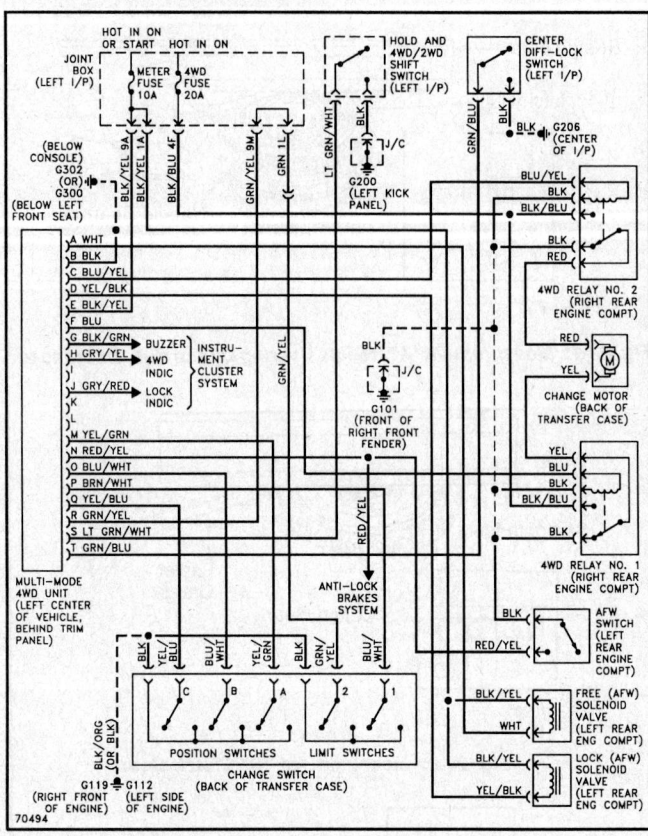

Fig. 27: Transfer Case Wiring Diagram (1995 MPV)

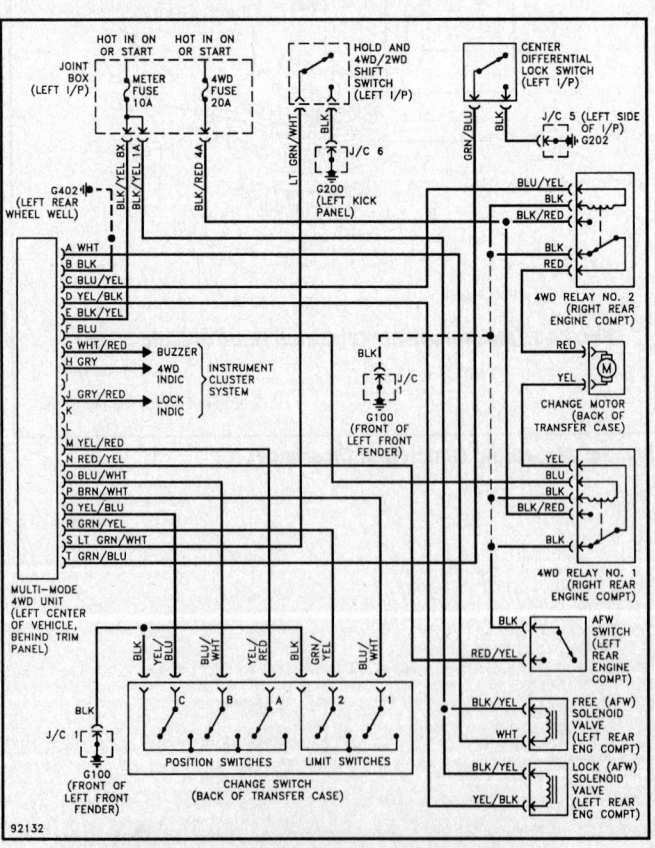

Fig. 28: Transfer Case Wiring Diagram (1996 MPV)

Montero, Pickup

APPLICATION

APPLICATION

Application & Model	Transfer Case Model
Montero	
V4AW3 Transmission	V4AW3-7
V4AW2 Transmission	V4AW2-7
V5MT1 Transmission	V5MT1-6
1995 Pickup	V5MT1-2

DESCRIPTION

Transfer case is a part-time, 2-speed unit with a 3-piece aluminum case. Transfer case has a floor-mounted shifter and integral speedometer gear. In Montero a Viscous Coupling Unit (VCU) and center differential allows 2WD-to-4WD shifting at speeds under 62 MPH and full-time 4WD operation.

WARNING: When battery is disconnected, vehicles equipped with computers may lose memory data. When battery power is restored, driveability problems may exist on some vehicles. These vehicles may require a relearn procedure. See COMPUTER RELEARN PROCEDURES in APPLICATIONS & IDENTIFICATION section.

TESTING

4WD INDICATOR CONTROL UNIT (MONTERO)

The 4WD indicator control unit is located behind radio or CD player. Remove 4WD indicator control unit and disconnect harness. Back-probe harness connector and measure voltage between terminal No. 8 (ground) and each respective terminal. See Fig. 1.

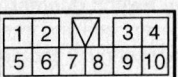

CONTROL UNIT SIDE

NOTE: Battery positive voltage marked with (*) is 1-2 volts lower than actual battery positive voltage.

Terminal No.	Inspection item		Inspection condition			Terminal voltage
3	Ignition switch (IG2)		Ignition switch (IG2)		OFF	0 V
					ON	Battery positive voltage
4	Combination meter (4WD indicator lamp)	Center differential lock indicator lamp	Ignition switch: ON	Transfer lever position	4H	Battery positive voltage
					4HLc	Less than 1.5V
10		Front wheel lamp	Ignition switch: ON		In 2WD	0 V
					In 4WD	Battery positive voltage*
9		Rear wheel lamp	Ignition switch: ON	Transfer lever position	N	0 V
					4HLc, 4LLc	Battery positive voltage*
6	Free-wheel engage switch		Ignition switch: ON		In 2WD	Battery positive voltage*
					In 4WD	0 V
1	HI/LOW detection switch		Ignition switch: ON	Transfer lever position	N	Battery positive voltage*
					4HLc, 4LLc	0 V
2	4WD operation detection switch		Ignition switch: ON	Transfer lever position	2H	Battery positive voltage*
					4H	0 V
5	Center differential lock detection switch		Ignition switch: ON	Transfer lever position	4H	Battery positive voltage*
					4HLc	0 V
7	Center differential lock operation detection switch		Ignition switch: ON	Transfer lever position	4H	Battery positive voltage*
					4HLc	0 V

93J25576

Courtesy of Mitsubishi Motor Sales of America.

Fig. 1: 4WD Indicator Control Unit Testing (Montero)

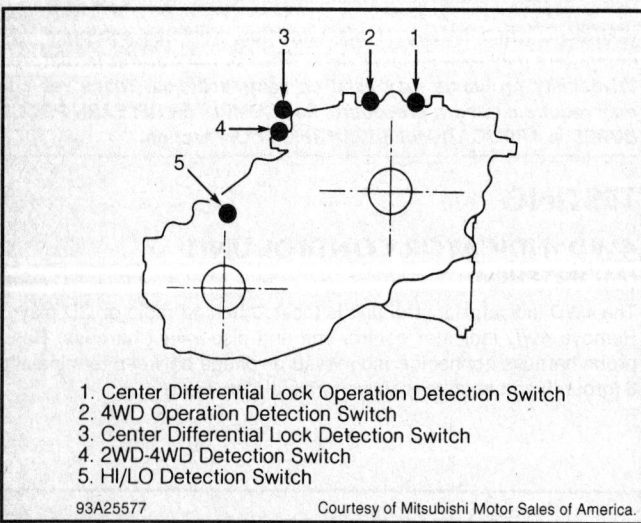

1. Center Differential Lock Operation Detection Switch
2. 4WD Operation Detection Switch
3. Center Differential Lock Detection Switch
4. 2WD-4WD Detection Switch
5. HI/LO Detection Switch

93A25577   Courtesy of Mitsubishi Motor Sales of America.

Fig. 2: Detection Switch Testing Locations (Montero)

DETECTION SWITCH

NOTE: With switch removed, check continuity between switch connector terminal and switch body. With switch installed, check continuity between switch connector terminal and transfer case.

4WD Indicator Light Switch (Pickup) – Remove switch. *See Fig. 3.* Check continuity between connector terminal and switch body. With switch end pressed, continuity should not exist. With switch end released, continuity should exist.

Center Differential Lock Operation Detection Switch (Montero) – Check continuity between Brown wire connector terminal and transfer case. With transfer control lever in "4H" position, continuity should not exist. With transfer control lever in "4HLc" position, continuity should exist. *See Fig. 2.*

4WD Operation Detection Switch (Montero) – Check continuity between Black wire connector terminal and transfer case. With transfer control lever in "2H" position, continuity should not exist. With transfer control lever in "4H" position, continuity should exist. *See Fig. 2.*

Center Differential Lock Detection Switch (Montero) – Check continuity between Brown wire connector terminal and transfer case. With transfer control lever in "4H" position, continuity should not exist. With transfer control lever in "4HLc" position, continuity should exist. *See Fig. 2.*

2WD-4WD Detection Switch (Montero) – Check continuity between Black wire connector terminal and transfer case. With transfer control lever in "4H" position, continuity should not exist. With transfer control lever in "2H" position, continuity should exist. *See Fig. 2.*

HI/LO Detection Switch (Montero) – Check continuity between White wire connector terminal and transfer case. With transfer control lever in "N" (between "4HLc" and "4LLc") position, continuity should not

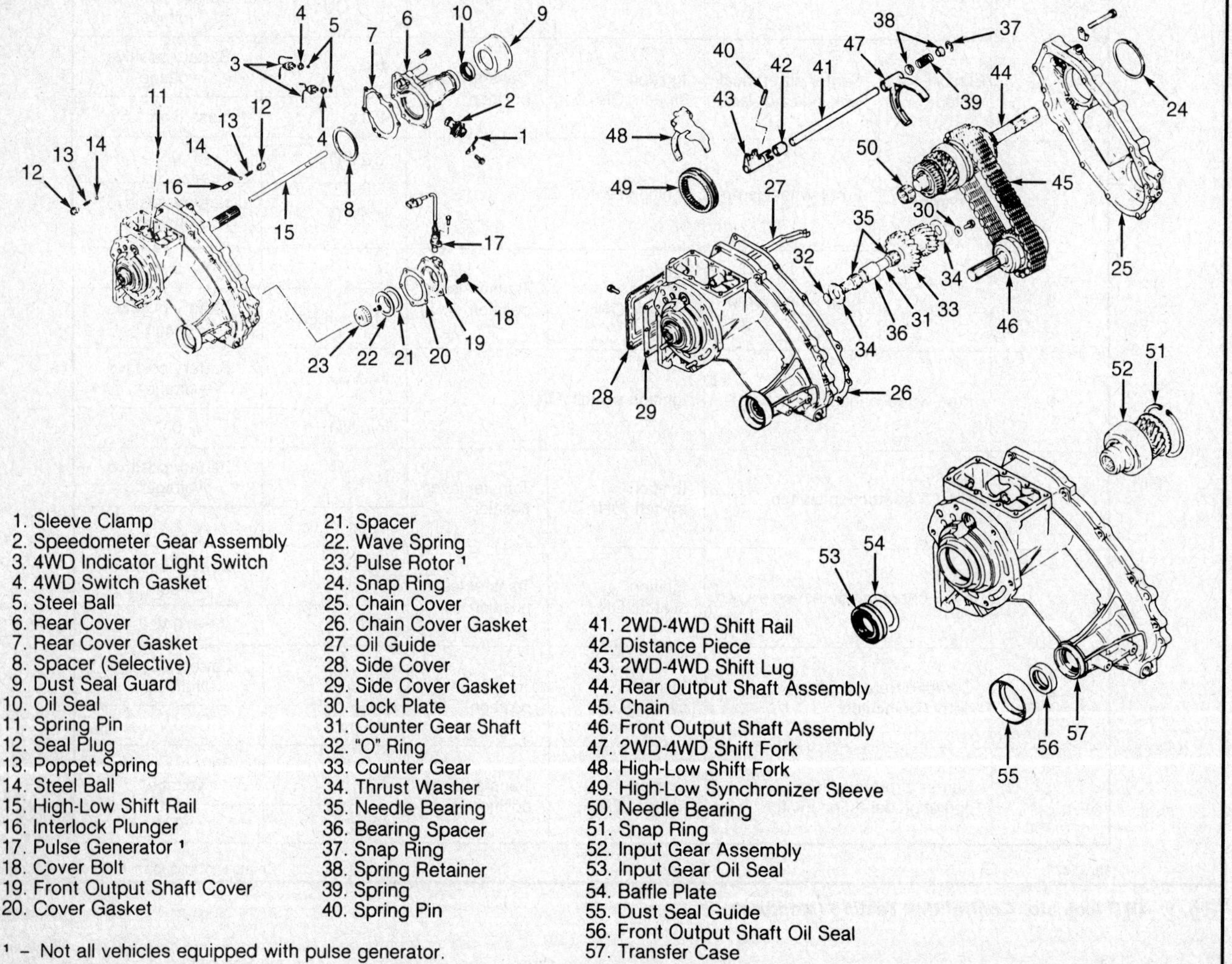

1. Sleeve Clamp
2. Speedometer Gear Assembly
3. 4WD Indicator Light Switch
4. 4WD Switch Gasket
5. Steel Ball
6. Rear Cover
7. Rear Cover Gasket
8. Spacer (Selective)
9. Dust Seal Guard
10. Oil Seal
11. Spring Pin
12. Seal Plug
13. Poppet Spring
14. Steel Ball
15. High-Low Shift Rail
16. Interlock Plunger
17. Pulse Generator [1]
18. Cover Bolt
19. Front Output Shaft Cover
20. Cover Gasket
21. Spacer
22. Wave Spring
23. Pulse Rotor [1]
24. Snap Ring
25. Chain Cover
26. Chain Cover Gasket
27. Oil Guide
28. Side Cover
29. Side Cover Gasket
30. Lock Plate
31. Counter Gear Shaft
32. "O" Ring
33. Counter Gear
34. Thrust Washer
35. Needle Bearing
36. Bearing Spacer
37. Snap Ring
38. Spring Retainer
39. Spring
40. Spring Pin
41. 2WD-4WD Shift Rail
42. Distance Piece
43. 2WD-4WD Shift Lug
44. Rear Output Shaft Assembly
45. Chain
46. Front Output Shaft Assembly
47. 2WD-4WD Shift Fork
48. High-Low Shift Fork
49. High-Low Synchronizer Sleeve
50. Needle Bearing
51. Snap Ring
52. Input Gear Assembly
53. Input Gear Oil Seal
54. Baffle Plate
55. Dust Seal Guide
56. Front Output Shaft Oil Seal
57. Transfer Case

[1] – Not all vehicles equipped with pulse generator.

93B25578   Courtesy of Mitsubishi Motor Sales of America.

Fig. 3: Exploded View Of Transfer Case (V5MT1-2)

exist. With transfer control lever in "4HLc" position, continuity should exist. With transfer control lever in "4LLc" position, continuity should exist. *See Fig. 2.*

REMOVAL & INSTALLATION

Removal – 1) Remove negative battery cable. Remove transfer case skid plate (if equipped). Scribe alignment marks and remove both drive shafts. Drain oil from transfer case. Disconnect wiring harness from back-up light switch, all 4WD switches and any other electrical connectors (if equipped).

2) Disconnect speedometer cable from drive. Unclip cable from case. Place transfer case shifter in "2H" position and transmission in Neutral. Remove 6 bolts holding control lever assembly. Remove control lever assembly and gasket.

3) Remove select plunger bore plug at right side of case. Remove select spring and plunger. Remove change shifter spring pin. Remove change shifter. Remove transfer case mount. Remove 4 bolts and 2 nuts holding transfer case to adapter. Remove transfer case from vehicle.

Installation – 1) Position transmission shifter in Neutral and transfer case lever in "2H" position. Install neutral return plungers and springs in holes on top of adapter. Tighten plug until it is flush with adapter surface. Cover plug threads with sealant.

2) Coat inside of change shifter with grease. Ensure change shifter pin protrudes 1/8" above change shifter when installed. Mount detent plunger spring and install plug (if equipped). To complete installation, reverse removal procedure. Fill transfer case with API GL-4 or higher 75W-90 or 75W-85W gear oil.

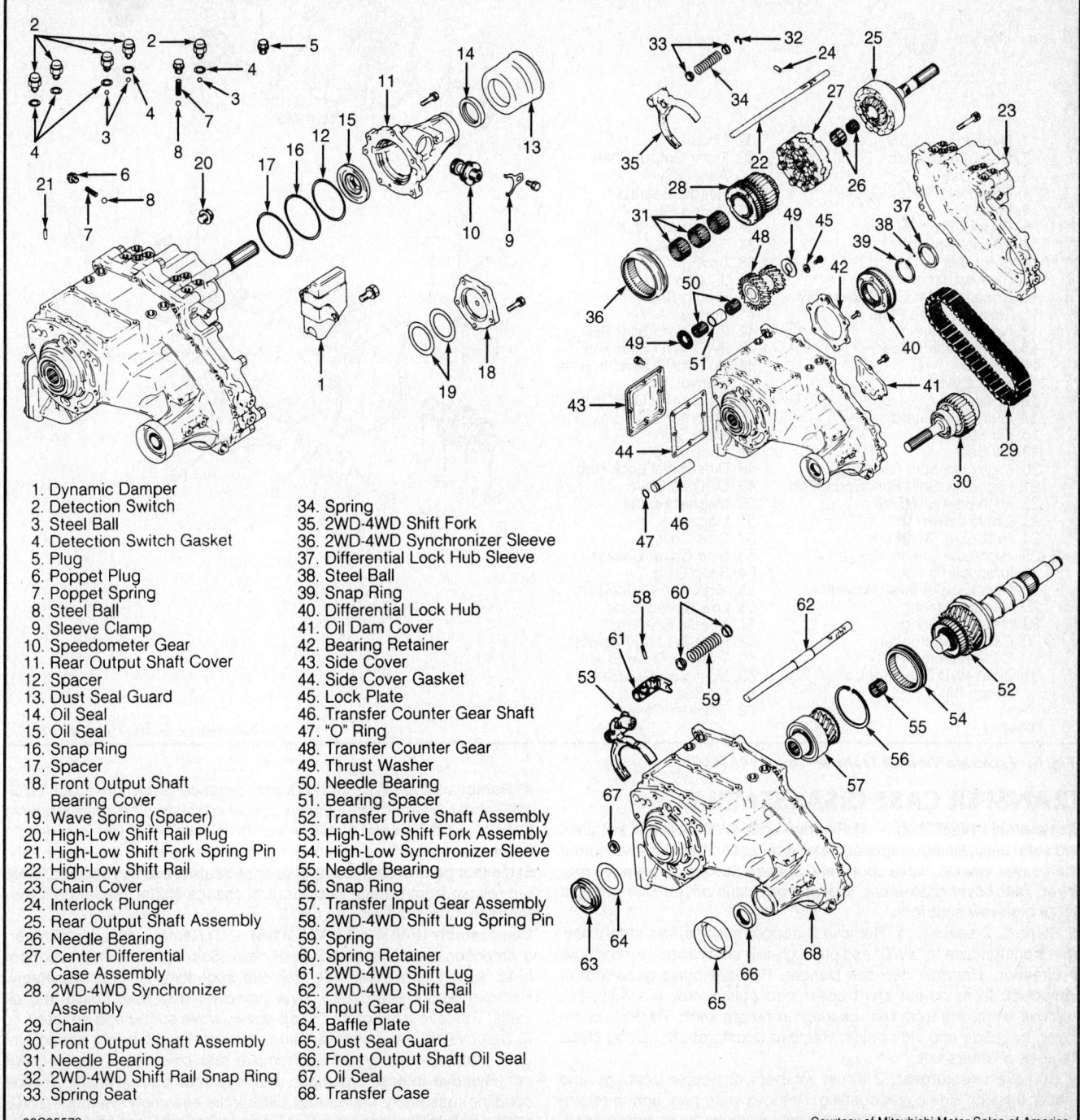

1. Dynamic Damper
2. Detection Switch
3. Steel Ball
4. Detection Switch Gasket
5. Plug
6. Poppet Plug
7. Poppet Spring
8. Steel Ball
9. Sleeve Clamp
10. Speedometer Gear
11. Rear Output Shaft Cover
12. Spacer
13. Dust Seal Guard
14. Oil Seal
15. Oil Seal
16. Snap Ring
17. Spacer
18. Front Output Shaft Bearing Cover
19. Wave Spring (Spacer)
20. High-Low Shift Rail Plug
21. High-Low Shift Fork Spring Pin
22. High-Low Shift Rail
23. Chain Cover
24. Interlock Plunger
25. Rear Output Shaft Assembly
26. Needle Bearing
27. Center Differential Case Assembly
28. 2WD-4WD Synchronizer Assembly
29. Chain
30. Front Output Shaft Assembly
31. Needle Bearing
32. 2WD-4WD Shift Rail Snap Ring
33. Spring Seat
34. Spring
35. 2WD-4WD Shift Fork
36. 2WD-4WD Synchronizer Sleeve
37. Differential Lock Hub Sleeve
38. Steel Ball
39. Snap Ring
40. Differential Lock Hub
41. Oil Dam Cover
42. Bearing Retainer
43. Side Cover
44. Side Cover Gasket
45. Lock Plate
46. Transfer Counter Gear Shaft
47. "O" Ring
48. Transfer Counter Gear
49. Thrust Washer
50. Needle Bearing
51. Bearing Spacer
52. Transfer Drive Shaft Assembly
53. High-Low Shift Fork Assembly
54. High-Low Synchronizer Sleeve
55. Needle Bearing
56. Snap Ring
57. Transfer Input Gear Assembly
58. 2WD-4WD Shift Lug Spring Pin
59. Spring
60. Spring Retainer
61. 2WD-4WD Shift Lug
62. 2WD-4WD Shift Rail
63. Input Gear Oil Seal
64. Baffle Plate
65. Dust Seal Guard
66. Front Output Shaft Oil Seal
67. Oil Seal
68. Transfer Case

93C25579

Courtesy of Mitsubishi Motor Sales of America.

Fig. 4: Exploded View Of Transfer Case (V4AW2-7 & V5MT1-6)

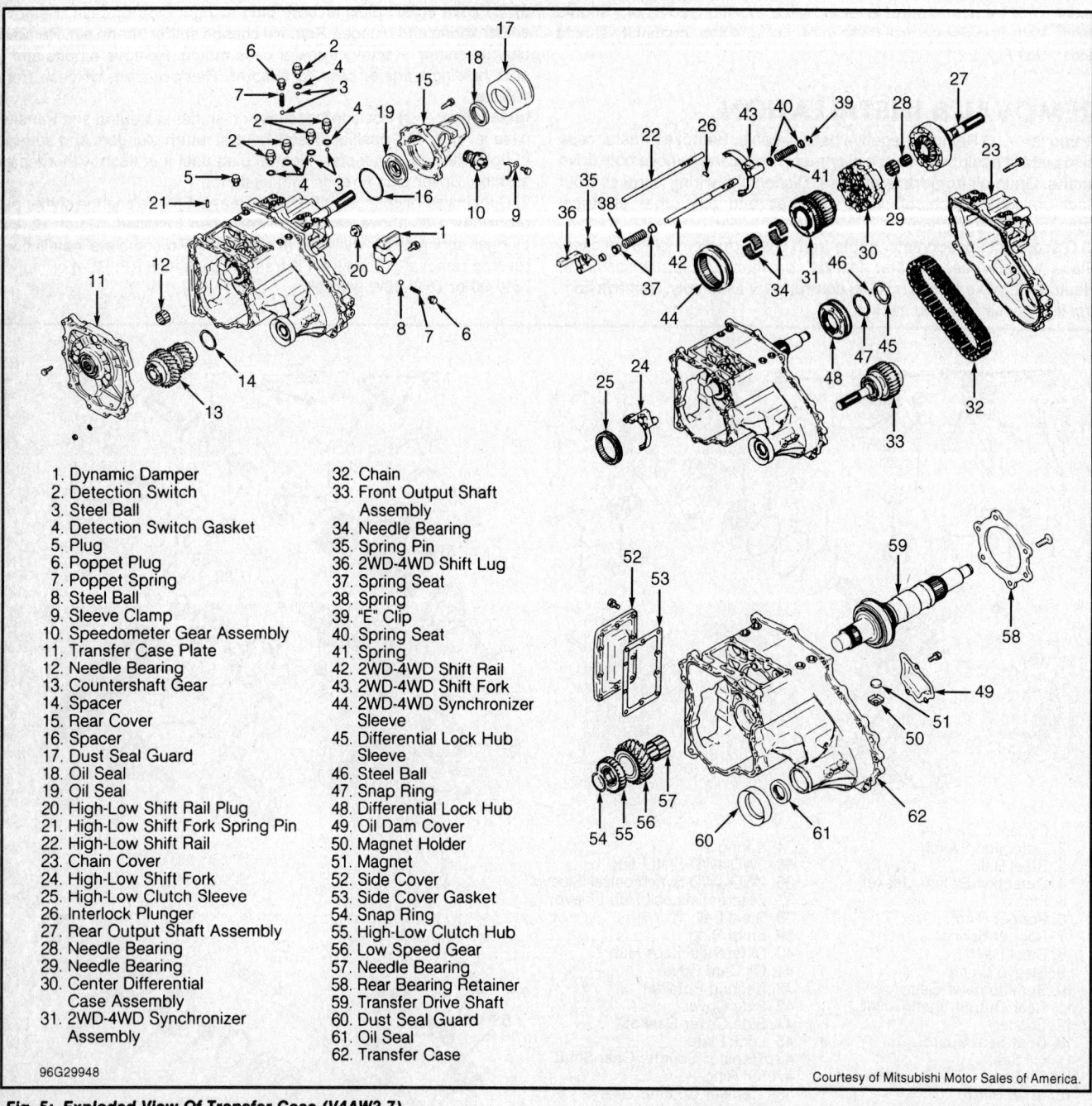

1. Dynamic Damper
2. Detection Switch
3. Steel Ball
4. Detection Switch Gasket
5. Plug
6. Poppet Plug
7. Poppet Spring
8. Steel Ball
9. Sleeve Clamp
10. Speedometer Gear Assembly
11. Transfer Case Plate
12. Needle Bearing
13. Countershaft Gear
14. Spacer
15. Rear Cover
16. Spacer
17. Dust Seal Guard
18. Oil Seal
19. Oil Seal
20. High-Low Shift Rail Plug
21. High-Low Shift Fork Spring Pin
22. High-Low Shift Rail
23. Chain Cover
24. High-Low Shift Fork
25. High-Low Clutch Sleeve
26. Interlock Plunger
27. Rear Output Shaft Assembly
28. Needle Bearing
29. Needle Bearing
30. Center Differential
    Case Assembly
31. 2WD-4WD Synchronizer
    Assembly

32. Chain
33. Front Output Shaft
    Assembly
34. Needle Bearing
35. Spring Pin
36. 2WD-4WD Shift Lug
37. Spring Seat
38. Spring
39. "E" Clip
40. Spring Seat
41. Spring
42. 2WD-4WD Shift Rail
43. 2WD-4WD Shift Fork
44. 2WD-4WD Synchronizer
    Sleeve
45. Differential Lock Hub
    Sleeve
46. Steel Ball
47. Snap Ring
48. Differential Lock Hub
49. Oil Dam Cover
50. Magnet Holder
51. Magnet
52. Side Cover
53. Side Cover Gasket
54. Snap Ring
55. High-Low Clutch Hub
56. Low Speed Gear
57. Needle Bearing
58. Rear Bearing Retainer
59. Transfer Drive Shaft
60. Dust Seal Guard
61. Oil Seal
62. Transfer Case

96G29948

Courtesy of Mitsubishi Motor Sales of America.

Fig. 5: Exploded View Of Transfer Case (V4AW3-7)

TRANSFER CASE DISASSEMBLY

Disassembly (V5MT1-2) – **1)** Remove both 4WD indicator switches and steel balls. Remove speedometer gear assembly. Remove output shaft cover, gasket, wave spring and spacer. *See Fig. 3.* Remove rear cover, rear cover gasket and spacer from chain cover. Drive roll pin out of high-low shift fork.

2) Remove 2 seal plugs. Remove 2 poppet springs and steel balls. Shift transfer case to "4WD" and pull high-low shift rail out, in rear cover direction. Remove interlock plunger. Remove pulse generator (if equipped), front output shaft cover and pulse rotor (if equipped). Remove snap ring from rear bearing on output shaft. Remove chain cover, oil guide and side cover. Remove countershaft locking plate. Remove countershaft.

3) Remove countergear, 2 thrust washers, 2 needle bearings and spacer through side cover opening. Remove snap ring, spring retainers and spring from 2WD-4WD shift rail. Remove front output shaft, rear output shaft and chain as assembly.

4) Remove 2WD-4WD shift fork and distance piece. Drive out 2WD-4WD shift rail spring pin. Remove 2WD-4WD shift rail and lug. Remove high-low shift fork and high-low synchronizer sleeve. Remove needle bearing and snap ring from input gear. Remove input gear assembly.

5) If either control shaft or input gear oil seals are to be replaced, drive out roll pin from transmission control change shifter. Separate transfer case from adapter. *See Fig. 3.*

Disassembly (V4AW2-7 & V5TM1-6) – **1)** Remove dynamic damper, 5 detection switches and 3 steel balls. *See Fig. 4.* Remove poppet plug, spring and steel ball. Remove speedometer gear assembly. Remove output shaft rear cover, spacers, dust seal guard and oil seals. Remove front output shaft cover, wave spring and spacer.

2) Remove high-low shift rail plug and high-low shift fork spring pin. Shift transfer case to "4WD". Remove rear cover and high-low shift rail. Remove interlock plunger. Remove rear output shaft (viscous coupling) assembly and center differential assembly. Remove 2WD-4WD synchronizer assembly, chain and front output shaft from transmission as a unit. With White paint make match marks in grooves of

2WD-4WD synchronizer in 3 places. With White paint make match marks on spline projections of 2WD-4WD synchronizer sleeve in 3 places. Refer to match marks during reassembly.

3) Remove snap ring, spring seat, spring, 2WD-4WD shift fork and 2WD-4WD synchronizer sleeve. Remove differential lock hub, oil dam cover and bearing retainer. Remove side cover and gasket. Remove transfer counter gear shaft, transfer counter gear, thrust washer, needle bearings and spacer. Remove transfer drive shaft assembly. Remove high-low shift fork assembly and clutch sleeve. Remove transfer input gear assembly.

4) Remove 2WD-4WD shift lug spring pin, spring, spring retainer 2WD-4WD shift lug and shift rail. Remove input gear oil seal, baffle plate, dust seal guard and front output shaft oil seal. *See Fig. 4.*

Disassembly (V4AW3-7) – **1)** Remove dynamic damper, 5 detection switches and 3 steel balls. *See Fig. 5.* Remove poppet plug, spring and steel ball. Remove speedometer gear assembly.

2) Remove transfer case plate and needle bearing. Remove countershaft gear. Remove output shaft rear cover, spacers, dust seal guard and oil seals. Remove front output shaft cover, wave spring and spacer.

3) Remove high-low shift rail plug and high-low shift fork spring pin. Shift transfer case to "4WD". Remove rear cover and high-low shift rail. Remove chain cover. Remove high-low shift fork and sleeve.

4) Remove interlock plunger. Remove rear output shaft (viscous coupling) assembly and center differential assembly. Remove 2WD-4WD synchronizer assembly, chain and front output shaft from transmission as a unit.

5) With White paint make match marks in grooves of 2WD-4WD synchronizer in 3 places. With White paint make match marks on spline projections of 2WD-4WD synchronizer sleeve in 3 places. Refer to match marks during reassembly.

6) Remove spring pin and 2WD-4WD shift lug. Remove snap ring, spring seat, spring, 2WD-4WD shift fork and 2WD-4WD synchronizer sleeve. Remove differential lock hub, oil dam cover and bearing retainer. Remove side cover and gasket.

7) Remove snap ring and high-low clutch hub. Remove low speed gear and transfer drive shaft. Remove input gear oil seal, dust seal guard and front output shaft oil seal. *See Fig. 5.*

COMPONENT DISASSEMBLY & REASSEMBLY

OUTPUT SHAFT ASSEMBLY (MONTERO)

Disassembly & Reassembly (Rear Shaft) – Remove snap ring and press ball bearing off without putting pressure on vicious coupling. Remove viscous coupling. To install, reverse removal procedure. When installing new snap ring, select thickest ring that will fit into groove. Acceptable clearance is 0-.003" (0-.08 mm).

Disassembly & Reassembly (Front Shaft) – Remove front bearing. Remove rear bearing. To install reverse removal procedure.

OUTPUT SHAFT ASSEMBLY (V5MT1-2)

Disassembly – **1)** Remove snap ring from rear of output shaft. Remove high-low synchronizer hub by hand or when low speed gear is pressed off. Remove bearing spacer and needle bearing. Remove staking from lock nut on rear output shaft. *See Fig. 6.*

2) Remove lock nut. Remove ball bearing from below lock nut. Remove sprocket spacer and steel ball. Remove drive sprocket, 2 needle bearings, sprocket sleeve and steel ball. Remove 2WD-4WD synchronizer sleeve, hub, stopper plate and ball bearing.

Reassembly – **1)** Press ball bearing and stopper plate on front output shaft, pushing against inner race. After fitting, ensure bearing rotates smoothly. Install 2WD-4WD synchronizer hub and sleeve. Ensure hub and sleeve face correct direction. Install steel ball (for sprocket sleeve positioning) on rear output shaft. Install sprocket sleeve.

2) Install 2 needle bearings on outer circumference of sprocket sleeve. Install drive sprocket. Install steel ball and sprocket spacer. Install ball bearing (press may not be needed as bearing may be loose). Check for smooth rotation.

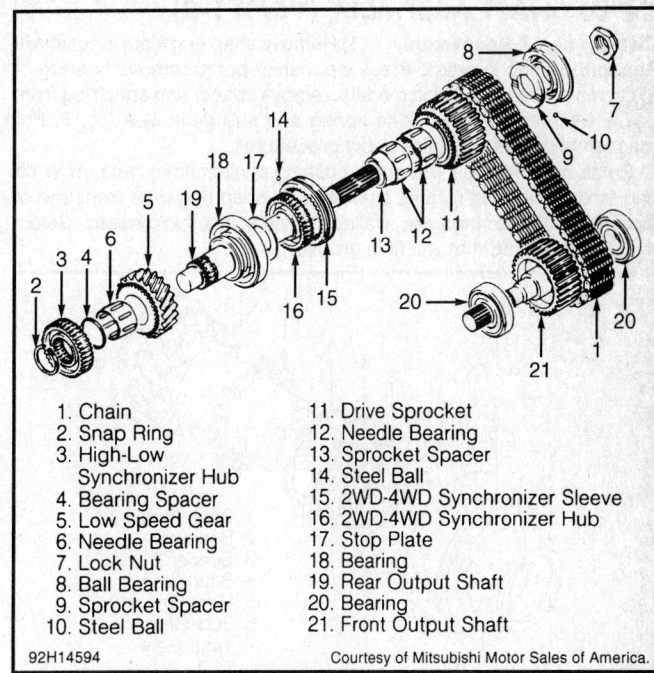

1. Chain
2. Snap Ring
3. High-Low Synchronizer Hub
4. Bearing Spacer
5. Low Speed Gear
6. Needle Bearing
7. Lock Nut
8. Ball Bearing
9. Sprocket Spacer
10. Steel Ball
11. Drive Sprocket
12. Needle Bearing
13. Sprocket Spacer
14. Steel Ball
15. 2WD-4WD Synchronizer Sleeve
16. 2WD-4WD Synchronizer Hub
17. Stop Plate
18. Bearing
19. Rear Output Shaft
20. Bearing
21. Front Output Shaft

92H14594   Courtesy of Mitsubishi Motor Sales of America.

Fig. 6: Exploded View Of Output Shaft Assembly (V5MT1-2)

3) Tighten lock nut to specification. See TORQUE SPECIFICATIONS. Stake lock nut with punch. After lock nut is tightened, ensure drive sprocket rotates smoothly. Install needle bearing, thrust washer and low speed gear on rear of rear output shaft.

4) Install needle bearing, thrust washer and low speed gear on rear output shaft. Mount high-low synchronizer hub. Ensure hub faces correct direction.

5) Mount high-low synchronizer hub snap ring on front end of rear output shaft. Selective fit snap rings are available in 5 thicknesses. Use thickest snap ring that will fit into output shaft groove. Acceptable clearance is 0-.003" (0-.08 mm). *See Fig. 6.*

TRANSFER CASE PLATE (V4AW3-7)

Disassembly & Reassembly – Remove bearing retainer bolts and bearing retainer. Remove input transfer gear. Remove oil seal and baffle plate. *See Fig. 7.* To reassemble, reverse disassembly procedure. Apply Sealant (MD997740) to bearing retainer bolt threads before installing. Torque bearing retainer bolts to 14 ft. lbs. (19 N.m).

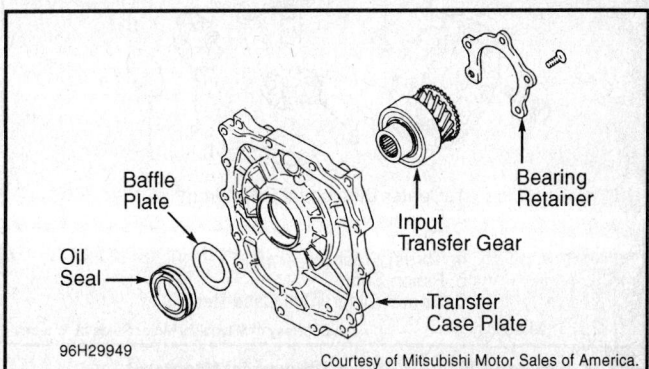

Baffle Plate

Oil Seal

Input Transfer Gear

Bearing Retainer

Transfer Case Plate

96H29949   Courtesy of Mitsubishi Motor Sales of America.

Fig. 7: Exploded View Of Transfer Case Plate (V4AW3-7)

TRANSFER DRIVE SHAFT (MONTERO)

Disassembly & Reassembly – Remove snap ring, high-low synchronizer hub and low speed gear. Remove bearing spacer, needle bearing and ball bearing. To assemble, reverse disassembly procedure. Use thickest snap ring that will fit into output shaft groove. Acceptable clearance is 0-.0024" (0-.06 mm).

TRANSFER CASES
Mitsubishi (Cont.)

INPUT SHAFT ASSEMBLY (V5MT1-2)

Disassembly & Reassembly – **1)** Remove snap ring from input shaft. Support bearing in press. Press input shaft out to remove bearing.

2) On manual transmission models, remove spacer and snap ring from below bearing. Remove cone spring and sub gear. *See Fig. 8.* For reassembly, reverse disassembly procedures.

3) Press bearing into input shaft, pushing against inner race. After fitting, ensure bearing rotates smoothly. Fit snap ring over front end of input shaft. Snap rings are available in selective thicknesses. Select thickest snap ring that will fit in groove.

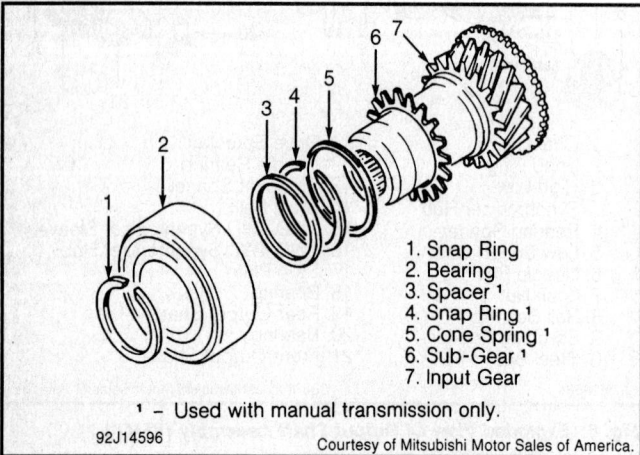

1. Snap Ring
2. Bearing
3. Spacer [1]
4. Snap Ring [1]
5. Cone Spring [1]
6. Sub-Gear [1]
7. Input Gear

[1] – Used with manual transmission only.

92J14596   Courtesy of Mitsubishi Motor Sales of America.

Fig. 8: Exploded View Of Input Shaft Assembly (V5MT1-2)

CENTER DIFFERENTIAL CASE (MONTERO)

Disassembly & Reassembly – Separate center differential case front from rear case. Remove pinion shaft, pinions, thrust washers and dowel pins. Inspect for excessive wear and replace parts as needed. Align dowel pins and match marks on outer case circumferences. Assemble front and rear center differential cases. See TORQUE SPECIFICATIONS. *See Fig. 9.*

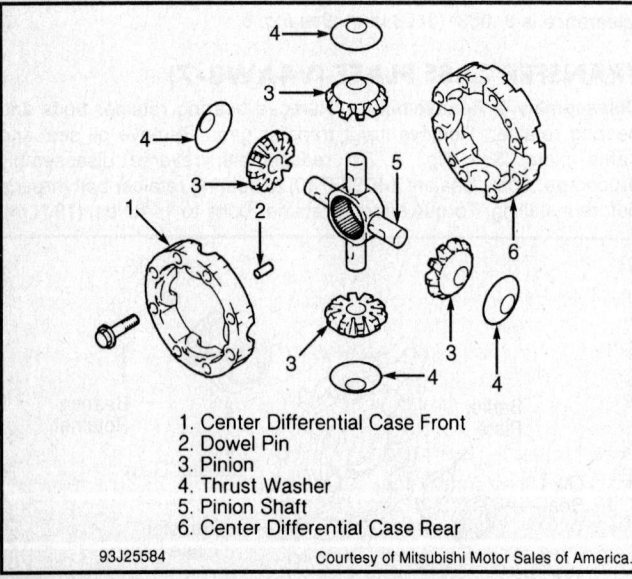

1. Center Differential Case Front
2. Dowel Pin
3. Pinion
4. Thrust Washer
5. Pinion Shaft
6. Center Differential Case Rear

93J25584   Courtesy of Mitsubishi Motor Sales of America.

Fig. 9: Exploded View Of Center Differential (Montero)

2WD-4WD SYNCHRONIZER (MONTERO)

Disassembly – **1)** Remove snap ring, 2WD-4WD synchronizer hub and synchronizer spring. *See Fig. 10.* Remove outer synchronizer ring, synchronizer cone and inner synchronizer ring.

2) Remove drive sprocket and needle bearing from front drive pinion. Inspect inner and outer synchronizer rings and cone for excessive wear. Install inner and outer synchronizer rings and cone onto drive sprocket.

3) Measure distance between drive sprocket and outer synchronizer. If distance is less than .0118" (.300 mm) replace synchronizer parts as a set.

Reassembly – **1)** Install drive sprocket and needle bearing onto front drive pinion. Apply transfer case gear oil to contacting surfaces of inner and outer synchronizer rings and synchronizer cone. Install inner and outer synchronizer rings and synchronizer cone.

2) Install synchronizer spring, 2WD-4WD synchronizer hub and snap ring to complete assembly. When installing new snap ring, select thickest ring that will fit into groove. Acceptable snap ring clearance is 0-.003" (0-.080 mm).

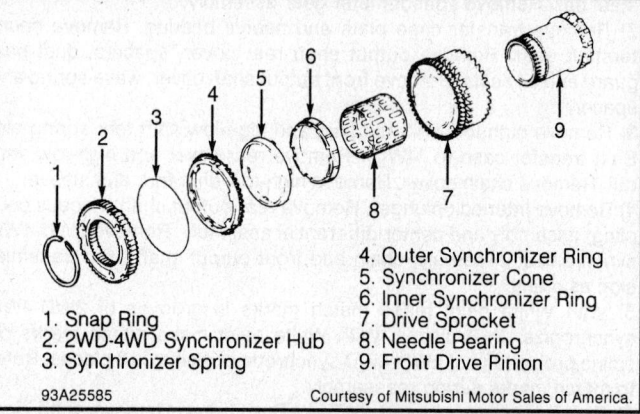

1. Snap Ring
2. 2WD-4WD Synchronizer Hub
3. Synchronizer Spring
4. Outer Synchronizer Ring
5. Synchronizer Cone
6. Inner Synchronizer Ring
7. Drive Sprocket
8. Needle Bearing
9. Front Drive Pinion

93A25585   Courtesy of Mitsubishi Motor Sales of America.

Fig. 10: Exploded View Of 2WD-4WD Synchronizer (Montero)

TRANSFER CASE REASSEMBLY

NOTE: ALWAYS replace all gaskets, oil seals, snap rings and spring pins with new parts. Coat both sides of gaskets and bolt threads with appropriate sealant. Lubricate all sliding and rotating parts with transfer case gear oil before assembling.

Reassembly (V5MT1-2) – **1)** Install input gear and front output shaft oil seals into transfer case housing. Pack grease between lips of seals and press seal circumference uniformly.

2) Install input gear assembly in transfer case. *See Figs. 3 and 8.* Input gear assembly snap ring is available in selective thicknesses. Use thickest snap ring that will fit into input shaft groove. Allowed snap ring clearance is 0-.0024" (0-.060 mm).

3) Insert needle bearing onto rear output shaft assembly. Install high-low synchronizer sleeve and shift fork. Install 2WD-4WD shift fork. Engage chain securely on front and rear output shaft sprockets. Assemble 2WD-4WD synchronizer sleeve with 2WD-4WD shift fork. Install assembly over 2WD-4WD shift rail. Install front and rear output shafts with chain as an assembly.

4) Install 2WD-4WD shift lug, distance piece, 2WD-4WD shift rail and spring pin. Ensure slit in spring pin is in line with 2WD-4WD shift rail. Install 2 spring retainers with spring on 2WD-4WD shift rail. Install snap ring to end of 2WD-4WD shift rail. *See Fig. 3.*

5) Insert 2 needle bearings and spacer into countergear. Install one thrust washer at each end of countergear. Ensure tab on thrust washers fits into groove of transfer case. Install countergear shaft assembly with "O" ring.

6) Install side cover and gasket. Install oil guide. Apply sealant to both sides of gasket and install gasket and chain cover. Ensure oil guide end fits into chain cover opening. Fit snap ring into groove of rear bearing on rear output shaft. Tighten bolts to specification. See TORQUE SPECIFICATIONS.

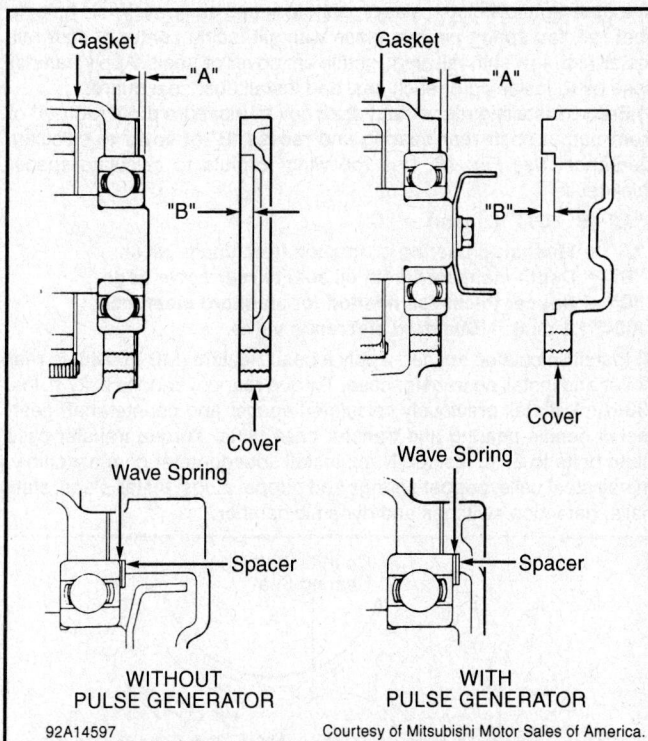

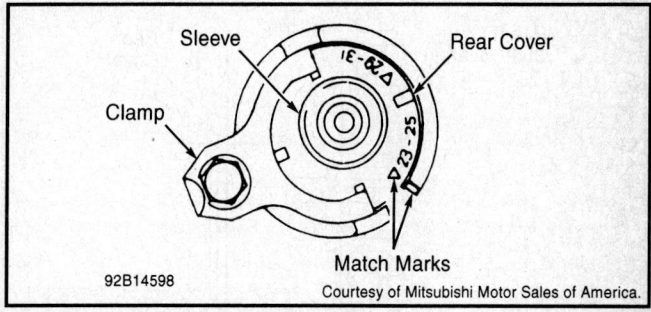

Fig. 12: Aligning Speedometer Sleeve

Fig. 11: Measuring Rear Output Shaft Bearing Clearance (V5MT1-2)

7) Install interlock plunger. Shift 2WD-4WD shift rail to 4WD position. Install high-low shift rail through high-low shift fork in case. Install 2 poppet balls and springs. Install seal plugs. When installing poppet springs, smaller end must be toward ball.

8) On models with pulse generator, install pulse rotor, wave spring and spacer. Measure protrusion "A" of front output shaft rear bearing and recess "B" of cover and calculate clearance. See Fig. 11. If clearance is greater than .079" (2.0 mm), select and install spacer to bring clearance within specification. If clearance is less than .079" (2.0 mm), use wave spring alone. Apply sealant to both sides of gasket and install gasket and cover. Install pulse generator (if equipped).

9) On all models, align high-low shift fork and shift rail spring holes and drive in roll pin with punch. Roll pin should be installed with slit on center line of shift rail. Install wave spring on rear of rear output shaft bearing. Apply sealant to both sides of rear cover gasket. Install gasket and cover.

10) Check output shaft end play. Measure protrusion "A" of rear output shaft rear bearing and recess "B" of cover and calculate clearance. Ensure end play is 0-.004" (0-.10 mm). Apply sealant to both sides of gasket and install gasket and cover. See Fig. 11.

11) Install speedometer sleeve assembly in rear cover. Align match mark on speedometer sleeve assembly in rear cover. See Fig. 12. Align match mark on speedometer sleeve with mark on case according to number of teeth on speedometer driven gear. Install speedometer driven gear sleeve clamp and tighten bolt to specification. Install both 4WD indicator light switches with steel balls. See TORQUE SPECIFICATIONS.

Reassembly (V4AW2-7 & V5MT1-6) – 1) Install input gear and front output shaft oil seals into transfer case housing. Install transfer input gear assembly baffle plate and input gear seal. See Fig. 4. Pack grease between lips of seals and press seal circumference uniformly.

2) Install 2WD-4WD shift lug into transfer case. Install spring retainer and spring to shift rail and install into shift lug. Press on shift rail to align spring pin holes in shift rail and shift lug. While holding shift rail, tap spring pin into place with slit facing center of shift rail.

3) Install transfer input gear assembly and snap ring. Select thickest snap ring that will fit into groove. Allowed snap ring clearance is 0-.0024" (0-.060 mm). Insert needle bearing onto transfer drive shaft

assembly. Install high-low synchronizer sleeve and shift fork assembly. Install transfer drive shaft assembly.

4) Install transfer countergear shaft thrust washers, needle bearings, bearing spacer and transfer countergear. Install one thrust washer at each end of transfer countergear. Ensure tab on thrust washers fits into groove of transfer case. Install counter gear shaft from transmission case side so lock plate groove is aligned with lock plate. Install lock plate. Install side cover and gasket.

5) Install bearing retainer. If reusing bearing retainer bolts, apply Stud Locking Compound (3M 4170) to threads. Install oil dam cover. Install differential lock hub, snap ring, steel ball and sleeve. Select thickest snap ring that will fit into groove. Allowed snap ring clearance is 0-.003" (0-.08 mm). Install 2WD-4WD synchronizer sleeve, 2WD-4WD shift fork, spring, spring seat and 2WD-4WD shift rail snap ring.

6) Assemble front output shaft assembly, chain and 2WD-4WD synchronizer assembly. Align match marks made during disassembly. Link chain tightly onto 2WD-4WD synchronizer and front output shaft sprockets. Install both sprockets and chain to transfer case at same time, while keeping them as far apart as possible.

7) Install center differential case assembly, rear output shaft assembly needle bearings and rear output shaft assembly. Install interlock plunger so it does not interfere with 2WD-4WD shift rail. Evenly apply sealant to chain cover and install chain cover.

8) Install high-low shift rail through high-low shift rail hole into shift fork. Align spring pin holes in high-low shift rail and shift fork. Tap in spring pin so slit is facing shift rail shaft center. Install and tighten high-low shift rail plug to specification. See TORQUE SPECIFICATIONS.

9) Before installing front output shaft cover, measure protrusion "A" of front output shaft rear bearing and recess "B" of cover and calculate clearance. See Fig. 13. If clearance is greater than .079" (2.0 mm), select and install spacer to bring clearance within specification. If clearance is less than .079" (2.0 mm), use wave spring alone. Apply sealant to both sides of gasket and install gasket and cover. Apply Stud Locking Compound (3M 4170) to bolts and tighten to specification. See TORQUE SPECIFICATIONS.

10) Install rear output shaft ball bearing snap ring. Measure clearance between chain cover and snap ring. Add .0008-.0039" (.02-.10 mm) to clearance measured and install spacer of similar thickness. Install rear output shaft oil seal (apply grease to lip of seal). Install rear cover oil seal (apply grease to lip of seal).

11) Before installing rear cover, snap ring and spacer thicknesses must be determined. Measure protrusion of rear output shaft bearing. Measure inset of both stages of cover. Subtract inset recess from rear bearing protrusion. Select a snap ring which adjusts difference between inset recess and rear bearing protrusion, and spacer thickness to 0-.004" (0-0.10 mm). Evenly apply sealant to rear cover and install cover. Tighten bolts to specification. See TORQUE SPECIFICATIONS.

12) Install speedometer gear, ensuring mating marks match according to number of gear teeth. Install speedometer gear sleeve clamp and tighten bolt to specification. See Fig. 12.

13) Apply sealant to poppet plug threads. Install poppet steel balls, springs and poppet plugs and tighten to specification. Install detection switches, steel balls and gaskets. See Fig. 14. Install dynamic damper and tighten bolts to specification.

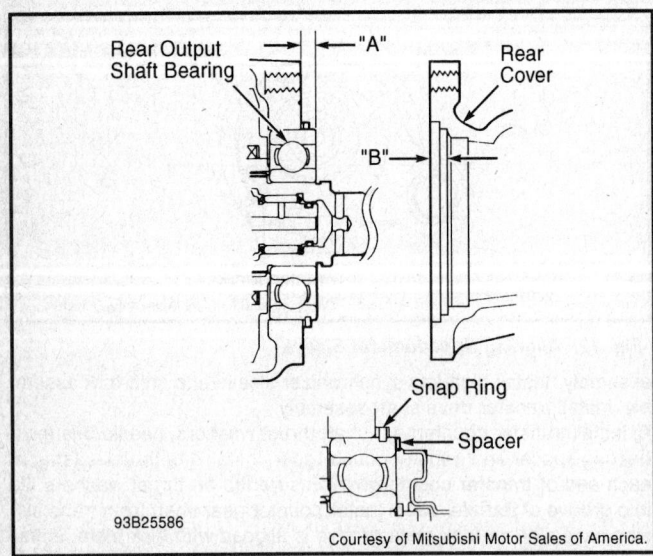

Fig. 13: Measuring Rear Output Shaft Bearing Clearance (V4AW2-7 & V5MT1-6 Is Shown, V4AW3-7 Is Similar)

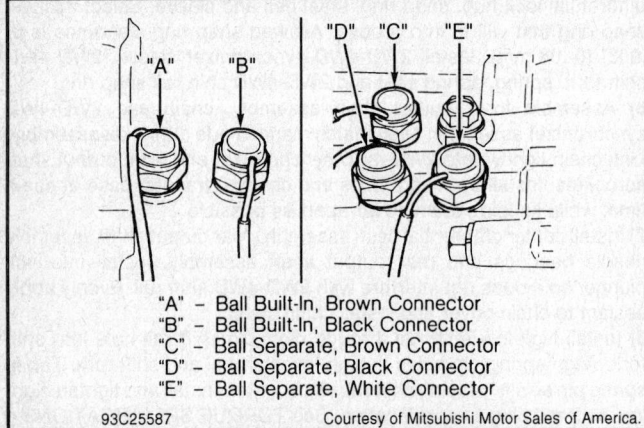

"A" – Ball Built-In, Brown Connector
"B" – Ball Built-In, Black Connector
"C" – Ball Separate, Brown Connector
"D" – Ball Separate, Black Connector
"E" – Ball Separate, White Connector

Fig. 14: Installation Of Detection Switches (Montero)

Reassembly (V4AW3-7) – 1) Before reassembly, place 2 pieces of solder on transfer case. See Fig. 15. Install countershaft gear and transfer case plate. Torque transfer case plate bolts to 27 ft. lbs. (36 N.m). Remove transfer case plate and countershaft gear. Remove solder pieces and measure thickness. Select a spacer to obtain a 0-.006" (0-.15 mm) end play.

2) Install front output shaft oil seal into transfer case housing. Apply transfer case gear oil to oil seal lip and install dust seal guard. Install transfer drive shaft. See Fig. 5. Apply Stud Locking Compound (3M 4170) to bearing retainer bolts and install bearing retainer. Torque bearing retainer bolts to 14 ft. lbs. (19 N.m).

3) Install needle bearing, low speed gear, high-low clutch hub and snap ring. Select snap ring to obtain a 0-.0031" (0-.08 mm) end play value. Install side cover gasket, side cover and torque bolts to 80 INCH lbs. (9 N.m). Install magnet holder and magnet. Install oil dam cover and torque bolts to 80 INCH lbs. (9 N.m).

4) Install differential lock hub and snap ring onto transfer drive shaft. Select snap ring to obtain a 0-.0031" (0-.08 mm) end play value. Install steel ball and sleeve. Install 2WD-4WD synchronizer sleeve, shift fork and shift rail. Install spring seats and springs. Install 2WD-4WD shift lug onto shift rail. While holding shift rail, tap spring pin into place with slit facing center of shift rail.

5) Install front output shaft. Using reference marks made during disassembly, 2WD-4WD synchronizer and chain. Install center differential case, needle bearings and rear output shaft. Install interlock plunger and ensure it does not interfere with 2WD-4WD shift rail. Apply a consistent bead of Sealant (MD997740) to chain cover and install. Torque chain cover bolts to 27 ft. lbs. (36 N.m).

6) Install high-low clutch sleeve, shift fork and shift rail. While holding shift rail, tap spring pin into place with slit facing center of shift rail. Install high-low shift rail plug. Install rear cover oil seals. Apply transfer case oil to inside lip of each seal and install dust seal guard.

7) Before installing rear output shaft cover, measure protrusion "A" of front output shaft rear bearing and recess "B" of cover to calculate clearance. See Fig. 13. Use following formula to calculate spacer thickness:

"A"-"B"-.004" (.1 mm) = "C"

"A" = Measured bearing protrusion from chain cover.
"B" = Depth measured from oil seal to rear cover edge.
"C" = Spacer thickness needed for standard clearance.
.004" (.1 mm) = Standard clearance value.

8) Install calculated spacer. Apply a bead Sealant (MD997740) to rear cover and install on transfer case. Torque rear cover bolts to 27 ft. lbs. (36 N.m). Install previously calculated spacer and countershaft gear. Install needle bearing and transfer case plate. Torque transfer case plate bolts to 27 ft. lbs. (36 N.m). Install speedometer gear assembly. Install steel balls, poppet springs and poppet plugs. Install plugs, steel balls, detection switches and dynamic damper.

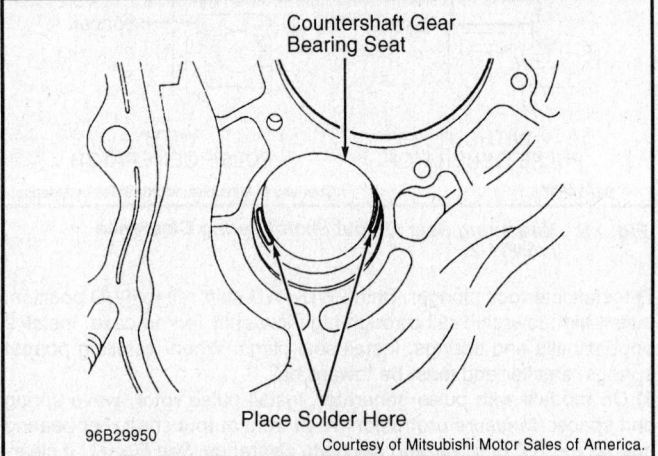

Fig. 15: Locating Solder Position On Transfer Case

TORQUE SPECIFICATIONS
TORQUE SPECIFICATIONS

Application	Ft. Lbs. (N.m)
Adapter-To-Transfer Bearing Retainer	[1] 14 (19)
Case Nuts & Bolts	22-31 (30-42)
Center Differential Case Bolts	48 (65)
Chain Cover Bolt	22-31 (30-42)
Detection Switch	[1] 27 (36)
Drain Plug	22-26 (30-35)
Dynamic Damper	52 (70)
High-Low Shift Rail Plug	[1] 24 (33)
Interlock Plunger Plug	[1] 22-26 (30-35)
Lock Plate Bolts	11-16 (15-22)
Oil Dam Cover	[1] 14 (19)
Oil Filler Plug	22-26 (30-35)
Output Shaft Cover Bolt	11-16 (15-22)
Poppet Plug	[1] 27 (36)
Pulse Rotor Bolt	[2] 11-16 (15-22)
Rear Cover Bolt	11-16 (15-22)
Rear Output Shaft Lock Nut	74-96 (100-130)
Seal Plug	[2] 22-31 (30-42)
Speedometer Sleeve Clamp Bolt	11-16 (15-22)
Transfer Case Plate	[2] 27 (36)
4WD Indicator Light Switch	[2] 22 (33)

	INCH Lbs. (N.m)
Pulse Generator Bolt	[2] 89-106 (10-12)
Side Cover Bolt	71-89 (8-10)

[1] – Applies to Montero models only.
[2] – Applies to Pickup models only.

WIRING DIAGRAMS

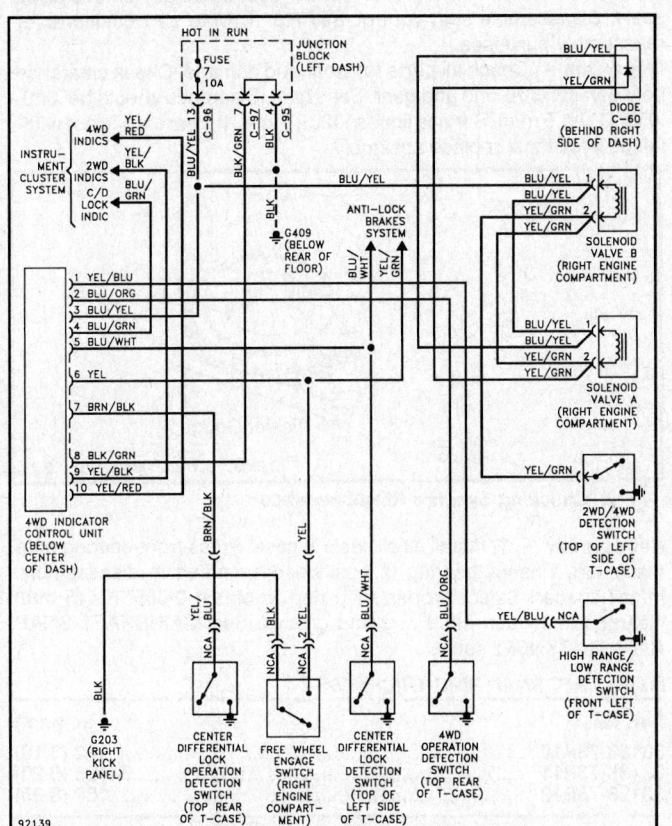

Fig. 16: Transfer Case Wiring Diagram (1995-96 Montero Active Trac)

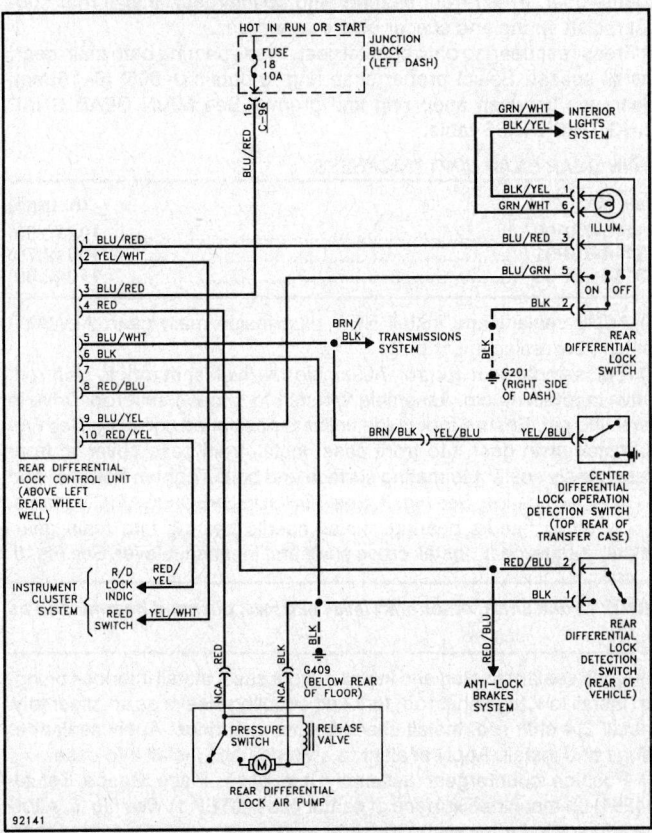

Fig. 17: Rear Differential Lock Wiring Diagram (1995 Montero)

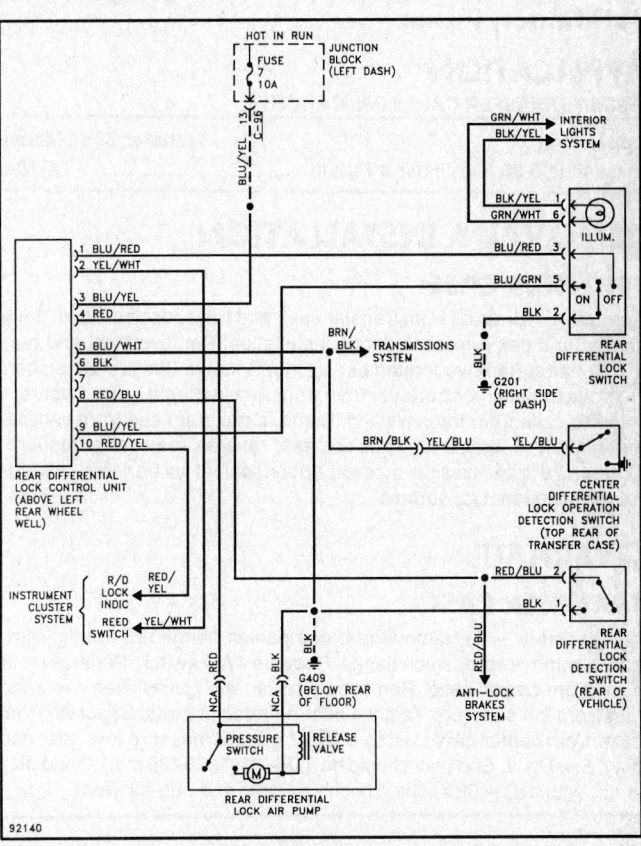

Fig. 18: Rear Differential Lock Wiring Diagram (1996 Montero)

Pathfinder, Pickup

APPLICATION

NISSAN TRANSFER CASE APPLICATION

Application	Transfer Case Model
Nissan 1995-96 Pathfinder & Pickup	TX-10A

REMOVAL & INSTALLATION

TRANSFER CASE

Removal – Drain oil from transfer case and transmission. Mark drive shafts for index reference during installation. Remove front and rear drive shafts. Remove torsion bar spring. Remove 2nd crossmember. Remove transfer control lever from transfer outer shift lever. Separate transfer case from transmission. Remove transfer case from vehicle.

Installation – To install transfer case, reverse removal procedure. On manual transmission models, apply sealant to transfer case-to-transmission mating surface.

OVERHAUL

TRANSFER CASE

Disassembly – **1)** Remove rear companion flange nut. Using 2-jaw puller, remove companion flange. Remove 4WD switch. Separate rear case from center case. Remove oil cover and gutter. Remove snap ring from 2-4 shift rod. Remove bearing retainer bolts. Separate front case from center case. Using a feeler gauge, measure low gear end play. See Fig. 1. End play should be .008-.014" (.20-.35 mm). If end play is not within specifications, check low gear and hub for wear.

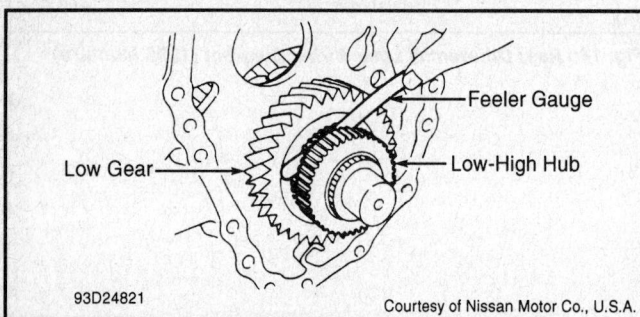

Fig. 1: Measuring Low Gear End Play

2) Remove snap ring from mainshaft, Using puller with bearing splitter, remove gear and low/high hub from mainshaft. Remove needle bearing. Note drive chain direction for reassembly purposes.

3) Using a soft-faced hammer, alternately tap front end of mainshaft and front drive shaft and remove assembly from case. Be careful not to bend drive chain. Remove all switches from front case. Remove check plugs, springs and balls. Drive out roll pin from outer shift lever and remove lever.

4) Remove inner shift lever lock pin. Remove cross shaft. Remove 2-4 shift rod. Remove low/high shift rod, fork and coupling sleeve as an assembly. Remove main gear needle bearing. Remove front case cover. Remove countergear and main gear. Mount mainshaft in soft-jawed vise. Mount dial indicator on front drive sprocket and measure front drive sprocket end play.

5) End play should be .008-.014 (.20-.35 mm). If end play is not within specifications, check sprocket and clutch gear for wear. Remove snap ring, speedometer drive gear and steel ball. Remove snap ring and spacer. Support front drive sprocket in blocks and press out mainshaft from sprocket, rear bearing and clutch gear as an assembly. Remove needle bearing. Remove bearing retainer, snap ring and spacer. Press off front bearing from mainshaft.

6) Using a puller, remove front drive shaft bearings. Press countergear front bearing off countergear. Remove sub-gear, spacer, and dish plate. Press countergear rear bearing off countergear. Remove

sub-gear, spacer and dish plate. Remove snap ring and spacer from main gear. Using a puller, remove main gear bearing. Remove all oil seals. Disassemble shift control. See Fig. 4. Note part positions for reassembly purposes.

Inspection – Check all parts for wear and damage. Check clearance between synchro ring and gear. See Fig. 2. Clearance should be .039-.059" (1.0-1.5 mm). Service limit is .020 (.5 mm). If clearance is not within specifications, replace assembly.

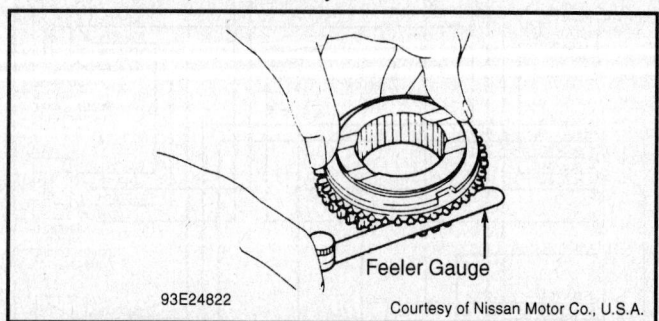

Fig. 2: Checking Synchro Ring Clearance

Reassembly – **1)** Install all oil seals in case. Press front bearing onto mainshaft. Ensure bearing is positioned as noted in disassembly. Install spacer. Select proper snap ring to obtain 0-006" (0-.15 mm) clearance between snap ring and groove. See MAINSHAFT SNAP RING THICKNESS table.

MAINSHAFT SNAP RING THICKNESS

Part No.	In. (mm)
33138-73P10	.122 (3.10)
33138-73P11	.126 (3.20)
33138-73P12	.130 (3.30)

2) Press front bearing onto front drive shaft. Press rear bearing onto drive shaft. Install front sub-gear, dish spring and spacer onto countergear. Press front bearing onto countergear. Install rear sub-gear, dish spring and spacer onto countergear.

3) Press rear bearing onto countergear. Press bearing onto main gear. Install spacer. Select proper snap ring to obtain 0-.006" (0-.15 mm) clearance between snap ring and groove. See MAIN GEAR SNAP RING THICKNESS table.

MAIN GEAR SNAP RING THICKNESS

Part No.	In. (mm)
33114-73P00	.102 (2.60)
33114-73P01	.106 (2.70)
33114-73P02	.110 (2.80)

4) Apply sealant and install NEW plug inside main gear. ALWAYS install new replacement plug

5) Reassemble shift control. Assemble low/high shift fork to shift rod. Drive in retaining pin. Assemble 2/4 shift fork to 2/4 shift rod. Drive in retaining pin. Ensure fork guide collar is positioned correctly. See Fig. 4. Install main gear into front case. Install front case cover to front case. Apply sealant to mating surface and bolts. Tighten bolts "A" and "B" to specification. See Fig. 3. See TORQUE SPECIFICATIONS table. Apply oil to needle bearing. Install needle bearing into main gear. Install countergear. Install cross shaft and inner shift lever. See Fig. 5.

NOTE: Cross shaft, outer shift lever and lock pin must be replaced as a set.

6) Apply sealant to plug and install in front case. Install interlock plunger. Install low/high shift rod, fork and coupling sleeve as an assembly. Install 2/4 shift rod. Install check balls and springs. Apply sealant to plugs and install. Apply sealant to switches and install into case.

7) Position countergear assembly into case. Place Gauge Set (J-34291) on machined surface of center case (STEP 1). See Fig. 5. Allow gauging cylinder to rest on top outer portion of countergear rear bearing (STEP 2). Lock gauging cylinder in place. Insert Gauging Plunger (J-34291-20) into cylinder. Place Gauging Assembly onto machined surface of front case assembly (STEP 3). Using a feeler gauge, measure distance between Gauging Cylinder (J-34291-5) and Gauging Plunger (J-34291-20). Select proper shim to obtain 0-008" (0-.2 mm) clearance. See COUNTERGEAR SHIM SELECTION table.

COUNTERGEAR SHIM SELECTION

Part No.	In. (mm)
33112-C6900	.004 (.10)
33112-C6901	.008 (.20)
33112-C6902	.012 (.30)
33112-C6903	.016 (.40)
33112-33G00	.020 (.50)
33112-33G01	.024 (.60)

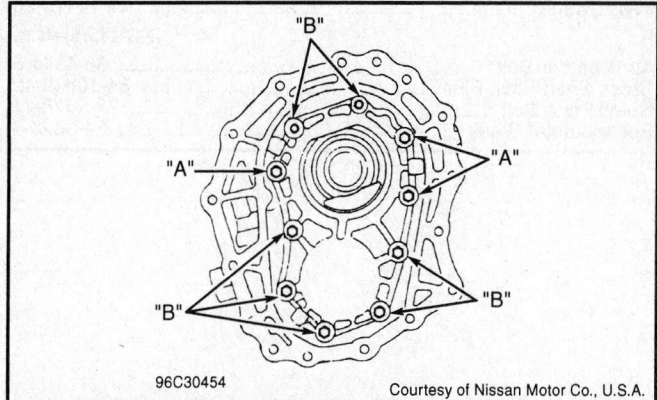

96C30454   Courtesy of Nissan Motor Co., U.S.A.

Fig. 3: Identifying Front Case Cover Bolts

8) Apply grease to selected shim. Position shim on countergear rear bearing. Apply gear oil to each part of front case. Using plastic

hammer, lightly tap mainshaft to install on center case. Install bearing retainer.

9) Position drive chain onto front drive sprocket and front drive shaft. Ensure drive chain placement is correct. Install assembly in center case. Install front drive shaft into case. Ensure shafts are aligned straight.

10) Apply gear oil to needle bearings. Install needle bearings into front drive sprocket. Rotate front drive sprocket to ease bearing installation. Install 2/4 coupling sleeve and shift fork. Ensure bevelled edge of coupling sleeve is facing gear.

11) Install shifting inserts and spring. Ensure spring side is facing gear. Install synchro ring. Install clutch gear and mainshaft rear bearing. Install spacer. Select proper size snap ring to obtain 0-.006" (0-.15 mm) clearance between snap ring and groove. See REAR BEARING SELECTIVE SNAP RING table.

12) Install steel ball, speedometer drive gear and retaining ring. Apply gear oil to low gear needle bearing. Install low gear and needle bearing. Install low-high hub and snap ring. Ensure low-high hub is positioned correctly.

13) Check low gear end play. *See Fig. 1.* Low gear end play should be .008-.014 (.20-.35 mm). If end play is not within specifications, check low-high hub and low gear for wear. Install front case onto center case. Apply sealant to mating surfaces.

REAR BEARING SELECTIVE SNAP RING

Part No.	In. (mm)
33138-73P20	.071 (1.80)
33138-73P21	.075 (1.90)
33138-73P22	.079 (2.00)
33138-73P23	.083 (2.10)
33138-73P24	.087 (2.20)

14) Install 2-4 shift rod snap ring. Install oil gutter and cover. Apply gear oil to all parts. Install rear case onto center case. Apply sealant to mating surfaces. Install 4WD switch. Install companion flanges.

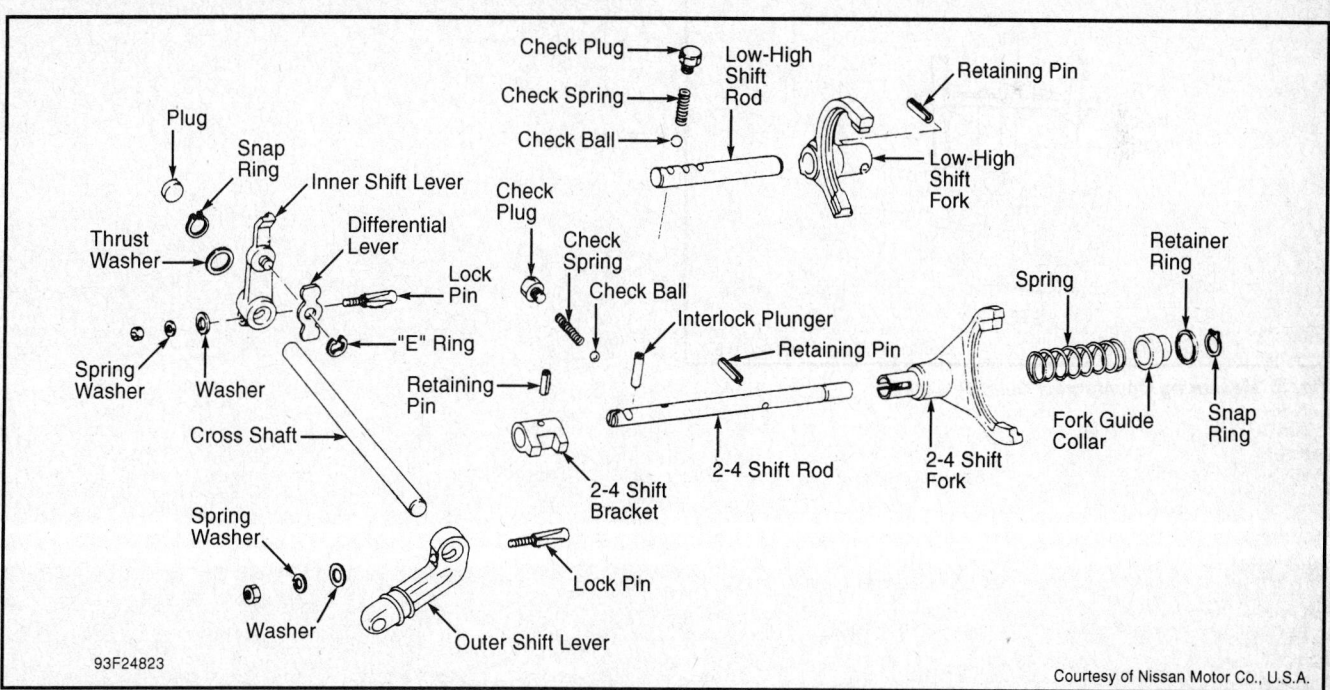

93F24823   Courtesy of Nissan Motor Co., U.S.A.

Fig. 4: Exploded View Of Shift Control Assembly

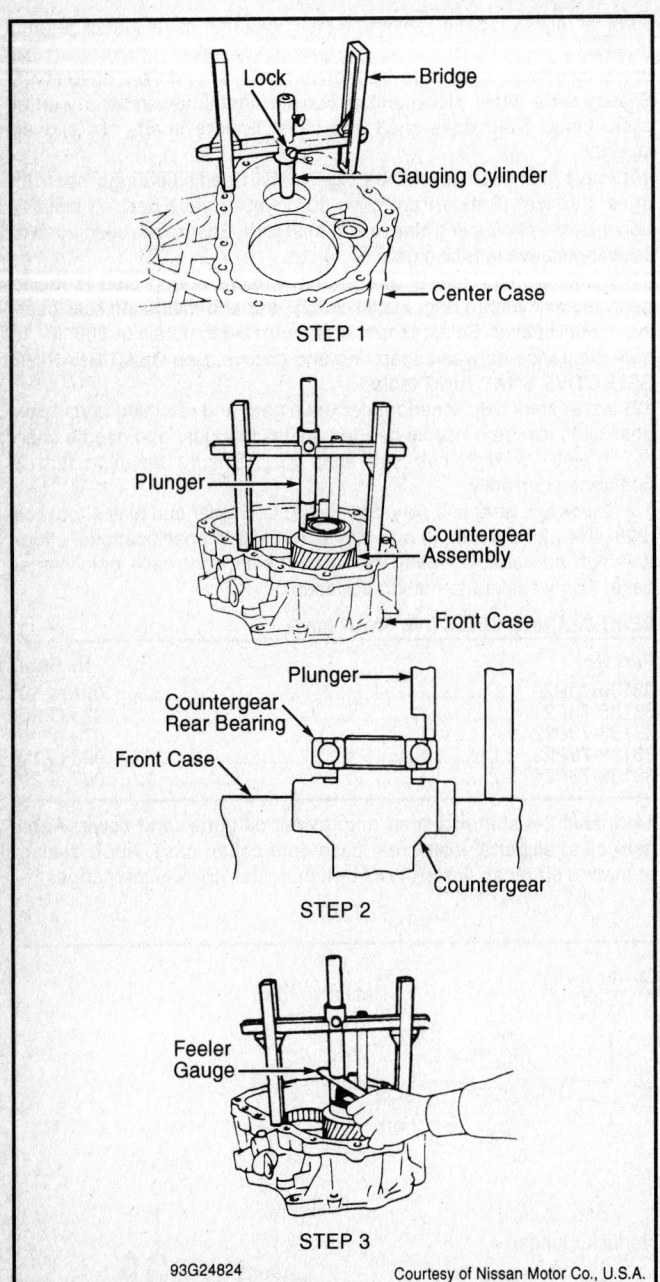

Fig. 5: Measuring Countergear Shim Thickness

93G24824   Courtesy of Nissan Motor Co., U.S.A.

TORQUE SPECIFICATIONS
TORQUE SPECIFICATIONS

Application	Ft. Lbs. (N.m)
Bearing Retainer Bolt	12-15 (16-21)
Check Plug	14-18 (19-25)
Companion Flange Nut	166-239 (226-324)
Control Lever Bracket Bolt	12-15 (16-21)
Control Lever-To-Outer Shift Lever Bolt	18-22 (25-30)
Crossmember Bolt	43-58 (59-78)
Drain & Fill Plug	18-25 (25-34)
Front Case Cover Bolt	14-16 (19-22)
Front Case-To-Center Case Bolt	20-27 (26-36)
Neutral Switch	11-14 (15-20)
Rear Case-To-Center Case Bolt	20-27 (26-36)
Transfer Case-To-Transmission Bolt	23-30 (31-41)
4WD Switch	11-14 (15-20)

	INCH Lbs. (N.m)
Air Breather Bolt	36-48 (4-5)
Cross Shaft Lock Pin	84-108 (9-12)
Guide Plate Bolt	72-96 (8-11)
Speedometer Sleeve	24-36 (3-4)

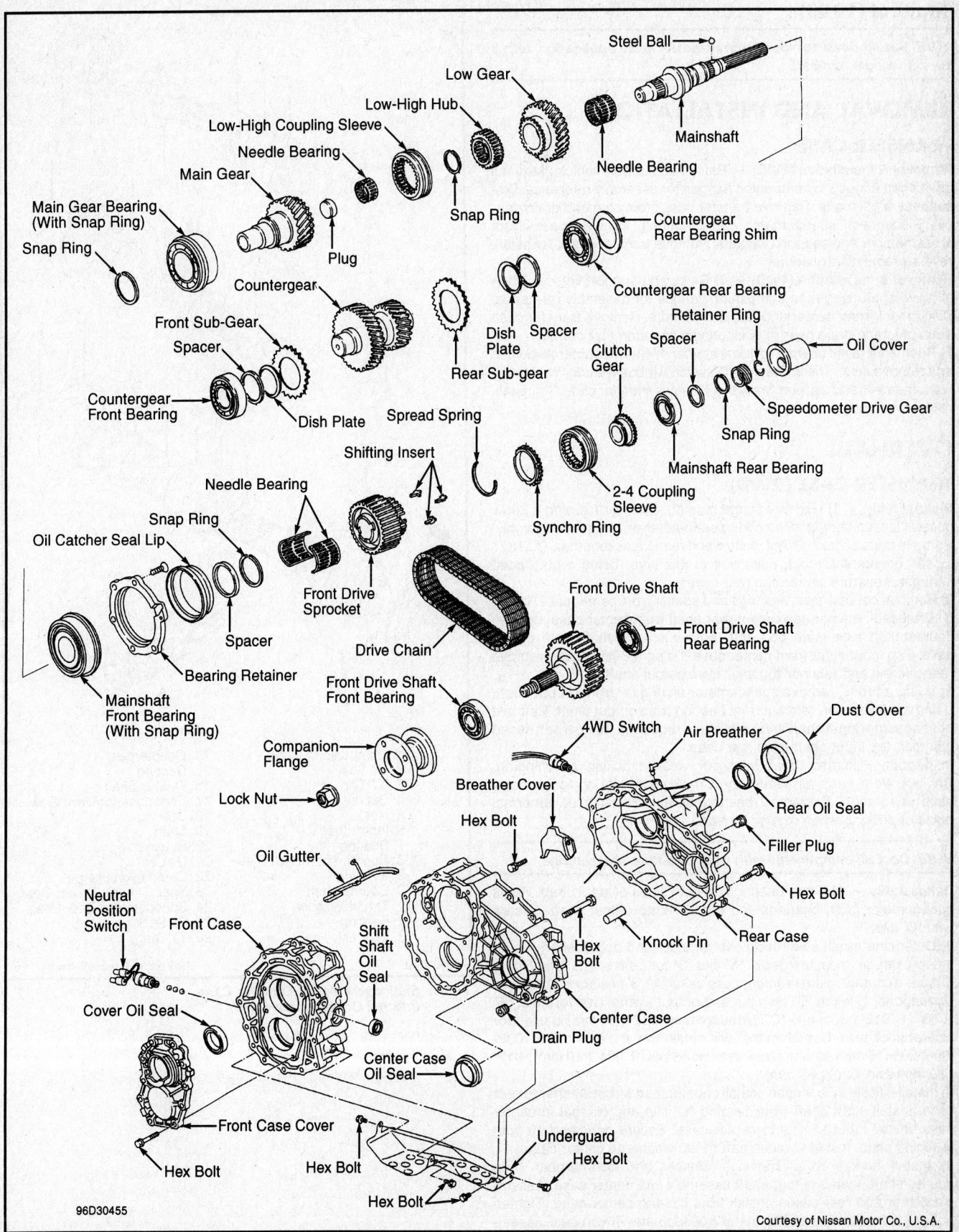

Fig. 6: Exploded View Of Transfer Case & Gear Assembly

96D30455

Courtesy of Nissan Motor Co., U.S.A.

Samurai (1995)

NOTE: Suzuki does not identify the transfer case application with a specific model number.

REMOVAL AND INSTALLATION

TRANSFER CASE

Removal & Installation (2WD) – Raise and support vehicle. Mark all drive shaft flanges to companion flanges for assembly reference. Disconnect drive shafts. Remove transfer case drain plug and drain gear oil. Disconnect speedometer cable. Unbolt transfer case from crossmember and support brackets. Remove transfer case. To install, reverse removal procedure.

Removal & Installation (4WD) – **1)** Raise and support vehicle. Mark all drive shaft flanges to companion flanges for assembly reference. Disconnect front, center and rear drive shafts. Remove transfer case drain plug and drain gear oil. Disconnect speedometer cable.

2) Push shift lever down and turn retainer 1/4 turn counterclockwise and remove lever. Disconnect 4WD switch. Unbolt transfer case from crossmember and support brackets. Remove transfer case. To install, reverse removal procedure.

OVERHAUL

TRANSFER CASE (2WD)

Disassembly – **1)** Remove flange nuts (2). *See Fig. 1.* Using a 2-jaw puller, remove flanges. Remove speedometer driven gear assembly. Remove bolts securing front, center and rear cases together. DO NOT loosen countershaft lock plate bolt at this time. Using a soft-faced hammer, separate center and rear cases.

2) Remove countergear, bearings and spacer from center case. Using a soft-faced hammer, tap output rear shaft from center case. Loosen countershaft lock plate bolt and remove countershaft from center case. Tap input shaft from center case. Using a 2-jaw puller, remove rear bearing and retainer together from output shaft.

3) Using a press, remove speedometer drive gear from output shaft. Using a 2-jaw puller, remove front bearing from output shaft. Remove bearings from input shaft and/or case (as required). Using a soft-faced hammer, tap input shaft from rear case.

Inspection – Inspect gear teeth for wear, cracking or chipping. Replace worn parts as necessary. Check each bearing for smoothness of rotation. Replace if bearing exhibits resistance, abnormal noise or sticking when rotated by hand.

NOTE: Coat all components with gear oil before reassembly.

Reassembly – **1)** Press bearings on both sides of input shaft. Press speedometer gear, bearings and retainer onto output shaft. Secure with "C" clip.

2) Determine thrust shim thickness for input and output shaft. Using a depth gauge, measure depth "A" and "B" for both shafts. *See Fig. 2.* Ensure accurate measurements are taken at 3 positions. Measure corresponding width "C" on input and output shafts. Use formula, "A" + "B" + .012" (.30 mm) - "C". Measurement .012" (.30 mm) is used for gasket thickness. Use shim that will obtain thrust clearance of .002-.006" (.05-.15 mm). Shims range in thicknesses of .004" (.10 mm), .012" (.30 mm) and .020" (.50 mm).

3) Install oil seal in rear case. Install countershaft thrust washer to rear case. Install input shaft front bearing "C" clip and oil seal in center case. Install input shaft into center case. Secure countershaft with retaining plate. Install countershaft thrust washer to center case.

4) Install needle roller bearings, spacer and countergear onto countershaft. Install output shaft assembly into center case. Assemble center and rear cases. Install front case to center case. Tighten bolts in a crisscross pattern. Install speedometer driven gear assembly. Install all companion flanges.

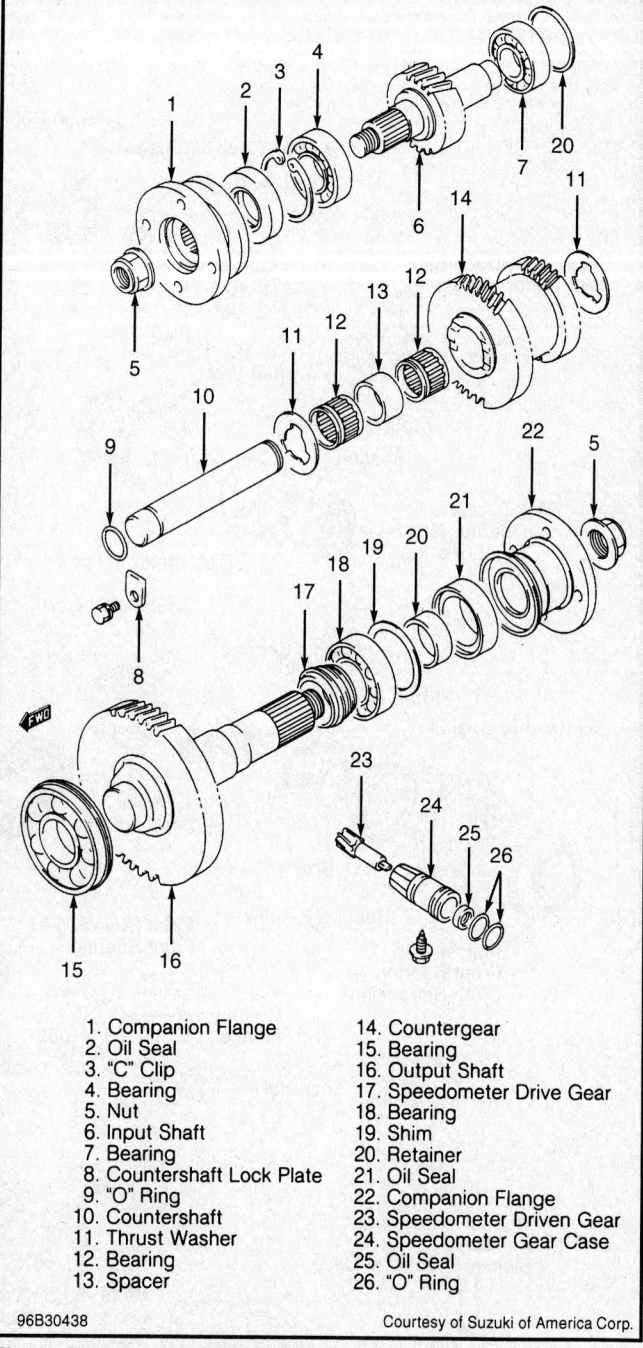

1. Companion Flange	14. Countergear
2. Oil Seal	15. Bearing
3. "C" Clip	16. Output Shaft
4. Bearing	17. Speedometer Drive Gear
5. Nut	18. Bearing
6. Input Shaft	19. Shim
7. Bearing	20. Retainer
8. Countershaft Lock Plate	21. Oil Seal
9. "O" Ring	22. Companion Flange
10. Countershaft	23. Speedometer Driven Gear
11. Thrust Washer	24. Speedometer Gear Case
12. Bearing	25. Oil Seal
13. Spacer	26. "O" Ring

96B30438 Courtesy of Suzuki of America Corp.

Fig. 1: Exploded View Of Transfer Case Internal Components (2WD)

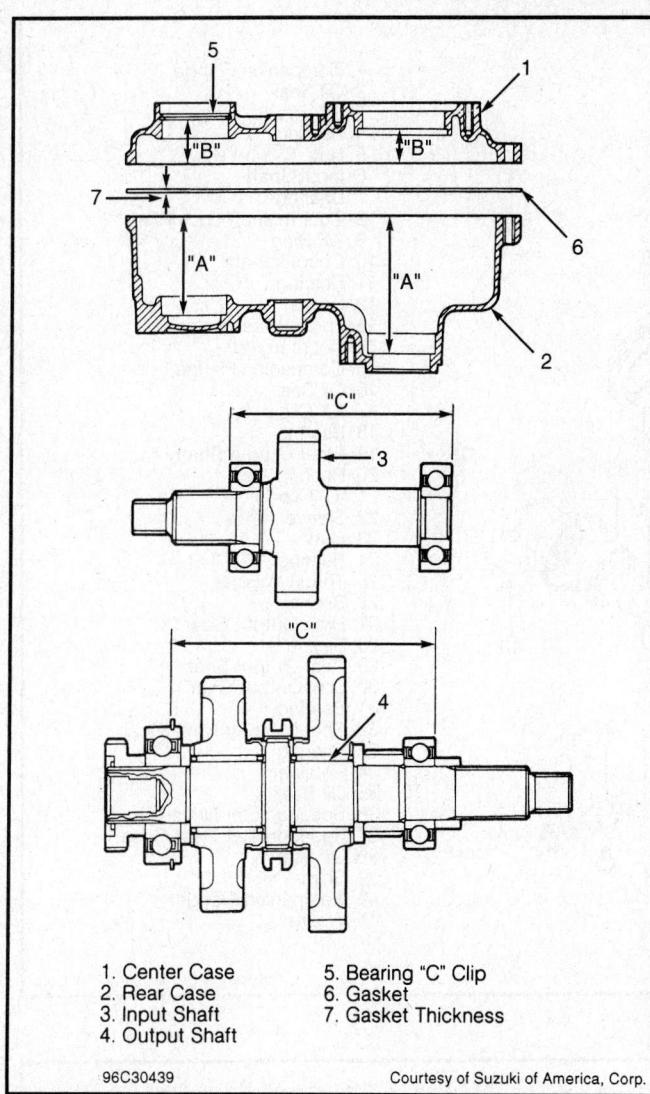

1. Center Case
2. Rear Case
3. Input Shaft
4. Output Shaft
5. Bearing "C" Clip
6. Gasket
7. Gasket Thickness

96C30439   Courtesy of Suzuki of America, Corp.

Fig. 2: Measuring Input & Output Shaft Thrust Clearances

TRANSFER CASE (4WD)

Disassembly – **1)** Remove flange nuts (3). See Fig. 3. Using a 2-jaw puller, remove flanges. Remove speedometer driven gear assembly. Remove 4WD indicator light switch. DO NOT misplace switch ball. Unbolt and remove front case. DO NOT loosen countershaft lock plate bolt at this time. Using a soft-faced hammer, drive out input shaft from front case.

2) Remove front case oil seal and "C" clip. Drive out bearing. Unbolt and separate center and rear transfer cases. Inspect gear teeth, internal teeth of clutch sleeve and gear clutch teeth. Replace any worn or damaged parts. Measure output shaft gear clearances. See Fig. 4. Standard clearance of low and high output gear is .007-.012" (.175-.325 mm). Service limit is .027" (.70 mm). If clearance is not within specifications, replace thrust washer.

3) DO NOT remove countershaft retaining plate from center case. Remove plug, spring and detent ball. Drive out roll pins from front drive shift shaft and reduction shift shaft. Remove shift forks and shift shafts. Ensure to remove remaining detent balls and spring.

4) Drive out rear output shaft from center case. Pull out countergear, bearings and spacer. Remove countershaft retaining plate and remove countershaft. Remove input shaft from center case.

5) Using a press, remove output shaft rear bearing. Remove speedometer drive gear, thrust washer, output low gear and needle bearing. Remove front drive hub and snap ring. Press off front bearing. If necessary, remove input bearing with a 2-jaw puller. See Fig. 3.

Inspection – Inspect condition of disassembled components. Replace any worn or damaged components. Measure length of detent springs. Standard spring length should be .933" (23.70 mm). Service limit is .866" (22.0 mm). If spring is not within specifications, replace. Check all bearings for pitting, scoring or any irregular wear. Replace as needed.

NOTE: Coat all components in gear oil before reassembly.

Reassembly – **1)** Press bearings on both sides of input shaft. Install output low gear with needle bearing on output shaft. Install thrust washer and speedometer drive gear. See Fig. 3. Press on bearing and retainer. Install output high gear and needle bearing. Install thrust washer. Press on bearing. Install clutch hub with sleeve and "C" clip.

2) Determine thrust shim thickness for input and output shaft. Using depth gauge, measure depth "A" and "B" for both shafts. See Fig. 2. Ensure accurate measurements are taken at 3 positions. Measure corresponding width "C" on input and output shafts. Use the following formula: "A" + "B" + .012" (.30 mm) - "C". Measurement .012" (.30 mm) is used for gasket thickness. Use shim that will obtain thrust clearance of .002-.006" (.05-.15 mm). Shims range in thicknesses of .004" (.10 mm), .012" (.30 mm) and .020" (.50 mm).

3) Install seal in rear case. Install countershaft thrust washer to rear case. Install input shaft front bearing snap ring and seal in center case. Install input shaft in center case. Secure countershaft with retaining plate. Install countershaft thrust washer to center case. Install countershaft with needle bearings, spacer and countergear.

4) Install output shaft assembly in center case. Install shift assembly. In center case, install spring, detent ball and front drive shift shaft. Install detent ball, reduction shift shaft, detent ball, spring and plug. Drive roll pins into shift forks to secure shift shafts.

5) Assemble center and rear cases. Tighten bolts in a crisscross pattern. Install snap ring and seal in front case. Install front case. Install speedometer driven gear assembly. Install 4WD switch and secure switch harness. Install all companion flanges.

TORQUE SPECIFICATIONS

TORQUE SPECIFICATIONS

Application	Ft. Lbs. (N.m)
Case Bolts	10-17 (14-23)
Companion Flange Nut	80-108 (108-146)
Countershaft Retainer Bolt	7-12 (10-16)
Crossmember Bolt	17-22 (23-30)
Drain & Filler Plug	14-20 (19-27)
Mounting Bracket Bolt	14-20 (19-27)
Transfer Case Mounting Nut	19-25 (26-34)

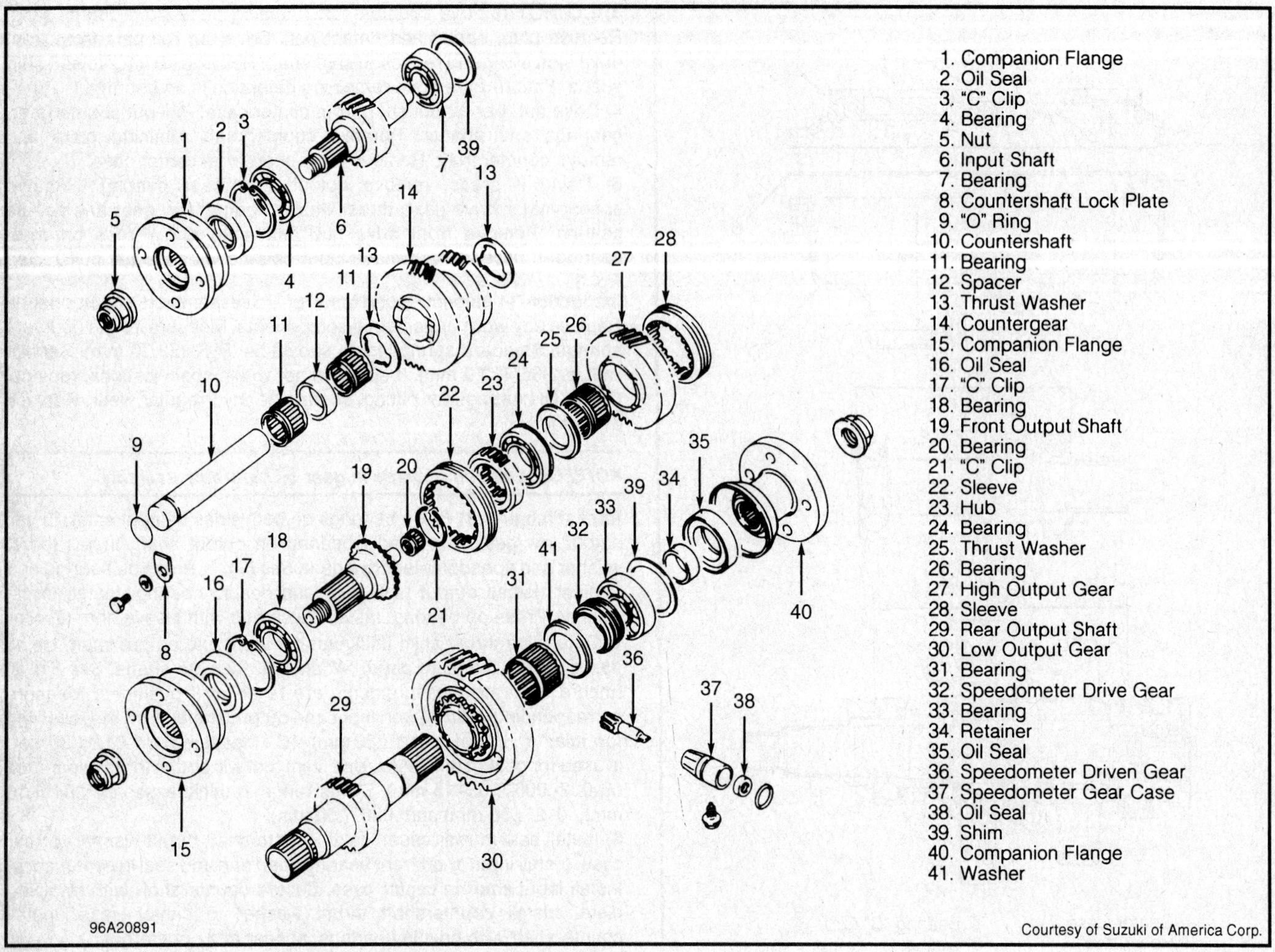

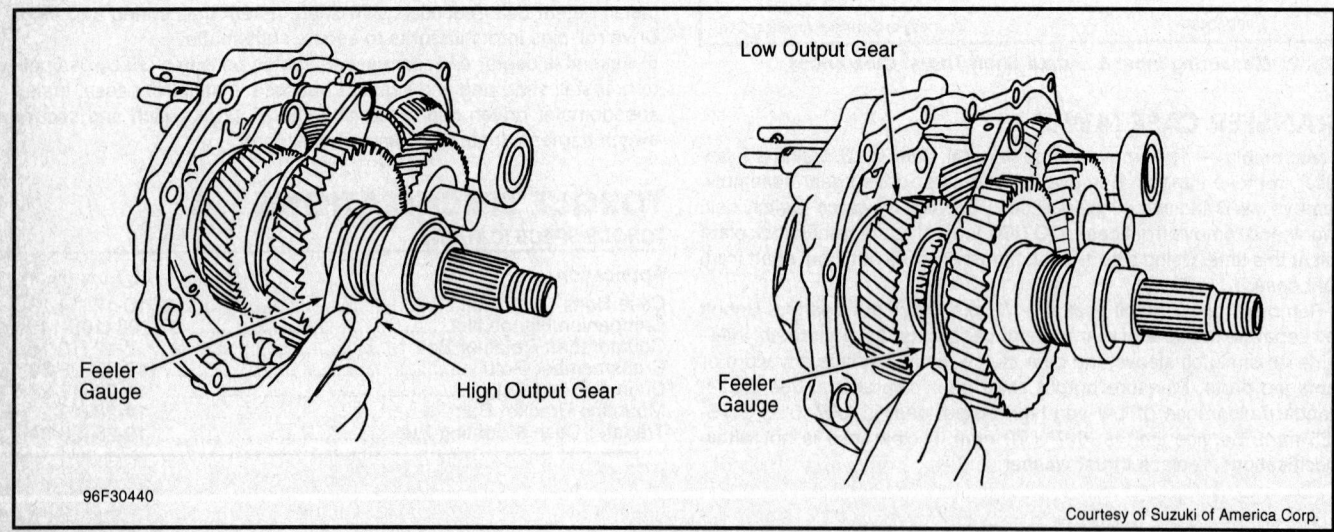

1. Companion Flange
2. Oil Seal
3. "C" Clip
4. Bearing
5. Nut
6. Input Shaft
7. Bearing
8. Countershaft Lock Plate
9. "O" Ring
10. Countershaft
11. Bearing
12. Spacer
13. Thrust Washer
14. Countergear
15. Companion Flange
16. Oil Seal
17. "C" Clip
18. Bearing
19. Front Output Shaft
20. Bearing
21. "C" Clip
22. Sleeve
23. Hub
24. Bearing
25. Thrust Washer
26. Bearing
27. High Output Gear
28. Sleeve
29. Rear Output Shaft
30. Low Output Gear
31. Bearing
32. Speedometer Drive Gear
33. Bearing
34. Retainer
35. Oil Seal
36. Speedometer Driven Gear
37. Speedometer Gear Case
38. Oil Seal
39. Shim
40. Companion Flange
41. Washer

96A20891

Courtesy of Suzuki of America Corp.

Fig. 3: Exploded View Of Transfer Case Internal Components (4WD)

Low Output Gear

Feeler Gauge

High Output Gear

Feeler Gauge

96F30440

Courtesy of Suzuki of America Corp.

Fig. 4: Measuring Output Gear Thrust Clearances

TRANSFER CASES
Toyota Land Cruiser & Lexus LX450

Lexus: LX450
Toyota: Land Cruiser

APPLICATION

TOYOTA TRANSFER CASE APPLICATION

Application	Transfer Case Model
1995-96 Land Cruiser	HF2AV
1996 Lexus LX450	HF2AV

DESCRIPTION & OPERATION

The HF2AV transfer case is an electronically controlled unit with mode changes (2WD-4WD) made by an electric motor operating the linkage. Mode selection is made through "CENTER DIFF LOCK" switch and shift lever "L" position, center differential lock control relay and motor actuator. Center differential lock indicated by "DIFF LOCK" light. Transfer transmits drive force from the transmission to front and rear wheels.

REMOVAL & INSTALLATION

TRANSFER CASE

Manufacturer does not supply information on separate procedures for removal and installation of transfer case. Transfer case is removed from transmission once complete assembly is removed from vehicle. See REMOVAL & INSTALLATION procedures in TRANSMISSION SERVICING section.

TESTING

ELECTRONIC COMPONENTS

NOTE: For component location, See Figs. 1 and 5.

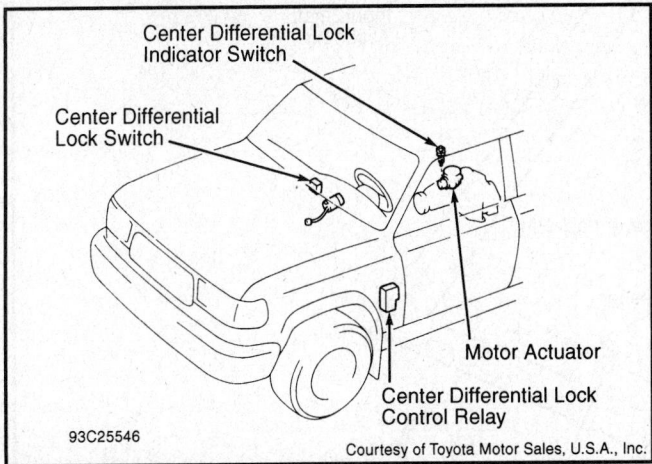

93C25546   Courtesy of Toyota Motor Sales, U.S.A., Inc.

Fig. 1: Identifying Differential Lock Components

Center Differential Lock Control Relay – Refer to RESISTANCE CONTINUITY CHECK for terminal testing. *See Fig. 2.* There is a diode between terminals No. 6 and 7. If circuit shows no continuity, perform voltage check. Apply battery voltage between terminals as specified and check circuit continuity as shown in VOLTAGE CONTINUITY CHECK. *See Fig. 2.* If circuit(s) are malfunctioning, replace relay.

Center Differential Lock Switch – 1) Inspect operation of switch (Non-ABS models). Start engine and shift transfer shift lever into "H" position. Check that center differential lock indicator light illuminates when center differential lock switch is pushed on. Ensure indicator light goes out when switch is pushed off.
2) Start engine and ensure switch is off. Ensure light only illuminates when transfer case shift lever is in "L" position. Intermittently, the light

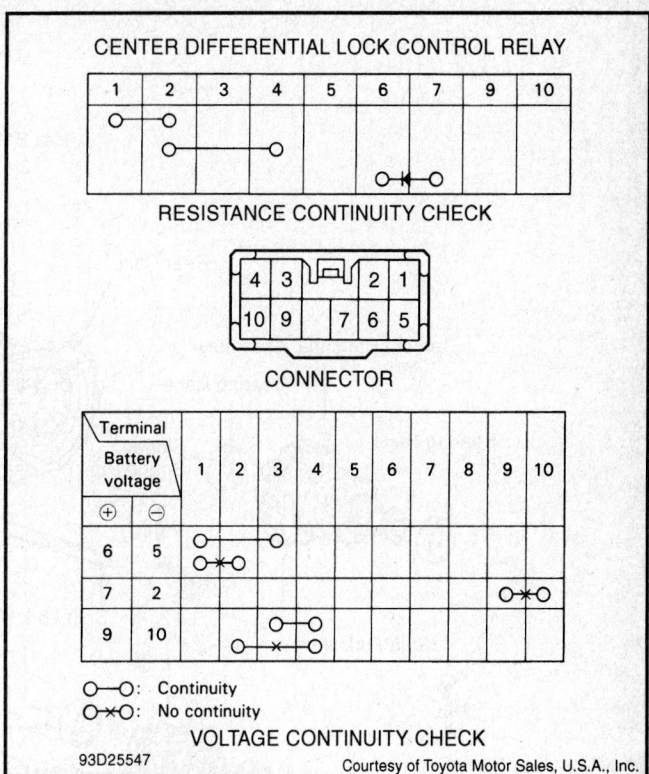

93D25547   Courtesy of Toyota Motor Sales, U.S.A., Inc.

Fig. 2: Continuity Checking Diagrams

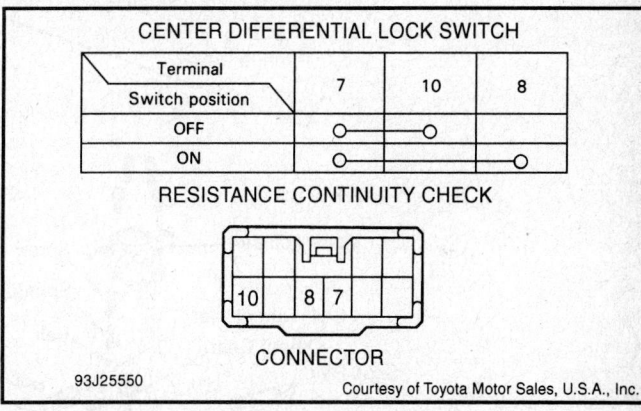

93J25550   Courtesy of Toyota Motor Sales, U.S.A., Inc.

Fig. 3: Checking Differential Lock Switch Continuity

will not go off unless the front wheels are in straight-ahead position and acceleration/deceleration is performed slowly. Check continuity between terminals. *See Fig. 3.* If continuity is not as shown, replace switch.

Motor Actuator – Using ohmmeter, measure resistance between terminals No. 2 and 3. *See Fig. 4.* Resistance should be .3-100 ohms. Measure resistance between terminals No. 2 or 3 and body ground. Resistance should be infinite (greater than 500 k/ohms). If resistance is not within specifications, replace motor actuator.

Transfer Indicator Switch – Connect ohmmeter between switch terminals. Push switch button and release. Continuity should be present with button pushed.

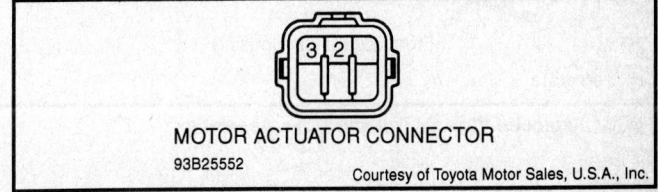

MOTOR ACTUATOR CONNECTOR
93B25552   Courtesy of Toyota Motor Sales, U.S.A., Inc.

Fig. 4: Identifying Motor Actuator Connector

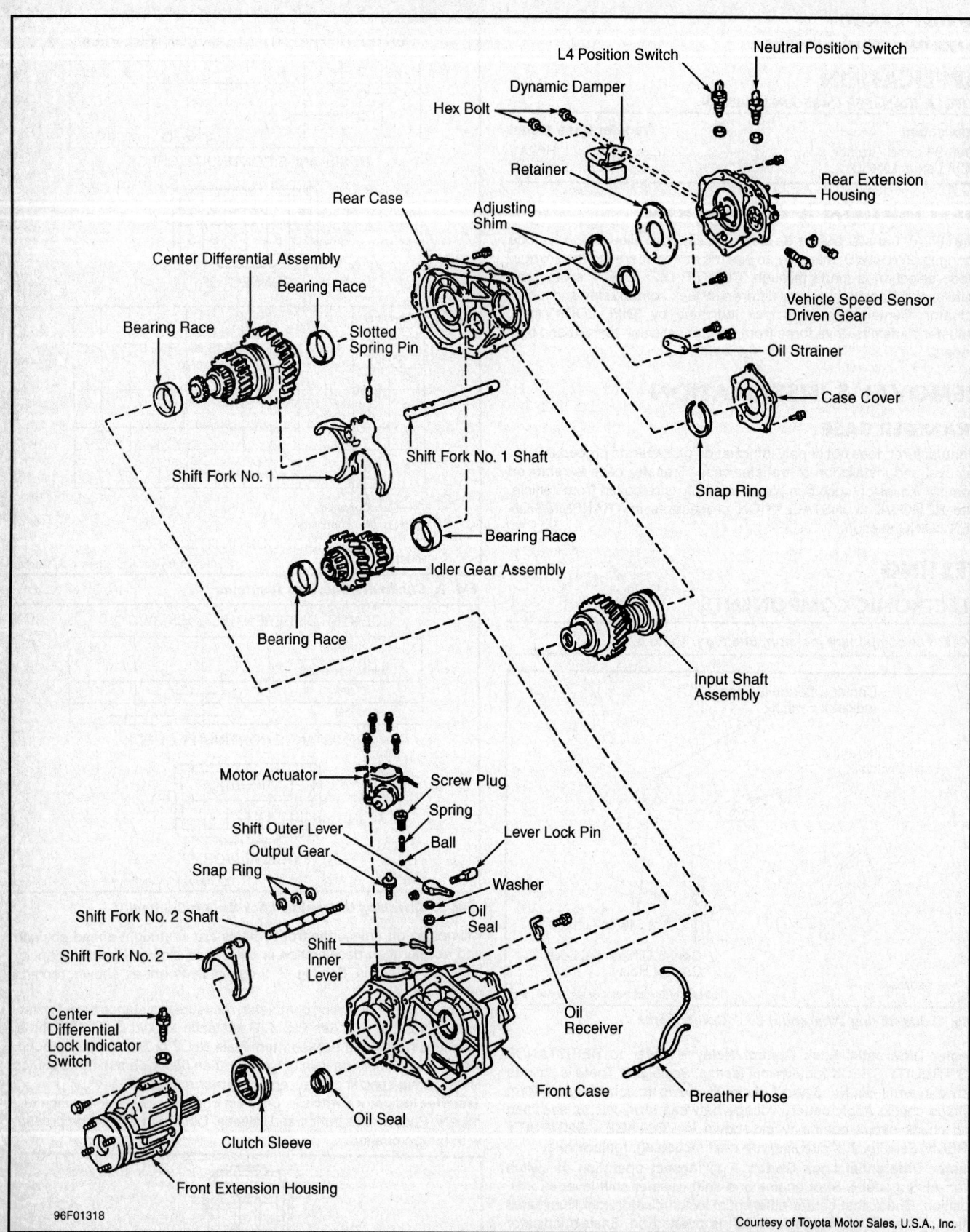

96F01318

Courtesy of Toyota Motor Sales, U.S.A., Inc.

Fig. 5: Exploded View Of Transfer Case Assembly

OVERHAUL

DISASSEMBLY

1) Remove breather hose. Remove dynamic damper. Remove motor actuator. Ensure transfer case is in locked position before removing actuator. Remove actuator output gear. Remove plug, spring and ball. Remove all indicator switches. *See Fig. 5.*

2) Remove front extension housing. Remove clutch sleeve, shift fork No. 2 and fork shaft. Remove rear extension housing. Remove retainer and 5 attaching bolts. Remove the adjusting shims. Remove oil strainer from rear case. Remove case cover. Remove snap ring from rear case. Unbolt and separate cases. Remove 2 bearing races from rear case. Remove input shaft assembly. Remove idle gear assembly, center differential assembly and shift fork No. 1 and shift fork No. 1 shaft assembly as single unit. *See Fig. 5.*

3) Remove inner and outer shift levers. Remove lever lock pin. Separate and remove levers. Replace shift lever and input shaft oil seal if necessary. Remove oil receiver from front case. Remove idler gear and output shaft bearing races from front case if necessary. Disassemble input shaft assembly. Remove snap ring. Support bearing and press out input shaft. Remove inner snap ring and support input gear. Press out input shaft. Support bearing and press out shaft. *See Fig. 6.*

4) Measure low gear idler thrust clearance. *See Fig. 7.* Clearance should be .005-.011" (.125-.275 mm). Using dial indicator, measure low idler gear radial movement (oil clearance). Clearance should be .0006-.0027" (.015-.068 mm).

5) Disassemble idler gear assembly. Using 2-jaw puller, remove front bearing. Using bearing splitter, press off rear bearing. Remove idler low gear and needle bearing. Remove high/low clutch sleeve.

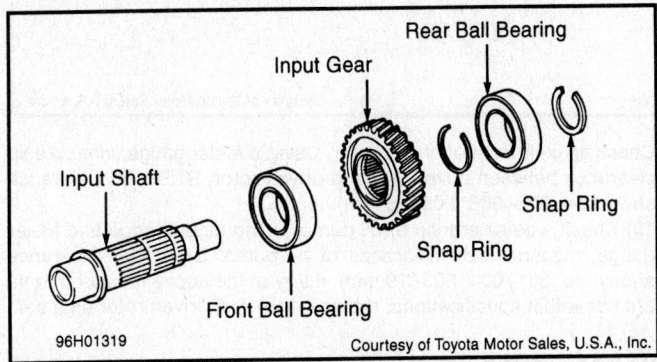

Fig. 6: **Identifying Input Shaft Components**

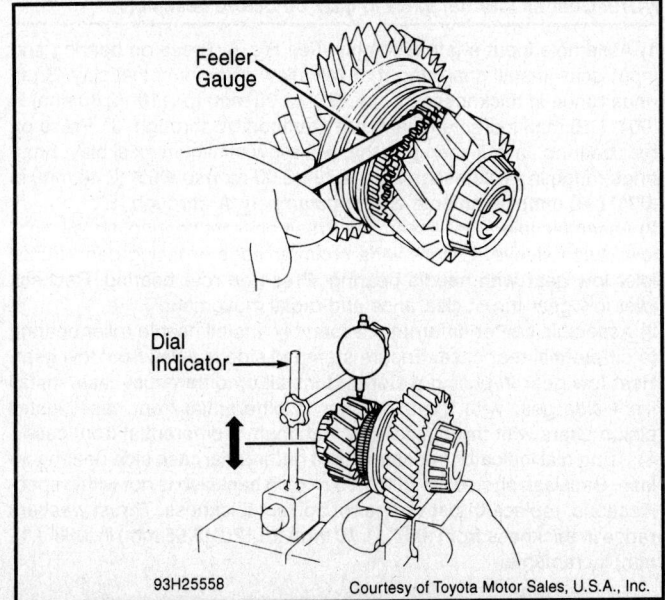

Fig. 7: **Measuring Idler Gear Assembly Thrust Clearances**

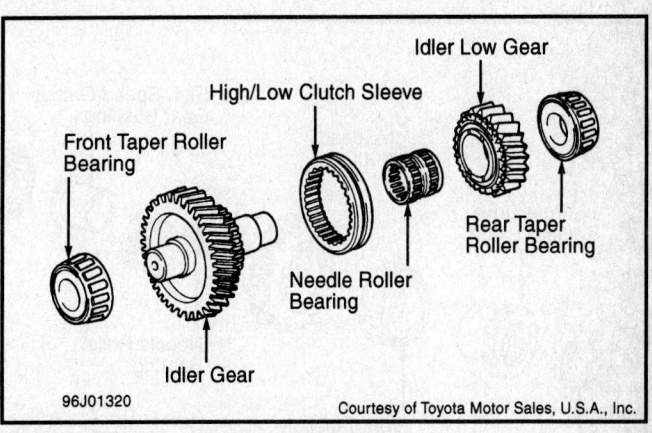

Fig. 8: **Identifying Idler Gear Components**

6) Disassemble differential assembly. Check high speed gear thrust clearance. *See Fig. 9.* Clearance should be .004-.010" (.10-.25 mm). Using dial indicator, measure high speed gear radial clearance (oil clearance). Clearance should be .0006-.0030" (.015-.071 mm).

7) Remove front snap ring. Using bearing splitter, support front drive gear piece and press out shaft. Press off front bearing. Remove high speed output gear and low clutch sleeve. Remove needle bearing. Remove high/low clutch sleeve assembly. Using bearing splitter, support clutch hub and press off high speed output gear bushing and clutch hub. *See Fig. 10.*

8) Remove 2 straight pins. Press off rear bearing. Unbolt and separate differential cases. Remove rear side gear with thrust washer. Remove pinion shaft straight pin. Remove pinion shaft, pinion gear and thrust washer. Remove front side gear with thrust washer. Using soft-faced hammer, remove low gear.

9) Disassemble front extension housing assembly. Remove drive clutch hub snap ring. Using 2 jaw puller, remove drive clutch hub. Using a soft-faced hammer, drive out front output shaft. Remove dust deflectors. Remove oil seal. Remove snap ring and bearing from housing. *See Fig. 11.*

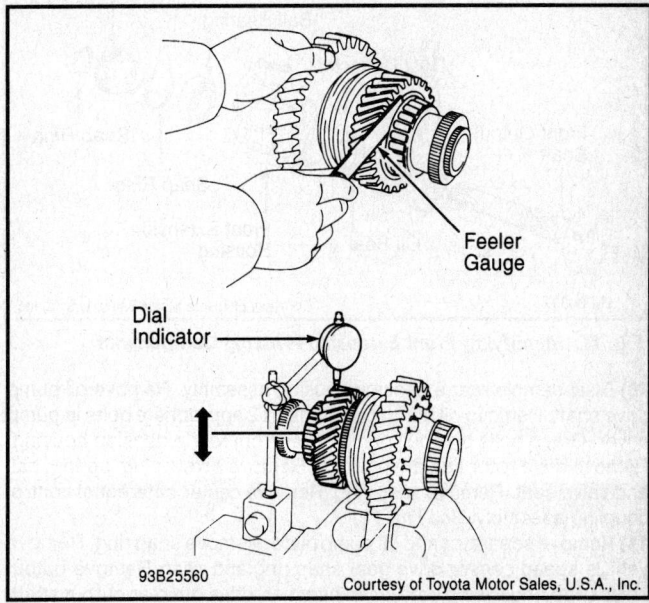

Fig. 9: **Measuring Differential Assembly Thrust Clearance**

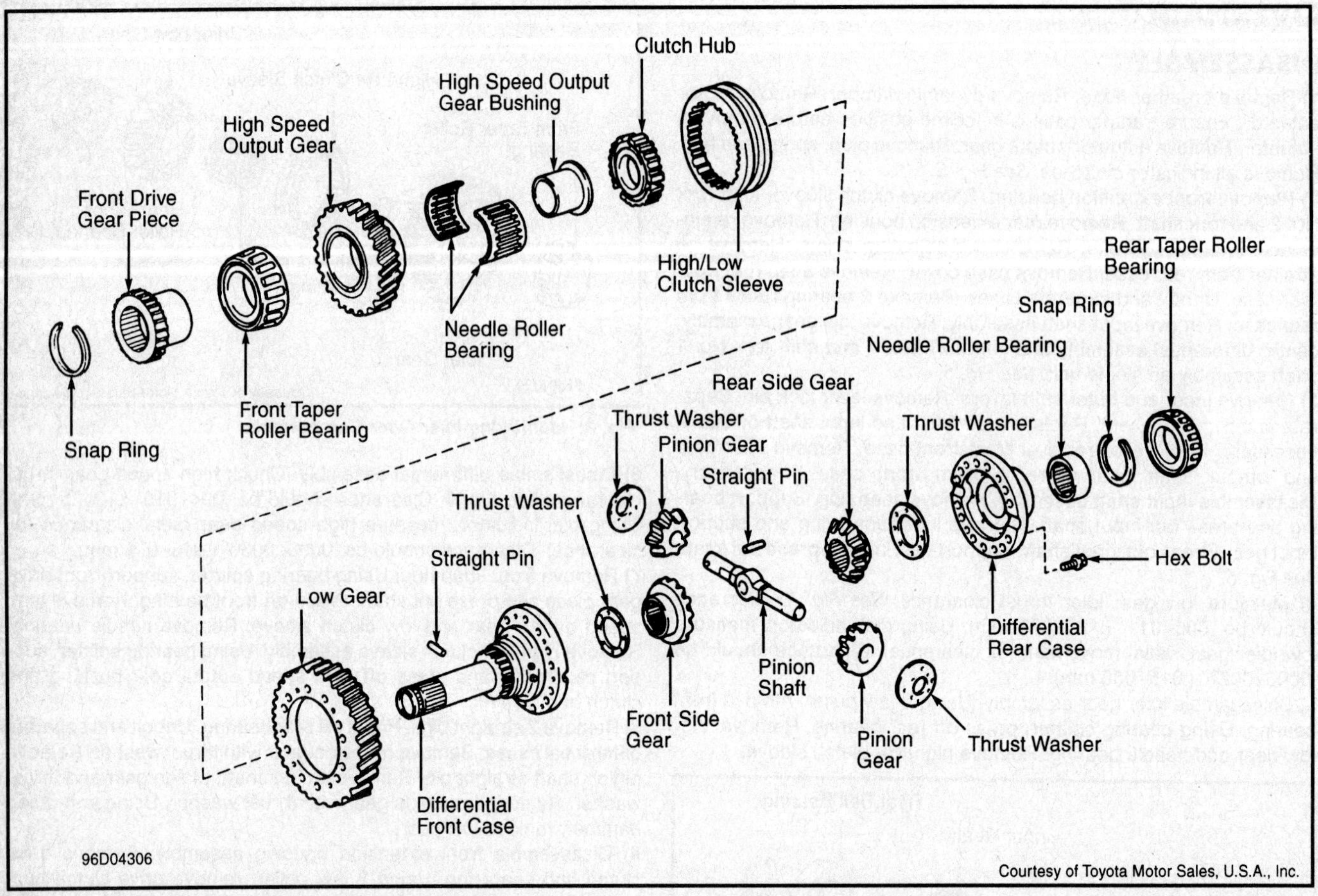

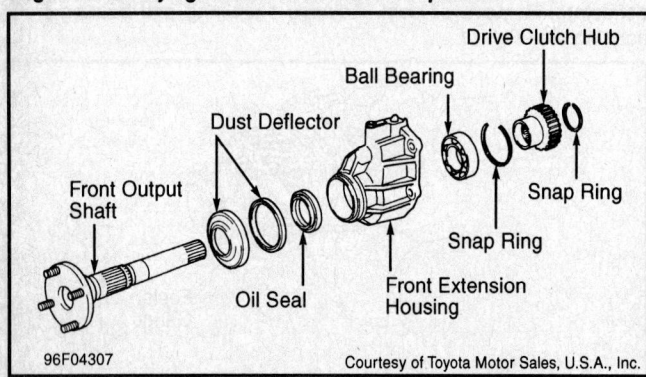

Fig. 10: Identifying Center Differential Components

96D04306

Courtesy of Toyota Motor Sales, U.S.A., Inc.

Fig. 11: Identifying Front Extension Housing Components

96F04307

Courtesy of Toyota Motor Sales, U.S.A., Inc.

10) Disassemble rear extension housing assembly. Remove oil pump drive shaft. Remove oil pump cover. Insert 2 appropriate bolts in pump cover. Grasp bolts and pull pump cover from rear extension housing. Remove drive rotor and driven rotor. Remove screw plug, spring, ball and valve seat. Remove snap ring. Remove center differential control coupling assembly. See Fig. 12.

11) Remove separator and oil pump plate. Remove snap ring. Remove vehicle speed sensor drive gear snap ring and gear. Remove output shaft snap ring. Using soft-faced hammer, drive out rear output shaft. Remove two seal rings from rear of output shaft. Remove dust deflectors. Remove oil seal. Remove snap ring, remove ball bearing from rear extension housing. Check oil pump clearances. Install oil pump drive and driven rotor.

12) Check body clearance of driven rotor. Using a feeler gauge, measure body clearance between driven rotor and extension housing, STEP "A". See Fig. 13. Clearance should be .003-.007" (.08-.17 mm).

Check tip clearance of driven rotor. Using a feeler gauge, measure tip clearance between drive rotor and driven rotor, STEP "B". Clearance should be .002-.006" (.05-.15 mm).

13) Check side clearance of oil pump. Using straightedge and feeler gauge, measure side clearance of oil pump, STEP "C". Clearance should be .001-.004" (.03-.10 mm). If any of the above measurements are not within specifications, replace drive and driven rotor as a set.

REASSEMBLY

NOTE: Coat all internal parts in gear oil before assembly.

1) Assemble input shaft assembly. See Fig. 6. Press on bearing and input gear. Install snap ring that will allow minimum axial play. Snap rings range in thicknesses from .079" (2.00 mm) to .110" (2.80 mm) in .004" (.10 mm) increments, and are stamped "A" through "J". Press on rear bearing. Install snap ring that will allow minimum axial play. Snap rings range in thicknesses from .079" (2.00 mm) to .095" (2.40 mm) in .004" (.10 mm) increments and are stamped "A" through "E".

2) Assemble idler gear assembly. Press on front bearing. Install high/low clutch sleeve. Ensure wide chamfer edge is facing gear. Install idler low gear with needle bearing. Press on rear bearing. Recheck idler low gear thrust clearance and radial movement.

3) Assemble center differential assembly. Install needle roller bearing to differential rear case. Ensure stamped side is away from low gear. Heat low gear in boiling water and install on differential case. Install front side gear with thrust washer in differential front case. Install pinion gears with thrust washers and shaft in differential front case.

4) Using dial indicator, measure front differential case side gear backlash. Backlash should be .002" (.05 mm). If backlash is not within specifications, replace thrust washer of correct thickness. Thrust washers range in thickness from .067" (1.70 mm) to .120" (3.05 mm) in .006" (.15 mm) increments.

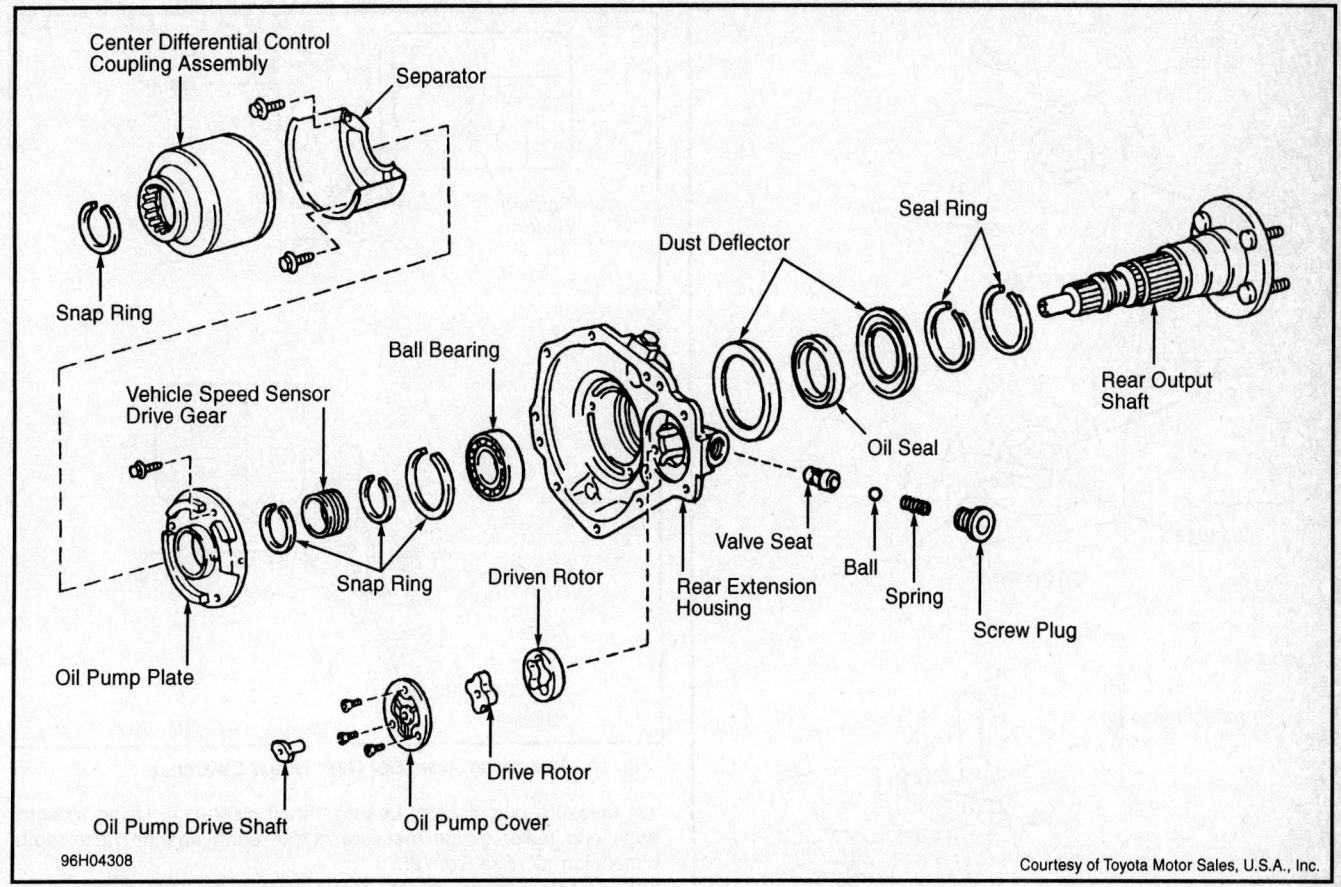

96H04308

Courtesy of Toyota Motor Sales, U.S.A., Inc.

Fig. 12: Identifying Rear Extension Housing Components

5) Using dial indicator, measure rear differential case side gear backlash. *See Fig. 14*. Backlash should be .002" (.05 mm). If backlash is not within specifications, replace thrust washer of correct thickness. Thrust washers range in thickness from .067" (1.70 mm) to .120" (3.05 mm) in .006" (.15 mm) increments.

6) Install straight pin through pinion shaft into front differential case. Install rear side gear with thrust washer. Install differential rear case and tighten bolts to 65 ft. lbs. (88 N.m). Turn pinion gears. Loosen differential case bolts and retighten bolts to 72 ft. lbs. (98 N.m).

7) Press rear bearing onto differential case. Press on clutch hub. Install straight pin. Press on high speed output gear bushing. Ensure bushing is properly aligned. Install straight pin. Install high/low clutch sleeve. Ensure wide chamfer edge is facing gear. Install high speed output gear with needle bearing.

8) Press on front bearing. Press on front drive gear piece. Install snap ring that will allow minimum axial play. Snap rings range in thickness from .071" (1.80 mm) to .110" (2.80 mm) in .004" (.10 mm) increments. Check high speed gear thrust clearance. *See Fig. 9*. Clearance should be .004-.010" (.10-.25 mm). Using dial indicator, measure high speed gear radial movement (oil clearance). Clearance should be .0006-.0030" (.015-.071 mm).

9) Assemble front extension housing. Install dust deflectors. Install ball bearing to front extension housing. Select and install snap ring that will allow minimum axial play. Snap rings are available marked "A" and "B" in measurements of .067" (1.7 mm) and .071" (1.8 mm). Drive in front output shaft. Press on drive clutch hub. Install snap ring that allows minimum axial play. Snap rings are available in thicknesses ranging from .071" (1.8 mm) to .087" (2.2 mm) in .005" (.10 mm) and are stamped "A" through "E".

10) Assemble rear extension housing. Install ball bearing to rear housing. Select and install snap ring that allows minimum axial play. Snap ring are stamped "A" and "B" in thicknesses of .067" (1.7 mm) and .071" (1.8 mm). Install dust deflectors and oil seal. *See Fig. 11*. Press in rear

output shaft. Install snap ring that allows minimum axial play. Snap rings available in thicknesses of .077" (1.95 mm) to .089" (2.25 mm) in .004" (.10 mm) increments. Snap rings are marked "1" through "4".

11) Install vehicle speed sensor drive gear and snap ring. Install oil pump plate and separator. Install valve seat, ball, spring and screw plug. Install drive and driven rotor. Ensure both rotors are properly indexed using alignment marks. Install oil pump cover. Ensure to align oil hole of rear extension housing and oil groove end of oil pump cover. Install oil pump drive shaft.

12) Install dust deflector to front case and front output shaft. Install ball bearing to front case. Select and install snap ring that allows minimum axial play. Snap rings are marked "A" and "B" in thicknesses of .067" (1.7 mm) and .071" (1.8 mm). Install oil seal. Install front output shaft and drive clutch hub. Install snap ring that allows minimum axial play. Snap rings are available in thicknesses of .071" (1.8 mm) to .087" (2.2 mm).

13) Install bearing races for output shaft and idler gear to front case. Install oil receiver in front case. Install outer and inner shift lever. Drive lock pin in outer lever and secure with nut. Install idle gear assembly, center differential assembly and shift fork No. 1 assembly as single unit in front case.

14) Using soft-faced hammer, install input shaft assembly in front case. Install oil strainer in rear case. Apply Three Bond (1281) sealant on case halves and assemble cases. Install input shaft bearing snap ring. Apply sealant to rear case cover and install.

15) Measure idler gear rear bearing thrust clearance. Using depth gauge, measure depth of idler gear rear bearing race, dimension "A". *See Fig. 15*. Apply pressure on bearing race when measuring. Using straightedge and feeler gauge, measure depth of oil pump cover, dimension "B".

16) Determine shim thickness from calculation, "A" + "B" + thrust clearance. Thrust clearance specification is .022-.049" (.0009-.0019 mm). See REAR IDLER GEAR BEARING SHIM SPECIFICATION table for necessary shim.

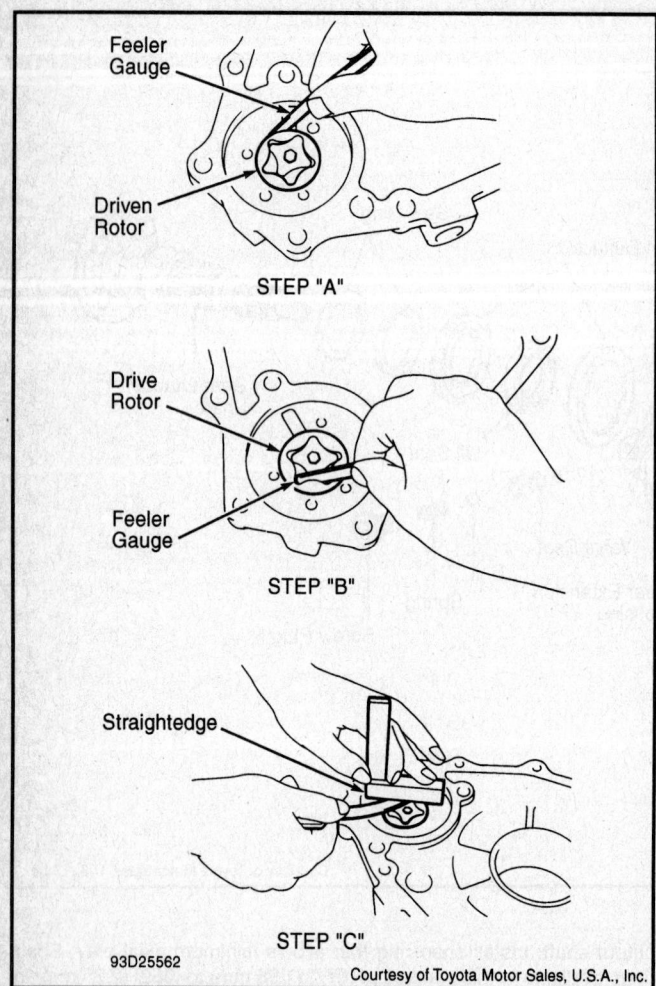

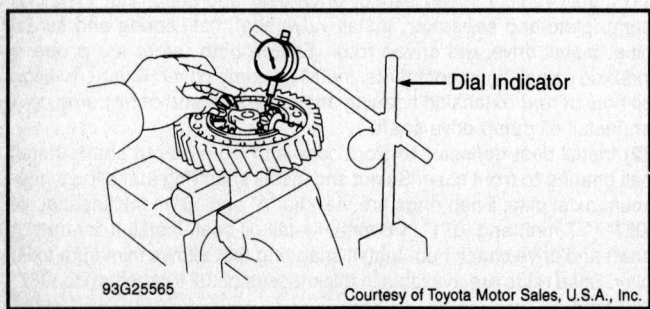

Fig. 13: Identifying Oil Pump Measuring Points

Fig. 14: Measuring Differential Backlash

REAR IDLER GEAR BEARING SHIM SPECIFICATION

Thickness In. (mm)	Stamped I.D. Code
.012 (.30)	2
.018 (.45)	3
.021 (.55)	13
.095 (2.4)	4
.102 (2.6)	5
.110 (2.8)	6
.118 (3.0)	7
.126 (3.2)	8
.134 (3.4)	9
.142 (3.6)	10
.150 (3.8)	11
.156 (4.0)	12

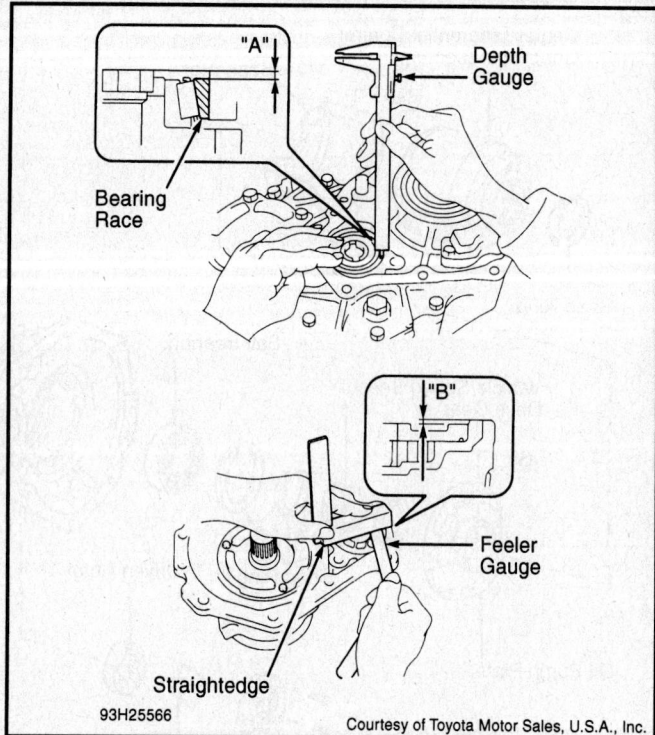

Fig. 15: Measuring Rear Idler Gear Thrust Clearance

17) Measure output shaft bearing thrust clearance. Using straightedge and feeler gauge measure output shaft bearing race depth, dimension "C". See Fig. 16.

18) Select correct thrust shim using calculation; Dimension "C" + .0006-.0015" (.014-.039 mm). See OUTPUT SHAFT BEARING SHIM SPECIFICATION table.

OUTPUT SHAFT BEARING SHIM SPECIFICATION

Thickness In. (mm)	Stamped
.012 (.30)	B
.018 (.45)	C
.022 (.55)	M
.039 (1.0)	D
.047 (1.2)	E
.055 (1.4)	F
.063 (1.6)	G
.071 (1.8)	H
.079 (2.0)	J
.087 (2.2)	K
.095 (2.4)	L

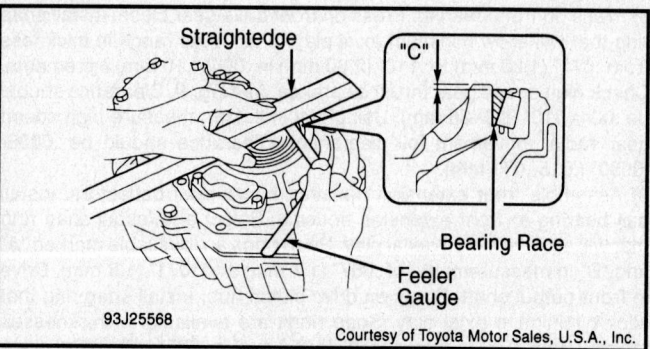

Fig. 16: Measuring Output Shaft Thrust Clearance

19) Install selected shims to idler gear and output shaft bearings. If using more than one shim, install thinner shim on bearing side. Install retainer to rear case. Apply Three Bond (1281) sealant to rear extension housing and install. Tighten bolts to specification. See TORQUE SPECIFICATIONS table. Install clutch sleeve, shift fork No. 2 and fork shaft No. 2.

20) Apply Three Bond (1281) sealant to front extension housing. Shift clutch sleeve into 4WD lock position and install housing. Install all indicator switches. Install ball, spring and screw plug through actuator case opening. Install actuator output gear. Apply Three Bond (1281) sealant to case and install motor actuator. Install dynamic damper. Install breather hose. *See Fig.5.* Tighten all fasteners to specification. See TORQUE SPECIFICATIONS table.

TORQUE SPECIFICATIONS

TORQUE SPECIFICATIONS

Application	Ft. Lbs. (N.m)
Actuator Screw Plug	14 (19)
Case Cover Bolt	27 (37)
Differential Case Bolt (Initial)	65 (88)
Differential Case Bolt (After Pinion Turned)	72 (98)
Dynamic Damper	27 (37)
Front Extension Housing Bolt	27 (37)
Indicator Switches	27 (37)
Motor Actuator Bolt	13 (18)
Oil Pump Screw Plug	14 (19)
Rear Case Retainer	28 (39)
Rear Extension Housing Bolt	28 (39)
Transfer Case Bolt	27 (37)

Application	INCH Lbs. (N.m)
Oil Pump Cover	43 (4.9)
Oil Pump Plate	43 (4.9)
Oil Receiver Bolt	108 (12)
Oil Strainer Bolt	43 (4.9)
Shift Lever Lock Pin Nut	108 (12)

WIRING DIAGRAMS

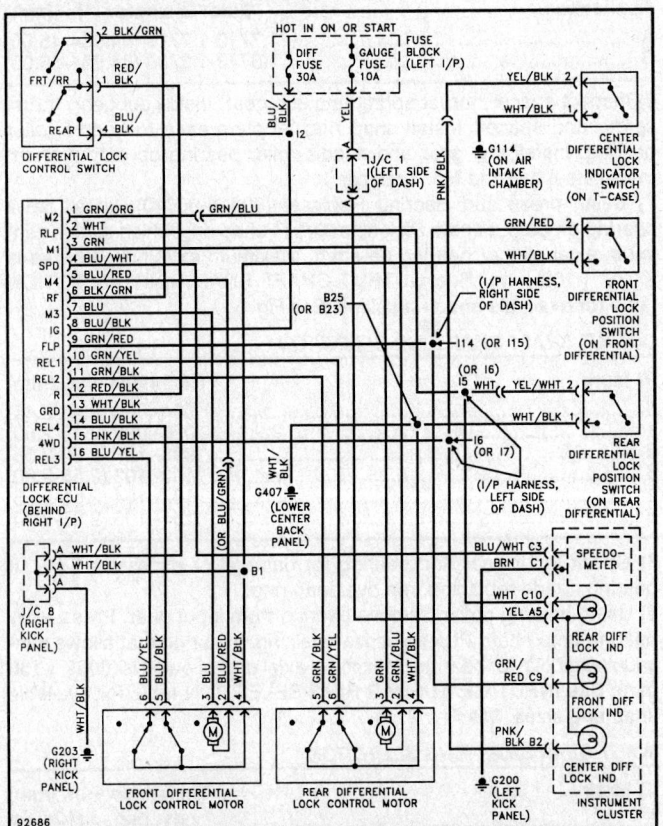

Fig. 17: *Front & Rear Differential Lockout Wiring Diagram (1995-96 Toyota Land Cruiser & Lexus LX 450)*

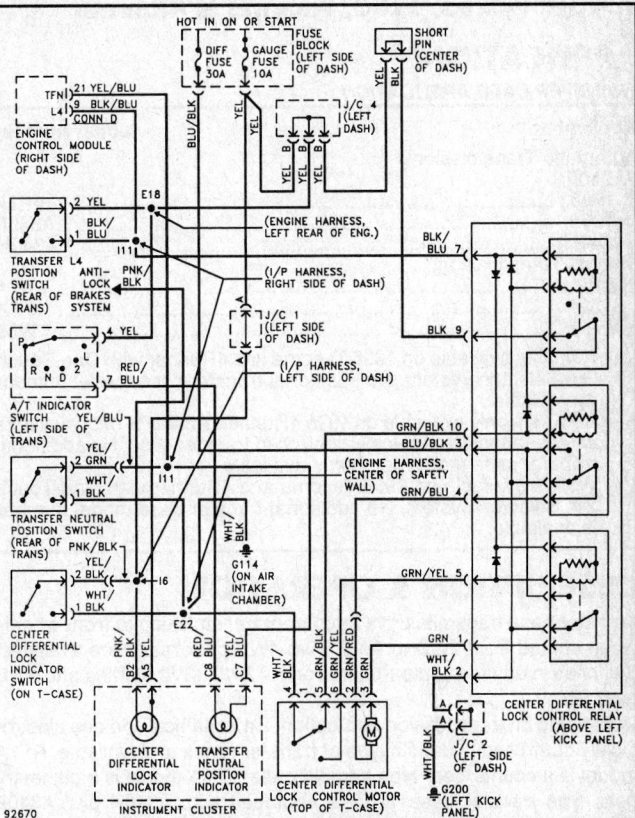

Fig. 18: *Center Differential Lockout Wiring Diagram (1995 Toyota Land Cruiser & Lexus LX 450)*

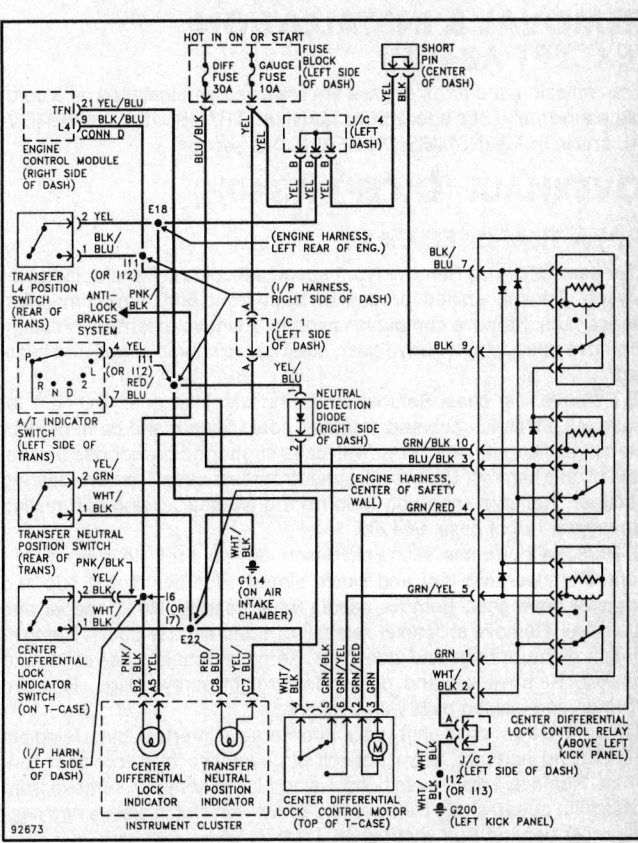

Fig. 19: *Center Differential Lockout Wiring Diagram (1996 Toyota Land Cruiser & Lexus LX 450)*

TRANSFER CASES
Toyota Pickup, T100, Tacoma & 4Runner

Toyota Pickup, T100, Tacoma & 4Runner

APPLICATION

TRANSFER CASE APPLICATION

Application	Model Number
Automatic Transmission	
A340F	
1995	VF1A
1996	[1] A340F
A340H	[2] A340H
Manual Transmission	
G58	RF1A
R150F	VF1A
W59	[3] W59

[1] – A340F is available on 1996 Tacoma and 4Runner with One-Touch 2-4 Selector System. No additional transfer case model number is available.

[2] – A340H is only available on 1995 4Runner. A340H is only available with 2-speed electronically controlled transfer case. No additional transfer case model number is available.

[3] – W59 is available on 1996 Tacoma and 4Runner with One-Touch 2-4 Selector System. No additional transfer case model number is available.

DESCRIPTION & OPERATION

Transfer case transmits drive force from transmission to front wheels when shifted from 2WD to 4WD. Two 4WD gear ratios are available. Switches in driver's compartment control 2WD/4WD shifting and 4WD gear ratios.

Depending on transmission application, 2 mechanical and one electronically controlled hydraulic type of transfer cases are available. RF1A model is a countergear type transfer case. VF1A model is a planetary gear type transfer case. Models equipped with A340H and A340F automatic transmission incorporate an electronically controlled 2-speed transfer case.

REMOVAL & INSTALLATION (EXCEPT A340H)

Transmission and transfer case are removed and installed as a complete assembly. See appropriate MANUAL TRANSMISSION REMOVAL article in TRANSMISSION SERVICING section.

OVERHAUL (EXCEPT A340H)

RF1A TRANSFER CASE

Disassembly – 1) Remove No. 1 speed sensor and transfer indicator switch. Loosen staked portion of both front and rear companion flange nuts. Remove companion flanges. Remove extension housing. Remove speedometer drive gear, steel ball, oil pump screw and bearing.

2) Remove rear case. Remove snap ring with idler gear. DO NOT let case fall, as clutch hub and steel ball could fall out and be damaged. Remove idler gear snap ring. With case supported on wooden blocks, use plastic hammer to drive idler gear from rear case. Remove bearing retainer. Remove snap ring from front drive gear. Using soft mallet, drive gear out of case. See Fig. 1.

3) Remove 2 oil pipes. Using pin punch, drive out roll pin in No. 1 shift fork. Remove shift fork and clutch sleeve. Remove clutch hub and transfer drive gear. Remove needle roller bearing, No. 2 spacer and steel ball. Remove shift lever retainer or transfer case cover. Remove detent plugs, springs and steel balls. Remove transfer case cover and gasket. Remove left and right side straight screw plugs. Remove springs and locking balls with a magnet.

4) Remove front drive shift fork shaft. Remove interlock pin. Using pin punch and hammer, drive out roll pin. Remove high-low shift fork shaft. Remove 4 front case bolts. Using plastic hammer, remove front case with output shaft. Remove No. 2 fork with clutch sleeve and needle roller bearing from input shaft.

5) Remove 2 snap rings from input gear and countergear. Place reduction gear case on wooden blocks. Using a plastic hammer, tap input gear and countergear out of reduction gear case. Remove output shaft bearing retainer. Remove snap ring from output shaft bearing.

Place front case on wooden blocks. Using a plastic hammer, tap output shaft from front case.

6) Remove snap ring from output shaft. Press out output shaft front bearing, No. 1 spacer and low gear. Remove steel ball and needle roller bearing from output shaft. Remove snap ring from low gear. Remove spacer, thrust spring and sub gear.

Inspection – 1) Measure oil clearance between transfer low gear and output shaft with needle roller bearing installed. Standard clearance should be .0004-.0022" (.010-.055 mm). Maximum clearance is .0030" (.075 mm). If clearance exceeds specification, replace low gear, needle roller bearing or output shaft.

2) Measure thrust clearance of transfer low gear with spacer and bearing installed on output shaft. DO NOT allow shaft of dial indicator to touch sub-gear while measuring thrust. Standard clearance should be .0039-.0098" (.10-.25 mm). Maximum clearance is .0118" (.30 mm). If clearance exceeds specification, replace spacer. See Fig. 3.

3) Using an arbor press, install ball, spacer, 2 needle roller bearings and transfer drive gear. DO NOT loosen ball. Measure oil clearance between transfer drive gear and output shaft with needle roller bearing installed. Standard clearance should be .0004-.0020" (.009-.051 mm). Maximum clearance is .0027" (.071 mm). If clearance exceeds specification, replace transfer drive gear, needle roller bearing or output shaft.

4) Measure thrust clearance of transfer drive gear on output shaft with spacer and clutch hub installed on shaft. Standard clearance should be .0035-.0106" (.089-.269 mm). Maximum clearance is .0126" (.320 mm). If clearance exceeds specification, replace spacer. Using an arbor press, remove ball, spacer, 2 needle roller bearings and transfer drive gear.

5) Measure clearance between hub sleeve and shift fork. Maximum clearance is .039" (1.00 mm). If clearance exceeds specification, replace shift fork or hub sleeve. Measure outer diameter of output shaft. See OUTPUT SHAFT MAXIMUM OUTER DIAMETER SPECIFICATIONS table. See Fig. 4. Measure shaft runout. Maximum runout is .0012" (.030 mm).

OUTPUT SHAFT MAXIMUM OUTER DIAMETER SPECIFICATIONS

Application	Outer Diameter – In. (mm)
A	1.7710-1.7717 (44.984-45.00)
B	1.3773-1.3780 (34.984-35.00)

6) Inspect spacer, thrust spring and sub gear. Install subgear, thrust spring and spacer. Install snap ring. Apply grease to needle roller bearing. Install low gear and needle roller bearing on output shaft. Install steel ball and No. 1 spacer.

7) Using press and Bearing Replacer (09316-60010), install NEW bearing on output shaft. Pick selective fit snap ring which allows minimum axial play of bearing on shaft. Maximum axial play allowed is .0039" (.100 mm). See OUTPUT SHAFT SNAP RING SELECTION table for available snap ring sizes. See Fig. 3.

OUTPUT SHAFT SNAP RING SELECTION

ID Mark	Thickness – In. (mm)
0	1.094-.096 (2.40-2.45)
1	.096-.098 (2.45-2.50)
2	.098-.100 (2.50-2.55)
3	.100-.102 (2.55-2.60)
4	.102-.104 (2.60-2.65)
5	.104-.106 (2.65-2.70)

8) Check input gear and bearing for damage or excessive wear. If bearing needs replacing, remove snap ring.

9) Using bearing puller, remove bearing from input gear. Press NEW bearing onto shaft. Pick selective retaining snap ring that allows minimum axial play of bearing. Maximum axial play allowed is .0059" (.150 mm). See INPUT GEAR SNAP RING SELECTION table for available snap ring sizes. See Fig. 2.

INPUT GEAR SNAP RING SELECTION

ID Mark	Thickness – In. (mm)
1	.081-.083 (2.05-2.10)
3	.085-.087 (2.15-2.20)
5	.089-.091 (2.25-2.30)

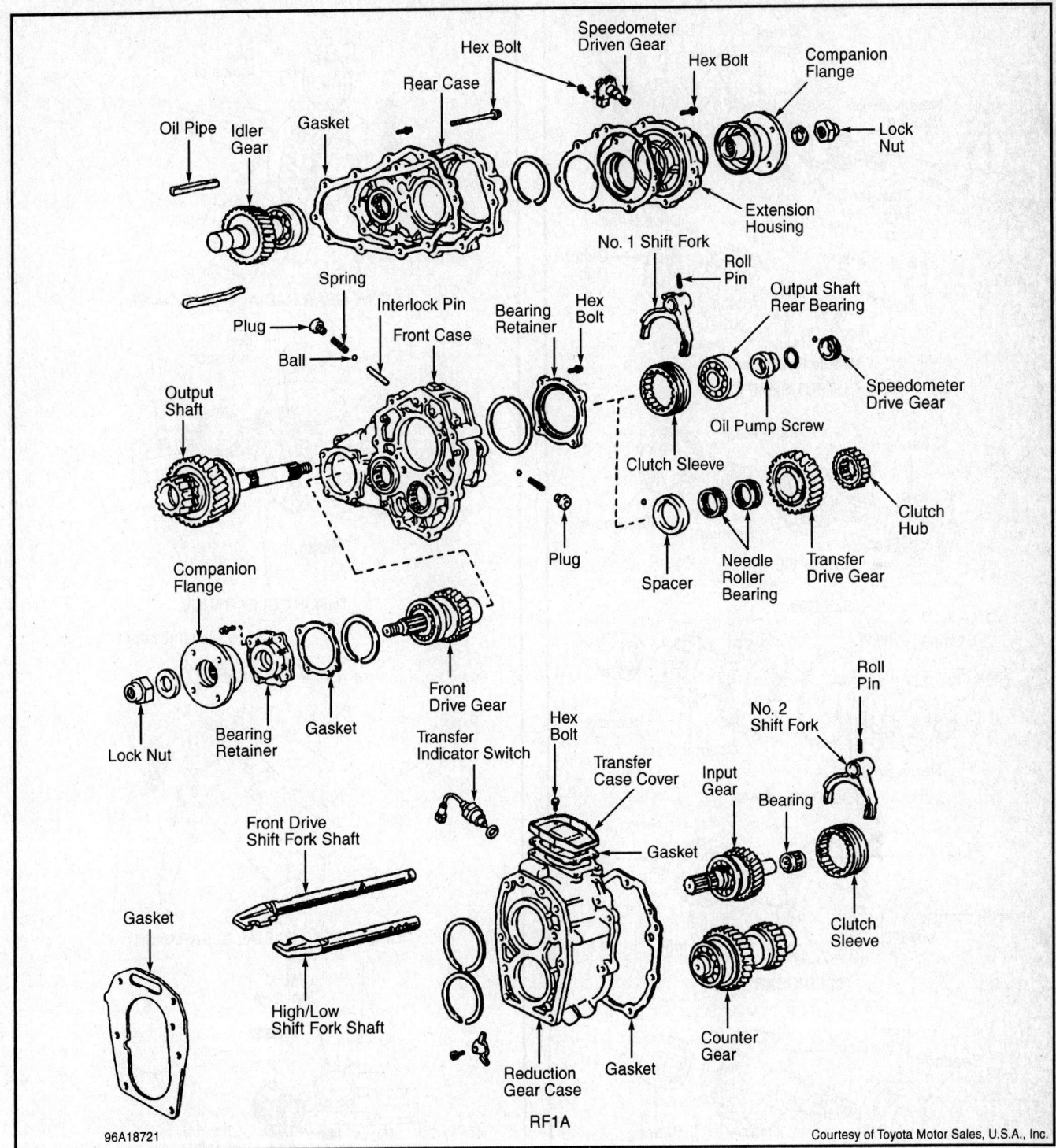

96A18721

RF1A

Courtesy of Toyota Motor Sales, U.S.A., Inc.

Fig. 1: Exploded View Of Transfer Case Components (RF1A)

10) Check countergear front bearing and sub-gear. Remove snap ring. Using press and bearing puller, remove countergear front bearing. Remove spacer, thrust spring and sub-gear. Install good sub-gear, thrust spring and spacer on countergear. *See Fig. 2.*

11) Using press and 32 mm socket, install NEW bearing on countergear. Install selective fit snap ring which allows minimum axial play of bearing on countergear shaft. Maximum axial play allowed is .0059" (.15 mm). See COUNTERGEAR SHAFT SNAP RING SELECTION table for available snap ring sizes. *See Fig. 2.*

COUNTERGEAR SHAFT SNAP RING SELECTION

ID Mark	Thickness – In. (mm)
1	.083-.085 (2.10-2.15)
3	.087-.089 (2.20-2.25)

12) Inspect rear countergear bearing and replace it (if necessary). Using Inside Bearing Puller (09612-30012), remove countergear rear bearing from front case. Install NEW bearing in front case.

13) Inspect idler gear and front bearing. If bearing needs replacement, use press sleeve to remove bearing from front case. Install NEW bearing in front case until it touches snap ring.

TRANSFER CASES
Toyota Pickup, T100, Tacoma & 4Runner (Cont.)

Thrust Spring
Bearing
Snap Ring
Sub-Gear
Spacer
Ball
Needle Roller Bearing
Snap Ring
Transfer Low Gear
Transfer Drive Gear
Output Shaft
Ball
Spacer
Clutch Hub
Needle Roller Bearing
OUTPUT SHAFT
Bearing
Input Gear
Snap Ring
Bearing
Hub Sleeve
INPUT GEAR
Sub-Gear
Bearing
Spacer
Snap Ring
Bearing
Counter Gear
Thrust Spring
COUNTER GEAR
Idler Gear
Snap Ring
Bearing
Bearing
IDLER GEAR
Front Drive Gear
Bearing
Bearing
FRONT DRIVE GEAR
96B18722
Courtesy of Toyota Motor Sales, U.S.A., Inc.

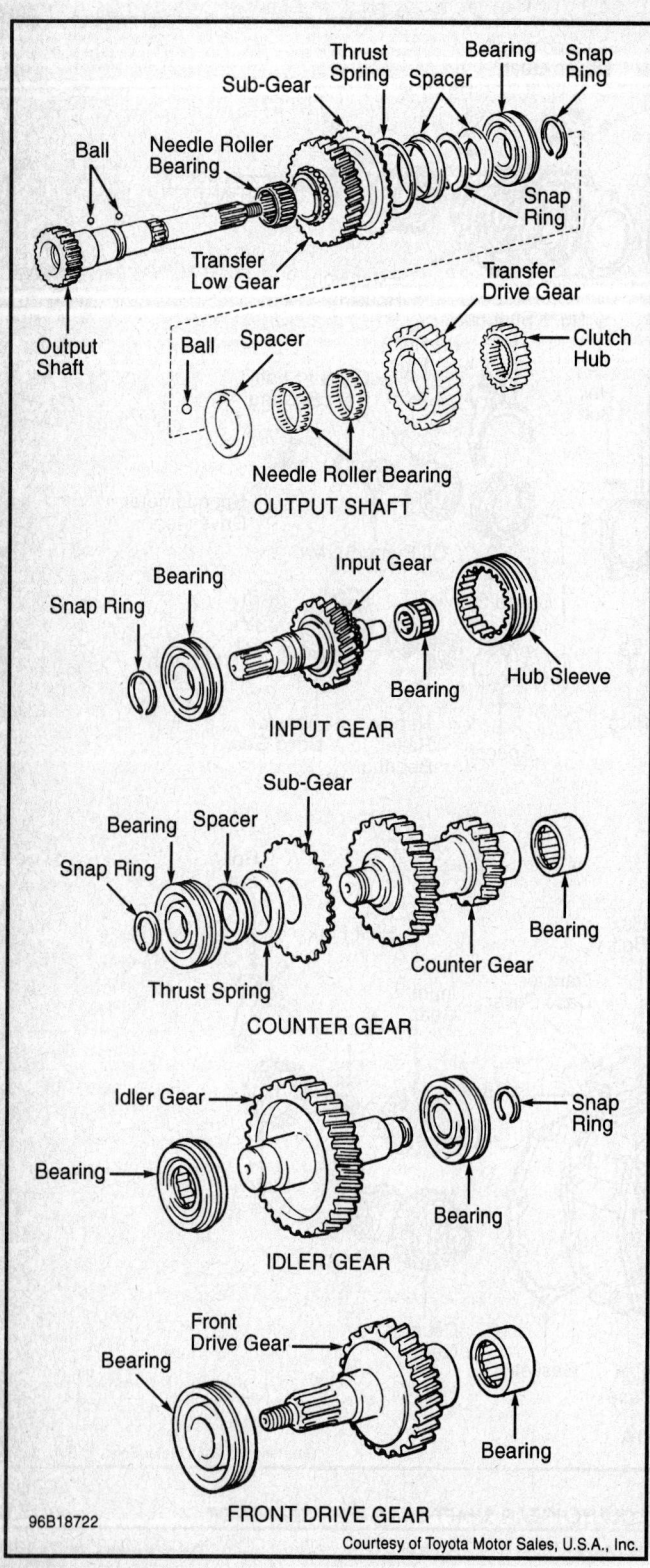

Fig. 2: Exploded View Of Transfer Case Shafts & Gears (RF1A)

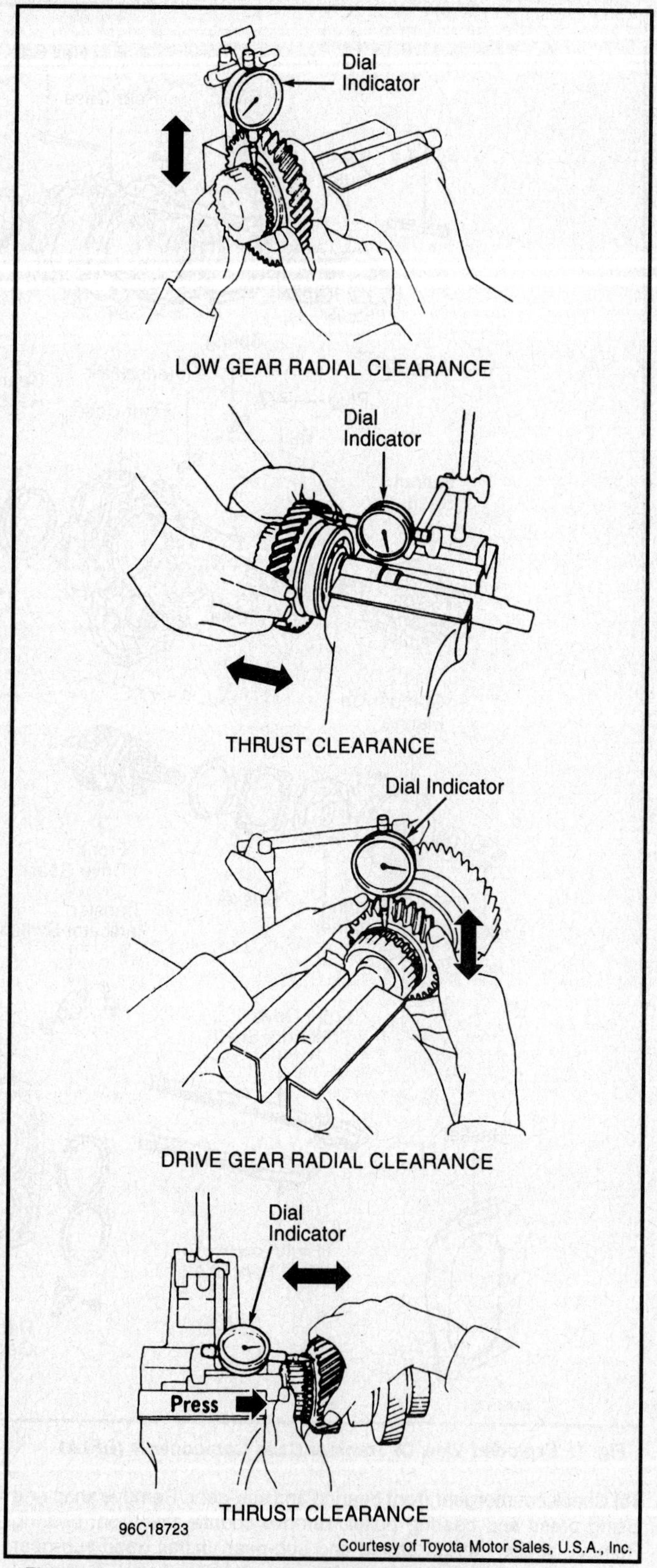

Dial Indicator
LOW GEAR RADIAL CLEARANCE
Dial Indicator
THRUST CLEARANCE
Dial Indicator
DRIVE GEAR RADIAL CLEARANCE
Dial Indicator
Press
THRUST CLEARANCE
96C18723
Courtesy of Toyota Motor Sales, U.S.A., Inc.

Fig. 3: Identifying Output Shaft Measuring Points

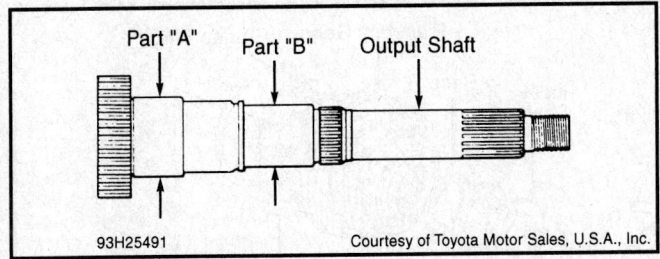

Fig. 4: Measuring Output Shaft Journal Diameter (RF1A)

14) If idler gear rear bearing needs replacement, remove snap ring. Press bearing off idler gear. Press NEW bearing onto idler gear. Install selective fit snap ring which allows minimum axial play of bearing on countergear shaft. Maximum axial play allowed is .0059" (.150 mm). See IDLER GEAR SNAP RING SELECTION table for available snap ring sizes. See Fig. 2.

IDLER GEAR SNAP RING SELECTION

ID Mark	Thickness – In. (mm)
A	.059-.061 (1.50-1.55)
B	.063-.065 (1.60-1.65)

15) Check front drive gear and bearing. Press damaged bearing off front drive gear. Install NEW bearing on front drive gear. If front drive gear rear bearing is defective, use inside bearing puller to remove bearing from rear case. Press NEW bearing into rear case. See Fig. 2.

16) Check oil seal at speedometer driven gear for wear or damage to sealing lips. If seal is damaged, use seal puller to remove oil seal. Install seal in sleeve so that face of seal is .79" (20.0 mm) below top edge of bore.

17) Check oil seals in extension housing for wear or damage to sealing lips. If either seal is damaged, use slide hammer with inside jaws to remove 2 seals. Install NEW seal for oil pump screw. Flat surface of this seal must face upward. Second seal in extension housing is output shaft oil seal.

18) Output shaft and front drive gear oil seals are identical except for certain markings. See Fig. 5. Identify output shaft oil seal by grooves which lean to right (clockwise) and by single arrow pointing in counterclockwise direction on this seal. Using Plug (09325-20010), install output shaft oil seal in extension housing.

19) Check oil seal at front drive gear for wear or damage to sealing lips. If seal is damaged, use Plug (09325-20010) to drive seal and dust cover out of front bearing retainer. Be sure to place retainer on wooden blocks to avoid damage to retainer surface while driving seal out.

20) Identify front drive gear oil seal by grooves which lean to left (counterclockwise), by double arrows pointing in clockwise direction and word FRONT on face of front drive gear oil seal. See Fig. 5. Using plug, install NEW oil seal with face at depth of .28" (7.0 mm) from front end of retainer. Install NEW dust cover using plug.

21) Using ohmmeter, check transfer indicator switch. When plunger is out, switch should be open and show no continuity. When plunger is in, switch should be closed and show continuity.

Reassembly – 1) Place front case on wooden blocks. Using plastic hammer, install output shaft to front case. Install roller bearing snap ring. Install bearing retainer on front case and tighten bolts to 13 ft. lbs. (18 N.m).

2) Place reduction gear case on wooden blocks. Using plastic hammer, install input gear and countergear in reduction gear case. Install input gear and countergear retaining snap rings. Install roller bearing on input shaft. Install No. 2 hub sleeve on input shaft. Install No. 2 shift fork on input shaft.

3) Place NEW gasket on front case. Install reduction gear case, with input gear and countergear, on front case. Install and tighten bolts to 27 ft. lbs. (37 N.m). Using plastic hammer, install front drive gear in front case. Install front drive gear snap ring. Place NEW gasket on front case. Lubricate oil seal lip with grease. Install front drive gear bearing retainer. Install and tighten bolts to 13 ft. lbs. (18 N.m). See Fig. 1.

4) Insert high-low shift fork shaft into No. 2 shift fork. Align slotted spring hole in shift fork with hole in shift shaft. Install interlock pin. Install front drive shift fork shaft with 2 grooves facing outward. Install ball and spring. Apply Three Bond (1344) sealer to plug threads. Install plug and tighten to 106 INCH lbs. (12 N.m). Repeat procedure with opposite ball, spring and plug.

5) Install steel locking ball and No. 2 spacer on output shaft. Install needle roller bearings, transfer lower gear and clutch hub. Install No. 1 shift fork and hub sleeve on front drive shift fork shaft. Align pin hole in fork with hole in shaft. Using pin punch, drive roll pin through fork and shaft. Install 2 oil pipes, positioned so that cut-out side faces upward.

6) Place rear case on wooden blocks. Using plastic hammer, drive idler gear into rear case. Install idler gear snap ring. Place NEW gasket on front case. Install rear case, together with idler gear, on front case. Install and tighten bolts "A" to 29 ft. lbs. (39 N.m) and bolts "B" to 27 ft lbs. (37 N.m). See Fig. 6. Install bearing, oil pump screw, locking bolt and speedometer drive gear. Using NEW gasket, install extension housing on rear case. Apply grease to 2 oil seals. Install extension housing bolts and tighten to 29 ft. lbs. (39 N.m).

7) Install transfer case cover with NEW gasket. Install and tighten bolts to 78 INCH lbs. (8.8 N.m). Install rear companion flange to output shaft. Apply Three Bond (1281) seal packing to output shaft and rear companion flange. Using Holding Tool (09330-00021), hold flange. Install washer and nut. Tighten nut to 91 ft. lbs. (123 N.m). Stake nut. Repeat procedure to install front companion flange to front drive gear. Install transfer indicator switch with washer. Tighten to 25 ft. lbs. (34 N.m). Install speed sensor and lock plate. Install and tighten bolt to 97 INCH lbs. (11 N.m).

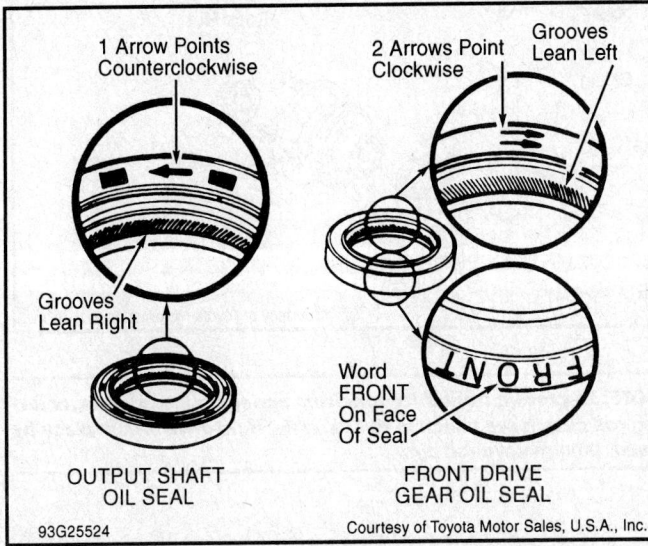

Fig. 5: Identifying Drive Gear Oil Seals

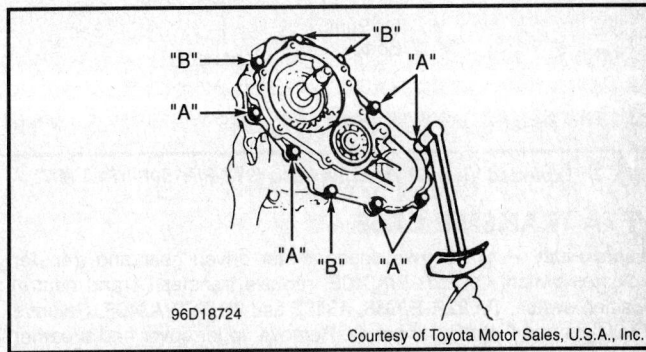

Fig. 6: Identifying Front & Rear Case Bolts

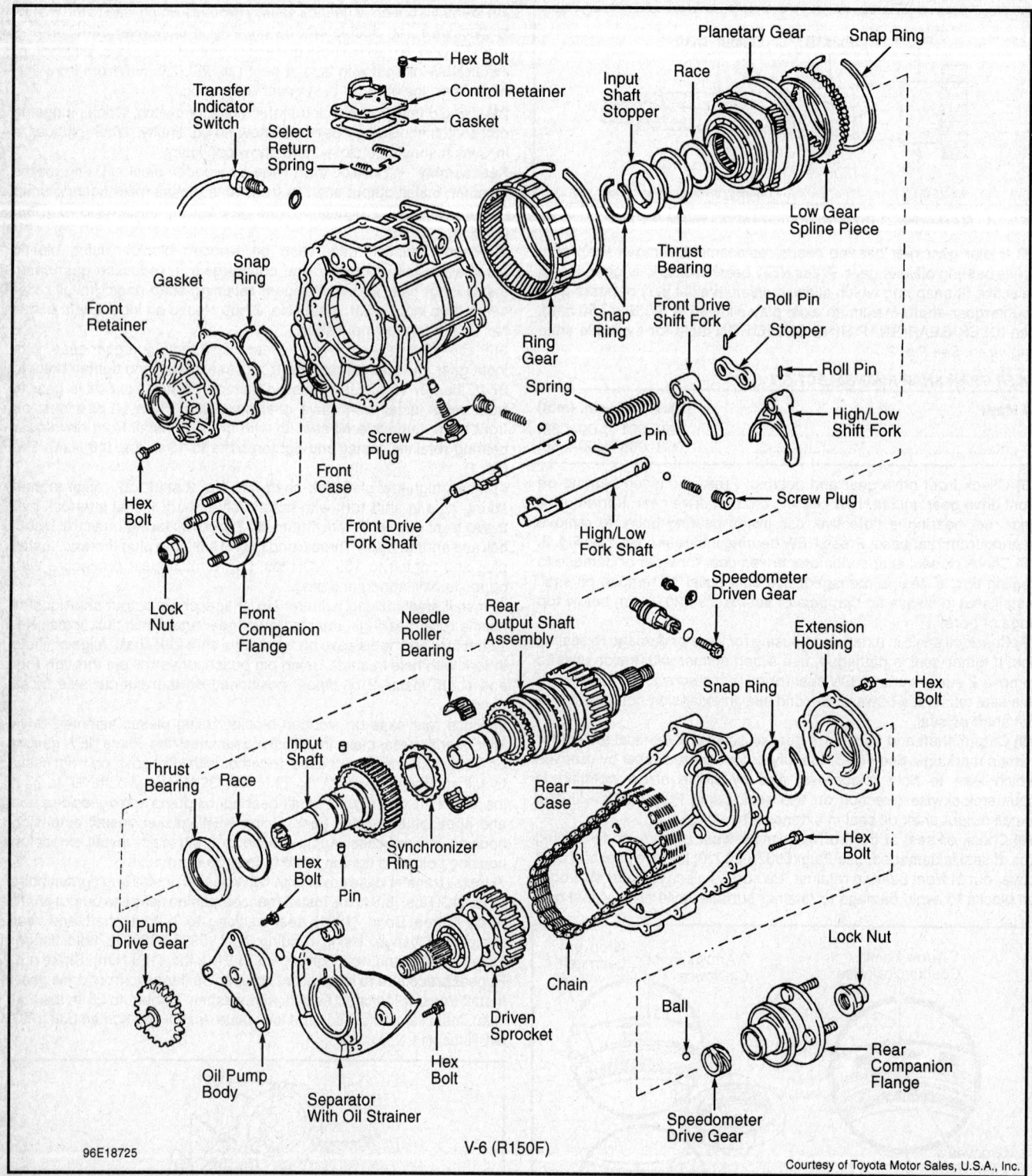

Fig. 7: Exploded View Of Transfer Case (3VZ-E/R150F-VF1A M/T)

VF1A TRANSFER CASE

Disassembly – 1) Remove speedometer driven gear and transfer indicator switch. On 22R-E/A340E, remove transfer L4 and neutral position switch. On 22R-E/G58, A340F and 3RZ-FE/A340F, Remove 2 roll pins and 2 shift gear heads. Remove upper cover and breather hose deflector. On 3VZ-E/R150F, remove control retainer. Remove select return spring from retainer. On all models, unstake and remove front and rear companion flange lock nuts. Remove front and rear companion flange. See Fig. 7, 8, 9, 10 or 11.

NOTE: To prevent front drive fork from springing loose when removing roll pins, leave punch in roll pin hole. Hold drive fork in place by hand, then remove roll pin.

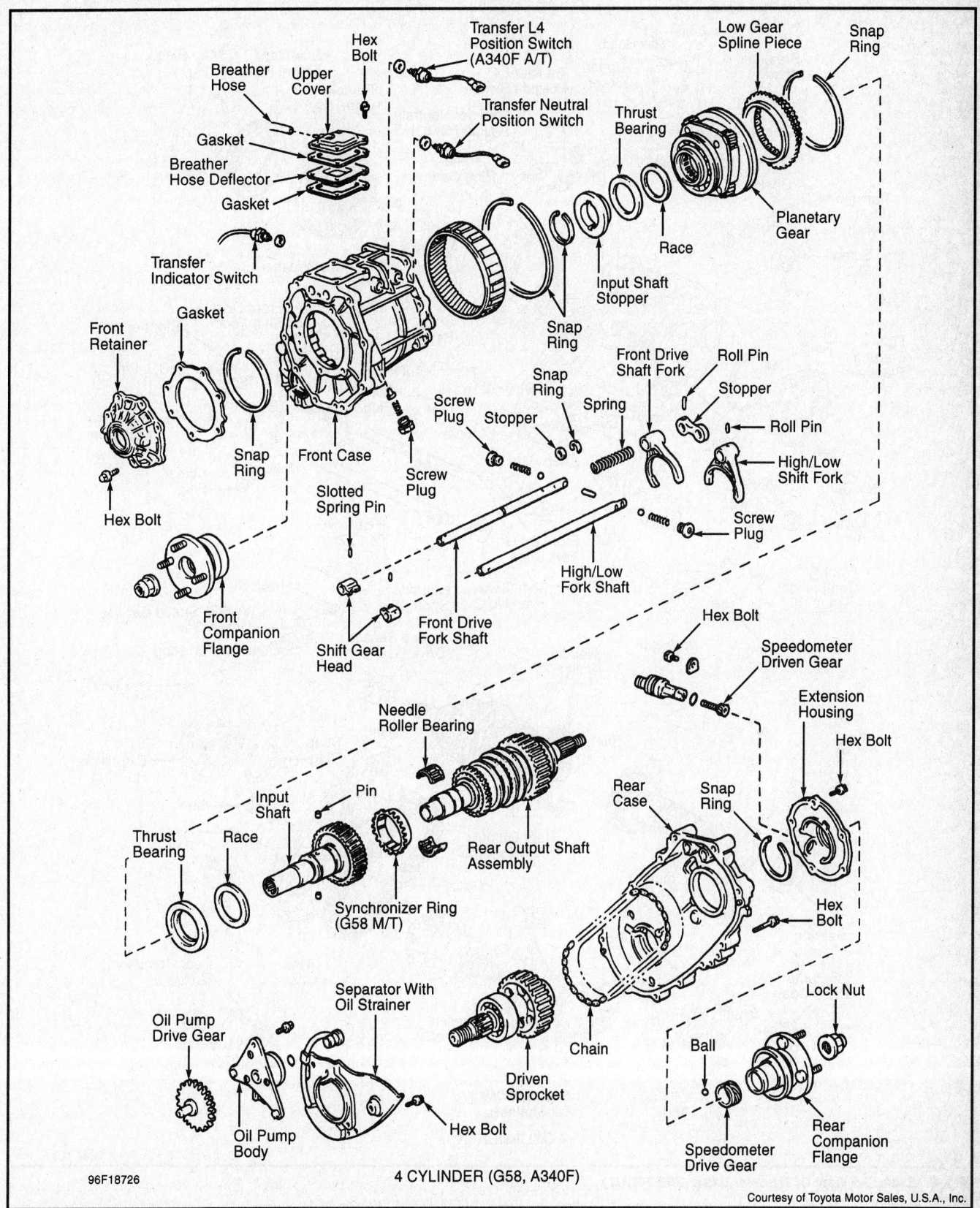

Fig. 8: Exploded View Of Transfer Case (22R-E/G58 & A340F-VF1A A/T)

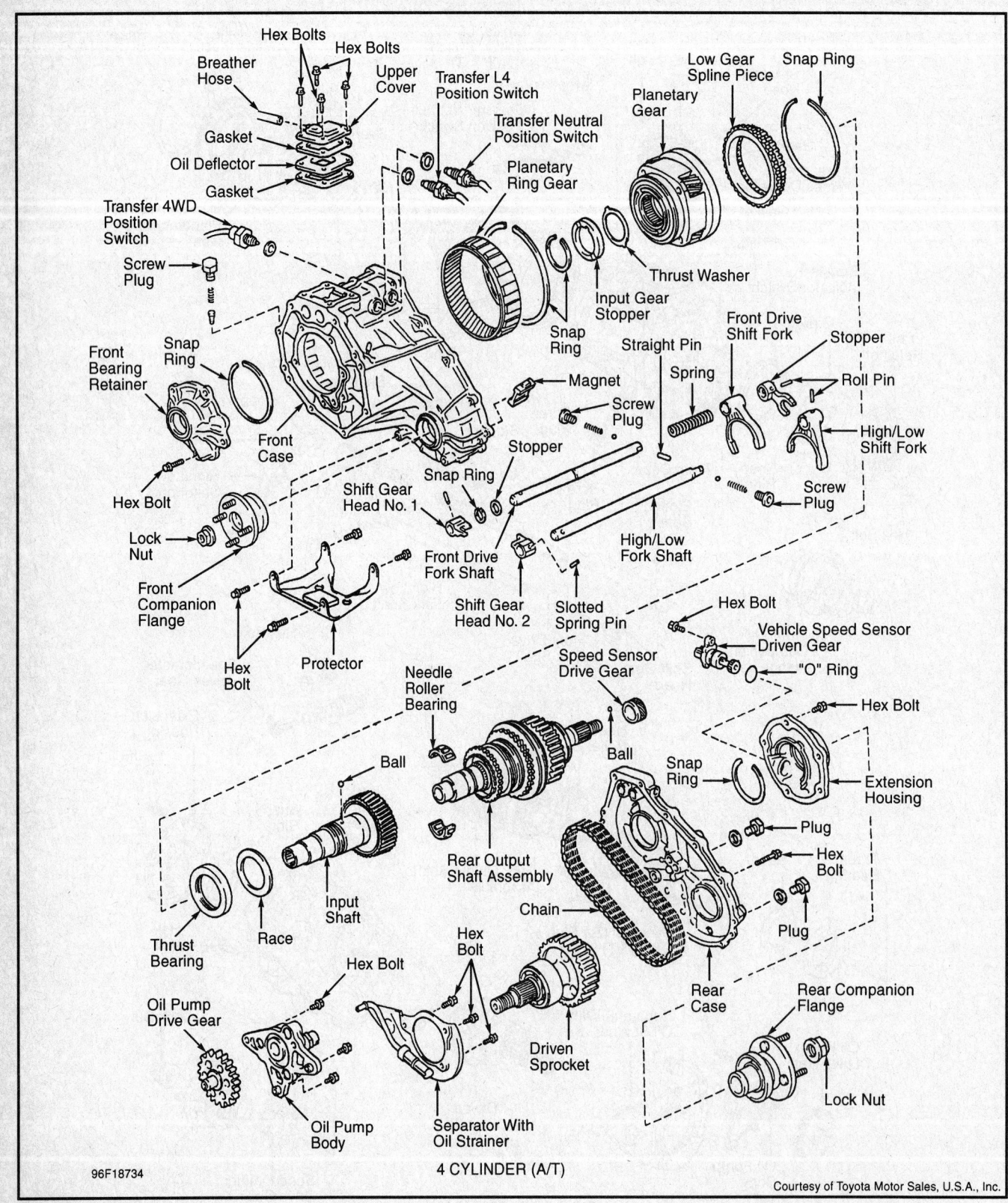

96F18734

4 CYLINDER (A/T)

Courtesy of Toyota Motor Sales, U.S.A., Inc.

Fig. 9: Exploded View Of Transfer Case (3RZ-FE A/T)

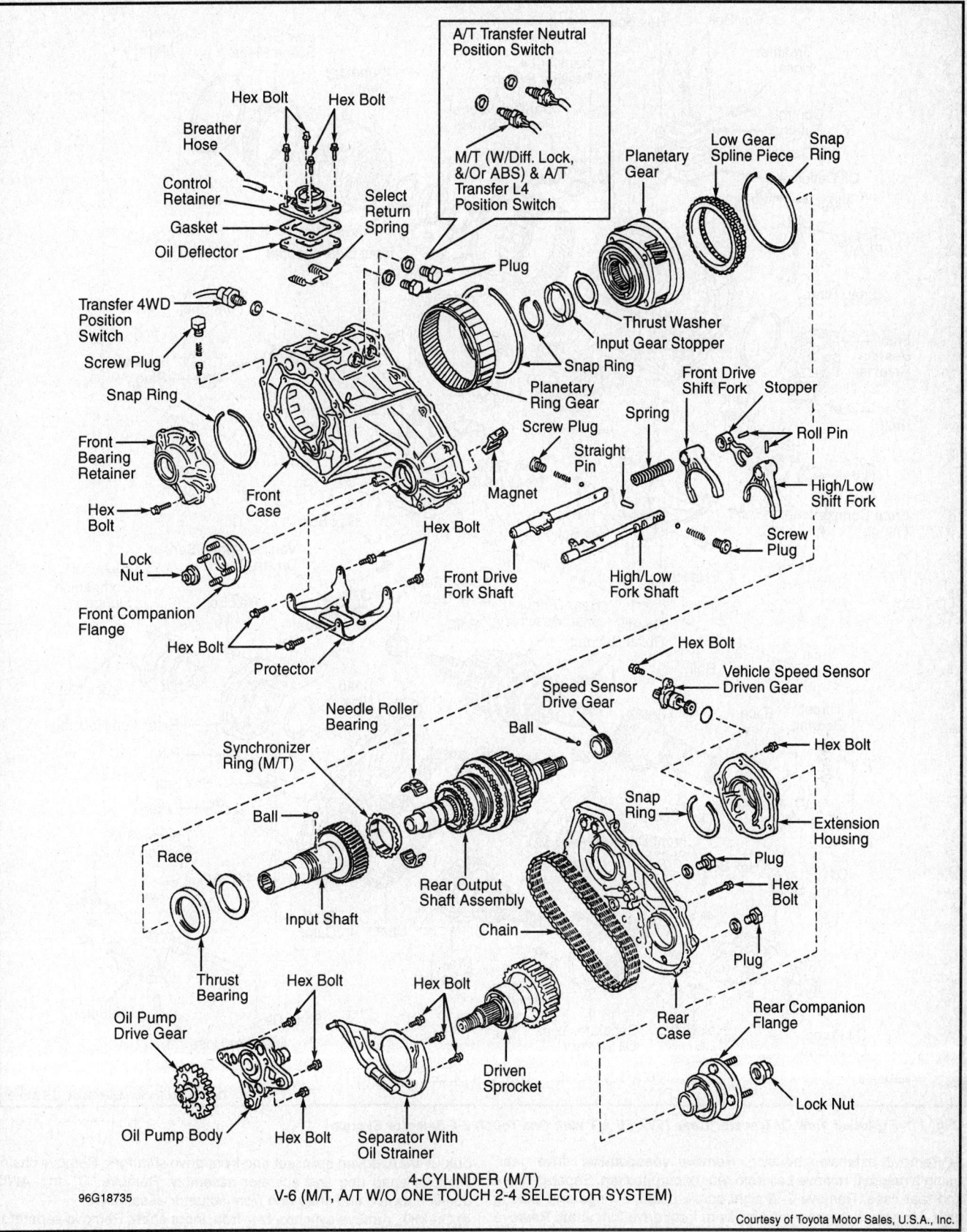

A/T Transfer Neutral Position Switch

M/T (W/Diff. Lock, &/Or ABS) & A/T Transfer L4 Position Switch

Hex Bolt Hex Bolt

Breather Hose

Control Retainer

Gasket

Oil Deflector

Select Return Spring

Plug

Planetary Gear

Low Gear Spline Piece

Snap Ring

Thrust Washer

Input Gear Stopper

Transfer 4WD Position Switch

Screw Plug

Snap Ring

Snap Ring

Planetary Ring Gear

Front Drive Shift Fork

Stopper

Roll Pin

Front Bearing Retainer

Screw Plug

Straight Pin

Spring

High/Low Shift Fork

Hex Bolt

Front Case

Magnet

Front Drive Fork Shaft

High/Low Fork Shaft

Screw Plug

Lock Nut

Front Companion Flange

Hex Bolt

Hex Bolt

Protector

Hex Bolt

Vehicle Speed Sensor Driven Gear

Needle Roller Bearing

Speed Sensor Drive Gear

Ball

Hex Bolt

Synchronizer Ring (M/T)

Ball

Snap Ring

Extension Housing

Ball

Race

Rear Output Shaft Assembly

Plug

Hex Bolt

Input Shaft

Chain

Plug

Thrust Bearing

Hex Bolt

Hex Bolt

Rear Case

Rear Companion Flange

Oil Pump Drive Gear

Driven Sprocket

Lock Nut

Oil Pump Body

Hex Bolt

Separator With Oil Strainer

4-CYLINDER (M/T)
V-6 (M/T, A/T W/O ONE TOUCH 2-4 SELECTOR SYSTEM)

96G18735

Courtesy of Toyota Motor Sales, U.S.A., Inc.

Fig. 10: Exploded View Of Transfer Case (3RZ-FE M/T, 5VZ-FE M/T & A/T With One-Touch 2-4 Selector System)

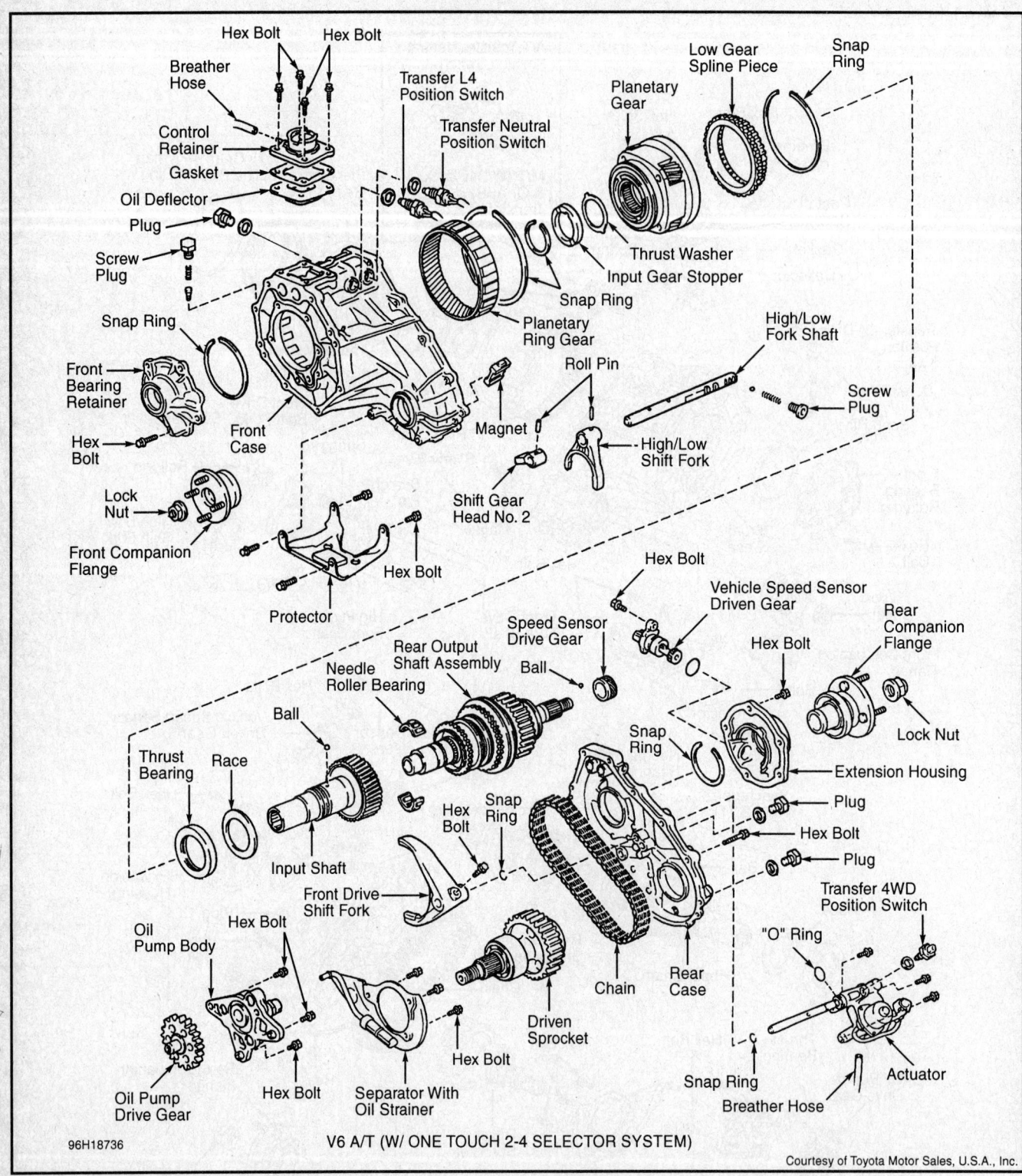

Fig. 11: Exploded View Of Transfer Case (5VZ-FE A/T With One-Touch 2-4 Selector System)

2) Remove extension housing. Remove speedometer drive gear. Using a magnet, remove ball from rear of output shaft. Separate front and rear case. Remove 2 straight screw plugs, springs and locking balls. Using punch, drive roll pins from front drive fork shaft. Remove front drive fork shaft, fork and spring. Remove high/low fork shaft, fork and stopper. Mount rear case in vise. Tap rear case with plastic hammer while pulling on output shaft. Remove rear output shaft, driven sprocket and chain.

3) On A/T with one-touch 2-4 selector system, Remove shift fork bolt and snap ring. Using a plastic hammer, tap rear case while pulling rear

output shaft, driven sprocket and front drive shift fork. Remove chain. Remove snap ring and actuator assembly. Remove "O" ring, 4WD position switch and snap ring from actuator assembly.

4) On M/T, remove synchronizer from input shaft. Remove separator with oil strainer and magnet if applicable. Remove oil pump body assembly and oil pump drive gear. Remove snap ring securing planetary gear assembly. Remove planetary gear assembly and input shaft. Remove snap ring and low gear spline piece. Remove needle roller bearing from input shaft.

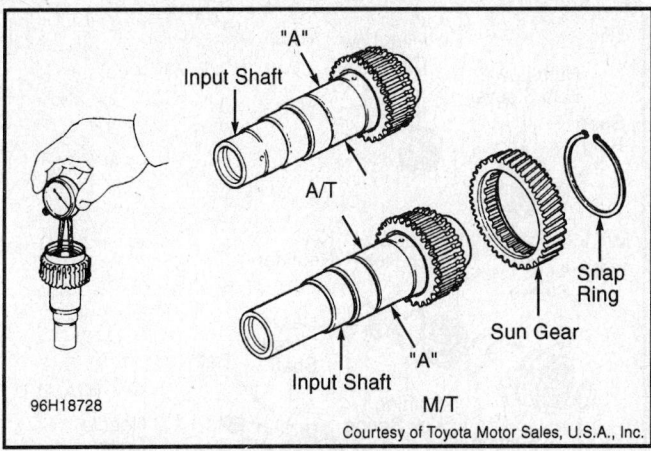

Fig. 12: Identifying Input Shaft Measuring Points & Components (VF1A)

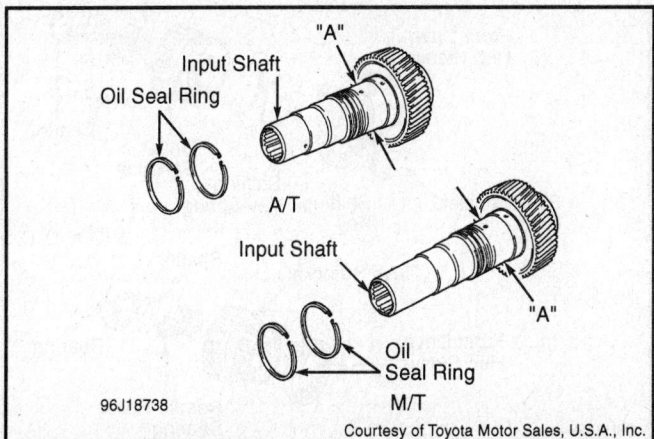

Fig. 13: Identifying Input Shaft Measuring Points & Components

5) Using snap ring pliers, remove input shaft stopper, thrust bearings and pins (or thrust washer and ball). Remove input shaft and race. Remove snap ring retaining planetary gear. Remove plug, spring and pin. Remove planetary gear.

Disassembly & Reassembly – 1) Visually inspect input shaft for grooves, damaged gear teeth and worn bearing journals. Remove snap ring and sun gear. Measure front bearing journal as indicated in figure. See Fig. 12 or 13. See INPUT SHAFT SPECIFICATIONS table. Using dial indicator, measure inside diameter of input shaft bushing at rear of input shaft. Replace input shaft if not within specifications or if it is damaged. On 1996 A340F, remove oil seal rings. Clean and inspect grooves. Reinstall rings. Ensure rings rotate smoothly.

2) Place synchronizer ring in recess at rear of input shaft. Press ring in and rotate to check braking action. Replace ring if it rotates freely. Repeat test with NEW synchronizer ring. If ring still rotates freely, replace input shaft. Holding ring firmly in place, check clearance between ring back and input shaft spline end. Replace input shaft if not within specification. Install sun gear and snap ring to input shaft. Replace oil seals as needed.

INPUT SHAFT SPECIFICATIONS

Application	In. (mm)
Front Bearing Journal Diameter (Minimum)	1.8736 (47.59)
Bushing Inside Diameter (Maximum)	1.5409 (39.14)
Synchronizer Ring Clearance	
1995-1996 VF1A	
Standard	.0452-.0728 (1.15-1.85)
Minimum	.031 (.80)
1996 A340F, Tacoma & 4Runner	
Standard	.04313-.0728 (1.5-1.85)
Minimum	.0315 (.80)

OIL PUMP BODY

Disassembly & Inspection – Install oil pump drive gear to drive rotor. Ensure drive rotor turns smoothly. Remove straight screw plug, spring, ball and seat. Remove "O" ring from seat. On 1996 Tacoma and 4Runner, Remove relief valve and "O" ring. Remove oil pump plate. Using feeler gauge, check body clearance of driven (outer) rotor. See OIL PUMP CLEARANCE SPECIFICATIONS table. Check tip clearance of both rotors. Using straightedge and feeler gauge, check side clearance of both rotors. If clearances are not as specified, replace oil pump. See Fig. 16.

Reassembly – Apply gear oil to both rotors and install. Install oil pump plate. Tighten torx screws to 65 INCH lbs. (7.4 N.m). Install NEW "O" ring to seat. Install seat, ball and spring. Apply Three Bond 1344 to straight plug threads. Install and tighten to 22 ft.lbs. (29 N.m). Install NEW "O" ring to relief valve, install and tighten to 21 ft. lbs (29 N.m). Install oil pump drive gear to drive rotor. Ensure that drive rotor turns smoothly. See Fig. 14 or 15.

OIL PUMP CLEARANCE SPECIFICATIONS

Application	In. (mm)
1995-1996 VF1A	
Driven Rotor-To-Body	.0039-.0063 (.10-.16)
Rotor Side	.0012-.0031 (.03-.08)
Rotor Tip	.0031-.0063 (.08-.16)
1996 A340F	
Driven Rotor To Body	.0035-.0063 (.09-.16)
Rotor Side	.0012-.0039 (.03-.10)
Rotor Tip	.0020-.0059 (.05-.15)

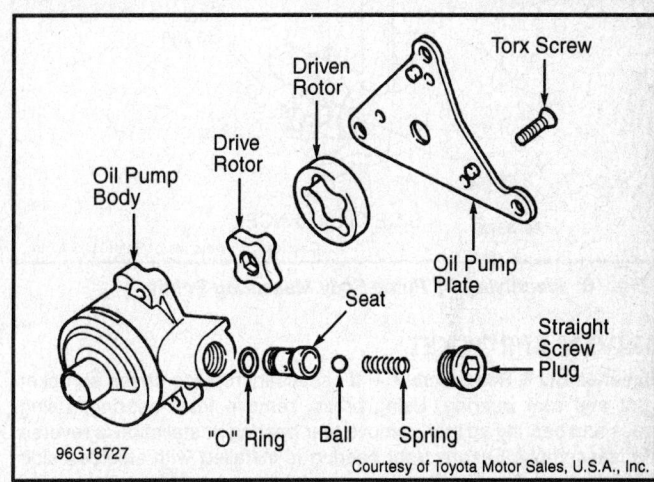

Fig. 14: Identifying Oil Pump Body Components (VF1A)

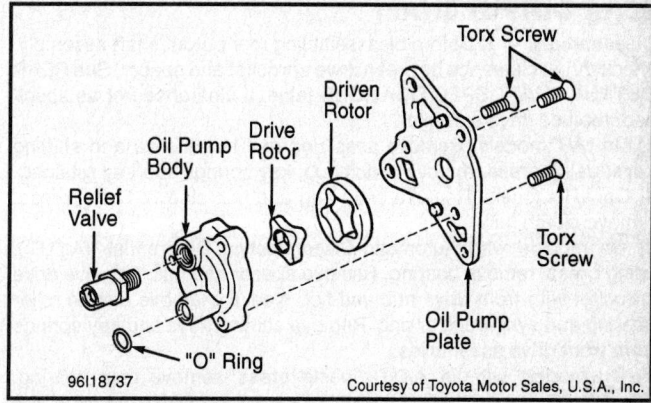

Fig. 15: Identifying Oil Pump Body Components (1996 A340F)

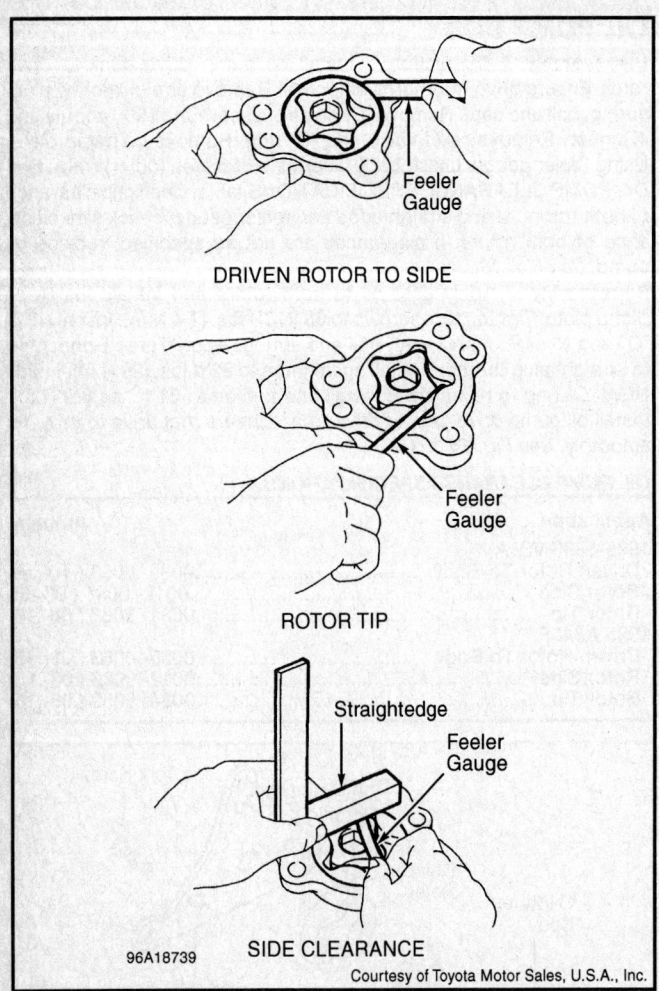

Fig. 16: Identifying Oil Pump Body Measuring Points

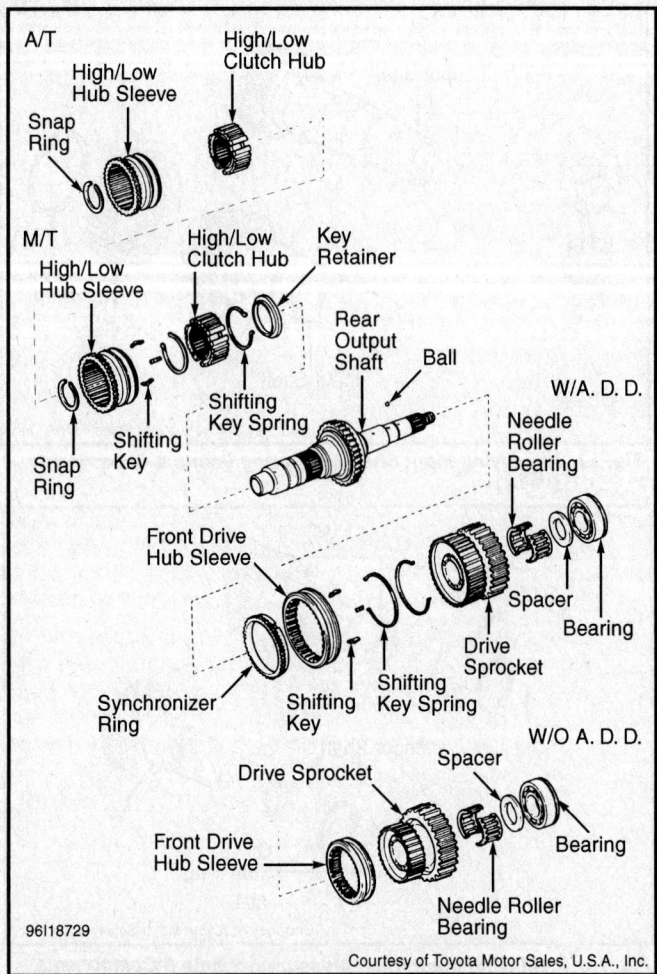

Fig. 17: Identifying Output Shaft Components

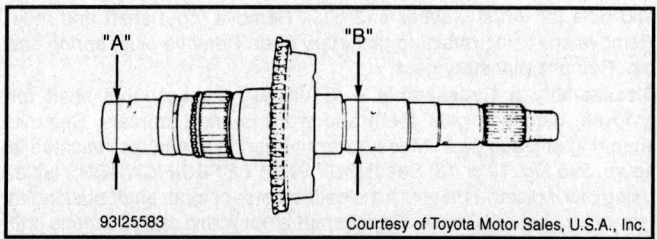

Fig. 18: Measuring Output Shaft Journal Diameters (VF1A & A340F)

DRIVEN SPROCKET

Disassembly & Reassembly – If necessary replace driven sprocket front and rear bearing. Using press, remove front bearing. Using press and bearing splitter, remove rear bearing. Installation is reverse of disassembly. Ensure front bearing is installed with shielded side towards gear. See Fig. 2.

REAR OUTPUT SHAFT

Disassembly – **1)** Before disassembling rear output shaft assembly, check thrust clearance between drive sprocket and spacer. See REAR OUTPUT SHAFT SPECIFICATIONS table. If clearance not as specified, replace drive sprocket.

2) On M/T models, Remove snap ring and hub sleeve and shifting keys. Using press, remove clutch hub, key springs and key retainer.

3) On A/T models, Remove snap ring and hub sleeve. Using press, remove clutch hub.

4) On models with Automatic Disconnecting Differential, (A.D.D.), using press, remove bearing. Remove spacer and ball. Remove drive sprocket with front drive hub and hub sleeve. Remove needle roller bearing and synchronizer ring. Remove shifting keys and key springs from front drive assemblies.

5) On models without A.D.D., using press, remove rear bearing. Remove spacer and ball. Remove drive sprocket with front drive hub and hub sleeve. Remove needle bearing. See Fig. 17.

Inspection – Check diameter of rear output shaft journal surfaces. See Fig. 18. Mount output shaft in vise. Using dial indicator, check oil clearance of drive sprocket. See REAR OUTPUT SHAFT SPECIFICATIONS table. If clearance not as specified, replace output shaft,

sprocket or roller needle bearings. Using a feeler gauge, measure clearance between front drive shift fork and hub sleeve. Check clearance between high/low shift fork and hub sleeve. If fork clearances are not as specified, replace fork or hub, as required.

REAR OUTPUT SHAFT SPECIFICATIONS

Applications	In. (mm)
1995-1996 VF1A	
Drive Sprocket Oil Clearance	.0004-.0022 (.010-.055)
Drive Sprocket Thrust Clearance	.0039-.0098 (.010-.25)
1996 A340F	
Drive Sprocket Oil Clearance	.0039-.0098 (.10-.25)
Drive sprocket Thrust Clearance	.0039-.0098 (.10-.25)
Output Shaft Journal Diameter (Minimum)	
A	1.1016 (27.98)
B	1.4561 (36.98)
Shift Fork-To-Hub Clearance (All-Maximum)	.039 (1.0)

Reassembly – 1) On models with A.D.D., install front drive hub sleeve onto clutch hub. Ensure hub sleeve is installed in correct direction. *See Fig. 17.* Install shifting keys and springs.

2) Apply gear oil to shaft and needle roller bearing. Install synchronizer ring. Install needle roller bearing in drive sprocket. Install drive sprocket with front drive hub sleeve. Place synchronizer ring on gear and align ring slots with shifting keys. Align spacer with ball and install. Using press, install rear bearing with outer race snap ring groove toward rear.

3) On models without A.D.D., Install front drive hub sleeve onto clutch hub. Ensure hub sleeve is installed in correct direction. *See Fig. 17.* Apply gear oil to shaft and needle roller bearing. Install needle roller bearing in drive sprocket. Install drive sprocket with front drive hub sleeve. Align spacer with ball and install. Using press, install rear bearing with outer race snap ring groove toward rear.

4) On all models, measure drive sprocket thrust clearance. Standard clearance is .0039-.0098" (.10-.25 mm).

5) On M/T models, Install clutch hub and shifting keys to hub sleeve. Install shifting key springs under shifting keys. Ensure end gaps are not in line. Drive in NEW key retainer. Using press, install high/low hub sleeve assembly.

6) On A/T models, install clutch hub to hub sleeve. Using press, install high/low hub sleeve assembly.

7) On all models, Select and install snap ring that allows minimal axial play. See HIGH/LOW SNAP RING THICKNESS table.

HIGH/LOW SNAP RING THICKNESS

Mark	In. (mm)
K	.0787-.0807 (2.00-2.05)
L	.0807-.0827 (2.05-2.10)
A	.0827-.0846 (2.10-2.15)
B	.0846-.0866 (2.15-2.20)
C	.0866-.0886 (2.20-2.25)
D	.0886-.0906 (2.25-2.30)
E	.0906-.0925 (2.30-2.35)
F	.0924-.0945 (2.35-2.40)
G	.0945-.0965 (2.40-2.45)
H	.0965-.0984 (2.45-2.50)
J	.0984-.1004 (2.50-2.55)

PLANETARY GEAR

Disassembly & Inspection – Inspect planetary pinion gear thrust clearance. On 1995-1996 VF1A, standard clearance is .0043-.0339" (.11-.86 mm). On 1996 A340F, standard clearance is .0043-.0031" (.11-.84 mm). Using dial indicator, measure radial clearance of planetary pinion gear. Standard clearance is .0004-.0015" (.009-.038 mm). If clearances exceeds maximum, replace planetary gear assembly. If necessary, replace planetary gear outer bearing. Remove snap ring. Using bearing splitter and press, remove bearing. To assemble, reverse disassembly procedure. Select and install snap ring that allows minimum axial play. See SNAP RING THICKNESS table. If necessary, replace planetary gear inner bearing. Using press, remove and install NEW bearing. Install to depth of .197-.220" (5.0-5.6). *See Fig. 7, 8, 9, 10 or 11.*

PLANETARY GEAR SNAP RING THICKNESS

Mark	In. (mm)
1	.0571-.0591 (1.45-1.50)
2	.0591-.0610 (1.50-1.55)
3	.0610-.0630 (1.55-1.60)
4	.0630-.0650 (1.60-1.65)
5	.0650-.0669 (1.65-1.70)

Reassembly – 1) Install planetary ring gear in front case. Apply sealant to plug. Install pin, spring and plug. Install snap ring. Ensure end gap of snap ring is aligned with upper side of case. Apply gear oil to thrust bearing and race and install in planetary gear assembly. Install input shaft in planetary gear assembly. Apply gear oil to thrust bearing and race and install on input shaft. Install 2 pins onto input shaft. Install input shaft stopper. Select and install a snap ring which will allow .0020-.0059" (.050-.150 mm) axial play. See INPUT SHAFT SNAP RING SELECTION table.

INPUT SHAFT SNAP RING SELECTION

ID Mark	Thickness In. (mm)
A	.0827-.0846 (2.10-2.15)
B	.0846-.0866 (2.15-2.20)
C	.0866-.0886 (2.20-2.25)
D	.0086-.0906 (2.25-2.30)
E	.0906-.0925 (2.30-2.35)
F	.0925-.0945 (2.35-2.40)
G	.0945-.0965 (2.40-2.45)
H	.0965-.0984 (2.45-2.50)
J	.0984-.1004 (2.50-2.55)
K	.1004-.1024 (2.55-2.60)
L	.1024-.1043 (2.60-2.65)
M	.1043-.1063 (2.65-2.70)
N	.1063-.1083 (2.70-2.75)
P	.1083-.1102 (2.75-2.80)
Q	.1192-.1122 (2.80-2.85)
R	.1122-.1142 (2.85-2.90)
S	.1142-.1161 (2.90-2.95)
T	.1161-.1181 (2.95-3.00)
U	.1181-.1201 (3.00-3.05)

NOTE: It may be necessary to heat front case to about 158°F (70°C) to install planetary gear and input shaft assembly.

2) Install needle roller bearing in input shaft. Place low gear spline piece in planetary gear and install snap ring. Ensure snap ring gap is NOT aligned with cut-out portion of planetary carrier. Install planetary gear and input shaft assembly in front case. Install snap ring. Install oil pump drive gear and body assembly. Lubricate "O" ring and install on oil strainer pipe. Install separator with oil strainer. Install magnet if applicable. *See Figs. 7, 8, 9, 10 or 11.*

NOTE: It may be necessary to heat rear case to about 158°F (70°C) to install rear output shaft.

3) Align synchronizer ring slots with shifting keys. Install ring on high-low clutch hub. On 1996 A340F with one-touch 2-4 selector system, Install NEW "O" ring with gear oil and install to 4WD position switch. Install to actuator assembly. Install actuator assembly and snap ring. Without one-touch 2-4 selector system, assemble rear output shaft, driven sprocket and chain. Mount rear case in vise. While pushing output shaft into rear case, tap case gently with plastic hammer. Install snap ring.

4) Place high/low shift fork in groove of hub sleeve. Install the fork shaft in rear case through shift fork and stopper. Apply gear oil to straight pin and insert into case hole. Place front drive shift fork in groove of hub sleeve. Install spring on fork shaft. Install the fork shaft in rear case through shift fork and stopper. Push front drive fork toward rear case to compress spring. Install roll pin while spring is compressed. Install roll pin through high/low fork and shaft.

5) With one-touch 2-4 selector system, install high low shift fork shaft into groove of clutch sleeve. Install shift fork and shift head No. 2. Install 2 roll pins.

6) Install straight screw plugs, springs and locking balls. Apply sealant to plug. Tighten plugs to specification. See TORQUE SPECIFICATIONS. Apply sealant to sealing surface of rear case. Shift high/low hub sleeve to low (rear) side. Assemble front and rear cases. Install bolts. Tighten bolts to specification.

7) Install ball and speedometer drive gear on rear output shaft. Apply sealant to sealing surface of extension housing. Install extension housing. Apply sealer to extension housing bolts. Install bolts and tighten to specification.

8) Apply gear oil to front companion flange inner surface. Install front companion flange to driven sprocket shaft. Using Holder (09330-00021) to prevent flange rotation, install and tighten lock nut to specification. Stake lock nut. Install rear companion flange in similar manner.

9) On V6 (G58 and A340F) models, install select return spring in control retainer. Using NEW gasket, install control retainer on front case. Tighten bolts to specification. On 4-cyl. (G58 and A340F) models, using NEW gasket, install case cover. Install upper cover and breather hose deflector. Install shift gear head No. 1 and No. 2. Using pin punch and hammer drive in 2 roll pins. Install protector if applicable. On all models, Install front retainer and NEW gasket to front case. Apply sealer to bolts. Install bolts and tighten to specification. *See Fig. 7, 8, 9, 10 or 11.*

10) Install transfer indicator switch. Install No. 1 speed sensor.

11) On 4-cyl. (A340F) models, install transfer L4 and neutral position switch. Ensure on all models, that input and output shafts rotate smoothly and shifting can be made to all positions.

REMOVAL & INSTALLATION (A340H)

NOTE: *Transfer case must be disassembled for removal from transmission case. See OVERHAUL (A340H).*

OVERHAUL (A340H)

TRANSFER CASE UNIT

Disassembly – 1) Remove temperature and speed sensors. Remove transfer case cooler line fittings. Remove transfer control shaft lever and park/neutral position switch. Remove transfer case oil cooler tubes. Remove No. 1 vehicle speed sensor. Remove driven gear from sensor and remove "O" ring. Disconnect and remove No. 2 vehicle speed sensor. Remove "O" ring. Remove transmission housing.

2) Remove transfer case oil pan. Disconnect No. 4 solenoid connector and transfer pressure switch. Remove valve body. Remove solenoid wiring stopper plate and solenoid wiring from transfer case. *See Fig. 19 or 20.*

3) Using hammer and chisel, loosen staked area of rear companion flange nut. Using Flange Holder (09339-00021), hold companion flange and remove nut. Remove front and rear companion flanges.

4) Remove extension housing and speedometer drive gear. Remove oil pump assembly. Remove chain cover bolts. Using plastic hammer, remove chain rear case. Remove sprocket snap ring. Remove drive chain, drive sprocket and driven shaft. *See Fig. 19.*

5) Remove chain oil receiver plate. Remove chain front case with front output shaft. Remove front output shaft from chain front case. Remove front drive clutch snap ring from output shaft. Lift front drive clutch from output shaft. Remove snap ring from front output shaft. Check pack clearance of transfer low speed brake. Clearance should be .0358-.0827" (.91-2.10 mm). If clearances are not within specifications, inspect discs.

6) Remove center support snap ring. Remove center support and low speed brake assembly. Remove front flange from case. Remove race and assembled bearing and race from sun gear.

7) Remove sun gear. Remove race and assembled bearing and race from direct clutch. Remove direct clutch snap ring. Remove direct clutch from case. Remove front support from transfer case. Remove assembled bearing and race from front support. Separate transfer case from transmission case. Remove snap ring and speed sensor rotor and key. Remove front snap ring. *See Fig. 20.*

NOTE: *Coat all components with ATF prior to installation. Clutch discs must be soaked in ATF for at least 15 minutes prior to installation. Coat thrust bearings and races with petroleum jelly before installation. See Fig. 21. Ensure ends of snap rings are not aligned with cut-out area of case. Ensure all apply gaskets are installed.*

Reassembly – 1) Install front snap ring, speed sensor rotor and snap ring. Apply Three Bond (1281) seal packing to transfer case. Confirm 2 gaskets are installed correctly. Install transfer case on transmission case. Tighten bolts to 25 ft. lbs. (34 N.m).

2) Install bearing and race on front support. Confirm apply gasket is installed correctly. Install front support and tighten bolts to 25 ft. lbs. (34 N.m). Install race on front support. *See Fig. 21.*

3) Install bearing and race on sun gear. Install sun gear into direct clutch. Mesh sun gear splines with disc tabs by rotating and pushing

sun gear. Install direct clutch and sun gear into case. Install bearing and race on direct clutch and sun gear. Install snap ring.

4) Install races on planetary gear and planetary ring gear. Install output shaft and planetary ring gear into case. Install low speed brake front flange to case. Install in order: disc, plate, disc, plate, disc, plate, disc, plate, disc, plate, disc, plate and disc. Install low speed brake rear flange. Install cushion plate with rounded end facing inward. *See Fig. 20.*

5) Install low speed brake piston return spring. Install bearing and race on center support. Align oil and bolt holes of center support and transfer case. Install center support. Push center support forward and install snap ring.

6) Measure low speed brake pack clearance between snap ring and flange. Pack clearance should be .0358-.0827" (.91-2.10 mm). If piston stroke is less than specification, check for improper installation of components. Repeat procedure. If piston stroke exceeds specification, different thickness flange must be installed. Flanges are available in the following thicknesses: .150" (3.80 mm), .157" (4.00 mm), .165" (4.20 mm), .173" (4.40 mm) and .181" (4.60 mm).

7) Install snap ring on output shaft. Install front drive clutch and snap ring. Mesh front output shaft splines with disc tabs by rotating and pushing front output shaft. Install front output shaft into front drive clutch.

8) Apply sealant to transfer case. Install chain front case to transfer case. Apply sealant to bolt threads. Install and tighten bolts to 25 ft. lbs. (34 N.m).

9) Apply sealant to chain oil receiver bolt threads. Install oil receiver to chain front case. Install and tighten bolts to 89 INCH lbs. (10 N.m). Install drive chain with drive sprocket and driven shaft. Install snap ring.

10) Apply sealant to chain rear case. Install chain rear case to front case. Install and tighten bolts to 25 ft. lbs. (34 N.m). Install transfer oil pump and tighten bolts to 22 ft. lbs. (16 N.m). *See Fig. 19.*

11) Install speedometer drive gear. Apply sealant to extension housing. Install extension housing to chain rear case. Tighten bolts to 25 ft. lbs. (34 N.m).

12) Install front and rear companion flanges, washers and NEW companion flange nuts. Using flange holder, tighten nuts to 90 ft. lbs. (123 N.m). Stake nuts to shaft.

13) Check for sound of operation for direct clutch, low speed brake and front drive clutch while applying low pressure compressed air into oil holes. If no noise occurs, check for improper installation of components.

14) Install parking lock pawl bracket. Tighten bolts to 65 INCH lbs. (7.4 N.m). Install solenoid wiring into transfer case. Install stopper plate. Align manual valve grooves to lever pin. Install transfer valve body and tighten bolts to 89 INCH lbs. (10 N.m). *See Fig. 22.* Connect No. 4 solenoid and transfer pressure switch connectors. Clamp wiring.

15) Install magnets in transfer oil pan. Apply seal packing Three Bond (1281) to oil pan. Apply sealant to threads of 3 bolts. *See Fig. 23.* Install oil pan and tighten bolts to 65 INCH lbs. (7.4 N.m).

16) Install speed sensor and stopper plate. Connect speed sensor wiring connector. Insert transfer position switch on manual valve lever shaft and temporarily tighten adjusting bolt. Install grommet and NEW lock washer. Install and tighten nut to 35 INCH lbs. (3.9 N.m). Using control shaft lever, shift lever into H4 position. Align basic line and switch groove. Tighten bolt to 115 INCH lbs. (13 N.m). Bend tabs on lock washer.

17) Install control shaft lever. Tighten to 12 ft. lbs. (16 N.m). Install NEW "O" rings to No. 1 and No. 2 vehicle speed sensor and install to case. Insert speedometer driven gear into sleeve. Install clip. Install sleeve to extension housing. Install lock plate with bolt. Tighten bolt to 12 ft. lbs. (16 N.m).

18) Install transfer case cooler line fittings and tighten to 21 ft. lbs. (29 N.m). Install oil cooler tubes and tube clamp bracket. Tighten to 25 ft. lbs. (34 N.m). Install tube clamp and tighten to 89 INCH lbs. (10 N.m). Install transmission and transfer fluid temperature sensors and tighten to 11 ft. lbs. (15 N.m). *See Fig. 19.*

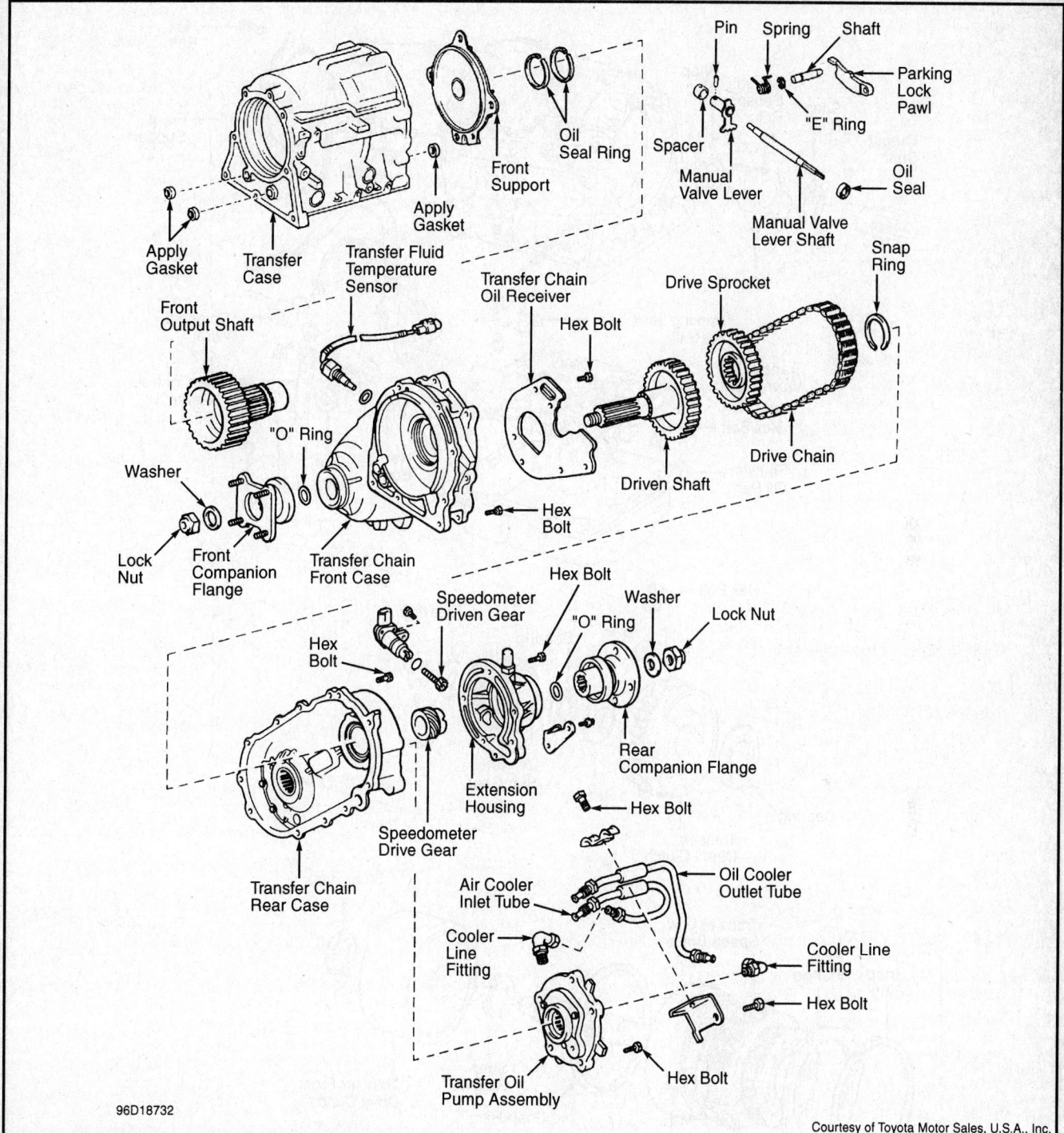

Fig. 19: Identifying Transfer Case Components (A340H)

DIRECT CLUTCH

Disassembly – 1) Remove snap ring from clutch drum. Remove flanges, discs and plates. Note location and number of components. Using an arbor press and Spring Compressor (09320-89010), compress piston return spring and remove snap ring. Remove piston return spring. *See Fig. 24.*

2) Place direct clutch on front support and carefully apply compressed air to piston supply port. Remove direct clutch piston. Remove 2 "O" rings from piston and one "O"ring from drum. *See Fig. 25.*

Inspection – 1) Clean all components (except discs) with solvent. Dry with low pressure compressed air. Inspect plates and discs for flaking or burnt areas. Clutch discs should be soaked in ATF for at least 15 minutes prior to installation.

2) Ensure check ball is free in direct clutch piston and direct clutch drum. Apply low pressure compressed air to clutch piston check ball area. Ensure check ball does not allow air to bleed through piston.

3) Measure inside diameter of direct clutch drum bushing. Replace direct clutch drum if bushing diameter exceeds 1.876" (47.65 mm).

Reassembly – 1) Coat NEW "O" rings with ATF and install on piston and drum. Place spring compressor on direct clutch piston. Carefully tap piston into clutch drum with plastic hammer.

Courtesy of Toyota Motor Sales, U.S.A., Inc.

96D18732

TRANSFER CASES
Toyota Pickup, T100, Tacoma & 4Runner (Cont.)

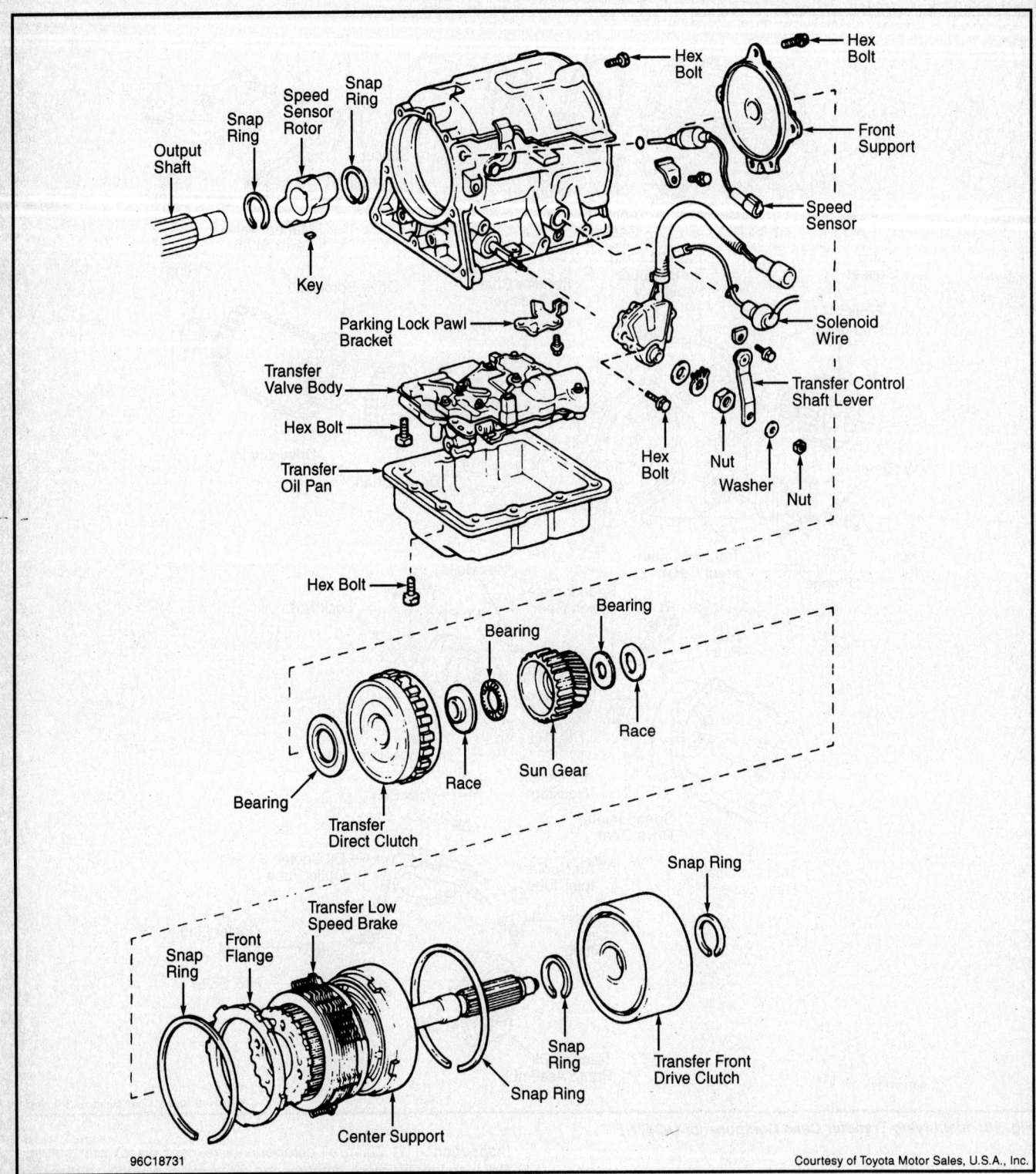

96C18731

Courtesy of Toyota Motor Sales, U.S.A., Inc.

Fig. 20: Identifying Transfer Case Assemblies (A340H)

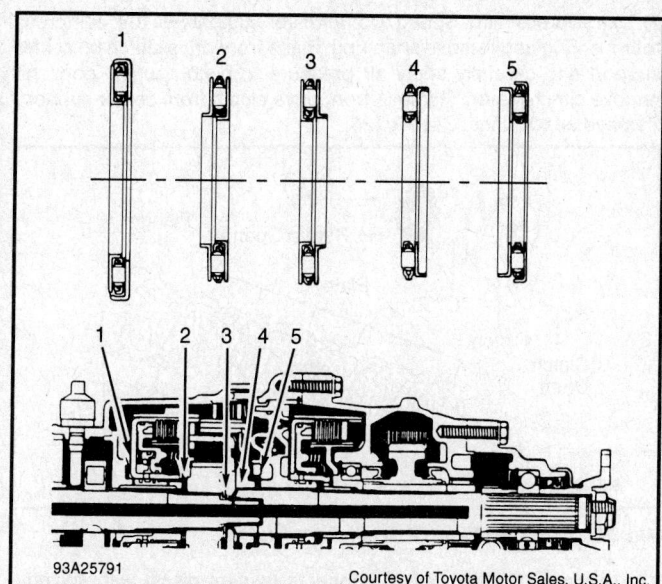

Fig. 21: Identifying Thrust Bearing Locations (A340H)

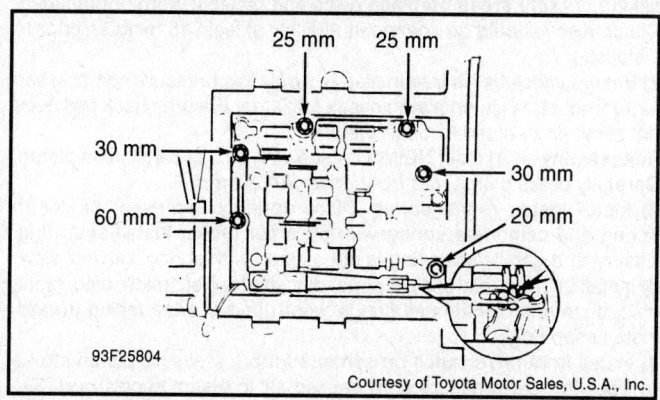

Fig. 22: Identifying Transfer Valve Body Mounting Bolts (A340H)

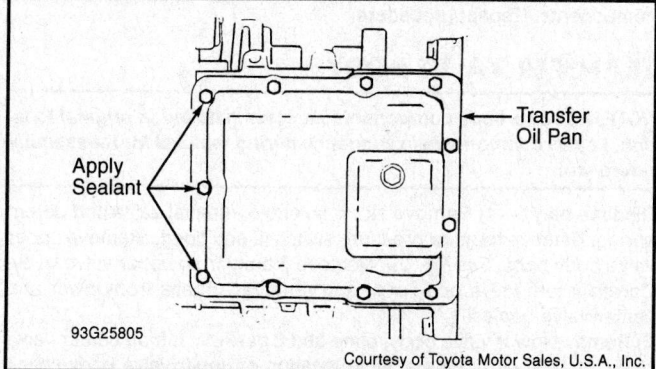

Fig. 23: Identifying Bolts Requiring Sealant (A340H)

2) Install piston return spring. Place spring compressor on spring retainer and compress spring with an arbor press. Install snap ring. Ensure end-gap of snap ring is not aligned with spring retainer claw.

3) Install in order: plate, disc, thick plate, disc, thin plate, disc, thin plate, disc, thin plate, disc, thin plate, and disc. *See Fig. 24.* Install flange with flat side facing clutch pack. Install snap ring.

4) Place direct clutch on front support. Measure direct clutch piston stroke. *See Fig. 25.* Piston stroke should be .0898-.1055" (2.28-2.68 mm). If piston stroke is less than specification, check for improper installation of components. Repeat procedure. If piston stroke exceeds specification, different thickness flange must be installed. Flanges are available in the following thicknesses: .154" (3.9 mm), .161" (4.1 mm), .169" (4.3 mm) and .177" (4.5 mm).

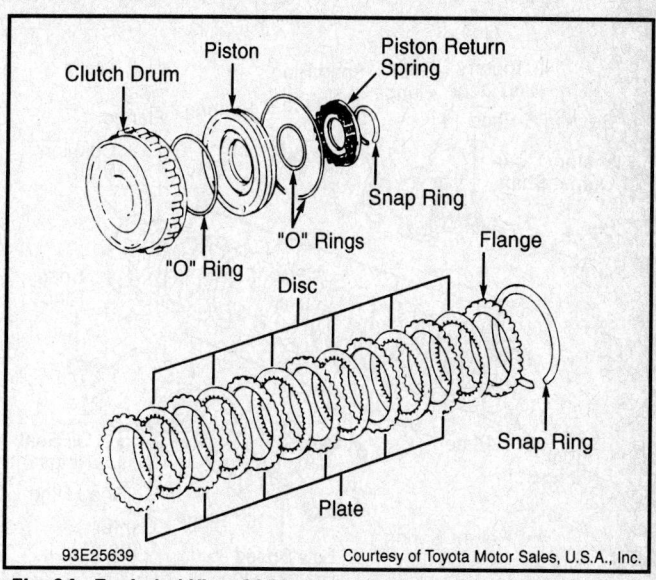

Fig. 24: Exploded View Of Direct Clutch Assembly (A340H)

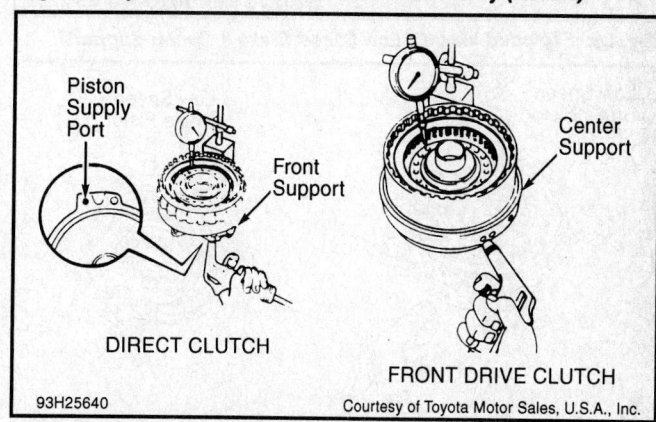

Fig. 25: Checking Direct & Front Drive Clutch Piston Stroke

LOW SPEED BRAKE & CENTER SUPPORT

Disassembly – 1) Remove center support from output shaft. Remove bearing from rear of center support. Remove bearing race from output shaft. *See Fig. 26.*

2) Remove piston return spring, cushion plate, rear flange, discs and plates. Note number and location of components. Remove planetary ring gear from output shaft.

3) Remove bearing and race from rear side of planetary gear. Remove snap ring from planetary ring gear. Remove planetary ring gear flange. Carefully apply air pressure to center support and remove low speed brake piston. Remove two "O" rings from piston and one "O" ring from center support. *See Fig. 26.* Remove oil seal rings from center support.

Inspection – 1) Clean all components (except discs) with solvent. Dry with low pressure compressed air. Inspect plates and discs for flaking or burnt areas. Discs should be soaked in ATF for at least 15 minutes prior to installation.

2) Ensure check balls are free in center support. Apply low pressure compressed air to center support check ball area. Ensure check balls do not allow air to bleed through piston.

3) Measure inside diameter of center support bushing, ring gear flange bushing and planetary gear bushing. See LOW SPEED BRAKE & CENTER SUPPORT SPECIFICATIONS table. If inside diameter is not as specified, replace component in question.

4) Measure planetary pinion gear thrust clearance. If clearance exceeds specification, replace planetary gear assembly.

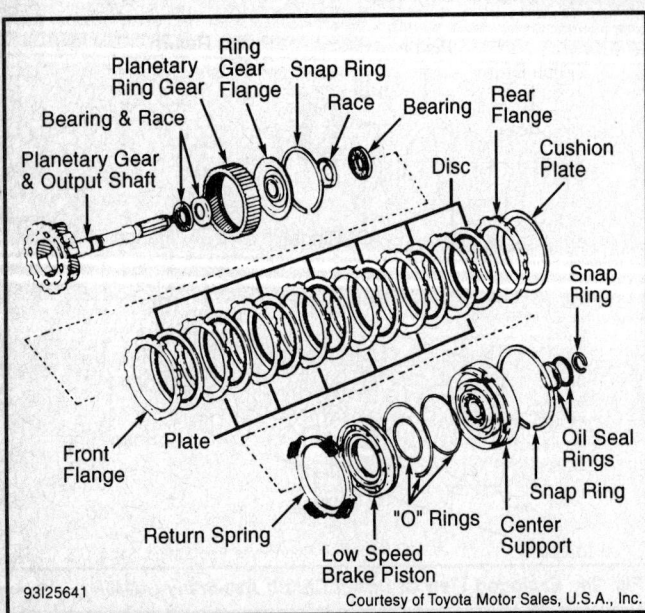

Fig. 26: *Exploded View Of Low-Speed Brake & Center Support*

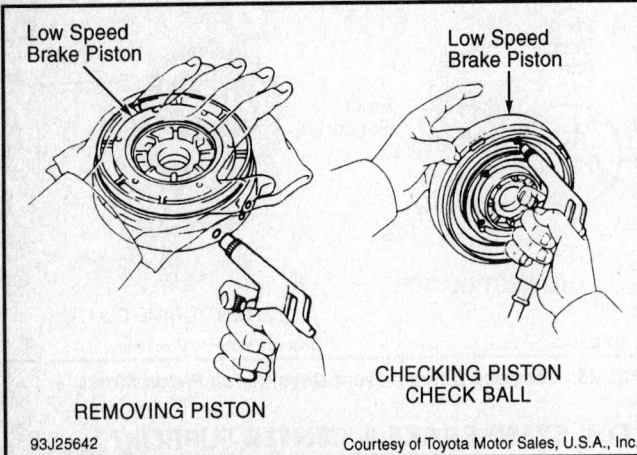

Fig. 27: *Removing & Checking Low-Speed Brake Piston*

LOW SPEED BRAKE & CENTER SUPPORT SPECIFICATIONS

Applications	In. (mm)
Center Support Bushing Diameter (Maximum)	1.3811 (35.08)
Ring Gear Flange Bushing Diameter (Maximum)	1.3811 (35.08)
Planetary Gear Bushing	.7118 (18.08)
Planetary Pinion Gear Thrust Clearance	
Standard	.0018-.0236 (.30-.60)
Maximum	.0394 (1.0)

Reassembly – 1) Coat 2 oil seal rings with ATF. Install oil seal rings to center support. Spread ends of oil seal rings apart to place rings in grooves on center support. Hook ends of oil seal rings together. Ensure oil seal rings rotate smoothly after installation.

2) Coat NEW "O" rings with ATF and install on low speed brake piston and center support. Carefully press low speed brake piston into center support.

3) Install planetary ring gear flange into planetary ring gear. Install snap ring. Install bearing and race to planetary gear. Install planetary ring gear to output shaft.

FRONT DRIVE CLUTCH

Disassembly – 1) Remove snap ring from clutch drum. Remove flanges, discs and plates. Note location and number of components.

2) Using press and Spring Compressor (09320-89010), compress return spring and remove snap ring. Place front drive clutch on center support and carefully apply air pressure to piston supply port and remove clutch piston. Remove front drive clutch from center support. Remove all "O" rings. *See Fig. 28.*

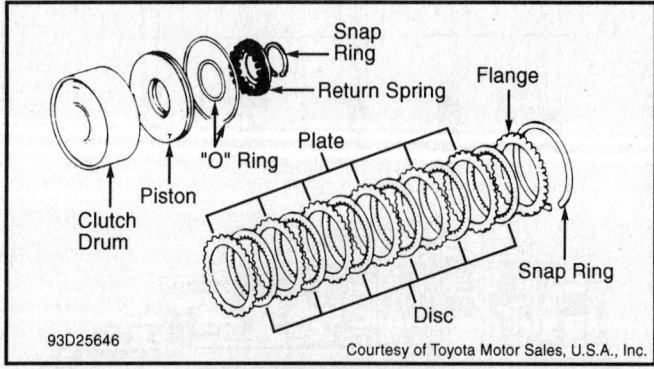

Fig. 28: *Exploded View Of Front Drive Clutch*

Inspection – 1) Clean all components (except discs) with solvent. Dry with low pressure compressed air. Inspect plates and discs for flaking or burnt areas. Replace discs and plates if worn or damaged. Clutch discs should be soaked in ATF for at least 15 minutes prior to installation.

2) Ensure check ball is free in piston. Apply low pressure compressed air to front drive clutch piston check ball area. Ensure check ball does not allow air to bleed through piston.

Reassembly – 1) Coat NEW "O" rings with ATF and install on piston. Carefully press piston into front drive clutch drum.

2) Install piston return spring. Place spring compressor on return spring and compress spring with an arbor press. Install snap ring. Ensure end-gap of snap ring is not aligned with spring retainer claw.

3) Install in order: plate, disc, plate, disc, plate, disc, plate, disc, plate, disc, plate and disc. Install flange with rounded edge facing inward. Install snap ring.

4) Install front drive clutch on center support. Measure piston stroke by applying low pressure compressed air to piston supply port. *See Fig. 28.* Piston stroke should be .0937-.1268" (2.38-3.22 mm). If piston stroke is not as specified, check for improper installation of components. Repeat procedure.

TRANSFER VALVE BODY

NOTE: All valve body components must be installed in original location. Lay all components in sequence during removal for reassembly reference.

Disassembly – 1) Remove No. 4 solenoid, manual valve and detent spring. Remove transfer pressure switch (if equipped). Remove upper valve body bolts. *See Fig. 29.* Remove 8 bolts from upper valve body. Carefully turn valve body over and remove 10 bolts from lower and center valve bodies.

2) Remove lower valve body, plate and 2 gaskets. Lift off center valve body, plate and 2 gaskets. Note location of upper valve body check balls and oil strainers. *See Fig. 30.*

3) Push inward on plugs to remove retainers. Remove retainers, plugs and valve body components from each valve body. *See Fig. 30.*

Inspection – 1) Clean all parts in solvent. Dry with compressed air. Ensure all valve body passages are clear. Ensure strainers are not damaged or clogged. Inspect valves for scoring or roughness.

2) Ensure valves slide freely in bores. Inspect valve springs for damage, squareness and collapsed coils. Measure spring free length. Replace spring if not within specification . See VALVE BODY SPRING SPECIFICATIONS table.

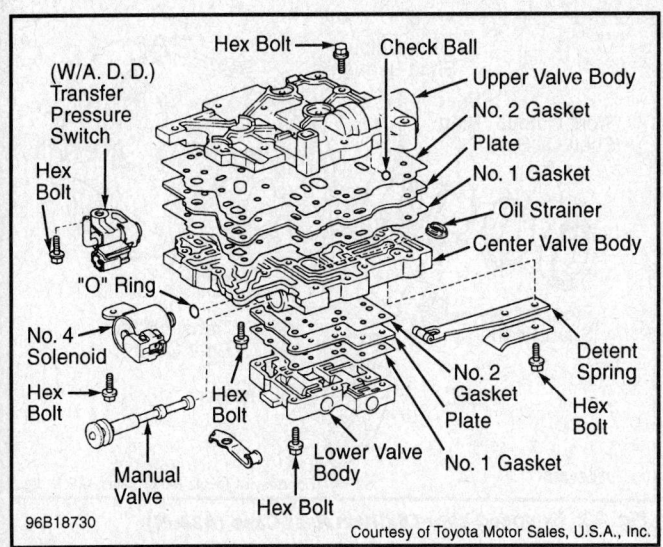

96B18730

Courtesy of Toyota Motor Sales, U.S.A., Inc.

Fig. 29: Identifying Valve Body Assemblies (A340H)

VALVE BODY SPRING SPECIFICATIONS

Spring Application	Color	Free Length In. (mm)
Center Valve Body		
Accumulator Control Valve	White	1.154 (29.3)
Low Shift Valve	Yellow	1.150 (29.2)
Low-High Relay Valve	Lt. Blue	1.248 (31.7)
Lower Valve Body		
Low-High Orifice Control Valve	Green	1.169 (29.7)
Low-High Shift Timing Valve	Red	1.303 (33.1)
Upper Valve Body		
Accumulator Valve	Blue	2.193 (55.7)

Reassembly – 1) Coat all components with ATF. To reassemble, reverse disassembly procedure. Ensure all valves slide freely in bores. Install check balls and strainers in correct location. *See Fig. 30.*
2) Reassemble valve body assembly using NEW gaskets. Ensure all holes of gaskets align with plates. Proper length bolts must be installed in designated locations. *See Fig. 31.* Install all bolts hand tight only. Tighten valve body bolts to 61 INCH lbs. (6.9 N.m).
3) Install detent spring. Tighten to 61 INCH lbs. (6.9 N.m). Insert manual valve. Ensure valve moves smoothly. Install No. 4 solenoid. Tighten bolt to 89 INCH lbs. (10 N.m). Install transfer pressure switch (if equipped). Tighten to 61 INCH lbs. (6.9 N.m).

TRANSFER CASE & FRONT SUPPORT

Disassembly – 1) Remove 3 apply circuit gasket seals (2 from front side and one from inside). Using chisel, cut spacer and remove from manual valve lever shaft. Using pin punch and hammer, drive out manual valve lever pin.
2) Slide manual valve lever shaft from case and remove manual valve lever. Remove oil seal from case. Remove spring, shaft and parking lock pawl. Remove "E" ring from shaft. Remove oil seal rings. *See Fig. 19.*
Inspection – 1) Clean components in solvent. Dry with compressed air. Ensure check ball is free in front support. Apply air pressure to lower port area of front support. Ensure check ball does not allow air to bleed through piston.
2) Measure inside diameter of front support bushing. Maximum inside diameter is 1.236" (31.4 mm). If inside diameter exceeds specification, replace front support.

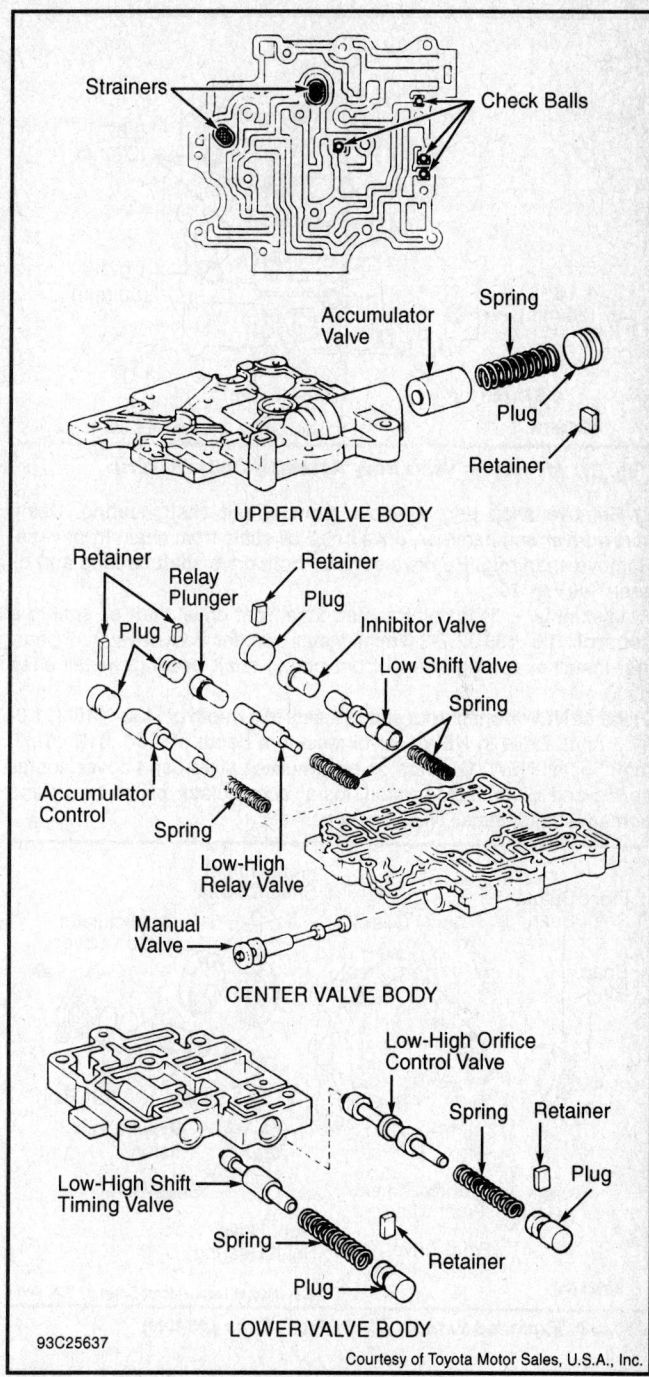

93C25637

Courtesy of Toyota Motor Sales, U.S.A., Inc.

Fig. 30: Exploded View Of Valve Bodies (A340H)

Reassembly – 1) Install oil seal rings on front support. DO NOT over expand rings during installation. Ensure oil seal rings rotate smoothly.
2) Install "E" ring to shaft. Install parking lock pawl, shaft and spring. Install manual valve lever oil seal. Lubricate seal lip.
3) Install NEW spacer to manual valve lever. Install manual valve lever shaft to case. Align spacer hole with manual valve lever hollow area. Stake spacer to lever. Ensure manual valve lever shaft turns smoothly. Install NEW apply gasket seals.

CHAIN FRONT CASE

Disassembly – 1) Remove 2 apply circuit gasket seals. Remove B4 accumulator piston cover. *See Fig. 32.* Place shop towel over accumulator piston. Apply low pressure compressed air to ports of apply gasket areas to remove accumulator piston and spring. Remove "O" rings from accumulator piston.

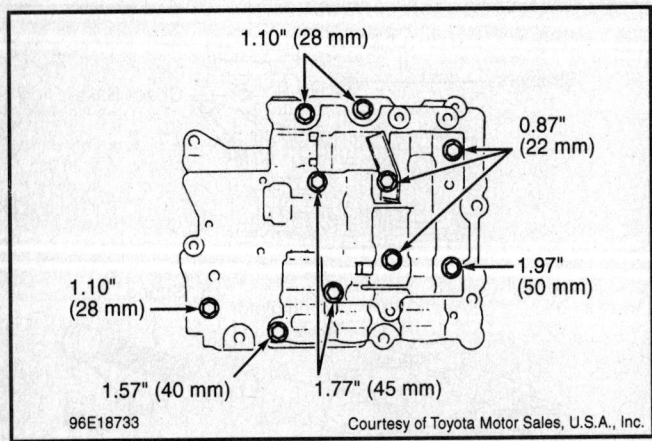

96E18733   Courtesy of Toyota Motor Sales, U.S.A., Inc.

Fig. 31: Identifying Valve Body Assembly Bolts (A340H)

2) Remove snap ring. Remove front output shaft bearing. Using screwdriver and hammer, drive out 2 oil seals from chain front case. Remove snap ring. Remove transfer front drive shaft bearing and oil seal. See Fig. 20.

Reassembly – 1) Install transfer case front drive shaft oil seal to a depth of .106-.130" (2.7-3.3 mm). Install transfer front drive shaft bearing. Install snap ring. Install front output shaft bearing. Install snap ring.

2) Install NEW front output shaft oil seal to a depth of .433-.445" (11.0-11.3 mm). Drive in NEW rear oil seal to a depth of .000-.012" (0-.30 mm). Install NEW "O" rings on accumulator piston and cover. Install spring and accumulator piston. Install accumulator piston cover and tighten 3 bolts. Install NEW apply gaskets.

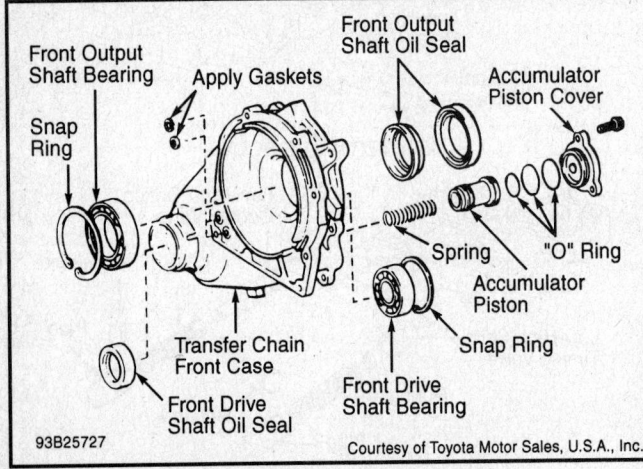

93B25727   Courtesy of Toyota Motor Sales, U.S.A., Inc.

Fig. 32: Exploded View Of Chain Front Case (A340H)

CHAIN REAR CASE

Disassembly – 1) Using screwdriver and hammer, drive out 2 front output shaft oil seals. Remove snap ring. Remove front output shaft bearing.

2) Using Bearing Remover/Installer (09608-12010) and an arbor press, press out front drive shaft bearing. Remove oil strainer from chain rear case. See Fig. 33.

Reassembly – 1) Apply sealant to oil strainer bolt threads. Install oil strainer. Tighten bolts to 61 INCH lbs. (6.9 N.m). Using bearing remover/installer, install front drive shaft bearing to a depth of .047-.071" (1.2-1.8 mm) below chain rear case surface.

2) Install front output shaft bearing. Install snap ring. Install NEW rear side front output shaft oil seals to a depth of .433-.445" (11.0-11.3 mm) below chain rear case. Using handle and seal installer, install front side front output shaft oil seals to a depth of .000-.012" (0-.30 mm) below chain rear case. Coat oil seal lips with grease.

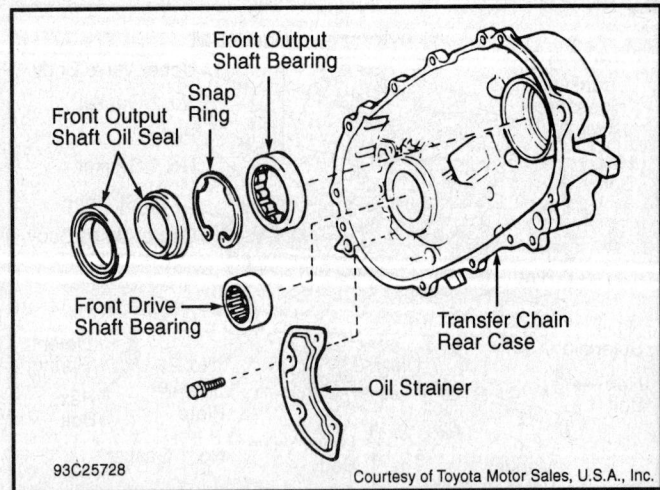

93C25728   Courtesy of Toyota Motor Sales, U.S.A., Inc.

Fig. 33: Exploded View Of Chain Rear Case (A340H)

TRANSFER OIL PUMP

Disassembly – Remove oil pump bolts. Remove oil pump body and plate from oil pump cover. Remove pressure relief valve and spring. See Fig. 34. Place reference mark on drive and driven gear. Remove gears.

Inspection – 1) Clean all components in solvent. Dry with compressed air. Install drive and driven gears in oil pump body.

2) Push driven gear to one side of oil pump body. Measure driven gear body clearance. Standard body clearance should be .0028-.0059" (.07-.15 mm). Maximum body clearance is .012" (.30 mm). If body clearance exceeds specification, replace drive gear, driven gear or pump body. See Fig. 35.

3) Measure between driven gear teeth and crescent shaped part of pump body. Standard tip clearance should be .0059-.0165" (.15-.42 mm). Maximum tip clearance is .024 (.60 mm). If tip clearance exceeds specification, replace drive gear, driven gear or pump body. See Fig. 35.

4) Using steel straightedge and feeler gauge, measure side clearance of both gears. Standard side clearance should be .0016-.0059" (.04-.15 mm). Maximum side clearance is .012" (.30 mm). If side clearance exceeds specification, replace drive gear, driven gear or pump body.

Reassembly – Coat driven and drive gears with ATF. Install oil pump gears so reference mark is aligned. Install pressure relief valve and spring. Install plate and oil pump body. Tighten bolts to 89 INCH lbs. (10 N.m).

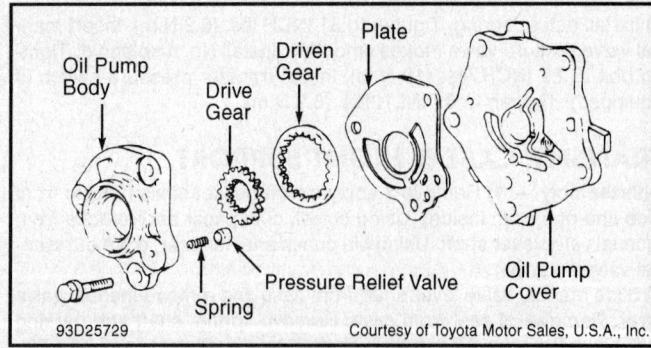

93D25729   Courtesy of Toyota Motor Sales, U.S.A., Inc.

Fig. 34: Exploded View Of Transfer Oil Pump (A340H)

EXTENSION HOUSING

If bearing is worn, replace extension housing assembly. Remove oil seal. Inspect bearing for damage. Install NEW oil seal to extension housing to a depth of .106-.130 (2.7-3.3 mm). Coat oil seal lip with grease.

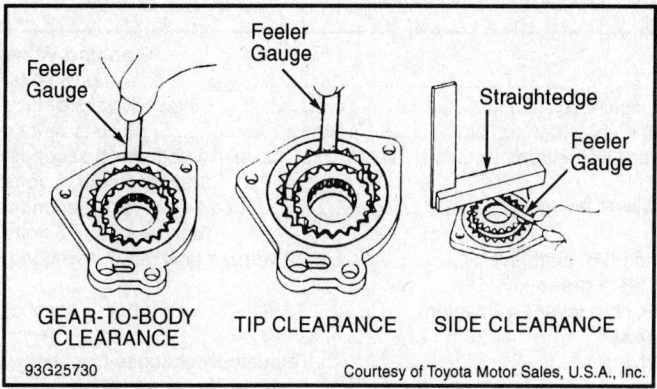

Fig. 35: *Measuring Oil Pump Clearance (A340H)*

TESTING

ELECTRONIC COMPONENTS

NOTE: *For component location, See Fig. 36.*

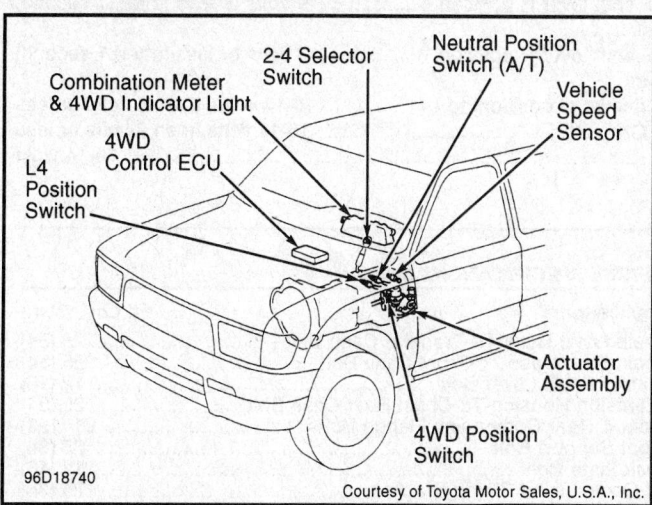

Fig. 36: *2-4 Selector System Component Location*

Selector Switch – Check for continuity at selector switch. With switch in OFF position, connect tester at terminals No. 1 and No. 2. No continuity should exist. With Switch in ON position, continuity should be present. *See Fig. 37.*

Actuator – **1)** Using an ohmmeter, measure resistance between terminals No. 2 and 3. Standard resistance is .3-100 ohms. *See Fig 38.*
2) Using an ohmmeter, measure resistance between terminals No. 2 or 3 and body ground. Standard resistance is more than 500 k/ohms. If resistance values are not as specified, replace the actuator assembly.
3) Check Actuator operation. Connect positive lead from battery to terminal No. 2 and negative lead to terminal No. 3. Ensure actuator fork shaft moves to 2WD Position. Connect positive lead from battery to terminal No. 3 and negative lead to terminal No. 2. Ensure actuator fork shaft moves to 4WD position. If operation is not as specified, replace actuator assembly.
4) Check actuator limit switch continuity. Connect positive lead from battery to terminal No. 2 and negative lead to terminal No. 3. Connect positive lead from ohmmeter to terminal No. 5 and negative lead to terminal No. 4. Ensure that there is continuity between terminals No. 4 and 5.

5) Connect positive lead from battery to terminal No. 3 and negative lead to terminal No. 2. Connect positive lead from ohmmeter to terminal No. 6 and negative lead to terminal No. 4. Ensure that there is continuity between terminals No. 4 and 6. If continuity is not as specified, replace actuator assembly.

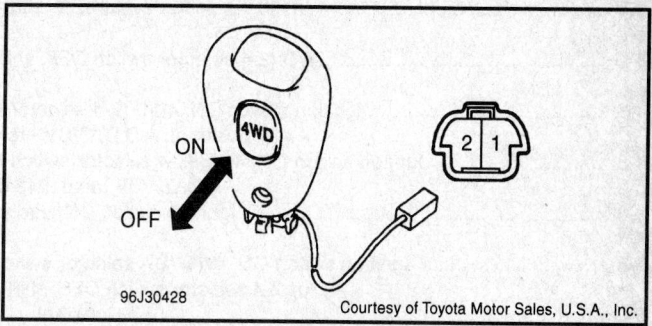

Fig. 37: *Identifying Selector Switch connector*

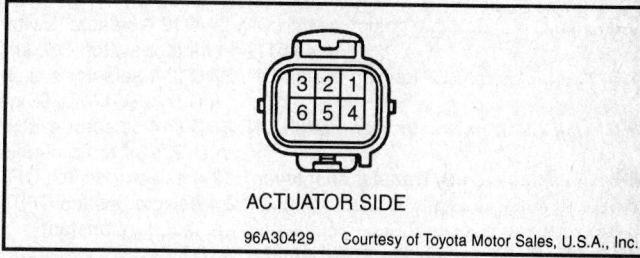

Fig. 38: *Identifying Actuator Plug Terminals*

Vehicle Speed Sensor (VSS) – Connect positive lead from battery to terminal No. 1 and negative lead to terminal No. 2. Connect positive lead from speedometer tester to terminal No. 3 and negative lead to terminal No. 2. Rotate shaft. Ensure there is a voltage change from approximately 0 volts to 11 volts or more between terminals No. 2 and 3. Voltage change should be 4 times for every revolution of speed sensor shaft. If operation is not as specified, replace sensor.
4WD Indicator Light – Disconnect connector from 4WD indicator switch. Connect switch terminal No. 2 to body ground. Turn ignition switch ON. Ensure bulb lights up. If operation is not as specified, check bulb.
4WD Control ECU – Connect wire harness side connector to ECU and inspect wire harness side connector from backside. *See Fig. 39.* See STANDARD VALUE OF ECU TERMINAL table for specifications.

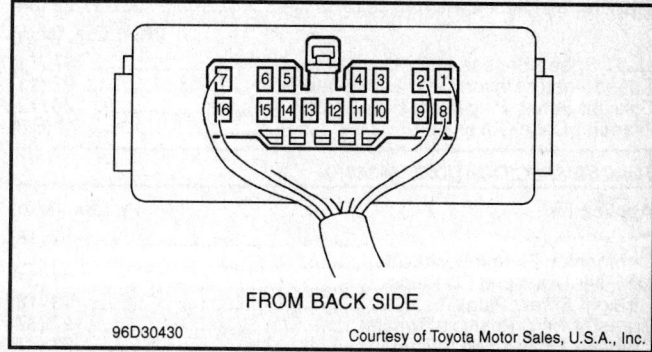

Fig. 39: *Identifying 4WD Control ECU (1996 4Runner & Tacoma)*

STANDARD VALUE OF ECU TERMINAL

Terminal No.	Condition	Standard Value
1-8	Engine Running, then 2WD to 4WD (4WD indicator light ON)	12-16 volts, then 1.2 volts or less
3-2	Ignition switch ON (2WD)	.5 volts or less
3-2	4WD (2-4 selector switch ON, shift lever L4 Position)	10-14 volts for 5 seconds, then less than .5 volts
3-2	4WD (2-4 selector switch OFF, shift lever H Position)	10-14 volts for 5 seconds, then less than .5 volts
4-8	Ignition switch ON, 4WD (2-4 selector switch ON, shift lever. in H position), A.D.D.[1] VSV[2] temp. 68 degrees	9 volts or less (after .1 second)
4-8	Ignition switch ON, 4WD (2-4 selector switch OFF, shift lever L4 Position), A.D.D. VSV temp. 248 degrees	13 volts or less (after .1 second)
5-8	Ignition switch ON, during driving	Repeatedly changes from below .5 volts or less to 4 volts or more
6-8	Ignition switch ON, 4WD (2-4 selector switch ON, shift lever H position or 2-4 selector switch OFF, shift lever L4 position	2 volts or less
8-Ground	Constant	Continuity
9-8	Ignition switch ON, 4WD (2-4 selector switch ON or shift lever L4 position) to 2WD (2-4 selector switch OFF, shift lever L4 position)	.5 volts or less, then 10-14 volts, then .5 volts (after 5 seconds)
10-8	Ignition switch ON, 2WD (2-4 selector switch Off shift lever H position) to 4WD (2-4 selector switch ON, shift lever L4 position	.5 volts or less, then 10-14 volts then .5 volts (after 5 seconds)
11-8	Ignition switch ON, 2WD (2-4 selector switch OFF shift lever H position. A.D.D. VSV temp. 68 degrees	9 volts or less (after .1 second)
11-8	Ignition switch ON, 2WD (2-4 selector switch OFF shift lever H position. A.D.D. VSV temp. 248 degrees	13 volts or less (after .1 second)
14-8	Transfer shift lever H (2-4 selector switch OFF, shift lever H position) to L4	10-14 volts, then .5 volts or less
15-8	2-4 selector switch OFF then ON	10-14 volts, then 2 volts or less
16-8	Constant	10-14 volts

[1] – Automatic Disconnecting Differential
[2] – Vacuum Switching Valve

TORQUE SPECIFICATIONS

TORQUE SPECIFICATIONS (RF1A & VF1A)

Application	Ft. Lbs. (N.m)
Bearing Control Retainer	13 (18)
Extension Housing-To-Rear Case Bolt	29 (39)
Front Case-To-Rear Case Bolt	29 (39)
Front Drive Gear Bearing Retainer Bolt	13 (18)
Oil Pump Body	14 (19)
Oil Strainer/Separator	13 (18)
Output Shaft-To-Companion Flange Nut	91 (123)
Rear Case "A" Bolts	29 (39)
Rear Case "B" Bolts	27 (37)
Reduction Gear Case-To-Front Case Bolt	29 (39)
Retainer-To-Front Case Bolt	13 (18)
Transfer Indicator Switch	25 (34)

	INCH Lbs. (N.m)
No. 1 Speed Sensor	97 (11)
Speedometer Driven Gear Lock Plate Bolt	97 (11)
Straight Screw Plug (Shift Fork Shaft)	106 (12)
Transfer Case Cover Bolt	78 (8.8)

TORQUE SPECIFICATIONS (A340F)

Application	Ft. Lbs. (N.m)
Case Protector	13 (18)
Companion Flange Lock Nuts	87 (118)
Oil Filler Drain and Fill Plugs	27 (37)
Straight Screw Plugs	13 (18)
Transfer 4WD Position Switch	27 (37)
Transfer L4 Position Switch	27 (37)
Transfer Neutral Poaition Switch	27 (37)
Upper Cover	13 (18)

	INCH Lbs. (N.m)
Extension Housing Cover	106 (12)
Front Bearing Container	97 (11)
Oil Pump Body	69 (7.4)
Oil Separator/Strainer	69 (7.4)
Vehicle Speed Sensor	97 (11)

TORQUE SPECIFICATIONS (A340H)

Application	Ft. Lbs. (N.m)
Chain Front Case-To-Transfer Case Bolt	25 (34)
Chain Rear Case-To-Front Case Bolt	25 (34)
Control Shaft Lever Bolt	12 (16)
Extension Housing-To-Chain Rear Case Bolt	25 (34)
Front & Rear Companion Flange Bolts	91 (123)
Front Support Bolt	25 (34)
Lock Plate Bolt	12 (16)
Oil Cooler Tube Clamp Bracket	25 (34)
Oil Pump Assembly	2 (16)
Transfer Case-To-Transmission Case Bolt	25 (34)
Transfer Fluid Temperature Sensor	11 (15)
Transfer Oil Pump-To-Chain Rear Case Bolt	12 (16)
Transfer Side Unions	21 (29)

	INCH Lbs. (N.m)
Chain Oil Receiver-To-Chain Front Case Bolt	89 (10)
Detent Spring-To-Valve Body Bolt	61 (6.9)
No. 4 Solenoid-To-Valve Body Bolt	89 (10)
Oil Cooler Tube Clamp	89 (10)
Oil Pan Bolt	65 (7.4)
Oil Pump Body Bolt	89 (10)
Oil Strainer Bolt	61 (6.9)
Parking Lock Pawl Bracket Bolt	61 (6.9)
Transfer Position Switch Nut	35 (3.9)
Transfer Position Switch Bolt	115 (13)
Transfer Pressure Switch-To-Valve Body Bolt	61 (6.9)
Transfer Valve Body Bolt	61 (6.9)
Valve Body-To-Transfer Case Bolt	89 (10)

WIRING DIAGRAMS

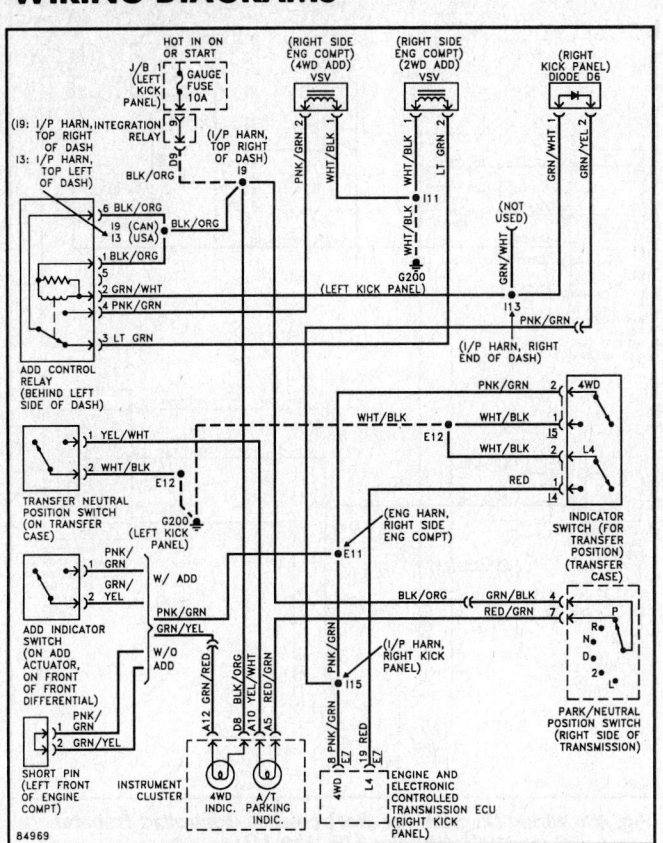

Fig. 40: *Wiring Diagram For Electronically Controlled Transfer Case (1995 Pickup 2.4L With A/T)*

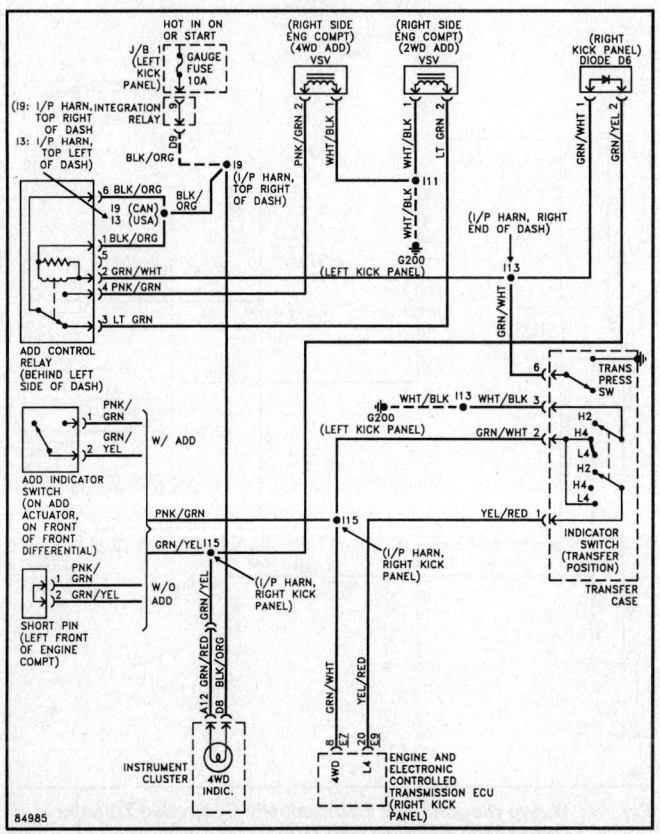

Fig. 41: *Wiring Diagram For Electronically Controlled Transfer Case (1995 Pickup 3.0L With A/T)*

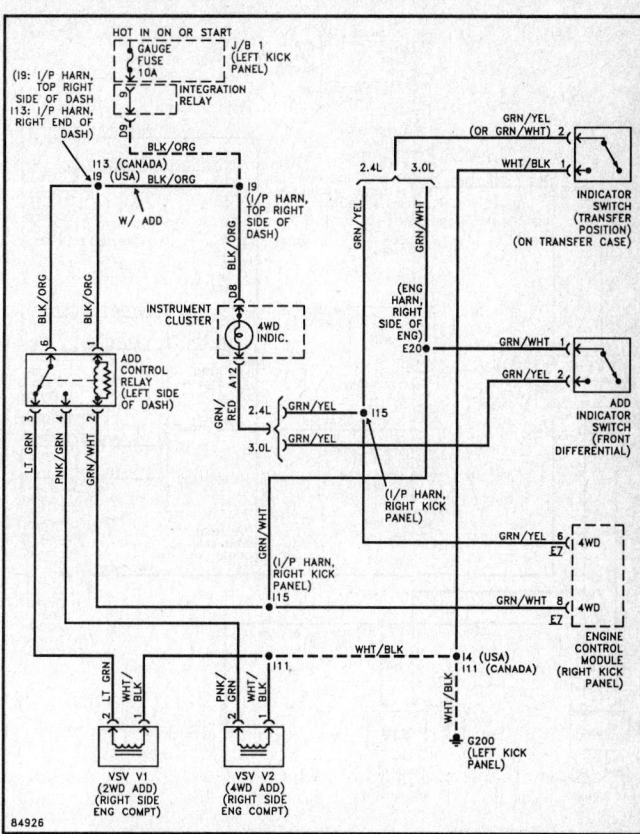

Fig. 42: *Wiring Diagram For Electronically Controlled Transfer Case (1995 Pickup With M/T)*

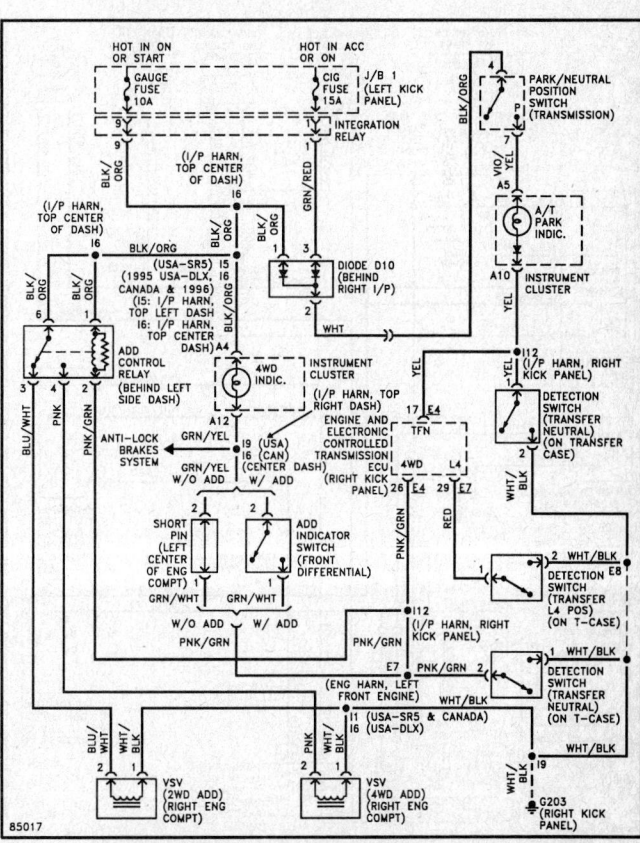

Fig. 43: *Wiring Diagram For Electronically Controlled Transfer Case (1995-96 T100 With A/T)*

TRANSFER CASES
Toyota Pickup, T100, Tacoma & 4Runner (Cont.)

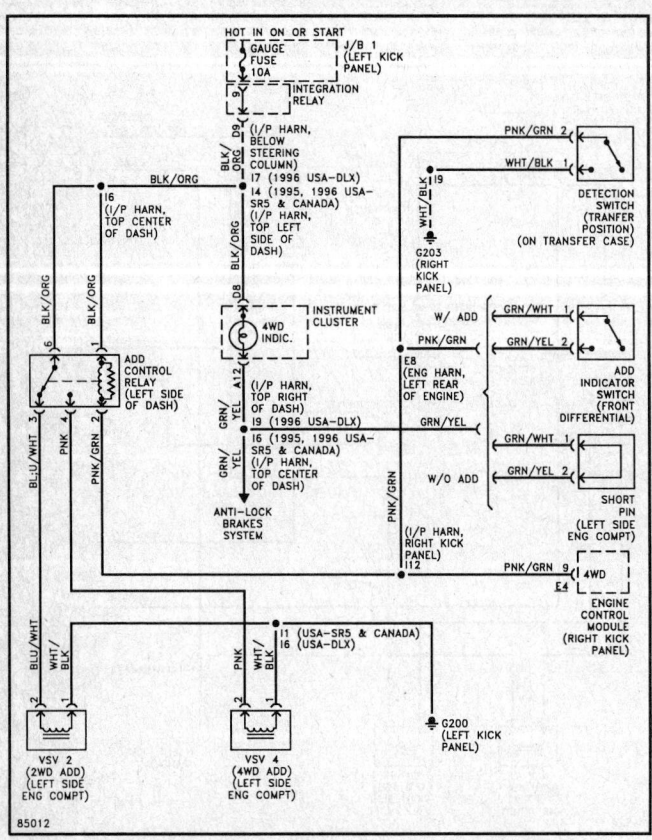

Fig. 44: *Wiring Diagram For Electronically Controlled Transfer Case (1995-96 T100 With M/T)*

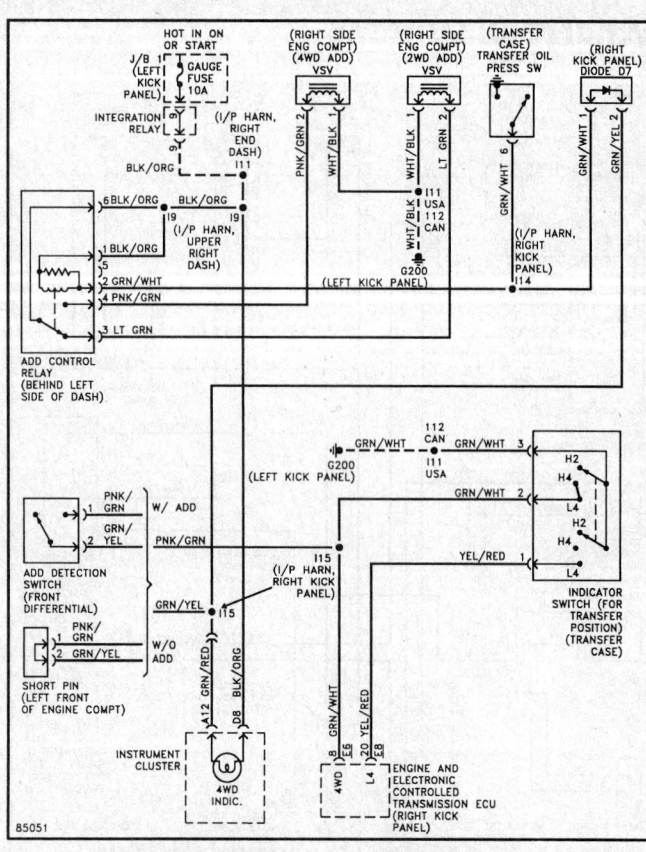

Fig. 46: *Wiring Diagram For Electronically Controlled Transfer Case (1995 4Runner 3.0L With A/T)*

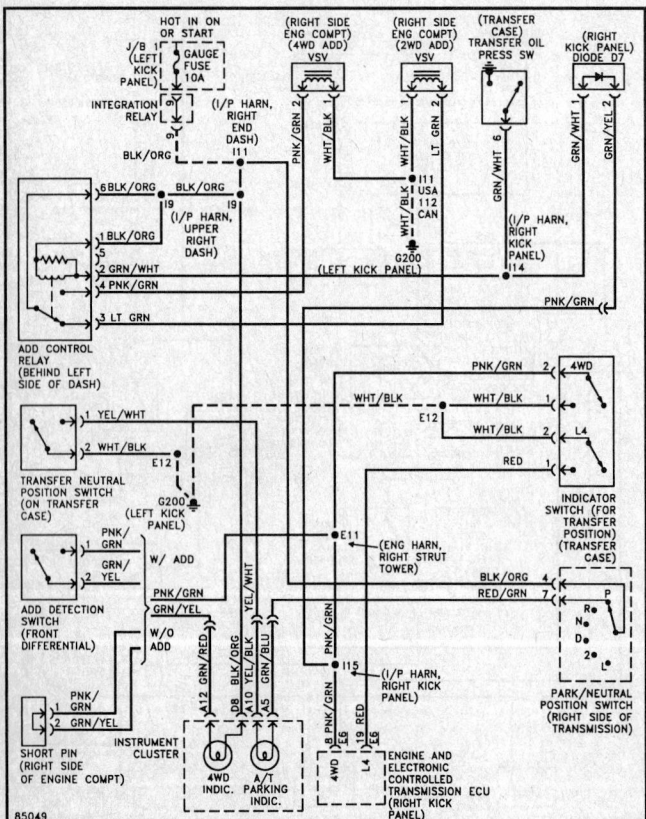

Fig. 45: *Wiring Diagram For Electronically Controlled Transfer Case (1995 4Runner 2.4L With A/T)*

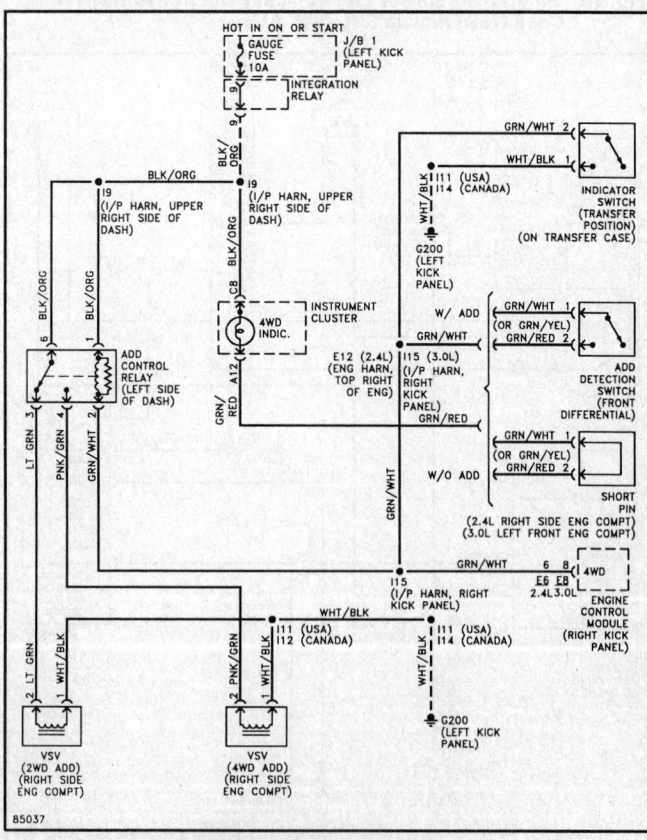

Fig. 47: *Wiring Diagram For Electronically Controlled Transfer Case (1995 4Runner With M/T)*

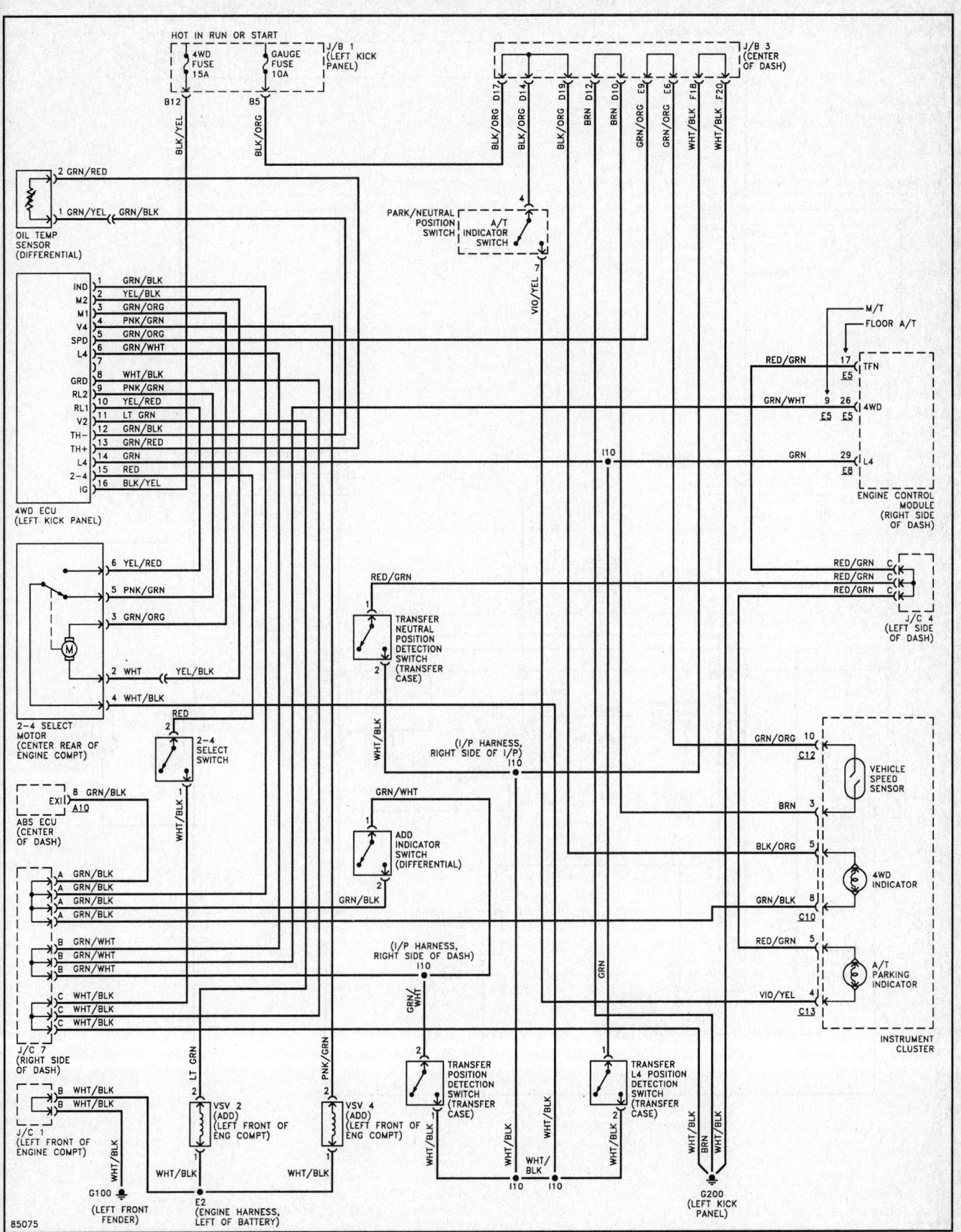

Fig. 48: *Wiring Diagram For Electronically Controlled Transfer With 2-4 Select Switch Case (1995-96 Tacoma With A/T)*

85075

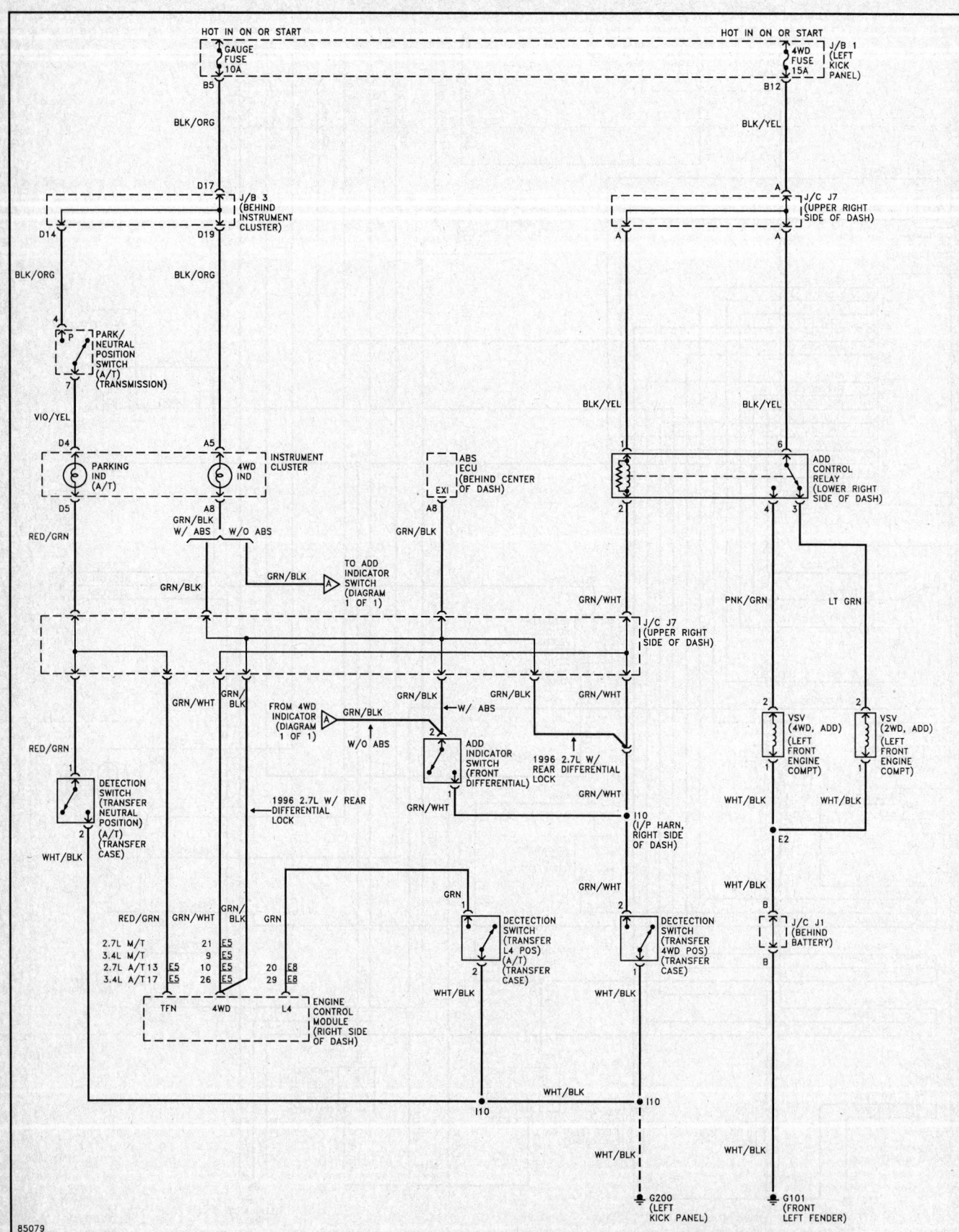

Fig. 49: Wiring Diagram For Electronically Controlled Transfer Without 2-4 Select Switch Case (1995-96 Tacoma With A/T)

85079

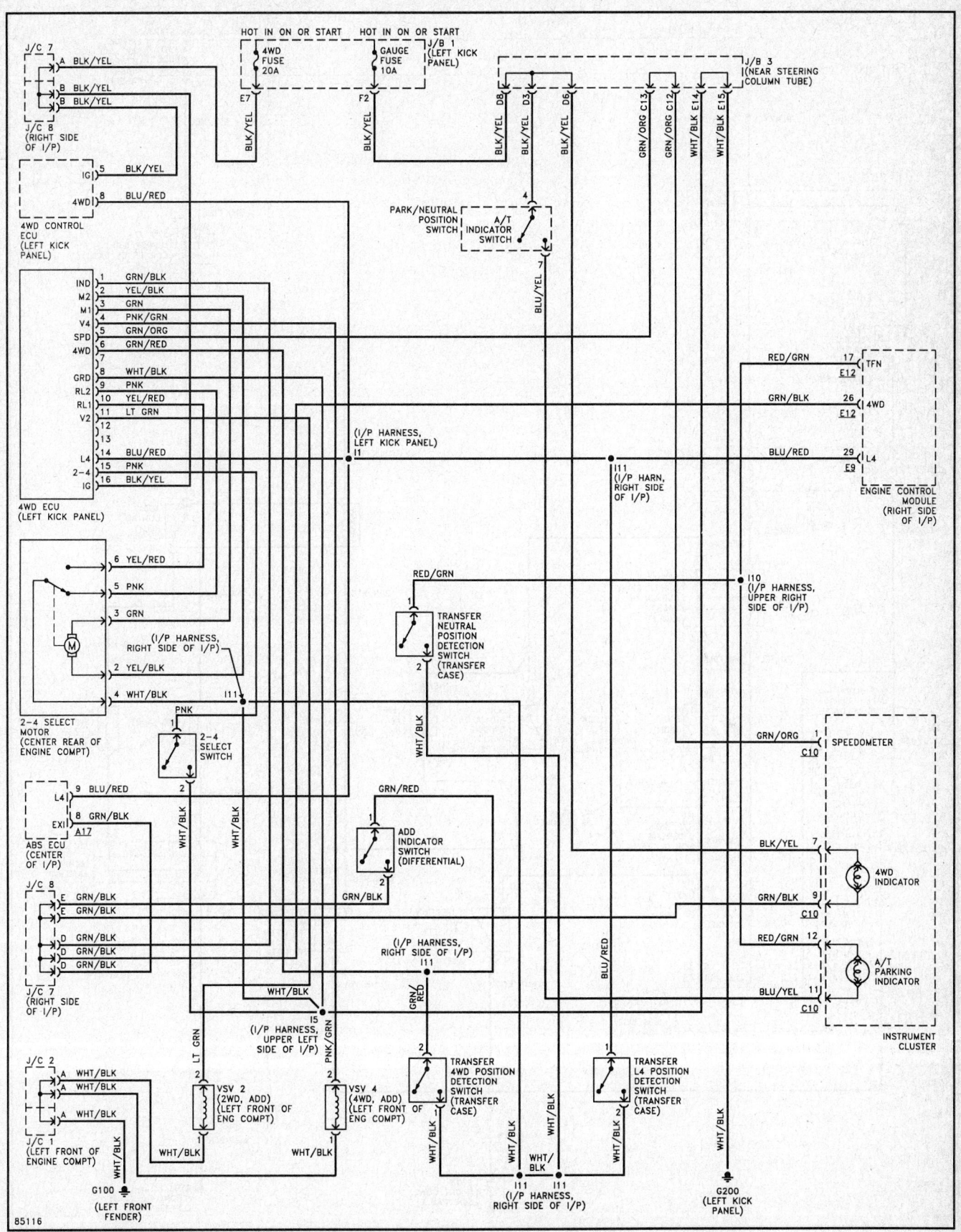

Fig. 50: Wiring Diagram For Electronically Controlled Transfer With 2-4 Select Switch Case (1996 4Runner)

TRANSFER CASES
Toyota Pickup, T100, Tacoma & 4Runner (Cont.)

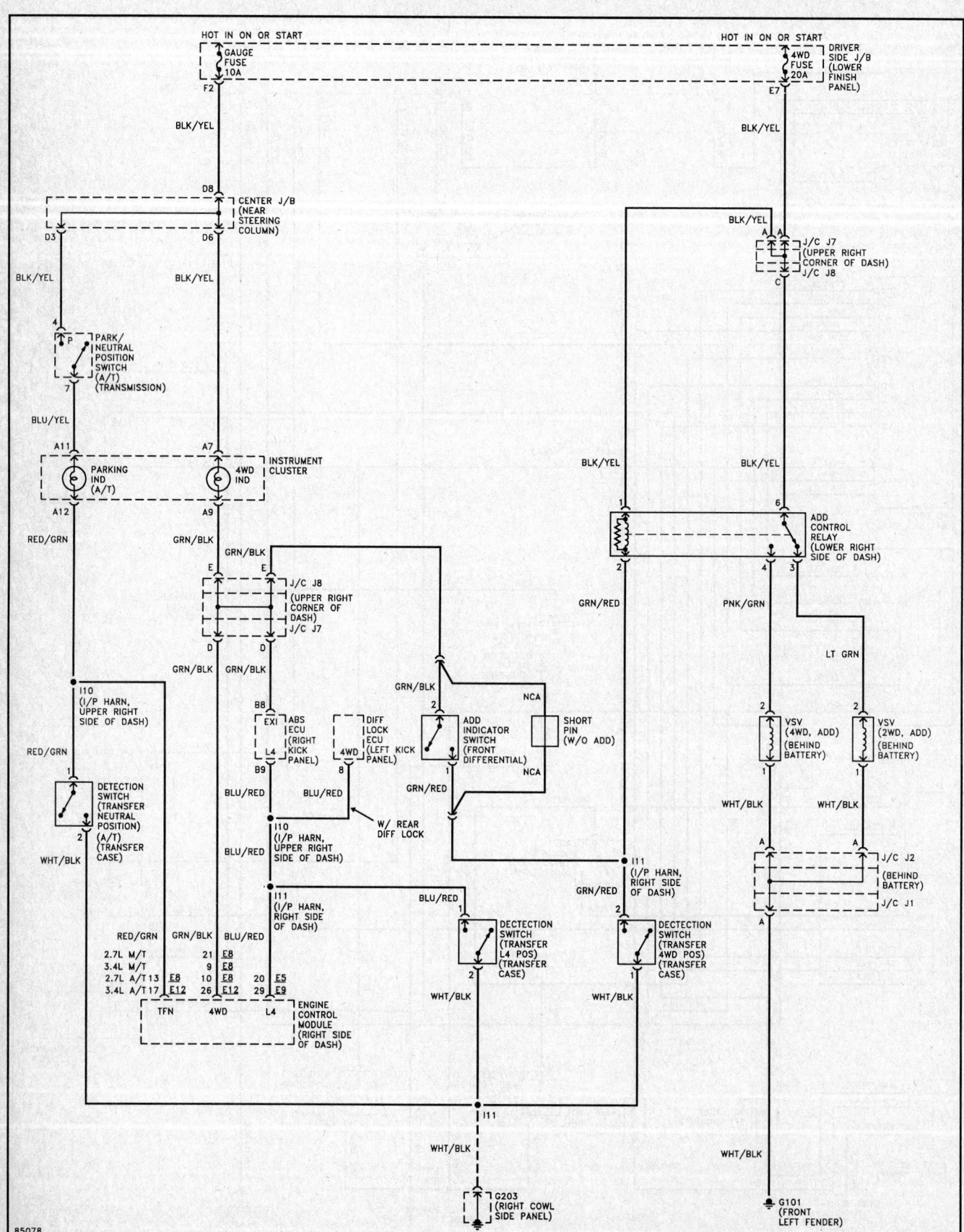

Fig. 51: *Wiring Diagram For Electronically Controlled Transfer Without 2-4 Select Switch Case (1996 4Runner)*

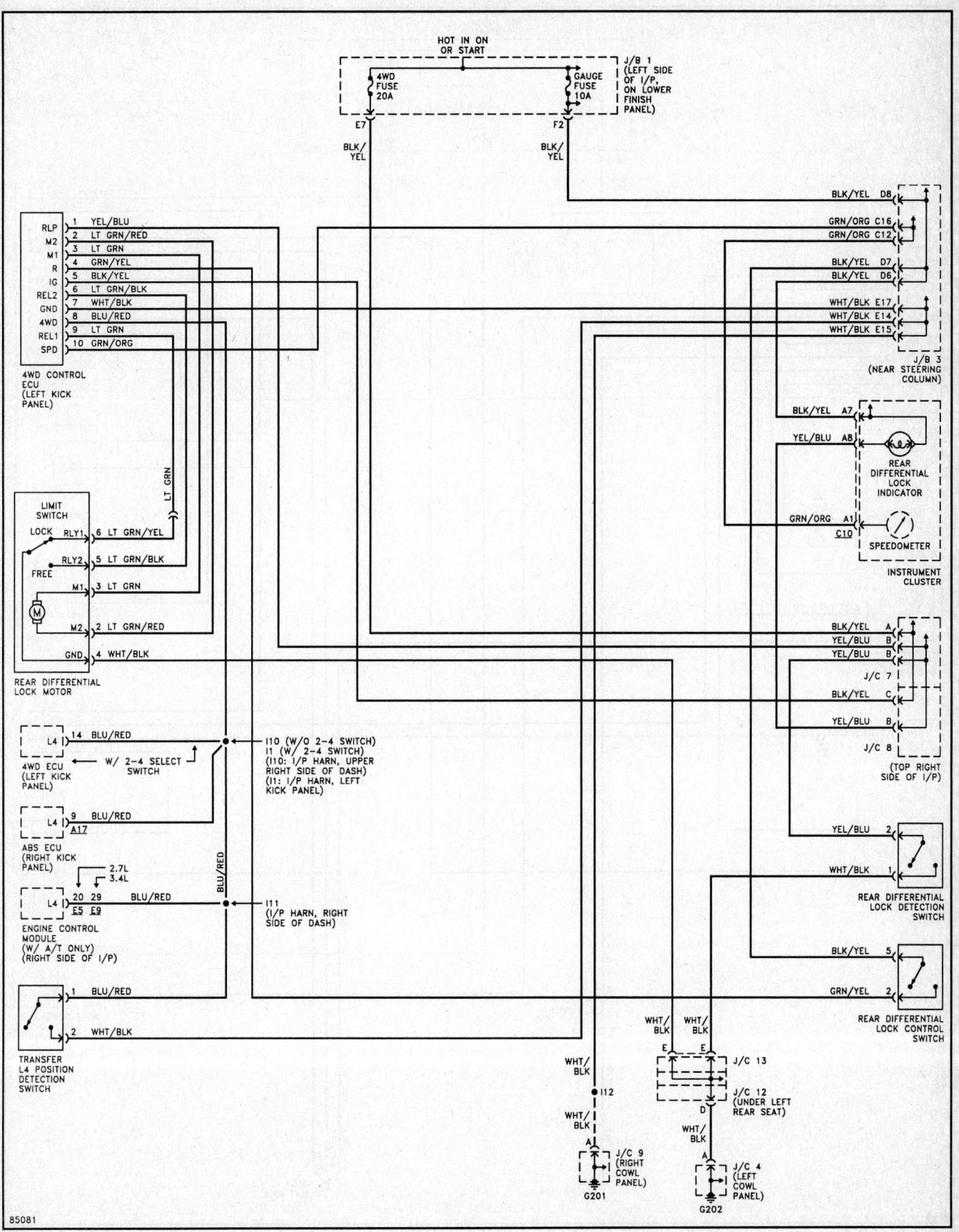

Fig. 52: *Wiring Diagram For Rear Differential Lock Case (1996 4Runner)*

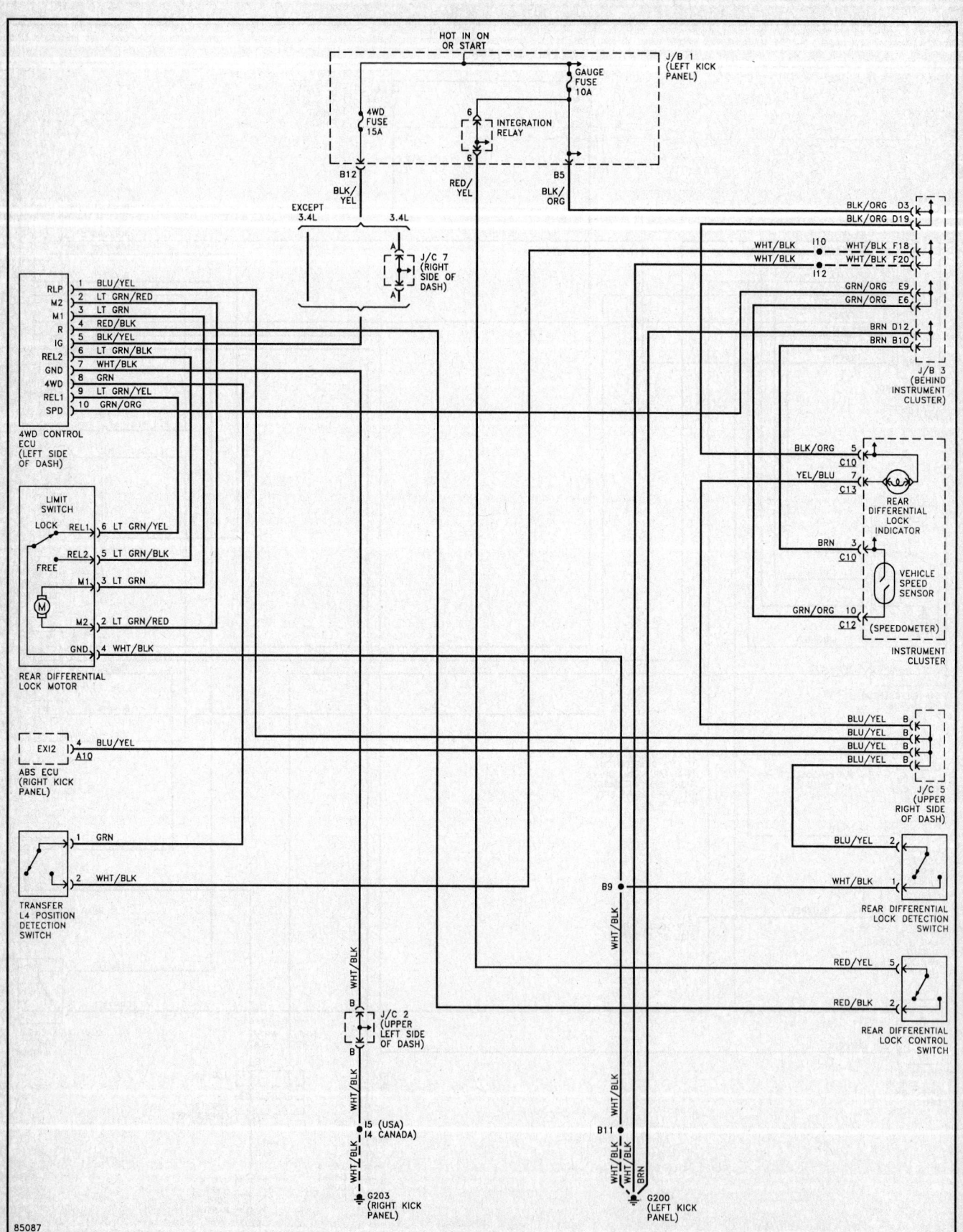

Fig. 53: *Wiring Diagram For Rear Differential Lock Case (1996 Tacoma)*

Previa

APPLICATION

TOYOTA TRANSFER CASE APPLICATION

Application	Transfer Case Model
1995-96 Previa	TF1AV

DESCRIPTION & OPERATION

The Toyota TF1AV transfer case delivers full time all wheel drive. The planetary gear in the center differential equally distributes engine power to front and rear propeller shafts. The center differential is equipped with a limited slip differential (LSD) which compensates for any difference in rotation in front and rear wheels.

TRANSFER CASE

REMOVAL & INSTALLATION

Manufacturer does not supply information on separate procedures for removal and installation of transfer case. Transfer case is removed from transmission once complete assembly is removed from vehicle. See REMOVAL & INSTALLATION procedures in TRANSMISSION SERVICING section.

OVERHAUL

Disassembly – 1) Remove vehicle speed sensor. Remove oil pump body. Using a magnet, remove 2 straight pins from input shaft. Using 2-jaw puller, remove drive shaft dust deflector. Unstake companion flange lock nut. Secure companion flange from turning using Holder (09330-00021). Remove companion flange.

2) Remove vehicle speed sensor drive gear from companion flange. Remove dust deflector. Remove extension housing. Remove snap ring. Unbolt and separate front and rear case. Remove oil separator from rear case with Torx (T30) socket. Using a plastic hammer, tap front output shaft. Remove front drive chain, front output shaft and rear output shaft. Separate front drive chain, front output shaft and rear output shaft. See Fig. 1.

3) Remove snap ring remove input shaft and planetary ring gear. Remove oil separator, oil strainer and oil receiver. 1995 oil separator and strainer are one unit.

4) Inspect condition of front output shaft bearings. Ensure bearings are free from pitting, scoring or overheating. Check for smooth operation. If bearings require replacement, remove snap ring and remove with press. See Fig. 2.

5) Disassemble rear output shaft. Using 2-jaw puller, remove bearing. Using bearing splitter, support clutch hub and press out shaft.

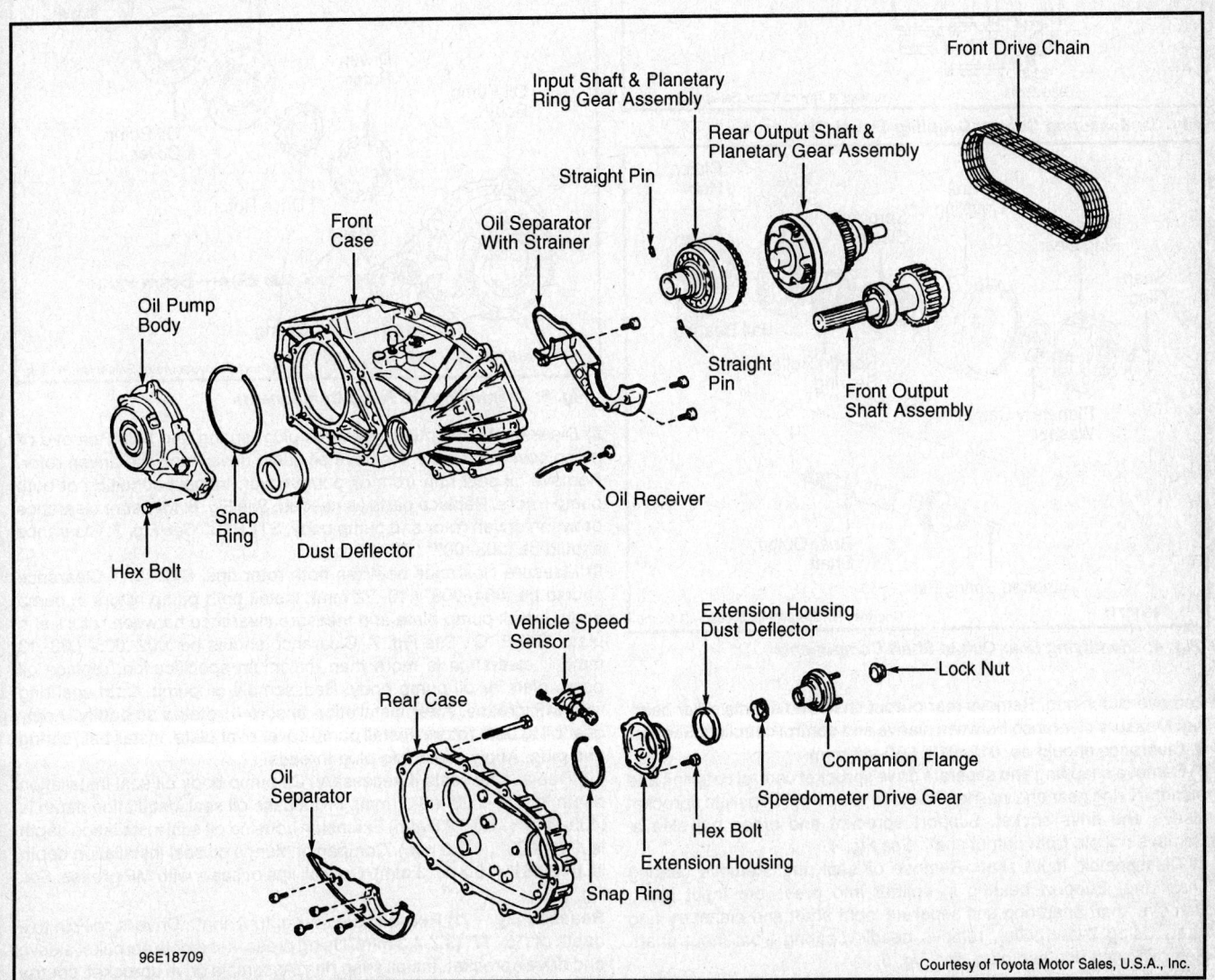

96E18709

Courtesy of Toyota Motor Sales, U.S.A., Inc.

Fig. 1: Exploded View Of Transfer Case

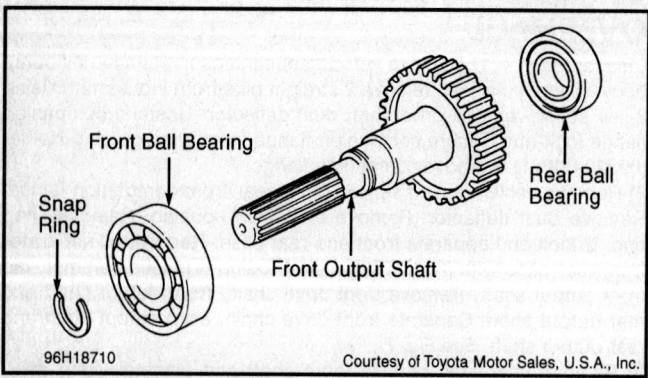

96H18710   Courtesy of Toyota Motor Sales, U.S.A., Inc.

Fig. 2: Identifying Front Output Shaft Components

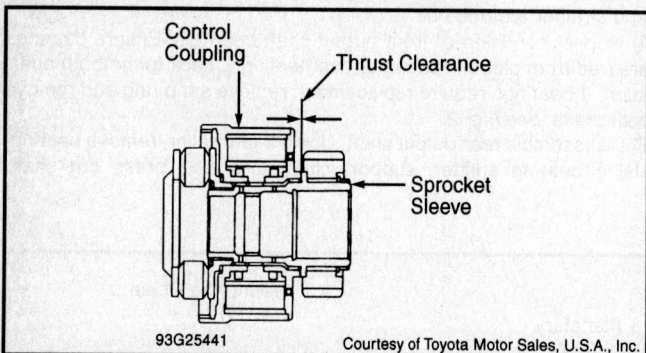

93G25441   Courtesy of Toyota Motor Sales, U.S.A., Inc.

Fig. 3: Measuring Control Coupling Thrust Clearance

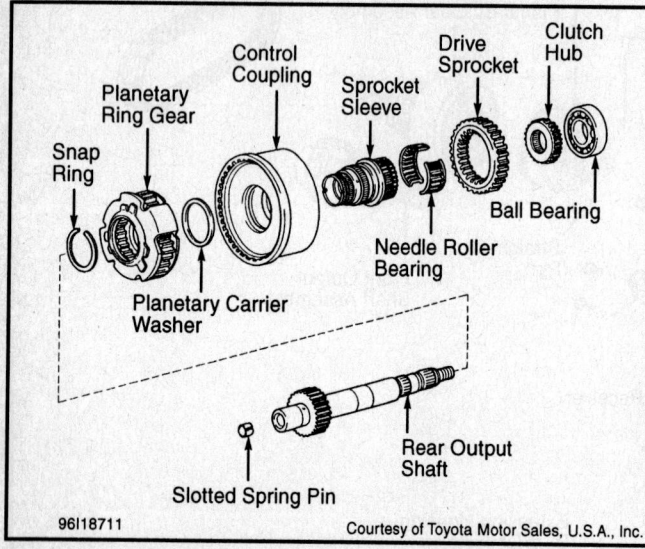

96I18711   Courtesy of Toyota Motor Sales, U.S.A., Inc.

Fig. 4: Identifying Rear Output Shaft Components

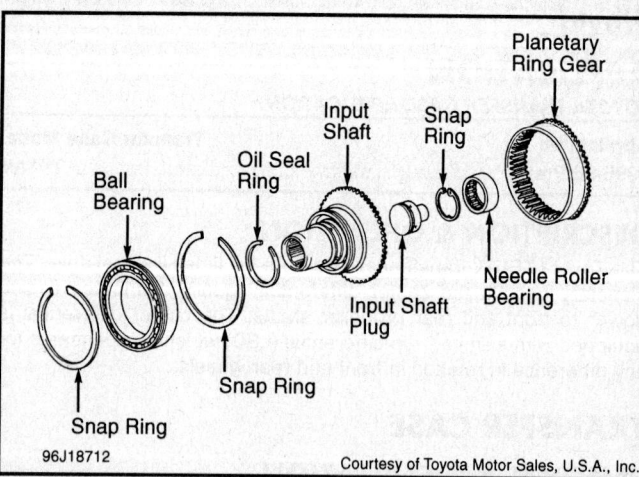

96J18712   Courtesy of Toyota Motor Sales, U.S.A., Inc.

Fig. 5: Identifying Input Shaft Components

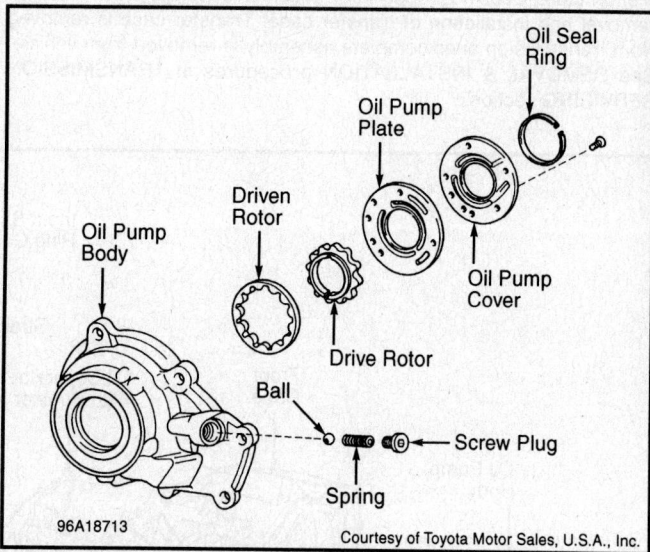

96A18713   Courtesy of Toyota Motor Sales, U.S.A., Inc.

Fig. 6: Identifying Oil Pump Components

Remove clutch hub. Remove rear output shaft and needle roller bearing. Measure clearance between sleeve and control coupling. See Fig. 3. Clearance should be .012-.018" (.30-.45 mm).

6) Remove snap ring and separate drive sprocket control coupling and planetary ring gear and washer. Remove snap ring. Separate sprocket sleeve and drive socket. Support sprocket and press out sleeve. Remove roll pin from output shaft. See Fig. 4.

7) Disassemble input shaft. Remove oil seal ring. Remove bearing snap ring. Support bearing in splitter and press out input shaft. Remove shaft snap ring and separate input shaft and planetary ring gear. Using 2-jaw puller, remove needle bearing from input shaft. Remove snap ring and plug. See Fig. 5.

8) Disassemble oil pump. Remove plug, spring and ball. Remove oil pump cover and plate. Remove oil pump drive rotor and driven rotor. Remove oil seal ring from oil pump cover. Inspect condition of both pump rotors. Replace parts as needed. See Fig. 6. Measure clearance between driven rotor and pump body, STEP "B". See Fig. 7. Clearance should be .003-.007" (.08-.17 mm).

9) Measure clearance between both rotor tips, STEP "A". Clearance should be .004-.009" (.10-.22 mm). Install both pump rotors in pump body. Install pump plate and measure clearance between rotors and plate, STEP "C". See Fig. 7. Clearance should be .002-.005" (.03-.13 mm). If clearance is more than maximum specification, replace oil pump plate or oil pump body. Reassemble oil pump. Coat seal ring with MP grease. After installation ensure it rotates smoothly. Apply gear oil to both rotors. Install pump cover over plate. Install ball, spring and plug. Apply sealant to plug threads.

10) Replace oil seals if necessary. Oil pump body oil seal installation depth is .012-.028" (.3-.7 mm). Front case oil seal installation depth is .433-.427" (11.0-12.0 mm) Extension housing oil seal installation depth is .024-.039" (.6-1.0 mm). Companion flange oil seal installation depth is .642-681" (16.3-17.3 mm). Coat all lips of seals with MP grease. See Fig. 8.

Reassembly – 1) Reassemble rear output shaft. Drive in roll pin to a depth of .15-.17" (3.7-4.3 mm). Using press, assemble sprocket sleeve and drive sprocket. Install snap ring. Assemble drive sprocket, control

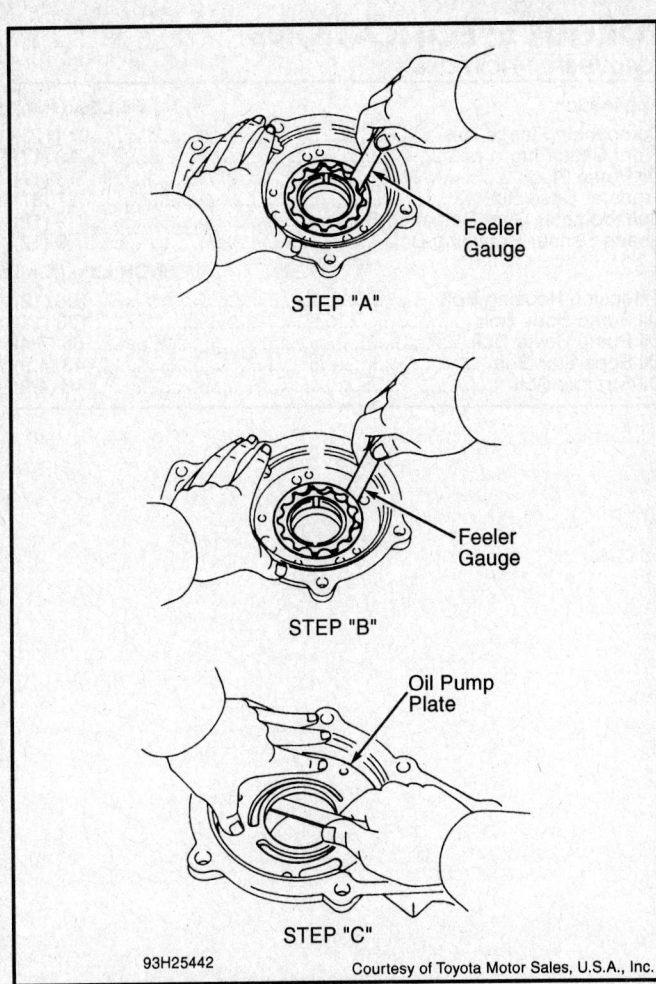

Fig. 7: Measuring Oil Pump Clearances

coupling, thinnest washer and planetary ring gear. Select snap ring that allows minimum axial play. Snap rings are available in thicknesses from .061" (1.55 mm) to .069" (1.75 mm) in .020" (.05 mm) increments. Snap rings are marked "A" through "E". See Fig. 4.

2) Measure control coupling thrust clearance. Clearance should be .0118-.0177" (.30-.45 mm). If clearance is not within specification, disassemble control coupling and planetary ring gear and install thrust washer of a different thickness. Thrust washers range in thicknesses of .051" (1.30 mm) to .071" (1.80 mm) in .004" (.10 mm) increments. Thrust washers are marked "A" through "F".

3) Apply gear oil to needle roller bearing. Install needle roller bearing in the sprocket sleeve. Install rear output shaft. Install clutch hub. Install ball bearing.

4) Assemble front output shaft. Coat all sliding and rotating parts with gear oil. Install rear bearing with shielded side toward gear. Install front ball bearing with shielded side toward gear. Install snap ring that allows minimum axial play. Snap rings range in thicknesses from .077" (1.95 mm) to .098 " (2.50 mm) in .02 (.05 mm) increments. Snap rings are marked "1" through "12". See Fig. 2.

5) Assemble input shaft. Replace plug "O" ring and install plug. Ensure "O" ring is coated with lubricant. Install snap ring. Install needle roller bearing in shaft to a depth of .329-.352" (8.35-8.95 mm). Assemble input shaft and planetary ring. Install snap ring. Install ball bearing. Select and install snap ring that allows minimum axial play. Snap rings range in thicknesses of .057" (1.45 mm) to .065" (1.65 mm) in .002" (.05 mm) increments. Snap rings are marked "1" through "5". Coat oil seal ring with MP grease and install onto input shaft. Ensure oil seal ring rotates freely. See Fig. 5.

6) Install oil separator with oil strainer and oil receiver in front case. Install input shaft and planetary gear assembly. Secure input shaft assembly in case with snap ring. Assemble front drive chain, rear output shaft, front output shaft.

7) Install assembled components together in front case. Use soft faced hammer to fully seat input and output shaft assemblies. Install oil separator in rear case. Apply Three Bond (1281) sealant to case halves and assemble. Tighten bolts to specifications. See TORQUE SPECIFICATIONS table.

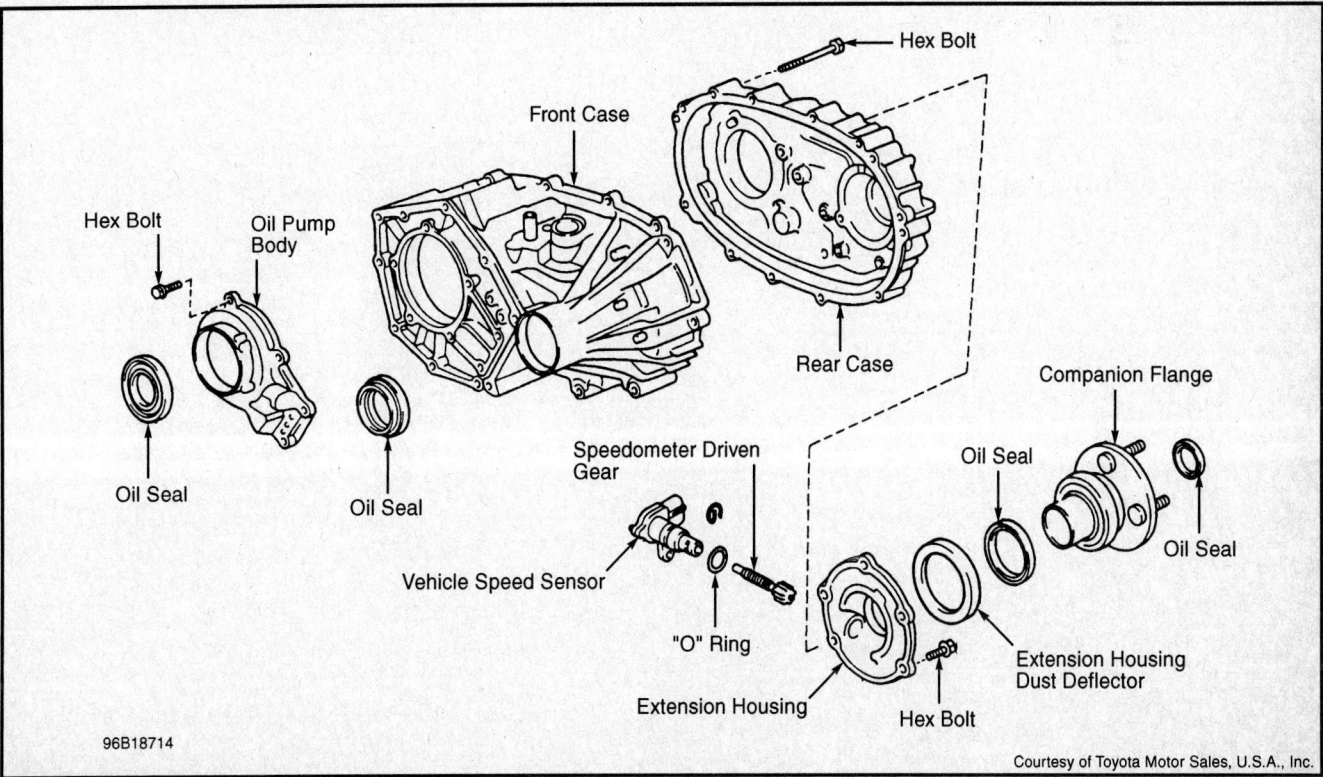

Fig. 8: Identifying Oil Seal Locations

8) Install snap ring to rear output shaft bearing. Install extension housing. Install extension housing dust deflector. Install speedometer drive gear to companion flange. Install companion flange. Tighten lock nut to 91 ft. lbs. (123 N.m). Stake lock nut. Install dust deflector.

9) Install 2 straight pins on input shaft. Apply sealant to oil pump body and install oil pump. Ensure that input shaft and output shafts rotate smoothly. Install vehicle speed sensor assembly. *See Fig. 1.*

TORQUE SPECIFICATIONS
TORQUE SPECIFICATIONS

Application	Ft. Lbs. (N.m)
Companion Flange Nut	91 (123)
Front Case Plug	13 (17)
Oil Pump Plug	13 (17)
Transfer Case Bolt	27 (37)
Speedometer Gear Retaining Bolt	9 (12)
Speed Sensor Retaining Bolt	9 (12)
	INCH Lbs. (N.m)
Extension Housing Bolt	108 (12)
Oil Pump Body Bolt	108 (12)
Oil Pump Cover Bolt	65 (7.4)
Oil Separator Bolt	43 (4.9)
Oil Strainer Bolt	43 (4.9)

RAV4

APPLICATION

TOYOTA TRANSFER CASE APPLICATION

Application	[1] Model Number
RAV4 (1996)	A-540H

[1] – Identifies transmission code. No additional transfer case model number information is available.

TRANSFER CASE

REMOVAL & INSTALLATION

Manufacturer does not supply information on separate procedures for removal and installation of transfer case. Transfer case is removed from transmission once complete assembly is removed from vehicle. See REMOVAL & INSTALLATION procedures in TRANSMISSION SERVICING.

ELECTRONIC TESTING

CENTER DIFFERENTIAL CLUTCH CONTROL SOLENOID

CAUTION: Perform test at normal operating fluid temperature of 122-176°F (50-80°C).

1) Ensure transmission fluid is at operating temperature. Block wheels. Remove transfer valve body cover plug and install pressure gauge. *See Fig. 1.*
2) Start vehicle and accelerate 50 percent or more in Park. Ensure center differential clutch control pressure is more than 42 psi (3.0 kg/cm²). Release accelerator. Ensure center differential clutch control pressure is 1.4 psi (0.1 kg/cm²) or less at idle. If pressure is not as specified, go to next step.
3) Install a 24 watt bulb in jumper wire connected between positive battery terminal and control solenoid terminal No. 1. Connect jumper wire between negative battery terminal and control solenoid terminal No. 3 to activate solenoid. *See Fig. 1.* Measure center differential clutch control pressure at idle. See CONTROL SOLENOID PRESSURE SPECIFICATIONS table.

CAUTION: DO NOT maintain stall speed RPM for more than 5 seconds.

4) Measure center differential clutch control pressure at stall speed. Connect tachometer to vehicle and ensure it is visible to driver. Apply parking and service brakes. Start engine. Position transmission in "D" range. Fully depress accelerator pedal. Immediately note highest engine RPM. DO NOT perform test longer than 5 seconds. Stall speed should be 2250-2550 RPM.
5) If pressures exceed specifications in all ranges, center differential clutch control valve or control solenoid is defective.
6) If pressures are lower than specifications in all ranges, oil pump, differential clutch control valve or control solenoid is defective.
7) If pressure is lower than specifications at stall speed with control solenoid on, control solenoid is defective.
8) If pressure is higher or lower than specifications when jumper wires are connected, differential clutch control valve or control solenoid is defective.

CONTROL SOLENOID PRESSURE SPECIFICATIONS

Engine Speed	Pressure psi (kg/cm²)
Idle Speed	53-61 (3.7-4.3)
Stall Speed	
With Solenoid On	192-225 (13.5-15.8)
With Solenoid Off	107-125 (7.5-8.8)

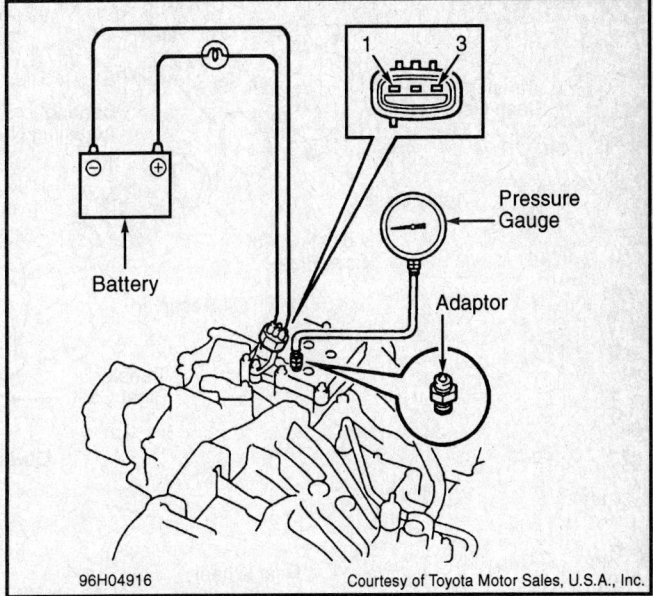

96H04916   Courtesy of Toyota Motor Sales, U.S.A., Inc.

Fig. 1: Checking Center Differential Clutch Control Solenoid Pressure

OVERHAUL

DISASSEMBLY & REASSEMBLY

Disassembly (Transfer Case) – 1) Remove mode select lever and rod (if equipped). Remove rear wheel speed sensor. Remove "O" ring from speed sensor. Remove dynamic damper (if equipped). *See Fig. 2.*
2) Remove dust deflector from extension housing. Remove 4 bolts. Remove "O" ring from housing. Using Seal Puller (09308-00010), remove extension housing oil seal.
3) Remove 5 bolts from transfer right case retainer. Using plastic hammer, remove right case retainer. Remove "O" ring and apply gasket from retainer. Remove 3 bolts and transfer inspection hole cover.
4) Using Lock Nut Wrench (09326-20011) and spring tension gauge, measure driven pinion preload and backlash between driven pinion and ring gear. Driven pinion preload at starting point is 2.0-3.1 lbs. (.9-1.4 kg).
5) Using lock nut wrench and spring gauge, measure total preload. Total preload at starting point is 1.1-2.0 lbs. (.5-.9 kg). Add driven pinion preload. Using dial indicator, measure ring gear backlash. Backlash should be .0051-.0071" (.130-.180 mm).
6) Remove driven pinion bearing cage. Remove "O" ring and shims from bearing cage. Remove transfer right case. Remove center differential assembly. Remove apply gasket from left case.
7) Remove oil pump driven gear and strainer. Remove "O" ring from oil pump strainer. Remove adjusting nut lock plate. Remove "O" ring from bolt.
8) Using Adjusting Nut Wrench (09318-12010), remove adjusting nut and oil reserver from right case. Remove outer race with a brass bar and hammer. Using Oil Seal Puller (09308-00010), remove outer race and plate washer. Remove left case oil seal.

Disassembly (Transfer Case Driven Pinion Bearing Cage) –
1) Using chisel and hammer, unstake lock nut. Using Lock Nut Wrench (09326-20011), remove lock nut. Use soft jaws for holding driven pinion in vise.
2) Remove driven pinion, rear side bearing and spacer with arbor press. Using Bearing Remover (09950-00020), remove front side bearing. Using brass bar and hammer, remove bearing outer races. *See Fig. 3.*

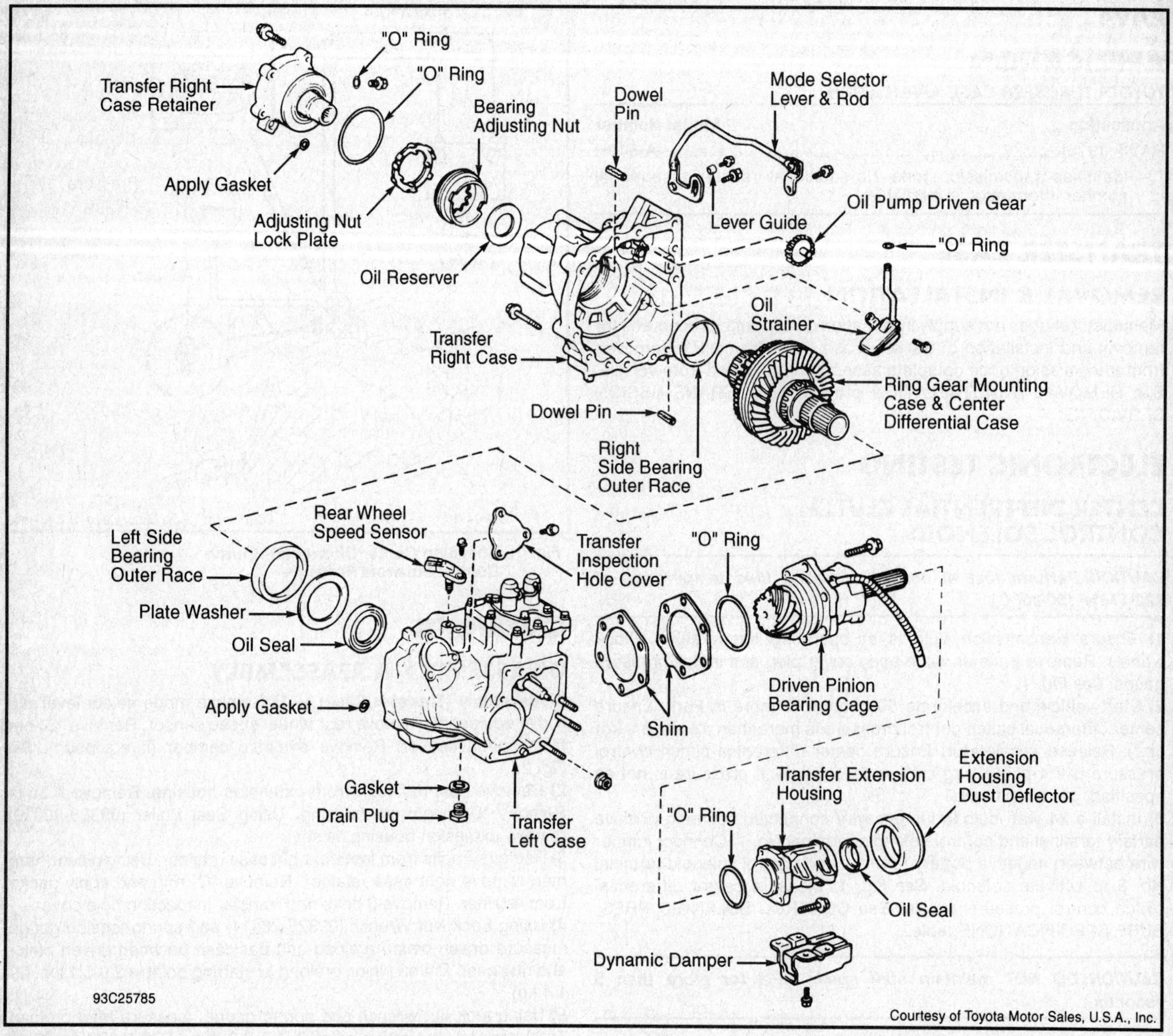

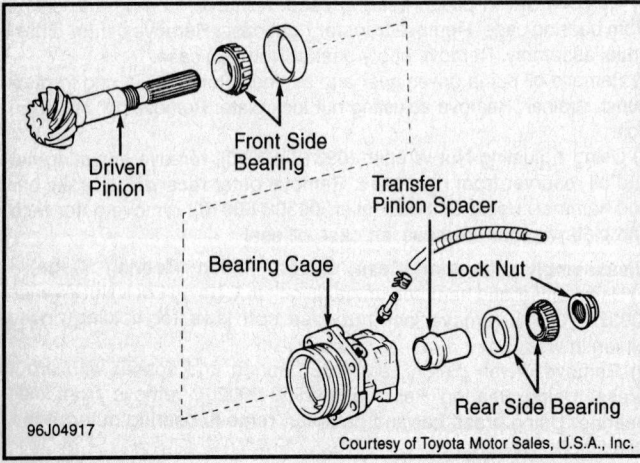

"O" Ring
"O" Ring
Transfer Right Case Retainer
Apply Gasket
Adjusting Nut Lock Plate
Oil Reserver
Bearing Adjusting Nut
Transfer Right Case
Dowel Pin
Mode Selector Lever & Rod
Lever Guide
Oil Pump Driven Gear
"O" Ring
Oil Strainer
Ring Gear Mounting Case & Center Differential Case
Dowel Pin
Right Side Bearing Outer Race

Left Side Bearing Outer Race
Plate Washer
Oil Seal
Apply Gasket
Gasket
Drain Plug
Transfer Left Case
Rear Wheel Speed Sensor
Transfer Inspection Hole Cover
"O" Ring
Shim
Driven Pinion Bearing Cage

"O" Ring
Transfer Extension Housing
Extension Housing Dust Deflector
Oil Seal
Dynamic Damper

93C25785

Courtesy of Toyota Motor Sales, U.S.A., Inc.

Fig. 2: Exploded View Of Transfer Case Components

Driven Pinion
Front Side Bearing
Bearing Cage
Transfer Pinion Spacer
Lock Nut
Rear Side Bearing

96J04917

Courtesy of Toyota Motor Sales, U.S.A., Inc.

Fig. 3: Exploded View Of Transfer Driven Pinion Bearing Cage

Reassembly – 1) Use Bearing Tool (099050-60020) to install front side bearing outer race to bearing cage. Using Bearing Replacer (09950-60010), install rear side bearing outer race. Using Bearing Replacer (09506-35010), install front side bearing. Install NEW spacer to driven pinion.

2) Install bearing cage to driven pinion. Using bearing replacer, install rear side bearing to driven pinion. Adjust drive pinion preload. Using Lock Nut Wrench (09326-20011) and torque wrench, tighten nut to 72 ft. lbs. (98 N.m).

3) Using lock nut wrench and spring tension gauge, measure preload. Rotate driven pinion counterclockwise and clockwise several times to allow bearings to settle. Measure preload of driven pinion at starting point. Preload with new bearing is 4.0-6.4 lbs. (1.8-2.9 kg). With used bearing, preload should be 2.0-3.1 lbs. (.9-1.4 kg).

4) If preload exceeds specification, replace bearing spacer. If preload is less than specification, retighten nut 5-10 degrees at a time until specified preload is reached.

5) If maximum torque is exceeded by retightening nut, replace bearing spacer. Repeat preload procedure. DO NOT back off pinion nut to reduce preload. Maximum nut torque is 174 ft. lbs. (235 N.m). Stake lock nut.

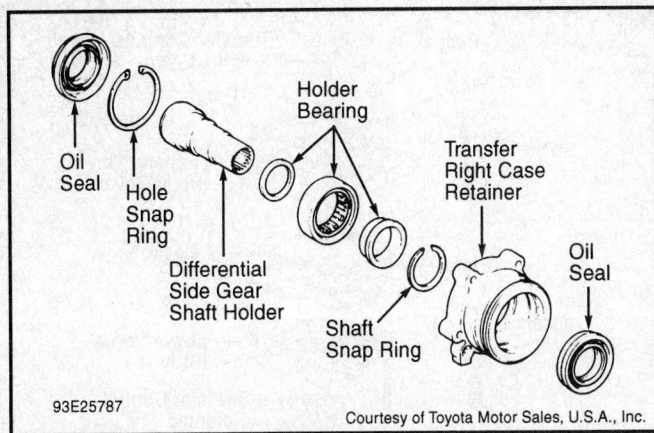

93E25787

Courtesy of Toyota Motor Sales, U.S.A., Inc.

Fig. 4: Exploded View Of Transfer Right Case Retainer

Disassembly (Transfer Right Case Retainer) – Using a screwdriver, remove oil seal. Remove snap ring. Remove side gear shaft holder with a plastic hammer. Remove snap ring. Using an arbor press, remove holder bearing. Remove oil seal. See Fig. 4.

Reassembly – Using Bearing Replacer (09226-10010) and an arbor press, install holder bearing. Install snap ring. Install side gear shaft holder. Install snap ring. Coat oil seal lip with grease. Using a hammer and Bearing Replacer (09316-60010), install left side oil seal. Using hammer and Seal Replacer (09608-32010), install right side oil seal.

Disassembly (Transfer Right Case) – Check oil pump operation. Oil pump should turn smoothly with oil pump driven gear. Remove 3 bolts and oil pump driven gear stopper. Remove oil pump cover, drive rotor and driven rotor. Remove relief valve and spring. See Fig. 5.

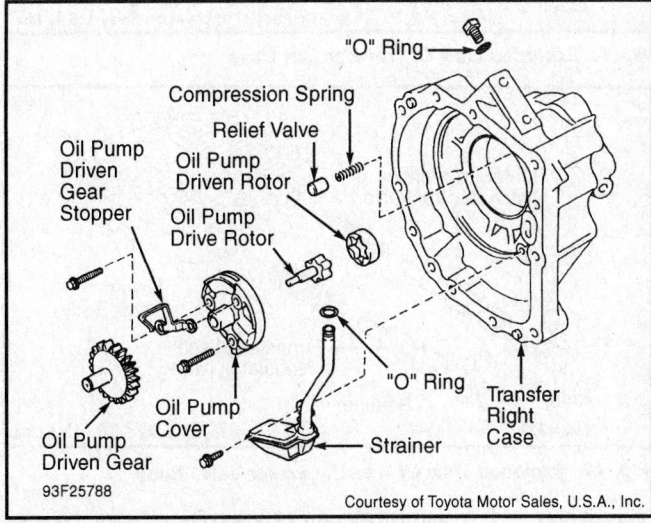

93F25788

Courtesy of Toyota Motor Sales, U.S.A., Inc.

Fig. 5: Exploded View Of Transfer Right Case

Reassembly – Install relief valve and spring. Install oil pump drive rotor and driven rotor. Align match marks on rotors. Install oil pump cover and driven gear stopper. Tighten 3 bolts to 69 INCH lbs. (7.8 N.m). Insert oil pump driven gear to drive rotor. Ensure drive rotor turns smoothly.

Disassembly (Ring Gear Mounting Case & Center Differential Case) –
1) Remove shaft snap ring. Remove oil pump drive gear. Place match marks on differential left and right case. Remove 12 bolts. Remove differential left case upward. See Fig. 6.
2) Place match marks on differential left case and ring gear. Using a plastic hammer, tap out ring gear. Remove "O" ring from case. Using Bearing Remover (09950-00020) and an arbor press, remove left case bearing.

3) Remove thrust washer. Remove center differential case assembly. Remove shaft snap rings. Remove spacer. Remove following parts from case: 4 pinion shafts, pinion shaft holder, 4 differential pinions, 4 pinion thrust washers, differential side left gear and side gear thrust washer.
4) Remove differential side right gear and conical spring washer. Note direction of conical spring washer for reassembly reference. Using bearing puller and an arbor press, remove right case bearing.

Reassembly – 1) Using Bearing Replacer (09316-12010) and Bearing Tool Set (09950-70010), press in right case bearing with an arbor press. Using bearing replacer and bearing tool set, press in left case bearing with an arbor press.
2) Clean contact surface of ring gear mounting left case. Heat ring gear to about 212°F (100°C) in an oil bath. DO NOT heat ring above 230°F (110°C). Clean contact surface of ring gear with cleaning solvent. Quickly install ring gear on ring gear mounting left case.
3) Install following parts to center differential case: side gear thrust washer, differential side left gear, 4 pinion thrust washers, 4 differential pinions, pinion shaft holder and 4 pinion shafts. Install spacer to center differential case. Using a dial indicator, measure side gear backlash while holding one pinion toward case. Backlash is .0020-.0079" (.050-.200 mm). If backlash exceeds specification, install correct thrust washer on side gears. See SIDE GEAR THRUST WASHER SPECIFICATIONS table for available thrust washer sizes.
4) Install differential side right gear. DO NOT install conical spring washer. Install center differential case. Install thrust washer. Align match marks on left and right cases. Install 12 bolts. Tighten to 72 ft. lbs. (97 N.m). DO NOT install "O" ring. Using a caliper, measure conical spring washer thickness. Measure thrust clearance of center differential case while holding ring gear mounting case. See Figs. 7 and 8.
5) See SIDE GEAR THRUST WASHER SPECIFICATIONS table. Select thrust washer which will ensure backlash is within specification. Install differential side gear and conical spring washer. Ensure correct direction of conical spring washer.
6) Install center differential case. Install correct thrust washer. Install NEW "O" ring on left case. Align match marks on right and left case. Install 12 bolts. Tighten to 72 ft. lbs. (97 N.m). Install oil pump drive gear. Install shaft snap ring.

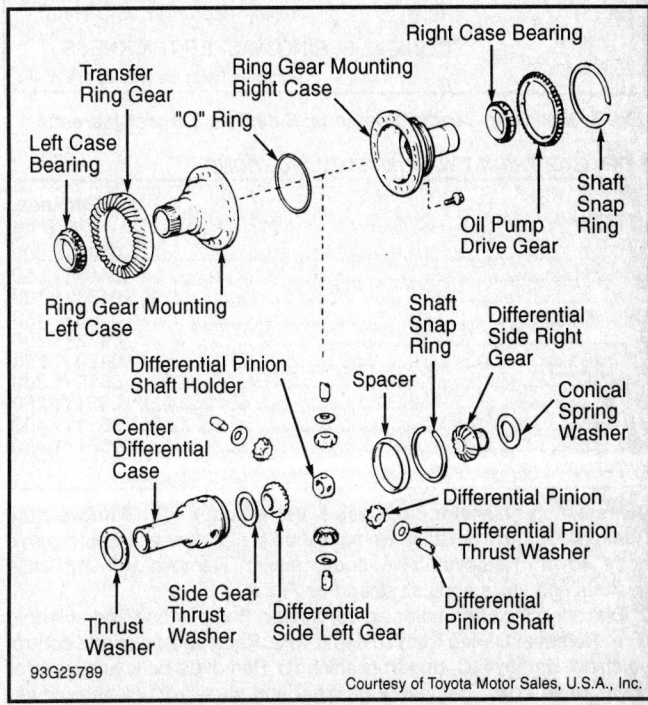

93G25789

Courtesy of Toyota Motor Sales, U.S.A., Inc.

Fig. 6: Exploded View Of Ring Gear Mounting & Center Differential Case

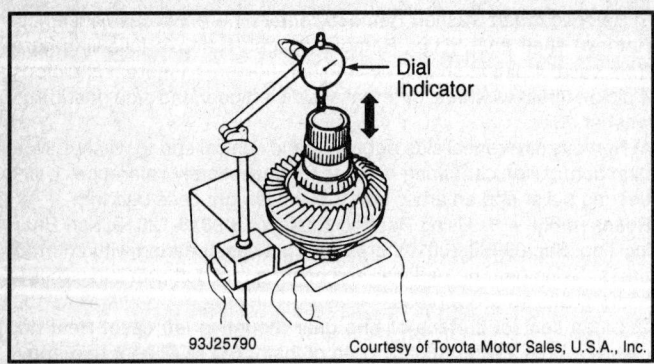

Fig. 7: Measuring Center Differential Thrust Clearance

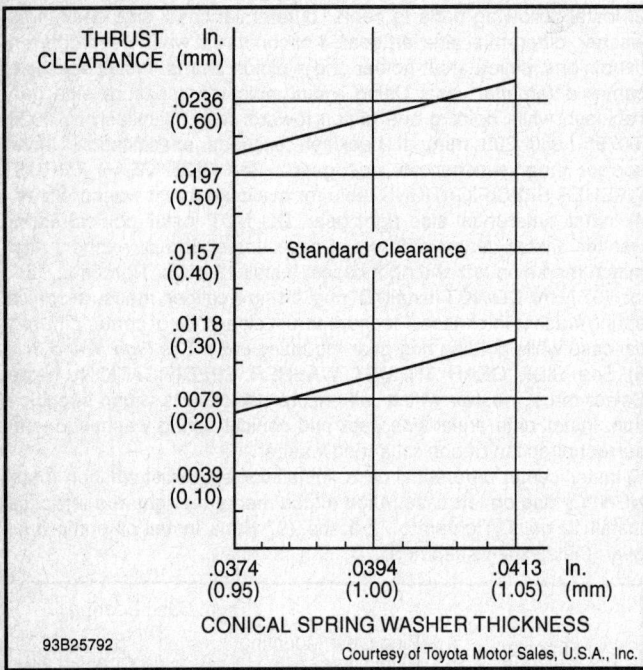

Fig. 8: Checking Center Differential Side Gear Thrust Clearance

SIDE GEAR THRUST WASHER SPECIFICATIONS

ID Mark	Thickness In. (mm)
A	.0394 (1.000)
B	.0413 (1.050)
C	.0433 (1.100)
D	.0453 (1.150)
E	.0472 (1.200)
F	.0492 (1.250)
G	.0512 (1.300)
H	.0531 (1.350)
J	.0551 (1.400)
K	.0571 (1.450)
L	.0591 (1.500)

Disassembly (Transfer Left Case & Valve Body) – **1)** Remove plug. Remove "O" ring from plug. Remove 8 bolts and remove transfer valve body cover. Remove valve body gasket. Remove transfer case gaskets and valve body strainer. *See Fig. 9.*
2) Disconnect control solenoid connector. Remove bolt and solenoid wire. Remove "O" ring from solenoid wire. Remove 2 bolts and control solenoid. Remove "O" ring from solenoid. Remove 6 bolts and transfer lower valve body. Remove 2 gaskets and plate from transfer lower valve body. *See Figs. 9 and 10.*

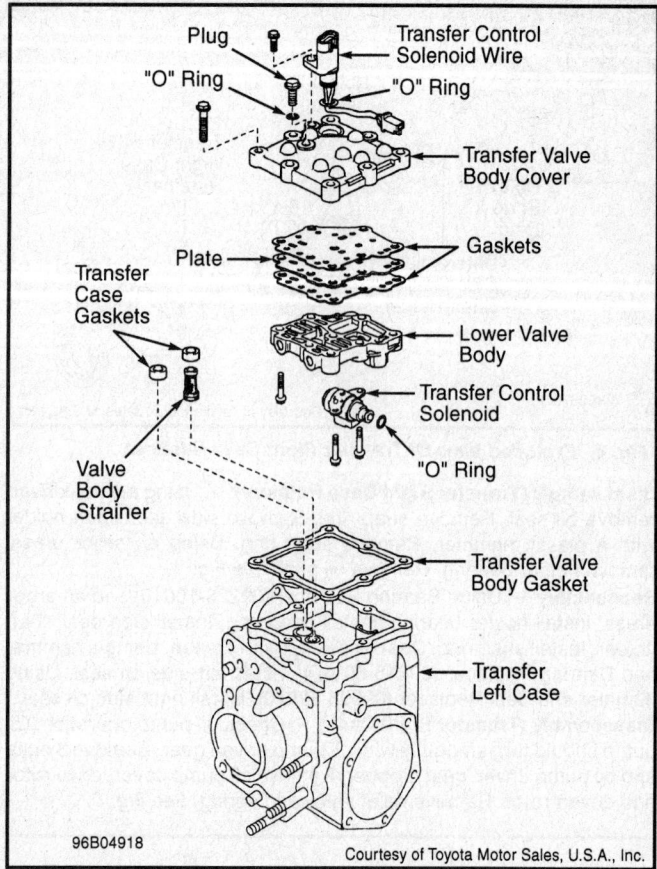

Fig. 9: Exploded View Of Transfer Left Case

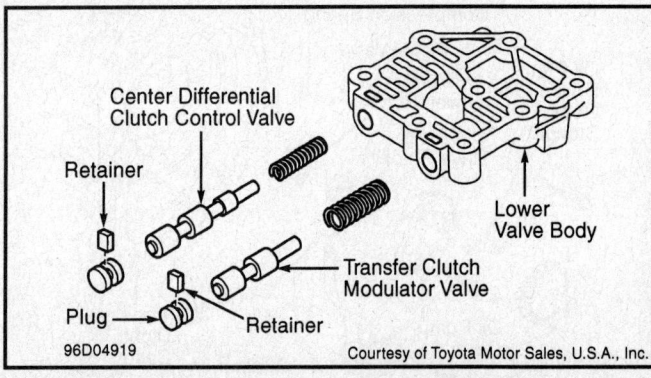

Fig. 10: Exploded View Of Transfer Lower Valve Body

Reassembly – **1)** Install NEW transfer lower valve body gaskets. Install plate. Ensure transfer lower valve body springs are installed in correct locations. See TRANSFER LOWER VALVE BODY SPRING SPECIFICATIONS table. Retainers are same height, width and thickness. Lower transfer lower valve body into place.
2) Install 6 bolts and tighten to 58 INCH lbs. (6.6 N.m). Install NEW "O" ring on control solenoid and coat with ATF. Install 2 bolts and control solenoid. Tighten bolts to 58 INCH lbs. (6.6 N.m).
3) Install NEW "O" ring on control solenoid wiring and coat with ATF. Install solenoid wiring and bolt. Tighten bolt to 58 INCH lbs. (6.6 N.m). Install solenoid connector.
4) Install NEW transfer case gaskets and valve body strainer. Install NEW transfer valve body gasket. Install transfer valve body cover. Tighten 8 bolts to 97 INCH lbs. (11 N.m). Install NEW "O" ring on plug and coat with ATF. Install plug and tighten to 65 INCH lbs. (7.4 N.m).

TRANSFER LOWER VALVE BODY SPRING SPECIFICATIONS

Spring	Free Length In. (mm)	No. Of Coils
Center Differential Clutch Control Valve	1.150 (29.20)	15.5
Transfer Clutch Modulator Valve	1.063 (27.00)	14.3

Reassembly (Transfer Case) – 1) Install case side plate washer. Using Bearing Replacer (09316-60010) and an arbor press, install case side outer race. Using bearing replacer and an arbor press, install right case side outer race. Install bearing adjusting nut and oil reserver until nut and reserver touch outer race. *See Fig. 2.*

2) Install shim(s) to driven pinion bearing cage assembly. Install same thickness shim(s) as removed. Install driven pinion bearing cage. Tighten to 29 ft. lbs. (39 N.m). DO NOT install "O" ring. Install ring gear mounting case and center differential case. Using a dial indicator, measure ring gear backlash. Backlash should be .0051-.0071" (.130-.180 mm). *See Fig. 11.* If backlash exceeds specification, install correct plate washer on ring gears. See RING GEAR PLATE WASHER SPEC-IFICATIONS table.

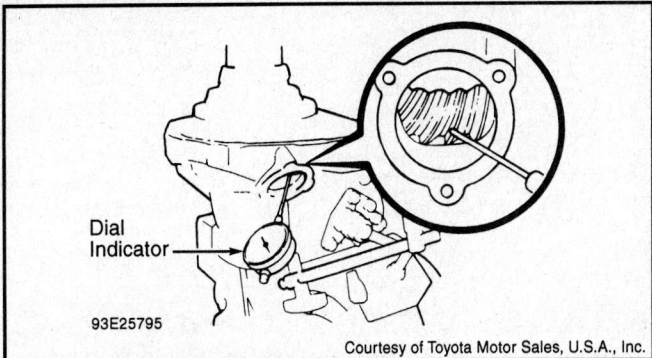

93E25795

Courtesy of Toyota Motor Sales, U.S.A., Inc.

Dial Indicator

Fig. 11: Measuring Ring Gear Backlash

RING GEAR PLATE WASHER SPECIFICATIONS

ID Mark	Thickness In. (mm)
71	.0839 (2.130)
72	.0850 (2.160)
73	.0862 (2.190)
74	.0874 (2.220)
75	.0886 (2.250)
76	.0898 (2.280)
77	.0909 (2.310)
78	.0921 (2.340)
79	.0933 (2.370)
80	.0945 (2.400)
81	.0957 (2.430)
82	.0969 (2.460)
83	.0980 (2.490)
84	.0992 (2.520)
85	.1004 (2.550)
86	.1016 (2.580)
87	.1028 (2.610)
88	.1039 (2.640)
89	.1051 (2.670)
90	.1063 (2.700)
91	.1075 (2.730)
92	.1087 (2.760)
93	.1098 (2.790)
94	.1110 (2.820)

3) Install transfer right case. DO NOT apply seal packing and gasket. Tighten bolts to 32 ft. lbs. (44 N.m). Using Lock Nut Wrench (09326-20011) and spring tension gauge, measure total preload. Total preload at starting point with new bearing is 2.9-3.1 lbs. (1.3-1.4 kg). With used bearing, preload should be 1.1-2.0 lbs. (.5-.9 kg).

4) Add drive pinion preload. Rotate drive pinion counterclockwise and clockwise several times. Using Adjusting Nut Wrench (09318-12010) and tighten wrench, adjust total preload by tightening bearing adjusting nut in small increments. Measure ring gear backlash. Backlash should be .0051-.0071" (.130-180 mm). If backlash exceeds specification, install correct plate washer on ring gear. See RING GEAR PLATE WASHER SPECIFICATIONS table.

5) Check tooth contact. Coat 3 or 4 teeth at 4 different positions on ring gear with Red lead. Rotate ring gear, and inspect teeth pattern. *See Fig. 12.* If teeth are not meshing properly, install proper shim and plate washer. See RING GEAR SHIM SPECIFICATIONS and RING GEAR PLATE WASHER SPECIFICATIONS tables.

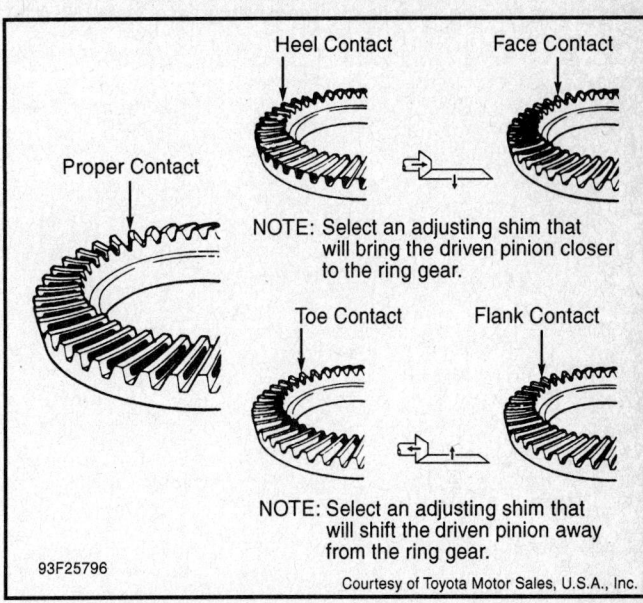

Heel Contact   Face Contact

Proper Contact

NOTE: Select an adjusting shim that will bring the driven pinion closer to the ring gear.

Toe Contact   Flank Contact

NOTE: Select an adjusting shim that will shift the driven pinion away from the ring gear.

93F25796

Courtesy of Toyota Motor Sales, U.S.A., Inc.

Fig. 12: Checking Ring Gear Tooth Contact

RING GEAR SHIM SPECIFICATIONS

ID Mark	Thickness In. (mm)
A	.0118 (.300)
B	.0130 (.330)
C	.0142 (.360)
D	.0154 (.390)
E	.0165 (.420)
F	.0177 (.450)
G	.0189 (.480)
H	.0201 (.510)
J	.0213 (.540)
K	.0224 (.570)

6) Remove transfer right case. Remove ring gear mounting case and center differential case. Remove driven pinion bearing cage assembly. Using Oil Seal Puller (09308-00010), remove outer race and plate washer.

7) Using Bearing Replacer (09316-60010), install NEW oil seal. Oil seal depth is .12" (3 mm). Coat lip of oil seal with grease. Install plate washer. Using Bearing Replacer (09316-60010) and an arbor press, install left case bearing outer race.

8) Coat "O" ring with gear oil and install on driven pinion bearing cage assembly. Install driven pinion bearing cage with adjusting shim to transfer left case. Install 6 bolts. Tighten bolts to 29 ft. lbs. (39 N.m). Install ring gear mounting case and center differential case.

9) Install NEW apply gasket to left case. Coat "O" ring with gear oil. Install "O" ring to oil pump strainer. Install strainer to transfer right case. Install bolts. Tighten to 48 INCH lbs. (5.4 N.m) Install oil pump driven gear. Apply Three Bond (1281) seal packing to left case. Install right case as soon as seal packing is applied. Install right case to left case. Install 10 bolts. Tighten to 32 ft. lbs. (44 N.m). Check total preload as shown in step 3).

10) Install lock plate so that projection from lock plate fits properly into groove of adjusting nut. When lock plate cannot be installed, tighten adjusting nut smallest amount possible. Coat NEW "O" ring with gear oil. Install "O" ring on lock bolt. Install and tighten lock nut to 62 INCH lbs. (7 N.m).

11) Apply seal packing Three Bond (1281) to left case. Install inspection hole cover as soon as seal packing is applied. Install hole cover to transfer left case. Install 3 bolts. Tighten to 12 ft. lbs. (16 N.m).

12) Coat NEW "O" ring with gear oil. Install "O" ring and NEW apply gasket. Install right case retainer to transfer right case. Install 5 bolts. Tighten bolts to 21 ft. lbs. (29 N.m).

13) Use Oil Plug (09325-20010) and a hammer to install NEW oil seal in extension housing. Coat lip of oil seal with grease. Install NEW "O" ring in extension housing. Install extension housing to driven pinion bearing cage. Install 4 bolts. Tighten to 18 ft. lbs. (25 N.m). Using a hammer, install dust deflector (if equipped). Install dynamic damper. Tighten to 18 ft. lbs. (25 N.m).

14) Install NEW "O" ring on speed sensor. Install speed sensor to transfer left case. Tighten to 48 INCH lbs. (5.4 N.m). Install transfer mode selector lever, rod and lever guide (if equipped). Tighten 2 lever bolts to 96 INCH lbs. (11 N.m). Tighten guide bolt to 48 INCH lbs. (5.4 N.m).

RAV4 (With M/T)

APPLICATION

TOYOTA TRANSFER CASE APPLICATION

Application	Transaxle Model
1996 RAV4	E250F 5-Speed

DESCRIPTION & OPERATION

CENTER DIFFERENTIAL LOCK SYSTEM

The center differential lock system enables vehicle to have traction to move vehicle when one of the 4 wheels, both front wheels or both rear wheels are off the ground or on a slippery surface.

Center differential lock system consists of control switch, differential lock control solenoids (vacuum switching valves), differential lock actuator, indicator light switch, and warning buzzer. See Fig. 1.

With control switch off, the center differential lock indicator light on instrument panel is off, along with vacuum switching valves No. 1 and 2. Vacuum switching valve No. 1 draws vacuum from vacuum tank to chamber "A" of the vacuum actuator. Vacuum switching valve No. 2 draws atmospheric air to chamber "B".

Under these conditions, the vacuum actuator diaphragm moves the rod, which moves the locking sleeve shift fork and shaft, which causes the locking sleeve to disengage from the case. See Fig. 6. During this time, the center differential warning buzzer will sound. When the locking sleeve is completely disengaged, the warning buzzer will turn off (free position).

REMOVAL & INSTALLATION

Manufacturer does not supply information on separate procedures for removal and installation of transfer case. Transfer case is removed from transmission once complete assembly is removed from vehicle. See REMOVAL & INSTALLATION procedures in TRANSMISSION SERVICING section.

TESTING

CENTER DIFFERENTIAL LOCK SYSTEM

1) Raise vehicle off ground so all 4 wheels can rotate. Apply parking brake and start engine. Turn center differential lock system on.
2) Depress clutch pedal and shift into 2nd gear. With engine idling, gradually engage the clutch and ensure engine stalls.
3) With parking brake and engine on, turn center differential lock system off. Depress clutch pedal and shift into 2nd gear. With engine idling, gradually engage the clutch and ensure front wheels rotate.

CENTER DIFFERENTIAL LOCK INDICATOR LIGHT

Turn ignition on. Ensure indicator light is off with center differential lock system off, and on with system on.

WARNING BUZZER

NOTE: *If the buzzer continues to sound, point the wheels straight ahead, accelerate or decelerate, or drive the vehicle in reverse to stop the buzzer.*

1) Start engine and ensure warning buzzer does not sound when center differential lock switch is turned on. Change position of vacuum hoses at vacuum switching valves.
2) Turn off center differential lock switch and ensure warning buzzer sounds. Change position of vacuum hoses at vacuum switching valves once again, and ensure buzzer stops. If buzzer operation is not as specified, check vacuum hoses.

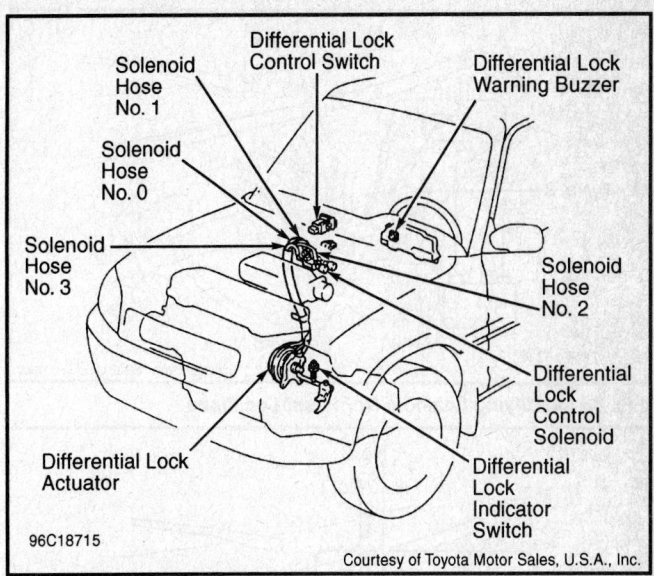

96C18715   Courtesy of Toyota Motor Sales, U.S.A., Inc.

Fig. 1: Identifying Differential Lock Components

ELECTRONIC COMPONENTS

NOTE: *For Component Location See Figs. 1 and 6.*

Differential Lock Control Switch – With switch in OFF (free) position, check for continuity between terminals No. 7 and 10. With switch in ON (lock) position, check for continuity between terminals No. 7 and 8. Check illumination circuit at terminals No. 2 and 3 for continuity. if continuity is not as specified, check bulb or replace switch. See Fig. 2.
Differential Lock Warning Buzzer – Remove combination meter. Remove differential lock warning buzzer. Apply battery voltage to buzzer. Ensure polarity matches. Ensure buzzer sounds.
Differential Lock Indicator Switch – With switch in free position, no continuity should be present between terminals. With switch pushed, continuity should be present. If continuity is not as specified, replace switch.

96D18716   Courtesy of Toyota Motor Sales, U.S.A., Inc.

Fig. 2: Identifying Differential Lock Control Terminals

Differential Lock Control Solenoid – Disconnect connector from solenoids No. 1 and No. 2. Check air flow to each port when battery positive voltage is applied and released from connector terminals of solenoid No. 1 and No. 2. With battery voltage applied to solenoid No. 1, port No. 2 should vent to atmosphere. Without battery voltage, flow should be between port No. 2 and No. 3. With battery voltage applied to solenoid No. 2, No. 0 should flow to No. 1. Without battery voltage, No. 1 should vent to atmosphere. See Figs. 3 and 4.

TRANSFER VACUUM ACTUATOR

NOTE: *If actuator operation is not as specified, replace actuator.*

Vacuum Tank – Disconnect solenoid hose No. 0, No. 2 and No. 3 from the solenoids. Plug No. 3 hose. Apply 20" hg. to hose No. 0. Vacuum drop in 15 second should be 1.77" hg or less.

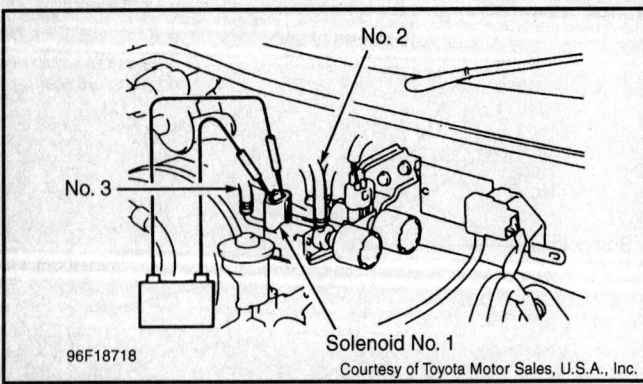

Fig. 3: Identifying Solenoid No. 1 Test Locations

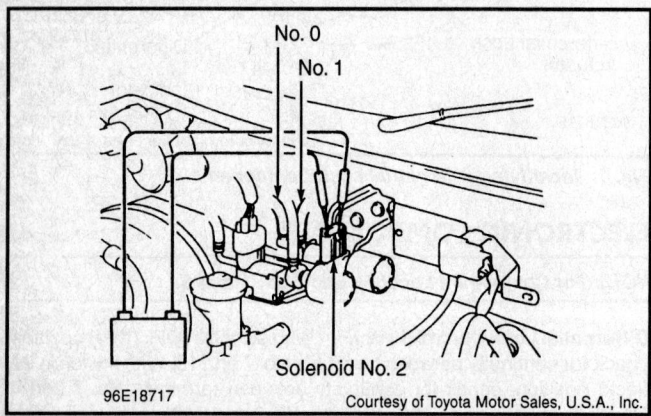

Fig. 4: Identifying Solenoid No. 2 Test Locations

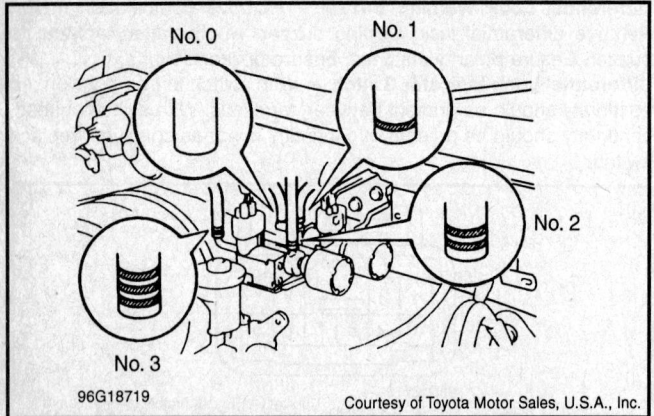

Fig. 5: Identifying Vacuum Hose Connections

Diaphragm (Lock Position Side) – Disconnect solenoid hoses No. 1 and No. 2 from solenoids. Apply 20" hg to hose No. 1. Within 15 seconds, vacuum drop should be 1.77" hg or less. Reinstall vacuum hoses to appropriate port. See Fig. 5.

Diaphragm (Free Position Side) – Disconnect solenoid hoses No. 0, No. 1, No. 2 and No. 3 from the solenoids. Plug No. 3 vacuum hose. Apply 20" hg of vacuum to No. 0 and No. 2 hoses simultaneously. Within 15 seconds, vacuum drop should be 1.77" hg or less. Reinstall vacuum hoses to appropriate ports. See Fig. 5.

OVERHAUL

Disassembly – 1) Remove dust boot. Remove dynamic dampener. Remove extension housing. Remove "O" ring from extension housing. Remove plug, differential lock indicator switch and right case oil seal. Measure driven pinion preload of backlash between driven pinion and pinion gear. Starting preload should be 2-3 lbs. (.9-1.4 kg). Measure total preload. Total driven pinion plus starting preload should be 1-2 lbs. (.5-.9 kg). See Fig. 6.

2) Remove transfer case inspection hole cover. Using a dial indicator, measure ring gear backlash. Backlash should be .005-.007" (.13-.18 mm). See Fig. 8. Remove transfer pinion bearing cage assembly. Remove "O" ring and adjusting shims from transfer pinion bearing cage. Remove shift fork, shift fork shaft and lock sleeve. Remove transfer right case. Remove ring gear mounting case assembly. Remove side gear shaft holder and snap ring from the right case. Press off differential side gear shaft holder. Remove adjusting nut lock plate. Remove shift fork shaft oil seal. Replace if necessary. See Fig. 6.

3) If necessary, replace extension housing oil seal. Oil seal installation depth should be .043-.075" (1.1-1.9 mm). Coat oil seal lip with MP grease. If necessary, replace side gear shaft holder bearing. Remove snap ring. Press bearing from shaft gear holder. Press new bearing and install snap ring. Remove oil pipe and cushion from left transfer case. Install new cushion. Replace oil pipe if needed. Remove bearing adjusting nut and outer race. Turn adjusting nut until it contacts lip of case. Press new bearing outer race until it almost touches bearing adjusting nut.

4) From left side case, drive out bearing race. Remove plate washer and replace with washer of same thickness. Press new bearing outer race.

Transfer Pinion Bearing Cage Disassembly & Reassembly – 1) Unstake lock nut. Using Special Socket (09326-20011) remove lock nut. Press transfer driven pinion from cage. Remove rear bearing and spacer. Replace driven pinion bearing if needed. Replace front and rear bearing outer races as needed. To replace, drive out outer races evenly and press in new races.

NOTE: Coat all sliding and rotating surfaces with gear oil before assembly.

2) Install new bearing spacer with smaller diameter facing upwards. Press rear bearing until pinion can move slightly. Using Special Tool (09326-20011), Install lock nut. Torque to 70 ft. lbs. (95 N.m). Torque without special tool to 80 ft. lbs. (108 N.m). Rotate driven pinion right and left 2 to 3 times to allow bearing to settle. Using spring tension gauge, measure preload. With new bearing, starting preload should be 4-6.4 lbs. (1.8-2.9 kg). Starting preload for a used bearing should be 1.1-2.0 lb. (.9-1.4 kg). If preload exceeds specifications, replace bearing spacer. If preload is less than specification, retighten nut at 5-10 degree increments until specified preload is reached. If maximum torque is exceeded while retightening nut, replace bearing spacer and repeat procedure. Do not back off pinion nut to reduce preload. Maximum torque with Special Tool (09326-20011) is 158 ft. lbs. (214 N.m). Maximum torque without special tool is 174 ft. lbs. (214 N.m). Stake lock nut. See Fig. 7.

Ring Gear Mounting Case Disassembly – 1) Using 2-jaw puller, remove ring gear mounting case side bearings. Using dial indicator, check ring gear runout. Maximum runout is .004" (0.1 mm). See Fig. 9. Place matchmarks on ring gear mounting case and transfer ring gear. Remove 12 bolts, tap out transfer ring gear.

Reassembly – 1) Install transfer ring gear. Heat ring gear to about 212° F (100° C) in boiling water. Clean contact surfaces with cleaning solvent. Quickly install ring gear to mounting case aligning matchmarks. Install bolts and torque to 71 ft. lbs. (97 N.m). Recheck ring gear runout.

NOTE: Coat all sliding and rotating surfaces with gear oil before assembly.

2) Install new mounting case side bearings. Install adjusting shim (same thickness as one removed) to transfer pinion bearing cage assembly. Install pinion bearing cage assembly to left transfer case. Torque bolts to 29 ft. lbs. (39 N.m). Do not install "O" ring. Install ring gear mounting case assembly to left transfer case. Using dial indicator, measure ring gear backlash. Backlash should be .005-.007 (.13-.18 mm). See Fig. 8. If backlash is not within specification, select plate washer which will ensure backlash is within specification. Plate washers are available in thicknesses of .0839" (2.13 mm) to .111" (2.82 mm) in .0012" (.03 mm) increments and are stamped "1" through "24". Backlash will change approximately .0008" (.02 mm) with every .0012" (.03 mm) change in shim thickness.

Notes

Notes

Notes

Notes

Notes

Notes

Notes

Notes

Notes

English-Metric Conversion Chart

CONVERSION FACTORS

Unit	To	Unit	Multiply By
LENGTH			
Millimeters	Inches		.03937
Inches	Millimeters		25.4
Meters	Feet		3.28084
Feet	Meters		.3048
Kilometers	Miles		.62137
Miles	Kilometers		1.60935
AREA			
Square Centimeters	Square Inches		.155
Square Inches	Square Centimeters		6.45159
VOLUME			
Cubic Centimeters	Cubic Inches		.06103
Cubic Inches	Cubic Centimeters		16.38703
Liters	Cubic Inches		61.025
Cubic Inches	Liters		.01639
Liters	Quarts		1.05672
Quarts	Liters		.94633
Liters	Pints		2.11344
Pints	Liters		.47317
Liters	Ounces		33.81497
Ounces	Liters		.02957

Unit	To	Unit	Multiply
WEIGHT			
Grams	Ounces		.035
Ounces	Grams		28.349
Kilograms	Pounds		2.20
Pounds	Kilograms		.45
WORK			
Centimeter Kilograms	Inch Pounds		.8
Inch Pounds	Centimeter Kilograms		1.15
Meter Kilograms	Foot Pounds		7.23
Foot Pounds	Newton Meters		1.3
PRESSURE			
Kilograms/Sq. Centimeter	Pounds/Sq. Inch		14.22
Pounds/Sq. Inch	Kilograms/Sq. Centimeter		.07
Bar	Pounds/Sq. Inch		14.
Pounds/Sq. Inch	Bar		.06
Atmosphere	Pounds/Sq. Inch		14.
Pounds/Sq. Inch	Atmosphere		.06
TEMPERATURE			
Centigrade Degrees	Fahrenheit Degrees		$(C° \times 9/5)$
Fahrenheit Degrees	Centigrade Degrees		$(F° - 32)$

Inches	Decimals	MM	Inches	Decimals	M
1/64	.016	.397	33/64	.516	13.0
1/32	.031	.794	17/32	.531	13.4
3/64	.047	1.191	35/64	.547	13.8
1/16	.063	1.588	9/16	.563	14.2
5/64	.078	1.984	37/64	.578	14.6
3/32	.094	2.381	19/32	.594	15.0
7/64	.109	2.778	39/64	.609	15.4
1/8	.125	3.175	5/8	.625	15.8
9/64	.141	3.572	41/64	.641	16.2
5/32	.156	3.969	21/32	.656	16.6
11/64	.172	4.366	43/64	.672	17.0
3/16	.188	4.763	11/16	.687	17.4
13/64	.203	5.159	45/64	.703	17.8
7/32	.219	5.556	23/32	.719	18.2
15/64	.234	5.953	47/64	.734	18.6
1/4	.250	6.350	3/4	.750	19.0
17/64	.266	6.747	49/64	.766	19.4
9/32	.281	7.144	25/32	.781	19.8
19/64	.297	7.541	51/64	.797	20.2
5/16	.313	7.938	13/16	.813	20.6
21/64	.328	8.334	53/64	.828	21.0
11/32	.344	8.731	27/32	.844	21.4
23/64	.359	9.128	55/64	.859	21.8
3/8	.375	9.525	7/8	.875	22.2
25/64	.391	9.922	57/64	.891	22.6
13/32	.406	10.319	29/32	.906	23.0
27/64	.422	10.716	59/64	.922	23.4
7/16	.438	11.113	15/16	.938	23.8
29/64	.453	11.509	61/64	.953	24.2
15/32	.469	11.906	31/32	.969	24.6
31/64	.484	12.303	63/64	.984	25.0
1/2	.500	12.700			